THE CRITICAL TRADITION

Classic Texts and Contemporary Trends

THE CRITICAL TRADITION

Classic Texts and Contemporary Trends

Third Edition

Edited by

David H. Richter

Queens College
of the City University of New York

BEDFORD/ST. MARTIN'S   **BOSTON ◆ NEW YORK**

For Bedford/St. Martin's

Executive Editor: Stephen A. Scipione
Developmental Editor: Jennifer Blanksteen
Senior Production Supervisor: Joe Ford
Production Associates: Christopher Gross, Matthew Hayes
Senior Marketing Manager: Jenna Bookin Barry
Project Management: DeMasi Design and Publishing Service
Cover Design: Donna L. Dennison
Composition: Macmillan India Ltd.
Printing and Binding: RR Donnelley & Sons Company

President: Joan E. Feinberg
Editorial Director: Denise B. Wydra
Editor in Chief: Karen S. Henry
Director of Marketing: Karen Melton Soeltz
Director of Editing, Design, and Production: Marcia Cohen
Manager, Publishing Services: Emily Berleth

Library of Congress Control Number: 2005921359

Manufactured in the United States of America.

2   1   0   9   8   7
f   e   d   c   b   a

For information, write: Bedford/St. Martin's, 75 Arlington Street, Boston, MA 02116   (617–399–4000)

ISBN: 0–312–41520–6
EAN: 978–0–312–41520–4

Acknowledgments
Acknowledgments and copyrights are continued at the back of the book on pages 2029–34, which constitute an extension of the copyright page.

Preface

The "canon of theory" introduces into the institutional context of literary pedagogy (the graduate seminar) a syllabus whose symptomatic function is to signify precisely methodological "rigor," rather than the taste or discrimination which for so long determined the ideological protocols of literary criticism. . . . Those authors or texts designated as "theoretical" are now increasingly capable of being introduced to students in traditional routinized forms, even by means of anthologies. — JOHN GUILLORY, *Cultural Capital* (1993)

THE FIRST WAVE

In the late 1960s, when I started teaching, literary criticism was primarily an arcane subspecialty of historical research, in which scholars quarreled about Philip Sidney's distinction between "poesy" and "poetry" or the relative influence of Horace and Longinus on Samuel Johnson. My own interest in literary theory as an ongoing as well as a historic concern, stimulated by University of Chicago professors Wayne Booth and Sheldon Sacks, Norman Maclean and Richard McKeon, then seemed a harmless oddity to most of my colleagues at Queens College. One of them, since guilty of a metacritical book himself, warned me authoritatively over lunch that I was wasting my time with theory because there was no future in it.

By then, of course, the revolution had already begun that would end by making critical theory the roiling pivot point of the profession of letters, the one topic the fans of Philip Roth and the devotees of Lady Mary Wroth might have in common. The turbulence and clash of ideas had begun decades before on the Continent, but those of us in the provinces, who read French and German haltingly and Russian not at all, didn't experience the explosion of theory until the mid-1970s, as structuralism and semiotics, deconstruction, Lacanian psychology, Althusserian Marxism, Russian formalism, phenomenology, and reception theory rode successive waves into our awareness. A profession that a few years before had been hacking out dozens of progressively less plausible ways of misreading *The Turn of the Screw* was now lit up with a rush of ideas, a dozen disparate systems with enormous philosophical reach and scope. Many of those systems were capable also of informing and channeling the social imperatives of women and minorities seeking a theoretical manifestation of their need for greater freedom and power. To academics like me the sense of liberation was palpable, echoing Wordsworth's sentiments about a revolution two hundred years past: "Great it was in that dawn to be alive / But to be young was very heaven."

The first edition of *The Critical Tradition* was conceived in the rush of that era, as a tool to help my own students and those like them all over the Americas, many of them innocent of philosophy of any sort, take tentative steps toward joining the magnificent conversation going on about them. Its aim was not merely to provide an anthology of contemporary theory, with examples of all the latest trends, but a book that could locate and present the sources of the new theory within Western intellectual history going back to Plato.

The revolution was, after all, reshaping our sense of intellectual history, forcing us to broaden our horizons. Anglo-American feminist theory, like that of Elaine Showalter and Sandra Gilbert, needed to be understood against the backdrop of Germaine de Staël, Virginia Woolf, Simone de Beauvoir, and other forebears who served either as sources of inspiration or as antagonists. Understanding Derrida required one to understand not only the theories of structuralism and semiotics against which he had reacted: he presumes in the reader the knowledge of Plato, Kant, Hegel, Nietzsche, and Heidegger, some of whom were comparative strangers to traditional literary criticism courses. On the other side, with the waning of the hegemony of New Critical explication, the differences between the various New Critics, like Allen Tate, John Crowe Ransom, and Cleanth Brooks, no longer seemed as profound as they once did, and the New Criticism itself receded to a trend within the larger formalist movement in the earlier part of the twentieth century that also comprehended such disparate theorists as Victor Shklovsky and R. S. Crane. An entire tradition of rhetorical theory going back to classical times, whose centrality depended on that of the New Criticism, was displaced. But original thinkers like Kenneth Burke, who had once been seen within the context of New Criticism, now assumed unique places in the pantheon.

THE SECOND WAVE: PRACTICES AND PIDGINS

Intellectual revolutions too have their Thermidors, and not long after *The Critical Tradition* appeared in 1989, it became clear that the era of Grand Theory was coming to an end. No longer did each year bring a rediscovered thinker with the significance of Bakhtin, a new theory with the impact of deconstruction. Theory had moved into a period of consolidation, when it was being used not for its own sake but to make possible a new sort of encounter with a text or a group of related texts. Critical practices that had emerged since the beginning of the revolution, engaged in "gender studies," "New Historicism," and, broadest of all, "cultural studies," began to dominate the graduate and undergraduate study of literature.

People began to engage in loose talk about the arrival of a post-theoretical age, and Terry Eagleton published a book titled *After Theory* (2003). But of course theory had not disappeared. The new critical discourses were so thoroughly imbued with contemporary theory that they were incomprehensible in isolation from their theoretical origins. Really coming to terms with the methodology behind the New Historicism involved reading all sorts of abstract texts: not only practitioners like Stephen Greenblatt and Jerome McGann but theorists like Clifford Geertz and Hayden White and Michel Foucault. And to do things properly one would have to read the theorists who had most influenced them: not only Clifford Geertz on the semiotics of culture, but also Max Weber and Emile Durkheim and Claude Lévi-Strauss; not only Hayden White on the tropics of history, but also Jacques Derrida and Ludwig Wittgenstein; not only Michel Foucault on the genealogies of power/knowledge, but also Martin Heidegger and the later Nietzsche. The bases for gender studies and cultural studies would be even wider and more diverse.

The process of consolidating and simplifying the elaborate and difficult Grand Theories into workable critical practices involved creating a pidgin, in much the same way people manage to communicate across language barriers by forming a *lingua franca* for trade and barter during interludes between hostilities. This critical pidgin was encouraged by the way universities avoided the creation of "schools" of like-minded thinkers such as those you find on the Continent, and instead filled slots so as to create the greatest possible diversity. English departments that had acquired a Lacanian or a reception theorist to be fashionable didn't feel the need of a breeding pair. This tendency to isolate individuals using a particular theoretical vocabulary from one another had the consequence that, while they could use their chosen critical language in all its purity in their own classroom and at conferences, they had to use some other sort of discourse to talk with their colleagues. The result was a carnival of jostling jargons, in which purity of rhetoric took second place to the pragmatics of discourse. A gender theorist like Judith Butler could derive her notions about sex and society from Foucault, but her rhetorical ploys might be taken from Derrida and J. L. Austin, and never mind that these thinkers might otherwise be strange bedfellows. An important innovator in postcolonial theory, such as Gayatri Spivak, was unlikely to talk purely like a feminist or a Marxist or a deconstructionist, but rather like a combination of all three.

If all this has given literary studies a sense of common purpose that we have lacked since the hegemony of the New Criticism, there are also potentially disturbing consequences. One problem is that pidgins are defective languages that suppress the more complex features of the different critical languages that compose them. Critical pidgins adopt terms without necessarily adopting the full philosophy out of which the terms emerge. When we try to say something for ourselves without understanding how each of those sets of ideas works, the result is often gobbledygook composed of different and irreconcilable terminologies. One reads "theory-damaged" discourse that sounds plausible but really makes no sense, like the following sentences taken from a recent book: "Bakhtin's reading of the process of self-realization is the opposite of Lacan's. If for Lacan there is an inevitable dismemberment of a total self, for Bakhtin there is a continual movement toward a self that is never total but always capable of further realization." It would take a long time to explain everything that is wrong with this formulation, though one might begin with the fact that in Lacan there is no "total self" to be dismembered except as an Imaginary construct. But the main problem lies not in such details but in the unexamined assumption that Bakhtin's use of the word *self* and Lacan's have enough in common to allow them to be juxtaposed in this way.

The only way to avoid this kind of muddle is to understand Bakhtin and Lacan in their own terms. Otherwise, we are at the mercy of hybrid practices with internal contradictions, formed from some elements that aspire to be "scientific" and empirical (such as structural linguistics) along with others that are deeply hostile to science and positivism (such as Foucault's genealogies of discursive practices); some elements that are humanistic and pluralistic (such as the work of Habermas), and others (such as Derrida's) that are profoundly distrustful of the relics of the Enlightenment. So while a synthesis of critical practices may have been desperately needed to correct the excesses of the era of Grand Theory, an understanding of theory is more desperately needed than ever to avoid the incoherence of an eclectic critical practice.

THE THIRD WAVE

In recent years these syncretic trends have continued to proliferate, as the study of literature has become just one area in a widening arena of textual criticism. Critical tools for studying literature have been applied to other artistic cultural productions like film and television, radio plays and comic books, painting and photography — and vice versa. Analytic approaches to narrative originally used to study novels and short stories have found application to medical case histories, or the narratives judges create in writing legal decisions. Historical movements in architecture and home furnishing — such as the eighteenth-century vogue in England and France for chinoiserie — are today thought of not as capricious episodes of fashion but as part of a larger cultural plenum shared with all the other fine and useful arts and determined by changes in trading relationships and other economic and social trends. Cultural studies has in fact turned back upon itself in ecocriticism, which attempts to understand how culture comes to define its opposite, nature, and to explore the changing relationship between civilization and the wild. Science studies, legal studies, business studies: new fields like these attempt to interrogate the paradigms of knowledge taught to and accepted by professionals in these areas. Most eclectic of all, perhaps, is the field of global studies, which uses every resource of the social sciences and humanities to analyze how the forces of power, money, and culture have shaped a planet that began to become one world since the voyages of discovery some five hundred years ago. The result of all this has been that, although institutional structures within academe have remained more or less stable — most professors still teach and most students still earn degrees within departments — my own research projects and those of most of my doctoral students, colleagues, and friends have become ever more interdisciplinary.

The other clear change of the last decade has been the demise of the traditional literary canon as a basis for the curriculum in humanities courses. The persistent attacks on the traditional canon as a gentleman's club for dead white European males provoked culture wars beginning in the 1980s, but those wars are over now. Research on the history of literary evaluation revealed that, despite the long-term agreement on the significance of Homer and the Bible, the canon of the vernacular literatures had always been in flux. Most teachers understood that there was no way to teach any permanent list as "the best that has been known and thought in the world," that the best we could do would be to teach different ways of reading whatever texts retained cultural importance today. The emphasis on the contemporary and the postmodern did not mean eliminating all the old favorites — indeed, Shakespeare and Jane Austen have as many followers as they ever had — but the culture of the university had approved so many new major writers, and so many new areas of study, that no one could rationally feel guilty any more about what got left out of the selection taken by undergraduate and graduate students. Our students, living in a postmodern culture that insistently recycles the cultural icons of the past, thus needed to read Defoe's *Robinson Crusoe* not only for its historical importance, but in order to understand Coetzee's *Foe* and Tournier's *Vendredi*, or Dickens' *Great Expectations* in order to understand the versions by Kathy Acker and Peter Carey.

With contemporary cultural value taking clear precedence over other versions of merit, the curriculum began to give greater attention to ethnic literatures, particularly by writers of African American, Asian, and Latino/Hispanic descent, and abroad to the contemporary literature of Africa, South Asia, and the Caribbean, where so much of the most innovative poetry and fiction of the last decades has been written. With this shift, postcolonial theory has become a major growth area. Originating in the politics of identity within nation-states carved out of European empires, postcolonial theory has since been applied to American literature (based on the view that the United States was formed by absorbing territories inhabited by other cultures in a process of internal colonization). The theory behind contemporary and historical ethnic studies has tended to borrow from postcolonial theory and its sources. But of course these studies are not limited to the contemporary: they can even be read back onto biblical texts, where the Israelites appear first as the conquering hegemons of Canaan, later as a conquered people at risk of cultural absorption by the Eastern empires of Babylon and Persia.

If most of the forces in the third wave of theory have been centrifugal — exploding the canon of literature, and viewing literature against the countless other arenas of life — at least one, cognitive psychology, seems to be seeking a new center within, in the activities of the human mind. Philology could reveal the poem and its patterns, and rhetoric could give us some inkling of how audiences reacted, but until recently the key aesthetic moment was a mystery, a "black box" whose workings were hidden to us. Experimental psychology, however, has begun to shine some light on mind and brain, how literary tropes (like metaphor) are involved in all cognition, how the aesthetic moment happens, and how literary texts engage and occasionally test the limits of cognitive functioning.

YET ANOTHER CRITICAL TRADITION

It was against this understanding of our current moment in the history of literary and cultural studies that I began this latest revision of *The Critical Tradition*. The chapter on the Canon and the Culture Wars, which had begun to seem of historical interest, has been replaced with a chapter on postmodernism engaging the various theories — economic, semiotic, psychological — illuminating this literary and cultural movement, and questioning whether postmodernism is here to stay and whether the program of modernity begun during the Enlightenment has reached its full promise.

Postcolonial theory has been broken out from its previous situation as one of several programs within cultural studies to a separate chapter. But since it shares with contemporary African American, Latino, and Asian studies the issues of cultural identity, nationality, liminality, and contact zones, I have incorporated all these into a single coherent chapter.

The volume, as before, is organized in two parts. Part One, Classic Texts, presents a history of criticism through seventy-two selections by fifty major critics from Plato through Susan Sontag. In this edition, new selections appear by Mary Wollstonecraft, Thomas Love Peacock, and W. E. B. Du Bois. Selections by J. L. Austin, whose ideas about speech acts and performativity have enlivened not only formalist studies but also studies of gender and ethnicity, have also been included among the classic texts. Some selections have been added to previous segments: A portion of *Phaedrus* has been added to the work of Plato; the Marx section has been expanded to include writings on alienation from the 1844 Manuscripts. Lovers of Nietzsche will be glad that we have supplemented *The Birth of Tragedy* with selections on aesthetics from his late work, *Twilight of the Idols*, and with his pivotal essay on language and culture, "On Truth and Lie in an Extra-Moral Sense," Freud has been expanded greatly, adding the passage on the Medusa's head that inspired Hélène Cixous, the literary essay on "The Uncanny," and key selections from *The Interpretation of Dreams*.

Part Two contains 110 readings grouped into ten chapters on contemporary critical trends. Chapters carried over from previous editions have been refurbished to include theorists we had previously neglected (Bertolt Brecht, Michel de Certeau, Slavoj Žižek) and now also include some essays that previously had merely been summarized in my introductory comments, such as Louis Althusser's analysis of Ideological State Apparatuses. Three essays using cognitive psychology have been incorporated into the existing chapter on reader-response theory. And, as mentioned earlier, there are two new chapters, Postcolonialism and Ethnic Studies, and Theorizing Postmodernism. Throughout, many more selections by women and persons of color have been incorporated — more, in fact, than appear in other anthologies of theory and criticism. We have also rethought the decision in the second edition to eliminate applications of theory to specific literary texts, so that the new edition includes full-scale applications of structuralism, deconstruction, reader-response, feminism and queer theory, cultural studies, and so on.

The major new feature in the third edition is the inclusion of short selections showing theorists in explicit dialogue with each other, sometimes as constructive critique (like Aijaz Ahmad's commentary on Fredric Jameson or Houston Baker's suggestions for Henry Louis Gates), sometimes in full attack mode (as with Frank Lentricchia's assault on the New Historicism and Martha Nussbaum's snarky review of Judith Butler). These dialogues were primarily intended to display literary and cultural theory as a theater of controversy, but they have also enabled us to include many important thinkers that could not otherwise be accorded a full selection. And let me mention in passing that these dialogues also appear in Part One, juxtaposing Leo Tolstoy with Plato, Barbara Herrnstein Smith with David Hume, and Raymond Williams with Percy Bysshe Shelley.

Other changes were made in direct response to what some fifty users of the previous edition requested. The survey of readers wanted more Saussure, Barthes, Derrida, and Lacan than we had previously offered, and we have hastened to oblige. We also listened and abridged when you said you didn't teach in their entirety some of the longer essays by Longinus and Dryden. We have corrected all the typos brought to my attention over the life of the previous edition. And there were dozens of other changes that the user of earlier editions will notice, including new essays by familiar authors as well as new exemplars of familiar modes of theory. All in all, something over half of the contents and editorial materials in the third edition of *The Critical Tradition* are new and, we are confident, enormously improved.

"THE DULL DUTY OF AN EDITOR"

Because the critical tradition contains such varied ideas in such complex relationships, extensive apparatus — what Alexander Pope disdained as "dull duty" — has been provided to make the works collected here easier to assimilate. *The Critical Tradition* begins with an introduction that explores the ways in which theorists have tried to chart the terrain of criticism. The first half of this introduction describes the ineluctable fourfold classifications of critical theories from M. H. Abrams's *The Mirror and the Lamp*, evaluates the powers and limitations of the Abrams map, its general biases and unspoken assumptions, and then discusses other quite different ways of mapping critical tasks and methods. New to the introduction is a section that focuses on the relation of theory to the sort of textual criticism and analysis students will find in their research into academic journals, with some practical advice on how to "unpack" the elaborate skein of theoretical assumptions that underlie and imbue literary discourse in what we ironically call our "post-theoretical" age.

In Part One of *The Critical Tradition*, each reading is prefaced with an extensive headnote that places the text within the context of the author's life and works, explores the key issues of each reading and its relationship with other readings, and occasionally analyzes troublesome twists in the argumentation. For the readings by contemporary academic theorists and critics composing Part Two, the biographical headnotes before each selection are necessarily briefer, but each of the ten chapters is prefaced by a substantial introduction. These introductions, addressed to the serious reader, cover the origins, the general approach, and the variations in theory and practice of each of the nine movements, and provide equivalent coverage for the issue under debate. Individual readings are analyzed primarily to mark out their place within larger critical trends. The introductions try to navigate between the Scylla of commentary that expresses only the prejudices of the editor and the Charybdis of neutralist mumbling that expresses nothing. The intent was to provide an even-handed overview of each critical movement or issue showing both its power and its limitations. Finally, following the headnotes to Part One and the introductions to Part Two, selected bibliographies direct the interested reader to further works by and about the authors and their critical approaches. The texts in both parts are annotated to save the reader's time in tracking down allusions, to highlight the cross-references between one text and another, and to fill in the argument where the text has been abridged.

Although Part Two sorts its selections into ten "schools" and "debates," it need hardly be said that even centrally placed "members" of a "school" swear no allegiance to its doctrines; despite the "fallacies" and "heresies" of the New Critics, there were no recorded excommunications. We need to bear in mind that some theorists bridge categories, as is becoming more and more usual these days. Pierre Bourdieu, one of the theoretical lights of cultural studies, is a Marxist sociologist, while Julia Kristeva, here represented as a feminist, has made major contributions to psychoanalysis and semiotics. Michel Foucault, influential everywhere these days, rightly appears in three chapters of the book, as a poststructuralist, as an influence on the New Historicism, and as a gender theorist. Fredric Jameson, America's foremost theorist of Marxism, has also contributed to debates on postcolonialism and postmodernism. Therefore, an additional table of contents that places theorists in alternative categories has been provided for Part Two. The book concludes with an index to proper names and major critical terms, which, together with the cross-references in the annotations, should help the reader understand the shifting skeins of influence upon which the critical tradition is built. "Let us now be told no more," as Samuel Johnson said with both weariness and pride, "of 'the dull duty of an editor.'"

ACKNOWLEDGMENTS

Although the title page might suggest a solo performance, no book the size and complexity of *The Critical Tradition* can be created alone. At every stage, from the initial impulse to produce the book to the final corrections in this revised edition, I have depended on the assistance and collaboration of colleagues within academia and publishing. At Bedford Books, first and foremost were Chuck Christensen and Joan Feinberg, who believed in the project and made it happen. Steve Scipione developed the first edition and worked out the myriad details that made it the teaching text it became, and Kathy Retan masterminded the adventurous revision that reshaped the book for the needs of the twenty-first century. The voluminous and candid dialogue between us (often grumpy on my side) gave me necessary perspective on my flippant prejudices and deep convictions and helped me recognize the difference between them. Aron Keesbury, Kathy's assistant, handled numerous details that came to my attention only when he caught and corrected my own errors and inadvertencies. For both editions, Elizabeth Schaaf headed the production crew that turned messy masses of manuscript into aesthetically pleasing objects, and Julie Sullivan undertook the unenviable task for the revision of threading a mass of new material with what was retained from the first edition, keeping continuity and consistency in the project. Having done it myself for the first edition, I am in a better position than most authors to appreciate the exhausting and intricate negotiations heroically performed by Margaret Hyre in procuring permissions for the second edition. For the third edition, I owe thanks again to Steve Scipione for helping me to imagine how the book might be improved as a pedagogical tool, and to Emily Berleth, who shouldered the task of guiding an even larger and more daunting manuscript through the production process. Thanks also are due to Linda DeMasi, the project manager, who struggled heroically with the logistical problems of a book being edited in the United States but typeset in India: through three sets of corrected page proofs she endured and ultimately prevailed. Jennifer Blanksteen deserves a sentence, indeed a paragraph, to herself: She not only cleared permissions (a task that can drive anyone crazy) but developed the book, conferring about the thousands of decisions that had to be made, under pressure of deadlines, with unfailing intelligence and energy, wit and good humor. She is one awesome lady, and I hope her daughters and husband — from whom our Herculean task constantly distracted her — continue to value her as she deserves. I am also indebted to Carrie Shanafelt, my brilliant and charming research assistant for Spring 2005, who contributed dozens of cogent and erudite headnotes, unacknowledged except here, that kept us from falling off schedule.

I am also thankful to the literary critics, theorists, and teachers of literary theory who, during the development of one or both editions, have provided helpful suggestions and pointed comments on the choice of contents and editorial materials. They include Beate Allert of Purdue University; Robert F. Barsky of Vanderbilt University; Raymond L. Baubles Jr., of Western Connecticut State University; Michael Beard of the University of North Dakota; Greg Bentley of Mississippi State University; Jill Benton of Pitzer College; Kathryn N. Benzel of the University of Nebraska, Kearney; Glen Brewster of Westfield State College; Theron Britt of the University of Memphis; Suzanne L. Bunkers of Mankato State University; William E. Cain of Wellesley College; Wes Chapman of Illinois Wesleyan University; Joseph J. Colavito of the University of Arizona; Glen Colburn of Morehead State University; Michael Colson of Allan Hancock College; Frederick Crews of the University of California, Berkeley; Ashley J. Cross of Manhattan College; Robert Denham of Roanoke College; Victoria deZwaan of Trent University; Joseph Dupras of the University of Alaska, Fairbanks; Bernard Duyfhuizen of the University of Wisconsin, Eau Claire; Neil Easterbrook of Texas Christian University; Marilyn Edelstein of Santa Clara University; Lee Erickson of Marshall University; Anne Fairbanks of Hastings College; Susan Felch of Calvin College; Thomas Ferraro of Duke University; Daniel Fineman of Occidental College; Jane Fisher of Canisius College; Peter Fitz of the University of Baltimore; Elizabeth Flynn of Michigan Technological University; Joseph Francavilla of Columbus State University; Dean Franco of Wake Forest University; Stephen Goldsmith of the University of California, Berkeley; Stephen Greenblatt of Harvard University; Marshall Gregory of Butler University; Robin Grey of the University of Illinois, Chicago; Susan Gubar of Indiana University Bloomington; Nira Gupta-Casale of Kean University; David Halliburton of Stanford University; Michael Hancher of the University of Minnesota; James Hans of Wake Forest University; Barbara Leah Harmon of Wellesley College; Lee Harrod of The College of New Jersey; Cary Henson of the University of Wisconsin, Oshkosh; Frank Hoffman of Susquehanna University; Norman N. Holland of the University of Florida; John R. Holmes of the Franciscan University of Steubenville; Harriet Hustis of The College of New Jersey; Earl Ingersoll of the State University of New York, Brockport; Michael C. Jordan of the University of St. Thomas; Linda Karell of Montana State University, Bozeman; Meegan Kennedy of Harvard University;

William Kenney of Manhattan College; Mark Koch of St. Mary's College; Catherine Gunther Kodat of Hamilton College; Augustus M. Kolich of St. Xavier University; Janet Sanders Land of Gardner-Webb University; Page R. Laws of Norfolk State University; L. B. Lebim of Lock Haven University; Pericles Lewis of Yale University; Mary Libertin of Shippensburg University of Pennsylvania; Lawrence Lipking of Northwestern University; Jun Liu of California State University, Los Angeles; Zhang Longxi of the University of California, Riverside; Carol Schaechterle Loranger of Wright State University; Paul Lukacs of Loyola College in Maryland; Kathleen Lundeen of Western Washington University; Steven Mailloux of the University of California, Irvine; Bruce Martin of Drake University; Felix Martínez-Bonati of Columbia University; Bill McCarron of East Texas State University; Janet McNew of Illinois Wesleyan University; Robert McRuer of George Washington University; Michael Meyer of the University of Connecticut, Storrs; Nancy K. Miller of the Graduate Center, City University of New York; Christian Moraru of the University of North Carolina, Greensboro; Eileen Morgan of the State University of New York, Oneonta; Bradford Mudge of the University of Colorado, Denver; Michael Murrin of the University of Chicago; James W. Newcomb of Memphis State University; Eric W. Nye of the University of Wyoming; Charles O'Neill of St. Thomas Aquinas College; Edward O'Shea of the State University of New York, Oswego; Windy C. Petrie of Colorado Christian University; Jan Plug of the University of Western Ontario; Mary Poovey of New York University; Ronald Primeau of Central Michigan University; Catherine Rainwater of St. Edward's University; Luz Elena Ramirez of California State University, San Bernardino; Herman Rapaport of Wayne State University; James A. W. Rembert of The Citadel; Michael Karl Ritchie of Arkansas Tech University; Lance Rivers of Lake Superior State University; Thomas M. Rivers of the University of Southern Indiana; John G. Roberts of the University of Rochester; Doug Robinson of the University of Mississippi; Lisa Schnell of the University of Vermont, Burlington; Michael Sexson of Montana State University; William Sheidley of the University of Southern Colorado; Faiza Shereen of the University of Dayton; Elaine Showalter of Princeton University; Anne B. Simpson of California State Polytechnic University, Pomona; Barbara Herrnstein Smith of Duke University; Mark Trevor Smith of Southwest Missouri State University; Jack Solomon of California State University, Northridge; James Sosnoski of Miami University; Patricia Meyer Spacks of the University of Virginia; Henry Staten of the University of Washington; Gary Lee Stonum of Case Western Reserve University; David Suchoff of Colby College; Susan Suleiman of Harvard University; James Sullivan of California State University at Los Angeles; Leon Surette of the University of Western Ontario; John Sykes of Wingate College; Brook Thomas of the University of California, Irvine; Calvin Thomas of Georgia State University; Jane Tompkins of Duke University; Steven Venturino of Loyola University; David Wagenknecht of Boston University; Jim Warren of Washington and Lee University; Michelle Warren of the University of Miami; Jack W. Weaver of Winthrop University; Keith Welsh of Webster University; David Willbern of the State University of New York, Buffalo; Dolora Chapelle Wojciehowski of the University of Texas, Austin; Steven J. Zani of Lamar University; and Clarisse Zimra of Southern

Illinois University, Carbondale. While all these scholars and teachers have influenced the book's form and content, I would like to single out for particular mention James Phelan of Ohio State University, who read the entire manuscript of the first edition, whose perceptive commentary helped me to clarify and rethink my entrenched opinions, and whose unfailing tact and generosity of spirit made his suggestions easy to take.

In addition to these participants in formal reviewing procedures, the table of contents and sections of the manuscript were read by friends whose formal or casual suggestions I have shamelessly incorporated. These include Don Bialostosky of Pennsylvania State University; Brian Corman of the University of Toronto (who told me all about Aphra); Bob Folkenflik of the University of California, Irvine; Susan K. Harris and William J. Harris of the University of Kansas; Donald McQuade of the University of California, Berkeley; Laura Wadenpfuhl of New Jersey City University (who never spared me); and my colleagues at Queens College and/or the Graduate Center of the City University of New York: Barbara Bowen (who talked about gender and cultural studies with me), Nancy Comley (who has read everything), Tom Hayes (who helped me with Lacan and Žižek), Carrie Hintz, David Kazanjian (who taught me how to teach Spivak), Bill Kelly, Steve Kruger (who put me straight about queer theory), Rich McCoy, Charles Molesworth, Tony O'Brien, Blanford Parker, Michael Sargent (who explained the *querelle*), Barbara Shollar, Chris Suggs, Joe Wittreich, and Susan Zimmerman. My research for the third edition was carried out at the British Library, the Mina Rees Library at the CUNY Graduate Center, the New York Public Library, the Rosenthal Library of Queens College, and, hey, over the Internet. The index was produced and compiled on my own little Dell computer, and you don't want to know.

In closing, I recall those who taught me literary theory at the University of Chicago, including Wayne Booth, Norman Mclean, and Elder Olson, in whose criticism courses I sat with varying degrees of comprehension. At times I hear also the ghostly voices of R. S. Crane and Richard McKeon, and of Shelly Sacks, who taught me the uses of theory. From the thousands of students in the undergraduate and graduate literary criticism courses I have taught at Queens College and the CUNY Graduate Center over the last twenty-five years, I have learned what was clear and what opaque about the theoretical texts we studied together. I have tried to put some of that knowledge to work in this book, but I plan to continue learning from them.

And finally, I dedicate this third edition of *The Critical Tradition* to Gabriel Richter, the boy I love, who once thought all Western philosophy but a footnote to Play-Doh, and is now reading cognitive theory and psychology at McGill. *Eheu fugaces labuntur anni . . .*

Contents

Part Two

CONTEMPORARY TRENDS IN LITERARY CRITICISM

747

INTRODUCTION

Everybody . . . would be willing to admit, as a general proposition, that the critical faculty is lower than the inventive. But is it true that criticism is really, in itself, a baneful and injurious employment?
> — MATTHEW ARNOLD, *The Function of Criticism at the Present Time* (1864)

What if criticism is a science as well as an art?
> — NORTHROP FRYE, *The Function of Criticism at the Present Time* (1949)

Criticism is not literature, and the pleasure of criticism is not the pleasure of literature. . . . But experience suggests that the two pleasures go together, and the pleasure of criticism makes literature and its pleasure the more readily accessible.
> — LIONEL TRILLING, preface to *Literary Criticism: An Introductory Reader* (1970)

The . . . general and well publicized curricular crisis of the "humanities" suggests that the ambivalence of theory with respect to the literary syllabus is itself related to long-term developments in the educational institution. For the "canon of theory" introduces into the institutional context of literary pedagogy . . . a syllabus whose symptomatic function is to signify precisely methodological "rigor," rather than the taste or discrimination which for so long determined the ideological protocols of literary criticism.
> — JOHN GUILLORY, *Cultural Capital* (1993)

In the Socratic dialogues of the early fourth century B.C.E., Plato raised skeptical questions about the value of art and literature that have provoked responses from artists and philosophers from Aristotle's day to our own. In striving to rescue poetry from the exile to which Socrates had condemned it, the defenders of literature have had to recast the questions Plato answered with such assurance. We are still asking the same questions today: What is the nature of the work of art? What are its sources in the artist, in the literary scene, in the society for which it is produced? What are its properties, uses, powers, and value? How is the nature of literature circumscribed by the properties of language itself, by the gender of the writer or the reader, by the intrinsic limitations of the human mind? What are literature's effects on individuals and on communities? Questions like these remain at the heart of the critical tradition. They have inspired an ongoing conversation that is continually modified by new voices from different cultural matrices, which join in with other critical languages, other norms, other views of the world. The proliferation in the past three decades of new critical theories and practices is a sign that the inquiring and speculative spirit of that critical tradition is thriving as never before. But the very abundance of voices and vocabularies can be intimidating to the newcomer seeking to enter the conversation.

The discussion that follows is intended as a guide to the two key problems of theoretical discourse: synthesis and analysis. The first is aimed at understanding the relationships of the great variety of critical theories to each other, drawing maps of the critical terrain, elucidating the various ways our ideas about the nature of literature and the tasks of criticism have been organized. Learning this terrain is the surest way to take one's own bearings and find one's own voice. The second is aimed at understanding how to take critical discourse apart, how to unpack the theoretical assumptions that lie underneath the surface — which, as we shall see, is something one can do best when already provided with a map.

MAPPING CRITICAL THEORIES

M. H. Abrams and the Traditional Classification

In his influential treatise on romantic views of art, *The Mirror and the Lamp* (1953), the literary historian M. H. Abrams distinguished among four different types of literary theories, and the map he drew of these distinctions is still valuable as a place to start thinking about the history of criticism.

Historically, the first type, the mimetic theories of classical antiquity, focused on the relationship between the outside world and the work of art. These theories posited that poetry could best be understood as an imitation, a representation, a copy of the physical world.

The second type, the rhetorical, emphasized the relationship between the work of art and its audience — either how the literary work should be formed to please and instruct its audience, or what that audience should be like in order to appreciate literature correctly. These theories held that to attain its proper effect, the poem must be shaped by both the poet's innate talent and the rules of art. Such theories, most popular during the later classical period, the Middle Ages, and the Renaissance, began to decline toward the end of the eighteenth century.

The third type, which Abrams called expressive, stressed the relationship between the work of art and the artist, particularly the special faculties of mind and soul that the artist brings to the act of creation. These theories proliferated during the late eighteenth and most of the nineteenth centuries.[1]

---

[1]Although it is possible to specify when mimetic, rhetorical, and expressive theories flourished, it must be understood that all three continue to be influential. Even when theory is not progressing along certain lines, the old questions are asked of new texts. Thus the movie reviewer who wonders whether *Braveheart* accurately depicts battle conditions in medieval Scotland is as much a mimetic critic as Aristotle.

The fourth type, which developed around the beginning of the twentieth century, played down the connections of the work of art with the exterior world, the audience, and the artist. These formal theories stressed the purely aesthetic relationship between the parts of a work of literature, analyzing its "themes" or "motifs" as if a literary text were a form of classical music or an abstract painting, and strove for a quasi-scientific objectivity. Such theories probably prevail today, since thousands of teachers and scholars who might deny allegiance to any theory actually adhere to formalist principles. In their explicit claims to possessing the highest truth about literature, however, formal theories now face a great deal of competition.

One version of the Abrams map might look like Figure 1. The world of criticism is not as clear or as neat as this diagram suggests. Abrams himself points out that a label such as "mimetic" or "expressive" indicates only the primary orientation of a theory: "Any reasonable theory takes account of all four elements." A mimetic theorist (such as Aristotle) might have much to say about how works of art affect an audience or about the artist, but his views often derive directly from his mimetic principles. When Aristotle suggests in *Poetics*, Chapter 4, for example, that poets of noble character took up the art of tragedy and those of baser character created comedy, his rationale is that nobler poets are better able to understand and then to imitate in poetic language the noble characters of tragedy. In this sense, Aristotle's mimetic orientation comes through even when he takes up the problem of poetic creativity.

Abrams's notion of critical orientation helps us distinguish the disparate rationales behind the same piece of conventional wisdom. A mimetic critic, for instance, might enjoin an aspiring poet to observe human nature well, the more accurately to imitate human actions in his poetry. A rhetorical critic might advise the poet in the very same words, but in order to prompt the poet to discover what pleases the various classes and age groups that comprise his audience. As the notes to Part One of

Figure 1

this collection show, the various dicta of Plato and Aristotle, shorn of their mimetic logic, reappear in the works of rhetorical, expressive, and objective critics to bolster markedly different arguments.

Each of these four orientations covers a great deal of ground, and the fact that two critics are both mimetic in orientation does not guarantee that they agree. Quite the contrary: Whereas critics with different principles merely tend to miss each other's points, those who share a theoretical orientation are likely to clash in an interesting and violent way. A brief consideration of Plato (p. 25), Aristotle (p. 55), and Plotinus (p. 109), three of the more influential mimetic critics, can reveal how some of these disagreements take shape.

Differences within Theoretical Orientations

Plato's view of art derives from a complicated metaphysics and a relatively simple notion of imitation. Imitation, for Plato, is the creation of an *eidolon*. The artist makes an "image" — a degraded copy — of the external world, which is analogous to the image formed in a mirror (it lasts longer than a mirror image, but, not being eternal, the difference is not significant). Plato's worldview is idealist, which means that he takes the material world, the world of the senses, to be a copy of an eternal world of Ideas. Works of art, in their turn, are copies of material things, and hence copies of copies. For Plato, art is therefore an activity inferior to artisanship (the making of useful objects), first, because art copies rather than creates a material object, and second, because an artist needs only to know the appearances of things, not their real nature. Plato also worried that imitation might weaken the individual spirit by arousing passion and corrupt the body politic through its distance from the truth.

Six centuries later, the Neoplatonic philosopher Plotinus developed a mimetic theory of art that generally conformed with that of Plato but drew vastly different conclusions about the value of art. In the idealism of Plotinus, although imitation is still basically copying, the artist imitates not the material world but the Ideas themselves. A sculptor carving a statue of Zeus makes not a marble copy of a flesh-and-blood man but a representation of what Power and Majesty might be like if those concepts could become visible. The Idea of Beauty resides within the artist, shaping his conceptions as it shapes all beauty in nature. For Plotinus, the artist is superior to the artisan because Beauty, the Idea informing the artist's craft, is higher than Utility, which informs that of the artisan. Whereas Plotinus accepted Plato's metaphysics and his notion of imitation, Plato's pupil Aristotle fundamentally disagreed with both. A materialist who did not believe in an eternal world of Ideas, Aristotle saw everything as subject to process, growth, and change. Poets, by imitating the process by which one state of affairs metamorphoses into another, capture in language the general principles of human action, which are among the most important things one can know. Nor is imitation merely copying: The poet, in imitating human action, purifies it of the dross of the accidental and the incidental, unifies it into a plot, beautifies it with expressive language, and molds it into a concrete whole with the capacity to command the emotions. Those feelings, aroused and guided by a complex imitation, can cleanse rather than weaken the individual, and can serve the state rather than harm it, by draining off passions and frustrations that might lead to political instability.

Just as mimetic thinkers could agree that art was primarily a matter of imitation but differ about what the world was like, what aspect of that world the artists imitated, and what sort of process imitation actually was, so rhetorical theorists also had their differences about the ends and means of artistic production. The main question for them was how to construct a work of art so that it would affect an audience properly. Horace (p. 82), one of the earliest and most influential of the rhetorical theorists, thought that poems should "either delight, or instruct, or if possible accomplish both ends at once," but later critics subtly redrew his specifications. For moralists like Dante (p. 120) or Samuel Johnson (p. 210), the more significant purpose was instruction, delight being merely a means to that didactic end. Sir Philip Sidney (p. 132) and John Dryden (p. 160) gave delight a more equal role. Although many theorists took "delight" and "instruction" as general and indivisible qualities to be sought in poetry, others elaborately classified the arts according to the varieties of pleasure and benefit that should reside in each.

And for which audience should the poet write? Horace's audience is apparently limited to the upper classes — the *senatores* and *equites* of the early Roman Empire; what the middle-class sellers of beans care about is not the concern of the aristocratic writer. Sidney assumes a universal contemporary audience, but there too the universe may be implicitly restricted to gentlemen — indeed, perhaps even English gentlemen, whom Sidney thinks provincial relative to those in Italy, even though they may be models of cultivation relative to those of Ireland and Scotland. Dryden's debaters in *An Essay of Dramatic Poesy* posit national audiences with specific national characteristics, not a strange move for a piece written during the Restoration, when King Charles and his court had arrived from a long exile in France. And in Samuel Johnson's analysis, Shakespeare's greatness inheres in his ability to affect people of other countries and much later eras. In the eighteenth century, when the question of taste had become an important one in literary theory, Horace's problem, the adaptation of work to audience, had, in effect, been inverted. For critics like David Hume (p. 231), the most important issue was not how poems should be shaped to please audiences but why some members of the audience were better adapted to appreciate the arts than others. (This is an issue that is not likely to come up until the audience for art has become split between different classes that have been educated in different ways.)

In similar fashion, expressive theorists concurred that art manifested the artist's sensibility even as they disputed the source of that sensibility. Many nineteenth-century Romantics agreed that the key faculty was the imagination — although they differed sharply on how that faculty worked. Later expressive theorists found the source of poetry in the artist's unconscious mind. For one group of psychological critics, the followers of Sigmund Freud (p. 497), a poem, like a dream, was the imagined fulfillment of an individual artist's unconscious wish; for another group, the followers of Carl Gustav Jung (p. 542), all art evinced archetypal imagery common to the entire human race. For critics like Northrop Frye (p. 691), the artist expresses the "dream of mankind," which is contained not in the collective unconscious but in a literary tradition that speaks through us all. For sociohistorical critics, followers of Karl Marx (p. 397) or Hippolyte Taine, artists inadvertently expressed the ideologies of their times, conveying their understanding of the world in ways determined by their position within the class struggle and their moment in history.

In the twentieth century, formalists have differed about both what sort of form should be sought and where it could be found. The New Critics discovered form in a dialectical thrust and counterthrust of themes; neo-Aristotelians in a complex linkage of plot, language, technique, and purpose; and structuralists and semioticians in repeated patterns of language. Just as in the eighteenth century, there is a split between those critics investigating the various principles of form within literature and those exploring the reader's capacity to discover form or to supply it when it is not to be found. These variations and developments within major critical orientations seem to embody the behavior of biological organisms that proliferate to fill up a new ecological niche. Once a mode like expressive criticism had become established, it was almost inevitable that every aspect of the poet's psyche, conscious and unconscious, would be held up to scrutiny as a source of the creative spirit. A more difficult question is why changes in critical orientation occur — why mimetic criticism gave way to rhetorical or rhetorical to expressive.

Such epochs seem to be analogous to scientific revolutions, described by Thomas Kuhn in *The Structure of Scientific Revolutions* (1962). Over one or two generations, the previous "paradigm," a vast structure of assumptions, principles, and methods, gives way and is replaced by another for a variety of reasons — new facts that need explaining, new theories that cannot be reconciled with the present paradigm, a scientific community that has lost intellectual cohesion over its basic principles. The causes of such "revolutions" in critical tradition, where Kuhn's model is less exact, might include the creation of new literary works and styles; shifts in the canon (the informal list of the literary works that are held to be significant); developments in the other arts, in philosophy, and in other humanistic disciplines; and changes in politics and society.

Changes in Theoretical Paradigms

The first critical revolution was when Plato and his doctrine of imitation displaced the Sophists, who saw literature as essentially a function of language. Because few writings of the Sophists have survived, too little is known about that revolution to hazard any explanation of Plato's triumph. The second major shift, from mimetic to rhetorical criticism, might have developed partly from a misreading of Aristotle's *Poetics*, a document of enormous authority, if one more respected than understood. (As late as the age of Dryden and Johnson, critics quoted — or misquoted — Aristotle while ignoring his central ideas, methods, and principles.) Though the *Poetics* views art as the imitation of human action, the product is not a simple copy. It differs from the natural process it represents in its form, its material (language instead of action), its technique, and its purpose. These four "causes," as Aristotle termed them, all contribute equally in defining the special character of a particular work of art. But one of them — purpose — is, so to speak, more equal than the rest, since it largely dictates the others. Purpose, for

Aristotle, refers to the potential capacity of a work to move human beings in a certain way, not its actual effect on an audience.

One can easily imagine, however, how internal purpose could be altered to external effect, and how the four-cause structure of Aristotelian imitation might be simplified to the means/end argument we find in Horace. There were surely external reasons as well for mimetic theories to give way to rhetorical ones. The development in late republican Rome of a publishing industry (using hand-copying), serving a far-flung and disparate literary audience, may have fostered a critical scene different from that of post-Periclean Athens, where the poet's audience was the tight-knit coterie within the polis.

The revolution from rhetorical to expressive criticism may also have been partly the result of social change. The reading public grew enormously in the eighteenth century as formerly illiterate classes became avid consumers of literature. The new cadres of less-educated readers made taste an issue in criticism as it had never been before. As theorists investigating taste examined the inner experience of readers, they found that the faculties behind good taste, the capacities that made ideal readers — delicate imagination, good sense, wide experience — were the same as those that made the best poets. Creation and appreciation were more closely allied than one might have supposed, for the audience passively reenacted what the poets had actively created. Poetic creativity was therefore a refined but not a mysterious process: It could be investigated and understood.

The twentieth-century shift from expressive to formal criticism was not a total revolution: Biographical, psychological, sociological, and myth criticism continued to develop alongside the several varieties of formalism. But in a sense, formalism grew out of the exhaustion of expressive criticism. Literature, once thought to grow organically from the artistic imagination, which, as Samuel Taylor Coleridge (p. 319) said, was "coexistent with the conscious will," was increasingly seen as deriving from forces beyond the artist's control (milieu, class, unconscious drives, the collective unconscious). The poet appeared to be less an agent and more a catalyst in the act of creation,[2] while at the same time, poetry, like music, painting, and sculpture, became increasingly abstract. And in the demotic twentieth century, audience reaction has seemed an even less plausible guide to art than in the eighteenth. The eighteenth-century split between refined and popular art, which had been partially repaired during the Victorian era, re-emerged in the 1890s to become an ongoing fixture of twentieth-century culture.

As a result, criticism was left with almost nowhere to go. With the principle of imitation stymied by the vogue of abstraction, the fashion of the impersonal artist nullifying the romantic appeal to expression, and the fragmented and unreliable audience undermining rhetorical criticism, the only avenue left was an appeal to pure form. These developments seem to have been felt all over Europe and America after World War I, and they culminated in a variety of formalist movements: Russian formalism,

---

[2]The cult of impersonality in poetry and of the poet as the catalyst will be found in the criticism of T. S. Eliot (p. 534), one of the founders of the New Criticism.

structuralism, the New Criticism, neo-Aristotelianism. Another factor, exterior to art and criticism, was the development of the modern university, within which departments of literature, structured like those of the natural and social sciences, may have sought for a comparably "objective" and "scientific" mode of literary study, which the varieties of formalism could supply.[3]

During the most recent revolution, which began in the years since Abrams drew up his map, many literary theorists have viewed literature as the free play of signifiers. In this view, words — the signifiers — no longer have an innocent connection to their meanings — the signified; and the relation of language and meaning is not transparent. Instead of testifying to the truth and beauty of the world, instead of expressing the personality (or impersonality) of the author, instead of delighting and instructing its audience, instead of presenting an abstract aesthetic form, language now expresses the circularity of meaning, contemplates the paradoxes of its own making. The text is no longer the poem isolated in the center of the diagram. Rather textuality — the condition of inscription within language — is implicated in all our knowledge of the world, of reading, of expression. History is no longer the inferior of poetry, as Aristotle thought, nor its master, as Karl Marx suggested. History cannot even be opposed to poetry, for both of them are equally texts; they may be seen as discursive practices, modes of power/knowledge that need to be analyzed using the rules of New Historicism and cultural studies. Thus we have returned full circle to the position of the Sophists, for whom everything was ruled by the art of rhetoric. A key question for the future of theory is whether the key topics of textuality, language, and discursive practice will remain at the center of critical study, or whether some new revolution may not lurk over the horizon.

Other Maps of the Critical Terrain

Abrams's map of the spectrum of critical theory is useful as far as it goes. But maps have a way of reducing the number of dimensions, inevitably distorting even as they clarify the actual landscape. The points of Abrams's compass should not be taken as natural, self-evident, or unquestionable. Like any other theoretical construct, Abrams's map includes areas of blindness as well as insight, and its limitations derive from its unstated assumptions. By differentiating between "rhetorical" and "objective" theories, for example, Abrams seems to presume that the text can have a meaning apart from what it means to its readers. In practice, however, many formalist critics have relied heavily for their analysis on what an "ideal" or "potential" reader would make of the text. Nor can Abrams's map comfortably accommodate forms of criticism (Marxist and otherwise) that view the text, author, and reader as determined, collectively or separately, by the processes of history. (Abrams may think that an author expresses his or her age, but while this will do for some forms of historical criticism, it will not adequately characterize neo-Marxist criticism, New Historicism, or cultural studies.)

[3]Cf. Richard Ohmann, *English in America* (New York: Oxford University Press, 1976), and Gerald Graff, *Professing Literature: An Institutional History* (Chicago: University of Chicago Press, 1987).

Another limitation of the Abrams map — or at least of how many readers have employed it — is the specious linearity it imposes upon the history of criticism. It seems to imply that mimetic thought was confined to classical antiquity and that everyone shifted from rhetorical to expressive criticism around the end of the eighteenth century. Not only did rhetorical criticism continue to be practiced throughout the nineteenth and twentieth centuries, but (as Robert Marsh has shown) one essential pattern of romantic criticism flourished during what is typically considered the neoclassical period. The prestige of the Abrams map should not mask the importance of other theorists and critics (such as James "Hermes" Harris or Walter Scott) whose work implicitly challenges Abrams's notion of historical succession.

One way of transcending the limitations of the Abrams map is by formulating other maps whose limitations are different. The Abrams map groups literary theories in terms of the critical principle on which each rests. Both R. S. Crane (p. 813) and Norman Friedman have, at different times, constructed a different sort of map to clarify the interrelationships of critical tasks and the variety of approaches to a given literary work. The form of these maps is not a group of adjacent territories but a series of concentric circles, with the work itself in the middle. A single composite map combining the essential features of both might look something like Figure 2 on page 10.

This map is one way of visualizing the relationship of various modes of literary interpretation to one another. Its bias is its suggestion that a poem is determined most intimately by the requirements of form, both its own organic shape and the institutional shapes that culture bequeaths to art. (For example, the terseness of a sonnet — its fourteen-line structure — is a formal issue.) As long as form accounts adequately for an aspect of a given work, no explanation need be sought elsewhere.

But when form is exhausted, one must turn directly to the poet, both to the poet's conscious life (biographical interpretation) and to the poet's unconscious fantasies and defenses (psychological interpretation). The circle is broader here, too, because what biographical and psychological interpretation reveals will cover the whole of the artist's work. Still broader modes of interpretation, sociological and historical, will link that work with others written by authors of the same class in the same era — or explain the differences among works written from different class perspectives and at different times. Broadest of all (and hence least explanatory of any given work) are interpretations based on human universals. One such universal is the collective unconscious of Carl Gustav Jung, whose archetypes are said to run through all imaginative literature and art. Another is the ethical wisdom that can give works of literature long-term significance across cultural boundaries.[4]

Neither of these maps of the critical tasks assigns an explicit spot to the most traditional job of the critic: judging the quality of a literary work. In effect, academic critics indicate their preferences by what they choose to spend their time interpreting (although

[4]For further discussion of this "concentric" map of critical theory, see R. S. Crane, "Questions and Answers in the Teaching of Literary Texts," in *The Idea of the Humanities,* vol 2. (Chicago: University of Chicago Press, 1966); and Norman Friedman, "Pluralism Exemplified: *Great Expectations* and *The Great Gatsby,*" in *Form and Meaning in Fiction* (Athens: University of Georgia Press, 1975).

Figure 2

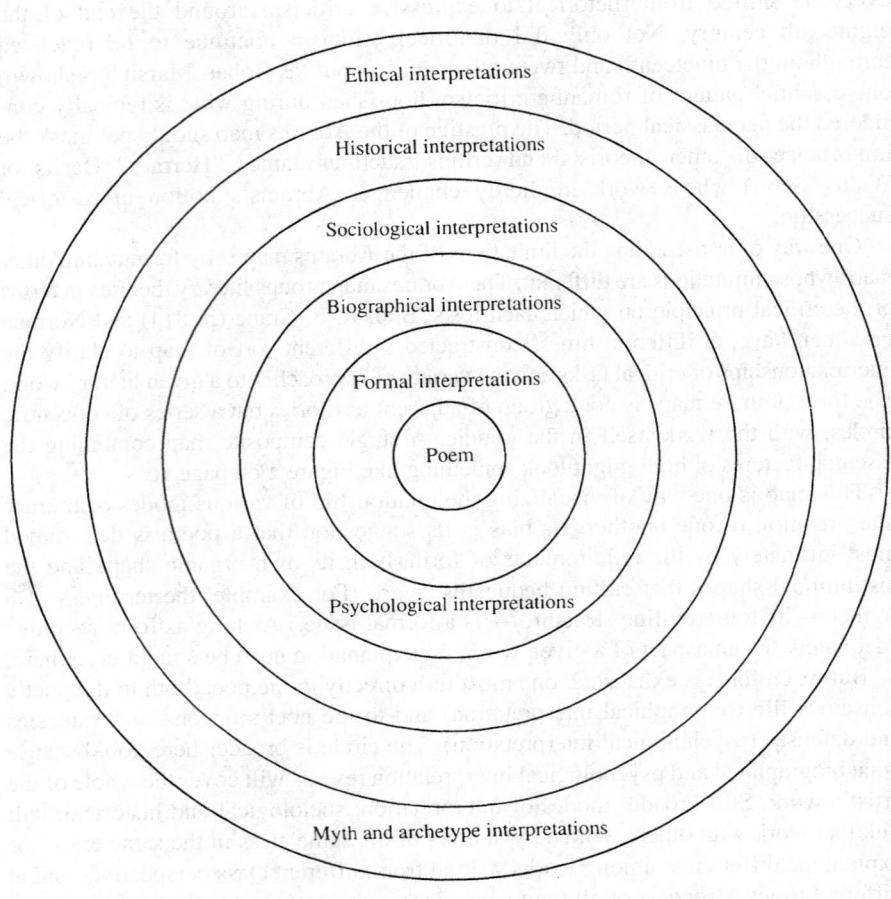

Ethical interpretations

Historical interpretations

Sociological interpretations

Biographical interpretations

Formal interpretations

Poem

Psychological interpretations

Myth and archetype interpretations

this implicit procedure is currently being questioned in a wide-ranging debate over the literary canon). And both maps, it will be noted, place the work in the center, thus implying that the text is the still and stable point around which the complex world of critical thought revolves — which seems reasonable enough, since it went unquestioned for over two thousand years. But this dogma is precisely what a good deal of audience-centered criticism is challenging today, and maps like those of Abrams and Crane/Friedman will be seen as seriously distortive by those who feel that the text is not a stable entity, or that it is determined by the reader. At the same time, any map that placed the reader in the center would be thought severely distorted by critics of many other persuasions. But how is a map to avoid a center?

Semantic Maps: Ideas about Method

One map of sufficient generality and neutrality might be derived from the semantics of Richard McKeon. It would group critics according to their methods, or modes of thought, rather than their central topic. Whereas the Abrams map groups Plato with Aristotle and Plotinus because of the centrality in all three of the principles of mimesis, the McKeon map would emphasize Plato's dialectical method — his habit of analogizing the structure of an upper realm (the world of Ideas) to a lower realm (the world of Matter). Aristotle does not work that way, though Plotinus does. Later critics with different principles, like the expressive critic Samuel Taylor Coleridge and the formal critic Cleanth Brooks (p. 797), adopted the same dialectical method.

Dialectic is one of four abstract methods of proceeding, which include the operational, the problematic, and the logistic, that McKeon calls modes of thought. Walter Davis, in *The Act of Interpretation*, has defined them succinctly: Dialectic is a method of assimilation to a model whereby comprehensive truths are approximated or embodied. Operational thought is a method of discrimination and postulation whereby arbitrary formulations are interpreted in order to distinguish the different legitimate perspectives on a topic. The problematic is a method of inquiry that separates questions into the distinct disciplines in which particular problems are determined and solved. Logistic thought is a method of composition in which irreducible least parts are put together by means of invariable laws.[5]

Dialectical thinkers, such as Plato and Georg Wilhelm Friedrich Hegel (p. 369), see the world as a bound and interconnected whole, with a lower realm (defined by terms like "becoming" or "consciousness") and an upper realm (that of "being" or "self-consciousness"). Such a pattern runs through all of reality, and each aspect of life — religion, politics, ethics, aesthetics — can be analyzed in the same way using analogous terms.

But where dialectical thought is intrinsically interdisciplinary, problematic thought is discipline-bound. Problematic thinkers, such as Aristotle and John Dewey, see the world as containing a number of irreconcilable things, and therefore find no single method that will answer all questions, no single set of terms that can be used to grapple with all problems. The initial task of problematic thinking is to separate disciplines according to their scope, determining their bounds and establishing a method of inquiry according to the nature of the discipline itself.

[5]Walter A. Davis, *The Act of Interpretation: A Critique of Literary Reason* (Chicago: University of Chicago Press, 1978), pp. 93–94. McKeon's grid is too complex to do justice to here, since it contains three other dimensions as well: A dialectical thinker might have comprehensive, simple, reflexive, or actional principles. There are also quadripartite distinctions for a thinker's organization and interpretation. The result is sixteen categories that generate 256 possible positions. McKeon's own mode of thought is, of course, operationalist — his grid is a way of talking about the relation among modes of discourse. Richard McKeon's clearest exposition of his semantics occurs in an essay called "Philosophic Semantics and Philosophic Discovery," widely circulated among his students but unpublished at his death. It was published posthumously in Richard P. McKeon, *Freedom and History and Other Essays*, ed. Zahava K. McKeon (Chicago: University of Chicago Press, 1990). See also his article, "Philosophy and Method," in *Journal of Philosophy* 48 (1951): 653–81; and "Imitation and Poetry," in his book *Thought, Action and Passion* (Chicago: University of Chicago Press, 1954). See also the exposition of McKeon in Walter A. Davis, "Critical Theory and Philosophic Method," in *The Act of Interpretation*, pp. 88–119.

Like dialectical thinkers, operational thinkers take a holistic view of the universe, but for them, the whole is determined not by the nature of things but by the way people view them and talk about them. There is no higher realm of being or truth: The way people see things is all there is. The role of operational thought, in Cicero or in Kenneth Burke (p. 633), is to clarify discourse, to reduce the ambiguities that arise from using common language to describe disparate perspectives.

Like problematic thinkers, logistic thinkers avoid the holistic; but unlike them, they have a single method, which is associated with but not limited to modern science: breaking down phenomena into their least parts and then discovering the laws by which those parts are interrelated. This method is clearest in sciences like chemistry and physics, which are concerned with particles and forces, but a logistic approach has also been made to politics (by Niccolò Machiavelli), ethics (by René Descartes and Thomas Hobbes), and social structure (by Claude Lévi-Strauss, p. 859).

Applied to literature, dialectical thought often takes poetry to be a mode of thinking, while problematic thought often takes it to be a mode of making. Operational thought considers literature as one of many forms of discourse; logistic thought considers literature as data in its scientific analysis of the parts of a text, confident that parts make up a whole. Another map might be created, in other words, gathering dialectical thinkers (like Plato, Plotinus, Coleridge, and Hegel) into one group, problematic thinkers (like Aristotle) into another, logistic thinkers (like Freud or Lévi-Strauss) into a third, and operational thinkers (like Alexander Pope, p. 198, and Kenneth Burke) into a fourth. This map would be more historically complicated than Abrams's since competing modes of thought would operate within a given age, but it would suggest some important linkages across the centuries that should not be ignored.[6]

It is useful to be able to refer to three maps rather than one, but in the long run, all maps are inadequate and none is wholly innocent. That is, any map, no matter how apparently objective and pluralistic, is certain to contain implicit assumptions congenial to some theorists and anathema to others. Abrams's map is that of a historical critic seeking a set of distinctions that will allow him to write a history of critical thought, particularly one that will help him make sense of the transition between the eighteenth century and the romantic age. Crane, the formalist, draws a map that puts formalism in the center, the implicit starting point for any further study of the text. McKeon's map, though contemporary with Abrams's, looks like something a structuralist might devise, with spatial vectors that replace linear causality. Maps are like Ludwig Wittgenstein's ladder in the *Tractatus Logico-Philosophicus* (1922): We can climb only with their assistance, but once we have ascended, we throw them to the ground. Once we outgrow the maps we are given, we learn to do without them — or do as our three mapmakers did: make our own.

---

[6]Applied to the critical revolution of the past three decades, the McKeon map might suggest that operational thought, hitherto one element among many, moved into the vanguard, as once dialectical Marxists began (after Louis Althusser, p. 1263) to consider history as a text rather than a force, as once logistical psychoanalysts began (after Jacques Lacan, p. 1122) to think of the unconscious as a mode of discourse rather than a hidden space. Similarly, the Derridean revolution consists, as Paul de Man (p. 882) has explicitly stated, in the displacement of grammar (in Ferdinand de Saussure's logistical approach, p. 841) by rhetoric.

Traditional literature courses typically impose a method and an order on the disparate texts of one period or one author. In contrast, a course in critical theory will often call into question the very myths of order the traditions of culture have handed down. The study of critical theory tends to raise the ultimate questions about literature and its relation to life without establishing an ultimate order, because the clash of one principle, one method, one logic with another cannot be evaded. To the extent that these oppositions are genuinely understood, we are unlikely to end by resolving their differences into a tidy and harmonious chorus. We can, however, set the voices at play, engage them in contrapuntal dialogue with each other, and enter that dialogue ourselves. And in discoursing with some of the most probing minds that have trained their gaze upon literature, we become participants in an ancient and exalted conversation.

UNPACKING CRITICAL THEORIES

Having first ascended to an overview of theory as a whole, we now need to descend to where theory meets practical criticism, where theory informs talk about literary texts, for there are some very practical reasons why those who want to study literature need to understand literary theory. Any research we do into a poem, a play, or a novel is certain to bring us into contact with contemporary critical essays, essays that, whether or not they explicitly support a particular literary theory, use theoretical vocabulary as a kind of shorthand to indicate the writer's critical assumptions.

At one time academic articles were expected to be written in a transparent language that could be easily understood by the educated layman, but today we need to be able to "unpack" the author's language to discover the theory or, more often, theories underlying the literary discourse. Even book reviews in popular magazines by non-academic writers can have us reaching for the dictionary of literary terms and make us grateful for whatever grounding in theory we have. For instance, in his *New Yorker* review of Colm Tóibín's novel about Henry James, John Updike raises issues about the recent vogue of the historical novel and the postmodern uses of the recorded past in ways that presume that the reader is familiar with theories of postmodernism such as those of Baudrillard (p. 1935) and Jameson (p. 1955) that we find in the final chapter of this book:

> Fiction about actual historical persons, so intrinsically conflicted and impure, feels like part of postmodernism's rampant eclecticism. True, examples exist before the twentieth century, in, say, Tolstoy's depiction of Napoleon and the Russian general Kutuzov in "War and Peace," and in the portraits of the poet Petronius, the emperor Nero, and the saint Peter in Sienkiewicz's "Quo Vadis?" But until truth became thoroughly relative, and image seized priority over fact, and the historical past became an attic full of potentially entertaining trinkets, the famous dead were allowed to rest in the record they left in their documents and documented deeds, in their letters and the accounts of their contemporaries.[7]

Articles in learned journals are even more explicitly steeped in theoretical discourses, and it may be even more difficult to unpack the structure of assumptions, because

---

[7]John Updike, "Silent Master," *The New Yorker* (June 28, 2004): 98.

today's critics are less likely to raise questions that are purely formalist, or purely Marxist, or purely psychoanalytic. More than likely we will discover that we need to unpack a complicated eclectic mixture of literary theories, such as we find in the following example, taken from a remarkable essay by Jay Ladin.[8] Here are the first four paragraphs, in which Ladin makes his intentions and his methods clear — to those who know how to read him:

"So Anthracite, to live": Emily Dickinson and American Literary History[9]

It was R. P. Blackmur who described the phrase "So Anthracite, to live" as "beyond bearing awkward to read" (42).[10] Even now, when we have had seven more decades to grow accustomed to Dickinson's peculiar diction, "So Anthracite, to live" is a shockingly awkward phrase, one of many in Dickinson's unruly oeuvre. Twentieth-century American poetry experiments with norm-defying diction, but how did a woman in the early 1860s come to write phrases such as "So Anthracite, to live"? To put it differently, how should American literary history account for Emily Dickinson?

For the most part, as Margaret Dickie points out, it hasn't. "[E]ven when she is acknowledged as a great writer, Dickinson has never found a central place in American literary history . . . Dickinson remains an anomaly . . . fit into a largely masculine history . . . as an eccentric woman isolated from the main concerns of the day" (186, 187).[11] Dickinson is fortunate to have achieved even anomaly status. Though the nineteenth century was a boom era for American women poets — as Paula Bennett notes, "by the last decades of the century, women poets were beginning to out-publish men even in the most exclusive and prestigious venues" — none but Dickinson have entered the canons of American literary history (216). Dickie argues that the marginalization of Dickinson and eclipse of other nineteenth-century women authors are symptoms of the same androcentric astigmatism and that allotting Dickinson a central role in American literary history will bring other women's achievements into proper focus: "[A] literary history that would include women writers should start with Dickinson and redo the conventional story by fitting literary history around the poet, considering both how she defines the period and how literary history might be redone if she were placed at its center" (187). But fitting American literary history around Dickinson is easier said than done, because both Dickinson's claim to a place in that history and her relegation to its margins derive in large part from the innovative approach to poetic language apparent in phrases such as "So Anthracite, to live" — an approach unparalleled among female (or, for that matter, male) nineteenth-century American poets.

For the most part, scholars have swerved around the question of how Dickinson's use of language relates to that of her contemporaries.[12] Studies that focus on Dickinson's language

[8]*Emily Dickinson Journal* 13, no. 1. (2004): 19–50. [Slightly revised by the author.]

[9]From Emily Dickinson's poem "More Life - went out - when He went," Fr415. [Ladin] [The number Fr415 refers to the numbering of Emily Dickenson's poems as established in the Ralph W. Franklin edition (Cambridge: Harvard University Press, 1999).]

[10]R. P. Blackmur, *Language as Gesture* (New York: Harcourt Brace, 1962).

[11]Margaret Dickie, "Emily Dickinson in History and Literary History," in *Challenging Boundaries: Gender and Periodization*, eds. Joyce W. Warren and Margaret Dickie (Athens: University of Georgia Press, 2000).

[12]Dickie's efforts to recenter American literary history focus on establishing Dickinson as a writer engaged with the major political event of her era — the Civil War. Like most content-oriented studies of Dickinson, Dickie says little about how Dickinson uses language. [Ladin]

tend either to treat her innovations as unique idiosyncrasies or to present her as a sort of wrinkle in time, a modernist poet born fifty or a hundred years early.[13] Both these approaches avoid relating Dickinson's poetics to those of her contemporaries; both isolate Dickinson from her milieu. Historicizing studies that locate Dickinson in cultural context generally ignore the peculiarity of Dickinson's poetic language.[14] Even studies that focus on aspects of Dickinson's poetics, such as Christine Ross' recent "Uncommon Measures," which places Dickinson's prosody in the context of practices promoted in nineteenth-century textbooks, tend to overlook her deviant diction.[15] But to move Dickinson to the center of American literary history — and, by extension, to fashion "a literary history that would include women writers" as central rather than peripheral figures — we must understand how Dickinson's "anomalous" treatment of language relates to the more normative language of her contemporaries. That is, we must read Dickinson's work as an example of, rather than an exception to, nineteenth-century women's poetry, before we can take up Dickie's challenge to "consider both how [Dickinson] defines the period and how literary history" — i.e., the history which leads to and through Dickinson into the feverish poetic innovation of the twentieth century — "might be redone if she were placed at its center."

To bring the common ground between Dickinson's treatment of language and that of her peers into focus, this essay, like many other recent studies of Dickinson, adapts concepts introduced by Mikhail Bakhtin for the study of novels to poetic analysis.[16] Specifically, I argue that Dickinson transfigures common nineteenth-century linguistic materials, themes and rhetorical modes into previously unheard-of diction such as "So Anthracite, to live" by tipping the balance of what Bakhtin calls "centripetal and centrifugal forces" from the centripetally-weighted modes characteristic of most nineteenth-century poetry to centrifugally-weighted modes that became a mainstay of twentieth-century American modernist poetry. Building on recent work by Paula Bennett, I argue that Dickinson's precociously modernist treatment of language represents not an isolated literary mutation, but a conscious engagement with — and reaction against — the flourishing mid-nineteenth-century American women's poetry scene. By examining Dickinson's early letters and poems, I show that Dickinson's precociously modernist configuration of centripetal and centrifugal forces evolved from a technique that Bakhtin calls "novelization" which was common in nineteenth-century prose, and had already been adapted to poetic uses by other nineteenth-century women poets by the 1850s, when Dickinson began to write seriously. Finally, I consider how American literary history looks when Dickinson is placed at its center, focusing on Dickinson's crucial but complex relation to the tradition of

---

[13]For example, Cristanne Miller's landmark study *Emily Dickinson: A Poet's Grammar* catalogues and analyzes the interpretive implications of Dickinson's idiosyncratic diction and punctuation with little attempt to relate Dickinson's techniques to those of other nineteenth-century poets. David Porter's *Dickinson: The Modern Idiom*, the most extended presentation of Dickinson in relation to twentieth-century modernist poetry, argues that Dickinson should be read as the "first practitioner" of "an extreme . . . American modernism" (1). [Ladin]

[14]See for example Domhnall Mitchell's fine *Emily Dickinson: Monarch of Perception*, which notes Dickinson's polysemy but does not address the difference between her poetic language and that of her contemporaries. [Ladin]

[15]For example, Ross' discussion of "My Reward for Being - was this" (Fr375) does not note the oddity of language such as "When Thrones - accost my Hands - / With 'Me - Miss - Me' - / I'll unroll - Thee -." [Ladin]

[16]Bakhtin-influenced scholars of poetry have long noted that Bakhtin's insistence that poetry is monoglossic does not hold true for many texts. Indeed, Gerald Bruns has suggested that American poetry is inherently heteroglossic. [Ladin]

American women's poetry, and the deep continuities between nineteenth-century American verse and the twentieth-century poetic practices that Dickinson's work prefigures.

The problem, as Ladin announces in his title, is the relationship of Emily Dickinson to American literary history. But Ladin begins with the observation, not of a literary historian, but of a New Critic, R. P. Blackmur, about the difficulty "beyond bearing" of Dickinson's poetic diction in the last line of her poem "More life – went out – when he went." This leads Ladin to the key paradox: Dickinson's use of language is "shocking" and "experimental," akin to the poetics of the modernist poets of the 1920s, such as T. S. Eliot, Ezra Pound, and Marianne Moore (who were the heroes of the New Critics). But to view Dickinson purely as a "precocious modernist" writing in the 1860s would be to isolate her from the literary history of her own period. Previous writers have found contemporary themes in Dickinson, such as the devastation of the Civil War, but have not accounted for her poetics. Ladin wants simultaneously to do justice to the originality of Dickinson's poetic techniques and to view her as a woman of her time.

Two other recent theoretical movements stand in the background of Ladin's problem, and have assisted Ladin with his quest: feminism and New Historicism (see respectively Chapters 7 and 6). Feminist scholarship like that of Paula Bennett has made us aware that women were publishing poetry in great volume in the important periodicals of the nineteenth century, and has unearthed once-forgotten female poets who were Emily Dickinson's peers in her own period. And the New Historicism has made clear that "history is textual" and that the writers of a given period are often responding not only to their peers in the literary world but also to genres at the margins of the literary (sermons, eulogies, legal tracts, advertisements). In the course of his essay, Ladin will quote a conventional eulogy on Abraham Lincoln by Phineas Gurley as one example of what Dickinson's obituary poem, "More life," was explicitly reacting against. And he will quote a poem by Sarah Louise Forten published in William Lloyd Garrison's *Liberator* as proof that Dickinson's radical poetics were not hers alone.

But the theorist who provides Ladin with the important tools for his mission is Mikhail Bakhtin (see the selection from "Discourse in the Novel," pp. 578–87). Bakhtin discusses how novelists of the nineteenth century, such as Charles Dickens, created their satirical narrative voices by importing and juxtaposing for comic effect catch phrases used by various trades and professions, by the classes and the masses. This discussion is Ladin's key to what Dickinson is doing. In effect, Ladin argues, Dickinson shifts this technique from prose to poetry, where the catch phrases belong to a disembodied voice rather than literary characters, and are juxtaposed within the confines of brief lyrics that react against the conventional sentiments of contemporary poetic discourse.

So in the article as a whole Ladin accounts for Dickinson as a writer of her time, in reacting against the conventional poetry of her day, and in using the techniques of the nineteenth-century comic novel, but also as a great original, in adapting those techniques to poetry. And he accounts for why Dickinson, despite her grounding in the nineteenth century, also appears to us as a precocious modernist: because the "centrifugal" qualities of Dickinson's poetry are similar to that of modernists like Eliot and Moore, even though those modernists came to their poetics through a different route.

Unpacking Ladin's essay is relatively easy because he is a lucid writer who is at great pains to indicate his sources and his critical affiliations. He also has a single key critical figure (Mikhail Bakhtin) at the center of his approach to Dickinson. But not all critical discourse is so lucid, or based on a single theoretical approach.

At the other end of the range, both of difficulty of the language and complexity of the argument, is the following passage, taken from the first pages of Gayatri Spivak's Introduction to Ranajit Guha's *Subaltern Studies*:[17]

The work of the Subaltern Studies group offers a theory of change. The insertion of India into colonialism is generally defined as a change from semi-feudalism into capitalist subjection. Such a definition theorizes the change within the great narrative of the modes of production and, by uneasy implication, within the narrative of the transition from feudalism to capitalism. Concurrently, this change is seen as the inauguration of politicization for the colonized. The colonial subject is seen as emerging from those parts of the indigenous elite which come to be loosely described as "bourgeois nationalist." The Subaltern Studies group seems to me to be revising this general definition and its theorization by proposing at least two things: first, that the moment(s) of change be pluralized and plotted as confrontations rather than transition (they would thus be seen in relation to histories of domination and exploitation rather than within the great modes-of-production narrative) and, secondly, that such changes are signaled or marked by a functional change in sign-systems. The most important functional change is from the religious to the militant. There are, however, many other functional changes in sign-systems indicated in these collections: from crime to insurgency, from bondsman to worker, and so on.

The most significant outcome of this revision or shift in perspective is that the agency of change is located in the insurgent or the "subaltern." A functional change in a sign-system is a violent event. Even when it is perceived as "gradual," or "failed," or yet "reversing itself," the change itself can only be operated by the force of a crisis. Yet, if the space for a change (necessarily also an addition) had not been there in the prior function of the sign-system, the crisis could not have made the change happen. The change in signification-function supplements the previous function. The Subaltern Studies collective scrupulously annotates this double movement.

They generally perceive their task as making a theory of consciousness or culture rather than specifically a theory of change. It is because of this, I think, that the force of crisis, *although never far from their argument*, is not systematically emphasized in their work, and sometimes disarmingly alluded to as "impingement," "combination," "getting caught up in a general wave," "circumstances for unification," "reasons for change," "ambiguity," "unease," "transit[ion]," "bringing into focus"; even as it is also described as "switch," "catching fire" and, pervasively, as "turning upside down" — all critical concept-metaphors that would indicate force. Indeed, a general sobriety of tone will not allow them to emphasize sufficiently that they are themselves bringing hegemonic historiography to crisis. This leads them to describe the clandestine operation of supplementarity as the inexorable speculative logic of the dialectic. In this they seem to me to do themselves a disservice, for, as self-professed dialecticians, they open themselves to older debates between spontaneity and consciousness or structure and history. Their actual practice, which I will argue, is closer to deconstruction, would put these oppositions into question. A theory of change as the site of the displacement of function between sign-systems — which is what they oblige me to read

[17]New York: Oxford University Press, 1988.

in them — is a theory of reading in the strongest possible general sense. The site of displacement of the function of signs is the name of reading as active transaction between past and future. This transactional reading as (the possibility of) action, even at its most dynamic, is perhaps what Antonio Gramsci meant by 'elaboration,' *e-laborare*, working out. If seen in this way, the work of the Subaltern Studies group repeatedly makes it possible for us to grasp that the concept-metaphor of the 'social text' is not the reduction of real life to the page of a book. My theoretical intervention is a modest attempt to remind us of this. (3–5)

The key to unpacking this difficult passage involves locating where Spivak stands in relation to the Subaltern Studies group she is introducing. Since she is writing an introduction to a collection of their essays, one might expect to find her in general agreement with them. But it is quite clear from the tone of the opening lines that her attitude seems to be one of critique rather than of univocal praise. Spivak would agree that, relative to the currently available histories of social change in India, Subaltern Studies offers a massive improvement, but all the same, Spivak is not entirely happy with the way the group has characterized the social history it chronicles and with its own efforts at historiography.

Even this may be difficult to pick up because the history books touching India and imperialism that most of us are likely to have actually read are not on the horizon of Spivak's essay. Standard "world studies" history textbooks discuss the colonization of India in the eighteenth century and its emancipation in the mid-twentieth century in terms that emphasize India as a land exploited but also modernized and given a set of enlightened civil institutions by Great Britain, and this story of colonization and emancipation is told in terms of the major personalities involved: John Clive and Warren Hastings, Gandhi and Nehru, and Mountbatten. This story, whatever its value, is not on Spivak's map at all.

The historiography against which Spivak views the Subaltern Studies group as an improvement is traditional Marxist historiography, which would inevitably represent the colonization of India in terms of what Spivak calls "the great narrative of modes of production," as a possession acquired and exploited by the burgeoning industrial capitalists of England, first because of the need for access to exotic imports (such as tea and spices) but later, as the nineteenth century progressed, as a captive market for the export of English industrial goods. Spivak talks of the "uneasy implication" of this narrative. What she is uneasy about is the fact that the protagonist of colonial history in Marx's grand narrative of modes of production is not the native Indian but the English bureaucrat and industrialist (who by pushing capitalism to its limits will bring about the proletarian revolution). The natives of India, within this narrative, are not agents, or as Spivak puts it, "subjects." They are mere objects, victims of exploitation, for most of the history of the Raj. Similarly, the story of the emancipation of India in the mid-twentieth century is the story of "bourgeois nationalists" seeking self-rule in order to exploit Indian workers themselves instead of having them exploited by industrialists living abroad, and the active agents will predictably be the elite classes of postcolonial India. Again there is no room for the masses.

Spivak goes on to claim that the Subaltern Studies group proposes to write a different history based on the ideas of the Marxist thinker Antonio Gramsci (1891–1937).

It was Gramsci who coined the term "subaltern" in the sense of the subject who is dominated by the physical power of the state and not merely by its ideological apparatus. (For further information, see the introduction to Marxist Criticism, p. 1198.) This revised history would allow a greater active role to the masses, would view them as "workers" with a collective or class consciousness rather than as "bondsmen" or slaves with at best an individual hatred for their owners or exploiters. Similarly, Gramsci would view their rebellions against the systems set up by the British as "insurgency" (collective opposition) instead of "crime" (individuals breaking laws). This in turn would allow the Subaltern Studies group to write what has been called "history from the bottom up": the emancipation of India would be viewed as the result of the efforts of the masses rather than as the victory of elite bourgeois leaders like Nehru.

Spivak is definitely in favor of "history from the bottom up," but she feels that the Subaltern Studies group is selling itself short by not comprehending that "a functional change in a sign system is a violent event." Even more revolutionary than the insurgency of the masses against the British Raj, for Spivak, is the crisis in historiography that the Subaltern Studies group is forcing upon Marxist thought. At bottom, her critique of Subaltern Studies is that it has not paid sufficient attention to the revolutionary implications of its own activities. Despite occasionally falling back into vague terms like "gradual" or "transition," the Subaltern Studies group has actually caused a change in the sign-systems of history.

Here Spivak is speaking as a deconstructionist rather than as a Marxist: a change in discourse is in this context a revolution more powerful than the storming of the Bastille. When she refers to the Subaltern Studies group's "theory of change . . . between sign-systems" as "a theory of reading," Spivak is appealing to Paul de Man's *Allegories of Reading*; when she refers to it as employing the "operation of supplementarity," Spivak is appealing to Jacques Derrida's *Of Grammatology*. In both cases she sees the rhetorical moves of deconstruction as evading "older debates" within Marxism (such as the debate about the value of class consciousness versus that of spontaneity), which she sees as leading nowhere. Spivak sees Gramsci's language as deconstructing the discourse of Karl Marx, and the changes in the language of history of the Subaltern Studies group as revolutionizing the narratives about subaltern insurgency.

This is only the start of a far more complex essay; later on, Spivak will critique the Subaltern Studies group in terms of the dilemmas about representing consciousness. When the educated historian writes about the activities of the illiterate masses (who necessarily cannot write their own history), it is the historian's thought process that necessarily takes over and thereby effaces the consciousness of those whose chronicler he is. And finally Spivak analyzes the even more intense dilemma of the representation of the Indian woman, and the way femininity operates within patriarchal Indian society. Spivak points out how "woman" (as the Othered subordinate to "man") becomes a metaphor for India as a whole, in the scheme of colonial social relations, and how that metaphor effaces, even more completely, the consciousness of actual Indian women.

At this point, if the unpacking has been a success, one can go back to the Spivak passage and understand its drift. But how does one do that for oneself? We can go back over the steps in the process, which can be generalized as follows:

1. *Identify the sources the writer is using.* In the case of Ladin, the key source, apart from Emily Dickinson herself, is Mikhail Bakhtin's "Discourse and the Novel," quoted in the fourth paragraph and discussed at length later in the essay. The New Critical reading of Blackmur is there primarily to demonstrate how challenging Dickinson's discourse could be even to critics who valorized modern poetry, and the various studies of Dickinson cited are primarily "touchstones" Ladin discusses to show that he is aware of previous work on American literary history and on Dickinson's poetics and that he is not repeating already published studies.

In the case of Spivak, the key sources are Gramsci and Marx, Derrida and de Man. And one of the things that makes Spivak so difficult to penetrate is that, of the four, only Gramsci is mentioned in Spivak's text. We are expected to understand that her general topic is Marxist historiography through Spivak's use of phrases that explicitly echo Marx's texts, like "capitalist subjection" and "great narrative of the modes of production." Similarly, although Spivak mentions "deconstruction," the name Derrida is not mentioned; we are expected to pick this up because terms like "supplement" and "supplementarity" connect up with Derrida's arguments about discourse in *Of Grammatology* (see the introduction to structuralism and deconstruction, p. 819).

How does the reader pick up covert references of that sort? One might as well be honest about the fact that writing like Spivak's can be obscure even to highly trained scholars. The reader of *The Critical Tradition*, however, will find by consulting the index that "supplement" leads one to Derrida, and that Gramsci is discussed at length in terms of his influence on Althusser and Eagleton. Even in Ladin's essay, it would not be obvious to everyone who R. P. Blackmur is or what set of ideas about poetry he stands for (Blackmur too can be found in the index to *The Critical Tradition*, and is identified as a New Critic on p. 754).

2. *Determine the writer's stance toward sources.* Ladin finds he needs to critique two varieties of Dickinson criticism: formal criticism that detaches Dickinson from history, as though one could be a modernist poet half a century before modernist poetry began to be written; and historical criticism that places Dickinson in her own time in terms of the subject matter touched on in her poetry, but does not bother to account for Dickinson's formal innovations, as though these were an unimportant part of her reputation. Ladin's critique is not mean-spirited or even snarky, but it makes clear that the question he is working on is one that should interest any serious reader of Dickinson. Ladin is not critical of either Dickinson or Bakhtin. His primary difficulty is in getting them together, since Bakhtin's discussion of "centrifugal" and "centripetal" writing in "Discourse and the Novel" is, as the title suggests, primarily aimed at explaining how prose fiction (including narrative poetry, such as Pushkin's *Eugene Onegin*) works as a speech act. Since Bakhtin does not discuss lyric poetry as such, and at one point suggests that the lyric is not dialogical, Ladin has to work

hard, in a key section of his article not reproduced here, to show that Bakhtin's ideas apply fruitfully to Dickinson.

Spivak's tone is quite different: She is making a "theoretical intervention" to "remind" the Subaltern Studies group of what is genuinely revolutionary about their historiography. Rather than considering them as misguided or wrong-headed, she thinks that they are going about things the right way but are theoretically woolly: They need to understand better than they do exactly how right they are. For Spivak, furthermore, the deconstructionists de Man and Derrida are also revolutionaries operating in the realm of discourse (Spivak's view, though, is not the only possible one: In the 1990s leftist writers attacked deconstruction as a politically suspect evasion of ideology). Despite her own commitment to Marxism, Spivak holds Marx's "grand narrative" at arm's length: For postcolonial theory, Marx needs to be revised or, as she would put it, deconstructed, by Gramsci in order to allow agency and a subject position to the "subaltern" under the Raj.

3. *Identify the writer's theoretical commitments.* At this point we are pretty well placed to understand where both Ladin and Spivak are coming from in the cited passages.

Ladin seems committed to a literary history that will do justice to both the content and form of the poetic text. Like some New Historicists, he understands the poet to be in dialogue with other cultural discourses in society, literary and otherwise, and understands that this dialogue may be a reaction against conventional utterances as well as a reproduction of those utterances. Taking poetry as a speech-act, Ladin finds the ideas of Mikhail Bakhtin useful in analyzing the ways in which a writer has travestied or re-accented the speech-acts of others, but has discarded Bakhtin's notion that this play of language has no place in lyric poetry.

Spivak, for her part, is a postcolonial theorist whose understanding of social change owes a great deal to the neo-Marxist Gramsci, who saw change occurring through social conflict at diverse zones of contact, and who stressed the agency of the subaltern fighting an insurgency against state power. Like the deconstructionists, she views textuality as a pervasive condition, and she sees the possibility for revolution in new forms of discourse, new ways of "reading" society as text. She is also concerned with the issue of who is allowed to speak for whom: how the subject position of oppressed classes can be effaced even by those from the literate elites who defend those classes, and how the subject position of women can be effaced by the men who presume to tell their story.

This three-step process is just one possible way of blazing a trail into criticism that depends crucially on rhetorical moves licensed by literary and cultural theory. But it should be clear from the analysis of Ladin and Spivak that any process of unpacking is going to depend at least in part on having maps of the critical terrain. To analyze we need to synthesize, but of course to read the texts that we will later synthesize we need to have analyzed them. It sounds like a vicious circle, where in order to understand anything we need first to have understood everything.

There is a name for this vicious circle — "the hermeneutic circle" — but it's actually a virtuous circle, or perhaps a spiral. We enter it every time we interpret any text, including the words you are reading right now, words that have countless meanings, individually and in combination — ask any dictionary. But as we grope for the overall intention, however crudely, we remove ambiguities, which in turn allows us to refine our sense of the whole, which eliminates more ambiguities, and so on.

And that power is what is working for us here, as our unpacking not only reveals the sense of criticism but helps us revise our maps of the terrain. Our prior sense of what Bakhtin is all about allows us to understand Jay Ladin, but reading Jay Ladin has also expanded and corrected our sense of what Bakhtin is all about. Unpacking criticism thus gives us a sense of the possible reach of theory that we couldn't have gotten from reading theory alone.

CLASSIC TEXTS IN LITERARY CRITICISM

Part One

CLASSIC TEXTS IN
LITERARY CRITICISM

Plato

ca. 427–347 B.C.E.

"All of Western philosophy is but a footnote to Plato," Alfred North Whitehead once said, and it is true in the sense that most of the historically significant issues with which philosophy has been concerned — the nature of being, the question of how we know things, the purposes of right action, the structure of an ordered society, the meaning of love and beauty — were issues that he raised. Later philosophers, including Plato's great pupil, Aristotle, have disagreed not only with his results but also with his ways of setting up the questions, and their argument with Plato makes up much of the history of thought. Nor have later thinkers always merely disagreed with and revised Plato: Century after century has witnessed a renaissance of his system of thought, most notably in the Neoplatonists of the second century C.E., the Cambridge Platonists of the latter seventeenth century, and the idealists of the romantic movement. Later thinkers, including Plotinus (p. 109), Sidney (p. 132), and Shelley (p. 344), directly take up Plato's challenge, but his shadow falls, as Whitehead said, over all of Western thought.

For contemporary readers the most difficult concept in Plato's thought is his *idealism* — the doctrine of a permanent realm of eternal Forms that shape our mutable material world. In a philosophy class students might be asked to contrast the "Idea of the Desk" — the concept of a thing to write on that also holds one's papers — with the physical object in the classroom. The former is timeless and pure, while the latter is time-bound: It came into being, exists for a time, will soon vanish. Nor is the material desk a *perfect* desk: Its very materiality precludes it. Presumably, the Idea of the Desk must have preceded the material desk and caused it, in effect, to be created. A carpenter who is not merely copying an existing desk must be working from some inner awareness of this Idea.

This approach is a time-honored way of introducing Plato's ideas, but it tends to lead our thought downward, to wondering, for example, whether there is a Platonic Idea of a pencil-shaving or of manure. Actually, despite their vulgarity, these are perfectly sound Platonic questions. The usual solution is to assume that formless things — mud, sawdust, and so on — have no Forms because they are in fact formless matter. The real problem is that the explanation removes Plato's ideas from common human thought. Few of us are acquainted, other than in theory, with the ideas of things like desks. Nor is it apparent at first glance that the Idea of a Desk is a higher or better thing than a material desk; it is certainly much harder to do one's work on.

It may be more helpful to think of a geometry class, where one operates with perfect circles, right angles, and parallel lines, and where one learns to prove theorems — or eternal truths — about them. It is understood that the diagrams drawn to illustrate the theorems, however neatly done, are imperfect representations of the lines and angles of the theorem. Here, on a mathematical level, one is working with the Ideal and the Material, and it is the Ideal — the proof, not the diagram — which counts. This may be why the door to Plato's school, the Academy, had a warning on it: "Let no one ignorant of geometry enter here." The mathematics prerequisite, so to speak, had a good reason: Those who had already wrestled with the Idea of the Right Triangle in proving the Pythagorean theorem were prepared to understand the higher ideas of Truth, Goodness, and Beauty that Plato believed shape all human knowledge, right action, artistic endeavor, and love.

Plato developed his idealism in reaction against the notions of the Sophists. They have a poor reputation today — the word *sophistry* testifies to that — but the original Sophists were not a set of quibblers but a diverse group of teachers of what we would now call rhetoric and composition, the language arts. Some of the major Sophists, like Gorgias and Lysias, are known today because Plato used them as debating opponents for his spokesman, Socrates. The Sophists claimed that their science of language could lead to the knowledge of truth and virtue. Against this, Plato thought it dangerous to suppose that the highest realities — Truth, Goodness, and Beauty — had the flickering impermanence of human words, and his world of ideas may derive from his fear that, like language, even matter could be shaped to cheat and deceive.

REPUBLIC, BOOK X

Book X is the most influential discussion of art in the Platonic canon. Its central thesis — that poets have no place in Plato's perfect state save as writers of hymns to the gods and songs in praise of great leaders — has stung devotees of the arts for the last two thousand years.

Book X is at the end of the *Republic,* the longest of the dialogues, which opens with the issue of whether Might makes Right. This harsh question leads Socrates and his two friends to consider the question, What is Justice? Socrates' hypothesis is that Justice is knowing one's place and performing its duties — but how can one know and act properly in the Athenian polis? This question leads Socrates to fashion a model state, a republic governed by a natural elite of guardians, in which it would be possible, as it is not in Athens, to understand one's place and its duties. But how should the guardians be educated to rule? They must learn a great many other things, but at the center of their training is philosophy. And it is in answering *this* question — of what does philosophy consist? — that Socrates presents his hierarchical portrait of the physical and mental universe: the myth of the divided line. In simplified form, the diagram Socrates draws looks like this:

MODES OF BEING	MODES OF MENTAL ACTIVITY
Ideas	Knowing
Mathematical Forms	Understanding
Material Things	Opinion
Images	Conjecture

The first horizontal line separates the eternal world of true Being from the world of Becoming, the material things that are begotten, born, and die. The vertical line separates modes of existence from the modes of thought appropriate to them. For Plato the word *know* applies only to Ideas, but about material animals, plants, and human artifacts we can at best hold correct opinions, and with respect to mere images we can only hazard guesses.

In this context, the discussion of art in Book X is logically sound. First of all, Plato identifies art as imitation, positing that what artists do (as they have claimed in the centuries before and after Plato) is hold the mirror up to nature: They copy the appearances of men, animals, and objects in the physical world. But if this is the case, then the artistic object is merely an image, slightly but not more meaningfully permanent than a reflection in a pool of water. And the intelligence that went into its creation need involve nothing more than conjecture. (Notice that Socrates is not being redundant when he twice proves the inferiority of art: The first time he proves the inferiority of the *mode of being* of art; the second, its inferiority as a *mode of mental activity*.) As a result, art cannot be justified as an activity worthy in its own right. The poets may stay as servants of the state if they teach piety and virtue, but the pleasures of art are condemned as inherently corrupting to citizens and guardians alike.

ION

Much of the *Ion* is reasonably consistent with the *Republic,* and a good deal more entertaining if we allow ourselves to enjoy the spectacle of Socrates exposing the vanity and pretensions of the none-too-bright performer for whom the dialogue is named. (The moment when Ion declares that he is the greatest general in Athens as well as its greatest rhapsode is made richer if one remembers that at the purported time of the discourse, Athens was fighting for its survival in the Peloponnesian War.) Here, as in the *Republic,* Socrates exposes the inferiority of art as a way of knowing.

Where *Ion* differs from the *Republic* is in the suggestion contained in the image of the magnet as a metaphor of divine inspiration. Just as a magnet attracts iron and passes that attraction along, so the muse inspires the artist, who inspires the interpreter, who inspires the audience. The chain runs from the god to Homer to Ion to the applauding citizens. If this view of art is true, then it is divine, not inferior stuff.

Reconciling this notion of art with the contrary position in *Republic*, Book X, has been attempted in a number of different ways. One way is to suppose that Plato changed his mind, but that would mean trying to discover which, the *Ion* or the *Republic,* is the later dialogue (we have only conjectural datings) and deciding whether his first or second thoughts were the more trustworthy.

Another possibility is to suppose that the *Ion* is an essentially ironic (as well as humorous) dialogue, and that Socrates does not seriously respect inspiration. The Greek word translated as "inspiration" is *enthousiasmós,* and its literal meaning is closer to "demonic possession" than to the English derivative "enthusiasm." It is hard to believe that the rationalistic Plato could commend such a state. But on the other side, Socrates *does* praise such an experience elsewhere, in the *Phaedrus,* the principal dialogue on love and beauty, where poetry finds its place along with prophecy and love as forms of divine madness, the gods' most precious gifts to humanity. There Socrates claims that the state of *enthousiasmós* allows a dim but gripping memory of the Ideas, the eternal Forms of Truth, Goodness, and Beauty, which the soul experienced directly prior to its incarnation. This doctrine is narrated as a myth, but it is surely not ironic in context.

Perhaps most plausibly, the discrepancies between *Ion* and *Republic* may be ascribed to their different contexts. In *Republic* Socrates is imagining a perfect state, one that must be designed to run without benefit of chance, luck, or divine intervention. Its rulers must therefore act rightly out of permanently dependable knowledge, not occasional inspiration. In the *Ion* Socrates is discoursing about the actual world, where poets may be generally foolish and ignorant, but can sometimes be heard to speak holy truths in tongues given them by the gods.

PHAEDRUS

The selection from the *Phaedrus* points up Plato's mistrust in writing. Socrates tells Phaedrus a myth from Egypt, the place where hieroglyphic writing was invented, in which the god of learning, Thoth, praises writing as an aid to fallible memory, and the ruler of the gods, Ammon, replies that, with writing as an aid, human memory is certain to decay. (We see this process today, as telephone memories make it unnecessary to recollect the numbers of even our closest friends, so we do not commit them to memory.) Socrates' deeper complaint is that writing is one step farther removed from human thought than spoken language is. We try to express exactly what we think. When we advance an argument in writing, we may be right or wrong, and our readers may or may not understand us correctly. Whether they agree or disagree, they cannot interrogate the written text, which has no "living soul" to give an answer. In oral discourse, our audience can ask us to go back, to retrace, can point up possible self-contradictions, and we can respond, try different expressions, to see if the conflict is in what we think or in different understandings of the words we have used. In this dialogue, the speakers can search for truth.

This in fact is what Phaedrus and Socrates have been doing throughout the dialogue. At the outset, Phaedrus is full of admiration for a text by Lysias, who has argued that, for prudential reasons, because lovers can act insanely and irrationally, a young man should choose as his lover an older man who is not in love with him rather than one who is. In response to Phaedrus, Socrates first produces a parody version of Lysias in which he suggests that such a text would more naturally be spoken by a wily lover, someone only pretending not to be in love. But suddenly Socrates stops this mode of attack in its tracks as he realizes that he is misleading Phaedrus, because, like Lysias's, his own speech presumes love to be nothing more than physical desire. The real truth, as Socrates argues in his speech of recantation, is that love is one of the gods' most precious gifts, and, if it be a form of madness in our mortal longing for transcendent Beauty within the physical world, its source is nonetheless divine. (Poetry, as Socrates mentions almost in passing, is yet another species of this divine madness.) The other truth Socrates arrives at is the truth about rhetoric: that while written discourse can be flashy and impressive, the way to search for the deepest truths is through oral discourse between people who care about each other.

This may be why Plato did not set down his philosophy in the usual form of a set of treatises but rather in dialogues. Indeed, in the Seventh Letter, Plato claims that he never wrote down his philosophy at all, because it could not be written down. What he seems to have meant is that the published dialogues represent philosophy as an *activity* rather than as a set of received doctrines. But Plato may also have meant the dialogues to *stimulate* philosophy: The dialogues cause us to philosophize as we read and reason and argue with the positions taken by Socrates and his interlocutors.

But if the liveliness and depth of the dialogues remains unequalled, their form creates problems of interpretation and consistency. At times we wonder whether Socrates is being serious or ironic, whether he always is speaking directly for Plato. And a position held in one dialogue may be renounced in another. Both these issues emerge in the *Republic*, Book X, and in the *Ion*.

Selected Bibliography

Cavarnos, Constantine. *Plato's Theory of Fine Art.* Athens: Astir, 1973.

Else, Gerald F. *Plato and Aristotle on Poetry.* Chapel Hill: University of North Carolina Press, 1986.

Fortenbaugh, William W. and Lewis Ayres, eds. *The Passionate Intellect: The Transformation of the Classical Traditions.* New Brunswick: Rutgers University Press, 1995.

Friedländer, Paul. *Plato.* New York: Pantheon, 1958–69.

Gadamer, Hans-Georg. "Plato und die Dichter." In *Platos Dialektische Ethik und andere Studien.* Hamburg: F. Meiner, 1968.

Gebauer, Gunter. *Mimesis: Culture — Art — Society.* Berkeley: University of California Press, 1995.

Greene, William Chase. "Plato's View of Poetry." *Harvard Studies in Classical Philology* 29 (1918): 1–75.

Grube, G. M. A. *Plato's Thought.* London: Methuen, 1935.

Gulley, Norman. *Plato's Theory of Knowledge.* London: Methuen, 1962.

Havelock, Eric. *Preface to Plato.* Cambridge: Harvard University Press, 1963.

Lodge, Rupert C. *Plato's Theory of Art.* New York: Humanities Press, 1953.

Marback, Richard. *Plato's Dream of Sophistry.* Columbia: University of South Carolina Press, 1999.

Murdoch, Iris. *The Fire and the Sun: Why Plato Banished the Artists.* Oxford: Clarendon Press, 1972.

Murray, James S. "Disputation, Deception and Dialectic: Plato on the True Rhetoric (Phaedrus 261–266)." *Philosophy and Rhetoric* 21, no. 4 (1988): 279–87.

Nightingale, Andrea Wilson. *Genres in Dialogue: Plato and the Construct of Philosophy.* Cambridge: Cambridge University Press, 1996.

Oates, Whitney J. *Plato's View of Art.* New York: Scribner, 1972.

Partee, Morriss Henry. *Plato's Poetics: The Authority of Beauty.* Salt Lake City: University of Utah Press, 1981.

Shorey, Paul. *What Plato Said.* Chicago: University of Chicago Press, 1933.

Sinaiko, Herman J. *Love, Knowledge and Discourse in Plato.* Chicago: University of Chicago Press, 1965.

Switzer, Robert. "The Topology of Madness: Philosophical Seduction in Plato's *Phaedrus.*" *Alif: Journal of Comparative Poetics* 14 (1994): 6–36.

Taylor, A. E. *Plato.* 1929; Ann Arbor: University of Michigan Press, 1960.

Republic, Book X

Of the many excellences which I perceive in the order of our State, there is none which upon reflection pleases me better than the rule about poetry.

To what do you refer?

To our refusal to admit the imitative kind of poetry, for it certainly ought not to be received; as I see far more clearly now that the parts of the soul have been distinguished.

What do you mean?

Speaking in confidence, for you will not denounce me to the tragedians and the rest of the imitative tribe, all poetical imitations are ruinous to the understanding of the hearers, unless as an antidote they possess the knowledge of the true nature of the originals.

Explain the purport of your remark.

Well, I will tell you, although I have always from my earliest youth had an awe and love of Homer which even now makes the words falter on my lips, for he seems to be the great captain and teacher of the whole of that noble tragic company; but a man is not to be reverenced more than the truth, and therefore I will speak out.

Very good, he said.

Listen to me then, or rather, answer me.

Put your question.

Can you give me a general definition of imitation? for I really do not myself understand what it professes to be.

A likely thing, then, that I should know.

There would be nothing strange in that, for the duller eye may often see a thing sooner than the keener.

Very true, he said; but in your presence, even if I had any faint notion, I could not muster courage to utter it. Will you inquire yourself?

Well then, shall we begin the inquiry at this point, following our usual method: Whenever a number of individuals have a common name, we assume that there is one corresponding idea or form: — do you understand me?

I do.

Let us take, for our present purpose, any instance of such a group; there are beds and tables in the world — many of each, are there not?

Yes.

But there are only two ideas or forms of such furniture — one the idea of a bed, the other of a table.

True.

And the maker of either of them makes a bed or he makes a table for our use, in accordance with the idea — that is our way of speaking in this and similar instances — but no artificer makes the idea itself: how could he?

Impossible.

And there is another artificer — I should like to know what you would say of him.

Who is he?

One who is the maker of all the works of all other workmen.

What an extraordinary man!

Wait a little, and there will be more reason for your saying so. For this is the craftsman who is able to make not only furniture of every kind, but all that grows out of the earth, and all living creatures, himself included; and besides these he can make earth and sky and the gods, and all the things which are in heaven or in the realm of Hades under the earth.

Translated by Benjamin Jowett. The speakers are Socrates and Glaucon.

He must be a wizard and no mistake.

Oh! you are incredulous, are you? Do you mean that there is no such maker or creator, or that in one sense there might be a maker of all these things but in another not? Do you see that there is a way in which you could make them all yourself?

And what way is this? he asked.

An easy way enough; or rather, there are many ways in which the feat might be quickly and easily accomplished, none quicker than that of turning a mirror round and round — you would soon enough make the sun and the heavens, and the earth and yourself, and other animals and plants, and furniture and all the other things of which we were just now speaking, in the mirror.

Yes, he said; but they would be appearances only.

Very good, I said, you are coming to the point now. And the painter too is, as I conceive, just such another — a creator of appearances, is he not?

Of course.

But then I suppose you will say that what he creates is untrue. And yet there is a sense in which the painter also creates a bed? Is there not?

Yes, he said, but here again, an appearance only.

And what of the maker of the bed? Were you not saying that he too makes, not the idea which according to our view is the real object denoted by the word bed, but only a particular bed?

Yes, I did.

Then if he does not make a real object he cannot make what *is,* but only some semblance of existence; and if anyone were to say that the work of the maker of the bed, or of any other workman, has real existence, he could hardly be supposed to be speaking the truth.

Not, at least, he replied, in the view of those who make a business of these discussions.

No wonder, then, that his work too is an indistinct expression of truth.

No wonder.

Suppose now that by the light of the examples just offered we inquire who this imitator is?

If you please.

Well then, here we find three beds: one existing in nature, which is made by God, as I think that we may say — for no one else can be the maker?

No one, I think.

There is another which is the work of the carpenter?

Yes.

And the work of the painter is a third?

Yes.

Beds, then, are of three kinds, and there are three artists who superintend them: God, the maker of the bed, and the painter?

Yes, there are three of them.

God, whether from choice or from necessity, made one bed in nature and one only; two or more such beds neither ever have been nor ever will be made by God.

Why is that?

Because even if He had made but two, a third would still appear behind them of which they again both possessed the form, and that would be the real bed and not the two others.

Very true, he said.

God knew this, I suppose, and He desired to be the real maker of a real bed, not a kind of bed, and therefore He created a bed which is essentially and by nature one only.

So it seems.

Shall we, then, speak of Him as the natural author or maker of the bed?

Yes, he replied; inasmuch as by the natural process of creation, He is the author of this and of all other things.

And what shall we say of the carpenter — is not he also the maker of a bed?

Yes.

But would you call the painter an artificer and maker?

Certainly not.

Yet if he is not the maker, what is he in relation to the bed?

I think, he said, that we may fairly designate him as the imitator of that which the others make.

Good, I said; then you call him whose product is third in the descent from nature, an imitator?

Certainly, he said.

And so if the tragic poet is an imitator, he too is thrice removed from the king and from the truth; and so are all other imitators.

That appears to be so.

Then about the imitator we are agreed. And what about the painter? — Do you think he tries to imitate in each case that which originally exists in nature, or only the creation of artificers?

The latter.

As they are or as they appear? you have still to determine this.

What do you mean?

I mean to ask whether a bed really becomes different when it is seen from different points of view, obliquely or directly or from any other point of view? Or does it simply appear different, without being really so? And the same of all things.

Yes, he said, the difference is only apparent.

Now let me ask you another question: Which is the art of painting designed to be — an imitation of things as they are, or as they appear — of appearance or of reality?

Of appearance, he said.

Then the imitator is a long way off the truth, and can reproduce all things because he lightly touches on a small part of them, and that part an image. For example: A painter will paint a cobbler, carpenter, or any other artisan, though he knows nothing of their arts; and, if he is a good painter, he may deceive children or simple persons when he shows them his picture of a carpenter from a distance, and they will fancy that they are looking at a real carpenter.

Certainly.

And surely, my friend, this is how we should regard all such claims: Whenever any one informs us that he has found a man who knows all the arts, and all things else that anybody knows, and every single thing with a higher degree of accuracy than any other man — whoever tells us this, I think that we can only retort that he is a simple creature who seems to have been deceived by some wizard or imitator whom he met, and whom he thought all-knowing, because he himself was unable to analyze the nature of knowledge and ignorance and imitation.

Most true.

And next, I said, we have to consider tragedy and its leader, Homer; for we hear some persons saying that these poets know all the arts; and all things human; where virtue and vice are concerned, and indeed all divine things too; because the good poet cannot compose well unless he knows his subject, and he who has not this knowledge can never be a poet. We ought to consider whether here also there may not be a similar illusion. Perhaps they may have come across imitators and been deceived by them; they may not have remembered when they saw their works that these were thrice removed from the truth, and could easily be made without any knowledge of the truth, because they are appearances only and not realities? Or, after all, they may be in the right, and good poets do really know the things about which they seem to the many to speak so well?

The question, he said, should by all means be considered.

Now do you suppose that if a person were able to make the original as well as the image, he would seriously devote himself to the image-making branch? Would he allow imitation to be the ruling principle of his life, as if he had nothing higher in him?

I should say not.

But the real artist, who had real knowledge of those things which he chose also to imitate, would be interested in realities and not in imitations; and would desire to leave as memorials of himself works many and fair; and, instead of being the author of encomiums, he would prefer to be the theme of them.

Yes, he said, that would be to him a source of much greater honor and profit.

Now let us refrain, I said, from calling Homer or any other poet to account regarding those arts to which his poems incidentally refer: We will not ask them, in case any poet has been a doctor and not a mere imitator of medical parlance, to show what patients have been restored to health by a poet, ancient or modern, as they were by Asclepius; or what disciples in medicine a poet has left behind him, like the Asclepiads. Nor shall we press the same question upon them about the other arts. But we have a right to know respecting warfare, strategy, the administration of States, and the education of man, which are the chiefest and noblest subjects of his poems, and we may fairly ask him about them. "Friend Homer," then we say to him, "if you are only in the second remove from truth in what you say of virtue, and not in the third — not an image maker, that is, by our definition, an imitator — and if you are able to discern what pursuits make men better or worse in private or public life, tell us what State was ever better governed by your help? The good order of Lacedaemon is due to Lycurgus, and many other cities great and small have been similarly benefited by others; but who says that you have been a good legislator to them and have done them any good? Italy and Sicily boast of Charondas, and there is Solon who is renowned among us; but what city has anything to say about you?" Is there any city which he might name?

I think not, said Glaucon; not even the Homerids themselves pretend that he was a legislator.

Well, but is there any war on record which was carried on successfully owing to his leadership or counsel?

There is not.

Or is there anything comparable to those clever improvements in the arts, or in other operations, which are said to have been due to men of practical genius such as Thales the Milesian or Anacharsis the Scythian?

There is absolutely nothing of the kind.

But, if Homer never did any public service, was he privately a guide or teacher of any? Had he in his lifetime friends who loved to associate with him, and who handed down to posterity a Homeric way of life, such as was established by Pythagoras who was especially beloved for this reason and whose followers are to this day conspicuous among others by what they term the Pythagorean way of life?

Nothing of the kind is recorded of him. For surely, Socrates, Creophylus, the companion of Homer, that child of flesh, whose name always makes us laugh, might be more justly ridiculed for his want of breeding, if what is said is true, that Homer was greatly neglected by him in his own day when he was alive?

Yes, I replied, that is the tradition. But can you imagine, Glaucon, that if Homer had really been able to educate and improve mankind — if he had been capable of knowledge and not been a mere imitator — can you imagine, I say, that he would not have attracted many followers, and been honored and loved by them? Protagoras of Abdera, and Prodicus of Ceos, and a host of others, have only to whisper to their contemporaries: "You will never be able to manage either your own house or your own State until you appoint us to be your ministers of education" — and this

ingenious device of theirs has such an effect in making men love them that their companions all but carry them about on their shoulders. And is it conceivable that the contemporaries of Homer, or again of Hesiod, would have allowed either of them to go about as rhapsodists, if they had really been able to help mankind forward in virtue? Would they not have been as unwilling to part with them as with gold, and have compelled them to stay at home with them? Or, if the master would not stay, then the disciples would have followed him about everywhere, until they had got education enough?

Yes, Socrates, that, I think, is quite true.

Then must we not infer that all these poetical individuals, beginning with Homer, are only imitators, who copy images of virtue and the other themes of their poetry, but have no contact with the truth? The poet is like a painter who, as we have already observed, will make a likeness of a cobbler though he understands nothing of cobbling; and his picture is good enough for those who know no more than he does, and judge only by colors and figures.

Quite so.

In like manner the poet with his words and phrases[1] may be said to lay on the colors of the several arts, himself understanding their nature only enough to imitate them; and other people, who are as ignorant as he is, and judge only from his words, imagine that if he speaks of cobbling, or of military tactics, or of anything else, in meter and harmony and rhythm, he speaks very well — such is the sweet influence which melody and rhythm by nature have. For I am sure that you know what a poor appearance the works of poets make when stripped of the colors which art puts upon them, and recited in simple prose. You have seen some examples?

Yes, he said.

They are like faces which were never really beautiful, but only blooming, seen when the bloom of youth has passed away from them?

Exactly.

Come now, and observe this point: The imitator or maker of the image knows nothing, we

[1] Or, "with his nouns and verbs." [Tr.]

have said, of true existence; he knows appearances only. Am I not right?

Yes.

Then let us have a clear understanding, and not be satisfied with half an explanation.

Proceed.

Of the painter we say that he will paint reins, and he will paint a bit?

Yes.

And the worker in leather and brass will make them?

Certainly.

But does the painter know the right form of the bit and reins? Nay, hardly even the workers in brass and leather who make them; only the horseman who knows how to use them — he knows their right form.

Most true.

And may we not say the same of all things?

What?

That there are three arts which are concerned with all things: one which uses, another which makes, a third which imitates them?

Yes.

And the excellence and beauty and rightness of every structure, animate or inanimate, and of every action of man, is relative solely to the use for which nature or the artist has intended them.

True.

Then beyond doubt it is the user who has the greatest experience of them, and he must report to the maker the good or bad qualities which develop themselves in use; for example, the flute player will tell the flute maker which of his flutes is satisfactory to the performer; he will tell him how he ought to make them, and the other will attend to his instructions?

Of course.

So the one pronounces with knowledge about the goodness and badness of flutes, while the other, confiding in him, will make them accordingly?

True.

The instrument is the same, but about the excellence or badness of it the maker will possess a correct belief, since he associates with one who knows, and is compelled to hear what he has to say; whereas the user will have knowledge?

True.

But will the imitator have either? Will he know from use whether or not that which he paints is correct or beautiful? or will he have right opinion from being compelled to associate with another who knows and gives him instructions about what he should paint?

Neither.

Then an imitator will no more have true opinion than he will have knowledge about the goodness or badness of his models?

I suppose not.

The imitative poet will be in a brilliant state of intelligence about the theme of his poetry?

Nay, very much the reverse.

And still he will go on imitating without knowing what makes a thing good or bad, and may be expected therefore to imitate only that which appears to be good to the ignorant multitude?

Just so.

Thus far then we are pretty well agreed that the imitator has no knowledge worth mentioning of what he imitates. Imitation is only a kind of play or sport, and the tragic poets, whether they write in iambic or in heroic verse,[2] are imitators in the highest degree?

Very true.

And now tell me, I conjure you — this imitation is concerned with an object which is thrice removed from the truth?

Certainly.

And what kind of faculty in man is that to which imitation makes its special appeal?

What do you mean?

I will explain: The same body does not appear equal to our sight when seen near and when seen at a distance?

True.

And the same objects appear straight when looked at out of the water, and crooked when in the water; and the concave becomes convex, owing to the illusion about colors to which the sight is liable. Thus every sort of confusion is revealed within us; and this is that weakness of the human mind on which the art of painting in

---

[2]Dramatists wrote in iambic verse and epic poets in dactylic hexameters — "heroic" verse.

light and shadow, the art of conjuring, and many other ingenious devices impose, having an effect upon us like magic.

True.

And the arts of measuring and numbering and weighing come to the rescue of the human understanding — there is the beauty of them — with the result that the apparent greater or less, or more or heavier, no longer have the mastery over us, but give way before the power of calculation and measuring and weighing?

Most true.

And this, surely, must be the work of the calculating and rational principle in the soul?

To be sure.

And often when this principle measures and certifies that some things are equal, or that some are greater or less than others, it is, at the same time, contradicted by the appearance which the objects present?

True.

But did we not say that such a contradiction is impossible — the same faculty cannot have contrary opinions at the same time about the same thing?

We did; and rightly.

Then that part of the soul which has an opinion contrary to measure can hardly be the same with that which has an opinion in accordance with measure?

True.

And the part of the soul which trusts to measure and calculation is likely to be the better one?

Certainly.

And therefore that which is opposed to this is probably an inferior principle in our nature?

No doubt.

This was the conclusion at which I was seeking to arrive when I said that painting or drawing, and imitation in general, are engaged upon productions which are far removed from truth, and are also the companions and friends and associates of a principle within us which is equally removed from reason, and that they have no true or healthy aim.

Exactly.

The imitative art is an inferior who from intercourse with an inferior has inferior offspring.

Very true.

And is this confined to the sight only, or does it extend to the hearing also, relating in fact to what we term poetry?

Probably the same would be true of poetry.

Do not rely, I said, on a probability derived from the analogy of painting; but let us once more go directly to that faculty of the mind with which imitative poetry has converse, and see whether it is good or bad.

By all means.

We may state the question thus: Imitation imitates the actions of men, whether voluntary or involuntary, on which, as they imagine, a good or bad result has ensued, and they rejoice or sorrow accordingly. Is there anything more?

No, there is nothing else.

But in all this variety of circumstances is the man at unity with himself — or rather, as in the instance of sight there was confusion and opposition in his opinions about the same things, so here also is there not strife and inconsistency in his life? Though I need hardly raise the question again, for I remember that all this has been already admitted; and the soul has been acknowledged by us to be full of these and ten thousand similar oppositions occurring at the same moment?

And we were right, he said.

Yes, I said, thus far we were right; but there was an omission which must now be supplied.

What was the omission?

Were we not saying that a good man, who has the misfortune to lose his son or anything else which is most dear to him, will bear the loss with more equanimity than another?

Yes, indeed.

But will he have no sorrow, or shall we say that although he cannot help sorrowing, he will moderate his sorrow?

The latter, he said, is the truer statement.

Tell me: will he be more likely to struggle and hold out against his sorrow when he is seen by his equals, or when he is alone in a deserted place?

The fact of being seen will make a great difference, he said.

When he is by himself he will not mind saying many things which he would be ashamed of anyone hearing, and also doing many things which he would not care to be seen doing?

True.

And doubtless it is the law and reason in him which bids him resist; while it is the affliction itself which is urging him to indulge his sorrow?

True.

But when a man is drawn in two opposite directions, to and from the same object, this, as we affirm, necessarily implies two distinct principles in him?

Certainly.

One of them is ready to follow the guidance of the law?

How do you mean?

The law would say that to be patient under calamity is best, and that we should not give way to impatience, as the good and evil in such things are not clear, and nothing is gained by impatience; also, because no human thing is of serious importance, and grief stands in the way of that which at the moment is most required.

What is most required? he asked.

That we should take counsel about what has happened, and when the dice have been thrown, according to their fall, order our affairs in the way which reason deems best; not, like children who have had a fall, keeping hold of the part struck and wasting time in setting up a howl, but always accustoming the soul forthwith to apply a remedy, raising up that which is sickly and fallen, banishing the cry of sorrow by the healing art.

Yes, he said, that is the true way of meeting the attacks of fortune.

Well then, I said, the higher principle is ready to follow this suggestion of reason?

Clearly.

But the other principle, which inclines us to recollection of our troubles and to lamentation, and can never have enough of them, we may call irrational, useless, and cowardly?

Indeed, we may.

Now does not the principle which is thus inclined to complaint, furnish a great variety of materials for imitation? Whereas the wise and calm temperament, being always nearly equable, is not easy to imitate or to appreciate when imitated, especially at a public festival when a promiscuous crowd is assembled in a theater. For the feeling represented is one to which they are strangers.

Certainly.

Then the imitative poet who aims at being popular is not by nature made, nor is his art intended, to please or to affect the rational principle in the soul; but he will appeal rather to the lachrymose and fitful temper, which is easily imitated?

Clearly.

And now we may fairly take him and place him by the side of the painter, for he is like him in two ways: first, inasmuch as his creations have an inferior degree of truth — in this, I say, he is like him; and he is also like him in being the associate of an inferior part of the soul; and this is enough to show that we shall be right in refusing to admit him into a State which is to be well ordered, because he awakens and nourishes this part of the soul, and by strengthening it impairs the reason. As in a city when the evil are permitted to wield power and the finer men are put out of the way, so in the soul of each man, as we shall maintain, the imitative poet implants an evil constitution, for he indulges the irrational nature which has no discernment of greater and less, but thinks the same thing at one time great and at another small — he is an imitator of images and is very far removed from the truth.

Exactly.

But we have not yet brought forward the heaviest count in our accusation: The power which poetry has of harming even the good (and there are very few who are not harmed) is surely an awful thing?

Yes, certainly, if the effect is what you say.

Hear and judge: The best of us, as I conceive, when we listen to a passage of Homer or one of the tragedians, in which he represents some hero who is drawling out his sorrows in a long oration, or singing, and smiting his breast — the best of us, you know, delight in giving way to sympathy, and are in raptures at the excellence of the poet who stirs our feelings most.

Yes, of course I know.

But when any sorrow of our own happens to us, then you may observe that we pride ourselves on the opposite quality — we would fain be quiet and patient; this is considered the manly part, and the other which delighted us in the recitation is now deemed to be the part of a woman.

Very true, he said.

Now can we be right in praising and admiring another who is doing that which any one of us would abominate and be ashamed of in his own person?

No, he said, that is certainly not reasonable.

Nay, I said, quite reasonable from one point of view.

What point of view?

If you consider, I said, that when in misfortune we feel a natural hunger and desire to relieve our sorrow by weeping and lamentation, and that this very feeling which is starved and suppressed in our own calamities is satisfied and delighted by the poets; the better nature in each of us, not having been sufficiently trained by reason or habit, allows the sympathetic element to break loose because the sorrow is another's; and the spectator fancies that there can be no disgrace to himself in praising and pitying anyone who, while professing to be a brave man, gives way to untimely lamentation; he thinks that the pleasure is a gain, and is far from wishing to lose it by rejection of the whole poem. Few persons ever reflect, as I should imagine, that the contagion must pass from others to themselves. For the pity which has been nourished and strengthened in the misfortunes of others is with difficulty repressed in our own.

How very true!

And does not the same hold also of the ridiculous? There are jests which you would be ashamed to make yourself, and yet on the comic stage, or indeed in private, when you hear them, you are greatly amused by them, and are not at all disgusted at their unseemliness; the case of pity is repeated; there is a principle in human nature which is disposed to raise a laugh, and this, which you once restrained by reason because you were afraid of being thought a buffoon, is now let out again; and having stimulated the risible faculty at the theater, you are betrayed unconsciously to yourself into playing the comic poet at home.

Quite true, he said.

And the same may be said of lust and anger and all the other affections, of desire and pain and pleasure, which are held to be inseparable from every action — in all of them poetry has a like effect; it feeds and waters the passions instead of drying them up; she lets them rule, although they ought to be controlled if mankind are ever to increase in happiness and virtue.

I cannot deny it.

Therefore, Glaucon, I said, whenever you meet with any of the eulogists of Homer declaring that he has been the educator of Hellas, and that he is profitable for education and for the ordering of human things, and that you should take him up again and again and get to know him and regulate your whole life according to him, we may love and honor those who say these things — they are excellent people, as far as their lights extend; and we are ready to acknowledge that Homer is the greatest of poets and first of tragedy writers; but we must remain firm in our conviction that hymns to the gods and praises of famous men are the only poetry which ought to be admitted into our State. For if you go beyond this and allow the honeyed Muse to enter, either in epic or lyric verse, not law and the reason of mankind, which by common consent have ever been deemed best, but pleasure and pain will be the rulers in our State.

That is most true, he said.

And now since we have reverted to the subject of poetry, let this our defense serve to show the reasonableness of our former judgment in sending away out of our State an art having the tendencies which we have described; for reason constrained us. But that she may not impute to us any harshness or want of politeness, let us tell her that there is an ancient quarrel between philosophy and poetry; of which there are many proofs, such as the saying of "the yelping hound howling at her lord," or of one "mighty in the vain talk of fools," and "the mob of sages circumventing Zeus," and the "subtle thinkers who are beggars after all,"[3] and there are innumerable other signs of ancient enmity between them. Notwithstanding this, let us assure the poetry which aims at pleasure, and the art of imitation, that if she will only prove her title to exist in a well-ordered State we shall be delighted to receive her — we are very conscious of her charms; but it would not be right on that account to betray the truth. I dare say, Glaucon,

---

[3]Socrates is alluding to various proverbs, otherwise unknown, denigrating both poets and philosophers.

that you are as much charmed by her as I am, especially when she appears in Homer?

Yes, indeed, I am greatly charmed.

Shall I propose, then, that she be allowed to return from exile, but upon this condition only — that she make a defense of herself in some lyrical or other meter?

Certainly.

And we may further grant to those of her defenders who are lovers of poetry and yet not poets the permission to speak in prose on her behalf: let them show not only that she is pleasant but also useful to States and to human life, and we will listen in a kindly spirit; for we shall surely be the gainers if this can be proved, that there is a use in poetry as well as a delight?

Certainly, he said, we shall be the gainers.

If her defense fails, then, my dear friend, like other persons who are enamored of something, but put a restraint upon themselves when they think their desires are opposed to their interests, so too must we after the manner of lovers give her up, though not without a struggle. We too are inspired by that love of such poetry which the education of noble States has implanted in us, and therefore we shall be glad if she appears at her best and truest; but so long as she is unable to make good her defense, this argument of ours shall be a charm to us, which we will repeat to ourselves while we listen to her strains; that we may not fall away into the childish love of her which captivates the many. At all events we are well aware that poetry, such as we have described, is not to be regarded seriously as attaining to the truth; and he who listens to her, fearing for the safety of the city which is within him, should be on his guard against her seductions and make our words his law.

Yes, he said, I quite agree with you.

Yes, I said, my dear Glaucon, for great is the issue at stake, greater than appears, whether a man is to be good or bad. And what will any one be profited if under the influence of honor or money or power, aye, or under the excitement of poetry, he neglect justice and virtue?

Yes, he said; I have been convinced by the argument, as I believe that anyone else would have been.

Ion

SOCRATES: Welcome, Ion! And whence come you now to pay us a visit? From your home in Ephesus?

ION: No, Socrates, I come from Epidaurus and the festival of Asclepius.[1]

SOCRATES: What! Do the citizens of Epidaurus, in honoring the god, have a contest between rhapsodes[2] too?

ION: Indeed they do. They have every sort of musical competition.

SOCRATES: So? And did you compete? And how did you succeed?

ION: We carried off first prize, Socrates.

SOCRATES: Well done! See to it, now, that we win the Panathenaea also.

ION: It shall be so, God willing.

SOCRATES: I must say, Ion, I am often envious of you rhapsodists in your profession. Your art requires of you always to go in fine array, and look as beautiful as you can, and meanwhile you must be conversant with many excellent poets, and especially with Homer, the best and most divine of all. You have to understand his thought, and not merely learn his lines. It is an enviable lot! In fact, one never could be a rhapsode if one did not comprehend the utterances of the poet, for the rhapsode must become an interpreter of the poet's thought to

---

Translated by Lane Cooper.

[1]Greek god of medicine; his festival, like that of other minor divinities connected with Apollo, was the occasion for artistic performances and competitions.

[2]Professionals who delivered recitations of poetry, especially of Homer and the other epic poets.

those who listen, and to do this well is quite impossible unless one knows just what the poet is saying. All that, of course, will excite one's envy.

ION: What you say is true, Socrates; to me, at all events, this aspect of the art has given the most concern. And I judge that I, of all men, have the finest things to say on Homer, that neither Metrodorus of Lampsacus, nor Stesimbrotus of Thasos, nor Glaucon, nor anyone else who ever lived, had so many reflections, or such fine ones, to present on Homer as have I.

SOCRATES: That is pleasant news, Ion, for obviously you will not begrudge me a display of your talent.

ION: Not at all. And, Socrates, it really is worthwhile to hear how well I have embellished Homer. In my opinion I deserve to be crowned with a wreath of gold by the Homeridae.[3]

SOCRATES: Another time I shall find leisure to hear your recitation. At the moment do but answer me so far. Are you skilled in Homer only, or in Hesiod and Archilochus as well?

ION: No, only in regard to Homer; to me that seems enough.

SOCRATES: Is there any point on which both Homer and Hesiod say the same thing?

ION: Indeed, I think so; there are many cases of it.

SOCRATES: In those cases, then, would you interpret what Homer says better than what Hesiod says?

ION: In the cases where they say the same, Socrates, I should do equally well with both.

SOCRATES: But what about the cases where they do not say the same? For example, take the art of divination; Homer and Hesiod both speak of it.

ION: Quite so.

SOCRATES: Well then, where they say the same on the art of divination, and where they differ on it, would you interpret better what these two poets say, or would one of the diviners, one of the good ones, do so?

ION: One of the diviners.

SOCRATES: But suppose you were a diviner. If you were competent to explain the passages where they agree, would you not be competent to explain as well the passages where they differ?

ION: Manifestly, yes.

SOCRATES: How is it, then, that you are skilled in Homer, but not in Hesiod or the other poets? Does Homer treat of matters different from those that all the other poets treat of? Wasn't his subject mainly war, and hasn't he discussed the mutual relations of men good and bad, or the general run as well as special craftsmen, the relations of the gods to one another and to men, as they forgather, the phenomena of the heavens and occurrences in the underworld, and the birth of gods and heroes? Are not these the subjects Homer dealt with in his poetry?

ION: What you say is true, Socrates.

SOCRATES: And what about the other poets? Haven't they dealt with these same themes?

ION: Yes, but, Socrates, not in the same way.

SOCRATES: How so? In a worse way than he?

ION: Far worse.

SOCRATES: He in a better way?

ION: Better indeed, I warrant you.

SOCRATES: Well now, Ion darling, tell me. When several persons are discussing number, and one of them talks better than the rest, there will be someone who distinguishes the good speaker?

ION: I agree.

SOCRATES: It will be the same one who distinguishes those who are speaking badly, or will it be another?

ION: No doubt the same.

SOCRATES: And this will be the one who knows the art of numbers?

ION: Yes.

SOCRATES: Tell me. When several are discussing diet, and what foods are wholesome, and one of them speaks better than the rest, will a given person see the excellence of the best speaker, and another the inferiority of the worst, or will the same man distinguish both?

ION: Obviously, I think, the same.

SOCRATES: Who is he? What is he called?

ION: The doctor.

SOCRATES: We may therefore generalize, and say: When several persons are discussing a given subject, the man who can distinguish the one who is talking well on it, and the one who is talking

<hr>

[3]A group of poets who claimed descent from Homer, or more generally in this case, the admirers of Homer.

badly, will always be the same. Or, if he does not recognize the one who is talking badly, then, clearly, neither will he recognize the one who is talking well, granted that the subject is the same.

ION: That is so.

SOCRATES: Then the same man will be skilled with respect to both?

ION: Yes.

SOCRATES: Now you assert that Homer and the other poets, among them Hesiod and Archilochus, all treat of the same subjects, yet not all in the same fashion, but the one speaks well, and the rest of them speak worse.

ION: And what I say is true.

SOCRATES: Then you, if you can recognize the poet who speaks well, could also recognize the poets who speak worse, and see that they speak worse.

ION: So it seems.

SOCRATES: Well then, my best of friends, when we say that Ion has equal skill in Homer and all other poets, we shall not be mistaken. It must be so, since you yourself admit that the same man will be competent to judge of all who speak of the same matters, and that the poets virtually all deal with the same subjects.

ION: Then what can be the reason, Socrates, for my behavior? When anyone discusses any other poet, I pay no attention, and can offer no remark of any value. I frankly doze. But whenever anyone mentions Homer, immediately I am awake, attentive, and full of things to say.

SOCRATES: The riddle is not hard to solve, my friend. No, it is plain to everyone that not from art and knowledge comes your power to speak concerning Homer. If it were art that gave you power, then you could speak about all the other poets as well. There is an art of poetry as a whole? Am I not right?

ION: Yes.

SOCRATES: And is not the case the same with any other art you please, when you take it as a whole? The same method of inquiry holds for all the arts? Do you want some explanation, Ion, of what I mean by that?

ION: Yes, Socrates, upon my word I do. It gives me joy to listen to you wise men.

SOCRATES: I only wish you were right in saying that, Ion. But "wise men"! That means you, the rhapsodists and actors, and the men whose poems you chant, while I have nothing else to tell besides the truth, after the fashion of the ordinary man. For example, take the question I just now asked you. Observe what a trivial and commonplace remark it was that I uttered, something anyone might know, when I said that the inquiry is the same whenever one takes an art in its entirety. Let us reason the matter out. There is an art of painting taken as a whole?

ION: Yes.

SOCRATES: And there are and have been many painters, good and bad?

ION: Yes indeed.

SOCRATES: Now, take Polygnotus, son of Aglaophon. Have you ever seen a man with the skill to point out what is good and what is not in the works of Polygnotus, but without the power to do so in the works of other painters? A man who, when anybody shows the works of other painters, dozes off, is at a loss, has nothing to suggest, but when he has to express a judgment on one particular painter, say Polygnotus or anyone else you choose, wakes up, and is attentive, and is full of things to say?

ION: No, on my oath, I never saw the like.

SOCRATES: Or, again, take sculpture. Have you ever seen a man with the skill to judge the finer works of Daedalus, son of Metion, or of Epeus, son of Panopeus, or of Theodorus of Samos, or the works of any other single sculptor, but, confronted by the works of other sculptors, is at a loss, and dozes off, without a thing to say?

ION: No, on my oath, I never saw one.

SOCRATES: Yet further, as I think, the same is true of playing on the flute, and on the harp, and singing to the harp, and rhapsody. You never saw a man with the skill to judge of Olympus, of Thamyras, or of Orpheus, or of Phemius, the rhapsodist at Ithaca, but is at a loss, has no remark to make concerning Ion the Ephesian, and his success or failure in reciting.

ION: On that I cannot contradict you, Socrates. But of this thing I am conscious, that I excel all men in speaking about Homer, and on him have much to say, and that everybody else avers I do it well, but on the other poets I do not. Well then, see what that means.

SOCRATES: I do see, Ion, and in fact will proceed to show you what to my mind it betokens.

As I just now said, this gift you have of speaking well on Homer is not an art; it is a power divine, impelling you like the power in the stone Euripides called the magnet, which most call "stone of Heraclea." This stone does not simply attract the iron rings, just by themselves; it also imparts to the rings a force enabling them to do the same thing as the stone itself, that is, to attract another ring, so that sometimes a chain is formed, quite a long one, of iron rings, suspended from one another. For all of them, however, their power depends upon that loadstone. Just so the Muse. She first makes men inspired, and then through these inspired ones others share in the enthusiasm, and a chain is formed, for the epic poets, all the good ones, have their excellence, not from art, but are inspired, possessed, and thus they utter all these admirable poems. So is it also with the good lyric poets; as the worshiping Corybantes[4] are not in their senses when they dance, so the lyric poets are not in their senses when they make these lovely lyric poems. No, when once they launch into harmony and rhythm, they are seized with the Bacchic transport, and are possessed — as the bacchants, when possessed, draw milk and honey from the rivers, but not when in their senses. So the spirit of the lyric poet works, according to their own report. For the poets tell us, don't they, that the melodies they bring us are gathered from rills that run with honey, out of glens and gardens of the Muses, and they bring them as the bees do honey, flying like the bees? And what they say is true, for a poet is a light and winged thing, and holy, and never able to compose until he has become inspired, and is beside himself, and reason is no longer in him. So long as he has this in his possession, no man is able to make poetry or to chant in prophecy. Therefore, since their making is not by art, when they utter many things and fine about the deeds of men, just as you do about Homer, but is by lot divine — therefore each is able to do well only that to which the Muse has impelled him — one to make dithyrambs, another panegyric odes, another choral songs, another epic poems, another iambs. In all the rest, each one of them is poor, for not by art do they utter these, but by power divine, since if it were by art that they knew how to treat one subject finely, they would know how to deal with all the others too. Herein lies the reason why the deity has bereft them of their senses, and uses them as ministers, along with soothsayers and godly seers; it is in order that we listeners may know that it is not they who utter these precious revelations while their mind is not within them, but that it is the god himself who speaks, and through them becomes articulate to us. The most convincing evidence of this statement is offered by Tynnichus of Chalcis. He never composed a single poem worth recalling, save the song of praise which everyone repeats, wellnigh the finest of all lyrical poems, and absolutely what he called it, an "Invention of the Muses." By this example above all, it seems to me, the god would show us, lest we doubt, that these lovely poems are not of man or human workmanship, but are divine and from the gods, and that the poets are nothing but interpreters of the gods, each one possessed by the divinity to whom he is in bondage. And to prove this, the deity on purpose sang the loveliest of all lyrics through the most miserable poet. Isn't it so, Ion? Don't you think that I am right?[5]

ION: You are indeed, I vow! Socrates, your words in some way touch my very soul, and it does seem to me that by dispensation from above good poets convey to us these utterances of the gods.

SOCRATES: Well, and you rhapsodists, again, interpret the utterances of the poets?

ION: There also you are right.

SOCRATES: Accordingly, you are interpreters of interpreters?

ION: Undeniably.

SOCRATES: Wait now, Ion; tell me this. And answer frankly what I ask you. Suppose you are reciting epic poetry well, and thrill the spectators most deeply. You are chanting, say, the story of Odysseus as he leaped up to the dais, unmasked himself to the suitors, and poured the arrows out before his feet, or of Achilles rushing upon Hector, or one of the pitiful passages, about

---

[4]Female worshippers of Dionysus whose rites drove them to frenzy; cf. Euripides, *The Bacchae.*

[5]In the preceding speech, the language spoken by Socrates takes on the rhythms of the dithyramb — the traditional hymn to Dionysus — as though he himself were in an inspired state.

Andromache, or Hecuba, or Priam. When you chant these, are you in your senses? Or are you carried out of yourself, and does not your soul in an ecstasy conceive herself to be engaged in the actions you relate, whether they are in Ithaca, or Troy, or wherever the story puts them?

ION: How vivid, Socrates, you make your proof for me! I will tell you frankly that whenever I recite a tale of pity, my eyes are filled with tears, and when it is one of horror or dismay, my hair stands up on end with fear, and my heart goes leaping.

SOCRATES: Well now, Ion, what are we to say of a man like that? There he is, at a sacrifice or festival, got up in holiday attire, adorned with golden chaplets, and he weeps, though he has lost nothing of his finery. Or he recoils with fear, standing in the presence of more than twenty thousand friendly people, though nobody is stripping him or doing him damage. Shall we say that the man is in his senses?

ION: Never, Socrates, upon my word. That is strictly true.

SOCRATES: Now then, are you aware that you produce the same effects in most of the spectators too?

ION: Yes, indeed, I know it very well. As I look down at them from the stage above, I see them, every time, weeping, casting terrible glances, stricken with amazement at the deeds recounted. In fact, I have to give them very close attention, for if I set them weeping, I myself shall laugh when I get my money, but if they laugh, it is I who have to weep at losing it.

SOCRATES: Well, do you see that the spectator is the last of the rings I spoke of, which receive their force from one another by virtue of the loadstone? You, the rhapsodist and actor, are the middle ring, and the first one is the poet himself. But it is the deity who, through all the series, draws the spirit of men wherever he desires, transmitting the attractive force from one into another. And so, as from the loadstone, a mighty chain hangs down, of choric dancers, masters of the chorus, undermasters, obliquely fastened to the rings which are suspended from the Muse. One poet is suspended from one Muse, another from another; we call it being "possessed," but the fact is much the same, since he is *held*. And from these primary rings, the poets, others are in turn suspended, some attached to this one, some to that, and are filled with inspiration, some by Orpheus, others by Musaeus. But the majority are possessed and held by Homer, and, Ion, you are one of these, and are possessed by Homer. And whenever anyone chants the work of any other poet, you fall asleep, and haven't a thing to say, but when anybody gives tongue to a strain of this one, you are awake at once, your spirit dances, and you have much to say, for not by art or science do you say of Homer what you say, but by dispensation from above and by divine possession. So the worshiping Corybantes have a lively feeling for that strain alone which is of the deity by whom they are possessed, and for that melody are well supplied with attitudes and utterances, and heed no others. And so it is with you, Ion. When anyone mentions Homer, you are ready, but about the other poets you are at a loss. You ask me why you are ready about Homer and not about the rest. Because it is not by art but by lot divine that you are eloquent in praise of Homer.

ION: Well put, I grant you, Socrates. And yet I should be much surprised if by your argument you succeeded in convincing me that I am possessed or mad when I praise Homer. Nor do I think that you yourself would find me so if you heard me speaking upon Homer.

SOCRATES: And indeed I wish to hear you, but not until you have answered me as follows. On what point in Homer do you speak well? Not on all points, I take it.

ION: I assure you, Socrates, I do it on every point, without exception.

SOCRATES: Yet not, I fancy, on those matters of which you happen to be ignorant, but Homer tells of?

ION: And the matters Homer tells of, and I do not know, what are they?

SOCRATES: Why, does not Homer in many passages speak of arts, and have much to say about them? About driving a chariot, for instance; if I can recollect the lines, I'll repeat them to you.

ION: No, let me do it, for I know them.

SOCRATES: Then recite for me what Nestor says to Antilochus, his son, where he warns him to be careful at the turning post, in the lay of the horse race in honor of Patroclus.

ION:

Thyself lean slightly in the burnished car
To the left of them, then call upon the off horse
With goad and voice; with hand give him free rein.
And at the post let the near horse come so close
That the nave of the well-wrought wheel shall seem
To graze the stone. Which yet beware to strike![6]

SOCRATES: That will do. Now, Ion, in these lines, which will be more capable of judging whether Homer speaks aright or not, a doctor or a charioteer?

ION: The charioteer, do doubt.

SOCRATES: Because that is his art, or for some other reason?

ION: No, because it is his art.

SOCRATES: Each separate art, then, has had assigned to it by the deity the power of knowing a particular occupation? I take it that what we know by the pilot's art we do not know by the art of medicine as well.

ION: No indeed.

SOCRATES: And what we know by medical art we do not know by the builder's art as well.

ION: No indeed.

SOCRATES: Well, and so it is with all the arts? What we know by one of them, we do not know by another? But before you answer that, just tell me this. Do you allow a distinction between arts? One differs from another?

ION: Yes.

SOCRATES: Now with me the mark of differentiation is that one art means the knowledge of one kind of thing, another art the knowledge of another, and so I give them their respective names. Do you do that?

ION: Yes.

SOCRATES: If they meant simply knowledge of the same things, why should we distinguish one art from another? Why call them different, when both would give us the same knowledge? For example, take these fingers. I know that there are five of them, and you know the same as I about them. Suppose I asked you if we knew this same matter, you and I, by the same art, that of arithmetic, or by different arts. I fancy you would hold that we knew it by the same?

ION: Yes.

SOCRATES: Then tell me now what just a little while ago I was on the point of asking you. Does that seem true to you of all the arts — that, necessarily, the same art makes us know the same, another art not the same, but, if it really is another art, it must make us know something else?

ION: That is my opinion, Socrates.

SOCRATES: Well then, if one does not possess a given art, one will not be capable of rightly knowing what belongs to it in word or action?

ION: That is true.

SOCRATES: Then, in the lines which you recited, which will have the better knowledge whether Homer speaks aright or not, you or a charioteer?

ION: The charioteer.

SOCRATES: Doubtless because you are a rhapsode, and not a charioteer?

ION: Yes.

SOCRATES: The rhapsode's art is different from the charioteer's?

ION: Yes.

SOCRATES: If it is another art, then, it is a knowledge also about other matters.

ION: Yes.

SOCRATES: Now what about the passage in which Homer tells how Hecamede, Nestor's concubine, gave the wounded Machaon the broth to drink? The passage runs something like this:

She grated goat's-milk cheese in Pramnian wine,
With brazen grater, adding onion as a relish to the brew.[7]

On the question whether Homer here speaks properly or not, is it for the art of the physician, or the rhapsode's art, to discriminate aright?

ION: The art of the physician.

SOCRATES: What of this? The passage in which Homer says:

She plunged to the bottom like a leaden sinker
Which, mounted on the horntip from a field ox,
Speeds its way bringing mischief to voracious fish.[8]

[6] *Iliad* 23:335. [Tr.]

[7] *Iliad* 11:639–40. [Tr.]
[8] *Iliad* 24:80–82. [Tr.]

What shall we say? Is it rather for the art of fishing, or the rhapsode's art, to decide on what the verses mean, and whether they are good or not?

ION: Obviously, Socrates, it is for the art of fishing.

SOCRATES: Reflect now. Suppose that you were questioning, and asked me, "Now, Socrates, you find it is for these several arts to judge in Homer, severally, what appertains to each of them. Come then, pick me out the passages concerning the diviner, and the diviner's art, the kind of things that appertain to him, regarding which he must be able to discern whether the poetry is good or bad?" Observe how easily and truly I can answer you. The poet does, in fact, treat of this matter in the *Odyssey* too — for example, when a scion of Melampus, the diviner Theoclymenus, says to the wooers:

> Ah, wretched men, what bane is this ye suffer?
>> Shrouded in night
> Are your heads and your faces and your limbs
>> below,
> And kindled is the voice of wailing, and cheeks
>> are wet with tears.
> And the porch is full of ghosts; the hall is full of
>> them,
> Hastening hellward beneath the gloom, and the
>> sun
> Has perished out of heaven, and an evil mist
>> infolds the world.[9]

And he treats of it in many places in the *Iliad* — for instance, in the lay of the battle at the wall. There he says:

> For, as they were eager to pass over, a bird approached them,
> An eagle of lofty flight, skirting the host on the
>> left,
> And in its talons bearing a monstrous blood-red
>> serpent,
> Still alive and struggling; nor had it yet forgot the
>> joy of battle.
> Writhing back, it smote the bird that held it, upon
>> the breast
> Beside the neck, and the bird did cast it from him,
> In the agony of pain, to the earth,
> And dropped it in the middle of the throng.
> And, with a cry, himself went flying on the gusty
>> wind.[10]

[9] *Odyssey* 20:351–56. [Tr.]
[10] *Iliad* 12:200–08. [Tr.]

These passages, I contend, and others like them, appertain to the diviner to examine and to judge.

ION: And, Socrates, you are right.

SOCRATES: And you are right too, Ion, when you say so. Come now, you do for me what I have done for you. From both the *Odyssey* and *Iliad* I picked out for you the passages belonging to the doctor, the diviner, and the fisherman; now you likewise, since you are better versed than I in Homer, pick out for me the sort of passages, Ion, that concern the rhapsode and the rhapsode's art, the passages it befits the rhapsode, above all other men, to examine and to judge.

ION: *All* passages, Socrates, is what I say.

SOCRATES: Surely, Ion, you don't mean *all!* Are you really so forgetful? Indeed, it would ill become a man who is a rhapsode to forget.

ION: Why? What am I forgetting?

SOCRATES: Don't you remember how you stated that the art of the rhapsode was different from the charioteer's?

ION: I remember.

SOCRATES: Well, and you admitted also that, being different, it had another field of knowledge?

ION: Yes.

SOCRATES: Well then, by your own account the art of rhapsody will not know everything, nor the rhapsode either.

ION: The exceptions, Socrates, are doubtless only such matters as that.

SOCRATES: In "such matters" you must include approximately all the other arts. Well, as the rhapsode does not know the subject matter of them all, what sort of matters *will* he know?

ION: The kind of thing, I judge, that a man would say, and a woman would say, and a slave and a free man, a subject and a ruler — the suitable thing for each.

SOCRATES: You mean, the rhapsode will know better what the ruler of a ship in a storm at sea should say than will the pilot?

ION: No, in that case the pilot will know better.

SOCRATES: But suppose it is the ruler of a sick man. Will the rhapsode know better what the ruler should say than will the doctor?

ION: No, not in that case, either.

SOCRATES: But you say, "the kind of speech that suits a slave."

ION: Yes.

SOCRATES: You mean, for instance, if the slave is a cowherd, it is not he who will know what one should say to quiet angry cattle, but the rhapsode?

ION: Surely not.

SOCRATES: Well, "the kind of speech that suits a woman" — one who spins — about the working up of wool?

ION: No.

SOCRATES: Well, the rhapsodist will know "the kind of speech that suits a man" — a general exhorting his soldiers?

ION: Yes! that is the sort of thing the rhapsodist will know.

SOCRATES: What! Is the rhapsode's art the general's?

ION: At all events I ought to know the kind of speech a general should make.

SOCRATES: Indeed, you doubtless have the talents of a general, Ion! And suppose you happened to have skill in horsemanship, along with skill in playing on the lyre, you would know when horses were well or badly ridden, but if I asked you, "By which art, Ion, do you know that horses are well managed — is it because you are a horseman, or because you play the lyre?" What answer would you give me?

ION: I should say, "It is by my skill as horseman."

SOCRATES: Then, too, if you were picking out good players on the lyre, you would admit that you discerned them by your art in playing the lyre, and not by your art as horseman?

ION: Yes.

SOCRATES: But when you know of military matters, do you know them because you are competent as a general, or as a rhapsode?

ION: I cannot see a bit of difference.

SOCRATES: What, no difference, you say? You mean to call the art of the rhapsode and the art of the general a single art, or two?

ION: To me, there is a single art.

SOCRATES: And so, whoever is an able rhapsode is going to be an able general as well?

ION: Unquestionably, Socrates.

SOCRATES: And then, whoever happens to be an able general is an able rhapsode too.

ION: No, I do not think that holds.

SOCRATES: But you think the other does? That whoever is an able rhapsode is an able general too?

ION: Absolutely!

SOCRATES: Well, and you are the ablest rhapsodist in Greece?

ION: Yes, Socrates, by far.

SOCRATES: And the ablest general, Ion? The ablest one in Greece?

ION: You may be sure of it, for, Socrates, I learned this also out of Homer.

SOCRATES: Then, Ion, how in heaven's name is this? You are at once the ablest general and ablest rhapsodist among the Greeks, and yet you go about Greece performing as a rhapsode, but not as general. What think you? The Greeks are in great need of a rhapsode adorned with a wreath of gold, and do not need a general at all?[11]

ION: It is because my native city, Socrates, is under your dominion, and your military rule, and has no need whatever of a general. As for yours and Lacedaemon, neither would choose me for general; you think yourselves sufficient to yourselves.

SOCRATES: Excellent Ion, you know who Apollodorus is, of Cyzicus, don't you?

ION: What might he be?

SOCRATES: The man whom the Athenians at various times have chosen for their general, although he is an alien. The same is true of Phanosthenes of Andros, and Heraclides of Clazomenae, also aliens, who nevertheless, when they had shown their competence, were raised to the generalship by the city, and put in other high positions. And Ion of Ephesus, will she not elect him general, and accord him honors, if his worth becomes apparent? Why, you inhabitants of Ephesus are originally Athenians, are you not, and Ephesus is a city inferior to none? But the fact is, Ion, that if you are right, if it really is by art and knowledge that you are able to praise Homer, then you do me wrong. You assure me that you have much fine knowledge about Homer, and you keep offering to display it, but you are deceiving me. Far from giving the display, you will not even tell me what subject it is on which you are so able, though all this while I have been

---

[11]The dialogue occurs during the Peloponnesian War, which Athens eventually lost to Sparta.

entreating you to tell. No, you are just like Proteus; you twist and turn, this way and that, assuming every shape, until finally you elude my grasp and reveal yourself as a general. And all in order not to show how skilled you are in the lore concerning Homer! So if you are an artist, and, as I said just now, if you only promised me a display on Homer in order to deceive me, then you are at fault. But if you are not an artist, if by lot divine you are possessed by Homer, and so, knowing nothing, speak many things and fine about the poet, just as I said you did, then you do no wrong. Choose, therefore, how you will be called by us, whether we shall take you for a man unjust, or for a man divine.

ION: The difference, Socrates, is great. It is far lovelier to be deemed divine.

SOCRATES: This lovelier title, Ion, shall be yours, to be in our minds divine, and not an artist, in praising Homer.

From *Phaedrus*

SOCRATES: I have heard a tradition of the ancients, whether true or not they only know; although if we had found the truth ourselves, do you think that we should care much about the opinions of men?

PHAEDRUS: Your question needs no answer; but I wish that you would tell me what you say that you have heard.

SOCRATES: At the Egyptian city of Naucratis,[1] there was a famous old god, whose name was Theuth; the bird which is called the Ibis is sacred to him, and he was the inventor of many arts, such as arithmetic and calculation and geometry and astronomy and draughts and dice, but his great discovery was the use of letters. Now in those days the god Thamus[2] was the king of the whole country of Egypt; and he dwelt in that great city of Upper Egypt which the Hellenes call Egyptian Thebes, and the god himself is called by them Ammon. To him came Theuth and showed his inventions, desiring that the other Egyptians might be allowed to have the benefit of them; he enumerated them, and Thamus enquired about their several uses, and praised some of them and censured others, as he approved or disapproved them. It would take a long time to repeat all that Thamus said to Theuth in praise or blame of the various arts. But when they came to letters, This, said Theuth, will make the Egyptians wiser and give them better memories; it is a specific both for the memory and for the wit. Thamus replied: O most ingenious Theuth, the parent or inventor of an art is not always the best judge of the utility or inutility of his own inventions to the users of them. And in this instance, you who are the father of letters, from a paternal love of your own children have been led to attribute to them a quality which they cannot have; for this discovery of yours will create forgetfulness in the learners' souls, because they will not use their memories; they will trust to the external written characters and not remember of themselves. The specific which you have discovered is an aid not to memory, but to reminiscence, and you give your disciples not truth, but only the semblance of truth; they will be hearers of many things and will have learned nothing; they will appear to be omniscient and will generally know nothing; they will be tiresome company, having the show of wisdom without reality.

PHAEDRUS: Yes, Socrates, you can easily invent tales of Egypt, or of any other country.

Translated by Benjamin Jowett.
[1] A Greek trading colony in the Nile Delta founded in the seventh century B.C.E.
[2] Theuth and Thamus are better known as the Egyptian gods Thoth and Ammon, the god of learning and the god of power.

SOCRATES: There was a tradition in the temple of Dodona[3] that oaks first gave prophetic utterances. The men of old, unlike in their simplicity to young philosophy, deemed that if they heard the truth even from 'oak or rock,' it was enough for them; whereas you seem to consider not whether a thing is or is not true, but who the speaker is and from what country the tale comes.

PHAEDRUS: I acknowledge the justice of your rebuke; and I think that the Theban[4] is right in his view about letters.

SOCRATES: He would be a very simple person, and quite a stranger to the oracles of Thamus or Ammon, who should leave in writing or receive in writing any art under the idea that the written word would be intelligible or certain; or who deemed that writing was at all better than knowledge and recollection of the same matters?

PHAEDRUS: That is most true.

SOCRATES: I cannot help feeling, Phaedrus, that writing is unfortunately like painting; for the creations of the painter have the attitude of life, and yet if you ask them a question they preserve a solemn silence. And the same may be said of speeches. You would imagine that they had intelligence, but if you want to know anything and put a question to one of them, the speaker always gives one unvarying answer. And when they have been once written down they are tumbled about anywhere among those who may or may not understand them, and know not to whom they should reply, to whom not: and, if they are maltreated or abused, they have no parent to protect them; and they cannot protect or defend themselves.

PHAEDRUS: That again is most true.

SOCRATES: Is there not another kind of word or speech far better than this, and having far greater power — a son of the same family, but lawfully begotten?

PHAEDRUS: Whom do you mean, and what is his origin?

SOCRATES: I mean an intelligent word graven in the soul of the learner, which can defend itself, and knows when to speak and when to be silent.

PHAEDRUS: You mean the living word of knowledge which has a soul, and of which the written word is properly no more than an image?

SOCRATES: Yes, of course that is what I mean. And now may I be allowed to ask you a question: Would a husbandman, who is a man of sense, take the seeds, which he values and which he wishes to bear fruit, and in sober seriousness plant them during the heat of summer, in some garden of Adonis,[5] that he may rejoice when he sees them in eight days appearing in beauty? at least he would do so, if at all, only for the sake of amusement and pastime. But when he is in earnest he sows in fitting soil, and practices husbandry, and is satisfied if in eight months the seeds which he has sown arrive at perfection?

PHAEDRUS: Yes, Socrates, that will be his way when he is in earnest; he will do the other, as you say, only in play.

SOCRATES: And can we suppose that he who knows the just and good and honorable has less understanding, than the husbandman, about his own seeds?

PHAEDRUS: Certainly not.

SOCRATES: Then he will not seriously incline to 'write' his thoughts 'in water' with pen and ink, sowing words which can neither speak for themselves nor teach the truth adequately to others?

PHAEDRUS: No, that is not likely.

SOCRATES: No, that is not likely — in the garden of letters he will sow and plant, but only for the sake of recreation and amusement; he will write them down as memorials to be treasured against the forgetfulness of old age, by himself, or by any other old man who is treading the same path. He will rejoice in beholding their tender growth; and while others are refreshing their souls with banqueting and the like, this will be the pastime in which his days are spent.

---

[3]Site of the most ancient temple to Zeus, whose priests gave out oracles based on the leaves of the sacred oak tree.
[4]Thamus/Ammon.

[5]In the midsummer festival of Adonis (the mortal but annually resurrected lover of Aphrodite), women planted seeds in baskets or shallow bowls on rooftops, and watered them daily. The plants, which sprouted quickly, were thrown into the sea on the eighth day, along with an image of the dead Adonis.

PHAEDRUS: A pastime, Socrates, as noble as the other is ignoble, the pastime of a man who can be amused by serious talk, and can discourse merrily about justice and the like.

SOCRATES: True, Phaedrus. But nobler far is the serious pursuit of the dialectician, who, finding a congenial soul, by the help of science sows and plants therein words which are able to help themselves and him who planted them, and are not unfruitful, but have in them a seed which others brought up in different soils render immortal, making the possessors of it happy to the utmost extent of human happiness.

PHAEDRUS: Far nobler, certainly.

SOCRATES: And now, Phaedrus, having agreed upon the premises we may decide about the conclusion.

PHAEDRUS: About what conclusion?

SOCRATES: About Lysias,[6] whom we censured, and his art of writing, and his discourses, and the rhetorical skill or want of skill which was shown in them — these are the questions which we sought to determine, and they brought us to this point. And I think that we are now pretty well informed about the nature of art and its opposite.

PHAEDRUS: Yes, I think with you; but I wish that you would repeat what was said.

SOCRATES: Until a man knows the truth of the several particulars of which he is writing or speaking, and is able to define them as they are, and having defined them again to divide them until they can be no longer divided, and until in like manner he is able to discern the nature of the soul, and discover the different modes of discourse which are adapted to different natures, and to arrange and dispose of them in such a way that the simple form of speech may be addressed to the simpler nature, and the complex and composite to the more complex nature — until he has accomplished all this, he will be unable to handle arguments according to rules of art, as far as their nature allows them to be subjected to art, either for the purpose of teaching or persuading — such is the view which is implied in the whole preceding argument.

PHAEDRUS: Yes, that was our view, certainly.

SOCRATES: Secondly, as to the censure which was passed on the speaking or writing of discourses, and how they might be rightly or wrongly censured — did not our previous argument show — ?

PHAEDRUS: Show what?

SOCRATES: That whether Lysias or any other writer that ever was or will be, whether private man or statesman, proposes laws and so becomes the author of a political treatise, fancying that there is any great certainty and clearness in his performance, the fact of his so writing is only a disgrace to him, whatever men may say. For not to know the nature of justice and injustice, and good and evil, and not to be able to distinguish the dream from the reality, cannot in truth be otherwise than disgraceful to him, even though he have the applause of the whole world.

PHAEDRUS: Certainly.

SOCRATES: But he who thinks that in the written word there is necessarily much which is not serious, and that neither poetry nor prose, spoken or written, is of any great value, if, like the compositions of the rhapsodes,[7] they are only recited in order to be believed, and not with any view to criticism or instruction; and who thinks that even the best of writings are but a reminiscence of what we know, and that only in principles of justice and goodness and nobility taught and communicated orally for the sake of instruction and graven in the soul, which is the true way of writing, is there clearness and perfection and seriousness, and that such principles are a man's own and his legitimate offspring; — being, in the first place, the word which he finds in his own bosom; secondly, the brethren and descendants and relations of his idea which have been duly implanted by him in the souls of others; — and who cares for them and no others — this is the right sort of man; and you and I, Phaedrus, would pray that we may become like him.

---

[6]Athenian sophist (459–380 B.C.E.) Thirty-four of whose orations are still extant. His oration on love, analyzed and refuted in the Phaedrus, argued that a beloved should yield to someone not in love with him, not to a lover.

[7]Performers who recited poetry, particularly the works of Homer.

PHAEDRUS: That is most assuredly my desire and prayer.

SOCRATES: And now the play is played out; and of rhetoric enough. Go and tell Lysias that to the fountain and school of the Nymphs[8] we went down, and were bidden by them to convey a message to him and to other composers of speeches — to Homer and other writers of poems, whether set to music or not; and to Solon and others who have composed writings in the form of political discourses which they would term laws — to all of them we are to say that if their compositions are based on knowledge of the truth, and they can defend or prove them, when they are put to the test, by spoken arguments, which leave their writings poor in comparison of them, then they are to be called, not only poets, orators, legislators, but are worthy of a higher name, befitting the serious pursuit of their life.

PHAEDRUS: What name would you assign to them?

SOCRATES: Wise, I may not call them; for that is a great name which belongs to God alone, — lovers of wisdom or philosophers is their modest and befitting title.

[8]The stream of Ilissus, where Socrates' conversation with Phaedrus begins, and where, according to legend, Boreas (the North Wind) was supposed to have carried off the nymph Orythia.

❖ DIALOGUE WITH PLATO

Leo Tolstoy

1828–1910

Born at Yasnaya Polyana, Russia, Count Leo Nikolaievich Tolstoy enjoyed a dissipated youth before enlisting in the army to reform himself. There he began to write, partly to relieve the boredom of guard duty in the Caucasus, publishing sketches and stories starting in 1852. Back on his estate, he began to plan out his vast epic of Napoleonic Russia, *War and Peace*, which was completed in 1869; his more concentrated psychological tragedy, *Anna Karenina*, was published in 1877. That year Tolstoy experienced a spiritual crisis, repudiated his previous work with the exception of two short stories, and devoted himself rigorously to the doctrines of quietism (non-resistance to evil) and the social improvement of mankind.

What Is Art? may be, as Ernest J. Simmons, a scholar of Russian literature, has said, "the most immodest contribution to aesthetics ever written." Composed at white heat in 1897, it is the fruit of Tolstoy's speculations since the 1850s about the nature of art. Except for Tolstoy's biographers, few commentators have been charitable to *What Is Art?*, partly because Tolstoy himself is so dismissive of all previous aesthetic thought and partly because the conclusions to which he comes put most of the masterpieces of painting, music, and literature (including Tolstoy's own) into the vast category of bad art. In fact, Tolstoy's notions about art have an admirable consistency, and they are important if only because they voice a theory one needs to learn how to argue with.

Tolstoy begins by rejecting most of the central aesthetic principles of the nineteenth century. He is mystified by Hegel's idea that art is a necessary road to Absolute Spirit, and equally mystified by philosophers' use of the idea of beauty. The various definitions of beauty either lead in a circle (e.g., "beauty is that which pleases without exciting desire") or culminate in the notion of taste, which is unsatisfactory because people's tastes differ, so that any aesthetic based on taste would have to be specific to a particular class, and hence, insufficiently universal. At this point, Tolstoy presents his own idea of art:

> To evoke in oneself a feeling that one has once experienced and having evoked it in oneself then by means of movements, lines, colors, sounds or forms expressed in words, so to transmit that feeling that others experience the same feeling — that is the activity of art.
>
> Art is a human activity consisting in this, that one man consciously by means of certain external signs, hands on to others feelings he has lived through, and that others are infected by these feelings and also experience them.
>
> Art is not, as the metaphysicians say, the manifestation of some mysterious Idea of beauty or God; it is not, as the aesthetic physiologists say, a game in which man lets off his excess of stored-up energy; it is not the expression of man's emotions by external signs; it is not the production of pleasing objects; and, above all, it is not pleasure; but it is a means of union among men joining them together in the same feelings, and indispensable for the life and progress towards well-being of individuals and humanity. (Ch. 5)

If art is a form of infection, then there are two criteria for value, one internal and the other external. The internal criterion is *efficacy:* the best art will be that which infects us most strongly, and this, Tolstoy said, depends upon "(1) the greater or lesser individuality of the feeling transmitted; (2) on the greater or lesser clearness with which the feeling is transmitted; (3) on the sincerity of the artist" (Ch. 15).

More significant to Tolstoy was the external criterion for quality of art: the subject matter, which would determine the specific feelings that were communicated. The better the feelings according to some criterion of value, the better the art. Tolstoy does not pause to justify which are the best feelings. He merely suggests that every society has what he calls a "religious ideal," which becomes the repository of its most cherished values. (Tolstoy emphatically does not mean the ideal of any specific *organized* religion, since he was inveterately hostile to all religious cults as coming between man and God.) This value system Tolstoy locates in "Christianity in its true meaning" — what is today called the Judeo-Christian tradition of human brotherhood.

Once he has located the values which art should infect us with, Tolstoy is forced to distinguish invidiously between the upper class art of his time, whose infectious feelings were those to which the upper class are devoted — pride, sensuality, and ennui — and universal art, which serves *"to unite men with God and with one another."*

Here he distinguishes once more between the "higher, positive" kind of true art, which actively transmits the message of human brotherhood (and he gives a list that includes Dickens's *A Christmas Carol* and Eliot's *Adam Bede*), and a "lower, negative kind," which conveys universal feelings, if not the feeling of universality (the list here includes *Don Quixote* and Molière's comedies).

Had Tolstoy stopped here, he might have found general agreement with his thesis, but he also felt compelled to point out the negative consequence of his theory, which is that most of the artistic works beloved of the intelligentsia are, in his terms, bad art. Shakespeare's plays, for example, in that his characters speak a language never spoken by normal people and unintelligible to the normal people of the present day, work to divide rather than unite humankind. The same would be true of music, like Beethoven's *Ninth Symphony,* since, regardless of its explicit message, the medium in which it is expressed is such as to be unintelligible to most people. (A simple folksong or a lullaby would for Tolstoy be considered better art.) If Tolstoy was brutal, he was also consistent enough to consign most of his own works to the dustbin: He repudiated *War and Peace* and *Anna Karenina* as bad art, and excepted from the general condemnation only two of his stories: "God Sees the Truth but Waits" and "A Captive in the Caucasus."

The difficulties with *What Is Art?* have less to do with consistency than with the theory's external plausibility and internal coherence. It is questionable, for instance, whether feelings of pride, sensuality, and ennui are found only among the upper classes or whether modern culture has not made them universal. Similarly, Tolstoy's assumption that a folksong is more universal than a Beethoven symphony needs to be examined: The folksong, like the symphony, is informed by a Western scale and strophic form that may not be intelligible to a different musical culture (Indonesians, for example, or Hopi Indians). On the other side, Tolstoy (who was not musical) tended to overestimate the amount of cultural training required to appreciate a symphony. Internally, there are difficulties with the "infection" theory that Tolstoy did not anticipate. For one thing, the criterion of *sincerity* of feeling is one that cannot be tested: We know what a work has communicated to us but cannot know whether it is the same thing the artist experienced or indeed whether the artist experienced anything at all. In fact, the central notion implicit in Tolstoy's infection metaphor — the idea that art instills identical feelings into its whole audience — is equally untestable, since we cannot cross-compare the feelings of everyone who has experienced and will experience a specific work. These problems do not devastate Tolstoy's theory: They are objections that can be answered. But it is interesting to note what different questions arise when a moral critique of art (begun by Plato) is couched, as Tolstoy's version is, in the post-Romantic aesthetic tradition that art is a form not of imitation but of self-expression.

Selected Bibliography

Allen, James Sloan, "Tolstoy's Prophecy: *What Is Art?* Today." *New Criterion* 17 (December 1998): 15–20.

Bayley, John. *Tolstoy and the Novel*. London: Chatto and Windus, 1966.

Farrell, James T. *Literature and Morality*. New York: Vanguard Press, 1947.

Garrod, H. W. *Tolstoi's Theory of Art*. Oxford: Clarendon Press, 1935.

Jones, Malcolm, ed. *New Essays on Tolstoy*. Cambridge and New York: Cambridge University Press, 1978.

Kasulke, Maren S. "A Case of Well-Concealed Indebtedness: L. N. Tolstoy's Rejection of Kantian Beauty in *What Is Art?*" *Canadian Review of Comparative Literature* 27, nos. 1–2 (2000): 25–50.

Macy, John A. "Tolstoi's Moral Theory of Art." *Century Magazine* 62 (1901): 298–307.

Maude, Aylmer. *Tolstoi on Art and Its Critics*. London: H. Milford, 1925.

Perosa, Sergio. "James, Tolstoy, and the Novel." *Revue de Littérature Comparée* 53 (1983): 359–68.

Steiner, George. *Tolstoy or Dostoyevsky: An Essay in Contrast*. London: Faber and Faber, 1960.

Tolstoy, Lev Nikolaievich. *What Is Art?* Trans. Aylmer Maude. New York: T. Y. Crowell, 1898.

Troyat, Henri. *Tolstoy*. Garden City, NY: Doubleday, 1967.

From *What Is Art?*

How in the subject-matter of art are we to decide what is good and what is bad?

Art like speech is a means of communication and therefore of progress, that is, of the movement of humanity forward toward perfection. Speech renders accessible to men of the latest generations all the knowledge discovered by the experience and reflection both of preceding generations and of the best and foremost men of their own times; art

Translated by Aylmer Maude.

renders accessible to men of the latest generations all the feelings experienced by their predecessors and also those felt by their best and foremost contemporaries. And as the evolution of knowledge proceeds by truer and more necessary knowledge dislodging and replacing what was mistaken and unnecessary, so the evolution of feeling proceeds by means of art — feelings less kind and less necessary for the well-being of mankind being replaced by others kinder and more needful for that end. That is the purpose of art. And speaking now of the feelings which are its subject-matter, the more art fulfills that purpose the better the art, and the less it fulfills it the worse the art.

The appraisement of feelings (that is, the recognition of one or other set of feelings as more or less good, more or less necessary for the well-being of mankind) is effected by the religious perception of the age. . . .

The art of our time should be appraised differently from former art chiefly in this, that the art of our time, that is, Christian art (basing itself on a religious perception which demands the union of man), excludes from the domain of art good in its subject matter, everything transmitting exclusive feelings which do not unite men but divide them. It relegates such work to the category of art that is bad in its subject matter; while on the other hand it includes in the category of art that is good in subject matter a section not formerly admitted as deserving of selection and respect, namely, universal art transmitting even the most trifling and simple feelings if only they are accessible to all men without exception, and therefore unite them. Such art cannot but be esteemed good in our time, for it attains the end which Christianity, the religious perception of our time, sets before humanity.

Christian art either evokes in men feelings which through love of God and of one's neighbor draw them to closer and ever closer union and make them ready for, and capable of, such union; or evokes in them feelings which show them that they are already united in the joys and sorrows of life. And therefore the Christian art of our time can be and is of two kinds: first, art transmitting feelings flowing from a religious perception of man's position in the world in relation to God and to his neighbor — religious art in the limited meaning of the term; and secondly, art transmitting the simplest feelings of common life, but such always as are accessible to all men in the whole world — the art of common life — the art of the people — universal art. Only these two kinds of art can be considered good art in our time.

The first, religious art — transmitting both positive feelings of love of God and one's neighbor, and negative feelings of indignation and horror at the violation of love — manifests itself chiefly in the form of words, and to some extent also in painting and sculpture: the second kind, universal art, transmitting feelings accessible to all, manifests itself in

words, in painting, in sculpture, in dances, in architecture, and most of all in music.

If I were asked to give modern examples of each of these kinds of art, then as examples of the highest art flowing from love of God and man (both of the higher, positive, and of the lower, negative kind), in literature I should name *The Robbers* by Schiller; Victor Hugo's *Les Pauvres Gens* and *Les Misérables;* the novels and stories of Dickens — *The Tale of Two Cities, The Christmas Carol, The Chimes,* and others — *Uncle Tom's Cabin;* Dostoyevsky's works — especially his *Memoirs from the House of Death* — and *Adam Bede* by George Eliot.

In modern painting, strange to say, works of this kind, directly transmitting the Christian feeling of love of God and of one's neighbor, are hardly to be found, especially among the works of the celebrated painters. There are plenty of pictures treating of the Gospel stories; these however, while depicting historical events with great wealth of detail, do not and cannot transmit religious feelings not possessed by their painters. There are many pictures treating of the personal feelings of various people, but of pictures representing great deeds of self-sacrifice and Christian love there are very few, and what there are are principally by artists who are not celebrated, and they are for the most part not pictures but merely sketches. Such for instance is the drawing by Kramskoy (worth many of his finished pictures), showing a drawing-room with a balcony past which troops are marching in triumph on their return from the war. On the balcony stands a wet-nurse holding a baby, and a boy. They are admiring the procession of the troops, but the mother, covering her face with a handkerchief, has fallen back on the sofa sobbing. Such also is the picture by Walter Langley to which I have already referred, and such again is a picture by the French artist Morlon, depicting a lifeboat hastening in a heavy storm to the relief of a steamer that is being wrecked. Approaching these in kind are pictures which represent the hard-working peasant with respect and love. Such are the pictures by Millet and particularly his drawing, *The Man with the Hoe,* also pictures in this style by Jules Breton, Lhermitte, Defregger, and others. As examples of pictures evoking indignation and horror at the violation of love of God and man, Gay's picture *Judgment* may serve, and also Leizen-Mayer's *Signing the Death*

Warrant. But there are very few of this kind also. Anxiety about the technique and the beauty of the picture for the most part obscures the feeling. For instance, Gérôme's *Pollice Verso* expresses, not so much horror at what is being perpetrated as attraction by the beauty of the spectacle.[1]

To give examples from the modern art of our upper classes, of art of the second kind: good universal art, or even of the art of a whole people, is yet more difficult, especially in literature and music. If there are some works which by their inner contents might be assigned to this class (such as *Don Quixote,* Molière's comedies, *David Copperfield* and *The Pickwick Papers* by Dickens, Gogol's and Pushkin's tales, and some things of Maupassant's), these works for the most part — owing to the exceptional nature of the feelings they transmit, and the superfluity of special details of time and locality, and above all on account of the poverty of their subject matter in comparison with examples of universal ancient art (such, for instance, as the story of Joseph) — are comprehensible only to people of their own circle. That Joseph's brethren, being jealous of his father's affection, sell him to the merchants; that Potiphar's wife wishes to tempt the youth; that having attained to highest station he takes pity on his brothers, including Benjamin the favorite — these and all the rest are feelings accessible alike to a Russian peasant, a Chinese, an African, a child, or an old man, educated or uneducated; and it is all written with such restraint, is so free from any superfluous detail, that the story may be told to any circle and will be equally comprehensible and touching to everyone. But not such are the feelings of Don Quixote or of Molière's heroes (though Molière is perhaps the most universal, and therefore the most excellent, artist of modern times), nor of Pickwick and his friends. These feelings are not common to all men but very exceptional, and therefore to make them contagious the authors have surrounded them with abundant details of time and place. And this abundance of detail makes the stories difficult of comprehension to all who do not live within reach of the conditions described by the author.

[1]In this picture the spectators in the Roman Amphitheater are turning down their thumbs to show that they wish the vanquished gladiator to be killed. [Tr.]

The author of the novel of Joseph did not need to describe in detail, as would be done nowadays, the blood-stained coat of Joseph, the dwelling and dress of Jacob, the pose and attire of Potiphar's wife, and how adjusting the bracelet on her left arm she said, "Come to me," and so on, because the content of feeling in this novel is so strong that all details except the most essential — such as that Joseph went out into another room to weep — are superfluous and would only hinder the transmission of emotion. And therefore this novel is accessible to all men, touches people of all nations and classes young and old, and has lasted to our times and will yet last for thousands of years to come. But strip the best novels of our time of their details and what will remain? . . .

Beethoven's *Ninth Symphony* is considered a great work of art. To verify its claim to be such I must first ask myself whether this work transmits the highest religious feeling? I reply in the negative, since music in itself cannot transmit those feelings; and therefore I ask myself next: Since this work does not belong to the highest kind of religious art, has it the other characteristic of the good art of our time — the quality of uniting all men in one common feeling — does it rank as Christian universal art? And again I have no option but to reply in the negative; for not only do I not see how the feelings transmitted by this work could unite people not specially trained to submit themselves to its complex hypnotism, but I am unable to imagine to myself a crowd of normal people who could understand anything of this long, confused, and artificial production, except short snatches which are lost in a sea of what is incomprehensible. And therefore, whether I like it or not, I am compelled to conclude that this work belongs to the rank of bad art. It is curious to note in this connexion, that attached to the end of this very symphony is a poem of Schiller's[2] which (though somewhat obscurely) expresses this very thought, namely that feeling (Schiller speaks only of the feeling of gladness) unites people and evokes love in them. But though this poem is sung at the end of the symphony, the music does not accord with the thought expressed in the verses; for the music is exclusive and does not unite all men, but unites only a few, dividing them off from the rest of mankind.

[2]The "Ode to Joy."

Aristotle

384–322 B.C.E.

Unlike his teacher Plato, who was a native-born Athenian aristocrat, Aristotle was a *metic* — a foreigner with a green card, as it were — the son of a doctor from Thrace. Aristotle's origins may help explain why Plato's idealism had so little ultimate appeal for him. As a skilled biologist from Macedonia, an impoverished military state, Aristotle may have been loath to dismiss physical reality as an illusion. Certainly for Aristotle the universal *processes* of nature, the eternal laws of change, were not mere signs of the mutable, inferior character of the world of Becoming compared with the unalterable world of Ideas. They possessed immense significance.

Aristotle spent many years in Plato's Academy, learning its philosophy and its methods of argumentation, but his own school, the Lyceum, rejected Plato's idealism in favor of a materialism that investigated every aspect of the physical world. If Plato is the father of Western philosophy, Aristotle is the father of most of the sciences. Although Aristotle was often wildly wrong about details (Galileo's disproof of his speculations on gravity is the most famous instance), his systematizing of thought made science as we know it possible.

Aristotle's immense philosophical output may be divided into treatises on three types of science: the *theoretical* sciences, like logic or physics, which aimed at improving thought itself — one's general ideas on a particular subject; the *practical* sciences, like ethics and politics, whose goal lay in the realm of human action; and the *productive* sciences, like rhetoric and poetics, whose purpose was in making something. Here already, one can see a major difference from Plato, whose *Republic* combined speculation on metaphysics, ethics, politics, music, poetry, and much else. For Plato, thought was *holistic:* all was ultimately One and could be known through one dialectical method. For Aristotle, the world was not One but Many, and investigating it meant adapting one's methods and principles to the subject under consideration. This is the *problematic* method, and it is rare in the history of philosophy, where most thinkers have preferred universal dialectic to institutionalized improvisation. At the same time, Aristotle's mode of organization has clearly prevailed over Plato's in the structure of the modern university, where specialized departments of physics, psychology, literature, and music pursue their disparate disciplines by different methodologies.

Textual scholars believe the *Poetics* to be what is technically termed an *esoteric* treatise — it was circulated privately, within the Lyceum — rather than an *exoteric* one meant for general publication. It can be compared to teacher's lecture notes, brief and pointed, but meant to be filled out with further examples and arguments during presentation. Where the text seems dogmatic or disconnected or downright obscure, we should be tolerant — this was not the form in which Aristotle's students received it. There are other sources of obscurity, of course, the usual gaps that appear in transmitting and translating a verbal text more than two thousand years old. In Chapter 6, for example, Aristotle tells us that he will speak of comedy later, but never returns to the subject. It has been presumed for centuries that the treatise on comedy was a second book of the *Poetics* that had been lost forever. Recently a manuscript has turned up containing what some scholars believe to be fragments of the lost *Poetics II,* but whether the fragments are genuinely Aristotelian or not is still undecided.

ORGANIZATION AND METHOD

As a treatise on productive science, the *Poetics* takes as its topic the making of a work of art, specifically a dramatic or epic tragedy. Although the *Poetics* was later misread as a how-to manual, Aristotle was only presenting the general *principles* of dramatic construction as they applied to the poetry and theater of his age; he was not dispensing tips for the practicing tragedian. Later critics attacked the drama of their day for not conforming to Aristotle's rules, often without understanding the reasons behind his general statements or the highly empirical basis of the *Poetics*. It would be as much a mistake to fault Aristotle for not being able to anticipate every development in the drama over the last two millennia.

Productive science relies on Aristotle's method of four-cause analysis, in which an artifact is defined by its shape (the formal cause), its composition (the material cause), its manner of construction (the efficient cause), and its end or purpose (the final cause).[1] Thus, in the poetics of hammers, that tool might be defined by its shape (a long handle to give leverage, a flat striking surface), its materials (hard metal for the head, light but strong wood or plastic for the handle), its manner of construction (the relation and attachments of the parts), and its purpose (pounding nails). In defining a dramatic or epic tragedy, the same method of definition is used. Here the material is language, rhythm, and harmony; the form is the imitation of a serious action; the manner is dramatic or narrative (as the case may be); and the end is the *katharsis* of pity and fear (about which more will be said later). The first four chapters of the *Poetics* discuss the causes of tragedy (among the other arts) and prepare the reader for the famous definition of tragedy in Chapter 6.

(Note that Aristotle never formally defines more general categories like *poetry* or *drama*. For him these are not legitimate genres. They are not definable because they do not have all their causes in common. Those things called poetry are similar in formal and material causes; those called drama in formal, material, and efficient causes; but because they do not have similar final causes, they remain congeries of many things rather than one definite species. Aristotle is a genre critic, in other words, not by choice but because of the demands of his systematic method.)

Having defined tragedy, Aristotle analyzes its qualitative parts (plot, character, thought, diction, song, and spectacle), and then examines each part successively, beginning with the most important — plot. Nearly half of the *Poetics* is devoted to the analysis of plot, and here again the same four-cause organization is used. Aristotle considers plot *form* (its general character, length, relation to history, the course of the action, and so on), plot *materials* (devices like recognition and reversal or the tragic deed), and plot *handling*. All these technical issues are

[1]The method of analysis is itself discussed in the *Posterior Analytics,* one of Aristotle's major treatises on logic.

explained ultimately in terms of the *purpose* of plot, the *katharsis.* In Chapter 13, he argues deductively that *hamartia* — the tragic protagonist's character flaw — derives directly from the nature of the tragic emotions of pity and fear. Later he moves from plot to the formal and material aspects of character, thought, and so on. Throughout, his method is rigorous, though what remains of the *Poetics* is not complete and there are occasional interruptions or interpolations (like Chapter 12).

ARISTOTELIAN IMITATION

Although Aristotle, like Plato, considers poetry a form of mimetic art, he surprisingly does not think that art itself is necessarily or essentially imitative. (Thus without having experienced abstract art or even discussing it, he does not preclude its possibility.)[2] Another surprise is the title of the treatise, since the word *poētikēs* in Greek means "things that are made or crafted." The point is that for Aristotle, poetic art is not, as Plato thought, merely copying: It is a creative act.

One reason poetics cannot be simple copying is that art involves the translation of reality into another medium. Just as the portrait sculptor translates the human countenance into clay or stone, the poet translates action into language. Nor can the poet merely translate his materials raw. Even if he does not invent his plots but takes them, as many Greek tragedians did, from the historical or mythological record, he selectively reshapes the action to make it more universal, and thus more powerfully tragic. Divesting the historical action of the accidental and the incidental,[3] he pares away unnecessary prologue until he has a probable sequence of actions leading inexorably to the protagonist's doom. If this is done well, the bare summary of a tragic plot should have something of the tragic effect. After he has constructed the plot, he must compose it verbally using extraordinary, "embellished" language and compose it visually for the stage. The whole process is a complex one — of making, not of mere imitation — that requires keeping the ultimate end in constant view.

For Plato, that artists were not always faithful to the truth counted against them; for Aristotle, artists must disregard incidental facts to search for deeper *universal* truths. For Plato, Pygmalion's statue, which came to life, would be the transcendent triumph of art; for Aristotle, a statue that was merely true to life would not be art at all.

KATHARSIS

One of the most controversial passages in the *Poetics* is contained in the passage on the final cause of tragedy: The play, "through incidents arousing pity and fear effects

---

[2]In the sentence where Aristotle tells us that poetry is a form of imitation, he uses not the usual verb *eimi* ("be") but rather *tugkhanō,* "happen to be."

[3]"Poetry . . . is more philosophical and more significant than history, for poetry is more concerned with the universal, and history more with the individual." This is a crucial passage in the *Poetics* (see p. 65). The issue for Aristotle seems to be that we can learn more from the universal principles that poets must abstract in creating their plots than from the messy, contingent realities the historian is forced to deal with. This is the paradox behind the saying "Truth is stranger than fiction." Precisely — the poets who create fictions must jettison the strange accidents that shape the events of this world.

their *katharsis.*"[4] But what does *katharsis* mean and what is "katharted"? Three possible translations of *katharsis* are "clarification," "purification," and "purgation"; and what is clarified, purified, or purged must be either the "incidents" or the emotions of "pity and fear."

According to the classical scholar Leon Golden, *katharsis* means "clarification," and it is the tragic *incidents* that are clarified: The process of poetic imitation, by stripping all accident and contingency from the tragic fall of the noble protagonist, reveals as clearly as possible how such things can happen. Tragedy here has an educative function. The "purification" theory, which has a long history beginning with the Renaissance theorists Lodovico Castelvetro and Francesco Robortello, suggests that tragedy has the function of tempering (or hardening) the emotions by revealing to the audience the proper objects of pity and fear.

The oldest theory holds that *katharsis* means "purgation," the violent driving-out of the emotions of pity and fear. This theory is supported by the only other instance in which Aristotle uses *katharsis* in the context of the arts, in a passage from the *Politics:*

> Music should be studied . . . for the sake of . . . many benefits . . . [one of which is] purgation (the word purgation we use at present without any explanation, but when hereafter we speak of poetry we will treat the subject with more precision). For feelings such as pity and fear, or, again, enthusiasm, exist very strongly in some souls, and have more or less influence over all. Some persons fall into a religious frenzy, whom we see . . . when they have used the sacred melodies, restored as though they had found healing and purgation. Those who are influenced by pity or fear, and every emotional nature, must have a like experience, and others in so far as each is susceptible to such emotions, and all are in a manner purged and their souls lightened and delighted. (*Politics* 1341^b 35 to 1342^a 15)

Aristotle thought that the *Poetics* would clarify the *Politics* rather than the other way around, but the context of this passage is clear enough: Unpleasant feelings may be relieved through music or poetry. When the experience is over, the soul is "lightened and delighted." After seeing a performance of *Oedipus the King* or *King Lear,* spectators are no longer gripped by pity and fear; rather they are exhausted, cleansed, emptied of emotion. The primary meaning of the word *katharsis,* preserved in the English cognate "cathartic," is the action of a powerful laxative. A doctor's son, Aristotle perhaps could not resist using a familiar medical metaphor for the experience.

Selected Bibliography

Belfiore, Elizabeth. *Tragic Pleasures: Aristotle on Plot and Emotion.* Princeton: Princeton University Press, 1992.

Butcher, S. H. *Aristotle's Theory of Poetry and Fine Art.* New York: Macmillan, 1902.

Cooper, Lane. *The Poetics of Aristotle: Its Meaning and Influence.* 1923; New York: Cooper Square, 1963.

Cronk, Nicholas. "Aristotle, Horace and Longinus: The Conception of Reader Response." In *The Cambridge History of Literary Criticism, III: The Renaissance,* ed. Glyn P. Norton, 199–204. Cambridge: Cambridge University Press, 1999.

[4]Editor's literal translation.

Else, Gerald F. *Aristotle's Poetics: The Argument.* Cambridge: Harvard University Press, 1957.

———. *Plato and Aristotle on Poetry.* Chapel Hill: University of North Carolina Press, 1986.

Fergusson, Francis. "On the *Poetics.*" *Tulane Drama Review* 4 (1960): 23–32.

House, Humphrey. *The Poetics of Aristotle in England.* London: R. Hart-Davis, 1956.

Lucas, F. L. *Tragedy: Serious Drama in Relation to Aristotle's Poetics.* New York: Macmillan, 1958.

Modrak, Deborah K. W. *Aristotle: The Power of Perception.* Chicago: University of Chicago Press, 1987.

———. *Aristotle's Theory of Language and Meaning.* Cambridge: Cambridge University Press, 2001.

Olson, Elder. *Aristotle's Poetics and English Literature.* Chicago: University of Chicago Press, 1965.

———. "The Poetic Method of Aristotle: Its Powers and Limitations." In *On Value Judgments in the Arts and Other Essays.* Chicago: University of Chicago Press, 1976.

Rorty, Amelie Oksenberg, ed. *Essays on Aristotle's Poetics.* Princeton: Princeton University Press, 1992.

From *Poetics*

I

Let us discuss the art of poetry, itself, and its species, describing the character of each of them, and how it is necessary to construct plots if the poetic composition is to be successful and, furthermore, the number and kind of parts to be found in the poetic work, and as many other matters as are relevant. Let us follow the order of nature, beginning with first principles.

Now epic poetry, tragedy, comedy, dithyrambic poetry, and most forms of flute and lyre playing all happen to be, in general, imitations, but they differ from each other in three ways: either because the imitation is carried on by different means or because it is concerned with different kinds of objects or because it is presented, not in the same, but in a different manner.

For just as some artists imitate many different objects by using color and form to represent them (some through art, others only through habit), other artists imitate through sound, as indeed, in the arts mentioned above; for all these accomplish imitation through rhythm and speech and harmony, making use of these elements separately or in combination. Flute playing and lyre playing, for example, use harmony and rhythm alone; and this would also be true of any other arts (for example, the art of playing the shepherd's pipe) that are similar in character to these. Dancers imitate by using rhythm without harmony, since they imitate characters, emotions, and actions by rhythms that are arranged into dance-figures.

The art that imitates by words alone, in prose and in verse, and in the latter case, either combines various meters or makes use of only one, has been nameless up to the present time. For we cannot assign a common name to the mimes of Sophron and Xenarchus and the Socratic dialogues; nor would we have a name for such an imitation if someone should accomplish it through trimeters or elegiacs or some other such meter, except that the public at large by joining the term "poet" to a meter gives writers such names as "elegiac poets" and "epic poets." Here the public classifies all those who write in meter as poets and completely misses the point that the

Translated by Leon Golden.

capacity to produce an imitation is the essential characteristic of the poet. The public is even accustomed to apply the name "poet" to those who publish a medical or scientific treatise in verse, although Homer has nothing at all in common with Empedocles except the meter. It is just to call Homer a poet, but we must consider Empedocles a physicist rather than a poet.

And in the same way, if anyone should create an imitation by combining all the meters as Chairemon did when he wrote *The Centaur,* a rhapsody composed by the use of all the meters, he must also be designated a poet. Concerning these matters let us accept the distinctions we have just made.

There are some arts that use all the means that have been discussed, namely, rhythm and song and meter, as in the writing of dithyrambs and nomic poetry[1] and in tragedy and comedy. A difference is apparent here in that some arts use all the various elements at the same time, whereas others use them separately. These, then, are what I call the differences in the artistic means through which the imitation is accomplished.

2

Artists imitate men involved in action and these must either be noble or base since human character regularly conforms to these distinctions, all of us being different in character because of some quality of goodness or evil. From this it follows that the objects imitated are either better than or worse than or like the norm. We find confirmation of this observation in the practice of our painters. For Polygnotus represents men as better, Pauson as worse, and Dionysius as like the norm.[2] It is clear that each of the above-mentioned forms of imitation will manifest differences of this type and will be different through its choosing, in this way, a different kind of object

to imitate. Even in dancing, flute-playing, and lyre-playing it is possible for these differences to exist, and they are seen also in prose, and in verse that does not make use of musical accompaniment, as is shown by the fact that Cleophon represents men like the norm, Homer as better, and both Hegemon the Thasian (who was the first writer of parodies) and Nicochares, the author of the *Deiliad,* as worse.[3] The same situation is found in dithyrambic and nomic poetry,[4] as we see in the way Timotheus and Philoxenus handled the Cyclops theme.[5] It is through the same distinction in objects that we differentiate comedy from tragedy, for the former takes as its goal the representation of men as worse, the latter as better, than the norm.

3

There is, finally, a third factor by which we distinguish imitations, and that is the manner in which the artist represents the various types of object. For, using the same means and imitating the same kinds of object, it is possible for the poet on different occasions to narrate the story (either speaking in the person of one of his characters as Homer does or in his own person without changing roles)[6] or to have the imitators performing and acting out the entire story.

[3]Not much is known about the poets other than Homer mentioned here. Cleophon was a dramatic or epic writer; a small fragment of a parody of Hegemon of Thasos is preserved in Athenaeus; we have no further certain information about Nicochares. [Tr.]

[4]There is a lacuna in the text at this point where the name of another writer of nomic poetry was probably mentioned. [Tr.]

[5]Timotheus was a dithyrambic poet who lived in Miletus from 450 to 360 B.C.; Philoxenus was a dithyrambic poet who lived in Cythera from 436 to 380 B.C. [Tr.]

[6]The translation given of this phrase is based on the traditional text, which has been accepted by Butcher, Hardy, and Kassel. On philosophical and linguistic grounds, Bywater prefers to emend the text of the passage so that it reads as follows: "Given both the same means and the same kind of object for imitation, one may either (1) speak at one moment in narrative and at another in an assumed character, as Homer does; or (2) one may remain the same throughout, without any such change; or (3) the imitators may represent the whole story dramatically, as though they were actually doing the things described." [Tr.]

[1]The dithyramb was originally a choral ode sung in honor of Dionysus, whereas nomic poetry was originally concerned with texts taken from the epic and was presented with a flute or lyre accompaniment. [Tr.]

[2]Polygnotus was one of the great painters of the fifth century B.C. Neither Pauson nor Dionysius are identified with certainty. [Tr.]

As we said at the beginning, imitations are to be distinguished under these three headings: means, object, and manner. Thus, in one way, Sophocles is the same kind of imitative artist as Homer, since they both imitate noble men; but in another sense, he resembles Aristophanes, since they both imitate characters as acting and dramatizing the incidents of the story. It is from this, some tell us, that these latter kinds of imitations are called "dramas" because they present characters who "dramatize" the incidents of the plot.

By the way, it is also for this reason that the Dorians claim to be the originators of both tragedy and comedy. The Megarians — both those in Megara itself, who assert that comedy arose when democracy was established among them, and those Megarians in Sicily, who point out that their poet Epicharmus far antedates Chionides and Magnes[7] — claim to have originated comedy; in addition, some of the Dorians in the Peloponnesus claim to be the originators of tragedy. As proof of their contentions, they cite the technical terms they use for these art forms; for they say that they call the towns around their city *komai,* but that the Athenians call their towns *demoi.* By this they argue that the root of the name "comedian" is not derived from *komazein* [the word for "reveling"] but from *komai* [their word for the towns] that the comic artists visited in their wanderings after they had been driven in disgrace from the city. In support of their claim to be the originators of "drama," they point out that the word for "doing" is *dran* in their dialect, whereas Athenians use the word *prattein* for this concept.

Concerning the number and kind of distinctions that characterize "imitations," let us accept what has been said above.

4

Speaking generally, the origin of the art of poetry is to be found in two natural causes. For the

process of imitation is natural to mankind from childhood on: Man is differentiated from other animals because he is the most imitative of them, and he learns his first lessons through imitation, and we observe that all men find pleasure in imitations. The proof of this point is what actually happens in life. For there are some things that distress us when we see them in reality, but the most accurate representations of these same things we view with pleasure — as, for example, the forms of the most despised animals and of corpses. The cause of this is that the act of learning is not only most pleasant to philosophers but, in a similar way, to other men as well, only they have an abbreviated share in this pleasure. Thus men find pleasure in viewing representations because it turns out that they learn and infer what each thing is — for example, that this particular object is that kind of object; since if one has not happened to see the object previously, he will not find any pleasure in the imitation qua imitation but rather in the workmanship or coloring or something similar.

Since imitation is given to us by nature, as are harmony and rhythm (for it is apparent that meters are parts of the rhythms), men, having been naturally endowed with these gifts from the beginning and then developing them gradually, for the most part, finally created the art of poetry from their early improvisations.

Poetry then diverged in the directions of the natural dispositions of the poets. Writers of greater dignity imitated the noble actions of noble heroes; the less dignified sort of writers imitated the actions of inferior men, at first writing invectives as the former writers wrote hymns and encomia. We know of no "invective" by poets before Homer, although it is probable that there were many who wrote such poems; but it is possible to attribute them to authors who came after Homer — for example, the *Margites* of Homer himself, and other such poems. In these poems, the fitting meter came to light, the one that now bears the name "iambic" [i.e., invective] because it was originally used by men to satirize each other. Thus, of our earliest writers, some were heroic and some iambic poets. And just as Homer was especially the poet of noble actions (for he not only handled these well but he also made his

[7]Not much is known, beyond what Aristotle tells us in the *Poetics,* about these three comic writers who lived in the early part of the fifth century B.C. [Tr.]

imitations dramatic), so also he first traced out the form of comedy by dramatically presenting not invective but the ridiculous. For his *Margites* has the same relation to comedy as the *Iliad* and *Odyssey* have to tragedy. But when tragedy and comedy began to appear, poets were attracted to each type of poetry according to their individual natures, one group becoming writers of comedies in place of iambics, and the other, writers of tragedies instead of epics because these genres were of greater importance and more admired than the others.

Now then, the consideration of whether or not tragedy is by now sufficiently developed in its formal elements, judged both in regard to its essential nature and in regard to its public performances, belongs to another discussion. What is relevant is that it arose, at first, as an improvisation (both tragedy and comedy are similar in this respect) on the part of those who led the dithyrambs, just as comedy arose from those who led the phallic songs that even now are still customary in many of our cities. Tragedy, undergoing many changes (since our poets were developing aspects of it as they emerged), gradually progressed until it attained the fulfillment of its own nature. Aeschylus was the first to increase the number of actors from one to two; he also reduced the role of the chorus and made the dialogue the major element in the play. Sophocles increased the number of actors to three and introduced scene painting. Then tragedy acquired its magnitude. Thus by developing away from a satyr-play of short plots and absurd diction, tragedy achieved, late in its history, a dignified level. Then the iambic meter took the place of the tetrameter. For the poets first used the trochaic tetrameter because their poetry was satyric and very closely associated with dance; but when dialogue was introduced, nature itself discovered the appropriate meter. For the iambic is the most conversational of the meters — as we see from the fact that we speak many iambs when talking to each other, but few [dactylic] hexameters, and only when departing from conversational tone. Moreover, the number of episodes was increased. As to the other elements by which, we are told, tragedy was embellished, we must consider them as having been mentioned by us. For it would

probably be an enormous task to go through each of these elements one by one.

5

As we have said, comedy is an imitation of baser men. These are characterized not by every kind of vice but specifically by "the ridiculous," which is a subdivision of the category of "deformity." What we mean by "the ridiculous" is some error or ugliness that is painless and has no harmful effects. The example that comes immediately to mind is the comic mask, which is ugly and distorted but causes no pain.

Now then, the successive changes in the history of tragedy and the men who brought them about have been recorded; but the analogous information about the history of comedy is lacking because the genre was not treated, at the beginning, as a serious art form. It was only recently that the archons began to grant choruses to the comic poets; until then, the performers were all volunteers. And it was only after comedy had attained some recognizable form that we began to have a record of those designated as "comic poets." Who introduced masks or prologues, who established the number of actors, and many other matters of this type, are unknown. The creation of plots came first from Sicily, where it is attributed to Epicharmus and Phormis; and it was first Crates among the Athenian poets who departed from iambic [or invective] poetry and began to write speeches and plots of a more universal nature.

Now epic poetry follows the same pattern as tragedy insofar as it is the imitation of noble subjects presented in an elevated meter. But epic differs from tragedy in that it uses a single meter, and its manner of presentation is narrative. And further, there is a difference in length. For tragedy attempts, as far as possible, to remain within one circuit of the sun or, at least, not depart from this by much. Epic poetry, however, has no limit in regard to time, and differs from tragedy in this respect; although at first the poets proceeded in tragedy in the same way as they did in epic. Some of the parts of a poem are common to both tragedy and epic, and some belong to tragedy alone. Therefore, whoever can judge what is good and bad in tragedy can also do this in regard to epic. For whatever parts epic poetry has, these are also found in tragedy; but, as we have said, not all of the parts of tragedy are found in epic poetry.

6

We shall speak about the form of imitation that is associated with hexameter verse and about comedy later.[8] Let us now discuss tragedy, bringing together the definition of its essence that has emerged from what we have already said. Tragedy is, then, an imitation of a noble and complete action, having the proper magnitude;[9] it employs language that has been artistically enhanced by each of the kinds of linguistic adornment, applied separately in the various parts of the play; it is presented in dramatic, not narrative form, and achieves, through the representation of pitiable and fearful incidents, the catharsis of such pitiable and fearful incidents. I mean by "language that has been artistically enhanced," that which is accompanied by rhythm and harmony and song; and by the phrase "each of the kinds of linguistic adornment applied separately in the various parts of the play," I mean that some parts are accomplished by meter alone and others, in turn, through song.

And since [in drama] agents accomplish the imitation by acting the story out, it follows, first of all, that the arrangement of the spectacle should be, of necessity, some part of the tragedy as would be melody and diction, also; for these are the means through which the agents accomplish the imitation. I mean by diction the act, itself, of making metrical compositions, and by

melody, what is completely obvious. Since the imitation is of an action and is accomplished by certain agents, the sort of men these agents are is necessarily dependent upon their "character" and "thought." It is, indeed, on the basis of these two considerations that we designate the quality of actions, because the two natural causes of human action are thought and character. It is also in regard to these that the lives of all turn out well or poorly. For this reason we say that tragic plot is an imitation of action.

Now I mean by the plot the arrangement of the incidents, and by character that element in accordance with which we say that agents are of a certain type; and by thought I mean that which is found in whatever things men say when they prove a point or, it may be, express a general truth. It is necessary, therefore, that tragedy as a whole have six parts in accordance with which, as a genre, it achieves its particular quality. These parts are plot, character, diction, thought, spectacle, and melody. Two of these parts come from the means by which the imitation is carried out; one from the manner of its presentation, and three from the objects of the imitation. Beyond these parts there is nothing left to mention. Not a few poets, so to speak, employ these parts; for indeed, every drama [theoretically] has spectacle, character, plot, diction, song, and thought.

The most important of these parts is the arrangement of the incidents; for tragedy is not an imitation of men, per se, but of human action and life and happiness and misery. Both happiness and misery consist in a kind of action; and the end of life is some action, not some quality.[10] Now according to their characters men have certain qualities; but according to their actions they are happy or the opposite. Poets do not, therefore, create action in order to imitate character; but character is included on account of the action. Thus the end of tragedy is the presentation of the individual incidents and of the plot; and the end is, of course, the most significant thing of all. Furthermore, without action tragedy would be

<hr/>

[8]Aristotle discusses the epic in Chs. 23 and 24, but the section of the *Poetics* dealing with comedy seems to have been written but lost. Various Aristotelian scholars (including Lane Cooper and Elder Olson) have attempted to reconstruct what a poetics of comedy would be like.

[9]There is no word in the Greek text for "proper," but I have followed the practice of several other translators who add a modifier to the term "magnitude" where it is logically warranted. The term "representation" has also been added to the final clause of this sentence because of Aristotle's insistence that the pleasure of tragedy is achieved *through imitation* (Ch. 14, ll. 18–19). See L. Golden, "Catharsis," *TAPA* 93 (1962): 58. [Tr.]

[10]The text is corrupt here. The translation follows an emendation suggested by Vahlen and accepted by Bywater and Hardy. [Tr.]

impossible, but without character it would still be possible. This point is illustrated both by the fact that the tragedies of many of our modern poets are characterless, and by the fact that many poets, in general, experience this difficulty. Also, to take an example from our painters, Zeuxis illustrates the point when compared to Polygnotus; for Polygnotus is good at incorporating character into his painting, but the work of Zeuxis shows no real characterization at all. Furthermore, if someone arranges a series of speeches that show character and are well-constructed in diction and thought, he will not, by this alone, achieve the end of tragedy; but far more will this be accomplished by the tragedy that employs these elements rather inadequately but, nevertheless, has a satisfactory plot and arrangement of incidents. In addition to the arguments already given, the most important factors by means of which tragedy exerts an influence on the soul are parts of the plot, the reversal, and the recognition. We have further proof of our view of the importance of plot in the fact that those who attempt to write tragedies are able to perfect diction and character before the construction of the incidents, as we see, for example, in nearly all of our early poets.

The first principle, then, and to speak figuratively, the soul of tragedy, is the plot; and second in importance is character. A closely corresponding situation exists in painting. For if someone should paint by applying the most beautiful colors, but without reference to an overall plan, he would not please us as much as if he had outlined the figure in black and white. Tragedy, then, is an imitation of an action; and it is, on account of this, an imitation of men acting.

Thought is the third part of tragedy and is the ability to say whatever is pertinent and fitting to the occasion, which, in reference to the composition of speeches, is the essential function of the arts of politics and rhetoric. As proof of this we point out that our earlier poets made their characters speak like statesmen, and our contemporary poets make them speak like rhetoricians. Now character is that part of tragedy which shows an individual's purpose by indicating, in circumstances where it is not clear, what sort of things he chooses or rejects. Therefore those speeches do not manifest character in which there is absolutely nothing that the speaker chooses or rejects. Thought we find in those speeches in which men show that something is or is not, or utter some universal proposition.

The fourth literary part is diction, and I mean by diction, as has already been said, the expression of thoughts through language which, indeed, is the same whether in verse or prose.

Of the remaining parts, melody is the greatest of the linguistic adornments; and spectacle, to be sure, attracts our attention but is the least essential part of the art of poetry. For the power of tragedy is felt even without a dramatic performance and actors. Furthermore, for the realization of spectacle, the art of the costume designer is more effective than that of the poet.

7

Now that we have defined these terms, let us discuss what kind of process the arrangement of incidents must be, since this is the first and most important element of tragedy. We have posited that tragedy is the imitation of a complete and whole action having a proper magnitude. For it is possible for something to be a whole and yet not have any considerable magnitude. To be a whole is to have a beginning and a middle and an end. By a "beginning" I mean that which is itself not, by necessity, after anything else but after which something naturally is or develops. By an "end" I mean exactly the opposite: that which is naturally after something else, either necessarily or customarily, but after which there is nothing else. By a "middle" I mean that which is itself after something else and which has something else after it. It is necessary, therefore, that well-constructed plots not begin by chance, anywhere, nor end anywhere, but that they conform to the distinctions that have been made above.

Furthermore, for beauty to exist, both in regard to a living being and in regard to any object that is composed of separate parts, not only must there be a proper arrangement of the component elements, but the object must also be of a magnitude that is not fortuitous. For beauty is determined by magnitude and order; therefore, neither would a very small animal be beautiful (for one's view of the animal is not clear, taking place, as it does, in an almost unperceived length of time), nor is a very large animal beautiful (for then one's view does not occur all at once, but, rather, the unity and wholeness of the animal are lost to the viewer's sight as would happen, for example, if we should come across an animal a thousand miles in length). So that just as it is necessary in regard to bodies and animals for there to be a proper magnitude — and this is the length that can easily be perceived at a glance — thus, also, there must be a proper length in regard to plots, and this is one that can be easily taken in by the memory. The limit of length in regard to the dramatic contests and in terms of the physical viewing of the performance is not a matter related to the art of poetry. For if it were necessary for a hundred tragedies to be played, they would be presented by timing them with water clocks as we are told happened on some occasions in the past. The limit, however, that is set in regard to magnitude by the very nature of the subject itself is that whatever is longer (provided it remains quite clear) is always more beautiful. To give a general rule, we say that whatever length is required for a change to occur from bad fortune to good or from good fortune to bad through a series of incidents that are in accordance with probability or necessity, is a sufficient limit of magnitude.

8

A plot is a unity not, as some think, merely if it is concerned with one individual, for in some of the many and infinitely varied things that happen to any one person, there is no unity. Thus, we must assert, there are many actions in the life of a single person from which no overall unity of action emerges. For this reason all those poets seem to have erred who have written a *Heracleid* and a *Theseid* and other poems of this type; for they think that since Heracles was one person it is appropriate for his story to be one story. But Homer, just as he was superior in other respects, also seems to have seen this point well, whether through his technical skill or his native talent, since in making the *Odyssey* he did not include all the things that ever happened to Odysseus. (For example, it happened that Odysseus was wounded on Parnassus and that he

feigned madness at the time of the call to arms; but between these two events there is no necessary or probable relation.) Homer, rather, organized the *Odyssey* around one action of the type we have been speaking about and did the same with the *Iliad*. Necessarily, then, just as in other forms of imitation, one imitation is of one thing, so also, a plot, since it is an imitation of an action, must be an imitation of an action that is one and whole. Moreover, it is necessary that the parts of the action be put together in such a way that if any one part is transposed or removed, the whole will be disordered and disunified. For that whose presence or absence has no evident effect is not part of the whole.

9

It is apparent from what we have said that it is not the function of the poet to narrate events that have actually happened, but rather, events such as might occur and have the capability of occurring in accordance with the laws of probability or necessity. For the historian and the poet do not differ by their writing in prose or verse (the works of Herodotus might be put into verse but they would, nonetheless, remain a form of history both in their metrical and prose versions). The difference, rather, lies in the fact that the historian narrates events that have actually happened, whereas the poet writes about things as they might possibly occur. Poetry, therefore, is more philosophical and more significant than history, for poetry is more concerned with the universal, and history more with the individual. By the universal I mean what sort of man turns out to say or do what sort of thing according to probability or necessity — this being the goal poetry aims at, although it gives individual names to the characters whose actions are imitated. By the individual I mean a statement telling, for example, "what Alcibiades did or experienced."

Now then, this point has already been made clear in regard to comedy; for the comic poets, once they have constructed the plot through probable incidents, assign any names that happen to occur to them, and they do not follow the procedure of the iambic poets who write about specific individuals. In regard to tragedy, however, our poets cling to the names of the heroes of the past on the principle that whatever is clearly capable of happening is readily believable. We cannot be sure that whatever has not yet happened is possible; but it is apparent that whatever has happened is also capable of happening for, if it were not, it could not have occurred. Nevertheless in some tragedies one or two of the names are well known and the rest have been invented for the occasion; in others not even one is well known, for example, Agathon's *Antheus*,[11] since in this play both the incidents and the names have been invented, and nonetheless they please us. Thus we must not seek to cling exclusively to the stories that have been handed down and about which our tragedies are usually written. It would be absurd, indeed, to do this since the well-known plots are known only to a few, but nevertheless please everyone. It is clear then from these considerations that it is necessary for the poet to be more the poet of his plots than of his meters, insofar as he is a poet because he is an imitator and imitates human actions. If the poet happens to write about things that have actually occurred, he is no less the poet for that. For nothing prevents some of the things that have actually occurred from belonging to the class of the probable or possible, and it is in regard to this aspect that he is the poet of them.

Of the simple plots and actions the episodic are the worst; and I mean by episodic a plot in which the episodes follow each other without regard for the laws of probability or necessity. Such plots are constructed by the inferior poets because of their own inadequacies, and by the good poets because of the actors. For since they are writing plays that are to be entered in contests (and so stretch the plot beyond its capacity) they are frequently forced to distort the sequence of action.

Since the imitation is not only a complete action but is also of fearful and pitiable incidents, we must note that these are intensified when they occur unexpectedly, yet because of one another. For there is more of the marvelous

in them if they occur this way than if they occurred spontaneously and by chance. Even in regard to coincidences, those seem to be most astonishing that appear to have some design associated with them. We have an example of this in the story of the statue of Mitys in Argos killing the man who caused Mitys' death by falling upon him as he was a spectator at a festival.[12] The occurrence of such an event, we feel, is not without meaning and thus we must consider plots that incorporate incidents of this type to be superior ones.

10

Plots are divided into the simple and the complex, for the actions of which the plots are imitations are naturally of this character. An action that is, as has been defined, continuous and unified I call simple when its change of fortune arises without reversal and recognition, and complex when its change of fortune arises through recognition or reversal or both. Now these aspects of the plot must develop directly from the construction of the plot itself, so that they occur from prior events either out of necessity or according to the laws of probability. For it makes quite a difference whether they occur *because* of those events or merely *after* them.

11

Reversal is the change of fortune in the action of the play to the opposite state of affairs, just as has been said; and this change, we argue, should be in accordance with probability and necessity. Thus, in the *Oedipus* the messenger comes to cheer Oedipus and to remove his fears in regard to his mother; but by showing him who he actually is he accomplishes the very opposite effect. And in *Lynceus,* Lynceus is being led away to die and Danaus is following to kill him; but it turns out, because of the action that has taken place, that Danaus dies and Lynceus is saved. Recognition, as the same indicates, is a change from ignorance to knowledge, bringing about either a state of

---

[11]Agathon was a late fifth-century B.C. tragic poet whose work has not survived except in fragments. He appears, prominently, in Plato's *Symposium*. [Tr.]

[12]I have followed Butcher's, Hardy's, and Bywater's interpretation of this passage. Others, however, understand the phrase to mean "when he was looking at the statue." [Tr.]

friendship or one of hostility on the part of those who have been marked out for good fortune or bad. The most effective recognition is one that occurs together with reversal, for example, as in the *Oedipus*. There are also other kinds of recognition for, indeed, what we have said happens, in a way, in regard to inanimate things, even things of a very causal kind; and it is possible, further, to "recognize" whether someone has or has not done something. But the type of recognition that is especially a part of the plot and the action is the one that has been mentioned. For such a recognition and reversal will evoke pity or fear, and we have defined tragedy as an imitation of actions of this type; and furthermore, happiness and misery will appear in circumstances of this type. Since this kind of recognition is of persons, some recognitions that belong to this class will merely involve the identification of one person by another when the identity of the second person is clear; on other occasions it will be necessary for there to be a recognition on the part of both parties: for example, Iphigenia is recognized by Orestes from her sending of the letter; but it is necessary that there be another recognition of him on her part.

Now then, these are two parts of the plot, reversal and recognition, and there is also a third part, suffering. Of these, reversal and recognition have been discussed; the incident of suffering results from destructive or painful action such as death on the stage, scenes of very great pain, the infliction of wounds, and the like.

12

The parts of tragedy that we must view as formal elements we have discussed previously; looking at the quantitative aspect of tragedy and the parts into which it is divided in this regard, the following are the distinctions to be made: prologue, episode, exode, and the choral part, which is divided into parode and stasimon. These are commonly found in all plays, but only in a few are found songs from the stage and *kommoi*. The prologue is the complete section of a tragedy before the parode of the chorus; an episode is the complete section of a tragedy between complete choric songs; the exode is the complete section of a tragedy after which there is no song of the

chorus. Of the choral part, the parode is the entire first speech of the chorus, the stasimon is a song of the chorus without anapests and trochees, and a *kommos* is a lament sung in common by the chorus and the actors. The parts of tragedy that we must view as formal elements we have discussed previously; the above distinctions have been made concerning the quantitative aspects of tragedy, and the parts into which it is divided in this regard.

13

What goals poets must aim at, which difficulties they must be wary of when constructing their plots, and how the proper function of tragedy is accomplished are matters we should discuss after the remarks that have just been made.

Since the plots of the best tragedies must be complex, not simple, and the plot of a tragedy must be an imitation of pitiable and fearful incidents (for this is the specific nature of the imitation under discussion), it is clear, first of all, that unqualifiedly good human beings must not appear to fall from good fortune to bad; for that is neither pitiable nor fearful; it is, rather, repellent. Nor must an extremely evil man appear to move from bad fortune to good fortune for that is the most untragic situation of all because it has none of the necessary requirements of tragedy; it both violates our human sympathy and contains nothing of the pitiable or fearful in it. Furthermore, a villainous man should not appear to fall from good fortune to bad. For, although such a plot would be in accordance with our human sympathy, it would not contain the necessary elements of pity and fear; for pity is aroused by someone who undeservedly falls into misfortune, and fear is evoked by our recognizing that it is someone like ourselves who encounters this misfortune (pity, as I say, arising for the former reason, fear for the latter). Therefore the emotional effect of the situation just mentioned will be neither pitiable nor fearful. What is left, after our considerations, is someone in between these extremes. This would be a person who is neither perfect in virtue and justice, nor one who falls into misfortune through vice and depravity; but rather, one who succumbs through some miscalculation. He must also be a person who enjoys great reputation and good fortune, such as Oedipus, Thyestes, and other illustrious men from similar families. It is necessary, furthermore, for the well-constructed plot to have a single rather than a double construction, as some urge, and to illustrate a change of fortune not from bad fortune to good but, rather, the very opposite, from good fortune to bad, and for this to take place not because of depravity but through some great miscalculation on the part of the type of person we have described (or a better rather than a worse one).

A sign of our point is found in what actually happens in the theater. For initially, our poets accepted any chance plots; but now the best tragedies are constructed about a few families, for example, about Alcmaeon, Oedipus, Orestes, Meleager, Thyestes, Telephon, and any others who were destined to experience, or to commit, terrifying acts. For as we have indicated, artistically considered, the best tragedy arises from this kind of plot. Therefore, those critics make the very mistake that we have been discussing who blame Euripides because he handles the material in his tragedies in this way, and because many of his plots end in misfortune. For this is, indeed, the correct procedure, as we have said. The very great proof of this is that on the stage and in the dramatic contests such plays appear to be the most tragic, if they are properly worked out; and Euripides, even if in other matters he does not manage things well, nevertheless appears to be the most tragic of the poets. The second ranking plot, one that is called first by some, has a double structure of events, as in the *Odyssey,* ending in opposite ways for the better and worse characters. It seems to be first on account of the inadequacy of the audience. For our poets trail along writing to please the tastes of the audience. But this double structure of events involves a pleasure that is not an appropriate pleasure of tragedy but rather of comedy. For in comedy, whoever are the greatest enemies in the story — for example, Orestes and Aegisthus — becoming friends at the end, go off together, and no one is killed by anyone.

14

Pity and fear can arise from the spectacle and also from the very structure of the plot, which is the superior way and shows the better poet. The poet should construct the plot so that even if the action is not performed before spectators, one who merely hears the incidents that have occurred both shudders and feels pity from the way they turn out. That is what anyone who hears the plot of the *Oedipus* would experience. The achievement of this effect through the spectacle does not have much to do with poetic art and really belongs to the business of producing the play. Those who use the spectacle to create not the fearful but only the monstrous have no share in the creation of tragedy; for we should not seek every pleasure from tragedy but only the one proper to it.

Since the poet should provide pleasure from pity and fear through imitation, it is apparent that this function must be worked into the incidents. Let us try to understand what type of occurrences appear to be terrifying and pitiable. It is, indeed, necessary that any such action occur either between those who are friends or enemies to each other, or between those who have no relationship, whatsoever, to each other. If an enemy takes such an action against an enemy, there is nothing pitiable in the performance of the act or in the intention to perform it, except the suffering itself. Nor would there be anything pitiable if neither party had any relationship with the other. But whenever the tragic incidents occur in situations involving strong ties of affection — for example, if a brother kills or intends to kill a brother or a son a father or a mother a son or a son a mother or commits some equally terrible act — there will be something pitiable. These situations, then, are the ones to be sought. Now, it is not possible for a poet to alter completely the traditional stories. I mean, for example, the given fact that Clytemnestra dies at the hands of Orestes, and Eriphyle at the hands of Alcmaeon; but it is necessary for the poet to be inventive and skillful in adapting the stories that have been handed down. Let us define more clearly what we mean by the skillful adaptation of a story. It is possible for the action to occur, as our early poets handled it, with the characters knowing and understanding what they are doing, as indeed Euripides makes Medea kill her children. It is also possible to have the deed done with those who accomplish the terrible deed in ignorance of the identity of their victim, only later recognizing the relationship as in Sophocles' *Oedipus*. The incident, here, is outside the plot, but we find an example of such an incident in the play itself, in the action of Astydamas's *Alcmaeon* or of Telegonus in the *Wounded Odysseus*;[13] and there is further a third type in addition to these that involves someone who intends to commit some fatal act through ignorance of his relationship to another person but recognizes this relationship before doing it. Beyond these possibilities, there is no other way to have an action take place. For it is necessary either to do the deed or not and either knowingly or in ignorance.

Of these possibilities, the case in which one knowingly is about to do the deed and does not is the worst; for it is repellent and not tragic because it lacks the element of suffering. Therefore, no one handles a situation this way, except rarely; for example, in the *Antigone*, Haemon is made to act in this way toward Creon. To do the deed knowingly is the next best way. Better than this is the case where one does the deed in ignorance and after he has done it recognizes his relationship to the other person. For the repellent aspect is not present, and the recognition is startling. But the most effective is the final type, for example, in the *Cresphontes*, where Merope is going to kill her son and does not, but, on the contrary, recognizes him, and in the *Iphigenia*, where a sister is involved in a similar situation with a brother, and in the *Helle*, where a son who is about to surrender his mother recognizes her.[14]

It is for this reason that, as we have said previously, tragedies are concerned with a few families. For proceeding not by art, but by trial and error, poets learned how to produce the appropriate effect in their plots. They are compelled, therefore, to return time and again to that number of families in which these terrifying events have occurred. We have now spoken sufficiently about the construction of the incidents and of what type the plot must be.

15

In regard to character, there are four points to be aimed at. First and foremost, character should be good. If a speech or action has some choice connected with it, it will manifest character, as has been said, and the character will be good if the choice is good. Goodness is possible for each class of individuals. For, both a woman and a slave have their particular virtues even though the former of these is inferior to a man, and the latter is completely ignoble.[15] Second, character must be appropriate. For it is possible for a person to be manly in terms of character, but it is not appropriate for a woman to exhibit either this quality or the intellectual cleverness that is associated with men. The third point about character is that it should be like reality, for this is different from making character virtuous and making it appropriate, as we have defined these terms. The fourth aspect of character is consistency. For even if it is an inconsistent character who is the subject of the imitation (I refer to the model that suggested the kind of character being imitated), it is nevertheless necessary for him to be consistently inconsistent. We have an example of unnecessarily debased character in the figure of Menelaus in the *Orestes*, of unsuitable and inappropriate character in the lament of Odysseus in the *Scylla* and the speech of Melanippe, and of inconsistency of character in *Iphigenia at Aulis* where the heroine's role as a suppliant does not fit in with her character as it develops later in the play.

In character, as in the construction of the incidents, we must always seek for either the necessary or the probable, so that a given type of person says or does certain kinds of things, and one event

---

[13]Astydamas was a fourth-century B.C. poet; the *Wounded Odysseus* may have been a play by Sophocles. [Tr.]

[14]The *Cresphontes* and the *Iphigenia*, the former no longer extant, are plays by Euripides. We have no further information concerning the *Helle*. [Tr.]

[15]Aristotle's word for "good" here, *chrēstēn*, means "valuable" rather than "noble." Aristotle is distinguishing between the intrinsic value of personages (he considered women and slaves to be inferior beings) and the instrumental value of their ethical choices to the drama in which they figure. Aristotle's point is that character must serve the ends of the drama, and that *motiveless* choice, which has no effect on the action — like Menelaus's cowardice in Euripides' *Orestes* — is to be avoided.

follows another according to necessity or probability. Thus, it is apparent that the resolutions of the plots should also occur through the plot itself and not by means of the deus ex machina, as in the *Medea,* and also in regard to the events surrounding the department of the fleet in the *Iliad.* The deus ex machina must be reserved for the events that lie outside the plot, either those that happened before it that are not capable of being known by men, or those that occur after that need to be announced and spoken of beforehand. For we grant to the gods the power of seeing all things. There should, then, be nothing improbable in the action; but if this is impossible, it should be outside the plot as, for example, in Sophocles' *Oedipus.*

Because tragedy is an imitation of the nobler sort of men it is necessary for poets to imitate good portrait painters. For even though they reproduce the specific characteristics of their subjects and represent them faithfully, they also paint them better than they are. Thus, also, the poet imitating men who are prone to anger or who are indifferent or who are disposed in other such ways in regard to character makes them good as well, even though they have such characteristics, just as Agathon[16] and Homer portray Achilles.

It is necessary to pay close attention to these matters and, in addition, to those that pertain to the effects upon an audience that follow necessarily from the nature of the art of poetry. For, indeed, it is possible frequently to make mistakes in regard to these. We have spoken sufficiently about these matters in our published works.

16

What we mean by "recognition" we have indicated previously. Of the kinds of recognition that occur, there is one, first of all, that is least artistic, which poets mainly use through the poverty of their inspiration. This is the form of recognition that is achieved through external signs; some of these are birthmarks, for example, "the spearhead which the Earth-born are

---

[16]I have followed Butcher, Hardy, and Bywater in reading the name of the tragic poet here. Other scholars accept a manuscript reading of the word meaning "good." [Tr.]

accustomed to bear," or the "stars" such as Carcinus wrote about in his *Thyestes.* Then there are characteristics that we acquire after birth. Of these some are found on the body, for example, scars; and others are external to the body, such as necklaces, and as another example, the ark through which the recognition is accomplished in the *Tyro.* It is also possible to employ these recognitions in better and worse ways; for example, Odysseus was recognized through his scar in one way by the nurse and in another way by the swineherds. Now those recognitions are less artistic that depend on signs as proof, as well as all that are similar to these; but those that derive from the reversal of action, as in the Bath Scene of the *Odyssey,* are better.

In second place come those recognitions that have been contrived for the occasion by the poet and are therefore inartistic. For example, the way Orestes in the *Iphigenia* makes known that he is Orestes; for Iphigenia made herself known through the letter, but he himself says what the poet wishes him to say but not what the plot requires. Therefore this type of recognition is rather close to the error that has already been mentioned; for it would have been just as possible for him to carry tokens with him. Another example of this type of recognition is the use of the "voice of the shuttle" in the *Tereus* of Sophocles.

The third type arises from our being stimulated by something that we see to remember an event that has an emotional significance for us. This type of recognition occurs in the *Cyprioe* of Dicaeogenes where the sight of the painting brings forth tears, and also in the story of Alcinous where Odysseus hears the lyre player and, reminded of his past fortunes, weeps; in both instances, it was by their emotional reactions that the characters were recognized.

The fourth type of recognition occurs through reasoning, for example, in the *Choëphoroe* it is achieved by the deduction: Someone like me has come; there is no one resembling me except Orestes; he, therefore, has come. Another recognition of this type was suggested by Polyidus the Sophist in regard to Iphigenia; for it was reasonable for Orestes to infer that, since his sister was sacrificed, he was also going to be sacrificed. Again, in the *Tydeus* of Theodectes, the deduction is made that he who had come to find a son was, himself, to perish. Another example is in the *Phinidae* where the women, when they had seen the place, inferred their destiny: that since they had been exposed there, they were fated to die there.

There is also a type of composite recognition from false reasoning on the part of another character,[17] for example, in the story of Odysseus, the False Messenger; for he said that he would know the bow that he had not seen, but it is false reasoning to suppose through this that he *would* recognize it again (as if he had seen it before).[18]

The best recognition is the one that arises from the incidents themselves, striking us, as they do, with astonishment through the very probability of their occurrence as, for example, in the action of the *Oedipus* of Sophocles and in the *Iphigenia*, where it is reasonable for the heroine to wish to dispatch a letter. Such recognitions alone are accomplished without contrived signs and necklaces. The second-best type of recognition is the one that is achieved by reasoning.

17

In constructing plots and working them out with diction, the poet must keep the action as much as possible before his eyes. For by visualizing the events as distinctly as he can, just as if he were present at their actual occurrence, he will discover what is fitting for his purpose, and there will be the least chance of incongruities escaping his notice. A sign of this is found in the criticism that is made of Carcinus. For Amphiarus is coming back from the temple, a point that would have escaped the audience's notice if it had not actually seen it; and on the stage, the play failed

because the audience was annoyed at this incongruity.[19]

As much as is possible the poet should also work out the action with gestures. For, given poets of the same natural abilities, those are most persuasive who are involved in the emotions they imitate; for example, one who is distressed conveys distress, and one who is enraged conveys anger most truly. Therefore, the art of poetry is more a matter for the well-endowed poet than for the frenzied one. For poets marked by the former characteristic can easily change character, whereas those of the latter type are possessed.

In regard to arguments, both those that already are in existence and those he himself invents, the poet should first put them down in universal form and then extend them by adding episodes. I mean that the poet should take a general view of the action of the play, like, for example, the following general view of the *Iphigenia:* A young girl had been sacrificed and had disappeared in a way that was obscure to the sacrificers. She settled in another country in which it was the custom to sacrifice strangers to the goddess, and she came to hold the priesthood for this sacrifice. Later, it turned out that the brother of the priestess came to this country (the fact that the god, for some reason, commanded him to come is outside the argument; the purpose of his coming is outside of the plot). When he came he was seized, and on the point of being sacrificed he made himself known, either as Euripides handled the situation or as Polyidus arranged it, by his saying, in a very reasonable way, that not only had it been necessary for his sister to be sacrificed but also for him; and from this came his deliverance. After this, when the names have already been assigned, it is necessary to complete the episodes. The episodes must be appropriate, as, for example, the madness of Orestes through which he was captured and his deliverance through purification.

In drama, the episodes are short, but epic achieves its length by means of them. For the argument of the *Odyssey* is not long: A certain man is away from home for many years, closely

---

[17]I have followed Bywater in accepting an emendation meaning "another" in place of the manuscript reading "audience" followed by Kassel and Hardy. [Tr.]

[18]In this passage, Bywater notes that, "both text and interpretation here are in the highest degree doubtful." I have followed his interpretation of this difficult passage. Except for the *Choëphoroe,* we do not have any information about the plays mentioned in the previous paragraph. [Tr.]

[19]Carcinus was a fifth-century B.C. tragic poet; nothing further is known of the play mentioned here. [Tr.]

watched by Poseidon but otherwise completely alone. His family at home continually faces a situation where his possessions are being squandered by the suitors who plot against his son. Storm-driven, he arrives home and, having made certain people acquainted with him, he attacks the suitors and, while destroying his enemies, is himself saved. This is the essence of the story; everything else is episode.

18

In every tragedy, we find both the complication and the resolution of the action. Frequently some matters outside the action together with some within it comprise the complication, and the rest of the play consists of the resolution. By complication I mean that part of the play from the beginning up to the first point at which the change occurs to good or to bad fortune. By resolution I mean the part of the play from the beginning of the change in fortune to the end of the play. For example, in the *Lynceus* of Theodectes, the complication comprises everything done before the action of the play begins and the seizing of the child, and, in turn, of the parents; the resolution comprises all that happens from the accusation of murder to the end of the play.[20]

There are four kinds of tragedy (for that number of parts has been mentioned): the complex, which consists wholly in reversal and recognition; the tragedies of suffering, for example, the *Ajaxes* and *Ixions* that have been written; the tragedies of character, for example, the *Phthiotian Women* and the *Peleus*.[21] And a fourth type [the tragedy of spectacle], for example, is *The Daughters of Phorcis* and *Prometheus*[22] and

those plays that take place in Hades. Now it is necessary to attempt, as much as possible, to include all elements in the play, but if that is not possible, then as many as possible and certainly the most important ones. This is especially so now, indeed, when the public unjustly criticizes our poets. For although there have been poets who were outstanding in regard to each kind of tragedy, the public now demands that one man be superior to the particular virtue of each of his predecessors.

It is correct to speak of a tragedy as different from or similar to another one on the basis of its plot more than anything else: that is, in regard to an action having the same complication and resolution. Many poets are skillful in constructing their complications, but their resolutions are poor. It is, however, necessary for both elements to be mastered.

The poet, as has frequently been said, must remember not to make a tragedy out of an epic body of incidents (by which I mean a multiple plot), [as would be the case], for example, if someone should construct a plot out of the entire *Iliad*. For, there, because of the length, the parts take on the appropriate magnitude, but the same plot used in the drama turns out quite contrary to one's expectations. A sign of this is that so many as have written about the entire destruction of Troy (and not of sections of it, as Euripides) or about the entire story of Niobe (and not just a part, as Aeschylus) either completely fail on stage or do badly, since even Agathon failed for this reason alone. But in their reversals and in their simple plots, these poets aim with marvelous accuracy at the effects that they wish for: that is, whatever is tragic and touches our human sympathy. This occurs whenever a clever but evil person is deceived, as Sisyphus, or a brave but unjust man is defeated. Such an event is probable, as Agathon says, because it is probable for many things to occur contrary to probability.

It is necessary to consider the chorus as one of the actors and as an integral part of the drama; its involvement in the action should not be in Euripides' manner but in Sophocles'. In the hands of our later poets, the songs included in the play are no more a part of that particular plot than they

---

[20]The text is in dispute here. Bywater, following a suggestion of Susemihl, translates the passage 1456ª, 7–10, at this point in the text. Butcher, Hardy, and Kassel retain the traditional reading that I have followed in my translation. [Tr.]

[21]*The Phthiotian Women* and *Peleus,* neither now extant, were probably written by Sophocles. The *Lynceus,* mentioned above and at 1. 9 in Ch. 11, is also no longer extant. [Tr.]

[22]*The Daughters of Phorcis* and *Prometheus* are both by Aeschylus; Bywater identifies them as lost satyr-plays and does not connect the latter play with the famous *Prometheus Bound.* [Tr.]

are of any other tragedy. They have been sung, therefore, as inserted pieces from the time Agathon first introduced this practice. And yet what difference does it make whether one sings an inserted song or adopts a speech or a whole episode from one play into another?

19

We have already spoken about other matters; it remains for us to discuss diction and thought. Concerning thought, let it be taken as given what we have written in the *Rhetoric,* for this is more appropriately a subject of that discipline. All those matters pertain to thought that must be presented through speech; and they may be subdivided into proof and refutation and the production of emotional effect, for example, pity or fear or anger or other similar emotions. Indications of the importance or insignificance of anything also fall under this heading. It is clear that we must employ thought also in actions in the same ways [as in speech] whenever we aim at the representation of the pitiable, the terrible, the significant, or the probable, with the exception of this one difference — that the effects arise in the case of the incidents without verbal explanation, whereas in the speech they are produced by the speaker and arise because of the speech. For what would be the function of the speaker if something should appear in the way that is required without being dependent on the speech?

Concerning diction one kind of study involves the forms of diction that are investigated by the art of elocution and are the concern of the individual who considers this his guiding art, for example, what a command is and what a prayer is, what a statement is, and threat and question and answer and any other such matters. For in regard to the knowledge or ignorance of these matters, no censure worth taking seriously can be made against the art of poetry. Why should any one accept as an error Protagoras's censure of Homer on the grounds that when he said, "Sing, O goddess, of the wrath . . ." he gave a command, although he really wished to utter a prayer. For Protagoras says to order someone to do something or not is a command. Let us, therefore,

disregard such a consideration as being a principle of some other art, not the art of poetry.

20

The following parts comprise the entire scope of diction: letter, syllable, connective, noun, verb, inflection, and sentence. A letter is an indivisible sound; not every such sound is a letter, however, but only one from which a compound sound can be constructed. For I would call none of the individual sounds uttered by wild animals letters. The subdivisions of this category of "letters" are vowel, semivowel, and mute. A vowel is a sound that is audible without the contact of any of the physical structures of the mouth,[23] a semivowel is a sound that is audible with the contact of some of the physical structures of the mouth, for example, the *S* and *R* sounds; and a mute is a letter produced by the contact of the physical structures of the mouth, but inaudible in itself, although it becomes audible when it is accompanied by letters that are sounded, for example, the *G* and *D* sounds. These letters differ in the positions taken by the mouth to produce them, in the places in the mouth where they are produced, in aspiration and smoothness, in being long or short and, furthermore, in having an acute, grave, or middle [circumflex] pitch accent. The detailed investigation concerning these matters belongs to the study of metrics.

A syllable is a nonsignificant sound constructed from a mute and a vowel. For, indeed, *GR* without an *A* is a syllable and also with it, for example, *GRA.* However, it is the business of the art of metrics also to investigate distinctions in this area.[24]

A connective is a nonsignificant sound that neither hinders nor promotes the creation of one significant sound from many sounds and that it is

---

[23]I have followed Butcher and Hardy in seeing this passage as a reference to the physical means of producing speech. Bywater disputes this interpretation and argues that the ambiguous term *prosbole* does not refer to the impact of the physical structures of the mouth but to the addition of one letter to another. [Tr.]

[24]The passage that begins here is corrupt and contains many difficulties of interpretation. [Tr.]

not appropriate to place at the beginning of a speech that stands independently, for example, *men, dē, toi, de.* Or it is a nonsignificant sound that is naturally able to make one significant sound from a number of sounds, for example, *amphi, peri,* and others like them. There is also a kind of connective that is a nonsignificant sound that shows the beginning, end, or division of a sentence and that may naturally be placed at either end or in the middle of a sentence.

A noun is a compound significant sound, not indicating time, no part of which is significant by itself. For in compound nouns we do not consider each part of the compound as being significant in itself; for example, in the name "Theodore" the root *dor* [gift] has no significance.

A verb is a compound significant sound indicating time, no part of which is significant by itself in the same way as has been indicated in regard to nouns. For "man" or "white" do not tell us anything about "when"; but "he goes" or "he has gone" indicate the present and the past.

Inflection is a characteristic of a noun or verb signifying the genitive or dative relation, or other similar ones, or indicating the singular or plural, that is, man or men, or is concerned with matters that fall under the art of elocution, for example, questions and commands; for the phrases, "Did he go?" or "Go!" involve inflections of the verb in regard to these categories.

A speech is a compound, significant sound some of whose parts are significant by themselves. For not every speech is composed of verbs and nouns but it is possible to have a speech without verbs (for example, the definition of man). However, part of the speech will always have some significance, for example, "Cleon" in the phrase "Cleon walks." A speech is a unity in two ways. Either it signifies one thing or it is a unity through the joining together of many speeches. For example, the *Iliad* is a unity by the process of joining together many speeches, and the definition of man by signifying one thing.

21

Nouns are either simple, by which I mean constructed solely from nonsignificant elements, for example *gē* [earth], or compound. This latter category is divided into nouns that are constructed from both significant and nonsignificant elements (except that neither element is significant within the compound word itself) and nouns that are composed solely out of significant elements. Nouns may also be made up of three, four, or more parts, for example, many of the words in the Massilian vocabulary, such as Hermocaicoxanthus. . . .[25]

Every word is either standard, or is a strange word, or is a metaphor, or is ornamental, or is a coined word, or is lengthened, or contracted, or is altered in some way. I mean by standard, words that everyone uses, and by a strange word, one that foreigners use. Thus, it is apparent, the same word can be both strange and ordinary but not, of course, to the same persons. The word *sigunon* [spear] is ordinary for the Cyprians and strange to us.

Metaphor is the transference of a name from the object to which it has a natural application; this transference can take place from genus to species or species to genus or from species to species or by analogy. I mean by "from genus to species," for example, "This ship of mine stands there." For to lie at anchor is a species of standing. An example of the transference from species to genus, "Odysseus has truly accomplished a myriad of noble deeds." For a myriad is the equivalent of "many," for which the poet now substitutes this term. An example of the transference from species to species is "having drawn off life with a sword" and also "having cut with unyielding bronze." For here to draw off is to cut and to cut is called to draw off, for both are subdivisions of "taking away."

I mean by "transference by analogy" the situation that occurs whenever a second element is related to a first as a fourth is to a third. For the poet will then use the fourth in place of the second or the second in place of the fourth, and sometimes poets add the reference to which the transferred term applies. I mean, for example, that a cup is related to Dionysus as a shield is to Ares. The poet will, therefore, speak of the cup as the

[25]There is a lacuna in the text here. Some editors accept Diel's conjecture, "praying to father Zeus," as the completion of this line. [Tr.]

shield of Dionysus and the shield as the cup of Ares. The same situation occurs in regard to the relation of old age to life and evening to day. A poet will say that evening is the old age of day, or however Empedocles expressed it, and that old age is the evening of life or the sunset of life. In some situations, there is no regular name in use to cover the analogous relation, but nevertheless the related elements will be spoken of by analogy; for example, to scatter seed is to sow, but the scattering of the sun's rays has no name. But the act of sowing in regard to grain bears an analogous relation to the sun's dispersing of its rays, and so we have the phrase "sowing the god-created fire."

It is also possible to use metaphor in a different way by applying the transferred epithet and then denying some aspect that is proper to it — for example, if one should call the shield not the cup of Ares but the wineless cup.[26] A coined word is one that is not in use among foreigners but is the invention of the poet. There seem to be some words of this type, for example, horns [*kerata*] called "sprouters" [*ernuges*], and a priest [*iereus*] called "supplicator" [*arētēr*].

A word may be lengthened or contracted. It is lengthened if it makes use of a longer vowel than is usual for it, or a syllable is inserted in it; and it is contracted if any element is removed from it. An example of lengthening is *poleōs* to *polēos* and *Pēleidou* to *Pēlēiadeō;* an example of contraction is *krī* and *dō* and *ops* in *"mia ginetai amphoterōn ops."*

A word is altered whenever a poet utilizes part of the regular name for the object he is describing and invents part anew, for example, in the phrase *"deksiteron kata mazon"* the use of *deksiteron* in place of *deksion.*[27]

Nouns are subdivided into masculine, feminine, and neuter. Those are masculine that end in nu, rho, and sigma and in the two letters psi and ksi that are constructed in combination with sigma. Those nouns are feminine that end in the vowels that are always long, the eta and omega, and that end (in regard to the vowels subject to lengthening) in the lengthened alpha. Thus it turns out that there are an equal number of terminations for masculine and feminine nouns since psi and ksi are subdivisions of sigma. No noun ends in a mute nor in a short vowel. Only three end in iota, *meli, kommi, peperi,* and five end in upsilon. Neuter nouns end in these vowels and in nu and sigma.

22

Diction achieves its characteristic virtue in being clear but not mean. The clearest style results from the use of standard words; but it is also mean, as can be seen in the poetry of Cleophon and Sthenelus. A really distinguished style varies ordinary diction through the employment of unusual words. By unusual I mean strange words and metaphor and lengthened words and everything that goes beyond ordinary diction. But if someone should write exclusively in such forms the result would either be a riddle or a barbarism. A riddle will result if someone writes exclusively in metaphor; and a barbarism will result if there is an exclusive use of strange words. For it is in the nature of a riddle for one to speak of a situation that actually exists in an impossible way. Now it is not possible to do this by the combination of strange words; but it can be done by metaphor, for example, "I saw a man who welded bronze on another man by fire," and other metaphors like this. A statement constructed exclusively from strange words is a barbarism.

It is therefore necessary to use a combination of all these forms. The employment of strange words and metaphor and ornamental words and the other forms of speech that have been mentioned will prevent the diction from being ordinary and mean; and the use of normal speech will keep the diction clear. The lengthening and contraction of words and alterations in them contribute in no small measure to the diction's clarity and its elevation above ordinary diction. For because such words are different they will prevent the diction from being ordinary through their contrast with the ordinary expression; and

[26]Editors have noted that a definition of the term "ornamental word" belongs in the text at this point, although it is missing from the manuscripts. [Tr.]

[27]The phrase quoted comes from the *Iliad* 5:393 and means "at her right breast." Two words meaning "right" are quoted to illustrate Aristotle's point here. [Tr.]

because they have a share in the customary word, they will keep the diction clear.

Thus, the criticism is not well-taken on the part of those who censure this way of using language and who mock the poet, as the elder Euclid did, on the grounds that it is easy to write poetry if you are allowed to lengthen forms as much as you want; Euclid composed a satiric verse in the very words he used, *Epicharēn eidon Marathōnade badizonta* and *ouk an g'eramenos ton ekeinou elleboron.*[28]

Now then, the employment of the technique of lengthening in excess is ridiculous, and moderation is a quality that is commonly needed in all aspects of diction. For, indeed, if one employs metaphors and strange words and other forms in an inappropriate way and with intended absurdity, he can also accomplish the same effect. When the ordinary words are inserted in the verse, it can be seen how great a difference the appropriate use of lengthening makes in epic poetry. If someone should also change the strange words and metaphors and other forms to ordinary words, he would see the truth of what we have said. For example, Aeschylus and Euripides wrote the same iambic line, but Euripides changed one word and instead of using a standard one employed a strange one; his line thus has an elegance to it, whereas the other is mean. For Aeschylus wrote in his *Philoctetes:*

phagediana hē mou sarkas esthiei podos
[this cancerous sore eats the flesh of my leg].

Euripides in place of "eats" substitutes *thoinatai* [feasts upon]. A similar situation would occur in the line

nun de m'eōn oligos te kai outidanos kai aeikēs[29]

if someone should substitute the ordinary words

nun de m'eōn mikros te kai asthenikos kai aeidēs

or if we changed the line

diphron aeikelion katatheis oligēn te trapezan[30]

to

diphron moxtheron katatheis mikran te trapezan

or for *ēiones booōsin*, we substituted *ēiones krazousin.*[31] Furthermore, Ariphrades mocked the tragedians because no one would use their style in conversation; for example, the word order *dōmatōn apo* in place of *apo dōmatōn,* and the word *sethen,* and the phrase *egō de nin,* and the word order *Achilleōs peri* in place of *peri Achilleōs,* and many other similar expressions. For he missed the point that the virtue of all these expressions is that they create an unusual element in the diction by their not being in ordinary speech.

It is a matter of great importance to use each of the forms mentioned in a fitting way, as well as compound words and strange ones, but by far the most important matter is to have skill in the use of metaphor. This skill alone it is not possible to obtain from another, and it is, in itself, a sign of genius. For the ability to construct good metaphors implies the ability to see essential similarities.

In regard to words, compounds are especially suitable for dithyrambs, strange words for heroic verse, and metaphors for iambic verse; in heroic verse all the forms mentioned are serviceable; but in iambic verse, because as much as possible it imitates conversation, only those words are appropriate that might be used in prose.

Of this nature are standard words, metaphors, and ornamental words.

Now, then, concerning tragedy and the imitation that is carried out in action, let what has been said suffice.

---

[28]This passage offers a number of difficulties in text and interpretation. The essential point is that the prosaic lines quoted can be technically turned into verse if enough licenses are allowed. The first phrase may be translated "I saw Epichares going to Marathon." The text of the second phrase is corrupt and does not have a clear meaning as it stands. [Tr.]

[29]A passage quoted from *Odyssey* 9:515, meaning "someone small, worthless, and unseemly." [Tr.]

[30]A passage quoted from *Odyssey* 20:259, meaning "having set down [for him] an unseemly chair and a small table." [Tr.]

[31]A passage quoted from *Iliad* 17:265, meaning "the shores cry out." [Tr.]

Concerning that form of verse imitation that is narrative, it is necessary to construct the plot as in tragedy in a dramatic fashion, and concerning a single action that is whole and complete (having a beginning, middle, and end) so that, like a single integrated organism, it achieves the pleasure natural to it.

The composition of incidents should not be similar to that found in our histories, in which it is necessary to show not one action but one period of time and as many things as happened in this time, whether they concern one man or many, and whether or not each of these things is related to the others. For just as there occurred in the same period of time a sea battle at Salamis and a battle with the Carthaginians in Sicily, but these did not at all lead to a common goal, thus also in the sequence of time, occasionally one event happens after another without there being a common goal to join them.

However, almost all the poets commit this error. Also in this, then, Homer would appear to be of exceptional skill in relation to other poets, as we have already said, since he did not attempt to write about the complete war, although it had a beginning and end; for that would have been a very large subject and could not have been taken in easily in a single view; or even if its magnitude were moderate, the story still would be tangled because of the diversity of incidents. But note how although treating only one part of the war, he also introduces many of the other episodes in the war, for example, the catalogue of ships and others, by which he gives variety to his poem. Others write about one man and about one period and one action with diverse parts, for example, the poet who wrote the *Cypria* and the *Little Iliad*. Therefore from the *Iliad* and *Odyssey* one or two tragedies apiece are constructed; but from the *Cypria* many tragedies are constructed and from the *Little Iliad* eight, for example, *The Award of the Arms, Philoctetes, Neoptolemus, Eurypylus, The Beggar, The Laconian Woman, The Sack of Troy, The Return Voyage,* and a *Sinon,* and a *Women of Troy.*[32]

[32]Butcher and Kassel bracket the names of the last two plays as being later additions to the original text of the *Poetics.* [Tr.]

Moreover, it is necessary for epic poetry to exhibit the same characteristic forms as tragedy; for it is either simple or complex, displays character or suffering, and is composed of the same parts, with the exception of song and spectacle. In epic, there is also a necessity for reversals, recognitions, and the depiction of suffering. Here too, thought and diction must be handled with skill. Homer used all these elements first and in a proper way. For each of his poems is well constructed; the *Iliad* is simple and exhibits suffering, whereas the *Odyssey* is complex (for there is recognition throughout) and shows character. In addition to these matters, Homer outstrips all others in diction and thought.

Epic differs from tragedy in regard to the length of the plot, and the meter. The sufficient limit of length has been mentioned, for we have noted that it must be possible to take in the plot's beginning and end in one view. This would occur if the plots were shorter than those of the old epics but would extend to the length of the number of tragedies that are designated for one performance. For the purpose of extending its length, epic poetry has a very great capacity that is specifically its own, since it is not possible in tragedy to imitate many simultaneous lines of action but only that performed by the actors on the stage. But because of the narrative quality of epic it is possible to depict many simultaneous lines of action that, if appropriate, become the means of increasing the poem's scope. This has an advantage in regard to the elegance of the poem and in regard to varying the interest of the audience and for constructing a diverse sequence of episodes. For the rapid overloading of tragedies with the same kind of incident is what makes tragedies fail.

The heroic meter has been found appropriate to epic through practical experience. If someone should write a narrative imitation in another meter, or in a combination of meters, we would feel it to be inappropriate. For the heroic is the stateliest and most dignified meter, and therefore it is especially receptive to strange words and metaphors, for narrative poetry in this regard is exceptional among the forms of imitation; the iambic and the trochaic tetrameter are expressive of motion, the latter being a dance meter and the former displaying the quality of action. Furthermore, it makes a very strange impression if someone combines these meters as Chairemon did. Therefore, no one has written a long poem in a meter other than the heroic; but, as we said, nature herself teaches us to choose the appropriate meter.

Homer deserves praise for many qualities and, especially, because alone of the poets he is not ignorant of the requirements of his craft. For it is necessary for the poet himself to speak in his own person in the poem as little as possible, because he is not fulfilling his function as an imitator when he appears in this way. Now the other poets are themselves active performers throughout the poem, and they perform their imitative function infrequently and in regard to only a few objects. Homer, on the other hand, when he has made a brief prelude immediately brings in a man or woman or some other character; and all his figures are expressive of character, and none lacks it.

Now then, it is necessary in tragedy to create the marvelous, but the epic admits, even more, of the irrational, on which the marvelous especially depends, because the audience does not see the person acting. The whole business of the pursuit of Hector would appear ridiculous on the stage with some men standing about and not pursuing and Achilles nodding at them to keep them back; but in the narrative description of epic, this absurdity escapes notice.

The marvelous is pleasant, and the proof of this is that everyone embellishes the stories he tells as if he were adding something pleasant to his narration. Homer has especially taught others how it is necessary to lie, and this is through the employment of false reasoning. For whenever one event occurs or comes into existence and is naturally accompanied by a second event, men think that whenever this second event is present the first one must also have occurred or have come into existence. This, however, is a fallacy. Therefore, if the first event mentioned is false but there is another event that must occur or come into existence when the first event occurs, we feel compelled to join the two events in our thought. For our mind, through knowing that the second

event is true, falsely reasons that the first event must have occurred or have come into existence also. There is an example of this type of fallacy in the Bath Scene in the *Odyssey*.

The use of impossible probabilities is preferable to that of unpersuasive possibilities. We must not construct plots from irrational elements, and we should especially attempt not to have anything irrational at all in them; but if this is not possible, the irrational should be outside the plot (as in Oedipus's ignorance of how Laius died); it should not be in the drama itself, as occurs in the *Electra* concerning those who bring news of the Pythian games, or in the *Mysians,* concerning the man who has come from Tegea to Mysia without speaking. To say that without the use of such incidents the plot would have been ruined is ridiculous. For it is necessary, right from the beginning, not to construct such plots.

If the poet takes such a plot and if it appears to admit of a more probable treatment, the situation is also absurd,[33] since it is clear that even the improbable elements in the *Odyssey* concerning the casting ashore of Odysseus would not be bearable if a poor poet had written them. Here the poet conceals the absurdity by making it pleasing through his other skillful techniques. It is necessary to intensify the diction only in those parts of the poem that lack action and are unexpressive of character and thought. For too brilliant a diction conceals character and thought.

25

Concerning the number and character of the problems that lead to censure in poetry and the ways in which this censure must be met, the following considerations would be apparent to those who study the question. Since the poet is an imitator, like a painter or any maker of likenesses, he must carry out his imitations on all occasions in one of three possible ways. Thus, he must imitate the

[33]Butcher and Hardy, following a different punctuation of the text, interpret this passage to mean that it is possible to admit some element of the irrational to the plot; others feel that the Greek text does not make adequate sense as it stands. I have followed Bywater's punctuation and interpretation of this passage. [Tr.]

things that were in the past, or are now, or that people say and think to be or those things that ought to be. The poet presents his imitation in standard diction, as well as in strange words and metaphors and in many variations of diction, for we grant this license to poets. In addition to this, there is not the same standard of correctness for politics and poetry, nor for any other art and poetry. In regard to poetry itself, two categories of error are possible, one essential, and one accidental. For if the poet chose to imitate but imitated incorrectly through lack of ability,[34] the error is an essential one; but if he erred by choosing an incorrect representation of the object (for example, representing a horse putting forward both right hooves) or made a technical error, for example, in regard to medicine or any other art, or introduced impossibilities of any sort, the mistake is an accidental, not an essential, one.

As a result, we must meet the criticisms of the problems encountered in poetry by taking these points into consideration. First, in regard to the problems that are related to the essential nature of art: if impossibilities have been represented, an error has been made; but it may be permissible to do this if the representation supports the goal of the imitation (for the goal of an imitation has been discussed) and if it makes the section in which it occurs, or another part of the poem, more striking. An example of such a situation is the pursuit of Hector in the *Iliad*. If, indeed, the goal of the imitation admits of attainment as well, or better, when sought in accordance with technical requirements, then it is incorrect to introduce the impossible. For, if it is at all feasible, no error should be committed at all. Further, we must ascertain whether an error originates from an essential or an accidental aspect of the art. For it is a less important matter if the artist does not know that a hind does not have horns than if he is unskillful in imitating one. In addition, the criticism that a work of art is not a truthful representation can be met by the argument that it represents the situation as it should be. For example, Sophocles said that he himself created characters

such as should exist, whereas Euripides created ones such as actually do exist. If neither of the above is the case, the criticism must be met by reference to men's opinions, for example, in the myths that are told about the gods. For, perhaps, they do not describe a situation that is better than actuality, nor a true one, but they are what Xenophanes said of them — in accordance, at any rate, with men's opinions. Perhaps the situation described by the artist is not better than actuality but was one that actually existed in the past, for example, the description of the arms that goes, "The spears were standing upright on their butt spikes"; for once this was customary, as it is now among the Illyrians. Now to judge the nobility or ignobility of any statement made or act performed by anyone, we must not only make an investigation into the thing itself that has been said or done, considering whether it is noble or ignoble, but we must also consider the one who does the act or says the words in regard to whom, when, by what means, and for what purpose he speaks or acts — for example, whether the object is to achieve a greater good or to avoid a greater evil.

We must meet some kinds of criticism by considering the diction, for example, by reference to the use of a strange word, as in the phrase, *ouréas men prôton*.[35] The word *oureas* here could cause some difficulty because perhaps the poet does not mean mules but guards. Dolon's statement, "I who was badly formed,"[36] has a similar difficulty involved in it; for he does not mean that he was misshapen in body but that he was ugly, because the Cretans use *eueidēs* [of fair form] to denote "handsome." A difficulty might arise in the phrase "mix the drink purer,"[37] which does not mean stronger, as if for drunkards, but faster. Difficulties arise in thoughts that are expressed in metaphors, for example, "All the gods and men slept the entire night through," which is said at the same time as "When truly he turned his gaze upon the Trojan plain, and hears the sound of flutes and pipes." "All" is used here metaphorically in place of "many," since "all" is some

---

[34]There is a lacuna in the text here that I have filled by translating Bywater's suggested reading, *hēmarte de di'*. [Tr.]

[35]Quoted from *Iliad* 1:50. The phrase means "first of all, the mules." [Tr.]
[36]Quoted from *Iliad* 10:316. [Tr.]
[37]Quoted from *Iliad* 11:202. [Tr.]

division of "many." The phrase "alone, she has no share"[38] shows a similar use of metaphor, since the best-known one is "alone." A problem may arise from the use of accent; Hippias the Thasian solved such a problem in the phrase, *didomen de oi* and similarly, in the phrase, *to men hoi katapythetai ombrō*.[39] Some difficulties are solved through punctuation, for example, in Empedocles' statement that "Suddenly things became mortal that had previously learned to be immortal and things unmixed before mixed."[40] Some problems are solved by reference to ambiguities, for example, "more than two-thirds of night has departed" because "more" is ambiguous here.[41] Some difficulties are met by reference to customary usages in our language. Thus, we call "wine" the mixture of water and wine; and it is with the same justification that the poet writes of "a greave of newly wrought tin"; and iron workers are called *chalkeas,* literally, copper smiths; and it is for this reason that Ganymede is called the wine pourer of Zeus, although the gods do not drink wine. This would also be justified through metaphor.

Whenever a word seems to signify something contradictory, we must consider how many different meanings it might have in the passage quoted; for example, in the phrase "the bronze spear was held there," we must consider how many different senses of "to be held" are possible, whether by taking it in this way or that one might best understand it. The procedure is opposite to the one that Glaucon mentions in which people make an unreasonable prior assumption and, having themselves made their decree, they draw their conclusions, and then criticize the poet as if he had said whatever they think he has said if it is opposed to their thoughts. We have had this experience in regard to discussion of the character Icarius.[42] People assume that he was a Spartan; but then it appears ridiculous that Telemachus did not meet him in Sparta when he visited there. Perhaps the situation is as the Cephallenians would have it, for they say that Odysseus married amongst them and that there was an Icadius involved, but no Icarius. Thus, it is probable that the difficulty has arisen through a mistake.

Speaking generally, the impossible must be justified in regard to the requirements of poetry, or in regard to what is better than actuality, or what, in the opinion of men, is held to be true. In regard to the art of poetry, we must prefer a persuasive impossibility to an unpersuasive possibility. Perhaps it is impossible[43] for the kind of men Zeuxis painted to exist; but they illustrate what is better than the actual. For whatever is a model must express superior qualities. The irrational must be justified in regard to what men say and also on the grounds that it is, sometimes, not at all irrational. For it is reasonable that some things occur contrary to reason.

We must consider contradictions in the same way as the refutation of arguments is carried on: that is, with reference to whether the same object is involved, and in the same relationship, and in the same sense, so that the poet, indeed, has contradicted himself in regard to what he himself says or what a sensible person might assume. There is justifiable censure for the presence of irrationality and depravity where, there being no necessity for them, the poet makes no use of them, as Euripides' handling of Aegeus in the *Medea* (in regard to the irrational) or in the same poet's treatment of the character of Menelaus in the *Orestes* (in regard to depravity). Criticisms of poetry, then, derive from five sources: either that the action is impossible or that it is irrational or that it is morally harmful or that it is contradictory or that it contains technical errors. The answers to these

---

[38]Quoted from *Iliad* 18:489. [Tr.]

[39]The problem here is that words that are spelled the same way, when given different accents, change their meaning. In the first phrase quoted, *didomen* can be either a present indicative or an infinitive used as an imperative, depending on the way in which it is accented; in the second phrase, *ou* can be either a relative pronoun or a negative adverb, depending on the way in which it is accented. [Tr.]

[40]The problem treated here is the effect that punctuation has on the meaning of a sentence. Thus, by means of different punctuations the word "before" in Empedocles' statement could be referred either to the phrase that precedes it, "things unmixed," or to the word that follows it, "mixed." [Tr.]

[41]The word "more" has a form in Greek that can also be translated as "full." [Tr.]

[42]In Homer, Icarius is Penelope's father. [Tr.]

[43]Translating *kai ei adunaton,* suggested by Vahlen to fill a lacuna in the text at this point. [Tr.]

criticisms must be sought from the solutions, twelve in number, that we have discussed.

26

The problem of whether epic or tragedy is the better type of imitation might be raised. For if whatever is less common is better, that art would be superior that is directed at the more discriminating audience; and it is very clear that the art that imitates every detail is common. For on the grounds that the audience does not see the point unless they themselves add something, the actors make quite a commotion; for example, the poorer sort of flute players roll about the stage if they must imitate a discus throw and drag their leader about if they are playing the *Scylla*. Now tragedy is considered to be of the same character that our older actors attribute to their successors; for, indeed, Mynescus called Callippides an ape on the grounds of overacting, and such an opinion was also held about Pindarus. As these two types of actor are related to each other, so the whole art of tragedy is thought to be related to epic by some people, who then conclude that epic is oriented toward a reasonable audience that does not at all require gestures, but that tragedy is disposed toward a less sophisticated audience. If, then, tragedy is directed toward a more common audience, it would be clear that it is the inferior art form.

Now then, first, this accusation is made against the art of acting, not poetry, since it is possible to overdo gestures both in epic recitations as Sosistratus did, and in song competitions as Mnasitheus the Opuntian did. Then, too, not every movement is to be rejected, if dancing indeed is not to be condemned, but only the movements of the ignoble, a point that was criticized in Callippides and now in others, since, it was charged, they were not representing freeborn women. Further, tragedy even without action achieves its function just as epic does; for its character is apparent simply through reading. If, then, tragedy is better in other respects, this defect is not essential to it. We argue, next, that it *is* better since it contains all of the elements that

epic has (for it is even possible to use epic meter in tragedy) and, further, it has no small share in music and in spectacle, through which pleasure is very distinctly evoked. Tragedy also provides a vivid experience in reading as well as in actual performance. Further, in tragedy the goal of the imitation is achieved in a shorter length of time (for a more compact action is more pleasant than one that is much diluted). I mean, for example, the situation that would occur if someone should put Sophocles' *Oedipus* into an epic as long as the *Iliad*. Further, the imitation of an epic story is less unified than that of tragedy (a proof of this is that a number of tragedies can be derived from any one epic). So that if epic poets write a story with a single plot, that plot is either presented briefly and appears to lack full development, or, if it follows the accustomed length of epic, it has a watered-down quality (I mean, for example, if the epic should be composed of very many actions in the same way as the *Iliad* and *Odyssey* have many such elements that also have magnitude in themselves). And yet these poems are constructed in the best possible way and are, as much as possible, the imitations of a single action.

If, then, tragedy is superior in all these areas and, further, in accomplishing its artistic effect (for it is necessary that these genres create not any chance pleasure, but the one that has been discussed as proper to them), it is apparent that tragedy, since it is better at attaining its end, is superior to epic.

Now then, we have expressed our view of tragedy and epic, both in general, and in their various species, and of the number and differences in their parts, as well as of some of the causes of their effectiveness or ineffectiveness, and the criticisms that can be directed against them, and the ways in which these criticisms must be answered. . . .[44]

---

[44]One of our manuscripts, Riccardianus 46, continues the text briefly at this point. The continuation seems to read, "Now as to iambic poetry and comedy. . . ." [Tr.]

Horace

65–8 B.C.E.

Quintus Horatius Flaccus was the son of a freed slave but received an excellent education in the private academies of Rome. Following the assassination of Julius Caesar, Horace fought in the ill-fated army of Marcus Brutus but was allowed to return to Rome at the amnesty. He served for a time as a clerk in government offices, but his talent as a poet and satirist came to the attention of Virgil, who introduced him to the renowned Roman patron Maecenas. Maecenas provided Horace with encouragement and money, and ultimately, the farm in the Sabine hills to which he retired.

The *Ars Poetica (The Art of Poetry)*, also known as the *Epistle to the Pisos*, was composed as a letter of advice in verse to the two sons of Lucius Calpurnius Piso, both of whom had poetic ambitions. Because it is a verse letter, it lacks the careful composition and exhaustive organization of a treatise on the art of poetry; Horace's aim was to blend witty reminders and sage maxims in an entertaining way.

Like Pope's *Essay on Criticism* (p. 199), the *Ars Poetica* contains dozens of lines and phrases that passed into the Latin language (and to an extent into English) as proverbs or catch phrases. We still speak of "purple patches" in prose, a phrase Horace coined. *Bonus dormitat Homerus* is the familiar "even Homer sometimes nods." *Parturiunt montes, nascetur ridiculus mus* (the mountains labor, giving birth to a ridiculous mouse) has become an adage for any pretentious activity. (The meaning of some of Horace's maxims has become garbled over the years: *Ut pictura poesis* [a poem is like a picture] was Horace's way of saying that some poems repay close scrutiny while others appeal through their broad outlines; it has been misinterpreted to suggest that Horace saw spatial form in poetry.)

To a reader expecting system, the organization of the *Ars Poetica* can be baffling. It is traditionally divided into three parts: lines 1–41 of the Latin original are on *poesis* or subject matter; lines 42–294 on *poema* or technique; and lines 295–476 on *poeta* or the poet. But in fact, Horace's wildfire ideas always outrace any system or organization that can be devised, and the reader should be prepared for rapid and unexpected transitions from one topic to another.

In the Middle Ages and the Renaissance, the *Ars Poetica* was often regarded as a commentary on Aristotle's *Poetics*. Though undoubtedly Horace had read Aristotle and occasionally echoes some of his remarks, the two thinkers have little in common. Where Aristotle suggests that tragedy uses iambic meter because it is closest to natural human speech, Horace offers two other rationales: literary tradition and the fact that iambics are better able to drown out a noisy and inattentive audience. Aristotle's explanation derives from his principle of *mimesis,* Horace's from his understanding of the expectations and the physical boisterousness of the *audience*.

Although Horace pays lip service to *mimesis* from time to time, what is really important to him is audience response. The poet should stick to traditional subjects, he tells us, but treat them in a new way. Poetic language should be novel, but not too novel — and the only way of judging the mean here is by closely observing the audience and the literary marketplace. Regardless of his innate genius, the poet must learn his art, especially the conventions that guide his audience in their expectations. Some of these, like the use of iambics in drama, may be more than mere conventions: They may reflect enduring aspects of human nature. Others, like Horace's dictum that a tragedy should have neither more nor less than five acts, were pure formalities. From Horace's point of view, such a distinction makes no difference, and indeed, he does not differentiate between rules and conventions. All alike need to be observed if the poet is to succeed in gaining a hearing from a fastidious and often captiously critical audience.

At the center of the *Ars Poetica* is Horace's statement of the ultimate aim of poetry: *aut prodesse aut delectare,* to teach or to delight — or both if possible, because the poet's audience, made up of diverse types, will require both: the *equites,* the knightly class, insist upon amusement, while the *senatores* want profitable lessons. The poet must understand their demands — and even those of the middle classes, the "roast-beans-and-chestnuts crowd" who applaud what is simple and exciting.

Like Aristotle, Horace assumes that different genres have their proper subject matter, technical devices, and effects; for example, that tragedy will concern dire events, be written in the highest style, and cause the audience to weep. But while for Aristotle, genres come into existence as if by the laws of nature and are scientifically comprehensible as emergent outgrowths of natural human impulses, for Horace genres do not have to make sense: They are just *there.* They exist, by accident as far as he is concerned, as predefined parts of the literary scene into which the poet comes, and the poet learns their rules as any prudent traveler in a strange country would learn the laws.

Unlike Plato and Aristotle, Horace is very much the worldly philosopher, and it is possible to misunderstand and cheapen the values by which he operates. Though Horace tells us that the successful author's book "will bring in money for Sosius and Son" — the Roman family that ran an operation copying manuscripts much in demand — he is not a prostitute producing verses to order. It is not vulgar commercial success Horace worships. For Horace, the author's reward is not money but fame. His ambition is to be read and praised, his terror to be ignored or laughed at. For Horace the poet was not a private man, but a public servant, like a successful statesman or ruler; both wore their laurels with pride, and their rewards came from the same public source.

Selected Bibliography

Brink, C. O. *Horace on Poetry.* Cambridge: Cambridge University Press, 1963.

D'Alton, J. F. *Horace and His Age.* London: Longmans Green, 1917.

Dettmer, Helena. *Horace: A Study in Structure.* Hildesheim and New York: Olms-Weidmann, 1983.

Freudenberg, Kirk. *The Walking Muse: Horace on the Theory of Satire.* Princeton: Princeton University Press, 1993.

Frischer, Bernard. *Shifting Paradigms: New Approaches to Horace's* Ars Poetica. Atlanta: Scholars Press, 1991.

Goad, Caroline. *Horace in the English Literature of the Eighteenth Century.* New Haven: Yale University Press, 1918.

Hack, R. K. "The Doctrine of Literary Forms." *Harvard Studies in Classical Philology* 27 (1916): 1–65.

Hardison, O. B., and Leon Golden, eds. *Horace for Students of Literature: The Ars Poetica and Its Tradition.* Gainesville: University Press of Florida, 1995.

Herrick, Marvin T. *The Fusion of Horatian and Aristotelian Literary Criticism.* Urbana: University of Illinois Press, 1946.

Perrot, Jacques. *Horace.* New York: New York University Press, 1964.

Showerman, Grant. *Horace and His Influence.* London: Longmans Green, 1922.

Stack, Frank. *Pope and Horace: Studies in Imitation.* Cambridge and New York: Cambridge University Press, 1985.

West, David. *Reading Horace.* Edinburgh: Edinburgh University Press, 1967.

Wood, Allen G. *Literary Satire and Theory: A Study of Horace, Boileau, and Pope.* New York: Garland, 1985.

The Art of Poetry

Humano capiti cervicem pictor equinam

Suppose you'd been asked to come for a private view
Of a painting wherein the artist had chosen to join
To a human head the neck of a horse, and gone on
To collect some odds and ends of arms and legs
And plaster the surface with feathers of differing
   colors,
So that what began as a lovely woman at the top
Tapered off into a slimy, discolored fish —
Could you keep from laughing, my friends? Believe
   me, dear Pisos,
Paintings like these look a lot like the book of a writer
Whose weird conceptions are just like a sick man's
   dreams,
So that neither the head nor the foot can be made to
   apply
To a single uniform shape. "But painters and poets
Have always been equally free to try anything."
We writers know that, and insist that such license be
   ours,
And in turn extend it to others — but not to the extent
Of mating the mild with the wild, so that snakes are
   paired
With birds, and tigers with lambs.

                    To works that begin
On a stately note and promise more grandeur to come
A couple of colorful patches are artfully stitched

To shimmer and shine, some sequins like these, for
   instance,
When the altar or grove of Diana, or perhaps it's a
   rainbow,
Or the Rhine is being described: "The sinuous stream
Rustles daintily, tastefully, on midst the sylvan
   scene."
But you put it in just the wrong place! You draw cy-
   press trees
Particularly well? But you're paid to hit off the
   likeness
Of the desperate sailor swimming away from his
   shipwreck!
This thing began as a wine jar: how come it comes
Off the wheel at last as a milk jug? Make what you
   want,
So long as it's one and the same, complete and entire.

O father, and sons who deserve a father like yours,
We poets are too often tricked into trying to achieve
A particular kind of perfection: I studiously try
To be brief, and become obscure; I try to be smooth,
And my vigor and force disappear; another assures us
Of something big which turns out to be merely
   pompous.
Another one crawls on the ground because he's too
   safe,
Too much afraid of the storm. The poet who strives
To vary his single subject in wonderful ways
Paints dolphins in woods and foaming boars on the
   waves.

Translated by Smith Palmer Bovie.

Avoiding mistakes, if awkwardly done, leads to error.
Nearby the gladiators' school there's a craftsman
 who molds
In bronze with special skill the lifelike shapes
Of fingernails and straying strands of hair,
But the whole result of his work is much less happy:
He can't represent the figure complete and entire.
If I were to try to cast a good piece of writing,
I'd no more prefer to be like this fellow than live
With my nose at an angle, no matter how much
 admired
I was for my coal-black hair and coal-black eyes.

Take up a subject equal to your strength, O writers,
And mull over well what loads your shoulders will
 bear,
And what they will not. The man who chooses a
 subject
He can really manage won't be at a loss for the words
Or the logical order they go in. As for order itself,
Its power and charm consist, if I'm not mistaken,
In saying just then what ought to be said at that point,
Putting some things off, leaving others out, for the
 present:
The author of the promised work must choose and
 discard.

In weaving your words, make use of care and good
 taste:
You've done it right, if a clever connection of phrases
Makes a good old word look new. If you have to
 display
Some recondite matter in brand-new terms, you can
 forge
Words never heard in the pre-tunic days of Cethegus;
License is given, on condition that you use it with
 care.
New-fashioned words, just coined, will soon gain
 currency,
If derived from a Grecian source, *and* in small
 amounts.
Will the Roman refuse the license to Vergil and
 Varius
And grant it to Plautus and Caecilius?[1] And why
 should I

Be refused the right to put in my bit, if I can,
When the language of Ennius and Cato enriched the
 speech
Of our native land and produced some new terms for
 things?
It has always been granted, and always will be, to
 produce
Words stamped with the date of the present. As trees
 change their leaves
When each year comes to its end, and the first fall
 first,
So the oldest words die first and the newborn thrive
In the manner of youth, and enjoy life. All that we are
And have is in debt to death, as are all our
 projects:[2]
The Portus Julius where Neptune is at home on the
 land
And protects our ships from his storms — a princely
 achievement;
The Pontine marshes, inhabitable only for boats
And plagues in the past, but now a food-bearing land
That feels the weight of the plow and feeds nearby
 towns;
The straightening-out of the Tiber that used to wreak
 havoc
On fields of grain but has now learned to mend its
 ways —
All these projects, whatever men make, will perish,
And the fame and dignity of speech are equally
 mortal.
Much that has once dropped out will be born again,
And much of our language now held in high repute
Will fall to the ground if UTILITY so decrees,
With which rests the final decision, the ultimate
 standard,
The legal existence, of speech.
                    Homer has showed us
The meter to use to describe sad wars and great deeds
Of kings and princes. The uneven couplet that joined
One verse to another was first adapted to grief,
But elegy easily turned into epigrammatic
Couplets expressive of thanks for prayers
 answered.
Who wrote these first little couplets? The critics are
 STILL

[1]Horace's point is that Plautus and Caecilius, a century earlier, had made new Latin words out of good Greek ones, but his contemporaries Virgil and Varius were being criticized for the same artistic license.

[2]The creation of a sheltered harbor at Ostia, the draining of the Pontine marshes, and the straightening of the Tiber were three of Augustus's great civic achievements.

Disputing the subject; the case is still on the books.
Fury equipped Archilochus[3] with his iambics:
The foot slipped into the comic sock as neatly
As into the tragic boot, so dramatists used it
To make their dialogue heard, even over the noise
The audience was making — the rhythm of
  purposeful action.
The muse entrusted to lyric verse the accounts
Of gods and the children of gods, of a winning boxer,
Of a prize-winning race horse, the laments of young
  lads in love,
The intoxicating freedom of wine. If I can't observe
These distinctions of form and tone, do I really
  deserve
To be hailed as a poet? Why, from a false sense of
  shame,
Do I prefer being ignorant to learning? A good comic
  sequence
Just won't submit to treatment in the meters of
  tragedy.
Likewise, Thyestes' feast[4] resents being told
In strains more nearly like those that comedy needs
In the vein of everyday life. Let each of the styles
Be assigned to the places most proper for it to
  maintain.
Of course, now and then even comedy raises her
  voice:
Angry old Chremes swells up like a supersorehead;
And the Tragedy of Telephus, the Plight of Peleus,
  stoop
To the muse of prose for words of grief when, poor
Or exiled, either hero discards the bombast
That jars on our ears and his wordsafootandahalflong,
To let his lament wing its way to the hearer's heart.

It isn't enough for poems to be things of beauty:
Let them STUN the hearer and lead his heart where
  they will.
A man's face is wreathed in smiles when he sees
  someone smile;
It twists when he sees someone cry; if you expect *me*
To burst into tears, you have to feel sorrow yourself.
Then your woes will fasten on me, O Telephus,
  Peleus;

If you speak incongruous lines, I'll snooze or I'll
  giggle.
Touching words most become the sorrowful
  countenance,
Blistering threats the enraged, playful remarks
The cheerful, suitably dignified speech the severe.
For nature first forms us, deep in our hearts, to
  respond
To the changing guise of our fortunes; she makes us
  take heart
Or drives us wild or bends us down to the ground
And let us writhe over inconsolable grief;
Then she brings these emotions out by using the
  tongue
To interpret them. If a speaker's words don't accord
With his fortunes, the Roman knights and those
  wretched wights
Who bought only standing room will both rock the
  house
With uproarious laughter. It will make a great deal of
  difference
Who's speaking: a god or a hero, a wise old man,
Or a fervent fellow in the flower of youth, or a
  matron,
A *powerful* matron, a busy old nurse, or a merchant,
A wandering merchant, or a man who farms the
  green field,
Or the Colchian or Assyrian type, or a man bred at
  Thebes,
A man bred at Argos.
                      You should either stick to tradition
Or invent a consistent plot. If you bring back
  Achilles,
Have him say how laws don't apply to him, have
  prowess
Prevail over status, make him ruthless, impatient and
  fierce,
And ANGRY! Let Medea be wild, inconquerably so,
Ino tearful, Io "lost"; let Ixion
Go back on his word; let Orestes be sadly depressed.
If it's something as yet untried you put on the stage
And you dare construct a new character, you must
  keep
To the end the same sort of person you started out
  with,
And make your portrayal consistent.
                          It's hard to write
Of familiar concerns in a new and original way.
You're better off telling the story of Troy in five acts

---

[3]Greek satiric poet of the sixth century B.C.E.
[4]As an act of revenge, Atreus served a feast to his brother
Thyestes, consisting of Thyestes' own children.

Than being the first to foist something new and
  untried
On the world. In the public domain you'll have pri-
  vate rights
If you keep from loitering around the most common
  places
And from dawdling on the easiest path, and take
  pains to refrain
From translating faithfully word for word, and don't
  leap
Right down the close-scooped well of the source you
  draw on,
Precluded by shame or the laws of your task from
  lifting
Your foot up over the edge. And don't begin
As the Cyclic poet once did: "And now I shall sing
Of the fortune of Priam and famous war of that king."
What could issue from the mouth that made such an
  opening?
Mountains will labor, a funny little mouse will be
  born.
To take on less is a much more sensible labor:

"Tell me, O Muse, of the man who, after Troy fell,
Came to know well all manner of cities and men."[5]

This writer plans to send up not smoke from the
  flames
But light from the smoke, to deliver some marvelous
  events:
Antiphates' giants, Scylla, Charybdis, the Cyclops.
Diomedes' return is not traced back to begin
With Meleager's death. The Trojan War doesn't start
With the egg of the twins.[6] He is eager to get to the
  point
And hurries the reader along to the middle of things,
As if they were already known, and simply leaves out
Whatever he thinks he can't bring off shining and
  clear,
And devises so well, intermingling the true and the
  false,
That the middle part fits with the first, the last with
  the middle.

---

[5]The opening lines of Homer's *Odyssey*.
[6]Meleager, Diomedes' uncle, died before he was born.
Helen of Troy was born from one of Leda's eggs; her twin
brothers Castor and Polydeukes were born from the other.

Now hear what I and the rest of your listeners expect
If you want them to sit there and wait till the curtain
  comes down
And the cantor intones "*vos plaudite*[7] . . . now is the
  time."
Make careful note of the way each age group
  behaves,
And apply the right tone to their changeable natures
  and years.
The child who by now knows how to reel off his
  words,
And plant his feet squarely beneath him, likes most of
  all
To play with his friends; he flies into rage like a flash
And forgets it equally fast, and changes every hour.
The beardless youth, finally free of his guardian,
Rejoices in horse and hounds and the sun-drenched
  grass
Of the Campus Martius: he is putty in your hands to
  mold
To evil courses, resentful of warning advisers;
Slow to provide for his needs but recklessly fast
To spend his money, enthusiastic, intense,
But quick to transfer his affections. As his interests
  change,
The man is seen in the manly style of his life:
He looks for wealth and for friends, is a slave to
  success,
Is wary of making a move he will soon be concerned
To undo. A great many troubles harass the old man,
Either because he keeps on trying for gain
And yet won't touch what he has, worried and afraid
To use it, or perhaps because in all that he does
He's slow and phlegmatic, and keeps postponing his
  pleasures,
Conscious of the rainy days he should be prepared
  for,
"Difficult," always complaining, ready to praise
The good old days when he was a boy and reprove
And disapprove of the young. As the years come
  along,
They bring along much that is fine; as they disappear,
They take many fine things away. In portraying our
  roles,
We will dwell on the matters best suited and best
  attached

---

[7]"Applaud."

To the age in question, and not let the old men's parts
Be assigned to a youth or the manly parts to a boy.

The events are either enacted on stage or described
As having occurred. But things entrusted to the ear
Impress our minds less vividly than what is exposed
To our trustworthy eyes so that a viewer informs
    himself
Of precisely what happened. Still, you are not to
    show
On stage what ought to take place backstage: remove
From our eyes the substance of things an eloquent
    messenger
Will soon be ready to state in person. Medea
Must not butcher her boys in front of the people;
Unspeakable Atreus should not cook up human flesh
Before our eyes, nor should Procne change into a
    bird,
Or Cadmus into a snake. Whatsoever such stuff
You *show* me, I won't believe it, I'll simply detest it.

The play that expects to be asked for another
    performance
Once it's been given, should be just five acts long,
No more, no less. A god must not intervene
Unless the action tangles itself in such knots
That only a divine deliverer can work the denoue-
    ment;
A fourth actor should not try to come forward to
    speak.[8]

The chorus should be handled as one of the actors
    and play
An important part, singing between episodes
What advances the plot and fits in well with the
    action.
Let it favor the good and offer them friendly advice,
Control the wrathful and develop a fondness for
    soothing
With quiet words the fearful in heart. Let it praise
    plain living,
The blessings of justice, the laws, and the doors left
    open
By Peace. Let the chorus respect the secrets it's told.

Let it pray to the gods, devoutly imploring that
    fortune
Return to the unhappy low and depart from the proud.

The present-day brass-bound flute produces a tone
That rivals the trumpet's, unlike the primitive pipe,
With its thin, clear tone and one or two stops, war-
    bling woodnotes
To give the chorus the pitch, and provide an accom-
    paniment —
A sound that could nevertheless carry in the
    uncrowded halls
When virtuous, decent, well-behaved folk came
    together.
But after a victorious people began to acquire
More land, and surround their cities with larger walls,
And drink to the Genius in broad daylight without
    shame,
More license entered the rhythms and modes of the
    music.
How could these rough country types be expected to
    judge,
Just off from work, mixed in with the city crowd,
The uncouth sitting next to the wealthy? And so the
    flute player
Added movement and gesture to the primitive style
And fluttered his robe as he strutted around the stage.
New notes increased the restricted range of the lyre,
And unrestrained wit produced a new form of
    eloquence,
So that even the thought, which had been such a fine
    detective
Of useful clues and prophet of future events,
Now resembled the unclear, ambiguous dictates of
    Delphi.

The writer who vied for the paltry prize of a goat
With tragic song, soon bared shaggy satyrs to view
On the stage, coarsely probing for laughs without los-
    ing dignity —
Some pleasant device and novel attraction like this
Being all that could make the spectator stay on and
    watch
After having fulfilled the ritual rites of the occasion,
And drunk a good bit, and been freed from the nor-
    mal restraints.
But those laughing, bantering satyrs will have to be
    told
To transform the mood from the grave to the gay with
    some care

---

[8]Latin and Greek plays had more than three characters, but
by convention, no more than three speaking actors in addition
to the chorus were allowed on stage at the same time. See
Aristotle's *Poetics,* Ch. 4.

And not let a god or a hero, previously seen
Coming out from his palace clad in royal crimson and
    gold,
Move into a dingy shack and a low way of talking
Or, avoiding the depths, climb too fantastically high.
For tragedy, not condescending to mouth low lines,
Joins the satyrs but briefly, and not without some
    hesitation,
Like a matron commanded to dance on a festive
    occasion.
I assure you, good Pisos, if I write a satyr play,
I will not use only commonplace nouns and verbs
Or "plain words," nor try to depart from the tragic
    tone
To the point where it makes no difference whether
    Davus is speaking
With maudlin Pythias (who's just swiped some
    dough from old Simo)
Or Silenus, tutor and guide to his heavenly ward.[9]
I shall set my sights on familiar things: anyone
Will think he can do as well but will soon find he can't
When he tries it and sweats and strains to bring it off.
The order and inner coherence and careful connection
Are what make your writing take hold: your major
    success
Consists in mastering the language that is common to
    all.
I incline to believe that when fauns trot in from the
    woods,
They ought not to act as if they were reared in the
    gutter
And virtually lived in the Forum, with citified ways
And prettified lays like those of young-bloods-about-
    town,
Or resort to indecent remarks and crack dirty jokes.
The better-class patrons may take offense (the
    freeborn,
The knights, the wealthy) and refuse to award the
    crown,
As it were, unwilling to see in a favorable light
What the roast-beans-and-chestnuts[10] crowd find so
    entertaining.

A short syllable followed by a long is of course an
    iambus.

It moves along fast, so a verse consisting of six
Full-fledged iambic stresses has come to be known
As iambic trimeter. But recently, to come to our ears
More slowly and solemnly, father Iambus adopted
A firm-footed son, the spondee. Affable and kind
Though he was, the iambus did not admit the young
    man
On equal terms into this partnership, but reserved
The second and fourth foot all for himself. This
    iambus
Appears but rarely in the "fine old" trimeters of
    Accius,
And the spondaic stress in the lines which Ennius
    heavily
Launched on the stage is a sign of hasty production
Or a fault to be chalked up to careless ignorance of
    style.
Not every critic can spot the lines that don't quite
    scan right,
And Roman poets have been granted too much
    indulgence.
Shall I therefore run wild and write without any
    restrictions
Or consider that everyone is bound to see my
    mistakes
And cautiously keep well within the bounds of
    indulgence?
I may have avoided the fault without rating praise.
Thumb through your Greek examples by day and by
    night!
Your ancestors praised both the wit and rhythms of
    Plautus?
For admiring both of these things they were *too*
    tolerant,
Not to say dense, if you and I can distinguish
A crudeness in phrasing from lapidary strength of
    wit,
And catch the legitimate beat with our fingers and
    ears.

Thespis is said to have discovered the unknown style
Of the tragic muse, and to have carted his plays
    about,
With actors singing the lines and performing the
    parts,
Their faces smeared with a paste concocted from
    wine lees —
So they trudged around in road shows, reveling in
    tragedy.

[9]Davus outwits Simo in Terence's *Andria;* Pythias is a
character from his *Eunuchus;* Silenus was the tutor of the god
Bacchus.
[10]Snacks sold outside Roman theaters.

Aeschylus thought up the masks and distinctive
    costumes;
He built the first stage on a platform of several small
    boards
And taught his actors a lofty manner of speech
And a stately, high-booted stride. These tragic arts
Were succeeded by Old Comedy, whose many good
    points
Should be noted. From freedom that form declined
    into license
And fell upon violent ways that required regulation.
The law was obeyed and the chorus then lapsed into
    silence,
Deprived of its right to insult and abuse its victims.

Our Roman poets have left no style untried
And have not been the least deserving when they
    have dared
To desert the traces of Greece and dwell on affairs
Originating here among us, on our native designs,
Whether tragic or comic. Latium would be as
    triumphant
In language as in character and military might
If a single one of her poets could endure the effort
And time-consuming, slow discipline of the file.
Oh, descendants of Numa, turn your backs on the
    poem
Which many a day and many a diligent erasure
Have not corrected, which a sensitive, newly-pared
    nail
Has not run over and checked, at the least, ten times.

Because Democritus held that *genius was all*
And the miserable practice of art far inferior to it,
And denied that sensible poets rated a place
On Helicon's heights,[11] most poets neglect their
    appearance —
They won't cut their nails or their beards, they won't
    take a bath,
They wander off somewhere alone. For surely the
    name
And the fame of the poet will attach itself to that
    dome
Which has never entrusted itself to the shears of
    Licinus,[12]
Which trips for treatment to three times as many
    psychiatrists

[11]Helicon was the mountain sacred to the Muses.
[12]A well-known Roman barber.

As even Switzerland harbors have failed to set
    straight.[13]
What a fool am I to purge myself of my bile
Seasonably, every spring! If I'd only refrained,
I'd be unsurpassed as a poet. But perhaps it's not
    worth it
To lose your head and then write verses instead,
So I'll play the whetstone's part, giving edge to the
    steel,
Without being able to cut. And though I write
    nothing,
I'll point out the writer's mission and function and
    show
Him where his best material lies and what
Nurtures and shapes the poet, what best accords
With his role, what worst, where the right path goes,
    and the wrong.

The principal source of all good writing is wisdom.
The Socratic pages will offer you ample material,
And with the matter in hand, the words will be quick
    to follow.
A man who has learned what is owing to country and
    friends,
The love that is due a parent, a brother, a guest,
What the role of a judge or senator chiefly requires,
What part is played by the general sent off to war,
Will surely know how to write the appropriate lines
For each of his players. I will bid the intelligent
    student
Of the imitative art to look to the model of life
And see how men act, to bring his speeches alive.
At times a play of no particular merit,
Artistically lacking in strength and smoothness of
    finish
But with vivid examples of character drawn true to
    life,
Will please the audience and hold their attention
    better
Than tuneful trifles and verses empty of thought.

[13]*Psychiatrists ... Switzerland*: The translator here
indulges in an anachronism to avoid a complicated explanation. The geographical reference in Horace's Latin is not to
Switzerland but to Antycra, a town famous for producing
black hellebore, a poisonous plant that, in legend, was used by
the physician Melampus to cure the madness of three daughters of the King of Argos. Horace's general point is that
poets, supposed to be men of genius, affect to be both uncouth
and mad.

To the Greeks the muse gave genius, the Greeks she
    endowed
With eloquent speech and greed for nothing but
    praise.
Our Roman lads learn arithmetic and divide
The unit into its hundreds. "The Son of
    Albinus —
You here today? All right, your turn to recite!
Subtract a twelfth from five-twelfths, and what have
    you left?
Come on, Albinus Minus — don't think so hard!"
"One-third, Sir." "Fine! You'll keep track of your
    money, you will.
Now take that original sum and add on a twelfth.
How much?" "One-half." When once the corrosive
    concern
For petty cash has tainted our minds, can we hope to
    write poems
To be oiled with cedar and kept in smooth cypress
    cases?

Poets would either delight or enlighten the reader,
Or say what is both amusing and really worth using.
But when you instruct, be brief, so the mind can
    clearly
Perceive and firmly retain. When the mind is full,
Everything else that you say just trickles away.
Fictions that border on truth will generate pleasure,
So your play is not to expect automatic assent
To whatever comes into its head, nor to draw forth a
    child
Still alive from Lamia's stomach after she's dined.
Our elders will chase off the stage what is merely
    delightful;
Our young bloods will pass up the works that merely
    make sense.
He wins every vote who combines the sweet and the
    useful,
Charming the reader and warning him equally well.
This book will bring in money for Sosius and Son,
Booksellers, travel across the sea, and extend
Its author's fame a long distance into the future.

There still may be some oversights, and we may be
    willing
To overlook them, for the string won't always play
    back
What the hand had in mind: quite often you ask for a
    flat

And get back a sharp. You brandish your bow at the
    target,
But the arrow won't always fly home. If happy
    effects
Figure more, I won't take offense at the few bad
    spots
Which either carelessness let slip onto the page
Or human nature took too little pains to avert.
And what's the truth here? If a slave who copies out
    books
Keeps making the same mistake no matter how often
He's warned, he can't be excused; if a harpist keeps
    striking
The same wrong note, he'll be laughed at. I would
    reserve
The role of Choerilus for poets who strike something
    good[14]
Two or three times in the course of a largely flawed
    work,
Which makes me laugh as a matter of sheer
    amazement.
Good Homer sometimes nods, which gives me a
    jerk —
But sleep may well worm its way into any long work!

A poem is much like a painting: one will please more
If you see it close up, another if seen from a distance;
One prefers being viewed in the shade, while the
    other
Prefers being seen in broad daylight and doesn't
    shrink back
From the piercing glance of the critic. One pleased
    once;
The other will always please, though it's called for
    ten times.

Let me say to the older of you two boys, and remind
You to take it to heart, no matter how wise you
    may be
And well directed to the right by your father's voice:
The doctrine of the mean does not correctly apply
To all things, but rather to a few quite definite
    matters.
The average lawyer, consultant or trial attorney,

[14]Choerilus was an epic poet of the fourth century B.C.E.
who was offered a piece of gold by Alexander the Great for
every *good* verse celebrating his victories. He died poor.

May lack Messalla's delivery, may not know as much
As Aulus Cascellius, and still be of no little worth.
But men and gods and booksellers WON'T PUT UP
WITH SECOND-RATE POETS. If the orchestra playing
    at dinner
Is all out of tune, if the ointment offered each guest
Is lumpy, if sour Sardinian honey is served
With the poppy seeds, the party is spoiled all the
    more;
It could have gone on perfectly, simply without them.
So a poem, designed and destined to afford the soul
Genuine pleasure, if it falls somewhat short of the
    top,
Sinks right down to the bottom. If a man can't play,
He avoids the weapons drill going on in the Campus.
And if he can't handle the ball or discus or hoop,
He stands off, lest he provoke the justified laughter
Of spectators crowded around and forming the circle.
But someone who doesn't know how dares fashion
    verses.
Why not? He's free, freeborn, in fact, and his income
Is rated at a knightly sum, has a fine reputation.

But you, my dear fellow, will refrain from speaking
    or acting
Without Minerva's consent? That shows good
    judgment
And a sound attitude. If you ever do write something,
    though,
Be sure to expose it to such ears as Tarpa the
    Censor's,
And your father's, and mine. Then put the parchment
    away
For a good nine years! What you haven't yet
    published
You can always destroy, but once a word is let go,
It can't be called back.
                    When primitive men roamed the forests,
Orpheus, the sacred interpreter of heavenly will,
Turned them away from killing and living like beasts
And hence is said to have tamed wild lions and tigers.
Amphion is said, as founder of the city of Thebes,
To have moved the stones and led them wherever he
    wished
By the sound of his lyre and the winning appeal of his
    voice.
This was the wisdom of former times: to distinguish
Public from private concerns and sacred from
    common,

To forbid impromptu liaisons and make rules for
    marriage,
To build towns and carve out the laws on pillars of
    wood.
The poets who taught by expressing these things were
    acclaimed:
They and their works were considered divine. After
    them,
Tyrtaeus and Homer won wide renown by sharpening
Masculine minds to a warlike pitch with their poems.
Oracles were uttered in song, and a way of life
Pointed out, along gnomic lines. The favor of kings
Was courted in verse, and festival joy was found
As the suitable end to periods of long, hard
    work —
Lest you make excuses for Apollo, the god of song,
Or the muse so skilled with the lyre.
                              The question is raised
Whether nature or art makes a poem deserving of
    praise.
I fail to see what good either learning can be
Which is not veined with natural wealth or primitive
    genius.
Each needs the other's help and friendly alliance.
The racer who wants to win has learned, as a boy,
To strain and train, shiver and sweat, stay away
From women and wine. The flute player who gets to
    play
At the Pythian games has long since studied and
    shuddered
In the presence of his teacher. Today, it's enough just
    to say:
"I PEN these marvelous POEMS — I'm a Creative
    Person.
The last one's a dirty shirt. I won't get left back,
Admitting I just don't know what I've never yet
    learned."

Like the auctioneer who collects a crowd for a sale,
The poet with property or money put out in loans
Is ordering flatterers to make a profit from him.
But when he can serve a nice little dinner for friends,
Or put up the bail for a poor man who's not a good
    risk,
Or rescue one held in the gloomy grip of the law,
I'll marvel if the lucky man can always distinguish
    the false friend from the true.
                              And if you have given,

Or intend to give, a present to someone, don't take
him
To hear, still glowing with joy, some verses you've
written.
He'll shout out "Fine! Oh, *excellent! How superb!*"
Go pale at the sombre parts, even squeeze out a drop
Of dew from his friendly eyes, and pound on the
ground
With his foot to keep time, and dance a bit for sheer
joy.
Just as hired mourners often behave much better at
funerals
Than those sincerely bereaved, so the man who
pretends
Makes more perpetual emotion than your honest
admirer.
Kings are said to ply with drink after drink
And put through the ordeal by wine the man they
would test
As worthy of the royal friendship. And if you would
write,
Don't ever forget: there's a motive concealed in the
fox.

If you read something out to Quintilius,[15] he'd usu-
ally say,
"You could straighten out *this,* or *that.*" And if, after
trying
Two or three times with no luck, you'd said you
could *not*
Improve on the passage, he'd tell you to strike it right
out
And hand back to the anvil those verses that came out
so bent,
To be hammered into shape once again. Then, if you
preferred
Standing by your mistake to changing it, he'd waste
not a word
Or an ounce of energy more, and not interfere
With your loving, alone and unrivaled, yourself and
your work.
The fair-minded, thoughtful man will reproach the
verses
That come out spineless and flat, find fault with the
clumsy

And rhythmically harsh; with a straight black stroke
of the pen
He will line out disorganized parts; your elegant
effects
He will simply cut out; he will force you to let in
more light
On the dark passages, point out ambiguous phrasing,
And note what ought to be changed, a real Richard
Bentley,[16]
Who won't stop to say, "But why should I harass a
friend
With these minor repairs?" These minor repairs will
create
A major disaster, once that friend is exposed
To a hostile reception and unfriendly jeers in public.

The mad poet only makes sensible people avoid him
And fear to touch him, as if he were plagued by the
itch
Or the royal disease of jaundice (yellow as gold
And worth a king's ransom to cure) or St. Vitus'
dance
Or lunatic frenzy. Kids chase after and taunt him.
With his head held high, he strolls off belching his
lines,
And then if he falls down a well or into a pit —
Like a fowler whose eyes are steadily trained on the
merles —
He may yell long and loud for help: "To the rescue!
This way,
Fellow citizens!" None will care to come pull him
out.
And if someone *should have* the urge to lend him a
hand
And let down a rope, I will say, "But how do you
know
He hasn't intentionally thrown himself in and *doesn't
Want* to be saved?" and then I will tell of the death
Of the Sicilian poet. Because Empedocles wished
To be thought an immortal god, he leaped into Etna,
This cool customer, to his fiery fate. We are left
To conclude that poetic justice or poetic license
Includes suicide. To save some person from death

---

[15]A Roman critic of the second century B.C.E.; Horace is
using the name to denote some man of taste.

[16]Another anachronism by the translator. Bentley
(1662–1742) was a British critic who corrected Pope's translation of Homer. Horace's Latin refers to Aristarchus of
Samothrace (220–143 B.C.E.), who wrote scholarly commentary on Homer.

Against his will is just as wrong as to kill him.
This isn't the first time it's happened, and if he's
    pulled out,
He will not necessarily be made over into a man
And put aside his desire for a memorable end.

It's not quite clear what drove him to write, in the
    first place —
Did he sprinkle his well-wrought urine on ancestral
    ashes?
Or blasphemously joggle the ground at some sacred
    spot?

At any rate, he's got it bad; and, bold as a bear,
If he's strong enough to have smashed in the fretwork
    of bars
That kept him confined to his cage, he's on a
    rampage,
Stampeding unlearned and learned alike, in his rage
To recite. Once he's caught you, he'll hang on with
    all his might;
The leech just clings to your skin and never gives in
Until bloated with blood; *he'll* never run out of breath
But will read you and read you and read you and read
    you to death.

Longinus

First Century C.E.

One of the most controversial aspects of "On the Sublime" has been its authorship. The oldest manuscript, from the tenth century, calls the author "Dionysius Longinus." The name is too apt to be true. Each of its two halves belongs to a great Greco-Roman philosopher, Dionysius of Halicarnassus (who wrote under Augustus Caesar) and Cassius Longinus (who died nearly three centuries later, in 273 C.E.). But neither of these men is a plausible candidate to have written "On the Sublime." The literary opinions of Longinus are inconsistent with those of Dionysius, while Cassius Longinus, who wrote during the most brutally chaotic period of the Empire, is unlikely to have penned Chapter 44, which discusses the causes of literary decline in an era of universal peace.

The style and historical allusions suggest a date during the quiet reigns of Nerva and Trajan, toward the end of the first century. The quotation in Chapter 9 from the Old Testament book of Genesis would be an extraordinary allusion for a pagan author to make, and it has been suggested that Longinus may have been either a Hellenized Jew (perhaps of the circle of Philo Judaeus[1]) or a Greek with Jewish connections.

Unlike Plato, who concerned himself with common features of artistic works in general, Longinus is interested in a special quality, sublimity or elevation, which is possessed by some works but not others. Unlike Aristotle, whose poetics dealt with the particular characteristics of different literary forms, Longinus's sublimity is a quality that transcends generic boundaries. It can be found in drama or epic or lyric — or even in rhetoric or history or theology. Longinus's approach might be called "qualitative criticism," and it constitutes the third enduring method of literary theory, with descendants from Burke to Bakhtin. "On the Sublime" is related in one sense to the rhetorical criticism of Horace and others — its principal topics seem to be author, work, and audience — but where Horace differentiated between a high, a middle, and a low style, Longinus is concerned only with the first. And Longinus is far more methodical in exploring his more limited subject than Horace.

The argument of "On the Sublime" can be easily outlined. In Chapters 1 and 2 Longinus defines the Sublime as that quality within a discourse that produces "not persuasion but transport" (*ekstasis*) within the audience. He then questions whether there is such an art — whether it is purely a matter of inspiration or whether there are basic principles at work. Much of the actual argument itself has been lost, but from the rest of the essay, which presents five components of the art, it is clear on which side Longinus comes down. In Chapters 3 through 7, Longinus discusses the traps that lie on all sides of the target, those faults in literature that result from trying for the sublime and missing the mark. There are faults of commission, such as

[1]Philo may be the "philosopher" in Ch. 44 whom Longinus attempts to confute.

trying too hard (bombast, pedantry, hysteria), and there are faults of omission, such as frigidity of tone.

In Chapter 8, Longinus outlines the remainder of his essay, which successively treats the five sources (beyond language itself) of the Sublime. First are high thoughts (Chapters 9–15) and second, strong passions (not included but promised in a separate treatise), both of which are innate within the artist. Next are rhetorical figures (Chapters 16–29), then noble diction (Chapters 30–38 and 43), and finally, elevated composition (Chapters 39–42), all of which are the product of art and must be learned.

Just as important as Longinus's systematic method is the clarity and vigor with which he pursues it. He always has an apt quotation ready to exemplify a literary fault or grace, and for a judicial critic, there is nothing mean-spirited about his tone or temper.

Longinus's treatise "On the Sublime" was not influential in its own time. Its importance dates only from the Renaissance; it was published by Francesco Robortello in 1554 and translated by Nicolas Boileau in 1674. Soon thereafter it became common property, and poet-critics like John Dryden drew upon its central issues. During the eighteenth century, the Sublime was considered to be of great significance in opposition to the beautiful (a dichotomy treated by Edmund Burke, Immanuel Kant, and many others), and Longinus's brilliance as a critic was much appreciated. In his *Essay on Criticism*, Alexander Pope conveys the typical Augustan sentiments about the author of "On the Sublime":

> Thee, bold Longinus! all the Nine inspire,
> And bless their critic with a poet's fire:
> An ardent judge, who, zealous in his trust,
> With warmth gives sentence, yet is always just;
> Whose own example strengthens all his laws;
> And is himself that great Sublime he draws.

But Longinus was more admired than imitated in the eighteenth century — except on one occasion by Pope, who wrote a travesty of "On the Sublime" in "The Art of Sinking in Poetry," explaining (with delicious examples from contemporary works) the sources of the quality of Bathos. In the nineteenth century, his overt influence and reputation declined somewhat, perhaps owing to his antidemocratic political beliefs, but his method of qualitative criticism was paradoxically revived in thinkers like Matthew Arnold (*The Study of Poetry*, p. 429), Walter Pater, and most recently Mikhail Bakhtin.

Selected Bibliography

Apfel, Henrietta Veit. *Literary Quotation and Allusion in Demetrius' Peri hermeneias and Longinus' Peri hypsos.* New York: Columbia University Library, 1935.

Ashfield, Andrew, and Peter De Bolla. *The Sublime: A Reader.* Cambridge: Cambridge University Press, 1993.

Brody, Jules. *Boileau and Longinus.* Geneva: Droz, 1953.

Davidson, Hugh M. "The Literary Arts of Longinus and Boileau." In *Studies in Seventeenth-Century French Literature*, ed. Jean Demonest. Ithaca: Cornell University Press, 1962.

Fuhrmann, Manfred. *Die Dichtungstheorie der Antike*. Darmstadt: Wissenschaftliche Buchgesellschaft, 1993.
Guerlac, Suzanne, and Frances Ferguson. "Longinus and the Subject of the Sublime." *New Literary History*, 16:2 (Winter 1985): 275–97.
Henn, T. R. *Longinus and English Criticism*. Cambridge: Cambridge University Press, 1934.
Marin, Demetrio St. *Bibliography of the Essay on the Sublime*. N.p. 1967.
Olson, Elder. "The Argument of Longinus's *On the Sublime*." In *On Value Judgments in the Arts and Other Essays*. Chicago: University of Chicago Press, 1976.
Rosenberg, Alfred. *Longinus in England*. Berlin: Meyer und Müller, 1937.
Russell, D. A., ed. *"Longinus" on the Sublime*. Oxford: Clarendon Press, 1964.

From *On the Sublime*

I

You will remember, my dear Postumius Terentianus, that when we examined together the treatise of Caecilius on the Sublime, we found that it fell below the dignity of the whole subject, while it failed signally to grasp the essential points, and conveyed to its readers but little of that practical help which it should be a writer's principal aim to give. In every systematic treatise two things are required. The first is a statement of the subject; the other, which although second in order ranks higher in importance, is an indication of the methods by which we may attain our end. Now Caecilius seeks to show the nature of the sublime by countless instances as though our ignorance demanded it, but the consideration of the means whereby we may succeed in raising our own capacities to a certain pitch of elevation he has, strangely enough, omitted as unnecessary. 2. However, it may be that the man ought not so much to be blamed for his shortcomings as praised for his happy thought and his enthusiasm. But since you have urged me, in my turn, to write a brief essay on the sublime for your special gratification, let us consider whether the views I have formed contain anything which will be of use to public men. You will yourself, my friend, in accordance with your nature and with what is fitting, join me in appraising each detail with the utmost regard for truth; for he answered well who, when asked in what qualities we resemble

Translated by W. Rhys Roberts.

the gods, declared that we do so in benevolence and truth. 3. As I am writing to you, my good friend, who are well versed in literary studies, I feel almost absolved from the necessity of premising at any length that sublimity is a certain distinction and excellence in expression, and that it is from no other source than this that the greatest poets and writers have derived their eminence and gained an immortality of renown. 4. The effect of elevated language upon an audience is not persuasion but transport. At every time and in every way imposing speech, with the spell it throws over us, prevails over that which aims at persuasion and gratification. Our persuasions we can usually control, but the influences of the sublime bring power and irresistible might to bear, and reign supreme over every hearer. Similarly, we see skill in invention, and due order and arrangement of matter, emerging as the hard-won result not of one thing nor of two, but of the whole texture of the composition, whereas Sublimity flashing forth at the right moment scatters everything before it like a thunderbolt, and at once displays the power of the orator in all its plenitude. But enough; for these reflections, and others like them, you can, I know well, my dear Terentianus, yourself suggest from your own experience.

2

First of all, we must raise the question whether there is such a thing as an art of the sublime or lofty. Some hold that those are entirely in error who would bring such matters under the precepts of art. A lofty tone, says one, is innate, and does not come by teaching; nature is the only art that can compass it. Works of nature are, they think, made worse and altogether feebler when wizened by the rules of art. 2. But I maintain that this will be found to be otherwise if it be observed that, while nature as a rule is free and independent in matters of passion and elevation, yet is she wont not to act at random and utterly without system. Further, nature is the original and vital underlying principle in all cases, but system can define limits and fitting seasons, and can also contribute the safest rules for use and practice. Moreover, the expression of the sublime is more exposed to danger when it goes its own way without the guidance of knowledge — when it is suffered to be unstable and unballasted — when it is left at the mercy of mere momentum and ignorant audacity. It is true that it often needs the spur, but it is also true that it often needs the curb. 3. Demosthenes expresses the view, with regard to human life in general, that good fortune is the greatest of blessings, while good counsel, which occupies the second place, is hardly inferior in importance, since its absence contributes inevitably to the ruin of the former. This we may apply to diction, nature occupying the position of good fortune, art that of good counsel. Most important of all, we must remember that the very fact that there are some elements of expression which are in the hands of nature alone, can be learnt from no other source than art. If, I say, the critic of those who desire to learn were to turn these matters over in his mind, he would no longer, it seems to me, regard the discussion of the subject as superfluous or useless. . . .

3

Quell they the oven's far-flung splendour-glow!
Ha, let me but one hearth-abider mark —
One flame-wreath torrent-like I'll whirl on high;
I'll burn the roof, to cinders shrivel it —
Nay, now my chant is not of noble strain.[1]

[1]Aeschylus, *Oreithia*.

Such things are not tragic but pseudo-tragic — "flame-wreaths," and "belching to the sky," and Boreas represented as a "flute-player," and all the rest of it. They are turbid in expression and confused in imagery rather than the product of intensity, and each one of them, if examined in the light of day, sinks little by little from the terrible into the contemptible. But since even in tragedy, which is in its very nature stately and prone to bombast, tasteless tumidity is unpardonable, still less, I presume, will it harmonize with the narration of fact. 2. And this is the ground on which the phrases of Gorgias of Leontini are ridiculed when he describes Xerxes as the "Zeus of the Persians" and vultures as "living tombs." So is it with some of the expressions of Callisthenes which are not sublime but high-flown, and still more with those of Cleitarchus, for the man is frivolous and blows, as Sophocles has it,

On pigmy hautboys: mouthpiece have they none.

Other examples will be found in Amphicrates and Hegesias and Matris, for often when these writers seem to themselves to be inspired they are in no true frenzy but are simply trifling. 3. Altogether, tumidity seems particularly hard to avoid. The explanation is that all who aim at elevation are so anxious to escape the reproach of being weak and dry that they are carried, as by some strange law of nature, into the opposite extreme. They put their trust in the maxim that "failure in a great attempt is at least a noble error." 4. But evil are the swellings, both in the body and in diction, which are inflated and unreal, and threaten us with the reverse of our aim; for nothing, say they, is drier than a man who has the dropsy. While tumidity desires to transcend the limits of the sublime, the defect which is termed puerility is the direct antithesis of elevation, for it is utterly low and mean and in real truth the most ignoble vice of style. What, then, is this puerility? Clearly, a pedant's thoughts, which begin in learned trifling and end in frigidity. Men slip into this kind of error because, while they aim at the uncommon and elaborate and most of all at the attractive, they drift unawares into the tawdry and affected. 5. A third, and closely allied, kind of defect in matters of passion is that which Theodorus used to call *parenthyrsus*. By this is meant unseasonable and empty passion, where no passion is required, or immoderate, where moderation is needed. For men are often carried away, as if by intoxication, into displays of emotion which are not caused by the nature of the subject, but are purely personal and wearisome. In consequence they seem to hearers who are in no wise affected to act in an ungainly way. And no wonder; for they are beside themselves, while their hearers are not. But the question of the passions we reserve for separate treatment.

4

Of the second fault of which we have spoken — frigidity — Timaeus supplies many examples. Timaeus was a writer of considerable general ability, who occasionally showed that he was not incapable of elevation of style. He was learned and ingenious, but very prone to criticize the faults of others while blind to his own. Through his passion for continually starting novel notions, he often fell into the merest childishness. 2. I will set down one or two examples only of his manner, since the greater number have been already appropriated by Caecilius. In the course of a eulogy on Alexander the Great, he describes him as "the man who gained possession of the whole of Asia in fewer years than it took Isocrates to write his *Panegyric* urging war against the Persians." Strange indeed is the comparison of the man of Macedon with the rhetorician. How plain it is, Timaeus, that the Lacedaemonians, thus judged, were far interior to Isocrates in prowess, for they spent thirty years in the conquest of Messene, whereas he composed his *Panegyric* in ten. 3. Consider again the way in which he speaks of the Athenians who were captured in Sicily. "They were punished because they had acted impiously towards Hermes and mutilated his images, and the infliction of punishment was chiefly due to Hermocrates the son of Hermon, who was descended, in the paternal line, from the outraged god." I am surprised, beloved Terentianus, that he does not write with regard to the despot Dionysius that "Dion and Heracleides deprived him of his sovereignty because he had acted impiously towards Zeus and Heracles." 4. But why speak of Timaeus when even those

heroes of literature, Xenophon and Plato, though trained in the school of Socrates, nevertheless sometimes forget themselves for the sake of such paltry pleasantries? Xenophon writes in the *Polity of the Lacedaemonians:* "You would find it harder to hear their voice than that of busts of marble, harder to deflect their gaze than that of statues of bronze; you would deem them more modest than the very maidens in their eyes."[2]

It was worthy of an Amphicrates and not of a Xenophon to call the pupils of our eyes "modest maidens." Good heavens, how strange it is that the pupils of the whole company should be believed to be modest notwithstanding the common saying that the shamelessness of individuals is indicated by nothing so much as the eyes! "Thou sot, that hast the eyes of a dog," as Homer has it.[3] 5. Timaeus, however, has not left even this piece of frigidity to Xenophon, but clutches it as though it were hid treasure. At all events, after saying of Agathocles that he abducted his cousin, who had been given in marriage to another man, from the midst of the nuptial rites, he asks, "Who could have done this had he not had wantons, in place of maidens, in his eyes?" 6. Yes, and Plato (usually so divine) when he means simply *tablets* says, "They shall write and preserve *cypress memorials* in the temples."[4]

And again, "As touching walls, Megillus, I should hold with Sparta that they be suffered to lie asleep in the earth and not summoned to arise."[5] The expression of Herodotus to the effect that beautiful women are "eye-smarts" is not much better.[6] This, however, may be condoned in some degree since those who use this particular phrase in his narrative are barbarians and in their cups, but not even in the mouths of such characters is it well that an author should suffer, in the judgment of posterity, from an unseemly exhibition of triviality.

[2]Xenophon, *On the Government of the Lacedaimonians* 3:5. [Tr.]
[3]Homer, *Iliad* 1:225. [Tr.]
[4]Plato, *Laws* 5:741c. [Tr.]
[5]Plato, *Laws* 6:778d [Tr.]
[6]Herodotus, *History* 5:18. [Tr.]

5

All these ugly and parasitical growths arise in literature from a single cause, that pursuit of novelty in the expression of ideas which may be regarded as the fashionable craze of the day. Our defects usually spring, for the most part, from the same sources as our good points. Hence, while beauties of expression and touches of sublimity, and charming elegances withal, are favorable to effective composition, yet these very things are the elements and foundation, not only of success, but also of the contrary. Something of the kind is true also of variations and hyperboles and the use of the plural number, and we shall show subsequently the dangers to which these seem severally to be exposed. It is necessary now to seek and to suggest means by which we may avoid the defects which attend the steps of the sublime.

6

The best means would be, my friend, to gain, first of all, clear knowledge and appreciation of the true sublime. The enterprise is, however, an arduous one. For the judgment of style is the last and crowning fruit of long experience. Nonetheless, if I must speak in the way of precept, it is not impossible perhaps to acquire discrimination in these matters by attention to some such hints as those which follow.

7

You must know, my dear friend, that it is with the sublime as in the common life of man. In life nothing can be considered great which it is held great to despise. For instance, riches, honors, distinctions, sovereignties, and all other things which possess in abundance the external trappings of the stage, will not seem, to a man of sense, to be supreme blessings, since the very contempt of them is reckoned good in no small degree, and in any case those who could have them, but are high-souled enough to disdain them, are more admired than those who have them. So also in the case of sublimity in poems and prose writings, we must consider whether some supposed examples have not simply the appearance of elevation with many idle accretions, so

that when analyzed they are found to be mere vanity — objects which a noble nature will rather despise than admire. 2. For, as if instinctively, our soul is uplifted by the true sublime; it takes a proud flight, and is filled with joy and vaunting, as though it had itself produced what it has heard. 3. When therefore, a thing is heard repeatedly by a man of intelligence, who is well versed in literature, and its effect is not to dispose the soul to high thoughts, and it does not leave in the mind more food for reflection than the words seem to convey, but falls, if examined carefully through and through, into disesteem, it cannot rank as true sublimity because it does not survive a first hearing. For that is really great which bears a repeated examination, and which it is difficult or rather impossible to withstand, and the memory of which is strong and hard to efface. 4. In general, consider those examples of sublimity to be fine and genuine which please all and always. For when men of different pursuits, lives, ambitions, ages, languages, hold identical views on one and the same subject, then that verdict which results, so to speak, from a concert of discordant elements makes our faith in the object of admiration strong and unassailable.

8

There are, it may be said, five principal sources of elevated language. Beneath these five varieties there lies, as though it were a common foundation, the gift of discourse, which is indispensable. First and most important is the power of forming great conceptions, as we have elsewhere explained in our remarks on Xenophon. Secondly, there is vehement and inspired passion. These two components of the sublime are for the most part innate. Those which remain are partly the product of art. The due formation of figures deals with two sorts of figures, first those of thought and secondly those of expression. Next there is noble diction, which in turn comprises choice of words, and use of metaphors, and elaboration of language. The fifth cause of elevation — one which is the fitting conclusion of all that have preceded it — is dignified and elevated composition. Come now, let us consider what is involved in each of these varieties, with this one remark by way of preface, that

Caecilius has omitted some of the five divisions, for example, that of passion. 2. Surely he is quite mistaken if he does so on the ground that these two, sublimity and passion, are a unity, and if it seems to him that they are by nature one and inseparable. For some passions are found which are far removed from sublimity and are of a low order, such as pity, grief and fear; and on the other hand there are many examples of the sublime which are independent of passion, such as the daring words of Homer with regard to the Aloadae, to take one out of numberless instances,

> Yea, Ossa in fury they strove to upheave on Olympus on high,
> With forest-clad Pelion above, that thence they might step to the sky.[7]

And so of the words which follow with still greater force:

> Ay, and the deed had they done.

3. Among the orators, too, eulogies and ceremonial and occasional addresses contain on every side examples of dignity and elevation, but are for the most part void of passion. This is the reason why passionate speakers are the worst eulogists, and why, on the other hand, those who are apt in encomium are the least passionate. 4. If, on the other hand, Caecilius thought that passion never contributes at all to sublimity, and if it was for this reason that he did not deem it worthy of mention, he is altogether deluded. I would affirm with confidence that there is no tone so lofty as that of genuine passion, in its right place, when it bursts out in a wild gust of mad enthusiasm and as it were fills the speaker's words with frenzy.

9

Now the first of the conditions mentioned, namely elevation of mind, holds the foremost rank among them all. We must, therefore, in this case also, although we have to do rather with an endowment than with an acquirement, nurture our souls (as far as that is possible) to thoughts sublime, and make them always pregnant, so to say, with noble inspiration. 2. In what way, you may ask, is this to be done? Elsewhere I have written as follows: "Sublimity is the echo of a great soul." Hence also a bare idea, by itself and without a spoken word, sometimes excites admiration just because of the greatness of soul implied. Thus the silence of Ajax in the Underworld is great and more sublime than words.[8] 3. First, then, it is absolutely necessary to indicate the source of this elevation, namely, that the truly eloquent must be free from low and ignoble thoughts. For it is not possible that men with mean and servile ideas and aims prevailing throughout their lives should produce anything that is admirable and worthy of immortality. Great accents we expect to fall from the lips of those whose thoughts are deep and grave. 4. Thus it is that stately speech comes naturally to the proudest spirits. [You will remember the answer of] Alexander to Parmenio when he said "For my part I had been well content."[9] . . .

. . . the distance from earth to heaven; and this might well be considered the measure of Homer no less than of Strife. 5. How unlike to this the expression which is used of Sorrow by Hesiod, if indeed the *Shield* is to be attributed to Hesiod:

> Rheum from her nostrils was trickling.[10]

The image he has suggested is not terrible but rather loathsome. Contrast the way in which Homer magnifies the higher powers:

> And far as a man with his eyes through the sea-line haze may discern,
> On a cliff as he sitteth and gazeth away o'er the wine-dark deep,
> So far at a bound do the loud-neighing steeds of the Deathless leap.[11]

He makes the vastness of the world the measure of their leap. The sublimity is so overpowering as naturally to prompt the exclamation that if the divine steeds were to leap thus twice in succession they would pass beyond the confines of the

---

[7]Homer, *Odyssey* 11:315–16. [Tr.]

[8]Homer, *Odyssey* 11:543. [Tr.]
[9]From Arrian's *Anabasis of Alexander*. A lacuna in the manuscript follows.
[10]Hesiod, *The Shield of Heracles*, 267. [Tr.]
[11]Homer, *Iliad* 5:770–72. [Tr.]

world. 6. How transcendent also are the images in the Battle of the Gods:

Far round wide heaven and Olympus echoed his
　clarion of thunder;
And Hades, king of the realm of shadows, quaked
　thereunder.
And he sprang from his throne, and he cried aloud
　in the dread of his heart
Lest o'er him earth-shaker Poseidon should cleave
　the ground apart,
And revealed to Immortals and mortals should
　stand those awful abodes,
Those mansions ghastly and grim, abhorred of the
　very Gods.[12]

You see, my friend, how the earth is torn from its foundations, Tartarus itself is laid bare, the whole world is upturned and parted asunder, and all things together — heaven and hell, things mortal and things immortal — share in the conflict and the perils of that battle!

7. But although these things are awe-inspiring, yet from another point of view, if they be not taken allegorically, they are altogether impious, and violate our sense of what is fitting. Homer seems to me, in his legends of wounds suffered by the gods, and of their feuds, reprisals, tears, bonds, and all their manifold passions, to have made, as far as lay within his power, gods of the men concerned in the Siege of Troy, and men of the gods. But whereas we mortals have death as the destined haven of our ills if our lot is miserable, he portrays the gods as immortal not only in nature but also in misfortune. 8. Much superior to the passages respecting the Battle of the Gods are those which represent the divine nature as it really is — pure and great and undefiled; for example, what is said of Poseidon in a passage fully treated by many before ourselves:

Her far-stretching ridges, her forest-trees, quaked
　in dismay,
And her peaks, and the Trojans' town, and the
　ships of Achaia's array,
Beneath his immortal feet, as onward Poseidon
　strode.

Then over the surges he drave: leapt sporting
　before the God
Sea-beasts that uprose all around from the depths,
　for their king they knew,
And for rapture the sea was disparted, and onward
　the car-steeds flew.[13]

9. Similarly, the legislator of the Jews, no ordinary man, having formed and expressed a worthy conception of the might of the Godhead, writes at the very beginning of his Laws, "God said," — what? "Let there be light, and there was light; let there be land, and there was land."[14] 10. Perhaps I shall not seem tedious, my friend, if I bring forward one passage more from Homer — this time with regard to the concerns of *men* — in order to show that he is wont himself to enter into the sublime actions of his heroes. In his poem the battle of the Greeks is suddenly veiled by mist and baffling night. Then Ajax, at his wits' end, cries:

Zeus, Father, yet save thou Achaia's sons from be-
　neath the gloom,
And make clear day, and vouchsafe unto us with
　our eyes to see!
So it be but in light, destroy us![15]

That is the true attitude of an Ajax. He does not pray for life, for such a petition would have ill beseemed a hero. But since in the hopeless darkness he can turn his valor to no noble end, he chafes at his slackness in the fray and craves the boon of immediate light, resolved to find a death worthy of his bravery, even though Zeus should fight in the ranks against him. 11. In truth, Homer in these cases shares the full inspiration of the combat, and it is neither more nor less than true of the poet himself that

Mad rageth he as Arês the shaker of spears, or as
　mad flames leap
Wild-wasting from hill unto hill in the folds of a
　forest deep,
And the foam-froth fringeth his lips.[16]

[12]Homer, *Iliad* 20:61–65. [Tr.]

[13]Homer, *Iliad* 13:18–19, 27–29. The second line belongs at the beginning of the last quotation; it is *Iliad* 20:60.

[14]Genesis 1:3, slightly misquoted.

[15]Homer, *Iliad* 17:645–47. [Tr.]

[16]Homer, *Iliad* 15:605–7. [Tr.]

He shows, however, in the Odyssey (and this further observation deserves attention on many grounds) that, when a great genius is declining, the special token of old age is the love of marvelous tales. 12. It is clear from many indications that the Odyssey was his second subject. A special proof is the fact that he introduces in that poem remnants of the adventures before Ilium as episodes, so to say, of the Trojan War. And indeed, he there renders a tribute of mourning and lamentation to his heroes as though he were carrying out a long-cherished purpose. In fact, the Odyssey is simply an epilogue to the Iliad:

> There lieth Ajax the warrior wight, Achilles is
> there,
> There is Patroclus, whose words had weight as a
> God he were;
> There lieth mine own dear son.[17]

13. It is for the same reason, I suppose, that he has made the whole structure of the Iliad, which was written at the height of his inspiration, full of action and conflict, while the Odyssey for the most part consists of narrative, as is characteristic of old age. Accordingly, in the Odyssey Homer may be likened to a sinking sun, whose grandeur remains without its intensity. He does not in the Odyssey maintain so high a pitch as in those poems of Ilium. His sublimities are not evenly sustained and free from the liability to sink; there is not the same profusion of accumulated passions, nor the supple and oratorical style, packed with images drawn from real life. You seem to see henceforth the ebb and flow of greatness, and a fancy roving in the fabulous and incredible, as though the ocean were withdrawing into itself and were being laid bare within its own confines. 14. In saying this I have not forgotten the tempests in the Odyssey and the story of the Cyclops and the like. If I speak of old age, it is nevertheless the old age of Homer. The fabulous element, however, prevails throughout this poem over the real. The object of this digression has been, as I said, to show how easily great natures in their decline are sometimes diverted into absurdity, as in the incident of the wine-skin and of the men who were fed like swine by Circe (*whining porkers,* as Zoilus called them), and of Zeus like a nestling nurtured by the doves, and of the hero who was without food for ten days upon the wreck, and of the incredible tale of the slaying of the suitors.[18] For what else can we term these things than veritable dreams of Zeus? 15. These observations with regard to the Odyssey should be made for another reason — in order that you may know that the genius of great poets and prose-writers, as their passion declines, finds its final expression in the delineation of character. For such are the details which Homer gives, with an eye to characterization, of life in the home of Odysseus; they form as it were a comedy of manners.

10

Let us next consider whether we can point to anything further that contributes to sublimity of style. Now, there inhere in all things by nature certain constituents which are part and parcel of their substance. It must needs be, therefore, that we shall find one source of the sublime in the systematic selection of the most important elements, and the power of forming, by their mutual combination, what may be called one body. The former process attracts the hearer by the choice of the ideas, the latter by the aggregation of those chosen. For instance, Sappho everywhere chooses the emotions that attend delirious passion from its accompaniments in actual life. Wherein does she demonstrate her supreme excellence? In the skill with which she selects and binds together the most striking and vehement circumstances of passion:

> 2. Peer of Gods he seemeth to me, the blissful
> Man who sits and gazes at thee before him,
> Close beside thee sits, and in silence hears thee
> Silverly speaking,
> Laughing love's low laughter. Oh this, this only
> Stirs the troubled heart in my breast to tremble!

[18]Five incidents from the *Odyssey.* The Cyclops at 9:192; Aiolos's wineskin at 10:17; the metamorphosis at 10:237; Zeus's doves at 12:62; Odysseus's fast at 12:447; the slaying of the suitors at 22:79–380.

[17]Homer, *Odyssey* 3:109–11. [Tr.]

For should I but see thee a little moment,
    Straight is my voice hushed;
Yea, my tongue is broken, and through and
    through me
'Neath the flesh impalpable fire runs tingling;
Nothing see mine eyes, and a noise of roaring
    Waves in my ear sounds;
Sweat runs down in rivers, a tremor seizes
All my limbs, and paler than grass in autumn,
Caught by pains of menacing death, I falter,
    Lost in the love-trance.

3. Are you not amazed how at one instant she summons, as though they were all alien from herself and dispersed, soul, body, ears, tongue, eyes, color? Uniting contradictions, she is, at one and the same time, hot and cold, in her senses and out of her mind, for she is either terrified or at the point of death. The effect desired is that not one passion only should be seen in her, but a concourse of the passions. All such things occur in the case of lovers, but it is, as I said, the selection of the most striking of them and their combination into a single whole that has produced the singular excellence of the passage. In the same way Homer, when describing tempests, picks out the most appalling circumstances. 4. The author of the *Arimaspeia* thinks to inspire awe in the following way:

A marvel exceeding great is this withal to my
    soul —
Men dwell on the water afar from the land, where
    deep seas roll.
Wretches are they, for they reap but a harvest of
    travail and pain,
Their eyes on the stars ever dwell, while their
    hearts abide in the main.
Often, I ween, to the Gods are their hands upraised
    on high,
And with hearts in misery heavenward-lifted in
    prayer do they cry.

It is clear, I imagine, to everybody that there is more elegance than terror in these words. 5. But what says Homer? Let one instance be quoted from among many:

And he burst on them like as a wave swift-rushing
    beneath black clouds,
Heaved huge by the winds, bursts down on a ship,
    and the wild foam shrouds

From the stem to the stern her hull, and the storm-
    blast's terrible breath
Roars in the sail, and the heart of the shipmen
    shuddereth
In fear, for that scantly upborne are they now from
    the clutches of death.[19]

6. Aratus has attempted to convert this same expression to his own use:

And a slender plank averteth their death.

Only, he has made it trivial and neat instead of terrible. Furthermore, he has put bounds to the danger by saying *A plank keeps off death.* After all, it *does* keep it off. Homer, however, does not for one moment set a limit to the terror of the scene, but draws a vivid picture of men continually in peril of their lives, and often within an ace of perishing with each successive wave. Moreover, he has in the words ʽυπὲκ θανάτοιο, forced into union, by a kind of unnatural compulsion, prepositions not usually compounded.[20] He has thus tortured his line into the similitude of the impending calamity, and by the constriction of the verse has excellently figured the disaster, and almost stamped upon the expression the very form and pressure of the danger, ʽυπὲκ θανάτοιο φέρονται. 7. This is true also of Archilochus in his account of the shipwreck, and of Demosthenes in the passage which begins "It was evening," where he describes the bringing of the news.[21] The salient points they selected, one might say, according to merit and massed them together, inserting in the midst nothing frivolous, mean, or trivial. For these faults mar the effect of the whole, just as though they introduced chinks or fissures into stately and co-ordered edifices, whose walls are compacted by their reciprocal adjustment.

II

An allied excellence to those already set forth is that which is termed *amplification.* This figure is employed when the narrative or the course of a

[19]Homer, *Iliad* 15:624–28. [Tr.]
[20]The point is that Homer has created an unusual compound word — *hypek,* out of *hyper* ("up") and *ek* ("out of"): "up out of death."
[21]Demosthenes, *On the Crown,* 169. [Tr.]

forensic argument admits, from section to section, of many starting points and many pauses, and elevated expressions follow, one after the other, in an unbroken succession and in an ascending order. 2. And this may be effected either by way of the rhetorical treatment of commonplaces, or by way of intensification (whether events or arguments are to be strongly presented), or by the orderly arrangement of facts or of passions; indeed, there are innumerable kinds of amplification. Only, the orator must in every case remember that none of these methods by itself, apart from sublimity, forms a complete whole, unless indeed where pity is to be excited or an opponent to be disparaged. In all other cases of amplification, if you take away the sublime, you will remove as it were the soul from the body. For the vigor of the amplification at once loses its intensity and its substance when not resting on a firm basis of the sublime. 3. Clearness, however, demands that we should define concisely how our present precepts differ from the point under consideration a moment ago, namely the marking-out of the most striking conceptions and the unification of them; and wherein, generally, the sublime differs from amplification.

12

Now the definition given by the writers on rhetoric does not satisfy me. Amplification is, say they, discourse which invests the subject with grandeur. This definition, however, would surely apply in equal measure to sublimity and passion and figurative language, since they too invest the discourse with a certain degree of grandeur. The point of distinction between them seems to me to be that sublimity consists in elevation, while amplification embraces a multitude of details. Consequently, sublimity is often comprised in a single thought, while amplification is universally associated with a certain magnitude and abundance. 2. Amplification (to sum the matter up in a general way) is an aggregation of all the constituent parts and topics of a subject, lending strength to the argument by dwelling upon it, and differing herein from proof that, while the latter demonstrates the matter under investigation. . . .

With his vast riches Plato swells, like some sea, into a greatness which expands on every side. 3. Wherefore it is, I suppose, that the orator in his utterance shows, as one who appeals more to the passions, all the glow of a fiery spirit. Plato, on the other hand, firm-planted in his pride and magnificent stateliness, cannot indeed be accused of coldness, but he has not the same vehemence. 4. And it is in these same respects, my dear friend Terentianus, that it seems to me (supposing always that we Greeks are allowed to have an opinion upon the point) that Cicero differs from Demosthenes in elevated passages. For the latter is characterized by sublimity which is for the most part rugged, Cicero by profusion. Our orator,[22] owing to the fact that in his vehemence — aye, and in his speed, power and intensity — he can as it were consume by fire and carry away all before him, may be compared to a thunderbolt or flash of lightning. Cicero, on the other hand, it seems to me, after the manner of a widespread conflagration, rolls on with all-devouring flames, having within him an ample and abiding store of fire, distributed now at this point now at that, and fed by an unceasing succession. 5. This, however, you will be better able to decide; but the great opportunity of Demosthenes' high-pitched elevation comes where intense utterance and vehement passion are in question, and in passages in which the audience is to be utterly enthralled. The profusion of Cicero is in place where the hearer must be flooded with words, for it is appropriate to the treatment of commonplaces, and to perorations for the most part and digressions, and to all descriptive and declamatory passages, and to writings on history and natural science, and to many other departments of literature.

13

To return from my digression. Although Plato thus flows on with noiseless stream, he is nonetheless elevated. You know this because you have read the *Republic* and are familiar with his

---

[22]Demosthenes. He is "our" orator because Longinus is a Greek writing to a Roman.

manner. "Those," says he, "who are destitute of wisdom and goodness and are ever present at carousals and the like are carried on the downward path, it seems, and wander thus throughout their life. They never look upwards to the truth, nor do they lift their heads, nor enjoy any pure and lasting pleasure, but like cattle they have their eyes ever cast downwards and bent upon the ground and upon their feeding-places, and they graze and grow fat and breed, and through their insatiate desire of these delights they kick and butt with horns and hoofs of iron and kill one another in their greed."[23]

2. This writer shows us, if only we were willing to pay him heed, that another way (beyond anything we have mentioned) leads to the sublime. And what, and what manner of way, may that be? It is the imitation and emulation of previous great poets and writers. And let this, my dear friend, be an aim to which we steadfastly apply ourselves. For many men are carried away by the spirit of others as if inspired, just as it is related of the Pythian priestess when she approaches the tripod, where there is a rift in the ground which (they say) exhales divine vapor. By heavenly power thus communicated she is impregnated and straightway delivers oracles in virtue of the afflatus. Similarly from the great natures of the men of old there are borne in upon the souls of those who emulate them (as from sacred caves) what we may describe as *effluences,* so that even those who seem little likely to be possessed are thereby inspired and succumb to the spell of the others' greatness. 3. Was Herodotus alone a devoted imitator of Homer? No, Stesichorus even before his time, and Archilochus, and above all Plato, who from the great Homeric source drew to himself innumerable tributary streams. And perhaps we should have found it necessary to prove this, point by point, had not Ammonius and his followers selected and recorded the particulars. 4. This proceeding is not plagiarism; it is like taking an impression from beautiful forms or figures or other works of art. And it seems to me that there would not have been so fine a bloom of perfection on Plato's philosophical doctrines, and that he

would not in many cases have found his way to poetical subject matter and modes of expression, unless he had with all his heart and mind struggled with Homer for the primacy, entering the lists like a young champion matched against the man whom all admire, and showing perhaps too much love of contention and breaking a lance with him as it were, but deriving some profit from the contest nonetheless. For, as Hesiod says, "This strife is good for mortals."[24] And in truth that struggle for the crown of glory is noble and best deserves the victory in which even to be worsted by one's predecessors brings no discredit.

14

Accordingly it is well that we ourselves also, when elaborating anything which requires lofty expression and elevated conception, should shape some idea in our minds as to how perchance Homer would have said this very thing, or how it would have been raised to the sublime by Plato or Demosthenes or by the historian Thucydides. For those personages, presenting themselves to us and inflaming our ardor and as it were illumining our path, will carry our minds in a mysterious way to the high standards of sublimity which are imaged within us. 2. Still more effectual will it be to suggest this question to our thoughts, "What sort of hearing would Homer, had he been present, or Demosthenes have given to this or that when said by me, or how would they have been affected by the other?" For the ordeal is indeed a severe one, if we presuppose such a tribunal and theater for our own utterances, and imagine that we are undergoing a scrutiny of our writings before these great heroes, acting as judges and witnesses. 3. A greater incentive still will be supplied if you add the question, "In what spirit will each succeeding age listen to me who have written thus?" But if one shrinks from the very thought of uttering aught that may transcend the term of his own life and time, the conceptions of his mind must necessarily be incomplete, blind, and as it were untimely born, since they are by no means brought to the perfection needed to ensure a futurity of fame.

[23]Plato, *Republic* 9:586a. [Tr.]

[24]Hesiod, *Works and Days,* 24. [Tr.]

44

It remains however (as I will not hesitate to add, in recognition of your love of knowledge) to clear up, my dear Terentianus, a question which a certain philosopher has recently mooted. "I wonder," he says, "as no doubt do many others, how it happens that in our time there are men who have the gift of persuasion to the utmost extent, and are well fitted for public life, and are keen and ready, and particularly rich in all the charms of language, yet there no longer arise really lofty and transcendent natures unless quite exceptionally. So great and worldwide a dearth of high utterance attends our age." 2. "Can it be," he continued, "that we are to accept the trite explanation that democracy is the kind nursing-mother of genius, and that literary power may be said to share its rise and fall with democracy and democracy alone? For freedom, it is said, has power to feed the imaginations of the lofty-minded and to inspire hope, and where it prevails there spreads abroad the eagerness of mutual rivalry and the emulous pursuit of the foremost place. 3. Moreover, owing to the prizes which are open to all under popular government, the mental excellences of the orator are continually exercised and sharpened, and as it were rubbed bright, and shine forth (as it is natural they should) with all the freedom which inspires the doings of the state. Today," he went on, "we seem in our boyhood to learn the lessons of a righteous servitude, being all but enswathed in its customs and observances, when our thoughts are yet young and tender, and never tasting the fairest and most productive source of eloquence (by which," he added, "I mean freedom), so that we emerge in no other guise than that of sublime flatterers." 4. This is the reason, he maintained, why no slave ever becomes an orator, although all other faculties may belong to menials. In the slave there immediately burst out signs of fettered liberty of speech, of the dungeon as it were, of a man habituated to buffetings. 5. "For the day of slavery," as Homer has it, "takes away half our manhood."[25] "Just as," he proceeded, "the cages (if what I hear

is true) in which are kept the Pygmies, commonly called *nani,* not only hinder the growth of the creatures confined within them, but actually attenuate them through the bonds which beset their bodies, so one has aptly termed all servitude (though it be most righteous) the cage of the soul and a public prisonhouse." 6. I answered him thus: "It is easy, my good sir, and characteristic of human nature, to find fault with the age in which one lives. But consider whether it may not be true that it is not the world's peace that ruins great natures, but far rather this war illimitable which holds our desires in its grasp, aye, and further still those passions which occupy as with troops our present age and utterly harry and plunder it. For the love of money (a disease from which we all now suffer sorely) and the love of pleasure make us their thralls, or rather, as one may say, drown us body and soul in the depths, the love of riches being a malady which makes men petty, and the love of pleasure one which makes them most ignoble. 7. On reflection I cannot discover how it is possible for us, if we value boundless wealth so highly, or (to speak more truly) deify it, to avoid allowing the entrance into our souls of the evils which are inseparable from it. For vast and unchecked wealth is accompanied, in close conjunction and step for step as they say, by extravagance, and as soon as the former opens the gates of cities and houses, the latter immediately enters and abides. And when time has passed the pair build nests in the lives of men, as the wise say, and quickly give themselves to the rearing of offspring, and breed ostentation, and vanity, and luxury, no spurious progeny of theirs, but only too legitimate. If these children of wealth are permitted to come to maturity, straightway they beget in the soul inexorable masters — insolence, and lawlessness, and shamelessness. 8. This must necessarily happen, and men will no longer lift up their eyes or have any further regard for fame, but the ruin of such lives will gradually reach its complete consummation and sublimities of soul fade and wither away and become contemptible, when men are lost in admiration of their own mortal parts and omit to exalt that which is immortal. 9. For a man who has once accepted a bribe for a judicial decision cannot be an unbiased and upright judge of what is just and honorable (since

[25]Homer, *Odyssey* 17:322. [Tr.]

to the man who is venal his own interests must seem honorable and just), and the same is true where the entire life of each of us is ordered by bribes, and huntings after the death of others, and the laying of ambushes for legacies, while gain from any and every source we purchase — each one of us — at the price of life itself, being the slaves of pleasure. In an age which is ravaged by plagues so sore, is it possible for us to imagine that there is still left an unbiased and incorruptible judge of works that are great and likely to reach posterity, or is it not rather the case that all are influenced in their decisions by the passion for gain? 10. Nay, it is perhaps better for men like ourselves to be ruled than to be free, since our appetites, if let loose without restraint upon our neighbors like beasts from a cage, would set the world on fire with deeds of evil. 11. Summing up, I maintained that among the banes of the natures which our age produces must be reckoned that half-heartedness in which the life of all of us with few exceptions is passed, for we do not labor or exert ourselves except for the sake of praise and pleasure, never for those solid benefits which are a worthy object of our own efforts and the respect of others. 12. But "'tis best to leave these riddles unresolved,"[26] and to proceed to what next presents itself, namely the subject of the Passions, about which I previously undertook to write in a separate treatise. These form, as it seems to me, a material part of discourse generally and of the Sublime itself.

[26]Euripides, *Electra*, 379. [Tr.]

Plotinus

204?–270 C.E.

Plotinus, the greatest of the Neoplatonists, was born of Roman parents in the Egyptian city of Lycopolis. To one who has read Plato, Plotinus's ideas will be alternately familiar and strange. What is familiar is his metaphysics, the structure of the universe. Like Plato, Plotinus posits an Ideal world (which he calls *ekei,* "There") as the paradigm for the physical world here below. What is strange is encountering these ideas unaccompanied by the classical clarity of Plato. Like other Neoplatonists Plotinus derives not only from Plato but also from the Gnostics of Alexandria and the Eastern Mystery cults of Dionysus or Mithras. He gives the impression of an improbable combination of Plato and Zen: This is inaccurate historically, but there is an oriental flavor to his thought.

Plotinus's thought is based on the higher Ideas, which he views in a complex hierarchy. At the top is The One, the principle of existence itself, Plotinus's God-term. The One gives rise to the Intellectual-Principle, by which things are knowable and differentiable; the Intellectual-Principle is the basis of beauty in the universe. Similarly the Intellectual-Principle gives rise to the All-Soul, which is the paradigm for consciousness here below. In his treatise "On the Intellectual Beauty," Plotinus explains that the Greek gods Ouranos, Kronos, and Zeus are myths of these three basic Ideas, though the Ideas give birth one to the other not through temporal but through logical priority. Below the All-Soul is the Nature-Principle, and it is this that gives rise to matter in all its diverse forms.

Plotinus is not primarily an aesthetician, and when he discusses art, he generally thinks first about painting and sculpture rather than about poetry. Nevertheless, his ideas are a useful adjunct to Plato's because, unlike Plato, Plotinus is basically sympathetic to art. For Plotinus as for Plato, the artist imitates but does not *necessarily* copy the things of this world. The artist may represent his grasp of an Idea within the medium of his art: "Thus Phidias wrought the [Olympian] *Zeus* upon no model among things of sense but by apprehending what form Zeus must take if he chose to become manifest to sight." Art at its best can be a way of knowing the Ideas. In fact, it is the artist's grasp of higher things that lends quality to his or her work.

This does not mean, however, that the artist should be a mathematician or a philosopher, for art does not derive from reason. Like Benedetto Croce at the beginning of the twentieth century, Plotinus insists that the work of art exists primarily as the intuition of the artist and is known prior to reason. (Plotinus calls it "one totality . . . a unity working out into detail . . . a distinct image, . . . not an aggregate of discursive reasoning and detailed willing.") Beauty exists in its highest degree only There, in lesser degree as the intuition within the soul of the artist, and in still lesser degree ("insofar as it has subdued the resistance of the material") in the concrete and physical work the artist makes. But even natural beauty is primarily a quality of soul: Even beautiful women, Plotinus suggests, are beautiful only insofar as their flesh projects a beautiful spirit.

The most mystical part of "On the Intellectual Beauty" is found in sections 10 and 11, where Plotinus discusses a series of spiritual exercises that help to bring the world of There within the self. Thus, he says, "a man filled with a god — possessed by Apollo or by one of the Muses — need no longer look outside for his vision of the divine being; it is but finding the strength to see divinity within." In the *Ion* Plato discussed *enthousiasmós,* or inspiration, as a form of possession given to favored mortals; for Plotinus this mystical state of unity with the Divine lies within the reach of everyone.

In the first stage of mystical union, the Divine invades the subject as a glorified self-image. In its final stages, the self fades out completely as the subject becomes completely identified with divine power and will. This process may suggest why egoism and temperament are so often found in the incomplete artist, and why the most supreme creators — Shakespeare, Rembrandt, Mozart — seem to show in their art not mere personality but rather a transcendent objectivity and clarity.

Selected Bibliography

Armstrong, A. H. *The Architecture of the Intelligible Universe in the Philosophy of Plotinus.* Cambridge: Cambridge University Press, 1940.

Asti Vera, Carlos. *Arte y realidad en la estetica de Plotino.* San Antonio de Padua: Ediciones Castaneda, 1978.

Atkinson, M. J. *A Commentary on Plotinus.* New York: Oxford University Press, 1983.

Bishop, Donald. *Mysticism and the Mystical Experience.* Selinsgrove, PA: Susquehanna University Press, 1995.

Blumenthal, H. J. *Plotinus's Psychology: His Doctrines of the Embodied Soul.* The Hague: Nijhoff, 1971.

Deck, John N. *Nature, Contemplation and the One.* Toronto: University of Toronto Press, 1967.

Gerson, Lloyd. *Cambridge Companion to Plotinus.* Cambridge: Cambridge University Press, 1996.

Harris, R. Baines. *The Structure of Being: A Neoplatonic Approach.* Norfolk: International Society for Neoplatonic Studies, 1982.

Inge, William R. *The Philosophy of Plotinus.* 1918; Hamden, CT: Greenwood, 1968.

Mead, G. R. S. *The Spiritual World of Plotinus.* London: Quest, 1920.

O'Daly, Gerard. *Plotinus's Philosophy of the Self.* New York: Barnes and Noble, 1973.

Rappe, Sara. *Reading Neoplatonism: Non-Discursive Thinking in the Texts of Plotinus, Proclus, and Damascius.* Cambridge: Cambridge University Press, 2000.

Underhill, Evelyn. "The Mysticism of Plotinus." *Quarterly Review* 231 (1919): 479–97.

Wallis, R. T. *Neoplatonism.* London: Duckworth, 1995.

On the Intellectual Beauty

I

It is a principle with us that one who has attained to the vision of the Intellectual Beauty and grasped the beauty of the Authentic Intellect will be able also to come to understand the Father and Transcendent of that Divine Being. It concerns us, then, to try to see and say, for ourselves and as far as such matters may be told, how the Beauty of the divine Intellect and of the Intellectual Kosmos may be revealed to contemplation.

Let us go to the realm of magnitudes: Suppose two blocks of stone lying side by side: one is unpatterned, quite untouched by art; the other has been minutely wrought by the craftsman's hands into some statue of god or man, a Grace or a Muse, or if a human being, not a portrait but a creation in which the sculptor's art has concentrated all loveliness.

Now it must be seen that the stone thus brought under the artist's hand to the beauty of form is beautiful not as stone — for so the crude block would be as pleasant — but in virtue of the form or idea introduced by the art. This form is not in the material; it is in the designer before ever it enters the stone; and the artificer holds it not by his equipment of eyes and hands but by his participation in his art. The beauty, therefore, exists in a far higher state in the art; for it does not come over integrally into the work; that original beauty is not transferred; what comes over is a derivative and a minor: and even that shows itself upon the statue not integrally and with entire realization of intention but only insofar as it has subdued the resistance of the material.

Art, then, creating in the image of its own nature and content, and working by the Idea or Reason-Principle of the beautiful object it is to produce, must itself be beautiful in a far higher and purer degree since it is the seat and source of that beauty, indwelling in the art, which must naturally be more complete than any comeliness of the external. In the degree in which the beauty is diffused by entering into matter, it is so much the weaker than that concentrated in unity; everything that reaches outwards is the less for it, strength less strong, heat less hot, every power less potent, and so beauty less beautiful.

Then again every prime cause must be, within itself, more powerful than its effect can be: the musical does not derive from an unmusical source but from music; and so the art exhibited in the material work derives from an art yet higher.

Still the arts are not to be slighted on the ground that they create by imitation of natural objects; for, to begin with, these natural objects are themselves imitations; then we must recognize that they give no bare reproduction of the thing seen but go back to the Ideas from which Nature itself derives, and, furthermore, that much of their work is all their own; they are holders of beauty and add where nature is lacking. Thus Phidias wrought the Zeus upon no model among things of sense but by apprehending what form Zeus must take if he chose to become manifest to sight.[1]

2

But let us leave the arts and consider those works produced by Nature and admitted to be naturally beautiful which the creations of art are charged with imitating, all reasoning life and unreasoning things alike, but especially the consummate among them, where the moulder and maker has subdued the material and given the form he desired. Now what is the beauty here?[2] It has nothing to do with the blood or the menstrual process: either there is also a color and form apart from all this or there is nothing unless sheer ugliness or (at best) a bare recipient, as it were the mere Matter of beauty.

Translated by Stephen McKenna.

---

[1] Here Plotinus distinguishes his position from Plato's in the *Republic,* where the artist was said to imitate material objects, not ideas.

[2] Plotinus continues his argument that Beauty resides in ideal form rather than in matter or in the process of origin.

Whence shone forth the beauty of Helen, battle-sought; or of all those women like in loveliness to Aphrodite; or of Aphrodite herself; or of any human being that has been perfect in beauty; or of any of these gods manifest to sight, or unseen but carrying what would be beauty if we saw?

In all these is it not the Idea, something of that realm but communicated to the produced from within the producer just as in works of art, we held, it is communicated from the arts to their creations? Now we can surely not believe that, while the made thing and the Idea thus impressed upon Matter are beautiful, yet the Idea not so alloyed but resting still with the creator — the Idea primal, immaterial, firmly a unity — is not Beauty.

If material extension were in itself the ground of beauty, then the creating principle, being without extension, could not be beautiful: but beauty cannot be made to depend upon magnitude since, whether in a large object or a small, the one Idea equally moves and forms the mind by its inherent power. A further indication is that as long as the object remains outside us we know nothing of it; it affects us by entry; but only as an Idea can it enter through the eyes which are not of scope to take an extended mass: we are, no doubt, simultaneously possessed of the magnitude which, however, we take in not as mass but by an elaboration upon the presented form.

Then again the principle producing the beauty must be, itself, ugly, neutral or beautiful: ugly, it could not produce the opposite; neutral, why should its product be the one rather than the other? The Nature, then, which creates things so lovely must be itself of a far earlier beauty; we, undisciplined in discernment of the inward, knowing nothing of it, run after the outer, never understanding that it is the inner which stirs us; we are in the case of one who sees his own reflection but not realizing whence it comes goes in pursuit of it.

But that the thing we are pursuing is something different and that the beauty is not in the concrete object is manifest from the beauty there is in matters of study, in conduct and custom; briefly in soul or mind. And it is precisely here that the greater beauty lies, perceived whenever you look to the wisdom in a man and delight in it, not wasting attention on the face, which may be hideous, but passing all appearance by and catching only at the inner comeliness, the truly personal; if you are still unmoved and cannot acknowledge beauty under such conditions, then looking to your own inner being you will find no beauty to delight you and it will be futile in that state to seek the greater vision, for you will be questing it through the ugly and impure.

This is why such matters are not spoken of to everyone; you, if you are conscious of beauty within, remember.

3

Thus there is in the Nature-Principle itself an Ideal archetype of the beauty that is found in material forms and, of that archetype again, the still more beautiful archetype in Soul, source of that in Nature. In the proficient soul this is brighter and of more advanced loveliness: adorning the soul and bringing to it a light from that greater light which is beauty primally, its immediate presence sets the soul reflecting upon the quality of this prior, and archetype which has no such entries, and is present nowhere but remains in itself alone, and thus is not even to be called a Reason-Principle but is the creative source of the very first Reason-Principle, which is the Beauty to which Soul serves as Matter.

This prior, then, is the Intellectual-Principle, the veritable, abiding and not fluctuant since not taking intellectual quality from outside itself. By what image thus, can we represent it? We have nowhere to go but to what is less. Only from itself can we take an image of it; that is, there can be no representation of it, except in the sense that we represent gold by some portion of gold — purified, either actually or mentally, if it be impure — insisting at the same time that this is not the total thing gold, but merely the particular gold of a particular parcel. In the same way we learn in this matter from the purified Intellect in ourselves or, if you like, from the gods and the glory of the Intellect in them.

For assuredly all the gods are august and beautiful in a beauty beyond our speech. And what makes them so? Intellect; and especially Intellect operating within them (the divine sun and stars) to visibility. It is not through the loveliness of their corporeal forms: even those that have body are not gods by that beauty; it is in virtue of Intellect that they, too, are gods, and as gods beautiful. They do not veer between wisdom and folly: in the immunity of Intellect unmoving and pure, they are wise always, all-knowing, taking cognizance not of the human but of their own being and of all that lies within the contemplation of Intellect. Those of them whose dwelling is in the heavens are ever in this meditation — what task prevents them? — and from afar they look, too, into that further heaven by a lifting of the head. The Gods belonging to that higher Heaven itself, they whose station is upon it and in it, see and know in virtue of their omnipresence to it. For all There is heaven; earth is heaven, and sea heaven; and animal and plant and man; all is the heavenly content of that heaven: and the Gods in it, despising neither men nor anything else that is there where all is of the heavenly order, traverse all that country and all space in peace.

4

To "live at ease" is There;[3] and to these divine beings verity is mother and nurse, existence and sustenance; all that is not of process but of authentic being they see, and themselves in all: for all is transparent, nothing dark, nothing resistant; every being is lucid to every other in breadth and depth; light runs through light. And each of them contains all within itself, and at the same time sees all in every other, so that everywhere there is all, and all is all and each all, and infinite the glory. Each of them is great; the small is great; the sun, There, is all the stars; and every star, again, is all the stars and sun. While some one manner of being is dominant in each, all are mirrored in every other.

Movement There is pure (as self-caused) for the moving principle is not a separate thing to complicate it as it speeds.

So, too, Repose is not troubled, for there is no admixture of the unstable; and the Beauty is all

---

[3]Just as "There" is Plotinus's term for the transcendent realm within and beyond matter, "Here" or "our realm" is the world of matter and time.

beauty since it is not merely resident (as an attribute or addition) in some beautiful object. Each There walks upon no alien soil; its place is its essential self; and, as each moves, so to speak, toward what is Above, it is attended by the very ground from which it starts: there is no distinguishing between the Being and the Place; all is Intellect, the Principle and the ground on which it stands, alike. Thus we might think that our visible sky (the ground or place of the stars), lit, as it is, produces the light which reaches us from it, though of course this is really produced by the stars (as it were, by the Principles of light alone not also by the ground as the analogy would require).

In our realm all is part rising from part and nothing can be more than partial; but There each being is an eternal product of a whole and is at once a whole and an individual manifesting as part but, to the keen vision There, known for the whole it is.

The myth of Lynceus seeing into the very deeps of the earth tells us of those eyes in the divine. No weariness overtakes this vision which yet brings no such satiety as would call for its ending; for there never was a void to be filled so that, with the fullness and the attainment of purpose, the sense of sufficiency be induced: nor is there any such incongruity within the divine that one Being there could be repulsive to another: and of course all There are unchangeable. This absence of satisfaction means only a satisfaction leading to no distaste for that which produces it; to see is to look the more, since for them to continue in the contemplation of an infinite self and of infinite objects is but to acquiesce in the bidding of their nature.

Life, pure, is never a burden; how then could there be weariness There where the living is most noble? That very life is wisdom, not a wisdom built up by reasonings but complete from the beginning, suffering no lack which could set it inquiring, a wisdom primal, unborrowed, not something added to the Being, but its very essence. No wisdom, thus, is greater; this is the authentic knowing, assessor to the divine Intellect as projected into manifestation simultaneously with it; thus, in the symbolic saying, Justice is assessor to Zeus.

(Perfect wisdom) for all the Principles of this order, dwelling There, are as it were visible images projected from themselves, so that all becomes an object of contemplation to contemplators immeasurably blessed. The greatness and power of the wisdom There we may know from this, that it embraces all the real Beings, and has made all and all follow it, and yet that it is itself those beings, which sprang into being with it, so that all is one and the essence There is wisdom. If we have failed to understand, it is that we have thought of knowledge as a mass of theorems and an accumulation of propositions, though that is false even for our sciences of the sense-realm. But in case this should be questioned, we may leave our own sciences for the present, and deal with the knowing in the Supreme at which Plato glances where he speaks of "that knowledge which is not a stranger in something strange to it" — though in what sense, he leaves us to examine and declare, if we boast ourselves worthy of the discussion. This is probably our best starting point.

5

All that comes to be, work of nature or of craft, some wisdom has made: everywhere a wisdom presides at a making.

No doubt the wisdom of the artist may be the guide of the work; it is sufficient explanation of the wisdom exhibited in the arts; but the artist himself goes back, after all, to that wisdom in Nature which is embodied in himself; and this is not a wisdom built up of theorems but one totality, not a wisdom consisting of manifold detail coordinated into a unity but rather a unity working out into detail.

Now, if we could think of this as the primal wisdom, we need look no further, since, at that, we have discovered a principle which is neither a derivative nor a "stranger in something strange to it." But if we are told that, while this Reason-Principle is in Nature, yet Nature itself is its source, we ask how Nature came to possess it; and, if Nature derived it from some other source, we ask what that other source may be; if, on the contrary, the principle is self-sprung, we need look no further: but if (as we assume) we are referred to the Intellectual-Principle, we must make clear whether the Intellectual-Principle engendered the wisdom: if we learn that it did, we ask whence: if from itself, then inevitably, it is itself Wisdom.

The true Wisdom, then (found to be identical with the Intellectual-Principle) is Real Being; and Real Being is Wisdom; it is wisdom that gives value to Real Being; and Being is Real in virtue of its origin in wisdom. It follows that all forms of existence not possessing wisdom are, indeed, Beings in right of the wisdom which went to their forming, but, as not in themselves possessing it, are not Real Beings.

We cannot therefore think that the divine Beings of that sphere, or the other supremely blessed There, need look to our apparatus of science: all of that realm (the very Beings themselves), all is noble image, such images as we may conceive to lie within the soul of the wise — but There not as inscription but as authentic existence. The ancients had this is mind when they declared the Ideas to be Beings, Essentials.

6

Similarly, as it seems to me, the wise of Egypt — whether in precise knowledge or by a prompting of nature — indicated the truth where, in their effort toward philosophical statement, they left aside the writing forms that take in the detail of words and sentences — those characters that represent sounds and convey the propositions of reasoning — and drew pictures instead, engraving in the temple inscriptions a separate image for every separate item: thus they exhibited the mode in which the Supreme goes forth.

For each manifestation of knowledge and wisdom is a distinct image, an object in itself, an immediate unity, not an aggregate of discursive reasoning and detailed willing. Later, from this wisdom in unity there appears, in another form of being, an image, already less compact, which announces the original in an outward stage and seeks the causes by which things are such that the wonder rises how a generated world can be so excellent.

For one who knows must declare his wonder that this Wisdom, while not itself containing the causes by which Being exists and takes such excellence, yet imparts them to the entities produced in Being's realm. This excellence, whose necessity is scarcely or not at all manifest to search, exists, if we could but find it out, before all searching and reasoning.

What I say may be considered in one chief thing, and thence applied to all the particular entities.

7

Consider the universe: we are agreed that its existence and its nature come to it from beyond itself; are we, now, to imagine that its maker first thought it out in detail — the earth, and its necessary situation in the middle; water and, again, its position as lying upon the earth; all the other elements and objects up to the sky in due place and order; living beings with their appropriate forms as we know them, their inner organs and their outer limbs — and that having thus appointed every item beforehand, he then set about the execution?

Such designing was not even possible; how could the plan for a universe come to one that had never looked outward? Nor could he work on material gathered from elsewhere as our craftsmen do, using hands and tools; feet and hands are of the later order.

One way, only, remains: all things must exist in something else; of that prior — since there is no obstacle, all being continuous within the realm of reality — there has suddenly appeared a sign, an image, whether given forth directly or through the ministry of soul or of some phase of soul, matters nothing for the moment: thus the entire aggregate of existence springs from the divine world, in greater beauty There because There unmingled but mingled here.

From the beginning to end all is gripped by the Forms of the Intellectual Realm: Matter itself is held by the Ideas of the elements and to these Ideas are added other Ideas and others again, so that it is hard to work down to crude Matter beneath all that sheathing of Idea. Indeed since Matter itself is, in its degree, an Idea — the lowest — all this universe is Idea and there is nothing that is not Idea as the archetype was. And all is made silently, since nothing had part in the making but Being and Idea — a further reason why creation went without toil. The Exemplar was the Idea of an All, and so an All must come into being.

Thus nothing stood in the way of the Idea, and even now it dominates, despite all the clash of things: the creation is not hindered on its way even now; it stands firm in virtue of being All. To me, moreover, it seems that if we ourselves were archetypes, Ideas, veritable Being, and the Idea with which we construct here were our veritable Essence, then our creative power too would toillessly effect its purpose: as man now stands, he does not produce in his work a true image of himself: become man, he has ceased to be the All; ceasing to be man — we read — "he soars aloft and administers the Kosmos entire"; restored to the All he is maker of the All.

But — to our immediate purpose — it is possible to give a reason why the earth is set in the midst and why it is round and why the ecliptic runs precisely as it does, but, looking to the creating principle, we cannot say that because this was the way, therefore things were so planned: we can say only that because the All is what it is, therefore there is a total of good; the causing principle, we might put it, reached the conclusion before all formal reasoning and not from any premises, not by sequence or plan but before either, since all of that order is later, all reason, demonstration, persuasion.

Since there is a Source, all the created must spring from it and in accordance with it; and we are rightly told not to go seeking the causes impelling a Source to produce, especially when this is the perfectly sufficient Source and identical with the Term: a Source which is Source and Term must be the All-Unity, complete in itself.

8

This then is Beauty primally: it is entire and omnipresent as an entirety; and therefore in none of its parts or members lacking in beauty; beautiful thus beyond denial. Certainly it cannot be anything (be, for example, Beauty) without being wholly that thing; it can be nothing which it is to possess partially or in which it utterly fails (and therefore it must entirely be Beauty entire).

If this principle were not beautiful, what other could be? Its prior does not deign to be beautiful; that which is the first to manifest itself — Form and object of vision to the intellect — cannot but be lovely to see. It is to indicate this that Plato, drawing on something well within our observation, represents the Creator as approving the work he has achieved: the intention is to make us feel the lovable beauty of the autotype and of the Divine Idea; for to admire a representation is to admire the original upon which it was made.

It is not surprising if we fail to recognize what is passing within us: lovers, and those in general that admire beauty here, do not stay to reflect that it is to be traced, as of course it must be, to the Beauty There. That the admiration of the Demiurge is to be referred to the Ideal Exemplar is deliberately made evident by the rest of the passage: "He admired; and determined to bring the work into still closer likeness with the Exemplar:" he makes us feel the magnificent beauty of the Exemplar by telling us that the Beauty sprung from this world is, itself, a copy from That.[4]

And indeed if the divine did not exist, the transcendently beautiful, in a beauty beyond all thought, what could be lovelier than the things we see? Certainly no reproach can rightly be brought against this world save only that it is not That.

9

Let us, then, make a mental picture of our universe: each member shall remain what it is, distinctly apart; yet all is to form, as far as possible, a complete unity so that whatever comes into view shall show as if it were the surface of the orb over all, bringing immediately with it the vision, on the one plane, of the sun and of all the stars with earth and sea and all living things as if exhibited upon a transparent globe.

Bring this vision actually before your sight, so that there shall be in your mind the gleaming representation of a sphere, a picture holding all the things of the universe moving or in repose or (as in reality) some at rest, some in motion. Keep this sphere before you, and from it image another, a

sphere stripped of magnitude and of spatial differences; cast out your inborn sense of Matter, taking care not merely to attenuate it: call on God, maker of the sphere whose image you now hold, and pray Him to enter. And may He come bringing His own Universe with all the Gods that dwell in it — He who is the one God and all the gods, where each is all, blending into a unity, distinct in powers but all one god in virtue of that one divine power of many facets.

More truly, this is the one God who is all the gods; for, in the coming to be of all those, this, the one, has suffered no diminishing. He and all have one existence, while each again is distinct. It is distinction by state without interval: there is no outward form to set one here and another there and to prevent any from being an entire identity; yet there is no sharing of parts from one to another. Nor is each of those divine wholes a power in fragment, a power totaling to the sum of the measurable segments: the divine is one all-power, reaching out to infinity, powerful to infinity: and so great is God that his very members are infinites. What place can be named to which He does not reach?

Great, too, is this firmament of ours and all the powers constellated within it, but it would be greater still, unspeakably, but that there is inbound in it something of the petty power of body; no doubt the powers of fire and other bodily substances might themselves be thought very great, but in fact, it is through their failure in the true power that we see them burning, destroying, wearing things away, and slaving toward the production of life; they destroy because they are themselves in process of destruction, and they produce because they belong to the realm of the produced.

The power in that other world has merely Being and Beauty of Being. Beauty without Being could not be, nor Being voided of Beauty: abandoned of Beauty, Being loses something of its essence. Being is desirable because it is identical with Beauty; and Beauty is loved because it is Being. How then can we debate which is the cause of the other, where the nature is one? The very figment of Being needs some imposed image of Beauty to make it possible, and even to ensure its existence; it exists to the degree in which it has taken some share in the beauty of Idea; and the more deeply it has drawn on this, the less

[4]The Demiurge is the creator of the world in Plato's *Timaeus*, 40.

imperfect it is, precisely because the nature which is essentially the beautiful has entered into it the more intimately.

10

This is why Zeus, although the oldest of the gods and their sovereign, advances first (in the Phaidros myth) toward that vision, followed by gods and demigods and such souls as are of strength to see.[5] That Being appears before them from some unseen place and rising loftily over them pours its light upon all things, so that all gleams in its radiance; it upholds some beings, and they see; the lower are dazzled and turn away, unfit to gaze upon that sun, the trouble falling the more heavily on those most remote.

Of those looking upon that Being and its content, and able to see, all take something but not all the same vision always: intently gazing, one sees the fount and principle of Justice, another is filled with the sight of Moral Wisdom, the original of that quality as found, sometimes at least, among men, copied by them in their degree from the divine virtue which, covering all the expanse, so to speak, of the Intellectual Realm is seen, last attainment of all, by those who have known already many splendid visions.

The gods see, each singly and all as one. So, too, the souls; they see all There in right of being sprung, themselves, of that universe and therefore including all from beginning to end and having their existence There if only by that phase which belongs inherently to the Divine, though often too they are There entire, those of them that have not incurred separation.

This vision Zeus takes and it is for such of us, also, as share his love and appropriate our part in the Beauty There, the final object of all seeing, the entire beauty upon all things; for all There sheds radiance, and floods those that have found their way thither so that they too become beautiful; thus it will often happen that men climbing heights where the soil has taken a yellow glow will themselves appear so, borrowing color from the place on which they move. The color flowering on that

other height we speak of is Beauty; or rather all There is light and beauty, through and through, for the beauty is no mere bloom upon the surface.

To those that do not see entire, the immediate impression is alone taken into account; but those drunken with this wine, filled with the nectar, all their soul penetrated by this beauty, cannot remain mere gazers: no longer is there a spectator outside gazing on an outside spectacle; the cleareyed hold the vision within themselves, though, for the most part, they have no idea that it is within but look toward it as to something beyond them and see it is an object of vision caught by the direction of the will.

All that one sees as a spectacle is still external; one must bring the vision within and see no longer in that mode of separation but as we know ourselves; thus a man filled with a god — possessed by Apollo or by one of the Muses — need no longer look outside for his vision of the divine being; it is but finding the strength to see divinity within.[6]

11

Similarly any one, unable to see himself, but possessed by that God, has but to bring that divine-within before his consciousness and at once he sees an image of himself, himself lifted to a better beauty: now let him ignore that image, lovely though it is, and sink into a perfect self-identity, no such separation remaining; at once he forms a multiple unity with the God silently present; in the degree of his power and will, the two become one; should he turn back to the former duality, still he is pure and remains very near to the God; he has but to look again and the same presence is there.

This conversion brings gain: at the first stage, that of separation, a man is aware of self; but retreating inward, he becomes possessor of all; he puts sense away behind him in dread of the separated life and becomes one in the Divine; if he plans to see in separation, he sets himself outside.

The novice must hold himself constantly under some image of the Divine Being and seek

---

[5]This is part of the myth of the soul in Plato's *Phaedrus*, p. 46.

[6]Here Plotinus gives a very different account of inspiration than Plato in the *Ion*: the source of *enthousiasmós* is within, not outside the poet.

in the light of a clear conception; knowing thus, in a deep conviction, whither he is going — into what a sublimity he penetrates — he must give himself forthwith to the inner and, radiant with the Divine Intellections (with which he is now one), be no longer the seer, but, as that place has made him, the seen.

Still, we will be told, one cannot be in beauty and yet fail to see it. The very contrary: to see the divine as something external is to be outside of it; to become it is to be most truly in beauty: since sight deals with the external, there can here be no vision unless in the sense of identification with the object.

And this identification amounts to a self-knowing, a self-consciousness, guarded by the fear of losing the self in the desire of a too wide awareness.

It must be remembered that sensations of the ugly and evil impress us more violently than those of what is agreeable and yet leave less knowledge as the residue of the shock: sickness makes the rougher mark, but health, tranquilly present, explains itself better; it takes the first place, it is the natural thing, it belongs to our being; illness is alien, unnatural and thus makes itself felt by its very incongruity, while the other conditions are native and we take no notice. Such being our nature, we are most completely aware of ourselves when we are most completely identified with the object of our knowledge.

This is why in that other sphere, when we are deepest in that knowledge by intellection, we are aware of none; we are expecting some impression on sense, which has nothing to report since it has seen nothing and never could in that order see anything. The unbelieving element is sense; it is the other, the Intellectual-Principle, that sees; and if this too doubted, it could not even credit its own existence, for it can never stand away and with bodily eyes apprehend itself as a visible object.

12

We have told how this vision is to be procured, whether by the mode of separation or in identity: now, seen in either way, what does it give to report?

The vision has been of God in travail of a beautiful offspring, God engendering a universe within himself in a painless labor and — rejoiced in what he has brought into being, proud of his children — keeping all closely by Him, for the pleasure He has in his radiance and in theirs.

Of this offspring — all beautiful, but most beautiful those that have remained within — only one has become manifest without; from him (Zeus, sovereign over the visible universe) the youngest born, we may gather, as from some image, the greatness of the Father and of the Brothers that remain within the Father's house.

Still the manifested God cannot think that he has come forth in vain from the father; for through him another universe has arisen, beautiful as the image of beauty, and it could not be lawful that Beauty and Being should fail of a beautiful image.

This second Kosmos at every point copies the archetype: it has life and being in copy, and has beauty as springing from that diviner world. In its character of image it holds, too, that divine perpetuity without which it would only at times be truly representative and sometimes fail like a construction of art; for every image whose existence lies in the nature of things must stand during the entire existence of the archetype.

Hence it is false to put an end to the visible sphere as long as the Intellectual endures, or to found it upon a decision taken by its maker at some given moment.

That teaching shirks the penetration of such a making as is here involved: it fails to see that as long as the Supreme is radiant there can be no failing of its sequel but, that existing, all exists. And — since the necessity of conveying our meaning compels such terms — the Supreme has existed forever and forever will exist.

13

The God fettered (as in the Kronos Myth) to an unchanging identity leaves the ordering of this universe to his son (to Zeus), for it could not be in his character to neglect his rule within the divine sphere, and, as though sated with the Authentic-Beauty, seek a lordship too recent and too poor for his might. Ignoring this lower world, Kronos

(Intellectual-Principle) claims for his own father (Ouranos, the Absolute, or One) with all the upward-tending between them: and he counts all that tends to the inferior, beginning from his son (Zeus, the All-Soul), as ranking beneath him. Thus he holds a midposition determined on the one side by the differentiation implied in the severance from the very highest and, on the other, by that which keeps him apart from the link between himself and the lower: he stands between a greater father and an inferior son. But since that father is too lofty to be thought of under the name of Beauty, the second God remains the primally beautiful.[7]

[7]Plotinus presents the traditional succession of the Greek gods — Ouranos, Kronos, and Zeus — as an allegory of the philosophical relationship between the One, the Intellectual-Principle, and the All-Soul, which generates the Nature-Principle. The transcendent idea of Intellectual Beauty thus mediates between the incomprehensible One and the forms of beauty we can apprehend in matter.

Soul also has beauty, but is less beautiful than Intellect as being its image and therefore, though beautiful in nature, taking increase of beauty by looking to that original. Since then the All-Soul — to use the more familiar term — since Aphrodite herself is so beautiful, what name can we give to that other? If Soul is so lovely in its own right, of what quality must that prior be? And since its being is derived, what must that power be from which the Soul takes the double beauty, the borrowed and the inherent?

We ourselves possess beauty when we are true to our own being; our ugliness is in going over to another order; our self-knowledge, that is to say, is our beauty; in self-ignorance we are ugly.

Thus beauty is of the Divine and comes Thence only.

Do these considerations suffice to a clear understanding of the Intellectual Sphere or must we make yet another attempt by another road?

Dante Alighieri

1265–1321

Dante Alighieri was born in Florence, the son of Alighiero Alighieri of the lesser nobility. His mother died when Dante was quite young, and his father, whom Dante mentions seldom and then only formally, remarried and produced a large second family. Dante was well educated, probably by the Franciscans; his rhetoric tutor was Brunetto Latini. Around 1285, Dante married Gemma Donati, by whom he had two sons and two daughters. Gemma's influence on his life pales, however, beside the radiance of another Florentine noblewoman, Bice Portinari, whom Dante dubbed "Beatrice," the bringer of blessing. Dante's contacts with Beatrice (who married Simone dei Bardi) were undoubtedly few and platonic in the years before her death in 1290, but she became his lifelong Muse and his guide through Paradise in the *Commedia*.

Although Dante experimented with verse in his twenties (under the influence of the poet Guido Cavalcanti), his life was devoted to public affairs: He fought in 1289 in the battle of Campaldino, spoke in the Florentine assembly, and became one of the six priors of Florence. While Dante was away from Florence on a diplomatic mission in 1300, factional warfare broke out; a rival party came to power and convicted Dante in absentia of graft and corruption in office. Under sentence of death if he returned, Dante spent the rest of his life abroad, where he learned "how salt is the bread of exile and how steep the stairs of another." Except for the *Vita Nuova*, which was written in Florence in 1292, most of Dante's works are the product of his exile, including the *Convivio* ("The Banquet," 1304–08), the *De Monarchia* (1308), and his masterpiece the *Commedia* (1306–14) — "Divina" was added by its readers. Dante's literary life was spent wandering between Verona (where his patrons included Can Grande della Scala) and other intellectual centers such as Bologna and Paris. He finally settled in Ravenna, where he died in 1321.

Dante's letter to Can Grande is the most familiar exposition of medieval semiotic theory; the ideas are not original with Dante, but have a long and distinguished history. In the sixth century, St. Augustine had claimed in *Of the Value of Belief* that the Old Testament was to be interpreted as "history, etiology, analogy, and allegory." During the Middle Ages, the Hebrew bible was interpreted not only as the literal history of the Israelites, but as prefiguring events in the life of Christ. And in the thirteenth century, St. Thomas Aquinas's *Summa Theologica* had codified this mode of interpreting scripture:

> That first signification whereby words signify things belongs to the first sense, the historical. . . . That signification whereby things signified by words have themselves also a signification is called the spiritual sense. . . . Now this spiritual sense has a threefold division. . . . So far as the things of the Old Law signify the things of the New Law, there is the allegorical sense. . . . So far as the things done in Christ . . . are signs of what we ought to do, there is the moral sense. . . . But so far as they signify what relates to eternal glory, there is the anagogical sense.

Dante's principal innovation, if indeed it is an innovation, is in applying these principles of symbolic meaning to something other than sacred scripture — to his

Commedia, a poetical work written in the "vulgar" language of common speech. Some medievalists (the followers of D. W. Robertson) have suggested that this multivalent mode of reading was part of the freight of medieval literacy, and that even apparently secular texts (like Chaucer's *Canterbury Tales*, or Boccaccio's *Decameron*) were automatically read in this manner. Whether this was actually the case is controversial, but certainly with the coming of the Renaissance, this mode of reading began to fade away, and the notion that all literature was potentially ambiguous — indeed, that the mark of literature was ambiguity and multiplicity of interpretation — would not return until Northrop Frye (p. 691) and William Empson in the middle of the twentieth century.

Selected Bibliography

Alighieri, Dante. *The Divine Comedy*. Translated and with a commentary by Charles S. Singleton. Princeton: Princeton University Press, 1970–75.

Dunbar, Helen Flanders. *Symbolism in Medieval Thought*. New Haven: Yale University Press, 1929.

Ginsberg, Warren. *Dante's Aesthetics of Being*. Ann Arbor: University of Michigan Press, 1999.

Hollander, Robert. *Allegory in Dante's Commedia*. Princeton: Princeton University Press, 1969.

Kirkpatrick, Robin. *Dante's Paradiso and the Limitations of Modern Criticism: A Study of Style and Poetic Theory*. Cambridge: Cambridge University Press, 1978.

Pietrobono, Luigi. "L'epistola a Can Grande." *Giornale dantesco* 4 (1939): 3–51.

Saley, John V. *Dante and the English Romantics*. New York: Columbia University Library, 1960.

Singleton, Charles S. *Dante Studies*. 2 vols. Cambridge: Harvard University Press, 1954–58.

Tock, J. F. *L'etterno piacer: Aesthetic Ideas in Dante*. Oxford: Clarendon Press, 1984.

Toynbee, Paget Jackson. *Dante in English Literature from Chaucer to Cary*. 2 vols. London: Methuen, 1909.

From *Letter to Can Grande della Scala*

5. As the Philosopher says in the second book of the *Metaphysics*, "As a thing is with respect to being, so it is with respect to truth";[1] and the reason for this is that the truth concerning a thing, which consists in the truth as its subject, is the perfect image of the thing as it is. And so, of all things which have being, some are such that they have absolute being in themselves, others such that their being is dependent upon a relationship with something else: they exist at the same time with something which is their correlative, as is the case with father and son, master and servant, double and half, the whole and the parts, and many other such things. Because such things depend for their being upon another thing, it follows that their truth would depend upon the truth of the other; not knowing the "half," its "double" could not be understood, and so with the other cases.

Translated by Robert S. Haller.
[1]Aristotle, *Metaphysics* 2.1 [Tr.]

6. Therefore, if one should wish to present an introduction to a part of a work, it is necessary to present some conception of the whole work of which it is a part. For this reason I, who wish to present something in the form of an introduction to the above-mentioned part of the whole *Comedy*,[2] have decided to preface it with some discussion of the whole work, in order to make the approach to the part easier and more complete. There are six questions, then, which should be asked at the beginning about any doctrinal work: what is its subject, its form, its agent, its end, the title of the book, and its branch of philosophy. In three cases the answers to these questions will be different for the part of the work I propose to give you than for the whole, that is, in the cases of its subject, form, and title, while in the other three, as will be clear upon inspection, they will be the same. Thus these first three should be specifically asked in a discussion of the whole work, after which the way will be clear for an introduction to the part. Let us, then, ask the last three questions not only about the whole but also about the offered part itself.

7. For the clarification of what I am going to say, then, it should be understood that there is not just a single sense in this work: it might rather be called *polysemous,* that is, having several senses. For the first sense is that which is contained in the letter, while there is another which is contained in what is signified by the letter. The first is called literal, while the second is called allegorical, or moral or anagogical. And in order to make this manner of treatment clear, it can be applied to the following verses: "When Israel went out of Egypt, the house of Jacob from a barbarous people, Judea was made his sanctuary, Israel his dominion."[3] Now if we look at the letter alone, what is signified to us is the departure of the sons of Israel from Egypt during the time of Moses; if at the allegory, what is signified to us is our redemption through Christ; if at the moral sense, what is signified to us is the conversion of the soul from the sorrow and misery of sin to the state of grace; if at the anagogical, what is signified to us is the departure of the sanctified soul from bondage to the corruption of this world into the freedom of eternal glory. And although these mystical senses are called by various names, they may all be called allegorical, since they are all different from the literal or historical. For allegory is derived from the Greek *alleon,* which means in Latin *alienus* ("belonging to another") or *diversus* ("different").

8. This being established, it is clear that the subject about which these two senses play must also be twofold. And thus it should first be noted what the subject of the work is when taken according to the letter, and then what its subject is when understood allegorically. The subject of the whole work, then, taken literally, is the state of souls after death, understood in a simple sense; for the movement of the whole work turns upon this and about this. If on the other hand the work is taken allegorically, the subject is man, in the exercise of his free will, earning or becoming liable to the rewards or punishments of justice.

9. And the form is twofold: the form of the treatise and the form of the treatment. The form of the treatise is threefold, according to its three kinds of divisions. The first division is that which divides the whole work into three canticles. The second is that which divides each canticle into cantos. The third, that which divides the cantos into rhymed units. The form or manner of treatment is poetic, fictive, descriptive, digressive, and transumptive, and it as well consists in definition, division, proof, refutation, and the giving of examples.

10. The title of the work is, "Here begins the Comedy of Dante Alighieri, a Florentine by birth but not in character." To understand the title, it must be known that comedy is derived from *comos,* "a village," and from *oda,* "a song," so that a comedy is, so to speak, "a rustic song." Comedy, then, is a certain genre of poetic narrative differing from all others. For it differs from tragedy in its matter, in that tragedy is tranquil and conducive to wonder at the beginning, but foul and conducive to horror at the end, or catastrophe, for which reason it is derived from *tragos,* meaning "goat," and *oda,* making it, as it were, a "goat song," that is, foul as a goat is foul. This is evident in Seneca's tragedies. Comedy, on

---

[2]His *Divine Comedy.*
[3]Psalm 113:1–2 (114:1–2 in the King James version). [Tr.]

the other hand, introduces a situation of adversity, but ends its matter in prosperity, as is evident in Terence's comedies. And for this reason some writers have the custom of saying in their salutations, by way of greeting, "a tragic beginning and a comic ending to you." And, as well, they differ in their manner of speaking. Tragedy uses an elevated and sublime style, while comedy uses an unstudied and low style, which is what Horace implies in the *Art of Poetry* where he allows comic writers occasionally to speak like the tragic, and also the reverse of this:

> Yet sometimes even comedy elevates its voice,
> and angry Chremes rages in swelling tones;
> and in tragedy Telephus and Peleus often lament
> in prosaic speeches. . . .[4]

So from this it should be clear why the present work is called the *Comedy*. For, if we consider the matter, it is, at the beginning, that is, in Hell, foul and conducive to horror, but at the end, in Paradise, prosperous, conducive to pleasure, and welcome. And if we consider the manner of speaking, it is unstudied and low, since its speech is the vernacular, in which even women communicate. There are, besides these, other genres of poetic narrative, such as pastoral verse, elegy, satire, and the hymn of thanksgiving, as could also be gathered from Horace in his *Art of Poetry*. But there is no purpose to discussing these at this time.

11. Now it can be explained in what manner the part I have offered you may be assigned a subject. For if the subject of the whole work, on the literal level, is the state of souls after death, in an absolute, not in a restricted sense, then the subject of this part is the same state, but restricted to the state of blessed souls after death. And if the subject of the whole work, considered allegorically, is man, through exercise of free will, earning or becoming liable to the rewards or punishments of justice, then it is evident that the subject in this part is restricted to man's becoming eligible, to the extent he has earned them, for the rewards of justice.

12. And in the same manner the form of this part follows from the form ascribed to the whole. For if the form of the whole treatise is threefold, then the form in this part is twofold, that is, the division into cantos and into rhymed units. This part could not have the first division as its form, since this part itself is [a product] of the first division.

13. The title of the book also follows; for while the title of the whole book is, as was said earlier, "Here begins the Comedy, etc.," the title of this part is, "Here begins the third canticle of Dante's *Comedy*, etc., which is called *Paradise*."

14. Having settled these three questions, where the answer was different for the part than for the whole, it remains to deal with the other three, where the answers will not be different for either the part or the whole. The agent, then, in the whole and in the part, is he who has been mentioned above; and he is clearly so throughout.

15. The end of the whole and of the part could be multiple, that is, both immediate and ultimate. But, without going into details, it can be briefly stated that the end of the whole as of the part is to remove those living in this life from the state of misery and to lead them to the state of happiness.

16. The branch of philosophy which determines the procedure of the work as a whole and in this part is moral philosophy, or ethics, inasmuch as the whole and this part have been conceived for the sake of practical results, not for the sake of speculation. So even if some parts or passages are treated in the manner of speculative philosophy, this is not for the sake of the theory, but for a practical purpose, following that principle which the Philosopher advances in the second book of the *Metaphysics*, that "practical men sometimes speculate about things in their particular and temporal relations."[5]

---

[4]Horace, *Art of Poetry*, 93–96. [Tr.] See Horace, p. 86.

[5]Aristotle, *Metaphysics* 2.1.

Christine de Pisan

1365–ca. 1431

Christine de Pisan, one of the most remarkable literary women of the Middle Ages, was born in Venice, daughter of civil councillor Tommaso di Benvenuto da Pizzano, a citizen of both scientific and medical accomplishments. Shortly after Christine's birth, Tommaso became Court Astrologer to Charles V of France, a position he held until Charles's death in 1380. During the quarrelsome regency at the time of the minority of Charles VI, Tommaso's salary and perquisites were cut, the family's fortunes declined, and, after a long illness, he died around 1385. Meanwhile, however, Christine had received a literary education at court that would have been unusual for a nobleman of the time, much less a woman.[1] This was owing to her father's encouragement, but over her mother's protests; as Christine put it in *The City of Ladies* (1405), "Your father, who was a great scientist and philosopher, did not believe that women were worth less by knowing science; rather . . . he took great pleasure from seeing your inclination to learning. The feminine opinion of your mother, however, who worked to keep you busy with spinning and silly girlishness . . . was the major obstacle" (II.37.4).[2] In 1380, Christine was married — apparently happily — to a rising young courtier from Picardy, Estienne de Castel, notary to the King, by whom she had three children, including at least one son and one daughter who survived into adulthood. Estienne, traveling with the court to Beauvais, died during an epidemic in 1390, leaving Christine to deal with the responsibility of her mother and three children while Estienne's inheritance was tied up in legal disputes. She had to go to work, and the work she chose was literature. For more than two decades starting around 1393, Christine was what today would be called a professional writer, working in most of the dominant prose and poetical genres of her day: lyric and narrative poetry, penitential psalms and proverbs, biography and history, literary criticism; as well she produced a courtesy manual and even an essay on military strategy compiled from classical authors. She tended to give her personal slant to conventional forms: Her poem on the mutability of fortune, for example, in addition to giving well-known cases of historical figures raised and then thrown down by Fortune's Wheel, presents her own life as a case in point.

Christine was an exceptionally successful writer. Her patrons included King Charles VI of France, for whom she wrote a biography of his father, Louis the dauphin; Charles King of Navarre; Jean duc de Berry; and Charles the Bold and Jean Sans Peur, dukes of Burgundy; and she was invited to the courts of London and Milan. Her works were translated into English, Italian, and other vernacular languages, and she carefully supervised, as few vernacular writers had done, the

---

[1]Christine wrote exclusively in the French vernacular, but must have known how to read Latin in order to participate in the fifteenth-century debate known as the *Querelle de la Rose,* from which the following selection is taken.

[2]Christine de Pisan. *The Book of the City of Ladies.* Translated and with an introduction by Earl Jeffrey Richards (New York: Persea, 1982), II.37.4.

illumination of her manuscripts. Christine seems to have fallen silent around the time of the Burgundian massacres at Paris in 1418, and she is thought to have secluded herself in her daughter's convent, St. Louis de Poissy. But she emerged once more to write *La Ditié de Jehanne d'Arc* (1429), the only celebratory poem on Joan of Arc written in Joan's lifetime. After this there is only silence, and it is supposed that Christine died at Poissy around 1431.

The *Querelle de la Rose*, a literary debate that took place in the opening years of the fifteenth century, pitted Christine and her powerful ally Jean Gerson, the chancellor of the University of Paris, against the humanist royal secretaries Gontier and Pierre Col and Jean de Montreuil, provost of Lille, in a moralistic attack on the literary quality and effect of the *Roman de la Rose*, one of the masterworks of the Middle Ages. Enormously influential on Chaucer and his contemporaries, the *Roman de la Rose* (or *Romance of the Rose*), is an allegorical love poem begun around 1225 by Guillaume de Lorris and completed and augmented around 1275 by Jean de Meun, which describes the ultimately successful quest of a lover for the mystical and fleshly Rose. As usual, time has been on the side of the *Rose*'s defenders, rather than the moralists, and it may not be easy to understand what so disturbed Christine and Gerson. Christine seems to view her society as spiritually adrift and to attribute this lack of standards in part to the popularity of attractive but immoral literature. As E. J. Richards puts it, "The French court was left to its own devices during the frequent spells of insanity which plagued Charles VI. Charles' queen, Isabella of Bavaria, led a licentious and frivolous existence. Not surprisingly, Christine and Gerson connected the immorality of their day with the popularity of the *Rose*."[3]

For Christine, the *Rose* was also threatening because it reinforced the dominant misogyny of the Middle Ages, representing women as unchaste objects of desire. Men get away with such misrepresentation, Christine says, because they own the pen and thus "can tell endless tales and keep the best parts for themselves" with impunity; "my answer is that women did not write these books.... They know they stand wrongfully accused. If women had written these books, I know full well the matter would have been handled differently." Christine finds the *Rose* shameful, not merely for its sexual frankness, but for the manners and morals it attributes to women.

In her later, more explicitly feminist treatise, *The Book of the City of Ladies*, written as an antidote to Ovid's *Remedia amoris* and to Boccaccio's stories in *De mulieribus claris*, Christine sets forth representations of admirable women from the present as well as legendary times, middle-class dames as well as noblewomen and queens. The treatise is not merely a defense of women against the standard masculine accusations, but a reinscription of femininity suggesting that standard male virtues — including learning, bravery, leadership, and magnanimity — are not limited to men at all, that women have been capable of them in the past and would be so more frequently were their opportunities less limited by restrictive social roles. By the end of her life, Christine found her vision of the ideal woman embodied in Joan of Arc, whom she represented as a chaste but heroic girl whose courage and fortitude could lead France to secular and spiritual salvation.

[3]From E. J. Richards's introduction to *The Book of the City of Ladies* (New York: Persea, 1982), pp. 31–32.

Selected Bibliography

Altmann, Barbara K., Deborah L. McGrady, and Charity Cannon Willard. *Christine de Pizan: A Casebook.* New York: Routledge, 2003.

Baird, Joseph L. and John R. Kane, eds. *La Querelle de la Rose: Letters and Documents.* Chapel Hill: North Carolina Studies in Romance Languages and Literatures, 1978.

Brown-Grant, Rosalind. *Christine de Pizan and the Moral Defense of Women: Reading Beyond Genre.* Cambridge Studies in Medieval Literature 40. Cambridge: Cambridge University Press, 1999.

Christine de Pisan. *Oeuvres Poetiques,* ed. Maurice Roy. 3 vols. 1886; New York: Johnson Reprint Corporation, 1965.

———. *The Book of the City of Ladies.* Translated and with an introduction by Earl Jeffrey Richards. New York: Persea, 1982.

Kelly, F. Douglas. "Reflections on the Role of Christine de Pisan as a Feminist Writer." *Sub-Stance* 2 (1972): 63–71.

McLeod, Enid. *The Order of the Rose: The Life and Ideas of Christine de Pizan.* Totowa, NJ: Rowman and Littlefield, 1976.

Quilligan, Maureen. *The Allegory of Female Authority: Christine de Pizan's Cité de Dames.* Ithaca: Cornell University Press, 1991.

Willard, Charity Cannon. *Christine de Pizan: Her Life and Works.* New York: Persea, 1984.

Yenal, Edith. *Christine de Pisan: A Bibliography.* Metuchen, NJ: Scarecrow Press, 1989.

From *La Querelle de la Rose*

To the very competent and wise person, Master John,[1] Secretary of the King our Lord and Provost of Lisle.

Reverence, honor, and due respect to you, Lord Provost of Lisle, esteemed Master, sage in morals, lover of knowledge, steeped in learning, and expert in rhetoric; from me, Christine de Pisan, a woman weak in understanding and inadequate in learning — for which things may your sagacity not hold in scorn the smallness of my reasons; rather may it take into account my feminine weakness. It has pleased you out of your goodness (for which I say thanks) to send me a small treatise expressed in fine language and true-seeming reasons. Your treatise was written, as I gather from your own words, to oppose critics of certain parts of the *Roman de la Rose,* to give firm support to the work, and to approve it and its authors, and in particular Meun.[2] Having read and considered your letter and having understood it, within the limits of my ability, I disagreed with your remarks and shared the opinion of the learned man to whom your letter was addressed. Therefore, although your letter was not addressed to me and did not require a reply, nevertheless I wish to say, to divulge, and to maintain openly that (saving your good grace) you are in grave error to give such lavish and unjustified praise to Meun's book — one which could better be called plain idleness[3] than useful work, in my judgment.

Translated by Joseph L. Baird and John R. Kane.

[1]Christine writes "Jehan Johannes," which was a frequent designation for Jean de Montreuil. [Trs.]

[2]Montreuil's original treatise, the first document in the debate known as *La Querelle de la Rose,* has been lost.

[3]Christine's word here is *oisiueté.* Is this not a half-amused allusion to Lady *Oiseuse,* keeper of the wicket gate of the garden in the *Roman de la Rose*? Not only is the garden to be condemned, *because* it is kept by Lady Idleness, but also the entire romance, which, for all the effort and industry that went into it, is mere trifling "idleness." [Trs.]

You severely criticize his opponents and say, "that a great thing is therein to be understood," "that what a third party says gives a better testimony," "has constructed and erected through great study and at great length." Yet may my daring to repudiate and find fault with an author so worthy and so subtle not seem presumption in me. Rather, take heed of the firm conviction which has moved me to oppose some opinions contained in your letter. In truth, a mere assertion not justified by law can be re-argued without prejudice. I am not, I confess, learned nor schooled in the subtle language, which would make my arguments dazzling, a language which you indeed can display with a fine array of carefully polished words. Nevertheless, I will not hesitate to express my opinion bluntly in the vernacular, although I may not be able to express myself elegantly.

But why did I say before that Meun's work could best be called idleness? Certainly, it seems to me that any trivial thing, even though it is treated, composed, and accomplished with great labor and difficulty, can be called idle, or worse than idle, insofar as evil follows from it. Yet because of the great and widespread fame of the said romance, I had long desired to read it, and once I had gained the knowledge to understand subtle matters somewhat, I did read and consider it at length, to the best of my ability. It is true that the subject matter did not please me in certain parts and so I skipped over it as quickly as a cock over hot embers; therefore, I have not read it in every detail. Nevertheless, some things have remained in my memory which my judgment strongly condemned, and still cannot approve, despite the contrary praise of other people. It is quite true that my small understanding finds great prettiness there; in some parts, he expresses himself very well indeed, using beautiful terms and graceful leonine rhyme. He could not have treated his subject more subtly or more skillfully. But I agree with the opinion (which you clearly oppose, it seems to me) that he speaks too dishonorably in some parts of the *Roman de la Rose*, even when he speaks through the character he calls Reason, who names the secret members plainly by name. You, in fact, support Meun and say that such frankness is perfectly reasonable, maintaining that in the things God has made there is no

ugliness, and consequently no need to eschew their names. To this I say and confess that truly God created all things pure and clean coming from himself and that in the State of Innocence it would not have been wrong to name them; but by the pollution of sin man became impure, and his original sin has remained with us, as Holy Scripture testifies. I can make this clear by a comparison: God made Lucifer beautiful above all the angels and gave him a very solemn and beautiful name, but then Lucifer was reduced by his sin to horrible ugliness; whereupon, the name, albeit very beautiful in itself, now, because of the impression of the person, creates horror in those who hear it.

Further, you point out that Jesus Christ calls the women sinners *meretrix*,[4] etc. But I can explain to you why he called them by that name, because the name *meretrix* is not particularly dishonorable to utter considering the vileness of the thing named, and, in fact, it could have been more basely said even in Latin. Thus should modesty be respected when speaking publicly of things about which Nature herself is ashamed. Saving your reverence and the author's, I say that you commit great wrong against the noble virtue of modesty, which by its nature bridles indecency and dishonorable conduct in words and deeds. Holy Scripture makes clear in many places that this is a great wrong, outside the range of decent conduct and good morals. Moreover, I affirm that the indecent name should not be avoided by substituting the word "relics" for it. I suggest to you that the name does not make the thing dishonorable, but the thing, the name. Therefore, in my humble opinion, one should speak about such matters soberly and only when necessary, as in certain particular cases, such as sickness or other genuine need. Just as our first parents hid their private parts instinctively, so ought we to do in deed and in word.

Further, I cannot be silent about a subject that so displeases me: that the function of Reason, whom he even calls the daughter of God, should be to propound such a dictum as the one I found in the chapter where Reason says to the Lover,

[4]See Matthew XXI.31–32; Luke XV.30. [Trs.] *Meretrix* is Latin for prostitute.

"In the amorous war, it is better to deceive than to be deceived." And truly, Master Jean de Meun, I dare say that Reason denied her heavenly father in that teaching, for He taught an utterly different doctrine. If you hold one of these two to be better than the other, it would follow that both are good, and this cannot be. I hold a contrary opinion: it is far less evil, clearly, to be deceived than to deceive.

Further, let us consider the subject matter or choice of words, which many people find reprehensible. Dear Lord! What horrible stuff! What an affront to honor! What reprehensible teachings recorded in the chapter about the Old Woman! In God's name, what can one find there but sophistical exhortations filled with ugliness and things horrible to recall? Ha, you who have beautiful daughters! If you really want to introduce them to the honorable life, give them, give them, I say, this book so that they may learn from the *Roman de la Rose* ways to distinguish Good from Evil — what am I saying! — rather Evil from Good! To what purpose or to what profit is it that the hearers of this book have their ears assailed by so much sinfulness?

Then, in the chapter about Jealousy, my God, what great good can be observed there! What need to record the dishonorable things and the shameful words, which are common enough in the mouths of the unfortunate people impassioned by this sickness! What good example or preparation for life could this be? And the wickedness which is there recorded of women! Many people attempt to excuse him by saying that it is the Jealous Man who speaks and that in truth Meun does no more than God himself did when He spoke through the mouth of Jeremiah! But whatever lying additions he may have made, he certainly could not have rendered worse or abased the condition of women more! Ha! When I remember the deceits, the hypocrisies, and the conduct dissembled within marriage and outside it, which one can find in this book — certainly, I consider these to be beautiful and edifying tales for one to hear!

Further, what great marvels does the character that he calls Genius the priest say! Surely, the works of Nature would have completely fallen into disuse long since, if he had not so greatly recommended them! But, my God, who could show or convince me what profit there is in the great argument full of vituperation that he calls a sermon (as if to deride holy preaching), which, he says, Genius delivers? It contains too many dishonorable things, names, sophistical words, fanning the flames of those secrets of Nature which ought to be left tacit and not named. Moreover, the "sermon" is superfluous, for a work which is of the very order of Nature cannot, obviously, fail. If it were not so, then it would be good for the maintenance of human generation to invent and say exciting and inflaming words and terms in order to stimulate man to continue that work.

Yet the author does more, if I remember well; for the life of me I can't understand to what purpose. For in the said sermon he adduces, as a comparison, paradise and its joys. He says truly enough that the virtuous will go to that place, but he concludes that everyone, men and women alike, should know how to perform and exercise the functions of Nature; nor in this does he make any exception of law, as if he wished to say, and indeed says plainly, that they will all be saved. And by this it appears that he wishes to maintain that the sin of lechery is nothing, rather a virtue, which is error and against the law of God. Ha! what seed and what doctrine! What great good can come of it! I believe that many have left the world because of it and entered religion, or become hermits because of that holy message, or come out of the evil life and been saved by such exhortation! Certainly (I dare say it, no matter whom it offends), this never came from anywhere but a heart corrupted and abandoned to dissolution and vice, which can be cause of great sin and unbecoming conduct.

And again, for God's sake, let us look a little further to see what profit there can possibly be in his excessive, impetuous, and most untruthful criticism and denigration of women as exceedingly wicked creatures! He declares that their conduct is filled with all manner of perversity, with which condemnations, even with all the give and take among his characters, he cannot fully gorge himself. For if you wish to tell me that the Jealous Man does this as a man overcome by passion, I fail to see how he fulfills the teaching of Genius, for Genius so fully recommends and exhorts men to bed them and to perform the act which he praises so highly. And this Genius, more than any of the characters, makes great attacks on women, saying, in fact, "Flee, flee, flee from the deadly serpent."[5] Then he declares that men should pursue them unremittingly. Here is a glaring contradiction, evilly intended: to order men to flee what he wishes them to pursue, and to pursue what he wishes them to flee. But since women are so perverse, he ought not to command men to approach them at all. For he who fears a problem ought to eschew it. And it is for this reason that he so strongly forbids a man to tell his secret to a woman, who is so eager to know it (as he records), although I simply do not know where the devil he found so much nonsense and so many useless words, which are there laid out by a long process. But I pray all those who truly hold this teaching authentic and put so much faith in it, that they kindly tell me how many men they have seen accused, killed, hanged, and publicly rebuked by the accusations of their women? I think you will find them few and far between. Nevertheless, it would be good and praiseworthy counsel for a man to keep his affairs to himself for the greatest security, for he who does so is rich above all men. Indeed, not long ago I heard tell of a man who was accused and hanged on account of having revealed himself to a friend whom he trusted. But I think that few have come before a judge with accusations or complaints of such horrible evil, such disloyalties, and such wickedness which he says women know how to commit so maliciously and underhandedly. It is indeed secret when nobody sees it. As I have said previously on this subject in my work called "L'Epistre au Dieu d'Amours," where are those countries and kingdoms which have been ruined by the great evils of women? If it be not presumptuous, let us speak of the great crimes that one can attribute to even the worst and most deceitful of women. What do they do? In what ways do they deceive you? If they ask you for money from your purse, which they cannot get from you by a ruse or cannot take themselves, do not give it to them if you do not wish to. And if you say that they have made a fool of you, don't let them. Do they go into your house

to woo, pursue, or rape you? It would be good to know how they deceive you. And, besides, he speaks superficially and wrongly about married women who deceive their husbands in this way, for he could know nothing of the married state by experience, and therefore he spoke of it only in generalities. I do not understand what good purpose this can serve or what good can come of it, save to impede the good and peace that is in marriage, and to render the husbands who hear so much babbling and extravagance (if they believe such things) suspicious and less affectionate toward their wives. God, what exhortation! How profitable it is! But truly since he blamed all women in general, I am constrained to believe that he never had acquaintance of, or regular contact with, any honorable or virtuous woman. But by having resort to many dissolute women of evil life (as lechers commonly do), he thought, or feigned to know, that all women were of that kind; for he had known no others. And if he had blamed only the dishonorable ones and counseled men to flee them, it would have been a good and just teaching. But no, without exception he accuses them all. But if, beyond all the bounds of reason, the author took it upon himself to accuse or judge them without justification, the ones accused ought not to be blamed for it. Rather, he should be blamed who carried his argument to the point where it was simply not true, since the contrary is so obvious. For if he and all his henchmen had sworn it in this matter (let no one take offense), there have been, there are, and there will be more virtuous women, more honorable, better bred, and even more learned, and from whom more great good has come forth into the world than ever did from his person. Similarly, there have been women well schooled in worldly conduct and virtuous morals, and many who have effected a reconciliation with their husbands and have borne their concerns and their secrets and their passions calmly and discreetly, despite the fact that their husbands were crude and brutish toward them. One finds proof enough of this in the Bible and in other ancient histories, women such as Sarah, Rebecca, Esther, Judith, and many others. And even in our own time we have seen in France many virtuous women, great ladies and others of our ladies of France: the holy devout

[5]Cf. Vergil, *Bucolica*, III.92–93. [Trs.]

Queen Jeanne; Queen Blanche; the Duchess of Orleans, daughter of the King of France; the Duchess of Anjou, who is now called Queen of Sicily; and many others — all of whom had such great beauty, chastity, honor, and wisdom. And also women of lesser rank, like Madame de la Ferté, wife of Monsieur Pierre de Craon, who did much that was praiseworthy; besides many others, whom I pass over for lack of time.

And do not believe or let anyone else think, dear Sir, that I have written this defense, out of feminine bias, merely because I am a woman. For, assuredly, my motive is simply to uphold the pure truth, since I know by experience that the truth is completely contrary to those things I am denying. And it is precisely because I am a woman that I can speak better in this matter than one who has not had the experience, since he speaks only by conjecture and by chance. But above all these things, pray let us consider what the aim of the aforementioned treatise is; for as the proverb says, "By the intent a case is concluded." Thus may be seen and noted what can be profitable in that excessively horrible and shameful conclusion.[6] I call it shameful and so very dishonorable that I dare say that nobody who loves virtue and honor will hear it without being totally confounded by shame and abomination at hearing described, expressed, and distorted in dishonorable fictions what modesty and reason should restrain well-bred folk from even thinking about. Yet, further, I dare say that even the goliards[7] would have been horrified to read or hear it in public, in decent places, and before people whom they would have considered virtuous. But who could praise a work which can be neither read nor quoted at the table of queens, of princesses, and of worthy women, who would surely, on hearing it, be constrained to cover their blushing faces?

And if you wish to excuse him by saying that by means of a pretty novelty it pleases him to put the purpose of love through such figures, I answer

you that in this work he tells us nothing new. Does one not know how men normally behave with women? If he had told us something about bears or lions or birds or other strange creatures, this would have been matter for laughing on account of the fable, but there is no novelty in this that he tells us. And certainly it could have been done more pleasantly, far more agreeably and by means of more courteous terms, a method which would have been more pleasing to handsome and decent lovers and to every other virtuous person.

Thus, without being more prolix, although a great deal more could be said, and said better, I do not know how, according to my small capacity and weak judgment, to consider this book useful in any way. But it seems so very manifest to me that a great labor was expended on it which produced nothing of value, although my judgment concedes that Master Jean de Meun was a very great, learned, and eloquent clerk. But he would have been able to produce so much better a work, more profitable, and of higher sentiment, if he had applied himself to it, and that he did not do so is great loss. I suppose, however, that perhaps the great carnality with which he was filled caused him to abandon himself to desire rather than to the good of his soul, for by one's actions generally the inclinations are known. Notwithstanding, I do not condemn the *Roman de la Rose* entirely, for it does indeed contain some good things, and its style is poetically pleasing, but therein lies the greater peril, for the more authentic the good the more faith one puts in the evil. And in this way many learned men have sometimes sown great errors by intermingling good and evil and by covering the errors over with truth and virtue. Thus if his priest Genius can say, "Flee, flee woman, the evil serpent hidden in the grass"; I can say, "Flee, flee the malice concealed in the shadow of goodness and virtue."

Therefore, I say this in conclusion to you, dear Sir, and to all your allies who praise this work so highly and make so much of it that you dare and presume to minimize almost all other works by comparison — I say that it does not merit such praise (saving your good grace) and that you do great wrong to the more deserving works. For a work without usefulness, contributing nothing to the general or personal good (even though we

---

[6]Christine refers here, of course, to the thinly veiled description of the sexual act which concludes the *Roman de la Rose*. [Trs.]

[7]The goliards were satiric poets of the thirteenth and fourteenth centuries.

concede it to be delightful, the fruit of great work and labor), in no way deserves praise. And as in former times the triumphant Romans would not attribute praise or honor to anything if it was not to the utility of the Republic, let us look to their example to see whether we can crown this Romance. But having considered the aforementioned things and numerous others we have touched on, I consider it more fitting to bury it in fire than to crown it with laurel, although you call it a mirror of good living and, for men of all classes, an example of good social conduct and of the wise, moral life. But to the contrary (saving your grace) I call it an exhortation to vice, a comfort to dissolute life, a doctrine full of deception, the way to damnation, a public defamer, the cause of suspicion and misbelieving, the shame of many people, and possibly the occasion of heresy. But I know well that you will excuse it by replying to me that therein he enjoins man to do the good but to eschew the evil. But my reasoning is better, for I can show that there is no point in reminding human nature, which is naturally inclined to evil, that it limps on one foot, in the hope that it will then walk straighter. Do you wish to speak of all the good which can be found in this book? Certainly, far more virtuous things, eloquently expressed, closer to the truth, and more profitable to the decorous and moral life can be found in many other books — books written by certain philosophers and by teachers of our faith, like Aristotle, Seneca, St. Paul, St. Augustine, and others, as you well know. For these testify and teach how to pursue virtue and flee vice more clearly and plainly than Master Jean de Meun has ever been able to do. But such teachings are not usually heard or remembered by fleshly men. They are like the thirsty invalid who, when the doctor permits him to drink, does so gladly and excessively, for the lust for drinking leads him to believe that now it will do him no harm.[8] If by God's grace you were restored to the light and purity of a clear conscience, freed from the stain and pollution of sin or any sinful intent, and purged by the prick of contrition which reveals the secrets of conscience and condemns self-will — and may God grant it to you and to all others — then you would be more receptive to truth and thus would make a different judgment of the *Rose;* perhaps you would wish that you had never seen it. So much suffices. And may it not be imputed to me as folly, arrogance, or presumption, that I, a woman, should dare to reproach and call into question so subtle an author, and to diminish the stature of his work, when he alone, a man, has dared to undertake to defame and blame without exception an entire sex.

---

[8] The passage is somewhat difficult to translate, because the comparison contains only its first term and is not completely worked out. Cf. Ovid, *Amores*, III.iv.18. [Trs.]

Sir Philip Sidney

1554–1586

As a skilled courtier, scholar, soldier, and poet, Philip Sidney was the pattern of the English Renaissance gentleman. After attending Shrewsbury School and Christ Church College at Oxford, and making a grand tour of the continent, he established himself at Elizabeth's court, where he joined the faction led by one of the Queen's favorites, his uncle Robert Dudley, Earl of Leicester. Sidney ended his short life as military governor in Flanders during the Dutch wars. His heroic death at the battle of Zutphen was the stuff of legend: Sidney is said to have courteously declined water and medical attention in favor of a lowlier fellow soldier, a deed that made him a model of the chivalric ideal. But notwithstanding his nobility of birth and spirit, Sidney's unique talents and personality would have procured him success and fame. His *Arcadia* (1593), a romance alternating prose with poetry, established a tradition for the English pastoral; it was a best-seller for over two centuries and was crucial to the development of the English novel. And his *Apology for Poetry,* written in 1583 and published in 1595, was the first significant piece of literary criticism in the English language. (The essay is also known as *The Defence of Poetry,* the title of a slightly earlier version.)

The occasion of *An Apology for Poetry* was to refute *The Schoole of Abuse* (1579), a moralistic attack on poetry written by Puritan minister Stephen Gosson and dedicated (without leave) to Sidney himself. In constructing his *apologia* — Greek for a legal defense — Sidney addressed himself less to Gosson than to Plato, whose *Republic* provides most of the ammunition the Puritan divine expended against poetry. Sidney's *Apology* is structured according to the principles of medieval rhetoric like a good legal brief, with an introduction that draws the reader into the case while offering reassurance of the ethical rightness of the speaker, a central argumentative section, a set of answers to objections, and a glowing peroration. The contemporary reader must have patience, however, with the slow Senecan amble of Sidney's sentences. They were formed before muscularity became the mainstay of English prose. The reader who gets lost will be glad of another characteristic of Renaissance prose: Sidney signals all his transitions with a rapid and elegant summary of the preceding section.

Sidney opens the systematic section of the *Apology* with a definition of poetry, which he calls "an art of imitation, for so Aristotle termeth it in his word *mimesis,* that is to say, a representing, counterfeiting, or figuring forth. . . ." The definition suggests an affinity with Aristotle that is more apparent than real, for Sidney concludes with the Horatian phrase ". . . with this end, to teach and delight." Like many Renaissance theorists, Sidney appeals to mimesis not because it is a crucial principle, but in order to set limits to his subject. He wants to differentiate that class of poetry he will discuss, fictions based on human action, from hymns and psalms on the one hand and philosophy or history or natural science written in verse on the other. The distinction is needed: The two latter types of poetry were not under attack as were fictions. But the end, "to teach and delight," is the pivotal phrase.

Sidney's world, like Plato's, is structured hierarchically and holistically. Like Plato also, he sees the sciences and arts all directed to a single end, "the mistress-knowledge, by the Greeks called *architectonike,* which stands . . . in the knowledge of a man's self, in the ethic and politic consideration, with the end of well doing and not of well knowing only." Horsemanship — the art Sidney begins his *Apology* by mentioning — is no end in itself but serves the art of the soldier, just as the soldier's art serves the statesman's; the ultimate goal is right action.

The arts are judged by their distance from that architectonic goal: the closer, the higher. Thus divinity, Sidney concedes, must be the highest of the sciences, and with this no merely earthly art, including poetry, can compete. It is only against the other major sublunary disciplines — law, history, and philosophy — that Sidney pits the poets. Which of these arts will best serve to make men better? Once the question is so phrased, poetry excels. For law at best keeps us from evil: Its function is not to make us good. Ethical philosophy will help us with the moral distinctions, but philosophy, although it teaches us what virtue is, will not *move* us to virtuous action. History occasionally teaches sound moral lessons — yet just as often its examples are immoral: how the evil triumphed or the virtuous were slain. Only poetry always provides poetic justice to move us to virtuous action, and by the pleasure it gives, move us to go on reading it. Poetry does not merely teach and delight; for Sidney it delights *in order to* teach.

Sidney's aesthetic principle, then, is Horatian, while his metaphysics owes much to Plato. Because of this, whenever he quotes and glosses Aristotle, he subtly alters and distorts his meaning. On page 143, for instance, Sidney argues for the poets and against the claims of history by quoting *Poetics,* Chapter 9, that "poetry is *philosophoteron* and *spoudaioteron,* that is to say, it is more philosophical and more studiously serious than history. . . . because poesy dealeth with *katholou,* that is to say, with the universal consideration, and the history with *kathekaston,* the particular. . . ." The quotation is accurate as far as it goes, but within the same paragraph, Sidney loses track of the distinction between the universal and the particular, substituting one more consistent with his basic Platonism between the *ideal* and the *real.* ("But if the question be . . . whether it be better to have it set down as it should be, or as it was, then certainly is more doctrinable [instructive] the feigned Cyrus in Xenophon than the true Cyrus in Justin. . . .")

The central argument in Sidney is based on poetry's "works and parts" — Elizabethan English for its *effects* and *genres.* After he has shown the superiority of poetry to law, history, and philosophy, he reviews the major genres of poetry to show that they are all instructive, or at least not injurious.

That done, Sidney runs through Gosson's four major objections to poetry in *The Schoole of Abuse.* The first, that there are more fruitful arts than poetry, his main argument has already disposed of. The second is an objection to fiction in general: that poets by the very nature of their trade must be liars. Here Sidney claims benefit of poetic license: that "the poet nothing affirmeth"; fictions are not asserted or received as verifiable truth and therefore can never deceive, as the statements of the historian or the scientist might.

The third objection, that "poetry abuseth man's wit," Sidney turns on its head. He admits that immoral poetry and fictions exist, but these constitute an abuse of the art, not a reflection of its deepest nature. In fact, the possible damage poetry may do, if its ends are perverted, is a reflection of poetry's importance — just as the improper use of the art of medicine will lead to illness and death. The fourth, that the poets were banished from Plato's republic, Sidney refutes with arguments ad hominem — that Plato, as a philosopher, was naturally in competition with the poets. While Sidney also expresses shock at Plato's frank discussions of homoerotic love (in the *Phaedrus* and the *Symposium*), in truth he wants Plato on his side, not on Gosson's, and his most serious argument here is that Plato banished poetry not because it was evil in its nature but only to avoid its possible abuses — such as the teaching of falsehoods about the nature of God. He thus assimilates the last objection to the previous one.

For many, the most interesting section of the *Apology for Poetry* is Sidney's digression on the arts in contemporary England, which he considered to be in a bad way. Applying the strict standards of Renaissance poetics to home-grown English verse and drama, Sidney finds most of his fellow poets admirable for their natural genius but lamentably ignorant about the rules and regulations that Horatian aesthetics had down the centuries evolved for literary art. Several of Sidney's accusations about the English theater — its neglect of the three unities of time, place, and action; mixing of comic scenes into tragedy, polluting genres that ought to be kept pure; indecorous portrayal of violence on the stage — will be debated nearly a century later in Dryden's *An Essay of Dramatic Poesy* (p. 163) and laid to rest after another century in Johnson's "Preface to *Shakespeare*" (p. 216). What Sidney thought to be immutable laws of art came to be seen, more and more, as mere conventions, useful in their day but no longer valid.

Sidney and his strictures on the artist's need for study and practice may seem pedantic unless we remember what was always before the well-traveled Sidney's eyes: how recently England had emerged from provincial barbarism into the sunlight of Elizabethan courtliness, and how much the English still needed to learn from the older cultures of Europe and the classical world. If these are the broad outlines of the *Apology,* this critical work repays close study as well. An undergraduate in one of my recent classes, Janet Strunk, noted that the word "poesy" itself switches gender in the course of the essay, and with the aid of a computer file of the essay we were able to confirm that, seven times referred to as "he" in the earlier sections of the essay, "poesy" becomes a "she" for Sidney three times toward its end.[1] Is this abstract gender-bending one more aspect of the Elizabethan fascination with cross-dressing, with which Sidney himself plays in the *Arcadia*? Or is it simply the argumentative context that dictates gender here? At the outset of the essay, poetry is portrayed as engaged in a contest to prove its excellence and virtue against rival sciences like philosophy and history, and, like a participant in one of the formal Elizabethan tournaments, must be gendered masculine. By the end of the essay,

[1]For example, "But I list not to defend poesy with the help of her underling historiography" (p. 154); "Sweet Poesy, that hath anciently had kings . . . not only to favor poets, but to be poets; and of our nearer times can present for her patrons a Robert, king of Sicily . . ." (p. 154); "[drama] like an unmannerly daughter showing a bad education, causeth her mother poesy's honesty to be called in question" (p. 157). In the early part of the *Apology,* we often get sentences like this: "Nay truly, though I yield that poesy may not only be abused, but that, being abused, by the reason of his sweet charming force, it can do more hurt than any other army of words" (p. 151).

though, poesy has become not the contender but what is contended for, the prize for which England's writers strive against those of other nations, the feminine reward of masculine valor. Such hidden metaphors remind us, if we needed such reminding, that the *Apology* was written by the Elizabethan age's foremost lyric poet, who could not help bringing his talents and wit into everything he did.

Selected Bibliography

Curtright, Travis. "Sidney's Defense of Poetry: Ethos and the Ideas." *Ben Jonson Journal* 10 (2003): 101–15.

Devereux, James A. "The Meaning of Delight in Sidney's Defense of Poesy." *Studies in the Literary Imagination* 15 (1982): 85–97.

Jacobson, Daniel. "Sir Philip Sidney's Dilemma: On the Ethical Function of Narrative Art." *Journal of Aesthetics and Art Criticism* 54, no. 4 (1996): 327–36.

Levao, Ronald. *Renaissance Minds and Their Fictions: Cusanus, Sidney, Shakespeare.* Berkeley: University of California Press, 1985.

Mason, H. A. "An Introduction to Literary Criticism by Way of Sidney's Apologie for Poetrie." *Cambridge Quarterly* 12, no. 2–3 (1984): 79–173.

McCoy, Richard C. *Sir Philip Sidney: Rebellion in Arcadia.* New Brunswick: Rutgers University Press, 1979.

Myrick, Kenneth Orne. *Sir Philip Sidney as a Literary Craftsman.* Cambridge: Harvard University Press, 1935.

Robinson, Forrest Glen. *The Shape of Things Known: Sidney's Apology in Its Philosophical Tradition.* Cambridge: Harvard University Press, 1972.

Spingarn, J. E. *A History of Literary Criticism in the Renaissance.* New York: Columbia University Press, 1912.

Stump, Donald V. "Sidney's Concept of Tragedy in the Apology and the Arcadia." *Studies in Philology* 79 (1982): 78–99.

Ulreich, John C., Jr. "Poets Only Deliver: Sidney's Conception of Mimesis." *Studies in the Literary Imagination* 15 (1982): 67–84.

Weiner, Andrew D. *Sir Philip Sidney and the Poetics of Protestantism.* Minneapolis: University of Minnesota Press, 1978.

An Apology for Poetry

When the right virtuous Edward Wotton and I were at the Emperor's Court together, we gave ourselves to learn horsemanship of John Pietro Pugliano, one that with great commendation had the place of an esquire in his stable. And he, according to the fertileness of the Italian wit, did not only afford us the demonstration of his practice, but sought to enrich our minds with the contemplations there which he thought most precious. But with none I remember mine ears were at any time more loaden, than when (either angered with slow payment, or moved with our learnerlike admiration) he exercised his speech in the praise of his faculty. He said soldiers were the noblest estate of mankind, and horsemen the noblest of soldiers. He said they were the masters of war and ornaments of peace; speedy goers and strong abiders; triumphers both in camps and courts. Nay, to so unbelieved a point he proceeded, as that no earthly thing bred such wonder to a prince as to be a good horseman. Skill of government was but a *pedenteria*[1] in comparison. Then would he add certain praises, by telling what a peerless beast a horse was, the only serviceable courtier without flattery, the beast of most beauty, faithfulness, courage, and such more, that, if I had not been a piece of a logician before I came to him, I think he would have persuaded me to have wished myself a horse. But thus much at least with his no few words he drove into me, that self-love is better than any gilding to make that seem gorgeous wherein ourselves are parties. Wherein, if Pugliano's strong affection and weak arguments will not satisfy you, I will give you a nearer example of myself, who (I know not by what mischance) in these my not old years and idlest times having slipped into the title of a poet, am provoked to say something unto you in the defense of that my unelected vocation, which if I handle with more good will than good reasons, bear with me, since the scholar is to be pardoned that followeth the steps of his master. And yet I must say that, as I have just cause to make a pitiful defense of poor Poetry, which from almost the highest estimation of learning is fallen to be the laughingstock of children, so have I need to bring some more available proofs, since the former is by no man barred of his deserved credit, the silly latter hath had even the names of philosophers used to the defacing of it, with great danger of civil war among the Muses.

And first, truly, to all them that professing learning inveigh against poetry may justly be objected, that they go very near to ungratefulness, to seek to deface that which, in the noblest nations and languages that are known, hath been the first light-giver to ignorance, and first nurse, whose milk by little and little enabled them to feed afterwards of tougher knowledges. And will they now play the hedgehog that, being received into the den, drove out his host, or rather the vipers, that with their birth kill their parents? Let learned Greece in any of her manifold sciences able to show me one book before Musaeus, Homer, and Hesiod, all three nothing else but poets. Nay, let any history be brought that can say any writers were there before them, if they were

not men of the same skill, as Orpheus, Linus, and some other are named, who, having been the first of that country that made pens deliverers of their knowledge to their posterity, may justly challenge to be called their fathers in learning, for not only in time they had this priority (although in itself antiquity be venerable) but went before them, as causes to draw with their charming sweetness the wild untamed wits to an admiration of knowledge, so, as Amphion was said to move stones with his poetry to build Thebes, and Orpheus to be listened to by beasts—indeed stony and beastly people.[2] So among the Romans were Livius Andronicus, and Ennius. So in the Italian language the first that made it aspire to be a treasure-house of science were the poets Dante, Boccaccio, and Petrarch. So in our English were Gower and Chaucer.

After whom, encouraged and delighted with their excellent foregoing, others have followed, to beautify our mother tongue, as well in the same kind as in other arts. This did so notably show itself that the philosophers of Greece durst not a long time appear to the world but under the masks of poets. So Thales, Empedocles, and Parmenides sang their natural philosophy in verses; so did Pythagoras and Phocylides their moral counsels; so did Tyrtaeus in war matters, and Solon in matters of policy: or rather, they, being poets, did exercise their delightful vein in those points of highest knowledge, which before them lay hid to the world. For that wise Solon was directly a poet it is manifest, having written in verse the notable fable of the Atlantic Island, which was continued by Plato.

And truly, even Plato, whosoever well considereth shall find that in the body of his work, though the inside and strength were philosophy, the skin as it were and beauty depended most of poetry: for all standeth upon dialogues, wherein he feigneth many honest burgesses of Athens to speak of such matters, that, if they had been set on the rack, they would never have confessed them, besides his poetical describing the circumstances of their meetings, as the well ordering of a banquet, the delicacy of a walk, with interlacing mere

---

[1]Pedantry: useless book-learning.

[2]Sidney's notion of poetry's power derives from Horace's *Art of Poetry*. See p. 92.

—claim Plato is also a poet (para. 3)

tales, as Gyges' ring, and others, which who knoweth not to be flowers of poetry did never walk into Apollo's garden.[3]

And even historiographers (although their lips sound of things done, and verity be written in their foreheads) have been glad to borrow both fashion and perchance weight of poets. So Herodotus entitled his history by the name of the nine Muses;[4] and both he and all the rest that followed him either stole or usurped of poetry their passionate describing of passions, the many particularities of battles, which no man could affirm, or, if that be denied me, long orations put in the mouths of great kings and captains, which it is certain they never pronounced. So that, truly, neither philosopher nor historiographer could at the first have entered into the gates of popular judgments, if they had not taken a great passport of poetry, which in all nations at this day, where learning flourisheth not, is plain to be seen, in all which they have some feeling of poetry. In Turkey, besides their lawgiving divines, they have no other writers but poets. In our neighbor country Ireland, where truly learning goeth very bare, yet are their poets held in a devout reverence. Even among the most barbarous and simple Indians where no writing is, yet have they their poets, who make and sing songs, which they call *areytos,* both of their ancestors' deeds and praises of their gods — a sufficient probability that, if ever learning come among them, it must be by having their hard dull wits softened and sharpened with the sweet delights of poetry. For until they find a pleasure in the exercises of the mind, great promises of much knowledge will little persuade them that know not the fruits of knowledge. In Wales, the true remnant of the ancient Britons, as there are good authorities to show the long time they had poets, which they called bards, so through all the conquests of Romans, Saxons, Danes, and Normans, some of whom did seek to ruin all memory of learning from among them, yet do their poets, even to this day, last; so as it is not more notable in soon beginning than in long continuing. But since the authors of most of our sciences were the Romans, and before them the Greeks, let us a little stand upon their authorities, but even so far as to see what names they have given unto this now scorned skill.

Among the Romans a poet was called *vates,* which is as much as a diviner, foreseer, or prophet, as by his conjoined words *vaticinium* and *vaticinari* is manifest: so heavenly a title did that excellent people bestow upon this heart-ravishing knowledge. And so far were they carried into the admiration thereof, that they thought in the chanceable hitting upon any such verses great foretokens of their following fortunes were placed. Whereupon grew the word of *sortes Virgilianae*[5] when, by sudden opening Virgil's book, they lighted upon any verse of his making: whereof the histories of the emperors' lives are full, as of Albinus, the governor of our island, who in his childhood met with this verse, *"Arma amens capio nec sat rationis in armis";*[6] and in his age performed it: which, although it were a very vain and godless superstition, as also it was to think that spirits were commanded by such verses — whereupon this word charms, derived of *carmina,*[7] cometh — so yet serveth it to show the great reverence those wits were held in. And altogether not without ground, since both the Oracles of Delphos and Sibylla's prophecies were wholly delivered in verses. For that same exquisite observing of number and measure in words, and that high flying liberty of conceit proper to the poet, did seem to have some divine force in it.

And may not I presume a little further, to show the reasonableness of this word *vates,* and say that the holy David's Psalms are a divine poem? If I do, I shall not do it without the testimony of great learned men, both ancient and modern. But even the name Psalms will speak for me, which, being interpreted, is nothing but "songs"; then that it is fully written in meter, as all learned Hebricians agree, although the rules be not yet

---

[3] The myth of Gyges' ring appears in *Republic,* Book II, and other myths appear in other dialogues; Plato also occasionally writes prose that modulates into dithyrambic verse, as in the *Ion* and the *Phaedrus.*

[4] Each of the nine books of Herodotus's *History* is titled with the name of one of the Muses.

[5] The Virgilian lots: a method of fortune-telling using a random passage from the *Aeneid.*

[6] "Insane, I seize my weapons; there's no sense in weapons. . . ." *Aeneid* 2:314.

[7] Songs.

fully found; lastly and principally, his handling his prophecy, which is merely poetical. For what else is the awaking his musical instruments, the often and free changing of persons, his notable *prosopopeias,*[8] when he maketh you, as it were, see God coming in his majesty, his telling of the beasts' joyfulness, and hills' leaping, but a heavenly poesy, wherein almost he showeth himself a passionate lover of that unspeakable and everlasting beauty to be seen by the eyes of the mind, only cleared by faith? But truly now having named him, I fear me I seem to profane that holy name, applying it to poetry, which is among us thrown down to so ridiculous an estimation. But they that with quiet judgments will look a little deeper into it, shall find the end and working of it such, as, being rightly applied, deserveth not to be scourged out of the church of God.

But now, let us see how the Greeks named it, and how they deemed of it. The Greeks called him a "poet" which name hath, as the most excellent, gone through other languages. It cometh of this word *poiein,* which is "to make": wherein, I know not whether by luck or wisdom, we Englishmen have met with the Greeks in calling him a *maker:* which name, how high and incomparable a title it is, I had rather were known by marking the scope of other sciences than by my partial allegation.

There is no art delivered to mankind that hath not the works of nature for his principal object, without which they could not consist, and on which they so depend, as they become actors and players, as it were, of what nature will have set forth. So doth the astronomer look upon the stars, and, by that he seeth, setteth down what order nature hath taken therein. So do the geometrician and arithmetician in their diverse sorts of quantities. So doth the musician in times tell you which by nature agree, which not. The natural philosopher thereon hath his name, and the moral philosopher standeth upon the natural virtues, vices, and passions of man; and "follow nature" (saith he) "therein, and thou shalt not err." The lawyer saith what men have determined; the historian what men have done. The grammarian speaketh only of the rules of speech; and the

[8]Personifications.

rhetorician and logician, considering what in nature will soonest prove and persuade, thereon give artificial rules, which still are compassed within the circle of a question according to the proposed matter. The physician weigheth the nature of a man's body, and the nature of things helpful or hurtful unto it. And the metaphysic, though it be in the second and abstract notions, and therefore be counted supernatural, yet doth he indeed build upon the depth of nature. Only the poet, disdaining to be tied to any such subjection, lifted up with the vigor of his own invention, doth grow in effect another nature, in making things either better than nature bringeth forth, or, quite anew, forms such as never were in nature, as the Heroes, Demigods, Cyclopes, Chimeras, Furies, and such like: so as he goeth hand in hand with nature, not enclosed within the narrow warrant of her gifts, but freely ranging only within the zodiac of his own wit.

Nature never set forth the earth in so rich tapestry as divers poets have done — neither with pleasant rivers, fruitful trees, sweet-smelling flowers, nor whatsoever else may make the too much loved earth more lovely. Her world is brazen, the poets only deliver a golden. But let those things alone, and go to man — for whom as the other things are, so it seemeth in him her uttermost cunning is employed — and know whether she have brought forth so true a lover as Theagenes, so constant a friend as Pylades, so valiant a man as Orlando, so right a prince as Xenophon's Cyrus, so excellent a man every way as Virgil's Aeneas. Neither let this be jestingly conceived, because the works of the one be essential, the other in imitation or fiction; for any understanding knoweth the skill of the artificer standeth in that idea or foreconceit of the work, and not in the work itself. And that the poet hath that idea is manifest, by delivering them forth in such excellency as he hath imagined them. Which delivering forth also is not wholly imaginative, as we are wont to say by them that build castles in the air: but so far substantially it worketh, not only to make a Cyrus, which had been but a particular excellency, as nature might have done, but to bestow a Cyrus upon the world, to make many Cyruses, if they will learn aright why and how that maker made him.

Neither let it be deemed too saucy a comparison to balance the highest point of man's wit with the efficacy of nature; but rather give right honor to the heavenly Maker of that maker, who, having made man to his own likeness, set him beyond and over all the works of that second nature: which in nothing he showeth so much as in poetry, when with the force of a divine breath he bringeth things forth far surpassing her doings, with no small argument to the incredulous of that first accursed fall of Adam, since our erected wit maketh us know what perfection is, and yet our infected will keepeth us from reaching unto it. But these arguments will by few be understood, and by fewer granted. Thus much (I hope) will be given me, that the Greeks with some probability of reason gave him the name above all names of learning. Now let us go to a more ordinary opening of him, that the truth may be more palpable: and so I hope, though we get not so unmatched a praise as the etymology of his names will grant, yet his very description, which no man will deny, shall not justly be barred from a principal commendation.

Poesy therefore is an art of imitation, for so Aristotle termeth it in his word *mimesis*,[9] that is to say, a representing, counterfeiting, or figuring forth — to speak metaphorically, a speaking picture; with this end, to teach and delight.[10] Of this have been three several kinds. The chief, both in antiquity and excellency, were they that did imitate the inconceivable excellencies of God. Such were David in his Psalms; Solomon in his Song of Songs, in his Ecclesiastes, and Proverbs; Moses and Deborah in their Hymns; and the writer of Job, which, beside other, the learned Emanuel Tremellius and Franciscus Junius do entitle the poetical part of the Scripture. Against these none will speak that hath the Holy Ghost in due holy reverence.

In this kind, though in a full wrong divinity, were Orpheus, Amphion, Homer in his *Hymns,* and many other, both Greeks and Romans, and this poesy must be used by whosoever will follow St. James's counsel in singing psalms when they are merry, and I know is used with the fruit of comfort by some, when, in sorrowful pangs of their death-bringing sins, they find the consolation of the never-leaving goodness.

The second kind is of them that deal with matters, philosophical: either moral, as Tyrtaeus, Phocylides, and Cato; or natural, as Lucretius and Virgil's *Georgics;* or astronomical, as Manilius and Pontanus; or historical, as Lucan; which who mislike, the fault is in their judgments quite out of taste, and not in the sweet food of sweetly uttered knowledge. But because this second sort is wrapped within the fold of the proposed subject, and takes not the course of his own invention, whether they properly be poets or no let grammarians dispute; and go to the third, indeed right poets, of whom chiefly this question ariseth, betwixt whom and these second is such a kind of difference as betwixt the meaner sort of painters, who counterfeit only such faces as are set before them, and the more excellent, who, having no law but wit, bestow that in colors upon you which is fittest for the eye to see, as the constant though lamenting look of Lucretia, when she punished in herself another's fault.

Wherein he painteth not Lucretia whom he never saw, but painteth the outward beauty of such a virtue. For these third be they which most properly do imitate to teach and delight, and to imitate borrow nothing of what is, hath been, or shall be; but range, only reined with learned discretion, into the divine consideration of what may be, and should be. These be they that, as the first and most noble sort may justly be termed *vates,* so these are waited on in the excellentest languages and best understandings, with the foredescribed name of poets; for these indeed do merely make to imitate, and imitate both to delight and teach, and delight to move men to take that goodness in hand, which without delight they would fly as from a stranger, and teach, to make them know that goodness whereunto they are moved: which being the noblest scope to which ever any learning was directed, yet want there not idle tongues to bark at them. These be subdivided into sundry more special denominations. The most notable be the heroic, lyric, tragic, comic, satiric, iambic, elegiac, pastoral, and certain others, some of these being termed according to the matter they deal with, some by the sorts of verses they liked best to write

[9]Aristotle, *Poetics,* Ch. I; see p. 59.
[10]Horace, *Art of Poetry;* see p. 91.

in; for indeed the greatest part of poets have appareled their poetical inventions in that numbrous kind of writing which is called verse — indeed but appareled, verse being but an ornament and no cause to poetry, since there have been many most excellent poets that never versified, and now swarm many versifiers that need never answer to the name of poets. For Xenophon, who did imitate so excellently as to give us *effigiem iusti imperii,* "the portraiture of a just empire," under name of Cyrus (as Cicero saith of him), made therein an absolute heroical poem.[11]

So did Heliodorus in his sugared invention of that picture of love in *Theagenes and Chariclea;* and yet both these writ in prose: which I speak to show that it is not rhyming and versing that maketh a poet — no more than a long gown maketh an advocate, who though he pleaded in armor should be an advocate and no soldier.[12] But it is that feigning notable images of virtues, vices, or what else, with that delightful teaching, which must be the right describing note to know a poet by, although indeed the senate of poets hath chosen verse as their fittest raiment, meaning, as in matter they passed all in all, so in manner to go beyond them — not speaking (table talk fashion or like men in a dream) words as they chanceably fall from the mouth, but peising[13] each syllable of each word by just proportion according to the dignity of the subject.

Now therefore it shall not be amiss first to weigh this latter sort of poetry by his works, and then by his parts,[14] and, if in neither of these anatomies he be condemnable, I hope we shall obtain a more favorable sentence. This purifying of wit, this enriching of memory, enabling of judgment, and enlarging of conceit, which commonly we call learning, under what name soever it come forth, or to what immediate end soever it be directed, the final end is to lead and draw us to as high a perfection as our degenerate souls, made worse by their clayey lodgings, can be capable of.

This, according to the inclination of the man, bred many formed impressions. For some that thought this felicity principally to be gotten by knowledge and no knowledge to be so high and heavenly as acquaintance with the stars, gave themselves to astronomy; others, persuading themselves to be demigods if they knew the causes of things, became natural and supernatural philosophers; some an admirable delight drew to music; and some the certainty of demonstration to the mathematics. But all, one and other, having this scope — to know, and by knowledge to lift up the mind from the dungeon of the body to the enjoying his own divine essence. But when by the balance of experience it was found that the astronomer looking to the stars might fall into a ditch, that the inquiring philosopher might be blind in himself, and the mathematician might draw forth a straight line with a crooked heart, then, lo, did proof, the overruler of opinions, make manifest that all these are but serving sciences, which, as they have each a private end in themselves, so yet are they all directed to the highest end of the mistress-knowledge, by the Greeks called *architectonike,*[15] which stands (as I think) in the knowledge of a man's self, in the ethic and politic consideration, with the end of well doing and not of well knowing only — even as the saddler's next end is to make a good saddle, but his farther end to serve a nobler faculty, which is horsemanship; so the horseman's to soldiery, and the soldier not only to have the skill, but to perform the practice of a soldier. So that, the ending end of all earthly learning being virtuous action, those skills, that most serve to bring forth that, have a most just title to be princes over all the rest. Wherein we can show the poet's nobleness, by setting him before his other competitors, among whom as principal challengers step forth the moral philosophers, whom, me thinketh, I see coming towards me with a sullen gravity, as though they could not abide vice by daylight, rudely clothed for to witness outwardly their contempt of outward things, with books in their hands against glory, whereto they set their names, sophistically speaking against subtlety, and angry with any man in

---

[11]Sidney is praising Xenophon's *Cyropaedia,* or *Education of Cyrus.*

[12]Cf. Aristotle, *Poetics,* Ch. 9; see p. 65.

[13]Weighing, evaluating.

[14]"Works" and "parts" are, in modern English, effects and genres.

[15]In Aristotle, the controlling principle of something. For Sidney, the ultimate end of knowledge is the Greek ideal of *sophrosyne:* self-knowledge and self-mastery.

whom they see the foul fault of anger. These men casting largesse as they go of definitions, divisions, and distinctions, with a scornful interrogative do soberly ask whether it be possible to find any path so ready to lead a man to virtue as that which teacheth what virtue is — and teacheth it not only by delivering forth his very being, his causes, and effects, but also by making known his enemy, vice (which must be destroyed), and his cumbersome servant, passion (which must be mastered), by showing the generalities that containeth it, and the specialties that are derived from it; lastly, by plain setting down, how it extendeth itself out of the limits of a man's own little world to the government of families, and maintaining of public societies.

The historian scarcely giveth leisure to the moralist to say so much, but that he, laden with old mouse-eaten records, authorizing himself (for the most part) upon other histories, whose greatest authorities are built upon the notable foundation of hearsay; having much ado to accord differing writers and to pick truth out of partiality; better acquainted with a thousand years ago than with the present age, and yet better knowing how this world goeth than how his own wit runneth; curious for antiquities and inquisitive of novelties; a wonder to young folks and a tyrant in table talk, denieth, in a great chafe, that any man for teaching of virtue, and virtuous actions, is comparable to him. "I am *lux vitae, temporum magistra, vita memoriae, nuntia vetustatis,*" &c.[16]

The philosopher (saith he)

teacheth a disputative virtue, but I do an active. His virtue is excellent in the dangerless Academy of Plato, but mine showeth forth her honorable face in the battles of Marathon, Pharsalia, Poitiers, and Agincourt. He teacheth virtue by certain abstract considerations, but I only bid you follow the footing of them that have gone before you. Old-aged experience goeth beyond the fine-witted philosopher, but I give the experience of many ages. Lastly, if he make the song book, I put the learner's hand to the lute; and if he be the guide, I am the light.

Then would he allege you innumerable examples, conferring story by story, how much the wisest senators and princes have been directed by the credit of history, as Brutus, Alphonsus of Aragon, and who not, if need be? At length the long line of their disputation maketh a point in this, that the one giveth the precept, and the other the example.

Now, whom shall we find (since the question standeth for the highest form in the school of learning) to be moderator? Truly, as me seemeth, the poet; and if not a moderator, even the man that ought to carry the title from them both, and much more from all other serving sciences. Therefore compare we the poet with the historian, and with the moral philosopher; and, if he go beyond them both, no other human skill can match him. For as for the Divine, with all reverence it is ever to be excepted, not only for having his scope as far beyond any of these as eternity exceedeth a moment, but even for passing each of these in themselves.

And for the lawyer, though Jus be the daughter of justice, and justice the chief of virtues, yet because he seeketh to make men good rather *formidine poenae* than *virtutis amore,*[17] or, to say righter, doth not endeavor to make men good, but that their evil hurt not others, having no care, so he be a good citizen, how bad a man he be: therefore, as our wickedness maketh him necessary, and necessity maketh him honorable, so is he not in the deepest truth to stand in rank with these who all endeavor to take naughtiness away, and plant goodness even in the secretest cabinet of our souls. And these four are all that any way deal in that consideration of men's manners, which being the supreme knowledge, they that best breed it deserve the best commendation.

The philosopher therefore and the historian are they which would win the goal, the one by precept, the other by example. But both, not having both, do both halt. For the philosopher, setting down with thorny argument the bare rule, is so hard of utterance, and so misty to be conceived, that one that hath no other guide but his shall wade in him till he be old before he shall find

---

[16]"The light of life, the master of the times, the life of memory, the messenger of antiquity." Cicero, *On Oratory* 2.9:36.

[17]Rather through fear of punishment than through love of virtue.

sufficient cause to be honest. For his knowledge standeth so upon the abstract and general, that happy is that man who may understand him, and more happy that can apply what he doth understand.

On the other side, the historian, wanting the precept, is so tied, not to what should be but to what is, to the particular truth of things and not to the general reason of things, that his example draweth no necessary consequence, and therefore a less fruitful doctrine.

Now doth the peerless poet perform both: for whatsoever the philosopher saith should be done, he giveth a perfect picture of it in someone by whom he presupposeth it was done; so as he coupleth the general notion with the particular example. A perfect picture I say, for he yieldeth to the powers of the mind an image of that whereof the philosopher bestoweth but a wordish description: which doth neither strike, pierce, nor possess the sight of the soul so much as that other doth.

For as in outward things, to a man that had never seen an elephant or a rhinoceros, who should tell him most exquisitely all their shapes, color, bigness, and particular marks, or of a gorgeous palace the architecture, with declaring the full beauties might well make the hearer able to repeat, as it were by rote, all he had heard, yet should never satisfy his inward conceits with being witness to itself of a true lively knowledge: but the same man, as soon as he might see those beasts well painted, or the house well in model, should straightways grow, without need of any description, to a judicial comprehending of them: so no doubt the philosopher with his learned definition — be it of virtue, vices, matters of public policy or private government — replenisheth the memory with many infallible grounds of wisdom, which, notwithstanding, lie dark before the imaginative and judging power, if they be not illuminated or figured forth by the speaking picture of poesy.

Tully[18] taketh much pains, and many times not without poetical helps, to make us know the force love of our country hath in us. Let us but hear old Anchises speaking in the midst of Troy's flames, or see Ulysses in the fullness of all Calypso's delights bewail his absence from barren and beggarly Ithaca. Anger, the Stoics say, was a short madness: let but Sophocles bring you Ajax on a stage, killing and whipping sheep and oxen, thinking them the army of Greeks, with their chieftains Agamemnon and Menelaus, and tell me if you have not a more familiar insight into anger than finding in the schoolmen his genus and difference. See whether wisdom and temperance in Ulysses and Diomedes, valor in Achilles, friendship in Nisus and Euryalus, even to an ignorant man carry not an apparent shining, and, contrarily, the remorse of conscience in Oedipus, the soon repenting pride of Agamemnon, the self-devouring cruelty in his father Atreus, the violence of ambition in the two Theban brothers, the soursweetness of revenge in Medea, and, to fall lower, the Terentian Gnatho and our Chaucer's Pandar so expressed that we now use their names to signify their trades; and finally, all virtues, vices, and passions so in their own natural seats laid to the view, that we seem not to hear of them, but clearly to see through them. But even in the most excellent determination of goodness, what philosopher's counsel can so readily direct a prince, as the feigned Cyrus in Xenophon; or a virtuous man in all fortunes, as Aeneas in Virgil; or a whole commonwealth, as the way of Sir Thomas More's *Utopia*? I say the way, because where Sir Thomas More erred, it was the fault of the man and not of the poet, for that way of patterning a commonwealth was most absolute, though he perchance hath not so absolutely performed it. For the question is, whether the feigned image of poesy or the regular instruction of philosophy hath the more force in teaching: wherein if the philosophers have more rightly showed themselves philosophers than the poets have attained to the high top of their profession, as in truth, *"mediocribus esse poetis, / Non dii, non homines, non concessere columnae"*;[19] it is, I say again, not the fault of the art, but that by few men that art can be accomplished.

Certainly, even our Saviour Christ could as well have given the moral commonplaces of uncharitableness and humbleness as the divine narration of Dives and Lazarus; or of disobedience and mercy, as that heavenly discourse of the

[18]Cicero.

[19]"But men and gods and booksellers won't put up / With second-rate poets." Horace, *Art of Poetry;* see p. 92.

- Christ used poetic parables, not philosophical instruction lost child and the gracious father; but that his through-searching wisdom knew the estate of Dives burning in hell, and of Lazarus being in Abraham's bosom, would more constantly (as it were) inhabit both the memory and judgment. Truly, for myself, meseems I see before my eyes the lost child's disdainful prodigality, turned to envy a swine's dinner: which by the learned divines are thought not historical acts, but instructing parables. For conclusion, I say the philosopher teacheth, but he teacheth obscurely, so as the learned only can understand him; that is to say, he teacheth them that are already taught. But the poet is the food for the tenderest stomachs, the poet is indeed the right popular philosopher, whereof Aesop's tales give good proof: whose pretty allegories, stealing under the formal tales of beasts, make many, more beastly than beasts, begin to hear the sound of virtue from these dumb speakers.

But now may it be alleged that, if this imagining of matters be so fit for the imagination, then must the historian needs surpass, who bringeth you images of true matters, such as indeed were done, and not such as fantastically or falsely may be suggested to have been done. Truly, Aristotle himself, in his discourse of poesy, plainly determineth this question, saying that poetry is *philosophoteron* and *spoudaioteron,* that is to say, it is more philosophical and more studiously serious than history. His reason is, because poesy dealeth with *katholou,* that is to say, with the universal consideration, and the history with *kathekaston,* the particular: "now," saith he, "the universal weighs what is fit to be said or done, either in likelihood or necessity (which the poesy considereth in his imposed names), and the particular only marks whether Alcibiades did, or suffered, this or that."[20] Thus far Aristotle: which reason of his (as all his) is most full of reason. For indeed, if the question were whether it were better to have a particular act truly or falsely set down, there is no doubt which is to be chosen, no more than whether you had rather have Vespasian's picture right as he was, or at the painter's pleasure nothing resembling. But if the question be for your own use and learning, whether it be better to have it set down as it should be, or as it was, then certainly is more doctrinable the feigned Cyrus in Xenophon than the true Cyrus in Justin, and the feigned Aeneas in Virgil than the right Aeneas in Dares Phrygius.[21]

As to a lady that desired to fashion her countenance to the best grace, a painter should more benefit her to portrait a most sweet face, writing Canidia upon it, than to paint Canidia as she was, who, Horace sweareth, was foul and ill favored.

If the poet do his part aright, he will show you in Tantalus, Atreus, and such like, nothing that is not to be shunned; in Cyrus, Aeneas, Ulysses, each thing to be followed; where the historian, bound to tell things as things were, cannot be liberal (without he will be poetical) of a perfect pattern, but, as in Alexander or Scipio himself, show doings, some to be liked, some to be misliked. And then how will you discern what to follow but by your own discretion, which you had without reading Quintus Curtius? And whereas a man may say, though in universal consideration of doctrine the poet prevaileth, yet that the history, in his saying such a thing was done, doth warrant a man more in that he shall follow.

The answer is manifest: that if he stand upon that *was* — as if he should argue, because it rained yesterday, therefore it should rain today — then indeed it hath some advantage to a gross conceit; but if he know an example only informs a conjectured likelihood, and so go by reason, the poet doth so far exceed him, as he is to frame his example to that which is most reasonable, be it in warlike, politic, or private matters; where the historian in his bare *was* hath many times that which we call fortune to overrule the best wisdom. Many times he must tell events whereof he can yield no cause: or, if he do, it must be poetical. For that a feigned example hath as much force to teach as a true example (for as for to move, it is clear, since the feigned may be tuned to the highest key of passion), let us take one example wherein a poet and a historian do concur.

[20]Aristotle, *Poetics,* Ch. 9; see p. 65.

[21]A slippage of terms characteristic of Sidney has just occurred. Aristotle's distinction between the universal and the particular has just become a distinction between the ideal and the real, which will support Sidney's defense of the moral function of poetry.

Herodotus and Justin do both testify that Zopyrus, King Darius's faithful servant, seeing his master long resisted by the rebellious Babylonians, feigned himself in extreme disgrace of his king: for verifying of which, he caused his own nose and ears to be cut off, and so flying to the Babylonians, was received, and for his known valor so far credited, that he did find means to deliver them over to Darius. Much like matter doth Livy record of Tarquinius and his son. Xenophon excellently feigneth such another stratagem performed by Abradates in Cyrus's behalf. Now would I fain know, if occasion be presented unto you to serve your prince by such an honest dissimulation, why you do not as well learn it of Xenophon's fiction as of the other's verity — and truly so much the better, as you shall save your nose by the bargain; for Abradates did not counterfeit so far. So then the best of the historian is subject to the poet; for whatsoever action, or faction, whatsoever counsel, policy, or war stratagem the historian is bound to recite, that may the poet (if he list) with his imitation make his own, beautifying it both for further teaching, and more delighting, as it pleaseth him, having all, from Dante's heaven to his hell, under the authority of his pen. Which if I be asked what poets have done so, as I might well name some, yet say I, and say again, I speak of the art, and not of the artificer.

Now, to that which commonly is attributed to the praise of histories, in respect of the notable learning is gotten by marking the success, as though therein a man should see virtue exalted and vice punished — truly that commendation is peculiar to poetry, and far off from history. For indeed poetry ever setteth virtue so out in her best colors, making Fortune her well-waiting handmaid, that one must needs be enamored of her. Well may you see Ulysses in a storm, and in other hard plights; but they are but exercises of patience and magnanimity, to make them shine the more in the near-following prosperity. And of the contrary part, if evil men come to the stage, they ever go out (as the tragedy writer answered to one that misliked the show of such persons) so manacled as they little animate folks to follow them. But the historian, being captived to the truth of a foolish world, is many times a terror from well doing, and an encouragement to unbridled wickedness.

For see we not valiant Miltiades rot in his fetters: the just Phocion and the accomplished Socrates put to death like traitors; the cruel Severus live prosperously; the excellent Severus miserably murdered; Sylla and Marius dying in their beds; Pompey and Cicero slain then, when they would have thought exile a happiness?

See we not virtuous Cato driven to kill himself, and rebel Caesar so advanced that his name yet, after 1,600 years, lasteth in the highest honor? And mark but even Caesar's own words of the forenamed Sylla (who in that only did honestly, to put down his dishonest tyranny). *Literas nescivit,*[22] as if want of learning caused him to do well. He meant it not by poetry, which, not content with earthly plagues, deviseth new punishments in hell for tyrants, nor yet by philosophy, which teacheth *Occidendos esse;*[23] but no doubt by skill in history, for that indeed can afford your Cypselus, Periander, Phalaris, Dionysius, and I know not how many more of the same kennel, that speed well enough to their abominable injustice or usurpation. I conclude, therefore, that he excelleth history, not only in furnishing the mind with knowledge, but in setting it forward to that which deserveth to be called and accounted good: which setting forward, and moving to well doing, indeed setteth the laurel crown upon the poet as victorious, not only of the historian, but over the philosopher, howsoever in teaching it may be questionable.

For suppose it be granted (that which I suppose with great reason may be denied) that the philosopher, in respect of his methodical proceeding, doth teach more perfectly than the poet, yet do I think that no man is so much *philophilosophos*[24] as to compare the philosopher, in moving, with the poet.

And that moving is of a higher degree than teaching, it may by this appear, that it is well-nigh the cause and the effect of teaching. For who will be taught, if he be not moved with desire to be taught, and what so much good doth that teaching

[22]He did not know literature.
[23]They must be put to death.
[24]A lover of philosophy.

bring forth (I speak still of moral doctrine) as that it moveth one to do that which it doth teach? For, as Aristotle saith, it is not *gnosis* but *praxis*[25] must be the fruit. And how *praxis* cannot be, without being moved to practice, it is no hard matter to consider.

The philosopher showeth you the way, he informeth you of the particularities, as well of the tediousness of the way, as of the pleasant lodging you shall have when your journey is ended, as of the many by-turnings that may divert you from your way. But this is to no man but to him that will read him, and read him with attentive studious painfulness; which constant desire whosoever hath in him, hath already passed half the hardness of the way, and therefore is beholding to the philosopher but for the other half. Nay truly, learned men have learnedly thought that where once reason hath so much over-mastered passion as that the mind hath a free desire to do well, the inward light each mind hath in itself is as good as a philosopher's book; seeing in nature we know it is well to do well, and what is well and what is evil, although not in the words of art which philosophers bestow upon us. For out of natural conceit the philosophers drew it; but to be moved to do that which we know, or to be moved with desire to know, *Hoc opus, hic labor est.*[26]

Now therein of all sciences (I speak still of human, and according to the humane conceits) is our poet the monarch. For he doth not only show the way, but giveth so sweet a prospect into the way, as will entice any man to enter into it. Nay, he doth, as if your journey should lie through a fair vineyard, at the first give you a cluster of grapes, that, full of that taste, you may long to pass further. He beginneth not with obscure definitions, which must blur the margent[27] with interpretations, and load the memory with doubtfulness; but he cometh to you with words set in delightful proportion, either accompanied with, or prepared for, the well-enchanting skill of music; and with a tale forsooth he cometh unto you, with a tale which holdeth children from play, and old men from the chimney corner. And, pretending no more, doth intend the winning of the mind with wickedness to virtue: even as the child is often brought to take most wholesome things by hiding them in such other as have a pleasant taste: which, if one should begin to tell them the nature of aloes or rhubarb they should receive, would sooner take their physic at their ears than at their mouth. So is it in men (most of which are childish in the best things, till they be cradled in their graves): glad they will be to hear the tales of Hercules, Achilles, Cyrus, and Aeneas; and, hearing them, must needs hear the right description of wisdom, valor, and justice; which, if they had been barely, that is to say philosophically, set out, they would swear they be brought to school again.

That imitation whereof poetry is, hath the most conveniency to nature of all other, insomuch that, as Aristotle saith, those things which in themselves are horrible, as cruel battles, unnatural monsters, are made in poetical imitation delightful. Truly, I have known men, that even with reading *Amadis de Gaule* (which God knoweth wanteth much of a perfect poesy) have found their hearts moved to the exercise of courtesy, liberality, and especially courage.

Who readeth Aeneas carrying old Anchises on his back, that wisheth not it were his fortune to perform so excellent an act? Whom do not the words of Turnus move, the tale of Turnus having planted his image in the imagination? — *"Fugientem haec terra videbit? / Usque adeone mori miserum est?"*[28] Where the philosophers, as they scorn to delight, so must they be content little to move, saving wrangling whether virtue be the chief or the only good, whether the contemplative or the active life do excel: which Plato and Boethius well knew, and therefore made Mistress Philosophy very often borrow the masking raiment of Poesy. For even those hardhearted evil men who think virtue a school name, and know no other good but *indulgere genio,*[29] and therefore despise the austere admonitions of the

---

[25]Not abstract knowledge but action.

[26]"That is the labor, that is the task." Virgil, *Aeneid* 6: 129.

[27]The margins of the page, where the notes to a text were then placed.

[28]"And shall the land see me fleeing? And after all, is death so sad a thing?" *Aeneid* 12:645–46.

[29]To indulge one's nature.

philosopher, and feel not the inward reason they stand upon, yet will be content to be delighted — which is all the good fellow poet seemeth to promise — and so steal to see the form of goodness, which seen they cannot but love ere themselves be aware, as if they took a medicine of cherries. Infinite proofs of the strange effects of his poetical invention might be alleged; only two shall serve, which are so often remembered as I think all men know them.

The one of Menenius Agrippa, who, when the whole people of Rome had resolutely divided themselves from the Senate, with apparent show of utter ruin, though he were (for that time) an excellent orator, came not among them upon trust of figurative speeches or cunning insinuations, and much less with farfetched maxims of philosophy, which (especially if they were Platonic) they must have learned geometry before they could well have conceived; but forsooth he behaves himself like a homely and familiar poet. He telleth them a tale, that there was a time when all the parts of the body made a mutinous conspiracy against the belly, which they thought devoured the fruits of each other's labor: they concluded they would let so unprofitable a spender starve. In the end, to be short (for the tale is notorious, and as notorious that it was a tale), with punishing the belly they plagued themselves. This applied by him wrought such effect in the people, as I never read that ever words brought forth but then so sudden and so good an alteration; for upon reasonable conditions a perfect reconcilement ensured. The other is of Nathan the Prophet, who, when the holy David had so far forsaken God as to confirm adultery with murder, when he was to do the tenderest office of a friend, in laying his own shame before his eyes, sent by God to call again so chosen a servant, how doth he it but by telling of a man whose beloved lamb was ungratefully taken from his bosom? — the application most divinely true, but the discourse itself feigned. Which made David (I speak of the second and instrumental cause) as in a glass to see his own filthiness, as that heavenly Psalm of Mercy well testifieth.

By these, therefore, examples and reasons, I think it may be manifest that the poet, with that same hand of delight, doth draw the mind more effectually than any other art doth: and so a conclusion not unfitly ensueth, that, as virtue is the most excellent resting place for all worldly learning to make his end of, so poetry, being the most familiar to teach it, and most princely to move towards it, in the most excellent work is the most excellent workman. But I am content not only to decipher him by his works (although works in commendation or dispraise must ever hold an high authority), but more narrowly will examine his parts: so that, as in a man, though all together may carry a presence full of majesty and beauty, perchance in some one defectious piece we may find a blemish. Now in his parts, kinds, or species (as you list to term them), it is to be noted that some poesies have coupled together two or three kinds, as tragical and comical, whereupon is risen the tragicomical. Some, in the like manner, have mingled prose and verse, as Sannazzaro and Boethius. Some have mingled matters heroical and pastoral. But that cometh all to one in this question, for, if severed they be good, the conjunction cannot be hurtful. Therefore, perchance forgetting some, and leaving some as needless to be remembered, it shall not be amiss in a word to cite the special kinds, to see what faults may be found in the right use of them.

Is it then the pastoral poem which is misliked? For perchance where the hedge is lowest they will soonest leap over. Is the poor pipe disdained, which sometime out of Melibaeus's mouth can show the misery of people under hard lords or ravening soldiers, and again, by Tityrus, what blessedness is derived to them that lie lowest from the goodness of them that sit highest; sometimes, under the pretty tales of wolves and sheep, can include the whole considerations of wrongdoing and patience; sometimes show that contention for trifles can get but a trifling victory; where perchance a man may see that even Alexander and Darius, when they strave who should be cock of this world's dunghill, the benefit they got was that the afterlivers may say, *"Haec memini et victum frustra contendere Thirsin: / Ex illo Coridon, Coridon est tempore nobis"*?[30]

[30]"I remember those things, and that conquered Thyrsis strove in vain; Since then Corydon is for us Corydon." Virgil, *Eclogues* 7:69–70.

Or is it the lamenting elegiac, which in a kind heart would move rather pity than blame, who bewails with the great philosopher Heraclitus the weakness of mankind and the wretchedness of the world; who surely is to be praised, either for compassionate accompanying just causes of lamentation, or for rightly pointing out how weak be the passions of woefulness? Is it the bitter but wholesome iambic, which rubs the galled mind, in making shame the trumpet of villainy with bold and open crying out against naughtiness? Or the satiric, who *"omne vafer vitium ridenti tangit amico"*;[31] who sportingly never leaveth until he make a man laugh at folly, and, at length ashamed, to laugh at himself, which he cannot avoid, without avoiding the folly; who, while *"circum praecordia ludit,"*[32] giveth us to feel how many headaches a passionate life bringeth us to; how, when all is done, *"est Ulubris animus si nos non deficit aequus?"*[33]

No, perchance it is the comic, whom naughty play-makers and stage-keepers have justly made odious. To the argument of abuse I will answer after. Only thus much now is to be said, that the comedy is an imitation of the common errors of our life, which he representeth in the most ridiculous and scornful sort that may be, so as it is impossible that any beholder can be content to be such a one.

Now, as in geometry the oblique must be known as well as the right, and in arithmetic the odd as well as the even, so in the actions of our life who seeth not the filthiness of evil wanteth a great foil to perceive the beauty of virtue. This doth the comedy handle so in our private and domestical matters, as with hearing it we get as it were an experience, what is to be looked for of a niggardly Demea, of a crafty Davus, of a flattering Gnatho, of a vainglorious Thraso; and not only to know what effects are to be expected, but to know who be such, by the signifying badge given them by the comedian. And little reason

hath any man to say that men learn evil by seeing it so set out; since, as I said before, there is no man living but, by the force truth hath in nature, no sooner seeth these men play their parts, but wisheth them in *pistrinum*;[34] although perchance the sack of his own faults lie so behind his back that he seeth not himself dance the same measure; whereto yet nothing can more open his eyes than to find his own actions contemptibly set forth. So that the right use of comedy will (I think) by nobody be blamed, and much less of the high and excellent tragedy, that openeth the greatest wounds, and showeth forth the ulcers that are covered with tissue; that maketh kings fear to be tyrants, and tyrants manifest their tyrannical humors; that, with stirring the affects of admiration and commiseration, teacheth the uncertainty of this world, and upon how weak foundations gilden roofs are builded; that maketh us know, *"Qui sceptra saevus duro imperio regit, / Timet timentes, metus in auctorem redit."*[35]

But how much it can move, Plutarch yieldeth a notable testimony of the abominable tyrant Alexander Pheraeus, from whose eyes a tragedy, well made and represented, drew abundance of tears, who, without all pity, had murdered infinite numbers, and some of his own blood, so as he, that was not ashamed to make matters for tragedies, yet could not resist the sweet violence of a tragedy.

And if it wrought no further good in him, it was that he, in despite of himself, withdrew himself from hearkening to that which might mollify his hardened heart. But it is not the tragedy they do mislike; for it were too absurd to cast out so excellent a representation of whatsoever is most worthy to be learned. Is it the lyric that most displeaseth, who with his tuned lyre, and well-accorded voice, giveth praise, the reward of virtue, to virtuous acts, who gives moral precepts, and natural problems, who sometimes raiseth up his voice to the height of the heavens, in singing the lauds of the immortal God? Certainly, I must confess my own barbarousness, I never heard the

[31]"The rogue touches every vice while making his friend laugh." Persius, *Satires* I:116–17.

[32]"He plays about the heartstrings." From the passage above.

[33]"Happiness is to be found, even in Ulubrae [a dead city], so long as we don't lose our sense of proportion." Horace, *Epistles* I.11:30.

[34]A treadmill for slaves.

[35]"The savage ruler who wields the sceptre with a hard hand / Fears the timid, and thus fear returns to its author." Seneca, *Oedipus*, 705–06.

old song of Percy and Douglas that I found not my heart moved more than with a trumpet; and yet is it sung but by some blind crowder, with no rougher voice than rude style; which, being so evil appareled in the dust and cobwebs of that uncivil age, what would it work, trimmed in the gorgeous eloquence of Pindar? In Hungary I have seen it the manner at all feasts, and other such meetings, to have songs of their ancestors' valor; which that right soldierlike nation think the chiefest kindlers of brave courage. The incomparable Lacedaemonians did not only carry that kind of music ever with them to the field, but even at home, as such songs were made, so were they all content to be the singers of them, when the lusty men were to tell what they did, the old men what they had done, and the young men what they would do. And where a man may say that Pindar many times praiseth highly victories of small moment, matters rather of sport than virtue; as it may be answered, it was the fault of the poet, and not of the poetry, so indeed the chief fault was in the time and custom of the Greeks, who set those toys at so high a price that Philip of Macedon reckoned a horse race won at Olympus among his three fearful felicities. But as the inimitable Pindar often did, so is that kind most capable and most fit to awake the thoughts from the sleep of idleness, to embrace honorable enterprises.

There rests the heroical, whose very name (I think) should daunt all backbiters; for by what conceit can a tongue be directed to speak evil of that which draweth with it no less champions than Achilles, Cyrus, Aeneas, Turnus, Tydeus, and Rinaldo? Who doth not only teach and move to a truth, but teacheth and moveth to the most high and excellent truth; who maketh magnanimity and justice shine throughout all misty fearfulness and foggy desires; who, if the saying of Plato and Tully be true, that who could see virtue would be wonderfully ravished with the love of her beauty — this man sets her out to make her more lovely in her holiday apparel, to the eye of any that will deign not to disdain until they understand. But if anything be already said in the defense of sweet Poetry, all concurreth to the maintaining the heroical, which is not only a kind, but the best and most accomplished kind of

poetry.[36] For as the image of each action stirreth and instructeth the mind, so the lofty image of such worthies most inflameth the mind with desire to be worthy, and informs with counsel how to be worthy. Only let Aeneas be worn in the tablet of your memory, how he governeth himself in the ruin of his country, in the preserving his old father, and carrying away his religious ceremonies, in obeying the god's commandment to leave Dido, though not only all passionate kindness, but even the human consideration of virtuous gratefulness, would have craved other of him; how in storms, how in sports, how in war, how in peace, how a fugitive, how victorious, how besieged, how besieging, how to strangers, how to allies, how to enemies, how to his own; lastly, how in his inward self, and how in his outward government, and I think, in a mind not prejudiced with a prejudicating humor, he will be found in excellency fruitful, yea, even as Horace saith, *"melius Chrysippo et Crantore."*[37]

But truly I imagine it falleth out with these poet-whippers, as with some good women, who often are sick, but in faith they cannot tell where. So the name of poetry is odious to them, but neither his cause nor effects, neither the sum that contains him nor the particularities descending from him, give any fast handle to their carping dispraise.

Since then poetry is of all human learning the most ancient and of most fatherly antiquity, as from whence other learnings have taken their beginnings; since it is so universal that no learned nation doth despise it, nor no barbarous nation is without it; since both Roman and Greek gave divine names unto it, the one of *prophesying,* the other of *making,* and that indeed that name of *making* is fit for him, considering that whereas other arts retain themselves within their subject, and receive, as it were, their being from it, the poet only bringeth his own stuff, and doth not

---

[36]It was characteristic of Renaissance criticism to favor epic over tragedy — unlike Aristotle, who in *Poetics,* Ch. 26, had favored the concise tragedy over the full-blown epic.

[37]"Better than Chrysippus and Crantor." Horace, *Epistles* I.2:4. Horace claims that Homer teaches virtue better than the above-mentioned two philosophers.

learn a conceit out of a matter, but maketh matter for a conceit; since neither his description nor his end containeth any evil, the thing described cannot be evil; since his effects be so good as to teach goodness and to delight the learners; since therein (namely in moral doctrine, the chief of all knowledges) he doth not only far pass the historian, but, for instructing, is well-nigh comparable to the philosopher, and, for moving, leaves him behind him; since the Holy Scripture (wherein there is no uncleanness) hath whole parts in it poetical, and that even our Saviour Christ vouchsafed to use the flowers of it; since all his kinds are not only in their united forms but in their severed dissections fully commendable; I think (and think I think rightly) the laurel crown appointed for triumphing captains doth worthily (of all other learnings) honor the poet's triumph. But because we have ears as well as tongues, and that the lightest reasons that may be will seem to weigh greatly, if nothing be put in the counter-balance, let us hear, and, as well as we can, ponder, what objections may be made against this art, which may be worthy either of yielding or answering.

First, truly I note not only in these *myso-mousoi*, "poet-haters," but in all that kind of people who seek a praise by dispraising others, that they do prodigally spend a great many wandering words in quips and scoffs, carping and taunting at each thing, which, by stirring the spleen, may stay the brain from a thorough beholding the worthiness of the subject.

Those kind of objections, as they are full of very idle easiness, since there is nothing of so sacred a majesty but that an itching tongue may rub itself upon it, so deserve they no other answer, but, instead of laughing at the jest, to laugh at the jester. We know a playing wit can praise the discretion of an ass, the comfortableness of being in debt, and the jolly commodity of being sick of the plague. So of the contrary side, if we will turn Ovid's verse, *"Ut lateat virtus proximitate mali,"* that "good lie hid in nearness of the evil," Agrippa will be as merry in showing the vanity of science as Erasmus was in commending of folly. Neither shall any man or matter escape some touch of these smiling railers. But for Erasmus and Agrippa, they had another foundation than the superficial part would promise.

Marry, these other pleasant faultfinders, who will correct the verb before they understand the noun, and confute others' knowledge before they confirm their own, I would have them only remember that scoffing cometh not of wisdom; so as the best title in true English they get with their merriments is to be called good fools, for so have our grave forefathers ever termed that humorous kind of jesters. But that which giveth greatest scope to their scorning humors is rhyming and versing. It is already said (and, as I think truly said) it is not rhyming and versing that maketh poesy. One may be a poet without versing, and a versifier without poetry. But yet presuppose it were inseparable (as indeed it seemeth Scaliger judgeth) truly it were an inseparable commendation.[38] For if *oratio* next to *ratio*, "speech" next to "reason," be the greatest gift bestowed upon mortality, that cannot be praiseless which doth most polish that blessing of speech; which considers each word, not only (as a man may say) by his forcible quality, but by his best measured quantity, carrying even in themselves a harmony (without, perchance, number, measure, order, proportion be in our time grown odious). But lay aside the just praise it hath, by being the only fit speech for music (music, I say, the most divine striker of the senses), thus much is undoubtedly true, that if reading be foolish without remembering, memory being the only treasurer of knowledge, those words which are fittest for memory are likewise most convenient for knowledge.

Now, that verse far exceedeth prose in the knitting up of the memory, the reason is manifest — the words (besides their delight, which hath a great affinity to memory) being so set as one word cannot be lost but the whole work fails; which accuseth itself, calleth the remembrance back to itself, and so most strongly confirmeth it. Besides, one word so, as it were, begetting another, as, be it in rhyme or measured verse, by the former a man shall have a near guess to the follower: lastly, even they that have taught the art of memory have showed nothing so apt for it as a certain room divided into many places well and

---

[38]In his *Poetics,* Julius Caesar Scaliger claimed that what the poet made was verses; Aristotle identified the poet's primary product as the imitation of a human action.

AN APOLOGY FOR POETRY   **149**

thoroughly known. Now, that hath the verse in effect perfectly, every word having his natural seat, which seat must needs make the words remembered. But what needeth more in a thing so known to all men? Who is it that ever was a scholar that doth not carry away some verses of Virgil, Horace, or Cato, which in his youth he learned, and even to his old age serve him for hourly lessons? But the fitness it hath for memory is notably proved by all delivery of arts: wherein for the most part, from grammar to logic, mathematic, physic, and the rest, the rules chiefly necessary to be borne away are compiled in verses. So that, verse being in itself sweet and orderly, and being best for memory, the only handle of knowledge, it must be in jest that any man can speak against it. Now then go we to the most important imputations laid to the poor poets. For aught I can yet learn, they are these. First, that there being many other more fruitful knowledges, a man might better spend his time in them than in this. Secondly, that it is the mother of lies. Thirdly, that it is the nurse of abuse, infecting us with many pestilent desires, with a siren's sweetness drawing the mind to the serpent's tale of sinful fancy — and herein, especially, comedies give the largest field to ear (as Chaucer saith) — how both in other nations and in ours, before poets did soften us, we were full of courage, given to martial exercises, the pillars of manlike liberty, and not lulled asleep in shady idleness with poets' pastimes. And lastly, and chiefly, they cry out with an open mouth, as if they outshot Robin Hood, that Plato banished them out of his commonwealth.[39] Truly, this is much, if there be much truth in it. First, to the first, that a man might better spend his time is a reason indeed: but it doth (as they say) but *petere principium*:[40] for if it be, as I affirm, that no learning is so good as that which teacheth and moveth to virtue, and that none can both teach and move thereto so much as poetry, then is the conclusion manifest that ink and paper cannot be to a more profitable purpose employed. And certainly, though a man should grant their first assumption, it should follow

[39]Plato, *Republic,* see pp. 36–38.
[40]To beg the question — assume what one needs to prove.

(methinks) very unwillingly, that good is not good because better is better. But I still and utterly deny that there is sprung out of earth a more fruitful knowledge. To the second therefore, that they should be the principal liars, I answer paradoxically, but truly, I think truly, that of all writers under the sun the poet is the least liar, and, though he would, as a poet can scarcely be a liar. The astronomer, with his cousin the geometrician, can hardly escape, when they take upon them to measure the height of the stars.

How often, think you, do the physicians lie, when they aver things good for sicknesses, which afterwards send Charon a great number of souls drowned in a potion before they come to his ferry? And no less of the rest, which take upon them to affirm. Now, for the poet, he nothing affirms, and therefore never lieth. For, as I take it, to lie is to affirm that to be true which is false; so as the other artists, and especially the historian, affirming many things, can, in the cloudy knowledge of mankind, hardly escape from many lies. But the poet (as I said before) never affirmeth. The poet never maketh any circles about your imagination, to conjure you to believe for true what he writes. He citeth not authorities of other histories, but even for his entry calleth the sweet Muses to inspire into him a good invention; in truth, no laboring to tell you what is, or is not, but what should or should not be. And therefore, though he recount things not true, yet because he telleth them not for true, he lieth not — without we will say that Nathan lied in his speech, before alleged, to David; which as a wicked man durst scarce say, so think I none so simple would say that Aesop lied in the tales of his beasts: for who thinks that Aesop writ it for actually true were well worthy to have his name chronicled among the beasts he writeth of.

What child is there that, coming to a play, and seeing *Thebes* written in great letters upon an old door, doth believe that it is Thebes? If then a man can arrive, at that child's age, to know that the poets' persons and doings are but pictures what should be, and not stories what have been, they will never give the lie to things not affirmatively but allegorically and figuratively written. And therefore, as in history, looking for truth, they go away full fraught with falsehood, so in poesy, looking for fiction, they shall use the narration but as an imaginative ground plot of a profitable invention.

But hereto is replied, that the poets give names to men they write of, which argueth a conceit of an actual truth, and so, not being true, proves a falsehood. And doth the lawyer lie then, when under the names of John a Stile and John a Noakes he puts his case? But that is easily answered. Their naming of men is but to make their picture the more lively, and not to build any history; painting men, they cannot leave men nameless. We see we cannot play at chess but that we must give names to our chessmen; and yet, methinks, he were a very partial champion of truth that would say we lied for giving a piece of wood the reverend title of a bishop. The poet nameth Cyrus or Aeneas no other way than to show what men of their fames, fortunes, and estates should do.

Their third is, how much it abuseth men's wit, training it to wanton sinfulness and lustful love: for indeed that is the principal, if not the only, abuse I can hear alleged. They say the comedies rather teach than reprehend amorous conceits. They say the lyric is larded with passionate sonnets, the elegiac weeps the want of his mistress, and that even to the heroical Cupid hath ambitiously climbed. Alas, Love, I would thou couldst as well defend thyself as thou canst offend others. I would those on whom thou dost attend could either put thee away, or yield good reason why they keep thee. But grant love of beauty to be a beastly fault (although it be very hard, since only man, and no beast, hath that gift to discern beauty); grant that lovely name of Love to deserve all hateful reproaches (although even some of my masters the philosophers spent a good deal of their lamp-oil in setting forth the excellency of it); grant, I say, whatsoever they will have granted; that not only love, but lust, but vanity, but (if they list) scurrility, possesseth many leaves of the poets' books: yet think I, when this is granted, they will find their sentence may with good manners put the last words foremost, and not say that poetry abuseth man's wit, but that man's wit abuseth poetry.

For I will not deny but that man's wit may make poesy, which should be *eikastike,* which

some learned have defined, "figuring forth good things," to be *phantastike,* which doth, contrariwise, infect the fancy with unworthy objects, as the painter, that should give to the eye either some excellent perspective, or some fine picture, fit for building or fortification, or containing in it some notable example, as Abraham sacrificing his son Isaac, Judith killing Holofernes, David fighting with Goliath, may leave those, and please an ill-pleased eye with wanton shows of better hidden matters. But what, shall the abuse of a thing make the right use odious? Nay truly, though I yield that poesy may not only be abused, but that being abused, by the reason of his sweet charming force, it can do more hurt than any other army of words, yet shall it be so far from concluding that the abuse should give reproach to the abused, that contrariwise it is a good reason, that whatsoever, being abused, doth most harm, being rightly used (and upon the right use each thing conceiveth his title), doth most good.

Do we not see the skill of physic (the best rampire[41] to our often-assaulted bodies), being abused, teach poison, the most violent destroyer? Doth not knowledge of law, whose end is to even and right all things, being abused, grow the crooked fosterer of horrible injuries? Doth not (to go to the highest) God's word abused breed heresy, and his name abused become blasphemy? Truly, a needle cannot do much hurt, and as truly (with leave of ladies be it spoken) it cannot do much good. With a sword thou mayest kill thy father, and with a sword thou mayest defend thy prince and country. So that, as in their calling poets the fathers of lies they say nothing, so in this their argument of abuse they prove the commendation.

They allege herewith, that before poets began to be in price our nation hath set their heart's delight upon action, and not upon imagination, rather doing things worthy to be written, than writing things fit to be done. What that beforetime was, I think scarcely Sphinx can tell, since no memory is so ancient that hath the precedence of poetry. And certain it is that, in our plainest homeliness, yet never was the Albion nation without poetry. Marry, this argument, though it be leveled against poetry, yet is it indeed a chainshot against

[41]Rampart, defense.

all learning, or bookishness, as they commonly term it. Of such mind were certain Goths, of whom it is written that, having in the spoil of a famous city taken a fair library, one hangman, belike, fit to execute the fruits of their wits, who had murdered a great number of bodies, would have set fire to it. "No," said another very gravely, "take heed what you do, for while they are busy about these toys, we shall with more leisure conquer their countries."

⸱ This indeed is the ordinary doctrine of ignorance, and many words sometimes I have heard spent in it: but because this reason is generally against all learning, as well as poetry, or rather, all learning but poetry; because it were too large a digression to handle, or at least too superfluous (since it is manifest that all government of action is to be gotten by knowledge, and knowledge best by gathering many knowledges, which is reading), I only, with Horace, to him that is of that opinion, *"iubeo stultum esse libenter"*;[42] for as for poetry itself, it is the freest from this objection. For poetry is the companion of the camps.

I dare undertake, Orlando Furioso, or honest King Arthur, will never displease a soldier: but the quiddity of *ens* and *prima materia*[43] will hardly agree with a corselet. And therefore, as I said in the beginning, even Turks and Tartars are delighted with poets. Homer, a Greek, flourished before Greece flourished. And if to a slight conjecture a conjecture may be opposed, truly it may seem, that, as by him their learned men took almost their first light of knowledge, so their active men received their first motions of courage. Only Alexander's example may serve, who by Plutarch is accounted of such virtue, that fortune was not his guide but his footstool; whose acts speak for him, though Plutarch did not — indeed the Phoenix of warlike princes. This Alexander left his schoolmaster, living Aristotle, behind him, but took dead Homer with him. He put the philosopher Callisthenes to death for his seeming philosophical, indeed mutinous, stubbornness, but the chief thing he ever was heard to

wish for was that Homer had been alive. He well found he received more bravery of mind by the pattern of Achilles than by hearing the definition of fortitude: and therefore, if Cato misliked Fulvius for carrying Ennius with him to the field, it may be answered that, if Cato misliked it, the noble Fulvius liked it, or else he had not done it: for it was not the excellent Cato Uticensis (whose authority I would much more have reverenced), but it was the former, in truth a bitter punisher of faults, but else a man that had never well sacrificed to the Graces. He misliked and cried out upon all Greek learning, and yet, being eighty years old, began to learn it, belike fearing that Pluto understood not Latin. Indeed, the Roman laws allowed no person to be carried to the wars but he that was in the soldier's roll, and therefore, though Cato misliked his unmustered persons, he misliked not his work. And if he had, Scipio Nasica, judged by common consent the best Roman, loved him. Both the other Scipio brothers, who had by their virtues no less surnames than of Asia and Afric, so loved him that they caused his body to be buried in their sepulcher. So as Cato's authority being but against his person, and that answered with so far greater than himself, is herein of no validity. But now indeed my burden is great; now Plato's name is laid upon me, whom, I must confess, of all philosophers I have ever esteemed most worthy of reverence, and with great reason, since of all philosophers he is the most poetical. Yet if he will defile the fountain out of which his flowing streams have proceeded, let us boldly examine with what reasons he did it. First truly, a man might maliciously object that Plato, being a philosopher, was a natural enemy of poets. For indeed, after the philosophers had picked out of the sweet mysteries of poetry the right discerning true points of knowledge, they forthwith, putting it in method, and making a school art of that which the poets did only teach by a divine delightfulness, beginning to spurn at their guides, like ungrateful 'prentices, were not content to set up shops for themselves, but sought by all means to discredit their masters; which by the force of delight being barred them, the less they could overthrow them, the more they hated them. For indeed, they found for Homer seven cities strove who should have him for their

---

[42]"I ask him to be a fool as much as he likes." Horace, *Satires* I.1:63.
[43]The whatness of being and primal matter. Sidney uses scholastic terms here.

citizen; where many cities banished philosophers as not fit members to live among them. For only repeating certain of Euripides' verses, many Athenians had their lives saved of the Syracusians, when the Athenians themselves thought many philosophers unworthy to live.

Certain poets, as Simonides and Pindarus, had so prevailed with Hiero the First, that of a tyrant they made him a just king; where Plato could do so little with Dionysius, that he himself of a philosopher was made a slave. But who should do thus, I confess, should require the objections made against poets with like cavillation against philosophers; as likewise one should do that should bid one read *Phaedrus* or *Symposium* in Plato, or the discourse of love in Plutarch, and see whether any poet do authorize abominable filthiness, as they do. Again, a man might ask out of what commonwealth Plato did banish them. In sooth, thence where he himself alloweth community of women. So as belike this banishment grew not for effeminate wantonness, since little should poetical sonnets be hurtful when a man might have what woman he listed. But I honor philosophical instructions, and bless the wits which bred them: so as they be not abused, which is likewise stretched to poetry.

St. Paul himself, who yet, for the credit of poets, allegeth twice two poets, and one of them by the name of a prophet, setteth a watchword upon philosophy — indeed upon the abuse. So doth Plato upon the abuse, not upon poetry. Plato found fault that the poets of his time filled the world with wrong opinions of the gods, making light tales of that unspotted essence, and therefore would not have the youth depraved with such opinions. Herein may much be said; let this suffice: the poets did not induce such opinions, but did imitate those opinions already induced. For all the Greek stories can well testify that the very religion of that time stood upon many and many-fashioned gods, not taught so by the poets, but followed according to their nature of imitation. Who list may read in Plutarch the discourses of Isis and Osiris, of the cause why oracles ceased, of the divine providence, and see whether the theology of that nation stood not upon such dreams which the poets indeed superstitiously observed, and truly (since they had not the light

of Christ) did much better in it than the philosophers, who, shaking off superstition, brought in atheism. Plato therefore (whose authority I had much rather justly construe than unjustly resist) meant not in general of poets, in those words of which Julius Scaliger saith, *"Qua authoritate barbari quidam atque hispidi abuti velint ad poetas e republica exigendos"*;[44] but only meant to drive out those wrong opinions of the Deity (whereof now, without further law, Christianity hath taken away all the hurtful belief), perchance (as he thought) nourished by the then esteemed poets. And a man need go no further than to Plato himself to know his meaning: who, in his dialogue called *Ion,* giveth high and rightly divine commendation to poetry. So as Plato, banishing the abuse, not the thing, not banishing it, but giving due honor unto it, shall be our patron and not our adversary. For indeed I had much rather (since truly I may do it) show their mistaking of Plato (under whose lion's skin they would make an asslike braying against poesy) than go about to overthrow his authority; whom, the wiser a man is, the more just cause he shall find to have in admiration; especially since he attributeth unto poesy more than myself do, namely, to be a very inspiring of a divine force, far above man's wit, as in the afore-named dialogue is apparent.

Of the other side, who would show the honors have been by the best sort of judgments granted them, a whole sea of examples would present themselves: Alexanders, Caesars, Scipios, all favorers of poets; Laelius, called the Roman Socrates, himself a poet, so as part of *Heautontimorumenos*[45] in Terence was supposed to be made by him, and even the Greek Socrates, whom Apollo confirmed to be the only wise man, is said to have spent part of his old time in putting Aesop's fables into verses. And therefore, full evil should it become his scholar Plato to put such words in his master's mouth against poets. But what need more? Aristotle writes the *Art of Poesy:* and why, if it should not be written? Plutarch teacheth the use to be gathered of them, and how, if they should not be read? And who reads Plutarch's either history or philosophy,

[44]"Barbarous and rude men would abuse this authority to drive poets out of the republic." Scaliger, *Poetics* I:2.
[45]*The Self-Tormentor.*

shall find he trimmeth both their garments with guards of poesy. But I list not to defend poesy with the help of her underling historiography. Let it suffice that it is a fit soil for praise to dwell upon; and what dispraise may set upon it, is either easily overcome, or transformed into just commendation. So that, since the excellencies of it may be so easily and so justly confirmed, and the low-creeping objections so soon trodden down; it not being an art of lies, but of true doctrine; not of effeminateness, but of notable stirring of courage; not of abusing man's wit, but of strengthening man's wit; not banished, but honored by Plato; let us rather plant more laurels for to engarland our poets' heads (which honor of being laureate, as besides them only triumphant captains wear, is a sufficient authority to show the price they ought to be had in) than suffer the ill-favoring breath of such wrongspeakers once to blow upon the clear springs of poesy.

But since I have run so long a career in this matter, methinks, before I give my pen a full stop, it shall be but a little more lost time to inquire why England (the mother of excellent minds) should be grown so hard a stepmother to poets, who certainly in wit ought to pass all other, since all only proceedeth from their wit, being indeed makers of themselves, not takers of others. How can I but exclaim, *"Musa, mihi causas memora, quo numine laeso!"*[46] Sweet Poesy, that hath anciently had kings, emperors, senators, great captains, such as, besides a thousand others, David, Adrian, Sophocles, Germanicus, not only to favor poets, but to be poets; and of our nearer times can present for her patrons a Robert, king of Sicily, the great King Francis of France, King James of Scotland; such cardinals as Bembus and Bibbiena: such famous preachers and teachers as Beza and Melancthon; so learned philosophers as Fracastorius and Scaliger; so great orators as Pontanus and Muretus; so piercing wits as George Buchanan; so grave counselors as, besides many, but before all, that Hospital of France, than whom (I think) that realm never brought forth a more accomplished judgment, more firmly builded upon virtue — I say, these, with numbers of others, not only to read others' poesies, but to poetize for others' reading — that poesy, thus embraced in all other places, should only find in our time a hard welcome in England, I think the very earth lamenteth it, and therefore decketh our soil with fewer laurels than it was accustomed. For heretofore poets have in England also flourished, and, which is to be noted, even in those times when the trumpet of Mars did sound loudest. And now that an overfaint quietness should seem to strew the house for poets, they are almost in as good reputation as the mountebanks at Venice. Truly even that, as of the one side it giveth great praise to poesy, which like Venus (but to better purpose) hath rather be troubled in the net with Mars than enjoy the homely quiet of Vulcan; so serves it for a piece of a reason why they are less grateful to idle England, which now can scarce endure the pain of a pen. Upon this necessarily followeth, that base men with servile wits undertake it, who think it enough if they can be rewarded of the printer. And so as Epaminondas is said, with the honor of his virtue, to have made an office, by his exercising it, which before was contemptible, to become highly respected, so these, no more but setting their names to it, by their own disgracefulness disgrace the most graceful poesy. For now, as if all the Muses were got with child, to bring forth bastard poets, without any commission they do post over the banks of Helicon, till they make the readers more weary than posthorses, while, in the meantime, they, *"queis meliore luto finxit praecordia Titan,"*[47] are better content to suppress the outflowing of their wit, than, by publishing them, to be accounted knights of the same order. But I that, before ever I durst aspire unto the dignity, am admitted into the company of the paper-blurrers, do find the very true cause of our wanting estimation is want of desert, taking upon us to be poets in despite of Pallas. Now, wherein we want desert were a thankworthy labor to express: but if I knew, I should have mended myself. But I, as I never desired the title, so have I neglected the means to come by it. Only, overmastered by some thoughts, I yielded an inky tribute unto them. Marry, they that

[46]"Tell me the reason, Muse: what was the injury to her divinity?" Virgil, *Aeneid* I:8.

[47]"Whom the Titan has formed out of finer clay." Juvenal, *Satires* 14:35.

delight in poesy itself should seek to know what they do, and how they do, and, especially, look themselves in an unflattering glass of reason, if they be inclinable unto it. For poesy must not be drawn by the ears; it must be gently led, or rather it must lead; which was partly the cause that made the ancient-learned affirm it was a divine gift, and no human skill; since all other knowledges lie ready for any that hath strength of wit; a poet no industry can make, if his own genius be not carried unto it; and therefore is it an old proverb, *Orator fit, poeta nascitur*.[48] Yet confess I always that as the fertilest ground must be manured, so must the highest-flying wit have a Daedalus to guide him. That Daedalus, they say, both in this and in other, hath three wings to bear itself up into the air of due commendation: that is, art, imitation, and exercise. But these, neither artificial rules nor imitative patterns, we much cumber ourselves withal. Exercise indeed we do, but that very forebackwardly: for where we should exercise to know, we exercise as having known: and so is our brain delivered of much matter which never was begotten by knowledge. For, there being two principal parts — matter to be expressed by words and words to express the matter — in neither we use art or imitation rightly. Our matter is *quodlibet*[49] indeed, though wrongly performing Ovid's verse, *"Quicquid conabar dicere, versus erat"*:[50] never marshaling it into an assured rank, that almost the readers cannot tell where to find themselves.

Chaucer, undoubtedly, did excellently in his *Troilus and Cressida;* of whom, truly, I know not whether to marvel more, either that he in that misty time could see so clearly, or that we in this clear age walk so stumblingly after him. Yet had he great wants, fit to be forgiven in so reverent antiquity. I account the *Mirror of Magistrates* meetly furnished of beautiful parts, and in the Earl of Surrey's lyrics many things tasting of a noble birth, and worthy of a noble mind. The *Shepherd's Calendar* hath much poetry in his eclogues, indeed worthy the reading, if I be not deceived. That same framing of his style to an old rustic language I dare not allow, since neither Theocritus in Greek, Virgil in Latin, nor Sannazzaro in Italian did affect it. Besides these, do I not remember to have seen but few (to speak boldly) printed, that have poetical sinews in them: for proof whereof, let but most of the verses be put in prose, and then ask the meaning; and it will be found that one verse did but beget another, without ordering at the first what should be at the last; which becomes a confused mass of words, with a tingling sound of rhyme, barely accompanied with reason.

Our tragedies and comedies (not without cause cried out against), observing rules neither of honest civility nor of skillful poetry, excepting *Gorboduc* (again, I say, of those that I have seen), which notwithstanding, as it is full of stately speeches and well-sounding phrases, climbing to the height of Seneca's style, and as full of notable morality, which it doth most delightfully teach, and so obtain the very end of poesy, yet in truth it is very defectious in the circumstances, which grieveth me, because it might not remain as an exact model of all tragedies. For it is faulty both in place and time, the two necessary companions of all corporal actions.[51] For where the stage should always represent but one place, and the uttermost time presupposed in it should be, both by Aristotle's precept and common reason, but one day, there is both many days, and many places, inartificially[52] imagined. But if it be so in *Gorboduc,* how much more in all the rest, where you shall have Asia of the one side, and Afric of the other, and so many other underkingdoms, that the player, when he cometh in, must ever begin with telling where he is, or else the tale will not be conceived? Now ye shall have three ladies walk to gather flowers and then we must believe the stage to be a garden. By and by we hear news of shipwreck in the same place, and then we are to blame if we accept it not for a rock.

Upon the back of that comes out a hideous monster, with fire and smoke, and then the miserable beholders are bound to take it for a cave. While in the meantime two armies fly in, represented with four swords and bucklers, and

[48]The orator is made; the poet is born.
[49]An impromptu performance.
[50]"Whatever I tried to say was verse." Ovid, *Tristia* IV. 10:26.

[51]*Gorboduc* fails to satisfy the unities of place and time, which Sidney ascribes to Aristotle.
[52]Unartistically.

then what hard heart will not receive it for a pitched field? Now, of time they are much more liberal, for ordinary it is that two young princes fall in love. After many traverses, she is got with child, delivered of a fair boy; he is lost, groweth a man, falls in love, and is ready to get another child; and all this in two hours' space: which, how absurd it is in sense, even sense may imagine, and art hath taught, and all ancient examples justified, and, at this day, the ordinary players in Italy will not err in. Yet will some bring in an example of *Eunuchus*[53] in Terence, that containeth matter of two days, yet far short of twenty years. True it is, and so was it to be played in two days, and so fitted to the time it set forth. And though Plautus hath in one place done amiss, let us hit with him, and not miss with him. But they will say, How then shall we set forth a story, which containeth both many places and many times? And do they not know that a tragedy is tied to the laws of poesy, and not of history; not bound to follow the story, but, having liberty, either to feign a quite new matter, or to frame the history to the most tragical conveniency? Again, many things may be told which cannot be showed, if they know the difference betwixt reporting and representing. As, for example, I may speak (though I am here) of Peru, and in speech digress from that to the description of Calicut; but in action I cannot represent it without Pacolet's horse. And so was the manner the ancients took, by some nuncius[54] to recount things done in former time or other place. Lastly, if they will represent an history, they must not (as Horace saith) begin *ab ovo*,[55] but they must come to the principal point of that one action which they will represent. By example this will be best expressed. I have a story of young Polydorus, delivered for safety's sake, with great riches, by his father Priam to Polymnestor, king of Thrace, in the Trojan war time. He, after some years, hearing the overthrow of Priam, for to make the treasure his own, murdereth the child. The body of the child is taken up by Hecuba. She, the same day, findeth a slight to be revenged most cruelly of the tyrant. Where now would one of our tragedy writers begin, but with the delivery of the child? Then should he sail over into Thrace, and so spend I know not how many years, and travel numbers of places. But where doth Euripides? Even with the finding of the body, leaving the rest to be told by the spirit of Polydorus. This need no further to be enlarged; the dullest wit may conceive it. But besides these gross absurdities, how all their plays be neither right tragedies, nor right comedies, mingling kings and clowns, not because the matter so carrieth it, but thrust in clowns by head and shoulders, to play a part in majestical matters, with neither decency nor discretion, so as neither the admiration and commiseration, nor the right sportfulness, is by their mongrel tragicomedy obtained. I know Apuleius did somewhat so, but that is a thing recounted with space of time, not represented in one moment: and I know the ancients have one or two examples of tragicomedies, as Plautus hath *Amphitrio*. But, if we mark them well, we shall find that they never, or very daintily, match hornpipes and funerals. So falleth it out that, having indeed no right comedy, in that comical part of our tragedy we have nothing but scurrility, unworthy of any chaste ears, or some extreme show of doltishness, indeed fit to lift up a loud laughter, and nothing else: where the whole tract of a comedy should be full of delight, as the tragedy should be still maintained in a well-raised admiration. But our comedians think there is no delight without laughter; which is very wrong, for though laughter may come with delight, yet cometh it not of delight, as though delight should be the cause of laughter; but well may one thing breed both together. Nay, rather in themselves they have, as it were, a kind of contrariety: for delight we scarcely do but in things that have a conveniency to ourselves or to the general nature: laughter almost ever cometh of things most disproportioned to ourselves and nature. Delight hath a joy in it, either permanent or present. Laughter hath only a scornful tickling.

For example, we are ravished with delight to see a fair woman, and yet are far from being moved to laughter. We laugh at deformed creatures, wherein certainly we cannot delight. We delight in good chances, we laugh at mischances;

[53] Actually the *Self-Tormentor,* not the *Eunuch.*
[54] Messenger.
[55] "From the egg"; Horace praises Homer for not beginning his tale of the Trojan war with the egg from which Helen was hatched. See the *Art of Poetry,* p. 87.

we delight to hear the happiness of our friends, or country, at which he were worthy to be laughed at that would laugh. We shall, contrarily, laugh sometimes to find a matter quite mistaken and go down the hill against the bias, in the mouth of some such men, as for the respect of them one shall be heartily sorry, yet he cannot choose but laugh; and so is rather pained than delighted with laughter. Yet deny I not but that they may go well together. For as in Alexander's picture well set out we delight without laughter, and in twenty mad antics we laugh without delight, so in Hercules, painted with his great beard and furious countenance, in woman's attire, spinning at Omphale's commandment, it breedeth both delight and laughter. For the representing of so strange a power in love procureth delight: and the scornfulness of the action stirreth laughter. But I speak to this purpose, that all the end of the comical part be not upon such scornful matters as stirreth laughter only, but, mixed with it, that delightful teaching which is the end of poesy. And the great fault even in that point of laughter, and forbidden plainly by Aristotle, is that they stir laughter in sinful things, which are rather execrable than ridiculous; or in miserable, which are rather to be pitied than scorned.[56] For what is it to make folks gape at a wretched beggar, or a beggarly clown; or, against the law of hospitality, to jest at strangers, because they speak not English so well as we do? What do we learn, since it is certain *"Nil habet infelix paupertas durius in se, / Quam quod ridiculos homines facit"*?[57] But rather a busy loving courtier, a heartless threatening Thraso, a self-wise–seeming schoolmaster, an awry-transformed traveler — these if we saw walk in stage names, which we play naturally, therein were delightful laughter, and teaching delightfulness: as in the other, the tragedies of Buchanan do justly bring forth a divine admiration. But I have lavished out too many words of this play matter. I do it because, as they are excelling parts of poesy, so is there none so much used in England, and none can be more pitifully abused; which,

like an unmannerly daughter showing a bad education, causeth her mother poesy's honesty to be called in question. Other sorts of poetry almost have we none, but that lyrical kind of songs and sonnets: which, Lord, if he gave us so good minds, how well it might be employed, and with how heavenly fruit, both private and public, in singing the praises of the immortal beauty, the immortal goodness of that God who giveth us hands to write and wits to conceive; of which we might well want words, but never matter; of which we could turn our eyes to nothing, but we should ever have new budding occasions. But truly many of such writings as come under the banner of unresistible love, if I were a mistress, would never persuade me they were in love; so coldly they apply fiery speeches, as men that had rather read lovers' writings, and so caught up certain swelling phrases (which hang together like a man which once told me the wind was at northwest, and by south, because he would be sure to name winds enough), than that in truth they feel those passions, which easily (as I think) may be betrayed by that same forcibleness or *energia* (as the Greeks call it) of the writer. But let this be a sufficient though short note, that we miss the right use of the material point of poesy.

Now, for the outside of it, which is words, or (as I may term it) diction, it is even well worse. So is that honey-flowing matron eloquence appareled, or rather disguised, in a courtesanlike painted affectation: one time with so farfetched words, they may seem monsters, but must seem strangers, to any poor Englishman; another time, with coursing of a letter, as if they were bound to follow the method of a dictionary; another time, with figures and flowers, extremely winterstarved. But I would this fault were only peculiar to versifiers, and had not as large possession among prose-printers, and (which is to be marveled) among many scholars, and (which is to be pitied) among some preachers. Truly I could wish, if at least I might be so bold to wish in a thing beyond the reach of my capacity, the diligent imitators of Tully and Demosthenes (most worthy to be imitated) did not so much keep Nizolian paper books of their figures and phrases, as by attentive translation (as it were) devour them whole, and make them wholly theirs. For

---

[56]Sidney may be thinking of Ch. 5 of the *Poetics,* but this is not Aristotle's point there.

[57]"The worst thing about poverty is that it makes people ridiculous." Juvenal, *Satires* 2:152–53.

now they cast sugar and spice upon every dish that is served to the table, like those Indians, not content to wear earrings at the fit and natural place of the ears, but they will thrust jewels through their nose and lips, because they will be sure to be fine.

Tully, when he was to drive out Catiline, as it were with a thunderbolt of eloquence, often used that figure of repetition, *"Vivit. Vivit? Imo in Senatum venit,"* &c.[58] Indeed, inflamed with a well-grounded rage, he would have his words (as it were) double out of his mouth, and so do that artificially which we see men do in choler naturally. And we, having noted the grace of those words, hale them in sometime to a familiar epistle, when it were too much choler to be choleric. Now for similitudes in certain printed discourses, I think all herberists, all stories of beasts, fowls, and fishes are rifled up, that they come in multitudes to wait upon any of our conceits; which certainly is as absurd a surfeit to the ears as is possible: for the force of a similitude not being to prove anything to a contrary disputer, but only to explain to a willing hearer; when that is done, the rest is a most tedious prattling, rather overswaying the memory from the purpose whereto they were applied, than any whit informing the judgment, already either satisfied, or by similitudes not to be satisfied. For my part, I do not doubt, when Antonius and Crassus, the great forefathers of Cicero in eloquence, the one (as Cicero testifieth of them) pretended not to know art, the other not to set by it, because with a plain sensibleness they might win credit of popular ears; which credit is the nearest step to persuasion; which persuasion is the chief mark of oratory — I do not doubt (I say) that but they used these knacks very sparingly; which, who doth generally use, any man may see doth dance to his own music; and so be noted by the audience more careful to speak curiously than to speak truly.

Undoubtedly (at least to my opinion undoubtedly) I have found in divers small-learned courtiers a more sound style than in some professors of learning: of which I can guess no other cause, but that the courtier, following that which by practice he findeth fittest to nature, therein

(though he know it not) doth according to art, though not by art: where the other, using art to show art, and not to hide art (as in these cases he should do), flieth from nature, and indeed abuseth art.

But what? Methinks I deserve to be pounded for straying from poetry to oratory: but both have such an affinity in this wordish consideration, that I think this digression will make my meaning receive the fuller understanding — which is not to take upon me to teach poets how they should do, but only, finding myself sick among the rest, to show some one or two spots of the common infection grown among the most part of writers: that, acknowledging ourselves somewhat awry, we may bend to the right use both of matter and manner; whereto our language giveth us great occasion, being indeed capable of any excellent exercising of it. I know some will say it is a mingled language. And why not so much the better, taking the best of both the other? Another will say it wanteth grammar. Nay truly, it hath that praise, that it wanteth grammar: for grammar it might have, but it needs it not; being so easy of itself, and so void of those cumbersome differences of cases, genders, moods, and tenses, which I think was a piece of the Tower of Babylon's curse, that a man should be put to school to learn his mother tongue. But for the uttering sweetly and properly the conceits of the mind, which is the end of speech, that hath it equally with any other tongue in the world: and is particularly happy in compositions of two or three words together, near the Greek, far beyond the Latin: which is one of the greatest beauties can be in a language.

Now, of versifying there are two sorts, the one ancient, the other modern: the ancient marked the quantity of each syllable, and according to that framed his verse; the modern observing only number (with some regard of the accent), the chief life of it standeth in that like sounding of the words, which we call rhyme. Whether of these be the most excellent, would bear many speeches. The ancient (no doubt) more fit for music, both words and tune observing quantity, and more fit lively to express divers passions, by the low and lofty sound of the well-weighed syllable. The latter likewise, with his rhyme, striketh a certain music to the ear: and, in fine, since it doth delight,

---

[58]"He lives. Does he live? He even comes into the Senate."

though by another way, it obtains the same purpose: there being in either sweetness, and wanting in neither majesty. Truly the English, before any other vulgar language I know, is fit for both sorts: for, for the ancient, the Italian is so full of vowels that it must ever be cumbered with elisions; the Dutch so, of the other side, with consonants, that they cannot yield the sweet sliding fit for a verse; the French, in his whole language, hath not one word that hath his accent in the last syllable saving two, called *antepenultima;* and little more hath the Spanish: and, therefore, very gracelessly may they use dactyls. The English is subject to none of these defects.

Now, for the rhyme, though we do not observe quantity, yet we observe the accent very precisely: which other languages either cannot do, or will not do so absolutely. That *caesura,* or breathing place in the midst of the verse, neither Italian nor Spanish have, the French, and we, never almost fail of. Lastly, even the very rhyme itself the Italian cannot put in the last syllable, by the French named the "masculine rhyme," but still in the next to the last, which the French call the "female," or the next before that, which the Italians term *sdrucciola.* The example of the former is *buono:suono,* of the *sdrucciola, femina: semina.* The French, of the other side, hath both the male, as *bon:son,* and the female, as *plaise:taise,* but the *sdrucciola* he hath not: where the English hath all three, as *due:true, father:rather, motion:potion,* with much more which might be said, but that I find already the triflingness of this discourse is much too much enlarged. So that since the ever-praise-worthy poesy is full of virtue-breeding delightfulness, and void of no gift that ought to be in the noble name of learning; since the blames laid against it are either false or feeble; since the cause why it is not esteemed in England is the fault of poet-apes, not poets; since, lastly, our tongue is most fit to honor poesy, and to be honored by poesy; I conjure you all that have had the evil luck to read this ink-wasting toy of mine, even in the name of the nine Muses, no more to scorn the sacred mysteries of poesy, no more to laugh at the name of *poets,* as though they were next inheritors to fools, no more to jest at the reverent title of a *rhymer;* but to believe, with Aristotle, that they were the ancient treasurers of the Grecians' divinity; to believe, with Bembus,[59] that they were first bringers-in of all civility; to believe, with Scaliger, that no philosopher's precepts can sooner make you an honest man than the reading of Virgil; to believe, with Clauserus, the translator of Cornutus, that it pleased the heavenly Deity, by Hesiod and Homer, under the veil of fables, to give us all knowledge, logic, rhetoric, philosophy, natural and moral, and *Quid non?;*[60] to believe, with me, that there are many mysteries contained in poetry, which of purpose were written darkly, lest by profane wits it should be abused; to believe, with Landino, that they are so beloved of the gods that whatsoever they write proceeds of a divine fury; lastly, to believe themselves, when they tell you they will make you immortal by their verses.

Thus doing, your name shall flourish in the printers' shops; thus doing, you shall be of kin to many a poetical preface; thus doing, you shall be most fair, most rich, most wise, most all; you shall dwell upon superlatives. Thus doing, though you be *"libertino patre natus,"* you shall suddenly grow *"Herculea proles," "si quid mea carmina possunt."*[61] Thus doing, your soul shall be placed with Dante's Beatrix, or Virgil's Anchises. But if (fie of such a but) you be born so near the dull-making cataract of Nilus that you cannot hear the planetlike music of poetry, if you have so earth-creeping a mind that it cannot lift itself up to look to the sky of poetry, or rather, by a certain rustical disdain, will become such a mome as to be a momus of poetry; then, though I will not wish unto you the ass's ears of Midas, nor to be driven by a poet's verses (as Bubonax was) to hang himself, nor to be rhymed to death, as is said to be done in Ireland; yet thus much curse I must send you, in the behalf of all poets, that while you live, you live in love, and never get favor for lacking skill of a sonnet, and, when you die, your memory die from the earth for want of an epitaph.

[59]Pietro Bembo (1470–1547), Italian scholar and critic.
[60]What not?
[61]"Thus doing, though you be 'the son of a freed slave,' you shall suddenly grow 'Herculean offspring,' 'if my poems can do anything.'" The quotations are from Horace, Ovid, and Virgil.

John Dryden

1631–1700

Best known as the poet laureate of Charles II and James II, and as the satirical author of *Mac Flecknoe* (1682) and the political allegory *Absalom and Achitophel* (1681), Dryden was also one of the most successful of the Restoration dramatists, famous for comedies like *Marriage à-la-Mode* (1673); for tragedies like *All for Love* (1678); and for operatic melodramas, now long out of fashion, called "heroic plays." *An Essay of Dramatic Poesy* (1668) derives from Dryden's practical experience in all areas of the theater.

The *Essay* is neither a Platonic dialogue nor a treatise, but rather a formal debate on the drama among four speakers: Crites, Eugenius, Lisideius, and Neander. Although no one supposes that any such debate actually took place, the speakers have traditionally been identified with contemporary personages. Crites, whose name suggests his captiously critical air, may be Sir Robert Howard, Dryden's brother-in-law and sometime collaborator, with whom Dryden had publicly quarreled over the issue of rhyme in drama. Eugenius, which means "well-born," is probably Charles Sackville, Lord Buckhurst, Dryden's patron before his laureateship and an eminent Cavalier poet in his own right. Lisideius is Sir Charles Sedley (the name is a Latinized anagram of Sedley). And Neander (Greek for "new man") is Dryden himself, of middle-class origins. By using the debate form, Dryden gives the other side equal time (or nearly) but manages to reserve some of the best arguments for himself.

Like Jonathan Swift's *Battle of the Books, An Essay of Dramatic Poesy* might be thought of as one volley of the international controversy in the late seventeenth century over the relative value of the ancient and modern writers. Conservative thinkers like Swift felt that the ancients — Homer, Virgil, Juvenal — could never be surpassed, while others, enthusiastic about the advances in learning since the Renaissance, felt that by building upon the foundations of the past, the present might progress beyond it. ("Dwarfs who stand on the shoulders of giants may see farther than the giants themselves," said Isaac Newton, Dryden's contemporary and fellow Modern.) This context helps explain the debate between Crites and Eugenius on the merits of classical and modern drama.

But there was another even more topical concern. The London theaters, closed for twenty years during the Civil War and the Protectorate of Cromwell, had reopened only six years before, in 1662. The drama was beginning to revive, but the traditions of the Elizabethan and Jacobean stage had lapsed during the interregnum. It remained to be seen on what model the English stage would return. Would the new drama be built on the native Tudor-Stuart model and look to Shakespeare, Jonson, and Fletcher as exemplars? Or would the English stage imitate Racine and Corneille, who had created the elegant but rather formal drama of France, where Charles II and his cavaliers had spent most of the interregnum?

Underlying these topical concerns are a set of more abstract issues that divided Renaissance and neoclassical critics. One was the status of the so-called Three

Unities of Time, Place, and Action, a set of rules for drama supposedly derived from Aristotle and Horace.[1] Under Unity of Time, it was claimed that the plot of a drama might take up no more than a single day from the first incident to the last; ideally, according to Pierre Corneille, the plot of a drama should last no longer than the dramatic representation itself — two hours or so. Under Unity of Place, it was asserted that the plot should be laid in a single city, ideally in a single room. Unity of Action meant that everything in a drama should further a single plot and that subplots, like that of Gloucester and his sons in *King Lear,* were to be avoided.

A second issue was that of generic integrity: comedy and tragedy were considered mutually exclusive, and characters and speeches appropriate to the one would not be appropriate to the other. The gravediggers in *Hamlet* or Iago's bawdy jokes in *Othello* would thus be inappropriate. A third issue was that of decorum: All acts of violence, especially deaths, should be performed offstage and revealed to the audience through narration. These matters were arguably a part of both Greek and Roman dramatic practice, though only Horace comments on them.

As the debate is joined between Crites and Eugenius, and between Lisideius and Neander, the reader is forced to dwell on an all-subsuming question: What is the status of the Three Unities, Generic Integrity, and Stage Decorum? Are they rules of art that hold for the ages or are they merely artistic conventions? Beyond this there is the further question: If there is no real difference between conventions and rules, then how do artistic styles change? If conventions may be irresponsibly disregarded, how can art function without them?

An Essay of Dramatic Poesy, like Aristotle's *Poetics,* hinges on a definition, this time of a *play,* which Lisideius defines as "a just and lively image of human nature, representing its passions and humours, and the changes of fortune to which it is subject; for the delight and instruction of mankind." The derivation from Horace and the *Ars Poetica* appears clearly in the last clause. Crites objects that the definition is "*a genere et fine,*" that it states only general class and purpose, implying that it is too broad, since it could serve as a definition of a novel or poem as well.

Crites is correct but has missed the main ambiguity in the definition: The combatants have differing interpretations of the key words "just" and "lively." For Crites, an image is "just" when it has been constructed according to correct rules; for Neander, when it gives a faithful impression of the original. For Lisideius, "lively" takes its older meaning of *lifelike;* for Neander it means something more like *spirited.*

Another confusion seems to arise over just what "mankind" is: While some of the debaters seem to be absolutists, Neander is a critical relativist who feels that the French and the English will be delighted and instructed by very different sorts of

---

[1]Unity of Action is the only unity that is taken directly and unequivocally from Aristotle's *Poetics* (Ch. 8). Unity of Time may derive from one passage in *Poetics,* Ch. 5 ("Tragedy endeavors as far as possible to confine itself to a single revolution of the sun or to exceed this but slightly"), which is contradicted by another passage in *Poetics,* Ch. 7 ("The proper magnitude is comprised within such limits that the sequence of events, according to the law of probability or necessity, will admit of a change from bad fortune to good or from good to bad"). Unity of Place does not appear in Aristotle or Horace, but one could claim that it follows as a corollary from the Unities of Time and Action: A single action occurring within a single day could not possibly, in the days before automobiles and airplanes, take place over a very widespread area.

things. This is not to suggest that the debaters are quarreling over the meaning of terms; on the contrary their apparent unanimity on the definition masks genuine disagreements over what drama ought to be.

In the final debate, Crites and Neander square off directly over the use of rhymed verse in the drama, with Crites attacking the practice and Neander defending it. In this section, Neander concedes half his ground by admitting the inappropriateness of rhyme in comedy. (In fact, Dryden was later to recant his position and write his tragedies, including the popular *All for Love,* in blank verse.) Here as elsewhere, however, Neander applies his audience-centered criteria, arguing that rhyme may be used in tragic drama if it is used well and thereby gains the acceptance of the public, while Crites puts forth a pseudo-mimetic argument that the characters of a drama may not speak poetry since their counterparts in real life spoke prose.[2]

For many readers, the most fascinating section of *An Essay of Dramatic Poesy* is Neander's comparative discussion of Shakespeare, Jonson, and Fletcher, and his explication of Jonson's *Epicoene, or The Silent Woman.* Abstract argument recedes as a major poet responds to his great exemplars. It is interesting to see how tastes have changed — that Shakespeare was not so certainly the greatest of the Elizabethan dramatists in Dryden's day as he is today. It is also enlightening to watch the principles of rhetorical criticism applied by a sensitive critic, who was also his age's most versatile practicing playwright.

Selected Bibliography

Bredvold, Louis I. *The Intellectual Milieu of John Dryden.* Ann Arbor: University of Michigan Press, 1934.

Brown, Laura. "Dryden and the Imperial Imagination." In *The Cambridge Companion to John Dryden,* ed. Steven N. Zwicker, 59–74. Cambridge: Cambridge University Press, 2004.

Cole, Elmer Joseph. *The Consistency of John Dryden's Literary Criticism in Theory and Practice.* Albuquerque: New Mexico University Press, 1970.

Eliot, T. S. *John Dryden: The Poet, the Dramatist, the Critic; Three Essays.* New York: Haskell House, 1966.

Hume, Robert D. *Dryden's Criticism.* Ithaca: Cornell University Press, 1970.

Huntley, Frank Livingstone. *On Dryden's Essay of Dramatic Poesy.* Ann Arbor: University of Michigan Press, 1951.

Mishra, J. B. *John Dryden: His Theory and Practice of Drama.* New Delhi: Bahri Publications, 1978.

Pechter, Edward. *Dryden's Classical Theory of Literature.* London and New York: Cambridge University Press, 1975.

Trowbridge, Hoyt. "The Place of Rules in Dryden's Criticism." *Modern Philology* 44 (1946): 84–96.

Watson, George. *John Dryden: Of Dramatic Poesy and Other Critical Essays.* 2 vols. London: J. Dent, 1962.

[2]Neither Aristotle nor Horace had so argued, certainly, and it is not clear where such literal-minded mimesis would stop. Should the characters in *Julius Caesar* have spoken in Latin because their historical originals did?

From *An Essay of Dramatic Poesy*

It was that memorable day,[1] in the first summer of the late war, when our Navy engaged the Dutch: a day wherein the two most mighty and best appointed fleets which any age had ever seen, disputed the command of the greater half of the globe, the commerce of nations, and the riches of the universe. While these vast floating bodies, on either side, moved against each other in parallel lines, and our countrymen, under the happy conduct of his Royal Highness,[2] went breaking, by little and little, into the line of the enemies, the noise of the cannon from both navies reached our ears about the City; so that all men, being alarmed with it, and in a dreadful suspense of the event, which they knew was then deciding, every one went following the sound as his fancy led him; and leaving the town almost empty, some took towards the Park, some cross the river, others down it; all seeking the noise in the depth of silence.

Amongst the rest, it was the fortune of Eugenius, Crites, Lisideius and Neander,[3] to be in company together: three of them persons whom their wit and quality have made known to all the town: and whom I have chose to hide under these borrowed names, that they may not suffer by so ill a relation as I am going to make of their discourse.

Taking then a barge which a servant of Lisideius had provided for them, they made haste to shoot the bridge, and left behind them that great fall of waters which hindered them from hearing what they desired: after which, having disengaged themselves from many vessels which rode at anchor in the Thames, and almost blocked up the passage towards Greenwich, they ordered the watermen to let fall their oars more gently; and then every one favouring his own curiosity with a strict silence, it was not long ere they perceived the air to break about them like the noise of distant thunder, or of swallows in a chimney: those little undulations of sound, though almost vanishing before they reached them, yet still seeming to retain somewhat of their first horror which they had betwixt the fleets: after they had attentively listened till such time as the sound by little and little went from them; Eugenius lifting up his head, and taking notice of it, was the first who congratulated to the rest that happy omen of our nation's victory: adding, that we had but this to desire in confirmation of it, that we might hear no more of that noise which was now leaving the English coast. When the rest had concurred in the same opinion, Crites, a person of a sharp judgment, and somewhat too delicate a taste in wit, which the world have mistaken in him for ill nature, said, smiling to us, that if the concernment of this battle had not been so exceeding great, he could scarce have wished the victory at the price he knew he must pay for it, in being subject to the reading and hearing of so many ill verses as he was sure would be made on that subject. Adding, that no argument could scape some of those eternal rhymers, who watch a battle with more diligence than the ravens and birds of prey; and the worst of them surest to be first in upon the quarry, while the better able, either out of modesty writ not at all, or set that due value upon their poems, as to let them be often desired and long expected! There are some of those impertinent people of whom you speak, answered Lisideius, who to my knowledge are already so provided, either way, that they can produce not only a panegyric upon the victory, but, if need be, a funeral elegy on the Duke: wherein after they have crowned his valour with many laurels, they will at last deplore the odds under which he fell, concluding that his courage deserved a better destiny. All the company smiled at the conceit of Lisideius; but Crites, more eager than before, began to make particular exceptions against some writers, and said the public magistrate ought to send betimes to forbid them; and that it concerned the peace and quiet of all honest people, that ill poets should be as well silenced as seditious preachers. In my opinion, replied Eugenius, you

[1] June 3, 1665.
[2] James, Duke of York, the Lord Admiral, afterward James II.
[3] For the traditional ascriptions of these names, see p. 160.

pursue your point too far; for as to my own particular, I am so great a lover of poesy, that I could wish them all rewarded who attempt but to do well, at least I would not have them worse used than one of their brethren was by Sylla the dictator: *Quem in concione vidimus* (says Tully) *cum ei libellum malus poeta de populo subjecisset, quod epigramma in eum fecisset tantummodo alternis versibus longiusculis, statim ex iis rebus quas tunc vendebat jubere ei praemium tribui, sub ea conditione ne quid postea scriberet.*[4] I could wish with all my heart, replied Crites; that many whom we know were as bountifully thanked upon the same condition, that they would never trouble us again. For amongst others, I have a mortal apprehension of two poets, whom this victory with the help of both her wings will never be able to escape;[5] 'tis easy to guess whom you intend, said Lisideius, and without naming them, I ask you if one of them does not perpetually pay us with clenches[6] upon words and a certain clownish kind of raillery? If now and then he does not offer at a catachresis[7] or Clevelandism, wresting and torturing a word into another meaning: in fine, if he be not one of those whom the French would call *un mauvais buffon;* one who is so much a well-willer to the satire, that he intends at least, to spare no man; and though he cannot strike a blow to hurt any, yet he ought to be punished for the malice of the action; as our witches are justly hanged because they think themselves to be such: and suffer deservedly for believing they did mischief, because they meant it. You have described him, said Crites, so exactly, that I am afraid to come after you with my other extremity of poetry: he is one of those who having

had some advantage of education and converse, knows better than the other what a poet should be, but puts it into practice more unluckily than any man; his style and matter are everywhere alike; he is the most calm, peaceable writer you ever read: he never disquiets your passions with the least concernment, but still leaves you in as even a temper as he found you; he is a very Leveller in poetry, he creeps along with ten little words in every line,[8] and helps out his numbers with *For to,* and *Unto,* and all the pretty expletives he can find, till he drags them to the end of another line; while the sense is left tired half way behind it: he doubly starves all his verses, first for want of thought, and then of expression; his poetry neither has wit in it, nor seems to have it; like him in Martial.

Pauper videri Cinna vult, et est pauper:[9]

He affects plainness, to cover his want of imagination: when he writes the serious way, the highest flight of his fancy is some miserable antithesis, or seeming contradiction; and in the comic he is still reaching at some thin conceit, the ghost of a jest, and that too flies before him, never to be caught; these swallows which we see before us on the Thames, are the just resemblance of his wit: you may observe how near the water they stoop, how many proffers they make to dip, and yet how seldom they touch it: and when they do, 'tis but the surface: they skim over it but to catch a gnat, and then mount into the air and leave it. Well gentlemen, said Eugenius, you may speak your pleasure of these authors; but though I and some few more about the town may give you a peaceable hearing, yet assure yourselves, there are multitudes who would think you malicious and them injured: especially him whom you first described; he is the very Withers[10] of the City: they have bought more editions of his works than would serve to lay under all their pies at the Lord Mayor's Christmas. When his famous poem first came out in the year 1660, I have seen them

---

[4]"We have seen how, at a public meeting, when a bad poet among the people offered him an epigram made on himself, written in limping elegiacs, Sulla ordered that he be paid a reward from the booty on sale, provided that he never write again." Cicero, *Pro Archia Poeta* 10:25.

[5]It has been conjectured that Dryden's two poets were Richard Wild and Richard Flecknoe, respectively, who wrote on the battle. But the poets' faults seem to correspond to the two criteria of value in the subsequent definition of a play: The former poet's language fails to be just; the latter's, to be lively.

[6]Puns.

[7]Abuse of language. John Cleveland (1613–1658) tortured language in this way.

[8]Cf. Pope, *An Essay on Criticism:* "And ten low words oft creep in one dull line."

[9]"Cinna wishes to seem poor — and he is poor." Martial, *Epigrams* 8:19.

[10]"George Withers (1588–1667) was a Puritan poet.

reading it in the midst of change-time; nay so vehement they were at it, that they lost their bargain by the candles' ends: but what will you say, if he has been received amongst great persons; I can assure you he is, this day, the envy of one, who is lord in the art of quibbling; and who does not take it well, that any man should intrude so far into his province. All I would wish, replied Crites, is, that they who love his writings, may still admire him, and his fellow poet, *qui Bavium non odit,*[11] etc. is curse sufficient. And farther, added Lisideius, I believe there is no man who writes well, but would think he had hard measure, if their admirers should praise anything of his: *Nam quos contemnimus eorum quoque laudes contemnimus.*[12] There are so few who write well in this age, said Crites, that methinks any praises should be welcome; they neither rise to the dignity of the last age, nor to any of the Ancients; and we may cry out of the writers of this time, with more reason than Petronius of his, *Pace vestra liceat dixisse, primi omnium eloquentiam perdidistis:*[13] you have debauched the true old poetry so far, that nature, which is the soul of it, is not in any of your writings.

If your quarrel (said Eugenius) to those who now write, be grounded only on your reverence to antiquity, there is no man more ready to adore those great Greeks and Romans than I am: but on the other side, I cannot think so contemptibly of the age in which I live or so dishonourably of my own country, as not to judge we equal the Ancients in most kinds of poesy, and in some surpass them; neither know I any reason why I may not be as zealous for the reputation of our age, as we find the Ancients themselves were in reference to those who lived before them. For you hear your Horace saying,

Indignor quidquam reprehendi, non quia crasse compositum, illepideve putetur, sed quia nuper.

And after,

Si meliora dies, ut vina, poemata reddit,
scire velim pretium chartis quotus arroget annus?[14]

But I see I am engaging in a wide dispute, where the arguments are not like to reach close on either side; for poesy is of so large an extent, and so many both of the Ancients and Moderns have done well in all kinds of it, that in citing one against the other, we shall take up more time this evening, than each man's occasions will allow him: therefore I would ask Crites to what part of poesy he would confine his arguments, and whether he would defend the general cause of the Ancients against the Moderns, or oppose any age of the Moderns against this of ours?[15]

Crites a little while considering upon this demand, told Eugenius that if he pleased, he would limit their dispute to Dramatic Poesy; in which he thought it not difficult to prove, either that the Ancients were superior to the Moderns, or the last age to this of ours.

Eugenius was somewhat surprised, when he heard Crites make choice of the subject; for aught I see, said he, I have undertaken a harder province than I imagined; for though I never judged the plays of the Greek or Roman poets comparable to ours; yet on the other side those we now see acted, come short of many which were written in the last age: but my comfort is if we are overcome, it will be only by our own countrymen: and if we yield to them in this one part of poesy, we more surpass them in all the other; for in the epic or lyric way it will be hard for them to show us one such amongst them, as we have many now living, or who lately were. They can produce nothing so courtly writ, or which expresses so much the conversation of a gentleman, as Sir John Suckling; nothing so even, sweet, and flowing as Mr. Waller, nothing so majestic, so correct

---

[11]"Let whoever does not hate Bavius [love your songs, Maevius]." Virgil, *Eclogues* 3:90.
[12]"We despise the praise of those whom we despise."
[13]"If you will allow me to say so, you have killed the old eloquence." Petronius, *Satyricon,* 2.

[14]"I get angry when something is attacked, not for being coarse or clumsy, but for being new." and "If like wine, poems improve with age, how many years does it take for a poem to be ripe?" Horace, *Epistles* II.1:76–177 and 34–35.
[15]The periods in dispute are classical and modern literature — a traditional argument known as the *querelle des anciens et des modernes* — and within the modern age, the Elizabethan era and the contemporary period.

as Sir John Denham; nothing so elevated, so copious, and full of spirit, as Mr. Cowley; as for the Italian, French, and Spanish plays, I can make it evident, that those who now write, surpass them; and that the drama is wholly ours.

All of them were thus far of Eugenius' opinion, that the sweetness of English verse was never understood or practised by our fathers. Even Crites himself did not much oppose it: and every one was willing to acknowledge how much our poesy is improved, by the happiness of some writers yet living; who first taught us to mould our thoughts into easy and significant words, to retrench the superfluities of expression, and to make our rhyme so properly a part of the verse, that it should never mislead the sense, but itself be led and governed by it.

Eugenius was going to continue this discourse, when Lisideius told him that it was necessary, before they proceeded further, to take a standing measure of their controversy; for how was it possible to be decided who writ the best plays, before we know what a play should be? but, this once agreed on by both parties, each might have recourse to it, either to prove his own advantages, or to discover the failings of his adversary.

He had no sooner said this, but all desired the favour of him to give the definition of a play; and they were the more importunate, because neither Aristotle, nor Horace, nor any other, who had writ of that subject, had ever done it.

Lisideius, after some modest denials, at last confessed he had a rude notion of it; indeed rather a description than a definition, but which served to guide him in his private thoughts, when he was to make a judgement of what others writ: that he conceived a play ought to be, a just and lively image of human nature, representing its passions and humours, and the changes of fortune to which it is subject; for the delight and instruction of mankind.

This definition, though Crites raised a logical objection against it; that it was only *a genere et fine*,[16] and so not altogether perfect; was yet well received by the rest: and after they had given order to the watermen to turn their barge, and row softly, that they might take the cool of the evening in their return, Crites, being desired by the company to begin, spoke on behalf of the Ancients, in this manner:

If confidence presage a victory, Eugenius, in his own opinion, has already triumphed over the Ancients. Nothing seems more easy to him, than to overcome those whom it is our greatest praise to have imitated well: for we do not only build upon their foundations; but by their models. Dramatic poesy had time enough, reckoning from Thespis (who first invented it) to Aristophanes, to be born, to grow up, and to flourish in maturity. It has been observed of arts and sciences, that in one and the same century they have arrived to great perfection; and no wonder, since every age has a kind of universal genius, which inclines those that live in it to some particular studies: the work then being pushed on by many hands, must of necessity go forward.

Is it not evident, in these last hundred years (when the study of philosophy[17] has been the business of all the virtuosi in Christendom) that almost a new nature has been revealed to us? that more errors of the school have been detected, more useful experiments in philosophy have been made, more noble secrets in optics, medicine, anatomy, astronomy, discovered, than in all those credulous and doting ages from Aristotle to us? so true it is that nothing spreads more fast than science, when rightly and generally cultivated.

Add to this the more than common emulation that was in those times of writing well; which though it be found in all ages and all persons that pretend to the same reputation; yet poesy being then in more esteem than now it is, had greater honours decreed to the professors of it; and consequently the rivalship was more high between them; they had judges ordained to decide their merit, and prizes to reward it: and historians have been diligent to record of Aeschylus, Euripides, Sophocles, Lycophron, and the rest of them, both who they were that vanquished in these wars of the theatre, and how often they were crowned: while the Asian kings,

---

[16]"By genus and end": Crites is complaining that the definition is not restrictive enough, since it will serve to define poetry and prose fiction as well as drama. In fact, the problem is that the meaning of central terms — "just," "lively," and "representing" — is slippery.

[17]Natural philosophy; science.

and Grecian commonwealths scarce afforded them a nobler subject than the unmanly luxuries of a debauched court, or giddy intrigues of a factious city. *Alit aemulatio ingenia* (says Paterculus) *et nunc invidia, nunc admiratio incitationem accendit:* Emulation is the spur of wit, and sometimes envy, sometimes admiration quickens our endeavours.[18]

But now since the rewards of honour are taken away, that virtuous emulation is turned into direct malice; yet so slothful, that it contents itself to condemn and cry down others, without attempting to do better. 'Tis a reputation too unprofitable, to take the necessary pains for it; yet wishing they had it, that desire is incitement enough to hinder others from it. And this, in short, Eugenius, is the reason, why you have now so few good poets; and so many severe judges. Certainly, to imitate the Ancients well, much labour and long study is required: which pains, I have already shown, our poets would want encouragement to take, if yet they had ability to go through the work. Those Ancients have been faithful imitators and wise observers of that nature which is so torn and ill represented in our plays; they have handed down to us a perfect resemblance of her; which we, like ill copiers, neglecting to look on, have rendered monstrous, and disfigured. But, that you may know how much you are indebted to those your masters, and be ashamed to have so ill requited them, I must remember you that all the rules by which we practise the drama at this day, (either such as relate to the justness and symmetry of the plot; or the episodical ornaments, such as descriptions, narrations, and other beauties, which are not essential to the play) were delivered to us from the observations which Aristotle made, of those poets, who either lived before him, or were his contemporaries: we have added nothing of our own, except we have the confidence to say our wit is better; of which none boast in this our age, but such as understand not theirs. Of that book which Aristotle has left us περι τῆς Ποιητικῆς[19] Horace's *Art of Poetry* is an excellent comment, and, I believe, restores to us that second book of his concerning comedy, which is wanting in him.

Out of these two have been extracted the famous rules which the French call, *Des Trois Unités,* or, the three unities, which ought to be observed in every regular play; namely, of time, place, and action.[20]

The unity of time they comprehend in twenty-four hours, the compass of a natural day; or as near it as can be contrived. And the reason of it is obvious to every one; that the time of the feigned action, or fable of the play, should be proportioned as near as can be to the duration of that time in which it is represented; since therefore all plays are acted on the theatre in a space of time much within the compass of twenty-four hours, that play is to be thought the nearest imitation of nature, whose plot or action is confined within that time; and, by the same rule which concludes this general proportion of time, it follows, that all the parts of it are (as near as may be) to be equally sub-divided; namely, that one act take not up the supposed time of half a day, which is out of proportion to the rest, since the other four are then to be straitened within the compass of the remaining half. For it is unnatural that one act, which being spoke or written, is not longer than the rest, should be supposed longer by the audience. 'Tis therefore the poet's duty, to take care that no act should be imagined to exceed the time in which it is represented on the stage; and that the intervals and inequalities of time be supposed to fall out between the acts.

This rule of time how well it has been observed by the Ancients, most of their plays will witness. You see them in their tragedies (wherein to follow this rule, is certainly most difficult) from the very beginning of their plays, falling close into that part of the story which they intend for the action or principal object of it; leaving the former part to be delivered by narration: so that they set the audience, as it were, at the post where

[18]Velleius Paterculus, in the *Historia Romana* 1:17.
[19]The *Poetics.*

[20]The unity of Place is not explicitly mentioned in the *Poetics,* but it is implied by the constraints of the unities of Time and Action. If a tragedy "is confined to one revolution of the sun" then its single action cannot occur at widely separated places, given the limits of premodern transportation. But while Aristotle treats the unity of action as an essential matter of art, he treats the limitations of time in tragedy as a stage convention, with the length of plays regulated by such extraneous matters as dramatic competitions.

the race is to be concluded: and, saving them the tedious expectation of seeing the poet set out and ride the beginning of the course, they suffer you not to behold him, till he is in sight of the goal, and just upon you.

For the second unity, which is that of place, the Ancients meant by it, that the scene ought to be continued through the play, in the same place where it was laid in the beginning: for the stage, on which it is represented, being but one and the same place, it is unnatural to conceive it many; and those far distant from one another. I will not deny but by the variation of painted scenes, the fancy (which in these cases will contribute to its own deceit) may sometimes imagine it several places, with some appearance of probability; yet it still carries the greater likelihood of truth, if those places be supposed so near each other, as in the same town or city; which may all be comprehended under the larger denomination of one place: for a greater distance will bear no proportion to the shortness of time, which is allotted in the acting, to pass from one of them to another; for the observation of this, next to the Ancients, the French are to be most commended. They tie themselves so strictly to the unity of place, that you never see in any of their plays, a scene changed in the middle of an act: if the act begins in a garden, a street, or chamber, 'tis ended in the same place; and that you may know it to be the same, the stage is so supplied with persons that it is never empty all the time: he who enters second has business with him who was on before; and before the second quits the stage, a third appears who has business with him.

This Corneille[21] calls *La liaison des scènes,* the continuity or joining of the scenes; and 'tis a good mark of a well contrived play when all the persons are known to each other, and every one of them has some affairs with all the rest.

As for the third unity, which is that of action, the Ancients meant no other by it than what the logicians do by their *Finis,* the end or scope of any action: that which is the first in intention, and last in execution. Now the poet is to aim at one great and complete action, to the carrying on of

which all things in his play, even the very obstacles, are to be subservient; and the reason of this is as evident as any of the former.

For two actions equally laboured and driven on by the writer, would destroy the unity of the poem; it would be no longer one play, but two: not but that there may be many actions in a play, as Ben Jonson has observed in his *Discoveries;* but they must be all subservient to the great one, which our language happily expresses in the name of under-plots: such as in Terence's *Eunuch* is the difference and reconcilement of Thais and Phaedria, which is not the chief business of the play, but promotes the marriage of Charea and Chremes's sister, principally intended by the poet. There ought to be but one action, says Corneille, that is one complete action which leaves the mind of the audience in a full repose. But this cannot be brought to pass but by many other imperfect actions which conduce to it, and hold the audience in a delightful suspense of what will be.

If by these rules (to omit many other drawn from the precepts and practice of the Ancients) we should judge our modern plays, 'tis probable, that few of them would endure the trial. That which should be the business of a day, takes up in some of them an age; instead of one action they are the epitomes of a man's life; and for one spot of ground (which the stage should represent) we are sometimes in more countries than the map can show us.

But if we will allow the Ancients to have contrived well, we must acknowledge them to have written better; questionless we are deprived of a great stock of wit in the loss of Menander among the Greek poets, and of Caecilius, Affranius, and Varius, among the Romans: we may guess at Menander's excellency by the plays of Terence, who translated some of them: and yet wanted so much of him that he was called by C. Caesar the half-Menander; and may judge of Varius, by the testimonies of Horace, Martial, and Velleius Paterculus. 'Tis probable that these, could they be recovered, would decide the controversy; but so long as Aristophanes and Plautus are extant; while the tragedies of Euripides, Sophocles, and Seneca are in our hands, I can never see one of those plays which are now written, but it increases my admiration of the Ancients; and yet

---

[21]In the *Discours des trois unités* (1660).

I must acknowledge further, that to admire them as we ought, we should understand them better than we do. Doubtless many things appear flat to us, the wit of which depended on some custom or story which never came to our knowledge, or perhaps on some criticism in their language, which being so long dead, and only remaining in their books, 'tis not possible they should make us understand perfectly. To read Macrobius, explaining the propriety and elegancy of many words in Virgil, which I had before passed over without consideration, as common things, is enough to assure me that I ought to think the same of Terence; and that in the purity of his style (which Tully so much valued that he ever carried his works about him) there is yet left in him great room for admiration, if I knew but where to place it. In the mean time I must desire you to take notice, that the greatest man of the last age (Ben Jonson) was willing to give place to them in all things. He was not only a professed imitator of Horace, but a learned plagiary of all the others. You track him everywhere in their snow. If Horace, Lucan, Petronius Arbiter, Seneca, and Juvenal, had their own from him, there are few serious thoughts which are new in him. You will pardon me therefore if I presume he loved their fashion when he wore their clothes. But since I have otherwise a great veneration for him, and you, Eugenius, prefer him above all other poets, I will use no farther argument to you than his example. I will produce before you Father Ben, dressed in all the ornaments and colours of the Ancients, you will need no other guide to our party if you follow him; and whether you consider the bad plays of our age, or regard the good plays of the last, both the best and worst of the modern poets will equally instruct you to admire the Ancients.

Crites had no sooner left speaking, but Eugenius, who had waited with some impatience for it, thus began:

I have observed in your speech that the former part of it is convincing as to what the Moderns have profited by the rules of the Ancients, but in the latter you are careful to conceal how much they have excelled them. We own all the helps we have from them, and want neither veneration nor gratitude while we acknowledge that to overcome them we must make use of the advantages we have received from them; but to these assistances we have joined our own industry; for (had we sat down with a dull imitation of them) we might then have lost somewhat of the old perfection, but never acquired any that was new. We draw not therefore after their lines, but those of nature; and having the life before us, besides the experience of all they knew, it is no wonder if we hit some airs and features which they have missed. I deny not what you urge of arts and sciences, that they have flourished in some ages more than others; but your instance in philosophy makes for me; for if natural causes be more known now than in the time of Aristotle, because more studied, it follows that poesy and other arts may with the same pains arrive still nearer to perfection, and, that granted, it will rest for you to prove that they wrought more perfect images of human life than we; which, seeing in your discourse you have avoided to make good, it shall now be my task to show you some part of their defects, and some few excellencies of the Moderns; and I think there is none among us can imagine I do it enviously, or with purpose to detract from them; for what interest of fame or profit can the living lose by the reputation of the dead? On the other side, it is a great truth which Velleius Paterculus affirms, *Audita visis libentius laudamus; et praesentia invidia, praeterita admiratione prosequimur; et his nos obrui, illis instrui credimus:*[22] That praise or censure is certainly the most sincere which unbribed posterity shall give us.

Be pleased then in the first place to take notice, that the Greek poesy, which Crites has affirmed to have arrived to perfection in the reign of the Old Comedy,[23] was so far from it, that the distinction of it into acts was not known to them; or if it were, it is yet so darkly delivered to us that we cannot make it out.

All we know of it is from the singing of their chorus, and that too is so uncertain that in some of their plays we have reason to conjecture they

---

[22]"We praise more freely what we have heard about than what we have seen; we view the present with envy and the past with admiration; and we believe we are injured by the present and taught by the past." *Historia Romana* 2:92.

[23]The time of Aristophanes.

sung more than five times. Aristotle indeed divides the integral parts of a play into four.[24] First, the protasis or entrance, which gives light only to the characters of the persons, and proceeds very little into any part of the action: secondly, the epitasis, or working up of the plot where the play grows warmer; the design or action of it is drawing on, and you see something promising that it will come to pass: thirdly, the catastasis, called by the Romans, status, the height, and full growth of the play: we may call it properly the counterturn, which destroys that expectation, embroils the action in new difficulties, and leaves you far distant from that hope in which it found you, as you may have observed in a violent stream resisted by a narrow passage: it runs round to an eddy, and carries back the waters with more swiftness than it brought them on. Lastly, the catastrophe, which the Grecians called λύσις, the French *le dénouement*, and we the discovery or unravelling of the plot: there you see all things settling again upon their first foundations, and the obstacles which hindered the design or action of the play once removed, it ends with that resemblance of truth and nature, that the audience are satisfied with the conduct of it. Thus this great man delivered to us the image of a play, and I must confess it is so lively that from thence much light has been derived to the forming it more perfectly into acts and scenes; but what poet first limited to five the number of the acts I know not; only we see it so firmly established in the time of Horace, that he gives it for a rule in comedy; *Neu brevior quinto, neu sit productior actu:*[25] So that you see the Grecians cannot be said to have consummated this art; writing rather by entrances than by acts, and having rather a general indigested notion of a play, than knowing how and where to bestow the particular graces of it.

But since the Spaniards at this day allow but three acts, which they call *jornadas,* to a play, and the Italians in many of theirs follow them, when I condemn the Ancients, I declare it is not altogether because they have not five acts to every play, but because they have not confined themselves to one certain number; 'tis building an house without a model: and when they succeeded in such undertakings, they ought to have sacrificed to Fortune, not to the Muses.

Next, for the plot, which Aristotle called τὸ μῦθος, and often τῶν πραγμάτων σύνθεσις,[26] and from him the Romans *fabula,* it has already been judiciously observed by a late writer, that in their tragedies it was only some tale derived from Thebes or Troy, or at least something that happened in those two ages; which was worn so threadbare by the pens of all the epic poets, and even by tradition itself of the talkative Greeklings (as Ben Jonson calls them) that before it came upon the stage, it was already known to all the audience: and the people so soon as ever they heard the name of Oedipus, knew as well as the poet, that he had killed his father by a mistake, and committed incest with his mother, before the play; that they were now to hear of a great plague, an oracle, and the ghost of Laius: so that they sat with a yawning kind of expectation, till he was to come with his eyes pulled out, and speak a hundred or more verses in a tragic tone, in complaint of his misfortunes. But one Oedipus, Hercules, or Medea, had been tolerable; poor people they scaped not so good cheap: they had still the *chapon bouillé*[27] set before them, till their appetites were cloyed with the same dish, and the novelty being gone, the pleasure vanished: so that one main end of dramatic poesy in its definition, which was to cause delight, was of consequence destroyed.

In their comedies, the Romans generally borrowed their plots from the Greek poets; and theirs was commonly a little girl stolen or wandered from her parents, brought back unknown to the city, there got with child by some lewd young fellow; who, by the help of his servant, cheats his father, and when her time comes, to cry *Juno Lucina fer opem;*[28] one or other sees a little box

[24] Aristotle's discussion of the quantitative parts of tragedy occurs in *Poetics,* Ch. 12, where he differentiates the prologue, episode, exode, and choral ode. Later, in Ch. 18, he divides the play into the complication and the denouement. Neither of these corresponds to Eugenius's distinctions here.

[25] "The play that expects to be asked for another performance / Once it's been given, should be just five acts long." Horace, *Art of Poetry,* 189; see p. 88.

[26] The arrangement of the actions.

[27] Boiled capon.

[28] "Juno goddess of childbirth, help me!" Terence, *Andria* 3.1.15.

or cabinet which was carried away with her, and so discovers her to her friends, if some God do not prevent it, by coming down in a machine,[29] and taking the thanks of it to himself.

By the plot you may guess much of the characters of the persons. An old father who would willingly before he dies see his son well married; his debauched son, kind in his nature to his mistress, but miserably in want of money; a servant or slave, who has so much wit to strike in with him, and help to dupe his father, a braggadochio captain, a parasite, and a lady of pleasure.

As for the poor honest maid, on whom the story is built, and who ought to be one of the principal actors in the play, she is commonly a mute in it. She has the breeding of the old Elizabeth way, which was for maids to be seen and not to be heard; and it is enough you know she is willing to be married, when the fifth act requires it.

These are plots built after the Italian mode of houses, you see through them all at once; the characters are indeed the imitations of nature, but so narrow as if they had imitated only an eye or an hand, and did not dare to venture on the lines of a face, or the proportion of a body.

But in how straight a compass soever they have bounded their plots and characters, we will pass it by, if they have regularly pursued them, and perfectly observed those three unities of time, place, and action: the knowledge of which you say is derived to us from them. But in the first place give me leave to tell you, that the unity of place, however it might be practised by them, was never any of their rules. We neither find it in Aristotle, Horace, or any who have written of it, till in our age the French poets first made it a precept of the stage.[30] The unity of time, even Terence himself (who was the best and most regular of them) has neglected. His *Heautontimoroumenos* or *Self-Punisher* takes up visibly two days; says Scaliger, the two first acts concluding the first day, the three last the day ensuing; and Euripides, in tying himself to one day, has committed an absurdity never

to be forgiven him: for in one of his tragedies he has made Theseus go from Athens to Thebes, which was about forty English miles, under the walls of it to give battle, and appear victorious in the next act; and yet from the time of his departure to the return of the Nuntius, who gives the relation of his victory, Aethra and the chorus have but thirty-six verses; which is not for every mile a verse.

The like error is as evident in Terence's *Eunuch,* when Laches, the old man, enters by mistake into the house of Thais, where betwixt his exit and the entrance of Pythias, who comes to give ample relation of the disorders he has raised within, Parmeno who was left upon the stage, has not above five lines to speak: *C'est bien employer un temps si court,*[31] says the French poet, who furnished me with one of the observations; and almost all their tragedies will afford us examples of the like nature.

'Tis true, they have kept the continuity, or as you called it, *liaison des scènes* somewhat better: two do not perpetually come in together, talk and go out together; and other two succeed them, and do the same throughout the act, which the English call by the name of single scenes; but the reason is, because they have seldom above two or three scenes, properly so called, in every act; for it is to be accounted a new scene, not only every time the stage is empty, but every person who enters, though to others, makes it so; because he introduces a new business. Now the plots of their plays being narrow, and the persons few, one of their acts was written in a less compass than one of our well wrought scenes, and yet they are often deficient even in this. To go no further than Terence, you find in the *Eunuch* Antipho entering single in the midst of the third act, after Chremes and Pythias were gone off. In the same play you have likewise Dorias beginning the fourth act alone; and after she has made a relation of what was done at the soldiers' entertainment (which by the way was very inartificial) because she was presumed to speak directly to the audience, and to acquaint them with what was necessary to be known, but yet should have been so contrived by

---

[29]The *deus ex machina* of Horace's stricture.

[30]Eugenius forgets that the quintessentially English Philip Sidney condemns *Gorboduc* as "faulty both in place and time." See p. 155.

[31]"It's a good use of so short a time." Here and elsewhere, Dryden is paraphrasing Corneille's *Discours des trois unités.*

the poet as to have been told by persons of the drama to one another (and so by them to have come to the knowledge of the people) she quits the stage, and Phaedria enters next, alone likewise. He also give you an account of himself, and of his returning from the country, in monologue, to which unnatural way of narration Terence is subject in all his plays: In his *Adelphi* or Brothers, Syrus and Demea enter; after the scene was broken by the departure of Sostrata, Geta and Canthara; and indeed you can scarce look into any of his comedies, where you will not presently discover the same interruption.

But as they have failed both in laying of their plots, and in the management, swerving from the rules of their own art, by misrepresenting nature to us, in which they have ill-satisfied one intention of a play, which was delight, so in the instructive part they have erred worse: instead of punishing vice and rewarding virtue, they have often shown a prosperous wickedness, and an unhappy piety. They have set before us a bloody image of revenge in *Medea,* and given her dragons to convey her safe from punishment. A Priam and Astyanax murdered, and Cassandra ravished, and the lust and murder ending in the victory of him who acted them. In short, there is no indecorum in any of our modern plays, which if I would excuse, I could not shadow with some authority from the Ancients.

And one farther note of them let me leave you. Tragedies and comedies were not writ then as they are now, promiscuously, by the same person; but he who found his genius bending to the one, never attempted the other way. This is so plain, that I need not instance to you, that Aristophanes, Plautus, Terence, never any of them writ a tragedy; Aeschylus, Euripides, Sophocles, and Seneca, never meddled with comedy: the sock and buskin were not worn by the same poet: having then so much care to excel in one kind, very little is to be pardoned them if they miscarried in it; and this would lead me to the consideration of their wit, had not Crites given me sufficient warning not to be too bold in my judgement of it; because the languages being dead, and many of the customs and little accidents on which it depended, lost to us, we are not competent judges of it. But though I grant that here and there we may miss the application of a proverb or a custom, yet a thing well said will be wit in all languages; and though it may lose something in the translation, yet to him who reads it in the original, 'tis still the same; he has an idea of its excellency, though it cannot pass from his mind into any other expression or words than those in which he finds it. When Phaedria, in the *Eunuch,* had a command from his mistress to be absent two days; and encouraging himself to go through with it, said; *Tandem ego non illa caream, si opus sit, vel totum triduum?* Parmeno to mock the softness of his master, lifting up his hands and eyes, cries out as it were in admiration; *Hui! universum triduum!*[32] the elegancy of which *universum,* though it cannot be rendered in our language, yet leaves an impression on our souls: but this happens seldom in him, in Plautus oftener; who is infinitely too bold in his metaphors and coining words; out of which many times his wit is nothing, which questionless was one reason why Horace falls upon him so severely in those verses:

> Sed proavi nostri Plautinos et numeros, et
> laudavere sales, nimium patienter utrumque
> ne dicam stolide.[33]

For Horace himself was cautious to obtrude a new word on his readers, and makes custom and common use the best measure of receiving it into our writings.

> Multa renascentur quae nunc cecidere, cadentque
> quae nunc sunt in honore vocabula, si volet usus,
> quem penes, arbitrium est, et jus, et norma
> loquendi.[34]

The not observing this rule is that which the world has blamed in our satirist Cleveland; to

---

[32]"But cannot I manage to do without her, if I have to, for three whole days. . . . Alas, three entire days!" Terence, *Eunuch* 2.1.17–18.

[33]"Your ancestors praised both the wit and rhythms of Plautus? / For admiring both of these things they were *too* tolerant, / Not to say dense, if you and I can distinguish / A crudeness in phrasing from lapidary strength of wit . . ." Horace, *Art of Poetry,* 270–72; see p. 89.

[34]"All these projects, whatever men make, will perish, / And the fame and dignity of speech are equally mortal. / Much that has once dropped out will be born again, / And much of our language now held in high repute / Will fall to the ground if UTILITY so decrees, / With which rests the final decision, the ultimate standard, / The legal existence, of speech." Horace, *Art of Poetry,* 70–72; see p. 85.

express a thing hard and unnaturally, is his new way of elocution. 'Tis true, no poet but may sometimes use a catachresis, Virgil does it;

Mistaque ridenti colocasia fundet acantho.

In his Eclogue of Pollio, and in his 7th Æneid.

Mirantur et undae,
miratur nemus, insuetum fulgentia longe,
scuta virum fluvio, pictasque, innare carinas.

And Ovid once so modestly, that he asks leave to do it;

Si verbo audacia detur
haud metuam summi dixisse Palatia coeli.[35]

Calling the court of Jupiter by the name of Augustus's palace, though in another place he is more bold, where he says, *et longas visent capitolia pompas.*[36] But to do this always, and never be able to write a line without it, though it may be admired by some few pedants, will not pass upon those who know that wit is best conveyed to us in the most easy language; and is most to be admired when a great thought comes dressed in words so commonly received that it is understood by the meanest apprehensions, as the best meat is the most easily digested: but we cannot read a verse of Cleveland's without making a face at it, as if every word were a pill to swallow. He gives us many times a hard nut to break our teeth, without a kernel for our pains. So that there is this difference between his satires and Doctor Donne's, that the one gives us deep thoughts in common language, though rough cadence; the other gives us common thoughts in abstruse words: 'tis true, in some places his wit is independent of his words, as in that of the *Rebel Scot:*

Had Cain been Scot God would have changed his doom;
Not forced him wander, but confined him home,

Si sic omnia dixisset![37] This is wit in all languages: 'tis like Mercury, never to be lost or killed; and so that other:

For beauty like white-powder makes no noise,
And yet the silent hypocrite destroys.

You see the last line is highly metaphorical, but it is so soft and gentle that it does not shock us as we read it.

But, to return from whence I have digressed, to the consideration of the Ancients' writing and their wit, (of which by this time you will grant us in some measure to be fit judges,) though I see many excellent thoughts in Seneca, yet he, of them who had a genius most proper for the stage, was Ovid; he had a way of writing so fit to stir up a pleasing admiration and concernment, which are the objects of a tragedy, and to show the various movements of a soul combating between two different passions, that, had he lived in our age, or in his own could have writ with our advantages, no man but must have yielded to him; and therefore I am confident the *Medea* is none of his; for, though I esteem it for the gravity and sententiousness of it, which he himself concludes to be suitable to a tragedy, *Omne genus scripti gravitate tragaedia vincit,*[38] yet it moves not my soul enough to judge that he, who in the epic way wrote things so near the drama, as the story of Myrrha, of Caunus and Biblis, and the rest, should stir up no more concernment where he most endeavoured it. The masterpiece of Seneca I hold to be that scene in the *Troades,* where Ulysses is seeking for Astyanax to kill him. There you see the tenderness of a mother, so represented in Andromache, that it raises compassion to a high degree in the reader, and bears the nearest resemblance of anything in the tragedies of the Ancients, to the excellent scenes of passion in Shakespeare, or in Fletcher. For love-scenes you will find few among them, their tragic poets dealt not with that soft passion, but with lust, cruelty, revenge, ambition, and those bloody actions they produced; which were more capable of raising horror than compassion in an audience: leaving

---

[35]"The Egyptian bean, mixed with smiling acanthus, will flourish." (Virgil, *Eclogues* 4:20); "The waves and the woods wonder, shocked by the men's shining shields and by the painted ships." (Virgil, *Aeneid* 8:91–93); "If I were bold, I would not hesitate to call it the Palace of Heaven" (Ovid, *Metamorphoses* 1:175–76).

[36]"And Capitols view the long processions." Ovid, *Metamorphoses* 1:561.

[37]"If only he had always spoken thus!"
[38]"Tragedy surpasses in gravity all other kinds of writing." Ovid, *Tristia* 2:381.

love untouched, whose gentleness would have tempered them, which is the most frequent of all the passions, and which being the private concernment of every person, is soothed by viewing its own image in a public entertainment.

Among their comedies, we find a scene or two of tenderness, and that where you would least expect it, in Plautus; but to speak generally, their lovers say little, when they see each other, but *anima mea, vita mea;* ζωὴ καὶ ψυχὴ,[39] as the women in Juvenal's time used to cry out in the fury of their kindness: then indeed to speak sense were an offense. Any sudden gust of passion (as an ecstasy of love in an unexpected meeting) cannot better be expressed than in a word and a sigh, breaking one another. Nature is dumb on such occasions, and to make her speak, would be to represent her unlike herself. But there are a thousand other concernments of lovers, as jealousies, complaints, contrivances and the like, where not to open their minds at large to each other, were to be wanting to their own love, and to the expectation of the audience who watch the movements of their minds, as much as the changes of their fortunes. For the imaging of the first is properly the work of a poet, the latter he borrows of the historian.

Eugenius was proceeding in that part of his discourse, when Crites interrupted him. I see, said he, Eugenius and I are never like to have this question decided betwixt us; for he maintains the Moderns have acquired a new perfection in writing; I can only grant they have altered the mode of it. Homer described his heroes men of great appetites, lovers of beef broiled upon the coals, and good fellows; contrary to the practice of the French romances, whose heroes neither eat, nor drink, nor sleep, for love. Virgil makes Aeneas a bold avower of his own virtues,

Sum pius Aeneas fama super aethera notus;[40]

which in the civility of our poets is the character of a fanfaron or Hector: for with us the knight takes occasion to walk out, or sleep, to avoid the vanity of telling his own story, which the trusty squire is ever to perform for him. So in their love scenes, of which Eugenius spoke last, the Ancients were more hearty, we more talkative: they writ love as it was then the mode to make it, and I will grant thus much to Eugenius, that perhaps one of their poets, had he lived in our age,

Si foret hoc nostrum fato delapsus in aevum,[41]

(as Horace says of Lucilius) he had altered many things; not that they were not natural before, but that he might accommodate himself to the age in which he lived; yet in the mean time we are not to conclude anything rashly against those great men, but preserve to them the dignity of masters, and give that honour to their memories, (*Quos libitina sacravit*[42];) part of which we expect may be paid to us in future times.

This moderation of Crites, as it was pleasing to all the company, so it put an end to that dispute; which, Eugenius, who seemed to have the better of the argument, would urge no farther: but Lisideius after he had acknowledged himself of Eugenius's opinion concerning the Ancients, yet told him he had forborne, till his discourse were ended, to ask him why he preferred the English plays above those of other nations? and whether we ought not to submit our stage to the exactness of our next neighbours?

Though, said Eugenius, I am at all times ready to defend the honour of my country against the French, and to maintain, we are as well able to vanquish them with our pens as our ancestors have been with their swords, yet, if you please, added he, looking upon Neander, I will commit this cause to my friend's management; his opinion of our plays is the same with mine: and besides, there is no reason, that Crites and I, who have now left the stage, should re-enter so suddenly upon it; which is against the laws of comedy.

If the question had been stated, replied Lisideius, who had writ best, the French or English forty years ago, I should have been of your opinion, and adjudged the honour to our own

---

[39]"My soul, my life, life and soul." Cf. Juvenal, *Satires* 6:195.

[40]"I am pious Aeneas, renowned above the heavens." Virgil, *Aeneid* 1:378–89.

[41]"If Fate had dropped him into this era of ours." Horace, *Satires* I.9:68.

[42]"Whom the Goddess of funerals has sanctified." Horace, *Epistles* II.1:9.

nation; but since that time (said he, turning towards Neander) we have been so long together bad Englishmen, that we had not leisure to be good poets; Beaumont, Fletcher, and Jonson (who were only capable of bringing us to that degree of perfection which we have) were just then leaving the world; as if in an age of so much horror, wit and those milder studies of humanity, had no farther business among us. But the Muses, who ever follow peace, went to plant in another country; it was then, that the great Cardinal of Richelieu began to take them into his protection; and that, by his encouragement, Corneille and some other Frenchmen reformed their theatre, (which before was as much below ours as it now surpasses it and the rest of Europe); but because Crites, in his discourse for the Ancients, has prevented me, by observing many rules of the stage, which the Moderns have borrowed from them, I shall only, in short, demand of you, whether you are not convinced that of all nations the French have best observed them? In the unity of time you find them so scrupulous, that it yet remains a dispute among their poets, whether the artificial day of twelve hours more or less, be not meant by Aristotle, rather than the natural one of twenty-four; and consequently whether all plays ought not to be reduced into that compass? This I can testify, that in all their dramas writ within these last twenty years and upwards, I have not observed any that have extended the time to thirty hours: in the unity of place they are full as scrupulous, for many of their critics limit it to that very spot of ground where the play is supposed to begin; none of them exceed the compass of the same town or city.

The unity of action in all their plays is yet more conspicuous, for they do not burden them with under-plots, as the English do, which is the reason why many scenes of our tragi-comedies carry on a design that is nothing of kin to the main plot; and that we see two distinct webs in a play, like those in ill-wrought stuffs; and two actions, that is, two plays carried on together, to the confounding of the audience, who, before they are warm in their concernments for one part, are diverted to another; and by that means espouse the interest of neither. From hence likewise it arises that the one half of our actors are not known to the other. They keep their distances as if they were Montagues and Capulets, and seldom begin an acquaintance till the last scene of the fifth act, when they are all to meet upon the stage. There is no theatre in the world has anything so absurd as the English tragi-comedy, 'tis a drama of our own invention, and the fashion of it is enough to proclaim it so; here a course of mirth, there another of sadness and passion; a third of honour, and fourth a duel. Thus in two hours and a half we run through all the fits of Bedlam. The French afford you as much variety on the same day, but they do it not so unseasonably, or *mal à propos* as we. Our poets present you the play and the farce together, and our stages still retain somewhat of the original civility of the Red Bull;

> Atque ursum et pugiles media inter carmina poscunt.[43]

The end of tragedies or serious plays, says Aristotle, is to beget admiration, compassion, or concernment;[44] but are not mirth and compassion things incompatible? and is it not evident that the poet must of necessity destroy the former by intermingling of the latter? that is, he must ruin the sole end and object of his tragedy to introduce somewhat that is forced in to it; and is not of the body of it. Would you not think that physician mad, who having prescribed a purge, should immediately order you to take restringents?

But to leave our plays, and return to theirs, I have noted one great advantage they have had in the plotting of their tragedies; that is, they are always grounded upon some known history: according to that of Horace, *ex noto fictum carmen sequar*[45]; and in that they have so imitated the Ancients, that they have surpassed them. For the Ancients, as was observed before, took for the foundation of their plays some poetical fiction, such as under that consideration could move but little concernment in the audience, because they already knew the event of it. But the French goes farther;

[43]"They ask for a bear and boxers in the middle of the play." Horace, *Epistles* II.1:185–86.
[44]Aristotle mentions pity and fear, which may correspond to "compassion" and "concernment."
[45]"I shall set my sights on familiar things." Horace, *Art of Poetry,* 240; see p. 89.

Atque ita mentitur; sic veris falsa remiscet,
primo ne medium, medio ne discrepet imum.[46]

He so interweaves truth with probable fiction,
that he puts a pleasing fallacy upon us; mends the
intrigues of fate, and dispenses with the severity
of history, to reward that virtue which has been
rendered to us there unfortunate. Sometimes the
story has left the success so doubtful, that the
writer is free, by the privilege of a poet, to take
that which of two or more relations will best suit
with his design. As for example, in the death of
Cyrus, whom Justin and some others report to
have perished in the Scythian war, but Xenophon
affirms to have died in his bed of extreme old age.
Nay more, when the event is past dispute, even
then we are willing to be deceived, and the poet,
if he contrives it with appearance of truth, has all
the audience of his party; at least during the time
his play is acting: so naturally we are kind to
virtue, when our own interest is not in question,
that we take it up as the general concernment of
mankind. On the other side, if you consider the
historical plays of Shakespeare, they are rather so
many chronicles of kings, or the business many
times of thirty or forty years, cramped into a representation of two hours and an half, which is not
to imitate or paint nature, but rather to draw her in
miniature, to take her in little, to look upon her
through the wrong end of a perspective, and
receive her images not only much less, but infinitely more imperfect than the life: this, instead of
making a play delightful, renders it ridiculous.

Quodcumque ostendis mihi sic, incredulus odi.[47]

For the spirit of man cannot be satisfied but with
truth, or at least verisimility; and a poem is to contain, if not τὰ ἔτυμα, yet ἐτύμοισιν ὁμοῖα,[48] as
one of the Greek poets has expressed it.

Another thing in which the French differ from
us and from the Spaniards, is that they do not

embarrass, or cumber themselves with too much
plot: they only represent so much of a story as
will constitute one whole and great action sufficient for a play; we, who undertake more, do but
multiply adventures; which, not being produced
from one another, as effects from causes, but
barely following, constitute many actions in the
drama, and consequently make it many plays.

But by pursuing closely one argument, which
is not cloyed with many turns, the French have
gained more liberty for verse, in which they write:
they have leisure to dwell on a subject which
deserves it; and to represent the passions (which
we have acknowledged to be the poet's work)
without being hurried from one thing to another,
as we are in the plays of Calderón, which we have
seen lately upon our theatres, under the name of
Spanish plots.[49] I have taken notice but of one
tragedy of ours, whose plot has that uniformity
and unity of design in it which I have commended
in the French; and that is *Rollo*, or rather, under
the name of *Rollo*, the story of Bassianus and Geta
in Herodian; there indeed the plot is neither large
nor intricate, but just enough to fill the minds of
the audience, not to cloy them. Besides, you see it
founded upon the truth of history, only the time of
the action is not reducible to the strictness of the
rules; and you see in some places a little farce
mingled, which is below the dignity of the other
parts; and in this all our poets are extremely pec-
cant, even Ben Jonson himself in *Sejanus* and
Catiline has given us this oleo of a play: this
unnatural mixture of comedy and tragedy, which
to me sounds just as ridiculously as the history of
David with the merry humours of goliath. In
Sejanus you may take notice of the scene betwixt
Livia and the physician, which is a pleasant satire
upon the artificial helps of beauty. In *Catiline* you
may see the parliament of women; the little envies
of them to one another; and all that passes betwixt
Curio and Fulvia, scenes admirable in their kind,
but of an ill mingle with the rest.

But I return again to the French writers who, as
I have said, do not burden themselves too much
with plot, which has been reproached to them by
an ingenious person of our nation as a fault, for he

46". . . and simply leaves out / Whatever he thinks he can't
bring off shining and clear, / And devises so well, intermingling the true and the false. / That the middle part fits with the
first, the last with the middle." Horace, *Art of Poetry,*151–52;
see p. 87.
47"Whatsoever such stuff / You *show* me, I won't believe
it, I'll simply detest it." Horace, *Art of Poetry,* 188; see p. 88.
48"The truth"; "things like the truth." Homer, *Odyssey*
19:203.

49Dryden himself was to adapt Calderón in *An Evening's
Love* (1668).

says they commonly make but one person considerable in a play; they dwell on him, and his concernments, while the rest of the persons are only subservient to set him off. If he intends this by it, that there is one person in the play who is of greater dignity than the rest, he must tax, not only theirs, but those of the Ancients, and which he would be loth to do, the best of ours; for 'tis impossible but that one person must be more conspicuous in it than any other, and consequently the greatest share in the action must devolve on him. We see it so in the management of all affairs; even in the most equal aristocracy, the balance cannot be so justly poised, but someone will be superior to the rest, either in parts, fortune, interest, or the consideration of some glorious exploit, which will reduce the greatest part of business into his hands.

But, if he would have us to imagine that in exalting one character the rest of them are neglected, and that all of them have not some share or other in the action of the play, I desire him to produce any of Corneille's tragedies, wherein every person (like so many servants in a well governed family) has not some employment, and who is not necessary to the carrying on of the plot, or at least to your understanding it.

There are indeed some protatic[50] persons in the Ancients, whom they make use of in their plays, either to hear, or give the relation: but the French avoid this with great address, making their narrations only to, or by such, who are some way interested in the main design. And now I am speaking of relations, I cannot take a fitter opportunity to add this in favour of the French, that they often use them with better judgement and more *à propos* than the English do. Not that I commend narrations in general, but there are two sorts of them; one of those things which are antecedent to the play, and are related to make the conduct of it more clear to us, but, 'tis a fault to choose such subjects for the stage as will force us on that rock; because we see they are seldom listened to by the audience, and that is many times the ruin of the play: for, being once let pass without attention, the audience can never recover themselves to

understand the plot; and indeed it is somewhat unreasonable that they should be put to so much trouble as, that to comprehend what passes in their sight, they must have recourse to what was done, perhaps, ten or twenty years ago.

But there is another sort of relations, that is, of things happening in the action of the play, and supposed to be done behind the scenes, and this is many times both convenient and beautiful: for, by it the French avoid the tumult, to which we are subject in England, by representing duels, battles, and the like, which renders our stage too like the theatres where they fight prizes. For what is more ridiculous than to represent an army with a drum and five men behind it; all which, the hero of the other side is to drive in before him, or to see a duel fought, and one slain with two or three thrusts of the foil, which we know are so blunted, that we might give a man an hour to kill another in good earnest with them.

I have observed that in all our tragedies, the audience cannot forbear laughing when the actors are to die; 'tis the most comic part of the whole play. All passions may be lively[51] represented on the stage, if to the well-writing of them the actor supplies a good commanded voice, and limbs that move easily, and without stiffness; but there are many actions which can never be imitated to a just height: dying especially is a thing which none but a Roman gladiator could naturally perform on the stage when he did not imitate or represent, but do it; and therefore it is better to omit the representation of it.

The words of a good writer which describe it lively, will make a deeper impression of belief in us than all the actor can insinuate into us, when he seems to fall dead before us; as a poet in the description of a beautiful garden, or a meadow, will please our imagination more than the place itself can please our sight. When we see death represented we are convinced it is but fiction; but when we hear it related, our eyes (the strongest witnesses) are wanting, which might have undeceived us; and we are all willing to favour the sleight when the poet does not too grossly impose on us. They therefore who imagine these relations would make no concernment in the audience, are

[50]Introductory: like the Watchman in Aeschylus's *Agamemnon*.

[51]In a lifelike manner.

deceived, by confounding them with the other, which are of things antecedent to the play; those are made often in cold blood (as I may say) to the audience; but these are warmed with our concernments, which were before awakened in the play. What the philosophers say of motion, that, when it is once begun, it continues of itself, and will do so to eternity without some stop put to it,[52] is clearly true on this occasion; the soul being already moved with the characters and fortunes of those imaginary persons, continues going of its own accord, and we are no more weary to hear what becomes of them when they are not on the stage, than we are to listen to the news of an absent mistress. But it is objected, that if one part of the play may be related, then why not all? I answer, some parts of the action are more fit to be represented, some to be related. Corneille says judiciously, that the poet is not obliged to expose to view all particular actions which conduce to the principal: he ought to select such of them to be seen which will appear with the greatest beauty, either by the magnificence of the show, or the vehemence of passions which they produce, or some other charm which they have in them, and let the rest arrive to the audience by narration. 'Tis a great mistake in us to believe the French present no part of the action on the stage: every alteration or crossing of a design, every new sprung passion, and turn of it, is a part of the action, and much the noblest, except we conceive nothing to be action till the players come to blows; as if the painting of the hero's mind were not more properly the poet's work than the strength of his body. Nor does this anything contradict the opinion of Horace, where he tells us,

Segnius irritant animos demissa per aurem,
quam quae sunt oculis subjecta fidelibus. —

For he says immediately after,

Non tamen intus
digna geri promes in scenam, multaque tolles
ex oculis, quae mox narret facundia praesens.

Among which many he recounts some.

Nec pueros coram populo Medea trucidet,
aut in avem Progne mutetur, Cadmus in anguem,
etc.[53]

That is, those actions which by reason of their cruelty will cause aversion in us, or by reason of their impossibility unbelief, ought either wholly to be avoided by a poet, or only delivered by narration. To which, we may have leave to add such as to avoid tumult, (as was before hinted) or to reduce the plot into a more reasonable compass of time, or for defect of beauty in them, are rather to be related than presented to the eye. Examples of all these kinds are frequent, not only among all the Ancients, but in the best received of our English poets. We find Ben Jonson using them in his *Magnetic Lady,* where one comes out from dinner, and relates the quarrels and disorders of it to save the indecent appearance of them on the stage, and to abbreviate the story: and this in express imitation of Terence, who had done the same before him in his *Eunuch,* where Pythius makes the like relation of what had happened within at the soldiers' entertainment. The relations likewise of Sejanus's death, and the prodigies before it are remarkable; the one of which was hid from sight to avoid the horror and tumult of the representation; the other to shun the introducing of things impossible to be believed. In that excellent play, *The King and No King,* Fletcher goes yet farther; for the whole unravelling of the plot is done by narration in the fifth act, after the manner of the Ancients; and it moves great concernment in the audience, though it be only a relation of what was done many years before the play. I could multiply other instances, but these are sufficient to prove that there is no error in choosing a subject which requires this

[52]Dryden is not quoting Newton's first law of motion before it was announced; he is probably echoing Descartes's *Principia Philosophiae,* which had just been translated into English.

[53]"But things entrusted to the ear / Impress our minds less vividly than what is exposed / To our trustworthy eyes so that a viewer informs himself / Of precisely what happened. Still, you are not to show / On stage what ought to take place backstage: remove / From our eyes the substance of things . . . / Medea / must not butcher her boys in front of the people; / Unspeakable Atreus should not cook up human flesh / Before our eyes, nor should Procne change into a bird, / Or Cadmus into a snake." Horace, *Art of Poetry,* 180–87; see p. 88.

sort of narrations; in the ill-management of them, there may.

But I find I have been too long in this discourse since the French have many other excellencies not common to us; as that you never see any of their plays end with a conversion, or simple change of will, which is the ordinary way which our poets use to end theirs. It shows little art in the conclusion of a dramatic poem, which they who have hindered the felicity during the four acts, desist from it in the fifth without some powerful cause to take them off their design; and though I deny not but such reasons may be found, yet it is a path that is cautiously to be trod, and the poet is to be sure he convinces the audience that the motive is strong enough. As for example, the conversion of the usurer in *The Scornful Lady,* seems to me a little forced; for being a usurer, which implies a lover of money to the highest degree of covetousness (and such the poet has represented him) the account he gives for the sudden change is that he has been duped by the wild young fellow, which in reason might render him more wary another time, and make him punish himself with harder fare and coarser clothes to get up again what he had lost: but that he should look on it as a judgement, and so repent, we may expect to hear in a sermon, but I should never endure it in a play.

I pass by this; neither will I insist on the care they take, that no person after his first entrance shall ever appear, but the business which brings him upon the stage shall be evident: which rule if observed, must needs render all the events in the play more natural; for there you see the probability of every accident, in the cause that produced it; and that which appears chance in the play will seem so reasonable to you, that you will there find it almost necessary; so that in the exit of the actor you have a clear account of his purpose and design in the next entrance: (though, if the scene be well wrought, the event will commonly deceive you) for there is nothing so absurd, says Corneille, as for an actor to leave the stage, only because he has no more to say.

I should now speak of the beauty of their rhyme, and the just reason I have to prefer that way of writing in tragedies before ours in blank verse; but because it is partly received by us, and therefore not altogether peculiar to them, I will say no more of it in relation to their plays. For our own I doubt not but it will exceedingly beautify them, and I can see but one reason why it should not generally obtain, that is, because our poets write so ill in it. This indeed may prove a more prevailing argument than all others which are used to destroy it, and therefore I am only troubled when great and judicious poets, and those who are acknowledged such, have writ or spoke against it; as for others they are to be answered by that one sentence of an ancient author.

> Sed ut primo ad consequendos eos quos priores ducimus accendimur, itaubi aut praeteriri, aut aequari eos posse desperavimus, studium cum spe senescit: quod, scilicet, assequi non potest, sequi desinit; praeteritoque eo in quo eminere non possumus, aliquid in quo nitamur conquirimus.[54]

Lisideius concluded in this manner; and Neander after a little pause thus answered him.

I shall grant Lisideius, without much dispute, a great part of what he has urged against us; for I acknowledge that the French contrive their plots more regularly, and observe the laws of comedy, and decorum of the stage (to speak generally) with more exactness than the English. Farther, I deny not but he has taxed us justly in some irregularities of ours which he has mentioned; yet, after all, I am of opinion that neither our faults nor their virtues are considerable enough to place them above us.

For the lively imitation of nature being in the definition of a play, those which best fulfill that law ought to be esteemed superior to the others. 'Tis true, those beauties of the French poesy are such as will raise perfection higher where it is, but are not sufficient to give it where it is not: they are indeed the beauties of a statue, but not of a man, because not animated with the soul of poesy, which is imitation of humour and passions: and this Lisideius himself, or any other, however

---

[54]"At first we burn to excel those whom we think our leaders, but when we despair of surpassing them or even equalling them, our enthusiasm weakens with our hope; when it cannot overtake, it ceases to follow; putting away what we cannot excel in, we seek another outlet for our efforts." Velleius Paterculus, *Historia Romana* I:17.

biased to their party, cannot but acknowledge, if he will either compare the humours of our comedies, or the characters of our serious plays with theirs. He who will look upon theirs which have been written till these last ten years or thereabouts, will find it an hard matter to pick out two or three passable humours amongst them. Corneille himself, their arch-poet, what has he produced except *The Liar,* and you know how it was cried up in France; but when it came upon the English stage, though well translated, and that part of Dorant acted to so much advantage as I am confident it never received in its own country, the most favourable to it would not put it in competition with many of Fletcher's or Ben Jonson's. In the rest of Corneille's comedies you have little humour; he tells you himself his way is first to show two lovers in good intelligence with each other; in the working up of the play to embroil them by some mistake, and in the latter end to clear it, and reconcile them.

But of late years Molière, the younger Corneille, Quinault, and some others, have been imitating afar off the quick turns and graces of the English stage. They have mixed their serious plays with mirth, like our tragi-comedies, since the death of Cardinal Richelieu, which Lisideius and many others not observing, have commended that in them for a virtue which they themselves no longer practise. Most of their new plays are like some of ours, derived from the Spanish novels. There is scarce one of them without a veil, and a trusty Diego,[55] who drolls much after the rate of the *Adventures.* But their humours, if I may grace them with that name, are so thin sown that never above one of them comes up in any play. I dare take upon me to find more variety of them in some one play of Ben Jonson's than in all theirs together: as he who has seen the *Alchemist, The Silent Woman,* or *Bartholomew Fair,* cannot but acknowledge with me.

I grant the French have performed what was possible on the ground-work of the Spanish plays; what was pleasant before, they have made regular; but there is not above one good play to be writ on all those plots; they are too much alike to please often, which we need not the experience of our own stage to justify. As for their new way of mingling mirth with serious plot, I do not with Lisideius condemn the thing, though I cannot approve their manner of doing it. He tells us we cannot so speedily recollect ourselves after a scene of great passion and concernment, as to pass to another of mirth and humour, and to enjoy it with any relish: but why should he imagine the soul of man more heavy than his senses? Does not the eye pass from an unpleasant object to a pleasant in a much shorter time than is required to this? and does not the unpleasantness of the first commend the beauty of the latter? The old rule of logic might have convinced him, that contraries when placed near, set off each other. A continued gravity keeps the spirit too much bent; we must refresh it sometimes, as we bait in a journey, that we may go on with greater ease. A scene of mirth mixed with tragedy has the same effect upon us which our music has betwixt the acts, which we find a relief to us from the best plots and language of the stage, if the discourses have been long. I must therefore have stronger arguments ere I am convinced, that compassion and mirth in the same subject destroy each other, and in the mean time cannot but conclude, to the honour of our nation, that we have invented, increased and perfected a more pleasant way of writing for the stage than was ever known to the Ancients or Moderns of any nation, which is tragi-comedy.

And this leads me to wonder why Lisideius and many others should cry up the barrenness of the French plots above the variety and copiousness of the English. Their plots are single, they carry on one design which is pushed forward by all the actors, every scene in the play contributing and moving towards it. Our plays besides the main design, have under-plots or by-concernments, of less considerable persons, and intrigues, which are carried on with the motion of the main plot: as they say the orb of the fixed stars, and those of the planets, though they have motions of their own, are whirled about by the motion of the *primum mobile,* in which they are contained: that similitude expresses much of the English stage, for if contrary motions may be found in nature to agree; if a planet can go east and west at the same time, one way by virtue of his own motion, the other by

---

[55]Neander is alluding to a comic servant, Diego, in Samuel Tuke's *Adventures of Five Hours.*

the force of the first mover, it will not be difficult to imagine how the under-plot, which is only different, not contrary to the great design, may naturally be conducted along with it.

Eugenius[56] has already shown us, from the confession of the French poets, that the unity of action is sufficiently preserved if all the imperfect actions of the play are conducing to the main design: but when those petty intrigues of a play are so ill ordered, that they have no coherence with the other, I must grant that Lisideius has reason to tax that want of due connexion; for coordination in a play is as dangerous and unnatural as in a state. In the mean time he must acknowledge our variety, if well ordered, will afford a greater pleasure to the audience.

As for his other argument, that by pursuing one single theme they gain an advantage to express and work up the passions, I wish any example he could bring from them would make it good: for I confess their verses are to me the coldest I have ever read. Neither indeed is it possible for them, in the way they take, so to express passion, as that the effects of it should appear in the concernment of an audience, their speeches being so many declamations, which tire us with the length; so that instead of persuading us to grieve for their imaginary heroes, we are concerned for our own trouble, as we are in tedious visits of bad company; we are in pain till they are gone. When the French stage came to be reformed by Cardinal Richelieu, those long harangues were introduced, to comply with the gravity of a churchman. Look upon the *Cinna* and the *Pompey,* they are not so properly to be called plays, as long discourses of reason of state: and *Polyeucte* in matters of religion is as solemn as the long stops upon our organs. Since that time it is grown into a custom, and their actors speak by the hourglass, like our parsons; nay, they account it the grace of their parts, and think themselves disparaged by the poet, if they may not twice or thrice in a play entertain the audience with a speech of an hundred or two hundred lines. I deny not but this may suit well enough with the French; for as we, who are a more sullen people, come to be diverted at

our plays; so they who are of an airy and gay temper come thither to make themselves more serious. And this I conceive to be one reason why comedies are more pleasing to us, and tragedies to them. But to speak generally, it cannot be denied that short speeches and replies are more apt to move the passions, and beget concernment in us than the other: for it is unnatural for any one in a gust of passion to speak long together, or for another in the same condition, to suffer him, without interruption. Grief and passion are like floods raised in little brooks by a sudden rain; they are quickly up, and if the concernment be poured unexpectedly in upon us, it overflows us. But a long sober shower gives them leisure to run out as they came in, without troubling the ordinary current. As for comedy, repartee is one of its chiefest graces; the greatest pleasure of the audience is a chase of wit kept up on both sides, and swiftly managed. And this our forefathers, if not we, have had in Fletcher's plays, to a much higher degree of perfection than the French poets can, reasonably, hope to reach.

There is another part of Lisideius's discourse, in which he has rather excused our neighbours than commended them; that is, for aiming only to make one person considerable in their plays. 'Tis very true what he has urged, that one character in all plays, even without the poet's care, will have advantage of all the others; and that the design of the whole drama will chiefly depend on it. But this hinders not that there may be more shining characters in the play: many persons of a second magnitude, nay, some so very near, so almost equal to the first, that greatness may be opposed to greatness, and all the persons be made considerable, not only by their quality, but their action. 'Tis evident that the more the persons are, the greater will be the variety of the plot. If then the parts are managed so regularly that the beauty of the whole be kept entire, and that the variety become not a perplexed and confused mass of accidents, you will find it infinitely pleasing to be led in a labyrinth of design, where you see some of your way before you, yet discern not the end till you arrive at it. And that all this is practicable, I can produce for examples many of our English plays: as *The Maid's Tragedy, The Alchemist, The Silent Woman:* I was going to have named

---

[56]Crites; see p. 168.

The Fox, but that the unity of design seems not exactly observed in it; for there appear two actions in the play; the first naturally ending with the fourth act; the second forced from it in the fifth: which yet is the less to be condemned in him, because the disguise of Volpone, though it suited not with his character as a crafty or covetous person, agreed well enough with that of a voluptuary: and by it the poet gained the end at which he aimed, the punishment of vice, and the reward of virtue, both which that disguise produced. So that to judge equally of it, it was an excellent fifth act, but not so naturally proceeding from the former.

But to leave this, and pass to the latter part of Lisideius's discourse, which concerns relations, I must acknowledge with him, that the French have reason to hide that part of the action which would occasion too much tumult on the stage, and to choose rather to have it made known by narration to the audience. Farther I think it very convenient, for the reasons he has given, that all incredible actions were removed; but, whether custom has so insinuated itself into our countrymen, or nature has so formed them to fierceness, I know not; but they will scarcely suffer combats and other objects of horror to be taken from them. And indeed, the indecency of tumults is all which can be objected against fighting. For why may not our imagination as well suffer itself to be deluded with the probability of it, as with any other thing in the play? For my part, I can with as great ease persuade myself that the blows are given in good earnest, as I can, that they who strike them are kings or princes, or those persons which they represent. For objects of incredibility I would be satisfied from Lisideius, whether we have any so removed from all appearance of truth as are those of Corneille's *Andromède?* A play which has been frequented the most of any he has writ? If the Perseus, or the son of an heathen god, the Pegasus and the monster were not capable to choke a strong belief, let him blame any representation of ours hereafter. Those indeed were objects of delight; yet the reason is the same as to the probability: for he makes it not a ballet or masque, but a play, which is to resemble truth. But for death, that it ought not to be represented, I have besides the arguments alleged by Lisideius, the authority of Ben Jonson, who has forborne it in his tragedies; for both the death of Sejanus and Catiline are related: though in the latter I cannot but observe one irregularity of that great poet: he has removed the scene in the same act, from Rome to Catiline's army, and from thence again to Rome; and besides, has allowed a very inconsiderable time, after Catiline's speech, for the striking of the battle, and the return of Petreius, who is to relate the event of it to the Senate: which I should not animadvert on him, who was otherwise a painful observer of τὸ πρέπον, or the decorum of the stage, if he had not used extreme severity in his judgement on the incomparable Shakespeare for the same fault. To conclude on this subject of relations, if we are to be blamed for showing too much of the action, the French are as faulty for discovering too little of it: a mean betwixt both should be observed by every judicious writer, so as the audience may neither be left unsatisfied by not seeing what is beautiful, or shocked by beholding what is either incredible or indecent. I hope I have already proved in this discourse, that though we are not altogether so punctual as the French, in observing the laws of comedy; yet our errors are so few and little, and those things wherein we excel them so considerable, that we ought of right to be preferred before them. But what will Lisideius say if they themselves acknowledge they are too strictly bounded by those laws, for breaking which he has blamed the English? I will allege Corneille's words, as I find them in the end of his Discourse of the three unities; *Il est facile aux speculatifs d'estre sevères,* etc. ''Tis easy for speculative persons to judge severely; but if they would produce to public view ten or twelve pieces of this nature, they would perhaps give more latitude to the rules than I have done, when by experience they had known how much we are limited and constrained by them, and how many beauties of the stage they banished from it.' To illustrate a little what he has said; by their servile observations of the unities of time and place, and integrity of scenes, they have brought on themselves that dearth of plot, and narrowness of imagination, which may be observed in all their plays. How many beautiful accidents might naturally happen in two or three days, which cannot arrive with any probability in the compass of twenty-four hours? There is time to be allowed also for maturity of design, which amongst great and prudent persons, such as are often represented in tragedy, cannot, with any likelihood of truth, be brought to pass at so short a warning. Farther, by tying themselves strictly to the unity of place, and unbroken scenes, they are forced many times to omit some beauties which cannot be shown where the act began; but might, if the scene were interrupted, and the stage cleared for the persons to enter in another place; and therefore the French poets are often forced upon absurdities: for if the act begins in a chamber, all the persons in the play must have some business or other to come thither, or else they are not to be shown that act, and sometimes their characters are very unfitting to appear there; as, suppose it were the king's bedchamber, yet the meanest man in the tragedy must come and dispatch his business there, rather than in the lobby or courtyard, (which is fitter for him) for fear the stage should be cleared, and the scenes broken. Many times they fall by it into a greater inconvenience; for they keep their scenes unbroken, and yet change the place; as in one of their newest plays where the act begins in the street. There a gentleman is to meet his friend; he sees him with his man, coming out from his father's house; they talk together, and the first goes out: the second, who is a lover, has made an appointment with his mistress; she appears at the window, and then we are to imagine the scene lies under it. This gentleman is called away, and leaves his servant with his mistress: presently her father is heard from within; the young lady is afraid the serving-man should be discovered, and thrusts him into a place of safety, which is supposed to be her closet. After this, the father enters to the daughter, and now the scene is in a house: for he is seeking from one room to another for this poor Philipin, or French Diego, who is heard from within, drolling and breaking many a miserable conceit on the subject of his sad condition. In this ridiculous manner the play goes forward, the stage being never empty all the while: so that the street, the window, the two houses, and the closet, are made to walk about, and the persons to stand still. Now what, I beseech you, is more easy than to write a regular French play, or more difficult than to write an irregular English one, like those of Fletcher, or of Shakespeare?

If they content themselves as Corneille did, with some flat design, which, like an ill riddle, is found out ere it be half proposed, such plots we can make every way regular as easily as they: but whenever they endeavour to rise to any quick turns and counterturns of plot, as some of them have attempted, since Corneille's plays have been less in vogue, you see they write as irregularly as we, though they cover it more speciously. Hence the reason is perspicuous, why no French plays, when translated, have, or ever can, succeed on the English stage. For, if you consider the plots, our own are fuller of variety; if the writing, ours are more quick and fuller of spirit: and therefore 'tis a strange mistake in those who decry the way of writing plays in verse, as if the English therein imitated the French. We have borrowed nothing from them; our plots are weaved in English looms: we endeavour therein to follow the variety and greatness of characters which are derived to us from Shakespeare and Fletcher. The copiousness and well-knitting of the intrigues we have from Jonson, and for the verse itself we have English precedents of elder date than any of Corneille's plays (not to name our old comedies before Shakespeare, which were all writ in verse of six feet, or Alexandrines, such as the French now use). I can show in Shakespeare, many scenes of rhyme together, and the like in Ben Jonson's tragedies: in *Catiline* and *Sejanus* sometimes thirty or forty lines; I mean besides the chorus, or the monologues, which by the way, showed Ben no enemy to this way of writing, especially if you read his *Sad Shepherd,* which goes sometimes on rhyme, sometimes on blank verse, like an horse who eases himself on trot and amble. You find him likewise commending Fletcher's pastoral of *The Faithful Shepherdess;* which is for the most part rhyme, though not refined to that purity to which it hath since been brought. And these examples are enough to clear us from a servile imitation of the French.

But to return whence I have digressed, I dare boldly affirm these two things of the English drama: first, that we have many plays of ours as regular as any of theirs; and which, besides, have more variety of plot and characters: and secondly, that in most of the irregular plays of Shakespeare or Fletcher (for Ben Jonson's are for the most part regular) there is a more masculine fancy and greater spirit in the writing, than there is in any of the French. I could produce even in Shakespeare's and Fletcher's works, some plays which are almost exactly formed; as *The Merry Wives of Windsor,* and *The Scornful Lady:* but because (generally speaking) Shakespeare, who writ first, did not perfectly observe the laws of comedy, and Fletcher, who came nearer to perfection, yet through carelessness made many faults, I will take the pattern of a perfect play from Ben Jonson, who was a careful and learned observer of the dramatic laws, and from all his comedies I shall select *The Silent Woman;* of which I will make a short examen, according to those rules which the French observe.

As Neander was beginning to examine *The Silent Woman,* Eugenius, earnestly regarding him; I beseech you, Neander, said he, gratify the company and me in particular so far, as before you speak of the play, to give us a character of the author; and tell us frankly your opinion, whether you do not think all writers, both French and English, ought to give place to him?

I fear, replied Neander, that in obeying your commands I shall draw some envy on myself. Besides, in performing them, it will be first necessary to speak somewhat of Shakespeare and Fletcher, his rivals in poesy, and one of them, in my opinion, at least his equal, perhaps his superior.

To begin with Shakespeare; he was the man who of all modern, and perhaps ancient poets, had the largest and most comprehensive soul. All the images of nature were still present to him, and he drew them not laboriously, but luckily: when he describes anything, you more than see it, you feel it too. Those who accuse him to have wanted learning, give him the greater commendation: he was naturally learned; he needed not the spectacles of books to read nature; he looked inwards, and found her there. I cannot say he is everywhere alike; were he so, I should do him injury to compare him with the greatest of mankind. He is many times flat, insipid; his comic wit degenerating into clenches, his serious swelling into bombast. But he is always great, when some great occasion is presented to him: no man can say he ever had a fit subject for his wit, and did not then raise himself as high above the rest of poets.

Quantum lenta solent inter viburna cupressi.[57]

The consideration of this made Mr. Hales of Eton say that there was no subject of which any poet ever writ, but he would produce it much better done in Shakespeare; and however others are now generally preferred before him, yet the age wherein he lived, which had contemporaries with him, Fletcher and Jonson, never equalled them to him in their esteem. And in the last king's Court, when Ben's reputation was at highest, Sir John Suckling, and with him the greater part of the courtiers, set our Shakespeare far above him.

Beaumont and Fletcher of whom I am next to speak, had with the advantage of Shakespeare's wit, which was their precedent, great natural gifts, improved by study, Beaumont especially being so accurate a judge of plays, that Ben Jonson while he lived, submitted all his writings to his censure, and 'tis thought, used his judgement in correcting, if not contriving all his plots. What value he had for him, appears by the verse he writ to him; and therefore I need speak no farther of it. The first play that brought Fletcher and him in esteem was their *Philaster,* for before that, they had written two or three very unsuccessfully: as the like is reported of Ben Jonson, before he writ *Every Man in His Humour.* Their plots were generally more regular than Shakespeare's, especially those which were made before Beaumont's death; and they understood and imitated the conversation of gentlemen much better; whose wild debaucheries, and quickness of wit in repartees, no poet before them could paint as they have done. Humour which Ben Jonson derived from particular persons, they made it not their business to describe. They represented all the passions very lively, but above all, love. I am apt to believe the English language in them arrived to its highest perfection; what words have since been taken in, are rather superfluous than ornamental. Their plays are now the most pleasant and frequent entertainments of the stage, two of theirs being acted through the

---

[57]"As cypresses usually do among bending osiers." Virgil, *Eclogues* 1:25.

year for one of Shakespeare's or Jonson's: the reason is, because there is a certain gaiety in their comedies, and pathos in their more serious plays, which suits generally with all men's humours. Shakespeare's language is likewise a little obsolete, and Ben Jonson's wit comes short of theirs.

As for Jonson, to whose character I am now arrived, if we look upon him while he was himself, (for his last plays were but his dotages) I think him the most learned and judicious writer which any theatre ever had. He was a most severe judge of himself as well as others. One cannot say he wanted wit, but rather that he was frugal of it. In his works you find little to retrench or alter. Wit and language, and humour also in some measure we had before him; but something of art was wanting to the drama till he came. He managed his strength to more advantage than any who preceded him. You seldom find him making love in any of his scenes, or endeavouring to move the passions; his genius was too sullen and saturnine to do it gracefully, especially when he knew he came after those who had performed both to such an height. Humour was his proper sphere, and in that he delighted most to represent mechanic[58] people. He was deeply conversant in the Ancients, both Greek and Latin, and he borrowed boldly from them. There is scarce a poet or historian among the Roman authors of those times whom he has not translated in *Sejanus* and *Catiline*. But he has done his robberies so openly, that one may see he fears not to be taxed by any law. He invades authors like a monarch, and what would be theft in other poets, is only victory in him. With the spoils of these writers he so represents old Rome to us, in its rites, ceremonies and customs, that if one of their poets had written either of his tragedies, we had seen less of it than in him. If there was any fault in his language, 'twas that he weaved it too closely and laboriously, in his comedies especially: perhaps too, he did a little too much Romanize our tongue, leaving the words which he translated almost as much Latin as he found them: wherein though he learnedly followed their language, he did not enough comply with the idiom of ours. If I would compare him with Shakespeare, I must

acknowledge him the more correct poet, but Shakespeare the greater wit. Shakespeare was the Homer, or father of our dramatic poets; Jonson was the Virgil, the pattern of elaborate writing. I admire him, but I love Shakespeare. To conclude of him, as he has given us the most correct plays, so in the precepts which he has laid down in his *Discoveries,* we have as many and profitable rules for perfecting the stage as any wherewith the French can furnish us.

Having thus spoken of the author, I proceed to the examination of his comedy, *The Silent Woman.*

EXAMEN OF *THE SILENT WOMAN*

To begin first with the length of the action, it is so far from exceeding the compass of a natural day, that it takes not up an artificial one. 'Tis all included in the limits of three hours and an half, which is no more than is required for the presentment on the stage. A beauty perhaps not much observed; if it had, we should not have looked on the Spanish translation of *Five Hours* with so much wonder. The scene of it is laid in London; the latitude of place is almost as little as you can imagine, for it lies all within the compass of two houses, and after the first act, in one.[59] The continuity of scenes is observed more than in any of our plays, except his own *Fox* and *Alchemist.* They are not broken above twice or thrice at most in the whole comedy, and in the two best of Corneille's plays, the *Cid* and *Cinna,* they are interrupted once. The action of the play is entirely one; the end or aim of which is the settling Morose's estate on Dauphine. The intrigue of it is the greatest and most noble of any pure unmixed comedy in any language: you see in it many persons of various characters and humours, and all delightful; as first, Morose, or an old man, to whom all noise but his own talking is offensive. Some who would be thought critics, say this humour of his is forced: but to remove that objection, we may consider him first to be naturally of a delicate hearing, as many are to whom all sharp

---

[58]Low, vulgar.

[59]There are actually six different locations, and the action of the play takes up more than twelve hours, or more than an "artificial" day.

sounds are unpleasant; and secondly, we may attribute much of it to the peevishness of his age, or the wayward authority of an old man in his own house, where he may make himself obeyed; and to this the poet seems to allude in his name, Morose. Beside this, I am assured from divers persons, that Ben Jonson was actually acquainted with such a man, one altogether as ridiculous as he is here represented. Others say it is not enough to find one man of such an humour; it must be common to more, and the more common the more natural. To prove this, they instance in the best of comical characters, Falstaff. There are many men resembling him; old, fat, merry, cowardly, drunken, amorous, vain, and lying. But to convince these people, I need but tell them, that humour is the ridiculous extravagance of conversation, wherein one man differs from all others. If then it be common, or communicated to many, how differs it from other men's? or what indeed causes it to be ridiculous so much as the singularity of it? As for Falstaff, he is not properly one humour, but a miscellany of humours or images, drawn from so many several men; that wherein he is singular is his wit, or those things he says, *praeter expectatum,* unexpected by the audience; his quick evasions when you imagine him surprised, which as they are extremely diverting of themselves, so receive a great addition from his person; for the very sight of such an unwieldy old debauched fellow is a comedy alone. And here having a place so proper for it, I cannot but enlarge somewhat upon this subject of humour into which I am fallen. The Ancients had little of it in their comedies; for the τὸ γελοῖον,[60] of the Old Comedy, of which Aristophanes was chief, was not so much to imitate a man, as to make the people laugh at some odd conceit, which had commonly somewhat of unnatural or obscene in it. Thus when you see Socrates brought upon the stage you are not to imagine him made ridiculous by the imitation of his actions, but rather by making him perform something very unlike himself, something so childish and absurd, as by comparing it with the gravity of the true Socrates, makes

a ridiculous object for the spectators. In their New Comedy which succeeded, the poets sought indeed to express the ἦθος, as in their tragedies the πάθος of mankind.[61] But this ἦθος contained only the general characters of men and manners; as old men, lovers, serving-men, courtesans, parasites, and such other persons as we see in their comedies; all which they made alike: that is, one old man or father; one lover, one courtesan so like another, as if the first of them had begot the rest of every sort: *ex homine hunc natum dicas.*[62] The same custom they observed likewise in their tragedies. As for the French, though they have the word *humeur* among them, yet they have small use of it in their comedies, or farces; they being but ill imitations of the *ridiculum,* or that which stirred up laughter in the Old Comedy. But among the English 'tis otherwise, whereby humour is meant some extravagant habit, passion, or affection, particular (as I said before) to some one person, by the oddness of which, he is immediately distinguished from the rest of men; which being lively and naturally represented, most frequently begets that malicious pleasure in the audience which is testified by laughter, as all things which are deviations from customs are ever the aptest to produce it, though by the way this laughter is only accidental, as the person represented is fantastic or bizarre. But pleasure is essential to it, as the imitation of what is natural. The description of these humours, drawn from the knowledge and observation of particular persons, was the peculiar genius and talent of Ben Jonson; to whose play I now return.

Besides Morose, there are at least nine or ten different characters and humours in *The Silent Woman,* all which persons have several concernments of their own, yet are all used by the poet, to the conducting of the main design of perfection. I shall not waste time in commending the writing of this play, but I will give you my opinion, that there is more wit and acuteness of fancy in it than in any of Ben Jonson's. Besides, that he has here described the conversation of gentlemen in the

---

[60]The ridiculous.

[61]*Ethos* in Aristotle is "character": *pathos* is "suffering" — in particular the tragic deed.

[62]"You'd say the spit and image." Terence, *Eunuch,* 460.

persons of Truewit, and his friends, with more gaiety, air and freedom, than in the rest of his comedies. For the contrivance of the plot, 'tis extreme elaborate, and yet withal easy; for the λύσις, or untying of it, 'tis so admirable, that when it is done, no one of the audience would think the poet could have missed it; and yet it was concealed so much before the last scene, that any other way would sooner have entered into your thoughts. But I dare not take upon me to commend the fabric of it, because it is altogether so full of art, that I must unravel every scene in it to commend it as I ought. And this excellent contrivance is still the more to be admired, because 'tis comedy where the persons are only of common rank, and their business private, not elevated by passions or high concernments as in serious plays. Here everyone is a proper judge of all he sees; nothing is represented but that with which he daily converses: so that by consequence all faults lie open to discovery, and few are pardonable. 'Tis this which Horace has judiciously observed:

Creditur ex medio quia res arcessit habere
sudoris minimum, sed habet Comedia tanto
plus oneris, quanto veniae minus. — [63]

But our poet, who was not ignorant of these difficulties, has made use of all advantages, as he who designs a large leap takes his rise from the highest ground. One of these advantages is that which Corneille has laid down as the greatest which can arrive to any poem, and which he himself could never compass above thrice in all his plays, viz., the making choice of some signal and long-expected day, whereon the action of the play is to depend. This day was that designed by Dauphine for the settling of his uncle's estate upon him; which to compass he contrives to marry him. That the marriage had been plotted by him long beforehand is made evident by what he tells Truewit in the second act, that in one moment he had destroyed what he had been raising many months.

[63]"One might think that Comedy takes less work because its matter comes from daily life, but it takes more because less allowance is made." Horace, *Epistles* II.1:168–70.

There is another artifice of the poet, which I cannot here omit, because by the frequent practice of it in his comedies, he has left it to us almost as a rule, that is, when he has any character or humour wherein he would show a *coup de maistre,* or his highest skill; he recommends it to your observation by a pleasant description of it before the person first appears. Thus, in *Bartholomew Fair* he gives you the pictures of Numps and Cokes, and in this those of Daw, Lafoole, Morose, and the Collegiate Ladies; all which you hear described before you see them. So that before they come upon the stage you have a longing expectation of them, which prepares you to receive them favourably; and when they are there, even from their first appearance you are so far acquainted with them, that nothing of their humour is lost to you.

I will observe yet one thing further of this admirable plot; the business of it rises in every act. The second is greater than the first, the third than the second, and so forward to the fifth. There too you see, till the very last scene, new difficulties arising to obstruct the action of the play; and when the audience is brought into despair that the business can naturally be effected, then, and not before, the discovery is made. But that the poet might entertain you with more variety all this while, he reserves some new characters to show you, which he opens not till the second and third act. In the second Morose, Daw, the Barber and Otter; in the third the Collegiate Ladies, all which he moves afterwards in by-walks, or under-plots, as diversions to the main design, lest it should grow tedious, though they are still naturally joined with it, and somewhere or other subservient to it. Thus, like a skilful chess-player, by little and little he draws out his men, and makes his pawns of use to his greater persons.

If this comedy, and some others of his, were translated into French prose (which would now be no wonder to them, since Molière has lately given them plays out of verse which have not displeased them) I believe the controversy would soon be decided betwixt the two nations, even making them the judges. But we need not call our heroes to our aid. Be it spoken to the honour of the English, our nation can never want in any age such who are able to dispute the empire of wit with any people in the universe. And though the fury of a civil war, and power, for twenty years together, abandoned to a barbarous race of men, enemies of all good learning, had buried the muses under the ruins of monarchy, yet with the restoration of our happiness, we see revived poesy lifting up its head, and already shaking off the rubbish which lay so heavy on it. We have seen since his majesty's return, many dramatic poems which yield not to those of any foreign nation, and which deserve all laurels but the English. I will set aside flattery and envy. It cannot be denied but we have had some little blemish either in the plot or writing of all those plays which have been made within these seven years: (and perhaps there is no nation in the world so quick to discern them, or so difficult to pardon them, as ours:) yet if we can persuade ourselves to use the candour of that poet, who (though the most severe of critics) has left us this caution by which to moderate our censures;

— Ubi plura nitent in carmine non ego paucis offendar maculis.[64]

If in consideration of their many and great beauties, we can wink at some slight, and little imperfections; if we, I say, can be thus equal to ourselves, I ask no favour from the French. And if I do not venture upon any particular judgement of our late plays, 'tis out of the consideration which an ancient writer gives me; *Vivorum, ut magna admiratio, ita censura difficilis:* betwixt the extremes of admiration and malice, 'tis hard to judge uprightly of the living. Only I think it may be permitted me to say, that as it is no lessening to us to yield to some plays, and those not many of our own nation in the last age, so can it be no addition to pronounce of our present poets that they have far surpassed all the Ancients, and the modern writers of other countries. . . .

[64] "If happy effects / Figure more, I won't take offense at the few bad spots." Horace, *Art of Poetry,* 352; see p. 91.

Aphra Behn
1640?–1689

Aphra Behn is considered the first Englishwoman to have lived by her pen, but her birthplace and maiden name and many of the facts of her life are still either cloaked in darkness or subjects of controversy. One theory has it that she was born Aphra Johnson, daughter of the barber Bartholomew Johnson of the cathedral town of Canterbury, and that she came by her education through the aristocratic Colepeper family when her mother became wet nurse to one of its children. Another is that she was the "Ayfara" born the same year to John and Amy Amis (of unknown occupation) in Wye. And it is generally agreed that she traveled at some time between 1658 and 1663 to Surinam (now the independent country of Suriname) on the north equatorial coast of South America, which until its loss to the Dutch in 1665 had been a British colony. She stayed in Surinam at the plantation of the governor-general, Lord Willoughby, and there collected the factual background for her most famous narrative, *Oroonoko, or The Royal Slave* (published 1688), including the names and personal habits of the ruling gentry. She apparently brought back to England a cloak of feathers of native manufacture, which was used as a costume in a Dryden play. Yet there is no evidence that her father, like that of the narrator of *Oroonoko,* had been appointed lieutenant-governor of the colony.

On her return to England (she said she was eighteen but may have been somewhat older), she married a merchant of Dutch extraction named Behn, and she was known by that name from then on. Behn himself does not appear in her later writings, and some have surmised that he may have died or separated from Aphra before 1666. She had, along with her verbal ability and skill at intrigue, a connection to the government through the theatrical producer Thomas Killigrew. As a result of his recommendation, Aphra Behn had a personal interview with Charles II and was sent by Charles's foreign minister, Lord Arlington, to spy for England in Antwerp. Behn brought back and transmitted intelligence gathered by others about Admiral de Wit's plans to assault English vessels in their harbors at the outset of the Second Dutch War (1665–67). Her information might have been valuable had it been credited. It was disregarded, however, and Behn found herself seriously in debt because she wrongly believed that the Crown would pay the expenses she incurred in its service. In the late 1660s, Behn was jailed in debtor's prison, but she was soon bailed out, and began her literary career as a playwright around 1670.

Her plays, mainly comedies of intrigue like those of George Etherege and William Wycherley, were performed primarily by Killigrew's "King's Company" during the next two decades. Behn kept herself very busy, as was required in an age when the playwright's "royalties" were the receipts from the third night's performance and irregular "author's nights" thereafter — a risky business when many plays did not run even three nights. At least thirteen of her plays were produced between 1670 and 1687. Her works for the theater include *The Forced Marriage* (1670); *The Dutch Lover* (1673); *Abdelazar; or, The Moor's Revenge* (1676); *The*

Rover; or, The Banished Cavalier, Part I (1677); *Sir Patient Fancy* (1678); *The Feign'd Courtesans; or, A Night's Intrigue* (1679); *The Roundheads; or, The Good Old Cause* (1681); *The Rover, Part II* (1681); *The City Heiress; or, Sir Timothy Treat-all* (1682); *The Lucky Chance; or, An Alderman's Bargain* (ca. 1686); and *The Widow Ranter,* the first British play set in America (published posthumously in 1690).

Though some of Behn's plays have been successfully revived, as in recent London productions of *The Rover* and *The Lucky Chance,* today Behn is better known as an innovator in prose fiction who created the "factual fictions" that Daniel Defoe was later to bring to greater perfection. The narrative of *Oroonoko, or The Royal Slave* is filled with the sort of gritty, concrete details that suggest the narrator was an eyewitness to real happenings. Its ideology is equally surprising for its day: *Oroonoko* is intensely anti-imperialistic, attacking the base venality and cruelty of the European colonists and settlers. Indeed, the novel was instrumental in establishing the convention of the "noble savage," which dominated Western culture in the era of Rousseau. On the other hand, *Oroonoko* was not in any sense (as it has frequently been called) an antislavery novel. The novel takes the institution of slavery for granted; its African hero himself captures and sells others into slavery, and resents only that he, a prince, has been tricked into bondage. Behn's other stories and novels include *Love Letters Between a Noble-Man and His Sister* (1684), a reconstruction of the scandal surrounding a Whig lord who had eloped with his sister-in-law; and *The Fair Jilt* (1688), based upon an incident Behn observed in The Hague in the 1660s. Behn also published her *Poems on Several Occasions* in 1684. Behn's health began to fail in the early 1680s and she died in 1689, the year of the Glorious Revolution; she is buried in Westminster Abbey.

Behn's Preface to *The Lucky Chance* focuses on the charges of obscenity laid against her by envious fellow poets who, she claims, maliciously wish to tear down anything of quality that would threaten the success of their own plays. Her witty response deflates the hypocrisy of her fellow wits, but it is also interesting as an illustration of how an individual text was attacked and defended in an age when literature was considered a form of rhetoric, thus having an immediate relation with the audience. When every member of an audience is a qualified judge, but community standards are not really univocal or agreed upon, where stretching the permissible limits of a genre gains an enthusiastic audience until "going over the top" loses it, the successful dramatist is caught between the Scylla of recurrent moral outrage and the Charybdis of an audience's craving for the new.

Behn's rhetoric, despite the unfamiliar language in which it is couched, should remind us of twentieth-century issues. Like a Hollywood director accused of bringing sex or violence to a new level of offensiveness in a film, Behn insists that the outrageousness of her text is essentially that of the genre within which it works, that comedies of intrigue require offstage extramarital sex. Behn maintains that the much-criticized moment in the play where "Mr. Leigh opens his *Night Gown,* when he comes into the Bride-chamber," was an actor's improvisation, rather than her own stage direction. She also argues that *The Lucky Chance* was previewed and judged (given perhaps the equivalent of today's PG-13 rating) by the most authoritative persons, including the "rating board" of Davenant, L'Estrange, and Killigrew, and, in case their masculine sensibilities might be expected to be a bit coarse, that it was vetted before publication by "several Ladys of very great Quality, and unquestioned Fame," who considered it harmless fun. Equally modern is Behn's claim that, as a woman writer, she has been singled out for attacks on the decency of her plays, and that similar scrutiny is not accorded to equally outrageous texts by her male contemporaries — such as *Limberham* by poet laureate John Dryden. Behn's feminist successors would hardly be in agreement with Behn's claim that "the poet in me" is "my Masculine Part": but they would surely be sympathetic to her plea that women competing with men be judged by the same standards.

Behn seems more intensely feminist in the Preface to her quarto edition of *The Dutch Lover* (1673), where she takes on the "phlegmatick, white, ill-favour'd, wretched Fop" who complained on opening night "that they were to expect a woful Play, God damn him, for it was a woman's." Like her near-contemporary, Mary Astell, Behn presumes that women are "as capable of knowledge, of whatever sort" as men, if granted the same access to education. But given the male audience for her plays, she does not argue this directly, stressing instead that education is hardly a playwright's first requirement. The "immortal Shakespeare" had no more learning himself "than often falls to women's share," and even the more educated Ben Jonson "was no such Rabbi neither." Those who most overestimate the poet's need for learning are often, she suggests, those who have absorbed the least education themselves. Given that native genius and invention are more important than learning and the rules of art, there is little bar to women excelling in the arts: ". . . except our most unimitable Laureat [John Dryden] . . . I know of none that write . . . but that a woman may well hope to reach their greatest heights," says Behn. If in those words she was immodestly thinking of herself, as one may suspect, most of today's readers would agree that Behn achieved those heights.

Selected Bibliography

Chibka, Robert L. "'Oh! Do Not Fear a Woman's Invention': Truth, Falsehood and Fiction in Aphra Behn's *Oroonoko*." *Texas Studies in Literature and Language* 30 (1988): 510–37.

Duffy, Maureen. *The Passionate Shepherdess: Aphra Behn, 1640–1689*. London: Cape, 1977.

Goreau, Angeline. *Reconstructing Aphra: A Social Biography of Aphra Behn*. New York: Dial Press, 1980.

Huttner, Heidi, ed. *Rereading Aphra Behn: History, Theory and Criticism*. Charlottesville: University Press of Virginia, 1993.

O'Donnell, Mary Ann. "Tory Wit and Unconventional Woman: Aphra Behn." In *Women Writers of the Seventeenth Century*, eds. Katharina M. Wilson and Frank J. Warnke, 349–72. Athens: University of Ohio Press, 1989.

Todd, Janet, ed. *Aphra Behn Studies*. New York and London: Cambridge University Press, 1996.

An Epistle to the Reader
from *The Dutch Lover*

Good, Sweet, Honey, Sugar-Candied READER,

Which I think is more than anyone has called you yet, I must have a word or two with you before you do advance into the Treatise; but 'tis not to beg your pardon for diverting you from your affairs, by such an idle Pamphlet as this is, for I presume you have not much to do and therefore are to be obliged to me for keeping you from worse employment, and if you have a better you may get you gone about your business: but if you will misspend your Time, pray lay the fault upon yourself; for I have dealt pretty fairly in the matter, told you in the Title Page what you are to expect within. Indeed, had I hung a sign of the Immortality of the Soul, of the Mystery of Godliness, or of Ecclesiastical Policie, and then had treated you with Indiscerpibility and Essential Spissitude (words, which though I am no competent Judge of, for want of Languages, yet I fancy strongly ought to mean just nothing) with a company of Apocryphal midnight Tales cull'd out of the choicest Insignificant Authors; If I had only proved in Folio that Appolonius was a naughty knave, or had presented you with two or three of the worst principles transcrib'd out of the peremptory and ill-natur'd (though prettily ingenious) Doctor of Malmsbury undigested and ill-manag'd by a silly, saucy, ignorant, impertinent, ill educated Chaplain I were then indeed sufficiently in fault; but having inscrib'd Comedy on the beginning of my Book, you may guess pretty near what penny-worths you are like to have, and ware your money and your time accordingly. I would not yet be understood to lessen the dignity of Playes, for surely they deserve a place among the middle if not the better sort of Books; for I have heard the most of that which bears the name of Learning, and which has abused such quantities of Ink and Paper, and continually employs so many ignorant, unhappy souls for ten, twelve, twenty years in the University (who yet poor wretches think they are doing something all the while) as Logick etc. and several other things (that shall be nameless lest I misspell them) are much more absolutely nothing than the errantest Play that e'er was writ. Take notice, Reader, I do not assert this purely upon my own knowledge, but I think I have known it very fully prov'd, both sides being fairly heard, and even some ingenious opposers of it most abominably baffl'd in the Argument: Some of which I have got so perfectly by rote, that if this were a proper place for it, I am apt to think myself could almost make it clear; and as I would not undervalue Poetry, so neither am I altogether of their judgement who believe no wisdom in the world beyond it. I have often heard indeed (and read) how much the World was anciently oblig'd to it for most of that which they call'd Science, which my want of letters makes me less assured of than others happily may be: but I have heard some wise men say that no considerable part of useful knowledge was this way communicated, and on the other way, that it hath serv'd to propogate so many idle superstitions, as all the benefits it hath or can be guilty of, can never make sufficient amends for; which unaided by the unlucky charms of Poetry, could never have possest a thinking Creature such as man. However true this is, I am myself well able to affirm that none of all our English Poets, and least the Dramatique (so I think you call them) can be justly charg'd with too great reformation of men's minds or manners, and for that I may appeal to general experiment, if those who are the most assiduous Disciples of the Stage, do not make the fondest and the lewdest Crew about this Town; for if you should unhappily converse them through the year, you will not find one Dram of sense amongst a Club of them, unless you will allow for such a little Link-Boy's[1] Ribaldry thick larded with unseasonable oaths & impudent defiance of God, and all things serious; and that at

---

[1]A boy hired to carry a "link" (a torch made of tow dipped in pitch) to light his employer through the otherwise unlit streets. As observers of the nocturnal habits of the dissipated men and women of Charles II's London, link-boys could be expected to have seen everything and to have a street-wise sense of humor about it all.

such a senseless damn'd unthinking rate, as, if 'twere well distributed, would spoil near half the Apothecaries trade, and save the sober people of the Town the charge of Vomits; And it was smartly said (how prudently I cannot tell) by a late learned Doctor, who, though himself no great asserter of a Deity, (as you'll believe by that which follows) yet was observed to be continually persuading of this sort of men (if I for once may call them so) of the necessity and truth of our Religion; and being ask'd how he came to bestir himself so much this way, made answer that it was because their ignorance and indiscreet debauch made them a scandal to the profession of Atheism. And for their wisdom and design I never knew it reach beyond the invention of some notable expedient, for the speedier ridding them of their Estate, (a devilish clog to Wit and Parts), than other grouling Mortals know, or battering half-a-dozen fair new Windows in a Morning after their debauch, whilst the dull unjantee[2] Rascal they belong to is fast asleep. But I'll proceed no farther in their character, because that miracle of Wit (in spite of Academick frippery) the mighty Echard[3] hath already done it to my satisfaction; and whoever undertakes a Supplement to anything he hath discourst, had better for their reputation be doing nothing.

Besides this Theam is worn too thread-bare by the whiffling would-be Wits of the Town, and of both the stone-blind-eyes of the Kingdom. And therefore to return to that which I before was speaking of, I will have leave to say that in my judgement the increasing number of our latter Plays have not done much more towards the amending of men's Morals, or their Wit, than hath the frequent Preaching, which this last age hath been pester'd with, (indeed without all Controversie they have done less harm) nor can I once imagine what temptation anyone can have to expect it from them; for sure I am no Play was ever writ with that design. If you consider Tragedy, you'll find their best of Characters

unlikely patterns for a wise man to pursue: For he that is the Knight of the Play, no sublunary feats must serve his Dulcinea; for if he can't bestrid the Moon, he'll ne'er make good his business to the end, and if he chance to be offended, he must without considering right or wrong confound all things he meets, and put you half-a-score likely tall fellows into each pocket; and truly if he come not something near this Pitch I think the Tragedy's not worth a farthing; for Playes were certainly intended for the exercising of men's passions not their understandings, and he is infinitely far from wise that will bestow one moment's meditation on such things: And as for Comedie, the finest folks you meet with there are still unfitter for your imitation, for though within a leaf or two of the Prologue, you are told that they are people of Wit, good Humour, good Manners, and all that: yet if the Authors did not kindly add their proper names, you'd never know them by their Characters; for whatsoe'er's the matter, it hath happen'd so spightfully in several Playes, which have been prettie well received of late, that even those persons that were meant to be the ingenious Censors of the Play, have either prov'd the most debauch'd, or most unwittie people in the Company: nor is this error very lamentable, since as I take it Comedie was never meant, either for a converting or a conforming Ordinance: In short, I think a Play the best divertisement that wise men have: but I do also think them nothing so who do discourse as formallie about the rules of it, as if 'twere the grand affair of humane life. This being my opinion of Plays, I studied only to make this as entertaining as I could, which whether I have been successful in, my gentle Reader, you may for your shilling judge. To tell you my thoughts of it, were to little purpose, for were they very ill, you may be sure I would not have expos'd it; nor did I so till I had first consulted most of those who have a reputation for judgement of this kind; who were at least so civil (if not kind) to it as did encourage me to venture it upon the Stage, and in the Press: Nor did I take their single word for it, but us'd their reasons as a confirmation of my own.

Indeed that day 'twas Acted first, there comes me into the Pit, a long, lither, phlegmatick, white, ill-favour'd, wretched Fop, an Officer in

[2]Variant of "unjaunty," characterizing the stay-at-home sleepers, as opposed to the hellraisers battering their windows at dawn.

[3]Probably Laurence Echard, author of a contemporary *History of England*.

Masquerade newly transported with a Scarf & Feather out of France, a sorry Animal that has nought else to shield it from the uttermost contempt of all mankind, but that respect which we afford to Rats and Toads, which though we do not well allow to live, yet when considered as a part of God's Creation, we make honourable mention of them. A thing, Reader — but no more of such a Smelt: This thing, I tell ye, opening that which serves it for a mouth, out issued such a noise as this to those that sate about it, that they were to expect a woful Play, God damn him, for it was a woman's. Now how this came about I am not sure, but I suppose he brought it piping hot from some who had with him the reputation of a villanous Wit: for Creatures of his size of sense talk without all imagination, such scraps as they pick up from other folks. I would not for a world be taken arguing with such a propertie as this; but if I thought there were a man of any tolerable parts, who could upon mature deliberation distinguish well his right hand from his left, and justly state the difference between the number of sixteen and two, yet had this prejudice upon him; I would take a little pains to make him know how much he errs. For waving the examination why women having equal education with men, were not as capable of knowledge, of whatsoever sort as well as they: I'll only say as I have touch'd before, that Plays have no great room for that which is men's great advantage over women, that is Learning; We all well know that the immortal Shakespeare's Plays (who was not guilty of much more of this than often falls to women's share) have better pleas'd the World than Johnson's works, though by the way 'tis said that Benjamin was no such Rabbi neither, for I am inform'd that his Learning was but Grammar high; (sufficient indeed to rob poor Salust of his best orations) and it hath been observ'd that they are apt to admire him most confoundedly, who have just such a scantling of it as he had; and I have seen a man the most severe of Johnson's Sect, sit with his Hat remov'd less than a hair's breadth from one sullen posture for almost three hours at *The Alchymist;* who at that excellent Play of *Harry the Fourth* (which yet I hope is far enough from Farce) hath very hardly kept his Doublet whole; but affectation hath always had a greater share both in the action

and discourse of men than truth and judgement have; and for our Modern ones, except our most unimitable Laureat, I dare to say I know of none that write at such a formidable rate, but that a woman may well hope to reach their greatest heights. Then for their musty rules of Unity, and God knows what besides, if they meant anything, they are enough intelligible and as practible by a woman; but really methinks they that disturb their heads with any other rule of Playes besides the making them pleasant, and avoiding of scurrility, might much better be employed in studying how to improve men's too imperfect knowledge of that ancient English Game which hight long Laurence:[4] And if Comedy should be the picture of ridiculous mankind I wonder anyone should think it such a sturdy task, whilst we are furnish'd with such precious Originals as him I lately told you of; if at least that Character do not dwindle into Farce, and so become too mean an entertainment for those persons who are us'd to think. Reader, I have a complaint or two to make to you and I have done; Know then that this Play was hugely injur'd in the Acting, for 'twas done so imperfectly as never any was before, which did more harm to this than it could have done to any of another sort; the Plot being busie (though I think not intricate) and so requiring a continual attention, which being interrupted by the intolerable negligence of some that acted in it, must needs much spoil the beauty on't. My Dutch Lover spoke but little of what I intended for him, but supplied it with a great deal of idle stuff, which I was wholly unacquainted with until I had heard it first from him; so that Jack-pudding ever us'd to do: which though I knew before, I gave him yet the Part, because I knew him so

[4]Janet Todd's new edition of Aphra Behn's works defines a "Long Lawrence" as an instrument marked with signs about three inches long like a short ruler or totem with eight sides. Each side had a different set of markings of strokes, zigzags, and crosses. The ancient English game with the same name was played (particularly at Christmas), by rolling the Long Lawrence; each player would win or lose pins or tokens according to which side came up. The name itself may have come from the marks on the instrument, which resembled the bars of a gridiron, on which St. Lawrence was martyred. Todd cites Alice Bertha Gomme, *The Traditional Games of England, Scotland, and Ireland* (1894).

acceptable to most o'th' lighter Periwigs about the Town, and he indeed did vex me so, I could almost be angry: Yet, but Reader, you remember, I suppose, a fusty piece of Latine[5] that has past from hand to hand this thousand years they say (and how much longer I can't tell) in favour of the

[5]The "fusty bit of Latine . . . in favour of the dead" is probably the proverb "De mortuis nil nisi bonum": Of the dead speak nothing but good. The application is to Edward Angel, the actor who played the male lead in *The Dutch Lover* and whose ad-libbing of lines and vulgar stage business caused the scandal Behn is discussing: Angel had died in the interval between the production and publication of the play.

dead. I intended him a habit much more notably ridiculous, which if ever it be important was so here, for many of the Scenes in the three last Acts depended upon the mistakes of the Colonel for Haunce, which the ill-favour'd likeness of their Habits is suppos'd to cause. Lastly my Epilogue was promis'd me by a Person who had surely made it good, if any, but he failing of his word, deput'd one, who has made it as you see, and to make out your penyworth you have it here. The Prologue is by misfortune lost. Now, Reader, I have eas'd my mind of all I had to say, and so sans farther complyment, Adieu.

Preface to *The Lucky Chance*

The little Obligation I have to some of the witty Sparks and Poets of the Town, has put me on a Vindication of this Comedy from those Censures that Malice, and ill Nature have thrown upon it, tho in vain: The Poets I heartily excuse, since there is a sort of Self-Interest in their Malice, which I shou'd rather call a witty Way they have in this Age, of Railing at every thing they find with pain successful, and never to shew good Nature and speak well of any thing; but when they are sure 'tis damn'd, then they afford it that worse Scandal, their Pity. And nothing makes them so thorough-stitcht an Enemy as a full Third Day,[1] that's Crime enough to load it with all manner of Infamy; and when they can no other way prevail with the Town, they charge it with the old never failing Scandal — That 'tis not fit for the Ladys: As if (if it were as they falsly give it out) the Ladys were oblig'd to hear Indecencys only from their Pens and Plays and some of them have ventur'd to treat 'em as Coursely as 'twas possible, without the least Reproach from them; and in some of their most Celebrated Plays have entertained 'em with things, that if I should here strip from their Wit and Occasion that conducts 'em in and makes them

proper, their fair Cheeks would perhaps wear a natural Colour at the reading them: yet are never taken Notice of, because a Man writ them, and they may hear that from them they blush at from a Woman — But I make a Challenge to any Person of common Sense and Reason — that is not wilfully bent on ill Nature, and will in spight of Sense wrest a double *Entendre* from every thing, lying upon the Catch for a Jest or a Quibble, like a Rook for a Cully;[2] but any unprejudic'd Person that knows not the Author, to read any of my Comedy's and compare 'em with others of this Age, and if they find one Word that can offend the chastest Ear, I will submit to all their peevish Cavills; but Right or Wrong they must be Criminal because a Woman's; condemning them without having the Christian Charity, to examine whether it be guilty or not, with reading, comparing, or thinking; the Ladies taking up any Scandal on Trust from some conceited Sparks, who will in spight of Nature be Wits and *Beaus;* then scatter it for Authentick all over the Town and Court, poysoning of others Judgements with their false Notions, condemning it to worse than Death, Loss of Fame. And to fortifie their Detraction, charge me with all the Plays that have ever been offensive; though I wish with all their Faults I had been the Author of some of those they have honour'd me with.

[1]Restoration playwrights were paid not by a fixed royalty but by the receipts of the third night of the production (and other subsequently declared author's nights). When a play did not run a full three days, the author received nothing.

[2]Like a cheat for his victim.

For the farther Justification of this Play; it being a Comedy of Intrigue Dr. *Davenant* out of Respect to the Commands he had from Court, to take great Care that no Indecency should be in Plays, sent for it and nicely look't it over, putting out anything he but imagin'd the Criticks would play with. After that, Sir *Roger L'Estrange* read it and licens'd it, and found no such Faults as 'tis charg'd with: Then Mr. *Killigrew*, who more severe than any, from the strict Order he had, perus'd it with great Circumspection; and lastly the Master Players, who you will I hope in some Measure esteem Judges of Decency and their own Interest, having been so many Years Prentice to the Trade of Judging.

I say, after all these Supervisors the Ladys may be convinc'd, they left nothing that could offend, and the Men of their unjust Reflections on so many Judges of Wit and Decencys. When it happens that I challenge any one, to point me out the least Expression of what some have made their Discourse, they cry, *That Mr. Leigh opens his Night Gown, when he comes into the Bride-chamber;* if he do, which is a Jest of his own making, and which I never saw, I hope he has his Cloaths on underneath? And if so, where is the Indecency? I have seen in that admirable Play of *Oedipus,*[3] the Gown open'd wide, and the Man shown in his Drawers and Waist coat, and never thought it an Offence before. Another crys, *Why we know not what they mean, when the Man takes a Woman off the Stage, and another is thereby cuckolded;* is that any more than you see in the most Celebrated of your Plays? as the *City Politicks,*[4] the *Lady Mayoress,* and the *Old*

Lawyers Wife, who goes with a Man she never saw before, and comes out again the joyfull'st Woman alive, for having made her Husband a Cuckold with such Dexterity, and yet I see nothing unnatural nor obscene: 'tis proper for the Characters. So in that lucky Play of the *London Cuckolds,* not to recite Particulars. And in that good Comedy of *Sir Courtly Nice,* the *Taylor to the young Lady* — in the fam'd Sir *Fopling Dorimont* and *Bellinda,* see the very Words — in *Valentinian,* see the Scene between the *Court Bawds.* And *Valentinian* all loose and ruffld a Moment after the Rape, and all this you see without Scandal, and a thousand others The *Moor of Venice* in many places. The *Maids Tragedy* — see the Scene of undressing the Bride, and between the *King* and *Amintor,* and after between the *King* and *Evadne* — All these I Name as some of the best Plays I know; If I should repeat the Words exprest in these Scenes I mention, I might justly be charg'd with course ill Manners, and very little Modesty, and yet they so naturally fall into the places they are designed for, and so are proper for the Business, that there is not the least Fault to be found with them; though I say those things in any of mine wou'd damn the whole Peice, and alarm the Town. Had I a Day or two's time, as I have scarce so many Hours to write this in (the Play, being all printed off and the Press waiting,) I would sum up all your Beloved Plays, and all the Things in them that are past with such Silence by; because written by Men: such Masculine Strokes in me, must not be allow'd. I must conclude those Women (if there be any such) greater Critics in that sort of Conversation than my self, who find any of that sort in mine, or any thing that can justly be reproach't. But 'tis in vain by dint of Reason or Comparison to convince the obstinate Criticks, whose Business is to find Fault, if not by a loose and gross Imagination to create them, for they must either find the Jest, or make it; and those of this sort fall to my share, they find Faults of another kind for the Men Writers. And this one thing I will venture to say, though against my Nature, because it has a Vanity in it: That had the Plays I have writ come forth under any Mans Name, and never known to have been mine; I appeal to all unbyast Judges of Sense, if they had not said that Person had made as many good

[3]This would have to be the John Dryden / Nathaniel Lee version of 1679, based on Seneca, not the original play by Sophocles. In Act 2, scene 1, there is a stage direction: "Oedipus enters walking asleep in his shirt." This was not a joke or funny business, merely sleepwear of the day. Behn cites it for her own purpose, to ridicule the idea that an actor appearing without his coat must be obscene.

[4]Behn refers to several plays in this passage. *City Politicks:* a comedy by John Crowne (1683). *The London Cuckolds:* a comedy by Edward Ravenscroft (1682). *Sir Courtly Nice:* a comedy by John Crowne (1685). *Sir Fopling:* Behn alludes to *The Man of Mode, or Sir Fopling Flutter,* a classic Restoration comedy by George Etherege (1676). *Valentinian:* a tragedy by John Fletcher (performed 1610–14, published 1647). *The Moor of Venice:* the subtitle of Shakespeare's *Othello* (1602–4). *The Maid's Tragedy:* a tragedy by Francis Beaumont and John Fletcher (1610–11).

Comedies, as any one Man that has writ in our Age; but a Devil on't the Woman damns the Poet.

Ladies, for its further Justification to you, be pleas'd to know, that the first Copy of this Play was read by several Ladys of very great Quality, and unquestioned Fame, and received their most favourable Opinion, not one charging it with the Crime, that some have been pleas'd to find in the Acting. Other Ladys who saw it more than once, whose Quality and Vertue can sufficiently justifie any thing they design to favour, were pleas'd to say, they found an Entertainment in it very far from scandalous; and for the Generality of the Town, I found by my Receipts it was not thought so Criminal. However, that shall not be an Incouragement to me to trouble the Criticks with new Occasion of affronting me, for endeavouring at least to divert; and at this rate, both the few Poets that are left, and the Players who toil in vain will be weary of their Trade.

I cannot omit to tell you, that a Wit of the Town, a Friend of mine at *Wills* Coffee House, the first Night of the Play, cry'd it down as much as in him lay, who before had read it and assured me he never saw a prettier Comedy. So complaisant one pestilent Wit will be to another, and in the full Cry make his Noise too; but since 'tis to the witty Few I speak, I hope the better Judges will take no Offence, to whom I am oblig'd for better Judgments; and those I hope will be so kind to me, knowing my Conversation not at all addicted to the Indecencys alledged, that I would much less practice it in a Play, that must stand the Test of the censoring World. And I must want common Sense, and all the Degrees of good Manners, renouncing my Fame, all Modesty and Interest for a silly Sawcy fruitless Jest, to make Fools laugh, and Women blush, and wise Men asham'd; My self all the while, if I had been guilty of this Crime charg'd to me, remaining the only stupid, insensible. Is this likely, is this reasonable to be believ'd by any body, but the wilfully blind? All I ask, is the Priviledge for my Masculine Part the Poet in me, (if any such you will allow me) to tread in those successful Paths my Predecessors have so long thriv'd in, to take those Measures that both the Ancient and Modern Writers have set me, and by which they have pleas'd the World so well: If I must not, because of my Sex, have this Freedom, but that you will usurp all to your selves; I lay down my Quill, and you shall hear no more of me, no not so much as to make Comparisons, because I will be kinder to my Brothers of the Pen, than they have been to a defenceless Woman; for I am not content to write for a Third day only. I value Fame as much as if I had been born a *Hero;* and if you rob me of that, I can retire from the ungrateful World, and scorn its fickle Favours.

Alexander Pope

1688–1744

Born into a Roman Catholic family in the year the last Catholic monarch of England, James II, was forced to abdicate his throne, Alexander Pope was legally barred from a university education and from many careers. From his wet nurse he caught a severe case of spinal tuberculosis, which left him dwarfed, twisted, and delicate of constitution. Nevertheless, with the private education provided by his father, a well-to-do merchant of London just retired to Windsor Forest, Pope crafted himself into the prodigy and soon into the poet of eighteenth-century England, its laureate in all but name. His translations of the *Iliad* and the *Odyssey* (1720 and 1725) not only made him a fortune in royalties, they set the poetic standard for the age; his *Essay on Man* (1733) became its optimistic and rationalistic creed. What has best survived, however, are his satires, delicate fantasies like *The Rape of the Lock* (1714), or vitriolic diatribes like *An Epistle to Dr. Arbuthnot* (1735) and the *Dunciad* (1728–43).

The *Essay on Criticism*, published in 1711 and written possibly as early as 1707, belongs to Pope's earliest years, when he "lisp'd in numbers, and the numbers came." It would be astonishing for any nineteen-year-old, however learned, to make an original contribution to literary theory, and in fact, the *Essay on Criticism* is original only in that it is addressed to critics rather than to poets. But since Pope considered it the critic's first duty to endeavor to comprehend fully and disinterestedly the poem's form, matter, and end, the *Essay* easily and often shifts its focus from qualities of criticism to qualities of poetry. Pope's central ideas are the standard poetic notions of the Augustan Age, drawn from a variety of classical and Renaissance sources — from Horace and Quintilian to Boileau and Dryden — but these well-worn truths he imbues with a clarity and brilliance of expression.

The central and recurring image of the *Essay on Criticism* is that of the eternal war between critics, who judge according to a rigid system of regulations, and poets, hemmed in by such rules and longing to soar. By and large, although Pope presents the poets' perspective, he sides with the critics. While he insists that "Some beauties yet no precepts can declare / For there's a happiness as well as care," and admits that poets can through genius "snatch a grace beyond the reach of art," he also warns them that remorseless criticism will justly clip their wings should they depart from the precedent of the rules and practices of the ancients. The critics come in for a lashing in Part II, where they are attacked for partial readings, partial both in the sense that their praise and blame depend on the congruence of their party politics with that of the poet, and in the sense that they take only a single aspect of a poem into account without understanding its end or how it relates to the chosen means. Pope's demonstrations of prosody and imagery here have become classic citations.

Pope's tendency to use his central terms in a variety of related but distinct ways can be confusing. "Nature" is sometimes used to signify the objective world of creation and other times to mean human nature or the instinctual basis of our humanity. "Art" can be opposed to "Nature" in any of the following senses: It can be the world of human invention, as opposed to that of divine creation; it can be technique and craft, as opposed to creative instinct; it can be the rules behind a skill, as opposed to the skill itself; it can be (as in its usual modern meaning) the class of objects created by human intelligence and creativity. "Wit" is even more ambiguous than "Art" and "Nature" and can partake of either realm: It may mean "sense" or "intelligence" or "verbal facility" or "genius" or "creative power," or it may signify a person with any of these qualities — or just an educated person in general. These shifts, which are not announced, can create an immense and bewildering compression of meaning. When Pope claims that nature is "at once the source, and end, and test of Art," he may be using both Nature and Art in three different senses. Context is a guide here, and fortunately, the context is enhanced by Pope's tendency to repeat each of his ideas at least once before moving on to the next.

What may be more problematic for the reader is Pope's tendency to draw a distinction only to collapse it later on. Like Sidney, Pope suggests that the poet requires natural genius, a knowledge of the rules of art, and an education based on the classics to provide models for imitation. But art and nature, creation and imitation, turn out to be false dichotomies. The rules of art remain "Nature still, but Nature methodiz'd"; Virgil discovers that imitating Nature and imitating Homer are "the same." Pope in 1711 is content to leave such contradictions unresolved as poetic paradoxes; in later hands, like those of David Hume and Immanuel Kant, these issues will recur as evidence of inward mental structures common to humanity.

Selected Bibliography

Empson, William. "'Wit' in the *Essay on Criticism*." *Hudson Review* 2 (1950): 559–77.
Fenner, Arthur, Jr. "The Unity of Pope's *Essay on Criticism*." *Philological Quarterly* 39 (1960): 435–56.
Griffin, Dustin. *Alexander Pope: The Poet in the Poems*. Princeton: Princeton University Press, 1978.
Hooker, E. N. "Pope on Wit: The Essay on Criticism." *Hudson Review* 2 (1950): 84–100.
Stack, Frank. *Pope and Horace: Studies in Imitation*. Cambridge and New York: Cambridge University Press, 1985.
Warren, Austin. *Pope as Critic and Humanist*. Princeton: Princeton University Press, 1929.
Wood, Allen G. *Literary Satire and Theory: A Study of Horace, Boileau, and Pope*. New York: Garland, 1985.

An Essay on Criticism

— *Si quid novisti rectius istis,*
   Candidus imperti; si non, his utere mecum.[1]

[1]"If you know better maxims, impart them to me; if not, use these with me." Horace, *Epistles* 6:1.

PART I

'Tis hard to say, if greater want of skill
Appear in writing or in judging ill;
But of the two less dangerous is the offense
To tire our patience than mislead our sense.

Some few in that, but numbers err in this,
Ten censure wrong for one who writes amiss;
A fool might once himself alone expose,
Now one in verse makes many more in prose.

'Tis with our judgments as our watches, none
Go just alike, yet each believes his own.
In poets as true genius is but rare,
True taste as seldom is the critic's share;
Both must alike from Heaven derive their light,
These born to judge, as well as those to write.
Let such teach others who themselves excel,
And censure freely who have written well.
Authors are partial to their wit,[2] 'tis true.
But are not critics to their judgment too?

Yet if we look more closely, we shall find
Most have the seeds of judgment in their mind:
Nature affords at least a glimmering light;
The lines, though touched but faintly, are drawn
    right.
But as the slightest sketch, if justly traced,
Is by ill coloring but the more disgraced,
So by false learning is good sense defaced:
Some are bewildered in the maze of schools,[3]
And some made coxcombs Nature meant but
    fools.
In search of wit these lose their common sense,
And then turn critics in their own defense:
Each burns alike, who can, or cannot write,
Or with a rival's or an eunuch's spite.
All fools have still an itching to deride,
And fain would be upon the laughing side.
If Maevius[4] scribble in Apollo's spite,
There are who judge still worse than he can
    write.

Some have at first for wits, then poets passed,
Turned critics next, and proved plain fools at
    last.
Some neither can for wits nor critics pass,
As heavy mules are neither horse nor ass.
Those half-learn'd witlings, numerous in our
    isle,
As half-formed insects on the banks of Nile;[5]
Unfinished things, one knows not what to call,

Their generation's so equivocal:
To tell[6] them would a hundred tongues require,
Or one vain wit's, that might a hundred tire.

But you who seek to give and merit fame,
And justly bear a critic's noble name,
Be sure yourself and your own reach to know,
How far your genius, taste, and learning go;
Launch not beyond your depth, but be discreet,
And mark that point where sense and dullness
    meet.
Nature to all things fixed the limits fit,
And wisely curbed proud man's pretending wit.
As on the land while here the ocean gains,
In other parts it leaves wide sandy plains;
Thus in the soul while memory prevails,
The solid power of understanding fails;
Where beams of warm imagination play,
The memory's soft figures melt away.
One Science[7] only will one genius fit,
So vast is art, so narrow human wit.[8]
Not only bounded to peculiar arts,
But oft in those confined to single parts.
Like kings we lose the conquests gained before,
By vain ambition still to make them more;
Each might his several province well command,
Would all but stoop to what they understand.

First follow Nature, and your judgment frame
By her just standard, which is still the same;
Unerring Nature, still divinely bright,
One clear, unchanged, and universal light,
Life, force, and beauty must to all impart,
At once the source, and end, and test of art.
Art from that fund each just supply provides,
Works without show, and without pomp pre-
    sides.
In some fair body thus the informing soul
With spirits feeds, with vigor fills the whole,
Each motion guides, and every nerve sustains;
Itself unseen, but in the effects remains.
Some, to whom Heaven in wit has been profuse,
Want as much more to turn it to its use;
For wit[9] and judgment often are at strife,
Though meant each other's aid, like man and
    wife.

[2]Artistic genius.
[3]Scholastic learning.
[4]A legendarily bad poet, known only through contemptuous references by both Virgil and Horace.
[5]Insects were supposed to be spontaneously generated by river mud and other similar matter.

[6]Count.
[7]Branch of knowledge.
[8]Here, mental power.
[9]Here, imagination.

'Tis more to guide than spur the Muse's steed,[10]
Restrain his fury than provoke his speed;
The wingéd courser, like a generous horse,
Shows most true mettle when you check his
    course.
    Those rules of old discovered, not devised,
Are Nature still, but Nature methodized;
Nature, like liberty, is but restrained
By the same laws which first herself ordained.
    Hear how learn'd Greece her useful rules in-
    dites,
When to repress and when indulge our flights:
High on Parnassus'[11] top her sons she showed,
And pointed out those arduous paths they trod;
Held from afar, aloft, the immortal prize,
And urged the rest by equal steps to rise.
Just precepts thus from great examples given,
She drew from them what they derived from
    Heaven.
The generous critic fanned the poet's fire,
And taught the world with reason to admire.
Then criticism the Muse's handmaid proved,
To dress her charms, and make her more
    beloved:
But following wits from that intention strayed,
Who could not win the mistress, wooed the
    maid;
Against the poets their own arms they turned,
Sure to hate most the men from whom they
    learned.
So modern 'pothecaries, taught the art
By doctors' bills to play the doctor's part,
Bold in the practice of mistaken rules,
Prescribe, apply, and call their masters fools.[12]
Some on the leaves of ancient authors prey,
Nor time nor moths e'er spoiled so much as they.
Some dryly plain, without invention's aid,
Write dull receipts[13] how poems may be made.
These leave the sense their learning to display,
And those explain the meaning quite away.
    You then whose judgment the right course
    would steer,
Know well each ancient's proper character;

His fable, subject, scope in every page;
Religion, country, genius of his age:
Without all these at once before your eyes,
Cavil you may, but never criticize.
Be Homer's works your study and delight,
Read them by day, and meditate by night;
Thence form your judgment, thence your max-
    ims bring,
And trace the Muses upward to their spring.
Still with itself compared, his text peruse;
And let your comment be the Mantuan Muse.[14]
    When first young Maro in his boundless mind
A work to outlast immortal Rome designed,
Perhaps he seemed above the critic's law,
And but from Nature's fountains scorned to
    draw;
But when to examine every part he came,
Nature and Homer were, he found, the same.
Convinced, amazed, he checks the bold design, ⎤
And rules as strict his labored work confine ⎬
As if the Stagirite[15] o'erlooked each line. ⎦
Learn hence for ancient rules a just esteem;
To copy Nature is to copy them.
    Some beauties yet no precepts can declare,
For there's a happiness as well as care.[16]
Music resembles poetry, in each ⎤
Are nameless graces which no methods teach, ⎬
And which a master hand alone can reach. ⎦
If, where the rules not far enough extend
(Since rules were made but to promote their end)
Some lucky license answers to the full
The intent proposed, that license is a rule.
Thus Pegasus, a nearer way to take,
May boldly deviate from the common track.
From vulgar bounds with brave disorder part,
And snatch a grace beyond the reach of art,
Which without passing through the judgment,
    gains
The heart, and all its end at once attains.
In prospects thus, some objects please our eyes, ⎤
Which out of Nature's common order rise, ⎬
The shapeless rock, or hanging precipice. ⎦
Great wits sometimes may gloriously offend,
And rise to faults true critics dare not mend;

[10]Pegasus, the winged horse associated with the Muses.
[11]Hill where the Muses gathered.
[12]Pope refers to a contemporary dispute between doctors
and druggists, who were invading each other's territories.
[13]Recipes.

[14]Virgil, born in Mantua: his last name, mentioned in the
next line, was Maro.
[15]Aristotle, born in Stagira.
[16]Beauty that transcends the taking of pains.

But though the ancients thus their rules invade
(As kings dispense with laws themselves have
    made)
Moderns, beware! or if you must offend
Against the precept, ne'er transgress its end;
Let it be seldom, and compelled by need;
And have at least their precedent to plead.
The critic else proceeds without remorse,
Seizes your fame, and puts his laws in force.

    I know there are, to whose presumptuous
      thoughts
Those freer beauties, even in them, seem faults.
Some figures monstrous and misshaped appear,
Considered singly, or beheld too near,
Which, but proportioned to their light or place,
Due distance reconciles to form and grace.[17]
A prudent chief not always must display
His powers in equal ranks and fair array,
But with the occasion and the place comply,
Conceal his force, nay seem sometimes to fly.
Those oft are stratagems which errors seem,
Nor is it Homer nods, but we that dream.[18]

    Still green with bays each ancient altar stands
Above the reach of sacrilegious hands,
Secure from flames, from envy's fiercer rage,
Destructive war, and all-involving age.
See, from each clime the learn'd their incense
    bring!
Here in all tongues consenting paeans ring!
In praise so just let every voice be joined,
And fill the general chorus of mankind.
Hail, bards triumphant! born in happier days,
Immortal heirs of universal praise!
Whose honors with increase of ages grow,
As streams roll down, enlarging as they flow;
Nations unborn your mighty names shall sound,
And worlds applaud that must not yet be found!
Oh, may some spark of your celestial fire,
The last, the meanest of your sons inspire
(That on weak wings, from far, pursues your
    flights,

Glows while he reads, but trembles as he writes)
To teach vain wits a science little known,
To admire superior sense, and doubt their own!

PART II

    Of all the causes which conspire to blind
Man's erring judgment, and misguide the mind,
What the weak head with strongest bias rules,
Is pride, the never-failing vice of fools.
Whatever Nature has in worth denied,
She gives in large recruits of needful pride;
For as in bodies, thus in souls, we find
What wants in blood and spirits swelled with
    wind:
Pride, where wit fails, steps in to our defense,
And fills up all the mighty void of sense.
If once right reason drives that cloud away,
Truth breaks upon us with resistless day.
Trust not yourself: but your defects to know,
Make use of every friend — and every foe.

    A little learning is a dangerous thing;
Drink deep, or taste not the Pierian spring.[19]
There shallow draughts intoxicate the brain,
And drinking largely sobers us again.
Fired at first sight with what the Muse imparts,
In fearless youth we tempt the heights of arts,
While from the bounded level of our mind
Short views we take, nor see the lengths behind;
But more advanced, behold with strange surprise
New distant scenes of endless science rise!
So pleased at first the towering Alps we try,
Mount o'er the vales, and seem to tread the sky,
The eternal snows appear already past,
And the first clouds and mountains seem the last;
But, those attained, we tremble to survey
The growing labors of the lengthened way,
The increasing prospect tires our wandering
    eyes,
Hills peep o'er hills, and Alps on Alps arise!

    A perfect judge will read each work of wit
With the same spirit that its author writ:
Survey the whole, nor seek slight faults to find
Where Nature moves, and rapture warms the
    mind;
Nor lose, for that malignant dull delight,
The generous pleasure to be charmed with wit.

---

[17]Pope alludes to the "ut pictura poesis" passage in Horace's *Art of Poetry,* which stresses that some poems, like some paintings, need to be looked at from afar, not scrutinized in detail.

[18]Where Horace claims in the *Art of Poetry* to be "indignant even when it is the great Homer who falls asleep on the job," Pope suggests that the critic rather than the poet may be at fault.

[19]Pieria, near Mt. Olympus, was sacred to the Muses.

But in such lays as neither ebb nor flow,
Correctly cold, and regularly low,
That, shunning faults, one quiet tenor keep,
We cannot blame indeed — but we may sleep.
In wit, as nature, what affects our hearts
Is not the exactness of peculiar parts;
'Tis not a lip, or eye, we beauty call,
But the joint force and full result of all.
Thus when we view some well-proportioned dome[20]
(The world's just wonder, and even thine, O Rome!),
No single parts unequally surprise,
All comes united to the admiring eyes:
No monstrous height, or breadth, or length appear;
The whole at once is bold and regular.
Whoever thinks a faultless piece to see,
Thinks what ne'er was, nor is, nor e'er shall be.
In every work regard the writer's end,
Since none can compass more than they intend;
And if the means be just, the conduct true,
Applause, in spite of trivial faults, is due.
As men of breeding, sometimes men of wit,
To avoid great errors must the less commit,
Neglect the rules each verbal critic lays,
For not to know some trifles is a praise.
Most critics, fond of some subservient art,
Still make the whole depend upon a part:
They talk of principles, but notions prize,
And all to one loved folly sacrifice.
    Once on a time La Mancha's knight,[21] they say,
A certain bard encountering on the way,
Discoursed in terms as just, with looks as sage,
As e'er could Dennis,[22] of the Grecian stage;
Concluding all were desperate sots and fools
Who durst depart from Aristotle's rules.
Our author, happy in a judge so nice,
Produced his play, and begged the knight's advice;
Made him observe the subject and the plot,

The manners, passions, unities; what not?
All which exact to rule were brought about,
Were but a combat in the lists left out.
"What! leave the combat out?" exclaims the knight.
"Yes, or we must renounce the Stagirite."
"Not so, by Heaven!" he answers in a rage,
"Knights, squires, and steeds must enter on the stage."
"So vast a throng the stage can ne'er contain."
"Then build a new, or act it in a plain."
    Thus critics of less judgment than caprice,
Curious,[23] not knowing, not exact, but nice,
Form short ideas, and offend in arts
(As most in manners), by a love to parts.
    Some to conceit[24] alone their taste confine,
And glittering thoughts struck out at every line;
Pleased with a work where nothing's just or fit,
One glaring chaos and wild heap of wit.
Poets, like painters, thus unskilled to trace
The naked nature and the living grace,
With gold and jewels cover every part,
And hide with ornaments their want of art.
    True wit is Nature to advantage dressed,
What oft was thought, but ne'er so well expressed;
Something whose truth convinced at sight we find,
That gives us back the image of our mind.
As shades more sweetly recommend the light,
So modest plainness sets off sprightly wit;
For works may have more wit than does them good,
As bodies perish through excess of blood.
    Others for language all their care express,
And value books, as women men, for dress.
Their praise is still — the style is excellent;
The sense they humbly take upon contént.[25]
Words are like leaves; and where they most abound,
Much fruit of sense beneath is rarely found.
False eloquence, like the prismatic glass,
Its gaudy colors spreads on every place;
The face of Nature we no more survey,

[20]Of St. Peter's Basilica.
[21]Don Quixote. The episode is not in Cervantes but in a sequel written under the name of Alonzo Fernandez de Avellaneda and translated into English around 1705.
[22]John Dennis (1657–1734), a playwright and critic who had argued for the application of classical rules to the English stage.

[23]Pedantically careful; "nice" in the same line means "overrefined."
[24]Figures of speech.
[25]On faith.

All glares alike, without distinction gay.
But true expression, like the unchanging sun,
Clears and improves whate'er it shines upon;
It gilds all objects, but it alters none.
Expression is the dress of thought, and still
Appears more decent as more suitable.
A vile conceit in pompous words expressed
Is like a clown in regal purple dressed:
For different styles with different subjects sort,
As several garbs with country, town, and court.
Some by old words to fame have made pretense,
Ancients in phrase, mere moderns in their sense.
Such labored nothings, in so strange a style,
Amaze the unlearn'd, and make the learned
    smile;
Unlucky as Fungoso[26] in the play,
These sparks with awkward vanity display
What the fine gentleman wore yesterday;
And but so mimic ancient wits at best,
As apes our grandsires in their doublets dressed.
In words as fashions the same rule will hold,
Alike fantastic if too new or old:
Be not the first by whom the new are tried,
Nor yet the last to lay the old aside.
    But most by numbers[27] judge a poet's song,
And smooth or rough with them is right or
    wrong.
In the bright Muse though thousand charms con-
    spire,
Her voice is all these tuneful fools admire,
Who haunt Parnassus but to please their ear,
Not mend their minds; as some to church repair,
Not for the doctrine, but the music there.
These equal syllables alone require,
Though oft the ear the open vowels tire,
While expletives their feeble aid do join,
And ten low words oft creep in one dull line:
While they ring round the same unvaried chimes,
With sure returns of still expected rhymes;
Where'er you find "the cooling western breeze,"
In the next line, it "whispers through the trees";
If crystal streams "with pleasing murmurs
    creep,"
The reader's threatened (not in vain) with
    "sleep";

Then, at the last and only couplet fraught
With some unmeaning thing they call a thought,
A needless Alexandrine[28] ends the song
That, like a wounded snake, drags its slow length
    along.
Leave such to tune their own dull rhymes, and
    know
What's roundly smooth or languishingly slow;
And praise the easy vigor of a line
Where Denham's strength and Waller's sweet-
    ness join.
True ease in writing comes from art, not chance,
As those move easiest who have learned to
    dance.
'Tis not enough no harshness gives offense,
The sound must seem an echo to the sense.
Soft is the strain when Zephyr gently blows,
And the smooth stream in smoother numbers
    flows;
But when loud surges lash the sounding shore,
The hoarse, rough verse should like the torrent
    roar.
When Ajax strives some rock's vast weight to
    throw,
The line too labors, and the words move slow;
Not so when swift Camilla[29] scours the plain,
Flies o'er the unbending corn, and skims along
    the main.
Hear how Timotheus'[30] varied lays surprise,
And bid alternate passions fall and rise!
While at each change the son of Libyan Jove
Now burns with glory, and then melts with love;
Now his fierce eyes with sparkling fury glow,
Now sighs steal out, and tears begin to flow:
Persians and Greeks like turns of nature found
And the world's victor stood subdued by sound!
The power of music all our hearts allow,
And what Timotheus was is Dryden now.
    Avoid extremes; and shun the fault of such
Who still are pleased too little or too much.

[26]A character in Ben Jonson's *Every Man out of His
Humour* (1599).

[27]Prosody.

[28]Line of iambic hexameter, usually broken in the middle.

[29]Camilla was an Amazonian warrior allied to Turnus in
Virgil's *Aeneid.*

[30]Pope retells the story of Dryden's *Alexander's Feast:*
how Alexander the Great's bard, Timotheus, was able to subdue the conqueror of the world through his art. The "son of
Libyan Jove" is Alexander, who claimed descent from
Ammon after conquering Egypt.

At every trifle scorn to take offense:
That always shows great pride, or little sense.
Those heads, as stomachs, are not sure the best,
Which nauseate all, and nothing can digest.
Yet let not each gay turn thy rapture move;
For fools admire, but men of sense approve:
As things seem large which we through mists
   descry,
Dullness is ever apt to magnify.

Some foreign writers, some our own despise;
The ancients only, or the moderns prize.
Thus wit, like faith, by each man is applied
To one small sect, and all are damned beside.
Meanly they seek the blessing to confine,
And force that sun but on a part to shine,
Which not alone the southern wit sublimes,
But ripens spirits in cold northern climes;
Which from the first has shone on ages past,
Enlights the present, and shall warm the last;
Though each may feel increases and decays,
And see now clearer and now darker days.
Regard not then if wit be old or new,
But blame the false and value still the true.

Some ne'er advance a judgment of their own,
But catch the spreading notion of the town;
They reason and conclude by precedent,
And own stale nonsense which they ne'er invent.
Some judge of authors' names, not works, and
   then
Nor praise nor blame the writings, but the men.
Of all this servile herd the worst is he
That in proud dullness joins with quality,
A constant critic at the great man's board,
To fetch and carry nonsense for my lord.
What woeful stuff this madrigal would be
In some starved hackney sonneteer or me!
But let a lord once own the happy lines,
How the wit brightens! how the style refines!
Before his sacred name flies every fault,
And each exalted stanza teems with thought!

The vulgar thus through imitation err;
As oft the learn'd by being singular;
So much they scorn the crowd, that if the throng
By chance go right, they purposely go wrong.
So schismatics the plain believers quit,
And are but damned for having too much wit.
Some praise at morning what they blame at
   night,
But always think the last opinion right.

A Muse by these is like a mistress used,
This hour she's idolized, the next abused;
While their weak heads like towns unfortified,
'Twixt sense and nonsense daily change their
   side.
Ask them the cause; they're wiser still, they say;
And still tomorrow's wiser than today.
We think our fathers fools, so wise we grow;
Our wiser sons, no doubt, will think us so.
Once school divines[31] this zealous isle o'er-
   spread;
Who knew most sentences was deepest read.
Faith, Gospel, all seemed made to be disputed,
And none had sense enough to be confuted.
Scotists and Thomists now in peace remain
Amidst their kindred cobwebs in Duck Lane.[32]
If faith itself has different dresses worn,
What wonder modes in wit should take their
   turn?
Oft, leaving what is natural and fit,
The current folly proves the ready wit;
And authors think their reputation safe,
Which lives as long as fools are pleased to laugh.

Some valuing those of their own side or mind,
Still make themselves the measure of mankind:
Fondly[33] we think we honor merit then,
When we but praise ourselves in other men.
Parties in wit attend on those of state,
And public faction doubles private hate.
Pride, Malice, Folly against Dryden rose,
In various shapes of parsons, critics, beaux;
But sense survived, when merry jests were past;
For rising merit will buoy up at last.
Might he return and bless once more our eyes,
New Blackmores and new Milbourns must
   arise.[34]
Nay, should great Homer lift his awful head,
Zoilus[35] again would start up from the dead.
Envy will merit, as its shade, pursue,
But like a shadow, proves the substance true;
For envied wit, like Sol eclipsed, makes known
The opposing body's grossness, not its own.

[31]Scholastic theologians.
[32]Street of used bookstores.
[33]Foolishly.
[34]Richard Blackmore had attacked Dryden's dramas, Luke Milbourn his translation of the *Aeneid*.
[35]Zoilus was a severe critic of Homer of the fourth century B.C.E.

When first that sun too powerful beams displays,
It draws up vapors which obscure its rays;
But even those clouds at last adorn its way,
Reflect new glories, and augment the day.

Be thou the first true merit to befriend;
His praise is lost who stays till all commend.
Short is the date, alas! of modern rhymes,
And 'tis but just to let them live betimes.
No longer now that golden age appears,
When patriarch wits survived a thousand years:
Now length of fame (our second life) is lost,
And bare threescore is all even that can boast;
Our sons their fathers' failing language see,
And such as Chaucer is shall Dryden be.[36]
So when the faithful pencil has designed
Some bright idea of the master's mind,
Where a new world leaps out at his command,
And ready Nature waits upon his hand;
When the ripe colors soften and unite,
And sweetly melt into just shade and light;
When mellowing years their full perfection give,
And each bold figure just begins to live,
The treacherous colors the fair art betray,
And all the bright creation fades away!

Unhappy wit, like most mistaken things,
Atones not for that envy which it brings.
In youth alone its empty praise we boast,
But soon the short-lived vanity is lost;
Like some fair flower the early spring supplies,
That gaily blooms, but even in blooming dies,
What is this wit, which must our cares employ?
The owner's wife, that other men enjoy;
Then most our trouble still when most admired,
And still the more we give, the more required;
Whose fame with pains we guard, but lose with
    ease,
Sure some to vex, but never all to please;
'Tis what the vicious fear, the virtuous shun,
By fools 'tis hated, and by knaves undone!

If wit so much from ignorance undergo,
Ah, let not learning too commence its foe!
Of old those met rewards who could excel,
And such were praised who but endeavored well;
Though triumphs were to generals only due,
Crowns were reserved to grace the soldiers too.

Now they who reach Parnassus' lofty crown
Employ their pains to spurn some others down;
And while self-love each jealous writer rules,
Contending wits become the sport of fools;
But still the worst with most regret commend,
For each ill author is as bad a friend.
To what base ends, and by what abject ways,
Are mortals urged through sacred[37] lust of
    praise!
Ah, ne'er so dire a thirst of glory boast,
Nor in the critic let the man be lost!
Good nature and good sense must ever join;
To err is human, to forgive divine.

But if in noble minds some dregs remain
Nor yet purged off, of spleen and sour disdain,
Discharge that rage on more provoking crimes,
Nor fear a dearth in these flagitious[38] times.
No pardon vile obscenity should find,
Though wit and art conspire to move your mind;
But dullness with obscenity must prove
As shameful sure as impotence in love.
In the fat age of pleasure, wealth, and ease
Sprung the rank weed, and thrived with large in-
    crease:
When love was all an easy monarch's[39] care,
Seldom at council, never in a war;
Jilts[40] ruled the state, and statesmen farces writ;
Nay, wits had pensions, and young lords had wit;
The fair sat panting at a courtier's play,
And not a mask[41] went unimproved away;
The modest fan was lifted up no more,
And virgins smiled at what they blushed before.
The following license of a foreign reign[42]
Did all the dregs of bold Socinus drain;
Then unbelieving priests reformed the nation,
And taught more pleasant methods of salvation;
Where Heaven's free subjects might their rights
    dispute,
Lest God himself should seem too absolute;

---

[37]Accursed.
[38]Wicked.
[39]Charles II (reigned 1660–85).
[40]Charles's mistresses.
[41]Women wearing a vizard mask, whose concealment
allowed one to behave immorally without scandal.
[42]The reign of William III (1689–1701), who came from
Holland. Socinus, in the next line, was the name of two
Renaissance Italian theologians whose doctrines denied the
divinity of Christ and the efficacy of the Atonement.

[36]The Middle English in which Chaucer wrote had become
unintelligible by Pope's time.

Pulpits their sacred satire learned to spare,
And Vice admired to find a flatterer there!
Encouraged thus, wit's Titans braved the skies,
And the press groaned with licensed blas-
    phemies.
These monsters, critics! with your darts engage,
Here point your thunder, and exhaust your rage!
Yet shun their fault, who, scandalously nice,
Will needs mistake an author into vice;
All seems infected that the infected spy,
As all looks yellow to the jaundiced eye.

PART III

Learn then what morals Critics ought to show,
For 'tis but half a judge's task to know.
'Tis not enough Taste, Judgment, Learning join;
In all you speak let Truth and Candour shine;
That not alone what to your Sense is due
All may allow, but seek your friendship too.
    Be silent always when you doubt your Sense,
And speak, tho' sure, with seeming diffidence.
Some positive persisting fops we know,
Who if once wrong will needs be always so;
But you with pleasure own your errors past,
And make each day a critique on the last.
    'Tis not enough your counsel still be true;
Blunt truths more mischief than nice falsehoods
    do.
Men must be taught as if you taught them not,
And things unknown proposed as things forgot.
Without good breeding truth is disapprov'd;
That only makes superior Sense belov'd.
    Be niggards of advice on no pretence,
For the worst avarice is that of Sense.
With mean complacence ne'er betray your trust,
Nor be so civil as to prove unjust.
Fear not the anger of the wise to raise;
Those best can bear reproof who merit praise.
    'Twere well might critics still this freedom
    take,
But Appius[43] reddens at each word you speak,
And stares tremendous, with a threat'ning eye,
Like some fierce tyrant in old tapestry.
Fear most to tax an honourable fool,
Whose right it is, uncensured to be dull:

Such without Wit, are poets when they please,
As without Learning they can take degrees.[44]
Leave dangerous truths to unsuccessful satires,
And flattery to fulsome dedicators;
Whom, when they praise, the world believes no
    more
Than when they promise to give scribbling o'er.
'Tis best sometimes your censure to restrain,
And charitably let the dull be vain;
Your silence there is better than your spite,
For who can rail so long as they can write?
Still humming on their drowsy course they keep,
And lash'd so long, like tops, are lash'd asleep.
False steps but help them to renew the race,
As, after stumbling, jades will mend their pace.
What crowds of these, impenitently bold,
In sounds and jingling syllables grown old,
Still run on poets, in a raging vein,
Ev'n to the dregs and squeezings of the brain,
Strain out the last dull dropping of their sense,
And rhyme with all the rage of impotence!
    Such shameless bards we have; and yet 'tis
        true
There are as mad abandon'd critics too.
The bookful blockhead ignorantly read,
With loads of learned lumber in his head,
With his own tongue still edifies his ears,
And always list'ning to himself appears.
All books he reads, and all he reads assails,
From Dryden's Fables down to Durfey's Tales.[45]
With him most authors steal their works, or buy;
Garth did not write his own Dispensary.[46]
Name a new play, and he's the poet's friend;
Nay, show'd his faults — but when would poets
    mend?
No place so sacred from such fops is barr'd,
Nor is Paul's church more safe than Paul's
    churchyard:[47]
Nay, fly to altars, there they'll talk you dead;
For fools rush in where angels fear to tread.
Distrustful sense with modest caution speaks,

[43]See n. 22. Dennis wrote an unsuccessful play, *Appius and Virginia* (1709).

[44]Sons of peers were allowed to take degrees at Oxford and Cambridge without meeting the usual requirements.
[45]Thomas Durfey (1653–1723), author of popular songs, tales, plays, and other entertainments.
[46]Samuel Garth (1661–1719), physician-poet who wrote a didactic poem called "The Dispensary."
[47]Where booksellers plied their trade.

It still looks home, and short excursions makes;
But rattling nonsense in full volleys breaks
And never shock'd, and never turn'd aside,
Bursts out, resistless, with a thund'ring tide.

But where's the man who counsel can bestow,
Still pleas'd to teach, and yet not proud to know?
Unbiass'd or by favour or by spite;
Not dully prepossess'd nor blindly right;
Tho' learn'd, well bred, and tho' well bred sin-
cere;
Modestly bold, and humanly severe;
Who to a friend his faults can freely show,
And gladly praise the merit of a foe;
Bless'd with a taste exact, yet unconfin'd,
A knowledge both of books and humankind;
Gen'rous converse; a soul exempt from pride;
And love to praise, with reason on his side?
Such once were critics; such the happy few
Athens and Rome in better ages knew.
The mighty Stagyrite first left the shore,
Spread all his sails, and durst the deeps explore;
He steer'd securely, and discover'd far,
Led by the light of the Mæonian star.[48]
Poets, a race long unconfin'd and free,
Still fond and proud of savage liberty,
Receiv'd his laws, and stood convinc'd 'twas fit
Who conquer'd Nature should preside o'er Wit.

Horace still charms with graceful negligence,
And without method talks us into sense;
Will, like a friend, familiarly convey
The truest notions in the easiest way.
He who, supreme in judgment as in wit,
Might boldly censure as he boldly writ,
Yet judg'd with coolness, though he sung with
fire;
His precepts teach but what his works inspire.
Our critics take a contrary extreme,
They judge with fury, but they write with
phlegm;
Nor suffers Horace more in wrong translations
By Wits, than Critics in as wrong quotations.
See Dionysius[49] Homer's thoughts refine,
And call new beauties forth from ev'ry line!

Fancy and art in gay Petronius[50] please,
The Scholar's learning with the courtier's ease.
In grave Quintilian's[51] copious work we find
The justest rules and clearest method join'd.
Thus useful arms in magazines we place,
All ranged in order, and disposed with grace;
But less to please the eye then arm the hand,
Still fit for use, and ready at command.

Thee, bold Longinus! all the Nine[52] inspire,
And bless their critic with a poet's fire:
An ardent judge, who, zealous in his trust,
With warmth gives sentence, yet is always just;
Whose own example strengthens all his laws,
And is himself that great sublime he draws.

Thus long succeeding critics justly reign'd,
License repress'd, and useful laws ordain'd:
Learning and Rome alike in empire grew,
And arts still follow'd where her eagles flew;
From the same foes at last both felt their doom,
And the same age saw learning fall and Rome.
With tyranny then superstition join'd,
As that the body, this enslaved the mind;
Much was believ'd, but little understood,
And to be dull was construed to be good;
A second deluge learning thus o'errun,
And the monks finish'd what the Goths begun.

At length Erasmus, that great injur'd name,
(The glory of the priesthood and the shame!)
Stemm'd the wild torrent of a barb'rous age,
And drove those holy Vandals off the stage.

But see! each Muse in Leo's[53] golden days
Starts from her trance, and trims her wither'd
bays.
Rome's ancient genius, o'er its ruins spread,
Shakes off the dust, and rears his rev'rend head.
Then sculpture and her sister arts revive;
Stones leap'd to form, and rocks began to live;
With sweeter notes each rising temple rung;
A Raphael painted and a Vida[54] sung:
Immortal Vida! on whose honour'd brow

[48]Homer, whose birthplace, according to tradition, was Maeonia.
[49]Dionysius of Halicarnassus (first century B.C.E.), literary critic and historian.

[50]Petronius Arbiter (?–65 C.E.), author of the *Satyricon*.
[51]Quintilian (35–95), rhetorician and author of *Institutio Oratoria*.
[52]The nine Muses.
[53]Leo X, originally Giovanni de' Medici (1475–1521), whose pontificate was "golden" from the artistic commissions given out.
[54]Marco Girolamo Vida (1480–1566), Italian critic, poet, and author of *De arte poetica*.

The poet's bays and critic's ivy grow:
Cremona now shall ever boast thy name,
As next in place to Mantua,[55] next in fame!
    But soon by impious arms from Latium
    chased,
Their ancient bounds the banish'd Muses pass'd;
Thence arts o'er all the northern world advance,
But critic learning flourish'd most in France;
The rules a nation born to serve obeys,
And Boileau[56] still in right of Horace sways.
But we, brave Britons, foreign laws despised,
And kept unconquer'd and uncivilized;
Fierce for the liberties of wit, and bold,
We still defied the Romans, as of old.
Yet some there were, among the sounder few
Of those who less presumed and better knew,
Who durst assert the juster ancient cause,
And here restor'd Wit's fundamental laws.
Such was the Muse whose rules and practice tell
"Nature's chief masterpiece is writing well."[57]
Such was Roscommon,[58] not more learn'd than
    good,

With manners gen'rous as his noble blood;
To him the wit of Greece and Rome was known,
And every author's merit but his own.
Such late was Walsh[59] — the Muse's judge and
    friend,
Who justly knew to blame or to commend;
To failings mild but zealous for desert,
The clearest head, and the sincerest heart.
This humble praise, lamented Shade! receive;
This praise at least a grateful Muse may give:
The Muse whose early voice you taught to sing,
Prescribed her heights, and pruned her tender
    wing,
(Her guide now lost), no more attempts to rise,
But in low numbers short excursions tries;
Content if hence th' unlearn'd their wants may
    view,
The learn'd reflect on what before they knew;
Careless of censure, nor too fond of fame;
Still pleas'd to praise, yet not afraid to blame;
Averse alike to flatter or offend;
Not free from faults, nor yet too vain to mend.

---

[55]Birthplace of Virgil.
[56]Nicolas Boileau-Despréaux (1636–1711), French poet and critic, whose *Art poétique* is one of the sources of Pope's ideas.
[57]From Buckingham's "Essay on Poetry."
[58]Wentworth Dillon, Earl of Roscommon (1633–1685), poet, critic, and translator of Horace.

[59]William Walsh (1663–1708), Pope's friend, who had advised the young poet that he could make his mark by striving for correctness.

Samuel Johnson

1709–1784

Samuel Johnson, the "Great Cham of Literature," is the magisterial personality that dominates the late eighteenth century in England with his insistent moralism, his unflappable common sense, and his tragic vision of life. The only son of a provincial book dealer, whose formal education came to an end after an impecunious year at Oxford, Johnson made himself into the most broadly learned man of his age.

He arrived in London in 1737, just around the time the system of patrician patronage (which had supported John Dryden so well) was giving way to the one familiar today, in which authors bargain with publishers for their material support. In his thirties, Johnson joined the army of hack writers who eked out their living by producing for the Grub Street booksellers the journalism, travel books, occasional essays, translations, and histories for which the new middle-class reading public hankered. From 1747 to 1755, in sickness and sorrow, Johnson labored virtually alone on his massive *Dictionary of the English Language;* its appearance made Johnson's reputation, became the standard dictionary for over half a century, and helped to standardize the chaotic English tongue. He wrote major works in every important literary genre of his age: They include satirical poems like "London" (1739) and "The Vanity of Human Wishes" (1749); the fable *Rasselas* (1759); the tragedy *Irene* (1749); weekly essays for *The Rambler* (1750–52), *The Adventurer* (1753–54), and *The Idler* (1758–60); an authoritative edition of Shakespeare (1763); and a massive series of biographical and critical essays, *Lives of the Poets*, on all the significant English writers of the seventeenth and eighteenth centuries (1779–81).

Johnson's criticism, like that of Sidney and Dryden and most of his own contemporaries, derives its principles from Horace: He conceives of the literary work as a piece of rhetoric to be judged by the impact it makes upon the audience. But those trying to place Johnson within the broad spectrum of rhetorical criticism should note that he takes the didactic purpose of literature far more seriously than either Horace or Dryden, and that his insistence on the universal character of poetry differentiates him from such Platonizing critics as Sidney.

"The end of writing is to instruct; the end of poetry is to instruct by pleasing," he declared in his Preface to *Shakespeare*, and this *locus classicus* dominates the rest of his theory. Didacticism is surely the keynote in his essay on the novel in *The Rambler*, No. 4 (1750). While Johnson admits that literature should imitate life, and that the novel is therefore an improvement over the romance, he sees no reason why writers should not be selective about what aspects of life they choose to imitate. The plots of novels should end with poetic justice, and in presenting characters, novelists should strive to exhibit "the most perfect idea of virtue" in their heroes, not to present characters at once fascinating and deeply flawed. The date of the essay suggests that Johnson may have been reacting specifically to Fielding's *Tom Jones* (1749) and its scapegrace hero, but the viewpoint he presents is not topical, and it was one with which his entire age was in sympathy.

If the aim of poetry is "to instruct by pleasing," then we might inquire how that is brought about. The answer, also found in the Preface to *Shakespeare*, runs briefly thus: "Nothing can please many, and please long, but just representations of general nature." Poetry must be deeply true to life, not because art is a matter of imitation, but because the truth of accurate representation holds us longer than any artful fancy could: "The pleasures of sudden wonder are soon exhausted, and the mind can only repose on the stability of truth."

Precisely what Johnson means by "general nature" is glossed in *Rasselas*, Chapter 10, where Imlac tells the Prince that "the business of the poet . . . is to examine, not the individual, but the species; to remark general properties and large appearances: he does not number the streaks of the tulip. . . . He . . . must neglect the minuter discriminations, which one may have remarked, and another have neglected, for those characteristics which are alike obvious to vigilance and carelessness." Johnson's insistence on the universality of poetry is very similar to Aristotle's, but his point is Horatian: If the literary work is to please a universal audience it must deal broadly with the world we all know, not with special issues of interest to a few.

From Johnson's universalizing perspective, the old topics of rhetorical criticism — the three unities, generic integrity, decorum of the stage — finally recede to the status of mere conventions, and conventions that were not those of Shakespeare's era. With all due reverence to the venerable antiquity of these doctrines, Johnson refutes their assumptions so thoroughly that it becomes difficult to see how they influenced so many for so long. At every point, Johnson insists that "there is always an appeal open from criticism to nature," and the old dogmas wither in the brutal spotlight of Johnson's common sense. The unities of time and place, he says, derive from "the supposed necessity of making the drama credible"; but in fact, no one in the audience believes for an instant that the things happening on stage are actually occurring. The audience's enjoyment indeed depends upon their sense that they are watching fiction. Critics have claimed that by mixing comic with tragic scenes, the passions are interrupted and the drama is deprived of emotional force. This reasoning, Johnson insinuates, is "so specious [attractive] that it is received as true even by those who in daily experience feel it to be false." To critics who object to the apparent indecorum of Shakespeare's presenting King Claudius of Denmark as a drunkard, Johnson scoffs that "these are the petty cavils of petty minds."

Those who are accustomed to believe that Shakespeare could do no wrong may be surprised by Johnson's strictly judicial appraisal of the bard's faults and virtues. Johnson's didactic streak, in fact, is offended by Shakespeare's amorality, and Shakespeare's greatness is rescued only by his surpassing universality and trueness to life. In his stray judgments on Shakespeare, however, Johnson can be very shrewd — as when he states that Shakespeare's "tragedy seems to be skill, his comedy to be instinct."

The pleasures of reading Johnson's criticism are not merely intellectual. In his hands criticism becomes literature, delighting as well as instructing, and the source of the pleasure is Johnson's unique personality. We value his wisdom as much as his learning, and his tragic vision as much as his ebullient combativeness. He speaks of readers "willing to be thought wicked, if they may be allowed to be wits," and of writers who "are willing to hope from posterity what the present age refuses, and flatter themselves that the regard which is yet denied by envy, will be at last bestowed by time." He refers to the way "the common satiety of life sends us all in quest" of fantastic but worthless novelties; and reminds us that love "is only one of many passions, and . . . has no great influence upon the sum of life." It is then that we sense the presence of the very human sage who felt so deeply "The Vanity of Human Wishes."

Selected Bibliography

Bate, Walter Jackson. *The Achievement of Samuel Johnson*. Chicago: University of Chicago Press, 1978.

Battersby, James L. *Rational Praise and Natural Lamentation: Johnson, Lycidas and Principles of Criticism*. Rutherford, NJ: Fairleigh Dickinson University Press, 1980.

Damrosch, Leopold. *The Uses of Johnson's Criticism*. Charlottesville: University Press of Virginia, 1976.

Fussell, Paul. *Samuel Johnson and the Life of Writing*. New York: Norton, 1986.

Hagstrum, Jean H. *Samuel Johnson's Literary Criticism*. 1952; Chicago: University of Chicago Press, 1967.

Jenkins, Ralph Eugene. *Some Sources of Samuel Johnson's Literary Criticism*. Austin: University of Texas Press, 1969.

Keast, W. R. "Theoretical Foundations of Johnson's Criticism." In *Critics and Criticism: Ancient and Modern*, ed. R. S. Crane. Chicago: University of Chicago Press, 1952.

Mahoney, John L. "The True Story: Poetic Law and License in Johnson's Criticism." In *Ideas, Æsthetics, and Inquiries in the Early Modern Era*, vol. 6, ed. Kevin L. Cope, 185–98. New York: AMS Press, 2001.

Smallwood, Philip. *Johnson's Critical Presence: Image, History, Judgment*. Aldershot, England: Ashgate, 2003.

Stock, R. D. *Samuel Johnson and Neoclassical Dramatic Theory: The Literary Content of the "Preface to Shakespeare."* Lincoln: University of Nebraska Press, 1973.

The Rambler, No. 4

Simul et jucunda et idonea dicere vitæ.

—HORACE, *Ars Poetica,* 334

And join both profit and delight in one — CREECH

The works of fiction, with which the present generation seems more particularly delighted, are such as exhibit life in its true state, diversified only by accidents that daily happen in the world, and influenced by passions and qualities which are really to be found in conversing with mankind.

This kind of writing may be termed not improperly the comedy of romance, and is to be conducted nearly by the rules of comic poetry. Its province is to bring about natural events by easy means, and to keep up curiosity without the help of wonder: it is therefore precluded from the machines and expedients of the heroic romance, and can neither employ giants to snatch away a lady from the nuptial rites, nor knights to bring her back from captivity; it can neither bewilder its personages in deserts, nor lodge them in imaginary castles.

I remember a remark made by Scaliger[1] upon Pontanus, that all his writings are filled with the same images; and that if you take from him his

[1] Julius Caesar Scaliger, *Poetics* 5:4.

lilies and his roses, his satyrs and his dryads, he will have nothing left that can be called poetry. In like manner almost all the fictions of the last age will vanish, if you deprive them of a hermit and a wood, a battle and a shipwreck.

Why this wild strain of imagination found reception so long in polite and learned ages, it is not easy to conceive; but we cannot wonder that while readers could be procured, the authors were willing to continue it; for when a man had by practice gained some fluency of language, he had no further care than to retire to his closet, let loose his invention, and heat his mind with incredibilities; a book was thus produced without fear of criticism, without the toil of study, without knowledge of nature, or acquaintance with life.

The task of our present writers is very different; it requires, together with that learning which is to be gained from books, that experience which can never be attained by solitary diligence, but must arise from general converse and accurate observation of the living world. Their performances have, as Horace expresses it, *plus oneris quantum veniæ minus*, little indulgence, and therefore more difficulty.[2] They are engaged in portraits of which every one knows the original, and can detect any deviation from exactness of resemblance. Other writings are safe, except from the malice of learning, but these are in danger from every common reader; as the slipper ill executed was censured by a shoemaker who happened to stop in his way at the Venus of Apelles.[3]

But the fear of not being approved as just copiers of human manners, is not the most important concern that an author of this sort ought to have before him. These books are written chiefly to the young, the ignorant, and the idle, to whom they serve as lectures of conduct, and introductions into life. They are the entertainment of minds unfurnished with ideas, and therefore easily susceptible of impressions; not fixed by principles, and therefore easily following the current of fancy; not informed by experience, and consequently open to every false suggestion and partial account.

That the highest degree of reverence should be paid to youth, and that nothing indecent should be suffered to approach their eyes or ears, are precepts extorted by sense and virtue from an ancient writer, by no means eminent for chastity of thought. The same kind, though not the same degree, of caution, is required in every thing which is laid before them, to secure them from unjust prejudices, perverse opinions, and incongruous combinations of images.

In the romances formerly written, every transaction and sentiment was so remote from all that passes among men, that the reader was in very little danger of making any applications to himself; the virtues and crimes were equally beyond his sphere of activity; and he amused himself with heroes and with traitors, deliverers and persecutors, as with beings of another species, whose actions were regulated upon motives of their own, and who had neither faults nor excellencies in common with himself.

But when an adventurer is levelled with the rest of the world, and acts in such scenes of the universal drama, as may be the lot of any other man; young spectators fix their eyes upon him with closer attention, and hope, by observing his behaviour and success, to regulate their own practices, when they shall be engaged in the like part.

For this reason these familiar histories may perhaps be made of greater use than the solemnities of professed morality, and convey the knowledge of vice and virtue with more efficacy than axioms and definitions. But if the power of example is so great as to take possession of the memory by a kind of violence, and produce effects almost without the intervention of the will, care ought to be taken, that, when the choice is unrestrained, the best examples only should be exhibited; and that which is likely to operate so strongly, should not be mischievous or uncertain in its effects.

The chief advantage which these fictions have over real life is, that their authors are at liberty, though not to invent, yet to select objects, and to cull from the mass of mankind, those individuals upon which the attention ought most to be employed; as a diamond, though it cannot be made, may be polished by art, and placed in such a situation, as to display that lustre which before was buried among common stones.

[2]Horace, *Epistles* II.1:70.
[3]Pliny, *Natural History* 35:84–85.

It is justly considered as the greatest excellency of art, to imitate nature; but it is necessary to distinguish those parts of nature, which are most proper for imitation: greater care is still required in representing life, which is so often discoloured by passion, or deformed by wickedness. If the world be promiscuously described, I cannot see of what use it can be to read the account; or why it may not be as safe to turn the eye immediately upon mankind as upon a mirror which shows all that presents itself without discrimination.

It is therefore not a sufficient vindication of a character, that it is drawn as it appears; for many characters ought never to be drawn: nor of a narrative, that the train of events is agreeable to observation and experience; for that observation which is called knowledge of the world, will be found much more frequently to make men cunning than good. The purpose of these writings is surely not only to show mankind, but to provide that they may be seen hereafter with less hazard; to teach the means of avoiding the snares which are laid by Treachery for Innocence, without infusing any wish for that superiority with which the betrayer flatters his vanity; to give the power of counteracting fraud, without the temptation to practise it; to initiate youth by mock encounters in the art of necessary defence, and to increase prudence without impairing virtue.

Many writers, for the sake of following nature, so mingle good and bad qualities in their principal personages, that they are both equally conspicuous; and as we accompany them through their adventures with delight, and are led by degrees to interest ourselves in their favour, we lose the abhorrence of their faults, because they do not hinder our pleasure, or, perhaps, regard them with some kindness, for being united with so much merit.

There have been men indeed splendidly wicked, whose endowments threw a brightness on their crimes, and whom scarce any villainy made perfectly detestable, because they never could be wholly divested of their excellencies; but such have been in all ages the great corrupters of the world, and their resemblance ought no more to be preserved, than the art of murdering without pain.

Some have advanced, without due attention to the consequences of this notion, that certain virtues have their correspondent faults, and therefore that to exhibit either apart is to deviate from probability. Thus men are observed by Swift to be "grateful in the same degree as they are resentful." This principle, with others of the same kind, supposes man to act from a brute impulse, and pursue a certain degree of inclination, without any choice of the object; for, otherwise, though it should be allowed that gratitude and resentment arise from the same constitution of the passions, it follows not that they will be equally indulged when reason is consulted; yet, unless that consequence be admitted, this sagacious maxim becomes an empty sound, without any relation to practice or to life.

Nor is it evident, that even the first motions to these effects are always in the same proportion. For pride, which produces quickness of resentment, will obstruct gratitude, by unwillingness to admit that inferiority which obligation implies; and it is very unlikely that he who cannot think he receives a favour, will acknowledge or repay it.

It is of the utmost importance to mankind, that positions of this tendency should be laid open and confuted; for while men consider good and evil as springing from the same root, they will spare the one for the sake of the other, and in judging, if not of others at least of themselves, will be apt to estimate their virtues by their vices. To this fatal error all those will contribute, who confound the colours of right and wrong, and instead of helping to settle their boundaries, mix them with so much art, that no common mind is able to disunite them.

In narratives where historical veracity has no place, I cannot discover why there should not be exhibited the most perfect idea of virtue; of virtue not angelical, nor above probability, for what we cannot credit, we shall never imitate, but the highest and purest that humanity can reach, which, exercised in such trials as the various revolutions of things shall bring upon it, may, by conquering some calamities, and enduring others, teach us what we may hope, and what we can perform. Vice, for vice is necessary to be shown, should always disgust; nor should the graces of gaiety, or the dignity of courage, be so united with it, as to reconcile it to the mind. Wherever it appears, it should raise hatred by the malignity of its practices, and contempt by the meanness of its stratagems: for while it is supported by either parts or spirit, it will be seldom heartily abhorred. The Roman tyrant was content to be hated, if he was but feared; and there are thousands of the readers of romances willing to be thought wicked, if they may be allowed to be wits. It is therefore to be steadily inculcated, that virtue is the highest proof of understanding, and the only solid basis of greatness; and that vice is the natural consequence of narrow thoughts; that it begins in mistake, and ends in ignominy.

Rasselas, Chapter 10

IMLAC'S HISTORY CONTINUED

"Wherever I went, I found that Poetry was considered as the highest learning, and regarded with a veneration somewhat approaching to that which man would pay to the Angelick Nature. And it yet fills me with wonder, that, in almost all countries, the most ancient poets are considered as the best: whether it be that every other kind of knowledge is an acquisition gradually attained, and poetry is a gift conferred at once; or that the first poetry of every nation surprised them as a novelty, and retained the credit by consent which it received by accident at first: or whether the province of poetry is to describe Nature and Passion, which are always the same, and the first writers took possession of the most striking objects for description, and the most probable occurrences for fiction, and left nothing to those that followed them, but transcription of the same events, and new combinations of the same images. Whatever be the reason, it is commonly observed that the early writers are in possession of nature, and their followers of art: that the first excel in strength and invention, and the latter in elegance and refinement.

"I was desirous to add my name to this illustrious fraternity. I read all the poets of Persia and Arabia, and was able to repeat by memory the volumes that are suspended in the mosque of Mecca. But I soon found that no man was ever great by imitation. My desire of excellence impelled me to transfer my attention to nature and to life. Nature was to be my subject, and men to be my auditors: I could never describe what I had not seen: I could not hope to move those with delight of terrour, whose interests and opinions I did not understand.

"Being now resolved to be a poet, I saw every thing with a new purpose; my sphere of attention was suddenly magnified: no kind of knowledge was to be overlooked. I ranged mountains and deserts for images and resemblances, and pictured upon my mind every tree of the forest and flower of the valley. I observed with equal care the crags of the rock and the pinnacles of the palace. Sometimes I wandered along the mazes of the rivulet, and sometimes watched the changes of the summer clouds. To a poet nothing can be useless. Whatever is beautiful, and whatever is dreadful, must be familiar to his imagination: he must be conversant with all that is awfully vast or elegantly little. The plants of the garden, the animals of the wood, the minerals of the earth, and meteors of the sky, must all concur to store his mind with inexhaustible variety: for every idea is useful for the inforcement or decoration of moral or religious truth; and he, who knows most, will have most power of diversifying his scenes, and of gratifying his reader with remote allusions and unexpected instruction.

"All the appearances of nature I was therefore careful to study, and every country which I have surveyed has contributed something to my poetical powers."

"In so wide a survey, said the prince, you must surely have left much unobserved. I have lived, till now, within the circuit of these mountains, and yet cannot walk abroad without the sight of something which I had never beheld before, or never heeded."

"The business of a poet, said Imlac, is to examine, not the individual, but the species; to remark general properties and large appearances: he does not number the streaks of the tulip, or describe the different shades in the verdure of the forest. He is to exhibit in his portraits of nature such prominent and striking features, as recal the original to every mind; and must neglect the minuter discriminations, which one may have remarked, and another have neglected, for those characteristicks which are alike obvious to vigilance and carelessness.

"But the knowledge of nature is only half the task of a poet; he must be acquainted likewise with all the modes of life. His character requires that he estimate the happiness and misery of every condition; observe the power of all the passions in all their combinations, and trace the changes of the human mind as they are modified by various institutions and accidental influences of climate or custom, from the spriteliness of infancy to the despondence of decrepitude. He must divest himself of the prejudices of his age or country; he must consider right and wrong in their abstracted and invariable state; he must disregard present laws and opinions, and rise to general and transcendental truths, which will always be the same: he must therefore content himself with the slow progress of his name; contemn the applause of his own time, and commit his claims to the justice of posterity. He must write as the interpreter of nature, and the legislator of mankind, and consider himself as presiding over the thoughts and manners of successive generations; as a being superior to time and place. His labour is not yet at an end: he must know many languages and many sciences; and, that his stile may be worthy of his thoughts, must, by incessant practice, familiarize to himself every delicacy of speech and grace of harmony."

From *Preface to Shakespeare*

That praises are without reason lavished on the dead, and that the honours due only to excellence are paid to antiquity, is a complaint likely to be always continued by those, who, being able to add nothing to truth, hope for eminence from the heresies of paradox; or those, who, being forced by disappointment upon consolatory expedients, are willing to hope from posterity what the present age refuses, and flatter themselves that the regard which is yet denied by envy, will be at last bestowed by time.

Antiquity, like every other quality that attracts the notice of mankind, has undoubtedly votaries that reverence it, not from reason, but from prejudice. Some seem to admire indiscriminately whatever has been long preserved, without considering that time has sometimes cooperated with chance; all perhaps are more willing to honour past than present excellence; and the mind contemplates genius through the shades of age, as the eye surveys the sun through artificial opacity. The great contention of criticism is to find the faults of the moderns, and the beauties of the ancients. While an author is yet living we estimate his powers by his worst performance, and when he is dead we rate them by his best.

To works, however, of which the excellence is not absolute and definite, but gradual and comparative; to works not raised upon principles demonstrative and scientific, but appealing wholly to observation and experience, no other test can be applied than length of duration and continuance of esteem. What mankind have long possessed they have often examined and compared, and if they persist to value the possession, it is because frequent comparisons have confirmed opinion in its favour. As among the works of nature no man can properly call a river deep or a mountain high, without the knowledge of many mountains and many rivers; so in the productions of genius, nothing can be styled excellent till it has been compared with other works of the same kind. Demonstration immediately displays its power, and has nothing to hope or fear from the flux of years; but works tentative and experimental must be estimated by their proportion to the general and collective ability of man, as it is discovered in a long succession of endeavours. Of the first building that was raised, it might be with certainty determined that it was round or square, but whether it was spacious or lofty must have been referred to time. The Pythagorean scale of numbers was at once discovered to be perfect; but the poems of Homer we yet know not to transcend the common limits of human intelligence, but by remarking, that nation after nation, and century after century, has been able to do little more than transpose his incidents, new name his characters, and paraphrase his sentiments.

The reverence due to writings that have long subsisted arises therefore not from any credulous confidence in the superior wisdom of past ages, or gloomy persuasion of the degeneracy of mankind, but is the consequence of acknowledged and indubitable positions, that what has been longest known has been most considered, and what is most considered is best understood.

The Poet, of whose works I have undertaken the revision, may now begin to assume the dignity of an ancient, and claim the privilege of established fame and prescriptive veneration. He has long outlived his century, the term commonly fixed as the test of literary merit. Whatever advantages he might once derive from personal allusions, local customs, or temporary opinions, have for many years been lost; and every topic of merriment or motive of sorrow, which the modes of artificial life afforded him, now only obscure the scenes which they once illuminated. The effects of favour and competition are at an end; the tradition of his friendships and his enmities has perished; his works support no opinion with arguments, nor supply any faction with invectives; they can neither indulge vanity nor gratify malignity, but are read without any other reason than the desire of pleasure, and are therefore praised only as pleasure is obtained; yet, thus unassisted by interest or passion, they have passed through variations of taste and changes of manners, and, as they devolved from one generation to another, have received new honours at every transmission.

But because human judgement, though it be gradually gaining upon certainty, never becomes infallible; and approbation, though long continued, may yet be only the approbation of prejudice or fashion; it is proper to inquire, by what peculiarities of excellence Shakespeare has gained and kept the favour of his countrymen.

Nothing can please many, and please long, but just representations of general nature. Particular manners can be known to few, and therefore few only can judge how nearly they are copied. The irregular combinations of fanciful invention may delight a while, by that novelty of which the common satiety of life sends us all in quest; but the pleasures of sudden wonder are soon exhausted, and the mind can only repose on the stability of truth.

Shakespeare is above all writers, at least above all modern writers, the poet of nature; the poet that holds up to his readers a faithful mirror of manners and of life. His characters are not modified by the customs of particular places, unpractised by the rest of the world; by the peculiarities of studies or professions, which can operate but upon small numbers; or by the accidents of transient fashions or temporary opinions: they are the genuine progeny of common humanity, such as the world will always supply, and observation will always find. His persons act and speak by the influence of those general passions and principles by which all minds are agitated, and the whole system of life is continued in motion. In the writings of other poets a character is too often an individual; in those of Shakespeare it is commonly a species.

It is from this wide extension of design that so much instruction is derived. It is this which fills the plays of Shakespeare with practical axioms and domestic wisdom. It was said of Euripides, that every verse was a precept; and it may be said of Shakespeare, that from his works may be collected a system of civil and economical prudence.

Yet his real power is not shown in the splendour of particular passages, but by the progress of his fable, and the tenor of his dialogue; and he that tries to recommend him by select quotations, will succeed like the pedant in *Hierocles*, who, when he offered his house to sale, carried a brick in his pocket as a specimen.

It will not easily be imagined how much Shakespeare excels in accommodating his sentiments to real life, but by comparing him with other authors. It was observed of the ancient schools of declamation, that the more diligently they were frequented, the more was the student disqualified for the world, because he found nothing there which he should ever meet in any other place. The same remark may be applied to every stage but that of Shakespeare. The theatre, when it is under any other direction, is peopled by such characters as were never seen conversing in a language which was never heard, upon topics which will never arise in the commerce of mankind. But the dialogue of this author is often so evidently determined by the incident which produces it, and is pursued with so much ease and simplicity, that it seems scarcely to claim the merit of fiction, but to have been gleaned by diligent selection out of common conversation, and common occurrences.

Upon every other stage the universal agent is love, by whose power all good and evil is distributed, and every action quickened or retarded. To bring a lover, a lady and a rival into the fable; to entangle them in contradictory obligations, perplex them with oppositions of interest, and harass them with violence of desires inconsistent with each other; to make them meet in rapture and part in agony; to fill their mouths with hyperbolical joy and outrageous sorrow; to distress them as nothing human ever was distressed; to deliver them as nothing human ever was delivered, is the business of a modern dramatist. For this probability is violated, life is misrepresented, and language is depraved. But love is only one of many passions, and as it has no great influence upon the sum of life, it has little operation in the dramas of a poet, who caught his ideas from the living world, and exhibited only what he saw before him. He knew, that any other passion, as it was regular or exorbitant, was a cause of happiness or calamity.

Characters thus ample and general were not easily discriminated and preserved, yet perhaps no poet ever kept his personages more distinct from each other. I will not say with Pope[1] that every speech may be assigned to the proper speaker, because many speeches there are which have nothing characteristical; but perhaps, though some may be equally adapted to every person, it will be difficult to find any that can be properly transferred from the present possessor to another claimant. The choice is right, when there is reason for choice.

Other dramatists can only gain attention by hyperbolical or aggravated characters, by fabulous and unexampled excellence or depravity, as the writers of barbarous romances invigorated the reader by a giant and a dwarf; and he that should form his expectations of human affairs from the play, or from the tale, would be equally deceived. Shakespeare has no heroes; his scenes are occupied only by men, who act and speak as the reader thinks that he should himself have spoken or acted on the same occasion. Even where the agency is supernatural the dialogue is level with life. Other writers disguise the most natural passions and most frequent incidents; so that he who contemplates them in the book will not know them in the world; Shakespeare approximates the remote, and familiarizes the wonderful; the event which he represents will not happen, but if it were possible, its effects would probably be such as he has assigned; and it may be said, that he has not only shown human nature as it acts in real exigencies, but as it would be found in trials, to which it cannot be exposed.

This therefore is the praise of Shakespeare, that his drama is the mirror of life; that he who has mazed his imagination, in following the phantoms which other writers raise up before him, may here be cured of his delirious ecstasies, by reading human sentiment in human language; by scenes from which a hermit may estimate the transactions of the world, and a confessor predict the progress of the passions.

His adherence to general nature has exposed him to the censure of critics, who form their

[1]In Pope's Preface to his 1725 edition of Shakespeare.

judgements upon narrower principles. Dennis and Rhymer think his Romans not sufficiently Roman; and Voltaire censures his kings as not completely royal.[2] Dennis is offended, that Menenius, a senator of Rome, should play the buffoon; and Voltaire perhaps thinks decency violated when the Danish usurper is represented as a drunkard. But Shakespeare always makes nature predominate over accident; and if he preserves the essential character, is not very careful of distinctions superinduced and adventitious. His story requires Romans or kings, but he thinks only on men. He knew that Rome, like every other city, had men of all dispositions; and wanting a buffoon, he went into the senate-house for that which the senate-house would certainly have afforded him. He was inclined to show a usurper and a murderer not only odious but despicable; he therefore added drunkenness to his other qualities, knowing that kings love wine like other men, and that wine exerts its natural power upon kings. These are the petty cavils of petty minds; a poet overlooks the casual distinction of country and condition, as a painter, satisfied with the figure, neglects the drapery.

The censure which he has incurred by mixing comic and tragic scenes, as it extends to all his works, deserves more consideration. Let the fact be first stated, and then examined.

Shakespeare's plays are not in the rigorous and critical sense either tragedies or comedies, but compositions of a distinct kind; exhibiting the real state of sublunary nature, which partakes of good and evil, joy and sorrow, mingled with endless variety of proportion and innumerable modes of combination; and expressing the course of the world, in which the loss of one is the gain of another; in which, at the same time, the reveller is hasting to his wine, and the mourner burying his friend; in which the malignity of one is sometimes defeated by the frolic of another; and many mischiefs and many benefits are done and hindered without design.

Out of this chaos of mingled purposes and casualties the ancient poets, according to the laws which custom had prescribed, selected some the crimes of men, and some their absurdities; some the momentous vicissitudes of life, and some the lighter occurrences; some the terrors of distress, and some the gaieties of prosperity. Thus rose the two modes of imitation, known by the names of *tragedy* and *comedy*, compositions intended to promote different ends by contrary means, and considered as so little allied, that I do not recollect among the Greeks or Romans a single writer who attempted both.

Shakespeare has united the powers of exciting laughter and sorrow not only in one mind but in one composition. Almost all his plays are divided between serious and ludicrous characters, and, in the successive evolutions of the design, sometimes produce seriousness and sorrow, and sometimes levity and laughter.

That this is a practice contrary to the rules of criticism will be readily allowed; but there is always an appeal open from criticism to nature. The end of writing is to instruct; the end of poetry is to instruct by pleasing. That the mingled drama may convey all the instruction of tragedy or comedy cannot be denied, because it includes both in its alternations of exhibition, and approaches nearer than either to the appearance of life, by showing how great machinations and slender designs may promote or obviate one another, and the high and the low co-operate in the general system by unavoidable concatenation.

It is objected, that by this change of scenes the passions are interrupted in their progression, and that the principal event, being not advanced by a due gradation of preparatory incidents, wants at last the power to move, which constitutes the perfection of dramatic poetry. This reasoning is so specious, that it is received as true even by those who in daily experience feel it to be false. The interchanges of mingled scenes seldom fail to produce the intended vicissitudes of passion. Fiction cannot move so much, but that the attention may be easily transferred; and though it must be allowed that pleasing melancholy be sometimes interrupted by unwelcome levity, yet let it be considered likewise, that melancholy is often not pleasing, and that the disturbance of one man

[2]Johnson refers to John Dennis's *Essay on the Genius and Writings of Shakespeare* (1713); Thomas Rymer's *A Short View of Tragedy* (1692); and Voltaire's *Dissertation sur la tragédie ancienne et moderne* (1749) and *Appel à toutes les nations de l'Europe* (1761).

may be the relief of another; that different auditors have different habitudes; and that, upon the whole, all pleasure consists in variety.

The players, who in their edition[3] divided our author's works into comedies, histories, and tragedies, seem not to have distinguished the three kinds, by any very exact or definite ideas.

An action which ended happily to the principal persons, however serious or distressful through its intermediate incidents, in their opinion constituted a comedy. This idea of a comedy continued long amongst us, and plays were written, which, by changing the catastrophe, were tragedies today and comedies tomorrow.

Tragedy was not in those times a poem of more general dignity or elevation than comedy; it required only a calamitous conclusion, with which the common criticism of that age was satisfied, whatever lighter pleasure it afforded in its progress.

History was a series of actions, with no other than chronological succession, independent on each other, and without any tendency to introduce or regulate the conclusion. It is not always very nicely distinguished from tragedy. There is not much nearer approach to unity of action in the tragedy of *Antony and Cleopatra*, than in the history of *Richard the Second*. But a history might be continued through many plays; as it had no plan, it had no limits.

Through all these denominations of the drama, Shakespeare's mode of composition is the same; an interchange of seriousness and merriment, by which the mind is softened at one time, and exhilarated at another. But whatever be his purpose, whether to gladden or depress, or to conduct the story, without vehemence or emotion, through tracts of easy and familiar dialogue, he never fails to attain his purpose; as he commands us, we laugh or mourn, or sit silent with quiet expectation, in tranquillity without indifference.

When Shakespeare's plan is understood, most of the criticisms of Rhymer and Voltaire vanish away. The play of *Hamlet* is opened, without impropriety, by two sentinels; Iago bellows at Brabantio's window, without injury to the scheme of the play, though in terms which a modern audience would not easily endure; the character of Polonius is seasonable and useful; and the grave-diggers themselves may be heard with applause.

Shakespeare engaged in the dramatic poetry with the world open before him; the rules of the ancients were yet known to few; the public judgement was unformed; he had no example of such fame as might force him upon imitation, nor critics of such authority as might restrain his extravagance. He therefore indulged his natural disposition, and his disposition, as Rhymer has remarked, led him to comedy. In tragedy he often writes with great appearance of toil and study, what is written at last with little felicity; but in his comic scenes, he seems to produce without labour, what no labour can improve. In tragedy he is always struggling after some occasion to be comic, but in comedy he seems to repose, or to luxuriate, as in a mode of thinking congenial to his nature. In his tragic scenes there is always something wanting, but his comedy often surpasses expectation or desire. His comedy pleases by the thoughts and the language, and his tragedy for the greater part by incident and action. His tragedy seems to be skill, his comedy to be instinct.

The force of his comic scenes has suffered little diminution from the changes made by a century and a half, in manners or in words. As his personages act upon principles arising from genuine passion, very little modified by particular forms, their pleasures and vexations are communicable to all times and to all places; they are natural, and therefore durable; the adventitious peculiarities of personal habits, are only superficial dies, bright and pleasing for a little while, yet soon fading to a dim tinct, without any remains of former lustre; but the discriminations of true passion are the colours of nature; they pervade the whole mass, and can only perish with the body that exhibits them. The accidental compositions of heterogeneous modes are dissolved by the chance which combined them; but the uniform simplicity of primitive qualities neither admits increase, nor suffers decay. The sand heaped by one flood is scattered by another, but the rock always continues in its place. The stream of time,

[3]John Heminges and Henry Condell, who edited the First Folio in 1623.

which is continually washing the dissoluble fabrics of other poets, passes without injury by the adamant of Shakespeare.

If there be, what I believe there is, in every nation, a style which never becomes obsolete, a certain mode of phraseology so consonant and congenial to the analogy and principles of its respective language as to remain settled and unaltered; this style is probably to be sought in the common intercourse of life, among those who speak only to be understood, without ambition of elegance. The polite are always catching modish innovations, and the learned depart from established forms of speech, in hope of finding or making better; those who wish for distinction forsake the vulgar, when the vulgar is right; but there is a conversation above grossness and below refinement, where propriety resides, and where this poet seems to have gathered his comic dialogue. He is therefore more agreeable to the ears of the present age than any other author equally remote, and among his other excellencies deserves to be studied as one of the original masters of our language.

These observations are to be considered not as unexceptionably constant, but as containing general and predominant truth. Shakespeare's familiar dialogue is affirmed to be smooth and clear, yet not wholly without ruggedness or difficulty; as a country may be eminently fruitful, though it has spots unfit for cultivation. His characters are praised as natural, though their sentiments are sometimes forced, and their actions improbable; as the earth upon the whole is spherical, though its surface is varied with protuberances and cavities.

Shakespeare with his excellencies has likewise faults, and faults sufficient to obscure and overwhelm any other merit. I shall show them in the proportion in which they appear to me, without envious malignity or superstitious veneration. No question can be more innocently discussed than a dead poet's pretensions to renown; and little regard is due to that bigotry which sets candour higher than truth.

His first defect is that to which may be imputed most of the evil in books or in men. He sacrifices virtue to convenience, and is so much more careful to please than to instruct, that he seems to write without any moral purpose. From his writings indeed a system of social duty may be selected, for he that thinks reasonably must think morally; but his precepts and axioms drop casually from him; he makes no just distribution of good or evil, nor is always careful to show in the virtuous a disapprobation of the wicked; he carries his persons indifferently through right and wrong, and at the close dismisses them without further care, and leaves their examples to operate by chance. This fault the barbarity of his age cannot extenuate; for it is always a writer's duty to make the world better, and justice is a virtue independent on time or place.

The plots are often so loosely formed, that a very slight consideration may improve them, and so carelessly pursued, that he seems not always fully to comprehend his own design. He omits opportunities of instructing or delighting which the train of his story seems to force upon him, and apparently rejects those exhibitions which would be more affecting, for the sake of those which are more easy.

It may be observed, that in many of his plays the latter part is evidently neglected. When he found himself near the end of his work, and in view of his reward, he shortened the labour to snatch the profit. He therefore remits his efforts where he should most vigorously exert them, and his catastrophe is improbably produced or imperfectly represented.

He had no regard to distinction of time or place, but gives to one age or nation, without scruple, the customs, institutions, and opinions of another, at the expense not only of likelihood, but of possibility. These faults Pope has endeavoured, with more zeal than judgement, to transfer to his imagined interpolators. We need not wonder to find Hector quoting Aristotle,[4] when we see the loves of Theseus and Hippolyta combined with the Gothic mythology of fairies. Shakespeare, indeed, was not the only violator of chronology, for in the same age Sidney, who wanted not the advantages of learning, has, in his *Arcadia*, confounded the pastoral with the feudal

[4] In *Troilus and Cressida*, II.ii:166–67.

times, the days of innocence, quiet and security, with those of turbulence, violence, and adventure.

In his comic scenes he is seldom very successful, when he engages his characters in reciprocations of smartness and contests of sarcasm; their jests are commonly gross, and their pleasantry licentious; neither his gentlemen nor his ladies have much delicacy, nor are sufficiently distinguished from his clowns by any appearance of refined manners. Whether he represented the real conversation of his time is not easy to determine; the reign of Elizabeth is commonly supposed to have been a time of stateliness, formality and reserve; yet perhaps the relaxations of that severity were not very elegant. There must, however, have been always some modes of gaiety preferable to others, and a writer ought to choose the best.

In tragedy his performance seems constantly to be worse, as his labour is more. The effusions of passion which exigence forces out are for the most part striking and energetic; but whenever he solicits his invention, or strains his faculties, the offspring of his throes is tumour, meanness, tediousness, and obscurity.

In narration he affects a disproportionate pomp of diction, and a wearisome train of circumlocution, and tells the incident imperfectly in many words, which might have been more plainly delivered in few. Narration in dramatic poetry is naturally tedious, as it is unanimated and inactive, and obstructs the progress of the action; it should therefore always be rapid, and enlivened by frequent interruption. Shakespeare found it an encumbrance, and instead of lightening it by brevity, endeavoured to recommend it by dignity and splendour.

His declamations or set speeches are commonly cold and weak, for his power was the power of nature; when he endeavoured, like other tragic writers, to catch opportunities of amplification, and instead of inquiring what the occasion demanded, to show how much his stores of knowledge could supply, he seldom escapes without the pity or resentment of his reader.

It is incident to him to be now and then entangled with an unwieldy sentiment, which he cannot well express, and will not reject; he struggles with it a while, and if it continues stubborn, comprises it in words such as occur, and leaves it to be disentangled and evolved by those who have more leisure to bestow upon it.

Not that always where the language is intricate the thought is subtle, or the image always great where the line is bulky; the equality of words to things is very often neglected, and trivial sentiments and vulgar ideas disappoint the attention, to which they are recommended by sonorous epithets and swelling figures.

But the admirers of this great poet have never less reason to indulge their hopes of supreme excellence, than when he seems fully resolved to sink them in dejection, and mollify them with tender emotions by the fall of greatness, the danger of innocence, or the crosses of love. He is not long soft and pathetic without some idle conceit, or contemptible equivocation. He no sooner begins to move, than he counteracts himself; and terror and pity, as they are rising in the mind, are checked and blasted by sudden frigidity.

A quibble is to Shakespeare, what luminous vapours are to the traveller; he follows it at all adventures, it is sure to lead him out of his way, and sure to engulf him in the mire. It has some malignant power over his mind, and its fascinations are irresistible. Whatever be the dignity or profundity of his disquisition, whether he be enlarging knowledge or exalting affection, whether he be amusing attention with incidents, or enhancing it in suspense, let but a quibble spring up before him, and he leaves his work unfinished. A quibble is the golden apple for which he will always turn aside from his career, or stoop from his elevation. A quibble, poor and barren as it is, gave him such delight, that he was content to purchase it, by the sacrifice of reason, propriety and truth. A quibble was to him the fatal Cleopatra for which he lost the world, and was content to lose it.

It will be thought strange, that, in enumerating the defects of this writer, I have not yet mentioned his neglect of the unities; his violation of those laws which have been instituted and established by the joint authority of poets and of critics.

For his other deviations from the art of writing, I resign him to critical justice, without making any other demand in his favour, than that which must be indulged to all human excellence; that his virtues be rated with his failings: but, from the censure which his irregularity may bring upon him, I shall, with due reverence to that learning which I must oppose, adventure to try how I can defend him.

His histories, being neither tragedies nor comedies, are not subject to any of their laws; nothing more is necessary to all the praise which they expect, than that the changes of action be so prepared as to be understood, that the incidents be various and affecting, and the characters consistent, natural and distinct. No other unity is intended, and therefore none is to be sought.

In his other works he has well enough preserved the unity of action. He has not, indeed, an intrigue regularly perplexed and regularly unravelled; he does not endeavour to hide his design only to discover it, for this is seldom the order of real events, and Shakespeare is the poet of nature: but his plan has commonly what Aristotle requires, a beginning, a middle, and an end;[5] one event is concatenated with another, and the conclusion follows by easy consequence. There are perhaps some incidents that might be spared, as in other poets there is much talk that only fills up time upon the stage; but the general system makes gradual advances, and the end of the play is the end of expectation.

To the unities of time and place he has shown no regard, and perhaps a nearer view of the principles on which they stand will diminish their value, and withdraw from them the veneration which, from the time of Corneille,[6] they have very generally received, by discovering that they have given more trouble to the poet, than pleasure to the auditor.

The necessity of observing the unities of time and place arises from the supposed necessity of making the drama credible. The critics hold it impossible, that an action of months or years can be possibly believed to pass in three hours; or that the spectator can suppose himself to sit in the theatre, while ambassadors go and return between distant kings, while armies are levied and towns besieged, while an exile wanders and returns, or till he whom they saw courting his mistress, shall lament the untimely fall of his son. The mind revolts from evident falsehood, and fiction loses its force when it departs from the resemblance of reality.

From the narrow limitation of time necessarily arises the contraction of place. The spectator, who knows that he saw the first act at Alexandria, cannot suppose that he sees the next at Rome, at a distance to which not the dragons of Medea could, in so short a time, have transported him; he knows with certainty that he has not changed his place; and he knows that place cannot change itself; that what was a house cannot become a plain; that what was Thebes can never be Persepolis.

Such is the triumphant language with which a critic exults over the misery of an irregular poet, and exults commonly without resistance or reply. It is time therefore to tell him, by the authority of Shakespeare, that he assumes, as an unquestionable principle, a position which, while his breath is forming it into words, his understanding pronounces to be false. It is false, that any representation is mistaken for reality; that any dramatic fable in its materiality was ever credible, or, for a single moment, was ever credited.

The objection arising from the impossibility of passing the first hour at Alexandria, and the next at Rome, supposes, that when the play opens, the spectator really imagines himself at Alexandria, and believes that his walk to the theatre has been a voyage to Egypt, and that he lives in the days of Antony and Cleopatra. Surely he that imagines this may imagine more. He that can take the stage at one time for the palace of the Ptolemies, may take it in half an hour for the promontory of Actium. Delusion, if delusion be admitted, has no certain limitation; if the spectator can be once persuaded, that his old acquaintance are Alexander and Caesar, that a room illuminated with candles is the plain of Pharsalia, or the bank of Granicus, he is in a state of elevation above the reach of reason, or of truth, and from the heights of empyrean poetry, may despise the circumscriptions of terrestrial nature. There is no reason why a mind thus wandering in ecstasy should count the

[5]Aristotle, *Poetics*, Ch. 7; see p. 64.

[6]Pierre Corneille's *Discours des trois unités* was published in 1660. For other discussions of the three unities, see the selections from Sidney and Dryden.

clock, or why an hour should not be a century in that calenture[7] of the brains that can make the stage a field.

The truth is, that the spectators are always in their senses, and know, from the first act to the last, that the stage is only a stage, and that the players are only players. They came to hear a certain number of lines recited with just gesture and elegant modulation. The lines relate to some action, and an action must be in some place; but the different actions that complete a story may be in places very remote from each other; and where is the absurdity of allowing that space to represent first Athens, and then Sicily, which was always known to be neither Sicily nor Athens, but a modern theatre?

By supposition, as place is introduced time may be extended; the time required by the fable elapses for the most part between the acts; for, of so much of the action as is represented, the real and poetical duration is the same. If, in the first act, preparations for war against Mithridates are represented to be made in Rome, the event of the war may without absurdity, be represented, in the catastrophe, as happening in Pontus; we know that there is neither war, nor preparation for war; we know that we are neither in Rome nor Pontus; that neither Mithridates nor Lucullus are before us. The drama exhibits successive imitations of successive actions, and why may not the second imitation represent an action that happened years after the first; if it be so connected with it, that nothing but time can be supposed to intervene. Time is, of all modes of existence, most obsequious to the imagination; a lapse of years is as easily conceived as a passage of hours. In contemplation we easily contract the time of real actions, and therefore willingly permit it to be contracted when we only see their imitation.

It will be asked, how the drama moves, if it is not credited. It is credited with all the credit due to a drama. It is credited, whenever it moves, as a just picture of a real original; as representing to the auditor what he would himself feel, if he were to do or suffer what is there feigned to be suffered or to be done. The reflection that strikes the heart is not, that the evils before us are real evils, but that they are evils to which we ourselves may be exposed. If there be any fallacy, it is not that we fancy the players, but that we fancy ourselves unhappy for a moment; but we rather lament the possibility than suppose the presence of misery, as a mother weeps over her babe, when she remembers that death may take it from her. The delight of tragedy proceeds from our consciousness of fiction; if we thought murders and treasons real, they would please no more.

Imitations produce pain or pleasure, not because they are mistaken for realities, but because they bring realities to mind. When the imagination is recreated by a painted landscape, the trees are not supposed capable to give us shade, or the fountains coolness; but we consider, how we should be pleased with such fountains playing beside us, and such woods waving over us. We are agitated in reading the history of *Henry the Fifth*, yet no man takes his book for the field of Agincourt. A dramatic exhibition is a book recited with concomitants that increase or diminish its effect. Familiar comedy is often more powerful in the theatre, than on the page; imperial tragedy is always less. The humour of Petruchio may be heightened by grimace; but what voice or what gesture can hope to add dignity or force to the soliloquy of Cato?

A play read, affects the mind like a play acted. It is therefore evident, that the action is not supposed to be real, and it follows that between the acts a longer or shorter time may be allowed to pass, and that no more account of space or duration is to be taken by the auditor of a drama, than by the reader of a narrative, before whom may pass in an hour the life of a hero, or the revolutions of an empire.

Whether Shakespeare knew the unities, and rejected them by design, or deviated from them by happy ignorance, it is, I think, impossible to decide, and useless to inquire. We may reasonably suppose, that, when he rose to notice, he did not want the counsels and admonitions of scholars and critics, and that he at last deliberately persisted in a practice, which he might have begun by chance. As nothing is essential to the fable, but unity of action, and as the unities of time and place arise evidently from false assumptions, and, by circumscribing the extent of the drama, lessen

[7]Fever.

its variety, I cannot think it much to be lamented, that they were not known by him, or not observed: nor, if such another poet could arise, should I very vehemently reproach him, that his first act passed at Venice, and his next in Cyprus. Such violations of rules merely positive, become the comprehensive genius of Shakespeare, and such censures are suitable to the minute and slender criticism of Voltaire:

> Non usque adeo permiscuit imis
> Longus summa dies, ut non, si voce Metelli
> Serventur leges, malint a Cæsare tolli.[8]

Yet when I speak thus slightly of dramatic rules, I cannot but recollect how much wit and learning may be produced against me; before such authorities I am afraid to stand, not that I think the present question one of those that are to be decided by mere authority, but because it is to be suspected, that these precepts have not been so easily received but for better reasons than I have yet been able to find. The result of my inquiries, in which it would be ludicrous to boast of impartiality, is, that the unities of time and place are not essential to a just drama, that though they may sometimes conduce to pleasure, they are always to be sacrificed to the nobler beauties of variety and instruction; and that a play, written with nice observation of critical rules, is to be contemplated as an elaborate curiosity, as the product of superfluous and ostentatious art, by which is shown, rather what is possible, than what is necessary.

He that, without diminution of any other excellence, shall preserve all the unities unbroken, deserves the like applause with the architect, who shall display all the orders of architecture in a citadel, without any deduction from its strength; but the principal beauty of a citadel is to exclude the enemy; and the greatest graces of a play, are to copy nature and instruct life.

Perhaps, what I have here not dogmatically but deliberately written, may recall the principles of the drama to a new examination. I am almost frightened at my own temerity; and when I estimate the fame and the strength of those that maintain the

contrary opinion, am ready to sink down in reverential silence; as Æneas withdrew from the defence of Troy, when he saw Neptune shaking the wall, and Juno heading the besiegers.[9]

Those whom my arguments cannot persuade to give their approbation to the judgement of Shakespeare, will easily, if they consider the condition of his life, make some allowance for his ignorance.

Every man's performances, to be rightly estimated, must be compared with the state of the age in which he lived, and with his own particular opportunities; and though to the reader a book be not worse or better for the circumstances of the author, yet as there is always a silent reference of human works to human abilities, and as the inquiry, how far man may extend his designs, or how high he may rate his native force, is of far greater dignity than in what rank we shall place any particular performance, curiosity is always busy to discover the instruments, as well as to survey the workmanship, to know how much is to be ascribed to original powers, and how much to casual and adventitious help. The palaces of Peru or Mexico were certainly mean and incommodious habitations, if compared to the houses of European monarchs; yet who could forbear to view them with astonishment, who remembered that they were built without the use of iron?

The English nation, in the time of Shakespeare, was yet struggling to emerge from barbarity. The philology of Italy had been transplanted hither in the reign of Henry the Eighth; and the learned languages had been successfully cultivated by Lilly, Linacre and More; by Pole, Cheke, and Gardiner; and afterwards by Smith, Clerk, Haddon, and Ascham.[10] Greek was now taught to boys in the principal schools; and those

---

[8]"So long a time has not passed that the laws themselves would not prefer to be broken by Caesar than supported by Metellus." Lucan, *Pharsalia* 3:138–40.

[9]Virgil, *Aeneid* 2:610–15.

[10]Johnson's honor roll of Renaissance humanists includes William Lily, the author of a Latin grammar; Thomas Linacre, a Greek scholar; Thomas More, author of *Utopia* and other Latin works; Reginald Pole and Stephen Gardiner, scholar-statesmen who served Henry VIII and Mary Tudor; Sir John Cheke, who taught Greek at Cambridge; Sir Thomas Smith and Walter Haddon, who taught at Cambridge; John Clerk, who was Wolsey's chaplain; and Roger Ascham, who was tutor to Elizabeth and the author of *Toxophilus*.

who united elegance with learning, read, with great diligence, the Italian and Spanish poets. But literature was yet confined to professed scholars, or to men and women of high rank. The public was gross and dark; and to be able to read and write, was an accomplishment still valued for its rarity.

Nations, like individuals, have their infancy. A people newly awakened to literary curiosity, being yet unacquainted with the true state of things, knows not how to judge of that which is proposed as its resemblance. Whatever is remote from common appearance is always welcome to vulgar, as to childish credulity; and of a country unenlightened by learning, the whole people is the vulgar. The study of those who then aspired to plebeian learning was laid out upon adventures, giants, dragons, and enchantments. *The Death of Arthur*[11] was the favourite volume.

The mind, which has feasted on the luxurious wonders of fiction, has no taste of the insipidity of truth. A play which imitated only the common occurrences of the world, would upon the admirers of *Palmerin* and *Guy of Warwick*, have made little impression; he that wrote for such an audience was under the necessity of looking round for strange events and fabulous transactions, and that incredibility, by which maturer knowledge is offended, was the chief recommendation of writings, to unskilful curiosity.

Our author's plots are generally borrowed from novels, and it is reasonable to suppose, that he chose the most popular, such as were read by many, and related by more; for his audience could not have followed him through the intricacies of the drama, had they not held the thread of the story in their hands.

The stories, which we now find only in remoter authors, were in his time accessible and familiar. The fable of *As You Like It*, which is supposed to be copied from Chaucer's *Gamelyn*,[12] was a little pamphlet of those times; and old Mr. Cibber[13] remembered the tale of *Hamlet* in plain English

prose, which the critics have now to seek in *Saxo Grammaticus*.[14]

His English histories he took from English chronicles and English ballads; and as the ancient writers were made known to his countrymen by versions, they supplied him with new subjects; he dilated some of Plutarch's lives into plays, when they had been translated by North.[15]

His plots, whether historical or fabulous, are always crowded with incidents, by which the attention of a rude people was more easily caught than by sentiment or argumentation; and such is the power of the marvellous even over those who despise it, that every man finds his mind more strongly seized by the tragedies of Shakespeare than of any other writer; others please us by particular speeches, but he always makes us anxious for the event, and has perhaps excelled all but Homer in securing the first purpose of a writer, by exciting restless and unquenchable curiosity, and compelling him that reads his work to read it through.

The shows and bustle with which his plays abound, have the same original. As knowledge advances, pleasure passes from the eye to the ear, but returns, as it declines, from the ear to the eye. Those to whom our author's labours were exhibited had more skill in pomps or processions than in poetical language, and perhaps wanted some visible and discriminated events, as comments on the dialogue. He knew how he should most please; and whether his practice is more agreeable to nature, or whether his example has prejudiced the nation, we still find that on our stage something must be done as well as said, and inactive declamation is very coldly heard, however musical or elegant, passionate or sublime.

Voltaire expresses his wonder, that our author's extravagances are endured by a nation, which has seen the tragedy of *Cato*. Let him be answered, that Addison speaks the language of poets, and Shakespeare, of men. We find in *Cato* innumerable beauties which enamour us of its author, but we see nothing that acquaints us with human sentiments or human actions; we place it with the fairest and the noblest progeny which

[11]Sir Thomas Malory's *Morte D'Arthur*.
[12]A tale once attributed to Chaucer.
[13]Colley Cibber (1671–1757). The book referred to is *History of Hamblet* published in 1608, too late to be the source of Shakespeare's play.

[14]Saxo Grammaticus's *Historia Danica* (1514).
[15]In 1579.

judgement propagates by conjunction with learning, but *Othello* is the vigorous and vivacious offspring of observation impregnated by genius. *Cato* affords a splendid exhibition of artificial and fictitious manners, and delivers just and noble sentiments, in diction easy, elevated and harmonious, but its hopes and fears communicate no vibration to the heart; the composition refers us only to the writer; we pronounce the name of *Cato*, but we think on Addison.

The work of a correct and regular writer is a garden accurately formed and diligently planted, varied with shades, and scented with flowers; the composition of Shakespeare is a forest, in which oaks extend their branches, and pines tower in the air, interspersed sometimes with weeds and brambles, and sometimes giving shelter to myrtles and to roses; filling the eye with awful pomp, and gratifying the mind with endless diversity. Other poets display cabinets of precious rarities, minutely finished, wrought into shape, and polished unto brightness. Shakespeare opens a mine which contains gold and diamonds in unexhaustible plenty, though clouded by incrustations, debased by impurities, and mingled with a mass of meaner minerals.

It has been much disputed, whether Shakespeare owed his excellence to his own native force, or whether he had the common helps of scholastic education, the precepts of critical science, and the examples of ancient authors.

There has always prevailed a tradition, that Shakespeare wanted learning, that he had no regular education, nor much skill in the dead languages. Jonson, his friend, affirms, that "he had small Latin, and no Greek";[16] who, besides that he had no imaginable temptation to falsehood, wrote at a time when the character and acquisitions of Shakespeare were known to multitudes. His evidence ought therefore to decide the controversy, unless some testimony of equal force could be opposed.

Some have imagined, that they have discovered deep learning in many imitations of old writers; but the examples which I have known urged, were drawn from books translated in his time; or were such easy coincidences of thought, as will happen to all who consider the same subjects; or such remarks on life or axioms of morality as float in conversation, and are transmitted through the world in proverbial sentences.

I have found it remarked, that, in this important sentence, "Go before, I'll follow," we read a translation of, *I prae, sequar.* I have been told, that when Caliban, after a pleasing dream, says, "I cry'd to sleep again," the author imitates Anacreon, who had, like every other man, the same wish on the same occasion.

There are a few passages which may pass for imitations, but so few, that the exception only confirms the rule; he obtained them from accidental quotations, or by oral communication, and as he used what he had, would have used more if he had obtained it.

The *Comedy of Errors* is confessedly taken from the *Menæchmi* of Plautus; from the only play of Plautus which was then in English.[17] What can be more probable, than that he who copied that, would have copied more; but that those which were not translated were inaccessible?

Whether he knew the modern languages is uncertain. That his plays have some French scenes proves but little; he might easily procure them to be written, and probably, even though he had known the language in the common degree, he could not have written it without assistance. In the story of *Romeo and Juliet* he is observed to have followed the English translation, where it deviates from the Italian; but this on the other part proves nothing against his knowledge of the original. He was to copy, not what he knew himself, but what was known to his audience.

It is most likely that he had learned Latin sufficiently to make him acquainted with construction, but that he never advanced to an easy perusal of the Roman authors. Concerning his skill in modern languages, I can find no sufficient ground of determination; but as no imitations of French or Italian authors have been discovered, though the Italian poetry was then high in esteem, I am inclined to believe, that he read little more than English, and chose for his fables only such tales as he found translated.

[16]In the verses prefaced to the First Folio.

[17]The 1595 translation of *Menaechmi* by W. W. probably postdates Shakespeare's *Comedy of Errors.*

That much knowledge is scattered over his works is very justly observed by Pope, but it is often such knowledge as books did not supply. He that will understand Shakespeare, must not be content to study him in the closet, he must look for his meaning sometimes among the sports of the field, and sometimes among the manufactures of the shop.

There is however proof enough that he was a very diligent reader, nor was our language then so indigent of books, but that he might very liberally indulge his curiosity without excursion into foreign literature. Many of the Roman authors were translated, and some of the Greek; the reformation had filled the kingdom with theological learning; most of the topics of human disquisition had found English writers; and poetry had been cultivated, not only with diligence, but success. This was a stock of knowledge sufficient for a mind so capable of appropriating and improving it.

But the greater part of his excellence was the product of his own genius. He found the English stage in a state of the utmost rudeness; no essays either in tragedy or comedy had appeared, from which it could be discovered to what degree of delight either one or other might be carried. Neither character nor dialogue were yet understood. Shakespeare may be truly said to have introduced them both amongst us, and in some of his happier scenes to have carried them both to the utmost height.

By what gradations of improvement he proceeded, is not easily known; for the chronology of his works is yet unsettled. Rowe is of opinion, that

> perhaps we are not to look for his beginning, like those of other writers, in his least perfect works; art had so little, and nature so large a share in what he did, that for ought I know, [says he] the performances of his youth, as they were the most vigorous, were the best.[18]

But the power of nature is only the power of using to any certain purpose the materials which diligence procures, or opportunity supplies. Nature gives no man knowledge, and when images are collected by study and experience, can only assist in combining or applying them. Shakespeare, however favoured by nature, could impart only what he had learned; and as he must increase his ideas, like other mortals, by gradual acquisition, he, like them, grew wiser as he grew older, could display life better, as he knew it more, and instruct with more efficacy, as he was himself more amply instructed.

There is a vigilance of observation and accuracy of distinction which books and precepts cannot confer; from this almost all original and native excellence proceeds. Shakespeare must have looked upon mankind with perspicacity, in the highest degree curious and attentive. Other writers borrow their characters from preceding writers, and diversify them only by the accidental appendages of present manners; the dress is a little varied, but the body is the same. Our author had both matter and form to provide; for except the characters of Chaucer, to whom I think he is not much indebted, there were no writers in English, and perhaps not many in other modern languages, which showed life in its native colours.

The contest about the original benevolence or malignity of man had not yet commenced. Speculation had not yet attempted to analyse the mind, to trace the passions to their sources, to unfold the seminal principles of vice and virtue, or sound the depths of the heart for the motives of action. All those inquiries, which from that time that human nature became the fashionable study, have been made sometimes with nice discernment, but often with idle sublety, were yet unattempted. The tales, with which the infancy of learning was satisfied, exhibited only the superficial appearances of action, related the events but omitted the causes, and were formed for such as delighted in wonders rather than in truth. Mankind was not then to be studied in the closet; he that would know the world, was under the necessity of gleaning his own remarks, by mingling as he could in its business and amusements.

Boyle congratulated himself upon his high birth, because it favoured his curiosity, by facilitating his access. Shakespeare had no such advantage; he came to London a needy adventurer, and lived for a time by very mean employments. Many

---

[18]Nicholas Rowe, *Some Account of the Life &c of Mr. William Shakespeare* (1709).

works of genius and learning have been performed in states of life, that appear very little favourable to thought or to inquiry; so many, that he who considers them is inclined to think that he sees enterprise and perseverance predominating over all external agency, and bidding help and hindrance vanish before them. The genius of Shakespeare was not to be depressed by the weight of poverty, not limited by the narrow conversation to which men in want are inevitably condemned; the incumbrances of his fortune were shaken from his mind, "as dewdrops from a lion's mane."[19]

Though he had so many difficulties to encounter, and so little assistance to surmount them, he has been able to obtain an exact knowledge of many modes of life, and many casts of native dispositions; to vary them with great multiplicity; to mark them by nice distinctions; and to show them in full view by proper combinations. In this part of his performances he had none to imitate, but has himself been imitated by all succeeding writers; and it may be doubted, whether from all his successors more maxims of theoretical knowledge, or more rules of practical prudence, can be collected, than he alone has given to his country.

Nor was his attention confined to the actions of men; he was an exact surveyor of the inanimate world; his descriptions have always some peculiarities, gathered by contemplating things as they really exist. It may be observed, that the oldest poets of many nations preserve their reputation, and that the following generations of wit, after a short celebrity, sink into oblivion. The first, whoever they be, must take their sentiments and descriptions immediately from knowledge; the resemblance is therefore just, their descriptions are verified by every eye, and their sentiments acknowledged by every breast. Those whom their fame invites to the same studies, copy partly them, and partly nature, till the books of one age gain such authority, as to stand in the place of nature to another, and imitation, always deviating a little, becomes at last capricious and casual. Shakespeare, whether life or nature be his subject, shows plainly, that he has seen with his own eyes; he gives the image which he receives, not

weakened or distorted by the intervention of any other mind; the ignorant feel his representations to be just, and the learned see that they are complete.

Perhaps it would not be easy to find any author, except Homer, who invented so much as Shakespeare, who so much advanced the studies which he cultivated, or effused so much novelty upon his age or country. The form, the characters, the language, and the shows of the English drama are his. He seems, says Dennis,

> to have been the very original of our *English* tragical harmony, that is, the harmony of blank verse, diversified often by dissyllable and trissyllable terminations. For the diversity distinguishes it from heroic harmony, and by bringing it nearer to common use makes it more proper to gain attention, and more fit for action and dialogue. Such verse we make when we are writing prose; we make such verse in common conversation.[20]

I know not whether this praise is rigorously just. The dissyllable termination, which the critic rightly appropriates to the drama, is to be found, though, I think, not in *Gorboduc* which is confessedly before our author; yet in *Hieronimo*,[21] of which the date is not certain, but which there is reason to believe at least as old as his earliest plays. This however is certain, that he is the first who taught either tragedy or comedy to please, there being no theatrical piece of any older writer, of which the name is known, except to antiquaries and collectors of books, which are sought because they are scarce, and would not have been scarce, had they been much esteemed.

To him we must ascribe the praise, unless Spenser may divide it with him, of having first discovered to how much smoothness and harmony the English language could be softened. He has speeches, perhaps sometimes scenes, which have all the delicacy of Rowe, without his effeminacy. He endeavours indeed commonly to strike by the force and vigour of his dialogue, but he never executes his purpose better, than when he tries to soothe by softness.

[19]*Troilus and Cressida*, III.iii.224.

[20]In *Essay on the Genius and Writings of Shakespeare*, II:4–5.
[21]Thomas Kyd's *Spanish Tragedy* (1592).

Yet it must be at last confessed that as we owe every thing to him, he owes something to us; that, if much of his praise is paid by perception and judgement, much is likewise given by custom and veneration. We fix our eyes upon his graces, and turn them from his deformities, and endure in him what we should in another loathe or despise. If we endured without praising, respect for the father of our drama might excuse us; but I have seen, in the book of some modern critic, a collection of anomalies, which show that he has corrupted language by every mode of depravation, but which his admirer has accumulated as a monument of honour.

He has scenes of undoubted and perpetual excellence, but perhaps not one play, which, if it were now exhibited as the work of a contemporary writer, would be heard to the conclusion. I am indeed far from thinking, that his works were wrought to his own ideas of perfection; when they were such as would satisfy the audience, they satisfied the writer. It is seldom that authors, though more studious of fame than Shakespeare, rise much above the standard of their own age; to add a little to what is best will always be sufficient for present praise, and those who find themselves exalted into fame, are willing to credit their encomiasts, and to spare the labour of contending with themselves.

It does not appear, that Shakespeare thought his works worthy of posterity, that he levied any ideal tribute upon future times, or had any further prospect, than of present popularity and present profit. When his plays had been acted, his hope was at an end; he solicited no addition of honour from the reader. He therefore made no scruple to repeat the same jests in many dialogues, or to entangle different plots by the same knot of perplexity, which may be at least forgiven him, by those who recollect, that of Congreve's four comedies, two are concluded by a marriage in a mask, by a deception, which perhaps never happened, and which, whether likely or not, he did not invent.[22]

So careless was this great poet of future fame, that, though he retired to ease and plenty, while he was yet little "declined into the vale of years,"[23] before he could be disgusted with fatigue, or disabled by infirmity, he made no collection of his works, nor desired to rescue those that had been already published from the depravations that obscured them, or secure to the rest a better destiny, by giving them to the world in their genuine state.

[22]*The Old Bachelor* and *Love for Love.*
[23]*Othello,* III.iii.269–70.

David Hume

1711–1776

David Hume was one of the major figures of the Scottish Enlightenment, a group of skeptical, empiricist thinkers that also included the economist Adam Smith and the political philosophers Adam Ferguson and Francis Hutcheson. Hume's earliest work, the *Treatise of Human Nature* (1739), upon its appearance, as Hume put it, "fell dead-born from the press." It is, however, the centerpiece of all the philosopher's thought: His more successful later works, the *Enquiry Concerning Human Understanding* (1748), the *Enquiry Concerning the Principles of Morals* (1752), and his political essays all find their origin here.

Hume's last published work, the posthumous *Dialogues on Natural Religion* (1779), was a brilliantly ironic dramatic performance in which the skeptical Philo — a character identifiable with Hume himself — defeats two opponents, one propounding the mysteries of revealed religion, the other a deistical "natural religion" of the sort found in Pope's *Essay on Man*. In his private life, Hume was an infidel and an atheist. James Boswell, Samuel Johnson's biographer, was present at Hume's death, and he reports that the philosopher died calmly and quietly without any belief in God or in the comforts of religion. This was something remarkable in his time: When the pious Johnson heard Boswell tell of this, he scoffed and refused to believe it.

Hume wrote few essays on the principles of art and aesthetics, except where they intersected his central interest in the workings of the human mind. The essay *Of the Standard of Taste* (published in 1757 as part of *Four Dissertations*) is an attempt to refine the century's growing interest in the psychology of the audience's response to literature and the other arts. (This is Horatian rhetorical criticism stood on its head: Instead of discussing the qualities poems should have, given the characteristics of an audience, the aestheticians of taste discuss the qualities that readers should possess, given a body of classic literature.) Hume, in other words, is interested in the same issue as Pope in his *Essay on Criticism:* What makes a good reader? But where Pope simply assumes that one reader or critic's assessment of a work of art can be rationally said to be better than another's, Hume subjects such questions to strict philosophical scrutiny.

The first twelve paragraphs of Hume's essay are written in his most subtle style and repay close examination. Hume begins by separating "taste" from "opinion." We hold opinions upon matters of fact; we have taste with regard to the arts. Furthermore, when we differ in our opinions, it is likely to be over generalities rather than particulars. (For example, two people might disagree over whether the United States ought to be called a democracy or a republic, though they might agree entirely about how laws are made and carried out.) When our sentiments differ on a matter of taste, however, according to Hume we tend to agree on the generalities but disagree over how to apply them. We will agree, for example, that elegance is a virtue in writing and coldness a fault; but the work you are damning for its chilliness of spirit, I may be applauding for its elegant form.

So far, so good. But now Hume embarks upon what looks like a digression into moral questions. "Those who found morality on sentiment more than on reason" (and Hume is one of these) tend to link up ethics with aesthetics here as an area in which we agree on our general principles but disagree on particular cases. We may agree that courage is a virtue and that rashness and cowardice are vices, but whether an individual act was courageous or rash may depend on who is doing the labeling.

The purpose of the digression becomes clear in the sixth paragraph: "It is natural for us to seek a standard of taste; a rule by which the various sentiments of men may be reconciled. . . ." In the field of ethics the need for a standard is obvious; indeed, societies set up massive institutions, courts of law and equity, to make sure that there is a clear standard of conduct, to reconcile our moral sentiments or, at least, to decide in favor of one sentiment and against another. And so it must be in aesthetics: We would seek a standard of taste — if such a standard is possible.

But *is* it possible? We all know the proverb *de gustibus non est disputandum:* there is no disputing about tastes. The argument for this position, which Hume endeavors to refute, runs as follows. Opinions and judgments are objective: They refer to something outside themselves and can thus be proven right or wrong. If a person looks at a painting and guesses that it measures three feet by five, we can take a tape measure and discover whether the guess is right or wrong. But sentiments are different. A sentiment is subjective: It states a relation between the perceiving subject and an object outside. The relation exists in the human consciousness, and we cannot second-guess it from outside. If a man looks at a painting and experiences it as beautiful, he cannot be wrong. If another man looks at the same painting and experiences it as ugly, he too is right. Beauty, as the saying goes, lies in the eye of the beholder. If the beholders disagree, there exists no intersubjective standard that can mediate between them, no standard of taste.

The obvious way out of this would be to deny that beauty is merely subjective. If beauty were a quality within things themselves, then it would be possible in principle to compare two works of art objectively. (Plato, for instance, takes Beauty to be an Idea in which any work of art or nature participates to greater or lesser extent. For Plato there is clearly an objective standard of taste.) But Hume has already foreclosed this escape by claiming that sentiments of taste are essentially different from opinions on matters of fact. Any standard of taste will have to be a subjective standard.

Hume's first step toward such a solution is to point out that wide and varied as our disagreements on taste are, they are not so wide as they look. We may differ as to whether Shakespeare or Milton is the greater poet, but we don't differ over whether Shakespeare's sonnets are greater than the jingles in greeting cards. We may differ as to whether Rembrandt is greater than Michelangelo, yet we don't differ over whether a Rembrandt is more beautiful than a lump of mud. When two geniuses are at nearly the same level, we find it difficult to adjudicate their respective claims; if anybody defended the superiority of the greeting-card lyric or the lump of mud, we would assume he or she was either not being serious or not to be taken seriously. But to do this is to assume the existence of a standard of taste that is capable of making at least the coarsest of judgments.

Hume also appeals to the existence of rules of art. Whatever their value, such rules are not provable a priori, like a mathematical theorem. They are empirical rules, codifications of the "experience and . . . observation of the common sentiments of human nature." We cannot deny that such common sentiments exist; otherwise, how would we account for the way classic works of art have moved humanity from generation to generation? But the key point is that such "common sentiments" exist because there is a definable "human nature." Humankind, despite our wide variation, is cut to a pattern, and so a norm can be defined. There are thus "general principles of approbation and blame" deriving from the "operations of the mind. Some particular forms or qualities, from the original structures of the internal fabric [of the brain], are calculated to please, and others displease; and if they fail of their effect in any particular instance, it is from some apparent defect or imperfection in the organ."

In effect Hume's aesthetic norm is like the norm of human vision. The norm is a standard of perfection for the organism, but it is not the average: Most of us do not have 20/20 vision, and most of us do not possess the standard of taste. And just as we would defer, in our attempts to read a distant sign, to someone with better vision, we should defer in our sentiments to those closer to the standard of taste.

From the thirteenth through the twenty-second paragraph, Hume attempts to define the qualities that the man of taste needs and the corresponding defects that keep most of us from attaining perfect aesthetic vision. He concludes that the man who combines exquisite sensitivity with freedom from prejudice, long experience, the habit of comparison, and massive good sense is the rare character who will embody the standard of taste.

But how does one find such a character and how does one tell a true claimant to the standard of taste from an imposter? We would seem to be back in the same skeptical swamp where we started. But though problems still remain, we have in fact advanced in some real way. For the issue of whether A or B is in accord with the existing standard of taste is now a factual question, not one of judgment. And critic X can be compared with critic Y in terms of the five qualities that Hume finds make good readers. For instance, a sensitive reader will see subtleties in a poem that a less sensitive reader will ignore unless they are pointed out. And experience, freedom from prejudice, and general good sense are reasonably objectifiable qualities. Good critics, like good artists, make themselves known to us by appealing to what is best in our common human nature.

The penultimate section of Hume's essay suggests areas where the writ of the standard fails to run, places where the differing sentiments of men may *not* be reconcilable. One area is the generation gap. As Hume says, "At twenty, Ovid may be the favorite author; Horace at forty; and perhaps Tacitus at fifty." A second moot area is nationality. Though they may understand the nature of his greatness, few Americans can take the unaffected pleasure in reading Racine that the French can — nor do the French ever seem to comprehend what the English-speaking world sees in Shakespeare.

The final question Hume takes up is that of the factors by which the passage of time alters our perspectives on literature. Some changes, like advances in science or a shift in the dominant religion, cause no problems. We take no less pleasure in Homer because his scientific ideas have been superseded or because his characters worship pagan gods. On the other hand, changes in morality from his time to ours may be problematic. The brutality of Achilles and the casual way Odysseus breaks his oaths for personal advantage may affront our modern sensibilities — and Hume thinks we would not be wrong to be upset. The other manifestation that can upset the otherwise tolerant Hume is religious superstition; he objects to Catholic propaganda in Racine and Corneille, and even more to the easy mixture of the religious and the secular in medieval authors like Boccaccio and Petrarch. These are not the most important sections of *The Standard of Taste* but it is interesting to see what made Hume the infidel wince.

Selected Bibliography

Brunet, Olivier. *Philosophie et esthetique chez David Hume*. Paris: A.-G. Nizet, 1965.

Brunius, Teddy. *David Hume on Criticism*. Stockholm: Almqvist and Wiksell, 1952.

Levinson, Jerrold. "Hume's Standard of Taste: The Real Problem." *Journal of Aesthetics and Art Criticism* 60, no. 3 (2002): 227–38.

Mall, Ram Adhar. *Naturalism and Criticism*. The Hague: Nijhoff, 1975.

Mossner, E. C. *The Life of David Hume*. Edinburgh: Nelson, 1954.

Murphy, Richard T. *Hume and Husserl: Towards Radical Subjectivism*. The Hague and Boston: Nijhoff, 1980.

Roelofs, Monique. "A Pearl's Pleasures and Perils: The Detail at the Foundation of Taste." *Differences: A Journal of Feminist Cultural Studies* 14, no. 3 (2003): 57–88.

Smith, N. K. *The Philosophy of David Hume*. London: Macmillan, 1941.

Wilbanks, Jan. *Hume's Theory of Imagination*. The Hague: Mouton, 1968.

Of the Standard of Taste

The great variety of taste, as well as of opinion, which prevails in the world, is too obvious not to have fallen under everyone's observation. Men of the most confined knowledge are able to remark a difference of taste in the narrow circle of their acquaintance, even where the persons have been educated under the same government, and have early imbibed the same prejudices. But those, who can enlarge their view to contemplate distant nations and remote ages, are still more surprised at the great inconsistence and contrariety. We are apt to call barbarous whatever departs widely from our own taste and apprehension: but soon find the epithet of reproach retorted on us. And the highest arrogance and self-conceit is at last startled, on observing an equal assurance on all sides, and scruples, amidst such a contest of sentiment, to pronounce positively in its own favor.

As this variety of taste is obvious to the most careless inquirer; so will it be found, on examination, to be still greater in reality than in appearance. The sentiments of men often differ with regard to beauty and deformity of all kinds, even while their general discourse is the same. There are certain terms in every language, which import blame, and others praise; and all men, who use the same tongue, must agree in their application of them. Every voice is united in applauding elegance, propriety, simplicity, spirit in writing; and in blaming fustian, affectation, coldness, and a false brilliancy: but when critics come to particulars, this seeming unanimity vanishes; and it is found, that they had affixed a very different meaning to their expressions. In all matters of opinion and science, the case is opposite: The difference among men is there oftener found to lie in generals than in particulars; and to be less in reality than in appearance. An explanation of the terms commonly ends the controversy; and the disputants are surprised to find, that they had been quarreling, while at bottom they agreed in their judgment.

Those who found morality on sentiment, more than on reason are inclined to comprehend ethics under the former observation, and to maintain, that, in all questions, which regard conduct and manners, the difference among men is really greater than at first sight it appears. It is indeed obvious that writers of all nations and all ages concur in applauding justice, humanity, magnanimity, prudence, veracity; and in blaming the opposite qualities. Even poets and other authors, whose compositions are chiefly calculated to please the imagination, are yet found, from Homer down to Fénelon,[1] to inculcate the same moral precepts, and to bestow their applause and blame on the same virtues and vices. This great unanimity is usually ascribed to the influence of plain reason; which, in all these cases, maintains similar sentiments in all men, and prevents those controversies, to which the abstract sciences are so much exposed. So far as the unanimity is real, this account may be admitted as satisfactory: but we must also allow that some part of the seeming harmony in morals may be accounted for from the very nature of language. The word *virtue*, with its equivalent in every tongue, implies praise; as that of *vice* does blame: And no one, without the most obvious and grossest impropriety, could affix reproach to a term, which in general acceptation is understood in a good sense; or bestow applause, where the idiom requires disapprobation. Homer's general precepts, where he delivers any such, will never be controverted; but it is obvious, that, when he draws particular pictures of manners, and represents heroism in Achilles and prudence in Ulysses, he intermixes a much greater degree of ferocity in the former, and of cunning and fraud in the latter, than Fénelon would admit of. The sage Ulysses in the Greek poet seems to delight in lies and fictions, and often employs them without any necessity or

even advantage: But his more scrupulous son, in the French epic writer, exposes himself to the most imminent perils, rather than depart from the most exact line of truth and veracity.

The admirers and followers of the Alcoran[2] insist on the excellent moral precepts interspersed throughout that wild and absurd performance. But it is to be supposed, that the Arabic words, which correspond to the English, equity, justice, temperance, meekness, charity, were such as, from the constant use of that tongue, must always be taken in a good sense; and it would have argued the greatest ignorance, not of morals, but of language, to have mentioned them with any epithets, besides those of applause and approbation. But would we know, whether the pretended prophet had really attained a just sentiment of morals? Let us attend to his narration; and we shall soon find, that he bestows praise on such instances of treachery, inhumanity, cruelty, revenge, bigotry, as are utterly incompatible with civilized society. No steady rule of right seems there to be attained to; and every action is blamed or praised, so far only as it is beneficial or hurtful to the true believers.

The merit of delivering true general precepts in ethics is indeed very small. Whoever recommends any moral virtues, really does no more than is implied in the terms themselves. That people, who invented the word *charity,* and used it in a good sense, inculcated more clearly and much more efficaciously, the precept, "be charitable," than any pretended legislator or prophet, who should insert such a maxim in his writings. Of all expressions, those, which, together with their other meaning, imply a degree either of blame or approbation, are the least liable to be perverted or mistaken.

It is natural for us to seek a standard of taste; a rule by which the various sentiments of men may be reconciled; at least, a decision afforded, confirming one sentiment, and condemning another.

There is a species of philosophy, which cuts off all hope of success in such an attempt, and represents the impossibility of ever attaining any standard of taste. The difference, it is said, is very wide between judgment and sentiment. All

[1]François de Salignac de la Mothe Fénelon, who wrote a novel, *Télémaque* (1699) as a continuation of Book 4 of Homer's *Odyssey*.

[2]The Koran.

sentiment is right; because sentiment has a reference to nothing beyond itself, and is always real, wherever a man is conscious of it. But all determinations of the understanding are not right; because they have a reference to something beyond themselves, to wit, real matter of fact; and are not always conformable to that standard. Among a thousand different opinions which different men may entertain of the same subject, there is one, and but one, that is just and true; and the only difficulty is to fix and ascertain it. On the contrary, a thousand different sentiments, excited by the same object, are all right: because no sentiment represents what is really in the object. It only marks a certain conformity or relation between the object and the organs or faculties of the mind; and if that conformity did not really exist, the sentiment could never possibly have being. Beauty is no quality in things themselves: it exists merely in the mind which contemplates them; and each mind perceives a different beauty. One person may even perceive deformity, where another is sensible of beauty; and every individual ought to acquiesce in his own sentiment, without pretending to regulate those of others. To seek the real beauty, or real deformity, is as fruitless an inquiry, as to pretend to ascertain the real sweet or real bitter. According to the disposition of the organs, the same object may be both sweet and bitter; and the proverb has justly determined it to be fruitless to dispute concerning tastes. It is very natural, and even quite necessary, to extend this axiom to mental, as well as bodily taste; and thus common sense, which is so often at variance with philosophy, especially with the skeptical kind, is found, in one instance at least, to agree in pronouncing the same decision.

But though this axiom, by passing into a proverb, seems to have attained the sanction of common sense; there is certainly a species of common sense which opposes it, at least serves to modify and restrain it. Whoever would assert an equality of genius and elegance between Ogilby[3] and Milton, or Bunyan and Addison, would be thought to defend no less an extravagance, than if

he had maintained a molehill to be as high as Tenerife,[4] or a pond as extensive as the ocean. Though there may be found persons, who give the preference to the former authors, no one pays attention to such a taste; and we pronounce without scruple the sentiment of these pretended critics to be absurd and ridiculous. The principle of the natural equality of tastes is then totally forgot, and while we admit it on some occasions, where the objects seem near an equality, it appears an extravagant paradox, or rather a palpable absurdity, where objects so disproportioned are compared together.

It is evident that none of the rules of composition are fixed by reasoning *a priori,* or can be esteemed abstract conclusions of the understanding, from comparing those habitudes and relations of ideas, which are eternal and immutable. Their foundation is the same with that of all the practical sciences, experience; nor are they anything but general observations, concerning what has been universally found to please in all countries and in all ages. Many of the beauties of poetry and even of eloquence are founded on falsehood and fiction, on hyperboles, metaphors, and an abuse or perversion of terms from their natural meaning. To check the sallies of the imagination, and to reduce every expression to geometrical truth and exactness, would be the most contrary to the laws of criticism; because it would produce a work, which, by universal experience, has been found the most insipid and disagreeable. But though poetry can never submit to exact truth, it must be confined by rules of art, discovered to the author either by genius or observation. If some negligent or irregular writers have pleased, they have not pleased by their transgressions of rule or order, but in spite of these transgressions: They have possessed other beauties, which were conformable to just criticism; and the force of these beauties has been able to overpower censure, and give the mind a satisfaction superior to the disgust arising from the blemishes.

---

[3]John Ogilby (1600–1676), a Scottish poet who, like Milton, but less successfully, tried his hand at epic. In Hume's day the comparison of Bunyan with Addison was as clear as

that of Ogilby with Milton: The former in both pairings was considered a far inferior popular writer. Two hundred years later, Hume's preference for Addison seems less self-explanatory.

[4]A mountain in the Canary Islands.

Ariosto[5] pleases; but not by his monstrous and improbable fictions, by his bizarre mixture of the serious and comic styles, by the want of coherence in his stories, or by the continual interruptions of his narration. He charms by the force and clearness of his expression, by the readiness and variety of his inventions, and by his natural pictures of the passions, especially those of the gay and amorous kind: And however his faults may diminish our satisfaction, they are not able entirely to destroy it. Did our pleasure really arise from those parts of his poem, which we denominate faults, this would be no objection to criticism in general: It would only be an objection to those particular rules of criticism, which would establish such circumstances to be faults, and would represent them as universally blamable. If they are found to please, they cannot be faults; let the pleasure, which they produce, be ever so unexpected and unaccountable.

But though all the general rules of art are founded only on experience and on the observation of the common sentiments of human nature, we must not imagine, that, on every occasion, the feelings of men will be conformable to these rules. Those finer emotions of the mind are of a very tender and delicate nature, and require the concurrence of many favorable circumstances to make them play with facility and exactness, according to their general and established principles. The least exterior hindrance to such small springs, or the least internal disorder, disturbs their motion, and confounds the operation of the whole machine. When we would make an experiment of this nature, and would try the force of any beauty or deformity, we must choose with care a proper time and place, and bring the fancy to a suitable situation and disposition. A perfect serenity of mind, a recollection of thought, a due attention to the object; if any of these circumstances be wanting, our experiment will be fallacious, and we shall be unable to judge of the catholic and universal beauty. The relation, which nature has placed between the form and the sentiment, will at least be more obscure; and it will require greater accuracy to trace and discern it.

[5]Ludovico Ariosto was the author of the fanciful epic, *Orlando Furioso* (1516).

We shall be able to ascertain its influence not so much from the operation of each particular beauty, as from the durable admiration, which attends those works, that have survived all the caprices of mode and fashion, all the mistakes of ignorance and envy.

The same Homer, who pleased at Athens and Rome two thousand years ago, is still admired at Paris and at London. All the changes of climate, government, religion, and language, have not been able to obscure his glory. Authority or prejudice may give a temporary vogue to a bad poet or orator; but his reputation will never be durable or general. When his compositions are examined by posterity or by foreigners, the enchantment is dissipated, and his faults appear in their true colors. On the contrary, a real genius, the longer his works endure, and the more wide they are spread, the more sincere is the admiration which he meets with. Envy and jealousy have too much place in a narrow circle; and even familiar acquaintance with his person may diminish the applause due to his performances: but when these obstructions are removed, the beauties, which are naturally fitted to excite agreeable sentiments, immediately display their energy; and while the world endures, they maintain their authority over the minds of men.

It appears then, that, amidst all the variety and caprice of taste, there are certain general principles of approbation or blame, whose influence a careful eye may trace in all operations of the mind. Some particular forms or qualities, from the original structures of the internal fabric, are calculated to please, and others displease; and if they fail of their effect in any particular instance, it is from some apparent defect or imperfection in the organ. A man in a fever would not insist on his palate as able to decide concerning flavors; nor would one, affected with the jaundice, pretend to give a verdict with regard to colors. In each creature, there is a sound and defective state; and the former alone can be supposed to afford us a true standard of taste and sentiment. If, in the sound state of the organ, there be an entire or a considerable uniformity of sentiment among men, we may thence derive an idea of the perfect beauty; in like manner as the appearance of objects in daylight, to the eye of a man in health, is denominated their true and real color, even while color is allowed to be merely a phantasm of the senses.

Many and frequent are the defects in the internal organs which prevent or weaken the influence of those general principles, on which depends our sentiment of beauty or deformity. Though some objects, by the structure of the mind, be naturally calculated to give pleasure, it is not to be expected, that in every individual the pleasure will be equally felt. Particular incidents and situations occur, which either throw a false light on the objects, or hinder the true from conveying to the imagination the proper sentiment and perception.

One obvious cause, why many feel not the proper sentiment of beauty, is the want of that delicacy of imagination, which is requisite to convey a sensibility of those finer emotions. This delicacy everyone pretends to: everyone talks of it; and would reduce every kind of taste or sentiment to its standard. But as our intention in this essay is to mingle some light of the understanding with the feeling of sentiment, it will be proper to give a more accurate definition of delicacy, than has hitherto been attempted. And not to draw our philosophy from too profound a source, we shall have recourse to a noted story in *Don Quixote*.

"It is with good reason," says Sancho to the squire with the great nose, "that I pretend to have a judgment in wine: this is a quality hereditary in our family. Two of my kinsmen were once called to give their opinion of a hogshead, which was supposed to be excellent, being old and of a good vintage. One of them tastes it; considers it; and after mature reflection pronounces the wine to be good, were it not for a small taste of leather, which he perceived in it. The other, after using the same precautions, gives also his verdict in favor of the wine; but with the reserve of a taste of iron, which he could easily distinguish. You cannot imagine how much they were both ridiculed for their judgment. But who laughed in the end? On emptying the hogshead, there was found at the bottom, an old key with a leathern thong tied to it."

The great resemblance between mental and bodily taste will easily teach us to apply this story. Though it be certain that beauty and deformity, more than sweet and bitter, are not qualities in objects, but belong entirely to the sentiment, internal or external; it must be allowed, that there are certain qualities in objects, which are fitted by nature to produce those particular feelings. Now as these qualities may be found in a small degree, or may be mixed and confounded with each other, it often happens, that the taste is not affected with such minute qualities, or is not able to distinguish all the particular flavors, amidst the disorder, in which they are presented. Where the organs are so fine, as to allow nothing to escape them; and at the same time so exact as to perceive every ingredient in the composition: this we call delicacy of taste, where we employ these terms in the literal or metaphorical sense. Here then the general rules of beauty are of use; being drawn from established models, and from the observation of what pleases or displeases, when presented singly and in a high degree: and if the same qualities, in a continued composition and in a smaller degree, affect not the organs with a sensible delight or uneasiness, we exclude the person from all pretensions to this delicacy. To produce these general rules or avowed patterns of composition is like finding the key with the leathern thong; which justified the verdict of Sancho's kinsmen, and confounded those pretended judges who had condemned them. Though the hogshead had never been emptied, the taste of the one was still equally delicate, and that of the other equally dull and languid: but it would have been more difficult to have proved the superiority of the former, to the conviction of every bystander. In like manner, though the beauties of writing had never been methodized, or reduced to general principles; though no excellent models had ever been acknowledged; the different degrees of taste would still have subsisted, and the judgment of one man been preferable to that of another; but it would not have been so easy to silence the bad critic, who might always insist upon his particular sentiment, and refuse to submit to his antagonist. But when we show him an avowed principle of art; when we illustrate this principle by examples, whose operation, from his own particular taste, he acknowledges to be conformable to the principle; when we prove, that the same principle may be applied to the present case, where he did not perceive or feel its influence: he must conclude, upon the whole, that the fault lies in himself, and that he wants the delicacy, which is requisite to make him sensible of every beauty and every blemish, in any composition or discourse.

It is acknowledged to be the perfection of every sense or faculty, to perceive with exactness its most minute objects, and allow nothing to escape its notice and observation. The smaller the objects are, which become sensible to the eye, the finer is that organ, and the more elaborate its make and composition. A good palate is not tried by strong flavors; but by a mixture of small ingredients, where we are still sensible of each part, notwithstanding its minuteness and its confusion with the rest. In like manner, a quick and acute perception of beauty and deformity must be the perfection of our mental taste; nor can a man be satisfied with himself while he suspects, that any excellence or blemish in a discourse has passed him unobserved. In this case, the perfection of the man, and the perfection of the sense or feeling, are found to be united. A very delicate palate, on many occasions, may be a great inconvenience both to a man himself and to his friends: but a delicate taste of wit or beauty must always be a desirable quality; because it is the source of all the finest and most innocent enjoyments, of which human nature is susceptible. In this decision the sentiments of all mankind are agreed. Wherever you can ascertain a delicacy of taste, it is sure to meet with approbation; and the best way of ascertaining it is to appeal to those models and principles, which have been established by the uniform consent and experience of nations and ages.

But though there be naturally a wide difference in point of delicacy between one person and another, nothing tends further to increase and improve this talent, than practice in a particular art, and the frequent survey or contemplation of a particular species of beauty. When objects of any kind are first presented to the eye or imagination, the sentiment, which attends them, is obscure and confused; and the mind is, in a great measure, incapable of pronouncing concerning their merits or defects. The taste cannot perceive the several excellences of the performance; much less distinguish the particular character of each excellency, and ascertain its quality and degree. If it pronounce the whole in general to be beautiful or deformed, it is the utmost that can be expected; and even this judgment, a person, so unpracticed, will be apt to deliver with great hesitation and reserve. But allow him to acquire experience in those objects, his feeling becomes more exact and nice: he not only perceives the beauties and defects of each part, but marks the distinguishing species of each quality, and assigns it suitable praise or blame. A clear and distinct sentiment attends him through the whole survey of the objects; and he discerns that very degree and kind of approbation or displeasure, which each part is naturally fitted to produce. The mist dissipates, which seemed formerly to hang over the object: the organ acquires greater perfection in its operations; and can pronounce, without danger of mistake, concerning the merits of every performance. In a word, the same address and dexterity, which practice gives to the execution of any work, is also acquired by the same means, in the judging of it.

So advantageous is practice to the discernment of beauty, that, before we can give judgment on any work of importance, it will even be requisite, that that very individual performance be more than once perused by us, and be surveyed in different lights with attention and deliberation. There is a flutter or hurry of thought which attends the first perusal of any piece, and which confounds the genuine sentiment of beauty. The relation of the parts is not discerned: the true characters of style are little distinguished: the several perfections and defects seem wrapped up in a species of confusion, and present themselves indistinctly to the imagination. Not to mention, that there is a species of beauty, which, as it is florid and superficial, pleases at first; but being found incompatible with a just expression either of reason or passion, soon palls upon the taste, and is then rejected with disdain, at least rated at much lower value.

It is impossible to continue in the practice of contemplating any order of beauty, without being frequently obliged to form comparisons between the several species and degrees of excellence, and estimating their proportion to each other. A man, who has had no opportunity of comparing the different kinds of beauty, is indeed totally unqualified to pronounce an opinion with regard to any object presented to him. By comparison alone we fix the epithets of praise or blame, and learn how to assign the due degree of each. The coarsest daubing contains a certain luster of colors and exactness of imitation, which are so far beauties, and would affect the mind of a peasant or Indian with the highest admiration. The most vulgar ballads are not entirely destitute of harmony or nature; and none but a person, familiarized to superior beauties, would pronounce their numbers harsh, or narration uninteresting. A great inferiority of beauty gives pain to a person conversant in the highest excellence of the kind, and is for that reason pronounced a deformity: as the most finished object, with which we are acquainted, is naturally supposed to have reached the pinnacle of perfection, and to be entitled to the highest applause. One accustomed to see, and examine, and weigh the several performances, admired in different ages and nations, can only rate the merits of a work exhibited to his view, and assign its proper rank among the productions of genius.

But to enable a critic the more fully to execute this undertaking, he must preserve his mind free from all prejudice, and allow nothing to enter into his consideration, but the very object which is submitted to his examination. We may observe, that every work of art, in order to produce its due effect on the mind, must be surveyed in a certain point of view, and cannot be fully relished by persons, whose situation, real or imaginary, is not conformable to that which is required by the performance. An orator addresses himself to a particular audience, and must have a regard to their particular genius, interest, opinions, passions, and prejudices; otherwise he hopes in vain to govern their resolutions, and inflame their affections. Should they even have entertained some prepossessions against him, however unreasonable, he must not overlook this disadvantage; but, before he enters upon the subject, must endeavor to conciliate their affection, and acquire their good graces. A critic of a different age or nation, who should peruse this discourse, must have all these circumstances in his eye, and must place himself in the same situation as the audience, in order to form a true judgment of the oration. In like manner, when any work is addressed to the public, though I should have a friendship or enmity with the author, I must depart from this situation; and considering myself as a man in general, forget, if possible, my individual being and my peculiar circumstances. A person influenced by prejudice, complies not with this condition; but obstinately maintains his natural position, without placing himself in that point of view, which the performance supposes. If the work be addressed to persons of a different age or nation, he makes no allowance for their peculiar views and prejudices; but, full of the manners of his own age and country, rashly condemns what seemed admirable in the eyes of those for whom alone the discourse was calculated. If the work be executed for the public, he never sufficiently enlarges his comprehension, or forgets his interest as a friend or enemy, as a rival or commentator. By this means, his sentiments are perverted; nor have the same beauties and blemishes the same influence upon him, as if he had imposed a proper violence on his imagination, and had forgotten himself for a moment. So far his taste evidently departs from the true standard; and of consequence loses all credit and authority.

It is well known, that in all questions, submitted to the understanding, prejudice is destructive of sound judgment, and perverts all operations of the intellectual faculties; it is no less contrary to good taste; nor has it less influence to corrupt our sentiment of beauty. It belongs to good sense to check its influence in both cases; and in this respect, as well as in many others, reason, if not an essential part of taste, is at least requisite to the operations of this latter faculty. In all the nobler productions of genius, there is a mutual relation and correspondence of parts; nor can either the beauties or blemishes be perceived by him, whose thought is not capacious enough to comprehend all those parts, and compare them with each other, in order to perceive the consistence and uniformity of the whole. Every work of art has also a certain end or purpose, for which it is calculated; and is to be deemed more or less perfect, as it is more or less fitted to attain this end. The object of eloquence is to persuade, of history to instruct, of poetry to please by means of the passions and the imagination. These ends we must carry constantly in our view, when we peruse any performance; and we must be able to judge how far the means employed are adapted to their respective purposes. Besides every kind of composition, even the most poetical, is nothing but a chain of propositions and reasonings; not always, indeed, the justest and most exact, but still plausible and specious, however disguised by the coloring of the imagination. The persons introduced in tragedy and epic poetry, must be represented as reasoning, and thinking, and concluding, and acting, suitably to their character and circumstances; and without judgment, as well as taste and invention, a poet can never hope to succeed in so delicate an undertaking. Not to mention, that the same excellence of faculties which contributes to the improvement of reason, the same clearness of conception, the same exactness of distinction, the same vivacity of apprehension, are essential to the operations of true taste, and are its infallible concomitants. It seldom, or never happens, that a man of sense, who has experience in any art, cannot judge of its beauty; and it is no less rare to meet with a man who has a just taste without a sound understanding.

Thus, though the principles of taste be universal, and, nearly, if not entirely the same in all men; yet few are qualified to give judgment on any work of art, or establish their own sentiment as the standard of beauty. The organs of internal sensation are seldom so perfect as to allow the general principles their full play, and produce a feeling correspondent to those principles. They either labor under some defect, or are vitiated by some disorder; and by that means, excite a sentiment, which may be pronounced erroneous. When the critic has no delicacy, he judges without any distinction, and is only affected by the grosser and more palpable qualities of the object: the finer touches pass unnoticed and disregarded. Where he is not aided by practice, his verdict is attended with confusion and hesitation. Where no comparison has been employed, the most frivolous beauties, such as rather merit the name of defects, are the objects of his admiration. Where he lies under the influence of prejudice, all his natural sentiments are perverted. Where good sense is wanting, he is not qualified to discern the beauties of design and reasoning, which are the highest and most excellent. Under some or other of these imperfections, the generality of men labor; and hence a true judge in the finer arts is observed, even during the most polished ages, to be so rare a character: strong sense, united to delicate sentiment, improved by practice, perfected by comparison, and cleared of all prejudice, can alone entitle critics to this valuable character; and the joint verdict of such, wherever they are to be found, is the true standard of taste and beauty.

But where are such critics to be found? By what marks are they to be known? How distinguish them from pretenders? These questions are embarrassing; and seem to throw us back into the same uncertainty, from which, during the course of this essay, we have endeavored to extricate ourselves.

But if we consider the matter aright, these are questions of fact, not of sentiment. Whether any particular person be endowed with good sense and a delicate imagination, free from prejudice, may often be the subject of dispute, and be liable to great discussion and inquiry: But that such a character is valuable and estimable will be agreed in by all mankind. Where these doubts occur, men can do no more than in other disputable questions, which are submitted to the understanding: they must produce the best arguments, that their invention suggests to them; they must acknowledge a true and decisive standard to exist somewhere, to wit, real existence and matter of fact; and they must have indulgence to such as differ from them in their appeals to this standard. It is sufficient for our present purpose, if we have proved, that the taste of all individuals is not upon an equal footing, and that some men in general, however difficult to be particularly pitched upon, will be acknowledged by universal sentiment to have a preference above others.

But in reality the difficulty of finding, even in particulars, the standard of taste, is not so great as it is represented. Though in speculation, we may readily avow a certain criterion in science and deny it in sentiment, the matter is found in practice to be much more hard to ascertain in the former case than in the latter. Theories of abstract philosophy, systems of profound theology, have prevailed during one age: in a successive period, these have been universally exploded: their absurdity has been detected: other theories and systems have supplied their place, which again gave place to their successors: and nothing has been experienced more liable to the revolutions of chance and fashion than these pretended decisions of science. The case is not the same with beauties of eloquence and poetry. Just expressions of passion and nature are sure, after a little time, to gain public applause, which they maintain forever. Aristotle, and Plato, and Epicurus, and Descartes, may successively yield to each other: but Terence and Virgil maintain a universal, undisputed empire over the minds of men. The abstract philosophy of Cicero has lost its credit: the vehemence of his oratory is still the object of our admiration.

Though men of delicate taste be rare, they are easily to be distinguished in society, by the soundness of their understanding and the superiority of their faculties above the rest of mankind. The ascendant, which they acquire, gives a prevalence to that lively approbation, with which they receive any productions of genius, and renders it generally predominant. Many men, when left to themselves, have but a faint and dubious perception of beauty, who yet are capable of relishing any fine stroke, which is pointed out to them. Every convert to the admiration of the real poet or orator is the cause of some new conversion. And though prejudices may prevail for a time, they never unite in celebrating any rival to the true genius, but yield at last to the force of nature and just sentiment. Thus, though a civilized nation may easily be mistaken in the choice of their admired philosopher, they never have been found long to err, in their affection for a favorite epic or tragic author.

But notwithstanding all our endeavors to fix a standard of taste, and reconcile the discordant apprehensions of men, there still remain two sources of variation, which are not sufficient indeed to confound all the boundaries of beauty and deformity, but will often serve to produce a difference in the degrees of our approbation or blame. The one is the different humors of particular men; the other, the particular manners and opinions of our age and country. The general principles of taste are uniform in human nature: where men vary in their judgments, some defect or perversion in the faculties may commonly be remarked;

proceeding either from prejudice, from want of practice, or want of delicacy; and there is just reason for approving one taste, and condemning another. But where there is such a diversity in the internal frame or external situation as is entirely blameless on both sides, and leaves no room to give one the preference above the other; in that case a certain degree of diversity in judgment is unavoidable, and we seek in vain for a standard, by which we can reconcile the contrary sentiments.

A young man, whose passions are warm, will be more sensibly touched with amorous and tender images, than a man more advanced in years, who takes pleasure in wise, philosophical reflections concerning the conduct of life and moderation of the passions. At twenty, Ovid may be the favorite author; Horace at forty; and perhaps Tacitus at fifty. Vainly would we, in such cases, endeavor to enter into the sentiments of others, and divest ourselves of those propensities, which are natural to us. We choose our favorite author as we do our friend, from a conformity of humor and disposition. Mirth or passion, sentiment or reflection; whichever of these most predominates in our temper, it give us a peculiar sympathy with the writer who resembles us.

One person is more pleased with the sublime; another with the tender; a third with raillery. One has a strong sensibility to blemishes, and is extremely studious of correctness: another has a more lively feeling of beauties, and pardons twenty absurdities and defects for one elevated or pathetic stroke. The ear of this man is entirely turned toward conciseness and energy; that man is delighted with a copious, rich, and harmonious expression. Simplicity is affected by one; ornament by another. Comedy, tragedy, satire, odes, have each its partisans, who prefer that particular species of writing to all others. It is plainly an error in a critic, to confine his approbation to one species or style of writing, and condemn all the rest. But it is almost impossible not to feel a predilection for that which suits our particular turn and disposition. Such preferences are innocent and unavoidable, and can never reasonably be the object of dispute, because there is no standard, by which they can be decided.

For a like reason, we are more pleased, in the course of our reading, with pictures and characters, that resemble objects which are found in our own age or country, than with those which describe a different set of customs. It is not without some effort, that we reconcile ourselves to the simplicity of ancient manners, and behold princesses carrying water from the spring, and kings and heroes dressing their own victuals. We may allow in general, that the representation of such manners is no fault in the author, nor deformity in the piece; but we are not so sensibly touched with them. For this reason, comedy is not easily transferred from one age or nation to another. A Frenchman or Englishman is not pleased with the *Andria* of Terence, or *Clitia* of Machiavel; where the fine lady, upon whom all the play turns, never once appears to the spectators, but is always kept behind the scenes, suitably to the reserved humor of the ancient Greeks and modern Italians. A man of learning and reflection can make allowance for these peculiarities of manners; but a common audience can never divest themselves so far of their usual ideas and sentiments, as to relish pictures which in no wise resemble them.

But here there occurs a reflection, which may, perhaps, be useful in examining the celebrated controversy concerning ancient and modern learning; where we often find the one side excusing any seeming absurdity in the ancients from the manners of the age, and the other refusing to admit this excuse, or at least, admitting it only as an apology for the author, not for the performance. In my opinion, the proper boundaries in this subject have seldom been fixed between the contending parties. Where any innocent peculiarities of manners are represented, such as those above mentioned, they ought certainly to be admitted; and a man, who is shocked with them, gives an evident proof of false delicacy and refinement. The poet's monument more durable than brass must fall to the ground like common brick or clay, were men to make no allowance for the continual revolutions of manners and customs, and would admit of nothing but what was suitable to the prevailing fashion. Must we throw aside the pictures of our ancestors, because of their ruffs and farthingales? But where the ideas of morality and decency alter from one age to another, and where vicious manners are described, without being marked with the proper

characters of blame and disapprobation; this must be allowed to disfigure the poem, and to be a real deformity. I cannot, nor is it proper I should, enter into such sentiments; and however I may excuse the poet, on account of the manners of his age, I never can relish the composition. The want of humanity and of decency, so conspicuous in the characters drawn by several of the ancient poets, even sometimes by Homer and the Greek tragedians, diminishes considerably the merit of their noble performances, and gives modern authors an advantage over them. We are not interested in the fortunes and sentiments of such rough heroes: we are displeased to find the limits of vice and virtue so much confounded: and whatever indulgence we may give to the writer on account of his prejudices, we cannot prevail on ourselves to enter into his sentiments, or bear an affection to characters, which we plainly discover to be blamable.

The case is not the same with moral principles, as with speculative opinions of any kind. These are in continual flux and revolution. The son embraces a different system from the father. Nay, there scarcely is any man, who can boast of great constance and uniformity in this particular. Whatever speculative errors may be found in the polite writings of any age or country, they detract but little from the value of those compositions. There needs but a certain turn of thought or imagination to make us enter into all the opinions, which then prevailed, and relish the sentiments or conclusions derived from them. But a very violent effort is requisite to change our judgment of manners, and excite sentiments of approbation or blame, love or hatred, different from those to which the mind from long custom has been familiarized. And where a man is confident of the rectitude of that moral standard, by which he judges, he is justly jealous of it, and will not pervert the sentiments of his heart for a moment, in complaisance to any writer whatsoever.

Of all speculative errors, those, which regard religion, are the most excusable in compositions of genius; nor is it ever permitted to judge of the civility or wisdom of any people, or even of single persons, by the grossness or refinement of their theological principles. The same good sense, that directs men in the ordinary occurrences of life, is not harkened to in religious matters, which are supposed to be placed altogether above the cognizance of human reason. On this account, all the absurdities of the pagan system of theology must be overlooked by every critic, who would pretend to form a just notion of ancient poetry; and our posterity, in their turn, must have the same indulgence to their forefathers. No religious principles can ever be imputed as a fault to any poet, while they remain merely principles, and take no such strong possession of his heart, as to lay him under the imputation of bigotry or superstition. Where that happens, they confound the sentiments of morality, and alter the natural boundaries of vice and virtue. They are therefore eternal blemishes, according to the principle above mentioned; nor are the prejudices and false opinions of the age sufficient to justify them.

It is essential to the Roman Catholic religion to inspire a violent hatred of every other worship, and to represent all pagans, Mahometans, and heretics as the objects of divine wrath and vengeance. Such sentiments, though they are in reality very blamable, are considered as virtues by the zealots of that communion, and are represented in their tragedies and epic poems as a kind of divine heroism. This bigotry has disfigured two very fine tragedies of the French theater, *Polyeucte* and *Athalie;*[6] where an intemperate zeal

[6]Plays by Corneille and Racine, respectively. The dialogue Hume quotes is from the latter.

for particular modes of worship is set off with all the pomp imaginable, and forms the predominant character of the heroes. "What is this," says the sublime Joad to Josabet, finding her in discourse with Mathan, the priest of Baal, "does the daughter of David speak to this traitor? Are you not afraid, lest the earth should open and pour forth flames to devour you both? Or lest these holy walls should fall and crush you together? What is his purpose? Why comes that enemy of God hither to poison the air, which we breathe, with his horrid presence?" Such sentiments are received with great applause on the theater of Paris; but at London the spectators would be full as much pleased to hear Achilles tell Agamemnon, that he was a dog in his forehead, and a deer in his heart, or Jupiter threaten Juno with a sound drubbing, if she will not be quiet.

Religious principles are also a blemish in any polite composition, when they rise up to superstition, and intrude themselves into every sentiment, however remote from any connection with religion. It is no excuse for the poet, that the customs of his country had burthened life with so many religious ceremonies and observances, that no part of it was exempt from that yoke. It must forever be ridiculous in Petrarch to compare his mistress Laura, to Jesus Christ. Nor is it less ridiculous in that agreeable libertine, Boccace, very seriously to give thanks to God Almighty and the ladies, for their assistance in defending him against his enemies.

Barbara Herrnstein Smith

b. 1932

Barbara Herrnstein Smith is a scholar of aesthetics, literary theory, and linguistic theory. Born in New York City, Smith took her B.A. (1954), M.A. (1955), and Ph.D. (1965) in English and American litera-ture at Brandeis University in Massachusetts. She has been an instructor at the Sanz School of Languages in Washington, D.C. (1956–57), a member of the literature faculty at Bennington College (1962–74), and a professor at the University of Pennsylvania (1974–87), where in 1979 she was named director of the Center for the Study of Art and Symbolic Behavior, and in 1980 University Professor of English and communications. Smith has been a fellow of (1970–71) and a consultant for (1974) the National Endowment of the Humanities as well as a Guggenheim fellow (1977–78) and a chair of the Modern Language Association (1987–88). Currently she is Braxton Craven professor of Comparative Literature and English at Duke University. Most of Smith's publications have been academic articles. Her books include Poetic Closure: A Study of How Poems End, *which won the Christian Gauss Award and the Explicator Award for 1968,* On the Margins of Discourse: The Relation of Literature to Language *(1978),* Contingencies of Value: Alternative Perspectives for Critical Theory *(1988), and* The Politics of Liberal Education *(ed., with Darryl Gless, 1991). "Contingencies of Value" is from* Critical Inquiry *10 (1983). In "Contingencies of Value," Barbara Herrnstein Smith attempts to cut the ground from beneath David Hume's feet, arguing that, where aesthetic judgments are concerned, the relatively similar physical constitutions we all share shrink to insignificance when we consider the immense dif-ferences in culture. But she also suggests that nothing very much has been lost if we give up on the notion of a uniquely valid standard of taste, and inquire instead about the various interests that aes-thetic judgments serve.*

From *Contingencies of Value*

Given a more sophisticated formulation, Hume's belief that the individual experience of "beauty" can be related to "forms" and "qualities" that grat-ify human beings "naturally" by virtue of certain physiological structures and psychological mech-anisms is probably not altogether without founda-tion.[1] Taken as a ground for the justification

[1]The discipline of "empirical aesthetics" has been developed out of precisely such a belief. For a recent survey and discussion of its findings, see Hans and Shulamith Kreitler, *Psychology of the Arts* (Durham, N.C.: Duke University Press, 1972). [Smith]

of normative claims, however, and transformed accordingly into a model of standards-and-devia-tions, it obliged him (as it did and does many oth-ers) to interpret as so many instances of individual pathology what are, rather, the variable products of the interaction between, on the one hand, cer-tain *relatively* uniform innate structures, mecha-nisms, and tendencies and, on the other, innumer-able cultural and contextual variables as well as other individual variables — the latter including particulars of personal history, temperament, age, and so forth. What produces evaluative consensus, such as it is, is not the healthy functioning of universal organs but the playing out of the *same* dynamics and variable contingencies that produce evaluative divergences. . . .

There is a tenacious conviction among those who argue these questions that unless one judgment can be said or shown to be more "valid" than another, then all judgments must be "equal" or "equally valid." Indeed, it is the horror or apparent absurdity of such egalitarianism that commonly gives force to the charge that "relativism" produces social chaos or is a logically untenable position. While the radical contingency of all value certainly does imply that no value judgment can be more valid than another in the sense of being a more accurate statement of *the* value of an object (for the latter concept then becomes vacuous), it does not follow that all value judgments are equal or equally valid. On the contrary, what does follow is that the concept of "validity" is *inappropriate* with regard to evaluations and that there is no nontrivial parameter with respect to which they *could* be "equal." This is not to say that no evaluations can be better or worse than others. What must be emphasized, however, is that the value — the "goodness" or "badness" — of an evaluation, like that of anything else (including any other type of utterance), is *itself* contingent, and thus a matter not of its abstract "truth-value" but of how well it performs various desired/able functions for the various people who may at any time be concretely involved with it. In the case of an aesthetic evaluation, these people will always include the evaluator, who will have his or her own particular interest in the various effects of the judgments s/he produces, and may also include anyone from the artist to a potential publisher or patron, various current or future audiences of the work, and perhaps someone who just likes to know what's going on and what other people think is going on. Each of them will have his or her own interest in the evaluation, and it will be better or worse for each of them in relation to a different set of desired/able functions. What all this suggests is that the obsessive debates over the cognitive substance, logical status, and "truth-value" of aesthetic judgments are not only unresolvable in the terms given but, strictly speaking, pointless.

Immanuel Kant

1724–1804

It is an irony of the history of philosophy that the most revolutionary thinker of the eighteenth century, an unwitting founder of the romantic movement, should have lived a life whose restriction and regularity were the stuff of legend. Immanuel Kant, son of a saddlemaker, was born and educated in the Prussian seaport of Königsberg, became professor of philosophy at the university, and died without traveling more than forty miles from his birthplace. His self-discipline was so stringent and his routine so invariable that Königsbergers reputedly set their watches by him: He was awakened daily at five A.M., read for two hours, lectured to his students for two hours, wrote for two hours, and then went to a restaurant for his midday meal, where, at the height of his fame, crowds of strangers would gather to see and hear him.

Kant began his career as a scientist rather than a metaphysician (his collected works include treatises on earthquakes and lunar volcanoes), and he may have turned to philosophy to determine for himself the boundaries between the physical questions that may result in positive knowledge and the moral and aesthetic questions that can only produce further speculation.

In his *Critique of Pure Reason* (1781), Kant shifted the entire basis of our understanding of perception by showing how the mind, previously considered a passive receptor of objective sense data, instead actively *creates* the sensual world of which we are conscious. But because each mind has essentially the same equipment and performs the same operations, and because these creative operations occur prior to consciousness, we are able — in fact, we are forced — to experience the world of the senses as though it were objectively present. This theory of the mind has had immense influence on critical theory. (See the headnote for Samuel Taylor Coleridge on p. 319 for a fuller discussion of Kant's theory of perception.) In his *Critique of Judgment* (1790), Kant takes a similar tack. Just as the sensual world is the product of our subjective mental processes rather than of objective features, so our judgments of beauty are also subjective. The beauty of a work of art or a natural landscape exists nowhere but in the eye of the beholder. Yet because of their special qualities, aesthetic judgments seem to have an objective character and to reflect universal rather than individual concerns.

Kant has an unenviable reputation as one of the most perversely difficult of philosophers. His language tends to be abstract, it is true, but he proceeds slowly and delights in giving examples. The major problem readers often have with the *Critique of Judgment* involves their misunderstanding of the exact nature of the questions Kant is trying to answer. He is not trying, as Plato might have done, to define the essence of Beauty, since for him, such essences have no meaning. Nor is he concerned, as Aristotle was, to note what features good works of art have in common. His interest is in the mind, not in the object: He is more of a psychologist than a metaphysician. His overriding question might be paraphrased as follows: When a person looks at a flower or listens to a symphony and experiences it as beautiful, what propositions does that moment of aesthetic judgment strictly entail? When someone looks at Velasquez's *Las Meninas* and exclaims in aesthetic delight, what mental experience is implicit in that exclamation? Kant analyzes that mental experience in a vigorous and systematic way, by running it through his list of categories (Quality, Quantity, Relation, Modality).

The first issue is Quality: What sort of mental process underlies the judgment that a work of art or of nature is beautiful? Here Kant distinguishes beauty from two other types of judgments, those of utility and ethical goodness. Something is useful when it is good for an individual (though it may not benefit anybody else); ethically good things — virtuous actions — are universally beneficial, since it is to each person's collective advantage that everyone act justly. But to judge something as beautiful is to approve of it *freely,* without considering individual or collective interests. (Obviously some works of art — like a Frank Lloyd Wright house — can be functional as well as beautiful, but the judgment of beauty, strictly speaking, has nothing to do with function.) Personal satisfaction in a thing of beauty, therefore, is entirely *disinterested.*

The second issue is Quantity. Some judgments we make — that something is *pleasant,* for example — are *singular:* We apply them purely as individuals. Someone might enjoy raspberries but without any sense that others should agree; if a friend says he detests raspberries, a rational reaction is "All the more for me!" Other judgments are *universal:* We apply them as individuals but with a sense that our judgment holds for all humankind. Ethical judgments are universal in this sense. If we are morally outraged at, for example, the Iranian persecution of the Baha'i faith, our judgment is combined with a sense that everyone ought to agree with us. According to Kant, the judgment of taste is *universal,* like moral judgments, not *singular,* like the judgment that something is pleasant; for to judge a thing as beautiful is also to *impute* that judgment implicitly to everyone else. Kant is not saying that aesthetic judgments are *in practice* universal, that everyone in fact agrees about what is and is not beautiful; he knew as well as Hume that human tastes differ enormously. His point is only that the *disinterested* quality of our sense of beauty makes us feel that, since there is nothing peculiar about us or our situation, everyone similarly placed ought to make the same judgment.

The third issue in the judgment of taste has to do with the "relations of purposes" inherent in it, which is the closest Kant comes to talking about the nature of beauty. His contemporaries had proposed that beauty was a matter of simple charm (Winckelmann) or the contemplation of perfection (Wolff). Kant disagreed: For him the central experience in a beautiful object is the form of "purposiveness without purpose" (*Zweckmässigkeit ohne Zweck*). That is, works of art and natural beauty evince relationships of parts to whole or means to end that are *like* artifacts that have purposes. The intricacy of the interaction of themes in a Bach fugue or the pattern of petals in a chrysanthemum is like the patterned intricacy of a precisely tooled machine; but the machine is made to serve another end — an exterior purpose — while the formal purposiveness in the fugue or the flower is an end in itself. However, Kant is never talking about what is objectively *in* the object we find beautiful. He is talking about the psychological experience of judgment and this sense of purposiveness-without-purpose as something that takes hold within us.

Kant's thesis under his final category, Modality, seems to follow from all that has gone before: Taste is an *exemplary* judgment. By this Kant means that our aesthetic feelings do not seem to be merely random; rather, they feel as though they were the *necessary* consequence of a rule, but one we cannot state. Our sense of beauty seems to be formed prior to conceptual knowledge, and its basis seems to be common sense. As a result, there can be (indeed, must be) disagreements about taste. But, as the proverb states, there cannot be *disputations* about taste, since there are no general, a priori principles to which we can rationally appeal.

In the second book, Kant takes up another common topic of late eighteenth-century aesthetics: the differences between the beautiful and the sublime. Consistently, Kant's interest is in psychological processes rather than in realities; he is less concerned to explain what things we consider sublime than to help us understand the motions of the mind when we experience it. Motion is important here, for the sublime is psychologically *dynamic,* while the beautiful is a matter of restful contemplation.

The movement of the mind that constitutes the sublime resembles one or the other of two mental acts: cognition or desire. But herein lies the paradox. We judge something to be sublime precisely when cognition fails — when in looking up into the starry sky, for instance, we experience a height, or depth, or magnitude that defies reason or is beyond our power to comprehend. On the other hand, it may be that the principles of rational desire are overthrown. When we contemplate something horrible and dangerous, like rocky cliffs or a storm at sea, and yet manage to stifle the imaginative desire to flee, we also experience the sublime. This means that the sublime depends on human reason, with its attendant limitations. An angelic or divine mind could experience the beautiful, as Kant defines it, but an omnipotent and omniscient God could not find his own handiwork sublime.

In Section 49, near the end of the *Critique of Judgment,* Kant shifts his interest from the (chiefly) eighteenth-century issue of *taste* to the quintessentially romantic issue of *genius,* from the psychological qualities involved in the reception of beauty to those involved in its creation.[1] His discussion is not developed at great length or in detail, but one can see in it many of the ideas that later German critics, such as Schiller, were to take up and that students of German philosophy, such as Coleridge, were to import into the English tradition.

Here we begin with Kant's presentation of the imagination as the primary mental faculty in genius, and one that is primarily *creative and intuitive* rather than *rational and cognitive.* The imagination indulges in the free play of spirit, breaking the laws that bind rational thought (though it follows laws of its own) and "creating another

---

[1]Kant here also shifts his attention away from the beauty of nature to that of art. Where Hume's essay on taste had taken the response of the spectator to *art* (especially poetry) as the typical moment of aesthetic judgment, Kant instead presented taste as the response to nature ("flowers," he says, "are typical free beauties"). Perhaps this is because in nature the forms of animals, plants, and landscapes seem clearly ends in themselves and our response to them almost unconditioned by social motives.

nature . . . out of the material that actual nature gives it." Genius consists of the ability to seize and make concrete this free play of spirit and then to embody it in a material that will make it universally communicable. In this final process, the imagination must work unfettered yet somehow under the control of the understanding. This enables the creator to get *outside* the creative process in order to assess the product of the imagination as it would appear to the spirit of another. Artists must therefore be at once creators and consumers: They must approach their creations from the outside, via their faculty of taste, to shape and mold them into proper form.

But on the other side, the consumer of art must also be, potentially, at least, a producer, because the product of the artist's free play is what Kant calls an *aesthetical idea.* Unlike a *rational idea,* an aesthetical idea calls up the faculty of cognition only to defeat it by employing more thought in the representation than we can clearly grasp. To comprehend aesthetical ideas embodied in a poem or painting requires the free play of the listener's or viewer's imagination as well.

In a sense, however, Kant had appealed to this free play of the spirit even in the earlier sections of the *Critique of Judgment* — particularly when he defined beauty as a product of the subjective sense of purposiveness (rational structure) cut loose from purpose itself. How could it be anything but a free play of the mind, untrammeled by the usually utilitarian (or ethical) notions of purpose, that could succeed in thus divorcing form from goal.

Selected Bibliography

Allison, Henry E. *Kant's Theory of Taste: A Reading of the Critique of Aesthetic Judgment.* Cambridge: Cambridge University Press, 2001.

Cassirer, H. W. *Commentary on Kant's Critique of Judgment.* London: Methuen, 1938.

Cohen, Ted, and Paul Guyer, eds. *Essays in Kant's Aesthetics.* Chicago: University of Chicago Press, 1982.

Coleman, Francis X. J. *The Harmony of Reason: A Study in Kant's Aesthetics.* Pittsburgh: University of Pittsburgh Press, 1974.

Crawford, Donald W. *Kant's Aesthetic Theory.* Madison: University of Wisconsin Press, 1974.

Gasché, Rodolphe, Mieke Bal, and Hent de Vries. *The Idea of Form: Rethinking Kant's Aesthetics.* Stanford: Stanford University Press, 2003.

Guyer, Paul. *Kant and the Claims of Taste.* Cambridge: Harvard University Press, 1979.

Jaspers, Karl. *Kant.* Munich: R. Piper, 1975.

McCloskey, Mary A. *Kant's Aesthetic.* Basingstoke, Hampshire: Macmillan, 1987.

Richardson, Robert Allan. *Aesthetics and Freedom: A Critique of Kant's Analysis of Beauty.* New Haven: Yale University Press, 1969.

Rogerson, Kenneth F. *Kant's Aesthetics: The Roles of Form and Expression.* Lanham, MD: University Press of America, 1986.

Schaper, Eva. *Studies in Kant's Aesthetics.* Edinburgh: University of Edinburgh Press, 1979.

Zimmerman, R. L. "Kant: The Aesthetic Judgment." *Journal of Aesthetics and Art Criticism* 21 (1963): 333–44.

From *Critique of Judgment*

First Book.
Analytic of the Beautiful

FIRST MOMENT. OF THE JUDGMENT OF TASTE,[1] ACCORDING TO QUALITY

1. The Judgment of Taste Is Aesthetical

In order to distinguish whether anything is beautiful or not, we refer the representation, not by the understanding to the object for cognition, but by the imagination (perhaps in conjunction with the understanding) to the subject and its feeling of pleasure or pain. The judgment of taste is therefore not a judgment of cognition, and is consequently not logical but aesthetical, by which we understand that whose determining ground can be *no other than subjective*. Every reference of representations, even that of sensations, may be objective (and then it signifies the real element of an empirical representation), save only the reference to the feeling of pleasure and pain, by which nothing in the object is signified, but through which there is a feeling in the subject as it is affected by the representation.

To apprehend a regular, purposive building by means of one's cognitive faculty (whether in a clear or a confused way of representation) is something quite different from being conscious of this representation as connected with the sensation of satisfaction. Here the representation is altogether referred to the subject and to its feeling of life, under the name of the feeling of pleasure or pain. This establishes a quite separate faculty of distinction and of judgment, adding nothing to cognition, but only comparing the given representation in the subject with the whole faculty of representations, of which the mind is conscious in the feeling of its state. Given representations in a judgment can be empirical (consequently, aesthetical); but the judgment which is formed by means of them is logical, provided they are referred in the judgment to the object. Conversely, if the given representations are rational, but are referred in a judgment simply to the subject (to its feeling), the judgment is so far always aesthetical.

2. The Satisfaction Which Determines the Judgment of Taste Is Disinterested

The satisfaction which we combine with the representation of the existence of an object is called "interest." Such satisfaction always has reference to the faculty of desire, either as its determining ground or as necessarily connected with its determining ground. Now when the question is if a thing is beautiful, we do not want to know whether anything depends or can depend on the existence of the thing, either for myself or for anyone else, but how we judge it by mere observation (intuition or reflection). If anyone asks me if I find that palace beautiful which I see before me, I may answer: I do not like things of that kind which are made merely to be stared at. Or I can answer like that Iroquois Sachem, who was pleased in Paris by nothing more than by the cook shops. Or again, after the manner of Rousseau, I may rebuke the vanity of the great who waste the sweat of the people on such superfluous things. In fine, I could easily convince myself that if I found myself on an uninhabited island without the hope of ever again coming among men, and could conjure up just such a splendid building by my mere wish, I should not even give myself the trouble if I had a sufficiently comfortable hut. This may all be admitted and approved, but we are not now talking of this. We wish only to know if this mere representation of the object is accompanied in me with satisfaction, however indifferent I may be as regards the existence of the object of this

---

Translated by J. H. Bernard.

[1]The definition of "taste" which is laid down here is that it is the faculty of judging of the beautiful. But the analysis of judgments of taste must show what is required in order to call an object beautiful. The moments to which this judgment has regard in its reflection I have sought in accordance with the guidance of the logical functions of judgment (for in a judgment of taste a reference to the understanding is always involved). I have considered the moment of quality first because the aesthetical judgment upon the beautiful first pays attention to it. [Kant]

representation. We easily see that, in saying it is *beautiful* and in showing that I have taste, I am concerned, not with that in which I depend on the existence of the object, but with that which I make out of this representation in myself. Everyone must admit that a judgment about beauty, in which the least interest mingles, is very partial and is not a pure judgment of taste. We must not be in the least prejudiced in favor of the existence of the things, but be quite indifferent in this respect, in order to play the judge in things of taste.

We cannot, however, better elucidate this proposition, which is of capital importance, than by contrasting the pure disinterested[2] satisfaction in judgments of taste with that which is bound up with an interest, especially if we can at the same time be certain that there are no other kinds of interest than those which are to be now specified.

3. The Satisfaction in the Pleasant Is Bound Up with Interest

That which pleases the senses in sensation is "pleasant." Here the opportunity presents itself of censuring a very common confusion of the double sense which the word "sensation" can have, and of calling attention to it. All satisfaction (it is said or thought) is itself sensation (of a pleasure). Consequently everything that pleases is pleasant because it pleases (and according to its different degrees or its relations to other pleasant sensations it is *agreeable, lovely, delightful, enjoyable,* etc.). But if this be admitted, then impressions of sense which determine the inclination, fundamental propositions of reason which determine the will, mere reflective forms of intuition which determine the judgment, are quite the same as regards the effect upon the feeling of pleasure. For this would be pleasantness in the sensation of one's state; and since in the end all the operations of our faculties must issue in the

practical and unite in it as their goal, we could suppose no other way of estimating things and their worth than that which consists in the gratification that they promise. It is of no consequence at all how this is attained, and since then the choice of means alone could make a difference, men could indeed blame one another for stupidity and indiscretion, but never for baseness and wickedness. For thus they all, each according to his own way of seeing things, seek one goal, that is, gratification.

If a determination of the feeling of pleasure or pain is called sensation, this expression signifies something quite different from what I mean when I call the representation of a thing (by sense, as a receptivity belonging to the cognitive faculty) sensation. For in the latter case the representation is referred to the object, in the former simply to the subject, and is available for no cognition whatever, not even for that by which the subject *cognizes* itself.

In the above elucidation we understand by the word "sensation" an objective representation of sense; and, in order to avoid misinterpretation, we shall call that which must always remain merely subjective and can constitute absolutely no representation of an object by the ordinary term "feeling." The green color of the meadows belongs to *objective* sensation, as a perception of an object of sense; the pleasantness of this belongs to *subjective* sensation by which no object is represented, i.e., to feeling, by which the object is considered as an object of satisfaction (which does not furnish a cognition of it).

Now that a judgment about an object by which I describe it as pleasant expresses an interest in it, is plain from the fact that by sensation it excites a desire for objects of that kind; consequently the satisfaction presupposes, not the mere judgment about it, but the relation of its existence to my state, so far as this is affected by such an object. Hence we do not merely say of the pleasant, *it pleases,* but, *it gratifies.* I give to it no mere assent, but inclination is aroused by it; and in the case of what is pleasant in the most lively fashion there is no judgment at all upon the character of the object, for those persons who always lay themselves out for enjoyment (for that is the word describing intense gratification) would fain dispense with all judgment.

---

[2]A judgment upon an object of satisfaction may be quite *disinterested,* but yet very *interesting,* i.e., not based upon an interest, but bringing an interest with it; of this kind are all pure moral judgments. Judgments of taste, however, do not in themselves establish any interest. Only in society is it *interesting* to have taste; the reason of this will be shown in the sequel. [Kant]

4. The Satisfaction in the Good Is Bound Up with Interest

Whatever by means of reason pleases through the mere concept is *good*. That which pleases only as a means we call *good for something* (the useful), but that which pleases for itself is *good in itself*. In both there is always involved the concept of a purpose, and consequently the relation of reason to the (at least possible) volition, and thus a satisfaction in the *presence* of an object or an action, i.e., some kind of interest.

In order to find anything good, I must always know what sort of a thing the object ought to be, i.e., I must have a concept of it. But there is no need of this to find a thing beautiful. Flowers, free delineations, outlines intertwined with one another without design and called conventional foliage, have no meaning, depend on no definite concept, and yet they please. The satisfaction in the beautiful must depend on the reflection upon an object, leading to any concept (however indefinite), and it is thus distinguished from the pleasant, which rests entirely upon sensation.

It is true, the pleasant seems in many cases to be the same as the good. Thus people are accustomed to say that all gratification (especially if it lasts) is good in itself, which is very much the same as to say that lasting pleasure and the good are the same. But we can soon see that this is merely a confusion of words, for the concepts which properly belong to these expressions can in no way be interchanged. The pleasant, which, as such, represents the object simply in relation to sense, must first be brought by the concept of a purpose under principles of reason, in order to call it good, as an object of the will. But that there is involved a quite different relation to satisfaction in calling that which gratifies at the same time *good* may be seen from the fact that, in the case of the good, the question always is whether it is mediately or immediately good (useful or good in itself); but on the contrary in the case of the pleasant, there can be no question about this at all, for the word always signifies something which pleases immediately. (The same is applicable to what I call beautiful.)

Even in common speech men distinguish the pleasant from the good. Of a dish which stimulates the taste by spices and other condiments we say unhesitatingly that it is pleasant, though it is at the same time admitted not to be good; for though it immediately *delights* the senses, yet mediately, i.e., considered by reason which looks to the after results, it displeases. Even in the judging of health we may notice this distinction. It is immediately pleasant to everyone possessing it (at least negatively, i.e., as the absence of all bodily pains). But in order to say that it is good, it must be considered by reason with reference to purposes, viz., that it is a state which makes us fit for all our business. Finally, in respect of happiness, everyone believes himself entitled to describe the greatest sum of the pleasantness of life (as regards both their number and their duration) as a true, even as the highest, good. However, reason is opposed to this. Pleasantness is enjoyment. And if we were concerned with this alone, it would be foolish to be scrupulous as regards the means which procure it for us, or to care whether it is obtained passively by the bounty of nature or by our own activity and work. But reason can never be persuaded that the existence of a man who merely lives for *enjoyment* (however busy he may be in this point of view) has a worth in itself, even if he at the same time is conducive as a means to the best enjoyment of others and shares in all their gratifications by sympathy. Only what he does, without reference to enjoyment, in full freedom and independently of what nature can procure for him passively, gives an absolute worth to his presence in the world as the existence of a person; and happiness, with the whole abundance of its pleasures, is far from being an unconditioned good.[3]

However, notwithstanding all this difference between the pleasant and the good, they both agree in this that they are always bound up with an interest in their object; so are not only the pleasant (§ 3), and the mediate good (the useful) which is pleasing as a means toward pleasantness

---

[3]An obligation to enjoyment is a manifest absurdity. Thus the obligation to all actions which have merely enjoyment for their aim can only be a pretended one, however spiritually it may be conceived (or decked out), even if it is a mystical, or so-called heavenly, enjoyment. [Kant]

somewhere, but also that which is good absolutely and in every aspect, viz., moral good, which brings with it the highest interest. For the good is the object of will (i.e., of a faculty of desire determined by reason). But to wish for something and to have a satisfaction in its existence, i.e., to take an interest in it, are identical.

5. Comparison of the Three Specifically Different Kinds of Satisfaction

The pleasant and the good have both a reference to the faculty of desire, and they bring with them, the former a satisfaction pathologically conditioned (by impulses, *stimuli*), the latter a pure practical satisfaction which is determined not merely by the representation of the object but also by the represented connection of the subject with the existence of the object. It is not merely the object that pleases, but also its existence. On the other hand, the judgment of taste is merely *contemplative;* i.e., it is a judgment which, indifferent as regards the existence of an object, compares its character with the feeling of pleasure and pain. But this contemplation itself is not directed to concepts; for the judgment of taste is not a cognitive judgment (either theoretical or practical), and thus is not *based* on concepts, nor has it concepts as its *purpose.*

The pleasant, the beautiful, and the good designate then three different relations of representations to the feeling of pleasure and pain, in reference to which we distinguish from one another objects or methods of representing them. And the expressions corresponding to each, by which we mark our complacency in them, are not the same. That which *gratifies* a man is called *pleasant;* that which merely *pleases* him is *beautiful;* that which is *esteemed* or *approved* by him, i.e., that to which he accords an objective worth, is *good.* Pleasantness concerns irrational animals also, but beauty only concerns men, i.e., animal, but still rational, beings — not merely *qua* rational (e.g., spirits), but *qua* animal also — and the good concerns every rational being in general. This is a proposition which can only be completely established and explained in the sequel. We may say that, of all these three kinds of satisfaction, that of taste in the beautiful is alone a disinterested and *free* satisfaction; for no interest, either of sense or of reason, here forces our assent. Hence we may say of satisfaction that it is related in the three aforesaid cases to *inclination,* to *favor,* or to *respect.* Now *favor* is the only free satisfaction. An object of inclination and one that is proposed to our desire by a law of reason leave us no freedom in forming for ourselves anywhere an object of pleasure. All interest presupposes or generates a want, and, as the determining ground of assent, it leaves the judgment about the object no longer free.

As regards the interest of inclination in the case of the pleasant, everyone says that hunger is the best sauce, and everything that is eatable is relished by people with a healthy appetite; and thus a satisfaction of this sort shows no choice directed by taste. It is only when the want is appeased that we can distinguish which of many men has or has not taste. In the same way there may be manners (conduct) without virtue, politeness without good will, decorum without modesty, etc. For where the moral law speaks there is no longer, objectively, a free choice as regards what is to be done; and to display taste in its fulfillment (or in judging of another's fulfillment of it) is something quite different from manifesting the moral attitude of thought. For this involves a command and generates a want, while moral taste only plays with the objects of satisfaction, without attaching itself to one of them.

Explanation of the Beautiful Resulting from the First Moment

Taste is the faculty of judging of an object or a method of representing it by an *entirely disinterested* satisfaction or dissatisfaction. The object of such satisfaction is called *beautiful.*[4]

---

[4]Ueberweg points out (*History of Philosophy, II,* 528, English translation) that Mendelssohn had already called attention to the disinterestedness of our satisfaction in the beautiful. "It appears," says Mendelssohn, "to be a particular mark of the beautiful, that it is contemplated with quiet satisfaction, that it pleases, even though it be not in our possession, and even though we be never so far removed from the desire to put it to our use." But, of course, as Ueberweg remarks, Kant's conception of disinterestedness extends far beyond the idea of merely not desiring to possess the object. [Tr.]

SECOND MOMENT. OF THE JUDGMENT OF TASTE, ACCORDING TO QUANTITY

6. The Beautiful Is That Which Apart from Concepts Is Represented as the Object of a Universal Satisfaction

This explanation of the beautiful can be derived from the preceding explanation of it as the object of an entirely disinterested satisfaction. For the fact of which everyone is conscious, that the satisfaction is for him quite disinterested, implies in his judgment a ground of satisfaction for all men. For since it does not rest on any inclination of the subject (nor upon any other premeditated interest), but since the person who judges feels himself quite *free* as regards the satisfaction which he attaches to the object, he cannot find the ground of this satisfaction in any private conditions connected with his own subject, and hence it must be regarded as grounded on what he can presuppose in every other person. Consequently he must believe that he has reason for attributing a similar satisfaction to everyone. He will therefore speak of the beautiful as if beauty were a characteristic of the object and the judgment logical (constituting a cognition of the object by means of concepts of it), although it is only aesthetical and involves merely a reference of the representation of the object to the subject. For it has this similarity to a logical judgment that we can presuppose its validity for all men. But this universality cannot arise from concepts; for from concepts there is no transition to the feeling of pleasure or pain (except in pure practical laws, which bring an interest with them such as is not bound up with the pure judgment of taste). Consequently the judgment of taste, accompanied with the consciousness of separation from all interest, must claim validity for every man, without this universality depending on objects. That is, there must be bound up with it a title to subjective universality.

7. Comparison of the Beautiful with the Pleasant and the Good by Means of the Above Characteristic

As regards the pleasant, everyone is content that his judgment, which he bases upon private feeling and by which he says of an object that it pleases him, should be limited merely to his own person. Thus he is quite contented that if he says, "Canary wine is pleasant," another man may correct his expression and remind him that he ought to say, "It is pleasant *to me*." And this is the case not only as regards the taste of the tongue, the palate, and the throat, but for whatever is pleasant to anyone's eyes and ears. To one, violet color is soft and lovely; to another, it is washed out and dead. One man likes the tone of wind instruments, another that of strings. To strive here with the design of reproving as incorrect another man's judgment which is different from our own, as if the judgments were logically opposed, would be folly. As regards the pleasant, therefore, the fundamental proposition is valid: *Everyone has his own taste* (the taste of sense).

The case is quite different with the beautiful. It would (on the contrary) be laughable if a man who imagined anything to his own taste thought to justify himself by saying: "The object (the house we see, the coat that person wears, the concert we hear, the poem submitted to our judgment) is beautiful *for me*." For he must not call it *beautiful* if it merely pleases him. Many things may have for him charm and pleasantness — no one troubles himself at that — but if he gives out anything as beautiful, he supposes in others the same satisfaction; he judges not merely for himself, but for everyone, and speaks of beauty as if it were a property of things. Hence he says "the *thing* is beautiful"; and he does not count on the agreement of others with this his judgment of satisfaction, because he has found this agreement several times before, but he *demands* it of them. He blames them if they judge otherwise and he denies them taste, which he nevertheless requires from them. Here, then, we cannot say that each man has his own particular taste. For this would be as much as to say that there is no taste whatever, i.e., no aesthetical judgment which can make a rightful claim upon everyone's assent.

At the same time we find as regards the pleasant that there is an agreement among men in their judgments upon it in regard to which we deny taste to some and attribute it to others, by this not meaning one of our organic senses, but a faculty of judging in respect of the pleasant generally. Thus we say of a man who knows how to entertain his guests with pleasures (of enjoyment for all the senses), so that they are all pleased, "he has taste." But here the universality is only taken comparatively; and there emerge rules which are only *general* (like all empirical ones), and not *universal,* which latter the judgment of taste upon the beautiful undertakes or lays claim to. It is a judgment in reference to sociability, so far as this rests on empirical rules. In respect of the good it is true that judgments make rightful claim to validity for everyone; but the good is represented only *by means of a concept* as the object of a universal satisfaction, which is the case neither with the pleasant nor with the beautiful.

8. The Universality of the Satisfaction Is Represented in a Judgment of Taste Only as Subjective

This particular determination of the universality of an aesthetical judgment, which is to be met with in a judgment of taste, is noteworthy, not indeed for the logician, but for the transcendental philosopher. It requires no small trouble to discover its origin, but we thus detect a property of our cognitive faculty which without this analysis would remain unknown.

First, we must be fully convinced of the fact that in a judgment of taste (about the beautiful) the satisfaction in the object is imputed to *everyone,* without being based on a concept (for then it would be the good). Further, this claim to universal validity so essentially belongs to a judgment by which we describe anything as *beautiful* that, if this were not thought in it, it would never come into our thoughts to use the expression at all, but everything which pleases without a concept would be counted as pleasant. In respect of the latter, everyone has his own opinion; and no one assumes in another agreement with his judgment of taste, which is always the case in a judgment of taste about beauty. I may call the first the taste of sense, the second the taste of reflection, so far as the first lays down mere private judgments and the second judgments supposed to be generally valid (public), but in both cases aesthetical (not practical) judgments about an object merely in respect of the relation of its representation to the feeling of pleasure and pain. Now here is

something strange. As regards the taste of sense, not only does experience show that its judgment (of pleasure or pain connected with anything) is not valid universally, but everyone is content not to impute agreement with it to others (although actually there is often found a very extended concurrence in these judgments). On the other hand, the taste of reflection has its claim to the universal validity of its judgments (about the beautiful) rejected often enough, as experience teaches, although it may find it possible (as it actually does) to represent judgments which can demand this universal agreement. In fact it imputes this to everyone for each of its judgments of taste, without the persons that judge disputing as to the possibility of such a claim, although in particular cases they cannot agree as to the correct application of this faculty.

Here we must, in the first place, remark that a universality which does not rest on concepts of objects (not even on empirical ones) is not logical but aesthetical; i.e., it involves no objective quantity of the judgment, but only that which is subjective. For this I use the expression *general validity,* which signifies the validity of the reference of a representation, not to the cognitive faculty, but to the feeling of pleasure and pain for every subject. (We can avail ourselves also of the same expression for the logical quantity of the judgment, if only we prefix "objective" to "universal validity," to distinguish it from that which is merely subjective and aesthetical.)

A judgment with *objective universal validity* is also always valid subjectively; i.e., if the judgment holds for everything contained under a given concept, it holds also for everyone who represents an object by means of this concept. But from a *subjective universal validity,* i.e., aesthetical and resting on no concept, we cannot infer that which is logical because that kind of judgment does not extend to the object. But, therefore, the aesthetical universality which is ascribed to a judgment must be of a particular kind, because it does not unite the predicate of beauty with the concept of the object, considered in its whole logical sphere, and yet extends it to the whole sphere of judging persons.

In respect of logical quantity, all judgments of taste are *singular* judgments. For because I must refer the object immediately to my feeling of pleasure and pain, and that not by means of concepts, they cannot have the quantity of objective generally valid judgments. Nevertheless, if the singular representation of the object of the judgment of taste, in accordance with the conditions determining the latter, were transformed by comparison into a concept, a logically universal judgment could result therefrom. E.g., I describe by a judgment of taste the rose that I see as beautiful. But the judgment which results from the comparison of several singular judgments, "Roses in general are beautiful," is no longer described simply as aesthetical, but as a logical judgment based on an aesthetical one. Again the judgment, "The rose is pleasant" (to use) is, although aesthetical and singular, not a judgment of taste but of sense. It is distinguished from the former by the fact that the judgment of taste carries with it an *aesthetic quantity* of universality, i.e., of validity for everyone, which cannot be found in a judgment about the pleasant. It is only judgments about the good which, although they also determine satisfaction in an object, have logical and not merely aesthetical universality, for they are valid of the object as cognitive of it, and thus are valid for everyone.

If we judge objects merely according to concepts, then all representation of beauty is lost. Thus there can be no rule according to which anyone is to be forced to recognize anything as beautiful. We cannot press [upon others] by the aid of any reasons or fundamental propositions our judgment that a coat, a house, or a flower is beautiful. People wish to submit the object to their own eyes, as if the satisfaction in it depended on sensation; and yet, if we then call the object beautiful, we believe that we speak with a universal voice, and we claim the assent of everyone, although on the contrary all private sensation can only decide for the observer himself and his satisfaction.

We may see now that in the judgment of taste nothing is postulated but such a *universal voice,* in respect of the satisfaction without the intervention of concepts, and thus the *possibility* of an aesthetical judgment that can, at the same time, be regarded as valid for everyone. The judgment of taste itself does not *postulate* the agreement of everyone (for that can only be done by a logically universal judgment because it can adduce reasons); it only *imputes* this agreement to everyone, as a case of the rule in respect of which it expects, not confirmation by concepts, but assent from others. The universal voice is, therefore, only an idea (we do not yet inquire upon what it rests). It may be uncertain whether or not the man who believes that he is laying down a judgment of taste is, as a matter of fact, judging in conformity with that idea; but that he refers his judgment thereto, and consequently that it is intended to be a judgment of taste, he announces by the expression "beauty." He can be quite certain of this for himself by the mere consciousness of the separating off everything belonging to the pleasant and the good from the satisfaction which is left; and this is all for which he promises himself the agreement of everyone — a claim which would be justifiable under these conditions, provided only he did not often make mistakes, and thus lay down an erroneous judgment of taste. . . .

Explanation of the Beautiful
Resulting from the Second Moment

The *beautiful* is that which pleases universally without requiring a concept.

THIRD MOMENT. OF JUDGMENTS OF TASTE, ACCORDING TO THE RELATION OF THE PURPOSES WHICH ARE BROUGHT INTO CONSIDERATION IN THEM

10. Of Purposiveness in General

If we wish to explain what a purpose is according to its transcendental determinations (without presupposing anything empirical like the feeling of pleasure), we say that the purpose is the object of a concept, insofar as the concept is regarded as the cause of the object (the real ground of its possibility); and the causality of a *concept* in respect of its *object* is its purposiveness (*forma finalis*). Where then not merely the cognition of an object but the object itself (its form and existence) is thought as an effect only possible by means of the concept of this latter, there we think a purpose.

The representation of the effect is here the determining ground of its cause and precedes it. The consciousness of the causality of a representation, for *maintaining* the subject in the same state, may here generally denote what we call pleasure; while on the other hand pain is that representation which contains the ground of the determination of the state of representations into their opposite of restraining or removing them.[5]

The faculty of desire, so far as it is determinable to act only through concepts, i.e., in conformity with the representation of a purpose, would be the will. But an object, or a state of mind, or even an action is called purposive, although its possibility does not necessarily presuppose the representation of a purpose, merely because its possibility can be explained and conceived by us only so far as we assume for its ground a causality according to purposes, i.e., in accordance with a will which has regulated it according to the representation of a certain rule. There can be, then, purposiveness without purpose, so far as we do not place the causes of this form in a will, but yet can only make the explanation of its possibility intelligible to ourselves by deriving it from a will. Again, we are not always forced to regard what we observe (in respect of its possibility) from the point of view of reason. Thus we can at least observe a purposiveness according to form, without basing it on a purpose (as the material of the *nexus finalis*), and remark it in objects, although only by reflection.

11. The Judgment of Taste Has Nothing at Its Basis but the Form of the Purposiveness of an Object (or of Its Mode of Representation)

Every purpose, if it be regarded as a ground of satisfaction, always carries with it an interest — as the determining ground of the judgment — about the object of pleasure. Therefore no subjective purpose can lie at the basis of the judgment

---

[5]Mr. Herbert Spencer expresses much more concisely what Kant has in his mind here. "Pleasure . . . is a feeling which we seek to bring into consciousness and retain there; pain is . . . a feeling which we seek to get out of consciousness and to keep out." *Principles of Psychology,* 125. [Tr.]

of taste. But also the judgment of taste can be determined by no representation of an objective purpose, i.e., of the possibility of the object itself in accordance with principles of purposive combination, and consequently by no concept of the good, because it is an aesthetical and not a cognitive judgment. It therefore has to do with no *concept* of the character and internal or external possibility of the object by means of this or that cause, but merely with the relation of the representative powers to one another, so far as they are determined by a representation.

Now this relation in the determination of an object as beautiful is bound up with the feeling of pleasure, which is declared by the judgment of taste to be valid for everyone; hence a pleasantness merely accompanying the representation can as little contain the determining ground of the judgment as the representation of the perfection of the object and the concept of the good can. Therefore it can be nothing else than the subjective purposiveness in the representation of an object without any purpose (either objective or subjective), and thus it is the mere form of purposiveness in the representation by which an object is *given* to us, so far as we are conscious of it, which constitutes the satisfaction that we without a concept judge to be universally communicable; and, consequently, this is the determining ground of the judgment of taste.

12. The Judgment of Taste Rests on A Priori *Grounds*

To establish *a priori* the connection of the feeling of a pleasure or pain as an effect, with any representation whatever (sensation or concept) as its cause, is absolutely impossible, for that would be a particular causal relation which (with objects of experience) can always only be cognized *a posteriori* and through the medium of experience itself. We actually have, indeed, in the *Critique of Practical Reason,* derived from universal moral concepts *a priori* the feeling of respect (as a special and peculiar modification of feeling which will not strictly correspond either to the pleasure or the pain that we get from empirical objects). But there we could go beyond the bounds of experience and call in a causality which rested on a supersensible attribute of the subject, viz., freedom. And even there, properly speaking, it was not this *feeling* which we derived from the idea of the moral as cause, but merely the determination of the will. But the state of mind which accompanies any determination of the will is in itself a feeling of pleasure and identical with it, and therefore does not follow from it as its effect. This last must only be assumed if the concept of the moral as a good precedes the determination of the will by the law, for in that case the pleasure that is bound up with the concept could not be derived from it as from a mere cognition.

Now the case is similar with the pleasure in aesthetical judgments, only that here it is merely contemplative and does not bring about an interest in the object, while on the other hand in the moral judgment it is practical.[6] The consciousness of the mere formal purposiveness in the play of the subject's cognitive powers, in a representation through which an object is given, is the pleasure itself, because it contains a determining ground of the activity of the subject in respect of the excitement of its cognitive powers, and therefore an inner causality (which is purposive) in respect of cognition in general, without however being limited to any definite cognition, and consequently contains a mere form of the subjective purposiveness of a representation in an aesthetical judgment. This pleasure is in no way practical, neither like that arising from the pathological ground of pleasantness, nor that from the intellectual ground of the presented good. But yet it involves causality, viz., of *maintaining* without further design the state of the representation itself and the occupation of the cognitive powers. We *linger* over the contemplation of the beautiful because this contemplation strengthens and

<hr>

[6]Cf. *Metaphysic of Morals*, Introduction I. "The pleasure which is necessarily bound up with the desire (of the object whose representation affects feeling) may be called *practical* pleasure, whether it be cause or effect of the desire. On the contrary, the pleasure which is not necessarily bound up with the desire of the object, and which, therefore, is at bottom not a pleasure in the existence of the object of the representation, but clings to the representation only, may be called mere contemplative pleasure or *passive satisfaction*. The feeling of the latter kind of pleasure we call *taste*." [Tr.]

reproduces itself, which is analogous to (though not of the same kind as) that lingering which takes place when a physical charm in the representation of the object repeatedly arouses the attention, the mind being passive. . . .

16. The Judgment of Taste, by Which an Object Is Declared to Be Beautiful Under the Condition of a Definite Concept, Is Not Pure

There are two kinds of beauty: free beauty (*pulchritudo vaga*), or merely dependent beauty (*pulchritudo adhaerens*). The first presupposes no concept of what the object ought to be; the second does presuppose such a concept and the perfection of the object in accordance therewith. The first is called the (self-subsistent) beauty of this or that thing; the second, as dependent upon a concept (conditioned beauty), is ascribed to objects which come under the concept of a particular purpose.

Flowers are free natural beauties. Hardly anyone but a botanist knows what sort of a thing a flower ought to be; and even he, though recognizing in the flower the reproductive organ of the plant, pays no regard to this natural purpose if he is passing judgment on the flower by taste. There is, then, at the basis of this judgment no perfection of any kind, no internal purposiveness, to which the collection of the manifold is referred. Many birds (such as the parrot, the hummingbird, the bird of paradise) and many seashells are beauties in themselves, which do not belong to any object determined in respect of its purpose by concepts, but please freely and in themselves. So also delineations *à la grecque,* foliage for borders or wall papers, mean nothing in themselves; they represent nothing — no object under a definite concept — and are free beauties. We can refer to the same class what are called in music phantasies (i.e., pieces without any theme), and in fact all music without words.

In the judging of a free beauty (according to the mere form), the judgment of taste is pure. There is presupposed no concept of any purpose which the manifold of the given object is to serve, and which therefore is to be represented in it. By such a concept the freedom of the imagination which disports itself in the contemplation of the figure would be only limited.

But human beauty (i.e., of a man, a woman, or a child), the beauty of a horse, or a building (be it church, palace, arsenal, or summer house), presupposes a concept of the purpose which determines what the thing is to be, and consequently a concept of its perfection; it is therefore adherent beauty. Now as the combination of the pleasant (in sensation) with beauty, which properly is only concerned with form, is a hindrance to the purity of the judgment of taste, so also is its purity injured by the combination with beauty of the good (viz., that manifold which is good for the thing itself in accordance with its purpose).

We could add much to a building which would immediately please the eye if only it were not to be a church. We could adorn a figure with all kinds of spirals and light but regular lines, as the New Zealanders do with their tattooing, if only it were not the figure of a human being. And again this could have much finer features and a more pleasing and gentle cast of countenance provided it were not intended to represent a man, much less a warrior.

Now the satisfaction in the manifold of a thing in reference to the internal purpose which determines its possibility is a satisfaction grounded on a concept; but the satisfaction in beauty is such as presupposes no concept, but is immediately bound up with the representation through which the object is given (not through which it is thought). If now the judgment of taste in respect of the beauty of a thing is made dependent on the purpose in its manifold, like a judgment of reason, and thus limited, it is no longer a free and pure judgment of taste.

It is true that taste gains by this combination of aesthetical with intellectual satisfaction, inasmuch as it becomes fixed; and though it is not universal, yet in respect to certain purposively determined objects it becomes possible to prescribe rules for it. These, however, are not rules of taste, but merely rules for the unification of taste with reason, i.e., of the beautiful with the good, by which the former becomes available as an instrument of design in respect of the latter. Thus the tone of mind which is self-maintaining and of subjective universal validity is subordinated to the way of thinking which can be maintained only by painful resolve, but is of objective universal validity. Properly speaking, however, perfection gains nothing by beauty, or beauty by perfection; but when we compare the representation by which an object is given to us with the object (as regards what it ought to be) by means of a concept, we cannot avoid considering along with it the sensation in the subject. And thus when both states of mind are in harmony our *whole faculty* of representative power gains.

A judgment of taste, then, in respect of an object with a definite internal purpose, can only be pure if either the person judging has no concept of this purpose or else abstracts from it in his judgment. Such a person, although forming an accurate judgment of taste in judging of the object as free beauty, would yet by another who considers the beauty in it only as a dependent attribute (who looks to the purpose of the object) be blamed and accused of false taste, although both are right in their own way — the one in reference to what he has before his eyes, the other in reference to what he has in his thought. By means of this distinction we can settle many disputes about beauty between judges of taste, by showing that the one is speaking of free, the other of dependent, beauty — that the first is making a pure, the second an applied, judgment of taste. . . .

Explanation of the Beautiful
Derived from This Third Moment

Beauty is the form of the *purposiveness* of an object, so far as this is perceived in it *without any representation of a purpose.*[7]

---

[7] It might be objected to this explanation that there are things in which we see a purposive form without cognizing any purpose in them, like the stone implements often gotten from old sepulchral tumuli with a hole in them, as if for a handle. These, although they plainly indicate by their shape a purposiveness of which we do not know the purpose, are nevertheless not described as beautiful. But if we regard a thing as a work of art, that is enough to make us admit that its shape has reference to some design and definite purpose. And hence there is no immediate satisfaction in the contemplation of it. On the other hand a flower, e.g., a tulip, is regarded as beautiful, because in perceiving it we find a certain purposiveness which, in our judgment, is referred to no purpose at all. [Kant]

FOURTH MOMENT. OF THE JUDGMENT OF TASTE, ACCORDING TO THE MODALITY OF THE SATISFACTION IN THE OBJECT

18. What the Modality in a Judgment of Taste Is

I can say of every representation that it is at least *possible* that (as a cognition) it should be bound up with a pleasure. Of a representation that I call *pleasant* I say that it *actually* excites pleasure in me. But the *beautiful* we think as having a *necessary* reference to satisfaction. Now this necessity is of a peculiar kind. It is not a theoretical objective necessity, in which case it would be cognized *a priori* that everyone *will feel* this satisfaction in the object called beautiful by me. It is not a practical necessity, in which case, by concepts of a pure rational will serving as a rule for freely acting beings, the satisfaction is the necessary result of an objective law and only indicates that we absolutely (without any further design) ought to act in a certain way. But the necessity which is thought in an aesthetical judgment can only be called exemplary, i.e., a necessity of the assent of *all* to a judgment which is regarded as the example of a universal rule that we cannot state. Since an aesthetical judgment is not an objective cognitive judgment, this necessity cannot be derived from definite concepts and is therefore not apodictic. Still less can it be inferred from the universality of experience (of a complete agreement of judgments as to the beauty of a certain object). For not only would experience hardly furnish sufficiently numerous vouchers for this, but also, on empirical judgments, we can base no concept of the necessity of these judgments.

19. The Subjective Necessity, Which We Ascribe to the Judgment of Taste, Is Conditioned

The judgment of taste requires the agreement of everyone, and he who describes anything as beautiful claims that everyone *ought* to give his approval to the object in question and also describe it as beautiful. The *ought* in the aesthetical judgment is therefore pronounced in accordance with all the data which are required for judging, and yet is only conditioned. We ask for the agreement of everyone else, because we have for it a ground that is common to all; and we could count on this agreement, provided we were always sure that the case was correctly subsumed under that ground as rule of assent.

20. The Condition of Necessity Which a Judgment of Taste Asserts Is the Idea of a Common Sense

If judgments of taste (like cognitive judgments) had a definite objective principle, then the person who lays them down in accordance with this latter would claim an unconditioned necessity for his judgment. If they were devoid of all principle, like those of the mere taste of sense, we would not allow them in thought any necessity whatever. Hence they must have a subjective principle which determines what pleases or displeases only by feeling and not by concepts, but yet with universal validity. But such a principle could only be regarded as a *common sense,* which is essentially different from common understanding which people sometimes call common sense (*sensus communis*); for the latter does not judge by feeling but always by concepts, although ordinarily only as by obscurely represented principles.

Hence it is only under the presupposition that there is a common sense (by which we do not understand an external sense, but the effect resulting from the free play of our cognitive powers) — it is only under this presupposition, I say, that the judgment of taste can be laid down. . . .

Explanation of the Beautiful Resulting from the Fourth Moment

The *beautiful* is that which without any concept is cognized as the object of a *necessary* satisfaction.

GENERAL REMARK ON THE FIRST SECTION OF THE ANALYTIC

If we seek the result of the preceding analysis, we find that everything runs up into this concept of taste — that it is a faculty for judging an object in reference to the imagination's *free conformity to law*. Now, if in the judgment of taste the imagination must be considered in its freedom, it is in the first place not regarded as reproductive, as it is subject to the laws of association, but as productive and spontaneous (as the author of arbitrary forms of possible intuition). And although in the apprehension of a given object of sense it is tied to a definite form of this object and so far has no free play (such as that of poetry), yet it may readily be conceived that the object can furnish it with such a form containing a collection of the manifold as the imagination itself, if it were left free, would project in accordance with the *conformity to law of the understanding* in general. But that the *imaginative power* should be *free* and yet *of itself conformed to law,* i.e., bringing autonomy with it, is a contradiction. The understanding alone gives the law. If, however, the imagination is compelled to proceed according to a definite law, its product in respect of form is determined by concepts as to what it ought to be. But then, as is above shown, the satisfaction is not that in the beautiful, but in the good (in perfection, at any rate in mere formal perfection), and the judgment is not a judgment of taste. Hence it is a conformity to law without a law; and a subjective agreement of the imagination and understanding — without such an objective agreement as there is when the representation is referred to a definite concept of an object — can subsist along with the free conformity to law of the understanding (which is also called purposiveness without purpose) and with the peculiar feature of a judgment of taste.

Now geometrically regular figures, such as a circle, a square, a cube, etc., are commonly adduced by critics of taste as the simplest and most indisputable examples of beauty, and yet they are called regular because we can only represent them by regarding them as mere presentations of a definite concept which prescribes the rule of the figure (according to which alone it is possible). One of these two must be wrong, either that judgment of the critic which ascribes beauty to the said figures, or ours which regards purposiveness apart from a concept as requisite for beauty.

Hardly anyone will say that a man must have taste in order that he should find more satisfaction in a circle than in a scrawled outline, in an equilateral and equiangular quadrilateral than in which is oblique, irregular, and as it were deformed, for this belongs to the ordinary understanding and is not taste at all. Where, e.g., our design is to judge of the size of an area or to make intelligible the relation of the parts of it, when divided, to one another and to the whole, then regular figures and those of the simplest kind are needed, and the satisfaction does not rest immediately on the aspect of the figure, but on its availability for all kinds of possible designs. A room whose walls form oblique angles, or a parterre of this kind, even every violation of symmetry in the figure of animals (e.g., being one-eyed), of buildings, or of flower beds, displeases because it contradicts the purpose of the thing, not only practically in respect of a definite use of it, but also when we pass judgment on it as regards any possible design. This is not the case in the judgment of taste, which when pure combines satisfaction or dissatisfaction — without any reference to its use or to a purpose — with the mere *consideration* of the object.

The regularity which leads to the concept of an object is indeed the indispensable condition (*conditio sine qua non*) for grasping the object in a single representation and determining the manifold in its form. This determination is a purpose in respect of cognition, and in reference to this it is always bound up with satisfaction (which accompanies the execution of every, even problematical, design). There is here, however, merely the approval of the solution satisfying a problem, and not a free and indefinite purposive entertainment of the mental powers with what we call beautiful, where the understanding is at the service of imagination, and not *vice versa.*

In a thing that is only possible by means of design — a building, or even an animal — the regularity consisting in symmetry must express the unity of the intuition that accompanies the concept of purpose, and this regularity belongs to cognition. But where only a free play of the representative powers (under the condition, however, that the understanding is to suffer no shock thereby) is to be kept up, in pleasure gardens, room decorations, all kinds of tasteful furniture, etc., regularity that shows constraint is avoided as much as possible. Thus in the English taste in gardens or in bizarre taste in furniture, the freedom of the imagination is pushed almost near to the grotesque, and in this separation from every constraint of rule we have the case where taste can display its greatest perfection in the enterprises of the imagination.

All stiff regularity (such as approximates to mathematical regularity) has something in it repugnant to taste; for our entertainment in the contemplation of it lasts for no length of time, but it rather, insofar as it has not expressly in view cognition or a definite practical purpose, produces weariness. On the other hand, that with which imagination can play in an unstudied and purposive manner is always new to us, and one does not get tired of looking at it. Marsden, in his description of Sumatra, makes the remark that the free beauties of nature surround the spectator everywhere and thus lose their attraction for him.[8] On the other hand, a pepper garden, where the stakes on which this plant twines itself form parallel rows, had much attractiveness for him if he met with it in the middle of a forest. And he hence infers that wild beauty, apparently irregular, only pleases as a variation from the regular beauty of which one has seen enough. But he need only have made the experiment of spending one day in a pepper garden to have been convinced that, if the understanding has put itself in accordance with the order that it always needs by means of regularity, the object will not entertain for long — nay, rather it will impose a burdensome constraint upon the imagination. On the other hand, nature, which there is prodigal in its variety even to luxuriance, that is subjected to no constraint of artificial rules, can supply constant food for taste. Even the song of birds, which we can bring under no musical rule, seems to have more freedom, and therefore more for taste, than a song of a human being which is produced in accordance with all the rules of music; for we very much sooner weary of the latter if it is repeated often and at length. Here, however, we probably confuse our participation in the mirth of a little creature that we love with the beauty of its song, for

[8]W. Marsden, *The History of Sumatra* (London, 1783), p. 113. [Tr.]

if this were exactly imitated by man (as sometimes the notes of the nightingale are), it would seem to our ear quite devoid of taste.

Again, beautiful objects are to be distinguished from beautiful views of objects (which often on account of their distance cannot be more clearly cognized). In the latter case taste appears, not so much in what the imagination *apprehends* in this field, as in the impulse it thus gets to *fiction,* i.e., in the peculiar fancies with which the mind entertains itself, while it is continually being aroused by the variety which strikes the eye. An illustration is afforded, e.g., by the sight of the changing shapes of a fire on the hearth or of a rippling brook; neither of these has beauty, but they bring with them a charm for the imagination because they entertain it in free play.

Second Book.
Analytic of the Sublime

23. Transition from the Faculty Which Judges of the Beautiful to That Which Judges of the Sublime

The beautiful and the sublime agree in this that both please in themselves. Further, neither presupposes a judgment of sense nor a judgment logically determined, but a judgment of reflection. Consequently the satisfaction belonging to them does not depend on a sensation, as in the case of the pleasant, nor on a definite concept, as in the case of the good; but it is nevertheless referred to concepts, although indeterminate ones. And so the satisfaction is connected with the mere presentation of the object or with the faculty of presentation, so that in the case of a given intuition this faculty or the imagination is considered as in agreement with the *faculty of concepts* of understanding or reason, regarded as promoting these latter. Hence both kinds of judgments are *singular,* and yet announce themselves as universally valid for every subject; although they lay claim merely to the feeling of pleasure, and not to any cognition of the object.

But there are also remarkable differences between the two. The beautiful in nature is connected with the form of the object, which consists in having definite boundaries. The sublime, on the other hand, is to be found in a formless object, so far as in it or by occasion of it *boundlessness* is represented, and yet its totality is also present to thought. Thus the beautiful seems to be regarded as the presentation of an indefinite concept of understanding, the sublime as that of a like concept of reason. Therefore the satisfaction in the one case is bound up with the representation of *quality,* in the other with that of *quantity.* And the latter satisfaction is quite different in kind from the former, for the beautiful directly brings with it a feeling of the furtherance of life, and thus is compatible with charms and with the play of the imagination. But the feeling of the sublime is a pleasure that arises only indirectly; viz., it is produced by the feeling of a momentary checking of the vital powers and a consequent stronger outflow of them, so that it seems to be regarded as emotion — not play, but earnest in the exercise of the imagination. Hence it is incompatible with physical charm; and as the mind is not merely attracted by the object but is ever being alternately repelled, the satisfaction in the sublime does not so much involve a positive pleasure as admiration or respect, which rather deserves to be called negative pleasure.

But the inner and most important distinction between the sublime and beautiful is, certainly, as follows. (Hence, as we are entitled to do, we only bring under consideration in the first instance the sublime in natural objects, for the sublime of art is always limited by the conditions of agreement with nature.) Natural beauty (which is independent) brings with it a purposiveness in its form by which the object seems to be, as it were, preadapted to our judgment, and thus constitutes in itself an object of satisfaction. On the other hand, that which excites in us, without any reasoning about it, but in the mere apprehension of it, the feeling of the sublime may appear, as regards its form, to violate purpose in respect of the judgment, to be unsuited to our presentative faculty, and as it were to do violence to the imagination; and yet it is judged to be only the more sublime.

Now we may see from this that, in general, we express ourselves incorrectly if we call any *object of nature* sublime, although we can quite correctly call many objects of nature beautiful. For how can that be marked by an expression of

approval which is apprehended in itself as being a violation of purpose? All that we can say is that the object is fit for the presentation of a sublimity which can be found in the mind, for no sensible form can contain the sublime properly so-called. This concerns only ideas of the reason which, although no adequate presentation is possible for them, by this inadequateness that admits of sensible presentation are aroused and summoned into the mind. Thus the wide ocean, disturbed by the storm, cannot be called sublime. Its aspect is horrible; and the mind must be already filled with manifold ideas if it is to be determined by such an intuition to a feeling itself sublime, as it is incited to abandon sensibility and to busy itself with ideas that involve higher purposiveness.

Independent natural beauty discovers to us a technique of nature which represents it as a system in accordance with laws, the principle of which we do not find in the whole of our faculty of understanding. That principle is the principle of purposiveness, in respect of the use of our judgment in regard to phenomena, which requires that these must not be judged as merely belonging to nature in its purposeless mechanism, but also as belonging to something analogous to art. It therefore actually extends, not indeed our cognition of natural objects, but our concept of nature, which is now not regarded as mere mechanism but as art. This leads to profound investigations as to the possibility of such a form. But in what we are accustomed to call sublime there is nothing at all that leads to particular objective principles and forms of nature corresponding to them; so far from it that, for the most part, nature excites the ideas of the sublime in its chaos or in its wildest and most irregular disorder and desolation, provided size and might are perceived. Hence, we see that the concept of the sublime is not nearly so important or rich in consequences as the concept of the beautiful; and that, in general, it displays nothing purposive in nature itself, but only in that possible use of our intuitions of it by which there is produced in us a feeling of a purposiveness quite independent of nature. We must seek a ground external to ourselves for the beautiful of nature, but seek it for the sublime merely in ourselves and in our attitude of thought, which introduces sublimity into the representation of nature.

This is a very needful preliminary remark, which quite separates the ideas of the sublime from that of a purposiveness of *nature* and makes the theory of the sublime a mere appendix to the aesthetical judging of that purposiveness, because by means of it no particular form is represented in nature, but there is only developed a purposive use which the imagination makes of its representation.

24. *Of the Divisions of an Investigation into the Feeling of the Sublime*

As regards the division of the moments of the aesthetical judging of objects in reference to the feeling of the sublime, the Analytic can proceed according to the same principle as was adopted in the analysis of judgments of taste. For as an act of the aesthetical reflective judgment, the satisfaction in the sublime must be represented just as in the case of the beautiful — according to *quantity* as universally valid, according to *quality* as devoid of *interest,* according to *relation* as subjective purposiveness, and according to *modality* as necessary. And so the method here will not diverge from that of the preceding section, unless indeed we count it a difference that in the case where the aesthetical judgment is concerned with the form of the object we began with the investigation of its quality, but here, in view of the formlessness which may belong to what we call sublime, we will begin with quantity, as the first moment of the aesthetical judgment as to the sublime. The reason for this may be seen from the preceding paragraph.

But the analysis of the sublime involves a division not needed in the case of the beautiful, viz., a division into the *mathematically* and the *dynamically sublime.*

For the feeling of the sublime brings with it as its characteristic feature a *movement* of the mind bound up with the judging of the object, while in the case of the beautiful taste presupposes and maintains the mind in *restful* contemplation. Now this movement ought to be judged as subjectively purposive (because the sublime pleases us), and thus it is referred through the imagination either to the *faculty of cognition* or *of desire.* In either reference the purposiveness of the given representation ought to be judged only in respect of this *faculty* (without purpose or interest), but in the first case, it is ascribed to the object as a *mathematical* determination of the imagination, in the second as *dynamical.* And hence we have this twofold way of representing the sublime.

A. OF THE MATHEMATICALLY SUBLIME

25. *Explanation of the Term Sublime*

We call that *sublime* which is *absolutely great.* But to be great and to be a great something are quite different concepts (*magnitudo* and *quantitas*). In like manner to say simply (*simpliciter*) that anything is *great* is quite different from saying that it is *absolutely great* (*absolute, non comparative magnum*). The latter is *what is great beyond all comparison.* What now is meant by the expression that anything is great or small or of medium size? It is not a pure concept of understanding that is thus signified; still less is it an intuition of sense; and just as little is it a concept of reason, because it brings with it no principle of cognition. It must therefore be a concept of judgment or derived from one, and a subjective purposiveness of the representation in reference to the judgment must lie at its basis. That anything is a magnitude (*quantum*) may be cognized from the thing itself, without many comparisons of it with other things, viz., if there is a multiplicity of the homogeneous constituting one thing. But to cognize *how great* it is always requires some other magnitude as a measure. But because the judging of magnitude depends, not merely on multiplicity (number), but also on the magnitude of the unit (the measure), and since, to judge of the magnitude of this latter again requires another as measure with which it may be compared, we see that the determination of the magnitude of phenomena can supply no absolute concept whatever of magnitude, but only a comparative one.

If now I say simply that anything is great, it appears that I have no comparison in view, at least none with an objective measure, because it is thus not determined at all how great the object is. But although the standard of comparison is merely subjective, yet the judgment nonetheless claims universal assent; "this man is beautiful" and "he is tall" are judgments, not limited merely to the judging subject, but, like theoretical judgments, demanding the assent of everyone.

In a judgment by which anything is designated simply as great, it is not merely meant that the object has a magnitude, but that this magnitude is superior to that of many other objects of the same kind, without, however, any exact determination of this superiority. Thus there is always at the basis of our judgment a standard which we assume as the same for everyone; this, however, is not available for any logical (mathematically definite) judging of magnitude, but only for aesthetical judging of the same, because it is a merely subjective standard lying at the basis of the reflective judgment upon magnitude. It may be empirical, as, e.g., the average size of the men known to us, of animals of a certain kind, trees, houses, mountains, etc. Or it may be a standard given *a priori* which, through the defects of the judging subject, is limited by the subjective conditions of presentation *in concreto,* as, e.g., in the practical sphere, the greatness of a certain virtue or of the public liberty and justice in a country, or, in the theoretical sphere, the greatness of the accuracy or the inaccuracy of an observation or measurement that has been made, etc.

Here it is remarkable that, although we have no interest whatever in an object — i.e., its existence is indifferent to us — yet its mere size, even if it is considered as formless, may bring a satisfaction with it that is universally communicable and that consequently involves the consciousness of a subjective purposiveness in the use of our cognitive faculty. This is not indeed a satisfaction in the object (because it may be formless), as in the case of the beautiful, in which the reflective judgment finds itself purposively determined in reference to cognition in general, but a satisfaction in the extension of the imagination by itself.

If (under the above limitation) we say simply of an object "it is great," this is no mathematically definite judgment, but a mere judgment of reflection upon the representation of it, which is subjectively purposive for a certain use of our cognitive powers in the estimation of magnitude; and we always then bind up with the representation a kind of respect, as also a kind of contempt, for what we simply call "small." Further, the judging of things as great or small extends to everything, even to all their characteristics; thus we describe beauty as great or small. The reason of this is to be sought in the fact that whatever we present in intuition according to the precept of the judgment (and thus represent aesthetically) is always a phenomenon, and thus a quantum.

But if we call anything, not only great, but absolutely great in every point of view (great beyond all comparison), i.e., sublime, we soon see that it is not permissible to seek for an adequate standard of this outside itself, but merely in itself. It is a magnitude which is like itself alone. It follows hence that the sublime is not to be sought in the things of nature, but only in our ideas; but in which of them it lies must be reserved for the "Deduction."

The foregoing explanation can be thus expressed: *The sublime is that in comparison with which everything else is small.* Here we easily see that nothing can be given in nature, however great it is judged by us to be, which could not, if considered in another relation, be reduced to the infinitely small; and conversely there is nothing so small which does not admit of extension by our imagination to the greatness of a world if compared with still smaller standards. Telescopes have furnished us with abundant material for making the first remark, microscopes for the second. Nothing, therefore, which can be an object of the senses is, considered on this basis, to be called sublime. But because there is in our imagination a striving toward infinite progress and in our reason a claim for absolute totality, regarded as a real idea, therefore this very inadequateness for that idea in our faculty for estimating the magnitude of things of sense excites in us the feeling of a supersensible faculty. And it is not the object of sense, but the use which the judgment naturally makes of certain objects on behalf of this latter feeling that is absolutely great, and in comparison every other use is small. Consequently it is the state of mind produced by a certain representation with which the reflective judgment is occupied, and not the object, that is to be called sublime.

We can therefore append to the preceding formulas explaining the sublime this other: *The sublime is that, the mere ability to think which shows a faculty of the mind surpassing every standard of sense. . . .*

27. Of the Quality of the Satisfaction in Our Judgments upon the Sublime

The feeling of our incapacity to attain to an idea *which is a law for us* is *respect.* Now the idea of the comprehension of every phenomenon that can be given us in the intuition of a whole is an idea prescribed to us by a law of reason, which recognizes no other measure, definite, valid of everyone, and invariable, than the absolute whole. But our imagination, even in its greatest efforts, in respect of that comprehension which we expect from it of a given object in a whole of intuition (and thus with reference to the presentation of the idea of reason) exhibits its own limits and inadequacy, although at the same time it shows that its destination is to make itself adequate to this idea regarded as a law. Therefore the feeling of the sublime in nature is respect for our own destination, which, by a certain subreption, we attribute to an object of nature (conversion of respect for the idea of humanity in our own subject into respect for the object). This makes intuitively evident the superiority of the rational determination of our cognitive faculties to the greatest faculty of our sensibility.

The feeling of the sublime is therefore a feeling of pain arising from the want of accordance between the aesthetical estimation of magnitude formed by the imagination and the estimation of the same formed by reason. There is at the same time a pleasure thus excited, arising from the correspondence with rational ideas of this very judgment of the inadequacy of our greatest faculty of sense, in so far as it is a law for us to strive after these ideas. In fact it is for us a law (of reason) and belongs to our destination to estimate as small, in comparison with ideas of reason, everything which nature, regarded as an object of sense, contains that is great for us; and that which arouses in us the feeling of this supersensible destination agrees with that law. Now the greatest effort of the imagination in the presentation of the unit for the estimation of magnitude indicates a reference to something *absolutely great,* and consequently a reference to the law of reason, which bids us take this alone as our highest measure of magnitude. Therefore the inner perception of the inadequacy of all sensible standards for rational estimation of magnitude indicates a correspondence with rational laws; it involves a pain, which arouses in us the feeling of our supersensible destination, according to which it is purposive and therefore pleasurable to find every standard of sensibility inadequate to the ideas of understanding.

The mind feels itself *moved* in the representation of the sublime in nature, while in aesthetical judgments about the beautiful it is in *restful* contemplation. This movement may (especially in its beginning) be compared to a vibration, i.e., to a quickly alternating attraction toward, and repulsion from, the same object. The transcendent (toward which the imagination is impelled in its apprehension of intuition) is for the imagination like an abyss in which it fears to lose itself; but for the rational idea of the supersensible it is not transcendent, but in conformity with law to bring about such an effort of the imagination, and consequently here there is the same amount of attraction as there was of repulsion for the mere sensibility. But the judgment itself always remains in this case only aesthetical, because, without having any determinate concept of the object at its basis, it merely represents the subjective play of the mental powers (imagination and reason) as harmonious through their very contrast. For just as imagination and *understanding,* in judging of the beautiful, generate a subjective purposiveness of the mental powers by means of their harmony, so in this case imagination and *reason* do so by means of their conflict. That is, they bring about a feeling that we possess pure self-subsistent reason, or a faculty for the estimation of magnitude, whose superiority can be made intuitively evident only by the inadequacy of that faculty imagination which is itself unbounded in the presentation of magnitudes (of sensible objects).

The measurement of a space (regarded as apprehension) is at the same time a description of it, and thus an objective movement in the act of imagination and a progress. On the other hand, the comprehension of the manifold in the unity — not of thought but of intuition — and consequently the comprehension of the successively apprehended elements in one glance is a regress which annihilates the condition of time in this progress of the imagination and makes *coexistence* intuitible. It is therefore (since the time series is a condition of the internal sense and of an intuition) and subjective movement of the imagination, by which it does violence to the internal sense; this must be the more noticeable, the greater the quantum in which the imagination comprehends in one intuition. The effort, therefore, to receive in one single intuition a measure for magnitude that requires a considerable time to apprehend is a kind of representation which, subjectively considered, is contrary to purpose; but objectively, as requisite for the estimation of magnitude, it is purposive. Thus that very violence which is done to the subject through the imagination is judged as purposive *in reference to the whole determination* of the mind.

The *quality* of the feeling of the sublime is that it is a feeling of pain in reference to the faculty by which we judge aesthetically of an object, which pain, however, is represented at the same time as purposive. This is possible through the fact that the very incapacity in question discovers the consciousness of an unlimited faculty of the same subject, and that the mind can only judge of the latter aesthetically by means of the former.

In the logical estimation of magnitude, the impossibility of ever arriving at absolute totality, by means of the progress of the measurement of things of the sensible world in time and space, was cognized as objective, i.e., as an impossibility of *thinking* the infinite as entirely given, and not as merely subjective or that there was only an incapacity to *grasp* it. For there we have not to do with the degree of comprehension in an intuition, regarded as a measure, but everything depends on a concept of number. But in aesthetical estimation of magnitude, the concept of number must disappear or be changed, and the comprehension of the imagination in reference to the unit of measure (thus avoiding the concepts of a law of the successive production of concepts of magnitude) is alone purposive for it. If now a magnitude almost reaches the limit of our faculty of comprehension in an intuition, and yet the imagination is invited by means of numerical magnitudes (in respect of which we are conscious that our faculty is unbounded) to aesthetical comprehension in a greater unit, then we mentally feel ourselves confined aesthetically within bounds. But nevertheless the pain in regard to the necessary extension of the imagination for accordance with that which is unbounded in our faculty of reason, viz., the idea of the absolute whole, and consequently the very unpurposiveness of the faculty of imagination for rational ideas and the arousing of them, are represented as purposive. Thus it is that the aesthetical judgment itself is subjectively purposive for the reason as the source of ideas, i.e., as the source of an intellectual comprehension for which all aesthetical comprehension is small, and there accompanies the reception of an object as sublime a pleasure, which is only possible through the medium of a pain.

B. OF THE DYNAMICALLY SUBLIME IN NATURE

28. Of Nature Regarded as Might

Might is that which is superior to great hindrances. It is called *dominion* if it is superior to the resistance of that which itself possesses might. Nature, considered in an aesthetical judgment as might that has no dominion over us, is *dynamically sublime*.

If nature is to be judged by us as dynamically sublime, it must be represented as exciting fear (although it is not true conversely that every object which excites fear is regarded in our aesthetical judgment as sublime). For in aesthetical judgments (without the aid of concepts) superiority to hindrances can only be judged according to the greatness of the resistance. Now that which we are driven to resist is an evil and, if we do not find our faculties a match for it, is an object of fear. Hence nature can be regarded by the aesthetical judgment as might, and consequently as dynamically sublime, only so far as it is considered an object of fear.

But we can regard an object as *fearful* without being afraid *of* it, viz., if we judge of it in such a way that we merely *think* a case in which we would wish to resist it and yet in which all resistance would be altogether vain. Thus the virtuous man fears God without being afraid of Him, because to wish to resist Him and His commandments he thinks is a case that *he* need not apprehend. But in every such case that he thinks as not impossible, he cognizes Him as fearful.

He who fears can form no judgment about the sublime in nature, just as he who is seduced by inclination and appetite can form no judgment about the beautiful. The former flies from the sight of an object which inspires him with awe, and it is impossible to find satisfaction in a terror that is seriously felt. Hence the pleasurableness arising from the cessation of an uneasiness is *a state of joy*. But this, on account of the deliverance from danger which is involved, is a state of joy when conjoined with the resolve that we shall no more be exposed to the danger; we cannot willingly look back upon our sensations of danger, much less seek the occasion for them again.

Bold, overhanging, and as it were threatening rocks; clouds piled up in the sky, moving with lightning flashes and thunder peals; volcanoes in all their violence of destruction; hurricanes with their track of devastation; the boundless ocean in a state of tumult; the lofty waterfall of a mighty river, and such like — these exhibit our faculty of resistance as insignificantly small in comparison with their might. But the sight of them is the more attractive, the more fearful it is, provided only that we are in security; and we willingly call these objects sublime, because they raise the energies of the soul above their accustomed height and discover in us a faculty of resistance of a quite different kind, which gives us courage to measure ourselves against the apparent almightiness of nature.

Now, in the immensity of nature and in the insufficiency of our faculties to take in a standard proportionate to the aesthetical estimation of the magnitude of its *realm,* we find our own limitation, although at the same time in our rational faculty we find a different, nonsensuous standard, which has that infinity itself under it as a unity, in comparison with which everything in nature is small, and thus in our mind we find a superiority to nature even in its immensity. And so also the irresistibility of its might, while making us recognize our own physical impotence, considered as beings of nature, discloses to us a faculty of judging independently of and a superiority over nature,

on which is based a kind of self-preservation entirely different from that which can be attacked and brought into danger by external nature. Thus humanity in our person remains unhumiliated, though the individual might have to submit to this dominion. In this way nature is not judged to be sublime in our aesthetical judgments insofar as it excites fear, but because it calls up that power in us (which is not nature) of regarding as small the things about which we are solicitous (goods, health, and life), and of regarding its might (to which we are no doubt subjected in respect of these things) as nevertheless without any dominion over us and our personality to which we must bow where our highest fundamental propositions, and their assertion or abandonment, are concerned. Therefore nature is here called sublime merely because it elevates the imagination to a presentation of those cases in which the mind can make felt the proper sublimity of its destination, in comparison with nature itself.

This estimation of ourselves loses nothing through the fact that we might regard ourselves as safe in order to feel this inspiriting satisfaction and that hence, as there is no seriousness in the danger, there might be also (as might seem to be the case) just as little seriousness in the sublimity of our spiritual faculty. For the satisfaction here concerns only the *destination* of our faculty which discloses itself in such a case, so far as the tendency to this destination lies in our nature, while its development and exercise remain incumbent and obligatory. And in this there is truth and reality, however conscious the man may be of his present actual powerfulness, when he turns his reflection to it.

No doubt this principle seems to be too far-fetched and too subtly reasoned, and consequently seems to go beyond the scope of an aesthetical judgment; but observation of men proves the opposite and shows that it may lie at the root of the most ordinary judgments, although we are not always conscious of it. For what is that which is, even to the savage, an object of the greatest admiration? It is a man who shrinks from nothing, who fears nothing, and therefore does not yield to danger, but rather goes to face it vigorously with the most complete deliberation. Even in the most highly civilized state this peculiar veneration for the soldier remains, though only under the condition that he exhibit all the virtues of peace, gentleness, compassion, and even a becoming care for his own person; because even by these it is recognized that his mind is unsubdued by danger. Hence whatever disputes there may be about the superiority of the respect which is to be accorded them, in the comparison of a statesman and a general, the aesthetical judgment decides for the latter. War itself, if it is carried on with order and with a sacred respect for the rights of citizens, has something sublime in it, and makes the disposition of the people who carry it on thus only the more sublime, the more numerous are the dangers to which they are exposed and in respect of which they behave with courage. On the other hand, a long peace generally brings about a predominant commercial spirit and, along with it, low selfishness, cowardice, and effeminacy, and debases the disposition of the people.

It appears to conflict with this solution of the concept of sublime, so far as sublimity is ascribed to might, that we are accustomed to represent God as presenting Himself in His wrath and yet in His sublimity, in the tempest, the storm, the earthquake, etc.; and that it would be foolish and criminal to imagine a superiority of our minds over these works of His and, as it seems, even over the designs of such might. Hence it would appear that no feeling of the sublimity of our own nature, but rather subjection, abasement, and a feeling of complete powerlessness, is a fitting state of mind in the presence of such an object; and this is generally bound up with the idea of it during natural phenomena of this kind. In religion in general, prostration, adoration with bent head, with contrite, anxious demeanor and voice, seems to be the only fitting behavior in presence of the Godhead, and hence most peoples have adopted and still observe it. But this state of mind is far from being necessarily bound up with the idea of the *sublimity* of a religion and its object. The man who is actually afraid, because he finds reasons for fear in himself, while conscious by his culpable disposition of offending against a might whose will is irresistible and at the same time just, is not in the frame of mind for admiring the divine greatness. For this a mood of calm contemplation and a quiet free judgment are needed. Only if he is conscious of an upright disposition pleasing to God do those operations of might serve to awaken in him the idea of the sublimity of this Being, for then he recognizes in himself a sublimity of disposition conformable to His will; and thus he is raised above the fear of such operations of nature, which he no longer regards as outbursts of His wrath. Even humility, in the shape of a stern judgment upon his own faults — which otherwise, with a consciousness of good intentions, could be easily palliated from the frailty of human nature — is a sublime state of mind, consisting in a voluntary subjection of himself to the pain of remorse, in order that the causes of this may be gradually removed. In this way religion is essentially distinguished from superstition. The latter establishes in the mind, not reverence for the sublime, but fear and apprehension of the all-powerful Being to whose will the terrified man sees himself subject, without according Him any high esteem. From this nothing can arise but a seeking of favor and flattery, instead of a religion which consists in a good life.[9]

Sublimity, therefore, does not reside in anything of nature, but only in our mind, in so far as we can become conscious that we are superior to nature within, and therefore also to nature without us (so far as it influences us). Everything that excites this feeling in us, e.g., the *might* of nature which calls forth our forces, is called then (although improperly) sublime. Only by supposing this idea in ourselves and in reference to it are we capable of attaining to the idea of the sublimity of that Being which produces respect in us, not merely by the might that it displays in nature, but rather by means of the faculty which resides in us of judging it fearlessly and of regarding our destination as sublime in respect of it. . . .

---

[9]In the *Philosophical Theory of Religion*, Pt. I (Abbott's trans., p. 360), Kant, as here, divides "all religions into two classes — *favor-seeking* religion (mere worship) and *moral* religion, that is, the religion *of a good life*"; and he concludes that "amongst all the public religions that have ever existed the Christian alone is moral." [Tr.]

49. Of the Faculties of the Mind That Constitute Genius

We say of certain products of which we expect that they should at least in part appear as beautiful art, they are without *spirit,*[10] although we find nothing to blame in them on the score of taste. A poem may be very neat and elegant, but without spirit. A history may be exact and well arranged, but without spirit. A festal discourse may be solid and at the same time elaborate, but without spirit. Conversation is often not devoid of entertainment, but it is without spirit; even of a woman we say that she is pretty, an agreeable talker, and courteous, but without spirit. What then do we mean by spirit?

Spirit, in an aesthetical sense, is the name given to the animating principle of the mind. But that by means of which this principle animates the soul, the material which it applies to that purpose, is what puts the mental powers purposively into swing, i.e., into such a play as maintains itself and strengthens the mental powers in their exercise.

Now I maintain that this principle is no other than the faculty of presenting *aesthetical ideas.* And by an aesthetical idea I understand that representation of the imagination which occasions much thought, without however any definite thought, i.e., any *concept,* being capable of being adequate to it; it consequently cannot be completely compassed and made intelligible by language. We easily see that it is the counterpart (pendant) of a *rational idea,* which conversely is a concept to which no *intuition* (or representation of the imagination) can be adequate.

The imagination (as a productive faculty of cognition) is very powerful in creating another nature, as it were, out of the material that actual nature gives it. We entertain ourselves with it when experience becomes too commonplace, and by it we remold experience, always indeed in accordance with analogical laws, but yet also in accordance with principles which occupy a higher place in reason (laws, too, which are just as natural to us as those by which understanding comprehends empirical nature). Thus we feel our freedom from the law of association (which attaches to the empirical employment of imagination), so that the material supplied to us by nature in accordance with this law can be worked up into something different which surpasses nature.

Such representations of the imagination we may call *ideas,* partly because they at least strive after something which lies beyond the bounds of experience and so seek to approximate to a presentation of concepts of reason (intellectual ideas), thus giving to the latter the appearance of objective reality, but especially because no concept can be fully adequate to them as internal intuitions. The poet ventures to realize to sense,[11] rational ideas of invisible beings, the kingdom of the blessed, hell, eternity, creation, etc.; or even if he deals with things of which there are examples in experience — e.g., death, envy and all vices, also love, fame, and the like — he tries, by means of imagination, which emulates the play of reason in its quests after a maximum, to go beyond the limits of experience and to present them to sense with a completeness of which there is no example in nature. This is properly speaking the art of the poet, in which the faculty of aesthetical ideas can manifest itself in its entire strength. But this faculty, considered in itself, is properly only a talent (of the imagination).

If now we place under a concept a representation of the imagination belonging to its presentation, but which occasions in itself more thought than can ever be comprehended in a definite concept and which consequently aesthetically enlarges the concept itself in an unbounded fashion, the imagination is here creative, and it brings the faculty of intellectual ideas (the reason) into movement; i.e., by a representation more thought (which indeed belongs to the concept of the object) is occasioned than can in it be grasped or made clear.

Those forms which do not constitute the presentation of a given concept itself but only, as approximate representations of the imagination, express the consequences bound up with it and its relationship to other concepts, are called

---

[10]In English we would rather say "without soul," but I prefer to translate *"Geist"* consistently by "spirit," to avoid the confusion of it with *"Seele."* [Tr.]

[11]Ventures to make real for the senses.

(aesthetical) *attributes* of an object whose concept as a rational idea cannot be adequately presented. Thus Jupiter's eagle with the lightning in its claws is an attribute of the mighty king of heaven, as the peacock is of his magnificent queen. They do not, like *logical attributes,* represent what lies in our concepts of the sublimity and majesty of creation, but something different, which gives occasion to the imagination to spread itself over a number of kindred representations that arouse more thought than can be expressed in a concept determined by words. They furnish an *aesthetical idea,* which for that rational idea takes the place of logical presentation; and thus, as their proper office, they enliven the mind by opening out to it the prospect into an illimitable field of kindred representations. But beautiful art does this not only in the case of painting or sculpture (in which the term "attribute" is commonly employed); poetry and rhetoric also get the spirit that animates their works simply from the aesthetical attributes of the object, which accompany the logical and stimulate the imagination, so that it thinks more by their aid, although in an undeveloped way, than could be comprehended in a concept and therefore in a definite form of words. For the sake of brevity, I must limit myself to a few examples only.

When the great king in one of his poems expresses himself as follows:

> Oui, finissons sans trouble et mourons sans regrets,
> En laissant l'univers comblé de nos bienfaits.
> Ainsi l'astre du jour au bout de sa carriere,
> Répand sur l'horizon une douce lumière;
> Et les derniers rayons qu'il darde dans les airs,
> Sont les derniers soupirs qu'il donne à l'univers;[12]

he quickens his rational idea of a cosmopolitan disposition at the end of life by an attribute which the imagination (in remembering all the pleasures of a beautiful summer day that are recalled at its close by a serene evening) associates with that representation, and which excites a number of sensations and secondary representations for which no expression is found. On the other hand, an intellectual concept may serve conversely as an attribute for a representation of sense, and so can quicken this latter by means of the idea of the supersensible, but only by the aesthetical element, that subjectively attaches to the concept of the latter, being here employed. Thus, for example, a certain poet says, in his description of a beautiful morning:

> The sun arose
> As calm from virtue springs.

The consciousness of virtue, if we substitute it in our thoughts for a virtuous man, diffuses in the mind a multitude of sublime and restful feelings, and a boundless prospect of a joyful future, to which no expression that is measured by a definite concept completely attains.[13]

In a word, the aesthetical idea is a representation of the imagination associated with a given concept, which is bound up with such a multiplicity of partial representations in its free employment that for it no expression marking a definite concept can be found; and such a representation, therefore, adds to a concept much ineffable thought, the feeling of which quickens the cognitive faculties, and with language, which is the mere letter, binds up spirit also.

The mental powers, therefore, whose union (in a certain relation) constitutes genius are imagination and understanding. In the employment of the imagination for cognition, it submits to the constraint of the understanding and is subject to the

---

[12]"Yes, let us end without sadness and let us die without regrets, in leaving the world filled with our good deeds. So the day-star, at the end of its course, sheds a gentle light on the horizon; and the last rays that it darts into the air are the last sighs which it gives to the world." [Ed.] Barni quotes these lines as occurring in one of Frederick the Great's French poems: "Epitre au maréchal Keith, sur les vaines terreurs de la mort et les frayeurs d'une autre vie" [Letter to Marshal Keith on the Pointless Terror of Death and Fears of Another Life]; but I have not been able to verify his reference. Kant here translates them into German. [Tr.]

[13]Perhaps nothing more sublime was ever said and no sublimer thought ever expressed than the famous inscription on the Temple of Isis (Mother Nature): "I am all that is and that was and that shall be, and no mortal hath lifted my veil." Segner availed himself of this idea in a *suggestive* vignette prefixed to his *Natural Philosophy,* in order to inspire beforehand the pupil whom he was about to lead into that temple with a holy awe, which should dispose his mind to serious attention. [Kant] J. A. de Segner (1704–1777) was Professor of Natural Philosophy at Göttingen and the author of several scientific works of repute. [Tr.]

limitation of being conformable to the concept of the latter. On the contrary, in an aesthetical point of view it is free to furnish unsought, over and above that agreement with a concept, abundance of undeveloped material for the understanding, to which the understanding paid no regard in its concept but which it applies, though not objectively for cognition, yet subjectively to quicken the cognitive powers and therefore also indirectly to cognitions. Thus genius properly consists in the happy relation between these faculties, which no science can teach and no industry can learn, by which ideas are found for a given concept; and, on the other hand, we thus find for these ideas the expression by means of which the subjective state of mind brought about by them, as an accompaniment of the concept, can be communicated to others. The latter talent is, properly speaking, what is called spirit; for to express the ineffable element in the state of mind implied by a certain representation and to make it universally communicable — whether the expression be in speech or painting or statuary — this requires a faculty of seizing the quickly passing play of imagination and of unifying it in a concept (which is even on that account original and discloses a new rule that could not have been inferred from any preceding principles of examples) that can be communicated without any constraint of rules.

If, after this analysis, we look back to the explanation given above of what is called *genius,* we find: first, that it is a talent for art, not for science, in which clearly known rules must go beforehand and determine the procedure. Secondly, as an artistic talent it presupposes a definite concept of the product as the purpose, and therefore understanding; but it also presupposes a representation (although an indeterminate one) of the material, i.e., of the intuition, for the presentment of this concept, and, therefore a relation between the imagination and the understanding. Thirdly, it shows itself, not so much in the accomplishment of the proposed purpose in a presentment of a definite concept, as in the enunciation or expression of aesthetical ideas which contain abundant material for that very design; and consequently it represents the imagination as free from all guidance of rules and yet as purposive in reference to the presentment of the given concept. Finally, in the fourth place, the unsought, undesigned subjective purposiveness in the free accordance of the imagination with the legality of the understanding presupposes such a proportion and disposition of these faculties as no following of rules, whether of science or of mechanical imitation, can bring about, but which only the nature of the subject can produce.

In accordance with these suppositions, genius is the examplary originality of the natural gifts of a subject in the *free* employment of his cognitive faculties. In this way the product of a genius (as regards what is to be ascribed to genius and not to possible learning or schooling) is an example, not to be imitated (for then that which in it is genius and constitutes the spirit of the work would be lost), but to be followed by another genius, whom it awakens to a feeling of his own originality and whom it stirs so to exercise his art in freedom from the constraint of rules, that thereby a new rule is gained for art; and thus his talent shows itself to be exemplary. But because a genius is a favorite of nature and must be regarded by us as a rare phenomenon, his example produces for other good heads a school, i.e., a methodical system of teaching according to rules, so far as these can be derived from the peculiarities of the products of his spirit. For such persons beautiful art is so far imitation, to which nature through the medium of a genius supplied the rule.

But this imitation becomes a mere *aping* if the scholar *copies* everything down to the deformities, which the genius must have let pass only because he could not well remove them without weakening his idea. This mental characteristic is meritorious only in the case of a genius. A certain *audacity* in expression — and in general many a departure from common rules — becomes him well, but it is in no way worthy of imitation; it always remains a fault in itself which we must seek to remove, though the genius is, as it were, privileged to commit it, because the inimitable rush of his spirit would suffer from overanxious carefulness. *Mannerism* is another kind of aping, viz., of mere *peculiarity* (originality) in general, by which a man separates himself as far as possible from imitators, without however possessing the talent to be at the same time *exemplary.* There are indeed in general two ways (*modi*) in which such a man may put together his notions of expressing himself; the one is called a *manner* (*modus aestheticus*), the other a *method* (*modus logicus*). They differ in this, that the former has no other standard than the *feeling* of unity in the presentment, but the latter follows definite *principles;* hence the former alone avails for beautiful art. But an artistic product is said to show *mannerism* only when the exposition of the artist's idea is *founded* on its very singularity and is not made appropriate to the idea itself. The ostentatious (*précieux*), contorted, and affected manner adopted to differentiate oneself from ordinary persons (though devoid of spirit) is like the behavior of a man of whom we say that he hears himself talk, or who stands and moves about as if he were on a stage in order to be stared at; this always betrays a bungler.

Mary Wollstonecraft

1759–1797

The most important British feminist writer of the eighteenth century was born in London. Her grandfather, a prosperous silk weaver, had left her father a small fortune, with which he bought a farm in Yorkshire in 1768, setting himself up as gentry. But expensive habits, lack of experience at farming, and addiction to drink turned this venture into a failure. He sold the farm and returned to London in 1774, a pattern he then repeated with another farm in Wales. Wollstonecraft's childhood was embittered as much by the preference given her elder brother — who was formally educated for the law, whereas she and her sisters were left to scrape together learning as they could — as by her family's impoverishment and her father's drunken brutality. Her solace was two close friendships with intelligent women who assisted in her self-development: Jane Arden in Yorkshire and Fanny Blood in London.

For ten years from the age of nineteen, Wollstonecraft took on most of the jobs available to genteel women at that time: She served as companion to a rich trades-man's widow; she managed and taught in schools for young ladies at Islington and Stoke Newington; she was governess to the two daughters of Viscount Kingsborough. All the while she continued to educate herself, participating in con-versations with the men of letters with whom her work brought her into contact, and reading the literature and philosophy of the Enlightenment period, particularly that of Jean-Jacques Rousseau, whose work on education both inspired and outraged her. She also became aware of the pitfalls fate digs for women: Her sister Eliza was dev-astated by post-partum depression and lost custody of her child; her friend Fanny Blood died of childbed fever in the weeks following a premature childbirth.

Back in London, Wollstonecraft began her career as a writer, working primarily for Joseph Johnston, publisher of the liberal *Analytical Review*, and specializing pri-marily in works on education. *Thoughts on the Education of Daughters* (1787) was her first monograph; over the next two years she published a proto-feminist novel called *Mary*, a highly successful children's book, *Original Stories from Real Life* (1788), a reader for women, and book-length translations from both French and German on moral education. In 1790, the direction of her work changed. The par-liamentarian Edmund Burke published *Reflections on the Revolution in France*, in response to a pro-Jacobin sermon by Richard Price, a minister in Wollstonecraft's circle. Wollstonecraft responded swiftly with *A Vindication of the Rights of Men*, meeting Burke's personal attacks on Price with insinuations of her own, and argu-ing that the French Revolution was not to be judged by the momentary violence of the march on Versailles, but by the National Assembly's passage of the Declaration of Rights of Man and the Citizen.

Wollstonecraft quickly followed this success — which may, as William Godwin thought, have made her for a time "the most famous woman in the world" — with her most important work, *A Vindication of the Rights of Woman* (1792), from which a selection appears below. Wollstonecraft's central argument is that the traditional education of women has been in the art of pleasing men, and the accomplishments that women acquired — music and dancing, painting and penmanship — serve to make them decorative objects fit for a seraglio, but not to make them fit companions for intelligent men who want to converse on the important subjects of the day, like science and philosophy. Men have established their superiority by this arrangement, Wollstonecraft argues, but not their own felicity, since marriages would be happier if the partners were on an equal intellectual footing. And since not all women become wives, cared for by wealthy men, women should be encouraged to study other matters as well, like business, law, and politics, to become more useful citizens, in coeducational public schools supported by government funds. Wollstonecraft's controversial tract sold out two editions in a year and was widely attacked as well as defended (Horace Walpole called her "a hyena in petticoats").

In the years following the two *Vindications*, Wollstonecraft became involved in a series of intense romantic involvements: with the Swiss-German painter Henry Fuseli, whose wife objected to sharing him; with an American officer and adventurer named Gilbert Imlay, whom she met in France during the most violent phase of the French Revolution (and by whom she had a child out of wedlock, named Fanny, after her late friend); and with the philosopher and radical social critic William Godwin. Godwin had argued in his celebrated tract *Political Justice* (1793) that marriage and the family are regressive features of society, which should teach us to love each of our fellow citizens alike, and Wollstonecraft had argued that marriage under English law took away any rights women had to their property and their own persons. She was in fact hard at work on a second feminist novel, *Maria, or The Wrongs of Woman*, which delineates in scarifying detail the failure of English law and social practice to protect married women from violence, fraud, and patriarchal power. But she and Godwin had become lovers, and once Mary became pregnant, they were forced to break with principle and marry (in March 1797) because of the social and legal penalties their child would otherwise have had to bear. On August 30, 1797, Mary delivered a healthy girl, whom they named Mary; the child would one day marry the poet Shelley and achieve fame as the author of *Frankenstein*. But the placenta failed to deliver, puerperal fever set in, and Wollstonecraft died in London on September 10. After her death Godwin published an affectionate memoir of Wollstonecraft's life, and an edition of his late wife's unfinished novel, *Maria*.

Selected Bibliography

Conger, Syndy M. *Mary Wollstonecraft and the Language of Sensibility* (Rutherford, NJ: Fairleigh Dickinson UP, 1996).

Falco, Maria, ed. *Feminist Interpretations of Mary Wollstonecraft* (University Park: Penn State UP, 1996).

Kelly, Gary. *Revolutionary Feminism: The Mind and Career of Mary Wollstonecraft* (New York: St. Martin's, 1992).

Poovey, Mary. *The Proper Lady and the Woman Writer* (Chicago: U Chicago P, 1984).

Taylor, Barbara. *Mary Wollstonecraft and the Feminist Imagination* (New York: Cambridge UP, 2003).

Todd, Janet. *Mary Wollstonecraft: A Revolutionary Life* (New York: Columbia UP, 2000).
—— . *Mary Wollstonecraft: An Annotated Bibliography* (New York: Garland, 1976).
Todd, Janet, and Marilyn Butler, eds. *The Works of Mary Wollstonecraft* (7 vols; London: Pickering, 1989).
Wardle, Ralph, ed. *Collected Letters of Mary Wollstonecraft* (Ithaca: Cornell UP, 1979).

From *A Vindication of the Rights of Woman*

CHAPTER III: THE PREVAILING OPINION OF A SEXUAL CHARACTER DISCUSSED

Women, as well as despots, have now perhaps more power than they would have if the world, divided and subdivided into kingdoms and families, were governed by laws deduced from the exercise of reason; but in obtaining it, to carry on the comparison, their character is degraded, and licentiousness spread through the whole aggregate of society. The many become pedestal to the few. I, therefore, will venture to assert that till women are more rationally educated, the progress of human virtue and improvement in knowledge must receive continual checks. And if it be granted that woman was not created merely to gratify the appetite of man, or to be the upper servant who provides his meals and takes care of his linen, it must follow that the first care of those mothers or fathers who really attend to the education of females should be, if not to strengthen the body, at least not to destroy the constitution by mistaken notions of beauty and female excellence; nor should girls ever be allowed to imbibe the pernicious notion that a defect can, by any chemical process of reasoning, become an excellence. In this respect I am happy to find that the author of one of the most instructive books that our country has produced for children, coincides with me in opinion. I shall quote his pertinent remarks to give the force of his respectable authority to reason.[1,2]

But should it be proved that woman is naturally weaker than man, whence does it follow that it is

[1]A respectable old man gives the following sensible account of the method he pursued when educating his daughter: "I endeavoured to give both to her mind and body a degree of vigour which is seldom found in the female sex. As soon as she was sufficiently advanced in strength to be capable of the lighter labours of husbandry and gardening I employed her as my constant companion. Selene — for that was her name — soon acquired a dexterity in all these rustic employments which I considered with equal pleasure and admiration. If women are in general feeble both in body and mind it arises less from nature than from education. We encourage a vicious indolence and inactivity which we falsely call delicacy. Instead of hardening their minds by the severer principles of reason and philosophy, we breed them to useless arts which terminate in vanity and sensuality. In most of the countries which I had visited they are taught nothing of an higher nature than a few modulations of the voice or useless postures of the body; their time is consumed in sloth or trifles and trifles become the only pursuit capable of interesting them. We seem to forget that it is upon the qualities of the female sex that our own domestic comforts and the education of our children must depend. And what are the comforts or the education which a race of beings corrupted from their infancy and unacquainted with all the duties of life are fitted to bestow? To touch a musical instrument with useless skill, to exhibit their cultural or affected graces to the eyes of indolent and debauched young men, to dissipate their husband's patrimony in riotous and unnecessary expenses: these are the only arts cultivated by women in most of the polished nations I had seen. And the consequences are uniformly such as may be expected to proceed from such polluted sources — private and public servitude. But Selene's education was regulated by different views, and conducted upon severer principles — if that can be called severity which opens the mind to a sense of moral and religious duties, and most effectually arms it against the inevitable evils of life." — Mr. Day's *Sandford and Merton*, vol. iii. [Wollstonecraft]

[2]Thomas Day (1748–1789), a British follower of Rousseau, wrote *Sandford and Merton* (1783) as a didactic novel explicating his theories about education.

natural for her to labour to become still weaker than nature intended her to be? Arguments of this cast are an insult to common sense, and savour of passion. The divine right of husbands, like the divine right of kings, may, it is to be hoped, in this enlightened age, be contested without danger; and though conviction may not silence many boisterous disputants, yet, when any prevailing prejudice is attacked, the wise will consider, and leave the narrow-minded to rail with thoughtless vehemence at innovation. The mother who wishes to give true dignity of character to her daughter must, regardless of the sneers of ignorance, proceed on a plan diametrically opposite to that which Rousseau[3] has recommended with all the deluding charms of eloquence and philosophical sophistry, for his eloquence renders absurdities plausible, and his dogmatic conclusions puzzle, without convincing, those who have not ability to refute them. Throughout the whole animal kingdom every young creature requires almost continual exercise, and the infancy of children, conformable to this intimation, should be passed in harmless gambols that exercise the feet and hands, without requiring very minute direction from the head, or the constant attention of a nurse. In fact, the care necessary for self-preservation is the first natural exercise of the understanding, as little inventions to amuse the present moment unfold the imagination.

But these wise designs of nature are counteracted by mistaken fondness or blind zeal. The child is not left a moment to its own direction — particularly a girl — and thus rendered dependent. Dependence is called natural. To preserve personal beauty — woman's glory — the limbs and faculties are cramped with worse than Chinese bands,[4] and the sedentary life which they are condemned to live, whilst boys frolic in the open air, weakens the muscles and relaxes the nerves. As for Rousseau's remarks, which have since been echoed by several writers, that they have naturally, that is, from their birth, independent of

education, a fondness for dolls, dressing, and talking, they are so puerile as not to merit a serious refutation. That a girl, condemned to sit for hours together listening to the idle chat of weak nurses, or to attend at her mother's toilet, will endeavour to join the conversation, is, indeed, very natural; and that she will imitate her mother or aunts, and amuse herself by adorning her lifeless doll, as they do in dressing her, poor innocent babe! is undoubtedly a most natural consequence. For men of the greatest abilities have seldom had sufficient strength to rise above the surrounding atmosphere; and if the pages of genius have always been blurred by the prejudices of the age, some allowance should be made for a sex, who, like kings, always see things through a false medium. Pursuing these reflections, the fondness for dress, conspicuous in woman, may be easily accounted for, without supposing it the result of a desire to please the sex on which they are dependent. The absurdity, in short, of supposing that a girl is naturally a coquette, and that a desire connected with the impulse of nature to propagate the species, should appear even before an improper education has, by heating the imagination, called it forth prematurely, is so unphilosophical, that such a sagacious observer as Rousseau would not have adopted it, if he had not been accustomed to make reason give way to his desire of singularity, and truth to a favourite paradox. Yet thus to give a sex to mind was not very consistent with the principles of a man who argued so warmly, and so well, for the immortality of the soul. But what a weak barrier is truth when it stands in the way of an hypothesis! Rousseau respected — almost adored virtue — and yet he allowed himself to love with sensual fondness. His imagination constantly prepared inflammable fuel for his inflammable senses; but, in order to reconcile his respect for self-denial, fortitude, and those heroic virtues, which a mind like his could not coolly admire, he labours to invert the law of nature, and broaches a doctrine pregnant with mischief, and derogatory to the character of supreme wisdom. His ridiculous stories, which tend to prove that girls are naturally attentive to their persons, without laying any stress on daily example, are below contempt. And that a little miss should have such a correct taste as to neglect the pleasing amusement of

[3]Wollstonecraft alludes to the educational theories of the French philosopher Jean-Jacques Rousseau (1712–1778) as expressed in his novel *Émile, or Education* (1762).

[4]Alluding to the practice of binding the feet of aristocratic Chinese wives, which deformed the limbs so that the woman was unable to walk.

making O's, merely because she perceived that it was an ungraceful attitude, should be selected with the anecdotes of the learned pig.[5]

I have, probably, had an opportunity of observing more girls in their infancy than J. J. Rousseau. I can recollect my own feelings, and I have looked steadily around me; yet, so far from coinciding with him in opinion respecting the first dawn of the female character, I will venture to affirm, that a girl, whose spirits have not been damped by inactivity, or innocence tainted by false shame, will always be a romp, and the doll will never excite attention unless confinement allows her no alternative. Girls and boys, in short, would play harmlessly together, if the distinction of sex was not inculcated long before nature makes any difference. I will go further, and affirm, as an indisputable fact, that most of the women, in the circle of my observation, who have acted like rational creatures, or shown any vigour of intellect, have accidentally been allowed to run wild, as some of the elegant formers of the fair sex would insinuate.

The baneful consequences which flow from inattention to health during infancy and youth extend further than is supposed — dependence of body naturally produces dependence of mind; and how can she be a good wife or mother, the greater part of whose time is employed to guard against or endure sickness? Nor can it be expected that a woman will resolutely endeavour to strengthen her constitution and abstain from enervating indulgences, if artificial notions of beauty, and false descriptions of sensibility, have been early entangled with her motives of action. Most men are sometimes obliged to bear with bodily inconveniences, and to endure, occasionally, the inclemency of the elements; but genteel women are, literally speaking, slaves to their bodies, and glory in their subjection.

I once knew a weak woman of fashion, who was more than commonly proud of her delicacy and sensibility. She thought a distinguishing taste and puny appetite the height of all human perfection, and acted accordingly. I have seen this weak sophisticated being neglect all the duties of life, yet recline with self-complacency on a sofa, and boast of her want of appetite as a proof of delicacy that extended to, or, perhaps, arose from, her exquisite sensibility; for it is difficult to render intelligible such ridiculous jargon. Yet, at the moment, I have seen her insult a worthy old gentlewoman, whom unexpected misfortunes had made dependent on her ostentatious bounty, and who, in better days, had claims on her gratitude. Is it possible that a human creature could have become such a weak and depraved being, if, like the Sybarites,[6] dissolved in luxury, everything like virtue had not been worn away, or never impressed by precept, a poor substitute, it is true, for cultivation of mind, though it serves as a fence against vice?

Such a woman is not a more irrational monster than some of the Roman emperors, who were depraved by lawless power. Yet, since kings have been more under the restraint of law, and the curb, however weak, of honour, the records of history are not filled with such unnatural instances of folly and cruelty, nor does the despotism that kills virtue and genius in the bud, hover over Europe with that destructive blast which desolates Turkey, and renders the men, as well as the soil, unfruitful.[7]

Women are everywhere in this deplorable state; for, in order to preserve their innocence, as ignorance is courteously termed, truth is hidden from them, and they are made to assume an artificial character before their faculties have acquired any strength. Taught from their infancy that beauty is woman's sceptre, the mind shapes

[5]"I once knew a young person who learned to write before she learned to read, and began to write with her needle before she could use a pen. At first, indeed she took it into her head to make no letter than the O: this letter she was constantly making of all sizes and always the wrong way. Unluckily one day as she was intent on this employment, she happened to see herself in the looking-glass; when, taking a dislike to the constrained attitude in which she sat while writing she threw away her pen like another Pallas and determined against making the O any more. Her brother was also equally averse to writing; it was the confinement however and not the constrained attitude that most disgusted him." — Rousseau's *Emilius*. [Wollstonecraft]

[6]Someone devoted to pleasure and luxury.
[7]The Ottoman Empire, known for the prevalence of despotism and cruelty among its sultans, was in serious decline in the decades before the publication of Wollstonecraft's *Vindication*; under Sultan Abdul Hamid I (who ruled 1774–1789), several of its provinces rebelled against rule from Istanbul, and it lost territory, including the Crimea, to wars with Russia.

itself to the body, and roaming round its gilt cage, only seeks to adore its prison. Men have various employments and pursuits which engage their attention, and give a character to the opening mind; but women, confined to one, and having their thoughts constantly directed to the most insignificant part of themselves, seldom extend their views beyond the triumph of the hour. But were their understanding once emancipated from the slavery to which the pride and sensuality of man and their short-sighted desire, like that of dominion in tyrants, of present sway, has subjected them, we should probably read of their weaknesses with surprise. I must be allowed to pursue the argument a little further. Perhaps, if the existence of an evil being were allowed, who, in the allegorical language of Scripture, went about seeking whom he should devour,[8] he could not more effectually degrade the human character, than by giving a man absolute power.

This argument branches into various ramifications. Birth, riches, and every extrinsic advantage that exalt a man above his fellows, without any mental exertion, sink him in reality below them. In proportion to his weakness, he is played upon by designing men, till the bloated monster has lost all traces of humanity. And that tribes of men, like flocks of sheep, should quietly follow such a leader, is a solecism that only a desire of present enjoyment and narrowness of understanding can solve. Educated in slavish dependence, and enervated by luxury and sloth, where shall we find men who will stand forth to assert the rights of man, or claim the privilege of moral beings, who should have but one road to excellence? Slavery to monarchs and ministers, which the world will be long in freeing itself from, and whose deadly grasp stops the progress of the human mind, is not yet abolished.

Let not men then in the pride of power, use the same arguments that tyrannic kings and venal ministers have used, and fallaciously assert that woman ought to be subjected because she has always been so. But, when man, governed by reasonable laws, enjoys his natural freedom, let him despise woman, if she do not share it with him;

and, till that glorious period arrives, in descanting on the folly of the sex, let him not overlook his own.

Women, it is true, obtaining power by unjust means, by practicing or fostering vice, evidently lose the rank which reason would assign them, and they become either abject slaves or capricious tyrants. They lose all simplicity, all dignity of mind, in acquiring power, and act as men are observed to act when they have been exalted by the same means.

It is time to effect a revolution in female manners — time to restore to them their lost dignity — and make them, as a part of the human species, labour by reforming themselves to reform the world. It is time to separate unchangeable morals from local manners. If men be demi-gods, why let us serve them! And if the dignity of the female soul be as disputable as that of animals — if their reason does not afford sufficient light to direct their conduct whilst unerring instinct is denied — they are surely of all creatures the most miserable! and, bent beneath the iron hand of destiny, must submit to be a fair defect in creation. But to justify the ways of Providence respecting them, by pointing out some irrefragable reason for thus making such a large portion of mankind accountable and not accountable, would puzzle the subtilest casuist.

The only solid foundation for morality appears to be the character of the Supreme Being; the harmony of which arises from a balance of attributes, — and, to speak with reverence, one attribute seems to imply the necessity of another. He must be just, because He is wise; He must be good, because He is omnipotent. For to exalt one attribute at the expense of another equally noble and necessary, bears the stamp of the warped reason of man — the homage of passion. Man, accustomed to bow down to power in his savage state, can seldom divest himself of this barbarous prejudice, even when civilisation determines how much superior mental is to bodily strength; and his reason is clouded by these crude opinions, even when he thinks of the Deity. His omnipotence is made to swallow up, or preside over His other attributes, and those morals are supposed to limit His power irreverently, who think that it must be regulated by His wisdom. I disclaim that specious humility

[8]Wollstonecraft is alluding to I Peter 5:8.

which, after investigating nature, stops at the Author. The High and Lofty one, who inhabiteth eternity, doubtless possesses many attributes of which we can form no conception; but Reason tells me that they cannot clash with those I adore — and I am compelled to listen to her voice. It seems natural for man to search for excellence, and either to trace it in the object that he worships, or blindly to invest it with perfection, as a garment. But what good effect can the latter mode of worship have on the moral conduct of a rational being? He bends to power; he adores a dark cloud, which may open a bright prospect to him, to burst in angry, lawless fury, on his devoted head — he knows not why. And, supposing that the Deity acts from the vague impulse of an undirected will, man must also follow his own, or act according to rules, deduced from principles which he disclaims as irreverent. Into this dilemma have both enthusiasts and cooler thinkers fallen, when they laboured to free men from the wholesome restraints which a just conception of the character of God imposes.

It is not impious thus to scan the attributes of the Almighty: in fact, who can avoid it that exercises his faculties? For to love God as the fountain of wisdom, goodness, and power, appears to be the only worship useful to a being who wishes to acquire either virtue or knowledge. A blind unsettled affection may, like human passions, occupy the mind and warm the heart, whilst, to do justice, love mercy, and walk humbly with our God, is forgotten. I shall pursue this subject still further, when I consider religion in a light opposite to that recommended by Dr. Gregory,[9] who treats it as a matter of sentiment or taste.

To return from this apparent digression. It were to be wished that women would cherish an affection for their husbands, founded on the same principle that devotion ought to rest upon. No other firm base is there under heaven — for let them beware of the fallacious light of sentiment; too often used as a softer phrase for sensuality. It follows then, I think, that from their infancy women should either be shut up like Eastern princes, or educated in such a manner as to be able to think and act for themselves. Why do men halt between two opinions, and expect impossibilities? Why do they expect virtue from a slave, from a being whom the constitution of civil society has rendered weak, if not vicious? Still I know that it will require a considerable length of time to eradicate the firmly rooted prejudices which sensualists have planted; it will also require some time to convince women that they act contrary to their real interest on an enlarged scale, when they cherish or affect weakness under the name of delicacy, and to convince the world that the poisoned source of female vices and follies, if it be necessary, in compliance with custom, to use synonymous terms in a lax sense, has been the sensual homage paid to beauty: — to beauty of features; for it has been shrewdly observed by a German writer[10] that a pretty woman, as an object of desire, is generally allowed to be so by men of all descriptions; whilst a fine woman, who inspires more sublime emotions by displaying intellectual beauty, may be overlooked or observed with indifference, by those men who find their happiness in their gratification of their appetites. I foresee an obvious retort — whilst man remains such an imperfect being as he appears hitherto to have been, he will, more or less, be the slave of his appetites; and those women obtaining most power who gratify a predominant one, the sex is degraded by a physical, if not by a moral necessity.

This objection has, I grant, some force; but while such a sublime precept exists, as, "Be pure as your heavenly Father is pure";[11] it would seem that the virtues of man are not limited by the Being who alone could limit them; and that he may press forward without considering whether he steps out of his sphere by indulging such a noble ambition. To the wild billows it has been said, "Thus far shalt thou go, and no farther; and here shall thy proud waves be stayed."[12] Vainly then do they beat and foam, restrained by the power that confines the struggling planets in their orbits, matter yields to the great governing Spirit. But an immortal soul, not restrained by mechanical laws and struggling to free itself from the

[9]Dr. John Gregory (1724–1773) was the author of the widely read conduct book, *A Father's Legacy to His Daughters* (1774).

[10]Possibly Immanuel Kant's *Critique of Judgment* (1790).
[11]1 John 3:3.
[12]Job 38:11.

shackles of matter, contributes to, instead of disturbing, the order of creation, when, co-operating with the Father of spirits, it tries to govern itself by the invariable rule that, in a degree, before which our imagination faints, regulates the universe.

Besides, if women be educated for dependence, that is, to act according to the will of another fallible being, and submit, right or wrong, to power, where are we to stop? Are they to be considered as vicegerents allowed to reign over a small domain, and answerable for their conduct to a higher tribunal, liable to error? It will not be difficult to prove that such delegates will act like men subjected by fear, and make their children and servants endure their tyrannical oppression. As they submit without reason, they will, having no fixed rules to square their conduct by, be kind, or cruel, just as the whim of the moment directs; and we ought not to wonder if sometimes, galled by their heavy yoke, they take a malignant pleasure in resting it on weaker shoulders.

But, supposing a woman, trained up to obedience, be married to a sensible man, who directs her judgment without making her feel the servility of her subjection, to act with as much propriety by this reflected light as can be expected when reason is taken at secondhand, yet she cannot ensure the life of her protector; he may die and leave her with a large family. A double duty devolves on her; to educate them in the character of both father and mother; to form their principles and secure their property. But, alas! she has never thought, much less acted for herself. She has only learned to please[13] men, to depend gracefully on them; yet, encumbered with children, how is she to obtain another protector — a husband to supply the place of reason? A rational man, for we are not treading on romantic ground, though he may think her a pleasing docile creature, will not choose to marry a family for love, when the world contains many more pretty creatures. What is then to become of her? She either falls an easy prey to some mean fortune-hunter, who defrauds her children of their paternal inheritance, and renders her miserable; or becomes the victim of discontent and blind indulgence. Unable to educate her sons, or impress them with respect, — for it is not a play on words to assert, that people are never respected, though filling an important station, who are not respectable, — she pines under the anguish of unavailing impotent regret. The serpent's tooth enters into her very soul, and the vices of licentious youth bring her with sorrow, if not with poverty also, to the grave.

This is not an overcharged picture; on the contrary, it is a very possible case, and something similar must have fallen under every attentive eye. I have, however, taken it for granted, that she was well disposed, though experience shows, that the blind may as easily be led into a ditch as along the beaten road. But supposing, no very improbable conjecture, that a being only taught to please must still find her happiness in pleasing; what an example of folly, not to say vice, will she be to her innocent daughters! The mother will be lost in the coquette, and, instead of making friends of her daughters, view them with eyes askance, for they are rivals — rivals more cruel than any other, because they invite a comparison, and drive her from the throne of beauty, who has never thought of a seat on the bench of reason.

It does not require a lively pencil, or the discriminating outline of a caricature, to sketch the

[13]"In the union of the sexes, both pursue one common object, but not in the same manner. From their diversity in this particular, arises the first determinate difference between the moral relations of each. The one should be active and strong the other passive and weak; it is necessary the one should have both the power and the will and that the other should make little resistance. This principle being established it follows that woman is expressly formed to please the man: if the obligation be reciprocal also and the man ought to please in his turn it is not so immediately necessary: his great merit is in his power, and he pleases merely because he is strong. This I must confess is not one of the refined maxims of love; it is however one of the laws of nature prior to love itself. If woman be formed to please and be subjected to man, it is her place, doubtless, to render herself agreeable to him instead of challenging his passion. The violence of his desires depends on her charms; it is by means of these she should urge him to the exertion of those powers which nature hath given him. The most successful method of exciting them, is, to render such exertion necessary by resistance; as in that case self-love is added to desire and the one triumphs in the victory which the other is obliged to acquire. Hence arise the various modes of attack and defence between the sexes; the boldness of one sex and the timidity of the other; — and in a word that bashfulness and modesty with which nature hath armed the weak in order to subdue the strong." — Rousseau's *Emilius*. I shall make no other comment on this ingenious passage than just to observe that it is the philosophy of lasciviousness. [Wollstonecraft]

domestic miseries and petty vices which such a mistress of a family diffuses. Still she only acts as a woman ought to act, brought up according to Rousseau's system. She can never be reproached for being masculine, or turning out of her sphere; nay, she may observe another of his grand rules, and, cautiously preserving her reputation free from spot, be reckoned a good kind of woman. Yet in what respect can she be termed good? She abstains, it is true, without any great struggle, from committing gross crimes; but how does she fulfil her duties? Duties! in truth she has enough to think of to adorn her body and nurse a weak constitution.

With respect to religion, she never presumed to judge for herself; but conformed, as a dependent creature should, to the effects of a good education! These the virtues of man's helpmate![14]

I must relieve myself by drawing a different picture. Let fancy now present a woman with a tolerable understanding, for I do not wish to leave the line of mediocrity, whose constitution, strengthened by exercise, has allowed her body to acquire its full vigour; her mind, at the same time, gradually expanding itself to comprehend the moral duties of life, and in what human virtue and dignity consist. Formed thus by the discharge of the relative duties of her station, she marries from affection, without losing sight of prudence, and looking beyond matrimonial felicity, she secures her husband's respect before it is necessary to exert mean arts to please him and feed a dying flame, which nature doomed to expire when the object became familiar, when friendship and forbearance take place of a more ardent affection. This is the natural death of love, and domestic peace is not destroyed by struggles to prevent its extinction. I also suppose the husband to be virtuous; or she is still more in want of independent principles. Fate, however,

breaks this tie. She is left a widow, perhaps without a sufficient provision; but she is not desolate! The pang of nature is felt; but after time has softened sorrow into melancholy resignation, her heart turns to her children with redoubled fondness, and anxious to provide for them, affection gives a sacred heroic cast to her maternal duties. She thinks that not only the eye sees her virtuous efforts from whom all her comfort now must flow, and whose approbation is life; but her imagination, a little abstracted and exalted by grief, dwells on the fond hope that the eyes which her trembling hand closed, may still see how she subdues every wayward passion to fulfil the double duty of being the father as well as the mother of her children. Raised to heroism by misfortunes, she represses the first faint dawning of a natural inclination, before it ripens into love, and in the bloom of life forgets her sex — forgets the pleasure of an awakening passion, which might again have been inspired and returned. She no longer thinks of pleasing, and conscious dignity prevents her from priding herself on account of the praise which her conduct demands. Her children have her love, and her brightest hopes are beyond the grave, where her imagination often strays. I think I see her surrounded by her children, reaping the reward of her care. The intelligent eye meets hers, whilst health and innocence smile on their chubby cheeks, and as they grow up the cares of life are lessened by their grateful attention. She lives to see the virtues which she endeavoured to plant on principles, fixed into habits, to see her children attain a strength of character sufficient to enable them to endure adversity without forgetting their mother's example. The task of life thus fulfilled, she calmly waits for the sleep of death, and rising from the grave, may say — "Behold, Thou gavest me a talent, and here are five talents."[15]

I wish to sum up what I have said in a few words, for I here throw down my gauntlet, and deny the existence of sexual virtues, not excepting modesty. For man and woman, truth, if I understand the meaning of the word, must be the same; yet the fanciful female character, so prettily drawn by poets and novelists, demanding the sacrifice of

[14]"O how lovely, exclaims Rousseau, speaking of Sophia, is her ignorance! Happy is he who is destined to instruct her! She will never pretend to be the tutor of her husband but will be content to be his pupil. Far from attempting to subject him to her taste she will accommodate her self to his. She will be more estimable to him than if she was learned he will have a pleasure in instructing her." — Rousseau's *Emilius*. I shall content myself with simply asking how friendship can subsist when love expires between the master and his pupil. [Wollstonecraft]

[15]Wollstonecraft alludes to the parable of the talents, Matthew 25: 14–30.

truth and sincerity, virtue becomes a relative idea, having no other foundation than utility, and of that utility men pretend arbitrarily to judge, shaping it to their own convenience. Women, I allow, may have different duties to fulfill; but they are *human* duties, and the principles that should regulate the discharge of them, I sturdily maintain, must be the same. To become respectable, the exercise of their understanding is necessary, there is no other foundation for independence of character; I mean explicitly to say that they must only bow to authority of reason, instead of being the *modest* slaves of opinion. In the superior ranks of life how seldom do we meet with a man of superior abilities, or even common acquirements? The reason appears to me clear, the state they are born in was an unnatural one. The human character has ever been formed by the employments the individual, or class, pursues; and if the faculties are not sharpened by necessity, they must remain obtuse. The argument may fairly be extended to women; for, seldom occupied by serious business, the pursuit of pleasure gives that insignificancy to their character which renders the society of the *great* so insipid. The same want of firmness, produced by a similar cause, forces them both to fly from themselves to noisy pleasures, and artificial passions, till vanity takes place of every social affection, and the characteristics of humanity can scarcely be discerned. Such are the blessings of civil governments, as they are at present organised, that wealth and female softness equally tend to debase mankind, and are produced by the same cause; but allowing women to be rational creatures, they should be incited to acquire virtues which they may call their own, for how can a rational being be ennobled by anything that is not obtained by its *own* exertions?

Germaine de Staël
1766–1817

Born into a society that even today seems to exclude women systematically from many cultural and intellectual pursuits, Anne-Louise-Germaine Necker, Baronne de Staël-Holstein was the first French woman to become a writer of international importance. She was well placed to do so as the daughter of Jacques Necker, the Swiss banker and financier who was finance minister to Louis XVI from 1776 to 1781 and again at the fateful calling of the Estates General in 1788. Her mother, Suzanne Curchod, was an intellectual in her own right, a clergyman's daughter to whom the historian Edward Gibbon had in his youth been engaged.

Germaine de Staël's *Essay on Fictions* dates from 1795, just after her return from exile in England, and its primary examples — Richardson and Fielding — are taken from English literature rather than from that of her native country. The ideas in the essay, like much written during this period, represent an awkward transitional phase between Enlightenment and Romantic thinking. Parts of the essay sound like an apology for fiction in line with Sidney's *Apology for Poetry* by insisting upon the greater power of the novel over history to make a sustained moral impression upon us. He is not mentioned by name, but her primary antagonist seems to be Samuel Johnson, for although she adroitly concedes what she must, she parries his major attacks in *The Rambler,* No. 4 (p. 212), on the immorality of fiction.

Instead of agreeing that the subject proper to art is general nature, she insists upon the importance of *nuance,* the specific and particular emotional quality within events that makes them real for us. (The reality achieved by the elaboration of details does not, on the other hand, strike her as artistically interesting.) Even more directly she defends the object of Johnson's odium, Fielding's *Tom Jones,* for possessing "the most general moral of any novel" geared "to show the uncertainty of judgments founded on appearances, proving the superiority of natural and what we may call involuntary virtues over reputations based on mere respect for external etiquette."

If Germaine de Staël defends Fielding as a moral educator — which would be Sidney's or Dryden's or Johnson's criterion as well — her ethical values, and specifically her preference for nature and instinct over social convention, bring her closer to being the first spokeswoman for Romanticism. If, like a woman of the Enlightenment salons, she spoke for Truth, she also felt, like the major Romantics, that the highest truth was that of feeling and that such a truth needed nurturing. She defended the growing literature of passionate eloquence, from Pope's "Eloisa to Abelard" to Goethe's *Werther,* as serving a significant function in reconciling especially gifted individuals — sensitive, passionate, and isolated from society — to their place in the world. A generation later, Shelley, who was born the year de Staël published her essay on fiction, would term these sensitive beings — whose passions are Aeolian harps on which the world plays — the "unacknowledged legislators of the world."

De Staël's last important piece of literary criticism, *On Literature Considered in Relation to Social Institutions* (1800), is, theoretically speaking, her most ambitious work, breaking ground that would later be explored by Hyppolite Taine and Karl Marx.

If, as her translator Vivian Folkenflik suggests, the book helped establish the Romantic canon, it went beyond the Romantic view of literature as the verbal product of special psychological traits like fancy, imagination, and genius. For de Staël, literature, however fantastic, is a product of the society within which artists produce and audiences enjoy creations, and it takes its form from geography, history, and politics, which shape the "manners" out of which art springs. De Staël's sense of manners is not a matter of mere politenesses and grace, like knowing which fork to use when picking up your smoked salmon. For de Staël, manners are the way connections are formed in a society, how influence works, how the powerful are constrained, and whose voice counts and with whom: The notion of manners is similar to what Foucault, in a more extensive context, calls "power/knowledge" (see the introduction to New Historicism and Cultural Studies, p. 1320).

De Staël's assessment of French literature since the Revolution is subtly balanced for a returned emigrée: She understands the overrefinement of the French court of the ancien régime, and the way in which many artistic talents were lost on an audience that demanded not merely wit, but wit of a sort that could be learned only by thorough familiarity with the conventions of that court. But she also recognizes that, in breaking through all the rules that had bound polite society, the republican revolution in politics had produced a vulgarity that was even more brutal. The satire that had restrained the powerful under Louis XVI had lost its force under the corrupt *Directoire*.[1]

In Section 2.4 of *On Literature* ("On Women Writers," reproduced here), de Staël views the republican revolution from her own particular perspective. A small clique of intelligent refined women — including her own mother, Mme. Necker — had set the intellectual and moral tone for the court under Louis XVI; incapable of holding public office themselves, their disinterested judgment of the capability and honesty of courtiers and ministers carried weight. With the destruction of the discursive practices of the old régime, however, women had no place at all, belonging "neither to the natural nor the social order." Not despite but because of the democratic institutions being established, the intelligent and creative woman had become an object of hatred to men and of indifference to her fellow women. De Staël hoped that a French republic would eventually foster equality of education between men and women, correcting this injustice, but, from our perspective it is not clear whether two centuries of democracy have entirely changed how both men and women respond to the exceptional woman.

Selected Bibliography

Andrews, Wayne. *Germaine: A Portrait of Madame de Staël*. New York: Atheneum, 1963.

Duffy, Bella. *Madame de Staël*. Boston: Roberts Brothers, 1887.

Folkenflik, Vivian, ed. and trans. *An Extraordinary Woman: Selected Writings of Germaine de Staël*. New York: Columbia University Press, 1987.

Forsberg, Roberta. *Madame de Staël and the English*. New York: Astra Books, 1967.

Gutwirth, Madelyn. *Madame de Staël, Novelist: The Emergence of the Artist as Woman*. Urbana: University of Illinois Press, 1978.

[1]The five-man executive body that ruled France from the collapse of the Revolutionary government in 1795 to the consulate of Napoleon (1799).

Luppé, Robert de. *Les Idées littéraires de Madame de Staël et l'heritage des lumières.* Paris: J. Vrin, 1969.

Marso, Lori J. "Defending the Queen: Wollstonecraft and Staël on the Politics of Sensibility and Feminine Difference." *Eighteenth Century: Theory and Interpretation* 43, no. 1 (2002): 43–60.

Postgate, Helen B. Smith. *Madame de Staël.* New York: Twayne, 1968.

Van Tieghem, Paul, ed. *De la littérature, considérée dans ses rapports avec les institutions sociales. Edition critique.* 3 vols. Geneva: Droz, 1959.

Winegarten, Renee. *Madame de Staël.* Leamington Spa, Eng., and Dover, NH: Berg, 1985.

From *Essay on Fictions*

INTRODUCTION

Man's most valuable faculty is his imagination. Human life seems so little designed for happiness that we need the help of a few creations, a few images, a lucky choice of memories to muster some sparse pleasure on this earth and struggle against the pain of all our destinies — not by philosophical force, but by the more efficient force of distraction. The dangers of imagination have been discussed a good deal, but there is no point in looking up what impotent mediocrity and strict reason have said on this topic over and over again. The human race is not about to give up being stimulated, and anyone who has the gift of appealing to people's emotions is even less likely to give up the success promised by such talent. The number of necessary and evident truths is limited; it will never be enough for the human mind or heart. The highest honor may well go to those who discover such truths, but the authors of books producing sweet emotions or illusions have also done useful work for humanity. Metaphysical precision cannot be applied to man's affections and remain compatible with his nature. Beginnings are all we have on this earth — there is no limit. Virtue is actual and real, but happiness floats in space; anyone who tries to examine happiness inappropriately will destroy it, as we dissolve the brilliant images of the mist if we walk straight through them. And yet the advantage of fictions is not the pleasure they bring. If fictions please nothing but the eye, they do nothing but amuse; but if they touch our hearts, they can have a great influence on all our moral ideas. This talent may be the most powerful way there is of controlling behavior and enlightening the mind. Man has only two distinct faculties: reason and imagination. All the others, even feeling, are simply results or combinations of these two. The realm of fiction, like that of imagination, is therefore vast. Fictions do not find obstacles in passions: they make use of them. Philosophy may be the invisible power in control of fictions, but if she is the first to show herself, she will destroy all their magic.

When I talk about fictions, I will therefore be considering them from two perspectives of content and charm: this kind of writing may contain pleasure without useful purpose, but never vice versa. Fictions are meant to attract us; the more moral or philosophical the result one is trying to achieve, the more they have to be decked out with things to move us, leading us to the goal without advance warning. In mythological fictions I will consider only the poet's talent; these fictions could well be examined in the light of their religious influence, but such a point of view is absolutely foreign to my subject. I will be discussing the writings of the ancients according to the impression they create in our times, so my concern must be with their literary talent rather than their religious beliefs.

Fictions can be divided into three groups: (1) marvelous and allegorical fictions, (2) historical fictions, (3) fictions in which everything is both

Translated by Vivian Folkenflik.

invented and imitated, where nothing is true and everything is likely.

This topic should really be discussed in an extensive treatise including most existing literary works and involving thoughts on almost every topic, since the complete exposition of any one idea is connected to the whole chain of ideas. But I am only trying to prove that the most useful kind of fiction will be novels taking life as it is, with delicacy, eloquence, depth, and morality, and I have excluded everything irrelevant to that goal from this essay.[1] . . .

III

The third and last part of this essay must deal with the usefulness of natural fictions, as I call them, where everything is both invented and imitated, so that nothing is true but everything looks true to life. Tragedies with completely imaginary subjects will not be included here; they portray a more lofty nature, an extraordinary situation at an extraordinary level. The verisimilitude of such plays depends on events that are extremely rare, and morally applicable to very few people. Comedies and other dramas are in the theater what novels are to other fiction: their plots are taken from private life and natural circumstances. However, the conventions of the theater deprive us of the commentary which gives examples of reflections their individuality. Dramas are allowed to choose their characters among people other than kings and heroes, but they can show only broadly defined situations, because there is no time for nuance. And life is not concentrated like that — does not happen in contrasts — is not really theatrical in the way plays have to be written. Dramatic art has different effects, advantages, and means which might well be discussed separately,

but I think only the modern novel is capable of achieving the constant, accurate usefulness we can get from the picture of our ordinary, habitual feelings. People usually make a separate case of what they call philosophical novels; all novels should be philosophical, as they should all have a moral goal. Perhaps, however, we are not guided so inevitably toward this moral goal when all the episodes narrated are focused on one principal idea, exempting the author from all probability in the way one situation follows another. Each chapter then becomes a kind of allegory — its events are only there to illustrate the maxim at the end. The novels *Candide, Zadig,* and *Memnon,* while delightful in other respects, would be much more useful if they were not marvelous, if they offered an example instead of an emblem and if, as I say, the whole story did not have to relate to the same goal.[2] Such novels are at the same disadvantage as teachers: children never believe them, because they make everything that happens relate to the lesson at hand. Children unconsciously know already that there is less regularity than that in real life. Events are also invented in novels like Richardson's and Fielding's, where the author is trying to keep close to life by following with great accuracy the stages, developments, and inconsistencies of human history, and the way the results of experience always come down to the morality of actions and the advantages of virtue, nonetheless. In these novels, however, the feelings are so natural that the reader often believes he is being spoken to directly, with no artifice but the tactfulness of changing the names.

The art of novel-writing does not have the reputation it deserves because of a throng of bad writers overwhelming us with their colorless productions; in this genre, perfection may require the greatest genius, but mediocrity is well within everyone's grasp. This infinite number of colorless novels has almost used up the passion portrayed in them; one is terrified of finding the slightest resemblance in one's own life to the situations they describe. It has taken the very greatest masters to bring this genre back again, despite the writers who have degraded it. And others

[1] I have read several chapters of a book called *The Spirit of Religions,* by M. Benjamin Constant, which offers some extremely ingenious insights into this whole question. The world of letters and philosophers ought to insist that the author of so great a work finish it and publish it. [De Staël] Later published as *The Origin, Forms, and Development of Religion* (1824–1831). Benjamin Constant de Rebecque (1767–1830), known today chiefly for his autobiographical love story *Adolphe,* was the longtime companion of Mme. de Staël, and the father of her daughter Albertine. They collaborated on writing and on plans for the political reform of France. [Tr.]

[2] Tales by Voltaire: *Zadig* was published in 1747, *Memnon* in 1749, *Candide* in 1759. [Tr.]

have dragged it even lower by including disgusting scenes of vice. Despite the fact that fiction's main advantage is to gather around man everything in nature that might be useful to him as a lesson or model, some writers supposed we might have some kind of use for these detestable paintings of evil habits. As if such fictions could ever leave a heart that rejected them in the same state of purity as a heart that had never known them! The novel as we conceive of it, however — as we have a few examples of it — is one of the most beautiful creations of the human mind, and one of the most influential on individual morality, which is what ultimately determines the morality of the public.

There is a very good reason why public opinion does not have enough respect for the writing of good novels, however. This is because novels are considered to be exclusively devoted to the portrayal of love — the most violent, universal, and true passion of them all, but also the passion which inspires no interest at any other time of life than youth, since youth is all it influences. We may well believe that all deep and tender feelings belong to the nature of love, and that hearts which have neither known nor pardoned love cannot feel enthusiasm in friendship, devotion in misery, worship of one's parents, passion for one's children. One can feel respect for one's duties, but no delight or self-surrender in their accomplishment, if one has not loved with all the strength of one's soul, ceasing to be one's self to live entirely in another. The destiny of women and the happiness of men who are not called upon to govern empires often depend for the rest of their lives on the role they gave to the influence of love in their youth. Nevertheless, when people reach a certain age, they completely forget the impression love made on them. Their character changes; they devote themselves to other goals, other passions; and these new interests are what we should extend the subjects of novels to include. A new career would then be open to authors who have the talent to paint all the emotions of the human heart, and are able to use their intimate knowledge of it to involve us. Ambition, pride, greed, vanity could be the primary topic of novels which would have situations as varied as those arising from love, and fresher plots. Will people object that such a tableau of men's passions exists in history, and that we should look for it there? History does not reach the lives of private men, feelings and characters that do not result in public events. History does not act on you with sustained moral interest. Reality often fails to make an effect; and the commentary needed to make a lasting impression would stop the essential quick narrative pace, and give dramatic form to a work that should have a very different sort of merit. And the moral of history can never be completely clear. This may be because one cannot always show with any degree of certainty the inner feelings that punish the wicked in their prosperity and reward the virtuous in their misery, or perhaps because man's destiny is not completed in this life. Practical morality is founded on the advantages of virtue, but the reading of history does not always put it in the limelight.

Great historians (especially Tacitus) do try to attach some moral to every event they relate, making us envy the dying Germanicus, and hate Tiberius at the pinnacle of his grandeur.[3] But they can still portray only those feelings certified by facts. What stays with us from a reading of history is more likely to be the influence of talent, the brilliance of glory, the advantages of power, than the quiet, subtle, gentle morality which is the basis of individual happiness and the relationship between individuals. Everyone would think me ridiculous if I said I set no value on history, and that I preferred fictions — as if fictions did not arise from experience, and as if the delicate nuances shown in novels did not come from the philosophical results and mother-ideas presented by the great panorama of public events! However, the morality of history only exists in bulk. History gives constant results by means of the recurrence of a certain number of chances: its lessons apply to nations, not individuals. Its examples always fit nations, because if one considers them in a general way they are invariable; but it never explains the exceptions. These exceptions can seduce each man as an individual; the exceptional circumstances consecrated by history leave vast empty spaces into which the miseries and wrongs that make up most private destinies could easily fall.

[3]See Tacitus' *Annales*, 2.72; books 1 and 2. [Tr.]

On the other hand, novels can paint characters and feeling with such force and detail that they make more of an impression of hatred for vice and love for virtue than any other kind of reading. The morality of novels belongs more to the development of the internal emotions of the soul than to the events they relate. We do not draw a useful lesson from whatever arbitrary circumstance the author invents as punishment for the crime; what leaves its indelible mark on us comes from the truthful rendition of the scenes, the gradual process or sequence of wrongdoing, the enthusiasm for sacrifices, the sympathy for misfortune. Everything is so true to life in such novels that we have no trouble persuading ourselves that everything could happen just this way — not past history, but often, it seems, the history of the future.

Novels give a false idea of mankind, it has been said. This is true of bad novels, as it is true of paintings which imitate nature badly. When novels are good, however, nothing gives such an intimate knowledge of the human heart as these portrayals of the various circumstances of private life and the impressions they inspire. Nothing gives so much play to reflection, which finds much more to discover in details than in generalities. Memoirs would be able to do this if their only subjects were not, as in history, famous men and public events. If most men had the wit and good faith to give a truthful, clear account of what they had experienced in the course of their lives, novels would be useless — but even these sincere narratives would not have all the advantages of novels. We would still have to add a kind of dramatic effect to the truth; not deforming it, but condensing it to set it off. This is the art of the painter: far from distorting objects, it represents them in a way that makes them more immediately apprehended. Nature sometimes shows us things all on the same level, eliminating any contrasts; if we copy her too slavishly we become incapable of portraying her. The most truthful account is always an imitative truth: as a tableau, it demands a harmony of its own. However remarkable a true story may be for its nuances, feelings, and characters, it cannot interest us without the talent necessary for the composition of fiction. But despite our admiration for the genius that lets us penetrate the recesses of the human heart, it is impossible to bear all those minute details with which even the most famous novels are burdened. The author thinks they add to the picture's verisimilitude, blind to the fact that anything that slows down the interest destroys the only truth fiction has: the impression it produces. To put everything that happens in a room onstage is to destroy theatrical illusion completely. Novels have dramatic conventions also: the only thing necessary in an invention is what adds to the effect one is creating. If a glance, a movement, or an unnoticed circumstance helps paint a character or develop our understanding of a feeling, the simpler the means, the greater the merit in catching it — but a scrupulously detailed account of an ordinary event diminishes verisimilitude instead of increasing it. Thrown back on a positive notion of what is true by the kind of details that belong only to truth, you soon break out of the illusion, weary of being unable to find either the instruction of history or the interest of a novel.

The greatest power of fiction is its talent to touch us; almost all moral truths can be made tangible if they are shown in action. Virtue has so much influence on human happiness or misery that one can make most of life's situations depend on it. Some severe philosophers condemn all emotions, wanting moral authority to rule by a simple statement of moral duty. Nothing is less suited to human nature. Virtue must be brought to life if she is to fight the passions with any chance of winning; a sort of exaltation must be aroused for us to find any charm in sacrifice; misfortune must be embellished for us to prefer it to the great charm of guilty enticement; and the touching fictions which incite the soul to generous feelings make it unconsciously engage itself in a promise that it would be ashamed to retract in similar circumstances. But the more real power there is in fiction's talent for touching us, the more important it becomes to widen its influence to the passions of all ages, and the duties of all situations. The primary subject of novels is love, and characters who have nothing to do with it are present only as accessories. It would be possible to find a host of new subjects if one followed a different plan. *Tom Jones* has the most general moral of any novel: love appears in it as only one of many means of showing the philosophical result. The real aim of *Tom Jones* is to show the uncertainty of judgments founded on appearances, proving the superiority of natural and what we may call involuntary virtues over reputations based on mere respect for external etiquette. And this is one of the most useful, most deservedly famous of all novels. *Caleb Williams,* by Mr. Godwin, is a recent novel which, despite some tedious passages and oversights, seems to give a good idea of this inexhaustible genre.[4] Love plays no part in this fiction; the only motives for the action are the hero's unbridled passion for the world's respect and Caleb's overpowering curiosity, leading him to discover whether or not Falkland deserves the esteem he enjoys. We read this story with all the absorption inspired by romantic interest and the reflection commanded by the most philosophical tableau.

Some successful fictions do give pictures of life unrelated to love: several *Moral Tales* of Marmontel, a few chapters of *Sentimental Journey,* various anecdotes from the *Spectator* and other books on morality, some pieces taken from German literature, whose superiority is growing every day.[5] There is still, however, no new Richardson devoting himself to paint men's other passions in a novel completely exploring the progress and consequences of these passions. The success of such a work would come from the truth of its characters, the force of its contrasts and the energy of its situations, rather than from that feeling which is so easy to paint, so quick to arouse interest, pleasing women by what it makes them remember even if it cannot attract them by the greatness or novelty of the scenes it presents. What beautiful things we would find in the Lovelace of ambition![6] What philosophical developments, if we were eager to explain and analyze all the passions, as novels have already done for love! Let no one object that books on morality are enough to teach us a knowledge of our duties; such books cannot possibly go into all

the nuances of delicacy, or detail the myriad resources of the passions. We can glean a morality purer and higher from novels than from any didactic work on virtue; didactic works are so dry that they have to be too indulgent. Maxims have to be generally applicable, so they never achieve that heroic delicacy we may offer as a model but cannot reasonably impose as a duty. Where is the moralist who could say: "If your whole family wants you to marry a detestable man, and you are prompted by their persecution to give a few signs of the most innocent interest to the man you find attractive, you are going to bring death and dishonor upon yourself"? This, however, is the plot of *Clarissa;* this is what we read with admiration, without a word of protest to the author who touches us and holds us captive. What moralist would claim that it is better to abandon oneself to deep despair, the sort of despair that threatens life and disturbs the mind, rather than marry the most virtuous man in the world if his religion is different from your own? Well, we need not approve of the superstitious opinions of *Clementina,* but love struggling against a scruple of conscience and duty winning out over passion are a sight that moves and touches even loose-principled people who would have rejected such a conclusion disdainfully if it had been a maxim preceding the tableau instead of an effect that followed it.[7] In novels of a less sublime genre, there are so many subtle rules for women's conduct! We could support this opinion by quoting from masterpieces like *The Princess of Clèves, The Count of Comminge, Paul and Virginia, Cecilia,* most of the writings of Madame Riccoboni, *Caroline,* whose charm is felt by everyone, the touching episode of Caliste, the letters of Camilla, in which the mistakes of a woman and their miserable consequences give a more moral and severe picture than the spectacle of virtue itself, and many other French, English, and

---

[4]William Godwin published *Caleb Williams* in 1794. [Tr.]

[5]Jean-François Marmontel, *Moral Tales* (1761, 1789–1792); Laurence Sterne, *A Sentimental Journey* (1768); Joseph Addison and Richard Steele, *The Spectator* (1711–12). [Tr.]

[6]Lovelace is the hero-villain of Richardson's *Clarissa* (1748). [Tr.]

[7]Clementina is the Italian woman who renounces the eponymous hero of Richardson's *Sir Charles Grandison* (1754), enabling him to marry Harriet Byron. Prévost's translation retains Richardson's title, but Mme. de Staël sees Clementina as primary. For the influence of this character on Corinne, see Ellen Moers, *Literary Women* (Garden City, N.Y.: Doubleday, 1977), p. 306. [Tr.]

German works.[8] Novels have the right to offer the severest morality without revolting our hearts; they have captured feeling, the only thing that can successfully plead for indulgence. Pity for misfortune or interest in passion often win the struggle against books of morality, but good novels have the art of putting this emotion itself on their side and using it for their own ends.

There is still one serious objection to love stories: that they paint love in such a way as to arouse it, and that there are moments in life when this danger wins out over every kind of advantage. This drawback could not exist in novels about any other human passion, however. By recognizing the most fleeting symptoms of a dangerous inclination from the very beginning, one could turn oneself as well as others away from it. Ambition, pride, and avarice often exist without the least consciousness on the part of those they rule. Love feeds on the portrait of its own feelings, but the best way to fight the other passions is to make them be recognized. If the features, tricks, means, and results of these passions were as fully shown and popularized by novels as the history of love, society would have more trustworthy rules and more scrupulous principles about all the transactions of life. Even if purely philosophical writings could predict and detail all the nuances of actions, as do novels, dramatic morality would still have the great advantage of arousing indignant impulses, an exaltation of soul, a sweet melancholy — the various effects of fictional situations, and a sort of supplement to existence. This impression resembles the one we have of real facts we might have witnessed, but it is less distracting for the mind than the incoherent panorama of events around us, because it is always directed toward a single goal. Finally, there are men over whom duty has no influence,

and who could still be preserved from crime by developing within them the ability to be moved. Characters capable of adopting humanity only with the help of such a faculty of emotion, the physical pleasure of the soul, would naturally not deserve much respect; nevertheless, if the effect of these touching fictions became widespread enough among the people, it might give us some assurance that we would no longer have in our country those beings whose character poses the most incomprehensible moral problem that has ever existed. The gradual steps from the known to the unknown stop well before we reach any understanding of the emotions which rule the executioners of France. Neither events nor books can have developed in them the least trace of humanity, the memory of a single sensation of pity, any mobility within the mind itself for them to remain capable of that constant cruelty, so foreign to all the impulses of nature — a cruelty which has given mankind its first limitless concept, the complete idea of crime.

There are writings whose principal merit is the eloquence of passion, such as the "Epistle of Abelard" by Pope, *Werther,* the *Portuguese Letters,* and especially *The New Héloïse.*[9] The aim of such works is often moral, but what remains with us more than anything else is the absolute power of the heart. We cannot classify such novels. Every century has one soul and one genius capable of achieving this — it cannot be a genre, it cannot be a goal. Who would want to proscribe these miracles of the word, these deep impressions which satisfy all the emotions of the passionate? Readers enthusiastic about such talent are very few in number; these works always do their admirers good. Let ardent, sensitive souls admire them; they cannot make their language understood by anyone else. The feelings that disturb such beings are rarely understood; constantly condemned, they would believe themselves alone

---

[8]All these works are novels. *The Princess of Clèves* is by Mme. de La Fayette (1678); *The Count of Comminge* is by Mme. de Tencin (1735); *Paul and Virginia* is by Jacques-Henri Bernadin de Saint-Pierre (1787); *Cecilia* (1782) and *Camilla* (1796) are by Fanny Burney; Marie-Jeanne Riccoboni wrote a number of novels in the mid-eighteenth century. *Caroline* is probably *Caroline de Lichtfield,* by Isabelle de Montolieu (1785). Isabelle de Charrière, later Constant's intimate friend, wrote *Caliste* (1787). [Tr.]

[9]Alexander Pope's poem "Eloisa to Abelard" (1717); Johann Wolfgang von Goethe's *The Sorrows of Young Werther* (1774); *The Portuguese Letters,* said to have been written by a Portuguese nun to her lover, but probably written by the translator, Gabriel-Joseph de Guilleragues (1669); Jean-Jacques Rousseau's *Julie, or The New Héloïse* (1761). All of these are epistolary fictions. [Tr.]

in the world, they would soon hate their own nature for isolating them, if a few passionate, melancholy works did not make them hear a voice in the desert of life, letting them find in solitude a few rays of the happiness that escapes them in the middle of society. The pleasure of retreat is refreshing after the vain attempts of disappointed hope; far from this unfortunate creature, the entire universe may be in motion, but such eloquent, tender writing stays near him as his most faithful friend, the one who understands him best. Yes, a book must be right if it offers even one day's distraction from pain; it helps the best of men. Of course there are also sorrows that come from one's own character flaws, but so many of them come from superiority of mind or sensitivity of heart! and there are so many that would be easier to bear if one had fewer good qualities! I respect the suffering heart, even when it is unknown to me; I take pleasure in fictions whose only effect might be to comfort this heart by capturing its interest. In this life, which we pass through rather than feel, the distributor of the only real happiness of which human nature is capable would be someone who distracts man from himself and others, suspending the action of the passions by substituting independent pleasures for them — if the influence of his talent could only last.

On Women Writers

Unhappiness is like the black mountain of Bember, at the edge of the blazing kingdom of Lahor. As long as you are climbing it, you see nothing ahead of you but sterile rocks; but once you are at the peak, heaven is at your head, and at your feet the kingdom of Cashmere.
— *The Indian Hut,* by BERNADIN DE SAINT-PIERRE[1]

The existence of women in society is still uncertain in many ways. A desire to please excites their minds; reason recommends obscurity; and their triumphs and failures are equally and completely arbitrary.

I believe a day will come when philosophical legislators will give serious attention to the education of women, to the laws protecting them, to the duties which should be imposed on them, to the happiness which can be guaranteed them. At present, however, most women belong neither to the natural nor to the social order. What succeeds for some women is the ruin of others; their good points may do them harm, their faults may prove useful. One minute they are everything, the next nothing. Their destiny resembles that of freedmen under the emperors: if they try to gain any influence, this unofficial power is called criminal, while if they remain slaves their destiny is crushed.

It would no doubt be generally preferable for women to devote themselves entirely to the domestic virtues, but the peculiar thing about men's judgments of women is that they are much likelier to forgive women for neglecting these duties than for attracting attention by unusual talent. Men are quite willing to tolerate women's degradation of the heart, so long as it is accompanied by mediocrity of mind. The best behavior in the world can scarcely obtain forgiveness for real superiority.

I am now going to discuss the various causes of this peculiar phenomenon, beginning with the condition of women writers in monarchies, then in republics. I am interested in the differences these political situations make in the destinies of women who set their minds upon literary celebrity; I will then consider more generally the sort of happiness fame can promise these women.

In monarchies, women have ridicule to fear; in republics, hatred.

In a monarchy, the sense of the right and proper is so acute that any unusual act or impulse

[1]A novel published in 1790. [Tr.]

to change one's situation looks ridiculous right away. Anything your rank or position forces you to do finds a thousand admirers; everything you invent spontaneously, with no obligation, is judged severely and in advance. The jealousy natural to all men calms down only if you can apologize for success under cover of some obligation. Unless you cover fame itself with the excuse of your situation and practical interests, if people think your only motive is a need to distinguish yourself, you will annoy those whom ambition is leading in the same direction as yourself.

Men can always hide their vanity or their craving for applause under the appearance or reality of stronger, nobler passions; but women who write are generally assumed to be primarily inspired by a wish to show off their wit. As a result, the public is very reluctant to grant its approval, and the public's sense that women cannot do without this approval is precisely what tempts it to deny it. In every walk of life, as soon as a man sees your obvious need of him, his feelings for you almost always cool down. A woman publishing a book makes herself so dependent on public opinion that those who mete it out make her harshly aware of their power.

These general causes, acting more or less uniformly in all countries, are reinforced by various circumstances peculiar to the French monarchy. The spirit of chivalry, still lingering on in France, was opposed in some respects to the overeager cultivation of letters even by men; it must have aroused all the more dislike for women concentrating on literary studies and turning their thoughts away from their primary concern, the sentiments of the heart. The niceties of the code of honor might well make men averse from submitting themselves to the motley criticism attracted by publicity. How much more must they have disliked seeing the creatures entrusted to their protection — their wives, sisters, daughters — running the gauntlet of public criticism, or even giving the public the right to make a habit of talking about them!

Great talent could triumph over all these considerations, but it was still hard for women to bear reputations as authors nobly, simultaneously combining them with the independence of high rank and keeping up the dignity, grace, ease, and unself-consciousness that were supposed to distinguish their habitual style and manners.

Women were certainly allowed to sacrifice household occupations to a love of society and its pleasures; serious study, however, was condemned as pedantic. If from the very first moment one did not rise above the teasing which went on from all sides, this teasing would end by discouraging talent and poisoning the well of confidence and exaltation.

Some of these disadvantages are not found in republics, especially if one of the goals of the republic is the encouragement of enlightenment. It might perhaps be natural for literature to become women's portion in such a state, and for men to devote themselves entirely to higher philosophy.

The education of women has always followed the spirit of the constitutions established in free countries. In Sparta, women were accustomed to the exercises of war; in Rome, they were expected to have austere and patriotic virtues. If we want the moving principle of the French Republic to be the emulation of enlightenment and philosophy, it is only reasonable to encourage women to cultivate their minds, so that men can talk with them about ideas that would hold their interest.

Nevertheless, ever since the Revolution men have deemed it politically and morally useful to reduce women to a state of the most absurd mediocrity. They have addressed women only in a wretched language with no more delicacy than wit. Women have no longer any motive to develop their minds. This has been no improvement in manners or morality. By limiting the scope of ideas we have not succeeded in bringing back the simplicity of primitive life: the only result of less wit has been less delicacy, less respect for public opinion, fewer ways to endure solitude. And this applies to everything else in the current intellectual climate too: people invariably think that enlightenment is the cause of whatever is going wrong, and they want to make up for it by making reason go backward. Either morality is a false concept, or the more enlightened we are the more attached to morality we become.

If Frenchmen could give their wives all the virtues of Englishwomen, including retiring habits and a taste for solitude, they would do very well to prefer such virtues to the gifts of brilliant wit. All the French will manage to do this way, however, is to make their women read nothing, know nothing, and become incapable of carrying on a conversation with an interesting idea, or an apt expression, or eloquent language. Far from being kept at home by this happy ignorance, Frenchwomen unable to direct their children's education would become less fond of them. Society would become more necessary to these women — and also more dangerous, because no one could talk to them of anything but love, and this love would not even have the delicacy that can stand in for morality.

If such an attempt to make women completely insipid and frivolous ever succeeded, there would be several important losses to national morality and happiness. Women would have fewer ways to calm men's furious passions. They would no longer have any useful influence over opinion — and women are the ones at the heart of everything relating to humanity, generosity, delicacy. Women are the only human beings outside the realm of political interest and the career of ambition, able to pour scorn on base actions, point out ingratitude, and honor even disgrace if that disgrace is caused by noble sentiments. The opinion of society would no longer have any power over men's actions at all if there were no women left in France enlightened enough to make their judgments count, and imposing enough to inspire genuine respect.

I firmly believe that under the ancien régime, when opinion exerted such wholesome authority, this authority was the work of women distinguished by character and wit. Their eloquence was often quoted when they were inspired by some generous scheme or defending the unfortunate; if the expression of some sentiment demanded courage because it would offend those in power.

These are the same women who gave the strongest possible proofs of devotion and energy during the course of the Revolution.

Men in France will never be republican enough to manage without the independence and pride that comes naturally to women. Women may indeed have had too much influence on public affairs under the ancien régime; but they are no less dangerous when bereft of enlightenment, and therefore of reason. Their influence then turns to an inordinate craving for luxury, undiscerning choices, indelicate recommendations. Such women debase the men they love, instead of exalting them. And is the state the better off for it? Should the very limited risk of meeting a woman whose superiority is out of line with the destiny of her sex deprive the republic of France's reputation for the art of pleasing and living in society? Without any women, society can be neither agreeable nor amusing; with women bereft of wit, or the kind of conversational grace which requires the best education, society is spoiled rather than embellished. Such women introduce a kind of idiotic chatter and cliquish gossip into the conversation, alienating all the superior men and reducing brilliant Parisian gatherings to young men with nothing to do and young women with nothing to say.

We can find disadvantages to everything in life. There are probably disadvantages to women's superiority — and to men's; to the vanity of clever people; to the ambition of heroes; to the imprudence of kind hearts, the irritability of independent minds, the recklessness of courage, and so forth. But does that mean we should use all our energy to fight natural gifts, and direct our social institutions toward humbling our abilities? It is hardly as if there were some guarantee that such degradation would promote familial or governmental authority. Women without the wit for conversation or writing are usually just that much more skillful at escaping their duties. Unenlightened countries may not understand how to be free, but they are able to change their masters with some frequency.

Enlightening, teaching, and perfecting women together with men on the national and individual level: this must be the secret for the achievement of every reasonable goal, as well as the establishment of any permanent social or political relationships.

The only reason to fear women's wit would be some sort of scrupulous anxiety about their happiness. And indeed, by developing their rational minds one might well be enlightening them as to the misfortunes often connected with their fate; but that same reasoning would apply to the effect of enlightenment on the happiness of the human race in general, a question which seems to me to have been decided once and for all.

If the situation of women in civil society is so imperfect, what we must work toward is the improvement of their lot, not the degradation of their minds. For women to pay attention to the development of mind and reason would promote both enlightenment and the happiness of society in general. The cultivated education they deserve could have only one really unfortunate result: if some few of them were to acquire abilities distinguished enough to make them hungry for glory. Even this risk, however, would do society no harm, and would only be unfortunate for the very limited number of women whom nature might dedicate to the torture of useless superiority.

And if there were to be some woman seduced by intellectual celebrity and insistent on achieving it! How easy it would be to divert her, if she were caught in time! She could be shown the dreadful destiny to which she was on the verge of committing herself. Examine the social order, she would be told; you will soon see it up in arms against any woman trying to raise herself to the height of masculine reputation.

As soon as any woman is pointed out as a person of distinction, the general public is prejudiced against her. The common people judge according to a few common rules which can be followed without taking any risks. Whatever goes beyond the habitual immediately offends people who consider daily routine the safeguard of mediocrity. A superior man is enough to startle them; a superior woman, straying even farther from the beaten track, must surprise and annoy them even more. A distinguished man almost always has some important career as his field of action, so his talents may turn out to be useful to the interests of even those who least value the delights of the mind. The man of genius may become a man of power, so envious and silly people humor him. But a clever woman is only called upon to offer them new ideas of lofty sentiments, about which they could not care less; her celebrity seems to them much ado about nothing.

Even glory can be a source of reproach to a woman, because it contrasts with her natural destiny. Strict virtue condemns the celebrity even of something which is good in itself, because it damages the perfection of modesty. Men of wit are so astounded by the existence of women rivals that they cannot judge them with either an adversary's generosity or a protector's indulgence. This is a new kind of combat, in which men follow the laws of neither kindness nor honor.

Suppose, as a crowning misfortune, a woman were to acquire celebrity in a time of political dissension. People would think her influence unbounded, even if she had no influence at all; accuse her of all her friends' actions; and hate her for everything she loved. It is far preferable to attack a defenseless target than a dangerous one.

Nothing lends itself more quickly to vague assumptions than the dubious life of a woman with a famous name and an obscure career. An empty-witted man may inspire ridicule, a man of bad character may drop under the weight of contempt, a mediocre man may be cast aside — but everyone would much rather attack the unknown power they call a woman. When the plans of the ancients did not work out, they used to convince themselves that fate had thwarted them. Our modern vanity also prefers to attribute its failures to secret causes instead of to itself; in time of need, what stands in for fatality is the supposed power of famous women.

Women have no way to show the truth, no way to throw light on their lives. The public hears the lie; only their intimate friends can judge the truth. What real way is there for a woman to disprove slanderous accusations? A man who had been slandered lets his actions answer the universe, saying, "My life is a witness: it too must be heard."[2] But where can a woman find any such witness? A few private virtues, hidden favors, feelings locked into the narrow circle of her situation, writings which may make her known in places where she does not live, in times when she will no longer exist.

A man can refute calumny in his work itself, but self-defense is an additional handicap for women. For a woman to justify herself is a new

---

[2]"Ma vie est un témoin qu'il faut entendre aussi." Mme. de Staël may be quoting an alexandrine from French classical drama. [Tr.]

topic for gossip. Women feel there is something pure and delicate in their nature, quickly withered by the very gaze of the public. Wit, talent, passion in the soul may make them emerge from this mist which should always be surrounding them, but they will always yearn for it as their true refuge.

However distinguished women may be, the sight of ill will makes them tremble. Courageous in misfortune, they are cowards against dislike; thought uplifts them, but their character is still weak and sensitive. Most women whose superior abilities make them want renown are like Erminia dressed in armor.[3] Warriors see the helmet, the lance, the bright plume of feathers, and think they are up against strength, so they attack with violence; with the very first blows, they have struck at the heart.

Such injustices can not only spoil a woman's happiness and peace of mind, but also alienate even the most important objects of her affection. Who can be sure that a libelous portrayal will not strike at the truth of memory? Who knows

[3] In Tasso's *Jerusalem Delivered* (1581), the princess Erminia wears borrowed armor to seek her love Tancred in the Christian camp. [Tr.]

whether or not slanderers, having wreaked havoc with life, will rob death itself of the tender, regretful feelings that should be associated with the memory of a beloved woman?

So far I have portrayed only the unfairness of men: but what about the threat of injustice from other women? Do not women secretly arouse the malevolence of men? Do women ever form an alliance with a famous woman, sustaining her, defending her, supporting her faltering steps?

And that is still not all. Public opinion seems to release men from every duty toward a recognizably superior woman. Men can be ungrateful to her, unfaithful, even wicked, without making public opinion responsible for avenging her. "Is she not an extraordinary woman?" That says it all; she is abandoned to her own strength, and left to struggle with misery. She lacks both the sympathy inspired by a woman and the power protecting a man. Like the pariahs of India, such a woman parades her peculiar existence among classes she cannot belong to, which consider her as destined to exist on her own, the object of curiosity and perhaps a little envy: what she deserves, in fact, is pity.

Friedrich von Schiller

1759–1805

Friedrich von Schiller, who chafed at being thought the *second* greatest poet, dramatist, and thinker of the early phase of the German Romantic Movement, was the son
of an army doctor who had risen to the rank of captain and married the daughter of
an innkeeper. He was educated through the patronage of the Duke of Württemberg
at his military school and trained in his father's career of military medicine. While
still in school he published lyric poetry, and at eighteen he wrote his most romantic
tragedy, *Die Räuber* (published in 1781 and performed the next year). Despite the
fame *Die Räuber* brought him, Schiller's artistic career took a long time to become
established; his patron disapproved of and discouraged his literary ambitions, the
more so as his drama became infected with liberal politics.

Schiller escaped to another province and wrote the domestic tragedy *Kabale und
Liebe* (1784) and the political drama *Don Carlos* (1787), plays that are familiar to
operagoers from Verdi's *Luisa Miller* and *Don Carlo*. For most of the 1780s Schiller
worked in provincial capitals like Mannheim and Dresden without securing a satisfactory position. At Weimar in 1787, however, he turned from the drama of Spanish
politics — in *Don Carlos* — to its history, and began a study of the Dutch struggle
against Spanish rule in the sixteenth century and the subsequent Thirty Years' War
that destroyed the Spanish Empire. As a result, he won the patronage of the Duchess
of Weimar and Goethe's recommendation to a professorship, and was able to marry
Charlotte von Lengefeld.

In the 1790s, Schiller moved from history to philosophy, absorbing the then new
theories of Immanuel Kant and turning his hand to the aesthetic questions that
Kant's *Critique of Judgment* had raised. His criticism includes *On Tragic Art* (1792),
Letters on Aesthetic Development (1795), and *On Naive and Sentimental Poetry*
(published in the journal *Die Horen* in 1795–96 and collected in 1800).

Following his work on poetic theory, Schiller returned to its practice, and in the
late 1790s published his major ballads. At the end of his life, however, he went back
to his first love, the theater, writing a series of grandly tragic plays that developed
out of his studies of the past and out of his political vision of a free society. Drawing
on his history of the Thirty Years' War, Schiller developed a trilogy about the
upstart General Wallenstein (1798–99), which he followed with *The Maid of
Orleans* (1801), *The Bride of Messina* (1803), and *Wilhelm Tell* (1804). In chronic
ill-health for the last several decades of his life, Schiller died at Weimar in 1805.

Schiller's motivation for writing *On Naive and Sentimental Poetry* is closely
linked to his ambivalent feelings — a combination of envy and admiration — about
his great contemporary, Goethe. Schiller was struck by how different he was from
Goethe: He wrote with painful hesitations, Goethe with ease; he was chronically ill,
Goethe vigorous; he was from the middle classes and social encounters were difficult for him, while Goethe had an aristocrat's easy manners. Since Goethe was evidently a great master of letters, what was Schiller? In a letter to his friend Wilhelm

von Humboldt, Schiller said: "We shall be differently categorized, but in my most courageous moments I am convinced that our categories will not be subordinated to one another, but instead will be jointly assimilated to a higher ideal concept of the species." So long as Schiller thought of human nature as one thing, as Kant's notions in the *Critique of Judgment* would incline one to do, either he or Goethe would have to be the closer to its ideal, but the dichotomy he sees between the *naive* and the *sentimental* implicitly allowed both poets to be supreme, each in his category: Goethe as the type of the naive genius, Schiller himself as the type of the sentimental.

The central distinction between naive and sentimental poetry turns on the poet's basic temperament, and the relation of that temperament to nature, which was regarded by Schiller as an ideal. The naive poets (Schiller's chief examples are Homer and Shakespeare) *are* nature itself: Their character is that of a child, with a child's sweetness and simplicity, and with a child's cruelty.

> The childlike character that the genius imposes upon his works he likewise displays in his private life and morals. He is *chaste,* for this nature always is; but he is not *prudish,* for only decadence is prudish. He is *intelligent,* for nature can never be otherwise; but he is not *cunning,* for only art can be so. He is *true* to his characters and his inclinations, but not so much because he possesses principles as because nature, despite all fluctuations, always returns to its former state.... He is *modest,* ... because genius always remains a mystery to itself, but he is not fearful because he does not know the dangers of the path he travels. The genres of naive poetry are the classic genres of epic, tragedy, and comedy.

If the naive poets *are* nature, the sentimental poets, in contrast, *love* nature — love it as something they feel they lack, as something that complements their character. The genres of sentimental poetry take shape from the poet's response to this lack. If the sentimental poet takes up the subject of the world as it is, alienated from nature, the real contrary to the ideal, then the poetry will be some form of *satire —* punitive (like that of Juvenal or Swift) if the poet "dwells in the realm of the will," conscious of the need to make things better; or *playful* (like that of Horace and Sterne) if the poet dwells in the "realm of the understanding," where the world's problems can be contemplated without battling over them.

On the other hand, the poet may write about the ideal rather than the real; the result is *elegiac* poetry. The true *elegy* is produced when the subject is the ideal of the past compared with the fallen present. (Here Schiller's primary example is the German poet Klopstock, but he also mentions James Thomson's *The Seasons* and Edward Young's *Night Thoughts* — a masterpiece of the English "graveyard school"). Or the poet may produce an *idyll* (as in Rousseau's *Julie, or the New Héloïse*) if the ideal is presented *as though* it were contemporary.

Since both the naive and the sentimental have associated temperaments and genres, it is possible for a sentimental master to work in a naive genre (as Virgil's and Milton's work in the epic demonstrates). Goethe is analyzed here as the reverse case, a naive genius taking up (in *The Sorrows of Young Werther* and *Wilhelm Meister's Apprenticeship*) sentimental themes and genres: "fanatically unhappy love, sensitivity to nature, feeling for religion ... the gloomy, formless, melancholic Ossianic world." "This task," Schiller concedes, "appears to be completely new and of quite unique difficulty, for in the ancient and naive world a *theme* of this kind did not occur, whereas in the modern the *poet* would be lacking." Goethe's subject — Werther — is "a personality who embraces the ideal with burning feeling and abandons actuality in order to contend with an insubstantial infinitude, who seeks continuously outside himself for that which he destroys within himself, to whom only his dreams are real." He himself is of all modern poets the most childlike and naive, the "least removed from the sensuous truth of things."

Schiller's ideas in *On Naive and Sentimental Poetry* spring from those of Kant but have a tendency to bring a historical dimension into idealist aesthetics, as the poet's work responds to his age and synthesizes its approach to the eternal nature from which all springs. As such, he is one of the links between the thinking of Kant and the later trends in German idealism that culminate in Hegel.

Selected Bibliography

Grossmann, Walter. "The Idea of Cultural Evolution in Schiller's *Aesthetic Education*." *Germanic Review* 34 (1959): 39–49.

Hewitt, Mark Algee. "(Re)Zoning the Naïve: Schiller's Construction of Auto-Historiography." *European Romantic Review* 14, no.2 (2003): 197–203.

Hermand, Jost. "Schillers Abhandlung über naive und sentimentalische Dichtung im Lichte der deutschen Popularphilosophie der 18. Jahrhunderts." *PMLA* 79 (1964): 428–41.

Jones, Michael T. "Twilight of the Gods: The Greeks in Schiller and Lukács." *Germanic Review* 59 (1984): 49–56.

Lloyd, Tom. "Madame Roland and Schiller's Aesthetics." *Prose Studies* 9 (1986): 39–53.

Lukács, Georg. "Schillers Theorie der modernen Literatur." In *Goethe und Seinen Zeit*. Bern: A. Francke, 1947.

Miller, R. D. *A Study of Schiller's 'Letters on the Aesthetic Education of Man.'* Harrogate, Eng.: Duchy, 1986.

Schaper, Eva. "Towards the Aesthetic: A Journey with Friedrich Schiller." *British Journal of Aesthetics* 25 (1985): 153–68.

Sharpe, Leslie. "Schiller's Fragment 'Tragödie und Komödie.'" *Modern Language Review* 81 (1986): 116–17.

Wilm, Emil Carl. *The Philosophy of Schiller in Its Historic Relations*. Boston: Luce and Co., 1912.

From *On Naïve and Sentimental Poetry*

The poet, I said either *is* nature or he will *seek* her. The former is the naive, the latter the sentimental poet.

The poetic spirit is immortal and inalienable in mankind, it cannot be lost except together with humanity or with the capacity for it. For even if

Translated by Julius Elias.

man should separate himself by the freedom of his fantasy and his understanding from the simplicity, truth and necessity of nature, yet not only does the way back to her remain open always, but also a powerful and ineradicable impulse, the moral, drives him ceaselessly back to her, and it is precisely with this impulse that the poetic faculty stands in the most intimate relationship.

Even now, nature is the sole flame at which the poetic spirit nourishes itself; from her alone it draws its whole power, to her alone it speaks even in the artificial man entoiled by civilization. All other modes of expression are alien to the poetic spirit; hence, generally speaking, all so-called works of wit are quite misnamed poetic; although, for long, misled by the reputation of French literature, we have mistaken them as such. It is still nature, I say, even now in the artificial condition of civilization, in virtue of which the poetic spirit is powerful; but now it stands in quite another relation to nature.

So long as man is pure — not, of course, crude — nature, he functions as an undivided sensuous unity and as a unifying whole. Sense and reason, passive and active faculties, are not separated in their activities, still less do they stand in conflict with one another. His perceptions are not the formless play of chance, his thoughts not the empty play of the faculty of representation; the former proceed out of the law of *necessity*, the latter out of *actuality*. Once man has passed into the state of civilization and art has laid her hand upon him, that *sensuous* harmony in him is withdrawn, and he can now express himself only as a *moral* unity, i.e., as striving after unity. The correspondence between his feeling and thought which in his first condition *actually* took place, exists now only *ideally;* it is no longer within him, but outside of him, as an idea still to be realized, no longer as a fact in his life. If one now applies the notion of poetry, which is nothing but *giving mankind its most complete possible expression,* to both conditions, the result in the earlier state of natural simplicity is the completest possible *imitation of actuality* — at that stage man still functions with all his powers simultaneously as a harmonious unity and hence the whole of his nature is expressed completely in actuality; whereas now, in the state of civilization where that harmonious cooperation of his whole nature is only an idea, it is the elevation of actuality to the ideal or, amounting to the same thing, the *representation of the ideal,* that makes for the poet. And these two are likewise the only possible modes in which poetic genius can express itself at all. They are, as one can see, extremely different from one another, but there is a higher concept under which both can

be subsumed, and there should be no surprise if this concept should coincide with the idea of humanity.

This is not the place further to pursue these thoughts, which can only be expounded in full measure in a separate disquisition. But anyone who is capable of making a comparison, based on the spirit and not just on the accidental forms, between ancient and modern poets,[1] will be able readily to convince himself of the truth of the matter. The former move us by nature, by sensuous truth, by living presence; the latter by ideas.

This path taken by the modern poets is, moreover, that along which man in general, the individual as well as the race, must pass. Nature sets him at one with himself, art divides and cleaves him in two, through the ideal he returns to unity. But because the ideal is an infinitude to which he never attains, the civilized man can never become perfect in *his* own wise, while the natural man can in his. He must therefore fall infinitely short of the latter in perfection, if one heeds only the relation in which each stands to his species and to his maximum capacity. But if one compares the species with one another, it becomes evident that the goal to which man in civilization *strives* is infinitely preferable to that which he *attains* in nature. For the one obtains its value by the absolute achievement of a finite, the other by approximation to an infinite greatness. But only the latter possesses *degrees* and displays a *progress,* hence the relative worth of a man who is involved in civilization is in general never determinable, even though the same man considered as an individual necessarily finds himself at a disadvantage compared with one in whom nature functions in her utter perfection. But insofar as the ultimate object of mankind is not otherwise to be attained than by that progress, and man

[1]It is perhaps not superfluous to remark that if here the new poets are set over against the ancients, the difference of manner rather than of time is to be understood. We possess in modern times, even most recently, naive works of poetry in all classes, even if no longer of the purest kind and, among the old Latin, even among the Greek poets, there is no lack of sentimental ones. Not only in the same poet, even in the same work one often encounters both species combined, as, for example, in *The Sorrows of Young Werther,* and such creations will always produce the greater effects. [Schiller]

cannot progress other than by civilizing himself and hence passing over into the first category, there cannot therefore be any question to which of the two the advantage accrues with reference to that ultimate object.

The very same as has been said of the two different forms of humanity can likewise be applied to those species of poet corresponding to them.

Perhaps on this account one should not compare ancient with modern — naive with sentimental — poets either at all, or only by reference to some higher concept common to both (there is in fact such a concept). For clearly, if one has first abstracted the concept of those species one-sidedly from the ancient poets, nothing is easier, but nothing also more trivial, than to depreciate the moderns by comparison. If one calls poetry only that which in every age has affected simple nature uniformly, the result cannot be other than to deny the modern poets their title just where they achieve their most characteristic and sublimest beauty, since precisely here they speak only to the adherent of civilization and have nothing to say to simple nature.[2] Anyone whose temperament is not already prepared to pass beyond actuality into the realm of ideas will find the richest content empty appearance, and the loftiest flights of the poet exaggeration. It would not occur to a reasonable person to want to compare any modern with Homer where Homer excels, and it sounds ridiculous enough to find Milton or Klopstock honored with the title of a modern Homer. But just as little could any ancient poet, and least of all Homer, support the comparison with a modern poet in those aspects which most characteristically distinguish him.

[2]Molière, as a naive poet, is said to have left it in every case to the opinion of his chambermaid what should stand or fall in his comedies; it might also be wished that the masters of the French buskin had occasionally tried the same experiment with their tragedies. But I would not advise that a similar experiment be undertaken with Klopstock's *Odes,* with the finest passages in the *Messiade,* in *Paradise Lost,* in *Nathan the Wise,* or in many other pieces. Yet what am I saying? — the test has really been undertaken, and Molière's chambermaid chops logic back and forth in our critical literature, philosophical and belletristic journals and travel accounts, on poetry, art and the like, as easily, if in poorer taste, on German soil than on French, as only becomes the servants' hall of German literature. [Schiller]

The former, I might put it, is powerful through the art of finitude; the latter by the art of the infinite.

And for the very reason that the strength of the ancient artist (for what has been said here of the poet can, allowing for self-evident qualifications, be extended to apply to the fine arts generally) subsists in finitude, the great advantage arises which the plastic art of antiquity maintains over that of modern times, and in general the unequal value relationship in which the modern art of poetry and modern plastic art stand to both species of art in antiquity. A work addressed to the eye can achieve perfection only in finitude; a work addressed to the imagination can achieve it also through the infinite. In plastic art works the modern is little aided by his superiority in ideas; here he is obliged to *determine in space in the most precise way* the representation of his imagination and hence to compete with the ancient artists in precisely that quality in which they indisputably excel. In poetic works it is otherwise, and even if the ancient poets are victorious too in the simplicity of forms and in whatever is sensuously representable and *corporeal,* the modern can nonetheless leave them behind in richness of material in whatever is insusceptible of representation and ineffable, in a word, in whatever in the work of art is called *spirit.*

Since the naive poet only follows simple nature and feeling, and limits himself solely to imitation of actuality, he can have only a single relationship to his subject and in *this* respect there is for him no choice in his treatment. The varied impression of naive poetry depends (provided that one puts out of mind everything which in it belongs to the content, and considers that impression only as the pure product of the poetic treatment), it depends, I say, solely upon the various degrees of one and the same mode of feeling; even the variety of external forms cannot effect any alteration in the quality of that aesthetic impression. The form may be lyric or epic, dramatic or narrative: We can indeed be moved to a weaker or stronger degree, but (as soon as the matter is abstracted) never heterogeneously. Our feeling is uniformly the same, entirely composed of *one* element, so that we cannot differentiate within it. Even the difference of language and era changes nothing in this regard, for just this pure unity of its origin and of its effect is a characteristic of naive poetry.

The case is quite otherwise with the sentimental poet. He *reflects* upon the impression that objects make upon him, and only in that reflection is the emotion grounded which he himself experiences and which he excites in us. The object here is referred to an idea and his poetic power is based solely upon this referral. The sentimental poet is thus always involved with two conflicting representations and perceptions — with actuality as a limit and with his idea as infinitude; and the mixed feelings that he excites will always testify to this dual source.[3] Since in this case there is a plurality of principles it depends which of the two will *predominate* in the perception of the poet and in his representation, and hence a variation in the treatment is possible. For now the question arises whether he will tend more toward actuality or toward the ideal — whether he will realize the former as an object of antipathy or the latter as an object of sympathy. His presentation will, therefore, be either *satirical* or it will be (in a broader connotation of the word which will become clearer later) *elegiac;* every sentimental poet will adhere to one of these two modes of perception.

---

[3]Anyone who observes the impression that naive poetry makes on him and is able to separate from it that part which is due to the content will find this impression always joyous, always pure, always serene, even in the case of very pathetic objects; with sentimental poetry it will always be somewhat solemn and intense. This is because with naive accounts, regardless of their subject matter, we always rejoice in our imagination in the truth, in the living presence of the object, and seek nothing further beyond these; whereas with the sentimental we have to reconcile the representation of imagination with an idea of reason and hence always fluctuate between two different conditions. [Schiller]

William Wordsworth

1770–1850

William Wordsworth was born in Cockermouth, Cumberlandshire, the son of an attorney who was steward to a noble lord, and raised in the Lake District in north-west England among hills and lakes and their rustic inhabitants and sojourners, whom he would celebrate in his poetry. Though orphaned at thirteen, Wordsworth managed to attend St. John's College, Cambridge. Taking his degree in 1791, Wordsworth spent a year on the Continent absorbing the sights and the spirit of the French Revolution in its most idealistic phase. On his return to England, Wordsworth wrote *Descriptive Sketches* and met an admirer of that volume, Samuel Taylor Coleridge, who was to be a major poetical and intellectual influence. Together, Wordsworth and Coleridge (mostly Wordsworth) wrote *Lyrical Ballads* (1798), the premier volume of English Romanticism. Although the critics were harsh ("This will never do," Francis Jeffrey began in his notorious attack), the public was not, and a second edition was published in 1800, to which Wordsworth contributed a preface, his single major piece of literary criticism, reprinted here.[1]

Most of Wordsworth's best poetry was written in a single decade, 1797–1807; during this period he wrote not only *Lyrical Ballads* but *Poems in Two Volumes* (1807), including the "Intimations of Immortality" Ode, and *The Prelude* (1805, published 1850). By his forties, when he published *The Excursion* (1814), he was in decline, though he continued to write long into his eighth decade. In old age he had become an institution, and Queen Victoria appointed him poet laureate in 1843.

The Preface to *Lyrical Ballads* is a transitional work between the rhetorical/mimetic literary theory of the eighteenth century and the expressive theories of the nineteenth. As an argument it is at odds with itself. Part of the confusion derives from Wordsworth's revisions: Most of the original 1800 version of the Preface adheres to a mode of thought (though not, of course, a thesis) that Samuel Johnson would readily have understood, while the 1802 version and subsequent editions ally the essay with later expressive theories of literature.

The occasion of the Preface was Wordsworth's desire to defend two of the revolutionary aspects of *Lyrical Ballads*: their use of a plain style and their rustic subject matter. He does so by attacking the poetic diction of the latter eighteenth century as artificial and meaningless. His memorable analysis of Thomas Gray's "Sonnet on the Death of Mr. Richard West" demonstrates how little of that brief poem actually functions in making its elegiac impression.

When he discusses the subject and style of *Lyrical Ballads*, however, Wordsworth calls on the values the eighteenth century already revered. Why did he choose to write about "low and rustic life"? Because there "the essential passions of the heart find a better soil in which they can attain their maturity, are under less

---

[1]Reprinted here is the 1802 version of the Preface to *Lyrical Ballads,* which includes the "What is a poet?" section, among other revisions.

restraint," and because "the manners of rural life . . . are most easily comprehended; and are more durable." This recalls Johnson's dictum that the poet who wishes to become a classic should choose to imitate "general nature" rather than topical but evanescent manners. Why did Wordsworth choose to write in the plain style, and what is the role of the reader? "I have proposed to myself to imitate, and, as far as is possible, to adopt the very language of men. . . . to keep my reader in the company of flesh and blood, persuaded that by so doing I shall interest him." At the same time, he hopes to "enlighten the understanding" of the reader and "strengthen and purify" his affections. It sounds as if Wordsworth, however revolutionary his style and subject matter, were defending his poetic practice in the most traditional terms as an attempt to "please many and please long" by providing "just representations of general nature."

Wordsworth thus far seems to be claiming that in *Lyrical Ballads* he was imitating the manners, passions, and actions of rustic Englishmen for the delight and instruction of his audience, but the sections added in 1802 suggest a very different approach to poetry: That poetry is created less by representing what is in the outside world than by attending to the voice within. These passages focus on the poet and the genesis of poetry. But once he had defined poetry as "the spontaneous overflow of powerful feelings," it becomes necessary to explain how the feelings of his preferred humble rustics, such as Goody Blake and Harry Gill, can overflow from a university-educated son of a country lawyer. Wordsworth's solution is to posit for the poet a special internal makeup. The poet is "endued with more lively sensibility, more enthusiasm and tenderness . . . a greater knowledge of human nature, and a more comprehensive soul, than are supposed to be common among mankind." Most important, the poet can express "those thoughts and feelings which," voluntarily or not, "arise in him without immediate external excitement." At times the poet can "let himself slip into an entire delusion, and even confound and identify his own feelings with" those of the people he describes. The poet is thus able to internalize something he has seen and experienced and call it up in himself as though he were participating in it.

As he discusses the process of poetic imagination and composition, Wordsworth erodes the mimetic/rhetorical framework with which he has begun by claiming that the feeling will not be precisely the same when it is imaginatively "recollected in tranquillity" as in immediate experience: It will be purified, on the one hand, but it will "fall short" of reality on the other. The validity of the feeling the poet conveys therefore is not measurable by its accuracy, as a mimetic theory would suggest; it must be measured by a subjective, internal measure: The poet's "faith that no words, which *his* fancy or imagination can suggest, will be to be compared with those which are the emanations of reality and truth."

Wordsworth's theories of poetic diction would be criticized by his friend Coleridge (in *Biographia Literaria,* Ch. 17), his theory of poetic process and imagination refined and replaced by more sophisticated versions, and his vision of the high status and purposes of poetry superseded by the celestial ascending rhetoric of Shelley. But in the Preface to *Lyrical Ballads* Wordsworth created the first and one of the most lasting apologies for the Romantic Movement in poetry and for the expressive theory of literature that underpinned its other beliefs.

Selected Bibliography

Barstow, Marjorie Latta. *Wordsworth's Theory of Poetic Diction.* New Haven: Yale University Press, 1917.

Berman, Douglas Scott. "The 'Other' Wordsworth: Philosophy, Art, and the Pursuit of the 'Real' in the Preface to *Lyrical Ballads.*" *Concentric: Literary and Cultural Studies*, 27, no. 1 (2001): 111–28.

Clancey, Richard W. *Wordsworth's Classical Undersong: Education, Rhetoric and Poetic Truth.* New York: St. Martin's Press, 2000.

Hirsch, E. D. *Wordsworth and Schelling.* New Haven: Yale University Press, 1960.

Jackson, Wallace. *The Probable and the Marvelous: Blake, Wordsworth and the Eighteenth-Century Critical Tradition.* Athens: University of Georgia Press, 1978.

Jones, Henry John Franklin. *The Egotistical Sublime: A History of Wordsworth's Imagination.* London: Chatto and Windus, 1960.

Knapp, Steven. *Personification and the Sublime: Milton to Coleridge.* Cambridge: Harvard University Press, 1985.

Peacock, M. L., Jr. *Critical Opinions of William Wordsworth.* Baltimore: Johns Hopkins University Press, 1950.

Smith, Nowell C., ed. *Wordsworth's Literary Criticism.* Bristol, Eng.: Bristol Classical Press, 1980.

Thorpe, C. D. "The Imagination: Coleridge versus Wordsworth." *Philological Quarterly* 18 (1939): 1–18.

Wlecke, Albert O. *Wordsworth and the Sublime.* Berkeley: University of California Press, 1973.

Preface to *Lyrical Ballads*

The first volume of these poems has already been submitted to general perusal. It was published, as an experiment, which, I hoped, might be of some use to ascertain, how far, by fitting to metrical arrangement a selection of the real language of men in a state of vivid sensation, that sort of pleasure and that quantity of pleasure may be imparted, which a poet may rationally endeavour to impart.

I had formed no very inaccurate estimate of the probable effect of those poems: I flattered myself that they who should be pleased with them would read them with more than common pleasure: and, on the other hand, I was well aware, that by those who should dislike them they would be read with more than common dislike. The result has differed from my expectation in this only, that I have pleased a greater number, than I ventured to hope I should please.

For the sake of variety, and from a consciousness of my own weakness, I was induced to request the assistance of a friend, who furnished me with the poems of the *Ancient Mariner,* the "Foster-Mother's Tale," the *Nightingale,* and the poem entitled *Love.* I should not, however, have requested this assistance, had I not believed that the poems of my friend would in a great measure have the same tendency as my own, and that, though there would be found a difference, there would be found no discordance in the colours of our style; as our opinions on the subject of poetry do almost entirely coincide.

Several of my friends are anxious for the success of these poems from a belief, that, if the views with which they were composed were indeed realized, a class of poetry would be produced, well adapted to interest mankind permanently, and not unimportant in the multiplicity, and in the quality of its moral relations: and on this account they have advised me to prefix a systematic defence of the theory, upon which the poems were written. But I was unwilling to undertake the task, because I knew that on this occasion the reader would look coldly upon my arguments, since I might be suspected of having been principally influenced by the selfish and foolish hope of *reasoning* him into an approbation of these particular poems: and I was still more unwilling to undertake the task, because, adequately to display my opinions, and fully to enforce my arguments, would require a space wholly disproportionate to the nature of a preface. For to treat the subject with the clearness and coherence, of which I believe it susceptible, it would be necessary to give a full account of the present state of the public taste in this country, and to determine how far this taste is healthy or depraved; which, again, could not be determined, without pointing out, in what manner language and the human mind act and react on each other, and without retracing the revolutions, not of literature alone, but likewise of society itself. I have therefore altogether declined to enter regularly upon this defence; yet I am sensible, that there would be some impropriety in abruptly obtruding upon the public, without a few words of introduction, poems so materially different from those, upon which general approbation is at present bestowed.

It is supposed, that by the act of writing in verse an author makes a formal engagement that he will gratify certain known habits of association; that he not only thus apprizes the reader that certain classes of ideas and expressions will be found in his book, but that others will be carefully excluded. This exponent or symbol held forth by metrical language must in different eras of literature have excited very different expectations: for example, in the age of Catullus, Terence, and Lucretius and that of Statius or Claudian; and in our own country, in the age of Shakespeare and Beaumont and Fletcher, and that of Donne and Cowley, or Dryden, or Pope. I will not take upon me to determine the exact import of the promise which by the act of writing in verse an author, in the present day, makes to his reader; but I am certain, it will appear to many persons that I have not fulfilled the terms of an engagement thus voluntarily contracted. They who have been accustomed to the gaudiness and inane phraseology of many modern writers, if they persist in reading this book to its conclusion, will, no doubt, frequently have to struggle with feelings of strangeness and awkwardness: they will look round for poetry, and will be induced to inquire by what species of courtesy these attempts can be permitted to assume that title. I hope therefore the reader will not censure me, if I attempt to state what I have proposed to myself to perform; and also (as far as the limits of a preface will permit), to explain some of the chief reasons which have determined me in the choice of my purpose: that at least he may be spared any unpleasant feeling of disappointment, and that I myself may be protected from the most dishonourable accusation which can be brought against an author, namely, that of an indolence which prevents him from endeavouring to ascertain what is his duty, or, when his duty is ascertained, prevents him from performing it.

The principal object, then, which I proposed to myself in these poems was to choose incidents and situations from common life and to relate or describe them, throughout, as far as was possible, in a selection of language really used by men; and, at the same time, to throw over them a certain colouring of imagination, whereby ordinary things should be presented to the mind in an unusual way; and, further, and above all, to make these incidents and situations interesting by tracing in them, truly though not ostentatiously, the primary laws of our nature: chiefly, as far as regards the manner in which we associate ideas in a state of excitement. Low and rustic life was generally chosen, because in that condition, the essential passions of the heart find a better soil in which they can attain their maturity, are less under restraint, and speak a plainer and more emphatic language; because in that condition of life our elementary feelings co-exist in a state of greater simplicity, and, consequently, may be more accurately contemplated, and more forcibly communicated; because the manners of rural life germinate from those elementary feelings; and, from the necessary character of rural occupations, are most easily comprehended; and are more durable; and lastly, because in that condition the passions of men are incorporated with the beautiful and permanent forms of nature. The language, too, of these men is adopted (purified indeed from what appear to be its real defects, from all lasting and rational causes of dislike or disgust) because such men hourly communicate with the best objects from which the best part of language is originally derived; and because, from their rank in society and the sameness and narrow circle of their intercourse, being less under the influence of social vanity they convey their feelings and notions in simple and unelaborated expressions. Accordingly, such a language, arising out of repeated experience and regular feelings, is a more permanent, and a far more philosophical language, than that which is frequently substituted for it by poets, who think that they are conferring honour upon themselves and their art, in proportion as they separate themselves from the sympathies of men, and indulge in arbitrary and capricious habits of expression, in order to furnish food for fickle tastes, and fickle appetites, of their own creation.

I cannot, however, be insensible of the present outcry against the triviality and meanness both of thought and language, which some of my contemporaries have occasionally introduced into their metrical compositions; and I acknowledge, that this defect, where it exists, is more dishonourable to the writer's own character than false refinement or arbitrary innovation, though I should contend at the same time that it is far less pernicious in the sum of its consequences. From such verses the poems in these volumes will be found distinguished at least by one mark of difference, that each of them has a worthy *purpose*. Not that I mean to say, that I always began to write with a distinct purpose formally conceived; but I believe that my habits of meditation have so formed my feelings, as that my descriptions of such objects as strongly excite those feelings, will be found to carry along with them a *purpose*. If in this opinion I am mistaken, I can have little right to the name of a poet. For all good poetry is the spontaneous overflow of powerful feelings: but though this be true, poems to which any value can be attached, were never produced on any variety of subjects but by a man, who being possessed of more than usual organic sensibility, had also thought long and deeply. For our continued influxes of feeling are modified and directed by our thoughts, which are indeed the representatives of all our past

feelings; and, as by contemplating the relation of these general representatives to each other we discover what is really important to men, so, by the repetition and continuance of this act, our feelings will be connected with important subjects, till at length, if we be originally possessed of much sensibility, such habits of mind will be produced, that, by obeying blindly and mechanically the impulses of those habits, we shall describe objects, and utter sentiments, of such a nature and in such connection with each other, that the understanding of the being to whom we address ourselves, if he be in a healthful state of association, must necessarily be in some degree enlightened, and his affections ameliorated.

I have said that each of these poems has a purpose. I have also informed my reader what this purpose will be found principally to be: namely to illustrate the manner in which our feelings and ideas are associated in a state of excitement. But, speaking in language somewhat more appropriate, it is to follow the fluxes and refluxes of the mind when agitated by the great and simple affections of our nature. This object I have endeavoured in these short essays to attain by various means; by tracing the maternal passion through many of its more subtle windings, as in the poems of the *Idiot Boy* and the *Mad Mother;* by accompanying the last struggles of a human being, at the approach of death, cleaving in solitude to life and society, as in the poem of the "Forsaken Indian"; by showing, as in the stanzas entitled "We Are Seven," the perplexity and obscurity which in childhood attend our notion of death, or rather our utter inability to admit that notion; or by displaying the strength of fraternal, or to speak more philosophically, of moral attachment when early associated with the great and beautiful objects of nature, as in *The Brothers;* or, as in the incident of "Simon Lee," by placing my reader in the way of receiving from ordinary moral sensations another and more salutary impression than we are accustomed to receive from them. It has also been part of my general purpose to attempt to sketch characters under the influence of less impassioned feelings, as in the "Two April Mornings," "The Fountain," "The Old Man Travelling," "The Two Thieves," etc. characters of which the elements are simple, belonging rather to nature than to manners, such as exist now, and will probably always exist, and which from their constitution may be distinctly and profitably contemplated. I will not abuse the indulgence of my reader by dwelling longer upon this subject; but it is proper that I should mention one other circumstance which distinguishes these poems from the popular poetry of the day; it is this, that the feeling therein developed gives importance to the action and situation, and not the action and situation to the feeling. My meaning will be rendered perfectly intelligible by referring my reader to the poems entitled "Poor Susan" and the "Childless Father," particularly to the last stanza of the latter poem.

I will not suffer a sense of false modesty to prevent me from asserting, that I point my reader's attention to this mark of distinction, far less for the sake of these particular poems than from the general importance of the subject. The subject is indeed important! For the human mind is capable of being excited without the application of gross and violent stimulants; and he must have a very faint perception of its beauty and dignity who does not know this, and who does not further know, that one being is elevated above another, in proportion as he possesses this capability. It has therefore appeared to me, that to endeavour to produce or enlarge this capability is one of the best services in which, at any period, a writer can be engaged; but this service, excellent at all times, is especially so at the present day. For a multitude of causes, unknown to former times, are now acting with a combined force to blunt the discriminating powers of the mind, and unfitting it for all voluntary exertion to reduce it to a state of almost savage torpor. The most effective of these causes are the great national events which are daily taking place, and the increasing accumulation of men in cities, where the uniformity of their occupations produces a craving for extraordinary incident, which the rapid communication of intelligence hourly gratifies.[1] To this tendency of life and manners the literature and theatrical exhibitions of the country have conformed themselves. The invaluable works of our elder writers,

I had almost said the works of Shakespeare and Milton, are driven into neglect by frantic novels, sickly and stupid German tragedies, and deluges of idle and extravagant stories in verse.[2] — When I think upon this degrading thirst after outrageous stimulation, I am almost ashamed to have spoken of the feeble effort with which I have endeavoured to counteract it; and, reflecting upon the magnitude of the general evil, I should be oppressed with no dishonourable melancholy, had I not a deep impression of certain inherent and indestructible qualities of the human mind, and likewise of certain powers in the great and permanent objects that act upon it which are equally inherent and indestructible; and did I not further add to this impression a belief, that the time is approaching when the evil will be systematically opposed, by men of greater powers, and with far more distinguished success.

Having dwelt thus long on the subjects and aim of these poems, I shall request the reader's permission to apprize him of a few circumstances relating to their *style,* in order, among other reasons, that I may not be censured for not having performed what I never attempted. The reader will find that personifications of abstract ideas rarely occur in these volumes; and, I hope, are utterly rejected as an ordinary device to elevate the style, and raise it above prose. I have proposed to myself to imitate, and, as far as is possible, to adopt the very language of men; and assuredly such personifications do not make any natural or regular part of that language. They are, indeed, a figure of speech occasionally prompted by passion, and I have made use of them as such; but I have endeavoured utterly to reject them as a mechanical device of style, or as a family language which writers in metre seem to lay claim to by prescription. I have wished to keep my reader in the company of flesh and blood, persuaded that by so doing I shall interest him. I am, however, well aware that others who pursue a different track may interest him likewise; I do not interfere with their claim, I only wish to prefer a different claim

---

[1]Wordsworth refers to the French Revolution and the war between England and France that followed.

[2]Wordsworth alludes to the vogue of the Gothic novel, which lasted from the early 1790s until about 1825.

of my own. There will also be found in these volumes little of what is usually called poetic diction; I have taken as much pains to avoid it as others ordinarily take to produce it; this I have done for the reason already alleged, to bring my language near to the language of men, and further, because the pleasure which I have proposed to myself to impart is of a kind very different from that which is supposed by many persons to be the proper object of poetry. I do not know how without being culpably particular I can give my reader a more exact notion of the style in which I wished these poems to be written than by informing him that I have at all times endeavoured to look steadily at my subject, consequently, I hope that there is in these poems little falsehood of description, and that my ideas are expressed in language fitted to their respective importance. Something I must have gained by this practice, as it is friendly to one property of all good poetry, namely, good sense; but it has necessarily cut me off from a large portion of phrases and figures of speech which from father to son have long been regarded as the common inheritance of poets. I also have thought it expedient to restrict myself still further, having abstained from the use of many expressions, in themselves proper and beautiful, but which have been foolishly repeated by bad poets, till such feelings of disgust are connected with them as it is scarcely possible by any art of association to overpower.

If in a poem there should be found a series of lines, or even a single line, in which the language, though naturally arranged and according to the strict laws of metre, does not differ from that of prose, there is a numerous class of critics, who, when they stumble upon these prosaisms as they call them, imagine that they have made a notable discovery, and exult over the poet as over a man ignorant of his own profession. Now these men would establish a canon of criticism which the reader will conclude he must utterly reject, if he wishes to be pleased with these volumes. And it would be a most easy task to prove to him, that not only the language of a large portion of every good poem, even of the most elevated character, must necessarily, except with reference to the metre, in no respect differ from that of good prose, but likewise that some of the most interesting parts of the best poems will be found to be strictly the language of prose, when prose is well written. The truth of this assertion might be demonstrated by innumerable passages from almost all the poetical writings, even of Milton himself. I have not space for much quotation; but, to illustrate the subject in a general manner, I will here adduce a short composition of Gray, who was at the head of those who by their reasonings have attempted to widen the space of separation betwixt prose and metrical composition, and was more than any other man curiously elaborate in the structure of his own poetic diction.

In vain to me the smiling mornings shine,
And reddening Phoebus lifts his golden fire:
The birds in vain their amorous descant join,
Or cheerful fields resume their green attire:
These ears alas! for other notes repine;
A different object do these eyes require;
My lonely anguish melts no heart but mine;
And in my breast the imperfect joys expire;
Yet Morning smiles the busy race to cheer,
And new-born pleasure brings to happier men;
The fields to all their wonted tribute bear;
To warm their little loves the birds complain.
I fruitless mourn to him that cannot hear
And weep the more because I weep in vain.[3]

It will easily be perceived that the only part of this sonnet which is of any value is the lines printed in italics: it is equally obvious, that, except in the rhyme, and in the use of the single word "fruitless" for fruitlessly, which is so far a defect, the language of these lines does in no respect differ from that of prose.

By the foregoing quotation I have shown that the language of prose may yet be well adapted to poetry; and I have previously asserted that a large portion of the language of every good poem can in no respect differ from that of good prose. I will go further. I do not doubt that it may be safely affirmed, that there neither is, nor can be, any essential difference between the language of prose and metrical composition. We are fond of tracing the resemblance between poetry and painting, and, accordingly, we call them sisters: but where shall we find bonds of connection sufficiently

[3]Thomas Gray, "Sonnet on the Death of Mr. Richard West."

strict to typify the affinity betwixt metrical and prose composition? They both speak by and to the same organs; the bodies in which both of them are clothed may be said to be of the same substance, their affections are kindred and almost identical, not necessarily differing even in degree; poetry[4] sheds no tears "such as Angels weep," but natural and human tears; she can boast of no celestial ichor that distinguishes her vital juices from those of prose; the same human blood circulates through the veins of them both.

If it be affirmed that rhyme and metrical arrangement of themselves constitute a distinction which overturns what I have been saying on the strict affinity of metrical language with that of prose, and paves the way for other artificial distinctions which the mind voluntarily admits, I answer that the language of such poetry as I am recommending is, as far as is possible, a selection of the language really spoken by men; that this selection, wherever it is made with true taste and feeling, will of itself form a distinction far greater than would at first be imagined, and will entirely separate the composition from the vulgarity and meanness of ordinary life; and, if metre be super-added thereto, I believe that a dissimilitude will be produced altogether sufficient for the gratification of a rational mind. What other distinction would we have? Whence is it to come? And where is it to exist? Not, surely, where the poet speaks through the mouths of his characters: it cannot be necessary here, either for elevation of style, or any of its supposed ornaments: for, if the poet's subject be judiciously chosen, it will naturally, and upon fit occasion, lead him to passions the language of which, if selected truly and judiciously, must necessarily be dignified and variegated, and alive with metaphors and figures. I forbear to speak of an incongruity which would shock the intelligent reader, should the poet interweave any foreign

splendour of his own with that which the passion naturally suggests: it is sufficient to say that such addition is unnecessary. And, surely, it is more probable that those passages, which with propriety abound with metaphors and figures, will have their due effect, if, upon other occasions where the passions are of a milder character, the style also be subdued and temperate.

But, as the pleasure which I hope to give by the poems I now present to the reader must depend entirely on just notions upon this subject, and, as it is in itself of the highest importance to our taste and moral feelings, I cannot content myself with these detached remarks. And if, in what I am about to say, it shall appear to some that my labour is unnecessary, and that I am like a man fighting a battle without enemies, I would remind such persons, that, whatever may be the language outwardly holden by men, a practical faith in the opinions which I am wishing to establish is almost unknown. If my conclusions are admitted, and carried as far as they must be carried if admitted at all, our judgments concerning the works of the greatest poets both ancient and modern will be far different from what they are at present, both when we praise, and when we censure: and our moral feelings influencing, and influenced by these judgments will, I believe, be corrected and purified.

Taking up the subject, then, upon general grounds, I ask what is meant by the word poet? What is a poet? To whom does he address himself? And what language is to be expected from him? He is a man speaking to men: a man, it is true, endued with more lively sensibility, more enthusiasm and tenderness, who has a greater knowledge of human nature, and a more comprehensive soul, than are supposed to be common among mankind; a man pleased with his own passions and volitions, and who rejoices more than other men in the spirit of life that is in him; delighting to contemplate similar volitions and passions as manifested in the goings-on of the universe, and habitually impelled to create them where he does not find them. To these qualities he has added a disposition to be affected more than other men by absent things as if they were present; an ability of conjuring up in himself passions, which are indeed far from being the same as those

[4]I here use the word "poetry" (though against my own judgment) as opposed to the word prose, and synonymous with metrical composition. But much confusion has been introduced into criticism by this contradistinction of poetry and prose, instead of the more philosophical one of poetry and matter of fact, or science. The only strict antithesis to prose is metre; nor is this, in truth, a *strict* antithesis, because lines and passages of metre so naturally occur in writing prose, that it would be scarcely possible to avoid them, even were it desirable. [Wordsworth]

produced by real events, yet (especially in those parts of the general sympathy which are pleasing and delightful) do more nearly resemble the passions produced by real events, than any thing which, from the motions of their own minds merely, other men are accustomed to feel in themselves; whence, and from practice, he has acquired a greater readiness and power in expressing what he thinks and feels, and especially those thoughts and feelings which, by his own choice, or from the structure of his own mind, arise in him without immediate external excitement.

But, whatever portion of this faculty we may suppose even the greatest poet to possess, there cannot be a doubt but that the language which it will suggest to him, must, in liveliness and truth, fall far short of that which is uttered by men in real life, under the actual pressure of those passions, certain shadows of which the poet thus produces, or feels to be produced, in himself. However exalted a notion we would wish to cherish of the character of a poet, it is obvious, that, while he describes and imitates passions, his situation is altogether slavish and mechanical, compared with the freedom and power of real and substantial action and suffering. So that it will be the wish of the poet to bring his feelings near to those of the persons whose feelings he describes, nay, for short spaces of time perhaps, to let himself slip into an entire delusion, and even confound and identify his own feelings with theirs; modifying only the language which is thus suggested to him, by a consideration that he describes for a particular purpose, that of giving pleasure. Here, then, he will apply the principle on which I have so much insisted, namely, that of selection; on this he will depend for removing what would otherwise be painful or disgusting in the passion; he will feel that there is no necessity to trick out or to elevate nature: and, the more industriously he applies this principle, the deeper will be his faith that no words, which *his* fancy or imagination can suggest, will be to be compared with those which are the emanations of reality and truth.

But it may be said by those who do not object to the general spirit of these remarks, that, as it is impossible for the poet to produce upon all occasions language as exquisitely fitted for the passion as that which the real passion itself suggests, it is proper that he should consider himself as in the situation of a translator, who deems himself justified when he substitutes excellences of another kind for those which are unattainable by him; and endeavours occasionally to surpass his original, in order to make some amends for the general inferiority to which he feels that he must submit. But this would be to encourage idleness and unmanly despair. Further, it is the language of men who speak of what they do not understand; who talk of poetry as of a matter of amusement and idle pleasure; who will converse with us as gravely about a *taste* for poetry, as they express it, as if it were a thing as indifferent as a taste for rope-dancing, or frontiniac or sherry. Aristotle, I have been told, hath said, that poetry is the most philosophic of all writing:[5] it is so: its object is truth, not individual and local, but general, and operative; not standing upon external testimony, but carried alive into the heart by passion; truth which is its own testimony, which gives strength and divinity to the tribunal to which it appeals, and receives them from the same tribunal. Poetry is the image of man and nature. The obstacles which stand in the way of the fidelity of the biographer and historian, and of their consequent utility, are incalculably greater than those which are to be encountered by the poet who has an adequate notion of the dignity of his art. The poet writes under one restriction only, namely, that of the necessity of giving immediate pleasure to a human being possessed of that information which may be expected from him, not as a lawyer, a physician, a mariner, an astronomer or a natural philosopher, but as a man. Except this one restriction, there is no object standing between the poet and the image of things; between this, and the biographer and historian there are a thousand.

Nor let this necessity of producing immediate pleasure be considered as a degradation of the poet's art. It is far otherwise. It is an acknowledgment of the beauty of the universe, an acknowledgment the more sincere because it is not formal, but indirect; it is a task light and easy to him who looks at the world in the spirit of love: further, it is a homage paid to the native and

---

[5]Aristotle, *Poetics,* Ch. 9. One notes that Wordsworth misquotes Aristotle by hearsay.

naked dignity of man, to the grand elementary principle of pleasure, by which he knows, and feels, and lives, and moves. We have no sympathy but what is propagated by pleasure: I would not be misunderstood; but wherever we sympathize with pain it will be found that the sympathy is produced and carried on by subtle combinations with pleasure. We have no knowledge, that is, no general principles drawn from the contemplation of particular facts, but what has been built up by pleasure, and exists in us by pleasure alone. The man of science, the chemist and mathematician, whatever difficulties and disgusts they may have had to struggle with, know and feel this. However painful may be the objects with which the anatomist's knowledge is connected, he feels that his knowledge is pleasure; and where he has no pleasure he has no knowledge. What then does the poet? He considers man and the objects that surround him as acting and reacting upon each other, so as to produce an infinite complexity of pain and pleasure; he considers man in his own nature and in his ordinary life as contemplating this with a certain quantity of immediate knowledge, with certain convictions, intuitions, and deductions which by habit become of the nature of intuitions; he considers him as looking upon this complex scene of ideas and sensations, and finding every where objects that immediately excite in him sympathies which, from the necessities of his nature, are accompanied by an overbalance of enjoyment.

To this knowledge which all men carry about with them, and to these sympathies in which without any other discipline than that of our daily life we are fitted to take delight, the poet principally directs his attention. He considers man and nature as essentially adapted to each other, and the mind of man as naturally the mirror of the fairest and most interesting qualities of nature. And thus the poet, prompted by this feeling of pleasure which accompanies him through the whole course of his studies, converses with general nature with affections akin to those, which, through labour and length of time, the man of science has raised up in himself, by conversing with those particular parts of nature which are the objects of his studies. The knowledge both of the poet and the man of science is pleasure; but the knowledge of the one cleaves to us as a necessary part of our existence, our natural and unalienable inheritance; the other is a personal and individual acquisition, slow to come to us, and by no habitual and direct sympathy connecting us with our fellow-beings. The man of science seeks truth as a remote and unknown benefactor; he cherishes and loves it in his solitude: the poet, singing a song in which all human beings join with him, rejoices in the presence of truth as our visible friend and hourly companion. Poetry is the breath and finer spirit of all knowledge; it is the impassioned expression which is in the countenance of all science. Emphatically may it be said of the poet, as Shakespeare hath said of man, "that he looks before and after." He is the rock of defence of human nature; an upholder and preserver, carrying every where with him relationship and love. In spite of difference of soil and climate, of language and manners, of laws and customs, in spite of things silently gone out of mind and things violently destroyed, the poet binds together by passion and knowledge the vast empire of human society, as it is spread over the whole earth, and over all time. The objects of the poet's thoughts are every where; though the eyes and senses of man are, it is true, his favourite guides, yet he will follow wheresoever he can find an atmosphere of sensation in which to move his wings. Poetry is the first and last of all knowledge — it is as immortal as the heart of man. If the labours of men of science should ever create any material revolution, direct or indirect, in our condition, and in the impressions which we habitually receive, the poet will sleep then no more than at present, but he will be ready to follow the steps of the man of science, not only in those general indirect effects, but he will be at his side, carrying sensation into the midst of the objects of the science itself. The remotest discoveries of the chemist, the botanist, or mineralogist, will be as proper objects of the poet's art as any upon which it can be employed, if the time should ever come when these things shall be familiar to us, and the relations under which they are contemplated by the followers of these respective sciences shall be manifestly and palpably material to us as enjoying and suffering beings. If the time should ever come when what is now called science, thus familiarized to men, shall be ready to put on, as it were, a form of flesh and blood, the poet will lend his divine spirit to aid the transfiguration, and will welcome the being thus produced, as a dear and genuine inmate of the household of man. — It is not, then, to be supposed that any one, who holds that sublime notion of poetry which I have attempted to convey, will break in upon the sanctity and truth of his pictures by transitory and accidental ornaments, and endeavour to excite admiration of himself by arts, the necessity of which must manifestly depend upon the assumed meanness of his subject.

What I have thus far said applies to poetry in general; but especially to those parts of composition where the poet speaks through the mouths of his characters; and upon this point it appears to have such weight that I will conclude, there are few persons, of good sense, who would not allow that the dramatic parts of composition are defective, in proportion as they deviate from the real language of nature, and are coloured by a diction of the poet's own, either peculiar to him as an individual poet, or belonging simply to poets in general, to a body of men who, from the circumstance of their compositions being in metre, it is expected will employ a particular language.

It is not, then, in the dramatic parts of composition that we look for this distinction of language; but still it may be proper and necessary where the poet speaks to us in his own person and character. To this I answer by referring my reader to the description which I have before given of a poet. Among the qualities which I have enumerated as principally conducing to form a poet, is implied nothing differing in kind from other men, but only in degree. The sum of what I have there said is, that the poet is chiefly distinguished from other men by a greater promptness to think and feel without immediate external excitement, and a greater power in expressing such thoughts and feelings as are produced in him in that manner. But these passions and thoughts and feelings are the general passions and thoughts and feelings of men. And with what are they connected? Undoubtedly with our moral sentiments and animal sensations, and with the causes which excite these; with the operations of the elements and the appearances of the visible universe; with storm and sunshine, with the revolutions of the seasons, with cold and heat, with loss of friends and kindred, with injuries and resentments, gratitude and hope, with fear and sorrow. These, and the like, are the sensations and objects which the poet describes, as they are the sensations of other men, and the objects which interest them. The poet thinks and feels in the spirit of the passions of men. How, then, can his language differ in any material degree from that of all other men who feel vividly and see clearly? It might be *proved* that it is impossible. But supposing that this were not the case, the poet might then be allowed to use a peculiar language, when expressing his feelings for his own gratification, or that of men like himself. But poets do not write for poets alone, but for men. Unless therefore we are advocates for that admiration which depends upon ignorance, and that pleasure which arises from hearing what we do not understand, the poet must descend from this supposed height, and, in order to excite rational sympathy, he must express himself as other men express themselves. To this it may be added, that while he is only selecting from the real language of men, or, which amounts to the same thing, composing accurately in the spirit of such selection, he is treading upon safe ground, and we know what we are to expect from him. Our feelings are the same with respect to metre; for, as it may be proper to remind the reader, the distinction of metre is regular and uniform, and not like that which is produced by what is usually called poetic diction, arbitrary, and subject to infinite caprices upon which no calculation whatever can be made. In the one case, the reader is utterly at the mercy of the poet respecting what imagery or diction he may choose to connect with the passion, whereas, in the other, the metre obeys certain laws, to which the poet and reader both willingly submit because they are certain, and because no interference is made by them with the passion but such as the concurring testimony of ages has shown to heighten and improve the pleasure which co-exists with it.

It will now be proper to answer an obvious question, namely, why, professing these opinions, have I written in verse? To this, in addition to such answer as is included in what I have already said, I reply in the first place, because, however I may have restricted myself, there is still left open to me what confessedly constitutes the most valuable object of all writing whether in prose or verse, the great and universal passions of men, the most general and interesting of their occupations, and the entire world of nature, from which I am at liberty to supply myself with endless combinations of forms and imagery. Now, supposing for a moment that whatever is interesting in these objects may be as vividly described in prose, why am I to be condemned, if to such description I have endeavoured to superadd the charm which, by the consent of all nations, is acknowledged to exist in metrical language? To this, by such as are unconvinced by what I have already said, it may be answered, that a very small part of the pleasure given by poetry depends upon the metre, and that it is injudicious to write in metre, unless it be accompanied with the other artificial distinctions of style with which metre is usually accompanied, and that by such deviation more will be lost from the shock which will be thereby given to the reader's associations, than will be counterbalanced by any pleasure which he can derive from the general power of numbers. In answer to those who still contend for the necessity of accompanying metre with certain appropriate colours of style in order to the accomplishment of its appropriate end, and who also, in my opinion, greatly underrate the power of metre in itself, it might perhaps, as far as relates to these poems, have been almost sufficient to observe, that poems are extant, written upon more humble subjects, and in a more naked and simple style than I have aimed at, which poems have continued to give pleasure from generation to generation. Now, if nakedness and simplicity be a defect, the fact here mentioned affords a strong presumption that poems somewhat less naked and simple are capable of affording pleasure at the present day; and, what I wished *chiefly* to attempt, at present, was to justify myself for having written under the impression of this belief.

But I might point out various causes why, when the style is manly, and the subject of some importance, words metrically arranged will long continue to impart such a pleasure to mankind as he who is sensible of the extent of that pleasure will be desirous to impart. The end of poetry is to produce excitement in co-existence with an overbalance of pleasure. Now, by the supposition, excitement is an unusual and irregular state of the mind; ideas and feelings do not in that state succeed each other in accustomed order. But, if the words by which this excitement is produced are in themselves powerful, or the images and feelings have an undue proportion of pain connected with them, there is some danger that the excitement may be carried beyond its proper bounds. Now the co-presence of something regular, something to which the mind has been accustomed in various moods and in a less excited state, cannot but have great efficacy in tempering and restraining the passion by an inter-texture of ordinary feeling, and of feeling not strictly and necessarily connected with the passion. This is unquestionably true, and hence, though the opinion will at first appear paradoxical, from the tendency of metre to divest language in a certain degree of its reality, and thus to throw a sort of half consciousness of unsubstantial existence over the whole composition, there can be little doubt but that more pathetic situations and sentiments, that is, those which have a greater proportion of pain connected with them, may be endured in metrical composition, especially in rhyme, than in prose. The metre of the old ballads is very artless; yet they contain many passages which would illustrate this opinion, and, I hope, if the following poems be attentively perused, similar instances will be found in them. This opinion may be further illustrated by appealing to the reader's own experience of the reluctance with which he comes to the reperusal of the distressful parts of *Clarissa Harlowe,* or the *Gamester.*[6] While Shakespeare's writings, in the most pathetic scenes, never act upon us as pathetic beyond the bounds of pleasure — an effect which, in a much greater degree than might at first be imagined, is to be ascribed to small, but continual and regular impulses of pleasurable surprise from the metrical arrangement. — On the other hand (what it must be allowed will much more frequently happen) if the poet's words should be incommensurate with the passion, and inadequate to raise the reader to a

[6]Samuel Richardson's *Clarissa* (1747–48) and Edward Moore's *The Gamester* (1753).

height of desirable excitement, then, (unless the poet's choice of his metre has been grossly injudicious) in the feelings of pleasure which the reader has been accustomed to connect with metre in general, and in the feeling, whether cheerful or melancholy, which he has been accustomed to connect with that particular movement of metre, there will be found something which will greatly contribute to impart passion to the words, and to effect the complex end which the poet proposes to himself.

If I had undertaken a systematic defence of the theory upon which these poems are written, it would have been my duty to develop the various causes upon which the pleasure received from metrical language depends. Among the chief of these causes is to be reckoned a principle which must be well known to those who have made any of the arts the object of accurate reflection; I mean the pleasure which the mind derives from the perception of similitude in dissimilitude. This principle is the great spring of the activity of our minds, and their chief feeder. From this principle the direction of the sexual appetite, and all the passions connected with it take their origin: it is the life of our ordinary conversation; and upon the accuracy with which similitude in dissimilitude, and dissimilitude in similitude are perceived, depend our taste and our moral feelings. It would not have been a useless employment to have applied this principle to the consideration of metre, and to have shown that metre is hence enabled to afford much pleasure, and to have pointed out in what manner that pleasure is produced. But my limits will not permit me to enter upon this subject, and I must content myself with a general summary.

I have said that poetry is the spontaneous overflow of powerful feelings: it takes its origin from emotion recollected in tranquillity: the emotion is contemplated till by a species of reaction the tranquillity gradually disappears, and an emotion, kindred to that which was before the subject of contemplation, is gradually produced, and does itself actually exist in the mind. In this mood successful composition generally begins, and in a mood similar to this it is carried on; but the emotion, of whatever kind and in whatever degree, from various causes is qualified by various pleasures, so that in describing any passions whatsoever, which are voluntarily described, the mind will upon the whole be in a state of enjoyment. Now, if nature be thus cautious in preserving in a state of enjoyment a being thus employed, the poet ought to profit by the lesson thus held forth to him, and ought especially to take care, that whatever passions he communicates to his reader, those passions, if his reader's mind be sound and vigorous, should always be accompanied with an overbalance of pleasure. Now the music of harmonious metrical language, the sense of difficulty overcome, and the blind association of pleasure which has been previously received from works of rhyme or metre of the same or similar construction, an indistinct perception perpetually renewed of language closely resembling that of real life, and yet, in the circumstance of metre, differing from it so widely, all these imperceptibly make up a complex feeling of delight, which is of the most important use in tempering the painful feeling which will always be found intermingled with powerful descriptions of the deeper passions. This effect is always produced in pathetic and impassioned poetry; while, in lighter compositions, the ease and gracefulness with which the poet manages his numbers are themselves confessedly a principal source of the gratification of the reader. I might perhaps include all which it is *necessary* to say upon this subject by affirming, what few persons will deny, that, of two descriptions, either of passions, manners, or characters, each of them equally well executed, the one in prose and the other in verse, the verse will be read a hundred times where the prose is read once. We see that Pope by the power of verse alone, has contrived to render the plainest common sense interesting, and even frequently to invest it with the appearance of passion. In consequence of these convictions I related in metre the tale of *Goody Blake and Harry Gill,* which is one of the rudest of this collection. I wished to draw attention to the truth that the power of the human imagination is sufficient to produce such changes even in our physical nature as might almost appear miraculous. The truth is an important one; the fact (for it is a *fact*) is a valuable illustration of it. And I have the satisfaction of knowing that it has been communicated to many hundreds of people who would never have heard of it, had it not been narrated as a ballad, and in a more impressive metre than is usual in ballads.

Having thus explained a few of the reasons why I have written in verse, and why I have chosen subjects from common life, and endeavoured to bring my language near to the real language of men, if I have been too minute in pleading my own cause, I have at the same time been treating a subject of general interest; and it is for this reason that I request the reader's permission to add a few words with reference solely to these particular poems, and to some defects which will probably be found in them. I am sensible that my associations must have sometimes been particular instead of general, and that, consequently, giving to things a false importance, sometimes from diseased impulses I may have written upon unworthy subjects; but I am less apprehensive on this account, than that my language may frequently have suffered from those arbitrary connexions of feelings and ideas with particular words and phrases, from which no man can altogether protect himself. Hence I have no doubt, that, in some instances, feelings even of the ludicrous may be given to my readers by expressions which appeared to me tender and pathetic. Such faulty expressions, were I convinced they were faulty at present, and that they must necessarily continue to be so, I would willingly take all reasonable pains to correct. But it is dangerous to make these alterations on the simple authority of a few individuals, or even of certain classes of men; for where the understanding of an author is not convinced, or his feelings altered, this cannot be done without great injury to himself: for his own feelings are his stay and support, and, if he sets them aside in one instance, he may be induced to repeat this act till his mind loses all confidence in itself, and becomes utterly debilitated. To this it may be added, that the reader ought never to forget that he is himself exposed to the same errors as the poet, and perhaps in a much greater degree: for there can be no presumption in saying, that it is not probable he will be so well acquainted with the various stages of meaning through which words have passed, or with the fickleness or stability of the relations of particular ideas to each other; and above all, since he is so much less interested in the subject, he may decide lightly and carelessly.

Long as I have detained my reader, I hope he will permit me to caution him against a mode of false criticism which has been applied to poetry in which the language closely resembles that of life and nature. Such verses have been triumphed over in parodies of which Dr. Johnson's stanza is a fair specimen.

> I put my hat upon my head,
> And walked into the Strand,
> And there I met another man
> Whose hat was in his hand.

Immediately under these lines I will place one of the most justly admired stanzas of the "Babes in the Wood."

> These pretty Babes with hand in hand
> Went wandering up and down;
> But never more they saw the Man
> Approaching from the Town.

In both these stanzas the words, and the order of the words, in no respect differ from the most unimpassioned conversation. There are words in both, for example, "the Strand," and "the Town," connected with none but the most familiar ideas; yet the one stanza we admit as admirable, and the other as a fair example of the superlatively contemptible. Whence arises this difference? Not from the metre, not from the language, not from the order of the words; but the *matter* expressed in Dr. Johnson's stanza is contemptible. The proper method of treating trivial and simple verses to which Dr. Johnson's stanza would be a fair parallelism is not to say, this is a bad kind of poetry, or this is not poetry; but this wants sense; it is neither interesting in itself, nor can *lead* to any thing interesting; the images neither originate in that sane state of feeling which arises out of thought, nor can excite thought or feeling in the reader. This is the only sensible manner of dealing with such verses: Why trouble yourself about the species till you have previously decided upon the genus? Why take pains to prove that an ape is not a Newton when it is self-evident that he is not a man?

I have one request to make of my reader, which is, that in judging these poems he would decide by his own feelings genuinely, and not by reflection upon what will probably be the judgment of others. How common is it to hear a person say, "I myself do not object to this style of composition or this or that expression, but to such and such classes of people it will appear mean or ludicrous." This mode of criticism, so destructive of all sound unadulterated judgment, is almost universal: I have therefore to request, that the reader would abide independently by his own feelings, and that if he finds himself affected he would not suffer such conjectures to interfere with his pleasure.

If an author by any single composition has impressed us with respect for his talents, it is useful to consider this as affording a presumption, that, on other occasions where we have been displeased, he nevertheless may not have written ill or absurdly; and, further, to give him so much credit for this one composition as may induce us to review what has displeased us with more care than we should otherwise have bestowed upon it. This is not only an act of justice, but in our decisions upon poetry especially, may conduce in a high degree to the improvement of our own taste: for an *accurate* taste in poetry and in all the other arts, as Sir Joshua Reynolds has observed,[7] is an *acquired* talent, which can only be produced by thought and a long continued intercourse with the best models of composition. This is mentioned, not with so ridiculous a purpose as to prevent the most inexperienced reader from judging for himself (I have already said that I wish him to judge for himself), but merely to temper the rashness of decision, and to suggest, that, if poetry be a subject on which much time has not been bestowed, the judgment may be erroneous; and that in many cases it necessarily will be so.

I know that nothing would have so effectually contributed to further the end which I have in view as to have shown of what kind the pleasure is, and how that pleasure is produced, which is confessedly produced by metrical composition

essentially different from that which I have here endeavoured to recommend: for the reader will say that he has been pleased by such composition; and what can I do more for him? The power of any art is limited; and he will suspect, that, if I propose to furnish him with new friends, it is only upon condition of his abandoning his old friends. Besides, as I have said, the reader is himself conscious of the pleasure which he has received from such composition, composition to which he has peculiarly attached the endearing name of poetry; and all men feel an habitual gratitude, and something of an honourable bigotry for the objects which have long continued to please them: we not only wish to be pleased, but to be pleased in that particular way in which we have been accustomed to be pleased. There is a host of arguments on these feelings; and I should be the less able to combat them successfully, as I am willing to allow, that, in order entirely to enjoy the poetry which I am recommending, it would be necessary to give up much of what is ordinarily enjoyed. But, would my limits have permitted me to point out how this pleasure is produced, I might have removed many obstacles, and assisted my reader in perceiving that the powers of language are not so limited as he may suppose; and that it is possible that poetry may give other enjoyments, of a purer, more lasting, and more exquisite nature. This part of my subject I have not altogether neglected; but it has been less my present aim to prove, that the interest excited by some other kinds of poetry is less vivid, and less worthy of the nobler powers of the mind, than to offer reasons for presuming, that, if the object which I have proposed to myself were adequately attained, a species of poetry would be produced, which is genuine poetry; in its nature well adapted to interest mankind permanently, and likewise important in the multiplicity and quality of its moral relations.

From what has been said, and from a perusal of the poems, the reader will be able clearly to perceive the object which I have proposed to myself: he will determine how far I have attained this object; and, what is a much more important question, whether it be worth attaining; and upon the decision of these two questions will rest my claim to the approbation of the public.

[7]Wordsworth refers to Joshua Reynolds's *Discourses* on art, probably a passage in Discourse 12 (*Works,* 2:95. London: Cadell and Davies, 1797.)

Samuel Taylor Coleridge

1772–1834

Coleridge's father, a parson in rural Devonshire, died when his son was nine years old. Thereafter Coleridge was educated at Christ's Hospital school as a charity student and then at Jesus College, Cambridge, which he left in 1794 without a degree. He became involved with Robert Southey's protosocialist pantisocracy scheme and in 1795 married Southey's sister-in-law, Sara Fricker, with whom he was deeply unhappy. That same year he was introduced to William Wordsworth, and the two "lake poets" collaborated on the seminal Romantic work of *Lyrical Ballads* (1798), in which Coleridge published "The Rime of the Ancient Mariner." Although he had experimented with opium as early as 1797, Coleridge did not become fully addicted until 1803 and remained so until 1816, when Dr. James Gillman attempted, with some success, to wean him gradually from the drug. Coleridge published *Christabel and Other Poems,* including the title poem "Christabel" and "Kubla Khan," in 1816, and his critical testament, *Biographia Literaria,* in 1817. The latter, together with some of Coleridge's Shakespeare lectures, comprises some of the richest critical theory the English Romantic Movement produced.

Coleridge based his ideas about the nature of imagination and art on his reading in the late 1790s of Kant and Kant's student Schelling. To understand fully what Coleridge intends in the *Biographia Literaria* requires a short detour into the history of the philosophy of mind.

KANT AND THE MIND

Immanuel Kant's most difficult and important work is probably the *Critique of Pure Reason,* in which his central concern is the way the mind operates. Since we are necessarily unaware of many of the operations of the mind, Kant is forced to focus on the most fleeting of our sensations; in fact he must generate a large-scale set of abstract notions in order to account for the mental output of which we are aware. The debate about mind that Kant joined in the eighteenth century was in some ways much like the debate in post–World War II psychology between the behaviorists and the mentalists.

Nearly a century before Kant, John Locke, in the *Essay Concerning Human Understanding* (1690), had attempted to establish the ultimate behaviorist position. Locke posited that the mind is a *tabula rasa,* a blank slate upon which experience writes. All ideas are derived from two sources: sense experience and the ability of the mind to contemplate itself. Locke tried to show that one could explain the most complex notions of the mind as aggregations of simple ideas. All the mind has to be able to do, by and large, is to place current sensations in memory and recall them on demand, to form simple ideas by associating and comparing current with past sense data, and to be able to associate and compare the simple ideas that result to build up more complex ones. In Locke's notion, the mind is like a computer with data inputs (the senses), an information storage/retrieval system, and some very simple programs, endlessly iterated, to process and compare the data.

Locke's picture of the mind as a simple machine influenced the thought of the entire eighteenth century (the novelist Laurence Sterne based *Tristram Shandy* on the workings and misworkings of Lockean associationism). But over the course of the century, Locke's system came to seem less and less adequate to account for the world as we know it. One problem was that Locke's philosophy assumed a sharp distinction between the inner world of mind and the outer world of matter. But since, as the philosopher George Berkeley argued, we know the world of matter only through mind, skeptics might doubt the very existence of the material world.

Another problem (raised by David Hume) concerned causality, surely the most important of the simple ideas by which we make sense of the phenomenal world. When we say that event A caused event B, we minimally mean that A is included in the ground of being of B. But when we see (on a billiard table, for example) the red ball hit the white ball (A) and the white ball move into the pocket (B), it is not clear that we know this much. What we know is that two events show spatial contiguity (the balls touched) and temporal succession (B followed A). But spatial contiguity and temporal succession do not add up to causality. If a baseball player were to scratch his nose and then hit a home run, would the scratching be thought the *cause* of the homer? Hume suggested that we attribute causality only where we have seen consistency of behavior. Only if there were a pattern in which nose-scratching led to home runs would we say that the former caused the latter; only on the basis of long experience with billiard balls do we say that the motion of the red ball causes that of the white. But this adds only subjective mental habit to the objective spatiotemporal contact we had before, and we seem just as far as ever from what we mean by cause.

Berkeley questioned the existence of the physical world that provides Locke's sense data and experience, and Hume raised doubts about whether the behavioristic mind Locke had assumed could effectually process its data in the way we know it does. The problem, it was becoming clear, was that the human mind had to be more complicated in its workings than Locke had thought. In fact, in order to account for what the mind can do, Kant was forced to attribute a great many more features of our sense of reality to the subjective mind.

For Kant, the external world consists of *noumena,* things whose existence we have to assume but about which we can form no clear idea. As the noumena impinge upon our senses, the mind actively (not passively as Locke claimed) processes the data into "representations." First the datum is marked with our identity — as *ours.* Then it is labeled for space and time — which for Kant were features of mind rather than of matter. Then it is run through the Kantian categories of the understanding and marked for quality, quantity, substance, relation, and so on. The noumena enter the mind; what emerges is phenomena, the world as it appears to us. For Kant, then, the phenomenal world is not *given;* it is *created* by us at every conscious moment through the processing system he calls the productive imagination. Since all minds contain the same mechanisms, we all perceive phenomena consistently and in roughly the same ways: The features of the outside world appear objectively real to us, although they are largely produced by the subjective workings of the mind.

COLERIDGE ON THE IMAGINATION

The above is a more elaborate explanation of what Coleridge is trying to say in a single enigmatic sentence of Chapter 13 of the *Biographia Literaria*. "The primary IMAGINATION I hold to be the living Power and prime Agent of all human Perception, and as a repetition in the finite mind of the eternal act of creation in the infinite I AM." What Kant had called the productive imagination, Coleridge renamed the primary: that mental faculty by which we create the world of our perceptions at each moment of consciousness. Just as God created the *noumena,* man creates the *phenomena.*

If the primary imagination is responsible for perception, the *secondary* imagination is responsible for art. It is, Coleridge says, "an echo" of the primary, and like an echo it is similar to but weaker than what it echoes. Like the primary imagination, it is a creative faculty, but even when the imagination operates it may not wholly displace the phenomenal world. Unlike the primary imagination, the power of the secondary imagination varies from individual to individual. Where the primary imagination creates the perceptual world without our desiring it, the secondary is "co-existing with," and at least partially responsive to, "the conscious will." It operates by dissolving, diffusing, dissipating the perceptual world and creating another world in its place — or at least minimally reshaping the perceptual world into a more idealized and unified picture. The more complete the process of dissolution and recreation, the more fantastic the art form produced; the less complete, the more realistic. Coleridge has thus accounted for the differences between his poetry and that of his friend Wordsworth.

At the end of Chapter 13, Coleridge differentiates between fancy and imagination. Imagination — the secondary imagination described above — is a fully creative activity that, in effect, produces a new perceptual world. Fancy, on the other hand, is an inferior activity, since it operates entirely within the usual perceptual world; it is an activity describable in purely Lockean terms as the willful conjunction of ideas that are normally distinct (like placing an elephant's head on the body of a camel).

COLERIDGE ON POEMS AND POETRY

In Chapter 14 Coleridge differentiates between *poem* and *poetry* — which are almost but not quite related as product is to process. The procedure by which Coleridge defines "poem" is laborious but not entirely lucid. The confusion largely stems from an internal conflict. On the one hand Coleridge wants to evaluate as he defines, to define the *legitimate* as opposed to the *mere* poem; on the other hand, he also knows well that the word *poem* is generally used to apply to any composition in verse — good, bad, or indifferent. In trying to have it both ways, Coleridge muddies his argument. First, he grudgingly concedes that mere rhyming mnemonics "may be given the name of poem." But the real process of definition is more involved.

In Coleridge's definition there are two criteria: "object" or purpose and "superficial form." A poem has as its immediate purpose "pleasure not truth" and is thus differentiated from history or science. And it is written in verse: rhyme or meter or both conjointly. In effect, Coleridge specifies the following outline for major genres of poetry and prose:

		IMMEDIATE OBJECT	
		PLEASURE	TRUTH
SUPERFICIAL FORM:			
RHYME AND/OR METER		Poem	Mnemonic
PROSE		Novel	History or science

This outline seems mechanical enough — but then Coleridge asks a revealing question: If we turned a work of prose fiction into verse, would that make it a poem? The superficial answer would be "yes," but Coleridge says it would not: "Nothing can permanently please, which does not contain in itself the reason why it is so, and not otherwise." In a genuine poem, the linguistic and ideological content justifies the "perpetual and distinct attention to each part" that meter excites in us. A novel versified might look like a poem, but it would be dreadful in effect, since its texture would not be tightly woven enough to bear up under the sort of attention we would give it *as verse*. In legitimate poems, on the other hand, form and content, structure and texture, are interconnected: They are designed to stand the intense scrutiny that meter provokes.

The broad principle to which Coleridge appeals is that of *organic form;* he discusses it at greater length in "Shakespeare's Judgment Equal to His Genius," where he contrasts the merely mechanical form that it is possible to impose upon materials with the organic form that grows out of the nature of the materials themselves. The "superficial" form in a genuine poem is, in fact, not superficial at all: It is an integral part of the poem's design.

Having defined "poem," Coleridge turns to "poetry," which to him is not a collective term for poems but an independent category. Poetry, he says, may be written in prose rather than in verse; and it may occur in works whose immediate object is truth rather than pleasure. More positively, his definition of poetry has "been in part anticipated in [some of the remarks] on the Fancy and Imagination": Less coyly, poetry is the verbal product of the "poetic genius" — the secondary imagination as defined in Chapter 13.

Long poems, Coleridge asserts, cannot be all poetry; conversely, much that is poetry is not in the form of a poem. In fact, so disparate are the two definitions that one might wonder why there needs to be *any* poetry whatever in the poem. The definitions only appear to be disconnected, however. What links them is Coleridge's concept of "organic form." If organic form is implicit in his definition of "poem," it is even more obvious that the distinction between organic and mechanical form is essentially that between imagination and fancy. Organicism is an essential characteristic of the workings of the secondary imagination in recreating an idealized, unified, and coherent fictive universe.

Selected Bibliography

Barth, J. Robert. *The Symbolic Imagination: Coleridge and the Romantic Tradition.* Princeton: Princeton University Press, 1977.

Christensen, Jerome. *Coleridge's Blessed Machine of Language.* Ithaca: Cornell University Press, 1981.

Corrigan, Timothy. *Coleridge, Language and Criticism.* Athens: University of Georgia Press, 1982.

Fogle, R. H. *The Idea of Coleridge's Criticism.* Berkeley: University of California Press, 1962.

Hamilton, Paul. *Coleridge's Poetics.* Oxford: Blackwell, 1983.

Harding, Anthony John. *Coleridge and the Inspired Word.* Kingston, Ont.: McGill-Queen's University Press, 1985.

Kooy, Michael John. *Coleridge, Schiller, and Aesthetic Education.* Basingstoke, Eng.: Palgrave, 2002.

Marks, Emerson. *Coleridge on the Language of Verse.* Princeton: Princeton University Press, 1981.

McKenzie, Gordon. *Organic Unity in Coleridge.* Berkeley: University of California Press, 1939.

Read, Herbert Edward. *Coleridge as a Critic.* London: Faber and Faber, 1949.

Richards, Ivor Armstrong. *Coleridge on Imagination,* 3rd ed. London: Routledge and Kegan Paul, 1962.

Sharma, L. S. *Coleridge: His Contribution to English Criticism.* New Delhi: Arnold-Heinemann, 1981.

Thorpe, C. D. "Coleridge as Aesthetician and Critic." *Journal of the History of Ideas* 1 (1944): 387–414.

Shakespeare's Judgment Equal to His Genius

The object which I was proceeding to attain in my last lecture was to prove that independently of his peculiar merits, which are hereafter to be developed, Shakespeare appears, from his poems alone, apart from his great works, to have possessed all the conditions of a true poet, and by this proof to do away, as far as may [be] in my power, the popular notion that he was a great dramatist by a sort of instinct, immortal in his own despite,

"Shakespeare's Judgment" was delivered as a lecture, probably around 1808. The text is compiled from Coleridge's notebooks.

and sinking below men of second- or third-rate character when he attempted aught beside the drama — even as bees construct their cells and manufacture their honey to admirable perfection, but would in vain attempt to build a nest. Now this mode of reconciling a compelled sense of inferiority with a feeling of pride, began in a few pedants, who having read that Sophocles was the great model of tragedy, and Aristotle the infallible dictator, and finding that the *Lear, Hamlet, Othello,* and the rest, were neither in imitation of Sophocles, nor in obedience to Aristotle — and not having (with one or two exceptions) the courage to affirm that the delight which their country received from generation to generation, in defiance of the alterations of circumstances and habits, was wholly groundless — it was a happy medium and refuge, to talk of Shakespeare as a sort of beautiful *lusus naturae*,[1] a delightful monster, — wild, indeed, without taste or judgment, but like the inspired idiots so much venerated in the East, uttering, amid the strangest follies, the sublimest truths. In nine places out of ten in which I find his awful name mentioned, it is with some epithet of "wild," "irregular," "pure child of nature," etc., etc., etc. If all this be true, we must submit to it; tho' to a thinking mind it cannot but be painful to find any excellence, merely human, thrown out of all human analogy, and thereby leaving us neither rules for imitation, nor motives to imitate. But if false, it is a dangerous falsehood; for it affords a refuge to secret self-conceit, — enables a vain man at once to escape his reader's indignation by general swoln panegyrics on Shakespeare, merely by his *ipse dixit*[2] to treat what he has not intellect enough to comprehend, or soul to feel, as contemptible, without assigning any reason, or referring his opinion to any demonstrated principle; and so has left Shakespeare as a sort of Tartarian Dalai Lama, adored indeed, and his very excrescences prized as relics, but with no authority, no real influence. I grieve that every late voluminous edition of his works would enable me to substantiate the present charge with a variety of facts one tenth of which would of themselves exhaust the time allotted to me. Every critic, who has or has not made a collection of black letter books — in itself a useful and respectable amusement — puts on the seven-league boots of self-opinion and strides at once from an illustrator into a supreme judge, and blind and deaf, fills his three-ounce phial at the waters of Niagara — and determines positively the greatness of the cataract to be neither more nor less than his three-ounce phial has been able to receive.

Not only a multitude of individuals but even whole nations [are] so enslaved to the habits of their education and immediate circumstances as not to judge disinterestedly even on those subjects, the very pleasure from which consists in their disinterestedness — subjects of taste and *belles lettres*. Instead of deciding concerning their own modes and customs by any rule of reason, nothing appears natural, becoming, or beautiful but what coincides with the accidents of their education. In this narrow circle individuals may attain exquisite discrimination, as the French critics have in their own literature, but a true critic can no man be without placing himself on some central point in which he can command the whole; i.e., some general rule, which, [as] founded in reason, or faculties common to all men, must therefore apply to all men.

This will not produce despotism, but on the contrary true tolerance. He will indeed require, as the spirit and substance of a work, something true in human nature, and independent of circumstances; but in the mode of applying it, he will estimate genius and judgement according to the felicity with which this imperishable soul has clothed and adapted itself to the age, place, and existing manners.

The error is reversing this by considering the circumstances as perpetual, to the neglect of the animating power.

The subject of the present lecture is no less than a question submitted to your understandings, emancipated from national prejudice: Are the plays of *Shakespeare* works of rude uncultivated genius, in which the splendor of the parts compensates, if aught can compensate, for the barbarous shapelessness and irregularity of the whole? To which not only the French critics, but even his own English admirers, say [yes]. Or is the form equally admirable with the matter, the judgment of the great poet not less deserving of our wonder than his genius? Or to repeat the question in other words, is Shakespeare a great dynamic poet on account only of those beauties and excellencies which he possesses in common with the ancients, but with diminished claims to our love and honor to the full extent of his difference from them? Or are these very differences additional proofs of poetic wisdom, at once results and symbols of living power as contrasted with lifeless mechanism, of free and rival originality as contradistinguished

[1]Freak of nature.
[2]Authority.

from servile imitation, or more accurately, [from] a blind copying of effects instead of a true imitation of the essential principles? Imagine not I am about to oppose genius to rules. No! the comparative value of these rules is the very cause to be tried. The spirit of poetry, like all other living powers, must of necessity circumscribe itself by rules, were it only to unite power with beauty. It must embody in order to reveal itself; but a living body is of necessity an organized one, — and what is organization, but the connection of parts to a whole, so that each part is at once end and means! This is no discovery of criticism; it is a necessity of the human mind — and all nations have felt and obeyed it, in the invention of metre and measured sounds as the vehicle and involucrum of poetry, itself a fellow-growth from the same life, even as the bark is to the tree.

No work of true genius dare want its appropriate form; neither indeed is there any danger of this. As it must not, so neither can it, be lawless! For it is even this that constitutes its genius — the power of acting creatively under laws of its own origination. How then comes it that not only single Zoili,[3] but whole nations have combined in unhesitating condemnation of our great dramatist, as a sort of African nature, fertile in beautiful monsters, as a wild heath where islands of fertility look greener from the surrounding waste, where the loveliest plants now shine out among unsightly weeds and now are choked by their parasitic growth, so intertwined that we cannot disentangle the weed without snapping the flower. In this statement I have had no reference to the vulgar abuse of Voltaire, save as far as his charges are coincident with the decisions of his commentators and (so they tell you) his almost idolatrous admirers. The true ground of the mistake, as has been well remarked by a continental critic,[4] lies in the confounding mechanical regularity with organic form. The form is mechanic when on any given material we impress a predetermined form, not necessarily arising out of the properties of the material, as when to a mass of wet clay we give whatever shape we wish it to retain when hardened. The organic form, on the other hand, is innate; it shapes as it develops itself from within, and the fullness of its development is one and the same with the perfection of its outward form. Such is the life, such the form. Nature, the prime genial artist, inexhaustible in diverse powers, is equally inexhaustible in forms. Each exterior is the physiognomy of the being within, its true image reflected and thrown out from the concave mirror. And even such is the appropriate excellence of her chosen poet, of our own Shakespeare, himself a nature humanized, a genial understanding directing self-consciously a power and an implicit wisdom deeper than consciousness.

[3]Zoilus was a captious critic of Homer around the fourth century B.C.E.

[4]August Wilhelm von Schlegel, from whose writings many of Coleridge's ideas derive.

From *Biographia Literaria*

From Chapter 13

The IMAGINATION then, I consider either as primary, or secondary. The primary IMAGINATION I hold to be the living Power and prime Agent of all human Perception, and as a repetition in the finite mind of the eternal act of creation in the infinite I AM. The secondary Imagination I consider as an echo of the former, co-existing with the conscious will, yet still as identical with the primary in the *kind* of its agency, and differing only in *degree,* and in the *mode* of its operation. It dissolves, diffuses, dissipates, in order to recreate; or where this process is rendered impossible, yet still at all events it struggles to idealize and to unify. It is essentially *vital,* even as all objects (*as* objects) are essentially fixed and dead.

FANCY, on the contrary, has no other counters to play with, but fixities and definites. The Fancy is indeed no other than a mode of Memory emancipated from the order of time and space; while it is blended with, and modified by that empirical phenomenon of the will, which we express by the word CHOICE. But equally with the ordinary memory the Fancy must receive all its materials ready made from the law of association.

Chapter 14

Occasion of the Lyrical Ballads, and the objects originally proposed — Preface to the second edition — The ensuing controversy, its causes and acrimony — Philosophic definitions of a poem and poetry with scholia.

During the first year that Mr. Wordsworth and I were neighbours,[1] our conversations turned frequently on the two cardinal points of poetry, the power of exciting the sympathy of the reader by a faithful adherence to the truth of nature, and the power of giving the interest of novelty by the modifying colors of imagination. The sudden charm, which accidents of light and shade, which moon-light or sun-set diffused over a known and familiar landscape, appeared to represent the practicability of combining both. These are the poetry of nature. The thought suggested itself (to which of us I do not recollect) that a series of poems might be composed of two sorts. In the one, the incidents and agents were to be, in part at least, supernatural; and the excellence aimed at was to consist in the interesting of the affections by the dramatic truth of such emotions, as would naturally accompany such situations, supposing them real. And real in *this* sense they have been to every human being who, from whatever source of delusion, has at any time believed himself under supernatural agency. For the second class, subjects were to be chosen from ordinary life; the characters and incidents were to be such, as will be found in every village and its vicinity, where there is a meditative and feeling mind to seek after them, or to notice them, when they present themselves.

In this idea originated the plan of the "Lyrical Ballads"; in which it was agreed, that my endeavours should be directed to persons and characters supernatural, or at least romantic; yet so as to transfer from our inward nature a human interest and a semblance of truth sufficient to procure for these shadows of imagination that willing suspension of disbelief for the moment, which constitutes poetic faith. Mr. Wordsworth, on the other hand, was to propose to himself as his object, to give the charm of novelty to things of every day, and to excite a feeling analogous to the supernatural, by awakening the mind's attention from the lethargy of custom, and directing it to the loveliness and the wonders of the world before us; an inexhaustible treasure, but for which, in consequence of the film of familiarity and selfish solicitude we have eyes, yet see not, ears that hear not, and hearts that neither feel nor understand.

With this view I wrote "The Ancient Mariner," and was preparing among other poems, "The Dark Ladie," and the "Christabel," in which I should have more nearly realized my ideal, than I had done in my first attempt. But Mr. Wordsworth's industry had proved so much more successful, and the number of his poems so much greater, that my compositions, instead of forming a balance, appeared rather an interpolation of heterogeneous matter. Mr. Wordsworth added two or three poems written in his own character, in the impassioned, lofty, and sustained diction, which is characteristic of his genius. In this form the "Lyrical Ballads" were published; and were presented by him, as an *experiment,* whether subjects, which from their nature rejected the usual ornaments and extra-colloquial style of poems in general, might not be so managed in the language of ordinary life as to produce the pleasureable interest, which it is the peculiar business of poetry to impart. To the second edition he added a preface of considerable length; in which, notwithstanding some passages of apparently a contrary import, he was understood to contend for the extension of this style to poetry of all kinds, and to reject as vicious and indefensible all phrases and forms of style that were not included in what he (unfortunately, I think, adopting an equivocal expression) called the language of *real* life. From this preface, prefixed to poems in which it was impossible to deny

[1] In 1797.

the presence of original genius, however mistaken its direction might be deemed, arose the whole long-continued controversy. For from the conjunction of perceived power with supposed heresy I explain the inveteracy and in some instances, I grieve to say, the acrimonious passions, with which the controversy has been conducted by the assailants.

Had Mr. Wordsworth's poems been the silly, the childish things, which they were for a long time described as being; had they been really distinguished from the compositions of other poets merely by meanness of language and inanity of thought; had they indeed contained nothing more than what is found in the parodies and pretended imitations of them; they must have sunk at once, a dead weight, into the slough of oblivion, and have dragged the preface along with them. But year after year increased the number of Mr. Wordsworth's admirers. They were found too not in the lower classes of the reading public, but chiefly among young men of strong sensibility and meditative minds; and their admiration (inflamed perhaps in some degree by opposition) was distinguished by its intensity, I might almost say, by its *religious* fervor. These facts, and the intellectual energy of the author, which was more or less consciously felt, where it was outwardly and even boisterously denied, meeting with sentiments of aversion to his opinions, and of alarm at their consequences, produced an eddy of criticism, which would of itself have borne up the poems by the violence, with which it whirled them round and round. With many parts of this preface, in the sense attributed to them, and which the words undoubtedly seem to authorize, I never concurred; but on the contrary objected to them as erroneous in principle, and as contradictory (in appearance at least) both to other parts of the same preface, and to the author's own practice in the greater number of the poems themselves. Mr. Wordsworth in his recent collection has, I find, degraded this prefatory disquisition to the end of his second volume, to be read or not at the reader's choice. But he has not, as far as I can discover, announced any change in his poetic creed. At all events, considering it as the source of a controversy, in which I have been honored more than I deserve by the frequent conjunction of my name with his, I think it expedient to declare once for all, in what points I coincide with his opinions, and in what points I altogether differ. But in order to render myself intelligible I must previously, in as few words as possible, explain my ideas, first, of a POEM; and secondly, of POETRY itself, in *kind,* and in *essence.*

The office of philosophical *disquisition* consists in just *distinction;* while it is the privilege of the philosopher to preserve himself constantly aware, that distinction is not division. In order to obtain adequate notions of any truth, we must intellectually separate its distinguishable parts; and this is the technical *process* of philosophy. But having so done, we must then restore them in our conceptions to the unity, in which they actually co-exist; and this is the *result* of philosophy. A poem contains the same elements as a prose composition; the difference therefore must consist in a different combination of them, in consequence of a different object being proposed. According to the difference of the object will be the difference of the combination. It is possible, that the object may be merely to facilitate the recollection of any given facts or observations by artificial arrangement; and the composition will be a poem, merely because it is distinguished from prose by metre, or by rhyme, or by both conjointly. In this, the lowest sense, a man might attribute the name of a poem to the well-known enumeration of the days in the several months;

Thirty days hath September,
April, June, and November, &c.

and others of the same class and purpose. And as a particular pleasure is found in anticipating the recurrence of sounds and quantities, all compositions that have this charm superadded, whatever be their contents, *may* be entitled poems.

So much for the superficial *form.* A difference of object and contents supplies an additional ground of distinction. The immediate purpose may be the communication of truths; either of truth absolute and demonstrable, as in works of science; or of facts experienced and recorded, as in history. Pleasure, and that of the highest and most permanent kind, may *result* from the *attainment* of the end; but it is not itself the immediate end. In other works the communication of pleasure may be the immediate purpose; and though truth, either moral or intellectual, ought to be the *ultimate* end, yet this will distinguish the character of the author, not the class to which the work belongs. Blest indeed is that state of society, in which the immediate purpose would be baffled by the perversion of the proper ultimate end; in which no charm of diction or imagery could exempt the Bathyllus even of an Anacreon, or the Alexis of Virgil, from disgust and aversion![2]

But the communication of pleasure may be the immediate object of a work not metrically composed; and that object may have been in a high degree attained, as in novels and romances. Would then the mere superaddition of metre, with or without rhyme, entitle *these* to the name of poems? The answer is, that nothing can permanently please, which does not contain in itself the reason why it is so, and not otherwise. If metre be superadded, all other parts must be made consonant with it. They must be such, as to justify the perpetual and distinct attention to each part, which an exact correspondent recurrence of accent and sound are calculated to excite. The final definition then, so deduced, may be thus worded. A poem is that species of composition, which is opposed to works of science, by proposing for its *immediate* object pleasure, not truth; and from all other species (having *this* object in common with it) it is discriminated by proposing to itself such delight from the *whole*, as is compatible with a distinct gratification from each component *part*.

Controversy is not seldom excited in consequence of the disputants attaching each a different meaning to the same word; and in few instances has this been more striking, than in disputes concerning the present subject. If a man chooses to call every composition a poem, which is rhyme, or measure, or both, I must leave his opinion uncontroverted. The distinction is at least competent to characterize the writer's intention. If it were subjoined, that the whole is likewise entertaining or affecting, as a tale, or as a series of interesting reflections, I of course admit this as another fit ingredient of a poem, and an additional

merit. But if the definition sought for be that of a *legitimate* poem, I answer, it must be one, the parts of which mutually support and explain each other; all in their proportion harmonizing with, and supporting the purpose and known influences of metrical arrangement. The philosophic critics of all ages coincide with the ultimate judgement of all countries, in equally denying the praises of a just poem, on the one hand, to a series of striking lines or distiches, each of which, absorbing the whole attention of the reader to itself, disjoins it from its context, and makes it a separate whole, instead of an harmonizing part; and on the other hand, to an unsustained composition, from which the reader collects rapidly the general result, unattracted by the component parts. The reader should be carried forward, not merely or chiefly by the mechanical impulse of curiosity, or by a restless desire to arrive at the final solution; but by the pleasureable activity of mind excited by the attractions of the journey itself. Like the motion of a serpent, which the Egyptians made the emblem of intellectual power; or like the path of sound through the air; at every step he pauses and half recedes, and from the retrogressive movement collects the force which again carries him onward. "Præcipitandus est *liber* spiritus," says Petronius Arbiter most happily.[3] The epithet, *liber,* here balances the preceding verb; and it is not easy to conceive more meaning condensed in fewer words.

But if this should be admitted as a satisfactory character of a poem, we have still to seek for a definition of poetry. The writings of PLATO, and Bishop TAYLOR, and the "Theoria Sacra" of BURNET, furnish undeniable proofs that poetry of the highest kind may exist without metre, and even without the contra-distinguishing objects of a poem. The first chapter of Isaiah (indeed a very large portion of the whole book) is poetry in the most emphatic sense; yet it would be not less irrational than strange to assert, that pleasure, and not truth, was the immediate object of the prophet. In short, whatever *specific* import we attach to the word, poetry, there will be found involved in it, as a necessary consequence, that a poem of any

---

[2]Anacreon's Ode 29 to Bathyllus, and Virgil's *Eclogue* 2.

[3]"The free spirit must be hurried onward." Petronius, *Satyricon,* 118.

length neither can be, nor ought to be, all poetry. Yet if an harmonious whole is to be produced, the remaining parts must be preserved *in keeping* with the poetry; and this can be no otherwise effected than by such a studied selection and artificial arrangement, as will partake of *one,* though not a *peculiar* property of poetry. And this again can be no other than the property of exciting a more continuous and equal attention than the language of prose aims at, whether colloquial or written.

My own conclusions on the nature of poetry, in the strictest use of the word, have been in part anticipated in the preceding disquisition on the fancy and imagination. What is poetry? is so nearly the same question with, what is a poet? that the answer to the one is involved in the solution of the other. For it is a distinction resulting from the poetic genius itself, which sustains and modifies the images, thoughts, and emotions of the poet's own mind.

The poet, described in *ideal* perfection, brings the whole soul of man into activity, with the subordination of its faculties to each other, according to their relative worth and dignity. He diffuses a tone and spirit of unity, that blends, and (as it were) *fuses,* each into each, by that synthetic and magical power, to which we have exclusively appropriated the name of imagination. This power, first put in action by the will and understanding, and retained under their irremissive, though gentle and unnoticed, controul (*laxis effertur habenis*)[4] reveals itself in the balance or reconciliation of opposite or discordant qualities: of sameness, with difference; of the general, with the concrete; the idea, with the image; the individual, with the representative; the sense of novelty and freshness, with old and familiar objects; a more than usual state of emotion, with more than usual order; judgement ever awake and steady self-possession, with enthusiasm and feeling profound or vehement; and while it blends and harmonizes the natural and the artificial, still subordinates art to nature; the manner to the matter; and our admiration of the poet to our sympathy with the poetry. "Doubtless," as Sir John Davies observes of the soul (and his words may with slight alteration be applied, and even more appropriately, to the poetic IMAGINATION)

> Doubtless this could not be, but that she turns
> Bodies to spirit by sublimation strange,
> As fire converts to fire the things it burns,
> As we our food into our nature change.
>
> From their gross matter she abstracts their forms,
> And draws a kind of quintessence from things;
> Which to her proper nature she transforms,
> To bear them light on her celestial wings.
>
> Thus does she, when from individual states
> She doth abstract the universal kinds;
> Which then re-clothed in divers names and fates
> Steal access through our senses to our minds.[5]

Finally, GOOD SENSE is the BODY of poetic genius, FANCY its DRAPERY, MOTION its LIFE, and IMAGINATION the SOUL that is everywhere, and in each; and forms all into one graceful and intelligent whole.

---

[4]"Carried on with slackened reins." Petrarch, *Epistola Barbato Sulmonensi,* 39.

[5]Sir John Davies, *Nosce Teipsum: Of the Soule of Man and the Immortality Thereof,* 4:11–13.

John Keats
1795–1821

John Keats was born in London, the son of a livery stableman who had married the stable-owner's daughter. He was educated in a private school at Enfield by Charles Cowden Clarke, later a friend to many of the second generation of Romantic poets, who encouraged Keats's love of reading and writing. Orphaned at fourteen with his mother's capital tied up in a chancery suit, Keats was apprenticed by his guardian to an apothecary-surgeon, and he studied medicine at Guy's Hospital in London until he was twenty-one. In London, Keats met Leigh Hunt, who gathered him into a politically radical circle of artists that included the poet Percy Bysshe Shelley, the essayist William Hazlitt, and the painter Benjamin Haydon. As soon as he was of age, Keats abandoned the medical profession to become a poet.

Keats's first books, *Poems* (1817) and *Endymion* (1818), were attacked, mainly by conservative enemies of Hunt. Stimulated more by his own scrutiny than by outside criticism, Keats refined his style and in 1819 wrote "The Eve of St. Agnes," "Lamia," the six Odes (on Psyche, Indolence, the Nightingale, the Grecian Urn, Melancholy, and Autumn), and "La Belle Dame sans Merci" — the quintessential lyrics of English Romanticism. In that year Keats also knew he was racing the clock: He had returned from a walking tour in the autumn of 1818 with an ulcerated throat and had enough medical training to foresee his own death from tuberculosis. Keats worked furiously at his fragmentary epic, *The Fall of Hyperion,* but in February 1820 he began to cough up blood and had serious hemorrhages later in the spring. That summer he left for the milder climate of Rome, but it was already too late. He died there on February 23, 1821, and is buried in the Protestant Cemetery.

Keats wrote no developed body of critical theory; his ideas — picked up from the intellectual atmosphere of the Romantics and completely unstructured by schools — appear as brilliant fragments in his personal letters to friends.

The letter to Benjamin Bailey reflects Keats's most idealistic phase. In it, Keats asserts that the product of the sensual intuition seems superior to the product of the rational intellect, and that what the imagination produces and records as Beauty is not illusion but "truth" — an authentic reality — "whether it existed before or not" in the material sense. Keats's first example of the authenticity of imagination — Adam's dream — comes from *Paradise Lost,* and seems to be a merely literary manifestation. But his second, when he asks Bailey to recall the way imagination reconstitutes the content of an old memory from a tiny stimulus, yet recaptures it more beautifully than it actually occurred, has become a major touchstone of Romantic aesthetics.

The same is true of the letter to his brothers George and Thomas Keats. Here we find Keats's classic definition of *negative capability:* "when man is capable of being in uncertainties, Mysteries, doubts, without any irritable reaching after fact & reason." The meaning of the phrase is clear enough, but its significance takes some teasing out from the context. Keats begins by contrasting two painful but beautiful works of art: Benjamin West's painting, *Death on the Pale Horse* and Shakespeare's

King Lear. Keats is only moderately pleased by the former, which lacks the intensity of Shakespeare's tragedy. The intensity of *Lear* seems to come from the "depth of speculation excited" in the audience that contemplates it. Shakespeare's work presents a vision of the pain and evil of life without attempting to comprehend and explain it; its raw presentation demands the intellectual and emotional participation of the viewer. But the West picture has already been processed through the artist's mind, and thus leaves less for the audience to do. Shakespeare possesses immense negative capability; West and the poet Coleridge (in the example at the end of the letter) are artists of a different kind. Keats's idea here may connect with Schiller's distinction between "naive" and "sentimental" writers; the naive Shakespeare presents the emotional object directly for the reader's consideration, whereas the sentimental West presents it filtered through his own private consciousness.

Selected Bibliography

Bate, Walter Jackson. *Negative Capability*. Cambridge: Harvard University Press, 1939.
Ende, Stuart A. *Keats and the Sublime*. New Haven: Yale University Press, 1976.
Ferris, David S. "Keats and the Aesthetics of Critical Knowledge: or, the Ideology of Studying Romanticism at the Present Time." In *Lessons of Romanticism: A Critical Companion*, ed. Thomas Pfau and Robert F. Gleckner, 103–25. Durham: Duke University Press, 1998.
Sharp, Ronald A. *Keats, Skepticism, and the Religion of Beauty*. Athens: University of Georgia Press, 1979.
Tate, Priscilla Weston. *From Innocence through Experience: Keats's Myth of the Poet*. Salzburg: Institut für Englische Sprache und Literatur, 1974.
Thekla, Sister. *The Disinterested Heart: The Philosophy of John Keats*. Newport Pagnell, Eng.: Greek Orthodox Monastery of the Assumption, 1973.
Thorpe, Clarence Dewitt. *The Mind of John Keats*. New York: Oxford University Press, 1926.

From a *Letter to Benjamin Bailey*

[November 22, 1817]

My dear Bailey,

. . . O I wish I was as certain of the end of all your troubles as that of your momentary start about the authenticity of the Imagination. I am certain of nothing but of the holiness of the Heart's affections and the truth of Imagination — What the imagination seizes as Beauty must be truth[1] — whether it existed before or not — for I have the same Idea of all our Passions as of Love they are all in their sublime, creative of essential Beauty — In a Word, you may know my favorite Speculation by my first Book and the little song I sent in my last[2] — which is a representation from the fancy of the probable mode of operating in these Matters — The Imagination may be compared to Adam's dream[3] — he awoke and found it truth. I am the more zealous in this affair, because I have never yet been able to perceive how any

[1]Cf. the last two lines of "Ode on a Grecian Urn": in both cases, "truth" seems to mean something like "authentic reality" rather than "verifiable fact."

[2]"O Sorrow" from *Endymion*.
[3]Milton, *Paradise Lost*, 8:460–90.

thing can be known for truth by consequitive reasoning — and yet it must be — Can it be that even the greatest Philosopher ever arrived at his goal without putting aside numerous objections — However it may be, O for a Life of Sensations rather than of Thoughts! It is "a Vision in the form of Youth" a Shadow of reality to come — and this consideration has further convinced me for it has come as auxiliary to another favorite Speculation of mine, that we shall enjoy ourselves here after by having what we called happiness on Earth repeated in a finer tone and so repeated — And yet such a fate can only befall those who delight in sensation rather than hunger as you do after Truth — Adam's dream will do here and seems to be a conviction that Imagination and its empyreal reflection is the same as human Life and its spiritual repetition. But as I was saying — the simple imaginative Mind may have its rewards in the repetition of its own silent Working coming continually on the spirit with a fine suddenness — to compare great things with small — have you never by being surprised with an old Melody — in a delicious place — by a delicious voice, felt over again your very speculations and surmises at the time it first operated on your soul — do you not remember forming to yourself the singer's face more beautiful than it was possible and yet with the elevation of the Moment you did not think so — even then you were mounted on the Wings of Imagination so high — that the Prototype must be here after — that delicious face you will see — What a time! I am continually running away from the subject — sure this cannot be exactly the case with a complex Mind — one that is imaginative and at the same time careful of its fruits — who would exist partly on sensation partly on thought — to whom it is necessary that years should bring the philosophic Mind[4] — such an one I consider your's and therefore it is necessary to your eternal

Happiness that you not only drink this old Wine of Heaven which I shall call the redigestion of our most ethereal Musings on Earth; but also increase in knowledge and know all things. I am glad to hear you are in a fair Way for Easter — you will soon get through your unpleasant reading and then! — but the world is full of troubles and I have not much reason to think myself pesterd with many — I think Jane or Marianne[5] has a better opinion of me than I deserve — for really and truly I do not think my Brothers illness connected with mine — you know more of the real Cause than they do — nor have I any chance of being rack'd as you have been — you perhaps at one time thought there was such a thing as Worldly Happiness to be arrived at, at certain periods of time marked out — you have of necessity from your disposition been thus led away — I scarcely remember counting upon any Happiness — I look not for it if it be not in the present hour — nothing startles me beyond the Moment. The setting sun will always set me to rights — or if a Sparrow come before my Window I take part in its existence and pick about the Gravel. The first thing that strikes me on hearing a Misfortune having befalled another is this. Well it cannot be helped. — he will have the pleasure of trying the resources of his spirit, and I beg now my dear Bailey that hereafter should you observe anything cold in me not to put it to the account of heartlessness but abstraction — for I assure you I sometimes feel not the influence of a Passion or Affection during a whole week — and so long this sometimes continues I begin to suspect myself and the genuiness of my feelings at other times — thinking them a few barren Tragedy-tears.

Your affectionate friend
John Keats —

[4]Keats is quoting Wordsworth's "Intimations of Immortality" ode.

[5]Jane and Marianne Reynolds, friends of Keats.

From a *Letter to George and Thomas Keats*

[December 21, 27 (?), 1817]

My dear Brothers

I must crave your pardon for not having written ere this. . . . I spent Friday evening with Wells[1] & went the next morning to see *Death on the Pale horse*. It is a wonderful picture, when West's age[2] is considered; But there is nothing to be intense upon; no women one feels mad to kiss; no face swelling into reality. The excellence of every Art is its intensity, capable of making all disagreeables evaporate, from their being in close relationship with Beauty & Truth — Examine King Lear & you will find this exemplified throughout; but in this picture we have unpleasantness without any momentous depth of speculation excited, in which to buy its repulsiveness — The picture is larger than Christ rejected — I dined with Haydon[3] the sunday after you left, & had a very pleasant day, I dined too (for I have been out too much lately) with Horace Smith & met his two Brothers with Hill & Kingston & one Du Bois,[4] they only served to convince me, how superior humour is to wit in respect to enjoyment — These men say things which make one start, without making one feel, they are all alike; their manners are alike; they all know fashionables; they have a mannerism in their very eating & drinking, in their mere handling a Decanter — They talked of Kean[5] & his low company — Would I were with that company instead of yours said I to myself! I know such like acquaintance will never do for me & yet I am going to Reynolds, on wednesday — Brown & Dilke[6] walked with me & back from the Christmas pantomime. I had not a dispute but a disquisition with Dilke, on various subjects; several things dovetailed in my mind, & at once it struck me, what quality went to form a Man of Achievement especially in Literature & which Shakespeare possessed so enormously — I mean *Negative Capability,* that is when man is capable of being in uncertainties, Mysteries, doubts, without any irritable reaching after fact & reason — Coleridge, for instance, would let go by a fine isolated verisimilitude caught from the Penetralium[7] of mystery, from being incapable of remaining content with half knowledge. This pursued through Volumes would perhaps take us no further than this, that with a great poet the sense of Beauty overcomes every other consideration, or rather obliterates all consideration.

Shelley's poem[8] is out & there are words about its being objected too, as much as Queen Mab was. Poor Shelley I think he has his Quota of good qualities, in sooth la!! Write soon to your most sincere friend & affectionate Brother

John

---

[1]Charles Wells, who had gone to school with Thomas Keats.

[2]Benjamin West (1738–1820) was seventy-nine when he painted *Death on the Pale Horse.*

[3]Benjamin Haydon, a painter who was a good friend of Keats.

[4]Literary figures of the day.

[5]Edmund Kean, the Shakespearean actor.

[6]John Hamilton Reynolds, Charles Armitage Brown, and Charles Wentworth Dilke were literary friends of Keats.

[7]Inner sanctum.

[8]*Laon and Cythna* (1817).

Thomas Love Peacock

1785–1866

Peacock was born in rural Dorsetshire; his father had been a successful glass merchant, his mother the daughter of a retired naval officer. He was educated in a private school until the age of twelve, and, with the rudiments of the ancient and modern languages in him, read voraciously for the rest of his life. As the nineteenth century began, he worked as a clerk in a London merchant banking firm, followed by a year as the secretary to the captain of HMS *Venerable*, which he called a "floating inferno." He went on to do geographical research discovering the source of the Thames. Peacock's ambition, though, was to become a poet, and he published slim volumes filled with romantic melancholy: *Palmyra* (1805), *The Genius of the Thames* (1810), and *The Philosophy of Melancholy* (1812). One youthful poem, "The Monks of St. Mark" (1804), sounds the satirical note that is most clearly associated with Peacock.

In 1812, Peacock met the poet Percy Bysshe Shelley and joined the Shelley circle at Bracknell, where he found much to admire in Shelley himself, and much to be amused by among his companions. As he later wrote, "I was sometimes irreverent enough to laugh at the fervour with which opinions utterly unconducive to any practical result were battled for as matters of the highest importance to the well-being of mankind."

Knowing Shelley may have convinced Peacock that he would never be in his friend's class as a poet, and Peacock was moved to take up a new genre that has been associated with him ever since, the conversation novel. Starting with *Headlong Hall* (1816), *Melincourt* (1817), *Nightmare Abbey* (1818), and concluding with *Crochet Castle* (1831), Peacock's prose fiction peopled a country house with guests who have bizarre opinions and ideas, and chronicled their comedic interactions over the short period of their stay. The novels are romans à clef — most of the characters can be identified with real people Peacock knew. For example, the metaphysical Mr. Flosky, in *Nightmare Abbey*, has his eldest son christened Emanuel Kant Flosky in imitation of Coleridge, whose eldest son was named Ernest Hartley Coleridge. Peacock steered clear of personal invective, but Coleridge and Robert Southey came in for some nasty attacks, while he displays his friend Shelley with only minor absurdities. Other creative writers were later to take up their own versions of the conversation novel, including George Meredith, Henry James, and Aldous Huxley.

The literary work for which Peacock is most famous is *The Four Ages of Poetry* (1820) and it is more famous for what it inspired — Shelley's *Defence of Poetry* (p. 346) — than for its own argument, which owes a great deal to the philosophers of the Enlightenment who posited that societies evolved through a series of stages. Like the societies described by eighteenth-century economist and philosopher Adam Smith, Peacock's vision of the stages of society — from primitive, to barbaric, then refined and finally decadent — locates his present day in the English "age of brass." Peacock's tone seems deadly serious, but the argument that an approaching "iron age" will see poetry neither needed nor wanted, coming from a would-be romantic poet, is a preposterous put-down — and Shelley would have known that Peacock's tongue was firmly in his cheek. Peacock's dismissal of poetry as an homage to power is wildly overstated, and his satire of romantic poetry, particularly its pretensions to novelty, seems primarily directed at the Lake Poets, rather than at Shelley and his circle. Since he was not personally stung, Shelley must have been moved by the pessimism of Peacock's final paragraph, which envisions poetry in an age of science as appealing to progressively fewer people of progressively lower intelligence until it reaches a state of ignominious degradation.

In 1819, Peacock joined the East India Company and worked as an examiner for that corporation until he retired in 1856. In 1820 he married Jane Gryffydh, a woman he had met in Wales eight years earlier during his search for the source of the Thames. They had three children, the first of whom became the first wife of George Meredith, who wrote the sonnet sequence *Modern Love* about her elopement with his friend Henry Wallis, her return, and her death. Peacock stopped writing poetry around the time he became a bureaucrat, but continued to write prose fiction, satirical and romantic, for many years. He concluded his writing career with his valuable 1858 memoirs of his friend Shelley, whose literary executor he had been, and with his last satirical conversation novel, *Gryll Grange* (1861). In his lonely old age, having become morbidly afraid of fires, Peacock died not long after a fire broke out in his bedroom, in 1866.

Selected Bibliography

Brett-Smith, H. F. B., and C. E. Jones, eds., *The Works of Thomas Love Peacock*. The Halliford Edition, 10 vols. London: Constable & Co.; New York: G. Wells, 1924–34.

Burns, Bryan. *The Novels of Thomas Love Peacock*. London: Croon Helm, 1985.

Hall, Jean. "The Divine and the Dispassionate Selves: Shelley's Defence and Peacock's 'The Four Ages of Poetry.'" *Keats-Shelley Journal* 41 (1992): 139–63.

Joukovsky, Nicholas A., ed. *The Letters of Thomas Love Peacock*. Oxford: Oxford University Press, 2001.

Mills, Howard. *Peacock: His Circle and His Age*. Cambridge: Cambridge University Press, 1969.

Prickett, Stephen. "Peacock's Four Ages Recycled." *British Journal of Aesthetics* 22, no. 2 (1982): 158–66.

The Four Ages of Poetry

Qui inter haec nutriuntur non magis sapere possunt, quam bene olere qui in culina habitant.
— PETRONIUS[1]

Poetry, like the world, may be said to have four ages, but in a different order: the first age of

[1]Petronius Arbiter, *Satyricon*, II: Those who are fed on these things can no more be wise than those who live in a kitchen can smell sweetly.

poetry being the age of iron; the second, of gold; the third, of silver; and the fourth, of brass.

The first, or iron age of poetry, is that in which rude bards celebrate in rough numbers the exploits of ruder chiefs, in days when every man is a warrior, and when the great practical maxim of every form of society, "to keep what we have and to catch what we can," is not yet disguised under names of justice and forms of law, but is the naked motto of the naked sword, which is the only judge and jury in every question of *meum* and *tuum*.[2] In these days, the only three trades flourishing (besides that of priest which flourishes always) are those of king, thief, and beggar: the beggar being for the most part a king deject, and the thief a king expectant. The first question asked of a stranger is, whether he is a beggar or a thief: the stranger, in reply, usually assumes the first, and awaits a convenient opportunity to prove his claim to the second appellation.

The natural desire of every man to engross to himself as much power and property as he can acquire by any of the means which might makes right, is accompanied by the no less natural desire of making known to as many people as possible the extent to which he has been a winner in this universal game. The successful warrior becomes a chief; the successful chief becomes a king: his next want is an organ to disseminate the fame of his achievements and the extent of his possessions; and this organ he finds in a bard, who is always ready to celebrate the strength of his arm, being first duly inspired by that of his liquor. This is the origin of poetry, which, like all other trades, takes its rise in the demand for the commodity, and flourishes in proportion to the extent of the market.

Poetry is thus in its origin panegyrical. The first rude songs of all nations appear to be a sort of brief historical notice, in a strain of tumid hyperbole, of the exploits and possessions of a few pre-eminent individuals. They tell us how many battles such a one has fought, how many helmets he has cleft, how many breastplates he has pierced, how many widows he has made, how much land he has appropriated, how many houses he has demolished for other people, what a large one he has built for himself, how much gold he has stowed away in it, and how liberally and plentifully he pays, feeds, and intoxicates the divine and immortal bards, the sons of Jupiter, but for whose everlasting songs the names of heroes would perish.

This is the first stage of poetry before the invention of written letters. The numerical modulation is at once useful as a help to memory, and pleasant to the ears of uncultured men, who are easily caught

by sound: and from the exceeding flexibility of the yet unformed language, the poet does no violence to his ideas in subjecting them to the fetters of number. The savage indeed lisps in numbers, and all rude and uncivilized people express themselves in the manner which we call poetical.[3]

The scenery by which he is surrounded, and the superstitions which are the creed of his age, form the poet's mind. Rocks, mountains, seas, unsubdued forests, unnavigable rivers, surround him with forms of power and mystery, which ignorance and fear have peopled with spirits, under multifarious names of gods, goddesses, nymphs, genii, and daemons. Of all these personages marvellous tales are in existence: the nymphs are not indifferent to handsome young men, and the gentlemen-genii are much troubled and very troublesome with a propensity to be rude to pretty maidens: the bard therefore finds no difficulty in tracing the genealogy of his chief to any of the deities in his neighbourhood with whom the said chief may be most desirous of claiming relationship.

In this pursuit, as in all others, some of course will attain a very marked pre-eminence; and these will be held in high honour, like Demodocus in the *Odyssey*, and will be consequently inflated with boundless vanity, like Thamyris in the *Iliad*.[4] Poets are as yet the only historians and chroniclers of their time, and the sole depositories of all the knowledge of their age; and though this knowledge is rather a crude congeries of traditional phantasies than a collection of useful truths, yet, such as it is, they have it to themselves. They are observing and thinking, while others are robbing and fighting: and though their object be nothing more than to secure a share of

---

[2] Property rights.

[3] Peacock's own poetry satirized these primative bards; his "War Song of Dinas Vawr" (1819), begins thus:

The mountain sheep are sweeter,
But the valley sheep are fatter;
We therefore deemed it meeter
To carry off the latter.
We made an expedition;
We met a host, and quelled it;
We forced a strong position,
And killed the men who held it.

[4] See *Odyssey* 8:43–92; *Iliad* 2:594–600.

the spoil, yet they accomplish this end by intellectual, not by physical, power: their success excites emulation to the attainment of intellectual eminence: thus they sharpen their own wits and awaken those of others, at the same time that they gratify vanity and amuse curiosity. A skilful display of the little knowledge they have gains them credit for the possession of much more which they have not. Their familiarity with the secret history of gods and genii obtains for them, without much difficulty, the reputation of inspiration; thus they are not only historians but theologians, moralists, and legislators: delivering their oracles *ex cathedra*,[5] and being indeed often themselves (as Orpheus and Amphion) regarded as portions and emanations of divinity: building cities with a song, and leading brutes with a symphony;[6] which are only metaphors for the faculty of leading multitudes by the nose.

The golden age of poetry finds its materials in the age of iron. This age begins when poetry begins to be retrospective; when something like a more extended system of civil polity is established; when personal strength and courage avail less to the aggrandizing of their possessor and to the making and marring of kings and kingdoms, and are checked by organized bodies, social institutions, and hereditary successions. Men also live more in the light of truth and within the interchange of observation; and thus perceive that the agency of gods and genii is not so frequent among themselves as, to judge from the songs and legends of the past time, it was among their ancestors. From these two circumstances, really diminished personal power, and apparently diminished familiarity with gods and genii, they very easily and naturally deduce two conclusions: 1st, That men are degenerated, and 2nd, That they are less in favour with the gods. The people of the petty states and colonies, which have now acquired stability and form, which owed their origin and first prosperity to the talents and courage of a single chief, magnify their founder through the mists of distance and tradition, and perceive him achieving wonders with a god or goddess always at his elbow. They find his name and his exploits thus magnified and accompanied in their traditionary songs, which are their only memorials. All that is said of him is in this character. There is nothing to contradict it. The man and his exploits and his tutelary deities are mixed and blended in one invariable association. The marvellous too is very much like a snowball: it grows as it rolls downward, till the little nucleus of truth which began its descent from the summit is hidden in the accumulation of superinduced hyperbole.

When tradition, thus adorned and exaggerated, has surrounded the founders of families and states with so much adventitious power and magnificence, there is no praise which a living poet can, without fear of being kicked for clumsy flattery, address to a living chief, that will not still leave the impression that the latter is not so great a man as his ancestors. The man must in this case be praised through his ancestors. Their greatness must be established, and he must be shown to be their worthy descendant. All the people of a state are interested in the founder of their state. All states that have harmonized into a common form of society, are interested in their respective founders. All men are interested in their ancestors. All men love to look back into the days that are past. In these circumstances traditional national poetry is reconstructed and brought like chaos into order and form. The interest is more universal: understanding is enlarged: passion still has scope and play: character is still various and strong: nature is still unsubdued and existing in all her beauty and magnificence, and men are not yet excluded from her observation by the magnitude of cities or the daily confinement of civic life: poetry is more an art: it requires greater skill in numbers, greater command of language, more extensive and various knowledge, and greater comprehensiveness of mind. It still exists without rivals in any other department of literature; and even the arts, painting and sculpture certainly, and music probably, are comparatively rude and imperfect. The whole field of intellect is its own. It has no rivals in history, nor in philosophy, nor in science. It is cultivated by the greatest intellects of the age, and listened to by all the rest.

[5]Literally "from the chair," this phrase denotes the most authoritative declarations of the Pope.

[6]According to legend, Amphion built Thebes "with a song" that sent the stones flying into their proper places, and Orpheus charmed the savage beasts with music.

This is the age of Homer, the golden age of poetry. Poetry has now attained its perfection: it has attained the point which it cannot pass: genius therefore seeks new forms for the treatment of the same subjects: hence the lyric poetry of Pindar and Alcaeus,[7] and the tragic poetry of Aeschylus and Sophocles.[8] The favour of kings, the honour of the Olympic crown, the applause of present multitudes, all that can feed vanity and stimulate rivalry, await the successful cultivator of this art, till its forms become exhausted, and new rivals arise around it in new fields of literature, which gradually acquire more influence as, with the progress of reason and civilization, facts become more interesting than fiction: indeed the maturity of poetry may be considered the infancy of history. The transition from Homer to Herodotus is scarcely more remarkable than that from Herodotus to Thucydides:[9] in the gradual dereliction of fabulous incident and ornamented language, Herodotus is as much a poet in relation to Thucydides as Homer is in relation to Herodotus. The history of Herodotus is half a poem: it was written while the whole field of literature yet belonged to the Muses, and the nine books of which it was composed were therefore of right, as well as of courtesy, superinscribed with their nine names.

Speculations, too, and disputes, on the nature of man and of mind; on moral duties and on good and evil; on the animate and inanimate components of the visible world; begin to share attention with the eggs of Leda and the horns of Io,[10] and to draw off from poetry a portion of its once undivided audience.

Then comes the silver age, or the poetry of civilized life. This poetry is of two kinds, imitative and original. The imitative consists in recasting, and giving an exquisite polish to, the poetry of the age of gold: of this Virgil is the most obvious and striking example.[11] The original is chiefly comic, didactic, or satiric: as in Menander, Aristophanes, Horace, and Juvenal.[12] The poetry of this age is characterized by an exquisite and fastidious selection of words, and a laboured and somewhat monotonous harmony of expression: but its monotony consists in this, that experience having exhausted all the varieties of modulation, the civilized poetry selects the most beautiful, and prefers the repetition of these to ranging through the variety of all. But the best expression being that into which the idea naturally falls, it requires the utmost labour and care so to reconcile the inflexibility of civilized language and the laboured polish of versification with the idea intended to be expressed, that sense may not appear to be sacrificed to sound. Hence numerous efforts and rare success.

This state of poetry is however a step towards its extinction. Feeling and passion are best painted in, and roused by, ornamental and figurative language; but the reason and the understanding are best addressed in the simplest and most unvarnished phrase. Pure reason and dispassionate truth would be perfectly ridiculous in verse, as we may judge by versifying one of Euclid's demonstrations. This will be found true of all dispassionate reasoning whatever, and all reasoning that requires comprehensive views and enlarged combinations. It is only the more tangible points of morality, those which command assent at once, those which have a mirror in every mind, and in which the severity of reason is warmed and rendered palatable by being mixed up with feeling and imagination, that are applicable even to what is called moral poetry: and as the sciences of morals and of mind advance towards perfection, as they become more enlarged and comprehensive in their

---

[7]Pindar and Alcaeus were Greek lyric poets of, respectively, the fifth and sixth centuries B.C.E.

[8]Both are of the fifth century B.C.E.

[9]Herodotus wrote his history of the Persian Wars around 440 B.C.E.; its nine books are not numbered but named after the nine muses. Thucydides wrote his history of the Pelopponesian War between 423 and 403 B.C.E.

[10]In Greek legend, Leda and Io were beloved by Zeus. Leda's eggs, fertilized by Zeus in the form of a swan, hatched into Castor, Polydeukes, Helen, and Clytemnaestra. Io was turned into a cow to protect her from the jealous rage of Hera, Zeus's wife.

[11]Virgil's *Aeneid* had been written in imitation of Homer's *Odyssey* and *Iliad*.

[12]Menander and Aristophanes were Greek comic playwrights; Horace and Juvenal were Roman satirists. Six centuries separate Aristophanes (who was born about 450 B.C.E) from Juvenal (who died about 140 C.E.).

views, as reason gains the ascendancy in them over imagination and feeling, poetry can no longer accompany them in their progress, but drops into the background, and leaves them to advance alone.

Thus the empire of thought is withdrawn from poetry, as the empire of facts had been before. In respect of the latter, the poet of the age of iron celebrates the achievements of his contemporaries; the poet of the age of gold celebrates the heroes of the age of iron; the poet of the age of silver re-casts the poems of the age of gold: we may here see how very slight a ray of historical truth is sufficient to dissipate all the illusions of poetry. We know no more of the men than of the gods of the *Iliad*; no more of Achilles than we do of Thetis; no more of Hector and Andromache than we do of Vulcan and Venus: these belong altogether to poetry; history has no share in them: but Virgil knew better than to write an epic about Caesar; he left him to Livy; and travelled out of the confines of truth and history into the old regions of poetry and fiction.[13]

Good sense and elegant learning, conveyed in polished and somewhat monotonous verse, are the perfection of the original and imitative poetry of civilized life. Its range is limited, and when exhausted, nothing remains but the *crambe repetita*[14] of commonplace, which at length becomes thoroughly wearisome, even to the most indefatigable readers of the newest new nothings.

It is now evident that poetry must either cease to be cultivated, or strike into a new path. The poets of the age of gold have been imitated and repeated till no new imitation will attract notice: the limited range of ethical and didactic poetry is exhausted: the associations of daily life in an advanced state of society are of very dry, methodical, unpoetical matters-of-fact: but there is always a multitude of listless idlers, yawning for amusement, and gaping for novelty: and the poet makes it his glory to be foremost among their purveyors.

Then comes the age of brass, which, by rejecting the polish and the learning of the age of silver, and taking a retrograde stride to the barbarisms and crude traditions of the age of iron, professes to return to nature and revive the age of gold. This is the second childhood of poetry. To the comprehensive energy of the Homeric Muse, which, by giving at once the grand outline of things, presented to the mind a vivid picture in one or two verses, inimitable alike in simplicity and magnificence, is substituted a verbose and minutely-detailed description of thoughts, passions, actions, persons, and things, in that loose rambling style of verse, which any one may write, *stans pede in uno*,[15] at the rate of two hundred lines in an hour. To this age may be referred all the poets who flourished in the decline of the Roman Empire. The best specimen of it, though not the most generally known, is the Dionysiaca of Nonnus, which contains many passages of exceeding beauty in the midst of masses of amplification and repetition.[16]

The iron age of classical poetry may be called the bardic; the golden, the Homeric; the silver, the Virgilian; and the brass, the Nonnic.

Modern poetry has also its four ages: but "it wears its rue with a difference."[17]

To the age of brass in the ancient world succeeded the dark ages, in which the light of the Gospel began to spread over Europe, and in which, by a mysterious and inscrutable dispensation, the darkness thickened with the progress of the light. The tribes that overran the Roman Empire brought back the days of barbarism, but with this difference, that there were many books in the world, many places in which they were preserved, and occasionally some one by whom they were read, who indeed (if he escaped being burned *pour l'amour de Dieu*[18]) generally lived an object of

---

[15]Latin for "standing on one foot."

[16]Nonnus's epic (in Greek) on Dionysus's journey to India and back was written around the beginning of the sixth century C.E.

[17]Peacock is quoting Ophelia's line in *Hamlet* (IV.v.179). Rue is worn "for remembrance," and it is worn "with a difference" by the English poets because their relation to their subject matter is not the same as the classical sequence of Greeks and Romans.

[18]French for "for the love of God."

[13]Peacock's point is that the humans of epic (Achilles, Hector, Andromache) are no less legendary, no more historical, than the gods of epic (Thetis, Vulcan, Venus). Virgil wrote his epic about the legendary founder of Rome, Aeneas, and not about his patron who ruled Rome, Augustus Caesar.

[14]Latin for "re-cooked cabbage."

mysterious fear, with the reputation of magician, alchemist, and astrologer. The emerging of the nations of Europe from this superinduced barbarism, and their settling into new forms of polity, was accompanied, as the first ages of Greece had been, with a wild spirit of adventure, which, cooperating with new manners and new superstitions, raised up a fresh crop of chimaeras, not less fruitful, though far less beautiful, than those of Greece. The semi-deification of women by the maxims of the age of chivalry, combining with these new fables, produced the romance of the middle ages. The founders of the new line of heroes took the place of the demi-gods of Grecian poetry. Charlemagne and his Paladins, Arthur and his knights of the round table, the heroes of the iron age of chivalrous poetry, were seen through the same magnifying mist of distance, and their exploits were celebrated with even more extravagant hyperbole. These legends, combined with the exaggerated love that pervades the songs of the troubadours, the reputation of magic that attached to learned men, the infant wonders of natural philosophy, the crazy fanaticism of the crusades, the power and privileges of the great feudal chiefs, and the holy mysteries of monks and nuns, formed a state of society in which no two laymen could meet without fighting, and in which the three staple ingredients of lover, prize-fighter, and fanatic, that composed the basis of the character of every true man, were mixed up and diversified, in different individuals and classes, with so many distinctive excellencies, and under such an infinite motley variety of costume, as gave the range of a most extensive and picturesque field to the two great constituents of poetry, love and battle.

From these ingredients of the iron age of modern poetry, dispersed in the rhymes of minstrels and the songs of the troubadours, arose the golden age, in which the scattered materials were harmonized and blended about the time of the revival of learning; but with this peculiar difference, that Greek and Roman literature pervaded all the poetry of the golden age of modern poetry, and hence resulted a heterogeneous compound of all ages and nations in one picture; an infinite licence, which gave to the poet the free range of the whole field of imagination and memory. This was carried very far by Ariosto,[19] but farthest of all by Shakespeare and his contemporaries, who used time and locality merely because they could not do without them, because every action must have its when and where: but they made no scruple of deposing a Roman Emperor by an Italian Count, and sending him off in the disguise of a French pilgrim to be shot with a blunderbuss by an English archer. This makes the old English drama very picturesque, at any rate, in the variety of costume, and very diversified in action and character; though it is a picture of nothing that ever was seen on earth except a Venetian carnival.

The greatest of English poets, Milton, may be said to stand alone between the ages of gold and silver, combining the excellencies of both; for with all the energy, and power, and freshness of the first, he united all the studied and elaborate magnificence of the second.

The silver age succeeded; beginning with Dryden, coming to perfection with Pope, and ending with Goldsmith, Collins, and Gray.

Cowper divested verse of its exquisite polish; he thought in metre, but paid more attention to his thoughts than to his verse. It would be difficult to draw the boundary of prose and blank verse between his letters and his poetry.

The silver age was the reign of authority; but authority now began to be shaken, not only in poetry but in the whole sphere of its dominion. The contemporaries of Gray and Cowper were deep and elaborate thinkers. The subtle scepticism of Hume, the solemn irony of Gibbon, the daring paradoxes of Rousseau, and the biting ridicule of Voltaire, directed the energies of four extraordinary minds to shake every portion of the reign of authority. Enquiry was roused, the activity of intellect was excited, and poetry came in for its share of the general result. The changes had been rung on lovely maid and sylvan shade, summer heat and green retreat, waving trees and sighing breeze, gentle swains and amorous pains, by versifiers who took them on trust, as meaning something very soft and tender, without much caring what: but with this

[19]Author of *Orlando Furioso* (1516), an epic about the days of Charlemagne.

general activity of intellect came a necessity for even poets to appear to know something of what they professed to talk of. Thomson and Cowper looked at the trees and hills which so many ingenious gentlemen had rhymed about so long without looking at them at all, and the effect of the operation on poetry was like the discovery of a new world. Painting shared the influence, and the principles of picturesque beauty were explored by adventurous essayists with indefatigable pertinacity. The success which attended these experiments, and the pleasure which resulted from them, had the usual effect of all new enthusiasms, that of turning the heads of a few unfortunate persons, the patriarchs of the age of brass, who, mistaking the prominent novelty for the all-important totality, seem to have ratiocinated much in the following manner: "Poetical genius is the finest of all things, and we feel that we have more of it than any one ever had. The way to bring it to perfection is to cultivate poetical impressions exclusively. Poetical impressions can be received only among natural scenes: for all that is artificial is anti-poetical. Society is artificial, therefore we will live out of society. The mountains are natural, therefore we will live in the mountains. There we shall be shining models of purity and virtue, passing the whole day in the innocent and amiable occupation of going up and down hill, receiving poetical impressions, and communicating them in immortal verse to admiring generations." To some such perversion of intellect we owe that egregious confraternity of rhymesters, known by the name of the Lake Poets; who certainly did receive and communicate to the world some of the most extraordinary poetical impressions that ever were heard of, and ripened into models of public virtue, too splendid to need illustration.[20] They wrote verses on a new principle; saw rocks and rivers in a new light; and remaining studiously ignorant of history, society, and human nature, cultivated the phantasy only at the expence of the memory and the reason; and contrived, though they

had retreated from the world for the express purpose of seeing nature as she was, to see her only as she was not, converting the land they lived in into a sort of fairy-land, which they peopled with mysticisms and chimaeras. This gave what is called a new tone to poetry, and conjured up a herd of desperate imitators, who have brought the age of brass prematurely to its dotage.

The descriptive poetry of the present day has been called by its cultivators a return to nature. Nothing is more impertinent than this pretension. Poetry cannot travel out of the regions of its birth, the uncultivated lands of semi-civilized men. Mr. Wordsworth, the great leader of the returners to nature, cannot describe a scene under his own eyes without putting into it the shadow of a Danish boy or the living ghost of Lucy Gray, or some similar phantastical parturition of the moods of his own mind.[21]

In the origin and perfection of poetry, all the associations of life were composed of poetical materials. With us it is decidedly the reverse. We know too that there are no Dryads in Hyde-park nor Naiads in the Regent's-canal. But barbaric manners and supernatural interventions are essential to poetry. Either in the scene, or in the time, or in both, it must be remote from our ordinary perceptions. While the historian and the philosopher are advancing in, and accelerating, the progress of knowledge, the poet is wallowing in the rubbish of departed ignorance, and raking up the ashes of dead savages to find gewgaws and rattles for the grown babies of the age. Mr. Scott digs up the poachers and cattle-stealers of the ancient border. Lord Byron cruises for thieves and pirates on the shores of the Morea and among the Greek Islands. Mr. Southey wades through ponderous volumes of travels and old chronicles, from which he carefully selects all that is false, useless, and absurd, as being essentially poetical; and when he has a commonplace book full of monstrosities, strings them into an epic. Mr. Wordsworth picks

---

[20]This is sarcastic: The Lake Poets (Wordsworth and Southey) began as enthusiasts for the French Revolution, then renounced their politics; Peacock, a liberal like his friend Shelley, would have found this reprehensible.

[21]Both "The Danish Boy" and "Lucy Gray" were published in the second (1800) edition of *Lyrical Ballads*, by Wordsworth; "Moods of My Own Mind" were poems published in 1807.

up village legends from old women and sextons; and Mr. Coleridge, to the valuable information acquired from similar sources, superadds the dreams of crazy theologians and the mysticisms of German metaphysics, and favours the world with visions in verse, in which the quadruple elements of sexton, old woman, Jeremy Taylor, and Emanuel Kant, are harmonized into a delicious poetical compound. Mr. Moore presents us with a Persian, and Mr. Campbell with a Pennsylvanian tale, both formed on the same principle as Mr. Southey's epics, by extracting from a perfunctory and desultory perusal of a collection of voyages and travels, all that useful investigation would not seek for and that common sense would reject.[22]

These disjointed relics of tradition and fragments of second-hand observation, being woven into a tissue of verse, constructed on what Mr. Coleridge calls a new principle (that is, no principle at all), compose a modern-antique compound of frippery and barbarism, in which the puling sentimentality of the present time is grafted on the misrepresented ruggedness of the past into a heterogeneous congeries of unamalgamating manners, sufficient to impose on the common readers of poetry, over whose understandings the poet of this class possesses that commanding advantage, which, in all circumstances and conditions of life, a man who knows something, however little, always possesses over one who knows nothing.

A poet in our times is a semi-barbarian in a civilized community. He lives in the days that are past. His ideas, thoughts, feelings, associations, are all with barbarous manners, obsolete customs, and exploded superstitions. The march of his intellect is like that of a crab, backward. The brighter the light diffused around him by the progress of reason, the thicker is the darkness of antiquated barbarism, in which he buries himself like a mole, to throw up the barren hillocks of his

Cimmerian[23] labours. The philosophic mental tranquillity which looks round with an equal eye on all external things, collects a store of ideas, discriminates their relative value, assigns to all their proper place, and from the materials of useful knowledge thus collected, appreciated, and arranged, forms new combinations that impress the stamp of their power and utility on the real business of life, is diametrically the reverse of that frame of mind which poetry inspires, or from which poetry can emanate. The highest inspirations of poetry are resolvable into three ingredients: the rant of unregulated passion, the whining of exaggerated feeling, and the cant of factitious sentiment: and can therefore serve only to ripen a splendid lunatic like Alexander, a puling driveller like Werter, or a morbid dreamer like Wordsworth.[24] It can never make a philosopher, nor a statesman, nor in any class of life a useful or rational man. It cannot claim the slightest share in any one of the comforts and utilities of life of which we have witnessed so many and so rapid advances. But though not useful, it may be said it is highly ornamental, and deserves to be cultivated for the pleasure it yields. Even if this be granted, it does not follow that a writer of poetry in the present state of society is not a waster of his own time, and a robber of that of others. Poetry is not one of those arts which, like painting, require repetition and multiplication, in order to be diffused among society. There are more good poems already existing than are sufficient to employ that portion of life which any mere reader and recipient of poetical impressions should devote to them, and these having been produced in poetical times, are far superior in all the characteristics of poetry to the artificial reconstructions of a few morbid ascetics in unpoetical times. To read the promiscuous rubbish of the present time to the exclusion of the select treasures of the past, is to

---

[22]Peacock is satirizing Walter Scott (*Minstrelsy of the Scottish Border*, 1803), Lord Byron (*The Giaour*, 1813), Robert Southey (*The Last of the Goths*, 1814), William Wordsworth (*The Excursion*, 1814), and Samuel Taylor Coleridge (the fantasy material is in "Rime of the Ancient Mariner" and "Christabel," both 1798; the metaphysics and theology are from *Biographia Literaria*, 1817). Peacock throws in for good measure the Irish Thomas Moore (*Lalla Rookh*, 1817) and the Scottish Thomas Campbell (*Gertrude of Wyoming*, 1817).

[23]Dark: Homer's Cimmerians, in Book 11 of the *Odyssey*, lived in a sunless land.
[24]"Werter" is the suicidal hero of Johann Wolfgang von Goethe's novel *The Sorrows of Young Werther* (1774), and Wordsworth is the English poet, but Alexander the "splendid lunatic" has not been satisfactorily identified. Possibly Peacock is referring to Czar Alexander I of Russia (1777–1825), whose liberal rule began to change around 1818.

substitute the worse for the better variety of the same mode of enjoyment.

But in whatever degree poetry is cultivated, it must necessarily be to the neglect of some branch of useful study: and it is a lamentable spectacle to see minds, capable of better things, running to seed in the specious indolence of these empty aimless mockeries of intellectual exertion. Poetry was the mental rattle that awakened the attention of intellect in the infancy of civil society: but for the maturity of mind to make a serious business of the playthings of its childhood, is as absurd as for a full-grown man to rub his gums with coral, and cry to be charmed to sleep by the jingle of silver bells.

As to that small portion of our contemporary poetry, which is neither descriptive, nor narrative, nor dramatic, and which, for want of a better name, may be called ethical, the most distinguished portion of it, consisting merely of querulous, egotistical rhapsodies, to express the writer's high dissatisfaction with the world and every thing in it, serves only to confirm what has been said of the semibarbarous character of poets, who from singing dithyrambics and "Io Triumphe," while society was savage, grow rabid, and out of their element, as it becomes polished and enlightened.

Now when we consider that it is not to the thinking and studious, and scientific and philosophical part of the community, not to those whose minds are bent on the pursuit and promotion of permanently useful ends and aims, that poets must address their minstrelsy, but to that much larger portion of the reading public, whose minds are not awakened to the desire of valuable knowledge, and who are indifferent to any thing beyond being charmed, moved, excited, affected, and exalted: charmed by harmony, moved by sentiment, excited by passion, affected by pathos, and exalted by sublimity: harmony, which is language on the rack of Procrustes;[25] sentiment, which is canting egotism in the mask of refined feeling; passion, which is the commotion of a weak and selfish mind; pathos, which is the whining of an unmanly

spirit; and sublimity, which is the inflation of an empty head: when we consider that the great and permanent interests of human society become more and more the main spring of intellectual pursuit; that in proportion as they become so, the subordinacy of the ornamental to the useful will be more and more seen and acknowledged; and that therefore the progress of useful art and science, and of moral and political knowledge, will continue more and more to withdraw attention from frivolous and unconducive, to solid and conducive studies: that therefore the poetical audience will not only continually diminish in the proportion of its number to that of the rest of the reading public, but will also sink lower and lower in the comparison of intellectual acquirement: when we consider that the poet must still please his audience, and must therefore continue to sink to their level, while the rest of the community is rising above it: we may easily conceive that the day is not distant, when the degraded state of every species of poetry will be as generally recognized as that of dramatic poetry has long been: and this not from any decrease either of intellectual power, or intellectual acquisition, but because intellectual power and intellectual acquisition have turned themselves into other and better channels, and have abandoned the cultivation and the fate of poetry to the degenerate fry of modern rhymesters, and their olympic judges, the magazine critics, who continue to debate and promulgate oracles about poetry, as if it were still what it was in the Homeric age, the all-in-all of intellectual progression, and as if there were no such things in existence as mathematicians, astronomers, chemists, moralists, metaphysicians, historians, politicians, and political economists, who have built into the upper air of intelligence a pyramid, from the summit of which they see the modern Parnassus[26] far beneath them, and, knowing how small a place it occupies in the comprehensiveness of their prospect, smile at the little ambition and the circumscribed perceptions with which the drivellers and mountebanks upon it are contending for the poetical palm and the critical chair.

[25]In Greek legend Procrustes was a bandit slain by Theseus. His practice, with travelers who fell into his clutches, was to "fit" them to his rack, cutting the feet off those who were longer, and stretching the limbs of those who were shorter till their joints dislocated.

[26]Mountain of the muses, associated with poetry.

Percy Bysshe Shelley

1792–1822

The most radical English poet since Milton, Percy Bysshe Shelley wrote in proud rebellion against his conservative and aristocratic roots: His grandfather was a landowning baronet, his father a member of Parliament. Shelley was educated at Eton and Oxford, from which he was sent down at the age of eighteen for publishing a tract advocating atheism. In London, he came under the influence of the philosopher William Godwin, whose *Political Justice* questioned the foundations of the English state. Though already married to Harriet Westbrook, Shelley fell in love with Godwin's daughter Mary, and in 1814 eloped with her to France; they were able to marry only after Harriet's suicide, in 1816. In financial straits and anathematized by the British public for his political opinions as well as his sexual immorality, Shelley moved to Italy the next year. There he wrote his most impressive works: *Prometheus Unbound* (1819), *The Masque of Anarchy* (1819), *Epipsychidion* (1821), and *Adonais* (1821). He had just embarked on his most ambitious poem, *The Triumph of Life,* when he drowned in July of 1822 in a boating accident in the Gulf of Spezia.

Like Sir Philip Sidney's *An Apology for Poetry,* Shelley's *A Defence of Poetry* (written in 1821, though not published until 1840) is a reply to Plato's attacks on mimetic art in *Republic,* Book X (p. 30). It should not be surprising that in the period after Kant and his successors, Shelley's riposte would depend on the notion of mental faculties and their powers. He thus begins the *Defence* with the parallel dialectical oppositions of *tò logizeín* and *tò poieîn,* reason and imagination, analysis and synthesis. His purpose is to refute Plato's attack on the mimetic artist as inferior to the artisan in knowledge and understanding by insisting that the poetic faculty is equal and complementary to logical reason.

The reader who scans *A Defence of Poetry* in search of a systematic approach to Romantic critical theory, however, will be disappointed. Although the essay begins austerely enough with what appears to be a set of logical distinctions, philosophical rigor is soon abandoned. Indeed, some readers may find Shelley's prose disjointed and contradictory, apparently unplanned in organization, at times almost incoherent. But if we set aside system and rigor and attend instead to Shelley's ideals and imagery, the essay yields an inspiring vision, rather like that at the conclusion of *Adonais,* of how the Romantic poets saw themselves and the place of poetry in human society. Perhaps the first and third sections of *A Defence of Poetry* (pp. 346–50 and 358–63) should be read as we read a lyric, through key metaphors.

The first of these metaphors likens the mind to an Aeolian lyre, struck to melody by the wind of its "external and internal impressions." Shelley develops this metaphor further: The mind produces not just melody but harmony as well, and the spontaneous song of the child is an expression of delight in this harmony, an effect the child prolongs by recalling its cause. It is here, deep in human nature, that Shelley locates the impulse to produce art, for poetry is nothing but the adult analogy to this process.

Toward the end of the *Defence,* in discussing the haphazard nature of poetic inspiration Shelley likens the mind of the poet to "a fading coal which some invisible influence, like an inconstant wind, awakens to transitory brightness." Again, the external world is like a wind, forcible but insubstantial, while the mind is like a physical object that can make light or heat or melody. Perhaps nothing suggests Shelley's deep affinity to Plato more than this; it is as if the mind and its ideas are real while the external physical world is not.

Shelley is most Platonic in opposition to his master. Where Plato ejected the poets from his Republic, Shelley makes them its masters, calling them "the unacknowledged legislators of the World." He begins with the idea that "every original language near to its source is in itself the chaos of a cyclic [i.e., epic] poem." We might think of poetry as a special use of language that arranges a harmony between sound and meaning, but all language does that. Whoever creates any new word or names any unnamed feature of the sensual world is, in effect, a poet. Language is everywhere a network of living, dying, and dead metaphors, statements of the likenesses between one aspect of experience and another. We talk of "the iron curtain," we play the game of "cat's cradle": Both are poetic metaphors. And language embalms metaphors in its etymologies: At one time the verb *transgress* literally signified "straying from the herd." In shaping language, the poets — these innovators of language, who are not necessarily identical with the canonized poets from Homer to Shelley himself — have in effect shaped human thought, and thus molded society and human relations.

But it is not enough for Shelley to find a poetic act somewhere behind any use of language. He claims that poetry, in any age removed from the primitive *source* of language, recaptures for humanity, by metaphor and harmony, the immediacy of life and experience, an immediacy that is lost by the use of logical, analytical thought and language. For Shelley, the world is veiled from human participation by dead thought and language, and it is the poets alone who are able to penetrate and "lift the veil from the hidden beauty of the world."

In the course of this argument the words *poetry* and *poet* shift their ground away from pure aesthetics. A poet is anyone who can synthesize a vision of the world and express that apprehended synthesis in language. Thus the great philosophers, Plato among them, are revealed to be nothing other than poets. And conversely, since poets' visions are necessarily of the eternal truths of the human spirit, Shakespeare, Dante, and Milton must be seen as "philosophers of the very loftiest power."

The development of these general ideas is interrupted by a long middle section (pp. 350–58), which was inspired less by Plato than by *The Four Ages of Poetry* (1820), a pamphlet by Shelley's friend, the satirist Thomas Love Peacock. Perhaps influenced by the Italian philosopher Giambattista Vico, Peacock posited a cyclical theory of the history of Western civilization: Both history and poetry had by then gone through two cycles with four phases in each.

Each cycle begins with an "age of iron," like the archaic period or the Middle Ages, when the poet is essentially a bard paid to flatter in verse the exploits of military chieftains. There follows an "age of gold," a tough but harmonious civilization, like Periclean Athens or Elizabethan England, which produces the finest poetry, the Homers and the Shakespeares. From then on, however, the increasing encroachment of scientific knowledge limits the scope of poetry. There arrives an "age of silver," a polished and classicizing civilization that gives rise to the Virgils and the Miltons and Popes. Finally comes the decadence of the "age of brass," in which poetry is mere nostalgic archaism, like the later Roman Empire — or the English Romantic period. At last, the destruction of civilization itself — the fall of the Roman Empire in the first cycle — puts an end to the decay and allows a new age of iron to begin. The bulk of *A Defence of Poetry* is a reply to Peacock's attack on Romantics and Romanticism, which takes the form of a progressive (rather than a cyclical) theory of history and of the poetry that grew up alongside (and in Shelley's view helped to form) political institutions.

Selected Bibliography

Bloom, Harold. *Shelley's Mythmaking*. New Haven: Yale University Press, 1959.
Damm, Robert F. *A Tale of Human Power: Art and Life in Shelley's Poetic Theory*. Oxford, OH: Miami University Press, 1970.
Gallagher, Catherine. "Formalism and Time." *Modern Language Quarterly* 61, no.1 (2000): 229–51.
Grabo, C. H. *The Magic Plant: The Growth of Shelley's Thought*. Chapel Hill: University of North Carolina Press, 1936.
Milnes, Tim. "Centre and Circumference: Shelley's Defence of Philosophy." *European Romantic Review* 15, no.1 (2004): 3–22.
Notopoulos, J. A. *The Platonism of Shelley*. Durham: Duke University Press, 1949.
Schulze, Earl J. *Shelley's Theory of Poetry: A Reappraisal*. The Hague: Mouton, 1966.
Shawcross, John, ed. *Shelley's Literary and Philosophical Criticism*. London: H. Frowde, 1909.
Solve, Melvin T. *Shelley: His Theory of Poetry*. Chicago: University of Chicago Press, 1927.

A Defence of Poetry

Or Remarks Suggested by an Essay Entitled "The Four Ages of Poetry"

According to one mode of regarding those two classes of mental action, which are called reason and imagination, the former may be considered as mind contemplating the relations borne by one thought to another, however produced; and the latter, as mind acting upon those thoughts so as to colour them with its own light, and composing from them, as from elements, other thoughts, each containing within itself the principle of its own integrity. The one is the τὸ ποιειν,[1] or the principle of synthesis, and has for its objects those forms which are common to universal nature and existence itself; the other is the τὸ λογιζειν,[2] or principle of analysis, and its action regards the relations of things, simply as relations; considering thoughts, not in their integral unity, but as the algebraical representations which conduct to certain general results. Reason is the enumeration of quantities already known; imagination is the perception of the

[1]Making.
[2]Reasoning.

value of those quantities, both separately and as a whole. Reason respects the differences, and imagination the similitudes of things. Reason is to Imagination as the instrument to the agent, as the body to the spirit, as the shadow to the substance.

Poetry, in a general sense, may be defined to be "the expression of the Imagination": and poetry is connate with the origin of man. Man is an instrument over which a series of external and internal impressions are driven, like the alternations of an ever-changing wind over an Æolian lyre, which move it by their motion to ever-changing melody. But there is a principle within the human being, and perhaps within all sentient beings, which acts otherwise than in the lyre, and produces not melody alone, but harmony, by an internal adjustment of the sounds or motions thus excited to the impressions which excite them. It is as if the lyre could accommodate its chords to the motions of that which strikes them, in a determined proportion of sound; even as the musician can accommodate his voice to the sound of the lyre. A child at play by itself will express its delight by its voice and motions; and every inflexion of tone and every gesture will bear exact relation to a corresponding antitype in the pleasurable impressions which awakened it; it will be the reflected image of that impression; and as the lyre trembles and sounds after the wind has died away, so the child seeks, by prolonging in its voice and motions the duration of the effect, to prolong also a consciousness of the cause. In relation to the objects which delight a child, these expressions are what poetry is to higher objects. The savage (for the savage is to ages what the child is to years) expresses the emotions produced in him by surrounding objects in a similar manner; and language and gesture, together with plastic or pictorial imitation, become the image of the combined effect of those objects, and of his apprehension of them. Man in society, with all his passions and his pleasures, next becomes the object of the passions and pleasures of man; an additional class of emotions produces an augmented treasure of expressions; and language, gesture, and the imitative arts, become at once the representation and the medium, the pencil and the picture, the chisel and the statue, the chord and the harmony. The social sympathies, or those laws from which as from its elements society results,

begin to develope themselves from the moment that two human beings coexist; the future is contained within the present as the plant within the seed; and equality, diversity, unity, contrast, mutual dependence, become the principles alone capable of affording the motives according to which the will of a social being is determined to action, inasmuch as he is social; and constitute pleasure in sensation, virtue in sentiment, beauty in art, truth in reasoning, and love in the intercourse of kind. Hence men, even in the infancy of society, observe a certain order in their words and actions, distinct from that of the objects and the impressions represented by them, all expression being subject to the laws of that from which it proceeds. But let us dismiss those more general considerations which might involve an enquiry into the principles of society itself, and restrict our view to the manner in which the imagination is expressed upon its forms.

In the youth of the world, men dance and sing and imitate natural objects, observing in these actions, as in all others, a certain rhythm or order. And, although all men observe a similar, they observe not the same order, in the motions of the dance, in the melody of the song, in the combinations of language, in the series of their imitations of natural objects. For there is a certain order or rhythm belonging to each of these classes of mimetic representation, from which the hearer and the spectator receive an intenser and purer pleasure than from any other: the sense of an approximation to this order has been called taste, by modern writers. Every man in the infancy of art, observes an order which approximates more or less closely to that from which this highest delight results: but the diversity is not sufficiently marked, as that its gradations should be sensible, except in those instances where the predominance of this faculty of approximation to the beautiful (for so we may be permitted to name the relation between this highest pleasure and its cause) is very great. Those in whom it exists in excess are poets, in the most universal sense of the word; and the pleasure resulting from the manner in which they express the influence of society or nature upon their own minds, communicates itself to others, and gathers a sort of reduplication from that community. Their language is vitally metaphorical; that is, it marks the before unapprehended relations of things, and perpetuates their apprehension, until the words which represent them, become through time signs for portions or classes of thoughts instead of pictures of integral thoughts; and then if no new poets should arise to create afresh the associations which have been thus disorganized, language will be dead to all the nobler purposes of human intercourse. These similitudes or relations are finely said by Lord Bacon to be "the same footsteps of nature impressed upon the various subjects of the world"[3] — and he considers the faculty which perceives them as the storehouse of axioms common to all knowledge. In the infancy of society every author is necessarily a poet, because language itself is poetry; and to be a poet is to apprehend the true and the beautiful, in a word the good which exists in the relation, subsisting, first between existence and perception, and secondly between perception and expression. Every original language near to its source is in itself the chaos of a cyclic poem: the copiousness of lexicography and the distinctions of grammar are the works of a later age, and are merely the catalogue and the form of the creations of Poetry.

But Poets, or those who imagine and express this indestructible order, are not only the authors of language and of music, of the dance and architecture and statuary and painting: they are the institutors of laws, and the founders of civil society and the inventors of the arts of life and the teachers, who draw into a certain propinquity with the beautiful and the true that partial apprehension of the agencies of the invisible world which is called religion. Hence all original religions are allegorical, or susceptible of allegory, and like Janus have a double face of false and true. Poets, according to the circumstances of the age and nation in which they appeared, were called in the earlier epochs of the world legislators or prophets: a poet essentially comprises and unites both these characters.[4] For he not only beholds intensely the present as it is, and discovers those laws according to which present things ought to be ordered, but he beholds the future in the present, and his thoughts are the germs of the

flower and the fruit of latest time. Not that I assert poets to be prophets in the gross sense of the word, or that they can foretell the form as surely as they foreknow the spirit of events: such is the pretence of superstition which would make poetry an attribute of prophecy, rather than prophecy an attribute of poetry. A Poet participates in the eternal, the infinite, and the one; as far as relates to his conceptions, time and place and number are not. The grammatical forms which express the moods of time, and the difference of persons and the distinction of place are convertible with respect to the highest poetry without injuring it as poetry, and the choruses of Æschylus, and the book of Job, and Dante's Paradise would afford, more than any other writings, examples of this fact, if the limits of this essay did not forbid citation. The creations of sculpture, painting, and music, are illustrations still more decisive.

Language, colour, form, and religious and civil habits of action are all the instruments and materials of poetry; they may be called poetry by that figure of speech which considers the effect as a synonime of the cause. But poetry in a more restricted sense expresses those arrangements of language, and especially metrical language, which are created by that imperial faculty, whose throne is curtained within the invisible nature of man. And this springs from the nature itself of language, which is a more direct representation of the actions and passions of our internal being, and is susceptible of more various and delicate combinations, than colour, form, or motion, and is more plastic and obedient to the controul of that faculty of which it is the creation. For language is arbitrarily produced by the Imagination and has relation to thoughts alone; but all other materials, instruments and conditions of art, have relations among each other, which limit and interpose between conception and expression. The former is as a mirror which reflects, the latter as a cloud which enfeebles, the light of which both are mediums of communication. Hence the fame of sculptors, painters and musicians, although the intrinsic powers of the great masters of these arts, may yield in no degree to that of those who have employed language as the hieroglyphic of their thoughts, has never equalled that of poets in the

---

[3]Francis Bacon, *The Advancement of Learning.* 3:1.
[4]Cf. Philip Sidney, *An Apology for Poetry;* see p. 135.

restricted sense of the term; as two performers of equal skill will produce unequal effects from a guitar and a harp. The fame of legislators and founders of religions, so long as their institutions last, alone seems to exceed that of poets in the restricted sense; but it can scarcely be a question whether, if we deduct the celebrity which their flattery of the gross opinions of the vulgar usually conciliates, together with that which belonged to them in their higher character of poets, any excess will remain.

We have thus circumscribed the meaning of the word Poetry within the limits of that art which is the most familiar and the most perfect expression of the faculty itself. It is necessary however to make the circle still narrower, and to determine the distinction between measured and unmeasured language; for the popular division into prose and verse is inadmissible in accurate philosophy.

Sounds as well as thoughts have relation both between each other and towards that which they represent, and a perception of the order of those relations has always been found connected with a perception of the order of the relations of thoughts. Hence the language of poets has ever affected a certain uniform and harmonious recurrence of sound, without which it were not poetry, and which is scarcely less indispensable to the communication of its influence, than the words themselves, without reference to that peculiar order. Hence the vanity of translation; it were as wise to cast a violet into a crucible that you might discover the formal principle of its colour and odour, as seek to transfuse from one language into another the creations of a poet. The plant must spring again from its seed or it will bear no flower — and this is the burthen of the curse of Babel.

An observation of the regular mode of the recurrence of this harmony in the language of poetical minds, together with its relation to music, produced metre, or a certain system of traditional forms of harmony of language. Yet it is by no means essential that a poet should accommodate his language to this traditional form, so that the harmony which is its spirit, be observed. The practise is indeed convenient and popular, and to be preferred, especially in such composition as includes much form and action: but every great poet must inevitably innovate upon the example of his predecessors in the exact structure of his peculiar versification. The distinction between poets and prose writers is a vulgar error. The distinction between philosophers and poets has been anticipated. Plato was essentially a poet — the truth and splendour of his imagery and the melody of his language is the most intense that it is possible to conceive. He rejected the measure of the epic, dramatic, and lyrical forms, because he sought to kindle a harmony in thoughts divested of shape and action, and he forbore to invent any regular plan of rhythm which would include, under determinate forms, the varied pauses of his style. Cicero sought to imitate the cadence of his periods but with little success. Lord Bacon was a poet.[5] His language has a sweet and majestic rhythm, which satisfies the sense, no less than the almost superhuman wisdom of his philosophy satisfies the intellect; it is a strain which distends, and then bursts the circumference of the hearer's mind, and pours itself forth together with it into the universal element with which it has perpetual sympathy. All the authors of revolutions in opinion are not only necessarily poets as they are inventors, nor even as their words unveil the permanent analogy of things by images which participate in the life of truth; but as their periods are harmonious and rhythmical and contain in themselves the elements of verse; being the echo of the eternal music. Nor are those supreme poets, who have employed traditional forms of rhythm on account of the form and action of their subjects, less capable of perceiving and teaching the truth of things, than those who have omitted that form. Shakespeare, Dante and Milton (to confine ourselves to modern writers) are philosophers of the very loftiest power.

A poem is the very image of life expressed in its eternal truth. There is this difference between a story and a poem, that a story is a catalogue of detached facts, which have no other bond of connexion than time, place, circumstance, cause and effect; the other is the creation of actions according to the unchangeable forms of human nature, as existing in the mind of the creator, which is itself the image of all other minds. The one is partial, and applies only to a definite period of time,

[5]See the *Filium Labyrinthi* and the *Essay on Death* particularly. [Shelley]

and a certain combination of events which can never again recur; the other is universal, and contains within itself the germ of a relation to whatever motives or actions have place in the possible varieties of human nature. Time, which destroys the beauty and the use of the story of particular facts, stript of the poetry which should invest them, augments that of Poetry, and for ever developes new and wonderful applications of the eternal truth which it contains. Hence epitomes have been called the moths of just history; they eat out the poetry of it. The story of particular facts is as a mirror which obscures and distorts that which should be beautiful: Poetry is a mirror which makes beautiful that which is distorted.

The parts of a composition may be poetical, without the composition as a whole being a poem. A single sentence may be considered as a whole though it be found in a series of unassimilated portions; a single word even may be a spark of inextinguishable thought. And thus all the great historians, Herodotus, Plutarch, Livy, were poets; and although the plan of these writers, especially that of Livy, restrained them from developing this faculty in its highest degree, they make copious and ample amends for their subjection, by filling all the interstices of their subjects with living images.

Having determined what is poetry, and who are poets, let us proceed to estimate its effects upon society.

Poetry is ever accompanied with pleasure: all spirits on which it falls, open themselves to receive the wisdom which is mingled with its delight. In the infancy of the world, neither poets themselves nor their auditors are fully aware of the excellence of poetry: for it acts in a divine and unapprehended manner, beyond and above consciousness; and it is reserved for future generations to contemplate and measure the mighty cause and effect in all the strength and splendour of their union. Even in modern times, no living poet ever arrived at the fulness of his fame; the jury which sits in judgement upon a poet, belonging as he does to all time, must be composed of his peers: it must be impanelled by Time from the selectest of the wise of many generations. A Poet is a nightingale, who sits in darkness and sings to cheer its own solitude with sweet sounds; his auditors are as men entranced by the melody of an unseen musician, who feel that they are moved and softened, yet know not whence or why. The poems of Homer and his contemporaries were the delight of infant Greece; they were the elements of that social system which is the column upon which all succeeding civilization has reposed. Homer embodied the ideal perfection of his age in human character; nor can we doubt that those who read his verses were awakened to an ambition of becoming like to Achilles, Hector and Ulysses: the truth and beauty of friendship, patriotism and persevering devotion to an object, were unveiled to the depths in these immortal creations: the sentiments of the auditors must have been refined and enlarged by a sympathy with such great and lovely impersonations, until from admiring they imitated, and from imitation they identified themselves with the objects of their admiration. Nor let it be objected, that these characters are remote from moral perfection, and that they can by no means be considered as edifying patterns for general imitation. Every epoch under names more or less specious has deified its peculiar errors; Revenge is the naked Idol of the worship of a semi-barbarous age; and Self-deceit is the veiled Image of unknown evil before which luxury and satiety lie prostrate. But a poet considers the vices of his contemporaries as the temporary dress in which his creations must be arrayed, and which cover without concealing the eternal proportions of their beauty. An epic or dramatic personage is understood to wear them around his soul, as he may the antient armour or the modern uniform around his body; whilst it is easy to conceive a dress more graceful than either. The beauty of the internal nature cannot be so far concealed by its accidental vesture, but that the spirit of its form shall communicate itself to the very disguise, and indicate the shape it hides from the manner in which it is worn. A majestic form and graceful motions will express themselves through the most barbarous and tasteless costume. Few poets of the highest class have chosen to exhibit the beauty of their conceptions in its naked truth and splendour; and it is doubtful whether the alloy of costume, habit, etc., be not necessary to temper this planetary music for mortal ears.

The whole objection however of the immorality of poetry rests upon a misconception of the manner in which poetry acts to produce the moral improvement of man. Ethical science arranges the elements which poetry has created, and propounds schemes and proposes examples of civil and domestic life: nor is it for want of admirable doctrines that men hate, and despise, and censure, and deceive, and subjugate one another. But Poetry acts in another and diviner manner. It awakens and enlarges the mind itself by rendering it the receptacle of a thousand unapprehended combinations of thought. Poetry lifts the veil from the hidden beauty of the world, and makes familiar objects be as if they were not familiar; it reproduces all that it represents, and the impersonations clothed in its Elysian light stand thenceforward in the minds of those who have once contemplated them, as memorials of that gentle and exalted content which extends itself over all thoughts and actions with which it coexists. The great secret of morals is Love; or a going out of our own nature, and an identification of ourselves with the beautiful which exists in thought, action, or person, not our own. A man, to be greatly good, must imagine intensely and comprehensively; he must put himself in the place of another and of many others; the pains and pleasures of his species must become his own. The great instrument of moral good is the imagination; and poetry administers to the effect by acting upon the cause. Poetry enlarges the circumference of the imagination by replenishing it with thoughts of ever new delight, which have the power of attracting and assimilating of their own nature all other thoughts, and which form new intervals and interstices whose void for ever craves fresh food. Poetry strengthens that faculty which is the organ of the moral nature of man, in the same manner as exercise strengthens a limb. A Poet therefore would do ill to embody his own conceptions of right and wrong, which are usually those of his place and time, in his poetical creations, which participate in neither. By this assumption of the inferior office of interpreting the effect, in which perhaps after all he might acquit himself but imperfectly, he would resign the glory in a participation in the cause. There was little danger that Homer, or any of the eternal poets, should have so far misunderstood themselves as to have abdicated this throne of their widest dominion. Those in whom the poetical faculty, though great, is less intense, as Euripides, Lucan, Tasso, Spenser, have frequently affected a moral aim, and the effect of their poetry is diminished in exact proportion to the degree in which they compel us to advert to this purpose.

Homer and the cyclic poets were followed at a certain interval by the dramatic and lyrical Poets of Athens, who flourished contemporaneously with all that is most perfect in the kindred expressions of the poetical faculty; architecture, painting, music, the dance, sculpture, philosophy, and we may add the forms of civil life. For although the scheme of Athenian society was deformed by many imperfections which the poetry existing in Chivalry and Christianity have erased from the habits and institutions of modern Europe; yet never at any other period has so much energy, beauty, and virtue, been developed; never was blind strength and stubborn form so disciplined and rendered subject to the will of man, or that will less repugnant to the dictates of the beautiful and the true, as during the century which preceded the death of Socrates. Of no other epoch in the history of our species have we records and fragments stamped so visibly with the image of the divinity in man. But it is Poetry alone, in form, in action, or in language, which has rendered this epoch memorable above all others, and the storehouse of examples to everlasting time. For written poetry existed at that epoch simultaneously with the other arts, and it is an idle enquiry to demand which gave and which received the light, which all as from a common focus have scattered over the darkest periods of succeeding time. We know no more of cause and effect than a constant conjunction of events: Poetry is ever found to coexist with whatever other arts contribute to the happiness and perfection of man. I appeal to what has already been established to distinguish between the cause and the effect.

It was at the period here adverted to, that the Drama had its birth; and however a succeeding writer may have equalled or surpassed those few great specimens of the Athenian drama which have been preserved to us, it is indisputable that the art itself never was understood or practised according to the true philosophy of it, as at Athens. For the Athenians employed language, action, music, painting, the dance, and religious institutions, to produce a common effect in the representation of the highest idealisms of passion and of power; each division in the art was made perfect in its kind by artists of the most consummate skill, and was disciplined into a beautiful proportion and unity one towards another. On the modern stage a few only of the elements capable of expressing the image of the poet's conception are employed at once. We have tragedy without music and dancing; and music and dancing without the highest impersonations of which they are the fit accompaniment, and both without religion and solemnity. Religious institution has indeed been usually banished from the stage. Our system of divesting the actor's face of a mask, on which the many expressions appropriated to his dramatic character might be moulded into one permanent and unchanging expression, is favourable only to a partial and inharmonious effect; it is fit for nothing but a monologue, where all the attention may be directed to some great master of ideal mimicry. The modern practice of blending comedy with tragedy, though liable to great abuse in point of practise, is undoubtedly an extension of the dramatic circle; but the comedy should be as in *King Lear*, universal, ideal, and sublime. It is perhaps the intervention of this principle which determines the balance in favour of *King Lear* against the *Œdipus Tyrannus* or the *Agamemnon*, or, if you will the trilogies with which they are connected;[6] unless the intense power of the choral poetry, especially that of the latter, should be considered as restoring the equilibrium. *King Lear*, if it can sustain this comparison, may be judged to be the most perfect specimen of the dramatic art existing in the world; in spite of the narrow conditions to which the poet was subjected by the ignorance of the philosophy of the Drama which has prevailed in modern Europe. Calderón in his religious *Autos*[7] has attempted to fulfil some of the high conditions of dramatic representation neglected by Shakespeare; such as the establishing a relation between the drama and religion, and the accommodating them to music and dancing; but he omits the observation of conditions still more important, and more is lost than gained by a substitution of the rigidly-defined and ever-repeated idealisms of a distorted superstition for the living impersonations of the truth of human passion.

But we digress. — The Author of the Four Ages of Poetry[8] has prudently omitted to dispute on the effect of the Drama upon life and manners. For, if I know the knight by the device of his shield, I have only to inscribe Philoctetes or Agamemnon or Othello[9] upon mine to put to flight the giant sophisms which have enchanted him, as the mirror of intolerable light, though on the arm of one of the weakest of the Paladins, could blind and scatter whole armies of necromancers and pagans. The connexion of scenic exhibitions with the improvement or corruption of the manners of men, has been universally recognized: in other words, the presence or absence of poetry in its most perfect and universal form has been found to be connected with good and evil in conduct and habit. The corruption which has been imputed to the drama as an effect, begins, when the poetry employed in its constitution ends: I appeal to the history of manners whether the periods of the growth of the one and the decline of the other have not corresponded with an exactness equal to any other example of moral cause and effect.

The drama at Athens, or wheresoever else it may have approached to its perfection, coexisted with the moral and intellectual greatness of the age. The tragedies of the Athenian poets are as mirrors in which the spectator beholds himself, under a thin disguise of circumstance, stript of all but that ideal perfection and energy which every one feels to be the internal type of all that he

---

[6] The *Agamemnon* by Aeschylus is the first play of the *Oresteia* trilogy. Sophocles' *Oedipus Tyrannos* is not part of an extant trilogy, though he wrote plays connected with the Oedipus story twenty years earlier (*Antigone*) and twenty years later (*Oedipus at Colonus*).

[7] The *autos* of the Spanish dramatist Calderón (1600–1681) were short religious allegorical dramas.
[8] Shelley's friend, Thomas Love Peacock (1785–1866).
[9] Tragic protagonists of Sophocles, Aeschylus, and Shakespeare, respectively.

loves, admires, and would become. The imagination is enlarged by a sympathy with pains and passions so mighty, that they distend in their conception the capacity of that by which they are conceived; the good affections are strengthened by pity, indignation, terror and sorrow; and an exalted calm is prolonged from the satiety of this high exercise of them into the tumult of familiar life; even crime is disarmed of half its horror and all its contagion by being represented as the fatal consequence of the unfathomable agencies of nature; error is thus divested of its wilfulness; men can no longer cherish it as the creation of their choice. In a drama of the highest order there is little food for censure or hatred; it teaches rather self-knowledge and self-respect. Neither the eye nor the mind can see itself, unless reflected upon that which it resembles. The drama, so long as it continues to express poetry, is as a prismatic and many-sided mirror, which collects the brightest rays of human nature and divides and reproduces them from the simplicity of these elementary forms, and touches them with majesty and beauty, and multiplies all that it reflects, and endows it with the power of propagating its like wherever it may fall.

But in periods of the decay of social life, the drama sympathizes with that decay. Tragedy becomes a cold imitation of the form of the great masterpieces of antiquity, divested of all harmonious accompaniment of the kindred arts; and often the very form misunderstood: or a weak attempt to teach certain doctrines, which the writer considers as moral truths; and which are usually no more than specious flatteries of some gross vice or weakness with which the author in common with his auditors are infected. Hence what has been called the classical and domestic drama. Addison's *Cato* is a specimen of the one; and would it were not superfluous to cite examples of the other! To such purposes Poetry cannot be made subservient. Poetry is a sword of lightning, ever unsheathed, which consumes the scabbard that would contain it. And thus we observe that all dramatic writings of this nature are unimaginative in a singular degree; they affect sentiment and passion: which, divested of imagination, are other names for caprice and appetite. The period in our own history of the grossest degradation of the drama is the reign of Charles II when all forms in which poetry had been accustomed to be expressed became hymns to the triumph of kingly power over liberty and virtue. Milton stood alone illuminating an age unworthy of him. At such periods the calculating principle pervades all the forms of dramatic exhibition, and poetry ceases to be expressed upon them. Comedy loses its ideal universality: wit succeeds to humour; we laugh from self-complacency and triumph instead of pleasure; malignity, sarcasm and contempt, succeed to sympathetic merriment; we hardly laugh, but we smile. Obscenity, which is ever blasphemy against the divine beauty in life, becomes, from the very veil which it assumes, more active if less disgusting: it is a monster for which the corruption of society for ever brings forth new food, which it devours in secret.

The drama being that form under which a greater number of modes of expression of poetry are susceptible of being combined than any other, the connexion of poetry and social good is more observable in the drama than in whatever other form: and it is indisputable that the highest perfection of human society has ever corresponded with the highest dramatic excellence; and that the corruption or the extinction of the drama in a nation where it has once flourished, is a mark of a corruption of manners, and an extinction of the energies which sustain the soul of social life. But, as Machiavelli says of political institutions, that life may be preserved and renewed, if men should arise capable of bringing back the drama to its principles. And this is true with respect to poetry in its most extended sense: all language, institution and form, require not only to be produced but to be sustained: the office and character of a poet participates in the divine nature as regards providence, no less than as regards creation.

Civil war, the spoils of Asia, and the fatal predominance first of the Macedonian, and then of the Roman arms were so many symbols of the extinction or suspension of the creative faculty in Greece. The bucolic writers, who found patronage under the lettered tyrants of Sicily and Egypt, were the latest representatives of its most glorious reign. Their poetry is intensely melodious; like the odour of the tuberose, it overcomes and sickens the spirit with excess of sweetness; whilst the poetry of the preceding age was as a meadow-gale of June which mingles the fragrance of all the flowers of the field, and adds a quickening and harmonizing spirit of its own which endows the sense with a power of sustaining its extreme delight. The bucolic and erotic delicacy in written poetry is correlative with that softness in statuary, music, and the kindred arts, and even in manners and institutions which distinguished the epoch to which we now refer. Nor is it the poetical faculty itself, or any misapplication of it, to which this want of harmony is to be imputed. An equal sensibility to the influence of the senses and the affections is to be found in the writings of Homer and Sophocles: the former especially has clothed sensual and pathetic images with irresistible attractions. Their superiority over these succeeding writers consists in the presence of those thoughts which belong to the inner faculties of our nature, not in the absence of those which are connected with the external; their incomparable perfection consists in an harmony of the union of all. It is not what the erotic writers have, but what they have not, in which their imperfection consists. It is not inasmuch as they were Poets, but inasmuch as they were not Poets, that they can be considered with any plausibility as connected with the corruption of their age. Had that corruption availed so as to extinguish in them the sensibility to pleasure, passion and natural scenery, which is imputed to them as an imperfection, the last triumph of evil would have been achieved. For the end of social corruption is to destroy all sensibility to pleasure; and therefore it is corruption. It begins at the imagination and the intellect as at the core, and distributes itself thence as a paralyzing venom, through the affections into the very appetites, until all become a torpid mass in which sense hardly survives. At the approach of such a period, Poetry ever addresses itself to those faculties which are the last to be destroyed, and its voice is heard, like the footsteps of Astræa, departing from the world.[10] Poetry ever communicates all the pleasure which men are capable of receiving: it is ever still the light of life; the source of whatever of beautiful, or generous, or true can

have place in an evil time. It will readily be confessed that those among the luxurious citizens of Syracuse and Alexandria who were delighted with the poems of Theocritus, were less cold, cruel and sensual than the remnant of their tribe. But corruption must have utterly destroyed the fabric of human society before Poetry can ever cease. The sacred links of that chain have never been entirely disjoined, which descending through the minds of many men is attached to those great minds, whence as from a magnet the invisible effluence is sent forth, which at once connects, animates and sustains the life of all. It is the faculty which contains within itself the seeds at once of its own and of social renovation. And let us not circumscribe the effects of the bucolic and erotic poetry within the limits of the sensibility of those to whom it was addressed. They may have perceived the beauty of those immortal compositions, simply as fragments and isolated portions: those who are more finely organized, or born in a happier age, may recognize them as episodes to that great poem, which all poets, like the co-operating thoughts of one great mind, have built up since the beginning of the world.

The same revolutions within a narrower sphere had place in antient Rome; but the actions and forms of its social life never seem to have been perfectly saturated with the poetical element. The Romans appear to have considered the Greeks as the selectest treasuries of the selectest forms of manners and of nature, and to have abstained from creating in measured language, sculpture, music or architecture, anything which might bear a particular relation to their own condition, whilst it should bear a general one to the universal constitution of the world. But we judge from partial evidence; and we judge perhaps partially. Ennius, Varro, Pacuvius, and Accius, all great poets, have been lost. Lucretius is in the highest, and Virgil in a very high sense, a creator. The chosen delicacy of the expressions of the latter is as a mist of light which conceals from us the intense and exceeding truth of his conceptions of nature. Livy is instinct with poetry. Yet Horace, Catullus, Ovid, and generally the other great writers of the Virgilian age, saw man and nature in the mirror of Greece. The institutions also and the religion of Rome were less poetical than those of Greece, as the shadow

[10]Astraea was the goddess of justice who fled Earth for Heaven once the reign of Zeus began.

is less vivid than the substance. Hence poetry in Rome, seemed to follow rather than accompany the perfection of political and domestic society. The true Poetry of Rome lived in its institutions; for whatever of beautiful, true and majestic they contained could have sprung only from the faculty which creates the order in which they consist. The life of Camillus, the death of Regulus; the expectation of the Senators, in their godlike state, of the victorious Gauls; the refusal of the Republic to make peace with Hannibal after the battle of Cannae, were not the consequences of a refined calculation of the probable personal advantage to result from such a rhythm and order in the shews of life, to those who were at once the poets and the actors of these immortal dramas. The imagination beholding the beauty of this order, created it out of itself according to its own idea: the consequence was empire, and the reward ever-living fame. These things are not the less poetry, *quia carent vate sacro.*[11] They are the episodes of the cyclic poem written by Time upon the memories of men. The Past, like an inspired rhapsodist, fills the theatre of everlasting generations with their harmony.

At length the antient system of religion and manners had fulfilled the circle of its revolution. And the world would have fallen into utter anarchy and darkness, but that there were found poets among the authors of the Christian and Chivalric systems of manners and religion, who created forms of opinion and action never before conceived; which, copied into the imaginations of men, became as generals to the bewildered armies of their thoughts. It is foreign to the present purpose to touch upon the evil produced by these systems: except that we protest, on the ground of the principles already established, that no portion of it can be imputed to the poetry they contain.

It is probable that the astonishing poetry of Moses, Job, David, Solomon and Isaiah had produced a great effect upon the mind of Jesus and his disciples. The scattered fragments preserved to us by the biographers of this extraordinary person, are all instinct with the most vivid poetry. But his doctrines seem to have been quickly distorted. At

a certain period after the prevalence of a system of opinions founded upon those promulgated by him, the three forms into which Plato had distributed the faculties of mind underwent a sort of apotheosis, and became the object of the worship of the civilized world. Here it is to be confessed that "Light seems to thicken," and

> The crow makes wing to the rooky wood,
> Good things of day begin to droop and drowze,
> And night's black agents to their preys do rouze.[12]

But mark how beautiful an order has sprung from the dust and blood of this fierce chaos! how the World, as from a resurrection, balancing itself on the golden wings of knowledge and of hope, has reassumed its yet unwearied flight into the Heaven of time. Listen to the music, unheard by outward ears, which is as a ceaseless and invisible wind, nourishing its everlasting course with strength and swiftness.

The poetry in the doctrines of Jesus Christ, and the mythology and institutions of the Celtic[13] conquerors of the Roman empire, outlived the darkness and the convulsions connected with their growth and victory, and blended themselves into a new fabric of manners and opinion. It is an error to impute the ignorance of the dark ages to the Christian doctrines or the predominance of the Celtic nations. Whatever of evil their agencies may have contained sprung from the extinction of the poetical principle, connected with the progress of despotism and superstition. Men, from causes too intricate to be here discussed, had become insensible and selfish: their own will had become feeble, and yet they were its slaves, and thence the slaves of the will of others: lust, fear, avarice, cruelty and fraud, characterised a race amongst whom no one was to be found capable of *creating* in form, language, or institution. The moral anomalies of such a state of society are not justly to be charged upon any class of events immediately connected with them, and those events are most entitled to our approbation which could dissolve it most expeditiously. It is unfortunate for those who cannot distinguish words from

[11]"Because they lack a sacred prophet/poet." Horace, *Odes* IV.9:28.

[12]Shakespeare, *Macbeth*, III.ii.50–53.

[13]Shelley uses "Celtic" to refer to Germanic tribes (like those Caesar fought), not the aboriginal inhabitants of the British Isles.

thoughts, that many of these anomalies have been incorporated into our popular religion.

It was not until the eleventh century that the effects of the poetry of the Christian and Chivalric systems began to manifest themselves. The principle of equality had been discovered and applied by Plato in his Republic, as the theoretical rule of the mode in which the materials of pleasure and of power produced by the common skill and labour of human beings ought to be distributed among them. The limitations of this rule were asserted by him to be determined only by the sensibility of each, or the utility to result to all. Plato, following the doctrines of Timæus and Pythagoras, taught also a moral and intellectual system of doctrine comprehending at once the past, the present, and the future condition of man. Jesus Christ divulged the sacred and eternal truths contained in these views to mankind, and Christianity, in its abstract purity, became the exoteric expression of the esoteric doctrines of the poetry and wisdom of antiquity. The incorporation of the Celtic nations with the exhausted population of the South, impressed upon it the figure of the poetry existing in their mythology and institutions. The result was a sum of the action and reaction of all the causes included in it; for it may be assumed as a maxim that no nation or religion can supersede any other without incorporating into itself a portion of that which it supersedes. The abolition of personal and domestic slavery, and the emancipation of women from a great part of the degrading restraints of antiquity were among the consequences of these events.

The abolition of personal slavery is the basis of the highest political hope that it can enter into the mind of man to conceive. The freedom of women produced the poetry of sexual love. Love became a religion, the idols of whose worship were ever present. It was as if the statues of Apollo and the Muses had been endowed with life and motion and had walked forth among their worshippers; so that earth became peopled by the inhabitants of a diviner world. The familiar appearance and proceedings of life became wonderful and heavenly; and a paradise was created as out of the wrecks of Eden. And as this creation itself is poetry, so its creators were poets; and language was the instrument of their art: "Galeotto fù il libro, e chi lo scrisse."[14] The Provençal Trouveurs, or inventors, preceded Petrarch, whose verses are as spells, which unseal the inmost enchanted fountains of the delight which is in the grief of Love. It is impossible to feel them without becoming a portion of that beauty which we contemplate: it were superfluous to explain how the gentleness and the elevation of mind connected with these sacred emotions can render men more amiable, more generous, and wise, and lift them out of the dull vapours of the little world of self. Dante understood the secret things of love even more than Petrarch. His *Vita Nuova* is an inexhaustible fountain of purity of sentiment and language: it is the idealized history of that period, and those intervals of his life which were dedicated to love. His apotheosis of Beatrice in Paradise and the gradations of his own love and her loveliness, by which as by steps he feigns himself to have ascended to the throne of the Supreme Cause, is the most glorious imagination of modern poetry. The acutest critics have justly reversed the judgement of the vulgar, and the order of the great acts of the "Divine Drama," in the measure of the admiration which they accord to the Hell, Purgatory and Paradise. The latter is a perpetual hymn of everlasting love. Love, which found a worthy poet in Plato alone of all the antients, has been celebrated by a chorus of the greatest writers of the renovated world; and the music has penetrated the caverns of society, and its echoes still drown the dissonance of arms and superstition. At successive intervals, Ariosto, Tasso, Shakespeare, Spenser, Calderón, Rousseau, and the great writers of our own age, have celebrated the dominion of love, planting as it were trophies in the human mind of that sublimest victory over sensuality and force. The true relation borne to each other by the sexes into which human kind is distributed has become less

[14]"That book was a Galeotto [legend of Sir Galahad], and so was he that wrote it." Dante, *Inferno* 5:137. The quotation is spoken by Francesca di Rimini, an adulterous wife Dante meets in Hell, who recounts how her affair with Paolo Malatesta began over a book of chivalric romance. Galahad introduced his uncle Lancelot to Queen Guinevere and so began their adulterous liaison; hence "Galeotto" in Italian can mean a go-between.

misunderstood; and if the error which confounded diversity with inequality of the powers of the two sexes has become partially recognized in the opinions and institutions of modern Europe, we owe this great benefit to the worship of which Chivalry was the law, and poets the prophets.

The poetry of Dante may be considered as the bridge thrown over the stream of time, which unites the modern and antient world. The distorted notions of invisible things which Dante and his rival Milton have idealized, are merely the mask and the mantle in which these great poets walk through eternity enveloped and disguised. It is a difficult question to determine how far they were conscious of the distinction which must have subsisted in their minds between their own creeds and that of the people. Dante at least appears to wish to mark the full extent of it by placing Riphæus, whom Virgil calls *justissimus unus,* in Paradise[15] and observing a most heretical caprice in his distribution of rewards and punishments. And Milton's poem contains within itself a philosophical refutation of that system of which, by a strange and natural antithesis, it has been a chief popular support. Nothing can exceed the energy and magnificence of the character of Satan as expressed in *Paradise Lost.* It is a mistake to suppose that he could ever have been intended for the popular personification of evil. Implacable hate, patient cunning, and a sleepless refinement of device to inflict the extremest anguish on an enemy, these things are evil; and although venial in a slave are not to be forgiven in a tyrant; although redeemed by much that ennobles his defeat in one subdued, are marked by all that dishonours his conquest in the victor. Milton's Devil as a moral being is as far superior to his God as one who perseveres in some purpose which he has conceived to be excellent in spite of adversity and torture, is to one who in the cold security of undoubted triumph inflicts the most horrible revenge upon his enemy, not from any mistaken notion of inducing him to repent of a perseverance in enmity, but with the alleged

design of exasperating him to deserve new torments. Milton has so far violated the popular creed (if this shall be judged to be a violation) as to have alleged no superiority of moral virtue to his God over his Devil. And this bold neglect of a direct moral purpose is the most decisive proof of the supremacy of Milton's genius. He mingled as it were the elements of human nature, as colours upon a single pallet, and arranged them into the composition of his great picture according to the laws of epic truth; that is, according to the laws of that principle by which a series of actions of the external universe and of intelligent and ethical beings is calculated to excite the sympathy of succeeding generations of mankind. The *Divina Commedia* and *Paradise Lost* have conferred upon modern mythology a systematic form; and when change and time shall have added one more superstition to the mass of those which have arisen and decayed upon the earth, commentators will be learnedly employed in elucidating the religion of ancestral Europe, only not utterly forgotten because it will have been stamped with the eternity of genius.

Homer was the first, and Dante the second epic poet: that is, the second poet the series of whose creations bore a defined and intelligible relation to the knowledge, and sentiment, and religion, and political conditions of the age in which he lived, and of the ages which followed it, developing itself in correspondence with their developement. For Lucretius had limed the wings of his swift spirit in the dregs of the sensible world; and Virgil, with a modesty which ill became his genius, had affected the fame of an imitator even whilst he created anew all that he copied; and none among the flock of mock-birds, though their notes were sweet, Apollonius Rhodius, Quintus Calaber Smyrnaeus, Nonnus, Lucan, Statius, or Claudian, have sought even to fulfil a single condition of epic truth. Milton was the third Epic Poet. For if the title of epic in its highest sense be refused to the *Æneid,* still less can it be conceded to the *Orlando Furioso,* the *Gerusalemme Liberata,* the *Lusiad,* or the *Fairy Queen.*

Dante and Milton were both deeply penetrated with the antient religion of the civilized world; and its spirit exists in their poetry probably in the same proportion as its forms survived in the unreformed

[15]"The one who is most just." Virgil, *Aeneid* 2:426. Dante finds him, to his surprise (since he was a pagan), in Paradise (*Paradiso* 20:67–69).

worship of modern Europe. The one preceded and the other followed the Reformation at almost equal intervals. Dante was the first religious reformer, and Luther surpassed him rather in the rudeness and acrimony, than in the boldness of his censures of papal usurpation. Dante was the first awakener of entranced Europe; he created a language in itself music and persuasion out of a chaos of inharmonious barbarisms. He was the congregator of those great spirits who presided over the resurrection of learning; the Lucifer[16] of that starry flock which in the thirteenth century shone forth from republican Italy, as from a heaven, into the darkness of the benighted world. His very words are instinct with spirit; each is as a spark, a burning atom of inextinguishable thought; and many yet lie covered in the ashes of their birth, and pregnant with a lightning which has yet found no conductor. All high poetry is infinite; it is as the first acorn, which contained all oaks potentially. Veil after veil may be undrawn, and the inmost naked beauty of the meaning never exposed. A great Poem is a fountain for ever overflowing with the waters of wisdom and delight; and after one person and one age has exhausted all its divine effluence which their peculiar relations enable them to share, another and yet another succeeds, and new relations are ever developed, the source of an unforeseen and an unconceived delight.

The age immediately succeeding to that of Dante, Petrarch, and Boccaccio, was characterized by a revival of painting, sculpture, music, and architecture. Chaucer caught the sacred inspiration, and the superstructure of English literature is based upon the materials of Italian invention.

But let us not be betrayed from a defence into a critical history of Poetry and its influence on Society. Be it enough to have pointed out the effects of poets, in the large and true sense of the word, upon their own and all succeeding times and to revert to the partial instances cited as illustrations of an opinion the reverse of that attempted to be established in the Four Ages of Poetry.

But poets have been challenged to resign the civic crown to reasoners and mechanists on another plea. It is admitted that the exercise of the imagination is most delightful, but it is alleged that of reason is more useful. Let us examine as the grounds of this distinction, what is here meant by Utility. Pleasure or good in a general sense, is that which the consciousness of a sensitive and intelligent being seeks, and in which when found it acquiesces. There are two kinds of pleasure, one durable, universal, and permanent; the other transitory and particular. Utility may either express the means of producing the former or the latter. In the former sense, whatever strengthens and purifies the affections, enlarges the imagination, and adds spirit to sense, is useful. But the meaning in which the Author of the Four Ages of Poetry seems to have employed the word utility is the narrower one of banishing the importunity of the wants of our animal nature, the surrounding men with security of life, the dispersing the grosser delusions of superstition, and the conciliating such a degree of mutual forbearance among men as may consist with the motives of personal advantage.

Undoubtedly the promoters of utility in this limited sense, have their appointed office in society. They follow the footsteps of poets, and copy the sketches of their creations into the book of common life. They make space, and give time. Their exertions are of the highest value so long as they confine their administration of the concerns of the inferior powers of our nature within the limits due to the superior ones. But whilst the sceptic destroys gross superstitions, let him spare to deface, as some of the French writers have defaced, the eternal truths charactered upon the imaginations of men. Whilst the mechanist abridges, and the political œconomist combines, labour, let them beware that their speculations, for want of correspondence with those first principles which belong to the imagination, do not tend, as they have in modern England, to exasperate at once the extremes of luxury and want. They have exemplified the saying, "To him that hath, more shall be given; and from him that hath not, the little that he hath shall be taken away."[17] The rich have become richer, and the poor have become poorer; and the vessel of the state is driven between the Scylla and Charybdis of anarchy and despotism. Such are the effects which must

---

[16]Shelley intends here the literal sense of "bearer of light."

[17]Matthew 25:29.

ever flow from an unmitigated exercise of the calculating faculty.

It is difficult to define pleasure in its highest sense; the definition involving a number of apparent paradoxes. For, from an inexplicable defect of harmony in the constitution of human nature, the pain of the inferior is frequently connected with the pleasures of the superior portions of our being. Sorrow, terror, anguish, despair itself are often the chosen expressions of an approximation to the highest good. Our sympathy in tragic fiction depends on this principle; tragedy delights by affording a shadow of the pleasure which exists in pain. This is the source also of the melancholy which is inseparable from the sweetest melody. The pleasure that is in sorrow is sweeter than the pleasure of pleasure itself. And hence the saying, "It is better to go to the house of mourning, than to the house of mirth."[18] Not that this highest species of pleasure is necessarily linked with pain. The delight of love and friendship, the extacy of the admiration of nature, the joy of the perception and still more of the creation of poetry is often wholly unalloyed.

The production and assurance of pleasure in this highest sense is true utility. Those who produce and preserve this pleasure are Poets or poetical philosophers.

The exertions of Locke, Hume, Gibbon, Voltaire, Rousseau,[19] and their disciples, in favour of oppressed and deluded humanity, are entitled to the gratitude of mankind. Yet it is easy to calculate the degree of moral and intellectual improvement which the world would have exhibited, had they never lived. A little more nonsense would have been talked for a century or two; and perhaps a few more men, women, and children, burnt as heretics. We might not at this moment have been congratulating each other on the abolition of the Inquisition in Spain. But it exceeds all imagination to conceive what would have been the moral condition of the world if neither Dante, Petrarch, Boccaccio, Chaucer, Shakespeare, Calderón, Lord Bacon, nor Milton, had ever existed; if Raphael and Michael Angelo had never been born; if the Hebrew poetry had never been translated; if a revival of the study of Greek literature had never taken place; if no monuments of antient sculpture had been handed down to us; and if the poetry of the religion of the antient world had been extinguished together with its belief. The human mind could never, except by the intervention of these excitements, have been awakened to the invention of the grosser sciences, and that application of analytical reasoning to the aberrations of society, which it is now attempted to exalt over the direct expression of the inventive and creative faculty itself.

We have more moral, political and historical wisdom, than we know how to reduce into practise; we have more scientific and œconomical knowledge than can be accommodated to the just distribution of the produce which it multiplies. The poetry in these systems of thought, is concealed by the accumulation of facts and calculating processes. There is no want of knowledge respecting what is wisest and best in morals, government, and political œconomy, or at least, what is wiser and better than what men now practise and endure. But we let "*I dare not* wait upon *I would,* like the poor cat i' the adage."[20] We want the creative faculty to imagine that which we know; we want the generous impulse to act that which we imagine; we want the poetry of life: our calculations have outrun conception; we have eaten more than we can digest. The cultivation of those sciences which have enlarged the limits of the empire of man over the external world, has, for want of the poetical faculty, proportionally circumscribed those of the internal world; and man, having enslaved the elements, remains himself a slave. To what but a cultivation of the mechanical arts in a degree disproportioned to the presence of the creative faculty, which is the basis of all knowledge, is to be attributed the abuse of all invention for abridging and combining labour, to the exasperation of the inequality of mankind? From what other cause has it arisen that the discoveries which should have lightened, have added a weight to the curse imposed on Adam? Poetry, and the principle of Self, of which money

[18]Ecclesiastes 7:2.

[19]I follow the classification adopted by the author of the Four Ages of Poetry. But Rousseau was essentially a poet. The others, even Voltaire, were mere reasoners. [Shelley]

[20]Shakespeare, *Macbeth,* I.vii:44–45.

is the visible incarnation, are the God and the Mammon of the world.

The functions of the poetical faculty are two-fold; by one it creates new materials of knowledge, and power and pleasure; by the other it engenders in the mind a desire to reproduce and arrange them according to a certain rhythm and order which may be called the beautiful and the good. The cultivation of poetry is never more to be desired than at periods when, from an excess of the selfish and calculating principle, the accumulation of the materials of external life exceed the quantity of the power of assimilating them to the internal laws of human nature. The body has then become too unwieldy for that which animates it.

Poetry is indeed something divine. It is at once the centre and circumference of knowledge; it is that which comprehends all science, and that to which all science must be referred. It is at the same time the root and blossom of all other systems of thought: it is that from which all spring, and that which adorns all; and that which, if blighted, denies the fruit and the seed, and withholds from the barren world the nourishment and the succession of the scions of the tree of life. It is the perfect and consummate surface and bloom of things; it is as the odour and the colour of the rose to the texture of the elements which compose it, as the form and the splendour of unfaded beauty to the secrets of anatomy and corruption. What were Virtue, Love, Patriotism, Friendship &c. — what were the scenery of this beautiful Universe which we inhabit — what were our consolations on this side of the grave — and what were our aspirations beyond it — if Poetry did not ascend to bring light and fire from those eternal regions where the owl-winged faculty of calculation dare not ever soar? Poetry is not like reasoning, a power to be exerted according to the determination of the will. A man cannot say, "I will compose poetry." The greatest poet even cannot say it: for the mind in creation is as a fading coal which some invisible influence, like an inconstant wind, awakens to transitory brightness: this power arises from within, like the colour of a flower which fades and changes as it is developed, and the conscious portions of our natures are unprophetic either of its approach or its departure. Could this influence be durable in its original purity and force, it is impossible to predict the greatness of the results: but when composition begins, inspiration is already on the decline, and the most glorious poetry that has ever been communicated to the world is probably a feeble shadow of the original conception of the poet. I appeal to the greatest Poets of the present day, whether it be not an error to assert that the finest passages of poetry are produced by labour and study. The toil and the delay recommended by critics can be justly interpreted to mean no more than a careful observation of the inspired moments, and an artificial connexion of the spaces between their suggestions by the intertexture of conventional expressions; a necessity only imposed by a limitedness of the poetical faculty itself. For Milton conceived the *Paradise Lost* as a whole before he executed it in portions. We have his own authority also for the Muse having "dictated" to him the "unpremeditated song,"[21] and let this be an answer to those who would allege the fifty-six various readings of the first line of the *Orlando Furioso*. Compositions so produced are to poetry what mosaic is to painting. This instinct and intuition of the poetical faculty is still more observable in the plastic and pictorial arts: a great statue or picture grows under the power of the artist as a child in the mother's womb, and the very mind which directs the hands in formation is incapable of accounting to itself for the origin, the gradations, or the media of the process.

Poetry is the record of the best and happiest moments of the happiest and best minds. We are aware of evanescent visitations of thought and feeling sometimes associated with place or person, sometimes regarding our own mind alone, and always arising unforeseen and departing unbidden, but elevating and delightful beyond all expression: so that even in the desire and the regret they leave, there cannot but be pleasure, participating as it does in the nature of its object. It is as it were the interpenetration of a diviner nature through our own; but its footsteps are like those of a wind over a sea, which the coming calm erases, and whose traces remain only as on the wrinkled sand which paves it. These and corresponding conditions of being are

[21]Milton, *Paradise Lost*, 9:21–24.

experienced principally by those of the most delicate sensibility and the most enlarged imagination; and the state of mind produced by them is at war with every base desire. The enthusiasm of virtue, love, patriotism, and friendship is essentially linked with these emotions; and whilst they last, self appears as what it is, an atom to a Universe. Poets are not only subject to these experiences as spirits of the most refined organization, but they can colour all that they combine with the evanescent hues of this etherial world; a word, a trait in the representation of a scene or a passion, will touch the enchanted chord, and reanimate, in those who have ever experienced these emotions, the sleeping, the cold, the buried image of the past. Poetry thus makes immortal all that is best and most beautiful in the world; it arrests the vanishing apparitions which haunt the interlunations of life, and veiling them or in language or in form sends them forth among mankind, bearing sweet news of kindred joy to those with whom their sisters abide — abide, because there is no portal of expression from the caverns of the spirit which they inhabit into the universe of things. Poetry redeems from decay the visitations of the divinity in man.

Poetry turns all things to loveliness; it exalts the beauty of that which is most beautiful, and it adds beauty to that which is most deformed: it marries exultation and horror, grief and pleasure, eternity and change; it subdues to union under its light yoke all irreconcilable things. It transmutes all that it touches, and every form moving within the radiance of its presence is changed by wondrous sympathy to an incarnation of the spirit which it breathes; its secret alchemy turns to potable gold the poisonous waters which flow from death through life; it strips the veil of familiarity from the world, and lays bare the naked and sleeping beauty which is the spirit of its forms.

All things exist as they are perceived: at least in relation to the percipient. "The mind is its own place, and of itself can make a heaven of hell, a hell of heaven."[22] But poetry defeats the curse which binds us to be subjected to the accident of surrounding impressions. And whether it spreads its own figured curtain or withdraws life's dark veil from before the scene of things, it equally creates for us a being within our being. It makes us the inhabitants of a world to which the familiar world is a chaos. It reproduces the common universe of which we are portions and percipients, and it purges from our inward sight the film of familiarity which obscures from us the wonder of our being. It compels us to feel that which we perceive, and to imagine that which we know. It creates anew the universe after it has been annihilated in our minds by the recurrence of impressions blunted by reiteration. It justifies that bold and true word of Tasso — *Non merita nome di creatore, se non Iddio ed il Poeta.*[23]

A Poet, as he is the author to others of the highest wisdom, pleasure, virtue and glory, so he ought personally to be the happiest, the best, the wisest, and the most illustrious of men. As to his glory, let Time be challenged to declare whether the fame of any other institutor of human life be comparable to that of a poet. That he is the wisest, the happiest, and the best, inasmuch as he is a poet, is equally incontrovertible: the greatest poets have been men of the most spotless virtue, of the most consummate prudence, and, if we could look into the interior of their lives, the most fortunate of men: and the exceptions, as they regard those who possessed the poetic faculty in a high yet inferior degree, will be found on consideration to confirm rather than destroy the rule. Let us for a moment stoop to the arbitration of popular breath, and usurping and uniting in our own persons the incompatible characters of accuser, witness, judge and executioner, let us decide without trial, testimony, or form, that certain motives of those who are "there sitting where we dare not soar"[24] are reprehensible. Let us assume that Homer was a drunkard, that Virgil was a flatterer, that Horace was a coward, that Tasso was a madman, that Lord Bacon was a peculator, that Raphael was a libertine, that Spenser was a poet laureate.[25] It is inconsistent with this

[22]Milton, *Paradise Lost*, 1:254–55.

[23]"Nobody merits the title of Creator save God and the Poet." The line is quoted thus in Serassi's *Life of Torquato Tasso.*

[24]Milton, *Paradise Lost*, 4:829.

[25]Poet laureate may seem an odd member of this sequence, unless we remember that the current laureate was Robert Southey, a personal and political enemy of Shelley's.

division of our subject to cite living poets, but Posterity has done ample justice to the great names now referred to. Their errors have been weighed and found to have been dust in the balance: if their sins "were as scarlet, they are now white as snow"; they have been washed in the blood of the mediator and the redeemer Time. Observe in what a ludicrous chaos the imputations of real or fictitious crime have been confused in the contemporary calumnies against poetry and poets; consider how little is, as it appears — or appears, as it is; look to your own motives, and judge not, lest ye be judged.

Poetry, as has been said, in this respect differs from logic, that it is not subject to the controul of the active powers of the mind, and that its birth and recurrence has no necessary connexion with consciousness or will. It is presumptuous to determine that these are the necessary conditions of all mental causation, when mental effects are experienced insusceptible of being referred to them. The frequent recurrence of the poetical power, it is obvious to suppose, may produce in the mind an habit or order and harmony correlative with its own nature and with its effects upon other minds. But in the intervals of inspiration, and they may be frequent without being durable, a poet becomes a man, and is abandoned to the sudden reflux of the influences under which others habitually live. But as he is more delicately organized than other men, and sensible to pain and pleasure, both his own and that of others, in a degree unknown to them, he will avoid the one and pursue the other with an ardour proportioned to this difference. And he renders himself obnoxious to calumny, when he neglects to observe the circumstances under which these objects of universal pursuit and flight have disguised themselves in one another's garments.

But there is nothing necessarily evil in this error, and thus cruelty, envy, revenge, avarice, and the passions purely evil, have never formed any portion of the popular imputations on the lives of poets.

I have thought it most favourable to the cause of truth to set down these remarks according to the order in which they were suggested to my mind by a consideration of the subject itself, instead of following that of the treatise that excited me to make them public. Thus although devoid of the formality of a polemical reply; if the view they contain be just, they will be found to involve a refutation of the Four Ages of Poetry, so far at least as regards the first division of the subject. I can readily conjecture what should have moved the gall of the learned and intelligent author of that paper; I confess myself like him unwilling to be stunned by the Theseids of the hoarse Codri of the day. Bavius and Mævius undoubtedly are, as they ever were, insufferable persons.[26] But it belongs to a philosophical critic to distinguish rather than confound.

The first part of these remarks has related to Poetry in its elements and principles; and it has been shewn, as well as the narrow limits assigned them would permit, that what is called poetry, in a restricted sense, has a common source with all other forms of order and of beauty according to which the materials of human life are susceptible of being arranged, and which is poetry in an universal sense.

The second part will have for its object an application of these principles to the present state of the cultivation of Poetry, and a defence of the attempt to idealize the modern forms of manners and opinion, and compel them into a subordination to the imaginative and creative faculty.[27] For the literature of England, an energetic developement of which has ever preceded or accompanied a great and free developement of the national will, has arisen as it were from a new birth. In spite of the low-thoughted envy which would undervalue contemporary merit, our own will be a memorable age in intellectual achievements, and we live among such philosophers and poets as surpass beyond comparison any who have appeared since the last national struggle for civil and religious liberty. The most unfailing herald, companion, and follower of the awakening of a great people to work a beneficial change in opinion or institution, is Poetry. At such periods there is an accumulation of the power of communicating and receiving intense and impassioned

---

[26]Codrus, Bavius, and Maevius are traditional examples of bad poets cited by Juvenal, Horace, and Virgil.
[27]The "second part" was never written.

conceptions respecting man and nature. The persons in whom this power resides, may often, as far as regards many portions of their nature, have little apparent correspondence with that spirit of good of which they are the ministers. But even whilst they deny and abjure, they are yet compelled to serve, the Power which is seated upon the throne of their own soul. It is impossible to read the compositions of the most celebrated writers of the present day without being startled with the electric life which burns within their words. They measure the circumference and sound the depths of human nature with a comprehensive and all-penetrating spirit, and they are themselves perhaps the most sincerely astonished at its manifestations, for it is less their spirit than the spirit of the age. Poets are the hierophants of an unapprehended inspiration, the mirrors of the gigantic shadows which futurity casts upon the present, the words which express what they understand not; the trumpets which sing to battle, and feel not what they inspire: the influence which is moved not, but moves. Poets are the unacknowledged legislators of the World.

Raymond Williams

1921–1988

Born to working-class parents in a Welsh border village, Raymond Williams was that rare creature, a Marxist intellectual with genuine proletarian roots. After serving in the British army from 1941 until the close of the war, Williams earned his M.A. from Trinity College, Cambridge, in 1946, and then attended Oxford, where he worked his way up the ladder of appointments. A professor of drama at Jesus College, Cambridge, until 1983, he was considered by many to be the preeminent Marxist literary critic and theorist of postwar Britain. In addition to his landmark study Culture and Society, 1780–1950 *(1958), and his masterpiece* The Country and the City *(1973), Williams wrote more than a dozen other books, including* The Long Revolution *(1961),* Drama from Ibsen to Brecht *(1969),* The English Novel from Dickens to Lawrence *(1970),* Keywords: A Vocabulary of Culture and Society *(1976),* Marxism and Literature *(1977),* The Sociology of Culture *(1982),* Writing in Society *(1983), and* Politics of Modernism *(1989), which was published in the year following his death.*

In this brief selection from his early book Culture and Society 1780–1950, *Raymond Williams gives us some perspective on Romantic literary theory, particularly that of Shelley, but touching also on Wordsworth, Coleridge, and Keats. Sympathetic to the plight of these poets, who in the midst of the Industrial Revolution were searching for a source of value that could counter the economic forces that were altering their England beyond recognition, Williams nevertheless views their ideological response as one that finally isolated them and literary culture in general from the broader popular culture they wished to imbue and inspire.*

The Romantic Artist
from *Culture and Society 1780–1950*

. . . The whole tradition can be summed up in one striking phrase used by Wordsworth, where the poet, the artist in general, is seen as

> an upholder and preserver, carrying every where with him relationship and love.[1]

[1] *Wordsworth's Poetical Works*, ed. Thomas Hutchinson (Oxford: Duckworth & Co., 1908), p. 938. See "Preface to *Lyrical Ballads*," p. 313.

Artists, in this mood, came to see themselves as agents of the "revolution for life," in their capacity as bearers of the creative imagination. Here, again, is one of the principal sources of the idea of Culture; it was on this basis that the association of the idea of the general perfection of humanity with the practice and study of the arts was to be made. For here, in the work of artists — "the first and last of all knowledge . . . as immortal as the heart of man" — was a practicable mode of access to that ideal of human perfection which was to be the centre of defence against the disintegrating tendencies of the age.

The emphasis on a general common humanity was evidently necessary in a period in which a new kind of society was coming to think of man as merely a specialized instrument of production. The emphasis on love and relationship was necessary not only within the immediate suffering but against the aggressive individualism and the primarily economic relationships which the new society embodied. Emphasis on the creative imagination, similarly, may be seen as an alternative construction of human motive and energy, in contrast with the assumptions of the prevailing political economy. This point is indeed the most interesting part of Shelley's *Defence*:

> Whilst the mechanist abridges, and the political economist combines, labour, let them beware that their speculations, for want of correspondence with those first principles which belong to the imagination, do not tend, as they have in modern England, to exasperate at once the extremes of luxury and want. . . . The rich have become richer, and the poor have become poorer; and the vessel of the state is driven between the Scylla and Charybdis of anarchy and despotism. Such are the effects which must ever flow from an unmitigated exercise of the calculating faculty.[2]

This is the general indictment which we can see already forming as a tradition, and the remedy is in the same terms:

> There is no want of knowledge respecting what is wisest and best in morals, government, and political economy, or at least, what is wiser and better than what men now practise or endure. But . . . we want the creative faculty to imagine that which we know; we want the generous impulse to act that which we imagine; we want the poetry of life: our calculations have outrun conception; we have eaten more than we can digest . . . Poetry, and the Principle of Self, of which money is the visible incarnation, are the God and Mammon of the world.[3]

The most obvious criticism of such a position as Shelley's is that, while it is wholly valuable to

present a wider and more substantial account of human motive and energy than was contained in the philosophy of industrialism, there are corresponding dangers in specializing this more substantial energy to the act of poetry, or of art in general. It is this specialization which, later, made much of this criticism ineffectual. The point will become clearer in the later stages of our enquiry, where it will be a question of distinguishing between the idea of culture as art and the idea of culture as a whole way of life. The positive consequence of the idea of art as a superior reality was that it offered an immediate basis for an important criticism of industrialism. The negative consequence was that it tended, as both the situation and the opposition hardened, to isolate art, to specialize the imaginative faculty to this one kind of activity, and thus to weaken the dynamic function which Shelley proposed for it. We have already examined certain of the factors which tended towards this specialization; it remains now to examine the growth of the idea of the artist as a "special kind of person."

The word *Art*, which had commonly meant "skill," became specialized during the course of the eighteenth century, first to "painting," and then to the imaginative arts generally. *Artist*, similarly, from the general sense of a skilled person, in either the "liberal" or the "useful" arts, had become specialized in the same direction, and had distinguished itself from *artisan* (formerly equivalent with *artist*, but later becoming what we still call, in the opposite specialized sense, a "skilled worker"), and of course from *craftsman*. The emphasis on skill, in the word, was gradually replaced by an emphasis on sensibility; and this replacement was supported by the parallel changes in such words as *creative* (a word which could not have been applied to art until the idea of the "superior reality" was forming), *original* (with its important implications of spontaneity and vitalism; a word, we remember, that Young[4] virtually

[2]See Shelley, "Defence of Poetry," p. 358–59.
[3]See Shelley, "Defence of Poetry," p. 359–60.

[4]Williams refers to "Conjectures on Original Composition" (1759) by poet Edward Young (1683–1765), one of the first critical essays to consider originality as the hallmark of literary genius.

contrasted with *art* in the sense of skill), and *genius* (which, because of its root association with the idea of *inspiration*, had changed from "characteristic disposition" to "exalted special ability," and took its tone in this from the other affective words). From *artist* in the new sense there were formed *artistic* and *artistical*, and these, by the end of the nineteenth century, had certainly more reference to "temperament" than to skill or practice. *Aesthetics*, itself a new word, and a product of the specialization, similarly stood parent to *aesthete*, which again indicated a "special kind of person."

The claim that the artist revealed a higher kind of truth is, as we have seen, not new in the Romantic period, although it received significant additional emphasis. The important corollary of the idea was, however, the conception of the artist's autonomy in this kind of revelation; his substantive element, for example, was now not faith but genius. In its opposition to the "set of rules," the autonomous claim is of course attractive. Keats puts it finely:

> The Genius of Poetry must work out its own salvation in a man: it cannot be matured by law and precept, but by sensation and watchfulness in itself. That which is creative must create itself.[5]

Our sympathy with this rests on the emphasis on a personal discipline, which is very far removed from talk of the "wild" or "lawless" genius. The difference is there, in Keats, in the emphasis on "the Genius of Poetry," which is impersonal as compared with the personal "genius." Coleridge put the same emphasis on law, with the same corresponding emphasis on autonomy:

> No work of true genius dare want its appropriate form; neither indeed is there any danger of this. As it must not, so neither can it, be lawless! For it is even this that constitutes its genius — the power of acting creatively under laws of its own origination.[6]

This is at once more rational and more useful for the making of art than the emphasis, at least as common in Romantic pamphleteering, on an "artless spontaneity." Of the Art (sensibility) which claims that it can dispense with art (skill) the subsequent years hold more than enough examples.

As literary theory, the emphases of Keats and Coleridge are valuable. The difficulty is that this kind of statement became entangled with other kinds of reaction to the problem of the artist's relations with society. The instance of Keats is most significant, in that the entanglement is less and the concentration more. If we complete the sentence earlier quoted from him we find:

> I have not the slightest feel of humility towards the public, or to anything in existence, — but the eternal Being, the Principle of Beauty, and the Memory of Great Men.[7]

This is characteristic, as is the famous affirmation:

> I am certain of nothing but of the holiness of the Heart's affections, and the truth of Imagination. What the Imagination seizes as Beauty must be truth — whether it existed before or not — for I have the same idea of all our passions as of Love; they are all, in their sublime, creative of essential Beauty. . . . The Imagination may be compared to Adam's dream — he awoke and found it truth.[8]

But the account of the artist's personality which Keats then gives is, in his famous phrase, that of "Negative Capability . . . when a man is capable of being in uncertainties, mysteries, doubts, without any irritable reaching after fact and reason."[9] Or again:

> Men of Genius are great as certain ethereal Chemicals operating on the Mass of neutral intellect — but they have not any individuality, any determined Character — I would call the top and head of those who have a proper self, Men of Power.[10]

It is certainly possible to see this emphasis on passivity as a compensatory reaction, but this is

---

[5] *Letters of John Keats*, ed. Forman, Letter 90, p. 223. The letter was written to J.A. Hessey, August 10, 1818 [Williams].

[6] See Coleridge, "Shakespeare's Judgment Equal to His Genius," p. 325.

[7] Op. cit., p. 130. [Williams].

[8] See Keats, "Letter to Benjamin Bailey," p. 331.

[9] See Keats, "Letter to George and Thomas Keats," p. 333.

[10] See Keats, "Letter to Benjamin Bailey."

less important than the fact that Keats's emphasis is on the poetic *process* rather than on the poetic *personality*. The theory of Negative Capability could degenerate into the wider and more popular theory of the poet as "dreamer," but Keats himself worked finely, in experience, to distinguish between "dreamer" and "poet," and if in the second *Hyperion* his formal conclusion is uncertain, it is at least clear that what he means by "dream" is something as hard and positive as his own skill. It is not from the fine discipline of a Keats that the loose conception of the romantic artist can be drawn.

Wordsworth, in the *Preface to Lyrical Ballads*, shows us most clearly how consideration of the poetic process became entangled with more general questions of the artist and society. In discussing his own theory of poetic language, he is in fact discussing communication. He asserts, reasonably and moderately, the familiar attitude to the Public:

> Such faulty expressions, were I convinced they were faulty at present, and that they must necessarily continue to be so, I would willingly take all reasonable pains to correct. But it is dangerous to make these alterations on the simple authority of a few individuals, or even of certain classes of men; for where the understanding of an Author is not convinced, or his feelings altered, this cannot be done without great injury to himself: for his own feelings are his stay and support.[11]

This has to be said on the one side, while at the same time Wordsworth is saying:

> The Poet thinks and feels in the spirit of human passions. How, then, can his language differ in any material degree from that of all other men who feel vividly and see clearly?[12]

And also:

> Among the qualities . . . enumerated as principally conducing to form a Poet, is implied nothing differing in kind from other men, but only in degree. . . . The Poet is chiefly distinguished from other men by a greater promptness to think and feel without immediate external excitement, and a greater power in expressing such thoughts and feelings as are produced in him in that manner. But these passions and thoughts and feelings are the general passions and thoughts and feelings of men.[13]

Of these chief distinctions, while the first is a description of a psychological type, the second is a description of a skill. While the two are held in combination, the argument is plausible. But in fact, under the tensions of the general situation, it became possible to dissociate them, and so to isolate the "artistic sensibility."

The matter is exceptionally complex, and what happened, under the stress of events, was a series of simplifications. The obstruction of a certain kind of experience was simplified to the obstruction of poetry, which was then identified with it and even made to stand for it as a whole. Under pressure, art became a symbolic abstraction for a whole range of general human experience: a valuable abstraction, because indeed great art has this ultimate power; yet an abstraction nevertheless, because a general social activity was forced into the status of a department or province, and actual works of art were in part converted into a self-pleading ideology. This description is not offered for purposes of censure; it is a fact, rather, with which we have to learn to come to terms. There is high courage, and actual utility, if also simplification, in Romantic claims for the imagination. There is courage, also, in the very weakness which, ultimately, we find in the special pleading of personality. In practice there were deep insights, and great works of art; but, in the continuous pressure of living, the free play of genius found it increasingly difficult to consort with the free play of the market, and the difficulty was not solved, but cushioned, by an idealization. The last pages of Shelley's *Defence of Poetry* are painful to read. The bearers of a high imaginative skill become suddenly the "legislators," at the very moment when they were being forced into

---

[11]See Wordsworth, "Preface to *Lyrical Ballads*," p. 317.
[12]See Wordsworth, "Preface to *Lyrical Ballads*," p. 314.

[13]See Wordsworth, "Preface to *Lyrical Ballads*," p. 314.

practical exile; their description as "unacknowledged," which, on the theory, ought only to be a fact to be accepted, carries with it also the felt helplessness of generation. Then Shelley at the same time claims that the Poet

> ought personally to be the happiest, the best, the wisest, and the most illustrious of men;[14]

where the emphasis, inescapably, falls painfully on the *ought*. The pressures, here personal as well as general, create, as a defensive reaction, the separation of poets from other men, and their classification into an idealized general person, "Poet" or "Artist," which was to be so widely and so damagingly received. The appeal, as it had to be, is beyond the living community, to the

> mediator and . . . redeemer, Time.[15]

Over the England of 1821 there had, after all, to be some higher Court of Appeal. We are not likely, when we remember the lives of any of these men, to be betrayed into the irritability of prosecution, but it is well, also, if we can avoid the irritability of defence. The whole action has passed into our common experience, to lie there, formulated and unformulated, to move and to be examined. "For it is less their spirit, than the spirit of the age."[16]

---

[14]See Shelley, "Defence of Poetry," p. 361.

[15]See Shelley, "Defence of Poetry," p. 362.
[16]See Shelley, "Defence of Poetry," p. 363.

Georg Wilhelm Friedrich Hegel
1770–1831

The central philosopher of modern nationalism was born the son of a civil servant in Stuttgart. Hegel is not known to have been a remarkable child. As a boy he played cards, learned to take snuff, and made a vast, painstakingly arranged collection of clippings and extracts from sources as varied as the classics and local newspapers. Hegel studied theology at Tübingen University without having much interest in it or, for that matter, much commitment to the mystical content of Christianity. After taking his Ph.D., he wrote (in advance of the demythologizer David Friedrich Strauss) a biography of Jesus, which considers him not as the son of God but as a human professor of ethics and religion whose contribution was to restore to Judaism the classical harmony between God and Man. Two friends from Tübingen assisted Hegel's early career: The poet Friedrich Hölderlin helped him to good posts as a private tutor, and the philosopher Friedrich von Schelling got him a course of lectures at the university at Jena.

There, in the first years of the nineteenth century, he developed his central ideas about mind, art, and the state. These years were dominated by the epoch-making figure of Napoleon, who carved the map of Europe with his sword, and whom Hegel saw as one of the "world-historical individuals" — his term for people who embodied the spirit of an age, and whose greatness came from the confluence of their private wills with the ineluctable movement of history. When Napoleon took Jena in a great battle in 1806, Hegel's sympathies were with the emperor rather than with the German states, which he saw as desperately in need of the same political reform and consolidation, through blood and iron, that the Revolution and Napoleon had given France. His political ideas became the watchwords of the second German Reich, of Bismarck and the Hohenzollern emperors.

But the battle — and the decade of war — had made Jena an uncomfortable place for the philosopher. Despite the publication of his revolutionary *Phenomenology of Spirit* (1807), Hegel was nearly bankrupt. He edited a newspaper and then took a post in Nuremberg as rector of a secondary school, the Aegidien-Gymnasium. There, at forty-two, he married a local girl of nineteen, who bore him two sons and with whom he had a happy and affectionate relationship.

Hegel continued his work at Nuremberg and, on the publication of his *Logic* (1812–16), was offered three secure professorships. Hegel went first to Heidelberg, where he brought out his *Encyclopaedia of the Philosophical Sciences* (1817). The following year, he accepted the chair of philosophy in Berlin, where he published his essay on *Philosophy of Right* (1821) as a guide to the burgeoning Prussian state and where he taught for the rest of his life.

By the late 1820s, Hegel had become the founder of a school of philosophy with a host of disciples and imitators. He was decorated by the king of Prussia and made rector of his university. Then in 1831, at the height of his fame, he died suddenly during a cholera epidemic. His death expanded rather than erased his influence, however. Most of his major works were derived from his class lectures at Berlin, and many of them were compiled after his death from his notes and those of his students.

These works were issued in nineteen volumes between 1832 and 1847; they include *The Philosophy of History, The Philosophy of Religion,* and *Aesthetics.* The selection that follows is taken from the *Introduction to the Philosophy of Art.* This was originally published posthumously in 1835 as the manuscript notes to Hegel's lectures on aesthetics. The lectures themselves were originally given in 1820, but were revised in 1823, 1826, and 1829.

Hegel's philosophy in its broadest sense presents the metamorphoses of the Spirit of the World from the beginning of history, when Man differentiated himself from the rest of Nature, to modern times. *The Phenomenology of Spirit* describes this evolution of mind from its most primitive stage, mere consciousness of an outside world, through the intermediate stages of consciousness-of-self, reason, spirit, and religion, to the ultimate realm of Absolute Knowledge.

Like Plato, Hegel is a holistic thinker. His later treatises on various subjects, like his posthumous lectures on politics, religion, and art, did not constitute a departure from the philosophy of mind in the *Phenomenology.* Rather, they showed how the spiritual evolution described in the *Phenomenology* had worked itself out in different areas of human experience. In each area, Hegel regarded the primitive oriental mode as engaged with substance at the expense of spirit, the intermediate classic mode as characterized by a harmony between body and spirit, and the modern mode as the culminating triumph of spirit over substance.

In politics, for example, Hegel saw the spiritual metamorphosis as the historical development of freedom. Politics originated in the alienation of man from nature, which required taming by collective action. The first solution was the patriarchal family, where all power and right are invested in the father, and the father is free to kill his wife or children if they disobey him. In the oriental world, patriarchal power was collectivized in the despotism of the ruler, who was a father to his subjects. In the empires of China and Persia, only one man was free: the emperor. This patriarchal form of government gave way to the democracy and aristocracy of Greece and Rome, where a whole class of people could be free, but whose freedom was based on the subjugation of slaves and foreigners. In the postclassical age — what Hegel called the German World — he foresaw the day when all men could be free, not as patriarchs or oriental despots or slave-owning aristocrats, but as mutual participants in an orderly freedom under law as subjects of an enlightened monarch.

In terms of religion, Hegel saw the faiths of the Orient — of China and India — as spiritually coherent with their despotic politics. The ancestor worship of China is its most obvious and direct manifestation. The later Confucian notion that the emperor rules under the mandate of T'ien, or Heaven, is only a slight deviation, since it reifies the magical forces of nature as operating through that individual. The Indian religions, Hinduism and Buddhism, represent the opposite reaction. Religion is a quietistic escape, through reincarnation and nirvana, from a despotism that, left intact on earth, is ignored as irrelevant or devalued as Maya (Illusion). Judaism too created a patriarchal God (like that of China) who was viewed as existing behind and transcending Nature (like the deities of India).

For Hegel the Greek religion was the next stage. Where the Orientals had portrayed spirit overwhelmed by substance, the Greeks found a balance between the two.

Their gods were anthropomorphic and human in their spiritual nature as well as in their physical forms. Having humanized the gods that lurked behind natural phenomena, the Greeks were free to trust nature. This confidence allowed them to develop a politics of trust in themselves rather than one of subjection to a semidivine despot. Christianity, the religion of the modern world, tips the balance from substance toward spirit. It combines the patriarchal despot inherited from Judaism (God the Creator) with an anthropomorphic deity (Jesus); but it adds the Holy Spirit, who incarnates the divine in the spirit of each man and ends the divorce of man from nature.

Each of these historical transformations is mediated by Hegel's "transcendental dialectic" — a well-known feature of his reasoning usually summarized by the triad of thesis, antithesis, and synthesis. An aspect of life becomes a thesis when it is abstracted from the background of nature and made into an absolute. Each Absolute calls into being its Other, the antithesis, which it negates and which in turn negates it. At length the conflict is mediated by a higher transcendent being that can resolve the negations and contradictions. The Judaic god, for example, is absolutized as God the Creator. He is thus defined by, and in opposition to, his creation, nature, including man, and is therefore outside nature and time, inhuman and incomprehensible. At the same time, nature and man are defined as barren of the divine. Thesis and antithesis negate each other. The synthesis mediating and transcending these negations was provided in Christianity through God the Son, who is human and natural as well as divine. Hegel's dialectic was later adopted by Karl Marx, who used it to support a materialistic theory of economics and society rather than an idealist approach to spiritual evolution.

Hegel's ideas on art must be seen in the context of both his dialectical method and his thinking on the histories of politics and religion, for in the *Phenomenology,* art is an aspect of religion (and vice versa) rather than a separate spiritual mode, and the collective expression of a society rather than of an individual voice. Although he was generally a follower of Kant's idealism, Hegel rejected Kant's aesthetic with its basis in natural beauty and its insistence on the purposelessness of the beautiful object. For Hegel, nature is beautiful only by analogy with art, and art is supremely useful to man, not as mere pleasure but for "its ability to represent in *sensuous form* even the highest ideas, bringing them thus nearer to . . . the senses, and to feeling." In the long run, perhaps in the last stage of human evolution toward absolute knowledge, art would be superseded by the more direct apprehension of ideas through philosophy. But far from being deceptive, as Plato thought, art serves to free "the true meaning of appearances from the show and deception of this bad and transient world."

If art is "the sensuous form of the idea," then it has two distinct ways of evolving: in the history of its forms — the modes of substance the idea inhabits — and through the history of the spirit itself. The latter gives Hegel his distinction between symbolic, classic, and romantic art. Each has its defects and virtues. Symbolic art (we should call it allegorical art) is typically the art of the oriental world, where substance is present in abundance but where the "spiritual idea has not yet found its adequate form." It can convey the sublime, as the pyramids do, although it has a spiritual quality that excludes the human, or it can merely degenerate into the grotesque. In classical art, as in Greek religion and politics, substance and spirit exist in full harmony in sculptures that express spiritual ideas "through the bodily form of man." But classic art, although perfect in its way, is limited to the contemplation of the merely human. Only romantic art can portray the greater spirituality of the divine. Here, though, the spirit outruns substance, giving the audience the sense of a meaning that extends beyond the power of matter to convey it.

In a second classification of artistic genres and forms, Hegel discusses the particular arts, categorizing them according to their relation to these movements of historical evolution. Architecture, the most massively physical of the arts, whose products dwarf the spectator, is clearly linked with the symbolic art of the oriental world while sculpture is obviously linked with the classic world. The romantic arts of the modern world are painting, music, and poetry, for they owe the least to substance and the most to spirit. Painting, like sculpture, is graphic, but a painting imposes a subjective point of view that sculpture — designed to be viewed in the round — cannot. And painting can represent whatever can be imagined — thoughts and feelings as well as plastic forms. Music is even more spiritual since it is insubstantial, but it still requires players and performance. Poetry alone is totally free of the requirements of substance.

Elsewhere, Hegel classifies poetic forms, viewing epic as the most objective and lyric as the most subjective of the poetic arts, and drama as the synthesis of the two. Like Aristotle, Hegel regarded tragedy as the highest of the arts, particularly because he felt that, at its best (as in Sophocles' *Antigone*), the tragic agon could be viewed not as a material struggle but as a battle for primacy between two ideas — an example of Hegel's own vision of spiritual evolution through the conflict of thesis and antithesis.

Selected Bibliography

Bungay, Stephen. *Beauty and Truth: A Study of Hegel's Aesthetics.* Oxford and New York: Oxford University Press, 1984.

Horn, András. *Kunst und Freiheit: Eine kritische Interpretation der Hegelische Asthetik.* The Hague: Nijhoff, 1969.

Kaminsky, Jack. *Hegel on Art: An Interpretation of Hegel's Aesthetics.* Albany: State University of New York Press, 1962.

Kaufmann, Walter. *Hegel: Reinterpretation, Texts, and Commentary.* Garden City, NY: Doubleday, 1965.

Kedney, John Steinfort. *Hegel's Aesthetics: A Critical Exposition.* Chicago: B. C. Griggs, 1892.

Knox, Israel. *The Aesthetic Theories of Kant, Hegel and Schopenhauer.* New York: Columbia University Press, 1936.

Pippin, Robert B. "What Was Abstract Art (from the Point of View of Hegel)" *Critical Inquiry* 29, no.1 (2002): 1–24.

Rajan, Tilottama. "How (Not) to Speak Properly: Writing 'German' Philosophy in Hegel's *Aesthetics.*" *CLIO: A Journal of Literature, History, and the Philosophy of History* 33, no.2 (2004): 119–42.

Stace, W. T. *The Philosophy of Hegel.* London: Macmillan, 1924.

Steinkraus, W., K. L. Schmitz, and J. O'Malley, eds. *Art and Logic in Hegel's Philosophy.* Atlantic Highlands, NJ: Humanities Press, 1980.

Sussman, Henry. *The Hegelian Aftermath: Readings in Hegel, Kierkegaard, Freud, Proust, and James.* Baltimore: Johns Hopkins University Press, 1982.

Teyssèdre, Bernard. *L'esthétique de Hegel.* Paris: Presses Universitaires de France, 1958.

Introduction to the Philosophy of Art

THE MEANING OF ART

The appropriate expression for our subject is the Philosophy of Art, or, more precisely, the Philosophy of Fine Arts. By this expression we wish to exclude the beauty of nature. In common life we are in the habit of speaking of beautiful color, a beautiful sky, a beautiful river, beautiful flowers, beautiful animals, and beautiful human beings. But quite aside from the question, which we wish not to discuss here, how far beauty may be predicated of such objects, or how far natural beauty may be placed side by side with artistic beauty, we must begin by maintaining that artistic beauty is higher than the beauty of nature. For the beauty of art is beauty born — and born again — of the spirit. And as spirit and its products stand higher than nature and its phenomena, by so much the beauty that resides in art is superior to the beauty of nature.

To say that spirit and artistic beauty stand higher than natural beauty, is to say very little, for "higher" is a very indefinite expression, which states the difference between them as quantitative and external. The "higher" quality of spirit and of artistic beauty does not at all stand in a merely relative position to nature. Spirit only is the true essence and content of the world, so that whatever is beautiful is truly beautiful only when it partakes of this higher essence and is produced by it. In this sense natural beauty appears only as a reflection of the beauty that belongs to spirit; it is an imperfect and incomplete expression of the spiritual substance.

Confining ourselves to artistic beauty, we must first consider certain difficulties. The first that suggests itself is the question whether art is at all worthy of a philosophic treatment. To be sure, art and beauty pervade, like a kindly genius, all the affairs of life, and joyously adorn all its inner and outer phases, softening the gravity and the burden of actual existence, furnishing pleasure for idle moments, and, where it can accomplish nothing positive, driving evil away by occupying its place. Yet, although art wins its way everywhere with its pleasing forms, from the crude adornment of the savages to the splendour of the temple with its marvellous wealth of decoration, art itself appears to fall outside the real aims of life. And though the creations of art cannot be said to be directly disadvantageous to the serious purposes of life, nay, on occasion actually further them by holding evil at bay, on the whole, art belongs to the relaxation and leisure of the mind, while the substantial interests of life demand its exertion. At any rate, such a view renders art a superfluity, though the tender and emotional influence which is wrought upon the mind by occupation with art is not thought necessarily detrimental, because effeminate.

There are others, again, who, though acknowledging art to be a luxury, have thought it necessary to defend it by pointing to the practical necessities of the fine arts and to the relation they bear to morality and piety. Very serious aims have been ascribed to art. Art has been recommended as a mediator between reason and sensuousness, between inclination and duty, as the reconcilor of all these elements constantly warring with one another. But it must be said that, by making art serve two masters, it is not rendered thereby more worthy of a philosophic treatment. Instead of being an end in itself, art is degraded into a means of appealing to higher aims, on the one hand, and to frivolity and idleness on the other.

Art considered as means offers another difficulty which springs from its form. Granting that art can be subordinated to serious aims and that the results which it thus produces will be significant, still the means used by art is deception, for beauty is appearance, its form is its life; and one must admit that a true and real purpose should not be achieved through deception. Even if a good end is thus, now and then, attained by art

Translated by Joseph Loewenberg

its success is rather limited, and even then deception cannot be recommended as a worthy means; for the means should be adequate to the dignity of the end, and truth can be produced by truth alone and not by deception and semblance.

It may thus appear as if art were not worthy of philosophic consideration because it is supposed to be merely a pleasing pastime; even when it pursues more serious aims it does not correspond with their nature. On the whole, it is conceived to serve both grave and light interests, achieving its results by means of deception and semblance.

As for the worthiness of art to be philosophically considered, it is indeed true that art can be used as a casual amusement, furnishing enjoyment and pleasure, decorating our surroundings, lending grace to the external conditions of life, and giving prominence to other objects through ornamentation. Art thus employed is indeed not an independent or free, but rather a subservient art. That art might serve other purposes and still retain its pleasure-giving function, is a relation which it has in common with thought. For science, too, in the hands of the servile understanding is used for finite ends and accidental means, and is thus not self-sufficient, but is determined by outer objects and circumstances. On the other hand, science can emancipate itself from such service and can rise in free independence to the pursuit of truth, in which the realization of its own aims is its proper function.

Art is not genuine art until it has thus liberated itself. It fulfils its highest task when it has joined the same sphere with religion and philosophy and has become a certain mode of bringing to consciousness and expression the divine meaning of things, the deepest interests of mankind, and the most universal truths of the spirit. Into works of art the nations have wrought their most profound ideas and aspirations. Fine Art often constitutes the key, and with many nations it is the only key, to an understanding of their wisdom and religion. This character art has in common with religion and philosophy. Art's peculiar feature, however, consists in its ability to represent in *sensuous form* even the highest ideas, bringing them thus nearer to the character of natural phenomena, to the senses, and to feeling. It is the height of a supra-sensuous world into which *thought* reaches, but it always appears to immediate consciousness and to present experience as an alien *beyond.* Through the power of philosophic thinking we are able to soar above what is merely *here,* above sensuous and finite experience. But spirit can heal the breach between the supra-sensuous and the sensuous brought on by its own advance; it produces out of itself the world of fine art as the first reconciling medium between what is merely external, sensuous, and transient, and the world of pure thought, between nature with its finite reality and the infinite freedom of philosophic reason.

Concerning the unworthiness of art because of its character as appearance and deception, it must be admitted that such criticism would not be without justice, if appearance could be said to be equivalent to falsehood and thus to something that ought not to be. Appearance is essential to reality; truth could not be, did it not shine through appearance. Therefore not appearance in general can be objected to, but merely the particular kind of appearance through which art seeks to portray truth. To charge the appearance in which art chooses to embody its ideas as deception, receives meaning only by comparison with the external world of phenomena and its immediate materiality, as well as with the inner world of sensations and feelings. To these two worlds we are wont, in our empirical work-a-day life, to attribute the value of actuality, reality, and truth, in contrast to art, which is supposed to be lacking such reality and truth. But, in fact, it is just the whole sphere of the empirical inner and outer world that is not the world of true reality; indeed it may be called a mere show and a cruel deception in a far stricter sense than in the case of art. Only beyond the immediacy of sense and of external objects is genuine reality to be found. Truly real is but the fundamental essence and the underlying substance of nature and of spirit, and the universal element in nature and in spirit is precisely what art accentuates and makes visible. This essence of reality appears also in the common outer and inner world, but it appears in the form of a chaos of contingencies, distorted by the immediateness of sense perception, and by the capriciousness and conditions, events, characters, etc. Art frees the true meaning of appearances from the show and deception of this bad and transient world, and invests it with a higher reality and a more genuine being than the things of ordinary life.

THE CONTENT AND IDEAL OF ART

The content of art is spiritual, and its form is sensuous; both sides art has to reconcile into a united whole. The first requirement is that the content, which art is to represent, must be worthy of artistic representation; otherwise we obtain only a bad unity, since a content not capable of artistic treatment is made to take on an artistic form, and a matter prosaic in itself is forced into a form quite opposed to its inherent nature.

The second requirement demands of the content of art that it shall be no abstraction. By this is not meant that it must be concrete, as the sensuous is alleged to be concrete in contrast to everything spiritual and intellectual. For everything that is genuinely true, in the realm of thought as well as in the domain of nature, is concrete, and has, in spite of universality, nevertheless, a particular and subjective character. By saying, for example, that God is simply One, the Supreme Being as such, we express thereby nothing but a lifeless abstraction of an understanding devoid of reason. Such a God, as indeed he is not conceived in his concrete truth, can furnish no content for art, least of all for plastic art. Thus the Jews and the Turks have not been able to represent their God, who is still more abstract, in the positive manner in which the Christians have represented theirs. For in Christianity God is conceived in his truth, and therefore concrete, as a person, as a subject, and, more precisely still, as Spirit. What he is as spirit appears to the religious consciousness as a Trinity of persons, which at the same time is One. Here the essence of God is the reconciled unity of universality and particularity, such unity alone being concrete. Hence, as a content in order to be true must be concrete in this sense, art demands the same concreteness; because a mere abstract idea, or an abstract universal, cannot manifest itself in a particular and sensuous unified form.

If a true and therefore concrete content is to have its adequate sensuous form and shape, this sensuous form must — this being the third requirement — also be something individual, completely concrete, and one. The nature of concreteness belonging to both the content and the representation of art, is precisely the point in which both can coincide and correspond to each other. The natural shape of the human body, for example, is a sensuous concrete object, which is perfectly adequate to represent the spiritual in its concreteness; the view should therefore be abandoned that an existing object from the external world is accidentally chosen by art to express a spiritual idea. Art does not seize upon this or that form either because it simply finds it or because it can find no other, but the concrete spiritual content itself carries with it the element of external, real, yes, even sensuous, representation. And this is the reason why a sensuous concrete object, which bears the impress of an essentially spiritual content, addresses itself to the inner eye; the outward shape whereby the content is rendered visible and imaginable aims at an existence only in our heart and mind. For this reason alone are content and artistic shape harmoniously wrought. The mere sensuously concrete external nature as such has not this purpose for its only origin. The gay and variegated plumage of the birds shines unseen, and their song dies away unheard; the torch-thistle which blossoms only for a night withers without having been admired in the wilds of southern forests; and these forests, groves of the most beautiful and luxuriant vegetation, with the most odorous and fragrant perfumes, perish and waste, no more enjoyed. The work of art is not so unconsciously self-immersed, but it is essentially a question, an address to the responsive soul, an appeal to the heart and to the mind.

Although the sensuous form in which art clothes its content is not accidental, yet it is not the highest form whereby the spiritually concrete may be grasped. A higher mode than representation through a sensuous form, is thought. True and rational thinking, though in a relative sense abstract, must not be one-sided, but concrete. How far a definite content can be adequately treated by art and how far it needs, according to its nature, a higher and more spiritual form, is a distinction which we see at once, if, for example, the Greek gods are compared with God as conceived in accordance with Christian notions. The Greek god is not abstract but individual, closely related to the natural human form. The Christian God is also a concrete personality, but he is purely spiritual, and can be known only as spirit and in spirit. His sphere of existence is therefore essentially inner knowledge, and not the outer natural shape through which he can be represented but imperfectly and not in the whole depth of his essence.

But the task of art is to represent a spiritual idea to direct contemplation in sensuous form, and not in the form of thought or of pure spirituality. The value and dignity of such representation lies in the correspondence and unity of the two sides, of the spiritual content and its sensuous embodiment, so that the perfection and excellency of art must depend upon the grade of inner harmony and union with which the spiritual idea and the sensuous form interpenetrate.

The requirement of the conformity of spiritual idea and sensuous form might at first be interpreted as meaning that any idea whatever would suffice, so long as the concrete form represented this idea and no other. Such a view, however, would confound the ideal of art with mere correctness, which consists in the expression of any meaning in its appropriate form. The artistic ideal is not to be thus understood. For any content whatever is capable, according to the standard of its own nature, of adequate representation, but yet it does not for that reason lay claim to artistic beauty in the ideal sense. Judged by the standard of ideal beauty, even such correct representation will be defective. In this connection we may remark that the defects of a work of art are not to be considered simply as always due to the incapacity of the artist; defectiveness of form has also its root in defectiveness of content. Thus, for instance, the Chinese, Indians, Egyptians, in their artistic objects, their representations of the gods, and their idols, adhered to formlessness, or to a vague and inarticulate form, and were not able to arrive at genuine beauty, because their mythological ideas, the content and conception of their works of art, were as yet vague and obscure. The more perfect in form works of art are, the more profound is the inner truth of their content and thought. And it is not merely a question of the greater or lesser skill with which the objects of external nature are studied and copied, for, in certain stages of artistic consciousness and

artistic activity, the misrepresentation and distortion of natural objects are not unintentional technical inexpertness and incapacity, but conscious alteration, which depends upon the content that is in consciousness, and is, in fact, demanded by it. We may thus speak of imperfect art, which, in its own proper sphere, may be quite perfect both technically and in other respects. When compared with the highest idea and ideal of art, it is indeed defective. In the highest art alone are the idea and its representation in perfect congruity, because the sensuous form of the idea is in itself the adequate form, and because the content, which that form embodies, is itself a genuine content.

The higher truth of art consists, then, in the spiritual having attained a sensuous form adequate to its essence. And this also furnishes the principle of division for the philosophy of art. For the Spirit, before it wins the true notion or meaning of its absolute essence, has to develop through a series of stages which constitute its very life. To this universal evolution there corresponds a development of the phases of art, under the form of which the Spirit — as artist — attains to a comprehension of its own meaning.

This evolution within the spirit of art has two sides. The development is, in the first place, a spiritual and universal one, insofar as a gradual series of definite conceptions of the universe — of nature, man, and God — finds artistic representation. In the second place, this universal development of art, embodying itself in sensuous form, determines definite modes of artistic expression and a totality of necessary distinctions within the sphere of art. These constitute the particular arts.

We have now to consider three definite relations of the spiritual idea to its sensuous expression.

SYMBOLIC ART

Art begins when the spiritual idea, being itself still indefinite and obscure and ill-comprehended, is made the content of artistic forms. As indefinite, it does not yet have that individuality which the artistic ideal demands; its abstractness and one-sidedness thus render its shape defective and whimsical. The first form of art is therefore rather a mere search after plasticity than a capacity of true representation. The spiritual idea has not yet found its adequate form, but is still engaged in striving and struggling after it. This form we may, in general, call the *symbolic* form of art; in such form the abstract idea assumes a shape in natural sensuous matter which is foreign to it; with this foreign matter the artistic creation begins, from which, however, it seems unable to free itself. The objects of external nature are reproduced unchanged, but at the same time the meaning of the spiritual idea is attached to them. They thus receive the vocation of expressing it, and must be interpreted as if the spiritual idea were actually present in them. It is indeed true that natural objects possess an aspect which makes them capable of representing a universal meaning, but in symbolic art a complete correspondence is not yet possible. In it the correspondence is confined to an abstract quality, as when, for example, a lion is meant to stand for strength.

This abstract relation brings also to consciousness the foreignness of the spiritual idea to natural phenomena. And the spiritual idea, having no other reality to express its essence, expatiates in all these natural shapes, seeks itself in their unrest and disproportion, but finds them inadequate to it. It then exaggerates these natural phenomena and shapes them into the huge and the boundless. The spiritual idea revels in them, as it were, seethes and ferments in them, does violence to them, distorts and disfigures them into grotesque shapes, and endeavors by the diversity, hugeness, and splendor of such forms to raise the natural phenomena to the spiritual level. For here it is the spiritual idea which is more or less vague and nonplastic, while the objects of nature have a thoroughly definite form.

The incongruity of the two elements to each other makes the relation of the spiritual idea to objective reality a negative one. The spiritual as a wholly inner element and as the universal substance of all things, is conceived unsatisfied with all externality, and in its *sublimity* it triumphs over the abundance of unsuitable forms. In this conception of sublimity the natural objects and the human shapes are accepted and left unaltered, but at the same time recognized as inadequate to their own inner meaning; it is this inner meaning which is glorified far and above every worldly content.

These elements constitute, in general, the character of the primitive artistic pantheism of the Orient, which either invests even the lowest objects with absolute significance, or forces all phenomena with violence to assume the expression of its world-view. This art becomes therefore bizarre, grotesque, and without taste, or it represents the infinite substance in its abstract freedom turning away with disdain from the illusory and perishing mass of appearances. Thus the meaning can never be completely molded into the expression, and, notwithstanding all the aspiration and effort, the incongruity between the spiritual idea and the sensuous form remains insuperable. This is, then, the first form of art — symbolic art with its endless quest, its inner struggle, its sphinxlike mystery, and its sublimity.

CLASSICAL ART

In the second form of art, which we wish to designate as the *classical,* the double defect of symbolic art is removed. The symbolic form is imperfect, because the spiritual meaning which it seeks to convey enters into consciousness in but an abstract and vague manner, and thus the congruity between meaning and form must always remain defective and therefore abstract. This double aspect disappears in the classical type of art; in it we find the free and adequate embodiment of the spiritual idea in the form most suitable to it, and with it meaning and expression are in perfect accord. It is classical art, therefore, which first affords the creation and contemplation of the completed ideal, realizing it as a real fact in the world.

But the congruity of idea and reality in classical art must not be taken in the formal sense of the agreement of a content with its external form; otherwise every photograph of nature, every picture of a countenance, landscape, flower, scene, etc., which constitutes the aim of a representation, would, through the conformity of content and form, be at once classical. The peculiarity of classical art, on the contrary, consists in its content being itself a concrete idea, and, as such, a concrete spiritual idea, for only the spiritual is a truly classical content. For a worthy object of such a content, Nature must be consulted as to whether she contains anything to which a spiritual attribute really belongs. It must be the World-Spirit itself that *invented* the proper form for the concrete spiritual ideal; the subjective mind — in this case the spirit of art — has only *found* it, and given it natural plastic existence in accordance with free individual spirituality. The form in which the idea, as spiritual and individual, clothes itself when revealed as a temporal phenomenon, is the *human form*. To be sure, personification and anthropomorphism have frequently been decried as a degradation of the spiritual; but art, insofar as its task is to bring before direct contemplation the spiritual in sensuous form, must advance to such anthropomorphism, for only in its body can mind appear in an adequately sensuous fashion. The migration of souls[1] is, in this respect, an abstract notion, and physiology should make it one of its fundamental principles that life has necessarily, in its evolution, to advance to the human shape as the only sensuous phenomenon appropriate to the mind.

The human body as portrayed by classical art is not represented in its mere physical existence, but solely as the natural and sensuous form and garb of mind; it is therefore divested of all the defects that belong to the merely sensuous and of all the finite contingencies that appertain to the phenomenal. But if the form must be thus purified in order to express the appropriate content, and, furthermore, if the conformity of meaning and expression is to be complete, the content which is the spiritual idea must be perfectly capable of being expressed through the bodily form of man, without projecting into another sphere beyond the physical and sensuous representation. The result is that Spirit is characterized as a particular form of mind, namely, as human mind, and not as simply absolute and eternal; but the absolute and eternal Spirit must be able to reveal and express itself in a manner far more spiritual.

This latter point brings to light the defect of classical art, which demands its dissolution and

---

[1]Hegel means the transmigration of souls into the bodies of other animals; this notion is "abstract" because it presumes that the soul has an ideal reality that allows it to be put into any earthly envelope.

its transition to a third and higher form, to wit, the *romantic* form of art.

ROMANTIC ART

The romantic form of art destroys the unity of the spiritual idea and its sensuous form, and goes back, though on a higher level, to the difference and opposition of the two, which symbolic art left unreconciled. The classical form of art attained, indeed, the highest degree of perfection which the sensuous process of art was capable of realizing; and, if it shows any defects, the defects are those of art itself, due to the limitation of its sphere. This limitation has its root in the general attempt of art to represent in sensuous concrete form the infinite and universal Spirit, and in the attempt of the classical type of art to blend so completely spiritual and sensuous existence that the two appear in mutual conformity. But in such a fusion of the spiritual and sensuous aspects Spirit cannot be portrayed according to its true essence, for the true essence of Spirit is its infinite subjectivity; and its absolute internal meaning does not lend itself to a full and free expression in the confinement of the bodily form as its only appropriate existence.

Now, romantic art dissolves the inseparable unity which is the ideal of the classical type, because it has won a content which goes beyond the classical form of art and its mode of expression. This content — if familiar ideas may be recalled — coincides with what Christianity declares to be true of God as Spirit, in distinction to the Greek belief in gods which constitutes the essential and appropriate subject for classical art. The concrete content of Hellenic art implies the unity of the human and divine nature, a unity which, just because it is merely *implied* and *immediate,* permits of a representation in an immediately visible and sensuous mold. The Greek god is the object of naïve contemplation and sensuous imagination; his shape is, therefore, the bodily shape of man; the circle of his power and his essence is individual and confined. To man the Greek god appears as a being and a power with whom he may *feel* a kinship and unity, but this kinship and unity are not reflected upon or raised into definite knowledge. The higher stage is the *knowledge* of this unconscious unity, which underlies the classical form of art and which it has rendered capable of complete plastic embodiment. The elevation of what is unconscious and implied into self-conscious knowledge brings about an enormous difference; it is the infinite difference which, for example, separates man from the animal. Man is an animal, but, even in his animal functions, does not rest satisfied with the potential and the unconscious as the animal does, but becomes conscious of them, reflects upon them, and raises them — as, for instance, the process of digestion — into self-conscious science. And it is thus that man breaks through the boundary of his merely immediate and unconscious existence, so that, just because he knows himself to be animal, he ceases in virtue of such knowledge to be animal, and, through such self-knowledge only, can characterize himself as mind or spirit.

If in the manner just described the unity of the human and divine nature is raised from an *immediate* to a *conscious* unity, the true mold for the reality of this content is no longer the sensuous, immediate existence of the spiritual, the bodily frame of man, but self-conscious and internal contemplation. For this reason Christianity, in depicting God as Spirit — not as particularized individual mind, but as absolute and universal Spirit — retires from the sensuousness of imagination into the sphere of inner being, and makes this, and not the bodily form, the material and mold of its content; and thus the unity of the human and divine nature is a conscious unity, capable of realization only by spiritual knowledge. The new content, won by this unity, is not dependent upon sensuous representation; it is now exempt from such immediate existence. In this way, however, romantic art becomes art which transcends itself, carrying on this process of self-transcendence within its own artistic sphere and artistic form.

Briefly stated, the essence of romantic art consists in the artistic object being the free, concrete, spiritual idea itself, which is revealed in its spirituality to the inner, and not the outer, eye. In conformity with such a content, art can, in a sense, not work for sensuous perception, but must aim at the inner mood, which completely fuses with its object, at the most subjective inner shrine, at the

heart, the feeling, which, as spiritual feeling, longs for freedom within itself and seeks and finds reconciliation only within the inner recesses of the spirit. This *inner* world is the content of romantic art, and as such an inner life, or as its reflection, it must seek embodiment. The inner life thus triumphs over the outer world — indeed, so triumphs over it that the outer world itself is made to proclaim its victory, through which the sensuous appearance sinks into worthlessness.

On the other hand, the romantic type of art, like every other, needs an external mode of expression. But the spiritual has now retired from the outer mode into itself, and the sensuous externality of form assumes again, as it did in symbolic art, an insignificant and transient character. The subjective, finite mind and will, the particularity and caprice of the individual, of character, action or of incident and plot, assume likewise the character they had in symbolic art. The external side of things is surrendered to accident and committed to the excesses of the imagination, whose caprice now mirrors existence as it is, now chooses to distort the objects of the outer world into a bizarre and grotesque medley, for the external form no longer possesses a meaning and significance, as in classical art, on its own account and for its own sake. Feeling is now everything. It finds its artistic reflection, not in the world of external things and their forms, but in its own expression; and in every incident and accident of life, in every misfortune, grief, and even crime, feeling preserves or regains its healing power of reconciliation.

Hence, the indifference, incongruity, and antagonism of spiritual idea and sensuous form, the characteristics of symbolic art, reappear in the romantic type, but with this essential difference. In the romantic realm, the spiritual idea, to whose defectiveness was due the defective forms of symbolic art, now reveals itself in its perfection within mind and feeling. It is by virtue of the higher perfection of the idea that it shuns any adequate union with an external form, since it can seek and attain its true reality and expression best within itself.

This, in general terms, is the character of the symbolic, classical, and romantic forms of art, which stand for the three relations of the spiritual idea to its expression in the realm of art. They consist in the aspiration after, and the attainment and transcendence of, the ideal as the true idea of beauty.

THE PARTICULAR ARTS

But, now, there inhere in the idea of beauty different modifications which art translates into sensuous forms. And we find a fundamental principle by which the several particular arts may be arranged and defined — that is, the species of art contain in themselves the same essential differences which we have found in the three general types of art. External objectivity, moreover, into which these types are molded by means of a sensuous and particular material, renders them independent and separate means of realizing different artistic functions, as far as each type finds its definite character in some one definite external material whose mode of portrayal determines its adequate realization.[2] Furthermore, the general types of art correspond to the several particular arts, so that they (the particular arts) belong each of them *specifically* to *one* of the general types of art. It is these particular arts which give adequate and artistic external being to the general types.

ARCHITECTURE

The first of the particular arts with which, according to their fundamental principle, we have to begin, is architecture. Its task consists in so shaping external inorganic nature that it becomes homogeneous with mind, as an artistic outer world. The material of architecture is matter itself in its immediate externality as a heavy mass subject to mechanical laws, and its forms remain the forms of inorganic nature, but are merely arranged and ordered in accordance with the

[2]Hegel's point is that while the art forms of architecture, sculpture, and poetry have intrinsic correspondences with the symbolic, the classical, and the romantic modalities of art, respectively, there nevertheless exist classical and romantic forms of architecture, symbolic and romantic forms of sculpture, symbolic and classical forms of poetry.

abstract rules of the understanding, the rules of symmetry. But in such material and in such forms the ideal as concrete spirituality cannot be realized; the reality which is represented in them remains, therefore, alien to the spiritual idea, as something external which it has not penetrated or with which it has but a remote and abstract relation. Hence the fundamental type of architecture is the *symbolical* form of art. For it is architecture that paves the way, as it were, for the adequate realization of the God, toiling and wrestling in his service with external nature, and seeking to extricate it from the chaos of finitude, and the abortiveness of chance. By this means it levels a space for the God, frames his external surroundings, and builds him his temple as the place for inner contemplation and for reflection upon the eternal objects of the spirit. It raises an enclosure around those gathered together, as a defense against the threatening of the wind, against rain, the thunderstorm, and wild beasts, and reveals the will to assemble, though externally, yet in accordance with the artistic form. A meaning such as this, the art of architecture is able to mold into its material and its forms with more or less success, according as the determinate nature of the content which it seeks to embody is more significant or more trivial, more concrete or more abstract, more deeply rooted within its inner being or more dim and superficial. Indeed, it may even advance so far as to endeavor to create for such meaning an adequate artistic expression with its material and forms, but in such an attempt it has already overstepped the bounds of its own sphere, and inclines towards sculpture, the higher phase of art. For the limit of architecture lies precisely in this, that it refers to the spiritual as an internal essence in contrast with the external forms of its art, and thus whatever is endowed with mind and spirit must be indicated as something other than itself.

SCULPTURE

Architecture, however, has purified the inorganic external world, has given it symmetric order, has impressed upon it the seal of mind, and the temple of the God, the house of his community, stands ready. Into this temple now enters the

God himself. The lightning-flash of individuality strikes the inert mass, permeates it, and a form no longer merely symmetrical, but infinite and spiritual, concentrates and molds its adequate bodily shape. This is the task of sculpture. Inasmuch as in it the inner spiritual element, which architecture can no more than hint at, completely abides with the sensuous form and its external matter, and as both sides are so merged into each other that neither predominates, sculpture has the *classical* form of art as its fundamental type. In fact, the sensuous realm itself can command no expression which could not be that of the spiritual sphere, just as, conversely, no spiritual content can attain perfect plasticity in sculpture which is incapable of being adequately presented to perception in bodily form. It is sculpture which arrests for our vision the spirit in its bodily frame, in immediate unity with it, and in an attitude of peace and repose; and the form in turn is animated by the content of spiritual individuality. Therefore the external sensuous matter is here not wrought, either according to its mechanical quality alone, as heavy mass, or in forms peculiar to inorganic nature, or as indifferent to color, etc., but in ideal forms of the human shape, and in the whole of the spatial dimensions. In this last respect sculpture should be credited with having first revealed the inner and spiritual essence in its eternal repose and essential self-possession. To such repose and unity with itself corresponds only that external element which itself persists in unity and repose. Such an element is the form taken in its abstract spatiality. The spirit which sculpture represents is that which is solid in itself, not variously broken up in the play of contingencies and passions; nor does its external form admit of the portrayal of such a manifold play, but it holds to this one side only, to the abstraction of space in the totality of its dimensions.

THE DEVELOPMENT OF
THE ROMANTIC ARTS

After architecture has built the temple and the hand of sculpture has placed inside it the statue of the God, then this sensuously visible God faces in the spacious halls of his house the *community*. The community is the spiritual, self-reflecting element in this sensuous realm, it is the animating subjectivity and inner life. A new principle of art begins with it. Both the content of art and the medium which embodies it in outward form now demand particularization, individualization, and the subjective mode of expressing these. The solid unity which the God possesses in sculpture breaks up into the plurality of inner individual lives, whose unity is not sensuous, but essentially ideal.

And now God comes to assume the aspect which makes him truly spiritual. As a hither-and-thither, as an alteration between the unity within himself and his realization in subjective knowledge and individual consciousness, as well as in the common and unified life of the man individuals, he is genuinely Spirit — the Spirit in his community. In his community God is released from the abstractness of a mysterious self-identity, as well as from the naïve imprisonment in a bodily shape, in which he is represented by sculpture. Here he is exalted into spirituality, subjectivity, and knowledge. For this reason the higher content of art is now this spirituality in its absolute form. But since what chiefly reveals itself in this stage is not the serene repose of God in himself, but rather his appearance, his being, and his manifestation to others, the objects of artistic representation are now the most varied subjective expressions of life and activity for their own sake, as human passions, deeds, events, and, in general, the wide range of human feeling, will, and resignation. In accordance with this content, the sensuous element must differentiate and show itself adequate to the expression of subjective feeling. Such different media are furnished by color, by the musical sound, and finally by the sound as the mere indication of inner intuitions and ideas; and thus as different forms of realizing the spiritual content of art by means of these media we obtain painting, music, and poetry. The sensuous media employed in these arts being individualized and in their essence recognized as ideal, they correspond most effectively to the spiritual content of art, and the union between spiritual meaning and sensuous expression develops, therefore, into greater intimacy than was possible in the case of architecture and sculpture. This intimate unity, however, is due wholly to the subjective side.

Leaving, then, the symbolic spirit and architecture and the classical ideal of sculpture behind, these new arts in which form and content are raised to an ideal level borrow their type from the *romantic* form of art, whose mode of expression they are most eminently fitted to voice. They form, however, a totality of arts, because the romantic type is the most concrete in itself.

PAINTING

The first art in this totality, which is akin to sculpture, is painting. The material which it uses for its content and for the sensuous expression of that content is visibility as such, in so far as it is individualized, viz., specified as color. To be sure, the media employed in architecture and sculpture are also visible and colored, but they are not, as in painting, visibility as such, not the simple light which contrasts itself with darkness and in combination with it becomes color. This visibility as a subjective and ideal attribute, requires neither, like architecture, the abstract mechanical form of mass which we find in heavy matter, nor, like sculpture, the three dimensions of sensuous space, even though in concentrated and organic plasticity, but the visibility which appertains to painting has its differences on a more ideal level, in the particular kind of color; and thus painting frees art from the sensuous completeness in space peculiar to material things only, by confining itself to a plane surface.

On the other hand, the content also gains in varied particularization. Whatever can find room in the human heart, as emotion, idea, and purpose, whatever it is able to frame into a deed, all this variety of material can constitute the many-colored content of painting. The whole range of particular existence, from the highest aspirations of the mind down to the most isolated objects of nature, can obtain a place in this art. For even finite nature, in its particular scenes and aspects, can here appear, if only some allusion to a spiritual element makes it akin to thought and feeling.

MUSIC

The second art in which the romantic form finds realization, on still a higher level than in painting, is music. Its material, though still sensuous, advances to a deeper subjectivity and greater specification. The idealization of the sensuous, music brings about by negating space. In music the indifferent extension of space whose appearance painting admits and consciously imitates is concentrated and idealized into a single point. But in the form of a motion and tremor of the material body within itself, this single point becomes a concrete and active process within the idealization of matter. Such an incipient ideality of matter which no longer appears under the spatial form, but as temporal ideality, is sound — the sensuous acknowledged as ideal, whose abstract visibility is transformed into audibility. Sound, as it were, exempts the ideal from its absorption in matter.

This earliest animation and inspiration of matter furnishes the medium for the inner and intimate life of the spirit, as yet on an indefinite level; it is through the tones of music that the heart pours out its whole scale of feelings and passions. Thus as sculpture constitutes the central point between architecture and the arts of romantic subjectivity, so music forms the center of the romantic arts, and represents the point of transition between abstract spatial sensuousness, which belongs to painting, and the abstract spirituality of poetry. Within itself music has, like architecture, an abstract quantitative relation, as a contrast to its inward and emotional quality; it also has as its basis a permanent law to which the tones with their combinations and successions must conform.[3]

POETRY

For the third and most spiritual expression of the romantic form of art, we must look to poetry. Its characteristic peculiarity lies in the power with which it subjugates to the mind and to its ideas

[3]Hegel refers to the mathematical basis of the diatonic scale and the laws of harmony and counterpoint that derive from it.

the sensuous element from which music and painting began to set art free. For sound, the one external medium of which poetry avails itself, is in it no longer a feeling of the tone itself, but is a sign which is, by itself, meaningless. This sign, moreover, is a sign of an idea which has become concrete, and not merely of indefinite feeling and of its *nuances* and grades. By this means the tone becomes the *word,* an articulate voice, whose function it is to indicate thoughts and ideas. The negative point to which music had advanced now reveals itself in poetry as the completely concrete point, as the spirit or the self-consciousness of the individual, which spontaneously unites the infinite space of its ideas with the time-element of sound. But this sensuous element which, in music, was still in immediate union with inner feelings and moods, is, in poetry, divorced from the content of consciousness, for in poetry the mind determines this content on its own account and for the sake of its ideas, and while it employs sound to express them, yet sound itself is reduced to a symbol without value or meaning. From this point of view sound may just as well be considered a mere letter, for the audible, like the visible, is now relegated to a mere suggestion of mind. Thus the genuine mode of poetic representation is the inner perception and the poetic imagination itself. And since all types of art share in this mode, poetry runs through them all, and develops itself independently in each. Poetry, then, is the universal art of the spirit which has attained inner freedom, and which does not depend for its realization upon external sensuous matter, but expatiates only in the inner space and inner time of the ideas and feelings. But just in this, its highest phase, art oversteps the bounds of its own sphere by abandoning the harmoniously sensuous mode of portraying the spirit and by passing from the poetry of imagination into the prose of thought.

SUMMARY

Such, then, is the organic totality of the several arts; the external art of architecture, the objective art of sculpture, and the subjective arts of painting, music, and poetry. The higher principle from which these are derived we have found in the types of art, the symbolic, the classical, and the romantic, which form the universal phases of the idea of beauty itself. Thus symbolic art finds its most adequate reality and most perfect application in architecture, in which it is self-complete, and is not yet reduced, so to speak, to the inorganic medium for another art. The classical form of art, on the other hand, attains its most complete realization in sculpture, while it accepts architecture only as forming an enclosure round its products and is as yet not capable of developing painting and music as absolute expressions of its meaning. The romantic type of art, finally, seizes upon painting, music, and poetry as its essential and adequate modes of expression. Poetry, however, is in conformity with all types of the beautiful and extends over them all, because its characteristic element is the aesthetic imagination, and imagination is necessary for every product of art, to whatever type it may belong.

Thus what the particular arts realize in individual artistic creations are, according to the philosophic conception, simply the universal types of the self-unfolding idea of beauty. Out of the external realization of this idea arises the wide Pantheon of art, whose architect and builder is the self-developing spirit of beauty, for the completion of which, however, the history of the world will require its evolution of countless ages.

Ralph Waldo Emerson

1803–1882

Emerson was the son of a Unitarian minister of Boston; he was educated at Boston Latin School and Harvard University and, after a brief and unhappy stint as a schoolmaster, returned to Cambridge to attend Harvard Divinity School. In 1826 he was licensed to preach and in 1829 was ordained as minister of the Second Church of Boston, where Cotton Mather had preached over a century before. In the same year he married Ellen Tucker, a young heiress who died of tuberculosis within sixteen months, leaving Emerson a widower with a legacy of over a thousand dollars a year and no pressing need to earn a living.

In the watershed year 1832, Emerson resigned his position at the Second Church because he had ceased to believe in the validity of the sacrament of the Lord's Supper and could no longer administer it. He embarked on an extended European tour, where he met the poets Wordsworth and Coleridge, and (most important for his intellectual development) Thomas Carlyle, who was to publicize Emerson in Britain and in return was publicized by Emerson in America.

In 1834, Emerson settled in the village of Concord, Massachusetts, where he married Lydia Jackson and began the quiet and orderly intellectual life that would continue for nearly fifty years. Although he believed in the theory that hard manual labor should be combined with scholarship, he found that work in the fields sapped his energies for his study. He also tried vegetarianism for a while but gave it up, since it seemed to be doing him no particular good. He wrote sermons at his farm and delivered them in enormously popular lectures on tours of Boston and the Northeast.

His first work, *Nature* (1836), though influenced by the mystical theology of Emmanuel Swedenborg, was essentially an American restatement of the idealistic and pantheist philosophy of Carlyle's *Sartor Resartus* (1834). It became the unofficial bible of the "Symposium" — an informal and occasional gathering of the American Transcendentalists, who included Bronson Alcott, Margaret Fuller, and Henry David Thoreau. His lectures appeared in print as *Essays* (1841), *Essays,* Second Series (1844), *Representative Men* (1850), and *The Conduct of Life* (1860). Like most Unitarians, Emerson was antislavery, as his journals of the 1850s reveal, but he steered clear of the abolitionist movement until it was too late for him to influence its course. After the Civil War, his writing declined as his once-prodigious memory began to fail, and the Sage of Concord gradually sank into senility at least a decade before his death.

"The Poet" is from Emerson's second series of *Essays,* and like many of his effusions, it preaches rather than analyzes its topic. "The Poet" quickly expands from its ostensible subject to include many of Emerson's central ideas, which strongly resemble the mystical views of Plotinus. Where Plotinus's god-term was "The One," Emerson's is the "Over-Soul," a pantheistic spiritual entity wherein everything living is united, the ultimate source of truth, goodness, and beauty. The universe itself, in its materiality, is merely a physical symbol, an emblem, of the Over-Soul. And the parts are as the whole: Each element in the material world is symbolic of spiritual truths.

Hence the centrality of the poet to Emerson's metaphysic, for the poet is, when working at full power, the individual who can transcend individuality, who through the professional manipulation of symbols and figures understands best the highest truths about the relationship between matter and spirit, which are to each other as the signifier is to the signified. Emerson consistently deals with poetry, as it was understood by Kant and Coleridge, as the product of the creative imagination. In this sense, any great spiritual thinker is a poet. Emerson's poet is not, however, the maker of *poems,* linguistic forms in measured language. His essay embodies instead, even more than Shelley's *Defence of Poetry,* a heaven-ascending compendium of romantic ideas about the poet as idealist.

Selected Bibliography

Buell, Lawrence. *Emerson.* Cambridge, MA: Belknap, 2003.

Foerster, Norman. *American Criticism: A Study in Literary Theory from Poe to the Present.* 1928; New York: Russell and Russell, 1962.

Hopkins, Vivian C. *Spires of Form: A Study of Emerson's Aesthetic Theory.* New York: Russell and Russell, 1965.

Matthiessen, F. O. *American Renaissance: Art and Expression in the Age of Emerson and Whitman.* New York: Oxford University Press, 1941.

Maulsby, David Lee. *Emerson: His Contribution to Literature.* Folcroft, PA: Folcroft Library Editions, 1973.

Michaud, Régis. *L'esthétique d'Emerson: La nature, l'art, l'histoire.* Paris: F. Alcan, 1927.

Paul, Sherman. *Emerson's Angle of Vision.* Cambridge: Harvard University Press, 1952.

Porte, Joel. *Representative Man: Emerson in His Time.* New York: Oxford University Press, 1979.

Porte, Joel, and Saundra Morris, eds. *The Cambridge Companion to Ralph Waldo Emerson.* Cambridge: Cambridge University Press, 1999.

Van Leer, David. *Emerson's Epistemology: The Argument of the Essays.* New York: Cambridge University Press, 1976.

Yoder, R. A. *Emerson and the Orphic Poet in America.* Berkeley: University of California Press, 1978.

The Poet

A moody child and wildly wise
Pursued the game with joyful eyes,
Which chose, like meteors, their way,
And rived the dark with private ray:
They overleapt the horizon's edge,
Searched with Apollo's privilege;
Through man, and woman, and sea, and star
Saw the dance of nature forward far;
Through worlds, and races, and terms, and times
Saw musical order, and pairing rhymes.[1]

Olympian bards who sung
Divine ideas below,
Which always find us young,
And always keep us so.[2]

Those who are esteemed umpires of taste are often persons who have acquired some knowledge of admired pictures or sculptures, and have an inclination for whatever is elegant; but if you inquire whether they are beautiful souls, and

[1]From Emerson's poem, "The Poet."

[2]From Emerson's "Ode to Beauty," lines 61–64.

whether their own acts are like fair pictures, you learn that they are selfish and sensual. Their cultivation is local, as if you should rub a log of dry wood in one spot to produce fire, all the rest remaining cold. Their knowledge of the fine arts is some study of rules and particulars, or some limited judgment of color or form, which is exercised for amusement or for show. It is a proof of the shallowness of the doctrine of beauty as it lies in the minds of our amateurs, that men seem to have lost the perception of the instant dependence of form upon soul. There is no doctrine of forms in our philosophy. We were put into our bodies, as fire is put into a pan to be carried about; but there is no accurate adjustment between the spirit and the organ, much less is the latter the germination of the former. So in regard to other forms, the intellectual men do not believe in any essential dependence of the material world on thought and volition. Theologians think it a pretty air-castle to talk of the spiritual meaning of a ship or a cloud, of a city or a contract, but they prefer to come again to the solid ground of historical evidence; and even the poets are contented with a civil and conformed manner of living, and to write poems from the fancy, at a safe distance from their own experience. But the highest minds of the world have never ceased to explore the double meaning, or shall I say the quadruple or the centuple of much more manifold meaning, of every sensuous fact; Orpheus, Empedocles, Heraclitus, Plato, Plutarch, Dante, Swedenborg, and the masters of sculpture, picture and poetry. For we are not pans and barrows, nor even porters of the fire and torch-bearers, but children of the fire, made of it, and only the same divinity transmuted and at two or three removes, when we know least about it. And this hidden truth, that the fountains whence all this river of Time and its creatures floweth are intrinsically ideal and beautiful, draws us to the consideration of the nature and functions of the Poet, or the man of Beauty; to the means and materials he uses, and to the general aspect of the art in the present time.

The breadth of the problem is great, for the poet is representative. He stands among partial men for the complete man, and apprises us not of his wealth, but of the common wealth. The young man reveres men of genius, because, to speak truly, they are more himself than he is. They receive of the soul as he also receives, but they more. Nature enhances her beauty, to the eye of loving men, from their belief that the poet is beholding her shows at the same time. He is isolated among his contemporaries by truth and by his art, but with this consolation in his pursuits, that they will draw all men sooner or later. For all men live by truth and stand in need of expression. In love, in art, in avarice, in politics, in labor, in games, we study to utter our painful secret. The man is only half himself, the other half is his expression.

Notwithstanding this necessity to be published, adequate expression is rare. I know not how it is that we need an interpreter, but the great majority of men seem to be minors, who have not yet come into possession of their own, or mutes, who cannot report the conversation they have had with nature. There is no man who does not anticipate a supersensual utility in the sun and stars, earth and water. These stand and wait to render him a peculiar service. But there is some obstruction or some excess of phlegm in our constitution, which does not suffer them to yield the due effect. Too feeble fall the impressions of nature on us to make us artists. Every touch should thrill. Every man should be so much an artist that he could report in conversation what had befallen him. Yet, in our experience, the rays or appulses have sufficient force to arrive at the senses, but not enough to reach the quick and compel the reproduction of themselves in speech. The poet is the person in whom these powers are in balance, the man without impediment, who sees and handles that which others dream of, traverses the whole scale of experience, and is representative of man, in virtue of being the largest power to receive and to impart.

For the universe has three children, born at one time, which reappear under different names in every system of thought, whether they be called cause, operation and effect; or, more poetically, Jove, Pluto, Neptune; or, theologically, the Father, the Spirit and the Son; but which we will call here the Knower, the Doer and the Sayer. These stand respectively for the love of truth, for the love of good, and for the love of beauty. These three are equal. Each is that which he is, essentially, so that he cannot be surmounted or analyzed, and each of these three has the power of the others latent in him and his own, patent.

The poet is the sayer, the namer, and represents beauty. He is a sovereign, and stands on the center. For the world is not painted or adorned, but is from the beginning beautiful; and God has not made some beautiful things, but Beauty is the creator of the universe. Therefore the poet is not any permissive potentate, but is emperor in his own right. Criticism is infested with a cant of materialism, which assumes that manual skill and activity is the first merit of all men, and disparages such as say and do not, overlooking the fact that some men, namely poets, are natural sayers, sent into the world to the end of expression, and confounds them with those whose province is action but who quit it to imitate the sayers. But Homer's words are as costly and admirable to Homer as Agamemnon's victories are to Agamemnon. The poet does not wait for the hero or the sage, but, as they act and think primarily, so he writes primarily what will and must be spoken, reckoning the others, though primaries also, yet, in respect to him, secondaries and servants; as sitters or models in the studio of a painter, or as assistants who bring building-materials to an architect.

For poetry was all written before time was, and whenever we are so finely organized that we can penetrate into that region where the air is music, we hear those primal warblings and attempt to write them down, but we lose ever and anon a word or a verse and substitute something of our own, and thus miswrite the poem. The men of more delicate ear write down these cadences more faithfully, and these transcripts, though imperfect, become the songs of the nations. For nature is as truly beautiful as it is good, or as it is reasonable, and must as much appear as it must be done, or be known. Words and deeds are quite indifferent modes of the divine energy. Words are also actions, and actions are a kind of words.

The sign and credentials of the poet are that he announces that which no man foretold. He is the true and only doctor; he knows and tells; he is the only teller of news, for he was present and privy to the appearance which he describes. He is a beholder of ideas and an utterer of the necessary and causal. For we do not speak now of men of poetical talents, or of industry and skill in meter, but of the true poet. I took part in a conversation the other day concerning a recent writer of lyrics, a man of subtle mind, whose head appeared to be a music-box of delicate tunes and rhythms, and whose skill and command of language we could not sufficiently praise. But when the question arose whether he was not only a lyrist but a poet, we were obliged to confess that he is plainly a contemporary, not an eternal man. He does not stand out of our low limitations, like a Chimborazo[3] under the line, running up from a torrid base through all the climates of the globe, with belts of the herbage of every latitude on its high and mottled sides; but this genius is the landscape-garden of a modern house, adorned with fountains and statues, with well-bred men and women standing and sitting in the walks and terraces. We hear, through all the varied music, the ground-tone of conventional life. Our poets are men of talents who sing, and not the children of music. The argument is secondary, the finish of the verses is primary.

For it is not meters, but a meter-making argument that makes a poem, — a thought so passionate and alive that like the spirit of a plant or an animal it has an architecture of its own, and adorns nature with a new thing. The thought and the form are equal in the order of time, but in the order of genesis the thought is prior to the form. The poet has a new thought; he has a whole new experience to unfold; he will tell us how it was with him, and all men will be the richer in his fortune. For the experience of each new age requires a new confession, and the world seems always waiting for its poet. I remember when I was young how much I was moved one morning by tidings that genius had appeared in a youth who sat near me at table. He had left his work and gone rambling none knew whither, and had written hundreds of lines, but could not tell whether that which was in him was therein told; he could tell nothing but that all was changed, — man, beast, heaven, earth and sea. How gladly we listened! how credulous! Society seemed to be compromised. We sat in the aurora of a sunrise which

[3]A mountain in Ecuador, near the equator ("under the line").

was to put out all the stars. Boston seemed to be at twice the distance it had the night before, or was much farther than that. Rome, — what was Rome? Plutarch and Shakespeare were in the yellow leaf, and Homer no more should be heard of. It is much to know that poetry has been written this very day, under this very roof, by your side. What! that wonderful spirit has not expired! These stony moments are still sparkling and animated! I had fancied that the oracles were all silent, and nature had spent her fires; and behold! all night, from every pore, these fine auroras have been streaming. Every one has some interest in the advent of the poet, and no one knows how much it may concern him. We know that the secret of the world is profound, but who or what shall be our interpreter, we know not. A mountain ramble, a new style of face, a new person, may put the key into our hands. Of course the value of genius to us is in the veracity of its report. Talent may frolic and juggle; genius realizes and adds. Mankind in good earnest have availed so far in understanding themselves and their work, that the foremost watchman on the peak announces his news. It is the truest word ever spoken, and the phrase will be the fittest, most musical, and the unerring voice of the world for that time.

All that we call sacred history attests that the birth of a poet is the principal event in chronology. Man, never so often deceived, still watches for the arrival of a brother who can hold him steady to a truth until he has made it his own. With what joy I begin to read a poem which I confide in as an inspiration! And now my chains are to be broken; I shall mount above these clouds and opaque airs in which I live, — opaque, though they seem transparent, — and from the heaven of truth I shall see and comprehend my relations. That will reconcile me to life and renovate nature, to see trifles animated by a tendency, and to know what I am doing. Life will no more be a noise; now I shall see men and women, and know the signs by which they may be discerned from fools and satans. This day shall be better than my birthday: then I became an animal; now I am invited into the science of the real. Such is the hope, but the fruition is postponed. Oftener it falls that this winged man, who will carry me into the heaven, whirls me into mists, then leaps and frisks about with me as it were from cloud to cloud, still affirming that he is bound heavenward; and I, being myself a novice, am slow in perceiving that he does not know the way into the heavens, and is merely bent that I should admire his skill to rise like a fowl or a flying fish, a little way from the ground or the water; but the all-piercing, all-feeding and ocular air of heaven that man shall never inhabit. I tumble down again soon into my old nooks, and lead the life of exaggerations as before, and have lost my faith in the possibility of any guide who can lead me thither where I would be.

But, leaving these victims of vanity, let us, with new hope, observe how nature, by worthier impulses, has insured the poet's fidelity to his office of announcement and affirming, namely by the beauty of things, which becomes a new and higher beauty when expressed. Nature offers all her creatures to him as a picture-language. Being used as a type, a second wonderful value appears in the object, far better than its old value; as the carpenter's stretched cord, if you hold your ear close enough, is musical in the breeze. "Things more excellent than every image," says Iamblichus,[4] "are expressed through images." Things admit of being used as symbols because nature is a symbol, in the whole, and in every part. Every line we can draw in the sand has expression; and there is no body without its spirit or genius. All form is an effect of character; all condition, of the quality of the life; all harmony, of health; and for this reason a perception of beauty should be sympathetic, or proper only to the good. The beautiful rests on the foundations of the necessary. The soul makes the body, as the wise Spenser teaches: —

So every spirit, as it is most pure,
And hath in it the more of heavenly light,
So it the fairer body doth procure
To habit in, and it more fairly dight,
With cheerful grace and amiable sight.
For, of the soul, the body form doth take,
For soul is form, and doth the body make.[5]

[4]Iamblichus was a fourth-century Neoplatonist.
[5]Edmund Spenser, "An Hymne in Honour of Beautie," 19:127–34.

Here we find ourselves suddenly not in a critical speculation but in a holy place, and should go very warily and reverently. We stand before the secret of the world, there where Being passes into Appearance and Unity into Variety.

The Universe is the externization of the soul. Wherever the life is, that bursts into appearance around it. Our science is sensual, and therefore superficial. The earth and the heavenly bodies, physics and chemistry, we sensually treat, as if they were self-existent; but these are the retinue of that Being we have. "The mighty heaven," said Proclus, "exhibits, in its transfigurations, clear images of the splendor of intellectual perceptions; being moved in conjunction with the unapparent periods of intellectual natures."[6] Therefore science always goes abreast with the just elevation of the man, keeping step with religion and metaphysics; or the state of science is an index of our self-knowledge. Since every thing in nature answers to a moral power, if any phenomenon remains brute and dark it is because the corresponding faculty in the observer is not yet active.

No wonder then, if these waters be so deep, that we hover over them with a religious regard. The beauty of the fable proves the importance of the sense; to the poet, and to all others; or, if you please, every man is so far a poet as to be susceptible of these enchantments of nature; for all men have the thoughts whereof the universe is the celebration. I find that the fascination resides in the symbol. Who loves nature? Who does not? Is it only poets, and men of leisure and cultivation, who live with her? No; but also hunters, farmers, grooms and butchers, though they express their affection in their choice of life and not in their choice of words. The writer wonders what the coachman or the hunter values in riding, in horses and dogs. It is not superficial qualities. When you talk with him he holds these at as slight a rate as you. His worship is sympathetic; he has no definitions, but he is commanded in nature by the living power which he feels to be there present. No imitation or playing of these things would content him; he loves the earnest of the north wind, of rain, of stone and wood and iron. A beauty not explicable is dearer than a beauty which we can see

to the end of. It is nature the symbol, nature certifying the supernatural, body overflowed by life which he worships with coarse but sincere rites.

The inwardness and mystery of this attachment drive men of every class to the use of emblems. The schools of poets and philosophers are not more intoxicated with their symbols than the populace with theirs. In our political parties, compute the power of badges and emblems. See the great ball which they roll from Baltimore to Bunker Hill! In the political processions, Lowell goes in a loom, and Lynn in a shoe, and Salem in a ship. Witness the cider-barrel, the log-cabin, the hickory-stick, the palmetto, and all the cognizances of party. See the power of national emblems. Some stars, lilies, leopards, a crescent, a lion, an eagle, or other figure which came into credit God knows how, on an old rag of bunting, blowing in the wind on a fort at the ends of the earth, shall make the blood tingle under the rudest or the most conventional exterior. The people fancy they hate poetry, and they are all poets and mystics!

Beyond the universality of the symbolic language we are apprised of the divineness of this superior use of things, whereby the world is a temple whose walls are covered with emblems, pictures and commandments of the Deity, — in this, that there is no fact in nature which does not carry the whole sense of nature; and the distinctions which we make in events and in affairs, of low and high, honest and base, disappear when nature is used as a symbol. Thought makes everything fit for use. The vocabulary of an omniscient man would embrace words and images excluded from polite conversation. What would be base, or even obscene, to the obscene, becomes illustrious, spoken in a new connection of thought. The piety of the Hebrew prophets purges their grossness. The circumcision is an example of the power of poetry to raise the low and offensive. Small and mean things serve as well as great symbols. The meaner the type by which a law is expressed, the more pungent it is, and the more lasting in the memories of men; just as we choose the smallest box or case in which any needful utensil can be carried. Bare lists of words are found suggestive to an imaginative and excited mind, as it is related of Lord Chatham that he was

[6]Proclus was a fifth-century Neoplatonist.

accustomed to read in Bailey's Dictionary when he was preparing to speak in Parliament. The poorest experience is rich enough for all the purposes of expressing thought. Why covet a knowledge of new facts? Day and night, house and garden, a few books, a few actions, serve us as well as would all trades and all spectacles. We are far from having exhausted the significance of the few symbols we use. We can come to use them yet with a terrible simplicity. It does not need that a poem should be long. Every word was once a poem. Every new relation is a new word. Also we use defects and deformities to a sacred purpose, so expressing our sense that the evils of the world are such only to the evil eye. In the old mythology, mythologists observe, defects are ascribed to divine natures, as lameness to Vulcan, blindness to Cupid, and the like, — to signify exuberances.

For as it is dislocation and detachment from the life of God that makes things ugly, the poet, who re-attaches things to nature and the Whole, — re-attaching even artificial things and violations of nature, to nature, by a deeper insight, — disposes very easily of the most disagreeable facts. Readers of poetry see the factory-village and the railway, and fancy that the poetry of the landscape is broken up by these; for these works of art are not yet consecrated in their reading; but the poet sees them fall within the great Order not less than the beehive or the spider's geometrical web. Nature adopts them very fast into her vital circles, and the gliding train of cars she loves like her own. Besides, in a centered mind, it signifies nothing how many mechanical inventions you exhibit. Though you add millions, and never so surprising, the fact of mechanics has not gained a grain's weight. The spiritual fact remains unalterable, by many or by few particulars; as no mountain is of any appreciable height to break the curve of the sphere. A shrewd country-boy goes to the city for the first time, and the complacent citizen is not satisfied with his little wonder. It is not that he does not see all the fine houses and know that he never saw such before, but he disposes of them as easily as the poet finds place for the railway. The chief value of the new fact is to enhance the great and constant fact of Life, which can dwarf any and every circumstance, and to which the belt of wampum and the commerce of America are alike.

The world being thus put under the mind for verb and noun, the poet is he who can articulate it. For though life is great, and fascinates and absorbs; and though all men are intelligent of the symbols through which it is named; yet they cannot originally use them. We are symbols and inhabit symbols; workmen, work, and tools, words and things, birth and death, all are emblems but we sympathize with the symbols, and being infatuated with the economical uses of things, we do not know that they are thoughts. The poet, by an ulterior intellectual perception, gives them a power which makes their old use forgotten, and puts eyes and a tongue into every dumb and inanimate object. He perceives the independence of the thought on the symbol, the stability of the thought, the accidency and fugacity of the symbol. As the eyes of Lynceus were said to see through the earth, so the poet turns the world to glass, and shows us all things in their right series and procession. For through that better perception he stands one step nearer to things, and sees the flowing or metamorphosis; perceives that thought is multiform; that within the form of every creature is a force impelling it to ascend into a higher form; and following with his eyes the life, uses the forms which express that life, and so his speech flows with the flowing of nature. All the facts of the animal economy, sex, nutriment, gestation, birth, growth, are symbols of the passage of the world into the soul of man, to suffer there a change and reappear a new and higher fact. He uses forms according to the life, and not according to the form. This is true science. The poet alone knows astronomy, chemistry, vegetation and animation, for he does not stop at these facts, but employs them as signs. He knows why the plain or meadow or space was strown with these flowers we call suns and moons and stars; why the great deep is adorned with animals, with men, and gods; for in every word he speaks he rides on them as the horses of thought.

By virtue of this science the poet is the Namer or Language-maker, naming things sometimes after their appearance, sometimes after their essence, and giving to every one its own name and not another's, thereby rejoicing the intellect, which delights in detachment or boundary. The poets made all the words, and therefore language is the archives of history, and, if we must say it, a sort of tomb of the muses. For though the origin of most of our words is forgotten, each word was at first a stroke of genius, and obtained currency because for the moment it symbolized the world to the first speaker and to the hearer. The etymologist finds the deadest word to have been once a brilliant picture. Language is fossil poetry. As the limestone of the continent consists of infinite masses of the shells of animalcules, so language is made up of images or tropes, which now, in their secondary use, have long ceased to remind us of their poetic origin. But the poet names the thing because he sees it, or comes one step nearer to it than any other. This expression or naming is not art, but a second nature, grown out of the first, as a leaf out of a tree. What we call nature is a certain self-regulated motion or change; and nature does all things by her own hands, and does not leave another to baptize her but baptizes herself; and this through the metamorphosis again. I remember that a certain poet[7] described it to me thus: —

Genius is the activity which repairs the decays of things, whether wholly or partly of a material and finite kind. Nature, through all her kingdoms, insures herself. Nobody cares for planting the poor fungus; so she shakes down from the gills of one agaric countless spores, any one of which, being preserved, transmits new billions of spores tomorrow or next day. The new agaric of this hour has a chance which the old one had not. This atom of seed is thrown into a new place, not subject to the accidents which destroyed its parent two rods off. She makes a man; and having brought him to ripe age, she will no longer run the risk of losing this wonder at a blow, but she detaches from him a new self, that the kind may be safe from accidents to which the individual is exposed. So when the soul of the poet has come to ripeness of thought, she detaches and sends away from it its poems or songs, — a fearless, sleepless, deathless progeny, which is not exposed to the accidents of the weary kingdom of time; a fearless, vivacious offspring, clad with wings (such was the virtue of the soul out of which they came) which carry them fast and far, and infix them irrecoverably into the hearts of men.

These wings are the beauty of a poet's soul. The songs, thus flying immortal from their mortal parent, are pursued by clamorous flights of censures, which swarm in far greater numbers and threaten to devour them; but these last are not winged. At the end of a very short leap they fall plump down and rot, having received from the souls out of which they came no beautiful wings. But the melodies of the poet ascend and leap and pierce into the deeps of infinite time.

So far the bard taught me, using his freer speech. But nature has a higher end, in the production of new individuals, than security, namely *ascension,* or the passage of the soul into higher forms. I knew in my younger days the sculptor who made the statue of the youth which stands in the public garden. He was, as I remember, unable to tell directly what made him happy or unhappy, but by wonderful indirections he could tell. He rose one day, according to his habit, before the dawn, and saw the morning break, grand as the eternity out of which it came, and for many days after, he strove to express this tranquillity, and lo! his chisel had fashioned out of marble the form of a beautiful youth, Phosphorus,[8] whose aspect is such that it is said all persons who look on it become silent. The poet also resigns himself to his mood, and that thought which agitated him is expressed, but *alter idem,*[9] in a manner totally new. The expression is organic, or the new type which things themselves take when liberated. As, in the sun, objects paint their images on the retina of the eye, so they, sharing the aspiration of the whole universe, tend to paint a far more delicate copy of their essence in his mind. Like the metamorphosis of things into higher organic forms is their change into melodies. Over everything stands its daemon or soul, and, as the form of the thing is reflected by the eye, so the soul of the thing is reflected by a melody. The sea, the mountain-ridge, Niagara, and every flower-bed, pre-exist, or super-exist, in precantations, which sail like odors in the air, and when any man goes by with an ear sufficiently fine, he overhears them and endeavors to write down the notes without diluting or depraving them. And herein is the

[7]The following passage is Emerson's own adaptation of Plato's *Phaedrus.*

[8]The morning star.
[9]The same thing in another way.

legitimation of criticism, in the mind's faith that the poems are a corrupt version of some text in nature with which they ought to be made to tally. A rhyme in one of our sonnets should not be less pleasing than the iterated nodes of a seashell, or the resembling difference of a group of flowers. The pairing of the birds is an idyl, not tedious as our idyls are; a tempest is a rough ode, without falsehood or rant; a summer, with its harvest sown, reaped and stored, is an epic song, subordinating how many admirably executed parts. Why should not the symmetry and truth that modulate these, glide into our spirits, and we participate the invention of nature?

This insight, which expresses itself by what is called Imagination, is a very high sort of seeing, which does not come by study, but by the intellect being where and what it sees; by sharing the path or circuit of things through forms, and so making them translucid to others. The path of things is silent. Will they suffer a speaker to go with them? A spy they will not suffer; a lover, a poet, is the transcendency of their own nature, — him they will suffer. The condition of true naming, on the poet's part, is his resigning himself to the divine *aura* which breathes through forms, and accompanying that.

It is a secret which every intellectual man quickly learns, that beyond the energy of his possessed and conscious intellect he is capable of a new energy (as of an intellect doubled on itself), by abandonment to the nature of things; that beside his privacy of power as an individual man, there is a great public power on which he can draw, by unlocking, at all risks, his human doors, and suffering the ethereal tides to roll and circulate through him; then he is caught up into the life of the Universe, his speech is thunder, his thought is law, and his words are universally intelligible as the plants and animals. The poet knows that he speaks adequately then only when he speaks somewhat wildly, or "with the flower of the mind"; not with the intellect used as an organ, but with the intellect released from all service and suffered to take its direction from its celestial life; or as the ancients were wont to express themselves, not with intellect alone but with the intellect inebriated by nectar. As the traveler who has lost his way throws his reins on his horse's neck and trusts to the instinct of the animal to find his road, so must we do with the divine animal who carries us through this world. For if in any manner we can stimulate this instinct, new passages are opened for us into nature; the mind flows into and through things hardest and highest, and the metamorphosis is possible.

This is the reason why bards love wine, mead, narcotics, coffee, tea, opium, the fumes of sandalwood and tobacco, or whatever other procurers of animal exhilaration. All men avail themselves of such means as they can, to add this extraordinary power to their normal powers; and to this end they prize conversation, music, pictures, sculpture, dancing, theaters, traveling, war, mobs, fires, gaming, politics, or love, or science, or animal intoxication, — which are several coarser or finer *quasi*-mechanical substitutes for the true nectar, which is the ravishment of the intellect by coming nearer to the fact. These are auxiliaries to the centrifugal tendency of a man, to his passage out into free space, and they help him to escape the custody of that body in which he is pent up, and of that jail-yard of individual relations in which he is enclosed. Hence a great number of such as were professionally expressers of Beauty, as painters, poets, musicians and actors, have been more than others wont to lead a life of pleasure and indulgence; all but the few who received the true nectar; and, as it was a spurious mode of attaining freedom, as it was an emancipation not into the heavens but into the freedom of baser places, they were punished for that advantage they won, by a dissipation and deterioration. But never can any advantage be taken of nature by a trick. The spirit of the world, the great calm presence of the Creator, comes not forth to the sorceries of opium or of wine. The sublime vision comes to the pure and simple soul in a clean and chaste body. That is not an inspiration, which we owe to narcotics, but some counterfeit excitement and fury. Milton says that the lyric poet may drink wine and live generously, but the epic poet, he who shall sing of the gods and their descent unto men, must drink water out of a wooden bowl. For poetry is not "Devil's wine," but God's wine. It is with this as it is with toys. We fill the hands and nurseries of our children with all manner of dolls, drums and horses; withdrawing their eyes from the plain face and sufficing objects of nature, the sun and moon, the animals, the water and stones, which should be their toys. So the poet's habit of living should be set on a key so low that the common influences should delight him. His cheerfulness should be the gift of the sunlight; the air should suffice for his inspiration, and he should be tipsy with water. That spirit which suffices quiet hearts, which seems to come forth to such from every dry knoll of sere grass, from every pine stump and half-imbedded stone on which the dull March sun shines, comes forth to the poor and hungry, and such as are of simple taste. If thou fill thy brain with Boston and New York, with fashion and covetousness, and wilt stimulate thy jaded senses with wine and French coffee, thou shalt find no radiance of wisdom in the lonely waste of the pine woods.

If the imagination intoxicates the poet, it is not inactive in other men. The metamorphosis excites in the beholder an emotion of joy. The use of symbols has a certain power of emancipation and exhilaration for all men. We seem to be touched by a wand which makes us dance and run about happily, like children. We are like persons who come out of a cave or cellar into the open air. This is the effect on us of tropes, fables, oracles and all poetic forms. Poets are thus liberating gods. Men have really got a new sense, and found within their world another world, or nest of worlds; for, the metamorphosis once seen, we divine that it does not stop. I will not now consider how much this makes the charm of algebra and the mathematics, which also have their tropes, but it is felt in every definition; as when Aristotle defines *space* to be an immovable vessel in which things are contained; — or when Plato defines a *line* to be a flowing point; or *figure* to be bound of solid; and many the like. What a joyful sense of freedom we have when Vitruvius announces the old opinion of artists that no architect can build any house well who does not know something of anatomy. When Socrates, in Charmides, tells us that the soul is cured of its maladies by certain incantations, and that these incantations are beautiful reasons, from which temperance is generated in souls; when Plato calls the world an animal, and Timaeus affirms that the plants also are animals; or affirms a man to be a heavenly tree, growing with his root, which is his head, upward; and, as George Chapman, following him, writes,

So in our tree of man, whose nervie root
Springs in his top; —

when Orpheus speaks of hoariness as "that white flower which marks extreme old age"; when Proclus calls the universe the statue of the intellect; when Chaucer, in his praise of "Gentilesse," compares good blood in mean condition to fire, which, though carried to the darkest house betwixt this and the mount of Caucasus, will yet hold its natural office and burn as bright as if twenty thousand men did it behold; when John saw, in the Apocalypse, the ruin of the world through evil, and the stars fall from heaven as the fig tree casteth her untimely fruit; when Aesop reports the whole catalogue of common daily relations through the masquerade of birds and beasts; — we take the cheerful hint of the immortality of our essence and its versatile habit and escapes, as when the gypsies say of themselves "it is in vain to hang them, they cannot die."

The poets are thus liberating gods. The ancient British bards had for the title of their order, "Those who are free throughout the world." They are free, and they make free. An imaginative book renders us much more service at first, by stimulating us through its tropes, than afterward when we arrive at the precise sense of the author. I think nothing is of any value in books excepting the transcendental and extraordinary. If a man is inflamed and carried away by his thought, to that degree that he forgets the authors and the public and heeds only this one dream which holds him like an insanity, let me read his paper, and you may have all the arguments and histories and criticism. All the value which attaches to Pythagoras, Paracelsus, Cornelius Agrippa, Cardan, Kepler, Swedenborg, Schelling, Oken, or any other who introduces questionable facts into his cosmogony, as angels, devils, magic, astrology, palmistry, mesmerism, and so on, is the certificate we have of departure from routine, and that here is a new witness. That also is the best success in conversation, the magic of liberty, which puts the world like a ball in our hands. How cheap even the liberty then seems; how mean to study, when an emotion communicates to the intellect the power to sap and upheave nature; how great the perspective! nations, times, systems, enter and disappear like threads in tapestry of large figure and many colors; dream delivers us to dream, and while the drunkenness lasts we will sell our bed, our philosophy, our religion, in our opulence.

There is good reason why we should prize this liberation. The fate of the poor shepherd, who, blinded and lost in the snowstorm, perishes in a drift within a few feet of his cottage door, is an emblem of the state of man. On the brink of the waters of life and truth, we are miserably dying. The inaccessibleness of every thought but that we are in, is wonderful. What if you come near to it; you are as remote when you are nearest as when you are farthest. Every thought is also a prison; every heaven is also a prison. Therefore we love the poet, the inventor, who in any form, whether in an ode or in an action or in looks and behavior, has yielded us a new thought. He unlocks our chains and admits us to a new scene.

This emancipation is dear to all men, and the power to impart it, as it must come from greater depth and scope of thought, is a measure of intellect. Therefore all books of the imagination endure, all which ascend to that truth that the writer sees nature beneath him, and uses it as his exponent. Every verse or sentence possessing this virtue will take care of its own immortality. The religions of the world are the ejaculations of a few imaginative men.

But the quality of the imagination is to flow, and not to freeze. The poet did not stop at the color or the form, but read their meaning; neither may he rest in this meaning, but he makes the same objects exponents of his new thought. Here is the difference betwixt the poet and the mystic, that the last nails a symbol to one sense, which was a true sense for a moment, but soon becomes old and false. For all symbols are fluxional; all language is vehicular and transitive, and is good, as ferries and horses are, for conveyance, not as farms and houses are, for homestead. Mysticism consists in the mistake of an accidental and individual symbol for an universal one. The morning-redness happens to be the favorite

meteor to the eyes of Jacob Behmen,[10] and comes to stand to him for truth and faith; and, he believes, should stand for the same realities to every reader. But the first reader prefers as naturally the symbol of a mother and child, or a gardener and his bulb, or a jeweler polishing a gem. Either of these, or of a myriad more, are equally good to the person to whom they are significant. Only they must be held lightly, and be very willingly translated into the equivalent terms which others use. And the mystic must be steadily told, — All that you say is just as true without the tedious use of that symbol as with it. Let us have a little algebra, instead of this trite rhetoric, — universal signs, instead of these village symbols, — and we shall both be gainers. The history of hierarchies seems to show that all religious error consisted in making the symbol too stark and solid, and was at last nothing but an excess of the organ of language.

Swedenborg, of all men in the recent ages, stands eminently for the translator of nature into thought. I do not know the man in history to whom things stood so uniformly for words. Before him the metamorphosis continually plays. Everything on which his eye rests, obeys the impulses of moral nature. The figs become grapes whilst he eats them. When some of his angels affirmed a truth, the laurel twig which they held blossomed in their hands. The noise which at a distance appeared like gnashing and thumping, on coming nearer was found to be the voice of disputants. The men in one of his visions, seen in heavenly light, appeared like dragons, and seemed in darkness; but to each other they appeared as men, and when the light from heaven shone into their cabin, they complained of the darkness, and were compelled to shut the window that they might see.

There was this perception in him which makes the poet or seer an object of awe and terror, namely that the same man or society of men may wear one aspect to themselves and their companions, and a

---

[10]Emerson probably means German mystic Jakob Böhme (1575–1624).

different aspect to higher intelligences. Certain priests, whom he describes as conversing very learnedly together, appeared to the children who were at some distance, like dead horses; and many the like misappearances. And instantly the mind inquires whether these fishes under the bridge, yonder oxen in the pasture, those dogs in the yard, are immutably fishes, oxen and dogs, or only so appear to me, and perchance to themselves appear upright men; and whether I appear as a man to all eyes. The Brahmins and Pythagoras propounded the same question, and if any poet has witnessed the transformation he doubtless found it in harmony with various experiences. We have all seen changes as considerable in wheat and caterpillars. He is the poet and shall draw us with love and terror, who sees through the flowing vest the firm nature, and can declare it.

I look in vain for the poet whom I describe. We do not with sufficient plainness or sufficient profoundness address ourselves to life, nor dare we chaunt our own times and social circumstance. If we filled the day with bravery, we should not shrink from celebrating it. Time and nature yield us many gifts, but not yet the timely man, the new religion, the reconciler, whom all things await. Dante's praise is that he dared to write his autobiography in colossal cipher, or into universality. We have had no genius in America, with tyrannous eye, which knew the value of our incomparable materials, and saw, in the barbarism and materialism of the times, another carnival of the same gods whose picture he so much admires in Homer; then in the Middle Age; then in Calvinism. Banks and tariffs, the newspaper and caucus, Methodism and Unitarianism, are flat and dull to dull people, but rest on the same foundations of wonder as the town of Troy and the temple of Delphi, and are as swiftly passing away. Our log-rolling, our stumps and their politics, our fisheries, our Negroes and Indians, our boasts and our repudiations, the wrath of rogues and the pusillanimity of honest men, the northern trade, the southern planting, the western clearing, Oregon and Texas, are yet unsung. Yet America is a poem in our eyes; its ample geography dazzles the imagination, and it will not wait long for meters. If I have not found that excellent combination of gifts in my countrymen which I seek, neither could I aid myself to fix the idea of the poet by reading now and then in Chalmers's collection of five centuries of English poets. These are wits more than poets, though there have been poets among them. But when we adhere to the ideal of the poets, we have our difficulties even with Milton and Homer. Milton is too literary, and Homer too literal and historical.

But I am not wise enough for a national criticism, and must use the old largeness a little longer, to discharge my errand from the muse to the poet concerning his art.

Art is the path of the creator to his work. The paths or methods are ideal and eternal, though few men ever see them; not the artist himself for years, or for a lifetime, unless he come into the conditions. The painter, the sculptor, the composer, the epic rhapsodist, the orator, all partake one desire, namely to express themselves symmetrically and abundantly, not dwarfishly and fragmentarily. They found or put themselves in certain conditions, as, the painter and sculptor before some impressive human figures; the orator into the assembly of the people; and the others in such scenes as each has found exciting to his intellect; and each presently feels the new desire. He hears a voice, he sees a beckoning. Then he is apprised, with wonder, what herds of daemons hem him in. He can no more rest; he says, with the old painter, "By God it is in me and must go forth of me." He pursues a beauty, half seen, which flies before him. The poet pours out verses in every solitude. Most of the things he says are conventional, no doubt; but by and by he says something which is original and beautiful. That charms him. He would say nothing else but such things. In our way of talking we say "That is yours, this is mine"; but the poet knows well that it is not his; that it is as strange and beautiful to him as to you; he would fain hear the like eloquence at length. Once having tasted this immortal ichor, he cannot have enough of it, and as an admirable creative power exists in these intellections, it is of the last importance that these things get spoken. What a little of all we know is said! What drops of all the sea of our science are baled up! and by what accident it is that these are exposed, when so many secrets sleep in nature! Hence the necessity of speech and song; hence these throbs and heart-beatings in the orator, at the door of the assembly, to the end namely that thought may be ejaculated as Logos, or Word.

Doubt not, O poet, but persist. Say "It is in me, and shall out." Stand there, balked and dumb, stuttering and stammering, hissed and hooted, stand and strive, until at last rage draw out of thee that *dream*-power which every night shows thee is thine own; a power transcending all limit and privacy, and by virtue of which a man is the conductor of the whole river of electricity. Nothing walks, or creeps, or grows, or exists, which must not in turn arise and walk before him as exponent of his meaning. Comes he to that power, his genius is no longer exhaustible. All the creatures by pairs and by tribes pour into his mind as into a Noah's ark, to come forth again to people a new world. This is like the stock of air for our respiration or for the combustion of our fireplace; not a measure of gallons, but the entire atmosphere if wanted. And therefore the rich poets, as Homer, Chaucer, Shakespeare, and Raphael, have obviously no limits to their works except the limits of their lifetime, and resemble a mirror carried through the street, ready to render an image of every created thing.

O poet! a new nobility is conferred in groves and pastures, and not in castles or by the swordblade any longer. The conditions are hard, but equal. Thou shalt leave the world, and know the muse only. Thou shalt not know any longer the times, customs, graces, politics, or opinions of men, but shall take all from the muse. For the time of towns is tolled from the world by funereal chimes, but in nature the universal hours are counted by succeeding tribes of animals and plants, and by growth of joy on joy. God wills also that thou abdicate a manifold and duplex life, and that thou be content that others speak for thee. Others shall be thy gentlemen and shall represent all courtesy and worldly life for thee; others shall do the great and resounding actions also. Thou shalt lie close hid with nature, and canst not be afforded to the Capitol or the Exchange. The world is full of renunciations and apprenticeships, and this is thine; thou must pass for a fool and a churl for a long season. This is the screen and sheath in which Pan has protected his well-beloved flower, and thou shalt be known only to thine own, and they shall console thee with tenderest love. And thou shalt not be able to rehearse the names of thy friends in thy verse, for an old shame before the holy ideal. And this is the reward; that the ideal shall be real to thee, and the impressions of the actual world shall fall like summer rain, copious, but not troublesome to thy invulnerable essence. Thou shalt have the whole land for thy park and manor, the sea for thy bath and navigation, without tax and without envy; the woods and the rivers thou shalt own, and thou shalt possess that wherein others are only tenants and boarders. Thou true land-lord! sea-lord! air-lord! Wherever snow falls or water flows, or birds fly, wherever day and night meet in twilight, wherever the blue heaven is hung by clouds or sown with stars, wherever are forms with transparent boundaries, wherever are outlets into celestial space, wherever is danger, and awe, and love, — there is Beauty, plenteous as rain, shed for thee, and though thou shouldst walk the world over, thou shalt not be able to find a condition inopportune or ignoble.

Karl Marx

1818–1883

Karl Marx, the chief philosopher and theorist of modern socialism, was born into a comfortable middle-class home in Trier, Germany. The son of a lawyer who converted from Judaism to Lutheranism, Marx studied law at Bonn and Berlin before turning to philosophy and taking his Ph.D. at Jena in 1841. He became editor of the *Rheinische Zeitung* in 1842, but his calls for radical reform led to its suppression in 1843. That same year he emigrated to Paris, where he began his lifelong partnership with Friedrich Engels, committed himself to socialism, and commenced his study of the works of the classical economists. Within a year he was expelled from France for his radical views, and he settled for the next three years in Brussels.

Marx's evolving theories, although recorded in 1846, were not published until 1932, as *The German Ideology.* In 1847 he joined the Communist League and with Engels wrote *The Communist Manifesto,* which was published in 1848 just before revolution swept the continent. Exiled from most European centers, in 1849 Marx settled permanently in London to a life of poverty, chronic illness, and arduous, unflagging devotion to the cause of world communism. *A Contribution to the Critique of Political Economy* was published in 1859, and the next twelve years saw the founding of the First International Working Men's Council (1864) and the publication of both the first volume of his monumental *Capital* (1867) and *The Civil War in France* (1871), an analysis of the brutally suppressed Paris Commune of 1871. Marx's last years, clouded by ill-health and by the deaths of his eldest daughter and wife, were less precarious financially owing to the pension that Engels settled on him in 1869.

Marx is usually classified as a "dialectical materialist." Like his teacher Hegel, Marx believed that historical transformations occur through a *dialectic* of thesis, antithesis, and synthesis, whereby each historical force calls into being its Other so that the two opposites negate each other and ultimately give rise to a third force, which transcends this opposition (see the headnote for Hegel, p. 369). But while Hegel was an idealist who believed in spiritual forces that bend and transform the material world, Marx was a materialist who contended that "it is not the consciousness of men that determines their being, but, on the contrary, their social being that determines their consciousness."

Marx argues in *The German Ideology* that the ultimate moving force of human history is economics, or perhaps one should use the older and broader term "political economy," since in Marxist thought the engine of change is a fusion of political and social as well as economic issues. Each society lives by certain "forces of production" — the methods and techniques by which it produces food, clothing, shelter, and the other necessities of life — and by the "social relations of production" these methods create. In an economy based on sheep-raising, for example, the shepherds work alone and relate primarily to the flock owner, while an economy based on manufacturing demands a division of labor, which in turn requires elaborate patterns of cooperation among workers and a hierarchy of managers. These modes of production and their accompanying social relations are the foundation *(Grundlage)* of a culture.

Marx posited that major historical changes occur not as a result of spiritual contradictions, as Hegel had thought, but because of economic ones. (It is in this sense that, as the cliché puts it, Marx stood Hegel on his head.) Feudalism, for example, was a relatively stable system as long as it was based on local agriculture; but as trade began to generate wealth, feudal rulers became rich and powerful by taxing it and secured their power by giving their towns and traders maximum freedom of action. By so doing, they created two rival centers of power, the feudal countryside and the bourgeois city. In the city, the merchants and manufacturers formed cooperative social relationships with one another and recognized their mutual class interests, which were not always in harmony with those of the agricultural feudatories. It was inevitable that eventually the bourgeoisie of the tightly organized city would gain ascendancy over the feudal lords, who were unaccustomed to cooperation. Conflict between feudal lords and the middle classes broke out most violently in bourgeois revolutions, like the English Civil War in the 1640s and the French Revolution of the 1790s. Marx devoted most of his efforts to demonstrating that capitalism was developing the same sorts of internal contradictions as feudalism and to predicting the course of the proletarian revolution that would displace it.

One of these key internal contradictions that flourish within capitalism, as Marx explained in the 1844 *Manuscripts*, involves the alienation of the worker. Workers depend on labor to provide the means to continue living, but the more dependent they become on this external factor, the less their lives belong to them. The products of their labor, too, belong to the capitalist, not to the workers. And Marx goes on to show that this alienation has a spiritual dimension as well: Laboring for themselves, workers affirm themselves, but in working for the capitalist, workers deny themselves. Work becomes a punishment they willingly inflict on themselves, a form of slavery from which they are free only while they are performing their animal functions of eating, sleeping, and reproducing themselves. They feel human only when they are behaving like animals, and like mere animals when they are working for their livelihood.

If the material foundation of a culture is economic, the spiritual superstructure *(Überbau)* finds expression in the culture's *ideology*. Marx used the term *ideology* to denote the culture's collective consciousness of its own being — comprising all its elaborate codes of law, politics, religion, art, and philosophy. By and large, the ideology of a society will be consistent with and supportive of its dominant material basis. One would expect, for example, that a society whose economy is based on herds of livestock (like that of the Old Testament Hebrews) would erect a paternalistic monarchy and believe in a fatherly God of their own profession ("The Lord is my shepherd; I shall not want"). This does not mean that art always expresses only the sentiments of the dominant class. All the implicit contradictions and conflicts within the economic base are likely to find some sort of expression within the ideological superstructure. For example, the aspiration of the capitalist middle classes to equality with the great lords emerges in literature as early as Chaucer's *Canterbury Tales,* in the Merchant's sentiment that tradesmen too may possess "gentilesse." But the term *ideology* in Marx's usage often has the connotation of "false consciousness," a set of illusions fostered by the dominant class in order to ensure social stability — and its own continued dominance. Marx was notoriously hostile to religious visions of equality in heaven that defused the proletarian desire for greater equality here on earth. Literature too might be "the opium of the people" to the extent that vicarious participation in the struggles of upper–middle-class life would undermine the natural solidarity of the working classes. Indeed, merely representing the world as it is as a coherent social structure has the conservative force of making the present into an icon: It implies that, since things are thus, they cannot be otherwise.

Art and literature are therefore dependent ideological features of the dominant socioeconomic system, changing as the base changes but usually reflecting the values of the hegemonic class. In part, this is true for obvious economic reasons: Making art is one way of earning a living and those who create art must flatter, or at least not affront, their patrons, those in a position to pay for it. Note, for example, the aristocratic bias of Shakespeare's plays in a day when theaters were licensed by the Crown and theatrical companies were sponsored by courtiers, or the fact that genre painting depicting bourgeois interiors with stunning detail arose in seventeenth-century Dutch society, which was dominated by merchants.

But beyond conscious pandering, there is Marx's broader assumption that individuals can only think the thoughts that are thinkable in their society. If Shakespeare regarded Jack Cade (in *2 Henry VI*) or the plebeian rebels of *Coriolanus* as bringers of chaos, chances are no one else in Shakespeare's still-feudal society could imagine how a democratic commonwealth might function. Similarly, Dickens was able to understand and represent the immense human misery produced by the Industrial Revolution and the gospel of wealth, but he was unable to envision any solution for that misery, other than a change of heart from acquisitiveness to benevolence on the part of wealthy capitalists.

On the other hand, in artistic matters at least, individuals can continue to think thoughts that their society no longer considers thinkable. Why the art of the distant past, based on social and political relationships that have long been superseded, should still have such an intense effect upon later audiences, is a question that long troubled Marx and his followers. The immense appeal of Greek art to the German middle class (including Marx) is one of the more perplexing issues Marx treats in the selection from *Contribution to a Critique of Political Economy.* It is a problem he solves as a collective case of emotional nostalgia: Just as our sentimental attachment to our own personal childhood depends on the fact that we will never have to live it over again, so Greek art reflects the idyllic childhood of the human race. For Marx, the lucidity and force of Greek literature and sculpture are captivating precisely because the hard life, the meager diet, the tyrants, and the slaves that produced it are things we no longer have to endure.

Selected Bibliography

Ahearn, Edward. *Marx and Modern Fiction*. New Haven: Yale University Press, 1989.

Berlin, Isaiah. *Karl Marx: His Life and Environment*, 4th ed. New York: Oxford University Press, 1996.

Demetz, Peter. *Marx, Engels, and the Poets: Origins of Marxist Literary Criticism*. Chicago: University of Chicago Press, 1967.

Dowling, William P. *Jameson, Althusser, Marx: An Introduction to The Political Unconscious*. Ithaca: Cornell University Press, 1984.

Foucault, Michel. *Remarks on Marx*. London: Autonomedia, 1991.

Kedourie, Elie. *Lectures on Hegel and Marx*. London: Blackwell, 1991.

Lifshitz, Mikhail. *The Philosophy of Art of Karl Marx*, 1933; London: Plato Press, 1973.

Marx, Karl, and Friedrich Engels. *Marx and Engels on Literature and Art*. St. Louis: Telos Press, 1973.

Mazlish, Bruce. *The Meaning of Karl Marx*. New York: Oxford University Press, 1984.

Wilson, H. T. *Marx's Critical-Dialectical Procedure*. New York: Routledge, 1990.

The Alienation of Labor[1] from *Economic and Philosophic Manuscripts of 1844*

In political economy[2] and its terminology, we have shown that the laborer sinks to the level of a commodity and indeed becomes the most miserable commodity possible, that the misery of the laborer stands in an inverse relationship to the power and size of his production, that the natural result of competition is the accumulation of capital in a few hands, which is the most frightening type of monopoly, that finally the difference between the ground-rentier[3] and the capitalist[4] as well as the difference between the farmer-renter and the factory laborer disappears and the entire society must fall into two classes: those with property and those propertyless souls who labor.

Political economy begins with the fact of private property. It does not explain this fact to us.

Translated by Richard Hooker.

[1] A note on terminology: Marx uses two terms to describe this phenomenon: *Entfremdung* (estrangement) and *Entäusserung* (alienation); these words are by and large interchangeable (the real title of this essay is "The Estrangement of Labor"). Estrangement means "dividing, separating" or "making strange or unfamiliar"; alienation means "making alien, making foreign." Estrangement of labor means "separating" labor from the laborer, separating the product of labor from the laborer, etc. Alienation of labor can be understood in largely the same terms: "making labor something foreign to the laborer," "making the product of labor something alien to the laborer."

[2] "Political economy" (in German: *Nationalökonomie*, "the economy of nations") is what we would call "macroeconomics," that is economics of large systems. The principal authors of political economy for Marx are Adam Smith, David Ricardo, David Hume, and Thomas Malthus.

[3] A "ground-rentier" for Marx is a person in a largely pre-industrial society who owns land and rents it out to people who produce goods from that land. Historically, in pre-industrial societies, land tends to accumulate in only a very few hands, and the bulk of people within these societies are renters. A ground-rentier is the prototype for the "capitalist" in an industrial society.

[4] The capitalist in European economics is understood as a person who accumulates the material of production, factories, raw materials, etc., and who pays laborers wages in order to produce various goods. The capitalist is essentially rational: he or she calculates the acquisition and disposal of materials and wage-labor in order to produce extra wealth, profit, which accumulates to the capitalist as a reward for accurate calculation.

It describes the material process of private property — by which it actually passes from hand to hand — in general, abstract formulas, which it then raises to the status of *laws*. It does not *understand* these laws, that is, it does not show how the existence of private property comes about. Political economy gives no explanation concerning the foundation of the division between labor and capital and between capital and land. When, for instance, it describes the relationship between wage-labor and the profit of capital, its fundamental point of departure is the interest of the capitalist, that is, it accepts as given what it should be explaining. In the same way, competition is used to explain everything. It is explained using external circumstances. How far these external, seemingly magical circumstances originate in a necessary process, political economy teaches us nothing. We have seen, that exchange itself appears to be some magical occurrence. The only wheels which political economy sets in motion are *greed* and *the war between the greedy: competition.* . . .

We have now to explain the real connections between private property, greed, the division of labor, capital, and land, the connection between exchange and competition, between value and the devaluation of humans, between monopoly and competition, etc., and between this entire estrangement and the money system. . . .

We must start our investigation from a *real* fact of political economy.

The laborer becomes poorer the more wealth he produces, indeed, the more powerful and wide-ranging his production becomes. The laborer becomes a cheaper commodity the more commodities he creates. With the *increase in value* of the world of things arises in direct proportion the *decrease of value* of human beings. Labor does not only produce commodities, it produces itself and the laborer as a *commodity*, and in relation to the level at which it produces commodities.[5]

This fact defines more than this: the object, which labor produces, its product, confronts the laborer as a strange thing, as a *power independent* of the producer. The product of labor is labor, which fixes itself in the object, it becomes a thing, it is the *objectification*[6] of labor. The "making real," or realization,[7] of labor is its objectification. The realization of labor appears in political economy as the "making unreal," or loss of reality[8] of, the laborer, objectification as the *loss of and slavery to the object*, appropriation as *estrangement*, as *alienation*.

The realization of labor manifests itself so much as a loss of reality, that the worker becomes unreal to the point that he starves to death. The objectification of labor manifests itself so much as a loss of objects, that the laborer is robbed of the most necessary objects, not only to maintain his own life, but even objects to labor with. Indeed, labor itself becomes an object, which only with the greatest effort and with random interruptions can be acquired. Appropriation of objects manifests itself so much as estrangement, that, the more objects the laborer produces, the fewer he can own and so he plunges deeper under the mastery of his product: capital.

In this definition — that the laborer is related to the *product of his labor* as a *strange, foreign* object, — lies all these consequences. For from this hypothesis the following becomes clear: the more the laborer labors, as well as the more powerful the alien, object world which he builds over himself becomes, the poorer he himself becomes, that is, his inner world, as he owns less. The same thing occurs in religion. The more people place in God, the less they retain in themselves. The laborer places his life in the object; but now it [his life] belongs less to him than to the object.

[5]What Marx is arguing is that wage-labor becomes something that can be bought and sold just like any other object. The more important products become, the less important humans as laborers become.

[6]*Vergegenständlichung*, often translated as "reification": "the making into a thing," that is, labor turned into an object. Labor becomes an object rather than a thing people do; as a result, the laborer becomes an object rather than a human being.

[7]*Verwirklichung*, meaning literally "the making real"; this is what the word "realization" means, that is, "making real."

[8]*Entwirklichung*, "making unreal"; this is the opposite of *Verwirklichung*, "the making real." In other words, labor "made real" in its product "makes unreal" the laborer; that is, the laborer is no longer a person who is laboring, but rather the products he or she produces. The products are more "valuable" than the people who produce them.

Therefore, the more this happens, the more deprived of objects the laborer becomes. What the product of his labor is, he is not. Therefore, the greater this product, the less he becomes. The alienation of the laborer in his product has this significance: since his labor is an object, not only does this labor become a separate existence, but it is also separate from him, independent, alien to his existence and a self-sufficient power which exists above him, that the life, which he has bestowed on the object, confronts him as something hostile and strange.

XXIII. Let us now treat more closely objectification, the production of the laborer and its estrangement, the loss of objects, its products.

The laborer can create nothing without nature, without the sensual, material world. It is the stuff on which labor realizes itself, on which it acts, and from which and with which it produces.

Just as nature provides the *means of life* for labor, in the sense that labor cannot live without objects, which it uses, but also it provides the *means of life* in a narrower sense, namely the means to sustain the physical existence of the *laborer*.

Therefore, the more the laborer through his labor appropriates the external world, sensuous nature, the more he deprives himself of the *means of life* in this double meaning: first, more and more the sensuous external world stops being an object proper to his labor, that is, to be a *means of life* to his labor; second: more and more the sensuous, external world stops being a *means of life* in the second sense: means to sustain the physical existence of the laborer.

In this double sense the worker becomes a slave to his objects; first: he receives an *object of labor*, that is, *labor*; and second: he receives a *means of subsistence*. In the first instance, he can exist as a laborer; in the second instance, he can exist as a *physical subject*. The result of this slavery is that he can maintain himself as a *physical subject* only if he is a *laborer*, and that he can maintain himself as a *laborer* only if he is a *physical subject*. . . .

Political economy hides completely the estrangement of labor in its real existence in that it does not treat the direct, unmediated *relationship between the* laborer *(labor) and production*. Labor produces wonderful works for the rich, but it produces poverty for the worker. It produces palaces, but hovels for the laborer. It produces beauty, but deformity for the laborer. It replaces labor with machines, but at the same time it throws the laborer into the most barbarous labor and at the same time makes the laborer into a machine. It produces intelligence and culture, but it produces senselessness and cretinism for the laborer.

The direct, unmediated relationship between labor and its product is the relationship between laborers and the objects of their production. The relationship between the wealthy man and the objects of production and to production itself is only a *consequence* of these primary relationships. And it, in fact, proves these primary relationships. We will treat these in later pages. Therefore, when we ask what the essential relationship of labor is, we are asking about the relationship of *labor* to production.

Up until this point, we have been treating the estrangement, the alienation of the laborer in only one sense, that is, his relationship to the products of his labor. But this estrangement displays itself not only in the products, but also in the *act of production*, in the *producing activity* itself. How can it happen that the laborer becomes estranged from the product of his activity if in the act of production he does not become estranged from himself? The product is only the sum of the activity, that is, production. If the product of labor is alienation, then production itself must be active alienation, the alienation of activity, the activity of alienation. In the estrangement of the objects of labor is summed up the estrangement, the alienation of the laboring activity itself. What then makes up the alienation of labor?

First, that labor is *alien* to the laborer, that is, that it does not make up his existence, that he does not affirm himself in his labor, but rather denies himself; he does not feel happy, but rather unhappy; he does not grow physically or mentally, but rather tortures his body and ruins his mind. The laborer feels himself first to be other than his labor and his labor to be other than himself. He is at home when he is not laboring, and when he is laboring he is not at home. His labor is not voluntary, but constrained, *forced labor*. Therefore, it does not meet a need, but rather it is a means to meet some need alien to it. Its estranged character becomes obvious when one sees that as soon as there is no physical or other coercion, labor is avoided like the plague. This alienated labor, this labor, in which human beings alienate themselves from themselves, is a labor of self-denial and self-torture. Finally, the alienation of labor manifests itself to the laborer in that this labor does not belong to him, but to someone else; it does not belong to him; while he is doing it he does not belong to himself, but to another. . . . the activity of the laborer is not his own activity. It belongs to someone else, it is the loss of his self.

The result, therefore, is that the human being (the laborer) does not feel himself to be free except in his animal functions: eating, drinking, and reproducing, at his best in his dwelling or in his clothing, etc., and in his human functions he is no more than an animal. The animal becomes human and the human becomes animal.

Eating, drinking, and reproducing, etc., are real human functions. However, in the abstraction which draws them out of the circle of other human activities and makes them the sole activity to be sought after, they are animal.

We have treated the act of the estrangement of practical, human activity, labor, as having two senses: 1.) The relationship of the laborer to the *product of labor* as a strange object having power over the laborer. This relationship is moreover a relationship to the sensuous, external world, in which the objects of nature confront the laborer as a dominating, strange, and hostile world. 2.) The relationship of labor as an *act of production* within labor itself. This relationship is a relationship of the laborer to his activity as if it were estranged, as if it didn't belong to him, activity as sorrow, strength as weakness, producing as emasculation, the laborer's *own* physical and mental energy, his individual life — what is life without activity? — is an activity which turns against him, does not depend on him, does not belong to him. This is *self-alienation*, where before we had the estrangement of the *thing*.

XXIV. We have now to demonstrate how a third aspect of *estranged labor* derives from these two.

Human beings . . . believe themselves to represent the real, living species, in that they believe themselves to be *universal*; they believe themselves to represent, therefore, a free being.

The life of the species, which applies to both humans and animals, consists in the physical, in which humans, just as animals, derive their life from inorganic nature, and the more universal man is in comparison to animals, the more universal is the sphere of inorganic nature, on which he lives. . . . Physically, human beings live only on the products of nature, whether they might appear in the form of food, heating, clothing, dwellings, etc. The universality of humanity manifests itself practically even in this universality, in which the whole of nature becomes the *inorganic* body of human beings, both inasmuch as it is 1.) a direct means for life, and 2.) the material, the object and the instrument of humanity's life-activity. Nature is the inorganic body of humanity insofar as it is not a human body. Humanity lives on nature, which means that nature is humanity's *body* with which it must remain in objective dialogue with or else perish. That the physical and mental life of human beings depends on nature has another sense: nature depends on itself since human beings are part of nature.

Estranged labor estranges human beings from 1.) nature and 2.) from themselves in their own active function, their life-activity, and from this, it estranges human beings from their *species*; estranged labor makes the *species-being* only the means for the individual life. First, it estranges the species life from the individual life, and second, it makes the individual life in its abstraction the purpose of the species life, even in its abstracted and estranged form.

First, labor appears to human beings, labor which is the *life-activity*, the *productive life* itself, only as a *means* to meet some need, the need of maintaining physical existence. The productive life is also the species life. It is life engendering life. In the art of life-activity lies the entire character of the species, its species-character, and the species-character of humanity consists of free, conscious activity. Life itself manifests itself as a *means of life*.

The animal is its own life-activity. It does not distinguish itself from it. It is *it*. Humanity makes its life-activity itself an object of will and consciousness. It has conscious life-activity. . . . Conscious life-activity distinguishes human beings from animals. . . . human life is an object that belongs to humanity, this is its species-being. For this reason its activity is free activity. Estranged labor reverses this relationship, so that human beings, because they have conscious being, make their life-activity, their *existence*, a means for existence. . . .

Estranged labor works thus:

3.) *the species-being of humanity*, in that nature and its mental species-property, confronts humanity as a strange existence, as a *means* to its *individual existence*. It estranges humanity from its own body, as it does the external, natural world, as it does his mental existence, his *human* existence.

4.) A direct consequence of the estrangement of the humans from the product of their labor, from their life-activity, from their species-being, is the *estrangement of humans* from *humans*. When a human confronts himself as a stranger, so he confronts another human as a stranger. The relationship of humans to their labor, to the product of their labor, and to themselves, is also the relationship of humans to each other, and to the labor of others and to the objects of others.

Moreover, this fact, that the individual is estranged from his species-being means that the individual is estranged from other individuals, since each of them is estranged from their own species-being.

The self-estrangement of individuals, in fact, every relationship in which individuals stand in relationship to themselves, is first realized in the relationship that individuals have with other individuals. Therefore, within the relationship of estranged labor, each individual treats others with the same standard and relative position that he finds himself in.

XXV. We began with a fact of political economy, the estrangement of the laborer and his production. We have produced the idea of this fact: *estranged, alienated* labor. We have analyzed this idea, therefore, we have analyzed a fact of political economy.

We must now see how this idea of estranged, alienated labor expresses and produces itself in actuality.

If the product of labor is foreign to me, if it confronts me as a foreign power, to whom, then, does it belong?

When my own activity does not belong to me, when it is a coerced activity, to whom then does it belong?

It belongs to a being *other* than myself.

Who is this being? . . .

This foreign being, to whom labor and the product of labor belong, in whose service labor and in whose benefit the product of labor is brought into existence, can only be another *human being*.

When the product of labor does not belong to the laborer, when a strange, foreign power confronts and dominates him, this can only be possible if it belongs *to a human being other than the laborer*. When his activity is agony to the laborer, it can only be a *delight* and joy to another. Not gods, not nature, but only human beings themselves can be this strange, foreign power over other human beings.

One should consider that in the proposition stated above man's relationship to himself is first and foremost an *objective, actual* relationship only through his relationship to other men. Therefore, if the product of his labor, of his labor turned into an object, is in relation to him a *foreign, hostile*, powerful, independent object, then his relation to it is such that it is an object mastered by a man foreign, hostile, powerful, and independent of him. If his own activity is for him an unfree activity, then he sees his activity as being done in the service, under the lordship, under the coercion and under the yoke of another man.

Every self-estrangement of people from themselves and from nature manifests itself in the relationship they establish between themselves, nature, and other humans differentiated from themselves. . . . In the practical, real world, self-estrangement can only manifest itself in the practical, real relationships between other people. The medium, through which estrangement arises, is itself *practical*. Through estranged labor, humans not only produce their relationship to the object and to the act of production as a power foreign and hostile to them, they produce also the relationship in which their production and their product stands in relationship to other humans as well as the relationship between themselves and other men. Just as the laborer gives birth to his own production as his reality, as his strife, just as he gives birth to his own product as a loss, as a product not to be owned by him, so he gives birth to the mastery of that man, who has produced nothing, over production and over the product. Just as he estranges himself from his own activity, so he confers ownership to a stranger over this activity which does not really belong to him.

We have until now treated only this relationship from the side of the laborer, and we shall later treat this relationship from the side of the non-laborer.

Therefore, through *estranged, alienated labor* the laborer gives birth to his relationship to his labor as something alien and external to him. This relationship of the laborer to his labor gives birth to the relationship of that labor to the capitalist, or whatever one wishes to name the "labor-master." *Private property* is also the product, the result, the natural consequence of *alienated labor*, of the alienated relationship of the laborer to nature and to himself.

Therefore, private property arises from the analysis of the idea of *alienated labor*, that is, of *alienated humanity*, of estranged labor, of estranged life, of *estranged* humanity.

In political economy we have derived this idea of *alienated labor* (of *alienated life*) as a result of the *circulation of private property*. But it is manifest in the analysis of this idea that even though private property appears as the ground, as the foundation of alienated labor, it is rather the consequence of it . . .

This explanation can shed light on several conflicts unsolved until now:

1.) Political economy begins with the notion that labor is the soul of production, yet it gives nothing to labor and everything to private property. . . . We now see, however, that this blatant contradiction is a contradiction of *estranged labor* with itself and that political economy only has drawn out the laws of estranged labor.

We can also see that wages and private property are identical: wages, which is the product, the object of labor, for which labor sells itself, are the necessary consequence of the estrangement of labor, just as in wage labor work itself is not an end in itself, but rather appears as a servant of the wage. . . .

XXVI. A coerced *rise in wages*, therefore . . . is nothing more than a better *salary for slaves* and would not recover for the laborer or for labor its human meaning and dignity.

Indeed, the *equality of salaries* . . . would only change the relationship of each laborer to his labor into the relationship of all humans to their labor. Society would then become an abstract capitalist.

Wages are an unmediated, direct result of estranged labor, and estranged labor is the unmediated, direct source of private property. If the one falls, the other must fall.

2.) From the relationship of estranged labor to private property follows the conclusion that the liberation of society from private property, etc., from servitude, expresses its *political* form in the *emancipation of the laborer*, and not only the emancipation of the laborer, for in the emancipation of the laborer is contained the emancipation of all humanity, and it contains this because the entirety of human servitude is involved in the relationship of the laborer to production and all relationships of servitude are only modifications and consequences of this primary relationship.

Consciousness Derived from Material Conditions from *The German Ideology*

The premises from which we begin are not arbitrary ones, not dogmas, but real premises from which abstraction can only be made in the imagination. They are the real individuals, their activity, and the material conditions under which they live, both those which they find already existing and those produced by their activity. These premises can thus be verified in a purely empirical way.

The first premise of all human history is, of course, the existence of living human individuals. Thus the first fact to be established is the physical organization of these individuals and their consequent relation to the rest of nature. Of course, we cannot here go either into the actual physical nature of man, or into the natural conditions in which man finds himself — geological, orohydrographical, climatic, and so on. The writing of history must always set out from these natural bases and their modification in the course of history through the action of man.

Men can be distinguished from animals by consciousness, by religion, or anything else you like. They themselves begin to distinguish themselves from animals as soon as they begin to *produce* their means of subsistence, a step which is conditioned by their physical organization. By producing their means of subsistence men are indirectly producing their actual material life.

The way in which men produce their means of subsistence depends first of all on the nature of the actual means they find in existence and have to reproduce. This mode of production must not be considered simply as being the reproduction of the physical existence of the individuals. Rather it is a definite form of activity of these individuals, a definite form of expressing their life, a definite *mode of life* on their part. As individuals express their life, so they are. What they are, therefore, coincides with their production, both with *what* they produce and with *how* they produce. The nature of individuals thus depends on the material conditions determining their production.

This production only makes its appearance with the increase of population. In its turn this presupposes the intercourse of individuals with one another. The form of this intercourse is again determined by production.

The relations of different nations among themselves depend upon the extent to which each has developed its productive forces, the division of labor, and internal intercourse.[1] This statement is generally recognized. But not only the relation of one nation to others, but also the whole internal structure of the nation itself depends on the stage of development reached by its production and its internal and external intercourse. How far the productive forces of a nation are developed is shown most manifestly by the degree to which the division of labor has been carried. Each new productive force, insofar as it is not merely a quantitative extension of productive forces already known, (for instance, the bringing into cultivation of fresh land), brings about a further development of the division of labor.

The division of labor inside a nation leads at first to the separation of industrial and commercial from agricultural labor, and hence to the separation of town and country and a clash of interests between them. Its further development leads to the separation of commercial from industrial labor. At the same time through the division of labor there develop further, inside these various branches, various divisions among the individuals cooperating in definite kinds of labor. The relative position of these individual groups is determined by the methods employed in

---

Translated by R. Pascal.

[1]Markets within the economy of the nation.

agriculture, industry, and commerce (patriarchalism, slavery, estates, classes). These same conditions are to be seen (given a more developed intercourse) in the relations of different nations to one another.

The various stages of development in the division of labor are just so many different forms of ownership; i.e., the existing stage in the division of labor determines also the relations of individuals to one another with reference to the material, instrument, and product of labor.

The first form of ownership is tribal ownership. It corresponds to the undeveloped stage of production, at which a people lives by hunting and fishing, by the rearing of beasts or, in the highest stage, agriculture. In the latter case it presupposes a great mass of uncultivated stretches of land. The division of labor is at this stage still very elementary and is confined to a further extension of the natural division of labor imposed by the family. The social structure is therefore limited to an extension of the family; patriarchal family chieftains; below them the members of the tribe; finally slaves. The slavery latent in the family only develops gradually with the increase of population, the growth of wants, and with the extension of external relations, of war or of trade.

The second form is the ancient communal and State ownership which proceeds especially from the union of several tribes into a city by agreement or by conquest, and which is still accompanied by slavery. Beside communal ownership we already find movable, and later also immovable, private property developing, but as an abnormal form subordinate to communal ownership. It is only as a community that the citizens hold power over their laboring slaves, and on this account alone, therefore, they are bound to the form of communal ownership. It is the communal private property which compels the active citizens to remain in this natural form of association over against their slaves. For this reason the whole structure of society based on this communal ownership, and with it the power of the people, decays in the same measure as immovable private property evolves. The division of labor is already more developed. We already find the antagonism of town and country; later the antagonism between those states which represent town interests and those which represent country, and inside the towns themselves the antagonism between industry and maritime commerce. The class relation between citizens and slaves is now completely developed.

The whole interpretation of history appears to be contradicted by the fact of conquest. Up till now violence, war, pillage, rape, and slaughter, etc. have been accepted as the driving force of history. Here we must limit ourselves to the chief points and take therefore only a striking example — the destruction of an old civilization by a barbarous people and the resulting formation of an entirely new organization of society. (Rome and the barbarians; Feudalism and Gaul; the Byzantine Empire and the Turks.) With the conquering barbarian people war itself is still, as hinted above, a regular form of intercourse, which is the more eagerly exploited as the population increases, involving the necessity of new means of production to supersede the traditional and, for it, the only possible, crude mode of production. In Italy it was, however, otherwise. The concentration of landed property (caused not only by buying-up and indebtedness but also by inheritance, since loose living being rife and marriage rare, the old families died out and their possessions fell into the hands of a few) and its conversion into grazing-land (caused not only by economic forces still operative today but by the importation of plundered and tribute-corn and the resultant lack of demand for Italian corn) brought about the almost total disappearance of the free population. The very slaves died out again and again, and had constantly to be replaced by new ones. Slavery remained the basis of the whole productive system. The plebeians, mid-way between freemen and slaves, never succeeded in becoming more than a proletarian rabble. Rome indeed never became more than a city; its connection with the provinces was almost exclusively political and could therefore easily be broken again by political events.

With the development of private property, we find here for the first time the same conditions which we shall find again, only on a more extensive scale, with modern private property. On the one hand the concentration of private property, which began very early in Rome (as the Licinian agrarian law[2] proves), and proceeded very rapidly from the time of the civil wars and especially under the Emperors; on the other hand, coupled with this, the transformation of the plebeian small peasantry into a proletariat, which, however, owing to its intermediate position between propertied citizens and slaves, never achieved an independent development.

The third form of ownership is feudal or estate-property. If antiquity started out from the town and its little territory, the Middle Ages started out from the country. This different starting-point was determined by the sparseness of the population at that time, which was scattered over a large area and which received no large increase from the conquerors. In contrast to Greece and Rome, feudal development therefore extends over a much wider field, prepared by the Roman conquests and the spread of agriculture at first associated with it. The last centuries of the declining Roman Empire and its conquest by the barbarians destroyed a number of productive forces; agriculture had declined, industry had decayed for want of a market, trade had died out or been violently suspended, the rural and urban population had decreased. From these conditions and the mode of organizations of the conquest determined by them, feudal property developed under the influence of the Germanic military constitution. Like tribal and communal ownership, it is based on a community; but the directly producing class standing over against it is not, as in the case of the ancient community, the slaves, but the enserfed small peasantry. As soon as feudalism is fully developed, there also arises antagonism to the towns. The hierarchical system of land ownership, and the armed bodies of retainers associated with it, gave the nobility power over the serfs. This feudal organization was, just as much as the ancient communal ownership, an association against a subjected producing class; but the form of association and the relation to the direct producers were different because of the different conditions of production.

This feudal organization of land-ownership had its counterpart in the towns in the shape of corporative property, the feudal organization of trades. Here property consisted chiefly in the labor of each individual person. The necessity for association against the organized robber-nobility, the need for communal covered markets in an age when the industrialist was at the same time a merchant, the growing competition of the escaped serfs swarming into the rising towns, the feudal structure of the whole country: these combined to bring about the guilds. Further, the gradually accumulated capital of individual craftsmen and their stable numbers, as against the growing population, evolved the relation of journeyman and apprentice, which brought into being in the towns a hierarchy similar to that in the country.

Thus the chief form of property during the feudal epoch consisted on the one hand of landed property with serf-labor chained to it, and on the other of individual labor with small capital commanding the labor of journeymen. The organization of both was determined by the restricted conditions of production — the small-scale and primitive cultivation of the land, and the craft type of industry. There was little division of labor in the heyday of feudalism. Each land bore in itself the conflict of town and country and the division into estates was certainly strongly marked; but apart from the differentiation of princes, nobility, clergy, and peasants in the country, and masters, journeymen, apprentices, and soon also the rabble of casual laborers in the towns, no division of importance took place. In agriculture it was rendered difficult by the strip-system, beside which the cottage industry of the peasants themselves emerged as another factor. In industry there was no division of labor at all in the individual trades themselves, and very little between them. The separation of industry and commerce was found already in existence in older towns; in the newer it only developed later, when the towns entered into mutual relations.

The grouping of larger territories into feudal kingdoms was a necessity for the landed nobility as for the towns. The organization of the ruling class, the nobility, had, therefore, everywhere a monarch at its head.

[2]A law dating to the early days of the Republic that prevented the dispersal of estates by providing that the eldest son inherited the landed property.

The fact is, therefore, that definite individuals who are productively active in a definite way enter into these definite social and political relations. Empirical observation must in each separate instance bring out empirically, and without any mystification and speculation, the connection of the social and political structure with production. The social structure and the State are continually evolving out of the life-process of definite individuals, but of individuals, not as they may appear in their own or other people's imagination, but as they really are; i.e., as they are effective, produce materially, and are active under definite material limits, presuppositions, and conditions independent of their will.

The production of ideas, of conceptions, of consciousness, is at first directly interwoven with the material activity and the material intercourse of men, the language of real life. Conceiving, thinking, the mental intercourse of men, appear at this stage as the direct efflux of their material behavior. The same applies to mental production as expressed in the language of the politics, laws, morality, religion, metaphysics of a people. Men are the producers of their conceptions, ideas, etc. — real, active men, as they are conditioned by a definite development of their productive forces and of the intercourse corresponding to these, up to its furthest forms. Consciousness can never be anything else than conscious existence, and the existence of men is their actual life-process. If in all ideology men and their circumstances appear upside down as in a *camera obscura*,[3] this phenomenon arises just as much from their historical life-process as the inversion

[3] Marx refers to the fact that the lens of a camera inverts the image while projecting it onto the plate or film.

of objects on the retina does from their physical life-process.

In direct contrast to German philosophy which descends from heaven to earth, here we ascend from earth to heaven. That is to say, we do not set out from what men say, imagine, conceive, nor from men as narrated, thought of, imagined, conceived, in order to arrive at men in the flesh. We set out from real, active men, and on the basis of their real life-process we demonstrate the development of the ideological reflexes and echoes of this life-process. The phantoms formed in the human brain are also, necessarily, sublimates of their material life-process, which is empirically verifiable and bound to material premises. Morality, religion, metaphysics, all the rest of ideology and their corresponding forms of consciousness, thus no longer retain the semblance of independence. They have no history, no development; but men, developing their material production and their material intercourse, alter, along with this their real existence, their thinking and the products of their thinking. Life is not determined by consciousness, but consciousness by life. In the first method of approach the starting point is consciousness taken as the living individual; in the second it is the real living individuals themselves, as they are in actual life, and consciousness is considered solely as *their* consciousness.

This method of approach is not devoid of premises. It starts out from the real premises and does not abandon them for a moment. Its premises are men, not in any fantastic isolation or abstract definition, but in their actual, empirically perceptible process of development under definite conditions. As soon as this active life-process is described, history ceases to be a collection of dead facts as it is with the empiricists (themselves still abstract), or an imagined activity of imagined subjects, as with the idealists.

On Greek Art in Its Time from *A Contribution to the Critique of Political Economy*

THE MODE OF PRODUCTION OF MATERIAL LIFE DETERMINES THE SOCIAL, POLITICAL, AND INTELLECTUAL PROCESSES OF LIFE

In the social production which men carry on they enter into definite relations that are indispensable and independent of their will; these relations of production correspond to a definite stage of development of their material forces of production. The sum total of these relations of production constitutes the economic structure of society — the real foundation, on which rises a legal and political superstructure and to which correspond definite forms of social consciousness. The mode of production in material life determines the social, political, and intellectual life processes in general. It is not the consciousness of men that determines their being, but, on the contrary, their social being that determines their consciousness. At a certain stage of their development, the material forces of production in society come in conflict with the existing relations of production or — what is but a legal expression for the same thing — with the property relations within which they have been at work before. From forms of development of the forces of production these relations turn into their fetters. Then begins an epoch of social revolution. With the change of the economic foundation the entire immense superstructure is more or less rapidly transformed. In considering such transformations a distinction should always be made between the material transformation of the economic conditions of production which can be determined with the precision of natural science, and the legal, political, religious, aesthetic, or philosophic — in short, ideological — forms in which men become conscious of this conflict and

Translated by Nahum Isaac Stone.

fight it out. Just as our opinion of an individual is not based on what he thinks of himself, so can we not judge of such a period of transformation by its own consciousness, on the contrary this consciousness must be explained rather from the contradictions of material life, from the existing conflict between the social forces of production and the relations of production. No social order ever disappears before all the productive forces for which there is room in it have been developed; and new higher relations of production never appear before the material conditions of their existence have matured in the womb of the old society itself. Therefore, mankind always sets itself only such tasks as it can solve; since, looking at the matter more closely, we will always find that the task itself arises only when the material conditions necessary for its solution already exist or are at least in the process of formation. In broad outlines we can designate the Asiatic, the ancient, the feudal, and the modern bourgeois modes of production as so many epochs in the progress of the economic formation of society. The bourgeois relations of production are the last antagonistic form of the social process of production — antagonistic not in the sense of individual antagonism, but of one arising from the social conditions of life of the individuals; at the same time the productive forces developing in the womb of bourgeois society create the material conditions for the solution of that antagonism. This social formation constitutes, therefore, the closing chapter of the prehistoric stage of human society.

It is well known that certain periods of highest development of art stand in no direct connection with the general development of society, nor with the material basis and the skeleton structure of its organization. Witness the example of the Greeks as compared with the modern nations or even Shakespeare. As regards certain forms of art, as e.g., the epos, it is admitted that they can never be produced in the world-epoch making form as soon as art as such comes into existence; in other words, that in the domain of art certain important forms of it are possible only at a low stage of its development. If that be true of the mutual relations of different forms of art within the domain of art itself, it is far less surprising that the same is true of the relation of art as a whole to the general development of society. The difficulty lies only in the general formulation of these contradictions. No sooner are they specified than they are explained. Let us take for instance the relation of Greek art and of that of Shakespeare's time to our own. It is a well-known fact that Greek mythology was not only the arsenal of Greek art, but also the very ground from which it had sprung. Is the view of nature and of social relations which shaped Greek imagination and Greek [art] possible in the age of automatic machinery, and railways, and locomotives, and electric telegraphs? Where does Vulcan come in as against Roberts & Co.; Jupiter, as against the lightning rod; and Hermes, as against the Credit Mobilier?[1] All mythology masters and dominates and shapes the forces of nature in and through the imagination; hence it disappears as soon as man gains mastery over the forces of nature. What becomes of the Goddess Fame side by side with Printing House Square?[2] Greek art presupposes the existence of Greek mythology; i.e., that nature and even the form of society are wrought up in popular fancy in an unconsciously artistic fashion. That is its material. Not, however, any mythology taken at random, nor any accidental

---

[1]Marx wittily compares ancient and modern institutions; Vulcan was the god of manufactures, while Roberts & Co. was a munitions maker; Jupiter controlled the lightning as now the lightning rod does; Hermes was the god of thieves, while the Credit Mobilier was a large financial institution.
[2]Where the London *Times* was printed.

unconsciously artistic elaboration of nature (including under the latter all objects, hence [also] society). Egyptian mythology could never be the soil or womb which would give birth to Greek art. But in any event [there had to be] a mythology. In no event [could Greek art originate] in a society which excludes any mythological explanation of nature, any mythological attitude towards it and which requires from the artists an imagination free from mythology.

Looking at it from another side: is Achilles possible side by side with powder and lead? Or is the *Iliad* at all compatible with the printing press and steam press? Does not singing and reciting and the muses necessarily go out of existence with the appearance of the printer's bar, and do not, therefore, disappear the prerequisites of epic poetry?

But the difficulty is not in grasping the idea that Greek art and epos are bound up with certain forms of social development. It rather lies in understanding why they still constitute with us a source of aesthetic enjoyment and in certain respects prevail as the standard and model beyond attainment.

A man can not become a child again unless he becomes childish. But does he not enjoy the artless ways of the child and must he not strive to reproduce its truth on a higher plane? Is not the character of every epoch revived perfectly true to nature in child nature? Why should the social childhood of mankind, where it had obtained its most beautiful development, not exert an eternal charm as an age that will never return? There are ill-bred children and precocious children. Many of the ancient nations belong to the latter class. The Greeks were normal children. The charm their art has for us does not conflict with the primitive character of the social order from which it had sprung. It is rather the product of the latter, and is rather due to the fact that the unripe social conditions under which the art arose and under which alone it could appear can never return.

Matthew Arnold
1822–1888

Matthew Arnold was born at Laleham, Middlesex, but in 1828 moved to Rugby, where his father Dr. Thomas Arnold, the sage and humane spirit of *Tom Brown's School Days,* had been appointed headmaster. Arnold went to Winchester, then to Rugby, to Balliol College of Oxford, and then to a fellowship at Oriel. In 1851 Arnold left academia, became an inspector of schools (a position he held for thirty-five years), and married Frances Lucy Wightman. His chief volumes of poetry were *Empedocles on Etna* (1852), *Poems* (1853), *Poems,* Second Series (1855), *Merope, a Tragedy* (1858), and *New Poems* (1867). His chief critical publications were *Essays in Criticism,* First Series (1865), *Culture and Anarchy* (1869), *Literature and Dogma* (1873), and *Essays in Criticism,* Second Series (1888). Arnold was elected professor of poetry at Oxford in 1857 and held the position for ten years. He died unexpectedly in 1888.

Some passages in Arnold's criticism have struck commentators as Aristotelian, notably a section from his preface to *Poems* (1853), which insists that human action, rather than the consciousness of the poet, is the true subject of poetry:

> What are the eternal objects of poetry, among all nations and at all times? They are actions; human actions; possessing an inherent interest in themselves, and which are to be communicated in an interesting manner by the art of the poet. Vainly will the latter imagine that he has everything in his power; that he can make an intrinsically inferior action ... delightful ... by his treatment of it.... I fearlessly assert that *Hermann and Dorothea, Childe Harold, Jocelyn, The Excursion,* leave the reader cold in comparison with the effect produced on him by the latter books of the *Iliad,* by the *Oresteia,* or by the episode of Dido....

If to know and to cite Aristotle is to be Aristotelian, then Arnold was one of the most loyal Aristotelians the nineteenth century produced. Indeed, in both of the essays included here, Arnold quotes or alludes to *Poetics,* Chapter 9, that poetry is a higher thing than history, because poetry is *philosophoteron kai spoudaioteron,* the more philosophical and more nobly serious human activity.

But in fact, Arnold's conception of literature is far from the gist and method of the *Poetics.* For Aristotle the poem's only duty is to be good in the way of its kind, and he resolutely differentiated between the genres of poetry and between poetry and all other forms of creativity. Aristotle's sense of the discreteness of activities and the primacy of form over content — both intellectual and spiritual — would be totally foreign to Arnold's way of thinking. For Arnold, form as an issue in itself never comes up.

Even the word *criticism* in "The Function of Criticism at the Present Time" (1864) is far broader than *literary* criticism: It denominates literature itself as a "criticism of life." Literature and literary criticism alike engage in a comprehensive critique of the entire culture. And while Arnold seems at times to be discussing literature as such, art is never for art's sake: Literature is of interest to him primarily as an index to and a banner of the society that produced it. In this sense Arnold is as holistic a critic as Plato in *Republic,* Book X. In another sense, however, Arnold entirely inverts Plato, for he views art as one possible salvation for an inhumane society rather than as a potential source of pollution in a utopia. Instead of being, as in Plato, a distorting mirror of reality, art for Arnold is one way of increasing the accuracy of one's spiritual vision — and a corrective for the illusions of political propaganda.

In one passage of "The Function of Criticism," for example, Arnold quotes some of the dithyrambically optimistic oratory of contemporary parliamentarians Charles Adderley and John Arthur Roebuck, who viewed Victorian society as not merely perfectible but as nearly perfected. Arnold responds not with a quotation from the classics but rather with a sordid newspaper paragraph about a "shocking child murder" committed at Nottingham by a workhouse girl named Wragg. Arnold asks us to imagine "the workhouse, the dismal Mapperly hills . . . the gloom, the smoke, the cold, the strangled illegitimate child. . . . And the final touch, — short, bleak, and inhuman: *Wragg is in custody.*" The passage is astonishing in a work of literary criticism. In a way, though, it is the center of the essay. This quotation represents the lowest level at which literature — the imaginative recreation of human existence — can be "criticism of life": minimally, by ironically exploding the pretenses of current ideology. But criticism of life has other phases. At its best literature can reawaken in us a sense of what it would mean to be fully human — a reawakening that Arnold sensed was needed more than ever in his mechanical age.

Because of what literature is capable of at its best, Arnold is concerned that we recognize what is best and not mistake cheaper merchandise for the genuine article. This form of elitism inspired "The Study of Poetry" (1880) and its doctrine of "touchstones" — lines of poetry that supposedly characterize the highest flights of the human spirit. When we hear a line of poetry, Arnold recommends that we compare it immediately to those lines in literature that are most sublime: "*In la sua voluntade è nostra pace*" from Dante's *Paradiso,* or "Absent thee from felicity awhile" from *Hamlet.*

As a method of literary criticism, "touchstonery" had been exploded a century before, in Johnson's *Preface to Shakespeare* (p. 216): "He that tries to recommend [Shakespeare] by select quotations, will succeed like the pedant in Hierocles, who, when he offered his house to sale, carried a brick in his pocket as a specimen." One problem with touchstonery is obvious: It valorizes the single, sublime line to the neglect of every other aspect of literature: plot, characterization, consistency of tone, originality of thought. Less obviously, perhaps, it devalues genres other than epic and tragedy. Within Arnold's essay itself it is clear that the comic genius of Chaucer must be placed below the soberer Milton, even below François Villon. The brilliant eighteenth-century wits who devoted themselves to satire and comedy fall, by Arnold's standard, below the salt.

While it would be hard to defend Arnold's touchstones as a mode of literary analysis, it is important to understand their historical significance as well as the general importance of the sublime in Arnold's thought. Arnold's age was also that of Charles Darwin and Herbert Spencer and David Friedrich Strauss. With science beginning to undermine the tenets of revealed religion, with philosophy becoming either too abstruse or too pragmatic to provide consolation and solace, Arnold felt that poetry could provide the new Word for which humanity was listening. "More and more," Arnold prophesies, "mankind will discover that we have to turn to poetry to interpret life for us, to console us, to sustain us. Without poetry, our science will appear incomplete; most of what now passes with us for religion and philosophy will be replaced by poetry." Culture would be grounded in literature, and Arnold was determined that if the culture was not to decline or vanish, that foundation would have to be revelatory of humanity's highest spiritual aspirations.

Arnold expected that the trends he saw would continue or accelerate, but as is usual with human affairs, this did not precisely happen. Revealed religion revived in the decade of Arnold's death, and the pendulum has swung back and forth several times since then. In many regions of America, Darwinian evolution is on the defensive, at least in the public schools, and one might as easily fear the possibility that religion might subvert science in the popular mind. But what has come to pass in the last few decades — a culture grounded not in poetry but in television and dedicated not to the sublime but to the lowest common denominator — might well have been Arnold's worst nightmare.

Selected Bibliography

Boutellier, Victor N. *Imaginative Reason: The Continuity of Arnold's Critical Effort.* Bern: Franke, 1977.

Buckley, Vincent. *Poetry and Morality: Studies in the Criticism of Matthew Arnold, T. S. Eliot, and F. R. Leavis.* London: Chatto and Windus, 1959.

Carroll, Joseph. *The Cultural Theory of Matthew Arnold.* Berkeley: University of California Press, 1982.

Donoghue, Denis. "Three Ways of Reading." *Southern Review* 34, no.2 (1998): 383–401.

Eells, John Shepard. *The Touchstones of Matthew Arnold.* New York: Bookman Associates, 1955.

Garrod, Heathcote William. *Poetry and the Criticism of Life.* New York: Russell and Russell, 1963.

Knickerbocker, William S. "Matthew Arnold's Theory of Poetry." *Sewanee Review* 33 (1925): 440–50.

Perkins, David. "Arnold and the Function of Literature." *ELH* 18 (1951): 287–309.

Stange, G. Robert. *Matthew Arnold: The Poet as Humanist.* Princeton: Princeton University Press, 1967.

Stone, Donald D. *Communications with the Future: Matthew Arnold in Dialogue.* Ann Arbor: University of Michigan Press, 1997.

Trilling, Lionel. *Matthew Arnold.* New York: Norton, 1939.

Wills, Anthony Aldwin. *Matthew Arnold's Literary and Religious Thought.* Stanford: Stanford University Press, 1968.

The Function of Criticism at the Present Time

Many objections have been made to a proposition which, in some remarks of mine on translating Homer, I ventured to put forth; a proposition about criticism, and its importance at the present day. I said: "Of the literature of France and Germany, as of the intellect of Europe in general, the main effort, for now many years, has been a critical effort; the endeavour, in all branches of knowledge, theology, philosophy, history, art, science, to see the object as in itself it really is." I added, that owing to the operation in English literature of certain causes, "almost the last thing for which one would come to English literature is just that very thing which now Europe most desires, — criticism"; and that the power and value of English literature was thereby impaired. More than one rejoinder declared that the importance I here assigned to criticism was excessive, and asserted the inherent superiority of the creative effort of the human spirit over its critical effort. And the other day, having been led by an excellent notice of Wordsworth[1] published in the *North British Review,* to turn again to his biography, I found, in the words of this great man, whom I, for one, must always listen to with the profoundest respect, a sentence passed on the critic's business, which seems to justify every possible disparagement of it. Wordsworth says in one of his letters:

> The writers in these publications [the Reviews], while they prosecute their inglorious employment,

can not be supposed to be in a state of mind very favourable for being affected by the finer influences of a thing so pure as genuine poetry.[2]

And a trustworthy reporter of his conversation quotes a more elaborate judgment to the same effect:

> Wordsworth holds the critical power very low, infinitely lower than the inventive; and he said today that if the quantity of time consumed in writing critiques on the works of others were given to original composition, of whatever kind it might be, it would be much better employed; it would make a man find out sooner his own level, and it would do infinitely less mischief. A false or malicious criticism may do much injury to the minds of others, a stupid invention, either in prose or verse, is quite harmless.[3]

It is almost too much to expect of poor human nature, that a man capable of producing some effect in one line of literature, should, for the greater good of society, voluntarily doom himself to impotence and obscurity in another. Still less is this to be expected from men addicted to the composition of the "false or malicious criticism," of which Wordsworth speaks. However, everybody would admit that a false or malicious criticism had better never have been written. Everybody, too, would be willing to admit, as a general proposition, that the critical faculty is lower than the inventive. But is it true that criticism is really, in itself, a baneful and injurious employment; is it true that all time given to writing critiques on the works of others would be much better employed if it were given to original composition, of whatever kind this may be? Is it true that Johnson had better have gone on producing more *Irenes* instead of writing his *Lives of the Poets;* nay, is it certain that Wordsworth himself was better

---

[1] I cannot help thinking that a practice, common in England during the last century, and still followed in France, of printing a notice of this kind,—a notice by a competent critic,—to serve as an introduction to an eminent author's works, might be revived among us with advantage. To introduce all succeeding editions of Wordsworth, Mr. Sharp's notice (it is permitted, I hope, to mention his name) might, it seems to me, excellently serve; it is written from the point of view of an admirer, nay, of a disciple, and that is right; but then the disciple must be also, as in this case he is, a critic, a man of letters, not, as too often happens, some relation or friend with no qualification for his task except affection for his author. [Arnold.] J. C. Shairp's "Wordsworth: The Man and Poet" appeared in *North British Review* 61 (1864): 1–54.

[2] Letter of January 12, 1816, to Bernard Barton in *The Letters of William and Dorothy Wordsworth* (ed. Ernest de Selincourt, revised by Mary Moorman and Alan G. Hill), 3: 269.
[3] William Knight, *Life of William Wordsworth* (1889) 3: 438.

employed in making his Ecclesiastical Sonnets than when he made his celebrated Preface, so full of criticism, and criticism of the works of others? Wordsworth was himself a great critic, and it is to be sincerely regretted that he has not left us more criticism; Goethe was one of the greatest of critics, and we may sincerely congratulate ourselves that he has left us so much criticism. Without wasting time over the exaggeration which Wordsworth's judgment on criticism clearly contains, or over an attempt to trace the causes, — not difficult I think to be traced, — which may have led Wordsworth to this exaggeration, a critic may with advantage seize an occasion for trying his own conscience, and for asking himself of what real service, at any given moment, the practice of criticism either is, or may be made, to his own mind and spirit, and to the minds and spirits of others.

The critical power is of lower rank than the creative. True; but in assenting to this proposition, one or two things are to be kept in mind. It is undeniable that the exercise of a creative power, that a free creative activity, is the highest function of man; it is proved to be so by man's finding in it his true happiness. But it is undeniable, also, that men may have the sense of exercising this free creative activity in other ways than in producing great works of literature or art; if it were not so, all but a very few men would be shut out from the true happiness of all men. They may have it in well-doing, they may have it in learning, they may have it even in criticizing. This is one thing to be kept in mind. Another is, that the exercise of the creative power in the production of great works of literature or art, however high this exercise of it may rank, is not at all epochs and under all conditions possible; and that therefore labour may be vainly spent in attempting it, which might with more fruit be used in preparing for it, in rendering it possible. This creative power works with elements, with materials; what if it has not those materials, those elements, ready for its use? In that case it must surely wait till they are ready. Now in literature, — I will limit myself to literature, for it is about literature that the question arises, — the elements with which the creative power works are ideas; the best ideas, on every matter which literature touches, current at the time. At any rate we may lay it down as certain that in modern literature no manifestation of the creative power not working with these can be very important or fruitful. And I say *current* at the time, not merely accessible at the time; for creative literary genius does not principally show itself in discovering new ideas; that is rather the business of the philosopher: the grand work of literary genius is a work of synthesis and exposition, not of analysis and discovery; its gift lies in the faculty of being happily inspired by a certain intellectual and spiritual atmosphere, by a certain order of ideas, when it finds itself in them; of dealing divinely with these ideas, presenting them in the most effective and attractive combinations, — making beautiful works with them, in short. But it must have the atmosphere, it must find itself amidst the order of ideas, in order to work freely; and these it is not so easy to command. This is why great creative epochs in literature are so rare; this is why there is so much that is unsatisfactory in the production of many men of real genius; because for the creation of a masterwork of literature two powers must concur, the power of the man and the power of the moment, and the man is not enough without the moment; the creative power has, for its happy exercise, appointed elements, and those elements are not in its own control.

Nay, they are more within the control of the critical power. It is the business of the critical power, as I said in the words already quoted, "in all branches of knowledge, theology, philosophy, history, art, science, to see the object as in itself it really is." Thus it tends, at last, to make an intellectual situation of which the creative power can profitably avail itself. It tends to establish an order of ideas, if not absolutely true, yet true by comparison with that which it displaces; to make the best ideas prevail. Presently these new ideas reach society, the touch of truth is the touch of life, and there is a stir and growth everywhere; out of this stir and growth come the creative epochs of literature.

Or, to narrow our range, and quit these considerations of the general march of genius and of society, considerations which are apt to become too abstract and impalpable, — everyone can see that a poet, for instance, ought to know life and the world before dealing with them in poetry; and life and the world being, in modern times, very complex things, the creation of a modern poet, to be worth much, implies a great critical effort behind it; else it must be a comparatively poor, barren, and short-lived affair. This is why Byron's poetry had so little endurance in it, and Goethe's so much; both Byron and Goethe had a great productive power, but Goethe's was nourished by a great critical effort providing the true materials for it, and Byron's was not; Goethe knew life and the world, the poet's necessary subjects, much more comprehensively and thoroughly than Byron. He knew a great deal more of them, and he knew them much more as they really are.

It has long seemed to me that the burst of creative activity in our literature, through the first quarter of this century, had about it, in fact, something premature; and that from this cause its productions are doomed, most of them, in spite of the sanguine hopes which accompanied and do still accompany them, to prove hardly more lasting than the productions of far less splendid epochs. And this prematureness comes from its having proceeded without having its proper data, without sufficient materials to work with. In other words, the English poetry of the first quarter of this century, with plenty of energy, plenty of creative force, did not know enough. This makes Byron so empty of matter, Shelley so incoherent, Wordsworth even, profound as he is, yet so wanting in completeness and variety. Wordsworth cared little for books, and disparaged Goethe. I admire Wordsworth, as he is, so much that I cannot wish him different; and it is vain, no doubt, to imagine such a man different from what he is, to suppose that he could have been different. But surely the one thing wanting to make Wordsworth an even greater poet than he is, — his thought richer, and his influence of wider application, — was that he should have read more books, among them, no doubt, those of that Goethe whom he disparaged without reading him.

But to speak of books and reading may easily lead to a misunderstanding here. It was not really books and reading that lacked to our poetry at this epoch; Shelley had plenty of reading, Coleridge had immense reading. Pindar and Sophocles — as we all say so glibly, and often with so little discernment of the real import of what we are saying — had not many books; Shakespeare was no deep reader. True; but in the Greece of Pindar and Sophocles, in the England of Shakespeare, the poet lived in a current of ideas in the highest degree animating and nourishing to the creative power; society was, in the fullest measure, permeated by fresh thought, intelligent and alive; and this state of things is the true basis for the creative power's exercise, — in this it finds its data, its materials, truly ready for its hand; all the books and reading in the world are only valuable as they are helps to this. Even when this does not actually exist, books and reading may enable a man to construct a kind of semblance of it in his own mind, a world of knowledge and intelligence in which he may live and work: this is by no means an equivalent, to the artist, for the nationally diffused life and thought of the epochs of Sophocles or Shakespeare, but, besides that it may be a means of preparation for such epochs, it does really constitute, if many share in it, a quickening and sustaining atmosphere of great value. Such an atmosphere the many-sided learning and the long and widely combined critical effort of Germany formed for Goethe, when he lived and worked. There was no national glow of life and thought there as in the Athens of Pericles, or the England of Elizabeth. That was the poet's weakness. But there was a sort of equivalent for it in the complete culture and unfettered thinking of a large body of Germans. That was his strength. In the England of the first quarter of this century, there was neither a national glow of life and thought, such as we had in the age of Elizabeth, nor yet a culture and a force of learning and criticism, such as were to be found in Germany. Therefore the creative power of poetry wanted, for success in the highest sense, materials and a basis; a thorough interpretation of the world was necessarily denied to it.

At first sight it seems strange that out of the immense stir of the French Revolution and its age should not have come a crop of works of genius equal to that which came out of the stir of the great productive time of Greece, or out of that of the Renascence, with its powerful episode the Reformation. But the truth is that the stir of the French Revolution took a character which essentially distinguished it from such movements as these. These were, in the main, disinterestedly intellectual and spiritual movements; movements in which the human spirit looked for its satisfaction in itself and in the increased play of its own activity: the French Revolution took a political, practical character. The movement which went on in France under the old régime, from 1700 to 1789, was far more really akin than that of the Revolution itself to the movement of the Renascence; the France of Voltaire and Rousseau told far more powerfully upon the mind of Europe than the France of the Revolution. Goethe reproached this last expressly with having "thrown quiet culture back."[4] Nay, and the true key to how much in our Byron, even in our Wordsworth, is this! — that they had their source in a great movement of feeling, not in a great movement of mind. The French Revolution, however, — that object of so much blind love and so much blind hatred, — found undoubtedly its motive-power in the intelligence of men and not in their practical sense; — this is what distinguishes it from the English Revolution of Charles the First's time; this is what makes it a more spiritual event than our Revolution, an event of much more powerful and worldwide interest, though practically less successful; — it appeals to an order of ideas which are universal, certain, permanent. 1789 asked of a thing, Is it rational? 1642 asked of a thing, Is it legal? Or, when it went furthest, Is it according to conscience? This is the English fashion; a fashion to be treated, within its own sphere, with the highest respect; for its success, within its own sphere, has been prodigious. But what is law in one place, is not law in another; what is law here today, is not law even here tomorrow; and as for conscience, what is binding on one man's conscience is not binding on another's; the old woman who threw her stool at the head of the surpliced minister in St. Giles's Church at Edinburgh[5] obeyed an impulse to which millions of the human race may be permitted to remain strangers. But the prescriptions of reason are absolute, unchanging, of universal validity; *to count by tens is the easiest way of counting,* — that is a proposition of which every one, from here to the Antipodes, feels the force; at least, I should say so, if we did not live in a country where it is not impossible that any morning we find a letter in *The Times* declaring that a decimal coinage is an absurdity.[6] That a whole nation should have been penetrated with an enthusiasm for pure reason, and with an ardent zeal for making its prescriptions triumph, is a very remarkable thing, when we consider how little of mind, or anything so worthy and quickening as mind, comes into the motives which alone, in general, impel great masses of men. In spite of the extravagant direction given to this enthusiasm, in spite of the crimes and follies in which it lost itself, the French Revolution derives from the force, truth, and universality of the ideas which took for its law, and from the passion with which it could inspire a multitude for these ideas, a unique and still living power; it is — it will probably long remain — the greatest, the most animating event in history. And, as no sincere passion for the things of the mind, even though it turns out in many respects an unfortunate passion, is ever quite thrown away and quite barren of good, France has reaped from hers one fruit — the natural and legitimate fruit, though not precisely the grand fruit she expected: she is the country in Europe where *the people* is most alive.

But the mania for giving an immediate political and practical application to all these fine ideas of the reason was fatal. Here an Englishman is in his element: on this theme we can all go on for hours. And all we are in the habit of saying on it has undoubtedly a great deal of truth. Ideas cannot be too much prized in and for themselves, cannot be too much lived with; but to transport them abruptly into the world of politics and practice, violently to revolutionize this world to their bidding, — that is quite another thing. There is the world of ideas and there is the world of practice; the French are often for suppressing the one and the English the other; but neither is to be suppressed. A member of the House of Commons said to me the other day: "That a thing is an

---

[4]In Goethe's "The Four Seasons: Spring."
[5]Jenny Geddes did this on July 23, 1637.

[6]A decimal coinage bill was introduced and withdrawn in 1863.

anomaly, I consider to be no objection to it what-ever." I venture to think he was wrong; that a thing is an anomaly *is* an objection to it, but absolutely and in the sphere of ideas: it is not necessarily, under such and such circumstances, or at such and such a moment, an objection to it in the sphere of politics and practice. Joubert has said beautifully: "C'est la force et la droit qui règlent toutes choses dans le monde; la force en attendant le droit." (Force and right are the governors of this world; force till right is ready.)[7] *Force till right is ready; and till right is ready, force, the existing order of things, is justified, is the legitimate ruler. But right is something moral, and implies inward recognition, free assent of the will; we are not ready for right, — *right,* so far as we are concerned, *is not ready,* — until we have attained this sense of seeing it and willing it. The way in which for us it may change and transform force, the existing order of things, and become, in its turn, the legitimate ruler of the world, should depend on the way in which, when our time comes, we see it and will it. Therefore for other people enamoured of their own newly discerned right, to attempt to impose it upon us as ours, and violently to substitute their right for our force, is an act of tyranny, and to be resisted. It sets at nought the second great half of our maxim, *force till right is ready.* This was the grand error of the French Revolution; and its movement of ideas, by quitting the intellectual sphere and rushing furiously into the political sphere, ran, indeed, a prodigious and memorable course, but produced no such intellectual fruit as the movement of ideas of the Renascence, and created, in opposition to itself, what I may call an *epoch of concentration.* The great force of that epoch of concentration was England; and the great voice of that epoch of concentration was Burke. It is the fashion to treat Burke's writings on the French Revolution as superannuated and conquered by the event; as the eloquent but unphilosophical tirades of bigotry and prejudice. I will not deny that they are often disfigured by the violence and passion of the moment, and that in some directions Burke's view was bounded, and his observation therefore at fault; but on the whole, and for those who can make the needful

[7]Jean Joubert, *Pensées* (1877), 2: 178.

corrections, what distinguishes these writings is their profound, permanent, fruitful, philosophical truth; they contain the true philosophy of an epoch of concentration, dissipate the heavy atmosphere which its own nature is apt to engender round it, and make its resistance rational instead of mechanical.

But Burke is so great because, almost alone in England, he brings thought to bear upon politics, he saturates politics with thought; it is his accident that his ideas were at the service of an epoch of concentration, not of an epoch of expansion; it is his characteristic that he so lived by ideas, and had such a source of them welling up within him, that he could float even an epoch of concentration and English Tory politics with them. It does not hurt him that Dr. Price and the Liberals were enraged with him; it does not even hurt him that George the Third and the Tories were enchanted with him. His greatness is that he lived in a world which neither English Liberalism nor English Toryism is apt to enter; — the world of ideas, not the world of catchwords and party habits. So far is it from being really true of him that he "to party gave up what was meant for mankind," that at the very end of his fierce struggle with the French Revolution, after all his invectives against its false pretensions, hollowness, and madness, with his sincere conviction of its mischievousness, he can close a memorandum on the best means of combating it, some of the last pages he ever wrote, — the *Thoughts on French Affairs,* in December 1791, — with these striking words:

The evil is stated, in my opinion, as it exists. The remedy must be where power, wisdom, and information, I hope, are more united with good intentions than they can be with me. I have done with this subject, I believe, for ever. It has given me many anxious moments for the last two years. *If a great change is to be made in human affairs, the minds of men will be fitted to it; the general opinions and feelings will draw that way. Every fear, every hope will forward it; and then they who persist in opposing this mighty current in human affairs, will appear rather to resist the decrees of Providence itself, than the mere designs of men. They will not be resolute and firm, but perverse and obstinate.*

That return of Burke upon himself has always seemed to me one of the finest things in English literature, or indeed in any literature. That is what I call living by ideas; when one side of a question has long had your earnest support, when all your feelings are engaged, when you hear all round you no language but one, when your party talks this language like a steam-engine and can imagine no other, — still to be able to think, still to be irresistibly carried, if so it be, by the current of thought to the opposite side of the question, and, like Balaam, to be unable to speak anything *but what the Lord has put in your mouth.*[8] I know nothing more striking, and I must add that I know nothing more un-English.

For the Englishman in general is like my friend the Member of Parliament, and believes, point-blank, that for a thing to be an anomaly is absolutely no objection to it whatever. He is like the Lord Auckland of Burke's day, who, in a memorandum on the French Revolution, talks of "certain miscreants, assuming the name of philosophers, who have presumed themselves capable of establishing a new system of society." The Englishman has been called a political animal, and he values what is political and practical so much that ideas easily become objects of dislike in his eyes, and thinkers "miscreants," because ideas and thinkers have rashly meddled with politics and practice. This would be all very well if the dislike and neglect confined themselves to ideas transported out of their own sphere, and meddling rashly with practice; but they are inevitably extended to ideas as such, and to the whole life of intelligence; practice is everything, a free play of the mind is nothing. The notion of the free play of the mind upon all subjects being a pleasure in itself, being an object of desire, being an essential provider of elements without which a nation's spirit, whatever compensations it may have for them, must, in the long run, die of inanition, hardly enters into an Englishman's thoughts. It is noticeable that the word *curiosity,* which in other languages is used in a good sense, to mean, as a high and fine quality of man's nature, just this disinterested love of a free play of the mind on all subjects, for its own sake, — it is noticeable, I say, that this word has in our language no sense of the

kind, no sense but a rather bad and disparaging one. But criticism, real criticism, is essentially the exercise of this very quality; it obeys an instinct prompting it to know the best that is known and thought in the world, irrespectively of practice, politics, and everything of the kind; and to value knowledge and thought as they approach this best, without the intrusion of any other considerations whatever. This is an instinct for which there is, I think, little original sympathy in the practical English nature, and what there was of it has undergone a long benumbing period of blight and suppression in the epoch of concentration which followed the French Revolution.

But epochs of concentration cannot well endure for ever; epochs of expansion, in the due course of things, follow them. Such an epoch of expansion seems to be opening in this country. In the first place all danger of a hostile forcible pressure of foreign ideas upon our practice has long disappeared; like the traveller in the fable, therefore, we begin to wear our cloak a little more loosely. Then, with a long peace, the ideas of Europe steal gradually and amicably in, and mingle, though in infinitesimally small quantities at a time, with our own notions. Then, too, in spite of all that is said about the absorbing and brutalizing influence of our passionate material progress, it seems to me indisputable that this progress is likely, though not certain, to lead in the end to an apparition of intellectual life; and that man, after he has made himself perfectly comfortable and has now to determine what to do with himself next, may begin to remember that he has a mind and that the mind may be made the source of great pleasure. I grant it is mainly the privilege of faith, at present, to discern this end to our railways, our business, and our fortune-making; but we shall see if, here as elsewhere, faith is not in the end the true prophet. Our ease, our travelling, and our unbounded liberty to hold just as hard and securely as we please to the practice to which our notions have given birth, all tend to beget an inclination to deal a little more freely with these notions themselves, to canvass them a little, to penetrate a little into their real nature. Flutterings of curiosity, in the foreign sense of the word, appear amongst us, and it is in

[8]Numbers 22:38.

these that criticism must look to find its account. Criticism first; a time of true creative activity, perhaps, — which, as I have said, must inevitably be preceded amongst us by a time of criticism, — hereafter, when criticism has done its work.

It is of the last importance that English criticism should clearly discern what rule for its course, in order to avail itself of the field now opening to it, and to produce fruit for the future, it ought to take. The rule may be summed up in one word, — *disinterestedness*. And how is criticism to show disinterestedness? By keeping aloof from practice; by resolutely following the law of its own nature, which is to be a free play of the mind on all subjects which it touches; by steadily refusing to lend itself to any of those ulterior, political, practical considerations about ideas which plenty of people will be sure to attach to them, which perhaps ought often to be attached to them, which in this country at any rate are certain to be attached to them quite sufficiently, but which criticism has really nothing to do with. Its business is, as I have said, simply to know the best that is known and thought in the world, and by in its turn making this known, to create a current of true and fresh ideas. Its business is to do this with inflexible honesty, with due ability; but its business is to do no more, and to leave alone all questions of practical consequences and applications, questions which will never fail to have due prominence given to them. Else criticism, besides being really false to its own nature, merely continues in the old rut which it has hitherto followed in this country, and will certainly miss the chance now given to it. For what is at present the bane of criticism in this country? It is that practical considerations cling to it and stifle it; it subserves interests not its own; our organs of criticism are organs of men and parties having practical ends to serve, and with them those practical ends are the first thing and the play of mind the second; so much play of mind as is compatible with the prosecution of those practical ends is all that is wanted. An organ like the *Revue des Deux Mondes*, having for its main function to understand and utter the best that is known and thought in the world, existing, it may be said, as just an organ for a free play of the mind, we have

not; but we have the *Edinburgh Review*, existing as an organ of the old Whigs, and for as much play of the mind as may suit its being that; we have the *Quarterly Review*, existing as an organ of the Tories, and for as much play of mind as may suit its being that; we have the *British Quarterly Review*, existing as an organ of the political Dissenters, and for as much play of mind as may suit its being that; we have *The Times*, existing as an organ of the common, satisfied, well-to-do Englishman, and for as much play of mind as may suit its being that. And so on through all the various fractions, political and religious, of our society; every fraction has, as such, its organ of criticism, but the notions of combining all fractions in the common pleasure of a free disinterested play of mind meets with no favour. Directly this play of mind wants to have more scope, and to forget the pressure of practical considerations a little, it is checked, it is made to feel the chain; we saw this the other day in the extinction, so much to be regretted, of the *Home and Foreign Review;* perhaps in no organ of criticism in this country was there so much knowledge, so much play of mind; but these could not save it: the *Dublin Review* subordinates play of mind to the practical business of English and Irish Catholicism, and lives. It must needs be that men should act in sects and parties, that each of these sects and parties should have its organ, and should make this organ subserve the interests of its action; but it would be well, too, that there should be a criticism, not the minister of these interests, not their enemy, but absolutely and entirely independent of them. No other criticism will ever attain any real authority or make any real way towards its end, — the creating a current of true and fresh ideas.

It is because criticism has so little kept in the pure intellectual sphere, has so little detached itself from practice, has been so directly polemical and controversial, that it has so ill accomplished, in this country, its best spiritual work; which is to keep man from a self-satisfaction which is retarding and vulgarizing, to lead him towards perfection, by making his mind dwell upon what is excellent in itself, and the absolute beauty and fitness of things. A polemical practical criticism makes men blind even to the ideal imperfection of their practice, makes them willingly assert its ideal perfection, in order the better to secure it against attack; and clearly this is narrowing and baneful for them. If they were reassured on the practical side, speculative considerations of ideal perfection they might be brought to entertain, and their spiritual horizon would thus gradually widen. Mr. Adderley says to the Warwickshire farmers:

> Talk of the improvement of breed! Why, the race we ourselves represent, the men and women, the old Anglo-Saxon race, are the best breed in the whole world. . . . The absence of a too enervating climate, too unclouded skies, and a too luxurious nature, has produced so vigorous a race of people, and has rendered us so superior to all the world.

Mr. Roebuck says to the Sheffeld cutlers:

> I look around me and ask what is the state of England? Is not property safe? Is not every man able to say what he likes? Can you not walk from one end of England to the other in perfect security? I ask you whether, the world over or in past history, there is anything like it? Nothing. I pray that our unrivalled happiness may last.[9]

Now obviously there is a peril for poor human nature in words and thoughts of each exuberant self-satisfaction, until we find ourselves safe in the streets of the Celestial City.

> Das wenige verschwindet leicht dem Blicke
> Der vorwärts sieht, wie viel noch übrig
> bleibt — [10]

says Goethe; the little that is done seems nothing when we look forward and see how much we have yet to do. Clearly this is a better line of reflection for weak humanity, so long as it remains on this earthly field of labour and trial.

But neither Mr. Adderley nor Mr. Roebuck is by nature inaccessible to considerations of this sort. They only lose sight of them owing to the controversial life we all lead, and the practical form which all speculation takes with us. They have in view opponents whose aim is not ideal, but practical; and in their zeal to uphold their own practice against these innovators, they go so far as even to attribute to this practice an ideal perfection. Somebody has been wanting to introduce a six-pound franchise, or to abolish church-rates, or to collect agricultural statistics by force, or to diminish local self-government. How natural, in reply to such proposals, very likely improper or ill-timed, to go a little beyond the mark and to say stoutly: "Such a race of people as we stand, so superior to all the world! The old Anglo-Saxon race, the best breed in the whole world! I pray that our unrivalled happiness may last! I ask you whether, the world over or in past history, there is anything like it?" And so long as criticism answers this dithyramb by insisting that the old Anglo-Saxon race would be still more superior to all others if it had no church-rates, or that our unrivalled happiness would last yet longer with a six-pound franchise, so long will the strain, "The best breed in the whole world!" swell louder and louder, everything ideal and refining will be lost out of sight, and both the assailed and their critics will remain in a sphere, to say the truth, perfectly unvital, a sphere in which spiritual progression is impossible. But let criticism leave church-rates and the franchise alone, and in the most candid spirit, without a single lurking thought of practical innovation, confront with our dithyramb this paragraph on which I stumbled in a newspaper immediately after reading Mr. Roebuck:

> A shocking child murder has just been committed at Nottingham. A girl named Wragg left the workhouse there on Saturday morning with her young illegitimate child. The child was soon afterwards found dead on Mapperly Hills, having been strangled. Wragg is in custody.[11]

Nothing but that; but, in juxtaposition with the absolute eulogies of Mr. Adderley and Mr. Roebuck, how eloquent, how suggestive are those few lines! "Our old Anglo-Saxon breed, the best in the whole world!" — how much that is harsh and ill-favoured there is in this best! Wragg! If we are to talk of ideal perfection, of "the best in the whole world," has anyone reflected what a touch of grossness in our race, what an original shortcoming in

---

[9]These speeches were reported in the London Times on September 17, 1863, and August 19, 1864, respectively.
[10]Goethe, Iphigenia on Tauris, I.ii.91–92.

[11]The crime was committed on September 10, 1864. Elizabeth Wragg was sentenced to twenty years in prison in March of the following year.

the more delicate spiritual perceptions, is shown by the natural growth amongst us of such hideous names, — Higginbottom, Stiggins, Bugg! In Ionia and Attica they were luckier in this respect than "the best race in the world"; by the Ilissus there was no Wragg, poor thing! And "our unrivalled happiness"; — what an element of grimness, bareness, and hideousness mixes with it and blurs it; the workhouse, the dismal Mapperly Hills, — how dismal those who have seen them will remember; — the gloom, the smoke, the cold, the strangled illegitimate child! "I ask you whether, the world over or in past history, there is anything like it?" Perhaps not, one is inclined to answer; but at any rate, in that case, the world is very much to be pitied. And the final touch, — short, bleak, and inhuman: *Wragg is in custody.* The sex lost in the confusion of our unrivalled happiness; or (shall I say?) the superfluous Christian name lopped off by the straightforward vigour of our old Anglo-Saxon breed! There is profit for the spirit in such contrasts as this; criticism serves the cause of perfection by establishing them. By eluding sterile conflict, by refusing to remain in the sphere where alone narrow and relative conceptions have any worth and validity, criticism may diminish its momentary importance, but only in this way has it a chance of gaining admittance for those wider and more perfect conceptions to which all its duty is really owed. Mr. Roebuck will have a poor opinion of an adversary who replies to his defiant songs of triumph only by murmuring under his breath, *Wragg is in custody;* but in no other way will these songs of triumph be induced gradually to moderate themselves, to get rid of what in them is excessive and offensive, and to fall into a softer and truer key.

It will be said that it is a very subtle and indirect action which I am thus prescribing for criticism, and that, by embracing in this manner the Indian virtue of detachment and abandoning the sphere of practical life, it condemns itself to a slow and obscure work. Slow and obscure it may be, but it is the only proper work of criticism. The mass of mankind will never have any ardent zeal for seeing things as they are; very inadequate ideas will always satisfy them. On these inadequate ideas reposes, and must repose, the general practice of the world. That is as much as saying that whoever sets himself to see things as they are

will find himself one of a very small circle; but it is only by this small circle resolutely doing its own work that adequate ideas will ever get current at all. The rush and roar of practical life will always have a dizzying and attracting effect upon the most collected spectator, and tend to draw him into its vortex; most of all will this be the case where that life is so powerful as it is in England. But it is only by remaining collected, and refusing to lend himself to the point of view of the practical man, that the critic can do the practical man any service; and it is only by the greatest sincerity in pursuing his own course, and by at last convincing even the practical man of his sincerity, that he can escape misunderstandings which perpetually threaten him.

For the practical man is not apt for fine distinctions, and yet in these distinctions truth and the highest culture greatly find their account. But it is not easy to lead a practical man — unless you reassure him as to your practical intentions, you have no chance of leading him — to see that a thing which he has always been used to look at from one side only, which he greatly values, and which, looked at from that side, quite deserves, perhaps, all the prizing and admiring which he bestows upon it, — that this thing, looked at from another side, may appear much less beneficent and beautiful, and yet retain all its claims to our practical allegiance. Where shall we find language innocent enough, how shall we make the spotless purity of our intentions evident enough, to enable us to say to the political Englishman that the British Constitution itself, which, seen from the practical side, looks such a magnificent organ of progress and virtue, seen from the speculative side, — which its compromises, its love of facts, its horror of theory, its studied avoidance of clear thoughts, — that, seen from this side, our august Constitution sometimes looks, — forgive me, shade of Lord Somers! — a colossal machine for the manufacture of Philistines? How is Cobbett to say this and not be misunderstood, blackened as he is with the smoke of a lifelong conflict in the field of political practice? how is Mr. Carlyle to say it and not be misunderstood, after his furious raid into this field with his *Latter-day Pamphlets?* how is Mr. Ruskin, after his pugnacious political economy? I say, the critic must keep out of the region of immediate practice in the political, social, humanitarian sphere, if he wants to make a beginning for that more free speculative treatment of things, which may perhaps one day make its benefits felt even in this sphere, but in a natural and thence irresistible manner.

Do what he will, however, the critic will still remain exposed to frequent misunderstandings, and nowhere so much as in this country. For here people are particularly indisposed even to comprehend that without this free disinterested treatment of things, truth and the highest culture are out of the question. So immersed are they in practical life, so accustomed to take all their notions from this life and its processes, that they are apt to think that truth and culture themselves can be reached by the processes of this life, and that it is an impertinent singularity to think of reaching them in any other. "We are all *terrae filii*,"[12] cries their eloquent advocate; "all Philistines together. Away with the notion of proceeding by any other course than the course dear to the Philistines; let us have a social movement, let us organize and combine a party to pursue truth and new thought, let us call it *the liberal party,* and let us all stick to each other, and back each other up. Let us have no nonsense about independent criticism, and intellectual delicacy, and the few and the many. Don't let us trouble ourselves about foreign thought; we shall invent the whole thing for ourselves as we go along: if one of us speaks well, applaud him; if one of us speaks ill, applaud him too; we are all in the same movement, we are all liberals, we are all in pursuit of truth." In this way the pursuit of truth becomes really a social, practical, pleasurable affair, almost requiring a chairman, a secretary, and advertisements; with the excitement of an occasional scandal, with a little resistance to give the happy sense of difficulty overcome; but, in general, plenty of bustle and very little thought. To act is so easy, as Goethe says; to think is so hard! It is true that the critic has many temptations to go with the stream, to make one of the party movement, one of these *terrae filii;* it seems ungracious to refuse to be a *terrae filius,* when so many excellent people are; but the critic's duty is to refuse, or, if resistance is

vain, at least to cry with Obermann: *Périssons en résistant.*[13]

How serious a matter it is to try and resist, I had ample opportunity of experiencing when I ventured some time ago to criticize the celebrated first volume of Bishop Colenso.[14] The echoes of the storm which was then raised I still, from time to time, hear grumbling round me. That storm arose out of a misunderstanding almost inevitable. It is a result of no little culture to attain to a clear perception that science and religion are two wholly different things; the multitude will for ever confuse them; but happily that is of no great real importance, for while the multitude imagines itself to live by its false science, it does really live by its true religion. Dr. Colenso, however, in his first volume did all he could to strengthen the confusion,[15] and to make it dangerous. He did this with the best intentions, I freely admit, and with the most candid ignorance that this was the natural effect of what he was doing; but, says Joubert, "Ignorance, which in matters of morals extenuates the crime, is itself, in intellectual matters, a crime of the first order."[16] I criticized Bishop Colenso's speculative confusion. Immediately there was a cry raised: "What is this? here is a liberal attacking a liberal. Do not you belong to the movement? are not you a friend of truth? Is not Bishop

---

[12]Children of earth.

[13]"Let us perish while resisting." Étienne de Sénancour, *Obermann* (1804).

[14]So sincere is my dislike to all personal attack and controversy, that I abstain from reprinting, at this distance of time from the occasion which called them forth, the essays in which I criticized Dr. Colenso's book; I feel bound, however, after all that has passed, to make here a final declaration of my sincere impenitence for having published them. Nay, I cannot forbear repeating yet once more, for his benefit and that of his readers, this sentence from my original remarks upon him: *There is truth of science and truth of religion; truth of science does not become truth of religion till it is made religious.* And I will add; Let us have all the science there is from the men of science; from the men of religion let us have religion. [Arnold] The essays in which Arnold criticized John William Colenso's *The Pentateuch and the Book of Joshua Critically Examined* (1863) were "The Bishop and the Philosopher" and "Dr. Stanley's Lectures on the Jewish Church," published in 1863.

[15]It has been said I make it "a crime against literary criticism and the higher culture to attempt to inform the ignorant." Need I point out that the ignorant are not informed by being confirmed in a confusion? [Arnold]

[16]Joubert, *Pensées*, 2:311.

Colenso in pursuit of truth? then speak with proper respect of his book. Dr. Stanley is another friend of truth, and you speak with proper respect of his book; why make these invidious differences? both books are excellent, admirable, liberal; Bishop Colenso's perhaps the most so, because it is the boldest, and will have the best practical consequences for the liberal cause. Do you want to encourage to the attack of a brother liberal his, and your, and our implacable enemies, the *Church and State Review* or the *Record,* — the High Church rhinoceros and the Evangelical hyaena? Be silent, therefore; or rather speak, speak as loud as ever you can, and go into ecstasies over the eighty and odd pigeons."

But criticism cannot follow this coarse and indiscriminate method. It is unfortunately possible for a man in pursuit of truth to write a book which reposes upon a false conception. Even the practical consequences of a book are to genuine criticism no recommendation of it, if the book is, in the highest sense, blundering. I see that a lady who herself, too, is in pursuit of truth, and who writes with great ability, but a little too much, perhaps, under the influence of the practical spirit of the English liberal movement, classes Bishop Colenso's book and M. Renan's[17] together, in her survey of the religious state of Europe, as facts of the same order, works, both of them, of "great importance"; "great ability, power, and skill"; Bishop Colenso's, perhaps, the most powerful; at least, Miss Cobbe[18] gives special expression to her gratitude that to Bishop Colenso "has been given the strength to grasp, and the courage to teach, truths of such deep import." In the same way, more than one popular writer has compared him to Luther. Now it is just this kind of false estimate which the critical spirit is, it seems to me, bound to resist. It is really the strongest possible proof of the low ebb at which, in England, the critical spirit is, that while the critical hit in the religious literature of Germany is Dr. Strauss's book,[19] in that of France M. Renan's book, the book of Bishop

Colenso is the critical hit in the religious literature of England. Bishop Colenso's book reposes on a total misconception of the essential elements of the religious problem, as that problem is now presented for solution. To criticism, therefore, which seeks to have the best that is known and thought on this problem, it is, however well meant, of no importance whatever. Mr. Renan's book attempts a new synthesis of the elements furnished to us by the Four Gospels. It attempts, in my opinion, a synthesis, perhaps premature, perhaps impossible, certainly not successful. Up to the present time, at any rate, we must acquiesce in Fleury's sentence on such recastings of the Gospel story: *Quiconque s'imagine la pouvoir mieux écrire, ne l'entend pas.*[20] M. Renan had himself passed by anticipation a like sentence on his own work, when he said: "If a new presentation of the character of Jesus were offered to me, I would not have it; its very clearness would be, in my opinion, the best proof of its insufficiency." His friends may with perfect justice rejoin that at the sight of the Holy Land, and of the actual scene of the Gospel story, all the current of M. Renan's thoughts may have naturally changed, and a new casting of that story irresistibly suggested itself to him; and that this is just a case for applying Cicero's maxim: Change of mind is not inconsistency — *nemo doctus unquam mutationem consilii inconstantiam dixit esse.*[21] Nevertheless, for criticism, M. Renan's first thought must still be the truer one, as long as his new casting so fails more fully to commend itself, more fully (to use Coleridge's happy phrase about the Bible) to *find* us. Still M. Renan's attempt is, for criticism, of the most real interest and importance, since, with all its difficulty, a fresh synthesis of the New Testament *data,* — not a making war on them, in Voltaire's fashion, not a leaving them out of mind, in the world's fashion, but the putting a new construction upon them, the taking them from under the old, adoptive, traditional, unspiritual point of view and placing them under a new one, — is the very essence of the religious problem, as now presented; and only by efforts in this direction can it receive a solution.

[17]Ernest Renan, *La Vie de Jesus* (1863).
[18]Frances Power Cobbe in *Broken Lights: An Inquiry into the Present Condition and Future Prospects of Religious Faith* (1864).
[19]David Friedrich Strauss's *Leben Jesus* (1835).

[20]"Whoever imagines himself able to write it better, does not understand it." Claude Fleury, *Ecclesiastical History* (1722).
[21]Cicero, *To Atticus* 16.17:3.

Again, in the same spirit in which she judges Bishop Colenso, Miss Cobbe, like so many earnest liberals of our practical race, both here and in America, herself sets vigorously about a positive reconstruction of religion, about making a religion of the future out of hand, or at least setting about making it; we must not rest, she and they are always thinking and saying, in negative criticism, we must be creative and constructive; hence we have such works as her recent *Religious Duty,* and works still more considerable, perhaps, by others, which will be in everyone's mind. These works often have much ability; they often spring out of sincere convictions, and a sincere wish to do good; and they sometimes, perhaps, do good. Their fault is (if I may be permitted to say so) one which they have in common with the British College of Health, in the New Road. Everyone knows the British College of Health; it is that building with the lion and the statue of the Goddess Hygeia before it; at least I am sure about the lion, though I am not absolutely certain about the goddess Hygeia. This building does credit, perhaps, to the resources of Dr. Morrison and his disciples; but it falls a good deal short of one's idea of which a British College of Health ought to be. In England, where we hate public interference and love individual enterprise, we have a whole crop of places like the British College of Health; the grand name without the grand thing. Unluckily, creditable to individual enterprise as they are, they tend to impair our taste by making us forget what more grandiose, noble, or beautiful character properly belongs to a public institution. The same may be said of the religions of the future of Miss Cobbe and others. Creditable, like the British College of Health, to the resources of their authors, they yet tend to make us forget what more grandiose, noble, or beautiful character properly belongs to religious constructions. The historic religions, with all their faults, have had this; it certainly belongs to the religious sentiment, when it truly flowers, to have this; and we impoverish our spirit if we allow a religion of the future without it. What then is the duty of criticism here? To take the practical point of view, to applaud the liberal movement and all its works, — its New Road religions of the future into the bargain, — for their general utility's sake? By no means; but to be perpetually dissatisfied with these works, while they perpetually fall short of a high and perfect ideal.

For criticism, these are elementary laws; but they never can be popular, and in this country they have been very little followed, and one meets with immense obstacles in following them. That is a reason for asserting them again and again. Criticism must maintain its independence of the practical spirit and its aim. Even with well-meant efforts of the practical spirit it must express dissatisfaction, if in the sphere of the ideal they seem impoverishing and limiting. It must not hurry on to the goal because of its practical importance. It must be patient, and know how to wait; and flexible, and know how to attach itself to things and how to withdraw from them. It must be apt to study and praise elements that for the fulness of spiritual perfection are wanted, even though they belong to a power which in the practical sphere may be maleficent. It must be apt to discern the spiritual shortcomings or illusions of powers that in the practical sphere may be beneficent. And this without any notion of favouring or injuring, in the practical sphere, one power or the other; without any notion of playing off, in this sphere, one power against the other. When one looks, for instance, at the English Divorce Court, — an institution which perhaps has its practical conveniences, but which in the ideal sphere is so hideous; an institution which neither makes divorce impossible nor makes it decent, which allows a man to get rid of his wife, or a wife of her husband, but makes them drag one another first, for the public edification, through a mire of unutterable infamy, — when one looks at this charming institution, I say, with its crowded benches, its newspaper-reports, and its money-compensations, this institution in which the gross unregenerate British Philistine has indeed stamped an image of himself, — one may be permitted to find the marriage-theory of Catholicism refreshing and elevating. Or when Protestantism, in virtue of its supposed rational and intellectual origin, gives the law to criticism too magisterially, criticism may and must remind it that its pretensions, in this respect, are illusive and do it harm; that the Reformation was a moral rather than an intellectual event; that Luther's theory of grace no more exactly reflects the mind of the spirit than Bossuet's philosophy of history[22] reflects it; and that there is no more antecedent probability of the Bishop of Durham's stock of ideas being agreeable to perfect reason than of Pope Pius the Ninth's. But criticism will not on that account forget the achievements of Protestantism in the practical and moral sphere; nor that, even in the intellectual sphere, Protestantism, though in a blind and stumbling manner, carried forward the Renascence, while Catholicism threw itself violently across its path.

I lately heard a man of thought and energy[23] contrasting the want of ardour and movement which he now found amongst young men in this country with what he remembered in his own youth, twenty years ago. "What reformers we were then!" he exclaimed; "what a zeal we had! how we canvassed every institution in Church and State, and were prepared to remodel them all on first principles!" He was inclined to regret, as a spiritual flagging, the lull which he saw. I am disposed rather to regard it as a pause in which the turn to a new mode of spiritual progress is being accomplished; everything was long seen, by the young and ardent amongst us, in inseparable connection with politics and practical life; we have pretty well exhausted the benefits of seeing things in this connection, we have got all that can be got by so seeing them. Let us try a more disinterested mode of seeing them; let us betake ourselves more to the serener life of the mind and spirit. This life, too, may have its excesses and dangers; but they are not for us at present. Let us think of quietly enlarging our stock of true and fresh ideas, and not, as soon as we get an idea or half an idea, be running out with it into the street, and trying to make it rule there. Our ideas will, in the end, shape the world all the better for maturing a little. Perhaps in fifty years' time it will in the English House of Commons be an objection to an institution that it is an anomaly, and my friend the Member of Parliament will shudder in

his grave. But let us in the meanwhile rather endeavour that in twenty years' time it may, in English literature, be an objection to a proposition that it is absurd. That will be a change so vast, that the imagination almost fails to grasp it. *Ab integro saeclorum nascitur ordo.*[24]

If I have insisted so much on the course which criticism must take where politics and religion are concerned, it is because, where these burning matters are in question, it is most likely to go astray. I have wished, above all, to insist on the attitude which criticism should adopt towards everything; on its right tone and temper of mind. Then comes the question as to the subject-matter which criticism should most seek. Here, in general, its course is determined for it by the idea which is the law of its being; the idea of a disinterested endeavour to learn and propagate the best that is known and thought in the world, and thus to establish a current of fresh and true ideas. By the very nature of things, as England is not all the world, much of the best that is known and thought in the world cannot be of English growth, must be foreign; by the nature of things, again, it is just this that we are least likely to know, while English thought is streaming in upon us from all sides, and takes excellent care that we shall not be ignorant of its existence; the English critic, therefore, must dwell much on foreign thought, and with particular heed on any part of it, which, while significant and fruitful in itself, is for any reason specially likely to escape him. Again, judging is often spoken of as the critic's one business, and so in some sense it is; but the judgment which almost insensibly forms itself in a fair and clear mind, along with fresh knowledge, is the valuable one; and thus knowledge, and ever fresh knowledge, must be the critic's great concern for himself; and it is by communicating fresh knowledge, and letting his own judgment pass along with it, — but insensibly, and in the second place not the first, as a sort of companion and clue, not as an abstract lawgiver, — that he will generally do most good to his readers.

[22]Jacques-Bénigne Boussuet, *Discourse on Universal History* (1681).

[23]Charles Thomas Baring, Bishop of Durham (1861–79).

[24]"Order is born from the renewal of the ages." Virgil, *Eclogues* 4:5.

Sometimes, no doubt, for the sake of establishing an author's place in literature, and his relation to a central standard (and if this is not done, how are we to get at our *best in the world?*) criticism may have to deal with a subject-matter so familiar that fresh knowledge is out of the question, and then it must be all judgment; an enunciation and detailed application of principles. Here the great safeguard is never to let oneself become abstract, always to retain an intimate and lively consciousness of the truth of what one is saying, and, the moment this fails us, to be sure that something is wrong. Still, under all circumstances, this mere judgment and application of principles is, in itself, not the most satisfactory work to the critic; like mathematics, it is tautological, and cannot well give us, like fresh learning, the sense of creative activity.

But stop, someone will say; all this talk is of no practical use to us whatever; this criticism of yours is not what we have in our minds when we speak of criticism; when we speak of critics and criticism, we mean critics and criticism of the current English literature of the day; when you offer to tell criticism its function, it is to this criticism that we expect you to address yourself. I am sorry for it, for I am afraid I must disappoint these expectations. I am bound by my own definition of criticism: *a disinterested endeavour to learn and propagate the best that is known and thought in the world.* How much of current English literature comes into this "best that is known and thought in the world"? Not very much, I fear; certainly less, at this moment, than of the current literature of France or Germany. Well, then, am I to alter my definition of criticism, in order to meet the requirements of a number of practising English critics, who, after all, are free in their choice of a business? That would be making criticism lend itself just to one of those alien practical considerations, which, I have said, are so fatal to it. One may say, indeed, to those who have to deal with the mass — so much better disregarded — of current English literature, that they may at all events endeavour, in dealing with this, to try it, so far as they can, by the standard of the best that is known and thought in the world; one may say, that to get anywhere near this standard, every critic should try and possess one great literature, at least, besides his own; and the more unlike his own; the better. But, after all, the criticism I am really concerned with, — the criticism which alone can much help us for the future, the criticism which, throughout Europe, is at the present day meant, when so much stress is laid on the importance of criticism and the critical spirit, — is a criticism which regards Europe as being, for intellectual and spiritual purposes, one great confederation, bound to a joint action and working to a common result; and whose members have, for their proper outfit, a knowledge of Greek, Roman, and Eastern antiquity, and of one another. Special, local, and temporary advantages being put out of account, that modern nation will in the intellectual and spiritual sphere make most progress, which most thoroughly carries out this programme. And what is that but saying that we too, all of us, as individuals, the more thoroughly we carry it out, shall make the more progress?

There is so much inviting us! — what are we to take? what will nourish us in growth towards perfection? That is the question which, with the immense field of life and of literature lying before him, the critic has to answer; for himself first, and afterwards for others. In this idea of the critic's business the essays brought together in the following pages have had their origin; in this idea, widely different as are their subjects, they have, perhaps, their unity.

I conclude with what I said in the beginning: to have the sense of creative activity is the great happiness and the great proof of being alive, and it is not denied to criticism to have it; but then criticism must be sincere, simple, flexible, ardent, ever widening its knowledge. Then it may have, in no contemptible measure, joyful sense of creative activity; a sense which a man of insight and conscience will prefer to what he might derive from a poor, starved, fragmentary, inadequate creation. And at some epochs no other creation is possible.

Still, in full measure, the sense of creative activity belongs only to genuine creation; in literature we must never forget that. But what true man of letters ever can forget it? It is no such common matter for a gifted nature to come into possession of a current of true and living ideas, and to produce amidst the inspiration of them, that we are likely to underrate it. The epochs of Aeschylus and Shakespeare make us feel their pre-eminence. In an epoch like those is, no doubt, the true life of a literature; there is the promised land, towards which criticism can only beckon.

That promised land it will not be ours to enter, and we shall die in the wilderness: but to have desired to enter it, to have saluted it from afar, is already, perhaps, the best distinction among contemporaries; it will certainly be the best title to esteem with posterity.

From *The Study of Poetry*

The future of poetry is immense, because in poetry, where it is worthy of its high destinies, our race, as time goes on, will find an ever surer and surer stay. There is not a creed which is not shaken, not an accredited dogma which is not shown to be questionable, not a received tradition which does not threaten to dissolve. Our religion has materialized itself in the fact, in the supposed fact; it has attached its emotion to the fact, and now the fact is failing it. But for poetry the idea is everything; the rest is a world of illusion, of divine illusion. Poetry attaches its emotion to the idea; the idea *is* the fact. The strongest part of our religion today is its unconscious poetry.[1]

Let me be permitted to quote these words of my own, as uttering the thought which should, in my opinion, go with us and govern us in all our study of poetry. In the present work it is the course of one great contributory stream to the world-river of poetry that we are invited to follow. We are here invited to trace the stream of English poetry. But whether we set ourselves, as here, to follow only one of the several streams that make the mighty river of poetry, or whether we seek to know them all, our governing thought should be the same. We should conceive of poetry worthily, and more highly than it has been the custom to conceive of it. We should conceive of it as capable of higher uses, and called to higher destinies, than those which in general men have assigned to it hitherto. More and more mankind will discover that we have to turn to poetry to interpret life for us, to console us, to

sustain us. Without poetry, our science will appear incomplete; and most of what now passes with us for religion and philosophy will be replaced by poetry. Science, I say, will appear incomplete without it. For finely and truly does Wordsworth call poetry "the impassioned expression which is in the countenance of all science,"[2] and what is a countenance without its expression? Again, Wordsworth finely and truly calls poetry "the breath and finer spirit of all knowledge": our religion, parading evidences such as those on which the popular mind relies now; our philosophy, pluming itself on its reasonings about causation and finite and infinite being; what are they but the shadows and dreams and false shows of knowledge? The day will come when we shall wonder at ourselves for having trusted to them, for having taken them seriously; and the more we perceive their hollowness, the more we shall prize "the breath and finer spirit of knowledge" offered to us by poetry.

But if we conceive thus highly of the destinies of poetry, we must also set our standard for poetry high, since poetry, to be capable of fulfilling such high destinies, must be poetry of a high order of excellence. We must accustom ourselves to a high standard and to a strict judgment. Sainte-Beuve relates that Napoleon one day said, when somebody was spoken of in his presence as a charlatan: "Charlatan as much as you please; but where is there *not* charlatanism?" — "Yes," answers Sainte-Beuve, "in politics, in the art of

[1]From the Introduction to *The Hundred Greatest Men* (1879).

[2]In "Preface to *Lyrical Ballads*"; see p. 313.

governing mankind, that is perhaps true. But in the order of thought, in art, the glory, the eternal honour is that charlatanism shall find no entrance; herein lies the inviolableness of that noble portion of man's being." It is admirably said, and let us hold fast to it. In poetry, which is thought and art in one, it is the glory, the eternal honour, that charlatanism shall find no entrance; that this noble sphere be kept inviolate and inviolable. Charlatanism is for confusing or obliterating the distinctions between excellent and inferior, sound and unsound or only half-sound, true and untrue or only half-true. It is charlatanism, conscious or unconscious, whenever we confuse or obliterate these. And in poetry, more than anywhere else, it is unpermissible to confuse or obliterate them. For in poetry the distinction between excellent and inferior, sound and unsound or only half-sound, true and untrue or only half-true, is of paramount importance. It is of paramount importance because of the high destinies of poetry. In poetry, as a criticism of life under the conditions fixed for such a criticism by the laws of poetic truth and poetic beauty, the spirit of our race will find, we have said, as time goes on and as other helps fail, its consolation and stay. But the consolation and stay will be of power in proportion to the power of the criticism of life. And the criticism of life will be of power in proportion as the poetry conveying it is excellent rather than inferior, sound rather than unsound or half-sound, true rather than untrue or half-true.

The best poetry is what we want; the best poetry will be found to have a power of forming, sustaining, and delighting us, as nothing else can. A clearer, deeper sense of the best in poetry, and of the strength and joy to be drawn from it, is the most precious benefit which we can gather from a poetical collection such as the present. And yet in the very nature and conduct of such a collection there is inevitably something which tends to obscure in us the consciousness of what our benefit should be, and to distract us from the pursuit of it. We should therefore steadily set it before our minds at the outset, and should compel ourselves to revert constantly to the thought of it as we proceed.

Yes; constantly, in reading poetry, a sense for the best, the really excellent, and of the strength and joy to be drawn from it, should be present in our minds and should govern our estimate of what we read. But this real estimate, the only true one, is liable to be superseded, if we are not watchful, by two other kinds of estimate, the historic estimate and the personal estimate, both of which are fallacious. A poet or a poem may count to us historically, they may count to us on grounds personal to ourselves, and they may count to us really. They may count to us historically. The course of development of a nation's language, thought, and poetry, is profoundly interesting; and by regarding a poet's work as a stage in this course of development we may easily bring ourselves to make it of more importance as poetry than in itself it really is, we may come to use a language of quite exaggerated praise in criticizing it; in short, to overrate it. So arises in our poetic judgments the fallacy caused by the estimate which we may call historic. Then, again, a poet or a poem may count to us on grounds personal to ourselves. Our personal affinities, likings, and circumstances have great power to sway our estimates of this or that poet's work, and to make us attach more importance to it as poetry than in itself it really possesses, because to us it is, or has been, of high importance. Here also we overrate the object of our interest, and apply to it a language of praise which is quite exaggerated. And thus we get the source of a second fallacy in our poetic judgments — the fallacy caused by an estimate which we may call personal.

Both fallacies are natural. It is evident how naturally the study of the history and development of a poetry may incline a man to pause over reputations and works once conspicuous but now obscure, and to quarrel with a careless public for skipping, in obedience to mere tradition and habit, from one famous name or work in its natural poetry to another, ignorant of what it misses, and of the reason for keeping what it keeps, and of the whole process of growth in its poetry. The French have become diligent students of their own early poetry, which they long neglected; the study makes many of them dissatisfied with their so-called classical poetry, the court-tragedy of the seventeenth century, a poetry which Pellisson long ago reproached with its want of the true poetic stamp, with its *politesse stérile et rampante*, but which nevertheless has reigned in France as absolutely as if it had been the perfection of classical poetry indeed. The dissatisfaction is natural; yet a lively and accomplished critic, M.Charles d'Héricault, the editor of Clément Marot, goes too far when he says that "the cloud of glory playing round a classic is a mist as dangerous to the future of a literature as it is intolerable for the purposes of history." "It hinders," he goes on, "it hinders us from seeing more than one single point, the culminating and exceptional point; the summary, fictitious and arbitrary, of a thought and of a work. It substitutes a halo for a physiognomy, it puts a statue where there was once a man, and, hiding from us all trace of the labour, the attempts, the weaknesses, the failures, it claims not study but veneration; it does not show us how the thing is done, it imposes upon us a model. Above all, for the historian this creation of classic personages is inadmissible; for it withdraws the poet from his time, from his proper life, it breaks historical relationships, it blinds criticism by conventional admiration, and renders the investigation of literary origins unacceptable. It gives us a human personage no longer, but a God seated immovable amidst His perfect work, like Jupiter on Olympus; and hardly will it be possible for the young student, to whom such work is exhibited at such a distance from him, to believe that it did not issue ready made from that divine head."

All this is brilliantly and tellingly said, but we must plead for a distinction. Everything depends on the reality of a poet's classic character. If he is a dubious classic, let us sift him; if he is a false classic, let us explode him. But if he is a real classic, if his work belongs to the class of the very best (for this is the true and right meaning of the word *classic, classical*), then the great thing for us is to feel and enjoy his work as deeply as ever we can, and to appreciate the wide difference between it and all work which has not the same high character. This is what is salutary, this is what is formative; this is the great benefit to be got from the study of poetry. Everything which interferes with it, which hinders it, is injurious. True, we must read our classic with open eyes, and not with eyes blinded with superstition; we must perceive when his work comes short, when it drops out of the class of the very best, and we must rate it, in such cases, at its proper value. But the use of this negative criticism is not in itself, it is entirely in its enabling us to have a clearer sense and a deeper enjoyment of what is truly excellent. To trace the labour, the attempts, the weaknesses, the failures of a genuine classic, to acquaint oneself with his time and his life and his historical relationships, is mere literary dilettantism unless it has that clear sense and deeper enjoyment for its end. It may be said that the more we know about a classic the better we shall enjoy him; and, if we lived as long as Methuselah and had all of us heads of perfect clearness and wills of perfect steadfastness, this might be true in fact as it is plausible in theory. But the case here is much the same as the case with the Greek and Latin studies of our schooldays. The elaborate philological groundwork which we require them to lay is in theory an admirable preparation for appreciating the Greek and Latin authors worthily. The more thoroughly we lay the groundwork, the better we shall be able, it may be said, to enjoy the authors. True, if time were not so short, and schoolboys' wits not so soon tired and their power of attention exhausted; only, as it is, the elaborate philological preparation goes on, but the authors are little known and less enjoyed. So with the investigator of "historic origins" in poetry. He ought to enjoy the true classic all the better for his investigations; he often is distracted from the enjoyment of the best, and with the less good he overbusies himself, and is prone to overrate it in proportion to the trouble which it has cost him.

The ideas of tracing historic origins and historical relationships cannot be absent from a compilation like the present. And naturally the poets to be exhibited in it will be assigned to those persons for exhibition who are known to prize them highly, rather than to those who have no special inclination towards them. Moreover, the very occupation with an author, and the business of exhibiting him, disposes us to affirm and amplify his importance. In the present work, therefore, we are sure of frequent temptation to adopt the historic estimate, or the personal estimate, and to forget the real estimate; which latter, nevertheless, we must employ if we are to make poetry yield us its full benefit. So high is that benefit, the benefit of clearly feeling and of deeply enjoying the really excellent, the truly classic in poetry, that we do well, I say, to set it fixedly before our minds as our object in studying poets and poetry, and to make the desire of attaining it the one principle to which, as the *Imitation*[3] says, whatever we may read or come to know, we always return. *Cum multa legeris et cognoveris, ad unum semper oportet redire principium.*

The historic estimate is likely in especial to affect our judgment and our language when we are dealing with ancient poets; the personal estimate when we are dealing with poets our contemporaries, or at any rate modern. The exaggerations due to the historic estimate are not in themselves, perhaps, of very much gravity. Their report hardly enters the general ear; probably they do not always impose even on the literary men who adopt them. But they lead to a dangerous abuse of language. So we hear Caedmon, amongst our own poets, compared to Milton. I have already noticed the enthusiasm of one accomplished French critic for "historic origins." Another eminent French critic, M. Vitet, comments upon that famous document of the early poetry of his nation, the *Chanson de Roland*. It is indeed a most interesting document. The *joculator* or *jongleur* Taillefer, who was with William the Conqueror's army at Hastings, marched before the Norman troops, so said the tradition, singing "of Charlemagne and of Roland and of Oliver, and of the vassals who died at Roncevaux"; and it is suggested that in the *Chanson de Roland* by one Turoldus or Théroulde, a poem preserved in a manuscript of the twelfth century in the Bodleian Library at Oxford, we have certainly the matter, perhaps even some of the words, of the chant which Taillefer sang. The poem has vigour and freshness; it is not without pathos. But M. Vitet is not satisfied with seeing in it a document of some poetic value, and of a very high historic and linguistic value; he sees in it a grand and beautiful work, a monument of epic genius. In its general design he finds the grandiose conception, in its details he finds the constant union of simplicity

with greatness, which are the marks, he truly says, of the genuine epic, and distinguish it from the artificial epic of literary ages. One thinks of Homer; this is the sort of praise which is given to Homer, and justly given. Higher praise there cannot well be, and it is the praise due to epic poetry of the highest order only and to no other. Let us try, then, the *Chanson de Roland* at its best. Roland, mortally wounded, lays himself down under a pine-tree, with his face turned towards Spain and the enemy —

> De plusurs choses a remembrer li prist,
> De tantes teres cume li bers cunquist,
> De dulce France, des humes de sun lign,
> De Carlemagne sun seignor ki l'nurrit.[4]

That is primitive work, I repeat, with an undeniable poetic quality of its own. It deserves such praise, and such praise is sufficient for it. But now turn to Homer —

> Ὣς φάτο· τοὺς δ' ἤδη κατέχεν φυσίζοος αἶα
> ἐν Λακεδαίμονι αὖθι, φίλη ἐν πατρίδι γαίη.[5]

We are here in another world, another order of poetry altogether; here is rightly due such supreme praise as that which M. Vitet gives to the *Chanson de Roland*. If our words are to have any meaning, if our judgments are to have any solidity, we must not heap that supreme praise upon poetry of an order immeasurably inferior.

Indeed there can be no more useful help for discovering what poetry belongs to the class of the truly excellent, and can therefore do us most good, than to have always in one's mind lines and expressions of the great masters, and to apply them as a touchstone to other poetry. Of course we are not to require this other poetry to resemble them; it may be very dissimilar. But if we have any tact we shall find them, when we have lodged them well in our minds, an infallible touchstone for detecting the presence or absence of high

---

[3]Thomas à Kempis, *The Imitation of Christ.*

[4]"Then began he to call many things to remembrance, — all the lands which his valour conquered, and pleasant France, and the men of his lineage, and Charlemagne his liege lord who nourished him." — *Chanson de Roland*, iii.939–42. [Arnold]

[5]"So said she; they long since in Earth's soft arms were reposing, / There, in their own dear land, their fatherland, Lacedaemon." *Iliad*, iii. 243, 244 (translated by Dr. Hawtrey). [Arnold]

poetic quality, and also the degree of this quality, in all other poetry which we may place beside them. Short passages, even single lines, will serve our turn quite sufficiently. Take the two lines which I have just quoted from Homer, the poet's comment on Helen's mention of her brothers; — or take his

Ἀ δειλώ τί σφῶϊ δόμεν Πηλῆϊ ἄνακτι
θνητῷ; ὑμεῖς δ' ἐστόν ἀγήρω τ' ἀθανάτω τε.
ἢ ἵνα δυστήνοισι μετ' ἀνδράσιν ἄλγε'
ἔχητον;[6]

the address of Zeus to the horses of Peleus; — or take finally his

Καί σέ, γέρον, τὸ πρὶν μὲν ἀκούομεν ὄλβιον
εἶναι.[7]

the words of Achilles to Priam, a suppliant before him. Take that incomparable line and a half of Dante, Ugolino's tremendous words —

Io no piangeva; sì dentro impietrai.
Piangevan elli . . .[8]

take the lovely words of Beatrice to Virgil —

Io son fatta da Dio, sua mercè, tale,
Che la vostra miseria non mi tange,
Nè fiamma d' esto incendio non m' assale . . .[9]

take the simple, but perfect, single line —

In la sua volontade è nostra pace.[10]

Take of Shakespeare a line or two of Henry the Fourth's expostulation with sleep —

Wilt thou upon the high and giddy mast
Seal up the ship-boy's eyes, and rock his brains
In cradle of the rude imperious surge . . .[11]

and take, as well, Hamlet's dying request to Horatio —

If thou didst ever hold me in thy heart,
Absent thee from felicity awhile,
And in this harsh world draw thy breath in pain
To tell my story . . .[12]

Take of Milton that Miltonic passage —

Darken'd so, yet shone
Above them all the archangel; but his face
Deep scars of thunder had intrench'd, and care
Sat on his faded cheek . . .[13]

add two such lines as —

And courage never to submit or yield
And what is else not to be overcome . . .[14]

and finish with the exquisite close to the loss of Proserpine, the loss

. . . which cost Ceres all that pain
To seek her through the world.[15]

These few lines, if we have tact and can use them, are enough even of themselves to keep clear and sound our judgments about poetry, to save us from fallacious estimates of it, to conduct us to a real estimate.

The specimens I have quoted differ widely from one another, but they have in common this: the possession of the very highest poetical quality. If we are thoroughly penetrated by their power, we shall find that we have acquired a sense enabling us, whatever poetry may be laid before us, to feel the degree in which a high poetical quality is present or wanting there. Critics give themselves great labour to draw out what in the abstract constitutes the characters of a high quality of poetry. It is much better simply to have recourse to concrete examples; — to take specimens of poetry of the high, the very highest quality, and to say: The characters of a high quality of poetry are what is expressed *there*. They are far better recognized by being felt in the verse of the

---

[6]"Ah, unhappy pair, why gave we you to King Peleus, to a mortal? but ye are without old age, and immortal. Was it that with men born in misery ye might have sorrow?" — *Iliad*, xvii. 443–45. [Arnold]

[7]"Nay, and thou too, old man, in former days wast, as we hear, happy." — *Iliad*, xxiv. 543. [Arnold]

[8]"I wailed not, so of stone grew I within; — *they* wailed." — *Inferno*, xxxiii. 39, 40. [Arnold]

[9]"Of such sort hath God, thanked be His mercy, made me, that your misery toucheth me not, neither doth the flame of this fire strike me." — *Inferno*, ii. 91–93. [Arnold]

[10]"In His will is our peace." — *Paradiso*, iii. 85. [Arnold]

[11]Shakespeare, *2 Henry IV*, III.i.18–20.

[12]Shakespeare, *Hamlet*, V.ii.357–60.

[13]Milton, *Paradise Lost*, 1:599–602.

[14]Milton, *Paradise Lost*, 1:108–9.

[15]Milton, *Paradise Lost*, 4:271–72.

master, than by being perused in the prose of the critic. Nevertheless if we are urgently pressed to give some critical account of them, we may safely, perhaps, venture on laying down, not indeed how and why the characters arise, but where and in what they arise. They are in the matter and substance of the poetry, and they are in its manner and style. Both of these, the substance and matter on the one hand, the style and manner on the other, have a mark, an accent, of high beauty, worth, and power. But if we are asked to define this mark and accent in the abstract, our answer must be: No, for we should thereby be darkening the question, not clearing it. The mark and accent are as given by the substance and matter of that poetry, by the style and manner of that poetry, and of all other poetry which is akin to it in quality.

Only one thing we may add as to the substance and matter of poetry, guiding ourselves by Aristotle's profound observation that the superiority of poetry over history consists in its possessing a higher truth and a higher seriousness (φιλοσοφώτερον καὶ σπουδαιότερον).[16] Let us add, therefore, to what we have said, this: that the substance and matter of the best poetry acquire their special character from possessing, in an eminent degree, truth and seriousness. We may add yet further, what is in itself evident, that to the style and manner of the best poetry their special

character, their accent, is given by their diction, and, even yet more, by their movement. And though we distinguish between the two characters, the two accents, of superiority, yet they are nevertheless vitally connected one with the other. The superior character of truth and seriousness, in the matter and substance of the best poetry, is inseparable from the superiority of diction and movement marking its style and manner. The two superiorities are closely related, and are in steadfast proportion one to the other. So far as high poetic truth and seriousness are wanting to a poet's matter and substance, so far also, we may be sure, will a high poetic stamp of diction and movement be wanting to his style and manner. In proportion as this high stamp of diction and movement, again, is absent from a poet's style and manner, we shall find, also, that high poetic truth and seriousness are absent from his substance and matter.

So stated, these are but dry generalities; their whole force lies in their application. And I could wish every student of poetry to make the application of them for himself. Made by himself, the application would impress itself upon his mind far more deeply than if made by me. Neither will my limits allow me to make any full application of the generalities above propounded; but in the hope of bringing out, at any rate, some significance in them, and of establishing an important principle more firmly by their means, I will, in the space which remains to me, follow rapidly from the commencement the course of our English poetry with them in my view.

[16]Aristotle, *Poetics,* Chapter 9.

Friedrich Nietzsche

1844–1900

Friedrich Wilhelm Nietzsche was born in 1844, the son of a Saxon pastor. He was educated at the universities of Bonn and Leipzig, took his degrees in philology, and was appointed professor at the University of Basel in 1869. One selection included here is from Nietzsche's first book, *The Birth of Tragedy from the Spirit of Music* (1872). *The Birth of Tragedy* is unusual among Nietzsche's works in having a sustained and coherent argument: In his later works, he intentionally became more and more aphoristic, conveying his thought in brief flashes and ironic hints. Because he died relatively young of complications from tertiary syphilis and because of nervous breakdowns in the decade before his death, some of his critics have suggested that he was incapable of sustained argument almost from the outset of his career. This is unfair to Nietzsche, who, like Plato, was in rebellion against the stultifying philosophical treatise. His aim was to stimulate thought in others, and for this he was willing to risk being misunderstood. As a result, he has been misunderstood as few philosophers ever have been. Nietzsche was neither nationalistic nor racist nor anti-Semitic, for example, so it is hideously ironic that less than a generation after his death, his ideas, perverted almost beyond recognition, were adopted as the pet philosophy of the Nazi regime.

If there is any central theme in Nietzsche's philosophy it is his opposition to the complacent Victorian faith in progress through a rationalistic reordering of society. He saw as basic to human nature darker motives (like the will-to-power) than his utilitarian contemporaries were willing to acknowledge, but he also saw the possibility of self-sacrifice and transcendence. These themes appear most strongly in his ecstatic tract, *Thus Spake Zarathustra* (1883–92), along with *The Joyful Wisdom* (1882) and *Beyond Good and Evil* (1886). Like Dostoevsky, Nietzsche was a reactionary whose insights into the obscene hunger of the human soul strikingly prefigured the discoveries of Freud.

APOLLO AND DIONYSUS

Nietzsche's essay begins with two opposed symbolic images: Apollo and Dionysus, dream and intoxication, plastic arts and music. The obvious question is why they should divide the aesthetic world between them. This dichotomy is best understood if we see Nietzsche as a follower — with many qualifications — of Arthur Schopenhauer. Schopenhauer's monumental treatise, *The World as Will and Idea* (1819), had posited that human life reverberates between the extremes of boredom and longing — most often the latter, given the competition among the many hungry wills inhabiting the universe. To be alive, Nietzsche agreed, was to be in a state of want: The image of Tantalus, forever groping at the desired food and drink beyond his grasp, was for Nietzsche an image of humankind. Existence was, in a word, tragic.

Nietzsche saw art as civilization's most effective means of coping with this tragedy of existence. Art works by taming dream and intoxication, two primitive methods of coping with the hungry will. In dream the hunger is satiated; in intoxication the self is obliterated. In dream (as Freud and many others had noted) we retreat into a fantasy world in which our desires are all fulfilled, as they cannot be in reality. In intoxication we do not lose our desires so much as we lose *ourselves:* When drunk, our sense of self — our awareness of an inside and an outside, of a consciousness differentiated from the Other — fades away as the ego is annihilated.

THE BIRTH, AND DEATH, AND REBIRTH, OF TRAGEDY

Most of Nietzsche's treatise is a historical essay on the development of Greek tragedy out of the religious ritual of Dionysus. It is startling to think that he developed this notion by an intuitive leap from a few hints in the classics, long before classical research established the religious origins and the ritual nature of the drama.

In the beginning was music, a chorus of dancing satyrs rhythmically, musically expressing their devotion to the god of intoxication, each Greek citizen losing his individuality within the satyr chorus. The choric dance then begins to include song, takes on language and, with it, the plastic images of Apollonian dream. For Nietzsche the essence of tragedy is now already present, before anything like a play exists, in the "Dionysiac chorus which again and again discharges itself in Apollonian images." Later still the god himself is impersonated by the choral leader, who becomes in effect the first actor. From here to the enactment of story and the addition of the second and third actors — to the drama of Aeschylus and Sophocles — it is only a short step: mere complications.

For Nietzsche, tragedy reaches its height with Aeschylus and Sophocles. Its essence in the fusion of Apollonian and Dionysiac impulses begins to be destroyed almost immediately thereafter. Nietzsche's villains are the individualism of Euripides and the rationalism of Socrates, which were consistent with the lyrics of Apollo but not with the music of Dionysus. Individualism and rationalism infected Greek civilization and the Roman and Western European civilizations that followed. Tragedy now began to explore the causes of the errors of highly placed individuals rather than expressing the essence of all human life. Even music itself began in the nineteenth century to become plastic and descriptive — Apollonian rather than Dionysian in character. This perversion of the tragic hit bottom, for Nietzsche, in the Italian opera.

The antidote for all this Nietzsche found in the music-dramas of Richard Wagner, who by 1871 had already written *Tristan und Isolde* and *Die Meistersinger* and had just produced *Das Rheingold* and *Die Walküre,* the first two segments of his massive cycle based on the *Nibelungenlied.* In Wagner's use of myth and universal types, and above all in his return of the leading role to the communal spirit of music rather than the individuation of the Apollonian image, Nietzsche saw the possibility for a rebirth of the healing qualities of art that had been lost when Greek tragedy declined. This enthusiasm with Wagner was to be short-lived. By the second edition of *The Birth of Tragedy,* Nietzsche had broken with Wagner, disgusted by his nationalism and the sickly spiritualism of his last opera, *Parsifal.*

APOLLO AND DIONYSUS REVISITED

It is interesting to see what happens to Nietzsche's views on the Apollonian and the Dionysian, on art and the artist, at the end of his career, as he returns to his critique of the aesthetic in the brilliant fragments of *Twilight of the Idols, or, How to Philosophize with a Hammer* (1889). Where Nietzsche had earlier opposed the Apollonian creation of dream images to the Dionysian musical intoxication, it seems that now art, from the perspective of both artist and audience, is purely a matter of *Rausch*, or intoxication, a psychological state of heightened awareness or excitement that can, of course, be produced by many things other than art. The Apollonian dream, when it comes up in fragment 10, becomes just one more aspect of this generalized intoxication. Both Apollo and Dionysus stand together, representing immediate sensation, as opposed to the asceticism, the dry logic, of the pure intellect, embodied here in the French moralist and philosopher Blaise Pascal (who takes the role of villain that Socrates had played in the earlier treatise). And curiously, Dionysian intoxication no longer has the function of delivering the individual from the prison of the self, but rather the opposite. Rather, by exciting the awareness, intoxication makes the individual more immediately present, both to the world of experience and to the experiencing self.

It is not entirely clear what has made Nietzsche change his mind so completely, but one possible clue is the way he reserves his bitterest and most contemptuous language, not for the intellectuals but for the moralists — and particularly for Christian moralists — who would deprive humanity of the freedom of the will, who would dry up the juices of life on earth, which come from immediate experience, in the name of an illusory life hereafter.

ON TRUTH AND LIE

It is a similar opposition, between the immediate experience and the concept, and the desperate search for a way outside the prison of the conceptual, that generates the extraordinary discussion of the nature of language in "On Truth and Lie." This essay was not published in Nietzsche's lifetime; like so many of his writings that have become central to contemporary thought, it is part of the huge *Nachlass*, the posthumous annex, to his public works. Scholars date "On Truth and Lie" to 1873, the year after *The Birth of Tragedy,* and one senses the kinship here in the explosive little fable with which Nietzsche begins the essay, which punctures the illusion that human life is special because of our cerebral cortex and our powerful intellect. In perspective, we are mere mayflies, and not very effective mayflies because of the way we have distanced ourselves from the immediate experience that our brief lives allow.

But there is no way back to immediate experience, because the human world is mediated through culture, which passes on previous experience in the form of language. It gives stability to our lives, a quick and easy way of understanding the world and therefore succeeding in the bitter struggle for existence — no god could help those who, deprived of language, would need to understand the world all by themselves. Language works precisely by depriving the things of the world of their individuality: a word like "leaf" can only stand for each and every leaf, regardless of shape, size, and color, by becoming a concept deprived of color, shape, and size. At most signifiers speak metaphorically or metonymically to a single aspect of the signified (a "serpent" twists, as the Latin verb *serpere* suggests); they cannot convey its essence. These metaphors are in that sense lies, but once they become structured into concepts, built into a framework that expresses the society's understanding of its world, they become truths:

> What, then, is truth? A mobile army of metaphors, metonyms, and anthropomorphisms — in short, a sum of human relations which have been enhanced, transposed, and embellished poetically and rhetorically, and which after long use seem firm, canonical, and obligatory to a people: truths are illusions about which one has forgotten that this is what they are; metaphors which are worn out and without sensuous power; coins which have lost their pictures and now matter only as metal, no longer as coins.

Or, as we might say: language thinks us. And cultures change, slowly, as this mobile army of metaphors change, as original thinkers conceive new relationships that later harden into new concepts. (Nietzsche clearly agrees with Shelley, that the poets are the "unacknowledged legislators of mankind.")

Nietzsche explores the ways language constitutes society for the masses by defining knowledge and apportioning power, but, in the last three paragraphs, he focuses not on the masses but on the original thinkers who create the new metaphors through aesthetic play, harvesting suffering but experiencing a kind of satisfaction unavailable to those who live by the "truth" of socially accepted concepts. For those with "free intellect," this conceptual grid is a mere "scaffolding and toy for the most audacious feats of the liberated intellect. And when it smashes this framework to pieces, throws it into confusion, and puts it back together in an ironic fashion, pairing the most alien things and separating the closest, it is demonstrating that . . . it will now be guided by intuitions rather than by concepts." That is clearly how Nietzsche conceived of his own job, anticipating by nearly a century Jacques Derrida's deconstruction of the metaphorical world inherent in language.

Selected Bibliography

Danto, Arthur. *Nietzsche as a Philosopher.* New York: Macmillan, 1965.

Donadio, Stephen. *Nietzsche, Henry James, and the Artistic Will.* New York: Oxford University Press, 1976.

Gilman, Sander L. *Nietzschean Parody: An Introduction to Reading Nietzsche.* Bonn: Bouvier Verlag, 1976.

Jaspers, Karl. *Nietzsche: An Introduction to the Understanding of His Philosophical Activity.* Tucson: University of Arizona Press, 1965.

Kaufmann, Walter. *Nietzsche: Philosopher, Psychologist, Antichrist,* 3rd ed. Princeton: Princeton University Press, 1968.

Kemal, Salim, Ivan Gaskell, and Daniel W. Conway. *Nietzsche, Philosophy, and the Arts.* Cambridge, Eng.: Cambridge University Press, 1998.

Klein, Wayne. *Nietzsche and the Promise of Philosophy.* Albany: State University of New York Press, 1997.

Ludovici, Anthony. *Nietzsche and Art.* Boston: J. W. Luce, 1912.

Megill, Allan. *Prophets of Extremity: Nietzsche, Heidegger, Foucault, Derrida.* Berkeley: University of California Press, 1985.

Nehamas, Alexander. *Nietzsche: Life as Literature.* Cambridge: Harvard University Press, 1985.

Silk, M. S. *Nietzsche on Tragedy.* Cambridge and New York: Cambridge University Press, 1981.

From *The Birth of Tragedy from the Spirit of Music*

I

Much will have been gained for esthetics once we have succeeded in apprehending directly — rather than merely *ascertaining* — that art owes its continuous evolution to the Apollonian-Dionysiac duality, even as the propagation of the species depends on the duality of the sexes, their constant conflicts and periodic acts of reconciliation. I have borrowed my adjectives from the Greeks, who developed their mystical doctrines of art through plausible *embodiments,* not through purely conceptual means. It is by those two art-sponsoring deities, Apollo and Dionysos, that we are made to recognize the tremendous split, as regards both origins and objectives, between the plastic, Apollonian arts and the non-visual art of music inspired by Dionysos. The two creative tendencies developed alongside one another, usually in fierce opposition, each by its taunts forcing the other to more energetic production, both perpetuating in a discordant concord that agon[1] which the term *art* but feebly denominates: until at last, by the thaumaturgy of an Hellenic act of will, the pair accepted the yoke of marriage and, in this condition, begot Attic tragedy, which exhibits the salient features of both parents.

To reach a closer understanding of both these tendencies, let us begin by viewing them as the separate art realms of *dream* and *intoxication,* two physiological phenomena standing toward one another in much the same relationship as the Apollonian and Dionysiac. It was in a dream, according to Lucretius, that the marvelous gods and goddesses first presented themselves to the minds of men. That great sculptor, Phidias, beheld in a dream the entrancing bodies of more-than-human beings, and likewise, if anyone had asked the Greek poets about the mystery of poetic creation, they too would have referred him to dreams and instructed him much as Hans Sachs instructs us in *Die Meistersinger:*

My friend, it is the poet's work
Dreams to interpret and to mark.
Believe me that man's true conceit
In a dream becomes complete:
All poetry we ever read
Is but true dreams interpreted.[2]

The fair illusion of the dream sphere, in the production of which every man proves himself an accomplished artist, is a precondition not only of all plastic art, but even, as we shall see presently, of a wide range of poetry. Here we enjoy an immediate apprehension of form, all shapes speak to us directly, nothing seems indifferent or redundant. Despite the high intensity with which these dream realities exist for us, we still have a residual sensation that they are illusions; at least such has been my experience — and the frequency, not to say normality, of the experience is borne out in many passages of the poets. Men of philosophical

Translated by Francis Golffing.
[1] Tragic struggle.

[2] Richard Wagner, *The Mastersingers of Nuremberg,* III.i.99–104.

disposition are known for their constant premonition that our everyday reality, too, is an illusion, hiding another, totally different kind of reality. It was Schopenhauer who considered the ability to view at certain times all men and things as mere phantoms or dream images to be the true mark of philosophic talent. The person who is responsive to the stimuli of art behaves toward the reality of dream much the way the philosopher behaves toward the reality of existence: he observes exactly and enjoys his observations, for it is by these images that he interprets life, by these processes that he rehearses it. Nor is it by pleasant images only that such plausible connections are made: the whole divine comedy of life, including its somber aspects, its sudden balkings, impish accidents, anxious expectations, moves past him, not quite like a shadow play — for it is he himself, after all, who lives and suffers through these scenes — yet never without giving a fleeting sense of illusion; and I imagine that many persons have reassured themselves amidst the perils of dream by calling out, "It is a dream! I want it to go on." I have even heard of people spinning out the causality of one and the same dream over three or more successive nights. All these facts clearly bear witness that our innermost being, the common substratum of humanity, experiences dreams with deep delight and a sense of real necessity. This deep and happy sense of the necessity of dream experiences was expressed by the Greeks in the image of Apollo. Apollo is at once the god of all plastic powers and the soothsaying god. He who is etymologically the "lucent" one, the god of light, reigns also over the fair illusion of our inner world of fantasy. The perfection of these conditions in contrast to our imperfectly understood waking reality, as well as our profound awareness of nature's healing powers during the interval of sleep and dream, furnishes a symbolic analogue to the soothsaying faculty and quite generally to the arts, which make life possible and worth living. But the image of Apollo must incorporate that thin line which the dream image may not cross, under penalty of becoming pathological, of imposing itself on us as crass reality: a discreet limitation, a freedom from all extravagant urges, the sapient tranquillity of the plastic god. His eye must be sunlike, in keeping with his origin. Even at those moments when he is angry and ill-tempered there lies upon him the consecration of fair illusion. In an eccentric way one might say of Apollo what Schopenhauer says, in the first part of *The World as Will and Idea,* of man caught in the veil of Maya:[3] "Even as on an immense, raging sea, assailed by huge wave crests, a man sits in a little rowboat trusting his frail craft, so, amidst the furious torments of this world, the individual sits tranquilly, supported by the *principium individuationis*[4] and relying on it." One might say that the unshakable confidence in that principle has received its most magnificent expression in Apollo, and that Apollo himself may be regarded as the marvelous divine image of the *principium individuationis,* whose looks and gestures radiate the full delight, wisdom, and beauty of "illusion."

In the same context Schopenhauer has described for us the tremendous awe which seizes man when he suddenly begins to doubt the cognitive modes of experience, in other words, when in a given instance the law of causation seems to suspend itself. If we add to this awe the glorious transport which arises in man, even from the very depths of nature, at the shattering of the *principium individuationis,* then we are in a position to apprehend the essence of Dionysiac rapture, whose closest analogy is furnished by physical intoxication. Dionysiac stirrings arise either through the influence of those narcotic potions of which all primitive races speak in their hymns, or through the powerful approach of spring, which penetrates with joy the whole frame of nature. So stirred, the individual forgets himself completely. It is the same Dionysiac power which in medieval Germany drove ever increasing crowds of people singing and dancing from place to place; we recognize in these St. John's and St. Vitus' dancers the bacchic choruses of the Greeks, who had their precursors in Asia Minor and as far back as Babylon and the orgiastic Sacaea.[5] There are people who, either from lack of experience or out of

---

[3]Illusion.

[4]"The principle of individuation": that which differentiates the Self from the Other, the ego from the outside world.

[5]The Babylonian "day of the false king" — a kind of Saturnalia.

sheer stupidity, turn away from such phenomena, and, strong in the sense of their own sanity, label them either mockingly or pityingly "endemic diseases." These benighted souls have no idea how cadaverous and ghostly their "sanity" appears as the intense throng of Dionysiac revelers sweeps past them.

Not only does the bond between man and man come to be forged once more by the magic of the Dionysiac rite, but nature itself, long alienated or subjugated, rises again to celebrate the reconciliation with her prodigal son, man. The earth offers its gifts voluntarily, and the savage beasts of mountain and desert approach in peace. The chariot of Dionysos is bedecked with flowers and garlands; panthers and tigers stride beneath his yoke. If one were to convert Beethoven's "Paean to Joy"[6] into a painting, and refuse to curb the imagination when that multitude prostrates itself reverently in the dust, one might form some apprehension of Dionysiac ritual. Now the slave emerges as a freeman; all the rigid, hostile walls which either necessity or despotism has erected between men are shattered. Now that the gospel of universal harmony is sounded, each individual becomes not only reconciled to his fellow but actually at one with him — as though the veil of Maya had been torn apart and there remained only shreds floating before the vision of mystical Oneness. Man now expresses himself through song and dance as the member of a higher community; he has forgotten how to walk, how to speak, and is on the brink of taking wing as he dances. Each of his gestures betokens enchantment; through him sounds a supernatural power, the same power which makes the animals speak and the earth render up milk and honey. He feels himself to be godlike and strides with the same elation and ecstasy as the gods he has seen in his dreams. No longer the *artist,* he has himself become a *work of art;* the productive power of the whole universe is now manifest in his transport, to the glorious satisfaction of the primordial One. The finest clay, the most precious marble — man — is here kneaded and hewn, and the chisel blows of the Dionysiac world artist are accompanied by the cry of the Eleusinian mystagogues: "Do you fall on your knees, multitudes, do you divine your creator?"[7]

III

In order to comprehend this we must take down the elaborate edifice of Apollonian culture stone by stone until we discover its foundations. At first the eye is struck by the marvelous shapes of the Olympian gods who stand upon its pediments, and whose exploits, in shining bas-relief, adorn its friezes. The fact that among them we find Apollo as one god among many, making no claim to a privileged position, should not mislead us. The same drive that found its most complete representation in Apollo generated the whole Olympian world, and in this sense we may consider Apollo the father of that world. But what was the radical need out of which that illustrious society of Olympian beings sprang?

Whoever approaches the Olympians with a different religion in his heart, seeking moral elevation, sanctity, spirituality, loving-kindness, will presently be forced to turn away from them in ill-humored disappointment. Nothing in these deities reminds us of asceticism, high intellect, or duty: we are confronted by luxuriant, triumphant *existence,* which deifies the good and the bad indifferently. And the beholder may find himself dismayed in the presence of such overflowing life and ask himself what potion these heady people must have drunk in order to behold, in whatever direction they looked, Helen laughing back at them, the beguiling image of their own existence. But we shall call out to this beholder, who had already turned his back: Don't go! Listen first to what the Greeks themselves have to say of this life, which spreads itself before you with such puzzling serenity. An old legend has it that King Midas hunted a long time in the woods for the wise Silenus, companion of Dionysos, without being able to catch him. When he had finally

---

[6]The setting of Schiller's "Ode to Joy" takes up most of the final movement of the Ninth Symphony.

[7]The Eleusinian Mysteries were a cult devoted to the goddess Persephone which celebrated the coming of winter and the return of spring; the quotation is from Schiller's "Ode to Joy."

caught him the king asked him what he considered man's greatest good. The daemon remained sullen and uncommunicative until finally, forced by the king, he broke into a shrill laugh and spoke: "Ephemeral wretch, begotten by accident and toil, why do you force me to tell you what it would be your greatest boon not to hear? What would be best for you is quite beyond your reach: not to have been born, not to *be*, to be *nothing*. But the second best is to die soon."

What is the relation of the Olympian gods to this popular wisdom? It is that of the entranced vision of the martyr to his torment.

Now the Olympian magic mountain[8] opens itself before us, showing us its very roots. The Greeks were keenly aware of the terrors and horrors of existence; in order to be able to live at all they had to place before them the shining fantasy of the Olympians. Their tremendous distrust of the titanic forces of nature: *Moira*,[9] mercilessly enthroned beyond the knowable world; the vulture which fed upon the great philanthropist Prometheus; the terrible lot drawn by wise Oedipus; the curse on the house of Atreus which brought Orestes to the murder of his mother: that whole Panic[10] philosophy, in short, with its mythic examples, by which the gloomy Etruscans perished, the Greeks conquered — or at least hid from view — again and again by means of this artificial Olympus. In order to live at all the Greeks had to construct these deities. The Apollonian need for beauty had to develop the Olympian hierarchy of joy by slow degrees from the original titanic hierarchy of terror, as roses are seen to break from a thorny thicket. How else could life have been borne by a race so hypersensitive, so emotionally intense, so equipped for suffering? The same drive which called art into being as a completion and consummation of existence, and as a guarantee of further existence, gave rise also to the Olympian realm which acted as a transfiguring mirror to the Hellenic will. The gods justified human life by living it themselves — the

only satisfactory theodicy[11] ever invented. To exist in the clear sunlight of such deities was now felt to be the highest good, and the only real grief suffered by Homeric man was inspired by the thought of leaving that sunlight, especially when the departure seemed imminent. Now it became possible to stand the wisdom of Silenus on its head and proclaim that it was the worst evil for man to die soon, and second worst for him to die at all. Such laments as arise now arise over short-lived Achilles, over the generations ephemeral as leaves, the decline of the heroic age. It is not unbecoming to even the greatest hero to yearn for an afterlife, though it be as a day laborer. So impetuously, during the Apollonian phase, does man's will desire to remain on earth, so identified does he become with existence, that even his lament turns to a song of praise.

It should have become apparent by now that the harmony with nature which we late-comers regard with such nostalgia, and for which Schiller has coined the cant term *naïve*,[12] is by no means a simple and inevitable condition to be found at the gateway to every culture, a kind of paradise. Such a belief could have been endorsed only by a period for which Rousseau's Emile was an artist and Homer just such an artist nurtured in the bosom of nature. Whenever we encounter "naïveté" in art, we are face to face with the ripest fruit of Apollonian culture — which must always triumph first over titans, kill monsters, and overcome the somber contemplation of actuality, the intense susceptibility to suffering, by means of illusions strenuously and zestfully entertained. But how rare are the instances of true naïveté, of that complete identification with the beauty of appearance! It is this achievement which makes Homer so magnificent — Homer, who, as a single individual, stood to Apollonian popular culture in the same relation as the individual dream artist to the oneiric capacity of a race and of nature generally. The naïveté of Homer must be viewed as a complete victory of Apollonian illusion. Nature often uses illusions of this sort in order to accomplish its secret purposes. The true goal is covered over by a phantasm. We stretch out our hands to

---

[8]The Zauberberg was the mountain where Venus lived, to which the troubador Tannhäuser was attracted in the medieval legend. Nietzsche uses it as a symbol for a fantasy world.

[9]Destiny.

[10]Relating to Pan, the god of Nature.

[11]Explanation of divine justice.

[12]See Schiller, "On Naive and Sentimental Poetry," p. 300.

the latter, while nature, aided by our deception, attains the former. In the case of the Greeks it was the will wishing to behold itself in the work of art, in the transcendence of genius; but in order so to behold itself its creatures had first to view themselves as glorious, to transpose themselves to a higher sphere, without having that sphere of pure contemplation either challenge them or upbraid them with insufficiency. It was in that sphere of beauty that the Greeks saw the Olympians as their mirror images; it was by means of that esthetic mirror that the Greek will opposed suffering and the somber wisdom of suffering which always accompanies artistic talent. As a monument to its victory stands Homer, the naïve artist.

IV

We can learn something about the naïve artist through the analogy of dream. We can imagine the dreamer as he calls out to himself, still caught in the illusion of his dream and without disturbing it, "This is a dream, and I want to go on dreaming," and we can infer, on the one hand, that he takes deep delight in the contemplation of his dream, and, on the other, that he must have forgotten the day, with its horrible importunity, so to enjoy his dream. Apollo, the interpreter of dreams, will furnish the clue to what is happening here. Although of the two halves of life — the waking and the dreaming — the former is generally considered not only the more important but the only one which is truly lived, I would, at the risk of sounding paradoxical, propose the opposite view. The more I have come to realize in nature those omnipotent formative tendencies and, with them, an intense longing for illusion, the more I feel inclined to the hypothesis that the original Oneness, the ground of Being, ever-suffering and contradictory, time and again has need of rapt vision and delightful illusion to redeem itself. Since we ourselves are the very stuff of such illusions, we must view ourselves as the truly nonexistent, that is to say, as a perpetual unfolding in time, space, and causality — what we label "empiric reality." But if, for the moment, we abstract from our own reality, viewing our empiric existence, as well as the existence of the world at large, as the *idea* of the original Oneness,

produced anew each instant, then our dreams will appear to us as illusions of illusions, hence as a still higher form of satisfaction of the original desire for illusion. It is for this reason that the very core of nature takes such a deep delight in the naïve artist and the naïve work of art, which likewise is merely the illusion of an illusion. Raphael, himself one of those immortal "naïve" artists, in a symbolic canvas has illustrated that reduction of illusion to further illusion which is the original act of the naïve artist and at the same time of all Apollonian culture. In the lower half of his *Transfiguration,* through the figures of the possessed boy, the despairing bearers, the helpless, terrified disciples, we see a reflection of original pain, the sole ground of being: "illusion" here is a reflection of eternal contradiction, begetter of all things. From this illusion there rises, like the fragrance of ambrosia, a new illusory world, invisible to those enmeshed in the first: a radiant vision of pure delight, a rapt seeing through wide-open eyes. Here we have, in a great symbol of art, both the fair world of Apollo and its substratum, the terrible wisdom of Silenus, and we can comprehend intuitively how they mutually require one another. But Apollo appears to us once again as the apotheosis of the *principium individuationis,* in whom the eternal goad of the original Oneness, namely its redemption through illusion, accomplishes itself. With august gesture the god shows us how there is need for a whole world of torment in order for the individual to produce the redemptive vision and to sit quietly in his rocking rowboat in mid-sea, absorbed in contemplation.

If this apotheosis of individuation is to be read in normative terms, we may infer that there is one norm only: the individual — or, more precisely, the observance of the limits of the individual: *sophrosyne.* As a moral deity Apollo demands self-control from his people and, in order to observe such self-control, a knowledge of self. And so we find that the esthetic necessity of beauty is accompanied by the imperatives, "Know thyself," and "Nothing too much." Conversely, excess and *hubris* come to be regarded as the hostile spirits of the non-Apollonian sphere, hence as properties of the pre-Apollonian era — the age of Titans — and the extra-Apollonian world, that is to say the world of the barbarians. It was because of his Titanic love of man that Prometheus had to be devoured by vultures; it was because of his extravagant wisdom which succeeded in solving the riddle of the Sphinx that Oedipus had to be cast into a whirlpool of crime: in this fashion does the Delphic god interpret the Greek past.

The effects of the Dionysiac spirit struck the Apollonian Greeks as titanic and barbaric; yet they could not disguise from themselves the fact that they were essentially akin to those deposed Titans and heroes. They felt more than that: their whole existence, with its temperate beauty, rested upon a base of suffering and *knowledge* which had been hidden from them until the reinstatement of Dionysos uncovered it once more. And lo and behold! Apollo found it impossible to live without Dionysos. The elements of titanism and barbarism turned out to be quite as fundamental as the Apollonian element. And now let us imagine how the ecstatic sounds of the Dionysiac rites penetrated ever more enticingly into that artificially restrained and discreet world of illusion, how this clamor expressed the whole outrageous gamut of nature — delight, grief, knowledge — even to the most piercing cry; and then let us imagine how the Apollonian artist with his thin, monotonous harp music must have sounded beside the demoniac chant of the multitude! The muses presiding over the illusory arts paled before an art which enthusiastically told the truth, and the wisdom of Silenus cried "Woe!" against the serene Olympians. The individual, with his limits and moderations, forgot himself in the Dionysiac vortex and became oblivious to the laws of Apollo. Indiscreet extravagance revealed itself as truth, and contradiction, a delight born of pain, spoke out of the bosom of nature. Wherever the Dionysiac voice was heard, the Apollonian norm seemed suspended or destroyed. Yet it is equally true that, in those places where the first assault was withstood, the prestige and majesty of the Delphic god appeared more rigid and threatening than before. The only way I am able to view Doric art and the Doric state[13] is as a perpetual military encampment of

the Apollonian forces. An art so defiantly austere, so ringed about with fortifications — an education so military and exacting — a polity so ruthlessly cruel — could endure only in a continual state of resistance against the titanic and barbaric menace of Dionysos.

Up to this point I have developed at some length a theme which was sounded at the beginning of this essay: how the Dionysiac and Apollonian elements, in a continuous chain of creations, and enhancing the other, dominated the Hellenic mind; how from the Iron Age, with its battles of Titans and its austere popular philosophy, there developed under the aegis of Apollo and Homeric world of beauty; how this "naïve" splendor was then absorbed once more by the Dionysiac torrent, and how, face to face, with this new power, the Apollonian code rigidified into the majesty of Doric art and contemplation. If the earlier phase of Greek history may justly be broken down into four major artistic epochs dramatizing the battle between the two hostile principles, then we must inquire further (lest Doric art appear to us as the acme and final goal of all these striving tendencies) what was the true end toward which that evolution moved. And our eyes will come to rest on the sublime and much lauded achievement of the dramatic dithyramb and Attic tragedy, as the common goal of both urges; whose mysterious marriage, after long discord, ennobled itself with such a child, at once Antigone and Cassandra.[14]

V

We are now approaching the central concern of our inquiry, which has as its aim an understanding of the Dionysiac-Apollonian spirit, or at least an intuitive comprehension of the mystery which made this conjunction possible. Our first question must be: where in the Greek world is the new seed first to be found which was later to develop into tragedy and the dramatic dithyramb? Greek antiquity gives us a pictorial clue when it represents in statues, on cameos, etc., Homer and Archilochus side by side as ancestors and torch-bearers of

[13]Sparta.

[14]The dutiful Antigone may represent the Apollonian principle, the possessed Cassandra the Dionysiac.

Greek poetry, in the certainty that only these two are to be regarded as truly original minds, from whom a stream of fire flowed onto the entire later Greek world. Homer, the hoary dreamer, caught in utter abstraction, prototype of the Apollonian naïve artist, stares in amazement at the passionate head of Archilochus, soldierly servant of the Muses, knocked about by fortune. All that more recent esthetics has been able to add by way of interpretation is that here the "objective" artist is confronted by the first "subjective" artist. We find this interpretation of little use, since to us the subjective artist is simply the bad artist, and since we demand above all, in every genre and range of art, a triumph over subjectivity, deliverance from the self, the silencing of every personal will and desire; since, in fact, we cannot imagine the smallest genuine art work lacking objectivity and disinterested contemplation. For this reason our esthetic must first solve the following problem: how is the lyrical poet at all possible as artist — he who, according to the experience of all times, always says "I" and recites to us the entire chromatic scale of his passions and appetites? It is this Archilochus who most disturbs us, placed there beside Homer, with the stridor of his hate and mockery, the drunken outbursts of his desire. Isn't he — the first artist to be called subjective — for that reason the veritable nonartist? How, then, are we to explain the reverence in which he was held as a poet, the honor done him by the Delphic oracle, that seat of "objective" art, in a number of very curious sayings?

Schiller has thrown some light on his own manner of composition by a psychological observation which seems inexplicable to himself without, however, giving him pause. Schiller confessed that, prior to composing, he experienced not a logically connected series of images but rather a *musical mood*. "With me emotion is at the beginning without clear and definite ideas; those ideas do not arise until later on. A certain musical disposition of mind comes first, and after follows the poetical idea." If we enlarge on this, taking into account the most important phenomenon of ancient poetry, by which I mean that union — nay identity — everywhere considered natural, between musician and poet (alongside which our modern poetry appears as the statue of a god without a head), then we may, on the basis of the esthetics adumbrated earlier, explain the lyrical poet in the following manner. He is, first and foremost, a Dionysiac artist, become wholly identified with the original Oneness, its pain and contradiction, and producing a replica of that Oneness as music, if music may legitimately be seen as a repetition of the world; however, this music becomes visible to him again, as in a dream similitude, through the Apollonian dream influence. That reflection, without image or idea, or original pain in music, with its redemption through illusion, now produces a second reflection as a single simile or example. The artist had abrogated his subjectivity earlier, during the Dionysiac phase: the image which now reveals to him his oneness with the heart of the world is a dream scene showing forth vividly, together with original pain, the original delight of illusion. The "I" thus sounds out of the depth of being; what recent writers on esthetics speak of as "subjectivity" is a mere figment. When Archilochus, the first lyric poet of the Greeks, hurls both his frantic love and his contempt at the daughters of Lycambes, it is not his own passion that we see dancing before us in an orgiastic frenzy: we see Dionysos and the maenads, we see the drunken reveler Archilochus, sunk down in sleep — as Euripides describes him for us in the *Bacchae*, asleep on a high mountain meadow, in the midday sun — and now Apollo approaches him and touches him with his laurel. The sleeper's enchantment through Dionysiac music now begins to emit sparks of imagery, poems which, at their point of highest evolution, will bear the name of tragedies and dramatic dithyrambs.

The sculptor, as well as his brother, the epic poet, is committed to the pure contemplation of images. The Dionysiac musician, himself imageless, is nothing but original pain and reverberation of the image. Out of this mystical process of unselving, the poet's spirit feels a whole world of images and similitudes arise, which are quite different in hue, causality, and pace from the images of the sculptor or narrative poet. While the latter lives in those images and only in them, with joyful complacence, and never tires of scanning them down to the most minute features, while even the image of angry Achilles is no more for him than an *image* whose irate countenance he enjoys with a dreamer's delight in appearance — so that this mirror of appearance protects him from complete fusion with his characters — the lyrical poet, on the other hand, himself becomes his images, his images are objectified versions of himself. Being the active center of that world he may boldly speak in the first person, only his "I" is not that of the actual waking man, but the "I" dwelling, truly and eternally, in the ground of being. It is through the reflections of that "I" that the lyric poet beholds the ground of being. Let us imagine, next, how he views himself too among these reflections — as nongenius, that is, as his own subject matter, the whole teeming crowd of his passions and intentions directed toward a definite goal; and when it now appears as though the poet and the nonpoet joined to him were one, and as though the former were using the pronoun "I," we are able to see through this appearance, which has deceived those who have attached the label "subjective" to the lyrical poet. The man Archilochus, with his passionate loves and hates, is really only a vision of genius, a genius who is no longer merely Archilochus but the genius of the universe, expressing its pain through the similitude of Archilochus the man. Archilochus, on the other hand, the subjectively willing and desiring human being, can never be a poet. Nor is it at all necessary for the poet to see only the phenomenon of the man Archilochus before him as a reflection of Eternal Being: the world of tragedy shows us to what extent the vision of the poet can remove itself from the urgent, immediate phenomenon.

Schopenhauer, who was fully aware of the difficulties the lyrical poet creates for the speculative esthetician, thought that he had found a solution, which, however, I cannot endorse. It is true that he alone possessed the means, in his profound philosophy of music, for solving this problem; and I think I have honored his achievement in these pages, I hope in his own spirit. Yet in the first part of *The World as Will and Idea* he characterizes the essence of song as follows:

> The consciousness of the singer is filled with the subject of will, which is to say with his own willing. That willing may either be a released, satisfied willing (joy), or, as happens more commonly, an inhibited willing (sadness). In either case there is

affect here: passion, violent commotion. At the same time, however, the singer is moved by the contemplation of nature surrounding him to experience himself as the subject of pure, unwilling ideation, and the unshakable tranquillity of that ideation becomes contrasted with the urgency of his willing, its limits, and its lacks. It is the experience of this contrast, or tug of war, which he expresses in his song. While we find ourselves in the lyrical condition, pure ideation approaches us, as it were, to deliver us from the urgencies of willing; we obey, yet obey for moments only. Again and again our willing, our memory of personal objectives, distracts us from tranquil contemplation, while, conversely, the next scene of beauty we behold will yield us up once more to pure ideation. For this reason we find in song and in the lyrical mood a curious mixture of willing (our personal interest in *purposes*) and pure contemplation (whose subject matter is furnished by our surroundings); relations are sought and imagined between these two sets of experiences. Subjective mood — the affection of the will — communicates its color to the purely viewed surroundings, and vice versa. All authentic song reflects a state of mind mixed and divided in this manner.

Who can fail to perceive in this description that lyric poetry is presented as an art never completely realized, indeed a hybrid whose essence is made to consist in an uneasy mixture of will and contemplation, i.e., the esthetic and the nonesthetic conditions? We, on our part, maintain that the distinction between subjective and objective, which even Schopenhauer still uses as a sort of measuring stick to distinguish the arts, has no value whatever in esthetics; the reason being that the subject — the striving individual bent on furthering his egoistic purposes — can be thought of only as an enemy to art, never as its source. But to the extent that the subject is an artist he is already delivered from individual will and has become a medium through which the True Subject celebrates. His redemption in illusion. For better or worse, one thing should be quite obvious to all of us: the entire comedy of art is not played for our own sakes — for our betterment or education, say — nor can we consider ourselves the true originators of that art realm; while on the other hand we have every right to view ourselves as esthetic projections of the veritable creator and derive such dignity as we possess from our status as art works. Only as an esthetic product can the world be justified to all eternity — although our consciousness of our own significance does scarcely exceed the consciousness a painted soldier might have of the battle in which he takes part. Thus our whole knowledge of art is at bottom illusory, seeing that as mere *knowers* we can never be fused with that essential spirit, at the same time creator and spectator, who has prepared the comedy of art for his own edification. Only as the genius in the act of creation merges with the primal architect of the cosmos can he truly know something of the eternal essence of art. For in that condition he resembles the uncanny fairy tale image which is able to see itself by turning its eyes. He is at once subject and object, poet, actor, and audience.

XIV

Let us now imagine Socrates' great Cyclops' eye — that eye which never glowed with the artist's divine frenzy — turned upon tragedy. Bearing in mind that he was unable to look with any pleasure into the Dionysiac abysses, what could Socrates see in that tragic art which to Plato seemed noble and meritorious? Something quite abstruse and irrational, full of causes without effects and effects seemingly without causes, the whole texture so checkered that it must be repugnant to a sober disposition, while it might act as dangerous tinder to a sensitive and impressionable mind. We are told that the only genre of poetry Socrates really appreciated was the Aesopian fable. This he did with the same smiling complaisance with which honest Gellert sings the praise of poetry in his fable of the bee and the hen:

> I exemplify the use of poetry:
> To convey to those who are a bit backward
> The truth in a simile.[15]

The fact is that for Socrates tragic art failed even to "convey the truth," although it did address itself to those who were "a bit backward," which is to say to nonphilosophers: a double reason for leaving it

alone.[16] Like Plato, he reckoned it among the beguiling arts which represent the agreeable, not the useful, and in consequence exhorted his followers to abstain from such unphilosophical stimulants. His success was such that the young tragic poet Plato burned all his writings in order to qualify as a student of Socrates. And while strong native genius might now and again manage to withstand the Socratic injunction, the power of the latter was still great enough to force poetry into entirely new channels.

A good example of this is Plato himself. Although he did not lag behind the naïve cynicism of his master in the condemnation of tragedy and of art in general, nevertheless his creative gifts forced him to develop an art form deeply akin to the existing form which he had repudiated. The main objection raised by Plato to the older art (that it was the imitation of an imitation and hence belonged to an even lower order of empiric reality) must not, at all costs, apply to the new genre; and so we see Plato intent on moving beyond reality and on rendering the idea which underlies it. By a detour Plato the thinker reached the very spot where Plato the poet had all along been at home, and from which Sophocles, and with him the whole poetic tradition of the past, protested such a change. Tragedy had assimilated to itself all the older poetic genres. In a somewhat eccentric sense the same thing can be claimed for the Platonic dialogue, which was a mixture of all the available styles and forms and hovered between narrative, lyric, drama, between prose and poetry, once again breaking through the old law of stylistic unity. The Cynic philosophers went even farther in that direction, seeking, by their utterly promiscuous style and constant alternation between verse and prose, to project their image of the "raving Socrates" in literature, as they sought to enact it in life. The Platonic dialogue was the lifeboat in which the shipwrecked older poetry saved itself, together with its numerous offspring. Crowded together in a narrow space, and timidly obeying their helmsman Socrates, they moved forward into a new era which never tired of looking at this fantastic spectacle. Plato has furnished for all posterity the pattern of a

---

[15]Christian Fürchtegott Gellert (1715–1769), poet and novelist of the German Enlightenment; the quotation is from *Poems and Fables* (1746–48).

[16]Nietzsche alludes to Socrates' final assessment of poetry in Plato's *Republic*, Book X; see p. 30.

new art form, the novel, viewed as the Aesopian fable raised to its highest power; a form in which poetry played the same subordinate role with regard to dialectic philosophy as that same philosophy was to play for many centuries with regard to theology. This, then, was the new status of poetry, and it was Plato who, under the pressure of daemonic Socrates, had brought it about.

It is at this point that philosophical ideas begin to entwine themselves about art, forcing the latter to cling closely to the trunk of dialectic. The Apollonian tendency now appears disguised as logical schematism, just as we found in the case of Euripides a corresponding translation of the Dionysiac affect into a naturalistic one. Socrates, the dialectical hero of the Platonic drama, shows a close affinity to the Euripidean hero, who is compelled to justify his actions by proof and counterproof, and for that reason is often in danger of forfeiting our tragic compassion. For who among us can close his eyes to the optimistic element in the nature of dialectics, which sees a triumph in every syllogism and can breathe only in an atmosphere of cool, conscious clarity? Once that optimistic element had entered tragedy, it overgrew its Dionysiac regions and brought about their annihilation and, finally, the leap into genteel domestic drama. Consider the consequences of the Socratic maxims: "Virtue is knowledge; all sins arise from ignorance; only the virtuous are happy" — these three basic formulations of optimism spell the death of tragedy. The virtuous hero must henceforth be a dialectician; virtue and knowledge, belief and ethics, be necessarily and demonstrably connected; Aeschylus' transcendental concept of justice be reduced to the brash and shallow principle of poetic justice with its regular *deus ex machina*.

What is the view taken of the chorus in this new Socratic-optimistic stage world, and of the entire musical and Dionysiac foundation of tragedy? They are seen as accidental features, as reminders of the origin of tragedy, which can well be dispensed with — while we have in fact come to understand that the chorus is the cause of tragedy and the tragic spirit. Already in Sophocles we find some embarrassment with regard to the chorus, which suggests that the Dionysiac floor of tragedy is beginning to give way. Sophocles no

longer dares to give the chorus the major role in the tragedy but treats it as almost on the same footing as the actors, as though it had been raised from the *orchestra* onto the *scene*. By so doing he necessarily destroyed its meaning, despite Aristotle's endorsement of this conception of the chorus. This shift in attitude, which Sophocles displayed not only in practice but also, we are told, in theory, was the first step toward the total disintegration of the chorus: a process whose rapid phases we can follow in Euripides, Agathon, and the New Comedy. Optimistic dialectics took up the whip of its syllogisms and drove music out of tragedy. It entirely destroyed the meaning of tragedy — which can be interpreted only as a concrete manifestation of Dionysiac conditions, music made visible, an ecstatic dream world.

Since we have discovered an anti-Dionysiac tendency antedating Socrates, its most brilliant exponent, we must now ask, "Toward what does a figure like Socrates point?" Faced with the evidence of the Platonic dialogues, we are certainly not entitled to see in Socrates merely an agent of disintegration. While it is clear that the immediate result of the Socratic strategy was the destruction of Dionysiac drama, we are forced, nevertheless, by the profundity of the Socratic experience to ask ourselves whether, in fact, art and Socratism are diametrically opposed to one another, whether there is really anything inherently impossible in the idea of a Socratic artist?

It appears that this despotic logician had from time to time a sense of void, loss, unfulfilled duty with regard to art. In prison he told his friends how, on several occasions, a voice had spoken to him in a dream, saying "Practice music, Socrates!"[17] Almost to the end he remained confident that his philosophy represented the highest art of the muses, and would not fully believe that a divinity meant to remind him of "common, popular music." Yet in order to unburden his conscience he finally agreed, in prison, to undertake that music which hitherto he had held in low esteem. In this frame of mind he composed a poem on Apollo and rendered several Aesopian fables in verse. What prompted him to these exercises was something very similar to that

[17]In Plato's *Phaedo*.

warning voice of his daimonion: an Apollonian perception that, like a barbarian king, he had failed to comprehend the nature of a divine effigy, and was in danger of offending his own god through ignorance. These words heard by Socrates in his dream are the only indication that he ever experienced any uneasiness about the limits of his logical universe. He may have asked himself: "Have I been too ready to view what was unintelligible to me as being devoid of meaning? Perhaps there is a realm of wisdom, after all, from which the logician is excluded? Perhaps art must be seen as the necessary complement of rational discourse?"

XIX

The best way to characterize the core of Socratic culture is to call it the culture of the opera. It is in this area that Socratism has given an open account of its intentions — a rather surprising one when we compare the evolution of the opera with the abiding Apollonian and Dionysiac truths. First I want to remind the reader of the genesis of the *stilo rappresentativo*[18] and of recitative. How did it happen that this operatic music, so wholly external and incapable of reverence, was enthusiastically greeted by an epoch which, not so very long ago, had produced the inexpressibly noble and sacred music of Palestrina? Can anyone hold the luxury and frivolity of the Florentine court and the vanity of its dramatic singers responsible for the speed and intensity with which the vogue of opera spread? I can explain the passion for a semi-musical declamation, at the same period and among the same people who had witnessed the grand architecture of Palestrina's harmonies (in the making of which the whole Christian Middle Ages had conspired), only by reference to an extra-artistic tendency. To the listener who desires to hear the words above the music corresponds the singer who speaks more than he sings, emphasizing the verbal pathos in a kind of half-song. By this emphasis he aids the understanding of the words and gets rid of the remaining half of music. There is a danger that now and again the music will preponderate, spoiling the pathos and clarity of his declamation, while conversely he is always under the temptation to discharge the music of his voice in a virtuoso manner. The pseudopoetic librettist furnishes him ample opportunity for this display in lyrical interjections, repetitions of words and phrases, etc., where the singer may give himself up to the purely musical element without consideration for the text. This constant alternation, so characteristic of the *stilo rappresentativo*, between emotionally charged, only partly sung declamation and wholly musical interjections, this rapid shift of focus between concept and imagination, on the one hand, and the musical response of the listener, on the other, is so completely unnatural, equally opposed to the Dionysiac and the Apollonian spirit, that one must conclude the origin of recitative to have lain outside any artistic instinct. Viewed in these terms, the recitative may be characterized as a mixture of epic and lyric declamation. And yet, since the components are so wholly disparate, the resulting combination is neither harmonious nor constant, but rather a superficial and mosaic-like conglutination, not without precedent in the realm of nature and experience. However, the inventors of recitative took a very different view of it. They, and their age with them, thought they had discovered the secret of ancient music, that secret which alone could account for the amazing feats of an Orpheus or an Amphion or, indeed, for Greek tragedy. They thought that by that novel style they had managed to resuscitate ancient Greek music in all its power; and, given the popular conception of the Homeric world as the primordial world, it was possible to embrace the illusion that one had at last returned to the paradisaical beginnings of mankind, in which music must have had that supreme purity, power, and innocence of which the pastoral poets wrote so movingly. Here we have touched the nerve center of opera, that genuinely modern genre. In it, art satisfies a strong need, but one that can hardly be called esthetic: a hankering for the idyll, a belief in the primordial existence of pure, artistically sensitive man. Recitative stood for the rediscovered language of

[18]A term characterizing the opera created in the late sixteenth century by the Florentine musical society known as the *Camerata*, in which dramatic recitative alternates with florid arias expressing emotion. Operas in the current repertory written in the *stilo rappresentativo* include Monteverdi's *L'Incoronazione di Poppaea* and Purcell's *Dido and Aeneas*.

that archetypal man, opera for the rediscovered country of that idyllic and heroically pure species, who in all their actions followed a natural artistic bent — who, no matter what they had to say, sang at least part of it, and who when their emotions were ever so little aroused burst into full song. It is irrelevant to our inquiry that the humanists of the time used the new image of the paradisaical artist to combat the old ecclesiastical notion of man as totally corrupt and damned; that opera thus represented the opposition dogma of man as essentially good, and furnished an antidote to that pessimism which, given the terrible instability of the epoch, naturally enlisted its strongest and most thoughtful minds. What matters here is our recognition that the peculiar attraction and thus the success of this new art form must be attributed to its satisfaction of a wholly unesthetic need: it was optimistic; it glorified man in himself; it conceived of man as originally good and full of talent. This principle of opera has by degrees become a menacing and rather appalling claim, against which we who are faced with present-day socialist movements cannot stop our ears. The "noble savage" demands his rights: what a paradisaical prospect!

There is still a further point in support of my contention that opera is built on the same principles as our Alexandrian culture. Opera is the product of the man of theory, the critical layman, not the artist. This constitutes one of the most disturbing facts in the entire history of art. Since the demand, coming from essentially unmusical people, was for a clear understanding of the words, a renascence of music could come about only through the discovery of a type of music in which the words lorded it over the counterpoint as a master over his servant. For were not the words nobler than the accompanying harmonic system, as the soul is nobler than the body? It was with precisely that unmusical clumsiness that the combinations of music, image, and word were treated in the beginning of opera, and in this spirit the first experiments in the new genre were carried out, even in the noble lay circles of Florence, by the poets and singers patronized by those circles. Inartistic man produces his own brand of art, precisely by virtue of his artistic impotence. Having not the faintest conception of the Dionysiac profundity of music, he transforms musical enjoyment into a rationalistic rhetoric of passion in the *stilo rappresentativo,* into a voluptuous indulgence of vocal virtuoso feats; lacking imagination, he must employ engineers and stage designers; being incapable of understanding the true nature of the artist, he invents an "artistic primitive" to suit his taste, i.e., a man who, when his passions are aroused, breaks into song and recites verses. He projects himself into a time when passion sufficed to produce songs and poems — as though mere emotion had ever been able to create art. There lies at the root of opera a fallacious conception of the artistic process, the idyllic belief that every sensitive man is at bottom an artist. In keeping with this belief, opera is the expression of dilettantism in art, dictating its rules with the cheerful optimism of the theorist.

If we were to combine the two tendencies conspiring at the creation of opera into one, we might speak of an idyllic tendency of opera. Here it would be well to refer back to Schiller's account. Nature and ideal, according to Schiller, are objects of grief when the former is felt to be lost, the latter to be beyond reach. But both may become objects of joy when they are represented as actual. Then the first will produce the elegy, in its strict sense, and the second the idyll, in its widest sense. I would like to point out at once the common feature of these two conceptions in the origin of opera: here the ideal is never viewed as unattained nor nature as lost. Rather, a primitive period in the history of man is imagined, in which he lay at the heart of nature and in this state of nature attained immediately the ideal of humanity through Edenic nobility and artistry. From this supposedly perfect primitive we are all said to derive; indeed, we are still his faithful replicas. All we need do in order to recognize ourselves in that primitive is to jettison some of our later achievements, such as our superfluous learning and excess culture. The educated man of the Renaissance used the operatic imitation of Greek tragedy to lead him back to that concord of nature and ideal, to an idyllic reality. He used ancient tragedy the way Dante used Virgil, to lead him to the gates of Paradise,[19] but from there on he went ahead on his own, moving from an imitation of

<hr/>

[19]In the *Divina Commedia* the pagan Virgil guided Dante through Hell and Purgatory, but handed him over to Beatrice at the gates of Paradise.

the highest Greek art form to a "restitution of all things," to a re-creation of man's original art world. What confidence and bonhomie these bold enterprises betokened, arising as they did in the very heart of theoretical culture! The only explanation lies in the comforting belief of the day that "essential man" is the perennially virtuous operatic hero, the endlessly piping or singing shepherd, who, if he should ever by chance lose himself for a spell, would inevitably recover himself intact; in the optimism that rises like a perfumed, seductive cloud from the depths of Socratic contemplation.

Opera, then, does not wear the countenance of eternal grief but rather that of joy in an eternal reunion. It expresses the complacent delight in an idyllic reality, or such, at least, as can be viewed as real at any moment. Perhaps people will one day come to *realize* that this supposititious reality is at bottom no more than a fantastic and foolish trifling, which should make anyone who pits against it the immense seriousness of genuine nature and of the true origins of man exclaim in disgust: "Away with that phantom!" And yet it would be self-delusion to think that, trivial as it is, opera can be driven off with a shout, like an apparition. Whoever wants to destroy opera must gird himself for battle with that Alexandrian cheerfulness that has furnished opera its favorite conceptions and whose natural artistic expression it is. As for art proper, what possible benefit can it derive from a form whose origins lie altogether outside the esthetic realm, a form which from a semimoral sphere has trespassed on the domain of art and can only at rare moments deceive us as to its hybrid origin? What sap nourishes this operatic growth if not that of true art? Are we not right in supposing that its idyllic seductions and Alexandrian blandishments may sophisticate the highest, the truly serious task of art (to deliver the eye from the horror of night, to redeem us by virtue of the healing balm of illusion, from the spastic motions of the will) into an empty and frivolous amusement? What becomes of the enduring Apollonian and Dionysiac truths in such a mixture of styles as we find in the *stilo rappresentativo*; where music acts the part of the servant, the text that of the master; where music is likened to the body, the text to the soul; where the ultimate goal is at best a periphrastic tone painting, similar to that found

in the new Attic dithyramb; where music has abrogated its true dignity as the Dionysiac mirror of the universe and seems content to be the slave of appearance, to imitate the play of phenomenal forms, and to stimulate an artificial delight by dallying with lines and proportions? To a careful observer this pernicious influence of opera on music recapitulates the general development of modern music. The optimism that presided at the birth of opera and of the society represented by opera has succeeded with frightening rapidity in divesting music of its grand Dionysiac meanings and stamping it with the trivial character in a *divertissement,*[20] a transformation only equaled in scope by that of Aeschylean man into jovial Alexandrian man.

If we have been justified in suggesting a connection between the disappearance of the Dionysiac spirit and the spectacular, yet hitherto unexplained, degeneration of the Greek species, with what high hopes must we greet the auspicious signs of the opposite development in our own era, namely the gradual reawakening of the Dionysiac spirit! The divine power of Heracles cannot languish for ever in the service of Omphale.[21] Out of the Dionysiac recesses of the German soul has sprung a power which has nothing in common with the presuppositions of Socratic culture and which that culture can neither explain nor justify. Quite the contrary, the culture sees it as something to be dreaded and abhorred, something infinitely potent and hostile. I refer to German music, in its mighty course from Bach to Beethoven, and from Beethoven to Wagner. How can the petty intellectualism of our day deal with this monster that has risen out of the infinite deeps? There is no formula to be found, in either the reservoir of operatic filigree and arabesque or the abacus of the fugue and contrapuntal dialectics, that will subdue this monster, make it stand and deliver. What a spectacle to see our estheticians beating the air with the butterfly nets of their pedantic slogans, in vain pursuit of that marvelously volatile musical genius, their movements sadly belying their standards of "eternal" beauty and grandeur! Look at these patrons of

[20]Diversion.
[21]In the legend, in atonement for killing Iphitus, Heracles was forced to wear women's clothes and learn to spin at the direction of Queen Omphale.

music for a moment at close range, as they repeat indefatigably: "Beauty! Beauty!" and judge for yourselves whether they really look like the beautiful darlings of nature, or whether it would not be more correct to say that they have assumed a disguise for their own coarseness, as esthetic pretext for their barren and jejune sensibilities — take the case of Otto Jahn.[22] But liars and prevaricators ought to watch their step in the area of German music. For amidst our degenerate culture music is the only pure and purifying flame, towards which and away from which all things move in a Heracleitean double motion.[23] All that is now called culture, education, civilization will one day have to appear before the incorruptible judge, Dionysos.

Let us now recall how the new German philosophy was nourished from the same sources, how Kant and Schopenhauer succeeded in destroying the complacent acquiescence of intellectual Socratism,[24] how by their labors an infinitely more profound and serious consideration of questions

of ethics and art was made possible — a conceptualized form, in fact, of Dionysiac wisdom. To what does this miraculous union between German philosophy and music point if not to a new mode of existence, whose precise nature we can divine only with the aid of Greek analogies? For us, who stand on the watershed between two different modes of existence, the Greek example is still of inestimable value, since it embodies the violent transition to a classical, rationalistic form of suasion; only, we are living through the great phases of Hellenism in reverse order and seem at this very moment to be moving backward from the Alexandrian age into an age of tragedy. And we can't help feeling that the dawn of a new tragic age is for the German spirit only a return to itself, a blessed recovery of its true identity. For an unconscionably long time powerful forces from the outside have compelled the German spirit, which had vegetated in barbaric formlessness, to subserve their forms. But at long last the German spirit may stand before the other nations, free of the leading strings of Romance culture — provided that it continues to be able to learn from the nation from whom to learn at all is a high and rare thing, the Greeks. And was there ever a time when we needed these supreme teachers more urgently than now, as we witness the rebirth of tragedy and are in danger of not knowing either whence it comes or whither it goes?

---

[22]Otto Jahn (1813–1869), a classicist and archeologist, was a contemporary of Neitzsche.

[23]Heracleitus, who believed that all matter was in flux, thought nevertheless that changes in one direction for one aspect of the universe were balanced by changes in the opposite direction for another.

[24]Nietzsche is suggesting that Kant and Schopenhauer made aesthetics a matter of pure intuition, replacing the rationalist aesthetics common since Horace.

On Truth and Lie in an Extra-Moral Sense

I

In some remote corner of the universe, this glittering expanse of countless solar systems, there once was a star on which clever animals invented knowledge. It was the most arrogant and deceitful minute in the "history of the world" — and yet, no more than a minute. After nature had taken a few breaths, the star froze, and the clever animals had to

die. One could make up such a fable and still not have illustrated adequately just how pitiful, how shadowy and fleeting, how purposeless and arbitrary the human intellect comes across in nature. Eternities passed without it; and when it is gone once more, nothing will have come to pass. That is because there exists no further mission for this intellect that would reach beyond human life. It is human, after all, and only its possessor and generator invests it with such grandeur, as if the world hinged upon it. If we could communicate

Translated by Harry Heuser.

with the mosquito, however, we would learn that it drifts through the air with the same self-importance, sensing within itself the flying center of this world. Nothing in nature is so abject or small that would not swell at once, like a hose, when slightly breathed upon by this power of knowledge; and just as every burden-carrying drudge wants an admirer, so the proudest of human beings, the philosopher, assumes that the eyes of the universe are telescopically directed on all sides toward his actions and thoughts.

It is curious that the intellect should bring this about, since it is merely an aid given to the most unfortunate, most delicate, most ephemeral beings so as to hold them in the here-and-now for a minute, a here-and-now from which they otherwise, without such provision, would have every reason to flee as quickly as Lessing's son.[1] That arrogance associated with knowing and feeling, a blinding fog spread over human eyes and senses, thus deceives man about the worth of existence by bearing in itself the most flattering estimation of knowledge. Its most general effect is deception; but even its most specific effects have something of the same character about them.

As a means for the preservation of the individual, the intellect unfolds its chief powers in disguise; for this is the means by which weaker, less robust individuals preserve themselves, given that waging the struggle for existence with horns or fangs is denied to them. In man this art of disguise reaches its peak: here, deception, flattery, lying and tricking, talking behind people's back, posing, living in borrowed splendor, wearing masks, the cloak of convention, play-acting before others and before oneself — in short, the constant fluttering around the one flame of vanity — is so much the rule and the law that almost nothing is more inconceivable than how an honest and pure urge for truth could have arisen among men. They are steeped in illusions and dream images; their eye merely glides across the surface of things and sees "forms"; their sensation leads nowhere to the truth, but is content to receive stimuli and to play, as it were, blind-man's-buff on the back of things. Throughout his life, moreover, man permits himself to be lied to, at night in his dreams, without any attempt of his moral sense to prevent this; but it is said that men have conquered snoring by sheer will power. What does man really know of himself? Could he even perceive himself just once, in full, laid out as if in an illuminated glass case! Does not nature conceal most everything from him, about his own body even, in order to keep him cast out and locked up in a proud trickster consciousness — away from the winding bowels, the rapid flow of the blood stream and the intricate quiverings of the fibers? She threw away the key; and woe to the fatal curiosity that managed once to peer through a crack in the chamber of consciousness, look outside and beneath, and get an inkling that, in the indifference of his ignorance, man rests on what is merciless, greedy, insatiable, and murderous as if suspended in dreams on a tiger's back. Under such circumstances, where in the world would this urge for truth come from!

In a natural state of things, in so far as he tries to maintain himself in opposition to others, the individual uses the intellect mostly for disguise alone. Yet because man, out of both need and boredom, wants to exist socially in the herd, he must secure peace and so strives to banish at least the utmost *bellum omni contra omnes*[2] from his world. This peace treaty carries with it something that looks like the first step toward the attainment of that mysterious urge for truth. At this point, namely, something is being set up that shall be "truth" hereafter; that is, a universally valid and binding designation for things is being invented. The legislature of language also provides the first laws of truth: for it is here that the contrast between truth and lie first comes into being. The liar uses the valid terms, the words, to make the unreal seem real. He says, for example, "I am rich," when the word "poor" would be just the right label for his condition. He abuses fixed conventions by arbitrary changes or even reversals of

---

[1]In a famous letter to Johann Joachim Eschenburg (December 31, 1778), the German poet and playwright Gotthold Ephraim Lessing relates the death of his day-old infant son, who "understood the world so well that he left it at the first opportunity."

[2]Latin for "war of each against all."

names. If he does this in a way that is self-serving and incidentally damaging to others, then society will no longer trust him and shut him out because of it. In doing so, men do not so much run away from being tricked as from the damage brought about by trickery: what they hate, also at this level, is basically not deception itself, but the disagreeable, inimical consequences of certain kinds of deceit. Man only desires the truth in a similarly restrictive sense: he longs for the pleasant, life-preserving consequences of truth, is indifferent to pure knowledge, which is not consequential, and even hostile to possibly harmful and destructive truths. Beyond this, what else can we say about the conventions of language? Are they perhaps products of knowledge, of a sense of truth? Do words and things correspond? Is language the adequate expression of all realities?

Only through forgetfulness can man ever reach the point of fancying he possesses a "truth" to the degree just described. If he does not want to make do with truth in the form of tautology, that is, with empty husks, then he will forever trade illusions for truths. What is a word? The image of a nerve stimulus in sound. Yet further to infer, from this nerve stimulus, a cause outside of us is already the result of a false and unwarranted application of the principle of sufficient reason. If the single deciding factors in the genesis of language and in the act of designating had been truth and certainty, respectively, then how could we say "the stone is hard," as if "hard" were otherwise known to us, and not just as an entirely subjective stimulation! We separate things according to gender, designating the tree as masculine and the plant as feminine.[3] What arbitrary assignments! How far beyond the canon of certainty! We speak of a "snake," a designation that captures nothing but the act of winding and could therefore also fit the worm.[4] What arbitrary differentiations! What one-sided preferences, now for this property of a thing and now for that! Set side by side, the different languages show that it is never truth, never adequate expression that matters when it comes to words; otherwise, there would not

be so many languages. The "thing in itself"[5] (which is what pure truth, without its consequences, would be) is entirely incomprehensible to the creator of language and not at all desirable to him. He designates only the relations of things to man and seeks the aid of the boldest metaphors to express them. Initially, a nerve stimulus is being transposed into an image: first metaphor! The image is reworked again in sound: second metaphor! And each time, the complete overleaping of a sphere, right into the middle of an entirely new and different one. Imagine a deaf man who has never had a sensation of sound and music: how he gazes in astonishment at Chladni's sound figures in the sand,[6] how he discovers their causes in the vibrations of the string, and how he will swear thereafter that he ought to know from this just what it is that men call "sound"! So it is with all of us when it comes to language. We believe we know something of the things themselves when we speak of trees, colors, snow, and flowers; and yet we possess nothing but metaphors of things, which do not at all agree with the original entities. Just as a sound turned into a sand figure, so the mysterious X of the thing in itself occurs first as a nerve stimulus, then as an image, and finally as a sound. In any case, logic does not seem to figure in the evolution of language; and the entire material with which the man of truth, the researcher or philosopher, later works and builds, is derived, if not from cloud-cuckoo-land, then certainly not from the essence of things.

Let us think further about the formation of concepts in particular. Every word immediately becomes a concept inasmuch as it is not intended to serve as a reminder of the original, unique, and thoroughly individualized experience to which it owes its birth, but is supposed to fit innumerable cases at once; cases that are more or less similar — which means, strictly speaking, never

---

[3] In German "tree" is masculine (*der Baum*) and "plant" is feminine (*die Pflanze*).

[4] The German word for snake (*Schlange*) derives from the verb *schlingen*, which means to twist.

[5] The term used by Immanuel Kant in the *Critique of Pure Reason* for a reality beyond our human categories of perception.

[6] Ernst Chladni (1756–1827), German scientist known as the "father of acoustics," covered glass plates with a thin layer of sand and set them vibrating using a violin bow or the powerful sound of a pipe organ, creating intricate patterns that were visual "metaphors" of the sound that produced them.

the same — thus a lot of unique ones. Every concept has its origin in equating things that are not the same. Just as it is certain that no leaf is ever entirely like another, so is it certain that the concept "leaf" is formed by an arbitrary shedding of these individual differences, by forgetting what is distinct. And it now gives rise to the idea that, apart from the leaves, there exists in nature the "leaf," some original after which all leaves are woven, marked, outlined, colored, curled, and painted, but by incompetent hands, so that no specimen has turned out to be a correct, reliable, and faithful image of the original. We call a person "honest." "Why did he act so honestly today?" we ask. Our answer tends to be: because of his honesty. Honesty! This in turn means that the leaf is the cause of leaves. After all, we know absolutely nothing of an essential quality called "honesty," but only the numerous individual — and thus unique — actions, which we equate by first omitting what is unlike and by calling them honest actions thereafter. Finally we formulate from them a *qualitas occulta*[7] with the name "honesty." Ignoring what is individual and real provides us with the concept as well as the form; whereas nature knows neither forms nor concepts, and therefore no species, but only an X inaccessible and undefinable for us. For our contrast of individual and species is anthropomorphic as well and does not originate in the essence of things, even though we do not venture to say that the one does not correspond with the other: that, after all, would be a dogmatic assertion and as such just as indemonstrable as its opposite.

What, then, is truth? A mobile army of metaphors, metonymies, and anthropomorphisms; in short, a sum of human relations which have been poetically and rhetorically heightened, transferred, and embellished, and which, after long usage, seem fixed, canonical, and binding to a people. Truths are illusions that we have forgotten are just that; metaphors that have become worn out and sensuously powerless; coins that have lost their image and are now being considered only as metal, no longer as coins. We still do not know where the

urge for truth stems from; for thus far we have heard only of the obligation that society imposes in order to exist. To be truthful means using the customary metaphors; that is, in moral terms, the obligation to lie according to a fixed convention, as a herd, in a style binding upon all. Now man forgets, of course, that this is how things stand for him. Unconsciously and after centuries of getting into the habit of it, he thus lies in the manner indicated and arrives, *through just this unconsciousness*, this very obliviousness, at his sense of truth. From the sense of obligation to call one thing "red," another "cold," and a third "mute" arises a moral impulse in regard to truth: through contrast with the liar, whom no one trusts and everyone excludes, man demonstrates for himself the venerability, reliability, and utility of truth. As a *rational* being, he now places his actions under the dominion of abstractions; he can no longer abide getting carried away by sudden perceptions[8] and by observations. He first generalizes all these perceptions into less colorful, cooler concepts on which to hitch the vehicle of his life and actions. Everything that distinguishes man from beast depends on this ability to distill perceptual metaphors into a schema, thus to decompose an image into a concept. For something is possible in the realm of these schemata which could never be managed under vivid first impressions: the construction of a pyramidal order according to castes and degrees; the creation of a new world of laws, privileges, subordinations, and strict boundaries which now confronts that other vivid world of first impressions as the more solid, more universal, more familiar, more human world, and therefore as the regulative and imperative one. Whereas each perception is individual and unique, therefore always able to escape all classification, the great edifice of concepts displays the rigid regularity of a Roman columbarium[9] and exhales in logic that strength and coolness which is peculiar to mathematics. Anyone touched

---

[7]Latin for "hidden quality"; scholastic philosophers "explained" properties of matter of whose causes they were ignorant by attributing them to a *qualitas occulta*.

[8]The German word here is *Anschauung*, which is difficult to translate: it can mean an intuition, a perception, or the impression a sensual experience leaves in the mind; I have chosen "perception" here but at other places indicated have translated it "intuition" or "observation." [Heuser]

[9]A memorial building provided with niches for urns containing human ashes.

by this coolness will scarcely believe that even the concept — bony, eight-cornered, and shiftable like a die — remains only as the residue of a metaphor, and that the illusion involved in the artistic transfer of a nerve stimulus into images is, if not the mother, then the grandmother of every single concept. In this conceptual game of dice, however, "truth" means using every die as it is marked, accurately counting its spots, creating correct rubrics, and never violating the order of groups and sequential rankings. Like the Romans and Etruscans, who cut up the heavens along rigid mathematical lines and confined in each space thus demarcated a god as within a *templum*,[10] so every people has its mathematically divided concept heaven, and hence understands it to be the demand of truth that each concept god be sought only within his own sphere. In this, one may well admire man as a tremendous genius of construction who succeeds in piling an endlessly complicated dome of concepts on movable foundations and, as it were, on running water. To be sure, in order to rest on such foundations, the construction must be built out of spider thread: delicate enough to be carried by the waves, strong enough not to be blown apart by every wind. As a genius of construction, man thus raises himself far above the bee, inasmuch as she builds with wax gathered from nature, whereas he uses the far more delicate stuff of concepts, which he must fabricate first from within himself. In this he is greatly to be admired, just not on account of his drive for truth or pure knowledge of things. When someone hides a thing behind a bush, then looks for it there and finds it again, there is not much to praise in such seeking and finding. Yet so it is with the search and discovery of "truth" within the precinct of reason. If I make up the definition of a mammal and, after inspecting a camel, declare "behold, a mammal," a truth is being brought to light all right, but it is of limited value. I mean, it is thoroughly anthropomorphic and contains not a single point that is "true in itself," real and universally valid irrespective of man. Basically, whoever searches for such truths is only looking for the metamorphosis of the world in man; he grapples with an understanding of the world as a human thing and at best

[10]Latin for the sphere of the heavens designated for a particular god, and for an earthly temple designated for worship.

ekes out a sense of assimilation. Just as the astrologer considered the stars in the service of man and in relation to his happiness and sorrow, such a searcher considers the entire world as an extension of man; as the infinitely broken reverberation of one primordial sound, of man; as a reproduced copy of one primordial image, of man. His method is to take man as the measure of all things, whereby he sets out from the error of believing that he has these things immediately before him, as pure objects. He therefore forgets the original perceptual metaphors *qua* metaphors and takes them to be the things in themselves.

Only by forgetting this primitive world of metaphor, only by hardening and stiffening the primal mass of images that gush in fervid fluency from the original wealth of human fantasy, only by means of an unconquerable faith that *this* sun, *this* window, *this* table is a truth in itself, in short, only by forgetting himself as subject, that is, as an *artistically creative subject*, does man live with any tranquility, security, and constancy. If he could escape the prison walls of his faith for only an instant, it would be over at once for his "self-assurance." It is already difficult enough for man to admit to himself that the insect or bird perceives a world entirely different from his, and that the question, which of those two perceptions of the world is more right than the other, is utterly meaningless because it would require a standard of right perception, a standard that does not exist. It seems to me, however, that the *right perception* — which would mean the adequate expression of an object in the subject — is a self-contradictory nonentity: for between two absolutely different spheres such as subject and object there is no causality, no correctness, no meaning; there is, at most, an *aesthetic* relation, I mean, a suggestive transference — a stammering translation into an entirely foreign language — which requires, in any case, a freely poetic, freely inventive medial sphere and mediating force. The word "appearance" holds many temptations, which is why I avoid it as much as possible; for it is not true that the essence of things appears in the empirical world. A painter without hands who tries to express as song the image he has in mind will always reveal more through this substitution of spheres than the empirical world reveals about the essence of things. Even the relationship of a nerve stimulus to the image produced is in itself not an imperative one. Yet when the same image is reproduced millions of times and handed down for many generations, ultimately to appear for all mankind at the same impulse, then it acquires for man the same significance as if it were the only necessary image and as if that relationship between the original nerve stimulus and the image were a strictly causal one—just as a dream, forever repeated, would surely be perceived and judged to be reality. Yet the hardening and stiffening of a metaphor does not at all vouch for its necessity and exclusive authority.

Anyone at home in such contemplations has no doubt felt a deep mistrust of all idealism of this kind whenever he has quite convinced himself of the eternal logical consistency, ubiquity, and infallibility of the laws of nature. He concludes that, however far we reach into the telescopic heights and microscopic depths of the world, everything here is certain, thorough, endless, according to law and devoid of gaps; science will forever be able to dig successfully in these shafts, and the findings will fit together without contradicting one another. How little does this resemble a product of fantasy; for if it were one, he reasons, the illusion and unreality of it ought to become detectable somewhere. The following should be said against this: if each of us had another, distinct kind of sense perception and could perceive things alternately only as a bird, a worm, or a plant, or if one of us saw a particular stimulus as red, another as blue, while a third even heard it as sound, then no one would speak of any such rule of law in nature, but understand it only as an extremely subjective construct. So, what is a law of nature to us at all? It is known to us not in itself, but only in its effects, in its relations to other laws of nature, which, in turn, are known to us only as sums of relations. All these relations, therefore, always refer to each other and are, in their essence, thoroughly incomprehensible to us. What is really known to us is only what we ourselves bring: time and space, that is, sequential relationships and numbers. All that is wondrous, however, all that so astonishes us about the laws of nature, that demands our explanation and might tempt us to a distrust of idealism, lies precisely and entirely within the mathematical strictness and inviolability of the concepts of time and space. Yet these we produce by and within ourselves with the same inevitability with which the spider spins. When forced to comprehend all things in forms like these alone, it is no longer surprising that we indeed comprehend nothing but these forms; because all of them have to bear the laws of number, and it is precisely number that is most astonishing about things. All the conformity to law that so impresses us in the course of the stars and in chemical processes basically coincides with those properties which we bring to things in order to impress ourselves. However, the result is that this artistic formation of metaphors, with which every sentiment begins for us, already presupposes such forms and is thus governed by them; only the steadfast endurance of these primal forms can explain how it is possible that the edifice of concepts could have been constituted from such metaphors; that is, as an imitation of temporal, spatial, and numerical relationships on the basis of metaphors.

2

As we have seen, what is originally at work on the construction of concepts is language; in later ages it is science. Just as the bee simultaneously constructs cells and fills them with honey, so science works unceasingly on this great columbarium of concepts, the graveyard of intuitions [*Anschauungen*], always building new and higher stories, shoring up, cleaning and renewing old cells, and, above all, trying hard to fill in this piled-up monstrosity of a framework and to fit the whole empirical world — that is to say, the anthropomorphic world — inside of it. Whereas the man of business fastens his life to reason and its concepts so as not to get swept away and lose himself, the researcher goes so far as to build his hut close to the tower of science in order to contribute to its construction and to find shelter beneath the existing bulwark. Indeed, he needs shelter: terrible forces are continually intruding on him and counter scientific "truth" with entirely different kinds of "truths," held up on shields bearing the most disparate of signs.

The urge to shape metaphors — that fundamental human drive one cannot discount for an instant, for one would thereby discount man himself — is not in truth conquered, is hardly restrained by the regular and rigid new world that is being constructed like a stronghold from its distilled products, the concepts. It seeks a new field and a different channel for its workings, and it finds them in myth and in art as a whole. It forever confuses the categories of concepts and their components by setting up new figures, metaphors, and metony-mies; it shows a constant desire to arrange the existing world of waking man as wildly irregular and non-consequentially disjointed, as stimulating and ever new as the world of dreams. In essence, it is only through this rigid and regular web of concepts that waking man becomes aware he is awake; and that is why he sometimes believes he is dreaming when this web of concepts is torn asunder by art. Pascal is right when he claims that if the same dream came to us each night, it would preoccupy us just as much as the things we see every day. "If a laborer were to dream for fully twelve hours every night that he was a king," says Pascal, "I believe he would be just as happy as a king who dreams for twelve hours every night that he is a laborer."[11] To a people as excited by myth as the ancient Greeks, whose myth supposed ever-active wonders, waking day is more akin to dream than to the day of the thinker sobered by science. If every tree may be a nymph, and speak; if virgins may be abducted by a god in the guise of a bull; and if the goddess Athena herself may suddenly be seen as she, accompanied by Peisistratus,[12] drives through the markets of Athens with a fine team of horses — as any true Athenian would have believed — then everything is possible at any moment, as in a dream, and all of nature enraptures man as if it were nothing but a masquerade of the gods, who were merely making sport by beguiling man with all these shapes.

Yet man himself has an indomitable tendency to give in to such deception and is positively enchanted with happiness when the rhapsodist tells him epic fairy tales as if true, or when the actor on the stage plays the king more royally than reality shows him to be. The intellect, that master of deception, is free as long as it can deceive without *doing harm*; relieved from the slave duty it otherwise performs, it thus celebrates its Saturnalia.[13] It is never more profuse, rich, and proud, more nimble and daring; with creative pleasure it makes a muddle of metaphors and shifts the boundary stones of abstractions, so that, for example, it calls the stream a moving path that carries man where he would otherwise walk. Now it has cast off the token of servitude: thus far engaged in cheerless activity, attempting to show a poor individual the ways and means of the existence he craves, like a servant who goes out to pillage and loot for his master, it now has become master and may wipe away the expression of want from its features. Whatever it now does no longer bears the mark of distortion, as before, but that of disguise. It copies human life, but takes it to be something good and seems quite content with it. That enormous scaffold and framework of concepts to which the needy man clings for dear life is merely a stage and plaything for the boldest feats of the liberated intellect; and when it smashes, jumbles, and ironically reassembles this framework, pairing what is most foreign and separating what is closest, it reveals that it has no use for such makeshifts of need and that it will no longer be guided by concepts, but by intuitions. There is no regular path which leads from these intuitions into the land of ghostly schemata, the land of abstractions. No word exists for them, man is speechless at their sight; or else he talks only in a great many forbidden metaphors and unheard-of phrasings so that by smashing and mocking the old conceptual barriers he might at least creatively approximate the impression of intuition in its mighty presence.

There are ages in which rational man and intuitive man stand side by side, the one in fear of intuition, the other with scorn for abstraction, the latter being just as irrational as the former is inartistic. Both desire to control life: the former by knowing how to meet the most principal needs

---

[11]Blaise Pascal (1623–1662), from his *Pensées*, section 386.

[12]In *Histories*, Book I, Herodotus tells the story of how, after the tyrant Peisistratus had been exiled from Athens in 566, he and his allies paid a tall, well-built woman to put on full armor and ride in a chariot through the streets, proclaiming "Athenians, give a hearty welcome to Peisistratus, whom Athena honors above all men." Believing she was the goddess herself, the Athenians invited Peisistratus to return.

[13]Roman holiday at the end of the calendar year in which distinctions of social rank were not observed.

with foresight, prudence, and regularity; the latter, by ignoring those needs, like a "too happy" hero,[14] and by accepting as real only a life in the guise of illusion and beauty. Wherever intuitive man once wields his weapons more forcefully and victoriously than his counterpart — as in ancient Greece, for instance — conditions are most favorable for shaping a culture and founding a dominion of art over life. The elements of disguise, the denial of pressing needs, the splendor of metaphorical observations [Anschauungen], and, above all, the immediacy of deception accompany all expressions of such a life. Neither house, nor gait, nor dress, nor clay jug betray that they are the inventions of a pressing need; it appears as though all of them were intended to express sublime joy, Olympian cloudlessness, and, so to speak, playing with serious things. A man guided by concepts and abstractions only staves off misery by such means, but does not wring happiness from them; and whereas he merely craves the greatest possible freedom from pain, the intuitive man, who stands in the midst of a culture, reaps from his intuitions not only a defense against misfortune, but a constant flow of light, cheer, and relief. To be sure, when he suffers, he suffers more intensely; he even suffers more frequently, since he does not understand how to learn from experience and instead keeps falling, over and over again, into the same ditch. In his sorrow, he is then just as irrational as in happiness: he wails loudly and without consolation. How differently, in the same misfortune, fares the stoical man who learns from experience and governs himself by concepts. He, who otherwise seeks nothing but sincerity, truth, freedom from deception, and protection against baffling attacks, now executes a masterpiece of deception, acting in his misfortune the way the other did in happiness. He wears no twitching and animated human face, but, as it were, a mask with a dignified symmetry of features. He does not cry out or even alter his voice; when it pours down on him from a real storm cloud, he wraps himself in his cloak and, with slow steps, walks away underneath it.

[14]Nietzsche's phrase alludes to the fearless, intuitive Siegfried in Wagner's *Götterdämmerung*. In Act III, scene ii, his brother-in-law Gunther says to Siegfried, "You are too happy, my hero," while Siegfried calls Gunther a "morose man."

From *Twilight of the Idols*

8

Towards a psychology of the artist. — For art to exist, for any sort of aesthetic or perception to exist, a certain physiological precondition is indispensable: *intoxication*. Intoxication must first have heightened the excitability of the entire machine: no art results before that happens. All kinds of intoxication, however different their origin, have the power to do this: above all, the intoxication of sexual excitement, the oldest and most primitive form of intoxication. Likewise the intoxication which comes in the train of all great desires, all strong emotions; the intoxication of feasting, of contest, of the brave deed, of victory, of all extreme agitation; the intoxication of cruelty; intoxication in destruction; intoxication under certain meteorological influences, for example the intoxication of spring; or under the influence of narcotics; finally the intoxication of the will, the intoxication of an overloaded and distended will. — The essence of intoxication is the feeling of plenitude and increased energy. From out of this feeling one gives to things, one *compels* them to take, one rapes them — one calls this procedure *Idealizing*. Let us get rid of a prejudice here: idealization does *not* consist, as is commonly believed, in a subtracting or deducting

Translated by R. J. Hollingdale

of the petty and secondary. A tremendous *expulsion* of the principal features rather is the decisive thing, so that thereupon the others too disappear.

9

In this condition one enriches everything out of one's own abundance: what one sees, what one desires, one sees swollen, pressing, strong, overladen with energy. The man in this condition transforms things until they mirror his power — until they are reflections of his perfection. This *compulsion* to transform into the perfect is — art. Even all that which he is not becomes for him nonetheless part of his joy in himself; in art, man takes delight in himself as perfection. — It would be permissible to imagine an antithetical condition, a specific anti-artisticality of instinct — a mode of being which impoverishes and attenuates things and makes them consumptive. And history is in fact rich in such anti-artists, in such starvelings of life, who necessarily have to take things to themselves, impoverish them, make them *leaner*. This is, for example, the case with the genuine Christian, with Pascal[1] for example: a Christian who is at the same time an artist *does not exist*. . . . Let no one be childish and cite Raphael[2] as an objection, or some homoeopathic Christian of the nineteenth century: Raphael said Yes, Raphael *did* Yes, consequently Raphael was not a Christian.

10

What is the meaning of the antithetical concepts *Apollinian* and *Dionysian*, both conceived as forms of intoxication, which I introduced into aesthetics?[3] — Apollinian intoxication alerts above all the eye, so that it acquires power of vision. The painter, the sculptor, the epic poet are visionaries *par excellence*. In the Dionysian state, on the other hand, the entire emotional system is alerted and intensified: so that it discharges all its powers of representation, imitation, transfiguration,

transmutation, every kind of mimicry and play-acting, conjointly. The essential thing remains the facility of the metamorphosis, the incapacity *not* to react (— in a similar way to certain types of hysterics, who also assume *any* role at the slightest instigation). It is impossible for the Dionysian man not to understand any suggestion of whatever kind, he ignores no signal from the emotions, he possesses to the highest degree the instinct for understanding and divining, just as he possesses the art of communication to the highest degree. He enters into every skin, into every emotion; he is continually transforming himself. — Music, as we understand it today, is likewise a collective arousal and discharging of the emotions, but for all that only a vestige of a much fuller emotional world of expression, a mere residuum of Dionysian histrionicism. To make music possible as a separate art one had to immobilize a number of senses, above all the muscular sense (at least relatively: for all rhythm still speaks to our muscles to a certain extent): so that man no longer straightway imitates and represents bodily everything he feels. Nonetheless, *that* is the true Dionysian normal condition, at least its original condition: music is the gradually-achieved specialization of this at the expense of the most closely related faculties.

II

The actor, the mime, the dancer, the musician, the lyric poet are fundamentally related in their instincts and essentially one, only gradually specialized and separated from one another — even to the point of opposition. The lyric poet stayed united longest with the musician, the actor with the dancer. — The *architect* represents neither a Dionysian nor an Apollinian condition: here it is the mighty act of will, the will which moves mountains, the intoxication of the strong will, which demands artistic expression. The most powerful men have always inspired the architects; the architect has always been influenced by power. Pride, victory over weight and gravity, the will to power, seek to render themselves visible in a building; architecture is a kind of rhetoric of power, now persuasive, even cajoling in form, now bluntly imperious. The highest feeling of power and security finds expression in that which possesses *grand style*. Power which no longer requires proving; which

---

[1]Blaise Pascal (1623–1662) French mathematician and philosopher.
[2]Raphael Sanzio or Santi of Urbino (1483–1520) Renaissance painter, in Nietzsche's time perhaps the most highly regarded of them all. His most famous works are The School of Athens and the Sistine Madonna, both in the Vatican.
[3]In the *Birth of Tragedy*.

disdains to please, which is slow to answer; which is conscious of no witnesses around it; which lives oblivious of the existence of any opposition; which reposes in *itself*, fatalistic, a law among laws: *that* is what speaks of itself in the form of grand style.

20

Nothing is beautiful, only man: on this piece of naivety rests all aesthetics, it is the *first* truth of aesthetics. Let us immediately add its second; nothing is ugly but *degenerate* man — the domain of aesthetic judgment is therewith defined. — Reckoned physiologically, everything ugly weakens and afflicts man. It recalls decay, danger, impotence: he actually suffers a loss of energy in its presence. The effect of the ugly can be measured with a dynamometer. Whenever man feels in any way depressed, he senses the proximity of something "ugly." His feeling of power, his will to power, his courage, his pride — they decline with the ugly, they increase with the beautiful. . . . In the one case as in the other *we draw a conclusion*: its premises have been accumulated in the instincts in tremendous abundance. The ugly is understood as a sign and symptom of degeneration; that which recalls degeneration, however remotely, produces in us the judgment "ugly." Every token of exhaustion, of heaviness, of age, of weariness, every kind of unfreedom, whether convulsive or paralytic, above all the smell, colour and shape of dissolution, of decomposition, though it be attenuated to the point of being no more than a symbol — all this calls forth the same reaction, the value judgment "ugly." A feeling of *hatred* then springs up; what is man then hating? But the answer admits of no doubt: the *decline of his type*. He hates then from out of the profoundest instinct of his species; there is, horror, foresight, profoundity, far-seeing vision in this hatred — it is the profoundest hatred there is. It is for its sake that art is *profound*.

24

L'art pour l'art[4] — The struggle against *purpose* in art is always a struggle against the *moralizing* tendency in art, against the subordination of art to morality. *L'art pour l'art* means: "the devil take

[4]French, "art for art's sake."

morality!" — But this very hostility betrays that moral prejudice is still dominant. When one has excluded from art the purpose of moral preaching and human improvement it by no means follows that art is completely purposeless, goalless, meaningless, in short *l'art pour l'art* — a snake biting its own tail. "Rather no purpose at all than a moral purpose!" — thus speaks mere passion. A psychologist asks on the other hand: what does all art do? does it not praise? does it not glorify? does it not select? does it not highlight? By doing all this it *strengthens* or *weakens* certain valuations. . . . Is this no more than an incidental? an accident? Something in which the instinct of the artist has no part whatever? Or is it not rather the prerequisite for the artist's being an artist at all. . . . Is his basic instinct directed towards art, or is it not rather directed towards the meaning of art, which is *life?* towards a *desideratum of life?* — Art is the great stimulus to life: how could it be thought purposeless, aimless, *l'art pour l'art?* One question remains: art also brings to light much that is ugly, hard, questionable in life — does it not thereby seem to suffer from life? — And there have indeed been philosophers who lent it this meaning: Schopenhauer taught that the whole object of art was to "liberate from the will," and he revered tragedy because its greatest function was to "dispose one to resignation." — But this — as I have already intimated — is pessimist's perspective and "evil eye" — : one must appeal to the artists themselves. *What does the tragic artist communicate of himself?* Does he not display precisely the condition of *fearlessness* in the face of the fearsome and questionable? — This condition itself is a high desideratum: he who knows it bestows on it the highest honours. He communicates it, he *has* to communicate it if he is an artist, a genius of communication. Bravery and composure in the face of a powerful enemy, great hardship, a problem that arouses aversion — it is this *victorious* condition which the tragic artist singles out, which he glorifies. In the face of tragedy the warlike in our soul celebrates its Saturnalias[5]: whoever is accustomed to suffering, whoever seeks out suffering, the *heroic* man extols his existence by means of tragedy — for him alone does the tragic poet pour this draught of sweetest cruelty. —

[5]Roman holiday when class distinctions are not observed.

Henry James

1843–1916

Born in America, partly formed by the French, and late in life naturalized a British subject, Henry James was a relentless experimentalist with technique and subject matter who brought a new sophistication to the art of fiction. His father, Henry James, Sr., an independently wealthy gentleman, was a philosopher and religious mystic who valued eccentricity in himself and in his offspring. Henry and his equally well-known elder brother, William, were educated at schools in England, France, Switzerland, and Germany as well as in their birthplace, New York City; their father believed that his sons could become themselves only by avoiding attachments to any master, school, place, or nation, and he also loathed the pragmatism and professionalism of the American educational system. The paradoxical result was that both Henry and William became ardent professionals — William a psychologist and philosopher, Henry a novelist and critic.

James began publishing stories in his twenties but did not find his true voice until he left America for good in 1875 to live in Paris and then settle in London. The fiction of his first period is often some variation on the "international theme" — the moral and spiritual gap between America and Europe. *The American* (1877), *Daisy Miller* (1878), and *Portrait of a Lady* (1881) made his reputation; today these works (especially the last) seem to mark a transition between the social chronicle of the nineteenth century and the twentieth-century novel of psychological realism. The novels of his middle years, like *The Princess Casamassima* (1886) and *The Tragic Muse* (1890), were less successful, and James's attempt to conquer the London stage with *Guy Domville* (1895) ended in disaster. James withdrew from London to the retirement of Lamb House in Rye, where he produced the three ambiguous and highly nuanced masterworks of his late period, *The Wings of the Dove* (1902), *The Ambassadors* (1903), and *The Golden Bowl* (1904). In the next decade, James turned from fiction to memoir, but the outbreak of World War I disturbed the quiet of his last years. As an expression of solidarity with the British cause during America's long neutrality, James applied for citizenship (granted in 1915) and worked at war relief, the exertions of which broke his own health. He died on February 26, 1916.

"The Art of Fiction" (1884) seems to promise a manual of techniques, but this is precisely what James is least willing to provide. The title in fact is not James's own but was taken from a lecture by Walter Besant, which proposed that "laws of fiction may be laid down and taught with as much precision and exactness as the laws of harmony, perspective, and proportion." While generously granting everything he can to Besant's claims, James — who had been trained as a painter — essentially disagrees that regulations and conventions in fiction comparable to those in painting and music could exist. "If there are exact sciences, there are also exact arts, and the grammar of painting is so much more definite that it makes the difference." And James might have said, *Vive la différence,* for most of the distinctions that had become current in the short history of the criticism of fiction struck him as mechanical and empty.

Even before the English novel existed as such, William Congreve in his preface to *Incognita* (1692) had contrasted the romance and the novel. Later critics differentiated novels of incident from novels of character. For James, these notions might make talking about the novel easier but would only make excellence in writing more difficult. "What is character," he asks, "but the determination of incident? What is incident but the illustration of character?" For James, the novel is intended to convey the felt impression of life — a seamless web of action and motive that could not be reduced to simple formulas. The only Besantine dictum James wholeheartedly endorses is the recommendation that the prospective novelist keep a notebook to record impressions.

Although James rejects all of Besant's particular recommendations, he agrees that fiction is indeed an art. Today, after Joyce and Woolf and James himself, this contention would seem to need no proof. But the Victorian novel had been created mainly by entertainers who made few claims for themselves and their trade, and the British public was used to retreating into three-volume narratives that guaranteed adventure and escape, a love story with a happy ending, and poetic justice for all. In "The Art of Fiction" James positions himself against this stultifying formula. He is also concerned to champion his own style of writing fiction, which was more subtle and inward than was common. More generally, however, he wants the novelist to have the freedom to experiment not just with subject matter and point of view but with moral issues that disturb and disquiet.

Since James sets himself squarely against the philistines, we might expect him, in the 1880s, to embrace either the naturalism of Émile Zola or the pure "art for art's sake" aestheticism of Walter Pater. In fact he enters neither camp. James holds to fairly traditional notions of realism; beauty of form is not to be pursued merely for its own sake but in the process of conveying a complex and authentic experience that rests on the contingencies of life. "Do not listen," he warns, "to those who would . . . persuade you that this heavenly messenger wings her way outside of life altogether, breathing a superfine air, and turning away her head from the truth of things." But at the same time, James does not, like Zola, expect the artist to present social conditions in a scientifically accurate way; he claimed, in fact, that Zola's deterministic philosophy "vitiated" his portraiture.

Ultimately, James's impatience with rules and formulas for fiction derives from a post-Romantic, expressive theory of art. "The deepest quality of a work of art will always be the quality of the mind of the producer. In proportion as that intelligence is fine will the novel . . . partake of the substance of beauty and truth." James's most heartfelt recommendation to the aspiring artist is not to watch his handling of point-of-view but to remain open to experience, to "be one of the people on whom nothing is lost." A fine intelligence will, he is confident, find or invent the techniques needed to realize the imagined vision, while a mechanical mind, using all the arts, will never produce something worthy of lasting fame.

Selected Bibliography

Beach, Joseph Warren. *The Method of Henry James*. Philadelphia: A. Saifer, 1954.

Cameron, J. M. "History, Realism, and the Work of Henry James." *English Studies in Canada* 10 (1984): 299–316.

Da Sousa Correa, Delia. "'The Art of Fiction': Henry James as Critic." In *The Nineteenth-Century Novel: Identities*, ed. Dennis Walder, 137–56. London: Routledge, 2001.

Daugherty, Sarah B. *The Literary Criticism of Henry James*. Athens: Ohio University Press, 1981.

During, Simon. "Henry James and Me." *MLN*, 118, no. 5 (2003): 1279–93.

Edel, Leon. *The Prefaces of Henry James*. Paris: Jouvé, 1931.

Hughes, Herbert Leland. *Theory and Practice in Henry James*. Ann Arbor: Edwards Bros., 1926.

Jackson, Wendell P. "Theory of the Creative Process in the 'Prefaces' of Henry James." In *Amid Visions and Revisions: Poetry and Criticism on Literature and the Arts,* ed. Burney J. Hillis, Baltimore: Morgan State University Press, 1985, pp. 59–64.

James, Henry. *The Art of the Novel: Critical Prefaces*. Introduction by R. P. Blackmur. New York: Scribner, 1934.

Roberts, Morris. *Henry James's Criticism*. Cambridge: Harvard University Press, 1929.

Veeder, William. "Image as Argument: Henry James and the Style of Criticism." *Henry James Review* 6 (1985): 172–81.

The Art of Fiction

I should not have affixed so comprehensive a title to these few remarks, necessarily wanting in any completeness upon a subject the full consideration of which would carry us far, did I not seem to discover a pretext for my temerity in the interesting pamphlet lately published under this name by Mr. Walter Besant.[1] Mr. Besant's lecture at the Royal Institution — the original form of his pamphlet — appears to indicate that many persons are interested in the art of fiction, and are not indifferent to such remarks, as those who practice it may attempt to make about it. I am therefore anxious not to lose the benefit of this favorable association, and to edge in a few words under cover of the attention which Mr. Besant is sure to have excited. There is something very encouraging in his having put into form certain of his ideas on the mystery of story-telling.

It is a proof of life and curiosity — curiosity on the part of the brotherhood of novelists as well

as on the part of their readers. Only a short time ago it might have been supposed that the English novel was not what the French call *discutable*. It had no air of having a theory, a conviction, a consciousness of itself behind it — of being the expression of an artistic faith, the result of choice and comparison. I do not say it was necessarily the worse for that; it would take much more courage than I possess to intimate that the form of the novel as Dickens and Thackeray (for instance) saw it had any taint of incompleteness. It was, however, *naïf* (if I may help myself out with another French word); and evidently if it be destined to suffer in any way for having lost its *naïveté* it has now an idea of making sure of the corresponding advantages. During the period I have alluded to there was a comfortable, good-humored feeling abroad that a novel is a novel, as a pudding is a pudding and that our only business with it could be to swallow it. But within a year or two, for some reason or other, there have been signs of returning animation — the era of discussion would appear to have been to a certain extent

[1]Victorian man of letters (1836–1901). Besant's lecture on the art of fiction was delivered on April 25, 1884.

opened. Art lives upon discussion, upon experiment, upon curiosity, upon variety of attempt, upon the exchange of views and the comparison of standpoints; and there is a presumption that those times when no one has anything particular to say about it, and has no reason to give for practice or preference, though they may be times of honor, are not times of development — are times, possibly even, a little of dullness. The successful application of any art is a delightful spectacle, but the theory too is interesting; and though there is a great deal of the latter without the former I suspect there has never been a genuine success that has not had a latent core of conviction. Discussion, suggestion, formulation, these things are fertilizing when they are frank and sincere. Mr. Besant has set an excellent example in saying what he thinks, for his part, about the way in which fiction should be written, as well as about the way in which it should be published; for his view of the "art," carried on into an appendix, covers that too. Other laborers in the same field will doubtless take up the argument, they will give it the light of their experience, and the effect will surely be to make our interest in the novel a little more what it had for some time threatened to fail to be — a serious, active, inquiring interest, under protection of which this delightful study may, in moments of confidence, venture to say a little more what it thinks of itself.

It must take itself seriously for the public to take it so. The old superstition about fiction being "wicked"[2] has doubtless died out in England; but the spirit of it lingers in a certain oblique regard directed toward any story which does not more or less admit that it is only a joke. Even the most jocular novel feels in some degree the weight of the proscription that was formerly directed against literary levity: the jocularity does not always succeed in passing for orthodoxy. It is still expected, though perhaps people are ashamed to say it, that a production which is after all only a "make-believe" (for what else is a "story"?) shall be in some degree apologetic — shall renounce the pretension of attempting really to represent

[2] Cf. Johnson's stricture in *The Rambler*, No. 4. see p. 212.

life. This, of course, any sensible, wide-awake story declines to do, for it quickly perceives that the tolerance granted to it on such a condition is only an attempt to stifle it disguised in the form of generosity. The old evangelical hostility to the novel, which was as explicit as it was narrow, and which regarded it as little less favorable to our immortal part than a stage play, was in reality far less insulting. The only reason for the existence of a novel is that it does attempt to represent life. When it relinquishes this attempt, the same attempt that we see on the canvas of the painter, it will have arrived at a very strange pass. It is not expected of the picture that it will make itself humble in order to be forgiven; and the analogy between the art of the painter and the art of novelist is, so far as I am able to see, complete. Their inspiration is the same, their process (allowing for the different quality of the vehicle) is the same, their success is the same. They may learn from each other, they may explain and sustain each other. Their cause is the same, and the honor of one is the honor of another. The Mahometans think a picture an unholy thing, but it is a long time since any Christian did, and it is therefore the more odd that in the Christian mind the traces (dissimulated though they may be) of a suspicion of the sister art should linger to this day. The only effectual way to lay it to rest is to emphasize the analogy to which I just alluded — to insist on the fact that as the picture is reality, so the novel is history. That is the only general description (which does it justice) that we may give of the novel. But history also is allowed to represent life; it is not, any more than painting, expected to apologize. The subject-matter of fiction is stored up likewise in documents and records, and if it will not give itself away, as they say in California, it must speak with assurance, with the tone of the historian. Certain accomplished novelists have a habit of giving themselves away which must often bring tears to the eyes of people who take their fiction seriously. I was lately struck, in reading over many pages of Anthony Trollope, with his want of discretion in this particular. In a digression, a parenthesis or an aside, he concedes to the reader that he and this trusting friend are only "making believe." He admits that the events he narrates have not really happened, and that he can give his narrative any turn the reader may like best.[3] Such a betrayal of a sacred office seems to me, I confess, a terrible crime; it is what I mean by the attitude of apology, and it shocks me every whit as much in Trollope as it would have shocked me in Gibbon or Macaulay. It implies that the novelist is less occupied in looking for the truth (the truth, of course I mean, that he assumes, the premises that we grant him, whatever they may be) than the historian, and in doing so it deprives him at a stroke of all his standing room. To represent and illustrate the past, the actions of men, is the task of either writer, and the only difference that I can see is, in proportion as he succeeds, to the honor of the novelist, consisting as it does in his having more difficulty in collecting his evidence, which is so far from being purely literary. It seems to me to give him a great character, the fact that he has at once so much in common with the philosopher and the painter; this double analogy is a magnificent heritage.

It is of all this evidently that Mr. Besant is full when he insists upon the fact that fiction is one of the *fine* arts, deserving in its turn of all the honors and emoluments that have hitherto been reserved for the successful profession of music, poetry, painting, architecture. It is impossible to insist too much on so important a truth, and the place that Mr. Besant demands for the work of the novelist may be represented, a trifle less abstractly, by saying that he demands not only that it shall be reputed artistic, but that it shall be reputed very artistic indeed. It is excellent that he should have struck this note, for his doing so indicates that there was need of it, that his proposition may be to many people a novelty. One rubs one's eyes at the thought; but the rest of Mr. Besant's essay confirms the revelation. I suspect in truth that it would be possible to confirm it still further, and that one would not be far wrong in saying that in addition to the people to whom it has never occurred that a novel ought to be artistic, there are a great many others who, if this principle were urged upon them, would be filled with an indefinable mistrust. They would find it difficult to

explain their repugnance, but it would operate strongly to put them on their guard. "Art," in our Protestant communities, where so many things have got so strangely twisted about, is supposed in certain circles to have some vaguely injurious effect upon those who make it an important consideration, who let it weigh in the balance. It is assumed to be opposed in some mysterious manner to morality, to amusement, to instruction. When it is embodied in the work of the painter (the sculptor is another affair!) you know what it is: it stands there before you, in the honesty of pink and green and a gilt frame; you can see the worst of it at a glance, and you can be on your guard. But when it is introduced into literature it becomes more insidious — there is danger of its hurting you before you know it. Literature should be either instructive or amusing, and there is in many minds an impression that these artistic preoccupations, the search for form, contribute to neither end, interfere indeed with both. They are too frivolous to be edifying, and too serious to be diverting; and they are moreover priggish and paradoxical and superfluous. That, I think, represents the manner in which the latent thought of many people who read novels as an exercise in skipping would explain itself if it were to become articulate. They would argue, of course, that a novel ought to be "good," but they would interpret this term in a fashion of their own, which indeed would vary considerably from one critic to another. One would say that being good means representing virtuous and aspiring characters, placed in prominent positions; another would say that it depends on a "happy ending," on a distribution at the last of prizes, pensions, husbands, wives, babies, millions, appended paragraphs, and cheerful remarks. Another still would say that it means being full of incident and movement, so that we shall wish to jump ahead, to see who was the mysterious stranger, and if the stolen will was ever found, and shall not be distracted from this pleasure by any tiresome analysis or "description." But they would all agree that the "artistic" idea would spoil some of their fun. One would hold it accountable for all the description, another would see it revealed in the absence of sympathy. Its hostility to a happy ending would be evident, and it might even in some cases render any

[3]James may be thinking about such addresses to the reader as the opening of Ch. 51 in *Barchester Towers,* where the narrator worries aloud about the difficulty of writing endings.

ending at all impossible. The "ending" of a novel is, for many persons, like that of a good dinner, a course of dessert and ices, and the artist in fiction is regarded as a sort of meddlesome doctor who forbids agreeable aftertastes. It is therefore true that this conception of Mr. Besant's of the novel as a superior form encounters not only a negative but a positive indifference. It matters little that as a work of art it should really be as little or as much of its essence to supply happy endings, sympathetic characters, and an objective tone, as if it were a work of mechanics: the association of ideas, however incongruous, might easily be too much for it if an eloquent voice were not sometimes raised to call attention to the fact that it is at once as free and as serious a branch of literature as any other.

Certainly this might sometimes be doubted in presence of the enormous number of works of fiction that appeal to the credulity of our generation, for it might easily seem that there could be no great character in a commodity so quickly and easily produced. It must be admitted that good novels are much compromised by bad ones, and that the field at large suffers discredit from overcrowding. I think, however, that this injury is only superficial, and that the superabundance of written fiction proves nothing against the principle itself. It has been vulgarized, like all other kinds of literature, like everything else today, and it has proved more than some kinds accessible to vulgarization. But there is as much difference as there ever was between a good novel and a bad one: the bad is swept with all the daubed canvases and spoiled marble into some unvisited limbo, or infinite rubbish-yard beneath the back-windows of the world, and the good subsists and emits its light and stimulates our desire for perfection. As I shall take the liberty of making but a single criticism of Mr. Besant, whose tone is so full of the love of his art, I may as well have done with it at once. He seems to me to mistake in attempting to say so definitely beforehand what sort of an affair the good novel will be. To indicate the danger of such an error as that has been the purpose of these few pages; to suggest that certain traditions on the subject, applied *a priori*, have already had much to answer for, and that the good health of an art which undertakes so immediately to reproduce life must demand that it be perfectly free. It lives upon exercise, and the very meaning of exercise is freedom. The only obligation to which in advance we may hold a novel, without incurring the accusation of being arbitrary, is that it be interesting. That general responsibility rests upon it, but it is the only one I can think of. The ways in which it is at liberty to accomplish this result (of interesting us) strike me as innumerable, and such as can only suffer from being marked out or fenced in by prescription. They are as various as the temperament of man, and they are successful in proportion as they reveal a particular mind, different from others. A novel is in its broadest definition a personal, a direct impression of life: that, to begin with, constitutes its value, which is greater or less according to the intensity of the impression. But there will be no intensity at all, and therefore no value, unless there is freedom to feel and say. The tracing of a line to be followed, of a tone to be taken, of a form to be filled out, is a limitation of that freedom and a suppression of the very thing that we are most curious about. The form, it seems to me, is to be appreciated after the fact: then the author's choice has been made, his standard has been indicated; then we can follow lines and directions and compare tones and resemblances. Then in a word we can enjoy one of the most charming of pleasures, we can estimate quality, we can apply the test of execution. The execution belongs to the author alone; it is what is most personal to him, and we measure him by that. The advantage, the luxury, as well as the torment and responsibility of the novelist, is that there is no limit to what he may attempt as an executant — no limit to his possible experiments, efforts, discoveries, successes. Here it is especially that he works, step by step, like his brother of the brush, of whom we may always say that he has painted his picture in a manner best known to himself. His manner is his secret, not necessarily a jealous one. He cannot disclose it as a general thing if he would; he would be at a loss to teach it to others. I say this with a due recollection of having insisted on the community of method of the artist who paints a picture and the artist who writes a novel. The painter *is* able to teach the rudiments of his practice, and it is possible, from the study of good work (granted the aptitude), both to learn how to paint and to learn how to write. Yet it remains true, without injury to the *rapprochement,* that the literary artists would be obliged to say to his pupil much more than the other, "Ah, well, you must do it as you can!" It is a question of degree, a matter of delicacy. If there are exact sciences, there are also exact arts, and the grammar of painting is so much more definite that it makes the difference.

I ought to add, however, that if Mr. Besant says at the beginning of his essay that the "laws of fiction may be laid down and taught with as much precision and exactness as the laws of harmony, perspective, and proportion," he mitigates what might appear to be an extravagance by applying his remark to "general" laws, and by expressing most of these rules in a manner with which it would certainly be unaccommodating to disagree. That the novelist must write from his experience, that his "characters must be real and such as might be met with in actual life"; that "a young lady brought up in a quiet country village should avoid descriptions of garrison life," and "a writer whose friends and personal experiences belong to the lower middle-class should carefully avoid introducing his characters into society"; that one should enter one's notes in a common-place book; that one's figures should be clear in outline; that making them clear by some trick of speech or of carriage is a bad method, and "describing them at length" is a worse one; that English Fiction should have a "conscious moral purpose"; that "it is almost impossible to estimate too highly the value of careful workmanship — that is, of style"; that "the most important point of all is the story," that "the story is everything": these are principles with most of which it is surely impossible not to sympathize. That remark about the lower middle-class writer and his knowing his place is perhaps rather chilling; but for the rest I should find it difficult to dissent from any one of these recommendations. At the same time, I should find it difficult positively to assent to them, with the exception, perhaps, of the injunction as to entering one's notes in a common-place book. They scarcely seem to me to have the quality that Mr. Besant attributes to the rules of the novelist — the "precision and exactness" of "the laws of harmony, perspective, and proportion."

They are suggestive, they are even inspiring, but they are not exact, though they are doubtless as much so as the case admits of: which is a proof of that liberty of interpretation for which I just contended. For the value of these different injunctions — so beautiful and so vague — is wholly in the meaning one attaches to them. The characters, the situation, which strike one as real will be those that touch and interest one most, but the measure of reality is very difficult to fix. The reality of Don Quixote or of Mr. Micawber is a very delicate shade; it is a reality so colored by the author's vision that, vivid as it may be, one would hesitate to propose it as a model: one would expose one's self to some very embarrassing questions on the part of a pupil. It goes without saying that you will not write a good novel unless you possess the sense of reality; but it will be difficult to give you a recipe for calling that sense into being. Humanity is immense, and reality has a myriad forms; the most one can affirm is that some of the flowers of fiction have the odor of it, and others have not; as for telling you in advance how your nosegay should be composed, that is another affair. It is equally excellent and inconclusive to say that one must write from experience; to our supposititious aspirant such a declaration might savor of mockery. What kind of experience is intended, and where does it begin and end? Experience is never limited, and it is never complete; it is an immense sensibility, a kind of huge spider-web of the finest silken threads suspended in the chamber of consciousness, and catching every air-borne particle in its tissue. It is the very atmosphere of the mind; and when the mind is imaginative — much more when it happens to be that of a man of genius — it takes to itself the faintest hints of life, it converts the very pulses of the air into revelations. The young lady living in a village has only to be a damsel upon whom nothing is lost to make it quite unfair (as it seems to me) to declare to her that she shall have nothing to say about the military. Greater miracles have been seen than that, imagination assisting, she should speak the truth about some of these gentlemen. I remember an English novelist, a woman of genius, telling me that she was much commended for the impression she had managed to give in one of her tales of the nature and way of life of the French Protestant youth.[4] She had been asked where she learned so much about his recondite being, she had been congratulated on her peculiar opportunities. These opportunities consisted in her having once, in Paris, as she ascended a staircase, passed an open door where, in the household of a *pasteur*,[5] some of the young Protestants were seated at table round a finished meal. The glimpse made a picture; it lasted only a moment, but that moment was experience. She had got her direct personal impression, and she turned out her type. She knew what youth was, and what Protestantism; she also had the advantage of having seen what it was to be French, so that she converted these ideas into a concrete image and produced a reality. Above all, however, she was blessed with the faculty which when you give it an inch takes an ell, and which for the artist is a much greater source of strength than any accident of residence or of place in the social scale. The power to guess the unseen from the seen, to trace the implication of things, to judge the whole piece by the pattern, the condition of feeling life in general so completely that you are well on your way to knowing any particular corner of it — this cluster of gifts may almost be said to constitute experience, and they occur in country and in town, and in the most differing stages of education. If experience consists of impressions, it may be said that impressions *are* experience, just as (have we not seen it?) they are the very air we breathe. Therefore, if I should certainly say to a novice, "Write from experience and experience only," I should feel that this was rather a tantalizing monition if I were not careful immediately to add, "Try to be one of the people on whom nothing is lost!"

I am far from intending by this to minimize the importance of exactness — of truth of detail. One can speak best from one's own taste, and I may therefore venture to say that the air of reality (solidity of specification) seems to me to be the supreme virtue of a novel — the merit on which all its other merits (including that conscious

[4]Probably *The Story of Elizabeth* by Anne Thackeray, Lady Ritchie.

[5]Minister.

moral purpose of which Mr. Besant speaks) helplessly and submissively depend. If it be not there they are all as nothing, and if these be there, they owe their effect to the success with which the author has produced the illusion of life. The cultivation of this success, the study of this exquisite process, form, to my taste, the beginning and the end of the art of the novelist. They are his inspiration, his despair, his reward, his torment, his delight. It is here in very truth that he competes with life; it is here that he competes with his brother the painter in *his* attempt to render the look of things, the look that conveys their meaning, to catch the color, the relief, the expression, the surface, the substance of the human spectacle. It is in regard to this that Mr. Besant is well inspired when he bids him take notes. He cannot possibly take too many, he cannot possibly take enough. All life solicits him, and to "render" the simplest surface, to produce the most momentary illusion is a very complicated business. His case would be easier, and the rule would be more exact, if Mr. Besant had been able to tell him what notes to take. But this, I fear, he can never learn in any manual; it is the business of his life. He has to take a great many in order to select a few, he has to work them up as he can, and even the guides and philosophers who might have most to say to him must leave him alone when it comes to the applications of precepts, as we leave the painter in communion with his palette. That his characters "must be clear in outline," as Mr. Besant says — he feels that down to his boots; but how he shall make them so is a secret between his good angel and himself. It would be absurdly simple if he could be taught that a great deal of "description" would make them so, or that on the contrary the absence of description and the cultivation of dialogue, or the absence of dialogue and the multiplication of "incident," would rescue him from his difficulties. Nothing, for instance, is more possible than that he be of a turn of mind for which this odd, literal opposition of description and dialogue, incident and description, has little meaning and light. People often talk of these things as if they had a kind of internecine distinctness, instead of melting into each other at every breath, and being intimately associated parts of one general effort of expression. I cannot imagine composition existing in a series of blocks, nor conceive, in any novel worth discussing at all, of a passage of description that is not in its intention narrative, a passage of dialogue that is not in its intention descriptive, a touch of truth of any sort that does not partake of the nature of incident, or an incident that derives its interest from any other source than the general and only source of the success of a work of art — that of being illustrative. A novel is a living thing, all one and continuous, like any other organism, and in proportion as it lives will it be found, I think, that in each of the parts there is something of each of the other parts. The critic who over the close texture of a finished work shall pretend to trace a geography of items will mark some frontiers as artificial, I fear, as any that have been known to history. There is an old-fashioned distinction between the novel of character and the novel of incident which must have cost many a smile to the intending fabulist who was keen about his work. It appears to me as little to the point as the equally celebrated distinction between the novel and the romance — to answer as little to any reality. There are bad novels and good novels, as there are bad pictures and good pictures; but that is the only distinction in which I see any meaning, and I can as little imagine speaking of a novel of character as I can imagine speaking of a picture of character. When one says picture one says of character, when one says novel one says of incident, and the terms may be transposed at will. What is character but the determination of incident? What is incident but the illustration of character? What is either a picture or a novel that is *not* of character? What else do we seek in it and find in it? It is an incident for a woman to stand up with her hand resting on a table and look out at you in a certain way; or if it be not an incident I think it will be hard to say what it is. At the same time it is an expression of character. If you say you don't see it (character in *that — allons donc!*[6]), this is exactly what the artist who has reasons of his own for thinking he *does* see it undertakes to show you. When a young man makes up his mind that he has not

[6]Get out of here!

faith enough after all to enter the church as he intended, that is an incident, though you may not hurry to the end of the chapter to see whether perhaps he doesn't change once more. I do not say that these are extraordinary or startling incidents. I do not pretend to estimate the degree of interest proceeding from them, for this will depend upon the skill of the painter. It sounds almost puerile to say that some incidents are intrinsically much more important than others, and I need not take this precaution after having professed my sympathy for the major ones in remarking that the only classification of the novel that I can understand is into that which has life and that which has it not.

The novel and the romance, the novel of incident and that of character — these clumsy separations appear to me to have been made by critics and readers for their own convenience, and to help them out of some of their occasional queer predicaments, but to have little reality or interest for the producer, from whose point of view it is of course that we are attempting to consider the art of fiction. The case is the same with another shadowy category which Mr. Besant apparently is disposed to set up — that of the "modern English novel"; unless indeed it be that in this matter he has fallen into an accidental confusion of standpoints. It is not quite clear whether he intends the remarks in which he alludes to it to be didactic or historical. It is as difficult to suppose a person intending to write a modern English as to suppose him writing an ancient English novel: that is a label which begs the question. One writes the novel, one paints the picture, of one's language and of one's time, and calling it modern English will not, alas! make the difficult task any easier. No more, unfortunately, will calling this or that work of one's fellow-artist a romance — unless it be, of course, simply for the pleasantness of the thing, as for instance when Hawthorne gave this heading to his story of *Blithedale*. The French, who have brought the theory of fiction to remarkable completeness, have but one name for the novel, and have not attempted smaller things in it, that I can see, for that. I can think of no obligation to which the "romancer" would not be held equally with the novelist; the standard of execution is equally high for each. Of course it is of execution that we are talking — that being the only point of a novel that is open to contention. This is perhaps too often lost sight of, only to produce interminable confusions and cross-purposes. We must grant the artist his subject, his idea, his *donnée:*[7] our criticism is applied only to what he makes of it. Naturally I do not mean that we are bound to like it or find it interesting: in case we do not our course is perfectly simple — to let it alone. We may believe that of a certain idea even the most sincere novelist can make nothing at all, and the event may perfectly justify our belief; but the failure will have been a failure to execute, and it is in the execution that the fatal weakness is recorded. If we pretend to respect the artist at all, we must allow him his freedom of choice, in the face, in particular cases, of innumerable presumptions that the choice will not fructify. Art derives a considerable part of its beneficial exercise from flying in the face of presumptions, and some of the most interesting experiments of which it is capable are hidden in the bosom of common things. Gustave Flaubert has written a story about the devotion of a servant-girl to a parrot,[8] and the production, highly finished as it is, cannot on the whole be called a success. We are perfectly free to find it flat, but I think it might have been interesting; and I, for my part, am extremely glad he should have written it; it is a contribution to our knowledge of what can be done — or what cannot. Ivan Turgenev has written a tale about a deaf and dumb serf and a lap-dog,[9] and the thing is touching, loving, a little masterpiece. He struck the note of life where Gustave Flaubert missed it — he flew in the face of a presumption and achieved a victory.

Nothing, of course, will ever take the place of the good old fashion of "liking" a work of art or not liking it: the most improved criticism will not abolish that primitive, that ultimate test. I mention this to guard myself from the accusation of intimating that the idea, the subject, of a novel or a picture, does not matter. It matters, to my sense, in the highest degree, and if I might put up a

prayer it would be that artists should select none but the richest. Some, as I have already hastened to admit, are much more remunerative than others, and it would be a world happily arranged in which persons intending to treat them should be exempt from confusions and mistakes. This fortunate condition will arrive only, I fear, on the same day that critics become purged from error. Meanwhile, I repeat, we do not judge the artist with fairness unless we say to him,

"Oh, I grant you your starting-point, because if I did not I should seem to prescribe to you, and heaven forbid I should take that responsibility. If I pretend to tell you what you must not take, you will call upon me to tell you then what you must take; in which case I shall be prettily caught. Moreover, it isn't till I have accepted your data that I can begin to measure you. I have the standard, the pitch; I have no right to tamper with your flute and then criticize your music. Of course I may not care for your idea at all; I may think it silly, or stale, or unclean; in which case I wash my hands of you altogether. I may content myself with believing that you will not have succeeded in being interesting, but I shall, of course, not attempt to demonstrate it, and you will be as indifferent to me as I am to you. I needn't remind you that there are all sorts of tastes: who can know it better? Some people, for excellent reasons, don't like to read about carpenters; others, for reasons even better, don't like to read about courtesans. Many object to Americans. Others (I believe they are mainly editors and publishers) won't look at Italians. Some readers don't like quiet subjects; others don't like bustling ones. Some enjoy a complete illusion, others the consciousness of large concessions. They choose their novels accordingly, and if they don't care about your idea they won't, *a fortiori,* care about your treatment."

So that it comes back very quickly, as I have said, to the liking: in spite of M. Zola, who reasons less powerfully than he represents, and who will not reconcile himself to this absoluteness of taste, thinking that there are certain things that people ought to like, and that they can be made to like. I am quite at a loss to imagine anything (at any rate in this matter of fiction) that people *ought* to like or to dislike. Selection will be sure to take

[7]What is given.
[8]*A Simple Heart.*
[9]*Mumu.*

care of itself, for it has a constant motive behind it. That motive is simply experience. As people feel life, so they will feel the art that is most closely related to it. This closeness of relation is what we should never forget in talking of the effort of the novel. Many people speak of it as a factitious, artificial form, a product of ingenuity, the business of which is to alter and arrange the things that surround us, to translate them into conventional, traditional moulds. This, however, is a view of the matter which carries us but a very short way, condemns the art to an eternal repetition of a few familiar *cliché*s, cuts short its development, and leads us straight up to a dead wall. Catching the very note and trick, the strange irregular rhythm of life, that is the attempt whose strenuous force keeps Fiction upon her feet. In proportion as in what she offers us we see life *without* rearrangement do we feel that we are touching the truth; in proportion as we see it *with* rearrangement do we feel that we are being put off with a substitute, a compromise and convention. It is not uncommon to hear an extraordinary assurance of remark in regard to this matter of rearranging, which is often spoken of as if it were the last word of art. Mr. Besant seems to me in danger of falling into the great error with his rather unguarded talk about "selection." Art is essentially selection, but it is a selection whose main care is to be typical, to be inclusive. For many people art means rose-colored window-panes, and selection means picking a bouquet for Mrs. Grundy.[10] They will tell you glibly that artistic considerations have nothing to do with the disagreeable, with the ugly; they will rattle off shallow commonplaces about the province of art and the limits of art till you are moved to some wonder in return as to the province and the limits of ignorance. It appears to me that no one can ever have made a seriously artistic attempt without becoming conscious of an immense increase — a kind of revelation — of freedom. One perceives in that case — by the light of a heavenly ray — that the province of art is all life, all feeling, all observation, all vision. As Mr. Besant so justly intimates, it is all experience. That is a sufficient answer to those who maintain

[10]Personification of prudery.

that it must not touch the sad things of life, who stick into its divine unconscious bosom little prohibitory inscriptions on the end of sticks, such as we see in public gardens — "It is forbidden to walk on the grass; it is forbidden to touch the flowers; it is not allowed to introduce dogs or to remain after dark; it is requested to keep to the right." The young aspirant in the line of fiction whom we continue to imagine will do nothing without taste, for in that case his freedom would be of little use to him; but the first advantage of his taste will be to reveal to him the absurdity of the little sticks and tickets. If he have taste, I must add, of course he will have ingenuity, and my disrespectful reference to that quality just now was not meant to imply that it is useless in fiction. But it is only a secondary aid; the first is a capacity of receiving straight impressions.

Mr. Besant has some remarks on the question of "the story" which I shall not attempt to criticize, though they seem to me to contain a singular ambiguity, because I do not think I understand them. I cannot see what is meant by talking as if there were a part of a novel which is the story and part of it which for mystical reasons is not — unless indeed the distinction be made in a sense in which it is difficult to suppose that any one should attempt to convey anything. "The story," if it represents anything, represents the subject, the idea, the *donnée* of the novel; and there is surely no "school" — Mr. Besant speaks of a school — which urges that a novel should be all treatment and no subject. There must assuredly be something to treat; every school is intimately conscious of that. This sense of the story being the idea, the starting-point, of the novel, is the only one that I see in which it can be spoken of as something different from its organic whole; and since in proportion as the work is successful the idea permeates and penetrates it, informs and animates it, so that every word and every punctuation-point contribute directly to the expression, in that proportion do we lose our sense of the story being a blade which may be drawn more or less out of its sheath. The story and the novel, the idea and the form, are the needle and thread, and I never heard of a guild of tailors who recommended the use of the thread without the needle, or the needle without the thread. Mr. Besant is not the only critic who may be observed to have spoken as if there were certain things in life which constitute stories, and certain others which do not. I find the same odd implication in an entertaining article in the *Pall Mall Gazette,* devoted, as it happens, to Mr. Besant's lecture. "The story is the thing!" says this graceful writer, as if with a tone of opposition to some other idea. I should think it was, as every painter who, as the time for "sending in" his picture looms in the distance, finds himself still in quest of a subject — as every belated artist not fixed about his theme will heartily agree. There are some subjects which speak to us and others which do not, but he would be a clever man who should undertake to give a rule — an *index expurgatorius* — by which the story and the no-story should be known apart. It is impossible (to me at least) to imagine any such rule which shall not be altogether arbitrary. The writer in the *Pall Mall* opposes the delightful (as I suppose) novel of *Margot la Balafrée* to certain tales in which "Bostonian nymphs" appear to have "rejected English dukes for psychological reasons."[11] I am not acquainted with the romance just designated, and can scarcely forgive the *Pall Mall* critic for not mentioning the name of the author, but the title appears to refer to a lady who may have received a scar in some heroic adventure. I am inconsolable at not being acquainted with this episode, but am utterly at a loss to see why it is a story when the rejection (or acceptance) of a duke is not, and why a reason, psychological or other, is not a subject when a cicatrix is. They are all particles of the multitudinous life with which the novel deals, and surely no dogma which pretends to make it lawful to touch the one and unlawful to touch the other will stand for a moment on its feet. It is the special picture that must stand or fall, according as it seem to possess truth or to lack it. Mr. Besant does not, to my sense, light up the subject by intimating that a story must, under penalty of not being a story, consist of "adventures." Why of adventures more than of green spectacles? He mentions a category of impossible things, and among them he places "fiction without adventure." Why without adventure, more than without matrimony, or celibacy, or parturition, or cholera, or

[11]Henry James's own *An International Episode* (1879). *Margot la Balafrée* (1884) is by Fortune de Boisgobey.

hydropathy, or Jansenism? This seems to me to bring the novel back to the hapless little *rôle* of being an artificial, ingenious thing — bring it down from its large, free character of an immense and exquisite correspondence with life. And what *is* adventure, when it comes to that and by what sign is the listening pupil to recognize it? It is an adventure — an immense one — for me to write this little article; and for a Bostonian nymph to reject an English duke is an adventure only less stirring, I should say, than for an English duke to be rejected by a Bostonian nymph. I see dramas within dramas in that, and innumerable points of view. A psychological reason is, to my imagination, an object adorably pictorial; to catch the tint of its complexion — I feel as if that idea might inspire one to Titianesque efforts. There are few things more exciting to me, in short, than a psychological reason, and yet, I protest, the novel seems to me the most magnificent form of art. I have just been reading, at the same time, the delightful story of *Treasure Island,* by Mr. Robert Louis Stevenson and, in a manner less consecutive, the last tale from M. Edmond de Goncourt, which is entitled *Chérie.* One of these works treats of murder, mysteries, islands of dreadful renown, hairbreadth escapes, miraculous coincidences and buried doubloons. The other treats of a little French girl who lived in a fine house in Paris, and died of wounded sensibility because no one would marry her. I call *Treasure Island* delightful, because it appears to me to have succeeded wonderfully in what it attempts; and I venture to bestow no epithet upon *Chérie,* which strikes me as having failed deplorably in what it attempts — that is in tracing the development of the moral consciousness of a child. But one of these productions strikes me as exactly as much of a novel as the other, and as having a "story" quite as much. The moral consciousness of a child is as much a part of life as the islands of the Spanish Main, and the one sort of geography seems to me to have those "surprises" of which Mr. Besant speaks quite as much as the other. For myself (since it comes back in the last resort, as I say, to the preference of the individual), the picture of the child's experience has the advantage that I can at successive steps (an immense luxury, near to the "sensual pleasure" of which Mr. Besant's critic in the *Pall Mall* speaks) say Yes or No, as it may be, to what the artist puts before me. I have been a child in fact, but I have been on a quest for a buried treasure only in supposition, and it is a simple accident that with M. de Goncourt I should have for the most part to say No. With George Eliot, when she painted that country with a far other intelligence, I always said Yes.

The most interesting part of Mr. Besant's lecture is unfortunately the briefest passage — his very cursory allusion to the "conscious moral purpose" of the novel. Here again it is not very clear whether he be recording a fact or laying down a principle; it is a great pity that in the latter case he should not have developed his idea. This branch of the subject is of immense importance, and Mr. Besant's few words point to considerations of the widest reach, not to be lightly disposed of. He will have treated the art of fiction but superficially who is not prepared to go every inch of the way that these considerations will carry him. It is for this reason that at the beginning of these remarks I was careful to notify the reader that my reflections on so large a theme have no pretension to be exhaustive. Like Mr. Besant, I have left the question of the morality of the novel till the last, and at the last I find I have used up my space. It is a question surrounded with difficulties, as witness the very first that meets us, in the form of a definite question, on the threshold. Vagueness, in such a discussion, is fatal, and what is the meaning of your morality and your conscious moral purpose? Will you not define your terms and explain how (a novel being a picture) a picture can be either moral or immoral? You wish to paint a moral picture or carve a moral statue: will you not tell us how you would set about it? We are discussing the Art of Fiction; questions of art are questions (in the widest sense) of execution; questions of morality are quite another affair, and will you not let us see how it is that you find it so easy to mix them up? These things are so clear to Mr. Besant that he has deduced from them a law which he sees embodied in English Fiction, and which is "a truly admirable thing and a great cause for congratulation." It is a great cause for congratulation indeed when such thorny problems become as smooth as silk. I may add that in so far as Mr. Besant perceives that in point of fact English Fiction has

addressed itself preponderantly to these delicate questions he will appear to many people to have made a vain discovery. They will have been positively struck, on the contrary, with the moral timidity of the usual English novelist; with his (or with her) aversion to face the difficulties with which on every side the treatment of reality bristles. He is apt to be extremely shy (whereas the picture that Mr. Besant draws is a picture of boldness), and the sign of his work, for the most part, is a cautious silence on certain subjects. In the English novel (by which of course I mean the American as well), more than in any other there is a traditional difference between that which people know and that which they agree to admit that they know, that which they see and that which they speak of, that which they feel to be a part of life and that which they allow to enter into literature. There is the great difference, in short, between what they talk of in conversation and what they talk of in print. The essence of moral energy is to survey the whole field, and I should directly reverse Mr. Besant's remark and say not that the English novel has a purpose, but that it has a diffidence. To what degree a purpose in a work of art is a source of corruption I shall not attempt to inquire; the one that seems to me least dangerous is the purpose of making a perfect work. As for our novel, I may say lastly on this score that as we find it in England today it strikes me as addressed in a large degree to "young people," and that this in itself constitutes a presumption that it will be rather shy. There are certain things which it is generally agreed not to discuss, not even to mention, before young people. That is very well, but the absence of discussion is not a symptom of the moral passion. The purpose of the English novel — "a truly admirable thing, and a great cause for congratulation" — strikes me therefore as rather negative.

There is one point at which the moral sense and the artistic sense lie very near together; that is in the light of the very obvious truth that the deepest quality of a work of art will always be the quality of the mind of the producer. In proportion as that intelligence is fine will the novel, the picture, the statue partake of the substance of beauty and truth. To be constituted of such elements is, to my vision, to have purpose enough. No good novel will ever proceed from a superficial mind; that seems to me an axiom which, for the artist in fiction, will cover all needful moral ground: If the youthful aspirant take it to heart it will illuminate for him many of the mysteries of "purpose." There are many other useful things that might be said to him, but I have come to the end of my article, and can only touch them as I pass. The critic in the *Pall Mall Gazette,* whom I have already quoted, draws attention to the danger, in speaking of the art of fiction, of generalizing. The danger that he has in mind is rather, I imagine, that of particularizing, for there are some comprehensive remarks which, in addition to those embodied in Mr. Besant's suggestive lecture, might without fear of misleading him be addressed to the ingenuous student. I should remind him first of the magnificence of the form that is open to him, which offers to sight so few restrictions and such innumerable opportunities. The other arts, in comparison, appear confined and hampered; the various conditions under which they are exercised are so rigid and definite. But the only condition that I can think of attaching to the composition of the novel is, as I have already said, that it be sincere. This freedom is a splendid privilege, and the first lesson of the young novelist is to learn to be worthy of it.

"Enjoy it as it deserves [I should say to him]; take possession of it, explore it to its utmost extent, publish it, rejoice in it. All life belongs to you, and do not listen either to those who would shut you up into corners of it and tell you that it is only here and there that art inhabits, or to those who would persuade you that this heavenly messenger wings her way outside of life altogether, breathing a superfine air, and turning away her head from the truth of things. There is no impression of life, no manner of seeing it and feeling it, to which the plan of the novelist may not offer a place; you have only to remember that talents so dissimilar as those of Alexandre Dumas and Jane Austen, Charles Dickens and Gustave Flaubert have worked in this field with equal glory. Do not think too much about optimism and pessimism; try and catch the color of life itself. In France today we see a prodigious effort (that of Émile Zola, to whose solid and serious work no explorer of the capacity of the novel can allude without respect), we see an extraordinary effort vitiated by a spirit of pessimism on a narrow basis. M. Zola is magnificent, but he strikes an English reader as ignorant; he has an air of working in the dark; if he had as much light as energy, his results would be of the highest value. As for the aberrations of a shallow optimism, the ground (of English fiction especially) is strewn with their brittle particles as with broken glass. If you must indulge in conclusions, let them have the taste of a wide knowledge. Remember that your first duty is to be as complete as possible — to make as perfect a work. Be generous and delicate and pursue the prize."

Oscar Wilde

1854–1900

Oscar Fingal O'Flahertie Wills Wilde was born in Dublin, the son of the surgeon Sir William Wilde and Jane Francesca Elgee, who wrote poetry under the name of "Speranza." Wilde was educated first at Trinity College, Dublin, and then at Magdalen College, Oxford. At Oxford he proclaimed himself a disciple of the art historians and critics John Ruskin and Walter Pater, and developed a reputation for eccentricity by wearing his hair long, dressing in velvet knee breeches, and collecting china, the aesthetic perfection of which he hoped to duplicate in himself. Wilde won the Newdigate prize for poetry in 1878 and published his first volume of verse in 1881. At twenty-seven, he was already a public figure, lampooned by W. S. Gilbert as the "aesthetic sham" Bunthorne in his comic opera *Patience* (1881), who suggests that to impress the ladies you should "walk down Piccadilly with a poppy or a lily in your med-i-ee-val hand." Wilde's successful response to public ridicule (still current a century later) was to take his notoriety on tour, lecturing in the United States on the gospel of "Art for Art's Sake" — a pure aestheticism that rejected the notion of art and aesthetics as morally uplifting or socially useful. His first play, *Vera, or The Nihilists,* was produced in New York during his 1882 lecture tour. Two years later he married Constance Lloyd, an Irish heiress, with whom he had two sons.

Wilde published a volume of fairy tales, *The Happy Prince,* in 1888, but his notoriety had a second blossoming with the publication of *The Picture of Dorian Gray* (1891), which was attacked viciously in the press for immorality. Although Wilde's preface insists on the independence of art from moral and social value, the story itself — a Victorian Gothic masterpiece — seems distinctly moral, indeed moralistic today, as an apologue explicating the difference between hedonism (a life lived for mere physical pleasure) and epicureanism (a life lived for spiritual intensity). The eternally beautiful hero, Dorian, is as horrifying a figure in his empty pursuit of pleasure as the portrait that graphically expresses the rotting of his soul. What probably upset the press more deeply than Wilde's philosophy were the unmistakable hints of homosexual feeling, the love that "dared not speak its name" in the 1890s, in his portrayal of the relationship between the Paterian epicure, Sir Henry Wotton, and the young hedonist, Dorian Gray. Partly despite his embattled character and partly because of it, Wilde's dramas of the 1890s, jewelled with witty and amoral epigrams, became the hits of the London stage: *Lady Windemere's Fan* (1892), *A Woman of No Importance* (1893), *An Ideal Husband* (1895), and *The Importance of Being Earnest* (1895) were successively and often simultaneously on show in the West End, while his tragedy, *Salomé* (1894), was being played in Paris with Sarah Bernhardt in the title role.

The crash came in 1895, just when Wilde was at the height of his popularity. Wilde had been publicly labeled a sodomite by the Marquess of Queensberry, the father of Wilde's younger lover Lord Alfred Douglas, and Wilde was forced by social pressure to sue Queensberry for libel. Queensberry defended the truth of his accusation and won the civil lawsuit. Wilde then faced criminal prosecution for immoral conduct; convicted, he received two years' imprisonment with hard labor in Reading Gaol. A wealthy darling of society when the scandal broke, he was bankrupt and abandoned when he was released from prison in 1898. He published his most effective poem, "The Ballad of Reading Gaol," after leaving prison, but both the theater and society — the two sites of his triumph — had shut their doors upon him forever. He left England for Paris, living under the name of Sebastian Melmoth, where he died of meningitis in 1900.

"The Decay of Lying" (1889) is Wilde's wittiest and freshest expression of the "art for art's sake" aesthetic that he had learned from Walter Pater. In this not-so-Platonic dialogue between two Victorian gentlemen, the earnest Cyril and the dandified Vivian, Wilde takes up the relationship between art and life, poetic and logical truth, that had been at the center of the aesthetics debate since Plato. With playful paradox and overstatement, Vivian, Wilde's raisonneur, offers up what is at bottom a version of Aristotle's answer to Plato: that art has only extraneous and incidental relations to politics, morality, and other social spheres; that it is an autonomous human activity with its own means and ends whose products can be judged only by its own rules. Wilde's position may at times appear extreme, but he was arguing in a utilitarian age that often took the most literal realism and the strictest conformity with the morality of the community as the hallmarks of successful art. These tests were not merely those of the journalistic worshippers of Mrs. Grundy:[1] We see them as well in literary geniuses like Zola and Tolstoy. (See in this context Tolstoy, "What Is Art?" p. 52.)

But though an Aristotelian rather than a Platonist by inclination, Wilde sees a grander role for art than mere independence. Like Shelley, who calls poets "the unacknowledged legislators of the World," Wilde views the canonical works of art as a collective book of instruction not only on proper thought and feeling but even on the nature of existence. In a crucial section, Vivian attempts to prove that all life — even the life of nature itself — is merely an imitation of art. He argues that people model themselves and their behavior on literary characters, falling in love like Juliet or committing suicide like Goethe's Werther. Even the beautiful brown fogs of the London autumn are, according to Vivian, the product of Impressionist painters like Monet and Whistler.

Vivian's statements are extreme and his examples sometimes perverse, but his most profound point — often made in contemporary poststructuralist thought — is that nature is known to us only through culture, which frames it and makes it comprehensible. Since one culture differs from another primarily through its art, it is indeed art that instructs and defines our sense of the natural world. The fogs of London may have been made up materially of coke and coal smoke mixed with water vapor, but the sense of their peculiar beauty can be traced to the Impressionists' taste for the vague and indefinite. Longer ago, the two-point perspective introduced by Italian Renaissance painters of the late fifteenth century permanently transformed the human sense of space.

[1]Personification of prudery.

In "The Decay of Lying" Wilde's speakers draw their examples from painting, where the relation between art and human vision may be clearest, but elsewhere Wilde extends his argument to other artistic forms. Music changes the human idea of time and relation, and poetry and drama the psychological sense of the self in relation to the world. Wilde's aestheticism is not merely a product of the purple nineties; rather, his vision of art as transvaluing all values is reminiscent of his predecessor Nietzsche, while his sense of culture as constituting the ground of our experience of the world we inhabit seems to foreshadow the ideas of Heidegger.

Selected Bibliography

Behrendt, Patricia F. *Oscar Wilde: Eros and Aesthetics.* New York: St. Martin's Press, 1991.

Brown, Julia Prewitt. *Cosmopoliton Criticism: Oscar Wilde's Philosophy of Art.* Charlottesville: University Press of Virginia, 1997.

Buckler, William E. "Wilde's 'Trumpet against the Gate of Dullness': 'The Decay of Lying.'" *English Literature in Transition* 33 (1990): 311–23.

Freedman, Jonathan, ed. *Oscar Wilde: A Collection of Critical Essays.* Englewood Cliffs, NJ: Prentice-Hall, 1995.

Gide, André. *Oscar Wilde: A Study.* New York: Gordon Press, 1975.

Hannon, Patrice. "Aesthetic Criticism, Useless Art." In *Critical Essays on Oscar Wilde,* ed. Regenia Gagnier. New York: G. K. Hall, 1991, pp. 186–201.

Murray, Isobel M. *Oscar Wilde.* New York: Oxford University Press, 1989.

Novitz, David. "Art, Life and Reality." *British Journal of Aesthetics* 30 (1990): 301–10.

Small, Ian. "Semiotics and Oscar Wilde's Accounts of Art." *British Journal of Aesthetics* 25 (1985): 50–56.

Wilde, Oscar. *The Artist as Critic: Critical Writings of Oscar Wilde,* ed. Richard Ellmann. Chicago: University of Chicago Press, 1968.

Zhang, Longxi. "The Critical Legacy of Oscar Wilde." In *Critical Essays on Oscar Wilde,* ed. Regenia Gagnier. New York: G. K. Hall, 1991, pp. 157–71.

The Decay of Lying

An observation

A Dialogue.
Persons: Cyril and Vivian.
Scene: the library of a country house in Nottinghamshire.

CYRIL (*coming in through the open window from the terrace*): My dear Vivian, don't coop yourself up all day in the library. It is a perfectly lovely afternoon. The air is exquisite. There is a mist upon the woods, like the purple bloom upon a plum. Let us go and lie on the grass, and smoke cigarettes, and enjoy Nature.

VIVIAN: Enjoy Nature! I am glad to say that I have entirely lost that faculty. People tell us that Art makes us love Nature more than we loved her before; that it reveals her secrets to us; and that after a careful study of Corot and Constable[1] we

[1]Jean-Baptiste Camille Corot (1796–1875) and John Constable (1776–1837) were nineteenth-century landscape painters, French and British, respectively.

see things in her that had escaped our observation. My own experience is that the more we study Art, the less we care for Nature. What Art really reveals to us is Nature's lack of design, her curious crudities, her extraordinary monotony, her absolutely unfinished condition. Nature has good intentions, of course, but, as Aristotle once said, she cannot carry them out. When I look at a landscape I cannot help seeing all its defects. It is fortunate for us, however, that Nature is so imperfect, as otherwise we should have had no art at all. Art is our spirited protest, our gallant attempt to teach Nature her proper place. As for the infinite variety of Nature, that is a pure myth. It is not to be found in Nature herself. It resides in the imagination, or fancy, or cultivated blindness of the man who looks at her.

CYRIL: Well, you need not look at the landscape. You can lie on the grass and smoke and talk.

VIVIAN: But Nature is so uncomfortable. Grass is hard and lumpy and damp, and full of dreadful black insects. Why, even Morris' poorest workman[2] could make you a more comfortable seat than the whole of Nature can. Nature pales before the furniture of "the street which from Oxford has borrowed its name,"[3] as the poet you love so much once vilely phrased it. I don't complain. If Nature had been comfortable, mankind would never have invented architecture, and I prefer houses to the open air. In a house we all feel of the proper proportions. Everything is subordinated to us, fashioned for our use and our pleasure. Egotism itself, which is so necessary to a proper sense of human dignity, is entirely the result of indoor life. Out of doors one becomes abstract and impersonal. One's individuality absolutely leaves one. And then Nature is so indifferent, so unappreciative. Whenever I am walking in the park here, I always feel that I am no more to her than the cattle that browse on the slope, or the burdock that blooms in the ditch. Nothing is more evident than that Nature hates Mind. Thinking is the most unhealthy thing in the world, and people die of it just as they die of any

other disease. Fortunately, in England at any rate, thought is not catching. Our splendid physique as a people is entirely due to our national stupidity. I only hope we shall be able to keep this great historic bulwark of our happiness for many years to come; but I am afraid that we are beginning to be over-educated; at least everybody who is incapable of learning has taken to teaching — that is really what our enthusiasm for education has come to. In the meantime, you had better go back to your wearisome uncomfortable Nature, and leave me to correct my proofs.

CYRIL: Writing an article! That is not very consistent after what you have just said.

VIVIAN: Who wants to be consistent? The dullard and the doctrinaire, the tedious people who carry out their principles to the bitter end of action, to the *reductio ad absurdum* of practice. Not I. Like Emerson, I write over the door of my library the word "Whim." Besides, my article is really a most salutary and valuable warning. If it is attended to, there may be a new Renaissance of Art.

CYRIL: What is the subject?

VIVIAN: I intend to call it "The Decay of Lying: A Protest."

CYRIL: Lying! I should have thought that our politicians kept up that habit.

VIVIAN: I assure you that they do not. They never rise beyond the level of misrepresentation, and actually condescend to prove, to discuss, to argue. How different from the temper of the true liar, with his frank, fearless statements, his superb irresponsibility, his healthy, natural disdain of proof of any kind! After all, what is a fine lie? Simply that which is its own evidence. If a man is sufficiently unimaginative to produce evidence in support of a lie, he might just as well speak the truth at once. No, the politicians won't do. Something may, perhaps, be urged on behalf of the Bar.[4] The mantle of the Sophist has fallen on its members. Their feigned ardours and unreal rhetoric are delightful. They can make the worse appear the better cause, as though they were fresh from Leontine schools,[5] and have been known to

---

[2]The poet and painter William Morris (1834–1896) also ran a very profitable business designing and manufacturing furniture and other household articles, starting in 1861.

[3]Oxford Street was in the late nineteenth century, as today, the middle-class shopping district of London.

[4]The legal profession.

[5]Wilde's reference is to the sixth-century theologian Leontius of Byzantium, known as the first scholastic philosopher, who adapted Aristotelian logic to theological problems.

wrest from reluctant juries triumphant verdicts of acquittal for their clients, even when those clients, as often happens, were clearly and unmistakeably innocent. But they are briefed by the prosaic, and are not ashamed to appeal to precedent. In spite of their endeavors, the truth will out. Newspapers, even, have degenerated. They may now be absolutely relied upon. One feels it as one wades through their columns. It is always the unreadable that occurs. I am afraid that there is not much to be said in favour of either the lawyer or the journalist. Besides, what I am pleading for is Lying in art. Shall I read you what I have written? It might do you a great deal of good.

CYRIL: Certainly, if you give me a cigarette. Thanks. By the way, what magazine do you intend it for?

VIVIAN: For the *Retrospective Review*. I think I told you that the elect had revived it.

CYRIL: Whom do you mean by "the elect"?

VIVIAN: Oh, The Tired Hedonists of course. It is a club to which I belong. We are supposed to wear faded roses in our button-holes when we meet, and to have a sort of cult for Domitian.[6] I am afraid you are not eligible. You are too fond of simple pleasures.

CYRIL: I should be black-balled on the ground of animal spirits, I suppose?

VIVIAN: Probably. Besides, you are a little too old. We don't admit anybody who is of the usual age.

CYRIL: Well, I should fancy you are all a good deal bored with each other.

VIVIAN: We are. That is one of the objects of the club. Now, if you promise not to interrupt too often, I will read you my article.

CYRIL: You will find me all attention.

VIVIAN (*reading in a very clear, musical voice*): "THE DECAY OF LYING: A PROTEST. — One of the chief causes that can be assigned for the curiously commonplace character of most of the literature of our age is undoubtedly the decay of Lying as an art, a science, and a social pleasure. The ancient historians gave us delightful fiction in the form of fact; the modern novelist presents us with dull facts under the guise of fiction. The Blue-Book[7] is rapidly becoming his ideal both for method and manner. He has his tedious '*document humain*,'[8] his miserable little '*coin de la création*,'[9] into which he peers with his microscope. He is to be found at the Librairie Nationale, or at the British Museum,[10] shamelessly reading up his subject. He has not even the courage of other people's ideas, but insists on going directly to life for everything, and ultimately, between encyclopædias and personal experience, he comes to the ground, having drawn his types from the family circle or from the weekly washerwoman, and having acquired an amount of useful information from which never, even in his most meditative moments, can he thoroughly free himself.

"The loss that results to literature in general from this false ideal of our time can hardly be overestimated. People have a careless way of talking about a 'born liar,' just as they talk about a 'born poet.' But in both cases they are wrong. Lying and poetry are arts — arts, as Plato[11] saw, not unconnected with each other — and they require the most careful study, the most disinterested devotion. Indeed, they have their technique, just as the more material arts of painting and sculpture have, their subtle secrets of form and colour, their craft-mysteries, their deliberate artistic methods. As one knows the poet by his fine music, so one can recognize the liar by his rich rhythmic utterance, and in neither case will the casual inspiration of the moment suffice. Here, as elsewhere, practice must precede perfection. But in modern days while the fashion of writing poetry has become far too common, and should, if possible, be discouraged, the fashion of lying has almost fallen into disrepute. Many a young man starts in life with a natural gift for exaggeration which, if nurtured in congenial and

---

[6]Roman emperor 81–96 C.E., known for his pathological cruelty and suspicion.

[7]The official reports of Parliament, which are issued in a dark blue paper cover, were often referred to as "Blue-Books" in the nineteenth century.

[8]"Story of human life."

[9]"Corner of existence."

[10]The Bibliotheque Nationale and British Museum are the national libraries of France and England, respectively.

[11]See introduction to Plato, p. 25.

sympathetic surroundings, or by the imitation of the best models, might grow into something really great and wonderful. But, as a rule, he comes to nothing. He either falls into careless habits of accuracy — "

CYRIL: My dear fellow!

VIVIAN: Please don't interrupt in the middle of a sentence. "He either falls into careless habits of accuracy, or takes to frequenting the society of the aged and the well-informed. Both things are equally fatal to his imagination, as indeed they would be fatal to the imagination of anybody, and in a short time he develops a morbid and unhealthy faculty of truth-telling, begins to verify all statements made in his presence, has no hesitation in contradicting people who are much younger than himself, and often ends by writing novels which are so like life that no one can possibly believe in their probability. This is no isolated instance that we are giving. It is simply one example out of many; and if something cannot be done to check, or at least to modify, our monstrous worship of facts, Art will become sterile, and Beauty will pass away from the land.

"Even Mr. Robert Louis Stevenson,[12] that delightful master of delicate and fanciful prose, is tainted with this modern vice, for we know

positively no other name for it. There is such a thing as robbing a story of its reality by trying to make it too true, and *The Black Arrow* is so inartistic as not to contain a single anachronism to boast of, while the transformation of Dr. Jekyll reads dangerously like an experiment out of the *Lancet*. As for Mr. Rider Haggard, who really has, or had once, the makings of a perfectly magnificent liar, he is now so afraid of being suspected of genius that when he does tell us anything marvellous, he feels bound to invent a personal reminiscence, and to put it into a footnote as a kind of cowardly corroboration. Nor are our other novelists much better. Mr. Henry James writes fiction as if it were a painful duty, and wastes upon mean motives and imperceptible 'points of view' his neat literary style, his felicitous phrases, his swift and caustic satire. Mr. Hall Caine, it is true, aims at the grandiose, but then he writes at the top of his voice. He is so loud that one cannot hear what he says. Mr. James Payn is an adept in the art of concealing what is not worth finding. He hunts down the obvious with the enthusiasm of a short-sighted detective. As one turns over the pages, the suspense of the author becomes almost unbearable. The horses of Mr. William Black's phaeton do not soar towards the sun. They merely frighten the sky at evening into violent chromolithographic effects. On seeing them approach, the peasants take refuge in dialect. Mrs. Oliphant prattles pleasantly about curates, lawn-tennis parties, domesticity, and other wearisome things. Mr. Marion Crawford has immolated himself upon the altar of local colour. He is like the lady in the French comedy who keeps talking about 'le beau ciel d'Italie.'[13] Besides, he has fallen into a bad habit of uttering moral platitudes. He is always telling us that to be good is to be good, and that to be bad is to be wicked. At times he is almost edifying. *Robert Elsmere* is of course a masterpiece — a masterpiece of the 'genre ennuyeux,'[14] the one form of literature that the English people seem to thoroughly enjoy. A thoughtful young friend of ours once told us that it reminded him of the sort of

---

[12] Vivian lists many of the most popular British fiction writers of the late nineteenth century, most of them nearly forgotten today. *The Black Arrow* (1888) is a historical romance by Robert Louis Stevenson (1850–1894), which is implicitly being compared with the more anachronistic (and exciting) *Treasure Island* (1883) and *Kidnapped* (1886). Sir Henry Rider Haggard (1856–1925) wrote fantasy adventure stories set in exotic locations, like *King Solomon's Mines* (1885) and *She* (1887). For Henry James, see introduction to James, p. 462. Thomas Henry Hall Caine (1853–1931) wrote many sensational novels including *The Shadow of a Crime* (1885) and *The Scapegoat* (1891). James Payn (1830–1898) published over a hundred novels including *By Proxy* (1878). William Black (1841–1898) was a Scottish novelist known best for *A Daughter of Heth* (1872). Margaret Oliphant (1828–1897) was a prolific journalist and novelist who is enjoying a revival today; her *Miss Marjoribanks* (1866) is currently in print. Francis Marion Crawford (1854–1909) was an American short story writer and novelist who set novels in exotic lands, basing the stories on the lives of people he met while traveling. *Robert Elsmere* (1888) is a novel by Mary Augusta (Mrs. Humphry) Ward (1851–1920); Wilde's special animus against this novel was that it represents the Oxford at which he had studied under Walter Pater.

[13] "The beautiful sky of Italy."
[14] "Boring kind."

conversation that goes on at a meat tea in the house of a serious Nonconformist family, and we can quite believe it. Indeed it is only in England that such a book could be produced. England is the home of lost ideas. As for that great and daily increasing school of novelists for whom the sun always rises in the East-End,[15] the only thing that can be said about them is that they find life crude, and leave it raw.

"In France, though nothing so deliberately tedious as *Robert Elsmere* has been produced, things are not much better. M. Guy de Maupassant,[16] with his keen mordant irony and his hard vivid style, strips life of the few poor rags that still cover her, and shows us foul sore and festering wound. He writes lurid little tragedies in which everybody is ridiculous; bitter comedies at which one cannot laugh for very tears. M. Zola,[17] true to the lofty principle that he lays down in one of his pronunciamentos on literature, 'L'homme de génie n'a jamais d'esprit,'[18] is determined to show that, if he has not got genius, he can at least be dull. And how well he succeeds! He is not without power. Indeed at times, as in *Germinal,* there is something almost epic in his work. But his work is entirely wrong from beginning to end, and wrong not on the ground of morals, but on the ground of art. From any ethical standpoint it is just what it should be. The author is perfectly truthful, and describes things exactly as they happen. What more can any moralist desire? We have no sympathy at all with the moral indignation of our time against M. Zola. It is simply the indignation of Tartuffe[19] on being exposed. But from the standpoint of art, what can be said in favour of the author of *L'Assommoir, Nana,* and *Pot-Bouille?* Nothing. Mr. Ruskin once described the characters in George Eliot's novels as being like the sweepings of a Pentonville omnibus, but M. Zola's characters are much worse. They have their dreary vices, and their drearier virtues. The record of their lives is absolutely without interest. Who cares what happens to them? In literature we require distinction, charm, beauty, and imaginative power. We don't want to be harrowed and disgusted with an account of the doings of the lower orders. M. Daudet[20] is better. He has wit, a light touch, and an amusing style. But he has lately committed literary suicide. Nobody can possibly care for Delobelle with his 'Il faut lutter pour l'art,'[21] or for Valmajour with his eternal refrain about the nightingale, or for the poet in *Jack* with his 'mots cruels,'[22] now that we have learned from *Vingt Ans de ma Vie littéraire* that these characters were taken directly from life. To us they seem to have suddenly lost all their vitality, all the few qualities they ever possessed. The only real people are the people who never existed, and if a novelist is base enough to go to life for his personages he should at least pretend that they are creations, and not boast of them as copies. The justification of a character in a novel is not that other persons are what they are, but that the author is what he is. Otherwise the novel is not a work of art. As for M. Paul Bourget,[23] the master of the *roman psychologique,*[24] he commits the error of imagining that the men and women of modern life are capable of being infinitely analysed for an innumerable series of chapters. In point of fact what is interesting about people in good society — and M. Bourget rarely moves out of the Faubourg St. Germain,[25] except to come to London, — is the mask that each one of them wears, not the reality that lies behind the mask. It is a humiliating confession, but we are all of us made out of the same stuff. In Falstaff there is something of Hamlet, in Hamlet there is not a

---

[15]The area of London east of the commercial district contained the poorest neighborhoods.

[16]French writer (1850–1893) famous for mordantly ironic short stories.

[17]Émile Zola (1840–1902), French author of dozens of naturalistic novels including *L'Assommoir (The Dram Shop,* 1877), *Nana* (1880), and *Pot-Bouille (The Stew,* 1882), which focused attention on the social problems of alcoholism, prostitution, and middle-class competitiveness, respectively.

[18]"The man of genius never has wit."

[19]Hypocritical anti-hero of Molière's comedy by the same name.

[20]Alphonse Daudet, French novelist and dramatist (1840–1897), who wrote *Jack* in 1876.

[21]"One must struggle for the sake of art."

[22]"Cruel words."

[23]French psychological novelist (1852–1935) best known for *Le Disciple* (1889).

[24]"Psychological novel."

[25]The most fashionable and aristocratic neighborhood in late nineteenth-century Paris.

little of Falstaff. The fat knight has his moods of melancholy, and the young prince his moments of coarse humour. Where we differ from each other is purely in accidentals: in dress, manner, tone of voice, religious opinions, personal appearance, tricks of habit, and the like. The more one analyses people, the more all reasons for analysis disappear. Sooner or later one comes to that dreadful universal thing called human nature. Indeed, as any one who has ever worked among the poor knows only too well, the brotherhood of man is no mere poet's dream, it is a most depressing and humiliating reality; and if a writer insists upon analysing the upper classes, he might just as well write of match-girls and costermongers[26] at once." However, my dear Cyril, I will not detain you any further just here. I quite admit that modern novels have many good points. All I insist on is that, as a class, they are quite unreadable.

CYRIL: That is certainly a very grave qualification, but I must say that I think you are rather unfair in some of your strictures. I like *The Deemster,* and *The Daughter of Heth,* and *Le Disciple,* and *Mr. Isaacs,*[27] and as for *Robert Elsmere* I am quite devoted to it. Not that I can look upon it as a serious work. As a statement of the problems that confront the earnest Christian it is ridiculous a antiquated. It is simply Arnold's *Literature and Dogma* with the literature left out. It is as much behind the age as Paley's *Evidences,*[28] or Colenso's[29] method of Biblical exegesis. Nor could anything be less impressive than the unfortunate hero gravely heralding a dawn that rose long ago, and so completely missing its true significance that he proposes to carry on the business of the old firm under the new name. On the other hand, it contains several clever caricatures, and a heap of delightful quotations, and Green's philosophy very pleasantly sugars the somewhat bitter

pill of the author's fiction. I also cannot help expressing my surprise that you have said nothing about the two novelists whom you are always reading, Balzac[30] and George Meredith.[31] Surely they are realists, both of them?

VIVIAN: Ah! Meredith! Who can define him? His style is chaos illumined by flashes of lightning. As a writer he has mastered everything except language: as a novelist he can do everything, except tell a story: as an artist he is everything, except articulate. Somebody in Shakespeare — Touchstone, I think — talks about a man who is always breaking his shins over his own wit, and it seems to me that this might serve as the basis for a criticism of Meredith's method. But whatever he is, he is not a realist. Or rather I would say that he is a child of realism who is not on speaking terms with his father. By deliberate choice he has made himself a romanticist. He has refused to bow the knee to Baal, and after all, even if the man's fine spirit did not revolt against the noisy assertions of realism, his style would be quite sufficient of itself to keep life at a respectful distance. By its means he has planted round his garden a hedge full of thorns, and red with wonderful roses. As for Balzac, he was a most remarkable combination of the artistic temperament with the scientific spirit. The latter he bequeathed to his disciples: the former was entirely his own. The difference between such a book as M. Zola's *L'Assommoir* and Balzac's *Illusions Perdues* is the difference between unimaginative realism and imaginative reality. "All Balzac's characters," said Baudelaire,[32] "are gifted with the same ardour of life that animated himself. All his fictions are as deeply coloured as dreams. Each mind is a weapon loaded to the muzzle with will. The very scullions have genius." A steady course of Balzac reduces our living friends to shadows, and our acquaintances

---

[26]People who peddle their wares out of street wagons.

[27]Cyril goes back up Vivian's list of losers: *The Deemster* is by Hall Caine, *The Daughter of Heth* by William Black, *Le Disciple* by Paul Bourget, *Mr. Isaacs* by Marion Crawford.

[28]William Paley (1743–1805), English theologian, published *Evidences of the Existence and Attributes of the Deity* in 1802.

[29]Bishop John William Colenso, author of *The Pentateuch and the Book of Joshua Critically Examined* (1863), attacked by Arnold; see p. 424.

[30]Honoré de Balzac (1799–1850), French author of at least ninety-five novels forming a "Comédie Humaine" depicting life from the Revolution to the 1840s.

[31]English novelist (1828–1909), author of over a dozen novels of which *The Ordeal of Richard Feverel* (1859) and *The Egoist* (1879) are the best known.

[32]Charles Baudelaire (1821–1867), French poet and critic; the quotation is, however, from his friend Theophile Gautier (1811–1872).

to the shadows of shades. His characters have a kind of fervent fiery-coloured existence. They dominate us, and defy scepticism. One of the greatest tragedies of my life is the death of Lucien de Rubempré.[33] It is a grief from which I have never been able to completely rid myself. It haunts me in my moments of pleasure. I remember it when I laugh. But Balzac is no more a realist than Holbein[34] was. He created life, he did not copy it. I admit, however, that he set far too high a value on modernity of form, and that, consequently, there is no book of his that, as an artistic masterpiece, can rank with *Salammbô* or *Esmond*, or *The Cloister and the Hearth*, or the *Vicomte de Bragelonne*.[35]

CYRIL: Do you object to modernity of form, then?

VIVIAN: Yes. It is a huge price to pay for a very poor result. Pure modernity of form is always somewhat vulgarising. It cannot help being so. The public imagine that, because they are interested in their immediate surroundings, Art should be interested in them also, and should take them as her subject-matter. But the mere fact that they are interested in these things makes them unsuitable subjects for Art. The only beautiful things, as somebody once said, are the things that do not concern us. As long as a thing is useful or necessary to us, or affects us in any way, either for pain or for pleasure, or appeals strongly to our sympathies, or is a vital part of the environment in which we live, it is outside the proper sphere of art. To art's subject-matter we should be more or less indifferent. We should, at any rate, have no preferences, no prejudices, no partisan feeling of any kind. It is exactly because Hecuba is nothing to us that her sorrows are such an admirable motive for a tragedy. I do not know anything in the whole history of literature sadder than the artistic career of Charles Reade. He wrote one beautiful book, *The Cloister and the Hearth*, a book as much above *Romola* as *Romola* is above *Daniel Deronda*,[36] and wasted the rest of his life in a foolish attempt to be modern, to draw public attention to the state of our convict prisons, and the management of our private lunatic asylums. Charles Dickens was depressing enough in all conscience when he tried to arouse our sympathy for the victims of the poor-law administration;[37] but Charles Reade, an artist, a scholar, a man with a true sense of beauty, raging and roaring over the abuses of contemporary life like a common pamphleteer or a sensational journalist, is really a sight for the angels to weep over. Believe me, my dear Cyril, modernity of form and modernity of subject-matter are entirely and absolutely wrong. We have mistaken the common livery of the age for the vesture of the Muses, and spend our days in the sordid streets and hideous suburbs of our vile cities when we should be out on the hillside with Apollo. Certainly we are a degraded race, and have sold our birthright for a mess of facts.

CYRIL: There is something in what you say, and there is no doubt that whatever amusement we may find in reading a purely modern novel, we have rarely any artistic pleasure in re-reading it. And this is perhaps the best rough test of what is literature and what is not. If one cannot enjoy reading a book over and over again, there is no use reading it at all. But what do you say about the return to Life and Nature? This is the panacea that is always being recommended to us.

VIVIAN: I will read you what I say on that subject. The passage comes later on in the article, but I may as well give it to you now: —

[33]Hero of Balzac's *Illusions perdues.*

[34]Hans Holbein the Younger (1497–1543), German portrait painter who sketched many of the nobles of Henry VIII's court.

[35]*Salammbô:* romantic historical novel set in the Orient (1863) by French novelist Gustave Flaubert (1821–1880). *Esmond: The History of Henry Esmond* (1852), historical novel set in the early eighteenth century by English novelist William Makepeace Thackeray (1811–1863). *The Cloister and the Hearth:* 1861 historical novel about the Dutch renaissance humanist Desiderius Erasmus by Charles Reade (1814–1884). *Vicomte de Bragelonne:* third novel (1848–1851) in the *Three Musketeers* trilogy by French novelist Alexandre Dumas the Elder (1802–1870), best known for containing the final segment concerning the Man in the Iron Mask.

[36]Two novels by George Eliot (1819–1880); *Romola* (1863) is a historical novel set in the late Renaissance Florence of Savonarola; *Daniel Deronda* (1876) is set in contemporary England and deals with (among other things) the Jewish Question.

[37]The effects of the Poor Law of 1834 were illustrated in Dickens's *Oliver Twist* (1837–39).

"The popular cry of our time is 'Let us return to Life and Nature; they will recreate Art for us, and send the red blood coursing through her veins; they will shoe her feet with swiftness and make her hand strong.' But, alas! we are mistaken in our amiable and well-meaning efforts. Nature is always behind the age. And as for Life, she is the solvent that breaks up Art, the enemy that lays waste her house."

CYRIL: What do you mean by saying that Nature is always behind the age?

VIVIAN: Well, perhaps that is rather cryptic. What I mean is this. If we take Nature to mean natural simple instinct as opposed to self-conscious culture, the work produced under this influence is always old-fashioned, antiquated, and out of date. One touch of Nature may make the whole world kin,[38] but two touches of Nature will destroy any work of Art. If, on the other hand, we regard Nature as the collection of phenomena external to man, people only discover in her what they bring to her. She has no suggestions of her own. Wordsworth went to the lakes, but he was never a lake poet. He found in stones the sermons he had already hidden there. He went moralizing about the district, but his good work was produced when he returned, not to Nature but to poetry. Poetry gave him "Laodamia," and the fine sonnets, and the great Ode, such as it is. Nature gave him "Martha Ray" and "Peter Bell," and the address to Mr. Wilkinson's spade.

CYRIL: I think that view might be questioned. I am rather inclined to believe in the "impulse from a vernal wood,"[39] though of course the artistic value of such an impulse depends entirely on the kind of temperament that receives it, so that the return to Nature would come to mean simply the advance to a great personality. You would agree with that, I fancy. However, proceed with your article.

VIVIAN (reading): "Art begins with abstract decoration with purely imaginative and pleasurable work dealing with what is unreal and non-existent. This is the first stage. Then Life becomes fascinated with this new wonder, and asks to be admitted into the charmed circle. Art takes life as part of her rough material, recreates it, and refashions it in fresh forms, is absolutely indifferent to fact, invents, imagines, dreams, and keeps between herself and reality the impenetrable barrier of beautiful style, of decorative or ideal treatment. The third stage is when Life gets the upper hand, and drives Art out into the wilderness. This is the true decadence, and it is from this that we are now suffering.

"Take the case of the English drama. At first in the hands of the monks Dramatic Art was abstract, decorative, and mythological. Then she enlisted Life in her service, and using some of life's external forms, she created an entirely new race of beings, whose sorrows were more terrible than any sorrow man has ever felt, whose joys were keener than lover's joys, who had the rage of the Titans and the calm of the gods, who had monstrous and marvellous sins, monstrous and marvellous virtues. To them she gave a language different from that of actual use, a language full of resonant music and sweet rhythm, made stately by solemn cadence, or made delicate by fanciful rhyme, jewelled with wonderful words, and enriched with lofty diction. She clothed her children in strange raiment and gave them masks, and at her bidding the antique world rose from its marble tomb. A new Cæsar stalked through the streets of risen Rome, and with purple sail and flute-led oars another Cleopatra passed up the river to Antioch. Old myth and legend and dream took shape and substance. History was entirely re-written, and there was hardly one of the dramatists who did not recognize that the object of Art is not simple truth but complex beauty. In this they were perfectly right. Art itself is really a form of exaggeration; and selection, which is the very spirit of art, is nothing more than an intensified mode of over-emphasis.

"But Life soon shattered the perfection of the form. Even in Shakespeare we can see the beginning of the end. It shows itself by the gradual breaking up of the blank-verse in the later plays, by the predominance given to prose, and by the over-importance assigned to characterisation. The passages in Shakespeare — and they are many — where the language is uncouth, vulgar, exaggerated, fantastic, obscene even, are entirely

[38]Shakespeare, *Troilus and Cressida*, III.iii.171.
[39]From Wordsworth's "The Tables Turned," line 21.

due to Life calling for an echo of her own voice, and rejecting the intervention of beautiful style, through which alone should Life be suffered to find expression. Shakespeare is not by any means a flawless artist. He is too fond of going directly to life, and borrowing life's natural utterance. He forgets that when Art surrenders her imaginative medium she surrenders everything. Goethe says, somewhere —

In der Beschränkung zeigt sich erst der Meister,

'It is in working within limits that the master reveals himself,' and the limitation, the very condition of any art is style. However, we need not linger any longer over Shakespeare's realism. *The Tempest* is the most perfect of palinodes.[40] All that we desired to point out was, that the magnificent work of the Elizabethan and Jacobean artists contained within itself the seeds of its own dissolution, and that, if it drew some of its strength from using life as rough material, it drew all its weakness from using life as an artistic method. As the inevitable result of this substitution of an imitative for a creative medium, this surrender of an imaginative form, we have the modern English melodrama. The characters in these plays talk on the stage exactly as they would talk off it; they have neither aspirations nor aspirates; they are taken directly from life and reproduce its vulgarity down to the smallest detail; they present the gait, manner, costume, and accent of real people; they would pass unnoticed in a third-class railway carriage. And yet how wearisome the plays are! They do not succeed in producing even that impression of reality at which they aim, and which is their only reason for existing. As a method, realism is a complete failure.

"What is true about drama and the novel is no less true about those arts that we call decorative arts. The whole history of these arts in Europe is the record of the struggle between Orientalism, with its frank rejection of imitation, its love of artistic convention, its dislike to the actual representation of any object in Nature, and our own imitative spirit. Wherever the former has been paramount, as in Byzantium, Sicily, and Spain, by actual contact, or in the rest of Europe by the influence of the Crusades, we have had beautiful and imaginative work in which the visible things of life are transmuted into artistic conventions, and the things that Life has not are invented and fashioned for her delight. But wherever we have returned to Life and Nature, our work has always become vulgar, common, and uninteresting. Modern tapestry, with its aërial effects, its elaborate perspective, its broad expanses of waste sky, its faithful and laborious realism, has no beauty whatsoever. The pictorial glass of Germany is absolutely detestable. We are beginning to weave possible carpets in England, but only because we have returned to the method and spirit of the East. Our rugs and carpets of twenty years ago, with their solemn depressing truths, their inane worship of Nature, their sordid reproductions of visible objects, have become, even to the Philistine, a source of laughter. A cultured Mahomedan once remarked to us, 'You Christians are so occupied in misinterpreting the fourth commandment that you have never thought of making an artistic application of the second.' He was perfectly right, and the whole truth of the matter is this: The proper school to learn art in is not Life but Art."

And now let me read you a passage which seems to me to settle the question very completely.

"It was not always thus. We need not say anything about the poets, for they, with the unfortunate exception of Mr. Wordsworth, have been really faithful to their high mission, and are universally recognized as being absolutely unreliable. But in the works of Herodotus,[41] who, in spite of the shallow and ungenerous attempts of modern sciolists to verify his history, may justly be called the 'Father of Lies'; in the published speeches of Cicero and the biographies of Suetonius; in Tacitus at his best; in Pliny's *Natural History*; in Hanno's *Periplus*; in all the early chronicles; in the Lives of the Saints; in Froissart and Sir Thomas Mallory; in the travels of Marco Polo; in Olaus Magnus, and Aldrovandus, and

[40] A palinode is a poem that retracts the poet's previous work.

[41] Vivian's list mixes imaginative histories from those of Herodotus, Greek historian of the fifth century B.C.E., to *The French Revolution* (1837) by Thomas Carlyle (1795–1881), with works of rhetoric, natural science, hagiography, historical novels (e.g., Defoe's 1722 *Journal of the Plague Year*). Sciolists are pedantic scholars.

Conrad Lycosthenes, with his magnificent *Prodigiorum et Ostentorum Chronicon*; in the autobiography of Benvenuto Cellini; in the memoirs of Casanuova; in Defoe's *History of the Plague*; in Boswell's *Life of Johnson*; in Napoleon's despatches, and in the works of our own Carlyle, whose *French Revolution* is one of the most fascinating historical novels ever written, facts are either kept in their proper subordinate position, or else entirely excluded on the general ground of dulness. Now, everything is changed. Facts are not merely finding a footing-place in history, but they are usurping the domain of Fancy, and have invaded the kingdom of Romance. Their chilling touch is over everything. They are vulgarising mankind. The crude commercialism of America, its materialising spirit, its indifference to the poetical side of things, and its lack of imagination and of high unattainable ideals, are entirely due to that country having adopted for its national hero a man, who according to his own confession, was incapable of telling a lie, and it is not too much to say that the story of George Washington and the cherry-tree[42] has done more harm, and in a shorter space of time, than any other moral tale in the whole of literature."

CYRIL: My dear boy!

VIVIAN: I assure you it is the case, and the amusing part of the whole thing is that the story of the cherry-tree is an absolute myth. However, you must not think that I am too despondent about the artistic future either of America or of our own country. Listen to this: —

"That some change will take place before this century has drawn to its close we have no doubt whatsoever. Bored by the tedious and improving conversation of those who have neither the wit to exaggerate nor the genius to romance, tired of the intelligent person whose reminiscences are always based upon memory, whose statements are invariably limited by probability, who is at any time liable to be corroborated by the merest Philistine who happens to be present, Society sooner or later must return to its lost leader, the cultured and fascinating liar. Who he was who

first, without ever having gone out to the rude chase, told the wondering cavemen at sunset how he had dragged the Megatherium from the purple darkness of its jasper cave, or slain the Mammoth in single combat and brought back its gilded tusks, we cannot tell, and not one of our modern anthropologists, for all their much-boasted science, has had the ordinary courage to tell us. Whatever was his name or race, he certainly was the true founder of social intercourse. For the aim of the liar is simply to charm, to delight, to give pleasure. He is the very basis of civilized society, and without him a dinner party, even at the mansions of the great, is as dull as a lecture at the Royal Society, or a debate at the Incorporated Authors, or one of Mr. Burnand's[43] farcical comedies.

"Nor will he be welcomed by society alone. Art, breaking from the prison-house of realism, will run to greet him, and will kiss his false, beautiful lips, knowing that he alone is in possession of the great secret of all her manifestations, the secret that Truth is entirely and absolutely a matter of style; while Life — poor, probable, uninteresting human life — tired of repeating herself for the benefit of Mr. Herbert Spencer,[44] scientific historians, and the compilers of statistics in general, will follow meekly after him, and try to produce, in her own simple and untutored way, some of the marvels of which he talks.

"No doubt there will always be critics who, like a certain writer in the *Saturday Review,* will gravely censure the teller of fairy tales for his defective knowledge of natural history, who will measure imaginative work by their own lack of any imaginative faculty, and will hold up their inkstained hands in horror if some honest gentleman, who has never been farther than the yew-trees of his own garden, pens a fascinating book of travels like Sir John Mandeville,[45] or, like great

[42]The fifth edition (1806) of Mason Locke Weems's *Life and Memorable Actions of George Washington* contained the fictionalized story about the cherry tree.

[43]Francis C. Burnand (knighted in 1910) was the editor of *Punch.*

[44]Spencer (1820–1903) developed theories that adapted Darwin's ideas about evolution through natural selection to societies.

[45]Sir John Mandeville (1300?–1372) was the author of a book of *Travels* written in Norman French between 1357 and 1371; it is a compilation of other travelers' tales into a single first-person narrative.

Raleigh,[46] writes a whole history of the world, without knowing anything whatsoever about the past. To excuse themselves they will try and shelter under the shield of him who made Prospero the magician, and gave him Caliban and Ariel as his servants, who heard the Tritons blowing their horns round the coral reefs of the Enchanted Isle, and the fairies singing to each other in a wood near Athens, who led the phantom kings in dim procession across the misty Scottish heath, and hid Hecate in a cave with the weird sisters. They will call upon Shakespeare — they always do — and will quote that hackneyed passage about Art holding the mirror up to Nature, forgetting that this unfortunate aphorism is deliberately said by Hamlet in order to convince the bystanders of his absolute insanity in all art-matters."

CYRIL: Ahem! Another cigarette, please.

VIVIAN: My dear fellow, whatever you may say, it is merely a dramatic utterance, and no more represents Shakespeare's real views upon art than the speeches of Iago represent his real views upon morals. But let me get to the end of the passage:

"Art finds her own perfection within, and not outside of, herself. She is not to be judged by any external standard of resemblance. She is a veil, rather than a mirror. She has flowers that no forests know of, birds that no woodland possesses. She makes and unmakes many worlds, and can draw the moon from heaven with a scarlet thread. Hers are the 'forms more real than living man,' and hers the great archetypes of which things that have existence are but unfinished copies. Nature has, in her eyes, no laws, no uniformity. She can work miracles at her will, and when she calls monsters from the deep they come. She can bid the almond tree blossom in winter, and send the snow upon the ripe cornfield. At her word the frost lays its silver finger on the burning mouth of June, and the winged lions creep out from the hollows of the Lydian hills. The dryads peer from the thicket as she passes by, and the brown fauns smile strangely at her when she comes near them. She has hawk-faced gods that worship her, and the centaurs gallop at her side."

CYRIL: I like that. I can see it. Is that the end?

VIVIAN: No. There is one more passage, but it is purely practical. It simply suggests some methods by which we could revive this lost art of Lying.

CYRIL: Well, before you read it to me, I should like to ask you a question. What do you mean by saying that life, "poor, probable, uninteresting human life," will try to reproduce the marvels of art? I can quite understand your objection to art being treated as a mirror. You think it would reduce genius to the position of a cracked looking-glass. But you don't mean to say that you seriously believe that Life imitates Art, that Life in fact is the mirror, and Art the reality?

VIVIAN: Certainly I do. Paradox though it may seem — and paradoxes are always dangerous things — it is none the less true that Life imitates art far more than Art imitates life. We have all seen in our own day in England how a certain curious and fascinating type of beauty, invented and emphasised by two imaginative painters,[47] has so influenced Life that whenever one goes to a private view or to an artistic salon one sees, here the mystic eyes of Rossetti's dream, the long ivory throat, the strange square-cut jaw, the loosened shadowy hair that he so ardently loved, there the sweet maidenhood of "The Golden Stair," the blossom-like mouth and weary loveliness of the "Laus Amoris," the passion-pale face of Andromeda, the thin hands and lithe beauty of the Vivien in "Merlin's Dream." And it has always been so. A great artist invents a type, and Life tries to copy it, to reproduce it in a popular form, like an enterprising publisher. Neither Holbein nor Vandyck found in England what they have given us. They brought their types with them, and Life with her keen imitative faculty set herself to supply the master with models. The Greeks, with their quick

[46]Sir Walter Raleigh (1554–1618) wrote a *History of the World* (1614) while in prison.

[47]Vivian gives a list of paintings by the Pre-Raphaelite artist (and poet) Dante Gabriel Rossetti (1828–1882). The other "imaginative painter" may be Sir Edward Coley Burne-Jones (1833–1898).

artistic instinct, understood this, and set in the bride's chamber the statue of Hermes or of Apollo, that she might bear children as lovely as the works of art that she looked at in her rapture or her pain. They knew that Life gains from Art not merely spirituality, depth of thought and feeling, soul-turmoil or soul-peace, but that she can form herself on the very lines and colours of art, and can reproduce the dignity of Pheidias as well as the grace of Praxiteles. Hence came their objection to realism. They disliked it on purely social grounds. They felt that it inevitably makes people ugly, and they were perfectly right. We try to improve the conditions of the race by means of good air, free sunlight, wholesome water, and hideous bare buildings for the better housing of the lower orders. But these things merely produce health, they do not produce beauty. For this, Art is required, and the true disciples of the great artist are not his studio-imitators, but those who become like his works of art, be they plastic as in the Greek days, or pictorial as in modern times; in a word, Life is Art's best, Art's only pupil.

As it is with the visible arts, so it is with literature. The most obvious and the vulgarest form in which this is shown is in the case of the silly boys who, after reading the adventures of Jack Sheppard or Dick Turpin,[48] pillage the stalls of unfortunate apple-women, break into sweet-shops at night, and alarm old gentlemen who are returning home from the city by leaping out on them in suburban lanes, with black masks and unloaded revolvers. This interesting phenomenon, which always occurs after the appearance of a new edition of either of the books I have alluded to, is usually attributed to the influence of literature on the imagination. But this is a mistake. The imagination is essentially creative and always seeks for a new form. The boy-burglar is simply the inevitable result of life's imitative instinct. He is Fact, occupied as Fact usually is, with trying to reproduce Fiction, and what we see in him is repeated on an extended scale throughout the whole of life. Schopenhauer has analyzed the pessimism that characterises modern thought, but

Hamlet invented it. The world has become sad because a puppet was once melancholy. The Nihilist, that strange martyr who has no faith, who goes to the stake without enthusiasm, and dies for what he does not believe in, is a purely literary product. He was invented by Tourgénieff, and completed by Dostoieffski.[49] Robespierre came out of the pages of Rousseau as surely as the People's Palace rose out of the *débris* of a novel. Literature always anticipates life. It does not copy it, but moulds it to its purpose. The nineteenth century, as we know it, is largely an invention of Balzac. Our Luciens de Rubempré, our Rastignacs, and De Marsays made their first appearance on the stage of the *Comédie Humaine*. We are merely carrying out, with footnotes and unnecessary additions, the whim or fancy or creative vision of a great novelist. I once asked a lady, who knew Thackeray intimately, whether he had had any model for Becky Sharp. She told me that Becky was an invention, but that the idea of the character had been partly suggested by a governess who lived in the neighbourhood of Kensington Square, and was the companion of a very selfish and rich old woman. I inquired what became of the governess, and she replied that, oddly enough, some years after the appearance of *Vanity Fair,* she ran away with the nephew of the lady with whom she was living, and for a short time made a great splash in society, quite in Mrs. Rawdon Crawley's style, and entirely by Mrs. Rawdon Crawley's methods. Ultimately she came to grief, disappeared to the Continent, and used to be occasionally seen at Monte Carlo and other gambling places. The noble gentleman from whom the same great sentimentalist drew Colonel Newcome died, a few months after *The Newcomes* had reached a fourth edition, with the word "Adsum" on his lips. Shortly after Mr. Stevenson published his curious psychological story of transformation, a friend of mine, called Mr. Hyde, was in the north of London, and being anxious to get to a railway station, took what he thought would

---

[48]Legendary British highwaymen of the eighteenth century.

[49]Nihilism was analyzed by Ivan Sergeievich Turgenev (1818–1883) in *Fathers and Sons* (1862) and by Fyodor Mikhailovich Dostoevsky (1821–1881) in *The Devils* (1871–72).

be a short cut, lost his way, and found himself in a network of mean, evil-looking streets. Feeling rather nervous he began to walk extremely fast, when suddenly out of an archway ran a child right between his legs. It fell on the pavement, he tripped over it, and trampled upon it. Being of course very much frightened and a little hurt, it began to scream, and in a few seconds the whole street was full of rough people who came pouring out of the houses like ants. They surrounded him, and asked him his name. He was just about to give it when he suddenly remembered the opening incident in Mr. Stevenson's story. He was so filled with horror at having realized in his own person that terrible and well written scene, and at having done accidently, though in fact, what the Mr. Hyde of fiction had done with deliberate intent, that he ran away as hard as he could go. He was, however, very closely followed, and finally he took refuge in a surgery, the door of which happened to be open, where he explained to a young assistant, who happened to be there, exactly what had occurred. The humanitarian crowd were induced to go away on his giving them a small sum of money, and as soon as the coast was clear he left. As he passed out, the name on the brass door-plate of the surgery caught his eye. It was "Jekyll." At least it should have been.

Here the imitation, as far as it went, was of course accidental. In the following case the imitation was self-conscious. In the year 1879, just after I had left Oxford, I met at a reception at the house of one of the Foreign Ministers a woman of very curious exotic beauty. We became great friends, and were constantly together. And yet what interested me most in her was not her beauty, but her character, her entire vagueness of character. She seemed to have no personality at all, but simply the possibility of many types. Sometimes she would give herself up entirely to art, turn her drawing-room into a studio, and spend two or three days a week at picture-galleries or museums. Then she would take to attending race-meetings, wear the most horsey clothes, and talk about nothing but betting. She abandoned religion for mesmerism, mesmerism for politics, and politics for the melodramatic excitements of philanthropy. In fact, she was a kind of Proteus, and as much a failure in all her transformations as was that wondrous sea-god when Odysseus laid hold of him. One day a serial began in one of the French magazines. At that time I used to read serial stories, and I well remember the shock of surprise I felt when I came to the description of the heroine. She was so like my friend that I brought her the magazine, and she recognized herself in it immediately, and seemed fascinated by the resemblance. I should tell you, by the way, that the story was translated from some dead Russian writer, so that the author had not taken his type from my friend. Well, to put the matter briefly, some months afterwards I was in Venice, and finding the magazine in the reading-room of the hotel, I took it up casually to see what had become of the heroine. It was a most piteous tale, as the girl had ended by running away with a man absolutely inferior to her, not merely in social station, but in character and intellect also. I wrote to my friend that evening about my views on John Bellini,[50] and the admirable ices at Florio's, and the artistic value of gondolas, but added a postscript to the effect that her double in the story had behaved in a very silly manner. I don't know why I added that, but I remember I had a sort of dread over me that she might do the same thing. Before my letter had reached her, she had run away with a man who deserted her in six months. I saw her in 1884 in Paris, where she was living with her mother, and I asked her whether the story had had anything to do with her action. She told me that she had felt an absolutely irresistible impulse to follow the heroine step by step in her strange and fatal progress, and that it was with a feeling of real terror that she had looked forward to the last few chapters of the story. When they appeared, it seemed to her that she was compelled to reproduce them in life, and she did so. It was a most clear example of this imitative instinct of which I was speaking, and an extremely tragic one.

However, I do not wish to dwell any further upon individual instances. Personal experience is

---

[50]"John" Bellini is Giovanni Bellini (1431–1515), Venetian artist and craftsman.

a most vicious and limited circle. All that I desire to point out is the general principle that Life imitates Art far more than Art imitates Life, and I feel sure that if you think seriously about it you will find that it is true. Life holds the mirror up to Art, and either reproduces some strange type imagined by painter or sculptor, or realizes in fact what has been dreamed in fiction. Scientifically speaking, the basis of life — the energy of life, as Aristotle would call it — is simply the desire for expression, and Art is always presenting various forms through which this expression can be attained. Life seizes on them and uses them, even if they be to her own hurt. Young men have committed suicide because Rolla did so, have died by their own hand because by his own hand Werther died. Think of what we owe to the imitation of Christ, of what we owe to the imitation of Cæsar.

CYRIL: The theory is certainly a very curious one, but to make it complete you must show that Nature, no less than Life, is an imitation of Art. Are you prepared to prove that?

VIVIAN: My dear fellow, I am prepared to prove anything.

CYRIL: Nature follows the landscape painter then, and takes her effects from him?

VIVIAN: Certainly. Where, if not from the Impressionists, do we get those wonderful brown fogs that come creeping down our streets, blurring the gas-lamps and changing the houses into monstrous shadows? To whom, if not to them and their master, do we owe the lovely silver mists that brood over our river, and turn to faint forms of fading grace curved bridge and swaying barge? The extraordinary change that has taken place in the climate of London during the last ten years is entirely due to this particular school of Art. You smile. Consider the matter from a scientific or a metaphysical point of view, and you will find that I am right. For what is Nature? Nature is no great mother who has borne us. She is our creation. It is in our brain that she quickens to life. Things are because we see them, and what we see, and how we see it, depends on the Arts that have influenced us. To look at a thing is very different from seeing a thing. One does not see anything until one sees its beauty. Then, and then only, does it come into existence. At present, people see fogs, not because there are fogs, but because poets and painters have taught them the mysterious loveliness of such effects. There may have been fogs for centuries in London. I dare say there were. But no one saw them, and so we do not know anything about them. They did not exist till Art had invented them. Now, it must be admitted, fogs are carried to excess. They have become the mere mannerism of a clique,[51] and the exaggerated realism of their method gives dull people bronchitis. Where the cultured catch an effect, the uncultured catch cold. And so, let us be humane, and invite Art to turn her wonderful eyes elsewhere. She has done so already, indeed. That white quivering sunlight that one sees now in France, with its strange blotches of mauve, and its restless violet shadows, is her latest fancy, and, on the whole, Nature reproduces it quite admirably. Where she used to give us Corots and Daubignys, she gives us now exquisite Monets and entrancing Pissarros. Indeed there are moments, rare, it is true, but still to be observed from time to time, when Nature becomes absolutely modern. Of course she is not always to be relied upon. The fact is that she is in this unfortunate position. Art creates an incomparable and unique effect, and, having done so, passes on to other things. Nature, upon the other hand, forgetting that imitation can be made the sincerest form of insult, keeps on repeating this effect until we all become absolutely wearied of it. Nobody of any real culture, for instance, ever talks now-a-days about the beauty of a sunset. Sunsets are quite old-fashioned. They belong to the time when Turner was the last note in art.[52] To admire them is a distinct sign of provincialism of temperament. Upon the other hand they go on. Yesterday evening Mrs. Arundel insisted on my going to the window, and looking at the glorious sky, as she called it. Of course I had to look at it. She is one of those absurdly pretty Philistines, to whom one can deny nothing. And what was it? It

[51]Wilde is gibing at his friend James Abbott McNeill Whistler (1834–1903), whose smoky paintings of London in fog began the fad of which he speaks.
[52]Joseph Mallord William Turner (1775–1851) was the last word in art in the 1840s.

was simply a very second-rate Turner, a Turner of a bad period, with all the painter's worst faults exaggerated and overemphasized. Of course, I am quite ready to admit that Life very often commits the same error. She produces her false Renés and her sham Vautrins, just as Nature gives us, on one day a doubtful Cuyp,[53] and on another a more than questionable Rousseau. Still, Nature irritates one more when she does things of that kind. It seems so stupid, so obvious, so unnecessary. A false Vautrin might be delightful. A doubtful Cuyp is unbearable. However, I don't want to be too hard on Nature. I wish the Channel, especially at Hastings, did not look quite so often like a Henry Moore,[54] grey pearl with yellow lights, but then, when Art is more varied, Nature will, no doubt, be more varied also. That she imitates Art, I don't think even her worst enemy would deny now. It is the one thing that keeps her in touch with civilized man. But have I proved my theory to your satisfaction?

CYRIL: You have proved it to my dissatisfaction, which is better. But even admitting this strange imitative instinct in Life and Nature, surely you would acknowledge that Art expresses the temper of its age, the spirit of its time, the moral and social conditions that surround it, and under whose influence it is produced.

VIVIAN: Certainly not! Art never expresses anything but itself. This is the principle of my new æsthetics; and it is this, more than that vital connection between form and substance, on which Mr. Pater[55] dwells, that makes music the type of all the arts. Of course, nations and individuals, with that healthy natural vanity which is the secret of existence, are always under the impression that it is of them that the Muses are talking, always trying to find in the calm dignity

of imaginative art some mirror of their own turbid passions, always forgetting that the singer of life is not Apollo, but Marsyas.[56] Remote from reality, and with her eyes turned away from the shadows of the cave,[57] Art reveals her own perfection, and the wondering crowd that watches the opening of the marvellous, many-petalled rose fancies that it is its own history that is being told to it, its own spirit that is finding expression in a new form. But it is not so. The highest art rejects the burden of the human spirit, and gains more from a new medium or a fresh material than she does from any enthusiasm for art, or from any lofty passion, or from any great awakening of the human consciousness. She develops purely on her own lines. She is not symbolic of any age. It is the ages that are her symbols.

Even those who hold that Art is representative of time and place and people, cannot help admitting that the more imitative an art is, the less it represents to us the spirit of its age. The evil faces of the Roman emperors look out at us from the foul porphyry and spotted jasper in which the realistic artists of the day delighted to work, and we fancy that in those cruel lips and heavy sensual jaws we can find the secret of the ruin of the Empire. But it was not so. The vices of Tiberius could not destroy that supreme civilization, any more than the virtues of the Antonines could save it. It fell for other, for less interesting reasons. The sibyls and prophets of the Sistine may indeed serve to interpret for some that new birth of the emancipated spirit that we call the Renaissance; but what do the drunken boors and brawling peasants of Dutch art tell us about the great soul of Holland? The more abstract, the more ideal an art is, the more it reveals to us the temper of its age. If we wish to understand a nation by means of its art, let us look at its architecture or its music.

CYRIL: I quite agree with you there. The spirit of an age may be best expressed in the abstract ideal arts, for the spirit itself is abstract and ideal. Upon the other hand, for the visible aspect of an

---

[53]René is the eponymous hero of vicomte Francois René de Chateaubriand's novella (1805); Vautrin is the Napoleon of crime in several novels by Balzac, including *Le Père Goriot* (1835). Aelbert Cuyp (1620–1691) was a Dutch painter of landscapes, often ones replete with recumbent cows.

[54]An English landscape artist known for seascapes (1831–1895).

[55]Walter Pater (1839–1894) said that "all art aspires to the condition of music" in *Studies in the History of the Renaissance* (1873).

[56]In Greek legend, Marsyas was the satyr who invented the flute; beaten in a contest of music with Apollo, he was flayed to death by the god.

[57]See introduction to Plato, p. 25.

age, for its look, as the phrase goes, we must of course go to the arts of imitation.

VIVIAN: I don't think so. After all, what the imitative arts really give us are merely the various styles of particular artists, or of certain schools of artists. Surely you don't imagine that the people of the Middle Ages bore any resemblance at all to the figures on mediæval stained glass, or in mediæval stone and wood carving, or on mediæval metal-work, or tapestries, or illuminated MSS.[58] They were probably very ordinary-looking people, with nothing grotesque, or remarkable, or fantastic in their appearance. The Middle Ages, as we know them in art, are simply a definite form of style, and there is no reason at all why an artist with this style should not be produced in the nineteenth century. No great artist ever sees things as they really are. If he did, he would cease to be an artist. Take an example from our own day. I know that you are fond of Japanese things. Now, do you really imagine that the Japanese people, as they are presented to us in art, have any existence? If you do, you have never understood Japanese art at all. The Japanese people are the deliberate self-conscious creation of certain individual artists. If you set a picture by Hokusai, or Hokkei, or any of the great native painters, beside a real Japanese gentleman or lady, you will see that there is not the slightest resemblance between them. The actual people who live in Japan are not unlike the general run of English people; that is to say, they are extremely commonplace, and have nothing curious or extraordinary about them. In fact the whole of Japan is a pure invention. There is no such country, there are no such people. One of our most charming painters went recently to the Land of the Chrysanthemum in the foolish hope of see-ing the Japanese. All he saw, all he had the chance of painting, were a few lanterns and some fans. He was quite unable to discover the inhabitants, as his delightful exhibition at Messrs. Dowdeswell's Gallery showed only too well. He did not know that the Japanese people are, as I have said, simply a mode of style, an exquisite fancy of art. And so, if you desire to see a Japanese effect, you will not

behave like a tourist and go to Tokio. On the con-trary, you will stay at home, and steep yourself in the work of certain Japanese artists, and then, when you have absorbed the spirit of their style, and caught their imaginative manner of vision, you will go some afternoon and sit in the Park or stroll down Piccadilly, and if you cannot see an absolutely Japanese effect there, you will not see it anywhere. Or, to return again to the past, take as another instance the ancient Greeks. Do you think that Greek art ever tells us what the Greek people were like? Do you believe that the Athenian women were like the stately dignified figures of the Parthenon frieze, or like those marvellous god-desses who sat in the triangular pediments of the same building? If you judge from the art, they cer-tainly were so. But read an authority, like Aristo-phanes for instance. You will find that the Athenian ladies laced tightly, wore high-heeled shoes, dyed their hair yellow, painted and rouged their faces, and were exactly like any silly fash-ionable or fallen creature of our own day. The fact is that we look back on the ages entirely through the medium of Art, and Art, very fortunately, has never once told us the truth.

CYRIL: But modern portraits by English painters, what of them? Surely they are like the people they pretend to represent?

VIVIAN: Quite so. They are so like them that a hundred years from now no one will believe in them. The only portraits in which one believes are portraits where there is very little of the sitter, and a very great deal of the artist. Holbein's drawings of the men and women of his time impress us with a sense of their absolute reality. But this is simply because Holbein compelled life to accept his conditions, to restrain itself within his limita-tions, to reproduce his type, and to appear as he wished it to appear. It is style that makes us believe in a thing — nothing but style. Most of our modern portrait painters are doomed to absolute oblivion. They never paint what they see. They paint what the public sees, and the pub-lic never sees anything.

CYRIL: Well, after that I think I should like to hear the end of your article.

VIVIAN: With pleasure. Whether it will do any good I really cannot say. Ours is certainly the

[58]Manuscripts.

dullest and most prosaic century possible. Why, even Sleep has played us false, and has closed up the gates of ivory, and opened the gates of horn.[59] The dreams of the great middle classes of this country, as recorded in Mr. Myers's[60] two bulky volumes on the subject and in the Transactions of the Psychical Society, are the most depressing things that I have ever read. There is not even a fine nightmare among them. They are commonplace, sordid, and tedious. As for the Church I cannot conceive anything better for the culture of a country than the presence in it of a body of men whose duty it is to believe in the supernatural, to perform daily miracles, and to keep alive that mythopœic faculty which is so essential for the imagination. But in the English Church a man succeeds, not through his capacity for belief, but through his capacity for disbelief. Ours is the only Church where the sceptic stands at the altar, and where St. Thomas is regarded as the ideal apostle.[61] Many a worthy clergyman, who passes his life in admirable works of kindly charity, lives and dies unnoticed and unknown; but it is sufficient for some shallow uneducated passman out of either University to get up in his pulpit and express his doubts about Noah's ark, or Balaam's ass, or Jonah and the whale, for half of London to flock to hear him, and to sit open-mouthed in rapt admiration at his superb intellect. The growth of common sense in the English Church is a thing very much to be regretted. It is really a degrading concession to a low form of realism. It is silly, too. It springs from an entire ignorance of psychology. Man can believe the impossible, but man can never believe the improbable. However, I must read the end of my article: —

"What we have to do, what at any rate it is our duty to do, is to revive this old art of Lying. Much of course may be done, in the way of educating the public, by amateurs in the domestic circle, at literary lunches, and at afternoon teas. But this is merely the light and graceful side of lying, such as was probably heard at Cretan dinner parties. There are many other forms. Lying for the sake of gaining some immediate personal advantage, for instance — lying with a moral purpose, as it is usually called — though of late it has been rather looked down upon, was extremely popular with the antique world. Athena laughs when Odysseus tells her 'his words of sly devising,' as Mr. William Morris phrases it, and the glory of mendacity illumines the pale brow of the stainless hero of Euripidean tragedy, and sets among the noble women of the past the young bride of one of Horace's most exquisite odes. Later on, what at first had been merely a natural instinct was elevated into a self-conscious science. Elaborate rules were laid down for the guidance of mankind, and an important school of literature grew up round the subject. Indeed, when one remembers the excellent philosophical treatise of Sanchez on the whole question, one cannot help regretting that no one has ever thought of publishing a cheap and condensed edition of the works of that great casuist. A short primer, 'When to Lie and How,' if brought out in an attractive and not too expensive a form, would no doubt command a large sale, and would prove of real practical service to many earnest and deep-thinking people. Lying for the sake of the improvement of the young, which is the basis of home education, still lingers amongst us, and its advantages are so admirably set forth in the early books of Plato's *Republic*[62] that it is unnecessary to dwell upon them here. It is a mode of lying for which all good mothers have peculiar capabilities, but it is capable of still further development, and has been sadly overlooked by the School Board. Lying for the sake of a monthly salary is of course well known in Fleet Street,[63] and the

---

[59]In the *Iliad*, Book 2, Zeus sends true dreams to men through the gate of horn, false dreams through the gate of ivory.

[60]Frederic William Henry Myers (1843–1901), English essayist, was a member of the Society for Psychical Research, and published a two-volume study of dreams, *Phantasms of the Living* (1886).

[61]The disciple Thomas, seeing the risen Christ, wanted to touch his wounds to assure his senses that what he saw was real.

[62]Plato suggests that the education of children in the Republic should be suited to their age, small children taught morality through fictions and fables until they are old enough for philosophy.

[63]Where London newspapers were published.

profession of a political leader-writer[64] is not without its advantages. But it is said to be a somewhat dull occupation, and it certainly does not lead to much beyond a kind of ostentatious obscurity. The only form of lying that is absolutely beyond reproach is Lying for its own sake, and the highest development of this is, as we have already pointed out, Lying in Art. Just as those who do not love Plato more than Truth cannot pass beyond the threshold of the Academe, so those who do not love Beauty more than Truth never know the inmost shrine of Art. The solid stolid British intellect lies in the desert sands like the Sphinx in Flaubert's marvellous tale, and fantasy, *La Chimère,* dances round it, and calls to it with her false, flute-toned voice. It may not hear her now, but surely some day, when we are all bored to death with the commonplace character of modern fiction, it will hearken to her and try to borrow her wings.

"And when that day dawns, or sunset reddens how joyous we shall all be! Facts will be regarded as discreditable, Truth will be found mourning over her fetters, and Romance, with her temper of wonder, will return to the land. The very aspect of the world will change to our startled eyes. Out of the sea will rise Behemoth and Leviathan, and sail round the high-pooped galleys, as they do on the delightful maps of those ages when books on geography were actually readable. Dragons will wander about the waste places, and the phœnix will soar from her nest of fire into the air. We shall lay our hands upon the basilisk, and see the jewel in the toad's head. Champing his gilded oats, the Hippogriff will stand in our stalls, and over our heads will float the Blue Bird singing of beautiful and impossible things, of things that are lovely and that never happen, of things that are not and that should be. But before this comes to pass we must cultivate the lost art of Lying."

CYRIL: Then we must certainly cultivate it at once. But in order to avoid making any error I want you to tell me briefly the doctrines of the new æsthetics.

VIVIAN: Briefly, then, they are these. Art never expresses anything but itself. It has an independent life, just as Thought has, and develops purely on its own lines. It is not necessarily realistic in an age of realism, nor spiritual in an age of faith. So far from being the creation of its time, it is usually in direct opposition to it, and the only history that it preserves for us is the history of its own progress. Sometimes it returns upon its footsteps, and revives some antique form, as happened in the archaistic movement of late Greek Art, and in the pre-Raphaelite movement of our own day. At other times it entirely anticipates its age, and produces in one century work that it takes another century to understand, to appreciate, and to enjoy. In no case does it reproduce its age. To pass from the art of a time to the time itself is the great mistake that all historians commit.

The second doctrine is this. All bad art comes from returning to Life and Nature, and elevating them into ideals. Life and Nature may sometimes be used as part of Art's rough material, but before they are of any real service to art they must be translated into artistic conventions. The moment Art surrenders its imaginative medium it surrenders everything. As a method Realism is a complete failure, and the two things that every artist should avoid are modernity of form and modernity of subject-matter. To us, who live in the nineteenth century, any century is a suitable subject for art except our own. The only beautiful things are the things that do not concern us. It is, to have the pleasure of quoting myself, exactly because Hecuba is nothing to us that her sorrows are so suitable a motive for a tragedy.[65] Besides, it is only the modern that ever becomes old-fashioned. M. Zola sits down to give us a picture of the Second Empire. Who cares for the Second Empire now? It is out of date. Life goes faster than Realism, but Romanticism is always in front of Life.

The third doctrine is that Life imitates Art far more than Art imitates Life. This results not merely from Life's imitative instinct, but from the fact that the self-conscious aim of Life is to find

[64]Editorial writer.

[65]Vivian alludes to Hamlet's line about the Player: "What's Hecuba to him or he to Hecuba/That he should weep for her?" Shakespeare, *Hamlet,* II.ii.593.

expression, and that Art offers it certain beautiful forms through which it may realize that energy. It is a theory that has never been put forward before, but it is extremely fruitful, and throws an entirely new light upon the history of Art.

It follows, as a corollary from this, that external Nature also imitates Art. The only effects that she can show us are effects that we have already seen through poetry, or in paintings. This is the secret of Nature's charm, as well as the explanation of Nature's weakness.

The final revelation is that Lying, the telling of beautiful untrue things, is the proper aim of Art. But of this I think I have spoken at sufficient length. And now let us go out on the terrace, where "droops the milk-white peacock like a ghost," while the evening star "washes the dusk with silver." At twilight nature becomes a wonderfully suggestive effect, and is not without loveliness, though perhaps its chief use is to illustrate quotations from the poets. Come! We have talked long enough.

Sigmund Freud

1856–1939

Sigmund Freud, the patriarch of psychoanalysis, was by no means primarily a literary critic, but his ideas have had a major influence on twentieth-century literary theory, and his influence has been as far-reaching on those who are outraged by his ideas as it has been on his disciples. (Freud's theory of the unconscious is given more complete exposition in the introduction to Psychoanalytic Theory in Part Two of this book, to which the reader is referred; see p. 1106.)

Freud was born in Moravia (now part of the Czech Republic) but lived most of his assiduous life in the imperial capital of Vienna, where he received his M.D. from the university in 1881. He studied under Charcot in Paris, and then with Josef Breuer in Vienna, where their collaborative investigations of the treatment of hysterical patients, though not well received by the rest of the profession, led Freud to devise his famed analytical technique, based on free association, to reveal the contents of the unconscious mind. Freud's epochal *The Interpretation of Dreams* (1900) and other ground-breaking studies met with much skeptical antagonism; nevertheless, by 1910 his fame had spread throughout Europe and had reached America.

A group calling itself "The International Psycho-Analytical Association" gathered around him, but by 1913 — the year Freud published *Totem and Taboo* — two of its most impressive members, Carl Jung and Alfred Adler, had resigned to form their own schools in protest against Freud's insistence on the primacy of infantile sexuality. During and after World War I, despite hardships that included agonizing jaw cancer, Freud continued to publish important work, notably *Beyond the Pleasure Principle* (1920) and *The Ego and the Id* (1923). His last year was spent in London, where he fled in 1938 after the Nazi invasion of Austria.

Freud's most important general discussion of art is "Creative Writers and Daydreaming"; it was delivered as a lecture in 1907 and published in 1908. Here Freud draws an analogy between nocturnal dreams, daytime fantasies, and the conscious constructions of literary artists, all of which he views as disguised versions of repressed wishes. Freud does not explain his method of dream-analysis fully in this brief essay (which had been contained in his earlier treatise, *The Interpretation of Dreams*), but the key to his explication is that what motivates the dream is the *pleasure principle,* in which one's unconscious desires are magically fulfilled. The unconscious wish for pleasure or power is the latent content of the dream. But the dream as it appears to the dreamer and is reported to the analyst consists of what Freud termed *manifest content* — it is a story that has, in effect, been censored by the defenses of the ego. One could say that latent content is to manifest content, as primary process (the basic urges and drives) is to secondary process (in which those urges and drives are shifted, filtered, sublimated, and altered into more socially acceptable forms). The analysis of a dream involves peeling back the ego-defenses that have distorted the wish in order to reveal the working of the primary process beneath.

In the sections on "The Dream-Work" included below from *The Interpretation of Dreams,* we can see some examples of how Freud approached the question of how dreams signify. What may seem most surprising is that Freud treats the unconscious psyche of the dreamer as a kind of poet. The raw fantasies that make up the latent content are transformed by substitutions and analogies, so as to disinfect them, so to speak, of the unacceptable content that the dreamer has to censor from awareness. What Freud calls "displacement" is a process similar to poetic metaphor, and the process can be recursively repeated to create a more complicated code, a signifying chain of metaphors of metaphors. If displacement corresponds to metaphor, condensation corresponds to poetic metonymy or synecdoche, where several different associations to the forbidden fantasy coalesce into a single complex vision. As with a poem, a dream operates on several levels: it represents the dreamer's history, but some of its elements may need to be interpreted symbolically. Visual symbols may need to be turned into words, that in turn need to be examined for puns and other verbal transformations.

Like nocturnal dreams, Freud believes, literature contains a latent and a manifest content. According to Freud, the primary process that lurks behind popular novels (for example, ranging from *The Godfather* to *The Bridges of Madison County*) obviously embodies the ambitious and erotic wishes to dominate others and to possess loved objects, wishes that formed during the Oedipal phase of childhood development. But those same drives underlie the greatest masterpieces, like *Emma* or *The Great Gatsby*. The differences between popular fiction and literature is not in the latent content but in the way the ego's defenses are marshalled. Freud suggests that "better" fiction contains the same Oedipal fantasies but that they are expressed in a form that is more carefully and elaborately defended. Because the form is less raw, the fantasy content is more acceptable to refined readers.

While Freud was once attacked by Jung (p. 542) for implying that the artist is sick, creating out of personal neurotic needs, it is now widely accepted that nearly all of us are at least slightly neurotic and that the artist's need to create comes not from any incapacitating lunacy but merely from a greater sensitivity to the lacks and dissatisfactions that plague us all. The primary objection to Freudian criticism of this sort is its insensitivity to aesthetic quality: Although Freud was personally deeply moved by art and literature, in his version of artistic creation, form itself enters the work of art merely as a sugar-coating that allows the reader to swallow the dose of fantasy more easily. Later analytic critics, like Peter Brooks, have tried to deal more constructively with this issue, although the function of artistic form remains one of the vexing questions within the psychoanalytic approach to literature. (See Brooks, p. 797.)

Freud also wrote several papers analyzing particular literary texts, including *The Merchant of Venice* and *King Lear*. But "The Uncanny" (1919, revised 1924), an analysis of the novella *The Sandman* (1817) by Ernst Theodor Amadeus Hoffmann, is probably the most complex and interesting of these papers. Freud takes off from Ernst Jentsch's 1906 article on the psychology of the uncanny, and his focus of interest here, unlike in "Creative Writers and Daydreaming," is not the poet, but the reader's experience of the text. Freud is not happy with Jentsch's conclusion about the uncanny, that it is all about the reader's uncertainty over whether what appears alive is in fact dead, or whether what appears to be dead is in fact alive. Jentsch's examples of the uncanny are people in the throes of an epileptic fit, or the insane, who appear to be mechanical objects rather than sentient humans; in his analysis, he adds the mechanical doll, Olympia, in Hoffman's *The Sandman*. Freud sees something else at work here, and approaches it first through language.

In the first section of the paper, Freud takes apart the word *unheimlich*, German for uncanny. Its opposite, *heimlich*, has two distinct meanings: what is homey or familiar (*heim* = home) and what is hidden or concealed (*geheim* = mystery). *Unheimlich* similarly has two meanings: what is unfamiliar and what has been inadvertently revealed. The contraries thus coalesce: the *heimlich* is known but also hidden and therefore unknown; the *unheimlich* is unknown but also revealed and therefore known. (These coalescing contraries also appear in English, in the overlapping meanings of the words "canny" and "uncanny.") For Freud, these contraries describe the process of repression (making the known unknown) and also the "return of the repressed" (where what we have attempted to repress comes to light).

Freud then shows how the plot of *The Sandman*, through three repeated stages, represents the narrative of the Oedipus complex. The Sandman who tears out children's eyes symbolizes Nathaniel's "evil" father who comes to castrate the son. Both Coppelius and Coppola take on this role, while the Father and Professor Spalanzani symbolize the "good" father Nathaniel wants to supplant. Olympia and Clara both symbolize the desired mother who is withheld from Nathaniel. What makes the story uncanny for readers, according to Freud, is that the story starts out as realistic, seemingly true, but we suddenly find ourselves in a dream world where what should be hidden (the repressed Oedipal struggle) is instead quite clearly revealed.

From this point Freud clarifies his position, expanding it, and also qualifying it. If the uncanny is the return of the repressed, then it must appear in other infantile psychic material that we repress. Uncanny stories about being buried alive relate to the wish to return to the womb, an "inter-uterine existence" that Freud calls "lascivious" because it involves fusion with the mother. Stories about doubles or döppelgangers may relate to the post-Oedipal creation of the superego, a "second self" that chides us about our sinful desires: the stories are usually about doubles that enact those desires while the protagonist stands about too repressed to act. And similarly, Freud analyzes other causes of the uncanny, haunted houses, revenants who return from death, severed hands with a will of their own. But Freud also discusses why this repressed material does not always strike us as uncanny in fictional form, what special literary qualities uncanny stories possess that force us to enter this forbidden world of fantasy without being aware of what we are doing.

Our last, very brief Freud selection is one of the few places where Freud interprets a single image from a Greek myth. Published posthumously in 1940, "Medusa's Head" is interesting primarily because of what it displays about Freud himself, and secondarily because of the feminist reaction to it. Freud analyzes the decapitated head as a symbol of female castration, a visual metaphor that connects with the moment "when a boy . . . catches sight of the female genitals . . . surrounded by hair . . . those of his mother." In childhood, the episode advances the Oedipal struggle, but is repressed; in adult life, the repressed returns when the decapitated female head is seen, an open mouth surrounded with snakes, an image of horror that "makes the spectator stiff." This in turn reminds Freud that the male erection can be displayed to ward off evil, and is comforting evidence that one has come through the Oedipal struggle intact. Today's reader may feel that Freud's penultimate comment — "I am not afraid of you. I defy you. I have a penis" — reveals rather more than we wanted to know about the sage of Vienna. Certainly Freud's discourse seems disconcertingly male-oriented. The myth takes the shape it does because of what boys discover; the stiffening response to horror is what men do to ward off an evil whose deep meaning is female sexuality. Women have no part in the struggle except as objects of the male gaze, or as demonic enemies who are designated victims. It seems appropriate that the French feminist Hélène Cixous has taken the image of a triumphantly laughing medusa as the aegis of the woman who, in spite of patriarchy, finds her own voice. (See Cixous, pp. 1643.)

Selected Bibliography

Bowie, Malcolm. *Psychoanalysis and the Future of Theory.* London: Blackwell, 1994.

Brenner, Charles. *An Elementary Textbook of Psychoanalysis.* New York: Anchor Books, 1974.

Freud, Sigmund. *The Standard Edition of the Complete Psychological Works.* 24 vols. London: Hogarth Press and the Institute for Psychoanalysis, 1940–68.

Gilman, Sander L., ed. *Introducing Psychoanalytic Theory.* New York: Brunner/Mazel, 1982.

Hoffman, Frederick J. *Freudianism and the Literary Mind.* New York: Greenwood, 1977.

Jones, Ernest. *Hamlet and Oedipus.* New York: Doubleday, 1949.

Kris, Ernst. *Psychoanalytic Exploration in Art.* New York: Schocken Books, 1962.

Royle, Nicholas. *The Uncanny.* New York: Routledge, 2003.

Sadoff, Dianne F. *Sciences of the Flesh: Representing Body and Subject in Psychoanalysis.* Stanford: Stanford University Press, 1998.

Thomas, Ronald R. *Dreams of Authority: Freud and the Fictions of the Unconscious.* Ithaca, NY: Cornell University Press.

The Dream-Work[1]
from *The Interpretation of Dreams*

Every attempt that has hitherto been made to solve the problem of dreams has dealt directly with their *manifest* content as it is presented in our memory. All such attempts have endeavored to arrive at an interpretation of dreams from their manifest content or (if no interpretation was attempted) to form a judgement as to their nature on the basis of that same manifest content. We are alone in taking something else into account. We have introduced a new class of psychical material between the manifest content of dreams and the conclusions of our inquiry: namely, their *latent* content, or (as we say) the "dream-thoughts," arrived at by means of our procedure. It is from these dream-thoughts and not from a dream's manifest content that we disentangle its meaning. We are thus presented with a new task which had

Translated by A. A. Brill.

[1]Lecture XI of Freud's *Introductory Lectures* (1916–17) deals with the dream-work on a much less extensive scale. This refers to the German publication *Vorlesungen zur Einführung indie Psychoanalyse.* (Wien: H. Heller, 1916–17). [Tr.]

no previous existence: the task, that is, of investigating the relations between the manifest content of dreams and the latent dream-thoughts, and of tracing out the processes by which the latter have been changed into the former.

The dream-thoughts and the dream-content are presented to us like two versions of the same subject-matter in two different languages. Or, more properly, the dream-content seems like a transcript of the dream-thoughts into another mode of expression, whose characters and syntactic laws it is our business to discover by comparing the original and the translation. The dream-thoughts are immediately comprehensible, as soon as we have learnt them. The dream-content, on the other hand, is expressed as it were in a pictographic script,[2] the characters of which have to be transposed individually into the language of the dream-thoughts. If we attempted to read these characters according to their pictorial value instead of according to their symbolic relation, we should clearly be led into error. Suppose I have a picture-puzzle, a rebus, in front of me. It depicts a house with a boat on its roof, a single letter of the alphabet, the figure of a running man whose head has been conjured away, and so on. Now I might be misled into raising objections and declaring that the picture as a whole and its component parts are nonsensical. A boat has no business to be on the roof of a house, and a headless man cannot run. Moreover, the man is bigger than the house; and if the whole picture is intended to represent a landscape, letters of the alphabet are out of place in it since such objects do not occur in nature. But obviously we can only form a proper judgement of the rebus if we put aside criticisms such as these of the whole composition and its parts and if, instead, we try to replace each separate element by a syllable or word that can be represented by that element in some way or other. The words which are put together in this way are no longer nonsensical but may form a poetical phrase of the greatest beauty and significance. A dream is a picture-puzzle of this sort and our predecessors in the field of dream-interpretation

have made the mistake of treating the rebus as a pictorial composition: and as such it has seemed to them nonsensical and worthless.

THE WORK OF CONDENSATION

The first thing that becomes clear to anyone who compares the dream-content with the dream-thoughts is that a work of *condensation* on a large scale has been carried out. Dreams are brief, meager and laconic in comparison with the range and wealth of the dream-thoughts. If a dream is written out it may perhaps fill half a page. The analysis setting out the dream-thoughts underlying it may occupy six, eight or a dozen times as much space. This relation varies with different dreams; but so far as my experience goes its direction never varies. As a rule one underestimates the amount of compression that has taken place, since one is inclined to regard the dream-thoughts that have been brought to light as the complete material, whereas if the work of interpretation is carried further it may reveal still more thoughts concealed behind the dream. I have already had occasion to point out that it is in fact never possible to be sure that a dream has been completely interpreted. Even if the solution seems satisfactory and without gaps, the possibility always remains that the dream may have yet another meaning. Strictly speaking, then, it is impossible to determine the amount of condensation.

There is an answer, which at first sight seems most plausible, to the argument that the great lack of proportion between the dream-content and the dream-thoughts implies that the psychical material has undergone an extensive process of condensation in the course of the formation of the dream. We very often have an impression that we have dreamt a great deal all through the night and have since forgotten most of what we dreamt. On this view, the dream which we remember when we wake up would only be a fragmentary remnant of the total dream-work; and this, if we could recollect it in its entirety, might well be as extensive as the dream-thoughts. There is undoubtedly some truth in this: there can be no question that dreams can be reproduced most accurately if we try to recall them as soon as we wake up and that our memory of them becomes more and more

[2]Form of writing in which each character pictorially represents a separate word (as in Chinese) rather than a syllable or a phoneme.

incomplete towards evening. But on the other hand it can be shown that the impression that we have dreamt a great deal more than we can reproduce is very often based on an illusion, the origin of which I shall discuss later. Moreover the hypothesis that condensation occurs during the dream-work is not affected by the possibility of dreams being forgotten, since this hypothesis is proved to be correct by the quantities of ideas which are related to each individual piece of the dream which has been retained. Even supposing that a large piece of the dream has escaped recollection, this may merely have prevented our having access to another group of dream-thoughts. There is no justification for supposing that the lost pieces of the dream would have related to the same thoughts which we have already reached from the pieces of the dream that have survived.[3]

In view of the very great number of associations produced in analysis to each individual element of the content of a dream, some readers may be led to doubt whether, as a matter of principle, we are justified in regarding as part of the dream-thoughts all the associations that occur to us during the subsequent analysis — whether we are justified, that is, in supposing that all these thoughts were already active during the state of sleep and played a part in the formation of the dream. Is it not more probable that new trains of thought have arisen in the course of the analysis which had no share in forming the dream? I can only give limited assent to this argument. It is no doubt true that some trains of thought arise for the first time during the analysis. But one can convince oneself in all such cases that these new connections are only set up between thoughts which were already linked in some other way in the dream-thoughts. The new connections are, as it were, loop-lines or short-circuits, made possible by the existence of other and deeper-lying connecting paths. It must be allowed that the great bulk of the thoughts which are revealed in analysis were already active during the process of forming the dream; for, after working through a string of thoughts which seem to have no connection with the formation of the dream, one suddenly comes upon one which is represented in its content and is indispensable for its interpretation, but which could not have been reached except by this particular line of approach. I may here recall the dream of the botanical monograph,[4] which strikes one as the product of an astonishing amount of condensation, even though I have not reported its analysis in full.

How, then, are we to picture psychical conditions during the period of sleep which precedes dreams? Are all the dream-thoughts present alongside one another? or do they occur in sequence? or do a number of trains of thought start out simultaneously from different centers and afterwards unite? There is no need for the present, in my opinion, to form any plastic idea of psychical conditions during the formation of dreams. It must not be forgotten, however, that we are dealing with an *unconscious* process of thought, which may easily be different from what we perceive during purposive reflection accompanied by consciousness.

The unquestionable fact remains, however, that the formation of dreams is based on a process of condensation. How is that condensation brought about?

When we reflect that only a small minority of all the dream-thoughts revealed are represented in the dream by one of their ideational elements, we might conclude that condensation is brought about by *omission*: that is, that the dream is not a faithful translation or a point-for-point projection of the dream-thoughts, but a highly incomplete and fragmentary version of them. This view, as we shall soon discover, is a most inadequate one. But we may take it as a provisional starting-point and go on to a further question. If only a few elements from the dream-thoughts find their way into the dream-content, what are the conditions which determine their selection? . . .

---

[3][Footnote added 1914:] The occurrence of condensation in dreams has been hinted at by many writers. Du Prel (1885, 85) has a passage in which he says it is absolutely certain that there has been a process of condensation of the groups of ideas in dreams. [Freud]

[4]Freud's own dream, in which he has written a learned article on a certain plant. "The book lies before me. I am just turning over a folded colored plate. A dried specimen of the plant, as though from a herbarium, is bound up with every copy."

THE WORK OF DISPLACEMENT

In making our collection of instances of condensation in dreams, the existence of another relation, probably of no less importance, had already become evident. It could be seen that the elements which stand out as the principal components of the manifest content of the dream are far from playing the same part in the dream-thoughts. And, as a corollary, the converse of this assertion can be affirmed: what is clearly the essence of the dream-thoughts need not be represented in the dream at all. The dream is, as it were, differently centered from the dream-thoughts — its content has different elements as its central point. Thus in the dream of the botanical monograph, for instance, the central point of the dream-content was obviously the element "botanical"; whereas the dream-thoughts were concerned with the complications and conflicts arising between colleagues from their professional obligations, and further with the charge that I was in the habit of sacrificing too much for the sake of my hobbies. The element "botanical" had no place whatever in this core of the dream-thoughts, unless it was loosely connected with it by an antithesis — the fact that botany never had a place among my favorite studies. In my patient's *Sappho* dream[5] the central position was occupied by climbing up and down and being up above and down below; the dream-thoughts, however, dealt with the dangers of sexual relations with people of an inferior social class. So that only a single element of the dream-thoughts seems to have found its way into the dream-content, though that element was expanded to a disproportionate extent. Similarly, in the dream of the may-beetles,[6] the topic of which was the relations of sexuality to cruelty, it is true that the factor of cruelty emerged in the dream-content; but it did so in another connection and without any mention of sexuality, that is to say, divorced from its context and consequently transformed into something extraneous. Once again, in my dream about my uncle,[7] the fair beard which formed its center-point seems to have had no connection in its meaning with my ambitious wishes which, as we saw, were the core of the dream-thoughts. Dreams such as these give a justifiable impression of "displacement." In complete contrast to these examples, we can see that in the dream of Irma's injection[8] the different elements were able to retain, during the process of constructing the dream, the approximate place which they occupied in the dream-thoughts. This further relation between the dream-thoughts and the dream-content, wholly variable as it is in its sense or direction, is calculated at first to create astonishment. If we are considering a psychical process in normal life and find that one of its several component ideas has been picked out and has acquired a special degree of vividness in consciousness, we usually regard this effect as evidence that a specially high amount of psychical value — some particular degree of interest — attaches to this predominant idea. But we now discover that, in the case of the different elements of the dream-thoughts, a value of this kind does not persist or is disregarded in the process of dream-formation. There is never any doubt as to which of the elements of the dream-thoughts have the highest psychical value; we learn that by direct judgement. In the course of the formation of a dream these essential elements, charged, as they are, with intense interest, may be treated as though they were of small value, and their place may be taken in the dream by other elements, of whose small value in the dream-thoughts there can be no question. At first sight it looks as though no attention whatever is paid to the psychical intensity[9] of the various ideas in

---

[5]A patient dreams that he is part of an acting company changing their clothes in an inn, some of whom are given rooms on the ground floor, some on the floor above.

[6]An elderly female patient dreams that "she had two may-beetles in a box and that she must set them free or they would suffocate." She opens the box and one flies out the open window, the other is crushed as she shuts the window casement.

[7]Freud's own dream, that a friend of his ("R") is his uncle, and that his face has a particularly distinctive blond beard.

[8]Freud's own dream, that a patient of his whom he had cured of hysterical symptoms is still unwell; he examines her and finds disease in her mouth, an infection originating in an injection, given by his friend Otto, who had used a dirty syringe.

[9]*Psychical* intensity or value or the degree of interest of an idea is of course to be distinguished from *sensory* intensity or the intensity of the image presented. [Freud]

making the choice among them for the dream, and as though the only thing considered is the greater or less degree of multiplicity of their determination. What appears in dreams, we might suppose, is not what is *important* in the dream-thoughts but what occurs in them several times over. But this hypothesis does not greatly assist our understanding of dream-formation, since from the nature of things it seems clear that the two factors of multiple determination and inherent psychical value must necessarily operate in the same sense. The ideas which are most important among the dream-thoughts will almost certainly be those which occur most often in them, since the different dream-thoughts will, as it were, radiate out from them. Nevertheless a dream can reject elements which are thus both highly stressed in themselves and reinforced from many directions, and can select for its content other elements which possess only the second of these attributes.

In order to solve this difficulty we shall make use of another impression derived from our inquiry [in the previous section] into the overdetermination of the dream-content. Perhaps some of those who have read that inquiry may already have formed an independent conclusion that the overdetermination of the elements of dreams is no very important discovery, since it is a self-evident one. For in analysis we start out from the dream-elements and note down all the associations which lead off from them; so that there is nothing surprising in the fact that in the thought-material arrived at in this way we come across these same elements with peculiar frequency. I cannot accept this objection; but I will myself put into words something that sounds not unlike it. Among the thoughts that analysis brings to light are many which are relatively remote from the kernel of the dream and which look like artificial interpolations made for some particular purpose. That purpose is easy to divine. It is precisely *they* that constitute a connection, often a forced and far-fetched one, between the dream-content and the dream-thoughts; and if these elements were weeded out of the analysis the result would often be that the component parts of the dream-content would be left not only without overdetermination but without any satisfactory determination at all.

We shall be led to conclude that the multiple determination which decides what shall be included in a dream is not always a primary factor in dream-construction but is often the secondary product of a psychical force which is still unknown to us. Nevertheless multiple determination must be of importance in choosing what particular elements shall enter a dream, since we can see that a considerable expenditure of effort is used to bring it about in cases where it does not arise from the dream-material unassisted.

It thus seems plausible to suppose that in the dream-work a psychical force is operating which on the one hand strips the elements which have a high psychical value of their intensity, and on the other hand, *by means of overdetermination*, creates from elements of low psychical value new values, which afterwards find their way into the dream-content. If that is so, *a transference and displacement of psychical intensities* occurs in the process of dream-formation, and it is as a result of these that the difference between the text of the dream-content and that of the dream-thoughts comes about. The process which we are here presuming is nothing less than the essential portion of the dreamwork; and it deserves to be described as "dream-displacement." Dream-displacement and dream-condensation are the two governing factors to whose activity we may in essence ascribe the form assumed by dreams.

Nor do I think we shall have any difficulty in recognizing the psychical force which manifests itself in the facts of dream-displacement. The consequence of the displacement is that the dream-content no longer resembles the core of the dream-thoughts and that the dream gives no more than a distortion of the dream-wish which exists in the unconscious. But we are already familiar with dream-distortion. We traced it back to the censorship which is exercised by one psychical agency in the mind over another.[10] Dream-displacement is one of the chief methods by which that distortion is achieved. *Is fecit cui profuit*.[11] We may assume, then, that dream-displacement comes about

---

[10]That is, the ego is using defense mechanisms against unacceptable images of desire coming from the id.

[11]The old legal tag: "He did the deed who gained by it." [Tr.]

through the influence of the same censorship — that is, the censorship of endopsychic defence.[12]

The question of the interplay of these factors — of displacement, condensation and overdetermination — in the construction of dreams, and the question which is a dominant factor and which a subordinate one — all of this we shall leave aside for later investigation. But we can state provisionally a second condition which must be satisfied by those elements of the dream-thoughts which make their way into the dream: *they must*

[12][Footnote added 1909:] Since I may say that the kernel of my theory of dreams lies in my derivation of dream-distortion from the censorship, I will here insert the last part of a story from *Phantasien eines Realisten* [*Phantasies of a Realist*] by "Lynkeus" (Vienna, 2nd edition, 1900 [1st edition, 1899]), in which I have found this principal feature of my theory once more expounded. [See above, postscript, 1909, to Chapter I, p. 94 f.; also Freud 1923f and 1932c.] The title of the story is "Traumen wie Wachen" ["Dreaming like Waking"]:

"About a man who has the remarkable attribute of never dreaming nonsense. . . .

"'This splendid gift of yours, for dreaming as though you were waking, is a consequence of your virtues, of your kindness, your sense of justice, and your love of truth; it is the moral serenity of your nature which makes me understand all about you.'

"'But when I think the matter over properly,' replied the other, 'I almost believe that everyone is made like me, and that no one at all ever dreams nonsense. Any dream which one can remember clearly enough to describe it afterwards — any dream, that is to say, which is not a fever-dream — must *always* make sense, and it cannot possibly be otherwise. For things that were mutually contradictory could not group themselves into a single whole. The fact that time and space are often thrown into confusion does not affect the true content of the dream, since no doubt neither of them are of significance for its real essence. We often do the same thing in waking life. Only think of fairy tales and of the many daring products of the imagination, which are full of meaning and of which only a man without intelligence could say: "This is nonsense for it's impossible."'

"'If only one always knew how to interpret dreams in the right way, as you have just done with mine!' said his friend.

"'That is certainly no easy task; but with a little attention on the part of the dreamer himself it should no doubt always succeed. — You ask why it is that for the most part it does *not* succeed? In your other people there seems always to be something that lies concealed in your dreams, something unchaste in a special and higher sense, a certain secret quality in your being which it is hard to follow. And that is why your dreams so often seem to be without meaning or even to be nonsense. But in the deepest sense this is not in the least so; indeed, it cannot be so at all — for it is always the same man, whether he is awake or dreaming.'" [Freud, (Tr.)]

escape the censorship imposed by resistance.[13] And henceforward in interpreting dreams we shall take dream-displacement into account as an undeniable fact.

THE MEANS OF REPRESENTATION IN DREAMS

In the process of transforming the latent thoughts into the manifest content of a dream we have found two factors at work: dream-condensation and dream-displacement. As we continue our investigation we shall, in addition to these, come across two further determinants which exercise an undoubted influence on the choice of the material which is to find access to the dream.

But first, even at the risk of appearing to bring our progress to a halt, I should like to take a preliminary glance at the processes involved in carrying out the interpretation of a dream. I cannot disguise from myself that the easiest way of making those processes clear and of defending their trustworthiness against criticism would be to take some particular dream as a sample, go through its interpretation (just as I have done with the dream of Irma's injection in my second chapter), and then collect the dream-thoughts which I have discovered and go on to reconstruct from them the process by which the dream was formed — in other words, to complete a dream-analysis by a dream-synthesis. I have in fact carried out that task for my own instruction on several specimens; but I cannot reproduce them here, since I am forbidden to do so for reasons connected with the nature of the psychical material involved — reasons which are of many kinds and which will be accepted as valid by any reasonable person. Such considerations interfered less in the *analysis* of dreams, since an analysis could be incomplete and nevertheless retain its value, even though it penetrated only a small way into the texture of the dream. But in the case of the *synthesis* of a dream I do not see how it can be convincing unless it is complete. I could only give a complete synthesis

[13]The first condition being that they must be overdetermined. (See p. 504.) [Tr.]

of dreams dreamt by people unknown to the reading public. Since however, this condition is fulfilled only by my patients, who are neurotics, I must postpone this part of my exposition of the subject till I am able — in another volume — to carry the psychological elucidation of neuroses to a point at which it can make contact with our present topic.[14]

My attempts at building up dreams by synthesis from the dream-thoughts have taught me that the material which emerges in the course of interpretation is not all of the same value. One part of it is made up of the essential dream-thoughts — those, that is, which completely replace the dream, and which, if there were no censorship of dreams, would be sufficient in themselves to replace it. The other part of the material is usually to be regarded as of less importance. Nor is it possible to support the view that all the thoughts of this second kind had a share in the formation of the dream. On the contrary, there may be associations among them which relate to events that occurred *after* the dream, between the times of dreaming and interpreting. This part of the material includes all the connecting paths that led from the manifest dream-content to the latent dream-thoughts, as well as the intermediate and linking associations by means of which, in the course of the process of interpretation, we came to discover these connecting paths.[15]

We are here interested only in the essential dream-thoughts. These usually emerge as a complex of thoughts and memories of the most intricate possible structure, with all the attributes of the trains of thought familiar to us in waking life. They are not infrequently trains of thought starting out from more than one center, though having points of contact. Each train of thought is almost invariably accompanied by its contradictory counterpart, linked with it by antithetical association.

The different portions of this complicated structure stand, of course, in the most manifold logical relations to one another. They can represent foreground and background, digressions and illustrations, conditions, chains of evidence and counter-arguments. When the whole mass of these dream-thoughts is brought under the pressure of the dream-work, and its elements are turned about, broken into fragments and jammed together — almost like pack-ice — the question arises of what happens to the logical connections which have hitherto formed its framework. What representation do dreams provide for "if," "because," "just as," "although," "either — or," and all the other conjunctions without which we cannot understand sentences or speeches?

In the first resort our answer must be that dreams have no means at their disposal for representing these logical relations between the dream-thoughts. For the most part dreams disregard all these conjunctions, and it is only the substantive content of the dream-thoughts that they take over and manipulate. The restoration of the connections which the dream-work has destroyed is a task which has to be performed by the interpretative process.

The incapacity of dreams to express these things must lie in the nature of the psychical material out of which dreams are made. The plastic arts of painting and sculpture labor, indeed, under a similar limitation as compared with poetry, which can make use of speech; and here

[14][Footnote added 1909:] Since writing the above words, I have published a complete analysis and synthesis of two dreams in my "Fragment of the Analysis of a Case of Hysteria" [Freud, 1905e (Sections II and III). See also the synthesis of the "Wolf Man's" dream in Section IV of Freud (1918b). — Added 1914:] Otto Rank's analysis "Ein Traum, der sich selbst deutet" ["A Dream which Interprets Itself," 1910], deserves mention as the most complete interpretation that has been published of a dream of considerable length. [Freud, (Tr.)]

[15]The last four sentences (beginning with "the other part of the material") date in their present form from 1919. In editions earlier than that, this passage ran as follows: "The other part of the material may be brought together under the term 'collaterals.' As a whole, they constitute the paths over which the true wish, which arises from the dream-thoughts, passes before becoming the dream-wish. The first set of these 'collaterals' consist in derivatives from the dream-thoughts proper; they are, schematically regarded, displacements from what is essential to what is inessential. A second set of them comprise the thoughts that connect these inessential elements

(which have become important owing to displacement) with one another, and extend from them to the dream-content. Finally, a third set consist in the associations and trains of thought by means of which the work of interpretation leads us from the dream-content to the second group of collaterals. It need not be supposed that the whole of this third set were necessarily also concerned in the formation of the dream." [Tr.]

once again the reason for their incapacity lies in the nature of the material which these two forms of art manipulate in their effort to express something. Before painting became acquainted with the laws of expression by which it is governed, it made attempts to get over this handicap. In ancient paintings small labels were hung from the mouths of the persons represented, containing in written characters the speeches which the artist despaired of representing pictorially.

At this point an objection may perhaps be raised in dispute of the idea that dreams are unable to represent logical relations. For there are dreams in which the most complicated intellectual operations take place, statements are contradicted or confirmed, ridiculed or compared, just as they are in waking thought. But here again appearances are deceitful. If we go into the interpretation of dreams such as these, we find that the whole of this *is part of the material of the dream-thoughts and is not a representation of intellectual work performed during the dream itself.* What is reproduced by the ostensible thinking in the dream is the *subject matter* of the dream-thoughts and not the *mutual relations between them*, the assertion of which constitutes thinking. I shall bring forward some instances of this. But the easiest point to establish in this connection is that all spoken sentences which occur in dreams and are specifically described as such are unmodified or slightly modified reproductions of speeches which are also to be found among the recollections in the material of the dream-thoughts. A speech of this kind is often no more than an allusion to some event included among the dream-thoughts, and the meaning of the dream may be a totally different one.

Nevertheless, I will not deny that critical thought-activity which is not a mere repetition of material in the dream-thoughts *does* have a share in the formation of dreams. I shall have to elucidate the part played by this factor at the end of the present discussion. It will then become apparent that this thought–activity is not produced by the dream-thoughts but by the dream itself after it has already, in a certain sense, been completed.

Provisionally, then, it may be said that the logical relations between the dream-thoughts are not given any separate representation in dreams.

For instance, if a contradiction occurs in a dream, it is either a contradiction of the dream itself or a contradiction derived from the subject-matter of one of the dream-thoughts. A contradiction in a dream can only correspond in an exceedingly indirect manner to a contradiction *between* the dream-thoughts. But just as the art of painting eventually found a way of expressing, by means other than the floating labels, at least the *intention* of the words of the personages represented — affection, threats, warnings, and so on — so too there is a possible means by which dreams can take account of some of the logical relations between their dream-thoughts, by making an appropriate modification in the method of representation characteristic of dreams. Experience shows that different dreams vary greatly in this respect. While some dreams completely disregard the logical sequence of their material, others attempt to give as full an indication of it as possible. In doing so dreams depart sometimes more and sometimes less widely from the text that is at their disposal for manipulation. Incidentally dreams vary similarly in their treatment of the *chronological* sequence of the dream-thoughts, if such a sequence has been established in the unconscious (as, for instance, in the dream of Irma's injection).

What means does the dream-work possess for indicating these relations in the dream-thoughts which it is so hard to represent? I will attempt to enumerate them one by one.

In the first place, dreams take into account in a general way the connection which undeniably exists between all the portions of the dream-thoughts by combining the whole material into a single situation or event. They reproduce *logical connection* by *simultaneity in time*. Here they are acting like the painter who, in a picture of the School of Athens or of Parnassus, represents in one group all the philosophers or all the poets. It is true that they were never in fact assembled in a single hall or on a single mountain-top; but they certainly form a group in the conceptual sense.

Dreams carry this method of reproduction down to details. Whenever they show us two elements close together, this guarantees that there is some specially intimate connection between what corresponds to them among the dream-thoughts.

In the same way, in our system of writing, "*ab*" means that the two letters are to be pronounced in a single syllable. If a gap is left between the "*a*" and the "*b*," it means that the "*a*" is the last letter of one word and the "*b*" is the first of the next one.[16] So, too, collocations in dreams do not consist of any chance, disconnected portions of the dream-material, but of portions which are fairly closely connected in the dream-thoughts as well.

For representing *causal relations* dreams have two procedures which are in essence the same. Suppose the dream-thoughts run like this: "Since this was so and so, such and such was bound to happen." Then the commoner method of representation would be to introduce the dependent clause as an introductory dream and to add the principal clause as the main dream. If I have interpreted aright, the temporal sequence may be reversed. But the more extensive part of the dream always corresponds to the principal clause. . . .

CONSIDERATIONS OF REPRESENTABILITY

We have been occupied so far with investigating the means by which dreams represent the relations between the dream-thoughts. In the course of this investigation, however, we have more than once touched upon the further topic of the general nature of the modifications which the material of the dream-thoughts undergoes for the purpose of the formation of a dream. We have learnt that material, stripped to a large extent of its relations, is submitted to a process of compression, while at the same time displacements of intensity between its elements necessarily bring about a psychical transvaluation of the material. The displacements we have hitherto considered turned out to consist in the replacing of some one particular idea by another in some way closely associated with it, and they were used to facilitate condensation in so far as, by their means, instead of *two* elements, a single common element intermediate between

them found its way into the dream. We have not yet referred to any other sort of displacement. Analyses show us, however, that another sort exists and that it reveals itself in a change in the *verbal expression* of the thoughts concerned. In both cases there is a displacement along a chain of associations; but a process of such a kind can occur in various psychical spheres, and the outcome of the displacement may in one case be that one element is replaced by another, while the outcome in another case may be that a single element has its *verbal form* replaced by another.

This second species displacement which occurs in dream-formation is not only of great theoretical interest but is also specially well calculated to explain the appearance of fantastic absurdity in which dreams are disguised. The direction taken by the displacement usually results in a colorless and abstract expression in the dream-thought being exchanged for a pictorial and concrete one. The advantage, and accordingly the purpose, of such a change jumps to the eyes. A thing that is pictorial is, from the point of view of a dream, a thing that is *capable of being represented*: it can be introduced into a situation in which abstract expressions offer the same kind of difficulties to representation in dreams as a political leading article[17] in a newspaper would offer to an illustrator. But not only representability, but the interests of condensation and the censorship as well, can be the gainers from this exchange. A dream-thought is unusable so long as it is expressed in an abstract form; but when once it has been transformed into pictorial language, constrasts and identifications of the kind which the dream-work requires, and which it creates if they are not already present, can be established more easily than before between the new form of expression and the remainder of the material underlying the dream. This is so because in every language concrete terms, in consequence of the history of their development, are richer in associations than conceptual ones. We may suppose that a good part of the intermediate work done during the formation of a dream, which seeks to reduce the dispersed dream-thoughts to the most succinct and unified expression possible,

---

[16]This simile is a favorite one of Freud's. He uses it . . . [in this essay] and again in the middle of Section I of the case history of Dora (1905c) It is possibly derived from a lyric of Goethe's ("Schwer in Waldes Busch") in which the same image occurs. [Tr.]

[17]Editorial.

proceeds along the line of finding appropriate verbal transformations for the individual thoughts. Any one thought, whose form of expression may happen to be fixed for other reasons, will operate in a determinant and selective manner on the possible forms of expression allotted to the other thoughts, and it may do so, perhaps, from the very start — as is the case in writing a poem. If a poem is to be written in rhymes, the second line of a couplet is limited by two conditions: it must express an appropriate meaning, and the expression of that meaning must rhyme with the first line. No doubt the best poem will be one in which we fail to notice the intention of finding a rhyme, and in which the two thoughts have, by mutual influence, chosen from the very start a verbal expression which will allow a rhyme to emerge with only slight subsequent adjustment.

In a few instances a change of expression of this kind assists dream-condensation even more directly, by finding a form of words which owing to its ambiguity is able to give expression to more than one of the dream-thoughts. In this way the whole domain of verbal wit is put at the disposal of the dream-work. There is no need to be astonished at the part played by words in dream-formation. Words, since they are the nodal points of numerous ideas, may be regarded as predestined to ambiguity; and the neuroses (e.g. in framing obsessions and phobias), no less than dreams, make unashamed use of the advantages thus offered by words for purposes of condensation and disguise. It is easy to show that dream-distortion too profits from displacement of expression. If one ambiguous word is used instead of two unambiguous ones the result is misleading; and if our everyday, sober method of expression is replaced by a pictorial one, our understanding is brought to a halt, particularly since a dream never tells us whether its elements are to be interpreted literally or in a figurative sense or whether they are to be connected with the material of the dream-thoughts directly or through the intermediary of some interpolated phraseology. In interpreting any dream-element it is in general doubtful

(a) whether it is to be taken in a positive or negative sense (as an antithetic relation),

(b) whether it is to be interpreted historically (as a recollection),

(c) whether it is to be interpreted symbolically, or

(d) whether its interpretation is to depend on its wording.

Yet, in spite of all this ambiguity, it is fair to say that the productions of the dream-work, which, it must be remembered, *are not made with the intention of being understood*, present no greater difficulties to their translators than do the ancient hieroglyphic scripts to those who seek to read them.

[Creative Writers and Daydreaming]

We laymen have always been intensely curious to know — like the cardinal who put a similar question to Ariosto[1] — from what sources that strange being, the creative writer, draws his material, and how he manages to make such an impression on us with it and to arouse in us emotions of which, perhaps, we had not even thought ourselves capable. Our interest is only heightened the more by the fact that, if we ask him, the writer himself gives us no explanation, or none that is satisfactory; and it is not at all weakened by our knowledge that not even the clearest insight into the determinants of his choice of material and into the nature of the art of creating imaginative form will ever help to make creative writers of *us*.

Translated by I. F. Grant-Duff.
[1]Ariosto dedicated the *Orlando Furioso* to Cardinal Ippolito d'Este, who said in response, "Where did you find so many stories?" [Freud]

If we could at least discover in ourselves or in people like ourselves an activity which was in some way akin to creative writing! An examination of it would then give us a hope of obtaining the beginnings of an explanation of the creative work of writers. And, indeed, there is some prospect of this being possible. After all, creative writers themselves like to lessen the distance between their kind and the common run of humanity; they so often assure us that every man is a poet at heart and that the last poet will not perish till the last man does.

Should we not look for the first traces of imaginative activity as early as in childhood? The child's best-loved and most intense occupation is with his play or games. Might we not say that every child at play behaves like a creative writer, in that he creates a world of his own, or, rather, rearranges the things of his world in a new way which pleases him? It would be wrong to think he does not take that world seriously; on the contrary, he takes his play very seriously and he expends large amounts of emotion on it. The opposite of play is not what is serious but what is real. In spite of all the emotion with which he cathects[2] his world of play, the child distinguishes it quite well from reality; and he likes to link his imagined objects and situations to the tangible and visible things of the real world. This linking is all that differentiates the child's "play" from "fantasying."

The creative writer does the same as the child at play. He creates a world of fantasy which he takes very seriously — that is, which he invests with large amounts of emotion — while separating it sharply from reality. Language has preserved this relationship between children's play and poetic creation. It gives the name of *Spiel* ["play"] to those forms of imaginative writing which require to be linked to tangible objects and which are capable of representation. It speaks of a *Lustspiel* or *Trauerspiel* ["comedy" or "tragedy"] and describes those who carry out the representation as *Schauspieler* ["players"]. The unreality of the writer's imaginative world, however, has very important consequences for the technique of his art; for many things which, if they were real, could

give no enjoyment, can do so in the play of fantasy, and many excitements which, in themselves, are actually distressing, can become a source of pleasure for the hearers and spectators at the performance of a writer's work.

There is another consideration for the sake of which we will dwell a moment longer on this contrast between reality and play. When the child has grown up and has ceased to play, and after he has been laboring for decades to envisage the realities of life with proper seriousness, he may one day find himself in a mental situation which once more undoes the contrast between play and reality. As an adult he can look back on the intense seriousness with which he once carried on his games in childhood, and, by equating his ostensibly serious occupations of today with his childhood games, he can throw off the too heavy burden imposed on him by life and win the high yield of pleasure afforded by *humor*.

As people grow up, then, they cease to play, and they seem to give up the yield of pleasure which they gained from playing. But whoever understands the human mind knows that hardly anything is harder for a man than to give up a pleasure which he has once experienced. Actually, we can never give anything up; we only exchange one thing for another. What appears to be a renunciation is really the formation of a substitute or surrogate. In the same way, the growing child, when he stops playing, gives up nothing but the link with real objects; instead of *playing*, he now *fantasies*. He builds castles in the air and creates what are called *daydreams*. I believe that most people construct fantasies at times in their lives. This is a fact which has long been overlooked and whose importance has therefore not been sufficiently appreciated.

People's fantasies are less easy to observe than the play of children. The child, it is true, plays by himself or forms a closed psychical system with other children for the purposes of a game; but even though he may not play his game in front of the grown-ups, he does not, on the other hand, conceal it from them. The adult, on the contrary, is ashamed of his fantasies and hides them from other people. He cherishes his fantasies as his most intimate possessions, and as a rule he would rather confess his misdeeds than tell anyone his

[2]Cathexis is the investment of *libido* energy in an activity.

fantasies. It may come about that for that reason he believes he is the only person who invents such fantasies and has no idea that creations of this kind are widespread among other people. This difference in the behavior of a person who plays and a person who fantasies is accounted for by the motives of these two activities, which are nevertheless adjuncts to each other.

A child's play is determined by wishes: in point of fact by a single wish — one that helps in his upbringing — the wish to be big and grown up. He is always playing at being "grown up," and in his games he imitates what he knows about the lives of his elders. He has no reason to conceal this wish. With the adult, the case is different. On the one hand, he knows that he is expected not to go on playing or fantasying any longer, but to act in the real world; on the other hand, some of the wishes which give rise to his fantasies are of a kind which it is essential to conceal. Thus he is ashamed of his fantasies as being childish and as being unpermissible.

But, you will ask, if people make such a mystery of their fantasying, how is it that we know such a lot about it? Well, there is a class of human beings upon whom, not a god, indeed, but a stern goddess — Necessity — has allotted the task of telling what they suffer and what things give them happiness. These are the victims of nervous illness, who are obliged to tell their fantasies, among other things, to the doctor by whom they expect to be cured by mental treatment. This is our best source of knowledge, and we have since found good reason to suppose that our patients tell us nothing that we might not also hear from healthy people.

Let us make ourselves acquainted with a few of the characteristics of fantasying. We may lay it down that a happy person never fantasies, only an unsatisfied one. The motive forces of fantasies are unsatisfied wishes, and every single fantasy is the fulfillment of a wish, a correction of unsatisfying reality. These motivating wishes vary according to the sex, character, and circumstances of the person who is having the fantasy; but they fall naturally into two main groups. They are either ambitious wishes, which serve to elevate the subject's personality; or they are erotic ones. In young women the erotic wishes predominate almost exclusively, for their ambition is as a rule absorbed by erotic trends. In young men egoistic and ambitious wishes come to the fore clearly enough alongside of erotic ones. But we will not lay stress on the opposition between the two trends; we would rather emphasize the fact that they are often united. Just as, in many altarpieces, the portrait of the donor is to be seen in a corner of the picture, so, in the majority of ambitious fantasies, we can discover in some corner or other the lady for whom the creator of the fantasy performs all his heroic deeds and at whose feet all his triumphs are laid. Here, as you see, there are strong enough motives for concealment; the well-brought-up young woman is only allowed a minimum of erotic desire, and the young man has to learn to suppress the excess of self-regard which he brings with him from the spoilt days of his childhood, so that he may find his place in a society which is full of other individuals making equally strong demands.

We must not suppose that the products of this imaginative activity — the various fantasies, castles in the air and daydreams — are stereotyped or unalterable. On the contrary, they fit themselves into the subject's shifting impressions of life, change with every change in his situation, and receive from every fresh active impression what might be called a "date-mark." The relation of a fantasy to time is in general very important. We may say that it hovers, as it were, between three times — the three moments of time which our ideation involves. Mental work is linked to some current impression, some provoking occasion in the present which has been able to arouse one of the subject's major wishes. From there it harks back to a memory of an earlier experience (usually an infantile one) in which this wish was fulfilled; and it now creates a situation relating to the future which represents a fulfillment of the wish. What it thus creates is a daydream or fantasy, which carries about it traces of its origin from the occasion which provoked it and from the memory. Thus past, present, and future are strung together, as it were, on the thread of the wish that runs though them.

A very ordinary example may serve to make what I have said clear. Let us take the case of a poor orphan boy to whom you have given the address of some employer where he may perhaps find a job. On his way there he may indulge in a daydream appropriate to the situation from which it arises. The content of his fantasy will perhaps be something like this. He is given a job, finds favor with his new employer, makes himself indispensable in the business, is taken into his employer's family, marries the charming young daughter of the house, and then himself becomes a director of the business, first as his employer's partner and then as his successor. In this fantasy, the dreamer has regained what he possessed in his happy childhood — the protecting house, the loving parents, and the first objects of his affectionate feelings. You will see from this example the way in which the wish makes use of an occasion in the present to construct, on the pattern of the past, a picture of the future.

There is a great deal more that could be said about fantasies; but I will only allude as briefly as possible to certain points. If fantasies become overluxuriant and overpowerful, the conditions are laid for an onset of neurosis or psychosis. Fantasies, moreover, are the immediate mental precursors of the distressing symptoms complained of by our patients. Here a broad bypath branches off into pathology.

I cannot pass over the relation of fantasies to dreams. Our dreams at night are nothing else than fantasies like these, as we can demonstrate from the interpretation of dreams. Language, in its unrivaled wisdom, long ago decided the question of the essential nature of dreams by giving the name of *daydreams* to the airy creations of fantasy. If the meaning of our dreams usually remains obscure to us in spite of this pointer, it is because of the circumstance that at night there also arise in us wishes of which we are ashamed; these we must conceal from ourselves, and they have consequently been repressed, pushed into the unconscious. Repressed wishes of this sort and their derivatives are only allowed to come to expression in a very distorted form. When scientific work had succeeded in elucidating this factor of *dream distortion*, it was no longer difficult to recognize that night dreams are wish-fulfillments in just the same way as daydreams — the fantasies which we all know so well.

So much for fantasies. And now for the creative writer. May we really attempt to compare the imaginative writer with the "dreamer in broad daylight," and his creations with daydreams? Here we must begin by making an initial distinction. We must separate writers who, like the ancient authors of epics and tragedies, take over their material ready-made, from writers who seem to originate their own material. We will keep to the latter kind, and, for the purposes of our comparison, we will choose not the writers most highly esteemed by the critics, but the less pretentious authors of novels, romances, and short stories, who nevertheless have the widest and most eager circle of readers of both sexes. One feature above all cannot fail to strike us about the creations of these story-writers: each of them has a hero who is the center of interest, for whom the writer tries to win our sympathy by every possible means and whom he seems to place under the protection of a special providence. If, at the end of one chapter of my story, I leave the hero unconscious and bleeding from severe wounds, I am sure to find him at the beginning of the next being carefully nursed and on the way to recovery; and if the first volume closes with the ship he is in going down in a storm at sea, I am certain, at the opening of the second volume, to read of his miraculous rescue — a rescue without which the story could not proceed. The feeling of security with which I follow the hero through his perilous adventures is the same as the feeling with which a hero in real life throws himself into the water to save a drowning man or exposes himself to the enemy's fire in order to storm a battery. It is the true heroic feeling, which one of our best writers has expressed in an inimitable phrase: "Nothing can happen to *me*!" It seems to me, however, that through this revealing characteristic of invulnerability we can immediately recognize His Majesty the Ego, the hero alike of every daydream and of every story.

Other typical features of these egocentric stories point to the same kinship. The fact that all the women in the novel invariably fall in love with the hero can hardly be looked on as a portrayal of reality, but it is easily understood as a necessary constituent of a daydream. The same is true of the fact that the other characters in the story are sharply divided into good and bad, in defiance of the variety of human characters that are to be observed in real life. The "good" ones are the helpers, while the "bad" ones are the enemies and rivals, of the ego which has become the hero of the story.

We are perfectly aware that very many imaginative writings are far removed from the model of the naive daydream; and yet I cannot suppress the suspicion that even the most extreme deviations from that model could be linked with it through an uninterrupted series of transitional cases. It has struck me that in many of what are known as "psychological" novels only one person — once again the hero — is described from within. The author sits inside his mind, as it were, and looks at the other characters from outside. The psychological novel in general no doubt owes its special nature to the inclination of the modern writer to split up his ego, by self-observation, into many part-egos, and, in consequence, to personify the conflicting currents of his own mental life in several heroes. Certain novels, which might be described as "eccentric," seem to stand in quite special contrast to the types of the daydream. In these, the person who is introduced as the hero plays only a very small active part; he sees the actions and sufferings of other people pass before him like a spectator. Many of Zola's later works belong to this category. But I must point out that the psychological analysis of individuals who are not creative writers, and who diverge in some respects from the so-called norm, has shown us analogous variations of the daydream, in which the ego contents itself with the role of spectator.

If our comparison of the imaginative writer with the daydreamer, and of poetical creation with the daydream, is to be of any value, it must, above all, show itself in some way or other fruitful. Let us, for instance, try to apply to these authors' works the thesis we laid down earlier concerning the relation between fantasy and the three periods of time and the wish which runs through them; and, with its help, let us try to study the connections that exist between the life of the writer and his works. No one has known, as a rule, what expectations to frame in approaching this problem; and often the connection has been thought of in much too simple terms. In the light of the insight we have gained from fantasies, we ought to expect the following state of affairs. A strong experience in the present awakens in the creative writer a memory of an earlier experience (usually belonging to his childhood) from which there now proceeds a wish which finds its fulfillment in the creative work. The work itself exhibits elements of the recent provoking occasion as well as of the old memory.

Do not be alarmed at the complexity of this formula. I suspect that in fact it will prove to be too exiguous a pattern. Nevertheless, it may contain a first approach to the true state of affairs; and, from some experiments I have made, I am inclined to think that this way of looking at creative writings may turn out not unfruitful. You will not forget that the stress it lays on childhood memories in the writer's life — a stress which may perhaps seem puzzling — is ultimately derived from the assumption that a piece of creative writing, like a daydream, is a continuation of, and a substitute for, what was once the play of childhood.

We must not neglect, however, to go back to the kind of imaginative works which we have to recognize, not as original creations, but as the refashioning of ready-made and familiar material. Even here, the writer keeps a certain amount of independence, which can express itself in the choice of material and in changes in it which are often quite extensive. Insofar as the material is already at hand, however, it is derived from the popular treasure-house of myths, legends, and fairy tales. The study of constructions of folk psychology such as these is far from being complete, but it is extremely probable that myths, for instance, are distorted vestiges of the wishful fantasies of whole nations, the *secular dreams* of youthful humanity.

You will say that, although I have put the creative writer first in the title of my paper, I have told you far less about him than about fantasies. I am aware of that, and I must try to excuse it by pointing to the present state of our knowledge. All I have been able to do is to throw out some encouragements and suggestions which, starting from the study of fantasies, lead on to the problem of the writer's choice of his literary material. As for the other problem — by what means the creative writer achieves the emotional effects in us that are aroused by his creations — we have as yet not touched on it at all. But I should like at least to point out to you the path that leads from our discussion of fantasies to the problems of poetical effects.

You will remember how I have said that the daydreamer carefully conceals his fantasies from other people because he feels he has reasons for being ashamed of them. I should now add that even if he were to communicate them to us he could give us no pleasure by his disclosures. Such fantasies, when we learn them, repel us or at least leave us cold. But when a creative writer presents his plays to us or tells us what we are inclined to take to be his personal daydreams, we experience a great pleasure, and one which probably arises from the confluence of many sources. How the writer accomplishes this is his innermost secret; the essential *ars poetica*[3] lies in the technique of overcoming the feeling of repulsion in us which is undoubtedly connected with the barriers that rise between each single ego and the others. We

[3] Art of poetry.

can guess two of the methods used by this technique. The writer softens the character of his egoistic daydreams by altering and disguising it, and he bribes us by the purely formal — that is, aesthetic — yield of pleasure which he offers us in the presentation of his fantasies. We give the name of an *incentive bonus,* or a *forepleasure,* to a yield of pleasure such as this, which is offered to us so as to make possible the release of still greater pleasure arising from deeper psychical sources. In my opinion, all the aesthetic pleasure which a creative writer affords us has the character of a forepleasure of this kind, and our actual enjoyment of an imaginative work proceeds from a liberation of tensions in our minds. It may even be that not a little of this effect is due to the writer's enabling us thenceforward to enjoy our own daydreams without self-reproach or shame. This brings us to the threshold of new, interesting, and complicated inquiries; but also, at least for the moment, to the end of our discussion.

The "Uncanny"

I

It is only rarely that a psycho-analyst feels impelled to investigate the subject of aesthetics, even when aesthetics is understood to mean not merely the theory of beauty but the theory of the qualities of feeling. He works in other strata of mental life and has little to do with the subdued emotional impulses which, inhibited in their aims and dependent on a host of concurrent factors, usually furnish the material for the study of aesthetics. But it does occasionally happen that he has to interest himself in some particular province of that subject; and this province usually proves to be a rather remote one, and one which has been neglected in the specialist literature of aesthetics.

The subject of the "uncanny"[1] is a province of this kind. It is undoubtedly related to what is

frightening — to what arouses dread and horror; equally certainly, too, the word is not always used in a clearly definable sense, so that it tends to coincide with what excites fear in general. Yet we may expect that a special core of feeling is present which justifies the use of a special conceptual term. One is curious to know what this common core is which allows us to distinguish as "uncanny" certain things which lie within the field of what is frightening.

As good as nothing is to be found upon this subject in comprehensive treatises on aesthetics, which in general prefer to concern themselves with what is beautiful, attractive and sublime — that is, with feelings of a positive nature — and with the circumstances and the objects that call them forth, rather than with the opposite feelings

Translated by James Strachey.
[1] The German word, translated throughout this paper by the English "uncanny," is "*unheimlich,*" literally "unhomely."

The English term is not, of course, an exact equivalent of the German one. [Tr.]

of repulsion and distress. I know of only one attempt in medico-psychological literature, a fertile but not exhaustive paper by Jentsch (1906). But I must confess that I have not made a very thorough examination of the literature, especially the foreign literature, relating to this present modest contribution of mine, for reasons which, as may easily be guessed, lie in the times in which we live;[2] so that my paper is presented to the reader without any claim to priority.

In his study of the "uncanny" Jentsch quite rightly lays stress on the obstacle presented by the fact that people vary so very greatly in their sensitivity to this quality of feeling. The writer of the present contribution, indeed, must himself plead guilty to a special obtuseness in the matter, where extreme delicacy of perception would be more in place. It is long since he has experienced or heard of anything which has given him an uncanny impression, and he must start by translating himself into that state of feeling, by awakening in himself the possibility of experiencing it. Still, such difficulties make themselves powerfully felt in many other branches of aesthetics; we need not on that account despair of finding instances in which the quality in question will be unhesitatingly recognized by most people.

Two courses are open to us at the outset. Either we can find out what meaning has come to be attached to the word "uncanny" in the course of its history; or we can collect all those properties of persons, things, sense-impressions, experiences and situations which arouse in us the feeling of uncanniness, and then infer the unknown nature of the uncanny from what all these examples have in common. I will say at once that both courses lead to the same result: the uncanny is that class of the frightening which leads back to what is known of old and long familiar. How this is possible, in what circumstances the familiar can become uncanny and frightening, I shall show in what follows. Let me also add that my investigation was actually begun by collecting a number of individual cases, and was only later confirmed by an examination of linguistic usage. In this discussion, however, I shall follow the reverse course.

The German word *unheimlich* is obviously the opposite of *heimlich* [homely], *heimisch* [native] — the opposite of what is familiar; and we are tempted to conclude that what is "uncanny" is frightening precisely because it is *not* known and familiar. Naturally not everything that is new and unfamiliar is frightening, however; the relation is not capable of inversion. We can only say that what is novel can easily become frightening and uncanny; some new things are frightening but not by any means all. Something has to be added to what is novel and unfamiliar in order to make it uncanny.

On the whole, Jentsch did not get beyond this relation of the uncanny to the novel and unfamiliar. He ascribes the essential factor in the production of the feeling of uncanniness to intellectual uncertainty; so that the uncanny would always, as it were, be something one does not know one's way about in. The better orientated in his environment a person is, the less readily will he get the impression of something uncanny in regard to the objects and events in it.

It is not difficult to see that this definition is incomplete, and we will therefore try to proceed beyond the equation "uncanny" = "unfamiliar." We will first turn to other languages. But the dictionaries that we consult tell us nothing new, perhaps only because we ourselves speak a language that is foreign. Indeed, we get an impression that many languages are without a word for this particular shade of what is frightening.

I should like to express my indebtedness to Dr. Theodor Reik for the following excerpts: —

LATIN: (K. E. Georges, *Deutschlateinisches Wörterbuch*, 1898). An uncanny place: *locus suspectus*; at an uncanny time of night: *intempesta nocte*.

GREEK: (Rost's and Schenkl's Lexikons). ξένος (i.e. strange, foreign).

ENGLISH: (from the dictionaries of Lucas, Bellows, Flügel and Muret-Sanders). Uncomfortable, uneasy, gloomy, dismal, uncanny, ghastly; (of a house) haunted; (of a man) a repulsive fellow.

FRENCH: (Sach-Villatte). *Inquiétant, sinistre, lugubre, mal à son aise.*

SPANISH: (Tollhausen, 1889). *Sospechoso, de mal agüero, lúgubre, siniestro.*

The Italian and Portuguese languages seem to content themselves with words which we should

[2]An allusion to the first World War only just concluded. [Tr.]

describe as circumlocutions. In Arabic and Hebrew "uncanny" means the same as "demonic," "gruesome."

Let us therefore return to the German language. In Daniel Sanders's *Wörterbuch der Deutschen Sprache* (1860, I, 729), the following entry, which I here reproduce in full, is to be found under the word "*heimlich*." I have laid stress on one or two passages by italicizing them.[3]

Heimlich, adj., subst. *Heimlichkeit* (pl. *Heimlichkeiten*): I. Also *heimelich, heimelig*, belonging to the house, not strange, familiar, tame, intimate, friendly, etc.

(*a*) (Obsolete) belonging to the house or the family, or regarded as so belonging (cf. Latin *familiaris*, familiar): *Die Heimlichen*, the members of the household; *Der heimliche Rat* (Gen. xli, 45; 2 Sam. xxiii. 23; I Chron. xii. 25; Wisd. viii. 4), now more usually *Geheimer Rat* [Privy Councillor].

(*b*) Of animals: tame, companionable to man. As opposed to wild, e.g., "Animals which are neither wild nor *heimlich*," etc. "Wild animals . . . that are trained to be *heimlich* and accustomed to men." "If these young creatures are brought up from early days among men they become quite *heimlich*, friendly" etc. — So also: "It (the lamb) is so *heimlich* and eats out of my hand." "Nevertheless, the stork is a beautiful, *heimlich* bird."

(*c*) Intimate, friendly comfortable; the enjoyment of quiet content, etc., arousing a sense of agreeable restfulness and security as in one within the four walls of his house.[4] "Is it still *heimlich* to you in your country where strangers are felling your woods?" "She did not feel too *heimlich* with him." "Along a high, *heimlich*, shady path . . ., beside a purling, gushing and babbling woodland brook." "To destroy the *Heimlichkeit* of the home." "I could not readily find another spot so intimate and *heimlich* as this." "We pictured it so comfortable, so nice, so cozy and *heimlich*." "In quiet *Heimlichkeit*, surrounded by close walls." "A careful housewife, who knows how to make a pleasing *Heimlichkeit* (*Häuslichkeit* [domesticity]) out of the smallest means." "The man who till recently had been so strange to him now seemed to him all the more

heimlich." "The protestant land-owners do not feel . . . *heimlich* among their catholic inferiors." "When it grows *heimlich* and still, and the evening quiet alone watches over your cell." "Quiet, lovely and *heimlich*, no place more fitted for their rest." "He did not feel at all *heimlich* about it." — Also, [in compounds] "The place was so peaceful, so lonely, so shadily-*heimlich*." "The in- and outflowing waves of the current, dreamy and lullaby-*heimlich*." Cf. in especial *Unheimlich* [see below]. Among Swabian Swiss authors in especial, often as a trisyllable: "How *heimelich* it seemed to Ivo again of an evening, when he was at home." "It was so *heimelig* in the house." "The warm room and the *heimelig* afternoon." "When a man feels in his heart that he is so small and the Lord so great — that is what is truly *heimelig*." "Little by little they grew at ease and *heimelig* among themselves." "Friendly *Heimeligkeit*." "I shall be nowhere more *heimelich* than I am here." "That which comes from afar . . . assuredly does not live quite *heimelig* (*heimatlich* [at home], *freundnachbarlich* [in a neighborly way]) among the people." "The cottage where he had once sat so often among his own people, so *heimelig*, so happy." "The sentinel's horn sounds so *heimelig* from the tower, and his voice invites so hospitably." "You go to sleep there so soft and warm, so wonderfully *heim'lig*." — *This form of the word deserves to become general in order to protect this perfectly good sense of the word from becoming obsolete through an easy confusion with II [see below]. Cf: "'The Zecks* [a family name] *are all "heimlich."'* (in sense II) *'"Heimlich"? . . . What do you understand by "heimlich"?' 'Well, . . . they are like a buried spring or a dried-up pond. One cannot walk over it without always having the feeling that water might come up there again.' 'Oh we call it "unheimlich"; you call it "heimlich." Well, what makes you think that there is something secret and untrustworthy about this family?'"* (Gutzkow).

(*d*) Especially in Silesia: gay, cheerful; also of the weather.

II. Concealed, kept from sight, so that others do not get to know of or about it, withheld from others. To do something *heimlich*, i.e. behind someone's back; to steal away *heimlich*; *heimlich* meetings and appointments; to look on with *heimlich* pleasure at someone's discomfiture; to sigh or weep *heimlich*; to behave *heimlich*, as though there was something to conceal; *heimlich* love-affair, love, sin; *heimlich* places (which good manners oblige us to conceal) (I Sam. v. 6). "The *heimlich* chamber" (privy) (2 Kings x. 27.). Also, "the *heimlich* chair." "To throw into pits or *Heimlichkeiten*." — "Led the steeds *heimlich*

---

[3]In the translation which follows in the text above, a few details, mainly giving the sources of the quotations, have been omitted. [Tr.]

[4]It may be remarked that the English "canny," in addition to its more usual meaning of "shrewd," can mean "pleasant," "cozy." [Tr.]

before Laomedon." — "As secretive, *heimlich*, deceitful and malicious towards cruel masters . . . as frank, open, sympathetic and helpful towards a friend in misfortune." "You have still to learn what is *heimlich* holiest to me." "The *heimlich* art" (magic). "Where public ventilation has to stop, there *heimlich* machinations begin." "Freedom is the whispered watchword of *heimlich* conspirators and the loud battle-cry of professed revolutionaries." "A holy, *heimlich* effect." "I have roots that are most *heimlich*. I am grown in the deep earth." "My *heimlich* pranks." "If he is not given it openly and scrupulously he may seize it *heimlich* and unscrupulously." "He had achromatic telescopes constructed *heimlich* and secretly." "Henceforth I desire that there should be nothing *heimlich* any longer between us." — To discover, disclose, betray someone's *Heimlichkeiten*; "to concoct *Heimlichkeiten* behind my back." "In my time we studied *Heimlichkeit*." "The hand of understanding can alone undo the powerless spell of the *Heimlichkeit* (of hidden gold)." "Say, where is the place of concealment . . . in what place of hidden *Heimlichkeit*?" "Bees, who make the lock of *Heimlichkeiten*" (i.e. sealing-wax). "Learned in strange *Heimlichkeiten*" (magic arts).

For compounds see above, Ic. Note especially the negative "*un-*": eerie, weird, arousing gruesome fear: "Seeming quite *unheimlich* and ghostly to him." "The *unheimlich*, fearful hours of night." "I had already long since felt an *unheimlich*, even gruesome feeling." "Now I am beginning to have an *unheimlich* feeling." . . . "Feels an *unheimlich* horror." "*Unheimlich* and motionless like a stone image." "The *unheimlich* mist called hill-fog." "These pale youths are *unheimlich* and are brewing heaven knows what mischief." " '*Unheimlich*' is the name for everything that ought to have remained . . . secret and hidden but has come to light" (Schelling). — "To veil the divine, to surround it with a certain *Unheimlichkeit*." — *Unheimlich* is not often used as opposite to meaning II (above).

What interests us most in this long extract is to find that among its different shades of meaning the word *heimlich* exhibits one which is identical with its opposite, *unheimlich*. What is *heimlich* thus comes to be *unheimlich*. (Cf. the quotation from Gutzkow: "We call it '*Unheimlich*'; you call it '*heimlich*.'") In general we are reminded that the word '*heimlich*' is not unambiguous, but belongs to two sets of ideas, which, without being contradictory, are yet very different: on the one hand it means what is familiar and agreeable, and

on the other, what is concealed and kept out of sight.[5] "*Unheimlich*" is customarily used, we are told, as the contrary only of the first signification of "*heimlich*," and not of the second. Sanders tells us nothing concerning a possible genetic connection between these two meanings of *heimlich*. On the other hand, we notice that Schelling says something which throws quite a new light on the concept of the *Unheimlich*, for which we were certainly not prepared. According to him, everything is *unheimlich* that ought to have remained secret and hidden but has come to light.

Some of the doubts that have thus arisen are removed if we consult Grimm's dictionary. (1877, 4, Part 2, 873 ff.)

We read:

Heimlich; adj. and adv. *vernaculus, occultus*; MHG. heimelîch, heimlîch.

(P. 874.) In a slightly different sense: "I feel *heimlich*, well, free from fear." . . .

[3] (*b*) *Heimlich* is also used of a place free from ghostly influences . . . familiar, friendly, intimate.

(P. 875: *β*) Familiar, amicable, unreserved.

4. *From the idea of "homelike," "belonging to the house," the further idea is developed of something withdrawn from the eyes of strangers, something concealed, secret; and this idea is expanded in many ways* . . .

(P. 876.) "On the left bank of the lake there lies a meadow *heimlich* in the wood." (Schiller, *Wilhelm Tell*, I. 4.) . . . Poetic license, rarely so used in modern speech . . . *Heimlich* is used in conjuction with a verb expressing the act of concealing: "In the secret of his tabernacle he shall hide me *heimlich*." (Ps. xxvii. 5.) . . . *Heimlich* parts of the human body, *pudenda* . . . "the men that died not were smitten on their *heimlich* parts." (I Samuel v. 12.) . . .

(*c*) Officials who give important advice which has to be kept secret in matters of state are called *heimlich* councillors; the adjective, according to modern usage, has been replaced by *geheim* [secret] . . . "Pharaoh called Joseph's name 'him to whom secrets are revealed' " (*heimlich* councillor). (Gen. xli. 45.)

(P. 878.) 6. *Heimlich*, as used of knowledge — mystic, allegorical: a *heimlich* meaning, *mysticus, divinus, occultus, figuratus*.

[5] According to the *Oxford English Dictionary*, a similar ambiguity attaches to the English "canny," which may mean not only "cozy" but also "endowed with occult or magical power." [Tr.]

(P. 878.) *Heimlich* in a different sense, as withdrawn from knowledge, unconscious . . . *Heimlich* also has the meanings of that which is obscure, inaccessible to knowledge . . . "Do you not see? They do not trust us; they fear the *heimlich* face of the Duke of Friedland." (Schiller, *Wallensteins Lager*, Scene 2.)

9. *The notion of something hidden and dangerous, which is expressed in the last paragraph, is still further developed, so that "heimlich" comes to have the meaning usually ascribed to "unheimlich."* Thus: "At times I feel like a man who walks in the night and believes in ghosts; every corner is *heimlich* and full of terrors for him." (Klinger, *Theater*, 3. 298.)

Thus *heimlich* is a word the meaning of which develops in the direction of ambivalence, until it finally coincides with its opposite, *unheimlich*. *Unheimlich* is in some way or other a sub-species of *heimlich*. Let us bear this discovery in mind, though we cannot yet rightly understand it, alongside of Schelling's[6] definition of the *Unheimlich*. If we go on to examine individual instances of uncanniness, these hints will become intelligible to us.

II

When we proceed to review the things, persons, impressions, events and situations which are able to arouse in us a feeling of the uncanny in a particularly forcible and definite form, the first requirement is obviously to select a suitable example to start on. Jentsch has taken as a very good instance "doubts whether an apparently animate being is really alive; or conversely, whether a lifeless object might not be in fact animate"; and he refers in this connection to the impression made by waxwork figures, ingeniously constructed dolls and automata. To these he adds the uncanny effect of epileptic fits, and of manifestations of insanity, because these excite in the spectator the impression of automatic, mechanical processes at work behind the ordinary appearance of mental activity. Without entirely accepting this author's view, we will take it as a starting-point for our own investigation because in what follows he reminds us of a writer who has succeeded in producing uncanny effects better than anyone else.

Jentsch writes: "In telling a story, one of the most successful devices for easily creating uncanny effects is to leave the reader in uncertainty whether a particular figure in the story is a human being or an automaton, and to do it in such a way that his attention is not focused directly upon his uncertainty, so that he may not be led to go into the matter and clear it up immediately. That, as we have said, would quickly dissipate the peculiar emotional effect of the thing. E. T. A. Hoffmann[7] has repeatedly employed this psychological artifice with success in his fantastic narratives."

This observation, undoubtedly a correct one, refers primarily to the story of "The Sand-Man" in Hoffmann's *Nachtstücken*,[8] which contains the original of Olympia, the doll that appears in the first act of Offenbach's opera, *Tales of Hoffmann*. But I cannot think — and I hope most readers of the story will agree with me — that the theme of the doll Olympia, who is to all appearances a living being, is by any means the only, or indeed the most important, element that must be held responsible for the quite unparalleled atmosphere of uncanniness evoked by the story. Nor is this atmosphere heightened by the fact that the author himself treats the episode of Olympia with a faint touch of satire and uses it to poke fun at the young man's idealization of his mistress. The main theme of the story is, on the contrary, something different, something which gives it its name, and which is always re-introduced at critical moments: it is the theme of the "Sand-Man" who tears out children's eyes.

This fantastic tale opens with the childhood recollections of the student Nathaniel. In spite of his present happiness, he cannot banish the memories associated with the mysterious and terrifying death of his beloved father. On certain evenings his mother used to send the children to

---

[6] In the original version of the paper (1919) only the name "Schleiermacher" was printed here, evidently in error. [Tr.]

[7] Ernst Theodor Amadeus Hoffmann (1776–1822), German romantic writer and composer, whose best known stories were used as plots for ballets (Tchaikovsky's *The Nutcracker*, Delibes' *The Sandman*) or operas (Offenbach's *Tales of Hoffmann*, taken from Hoffman's "The Devil's Elixir").

[8] A translation of "The Sand-Man" is included in *The Tales of Hoffmann*, ed. R. J. Hollingdale, New York: Penguin, 1990.

bed early, warnings them that "the Sand-Man was coming"; and, sure enough, Nathaniel would not fail to hear the heavy tread of a visitor, with whom his father would then be occupied for the evening. When questioned about the Sand-Man, his mother, it is true, denied that such a person existed except as a figure of speech; but his nurse could give him more definite information: "He's a wicked man who comes when children won't go to bed, and throws handfuls of sand in their eyes so that they jump out of their heads all bleeding. Then he puts the eyes in a sack and carries them off to the half-moon to feed his children. They sit up there in their nest, and their beaks are hooked like owls' beaks, and they use them to peck up naughty boys' and girls' eyes with."

Although little Nathaniel was sensible and old enough not to credit the figure of the Sand-Man with such gruesome attributes, yet the dread of him became fixed in his heart. He determined to find out what the Sand-Man looked like; and one evening, when the Sand-Man was expected again, he hid in his father's study. He recognized the visitor as the lawyer Coppelius, a repulsive person whom the children were frightened of when he occasionally came to a meal; and he now identified this Coppelius with the dreaded Sand-Man. As regards the rest of the scene, Hoffmann already leaves us in doubt whether what we are witnessing is the first delirium of the panic-stricken boy, or a succession of events which are to be regarded in the story as being real. His father and the guest are at work at a brazier with glowing flames. The little eavesdropper hears Coppelius call out: "Eyes here! Eyes here!" and betrays himself by screaming aloud. Coppelius seizes him and is on the point of dropping bits of red-hot coal from the fire into his eyes, and then of throwing them into the brazier, but his father begs him off and saves his eyes. After this the boy falls into a deep swoon; and a long illness brings his experience to an end. Those who decide in favor of the rationalistic interpretation of the Sand-Man will not fail to recognize in the child's fantasy the persisting influence of his nurse's story. The bits of sand that are to be thrown into the child's eyes turn into bits of red-hot coal from the flames; and in both cases they are intended to make his eyes jump out. In the course of another visit of the Sand-Man's, a year later, his father is killed in his study by an explosion. The lawyer Coppelius disappears from the place without leaving a trace behind.

Nathaniel, now a student, believes that he has recognized this phantom of horror from his childhood in an itinerant optician, an Italian called Giuseppe Coppola, who at his university town, offers him weather-glasses for sale. When Nathaniel refuses, the man goes on: "Not weather-glasses? not weather-glasses? also got fine eyes, fine eyes!" The student's terror is allayed when he finds that the proffered eyes are only harmless spectacles, and he buys a pocket spy-glass from Coppola. With its aid he looks across into Professor Spalanzani's house opposite and there spies Spalanzani's beautiful, but strangely silent and motionless daughter, Olympia. He soon falls in love with her so violently that, because of her, he quite forgets the clever and sensible girl to whom he is betrothed. But Olympia is an automaton whose clock-work has been made by Spalanzani and whose eyes have been put in by Coppola, the Sand-Man. The student surprises the two Masters quarrelling over their handiwork. The optician carries off the wooden eyeless doll; and the mechanician, Spalanzani, picks up Olympia's bleeding eyes from the ground and throws them at Nathaniel's breast, saying that Coppola had stolen them from the student. Nathaniel succumbs to a fresh attack of madness, and in his delirium his recollection of his father's death is mingled with his new experience. "Hurry up! hurry up! ring of fire!" he cries. "Spin about, ring of fire — Hurrah! Hurry up, wooden doll! lovely wooden doll, spin about —." He then falls upon the professor, Olympia's "father," and tries to strangle him.

Rallying from a long and serious illness, Nathaniel seems at last to have recovered. He intends to marry his betrothed, with whom he has become reconciled. One day he and she are walking through the city market-place, over which the high tower of the Town Hall throws its huge shadow. On the girl's suggestion, they climb the tower, leaving her brother, who is walking with them, down below. From the top, Clara's attention is drawn to a curious object moving along the street. Nathaniel looks at this thing through

Coppola's spy-glass, which he finds in his pocket, and falls into a new attack of madness. Shouting "Spin about, wooden doll!" he tries to throw the girl into the gulf below. Her brother, brought to her side by her cries, rescues her and hastens down with her to safety. On the tower above, the madman rushes round, shrieking "Ring of fire, spin about!" — and we know the origin of words. Among the people who begin to gather below there comes forward the figure of the lawyer Coppelius, who has suddenly returned. We may suppose that it was his approach, seen through the spy-glass, which threw Nathaniel into his fit of madness. As the onlookers prepare to go up and overpower the madman, Coppelius laughs and says: "Wait a bit; he'll come down of himself." Nathaniel suddenly stands still, catches sight of Coppelius, and with a wild shriek "Yes! 'Fine eyes — fine eyes'!" flings himself over the parapet. While he lies on the paving-stones with a shattered skull the Sand-Man vanishes in the throng.

This short summary leaves no doubt, I think, that the feeling of something uncanny is directly attached to the figure of the Sand-Man, that is, to the idea of being robbed of one's eyes, and that Jentsch's point of an intellectual uncertainty has nothing to do with the effect. Uncertainty whether an object is living or inanimate, which admittedly applied to the doll Olympia, is quite irrelevant in connection with this other, more striking instance of uncanniness. It is true that the writer creates a kind of uncertainty in us in the beginning by not letting us know, no doubt purposely, whether he is taking us into the real world or into a purely fantastic one of his own creation. He has, of course, a right to do either; and if he chooses to stage his action in a world peopled with spirits, demons and ghosts, as Shakespeare does in *Hamlet*, in *Macbeth* and, in a different sense, in *The Tempest* and *A Midsummer-Night's Dream*, we must bow to his decision and treat his setting as though it were real for as long as we put ourselves into his hands. But this uncertainty disappears in the course of Hoffmann's story, and we perceive that he intends to make us, too, look through the demon optician's spectacles or spy-glass — perhaps, indeed, that the author in his very own person once peered

through such an instrument. For the conclusion of the story makes it quite clear that Coppola the optician really *is* the lawyer Coppelius[9] and also, therefore, the Sand-Man.

There is no question therefore, of any intellectual uncertainty here: we know now that we are not supposed to be looking on at the products of a madman's imagination, behind which we, with the superiority of rational minds, are able to detect the sober truth; and yet this knowledge does not lessen the impression of uncanniness in the least degree. The theory of intellectual uncertainty is thus incapable of explaining that impression.

We know from psycho-analytic experience, however, that the fear of damaging or losing one's eyes is a terrible one in children. Many adults retain their apprehensiveness in this respect, and no physical injury is so much dreaded by them as an injury to the eye. We are accustomed to say, too, that we will treasure a thing as the apple of our eye. A study of dreams, phantasies and myths has taught us that anxiety about one's eyes, the fear of going blind, is often enough a substitute for the dread of being castrated. The self-blinding of the mythical criminal, Oedipus, was simply a mitigated form of the punishment of castration — the only punishment that was adequate for him by the *lex talionis*.[10] We may try on rationalistic grounds to deny that fears about the eye are derived from the fear of castration, and may argue that it is very natural that so precious an organ as the eye should be guarded by a proportionate dread. Indeed, we might go further and say that the fear of castration itself contains no other significance and no deeper secret than a justifiable dread of this rational kind. But this view does not account adequately for the substitutive relation between the eye and the male organ which is seen to exist in dreams and myths and phantasies; nor can it dispel the impression

[9] Frau Dr. Rank has pointed out the association of the name with "*copella*" = crucible, connecting it with the chemical operations that caused the father's death; and also with "*coppo*" = eye-socket. [Freud] Except in the first (1919) edition this footnote was attached, it seems erroneously, to the first occurrence of the name Coppelius on this page. [Tr.]

[10] Law of retribution.

that the threat of being castrated in especial excites a peculiarly violent and obscure emotion, and that this emotion is what first gives the idea of losing other organs its intense coloring. All further doubts are removed when we learn the details of their "castration complex" from the analysis of neurotic patients, and realize its immense importance in their mental life.

Moreover, I would not recommend any opponent of the psycho-analytic view to select this particular story of the Sand-Man with which to support his argument that anxiety about the eyes has nothing to do with the castration complex. For why does Hoffman bring the anxiety about eyes into such intimate connection with the father's death? And why does the Sand-Man always appear as a disturber of love? He separates the unfortunate Nathaniel from his betrothed and from her brother, his best friend; he destroys the second object of his love, Olympia, the lovely doll; and he drives him into suicide at the moment when he has won back his Clara and is about to be happily united to her. Elements in the story like these, and many others, seem arbitrary and meaningless so long as we deny all connection between fears about the eye and castration; but they become intelligible as soon as we replace the Sand-Man by the dreaded father at whose hands castration is expected.[11]

[11]In fact, Hoffmann's imaginative treatment of his material has not made such wild confusion of its elements that we cannot reconstruct their original arrangement. In the story of Nathaniel's childhood, the figures of his father and Coppelius represent the two opposites into which the father-imago is split by his ambivalence; whereas the one threatens to blind him — that is, to castrate him —, the other, the "good" father, intercedes for his sight. The part of the complex which is most strongly repressed, the death-wish against the "bad" father, finds expression in the death of the "good" father, and Coppelius is made answerable for it. This pair of fathers is represented later, in his student days, by Professor Spalanzani and Coppola the optician. The professor is in himself a member of the father-series, and Coppola is recognized as identical with Coppelius the lawyer. Just as they used before to work together over the secret brazier, so now they have jointly created the doll Olympia; the professor is even called the father of Olympia. This double occurrence of activity in common betrays them as divisions of the father-imago: both the mechanician and the optician were the father of Nathaniel (and

We shall venture, therefore, to refer the uncanny effect of the Sand-Man to the anxiety belonging to the castration complex of childhood. But having reached the idea that we can make an infantile factor such as this responsible for feelings of uncanniness, we are encouraged to see whether we can apply it to other instances of the uncanny. We find in the story of the Sand-Man the other theme on which Jentsch lays stress, of a doll which appears to be alive. Jentsch believes that a particularly favorable condition for awakening uncanny feelings is created when there is intellectual uncertainty whether an object is alive or not, and when an inanimate object becomes too much like an animate one. Now, dolls are of course rather closely connected with the childhood life. We remember that in their early games children do not distinguish at all sharply between living and inanimate objects, and that they are especially fond of treating their

of Olympia as well). In the frightening scene in childhood, Coppelius, after sparing Nathaniel's eyes, had screwed off his arms and legs as an experiment; that is, he had worked on him as a mechanician would on a doll. This singular feature, which seems quite outside the picture of the Sand-Man, introduces a new castration equivalent; but it also points to the inner identity of Coppelius with his later counterpart, Spalanzani the mechanician, and prepares us for the interpretation of Olympia. This automatic doll can be nothing else than a materialization of Nathaniel's feminine attitude towards his father in his infancy. Her fathers, Spalanzani and Coppola, are, after all, nothing but new editions, reincarnations of Nathaniel's pair of fathers. Spalanzani's otherwise incomprehensible statement that the optician has stolen Nathaniel's eyes (p. 519), so as to set them in the doll, now becomes significant as supplying evidence of the identity of Olympia and Nathaniel. Olympia is, as it were, a dissociated complex of Nathaniel's which confronts him as a person, and Nathaniel's enslavement to this complex is expressed in his senseless obsessive love of Olympia. We may with justice call love of this kind narcissistic, and we can understand why someone who has fallen victim to it should relinquish the real, external object of his love. The psychological truth of the situation in which the young man, fixated upon his father by his castration complex, becomes incapable of loving a woman, is amply proved by numerous analyses of patients whose story, though less fantastic, is hardly less tragic than that of the student Nathaniel.

Hoffmann was the child of an unhappy marriage. When he was three years old, his father left his small family, and was never united to them again. According to Grisebach, in his biographical introduction to Hoffmann's works, the writer's relation to his father was always a most sensitive subject with him. [Freud] dolls like live people. In fact, I have occasionally heard a woman patient declare that even at the age of eight she had still been convinced that her dolls would be certain to come to life if she were to look at them in a particular, extremely concentrated, way. So that here, too, it is not difficult to discover a factor from childhood. But, curiously enough, while the Sand-Man story deals with the arousing of an early childhood fear, the idea of a "living doll" excites no fear at all; children have no fear of their dolls coming to life, they may even desire it. The source of uncanny feelings would not, therefore, be an infantile fear in this case, but rather an infantile wish or even merely an infantile belief. There seems to be a contradiction here; but perhaps it is only a complication, which may be helpful to us later on.

Hoffmann is the unrivalled master of the uncanny in literature. His novel, *Die Elixire des Teufels* [*The Devil's Elixir*], contains a whole mass of themes to which one is tempted to ascribe the uncanny effect of the narrative;[12] but it is too obscure and intricate a story for us to venture upon a summary of it. Towards the end of the book the reader is told the facts, hitherto concealed from him, from which the action springs; with the result, not that he is at last enlightened, but that he falls into a state of complete bewilderment. The author has piled up too much material of the same kind. In consequence one's grasp of the story as a whole suffers, though not the impression it makes. We must content ourselves with selecting those themes of uncanniness which are most prominent, and with seeing whether they too can fairly be traced back to infantile sources. These themes are all concerned with the phenomenon of the "double," which appears in every shape and in every degree of development. Thus we have characters who are to be considered identical because they look alike. This relation is accentuated by mental processes leaping from one of these characters to another — by what we should call telepathy —, so that the one possesses knowledge, feelings and experience in common with the other. Or it is marked by the fact that the subject identifies himself with someone else, so that he is in doubt as to which his self is, or substitutes the extraneous self for his own. In other words, there is doubling, dividing and interchanging of the self. And finally there is the constant recurrence of the same thing[13] — the repetition of the same features or character-traits or vicissitudes, of the same crimes, or even the same names through several consecutive generations.

The theme of the "double" has been very thoroughly treated by Otto Rank (1914). He has gone into the connections which the "double" has with reflections in mirrors, with shadows, with guardian spirits, with the belief in the soul and with the fear of death; but he also lets in a flood of light on the surprising evolution of the idea. For the "double" was originally an insurance against the destruction of the ego, an "energetic denial of the power of death," as Rank says; and probably the "immortal" soul was the first "double" of the body. This invention of doubling as a preservation against extinction has its counterpart in the language of dreams, which is fond of representing castration by a doubling or multiplication of a genital symbol.[14] The same desire led the Ancient Egyptians to develop the art of making

---

[12]Under the rubric "Varia" in one of the issues of if the *Internationale Zeitschrift für Psychoanalyse* for 1919 (5, 308), the year in which the present paper was first published, there appears over the initials "S. F." a short note which it is not unreasonable to attribute to Freud. Its insertion here, though strictly speaking irrelevant, may perhaps be excused. The note is headed: "E.T.A. Hoffmann on the Function of Consciousness" and it proceeds: "In *Die Elixire des Teufels* (Part II, p. 210, in Hesse's edition) — a novel rich in masterly descriptions of pathological mental states — Schönfeld comforts the hero, whose consciousness is temporarily disturbed, with the following words: 'And what do you get out of it? I mean out of the particular mental function which we call consciousness, and which is nothing but the confounded activity of a damned toll-collector — excise-man — deputy-chief customs officer, who has set up his infamous bureau in our top story and who exclaims, whenever any goods try to get out: "Hi! hi! exports are prohibited . . . they must stay here . . . here, in this country. . . ."'"[Tr.]

[13]This phrase seems to be an echo from Nietzsche (e.g., from the last part of *Also Sprach Zarathustra*). In Chapter III of *Beyond the Pleasure Principle* (1920g), *Standard Ed.*, 18, 22, Freud puts a similar phrase "the perpetual recurrence of the same thing" into inverted commas. [Tr.]

[14]Cf. *The Interpretation of Dreams, Standard Ed.*, 5, 357. [Tr.]

images of the dead in lasting materials. Such ideas, however, have sprung from the soil of unbounded self-love, from the primary narcissism which dominates the mind of the child and of primitive man. But when this stage has been surmounted, the "double" reverses its aspect. From having been an assurance of immortality, it becomes the uncanny harbinger of death.

The idea of the "double" does not necessarily disappear with the passing of primary narcissism, for it can receive fresh meaning from the later stages of the ego's development. A special agency is slowly formed there, which is able to stand over against the rest of the ego, which has the function of observing and criticizing the self and of exercising a censorship within the mind, and which we become aware of as our "conscience." In the pathological case of delusions of being watched, this mental agency becomes isolated, dissociated from the ego, and discernible to the physician's eye. The fact that an agency of this kind exists, which is able to treat the rest of the ego like an object — the fact, that is, that man is capable of self-observation — renders it possible to invest the old idea of a "double" with a new meaning and to ascribe a number of things to it — above all, those things which seem to self-criticism to belong to the old surmounted narcissism of earliest times.[15]

But it is not only this latter material, offensive as it is to the criticism of the ego, which may be incorporated in the idea of a double. There are also all the unfulfilled but possible futures to which we still like to cling in fantasy, all the strivings of the ego which adverse external circumstances have crushed, and all our suppressed acts of volition which nourish in us the illusion of Free Will.[16] [Cf. Freud, 1901b, Chapter XII (B).]

But after having thus considered the *manifest* motivation of the figure of a "double," we have to admit that none of this helps us to understand the extraordinarily strong feeling of something uncanny that pervades the conception; and our knowledge of pathological mental processes enables us to add that nothing in this more superficial material could account for the urge towards defence which has caused the ego to project that material outward as something foreign to itself. When all is said and done, the quality of uncanniness can only come from the fact of the "double" being a creation dating back to a very early mental stage, long since surmounted — a stage, incidentally, at which it wore a more friendly aspect. The "double" has become a thing of terror, just as, after the collapse of their religion, the gods turned into demons.[17]

The other forms of ego-disturbance exploited by Hoffmann can easily be estimated along the same lines as the theme of the "double." They are a harking-back to particular phases in the evolution of the self-regarding feeling, a regression to a time when the ego had not yet marked itself off sharply from the external world and from other people. I believe that these factors are partly responsible for the impression of uncanniness, although it is not easy to isolate and determine exactly their share of it.

The factor of the repetition of the same thing will perhaps not appeal to everyone as a source of uncanny feeling. From what I have observed, this phenomenon does undoubtedly, subject to certain conditions and combined with certain circumstances, arouse an uncanny feeling, which, furthermore, recalls the sense of helplessness experienced in some dream-states. As I was walking, one hot summer afternoon, through the

---

[15]I believe that when poets complain that two souls dwell in the human breast, and when popular psychologists talk of the splitting of people's egos, what they are thinking of is this division (in the sphere of ego-psychology) between the critical agency and the rest of the ego, and not the antithesis discovered by psycho-analysis between the ego and what is unconscious and repressed. It is true that the distinction between these two antitheses is to some extent effaced by the circumstance that foremost among the things that are rejected by the criticism of the ego are derivatives of the repressed. [Freud] Freud had already discussed this critical agency at length in Section III of his paper on narcissism (1914c), and it was soon to be further expanded into the "ego-ideal" and "super-ego" in Chapter XI of his *Group Psychology* (1921c) and Chapter III of *The Ego and the Id* (1923b) respectively. [Tr.]

[16]In Ewers's *Der Student von Prag*, which serves as the starting-point of Rank's study on the "double," the hero has promised his beloved not to kill his antagonist in a duel. But on his way to the dueling ground he meets his "double," who has already killed his rival. [Freud]

[17]Heine, *Die Götter im Exil*. [Freud]

deserted streets of a provincial town in Italy which was unknown to me, I found myself in a quarter of whose character I could not long remain in doubt. Nothing but painted women were to be seen at the windows of the small houses, and I hastened to leave the narrow street at the next turning. But after having wandered about for a time without enquiring my way, I suddenly found myself back in the same street, where my presence was now beginning to excite attention. I hurried away once more, only to arrive by another *détour* at the same place yet a third time. Now, however, a feeling overcame me which I can only describe as uncanny, and I was glad enough to find myself back at the piazza I had left a short while before, without any further voyages of discovery. Other situations which have in common with my adventure an unintended recurrence of the same situation, but which differ radically from it in other respects, also result in the same feeling of helplessness and of uncanniness. So, for instance, when, caught in a mist perhaps, one has lost one's way in a mountain forest, every attempt to find the marked or familiar path may bring one back again and again to one and the same spot, which one can identify by some particular landmark. Or one may wander about in a dark, strange room, looking for the door or the electric switch, and collide time after time with the same piece of furniture — though it is true that Mark Twain succeeded by wild exaggeration in turning this latter situation into something irresistibly comic.[18]

If we take another class of things, it is easy to see that there, too, it is only this factor of involuntary repetition which surrounds what would otherwise be innocent enough with an uncanny atmosphere, and forces upon us the idea of something fateful and inescapable when otherwise we should have spoken only of "chance." For instance, we naturally attach no importance to the event when we hand in an overcoat and get a cloakroom ticket with the number, let us say, 62; or when we find that our cabin on a ship bears that number. But the impression is altered if two such events, each in itself indifferent, happen close

together — if we come across the number 62 several times in a single day, or if we begin to notice that everything which has a number — addresses, hotel rooms, compartments in railway trains — invariably has the same one, or at all events one which contains the same figures. We do feel this to be uncanny. And unless a man is utterly hardened and proof against the lure of superstition, he will be tempted to ascribe a secret meaning to this obstinate recurrence of a number; he will take it, perhaps, as an indication of the span of life allotted to him.[19] Or suppose one is engaged in reading the works of the famous physiologist, Hering, and within the space of a few days receives two letters from two different countries, each from a person called Hering, though one has never before had any dealings with anyone of that name. Not long ago an ingenious scientist (Kammerer, 1919) attempted to reduce coincidences of this kind to certain laws, and so deprive them of their uncanny effect. I will not venture to decide whether he has succeeded or not.

How exactly we can trace back to infantile psychology the uncanny effect of such similar recurrences is a question I can only lightly touch on in these pages; and I must refer the reader instead to another work,[20] already completed, in which this has been gone into in detail, but in a different connection. For it is possible to recognize the dominance in the unconscious mind of a "compulsion to repeat" proceeding from the instinctual impulses and probably inherent in the very nature of the instincts — a compulsion powerful enough to overrule the pleasure principle, lending to certain aspects of the mind their demonic character, and still very clearly expressed in the impulses of small children; a compulsion, too, which is responsible for a part of the course taken by the analysis of neurotic patients. All these considerations prepare us for the discovery that

---

[18]Mark Twain, *A Tramp Abroad*, London, 1880, I, 107. [Tr.]

[19]Freud had himself reached the age of 62 a year earlier, in 1918. [Tr.]

[20]This was published a year later as *Beyond the Pleasure Principle* (1920g). The various manifestations of the "compulsions to repeat" enumerated here are enlarged upon in Chapters II and III of that work. The "compulsion to repeat" had already been described by Freud as a clinical phenomenon, in a technical paper published five years earlier (1914g). [Tr.]

whatever reminds us of this inner "compulsion to repeat" is perceived as uncanny.

Now, however, it is time to turn from these aspects of the matter, which are in any case difficult to judge, and look for some undeniable instances of the uncanny, in the hope that an analysis of them will decide whether our hypothesis is a valid one.

In the story of "The Ring of Polycrates,"[21] the King of Egypt turns away in horror from his host, Polycrates, because he sees that his friend's every wish is at once fulfilled, his every care promptly removed by kindly fate. His host has become "uncanny" to him. His own explanation, that the too fortunate man has to fear the envy of the gods, seems obscure to us; its meaning is veiled in mythological language. We will therefore turn to another example in a less grandiose setting. In the case history of an obsessional neurotic,[22, 23] I have described how the patient once stayed in a hydropathic establishment[24] and benefited greatly by it. He had the good sense, however, to attribute his improvement not to the therapeutic properties of the water, but to the situation of his room, which immediately adjoined that of a very accommodating nurse. So on his second visit to the establishment he asked for the same room, but was told that it was already occupied by an old gentleman, whereupon he gave vent to his annoyance in the words: "I wish he may be struck dead for it." A fortnight later the old gentleman really did have a stroke. My patient thought this an "uncanny" experience. The impression of uncanniness would have been stronger still if less time had elapsed between his words and the untoward event, or if he had been able to report innumerable similar coincidences. As a matter of fact, he had no difficulty in producing coincidences of this sort; but then not only he but every obsessional neurotic I have observed has been able to relate analogous experiences. They are never surprised at their invariably running up against someone they have just been thinking of, perhaps for the first time for a long while. If they say one day "I haven't had any news of so-and-so for a long time," they will be sure to get a letter from him the next morning, and an accident or a death will rarely take place without having passed through their mind a little while before. They are in the habit of referring to this state of affairs in the most modest manner, saying that they have "presentiments" which "usually" come true.

One of the most uncanny and wide-spread forms of superstition is the dread of the evil eye, which has been exhaustively studied by the Hamburg oculist Seligmann (1910–11). There never seems to have been any doubt about the source of this dread. Whoever possesses something that is at once valuable and fragile is afraid of other people's envy, in so far as he projects on to them the envy he would have felt in their place. A feeling like this betrays itself by a look[25] even though it is not put into words; and when a man is prominent owing to noticeable, and particularly owing to unattractive, attributes, other people are ready to believe that his envy is rising to a more than usual degree of intensity and that this intensity will convert it into effective action. What is feared is thus a secret intention of doing harm, and certain signs are taken to mean that that intention has the necessary power at its command.

These last examples of the uncanny are to be referred to the principle which I have called "omnipotence of thoughts," taking the name from an expression used by one of my patients.[26] And now we find ourselves on familiar ground. Our analysis of instances of the uncanny has led us back to the old, animistic conception of the universe. This was characterized by the idea that the world was peopled with the spirits of human beings; by the subject's narcissistic overvaluation of his own mental processes; by the belief in the omnipotence of thoughts and the technique of magic based on that belief; by the attribution to various outside persons and things of carefully

---

[21]Schiller's poem based on Herodotus. [Tr.]

[22]"Notes upon a Case of Obsessional Neurosis" (1909*d*) [*Standard Ed.*, 10, 234]. [Freud]

[23]Freud's famous case of Ernest Lanzer, the "Rat Man," who has a neurotic fear that some rats would bore their way into the anus of a lady whom he admired and also into the anus of his (long-dead) father.

[24]A spa where one goes to drink medicinal waters.

[25]"The evil eye" in German is "*der böse Blick*," literally "the evil look." [Tr.]

[26]The obsessional patient referred to just above — the "Rat Man" (1909*d*), *Standard Ed.*, 10, 233f. [Tr.]

graded magical powers, or *"mana"*; as well as by all the other creations with the help of which man, in the unrestricted narcissism of that stage of development, strove to fend off the manifest prohibitions of reality. It seems as if each one of us has been through a phase of individual development corresponding to this animistic stage in primitive men, that none of us has passed through it without preserving certain residues and traces of it which are still capable of manifesting themselves, and that everything which now strikes us as "uncanny" fulfils the condition of touching those residues of animistic mental activity within us and bringing them to expression.[27]

At this point I will put forward two considerations which, I think, contain the gist of this short study. In the first place, if psycho-analytic theory is correct in maintaining that every affect belonging to an emotional impulse, whatever its kind, is transformed, if it is repressed, into anxiety, then among instances of frightening things there must be one class in which the frightening element can be shown to be something repressed which *recurs*. This class of frightening things would then constitute the uncanny; and it must be a matter of indifference whether what is uncanny was itself originally frightening or whether it carried some *other* affect. In the second place, if this is indeed the secret nature of the uncanny, we can understand why linguistic usage has extended *das Heimliche* [homely] into its opposite, *das Unheimliche* (p. 518); for this uncanny is in reality nothing new or alien, but something which is familiar and old-established in the mind and which has become alienated from it only through the process of repression. This reference to the factor of repression enables us, furthermore, to understand Schelling's definition (p. 517) of the uncanny as something which ought to have remained hidden but has come to light.

[27]Cf. my book *Totem and Taboo* (1912–13), Essay III, "Animism, Magic and the Omnipotence of Thoughts," where the following footnote will be found: "We appear to attribute an 'uncanny' quality to impressions that seek to confirm the omnipotence of thoughts and the animistic mode of thinking in general, after we have reached a stage at which, in our *judgement*, we have abandoned such beliefs." [*Standard Ed.*, 13, 86]. [Freud]

It only remains for us to test our new hypothesis on one or two more examples of the uncanny.

Many people experience the feeling in the highest degree in relation to death and dead bodies, to the return of the dead, and to spirits and ghosts. As we have seen (p. 515) some languages in use to-day can only render the German expression "an *unheimlich* house" by "a *haunted* house." We might indeed have begun our investigation with this example, perhaps the most striking of all, of something uncanny, but we refrained from doing so because the uncanny in it is too much intermixed with what is purely gruesome and is in part overlaid by it. There is scarcely any other matter, however, upon which our thoughts and feelings have changed so little since the very earliest times, and in which discarded forms have been so completely preserved under a thin disguise, as our relation to death. Two things account for our conservatism: the strength of our original emotional reaction to death and the insufficiency of our scientific knowledge about it. Biology has not yet been able to decide whether death is the inevitable fate of every living being or whether it is only a regular but yet perhaps avoidable event in life.[28] It is true that the statement "All men are mortal" is paraded in textbooks of logic as an example of a general proposition; but no human being really grasps it, and our unconscious has as little use now as it ever had for the idea of its own mortality.[29] Religions continue to dispute the importance of the undeniable fact of individual death and to postulate a life after death; civil governments still believe that they cannot maintain moral order among the living if they do not uphold the prospect of a better life hereafter as a recompense for mundane existence. In our great cities, placards announce lectures that undertake to tell us how to get into touch with the souls of the departed; and it cannot be denied that not a few of

[28]This problem figures prominently in *Beyond the Pleasure Principle* (1920g), on which Freud was engaged while writing the present paper. See *Standard Ed.*, 18, 44 ff. [Tr.]

[29]Freud had discussed the individual's attitude to death at greater length in the second part of his paper "Thoughts for the Times on War and Death" (1915b). [Tr.]

the most able and penetrating minds among our men of science have come to the conclusion, especially towards the close of their own lives, that a contact of this kind is not impossible. Since almost all of us still think as savages do on this topic, it is no matter for surprise that the primitive fear of the dead is still so strong within us and always ready to come to the surface on any provocation. Most likely our fear still implies the old belief that the dead man becomes the enemy of his survivor and seeks to carry him off to share his new life with him. Considering our unchanged attitude towards death, we might rather inquire what has become of the repression, which is the necessary condition of a primitive feeling recurring in the shape of something uncanny. But repression is there, too. All supposedly educated people have ceased to believe officially that the dead can become visible as spirits, and have made any such appearances dependent on improbable and remote conditions; their emotional attitude towards their dead, moreover, once a highly ambiguous and ambivalent one, has been toned down in the higher strata of the mind into an unambiguous feeling of piety.[30]

We have now only a few remarks to add — for animism, magic and sorcery, the omnipotence of thoughts, man's attitude to death, involuntary repetition and the castration complex comprise practically all the factors which turn something frightening into something uncanny.

We can also speak of a living person as uncanny, and we do so when we ascribe evil intentions to him. But that is not all; in addition to this we must feel that his intentions to harm us are going to be carried out with the help of special powers. A good instance of this is the "*Gettatore*,"[31] that uncanny figure of Romanic superstition which Schaeffer,[32] with intuitive poetic feeling and profound psycho-analytic understanding, has transformed into a sympathetic character in his *Josef Montfort*. But the question of these secret powers brings us back again to the realm of animism. It was the pious Gretchen's intuition that Mephistopheles possessed secret powers of this kind that made him so uncanny to her.

> Sie fühlt dass ich ganz sicher ein Genie,
> Vielleicht sogar der Teufel bin.[33]

The uncanny effect of epilepsy and of madness has the same origin. The layman sees in them the working of forces hitherto unsuspected in his fellow-men, but at the same time he is dimly aware of them in remote corners of his own being. The Middle Ages quite consistently ascribed all such maladies to the influence of demons, and in this their psychology was almost correct. Indeed, I should not be surprised to hear that psychoanalysis, which is concerned with laying bare these hidden forces, has itself become uncanny to many people for that very reason. In one case, after I had succeeded — though none too rapidly — in effecting a cure in a girl who had been an invalid for many years, I myself heard this view expressed by the patient's mother long after her recovery.

Dismembered limbs, a severed head, a hand cut off at the wrist, as in a fairy tale of Hauff's,[34, 35] feet which dance by themselves, as in the book by Schaeffer which I mentioned above — all these have something peculiarly uncanny about them, especially when, as in the last instance, they prove capable of independent activity in addition. As we already know, this kind of uncanniness springs from its proximity to the castration complex. To some people the idea of being buried alive by mistake is the most uncanny thing of all. And yet psycho-analysis has taught us that this terrifying fantasy is only a transformation of another fantasy which had originally nothing terrifying about it at all, but was qualified by a

---

[30]Cf. *Totem and Taboo* [*Standard Ed.*, 13, 66]. [Freud]

[31]Literally "thrower" (of bad luck), or "one who casts" (the evil eye). — Schaeffer's novel was published in 1918. [Tr.]

[32]Albrecht Schaeffer (1885–1950), German poet and novelist, author of the novel *Josef Montfort* (1922 [not 1918 per editor's note]).

[33]She feels that surely I'm a genius now, — Perhaps the very Devil indeed!
Goethe, *Faust*, Part I (Scene 16), (Bayard Taylor's translation). [Tr.]

[34]*Die Geschichte von der abgehauenen Hand* ("The Story of the Severed Hand"). [Tr.]

[35]Wilhelm Hauff (1802–1827), German collector of folktales.

certain lasciviousness — the fantasy, I mean, of intra-uterine existence.[36]

There is one more point of general application which I should like to add, though, strictly speaking, it has been included in what has already been said about animism and modes of working of the mental apparatus that have been surmounted; for I think it deserves special emphasis. This is that an uncanny effect is often and easily produced when the distinction between imagination and reality is effaced, as when something that we have hitherto regarded as imaginary appears before us in reality, or when a symbol takes over the full functions of the thing it symbolizes, and so on. It is this factor which contributes not a little to the uncanny effect attaching to magical practices. The infantile element in this, which also dominates the minds of neurotics, is the over-accentuation of psychical reality in comparison with material reality — a feature closely allied to the belief in the omnipotence of thoughts. In the middle of the isolation of war-time a number of the English *Strand Magazine* fell into my hands; and, among other somewhat redundant matter, I read a story about a young married couple who move into a furnished house in which there is a curiously shaped table with carvings of crocodiles on it. Towards evenings an intolerable and very specific smell begins to pervade the house; they stumble over something in the dark; they seem to see a vague form gliding over the stairs — in short, we are given to understand that the presence of the table causes ghostly crocodiles to haunt the place, or that the wooden monsters come to life in the dark, or something of the sort. It was a naïve enough story, but the uncanny feeling it produced was quite remarkable.

To conclude this collection of examples, which is certainly not complete, I will relate an instance taken from psychoanalytic experience; if it does not rest upon mere coincidence, it furnishes a beautiful confirmation of our theory of the uncanny. It often happens that neurotic men declare that they feel there is something uncanny about the female genital organs. This *unheimlich* place, however, is the entrance to the former *Heim* [home] of all human beings, to the place where each one of us lived once upon a time and in the beginning. There is a joking saying that "Love is home-sickness"; and whenever a man dreams of a place or a country and says to himself, while he is still dreaming: "this place is familiar to me, I've been here before," we may interpret the place as being his mother's genitals or her body.[37] In this case too, then the *unheimlich* is what was once *heimisch*, familiar; the prefix "*un*" ["un-"] is the token of repression.[38]

III

In the course of this discussion the reader will have felt certain doubts arising in his mind; and he must now have an opportunity of collecting them and bringing them forward.

It may be true that the uncanny [*unheimlich*] is something which is secretly familiar [*heimlich-heimisch*], which has undergone repression and then returned from it, and that everything that is uncanny fulfils this condition. But the selection of material on this basis does not enable us to solve the problem of the uncanny. For our proposition is clearly not convertible. Not everything that fulfils this condition — not everything that recalls repressed desires and surmounted modes of thinking belonging to the prehistory of the individual and of the race — is on that account uncanny.

Nor shall we conceal the fact that for almost every example adduced in support of our hypothesis one may be found which rebuts it. The story of the severed hand in Hauff's fairy tale [p. 527] certainly has an uncanny effect, and we have traced that effect back to the castration complex; but most readers will probably agree with me in judging that no trace of uncanniness is provoked by Herodotus's story of the treasure of

---

[36]See Section VIII of Freud's analysis of the "Wolf Man" (1918b), p. 101ff. [Tr.]

[37]Cf. *The Interpretation of Dreams* (1900a), *Standard Ed.*, 5, 399. [Tr.]
[38]See Freud's paper on "Negation" (1925h). [Tr.]

Rhampsinitus, in which the master-thief, whom the princess tries to hold fast by the hand, leaves his brother's severed hand behind with her instead. Again, the prompt fulfilment of the wishes of Polycrates [p. 525] undoubtedly affects us in the same uncanny way as it did the king of Egypt; yet our own fairy stories are crammed with instantaneous wish-fulfilments which produce no uncanny effect whatever. In the story of "The Three Wishes," the woman is tempted by the savory smell of a sausage to wish that she might have one too, and in an instant it lies on a plate before her. In his annoyance at her hastiness her husband wishes it may hang on her nose. And there it is, dangling from her nose. All this is very striking but not in the least uncanny. Fairy tales quite frankly adopt the animistic standpoint of the omnipotence of thoughts and wishes, and yet I cannot think of any genuine fairy story which has anything uncanny about it. We have heard that it is in the highest degree uncanny when an inanimate object — a picture or a doll — comes to life; nevertheless in Hans Andersen's stories the household utensils, furniture and tin soldiers are alive, yet nothing could well be more remote from the uncanny. And we should hardly call it uncanny when Pygmalion's beautiful statue comes to life.

Apparent death and the re-animation of the dead have been represented as most uncanny themes. But things of this sort too are very common in fairy stories. Who would be so bold as to call it uncanny, for instance, when Snow-White opens her eyes once more? And the resuscitation of the dead in accounts of miracles, as in the New Testament, elicits feelings quite unrelated to the uncanny. Then, too, the theme that achieves such an indubitably uncanny effect, the unintended recurrence of the same thing, serves other and quite different purposes in another class of cases. We have already come across one example [p. 524] in which it is employed to call up a feeling of the comic; and we could multiply instances of this kind. Or again, it works as a means of emphasis, and so on. And once more: what is the origin of the uncanny effect of silence, darkness and solitude? Do not these factors point to the part played by danger in the genesis of what is uncanny, notwithstanding that in children these same factors are the most frequent determinants of the expression of fear [rather than of the uncanny]? And are we after all justified in entirely ignoring intellectual uncertainty as a factor, seeing that we have admitted its importance in relation to death [pp. 526–27]?

It is evident therefore that we must be prepared to admit that there are other elements besides those which we have so far laid down as determining the production of uncanny feelings. We might say that these preliminary results have satisfied *psycho-analytic* interest in the problem of the uncanny, and that what remains probably calls for an *aesthetic* inquiry. But that would be to open the door to doubts about what exactly is the value of our general contention that the uncanny proceeds from something familiar which has been repressed.

We have noticed one point which may help us to resolve these uncertainties; nearly all the instances that contradict our hypothesis are taken from the realm of fiction, of imaginative writing. This suggests that we should differentiate between the uncanny that we actually experience and the uncanny that we merely picture or read about.

What is *experienced* as uncanny is much more simply conditioned but comprises far fewer instances. We shall find, I think, that it fits in perfectly with our attempt at a solution, and can be traced back without exception to something familiar that has been repressed. But here, too, we must make a certain important and psychologically significant differentiation in our material, which is best illustrated by turning to suitable examples.

Let us take the uncanny associated with the omnipotence of thoughts, with the prompt fulfilment of wishes, with secret injurious powers and with the return of the dead. The condition under which the feeling of uncanniness arises here is unmistakable. We — or our primitive forefathers — once believed that these possibilities were realities, and were convinced that they actually happened. Nowadays we no longer believe in them, we have *surmounted* these modes of thought; but we do not feel quite sure of our new beliefs, and the old ones still exist within us ready to seize upon any confirmation. As soon as something *actually happens* in our lives which seems to confirm the old, discarded beliefs we get a feeling of the uncanny; it is as though we were making a judgement something like this: "So, after all, it is *true* that one can kill a person by the mere wish!" or, "So the dead *do* live on and appear on the scene of their former activities!" and so on. Conversely, anyone who has completely and finally rid himself of animistic beliefs will be insensible to this type of the uncanny. The most remarkable coincidences of wish and fulfilment, the most mysterious repetition of similar experiences in a particular place or on a particular date, the most deceptive sights and suspicious noises — none of these things will disconcert him or raise the kind of fear which can be described as "a fear of something uncanny." The whole thing is purely an affair of "reality-testing," a question of the material reality of the phenomena.[39]

The state of affairs is different when the uncanny proceeds from repressed infantile complexes, from the castration complex, womb-fantasies, etc.; but experiences which arouse this

[39]Since the uncanny effect of a "double" also belongs to this same group it is interesting to observe what the effect is of meeting one's own image unbidden and unexpected. Ernst Mach has related two such observations in his *Analyse der Empfindungen* (1900, 3). On the first occasion he was not a little startled when he realized that the face before him was his own. The second time he formed a very unfavorable opinion about the supposed stranger who entered the omnibus, and thought "What a shabby-looking school-master that man is who is getting in!" — I can report a similar adventure. I was sitting alone in my *wagon-lit* compartment when a more than usually violent jolt of the train swung back the door of the adjoining washing-cabinet, and an elderly gentleman in a dressing-gown and a traveling cap came in. I assumed that in leaving the washing-cabinet, which lay between the two compartments, he had taken the wrong direction and come into my compartment by mistake. Jumping up with the intention of putting him right, I at once realized to my dismay that the intruder was nothing but my own reflection in the looking-glass on the open door. I can still recollect that I thoroughly disliked his appearance. Instead, therefore, of being *frightened* by our "doubles," both Mach and I simply failed to recognize them as such. Is it not possible, though, that our dislike of them was a vestigial trace of the archaic reaction which feels the "double" to be something uncanny? [Freud]

kind of uncanny feeling are not of very frequent occurrence in real life. The uncanny which proceeds from actual experience belongs for the most part to the first group [the group dealt with in the previous paragraph]. Nevertheless the distinction between the two is theoretically very important. Where the uncanny comes from infantile complexes the question of material reality does not arise; its place is taken by the psychical reality. What is involved is an actual repression of some content of thought and a return of this repressed content, not a cessation of *belief in the reality* of such a content. We might say that in the one case what had been repressed is a particular ideational content, and in the other the belief in its (material) reality. But this last phrase no doubt extends the term "repression" beyond its legitimate meaning. It would be more correct to take into account a psychological distinction which can be detected here, and to say that the animistic beliefs of civilized people are in a state of having been (to a greater or lesser extent) *surmounted* [rather than repressed]. Our conclusion could then be stated thus; an uncanny experience occurs either when infantile complexes which have been repressed are once more revived by some impression, or when primitive beliefs which have been surmounted seem once more to be confirmed. Finally, we must not let our predilection for smooth solutions and lucid exposition blind us to the fact that these two classes of uncanny experience are not always sharply distinguishable. When we consider that primitive beliefs are most intimately connected with infantile complexes, and are, in fact, based on them, we shall not be greatly astonished to find that the distinction is often a hazy one.

The uncanny as it is depicted in *literature*, in stories and imaginative productions, merits in truth a separate discussion. Above all, it is a much more fertile province than the uncanny in real life, for it contains the whole of the latter and something more besides, something that cannot be found in real life. The contrast between what has been repressed and what has been surmounted cannot be transposed on to the uncanny in fiction without profound modification; for the realm of fantasy depends for its effect on the fact that its content is not submitted to reality-testing. The somewhat paradoxical result is that *in the first place a great deal that is not uncanny in fiction would be so if it happened in real life; and in the second place that there are many more means of creating uncanny effects in fiction than there are in real life.*

The imaginative writer has this licence among many others, that he can select his world of representation so that it either coincides with the realities we are familiar with or departs from them in what particulars he pleases. We accept his ruling in every case. In fairy tales, for instance, the world of reality is left behind from the very start, and the animistic system of beliefs is frankly adopted. Wish-fulfilments, secret powers, omnipotence of thoughts, animation of inanimate objects, all the elements so common in fairy stories, can exert no uncanny influence here; for, as we have learnt, that feeling cannot arise unless there is a conflict of judgement as to whether things which have been "surmounted" and are regarded as incredible may not, after all, be possible; and this problem is eliminated from the outset by the postulates of the world of fairy tales. Thus we see that fairy stories, which have furnished us with most of the contradictions to our hypothesis of the uncanny, confirm the first part of our proposition — that in the realm of fiction many things are not uncanny which would be so if they happened in real life. In the case of these stories there are other contributory factors, which we shall briefly touch upon later.

The creative writer can also choose a setting which though less imaginary than the world of fairy tales does yet differ from the real world by admitting superior spiritual beings such as demonic spirits or ghosts of the dead. So long as they remain within their setting of poetic reality, such figures lose any uncanniness which they might possess. The souls in Dante's *Inferno*, or the supernatural apparitions in Shakespeare's *Hamlet, Macbeth* or *Julius Caesar*, may be gloomy and terrible enough, but they are no more really uncanny than Homer's jovial world of gods. We adapt our judgement to the imaginary reality imposed on us by the writer, and regard souls, spirits and ghosts as though their existence had the same validity as our own has in material reality. In this case too we avoid all trace of the uncanny.

The situation is altered as soon as the writer pretends to move in the world of common reality. In this case he accepts as well all the conditions operating to produce uncanny feelings in real life; and everything that would have an uncanny effect in reality has it in his story. But in this case he can even increase his effect and multiply it far beyond what could happen in reality, by bringing about events which never or very rarely happen in fact. In doing this he is in a sense betraying us to the superstitiousness which we have ostensibly surmounted; he deceives us by promising to give us the sober truth, and then after all overstepping it. We react to his inventions as we would have reacted to real experiences; by the time we have seen through his trick it is already too late and the author has achieved his object. But it must be added that his success is not unalloyed. We retain a feeling of dissatisfaction, a kind of grudge against the attempted deceit. I have noticed this particularly after reading Schnitzler's *Die Weissagung* [*The Prophecy*] and similar stories which flirt with the supernatural. However, the writer has one more means which he can use in order to avoid our recalcitrance and at the same time to improve his chances of success. He can keep us in the dark for a long time about the precise nature of the presuppositions on which the world he writes about is based, or he can cunningly and ingeniously avoid any definite information on the point to the last. Speaking generally, however, we find a confirmation of the second part of our proposition — that fiction presents more opportunities for creating uncanny feelings than are possible in real life.

Strictly speaking, all these complications relate only to that class of the uncanny which proceeds from forms of thought that have been surmounted. The class which proceeds from repressed complexes is more resistant and remains as powerful in fiction as in real experience, subject to one exception [see p. 532]. The uncanny belonging to the first class — that proceeding from forms of thought that have been surmounted — retains its character not only in experience but in fiction as well, so long as the setting is one of material reality; but where it is given an arbitrary and artificial setting in fiction, it is apt to lose that character.

We have clearly not exhausted the possibilities of poetic licence and the privileges enjoyed by story-writers in evoking or in excluding an uncanny feeling. In the main we adopt an unvarying passive attitude towards real experience and are subject to the influence of our physical environment. But the story-teller has a *peculiarly* directive power over us; by means of the moods he can put us into, he is able to guide the current of our emotions, to dam it up in one direction and make it flow in another, and he often obtains a great variety of effects from the same material. All this is nothing new, and has doubtless long since been fully taken into account by students of aesthetics. We have drifted into this field of research half involuntarily, through the temptation to explain certain instances which contradicted our theory of the causes of the uncanny. Accordingly we will now return to the examination of a few of those instances.

We have already asked (p. 528) why it is that the severed hand in the story of the treasure of Rhampsinitus has no uncanny effect in the way that the severed hand has in Hauff's story. The question seems to have gained in importance now that we have recognized that the class of the uncanny which proceeds from repressed complexes is the more resistant of the two. The answer is easy. In the Herodotus story our thoughts are concentrated much more on the superior cunning of the master-thief than on the feelings of the princess. The princess may very well have had an uncanny feeling, indeed she very probably fell into a swoon; but *we* have no

such sensations, for we put ourselves in the thief's place, not in hers. In Nestroy's farce, *Der Zerrissene* [*The Torn Man*],[40] another means is used to avoid any impression of the uncanny in the scene in which the fleeing man, convinced that he is a murderer, lifts up one trap-door after another and each time sees what he takes to be the ghost of his victim rising up out of it. He calls out in despair, "But I've only killed *one* man. Why this ghastly multiplication?" We know what went before this scene and do not share his error, so what must be uncanny to him has an irresistibly comic effect on us. Even a "real" ghost, as in Oscar Wilde's *Canterville Ghost*, loses all power of at least arousing *gruesome* feelings in us as soon as the author begins to amuse himself by being ironical about it and allows liberties to be taken with it. Thus we see how independent emotional effects can be of the actual subject-matter in the world of fiction. In fairy stories feelings of fear — including therefore uncanny feelings — are ruled out altogether. We understand this, and that is why we ignore any opportunities we find in them for developing such feelings.

Concerning the factors of silence, solitude and darkness (p. 529), we can only say that they are actually elements in the production of the infantile anxiety from which the majority of human beings have never become quite free. This problem has been discussed from a psycho-analytic point of view elsewhere.[41]

---

[40]Johann Nepomuc Nestroy (1801–1862) wrote *Der Zerrissene* (1845; the English translation is titled *A Man Full of Nothing*).

[41]See the discussion of children's fear of the dark in Section V of the third of Freud's *Three Essays* (1905d), *Standard Ed.*, 7, 224 n. [Tr.]

Medusa's Head[1]

We have not often attempted to interpret individual mythological themes, but an interpretation suggests itself easily in the case of the horrifying decapitated head of Medusa.

To decapitate = to castrate. The terror of Medusa is thus a terror of castration that is linked to the sight of something. Numerous analyses have made us familiar with the occasion for this: it occurs when a boy, who has hitherto been unwilling to believe the threat of castration, catches sight of the female genitals, probably those of an adult, surrounded by hair, and essentially those of his mother.

The hair upon Medusa's head is frequently represented in works of art in the form of snakes, and these once again are derived from the castration complex. It is a remarkable fact that, however frightening they may be in themselves, they nevertheless serve actually as a mitigation of the horror, for they replace the penis, the absence of which is the cause of the horror. This is a confirmation of the technical rule according to which a multiplication of penis symbols signifies castration.[2]

The sight of Medusa's head makes the spectator stiff with terror, turns him to stone. Observe that we have here once again the same transformation of affect! For becoming stiff means an erection. Thus in the original situation it offers consolation to the spectator: he is still in possession of a penis, and the stiffening reassures him of the fact.

This symbol of horror is worn upon her dress by the virgin goddess Athena.[3] And rightly so, for thus she becomes a woman who is unapproachable and repels all sexual desires — since she displays the terrifying genitals of the Mother. Since the Greeks were in the main strongly homosexual, it was inevitable that we should find among them a representation of woman as a being who frightens and repels because she is castrated.

If Medusa's head takes the place of a representation of the female genitals, or rather if it isolates their horrifying effects from their pleasure-giving ones, it may be recalled that displaying the genitals is familiar in other connections as an apotropaic[4] act. What arouses horror in oneself will produce the same effect upon the enemy against whom one is seeking to defend oneself. We read in Rabelais of how the Devil took to flight when the woman showed him her vulva.[5]

The erect male organ also has an apotropaic effect, but thanks to another mechanism. To display the penis (or any of its surrogates) is to say: "I am not afraid of you. I defy you. I have a penis." Here, then, is another way of intimidating the Evil Spirit.[6]

In order to seriously substantiate this interpretation it would be necessary to investigate the origin of this isolated symbol of horror in Greek mythology as well as parallels to it in other mythologies.[7]

---

[1]"Das Medusenhaupt." First published posthumously *Internationale Zeitschrift für Psychoanalyse Imago*, 25 (1940), 105; reprinted *Gesammelte Werke*, 17 (1941), 47. The manuscript is dated May 14, 1922, and appears to be a sketch for a more extensive work. The present translation, by James Strachey, is reprinted from *International Journal for Psycho-Analysis: Imago*, 22 (1941), 69 and *Collected Papers*, 5 (1950), 105. [Tr.]

[2]This is referred to in Freud's paper on "The 'Uncanny'" (1919h), middle of Section II. [Tr.]

[3]Athena was the Greek goddess of wisdom; Freud is alluding to the snaky decoration on her dress (the aegis) in the statue of Athena now in the Parthenon museum.

[4]Used for combating demons.

[5]See François Rabelais, *Gargantua and Pantagruel*, vol. 4, chapter 47.

[6]It may be worth quoting a footnote added by Freud to a paper of Stekel's, "Zur Psychologie des Exhibitionismus," in *Zentralbl. Psychoanal.*, 1 (1911), 495: "Dr. Stekel here proposes to derive exhibitionism from unconscious narcissistic motive forces. It seems to me probable that the same explanation can be applied to the apotropaic exhibiting found among the peoples of antiquity."[Tr.]

[7]The same topic was dealt with by Ferenczi (1923) in a very short paper which was itself briefly commented upon by Freud in his "Infantile Genital Organization of the Libido" (1923e). [Tr.]

T. S. Eliot

1888–1965

Thomas Stearns Eliot, America's most influential literary expatriate since Henry James, was born in St. Louis, Missouri, where his father was a businessman and his mother a locally renowned poet. He was educated at private schools in St. Louis and in Milton, Massachusetts, before entering Harvard, where he studied with the philosophers Bertrand Russell and George Santayana (from whom he may have derived the idea of the "objective correlative"), and the literary critic Irving Babbitt, from whom he absorbed an inveterate hostility to Romanticism. Eliot graduated from Harvard College in 1909 and spent most of the next five years in England working toward a Ph.D. in philosophy. He actually wrote his dissertation, on the English neo-idealist F. H. Bradley, but never returned to take his final orals. In 1914, he accepted a traveling fellowship to the University of Marburg but was stranded in England by the outbreak of World War I, stayed at Merton College, Oxford, and gradually came to make England his home. In 1915 he married Vivien Haigh-Wood, a beautiful and intelligent woman whose infidelities, emotional demands, and nervous instability made home life a misery for him; he eventually left her in 1933, and they lived apart until her death fourteen years later.

Eliot's poetic career seems to have dated from a year spent in France (1910–11), where his encounter with the French symbolists, especially Jules Laforgue, helped him to find his own voice. His first volume, *Prufrock and Other Observations* (1917), was a major contribution to the Modernist movement in poetry, characterized by the combination of hard clear images, mysterious and transcendent symbols, and an almost classical restraint of subjective feeling. In *The Waste Land* (1922), Eliot produced Modernism's epic of decay: an elegy upon the desiccation and near-death of the poet's own spirit with an odd Buddhistic conclusion ambiguously suggesting the hope of renewal and rebirth. The poem, written rapidly while Eliot was recovering from a nervous breakdown in a Swiss sanatorium, was tightened drastically by his friend Ezra Pound. Eliot found a more conventional source of solace and hope in his conversion to Anglo-Catholicism in 1927. Later poems included *Journey of the Magi* (1927), *Ash Wednesday* (1930), *Old Possum's Book of Practical Cats* (1939; adapted by Andrew Lloyd Webber into *Cats,* an international theatrical success in the 1980s and 1990s), and *Four Quartets* (1943). Eliot was also a successful playwright whose dry, menacing dialogue influenced postwar dramatists such as Harold Pinter. *The Cocktail Party* (1950), his most successful play, made Eliot a good deal of money from both the London and New York productions, though *Murder in the Cathedral* (1935), a verse tragedy on St. Thomas à Becket, may be the most durable and interesting of his dramas.

While he was gaining his reputation as a poet and playwright, Eliot worked first as a teacher of French and Latin, then as a clerk at Lloyds Bank, until he was made an editor at the publishing firm of Faber and Faber — which also subsidized the *Criterion,* a little magazine Eliot edited, and in which he published much of his critical writing. Eliot's criticism has been attacked as dry and pedantic, but at the time it was highly influential. Theoretical pieces like "Tradition and the Individual Talent" (1917) were manifestos of literary Modernism. But Eliot may have been more important as a tastemaker than as a theorist: His essays on Jacobean playwrights such as Philip Massinger and Thomas Middleton helped put a vanished generation of English drama back on the stage, while those on the metaphysical poets heralded a revival of interest in such then-neglected names as John Donne and George Herbert and such virtually forgotten figures as Thomas Traherne and Lancelot Andrewes.

Most of Eliot's major poetry and criticism was written before the end of World War II, though it could be argued that his most pleasant days were spent after the war, as an honored elder statesman of letters. In 1948 he was awarded both the Nobel Prize for literature and the British Order of Merit. At the age of 69 he married his secretary, Valerie Fletcher, who shared his last happy years. He died in 1965 and was buried in East Coker, the Somerset village from which his ancestors had emigrated to America.

Eliot's literary theory does not appear in total in any single book. His most celebrated passages usually occur within an appreciation of an author or a text, and to put all of them together would require reprinting quite a number of different essays. His famous definition of an "objective correlative," so important for the development of the New Criticism, appears in an essay on *Hamlet:*

> The only way of expressing emotion in the form of art is by finding an "objective correlative"; in other words a set of objects, a situation, a chain of events which shall be the formula of that *particular* emotion; such that when the external facts, which must terminate in sensory experience, are given, the emotion is immediately evoked.[1]

His theory of the dissociation of sensibility comes in the course of an essay on the metaphysical poets:

> . . . Something . . . had happened to the mind of England between the time of Donne or Lord Herbert of Cherbury and the time of Tennyson and Browning; it is the difference between the intellectual poet and the reflective poet. Tennyson and Browning are poets, and they think; but they do not feel their thought as immediately as the odour of a rose. A thought to Donne was an experience; it modified his sensibility. When a poet's mind is perfectly equipped for its work, it is constantly amalgamating disparate experience; the ordinary man's experience is chaotic, irregular, fragmentary. The latter falls in love, or reads Spinoza, and these two experiences have nothing to do with each other, or with the noise of the typewriter or the smell of cooking; in the mind of the poet these experiences are always forming new wholes.[2]

In context, the first quotation is designed to explain what is special about *Hamlet* — it is a play that is problematic precisely because the external causes of feeling do not match the internal effects; the second is designed to explain the characteristic tone of seventeenth-century poetry to readers whose notions of the poetic have been corrupted, in Eliot's view, by the dissociation of sensibility that set in

[1]T. S. Eliot, "Hamlet" (1919), in *Elizabethan Essays* (New York: Haskell House, 1964), p. 61.
[2]T. S. Eliot, "The Metaphysical Poets" (1921), in *Selected Prose of T. S. Eliot,* ed. Frank Kermode (New York: Harcourt, Brace and Jovanovich; Farrar, Straus and Giroux, 1975), p. 65.

with Milton and Dryden. Both of these ideas, however, also have direct bearing on the poetics of the Modernism that Eliot practiced. The doctrine of the objective correlative would lead to the sort of imagism practiced by both Eliot and Pound in their earliest poems, while the Modernists, just as much as Donne, were interested in exploring a varied range of the sensibilities. In addition to the heart's feelings, Eliot went on, "one must look into the cerebral cortex, the nervous system, and the digestive tracts."

"Tradition and the Individual Talent" is much more openly a manifesto for Modernism. In a voice that vacillates between a leaderly "we" and a modest "I," Eliot is clearly calling for a new "programme" for the *métier* of poetry. If the essay is a relatively difficult one, it is because of the ambiguities at the heart of what Eliot means by his two central terms, "tradition," which the poet is asked to cultivate, and "personality," which the poet must sacrifice.

Many creative writers are wary of immersing themselves in the tradition of English and American poetry because they fear that their own voices are not strong enough for the encounter and are likely to be lost in the process. Eliot argues the opposite: that a poet cannot become himself, cannot understand his own place in time, his own modernness, without an understanding of the past. As a result, the historical sense is "indispensable to anyone who would continue to be a poet beyond his twenty-fifth year" — Keats's age when he died. It is easy to understand the value Eliot places on tradition and on the historical sense that allows the poet to contemplate the current significance of the past.

What seems a bit mystical, however, is Eliot's claim that there is an "ideal order" in literary tradition.

> The existing monuments form an ideal order among themselves, which is modified by the introduction of the new (the really new) work of art among them. The existing order is complete before the new work arrives; for order to persist after the supervention of novelty, the *whole* existing order must be, if ever so slightly, altered; and so the relations, proportions, values of each work of art toward the whole are readjusted; and this is conformity between the old and the new.

Since Eliot never makes clear what the basis of the "ideal order" is — how this order is *ordered* — it remains unclear how the order can be perfect and complete both before and after the introduction of a new work. Nor is it clear of what this order is composed. It is not merely an anthology of celebrated texts, the current canon, but Eliot does not discuss how far removed a work can be from current fashion and yet remain within the tradition or how far down into popular culture the tradition reaches.

The difficulty with the issue of personality is not fuzziness but the apparent contradictions with other Eliot criticism. In "Tradition" Eliot seems to be suggesting that art is, or at least ought to be, essentially impersonal: that the tradition writes itself, as it were, using the poet as a catalyst for converting emotion and thought into poetry. But in an essay on Philip Massinger in 1920, Eliot suggests that personality is necessary for high art: "Marlowe's and Jonson's comedies . . . were, as great literature is, the transformation of a personality into a personal work of art. . . . Massinger is not simply a smaller personality: his personality hardly exists. He did not, out of his own personality, build a world of art, as Shakespeare and Marlowe and Jonson built."[3]

A careful reading finds a paradox here, but no real self-contradiction. Eliot (like Proust in *Contre Sainte-Beuve*) repudiates the post-Romantic notion that the self an artist expresses is the habitual self one presents in society to intimates, friends, and acquaintances. He postulates another deeper self that is responsible for the artist's unique vision of reality, and that lends that vision authority and general truth. The former "personality" is what the artist escapes from into art; the latter is the source of that art. These two definitions of "personality," which incidentally correspond to the "you" and "I" in that schizoid lyric, "The Love Song of J. Alfred Prufrock," are what Eliot puns on throughout the last section of "Tradition and the Individual Talent."

Selected Bibliography

Allan, Mowbray, *T. S. Eliot's Impersonal Theory of Poetry.* Lewisburg, PA: Bucknell University Press, 1974.

Austin, Allen. *T. S. Eliot: The Literary and Social Criticism.* Bloomington: Indiana University Press, 1971.

Brombert, Victor. *The Criticism of T. S. Eliot.* New Haven: Yale University Press, 1949.

Freed, Lewis. *T. S. Eliot: Aesthetics and History.* La Salle, IL: Open Court, 1962.

Frye, Northrop. *T. S. Eliot.* New York: Grove Press, 1963.

Habib, M. A. R. *The Early T. S. Eliot and Western Philosophy.* Cambridge: Cambridge University Press, 1999.

Lee, Brian. *Theory and Personality: The Significance of T. S. Eliot's Criticism.* London: Athlone Press, 1979.

Lu, Fei-Pai. *T. S. Eliot: The Dialectical Structure of His Theory of Poetry.* Chicago: University of Chicago Press, 1966.

Lucy, Sean. *T. S. Eliot and the Idea of Tradition.* London: Cohen and West, 1960.

Matthiessen, F. O. *The Achievement of T. S. Eliot.* New York: Oxford University Press, 1947.

Menand, Louis. *Discovering Modernism: T. S. Eliot and His Context.* New York: Oxford University Press, 1987.

Spurr, David. *Conflicts in Consciousness: T. S. Eliot's Poetry and Criticism.* Urbana: University of Illinois Press, 1983.

[3]T. S. Eliot, "Philip Massinger" (1920), in *Elizabethan Essays*, p. 171.

Tradition and the Individual Talent

I

In English writing we seldom speak of tradition, though we occasionally apply its name in deploring its absence. We cannot refer to "the tradition" or to "a tradition"; at most, we employ the adjective in saying that the poetry of so-and-so is "traditional" or even "too traditional." Seldom, perhaps, does the word appear except in a phrase of censure. If otherwise, it is vaguely approbative, with the implication, as to the work approved, of some pleasing archaeological reconstruction. You can hardly make the word agreeable in English ears without this comfortable reference to the reassuring science of archaeology.

Certainly the word is not likely to appear in our appreciations of living or dead writers. Every nation, every race, has not only its own creative, but its own critical turn of mind; and is even more oblivious of the shortcomings and limitations of its critical habits than of those of its creative genius. We know, or think we know, from the enormous mass of critical writing that has appeared in the French language the critical method or habit of the French; we only conclude (we are such unconscious people) that the French are "more critical" than we, and sometimes even plume ourselves a little with the fact, as if the French were the less spontaneous. Perhaps they are; but we might remind ourselves that criticism is as inevitable as breathing, and that we should be none the worse for articulating what passes in our minds when we read a book and feel an emotion about it, for criticizing our own minds in their work of criticism. One of the facts that might come to light in this process is our tendency to insist, when we praise a poet, upon those aspects of his work in which he least resembles anyone else. In these aspects or parts of his work we pretend to find what is individual, what is the peculiar essence of the man. We dwell with satisfaction upon the poet's difference from his predecessors, especially his immediate predecessors; we endeavor to find something that can be isolated in order to be enjoyed. Whereas if we approach a poet without this prejudice we shall often find not only the best, but the most individual parts of his work may be those in which the dead poets, his ancestors, assert their immortality most vigorously. And I do not mean the impressionable period of adolescence, but the period of full maturity.

Yet if the only form of tradition, of handing down, consisted in following the ways of the immediate generation before us in a blind or timid adherence to its successes, "tradition" should positively be discouraged. We have seen many such simple currents soon lost in the sand; and novelty is better than repetition. Tradition is a matter of much wider significance. It cannot be inherited, and if you want it you must obtain it by great labor. It involves, in the first place, the historical sense, which we may call nearly indispensable to anyone who would continue to be a poet beyond his twenty-fifth year; and the historical sense involves a perception, not only of the pastness of the past, but of its presence; the historical sense compels a man to write not merely with his own generation in his bones, but with a feeling that the whole of the literature of Europe from Homer and within it the whole of the literature of his own country has a simultaneous existence and composes a simultaneous order. This historical sense, which is a sense of the timeless as well as of the temporal and of the timeless and of the temporal together, is what makes a writer traditional. And it is at the same time what makes a writer most acutely conscious of his place in time, of his own contemporaneity.

No poet, no artist of any art, has his complete meaning alone. His significance, his appreciation is the appreciation of his relation to the dead poets and artists. You cannot value him alone; you must set him, for contrast and comparison, among the dead. I mean this as a principle of aesthetic, not merely historical, criticism. The necessity that he shall conform, that he shall cohere, is not one-sided; what happens when a new work of art is created is something that happens simultaneously to all the works of art which preceded it. The existing monuments form an ideal order among themselves, which is modified by the introduction of the new (the really new) work of art among them. The existing order is complete before the new work arrives; for order to persist after the supervention of novelty, the whole existing order must be, if ever so slightly, altered; and so the relations, proportions, values of each work of art toward the whole are readjusted; and this is conformity between the old and the new. Whoever has approved this idea of order, of the form of European, of English literature will not find it preposterous that the past should be altered by the present as much as the present is directed by the past. And the poet who is aware of this will be aware of great difficulties and responsibilities.

In a peculiar sense he will be aware also that he must inevitably be judged by the standards of the past. I say judged, not amputated, by them; not judged to be as good as, or worse or better than, the dead; and certainly not judged by the canons of dead critics. It is a judgment, a comparison, in which two things are measured by each other. To conform merely would be for the new work not really to conform at all; it would not be new, and would therefore not be a work of art. And we do not quite say that the new is more valuable because it fits in; but its fitting in is a test of its value — a test, it is true, which can only be slowly and cautiously applied, for we are none of us infallible judges of conformity. We say: It appears to conform, and is perhaps individual, or it appears individual, and may conform; but we are hardly likely to find that it is one and not the other.

To proceed to a more intelligible exposition of the relation of the poet to the past: he can neither take the past as a lump, an indiscriminate bolus, nor can he form himself wholly on one or two private admirations, nor can he form himself wholly upon one preferred period. The first course is inadmissible, the second is an important experience of youth, and the third is a pleasant and highly desirable supplement. The poet must be very conscious of the main current, which does not at all flow invariably through the most distinguished reputations. He must be quite aware of the obvious fact that art never improves, but that the material of art is never quite the same. He must be aware that the mind of Europe — the mind of his own country — a mind which he learns in time to be much more important than his own private mind — is a mind which changes, and that this change is a development which abandons nothing en route, which does not superannuate either Shakespeare, or Homer, or the rock drawing of the Magdalenian draftsmen.[1] That this development, refinement perhaps, complication certainly, is not, from the point of view of the artist, any improvement. Perhaps not even an improvement from the point of view of the psychologist or not to the extent which we imagine; perhaps only in the end based upon a complication in economics and machinery. But the difference between the present and the past is that the conscious present is an awareness of the past in a way and to an extent which the past's awareness of itself cannot show.

Someone said: "The dead writers are remote from us because we *know* so much more than they did." Precisely, and they are that which we know.

[1]The Cro-Magnon cave men.

I am alive to a usual objection to what is clearly part of my program for the métier of poetry. The objection is that the doctrine requires a ridiculous amount of erudition (pedantry), a claim which can be rejected by appeal to the lives of poets in any pantheon. It will even be affirmed that much learning deadens or perverts poetic sensibility. While, however, we persist in believing that a poet ought to know as much as will not encroach upon his necessary receptivity and necessary laziness, it is not desirable to confine knowledge to whatever can be put into a useful shape for examinations, drawing rooms, or the still more pretentious modes of publicity. Some can absorb knowledge, the more tardy must sweat for it. Shakespeare acquired more essential history from Plutarch than most men could from the whole British Museum. What is to be insisted upon is that the poet must develop or procure the consciousness of the past and that he should continue to develop this consciousness throughout his career.

What happens is a continual surrender of himself as he is at the moment to something which is more valuable. The progress of an artist is a continual self-sacrifice, a continual extinction of personality.

There remains to define this process of depersonalization and its relation to the sense of tradition. It is in this depersonalization that art may be said to approach the condition of science. I, therefore, invite you to consider, as a suggestive analogy, the action which takes place when a bit of finely filiated platinum is introduced into a chamber containing oxygen and sulfur dioxide.

II

Honest criticism and sensitive appreciation are directed not upon the poet but upon the poetry. If we attend to the confused cries of the newspaper critics and the susurrus of popular repetition that follows, we shall hear the names of poets in great numbers; if we seek not blue-book knowledge but the enjoyment of poetry, and ask for a poem, we shall seldom find it. I have tried to point out the importance of the relation of the poem to other poems by other authors, and suggested the conception of poetry as a living whole of all the poetry that has ever been written. The other aspect of this impersonal theory of poetry is the relation of the poem to its author. And I hinted, by an analogy, that the mind of the mature poet differs from that of the immature one not precisely in any valuation of "personality," not being necessarily more interesting, or having "more to say," but rather by being a more finely perfected medium in which special, or very varied, feelings are at liberty to enter into new combinations.

The analogy was that of the catalyst. When the two gases previously mentioned are mixed in the presence of a filament of platinum, they form sulfurous acid. This combination takes place only if the platinum is present; nevertheless the newly formed acid contains no trace of platinum, and the platinum itself is apparently unaffected; has remained inert, neutral, and unchanged. The mind of the poet is the shred of platinum. It may partly or exclusively operate upon the experience of the man himself; but, the more perfect the artist, the more completely separate in him will be the man who suffers and the mind which creates; the more perfectly will the mind digest and transmute the passions which are its material.

The experience, you will notice, the elements which enter the presence of the transforming catalyst, are of two kinds: emotions and feelings. The effect of a work of art upon the person who enjoys it is an experience different in kind from any experience not of art. It may be formed out of one emotion, or may be a combination of several; and various feelings, inhering for the writer in particular words or phrases or images, may be added to compose the final result. Or great poetry may be made without the direct use of any emotion whatever: composed out of feelings solely. Canto XV of the *Inferno* (Brunetto Latini) is a working up of the emotion evident in the situation; but the effect, though single as that of any work of art, is obtained by considerable complexity of detail. The last quatrain gives an image, a feeling attaching to an image, which "came," which did not develop simply out of what precedes, but which was probably in suspension in the poet's mind until the proper combination arrived for it to add itself to.[2] The poet's mind is in fact a receptacle for seizing and storing up numberless feelings, phrases, images, which remain there until all the particles which can unite to form a new compound are present together.

If you compare several representative passages of the greatest poetry you see how great is the variety of types of combination, and also how completely any semiethical criterion of "sublimity" misses the mark. For it is not the "greatness," the intensity, of the emotions, the components, but the intensity of the artistic process, the pressure, so to speak, under which the fusion takes place, that counts. The episode of Paolo and Francesca employs a definite emotion, but the intensity of the poetry is something quite different from whatever intensity in the supposed experience it may give the impression of. It is no more intense, furthermore, than Canto XXVI, the voyage of Ulysses, which has not the direct dependence upon an emotion. Great variety is possible in the process of transmutation of emotion: the murder of Agamemnon, or the agony of Othello, gives an artistic effect apparently closer to a possible original than the scenes from Dante. In the *Agamemnon,* the artistic emotion approximates to the emotion of an actual spectator; in *Othello* to the emotion of the protagonist himself. But the difference between art and the event is always absolute; the combination which is the murder of Agamemnon is probably as complex as that which is the voyage of Ulysses. In either case there has been a fusion of elements. The ode of Keats contains a number of feelings which have nothing particular to do with the nightingale, but which the nightingale, partly, perhaps, because of its attractive name, and partly because of its reputation, served to bring together.

The point of view which I am struggling to attack is perhaps related to the metaphysical theory of the substantial unity of the soul: for my meaning is, that the poet has, not a "personality" to express, but a particular medium, which is only a medium and not a personality, in which impressions and experiences combine in peculiar and unexpected ways. Impressions and experiences which are important for the man may take no place in the poetry, and those which become important in the poetry may play quite a negligible part in the man, the personality.

[2]"And seemed like one of those who over the flat / And open course in the fields beside Verona / Run for the green cloth; and he seemed, at that, / Not like a loser but like the winning runner." Dante, *Inferno* 15:121–24.

I will quote a passage which is unfamiliar enough to be regarded with fresh attention in the light — or darkness — of these observations:

> And now methinks I could e'en chide myself
> For doting on her beauty, though her death
> Shall be revenged after no common action.
> Does the silkworm expend her yellow labors
> For thee? For thee does she undo herself?
> Are lordships sold to maintain ladyships
> For the poor benefit of a bewildering minute?
> Why does yon fellow falsify highways,
> And put his life between the judge's lips,
> To refine such a thing — keeps horse and men
> To beat their valors for her? . . .[3]

In this passage (as is evident if it is taken in its context) there is a combination of positive and negative emotions: an intensely strong attraction toward beauty and an equally intense fascination by the ugliness which is contrasted with it and which destroys it. This balance of contrasted emotion is in the dramatic situation to which the speech is pertinent, but that situation alone is inadequate to it. This is, so to speak, the structural emotion, provided by the drama. But the whole effect, the dominant tone, is due to the fact that a number of floating feelings, having an affinity to this emotion by no means superficially evident, have combined with it to give us a new art emotion.

It is not in his personal emotions, the emotions provoked by particular events in his life, that the poet is in any way remarkable or interesting. His particular emotions may be simple, or crude, or flat. The emotion in his poetry will be a very complex thing, but not with the complexity of the emotions of people who have very complex or unusual emotions in life. One error, in fact, of eccentricity in poetry is to seek for new human emotions to express; and in this search for novelty in the wrong place it discovers the perverse. The business of the poet is not to find new emotions, but to use the ordinary ones and, in working them up into poetry, to express feelings which are not in actual emotions at all. And emotions which he has never experienced will serve his turn as well as those familiar to him. Consequently, we must believe that "emotion recollected in tranquility"[4] is an

inexact formula. For it is neither emotion, nor recollection, nor, without distortion of meaning, tranquility. It is a concentration, and a new thing resulting from the concentration, of a very great number of experiences which to the practical and active person would not seem to be experiences at all; it is a concentration which does not happen consciously or of deliberation. These experiences are not "recollected," and they finally unite in an atmosphere which is "tranquil" only in that it is a passive attending upon the event. Of course this is not quite the whole story. There is a great deal, in the writing of poetry, which must be conscious and deliberate. In fact, the bad poet is usually unconscious where he ought to be conscious, and conscious where he ought to be unconscious. Both errors tend to make him "personal." Poetry is not a turning loose of emotion, but an escape from emotion; it is not the expression of personality, but an escape from personality. But, of course, only those who have personality and emotions know what it means to want to escape from these things.

III

ὁ δὲ νοῦς ἴσως Θειότερον τὶ καὶ ἀπαθές ἔστιν.[5]

This essay proposes to halt at the frontier of metaphysics or mysticism, and confine itself to such practical conclusions as can be applied by the responsible person interested in poetry. To divert interest from the poet to the poetry is a laudable aim: for it would conduce to a juster estimation of actual poetry, good and bad. There are many people who appreciate the expression of sincere emotion in verse, and there is a smaller number of people who can appreciate technical excellence. But very few know when there is an expression of *significant* emotion, emotion which has its life in the poem and not in the history of the poet. The emotion of art is impersonal. And the poet cannot reach his impersonality without surrendering himself wholly to the work to be done. And he is not likely to know what is to be done unless he lives in what is not merely the present, but the present moment of the past; unless he is conscious, not of what is dead, but of what is already living.

---

[3]Cyril Tourneur, *The Revenger's Tragedy*, III.iv.
[4]Eliot is quoting Wordsworth's Preface to *Lyrical Ballads;* see p. 306.

[5]"The mind may be too divine and therefore unimpassioned." Heracleitus.

Carl Gustav Jung

1875–1961

Carl Gustav Jung, the founder of analytic psychology, was born in Switzerland. The son of a philologist and pastor, from a clan of many clergymen, Jung turned his back on the ministry to pursue philosophical and medical interests. He studied at Basel (1895–1900) and Zürich, where he earned his M.D. in 1902 after working under Eugen Bleuler at the Burghölzli Psychiatric Clinic.

In 1907 Jung met Freud and quickly became the intellectual "son" for whom Freud had long been looking. But in an Oedipal struggle that Freud doubtless appreciated, Jung rapidly and thoroughly shook off his master to declare an independent vision of the mind involving less the cure of symptomatic neurosis than the pursuit of a lifelong task: the achievement of individuation, including the harmonious wholeness of conscious and unconscious. The close collaboration ended in 1912, a year after Jung became president of the International Psycho-Analytical Association, and the year when he published the clearly un-Freudian *The Psychology of the Unconscious*. In 1933 Jung became professor of psychology at the Federal Polytechnical University in Zürich, and in 1943 professor of medical psychology at the University of Basel. Immensely prolific, Jung revised and reissued much of his work. His important books include *The Psychology of Dementia* (1906), *Psychological Types* (1921), and *Psychology and Alchemy* (1944). "On the Relation of Analytical Psychology to Poetry" was delivered to a German learned society as a lecture in 1922 and published later that year. "The Principal Archetypes" is from *Aion: Researches into the Phenomenology of the Self* (1951), a late work that tidily summarizes many of Jung's key ideas.

Jung took from Freud the notion of a structured unconscious mind, but beyond this the differences between them are profound. In Jung, the unconscious of Freud's writings is termed the "personal unconscious"; it is but a "thin layer" under the conscious mind, relatively accessible by tricks of free association and parapraxis, and therefore not of supreme significance. More important is the "collective unconscious," or racial memory, through which the spirit of the whole human species manifests itself. This deeper layer of the unconscious is not accessible through the techniques of analysis; we understand its existence through our profound response to universal symbols that appear both in dreams and in our waking lives.

Jung developed the idea of a racial memory through his study of anthropology and comparative mythology, sciences that were beginning to show interesting results by the first decade of the century. Studies like James Frazer's *The Golden Bough* (1890) had revealed striking similarities between the myths and rituals of primitive peoples around the globe, peoples who seemed to be too distant to have influenced each other directly. Jung's hypothesis was that direct influence was unnecessary, that the similar mythologies were merely differing manifestations of structures deep in the human unconscious.

These structures Jung termed *archetypes;* they manifest themselves not only in myth and in dreams but in the finished art of cultures like our own in the form of symbols. Jung distinguished very strictly between the archetype itself, as a purely psychic structure, and its images: the representations the archetype takes within the symbolic fantasies created by the individual, and which then reappear in various forms in art and literature. (Later thinkers strongly influenced by Jung, such as Northrop Frye (see p. 691) and Claude Lévi-Strauss (see p. 859), use the term "archetype" for what Jung would have called the "archetypal image.")

The archetypes and their symbols take the shape of various aspects of the Self. On the surface of the Self is the *Mask,* the face we show to the outside world. Beneath this is the *Shadow,* a demonic image of evil that represents the side of the Self that we reject. Beneath this is the *Anima,* the feminine side of the male Self, and the *Animus,* the correspondingly masculine side of the female Self. (The Animus, for males, becomes an image of the Father.) For men, the Anima, the Great Mother, is characteristically split in the shadow of the Shadow into the nurturing Mother, the tempting Whore, and the destroying Crone. Women, in turn, split the Animus into a Protector, a Lover, and a Destroying Angel. Finally there is the image of the *Spirit,* symbolized by a wise old man or woman. The four principal archetypes — Shadow, Anima, Animus, and Spirit — make up what Jung called the *Syzygy:* a quaternion composing a whole, the unified self of which people are in search. That very search for unity can take the archetypal form of the Quest, in which the Self journeys to encounter the various elements that make it up, thereby forming the relationships that constitute its individuality. The quest itself often culminates in another archetype, the Night-Sea-Journey, a voyage from life through death to a new rebirth.

In Jungian analysis, the patient recapitulates his life and looks for the ways in which symbols of the above-mentioned archetypes have been embodied within its texture. Similarly, Jungian criticism is generally involved with a search for the embodiment of these symbols within particular works of art. The pleasures of Jungian criticism often come in noting the parallels between one work and another; how, for example, Cora and Alice in *The Last of the Mohicans,* Rebecca and Rowena in *Ivanhoe,* Becky Sharp and Amelia Sedley in *Vanity Fair,* and Eustacia and Thomasin in *The Return of the Native* can all be read as variations on the Dark Lady and the White Lady — split versions of the Anima. On the other hand, since the archetypes can be found in all powerful literature, Jungian criticism can become a relatively monotonous and predictable approach, harping invariably on the same chord, finding the basic motifs of the Quest, the Shadow, and the Night-Sea-Journey in every text.

Selected Bibliography

Bodkin, Maud. *Archetypal Patterns in Poetry.* London: Oxford University Press, 1934.

Jung, Carl Gustav. *Complete Works.* 17 vols. Eds. Herbert Read, Michael Fordham, and Gerhard Adler. New York: Pantheon, 1953–.

Knapp, Bettina L. *Music, Archetype and the Writer: A Jungian View.* University College: Pennsylvania State University Press, 1988.

Rowland, Susan. *C. G. Jung and Literary Theory: The Challenge from Fiction.* Basingstoke, Eng. / New York: Macmillan–St. Martin's, 1999.

Sugg, Richard, ed. *Jungian Literary Criticism*. Evanston: Northwestern University Press, 1993.
Van Meurs, Jos. *Jungian Literary Criticism, 1920–1980: An Annotated Critical Bibliography of Works in English*. Metuchen, NJ: Scarecrow Press, 1988.
Walker, Steven F., and Robert A. Segal. *Jung and the Jungians on Myth: An Introduction*. London: Routledge, 2002.

On the Relation of Analytical Psychology to Poetry

In spite of its difficulty, the task of discussing the relation of analytical psychology to poetry affords me a welcome opportunity to define my views on the much debated question of the relations between psychology and art in general. Although the two things cannot be compared, the close connections which undoubtedly exist between them call for investigation. These connections arise from the fact that the practice of art is a psychological activity and, as such, can be approached from a psychological angle. Considered in this light, art, like any other human activity deriving from psychic motives, is a proper subject for psychology. This statement, however, involves a very definite limitation of the psychological viewpoint when we come to apply it in practice. Only that aspect of art which consists in the process of artistic creation can be a subject for psychological study, but not that which constitutes its essential nature. The question of what art is in itself can never be answered by the psychologist, but must be approached from the side of aesthetics.

A similar distinction must be made in the realm of religion. A psychological approach is permissible only in regard to the emotions and symbols which constitute the phenomenology of religion, but which do not touch upon its essential nature. If the essence of religion and art could be explained, then both of them would become mere subdivisions of psychology. This is not to say that such violations of their nature have not been

Translated by R. F. C. Hull.

attempted. But those who are guilty of them obviously forget that a similar fate might easily befall psychology, since its intrinsic value and specific quality would be destroyed if it were regarded as a mere activity of the brain, and were relegated along with the endocrine functions to a subdivision of physiology. This too, as we know, has been attempted.

Art by its very nature is not science, and science by its very nature is not art; both these spheres of the mind have something in reserve that is peculiar to them and can be explained only in its own terms. Hence when we speak of the relation of psychology to art, we shall treat only of that aspect of art which can be submitted to psychological scrutiny without violating its nature. Whatever the psychologist has to say about art will be confined to the process of artistic creation and has nothing to do with its innermost essence. He can no more explain this than the intellect can describe or even understand the nature of feeling. Indeed, art and science would not exist as separate entities at all if the fundamental difference between them had not long since forced itself on the mind. The fact that artistic, scientific, and religious propensities still slumber peacefully together in the small child, or that with primitives the beginnings of art, science, and religion coalesce in the undifferentiated chaos of the magical mentality, or that no trace of "mind" can be found in the natural instincts of animals — all this does nothing to prove the existence of a unifying principle which alone would justify a reduction of the one to the other. For if we go so far back into the history of the mind that the distinctions between its various fields of activity become altogether invisible, we do not reach an underlying principle of their unity, but merely an earlier, undifferentiated state in which no separate activities yet exist. But the elementary state is not an explanatory principle that would allow us to draw conclusions as to the nature of later, more highly developed states, even though they must necessarily derive from it. A scientific attitude will always tend to overlook the peculiar nature of these more differentiated states in favor of their causal derivation, and will endeavor to subordinate them to a general but more elementary principle.

These theoretical reflections seem to me very much in place today, when we so often find that works of art, and particularly poetry, are interpreted precisely in this manner, by reducing them to more elementary states. Though the material he works with and its individual treatment can easily be traced back to the poet's personal relations with his parents, this does not enable us to understand his poetry. The same reduction can be made in all sorts of other fields, and not least in the case of pathological disturbances. Neuroses and psychoses are likewise reducible to infantile relations with the parents, and so are a man's good and bad habits, his beliefs, peculiarities, passions, interests, and so forth. It can hardly be supposed that all these very different things must have exactly the same explanation, for otherwise we would be driven to the conclusion that they actually are the same thing. If a work of art is explained in the same way as a neurosis, then either the work of art is a neurosis or a neurosis is a work of art. This explanation is all very well as a play on words, but sound common sense rebels against putting a work of art on the same level as a neurosis. An analyst might, in an extreme case, view a neurosis as a work of art through the lens of his professional bias, but it would never occur to an intelligent layman to mistake a pathological phenomenon for art, in spite of the undeniable fact that a work of art arises from much the same psychological conditions as a neurosis. This is only natural, because certain of these conditions are present in every individual and, owing to the relative constancy of the human environment, are constantly the same, whether in the case of a nervous intellectual, a poet, or a normal human being. All have had parents, all have a father- or a mother-complex, all know about sex and therefore have certain common and typical human difficulties. One poet may be influenced more by his relation to his father, another by the tie to his mother, while a third shows unmistakable traces of sexual repression in his poetry. Since all this can be said equally well not only of every neurotic but of every normal human being, nothing specific is gained for the judgment of a work of art. At most our knowledge of its psychological antecedents will have been broadened and deepened.

The school of medical psychology inaugurated by Freud has undoubtedly encouraged the literary historian to bring certain peculiarities of a work of art into relations with the intimate, personal life of the poet. But this is nothing new in principle, for it has long been known that the scientific treatment of art will reveal the personal threads that the artist, intentionally or unintentionally, has woven into his work. The Freudian approach may, however, make possible a more exhaustive demonstration of the influences that reach back into earliest childhood and play their part in artistic creation. To this extent the psychoanalysis of art differs in no essential from the subtle psychological nuances of a penetrating literary analysis. The difference is at most a question of degree, though we may occasionally be surprised by indiscreet references to things which a rather more delicate touch might have passed over if only for reasons of tact. This lack of delicacy seems to be a professional peculiarity of the medical psychologist, and the temptation to draw daring conclusions easily leads to flagrant abuses. A slight whiff of scandal often lends spice to a biography, but a little more becomes a nasty inquisitiveness — bad taste masquerading as science. Our interest is insidiously deflected from the work of art and gets lost in the labyrinth of psychic determinants, the poet becomes a clinical case and, very likely, yet another addition to the curiosa of *psychopathia sexualis*.[1] But this means

[1]Sexual psychopathology.

that the psychoanalysis of art has turned aside from its proper objective and strayed into a province that is as broad as mankind, that is not in the least specific to the artist and has even less relevance to his art.

This kind of analysis brings the work of art into the sphere of general human psychology, where many other things besides art have their origin. To explain art in these terms is just as great a platitude as the statement that "every artist is a narcissist." Every man who pursues his own goal is a "narcissist" — though one wonders how permissible it is to give such wide currency to a term specifically coined for the pathology of neurosis. The statement therefore amounts to nothing; it merely elicits the faint surprise of a bon mot. Since this kind of analysis is in no way concerned with the work of art itself, but strives like a mole to bury itself in the dirt as speedily as possible, it always ends up in the common earth that unites all mankind. Hence its explanations have the same tedious monotony as the recitals which one daily hears in the consulting room.

The reductive method of Freud is a purely medical one, and the treatment is directed at a pathological or otherwise unsuitable formation which has taken the place of the normal functioning. It must therefore be broken down, and the way cleared for healthy adaptation. In this case, reduction to the common human foundation is altogether appropriate. But when applied to a work of art it leads to the results I have described. It strips the work of art of its shimmering robes and exposes the nakedness and drabness of *Homo sapiens,* to which species the poet and artist also belong. The golden gleam of artistic creation — the original object of discussion — is extinguished as soon as we apply to it the same corrosive method which we use in analyzing the fantasies of hysteria. The results are no doubt very interesting and may perhaps have the same kind of scientific value as, for instance, a post-mortem examination of the brain of Nietzsche, which might conceivably show us the particular atypical form of paralysis from which he died. But what would this have to do with *Zarathustra?* Whatever its subterranean background may have been, is it not a whole world in itself, beyond the human, all-too-human imperfections, beyond the world of migraine and cerebral atrophy?

I have spoken of Freud's reductive method but have not stated in what that method consists. It is essentially a medical technique for investigating morbid psychic phenomena, and it is solely concerned with the ways and means of getting round or peering through the foreground of consciousness in order to reach the psychic background, or the unconscious. It is based on the assumption that the neurotic patient represses certain psychic contents because they are morally incompatible with his conscious values. It follows that the repressed contents must have correspondingly negative traits — infantile-sexual, obscene, or even criminal — which make them unacceptable to consciousness. Since no man is perfect, everyone must possess such a background whether he admits it or not. Hence it can always be exposed if only one uses the technique of interpretation worked out by Freud.

In the short space of a lecture I cannot, of course, enter into the details of the technique. A few hints must suffice. The unconscious background does not remain inactive, but betrays itself by its characteristic effects on the contents of consciousness. For example, it produces fantasies of a peculiar nature, which can easily be interpreted as sexual images. Or it produces characteristic disturbances of the conscious processes, which again can be reduced to repressed contents. A very important source for knowledge of the unconscious contents is provided by dreams, since these are direct products of the activity of the unconscious. The essential thing in Freud's reductive method is to collect all the clues pointing to the unconscious background, and then, through the analysis and interpretation of this material, to reconstruct the elementary instinctual processes. Those conscious contents which give us a clue to the unconscious background are incorrectly called *symbols* by Freud. They are not true symbols, however, since according to his theory they have merely the role of *signs* or *symptoms* of the subliminal processes. The true symbol differs essentially from this, and should be understood as an expression of an intuitive idea that cannot yet be formulated in any other or better way. When Plato, for instance, puts the whole problem of the theory of knowledge in his parable of the cave,[2] or when Christ expresses the idea of the Kingdom of Heaven in parables, these are genuine and true symbols, that is, attempts to express something for which no verbal concept yet exists. If we were to interpret Plato's metaphor in Freudian terms we would naturally arrive at the uterus, and would have proved that even a mind like Plato's was still stuck on a primitive level of infantile sexuality. But we would have completely overlooked what Plato actually created out of the primitive determinants of his philosophical ideas; we would have missed the essential point and merely discovered that he had infantile-sexual fantasies like any other mortal. Such a discovery could be of value only for a man who regarded Plato as superhuman, and who can now state with satisfaction that Plato too was an ordinary human being. But who would want to regard Plato as a god? Surely only one who is dominated by infantile fantasies and therefore possesses a neurotic mentality. For him the reduction to common human truths is salutary on medical grounds, but this would have nothing whatever to do with the meaning of Plato's parable.

I have purposely dwelt on the application of medical psychoanalysis to works of art because I want to emphasize that the psychoanalytic method is at the same time an essential part of the Freudian doctrine. Freud himself by his rigid dogmatism has ensured that the method and the doctrine — in themselves two very different things — are regarded by the public as identical. Yet the method may be employed with beneficial results in medical cases without at the same time exalting it into a doctrine. And against this doctrine we are bound to raise vigorous objections. The assumptions it rests on are quite arbitrary. For example, neuroses are by no means exclusively caused by sexual repression, and the same holds true for psychoses. There is no foundation for saying that dreams merely contain repressed wishes whose moral incompatibility requires them to be disguised by a hypothetical dream-censor. The Freudian technique of interpretation, so far as it remains under the influence of its own one-sided and therefore erroneous hypotheses, displays a quite obvious bias.

In order to do justice to a work of art, analytical psychology must rid itself entirely of medical prejudice; for a work of art is not a disease, and consequently requires a different approach from the medical one. A doctor naturally has to seek out the causes of a disease in order to pull it up by the roots, but just as naturally the psychologist must adopt exactly the opposite attitude towards a work of art. Instead of investigating its typically human determinants, he will inquire first of all into its meaning, and will concern himself with its determinants only insofar as they enable him to understand it more fully. Personal causes have as much or as little to do with a work of art as the soil with the plant that springs from it. We can certainly learn to understand some of the plant's peculiarities by getting to know its habitat, and for the botanist this is an important part of his equipment. But nobody will maintain that everything essential has then been discovered about the plant itself. The personal orientation which the doctor needs when confronted with the question of etiology in medicine is quite out of place in dealing with a work of art, just because a work of art is not a human being, but is something suprapersonal. It is a thing and not a personality; hence it cannot be judged by personal criteria. Indeed, the special significance of a true work of art resides in the fact that it has escaped from the limitations of the personal and has soared beyond the personal concerns of its creator.

I must confess from my own experience that it is not at all easy for a doctor to lay aside his professional bias when considering a work of art and look at it with a mind cleared of the current biological causality. But I have come to learn that although a psychology with a purely biological orientation can explain a good deal about man in general, it cannot be applied to a work of art and still less to man as creator. A purely causalistic psychology is only able to reduce every human individual to a member of the species *Homo sapiens,* since its range is limited to what is transmitted by

[2]In Plato, *Republic,* Book VII.

heredity or derived from other sources. But a work of art is not transmitted or derived — it is a creative reorganization of those very conditions to which a causalistic psychology must always reduce it. The plant is not a mere product of the soil; it is a living, self-contained process which in essence has nothing to do with the character of the soil. In the same way, the meaning and individual quality of a work of art inhere within it and not in its extrinsic determinants. One might almost describe it as a living being that uses man only as a nutrient medium, employing his capacities according to its own laws and shaping itself to the fulfillment of its own creative purpose.

But here I am anticipating somewhat, for I have in mind a particular type of art which I still have to introduce. Not every work of art originates in the way I have just described. There are literary works, prose as well as poetry, that spring wholly from the author's intention to produce a particular result. He submits his material to a definite treatment with a definite aim in view; he adds to it and subtracts from it, emphasizing one effect, toning down another, laying on a touch of color here, another there, all the time carefully considering the overall result and paying strict attention to the laws of form and style. He exercises the keenest judgment and chooses his words with complete freedom. His material is entirely subordinated to his artistic purpose; he wants to express this and nothing else. He is wholly at one with the creative process, no matter whether he has deliberately made himself its spearhead, as it were, or whether it has made him its instrument so completely that he has lost all consciousness of this fact. In either case, the artist is so identified with his work that his intentions and his faculties are indistinguishable from the act of creation itself. There is no need, I think, to give examples of this from the history of literature or from the testimony of the artists themselves.

Nor need I cite examples of the other class of works which flow more or less complete and perfect from the author's pen. They come as it were fully arrayed into the world, as Pallas Athene sprang from the head of Zeus. These works positively force themselves upon the author; his hand is seized, his pen writes things that his mind contemplates with amazement. The work brings with it its own form; anything he wants to add is rejected, and what he himself would like to reject is thrust back at him. While his conscious mind stands amazed and empty before this phenomenon, he is overwhelmed by a flood of thoughts and images which he never intended to create and which his own will could never have brought into being. Yet in spite of himself he is forced to admit that it is his own self speaking, his own inner nature revealing itself and uttering things which he would never have entrusted to his tongue. He can only obey the apparently alien impulse within him and follow where it leads, sensing that his work is greater than himself, and wields a power which is not his and which he cannot command. Here the artist is not identical with the process of creation; he is aware that he is subordinate to his work or stands outside it, as though he were a second person; or as though a person other than himself had fallen within the magic circle of an alien will.

So when we discuss the psychology of art, we must bear in mind these two entirely different modes of creation, for much that is of the greatest importance in judging a work of art depends on this distinction. It is one that had been sensed earlier by Schiller, who as we know attempted to classify it in his concept of the *sentimental* and the *naive*.[3] The psychologist would call "sentimental" art *introverted* and the "naive" kind *extraverted*. The introverted attitude is characterized by the subject's assertion of his conscious intentions and aims against the demands of the object, whereas the extraverted attitude is characterized by the subject's subordination to the demands which the object makes upon him. In my view, Schiller's plays and most of his poems give one a good idea of the introverted attitude: the material is mastered by the conscious intentions of the poet. The extraverted attitude is illustrated by the second part of *Faust:* here the material is distinguished by its refractoriness. A still more striking example is Nietzsche's *Zarathustra*, where the author himself observed how "one became two."

From what I have said, it will be apparent that a shift of psychological standpoint has taken

[3]See Schiller, *On Naive and Sentimental Poetry*, p. 300.

place as soon as one speaks not of the poet as a person but of the creative process that moves him. When the focus of interest shifts to the latter, the poet comes into the picture only as a reacting subject. This is immediately evident in our second category of works, where the consciousness of the poet is not identical with the creative process. But in works of the first category the opposite appears to hold true. Here the poet appears to be the creative process itself, and to create of his own free will without the slightest feeling of compulsion. He may even be fully convinced of his freedom of action and refuse to admit that his work could be anything else than the expression of his will and ability.

Here we are faced with a question which we cannot answer from the testimony of the poets themselves. It is really a scientific problem that psychology alone can solve. As I hinted earlier, it might well be that the poet, while apparently creating out of himself and producing what he consciously intends, is nevertheless so carried away by the creative impulse that he is no longer aware of an "alien" will, just as the other type of poet is no longer aware of his own will speaking to him in the apparently "alien" inspiration, although this is manifestly the voice of his own self. The poet's conviction that he is creating in absolute freedom would then be an illusion: he fancies he is swimming, but in reality an unseen current sweeps him along.

This is not by any means an academic question, but is supported by the evidence of analytical psychology. Researchers have shown that there are all sorts of ways in which the conscious mind is not only influenced by the unconscious but actually guided by it. Yet is there any evidence for the supposition that a poet, despite his self-awareness, may be taken captive by his work? The proof may be of two kinds, direct or indirect. Direct proof would be afforded by a poet who thinks he knows what he is saying but actually says more than he is aware of. Such cases are not uncommon. Indirect proof would be found in cases where behind the apparent free will of the poet there stands a higher imperative that renews its peremptory demands as soon as the poet voluntarily gives up his creative activity, or that produces psychic complications whenever his work has to be broken off against his will.

Analysis of artists consistently shows not only the strength of the creative impulse arising from the unconscious, but also its capricious and willful character. The biographies of great artists make it abundantly clear that the creative urge is often so imperious that it battens on their humanity and yokes everything to the service of the work, even at the cost of health and ordinary human happiness. The unborn work in the psyche of the artist is a force of nature that achieves its end either with tyrannical might or with the subtle cunning of nature herself, quite regardless of the personal fate of the man who is its vehicle. The creative urge lives and grows in him like a tree in the earth from which it draws its nourishment. We would do well, therefore, to think of the creative process as a living thing implanted in the human psyche. In the language of analytical psychology this living thing is an *autonomous complex*. It is a split-off portion of the psyche, which leads a life of its own outside the hierarchy of consciousness. Depending on its energy charge, it may appear either as a mere disturbance of conscious activities or as a supraordinate authority which can harness the ego to its purpose. Accordingly, the poet who identifies with the creative process would be one who acquiesces from the start when the unconscious imperative begins to function. But the other poet, who feels the creative force as something alien, is one who for various reasons cannot acquiesce and is thus caught unawares.

It might be expected that this difference in its origins would be perceptible in a work of art. For in the one case it is a conscious product shaped and designed to have the effect intended. But in the other we are dealing with an event originating in unconscious nature; with something that achieves its aim without the assistance of human consciousness, and often defies it by willfully insisting on its own form and effect. We would therefore expect that works belonging to the first class would nowhere overstep the limits of comprehension, that their effect would be bounded by the author's intention and would not extend beyond it. But with works of the other class we would have to be prepared for something suprapersonal that transcends our understanding to the same degree that the author's consciousness was in abeyance during the process of creation. We would expect a strangeness of form and content, thoughts that can only be apprehended intuitively, a language pregnant with meanings, and images that are true symbols because they are the best possible expressions for something unknown — bridges thrown out towards an unseen shore.

These criteria are, by and large, corroborated in practice. Whenever we are confronted with a work that was consciously planned and with material that was consciously selected, we find that it agrees with the first class of qualities, and in the other case with the second. The example we gave of Schiller's plays, on the one hand, and *Faust II* on the other, or better still *Zarathustra*, is an illustration of this. But I would not undertake to place the work of an unknown poet in either of these categories without first having examined rather closely his personal relations with his work. It is not enough to know whether the poet belongs to the introverted or to the extraverted type, since it is possible for either type to work with an introverted attitude at one time, and an extraverted attitude at another. This is particularly noticeable in the difference between Schiller's plays and his philosophical writings, between Goethe's perfectly formed poems and the obvious struggle with his material in *Faust II,* and between Nietzsche's well-turned aphorisms and the rushing torrent of *Zarathustra*. The same poet can adopt different attitudes to his work at different times, and on this depends the standard we have to apply.

The question, as we now see, is exceedingly complicated, and the complication grows even worse when we consider the case of the poet who identifies with the creative process. For should it turn out that the apparently conscious and purposeful manner of composition is a subjective illusion of the poet, then his work would possess symbolic qualities that are outside the range of his consciousness. They would only be more difficult to detect, because the reader as well would be unable to get beyond the bounds of the poet's consciousness which are fixed by the spirit of the time. There is no Archimedean point outside his world by which he could lift his time-bound consciousness off its hinges and recognize the symbols hidden in the poet's work. For a symbol is the intimation of a meaning beyond the level of our present powers of comprehension.

I raise this question only because I do not want my typological classification to limit the possible significance of works of art which apparently mean no more than what they say. But we have often found that a poet who has gone out of fashion is suddenly rediscovered. This happens when our conscious development has reached a higher level from which the poet can tell us something new. It was always present in his work but was hidden in a symbol, and only a renewal of the spirit of the time permits us to read its meaning. It needed to be looked at with fresher eyes, for the old ones see in it only what they were accustomed to see. Experiences of this kind should make us cautious, as they bear out my earlier argument. But works that are openly symbolic do not require this subtle approach; their pregnant language cries out at us that they mean more than they say. We can put our finger on the symbol at once, even though we may not be able to unriddle its meaning to our entire satisfaction. A symbol remains a perpetual challenge to our thoughts and feelings. That probably explains why a symbolic work is so stimulating, why it grips us so intensely, but also why it seldom affords us a purely aesthetic enjoyment. A work that is manifestly not symbolic appeals much more to our aesthetic sensibility because it is complete in itself and fulfills its purpose.

What then, you may ask, can analytical psychology contribute to our fundamental problem, which is the mystery of artistic creation? All that we have said so far has to do only with the psychological phenomenology of art. Since nobody can penetrate to the heart of nature, you will not expect psychology to do the impossible and offer a valid explanation of the secret of creativity. Like every other science, psychology has only a modest contribution to make towards a deeper understanding of the phenomena of life, and is no nearer than its sister sciences to absolute knowledge.

We have talked so much about the meaning of works of art that one can hardly suppress a doubt as to whether art really "means" anything at all. Perhaps art has no "meaning," at least not as we understand meaning. Perhaps it is like nature, which simply *is* and "means" nothing beyond that. Is "meaning" necessarily more than mere interpretation — an interpretation secreted into something by an intellect hungry for meaning? Art, it has been said, is beauty, and "a thing of beauty is a joy forever."[4] It needs no meaning, for meaning has nothing to do with art. Within the sphere of art, I must accept the truth of this statement. But when I speak of the relation of psychology to art we are outside its sphere, and it is impossible for us not to speculate. We must interpret, we must find meanings in things, otherwise we would be quite unable to think about them. We have to break down life and events, which are self-contained processes, into meanings, images, concepts, well knowing that in doing so we are getting further away from the living mystery. As long as we ourselves are caught up in the process of creation, we neither see nor understand; indeed we ought not to understand, for nothing is more injurious to immediate experience than cognition. But for the purpose of cognitive understanding we must detach ourselves from the creative process and look at it from the outside; only then does it become an image that expresses what we are bound to call "meaning." What was a mere phenomenon before becomes something that in association with other phenomena has meaning, that has a definite role to play, serves certain ends, and exerts meaningful effects. And when we have seen all this we get the feeling of having understood and explained something. In this way we meet the demands of science.

When, a little earlier, we spoke of a work of art as a tree growing out of the nourishing soil, we might equally well have compared it to a child growing in the womb. But as all comparisons are lame, let us stick to the more precise terminology of science. You will remember that I described the nascent work in the psyche of the artists as an autonomous complex. By this we mean a psychic formation that remains subliminal until its energy-charge is sufficient to carry it over the threshold into consciousness. Its association with consciousness does not mean that it is assimilated, only that it is perceived; but it is not subject to conscious control, and can be neither inhibited nor voluntarily reproduced. Therein lies the autonomy of the complex: it appears and disappears in accordance with its own inherent tendencies, independently of the conscious will. The creative complex shares this peculiarity with every other autonomous complex. In this respect it offers an analogy with pathological processes, since these too are characterized by the presence of autonomous complexes, particularly in the case of mental disturbances. The divine frenzy of the artist comes perilously close to a pathological state, though the two things are not identical. The *tertium comparationis*[5] is the autonomous complex. But the presence of autonomous complexes is not in itself pathological, since normal people, too, fall temporarily or permanently under their domination. This fact is simply one of the normal peculiarities of the psyche, and for a man to be unaware of the existence of an autonomous complex merely betrays a high degree of unconsciousness. Every typical attitude that is to some extent differentiated shows a tendency to become an autonomous complex, and in most cases it actually does. Again, every instinct has more or less the character of an autonomous complex. In itself, therefore, an autonomous complex has nothing morbid about it; only when its manifestations are frequent and disturbing is it a symptom of illness.

How does an autonomous complex arise? For reasons which we cannot go into here, a hitherto unconscious portion of the psyche is thrown into activity, and gains ground by activating the adjacent areas of association. The energy needed for this is naturally drawn from consciousness — unless the latter happens to identify with the complex. But where this does not occur, the drain of energy produces what Janet calls an *abaissement du niveau mental*.[6] The intensity of conscious interests and activities gradually diminishes, leading either to apathy — a condition very common with artists — or to a regressive development of the conscious functions, that is, they revert to an infantile and archaic level and undergo something like a degeneration. The "inferior parts of the functions," as Janet calls them, push to the fore; the instinctual side of the personality prevails over the ethical, the infantile over the mature, and the

[4]Keats, "Endymion," I.

[5]Third element; the "middle term" or common factor between two disparate things.
[6]Lowering of mental level.

unadapted over the adapted. This too is something we see in the lives of many artists. The autonomous complex thus develops by using the energy that has been withdrawn from the conscious control of the personality.

But in what does an autonomous *creative* complex consist? Of this we can know next to nothing so long as the artist's work affords us no insight into its foundations. The work presents us with a finished picture, and this picture is amenable to analysis only to the extent that we can recognize it as a symbol. But if we are unable to discover any symbolic value in it, we have merely established that, so far as we are concerned, it means no more than what it says, or to put it another way, that it *is* no more than what it *seems* to be. I used the word *seems* because our own bias may prevent a deeper appreciation of it. At any rate we can find no incentive and no starting point for an analysis. But in the case of a symbolic work we should remember the dictum of Gerhard Hauptmann: "Poetry evokes out of words the resonance of the primordial word." The question we should ask, therefore, is: what primordial image lies behind the imagery of art?

This question needs a little elucidation. I am assuming that the work of art we propose to analyze, as well as being symbolic, has its source not in the *personal unconscious* of the poet, but in a sphere of unconscious mythology whose primordial images are the common heritage of mankind. I have called this sphere the *collective unconscious,* to distinguish it from the personal unconscious. The latter I regard as the sum total of all those psychic processes and contents which are capable of becoming conscious and often do, but are then suppressed because of their incompatibility and kept subliminal. Art receives tributaries from this sphere too, but muddy ones; and their predominance, far from making a work of art a symbol, merely turns it into a symptom. We can leave this kind of art without injury and without regret to the purgative methods employed by Freud.

In contrast to the personal unconscious, which is a relatively thin layer immediately below the threshold of consciousness, the collective unconscious shows no tendency to become conscious under normal conditions, nor can it be brought back to recollection by an analytical technique, since it was never repressed or forgotten. The collective unconscious is not to be thought of as a self-subsistent entity; it is no more than a potentiality handed down to us from primordial times in the specific form of mnemonic images or inherited in the anatomical structure of the brain. There are no inborn ideas, but there are inborn possibilities of ideas that set bounds to even the boldest fantasy and keep our fantasy activity within certain categories: *a priori* ideas, as it were, the existence of which cannot be ascertained except from their effects. They appear only in the shaped material of art as the regulative principles that shape it; that is to say, only by inferences drawn from the finished work can we reconstruct the age-old original of the primordial image.

The primordial image, or archetype, is a figure — be it a demon, a human being, or a process — that constantly recurs in the course of history and appears wherever creative fantasy is freely expressed. Essentially, therefore, it is a mythological figure. When we examine these images more closely, we find that they give form to countless typical experiences of our ancestors. They are, so to speak, the psychic residua of innumerable experiences of the same type. They present a picture of psychic life in the average, divided up and projected into the manifold figures of the mythological pantheon. But the mythological figures are themselves products of creative fantasy and still have to be translated into conceptual language. Only the beginnings of such a language exist, but once the necessary concepts are created they could give us an abstract, scientific understanding of the unconscious processes that lie at the roots of the primordial images. In each of these images there is a little piece of human psychology and human fate, a remnant of the joys and sorrows that have been repeated countless times in our ancestral history, and on the average follow ever the same course. It is like a deeply graven river-bed in the psyche, in which waters of life, instead of flowing along as before in a broad but shallow stream, suddenly swell into a mighty river. This happens whenever that particular set of circumstances is encountered which over long periods of time has helped to lay down the primordial image.

The moment when this mythological situation reappears is always characterized by a peculiar emotional intensity; it is as though chords in us were struck that had never resounded before, or as though forces whose existence we never suspected were unloosed. What makes the struggle for adaptation so laborious is the fact that we have constantly to be dealing with individual and atypical situations. So it is not surprising that when an archetypal situation occurs we suddenly feel an extraordinary sense of release, as though transported, or caught up by an overwhelming power. At such moments we are no longer individuals, but the race; the voice of all mankind resounds in us. The individual man cannot use his powers to the full unless he is aided by one of those collective representations we call ideals, which releases all the hidden forces of instinct that are inaccessible to his conscious will. The most effective ideals are always fairly obvious variants of an archetype, as is evident from the fact that they lend themselves to allegory. The ideal of the "mother country," for instance, is an obvious allegory of the mother, as is the "fatherland" of the father. Its power to stir us does not derive from the allegory, but from the symbolical value of our native land. The archetype here is the *participation mystique* of primitive man with the soil on which he dwells, and which contains the spirits of his ancestors.

The impact of an archetype, whether it takes the form of immediate experience or is expressed through the spoken word, stirs us because it summons up a voice that is stronger than our own. Whoever speaks in primordial images speaks with a thousand voices; he enthralls and overpowers, while at the same time he lifts the idea he is seeking to express out of the occasional and the transitory into the realm of the ever-enduring. He transmutes our personal destiny into the destiny of mankind, and evokes in us all those beneficent forces that ever and anon have enabled humanity to find a refuge from every peril and to outlive the longest night.

That is the secret of great art, and of its effect upon us. The creative process, so far as we are able to follow it at all, consists in the unconscious activation of an archetypal image, and in elaborating and shaping this image into the finished work. By giving it shape, the artist translates it into the language of the present, and so makes it possible for us to find our way back to the deepest springs of life. Therein lies the social significance of art: it is constantly at work educating the spirit of the age, conjuring up the forms in which the age is most lacking. The unsatisfied yearning of the artist reaches back to the primordial image in the unconscious which is best fitted to compensate the inadequacy and one-sidedness of the present. The artist seizes on this image, and in raising it from deepest unconsciousness he brings it into relation with conscious values, thereby transforming it until it can be accepted by the minds of his contemporaries according to their powers.

People and times, like individuals, have their own characteristic tendencies and attitudes. The very word *attitude* betrays the necessary bias that every marked tendency entails. Direction implies exclusion, and exclusion means that very many psychic elements that could play their part in life are denied the right to exist because they are incompatible with the general attitude. The normal man can follow the general trend without injury to himself; but the man who takes to the back streets and alleys because he cannot endure the broad highway will be the first to discover the psychic elements that are waiting to play their part in the life of the collective. Here the artist's relative lack of adaptation turns out to his advantage; it enables him to follow his own yearnings far from the beaten path, and to discover what it is that would meet the unconscious needs of his age. Thus, just as the onesidedness of the individual's conscious attitude is corrected by reactions from the unconscious, so art represents a process of self-regulation in the life of nations and epochs.

I am aware that in this lecture I have only been able to sketch out my views in the barest outline. But I hope that what I have been obliged to omit, that is to say their practical application to poetic works of art, has been furnished by your own thoughts, thus giving flesh and blood to my abstract intellectual frame.

The Principal Archetypes

THE EGO

Investigation of the psychology of the unconscious confronted me with facts which required the formulation of new concepts. One of these concepts is the *self.* The entity so denoted is not meant to take the place of the one that has always been known as the *ego,* but includes it in a supraordinate concept. We understand the ego as the complex factor to which all conscious contents are related. It forms, as it were, the center of the field of consciousness; and, insofar as this comprises the empirical personality, the ego is the subject of all personal acts of consciousness. The relation of a psychic content to the ego forms the criterion of its consciousness, for no content can be conscious unless it is represented to a subject.

With this definition we have described and delimited the *scope* of the subject. Theoretically, no limits can be set to the field of consciousness, since it is capable of indefinite extension. Empirically, however, it always finds its limit when it comes up against the *unknown.* This consists of everything we do not know, which, therefore, is not related to the ego as the center of the field of consciousness. The unknown falls into two groups of objects: those which are outside and can be experienced by the senses, and those which are inside and are experienced immediately. The first group comprises the unknown in the outer world; the second the unknown in the inner world. We call this latter territory the *unconscious.*

The ego, as a specific content of consciousness, is not a simple or elementary factor but a complex one which, as such, cannot be described exhaustively. Experience shows that it rests on two seemingly different bases: the *somatic* and the *psychic.* The somatic basis is inferred from the totality of endosomatic perceptions, which for their part are already of a psychic nature and are associated with the ego, and are therefore conscious. They are produced by endosomatic stimuli, only some of which cross the threshold of consciousness. A considerable proportion of these stimuli occur unconsciously, that is, subliminally. The fact that they are subliminal does not necessarily mean that their status is merely physiological, any more than this would be true of a psychic content. Sometimes they are capable of crossing the threshold, that is, of becoming perceptions. But there is no doubt that a large proportion of these endosomatic stimuli are simply incapable of consciousness and are so elementary that there is no reason to assign them a psychic nature — unless of course one favors the philosophical view that all life-processes are psychic anyway. The chief objection to this hardly demonstrable hypothesis is that it enlarges the concept of the psyche beyond all bounds and interprets the life-process in a way not absolutely warranted by the facts. Concepts that are too broad usually prove to be unsuitable instruments because they are too vague and nebulous. I have therefore suggested that the term "psychic" be used only where there is evidence of a will capable of modifying reflex or instinctual processes. Here I must refer the reader to my paper "On the Nature of the Psyche," where I have discussed this definition of the "psychic" at somewhat greater length.

The somatic basis of the ego consists, then, of conscious and unconscious factors. The same is true of the psychic basis: on the one hand the ego rests on the *total field of consciousness,* and on the other, on the *sum total of unconscious contents.* These fall into three groups: first, temporarily subliminal contents that can be reproduced voluntarily (memory); second, unconscious contents that cannot be reproduced voluntarily; third, contents that are not capable of becoming conscious at all. Group two can be inferred from the spontaneous irruption of subliminal contents into consciousness. Group three is hypothetical; it is a logical inference from the facts underlying group two. It contains contents which have *not yet* irrupted into consciousness, or which never will.

When I said that the ego "rests" on the total field of consciousness I do not mean that it

Translated by R. F. C. Hull.

consists of this. Were that so, it would be indistinguishable from the field of consciousness as a whole. The ego is only the latter's point of reference, grounded on and limited by the somatic factor described above.

Although its bases are in themselves relatively unknown and unconscious, the ego is a conscious factor par excellence. It is even acquired, empirically speaking, during the individual's lifetime. It seems to arise in the first place from the collision between the somatic factor and the environment, and, once established as a subject, it goes on developing from further collisions with the outer world and the inner.

Despite the unlimited extent of its bases, the ego is never more and never less than consciousness as a whole. As a conscious factor the ego could, theoretically at least, be described completely. But this would never amount to more than a picture of the *conscious personality;* all those features which are unknown or unconscious to the subject would be missing. A total picture would have to include these. But a total description of the personality is, even in theory, absolutely impossible, because the unconscious portion of it cannot be grasped cognitively. This unconscious portion, as experience has abundantly shown, is by no means unimportant. On the contrary, the most decisive qualities in a person are often unconscious and can be perceived only by others, or have to be laboriously discovered with outside help.

Clearly, then, the *personality as a total phenomenon* does not coincide with the ego, that is, with the conscious personality, but forms an entity that has to be distinguished from the ego. Naturally the need to do this is incumbent only on a psychology that reckons with the fact of the unconscious, but for such a psychology the distinction is of paramount importance. Even for jurisprudence it should be of some importance whether certain psychic facts are conscious or not — for instance, in adjudging the question of responsibility.

I have suggested calling the total personality which, though present, cannot be fully known, the *self.* The ego is, by definition, subordinate to the self and is related to it like a part to the whole. Inside the field of consciousness it has, as we say,

free will. By this I do not mean anything philosophical, only the well-known psychological fact of "free choice," or rather the subjective feeling of freedom. But, just as our free will clashes with necessity in the outside world, so also it finds its limits outside the field of consciousness in the subjective inner world, where it comes into conflict with the facts of the self. And just as circumstances or outside events "happen" to us and limit our freedom, so the self acts upon the ego like an *objective occurrence* which free will can do very little to alter. It is, indeed, well known that the ego not only can do nothing against the self, but is sometimes actually assimilated by unconscious components of the personality that are in the process of development and is greatly altered by them.

It is, in the nature of the case, impossible to give any general description of the ego except a formal one. Any other mode of observation would have to take account of the *individuality* which attaches to the ego as one of its main characteristics. Although the numerous elements composing this complex factor are, in themselves, everywhere the same, they are infinitely varied as regards clarity, emotional coloring, and scope. The result of their combination — the ego — is therefore, so far as one can judge, individual and unique, and retains its identity up to a certain point. Its stability is relative, because far-reaching changes of personality can sometimes occur. Alterations of this kind need not always be pathological; they can also be developmental and hence fall within the scope of the normal.

Since it is the point of reference for the field of consciousness, the ego is the subject of all successful attempts at adaptation so far as these are achieved by the will. The ego therefore has a significant part to play in the psychic economy. Its position there is so important that there are good grounds for the prejudice that the ego is the center of the personality, and that the field of consciousness is the psyche *per se.* If we discount certain suggestive ideas in Leibniz, Kant, Schelling, and Schopenhauer, and the philosophical excursions of Carus and von Hartmann, it is only since the end of the nineteenth century that modern psychology, with its inductive methods, has discovered the foundations of consciousness and proved empirically the existence of a psyche outside consciousness. With this discovery the position of the ego, till then absolute, became relativized; that is to say, though it retains its quality as the center of the field of consciousness, it is questionable whether it is the center of the personality. It is part of the personality but not the whole of it. As I have said, it is simply impossible to estimate how large or how small its share is; how free or how dependent it is on the qualities of this "extra-conscious" psyche. We can only say that its freedom is limited and its dependence proved in ways that are often decisive. In my experience one would do well not to underestimate its dependence on the unconscious. Naturally there is no need to say this to persons who already overestimate the latter's importance. Some criterion for the right measure is afforded by the psychic consequences of a wrong estimate, a point to which we shall return later on.

We have seen that, from the standpoint of the psychology of consciousness, the unconscious can be divided into three groups of contents. But from the standpoint of the psychology of the personality a twofold division ensues: an "extra-conscious" psyche whose contents are *personal,* and an "extra-conscious" psyche whose contents are *impersonal* and *collective.* The first group comprises contents which are integral components of the individual personality and could therefore just as well be conscious; the second group forms, as it were, an omnipresent, unchanging, and everywhere identical *quality or substrate of the psyche per se.* This is, of course, no more than a hypothesis. But we are driven to it by the peculiar nature of the empirical material, not to mention the high probability that the general similarity of psychic processes in all individuals must be based on an equally general and impersonal principle that conforms to law, just as the instinct manifesting itself in the individual is only the partial manifestation of an instinctual substrate common to all men.

THE SHADOW

Whereas the contents of the personal unconscious are acquired during the individual's lifetime, the contents of the collective unconscious are invariably archetypes that were present from the beginning. Their relation to the instincts has been discussed elsewhere.[1] The archetypes most clearly characterized from the empirical point of view are those which have the most frequent and the most disturbing influence on the ego. These are the *shadow,* the *anima,* and the *animus.*[2] The most accessible of these, and the easiest to experience, is the shadow, for its nature can in large measure be inferred from the contents of the personal unconscious. The only exceptions to this rule are those rather rare cases where the positive qualities of the personality are repressed, and the ego in consequence plays an essentially negative or unfavorable role.

The shadow is a moral problem that challenges the whole ego-personality, for no one can become conscious of the shadow without considerable moral effort. To become conscious of it involves recognizing the dark aspects of the personality as present and real. This act is the essential condition for any kind of self-knowledge, and it therefore, as a rule, meets with considerable resistance. Indeed, self-knowledge as a psychotherapeutic measure frequently requires much painstaking work extending over a long period.

Closer examination of the dark characteristics — that is, the inferiorities constituting the shadow — reveals that they have an *emotional* nature, a kind of autonomy, and accordingly an obsessive or, better, possessive quality. Emotion, incidentally, is not an activity of the individual but something that happens to him. Affects occur usually where adaptation is weakest, and at the same time they reveal the reason for its weakness, namely a certain degree of inferiority and the existence of a lower level of personality. On this lower level with its uncontrolled or scarcely controlled emotions one behaves more or less like a primitive, who is not only the passive victim of his affects but also singularly incapable of moral judgment.

---

[1] "Instinct and the Unconscious" and "On the Nature of the Psyche," pars. 397ff. [Jung]

[2] The contents of this and the following chapter are taken from a lecture delivered to the Swiss Society for Practical Psychology, in Zurich, 1948. The material was first published in the *Wiener Zeitschrift für Nervenheilkunde und deren Genzgebiete* I (1948): 4. [Jung]

Although, with insight and good will, the shadow can to some extent be assimilated into the conscious personality, experience shows that there are certain features which offer the most obstinate resistance to moral control and prove almost impossible to influence. These resistances are usually bound up with *projections,* which are not recognized as such, and their recognition is a moral achievement beyond the ordinary. While some traits peculiar to the shadow can be recognized without too much difficulty as one's own personal qualities, in this case both insight and good will are unavailing because the cause of the emotion appears to lie, beyond all possibility of doubt, in the *other person.* No matter how obvious it may be to the neutral observer that it is a matter of projections, there is little hope that the subject will perceive this himself. He must be convinced that he throws a very long shadow before he is willing to withdraw his emotionally-toned projections from their object.

Let us suppose that a certain individual shows no inclination whatever to recognize his projections. The projection-making factor then has a free hand and can realize its object — if it has one — or bring about some other situation characteristic of its power. As we know, it is not the conscious subject but the unconscious which does the projecting. Hence one meets with projections, one does not make them. The effect of projection is to isolate the subject from his environment, since instead of a real relation to it there is now only an illusory one. Projections change the world into the replica of one's own unknown face. In the last analysis, therefore, they lead to an autoerotic or autistic condition in which one dreams a world whose reality remains forever unattainable. The resultant *sentiment d'incomplétude*[3] and the still worse feeling of sterility are in their turn explained by projection as the malevolence of the environment, and by means of this vicious circle the isolation is intensified. The more projections are thrust in between the subject and the environment, the harder it is for the ego to see through its illusions. A forty-five-year-old patient who had suffered from a compulsion neurosis since he was

twenty and had become completely cut off from the world once said to me: "But I can never admit to myself that I've wasted the best twenty-five years of my life!"

It is often tragic to see how blatantly a man bungles his own life and the lives of others yet remains totally incapable of seeing how much the whole tragedy originates in himself, and how he continually feeds it and keeps it going. Not *consciously,* of course — for consciously he is engaged in bewailing and cursing a faithless world that recedes further and further into the distance. Rather, it is an unconscious factor which spins the illusions that veil his world. And what is being spun is a cocoon, which in the end will completely envelop him.

One might assume that projections like these, which are so very difficult if not impossible to dissolve, would belong to the realm of the shadow — that is, to the negative side of the personality. This assumption becomes untenable after a certain point, because the symbols that then appear no longer refer to the same but to the opposite sex, in a man's case to a woman and vice versa. The source of projections is no longer the shadow — which is always of the same sex as the subject — but a contrasexual figure. Here we meet the animus of a woman and the anima of a man, two corresponding archetypes whose autonomy and unconsciousness explain the stubbornness of their projections. Though the shadow is a motif as well known to mythology as anima and animus, it represents first and foremost the personal unconscious, and its content can therefore be made conscious without too much difficulty. In this it differs from anima and animus, for whereas the shadow can be seen through and recognized fairly easily, the anima and animus are much further away from consciousness and in normal circumstances are seldom if ever realized. With a little self-criticism one can see through the shadow — so far as its nature is personal. But when it appears as an archetype, one encounters the same difficulties as with anima and animus. In other words, it is quite within the bounds of possibility for a man to recognize the relative evil of his nature, but it is a rare and shattering experience for him to gaze into the face of absolute evil.

[3]Feeling of incompleteness.

THE SYZYGY: ANIMA AND ANIMUS

What, then, is this projection-making factor? The East calls it the "Spinning Woman"[4] — Maya, who creates illusion by her dancing. Had we not long since known it from the symbolism of dreams, this hint from the Orient would put us on the right track: the enveloping, embracing, and devouring element points unmistakably to the mother,[5] that is, to the son's relation to the real mother, to her imago, and to the woman who is to become a mother for him. His Eros is passive like a child's; he hopes to be caught, sucked in, enveloped, and devoured. He seeks, as it were, the protecting, nourishing, charmed circle of the mother, the condition of the infant released from every care, in which the outside world bends over him and even forces happiness upon him. No wonder the real world vanishes from sight!

If this situation is dramatized, as the unconscious usually dramatizes it, then there appears before you on the psychological stage a man living regressively, seeking his childhood and his mother, fleeing from a cold cruel world which denies him understanding. Often a mother appears beside him who apparently shows not the slightest concern that her little son should become a man, but who, with tireless and self-immolating effort, neglects nothing that might hinder him from growing up and marrying. You behold the secret conspiracy between mother and son, and how each helps the other to betray life.

Where does the guilt lie? With the mother, or with the son? Probably with both. The unsatisfied longing of the son for life and the world ought to be taken seriously. There is in him a desire to touch reality, to embrace the earth and fructify the field of the world. But he makes no more than a series of fitful starts, for his initiative as well as his staying power are crippled by the secret memory that the world and happiness may be had

as a gift — from the mother. The fragment of world which he, like every man, must encounter again and again is never quite the right one, since it does not fall into his lap, does not meet him half way, but remains resistant, has to be conquered, and submits only to force. It makes demands on the masculinity of a man, on his ardor, above all on his courage and resolution when it comes to throwing his whole being into the scales. For this he would need a faithless Eros, one capable of forgetting his mother and undergoing the pain of relinquishing the first love of his life. The mother, foreseeing this danger, has carefully inculcated into him the virtues of faithfulness, devotion, loyalty, so as to protect him from the moral disruption which is the risk of every life adventure. He has learnt these lessons only too well, and remains true to his mother. This naturally causes her the deepest anxiety (when, to her greater glory, he turns out to be a homosexual, for example) and at the same time affords her an unconscious satisfaction that is positively mythological. For, in the relationship now reigning between them, there is consummated the immemorial and most sacred archetype of the marriage of mother and son. What, after all, has commonplace reality to offer, with its registry offices, pay envelopes, and monthly rent, that could outweigh the mystic awe of the *hieros gamos?*[6] Or the star-crowned woman whom the dragon pursues, or the pious obscurities veiling the marriage of the Lamb?

This myth, better than any other, illustrates the nature of the collective unconscious. At this level the mother is both old and young, Demeter and Persephone, and the son is spouse and sleeping suckling rolled into one. The imperfections of real life, with its laborious adaptations and manifold disappointments, naturally cannot compete with such a state of indescribable fulfilment.

In the case of the son, the projection-making factor is identical with the mother-imago, and this is consequently taken to be the real mother. The projection can only be dissolved when the son sees that in the realm of his psyche there is an imago not only of the mother but of the daughter, the sister, the beloved, the heavenly goddess, and

---

[4]Erwin Rousselle, "Seelische Führung im lebenden Taoismus," Pl. I, pp. 150, 170. Rousselle calls the spinning woman the "animal soul." There is a saying that runs, "The spinner sets in motion." I have defined the anima as a personification of the unconscious. [Jung]

[5]Here and in what follows, the word "mother" is not meant in the literal sense but as a symbol of everything that functions as a mother. [Jung]

[6]Sacred marriage. Jung's allusions are to the book of Revelation.

the chthonic Baubo.[7] Every mother and every beloved is forced to become the carrier and embodiment of this omnipresent and ageless image, which corresponds to the deepest reality in a man. It belongs to him, this perilous image of Woman; she stands for the loyalty which in the interests of life he must sometimes forgo; she is the much needed compensation for the risks, struggles, sacrifices that all end in disappointment; she is the solace for all the bitterness of life. And, at the same time, she is the great illusionist, the seductress, who draws him into life with her Maya — and not only in life's reasonable and useful aspects, but into its frightful paradoxes and ambivalences where good and evil, success and ruin, hope and despair, counterbalance one another. Because she is his greatest danger she demands from a man his greatest, and if he has it in him she will receive it.

This image is "My Lady Soul," as Spitteler called her. I have suggested instead the term "anima," as indicating something specific, for which the expression "soul" is too general and too vague. The empirical reality summed up under the concept of the anima forms an extremely dramatic content of the unconscious. It is possible to describe this content in rational, scientific language, but in this way one entirely fails to express its living character. Therefore, in describing the living processes of the psyche, I deliberately and consciously give preference to a dramatic, mythological way of thinking and speaking, because this is not only more expressive but also more exact than an abstract scientific terminology, which is wont to toy with the notion that its theoretic formulations may one fine day be resolved into algebraic equations.

The projection-making factor is the anima, or rather the unconscious as represented by the anima. Whenever she appears, in dreams, visions, and fantasies, she takes on personified form, thus demonstrating that the factor she embodies possesses all the outstanding characteristics of a feminine being. She is not an invention of the conscious, but a spontaneous product of the unconscious. Nor is she a substitute figure for the mother.

On the contrary, there is every likelihood that the numinous qualities which make the mother-imago so dangerously powerful derive from the collective archetype of the anima, which is incarnated anew in every male child.

Since the anima is an archetype that is found in men, it is reasonable to suppose that an equivalent archetype must be present in women; for just as the man is compensated by a feminine element, so woman is compensated by a masculine one. I do not, however, wish this argument to give the impression that these compensatory relationships were arrived at by deduction. On the contrary, long and varied experience was needed in order to grasp the nature of anima and animus empirically. Whatever we have to say about these archetypes, therefore, is either directly verifiable or at least rendered probable by the facts. At the same time, I am fully aware that we are discussing pioneer work which by its very nature can only be provisional.

Just as the mother seems to be the first carrier of the projection-making factor for the son, so is the father for the daughter. Practical experience of these relationships is made up of many individual cases presenting all kinds of variations on the same basic theme. A concise description of them can, therefore, be no more than schematic.

Woman is compensated by a masculine element and therefore her unconscious has, so to speak, a masculine imprint. This results in a considerable psychological difference between men and women, and accordingly I have called the projection-making factor in women the animus, which means mind or spirit. The animus corresponds to the paternal Logos[8] just as the anima corresponds to the maternal Eros.[9] But I do not wish or intend to give these two intuitive concepts too specific a definition. I use Eros and Logos merely as conceptual aids to describe the fact that woman's consciousness is characterized more by the connective quality of Eros than by the discrimination and cognition associated with Logos. In men, Eros, the function of relationship, is usually less developed than Logos. In women, on the other hand, Eros is an expression of their true nature, while their Logos is

---

[7]The earth mother, symbol of the grave to which man goes.

[8]Reason.
[9]Love, desire.

often only a regrettable accident. It gives rise to misunderstandings and annoying interpretations in the family circle and among friends. This is because it consists of *opinions* instead of reflections, and by opinions I mean *a priori* assumptions that lay claim to absolute truth. Such assumptions, as everyone knows, can be extremely irritating. As the animus is partial to argument, he can best be seen at work in disputes where both parties know they are right. Men can argue in a very womanish way, too, when they are anima-possessed and have thus been transformed into the animus of their own anima. With them the question becomes one of personal vanity and touchiness (as if they were females); with women it is a question of *power*, whether of truth or justice or some other "ism" — for the dressmaker and hairdresser have already taken care of their vanity. The "Father" (i.e., the sum of conventional opinions) always plays a great role in female argumentation. No matter how friendly and obliging a woman's Eros may be, no logic on earth can shake her if she is ridden by the animus. Often the man has the feeling — and he is not altogether wrong — that only seduction or a beating or rape would have the necessary power of persuasion. He is unaware that this highly dramatic situation would instantly come to a banal and unexciting end if he were to quit the field and let a second woman carry on the battle (his wife, for instance, if she herself is not the fiery war horse). This sound idea seldom or never occurs to him, because no man can converse with an animus for five minutes without becoming the victim of his own anima. Anyone who still had enough sense of humor to listen objectively to the ensuing dialogue would be staggered by the vast number of commonplaces, misapplied truisms, clichés from newspapers and novels, shop-soiled platitudes of every description interspersed with vulgar abuse and brain-splitting lack of logic. It is a dialogue which, irrespective of its participants, is repeated millions and millions of times in all the languages of the world and always remains essentially the same.

This singular fact is due to the following circumstance: when animus and anima meet, the animus draws his sword of power and the anima ejects her poison of illusion and seduction. The outcome need not always be negative, since the two are equally likely to fall in love (a special instance of love at first sight). The language of love is of astonishing uniformity, using the well-worn formulas with the utmost devotion and fidelity, so that once again the two partners find themselves in a banal collective situation. Yet they live in the illusion that they are related to one another in the most individual way.

In both its positive and its negative aspects the anima/animus relationship is always full of "animosity," i.e., it is emotional, and hence collective. Affects lower the level of the relationship and bring it closer to the common instinctual basis, which no longer has anything individual about it. Very often the relationship runs its course heedless of its human performers, who afterwards do not know what happened to them.

Whereas the cloud of "animosity" surrounding the man is composed chiefly of sentimentality and resentment, in woman it expresses itself in the form of opinionated views, interpretations, insinuations, and misconstructions, which all have the purpose (sometimes attained) of serving the relation between two human beings. The woman, like the man, becomes wrapped in a veil of illusions by her demon-familiar, and, as the daughter who alone understands her father (that is, is eternally right in everything), she is translated to the land of sheep, where she is put to graze by the shepherd of her soul, the animus.

Like the anima, the animus too has a positive aspect. Through the figure of the father he expresses not only conventional opinion but — equally — what we call "spirit," philosophical or religious ideas in particular, or rather the attitude resulting from them. Thus the animus is a psychopomp, a mediator between the conscious and the unconscious and a personification of the latter. Just as the anima becomes, through integration, the Eros of consciousness, so the animus becomes a Logos; and in the same way that the anima gives relationship and relatedness to a man's consciousness, the animus gives to woman's consciousness a capacity for reflection, deliberation, and self-knowledge.

The effect of anima and animus on the ego is in principle the same. This effect is extremely difficult to eliminate because, in the first place, it is uncommonly strong and immediately fills the ego-personality with an unshakable feeling of rightness and righteousness. In the second place, the cause of the effect is projected and appears to lie in objects and objective situations. Both these characteristics can, I believe, be traced back to the peculiarities of the archetype. For the archetype, of course, exists *a priori*. This may possibly explain the often totally irrational yet undisputed and indisputable existence of certain moods and opinions. Perhaps these are so notoriously difficult to influence because of the powerfully suggestive effect emanating from the archetype. Consciousness is fascinated by it, held captive, as if hypnotized. Very often the ego experiences a vague feeling of moral defeat and then behaves all the more defensively, defiantly, and self-righteously, thus setting up a vicious circle which only increases its feeling of inferiority. The bottom is then knocked out of the human relationship, for, like megalomania, a feeling of inferiority makes mutual recognition impossible, and without this there is no relationship.

As I said, it is easier to gain insight into the shadow than into the anima or animus. With the shadow, we have the advantage of being prepared in some sort by our education, which has always endeavored to convince people that they are not one-hundred-per-cent pure gold. So everyone immediately understands what is meant by "shadow," "inferior personality," etc. And if he has forgotten, his memory can easily be refreshed by a Sunday sermon, his wife, or the tax collector. With the anima and animus, however, things are by no means so simple. Firstly, there is no moral education in this respect, and secondly, most people are content to be self-righteous and prefer mutual vilification (if nothing worse!) to the recognition of their projections. Indeed, it seems a very natural state of affairs for men to have irrational moods and women irrational opinions. Presumably this situation is grounded on instinct and must remain as it is to ensure that the Empedoclean game of the hate and love of the elements shall continue for all eternity. Nature is conservative and does not easily allow her courses to be altered; she defends in the most stubborn way the inviolability of the preserves where anima and animus roam. Hence it is much more difficult to become conscious of one's anima/animus projections than to acknowledge one's shadow side. One has, of course, to overcome certain moral obstacles, such as vanity, ambition, conceit, resentment, etc., but in the case of projections all sorts of purely intellectual difficulties are added, quite apart from the contents of the projection which one simply doesn't know how to cope with. And on top of all this there arises a profound doubt as to whether one is not meddling too much with nature's business by prodding into consciousness things which it would have been better to leave asleep.

Although there are, in my experience, a fair number of people who can understand without special intellectual or moral difficulties what is meant by anima and animus, one finds very many more who have the greatest trouble in visualizing these empirical concepts as anything concrete. This shows that they fall a little outside the usual range of experience. They are unpopular precisely because they seem unfamiliar. The consequence is that they mobilize prejudice and become taboo like everything else that is unexpected.

So if we set it up as a kind of requirement that projections should be dissolved, because it is wholesomer that way and in every respect more advantageous, we are entering upon new ground. Up till now everybody has been convinced that the idea "my father," "my mother," etc., is nothing but a faithful reflection of the real parent, corresponding in every detail to the original, so that when someone says "my father" he means no more and no less than what his father is in reality. This is actually what he supposes he does mean, but a supposition of identity by no means brings that identity about. This is where the fallacy of the *enkekalymmenos* ("the veiled one") comes in.[10] If one includes in the psychological equation X's picture of his father, which he takes for the real father, the equation will not work out, because the unknown quantity he has introduced does not tally with reality. X has overlooked the fact that his idea of a person consists, in the first place, of the possibly very incomplete picture he has received of the

[10]The fallacy, which stems from Eubulides the Megarian, runs: "Can you recognize your father?" Yes. "Can you recognize this veiled one?" No. "This veiled one is your father. Hence you can recognize your father and not recognize him." [Jung]

real person and, in the second place, of the subjective modifications he has imposed upon this picture. X's idea of his father is a complex quantity for which the real father is only in part responsible, an indefinitely larger share falling to the son. So true is this that every time he criticizes or praises his father he is unconsciously hitting back at himself, thereby bringing about those psychic consequences that overtake people who habitually disparage or overpraise themselves. If, however, X carefully compares his reactions with reality, he stands a chance of noticing that he has miscalculated somewhere by not realizing long ago from his father's behavior that the picture he has of him is a false one. But as a rule X is convinced that he is right, and if anybody is wrong it must be the other fellow. Should X have a poorly developed Eros, he will be either indifferent to the inadequate relationship he has with his father or else annoyed by the inconsistency and general incomprehensibility of a father whose behavior never really corresponds to the picture X has of him. Therefore X thinks he has every right to feel hurt, misunderstood, and even betrayed.

One can imagine how desirable it would be in such cases to dissolve the projection. And there are always optimists who believe that the golden age can be ushered in simply by telling people the right way to go. But just let them try to explain to these people that they are acting like a dog chasing its own tail. To make a person see the shortcomings of his attitude considerably more than mere "telling" is needed, for more is involved than ordinary common sense can allow. What one is up against here is the kind of fateful misunderstanding which, under ordinary conditions, remains forever inaccessible to insight. It is rather like expecting the average respectable citizen to recognize himself as a criminal.

I mention all this just to illustrate the order of magnitude to which the anima/animus projections belong, and the moral and intellectual exertions that are needed to dissolve them. Not all the contents of the anima and animus are projected, however. Many of them appear spontaneously in dreams and so on, and many more can be made conscious through active imagination. In this way we find that thoughts, feelings, and affects are alive in us which we would never have believed possible. Naturally, possibilities of this sort seem utterly fantastic to anyone who has not experienced them himself, for a normal person "knows what he thinks." Such a childish attitude on the part of the "normal person" is simply the rule, so that no one without experience in this field can be expected to understand the real nature of anima and animus. With these reflections one gets into an entirely new world of psychological experience, provided of course that one succeeds in realizing it in practice. Those who do succeed can hardly fail to be impressed by all that the ego does not know and never has known. This increase in self-knowledge is still very rare nowadays and is usually paid for in advance with a neurosis, if not with something worse.

The autonomy of the collective unconscious expresses itself in the figures of anima and animus. They personify those of its contents which, when withdrawn from projection, can be integrated into consciousness. To this extent, both figures represent *functions* which filter the contents of the collective unconscious through to the conscious mind. They appear or behave as such, however, only so long as the tendencies of the conscious and unconscious do not diverge too greatly. Should any tension arise, these functions, harmless till then, confront the conscious mind in personified form and behave rather like systems split off from the personality, or like part souls. This comparison is inadequate in so far as nothing previously belonging to the ego-personality has split off from it; on the contrary, the two figures represent a disturbing accretion. The reason for their behaving in this way is that though the *contents* of anima and animus can be integrated they themselves cannot, since they are archetypes. As such they are the foundation stones of the psychic structure, which in its totality exceeds the limits of consciousness and therefore can never become the object of direct cognition. Though the effects of anima and animus can be made conscious, they themselves are factors transcending consciousness and beyond the reach of perception and volition. Hence they remain autonomous despite the integration of their contents, and for this reason they should be borne constantly in mind. This is extremely important from the therapeutic standpoint, because constant observation pays the unconscious a tribute that more or less guarantees its co-operation. The unconscious as we know can never be "done with" once and for all. It is, in fact, one of the most important tasks of psychic hygiene to pay continual attention to the symptomatology of unconscious contents and processes, for the good reason that the conscious mind is always in danger of becoming one-sided, of keeping to well-worn paths and getting stuck in blind alleys. The complementary and compensating function of the unconscious ensures that these dangers, which are especially great in neurosis, can in some measure be avoided. It is only under ideal conditions, when life is still simple and unconscious enough to follow the serpentine path of instinct without hesitation or misgiving, that the compensation works with entire success. The more civilized, the more unconscious and complicated a man is, the less he is able to follow his instincts. His complicated living conditions and the influence of his environment are so strong that they drown the quiet voice of nature. Opinions, beliefs, theories, and collective tendencies appear in its stead and back up all the aberrations of the conscious mind. Deliberate attention should then be given to the unconscious so that the compensation can set to work. Hence it is especially important to picture the archetypes of the unconscious not as a rushing phantasmagoria of fugitive images but as constant, autonomous factors, which indeed they are.

Both these archetypes, as practical experience shows, possess a fatality that can on occasion produce tragic results. They are quite literally the father and mother of all the disastrous entanglements of fate and have long been recognized as such by the whole world. Together they form a divine pair,[11] one of whom, in accordance with his Logos nature, is characterized by *pneuma* and *nous*,[12] rather like Hermes with his ever-shifting hues, while the other, in accordance with her Eros nature, wears the features of Aphrodite, Helen (Selene), Persephone, and Hecate. Both of them are unconscious powers, "gods" in fact, as the ancient world quite rightly conceived them to be. To call them by this name is to give them that central position in the scale of psychological values which has always been theirs whether consciously acknowledged or not; for their power grows in proportion to the degree that they remain unconscious. Those who do not see them are in their hands, just as typhus epidemic flourishes best when its source is undiscovered. Even in Christianity the divine syzygy has not become obsolete, but occupies the highest place as Christ and his bride the Church.[13] Parallels like these prove extremely helpful in our attempts to find the right criterion for gauging the significance of these two archetypes. What we can discover about them from the conscious side is so slight as to be almost imperceptible. It is only when we throw light into the dark depths of the psyche and explore the strange and tortuous paths of human fate that it gradually becomes clear to us how immense is the influence wielded by these two factors that complement our conscious life.

Recapitulating, I should like to emphasize that the integration of the shadow, or the realization of the personal unconscious, marks the first stage in the analytic process, and that without it a recognition of anima and animus is impossible. The shadow can be realized only through a relation to a partner, and anima and animus only through a relation to a partner of the opposite sex, because only in such a relation do their projections become operative. The recognition of the anima gives rise, in a man, to a triad, one third of which is transcendent: the masculine subject, the opposing feminine subject, and the transcendent anima. With a woman the situation is reversed. The missing fourth element that would make the

---

[11]Naturally this is not meant as a psychological definition, let alone a metaphysical one. As I pointed out in "The Relations between the Ego and the Unconscious" (pars. 296ff.), the syzygy consists of three elements: the femininity pertaining to the man and the masculinity pertaining to the woman; the experience which man has of woman and vice versa; and, finally, the masculine and feminine archetypal image. The first element can be integrated into the personality by the process of conscious realization, but the last one cannot. [Jung]

[12]Spirit and mind.
[13]"For the Scripture says, God made man male and female; the male is Christ, the female is the Church." — Second Epistle of Clement to the Corinthians, xiv, 2 (*The Apostolic Fathers* [Loeb Classics], Vol. I, London, 1912, p. 151, trans. Kirsopp Lake). In pictorial representations, Mary often takes the place of the Church. [Jung]

triad a quaternity is, in a man, the archetype of the Wise Old Man, which I have not discussed here, and in a woman the Chthonic Mother. These four constitute a half immanent and half transcendent quaternity, an archetype which I have called the *marriage quaternio*.[14] The marriage quaternio

[14]"The Psychology of the Transference," pars. 425ff. [Jung]

provides a schema not only for the self but also for the structure of primitive society with its cross-cousin marriage, marriage classes, and division of settlements into quarters. The self, on the other hand, is a God-image, or at least cannot be distinguished from one. Of this the early Christian spirit was not ignorant, otherwise Clement of Alexandria could never have said that he who knows himself knows God.

W. E. B. Du Bois

1868–1963

The first African American intellectual leader, and the most militant and controversial civil rights leader before Martin Luther King, was born in Great Barrington, Massachusetts, soon after the ratification of the constitutional amendment abolishing slavery. William Edward Burghardt Du Bois was born free, and in fact his family on both sides had been free for generations. His mother, Mary Burghardt, had a grandfather who had been freed after fighting in the American Revolutionary War; his father, Alfred Du Bois, had fought in the Civil War. His father disappeared around the time of his birth, and Du Bois was raised by his mother with some assistance from his father's family. Du Bois attended public schools in Great Barrington, where he had his first personal experience of racial prejudice at the hands of a white female classmate, a "tall newcomer" who spurned him when he attempted to exchange "gorgeous" cards with her as with the others. Characteristically, as we read of the episode in Du Bois's *The Souls of Black Folk*, we feel the fresh sting of the young man's pain, but it is quickly reshaped into his mature meditation on the "double consciousness" of the African American, "this sense of always looking at one's self through the eyes of others," which Du Bois saw as one of the key conditions under which his race, striving for equality, would have to overcome.

Du Bois's own way of overcoming it was through education. An excellent student, he was sponsored by his neighbors to attend Fisk College in Nashville (now Fisk University), from which he went on to Harvard. There Du Bois studied with the pragmatist philosophers Josiah Royce, George Santayana, and William James; his 1890 commencement address on Jefferson Davis was cited in newspapers around the country. Du Bois did graduate work in history at Harvard, then at the Universität Friedrich Wilhelm in Berlin, returning to Harvard to complete his doctorate in 1896, with a dissertation on the efforts to suppress the African slave trade to the United States. Du Bois taught classics at Wilberforce College, then left to work at the University of Pennsylvania on a pioneering sociological study, *The Philadelphia Negro* (1899), which used field research to underpin its argument that racism was at the source of many of the social problems afflicting the colored communities, including crime, broken families, and unemployment. Unemployed himself after the conclusion of his study — since Penn would not offer an African American a position on the faculty — Du Bois moved to the South, to Atlanta University, where he taught from 1897 to 1910.

Around the turn of the century, as Du Bois was writing the influential essays that would appear in *The Souls of Black Folk*, the leading spokesman for African Americans was Booker T. Washington, a former slave who had organized the Tuskegee Institute, a teacher's college and school of industrial training in Alabama. Washington's message to his race, expressed in his 1895 Atlanta address, was to strive for economic equality, and, in the meanwhile, to forgo voting rights and accept second-class citizenship. Du Bois's sociological research had convinced him that white racism was the visible force behind the social, economic, and political plight of

African Americans, but he was at first moderate in his critique of Washington. Then, in 1899, the horrific lynching of Sam Hose near Atlanta became the "red ray" that radicalized Du Bois, and made him feel that African Americans needed another kind of leadership. In 1905, Du Bois began the Niagara Movement, an organization of educated African Americans devoted to the ideal of immediate political equality, in opposition to Washington's "Tuskegee Machine." Here he propagated the idea that the "talented tenth," the educated upper crust of African American society, owed it to the rest of their race to work selflessly for their collective advantage.

After a violent race riot in Springfield, Illinois, in 1909, Du Bois merged the Niagara Movement with that of northern liberal whites in what became the National Association for the Advancement of Colored People (NAACP). From 1910 through 1934, Du Bois was its most prominent officer and the editor of its magazine, *The Crisis*, a position that gave him an independent political pulpit to shape black public opinion. He flirted with socialism but supported the internationalist Woodrow Wilson, at a time when blacks usually voted for the party of Lincoln, and urged African Americans to "close ranks" with white America during World War I, despite the inequalities visited by racist practices on black soldiers. During the 1920s, he was a furious opponent of Marcus Garvey's "Back to Africa" movement, and considered himself a supporter of the Harlem Renaissance. It was in *The Crisis* that Du Bois published his 1925 speech, "Criteria of Negro Art" (published in 1926 and reprinted below). Du Bois takes it pretty much for granted that black men like Paul Laurence Dunbar and Countee Cullen have written superb poetry, recognized as such by critics white as well as black. His worry is about the effect of that on the white audience. Will the white world assume, once aware of the success of African Americans as writers, artists, and musicians, that the race problem has already been solved, that the political and economic inequalities of America have vanished? For that reason, Du Bois, argues, it is the duty of the Negro writer to portray the truth about their race, a truth that will include their struggle. At that time, when modernism was in flower, Du Bois's position that "all art is propaganda" stood in opposition to mainstream aesthetics, which saw art as an end in itself. Du Bois's critics included black intellectuals, including the "godfather" of the Harlem Renaissance, Alain Locke. Today, Du Bois's argument that one of the functions of art is to raise the social consciousness seems very current indeed.

By 1934, Du Bois's political position and that of the NAACP had diverged causing conflicts that he resolved by resigning and returning to Atlanta University. For the next ten years, Du Bois worked on a revisionist history of the Reconstruction era, a study on African and African American folkways, and his autobiography, *Dusk of Dawn* (1940). Retired from teaching in 1944, Du Bois returned to the NAACP, only to be expelled once more at the age of eighty, in 1948, for favoring the Progressive candidate, Henry Wallace, over the official NAACP candidate, Harry Truman. The last fifteen years of Du Bois's life are a chronicle of opposition, as he found himself drawn toward internationalist and Stalinist "front" organizations, and demonized by right-wing politicians. In 1961, responding to an invitation from Kwame Nkrumah, he emigrated to Ghana, where he renounced his American citizenship shortly before he died on August 27, 1963. It was ironically in the years of Du Bois's self-imposed exile that the militant civil rights movement came to fruition in the American South, and it was on the day after Du Bois's death that Martin Luther King addressed the March on Washington with his speech, "I Have a Dream."

Selected Bibliography

Andrews, William, ed. *Critical Essays on W. E. B. Du Bois*, Boston: G. K. Hall, 1985.

Byerman, Keith. *Seizing the Word: History, Art, and Self in the Work of W. E. B. Du Bois.* Athens: University Georgia Press, 1994.

DeMarco, Joseph P. *The Social Thought of W. E. B. Du Bois.* Lanham, MD: University Press of America, 1983.

Du Bois, W. E. B. *Complete Works*, ed. Herbert Aptheker. 32 vols. Millwood, NY: University Press of America, 1973–1986.

Hamilton, Virginia. *W. E. B. Du Bois: A Biography.* New York: Crowell, 1972.

Lewis, David Levering. *W. E. B. Du Bois: Biography of a Race.* New York: Henry Holt, 1994.

———. *W. E. B. Du Bois: The Fight for Equality and the American Century.* New York: Henry Holt, 2000.

Marable, Manning. *W. E. B. Du Bois: Black Radical Democrat.* Boston: Twayne, 1986.

Rampersad, Arnold. *The Art and Imagination of W. E. B. Du Bois.* Cambridge: Harvard University Press, 1976.

[On Double Consciousness] from *The Souls of Black Folk*

[B]eing a problem is a strange experience, — peculiar even for one who has never been anything else, save perhaps in babyhood and in Europe. It is in the early days of rollicking boyhood that the revelation first bursts upon one, all in a day, as it were. I remember well when the shadow swept across me. I was a little thing, away up in the hills of New England, where the dark Housatonic[1] winds between Hoosac and Taghkanic to the sea. In a wee wooden schoolhouse, something put it into the boys' and girls' heads to buy gorgeous visiting-cards — ten cents a package — and exchange. The exchange was merry, till one girl, a tall newcomer, refused my card, — refused it peremptorily, with a glance. Then it dawned upon

[1]The Housatonic River flows through the Berkshire hills past his hometown of Great Barrington, between the Taghkanic (Taconic) hills and Hoosac mountain.

me with a certain suddenness that I was different from the others; or like, mayhap, in heart and life and longing, but shut out from their world by a vast veil. I had thereafter no desire to tear down that veil, to creep through; I held all beyond it in common contempt, and lived above it in a region of blue sky and great wandering shadows. That sky was bluest when I could beat my mates at examination-time, or beat them at a foot-race, or even beat their stringy heads. Alas, with the years all this fine contempt began to fade; for the worlds I longed for, and all their dazzling opportunities, were theirs, not mine. But they should not keep these prizes, I said; some, all, I would wrest from them. Just how I would do it I could never decide: by reading law, by healing the sick, by telling the wonderful tales that swam in my head, — some way. With other black boys the strife was not so fiercely sunny: their youth shrunk into tasteless sycophancy, or into silent hatred of the pale world about them and mocking distrust of everything white; or wasted itself in a bitter cry, Why did God make me an outcast and a stranger in mine own house? The shades of the prison-house closed round about us all: walls strait and stubborn to the whitest, but relentlessly narrow, tall, and unscalable to sons of night who must plod darkly on in resignation, or beat unavailing palms against the stone, or steadily, half hopelessly, watch the streak of blue above.

After the Egyptian and Indian, the Greek and Roman, the Teuton and Mongolian, the Negro is a sort of seventh son, born with a veil,[2] and gifted with second-sight in this American world, — a world which yields him no true self-consciousness, but only lets him see himself through the revelation of the other world. It is a peculiar sensation, this double-consciousness, this sense of always looking at one's self through the eyes of others, of measuring one's soul by the tape of a world that looks on in amused contempt and pity. One ever feels his two-ness, — an American, a Negro; two souls, two thoughts, two unreconciled strivings; two warring ideals in one dark body, whose dogged strength alone keeps it from being torn asunder.

The history of the American Negro is the history of this strife, — this longing to attain self-conscious manhood, to merge his double self into a better and truer self. In this merging he wishes neither of the older selves to be lost. He would not Africanize America, for America has too much to teach the world and Africa. He would not bleach his Negro soul in a flood of white Americanism, for he knows that Negro blood has a message for the world. He simply wishes to make it possible for a man to be both a Negro and an American, without being cursed and spit upon by his fellows, without having the doors of Opportunity closed roughly in his face.

This, then, is the end of his striving: to be a co-worker in the kingdom of culture, to escape both death and isolation, to husband and use his best powers and his latent genius. These powers of body and mind have in the past been strangely wasted, dispersed, or forgotten. The shadow of a mighty Negro past flits through the tale of Ethiopia the Shadowy and of Egypt the Sphinx. Throughout history, the powers of single black men flash here and there like falling stars, and die sometimes before the world has rightly gauged their brightness. Here in America, in the few days since Emancipation, the black man's turning hither and thither in hesitant and doubtful striving has often made his very strength to lose effectiveness, to seem like absence of power, like weakness. And yet it is not weakness, — it is the contradiction of double aims. The double-aimed struggle of the black artisan — on the one hand to escape white contempt for a nation of mere hewers of wood and drawers of water,[3] and on the other hand to plough and nail and dig for a poverty-stricken horde — could only result in making him a poor craftsman, for he had but half a heart in either cause. By the poverty and ignorance of his people, the Negro minister or doctor was tempted toward quackery and demagogy; and by the criticism of the other world, toward ideals that made him ashamed of his lowly tasks. The would-be black savant was confronted by the paradox that the knowledge his people needed was a twice-told tale to his white neighbors, while the knowledge which would teach the white world was Greek to his own flesh and blood. The innate love of harmony and beauty that set the ruder souls of his people a-dancing and a-singing raised but confusion and doubt in the soul of the black artist; for the beauty revealed to him was the soul-beauty of a race which his larger audience despised, and he could not articulate the message of another people. This waste of double aims, this seeking to satisfy two unreconciled ideals, has wrought sad havoc with the courage and faith and deeds of ten thousand people, — has sent them often wooing false gods[4] and invoking false means of salvation, and at times has even seemed about to make them ashamed of themselves.

[2]In superstition, a seventh son and a child born with a caul (bluish skin from the afterbirth) over his face are supposed to have special supernatural gifts, including a dual soul, as well as extra senses that allow them to prophesy.

[3]Du Bois alludes to Joshua 9:23, where the Gibeonites are made into the slaves of the Israelites, to hew wood and draw water for the house of God.

[4]Du Bois alludes to Judges 2:17, about the Israelites who forsake the Lord and "went a whoring after other gods, and bowed themselves unto them,"

Criteria of Negro Art

I do not doubt but there are some in this audience who are a little disturbed at the subject of this meeting, and particularly at the subject I have chosen. Such people are thinking something like this: "How is it that an organization like this, a group of radicals trying to bring new things into the world, a fighting organization which has come up out of the blood and dust of battle, struggling for the right of black men to be ordinary human beings — how is it that an organization of this kind can turn aside to talk about Art? After all, what have we who are slaves and black to do with Art?"

Or perhaps there are others who feel a certain relief and are saying, "After all it is rather satisfactory after all this talk about rights and fighting to sit and dream of something which leaves a nice taste in the mouth."

Let me tell you that neither of these groups is right. The thing we are talking about tonight is part of the great fight we are carrying on and it represents a forward and an upward look — a pushing onward. You and I have been breasting hills, we have been climbing upward; there has been progress and we can see it day by day looking back along blood-filled paths. But as you go through the valleys and over the foothills, so long as you are climbing, the direction, — north, south, east or west, — is of less importance. But when gradually the vista widens and you begin to see the world at your feet and the far horizon, then it is time to know more precisely whither you are going and what you really want.

What do you want? What is the thing we are after? As it was phrased last night it had a certain truth: We want to be Americans, full-fledged Americans, with all the rights of other American citizens. But is that all? Do we want simply to be Americans? Once in a while through all of us there flashes some clairvoyance, some clear idea, of what America really is. We who are dark can see America in a way that white Americans can not. And seeing our country thus, are we satisfied with its present goals and ideals?

In the high school where I studied we learned most of Scott's "Lady of the Lake"[1] by heart. In after life once it was my privilege to see the lake. It was Sunday. It was quiet. You could glimpse the deer wandering in unbroken forests; you could hear the soft ripple of romance on the waters. Around me fell the cadence of that poetry of my youth. I fell asleep full of the enchantment of the Scottish border. A new day broke and with it came a sudden rush of excursionists. They were mostly Americans and they were loud and strident. They poured upon the little pleasure boat, — men with their hats a little on one side and drooping cigars in the wet corners of their mouths; women who shared their conversation with the world. They all tried to get everywhere first. They pushed other people out of the way. They made all sorts of incoherent noises and gestures so that the quiet home folk and the visitors from other lands silently and half-wonderingly gave way before them. They struck a note not evil but wrong. They carried, perhaps, a sense of strength and accomplishment, but their hearts had no conception of the beauty which pervaded this holy place.

If you tonight suddenly should become full-fledged Americans; if your color faded, or the color line here in Chicago was miraculously forgotten; suppose, too, you became at the same time rich and powerful; — what is it that you would want? What would you immediately seek? Would you buy the most powerful of motor cars and outrace Cook County? Would you buy the most elaborate estate on the North Shore? Would you be a Rotarian or a Lion or a What-not of the very last degree? Would you wear the most striking clothes, give the richest dinners and buy the longest press notices?

Even as you visualize such ideals you know in your hearts that these are not the things you really want. You realize this sooner than the average white American because, pushed aside as we have been in America, there has come to us not

[1]Sir Walter Scott (1771–1832) wrote the poem *Lady of the Lake* in 1810. [Huggins]

only a certain distaste for the tawdry and flamboyant but a vision of what the world could be if it were really a beautiful world; if we had the true spirit; if we had the Seeing Eye, the Cunning Hand, the Feeling Heart; if we had, to be sure, not perfect happiness, but plenty of good hard work, the inevitable suffering that always comes with life; sacrifice and waiting, all that — but, nevertheless, lived in a world where men know, where men create, where they realize themselves and where they enjoy life. It is that sort of a world we want to create for ourselves and for all America.

After all, who shall describe Beauty? What is it? I remember tonight four beautiful things: The Cathedral at Cologne,[2] a forest in stone, set in light and changing shadow, echoing with sunlight and solemn song; a village of the Veys[3] in West Africa, a little thing of mauve and purple, quiet, lying content and shining in the sun; a black and velvet room where on a throne rests, in old and yellowing marble, the broken curves of the Venus of Milo[4]; a single phrase of music in the Southern South — utter melody, haunting and appealing, suddenly arising out of night and eternity, beneath the moon.

Such is Beauty. Its variety is infinite, its possibility is endless. In normal life all may have it and have it yet again. The world is full of it; and yet today the mass of human beings are choked away from it, and their lives distorted and made ugly. This is not only wrong, it is silly. Who shall right this well-nigh universal failing? Who shall let this world be beautiful? Who shall restore to men the glory of sunsets and the peace of quiet sleep?

We black folk may help for we have within us as a race new stirrings; stirrings of the beginning of a new appreciation of joy, of a new desire to create, of a new will to be; as though in this morning of group life we had awakened from some sleep that at once dimly mourns the past and dreams a splendid future; and there has come the conviction that the Youth that is here today, the Negro Youth, is a different kind of Youth, because in some new way it bears this mighty prophecy on its breast, with a new realization of itself, with new determination for all mankind.

What has this Beauty to do with the world? What has Beauty to do with Truth and Goodness — with the facts of the world and the right actions of men? "Nothing," the artists rush to answer. They may be right. I am but an humble disciple of art and cannot presume to say. I am one who tells the truth and exposes evil and seeks with Beauty and for Beauty to set the world right. That somehow, somewhere eternal and perfect Beauty sits above Truth and Right I can conceive, but here and now and in the world in which I work they are for me unseparated and inseparable.

This is brought to us peculiarly when as artists we face our past as a people. There has come to us — and it has come especially through the man we are going to honor tonight[5] — a realization of that past, of which for long years we have been ashamed, for which we have apologized. We thought nothing could come out of that past which we wanted to remember; which we wanted to hand down to our children. Suddenly, this same past is taking on form, color and reality, and in a half shamefaced way we are beginning to be proud of it. We are remembering that the romance of the world did not die and lie forgotten in the Middle Age; that if you want romance to deal with you must have it here and now and in your own hands.

I once knew a man and woman. They had two children, a daughter who was white and a daughter who was brown; the daughter who was white married a white man; and when her wedding was preparing the daughter who was brown prepared to go and celebrate. But the mother said, "No!" and the brown daughter went into her room and turned on the gas and died. Do you want Greek tragedy swifter than that?

Or again, here is a little Southern town and you are in the public square. On one side of the square is the office of a colored lawyer and on all the other sides are men who do not like colored

---

[2]A Gothic cathedral in Germany. [Huggins]

[3]One of the Mandingo peoples of Senegal. [Huggins]

[4]The Venus de Milo, a Greek statue of the goddess Aphrodite carved 130–120 B.C.E., can be seen in the Louvre Museum in Paris.

[5]Carter Godwin Woodson, 12th Spingarn Medallist [Du Bois]. Professor Woodson (1875–1950), dean at Howard University and at West Virginia State College, was the author of dozens of books and articles on African American history and sociology, known as the "father of black history," and he inaugurated what is now known as Black History Month.

lawyers. A white woman goes into the black man's office and points to the white-filled square and says, "I want five hundred dollars now and if I do not get it I am going to scream."

Have you heard the story of the conquest of German East Africa? Listen to the untold tale: There were 40,000 black men and 4,000 white men who talked German. There were 20,000 black men and 12,000 white men who talked English. There were 10,000 black men and 400 white men who talked French. In Africa then where the Mountains of the Moon raised their white and snow-capped heads into the mouth of the tropic sun, where Nile and Congo rise and the Great Lakes swim, these men fought; they struggled on mountain, hill and valley, in river, lake and swamp, until in masses they sickened, crawled and died; until the 4,000 white Germans had become mostly bleached bones; until nearly all the 12,000 white Englishmen had returned to South Africa, and the 400 Frenchmen to Belgium and Heaven; all except a mere handful of the white men died; but thousands of black men from East, West and South Africa, from Nigeria and the Valley of the Nile, and from the West Indies still struggled, fought and died. For four years they fought and won and lost German East Africa; and all you hear about it is that England and Belgium conquered German Africa for the allies!

Such is the true and stirring stuff of which Romance is born and from this stuff come the stirrings of men who are beginning to remember that this kind of material is theirs, and this vital life of their own kind is beckoning them on.

The question comes next as to the interpretation of these new stirrings, of this new spirit: Of what is the colored artist capable? We have had on the part of both colored and white people singular unanimity of judgment in the past. Colored people have said: "The work must be inferior because it comes from colored people." White people have said: "It is inferior because it is done by colored people." But today there is coming to both the realization that the work of the black man is not always inferior. Interesting stories come to us. A professor in the University of Chicago read to a class that had studied literature a passage of poetry and asked them to guess the author. They guessed a goodly company from Shelley and Robert Browning down to Tennyson and Masefield. The author was Countée Cullen.[6] Or again the English critic John Drinkwater went down to a Southern seminary, one of the sort which "finishes" young white women of the South. The students sat with their wooden faces while he tried to get some response out of them. Finally he said, "Name me some of your Southern poets." They hesitated. He said finally, "I'll start out with your best: Paul Laurence Dunbar!"[7]

With the growing recognition of Negro artists in spite of the severe handicaps, one comforting thing is occurring to both white and black. They are whispering, "Here is a way out. Here is the real solution of the color problem. The recognition accorded Cullen, Hughes, Fauset, White[8] and others shows there is no real color line. Keep quiet! Don't complain! Work! All will be well!"

I will not say that already this chorus amounts to a conspiracy. Perhaps I am naturally too suspicious. But I will say that there are today a surprising number of white people who are getting great satisfaction out of these younger Negro writers because they think it is going to stop agitation of the Negro question. They say, "What is the use of your fighting and complaining; do the great thing and the reward is there." And many colored people are all too eager to follow this advice; especially those who are weary of the external struggle along the color line, who are afraid to fight and to whom the money of philanthropists and the alluring publicity are subtle and deadly bribes. They say, "What is the use of fighting? Why not show simply what we deserve and let the reward come to us?"

And it is right here that the National Association for the Advancement of Colored People comes upon the field, comes with its great call to

[6]African American poet (1903–1946). Percy Bysshe Shelley (1792–1822); Robert Browning (1812–1889); Alfred, Lord Tennyson (1809–1892); and John Masefield (1878–1967) were all English poets. [Huggins]
[7]African American poet (1872–1906). [Huggins] Dunbar was born in Dayton, Ohio, and never lived in the South, though both his parents had been slaves in Kentucky.
[8]Walter White (1893–1955), author and civil rights leader. Langston Hughes (1902–1967), poet, dramatist, and fiction writer. Jessie Redmon Fauset (1882–1961), editor and novelist. [Huggins]

a new battle, a new fight and new things to fight before the old things are wholly won; and to say that the Beauty of Truth and Freedom which shall some day be our heritage and the heritage of all civilized men is not in our hands yet and that we ourselves must not fail to realize.

There is in New York tonight a black woman molding clay by herself in a little bare room, because there is not a single school of sculpture in New York where she is welcome. Surely there are doors she might burst through, but when God makes a sculptor He does not always make the pushing sort of person who beats his way through doors thrust in his face. This girl is working her hands off to get out of this country so that she can get some sort of training.

There was Richard Brown.[9] If he had been white he would have been alive today instead of dead of neglect. Many helped him when he asked but he was not the kind of boy that always asks. He was simply one who made colors sing.

There is a colored woman in Chicago who is a great musician. She thought she would like to study at Fontainebleau this summer where Walter Damrosch[10] and a score of leaders of Art have an American school of music. But the application blank of this school says: "I am a white American and I apply for admission to the school."

We can go on the stage; we can be just as funny as white Americans wish us to be; we can play all the sordid parts that America likes to assign to Negroes; but for any thing else there is still a small place for us.

And so I might go on. But let me sum up with this: Suppose the only Negro who survived some centuries hence was the Negro painted by white Americans in the novels and essays they have written. What would people in a hundred years say of black Americans? Now turn it around. Suppose you were to write a story and put in it the kind of people you know and like and imagine. You might get it published and you might not. And the "might not" is still far bigger than the "might." The white publishers catering to white folk would say, "It is not interesting" — to white folk, naturally not. They want Uncle Toms, Topsies,[11] good "darkies" and clowns. I have in my office a story with all the earmarks of truth. A young man says that he started out to write and had his stories accepted. Then he began to write about the things he knew best about, that is, about his own people. He submitted a story to a magazine which said, "We are sorry, but we cannot take it." I sat down and revised my story, changing the color of the characters and the locale and sent it under an assumed name with a change of address and it was accepted by the same magazine that had refused it, the editor promising to take anything else I might send in providing it was good enough."

We have, to be sure, a few recognized and successful Negro artists; but they are not all those fit to survive or even a good minority. They are but the remnants of that ability and genius among us whom the accidents of education and opportunity have raised on the tidal waves of chance. We black folk are not altogether peculiar in this. After all, in the world at large, it is only the accident, the remnant, that gets the chance to make the most of itself; but if this is true of the white world it is infinitely more true of the colored world. It is not simply the great clear tenor of Ronald Hayes[12] that opened the ears of America. We have had many voices of all kinds as fine as his and America was and is as deaf as she was for years to him. Then a foreign land heard Hayes and put its imprint on him and immediately America with all its imitative snobbery woke up. We approved Hayes because London, Paris and Berlin approved him and not simply because he was a great singer.

[9]Richard Lonsdale Brown (1886–1915), an African American landscape artist raised in West Virginia, who was "discovered" by New York artist George de Forest Brush in 1911. Brown studied with Brush and was given a one-man show at the Ovington Gallery on Fifth Avenue the following year. According to John Cuthbert of West Virginia University (personal communication), Brown "subsequently studied for a year at the Robert Gould Shaw House in Boston. During this period he was a poster artist for W. E. B. Du Bois. He died of an unspecified illness while still in his twenties."

[10]German-American conductor and composer (1862–1950). [Huggins] Fontainebleau is a chateau built by French king Francois I in a forest about 40 miles southeast of Paris, and the site of artists' colonies since the sixteenth century.

[11]Uncle Tom and Topsy are characters from Harriet Beecher Stowe's *Uncle Tom's Cabin* (1852). [Huggins]

[12]Internationally acclaimed African American singer (1887–1976). [Huggins]

Thus it is the bounden duty of black America to begin this great work of the creation of Beauty, of the preservation of Beauty, of the realization of Beauty, and we must use in this work all the methods that men have used before. And what have been the tools of the artist in times gone by? First of all, he has used the Truth — not for the sake of truth, not as a scientist seeking truth, but as one upon whom Truth eternally thrusts itself as the highest handmaid of imagination, as the one great vehicle of universal understanding. Again artists have used Goodness — goodness in all its aspects of justice, honor and right — not for sake of an ethical sanction but as the one true method of gaining sympathy and human interest.

The apostle of Beauty thus becomes the apostle of Truth and Right not by choice but by inner and outer compulsion. Free he is but his freedom is ever bounded by Truth and Justice; and slavery only dogs him when he is denied the right to tell the Truth or recognize an ideal of Justice.

Thus all Art is propaganda and ever must be, despite the wailing of the purists. I stand in utter shamelessness and say that whatever art I have for writing has been used always for propaganda for gaining the right of black folk to love and enjoy. I do not care a damn for any art that is not used for propaganda. But I do care when propaganda is confined to one side while the other is stripped and silent.

In New York we have two plays: "White Cargo" and "Congo."[13] In "White Cargo" there is a fallen woman. She is black. In "Cargo" the fallen woman is white. In "White Cargo" the black woman goes down further and further and in "Congo" the white woman begins with degradation but in the end is one of the angels of the Lord.

You know the current magazine story: A young white man goes down to Central America and the most beautiful colored woman there falls in love with him. She crawls across the whole isthmus to get to him. The white man says nobly, "No." He goes back to his white sweetheart in New York.

In such cases, it is not the positive propaganda of people who believe white blood divine, infallible and holy to which I object. It is the denial of a similar right of propaganda to those who believe black blood is human, lovable and inspired with new ideals for the world. White artists themselves suffer from this narrowing of their field. They cry for freedom in dealing with Negroes because they have so little freedom in dealing with whites. DuBose Heyward writes "Porgy"[14] and writes beautifully of the black Charleston underworld. But why does he do this? Because he cannot do a similar thing for the white people of Charleston, or they would drum him out of town. The only chance he had to tell the truth of pitiful human degradation was to tell it of colored people. I should not be surprised if Octavius Roy Cohen[15] had approached the *Saturday Evening Post* and asked permission to write about a different kind of colored folk than the monstrosities he has created; but if he has, the *Post* has replied, "No. You are getting paid to write about the kind of colored people you are writing about."

In other words, the white public today demands from its artists, literary and pictorial, racial pre-judgment which deliberately distorts Truth and Justice, as far as colored races are concerned, and it will pay for no other.

On the other hand, the young and slowly growing black public still wants its prophets almost equally unfree. We are bound by all sorts of customs that have come down as second-hand soul clothes of white patrons. We are ashamed of sex and we lower our eyes when people will talk of it. Our religion holds us in superstition. Our worst side has been so shamelessly emphasized that we are denying we have or ever had a worst side. In all sorts of ways we are hemmed in and our new young artists have got to fight their way to freedom.

The ultimate judge has got to be you and you have got to build yourselves up into that wide judgment, that catholicity[16] of temper which is

[13]Or *Kongo* (1926) by Kilbourn Gordon and Chester DeVonde. *White Cargo: A Play of the Primitive* (1925) by Leon Gordon. [Huggins]

[14]A 1925 novel about southern African American life by DuBose Heyward (1885–1940). [Huggins]

[15]Cohen was an American magazine fiction writer (1891–1959) whose African American series characters included Epic Peters, a Pullman porter, and Florian Slappey, a private detective from Birmingham, Alabama, operating in Harlem.

[16]Universality.

going to enable the artist to have his widest chance for freedom. We can afford the Truth. White folk today cannot. As it is now we are handing everything over to a white jury. If a colored man wants to publish a book, he has got to get a white publisher and a white newspaper to say it is great; and then you and I say so. We must come to the place where the work of art when it appears is reviewed and acclaimed by our own free and unfettered judgment. And we are going to have a real and valuable and eternal judgment only as we make ourselves free of mind, proud of body and just of soul to all men.

And then do you know what will be said? It is already saying. Just as soon as true Art emerges; just as soon as the black artist appears, someone touches the race on the shoulder and says, "He did that because he was an American, not because he was a Negro; he was born here; he was trained here; he is not a Negro — what is a Negro anyhow? He is just human; it is the kind of thing you ought to expect."

I do not doubt that the ultimate art coming from black folk is going to be just as beautiful, and beautiful largely in the same ways, as the art that comes from white folk, or yellow, or red; but the point today is that until the art of the black folk compels recognition they will not be rated as human. And when through art they compel recognition then let the world discover if it will that their art is as new as it is old and as old as new.

I had a classmate once who did three beautiful things and died. One of them was a story of a folk who found fire and then went wandering in the gloom of night seeking again the stars they had once known and lost; suddenly out of blackness they looked up and there loomed the heavens; and what was it that they said? They raised a mighty cry: "It is the stars, it is the ancient stars, it is the young and everlasting stars!"

Mikhail Bakhtin

1895–1975

Nearly lost to the world because of Soviet political turbulence in the first half of the century, the literary and aesthetic theories of the Russian polymath Mikhail Bakhtin have, in the past two decades, exerted a spellbinding and fertile power over critical imaginations in North America and Europe. Born in Orel, Russia, Bakhtin attended the universities in Odessa and St. Petersburg. In 1920 he moved to the cultural center Vitebsk and in 1924 back to St. Petersburg (then renamed Leningrad), where he worked at the Historical Institute and became part of an intellectual circle that opposed itself to the then-fashionable philosophy of the neo-Kantian Hermann Cohen.[1]

Bakhtin's magisterial *Problems of Dostoevsky's Poetics* appeared in 1929, but its impact was stifled when a Stalinist purge sent its author into internal exile, probably because of his connections with Russian Orthodox "Old-Believers." During the next six precarious years on the border of Siberia, Bakhtin wrote the seminal essay "Discourse in the Novel" (later printed as one of the four essays in *The Dialogic Imagination*) and a study of the German *Bildungsroman* that was thought lost when it disappeared from a publishing house during the German invasion; fragments of it have since been recovered and are being translated. On his return from exile in 1936, Bakhtin was offered a position at the Mordovia State Teachers' College (later University) at Saransk, where he taught until his retirement in 1961. In 1940, Bakhtin submitted a dissertation on Rabelais but was unable to defend it until after the war; when he did defend it in 1946, the dissertation's very originality worked against its acceptance. Its acceptance in 1951 and eventual publication in 1965 (as *Rabelais and His World*) lifted Bakhtin's ideas from obscurity and made them available to the international scholarly community. One important vector for the spread of his fame was Julia Kristeva, who incorporated Bakhtin's ideas about intertextuality into her early structuralist work. Meanwhile Bakhtin, in declining health from osteomyelitis, which had plagued him all his life, was able to move from Saransk to Moscow in 1969. At the end of his life he gathered around him a group of students that reportedly included the daughter of then-KGB director Yuri Andropov. At the center rather than the periphery of Russia, and no longer in danger of being purged for heterodox views, he was finally able to publish many of the seminal pieces on the philosophy of language and theory of literature that he had written fifty years before. He died in Moscow in 1975.

Given his views on the social construction of languages and the literary codes based on language, Mikhail Bakhtin has been claimed as both a Marxist and a formalist. Part of the difficulty in categorizing his work stems from the still-disputed question of Bakhtin's contribution to three books published in the late 1920s by members of his philosophical circle. Bakhtin's thought clearly informs *Marxism and the Study of*

---

[1]Cohen, who worked at the University of Marburg, is almost unknown today; he is a significant figure in intellectual history, however, because his views inspired reaction by so many other literary/philosophical theorists, including Gadamer (see p. 718) and Heidegger (see p. 611).

Language (1929–30) and *Freudianism: A Critical Sketch* (1927) by V. N. Vološinov, and *The Formal Method in Literary Scholarship* (1928) by P. N. Medvedev. Some scholars have argued that Bakhtin actually wrote these attacks on Freudian psychology and formalist literary theory, publishing them, for some reason, under the names of his friends. But more recent evidence suggests that these Marxist texts of the Bakhtin circle owe their orthodox slant and dialectical argumentation to their titular authors. Without these texts as part of his canon, Bakhtin can be seen as a highly individualistic theorist concerned with problems similar to the ones that engrossed Shklovsky (see p. 774) and other formalists, such as Yuri Tynyanov.

At the center of Bakhtin's ideas is the principle usually translated as *heteroglossia* (in the original Russian: *raznorecie,* literally "the word of another"): the notion that the meaning of language is socially determined, that utterances reflect social values and depend for their meaning on their relation to other utterances. The idea is a familiar one in the purely linguistic context of speech-act theory: An imperative sentence can be an order, a command, a request, a plea, or a prayer, depending on who is talking to whom. We could say that Bakhtin — who was working on these ideas many years before the speech-act theorists Austin and Searle — essentially directs our attention to the *pragmatics* of literary discourse. He differentiates sharply between *dialogical* discourse, which explicitly or tacitly acknowledges the language of the Other, the controlling presence of a social context; and *monological* discourse, which tries to have its say in a vacuum. What many English and American critics find worth emulating in Bakhtin's criticism is the extraordinary sensitivity with which he succeeds in locating the various nuances — the responses to internal and external pressures — that go into the creation of dialogical fictional discourse.

But Bakhtin does not merely analyze literary pragmatics neutrally; he loathes single-voiced authoritative discourse, the unquestionable word that comes from above to dictate meaning. For Bakhtin, monologism denies the existence and validity of the Other, assuming an auditor to whom one speaks without needing to listen. Instead, Bakhtin valorizes dialogism and the types of discourse he calls *double-voiced (dvugolosnöe slovo),* in which a single sentence will bring into dialogue two or more different languages. What Bakhtin calls languages can be idiolects — the individualized discourse of a particular person — or various sorts of dialects, communication styles, or jargons characteristic of particular social groups: trades, professions, classes, parties, generations. The shifting planes of intention that can occur whenever one language meets another in a single discourse permit an exhilaratingly chaotic freedom of expression. Bakhtin particularly loves the various forms of parody, which mediate comically between an audience and a known prior discourse.

Thus, purity and clarity of speech, with clear levels of discourse of the sort Aristotle and Horace recommended, earn no points from Bakhtin. They suggest to him a closed and stratified society without freedom of thought, devoted to "terror, dogmatism, reverence, and piety." What he values instead is the Rabelaisian carnivalization of literature: the sociolinguistic fun-fair where, as in the medieval festival or carnival, rulers and ruled mix on equal terms in a parodic rout devoted to "ambivalent laughter, blasphemy, the profanation of everything sacred, full of debasing and obscenities, familiar contact with everyone and everything."

Bakhtin consequently valorizes the novel, where heteroglossia is practically unavoidable, to poetry, which is typically single-voiced.[2] And of course some novelists are more given to heteroglossia than others — at one point Bakhtin contrasts Tolstoy, whose multifarious characters nonetheless always express the author's dogmas, with Dostoevsky, who gives some of the most striking dialogue to characters whose ideas are anathema to him, like Svidrigaïlov and Ivan Karamazov. The existence of conversation and dialogue as such does not guarantee double-voiced discourse. On the other hand the voice of an authorial narrator, which one might expect to be entirely authoritative, may represent perspectives other than those of the characters of the fiction. Analyzing the narrator's voice in *Little Dorrit* in "Discourse and the Novel," reproduced below, Bakhtin makes us aware that Dickens's narrator is not a single univocal speaker but embodies, paradoxically at times, various linguistic strata embedded in Victorian society, the jargons of various trades and professions, the chatter of particular segments of society, and so on. Within these "heteroglot" utterances may be included direct authorial discourse, though within a complex passage it may be impossible to say whether a particular phrase belongs to the author or to an Other whose language he is re-accenting — and it may indeed be both at once.

Bakhtin's dialogism is the basis for a broader genre-criticism, which in turn is the basis for an innovative approach to literary history. But his notion of the languages competing within an individual's speech, the way one's discourse is at the same time the discourse of an Other, lies at the heart of his critical system.

The two selections reprinted here are both from *Discourse in the Novel*; in addition we have reproduced a convenient chart presenting the levels of dialogue within a discourse from *Problems in Dostoevsky's Poetics*.

Selected Bibliography

Bakhtin, Mikhail. *Rabelais and His World*. Cambridge: MIT Press, 1968.
———. *The Dialogic Imagination: Four Essays*. Austin: University of Texas Press, 1981.
———. *Problems of Dostoevsky's Poetics*. Minneapolis: University of Minnesota Press, 1984.
———. *Speech Genres, and Other Essays*. Austin: University of Texas Press, 1987.
———. *Art and Answerability: Early Philosophical Essays*. Austin: University of Texas Press, 1990.
Clark, Katerina, and Michael Holquist. *Mikhail Bakhtin*. Cambridge: Belknap Press of Harvard University, 1984.
Emerson, Caryl. *Bakhtin Across the Disciplines*. Evanston, IL: Northwestern University Press, 1995.
Holquist, Michael. *Dialogism: Bakhtin and His World*. London and New York: Routledge, 1990.
———. *Dialogism*. London: Routledge, 2002.
Medvedev, P. N. *The Formal Method in Literary Scholarship*. Baltimore: Johns Hopkins University Press, 1978.
Morson, Gary. *Bakhtin: Essays and Dialogues on His Work*. Chicago: University Press, 1986.

---

[2]This is not purely a question of genre. As Bakhtin himself points out, there are what he calls "novelized forms" within any genre. But historically the novel has lent itself to heteroglossia far more than lyric poetry has done.

Richter, David. "Dialogism and Poetry." *Studies in the Literary Imagination* (Spring 1990): 3–27.

Todorov, Tzvetan. *Mikhail Bakhtin: The Dialogical Principle.* Minneapolis: University of Minnesota Press, 1985.

Vološinov, V. N. *Marxism and the Philosophy of Language.* Cambridge: Harvard University Press, 1986.

The Topic of the Speaking Person
from *Discourse in the Novel*

Before, then, taking up the issue of the artistic representation of another's speech conceived as the image of a language, we should say something about the importance in extra-artistic areas of life and ideology of the topic of the speaking person and his discourse. While in the many forms available for transmitting another's speech outside the novel there is no defining concern for the images of a language, such forms are used in the novel for self-enrichment — but not before they are first transformed and subjected within it to the new holistic unity of the novel itself (and, conversely, novels have a powerful influence on the extra-artistic perception and transmission of another's discourse).

The topic of a speaking person has enormous importance in everyday life. In real life we hear speech about speakers and their discourse at every step. We can go so far as to say that in real life people talk most of all about what others talk about — they transmit, recall, weigh and pass judgment on other people's words, opinions, assertions, information; people are upset by others' words, or agree with them, contest them, refer to them and so forth. Were we to eavesdrop on snatches of raw dialogue in the street, in a crowd, in lines, in a foyer and so forth, we would hear how often the words "he says," "people say," "he said . . ." are repeated, and in the conversational

hurly-burly of people in a crowd, everything often fuses into one big "he says . . . you say . . . I say. . . ." Reflect how enormous is the weight of "everyone says" and "it is said" in public opinion, public rumor, gossip, slander and so forth. One must also consider the psychological importance in our lives of what others say about us, and the importance, for us, of understanding and interpreting these words of others ("living hermeneutics").

The importance of this motif is in no way diminished in the higher and better-organized areas of everyday communication. Every conversation is full of transmissions and interpretations of other people's words. At every step one meets a "quotation" or a "reference" to something that a particular person said, a reference to "people say" or "everyone says," to the words of the person one is talking with, or to one's own previous words, to a newspaper, an official decree, a document, a book and so forth. The majority of our information and opinions is usually not communicated in direct form as our own, but with reference to some indefinite and general source: "I heard," "It's generally held that . . . ," "It is thought that . . ." and so forth. Take one of the most widespread occurrences in our everyday life, conversations about some official meeting: they are all constructed on the transmission, interpretation and evaluation of various kinds of verbal performance, resolutions, the rejected and accepted corrections that are made to them and so forth. Thus talk goes on about speaking people and their words everywhere — this motif returns again and again; it either accompanies the development of the other

Translated by Caryl Emerson and Michael Holquist.

topics in everyday life, or directly governs speech as its leading theme.

Further examples of the significance of the topic of the speaking person in everyday life would be superfluous. We need only keep our ears open to the speech sounding everywhere around us to reach such a conclusion: in the everyday speech of any person living in society, no less than half (on the average) of all the words uttered by him will be someone else's words (consciously someone else's), transmitted with varying degrees of precision and impartiality (or more precisely, partiality).

It goes without saying that not all transmitted words belonging to someone else lend themselves, when fixed in writing, to enclosure in quotation marks. That degree of otherness and purity in another's word that in written speech would require quotation marks (as per the intention of the speaker himself, how he himself determines this degree of otherness) is required much less frequently in everyday speech.

Furthermore, syntactic means for formulating the transmitted speech of another are far from exhausted by the grammatical paradigms of direct and indirect discourse: the means for its incorporation, for its formulation and for indicating different degrees of shading are highly varied. This must be kept in mind if we are to make good our claim that of all words uttered in everyday life, no less than half belong to someone else.

The speaking person and his discourse are not, in everyday speech, subjects for artistic representation, but rather they are topics in the engaged transmission of practical information. For this reason everyday speech is not concerned with forms of representation, but only with means of *transmission*. These means, conceived both as a way to formulate verbally and stylistically another's speech and as a way to provide an interpretive frame, a tool for reconceptualization and re-accenting — from direct verbatim quotation in a verbal transmission to malicious and deliberately parodic distortion of another's word, slander — are highly varied.[1]

[1]There are different ways to falsify someone else's words while taking them to their furthest extreme, to reveal their *potential* content. Rhetoric, the art of argument, and "heuristics" explore this area somewhat. [Bakhtin]

The following must be kept in mind: that the speech of another, once enclosed in a context, is — no matter how accurately transmitted — always subject to certain semantic changes. The context embracing another's word is responsible for its dialogizing background, whose influence can be very great. Given the appropriate methods for framing, one may bring about fundamental changes even in another's utterance accurately quoted. Any sly and ill-disposed polemicist knows very well which dialogizing backdrop he should bring to bear on the accurately quoted words of his opponent, in order to distort their sense. By manipulating the effects of context, it is very easy to emphasize the brute materiality of another's words, and to stimulate dialogic reactions associated with such "brute materiality"; thus it is, for instance, very easy to make even the most serious utterance comical. Another's discourse, when introduced into a speech context, enters the speech that frames it not in a mechanical bond but in a chemical union (on the semantic and emotionally expressive level); the degree of dialogized influence, one on the other, can be enormous. For this reason we cannot, when studying the various forms for transmitting another's speech, treat any of these forms in isolation from the means for its contextualized (dialogizing) framing — the one is indissolubly linked with the other. The formulation of another's speech as well as its framing (and the context can begin preparing for the introduction of another's speech far back in the text) both express the unitary act of dialogic interaction with that speech, a relation determining the entire nature of its transmission and all the changes in meaning and accent that take place in it during transmission.

The speaking person and his discourse in everyday speech, we have said, serves as a *subject* for the engaged, practical transmission of information, and not as a *means* of representation. As a matter of fact, all everyday forms for transmitting another's discourse, as well as the changes in discourse connected with those forms — from subtle nuances in meaning and emphasis to gross externalized distortions of the verbal composition — are defined by this practical engagement. But this emphasis on engaged discourse does not exclude certain aspects of representability. In order to assess and divine the real meaning of others' words in everyday life, the following are surely of decisive significance: *who* precisely is speaking, and under *what* concrete circumstances? When we attempt to understand and make assessments in everyday life, we do not separate discourse from the personality speaking it (as we can in the ideological realm), because the personality is so materially present to us. And the entire speaking situation is very important: who is present during it, with what expression or mimicry is it uttered, with what shades of intonation? During everyday verbal transmission of another's words, the entire complex of discourse as well as the personality of the speaker may be expressed and even played with (in the form of anything from an exact replication to a parodic ridiculing and exaggeration of gestures and intonations). This representation is always subordinated to the tasks of practical, engaged transmission and is wholly determined by these tasks. This of course does not involve the artistic image of a speaking person and the artistic image of his discourse, and even less the image of a language. Nevertheless, everyday episodes involving the same person, when they become linked, already entail prose devices for the double-voiced and even double-languaged representation of another's words.

These conversations about speaking persons and others' words in everyday life do not go beyond the boundaries of the superficial aspects of discourse, the weight it carries in a specific situation; the deeper semantic and emotionally expressive levels of discourse do not enter the game. The topic of a speaking person takes on quite another significance in the ordinary ideological workings of our consciousness, in the process of assimilating our consciousness to the ideological world. The ideological becoming of a human being, in this view, is the process of selectively assimilating the words of others.

When verbal disciplines are taught in school, two basic modes are recognized for the appropriation and transmission — simultaneously — of another's words (a text, a rule, a model): "reciting by heart" and "retelling in one's own words." The latter mode poses on a small scale the task implicit in all prose stylistics: retelling a text in one's own words is to a certain extent a double-voiced narration of another's words, for indeed "one's own

words" must not completely dilute the quality that makes another's words unique; a retelling in one's own words should have a mixed character, able when necessary to reproduce the style and expressions of the transmitted text. It is this second mode used in schools for transmitting another's discourse, "retelling in one's own words," that includes within it an entire series of forms for the appropriation while transmitting of another's words, depending upon the character of the text being appropriated and the pedagogical environment in which it is understood and evaluated.

The tendency to assimilate others' discourse takes on an even deeper and more basic significance in an individual's ideological becoming, in the most fundamental sense. Another's discourse performs here no longer as information, directions, rules, models and so forth — but strives rather to determine the very bases of our ideological interrelations with the world, the very basis of our behavior; it performs here as *authoritative discourse,* and as *internally persuasive discourse.*

Both the authority of discourse and its internal persuasiveness may be united in a single word — one that is *simultaneously* authoritative and internally persuasive — despite the profound differences between these two categories of alien discourse. But such unity is rarely a given — it happens more frequently that an individual's becoming, an ideological process, is characterized precisely by a sharp gap between these two categories: in one, the authoritative word (religious, political, moral; the word of a father, of adults and of teachers, etc.) that does not know internal persuasiveness; in the other the internally persuasive word that is denied all privilege, backed up by no authority at all, and is frequently not even acknowledged in society (not by public opinion, nor by scholarly norms, nor by criticism), not even in the legal code. The struggle and dialogic interrelationship of these categories of ideological discourse are what usually determine the history of an individual ideological consciousness.

The authoritative word demands that we acknowledge it, that we make it our own; it binds us, quite independent of any power it might have to persuade us internally; we encounter it with its authority already fused to it. The authoritative word is located in a distanced zone, organically connected with a past that is felt to be hierarchically higher. It is, so to speak, the word of the fathers. Its authority was already *acknowledged* in the past. It is a *prior* discourse. It is therefore not a question of choosing it from among other possible discourses that are its equal. It is given (it sounds) in lofty spheres, not those of familiar contact. Its language is a special (as it were, hieratic) language. It can be profaned. It is akin to taboo, i.e., a name that must not be taken in vain.

We cannot embark here on a survey of the many and varied types of authoritative discourse (for example, the authority of religious dogma, or of acknowledged scientific truth or of a currently fashionable book), nor can we survey different degrees of authoritativeness. For our purposes only formal features for the transmission and representation of authoritative discourse are important, those common to all types and degrees of such discourse.

The degree to which a word may be conjoined with authority — whether the authority is recognized by us or not — is what determines its specific demarcation and individuation in discourse; it requires a *distance* vis-à-vis itself (this distance may be valorized as positive or as negative, just as our attitude toward it may be sympathetic or hostile). Authoritative discourse may organize around itself great masses of other types of discourses (which interpret it, praise it, apply it in various ways), but the authoritative discourse itself does not merge with these (by means of, say, gradual transitions); it remains sharply demarcated, compact and inert: it demands, so to speak, not only quotation marks but a demarcation even more magisterial, a special script, for instance.[2] It is considerably more difficult to incorporate semantic changes into such a discourse, even with the help of a framing context: its semantic structure is static and dead, for it is fully complete, it has but a single meaning, the letter is fully sufficient to the sense and calcifies it.

It is not a free appropriation and assimilation of the word itself that authoritative discourse

seeks to elicit from us; rather, it demands our unconditional allegiance. Therefore authoritative discourse permits no play with the context framing it, no play with its borders, no gradual and flexible transitions, no spontaneously creative stylizing variants on it. It enters our verbal consciousness as a compact and indivisible mass; one must either totally affirm it, or totally reject it. It is indissolubly fused with its authority — with political power, an institution, a person — and it stands and falls together with that authority. One cannot divide it up — agree with one part, accept but not completely another part, reject utterly a third part. Therefore the distance we ourselves observe vis-à-vis this authoritative discourse remains unchanged in all its projections: a playing with distances, with fusion and dissolution, with approach and retreat, is not here possible.

All these functions determine the uniqueness of authoritative discourse, both as a concrete means for formulating itself during transmission and as its distinctive means for being framed by contexts. The zone of the framing context must likewise be distanced — no familiar contact is possible here either. The one perceiving and understanding this discourse is a distant descendent; there can be no arguing with him.

These factors also determine the potential role of authoritative discourse in prose. Authoritative discourse can not be represented — it is only transmitted. Its inertia, its semantic finiteness and calcification, the degree to which it is hard-edged, a thing in its own right, the impermissibility of any free stylistic development in relation to it — all this renders the artistic representation of authoritative discourse impossible. Its role in the novel is insignificant. It is by its very nature incapable of being double-voiced; it cannot enter into hybrid constructions. If completely deprived of its authority it becomes simply an object, a *relic,* or *thing.* It enters the artistic context as an alien body, there is no space around it to play in, no contradictory emotions — it is not surrounded by an agitated and cacophonous dialogic life, and the context around it dies, words dry up. For this reason images of official-authoritative truth, images of virtue (of any sort: monastic, spiritual, bureaucratic, moral, etc.) have never been successful in the novel. It suffices to mention the hopeless

[2]Often the authoritative word is in fact a word spoken by another in a foreign language (cf. for example the phenomenon of foreign-language religious texts in most cultures). [Bakhtin]

attempts of Gogol and Dostoevsky in this regard.[3] For this reason the authoritative text always remains, in the novel, a dead quotation, something that falls out of the artistic context (for example, the evangelical texts in Tolstoy at the end of *Resurrection*).[4]

Authoritative discourses may embody various contents: authority as such, or the authoritativeness of tradition, of generally acknowledged truths, of the official line and other similar authorities. These discourses may have a variety of zones (determined by the degree to which they are distanced from the zone of contact) with a variety of relations to the presumed listener or interpreter (the apperceptive background presumed by the discourse, the degree of reciprocation between the two and so forth).

In the history of literary language, there is a struggle constantly being waged to overcome the official line with its tendency to distance itself from the zone of contact, a struggle against various kinds and degrees of authority. In this process discourse gets drawn into the contact zone, which results in semantic and emotionally expressive (intonational) changes: there is a weakening and degradation of the capacity to generate metaphors, and discourse becomes more reified, more concrete, more filled with everyday elements and so forth. All of this has been studied by psychology, but not from the point of view of its verbal formulation in possible inner monologues of developing human beings, the monologue that lasts a whole life. What confronts us is the complex problem presented by forms capable of expressing such a (dialogized) monologue.

When someone else's ideological discourse is internally persuasive for us and acknowledged by us, entirely different possibilities open up. Such discourse is of decisive significance in the evolution of an individual consciousness: consciousness awakens to independent ideological life precisely in a world of alien discourses surrounding it, and from which it cannot initially separate itself; the process of distinguishing between one's own and another's discourse, between one's own and another's thought, is activated rather late in development. When thought begins to work in an independent, experimenting and discriminating way, what first occurs is a separation between internally persuasive discourse and authoritarian enforced discourse, along with a rejection of those congeries of discourses that do not matter to us, that do not touch us.

Internally persuasive discourse — as opposed to one that is externally authoritative — is, as it is affirmed through assimilation, tightly interwoven with "one's own word."[5] In the everyday rounds of our consciousness, the internally persuasive word is half ours and half someone else's. Its creativity and productiveness consist precisely in the fact that such a word awakens new and independent words, that it organizes masses of our words from within, and that it does not remain in an isolated and static condition. It is not so much interpreted by us as it is further, that is, freely, developed, applied to new material, new conditions; it enters into interanimating relationships with new contexts. More than that, it enters into an intense interaction, a *struggle* with other internally persuasive discourses. Our ideological development is just such an intense struggle within us for hegemony among various available verbal and ideological points of view, approaches, directions and values. The semantic structure of an internally persuasive discourse is *not finite,* it is *open;* in each of the new contexts that dialogize it, this discourse is able to reveal ever newer *ways to mean.*

The internally persuasive word is either a contemporary word, born in a zone of contact with unresolved contemporaneity, or else it is a word that has been reclaimed for contemporaneity; such a word relates to its descendents as well as to its contemporaries as if *both* were contemporaries; what is constitutive for it is a special

---

[3]Bakhtin refers to Gogol's and Dostoevsky's failed attempts to represent the ideal of holiness they believed in — such as Father Zossima in the latter's *Brothers Karamazov.*

[4]When analyzing a concrete example of authoritative discourse in a novel, it is necessary to keep in mind the fact that purely authoritative discourse may, in another epoch, be internally persuasive; this is especially true where ethics are concerned. [Bakhtin]

[5]One's own discourse is gradually and slowly wrought out of others' words that have been acknowledged and assimilated, and the boundaries between the two are at first scarcely perceptible. [Bakhtin]

conception of listeners, readers, perceivers. Every discourse presupposes a special conception of the listener, of his apperceptive background and the degree of his responsiveness; it presupposes a specific distance. All this is very important for coming to grips with the historical life of discourse. Ignoring such aspects and nuances leads to a reification of the word (and to a muffling of the dialogism native to it).

All of the above determine the methods for formulating internally persuasive discourse during its transmission, as well as methods for framing it in contexts. Such methods provide maximal interaction between another's word and its context, for the dialogizing influence they have on each other, for the free and creative development of another's word, for a gradation of transitions. They serve to govern the play of boundaries, the distance between that point where the context begins to prepare for the introduction of another's word and the point where the word is actually introduced (its "theme" may sound in the text long before the appearance of the actual word). These methods account for other peculiarities as well, which also express the essence of the internally persuasive word, such as that word's semantic openness to us, its capacity for further creative life in the context of our ideological consciousness, its unfinishedness and the inexhaustibility of our further dialogic interaction with it. We have not yet learned from it all it might tell us; we can take it into new contexts, attach it to new material, put it in a new situation in order to wrest new answers from it, new insights into its meaning, and even wrest from it new words, of its *own* (since another's discourse, if productive, gives birth to a new word from us in response).

The means for formulating and framing internally persuasive discourse may be supple and dynamic to such an extent that this discourse may literally be *omnipresent* in the context, imparting to everything its own specific tones and from time to time breaking through to become a completely materialized thing, as another's word fully set off and demarcated (as happens in character zones). Such variants on the theme of another's discourse are widespread in all areas of creative ideological activity, and even in the narrowly scientific disciplines. Of such a sort is any gifted, creative exposition defining alien world views: such an exposition is always a free stylistic variation on another's discourse; it expounds another's thought in the style of that thought even while applying it to new material, to another way of posing the problem; it conducts experiments and gets solutions in the language of another's discourse.

In other less obvious instances we notice analogous phenomena. We have in mind first of all those instances of powerful influence exercised by another's discourse on a given author. When such influences are laid bare, the half-concealed life lived by another's discourse is revealed within the new context of the given author. When such an influence is deep and productive, there is no external imitation, no simple act of reproduction, but rather a further creative development of another's (more precisely, half-other) discourse in a new context and under new conditions.

In all these instances the important thing is not only forms for transmitting another's discourse, but the fact that in such forms there can always be found the embryonic beginnings of what is required for an artistic representation of another's discourse. A few changes in orientation and the internally persuasive word easily becomes an object of representation. For certain kinds of internally persuasive discourse can be fundamentally and organically fused with the image of a speaking person: ethical (discourse fused with the image of, let us say, a preacher), philosophical (discourse fused with the image of a wise man), sociopolitical (discourse fused with an image of a Leader). While creatively stylizing upon and experimenting with another's discourse, we attempt to guess, to imagine, how a person with authority might conduct himself in the given circumstances, the light he would cast on them with his discourse. In such experimental guesswork the image of the speaking person and his discourse become the object of creative, artistic imagination.[6]

[6]In Plato, Socrates serves as just such an artistic image of the wise man and teacher, an image employed for the purposes of experiment. [Bakhtin]

This process — experimenting by turning persuasive discourse into speaking persons — becomes especially important in those cases where a struggle against such images has already begun, where someone is striving to liberate himself from the influence of such an image and its discourse by means of objectification, or is striving to expose the limitations of both image and discourse. The importance of struggling with another's discourse, its influence in the history of an individual's coming to ideological consciousness, is enormous. One's own discourse and one's own voice, although born of another or dynamically stimulated by another, will sooner or later begin to liberate themselves from the authority of the other's discourse. This process is made more complex by the fact that a variety of alien voices enter into the struggle for influence within an individual's consciousness (just as they struggle with one another in surrounding social reality). All this creates fertile soil for experimentally objectifying another's discourse. A conversation with an internally persuasive word that one has begun to resist may continue, but it takes on another character: it is questioned, it is put in a new situation in order to expose its weak sides, to get a feel for its boundaries, to experience it physically as an object. For this reason stylizing discourse by attributing it to a person often becomes parodic, although not crudely parodic — since another's word, having been at an earlier stage internally persuasive, mounts a resistance to this process and frequently begins to sound with no parodic overtones at all. Novelistic images, profoundly double-voiced and double-languaged, are born in such a soil, seek to objectivize the struggle with all types of internally persuasive alien discourse that had at one time held sway over the author (of such a type, for instance, is Pushkin's Onegin or Lermontov's Pechorin).[7] At the heart of the *Prüfungsroman*[8] is the same kind of subjective struggle with internally persuasive, alien discourse, and just such a liberation from this discourse by turning it into an object. Another illustration of what we mean here is provided by the *Bildungsroman*,[9] but in such novels the maturation — a selecting, ideological process — is developed as a theme within the novel, whereas in the *Prüfungsroman* the subjectivity of the author himself remains outside the work.

The works of Dostoevsky, in such a view, can be seen to occupy an extraordinary and unique place. The acute and intense interaction of another's word is present in his novels in two ways. In the first place in his characters' language there is a profound and unresolved conflict with another's word on the level of lived experience ("another's word about me"), on the level of ethical life (another's judgment, recognition or nonrecognition by another) and finally on the level of ideology (the world views of characters understood as unresolved and unresolvable dialogue). What Dostoevsky's characters *say* constitutes an arena of never-ending struggle with others' words, in all realms of life and creative ideological activity. For this reason these utterances may serve as excellent models of the most varied forms for transmitting and framing another's discourse. In the second place, the works (the novels) in their entirety, taken as utterances of their *author,* are the same never-ending, internally unresolved dialogues among characters (seen as embodied points of view) and between the author himself and his characters; the characters' discourse is never entirely subsumed and remains free and open (as does the discourse of the author himself). In Dostoevsky's novels, the life experience of the characters and their discourse may be resolved as far as plot is concerned, but internally they remain incomplete and unresolved.[10]

The enormous significance of the motif of the speaking person is obvious in the realm of ethical and legal thought and discourse. The speaking person and his discourse is, in these areas, the major topic of thought and speech. All fundamental categories of ethical and legal inquiry and evaluation

---

[7]The antiheroes, respectively, of *Eugene Onegin* and *A Hero for Our Time.*

[8]Novel of testing.

[9]Novel of education.

[10]Cf. our book *Problems of Dostoevsky's Art* [*Problemy tvorčestva Dostoevskogo*], Leningrad, 1929 (in its second and third editions, *Problems of Dostoevsky's Poetics* [*Problemy poetiki Dostoevskogo*], Moscow, 1963, Moscow, 1972). This book contains stylistic analyses of characters' utterances, revealing various forms of transmission and contextual framing. [Bakhtin]

refer to speaking persons precisely as such: conscience (the "voice of conscience," the "inner word"), repentance (a free admission, a statement of wrongdoing by the person himself), truth and falsehood, being liable and not liable, the right to vote [*pravo golosa*] and so on. An independent, responsible and active discourse is *the* fundamental indicator of an ethical, legal and political human being. Challenges to this discourse, provocations of it, interpretations and assessments of it, the establishing of boundaries and forms for its activity (civil and political rights), the juxtaposing of various wills and discourses and so on — all these acts carry enormous weight in the realms of ethics and the law. It is enough to point out the role played in narrowly judicial spheres by formulation, analysis and interpretation of testimony, declarations, contracts, various documents and other forms of others' utterances; finally, of course, there is legal hermeneutics.

All this calls for further study. Juridical (and ethical) techniques have been developed for dealing with the discourse of another [after it has been uttered], for establishing authenticity, for determining degrees of veracity and so forth (for example, the process of notarizing and other such techniques). But problems connected with the methods used for formulating such kinds of discourse — compositional, stylistic, semantic and other — have not as yet been properly posed.

The problem of *confession* in cases being investigated for trial (what has made it necessary and what provokes it) has so far been interpreted only at the level of laws, ethics and psychology. Dostoevsky provides a rich body of material for posing this language (of discourse): the problem of a thought, a desire, a motivation that is authentic — as in the case of Ivan Karamazov, for instance — and how these problems are exposed in words; the role of the other in formulating discourse, problems surrounding an inquest and so forth.

The speaking person and his discourse, as subject of thought and speech, is of course treated in the ethical and legal realms only insofar as it contributes to the specific interests of these disciplines. All methods for transmitting, formulating and framing another's discourse are made subordinate to such special interests and orientations.

However, even there elements of an artistic representation of another's word are possible, especially in the ethical realm: for example, a representation of the struggle waged by the voice of conscience with other voices that sound in a man, the internal dialogism leading to repentance and so forth. Artistic prose, the novelistic element present in ethical tracts, especially in confessions, may be quite significant — for example, in Epictetus, Marcus Aurelius, Augustine and Petrarch we can detect the embryonic beginnings of the *Prüfungs-* and *Bildungsroman*.

Our motif carries even greater weight in the realm of religious thought and discourse (mythological, mystical and magical). The primary subject of this discourse is a being who speaks: a deity, a demon, a soothsayer, a prophet. Mythological thought does not, in general, acknowledge anything not alive or not responsive. Divining the will of a deity, of a demon (good or bad), interpreting signs of wrath or beneficence, tokens, indications and finally the transmission and interpretation of words directly spoken by a deity (revelation), or by his prophets, saints, soothsayers — all in all, the transmission and interpretation of the divinely inspired (as opposed to the profane) word are acts of religious thought and discourse having the greatest importance. All religious systems, even primitive ones, possess an enormous, highly specialized methodological apparatus (hermeneutics) for transmitting and interpreting various kinds of holy word.

The situation is somewhat different in the case of scientific thought. Here, the significance of discourse as such is comparatively weak. Mathematical and natural sciences do not acknowledge discourse as a subject in its own right. In scientific activity one must, of course, deal with another's discourse — the words of predecessors, the judgments of critics, majority opinion and so forth; one must deal with various forms for transmitting and interpreting another's word — struggle with an authoritative discourse, overcoming influences, polemics, references, quotations and so forth — but all this remains a mere operational necessity and does not affect the subject matter itself of the science, into whose composition the speaker and his discourse do not, of course, enter. The entire methodological apparatus of the mathematical and natural sciences is directed toward mastery over *mute objects, brute things,* that do not reveal themselves in words, that do not *comment on themselves.* Acquiring knowledge here is not connected with receiving and interpreting words or signs from the object itself under consideration.

In the humanities — as distinct from the natural and mathematical sciences — there arises the specific task of establishing, transmitting and interpreting the words of others (for example, the problem of sources in the methodology of the historical disciplines). And of course in the philological disciplines, the speaking person and his discourse is the fundamental object of investigation.

Philology has specific aims and approaches to its subject (the speaker and his discourse) that determine the ways it transmits and represents others' words (for example, discourse as an object of study in the history of language). However, within the limits of the humanities (and even of philology in the narrow sense) there is possible a twofold approach to another's word when it is treated as something we seek to understand.

The word can be perceived purely as an object (something that is, in its essence, a thing). It is perceived as such in the majority of the linguistic disciplines. In such a word-object even meaning becomes a thing: there can be no dialogic approach to such a word of the kind immanent to any deep and actual understanding. Understanding, so conceived, is inevitably abstract: it is completely separated from the living, ideological power of the word to mean — from its truth or falsity, its significance or insignificance, beauty or ugliness. Such a reified word-thing cannot be understood by attempts to penetrate its meaning dialogically: there can be no conversing with such a word.

In philology, however, a dialogic penetration into the word is obligatory (for indeed without it no sort of understanding is possible): dialogizing it opens up fresh aspects in the word (semantic aspects, in the broadest sense), which, since they were revealed by dialogic means, become more immediate to perception. Every step forward in our knowledge of the word is preceded by a "stage of genius" — *a sharpened dialogic relationship to the word* — that in turn uncovers fresh aspects within the word.

Precisely such an approach is needed, more concrete and that does not deflect discourse from its actual power to mean in real ideological life, an approach where objectivity of understanding is linked with dialogic vigor and a deeper penetration into discourse itself. No other approach is in fact possible in the area of poetics, or the history of literature (and in the history of ideologies in general) or to a considerable extent even in the philosophy of discourse: even the driest and flattest positivism in these disciplines cannot treat the word neutrally, as if it were a thing, but is obliged to initiate talk not only about words but in words, in order to penetrate their ideological meanings — which can only be grasped dialogically, and which include evaluation and response. The forms in which a dialogic understanding is transmitted and interpreted may, if the understanding is deep and vigorous, even come to have significant parallels with the double-voiced representations of another's discourse that we find in prose art. It should be noted that the novel always includes in itself the activity of coming to know another's word, a coming to knowledge whose process is represented in the novel.

Finally, a few words about the importance of our theme in the rhetorical genres. The speaker and his discourse is, indisputably, one of the most important subjects of rhetorical speech (and all other themes are inevitably implicated in the topic of discourse). In the rhetoric of the courts, for example, rhetorical discourse accuses or defends the subject of a trial, who is, of course, a speaker, and in so doing relies on his words, interprets them, polemicizes with them, creatively erecting *potential* discourses for the accused or for the defense (just such free creation of likely, but never actually uttered, words, sometimes whole speeches — "as he must have said" or "as he might have said" — was a device very widespread in ancient rhetoric); rhetorical discourse tries to outwit possible retorts to itself, it passes on and compiles the words of witnesses and so forth. In political rhetoric, for example, discourse can support some candidacy, represent the personality of a candidate, present and defend his point of view, his verbal statements, or in other cases protest against some decree, law, order, announcement, occasion — that is, protest against the specific verbal utterances toward which it is dialogically aimed.

Publicistic discourse also deals with the word itself and with the individual as its agent: it criticizes a speech, an article, a point of view; it polemicizes, exposes, ridicules and so forth. When it analyzes an act it uncovers its verbal motifs, the point of view in which it is grounded, it formulates such acts in words, providing them the appropriate emphases — ironic, indignant and so on. This does not mean, of course, that the rhetoric behind the word forgets that there are deeds, acts, a reality outside words. But such rhetoric has always to do with social man, whose most fundamental gestures are made meaningful ideologically through the word, or directly embodied in words.

The importance of another's speech as a subject in rhetoric is so great that the word frequently begins to cover over and substitute itself for reality; when this happens the word itself is diminished and becomes shallow. Rhetoric is often limited to purely verbal victories over the word; when this happens, rhetoric degenerates into a formalistic verbal play. But, we repeat, when discourse is torn from reality, it is fatal for the word itself as well: words grow sickly, lose semantic depth and flexibility, the capacity to expand and renew their meanings in new living contexts — they essentially die as discourse, for the signifying word lives beyond itself, that is, it lives by means of directing its purposiveness outward. The exclusive concentration on another's discourse as a subject does not, however, *in itself* inevitably indicate such a rupture between discourse and reality.

Rhetorical genres possess the most varied forms for transmitting another's speech, and for the most part these are intensely dialogized forms. Rhetoric relies heavily on the vivid re-accentuating of the words it transmits (often to the point of distorting them completely) that is accomplished by the appropriate framing context. Rhetorical genres provide rich material for studying a variety of forms for transmitting another's speech, the most varied means for formulating and framing such speech. Using rhetoric, even a representation of a speaker and his discourse of the sort one finds in prose art is possible — but the rhetorical double-voicedness of such images is usually not very deep: its roots do not extend to the dialogical essence of evolving language itself; it is not structured on authentic heteroglossia but on a mere diversity of voices; in most cases the double-voicedness of rhetoric is abstract and thus lends itself to formal, purely logical analysis of the ideas that are parceled out in

voices, an analysis that then exhausts it. For this reason it is proper to speak of a distinctive *rhetorical* double-voicedness, or, put another way, to speak of the double-voiced rhetorical transmission of another's word (although it may involve some artistic aspects), in contrast to the double-voiced *representation* of another's word in the novel with its orientation toward the *image of a language*.

Such, then, is the importance of the speaker and his discourse as a topic in all areas of everyday, as well as verbal-ideological, life. It might be said, on the basis of our argument so far, that in the makeup of almost every utterance spoken by a social person — from a brief response in a casual dialogue to major verbal-ideological works (literary, scholarly and others) — a significant number of words can be identified that are implicitly or explicitly admitted as someone else's, and that are transmitted by a variety of different means. Within the arena of almost every utterance an intense interaction and struggle between one's own and another's word is being waged, a process in which they oppose or dialogically interanimate each other. The utterance so conceived is a considerably more complex and dynamic organism than it appears when construed simply as a thing that articulates the intention of the person uttering it, which is to see the utterance as a direct, single-voiced vehicle for expression.

That one of the main subjects of human speech is discourse itself has not up to now been sufficiently taken into consideration, nor has its crucial importance been appreciated. There has been no comprehensive philosophical grasp of all the ramifications of this fact. The specific nature of discourse as a topic of speech, one that requires the transmission and reprocessing of another's word, has not been understood: one may speak of another's discourse only with the help of that alien discourse itself, although in the process, it is true, the speaker introduces into the other's words his own intentions and highlights the context of those words in his own way. To speak of discourse as one might speak of any other subject, that is, thematically, without any dialogized transmission of it, is possible only when such discourse is utterly reified, a thing; it is possible, for example, to talk about the word in such a way in grammar, where it is precisely the dead, thing-like shell of the word that interests us.

Heteroglossia in the Novel
from *Discourse in the Novel*

The compositional forms for appropriating and organizing heteroglossia in the novel, worked out during the long course of the genre's historical development, are extremely heterogeneous in their variety of generic types. Each such compositional form is connected with particular stylistic possibilities, and demands particular forms for the artistic treatment of the heteroglot "languages" introduced into it. We will pause here only on the most basic forms that are typical for the majority of novel types.

The so-called comic novel makes available a form for appropriating and organizing heteroglossia that is both externally very vivid and at the same time historically profound: its classic representatives in England were Fielding, Smollett, Sterne, Dickens, Thackeray and others, and in Germany Hippel and Jean Paul.

In the English comic novel we find a comic-parodic re-processing of almost all the levels of literary language, both conversational and written that were current at the time. Almost every novel we mentioned above as being a classic representative of this generic type is an encyclopedia of all strata and forms of literary language: depending on the subject being represented, the storyline parodically reproduces first the forms of parliamentary eloquence, then the eloquence of the court, or particular forms of parliamentary protocol, or court protocol, or forms used by reporters in newspaper articles, or the dry business language of the City, or the dealings of speculators, or the pedantic speech of scholars, or the high epic style, or the style of the hypocritical moral sermon or finally the way one or another concrete and socially determined personality, the subject of the story, happens to speak.

This usually parodic stylization of generic, professional and other strata of language is sometimes interrupted by the direct authorial word (usually as an expression of pathos, of Sentimental or idyllic sensibility), which directly embodies (without any refracting) semantic and axiological intentions of the author. But the primary source of language usage in the comic novel is a highly specific treatment of "common language." This "common language" — usually the average norm of spoken and written language for a given social group — is taken by the author precisely as the *common view*, as the verbal approach to people and things normal for a given sphere of society, as the *going point of view* and the *going value*. To one degree or another, the author distances himself from this common language, he steps back and objectifies it, forcing his own intentions to refract and diffuse themselves through the medium of this common view that has become embodied in language (a view that is always superficial and frequently hypocritical).

The relationship of the author to a language conceived as the common view is not static — it is always found in a state of movement and oscillation that is more or less alive (this sometimes is a rhythmic oscillation): the author exaggerates, now strongly, now weakly, one or another aspect of the "common language," sometimes abruptly exposing its inadequacy to its object and sometimes, on the contrary, becoming one with it, maintaining an almost imperceptible distance, sometimes even directly forcing it to reverberate with his own "truth," which occurs when the author completely merges his own voice with the common view. As a consequence of such a merger, the aspects of common language, which in the given situation had been parodically exaggerated or had been treated as mere things, undergo change. The comic style demands of the author a lively to-and-fro movement in his relation to language, it demands a continual shifting of the distance between author and language, so that first some, then other aspects of language are thrown into relief. If such were not the case the style would be monotonous or would require a greater individualization of the narrator — would, in any case, require a quite different means for introducing and organizing heteroglossia.

Against this same backdrop of the "common language," of the impersonal, going opinion, one can also isolate in the comic novel those parodic stylizations of generic, professional and other languages we have mentioned, as well as compact masses of direct authorial discourse — pathos-filled, moral-didactic, sentimental-elegiac or idyllic. In the comic novel the direct authorial word is thus realized in direct, unqualified stylizations of poetic genres (idyllic, elegiac, etc.) or stylizations of rhetorical genres (the pathetic, the moral didactic). Shifts from common language to parodying of generic and other languages and shifts to the direct authorial word may be gradual, or may be on the contrary quite abrupt. Thus does the system of language work in the comic novel.

We will pause for analysis on several examples from Dickens, from his novel *Little Dorrit*.

(1) The conference was held at four or five o'clock in the afternoon, when all the region of Harley Street, Cavendish Square, was resonant of carriage-wheels and double-knocks. It had reached this point when Mr. Merdle came home *from his daily occupation of causing the British name to be more and more respected in all parts of the civilized globe capable of appreciation of wholewide commercial enterprise and gigantic combinations of skill and capital.* For, though nobody knew with the least precision what Mr. Merdle's business was, except that it was to coin money, these were the terms in which everybody defined it on all ceremonious occasions, and which it was the last new polite reading of the parable of the camel and the needle's eye to accept without inquiry. [book 1, ch. 33]

The italicized portion represents a parodic stylization of the language of ceremonial speeches (in parliaments and at banquets). The shift into this style is prepared for by the sentence's construction, which from the very beginning is kept within bounds by a somewhat ceremonious epic tone. Further on — and already in the language of the author (and consequently in a different style) — the parodic meaning of the ceremoniousness of Merdle's labors becomes apparent: such a characterization turns out to be "another's speech," to be taken only in quotation marks ("these were the terms in which everybody defined it on all ceremonious occasions").

Thus the speech of another is introduced into the author's discourse (the story) in *concealed form*, that is, without any of the formal markers usually accompanying such speech, whether direct or indirect. But this is not just another's speech in the same "language" — it is another's

utterance in a language that is itself "other" to the author as well, in the archaicized language of oratorical genres associated with hypocritical official celebrations.

(2) In a day or two it was announced to all the town, that Edmund Sparkler, Esquire, son-in-law of the eminent Mr. Merdle of worldwide renown, was made one of the Lords of the Circumlocution Office; and proclamation was issued, to all true believers, that this admirable *appointment was to be hailed as a graceful and gracious mark of homage, rendered by the graceful and gracious Decimus, to that commercial interest which must ever in a great commercial country — and all the rest of it, with blast of trumpet.* So, bolstered by this mark of Government homage, the *wonderful* Bank and all the other *wonderful* undertakings went on and went up; and gapers came to Harley Street, Cavendish Square, only to look at the house where the golden wonder lived. [book 2, ch. 12]

Here, in the italicized portion, another's speech in another's (official-ceremonial) language is openly introduced as indirect discourse. But it is surrounded by the hidden, diffused speech of another (in the same official-ceremonial language) that clears the way for the introduction of a form more easily perceived *as* another's speech and that can reverberate more fully as such. The clearing of the way comes with the word "Esquire," characteristic of official speech, added to Sparkler's name; the final confirmation that this is another's speech comes with the epithet "wonderful." This epithet does not of course belong to the author but to that same "general opinion" that had created the commotion around Merdle's inflated enterprises.

(3) It was a dinner to provoke an appetite, though he had not had one. The rarest dishes, sumptuously cooked and sumptuously served; the choicest fruits, the most exquisite wines; marvels of workmanship in gold and silver, china and glass; innumerable things delicious to the senses of taste, smell, and sight, were insinuated into its composition. *O, what a wonderful man this Merdle, what a great man, what a master man, how blessedly and enviably endowed* — in one word, what a rich man! [book 2, ch. 12]

The beginning is a parodic stylization of high epic style. What follows is an enthusiastic glorification of Merdle, a chorus of his admirers in the form of the concealed speech of another (the italicized portion). The whole point here is to expose the real basis for such glorification, which is to unmask the chorus' hypocrisy: "wonderful," "great," "master," "endowed" can all be replaced by the single word "rich." This act of authorial unmasking, which is openly accomplished within the boundaries of a single simple sentence, merges with the unmasking of another's speech. The ceremonial emphasis on glorification is complicated by a second emphasis that is indignant, ironic, and this is the one that ultimately predominates in the final unmasking words of the sentence.

We have before us a typical double-accented, double-styled *hybrid construction*.

What we are calling a hybrid construction is an utterance that belongs, by its grammatical (syntactic) and compositional markers, to a single speaker, but that actually contains mixed within it two utterances, two speech manners, two styles, two "languages," two semantic and axiological belief systems. We repeat, there is no formal — compositional and syntactic — boundary between these utterances, styles, languages, belief systems; the division of voices and languages takes place within the limits of a single syntactic whole, often within the limits of a simple sentence. It frequently happens that even one and the same word will belong simultaneously to two languages, two belief systems that intersect in a hybrid construction — and, consequently, the word has two contradictory meanings, two accents (examples below). As we shall see, hybrid constructions are of enormous significance in novel style.[1]

(4) But Mr. Tite Barnacle was a buttoned-up man, and *consequently* a weighty one. [book 2, ch. 12]

The above sentence is an example of *pseudo-objective motivation*, one of the forms for concealing another's speech — in this example, the speech of "current opinion." If judged by the formal markers above, the logic motivating the sentence seems to belong to the author, i.e., he is formally at one with it; but in actual fact, the motivation lies within the subjective belief system of his characters, or of general opinion.

Pseudo-objective motivation is generally characteristic of novel style,[2] since it is one of the manifold forms for concealing another's speech in hybrid constructions. Subordinate conjunctions and link words ("thus," "because," "for the reason that," "in spite of" and so forth), as well as words used to maintain a logical sequence ("therefore," "consequently," etc.) lose their authorial intention, take on the flavor of someone else's language, become refracted or even completely reified.

Such motivation is especially characteristic of comic style, in which someone else's speech is dominant (the speech of concrete persons, or, more often, a collective voice).[3]

(5) As a vast fire will fill the air to a great distance with its roar, so the sacred flame which the mighty Barnacles had fanned caused the air to resound more and more with the name of Merdle. It was deposited on every lip, and carried into every ear. There never was, there never had been, there never again should be, such a man as Mr. Merdle. Nobody, as aforesaid, knew what he had done; but *everybody knew him to be the greatest that had appeared*. [book 2, ch. 13]

Here we have an epic, "Homeric" introduction (parodic, of course) into whose frame the crowd's glorification of Merdle has been inserted (concealed speech of another in another's language"). We then get direct authorial discourse; however, the author gives an objective tone to this "aside" by suggesting that "everybody knew" (the italicized portion). It is as if even the author himself did not doubt the fact.

(6) That illustrious man and great national ornament, Mr. Merdle, continued his shinning course. It began to be widely understood that one who had done society the admirable service *of making so much money out of it*, could not be suffered to remain a commoner. A baronetcy was spoken of with confidence; a peerage was frequently mentioned. [book 2, ch. 24]

We have here the same fictive solidarity with the hypocritically ceremonial general opinion of Merdle. All the epithets referring to Merdle in the

---

[1] For more detail on hybrid constructions and their significance, see ch. 4 of the present essay. [Bakhtin]

[2] Such a device is unthinkable in the epic. [Bakhtin]
[3] Cf. the grotesque pseudo-objective motivations in Gogol. [Bakhtin]

first sentences derive from general opinion, that is, they are the concealed speech of another. The second sentence — "it began to be widely understood," etc. — is kept within the bounds of an emphatically objective style, representing not subjective opinion but the admission of an objective and completely indisputable fact. The epithet "who had done society the admirable service" is completely at the level of common opinion, repeating its official glorification, but the subordinate clause attached to that glorification ("of making so much money out of it") are the words of the author himself (as if put in parentheses in the quotation). The main sentence then picks up again at the level of common opinion. We have here a typical hybrid construction, where the subordinate clause is in direct authorial speech and the main clause in someone else's speech. The main and subordinate clauses are constructed in different semantic and axiological conceptual systems.

The whole of this portion of the novel's action, which centers around Merdle and the persons associated with him, is depicted in the language (or more accurately, the languages) of hypocritically ceremonial common opinion about Merdle, and at the same time there is a parodic stylization of that everyday language of banal society gossip, or of the ceremonial language of official pronouncements and banquet speeches, or the high epic style or Biblical style. This atmosphere around Merdle, the common opinion about him and his enterprises, infects the positive heroes of the novel as well, in particular the sober Pancks, and forces him to invest his entire estate — his own, and Little Dorrit's — in Merdle's hollow enterprises.

> (7) Physician had engaged to break the intelligence in Harley Street. Bar could not at once return to his inveiglements of the most enlightened and remarkable jury he had ever seen in that box, with whom, he could tell his learned friend, no shallow sophistry would go down, and no unhappily abused professional tact and skill prevail (this was the way he meant to begin with them); so he said he would go too, and would loiter to and fro near the house while his friend was inside. [book 2, ch. 25, mistakenly given as ch. 15 in Russian text, Tr.]

Here we have a clear example of hybrid construction where within the frame of authorial speech (informative speech) — the beginning of a speech prepared by the lawyer has been inserted, "The Bar could not at once return to his inveiglements . . . of the jury . . . so he said he would go too. . . ." etc. — while this speech is simultaneously a fully developed epithet attached to the subject of the author's speech, that is, "jury." The word "jury" enters into the context of informative authorial speech (in the capacity of a necessary object to the word "inveiglements") as well as into the context of the parodic-stylized speech of the lawyer. The author's word "inveiglements" itself emphasizes the parodic nature of the re-processing of the lawyer's speech, the hypocritical meaning of which consists precisely in the fact that it would be impossible to inveigle such a remarkable jury.

> (8) It followed that Mrs. Merdle, as a woman of fashion and good breeding *who had been sacrificed to wiles of a vulgar barbarian* (for Mr. Merdle was found out from the crown of his head to the sole of his foot, the moment he was found out in his pocket), must be actively championed by her order for her order's sake. [book 2, ch. 33]

This is an analogous hybrid construction, in which the definition provided by the general opinion of society — "a sacrifice to the wiles of a vulgar barbarian" — merges with authorial speech, exposing the hypocrisy and greed of common opinion.

So it is throughout Dickens' whole novel. His entire text is, in fact, everywhere dotted with quotation marks that serve to separate out little islands of scattered direct speech and purely authorial speech, washed by heteroglot waves from all sides. But it would have been impossible actually to insert such marks, since, as we have seen, one and the same word often figures both as the speech of the author and as the speech of another — and at the same time.

Another's speech — whether as storytelling, as mimicking, as the display of a thing in light of a particular point of view, as a speech deployed first in compact masses, then loosely scattered, a speech that is in most cases impersonal ("common opinion," professional and generic languages) — is at none of these points clearly separated from authorial speech: the boundaries are deliberately flexible and ambiguous, often passing through a single syntactic whole, often through a simple sentence, and sometimes even dividing up the main parts of a sentence. This varied *play with the boundaries of speech types*, languages and belief systems is one most fundamental aspects of comic style.

Comic style (of the English sort) is based, therefore, on the stratification of common language and on the possibilities available for isolating from these strata, to one degree or another, one's own intentions, without ever completely merging with them. *It is precisely the diversity of speech, and not the unity of a normative shared language, that is the ground of style.* It is true that such speech diversity does not exceed the boundaries of literary language conceived as a linguistic whole (that is, language defined by abstract linguistic markers), does not pass into an authentic heteroglossia and is based on an abstract notion of language as unitary (that is, it does not require knowledge of various dialects or languages). However a mere concern for language is but the abstract side of the concrete and active (i.e., dialogically engaged) understanding of the living heteroglossia that has been introduced into the novel and artistically organized within it.

In Dickens' predecessors, Fielding, Smollett and Sterne, the men who founded the English comic novel, we find the same parodic stylization of various levels and genres of literary language, but the distance between these levels and genres is greater than it is in Dickens and the exaggeration is stronger (especially in Sterne). The parodic and objectivized incorporation into their work of various types of literary language (especially in Sterne) penetrates the deepest levels of literary and ideological thought itself, resulting in a parody of the logical and expressive structure of any ideological discourse as such (scholarly, moral and rhetorical, poetic) that is almost as radical as the parody we find in Rabelais.

Literary parody understood in the narrow sense plays a fundamental role in the way language is structured in Fielding, Smollett and Sterne (the Richardsonian novel is parodied by the first two, and almost all contemporary novel-types are parodied by Sterne). Literary parody serves to distance the author still further from language, to complicate still further his relationship to the literary language of his time, especially in the novel's own territory. The novelistic discourse dominating a given epoch is itself turned into an object and itself becomes a means for refracting new authorial intentions.

Literary parody of dominant novel-types plays a large role in the history of the European novel. One could even say that the most important novelistic models and novel-types arose precisely during this parodic destruction of preceding novelistic worlds. This is true of the work of Cervantes, Mendoza, Grimmelshausen, Rabelais, Lesage and many others.

In Rabelais, whose influence on all novelistic prose (and in particular the comic novel) was very great, a parodic attitude toward almost all forms of ideological discourse — philosophical, moral, scholarly, rhetorical, poetic and in particular the pathos-charged forms of discourse (in Rabelais, pathos almost always is equivalent to lie) — was intensified to the point where it became a parody of the very act of conceptualizing anything in language. We might add that Rabelais taunts the deceptive human word by a parodic destruction of syntactic structures, thereby reducing to absurdity some of the logical and expressively accented aspects of words (for example, predication, explanations and so forth). Turning away from language (by means of language, of course), discrediting any direct or unmediated intentionality and expressive excess (any "weighty" seriousness) that might adhere in ideological discourse, presuming that all language is conventional and false, maliciously inadequate to reality — all this achieves in Rabelais almost the maximum purity possible in prose. But the truth that might oppose such falsity receives almost no direct intentional and verbal expression in Rabelais, it does not receive its *own* word — it reverberates only in the parodic and unmasking accents in which the lie is present. Truth is restored by reducing the lie to an absurdity, but truth itself does not seek words; she is afraid to entangle herself in the word, to soil herself in verbal pathos.

Rabelais' "philosophy of the word" — a philosophy expressed not as much in direct utterances as in stylistic practice — has had enormous influence on all consequent novel prose and in particular of the great representative forms of the comic novel; with that in mind we bring forward the purely Rabelaisian formulation of Sterne's Yorick, which might serve as an epigraph to the history of the most important stylistic lines of development in the European novel:

> For aught I know there might be some mixture of unlucky wit at the bottom of such Fracas : — For, to speak the truth, Yorick had an invincible dislike and opposition in his nature to gravity; — not to gravity as such; — for where gravity was wanted, he would be the most grave or serious of mortal men for days and weeks together; — but he was an enemy to the affectation of it, and declared open war against it, only as it appeared a cloak for ignorance, or for folly; and then, whenever it fell his way, however sheltered and protected, he seldom gave it much quarter.
>
> Sometimes, in his wild way of talking, he would say, That gravity was an errant scoundrel; and he would add, — of the most dangerous kind too, — because a sly one; and that, he verily believed, more honest, well-meaning people were bubbled out of their goods and money by it in one twelve-month, than by pocket-picking and shop-lifting in seven. In the naked temper which a merry heart discovered, he would say, There was no danger, — but to itself: — whereas the very essence of gravity was design, and consequently deceit; — 'twas a taught trick to gain credit of the world for more sense and knowledge than a man was worth; and that, with all its pretensions, — it was no better, but often worse, than what a French wit had long ago defined it, — viz. A mysterious carriage of the body to cover the defects of the mind; — which definition of gravity, Yorick, with great imprudence, would say, deserved to be wrote in letters of gold. [Bakhtin does not locate citation; it is from *Tristram Shandy*, vol. I, ch. II, Tr.]

Close to Rabelais, but in certain respects even exceeding him in the decisive influence he had on all of novelistic prose, is Cervantes. The English comic novel is permeated through and through with the spirit of Cervantes. It is no accident that this same Yorick, on his deathbed, quotes the words of Sancho Panza.

While the attitude toward language and toward its stratification (generic, professional and otherwise) among the German comic writers, in Hippel and especially in Jean Paul, is basically of the Sternean type, it is raised — as it is in Sterne himself — to the level of a purely philosophical problem, the very possibility of literary and ideological speech as such. The philosophical and ideological element in an author's attitude toward his own language forces into the background the play between intention and the concrete, primarily generic and ideological levels of literary language (cf. the reflection of just this in the aesthetic theories of Jean Paul).[4]

Thus the stratification of literary language, its speech diversity, is an indispensable prerequisite for comic style, whose elements are projected onto different linguistic planes while at the same time the intention of the author, refracted as it passes through these planes, does not wholly give itself up to any of them. It is as if the author has no language of his own, but does possess his own style, his own organic and unitary law governing the way he plays with languages and the way his own real semantic and expressive intentions are refracted within them. Of course this play with languages (and frequently the complete absence of a direct discourse of his own) in no sense degrades the general, deep-seated intentionality, the overarching ideological conceptualization of the work as a whole.

In the comic novel, the incorporation of heteroglossia and its stylistic utilization is characterized by two distinctive features:

(1) Incorporated into the novel are a multiplicity of "language" and verbal-ideological belief systems — generic, professional, class-and-interest-group (the language of the nobleman, the farmer, the merchant, the peasant); tendentious, everyday (the languages of rumor, of society chatter, servants' language) and so forth, but these languages are, it is true, kept primarily within the limits of the literary written and conversational language; at the same time these languages are not, in most cases, consolidated into fixed persons (heroes, storytellers) but rather are incorporated in an impersonal form "from the

---

[4]Intellect as embodied in the forms and the methods of verbal and ideological thought (i.e., the linguistic horizon of normal human intellectual activity) becomes in Jean Paul something infinitely petty and ludicrous when seen in the light of "reason." His humor results from play with intellectual activity and its forms. [Bakhtin]

author," alternating (while ignoring precise formal boundaries) with direct authorial discourse.

(2) The incorporated languages and socio-ideological belief systems, while of course utilized to refract the author's intentions, are unmasked and destroyed as something false, hypocritical, greedy, limited, narrowly rationalistic, inadequate to reality. In most cases these languages — already fully formed, officially recognized, reigning languages that are authoritative and reactionary — are (in real life) doomed to death and displacement. Therefore what predominates in the novel are various forms and degrees of *parodic stylization* of incorporated languages, a stylization that, in the most radical, most Rabelaisian[5] representatives of this novel-type (Sterne and Jean Paul), verges on a rejection of any straightforward and unmediated seriousness (true seriousness is the destruction of all false seriousness, not only in its pathos-charged expression but in its Sentimental one as well);[6] that is, it limits itself to a principled criticism of the word as such.

[5]It is of course impossible in the strict sense to include Rabelais himself — either chronologically or in terms of his essential character — among the representatives of comic novelists. [Bakhtin]

[6]Nevertheless sentimentality and "high seriousness" is not completely eliminated (especially in Jean Paul). [Bakhtin]

From *Problems in Dostoevsky's Poetics*

Table 1

I. Direct, unmediated discourse directed exclusively toward its referential object, as an expression of the speaker's ultimate semantic authority

II. Objectified discourse (discourse of a represented person)

   1. With a predominance of sociotypical determining factors

   2. With a predominance of individually characteristic determining factors
         } Various degrees of objectification.

III. Discourse with an orientation toward someone else's discourse (double-voiced discourse)

   1. Unidirectional double-voiced discourse
      a. Stylization;
      b. Narrator's narration;
      c. Unobjectified discourse of a character who carries out (in part) the author's intentions;
      d. *Ich-Erzählung*
         } When objectification is reduced, these tend toward a fusion of voices, i.e., toward discourse of the first type.

   2. Vari-directional double-voiced discourse
      a. Parody with all its nuances;
      b. Parodistic narration;
      c. Parodistic *Ich-Erzählung*;
      d. Discourse of a character who is parodically represented;
      e. Any transmission of someone else's words with a shift in accent
         } When objectification is reduced and the other's idea activated, these become internally dialogized and tend to disintegrate into two discourses (two voices) of the first type.

Table I *(Contd.,)*

3. The active type (reflected discourse of another)
   a. Hidden internal polemic;
   b. Polemically colored autobiography and confession;
   c. Any discourse with a sideward glance at someone else's word;
   d. A rejoinder of a dialogue;
   e. Hidden dialogue

} The other discourse exerts influence from without; diverse forms of interrelationship with another's discourse are possible here, as well as various degrees of deforming influence exerted by one discourse on the other.

The table above from *Problems in Dostoevsky's Poetics* is Bakhtin's classification of monological and dialogical discourses. Type I is monological discourse directed at a listener, neither expecting nor desiring any reply. At its most rigid such discourse is anonymous (like the signs telling us that smoking is not permitted or to be quiet in the library). Type II is monological discourse but the speaker is characterized in two possible ways, as a particular person, whose views may or may not be authoritative, or as some general sort of person. (Such sociotypes speak to us from advertisements, for example: speakers dressed as doctors recommending an over-the-counter drug, speakers dressed as mechanics recommending a particular motor oil.) Type III discourse is dialogical, directed at an audience and expecting an appropriate response.

The three subtypes vary according to whether the speaker's relationship to the listener is merely implicit (subtype 1), whether the speaker's discourse explicitly parodies another discourse (subtype 2), or whether the listener's anticipated response already operates within the speaker's discourse (subtype 3). Dickens, like Dostoevsky, was a skilled practitioner of subtypes 2 and 3, as is shown in the analysis of *Little Dorrit* in "Heteroglossia in the Novel" (see p. 588). Bakhtin's own note on his table emphasizes that the classification should not be viewed as rigid or static. Actual discourses often move rapidly from one class to another and back again, and may even belong simultaneously to different classes or even types.

Virginia Woolf

1882–1941

The novelist and critic Virginia Woolf, one of the founders of literary modernism in fiction, was born in London. The daughter of the Victorian intellectual Sir Leslie Stephen, Woolf educated herself thoroughly using the resources of her father's library and friends. On her father's death in 1904, she moved to Gordon Square in the Bloomsbury neighborhood that houses the University of London and the British Museum. There she and her sister Vanessa gathered round them that coterie of artists and intellectuals that have become known as the "Bloomsbury Group." In 1912 she married the journalist and editor Leonard Woolf, and together in 1917 they founded the Hogarth Press, a small press distinguished for publishing not only her own work but that of authors such as D. H. Lawrence and T. S. Eliot, in addition to the English translations of Sigmund Freud. Woolf's early *The Voyage Out* (1915) and *Night and Day* (1919) prepared the way for her more ambitious, experimental *Jacob's Room* (1922) and the novels for which she is most admired, *Mrs. Dalloway* (1925), *To the Lighthouse* (1927), and *The Waves* (1931). Her other novels include *Orlando: A Biography* (1928), *The Years* (1937), and *Between the Acts* (1941). While Woolf was completing *Between the Acts* during the darkest days of World War II, it was expected that at any moment the German Wehrmacht would invade the Sussex coast not far from her home — an event Woolf knew would create incomprehensible havoc for England, her Jewish husband, and herself. The invasion never came off but at that time of crisis Woolf suffered a terrifying recurrence of the depression that had plagued her since childhood, and she drowned herself in the River Ouse.

While Woolf may be best known for her novels, she was also a prolific writer of critical essays, reviews, and autobiography: The complete edition of her essays will contain over one million words. Working rapidly for the journalistic deadlines of the weekly *Times Literary Supplement,* the *Nation and Athenaeum,* and T. S. Eliot's *Criterion,* Woolf took up in her writing individual authors, schools, and aspects of contemporary culture. Although her subjects were often dictated by journalistic assignment, she used them to explore her own central aesthetic beliefs about the bankruptcy of the realist literary tradition and the importance of what we today call *modernism.* This credo can be found in the two volumes of *The Common Reader* (1925 and 1932), in *The Death of the Moth* (1942), and in *Granite and Rainbow* (1958) published after her death. The selections below are taken from her well-known work of feminist theory, *A Room of One's Own* (1929).

Woolf takes her place in the world of literary criticism as both a modernist and a feminist, and as a feminist she is considerably more modern than her dates of birth and death might suggest. If the major feminist issues of the 1970s and 1980s were the critique of patriarchal culture and its attitudes toward women, the analysis of female creativity and the tradition of women's writing, and the analysis of *écriture féminine* (as French feminists termed the special quality of women's writing), the roots of all three can be found in Woolf's *A Room of One's Own.*

The most famous section of *A Room of One's Own* — a personal brief for women writers expanded from two lectures Woolf gave at Newnham and Girton Colleges — is that which traces the tragically wasted career of an imaginary "Shakespeare's sister," whose creativity and talent would have found no outlet in the society of the sixteenth century. This fictional history is the premise for a historical sketch of actual women writers and the difficulties they experienced in their work, from Aphra Behn, the first female dramatist to make a living by her pen, through the noble bluestockings of the eighteenth century, to the four major novelists of the nineteenth: Jane Austen, Emily and Charlotte Brontë, and George Eliot. In her manifesto, written in 1929, ten years after women received the vote and sixty-five years after the founding of the first women's college at Oxford, Woolf remains painfully conscious of the disparities that still exist between women and men. But she is convinced that the birth of a female Shakespeare, one with an "incandescent" spirit capable of unimpeded expression, is possible within the century — if the rest of her sisters work to prepare her way.

In the course of tracing the histories of women writers, Woolf touches on a great many issues taken up by later feminists. Her ironic commentary, set in the British Museum, on the way women have traditionally been defined and analyzed as inferiors by men previews the issues later raised by Simone de Beauvoir, Kate Millett, Mary Ellmann, and other images-of-women critics. Woolf's analysis of the women novelists of the nineteenth century — of how the adoption of a masculine prose by Charlotte Brontë and George Eliot hampered their expressiveness, and of how Austen succeeded in devising a feminine prose that allowed her to say what she needed to — anticipates current research on women's language and *écriture féminine*. And in her emphatic endorsement of Coleridge's claim that a great mind is androgynous, Woolf takes a stand on the most contested feminist question — whether there are distinct masculine and feminine modes of creativity — which would be attacked by critics like Showalter who are committed to the idea of a uniquely feminine poetics, and by French feminists such as Cixous (see p. 1643) and Irigaray exploring a more polymorphous sexuality.

But, in her feminism, Woolf is also very much the modernist, convinced that the key role of the artist is to create a world whose validity stands independent of the testimony and personal life of the artist herself. Like Eliot's catalytic creator, Woolf's must be impersonal and detached, with the ego shaping a sensibility but not expressing a personality. This vision accounts for some of Woolf's judgments on her major predecessors, the women who made the nineteenth-century novel what it was. Austen's delicacy and disinterestedness wins the highest acclaim, as does Emily Brontë's masterly creation of a transcendent Yorkshire world of pure poetic imagination. In *Jane Eyre,* however, Woolf spots the telltale signs of Charlotte Brontë's rage:

> She left her story, to which her entire devotion was due, to attend to some personal griev-
> ance. She remembered that she had been starved of her proper due of experience —
> she had been made to stagnate in a parsonage mending stockings when she wanted to
> wander free over the world. Her imagination swerved from indignation and we feel it

swerve. . . . The portrait of Rochester is drawn in the dark. We feel the influence of fear in it; just as we constantly feel an acidity which is the result of oppression, a buried suffering smouldering beneath her passion, a rancour which contracts those books, splendid as they are, with a spasm of pain.

As Woolf well understands, the root causes of Charlotte Brontë's aesthetic imperfections were social. It would take a miracle for any woman under the oppression of patriarchal society, deprived of the financial independence and quiet leisure that men often took for granted, to produce texts that transcend the creating self. Woolf closes her treatise by arguing that it will take the transformation of society, giving women the titular "room of one's own," to make a space where Shakespeare's future sisters can evolve.

Selected Bibliography

Banfield, Ann. *The Phantom Table: Woolf, Fry, Russell and the Epistemology of Modernism.* Cambridge: Cambridge University Press, 2000.

Bell, Quentin. *Virginia Woolf: A Biography.* New York: Harcourt, Brace and Jovanovich, 1972.

Black, Naomi. *Virginia Woolf as Feminist.* Ithaca: Cornell University Press, 2004.

Hanson, Clare. *Virginia Woolf.* London: Macmillan, 1994.

King, James. *Virginia Woolf.* New York: Norton, 1995.

Majumdar, Robin. *Virginia Woolf: An Annotated Bibliography of Criticism.* New York: Garland, 1976.

Marcus, Jane. *Art and Anger: Reading Like a Woman.* Columbus: Ohio State University Press, 1988.

Marder, Herbert. *Feminism and Art: A Study of Virginia Woolf.* Chicago: University of Chicago Press, 1968.

Moi, Toril. *Sexual/Textual Politics: Feminist Literary Theory.* London: Methuen, 1985.

Newman, Herta. *Virginia Woolf and Mrs. Brown: Toward a Realism of Uncertainty.* New York: Garland, 1996.

Rosenbaum, S. P. *Women and Fiction: The Manuscript Versions of A Room of One's Own.* Oxford: Blackwell, 1992.

Rosenman, Ellen Bayuk. *A Room of One's Own: Women Writers and the Politics of Creativity.* New York: Twayne, 1995.

Woolf, Virginia. *A Room of One's Own.* New York: Harcourt Brace, 1929.

———. *Three Guineas.* New York: Harcourt Brace, 1938.

———. *The Essays of Virginia Woolf,* ed. Andrew McNeillie. London: Hogarth Press, 1986–.

[Shakespeare's Sister]
from *A Room of One's Own*

Let me imagine, since facts are so hard to come by, what would have happened had Shakespeare had a wonderfully gifted sister, called Judith, let us say. Shakespeare himself went, very probably — his mother was an heiress — to the grammar school, where he may have learnt Latin — Ovid, Virgil and Horace — and the elements of grammar and logic. He was, it is well known, a wild boy who poached rabbits, perhaps shot a deer, and had, rather sooner than he should have done, to marry a woman in the neighborhood, who bore him a child rather quicker than was right. That escapade sent him to seek his fortune in London. He had, it seemed, a taste for the theatre; he began by holding horses at the stage door. Very soon he got work in the theatre, became a successful actor, and lived at the hub of the universe, meeting everybody, knowing everybody, practising his art on the boards, exercising his wits in the streets, and even getting access to the palace of the queen. Meanwhile his extraordinarily gifted sister, let us suppose, remained at home. She was as adventurous, as imaginative, as agog to see the world as he was. But she was not sent to school. She had no chance of learning grammar and logic, let alone of reading Horace and Virgil. She picked up a book now and then, one of her brother's perhaps, and read a few pages. But then her parents came in and told her to mend the stockings or mind the stew and not moon about with books and papers. They would have spoken sharply but kindly, for they were substantial people who knew the conditions of life for a woman and loved their daughter — indeed, more likely than not she was the apple of her father's eye. Perhaps she scribbled some pages up in an apple loft on the sly, but was careful to hide them or set fire to them. Soon, however, before she was out of her teens, she was to be betrothed to the son of a neighboring wool-stapler. She cried out that marriage was hateful to her, and for that she was severely beaten by her father. Then he ceased to scold her. He begged her instead not to hurt him, not to shame him in this matter of her marriage. He would give her a chain of beads or a fine petticoat, he said; and there were tears in his eyes. How could she disobey him? How could she break his heart? The force of her own gift alone drove her to it. She made up a small parcel of her belongings, let herself down by a rope one summer's night and took the road to London. She was not seventeen. The birds that sang in the hedge were not more musical than she was. She had the quickest fancy, a gift like her brother's, for the tune of words. Like him, she had a taste for the theatre. She stood at the stage door; she wanted to act, she said. Men laughed in her face. The manager — a fat, loose-lipped man — guffawed. He bellowed something about poodles dancing and women acting — no woman, he said, could possibly be an actress. He hinted — you can imagine what. She could get no training in her craft. Could she even seek her dinner in a tavern or roam the streets at midnight? Yet her genius was for fiction and lusted to feed abundantly upon the lives of men and women and the study of their ways. At last — for she was very young, oddly like Shakespeare the poet in her face, with the same grey eyes and rounded brows — at last Nick Greene the actor-manager took pity on her; she found herself with child by that gentleman and so — who shall measure the heat and violence of the poet's heart when caught and tangled in a woman's body? — killed herself one winter's night and lies buried at some cross-roads where the omnibuses now stop outside the Elephant and Castle.[1]

That, more or less, is how the story would run, I think, if a woman in Shakespeare's day had had Shakespeare's genius. But for my part, I agree with the deceased bishop, if such he was — it is unthinkable that any woman in Shakespeare's

---

[1]Public square in London on the south bank of the Thames.

day should have had Shakespeare's genius. For genius like Shakespeare's is not born among labouring, uneducated, servile people. It was not born in England among the Saxons and the Britons. It is not born today among the working classes. How, then, could it have been born among women whose work began, according to Professor Trevelyan,[2] almost before they were out of the nursery, who were forced to it by their parents and held to it by all the power of law and custom? Yet genius of a sort must have existed among women as it must have existed among the working classes. Now and again an Emily Brontë or a Robert Burns blazes out and proves its presence. But certainly it never got itself on to paper. When, however, one reads of a witch being ducked, of a woman possessed by devils, of a wise women selling herbs, or even of a very remarkable man who had a mother, then I think we are on the track of a lost novelist, a suppressed poet, of some mute and inglorious Jane Austen, some Emily Brontë who dashed her brains out on the moor or mopped and mowed about the highways crazed with the torture that her gift had put her to. Indeed, I would venture to guess that Anon, who wrote so many poems without signing them, was often a woman. It was a woman Edward Fitzgerald, I think, suggested who made the ballads and the folk-songs, crooning them to her children, beguiling her spinning with them, or the length of the winter's night.

This may be true or it may be false — who can say? — but what is true in it, so it seemed to me, reviewing the story of Shakespeare's sister as I had made it, is that any woman born with a great gift in the sixteenth century would certainly have gone crazed, shot herself, or ended her days in some lonely cottage outside the village, half witch, half wizard, feared and mocked at. For it needs little skill in psychology to be sure that a highly gifted girl who had tried to use her gift for poetry would have been so thwarted and hindered by other people, so tortured and pulled asunder by her own contrary instincts, that she must have lost her health and sanity to a certainty. No girl could have walked to London and stood at a stage door and forced her way into the presence of actor-managers without doing herself a violence and suffering an anguish which may have been irrational — for chastity may be a fetish invented by certain societies for unknown reasons — but were none the less inevitable. Chastity had then, it has even now, a religious importance in a woman's life, and has so wrapped itself round with nerves and instincts that to cut it free and bring it to the light of day demands courage of the rarest. To have lived a free life in London in the sixteenth century would have meant for a woman who was poet and playwright a nervous stress and dilemma which might well have killed her. Had she survived, whatever she had written would have been twisted and deformed, issuing from a strained and morbid imagination. And undoubtedly, I thought, looking at the shelf where there are no plays by women, her work would have gone unsigned. That refuge she would have sought certainly. It was the relic of the sense of chastity that dictated anonymity to women even so late as the nineteenth century. Currer Bell, George Eliot, George Sand, all the victims of inner strife as their writings prove, sought ineffectively to veil themselves by using the name of a man. Thus they did homage to the convention, which if not implanted by the other sex was liberally encouraged by them (the chief glory of a woman is not to be talked of, said Pericles, himself a much-talked-of man), that publicity in women is detestable. Anonymity runs in their blood. The desire to be veiled still possesses them. They are not even now as concerned about the health of their fame as men are, and, speaking generally, will pass a tombstone or a signpost without feeling an irresistible desire to cut their names on it, as Alf, Bert or Chas. must do in obedience to their instinct, which murmurs if it sees a fine woman go by, or even a dog, Ce chien est à moi.[3] And, of course, it may not be a dog, I thought, remembering Parliament Square, the Sieges Allee[4] and other avenues; it may be a piece

[2]George Macaulay Trevelyan (1876–1962), Regius professor of modern history at Cambridge, author of *England in the Age of Wycliffe* (1899) and *British History in the Nineteenth Century* (1922).

[3]The dog is mine.
[4]Broad avenue in Berlin.

of land or a man with curly black hair. It is one of the great advantages of being a woman that one can pass even a very fine negress without wishing to make an Englishwoman of her.

That woman, then, who was born with a gift of poetry in the sixteenth century, was an unhappy woman, a woman at strife against herself. All the conditions of her life, all her own instincts, were hostile to the state of mind which is needed to set free whatever is in the brain. But what is the state of mind that is most propitious to the act of creation, I asked. Can one come by any notion of the state that furthers and makes possible that strange activity? Here I opened the volume containing the Tragedies of Shakespeare. What was Shakespeare's state of mind, for instance, when he wrote *Lear* and *Antony and Cleopatra*? It was certainly the state of mind most favourable to poetry that there has ever existed. But Shakespeare himself said nothing about it. We only know casually and by chance that he "never blotted a line." Nothing indeed was ever said by the artist himself about his state of mind until the eighteenth century perhaps. Rousseau perhaps began it. At any rate, by the nineteenth century self-consciousness had developed so far that it was the habit for men of letters to describe their minds in confessions and autobiographies. Their lives also were written, and their letters were printed after their deaths. Thus, though we do not know what Shakespeare went through when he wrote *Lear,* we do know what Carlyle went through when he wrote the *French Revolution;* what Flaubert went through when he wrote *Madame Bovary;* what Keats was going through when he tried to write poetry against the coming of death and the indifference of the world.

And one gathers from this enormous modern literature of confession and self-analysis that to write a work of genius is almost always a feat of prodigious difficulty. Everything is against the likelihood that it will come from the writer's mind whole and entire. Generally material circumstances are against it. Dogs will bark; people will interrupt; money must be made; health will break down. Further, accentuating all these difficulties and making them harder to bear is the world's notorious indifference. It does not ask people to write poems and novels and histories; it does not need them. It does not care whether Flaubert finds the right word or whether Carlyle scrupulously verifies this or that fact. Naturally, it will not pay for what it does not want. And so the writer, Keats, Flaubert, Carlyle, suffers, especially in the creative years of youth, every form of distraction and discouragement. A curse, a cry of agony, rises from those books of analysis and confession. "Mighty poets in their misery dead" — that is the burden of their song. If anything comes through in spite of all this, it is a miracle, and probably no book is born entire and uncrippled as it was conceived.

But for women, I thought, looking at the empty shelves, these difficulties were infinitely more formidable. In the first place, to have a room of her own, let alone a quiet room or a sound-proof room, was out of the question, unless her parents were exceptionally rich or very noble, even up to the beginning of the nineteenth century. Since her pin money, which depended on the good will of her father, was only enough to keep her clothed, she was debarred from such alleviations as came even to Keats or Tennyson or Carlyle, all poor men, from a walking tour, a little journey to France, from the separate lodging which, even if it were miserable enough, sheltered them from the claims and tyrannies of their families. Such material difficulties were formidable; but much worse were the immaterial. The indifference of the world which Keats and Flaubert and other men of genius have found so hard to bear was in her case not indifference but hostility. The world did not say to her as it said to them, Write if you choose; it makes no difference to me. The world said with a guffaw, Write? What's the good of your writing?

[Austen–Brontë–Eliot]
from *A Room of One's Own*

Here, then, one had reached the early nineteenth century. And here, for the first time, I found several shelves given up entirely to the works of women. But why, I could not help asking, as I ran my eyes over them, were they, with very few exceptions, all novels? The original impulse was to poetry. The "supreme head of song" was a poetess. Both in France and in England the women poets precede the women novelists. Moreover, I thought, looking at the four famous names, what had George Eliot in common with Emily Brontë? Did not Charlotte Brontë fail entirely to understand Jane Austen? Save for the possibly relevant fact that not one of them had a child, four more incongruous characters could not have met together in a room — so much so that it is tempting to invent a meeting and a dialogue between them. Yet by some strange force they were all compelled, when they wrote, to write novels. Had it something to do with being born of the middle class, I asked; and with the fact, which Miss Emily Davies[1] a little later was so strikingly to demonstrate, that the middle-class family in the early nineteenth century was possessed only of a single sitting-room between them? If a woman wrote, she would have to write in the common sitting-room. And, as Miss Nightingale was so vehemently to complain, — "women never have an half hour . . . that they can call their own" — she was always interrupted. Still it would be easier to write prose and fiction there than to write poetry or a play. Less concentration is required. Jane Austen wrote like that to the end of her days. "How she was able to effect all this," her nephew writes in his Memoir, "is surprising, for she had no separate study to repair to, and most of the work must have been done in the general sitting-room, subject to all kinds of casual interruptions. She was careful that her occupation should not be suspected by servants or visitors or any persons beyond her own family party."[2] Jane Austen hid her manuscripts or covered them with a piece of blotting-paper. Then, again, all the literary training that a woman had in the early nineteenth century was training in the observation of character, in the analysis of emotion. Her sensibility had been educated for centuries by the influences of the common sitting-room. People's feelings were impressed on her; personal relations were always before her eyes. Therefore, when the middle-class woman took to writing, she naturally wrote novels, even though, as seems evident enough, two of the four famous women here named were not by nature novelists. Emily Brontë should have written poetic plays; the overflow of George Eliot's capacious mind should have spread itself when the creative impulse was spent upon history or biography. They wrote novels, however; one may even go further, I said, taking *Pride and Prejudice* from the shelf, and say that they wrote good novels. Without boasting or giving pain to the opposite sex, one may say that *Pride and Prejudice* is a good book. At any rate, one would not have been ashamed to have been caught in the act of writing *Pride and Prejudice*. Yet Jane Austen was glad that a hinge creaked, so that she might hide her manuscript before any one came in. To Jane Austen there was something discreditable in writing *Pride and Prejudice*. And, I wondered, would *Pride and Prejudice* have been a better novel if Jane Austen had not thought it necessary to hide her manuscript from visitors? I read a page or two to see; but I could not find any signs that her circumstances had harmed her work in the slightest. That, perhaps, was the chief miracle about it. Here was a woman about the year 1800 writing without hate, without bitterness, without fear, without protest, without preaching. That was how Shakespeare wrote, I thought,

---

[1]Sarah Emily Davies (1830–1921), British feminist responsible for the admission of women to University College, London (1870) and the foundation of Girton College, Cambridge (1873).

[2]*Memoir of Jane Austen*, by her nephew, James Edward Austen-Leigh. [Woolf]

looking at *Antony and Cleopatra;* and when people compare Shakespeare and Jane Austen, they may mean that the minds of both had consumed all impediments; and for that reason we do not know Jane Austen and we do not know Shakespeare, and for that reason Jane Austen pervades every word that she wrote, and so does Shakespeare. If Jane Austen suffered in any way from her circumstances it was in the narrowness of life that was imposed upon her. It was impossible for a woman to go about alone. She never travelled; she never drove through London in an omnibus or had luncheon in a shop by herself. But perhaps it was the nature of Jane Austen not to want what she had not. Her gift and her circumstances matched each other completely. But I doubt whether that was true of Charlotte Brontë, I said, opening *Jane Eyre* and laying it beside *Pride and Prejudice.*

I opened it at chapter twelve and my eye was caught by the phrase, "Anybody may blame me who likes." What were they blaming Charlotte Brontë for, I wondered? And I read how Jane Eyre used to go up on the roof when Mrs. Fairfax was making jellies and looked over the fields at the distant view. And then she longed — and it was for this that they blamed her — that "then I longed for a power of vision which might overpass that limit; which might reach the busy world, towns, regions full of life I had heard of but never seen: that then I desired more of practical experience than I possessed; more of intercourse with my kind, of acquaintance with variety of character than was here within my reach. I valued what was good in Mrs. Fairfax, and what was good in Adèle; but I believed in the existence of other and more vivid kinds of goodness, and what I believed in I wished to behold.

"Who blames me? Many, no doubt, and I shall be called discontented. I could not help it: the restlessness was in my nature; it agitated me to pain sometimes. . . .

"It is vain to say human beings ought to be satisfied with tranquillity: they must have action; and they will make it if they cannot find it. Millions are condemned to a stiller doom than mine, and millions are in silent revolt against their lot. Nobody knows how many rebellions ferment in the masses of life which people earth.

Women are supposed to be very calm generally: but women feel just as men feel; they need exercise for their faculties and a field for their efforts as much as their brothers do; they suffer from too rigid a restraint, too absolute a stagnation, precisely as men would suffer; and it is narrow-minded in their more privileged fellow-creatures to say that they ought to confine themselves to making puddings and knitting stockings, to playing on the piano and embroidering bags. It is thoughtless to condemn them, or laugh at them, if they seek to do more or learn more than custom has pronounced necessary for their sex.

"When thus alone I not unfrequently heard Grace Poole's laugh. . . ."

That is an awkward break, I thought. It is upsetting to come upon Grace Poole all of a sudden. The continuity is disturbed. One might say, I continued, laying the book down beside *Pride and Prejudice,* that the woman who wrote those pages had more genius in her than Jane Austen; but if one reads them over and marks that jerk in them, that indignation, one sees that she will never get her genius expressed whole and entire. Her books will be deformed and twisted. She will write in a rage where she should write calmly. She will write foolishly where she should write wisely. She will write of herself where she should write of her characters. She is at war with her lot. How could she help but die young, cramped and thwarted?

One could not but play for a moment with the thought of what might have happened if Charlotte Brontë had possessed say three hundred a year — but the foolish woman sold the copyright of her novels outright for fifteen hundred pounds; had somehow possessed more knowledge of the busy world, and towns and regions full of life; more practical experience, and intercourse with her kind and acquaintance with a variety of character. In those words she puts her finger exactly not only upon her own defects as a novelist but upon those of her sex at that time. She knew, no one better, how enormously her genius would have profited if it had not spent itself in solitary visions over distant fields; if experience and intercourse and travel had been granted her. But they were not granted; they were withheld; and we must accept the fact that all those good novels, *Villette,*

Emma, Wuthering Heights, Middlemarch, were written by women without more experience of life than could enter the house of a respectable clergyman; written too in the common sitting-room of that respectable house and by women so poor that they could not afford to buy more than a few quires of paper at a time upon which to write *Wuthering Heights* or *Jane Eyre.* One of them, it is true, George Eliot, escaped after much tribulation, but only to a secluded villa in St. John's Wood. And there she settled down in the shadow of the world's disapproval. "I wish it to be understood," she wrote, "that I should never invite any one to come and see me who did not ask for the invitation"; for was she not living in sin with a married man and might not the sight of her damage the chastity of Mrs. Smith or whoever it might be that chanced to call? One must submit to the social convention, and be "cut off from what is called the world." At the same time, on the other side of Europe, there was a young man living freely with this gipsy or with that great lady; going to the wars; picking up unhindered and uncensored all that varied experience of human life which served him so splendidly later when he came to write his books. Had Tolstoy lived at the Priory in seclusion with a married lady "cut off from what is called the world," however edifying the moral lesson, he could scarcely, I thought, have written *War and Peace.*

But one could perhaps go a little deeper into the question of novel-writing and the effect of sex upon the novelist. If one shuts one's eyes and thinks of the novel as a whole, it would seem to be a creation owning a certain looking-glass likeness to life, though of course with simplifications and distortions innumerable. At any rate, it is a structure leaving a shape on the mind's eye, built now in squares, now pagoda shaped, now throwing out wings and arcades, now solidly compact and domed like the Cathedral of Saint Sofia at Constantinople. This shape, I thought, thinking back over certain famous novels, starts in one the kind of emotion that is appropriate to it. But that emotion at once blends itself with others, for the "shape" is not made by the relation of stone to stone, but by the relation of human being to human being. Thus a novel starts in us all sorts of antagonistic and opposed emotions. Life conflicts with something that is not life. Hence the difficulty of coming to any agreement about novels, and the immense sway that our private prejudices have upon us. On the one hand, we feel You — John the hero — must live, or I shall be in the depths of despair. On the other, we feel, Alas, John, you must die, because the shape of the book requires it. Life conflicts with something that is not life. Then since life it is in part, we judge it as life. James is the sort of man I most detest, one says. Or, This is a farrago of absurdity. I could never feel anything of the sort myself. The whole structure, it is obvious, thinking back on any famous novel, is one of infinite complexity, because it is thus made up of so many different judgments, of so many different kinds of emotion. The wonder is that any book so composed holds together for more than a year or two, or can possibly mean to the English reader what it means for the Russian or the Chinese. But they do hold together occasionally very remarkably. And what holds them together in these rare instances of survival (I was thinking of *War and Peace*) is something that one calls integrity, though it has nothing to do with paying one's bills or behaving honourably in an emergency. What one means by integrity, in the case of the novelist, is the conviction that he gives one that this is the truth. Yes, one feels, I should never have thought that this could be so; I have never known people behaving like that. But you have convinced me that so it is, so it happens. One holds every phrase, every scene to the light as one reads — for Nature seems, very oddly, to have provided us with an inner light by which to judge of the novelist's integrity or disintegrity. Or perhaps it is rather that Nature, in her most irrational mood, has traced in invisible ink on the walls of the mind a premonition which these great artists confirm; a sketch which only needs to be held to the fire of genius to become visible. When one so exposes it and sees it come to life one exclaims in rapture, But this is what I have always felt and known and desired! And one boils over with excitement, and, shutting the book even with a kind of reverence as if it were something very precious, a stand-by to return to as long as one lives, one puts it back on the shelf, I said, taking *War and Peace* and putting it back in its place. If, on the other hand, these poor sentences that one takes and tests rouse first a quick and eager response with their bright colouring and their dashing gestures but there they stop: something seems to check them in their development: or if they bring to light only a faint scribble in that corner and a blot over there, and nothing appears whole and entire, then one heaves a sigh of disappointment and says, Another failure. This novel has come to grief somewhere.

And for the most part, of course, novels do come to grief somewhere. The imagination falters under the enormous strain. The insight is confused; it can no longer distinguish between the true and false; it has no longer the strength to go on with the vast labour that calls at every moment for the use of so many different faculties. But how would all this be affected by the sex of the novelist, I wondered, looking at *Jane Eyre* and the others. Would the fact of her sex in any way interfere with the integrity of a woman novelist — that integrity which I take to be the backbone of the writer? Now, in the passages I have quoted from *Jane Eyre*, it is clear that anger was tampering with the integrity of Charlotte Brontë the novelist. She left her story, to which her entire devotion was due, to attend to some personal grievance. She remembered that she had been starved of her proper due of experience — she had been made to stagnate in a parsonage mending stockings when she wanted to wander free over the world. Her imagination swerved from indignation and we feel it swerve. But there were many more influences than anger tugging at her imagination and deflecting it from its path. Ignorance, for instance. The portrait of Rochester is drawn in the dark. We feel the influence of fear in it; just as we constantly feel an acidity which is the result of oppression, a buried suffering smouldering beneath her passion, a rancour which contracts those books, splendid as they are, with a spasm of pain.

And since a novel has this correspondence to real life, its values are to some extent those of real life. But it is obvious that the values of women differ very often from the values which have been made by the other sex; naturally, this is so. Yet it is the masculine values that prevail. Speaking crudely, football and sport are "important"; the worship of fashion, the buying of clothes "trivial."

And these values are inevitably transferred from life to fiction. This is an important book, the critic assumes, because it deals with war. This is an insignificant book because it deals with the feelings of women in a drawing-room. A scene in a battlefield is more important than a scene in a shop — everywhere and much more subtly the difference of value persists. The whole structure, therefore, of the early nineteenth-century novel was raised, if one was a woman, by a mind which was slightly pulled from the straight, and made to alter its clear vision in deference to external authority. One has only to skim those old forgotten novels and listen to the tone of voice in which they were written to divine that the writer was meeting criticism; she was saying this by way of aggression, or that by way of conciliation. She was admitting that she was "only a woman," or protesting that she was "as good as a man." She met that criticism as her temperament dictated, with docility and diffidence, or with anger and emphasis. It does not matter which it was; she was thinking of something other than the thing itself. Down comes her book upon our heads. There was a flaw in the centre of it. And I thought of all the women's novels that lie scattered, like small pock-marked apples in an orchard, about the second-hand book shops of London. It was the flaw in the centre that had rotted them. She had altered her values in deference to the opinion of others.

But how impossible it must have been for them not to budge either to the right or to the left. What genius, what integrity it must have required in face of all that criticism, in the midst of that purely patriarchal society, to hold fast to the thing as they saw it without shrinking. Only Jane Austen did it and Emily Brontë. It is another feather, perhaps the finest, in their caps. They wrote as women write, not as men write. Of all the thousand women who wrote novels then, they alone entirely ignored the perpetual admonitions of the eternal pedagogue — write this, think that. They alone were deaf to that persistent voice, now grumbling, now patronising, now domineering, now grieved, now shocked, now angry, now avuncular, that voice which cannot let women alone, but must be at them, like some too conscientious governess, adjuring them, like Sir Egerton Brydges, to be refined; dragging even into the criticism of poetry criticism of sex;[3] admonishing them, if they would be good and win, as I suppose, some shiny prize, to keep within certain limits which the gentleman in question thinks suitable: ". . . female novelists should only aspire to excellence by courageously acknowledging the limitations of their sex."[4] That puts the matter in a nutshell, and when I tell you, rather to your surprise, that this sentence was written not in August 1828 but in August 1928, you will agree, I think, that however delightful it is to us now, it represents a vast body of opinion — I am not going to stir those old pools, I take only what chance has floated to my feet — that was far more vigorous and far more vocal a century ago. It would have needed a very stalwart young woman in 1828 to disregard all those snubs and chidings and promises of prizes. One must have been something of a firebrand to say to oneself, Oh, but they can't buy literature too. Literature is open to everybody. I refuse to allow you, Beadle though you are, to turn me off the grass. Lock up your libraries if you like; but there is no gate, no lock, no bolt that you can set upon the freedom of my mind.

But whatever effect discouragement and criticism had upon their writing — and I believe that they had a very great effect — that was unimportant compared with the other difficulty which faced them (I was still considering those early nineteenth-century novelists) when they came to set their thoughts on paper — that is that they had no tradition behind them, or one so short and partial that it was of little help. For we think back through our mothers if we are women. It is useless to go to the great men writers for help, however much one may go to them for pleasure. Lamb, Browne, Thackeray, Newman, Sterne, Dickens, De Quincey — whoever it may be — never

helped a woman yet, though she may have learnt a few tricks of them and adapted them to her use. The weight, the pace, the stride of a man's mind are too unlike her own for her to lift anything substantial from him successfully. The ape is too distant to be sedulous. Perhaps the first thing she would find, setting pen to paper, was that there was no common sentence ready for her use. All the great novelists like Thackeray and Dickens and Balzac have written a natural prose, swift but not slovenly, expressive but not precious, taking their own tint without ceasing to be common property. They have based it on the sentence that was current at the time. The sentence that was current at the beginning of the nineteenth century ran something like this perhaps: "The grandeur of their works was an argument with them, not to stop short, but to proceed. They could have no higher excitement or satisfaction than in the exercise of their art and endless generations of truth and beauty. Success prompts to exertion; and habit facilitates success." That is a man's sentence; behind it one can see Johnson, Gibbon and the rest. It was a sentence that was unsuited for a woman's use. Charlotte Brontë, with all her splendid gift for prose, stumbled and fell with that clumsy weapon in her hands. George Eliot committed atrocities with it that beggar description. Jane Austen looked at it and laughed at it and devised a perfectly natural, shapely sentence proper for her own use and never departed from it. Thus, with less genius for writing than Charlotte Brontë, she got infinitely more said. Indeed, since freedom and fullness of expression are of the essence of the art, such a lack of tradition, such a scarcity and inadequacy of tools, must have told enormously upon the writing of women. Moreover, a book is not made of sentences laid end to end, but of sentences built, if an image helps, into arcades or domes. And this shape too has been made by men out of their own needs for their own uses. There is no reason to think that the form of the epic or of the poetic play suits a woman any more than the sentence suits her. But all the older forms of literature were hardened and set by the time she became a writer. The novel alone was young enough to be soft in her hands — another reason, perhaps, why she wrote novels. Yet who shall say that even now

[3]"[She] has a metaphysical purpose, and that is a dangerous obsession, especially with a woman, for women rarely possess men's healthy love of rhetoric. It is a strange lack in the sex which is in other things more primitive and more materialistic." — *New Criterion,* June 1928. [Woolf]

[4]"If, like the reporter, you believe that female novelists should only aspire to excellence by courageously acknowledging the limitations of their sex (Jane Austen [has] demonstrated how gracefully this gesture can be accomplished). . . ." — *Life and Letters,* August 1928. [Woolf]

"the novel" (I give it inverted commas to mark my sense of the words' inadequacy), who shall say that even this most pliable of all forms is rightly shaped for her use? No doubt we shall find her knocking that into shape for herself when she has the free use of her limbs; and providing some new vehicle, not necessarily in verse, for the poetry in her. For it is the poetry that is still denied outlet. And I went on to ponder how a woman nowadays would write a poetic tragedy in five acts — would she use verse — would she not use prose rather?

[The Androgynous Vision] from *A Room of One's Own*

What does one mean by "the unity of the mind," I pondered, for clearly the mind has so great a power of concentrating at any point at any moment that it seems to have no single state of being. It can separate itself from the people in the street, for example, and think of itself as apart from them, at an upper window looking down on them. Or it can think with other people spontaneously, as, for instance, in a crowd waiting to hear some piece of news read out. It can think back through its fathers or through its mothers, as I have said that a woman writing thinks back through her mothers. Again if one is a woman one is often surprised by a sudden splitting off of consciousness, say in walking down Whitehall, when from being the natural inheritor of that civilisation, she becomes, on the contrary, outside of it, alien and critical. Clearly the mind is always altering its focus, and bringing the world into different perspectives. But some of these states of mind seem, even if adopted spontaneously, to be less comfortable than others. In order to keep oneself continuing in them one is unconsciously holding something back, and gradually the repression becomes an effort. But there may be some state of mind in which one could continue without effort because nothing is required to be held back. And this perhaps, I thought, coming in from the window, is one of them. For certainly when I saw the couple get into the taxi-cab the mind felt as if, after being divided, it had come together again in natural fusion. The obvious reason would be that it is natural for the sexes to cooperate. One has a profound, if irrational, instinct in favour of the theory that the union of man and woman makes for the greatest satisfaction, the most complete happiness. But the sight of the two people getting into the taxi and the satisfaction it gave me made me also ask whether there are two sexes in the mind corresponding to the two sexes in the body, and whether they also require to be united in order to get complete satisfaction and happiness. And I went on amateurishly to sketch a plan of the soul so that in each of us two powers preside, one male, one female; and in the man's brain, the man predominates over the woman, and in the woman's brain, the woman predominates over the man. The normal and comfortable state of being is that when the two live in harmony together, spiritually co-operating. If one is a man, still the woman part of the brain must have effect; and a woman also must have intercourse with the man in her. Coleridge perhaps meant this when he said that a great mind is androgynous.[1] It is when this fusion takes place that the mind is fully fertilised and uses all its faculties. Perhaps a mind that is purely masculine cannot create, any more than a mind that is purely feminine, I thought. But it would be well to test what one meant by man-womanly, and conversely by woman-manly, by pausing and looking at a book or two.

Coleridge certainly did not mean, when he said that a great mind is androgynous, that it is a mind that has any special sympathy with women; a mind

[1]See *Specimens of the Table Talk of S. T. Coleridge* (London, 1837) for September 1, 1832.

that takes up their cause or devotes itself to their interpretation. Perhaps the androgynous mind is less apt to make these distinctions than the single-sexed mind. He meant, perhaps, that the androgynous mind is resonant and porous; that it transmits emotion without impediment; that it is naturally creative, incandescent, and undivided. In fact one goes back to Shakespeare's mind as the type of the androgynous, of the man-womanly mind, though it would be impossible to say what Shakespeare thought of women. And if it be true that it is one of the tokens of the fully developed mind that it does not think specially or separately of sex, how much harder it is to attain that condition now than ever before. Here I came to the books by living writers, and there paused and wondered if this fact were not at the root of something that had long puzzled me. No age can ever have been as stridently sex-conscious as our own; those innumerable books by men about women in the British Museum are a proof of it. The Suffrage campaign[2] was no doubt to blame. It must have roused in men an extraordinary desire for self-assertion; it must have made them lay an emphasis upon their own sex and its characteristics which they would not have troubled to think about had they not been challenged. And when one is challenged, even by a few women in black bonnets, one retaliates, if one has never been challenged before, rather excessively. That perhaps accounts for some of the characteristics that I remember to have found here, I thought, taking down a new novel by Mr. A, who is in the prime of life and very well thought of, apparently, by the reviewers. I opened it. Indeed, it was delightful to read a man's writing again. It was so direct, so straightforward after the writing of women. It indicated such freedom of mind, such liberty of person, such confidence in himself. One had a sense of physical well-being in the presence of this well-nourished, well-educated, free mind, which had never been thwarted or opposed, but had had full liberty from birth to stretch itself in whatever way it liked. All this was admirable. But after reading a chapter or two a shadow seemed to lie across the page. It was a straight dark bar, a shadow shaped something like the letter "I." One began dodging this way and that to catch a glimpse of the landscape behind it. Whether that was indeed a tree or a woman walking I was not quite sure. Back one was always hailed to the letter "I." One began to be tired of "I." Not but what this "I" was a most respectable "I"; honest and logical; as hard as a nut, and polished for centuries by good teaching and good feeding. I respect and admire that "I" from the bottom of my heart. But — here I turned a page or two, looking for something or other — the worst of it is that in the shadow of the letter "I" all is shapeless as mist. Is that a tree? No, it is a woman. But . . . she has not a bone in her body, I thought, watching Phoebe, for that was her name, coming across the beach. Then Alan got up and the shadow of Alan at once obliterated Phoebe. For Alan had views and Phoebe was quenched in the flood of his views. And then Alan, I thought, has passions; and here I turned page after page very fast, feeling that the crisis was approaching, and so it was. It took place on the beach under the sun. It was done very openly. It was done very vigorously. Nothing could have been more indecent. But . . . I had said "but" too often. One cannot go on saying "but." One must finish the sentence somehow, I rebuked myself. Shall I finish it, "But — I am bored!" But why was I bored? Partly because of the dominance of the letter "I" and the aridity, which, like the giant beech tree, it casts within its shade. Nothing will grow there. And partly for some more obscure reason. There seemed to be some obstacle, some impediment of Mr. A's mind which blocked the fountain of creative energy and shored it within narrow limits. And remembering the lunch party at Oxbridge, and the cigarette ash and the Manx cat and Tennyson and Christina Rossetti all in a bunch, it seemed possible that the impediment lay there. As he no longer hums under his breath, "There has fallen a splendid tear from the passion-flower at the gate,"[3] when Phoebe crosses the

[2]Women in the United Kingdom asserted their right to vote in a campaign that lasted from 1866 to 1928. (Women over 30 were given the vote in 1918; the franchise was extended to women 21–29 in 1928.)

[3]From *Maud* (1862) by Alfred Lord Tennyson (1809–1892), lines 165–68. This famous passage goes on: "She is coming, my dove, my dear; She is coming, my life, my fate; / The red rose cries, 'She is near, she is near;' and the white rose weeps, 'She is late;' / The larkspur listens, 'I hear, I hear;' and the lily whispers, 'I wait.'"

beach, and she no longer replies, "My heart is like a singing bird whose nest is in a water'd shoot,"[4] when Alan approaches what can he do? Being honest as the day and logical as the sun, there is only one thing he can do. And that he does, to do him justice, over and over (I said, turning the pages) and over again. And that, I added, aware of the awful nature of the confession, seems somehow dull. Shakespeare's indecency uproots a thousand other things in one's mind, and is far from being dull. But Shakespeare does it for pleasure; Mr. A, as the nurses say, does it on purpose. He does it in protest. He is protesting against the equality of the other sex by asserting his own superiority. He is therefore impeded and inhibited and self-conscious as Shakespeare might have been if he too had known Miss Clough and Miss Davies.[5] Doubtless Elizabethan literature would have been very different from what it is if the woman's movement had begun in the sixteenth century and not in the nineteenth.

What, then, it amounts to, if this theory of the two sides of the mind holds good, is that virility has now become self-conscious — men, that is to say, are now writing only with the male side of their brains. It is a mistake for a woman to read them, for she will inevitably look for something that she will not find. It is the power of suggestion that one most misses, I thought, taking Mr. B the critic in my hand and reading, very carefully and very dutifully, his remarks upon the art of poetry. Very able they were, acute and full of learning; but the trouble was, that his feelings no longer communicated; his mind seemed separated into different chambers; not a sound carried from one to the other. Thus, when one takes a sentence of Mr. B into the mind it falls plump to the ground — dead; but when one takes a sentence of Coleridge into the mind, it explodes and gives birth to all kinds of other ideas, and that is the only sort of writing of which one can say that it has the secret of perpetual life.

But whatever the reason may be, it is a fact that one must deplore. For it means — here I had come to rows of books by Mr. Galsworthy and Mr. Kipling — that some of the finest works of our greatest living writers fall upon deaf ears. Do what she will a woman cannot find in them that fountain of perpetual life which the critics assure her is there. It is not only that they celebrate male virtues, enforce male values, and describe the world of men; it is that the emotion with which these books are permeated is to a woman incomprehensible. It is coming, it is gathering, it is about to burst on one's head, one begins saying long before the end. That picture will fall on old Jolyon's head; he will die of the shock; the old clerk will speak over him two or three obituary words; and all the swans on the Thames will simultaneously burst out singing. But one will rush away before that happens and hide in the gooseberry bushes, for the emotion which is so deep, so subtle, so symbolical to a man moves a woman to wonder. So with Mr. Kipling's officers who turn their backs; and his Sowers who sow the Seed; and his Men who are alone with their Work; and the Flag — one blushes at all these capital letters as if one had been caught eavesdropping at some purely masculine orgy. The fact is that neither Mr. Galsworthy nor Mr. Kipling has a spark of the woman in him. Thus all their qualities seem to a woman, if one may generalise, crude and immature. They lack suggestive power. And when a book lacks suggestive power, however hard it hits the surface of the mind it cannot penetrate within.

And in that restless mood in which one takes books out and puts them back again without looking at them I began to envisage an age to come of pure, of self-assertive virility, such as the letters of professors (take Sir Walter Raleigh's[6] letters, for instance) seem to forebode, and the rulers of Italy[7]

---

[4]The opening lines of "A Birthday" in *Goblin Market and Other Poems* (published in the same years as *Maud*, 1862), by Christina Rossetti (1830–1894), ending "Because the birthday of my life / Is come, my love is come to me."

[5]Anne Jemima Clough (1820–1892) and Emily Davies (1830–1921) were prominent in both the suffrage movement and the efforts to open Cambridge University to women. Clough served as principal of Newnham College; Davies raised money for the foundation of what eventually became Girton College.

[6]Not the Elizabethan explorer, but Sir Walter Alexander Raleigh (1861–1922), professor at Oxford and the author of dozens of studies on English literature.

[7]Benito Mussolini and his Fascist Party.

have already brought into being. For one can hardly fail to be impressed in Rome by the sense of unmitigated masculinity; and whatever the value of unmitigated masculinity upon the state, one may question the effect of it upon the art of poetry. At any rate, according to the newspapers, there is a certain anxiety about fiction in Italy. There has been a meeting of academicians whose object it is "to develop the Italian novel." "Men famous by birth, or in finance, industry or the Fascist corporations" came together the other day and discussed the matter, and a telegram was sent to the Duce expressing the hope "that the Fascist era would soon give birth to a poet worthy of it." We may all join in that pious hope, but it is doubtful whether poetry can come out of an incubator. Poetry ought to have a mother as well as a father. The Fascist poem, one may fear, will be a horrid little abortion such as one sees in a glass jar in the museum of some county town. Such monsters never live long, it is said; one has never seen a prodigy of that sort cropping grass in a field. Two heads on one body do not make for length of life.

However, the blame for all this, if one is anxious to lay blame, rests no more upon one sex than upon the other. All seducers and reformers are responsible, Lady Bessborough when she lied to Lord Granville;[8] Miss Davies when she told the truth to Mr. Greg.[9] All who have brought about a state of sex-consciousness are to blame, and it is they who drive me, when I want to stretch my faculties on a book, to seek it in that happy age, before Miss Davies and Miss Clough were born, when the writer used both sides of his mind equally. One must turn back to Shakespeare then, for Shakespeare was androgynous; and so was Keats and Sterne and Cowper and Lamb and Coleridge. Shelley perhaps was sexless. Milton and Ben Jonson had a dash too much of the male

in them. So had Wordsworth and Tolstoi. In our time Proust was wholly androgynous, if not perhaps a little too much of a woman. But that failing is too rare for one to complain of it, since without some mixture of the kind the intellect seems to predominate and the other faculties of the mind harden and become barren. However, I consoled myself with the reflection that this is perhaps a passing phase; much of what I have said in obedience to my promise to give you the course of my thoughts will seem out of date; much of what flames in my eyes will seem dubious to you who have not yet come of age.

Even so, the very first sentence that I would write here, I said, crossing over to the writing-table and taking up the page headed Women and Fiction, is that it is fatal for any one who writes to think of their sex. It is fatal to be a man or woman pure and simple; one must be woman-manly or man-womanly. It is fatal for a woman to lay the least stress on any grievance; to plead even with justice any cause; in any way to speak consciously as a woman. And fatal is no figure of speech; for anything written with that conscious bias is doomed to death. It ceases to be fertilised. Brilliant and effective, powerful and masterly, as it may appear for a day or two, it must wither at nightfall; it cannot grow in the minds of others. Some collaboration has to take place in the mind between the woman and the man before the act of creation can be accomplished. Some marriage of opposites has to be consummated. The whole of the mind must lie wide open if we are to get the sense that the writer is communicating his experience with perfect fullness. There must be freedom and there must be peace. Not a wheel must grate, not a light glimmer. The curtains must be close drawn, The writer, I thought, once his experience is over, must lie back and let his mind celebrate its nuptials in darkness. He must not look or question what is being done. Rather, he must pluck the petals from a rose or watch the swans float calmly down the river. And I saw again the current which took the boat and the undergraduate and the dead leaves; and the taxi took the man and the woman, I thought, seeing them come together across the street, and the current swept them away, I thought, hearing far off the roar of London's traffic, into that tremendous stream.

[8]Two well-born Regency lovers, Henrietta Spencer Ponsonby, Countess Bessborough (1761–1821), and Granville Leveson Gower, Earl Granville (1773–1846). The "lie" is in her letter to Granville, which Woolf quotes earlier: "I perfectly agree with you that no woman has any business to meddle with [politics] or any other serious business whatsoever, farther than giving her opinion (if she is ask'd)."
[9]Probably Walter Wilson Greg (1875–1959), known primarily as a textual editor of English literature, who is quoted earlier in A Room of One's Own: the "essentials of a woman's being are that they are supported by, and they minister to, men."

Martin Heidegger

1889–1976

Martin Heidegger, born in Messkirch in the German province of Basel, was educated at the University of Freiburg where he studied under the phenomenologist Edmund Husserl. Heidegger began teaching at Freiburg in 1915, left to become a *privatdozent* at Marburg in 1923, and returned as professor of philosophy to Freiburg the year after the publication of his magnum opus, *Being and Time* (1927).

Briefly, *Being and Time* represents human beings as isolated individuals thrown helplessly into worlds not of their own making, who understand existence only through their interactions with the worlds they inhabit. This mode of existence Heidegger called *Dasein,* a coinage that is usually translated as "Being-There" or "Being-in-the-World." If our *Dasein* involves being endlessly distracted by the trivial everyday struggles within a mass society, human beings nevertheless are driven relentlessly to seek *Sein* (true Being), a transcendent state in which the meaning of life would be clarified. But this quest is by its very nature absurd. In Heidegger's philosophy, no romantic transcendence to the higher level of Being is possible: The best we can attain is an authentic (*eigentlich*) existence. Authenticity is predicated on three interlocking issues: (1) dread, the nauseating sense that our own death is the only thing indisputably our own; (2) conscience, the sense that while we cannot choose the world into which we are thrown, we can always choose how we act within it; and (3) history, the subjective sense of the relation of our personal destiny to the fate of the other human beings among whom we live.

If all this sounds a bit like the tenets of French existentialism, that is no accident: While studying in Berlin in 1933, Jean-Paul Sartre was immensely influenced by Heidegger's *Being and Time.* But for Heidegger, the relation of the individual to others making up the world was important in different ways than for Sartre. Heidegger was certain this relation was being destroyed by the fragmentation of modern life and emphasized each individual's need for a homeland and a folk culture with which to identify. He was thus attracted not to the internationalist and socialist Left in Germany, but to the reactionary parties of the Right who stressed the uniqueness of the German *Volk.*

When the National Socialists took power in Germany in 1933, Heidegger successfully campaigned to be made rector of the university, a position that he resigned ten months later when it became clear that the Nazis were merely using him and that his program to restructure the university was not going to be implemented. Heidegger continued to teach at the university and, during the later years of the Reich, increasingly distanced himself from Hitler's methods and goals, claiming after the war to have in effect created an "intellectual resistance" in his classes. While questions have been raised about precisely what damage Heidegger did in the service of Nazism to his Jewish and socialist colleagues, he was certainly, at least during 1933–34, not simply an opportunistic timeserver but an enthusiastic supporter of the Nazis' racial ideas and political program. Even after the fall of Hitler,

Heidegger refused to apologize for his speeches and acts under the Nazi regime and unrepentently viewed the German people as a race of high destiny beset by two barbarian mass societies: the Soviet Union and the United States. He died in his home town of Messkirch in 1976.

Despite his political and racial views, Heidegger was — together with Ludwig Wittgenstein — one of the most important influences on twentieth-century philosophy. Curiously enough, those he has influenced most decisively have not been conservatives or reactionaries but have located their politics either on the radical Left (not only Jean-Paul Sartre but cultural theorist Michel Foucault) or the liberal Center (such as theologians Rudolf Bultmann, Karl Jaspers, and Paul Tillich; political philosopher Hannah Arendt; phenomenologist Hans-Georg Gadamer; and deconstructionist Jacques Derrida). Heidegger's radical critique of science and its rhetoric underlies the thought of philosophers of science Thomas S. Kuhn (*The Structure of Scientific Revolutions*, 1970) and Paul Feyerabend (*Against Method*, 1975). His principal message, on the nature of man and human experience and the vital role of language (including poetic language) in our understanding of the world, has inspired many who were deeply disgusted by his life and politics, and it continues to underlie much of contemporary criticism.

Heidegger's essay, "Hölderlin and the Essence of Poetry" (1936), uses touchstones within texts of the poet Friedrich Hölderlin (1770–1843) to develop the theory of poetry and language that he presents at greater length in "The Origin of the Work of Art" (1936). Here Hölderlin's Romantic lyrics, rediscovered early in the twentieth century, provide perfect "pointers" for the turns of Heidegger's thought because they combine an intense subjective inwardness with serene abstraction, like a combination of Shelley with Wallace Stevens. Heidegger is able to use phrases and lines from Hölderlin's poetry to convey some of the basic themes that he developed in *Being and Time* and never abandoned. For example, in a prose poem, Hölderlin's seemingly chance phrase, "but Man dwells in huts," reminds Heidegger of the alienation of our species from Nature. The need to make houses becomes, for Heidegger, a metaphor for the need to choose one's being, to determine with authenticity precisely who one is. But while the essay recapitulates many of the themes of *Being and Time*, Heidegger here seems more influenced by the later works of Nietzsche than by Husserl, his former teacher. It is aesthetics and language, rather than quotidian experience, that Heidegger portrays as the cornerstone on which the vision of life is built.

Heidegger viewed art as the bringing-into-being of something new, a new world. In part this means that a work of art opens new worlds to us in the usual sense, by exposing us to an aspect of human experience that we would not know otherwise. Some of us don't have access to a certain form of play of language, for example, till we experience the works of James Joyce or Vladimir Nabokov. But in part it means something more. When Heidegger asserts that "Poetry is the primitive language of a historical people," he is insisting on the way in which language itself can become a homeland. As a result of the work of the poet, Heidegger believes, art can function as the "homeland" that he felt mass culture was distancing us from; it can give back to us the beauty and truth of certain aspects of experience that modern culture treats as mere instrumentalities.

This may seem like a version of Romantic aesthetics — like Hegel's view of art as a bearer of truth, or Shelley's argument in *A Defense of Poetry* that "Poets are the unacknowledged legislators of the World" (see p. 363) — but Heidegger puts it this way: "The speech of the poet is establishment . . . in the sense of the firm basing of human existence on its foundation." In fact, Heidegger's formulation goes much farther than Hegel's or Shelley's. Those Romantic idealists view the Truth or Law borne by the work of art as an independent essence prior to all human thought, which is discovered by the spirit of the artist and then conveyed to mankind by means of the poem. But for Heidegger, there are no such essences prior to thinking. The truth *in* the work is the truth *of* the work; the truth happens when it comes into historical existence, in that contingent moment when the work is made, when the poem is written or the painting painted. And it "happens" again when we read or view and understand the poem or the painting.

At the center of the Hölderlin essay, Heidegger briefly takes up the question of Language: "Language is not a mere tool, one of the many which man possesses; on the contrary, it is only language that affords the very possibility of standing in the openness of the existent. Only where there is language, is there world. . . . Only where world predominates, is there history" (see pp. 616–17). These remarks about language as the ground-of-being of the truth that is poetry hint at something new, for they suggest that the most basic level of existence is no longer lonely *Dasein* (Being-in-the-World) but the collective conversation that forms human Language.

These hints are developed into major themes in Heidegger's later work, which, like Nietzsche's later work, grounds his vision of reality on aesthetics. In his later essays, including "Language" (1950), "A Dialogue on Language" (1953–54), and "The Way to Language" (1959), Language replaces *Dasein* as the bedrock from which the world is called into being; it is not *Dasein* that speaks to us but Language, whose mystical power of naming and showing calls the world into existence for us. In his essay, "Language," Heidegger insists that "We do not wish to ground language in something else that is not language itself."[1] And, in "The Nature of Language," Heidegger enigmatically follows out the implications of the poet Stefan Georg's line "Where word breaks off, nothing may be," and himself poetically suggests how language creates the universe we experience: "When the word is called the mouth's flower and its blossom, we hear the sound of language rising like the earth. From whence? From Saying in which it comes to pass that World is made to appear. The sound rings out in the resounding assembly call which, open to the Open, makes World appear in all things."[2] From here it is no distance at all to St. John's mystical vision of the Logos that is God.

[1]"Language." In *Poetry, Language and Thought*, p. 191.
[2]"The Nature of Language." In *On the Way to Language*, p. 101.

Selected Bibliography

Bourdieu, Pierre. *The Political Ontology of Martin Heidegger.* Stanford: Stanford University Press, 1991.

Davis, Walter A. *Inwardness and Existence: Subjectivity in Hegel, Heidegger, Marx, and Freud.* Madison: University of Wisconsin Press, 1989.

Foti, Veronique M. *Heidegger and the Poets: Poesis — Sophia — Techne.* New York: Humanities Press International, 1995.

Gadamer, Hans-Georg. *Heidegger's Ways.* Albany: State University of New York Press, 1994.

Heidegger, Martin. *Martin Heidegger: Existence and Being,* trans. Douglas Scott. Chicago: Henry Regnery, 1949.

———. *Being and Time,* trans. John Macquarrie and Edward Robinson, 1927. New York: Harper and Row, 1962.

———. *On the Way to Language,* trans. Peter D. Hertz. New York: Harper and Row, 1971.

———. *Poetry, Language and Thought,* trans. Albert Hofstadter. New York: Harper and Row, 1971.

Holland, Nancy J., and Patricia Huntington, eds. *Feminist Interpretations of Martin Heidegger.* University Park: Pennsylvania State University Press, 2001.

Lafont, Cristina, and Graham Harman. *Heidegger, Language, and World-Disclosure.* Cambridge: Cambridge University Press, 2000.

Megill, Alan. *Prophets of Extremity: Nietzsche, Heidegger, Foucault, Derrida.* Berkeley: University of California Press, 1985.

Ott, Hugo. *Martin Heidegger: A Political Life.* New York: Basic Books, 1993.

Rorty, Richard. *Philosophical Papers: Essays on Heidegger and Others,* vol. 2. New York and London: Cambridge University Press, 1991.

Sass, Hans-Martin. *Martin Heidegger: Bibliography and Glossary.* Bowling Green, OH: Bowling Green University Press, 1982.

Spanos, William V. *Heidegger and Criticism: Retrieving the Cultural Politics of Destruction.* Minneapolis: University of Minnesota Press, 1993.

Wolin, Richard, ed. *The Heidegger Controversy: A Critical Reader.* Cambridge: MIT Press, 1992.

Hölderlin and the Essence of Poetry

THE FIVE POINTERS

1. Writing poetry: "That most innocent of all occupations." (III, 377.)
2. "Therefore has language, most dangerous of possessions, been given to man . . . so that he may affirm what he is. . . ." (IV, 246.)
3. "Much has man learnt.
Many of the heavenly ones has he named,

Since we have been a conversation
And have been able to hear from one another." (IV, 343.)
4. "But that which remains, is established by the poets." (IV, 63.)
5. "Full of merit, and yet poetically, dwells Man on this earth." (VI, 25.)

Why has Hölderlin's work been chosen for the purpose of showing the essence of poetry? Why not Homer or Sophocles, why not Virgil or Dante,

Translated by Douglas Scott.

why not Shakespeare or Goethe? The essence of poetry is realised in the works of these poets too, and more richly even, than in the creative work of Hölderlin, which breaks off so early and abruptly.

This may be so. And yet Hölderlin has been chosen, and he alone. But generally speaking is it possible for the universal essence of poetry to be read off from the work of one single poet? Whatever is universal, that is to say, what is valid for many, can only be reached through a process of comparison. For this, one requires a sample containing the greatest possible diversity of poems and kinds of poetry. From this point of view Hölderlin's poetry is only one among many others. By itself it can in no way suffice as a criterion for determining the essence of poetry. Hence we fail in our purpose at the very outset. Certainly — so long as we take "essence of poetry" to mean what is gathered together into a universal concept, which is then valid in the same way for every poem. But this universal which thus applies equally to every particular, is always the indifferent, that essence which can never become essential.

Yet it is precisely this essential element of the essence that we are searching for — that which compels us to decide whether we are going to take poetry seriously and if so how, whether and to what extent we can bring with us the presuppositions necessary if we are to come under the sway of poetry.

Hölderlin has not been chosen because his work, one among many, realises the universal essence of poetry, but solely because Hölderlin's poetry was borne on by the poetic vocation to write expressly of the essence of poetry. For us Hölderlin is in a pre-eminent sense *the poet of the poet*. That is why he compels a decision.

But — to write about the poet, is this not a symptom of a perverted narcissism and at the same time a confession of inadequate richness of vision? To write about the poet, is that not a senseless exaggeration, something decadent and a blind alley?

The answer will be given in what follows. To be sure, the path by which we reach the answer is one of expediency. We cannot here, as would have to be done, expound separately each of Hölderlin's poems one after the other. Instead let us take only five pointers which the poet gave on the subject of poetry. The necessary order in these sayings and their inner connectedness ought to bring before our eyes the essential essence of poetry.

1

In a letter to his mother in January 1799, Hölderlin calls the writing of poetry "that most innocent of all occupations" (III, 377). To what extent is it the "most innocent"? Writing poetry appears in the modest guise of *play*. Unfettered, it invents its world of images and remains immersed in the realm of the imagined. This play thus avoids the seriousness of decisions, which always in one way or another create guilt. Hence writing poetry is completely harmless. And at the same time it is ineffectual; since it remains mere saying and speaking. It has nothing about it of action, which grasps hold directly of the real and alters it. Poetry is like a dream, and not reality; a playing with words, and not the seriousness of action. Poetry is harmless and ineffectual. For what can be less dangerous than mere speech? But in taking poetry to be the "most innocent of all occupations," we have not yet comprehended its essence. At any rate this gives us an indication of where we must look for it. Poetry creates its works in the realm and out of the "material" of language. What does Hölderlin say about language? Let us hear a second saying of the poet.

2

In a fragmentary sketch, dating from the same period (1800) as the letter just quoted, the poet says:

> But man dwells in huts and wraps himself in the bashful garment, since he is more fervent and more attentive too in watching over the spirit, as the priestess the divine flame; this is his understanding. And therefore he has been given arbitrariness, and to him, godlike, has been given higher power to command and to accomplish, and therefore has language, most dangerous of possessions, been given to man, so that creating, destroying, and perishing and returning to the ever-living, to the mistress and mother, he may affirm what he is — that he has inherited, learned from thee, thy most divine possession, all-preserving love. (IV, 246.)

Language, the field of the "most innocent of all occupations," is the "most dangerous of possessions." How can these two be reconciled? Let us put this question aside for the moment and consider the three preliminary questions: 1. Whose possession is language? 2. To what extent is it the most dangerous of possessions? 3. In what sense is it really a possession?

First of all we notice where this saying about language occurs: in the sketch for a poem which is to describe who man is, in contrast to the other beings of nature; mention is made of the rose, the swans, the stag in the forest (IV, 300 and 385). So, distinguishing plants from animals, the fragment begins: "But man dwells in huts."

And who then is man? He who must affirm what he is. To affirm means to declare; but at the same time it means: to give in the declaration a guarantee of what is declared. Man is *he* who he *is*, precisely in the affirmation of his own existence. This affirmation does not mean here an additional and supplementary expression of human existence, but it does in the process make plain the existence of man. But what must man affirm? That he belongs to the earth. This relation of belonging to consists in the fact that man is heir and learner in all things. But all these things are in conflict. That which keeps things apart in opposition and thus at the same time binds them together, is called by Hölderlin "intimacy." The affirmation of belonging to this intimacy occurs through the creation of a world and its ascent, and likewise through the destruction of a world and its decline. The affirmation of human existence and hence its essential consummation occurs through freedom of decision. This freedom lays hold of the necessary and places itself in the bonds of a supreme obligation. This bearing witness of belonging to all that is existent, becomes actual as history. In order that history may be possible, language has been given to man. It is one of man's possessions.

But to what extent is language the "most dangerous of possessions?" It is the danger of all dangers, because it creates initially the possibility of a danger. Danger is the threat to existence from what is existent. But now it is only by virtue of language at all that man is exposed to something manifest, which, *as* what is existent, afflicts and enflames man in his existence, and as what is non-existent deceives and disappoints. It is language which first creates the manifest conditions for menace and confusion to existence, and thus the possibility of the loss of existence, that is to say — danger. But language is not only the danger of dangers, but necessarily conceals in itself a continual danger for itself. Language has the task of making manifest in its work the existent, and of preserving it as such. In it, what is purest and what is most concealed, and likewise what is complex and ordinary, can be expressed in words. Even the essential word, if it is to be understood and so become a possession in common, must make itself ordinary. Accordingly it is remarked in another fragment of Hölderlin's: "Thou spokest to the Godhead, but this you have all forgotten, that the first-fruits are never for mortals, they belong to the gods. The fruit must become more ordinary, more everyday, and then it will be mortals' own." (IV, 238.) The pure and the ordinary are both equally something said. Hence the word as word never gives any direct guarantee as to whether it is an essential word or a counterfeit. On the contrary — an essential word often looks in its simplicity like an unessential one. And on the other hand that which is dressed up to look like the essential, is only something recited by heart or repeated. Therefore language must constantly present itself in an appearance which it itself attests, and hence endanger what is most characteristic of it, the genuine saying.

In what sense however is this most dangerous thing one of man's possessions? Language is his own property. It is at his disposal for the purpose of communicating his experiences, resolutions and moods. Language serves to give information. As a fit instrument for this, it is a "possession."[1] But the essence of language does not consist entirely in being a means of giving information. This definition does not touch its essential essence, but merely indicates an effect of its essence. Language is not a mere tool, one of the many which man possesses; on the contrary, it is only language that affords the very possibility of standing in the openness of the existent. Only where there is language, is there world, i.e., the

---

[1] The German word *"Gut,"* which has been translated throughout as "possession," also has the meaning of "a good thing"; it is thus related to the English word "goods" as in "goods and chattels." [Tr.]

perpetually altering circuit of decision and production, of action and responsibility, but also of commotion and arbitrariness, of decay and confusion. Only where world predominates, is there history. Language is a possession[2] in a more fundamental sense. It is good for the fact that (i.e., it affords a guarantee that) man can *exist* historically. Language is not a tool at his disposal, rather it is that event which disposes of the supreme possibility of human existence. We must first of all be certain of this essence of language, in order to comprehend truly the sphere of action of poetry and with it poetry itself. How does language become actual? In order to find the answer to this question, let us consider a third saying of Hölderlin's.

3

We come across this saying in a long and involved sketch for the unfinished poem which begins "Versöhnender, der du nimmergeglaubt . . ." (IV, 162ff. and 339ff.):

Much has man learnt.
Many of the heavenly ones has he named,
Since we have been a conversation
And have been able to hear from one another. (IV, 343.)

Let us first pick out from these lines the part which has a direct bearing on what we have said so far: "Since we have been a conversation . . ." We — mankind — are a conversation. The being of men is founded in language. But this only becomes actual in *conversation*. Nevertheless the latter is not merely a manner in which language is put into effect, rather it is only as conversation that language is essential. What we usually mean by language, namely, a stock of words and syntactical rules, is only a threshold of language. But now what is meant by "a conversation"? Plainly, the act of speaking with others about something. Then speaking also brings about the process of coming together. But Hölderlin says: "Since we have been a conversation and have been able to hear from one another." Being able to hear is not a mere consequence of speaking with one another,

on the contrary it is rather pre-supposed in the latter process. But even the ability to hear is itself also adapted to the possibility of the word and makes use of it. The ability to speak and the ability to hear are equally fundamental. We are a conversation — and that means: we can hear from one another. We are a conversation, that always means at the same time: we are a *single* conversation. But the unity of a conversation consists in the fact that in the essential word there is always manifest that one and the same thing on which we agree, and on the basis of which we are united and so are essentially ourselves. Conversation and its unity support our existence.

But Hölderlin does not say simply: we are a conversation — but: "Since we have been a conversation . . ." Where the human faculty of speech is present and is exercised, that is not by itself sufficient for the essential actualisation of language — conversation. Since when have we been a conversation? Where there is to be a *single* conversation, the essential word must be constantly related to the one and the same. Without this relation an argument too is absolutely impossible. But the one and the same can only be manifest in the light of something perpetual and permanent. Yet permanence and perpetuity only appear when what persists and is present begins to shine. But that happens in the moment when time opens out and extends. After man has placed himself in the presence of something perpetual, then only can he expose himself to the changeable, to that which comes and goes; for only the persistent is changeable. Only after "ravenous time" has been riven into present, past and future, does the possibility arise of agreeing on something permanent. We have been a single conversation since the time when it "is time." Ever since time arose, we have *existed* historically. Both — existence as a *single* conversation and historical existence — are alike ancient, they belong together and are the same thing.

Since we have been a conversation — man has learnt much and named many of the heavenly ones. Since language really became actual as conversation, the gods have acquired names and a world has appeared. But again it should be noticed: the presence of the gods and the appearance of the world are not merely a consequence of the

[2]See note 1. [Tr.]

actualisation of language, they are contemporaneous with it. And this to the extent that it is precisely in the naming of the gods, and in the transmutation of the world into word, that the real conversation, which we ourselves are, consists.

But the gods can acquire a name only by addressing and, as it were, claiming us. The word which names the gods is always a response to such a claim. This response always springs from the responsibility of a destiny. It is in the process by which the gods bring our existence to language, that we enter the sphere of the decision as to whether we are to yield ourselves to the gods or withhold ourselves from them.

Only now can we appreciate in its entirety what is meant by: "Since we have been a conversation . . ." Since the gods have led us into conversation, since time has been time, ever since then the basis of our existence has been a conversation. The proposition that language is the supreme event of human existence has through it acquired its meaning and foundation.

But the question at once arises: how does this conversation, which we are, begin? Who accomplishes this naming of the gods? Who lays hold of something permanent in ravenous time and fixes it in the word? Hölderlin tells us with the sure simplicity of the poet. Let us hear a fourth saying.

4

This saying forms the conclusion of the poem "Remembrance" and runs:

> But that which remains, is established by the poets.
> (IV. 63.)

This saying throws light on our question about the essence of poetry. Poetry is the act of establishing by the word and in the word. What is established in this manner? The permanent. But can the permanent be established then? Is it not that which has always been present? No! Even the permanent must be fixed so that it will not be carried away, the simple must be wrested from confusion, proportion must be set before what lacks proportion. That which supports and dominates the existent in its entirety must become manifest. Being must be opened out, so that the existent may appear. But this very permanent is

the transitory. "Thus, swiftly passing is everything heavenly; but not in vain." (IV, 163f.) But that this should remain, is "Entrusted to the poets as a care and a service" (IV, 145). The poet names the gods and names all things in that which they are. This naming does not consist merely in something already known being supplied with a name; it is rather that when the poet speaks the essential word, the existent is by this naming nominated as what it is. So it becomes known *as* existent. Poetry is the establishing of being by means of the word. Hence that which remains is never taken from the transitory. The simple can never be picked out immediately from the intricate. Proportion does not lie in what lacks proportion. We never find the foundation in what is bottomless. Being is never an existent. But, because the being and essence of things can never be calculated and derived from what is present, they must be freely created, laid down and given. Such a free act of giving is establishment.

But when the gods are named originally and the essence of things receives a name, so that things for the first time shine out, human existence is brought into a firm relation and given a basis. The speech of the poet is establishment not only in the sense of the free act of giving, but at the same time in the sense of the firm basing of human existence on its foundation.

If we conceive this essence of poetry as the establishing of being by means of the word, then we can have some inkling of the truth of that saying which Hölderlin spoke long after he had been received into the protection of the night of lunacy.

5

We find this fifth pointer in the long and at the same time monstrous poem which begins:

> In the lovely azure there flowers with its
> Metallic roof the church-tower. (VI, 24ff.)

Here Hölderlin says (line 32f.):

> Full of merit, and yet poetically, dwells
> Man on this earth.

What man works at and pursues is through his own endeavours earned and deserved. "Yet" — says Hölderlin in sharp antithesis, all this does not touch the essence of his sojourn on this earth, all this does not reach the foundation of human existence. The latter is fundamentally "poetic." But we now understand poetry as the inaugural naming of the gods and of the essence of things. To "dwell poetically" means: to stand in the presence of the gods and to be involved in the proximity of the essence of things. Existence is "poetical" in its fundamental aspect — which means at the same time: in so far as it is established (founded), it is not a recompense, but a gift.

Poetry is not merely an ornament accompanying existence, not merely a temporary enthusiasm or nothing but an interest and amusement. Poetry is the foundation which supports history, and therefore it is not a mere appearance of culture, and absolutely not the mere "expression" of a "culture-soul."

That our existence is fundamentally poetic, this cannot in the last resort mean that it is really only a harmless game. But does not Hölderlin himself, in the first pointer which we quoted, call poetry "That most innocent of all occupations?" How can this be reconciled with the essence of poetry as we are now revealing it? This brings us back to the question which we laid aside in the first instance. In now proceeding to answer this question, we will try at the same time to summarise and bring before the inner eye the essence of poetry and of the poet.

First of all it appeared that the field of action of poetry is language. Hence the essence of poetry must be understood through the essence of language. Afterwards it became clear that poetry is the inaugural naming of being and of the essence of all things — not just any speech, but that particular kind which for the first time brings into the open all that which we then discuss and deal with in everyday language. Hence poetry never takes language as a raw material ready to hand, rather it is poetry which first makes language possible. Poetry is the primitive language of a historical people. Therefore, in just the reverse manner, the essence of language must be understood through the essence of poetry.

The foundation of human existence is conversation, in which language does truly become actual. But primitive language is poetry, in which being is established. Yet language is the "most dangerous of possessions." Thus poetry is the most dangerous work — and at the same time the "most innocent of all occupations."

In fact — it is only if we combine these two definitions and conceive them as one, that we fully comprehend the essence of poetry.

But is poetry then truly the most dangerous work? In a letter to a friend, immediately before leaving on his last journey to France, Hölderlin writes:

> O Friend! The world lies before me brighter than it was, and more serious. I feel pleasure at how it moves onward, I feel pleasure when in summer "the ancient holy father with calm hand shakes lightnings of benediction out of the rosy clouds." For amongst all that I can perceive of God, this sign has become for me the chosen one. I used to be able to exult over a new truth, a better insight into that which is above us and around us, now I am frightened lest in the end it should happen with me as with Tantalus of old, who received more from the gods than he was able to digest. (V, 321.)

The poet is exposed to the divine lightnings. This is spoken of in the poem which we must recognise as the purest poetry about the essence of poetry, and which begins:

> When on festive days a countryman goes
> To gaze on his field, in the morning . . . (IV, 151ff.)

There, the last stanza says:

> Yet it behoves us, under the storms of God,
> Ye poets! with uncovered head to stand,
> With our own hand to grasp the very lightning-flash
> Paternal, and to pass, wrapped in song,
> The divine gift to the people.

And a year later, when he had returned to his mother's house, struck down with madness, Hölderlin wrote to the same friend, recalling his stay in France:

> The mighty element, the fire of heaven and the stillness of men, their life amid nature, and their limitation and contentment, have constantly seized me, and, as it is told of the heroes, I can truly say that I have been struck by Apollo. (V, 327.)

The excessive brightness has driven the poet into the dark. Is any further evidence necessary as to the extreme danger of his "occupation"? The very destiny itself of the poet tells everything. The passage in Hölderlin's "Empedocles" rings like a premonition:

He, through whom the spirit speaks, must leave betimes. (III, 154.)

And nevertheless: poetry is the "most innocent of all occupations," Hölderlin writes to this effect in his letter, not only in order to spare his mother, but because he knows that this innocent fringe belongs to the essence of poetry, just as the valley does to the mountain; for how could this most dangerous work be carried on and preserved, if the poet were not "cast out" ("Empedocles" III, 191) from everyday life and protected *against* it by the apparent harmlessness of his occupation?

Poetry looks like a game and yet it is not. A game does indeed bring men together, but in such a way that each forgets himself in the process. In poetry on the other hand, man is re-united on the foundation of his existence. There he comes to rest; not indeed to the seeming rest of inactivity and emptiness of thought, but to that infinite state of rest in which all powers and relations are active (cf. the letter to his brother, dated 1st January, 1799. III, 368f.).

Poetry rouses the appearance of the unreal and of dream in the face of the palpable and clamorous reality, in which we believe ourselves at home. And yet in just the reverse manner, what the poet says and undertakes to be, is the real. So Panthea, with the clairvoyance of a friend, declares of "Empedocles" (III, 78):

That he himself should be, is
What is life, and the rest of us are dreams of it.

So in the very appearance of its outer fringe the essence of poetry seems to waver and yet stands firm. In fact it is itself essentially establishment — that is to say: an act of firm foundation.

Yet every inaugural act remains a free gift, and Hölderlin hears it said: "Let poets be free as swallows" (IV, 168). But this freedom is not undisciplined arbitrariness and capricious desire, but supreme necessity.

Poetry, as the act of establishing being, is subject to a *two-fold* control. In considering these integral laws we first grasp the essence entire.

The writing of poetry is the fundamental naming of the gods. But the poetic word only acquires its power of naming, when the gods themselves bring us to language. How do the gods speak?

.... And signs to us from antiquity are the language of the gods. (IV, 135.)

The speech of the poet is the intercepting of these signs, in order to pass them on to his own people. This intercepting is an act of receiving and yet at the same time a fresh act of giving; for "in the first signs" the poet catches sight already of the completed message and in his word boldly presents what he has glimpsed, so as to tell in advance of the not-yet-fulfilled. So:

... the bold spirit, like an eagle
Before the tempests, flies prophesying
In the path of his advancing gods. (IV, 135.)

The establishment of being is bound to the signs of the gods. And at the same time the poetic word is only the interpretation of the "voice of the people." This is how Hölderlin names the sayings in which a people remembers that it belongs to the totality of all that exists. But often this voice grows dumb and weary. In general even it is not capable of saying of itself what is true, but has need of those who explain it. The poem which bears the title "Voice of the People," has been handed down to us in two versions. It is above all the concluding stanzas which are different, but the difference is such that they supplement one another. In the first version the ending runs:

Because it is pious, I honour for love of the heavenly ones
The people's voice, the tranquil,
Yet for the sake of gods and men
May it not always be tranquil too willingly! (IV, 141.)

And the second version is:

... and truly
Sayings are good, for they are a reminder
Of the Highest, yet something is also needed
To explain the holy sayings. (IV, 144.)

In this way the essence of poetry is joined on to the laws of the signs of the gods and of the voice of the people, laws which tend towards and away from each other. The poet himself stands between the former — the gods, and the latter — the people. He is one who has been cast out — out into that *Between,* between gods and men. But only and for the first time in this Between is it decided, who man is and where he is settling his existence. "Poetically, dwells man on this earth."

Unceasingly and ever more securely, out of the fullness of the images pressing about him and always more simply, did Hölderlin devote his poetic word to this realm of Between. And this compels us to say that he is the poet of the poet.

Can we continue now to suppose that Hölderlin is entangled in an empty and exaggerated narcissism due to inadequate richness of vision? Or must we recognize that this poet, from an excess of impetus, reaches out with poetic thought into the foundation and the midst of being. It is to *Hölderlin himself* that we must apply what he said of Oedipus in the late poem "In the lovely azure there flowers . . .":

> King Oedipus has one
> Eye too many perhaps. (VI, 26.)

Hölderlin writes poetry about the essence of poetry — but not in the sense of a timelessly valid concept. This essence of poetry belongs to a determined time. But not in such a way that it merely conforms to this time, as to one which is already in existence. It is that Hölderlin, in the act of establishing the essence of poetry, first determines a new time. It is the time of the gods that have fled *and* of the god that is coming. It is the time *of need,* because it lies under a double lack and a double Not: the No-more of the gods that have fled and the Not-yet of the god that is coming.

The essence of poetry, which Hölderlin establishes, is in the highest degree historical, because it anticipates a historical time; but as a historical essence it is the sole essential essence.

The time is needy and therefore its poet is extremely rich — so rich that he would often like to relax in thoughts of those that have been and in eager waiting for that which is coming and would like only to sleep in this apparent emptiness. But he holds his ground in the Nothing of this night. Whilst the poet remains thus by himself in the supreme isolation of his mission, he fashions truth, vicariously and therefore truly, for his people. The seventh stanza of the elegy "Bread and Wine" (IV, 123f.) tells of this. What it has only been possible to analyse here intellectually, is expressed there poetically.

> But Friend! we come too late. The gods are alive, it
>   is true,
> But up there above one's head in another world.
> Eternally they work there and seem to pay little
>   heed
> To whether we live, so attentive are the Heavenly
>   Ones.
> For a weak vessel cannot always receive them,
> Only now and then does man endure divine abun-
>   dance.
> Life is a dream of them. But madness
> Helps, like slumber and strengthens need and night,
> Until heroes enough have grown in the iron cradle,
> Hearts like, as before, to the Heavenly in power.
> Thundering they come. Meanwhile it often seems
> Better to sleep than to be thus without companions,
> To wait thus, and in the meantime what to do and say
> I know not, and what use are poets in a time of need?
> But, thou sayest, they are like the wine-god's holy
>   priests,
> Who go from land to land in the holy night.

Edmund Wilson

1895–1972

In a career spanning fifty years, from 1920 to 1970, Edmund Wilson came to be widely recognized as the leading man of letters in the United States. Raised in genteel circumstances in Red Bank, New Jersey, the son of the state's attorney general, Wilson attended Princeton University, where he became friends with F. Scott Fitzgerald, and where Christian Gauss, a legendary French professor, inspired him to embark on a career in letters. Wilson served as a reporter for the *New York Sun* before enlisting in the U.S. Army and fighting in France during World War I. After the demobilization, he wrote for *Vanity Fair* before becoming the literary editor of *The New Republic* in 1926. He was guilty of a novel (*I Thought of Daisy*, 1929), of other fiction (*Memoirs of Hecate County*, 1946), and five volumes of poetry, but it was the appearance of *Axel's Castle* in 1931 that established his reputation as a critic. His analysis of the function of symbolism in Yeats, Joyce, Proust, Eliot, and Stein and of the debt of the twentieth-century writers to the French Symbolist poets like Valéry and Rimbaud, showed American readers how to interpret the major modernist texts.

Wilson continued to write as a literary journalist throughout his life, and many of his books, including *The Triple Thinkers* (1938), *Classics and Commercials* (1950), and *The Bit Between My Teeth* (1965) are essentially compilations of his essays for publications like *The New Republic*, *The New Yorker*, and, at the end of his life, *The New York Review of Books*. They brought his sensibility to a wide variety of texts: *The Triple Thinkers*, for example, takes up Pushkin, Flaubert, Housman, John Jay Chapman, Bernard Shaw, Ben Jonson, and Henry James. Wilson was an essayist rather than a scholar, and he despised and condemned the postwar takeover of literary studies by the academic profession. A late book, *The Fruits of the MLA* (1967), bitterly attacks the dry scholarship of the Modern Language Association's professional critical editions of the American classics, which he felt intruded a misplaced scholasticism between the responsive lay reader and the text. (His own posthumous editions of Scott Fitzgerald's works, *The Last Tycoon* [1941] and *The Crack Up* [1945], are totally self-effacing.) Wilson himself was more stringently self-educated than most members of the academic profession. In addition to the French, German, Latin, and Greek that were the common property of educated professionals, Wilson taught himself enough Hebrew and Aramaic to have an educated opinion on the meaning and value of the Dead Sea Scrolls (*The Scrolls from the Dead Sea*, 1955, later revised as *Israel and the Dead Sea Scrolls*, 1978), and enough Russian to be able to bandy opinions with Vladimir Nabokov about the latter's translation of Pushkin's *Eugene Onegin*. His range of reference was enormous: a minor work, *Red, Black, Blond and Olive* (1956), examines the civilizations of the Zuni Indians, Haiti, Soviet Russia, and Israel.

Wilson was married four times; his third wife was the novelist and critic Mary McCarthy. His last years were enlivened by feuds not only with Nabokov and with the MLA but with the far more powerful U.S. Internal Revenue Service, who resented his refusal on principle to file income tax returns. He died in his mother's family home in Talcottville, New York. Since his death, he has remained a major figure in the literary landscape because of the posthumous publication of his correspondence with Nabokov, his other letters, and his diaries and journals.

In 1941 Wilson published *The Wound and the Bow*, a collection of essays on various writers linked by his vision of Philoctetes as a metaphor for the artist in Western society. Philoctetes, the legendary Greek archer, possessed a bow without which Troy could not be taken, but he also had a festering wound whose stench made him abhorrent to society; Wilson suggests that there is a necessary link between Philoctetes's bow and his wound, his godlike talent and his horrifying curse. Artists too, Wilson suggested, are necessary to redeem their societies, but their art comes out of wounds — neuroses — that often make them into social misfits and outcasts.

This is in effect the argument of the selection from "Dickens: The Two Scrooges" reprinted here. Wilson sees Dickens's transformation in the 1850s from the broadly comic entertainer to the devastating critic of the entire Victorian social system as driven by two factors: his need for a kind of love he was not getting out of his marriage with Kate Dickens, and his neurotic inability to accept and enjoy the social elevation and financial security that he had earned by his genius and his incessant labors. Despite the social and sexual themes here, one would not want to claim that Wilson was a sophisticated Marxist critic or Freudian analyst. Literature was for him a social text, but he had no dialectical method for analyzing the representations of ideology authors cannot help but create: for Wilson, as for the French literary historian Hippolyte Taine, the text was a complex product of the author's life, origins, and times. Nor did Wilson's Freudianism go much beyond the parlor variety of psychoanalysis. He was rather a broadly learned journalist who saw his job as bringing these Continental European ideas to the profoundly provincial American readers: wising us up. If we feel today that we *ought* to have read Kafka and Camus, Brecht and Mann, Dostoevsky and Gogol, whether we have actually done so or not, it is partly because of magisterial critics like Wilson, who assumed that these foreign objects should become part of the average American's furnished mind.

Selected Bibliography

Castronovo, David. *Edmund Wilson*. New York: Ungar, 1983.

Dabney, Lewis M. "Edmund Wilson and *The Wound and the Bow*." *Sewanee Review* 91 (1983): 155–65.

———, ed. *Edmund Wilson: Centennial Reflections*. Princeton: Princeton University Press, 1997.

Day, Frank. *Edmund Wilson: A Reference Guide*. New York: Garland, 1990.

Douglas, George H. "Edmund Wilson: The Man of Letters as Journalist." *Journal of Popular Culture* 15 (1981): 78–85.

Groth, Janet. *Edmund Wilson: A Critic for Our Time*. Athens: Ohio University Press, 1989.

Meyers, Jeffrey. *Edmund Wilson: A Biography*. New York: Houghton Mifflin, 1995.

Polan, Dana. "Last Intellectual, Lapsed Intellectual? The Ends of Edmund Wilson." *Boundary 2* 21 (1994): 247–65.

Wilson, Edmund. *Axel's Castle*, 1931; New York: Scribners, 1961.

———. *Edmund Wilson: The Man in Letters*. Ed. David Castronovo and Janet Groth. Athens: Ohio University Press, 2001.

———. *The Triple Thinkers*, 1938; New York: Oxford University Press, 1948.

From *Dickens: The Two Scrooges*

V

With *Little Dorrit* (1855–57), Dickens' next novel after *Bleak House* and *Hard Times*, we enter a new phase of his work. To understand it, we must go back to his life.

Dickens at forty had won everything that a writer could expect to obtain through his writings: his genius was universally recognized; he was fêted wherever he went; his books were immensely popular; and they had made him sufficiently rich to have anything that money can procure. He had partly made up for the education he had missed by traveling and living on the Continent and by learning to speak Italian and French. (Dickens' commentary on the continental countries is usually not remarkably penetrating; but he did profit very much from his travels abroad in his criticism of things in England. Perhaps no other of the great Victorian writers had so much the consciousness that the phenomena he was describing were of a character distinctively English.) Yet from the time of his first summer at Boulogne in 1853, he had shown signs of profound discontent and unappeasable restlessness; he suffered severely from insomnia and, for the first time in his life, apparently, worried seriously about his work. He began to fear that his vein was drying up.

I believe that Forster's[1] diagnosis — though it may not go to the root of the trouble — must here be accepted as correct. There were, he intimates, two things wrong with Dickens: a marriage which exasperated and cramped him and from which he had not been able to find relief, and a social maladjustment which his success had never straightened out.

The opportunities of the young Dickens to meet eligible young women had evidently been rather limited. That he was impatient to get married, nevertheless, is proved by his announcing his serious intentions to three girls in close succession. The second of these was Maria Beadnell, the original of Dora in *David Copperfield* and,

one supposes, of Dolly Varden, too, with whom he fell furiously in love, when he was eighteen and she nineteen. Her father worked in a bank and regarded Charles Dickens, the stenographer, as a young man of shabby background and doubtful prospects; Maria, who seems to have been rather frivolous and silly, was persuaded to drop her suitor — with the result for him which may be read in the letters, painful in their wounded pride and their backfiring of a thwarted will, which he wrote her after the break. This was one of the great humiliations of Dickens' early life (he was at that time twenty-one) and, even after he had liquidated it in a sense by depicting the futilities of David's marriage with Dora, the disappointment still seems to have troubled him and Maria to have remained at the back of his mind as the Ideal of which he had been cheated.

He lost very little time, however, in getting himself a wife. Two years after his rejection by Maria Beadnell, he was engaged to the daughter of George Hogarth, a Scotchman, who, as the law agent of Walter Scott and from having been mentioned in the *Noctes Ambrosianae*,[2] was invested with the prestige of having figured on the fringes of the Edinburgh literary world. He asked Dickens to write for the newspaper which he was editing at that time in London, and invited the young man to his house. There Dickens found two attractive daughters, and he married the elder, Catherine, who was twenty.[3] But the other daughter, Mary,

---

[1] John Forster (1812–1876) was Dickens's first biographer, in *The Life of Charles Dickens* (1872).

[2] Imaginary dialogues and discussions supposedly from nights spent at Ambrose's Tavern, written by John Wilson, John Gibson Lockhart, James Hogg, and other Edinburgh literary figures. These appeared in *Blackwood's Magazine* from 1822 to 1835.

[3] There were three Hogarth sisters significant to Dickens: Catherine Hogarth Dickens (1815–1879) was the eldest; the others were Mary Scott Hogarth (1819–1837), who came to live with Charles and Kate Dickens after their marriage and died in Dickens's arms of what was probably a heart condition; and Georgina Hogarth (1827–1917), who came to live with the Dickenses in 1842, at the age of 15, and who continued to run Dickens's household at Gad's Hill after his legal separation from Kate in 1858 until his death in 1870.

though too young for him to marry — she was only fifteen when he met her — had a strange hold on Dickens' emotions. When, after living with the Dickenses for a year after their marriage, she suddenly died in Dickens' arms, he was so overcome by grief that he stopped writing *Pickwick* for two months and insisted in an obsessed and morbid way on his desire to be buried beside her: "I can't think there ever was love like I bear her. . . . I have never had her ring off my finger day or night, except for an instant at a time, to wash my hands, since she died. I have never had her sweetness and excellence absent from my mind so long." In *The Old Curiosity Shop*, he apotheosized her as Little Nell. What basis this emotion may have had in the fashionable romanticism of the period or in some peculiar psychological pattern of Dickens', it is impossible on the evidence to say. But this passion for an innocent young girl is to recur in Dickens' life; and in the meantime his feeling for Mary Hogarth seems to indicate pretty clearly that even during the early years of his marriage he did not identify the Ideal with Catherine.

Catherine had big blue eyes, a rather receding chin and a sleepy and languorous look. Beyond this, it is rather difficult to get a definite impression of her. Dickens' terrible gallery of shrews who browbeat their amiable husbands suggests that she may have been a scold; but surely Dickens himself was no Joe Gargery or Gabriel Varden. We do not know much about Dickens' marriage. We know that, with the exception of his sister-in-law Georgina, Dickens grew to loathe the Hogarths, who evidently lived on him to a considerable extent; and we must assume that poor Catherine, in both intellect and energy, was a good deal inferior to her husband. He lived with her, however, twenty years, and, although it becomes clear toward the end that they were no longer particularly welcome, he gave her during that time ten children.

And if Dickens was lonely in his household, he was lonely in society, also. He had, as Forster indicates, attained a pinnacle of affluence and fame which made him one of the most admired and most sought-after persons in Europe without his really ever having created for himself a social position in England, that society *par excellence* where everybody had to have a definite one and where there was no rank reserved for the artist. He had gone straight, at the very first throw, from the poor tenement, the prison, the press table, to a position of imperial supremacy over the imaginations of practically the whole literate world; but in his personal associations, he cultivated the companionship of inferiors rather than — save, perhaps, for Carlyle — of intellectual equals. His behavior toward Society, in the capitalized sense, was rebarbative to the verge of truculence; he refused to learn its patter and its manners; and his satire on the fashionable world comes to figure more and more prominently in his novels. Dickens is one of the very small group of British intellectuals to whom the opportunity has been offered to be taken up by the governing class and who have actually declined that honor.

His attitude — which in the period we have been discussing was still that of the middle-class "Radical" opposing feudal precedent and privilege: Mr. Rouncewell, the ironmaster, backed against Sir Leicester Dedlock[4] — is illustrated by the curious story of his relations with Queen Victoria. In 1857, Dickens got up a benefit for the family of Douglas Jerrold,[5] in which he and his daughters acted. The Queen was asked to be one of the sponsors; and, since she was obliged to refuse any such request for fear of being obliged to grant them all, she invited Dickens to put on the play at the palace. He replied that he "did not feel easy as to the social position of my daughters, etc., at a Court under those circumstances," and suggested that the Queen might attend a performance which should be given for her alone. She accepted, and sent backstage between the acts asking Dickens to come and speak to her. "I replied that I was in my Farce dress, and must beg to be excused. Whereupon she sent again, saying that the dress 'could not be so ridiculous as that,' and repeating the request. I sent my duty in reply, but again hoped Her Majesty would have the kindness to excuse my presenting myself in a costume and appearance that were not my own. I was mighty

[4]Rouncewell and Dedlock are characters from *Bleak House* (1851).
[5]Douglas Jerrold (1803–1857) was a British journalist and dramatist.

glad to think, when I woke this morning, that I had carried the point." The next year he was approached on behalf of the Queen, who wanted to hear him read the *Christmas Carol*; but he expressed his "hope that she would indulge me by making one of some audience or other — for I thought an audience necessary to the effect." It was only in the last year of his life — and then only on what seems to have been the pretext on the Queen's part that she wanted to look at some photographs of the battlefields of the Civil War which Dickens had brought back from America — that an interview was finally arranged. Here the record of Dickens' lecture manager, George Dolby, supplements the account given by Forster. Dickens told Dolby that "Her Majesty had received him most graciously, and that, as Court etiquette requires that no one, in an ordinary interview with the sovereign, should be seated, Her Majesty had remained the whole time leaning over the head of a sofa. There was a little shyness on both sides at the commencement, but this wore away as the conversation proceeded." When Victoria regretted that it had not been possible for her ever to hear Dickens read, he replied that he had made his farewell to the platform; when she said that she understood this, but intimated that it would be gracious on Dickens' part so far to forget his resolve as to give her the pleasure of hearing him, he insisted that this would be impossible. Not impossible, perhaps, said the Queen, but inconsistent, no doubt — and she knew that he was the most consistent of men. Yet they parted on very good terms: she invited him to her next levee and his daughter to the drawing-room that followed. If there is some stickling for his dignity on Dickens' part here, there is evidently also some scruple on the Queen's.

To be caught between two social classes in a society of strict stratifications — like being caught between two civilizations, as James was, or between two racial groups, like Proust[6] — is an excellent thing for a novelist from the point of view of his art, because it enables him to dramatize contrasts and to study interrelations which the dweller in one world cannot know. Perhaps something of the sort was true even of Shakespeare, between the provincial bourgeoisie and the Court. Dostoevsky, who had a good deal in common with Dickens and whose career somewhat parallels his, is a conspicuous example of a writer who owes his dramatic scope at least partly to a social maladjustment. The elder Dostoevsky was a doctor and his family origins were obscure, so that his social position was poor in a Russia still predominantly feudal; yet he bought a country estate and sent his sons to a school for the children of the nobility. But the family went to pieces after the mother's death: the father took to drink and was murdered by his serfs for his cruelty. Dostoevsky was left with almost nothing, and he slipped down into that foul and stagnant underworld of the Raskólnikovs and Stavrógins of his novels.[7] Dickens' case had been equally anomalous: he had grown up in an uncomfortable position between the upper and the lower middle classes, with a dip into the proletariat and a glimpse of the aristocracy through their trusted upper servants. But this position, which had been useful to him as a writer, was to leave him rather isolated in English society. In a sense, there was no place for him to go and belong; he had to have people come to him.

And in the long run all that he had achieved could not make up for what he lacked. *Little Dorrit* and *Great Expectations* (1860–61), which follows it after *A Tale of Two Cities*, are full of the disillusion and discomfort of this period of Dickens' life. The treatment of social situations and the treatment of individual psychology have both taken turns distinctly new.

Dickens now tackles the Marshalsea again,[8] but on a larger scale and in a more serious way. It is as if he were determined once and for all to get

---

[6]Henry James was born an American but lived most of his life in England; Marcel Proust was half Jewish.

[7]Raskólnikov and Stavrógin are the protagonists of Dostoevsky's *Crime and Punishment* and *The Possessed*, respectively.

[8]The Marshalsea, in south London, was where Dickens's father, John Dickens, had been imprisoned for debt in 1824, and it is a key locale in *Little Dorrit*. But Wilson seems also to associate it with the character Wilkins Micawber of *David Copperfield*, who is imprisoned for debt but in the King's Bench, another prison south of the Thames.

the prison out of his system. The figure of his father hitherto has always haunted Dickens' novels, but he has never known quite how to handle it. In Micawber, he made him comic and lovable; in Skimpole, he made him comic and unpleasant — for, after all, the vagaries of Micawber always left somebody out of pocket, and there is another aspect of Micawber — the Skimpole aspect he presented to his creditors. But what kind of person, really, had John Dickens been in himself? How had the father of Charles Dickens come to be what he was? Even after it had become possible for Charles to provide for his father, the old man continued to be a problem up to his death in 1851. He got himself arrested again, as the result of running up a wine bill; and he would try to get money out of his son's publishers without the knowledge of Charles. Yet Dickens said to Forster, after his father's death: 'The longer I live, the better man I think him'; and *Little Dorrit* is something in the nature of a justification of John.

Mr. Dorrit is "a very amiable and very helpless middle-aged gentleman . . . a shy, retiring man, well-looking, though in an effeminate style, with a mild voice, curling hair, and irresolute hands — rings upon the fingers in those days — which nervously wandered to his trembling lip a hundred times in the first half-hour of his acquaintance with the jail." The arrival of the Dorrit family in prison and their gradual habituation to it are done with a restraint and sobriety never displayed by Dickens up to now. The incident in which Mr. Dorrit, after getting used to accepting tips in his role of the Father of the Marshalsea, suddenly becomes insulted when he is offered copper halfpence by a workman, has a delicacy which makes up in these later books for the ebb of Dickens' bursting exuberance. If it is complained that the comic characters in these novels, the specifically "Dickens characters," are sometimes mechanical and boring, this is partly, perhaps, for the reason that they stick out in an unnatural relief from a surface that is more quietly realistic. And there are moments when one feels that Dickens might be willing to abandon the "Dickens character" altogether if it were not what the public expected of him. In any case, the story of Dorrit is a closer and more thoughtful study than any that has gone before of what bad institutions make of men.

But there is also in *Little Dorrit* something different from social criticism. Dickens is no longer satisfied to anatomize the organism of society. The main symbol here is the prison (in this connection, Mr. Jackson's chapter is the best thing that has been written on *Little Dorrit*);[9] but this symbol is developed in a way that takes it beyond the satirical application of the symbol of the fog in *Bleak House* and gives it a significance more subjective. In the opening chapter, we are introduced, not to the debtors' prison, but to an ordinary jail for criminals, which, in the case of Rigaud and Cavalletto,[10] will not make the bad man any better or the good man any worse. A little later, we are shown an English business man[11] who has come back from many years in China and who finds himself in a London — the shut-up London of Sunday evening — more frightening, because more oppressive, than the thieves' London of *Oliver Twist*. " 'Heaven forgive me,' said he, 'and those who trained me. How I have hated this day!' There was the dreary Sunday of his childhood, when he sat with his hands before him, scared out of his senses by a horrible tract which commenced business with the poor child by asking him, in its title, why he was going to Perdition?" At last he gets himself to the point of going to see his mother, whom he finds as lacking in affection and as gloomy as he could have expected. She lives in a dark and funereal house with the old offices on the bottom floor, one of the strongholds of that harsh Calvinism plus hard business which made one of the mainstays of the Victorian Age; she lies paralyzed on "a black bier-like sofa," punishing herself and everyone else for some guilt of which he cannot discover the nature. The Clennam house is a jail, and they are in prison, too. So are the people in Bleeding Heart Yard, small tenement-dwelling shopkeepers and artisans, rack-rented by the patriarchal Casby; so is Merdle, the great swindler-financier,

[9]Thomas Alfred Jackson (1879–1955), author of *Charles Dickens: The Progress of a Radical* (1937).
[10]Prisoners in the jail at Marseilles, in Chapter 1 of *Little Dorrit*.
[11]Arthur Clennam, one of the protagonists of *Little Dorrit*.

imprisoned, like Kreuger or Insull,[12] in the vast scaffolding of fraud he has contrived, who wanders about in his expensive house — itself, for all its crimson and gold, as suffocating and dark as the Clennams' — afraid of his servants, unloved by his wife, almost unknown by his guests, till on the eve of the collapse of the edifice he quietly opens his veins in his bath.

At last, after twenty-five years of jail, Mr. Dorrit inherits a fortune and is able to get out of the Marshalsea. He is rich enough to go into Society; but all the Dorrits, with the exception of the youngest, known as "Little Dorrit," who has been born in the Marshalsea itself and has never made any pretensions, have been demoralized or distorted by the effort to remain genteel while tied to the ignominy of the prison. They cannot behave like the people outside. And yet that outside world is itself insecure. It is dominated by Mr. Merdle, who comes, as the story goes on, to be universally believed and admired — is taken up by the governing class, sent to Parliament, courted by lords. The Dorrits, accepted by Society, still find themselves in prison. The moral is driven home when old Dorrit, at a fashionable dinner, loses control of his wits and slips back into his character at the Marshalsea: " 'Born here,' he repeated, shedding tears. 'Bred here. Ladies and gentlemen, my daughter. Child of an unfortunate father, but — ha — always a gentleman. Poor, no doubt, but — hum — proud.' " He asks the company for "Testimonials," which had been what he had used to call his tips. (Dr. Manette, in *A Tale of Two Cities*, repeats this pattern with his amnesic relapses into the shoemaking he has learned in prison.) Arthur Clennam, ruined by the failure of Merdle, finally goes to the Marshalsea himself; and there at last he and Little Dorrit arrive at an understanding. The

[12]Real-life counterparts of Dickens's Merdle: Ivar Kreuger (1880–1932) was a Swedish industrialist and financier who committed suicide rather than settle with his creditors. Samuel Insull (1859–1938) was a Chicago industrialist who fled the United States after his bankruptcy in 1932 ruined thousands of stockholders; he was extradited and tried for fraud but acquitted on all charges. Dickens probably based Merdle on John Sadleir, a member of Parliament, stock promoter and forger, who committed suicide in 1856.

implication is that, prison for prison, a simple incarceration is an excellent school of character compared to the dungeons of Puritan theology, of modern business, of money-ruled Society, or of the poor people of Bleeding Heart Yard who are swindled and bled by all of these.

The whole book is much gloomier than *Bleak House*, where the fog is external to the characters and represents something removable, the obfuscatory elements of the past. The murk of *Little Dorrit* permeates the souls of the people, and we see more of their souls than in *Bleak House*. Arthur Clennam, with his broodings on his unloving mother, who turns out not to be his real mother (a poor doomed child of natural impulse, like Lady Dedlock's lover), is both more real and more depressing than Lady Dedlock. Old Dorrit has been spoiled beyond repair: he can never be rehabilitated like Micawber. There is not even a villain like Tulkinghorn to throw the odium on a predatory class: the official villain Blandois has no organic connection with the story save as a caricature of social pretense. (Though the illustrations suggest that he may have been intended as a sort of cartoon of Napoleon III, whose régime Dickens loathed — in which case the tie-up between Blandois and the Clennams may figure a close relationship between the shady financial interests disguised by the flashy façade of the Second Empire and the respectable business interests of British merchants, so inhuman behind their mask of morality. Blandois is crushed in the end by the collapse of the Clennams' house, as people were already predicting that Napoleon would be by that of his own.) The role of the Court of Chancery is more or less played by the Circumlocution Office and the governing-class family of Barnacles — perhaps the most brilliant thing of its kind in Dickens: that great satire on all aristocratic bureaucracies, and indeed on all bureaucracies, with its repertoire of the variations possible within the bureaucratic type and its desolating picture of the emotions of a man being passed on from one door to another. But the Circumlocution Office, after all, only influences the action in a negative way.

The important thing to note in *Little Dorrit* — which was originally to have been called *Nobody's Fault* — is that the fable is here presented from the point of view of imprisoning states of mind as much as from that of oppressive institutions. This is illustrated in a startling way by *The History of a Self-Tormentor*, which we find toward the end of the book. Here Dickens, with a remarkable pre-Freudian insight, gives a sort of case history of a woman imprisoned in a neurosis which has condemned her to the delusion that she can never be loved. There is still, to be sure, the social implication that her orphaned childhood and her sense of being slighted have been imposed on her by the Victorian attitude toward her illegitimate birth. But her handicap is now simply a thought-pattern, and from that thought-pattern she is never to be liberated.

Dickens' personal difficulties make themselves felt like an ache at the back of *Little Dorrit* — in which he represents his hero as reflecting: "Who has not thought for a moment, sometimes? — that it might be better to flow away monotonously, like the river, and to compound for its insensibility to happiness with its insensibility to pain." The strain of his situation with his wife had become particularly acute the year that the book was begun. Dickens had been very much excited that February to get a letter from Maria Beadnell,[13] now married. The readiness and warmth of his response shows how the old Ideal had lighted up again. He was on the point of leaving for Paris, and during his absence he looked forward eagerly to seeing her: he arranged to meet her alone. The drop in the tone of his letters after this meeting has taken place is blighting to poor Mrs. Winter. He had found her banal and silly, with the good looks of her girlhood gone. He put her into his new novel as Flora Finching, a sort of Dora Spenlow vulgarized and transmogrified into a kind of Mrs. Nickleby — that is, into another version of Dickens' unforgiven mother. It seems clear that the type of woman that Dickens is chiefly glorifying during the years from *Martin Chuzzlewit* through *Little Dorrit*: the devoted and self-effacing little mouse, who hardly aspires to be loved,

[13]After her breakup with Dickens, Maria Beadnell (1810–1886) had married a merchant named Henry Winter; Maria and Dickens met again, to his intense disappointment, on February 25, 1855.

derives from Georgina Hogarth, his sister-in-law. Georgina, who had been eight when Dickens was married, had come to womanhood in the Dickens household. Dickens grew fond of her, explaining that his affection was due partly to her resemblance to her dead sister. She gradually took over the care of the children, whom Dickens complained of their mother's neglecting; and became the real head of the household — creating a situation which is reflected in these heroines of the novels. The virtues of Ruth Pinch are brought out mainly through her relation to her brother Tom; Esther Summerson, who keeps house for Mr. Jarndyce but does not suspect that he wants to marry her, is suspended through most of *Bleak House* in a relation to him that is semi-filial; Little Dorrit is shown throughout in a sisterly and filial relation, and Arthur Clennam, before he figures as a lover, plays simply, like Mr. Jarndyce, the role of a protective and elderly friend. In the love of Little Dorrit and Clennam, there seems to be little passion, but a sobriety of resignation, almost a note of sadness: they "went down," Dickens says at the end, "into a modest life of usefulness and happiness," one of the objects of which was to be "to give a mother's care . . . to Fanny's [her sister's] neglected children no less than to their own."

These children of Dickens' — he now had nine — were evidently giving him anxiety. He used to grumble about their lack of enterprise; and it would appear from Mrs. Perugini's story, which trails off in a depressing record of their failures and follies and untimely deaths, that in general they did not turn out well. The ill-bred daughter and worthless son of Dorrit probably caricature Dickens' fears. Surely the Dorrits' travels on the Continent caricature the progress of the Dickenses. Old Dorrit's rise in the world is no rescue at the end of a fairy tale, as it would have been in one of the early novels. The point of the story is that this rise can be only a mockery: the Dorrits will always be what the Marshalsea has made them.

The theme of *Little Dorrit* is repeated in *Great Expectations* (1860–61). This second of Dickens' novels in which the hero tells his own story is like an attempt to fill in some of the things that have been left out of *David Copperfield*. The story is the reverse of the earlier one. David was a gentleman by birth, who by accident became a wage slave. Pip is a boy out of the blacksmith's shop, who by accident gets a chance to become a gentleman. He straightway turns into a mean little snob.

The formula of *Bleak House* is repeated, too. The solution of the puzzle is again Dickens' moral, here more bitterly, even hatefully, delivered. Pip owes his mysterious income to the convict whom, in his childhood, he befriended on the marshes. Abel Magwitch himself had been a wretched tinker's boy, who had "first become aware of [himself] a-thieving turnips for a living." Later he had been exploited by a gentlemanly rotter turned crook, who had left Magwitch to take the rap when they had both fallen into the hands of the law. The poor rascal had been impressed by the advantage that his companion's social status — he had been to the public school — had given him in the eyes of the court; and when Magwitch later prospered in New South Wales, he decided to make a gentleman of Pip. Thus Pip finds himself in a position very similar to Lady Dedlock's: the money that chains him to Magwitch will not merely associate him with a poverty and ignorance more abject than that from which he has escaped, but will put him under obligations to an individual who represents to him the dregs of the underworld, a man with a price on his head. Not only this; but the proud lady here — who has known Pip in his first phase and scorns him because she thinks him a common village boy — turns out to be the daughter of Magwitch and of a woman who has been tried for murder and who is now employed in the humble capacity of housekeeper by the lawyer who got her off.

The symbol here is the "great expectations" which both Pip and Estella entertain: they figure (Mr. T. A. Jackson has here again put his finger on the point) the Victorian mid-century optimism. Estella and Pip have both believed that they could count upon a wealthy patroness, the heiress of a now disused brewery, to make them secure against vulgarity and hardship. But the patroness vanishes like a phantom, and they are left with their leisure-class habits and no incomes to keep them up. They were originally to lose one another, too: the tragedies in Dickens' novels are coming more and more to seem irremediable. Estella was to marry for his money a brutal country squire, and Pip was never to see her again except for one brief meeting in London. Here is the last sentence of the ending that Dickens first wrote: "I was very glad afterwards to have had the interview; for, in her face, and in her voice, and in her touch, she gave me the assurance that suffering had been stronger than Miss Havisham's teaching, and had given her a heart to understand what my heart used to be."

This was to have been all, and it was perfect in tone and touch. But Bulwer Lytton[14] made Dickens change it to the ending we now have, in which Estella's husband gets killed and Pip and she are united. Dickens was still a public entertainer who felt that he couldn't too far disappoint his audience.

In *Little Dorrit* and *Great Expectations*, there is, therefore, a great deal more psychological interest than in Dickens' previous books. We are told what the characters think and feel, and even something about how they change. And here we must enter into the central question of the psychology of Dickens' characters.

The world of the early Dickens is organized according to a dualism which is based — in its artistic derivation — on the values of melodrama: there are bad people and there are good people, there are comics and there are characters played straight. The only complexity of which Dickens is capable is to make one of his noxious characters become wholesome, one of his clowns turn into a serious person. The most conspicuous example of this process is the reform of Mr. Dombey, who, as Taine[15] says, "turns into the best of fathers and spoils a fine novel." But the reform of Scrooge in *A Christmas Carol* shows the phenomenon in its purest form.

[14]Edward George Bulwer-Lytton, Victorian novelist and parliamentarian (1803–1873). A friend and colleague of Dickens's, he advised Dickens to change the ending of *Great Expectations* and Dickens later wrote that he "had stated his reasons so well that I have resumed the wheel and taken another turn at it." No one knows for sure what those reasons were: Wilson assumes that Dickens was simply courting popularity, but it has also been suggested that Dickens's original ending may have been too similar to that of Charles Lever's novel *A Day's Ride* (1861), which had been published in Dickens's own magazine, *All the Year Round*.

[15]Hippolyte Adolphe Taine (1828–1893), French literary historian.

We have come to take Scrooge so much for granted that he seems practically a piece of Christmas folklore; we no more inquire seriously into the mechanics of his transformation than we do into the transformation of the Beast in the fairy tale into the young prince that marries Beauty. Yet Scrooge represents a principle fundamental to the dynamics of Dickens' world and derived from his own emotional constitution. It was not merely that his passion for the theater had given him a taste for melodramatic contrasts; it was rather that the lack of balance between the opposite impulses of his nature had stimulated an appetite for melodrama. For emotionally Dickens *was* unstable. Allowing for the English restraint, which masks what the Russian expressiveness indulges and perhaps over-expresses, and for the pretenses of English biographers, he seems almost as unstable as Dostoevsky. He was capable of great hardness and cruelty, and not merely toward those whom he had cause to resent: people who patronized or intruded on him. On one occasion, in the presence of other guests, he ordered Forster out of his house over some discussion that had arisen at dinner; he was certainly not gentle with Maria Winter; and his treatment of Catherine suggests, as we shall see, the behavior of a Renaissance monarch summarily consigning to a convent the wife who has served her turn.[16] There is more of emotional reality behind Quilp in *The Old Curiosity Shop* than there is behind Little Nell. If Little Nell sounds pathetic today, Quilp has lost none of his fascination. He is ugly, malevolent, perverse; he delights in making mischief for its own sake; yet he exercises over the members of his household a power which is almost an attraction and which resembles what was known in Dickens' day as "malicious animal magnetism." Though Quilp is ceaselessly tormenting his wife and browbeating the boy who works for him, they never attempt to escape: they admire him, in a sense they love him.

So Dickens' daughter, Kate Perugini, who had destroyed a memoir of her father that she had written, because it gave "only half the truth," told

Miss Gladys Storey, the author of *Dickens and Daughter*, that the spell which Dickens had been able to cast on his daughters was so strong that, after he and their mother had separated, they had refrained from going to see her, though he never spoke to them about it, because they knew that he did not like it, and would even take music lessons in a house just opposite the one where she was living without daring to pay her a call. "'I loved my father,' said Mrs. Perugini, 'better than any man in the world — in a different way of course. . . . I loved him for his faults.'" And she added, as she rose and walked to the door: "my father was a wicked man — a very wicked man." But from the memoirs of his other daughter Mamie, who also adored her father and seems to have viewed him uncritically, we hear of his colossal Christmas parties, of the vitality, the imaginative exhilaration, which swept all the guests along. It is Scrooge bursting in on the Cratchits. Shall we ask what Scrooge would actually be like if we were to follow him beyond the frame of the story? Unquestionably he would relapse when the merriment was over — if not while it was still going on — into moroseness, vindictiveness, suspicion. He would, that is to say, reveal himself as the victim of a manic-depressive cycle, and a very uncomfortable person.

This dualism runs all though Dickens. There has always to be a good and a bad of everything: each of the books has its counterbalancing values, and pairs of characters sometimes counterbalance each other from the casts of different books. There has to be a good manufacturer, Mr. Rouncewell, and a bad manufacturer, Mr. Bounderby; a bad old Jew, Fagin, and a good old Jew, Riah; an affable lawyer who is really unscrupulous, Vholes, and a kindly lawyer who pretends to be unfeeling, Jaggers; a malicious dwarf, Quilp, and a beneficent dwarf, Miss Mowcher (though Dickens had originally intended her to be bad); an embittered and perverse illegitimate daughter, Miss Wade, the Self-Tormentor, and a sweet and submissive illegitimate daughter, Esther Summerson. Another example of this tendency is Dickens' habit, noted by Mr. Kingsmill,[17] of making the comic side of

[16]In May 1858, Charles and Catherine Dickens signed a separation agreement giving her a house and £600 per year; her sister Georgina continued at Dickens's house at Gad's Hill and raised his children.

[17]Hugh Kingsmill (1889–1949), author of *The Sentimental Journey: A Life of Charles Dickens* (1935).

his novels a kind of parody on the sentimental side. Pecksniff is a satire on that domestic sentiment which wells up so profusely in Dickens himself when it is a question of a story for the Christmas trade; the performances of the Vincent Crummleses provide a burlesque of the stagy plot upon which *Nicholas Nickleby* is based.

Dickens' difficulty in his middle period, and indeed more or less to the end, is to get good and bad together in one character. He had intended in *Dombey and Son* to make Walter Gay turn out badly, but hadn't been able to bring himself to put it through. In *Bleak House*, however, he had had Richard Carstone undergo a progressive demoralization. But the real beginnings of a psychological interest may be said to appear in *Hard Times*, which, though parts of it have the crudity of a cartoon, is the first novel in which Dickens tries to trace with any degree of plausibility the processes by which people become what they are. We are given a certain sympathetic insight into what has happened to the Gradgrind children; and the conversion of Mr. Gradgrind is very much better prepared for than that of Mr. Dombey. In *Great Expectations* we see Pip pass through a whole psychological cycle. At first, he is sympathetic, then by a more or less natural process he turns into something unsympathetic, then he becomes sympathetic again. Here the effects of both poverty and riches are seen from the inside in one person. This is for Dickens a great advance; and it is a development which, if carried far enough, would end by eliminating the familiar Dickens of the lively but limited stage characters, with their tag lines and their unvarying make-ups.

EDMUND WILSON

Kenneth Burke

1897–1993

Kenneth Duva Burke was born on May 5, 1897, in Pittsburgh, where he was educated through high school. He attended college at Ohio State University in Columbus and Columbia University in New York but did not take a degree; this has been amply made up for by the number of universities — over a dozen at last count — that have awarded him honorary doctorates. Burke worked as a researcher for the Laura Spelman Rockefeller Foundation, as the music critic for *The Dial* and *The Nation,* and as an editor for government publications, but his chief occupation during his long life was that of itinerant scholar and critic. Burke took literally dozens of academic appointments at prestigious institutions but most of them, except for an eighteen-year appointment at Bennington College from 1943 to 1961, itself broken by visiting appointments elsewhere, were for a year or two. In addition to writing dozens of critical and philosophical books, Burke was a poet from his eighteenth year, and his first publication (*The White Oxen,* 1924) was a collection of short stories. Burke was married twice, to two sisters, and had three daughters by the first marriage and two sons by the second.

Burke, who was a quirky and individualistic thinker, has often and for understandable reasons been mischaracterized as a New Critic strongly influenced by Marx and Freud. Of the same generation as Brooks and Wimsatt, Burke was interested, like the New Critics, in the poem as a verbal creation, or as he put it himself, "a dance of attitudes"; and like most twentieth-century thinkers from Lionel Trilling to William Empson, he was also interested in the two most revolutionary thinkers of the later Victorian era. Nevertheless, Burke was more a philosopher than a literary critic as such, and his ideas, although primarily applied to literature and to prose texts, range far beyond our purposes here: his vision of language and literature as forms of symbolic action.

Perhaps we should begin at a very general level, with Burke's famous definition of Man. Burke conceived of man not as *homo sapiens* but as *homo symbolicus,* the only being capable of using (and therefore misusing) symbols. Man is therefore also the "inventor of the negative," since negation is a product only of symbol systems: Nature may not abhor a vacuum, but only language can explore the absence of something in a world that knows only presence. Man is also "separated from his natural condition by instruments of his own making," so conditioned by language and the social aspects of life that are created within and through language that even his physiology has changed from that of the arboreal apes from which he descended. Man is also "goaded by the spirit of hierarchy," a characteristically less pleasant way of saying "moved by a sense of order."

Finally, Burke likes to say that man is "rotten with perfection," in that our sense of order leads us to carry out our ideas to the nth degree, regardless of the consequences. One obvious instance is Hitler's idea of racial purity. Carried out to perfection, and with full negativity, using the power that rigidly enforced hierarchies give to a leader, the symbolic enactment leads to the horrors of the Holocaust.

Although Burke's theory suggests that humanity has a drive to "perfect" such ideas in such a way, a utopian strain in Burke hopes that the strife between contrary symbol-systems (like capitalism and communism) can be indefinitely confined, with all our help, to symbolic battles, rather than exploding in that final negativity, nuclear annihilation.

The idea of conflict confined to a symbolic agon, a struggle of words, brings us back to Burke and literature. Saying something is another way of doing something. Essentially, Burke assumes that human beings write literature, just as they do everything else, in an effort to achieve some personal goal. Writing is itself a drama. Authors are *agents* who *act* within a certain *scene* (their environment) by means of a certain *agency* (writing) to achieve a *purpose*. These five terms — agent, act, scene, agency, and purpose — make up the Burkean *pentad;* their "ratios," or the relationships between the terms, are crucial to his criticism. Authors do not merely write as an end in itself, nor do they write for secular reasons — to make money or achieve fame. Rather, they select their particular subjects, topics, conflicts, for reasons that go beyond the secular, usually the purgation of their own sense of sinfulness, which leads to a sense of redemption within their lives. As Burke says in "Literature as Equipment for Living," there is no room for such a thing as "pure literature" of the sort the New Critics wished to analyze. Works of art are "equipment for living," "strategies for selecting enemies and allies, for socializing losses, for warding off the evil eye, for purification, propitiation, and desanctification, consolation and vengeance, admonition and exhortation, implicit commands or instructions of one sort or another."

As an example of how the poet may socialize a loss or give himself symbolic instructions, we could take Burke's analysis of Milton's "Lycidas" in *Attitudes toward History* (1937). While a New Critic like John Crowe Ransom considered "Lycidas" "a poem nearly anonymous" in its exquisite variants on the general themes of the pastoral elegy, Burke boldly commits the intentional fallacy, even takes the poem, with its evocation of the death and resurrection of a poet, as a personal prophecy. After writing "Lycidas," Burke claims,

> Milton travelled in 1638 and 1639. And for the next twenty years thereafter, with the exception of an occasional sonnet, he devoted all his energies to his polemic prose. These dates, coupled with the contents of the poem, would justify us in contending that "Lycidas" was the symbolic dying of his poetic self. . . . In "Lycidas" he testifies that he is holding his dead self in abeyance, and that it will rise again. . . . So the poet remained, for all his dying; and at the Restoration, after the political interregnum of Cromwell, he would be reborn. "Paradise Lost" is the fulfillment of his contract.[1]

Similarly, "The Rime of the Ancient Mariner" represents Coleridge's symbolic way of purging the guilt arising out of his failed marriage and his drug addiction, and of achieving an equally symbolic redemption. For Burke, the slain albatross can be equated with Sarah Coleridge, since they are "in the same equational cluster" — connected by similar imagery in "Mariner" and "The Aeolian Harp." Similarly, the watersnakes whom the mariner blesses as a part of nature connect with his drug addiction,

---

[1]Kenneth Burke, *Attitudes toward History,* 3rd ed. (Berkeley: University of California Press, 1984), p. 57.

which is referred to in a letter as "a scourge of ever restless, ever coiling and uncoiling serpents," while Coleridge feels "driven on from behind" — as the Mariner's ship is driven. In effect, Coleridge uses the poem to symbolically "bless" his drug addiction and "curse" his marriage — the scene of the poem itself involves a detained wedding-guest who misses the ceremony, and the poem ends by denigrating marriage in favor of the brotherhood of Nature and of humanity ("to walk together to the kirk, With a goodly company").

Not only may authors have their purgative/redemptive purposes, their societies also have them (and, we might add, the "affective" fallacy means as little to Burke as the "intentional" fallacy does). Burke's analysis of Shakespeare's *Coriolanus* in *Language as Symbolic Action* (1966) presents the hero of that play as the apotheosis of the aristocracy, with all the virtues and vices of the highborn — courage, pride, stoical fortitude, snobbery, family feeling — taken to the last extreme, "rotten with perfection," as Burke liked to put it. According to Burke, the action of the tragedy shapes everything toward the sacrifice of Coriolanus as a scapegoat — a symbolic destruction of the ultimate patrician enacted at a time when the strife between patrician and plebeian in English society was already becoming virulent, although it would not erupt into civil war for another three decades. The death of Coriolanus causes the reunification of Rome and symbolically allows the English Cavaliers and Roundheads, enemies-to-be, to join in unity in a purgative/redemptive experience.

Here and in the Milton example, Burke is characteristically cavalier in his use of the facts and delights in prophecy after-the-fact. One could pedantically object that Milton in 1637 could not have foreseen Cromwell and his secretaryship, that Coleridge was not fully addicted to laudanum at the time he wrote "The Ancient Mariner," that Shakespeare in 1609 could not have foreseen the Civil War. But the sort of conflict Burke is talking about always runs behind and above such facts: If Milton could not have predicted Cromwell, he certainly saw the conflict within himself between poetry and politics, and if Shakespeare could not have predicted the civil war that broke out twenty-five years after his death, he certainly understood the clash between classes within his own society. The same is true of Coleridge; even if one is not willing to claim (as Burke once did) that the poet was an *incipient* addict in 1796, there was surely a deep-seated and long-standing conflict in Coleridge between affections licensed by society (symbolized by the wedding in the poem) and affections that transcend and defy the social (like the Mariner's demonic bond with the watersnakes).

Burke's method of analyzing literature turns primarily on reducing the text to its scene of conflict, then viewing that conflict as symbolic of other conflicts within other scenes — within the poet's self, family, or society, including his or her relation with intellectual forebears or poetic rivals. The "scene" for which the poem is a grand metaphor can be psychological, economic, political, sociological, even theological. And as the example of Coleridge shows, Burke is willing to read other poems or letters onto the text under analysis. Everything is relevant.

If this allegorizing and psychologizing is utterly foreign to the formalist movements against which Burke defined his own poetics, he nevertheless resembles the New Critics in his concern for symbol, language, and imagery. The notion that themes essentially reside in clusters of images, that the associations of primary terms determine their psychic meaning, is close to the New Critical method. Nevertheless, the freewheeling Burke went considerably further than the New Critics were ever comfortable with in his "joycings" — puns, usually scatological, that reduce the high-flown meaning of a passage to a physiological level. Burke's analysis of Keats's "Ode on a Grecian Urn" in *A Grammar of Motives* (1945), reprinted here, is relatively decorous, but in the later *A Rhetoric of Motives* (1950), the "urn" is joyced to "urine," while the final sentiment, "Beauty is truth, truth beauty," is joyced to "Body is turd, turd body." Burke is not being childishly dirty-minded here. His point is that, in any poem so concerned with transcendence, the poet tends to repress the earthly and bodily functions that are being transcended; but what is repressed returns in language that, in distorted form, conveys what the poet has been avoiding talking about. In Burke conflict is unavoidable and language always takes over — that much is certain.

Selected Bibliography

Frank, Armin Paul. *Kenneth Burke.* New York: Twayne, 1969.

Heath, Robert L. "Kenneth Burke's Break with Formalism." *Quarterly Journal of Speech* 70 (1984): 132–43.

———. *Realism and Relativism: A Perspective on Kenneth Burke.* Macon, GA: Mercer University Press, 1986.

Henderson, Greig, and David Cratis Williams, eds. *Unending Conversations: New Writings by and about Kenneth Burke.* Carbondale: Southern Illinois University Press, 2001.

Rueckert, William H. *The Rhetoric of Rebirth: A Study of the Literary Theory and Critical Practice of Kenneth Burke.* Ann Arbor: University Microfilms, 1957.

———. *Kenneth Burke and the Drama of Human Relations,* 2nd ed. Berkeley: University of California Press, 1982.

Southwell, Samuel B. *Kenneth Burke and Martin Heidegger, with a Note Against Deconstruction.* Gainesville: University Presses of Florida, 1987.

Wolin, Ross. *The Rhetorical Imagination of Kenneth Burke.* Columbia: University of South Carolina Press, 2001.

White, Hayden, and Margaret Brose, eds. *Representing Kenneth Burke.* Baltimore: Johns Hopkins University Press, 1982.

Symbolic Action in a Poem by Keats

We are here set to analyze the "Ode on a Grecian Urn" as a viaticum that leads, by a series of transformations, into the oracle, "Beauty is truth, truth beauty." We shall analyze the Ode "dramatistically," in terms of symbolic action.

To consider language as a means of *information* or *knowledge* is to consider it epistemologically, semantically, in terms of "science." To consider it as a mode of *action* is to consider it in terms of "poetry." For a poem is an act, the symbolic act of the poet who made it — an act of such a nature that, in surviving as a structure or object, it enables us as readers to re-enact it.

"Truth" being the essential word of knowledge (science) and "beauty" being the essential word of art or poetry, we might substitute accordingly.

636   KENNETH BURKE

The oracle would then assert, "Poetry is science, science poetry." It would be particularly exhilarating to proclaim them one if there were a strong suspicion that they were at odds (as the assertion that "God's in his heaven, all's right with the world" is really a *counter*-assertion to doubts about God's existence and suspicions that much is wrong). It was the dialectical opposition between the "aesthetic" and the "practical," with "poetry" on one side and utility (business and applied science) on the other that was being ecstatically denied. The *relief* in this denial was grounded in the romantic philosophy itself, a philosophy which gave strong recognition to precisely the *contrast* between "beauty" and "truth."

Perhaps we might put it this way: If the oracle were to have been uttered in the first stanza of the poem rather than the last, its phrasing proper to that place would have been: "Beauty is *not* truth, truth *not* beauty." The five stanzas of successive transformation were necessary for the romantic philosophy of a romantic poet to transcend itself (raising its romanticism to a new order, or new dimension). An abolishing of romanticism through romanticism! (To transcend romanticism through romanticism is, when all is over, to restore in one way what is removed in another.)

But to the poem, step by step through the five stanzas.

As a "way in," we begin with the sweeping periodic sentence that, before the stanza is over, has swiftly but imperceptibly been transmuted in quality from the periodic to the breathless, a cross between interrogation and exclamation:

Thou still unravish'd bride of quietness,
  Thou foster-child of silence and slow time,
Sylvan historian, who canst thus express
  A flowery tale more sweetly than our rhyme:
What leaf-fring'd legend haunts about thy shape
  Of deities or mortals, or of both,
    In Tempe or the dales of Arcady?
What men or gods are these?   What maidens loth?
  What mad pursuit?   What struggle to escape?
What pipes and timbrels? What wild
    ecstasy?

Even the last quick outcries retain somewhat the quality of the periodic structure with which the stanza began. The final line introduces the subject of "pipes and timbrels," which is developed and then surpassed in Stanza II:

Heard melodies are sweet, but those unheard
  Are sweeter; therefore, ye soft pipes, play on;
Not to the sensual ear, but, more endear'd,
  Pipe to the spirit ditties of no tone:
Fair youth, beneath the trees, thou canst not leave
  Thy song, nor ever can those trees be bare;
    Bold Lover, never, never canst thou kiss,
Though winning near the goal — yet, do not grieve;
  She cannot fade, though thou hast not thy bliss,
    Forever wilt thou love, and she be fair!

If we had only the first stanza of this Ode, and were speculating upon it from the standpoint of motivation, we could detect there tentative indications of two motivational levels. For the lines express a doubt whether the figures on the urn are "deities or mortals" — and the motives of gods are of a different order from the motives of men. This bare hint of such a possibility emerges with something of certainty in the second stanza's development of the "pipes and timbrels" theme. For we explicitly consider a contrast between body and mind (in the contrast between "heard melodies," addressed "to the sensual ear," and "ditties of no tone," addressed "to the spirit").

Also, of course, the notion of inaudible sound brings us into the region of the mystic oxymoron (the term in rhetoric for "the figure in which an epithet of a contrary significance is added to a word: e.g., *cruel kindness; laborious idleness*"). And it clearly suggests a concern with the level of motives-behind-motives, as with the paradox of the prime mover that is itself at rest, being the unmoved ground of all motion and action. Here the poet whose sounds are the richest in our language is mediating upon *absolute* sound, the *essence* of sound, which would be soundless as the prime mover is motionless, or as the "principle" of sweetness would not be sweet, having transcended sweetness, or as the sub-atomic particles of the sun are each, in their isolate purity, said to be devoid of temperature.

Contrast Keats's unheard melodies with those of Shelley:

Music, when soft voices die,
Vibrates in the memory —
Odours, when sweet violets sicken,
Live within the sense they quicken.

Rose leaves, when the rose is dead,
Are heaped for the beloved's bed;
And so thy thoughts, when thou art gone,
Love itself shall slumber on.[1]

Here the futuristic Shelley is anticipating retrospection; he is looking forward to looking back. The form of thought is naturalistic and temporalistic in terms of *past* and *future*. But the form of thought in Keats is mystical, in terms of an *eternal present*. The Ode is striving to move beyond the region of becoming into the realm of *being*. (This is another way of saying that we are here concerned with two levels of motivation.)

In the last four lines of the second stanza, the state of immediacy is conveyed by a development peculiarly Keatsian. I refer not simply to translation into terms of the erotic, but rather to a quality of *suspension* in the erotic imagery, defining an eternal prolongation of the state just prior to fulfilment — not exactly arrested ecstasy, but rather an arrested pre-ecstasy.[2]

Suppose that we had but this one poem by Keats, and knew nothing of its author or its period, so that we could treat it only in itself, as a series of internal transformations to be studied in their development from a certain point, and without reference to any motives outside the Ode. Under such conditions, I think, we should require no further observations to characterize (from the standpoint of symbolic action) the main argument in the second stanza. We might go on to make an infinity of observations about the details of the stanza; but as regards major deployments we should deem it enough to note that the theme of "pipes and timbrels" is developed by the use of mystic oxymoron, and then surpassed (or given a development-atop-the-development) by the stressing of erotic imagery (that had been ambiguously adumbrated in the references to "maidens loth"

and "mad pursuit" of Stanza I). And we could note the quality of *incipience* in this imagery, its state of arrest not at fulfilment, but at the point just prior to fulfilment.

Add, now, our knowledge of the poem's place as an enactment in a particular cultural scene, and we likewise note in this second stanza a variant of the identification between death and sexual love that was so typical of nineteenth-century romanticism and was to attain its musical monument in the Wagnerian *Liebestod*.[3] On a purely dialectical basis, to die in love would be to be born to love (the lovers dying as individual identities that they might be transformed into a common identity). Adding historical factors, one can note the part that capitalist individualism plays in sharpening this consummation (since a property structure that heightens the sense of individual identity would thus make it more imperiously a "death" for the individual to take on the new identity made by a union of two). We can thus see why the love-death equation would be particularly representative of a romanticism that was the reflex of business.

Fortunately, the relation between private property and the love-death equation is attested on unimpeachable authority, concerning the effect of consumption and consummation in a "mutual flame":

So between them love did shine,
That the turtle saw his right
Flaming in the phoenix' sight;
Either was the other's mine.
Property was thus appall'd,
That the self was not the same;
Single nature's double name
Neither two nor one was called.[4]

The addition of fire to the equation, with its pun on sexual burning, moves us from purely dialectical considerations into psychological ones. In the lines of Shakespeare, fire is the third term, the ground term for the other two (the synthesis that ends the lovers' roles as thesis and antithesis). Less

---

[1]Shelley's poem is titled "To——" in the *Posthumous Poems* of 1824.

[2]Mr. G. Wilson Knight, in *The Starlit Dome*, refers to "that recurring tendency in Keats to image a posed form, a stillness suggesting motion, what might be called a 'tiptoe' effect." [Burke]

[3]The denouement of Wagner's *Tristan und Isolde* in which the lovers find their apotheosis in death.

[4]Shakespeare, "The Phoenix and the Turtle."

obviously, the same movement from the purely dialectical to the psychological is implicit in any imagery of a *dying* or a *falling* in common, which when woven with sexual imagery signalizes a "transcendent" sexual consummation. The figure appears in a lover's compliment when Keats writes to Fanny Brawne, thus:

> I never knew before, what such a love as you have made me feel, was; I did not believe in it; my Fancy was afraid of it lest it should burn me up. But if you will fully love me, though there may be some fire, 'twill not be more than we can bear when moistened and bedewed with pleasures.

Our primary concern is to follow the transformations of the poem itself. But to understand its full nature as a symbolic act, we should use whatever knowledge is available. In the case of Keats, not only do we know the place of this poem in his work and its time, but also we have material to guide our speculations as regards correlations between poem and poet. I grant that such speculations interfere with the symmetry of criticism as a game. (Criticism as a game is best to watch, I guess, when one confines himself to the single unit, and reports on its movements like a radio commentator broadcasting the blow-by-blow description of a prizefight.) But linguistic analysis has opened up new possibilities in the correlating of producer and product — and these concerns have such important bearing upon matters of culture and conduct in general that no sheer conventions or ideals of criticism should be allowed to interfere with their development.

From what we know of Keats's illness, with the peculiar inclination to erotic imaginings that accompany its fever (as with the writings of D. H. Lawrence) we can glimpse a particular bodily motive expanding and intensifying the lyric state in Keats's case. Whatever the intense *activity* of his thoughts, there was the material *pathos* of his physical condition. Whatever transformations of mind or body he experienced, his illness was there as a kind of constitutional substrate, whereby all aspects of the illness would be imbued with their derivation from a common ground (the phthisic fever thus being at one with the phthisic chill, for whatever the clear contrast between fever and chill, they are but modes of the same illness, the common underlying substance).

The correlation between the state of agitation in the poems and the physical condition of the poet is made quite clear in the poignant letters Keats wrote during his last illness. In 1819 he complains that he is "scarcely content to write the best verses for the fever they leave behind." And he continues: "I want to compose without this fever." But a few months later he confesses, "I am recommended not even to read poetry, much less write it." Or: "I must say that for 6 Months before I was taken ill I had not passed a tranquil day. Either that gloom overspre[a]d me or I was suffering under some passionate feeling, or if I turn'd to versify that exacerbated the poison of either sensation." Keats was "like a sick eagle looking at the sky," as he wrote of his mortality in a kindred poem, "On Seeing the Elgin Marbles."

But though the poet's body was a *patient,* the poet's mind was an *agent.* Thus, as a practitioner of poetry, he could *use* his fever, even perhaps encouraging, though not deliberately, esthetic habits that, in making for the perfection of his lines, would exact payment in the ravages of his body (somewhat as Hart Crane could write poetry only by modes of living that made for the cessation of his poetry and so led to his dissolution).

Speaking of agents, patients, and action here, we might pause to glance back over the centuries thus: in the Aristotelian grammar of motives, action has its reciprocal in passion, hence *passion* is the property of a *patient.* But by the Christian paradox (which made the martyr's action identical with his passion, as the accounts of the martyrs were called both Acts and Passionals), *patience* is the property of a moral *agent.* And this Christian view, as secularized in the philosophy of romanticism, with its stress upon creativeness, leads us to the possibility of a bodily suffering redeemed by a poetic act.

In the third stanza, the central stanza of the Ode (hence properly the fulcrum of its swing) we see the two motives, the action and the passion, in the process of being separated. The possibility raised in the first stanza (which was dubious whether the level of motives was to be human or divine), and developed in the second stanza (which contrasts the "sensual" and the "spirit"), becomes definitive in Stanza III:

Ah, happy, happy boughs! that cannot shed
    Your leaves, nor ever bid the Spring adieu;
And, happy melodist, unwearied,
    For ever piping songs for ever new;
More happy love! more happy, happy love!
    For ever warm and still to be enjoy'd,
        For ever panting, and for ever young;
All breathing human passion far above,
    That leaves a heart high-sorrowful and cloy'd,
        A burning forehead, and a parching tongue.

The poem as a whole makes permanent, or fixes in a state of arrest, a peculiar agitation. But within this fixity, by the nature of poetry as a progressive medium, there must be development. Hence, the agitation that is maintained throughout (as a mood absolutized so that it fills the entire universe of discourse) will at the same time undergo internal transformations. In the third stanza, these are manifested as a clear division into two distinct and contrasted realms. There is a transcendental fever, which is felicitous, divinely above "all breathing human passion." And this "leaves" the other level, the level of earthly fever, "a burning forehead and a parching tongue." From the bodily fever, which is a passion, and malign, there has split off a spiritual activity, a wholly benign aspect of the total agitation.

Clearly, a movement has been finished. The poem must, if it is well-formed, take a new direction, growing out of and surpassing the curve that has by now been clearly established by the successive stages from "Is there the possibility of two motivational levels?" through "there are two motivational levels" to "the 'active' motivational level 'leaves' the 'passive' level."

Prophesying, with the inestimable advantage that goes with having looked ahead, what should we expect the new direction to be? First, let us survey the situation. Originally, before the two strands of the fever had been definitely drawn apart, the bodily passion could serve as the scene or ground of the spiritual action. But at the end of the third stanza, we abandon the level of bodily passion. The action is "far above" the passion, it

"leaves" the fever. What then would this transcendent act require, to complete it?

It would require a scene of the same quality as itself. An act and a scene belong together. The nature of the one must be a fit with the nature of the other. (I like to call this the "scene-act ratio," or "dramatic ratio.") Hence, the act having now transcended its bodily setting, it will require, as its new setting, a transcendent scene. Hence, prophesying *post eventum*, we should ask that, in Stanza IV, the poem *embody* the transcendental act by endowing it with an appropriate scene.

The scene-act ratio involves a law of dramatic consistency whereby the quality of the act shares the quality of the scene in which it is enacted (the synecdochic relation of container and thing contained). Its grandest variant was in supernatural cosmogonies wherein mankind took on the attributes of gods by acting in cosmic scenes that were themselves imbued with the presence of godhead.[5]

Or we may discern the logic of the scene-act ratio behind the old controversy as to whether "God willed the good because it is good," or "the good is good because God willed it." This strictly theological controversy had political implications. But our primary concern here is with the *dramatistic* aspects of this controversy. For you will note that the whole issue centers in the problem of the *grounds* of God's creative act.

Since, from the purely dramatic point of view, every act requires a scene in which it takes place, we may note that one of the doctrines (that "God willed the good because it is good") is more symmetrical than the other. For by it, God's initial act of creation is itself given a ground, or scene (the objective existence of goodness, which was so real that God himself did not simply make it up, but acted in conformity with its nature when willing it to be the law of his creation). In the scholastic formulas taken over from Aristotle, God was defined as "pure act" (though this pure act was in turn the ultimate ground or *scene* of human acting

[5]In an article by Leo Spitzer, "*Milieu* and *Ambiance*: An Essay in Historical Semantics" (September and December 1942 numbers of *Philosophy and Phenomenological Research*), one will find a wealth of material that can be read as illustrative of "dramatic ratio." [Burke]

and willing). And from the standpoint of purely dramatic symmetry, it would be desirable to have some kind of "scene" even for God. This requirement is met, we are suggesting, in the doctrine that "God willed the good *because* it is good." For this word, "because," in assigning a reason for God's willing, gives us in principle a kind of scene, as we may discern in the pun of our word, "ground," itself, which indeterminately applies to either "place" or "cause."

If even theology thus responded to the pressure for dramatic symmetry by endowing God, as the transcendent act, with a transcendent scene of like quality, we should certainly expect to find analogous tactics in this Ode. For as we have noted that the romantic passion is the secular equivalent of the Christian passion, so we may recall Coleridge's notion that poetic action itself is a "dim analogue of Creation."[6] Keats in his way confronting the same dramatistic requirement that the theologians confronted in theirs, when he has arrived at his transcendent act at the end of Stanza III (that is, when the benign fever has split sway from the malign bodily counterpart, as a divorcing of spiritual action from sensual passion), he is ready in the next stanza for the imagining of a scene that would correspond in quality to the quality of the action as so transformed. His fourth stanza will concretize, or "materialize," the act, by dwelling upon its appropriate ground.

> Who are these coming to the sacrifice?
> To what green altar, O mysterious priest,
> Lead'st thou that heifer lowing at the skies,
>   And all her silken flanks with garlands drest?
> What little town, by river or sea shore,
>   Or mountain built with peaceful citadel,
> Is emptied of this folk, this pious morn?
> And, little town, thy streets for evermore
>   Will silent be; and not a soul to tell
>   Why thou art desolate, can e'er return.

It is a vision, as you prefer, of "death" or of "immortality." "Immortality," we might say, is the "good" word for "death," and must necessarily be

conceived in terms of death (the necessity that Donne touches upon when he writes, " . . . but thinke that I / Am, by being dead, immortall"). This is why, when discussing the second stanza, I felt justified in speaking of the variations of the love-death equation, though the poem spoke not of love and *death,* but of love *for ever.* We have a deathy-deathless scene as the corresponding ground of our transcendent act. The Urn itself, as with the scene upon it, is not merely an immortal act in our present mortal scene; it was originally an immortal act in a mortal scene quite different. The imagery, of sacrifice, piety, silence, desolation, is that of communication with the immortal or the dead.[7]

Incidentally, we might note that the return to the use of rhetorical questions in the fourth stanza serves well, on a purely technical level, to keep our contact with the mood of the opening stanza, a music that now but vibrates in the memory. Indeed, one even gets the impression that the form of the rhetorical question had never been abandoned; that the poet's questings had been couched as questions throughout. This is tonal felicity at its best, and something much like unheard tonal felicity. For the actual persistence of the rhetorical questions through these stanzas would have been wearisome, whereas their return now gives us an inaudible variation, by making us

---

[7]In imagery there is no negation, or disjunction. Logically, we can say, "this *or* that," "this, *not* that." In imagery we can but say "this *and* that," "this *with* that," "this-that," etc. Thus, imagistically considered, a commandment cannot be simply a proscription, but is also latently a provocation (a state of affairs that figures in the kind of stylistic scrupulosity and/or curiosity to which Gide's heroes have been particularly sensitive, as "thou shalt not . . . " becomes imaginatively transformed into "what would happen if . . . "). In the light of what we have said about the deathiness of immortality, and the relation between the erotic and the thought of a "dying," perhaps we might be justified in reading the last line of the great "Bright Star!" sonnet as naming states not simply alternative but also synonymous:

> And so live ever — or else swoon to death.

This use of the love-death equation is as startlingly paralleled in a letter to Fanny Brawne:

> I have two luxuries to brood over in my walks, your loveliness and the hour of my death. O that I could take possession of them both in the same moment. [Burke]

---

[6]Coleridge goes even further in *Biographia Literaria,* chapter 13; see p. 325.

feel that the exclamations in the second and third stanzas had been questions, as the questions in the first stanza had been exclamations.

But though a lyric greatly profits by so strong a sense of continuousness, or perpetuity, I am trying to stress the fact that in the fourth stanza we *come upon* something. Indeed, this fourth stanza is related to the three foregoing stanzas quite as the sestet is related to the octave in Keats's sonnet, "On First Looking into Chapman's Homer":

> Much have I travell'd in the realms of gold,
>   And many goodly states and kingdoms seen;
>   Round many western islands have I been
> Which bards in fealty to Apollo hold.
> Oft of one wide expanse had I been told
>   That deep-brow'd Homer ruled as his demesne;
>   Yet did I never breathe its pure serene
> Till I heard Chapman speak out loud and bold:
> Then felt I like some watcher of the skies
>   When a new planet swims into his ken;
> Or like stout Cortez when with eagle eyes
>   He stared at the Pacific — and all his men
> Look'd at each other with a wild surmise —
>   Silent, upon a peak in Darien.

I am suggesting that, just as the sestet in this sonnet, *comes upon a scene,* so it is with the fourth stanza of the Ode. In both likewise we end on the theme of silence; and is not the Ode's reference to the thing that "not a soul can tell" quite the same in quality as the sonnet's reference to a "wild surmise"?

Thus, with the Urn as viaticum (or rather, with the *poem* as viaticum, and *in the name* of the Urn), having symbolically enacted a kind of act that transcends our mortality, we round out the process by coming to dwell upon the transcendental ground of this act. The dead world of ancient Greece, as immortalized on an Urn surviving from that period, is the vessel of this deathy-deathless ambiguity. And we have gone dialectically from the "human" to the "divine" and thence to the "ground of the divine" (here tracing in poetic imagery the kind of "dramatistic" course we have considered, on the purely conceptual plane, in the theological speculations about the "grounds" for God's creative act). Necessarily, there must be certain inadequacies in the conception of this ground, precisely because of the fact that immortality can only be conceived in terms of death. Hence the reference to the "desolate" in a scene otherwise possessing the benignity of the eternal.

The imagery of pious sacrifice, besides its fitness for such thoughts of departure as when the spiritual act splits from the sensual pathos, suggests also a bond of communication between the levels (because of its immortal character in a mortal scene). And finally, the poem, in the name of the Urn, or under the aegis of the Urn, is such a bond. For we readers, by re-enacting it in the reading, use it as a viaticum to transport us into the quality of the scene which it depicts on its face (the scene containing as a fixity what the poem as act extends into a process). The scene *on* the Urn is really the scene *behind* the Urn; the Urn is literally the ground of this scene, but transcendentally the scene is the ground of the Urn. The Urn contains the scene out of which it arose.

We turn now to the closing stanza:

> O Attic shape! Fair attitude! with brede
>   Of marble men, and maidens overwrought,
> With forest branches and the trodden weed;
>   Thou, silent form, dost tease us out of thought
> As doth eternity: Cold Pastoral!
>   When old age shall this generation waste,
>   Thou shalt remain, in midst of other woe
> Than ours, a friend to man, to whom thou say'st,
>   "Beauty is truth, truth beauty," — that is all
>   Ye know on earth, and all ye need to know.

In the third stanza we were at a moment of heat, emphatically sharing an imagery of loves "panting" and "for ever warm" that was, in the transcendental order, companionate to "a burning forehead, and a parching tongue" in the order of the passions. But in the last stanza, as signalized in the marmorean utterance, "Cold Pastoral!" we have gone from transcendental fever to transcendental chill. Perhaps, were we to complete our exegesis, we should need reference to some physical step from phthisic chill, that we might detect here a final correlation between bodily passion and mental action. In any event we may note that, the mental action having departed from the bodily passion, the change from fever to chill is not a sufferance. For, as only the *benign* aspects of the fever had been left after the split, so it is a wholly benign chill on which the poem ends.[8]

I wonder whether anyone can read the reference to "brede of marble men and maidens overwrought" without thinking of "breed" for "brede" and "excited" for "overwrought." (Both expressions would thus merge notions of sexuality and craftsmanship, the erotic and the poetic.) As for the designating of the Urn as an "Attitude," it fits in admirably with our stress upon symbolic action. For an attitude is an arrested, or incipient *act* — not just an *object*, or *thing*.

Yeats, in *A Vision*, speaks of "the diagrams in Law's *Boehme*, where one lifts a paper to discover both the human entrails and the starry heavens." This equating of the deeply without and the deeply within (as also with Kant's famous remark) might well be remembered when we think of the sky that the "watcher" saw in Keats's sonnet. It is an internal sky, attained through meditations induced by the reading of a book. And so the oracle, whereby truth and beauty are proclaimed as one, would seem to derive from a profound inwardness.

Otherwise, without these introductory mysteries, "truth" and "beauty" were at odds. For whereas "beauty" had its fulfillment in romantic poetry, "truth" was coming to have its fulfillment in science, technological accuracy, accountancy, statistics, actuarial tables, and the like. Hence, without benefit of the rites which one enacts in a sympathetic reading of the Ode (rites that remove the discussion to a different level), the enjoyment of "beauty" would involve an esthetic kind of awareness radically in conflict with the kind of awareness deriving from the practical "truth." And as regards the tactics of the poem, this conflict would seem to be solved by "estheticizing" the true rather than by "verifying" the beautiful.

[8]In a letter to Fanny Brawne, Keats touches upon the fever-chill contrast in a passage that also touches upon the love-death equation, though here the chill figures in an untransfigured state:

> I fear that I am too prudent for a dying kind of Lover. Yet, there is a great difference between going off in warm blood like Romeo; and making one's exit like a frog in a frost. [Burke]

Earlier in our essay, we suggested reading "poetry" for "beauty" and "science" for "truth," with the oracle deriving its *liberating* quality from the fact that it is uttered at a time when the poem has taken us to a level where earthly contradictions do not operate. But we might also, in purely conceptual terms, attain a level where "poetry" and "science" cease to be at odds; namely: by translating the two terms into the "grammar" that lies behind them. That is: we could generalize the term "poetry" by widening it to the point where we could substitute for it the term "act." And we could widen "science" to the point where we could substitute "scene." Thus we have:

"beauty" equals "poetry" equals "act"
"truth" equals "science" equals "scene"

We would equate "beauty" with "act," because it is not merely a decorative thing, but an assertion, an affirmative, a creation, hence in the fullest sense an act. And we would equate "truth" or "science" with the "scenic" because science is a knowledge of *what is* — and *all that is* comprises the over-all universal *scene*. Our corresponding transcendence, then, got by "translation" into purely grammatical terms, would be: "Act is scene, scene act." We have got to this point by a kind of purely conceptual transformation that would correspond, I think, to the transformations of imagery leading to the oracle in the Ode.

"Act is scene, scene act." Unfortunately, I must break the symmetry a little. For poetry, as conceived in idealism (romanticism) could not quite be equated with *act,* but rather with *attitude*. For idealistic philosophies, with their stress upon the subjective, place primary stress upon the *agent* (the individual, ego, the will, etc.). It was medieval scholasticism that placed primary stress upon the *act*. And in the Ode the Urn (which is the vessel or representative of poetry) is called an "attitude," which is not outright an act, but an incipient or arrested act, a *state of mind*, the property of an *agent*. Keats, in calling the Urn an attitude, is *personifying* it. Or we might use the italicizing resources of dialectic by saying that for Keats, beauty (poetry) was not so much "the *act* of an agent" as it was "the act of an *agent*."

Perhaps we can re-enforce this interpretation by examining kindred strategies in Yeats, whose poetry similarly derives from idealistic, romantic sources. Indeed, as we have noted elsewhere,[9] Yeats's vision of immortality in his Byzantium poems but carries one step further the Keatsian identification with the Grecian Urn:

> Once out of nature I shall never take
> My bodily form from any natural thing,
> But such a form as Grecian goldsmiths make
> Of hammered gold and gold enamelling . . .

Here certainly the poet envisions immortality as "esthetically" as Keats. For he will have immortality as a golden bird, a fabricated thing, a work of Grecian goldsmiths. Here we go in the same direction as the "overwrought" Urn, but farther along in that direction.

The ending of Yeats's poem, "Among School Children," helps us to make still clearer the idealistic stress upon agent:

> Labour is blossoming or dancing where
> The body is not bruised to pleasure soul,
> Nor beauty torn out of its own despair,
> Nor blear-eyed wisdom out of midnight oil.
> O chestnut tree, great rooted blossomer,
> Are you the leaf, the blossom or the bole?
> O body swayed to music, O brightening glance,
> How can we know the dancer from the dance?

Here the chestnut tree (as personified agent) is the ground of unity or continuity for all its scenic manifestations; and with the agent (dancer) is merged the act (dance). True, we seem to have here a commingling of act, scene, and agent, all three. Yet it is the *agent* that is "foremost among the equals." Both Yeats and Keats, of course, were much more "dramatistic" in their thinking than romantic poets generally, who usually center their efforts upon the translation of *scene* into terms of *agent* (as the materialistic science that was the dialectical counterpart of romantic idealism preferred conversely to translate *agent* into terms of *scene,* or in other words, to treat "consciousness" in terms of "matter," the "mental" in terms of the "physical," "people" in terms of "environment").

---

[9]"On Motivation in Yeats" (*The Southern Review,* Winter 1942). [Burke]

To review briefly: The poem begins with an ambiguous fever which in the course of the further development is "separated out," splitting into a bodily fever and a spiritual counterpart. The bodily passion is the malign aspect of the fever, the mental action its benign aspect. In the course of the development, the malign passion is transcended and the benign active partner, the intellectual exhilaration, takes over. At the beginning, where the two aspects were ambiguously one, the bodily passion would be the "scene" of the mental action (the "objective symptoms" of the body would be paralleled by the "subjective symptoms" of the mind, the bodily state thus being the other or ground of the mental state). But as the two become separated out, the mental action transcends the bodily passion. It becomes an act in its own right, making discoveries and assertions not grounded in the bodily passion. And this quality of action, in transcending the merely physical symptoms of the fever, would thus require a different ground or scene, one more suited in quality to the quality of the transcendent act.

The transcendent act is concretized, or "materialized," in the vision of the "immortal" scene, the reference in Stanza IV to the original scene of the Urn, the "heavenly" scene of the dead, or immortal, Greece (the scene in which the Urn was originally enacted and which is also fixed on its face). To indicate the internality of this vision, we referred to a passage in Yeats relating the "depths" of the sky without to the depths of the mind within; and we showed a similar pattern in Keats's account of the vision that followed his reading of Chapman's Homer. We suggested that the poet is here coming upon a new internal sky, through identification with the Urn as act, the same sky that he came upon through identification with the enactments of Chapman's translation.

This transcendent scene is the level at which the earthly laws of contradiction no longer prevail. Hence, in the terms of this scene, he can proclaim the unity of truth and beauty (of science and art), a proclamation which he needs to make precisely because here was the basic split responsible for the romantic agitation (in both poetic and philosophic idealism). That is, it was gratifying to have the oracle proclaim the unity of poetry and science because the values of technology and business were causing them to be at odds. And from the perspective of a "higher level" (the perspective of a dead or immortal scene transcending the world of temporal contradictions) the split could be proclaimed once more a unity.

At this point, at this stage of exaltation, the fever has been replaced by chill. But the bodily passion has completely dropped out of account. All is now mental action. Hence, the chill (as in the ecstatic exclamation, "Cold Pastoral!") is proclaimed only in its benign aspect.

We may contrast this discussion with explanations such as a materialist of the Kretschmer school might offer. I refer to accounts of motivation that might treat disease as cause and poem as effect. In such accounts, the disease would not be "passive," but wholly active; and what we have called the mental action would be wholly passive, hardly more than an epiphenomenon, a mere symptom of the disease quite as are the fever and the chill themselves. Such accounts would give us no conception of the essential matter here, the intense linguistic activity.

Literature as Equipment for Living

Here I shall put down, as briefly as possible, a statement in behalf of what might be catalogued, with a fair degree of accuracy, as a *sociological* criticism of literature. Sociological criticism in itself is certainly not new. I shall here try to suggest what partially new elements or emphasis I think should be added to this old approach. And to make the "way in" as easy as possible, I shall begin with a discussion of proverbs.

I

Examine random specimens in *The Oxford Dictionary of English Proverbs.* You will note, I think, that there is no "pure" literature here. Everything is "medicine." Proverbs are designed for consolation or vengeance, for admonition or exhortation, for foretelling.

Or they name typical, recurrent situations. That is, people find a certain social relationship recurring so frequently that they must "have a word for it." The Eskimos have special names for many different kinds of snow (fifteen, if I remember rightly) because variations in the quality of snow greatly affect their living. Hence, they must "size up" snow much more accurately than we do.

And the same is true of social phenomena. Social structures give rise to "type" situations, subtle subdivisions of the relationships involved in competitive and coöperative acts. Many proverbs seek to chart, in more or less homey and picturesque ways, these "type" situations. I submit that such naming is done, not for the sheer glory of the thing, but because of its bearing upon human welfare. A different name for snow implies a different kind of hunt. Some names for snow imply that one should not hunt at all. And similarly, the names for typical, recurrent social situations are not developed out of "disinterested curiosity," but because the names imply a command (what to expect, what to look out for).

To illustrate with a few representative examples:

Proverbs designed for consolation: "The sun does not shine on both sides of the hedge at once." "Think of ease, but work on." "Little troubles the eye, but far less the soul." "The worst luck now, the better another time." "The wind in one's face makes one wise." "He that hath lands hath quarrels." "He knows how to carry the dead cock home." "He is not poor that hath little, but he that desireth much."

For vengeance: "At length the fox is brought to the furrier." "Shod in the cradle, barefoot in the stubble." "Sue a beggar and get a louse." "The higher the ape goes, the more he shows his tail." "The moon does not heed the barking of dogs." "He measures another's corn by his own bushel." "He shuns the man who knows him well." "Fools tie knots and wise men loose them."

Proverbs that have to do with foretelling (the most obvious are those to do with the weather): "Sow peas and beans in the wane of the moon, Who soweth them sooner, he soweth too soon." "When the wind's in the north, the skilful fisher goes not forth." "When the sloe tree is as white as a sheet, sow your barley whether it be dry or wet." "When the sun sets bright and clear, An easterly wind you need not fear. When the sun sets in a bank, A westerly wind we shall not want."

In short: "Keep your weather eye open": be realistic about sizing up today's weather, because your accuracy has bearing upon tomorrow's weather. And forecast not only the meteorological weather, but also the social weather: "When the moon's in the full, then wit's in the wane." "Straws show which way the wind blows." "When the fish is caught, the net is laid aside." "Remove an old tree, and it will wither to death." "The wolf may lose his teeth, but never his nature." "He that bites on every weed must needs light on poison." "Whether the pitcher strikes the stone, or the stone the pitcher, it is bad for the pitcher." "Eagles catch no flies." "The more laws, the more offenders."

In this foretelling category we might also include the recipes for wise living, sometimes moral, sometimes technical: "First thrive, and then wive." "Think with the wise but talk with the vulgar." "When the fox preacheth, then beware your geese." "Venture a small fish to catch a great one." "Respect a man, he will do the more."

In the class of "typical, recurrent situations" we might put such proverbs and proverbial expressions as: "Sweet appears sour when we pay." "The treason is loved but the traitor is hated." "The wine in the bottle does not quench thirst." "The sun is never the worse for shining on a dunghill." "The lion kicked by an ass." "The lion's share." "To catch one napping." "To smell a rat." "To cool one's heels."

By all means, I do not wish to suggest that this is the only way in which the proverbs could be classified. For instance, I have listed in the "foretelling" group the proverb, "When the fox preacheth, then beware your geese." But it could obviously be "taken over" for vindictive purposes. Or consider a proverb like, "Virtue flies from the heart of a mercenary man." A poor man might obviously use it either to console himself for being poor (the implication being, "Because I am poor in money I am rich in virtue") or to strike at another (the implication being, "When he got money, what else could you expect of him but deterioration?"). In fact, we could even say that such symbolic vengeance would itself be an aspect of solace. And a proverb like "The sun is never the worse for shining on a dunghill" (which I have listed under "typical recurrent situations") might as well be put in the vindictive category.

The point of issue is not to find categories that "place" the proverbs once and for all. What I want is categories that suggest their active nature. Here is no "realism for its own sake." Here is realism for promise, admonition, solace, vengeance, foretelling, instruction, charting, all for the direct bearing that such acts have upon matters of welfare.

2

Step two: Why not extend such analysis of proverbs to encompass the whole field of literature? Could the most complex and sophisticated works of art legitimately be considered somewhat as "proverbs writ large"? Such leads, if held admissible, should help us to discover important facts about literary organization (thus satisfying the requirements of technical criticism). And the kind of observation from this perspective should apply beyond literature to life in general (thus helping to take literature out of its separate bin and give it a place in a general "sociological" picture).

The point of view might be phrased in this way: Proverbs are *strategies* for dealing with *situations*. In so far as situations are typical and recurrent in a given social structure, people develop names for them and strategies for handling them. Another name for strategies might be *attitudes*.

People have often commented on the fact that there are *contrary* proverbs. But I believe that the above approach to proverbs suggests a necessary modification of that comment. The apparent contradictions depend upon differences in *attitude,* involving a correspondingly different choice of *strategy.* Consider, for instance, the *apparently* opposite pair: "Repentance comes too late" and "Never too late to mend." The first is admonitory. It says in effect: "You'd better look out, or you'll get yourself too far into this business." The second is consolatory, saying in effect: "Buck up, old man, you can still pull out of this."

Some critics have quarreled with me about my selection of the word "strategy" as the name for this process. I have asked them to suggest an alternative term, so far without profit. The only one I can think of is "method." But if "strategy" errs in suggesting to some people an overly *conscious* procedure, "method" errs in suggesting an overly "*methodical*" one. Anyhow, let's look at the documents:

Concise Oxford Dictionary: "Strategy: Movement of an army or armies in a campaign, art of so moving or disposing troops or ships as to impose upon the enemy the place and time and conditions for fighting preferred by oneself" (from a Greek word that refers to the leading of an army).

New English Dictionary: "Strategy: The art of projecting and directing the larger military movements and operations of a campaign."

André Cheron, *Traité Complet d'Echecs:* "On entend par stratégie les manoeuvres qui ont pour but la sortie et le bon arrangement des pièces."[1]

Looking at these definitions, I gain courage. For surely, the most highly alembicated and sophisticated work of art, arising in complex civilizations, could be considered as designed to organize and command the army of one's thoughts and images, and to so organize them that one "imposes upon the enemy the time and place and conditions for fighting preferred by oneself." One seeks to "direct the larger movements and operations" in one's campaign of living. One "maneuvers," and the maneuvering is an "art."

Are not the final results one's "strategy"? One tries, as far as possible, to develop a strategy whereby one "can't lose." One tries to change the rules of the game until they fit his own necessities. Does the artist encounter disaster? He will "make capital" of it. If one is a victim of competition, for instance, if one is elbowed out, if one is willy-nilly more jockeyed against than jockeying, one can by the solace and vengeance of art convert this very "liability" into an "asset." One tries to fight on his own terms, developing a strategy for imposing the proper "time, place, and conditions."

But one must also, to develop a full strategy, be *realistic.* One must *size things up* properly. One cannot accurately know how things *will be,* what is promising and what is menacing, unless he accurately knows how things *are.* So the wise strategist will not be content with strategies of merely a self-gratifying sort. He will "keep his weather eye open." He will not too eagerly "read into" a scene an attitude that is irrelevant to it. He won't sit on the side of an active volcano and "see" it as a dormant plain.

Often, alas, he will. The great allurement in our present popular "inspirational literature," for instance, may be largely of this sort. It is a strategy for easy consolation. It "fills a need," since there is always a need for easy consolation — and in an era of confusion like our own the need is especially keen. So people are only too willing to "meet a man halfway" who will *play down* the realistic naming of our situation and *play up* such strategies as make solace cheap. However, I should propose a reservation here. We usually take it for granted that people who consume our current output of books on "How to Buy Friends and Bamboozle Oneself and Other People"[2] are reading as *students* who will attempt applying the recipes given. Nothing of the sort. *The reading of a book on the attaining of success is in itself the symbolic attaining of that success.* It is *while they read* that these readers are "succeeding." I'll wager that, in by far the great majority of cases, such readers make no serious attempt to apply the book's recipes. The lure of the book resides in the fact that the reader, while reading it, is then living in the aura of success. What he wants is

---

[1]*Complete Treatise on Chess:* "Strategy signifies the maneuvers whose goal is attack and correct position."

[2]Burke is parodying Dale Carnegie's *How to Make Friends and Influence People* in particular, but the genre of the self-help book continues to thrive today.

easy success; and he gets it in symbolic form by the mere reading itself. To attempt applying such stuff in real life would be very difficult, full of many disillusioning problems.

Sometimes a different strategy may arise. The author may remain realistic, avoiding too easy a form of solace — yet he may get as far off the track in his own way. Forgetting that realism is an aspect for foretelling, he may take it as an end in itself. He is tempted to do this by two factors: (1) an *ill-digested* philosophy of science, leading him mistakenly to assume that "relentless" naturalistic "truthfulness" is a proper end in itself, and (2) a merely *competitive* desire to outstrip other writers by being "more realistic" than they. Works thus made "efficient" by tests of competition internal to the book trade are a kind of academicism not so named (the writer usually thinks of it as the *opposite* of academicism). Realism thus stepped up competitively might be distinguished from the proper sort by the name of "naturalism." As a way of "sizing things up," the naturalistic tradition tends to become as inaccurate as the "inspirational" strategy, though at the opposite extreme.

Anyhow, the main point is this: A work like *Madame Bovary* (or its homely American translation, *Babbitt*) is the strategic naming of a situation. It singles out a pattern of experience that is sufficiently representative of our social structure, that recurs sufficiently often *mutatis mutandis,* for people to "need a word for it" and to adopt an attitude towards it. Each work of art is the addition of a word to an informal dictionary (or, in the case of purely derivative artists, the addition of a subsidiary meaning to a word already given by some originating artist). As for *Madame Bovary,* the French critic Jules de Gaultier proposed to add it to our *formal* dictionary by coining the word "Bovarysme" and writing a whole book to say what he meant by it.

Mencken's book on *The American Language,* I hate to say, is splendid. I console myself with the reminder that Mencken didn't write it. Many millions of people wrote it, and Mencken was merely the amanuensis who took it down from their dictation. He found a true "vehicle" (that is, a book that could be greater than the author who wrote it). He gets the royalties, but the job was done by a collectivity. As you read that book, you see a people who were up against a new set of typical recurrent situations, situations typical of their business, their politics, their criminal organizations, their sports. Either there were no words for these in standard English, or people didn't know them, or they didn't "sound right." So a new vocabulary arose, to "give us a word for it." I see no reason for believing that Americans are unusually fertile in word-coinage. American slang was not developed out of some exceptional gift. It was developed out of the fact that new typical situations had arisen and people needed names for them. They had to "size things up." They had to console and strike, to promise and admonish. They had to describe for purposes of forecasting. And "slang" was the result. It is, by this analysis, simply *proverbs not so named,* a kind of "folk criticism."

3

With what, then, would "sociological criticism" along these lines be concerned? It would seek to codify the various strategies which artists have developed with relation to the naming of situations. In a sense, much of it would even be "timeless," for many of the "typical, recurrent situations" are not peculiar to our own civilization at all. The situations and strategies framed in Aesop's Fables, for instance, apply to human relations now just as fully as they applied in ancient Greece. They are, like philosophy, sufficiently "generalized" to extend far beyond the particular combination of events named by them in any one instance. They name an "essence." Or, we could say that they are on a "high level of abstraction." One doesn't usually think of them as "abstract," since they are usually so concrete in their stylistic expression. But they invariably aim to discern the "general behind the particular" (which would suggest that they are good Goethe).

The attempt to treat literature from the standpoint of situations and strategies suggests a variant of Spengler's notion of the "contemporaneous." By "contemporaneity" he meant corresponding stages of different cultures. For instance, if modern New York is much like decadent Rome, then we are "contemporaneous" with decadent Rome, or with some corresponding decadent city among the

Mayas, etc. It is in this sense that situations are "timeless," "non-historical," "contemporaneous." A given human relationship may be at one time named in terms of foxes and lions, if there are foxes and lions about; or it may now be named in terms of salesmanship, advertising, the tactics of politicians, etc. But beneath the change in particulars, we may often discern the naming of the one situation.

So sociological criticism, as here understood, would seek to assemble and codify this lore. It might occasionally lead us to outrage good taste, as we sometimes found exemplified in some great sermon or tragedy or abstruse work of philosophy the same strategy as we found exemplified in a dirty joke. At this point, we'd put the sermon and the dirty joke together, thus "grouping by situation" and showing the range of possible particularizations. In his exceptionally discerning essay, "A Critic's Job of Work," R. P. Blackmur says, "I think on the whole his (Burke's) method could be applied with equal fruitfulness to Shakespeare, Dashiell Hammett, or Marie Corelli."[3] When I got through wincing, I had to admit that Blackmur was right. This article is an attempt to say for the method what can be said. As a matter of fact, I'll go a step further and maintain: You can't properly put Marie Corelli and Shakespeare apart until you have first put them together. First genus, then differentia. The strategy in common is the genus. The *range* or *scale* or *spectrum* of particularizations is the differentia.

Anyhow, that's what I'm driving at. And that's why reviewers sometime find in my work "intuitive" leaps that are dubious as "science." They are not "leaps" at all. They are classifications, groupings, made on the basis of some strategic element common to the items grouped. They are neither more nor less "intuitive" than *any* grouping or classification of social events. Apples can be grouped with bananas as fruits, and they can be grouped with tennis balls as round. I am simply proposing, in the social sphere, a method of classification with reference to *strategies*.

The method has these things to be said in its favor: It gives definite insight into the organization of literary works; and it automatically breaks

[3] Richard P. Blackmur, "A Critic's Job of Work" (1935), published in *Language as Gesture* (1952).

down the barriers erected about literature as a specialized pursuit. People can classify novels by reference to three kinds, eight kinds, seventeen kinds. It doesn't matter. Students patiently copy down the professor's classification and pass examinations on it, because the range of possible academic classifications is endless. Sociological classification, as herein suggested, would derive its relevance from the fact that it should apply both to works of art and to social situations outside of art.

It would, I admit, violate current pieties, break down current categories, and thereby "outrage good taste." But "good taste" has become *inert*. The classifications I am proposing would be *active*. I think that what we need is active categories.

These categories will lie on the bias across the categories of modern specialization. The new alignment will outrage in particular those persons who take the division of faculties in our universities to be an exact replica of the way in which God himself divided up the universe. We have had the Philosophy of Being; and we have had the Philosophy of Becoming. In typical contemporary specialization, we have been getting the Philosophy of the Bin. Each of these mental localities has had its own peculiar way of life, its own values, even its own special idiom for seeing, thinking, and "proving." Among other things, a sociological approach should attempt to provide a reintegrative point of view, a broader empire of investigation encompassing the lot.

What would such sociological categories be like? They would consider works of art, I think, as strategies for selecting enemies and allies, for socializing losses, for warding off evil eye, for purification, propitiation, and desanctification, consolation and vengeance, admonition and exhortation, implicit commands or instructions of one sort or another. Art forms like "tragedy" or "comedy" or "satire" would be treated as *equipments for living,* that size up situations in various ways and in keeping with correspondingly various attitudes. The typical ingredients of such forms would be sought. Their relation to typical situations would be stressed. Their comparative values would be considered, with the intention of formulating a "strategy of strategies," the "overall" strategy obtained by inspection of the lot.

F. R. Leavis

1895–1978

Frank Raymond Leavis, a critic devoted to firm standards and implacable moralism, was born in Cambridge, England, and was educated there at the Perse School. Leavis survived his tenure as an ambulance bearer on the Western Front in World War I to become a lecturer at Emmanuel College, Cambridge, in 1925. He moved on to Downing College in 1932, where he was elected to a fellowship in 1936. He and his wife, the former Queenie Dorothy Roth, were the founding editors of *Scrutiny* (1932–53), a quarterly journal of criticism devoted to the advancement of their critical principles. Leavis retired from Downing College in 1962 to serve as a visiting professor of English at a number of universities, including those of York (1965–68), Wales (1969), and Bristol (1970). He received numerous honorary degrees, and in the year of his death was made a Companion of Honour.

It has been said that Leavis's early critical interest was in poetry (*New Bearings in English Poetry: A Study of the Contemporary Situation* [1932]; *Revaluation: Tradition and Development in English Poetry* [1936]) and that his later interest was in the novel (*The Great Tradition* [1948]; *D. H. Lawrence: Novelist* [1955]; *"Anna Karenina," and Other Essays* [1968]; *Dickens: The Novelist* [1971; with Q. D. Leavis]). But this generalization does not take into account his consistent preoccupation with criticism itself (*The Common Pursuit* [1952]) and with questions of teaching and the university (*Education and the University: A Sketch for an "English School"* [1943]; *Literature in Our Time and the University* [1969; based on the Clark Lectures of 1965]; *The Living Principle: "English" as a Discipline of Thought* [1975]). In fact one must go beyond these categories and see Leavis as one of the successors to Matthew Arnold in viewing literary study (as Arnold had viewed literature itself) as a form of the "criticism of life" that would pierce through the dominant ideology and allow a blind and mechanical age to know and redeem itself.

Like his German contemporary, Martin Heidegger, and like the American New Critics, Leavis viewed the world of the twentieth century as anomic and rudderless, drifting after World War I had destroyed any semblance of the old Victorian consensus. Although England, unlike Germany, had been victorious in the war, the aristocratic ideology of the military elite had been exposed as pernicious folly in the mud of the Flanders trenches. Organized religion, already in retreat in Arnold's day, failed to offer any coherent explanation for the disasters of the war, and the desperate hedonism of the 1920s testified both to the emptiness of modern life and the loss of faith in any of the codes that had regulated it. Leavis's messianic vision of literary studies was a response to this moment in history.

Was it possible for a small cadre of highly educated, deeply cultured individuals to counter the leveling forces of popular literature and middlebrow culture, to restore coherence to contemporary life? This was the mission Leavis and his students undertook. Together with his contemporaries at Cambridge, who included I. A. Richards (see p. 763) and William Empson, Leavis set up literary studies as a way of understanding the evolution of modern life in all its complexity and established the prestige of the literary degree as one that fitted the bearer for the highest offices. As Terry Eagleton has put it, "In the early 1920s it was desperately unclear why English was worth studying at all; by the early 1930s it had become a question of why it was worth wasting your time on anything else. English was not only a subject worth pursuing, but *the* supremely civilizing pursuit, the spiritual essence of the social formation."[1] Before Leavis, professors of literature had been gifted aesthetes and dilettantes or pedantic philological pedagogues; after Leavis, it was the aim of the literary scholar to bring his research to bear on sociopolitical issues and the conduct of cultural life. He was to guard and give exposition to the literary and cultural tradition that united the nation. From the perspective of the 1990s, it seems clear that although Leavis's own values for analyzing literature may no longer be fashionable, his vision of what the profession of letters was all about has not changed. And in this sense he may be the most influential British critic of the century.

Just as Matthew Arnold had endorsed "touchstones" for determining which literary texts (or stanzas, or single lines) possessed the "high seriousness" that would make them suitable for altering the consciousness of Victorians in need of standards of quality, so too Leavis's program included a re-evaluation of the course of English literature. Leavis got rid of the previously standard practice of studying all the literary texts of a century, regardless of their tendency, and substituted a smaller and denser canon of works he approved of, ones that engaged "properly" with the essential social and cultural issues. Literary figures who were interested in form more than content, in the beauties of language rather than its ideological uses, were downgraded. The mellifluous Tennyson was not to be preferred to the harsh, difficult Hopkins. The clever self-referentiality and aestheticism of Joyce ranked far below the prophetic visions and cultural radicalism of D. H. Lawrence. The recherché medievalism of Spenser and the idiosyncratic religiosity of Milton devalued them beneath Donne and Marvell. While a few of these judgments — like that on Joyce — were ultimately ignored, Leavis's influence in forming the canon for English and American readers at midcentury was enormous.

It is in this context of moral judgment and cultural politics that we need to place the following selection, from the first chapter of the revised edition of *The Great Tradition* (1960), in which Leavis identifies the few novelists of whose vision of life he wholeheartedly approves. It is not easy, at times, to discern the precise criteria Leavis uses to make his selection. One conservative comedic novelist (Austen) might be a leader of the canon, while another (Fielding) might be beyond the pale. Leavis at first dismissed Dickens as a "mere entertainer"; later he accepted him into the Great Tradition. What seems to garner Leavis's basic approval is a certain core of psychological realism, which is one common denominator in Eliot, James, and Conrad, as long as it is not wrecked by playfulness (as in Trollope and Thackeray), or by a deep pessimism (as in Hardy or Ford Madox Ford). Leavis was once challenged by René Wellek to give some sort of general exposition to his criteria of value, to move

[1]Terry Eagleton, *Literary Theory: An Introduction* (Minneapolis: University of Minnesota Press, 1983), p. 31.

beyond judgment to some sort of *theory* — and he declined. Theory as we know it was neither his forte nor his business: He was one of the great magisterial figures — the Samuel Johnson of the twentieth century — and his refusal to theorize in this age of theory is one mark of his peculiar place in the critical tradition.

Selected Bibliography

Bell, Michael. *F. R. Leavis.* New York and London: Routledge, 1988.

Bilan, R. P. *The Literary Criticism of F. R. Leavis.* London: Cambridge University Press, 1979.

Cordner, Christopher. "F. R. Leavis and the Moral in Literature." In *On Literary Theory and Philosophy,* ed. Richard Freadman and Lloyd Reinhardt. New York: St. Martin's Press, 1991, pp. 60–81.

Gregor, Ian. "F. R. Leavis and The Great Tradition." *Sewanee Review* 93 (1985): 434–46.

Kinch, M. B., William Baker, and John Kimber. *F. R. Leavis and Q. D. Leavis: An Annotated Bibliography.* New York: Garland, 1989.

MacKillop, Ian. *F. R. Leavis: A Life in Criticism.* New York: St. Martin's Press, 1977.

Robertson, P. J. *The Leavises on Fiction: A Historic Partnership.* New York: St. Martin's Press, 1981.

Samson, Anne. *F. R. Leavis.* Toronto: University of Toronto Press, 1992.

From *The Great Tradition*

> *... not dogmatically but deliberately ...*
> — JOHNSON, *Preface to Shakespeare*

The great English novelists are Jane Austen, George Eliot, Henry James, and Joseph Conrad — to stop for the moment at that comparatively safe point in history. Since Jane Austen, for special reasons, needs to be studied at considerable length, I confine myself in this book to the last three. Critics have found me narrow, and I have no doubt that my opening proposition, whatever I may say to explain and justify it, will be adduced in reinforcement of their strictures. It passes as fact (in spite of the printed evidence) that I pronounced Milton negligible, dismiss "the Romantics," and hold that, since Donne, there is no poet we need bother about except Hopkins and Eliot. The view, I suppose, will be as confidently attributed to me that, except

Jane Austen, George Eliot, James, and Conrad, there are no novelists in English worth reading.

The only way to escape misrepresentation is never to commit oneself to any critical judgment that makes an impact — that is, never to *say* anything. I still, however, think that the best way to promote profitable discussion is to be as clear as possible with oneself about what one sees and judges, to try and establish the essential discriminations in the given field of interest, and to state them as clearly as one can (for disagreement, if necessary). And it seems to me that in the field of fiction some challenging discriminations are very much called for; the field is so large and offers such insidious temptations to complacent confusions of judgment and to critical indolence. It is of the field of fiction belonging to Literature that I am thinking, and I am thinking in particular of the present vogue of the Victorian age. Trollope,

Charlotte Yonge, Mrs. Gaskell, Wilkie Collins, Charles Reade, Charles and Henry Kingsley, Marryat, Shorthouse[1] — one after another the minor novelists of that period are being commended to our attention, written up, and publicized by broadcast, and there is a marked tendency to suggest that they not only have various kinds of interest to offer but that they are living classics. (Are not they all in the literary histories?) There are Jane Austen, Mrs. Gaskell, Scott, "the Brontës,"[2] Dickens, Thackeray, George Eliot, Trollope, and so on, all, one gathers, classical novelists.

It is necessary to insist, then, that there are important distinctions to be made, and that far from all of the names in the literary histories really belong to the realm of significant creative achievement. And as a recall to a due sense of differences it is well to start by distinguishing the few really great — the major novelists who count in the same way as the major poets, in the sense that they not only change the possibilities of the art for practitioners and readers, but that they are significant in terms of the human awareness they promote; awareness of the possibilities of life.[3]

[1]The novelist who has not been revived is Disraeli. Yet, though he is not one of the great novelists, he is so alive and intelligent as to deserve permanent currency, at any rate in the trilogy *Coningsby, Sybil* and *Tancred:* his own interests as expressed in these books — the interests of a supremely intelligent politician who has a sociologist's understanding of civilization and its movement in his time — are so mature. [Leavis]

[2]See "Note: 'The Brontës'" [p. 658]. [Leavis]

[3]Characteristic of the confusion I am contending against is the fashion (for which the responsibility seems to go back to Virginia Woolf and Mr. E. M. Forster) of talking of *Moll Flanders* as a "great novel." Defoe was a remarkable writer, but all that need be said about him as a novelist was said by Leslie Stephen in *Hours in a Library* (First Series). He made no pretension to practising the novelist's art, and matters little as an influence. In fact, the only influence that need be noted is that represented by the use made of him in the nineteen-twenties by the practitioners of the fantastic *conte* (or pseudo-moral fable) with its empty pretence of significance.

Associated with this use of Defoe is the use that was made in much the same *milieu* of Sterne, in whose irresponsible (and nasty) trifling, regarded as in some way extraordinarily significant and mature, was found a sanction for attributing value to other trifling.

The use of Bunyan by T. F. Powys is quite another matter. It is a mark of the genuine nature of Mr. Powys's creative gift (his work seems to me not to have had due recognition) that

To insist on the pre-eminent few in this way is not to be indifferent to tradition; on the contrary, it is the way towards understanding what tradition is. "Tradition," of course, is a term with many forces — and often very little at all. There is a habit nowadays of suggesting that there is a tradition of "the English Novel," and that all that can be said of the tradition (that being its peculiarity) is that "the English Novel" can be anything you like. To distinguish the major novelists in the spirit proposed is to form a more useful idea of tradition (and to recognize that the conventionally established view of the past of English fiction needs to be drastically revised). It is in terms of the major novelists, those significant in the way suggested, that tradition, in any serious sense, has its significance.

To be important historically is not, of course, to be necessarily one of the significant few. Fielding deserves the place of importance given him in the literary histories, but he hasn't the kind of classical distinction we are also invited to credit him with. He is important not because he leads to Mr. J. B. Priestley but because he leads to Jane Austen, to appreciate whose distinction is to feel that life isn't long enough to permit of one's giving much time to Fielding or any to Mr. Priestley.

Fielding made Jane Austen possible by opening the central tradition of English fiction. In fact, to say that the English novel began with him is as reasonable as such propositions ever are. He completed the work begun by *The Tatler* and *The Spectator,* in the pages of which we see the drama turning into the novel — that this development should occur by way of journalism being in the natural course of things. To the art of presenting character and *moeurs*[4] learnt in that school (he

he has been able to achieve a kind of traditional relation to Bunyan — especially, of course, in *Mr. Weston's Good Wine.* Otherwise there is little that can be said with confidence about Bunyan as an influence. And yet we know him to have been for two centuries one of the most frequented of all classics, and in such a way that he counts immeasurably in the English-speaking consciousness. It is, perhaps, worth saying that his influence would tend strongly to reinforce the un-Flaubertian quality of the line of English classical fiction . . . as well as to co-operate with the Jonsonian tradition of morally significant typicality in characters. [Leavis]

[4]Manners.

himself, before he became a novelist, was both playwright and periodical essayist) he joined a narrative habit the nature of which is sufficiently indicated by his own phrase, "comic epic in prose." That the eighteenth century, which hadn't much lively reading to choose from, but had much leisure, should have found *Tom Jones* exhilarating is not surprising; nor is it that Scott, and Coleridge, should have been able to give that work superlative praise. Standards are formed in comparison, and what opportunities had they for that? But the conventional talk about the "perfect construction" of *Tom Jones* (the late Hugh Walpole brought it out triumphantly and you may hear it in almost any course of lectures on "the English Novel") is absurd. There can't be subtlety of organization without richer matter to organize, and subtler interests, than Fielding has to offer. He is credited with range and variety and it is true that some episodes take place in the country and some in Town, some in the churchyard and some in the inn, some on the high-road and some in the bed-chamber, and so on. But we haven't to read a very large proportion of *Tom Jones* in order to discover the limits of the essential interests it has to offer us. Fielding's attitudes, and his concern with human nature, are simple, and not such as to produce an effect of anything but monotony (on a mind, that is, demanding more than external action) when exhibited at the length of an "epic in prose." What he *can* do appears to best advantage in *Joseph Andrews*. *Jonathan Wild*, with its famous irony, seem to me mere hobbledehoydom (much as one applauds the determination to explode the gangster-hero), and by *Amelia* Fielding has gone soft.

We all know that if we want a more inward interest it is to Richardson we must go. And there is more to be said for Johnson's preference, and his emphatic way of expressing it at Fielding's expense, than is generally recognized. Richardson's strength in the analysis of emotional and moral states is in any case a matter of common acceptance; and *Clarissa* is a really impressive work. But it's no use pretending that Richardson can ever be made a current classic again. The substance of interest that he too has to offer is in its own way extremely limited in range and variety, and the demand he makes on the reader's time is in proportion — and absolutely — so immense as to be found, in general, prohibitive (though I don't know that I wouldn't sooner read through again *Clarissa* than *A la recherche du temps perdu*). But we can understand well enough why his reputation and influence should have been so great throughout Europe; and his immediately relevant historical importance is plain: he too is a major fact in the background of Jane Austen.

The social gap between them was too wide, however, for his work to be usable by her directly: the more he tries to deal with ladies and gentlemen, the more immitigably vulgar he is. It was Fanny Burney who, by transposing him into educated life, made it possible for Jane Austen to absorb what he had to teach her. Here we have one of the important lines of English literary history — Richardson–Fanny Burney–Jane Austen. It is important because Jane Austen is one of the truly great writers, and herself a major fact in the background of other great writers. Not that Fanny Burney is the only other novelist who counts in her formation; she read all there was to read, and took all that was useful to her — which wasn't only lessons.[5] In fact, Jane Austen, in her indebtedness to others, provides an exceptionally illuminating study of the nature of originality, and she exemplifies beautifully the relations of "the individual talent" to tradition. If the influences bearing on her hadn't comprised something fairly to be called tradition she couldn't have found herself and her true direction; but her relation to tradition is a creative one. She not only makes tradition for those coming after, but her achievement has for us a retroactive effect: as we look back beyond her we see in what goes before, and see because of her, potentialities and significances brought out in such a way that, for us, she creates the tradition we see leading down to her. Her work, like the work of all great creative writers, gives a meaning to the past.[6]

---

[5]For the relation of Jane Austen to other writers see the essay by Q. D. Leavis, "A Critical Theory of Jane Austen's Writings," in *Scrutiny* 10, no. 1. [Leavis]

[6]In the next four paragraphs, omitted here, Leavis discusses other critics who have seen the central tradition of the English novel beginning with Austen.

The great novelists in that tradition are all very much concerned with "form"; they are all very original technically, having turned their genius to the working out of their own appropriate methods and procedures. But the peculiar quality of their preoccupation with "form" may be brought out by a contrasting reference to Flaubert. Reviewing Thomas Mann's *Der Tod in Venedig*, D. H. Lawrence[7] adduces Flaubert as figuring to the world the "will of the writer to be greater than and undisputed lord over the stuff he writes." This attitude in art, as Lawrence points out, is indicative of an attitude in life — or towards life. Flaubert, he comments, "stood away from life as from a leprosy." For the later Aesthetic writers, who, in general, represent in a weak kind of way the attitude that Flaubert maintained with a perverse heroism, "form" and "style" are ends to be sought for themselves, and the chief preoccupation is with elaborating a beautiful style to apply to the chosen subject. There is George Moore, who in the best circles, I gather (from a distance), is still held to be among the very greatest masters of prose, though — I give my own limited experience for what it is worth — it is very hard to find an admirer who, being pressed, will lay his hand on his heart and swear he has read one of the "beautiful" novels through. "The novelist's problem is to evolve an orderly composition which is also a convincing picture of life" — this is the way an admirer of George Moore sees it. Lord David Cecil, attributing this way to Jane Austen, and crediting her with a superiority over George Eliot in "satisfying the rival claims of life and art," explains this superiority, we gather, by a freedom from moral preoccupations that he supposes her to enjoy. (George Eliot, he tells us, was a Puritan, and earnestly bent on instruction.)[8]

As a matter of fact, when we examine the formal perfection of *Emma,* we find that it can be appreciated only in terms of the moral preoccupations that characterize the novelist's peculiar interest in life. Those who suppose it to be an "aesthetic matter," a beauty of "composition" that is combined, miraculously, with "truth to life," can give no adequate reason for the view that *Emma* is a great novel, and no intelligent account of its perfection of form. It is in the same way true of the other great English novelists that their interest in their art gives them the opposite of an affinity with Pater and George Moore; it is, brought to an intense focus, an unusually developed interest in life. For, far from having anything of Flaubert's disgust or disdain or boredom, they are all distinguished by a vital capacity for experience, a kind of reverent openness before life, and a marked moral intensity.

It might be commented that what I have said of Jane Austen and her successors is only what can be said of any novelist of unqualified greatness. That is true. But there *is* — and this is the point — an English tradition, and these great classics of English fiction belong to it; a tradition that, in the talk about "creating characters" and "creating worlds," and the appreciation of Trollope and Mrs. Gaskell and Thackeray and Meredith and Hardy and Virginia Woolf, appears to go unrecognized. It is not merely that we have no Flaubert (and I hope I haven't seemed to suggest that a Flaubert is no more worth having than a George Moore). Positively, there is a continuity from Jane Austen. It is not for nothing that George Eliot admired her work profoundly, and wrote one of the earliest appreciations of it to be published. The writer whose intellectual weight and moral earnestness strike some critics as her handicap certainly saw in Jane Austen something more than an ideal contemporary of Lytton Strachey.[9] What one great original artist learns from another, whose genius and problems are necessarily very different, is the hardest kind of "influence" to define, even when we see it to have

---

[7] D. H. Lawrence, *Phoenix: The Posthumous Papers of D. H. Lawrence* (London: Heinemann, 1936), p. 308. [Leavis]

[8] She is a moralist and a highbrow, the two handicaps going together. "Her humour is less affected by her intellectual approach. Jokes, thank heaven, need not be instructive." — Lord David Cecil, *Early Victorian Novelists: Essays in Revaluation* (London: Constable, 1934), p. 299. [Leavis]

[9] It is perhaps worth insisting that Peacock is more than that too. He is not at all in the same class as the Norman Douglas of *South Wind* and *They Went.* In his ironical treatment of contemporary society and civilization he is seriously applying serious standards, so that his books, which are obviously not novels in the same sense as Jane Austen's, have a permanent life as light reading — indefinitely rereadable — for minds with mature interests. [Leavis]

been of the profoundest importance. The obvious manifestation of influence is to be seen in this kind of passage:

> A little daily embroidery had been a constant element in Mrs. Transome's life; that soothing occupation of taking stitches to produce what neither she nor any one else wanted, was then the resource of many a well-born and unhappy woman.

> In short, he felt himself to be in love in the right place, and was ready to endure a great deal of predominance, which, after all, a man could always put down when he liked. Sir James had no idea that he should ever like to put down the predominance of this handsome girl, in whose cleverness he delighted. Why not? A man's mind — what there is of it — has always the advantage of being masculine, — as the smallest birch-tree is of a higher kind than the most soaring palm — and even his ignorance is of a sounder quality. Sir James might not have originated this estimate; but a kind Providence furnishes the limpest personality with a little gum or starch in the form of tradition.[10]

The kind of irony here is plainly akin to Jane Austen's — though it is characteristic enough of George Eliot; what she found was readily assimilated to her own needs. In Jane Austen herself the irony has a serious background, and is no mere display of "civilization." George Eliot wouldn't have been interested in it if she hadn't perceived its full significance — its relation to the essential moral interest offered by Jane Austen's art. And here we come to the profoundest kind of influence, that which is not manifested in likeness. One of the supreme debts one great writer can owe another is the realization of unlikeness (there is, of course, no significant unlikeness without the common concern — and the common seriousness of concern — with essential human issues). One way of putting the difference between George Eliot and the Trollopes whom we are invited to consider along with her is to say that she was capable of understanding Jane Austen's greatness and capable of learning from her. And except for Jane Austen there was no novelist to learn from — none whose work had

[10]The passages are from *Middlemarch*.

any bearing on her own essential problems as a novelist.[11]

Is there no name later than Conrad's to be included in the great tradition? There is, I am convinced, one: D. H. Lawrence. Lawrence, in the English language, was the great genius of our time (I mean the age, or climatic phase, following Conrad's). It would be difficult to separate the novelist off for consideration, but it was in the novel that he committed himself to the hardest and most sustained creative labour, and he was, as a novelist, the representative of vital and significant development. He might, he has shown conclusively, have gone on writing novels with the kind of "character creation" and psychology that the conventional cultivated reader immediately appreciates — novels that demanded no unfamiliar effort of approach. He might — if his genius had let him. In nothing is the genius more manifest than in the way in which, after the great success — and *succès d'estime*[12] — of *Sons and Lovers* he gives up that mode and devotes himself to the exhausting toil of working out the new things, the developments, that as the highly conscious and intelligent servant of life he saw to be necessary. Writing to Edward Garnett of the work that was to become *Women in Love* he says: "It is *very* different from *Sons and Lovers:* written in another language almost. I shall be sorry if you don't like it, but am prepared. I shan't write in the same manner as *Sons and Lovers* again, I think — in that hard, violent style full of sensation and presentation."[13]

Describing at length what he is trying to do he says:

> You mustn't look in my novel for the old stable *ego* of the character. There is another *ego,* according to whose action the individual is unrecognizable, and passes through, as it were, allotropic states which it needs a deeper sense than any we've

[11]In the next passage, omitted here, Leavis continues to trace the line of development and influence through Henry James and Joseph Conrad and to discuss why Dickens, though a "great genius," is not a stimulus to an "adult mind."

[12]Recognition.

[13]*The Letters of D. H. Lawrence*, ed. Aldous Huxley (London: Heinemann, 1934), p. 172. [Leavis]

been used to exercise, to discover are states of the same single radically unchanged element. (Like as diamond and coal are the same pure simple element of carbon. The ordinary novel would trace the history of the diamond — but I say, "Diamond, what! This is carbon." And my diamond might be coal or soot, and my theme is carbon.) You must not say my novel is shaky — it is not perfect, because I am not expert in what I want to do. But it is the real thing, say what you like. And I shall get my reception, if not now, then before long. Again I say, don't look for the development of the novel to follow the lines of certain characters: the characters fall into the form of some other rhythmic form, as when one draws a fiddle-bow across a fine tray delicately sanded, the sand takes lines unknown.[14]

He is a most daring and radical innovator in "form," method, technique. And his innovations and experiments are dictated by the most serious and urgent kind of interest in life. This is the spirit of it:

> Do you know Cassandra in Aeschylus and Homer? She is one of the world's great figures, and what the Greeks and Agamemnon did to her is symbolic of what mankind has done to her since — raped and despoiled her, to their own ruin. It is not your brain that you must trust to, nor your will — but to that fundamental pathetic faculty for receiving the hidden waves that come from the depths of life, and for transferring them to the unreceptive world. It is something which happens below the consciousness, and below the range of the will — it is something which is unrecognizable and frustrated and destroyed.[15]

It is a spirit that, for all the unlikeness, relates Lawrence closely to George Eliot.[16] He writes, again, to Edward Garnett:[17]

> You see — you tell me I am half a Frenchman and one-eighth a Cockney. But that isn't it. I have very often the vulgarity and disagreeableness of the common people, as you say Cockney, and I may be a Frenchman. But primarily I am a passionately religious man, and my novels must be written from the depth of my religious experience. That I must

keep to, because I can only work like that. And my Cockneyism and commonness are only when the deep feeling doesn't find its way out, and a sort of jeer comes instead, and sentimentality and purplism. But you should see the religious, earnest, suffering man in me first, and then the flippant or common things after. Mrs. Garnett says I have no true nobility — with all my cleverness and charm. But that is not true. It is there, in spite of all the littlenesses and commonnesses.

It is this spirit, by virtue of which he can truly say that what he writes must be written from the depth of his religious experience, that makes him, in my opinion, so much more significant in relation to the past and future, so much more truly creative as a technical inventor, an innovator, a master of language, than James Joyce. I know that Mr. T. S. Eliot has found in Joyce's work something that recommends Joyce to him as positively religious in tendency (see *After Strange Gods*). But it seems plain to me that there is no organic principle determining, informing, and controlling into a vital whole, the elaborate analogical structure, the extraordinary variety of technical devices, the attempts at an exhaustive rendering of consciousness, for which *Ulysses* is remarkable, and which got it accepted by a cosmopolitan literary world as a new start. It is rather, I think, a dead end, or at least a pointer to disintegration — a view strengthened by Joyce's own development (for I think it significant and appropriate that *Work in Progress — Finnegans Wake,* as it became — should have engaged the interest of the inventor of Basic English).

It is true that we can point to the influence of Joyce in a line of writers to which there is no parallel issuing from Lawrence. But I find here further confirmation of my view. For I think that in these writers, in whom a regrettable (if minor) strain of Mr. Eliot's influence seems to me to join with that of Joyce, we have, insofar as we have anything significant, the wrong kind of reaction against liberal idealism.[18] I have in mind writers in whom Mr. Eliot has expressed an interest in strongly favourable terms: Djuna Barnes of *Nightwood,* Henry Miller, Lawrence Durrell of

---

[14]*Letters,* p. 198. [Leavis]
[15]*Letters,* p. 232. [Leavis]
[16]*Letters,* p. 190. [Leavis]
[17]Lawrence too has been called a Puritan. [Leavis]

[18]See D. H. Lawrence's *Fantasia of the Unconscious,* especially Ch. XI. [Leavis]

The Black Book. In these writers — at any rate in the last two (and the first seems to me insignificant) — the spirit of what we are offered affects me as being essentially a desire, in Laurentian phrase, to "do dirt" on life. It seems to me important that one should, in all modesty, bear one's witness in these matters. "One must speak for life and growth, amid all this mass of destruction and disintegration."[19] This is Lawrence, and it is the spirit of all his work. It is the spirit of the originality that gives his novels their disconcerting quality, and gives them the significance of works of genius.

I am not contending that he isn't, as a novelist, open to a great deal of criticism, or that his achievement is as a whole satisfactory (the potentiality being what it was). He wrote his later books far too hurriedly. But I know from experience that it is far too easy to conclude that his very aim and intention condemned him to artistic unsatisfactoriness. I am thinking in particular of two books at which he worked very hard, and in which he developed his disconcertingly original interests and approaches — *The Rainbow* and *Women in Love.* Reread, they seem to me astonishing works of genius, and very much more largely successful than they did when I read them (say) fifteen years ago. I still think that *The Rainbow* doesn't build up sufficiently into a whole. But I shouldn't be quick to offer my criticism of *Women in Love,* being pretty sure that I should in any case have once more to convict

[19] *The Letters of D. H. Lawrence,* p. 256. [Leavis]

myself of stupidity and habit-blindness on later rereading. And after these novels there comes, written, perhaps, with an ease earned by this hard work done, a large body of short stories and *nouvelles* that are as indubitably successful works of genius as any the world has to show.

I have, then, given my hostages. What I think and judge I have stated as responsibly and clearly as I can. Jane Austen, George Eliot, Henry James, Conrad, and D. H. Lawrence: the great tradition of the English novel is *there.*

NOTE: "THE BRONTËS"

It is tempting to retort that there is only one Brontë. Actually, Charlotte, though claiming no part in the great line of English fiction (it is significant that she couldn't see why any value should be attached to Jane Austen), has a permanent interest of a minor kind. She had a remarkable talent that enabled her to do something firsthand and new in the rendering of personal experience, above all in *Villette.*

The genius, of course, was Emily. I have said nothing about *Wuthering Heights* because that astonishing work seems to me a kind of sport. It may, all the same, very well have had some influence of an essentially undetectable kind: she broke completely, and in the most challenging way, both with the Scott tradition that imposed on the novelist a romantic resolution of his themes, and with the tradition coming down from the eighteenth century that demanded a plane-mirror reflection of the surface of "real" life. Out of her a minor tradition comes, to which belongs, most notably, *The House with the Green Shutters.*

Jean-Paul Sartre

1905–1980

As a philosopher, novelist, dramatist, and essayist, Jean-Paul Sartre is indelibly associated with existentialism, the ethical and humanistic movement that developed from the phenomenological thought of Edmund Husserl and Martin Heidegger (see p. 611). Sartre was born in Paris. His father died a year after his birth, and he was raised by his mother and his grandfather of the famous Schweitzer family in Paris and Meudon. He attended the prestigious Louis-le-Grand preparatory school and the Lycée Henri IV before training in philosophy at the École Normale Supérieure where he received his *agrégation* (postgraduate) degree in 1929, the same year as his lifelong companion, Simone de Beauvoir (see p. 673). He taught philosophy in various elite secondary schools until the outbreak of World War II in 1939. Caught in the German blitzkrieg, Sartre spent much of 1940–41 as a prisoner of war. When released, he joined the resistance and worked for the liberation of France as a journalist for underground publications. After the liberation of Paris in 1944, Sartre and de Beauvoir founded the prestigious literary and intellectual monthly, *Les Temps modernes* (1945–).

Sartre's existential philosophy grew out of his year of postgraduate study at the Institut Français in Berlin in 1933, where he became fascinated with the ideas of Heidegger and Husserl, using them as a springboard for his own work. Several shorter treatises culminated in his monumental *Being and Nothingness* (*L'Être et le néant,* 1943), whose title plays off that of Heidegger's 1927 treatise, *Being and Time.* In *Being and Nothingness,* Sartre distinguishes between things, which exist purely in themselves and can be essentialized (the *en-soi*), and human beings (the *pour-soi*). As human beings we have no essence to which we aspire: Ever-changing, we are always free to make ourselves what we are, negating what we currently are and do in favor of some other mode of action and existence. Indeed one should not say that we *are*, but rather that we *become.* Our existence is contingent, unfixed, dependent on our interactions with an ever-changing environment. To live in the world, to "become" in freedom, we are forced to project ourselves into the void of nothingness, the as-yet-nonexistent future. Unlike things, we are conscious of our own mortality, of a future in which we will not exist. This negation and projection involves the rejection of one way of existing and the choice of another, a choice we can never evade. The responsibility for conscious choice of what we shall become at every moment of existence produces in the authentic individual the feeling of *angst,* or existential dread. So terrifying is our freedom and responsibility that we are constantly tempted by what Sartre calls bad faith (*mauvaise foi*), comforting lies by which we reassure ourselves that we have been merely formed by circumstance, that our choices are predetermined by psychic or social forces beyond our control.

If Sartre's name became a household word, unlike those of his teachers, it was largely because he presented his ideas not only in philosophical treatises but in novels, such as *Nausea* (*La Nausée,* 1938) and *The Roads to Freedom* trilogy (*Les Chemins de la liberté,* 1945–49). His preferred genre, possibly because he felt humanity expresses its nature best through action, was the drama, and successful plays like *The Flies* (*Les Mouches*, 1943), *No Exit* (*Huis Clos*, 1945), *Dirty Hands* (*Les Mains sales*, 1948), and *The Condemned of Altona* (*Les Sequestrés d'Altona*, 1959) made adherents of people who would have been unlikely to read through even ten pages of *Being and Nothingness*.

After World War II, Sartre's principal interests were politics and literary criticism. Sartre was by temperament a leftist but had steered clear of Soviet-style communism until after the end of the war. It was precisely when the revelations of Stalin's mass murders and other crimes were shocking and repelling once-loyal party members that Sartre announced he wanted to align himself with the Soviets. This announcement led to a break between Sartre and other French intellectuals, like Raymond Aron and Albert Camus. Sartre returned to his original stance of distance from Russian communism after the brutal Soviet invasion of Hungary in 1956. His *Critique of Dialectical Reason* (*Critique de la raison dialectique*, 1960) presents his liberal Marxist vision of social action.

In the last two decades of his life, Sartre produced a fragmented literary autobiography in *The Words* (*Les Mots*, 1964) and a body of sustained literary biography, including *Saint Genet* (*Saint-Genet: Comédien et martyre*, 1963) and a lengthy study of Flaubert, *The Family Idiot* (*L'Idiot de la famille*, 1971–72). His major contribution to literary theory is the short volume *What Is Literature?* (*Qu'est-ce que la littérature?* 1947), which applies phenomenology and existentialism to questions of reading and writing but is also informed by Sartre's leftist social thought.

Toward the end of his life, Sartre fell further and further behind the shifts in French thought; he survived the height of his fame by about fifteen years, and Les Deux Magots, the left-bank cafe where he spent his afternoons, became a tourist site — and an intellectual backwater. Immediately after his death in 1980, his works went out of fashion with the intelligentsia and are only now returning to favor. In a sense, though, Sartre was never out of style in that his anti-essentialism — his insistence on absence and negation as the origin and bedrock of thought — profoundly influenced many later branches of French philosophy and psychology that reacted against his ideas, such as the neo-Freudianism of Jacques Lacan, the neo-Marxism of Louis Althusser, or the structuralism and poststructuralism of Roland Barthes and Jacques Derrida.

The Sartre of "Why Write?" elaborately considers the phenomenological position of the writer who creates from a deep sense of metaphysical absence. We who know that the physical world we animate with our perceptions will go on darkly after we are gone must write to make something that will survive us. We do this out of "the need of feeling that we are essential in relationship to the world." But writers are not alone with the rumblings of the void: The "world" we are essential to is that of the reader. But like Wolfgang Iser and Hans Robert Jauss of the school of Konstanz, who see the reader as performing the text (see the introduction to Reader-Response Theory, p. 962), Sartre sees the reader as at least equally necessary to the writer. In the process of reading, which Sartre says synthesizes the processes of "perception and creation," the reader completes what the writer has begun, in a re-invention that "would be as new and as original an act as the first invention."

Collaboration between reader and writer, after all, can be viewed under different enabling metaphors, and the politics of Sartre's literary phenomenology is uniquely his own. His fellow phenomenologist George Poulet saw the writer as "colonizing" the consciousness of the reader, who becomes a "prey" by temporarily abdicating his self-hood and individuality to the direction of the writer. The consciousness of the text is "inbreathed" by the reader whose consciousness it annexes, almost like the *daimonion* of Plato, which inspires the reader through a sort of divine possession. Unlike Poulet, Sartre characterizes the relation of writer and reader as the camaraderie of equals, each cherishing the freedom of the other as guaranteeing and enhancing his own.[1]

It is true that no earthly government has ever given its citizens anything but relative freedom, as opposed to the absolute existential freedom that is the tragic possession of every human being. Yet since "the author writes in order to address himself to the freedom of readers," since "he requires it in order to make his work exist," the politics of literature is a serious business. Not only is it in writers' interest *as writers* to work for the freedom of their societies, Sartre believes it is impossible for genuine writers to continue writing for readers whose minds and wills are enslaved by a totalitarian government. His historical example was Drieu la Rochelle, a collaborationist writer who attempted to produce a periodical review during the Nazi occupation of France: "The first few months he reprimanded, rebuked, and lectured his countrymen. No one answered him because no one was free to do so. He became irritated; he no longer *felt* his readers. . . . Finally, he kept still, gagged by the silence of others."

Selected Bibliography

Dobson, Andrew. *Jean-Paul Sartre and the Politics of Reason: A Theory of History.* New York and London: Cambridge University Press, 1993.

Hayman, Ronald. *Sartre: A Biography.* New York: Carroll and Graf, 1991.

Jameson, Fredric. *Sartre: The Origins of a Style.* New York: Columbia University Press, 1984.

LaCapra, Dominick. *A Preface to Sartre.* Ithaca: Cornell University Press, 1978.

McBride, William L. *Sartre and Existentialism: Philosophy, Politics, Ethics, the Psyche, Literature and Aesthetics.* New York: Garland, 1997.

McCulloch, Gregory. *Using Sartre: An Analytical Introduction to Early Sartrean Themes.* New York: Routledge, 1994.

Nordquist, Joan. *Jean-Paul Sartre: A Bibliography.* New York: Reference and Research Services, 1993.

Sartre, Jean-Paul. *What Is Literature?* New York: Philosophical Library, 1966.

———. *The Family Idiot: Gustave Flaubert, 1821–1857.* 5 vols. Trans. Carol Cosman. Chicago: University of Chicago Press, 1981–93.

———. *The Words.* New York: Random House, 1981.

Thody, Philip. *Jean-Paul Sartre.* New York: St. Martin's Press, 1992.

---

[1]Poulet feels that the abdication of the self is also the route to the fullest possible realization of the self. Similarly, Sartre sees reading as "a Passion, in the Christian sense of the word, that is, a freedom which resolutely puts itself into a state of passivity to obtain a transcendent effect by this sacrifice."

Why Write?

Each one has his reasons: for one, art is a flight; for another, a means of conquering. But one can flee into a hermitage, into madness, into death. One can conquer by arms. Why does it have to be *writing*, why does one have to manage his escapes and conquests by *writing*? Because, behind the various aims of authors, there is a deeper and more immediate choice which is common to all of us. We shall try to elucidate this choice, and we shall see whether it is not in the name of this very choice of writing that the engagement of writers must be required.

Each of our perceptions is accompanied by the consciousness that human reality is a "revealer," that is, it is through human reality that "there is" being, or, to put it differently, that man is the means by which things are manifested. It is our presence in the world which multiplies relations. It is we who set up a relationship between this tree and that bit of sky. Thanks to us, that star which has been dead for millennia, that quarter moon, and that dark river are disclosed in the unity of a landscape. It is the speed of our auto and our airplane which organizes the great masses of the earth. With each of our acts, the world reveals to us a new face. But, if we know that we are directors of being, we also know that we are not its producers. If we turn away from this landscape, it will sink back into its dark permanence. At least, it will sink back; there is no one mad enough to think that it is going to be annihilated. It is we who shall be annihilated, and the earth will remain in its lethargy until another consciousness comes along to awaken it. Thus, to our inner certainty of being "revealers" is added that of being inessential in relation to the thing revealed.

One of the chief motives of artistic creation is certainly the need of feeling that we are essential in relationship to the world. If I fix on canvas or in writing a certain aspect of the fields or the sea or a look on someone's face which I have disclosed, I am conscious of having produced them by condensing relationships, by introducing order where there was none, by imposing the unity of mind on the diversity of things. That is, I feel myself essential in relation to my creation. But this time it is the created object which escapes me; I can not reveal and produce at the same time. The creation becomes inessential in relation to the creative activity. First of all, even if it appears to others as definitive, the created object always seems to us in a state of suspension; we can always change this line, that shade, that word. Thus, it never *forces itself*. A novice painter asked his teacher, "When should I consider my painting finished?" And the teacher answered, "When you can look at it in amazement and say to yourself '*I'm* the one who did *that!*' "

Which amounts to saying "never." For it is virtually considering one's work with someone else's eyes and revealing what one has created. But it is self-evident that we are proportionally less conscious of the thing produced and more conscious of our productive activity. When it is a matter of pottery or carpentry, we work according to traditional norms, with tools whose usage is codified; it is Heidegger's famous "they" who are working with our hands. In this case, the result can seem to us sufficiently strange to preserve its objectivity in our eyes. But if we ourselves produce the rules of production, the measures, the criteria, and if our creative drive comes from the very depths of our heart, then we never find anything but ourselves in our work. It is we who have invented the laws by which we judge it. It is our history, our love, our gaiety that we recognize in it. Even if we should regard it without touching it any further, we never *receive* from it that gaiety or love. We put them into it. The results which we have obtained on canvas or paper never seem to us *objective*. We are too familiar with the processes of which they are the effects. These processes remain a subjective discovery; they are ourselves, our inspiration, our ruse, and when we seek to *perceive* our work, we create it again, we repeat mentally the operations which produced it; each of its aspects appears as a result.

Translated by Bernard Frechtman.

Thus, in the perception, the object is given as the essential thing and the subject as the inessential. The latter seeks essentiality in the creation and obtains it, but then it is the object which becomes the inessential.

This dialectic is nowhere more apparent than in the art of writing, for the literary object is a peculiar top which exists only in movement. To make it come into view a concrete act called reading is necessary, and it lasts only as long as this act can last. Beyond that, there are only black marks on paper. Now, the writer can not read what he writes, whereas the shoemaker can put on the shoes he has just made if they are his size, and the architect can live in the house he has built. In reading, one foresees; one waits. He foresees the end of the sentence, the following sentence, the next page. He waits for them to confirm or disappoint his foresights. The reading is composed of a host of hypotheses, of dreams followed by awakenings, of hopes and deceptions. Readers are always ahead of the sentence they are reading in a merely probable future which partly collapses and partly comes together in proportion as they progress, which withdraws from one page to the next and forms the moving horizon of the literary object. Without waiting, without a future, without ignorance, there is no objectivity.

Now the operation of writing involves an implicit quasi-reading which makes real reading impossible. When the words form under his pen, the author doubtless sees them, but he does not see them as the reader does, since he knows them before writing them down. The function of his gaze is not to reveal, by stroking them, the sleeping words which are waiting to be read, but to control the sketching of the signs. In short, it is a purely regulating mission, and the view before him reveals nothing except for slight slips of the pen. The writer neither foresees nor conjectures; he *projects*. It often happens that he awaits, as they say, the inspiration. But one does not wait for himself the way he waits for others. If he hesitates, he knows that the future is not made, that he himself is going to make it, and if he still does not know what is going to happen to his hero, that simply means that he has not thought about it, that he has not decided upon anything. The future is then a blank page, whereas the future of the reader is two hundred pages filled with words which separate him from the end. Thus, the writer meets everywhere only *his* knowledge, *his* will, *his* plans, in short, himself. He touches only his own subjectivity; the object he creates is out of reach; he does not create it *for himself*. If he rereads himself, it is already too late. The sentence will never quite be a thing in his eyes. He goes to the very limits of the subjective but without crossing it. He appreciates the effect of a touch, of an epigram, of a well-placed adjective, but it is the effect they will have on others. He can judge it, not feel it. Proust never discovered the homosexuality of Charlus, since he had decided upon it even before starting on his book. And if a day comes when the book takes on for its author a semblance of objectivity, it is that years have passed, that he has forgotten it, that its spirit is quite foreign to him, and doubtless he is no longer capable of writing it. This was the case with Rousseau when he reread the *Social Contract* at the end of his life.

Thus, it is not true that one writes for himself. That would be the worst blow. In projecting his emotions on paper, one barely manages to give them a languishing extension. The creative act is only an incomplete and abstract moment in the production of a work. If the author existed alone he would be able to write as much as he liked; the work as *object* would never see the light of day and he would either have to put down his pen or despair. But the operation of writing implies that of reading as its dialectical correlative and these two connected acts necessitate two distinct agents. It is the conjoint effort of author and reader which brings upon the scene that concrete and imaginary object which is the work of the mind. There is no art except for and by others.

Reading seems, in fact, to be the synthesis of perception and creation.[1] It supposes the essentiality of both the subject and the object. The object is essential because it is strictly transcendent, because it imposes its own structures, and because one must wait for it and observe it; but

[1]The same is true in different degrees regarding the spectator's attitude before other works of art (paintings, symphonies, statues, etc.). [Sartre]

the subject is also essential because it is required not only to disclose the object (that is, to make *there be* an object) but also so that this object might *be* (that is, to produce it). In a word, the reader is conscious of disclosing in creating, of creating by disclosing. In reality, it is not necessary to believe that reading is a mechanical operation and that signs make an impression upon him as light does on a photographic plate. If he is inattentive, tired, stupid, or thoughtless, most of the relations will escape him. He will never manage to "catch on" to the object (in the sense in which we see that fire "catches" or "doesn't catch"). He will draw some phrases out of the shadow, but they will seem to appear as random strokes. If he is at his best, he will project beyond the words a synthetic form, each phrase of which will be no more than a partial function: the "theme," the "subject," or the "meaning." Thus, from the very beginning, the meaning is no longer contained in the words, since it is he, on the contrary, who allows the signification of each of them to be understood; and the literary object, though realized *through* language, is never given *in* language. On the contrary, it is by nature a silence and an opponent of the word. In addition, the hundred thousand words aligned in a book can be read one by one so that the meaning of the work does not emerge. Nothing is accomplished if the reader does not put himself from the very beginning and almost without a guide at the height of this silence; if, in short, he does not invent it and does not then place there, and hold on to, the words and sentences which he awakens. And if I am told that it would be more fitting to call this operation a reinvention or a discovery, I shall answer that, first, such a reinvention would be as new and as original an act as the first invention. And, especially, when an object has never existed before, there can be no question of reinventing it or discovering it. For if the silence about which I am speaking is really the goal at which the author is aiming, he has, at least, never been familiar with it; his silence is subjective and anterior to language. It is the absence of words, the undifferentiated and lived silence of inspiration, which the word will then particularize, whereas the silence produced by the reader is an object. And at the very interior of this object there are more silences — which the author does not tell. It is a question of silences which are so particular that they could not retain any meaning outside of the object which the reading causes to appear. However, it is these which give it its density and its particular face.

To say that they are unexpressed is hardly the word; for they are precisely the inexpressible. And that is why one does not come upon them at any definite moment in the reading; they are everywhere and nowhere. The quality of the marvelous in *The Wanderer* (*Le Grand Meaulnes*), the grandiosity of *Armance,* the degree of realism and truth of Kafka's mythology, these are never given. The reader must invent them all in a continual exceeding of the written thing. To be sure, the author guides him, but all he does is guide him. The landmarks he sets up are separated by the void. The reader must unite them; he must go beyond them. In short, reading is directed creation.

On the one hand, the literary object has no other substance than the reader's subjectivity; Raskolnikov's waiting is my waiting which I lend him. Without this impatience of the reader he would remain only a collection of signs. His hatred of the police magistrate who questions him is my hatred which has been solicited and wheedled out of me by signs, and the police magistrate himself would not exist without the hatred I have for him via Raskolnikov. That is what animates him, it is his very flesh.

But on the other hand, the words are there like traps to arouse our feelings and to reflect them toward us. Each word is a path of transcendence; it shapes our feelings, names them, and attributes them to an imaginary personage who takes it upon himself to live them for us and who has no other substance than these borrowed passions; he confers objects, perspectives, and a horizon upon them.

Thus, for the reader, all is to do and all is already done; the work exists only at the exact level of his capacities; while he reads and creates, he knows that he can always go further in his reading, can always create more profoundly, and thus the work seems to him as inexhaustible and opaque as things. We would readily reconcile that "rational intuition" which Kant reserved to divine Reason with this absolute production of qualities, which, to the extent that they emanate from our subjectivity, congeal before our eyes into impermeable objectivities.

Since the creation can find its fulfillment only in reading, since the artist must entrust to another the job of carrying out what he has begun, since it is only through the consciousness of the reader that he can regard himself as essential to his work, all literary work is an appeal. To write is to make an appeal to the reader that he lead into objective existence the revelation which I have undertaken by means of language. And if it should be asked *to what* the writer is appealing, the answer is simple. As the sufficient reason for the appearance of the aesthetic object is never found either in the book (where we find merely solicitations to produce the object) or in the author's mind, and as his subjectivity, which he cannot get away from, cannot give a reason for the act of leading into objectivity, the appearance of the work of art is a new event which cannot *be explained* by anterior data. And since this directed creation is an absolute beginning, it is therefore brought about by the freedom of the reader, and by what is purest in that freedom. Thus, the writer appeals to the reader's freedom to collaborate in the production of his work.

It will doubtless be said that all tools address themselves to our freedom since they are the instruments of a possible action, and that the work of art is not unique in that. And it is true that the tool is the congealed outline of an operation. But it remains on the level of the hypothetical imperative. I may use a hammer to nail up a case or to hit my neighbor over the head. Insofar as I consider it in itself, it is not an appeal to my freedom; it does not put me face to face with it; rather, it aims at using it by substituting a set succession of traditional procedures for the free invention of means. The book does not serve my freedom; it requires it. Indeed, one cannot address himself to freedom as such by means of constraint, fascination, or entreaties. There is only one way of attaining it; first, by recognizing it, then, having confidence in it, and finally, requiring of it an act, an act in its own name, that is, in the name of the confidence that one brings to it.

Thus, the book is not, like the tool, a means for any end whatever; the end to which it offers itself is the reader's freedom. And the Kantian expression "finality without end"[2] seems to me quite inappropriate for designating the work of art. In fact, it implies that the aesthetic object presents only the appearance of a finality and is limited to soliciting the free and ordered play of the imagination. It forgets that the imagination of the spectator has not only a regulating function, but a constitutive one. It does not play; it is called upon to recompose the beautiful object beyond the traces left by the artist. The imagination can not revel in itself any more than can the other functions of the mind; it is always on the outside, always engaged in an enterprise. There would be finality without end if some object offered such a set ordering that it would lead us to suppose that it has one even though we can not ascribe one to it. By defining the beautiful in this way one can — and this is Kant's aim — liken the beauty of art to natural beauty, since a flower, for example, presents so much symmetry, such harmonious colors, and such regular curves, that one is immediately tempted to seek a finalist explanation for all these properties and to see them as just so many means at the disposal of an unknown end. But that is exactly the error. The beauty of nature is in no way comparable to that of art. The work of art *does not have* an end; there we agree with Kant. But the reason is that it is an end. The Kantian formula does not account for the appeal which resounds at the basis of each painting, each statue, each book. Kant believes that the work of art first exists as fact and that it is then seen. Whereas, it exists only if one *looks* at it and if it is first pure appeal, pure exigence to exist. It is not an instrument whose existence is manifest and whose end is undetermined. It presents itself as a task to be discharged; from the very beginning it places itself on the level of the categorical imperative. You are perfectly free to leave that book on the table. But if you open it, you assume responsibility for it. For freedom is not experienced by its enjoying its free subjective functioning, but in a creative act required by an imperative. This absolute end, this imperative which is transcendent yet acquiesced in, which freedom itself

[2]*Zweckmässigkeit ohne Zweck,* purposiveness without purpose. See Kant, p. 247.

adopts as its own, is what we call a value. The work of art is a value because it is an appeal.

If I appeal to my reader so that we may carry the enterprise which I have begun to a successful conclusion, it is self-evident that I consider him as a pure freedom, as an unconditioned activity; thus, in no case can I address myself to his passivity, that is, try to *affect* him, to communicate to him, from the very first, emotions of fear, desire, or anger. There are, doubtless, authors who concern themselves solely with arousing these emotions because they are foreseeable, manageable, and because they have at their disposal sure-fire means for provoking them. But it is also true that they are reproached for this kind of thing, as Euripides has been since antiquity because he had children appear on the stage. Freedom is alienated in the state of passion; it is abruptly engaged in partial enterprises; it loses sight of its task which is to produce an absolute end. And the book is no longer anything but a means for feeding hate or desire. The writer should not seek to *overwhelm;* otherwise he is in contradiction with himself; if he wishes to *make demands* he must propose only the task to be fulfilled. Hence, the character of pure presentation which appears essential to the work of art. The reader must be able to make a certain aesthetic withdrawal. This is what Gautier foolishly confused with "art for art's sake" and the Parnassians with the imperturbability of the artist. It is simply a matter of precaution, and Genet more justly calls it the author's politeness toward the reader. But that does not mean that the writer makes an appeal to some sort of abstract and conceptual freedom. One certainly creates the aesthetic object with feelings; if it is touching, it appears through our tears; if it is comic, it will be recognized by laughter. However, these feelings are of a particular kind. They have their origin in freedom; they are loaned. The belief which I accord the tale is freely assented to. It is a Passion, in the Christian sense of the word, that is, a freedom which resolutely puts itself into a state of passivity to obtain a certain transcendent effect by this sacrifice. The reader renders himself credulous; he descends into credulity which, though it ends by enclosing him like a dream, is at every moment conscious of being free. An effort is sometimes made to force the writer into

this dilemma: "Either one believes in your story, and it is intolerable, or one does not believe in it, and it is ridiculous." But the argument is absurd because the characteristic of aesthetic consciousness is to be a belief by means of engagement, by oath, a belief sustained by fidelity to one's self and to the author, a perpetually renewed choice to believe. I can awaken at every moment, and I know it; but I do not want to; reading is a free dream. So that all feelings which are exacted on the basis of this imaginary belief are like particular modulations of my freedom. Far from absorbing or masking it, they are so many different ways it has chosen to reveal itself to itself. Raskolnikov, as I have said, would only be a shadow, without the mixture of repulsion and friendship which I feel for him and which makes him live. But, by a reversal which is the characteristic of the imaginary object, it is not his behavior which excites my indignation or esteem, but my indignation and esteem which give consistency and objectivity to his behavior. Thus, the reader's feelings are never dominated by the object, and as no external reality can condition them, they have their permanent source in freedom; that is, they are all generous — for I call a feeling generous which has its origin and its end in freedom. Thus, reading is an exercise in generosity, and what the writer requires of the reader is not the application of an abstract freedom but the gift of his whole person, with his passions, his prepossessions, his sympathies, his sexual temperament, and his scale of values. Only this person will give himself generously; freedom goes through and through him and comes to transform the darkest masses of his sensibility. And as activity has rendered itself passive in order for it better to create the object, vice-versa, passivity becomes an act; the man who is reading has raised himself to the highest degree. That is why we see people who are known for their toughness shed tears at the recital of imaginary misfortunes; for the moment they have become what they would have been if they had not spent their lives hiding their freedom from themselves.

Thus, the author writes in order to address himself to the freedom of readers, and he requires it in order to make his work exist. But he does not stop there; he also requires that they return this confidence which he has given them, that they recognize his creative freedom, and that they in turn solicit it by a symmetrical and inverse appeal. Here there appears the other dialectical paradox of reading; the more we experience our freedom, the more we recognize that of the other; the more he demands of us, the more we demand of him.

When I am enchanted with a landscape, I know very well that it is not I who create it, but I also know that without me the relations which are established before my eyes among the trees, the foliage, the earth, and the grass would not exist at all. I know that I can give no reason for the appearance of finality which I discover in the assortment of hues and in the harmony of the forms and movements created by the wind. Yet, it exists; there it is before my eyes, and I can make *there be* being only if being already *is*. But even if I believe in God, I can not establish any passage, unless it be purely verbal, between the divine, universal solicitude and the particular spectacle which I am considering. To say that He made the landscape in order to charm me or that He made me the kind of person who is pleased by it is to take a question for an answer. Is the marriage of this blue and that green deliberate? How can I know? The idea of a universal providence is no guarantee of any particular intention, especially in the case under consideration, since the green of the grass is explained by biological laws, specific constants, and geographical determinism, while the reason for the blue of the water is accounted for by the depth of the river, the nature of the soil and the swiftness of the current. The assorting of the shades, if it is willed, can only be something *thrown into the bargain;* it is the meeting of two causal series, that is to say, at first sight, a fact of chance. At best, the finality remains problematic. All the relations we establish remain hypotheses; no end is proposed to us in the manner of an imperative, since none is expressly revealed as having been willed by a creator. Thus, our freedom is never *called forth* by natural beauty. Or rather, there is an appearance of order in the ensemble of the foliage, the forms, and the movements, hence, the illusion of a calling forth which seems to solicit this freedom and which disappears immediately when one regards it. Hardly have we begun to run our eyes over this arrangement, than the call disappears; we remain alone, free to tie up one color with another or with a third, to set up a relationship between the tree and the water or the tree and the sky, or the tree, the water and the sky. My freedom becomes caprice. To the extent that I establish new relationships, I remove myself further from the illusory objectivity which solicits me. I *muse* about certain motifs which are vaguely outlined by the things; the natural reality is no longer anything but a pretext for musing. Or, in that case, because I have deeply regretted that this arrangement which was momentarily perceived was not offered to me by somebody and consequently is not *real,* the result is that I fix my dream, that I transpose it to canvas or in writing. Thus, I interpose myself between the finality without end which appears in the natural spectacles and the gaze of other men. I transmit it to them. It becomes human by this transmission. Art here is a ceremony of the *gift* and the gift alone brings about the metamorphosis. It is something like the transmission of titles and powers in the matriarchate where the mother does not possess the names, but is the indispensable intermediary between uncle and nephew. Since I have captured this illusion in flight, since I lay it out for other men and have disengaged it and rethought it for them, they can consider it with confidence. It has become intentional. As for me, I remain, to be sure, at the border of the subjective and the objective without ever being able to contemplate the objective ordonnance which I transmit.

The reader, on the contrary, progresses in security. However far he may go, the author has gone farther. Whatever connections he may establish among the different parts of the book — among the chapters or the words — he has a guarantee, namely, that they have been expressly willed. As Descartes says, he can even pretend that there is a secret order among parts which seem to have no connection. The creator has preceded him along the way, and the most beautiful disorders are effects of art, that is, again order. Reading is induction, interpolation, extrapolation, and the basis of these activities rests on the reader's will, as for a long time it was believed that that of scientific induction rested on the divine will. A gentle force accompanies us and supports us from the first page to the last. That does not mean that we fathom the artist's intentions easily. They constitute, as we have said, the object of conjectures, and there is an *experience* of the reader; but these conjectures are supported by the great certainty we have that the beauties which appear in the book are never accidental. In nature, the tree and the sky harmonize only by chance; if, on the contrary, in the novel, the protagonists find themselves in a *certain* tower, in a *certain* prison, if they stroll in a *certain* garden, it is a matter both of the restitution of independent causal series (the character had a certain state of mind which was due to a succession of psychological and social events; on the other hand, he betook himself to a determined place and the layout of the city required him to cross a certain park) and of the expression of a deeper finality, for the park came into existence only *in order to* harmonize with a certain state of mind, to express it by means of things or to put it into relief by a vivid contrast, and the state of mind itself was conceived in connection with the landscape. Here it is causality which is appearance and which might be called "causality without cause," and it is the finality which is the profound reality. But if I can thus in all confidence put the order of ends under the order of causes, it is because by opening the book I am asserting that the object has its source in human freedom.

If I were to suspect the artist of having written out of passion and in passion, my confidence would immediately vanish, for it would serve no purpose to have supported the order of causes by the order of ends. The latter would be supported in its turn by a psychic causality and the work of art would end by re-entering the chain of determinism. Certainly I do not deny when I am reading that the author may be impassioned, nor even that he might have conceived the first plan of his work under the sway of passion. But his decision to write supposes that he withdraws somewhat from his feelings, in short, that he has transformed his emotions into free emotions as I do mine while reading him; that is, that he is in an attitude of generosity.

Thus, reading is a pact of generosity between author and reader. Each one trusts the other; each one counts on the other, demands of the other as much as he demands of himself. For this confidence is itself generosity. Nothing can force the author to believe that his reader will use his freedom; nothing can force the reader to believe that the author has used his. Both of them make a free decision. There is then established a dialectical going-and-coming; when I read, I make demands; if my demands are met, what I am then reading provokes me to demand more of the author, which means to demand of the author that he demand more of me. And, vice-versa, the author's demand is that I carry my demands to the highest pitch. Thus, my freedom, by revealing itself, reveals the freedom of the other.

It matters little whether the aesthetic object is the product of "realistic" art (or supposedly such) or "formal" art. At any rate, the natural relations are inverted; that tree on the first plane of the Cézanne painting first appears as the product of a causal chain. But the causality is an illusion; it will doubtless remain as a proposition as long as we look at the painting, but it will be supported by a deep finality; if the tree is placed in such a way, it is because the rest of the painting *requires* that this form and those colors be placed on the first plane. Thus, through the phenomenal causality, our gaze attains finality as the deep structure of the object, and, beyond finality, it attains human freedom as its source and original basis. Vermeer's realism is carried so far that at first it might be thought to be photographic. But if one considers the splendor of his texture, the pink and velvety glory of his little brick walls, the blue thickness of a branch of woodbine, the glazed darkness of his vestibules, the orange-colored flesh of his faces which are as polished as the stone of holy-water basins, one suddenly feels, in the pleasure that he experiences, that the finality is not so much in the forms or colors as in his material imagination. It is the very substance and temper of the things which here give the forms their reason for being. With this realist we are perhaps closest to absolute creation, since it is in the very passivity of the matter that we meet the unfathomable freedom of man.

The work is never limited to the painted, sculpted, or narrated object. Just as one perceives things only against the background of the world, so the objects represented by art appear against the background of the universe. On the background of the adventures of Fabrice[3] are the Italy of 1820, Austria, France, the sky and stars which the Abbé Blanis consults, and finally the whole earth. If the painter presents us with a field or a vase of flowers, his paintings are windows which are open on the whole world. We follow the red path which is buried among the wheat much farther than Van Gogh has painted it, among other wheat fields, under other clouds, to the river which empties into the sea, and we extend to infinity, to the other end of the world, the deep finality which supports the existence of the field and the earth. So that, through the various objects which it produces or reproduces, the creative act aims at a total renewal of the world. Each painting, each book, is a recovery of the totality of being. Each of them presents this totality to the freedom of the spectator. For this is quite the final goal of art: to recover this world by giving it to be seen as it is, but as if it had its source in human freedom. But, since what the author creates takes on objective reality only in the eyes of the spectator, this recovery is consecrated by the ceremony of the spectacle — and particularly of reading. We are already in a better position to answer the question we raised a while ago: the writer chooses to appeal to the freedom of other men so that, by the reciprocal implications of their demands, they may readapt the totality of being to man and may again enclose the universe within man.

If we wish to go still further, we must bear in mind that the writer, like all other artists, aims at giving his reader a certain feeling that is customarily called aesthetic pleasure, and which I would very much rather call aesthetic joy, and that this feeling, when it appears, is a sign that the work is achieved. It is therefore fitting to examine it in the light of the preceding considerations. In effect, this joy, which is denied to the creator, insofar as he creates, becomes one with the aesthetic consciousness of the spectator, that is, in the case under consideration, of the reader. It is a complex feeling but one whose structures and condition are inseparable from one another. It is identical, at first, with the recognition of a transcendent and absolute end which, for a moment, suspends the utilitarian round of ends-means and means-ends,[4] that is, of an appeal or, what amounts to the same thing, of a value. And the positional consciousness which I take of this value is necessarily accompanied by the non-positional consciousness of my freedom, since my freedom is manifested to itself by a transcendent exigency. The recognition of freedom by itself is joy, but this structure of non-thetical consciousness implies another: since, in effect, reading is creation, my freedom does not only appear to itself as pure autonomy but as creative activity, that is, it is not limited to giving itself its own law but perceives itself as being constitutive of the object. It is on this level that the phenomenon specifically is manifested, that is, a creation wherein the created object is given *as object* to its creator. It is the sole case in which the creator gets any enjoyment out of the object he creates. And the word enjoyment which is applied to the positional consciousness of the work read indicates sufficiently that we are in the presence of an essential structure of aesthetic joy. This positional enjoyment is accompanied by the non-positional consciousness of being essential in relation to an object perceived as essential. I shall call this aspect of aesthetic consciousness the feeling of security; it is this which stamps the strongest aesthetic emotions with a sovereign calm. It has its origin in the authentication of a strict harmony between subjectivity and objectivity. As, on the other hand, the aesthetic object is properly the world insofar as it is aimed at through the imaginary, aesthetic joy accompanies the positional consciousness that the world is a value, that is, a task proposed to human freedom. I shall call this the aesthetic modification of the human project, for, as usual, the world appears as the horizon of our situation, as the infinite distance which separates us from ourselves, as the synthetic totality of the given, as the undifferentiated ensemble of obstacles and implements — but never as a demand addressed to our freedom. Thus, aesthetic joy proceeds to this level of the consciousness which I take of recovering and

[3]In Stendhal's *Charterhouse of Parma* (1839).

[4]In *practical life* a means may be taken for an end as soon as one searches for it, and each end is revealed as a means of attaining another end. [Sartre]

internalizing that which is non-ego par excellence, since I transform the given into an imperative and the fact into a value. The world is *my task,* that is, the essential and freely accepted function of my freedom is to make that unique and absolute object which is the universe come into being in an unconditioned movement. And, thirdly, the preceding structures imply a pact between human freedoms, for, on the one hand, reading is a confident and exacting recognition of the freedom of the writer, and, on the other hand, aesthetic pleasure, as it is itself experienced in the form of a value, involves an absolute exigence in regard to others; every man, insofar as he is a freedom, feels the same pleasure in reading the same work. Thus, all mankind is present in its highest freedom; it sustains the being of a world which is both *its* world and the "external" world. In aesthetic joy the positional consciousness is an *image-making* consciousness of the world in its totality both as being and having to be, both as totally ours and totally foreign, and the more ours as it is the more foreign. The non-positional consciousness *really* envelops the harmonious totality of human freedoms insofar as it makes the object of a universal confidence and exigency.

To write is thus both to disclose the world and to offer it as a task to the generosity of the reader. It is to have recourse to the consciousness of others in order to make one's self be recognized as *essential* to the totality of being; it is to wish to live this essentiality by means of interposed persons; but, on the other hand, as the real world is revealed only by action, as one can feel himself in it only by exceeding it in order to change it, the novelist's universe would lack thickness if it were not discovered in a movement to transcend it. It has often been observed that an object in a story does not derive its density of existence from the number and length of the descriptions devoted to it, but from the complexity of its connections with the different characters. The more often the characters handle it, take it up, and put it down, in short, go beyond it toward their own ends, the more real will it appear. Thus, of the world of the novel, that is, the totality of men and things, we may say that in order for it to offer its maximum density the disclosure-creation by which the reader discovers it must also be an imaginary engagement in the action; in other words, the more disposed one is to change it, the more alive it will be. The error of realism has been to believe that the real reveals itself to contemplation, and that consequently one could draw an impartial picture of it. How could that be possible, since the very perception is partial, since by itself the naming is already a modification of the object? And how could the writer, who wants himself to be essential to this universe, want to be essential to the injustice which this universe comprehends? Yet, he must be; but if he accepts being the creator of injustices, it is in a movement which goes beyond them toward their abolition. As for me who reads, if I create and keep alive an unjust world, I can not help making myself responsible for it. And the author's whole art is bent on obliging me to *create* what he *discloses,* therefore to compromise myself. So both of us bear the responsibility for the universe. And precisely because this universe is supported by the joint effort of our two freedoms, and because the author, with me as medium, has attempted to integrate it into the human, it must appear truly *in itself,* in its very marrow, as being shot through and through with a freedom which has taken human freedom as its end, and if it is not really the city of ends that it ought to be, it must at least be a stage along the way; in a word, it must be a becoming and it must always be considered and presented not as a crushing mass which weighs us down, but from the point of view of its going beyond toward that city of ends. However bad and hopeless the humanity which it paints may be, the work must have an air of generosity. Not, of course, that this generosity is to be expressed by means of edifying discourses and virtuous characters; it must not even be premeditated, and it is quite true that fine sentiments to not make fine books. But it must be the very warp and woof of the book, the stuff out of which the people and things are cut; whatever the subject, a sort of essential lightness must appear everywhere and remind us that the work is never a natural datum, but an *exigence* and a *gift.* And if I am given this world with its injustices, it is not so that I might contemplate them coldly, but that I might animate them with my indignation, that I might disclose them and create them with their nature as injustices, that is, as abuses to be suppressed. Thus, the writer's universe will only reveal itself in all its depth to the examination, the admiration, and the indignation of the reader; and the generous love is a promise to maintain, and the generous indignation is a promise to change, and the admiration a promise to imitate; although literature is one thing and morality a quite different one, at the heart of the aesthetic imperative we discern the moral imperative. For, since the one who writes recognizes, by the very fact that he takes the trouble to write, the freedom of his readers, and since the one who reads, by the mere fact of his opening the book, recognizes the freedom of the writer, the work of art, from whichever side you approach it, is an act of confidence in the freedom of men. And since readers, like the author, recognize this freedom only to demand that it manifest itself, the work can be defined as an imaginary presentation of the world insofar as it demands human freedom. The result of which is that there is no "gloomy literature," since, however dark may be the colors in which one paints the world, he paints it only so that free men may feel their freedom as they face it. Thus, there are only good and bad novels. The bad novel aims to please by flattering, whereas the good one is an exigence and an act of faith. But above all, the unique point of view from which the author can present the world to those freedoms whose concurrence he wishes to bring about is that of a world to be impregnated always with more freedom. It would be inconceivable that this unleashing of generosity provoked by the writer could be used to authorize an injustice, and that the reader could enjoy his freedom while reading a work which approves or accepts or simply abstains from condemning the subjection of man by man. One can imagine a good novel being written by an American Negro even if hatred of the whites were spread all over it, because it is the freedom of his race that he demands through this hatred. And, as he invites me to assume the attitude of generosity, the moment I feel myself a pure freedom I can not bear to identify myself with a race of oppressors. Thus, I require of all freedoms that they demand the liberation of colored people against the white race and against myself insofar as I am a part of it, but nobody can suppose for a moment that it is possible to write a good novel in praise of anti-Semitism.[5] For, the moment I feel that my freedom is indissolubly linked with that of all other men, it can not be demanded of me that I use it to approve the enslavement of a part of these men. Thus, whether he is an essayist, a pamphleteer, a satirist, or a novelist, whether he speaks only of individual passions or whether he attacks the social order, the writer, a free man addressing free men, has only one subject — freedom.

Hence, any attempt to enslave his readers threatens him in his very art. A blacksmith can be affected by fascism in his life as a man, but not necessarily in his craft; a writer will be affected in both, and even more in his craft than in his life. I have seen writers, who before the war, called for fascism with all their hearts, smitten with sterility at the very moment when the Nazis were loading them with honors. I am thinking of Drieu la Rochelle in particular; he was mistaken, but he was sincere. He proved it. He had agreed to direct a Nazi-inspired review. The first few months he reprimanded, rebuked, and lectured his countrymen. No one answered him because no one was free to do so. He became irritated; he no longer *felt* his readers. He became more insistent, but no sign appeared to prove that he had been understood. No sign of hatred, nor of anger either; nothing. He seemed disoriented, the victim of a growing distress. He complained bitterly to the Germans. His articles had been superb; they became shrill. The moment arrived when he struck his breast; no echo, except among the bought journalists whom he despised. He handed in his resignation, withdrew it, again spoke, still in the desert. Finally, he kept still, gagged by the silence of others. He had demanded the enslavement of others, but in his crazy mind he must

---

[5]This last remark may arouse some readers. If so, I'd like to know a single good novel whose express purpose was to serve oppression, a single good novel which has been written against Jews, negroes, workers, or colonial people. "But if there isn't any, that's no reason why someone may not write one some day." But you then admit that you are an abstract theoretician. You, not I. For it is in the name of your abstract conception of art that you assert the possibility of a fact which has never come into being, whereas I limit myself to proposing an explanation for a recognized fact. [Sartre]

have imagined that it was voluntary, that it was still free. It came; the man in him congratulated himself mightily, but the writer could not bear it. While this was going on, others, who, happily, were in the majority, understood that the freedom of writing implies the freedom of the citizen. One does not write for slaves. The art of prose is bound up with the only regime in which prose has meaning, democracy. When one is threatened, the other is too. And it is not enough to defend them with the pen. A day comes when the pen is forced to stop, and the writer must then take up arms. Thus, however you might have come to it, whatever the opinions you might have professed, literature throws you into battle. Writing is a certain way of wanting freedom; once you have begun, you are engaged, willy-nilly.

Engaged in what? Defending freedom? That's easy to say. Is it a matter of acting as guardian of ideal values like Benda's clerk before the betrayal,[6] or is it concrete, everyday freedom which must be protected by our taking sides in political and social struggles? The question is tied up with another one, one very simple in appearance but which nobody ever asks himself: "For whom does one write?"

[6]The reference here is to Julien Benda's *La Trahison des clercs,* translated into English as *The Treason of the Intellectuals.* [Tr.]

Simone de Beauvoir
1908–1986

Simone-Lucie-Ernestine-Marie-Bertrand de Beauvoir was born and raised in a middle-class Parisian household that discouraged her interest in matters intellectual, but she went on to obtain a prestigious *agrégation* (postgraduate) degree in philosophy at the Sorbonne in 1929 and to write the influential feminist treatise, *The Second Sex* (*Le Deuxième sexe,* 1949). While she was preparing for her degree, she met Jean-Paul Sartre, who became her companion in a lifelong nonmarital union, though it was a partnership fraught with conflicts produced by, among other things, his persistent and pointed infidelities. They were also partners in the important intellectual journal *Les Temps modernes,* a monthly that she and Sartre began in 1945 and that she continued to edit and review after Sartre's death in 1980.

After taking her *agré,* Beauvoir taught philosophy for thirteen years in various schools, then decided to make her living by her pen, publishing novels, essays, and travel literature. Most of her novels focus on themes of freedom, responsibility, and angst — giving concrete exposition to the issues highlighted in existentialism, the philosophy espoused by Beauvoir and Sartre. (For a fuller discussion of the background of existentialism, see the introductions to Heidegger, p. 611, and Sartre, p. 659.) Her first novel, *She Came to Stay* (*L'Invitée,* 1943), for example, focuses on the problems of conscience produced by conflicts within a close familial group. It also reflects the emotional upheaval in the Beauvoir-Sartre *ménage* caused by the prolonged stay of Olga Kosakiewicz, a young girl that Sartre had "adopted." Her second, *The Blood of Others* (*Le Sang des autres,* 1945) raises the issue of causes and consequences: Must a French resistance fighter consider himself responsible for the reprisals carried out by the Nazis? Her later novel, *The Mandarins* (*Les Mandarins,* 1954), a probing portrait of the French literary and intellectual establishment after World War II, won the Prix Goncourt, an award presented by that very establishment.

Beginning at the age of fifty, Beauvoir turned from philosophical fiction to autobiography and memoir. *Memoirs of a Dutiful Daughter* (*Mémoires d'une jeune fille rangée,* 1958) explores her youth and rebellion; *The Prime of Life* (*La Force de l'age,* 1960) and *The Force of Circumstance* (*La Force des choses,* 1963) continue her story into her middle age. As she grew older, Beauvoir concerned herself more and more with the problems of aging and dying, which she addressed in *A Very Easy Death* (*Une Morte très douce,* 1964), which focuses on the death of her mother; she wrote about Sartre's last illness and death in *Adieux: A Farewell to Sartre* (*Cérémonies des adieux,* 1981).

Beauvoir's magnum opus, *The Second Sex,* is one of the most important texts for twentieth-century feminism, a broad and wide-ranging attempt to review and critique the social and psychological constructions that since the Bronze Age have defined "humanity" in terms of the capacities, ideologies, and desires of the male sex, and correspondingly have positioned women as protected — even at times worshipped — but inferior: "She is defined and differentiated with reference to man and not he with reference to her; she is the incidental, the inessential as opposed to the essential. He is the Subject, he is the Absolute — she is the Other."[1]

In terms of the existential philosophy that Beauvoir developed along with Jean-Paul Sartre, this "alterity" or Otherness means that a woman is implicitly defined as *en-soi* rather than *pour-soi:* a thing rather than a person, a means to some other end rather than an end-in-itself. If, as existentialist philosophy suggests, the freedom to define what one is through one's choices and acts is terrifyingly difficult to accept for men, Beauvoir argues that it is almost impossible for women, who internalize and help maintain a patriarchal belief that their essential nature is to exist for the sake of others.

For Beauvoir, the destiny of Woman to be the Other begins, though it does not end, with mammalian anatomy. Unlike the controlling female queens in bee and ant societies, or the choosy (and devouring) female arachnids, whose power depends on exteriorizing their reproductive maneuvers, the human female carries the fertilized ovum inside her — a growing being that is a part of her and yet not herself, a parasite whose significance to the survival of the species makes her body an object rather than a subject, something Other even to herself.[2] When at the dawn of history man began to till the soil, woman in her fecundity was like the Earth itself, and like the Earth was made to yield her harvest for his benefit.[3] The tool-making and tool-using capacity vested more significance in man's upper-body strength and less in woman's adaptivity and endurance. Once created, patriarchy required that property descend through the male line, which in turn demanded that virtuous women be passive, acquiescent, and above all chaste, to guarantee true genetic inheritance as strictly as possible in a species whose individuals can never truly know who their father is.

Beauvoir, like Hegel, sees the progress of civilization as bringing the individual closer and closer to the realization of his or her freedom, but she argues that while events like the French revolution liberated the masculine spirit from outmoded feudal social structures, the liberation of woman has been far slower in coming. She believes this is partly because women, however oppressed, are not a true class in Marx's sense: Restrictions on aristocratic women were imposed differently than on bourgeois or working-class women, and women could therefore gain no sense of common interest. The delay mainly results because women are epiphenomenal to the historically developing class struggle of men: Historical changes in women's status and choices — greater or less occupational or familial or sexual freedom — seem to depend not on what they want but on what men want of them.

In part III of *The Second Sex,* Beauvoir explores the ideological component of women's alterity: the way in which women are made to think of themselves as the Other, not by social rules or restrictions but by the myths through which societies construct the female consciousness. In "Myths: Of Women in Five Authors," Beauvoir exposes several myths that present women not as they are, but as projections

[1]Simone de Beauvoir, *The Second Sex* (New York: Random House, 1953), p. xix.

[2]Some contemporary feminists have been critical of Beauvoir's essentialization of female inferiority and of the implication of her argument that anatomy was always destiny.

[3]Beauvoir dismisses as "a myth" the theory of some anthropologists that an early Bronze-Age matriarchal society may have preceded the development of patriarchal society. The theory is based on texts like Aeschylus's *The Eumenides,* which presupposes that the patriarchal Olympian gods had recently displaced the rule of the female principles of Earth and Night.

of male needs, defined as whatever men need to complete themselves. These myths can be vulgar, as in Henri de Montherlant's casting of woman as mere "slimy" flesh with which man satiates himself sexually, or comparatively refined, as in D. H. Lawrence's vision of passive woman subordinating herself to the enabling transcendence of the Phallus. Or the myth can invert alterity, as in Paul Claudel's vision of woman as the holy channel through which the striving male soul may find the peace of God. Even Stendhal — who liked his women to have minds and hearts as well as bodies and souls, so that Beauvoir feels it is "a relief" to be able to talk about his complex and subtle creations — has his mythic woman. Stendhal's women — such as Madame de Rénal or la Sanseverina — are more complicated and intelligent than their male counterparts, but they are never the subject of the narrative in their own right: They are there as the Other to play their part in the maturation of the male subject, Julien Sorel or Fabrizio.[4]

The result of the construction of woman as an ideal, whatever her characteristics, Beauvoir argues, is to force women to choose between being a "woman" and being themselves. In her final section, she sees light at the end of the tunnel: In the dissatisfaction of contemporary men with the lack of womanliness of present-day women, Beauvoir senses that a parting of the ways has come and that the myth of femininity is not all-powerful. Her book itself gave a gigantic tug at that unstable ideological structure. Some present-day feminists would argue that it is necessary to go beyond Beauvoir's own dogmas, her own inherited essentialisms, such as the rigid dialectic between masculinity and femininity, but surely *The Second Sex* has a clear place on the map of today's feminist theory.

Selected Bibliography

Beauvoir, Simone de. *The Second Sex*. New York: Random House, 1953.
———. *All Said and Done*. New York: Marlowe, 1994.
Francis, Claude, and Fernande Gontier. *Simone de Beauvoir: A Life — A Love Story*. New York: St. Martin's Press, 1988.
Fullbrook, Kate, and Edward Fullbrook. *Simone de Beauvoir and Jean-Paul Sartre: The Remaking of the Twentieth-Century Legend*. New York: Basic Books, 1994.
Grosholz, Emily R., ed. *The Legacy of Simone de Beauvoir*. Oxford: Clarendon, 2004.
Keefe, Terry. *Simone de Beauvoir*. New York, St. Martin's Press, 1998.
Lundgren-Gothlin, Eva. *Sex and Existence: Simone de Beauvoir's* The Second Sex. Boston: University Press of New England, 1996.
Marks, Elaine, ed. *Critical Essays on Simone de Beauvoir*. Boston: G. K. Hall, 1987.
Moi, Toril. *Simone de Beauvoir: The Making of an Intellectual Woman*. London: Blackwell, 1994.
Pilardi, Jo-Ann. *Simone de Beauvoir Writing the Self: Philosophy Becomes Autobiography*. Westport, CT: Praeger, 1999.
Simons, Margaret A., ed. *Feminist Interpretations of Simone de Beauvoir*. University Park: Pennsylvania State University Press, 1995.

---

[4]Beauvoir's observations concerning Stendhal's novels are similar to what James Phelan has more recently argued about *A Farewell to Arms* — that the essential sexism of Hemingway's novel resides less in how Catherine Barkley is characterized than in the fact that the novel is structured so that the central tragedy is not her death but Frederic Henry's having to go on living without her. It is his loss, not hers, that counts.

Myths: Of Women in Five Authors

It is to be seen from these examples that each separate writer reflects the great collective myths: we have seen woman as *flesh;* the flesh of the male is produced in the mother's body and recreated in the embraces of the woman in love. Thus woman is related to *nature,* she incarnates it: vale of blood, open rose, siren, the curve of a hill, she represents to man the fertile soil, the sap, the material beauty and the soul of the world. She can hold the keys to *poetry;* she can be *mediatrix* between this world and the beyond: grace or oracle, star or sorceress, she opens the door to the supernatural, the surreal. She is doomed to *immanence;* and through her passivity she bestows peace and harmony — but if she declines this role, she is seen forthwith as a praying mantis, an ogress. In any case she appears as the *privileged Other,* through whom the subject fulfills himself: one of the measures of man, his counterbalance, his salvation, his adventure, his happiness.

But these myths are very differently orchestrated by our authors. The *Other* is particularly defined according to the particular manner in which the *One* chooses to set himself up. Every man asserts his freedom and transcendence — but they do not all give these words the same sense. For Montherlant[1] transcendence is a situation: he is the transcendent, he soars in the sky of heroes; woman crouches on earth, beneath his feet; it amuses him to measure the distance that separates him from her; from time to time he raises her up to him, takes her, and then throws her back; never does he lower himself down to her realm of slimy shadows. Lawrence[2] places transcendence in the phallus; the phallus is life and power only by grace of woman; immanence

is therefore good and necessary; the false hero who pretends to be above setting foot on earth, far from being a demigod, fails to attain man's estate. Woman is not to be scorned, she is deep richness, a warm spring; but she should give up all personal transcendence and confine herself to furthering that of her male. Claudel[3] asks her for the same devotion: for him, too, woman should maintain life while man extends its range through his activities; but for the Catholic all earthly affairs are immersed in vain immanence: the only transcendent is God; in the eyes of God the man in action and the woman who serves him are exactly equal; it is for each to surpass his or her earthly state: salvation is in all cases an autonomous enterprise. For Breton[4] the rank of the sexes is reversed; action and conscious thought, in which the male finds his transcendence, seem to Breton to constitute a silly mystification that gives rise to war, stupidity, bureaucracy, the negation of anything human; it is immanence, the pure, dark presence of the real, which is truth; true transcendence would be accomplished by a return to immanence. His attitude is the exact opposite of Montherlant's: the latter likes war because in war one gets rid of women; Breton venerates woman because she brings peace. Montherlant confuses mind and subjectivity — he refuses to accept the given universe; Breton thinks that mind is objectively present at the heart of the world; woman endangers Montherlant because she breaks his solitude; she is revelation for Breton because she tears him out of his subjectivity. As for Stendhal,[5] we have seen that for him woman hardly has a mystical value: he regards her as being, like man, a transcendent; for this humanist, free beings of

Translated by H. M. Parshley.

[1]Henri de Montherlant (1896–1972), antifeminist author of *Les Jeune filles* (1936), *Pitié pour les femmes* (1936), *Le Démon du bien* (1937), and *Les Lepreuses* (1939).

[2]D. H. Lawrence (1885–1930), author of *Sons and Lovers* (1913) and *Women in Love* (1920); Beauvoir's later discussion of "Kate" and "Don Cipriano" refers to his novel, *The Plumed Serpent* (1926).

[3]Paul Claudel (1868–1955), poet and playwright, author of *L'Annonce faite à Marie* (1912) and *Le Soulier de satin* (1937), which contains the salvation of Rodrigue by Prouhèze that Beauvoir refers to later.

[4]André Breton (1896–1966), surrealist poet and novelist, author of *Nadja* (1928) and *L'Amour fou* (1937).

[5]Marie-Henri Beyle (1783–1842), psychological novelist who wrote as Stendhal; his works include *Le Rouge et le noir* (1830) and *La Chartreuse de Parme* (1839).

both sexes fulfill themselves in their reciprocal relations; and for him it is enough if the *Other* be simply an other so that life may have what he calls "a pungent saltiness." He is not seeking a "stellar equilibrium," he is not fed on the bread of disgust; he is not looking for a miracle; he does not wish to be concerned with the cosmos or with poetry, but with free human beings.

More, Stendhal feels that he is himself a clear, free being. The others — and this is a most important point — pose as transcendents but feel themselves prisoners of a dark presence in their own hearts: they project this "unbreakable core of night" upon woman. Montherlant has an Adlerian complex, giving rise to his thick-witted bad faith: it is this tangle of pretensions and fears that he incarnates in woman; his disgust for her is what he dreads feeling for himself. He would trample underfoot, in woman, the always possible proof of his own insufficiency; he appeals to scorn to save him; and woman is the trench into which he throws all the monsters that haunt him. The life of Lawrence shows us that he suffered from an analogous though more purely sexual complex: in his works woman serves as a compensation myth, exalting a virility that the writer was none too sure of; when he describes Kate at Don Cipriano's feet, he feels as if he had won a male triumph over his wife, Frieda; nor does he permit his companion to raise any questions: if she were to oppose his aims he would doubtless lose confidence in them; her role is to reassure him. He asks of her peace, repose, faith, as Montherlant asks for certainty regarding his superiority: they demand what is missing in them. Claudel's lack is not that of self-confidence: if he is timid it is only in secret with God. Nor is there any trace of the battle of the sexes in his work. Man boldly assumes woman's weight; she is a possibility for temptation or for salvation. It would seem that for Breton man is true only through the mystery that is within him; it pleases him for Nadja to see that star toward which he moves and which is like "the heart of a heartless flower." In his dreams, his presentiments, the spontaneous flow of his stream of consciousness — in such activities, which escape the control of the will and the reason, he recognizes his true self; woman is the visible image of that veiled presence which is infinitely more essential than his conscious personality.

Stendhal is in tranquil agreement with himself; but he needs woman as she needs him in order to gather his diffuse existence into the unity of a single design and destiny: it is as though man reaches manhood for another; but still he needs to have the lending of the other's consciousness. Other males are too indifferent toward their fellows; only the loving woman opens her heart to her lover and shelters him there, wholly. Except for Claudel, who finds in God his preferred witness, all the writers we have considered expect that woman will cherish in them what Malraux[6] calls "this incomparable monster" known to themselves only. In cooperation or contest men face each other as generalized types. Montherlant is for his fellows a writer, Lawrence a doctrinaire, Breton a school principal, Stendhal a diplomat or man of wit; it is woman who reveals in one a magnificent and cruel prince, in another a disquieting faun, in this one a god or a sun or a being "black and cold as a man struck by lightning at the feet of the Sphinx,"[7] in the last a seducer, a charmer, a lover.

For each of them the ideal woman will be she who incarnates most exactly the *Other* capable of revealing him to himself. Montherlant, the solar spirit, seeks pure animality in her; Lawrence, the phallicist, asks her to sum up the feminine sex in general; Claudel defines her as a soul-sister; Breton cherishes Mélusine, rooted in nature, pinning his hope on the woman-child; Stendhal wants his mistress intelligent, cultivated, free in spirit and behavior: an equal. But the sole earthly destiny reserved for the equal, the woman-child, the soul-sister, the woman-sex, the woman-animal is always man! Whatever ego may seek himself through her, he can find himself only if she is willing to act as his crucible. She is required in every case to forget self and to love. Montherlant consents to have pity upon the woman who allows him to measure his virile potency; Lawrence addresses a burning hymn to the woman who gives up being herself for his sake; Claudel exalts the handmaid, the female servant,

---

[6]André Malraux (1901–76), novelist and political figure; his works include *La Condition humaine* (1933) and *Les Voix du silence* (1951).
[7]Breton's *Nadja.* [Beauvoir]

the devotee who submits to God in submitting to the male; Breton is in hopes of human salvation from woman because she is capable of total love for her child or her lover; and even in Stendhal the heroines are more moving than the masculine heroes because they give themselves to their passion with a more distraught violence; they help man fulfill his destiny, as Prouhèze contributes to the salvation of Rodrigue; in Stendhal's novels it often happens that they save their lovers from ruin, prison, or death. Feminine devotion is demanded as a duty by Montherlant and Lawrence; less arrogant, Claudel, Breton, and Stendhal admire it as a generous free choice; they wish for it without claiming to deserve it; but — except for the astounding Lamiel — all their works show that they expect from woman that altruism which Comte[8] admired in her and imposed upon her,

and which according to him constituted a mark at once of flagrant inferiority and of an equivocal superiority.

We could multiply examples, but they would invariably lead us to the same conclusions. When he describes woman, each writer discloses his general ethics and the special idea he has of himself; and in her he often betrays also the gap between his world view and his egotistical dreams. The absence or insignificance of the feminine element throughout the work of an author is in its own way symptomatic; but that element is extremely important when it sums up in its totality all the aspects of the Other, as happens with Lawrence. It remains important when woman is viewed simply as an other but the writer is interested in the individual adventure of her life, as with Stendhal; it loses importance in an epoch such as ours when personal problems of the individual are of secondary interest. Woman, however, as the other still plays a role to the extent that, if only to transcend himself, each man still needs to learn more fully what he is.

[8]Auguste Comte (1798–1857), French philosopher and sociologist, author of *Système de politique positive* (1851–54).

J. L. Austin
(1911–1960)

John Langshaw Austin was born in Lancaster, England, and educated at Balliol College at Oxford University, where he went on to teach philosophy at All Souls and Magdalen Colleges. During World War II, Austin served as an intelligence officer in the British Army, rising to the rank of lieutenant colonel; he was the chief coordinator for intelligence on the German coastal defenses before D-Day, and on the location of V-2 rocket launching sites within the Allied High Command, for which he was highly decorated by the French and American governments as well as his own. After the war, Austin returned to Magdalen College, Oxford, becoming the White Professor of Moral Philosophy in 1952.

Austin is a central figure in the "ordinary language" school of philosophy. Like the logical positivists of Cambridge, such as Ludwig Wittgenstein, the "ordinary language" philosophers opposed the cloudy conceptions of idealist metaphysics. But Austin and his school argued that it was the first task of philosophy to investigate how ordinary language was used by ordinary people in order to avoid creating categories that confuse rather than clarify thinking. For example, in *Sense and Sensibilia*, Austin took on philosophers like A. J. Ayer, who used phrases like "sense data" to refer to a part of the contents of people's minds in developing a theory of knowledge based on experience. Austin pointed out that Ayer used "sense data" indiscriminately to refer to things experienced and understood, things experienced but misunderstood (illusions) and things created entirely within the mind (delusions). Austin argued that any theory of knowledge that does not distinguish between things that are really there but appear different from what they are (optical illusions, like a highway that appears to be wet from a distance) and things that are not really there at all (like hallucinations) is not going to get very far. He also argued that we have to be careful with sentences like, "That looks like an airplane," because the word "looks" does not simply refer to a visual experience (you could not translate it as "I am having a visual experience of an airplane"). It rather signifies some doubt, caused by local conditions, such as fog, as to whether the speaker has correctly identified something that is definitely out there.

Austin's principal contribution to philosophy is termed speech-act theory, which he developed at Oxford in the early 1950s and presented as the William James lectures at Harvard in 1955 (the lectures were published posthumously in 1962 as *How to Do Things with Words*). The logical positivists had argued, as part of their program of eliminating metaphysics, that statements are meaningful only if they can be assessed as true or false, that is, that can be verified or falsified with respect to real matters of fact. "Brighton is south of London" is a true statement; "Brighton is north of London" is false. Meaningful statements have conditions for verification: if you want to test the truth of the statement "Yankee Stadium has 57,545 seats," you could go to the Bronx and count them. Statements may be good English but meaningless because they refer to what does not exist like "the present king of France is bald," or cannot be verified, like "Wagner's most sublime opera is *Parsifal*."

Austin argued to the contrary that there is a whole class of statements that cannot be verified as true or false but are enormously meaningful for ordinary users of language, statements like "I now pronounce you man and wife," or "I promise to help you out on Thursday" or "I agree to lend you my canoe." These are not sentences that assert the truth of a state of affairs; they are verbal actions. By words we thank hosts for invitations and condole with friends for their losses, we command our inferiors and entreat our superiors, we open and adjourn meetings, we find defendants guilty or not guilty, we make bets, we promise to love, honor, and cherish. These statements cannot be true or false but they have an analogous property: they have "felicity conditions," established by convention, within the society using the language, under which they are effective. For example, a marriage performed by actors as part of a play is not valid, only the chair of a meeting can adjourn it, a judge can sentence a defendant to prison only in a court of law.

Austin begins by distinguishing constative sentences (verifiable utterances) from these performative sentences, but ultimately he has to argue that all constatives are performatives: they assert or swear or report that a particular state of affairs is true, and as such are "doing" things just as much as sentences that promise or congratulate. They can also be performative in other senses as well. Speech acts are said to be "locutionary" (making a statement), "illocutionary" (having an intention), and "perlocutionary" (having an effect on an addressee). In a particular context, a sentence like "The door is open" could be all three: an assertion that the door is open, a hinted request or command by the speaker to close the door, and (if the listener takes the hint and closes it) an achieved intention. There are felicity conditions for the achieved intention — the listener has to be capable of closing the door and the speaker has to be socially dominant — but the key condition is that it be obvious to both speaker and listener that the door is open. Since people seldom announce obvious facts for no reason, the listener may conclude that the speaker is asking him to close the door.

Austin's theories of language were developed further by his student John Searle, among others, and have proven influential not only in purely philosophical contexts but in legal and sexual issues. (See the Introduction to Gender Studies and Queer Theory, p. 1617.)

Selected Bibliography

Austin, J. L. *Philosophical Papers*. Ed. J. O. Urmson and J. G. Warnock. Oxford: Clarendon Press, 1961; second edition, 1970.
—— . *Sense and Sensibilia*. Reconstructed by J. G. Warnock. Oxford: Clarendon Press, 1962.
Cavell, Stanley. *Philosophical Passages: Wittgenstein, Emerson, Austin, Derrida*. Cambridge, MA: Blackwell, 1995.
Felman, Shoshana. *The Scandal of the Speaking Body: Don Juan with J. L. Austin, or Seduction in Two Languages*. Stanford: Stanford University Press, 2002.
Graham, Keith. *J. L. Austin: A Critique of Ordinary Language Philosophy*. Hassocks, Sussex: Harvester Press, 1977.

[Constatives and Performatives]
from *How to Do Things with Words*

What I shall have to say here is neither difficult nor contentious; the only merit I should like to claim for it is that of being true, at least in parts. The phenomenon to be discussed is very widespread and obvious, and it cannot fail to have been already noticed, at least here and there, by others. Yet I have not found attention paid to it specifically.

It was for too long the assumption of philosophers that the business of a "statement" can only be to "describe" some state of affairs, or to "state some fact," which it must do either truly or falsely. Grammarians, indeed, have regularly pointed out that not all "sentences" are (used in making) statements:[1] there are, traditionally, besides (grammarians') statements, also questions and exclamations, and sentences expressing commands or wishes or concessions. And doubtless philosophers have not intended to deny this, despite some loose use of "sentence" for "statement." Doubtless, too, both grammarians and philosophers have been aware that it is by no means easy to distinguish even questions, commands, and so on from statements by means of the few and jejune grammatical marks available, such as word order, mood, and the like: though perhaps it has not been usual to dwell on the difficulties which this fact obviously raises. For how do we decide which is which? What are the limits and definitions of each?

But now in recent years, many things which would once have been accepted without question as "statements" by both philosophers and grammarians have been scrutinized with new care. This scrutiny arose somewhat indirectly — at least in philosophy. First came the view, not always formulated without unfortunate dogmatism, that a statement (of fact) ought to be "verifiable," and this led to the view that many

"statements" are only what may be called pseudo-statements. First and most obviously, many "statements" were shown to be, as Kant perhaps first argued systematically, strictly nonsense, despite an unexceptionable grammatical form: and the continual discovery of fresh types of nonsense, unsystematic though their classification and mysterious though their explanation is too often allowed to remain, has done on the whole nothing but good. Yet we, that is, even philosophers, set some limits to the amount of nonsense that we are prepared to admit we talk: so that it was natural to go on to ask, as a second stage, whether many apparent pseudo-statements really set out to be "statements" at all. It has come to be commonly held that many utterances which look like statements are either not intended at all, or only intended in part, to record or impart straightforward information about the facts: for example, "ethical propositions" are perhaps intended, solely or partly, to evince emotion or to prescribe conduct or to influence it in special ways. Here too Kant was among the pioneers. We very often also use utterances in ways beyond the scope at least of traditional grammar. It has come to be seen that many specially perplexing words embedded in apparently descriptive statements do not serve to indicate some specially odd additional feature in the reality reported, but to indicate (not to report) the circumstances in which the statement is made or reservations to which it is subject or the way in which it is to be taken and the like. To overlook these possibilities in the way once common is called the "descriptive" fallacy; but perhaps this is not a good name, as "descriptive" itself is special. Not all true or false statements are descriptions, and for this reason I prefer to use the word "Constative." Along these lines it has by now been shown piecemeal, or at least made to look likely, that many traditional philosophical perplexities have arisen through a mistake — the mistake of taking as straightforward statements of fact utterances which are

[1]It is, of course, not really correct that a sentence ever *is* a statement: rather, it is *used* in *making a statement*, and the statement itself is a "logical construction" out of the makings of statements. [Austin]

either (in interesting non-grammatical ways) nonsensical *or else* intended as something quite different.

Whatever we may think of any particular one of these views and suggestions, and however much we may deplore the initial confusion into which philosophical doctrine and method have been plunged, it cannot be doubted that they are producing a revolution in philosophy. If anyone wishes to call it the greatest and most salutary in its history, this is not, if you come to think of it, a large claim. It is not surprising that beginnings have been piecemeal, with *parti pris*,[2] and for extraneous aims; this is common with revolutions.

PRELIMINARY ISOLATION OF THE PERFORMATIVE[3]

The type of utterance we are to consider here is not, of course, in general a type of nonsense; though misuse of it can, as we shall see, engender rather special varieties of "nonsense." Rather, it is one of our second class — the masqueraders. But it does not by any means necessarily masquerade as a statement of fact, descriptive or constative. Yet it does quite commonly do so, and that, oddly enough, when it assumes its most explicit form. Grammarians have not, I believe, seen through this "disguise," and philosophers only at best incidentally.[4] It will be convenient, therefore, to study it first in this misleading form, in order to bring out its characteristics by contrasting them with those of the statement of fact which it apes.

We shall take, then, for our first examples some utterances which can fall into no hitherto recognized *grammatical* category save that of "statement," which are not nonsense, and which contain none of those verbal danger-signals which philosophers have by now detected or think they have detected (curious words like "good" or "all," suspect auxiliaries like "ought" or "can," and dubious constructions like the hypothetical): all will have, as it happens, humdrum verbs in the first person singular present indicative active.[5] Utterances can be found, satisfying these conditions, yet such that

A. they do not "describe" or "report" or con-state anything at all, are not "true or false"; and

B. the uttering of the sentences is, or is a part of, the doing of an action, which again would not *normally* be described as, or as "just," saying something.

This is far from being as paradoxical as it may sound or as I have meanly been trying to make it sound: indeed, the examples now to be given will be disappointing.

Examples:

(E. *a*) "I do (sc.[6] take this woman to be my lawful wedded wife)" — as uttered in the course of the marriage ceremony.[7]

(E. *b*) "I name this ship the *Queen Elizabeth*" — as uttered when smashing the bottle against the stern.

(E. *c*) "I give and bequeath my watch to my brother" — as occurring in a will.

(E. *d*) "I bet you sixpence it will rain tomorrow."

In these examples it seems clear that to utter the sentence (in, of course, the appropriate circumstances) is not to *describe* my doing of what I should be said in so uttering to be doing[8] or to state that I am doing it: it is to do it. None of the utterances cited is either true or false: I assert this as obvious and do not argue it. It needs argument no more than that "damn" is not true or false: it

---

[2]"Sides taken," i.e., prejudices.

[3]Everything said in these sections is provisional, and subject to revision in the light of later sections. [Austin]

[4]Of all people, jurists should be best aware of the true state of affairs. Perhaps some now are. Yet they will succumb to their own timorous function, that a statement of "the law" is a statement of fact. [Austin]

[5]Not without design: they are all "explicit" performatives, and of that prepotent class later called "exercitives." [Austin]

[6]Abbreviation for *scilicet*, meaning "leaving out" the phrase that follows in brackets.

[7][Austin realized that the expression "I do" is not used in the marriage ceremony too late to correct his mistake. We have let it remain in the text as it is philosophically unimportant that it is a mistake. J.O.U.] [Urmson, ed.]

[8]Still less anything that I have already done or have yet to do. [Austin]

may be that the utterance "serves to inform you" — but that is quite different. To name the ship *is* to say (in the appropriate circumstances) the words "I name, &c.." When I say, before the registrar or altar, &c., "I do," I am not reporting on a marriage: I am indulging in it.

What are we to call a sentence or an utterance of this type?[9] I propose to call it a *performative sentence* or a performative utterance, or, for short, "a performative." The term "performative" will be used in a variety of cognate ways and constructions, much as the term "imperative" is.[10] The name is derived, or course, from "perform," the usual verb with the noun "action": it indicates that the issuing of the utterance is the performing of an action — it is not normally thought of as just saying something.

A number of other terms may suggest themselves, each of which would suitably cover this or that wider or narrower class of performatives: for example, many performatives are *contractual* ("I bet") or *declaratory* ("I declare war") utterances. But no term in current use that I know of is nearly wide enough to cover them all. One technical term that comes nearest to what we need is perhaps "operative," as it is used strictly by lawyers in referring to that part, i.e. those clauses, of an instrument which serves to effect the transaction (conveyance or what not) which is its main object, whereas the rest of the document merely "recites" the circumstances in which the transaction is to be effected.[11] But "operative" has other meanings, and indeed is often used nowadays to mean little more than "important." I have preferred a new word, to which, though its etymology is not

irrelevant, we shall perhaps not be so ready to attach some preconceived meaning.

CAN SAYING MAKE IT SO?

Are we then to say things like this:

> "To marry is to say a few words," or
> "Betting is simply saying something"?

Such a doctrine sounds odd or even flippant at first, but with sufficient safeguards it may become not odd at all.

A sound initial objection to them may be this; and it is not without some importance. In very many cases it is possible to perform an act of exactly the same kind *not* by uttering words, whether written or spoken, but in some other way. For example, I may in some places effect marriage by cohabiting, or I may bet with a totalisator machine[12] by putting a coin in a slot. We should then, perhaps, convert the propositions above, and put it that "to say a few certain words is to marry" or "to marry is, in some cases, simply to say a few words" or "simply to say a certain something is to bet."

But probably the real reason why such remarks sound dangerous lies in another obvious fact, to which we shall have to revert in detail later, which is this. The uttering of the words is, indeed, usually a, or even *the*, leading incident in the performance of the act (of betting or what not), the performance of which is also the object of the utterance, but it is far from being usually, even if it is ever, the *sole* thing necessary if the act is to be deemed to have been performed. Speaking generally, it is always necessary that the *circumstances* in which the words are uttered should be in some way, or ways, *appropriate*, and it is very commonly necessary that either the speaker himself or other persons should *also* perform certain *other* actions, whether "physical" or "mental" actions or even acts of uttering further words. Thus, for naming the ship, it is essential that I should be the person appointed to name her, for (Christian) marrying, it is essential that I should not be already married with a wife living, sane and undivorced, and so on: for a bet to have been

---

[9]"Sentences" form a class of "utterances," which class is to be defined, so far as I am concerned, grammatically, though I doubt if the definition has yet been given satisfactorily. With performative utterances are constrasted, for example and essentially, "constative" utterances: to issue a constative utterance (i.e., to utter it with a historical reference) is to make a statement. To issue a performative utterance is, for example, to make a bet. See further below on "illocutions." [Austin]

[10]Formerly I used "performatory": but "performative" is to be preferred as shorter, less ugly, more tractable, and more traditional in formation. [Austin]

[11]I owe this observation to Professor H. L. A. Hart. [Austin]

[12]Slot machine.

made, it is generally necessary for the offer of the bet to have been accepted by a taker (who must have done something, such as to say "Done"), and it is hardly a gift if I say "I give it you" but never hand it over.

So far, well and good. The action may be performed in ways other than by a performative utterance, and in any case the circumstances, including other actions, must be appropriate. But we may, in objecting, have something totally different, and this time quite mistaken, in mind, especially when we think of some of the more awe-inspiring performatives such as "I promise to . . . ." Surely the words must be spoken "seriously" and so as to be taken "seriously"? This is, though vague, true enough in general — it is an important commonplace in discussing the purport of any utterance whatsoever. I must not be joking, for example, nor writing a poem. But we are apt to have a feeling that their being serious consists in their being uttered as (merely) the outward and visible sign, for convenience or other record or for information, of an inward and spiritual act: from which it is but a short step to go on to believe or to assume without realizing that for many purposes the outward utterance is a description, *true or false*, of the occurrence of the inward performance. The classic expression of this idea is to be found in the *Hippolytus* (l.612), where Hippolytus says

ἡ γλῶσσ' ὀμώμοχ', ἡ δὲ φρὴν ἀνωμοτὸς,

i.e., "my tongue swore to, but my heart (or mind or other backstage artiste)[13] did not."[14] Thus "I promise to . . ." obliges me — puts on record my spiritual assumption of a spiritual shackle.

It is gratifying to observe in this very example how excess of profundity, or rather solemnity, at once paves the way for immorality. For one who says "promising is not merely a matter of uttering words! It is an inward and spiritual act!" is apt to appear as a solid moralist standing out against a generation of superficial theorizers: we see him as he sees himself, surveying the invisible depths of ethical space, with all the distinction of a specialist in the *sui generis*.[15] Yet he provides Hippolytus with a let-out, the bigamist with an excuse for his "I do" and the welsher with a defence for his "I bet." Accuracy and morality alike are on the side of the plain saying that *our word is our bond*.

If we exclude such fictitious inward acts as this, can we suppose that any of the other things which certainly are normally required to accompany an utterance such as "I promise that . . ." or "I do (take this woman . . .)" are in fact described by it, and consequently do by their presence make it true or by their absence make it false? Well, taking the latter first, we shall next consider what we actually do say about the utterance concerned when one or another of its normal concomitants is *absent*. In no case do we say that the utterance was false but rather that the utterance — or rather the *act*,[16] e.g., the promise — was void, or given in bad faith, or not implemented, or the like. In the particular case of promising, as with many other performatives, it is appropriate that the person uttering the promise should have a certain intention, viz. here to keep his word: and perhaps of all concomitants this looks the most suitable to be that which "I promise" does describe or record. Do we not actually, when such intention is absent, speak of a "false" promise? Yet so to speak is *not* to say that the utterance "I promise that . . ." is false, in the sense that though he states that he does, he doesn't, or that though he describes he misdescribes — misreports. For he *does* promise: the promise here is not even *void*, though it is given *in bad faith*. His utterance is perhaps misleading, probably deceitful and doubtless wrong, but it is not a lie or a misstatement. At most we might make out a case for

---

[13]Austin's parentheses and footnote jokingly gloss the impossibility of translating the Greek word *phrên*, in the quoted line from Euripides' Hippolytus. The word originally meant "midriff," or "the parts about the heart or breast," which then was subsequently associated with various abstract notions like heart (as the seat of the passions), *mind*, *spirit*, and *will*.

[14]But I do not mean to rule out all the offstage performers—the lights men, the stage manager, even the prompter; I am objecting only to certain officious understudies, who would duplicate the play. [Austin]

[15]Something in a class by itself, unique.

[16]We deliberately avoid distinguishing these, precisely because the distinction is not in point. [Austin]

saying that it implies or insinuates a falsehood or a misstatement (to the effect that he does intend to do something): but that is a very different matter. Moreover, we do not speak of a false bet or a false christening; and that we *do* speak of a false promise need commit us no more than the fact that we speak of a false move. 'False' is not necessarily used of statements only.

[Speech Acts: Locutionary, Illocutionary, Perlocutionary] from *How to Do Things with Words*

In embarking on a programme of finding a list of explicit performative verbs, it seemed that we were going to find it not always easy to distinguish performative utterances from constative, and it therefore seemed expedient to go farther back for a while to fundamentals — to consider from the ground up how many senses there are in which to say something *is* to do something, or *in* saying something we do something, and even *by* saying something we do something. And we began by distinguishing a whole group of senses of "doing something" which are all included together when we say, what is obvious, that to say something is in the full normal sense to do something — which includes the utterance of certain noises, the utterance of certain words in a certain construction, and the utterance of them with a certain "meaning" in the favourite philosophical sense of that word, i.e., with a certain sense and with a certain reference.

The act of "saying something" in this full normal sense I call, i.e., dub, the performance of a locutionary act, and the study of utterances thus far and in these respects the study of locutions, or of the full units of speech. Our interest in the locutionary act is, of course, principally to make quite plain what it is, in order to distinguish it from other acts with which we are going to be primarily concerned. Let me add merely that, of course, a great many further refinements would be possible and necessary if we were to discuss it for its own sake — refinements of very great importance not merely to philosophers but to, say, grammarians and phoneticians.

We had made three rough distinctions between the phonetic act, the phatic act, and the rhetic act. The phonetic act is merely the act of uttering certain noises. The phatic act is the uttering of certain vocables or words, i.e., noises of certain types, belonging to and as belonging to, a certain vocabulary, conforming to and as conforming to a certain grammar. The rhetic act is the performance of an act of using those vocables with a certain more-or-less definite sense and reference. Thus "He said 'The cat is on the mat,'" reports a phatic act, whereas "He said that the cat was on the mat" reports a rhetic act. A similar contrast is illustrated by the pairs:

"He said 'The cat is on the mat,'" "He said (that) the cat was on the mat";

"He said 'I shall be there,'" "He said he would be there";

"He said 'Get out,'" "He told me to get out";

"He said 'Is it in Oxford or Cambridge?'";
   "He asked whether it was in Oxford or Cambridge."

To pursue this for its own sake beyond our immediate requirements, I shall mention some general points worth remembering:

(1) Obviously, to perform a phatic I must perform a phonetic act, or, if you like, in performing one I am performing the other (not, however, that phatic acts are a sub-class of phonetic acts; we defined the phatic act as the uttering of vocables *as* belonging to a certain vocabulary): but the converse is not true, for if a monkey makes a noise indistinguishable from "go" it is still not a phatic act.

(2) Obviously in the definition of the phatic act two things were lumped together: vocabulary and grammar. So we have not assigned a special name to the person who utters, for example, "cat thoroughly the if" or "the slithy toves did gyre." Yet a further point arising is the intonation as well as grammar and vocabulary.

(3) The phatic act, however, like the phonetic, is essentially mimicable, reproducible (including intonation, winks, gestures, &c.). One can mimic not merely the statement in quotation marks "She has lovely hair," but also the more complex fact that he said it like this: "She has lovely *hair*" (shrugs).

This is the "inverted commas" use of "said" as we get it in novels: every utterance can be just reproduced in inverted commas, or in inverted commas with "said he" or, more often, "said she," &c., after it.

But the rhetic act is the one we report, in the case of assertions, by saying "He said that the cat was on the mat," "He said he would go," "He said I was to go" (his words were "You are to go"). This is the so-called "indirect speech." If the sense or reference is *not* being taken as clear, then the whole or part is to be in quotation marks. Thus I might say: "He said I was to go to 'the minister,'" but he did not say which minister" or "I said that he was behaving badly and he replied that 'the higher you get the fewer.'" We cannot, however, always use "said that" easily: we would say "told to," "advise to," &c., if he used the imperative mood, or such equivalent phrases as "said I was to," "said I should," &c. Compare such phrases as "bade me welcome" and "extended his apologies."

I add one further point about the rhetic act: of course sense and reference (naming and referring) themselves are here ancillary acts performed in performing the rhetic act. Thus we may say "I meant by 'bank' . . ." and we say "by 'he' I was referring to . . . ." Can we perform a rhetic act without referring or without naming? In general it would seem that the answer is that we cannot, but there are puzzling cases. What is the reference in "all triangles have three sides"? Correspondingly, it is clear that we can perform a phatic act which is not a rhetic act, though not conversely. Thus we may repeat someone else's remark or mumble over some sentence, or we may read a Latin sentence without knowing the meaning of the words.

The question when one pheme or one rheme[1] is the *same* as another, whether in the "type" or "token" sense, and the question what is one single pheme or rheme, do not so much matter here. But, of course, it is important to remember that the same pheme, e.g., sentence, that is, tokens of the same type, may be used on different occasions of utterance with a different sense or reference, and so be a different rheme. When different phemes are used with the same sense and reference, we might speak of rhetically equivalent acts ("the same statement" in one sense) but not of the same rheme or rhetic acts (which are the same statement in another sense which involves using the same words).

The pheme is a unit of *language*: its typical fault is to be nonsense — meaningless. But the rheme is a unit of *speech;* its typical fault is to be vague or void or obscure, &c.

But though these matters are of much interest, they do not so far throw any light at all on our problem of the constative as opposed to the performative utterance. For example, it might be perfectly possible, with regard to an utterance, say "It is going to charge," to make entirely plain "what we were saying" in issuing the utterance, in all the senses so far distinguished, and yet not at all to have cleared up whether or not in issuing the utterance I was performing the act of *warning* or not. It may be perfectly clear what I mean by "It is going to charge" or "Shut the door," but not clear whether it is meant as a statement or warning, &c.

To perform a locutionary act is in general, we may say, also and *eo ipso*[2] to perform an *illocutionary* act, as I propose to call it. Thus in performing a locutionary act we shall also be performing such an act as:

asking or answering a question,
giving some information or an assurance or a warning,
announcing a verdict or an intention,
pronouncing sentence,

[1]In Austin's vocabulary a pheme is the object produced by a phatic act; a rheme is the object produced by a rhetic act.

[2]By its very nature.

making an appointment or an appeal or criticism,

making an identification or giving a description,

and the numerous like. (I am not suggesting that this is a clearly defined class by any means.) There is nothing mysterious about our *eo ipso* here. The trouble rather is the number of different senses of so vague an expression as "in what way are we using it" — this may refer even to a locutionary act, and further to perlocutionary acts to which we shall come in a minute. When we perform a locutionary act, we use speech: but in what way precisely are we using it on this occasion? For there are very numerous functions of or ways in which we use speech, and it makes a great difference to our act in some sense — sense (B) — in which way and which *sense* we were on this occasion "using" it. It makes a great difference whether we were advising, or merely suggesting, or actually ordering, whether we were strictly promising or only announcing a vague intention, and so forth. These issues penetrate a little but not without confusion into grammar (see above), but we constantly do debate them, in such terms as whether certain words (a certain locution) *had the force of* a question, or *ought to have been taken as* an estimate and so on.

I explained the performance of an act in this new and second sense as the performance of an "illocutionary" act, i.e., performance of an act *in* saying something as opposed to performance of an act *of* saying something; I call the act performed an "illocution" and shall refer to the doctrine of the different types of function of language here in question as the doctrine of "illocutionary forces."

It may be said that for too long philosophers have neglected this study, treating all problems as problems of "locutionary usage," and indeed that the "descriptive fallacy" mentioned in Lecture I commonly arises through mistaking a problem of the former kind for a problem of the latter kind. True, we are now getting out of this; for some years we have been realizing more and more clearly that the occasion of an utterance matters seriously, and that the words used are to some extent to be "explained" by the "context" in which they are designed to be or have actually been spoken in a linguistic interchange. Yet still perhaps we are too prone to give these explanations in terms of "the meanings of words." Admittedly we can use "meanings" also with reference to illocutionary force — "He meant it as an order," &c. But I want to distinguish *force* and meaning in the sense in which meaning is equivalent to sense and reference, just as it has become essential to distinguish sense and reference.

Moreover, we have here an illustration of the different uses of the expression, "uses of language," or "use of a sentence," &c. — "use" is a hopelessly ambiguous or wide word, just as is the word "meaning," which it has become customary to deride. But "use," its supplanter, is not in much better case. We may entirely clear up the "use of a sentence" on a particular occasion, in the sense of the locutionary act, without yet touching upon its use in the sense of an *illocutionary* act.

Before refining any further on this notion of the illocutionary act, let us contrast both the locutionary *and* the illocutionary act with yet a third kind of act.

There is yet a further sense (C) in which to perform a locutionary act, and therein an illocutionary act, may also be to perform an act of another kind. Saying something will often, or even normally, produce certain consequential effects upon the feelings, thoughts, or actions of the audience, or of the speaker, or of other persons: and it may be done with the design, intention, or purpose of producing them; and we may then say, thinking of this, that the speaker has performed an act in the nomenclature of which reference is made either (C. *a*), only obliquely, or even (C. *b*), not at all, to the performance of the locutionary or illocutionary act. We shall call the performance of an act of this kind the performance of a "perlocutionary" act, and the act performed, where suitable — essentially in cases falling under (C. *a*) — a "perlocution." Let us not yet define this idea any more carefully — of course it needs it — but simply give examples:

(E.1)

Act (A) or Locution
  He said to me "Shoot her!" meaning by "shoot" shoot and referring by "her" to *her*.

Act (B) or Illocution

He urged (or advised, ordered, &c.) me to shoot her.

Act (C. *a*) or Perlocution

He persuaded me to shoot her.

Act (C. *b*)

He got me to (or made me, &c.) shoot her.

(E.2)

Act (A) or Locution

He said to me, "You can't do that."

Act (B) or Illocution

He protested against my doing it.

Act (C. *a*) or Perlocution

He pulled me up, checked me.

Act (C. *b*)

He stopped me, he brought me to my senses, &c.

He annoyed me.

We can similarly distinguish the locutionary act "he said that . . ." from the illocutionary act "he argued that . . ." and the perlocutionary act "he convinced me that . . ."

It will be seen that the "consequential effects" here mentioned (see C. *a* and C. *b*) do not include a particular kind of consequential effects, those achieved, e.g., by way of committing the speaker as in promising, which come into the illocutionary act. Perhaps restrictions need making, as there is clearly a difference between what we feel to be the real production of real effects and what we regard as mere conventional consequences; we shall in any case return later to this.

We have here then roughly distinguished three kinds of acts — the locutionary, the illocutionary, and the perlocutionary. Let us make some general comments on these three classes, leaving them still fairly rough. The first three points will be about "the use of language" again.

(1) Our interest in these lectures is essentially to fasten on the second, illocutionary act and contrast it with the other two. There is a constant tendency in philosophy to elide this in favour of one or other of the other two. Yet it is distinct from both. We have already seen how the expressions "meaning" and "use of sentence" can blur the distinction between locutionary and illocutionary acts. We now notice that to speak of the "use" of language can likewise blur the distinction between the illocutionary and perlocutionary acts — so we will distinguish them more carefully in a minute. Speaking of the "use of 'language' for arguing or warning" looks just like speaking of "the use of 'language' for persuading, rousing, alarming"; yet the former may, for rough contrast, be said to be *conventional*, in the sense that at least it could be made explicit by the performative formula; but the latter could not. Thus we can say "I argue that" or "I warn you that" but we cannot say "I convince you that" or "I alarm you that." Further, we may entirely clear up whether someone was arguing or not without touching on the question whether he was convincing anyone or not.

(2) To take this farther, let us be quite clear that the expression "use of language" can cover other matters even more diverse than the illocutionary and perlocutionary acts and obviously quite diverse from any with which we are here concerned. For example, we may speak of the "use of language" *for* something, e.g. for joking; and we may use "in" in a way different from the illocutionary "in," as when we say "in saying 'p' I was joking" or "acting a part" or "writing poetry"; or again we may speak of "a poetical use of language" as distinct from "the use of language in poetry." These references to "use of language" have nothing to do with the illocutionary act. For example, if I say "Go and catch a falling star," it may be quite clear what both the meaning and the force of my utterance is, but still wholly unresolved which of these other kinds of things I may be doing. There are aetiolations,[3] parasitic uses, etc., various "not serious" and "not full normal" uses. The normal conditions of reference may be suspended, or no attempt made at a standard perlocutionary act, no attempt to make you do anything, as Walt Whitman does not seriously incite the eagle of liberty to soar.

(3) Furthermore, there may be some things we "do" in some connection with saying something which do not seem to fall, intuitively at least, exactly into any of these roughly defined classes, or else seem to fall vaguely into more than one; but any way we do not at the outset feel so clear that they are as remote from our three acts as would be joking or writing poetry. For example, *insinuating*,

[3]Things rendered pale or colorless.

as when we insinuate something in or by issuing some utterance, seems to involve some convention, as in the illocutionary act; but we cannot *say* "I insinuate . . .," and it seems like implying to be a clever effect rather than a mere act. A further example is evincing emotion. We may evince emotion in or by issuing an utterance, as when we swear; but once again we have no use here for performative formulas and the other devices of illocutionary acts. We might say that we use swearing[4] *for* relieving our feelings. We must notice that the illocutionary act is a conventional act: an act done as conforming to a convention.

The next three points that arise do so importantly because our acts are *acts*.

(4) Acts of all our three kinds necessitate, since they are the performing of actions, allowance being made for the ills that all action is heir to. We must systematically be prepared to distinguish between "the act of doing *x*," i.e., achieving *x*, and "the act of attempting to do *x*."

In the case of illocutions we must be ready to draw the necessary distinction, not noticed by ordinary language except in exceptional cases, between

(*a*) the act of attempting or purporting (or affecting or professing or claiming or setting up or setting out) to perform a certain illocutionary act, and

(*b*) the act of successfully achieving or consummating or bringing off such an act.

This distinction is, or should be, a commonplace of the theory of our language about "action" in general. But attention has been drawn earlier to its special importance in connexion with performatives: it is always possible, for example, to try to thank or inform somebody yet in different ways to fail, because he doesn't listen, or takes it as ironical, or wasn't responsible for whatever it was, and so on. This distinction will arise, as over any act, over locutionary acts too; but failures here will not be unhappinesses as there, but rather failures to get the words out, to express ourselves clearly, etc.

(5) Since our acts are actions, we must always remember the distinction between producing effects or consequences which are intended or unintended; and (i) when the speaker intends to produce an effect it may nevertheless not occur, and (ii) when he does not intend to produce it or intends not to produce it it may nevertheless occur. To cope with complication (i) we invoke as before the distinction between attempt and achievement; to cope with complication (ii) we invoke the normal linguistic devices of disclaiming (adverbs like "unintentionally" and so on) which we hold ready for general use in all cases of doing action.[5]

(6) Furthermore, we must, of course, allow that as actions they may be things that we do not exactly *do*, in the sense that we did them, say, under duress or in any other such way. Other ways besides in which we may not fully do the action are given in (2) above. We may, perhaps, add the cases given in (5) where we produce consequences by mistake, did not intend to do so.

(7) Finally we must meet the objection about our illocutionary and perlocutionary acts — namely that the notion of an act is unclear — by a general doctrine about action. We have the idea of an "act" as a fixed physical thing that we do, as distinguished from conventions and as distinguished from consequences. But

(*a*) the illocutionary act and even the locutionary act too involve conventions: compare with them the act of doing obeisance. It is obeisance only because it is conventional and it is done only because it is conventional. Compare also the distinction between kicking a wall and kicking a goal;

(*b*) the perlocutionary act always includes some consequences, as when we say "By doing *x* I was doing *y*": we do bring in a greater or less stretch of "consequences" always, some of which may be "unintentional." There is no restriction to the minimum physical act at all. That we can import an arbitrarily long stretch of what might also be called the "consequences" of our act into the nomenclature of the act itself is, or should be, a fundamental commonplace of the theory of our language about all "action" in general. Thus if

---

[5]This complication (ii), it may be pointed out, can of course also arise in the cases of both locutionary and illocutionary acts. I may say something or refer to something without meaning to, or commit myself unintentionally to a certain undertaking; for example, I may order someone to do something, when I did not intend to order him to do so. But it is in connection with perlocution that it is most prominent, as is also the distinction between attempt and achievement. [Austin]

---

[4]"Swearing" is ambiguous: I swear by Our Lady *is* to swear by Our Lady: but "Bloody" is not to swear by Our Lady. [Austin]

asked "What did he do?," we may reply either "He shot the donkey" or "He fired a gun" or "He pulled the trigger" or "He moved his trigger finger," and all may be correct. So, to shorten the nursery story of the endeavours of the old woman to drive her pig home in time to get her old man's supper, we may in the last resort say that the cat drove or got the pig, or made the pig get, over the stile.[6] If in

[6] Austin is alluding to the British folktale in which, to get her pig home the old woman has to persuade a long series of agents (a cat, a rat, a rope, a butcher, an ox, some water, a fire, a stick, and a dog) to act, each one on the one following, to get the pig over the stile.

such cases we mention both a B act (illocution) and a C act (perlocution) we shall say "*by* B-ing he C-ed" rather than "*in*-B-ing . . ." This is the reason for calling C a *per*locutionary act as distinct from an illocutionary act.

Next time we shall revert to the distinction between our three kinds of acts, and to the expressions "in" and "by doing *x* I am doing *y*," with a view to getting the three classes and their members and non-members somewhat clearer. We shall see that just as the locutionary act embraces doing many things at once to be complete, so may the illocutionary and perlocutionary acts.

Northrop Frye

1912–1991

In his native Canada, Northrop Frye's intellectual stature made him something of a national oracle and celebrity. In the world of literary theory and criticism, he was also a formidable and revered figure. Herman Northrop Frye was born in Sherbrooke, Quebec, received his B.A. from the University of Toronto in 1933, studied theology there at Emmanuel College, and was ordained a minister in 1936. He received an M.A. from Merton College, Oxford, in 1940. In 1948 he became a professor of English at Victoria College, Toronto; in 1959 principal of the college; and in 1967 he became the first University Professor at the University of Toronto. He wrote more than forty books, including *Fearful Symmetry* (1947), *Fables of Identity* (1963), *The Modern Century* (1967), *The Stubborn Structure* (1970), *The Critical Path* (1971), *The Secular Scripture* (1976), *The Great Code* (1982), and his last book, *Words with Power* (1990), which might be known as *The Great Code II*. His most celebrated work is *Anatomy of Criticism* (1957). "The Archetypes of Literature," first published in the *Kenyon Review* (vol. 8, 1951) and later reprinted in *Fables of Identity,* is, in Frye's words, "to some extent a summarized statement of the critical program" later expanded in *Anatomy of Criticism.*[1]

What is most distinctive about Northrop Frye's criticism is its metaphorical relationship to Jungian psychology. Frye was careful to disclaim any belief in a collective unconscious or racial memory, or the dependence of his literary theories upon any such belief. Indeed, Frye reads Jung only as one who has provided "a grammar of literary symbolism," as a textual critic rather than as a psychologist. Nevertheless, for Frye as for Jung, the power of literature comes out of its evocation of archetypes that have a permanent place in human life: the hero and the virgin, the witch and the magus, the quest and the journey, the open green world of the forest and the walled-off city.

But Frye sees mere mystification in Jung's notion that literature originates in a "collective unconscious" stored as racial memory within each individual. For Frye, literature originates in other literature, as stories are broken down into bits and reshaped into other stories. Many of these kernel structures of story arise naturally out of the cyclical patterns of life on a planet that spins circling the sun: The dualistic cycle of day and night, the sense of beginnings, maturation, ripeness, and death that come from the cycle of the agricultural seasons, and the slower parallel cycle that imitates the longer journey from birth to death that each individual and generation must follow. Each generation rewrites the stories of the past in ways that make sense for it, recycling a vast tradition over the ages. The great myths of the gods, created in the vast dream of mankind in an almost prehistoric past, are converted into legends of semidivine heroes, then into stories of people very much like ourselves.

Frye's "The Archetypes of Literature" (1951) promises in effect to go beyond the Jungian criticism of precursors such as Maud Bodkin by presenting not just

---

[1]Northrop Frye, *Fables of Identity: Studies in Poetic Mythology* (New York: Harcourt Brace and World, 1963), p. 1.

fragmentary insights but the "ground plan of a systematic and comprehensive development of criticism." What Frye eventually delivered was the encyclopaedic and highly influential study *Anatomy of Criticism* (1957), in which the schema of archetypal criticism is elaborated much further into an exhaustive mapping of the possibilities of literary form and content. Frye begins with a theory of *modes,* describing five levels of narrative (myth, legend, high mimetic, low mimetic, and ironic), which correspond to the stature and degree of freedom of action of the protagonist. For example, the tragic myth of the dying god of nature might descend to a legend in Malory's *Morte d'Arthur,* a high mimetic epic in Tennyson's *Idylls of the King,* a low mimetic novel in T. H. White's *The Once and Future King,* and an ironic parody in the film *Monty Python and the Holy Grail.*

A second theory of *symbols* differentiates five methods of symbolic interpretation, not unlike Dante's theory of polysemy: (1) In the *literal* approach to the symbol, the very shape of the signifier becomes important; (2) in the *descriptive* phase, the signifier is related to its signified — its usual meaning; (3) in the *formal* phase, the signifier is related to other similar signifiers in patterns of imagery; (4) in the *archetypal* phase, the signifier is related to its ritual significance; and (5) in the *anagogic* phase, the signifier becomes a monad, a symbolic universe in itself, a function of the total dream of mankind.

A third theory of *myth* elaborates on the relationships between comedy, romance, tragedy, and irony discussed in "The Archetypes of Literature," and categorizes them as twenty-four distinct variants on the monomyth of the quest. And finally, the theory of *genres* creates a schema for locating the various forms of presentation — lyric, drama, epos, and fiction — and divides the category of fiction into the forms of novel, romance, confession, and anatomy. Taken together, the four essays that constitute *Anatomy of Criticism* construct a multidimensional space in which one may locate the position of any work of literature and its relationship to any other.

Frye's *Anatomy of Criticism* comes close to fleshing out T. S. Eliot's remark that "the works of literature form an ideal order among themselves." In this direction, Frye seems to reach out toward the Structuralists, who were just beginning work on the Continent. Nevertheless, what is most original about Frye is the practical use he made of the theories of Jung, which is evident in "The Archetypes of Literature."

Selected Bibliography

Adamson, Joseph. *Northrop Frye: A Visionary Life.* London: InBook, 1993.

Boyd, David, and Imre Salusinszky, eds. *Rereading Frye: The Published and Unpublished Works.* Toronto: University of Toronto Press, 1999.

Denham, Robert D. *Northrop Frye: An Enumerative Bibliography.* Metuchen, NJ: Scarecrow Press, 1974.

——. *Northrop Frye: An Annotated Bibliography of Primary and Secondary Sources.* Toronto: University of Toronto Press, 1987.

——. *Northrop Frye: A Bibliography of His Published Writings 1931–2004.* Emory, VA: Iron Mountain, 2004.

Frye, Northrop. *Anatomy of Criticism: Four Essays.* Princeton: Princeton University Press, 1957.

——. *The Great Code: The Bible in Literature.* New York: Harcourt, Brace and Jovanovich, 1983.

Hart, Jonathan. *Northrop Frye: The Theoretical Imagination.* New York and London: Routledge, 1994.

Lee, Alvin A., and Robert D. Denham, eds. *The Legacy of Northrop Frye.* Toronto: University of Toronto Press, 1994.

Wang, Ning, ed. *Northrop Frye: Eastern and Western Perspectives.* Toronto: University of Toronto Press, 2003.

The Archetypes of Literature

I

Every organized body of knowledge can be learned progressively; and experience shows that there is also something progressive about the learning of literature. Our opening sentence has already got us into a semantic difficulty. Physics is an organized body of knowledge about nature, and a student of it says that he is learning physics, not that he is learning nature. Art, like nature, is the subject of a systematic study, and has to be distinguished from the study itself, which is criticism. It is therefore impossible to "learn literature": one learns about it in a certain way, but what one learns, transitively, is the criticism of literature. Similarly, the difficulty often felt in "teaching literature" arises from the fact that it cannot be done: the criticism of literature is all that can be directly taught. So while no one expects literature itself to behave like a science, there is surely no reason why criticism, as a systematic and organized study, should not be, at least partly, a science. Not a "pure" or "exact" science, perhaps, but these phrases form part of a nineteenth-century cosmology which is no longer with us. Criticism deals with the arts and may well be something of an art itself, but it does not follow that it must be unsystematic. If it is to be related to the sciences too, it does not follow that it must be deprived of the graces of culture.

Certainly criticism as we find it in learned journals and scholarly monographs has every characteristic of a science. Evidence is examined scientifically; previous authorities are used scientifically; fields are investigated scientifically; texts are edited scientifically. Prosody is scientific in structure; so is phonetics; so is philology. And yet in studying this kind of critical science the student becomes aware of a centrifugal movement carrying him away from literature. He finds that literature is the central division of the "humanities," flanked on one side by history and on the other by philosophy. Criticism so far ranks only as a subdivision of literature; and hence, for the systematic mental organization of the subject, the student has to turn to the conceptual framework of the historian for events, and to that of the philosopher for ideas. Even the more centrally placed critical sciences, such as textual editing, seem to be part of a "background" that recedes into history or some other nonliterary field. The thought suggests itself that the ancillary critical disciplines may be related to a central expanding pattern of systematic comprehension which has not yet been established, but which, if it were established, would prevent them from being centrifugal. If such a pattern exists, then criticism would be to art what philosophy is to wisdom and history to action.

Most of the central area of criticism is at present, and doubtless always will be, the area of commentary. But the commentators have little sense, unlike the researchers, of being contained within some sort of scientific discipline: they are chiefly engaged, in the words of the gospel hymn, in brightening the corner where they are. If we attempt to get a more comprehensive idea of what criticism is about, we find ourselves wandering over quaking bogs of generalities, judicious pronouncements of value, reflective comments, perorations to works of research, and other consequences of taking the large view. But this part of the critical field is so full of pseudo-propositions, sonorous nonsense that contains no truth and no falsehood, that it obviously exists only because criticism, like nature, prefers a waste space to an empty one.

The term "pseudo-proposition" may imply some sort of logical positivist attitude on my own part.[1] But I would not confuse the significant proposition with the factual one; nor should I consider it advisable to muddle the study of literature with a schizophrenic dichotomy between subjective-emotional and objective-descriptive aspects of meaning, considering that in order to produce any literary meaning at all one has to ignore this dichotomy. I say only that the principles by which one can distinguish a significant from a meaningless statement in criticism are not clearly defined. Our first step, therefore, is to recognize and get rid of meaningless criticism: that is, talking about literature in a way that cannot help to build up a systematic structure of knowledge. Casual value-judgments belong not to criticism but to the history of taste, and reflect, at best, only the social and psychological compulsions which prompted their utterance. All judgments in which the values are not based on literary experience but are sentimental or derived from religious or political prejudice may be regarded as casual. Sentimental judgments are usually based either on nonexistent categories or antitheses ("Shakespeare studied life, Milton books") or on a visceral reaction to the writer's personality. The literary chitchat which makes the reputations of poets boom and crash in an imaginary stock exchange[2] is pseudo-criticism. That wealthy investor Mr. Eliot, after dumping Milton on the market, is now buying him again; Donne has probably reached his peak and will begin to taper off; Tennyson may be in for a slight flutter but the Shelley stocks are still bearish. This sort of thing cannot be part of any systematic study, for a

systematic study can only progress: whatever dithers or vacillates or reacts is merely leisure-class conversation.

We next meet a more serious group of critics who say: the foreground of criticism is the impact of literature on the reader. Let us, then, keep the study of literature centripetal, and base the learning process on a structural analysis of the literary work itself. The texture of any great work of art is complex and ambiguous, and in unravelling the complexities we may take in as much history and philosophy as we please, if the subject of our study remains at the center. If it does not, we may find that in our anxiety to write about literature we have forgotten how to read it.

The only weakness in this approach is that it is conceived primarily as the antithesis of centrifugal or "background" criticism, and so lands us in a somewhat unreal dilemma, like the conflict of internal and external relations in philosophy. Antitheses are usually resolved, not by picking one side and refuting the other, or by making eclectic choices between them, but by trying to get past the antithetical way of stating the problem. It is right that the first effort of critical apprehension should take the form of a rhetorical or structural analysis of a work of art. But a purely structural approach has the same limitation in criticism that it has in biology. In itself it is simply a discrete series of analyses based on the mere existence of the literary structure, without developing any explanation of how the structure came to be what it was and what its nearest relatives are. Structural analysis brings rhetoric back to criticism, but we need a new poetics as well, and the attempt to construct a new poetics out of rhetoric alone can hardly avoid a mere complication of rhetorical terms into a sterile jargon. I suggest that what is at present missing from literary criticism is a co-ordinating principle, a central hypothesis which, like the theory of evolution in biology, will see the phenomena it deals with as parts of a whole. Such a principle, though it would retain the centripetal perspective of structural analysis, would try to give the same perspective to other kinds of criticism too.

The first postulate of this hypothesis is the same as that of any science: the assumption of total coherence. The assumption refers to the

---

[1]Logical positivists, like Ludwig Wittgenstein in the *Tractatus* (1922), believe that many "philosophical" questions are actually meaningless.

[2]Shocking as the admission may be, I was not aware when I wrote this that the same figure had appeared in Mr. Eliot's own essay, "What Is Minor Poetry?" [Frye]

science, not to what it deals with. A belief in an order of nature is an inference from the intelligibility of the natural sciences; and if the natural sciences ever completely demonstrated the order of nature they would presumably exhaust their subject. Criticism, as a science, is totally intelligible; literature, as the subject of a science, is, so far as we know, an inexhaustible source of new critical discoveries, and would be even if new works of literature ceased to be written. If so, then the search for a limiting principle in literature in order to discourage the development of criticism is mistaken. The assertion that the critic should not look for more in a poem than the poet may safely be assumed to have been conscious of putting there is a common form of what may be called the fallacy of premature teleology. It corresponds to the assertion that a natural phenomenon is as it is because Providence in its inscrutable wisdom made it so.

Simple as the assumption appears, it takes a long time for a science to discover that it is in fact a totally intelligible body of knowledge. Until it makes this discovery it has not been born as an individual science, but remains an embryo within the body of some other subject. The birth of physics from "natural philosophy" and of sociology from "moral philosophy" will illustrate the process. It is also very approximately true that the modern sciences have developed in the order of their closeness to mathematics. Thus physics and astronomy assumed their modern form in the Renaissance, chemistry in the eighteenth century, biology in the nineteenth and the social sciences in the twentieth. If systematic criticism, then, is developing only in our day, the fact is at least not an anachronism.

We are now looking for classifying principles lying in an area between two points that we have fixed. The first of these is the preliminary effort of criticism, the structural analysis of the work of art. The second is the assumption that there is such a subject as criticism, and that it makes, or could make, complete sense. We may next proceed inductively from structural analysis, associating the data we collect and trying to see larger patterns in them. Or we may proceed deductively, with the consequences that follow from postulating the unity of criticism. It is clear, of course,

that neither procedure will work indefinitely without correction from the other. Pure induction will get us lost in haphazard guessing; pure deduction will lead to inflexible and oversimplified pigeonholing. Let us now attempt a few tentative steps in each direction, beginning with the inductive one.

II

The unity of a work of art, the basis of structural analysis, has not been produced solely by the unconditioned will of the artist, for the artist is only its efficient cause:[3] it has form, and consequently a formal cause. The fact that revision is possible, that the poet makes changes not because he likes them better but because they are better, means that poems, like poets, are born and not made. The poet's task is to deliver the poem in as uninjured a state as possible, and if the poem is alive, it is equally anxious to be rid of him, and screams to be cut loose from his private memories and associations, his desire for self-expression, and all the other navel-strings and feeding tubes of his ego. The critic takes over where the poet leaves off, and criticism can hardly do without a kind of literary psychology connecting the poet with the poem. Part of this may be a psychological study of the poet, though this is useful chiefly in analyzing the failures in his expression, the things in him which are still attached to his work. More important is the fact that every poet has his private mythology, his own spectroscopic band or peculiar formation of symbols, of much of which he is quite unconscious. In works with characters of their own, such as dramas and novels, the same psychological analysis may be extended to the interplay of characters, though of course, literary psychology would analyze the behavior of such characters only in relation to literary convention.

[3]Here and later in this essay, Frye uses the Aristotelian terminology of the four causes (formal, material, efficient, and final) for the analysis of a manufactured object, but his use of the terminology is quite different from Aristotle's. For Aristotle, the material cause of a poem is language; for Frye, it is "the social conditions and cultural demands which produced it."

There is still before us the problem of the formal cause of the poem, a problem deeply involved with the question of genres. We cannot say much about genres, for criticism does not know much about them. A good many critical efforts to grapple with such words as "novel" or "epic" are chiefly interesting as examples of the psychology of rumor. Two conceptions of the genre, however, are obviously fallacious, and as they are opposite extremes, the truth must lie somewhere between them. One is the pseudo-Platonic conception of genres as existing prior to and independently of creation, which confuses them with mere conventions of form like the sonnet. The other is that pseudobiological conception of them as evolving species which turns up in so many surveys of the "development" of this or that form.

We next inquire for the origin of the genre, and turn first of all to the social conditions and cultural demands which produced it — in other words to the material cause of the work of art. This leads us into literary history, which differs from ordinary history in that its containing categories, "Gothic," "Baroque," "Romantic," and the like are cultural categories, of little use to the ordinary historian. Most literary history does not get as far as these categories, but even so we know more about it than about most kinds of critical scholarship. The historian treats literature and philosophy historically; the philosopher treats history and literature philosophically; and the so-called history of ideas approach marks the beginning of an attempt to treat history and philosophy from the point of view of an autonomous criticism.

But still we feel that there is something missing. We say that every poet has his own peculiar formation of images. But when so many poets use so many of the same images, surely there are much bigger critical problems involved than biographical ones. As Mr. Auden's brilliant essay *The Enchaféd Flood* shows, an important symbol like the sea cannot remain within the poetry of Shelley or Keats or Coleridge: it is bound to expand over many poets into an archetypal symbol of literature. And if the genre has a historical origin, why does the genre of drama emerge from medieval religion in a way so strikingly similar to the way it emerged from Greek religion centuries before? This is a problem of structure rather than

origin, and suggests that there may be archetypes of genres as well as of images.

It is clear that criticism cannot be systematic unless there is a quality in literature which enables it to be so, an order of words corresponding to the order of nature in the natural sciences. An archetype should be not only a unifying category of criticism, but itself a part of a total form, and it leads us at once to the question of what sort of total form criticism can see in literature. Our survey of critical techniques has taken us as far as literary history. Total literary history moves from the primitive to the sophisticated, and here we glimpse the possibility of seeing literature as a complication of a relatively restricted and simple group of formulas that can be studied in primitive culture. If so, then the search for archetypes is a kind of literary anthropology, concerned with the way that literature is informed by preliterary categories such as ritual, myth and folk tale. We next realize that the relation between these categories and literature is by no means purely one of descent, as we find them reappearing in the greatest classics — in fact there seems to be a general tendency on the part of great classics to revert to them. This coincides with a feeling that we have all had: that the study of mediocre works of art, however energetic, obstinately remains a random and peripheral form of critical experience, whereas the profound masterpiece seems to draw us to a point at which we can see an enormous number of converging patterns of significance. Here we begin to wonder if we cannot see literature, not only as complicating itself in time, but as spread out in conceptual space from some unseen center.

This inductive movement towards the archetype is a process of backing up, as it were, from structural analysis, as we back up from a painting if we want to see composition instead of brushwork. In the foreground of the grave-digger scene in *Hamlet,* for instance, is an intricate verbal texture, ranging from the puns of the first clown to the *danse macabre*[4] of the Yorick soliloquy, which we study in the printed text. One step back, and we are in the Wilson Knight and Spurgeon group of critics, listening to the steady rain of

[4]Dance of the dead.

images of corruption and decay.[5] Here too, as the sense of the place of this scene in the whole play begins to dawn on us, we are in the network of psychological relationships which were the main interest of Bradley.[6] But after all, we say, we are forgetting the genre: *Hamlet* is a play, and an Elizabethan play. So we take another step back into the Stoll and Shaw group and see the scene conventionally as part of its dramatic context.[7] One step more, and we can begin to glimpse the archetype of the scene, as the hero's *Liebestod*[8] and first unequivocal declaration of his love, his struggle with Laertes and the sealing of his own fate, and the sudden sobering of his mood that marks the transition to the final scene, all take shape around a leap into and return from the grave that has so weirdly yawned open on the stage.

At each stage of understanding this scene we are dependent on a certain kind of scholarly organization. We need first an editor to clean up the text for us, then the rhetorician and philologist, then the literary psychologist. We cannot study the genre without the help of the literary social historian, the literary philosopher and the student of the "history of ideas," and for the archetype we need a literary anthropologist. But now that we have got our central pattern of criticism established, all these interests are seen as converging on literary criticism instead of receding from it into psychology and history and the rest. In particular, the literary anthropologist who chases the source of the Hamlet legend from the pre-Shakespeare play[9] to Saxo, and from Saxo to nature-myths, is not running away from Shakespeare: he is drawing closer to the archetypal form which Shakespeare

recreated. A minor result of our new perspective is that contradictions among critics, and assertions that this and not that critical approach is the right one, show a remarkable tendency to dissolve into unreality. Let us now see what we can get from the deductive end.

III

Some arts move in time, like music; others are presented in space, like painting. In both cases the organizing principle is recurrence, which is called rhythm when it is temporal and pattern when it is spatial. Thus we speak of the rhythm of music and the pattern of painting; but later, to show off our sophistication, we may begin to speak of the rhythm of painting and the pattern of music. In other words, all arts may be conceived both temporally and spatially. The score of a musical composition may be studied all at once; a picture may be seen as the track of an intricate dance of the eye. Literature seems to be intermediate between music and painting: its words form rhythms which approach a musical sequence of sounds at one of its boundaries, and from patterns which approach the hieroglyphic or pictorial image at the other. The attempts to get as near to these boundaries as possible form the main body of what is called experimental writing. We may call the rhythm of literature the narrative, and the pattern, the simultaneous mental grasp of the verbal structure, the meaning or significance. We hear or listen to a narrative, but when we grasp a writer's total pattern we "see" what he means.

The criticism of literature is much more hampered by the representational fallacy than even the criticism of painting. That is why we are apt to think of narrative as a sequential representation of events in an outside "life," and of meaning as a reflection of some external "idea." Properly used as critical terms, an author's narrative is his linear movement; his meaning is the integrity of his completed form. Similarly an image is not merely a verbal replica of an external object, but any unit of a verbal structure seen as part of a total pattern or rhythm. Even the letters an author spells his words with form part of his imagery, though only in special cases (such as alliteration) would they call for critical notice. Narrative and

---

[5]Caroline Spurgeon and G. Wilson Knight, whose Shakespearean criticism involves the sorting of images into significant clusters.

[6]A. C. Bradley, in *Shakespearean Tragedy* (1904), discussed the relation of character and plot with great depth and subtlety.

[7]Elmer Edgar Stoll (1874–1950) was a historical critic of Shakespeare, author of *Shakespeare Studies* (1927) and *Art and Artifice in Shakespeare,* among many others. George Bernard Shaw, the playwright (1856–1950) wrote outrageous Shakespeare criticism, which has been collected by Edwin Wilson in *Shaw on Shakespeare* (1961).

[8]Love-death.

[9]The putative ur-*Hamlet* from which Shakespeare drew his plot.

meaning thus become respectively, to borrow musical terms, the melodic and harmonic contexts of the imagery.

Rhythm, or recurrent movement, is deeply founded on the natural cycle, and everything in nature that we think of as having some analogy with works of art, like the flower or the bird's song, grows out of a profound synchronization between an organism and the rhythms of its environment, especially that of the solar year. With animals some expressions of synchronization, like the mating dances of birds, could almost be called rituals. But in human life a ritual seems to be something of a voluntary effort (hence the magical element in it) to recapture a lost rapport with the natural cycle. A farmer must harvest his crop at a certain time of year, but because this is involuntary, harvesting itself is not precisely a ritual. It is the deliberate expression of a will to synchronize human and natural energies at that time which produces the harvest songs, harvest sacrifices and harvest folk customs that we call rituals. In ritual, then, we may find the origin of narrative, a ritual being a temporal sequence of acts in which the conscious meaning or significance is latent: it can be seen by an observer, but is largely concealed from the participators themselves. The pull of ritual is toward pure narrative, which, if there could be such a thing, would be automatic and unconscious repetition. We should notice too the regular tendency of ritual to become encyclopedic. All the important recurrences in nature, the day, the phases of the moon, the seasons and solstices of the year, the crises of existence from birth to death, get rituals attached to them, and most of the higher religions are equipped with a definitive total body of rituals suggestive, if we may put it so, of the entire range of potentially significant actions in human life.

Patterns of imagery, on the other hand, or fragments of significance, are oracular in origin, and derive from the epiphanic moment, the flash of instantaneous comprehension with no direct reference to time, the importance of which is indicated by Cassirer in *Myth and Language*.[10] By the time we get them, in the form of proverbs, riddles, commandments, and etiological folk tales, there is already a considerable element of narrative in them. They too are encyclopedic in tendency, building up a total structure of significance, or doctrine, from random and empiric fragments. And just as pure narrative would be an unconscious act, so pure significance would be an incommunicable state of consciousness, for communication begins by constructing narrative.

The myth is the central informing power that gives archetypal significance to the ritual and archetypal narrative to the oracle. Hence the myth *is* the archetype, though it might be convenient to say myth only when referring to narrative, and archetype when speaking of significance. In the solar cycle of the day, the seasonal cycle of the year, and the organic cycle of human life, there is a single pattern of significance, out of which myth constructs a central narrative around a figure who is partly the sun, partly vegetative fertility and partly a god or archetypal human being. The crucial importance of this myth has been forced on literary critics by Jung and Frazer[11] in particular, but the several books now available on it are not always systematic in their approach, for which reason I supply the following table of its phases:

1. The dawn, spring, and birth phase. Myths of the birth of the hero, of revival and resurrection, of creation and (because the four phases are a cycle) of the defeat of the powers of darkness, winter and death. Subordinate characters: the father and the mother. The archetype of romance and of most dithyrambic and rhapsodic poetry.[12]

2. The zenith, summer, and marriage or triumph phase. Myths of apotheosis, of the sacred marriage, and of entering into Paradise. Subordinate characters: the companion and the bride. The archetype of comedy, pastoral, and idyll.

3. The sunset, autumn, and death phase. Myths of fall, of the dying god, of violent death and sacrifice and of the isolation of the hero.

---

[10]Ernst Cassirer, neo-Kantian philosopher (1874–1945): *Myth and Language* (1925).

[11]Sir James Frazer, anthropologist, whose classic work, *The Golden Bough* (1890; 12-volume edition 1907–15), studied primitive myth in various cultures to argue the evolution of human thought from magic to religion and then to science.

[12]In *Anatomy of Criticism* (1957), Frye shifted romance to the summer season and comedy from summer to spring.

Subordinate characters: the traitor and the siren. The archetype of tragedy and elegy.

4. The darkness, winter, and dissolution phase. Myths of the triumph of these powers; myths of floods and the return of chaos, of the defeat of the hero, and Götterdämmerung[13] myths. Subordinate characters: the ogre and the witch. The archetype of satire (see, for instance, the conclusion of *The Dunciad*).

The quest of the hero also tends to assimilate the oracular and random verbal structures, as we can see when we catch the chaos of local legends that results from prophetic epiphanies consolidating into a narrative mythology of departmental gods. In most of the higher religions this in turn has become the same central quest-myth that emerges from ritual, as the Messiah myth became the narrative structure of the oracles of Judaism. A local flood may beget a folk tale by accident, but a comparison of flood stories will show how quickly such tales become examples of the myth of dissolution. Finally, the tendency of both ritual and epiphany to become encyclopedic is realized in the definitive body of myth which constitutes the sacred scriptures of religions. These sacred scriptures are consequently the first documents that the literary critic has to study to gain a comprehensive view of his subject. After he has understood their structure, then he can descend from archetypes to genres, and see how the drama emerges from the ritual side of myth and lyric from the epiphanic or fragmented side, while the epic carries on the central encyclopedic structure.

Some words of caution and encouragement are necessary before literary criticism has clearly staked out its boundaries in these fields. It is part of the critic's business to show how all literary genres are derived from the quest-myth, but the derivation is a logical one within the science of criticism: the quest-myth will constitute the first chapter of whatever future handbooks of criticism may be written that will be based on enough organized critical knowledge to call themselves "introductions" or "outlines" and still be able to live up to their titles. It is only when we try to expound the derivation chronologically that we find ourselves writing pseudo-prehistorical fictions and theories of mythological contact. Again, because psychology and anthropology are more highly developed sciences, the critic who deals with this kind of material is bound to appear, for some time, a dilettante of those subjects. These two phases of criticism are largely undeveloped in comparison with literary history and rhetoric, the reason being the later development of the sciences they are related to. But the fascination which *The Golden Bough* and Jung's book on libido symbols have for literary critics is not based on dilettantism, but on the fact that these books are primarily studies in literary criticism, and very important ones.

In any case the critic who is studying the principles of literary form has a quite different interest from the psychologist's concern with states of mind or the anthropologist's with social institutions. For instance: the mental response to narrative is mainly passive; to significance mainly active. From this fact Ruth Benedict's *Patterns of Culture* develops a distinction between "Apollonian" cultures based on obedience to ritual and "Dionysiac" ones based on a tense exposure of the prophetic mind to epiphany. The critic would tend rather to note how popular literature which appeals to the inertia of the untrained mind puts a heavy emphasis on narrative values, whereas a sophisticated attempt to disrupt the connection between the poet and his environment produces the Rimbaud type of *illumination,* Joyce's solitary epiphanies, and Baudelaire's conception of nature as a source of oracles. Also how literature, as it develops from the primitive to the self-conscious, shows a gradual shift of the poet's attention from narrative to significant values, this shift of attention being the basis of Schiller's distinction between naive and sentimental poetry.[14]

The relation of criticism to religion, when they deal with the same documents, is more complicated. In criticism, as in history, the divine is always treated as a human artifact. God for the critic, whether he finds him in *Paradise Lost* or the Bible, is a character in a human story; and for the critic all epiphanies are explained, not in

---

[13]Twilight of the gods.

[14]See Schiller, p. 298.

terms of the riddle of a possessing god or devil, but as mental phenomena closely associated in their origin with dreams. This once established, it is then necessary to say that nothing in criticism or art compels the critic to take the attitude of ordinary waking consciousness towards the dream or the god. Art deals not with the real but with the conceivable; and criticism, though it will eventually have to have some theory of conceivability, can never be justified in trying to develop, much less assume, any theory of actuality. It is necessary to understand this before our next and final point can be made.

We have identified the central myth of literature, in its narrative aspect, with the quest-myth. Now if we wish to see this central myth as a pattern of meaning also, we have to start with the workings of the subconscious where the epiphany originates, in other words in the dream. The human cycle of waking and dreaming corresponds closely to the natural cycle of light and darkness, and it is perhaps in this correspondence that all imaginative life begins. The correspondence is largely an antithesis: it is in daylight that man is really in the power of darkness, a prey to frustration and weakness; it is in the darkness of nature that the "libido" or conquering heroic self awakes. Hence art, which Plato called a dream for awakened minds, seems to have as its final cause the resolution of the antithesis, the mingling of the sun and the hero, the realizing of a world in which the inner desire and the outward circumstance coincide. This is the same goal, of course, that the attempt to combine human and natural power in ritual has. The social function of the arts, therefore, seems to be closely connected with visualizing the goal of work in human life. So in terms of significance, the central myth of art must be the vision of the end of social effort, the innocent world of fulfilled desires, the free human society. Once this is understood, the integral place of criticism among the other social sciences, in interpreting and systematizing the vision of the artist, will be easier to see. It is at this point that we can see how religious conceptions of the final cause of human effort are as relevant as any others to criticism.

The importance of the god or hero in the myth lies in the fact that such characters, who are conceived in human likeness and yet have more power over nature, gradually build up the vision of an omnipotent personal community beyond an indifferent nature. It is this community which the hero regularly enters in his apotheosis. The world of this apotheosis thus begins to pull away from the rotary cycle of the quest in which all triumph is temporary. Hence if we look at the quest-myth as a pattern of imagery, we see the hero's quest first of all in terms of its fulfillment. This gives us our central pattern of archetypal images, the vision of innocence which sees the world in terms of total human intelligibility. It corresponds to, and is usually found in the form of, the vision of the unfallen world or heaven in religion. We may call it the comic vision of life, in contrast to the tragic vision, which sees the quest only in the form of its ordained cycle.

We conclude with a second table of contents, in which we shall attempt to set forth the central pattern of the comic and tragic visions. One essential principle of archetypal criticism is that the individual and the universal forms of an image are identical, the reasons being too complicated for us just now. We proceed according to the general plan of the game of Twenty Questions, or, if we prefer, of the Great Chain of Being:

1. In the comic vision the *human* world is a community, or a hero who represents the wish-fulfillment of the reader. The archetype of images of symposium, communion, order, friendship, and love. In the tragic vision the human world is a tyranny or anarchy, or an individual or isolated man, the leader with his back to his followers, the bullying giant of romance, the deserted or betrayed hero. Marriage or some equivalent consummation belongs to the comic vision; the harlot, witch, and other varieties of Jung's "terrible mother"[15] belongs to the tragic one. All divine, heroic, angelic, or other superhuman communities follow the human pattern.

2. In the comic vision the *animal* world is a community of domesticated animals, usually a flock of sheep, or a lamb, or one of the gentler

---

[15]The negative projection of the *anima*. See Jung, p. 542.

birds, usually a dove. The archetype of pastoral images. In the tragic vision the animal world is seen in terms of beasts and birds of prey, wolves, vultures, serpents, dragons, and the like.

3. In the comic vision the *vegetable* world is a garden, grove or park, or a tree of life, or a rose or lotus. The archetype of Arcadian images, such as that of Marvell's green world or of Shakespeare's forest comedies. In the tragic vision it is a sinister forest like the one in *Comus* or at the opening of the *Inferno,* or a heath or wilderness, or a tree of death.

4. In the comic vision the *mineral* world is a city, or one building or temple, or one stone, normally a glowing precious stone — in fact, the whole comic series, especially the tree, can be conceived as luminous or fiery. The archetype of geometrical images: the "starlit dome"[16] belongs here. In the tragic vision the mineral world is seen in terms of deserts, rocks and ruins, or of sinister geometrical images like the cross.

5. In the comic vision the *unformed* world is a river, traditionally fourfold, which influenced the Renaissance image of the temperate body with its four humors.[17] In the tragic vision this world usually becomes the sea, as the narrative myth of dissolution is so often a flood myth. The combination of the sea and beast images gives us the leviathan and similar water-monsters.

Obvious as this table looks, a great variety of poetic images and forms will be found to fit it. Yeats's "Sailing to Byzantium," to take a famous example of the comic vision at random, has the city, the tree, the bird, the community of sages, the geometrical gyre and the detachment from the cyclic world. It is, of course, only the general comic or tragic context that determines the interpretation of any symbol: this is obvious with relatively neutral archetypes like the island, which may be Prospero's island or Circe's.[18]

Our tables are, of course, not only elementary but grossly oversimplified, just as our inductive approach to the archetype was a mere hunch. The important point is not the deficiencies of either procedure, taken by itself, but the fact that, somewhere and somehow, the two are clearly going to meet in the middle. And if they do meet, the ground plan of a systematic and comprehensive development of criticism has been established.

---

[16]Yeats's image of inanimate perfection in "Byzantium."
[17]The four humors were blood, bile, choler, and phlegm. Frye's notion of a fourfold balance is similar to Jung's quaternion; see p. 564.

[18]In Shakespeare's *The Tempest* and Homer's *Odyssey,* respectively.

Erich Auerbach

1892–1957

Erich Auerbach was born in Berlin in 1892 and was educated in the law before becoming in 1929 a professor of Romance philology at the University of Marburg. Auerbach was of the generation of German humanists, including Leo Spitzer and Robert Curtius, that developed the fields of comparative literature and history of ideas. In 1936, the year his Marburg colleague Martin Heidegger became chancellor of the University, Auerbach emigrated to Turkey, teaching at the State University of Istanbul.

It was there, deprived of his research library and assistants, that he wrote essays ranging widely from Homer and the Bible to Proust and Woolf that were collected into *Mimesis: The Representation of Reality in Western Literature* (1946; introductory chapter is reprinted here). Auerbach suggests in the "Epilogue" to *Mimesis* that, while the book has unavoidable flaws resulting from his lack of access to books, journals, and even to reliable critical editions of the texts he discusses, he would not have been bold enough to write such a wide-ranging study had they been available to him: "If it had been possible for me to acquaint myself with all the work that has been done on so many subjects, I might never have reached the point of writing" (p. 557). After World War II, Auerbach came to the United States, where he held the Sterling Professorship of Romance Languages at Yale until his death in 1957.

Mimesis is often celebrated as a model of pure literary interpretation and exegesis — as opposed to the products of contemporary literary theory — and indeed it is hard not to wonder at the seeming ease with which Auerbach finds passages and performs analyses that illuminate how certain texts (including Petronius, Gregory of Tours, the Chanson Roland, Dante, Boccaccio, Rabelais, Montaigne, Goethe, Schiller, Balzac, Stendhal, Flaubert, and Zola) purely express the ethos of their eras and cultures. Interestingly, the aim of Auerbach — to discover how discourse is defined by and evokes the cultures of the past — is precisely the aim of the New Historians and Cultural Studies proponents today.

Auerbach's literary-historical vision is far from the postmodern notions of Michel Foucault or Hayden White: It harkens back to the philosophies of Giambattista Vico and G. W. F. Hegel. Like Vico, Auerbach believes that history is not linear, but cyclical. In two different eras, classical Rome and neoclassical Europe, the culture had developed stratified style-systems, with very different languages for treating the "high," "middle," and "low" aspects of life. In both eras there had been a triumphant rebellion against the rigid distinctions of such systems marshalled in terms of a figural realism that incorporated the basest details in the service of the noblest and most significant narratives. Auerbach saw the revolt against the neoclassical ordering of literary styles at the beginning of the nineteenth century (which culminated in the novels of Balzac and Stendhal) not as a unique event but as a return of the rebellion against the classical ordering of styles made first by Augustine and, much later, by Dante.

Like Hegel, Auerbach believes this cyclical movement in history and culture is driven by the dialectical thrust of thesis and antithesis, which gives rise to a transcendent new synthesis. The *Odyssey* and the book of Genesis archetypally stand for the two different approaches to the representation of reality that Auerbach traces through nearly three millennia of history. For Auerbach, Homer presents reality as fixed and definite, lying on the surface, accessible through the selection of details used to sketch characters and events. In Homer past events not only shape the present situation, they also can be represented as present memory through the narrative vision. In the Bible, Auerbach believes, reality is implicit rather than explicit; the figural representation of the patriarchs and kings suggests that the interior truth of their histories is contained in a vision too vast to be expressed in words. Such figural vision therefore demands interpretation and exegesis, in which the individual event becomes iconic for a reality that recurs in later history and can only be fully contained in the mind of God. Auerbach returns to the contrast between Homer and the Bible in later chapters of *Mimesis*, as for example, when he contrasts the limited and static Roman narrative realism (exemplified by the layered details in the portrayal of Trimalchio's banquet in Petronius's *Satyricon*) with the richly implicit figural quality of the Gospels (where Peter's denials of Jesus demand engaged interpretation and complex exegesis precisely because they stand in themselves beyond any simple explanation). In still later chapters, Auerbach observes the recurrence of the same sorts of contrasts between the abstract or schematic and the figural modes of representation in different periods of literature up to that of high modernism. For example, Auerbach contrasts the abstract quality of medieval allegory (such as the *Roman de la Rose*) with the figural quality of Dante's vision of universal history in the *Commedia*. Or using examples from the later nineteenth century, Auerbach contrasts Zola's Petronian use of "low" detail in his *Rougon-Macquart* saga with the more figural treatment of humble life in the novels of Tolstoy and Dostoyevsky.

Auerbach's saga culminates in a discussion of Virginia Woolf's modernism that centers on a passage from *To the Lighthouse*. Auerbach sees Woolf's presentation of the rich meaning within the apparently insignificant moment as iconic of the beauty and goodness he envisions as emerging out of the horror of his own historical era:

> An economic and cultural leveling process is taking place. It is still a long way to a common life of mankind on earth, but the goal begins to be visible. And it is most concretely visible now in the unprejudiced, precise, interior and exterior representation of the random moment in the lives of different people. So the complicated process of dissolution which led to the fragmentation of the exterior action, to the reflection of consciousness, and to the stratification of time [as in Proust] seems to be tending toward a very simple solution (552–53).

This notion of literary modernism as the teleological endpoint of Old Testament realism is one testimony to the utopianism that underlies all of Auerbach's thought and that makes him such an attractive figure today.

Selected Bibliography

Auerbach, Erich. *Mimesis: The Representation of Reality in Western Literature.* Translated by Willard R. Trask. Princeton: Princeton University Press, 1953.
———. *Scenes from the Drama of European Literature: Six Essays.* New York: Meridian Books, 1959.

————. *Dante: Poet of the Secular World.* Translated by Ralph Manheim. Chicago: University of Chicago Press, 1961.

————. *Literary Language and Its Public in Late Latin Antiquity and in the Middle Ages.* Translated by Ralph Manheim. New York: Pantheon Books, 1965.

Bahti, Timothy. "Auerbach's *Mimesis:* Figural Structure and Historical Narrative." In *After Strange Texts,* ed. Gregory S. Jay and David L. Miller. Alabama University Press, 1985, pp. 125–48.

Bové, Paul. *Intellectuals in Power: A Genealogy of Critical Humanism.* New York: Columbia University Press, 1986.

Costa-Lima, Luiz. "Erich Auerbach: History and Metahistory." *New Literary History* 19 (1988): 467–99.

Damrosch, David. "Auerbach in Exile." *Comparative Literature* 47 (1995): 97–117.

Green, Geoffrey. *Literary Criticism and the Structures of History: Erich Auerbach and Leo Spitzer.* Lincoln: University of Nebraska Press, 1982.

Holquist, Michael. "The Last European: Erich Auerbach as Precursor in the History of Cultural Criticism." *Modern Language Quarterly* 54 (1993): 371–91.

Lerer, Seth, ed. *Literary History and the Challenge of Philology: The Legacy of Erich Auerbach.* Stanford: Stanford University Press, 1996.

Manheim, Ralph. "Bibliography of the Writings of Erich Auerbach." In *Literary Language and Its Public in Late Latin Antiquity and in the Middle Ages,* trans. Ralph Manheim. New York: Pantheon Books, 1965, pp. 343–68.

Said, Edward W. "Erich Auerbach, Critic of the Earthly World." *Boundary 2: An International Journal of Literature and Culture* 31 (2004): 11–34.

Sternberg, Meir, et al., eds. *Erich Auerbach and Literary Representation.* Special issue of *Poetics Today* 20 (1999): 3–77.

Odysseus' Scar

Readers of the *Odyssey* will remember the well-prepared and touching scene in book 19, when Odysseus has at last come home, the scene in which the old housekeeper Euryclea, who had been his nurse, recognizes him by a scar on his thigh. The stranger has won Penelope's good will; at his request she tells the housekeeper to wash his feet, which, in all old stories, is the first duty of hospitality toward a tired traveler. Euryclea busies herself fetching water and mixing cold with hot, meanwhile speaking sadly of her absent master, who is probably of the same age as the guest, and who perhaps, like the guest, is even now wandering somewhere, a stranger; and she remarks how astonishingly like him the guest looks. Meanwhile Odysseus, remembering his scar, moves back out of the light; he knows that, despite his efforts to hide his identity, Euryclea will now recognize him, but he wants at least to keep Penelope in ignorance. No sooner has the old woman touched the scar than, in her joyous surprise, she lets Odysseus' foot drop into the basin; the water spills over, she is about to cry out her joy; Odysseus restrains her with whispered threats and endearments; she recovers herself and conceals her emotion. Penelope, whose attention Athena's foresight had diverted from the incident, has observed nothing.

All this is scrupulously externalized and narrated in leisurely fashion. The two women express their feelings in copious direct discourse.

Translated by Willard R. Trask.

Feelings though they are, with only a slight admixture of the most general considerations upon human destiny, the syntactical connection between part and part is perfectly clear, no contour is blurred. There is also room and time for orderly, perfectly well-articulated, uniformly illuminated descriptions of implements, ministrations, and gestures; even in the dramatic moment of recognition, Homer does not omit to tell the reader that it is with his right hand that Odysseus takes the old woman by the throat to keep her from speaking, at the same time that he draws her closer to him with his left. Clearly outlined, brightly and uniformly illuminated, men and things stand out in a realm where everything is visible; and not less clear — wholly expressed, orderly even in their ardor — are the feelings and thoughts of the persons involved.

In my account of the incident I have so far passed over a whole series of verses which interrupt it in the middle. There are more than seventy of these verses — while to the incident itself some forty are devoted before the interruption and some forty after it. The interruption, which comes just at the point when the housekeeper recognizes the scar — that is, at the moment of crisis — describes the origin of the scar, a hunting accident which occurred in Odysseus' boyhood, at a boar hunt, during the time of his visit to his grandfather Autolycus. This first affords an opportunity to inform the reader about Autolycus, his house, the precise degree of the kinship, his character, and, no less exhaustively than touchingly, his behavior after the birth of his grandson; then follows the visit of Odysseus, now grown to be a youth; the exchange of greetings, the banquet with which he is welcomed, sleep and waking, the early start for the hunt, the tracking of the beast, the struggle, Odysseus' being wounded by the boar's tusk, his recovery, his return to Ithaca, his parents' anxious questions — all is narrated, again with such a complete externalization of all the elements of the story and of their interconnections as to leave nothing in obscurity. Not until then does the narrator return to Penelope's chamber, not until then, the digression having run its course, does Euryclea, who had recognized the scar before the digression began, let Odysseus' foot fall back into the basin.

The first thought of a modern reader — that this is a device to increase suspense — is, if not wholly wrong, at least not the essential explanation of this Homeric procedure. For the element of suspense is very slight in the Homeric poems; nothing in their entire style is calculated to keep the reader or hearer breathless. The digressions are not meant to keep the reader in suspense, but rather to relax the tension. And this frequently occurs, as in the passage before us. The broadly narrated, charming, and subtly fashioned story of the hunt, with all its elegance and self-sufficiency, its wealth of idyllic pictures, seeks to win the reader over wholly to itself as long as he is hearing it, to make him forget what had just taken place during the foot-washing. But an episode that will increase suspense by retarding the action must be so constructed that it will not fill the present entirely, will not put the crisis, whose resolution is being awaited, entirely out of the reader's mind, and thereby destroy the mood of suspense; the crisis and the suspense must continue, must remain vibrant in the background. But Homer — and to this we shall have to return later — knows no background. What he narrates is for the time being the only present, and fills both the stage and the reader's mind completely. So it is with the passage before us. When the young Euryclea (vv. 401ff.) sets the infant Odysseus on his grandfather Autolycus' lap after the banquet, the aged Euryclea, who a few lines earlier had touched the wanderer's foot, has entirely vanished from the stage and from the reader's mind.

Goethe and Schiller, who, though not referring to this particular episode, exchanged letters in April 1797 on the subject of "the retarding element" in the Homeric poems in general, put it in direct opposition to the element of suspense — the latter word is not used, but is clearly implied when the "retarding" procedure is opposed, as something proper to epic, to tragic procedure (letters of April 19, 21, and 22). The "retarding element," the "going back and forth" by means of episodes, seems to me, too, in the Homeric poems, to be opposed to any tensional and suspensive striving toward a goal, and doubtless Schiller is right in regard to Homer when he says that what he gives us is "simply the quiet existence and operation of things in accordance with their natures"; Homer's goal is "already present in every point of his progress." But both Schiller and Goethe raise Homer's procedure to the level of a law for epic poetry in general, and Schiller's words quoted above are meant to be universally binding upon the epic poet, in contradistinction from the tragic. Yet in both modern and ancient times, there are important epic works which are composed throughout with no "retarding element" in this sense but, on the contrary, with suspense throughout, and which perpetually "rob us of our emotional freedom" — which power Schiller will grant only to the tragic poet. And besides it seems to me undemonstrable and improbable that this procedure of Homeric poetry was directed by aesthetic considerations or even by an aesthetic feeling of the sort postulated by Goethe and Schiller. The effect, to be sure, is precisely that which they describe, and is, furthermore, the actual source of the conception of epic which they themselves hold, and with them all writers decisively influenced by classical antiquity. But the true cause of the impression of "retardation" appears to me to lie elsewhere — namely, in the need of the Homeric style to leave nothing which it mentions half in darkness and unexternalized.

The excursus upon the origin of Odysseus' scar is not basically different from the many passages in which a newly introduced character, or even a newly appearing object or implement, though it be in the thick of a battle, is described as to its nature and origin; or in which, upon the appearance of a god, we are told where he last was, what he was doing there, and by what road he reached the scene; indeed, even the Homeric epithets seem to me in the final analysis to be traceable to the same need for an externalization of phenomena in terms perceptible to the senses. Here is the scar, which comes up in the course of the narrative; and Homer's feeling simply will not permit him to see it appear out of the darkness of an unilluminated past; it must be set in full light, and with it a portion of the hero's boyhood — just as, in the *Iliad*, when the first ship is already burning and the Myrmidons finally arm that they may hasten to help, there is still time not only for the wonderful simile of the wolf, not only for the order of the Myrmidon host, but also for a detailed account of the ancestry of several subordinate leaders (16, vv. 155ff.). To be sure, the aesthetic effect thus produced was soon noticed and thereafter consciously sought; but the more original cause must have lain in the basic impulse of the Homeric style: to represent phenomena in a fully externalized form, visible and palpable in all their parts, and completely fixed in their spatial and temporal relations. Nor do psychological processes receive any other treatment: here too nothing must remain hidden and unexpressed. With the utmost fullness, with an orderliness which even passion does not disturb, Homer's personages vent their inmost hearts in speech; what they do not say to others, they speak in their own minds, so that the reader is informed of it. Much that is terrible takes place in the Homeric poems, but it seldom takes place wordlessly: Polyphemus talks to Odysseus; Odysseus talks to the suitors when he begins to kill them; Hector and Achilles talk at length, before battle and after; and no speech is so filled with anger or scorn that the particles which express logical and grammatical connections are lacking or out of place. This last observation is true, of course, not only of speeches but of the presentation in general. The separate elements of a phenomenon are most clearly placed in relation to one another; a large number of conjunctions, adverbs, particles, and other syntactical tools, all clearly circumscribed and delicately differentiated in meaning, delimit persons, things, and portions of incidents in respect to one another, and at the same time bring them together in a continuous and ever flexible connection; like the separate phenomena themselves, their relationships — their temporal, local, causal, final, consecutive, comparative, concessive, antithetical, and conditional limitations — are brought to light in perfect fullness; so that a continuous rhythmic procession of phenomena passes by, and never is there a form left fragmentary or half-illuminated, never a lacuna, never a gap, never a glimpse of unplumbed depths.

And this procession of phenomena takes place in the foreground — that is, in a local and temporal present which is absolute. One might think that the many interpolations, the frequent moving back and forth, would create a sort of perspective in time and place; but the Homeric style never gives any such impression. The way in which any impression of perspective is avoided can be clearly observed in the procedure for introducing episodes, a syntactical construction with which every reader of Homer is familiar; it is used in the passage we are considering, but can also be found in cases when the episodes are much shorter. To the word scar (v. 393) there is first attached a relative clause ("which once long ago a boar . . ."), which enlarges into a voluminous syntactical parenthesis; into this an independent sentence unexpectedly intrudes (v. 396: "A god himself gave him . . ."), which quietly disentangles itself from syntactical subordination, until, with verse 399, an equally free syntactical treatment of the new content begins a new present which continues unchallenged until, with verse 467 ("The old woman now touched it . . ."), the scene which had been broken off is resumed. To be sure, in the case of such long episodes as the one we are considering, a purely syntactical connection with the principal theme would hardly have been possible; but a connection with it through perspective would have been all the easier had the content been arranged with that end in view; if, that is, the entire story of the scar had been presented as a recollection which awakens in Odysseus' mind at this particular moment. It would have been perfectly easy to do; the story of the scar had only to be inserted two verses earlier, at the first mention of the word scar, where the motifs "Odysseus" and "recollection" were already at hand. But any such subjectivistic-perspectivistic procedure, creating a foreground and background, resulting in the present lying open to the depths of the past, is entirely foreign to the Homeric style; the Homeric style knows only a foreground, only a uniformly illuminated, uniformly objective present. And so the excursus does not begin until two lines later, when Euryclea has discovered the scar — the possibility for a perspectivistic connection no longer exists, and the story of the wound becomes an independent and exclusive present.

The genius of the Homeric style becomes even more apparent when it is compared with an equally ancient and equally epic style from a different world of forms. I shall attempt this comparison with the account of the sacrifice of Isaac, a homogeneous narrative produced by the so-called Elohist. The King James version translates the opening as follows (Genesis 22:1): "And it came to pass after these things, that God did tempt Abraham, and said to him, Abraham! and he said, Behold, here I am." Even this opening startles us when we come to it from Homer. Where are the two speakers? We are not told. The reader, however, knows that they are not normally to be found together in one place on earth, that one of them, God, in order to speak to Abraham, must come from somewhere, must enter the earthly realm from some unknown heights or depths. Whence does he come, whence does he call to Abraham? We are not told. He does not come, like Zeus or Poseidon, from the Aethiopians, where he has been enjoying a sacrificial feast. Nor are we told anything of his reasons for tempting Abraham so terribly. He has not, like Zeus, discussed them in set speeches with other gods gathered in council; nor have the deliberations in his own heart been presented to us; unexpected and mysterious, he enters the scene from some unknown height or depth and calls: Abraham! It will at once be said that this is to be explained by the particular concept of God which the Jews held and which was wholly different from that of the Greeks. True enough — but this constitutes no objection. For how is the Jewish concept of God to be explained? Even their earlier God of the desert was not fixed in form and content, and was alone; his lack of form, his lack of local habitation, his singleness, was in the end not only maintained but developed even further in competition with the comparatively far more manifest gods of the surrounding Near Eastern world. The concept of God held by the Jews is less a cause than a symptom of their manner of comprehending and representing things.

This becomes still clearer if we now turn to the other person in the dialogue, to Abraham. Where is he? We do not know. He says, indeed: Here I am — but the Hebrew word means only something like "behold me," and in any case is not meant to indicate the actual place where Abraham is, but a moral position in respect to God, who has called to him — Here am I awaiting thy command. Where he is actually, whether in Beersheba or elsewhere, whether indoors or in the open air, is not stated; it does not interest the narrator, the reader is not informed; and what Abraham was doing when God called to him is left in the same obscurity. To realize the difference, consider Hermes' visit to Calypso, for example, where command, journey, arrival and reception of the visitor, situation and occupation of the person visited, are set forth in many verses; and even on occasions when gods appear suddenly and briefly, whether to help one of their favorites or to deceive or destroy some mortal whom they hate, their bodily forms, and usually the manner of their coming and going, are given in detail. Here, however, God appears without bodily form (yet he "appears"), coming from some unspecified place — we only hear his voice, and that utters nothing but a name, a name without an adjective, without a descriptive epithet for the person spoken to, such as is the rule in every Homeric address; and of Abraham too nothing is made perceptible except the words in which he answers God: *Hinne-ni,* Behold me here — with which, to be sure, a most touching gesture expressive of obedience and readiness is suggested, but it is left to the reader to visualize it. Moreover the two speakers are not on the same level: if we conceive of Abraham in the foreground, where it might be possible to picture him as prostrate or kneeling or bowing with outspread arms or gazing upward, God is not there too: Abraham's words and gestures are directed toward the depths of the picture or upward, but in any case the undetermined, dark place from which the voice comes to him is not in the foreground.

After this opening, God gives his command, and the story itself begins: everyone knows it; it unrolls with no episodes in a few independent sentences whose syntactical connection is of the most rudimentary sort. In this atmosphere it is unthinkable that an implement, a landscape through which the travelers passed, the serving-men, or the ass, should be described, that their origin or descent or material or appearance or usefulness should be set forth in terms of praise; they do not even admit an adjective: they are serving-men, ass, wood, and knife, and nothing else, without an epithet; they are there to serve the end which God has commanded; what in other respects they were, are, or will be, remains in

darkness. A journey is made, because God has designated the place where the sacrifice is to be performed; but we are told nothing about the journey except that it took three days, and even that we are told in a mysterious way: Abraham and his followers rose "early in the morning" and "went unto" the place of which God had told him; on the third day he lifted up his eyes and saw the place from afar. That gesture is the only gesture, is indeed the only occurrence during the whole journey, of which we are told; and though its motivation lies in the fact that the place is elevated, its uniqueness still heightens the impression that the journey took place through a vacuum; it is as if, while he traveled on, Abraham had looked neither to the right nor to the left, had suppressed any sign of life in his followers and himself save only their footfalls.

Thus the journey is like a silent progress through the indeterminate and the contingent, a holding of the breath, a process which has no present, which is inserted, like a blank duration, between what has passed and what lies ahead, and which yet is measured: three days! Three such days positively demand the symbolic interpretation which they later received. They began "early in the morning." But at what time on the third day did Abraham lift up his eyes and see his goal? The text says nothing on the subject. Obviously not "late in the evening," for it seems that there was still time enough to climb the mountain and make the sacrifice. So "early in the morning" is given, not as an indication of time, but for the sake of its ethical significance; it is intended to express the resolution, the promptness, the punctual obedience of the sorely tried Abraham. Bitter to him is the early morning in which he saddles his ass, calls his serving-men and his son Isaac, and sets out; but he obeys, he walks on until the third day, then lifts up his eyes and sees the place. Whence he comes, we do not know, but the goal is clearly stated: Jeruel in the land of Moriah.[1]

[1]The particular spot called "Jeruel" appears in the Bible only in 2 Chronicles 20:16 as the wilderness site of a battle between Jehoshaphat, King of Judah and the Moabites and Edomites; it is not mentioned by the narrator of Genesis. Perhaps Auerbach intends the name Abraham subsequently gives to the particular mountain on which the sacrifice was to have taken place, called יהוה יראה in Hebrew

What place this is meant to indicate is not clear — "Moriah" especially may be a later correction of some other word. But in any case the goal was given, and in any case it is a matter of some sacred spot which was to receive a particular consecration by being connected with Abraham's sacrifice. Just as little as "early in the morning" serves as a temporal indication does "Jeruel in the land of Moriah" serve as a geographical indication; and in both cases alike, the complementary indication is not given, for we know as little of the hour at which Abraham lifted up his eyes as we do of the place from which he set forth — Jeruel is significant not so much as the goal of an earthly journey, in its geographical relation to other places, as through its special election, through its relation to God, who designated it as the scene of the act, and therefore it must be named.

In the narrative itself, a third chief character appears: Isaac. While God and Abraham, the serving-men, the ass, and the implements are simply named, without mention of any qualities or any other sort of definition, Isaac once receives an appositive; God says, "Take Isaac, thine only son, whom thou lovest." But this is not a characterization of Isaac as a person, apart from his relation to his father and apart from the story; he may be handsome or ugly, intelligent or stupid, tall or short, pleasant or unpleasant — we are not told. Only what we need to know about him as a personage in the action, here and now, is illuminated, so that it may become apparent how terrible Abraham's temptation is, and that God is fully aware of it. By this example of the contrary, we see the significance of the descriptive adjectives and digressions of the Homeric poems; with their indications of the earlier and as it were absolute existence of the persons described, they prevent the reader from concentrating exclusively on a present crisis; even when the most terrible things are occurring, they prevent the establishment of an overwhelming suspense. But here, in the story

of Abraham's sacrifice, the overwhelming suspense is present; what Schiller makes the goal of the tragic poet — to rob us of our emotional freedom, to turn our intellectual and spiritual powers (Schiller says "our activity") in one direction, to concentrate them there — is effected in this Biblical narrative, which certainly deserves the epithet epic.[2]

We find the same contrast if we compare the two uses of direct discourse. The personages speak in the Bible story too; but their speech does not serve, as does speech in Homer, to manifest, to externalize thoughts — on the contrary, it serves to indicate thoughts which remain unexpressed. God gives his command in direct discourse, but he leaves his motives and his purpose unexpressed; Abraham, receiving the command, says nothing and does what he has been told to do. The conversation between Abraham and Isaac on the way to the place of sacrifice is only an interruption of the heavy silence and makes it all the more burdensome. The two of them, Isaac carrying the wood and Abraham with fire and a knife, "went together." Hesitantly, Isaac ventures to ask about the ram, and Abraham gives the well-known answer. Then the text repeats: "So they went both of them together." Everything remains unexpressed.

It would be difficult, then, to imagine styles more contrasted than those of these two equally ancient and equally epic texts. On the one hand, externalized, uniformly illuminated phenomena, at a definite time and in a definite place, connected together without lacunae in a perpetual foreground; thoughts and feeling completely expressed; events taking place in leisurely fashion and with very little of suspense. On the other hand, the externalization of only so much of the phenomena as is necessary for the purpose of the narrative, all else left in obscurity; the decisive points of the narrative alone are emphasized, what lies between is nonexistent; time and place are undefined and call for interpretation; thoughts and feeling remain unexpressed, are only suggested by the silence and the fragmentary speeches; the

("Jehovahjireh" in the Authorized Version), properly translated "the Lord will see." Auerbach's coinage reverses the order of the original Hebrew, putting a different version of the "God" morpheme (el) at the end, and the "see" morpheme (yr'h) at the beginning.

[2]Schiller's notions of tragedy are presented in "On Tragic Art" and "On the Pleasure We Derive from Tragic Representation," both 1792.

whole, permeated with the most unrelieved suspense and directed toward a single goal (and to that extent far more of a unity), remains mysterious and "fraught with background."

I will discuss this term in some detail, lest it be misunderstood. I said above that the Homeric style was "of the foreground" because, despite much going back and forth, it yet causes what is momentarily being narrated to give the impression that it is the only present, pure and without perspective. A consideration of the Elohistic text teaches us that our term is capable of a broader and deeper application. It shows that even the separate personages can be represented as possessing "background"; God is always so represented in the Bible, for he is not comprehensible in his presence, as is Zeus; it is always only "something" of him that appears, he always extends into depths. But even the human beings in the Biblical stories have greater depths of time, fate, and consciousness than do the human beings in Homer; although they are nearly always caught up in an event engaging all their faculties, they are not so entirely immersed in its present that they do not remain continually conscious of what has happened to them earlier and elsewhere; their thoughts and feelings have more layers, are more entangled. Abraham's actions are explained not only by what is happening to him at the moment, nor yet only by his character (as Achilles' actions by his courage and his pride, and Odysseus' by his versatility and foresightedness), but by his previous history; he remembers, he is constantly conscious of, what God has promised him and what God has already accomplished for him — his soul is torn between desperate rebellion and hopeful expectation; his silent obedience is multilayered, has background. Such a problematic psychological situation as this is impossible for any of the Homeric heroes, whose destiny is clearly defined and who wake every morning as if it were the first day of their lives: their emotions, though strong, are simple and find expression instantly.

How fraught with background, in comparison, are characters like Saul and David! How entangled and stratified are such human relations as those between David and Absalom, between David and Joab! Any such "background" quality of the psychological situation as that which the story of Absalom's death and its sequel (II Samuel 18 and 19, by the so-called Jahvist) rather suggests than expresses, is unthinkable in Homer.[3] Here we are confronted not merely with the psychological processes of characters whose depth of background is veritably abysmal, but with a purely geographical background too. For David is absent from the battlefield; but the influence of his will and his feelings continues to operate, they affect even Joab in his rebellion and disregard for the consequences of his actions; in the magnificent scene with the two messengers, both the physical and psychological background is fully manifest, though the latter is never expressed. With this, compare, for example, how Achilles, who sends Patroclus first to scout and then into battle, loses almost all "presentness" so long as he is not physically present.[4] But the most important thing is the "multilayeredness" of the individual character; this is hardly to be met with in Homer, or at most in the form of a conscious hesitation between two possible courses of action; otherwise, in Homer, the complexity of the psychological life is shown only in the succession and alternation of emotions; whereas the Jewish writers are able to express the simultaneous existence of various layers of consciousness and the conflict between them.

The Homeric poems, then, though their intellectual, linguistic, and above all syntactical culture appears to be so much more highly developed, are yet comparatively simple in their picture of human

[3]The love-hate relationship between Saul and David, the first king of Israel and his worthier successor, is represented throughout the second half of 1 Samuel. In 2 Samuel 13, David's son Absalom kills David's firstborn son Amnon, who had raped Absalom's sister Tamar; subsequently Absalom leads a palace revolt against David that all but succeeds in displacing him; in 2 Samuel 18 Absalom is killed after a battle on the orders of David's general, Joab. Joab himself, though essential to David's security throughout his reign, is often treated by his monarch with contempt, and in 1 Kings 2:5, the dying David advises his son and successor Solomon to have Joab put to death. Auerbach is probably mistaken when he says that 2 Samuel 18 is "by the so-called Jahvist": it is part of what is usually called the "Court History of David" now generally believed to have been written somewhat before the J document of the Pentateuch.

[4]Patroclus obtains Achilles' permission to return to the fighting and achieves both his battle success and his death wound at the hands of Hector in Book 16 of the Iliad.

beings; and no less so in their relation to the real life which they describe in general. Delight in physical existence is everything to them, and their highest aim is to make that delight perceptible to us. Between battles and passions, adventures and perils, they show us hunts, banquets, palaces and shepherds' cots, athletic contests and washing days — in order that we may see the heroes in their ordinary life, and seeing them so, may take pleasure in their manner of enjoying their savory present, a present which sends strong roots down into social usages, landscape, and daily life. And thus they bewitch us and ingratiate themselves to us until we live with them in the reality of their lives; so long as we are reading or hearing the poems, it does not matter whether we know that all this is only legend, "make-believe." The oft-repeated reproach that Homer is a liar takes nothing from his effectiveness, he does not need to base his story on historical reality, his reality is powerful enough in itself; it ensnares us, weaving its web around us, and that suffices him. And this "real" world into which we are lured, exists for itself, contains nothing but itself; the Homeric poems conceal nothing, they contain no teaching and no secret second meaning. Homer can be analyzed, as we have essayed to do here, but he cannot be interpreted. Later allegorizing trends have tried their arts of interpretation upon him, but to no avail. He resists any such treatment; the interpretations are forced and foreign, they do not crystallize into a unified doctrine. The general considerations which occasionally occur (in our episode, for example, v. 360: that in misfortune men age quickly) reveal a calm acceptance of the basic facts of human existence, but with no compulsion to brood over them, still less any passionate impulse either to rebel against them or to embrace them in an ecstasy of submission.

It is all very different in the Biblical stories. Their aim is not to bewitch the senses, and if nevertheless they produce lively sensory effects, it is only because the moral, religious, and psychological phenomena which are their sole concern are made concrete in the sensible matter of life. But their religious intent involves an absolute claim to historical truth. The story of Abraham and Isaac is not better established than the story of Odysseus, Penelope, and Euryclea; both are legendary. But

the Biblical narrator, the Elohist, had to believe in the objective truth of the story of Abraham's sacrifice — the existence of the sacred ordinances of life rested upon the truth of this and similar stories.[5] He had to believe in it passionately; or else (as many rationalistic interpreters believed and perhaps still believe) he had to be a conscious liar — no harmless liar like Homer, who lied to give pleasure, but a political liar with a definite end in view, lying in the interest of a claim to absolute authority.

To me, the rationalistic interpretation seems psychologically absurd; but even if we take it into consideration, the relation of the Elohist to the truth of his story still remains a far more passionate and definite one than is Homer's relation. The Biblical narrator was obliged to write exactly what his belief in the truth of the tradition (or, from the rationalistic standpoint, his interest in the truth of it) demanded of him — in either case, his freedom in creative or representative imagination was severely limited; his activity was perforce reduced to composing an effective version of the pious tradition. What he produced, then, was not primarily oriented toward "realism" (if he succeeded in being realistic, it was merely a means, not an end); it was oriented toward truth. Woe to the man who did not believe it! One can perfectly well entertain historical doubts on the subject of the Trojan War or of Odysseus' wanderings, and still, when reading Homer, feel precisely the effects he sought to produce; but without believing in Abraham's sacrifice, it is possible to put the narrative of it to the use for which it was written. Indeed, we must go even further. The Bible's claim to truth is not only far

[5]The "Elohist" is a term that is sometimes used for the author of the E document, an important strand of Biblical narrative within Genesis, Exodus, and Numbers, probably written during the 9th century B.C.E. in the northern kingdom of Israel. (The name comes from the fact that in this document the deity is referred to as Elohim, usually translated "God." By contrast, the earlier J document, probably created several generations earlier in the southern kingdom of Judah, generally refers to the deity using the unvocalized word YHWH, usually translated "the LORD.") Genesis 22, in which the story of the sacrifice of Isaac takes place, is generally considered to have been written by the Elohist, although there has apparently been some conflation of the E and J texts at this point, since at verses 11 and 14–16, the deity is called YHWH.

more urgent than Homer's, it is tyrannical — it excludes all other claims. The world of the Scripture stories is not satisfied with claiming to be a historically true reality — it insists that it is the only real world, is destined for autocracy. All other scenes, issues, and ordinances have no right to appear independently of it, and it is promised that all of them, the history of all mankind, will be given their due place within its frame, will be subordinated to it. The Scripture stories do not, like Homer's, court our favor, they do not flatter us that they may please us and enchant us — they seek to subject us, and if we refuse to be subjected we are rebels.

Let no one object that this goes too far, that not the stories, but the religious doctrine, raises the claim to absolute authority; because the stories are not, like Homer's, simply narrated "reality." Doctrine and promise are incarnate in them and inseparable from them; for that very reason they are fraught with "background" and mysterious, containing a second, concealed meaning. In the story of Isaac, it is not only God's intervention at the beginning and the end, but even the factual and psychological elements which come between, that are mysterious, merely touched upon, fraught with background; and therefore they require subtle investigation and interpretation, they demand them. Since so much in the story is dark and incomplete, and since the reader knows that God is a hidden God, his effort to interpret it constantly finds something new to feed upon. Doctrine and the search for enlightenment are inextricably connected with the physical side of the narrative — the latter being more than simple "reality"; indeed they are in constant danger of losing their own reality, as very soon happened when interpretation reached such proportions that the real vanished.

If the text of the Biblical narrative, then, is so greatly in need of interpretation on the basis of its own content, its claim to absolute authority forces it still further in the same direction. Far from seeking, like Homer, merely to make us forget our own reality for a few hours, it seeks to overcome our reality: we are to fit our own life into its world, feel ourselves to be elements in its structure of universal history. This becomes increasingly difficult the further our historical environment is removed from

that of the Biblical books; and if these nevertheless maintain their claim to absolute authority, it is inevitable that they themselves be adapted through interpretative transformation. This was for a long time comparatively easy; as late as the European Middle Ages it was possible to represent Biblical events as ordinary phenomena of contemporary life, the methods of interpretation themselves forming the basis for such a treatment. But when, through too great a change in environment and through the awakening of a critical consciousness, this becomes impossible, the Biblical claim to absolute authority is jeopardized; the method of interpretation is scorned and rejected, the Biblical stories become ancient legends, and the doctrine they had contained, now dissevered from them, becomes a disembodied image.

As a result of this claim to absolute authority, the method of interpretation spread to traditions other than the Jewish. The Homeric poems present a definite complex of events whose boundaries in space and time are clearly delimited; before it, beside it, and after it, other complexes of events, which do not depend upon it, can be conceived without conflict and without difficulty. The Old Testament, on the other hand, presents universal history: it begins with the beginning of time, with the creation of the world, and will end with the Last Days, the fulfilling of the Covenant, with which the world will come to an end. Everything else that happens in the world can only be conceived as an element in this sequence; into it everything that is known about the world, or at least everything that touches upon the history of the Jews, must be fitted as an ingredient of the divine plan; and as this too became possible only by interpreting the new material as it poured in, the need for interpretation reaches out beyond the original Jewish-Israelitish realm of reality — for example to Assyrian, Babylonian, Persian, and Roman history; interpretation in a determined direction becomes a general method of comprehending reality; the new and strange world which now comes into view and which, in the form in which it presents itself, proves to be wholly unutilizable within the Jewish religious frame, must be so interpreted that it can find a place there. But this process nearly always also reacts upon the frame, which requires enlarging and modifying. The most striking piece of interpretation of this sort occurred in the first century of the Christian era, in consequence of Paul's mission to the Gentiles: Paul and the Church Fathers reinterpreted the entire Jewish tradition as a succession of figures prognosticating the appearance of Christ, and assigned the Roman Empire its proper place in the divine plan of salvation. Thus while, on the one hand, the reality of the Old Testament presents itself as complete truth with a claim to sole authority, on the other hand that very claim forces it to a constant interpretative change in its own content; for millennia it undergoes an incessant and active development with the life of man in Europe.

The claim of the Old Testament stories to represent universal history, their insistent relation — a relation constantly redefined by conflicts — to a single and hidden God, who yet shows himself and who guides universal history by promise and exaction, gives these stories an entirely different perspective from any the Homeric poems can possess. As a composition, the Old Testament is incomparably less unified than the Homeric poems, it is more obviously pieced together — but the various components all belong to one concept of universal history and its interpretation. If certain elements survived which did not immediately fit in, interpretation took care of them; and so the reader is at every moment aware of the universal religio-historical perspective which gives the individual stories their general meaning and purpose. The greater the separateness and horizontal disconnection of the stories and groups of stories in relation to one another, compared with the *Iliad* and the *Odyssey,* the stronger is their general vertical connection, which holds them all together and which is entirely lacking in Homer. Each of the great figures of the Old Testament, from Adam to the prophets, embodies a moment of this vertical connection. God chose and formed these men to the end of embodying his essence and will — yet choice and formation do not coincide, for the latter proceeds gradually, historically, during the earthly life of him upon whom the choice has fallen. How the process is accomplished, what terrible trials such a formation

inflicts, can be seen from our story of Abraham's sacrifice. Herein lies the reason why the great figures of the Old Testament are so much more fully developed, so much more fraught with their own biographical past, so much more distinct as individuals, than are the Homeric heroes. Achilles and Odysseus are splendidly described in many well-ordered words, epithets cling to them, their emotions are constantly displayed in their words and deeds — but they have no development, and their life-histories are clearly set forth once and for all. So little are the Homeric heroes presented as developing or having developed, that most of them — Nestor, Agamemnon, Achilles — appear to be of an age fixed from the very first. Even Odysseus, in whose case the long lapse of time and the many events which occurred offer so much opportunity for biographical development, shows almost nothing of it. Odysseus on his return is exactly the same as he was when he left Ithaca two decades earlier. But what a road, what a fate, lie between the Jacob who cheated his father out of his blessing and the old man whose favorite son has been torn to pieces by a wild beast! — between David the harp player, persecuted by his lord's jealousy, and the old king, surrounded by violent intrigues, whom Abishag the Shunnamite warmed in his bed, and he knew her not![6] The old man, of whom we know how he has become what he is, is more of an individual than the young man; for it is only during the course of an eventful life that men are differentiated into full individuality; and it is this history of a personality which the Old Testament presents to us as the formation undergone by those whom God has chosen to be examples. Fraught with their development, sometimes even aged to the verge of dissolution, they show a distinct stamp of individuality entirely foreign to the Homeric heroes.

[6] Jacob cheats his brother Esau out of his father Isaac's blessing in Genesis 27; Jacob's favorite son Joseph is misrepresented by his older brothers as having been torn to pieces by a wild beast in Genesis 37:33. The jealous persecution of the youthful court musician David by King Saul begins in 1 Samuel 18 and ends only with Saul's life; the aged David's failure to carnally know his bedmate Abishag the Shunnamite is recounted in 1 Kings 1.

Time can touch the latter only outwardly, and even that change is brought to our observation as little as possible; whereas the stern hand of God is ever upon the Old Testament figures; he has not only made them once and for all and chosen them, but he continues to work upon them, bends them and kneads them, and, without destroying them in essence, produces from them forms which their youth gave no grounds for anticipating. The objection that the biographical element of the Old Testament often springs from the combination of several legendary personages does not apply; for this combination is a part of the development of the text. And how much wider is the pendulum swing of their lives than that of the Homeric heroes! For they are bearers of the divine will, and yet they are fallible, subject to misfortune and humiliation — and in the midst of misfortune and in their humiliation their acts and words reveal the transcendent majesty of God. There is hardly one of them who does not, like Adam, undergo the deepest humiliation — and hardly one who is not deemed worthy of God's personal intervention and personal inspiration. Humiliation and elevation go far deeper and far higher than in Homer, and they belong basically together. The poor beggar Odysseus is only masquerading, but Adam is really cast down, Jacob really a refugee, Joseph really in the pit and then a slave to be bought and sold. But their greatness, rising out of humiliation, is almost superhuman and an image of God's greatness. The reader clearly feels how the extent of the pendulum's swing is connected with the intensity of the personal history — precisely the most extreme circumstances, in which we are immeasurably forsaken and in despair, or immeasurably joyous and exalted, give us, if we survive them, a personal stamp which is recognized as the product of a rich existence, a rich development. And very often, indeed generally, this element of development gives the Old Testament stories a historical character, even when the subject is purely legendary and traditional.

Homer remains within the legendary with all his material, whereas the material of the Old Testament comes closer and closer to history as the narrative proceeds; in the stories of David the historical report predominates. Here too, much that is legendary still remains, as for example the story of David and Goliath; but much — and the most essential — consists in things which the narrators knew from their own experience or from firsthand testimony. Now the difference between legend and history is in most cases easily perceived by a reasonably experienced reader. It is a difficult matter, requiring careful historical and philological training, to distinguish the true from the synthetic or the biased in a historical presentation; but it is easy to separate the historical from the legendary in general. Their structure is different. Even where the legendary does not immediately betray itself by elements of the miraculous, by the repetition of well-known standard motives, typical patterns and themes, through neglect of clear details of time and place, and the like, it is generally quickly recognizable by its composition. It runs far too smoothly. All cross-currents, all friction, all that is casual, secondary to the main events and themes, everything unresolved, truncated, and uncertain, which confuses the clear progress of the action and the simple orientation of the actors, has disappeared. The historical event which we witness, or learn from the testimony of those who witnessed it, runs much more variously, contradictorily, and confusedly; not until it has produced results in a definite domain are we able, with their help, to classify it to a certain extent; and how often the order to which we think we have attained becomes doubtful again, how often we ask ourselves if the data before us have not led us to a far too simple classification of the original events! Legend arranges its material in a simple and straightforward way; it detaches it from its contemporary historical context, so that the latter will not confuse it; it knows only clearly outlined men who act from few and simple motives and the continuity of whose feelings and actions remains uninterrupted. In the legends of martyrs, for example, a stiff-necked and fanatical persecutor stands over against an equally stiff-necked and fanatical victim; and a situation so complicated — that is to say, so real and historical — as that in which the "persecutor" Pliny finds himself in his celebrated letter to Trajan on the subject of the

Christians, is unfit for legend.[7] And that is still a comparatively simple case. Let the reader think of the history which we are ourselves witnessing; anyone who, for example, evaluates the behavior of individual men and groups of men at the time of the rise of National Socialism in Germany, or the behavior of individual peoples and states before and during the last war, will feel how difficult it is to represent historical themes in general, and how unfit they are for legend;[8] the historical comprises a great number of contradictory motives in each individual, a hesitation and ambiguous groping on the part of groups; only seldom (as in the last war) does a more or less plain situation, comparatively simple to describe, arise, and even such a situation is subject to division below the surface, is indeed almost constantly in danger of losing its simplicity; and the motives of all the interested parties are so complex that the slogans of propaganda can be composed only through the crudest simplification — with the result that friend and foe alike can often employ the same ones. To write history is so difficult that most historians are forced to make concessions to the technique of legend.

It is clear that a large part of the life of David as given in the Bible contains history and not legend. In Absalom's rebellion, for example, or in the scenes from David's last days, the contradictions and crossing of motives both in individuals and in the general action have become so concrete that it is impossible to doubt the historicity of the information conveyed. Now the men who composed the historical parts are often the same who edited the older legends too; their peculiar religious concept of man in history, which we have attempted to describe above, in no way led them to a legendary simplification of events; and so it is only natural that, in the legendary passages of the Old Testament, historical structure is frequently discernible — of course, not in the sense that the traditions are examined as to their credibility according to the methods of scientific criticism; but simply to the extent that the tendency to a smoothing down and harmonizing of events, to a simplification of motives, to a static definition of characters which avoids conflict, vacillation, and development, such as are natural to legendary structure, does not predominate in the Old Testament world of legend. Abraham, Jacob, or even Moses produces a more concrete, direct, and historical impression than the figures of the Homeric world — not because they are better described in terms of sense (the contrary is the case) but because the confused, contradictory multiplicity of events, the psychological and factual cross-purposes, which true history reveals, have not disappeared in the representation but still remain clearly perceptible. In the stories of David, the legendary, which only later scientific criticism makes recognizable as such, imperceptibly passes into the historical; and even in the legendary, the problem of the classification and interpretation of human history is already passionately apprehended — a problem which later shatters the framework of historical composition and completely overruns it with prophecy; thus the Old Testament, in so far as it is concerned with human events, ranges through all three domains: legend, historical reporting, and interpretative historical theology.

Connected with the matters just discussed is the fact that the Greek text seems more limited and more static in respect to the circle of personages involved in the action and to their political activity. In the recognition scene with which we began, there appears, aside from Odysseus and Penelope, the housekeeper Euryclea, a slave whom Odysseus' father Laertes had bought long before. She, like the swineherd Eumaeus, has

---

[7]The younger Pliny (Gaius Plinius Caecilius Secundus, C.E. 61–113), nephew of the more famous author of the *Natural History* who perished at the eruption of Pompeii, had been made governor of the province of Bithynia around 111 by the Roman emperor Trajan. During his fifteen months in office, Pliny was required to try persons accused of being Christians and execute those found guilty; inexperienced at this practice, he wrote to Trajan (*Epistola* 96) to confirm the emperor's approval of his course of action: pardoning those who denied or recanted, ignoring anonymous accusations, but sternly meting out the letter of the law to those who admitted their beliefs and refused to recant.

[8]The reader should be reminded that Auerbach was writing *Mimesis* while in self-imposed exile from his native Germany, which he had fled when the Nazis attempted to impose their ideology upon the University of Marburg, where he had taught.

spent her life in the service of Laertes' family; like Eumaeus, she is closely connected with their fate, she loves them and shares their interests and feelings. But she has no life of her own, no feelings of her own; she has only the life and feelings of her master. Eumaeus too, though he still remembers that he was born a freeman and indeed of a noble house (he was stolen as a boy), has, not only in fact but also in his own feeling, no longer a life of his own, he is entirely involved in the life of his masters. Yet these two characters are the only ones whom Homer brings to life who do not belong to the ruling class. Thus we become conscious of the fact that in the Homeric poems life is enacted only among the ruling class — others appear only in the role of servants to that class. The ruling class is still so strongly patriarchal, and still itself so involved in the daily activities of domestic life, that one is sometimes likely to forget their rank. But they are unmistakably a sort of feudal aristocracy, whose men divide their lives between war, hunting, marketplace councils, and feasting, while the women supervise the maids in the house. As a social picture, this world is completely stable; wars take place only between different groups of the ruling class; nothing ever pushes up from below. In the early stories of the Old Testament the patriarchal condition is dominant too, but since the people involved are individual nomadic or half-nomadic tribal leaders, the social picture gives a much less stable impression; class distinctions are not felt. As soon as the people completely emerges — that is, after the exodus from Egypt — its activity is always discernible, it is often in ferment, it frequently intervenes in events not only as a whole but also in separate groups and through the medium of separate individuals who come forward; the origins of prophecy seem to lie in the irrepressible politico-religious spontaneity of the people. We receive the impression that the movements emerging from the depths of the people of Israel-Judah must have been of a wholly different nature from those even of the later ancient democracies — of a different nature and far more elemental.

With the more profound historicity and the more profound social activity of the Old Testament text, there is connected yet another important distinction from Homer: namely, that a different conception of the elevated style and of the sublime is to be found here. Homer, of course, is not afraid to let the realism of daily life enter into the sublime and tragic; our episode of the scar is an example, we see how the quietly depicted, domestic scene of the foot-washing is incorporated into the pathetic and sublime action of Odysseus' homecoming. From the rule of the separation of styles which was later almost universally accepted and which specified that the realistic depiction of daily life was incompatible with the sublime and had a place only in comedy or, carefully stylized, in idyl — from any such rule Homer is still far removed. And yet he is closer to it than is the Old Testament. For the great and sublime events in the Homeric poems take place far more exclusively and unmistakably among the members of a ruling class; and these are far more untouched in their heroic elevation than are the Old Testament figures, who can fall much lower in dignity (consider, for example, Adam, Noah, David, Job); and finally, domestic realism, the representation of daily life, remains in Homer in the peaceful realm of the idyllic, whereas, from the very first, in the Old Testament stories, the sublime, tragic, and problematic take shape precisely in the domestic and commonplace: scenes such as those between Cain and Abel, between Noah and his sons, between Abraham, Sarah, and Hagar, between Rebekah, Jacob, and Esau, and so on, are inconceivable in the Homeric style. The entirely different ways of developing conflicts are enough to account for this. In the Old Testament stories the peace of daily life in the house, in the fields, and among the flocks, is undermined by jealousy over election and the promise of a blessing, and complications arise which would be utterly incomprehensible to the Homeric heroes. The latter must have palpable and clearly expressible reasons for their conflicts and enmities, and these work themselves out in free battles; whereas, with the former, the perpetually smouldering jealousy and the connection between the domestic and the spiritual, between the paternal blessing and the divine blessing, lead to daily life being permeated with the stuff of conflict, often with poison. The sublime influence of God here reaches so deeply into the everyday that the two realms of the sublime and the everyday are not only actually unseparated but basically inseparable.

We have compared these two texts, and, with them, the two kinds of style they embody, in order to reach a starting point for an investigation into the literary representation of reality in European culture. The two styles, in their opposition, represent basic types: on the one hand fully externalized description, uniform illumination, uninterrupted connection, free expression, all events in the foreground, displaying unmistakable meanings, few elements of historical development and of psychological perspective; on the other hand, certain parts brought into high relief, others left obscure, abruptness, suggestive influence of the unexpressed, "background" quality, multiplicity of meanings and the need for interpretation, universal-historical claims, development of the concept of the historically becoming, and preoccupation with the problematic.

Homer's realism is, of course, not to be equated with classical-antique realism in general; for the separation of styles, which did not develop until later, permitted no such leisurely and externalized description of everyday happenings; in tragedy especially there was no room for it; furthermore, Greek culture very soon encountered the phenomena of historical becoming and of the "multilayeredness" of the human problem, and dealt with them in its fashion; in Roman realism, finally, new and native concepts are added. We shall go into these later changes in the antique representation of reality when the occasion arises; on the whole, despite them, the basic tendencies of the Homeric style, which we have attempted to work out, remained effective and determinant down into late antiquity.

Since we are using the two styles, the Homeric and the Old Testament, as starting points, we have taken them as finished products, as they appear in the texts; we have disregarded everything that pertains to their origins, and thus have left untouched the question whether their peculiarities were theirs from the beginning or are to be referred wholly or in part to foreign influences. Within the limits of our purpose, a consideration of this question is not necessary; for it is in their full development, which they reached in early times, that the two styles exercised their determining influence upon the representation of reality in European literature.

Hans-Georg Gadamer

1900–2002

Hans-Georg Gadamer was born the son of a chemistry professor at the University of Breslau, the provincial capital of Silesia, which is now called Wroclow in Poland. Against his parents' wishes, Gadamer began to study philosophy at the University of Marburg. Studying under the Neo-Kantian philosophers Hermann Cohen[1] and Paul Natorp, Gadamer earned his doctorate at the age of twenty-two. He continued postgraduate work at Marburg and in 1923 came under the influence of Martin Heidegger, who had just arrived as a *privatdozent* and who remained Gadamer's friend for life.

Gadamer began teaching at Marburg in 1929 — around the time Heidegger left to take up the vacated chair of his teacher, Edmund Husserl — and was named professor of philosophy in 1937. In 1938 he moved to the University of Leipzig, where he stayed throughout the war years. He was appointed rector of the university in 1946 and helped rebuild after the damage caused by the war, but he left Leipzig (which was in the eastern sector) as the result of his growing dissatisfaction with and distrust of the communist government. In 1948 Gadamer went to Frankfurt and then to the University of Heidelberg, where he succeeded the theologian Karl Jaspers as chair of the department of philosophy, and where he trained the literary theorists Wolfgang Iser and Hans Robert Jauss, who founded a school of reader-response theory in Constanz.[2] Since retiring from Heidelberg in 1968, Gadamer has taught as a visiting professor all over the world, returning most often to Boston College. Gadamer died in 2002 at the remarkable age of 102, having lived in two different centuries.

The originality of Gadamer's thought, paradoxically enough, began when he came under the influence of Martin Heidegger. Heidegger, a student of the phenomenologist Edmund Husserl, was then working out the details of his major treatise, *Being and Time;* Gadamer adopted some of the same principles as Heidegger but developed them into what was primarily a theory of knowledge and interpretation, rather than a theory of being and action.

Gadamer's philosophical field is usually called "hermeneutics," from the Greek god Hermes who was associated with hidden writings, codes, and mysteries. Hermeneutics is a study of how people make interpretations out of encoded texts. The field dates back to the late eighteenth century when it was becoming clear that the most important text of all — the Judeo-Christian Bible — was a compilation of a number of sources by various authors who had quite disparate moral and literary intentions. It became quintessentially important for theologians, particularly Protestant theologians, to evaluate one interpretation or method of interpretation against another, in order to

---

[1]The relatively unknown Cohen seems to have played an instrumental part in the formation of some of the most important literary and philosophical thinkers of the twentieth century, including not only Gadamer and Martin Heidegger, who studied with him, but also Mikhail Bakhtin, who learned of his work through a Petersburg friend, Matvey Kagan. Interestingly, Cohen's best students reacted *against* his idealism, producing theories of worldly knowledge and action that contradicted it.

[2]See the introduction to Reader-Response Theory, p. 962.

develop a sense of how and how far interpretations of texts could be trusted. Today, of course, hermeneutics is a major issue in relation to secular literary as well as biblical texts: The question of whether it is possible to achieve an "objective" interpretation of a particular literary text, or to develop criteria by which one interpretation can be preferred to another, remains very much with us today.

The title of Gadamer's treatise, from which the following selection is taken, is *Truth and Method* (1960). It is an ironic title, in a way, because "truth" and "method" are the key terms of scientific thought after Descartes: The objective and inductive scientific methods are seen as the way to objective truth. The question Gadamer asked was whether the "human sciences" (art and literature, but also history and cultural studies) should be modeled on the natural sciences — whether you could find or create a method that would lead to truth in any discipline. His answer came out of his sense of human experience and of art's place in that experience. Gadamer agreed with Heidegger that our sense of experience is structured by our placement in time, the place into which we are thrown. He postulated that art is by nature a sort of game that we play, a game whose rules we learn as we go along and that changes us as we play it. Given the shifting, contingent position of the observing subject, Gadamer concluded that the search for objective truth in aesthetic interpretation based upon a special hermeneutical method was a fool's errand. We could never know what a text meant. The best we could achieve was what he called an "effective-historical understanding."

Gadamer entered the debate over hermeneutics in reaction to the post-Kantian hermeneutic theories associated with Friedrich Schleiermacher (1778–1841) and Wilhelm Dilthey (1833–1911). Schleiermacher argued that the interpreter's job is to place himself in the position of the author, to project himself into the author's subjectivity, and in that way try to understand not only the author's intended meaning, but also meanings that may not have been present to the author's consciousness. Dilthey saw more clearly than Schleiermacher that historical change was involved in the problem of finding an author's meaning, that the reader had to seek out the mental structures authors create in accordance with the demands of their worldviews, which are the worldviews of their age. Both Schleiermacher and Dilthey argued that the business of the interpreter of texts is to clear his or her mind of the prejudices and the mental detritus of the present age, so as to be able to enter, with a clean mental slate, the world of the author. For Gadamer, such a clean slate — the "reading-degree-zero" that Dilthey postulated — can never exist, because one's consciousness is defined by, and therefore cannot get outside of, the culture one inhabits. Objective truth is therefore impossible. When one exists in a world, one automatically perceives that world — and its texts — through the "horizon" of meaning that the culture of the present moment provides. Whereas Gadamer's metaphor of the "horizon" suggests the limit of vision imposed by one's physical position in *space*, he argues that our mental horizons are limited not by space but by our position in *time*.

The keys to interpretation, for Gadamer, are the very prejudices through which one reads. The English word *prejudice* has a pejorative cast, summoning up thoughts of a kangaroo court that judges and condemns before it has heard the facts.

But the German word Gadamer uses, *Vorurteilungen*, literally "fore-understandings," has nothing of this juridical flavor. Gadamer claims that without the fore-understanding our prejudices provide it would be impossible to achieve any effective-historical understanding of the past. For Gadamer, the voices of tradition and authority that can be barriers to scientific discovery are, in the human sciences, a part of what constitutes us as historical beings living in a world of time.

Interpretive reading, then, is a dialogical activity for Gadamer, in which the meaning-horizon of the reader and the meaning-horizon of the text impinge upon each other. We do not need a special scientific "method": we are always already fusing our own horizon with that of the text. When we read a text whose origins go back in time, we are often surprised, "brought up short," by what it says and the way it says it. When this happens, we enter into a dialogue with the text, asking questions and receiving answers in ways that begin to blend what Gadamer calls the "horizons" of the text and the "horizons" of the reader. Part of what links these two horizons is the force of a community of readers, a "tradition" of interpretation whose authority is earned by the wisdom and insight of those who have helped to constitute it. The force of such tradition is not absolute, but it inevitably conditions the kinds of issues we can raise and the kinds of questions we can ask.

As a result of our interaction with the text, we as readers not only come to understand the text better, we also come to understand ourselves better, in that we become more conscious of the historical place from which we interpret. We use the tradition, and in using it we remake it as something new. Consequently, the "prejudices" or "fore-understandings" through which we interpret texts of the past are not a fixed set of ideas but are themselves constituted and altered by our use of them.

All this seems to suggest a rigid division between the "human sciences," where truth is the product of an inevitably subjective interaction between text and reader, and the "hard sciences," which depend upon an objective scientific method, where the observer has no influence on what he or she observes. But phenomenological approaches to science, such as that of Thomas J. Kuhn, have suggested that the vaunted objectivity of science is only an enabling myth, and that something like Gadamer's notion of "fore-understanding" — in the shape of the "paradigms" that define scientific problems and the methodologies of their investigation — plays exactly the same role within scientific discovery that it does in historical or literary interpretation.

Selected Bibliography

Arnswald, Ulrich, and Jens Kertscher, eds. *Gadamer's Century: Essays in Honor of Hans-Georg Gadamer.* Cambridge: MIT Press, 2002.

Block, Ed, Jr. "Critical Perspectives on Hans-Georg Gadamer." *Renascence: Essays on Values in Literature* 56 (2004): 215–92.

Code, Lorraine, and Nancy Tuama, eds. *Feminist Interpretations of Hans-Georg Gadamer.* University Park: Pennsylvania State University Press, 2003.

Devereaux, Mary. "Can Art Save Us? A Meditation on Gadamer." *Philosophy and Literature* 15 (1991): 59–73.

Gadamer, Hans-Georg. *Truth and Method,* 1960; London: Sheed and Ward, 1975.

Holub, Robert C. *Reception Theory: A Critical Introduction.* London: Methuen, 1984.

Ingram, David. "Hermeneutics and Truth." In *Hermeneutics and Praxis,* ed. Robert Hollinger. Notre Dame: University of Notre Dame Press, 1985, pp. 32–53.

Misgeld, Dieter. "On Gadamer's Hermeneutics." In *Hermeneutics and Praxis,* ed. Robert Hollinger. Notre Dame: University of Notre Dame Press, 1985, pp. 143–70.

Palmer, L.M. "Gadamer and the Enlightenment's 'Prejudice against All Prejudices.' " *Clio* 22 (1993): 369–82.

Silverman, Hugh J., ed. *Gadamer and Hermeneutics.* London and New York: Routledge, 1991.

Weinsheimer, Joel. *Gadamer's Hermeneutics: A Reading of Truth and Method.* New Haven: Yale University Press, 1985.

———. *Philosophical Hermeneutics and Literary Theory.* New Haven: Yale University Press, 1991.

The Elevation of the Historicality of Understanding to the Status of Hermeneutical Principle

(A) THE HERMENEUTIC CIRCLE AND THE PROBLEM OF PREJUDICES

(i) Heidegger's Disclosure of the Fore-Structure of Understanding

Heidegger went into the problems of historical hermeneutics and criticism only in order to develop from it, for the purposes of ontology, the fore-structure of understanding.[1] Contrariwise, our question is how hermeneutics, once freed from the ontological obstructions of the scientific concept of objectivity, can do justice to the historicality of understanding. The way in which hermeneutics has traditionally understood itself is based on its character as art or technique.[2] This is true even of Dilthey's extension of hermeneutics to become an organon of the human sciences. It may be asked whether there is such a thing as this art or technique of understanding — we shall come back to the point. But at any rate we may inquire into the consequences that Heidegger's fundamental derivation of the circular structure of understanding from the temporality of Therebeing has for the hermeneutics of the human sciences. These consequences do not need to be such that a theory is applied to practice and the latter now be performed differently, i.e., in a way that is technically correct. They could also consist in a correction (and purification of inadequate manners) of the way in which constantly exercised understanding understands itself — a procedure that would benefit the art of understanding at most only indirectly.

Hence we shall examine once more Heidegger's description of the hermeneutical circle in order to use, for our own purpose, the new fundamental significance acquired here by the circular structure. Heidegger writes: "It is not to be reduced to the level of a vicious circle, or even of a circle which is merely tolerated. In the circle is hidden a positive possibility of the most primordial kind of knowing. To be sure, we genuinely take hold of this possibility only when, in our interpretation, we have understood that our first, last and constant

---

Translated by Garrett Burden and John Cumming.

[1] Heidegger, *Being and Time,* p. 312ff. [Gadamer]

[2] Cf. Schleiermacher's *Hermeneutik* (ed H. Kimmerle in *Abhandlungen der Heidelberger Akademie,* 1959, 2nd *Abhandlung*), which is explicitly committed to the old ideal of technique (p. 127, note: "I . . . hate it when theory does not go beyond nature and the bases of art, whose object it is.") [Gadamer]

task is never to allow our fore-having, fore-sight, and fore-conception to be presented to us by fancies and popular conceptions, but rather to make the scientific theme secure by working out these fore-structures in terms of the things themselves." (*Being and Time*)

What Heidegger works out here is not primarily a demand on the practice of understanding, but is a description of the way in which interpretation through understanding is achieved. The point of Heidegger's hermeneutical thinking is not so much to prove that there is a circle as to show that this circle possesses an ontologically positive significance. The description as such will be obvious to every interpreter who knows what he is about.[3] All correct interpretation must be on guard against arbitrary fancies and the limitations imposed by imperceptible habits of thought and direct its gaze "on the things themselves" (which, in the case of the literary critic, are meaningful texts, which themselves are again concerned with objects). It is clear that to let the object take over in this way is not a matter for the interpreter of a single decision, but is "the first, last and constant task." For it is necessary to keep one's gaze fixed on the thing throughout all the distractions that the interpreter will constantly experience in the process and which originate in himself. A person who is trying to understand a text is always performing an act of projecting. He projects before himself a meaning for the text as a whole as soon as some initial meaning emerges in the text. Again, the latter emerges only because he is reading the text with particular expectations in regard to a certain meaning. The working out of this fore-project, which is constantly revised in terms of what emerges as he penetrates into the meaning, is understanding what is there.

This description is, of course, a rough abbreviation of the whole. The process that Heidegger describes is that every revision of the fore-project is capable of projecting before itself a new project

of meaning, that rival projects can emerge side by side until it becomes clearer what the unity of meaning is, that interpretation begins with fore-conceptions that are replaced by more suitable ones. This constant process of new projection is the movement of understanding and interpretation. A person who is trying to understand is exposed to distraction from fore-meanings that are not borne out by the things themselves. The working-out of appropriate projects, anticipatory in nature, to be confirmed "by the things" themselves, is the constant task of understanding. The only "objectivity" here is the confirmation of a fore-meaning in its being worked out. The only thing that characterizes the arbitrariness of inappropriate fore-meanings is that they come to nothing in the working-out. But understanding achieves its full potentiality only when the fore-meanings that it uses are not arbitrary. Thus it is quite right for the interpreter not to approach the text directly, relying solely on the fore-meaning at once available to him, but rather to examine explicitly the legitimacy, i.e., the origin and validity, of the fore-meanings present within him.

This fundamental requirement must be seen as the radicalization of a procedure that in fact we exercise whenever we understand anything. Every text presents the task of not simply employing unexamined our own linguistic usage — or in the case of a foreign language the usage that we are familiar with from writers or from daily intercourse. We regard our task as rather that of deriving our understanding of the text from the linguistic usage of the time of the author. The question is, of course, to what extent this general requirement can be fulfilled. In the field of semantics, in particular, we are confronted with the problem of the unconscious nature of our own use of language. How do we discover that there is a difference between our own customary usage and that of the text?

I think we must say that it is generally the experience of being pulled up short by the text. Either it does not yield any meaning or its meaning is not compatible with what we had expected. It is this that makes us take account of possible difference in usage. It is a general presupposition that can be questioned only in particular cases that someone who speaks the same language as I

[3]Cf. E. Staiger's description, which is in accord with that of Heidegger, in *Die Kunst der Interpretation,* p. 11ff. I do not however, agree that the work of a literary critic begins only "when we are in the situation of a contemporary reader." This is something we never are, and yet we are capable of understanding, although we can never achieve a definite "personal or temporal identity" with the author. [Gadamer]

do uses the words in the sense familiar to me. The same thing is true in the case of a foreign language, i.e., that we all think we have a normal knowledge of it and assume this normal usage when we are reading a text.

What is true of the fore-meaning of usage, however, is equally true of the fore-meanings with regard to content with which we read texts, and which make up our fore-understanding. Here too we may ask how we can break the spell of our own notion that what is stated in a text will fit perfectly with my own meanings and expectations. On the contrary, what another person tells me, whether in conversation, letter, book or whatever, is generally thought automatically to be his own and not my opinion; and it is this that I am to take note of without necessarily having to share it. But this presupposition is not something that makes understanding easier, but harder, in that the fore-meanings that determine my own understanding can go entirely unnoticed. If they give rise to misunderstandings, how can misunderstandings of a text be recognized at all if there is nothing else to contradict? How can a text be protected from misunderstanding from the start?

If we examine the situation more closely, however, we find that meanings cannot be understood in an arbitrary way. Just as we cannot continually misunderstand the use of a word without its affecting the meaning of the whole, so we cannot hold blindly to our own fore-meaning of the thing if we would understand the meaning of another. Of course this does not mean that when we listen to someone or read a book we must forget all our fore-meanings concerning the content, and all our own ideas. All that is asked is that we remain open to the meaning of the other person or of the text. But this openness always includes our placing the other meaning in a relation with the whole of our own meanings or ourselves in a relation to it. Now it is the case that meanings represent a fluid variety of possibilities (when compared with the agreement presented by a language and a vocabulary), but it is still not the case that within this variety of what can be thought, i.e., of what a reader can find meaningful and hence expect to find, everything is possible, and if a person fails to hear what the other person is really saying, he will not be able to place correctly what he has misunderstood within the range of his own various expectations of meaning. Thus there is a criterion here also. The hermeneutical task becomes automatically a questioning of things and is always in part determined by this. This places hermeneutical work on a firm basis. If a person is trying to understand something, he will not be able to rely from the start on his own chance previous ideas, missing as logically and stubbornly as possible the actual meaning of the text until the latter becomes so persistently audible that it breaks through the imagined understanding of it. Rather, a person trying to understand a text is prepared for it to tell him something. That is why a hermeneutically trained mind must be, from the start, sensitive to the text's quality of newness. But this kind of sensitivity involves neither "neutrality" in the matter of the object nor the extinction of one's self, but the conscious assimilation of one's own fore-meanings and prejudices. The important thing is to be aware of one's own bias, so that the text may present itself in all its newness and thus be able to assert its own truth against one's own fore-meanings.

When Heidegger showed that what we call the "reading of what is there" is the fore-structure of understanding, this was, phenomenologically, completely correct. He also showed by an example the task that arises from this. In *Being and Time* he gave a concrete example, in the question of being, of the general statement that was, for him, a hermeneutical problem.[4] In order to explain the hermeneutical situation of the question of being in regard to fore-having, fore-sight and fore-conception, he critically applied his question, directed at metaphysics, to important turning-points in the history of metaphysics. Here he was actually doing simply what the historical, hermeneutical consciousness requires in every case. Methodologically conscious understanding will be concerned not merely to form anticipatory ideas, but to make them conscious, so as to check them and thus acquire right understanding from the things themselves. This is what Heidegger means when he talks about "securing" our scientific theme by deriving our fore-having, fore-sight and fore-conceptions from the things themselves.

[4]*Being and Time,* pp. 312ff. [Gadamer]

It is not, then, at all a case of safeguarding our-selves against the tradition that speaks out of the text but, on the contrary, to keep everything away that could hinder us in understanding it in terms of the thing. It is the tyranny of hidden prejudices that makes us deaf to the language that speaks to us in tradition. Heidegger's demonstration that the concept of consciousness in Descartes and of spirit in Hegel is still influenced by Greek substance-ontology, which sees being in terms of what is present and actual, undoubtedly goes beyond the self-understanding of modern meta-physics, yet not in an arbitrary, willful way, but on the basis of a fore-having that in fact makes this tradition intelligible by revealing the ontological premises of the concept of subjectivity. On the other hand, Heidegger discovers in Kant's critique of "dogmatic" metaphysics the idea of a meta-physics of the finite which is a challenge to his own ontological scheme. Thus he "secures" the scientific theme by framing it within the under-standing of tradition and so putting it, in a sense, at risk. This is the concrete form of the historical consciousness that is involved in understanding.

This recognition that all understanding inevitably involves some prejudice gives the hermeneutical problem its real thrust. By the light of this insight it appears that historicism, despite its critique of rationalism and of natural law phi-losophy, is based on the modern enlightenment and unknowingly shares its prejudices. And there is one prejudice of the enlightenment that is essential to it: the fundamental prejudice of the enlightenment is the prejudice against prejudice itself, which deprives tradition of its power.

Historical analysis shows that it is not until the enlightenment that the concept of prejudice acquires the negative aspect we are familiar with. Actually "prejudice" means a judgment that is given before all the elements that determine a sit-uation have been finally examined. In German legal terminology a "prejudice" is a provisional legal verdict before the final verdict is reached. For someone involved in a legal dispute, this kind of judgment against him affects his chances adversely. Accordingly, the French *préjudice,* as well as the Latin *praejudicium,* means simply "adverse effect," "disadvantage," "harm." But this negative sense is only a consecutive one. The negative consequence depends precisely on the positive validity, the value of the provisional decision as a prejudgment, which is that of any precedent.

Thus "prejudice" certainly does not mean a false judgment, but it is part of the idea that it can have a positive and a negative value. This is due clearly to the influence of the Latin *praejudicium.* There are such things as *préjugés légitimes.* This seems a long way from our current use of the word. The German *Vorurteil,* like English "preju-dice" and even more than the French *préjugé,* seems to have become limited in its meaning, through the enlightenment and its critique of reli-gion, and have the sense simply of an "unfounded judgment."[5] It is only its having a basis, a methodological justification (and not the fact that it may be actually correct) that gives a judgment its dignity. The lack of such a basis does not mean, for the enlightenment, that there might be other kinds of certainty, but rather that the judg-ment does not have any foundation in the facts themselves, i.e., that it is "unfounded." This is a conclusion only in the spirit of rationalism. It is the reason for the discrediting of prejudices and the claim by scientific knowledge completely to exclude them.

Modern science, in adopting this principle, is following the rule of Cartesian doubt of accepting nothing as certain which can in any way be doubted, and the idea of the method that adheres to this requirement. In our introductory observa-tions we have already pointed out how difficult it is to harmonize the historical knowledge that helps to shape our historical consciousness with this ideal and how difficult it is, for that reason, for the modern concept of method to grasp its true nature. This is the place to turn these negative statements into positive ones. The concept of the "prejudice" is where we can make a beginning. . . .

[5]Cf. Leo Strauss, *Die Religionskritik Spinozas,* p. 163: "The word 'prejudice' is the most suitable expression for the great aim of the enlightenment, the desire for free, untram-meled verification; the *Vorurteil* is the unambiguous polemical correlate of the very ambiguous word 'freedom.' " [Gadamer]

(B) PREJUDICES AS CONDITIONS OF UNDERSTANDING

(ii) The Classical Example

It is a lot to ask of the self-understanding of the human sciences to detach itself, in the whole of its activity, from the model of the natural sciences and to regard the historical movement of whatever it is concerned with not simply as an impairment of its objectivity, but as something of positive value. There are, however, in the recent development of the human sciences points at which reflection could start that would really do justice to the problem. The naive methodologism of historical research no longer dominates the field alone. The progress of inquiry is no longer universally seen within the framework of the expansion or penetration into new fields or material, but instead as the attaining of a higher stage of reflection in the problem. Even where this happens, thinking is still teleological, in terms of the progress of research, in a way appropriate to the scientist. But a hermeneutical consciousness is gradually growing which is infusing the attitude of inquiry with a spirit of self-criticism; this is true, above all, of those human sciences that have the oldest tradition. Thus the study of classical antiquity, after it had worked over the whole extent of the available transmitted texts, continually applied itself again, with more subtle questions, to the old favorite objects of its study. This introduced something of an element of self-criticism, in that it reflected on what constituted the real merit of its favorite objects. The concept of the classical, that since Droysen's[6] discovery of Hellenism had reduced historical thinking to a mere stylistic concept, now acquired a new scientific legitimacy.

It requires hermeneutical reflection of some sophistication to discover how it is possible for a normative concept such as that of the classical to acquire or regain its scientific legitimacy. For it follows from the self-understanding of historical consciousness that all normative significance of

the past is ultimately dissolved by the now sovereign historical reason. Only at the beginnings of historicism, as for example in Winckelmann's[7] epoch-making work, was the normative element still a real motive of historical research.

The concept of classical antiquity and of the classical, such as dominated pedagogical thought in particular, since the days of German classicism, had both a normative and an historical side. A particular stage in the historical development of man was thought to have produced a mature and perfect formation of man. This combination of a normative and an historical meaning in the concept goes back to Herder.[8] But Hegel[9] still preserved this combination, even though he gave it another emphasis in terms of the history of philosophy. Classical art retained its special excellence for him through being seen as the "religion of art." Since this is a form of the spirit that is past, it is exemplary only in a qualified sense. The fact that it is a past art testifies to the "past" character of art in general. Hegel used this to justify systematically the historicization of the concept of the classical and introduced that process of development that finally made the classical into a descriptive stylistic concept that describes the brief harmony of measure and fullness that comes between archaic rigidity and baroque dissolution. Since it became part of the aesthetic vocabulary of historical studies, the concept of the classical has preserved the reference to a normative content only in an unacknowledged way.

It was indicative of the start of historical self-criticism when classical studies started to examine themselves after the first world war in relation to a new humanism, and hesitantly again brought out the combination of the normative and

---

[6]Johann Gustav Droysen, German historian (1808–1884), author of celebrated histories of Alexander the Great (1833) and of Hellenism (1836–43).

[7]Johann Joachim Winckelmann, German archeologist (1717–1768), most famous for his *History of Ancient Art* (1764), which set up the ideal of Greek sculpture as noble simplicity and calm greatness.

[8]Johann Gottfried von Herder, German philosopher and philologist of the Romantic era (1744–1803). His *Ideas toward a Philosophy of History* sets up an evolutionary theory of history that prefigures Darwin's notions of adaptation to environment and struggle for existence.

[9]See the introduction to Hegel, p. 369.

the historical elements in "the classical."[10] It proved, however, impossible (although the attempt was made) to interpret the concept of the classical that arose in antiquity and was operative in the canonization of certain writers as if it had itself expressed the unity of a stylistic ideal.[11] On the contrary, the ancient concept was wholly ambiguous. When today we use "classic" as an historical stylistic concept that has a clear meaning by being set against what came before and after, this concept has become quite detached from the ancient one. The concept of the "classical" now signifies a period of time, the period of an historical development, but does not signify any suprahistorical value.

In fact, however, the normative element in the concept of the classical has never completely disappeared. It is still the basis of the idea of liberal education. The classicist is, rightly, not satisfied with simply applying to his texts the historical stylistic concept that has developed through the history of the plastic arts. The question that suggests itself, whether Homer is also "classical," shatters the historical stylistic category of the classical that is used in an analogy with the history of art — an instance of the fact that historical consciousness always includes more than it acknowledges of itself.

If we try to see what these implications mean, we might say that the classical is a truly historical category, precisely in that it is more than a concept of a period or an historical stylistic one and that yet it does not seek to be a suprahistorical concept of value. It does not refer to a quality that we assign to particular historical phenomena, but to a notable mode of "being historical," the historical process of preservation that, through the constant proving of itself, sets before us something that is true. It is not at all the case, as the historical mode of thought would have us believe,

that the value judgment through which something is dubbed classical was in fact destroyed by historical reflection and its criticism of all teleological constructions of the process of history. The value judgment that is implicit in the concept of the classical gains, rather, through this criticism a new, real legitimacy. The classical is what resists historical criticism because its historical dominion, the binding power of its validity that is preserved and handed down, precedes all historical reflection and continues through it.

To take the key example of the blanket concept of "classical antiquity," it is, of course, unhistorical to devalue the hellenistic as an age of the decline and fall of classicism, and Droysen has rightly emphasized its importance and its place within the continuity of history for the birth and spread of christianity. But he would not have needed to undertake this historical apologetic if there had not always been a prejudice in favor of the classical and if the culture of humanism had not held on to "classical antiquity" and preserved it within Western culture as the heritage of the past. The classical is fundamentally something quite different from a descriptive concept used by an objectivizing historical consciousness. It is a historical reality to which historical consciousness belongs and is subordinate. What we call "classical" is something retrieved from the vicissitudes of changing time and its changing taste. It can be approached directly, not through that, as it were, electric touch that sometimes characterizes a contemporary work of art and in which the fulfillment of an apprehension of meaning that surpasses all conscious expectation is instantaneously experienced. Rather it is a consciousness of something enduring, of significance that cannot be lost and is independent of all the circumstances of time, in which we call something "classical" — a kind of timeless present that is contemporaneous with every other age.

So the first thing about the concept of the classical (and this is wholly true of both the ancient and the modern use of the word) is the normative sense. But insofar as this norm is related retrospectively to a past entity that fulfilled and embodied it, it always contains a temporal quality that articulates it historically. So it was not surprising that, with the rise of historical reflection in

---

[10]The congress at Naumburg on the classical (1930), which was completely dominated by Werner Jaeger, is as much an example of this as the founding of the periodical *Die Antike*. Cf *Das Problem des Klassischen und die Antike* (1931). [Gadamer]

[11]Cf. the legitimate criticism that A. Körte made of the Naumburg lecture by J. Stroux, in the *Berichte der Sächsischen Akademie der Wissenchaften* 86, 1934, and my note in *Gnomon* 11 (1935), p. 612f. [Gadamer]

Germany which took as its standard the classicism of Winckelmann, an historical concept of a time or a period detached itself from what was regarded as classical in Winckelmann's sense and denoted a quite specific stylistic ideal and, in a historically descriptive way, also a time or period that fulfilled this ideal. From the distance of the Epigones, who set up the criterion, it becomes clear that this stylistic ideal was fulfilled at a particular past moment of the world's history. Accordingly, the concept of the classical came to be used in modern thought to describe the whole of "classical antiquity" when humanism proclaimed anew the exemplary nature of this antiquity. It was taking up an ancient usage, with some justification, for those ancient authors who were "discovered" by humanism were the same ones that, for the later period of antiquity, comprised the canon of classics.

They were preserved in the history of Western culture precisely because they became canonical as the writers of the "school." But it is easy to see how the historical stylistic concept was able to follow this usage. For although it is a normative consciousness that is behind this concept, it is still a retrospective element. It is an awareness of decline and distance that gives birth to the classical norm. It is not by accident that the concept of the classical and of classical style emerges in late periods. The *Dialogus* of Callimachus and Tacitus has been decisive in this connection.[12] But there is something else. Those authors who are regarded as classical are, as we know, always the representatives of particular literary genres. They were considered as the perfect fulfilment of the norm of that literary genre, an ideal that the

retrospective view of literary criticism makes plain. If we now examine these norms of literary genres historically, i.e., if we consider their history, then the classical is seen as the concept of a stylistic phase, of a climax that articulates the history of the genre in terms of before and after. Insofar as the climactic points in the history of genres come largely within the same brief period of time, the classical, within the totality of the historical development of classical antiquity, refers to such a period and thus also becomes a concept denoting a period: this concept fuses with the stylistic one.

As this kind of historical stylistic concept, the concept of the classical is capable of being extended to any "development" to which an immanent telos gives unity. And in fact all cultures have high periods, in which a particular civilization is marked by special achievements in all fields. Thus the general value concept of the classical becomes, via its particular historical fulfilment, again a general historical stylistic concept.

Although this is an understandable development, the historicization of the concept also involves its uprooting, and that is why historical consciousness, when it started to engage in self-criticism, reinstated the normative element in the concept of the classical and the historical uniqueness of its fulfilment. Every "new humanism" shares, with the first and oldest, the awareness of being directly committed to its model which, as something past, is unattainable and yet present. Thus there culminates in the classical a general character of historical being, preservation amid the ruins of time. It is the general nature of tradition that only that of the past which is preserved offers the possibility of historical knowledge. The classical, however, as Hegel says, is "that which signifies itself and hence also interprets itself."[13] But that means ultimately that the classical is what is preserved precisely because it signifies and interprets itself: i.e., that which speaks in such a way that it is not a statement about what is past, a mere testimony to something that still needs to be interpreted, but says something to the present as if it were said specially to it. What we

---

[12]Thus the *Dialogus de oratoribus,* rightly, received special attention in the Naumburg discussions on the classical. The reasons for the decline of rhetoric include the recognition of its former greatness, i.e., a normative awareness. B. Snell is correct when he points out that the historical stylistic concepts of "baroque," "archaic" etc all presuppose a relation to the normative concept of the classical and have only gradually lost their pejorative sense: "Wesen und Wirklichkeit des Menschen." *Festschrift für H. Plessner,* p. 333ff. [Gadamer] Callimachus was a Greek poet and grammarian who flourished around 250 B.C.E. Cornelius Tacitus, the great Roman historian (ca. 55–120), also wrote a *Dialogue on Orators* analyzing the causes of the decay of eloquence under the Roman empire.

[13]Hegel, *Ästhetik* II, 3. [Gadamer]

call "classical" does not first require the overcoming of historical distance, for in its own constant communication it does overcome it. The classical, then, is certainly "timeless," but this timelessness is a mode of historical being.

Of course this does not exclude the fact that works regarded as classical present tasks of historical understanding to a developed historical consciousness that is aware of the historical distance. It is not the aim of the historical consciousness to use the classical model in the direct way of Palladio or Corneille,[14] but to know it as an historical phenomenon that can be understood solely in terms of its own time. But this understanding will always be more than the mere historical construction of the past "world" to which the work belongs. Our understanding will always include consciousness of our belonging to that world. And correlative to this is the fact that the work belongs to our world.

This is just what the word "classical" means, that the duration of the power of a work to speak directly is fundamentally unlimited.[15] However much the concept of the classical expresses distance and unattainability and is part of cultural awareness, the phrase "classical culture" still expresses something of the continuing validity of the classical. Cultural awareness manifests an element of ultimate community and sharing in the world out of which a classical work speaks.

This discussion of the concept of the classical does not lay claim to any independent significance, but serves only to evoke a general question, namely: Does this kind of historical fusion of the past with the present that characterizes what is classical, ultimately lie at the base of the whole historical attitude as its effective substratum? Whereas romantic hermeneutics had taken

human nature as the unhistorical substratum of its theory of understanding and hence had freed the connatural interpreter from all historical limitations, the self-criticism of historical consciousness leads finally to seeing historical movement not only in process, but also in understanding itself. Understanding is not to be thought of so much as an action of one's subjectivity, but as the placing of oneself within a process of tradition, in which past and present are constantly fused. This is what must be expressed in hermeneutical theory, which is far too dominated by the idea of a process, a method.

(iii) The Hermeneutic Significance of Temporal Distance

Let us consider first how hermeneutics sets about its work. What follows for understanding from the hermeneutic condition of belonging to a tradition? We remember here the hermeneutical rule that we must understand the whole in terms of the detail and the detail in terms of the whole. This principle stems from ancient rhetoric, and modern hermeneutics has taken it and applied it to the art of understanding. It is a circular relationship in both cases. The anticipation of meaning in which the whole is envisaged becomes explicit understanding in that the parts, that are determined by the whole, themselves also determine this whole.

We know this from the learning of ancient languages. We learn that we must "construe" a sentence before we attempt to understand the individual parts of the sentence in their linguistic meaning. But this process of construing is itself already governed by an expectation of meaning that follows from the context of what has gone before. It is also necessary for this expected meaning to be adjusted if the text calls for it. This means, then, that the expectation changes and that the text acquires the unity of a meaning from another expected meaning. Thus the movement of understanding is constantly from the whole to the part and back to the whole. Our task is to extend in concentric circles the unity of the understood meaning. The harmony of all the details with the whole is the criterion of correct understanding. The failure to achieve this harmony means that understanding has failed.

[14]Andrea Palladio, Italian architect (1518–1580), produced an enormously influential four-volume folio on classical architecture that in the next century brought in the neoclassical style. Pierre Corneille, French playwright and critic (1606–1684), had a similarly classicizing impact on European drama.

[15]Friedrich Schlegel (*Fragmente*, Minor 20) draws the hermeneutical consequence: "A classical work of literature can never be completely understood. But those who are educated and educating themselves must always desire to learn more from it." [Gadamer]

Schleiermacher differentiated this hermeneutic circle of part and whole in both its objective and its subjective aspect. As the single word belongs within the total context of the sentence, so the single text belongs within the total context of a writer's work, and the latter within the whole of the particular literary genre or of literature. At the same time, however, the same text, as a manifestation of a creative moment, belongs to the whole of its author's inner life. Full understanding can take place only within this objective and subjective whole. Following this theory, Dilthey ... is applying to the historical world what has always been a principle of all textual interpretation: namely, that a text must be understood in terms of itself.

The question is, however, whether this is an adequate account of the circular movement of understanding. Here we must go back to the result of our analysis of Schleiermacher's hermeneutics. We may set aside Schleiermacher's ideas on subjective interpretation. When we try to understand a text, we do not try to recapture the author's attitude of mind but, if this is the terminology we are to use, we try to recapture the perspective within which he has formed his views. But this means simply that we try to accept the objective validity of what he is saying. If we want to understand, we shall try to make his arguments even more cogent. This happens even in conversation, so how much truer is it of the understanding of what is written down that we are moving in a dimension of meaning that is intelligible in itself and as such offers no reason for going back to the subjectivity of the author. It is the task of hermeneutics to clarify this miracle of understanding, which is not a mysterious communion of souls, but a sharing of a common meaning.

But even the objective side of this circle, as Schleiermacher describes it, does not reach the heart of the matter. We have seen that the goal of all communication and understanding is agreement concerning the object. Hence the task of hermeneutics has always been to establish agreement where it had failed to come about or been disturbed in some way. The history of hermeneutics can offer a confirmation of this if, for example, we think of Augustine, who sought to relate the christian gospel to the old testament, or of

early protestantism, which faced the same problem or, finally, the age of the enlightenment, when it is almost like a renunciation of agreement to seek to acquire "full understanding" of a text only by means of historical interpretation. It is something qualitatively new when romanticism and Schleiermacher ground a universal historical consciousness by no longer seeing the binding form of tradition, from which they come and in which they stand, as the firm foundation of all hermeneutical endeavor.

One of the immediate predecessors of Schleiermacher, Friedrich Ast,[16] still had a view of hermeneutical work that was markedly concerned with content, in that, for him, its purpose was to establish harmony between the world of classical antiquity and christianity, between a newly discovered genuine antiquity and the christian tradition. This is something new, in comparison with the enlightenment, in that this hermeneutics no longer accepts or rejects tradition in accord with the criterion of natural reason. But in its attempt to bring about a meaningful agreement between the two traditions to which it sees itself as belonging, this kind of hermeneutics is still pursuing the task of all preceding hermeneutics, namely to achieve in understanding agreement in content.

In going beyond the "particularity" of this reconciliation of the ancient classical world and christianity, Schleiermacher and, following him, nineteenth-century science, conceive the task of hermeneutics in a way that is formally universal. They were able to harmonize it with the natural sciences' ideal of objectivity, but only by ignoring the concentration of historical consciousness in hermeneutical theory.

Heidegger's description and existential account of the hermeneutic circle constitutes in contrast a decisive turning-point. The hermeneutic theory of the nineteenth century often spoke of the circular structure of understanding, but always within the framework of a formal relation of the part and the whole or its subjective reflex,

[16]Georg Anton Friedrich Ast, German philosopher (1778–1841), was best known as an editor of Plato and a critic of the Platonic canon.

the intuitive anticipation of the whole and its sub-sequent articulation in the parts. According to this theory, the circular movement of understanding runs backwards and forwards along the text and disappears when it is perfectly understood. This view of understanding culminated logically in Schleiermacher's theory of the divinatory act, by means of which one places oneself entirely within the writer's mind and from there resolves all that is strange and unusual about the text. As against this approach, Heidegger describes the circle in such a way that the understanding of the text remains permanently determined by the anticipatory movement of fore-understanding. The circle of the whole and the part is not dissolved in perfect understanding but, on the contrary, is most fully realized.

The circle, then, is not formal in nature, it is neither subjective nor objective, but describes understanding as the interplay of the movement of tradition and the movement of the interpreter. The anticipation of meaning that governs our understanding of a text is not an act of subjectivity, but proceeds from the communality that binds us to the tradition. But this is contained in our relation to tradition, in the constant process of education. Tradition is not simply a precondition into which we come, but we produce it ourselves, inasmuch as we understand, participate in the evolution of tradition and hence further determine it ourselves. Thus the circle of understanding is not a "methodological" circle, but describes an ontological structural element in understanding.

The significance of this circle, which is fundamental to all understanding, has a further hermeneutic consequence which I may call the "fore-conception of completion." But this, too, is obviously a formal condition of all understanding. It states that only what really constitutes a unity of meaning is intelligible. So when we read a text we always follow this complete presupposition of completion, and only when it proves inadequate, i.e., the text is not intelligible, do we start to doubt the transmitted text and seek to discover in what way it can be remedied. The rules of such textual criticism can be left aside, for the important thing to note is that their proper application cannot be detached from the understanding of the textual content.

The anticipation of completion that guides all our understanding is, then, always specific in content. Not only is an immanent unity of meaning guiding the reader assumed, but his understanding is likewise guided by the constant transcendent expectations of meaning which proceed from the relation to the truth of what is being said. Just as the recipient of a letter understands the news that it contains and first sees things with the eyes of the person who wrote the letter, i.e., considers what he writes as true, and is not trying to understand the alien meanings of the letter writer, so we understand texts that have been handed down to us on the basis of expectations of meaning which are drawn from our own anterior relation to the subject. And just as we believe the news reported by a correspondent because he was present or is better informed, we are fundamentally open to the possibility that the writer of a transmitted text is better informed than we are, with our previously formed meaning. It is only when the attempt to accept what he has said as true fails that we try to "understand" the text, psychologically or historically, as another's meaning.[17] The anticipation of completion, then, contains not only this formal element that a text should fully express its meaning, but also that what it says should be the whole truth.

We see here again that understanding means, primarily, to understand the content of what is said, and only secondarily to isolate and understand another's meaning as such. Hence the first of all hermeneutic requirements remains one's own fore-understanding, which proceeds from being concerned with the same subject. It is this that determines what unified meaning can be realized and hence the application of the anticipation of completion.[18]

[17]In a lecture on aesthetic judgment at a conference in Venice in 1958 I tried to show that it too, like historical judgment, is secondary in character and confirms the "anticipation of completion." (It appeared in the *Rivista di Estetica*, M A III, 1958, under the title "Zur Fragwürdigkeit des ästhetischen Bewusstseins"). [Gadamer]

[18]There is one exception to this anticipation of completion, namely the case of writing that is presenting something in disguise, e.g. a *roman à clef*. This presents one of the most difficult hermeneutical problems (cf the interesting remarks by Leo Strauss in *Persecution and the Art of Writing*). This

Thus the meaning of the connection with tradition, i.e., the element of tradition in our historical, hermeneutical attitude, is fulfilled in the fact that we share fundamental prejudices with tradition. Hermeneutics must start from the position that a person seeking to understand something has a relation to the object that comes into language in the transmitted text and has, or acquires, a connection with the tradition out of which the text speaks. On the other hand, hermeneutical consciousness is aware that it cannot be connected with this object in some self-evident, questioned way, as is the case with the unbroken stream of a tradition. There is a polarity of familiarity and strangeness on which hermeneutic work is based: only that this polarity is not to be seen, psychologically, with Schleiermacher, as the tension that conceals the mystery of individuality, but truly hermeneutically, i.e., in regard to what has been said: the language in which the text addresses us, the story that it tells us. Here too there is a tension. The place between strangeness and familiarity that a transmitted text has for us is that intermediate place between being an historically intended separate object and being part of a tradition. The true home of hermeneutics is in this intermediate area.

It follows from this intermediate position in which hermeneutics operates that its work is not to develop a procedure of understanding, but to clarify the conditions in which understanding takes place. But these conditions are not of the nature of a "procedure" or a method, which the interpreter must of himself bring to bear on the text, but rather they must be given. The prejudices and fore-meanings in the mind of the interpreter are not at his free disposal. He is not able to separate in advance the productive prejudices that make understanding possible from the prejudices that hinder understanding and lead to misunderstandings.

This separation, rather, must take place in the understanding itself, and hence hermeneutics must ask how it happens. But this means it must place in the foreground what has remained entirely peripheral in previous hermeneutics: temporal distance and its significance for understanding.

This point can be clarified by comparing it with the hermeneutic-theory of romanticism. We shall recall that the latter conceived understanding as the reproduction of an original production. Hence it was possible to say that one should be able to understand an author better than he understood himself. We examined the origin of this statement and its connection with the aesthetics of genius, but must now come back to it, as our present inquiry lends it a new importance.

That subsequent understanding is superior to the original production and hence can be described as superior understanding does not depend so much on the conscious realization that places him on the same level as the author (as Schleiermacher said), but denotes rather an inevitable difference between the interpreter and the author that is created by the historical distance between them. Every age has to understand a transmitted text in its own way, for the text is part of the whole of the tradition in which the age takes an objective interest and in which it seeks to understand itself. The real meaning of a text, as it speaks to the interpreter, does not depend on the contingencies of the author and whom he originally wrote for. It certainly is not identical with them, for it is always partly determined also by the historical situation of the interpreter and hence by the totality of the objective course of history. A writer like Chladenius, who does not yet see understanding in terms of history, is saying the same thing in a naive, ingenuous way when he says that an author does not need to know the real meaning of what he has written, and hence the interpreter can, and must, often understand more than he. But this is of fundamental importance. Not occasionally only, but always, the meaning of a text goes beyond its author. That is why understanding is not merely a reproductive, but always a productive attitude as well. Perhaps it is not correct to refer to this productive element in understanding as "superior understanding." For this phrase is, as we have

exceptional hermeneutical case is of special significance, in that it goes beyond interpretation of meaning in the same way as when historical source criticism goes back behind the tradition. Although the task here is not an historical, but an hermeneutical one, it can be performed only by using understanding of the subject as a key to discover what is behind the disguise — just as in conversation we understand irony to the extent to which we are in agreement on the subject with the other person. Thus the apparent exception confirms that understanding involves agreement. [Gadamer] shown, the application of a principle of criticism from the age of the enlightenment on the basis of the aesthetics of genius. Understanding is not, in fact, superior understanding, neither in the sense of superior knowledge of the subject because of clearer ideas, nor in the sense of fundamental superiority that the conscious has over the unconscious nature of creation. It is enough to say that we understand in a different way, if we understand at all.

This concept of understanding undoubtedly breaks right out of the circle drawn by romantic hermeneutics. Because what we are now concerned with is not individuality and what it thinks, but the objective truth of what is said, a text is not understood as a mere expression of life, but taken seriously in its claim to truth. That this is what is meant by "understanding" was once self-evident (we need only recall Chladenius).

But this dimension of the hermeneutical problem was discredited by historical consciousness and the psychological turn that Schleiermacher gave to hermeneutics, and could only be regained when the impasses of historicism appeared and led finally to the new development inspired chiefly, in my opinion, by Heidegger. For the hermeneutic importance of temporal distance could be understood only as a result of the ontological direction that Heidegger gave to understanding as an "existential" and of his temporal interpretation of the mode of being of there-being.

Time is no longer primarily a gulf to be bridged, because it separates, but it is actually the supportive ground of process in which the present is rooted. Hence temporal distance is not something that must be overcome. This was, rather, the naive assumption of historicism, namely that we must set ourselves within the spirit of the age, and think with its ideas and its thoughts, not with our own, and thus advance towards historical objectivity. In fact the important thing is to recognize the distance in time as a positive and productive possibility of understanding. It is not a yawning abyss, but is filled with the continuity of custom and tradition, in the light of which all that is handed down presents itself to us. Here it is not too much to speak of a genuine productivity of process. Everyone knows that curious impotence of our judgment where the distance in time has not given us sure criteria. Thus the judgment of contemporary works of art is desperately uncertain for the scientific consciousness. Obviously we approach such creations with the prejudices we are not in control of, presuppositions that have too great an influence over us for us to know about them; these can give to contemporary creations an extra resonance that does not correspond to their true content and their true significance. Only when all their relations to the present time have faded away can their real nature appear, so that the understanding of what is said in them can claim to be authoritative and universal.

It is this experience that has led to the idea in historical studies that objective knowledge can be arrived at only when there has been a certain historical distance. It is true that what a thing has to say, its intrinsic content, first appears only after it is divorced from the fleeting circumstances of its actuality. The positive conditions of historical understanding include the self-contained quality of an historical event, which allows it to appear as a whole, and its distance from the opinions concerning its import with which the present is filled. The implicit prerequisite of the historical method, then, is that the permanent significance of something can first be known objectively only when it belongs within a self-contained context. In other words, when it is dead enough to have only historical interest. Only then does it seem possible to exclude the subjective involvement of the observer. This is, in fact, a paradox, the epistemological counterpart to the old moral problem of whether anyone can be called happy before his death. Just as Aristotle showed what a sharpening of the powers of human judgment this kind of problem can bring about,[19] so hermeneutical reflection cannot fail to find here a sharpening of the methodological self-consciousness of science. It is true that certain hermeneutic requirements are automatically fulfilled when a historical context has become of no more than historical interest. Certain sources of error are automatically excluded. But it is questionable whether this is the end of the hermeneutical problem. Temporal distance has obviously another meaning than that of the quenching of our interest in the object. It lets the true meaning of the object emerge fully.

[19]*Eth Nic* I, 7. [Gadamer]

But the discovery of the true meaning of a text or a work of art is never finished; it is in fact an infinite process. Not only are fresh sources of error constantly excluded, so that the true meaning has filtered out of it all kinds of things that obscure it, but there emerge continually new sources of understanding, which reveal unsuspected elements of meaning. The temporal distance which performs the filtering process is not a closed dimension, but is itself undergoing constant movement and extension. And with the negative side of the filtering process brought about by temporal distance there is also the positive side, namely the value it has for understanding. It not only lets those prejudices that are of a particular and limited nature die away, but causes those that bring about genuine understanding to emerge clearly as such.

It is only this temporal distance that can solve the really critical question of hermeneutics, namely of distinguishing the true prejudices, by which we understand, from the false ones by which we misunderstand. Hence the hermeneutically trained mind will also include historical consciousness. It will make conscious the prejudices governing our own understanding, so that the text, as another's meaning, can be isolated and valued on its own. The isolation of a prejudice clearly requires the suspension of its validity for us. For so long as our mind is influenced by a prejudice, we do not know and consider it as a judgment. How then are we able to isolate it? It is impossible to make ourselves aware of it while it is constantly operating unnoticed, but only when it is, so to speak, stimulated. The encounter with a text from the past can provide this stimulus. For what leads to understanding must be something that has already asserted itself in its own separate validity. Understanding begins, as we have already said above,[20] when something addresses us. This is the primary hermeneutical condition. We now know what this requires, namely the fundamental suspension of our own prejudices. But all suspension of judgments and hence, a fortiori, of prejudices, has logically the structure of a question.

The essence of the question is the opening up, and keeping open, of possibilities. If a prejudice becomes questionable, in view of what another or a text says to us, this does not mean that it is simply set aside and the other writing or the other person accepted as valid in its place. It shows, rather, the naiveté of historical objectivism to accept this disregarding of ourselves as what actually happens. In fact our own prejudice is properly brought into play through its being at risk. Only through its being given full play is it able to experience the other's claim to truth and make it possible for he himself to have full play.[21]

The naiveté of so called historicism consists in the fact that it does not undertake this reflection, and in trusting to its own methodological approach forgets its own historicality. We must here appeal from a badly understood historical thinking to one that can better perform the task of understanding. True historical thinking must take account of its own historicality. Only then will it not chase the phantom of an historical object which is the object of progressive research, but learn to see in the object the counterpart of itself and hence understand both. The true historical object is not an object at all, but the unity of the one and the other, a relationship in which exist both the reality of history and the reality of historical understanding. A proper hermeneutics would have to demonstrate the effectivity of history within understanding itself. I shall refer to this as "effective-history." Understanding is, essentially, an effective-historical relation.

(iv) The Principle of Effective-History

The fact that the interest of the historian is directed not only towards the historical phenomenon and the work that has been handed down but also, secondarily, towards their effect in history (which also includes the history of research) is regarded in general as a mere supplement to the historical problematic that, from Hermann Grimm's *Raffael* to Gundolf and beyond, has given rise to many valuable insights. To this extent, effective-history is not new. But that this kind of effective-historical approach be required

[20]See p. 730.

[21]In this passage the author plays on the German expressions *ins Spiel bringen*, *auf dem Spiele stehen* and *sich ausspielen*. [Tr.]

every time that a work of art or an element of the tradition is led from the twilight region between tradition and history to be seen clearly and openly in terms of its own meaning — this is a new demand (addressed not to research, but to methodological consciousness itself) that proceeds inevitably from the analysis of historical consciousness.

It is not, of course, a hermeneutical requirement in the sense of the traditional concept of hermeneutics. I am not saying that historical inquiry should develop this effective-historical problematic that would be something separate from that which is concerned directly with the understanding of the work. The requirement is of a more theoretical kind. Historical consciousness must become aware that in the apparent immediacy with which it approaches a work of art or a tradition, there is also contained, albeit unrecognized and hence not allowed for, this other element. If we are trying to understand a historical phenomenon from the historical distance that is characteristic of our hermeneutical situation, we are always subject to the effects of effective-history. It determines in advance both what seems to us worth inquiring about and what will appear as an object of investigation, and we more or less forget half of what is really there — in fact, we miss the whole truth of the phenomenon when we take its immediate appearance as the whole truth.

In our understanding, which we imagine is so straightforward, we find that, by following the criterion of intelligibility, the other presents himself so much in terms of our own selves that there is no longer a question of self and other. Historical objectivism, in appealing to its critical method, conceals the involvement of the historical consciousness itself in effective-history. By the method of its foundational criticism it does away with the arbitrariness of cosy re-creations of the past, but it preserves its good conscience by failing to recognize those presuppositions — certainly not arbitrary, but still fundamental — that govern its own approach to understanding, and hence falls short of reaching that truth which, despite the finite nature of our understanding, could be reached. In this, historical objectivism resembles statistics, which are such an excellent means of propaganda because they let facts speak and hence simulate an objectivity that in reality depends on the legitimacy of the questions asked.

We are not saying, then, that effective-history must be developed as a new independent discipline ancillary to the human sciences, but that we should learn to understand ourselves better and recognize that in all understanding, whether we are expressly aware of it or not, the power of this effective-history is at work. When a naive faith in scientific method ignores its existence, there can be an actual deformation of knowledge. We know it from the history of science as the irrefutable proof of something that is obviously false. But looking at the whole situation, we see that the power of effective-history does not depend on its being recognized. This, precisely, is the power of history over finite human consciousness, namely that it prevails even where faith in method leads one to deny one's own historicality. The demand that we should become conscious of this effective-history is pressing because it is necessary for scientific consciousness. But this does not mean that it can be fulfilled in an absolute way. That we should become completely aware of effective-history is just as hybrid a statement as when Hegel speaks of absolute knowledge, in which history would become completely transparent to itself and hence be raised to the level of a concept. Rather, effective-historical consciousness is an element in the act of understanding itself and, as we shall see, is already operative in the choice of the right question to ask.

Effective-historical consciousness is primarily consciousness of the hermeneutical situation. To acquire an awareness of a situation is, however, always a task of particular difficulty. The very idea of a situation means that we are not standing outside it and hence are unable to have any objective knowledge of it.[22] We are always within the situation, and to throw light on it is a task that is never entirely completed. This is true also of the hermeneutic situation, i.e., the situation in which we find ourselves with regard to the tradition that we are trying to understand. The illumination of

[22]The structure of the concept of situation has been illuminated chiefly by K. Jaspers (*Die geistige Situation der Zeit*) and Erich Rothacker. [Gadamer]

this situation — effective-historical reflection — can never be completely achieved, but this is not due to a lack in the reflection, but lies in the essence of the historical being which is ours. To exist historically means that knowledge of oneself can never be complete. All self-knowledge proceeds from what is historically pre-given, what we call, with Hegel, "substance," because it is the basis of all subjective meaning and attitude and hence both prescribes and limits every possibility of understanding any tradition whatsoever in terms of its unique historical quality. This almost defines the aim of philosophical hermeneutics: its task is to move back along the path of Hegel's phenomenology of mind until we discover in all that is subjective the substantiality that determines it.

Every finite present has its limitations. We define the concept of "situation" by saying that it represents a standpoint that limits the possibility of vision. Hence an essential part of the concept of situation is the concept of "horizon." The horizon is the range of vision that includes everything that can be seen from a particular vantage point. Applying this to the thinking mind, we speak of narrowness of horizon, of the possible expansion of horizon, of the opening up of new horizons etc. The word has been used in philosophy since Nietzsche and Husserl[23] to characterize the way in which thought is tied to its finite determination, and the nature of the law of the expansion of the range of vision. A person who has no horizon is a man who does not see far enough and hence overvalues what is nearest to him. Contrariwise, to have an horizon means not to be limited to what is nearest, but to be able to see beyond it. A person who has an horizon knows the relative significance of everything within this horizon, as near or far, great or small. Similarly, the working out of the hermeneutical situation means the achievement of the right horizon of inquiry for the questions evoked by the encounter with tradition.

[23]Edmund Husserl's notion of the horizon, Gadamer explains earlier, "is not a rigid frontier, but something that moves with one and invites one to advance further." This subjective horizon intentionality, "which constitutes the unity and flow of experience, is paralleled by an equally comprehensive horizon intentionality on the objective side." (*Truth and Method*, p. 217).

In the sphere of historical understanding we also like to speak of horizons, especially when referring to the claim of historical consciousness to see the past in terms of its own being, not in terms of our contemporary criteria and prejudices, but within its own historical horizon. The task of historical understanding also involves acquiring the particular historical horizon, so that what we are seeking to understand can be seen in its true dimensions. If we fail to place ourselves in this way within the historical horizon out of which tradition speaks, we shall misunderstand the significance of what it has to say to us. To this extent it seems a legitimate hermeneutical requirement to place ourselves in the other situation in order to understand it. We may ask, however, whether this does not mean that we are failing in the understanding that is asked of us. The same is true of a conversation that we have with someone simply in order to get to know him, i.e., to discover his standpoint and his horizon. This is not a true conversation, in the sense that we are not seeking agreement concerning an object, but the specific contents of the conversation are only a means to get to know the horizon of the other person. Examples are oral examinations, or some kinds of conversation between doctor and patient. The historical consciousness is clearly doing something similar when it places itself within the situation of the past and hence is able to acquire the right historical horizon. Just as in a conversation, when we have discovered the standpoint and horizon of the other person, his ideas become intelligible, without our necessarily having to agree with him, the person who thinks historically comes to understand the meaning of what has been handed down, without necessarily agreeing with it, or seeing himself in it.

In both cases, in our understanding we have as it were, withdrawn from the situation of trying to reach agreement. He himself cannot be reached. By including from the beginning the other person's standpoint in what he is saying to us, we are making our own standpoint safely unattainable. We have seen, in considering the origin of historical thinking, that in fact it makes this ambiguous transition from means to ends, i.e., it makes an end of what is only a means. The text that is understood historically is forced to abandon its claim that it is uttering something true. We think we understand when we see the past from a historical standpoint, i.e., place ourselves in the historical situation and seek to reconstruct the historical horizon. In fact, however, we have given up the claim to find, in the past, any truth valid and intelligible for ourselves. Thus this acknowledgment of the otherness of the other, which makes him the object of objective knowledge, involves the fundamental suspension of his claim to truth.

The question is, however, whether this description really corresponds to the hermeneutical phenomenon. Are there, then, two different horizons here, the horizon in which the person seeking to understand lives, and the particular historical horizon within which he places himself? Is it a correct description of the art of historical understanding to say that we are learning to place ourselves within alien horizons? Are there such things as closed horizons, in this sense? We recall Nietzsche's complaint against historicism that it destroyed the horizon bounded by myth in which alone a culture is able to live.[24] Is the horizon of one's own present time ever closed in this way, and can a historical situation be imagined that has this kind of closed horizon?

Or is this a romantic reflection, a kind of Robinson Crusoe dream of the historical enlightenment, the fiction of an unattainable island, as artificial as Crusoe himself for the alleged primary phenomenon of the solus ipse? Just as the individual is never simply an individual, because he is always involved with others, so too the closed horizon that is supposed to enclose a culture is an abstraction. The historical movement of human life consists in the fact that it is never utterly bound to any one standpoint, and hence can never have a truly closed horizon. The horizon is, rather, something into which we move and that moves with us. Horizons change for a person who is moving. Thus the horizon of the past, out of which all human life lives and which exists in the form of tradition, is always in motion. It is not historical consciousness that first sets the surrounding horizon in motion. But in it this motion becomes aware of itself.

[24]Nietzsche, *Unzeitgemässe Betrachtungen* II, at the beginning. [Gadamer]

When our historical consciousness places itself within historical horizons, this does not entail passing into alien worlds unconnected in any way with our own, but together they constitute the one great horizon that moves from within and, beyond the frontiers of the present, embraces the historical depths of our self-consciousness. It is, in fact, a single horizon that embraces everything contained in historical consciousness. Our own past, and that other past towards which our historical consciousness is directed, help to shape this moving horizon out of which human life always lives, and which determines it as tradition.

Understanding of the past, then, undoubtedly requires an historical horizon. But it is not the case that we acquire this horizon by placing ourselves within a historical situation. Rather, we must always already have a horizon in order to be able to place ourselves within a situation. For what do we mean by "placing ourselves" in a situation? Certainly not just disregarding ourselves. This is necessary, of course, in that we must imagine the other situation. But into this other situation we must also bring ourselves. Only this fulfils the meaning of "placing ourselves." If we place ourselves in the situation of someone else, for example, then we shall understand him, ie become aware of the otherness, the indissoluble individuality of the other person, by placing ourselves in his position.

This placing of ourselves is not the empathy of one individual for another, nor is it the application to another person of our own criteria, but it always involves the attainment of a higher universality that overcomes, not only our own particularity, but also that of the other. The concept of the "horizon" suggests itself because it expresses the wide, superior vision that the person who is seeking to understand must have. To acquire a horizon means that one learns to look beyond what is close at hand — not in order to look away from it, but to see it better within a larger whole and in truer proportion. It is not a correct description of historical consciousness to speak, with Nietzsche, of the many changing horizons into which it teaches us to place ourselves. If we disregard ourselves in this way, we have no historical horizon. Nietzsche's view that historical study is deleterious to life is not directed, in fact, against historical consciousness as such, but against the self-alienation that it undergoes when it regards the method of modern historical science as its own true nature. We have already pointed out that a truly historical consciousness always sees its own present in such a way that it sees itself, as it sees the historically other, within the right circumstances. It requires a special effort to acquire an historical horizon. We are always affected, in hope and fear, by what is nearest to us, and hence approach, under its influence, the testimony of the past. Hence it is constantly necessary to inhibit the overhasty assimilation of the past to our own expectations of meaning. Only then will we be able to listen to the past in a way that enables it to make its own meaning heard.

We have shown above that this is a process of distinguishing. Let us consider what this idea of distinguishing involves. It is always reciprocal. Whatever is being distinguished must be distinguished from something which, in turn, must be distinguished from it. Thus all distinguishing also makes visible that from which something is distinguished. We have described this above as the operation of prejudices. We started by saying that a hermeneutical situation is determined by the prejudices that we bring with us. They constitute, then, the horizon of a particular present, for they represent that beyond which it is impossible to see. But now it is important to avoid the error of thinking that it is a fixed set of opinions and evaluations that determine and limit the horizon of the present, and that the otherness of the past can be distinguished from it as from a fixed ground.

In fact the horizon of the present is being continually formed, in that we have continually to test all our prejudices. An important part of this testing is the encounter with the past and the understanding of the tradition from which we come. Hence the horizon of the present cannot be formed without the past. There is no more an isolated horizon of the present than there are historical horizons. Understanding, rather, is always the fusion of these horizons which we imagine to exist by themselves. We know the power of this kind of fusion chiefly from earlier times and their naive attitude to themselves and their origin. In a tradition this process of fusion is continually going on, for there old and new continually grow together to make something of living value, without either being explicitly distinguished from the other.

If, however, there is no such thing as these horizons that are distinguished from one another, why do we speak of the fusion of horizons and not simply of the formation of the one horizon, whose bounds are set in the depths of tradition? To ask the question means that we are recognizing the special nature of the situation in which understanding becomes a scientific task, and that it is necessary to work out this situation as a hermeneutical situation. Every encounter with tradition that takes place within historical consciousness involves the experience of the tension between the text and the present. The hermeneutic task consists in not covering up this tension by attempting a naive assimilation but consciously bringing it out. This is why it is part of the hermeneutic approach to project an historical horizon that is different from the horizon of the present. Historical consciousness is aware of its own otherness and hence distinguishes the horizon of tradition from its own. On the other hand, it is itself, as we are trying to show, only something laid over a continuing tradition, and hence it immediately recombines what it has distinguished in order, in the unity of the historical horizon that it thus acquires, to become again one with itself.

The projecting of the historical horizon, then, is only a phase in the process of understanding, and does not become solidified into the self-alienation of a past consciousness, but is overtaken by our own present horizon of understanding. In the process of understanding there takes place a real fusing of horizons, which means that as the historical horizon is projected, it is simultaneously removed. We described the conscious act of this fusion as the task of the effective-historical consciousness. Although this task had been obscured by aesthetic historical positivism in the train of romantic hermeneutics, it is, in fact, the central problem of hermeneutics. It is the problem of application that exists in all understanding.

Susan Sontag

1933–2004

Susan Sontag was born in New York City but raised in Tucson, Arizona, and in Los Angeles. She began her college work at the University of California, Berkeley, but transferred to the University of Chicago, where she received her B.A. in philosophy in 1951, at the age of eighteen. She did graduate work in English and philosophy at Harvard, where she received her M.A., and further graduate study at Oxford and the Sorbonne. Sontag taught at Harvard, the University of Connecticut, Rutgers, and Columbia, but supported herself mainly through her books and periodical essays.

Though she resists being classified "primarily as an essayist," Sontag is usually regarded nevertheless as a literary and cultural critic, her two novels, shorter fiction, and screenplays notwithstanding. Like Lionel Trilling, Sontag seems to function as a cultural barometer. Her fiction, like his, seems to be generated by her cultural observations and critical ideas. But where Trilling was primarily concerned with demonstrating the continuity of the present with the past, Sontag — wrote from the sixties to the present, rather than in the forties and fifties — always appeared less concerned with the traditions than with the discontinuities of contemporary life.

One of Sontag's major roles, at the outset of her career at least, was as a conduit between America and Europe of avant-garde ideas and personalities. Theorists like Walter Benjamin and Roland Barthes, now canonical, were almost unknown in the United States when they were recommended by Sontag in 1964 as writers who "reveal the sensuous surface of art without mucking about in it" in Section 8 of "Against Interpretation." In other essays in the early 1960s, she called attention on this side of the Atlantic to writers like Nathalie Sarraute, Antonin Artaud, and Alain Robbe-Grillet.

But Sontag was not a typical literary critic. She did not wish to analyze and interpret a series of standard texts so much as to discuss the conditions for their appearance, and the cultural assumptions that underlie their production and their reception. The subjects that most appealed to her were the marginal areas of art, which sketch in the boundaries of a culture and its perceptions: the "camp" sensibility, the pornographic imagination, illness as metaphor, and photography as an art form. Despite the variety of topics, Sontag's work, according to Susan Jeffords, "is of a piece. . . . No matter what form they take, Sontag asks the same questions — about the construction and resolution of identity, about manipulation and violence as a basis for social and aesthetic encounters, about the structure and function of cultural interpretation, about the inspiration of those outside accepted social boundaries — hoping that new answers will appear as a byproduct of new form. It is paradigmatic of Sontag's position as a modernist that they do not." Although she was not a reader-response critic in any of the usual senses of the term (see the introduction to Reader-Response Theory, p. 962), Sontag was most strongly engaged by the question of how readers process texts, and by the cultural uses to which literature is put. This is the central concern in "Against Interpretation."

The core of the essay is the three short sentences in Section 5: "Real art has the capacity to make us nervous. By reducing the work of art to its content and then interpreting *that,* one tames the work of art. Interpretation makes art manageable, comfortable." Interpretation, for Sontag, was a vicious and cowardly form of translation, in which the work of art is stripped of its sensuous life and reduced to a bare statement, which is then processed through the categories of the various schools of criticism (Marxist, Freudian, Christian) into a message that is inevitably familiar, indeed always already known. Appreciative and analytical criticism — not the nasty judgmental kind — has thus become the most deadly enemy of art.

The reaction to "Against Interpretation" was predictably fierce, and not merely from the Freudians and Marxists whose oxen were explicitly gored. Representatives of the New Criticism, then enjoying its hegemony, objected that they had been making Sontag's point for her all along (in such essays as Cleanth Brooks's "The Heresy of Paraphrase"). In fact, Sontag's strictures would apply equally against the New Critics, who, while granting lip service to the primacy of form, had always treated poetry as a general statement (or pseudostatement) about the world, albeit an especially complex sort of statement, riffed by paradox, irony, ambiguity, and other tropes. In New Critical terminology, theme is a part of form — and thus Sontag's dichotomy of "form" and "content" might mislead one to think she favored that school of exegesis. In fact, for Sontag any *translation* of the text into other terms is a betrayal of that text, and the *thematization* of any text always reduces it to a subartistic level.

Since "Against Interpretation" was published, there have been at least a few faltering steps toward exploring the "erotics of art" Sontag mentions. In particular, much recent psychoanalytic theory (like that of Peter Brooks) have dropped the old dichotomy between latent and manifest content and attempted to discuss the form of the text as something other than a nicely wrapped container for fantasy and defense. Some New Historicist and cultural critics have moved beyond the representative quality and the political tendency of the text. Nevertheless, since translation and thematization have always been the mainstay of academic criticism, Sontag could be certain to find, in the pages of almost every scholarly journal today, specimens of the same destructive, spiritually impoverished interpretation she rejects.

Susan Sontag died as she had lived, with great fortitude, on December 28, 2004, after a long struggle with leukemia.

Selected Bibliography

Brooks, Peter. "Death of/as Metaphor." *Partisan Review* 46 (1979): 438–44.

Jeffords, Susan. "Susan Sontag." *Modern American Critics Since 1955*, ed. Gregory Jay. Detroit: Bruccoli-Clark-Layman, 1988.

Phillips, William. "Radical Styles." *Partisan Review* 36 (1969): 388–400.

Poague, Leland, and Kathy A. Parsons. *Susan Sontag: An Annotated Bibliography: 1948–1992.* New York: Garland, 2000.

Rollyson, Carl, and Lisa Paddock. *Susan Sontag; The Making of an Icon.* New York: Norton, 2000.

Roudiez, Leon S. "Susan Sontag: Against the Ideological Grain." *World Literature Today* 57 (1983): 219–23.

Rubin, Louis D., Jr. "Susan Sontag and the Camp Followers." *Sewanee Review* 82 (1974): 503–10.

Shaw, Peter. "Two Afterthoughts on Susan Sontag." *Encounter* 58/59 (1982): 38–40.

Against Interpretation

Content is a glimpse of something, an encounter like a flash. It's very tiny — very tiny, content.
 — WILLEM DE KOONING, in an interview

It is only shallow people who do not judge by appearances. The mystery of the world is the visible, not the invisible.
 — OSCAR WILDE, in a letter

1

The earliest *experience* of art must have been that it was incantatory, magical; art was an instrument of ritual. (Cf. the paintings in the caves at Lascaux, Altamira, Niaux, La Pasiega, etc.) The earliest *theory* of art, that of the Greek philosophers, proposed that art was mimesis, imitation of reality.

It is at this point that the peculiar question of the *value* of art arose. For the mimetic theory, by its very terms, challenges art to justify itself.

Plato, who proposed the theory, seems to have done so in order to rule that the value of art is dubious. Since he considered ordinary material things as themselves mimetic objects, imitations of transcendent forms or structures, even the best painting of a bed would be only an "imitation of an imitation." For Plato, art is neither particularly useful (the painting of a bed is no good to sleep on), nor, in the strict sense, true. And Aristotle's arguments in defense of art do not really challenge Plato's view that all art is an elaborate *trompe l'oeil*,[1] and therefore a lie. But he does dispute Plato's idea that art is useless. Lie or no, art has a certain value according to Aristotle because it is a form of therapy. Art is useful, after all, Aristotle counters, medicinally useful in that it arouses and purges dangerous emotions.[2]

In Plato and Aristotle, the mimetic theory of art goes hand in hand with the assumption that art is always figurative. But advocates of the mimetic theory need not close their eyes to decorative and abstract art. The fallacy that art is necessarily a "realism" can be modified or scrapped without ever moving outside the problems delimited by the mimetic theory.

The fact is, all Western consciousness of and reflection upon art have remained within the confines staked out by the Greek theory of art as mimesis or representation. It is through this theory that art as such — above and beyond given works of art — becomes problematic, in need of defense. And it is the defense of art which gives birth to the odd vision by which something we have learned to call "form" is separated off from something we have learned to call "content," and to the well-intentioned move which makes content essential and form accessory.

Even in modern times, when most artists and critics have discarded the theory of art as representation of an outer reality in favor of the theory of art as subjective expression, the main feature of the mimetic theory persists. Whether we conceive of the work of art on the model of a picture (art as a picture of reality) or on the model of a statement (art as the statement of the artist), content still comes first. The content may have changed. It may now be less figurative, less lucidly realistic. But it is still assumed that a work of art *is* its content. Or, as it's usually put today, that a work of art by definition says something. ("What X is saying is . . . ," "What X is trying to say is . . . ," "What X said is . . ." etc., etc.)

2

None of us can ever retrieve that innocence before all theory when art knew no need to justify itself, when one did not ask of a work of art what it *said* because one knew (or thought one knew) what it *did*. From now to the end of consciousness, we are stuck with the task of defending art. We can only quarrel with one or another means of defense. Indeed, we have an obligation to overthrow any means of defending and justifying art which becomes particularly obtuse or onerous or insensitive to contemporary needs and practice.

[1]Deception of the eye.
[2]Sontag conflates Aristotle's *Poetics* with the reference to *katharsis* in the *Politics,* quoted in the introduction to Aristotle; see p. 55.

This is the case, today, with the very idea of content itself. Whatever it may have been in the past, the idea of content is today mainly a hindrance, a nuisance, a subtle or not so subtle philistinism.

Though the actual developments in many arts may seem to be leading us away from the idea that a work of art is primarily its content, the idea still exerts an extraordinary hegemony. I want to suggest that this is because the idea is now perpetuated in the guise of a certain way of encountering works of art thoroughly ingrained among most people who take any of the arts seriously. What the overemphasis on the idea of content entails is the perennial, never consummated project of *interpretation*. And, conversely, it is the habit of approaching works of art in order to *interpret* them that sustains the fancy that there really is such a thing as the content of a work of art.

3

Of course, I don't mean interpretation in the broadest sense, the sense in which Nietzsche (rightly) says, "There are no facts, only interpretations." By interpretation, I mean here a conscious act of the mind which illustrates a certain code, certain "rules" of interpretation.

Directed to art, interpretation means plucking a set of elements (the X, the Y, the Z, and so forth) from the whole work. The task of interpretation is virtually one of translation. The interpreter says, Look, don't you see that X is really — or, really means — A? That Y is really B? That Z is really C?

What situation could prompt this curious project for transforming a text? History gives us the materials for an answer. Interpretation first appears in the culture of late classical antiquity, when the power and credibility of myth had been broken by the "realistic" view of the world introduced by scientific enlightenment. Once the question that haunts post-mythic consciousness — that of the *seemliness* of religious symbols — had been asked, the ancient texts were, in their pristine form, no longer acceptable. Then interpretation was summoned, to reconcile the ancient texts to "modern" demands. Thus, the Stoics, to accord with their view that the gods had to be moral, allegorized away the rude features of Zeus and his boisterous clan in Homer's epics. What Homer really designated by the adultery of Zeus with Leto, they explained, was the union between power and wisdom. In the same vein, Philo of Alexandria interpreted the literal historical narratives of the Hebrew Bible as spiritual paradigms. The story of the exodus from Egypt, the wandering in the desert for forty years, and the entry into the promised land, said Philo, was really an allegory of the individual soul's emancipation, tribulations, and final deliverance.[3] Interpretation thus presupposes a discrepancy between the clear meaning of the text and the demands of (later) readers. It seeks to resolve that discrepancy. The situation is that for some reason a text has become unacceptable; yet it cannot be discarded. Interpretation is a radical strategy for conserving an old text, which is thought too precious to repudiate, by revamping it. The interpreter, without actually erasing or rewriting the text, *is* altering it. But he can't admit to doing this. He claims to be only making it intelligible, by disclosing its true meaning. However far the interpreters alter the text (another notorious example is the Rabbinic and Christian "spiritual" interpretations of the clearly erotic Song of Songs), they must claim to be reading off a sense that is already there.

Interpretation in our own time, however, is even more complex. For the contemporary zeal for the project of interpretation is often prompted not by piety toward the troublesome text (which may conceal an aggression), but by an open aggressiveness, an overt contempt for appearances. The old style of interpretation was insistent, but respectful; it erected another meaning on top of the literal one. The modern style of interpretation excavates, and as it excavates, destroys; it digs "behind" the text, to find a subtext which is the true one. The most celebrated and influential modern doctrines, those of Marx and Freud, actually amount to elaborate systems of hermeneutics, aggressive and impious theories of interpretation. All observable phenomena are bracketed, in Freud's phrase, as *manifest content.* This manifest content must be probed and pushed

[3]Dante's redaction of Philo's system appears in his letter to Can Grande della Scala, p. 121.

aside to find the true meaning — the *latent content* — beneath.[4] For Marx, social events like revolutions and wars; for Freud, the events of individual lives (like neurotic symptoms and slips of the tongue) as well as texts (like a dream or a work of art) — all are treated as occasions for interpretation. According to Marx and Freud, these events only *seem* to be intelligible. Actually, they have no meaning without interpretation. To understand *is* to interpret. And to interpret is to restate the phenomenon, in effect to find an equivalent for it.

Thus, interpretation is not (as most people assume) an absolute value, a gesture of mind situated in some timeless realm of capabilities. Interpretation must itself be evaluated, within a historical view of human consciousness. In some cultural contexts, interpretation is a liberating act. It is a means of revising, of transvaluing, of escaping the dead past. In other cultural contexts, it is reactionary, impertinent, cowardly, stifling.

4

Today is such a time, when the project of interpretation is largely reactionary, stifling. Like the fumes of the automobile and of heavy industry which befoul the urban atmosphere, the effusion of interpretations of art today poisons our sensibilities. In a culture whose already classical dilemma is the hypertrophy of the intellect at the expense of energy and sensual capability, interpretation is the revenge of the intellect upon art.

Even more. It is the revenge of the intellect upon the world. To interpret is to impoverish, to deplete the world — in order to set up a shadow world of "meanings." It is to turn *the* world into *this* world. ("This world"! As if there were any other.)

The world, our world, is depleted, impoverished enough. Away with all duplicates of it, until we again experience more immediately what we have.

[4]See the introduction to Psychoanalytic Theory, p. 1106.

5

In most modern instances, interpretation amounts to the philistine refusal to leave the work of art alone. Real art has the capacity to make us nervous. By reducing the work of art to its content and then interpreting *that,* one tames the work of art. Interpretation makes art manageable, comfortable.

This philistinism of interpretation is more rife in literature than in any other art. For decades now, literary critics have understood it to be their task to translate the elements of the poem or play or novel or story into something else. Sometimes a writer will be so uneasy before the naked power of his art that he will install within the work itself — albeit with a little shyness, a touch of the good taste of irony — the clear and explicit interpretation of it. Thomas Mann is an example of such an overcooperative author. In the case of more stubborn authors, the critic is only too happy to perform the job.

The work of Kafka, for example, has been subjected to a mass ravishment by no less than three armies of interpreters. Those who read Kafka as a social allegory see case studies of the frustrations and insanity of modern bureaucracy and its ultimate issuance in the totalitarian state. Those who read Kafka as a psychoanalytic allegory see desperate revelations of Kafka's fear of his father, his castration anxieties, his sense of his own impotence, his thralldom to his dreams. Those who read Kafka as a religious allegory explain that K. in *The Castle* is trying to gain access to heaven, that Joseph K. in *The Trial* is being judged by the inexorable and mysterious justice of God. . . . Another *oeuvre* that has attracted interpreters like leeches is that of Samuel Beckett. Beckett's delicate dramas of the withdrawn consciousness — pared down to essentials, cut off, often represented as physically immobilized — are read as a statement about modern man's alienation from meaning or from God, or as an allegory of psychopathology.

Proust, Joyce, Faulkner, Rilke, Lawrence, Gide . . . one could go on citing author after author; the list is endless of those around whom thick encrustations of interpretation have taken hold. But it should be noted that interpretation is not simply the compliment that mediocrity pays to genius. It is, indeed, *the* modern way of understanding something, and is applied to works of every quality. Thus, in the notes that Elia Kazan published on his production of *A Streetcar Named Desire,* it becomes clear that, in order to direct the play, Kazan had to discover that Stanley Kowalski represented the sensual and vengeful barbarism that was engulfing our culture, while Blanche Du Bois was Western civilization, poetry, delicate apparel, dim lighting, refined feelings and all, though a little the worse for wear to be sure. Tennessee Williams's forceful psychological melodrama now became intelligible: it was *about* something, about the decline of Western civilization. Apparently, were it to go on being a play about a handsome brute named Stanley Kowalski and a faded mangy belle named Blanche Du Bois, it would not be manageable.

6

It doesn't matter whether artists intend, or don't intend, for their works to be interpreted. Perhaps Tennessee Williams thinks *Streetcar* is about what Kazan thinks it to be about. It may be that Cocteau in *The Blood of a Poet* and in *Orpheus* wanted the elaborate readings which have been given these films, in terms of Freudian symbolism and social critique. But the merit of these works certainly lies elsewhere than in their "meanings." Indeed, it is precisely to the extent that Williams's plays and Cocteau's films do suggest these portentous meanings that they are defective, false, contrived, lacking in conviction.

From interviews, it appears that Resnais and Robbe-Grillet consciously designed *Last Year at Marienbad* to accommodate a multiplicity of equally plausible interpretations. But the temptation to interpret *Marienbad* should be resisted. What matters in *Marienbad* is the pure, untranslatable, sensuous immediacy of some of its images, and its rigorous if narrow solutions to certain problems of cinematic form.

Again, Ingmar Bergman may have meant the tank rumbling down the empty night street in *The Silence* as a phallic symbol. But if he did, it was a foolish thought. ("Never trust the teller, trust the tale," said Lawrence.) Taken as a brute object, as an immediate sensory equivalent for the mysterious abrupt armored happenings going on inside the hotel, that sequence with the tank is the most striking moment in the film. Those who reach for a Freudian interpretation of the tank are only expressing their lack of response to what is there on the screen.

It is always the case that interpretation of this type indicates a dissatisfaction (conscious or unconscious) with the work, a wish to replace it by something else.

Interpretation, based on the highly dubious theory that a work of art is composed of items of content, violates art. It makes art into an article for use, for arrangement into a mental scheme of categories.

7

Interpretation does not, of course, always prevail. In fact, a great deal of today's art may be understood as motivated by a flight from interpretation. To avoid interpretation, art may become parody. Or it may become abstract. Or it may become ("merely") decorative. Or it may become non-art.

The flight from interpretation seems particularly a feature of modern painting. Abstract painting is the attempt to have, in the ordinary sense, no content; since there is no content, there can be no interpretation. Pop Art works by the opposite means to the same result; using a content so blatant, so "what it is," it, too, ends by being uninterpretable.

A great deal of modern poetry as well, starting from the great experiments of French poetry (including the movement that is misleadingly called Symbolism) to put silence into poems and to reinstate the *magic* of the word, has escaped from the rough grip of interpretation. The most recent revolution in contemporary taste in poetry — the revolution that has deposed Eliot and elevated Pound — represents a turning away from content in poetry in the old sense, an impatience with what made modern poetry prey to the zeal of interpreters.

I am speaking mainly of the situation in America, of course. Interpretation runs rampant here in those arts with a feeble and negligible avant-garde: fiction and the drama. Most American novelists and playwrights are really either journalists or gentlemen sociologists and psychologists. They are writing the literary equivalent of program music. And so rudimentary, uninspired, and stagnant has been the sense of what might be done with *form* in fiction and drama that even when the content isn't simply information, news, it is still peculiarly visible, handier, more exposed. To the extent that novels and plays (in America), unlike poetry and painting and music, don't reflect any interesting concern with changes in their form, these arts remain prone to assault by interpretation.

But programmatic avant-gardism — which has meant, mostly, experiments with form at the expense of content — is not the only defense against the infestation of art by interpretations. At least, I hope not. For this would be to commit art to being perpetually on the run. (It also perpetuates the very distinction between form and content which is, ultimately, an illusion.) Ideally, it is possible to elude the interpreters in another way, by making works of art whose surface is so unified and clean, whose momentum is so rapid, whose address is so direct that the work can be . . . just what it is. Is this possible now? It does happen in films, I believe. This is why cinema is the most alive, the most exciting, the most important of all art forms right now. Perhaps the way one tells how alive a particular art form is, is by the latitude it gives for making mistakes in it, and still being good. For example, a few of the films of Bergman — though crammed with lame messages about the modern spirit, thereby inviting interpretations — still triumph over the pretentious intentions of their director. In *Winter Light* and *The Silence,* the beauty and visual sophistication of the images subvert before our eyes the callow pseudo-intellectuality of the story and some of the dialogue. (The most remarkable instance of this sort of discrepancy is the work of D. W. Griffith.) In good films, there is always a directness that entirely frees us from the itch to interpret. Many old Hollywood films, like those of Cukor, Walsh, Hawks, and countless other directors, have this liberating anti-symbolic quality, no less than the best work of the new European

directors, like Truffaut's *Shoot the Piano Player* and *Jules and Jim,* Godard's *Breathless* and *Vivre Sa Vie,* Antonioni's *L'Avventura,* and Olmi's *The Fiancés.*

The fact that films have not been overrun by interpreters is in part due simply to the newness of cinema as an art. It also owes to the happy accident that films for such a long time were just movies; in other words, that they were understood to be part of mass, as opposed to high, culture, and were left alone by most people with minds. Then, too, there is always something other than content in the cinema to grab hold of, for those who want to analyze. For the cinema, unlike the novel, possesses a vocabulary of forms — the explicit, complex, and discussable technology of camera movements, cutting, and composition of the frame that goes into the making of a film.

8

What kind of criticism, of commentary on the arts, is desirable today? For I am not saying that works of art are ineffable, that they cannot be described or paraphrased. They can be. The question is how. What would criticism look like that would serve the work of art, not usurp its place?

What is needed, first, is more attention to form in art. If excessive stress on *content* provokes the arrogance of interpretation, more extended and more thorough descriptions of *form* would silence. What is needed is a vocabulary — a descriptive, rather than prescriptive, vocabulary — for forms.[5] The best criticism, and it is uncommon, is of this sort that dissolves considerations of content into those of form. On film, drama, and painting respectively, I can think of Erwin Panofsky's essay, "Style and Medium in the

[5]One of the difficulties is that our idea of form is spatial (the Greek metaphors for form are all derived from notions of space). This is why we have a more ready vocabulary of forms for the spatial than for the temporal arts. The exception among the temporal arts, of course, is the drama; perhaps this is because the drama is a narrative (i.e., temporal) form that extends itself visually and pictorially, upon a stage. . . . What we don't have yet is a poetics of the novel, any clear notion of the forms of narration. Perhaps film criticism will be the occasion of a breakthrough here, since films are primarily a visual form, yet they are also a subdivision of literature. [Sontag]

Motion Pictures," Northrop Frye's essay "A Conspectus of Dramatic Genres," Pierre Francastel's essay "The Destruction of a Plastic Space." Roland Barthes's book *On Racine* and his two essays on Robbe-Grillet are examples of formal analysis applied to the work of a single author. (The best essays in Erich Auerbach's *Mimesis,* like "The Scar of Odysseus," are also of this type.) An example of formal analysis applied simultaneously to genre and author is Walter Benjamin's essay, "The Story Teller: Reflections on the Works of Nicolai Leskov."

Equally valuable would be acts of criticism which would supply a really accurate, sharp, loving description of the appearance of a work of art. This seems even harder to do than formal analysis. Some of Manny Farber's film criticism, Dorothy Van Ghent's essay "The Dickens World: A View from Todgers,'" Randall Jarrell's essay on Walt Whitman are among the rare examples of what I mean. These are essays which reveal the sensuous surface of art without mucking about in it.

9

Transparence is the highest, most liberating value in art — and in criticism — today. Transparence means experiencing the luminousness of the thing in itself, of things being what they are. This is the greatness of, for example, the films of Bresson and Ozu and Renoir's *The Rules of the Game.*

Once upon a time (say, for Dante), it must have been a revolutionary and creative move to design works of art so that they might be experienced on several levels. Now it is not. It reinforces the principle of redundancy that is the principal affliction of modern life.

Once upon a time (a time when high art was scarce), it must have been a revolutionary and creative move to interpret works of art. Now it is not. What we decidedly do not need now is further to assimilate Art into Thought, or (worse yet) Art into Culture.

Interpretation takes the sensory experience of the work of art for granted, and proceeds from there. This cannot be taken for granted, now. Think of the sheer multiplication of works of art available to every one of us, superadded to the conflicting tastes and odors and sights of the urban environment that bombard our senses. Ours is a culture based on excess, on overproduction; the result is a steady loss of sharpness in our sensory experience. All the conditions of modern life — its material plenitude, its sheer crowdedness — conjoin to dull our sensory faculties. And it is in the light of the condition of our senses, our capacities (rather than those of another age), that the task of the critic must be assessed.

What is important now is to recover our senses. We must learn to *see* more, to *hear* more, to *feel* more.

Our task is not to find the maximum amount of content in a work of art, much less to squeeze more content out of the work than is already there. Our task is to cut back content so that we can see the thing at all.

The aim of all commentary on art now should be to make works of art — and, by analogy, our own experience — more, rather than less, real to us. The function of criticism should be to show *how it is what it is,* even *that it is what it is,* rather than to show *what it means.*

10

In place of a hermeneutics we need an erotics of art.

CONTEMPORARY TRENDS IN LITERARY CRITICISM

1

FORMALISMS: RUSSIAN FORMALISM, NEW CRITICISM, NEO-ARISTOTELIANISM

Habitualization devours works, clothes, furniture, one's wife, and the fear of war. . . . And art exists that one may recover the sensation of life; it exists to make one feel things, to make the stone stony. The purpose of art is to impart the sensation of things as they are perceived and not as they are known.
— VICTOR SHKLOVSKY

Finding its proper symbol, defined and refined by the participating metaphors, the theme becomes a part of the reality in which we live — an insight, rooted in and growing out of concrete experience, many-sided, three-dimensional.
— CLEANTH BROOKS

There are many questions that Aristotle's approach will not answer: questions about the spirit of tragedy throughout the ages, questions about how to rise from despair to faith, questions about how to use art to attack your enemies. . . . But you know there is no better cure for despair than rousing yourself and joining a great artist in his particular creative acts; there is no better proof of nobility than seeing a bit of it really work in a great piece of art; there is no more satisfactory proof of the existence of the good, the true and the beautiful than experiencing their fusion in the unique, particular achievement of a story. . . .
— WAYNE C. BOOTH

The three movements discussed here cover a vast amount of geographical ground (centered in Moscow, in London and Nashville, and in Chicago), and they have flourished over a long stretch of the present century, from just after World War I to the present day. Whether the theoretical territories inhabited by the formalists are seen as vast or confined depends on whether one looks at the positive ideas they have espoused or at their oppositions. All three versions of formalism proposed an "intrinsic" criticism that defined and addressed the specifically literary qualities in the text, and all three began in reaction to various forms of "extrinsic" criticism that viewed the text as either the product of social and historical forces or a document making an ethical statement. But no two of the three agreed on precisely what made a text "literary," what qualities of form, language, or content differentiated it from nonliterary discourse, or what the significance of literature was for humanity. There are major discrepancies among these three movements, as one might expect, but the divergences *within* each movement are almost as striking.

RUSSIAN FORMALISM

Of the three movements, Russian formalism had the briefest flowering. It originated in Moscow in 1915 with a group of linguists and stylisticians known as OPOYAZ (Society for the Study of Poetic Language), grew for about a decade in postrevolutionary Russia, and as a movement was finally eliminated for political reasons by Joseph Stalin and his henchman Andrey Zhdanov around 1930. Most of its members either formally recanted (as did Victor Shklovsky) or emigrated (like Roman Jakobson). Their publications, suppressed in the USSR, were lost to the West until Victor Erlich's pioneering study *Russian Formalism: History — Doctrine* (1955) and Tzvetan Todorov's 1965 translation of the formalists into French. Nevertheless, the ultimate influence of the formalists was considerable. Roman Jakobson carried their ideas west, first to the Prague Linguistic Circle (which included Jan Mukařovský), and then to Paris, where he and Claude Lévi-Strauss helped create the structuralist movement that flourished from the early 1960s.

The origins of Russian formalism and the New Criticism show some interesting parallels, largely because the two movements developed in opposition to the same two mainstream forms of contemporary criticism. On the one hand they rejected the historicism of academic criticism, which was seen as a tedious investigation of the circumstances of poetic creation pursued in the absence of any coherent notion of poetics itself. On the other, they despised the liberal "social criticism" of reformers who wished to use literature as a means of cultural progress. What the moralist Paul Elmer More was to the New Critics, nineteenth-century socialist critics like Vissarion Belinsky, Nikolay Chernyshevsky, and Nikolay Dobrolyubov were to the Russian formalists.

Serious divergences occurred, however. The New Critics were essentially allied with the imagist poets (including T. E. Hulme, T. S. Eliot, and Ezra Pound), who viewed poetry as a means of communicating, through image and symbol, what could not be said in prose. The poetics of the New Critics centered in semantics, and set the critic the task of decoding the text by explicating its tropes. The systems of individual New Critics largely differed over which of the principal figures of speech or thought — such as metaphor, irony, and ambiguity — was chosen as the master trope.

The Russian formalists began by refining but ultimately rejecting the work of a nineteenth-century philologist who might be seen as a prototype New Critic. Alexander Potebnya viewed imagery as the master trope distinguishing poetry from prose, which he regarded as two distinct ways of knowing the world. This theory was embraced by the symbolist poets (like Andrey Bely and Dmitry Merezhkovsky), who looked to art to produce a mystical form of knowledge. Potebnya was as much an exemplar as he was an opponent of the formalists; he had been concerned about the line dividing the literary from the nonliterary (an issue about which the social critics cared little), and he had defined literariness as a function of language, a point of view the formalists were also to embrace.

Potebnya is chiefly known today, however, through the attack on his ideas in Victor Shklovsky's manifesto of formalism, "Art as Technique," which takes issue with the narrowness of Potebnya's conception of art in elevating metaphor and symbolism, imagery, or any single trope to master status. From Shklovsky's perspective, the central difficulty with Potebnya's conception of poetry was its obsession with semantics, with the notion that the things poetry had to express were mystically different from those of prose. For Shklovsky, the chief function of art is not to lead us to a knowledge above and beyond the world but to restore our capacity to see a world to which use and habit have blinded us. "As perception becomes habitual, it becomes automatic," says Shklovsky, "and art exists that one may recover the sensation of life . . . . of things as they are perceived and not as they are known." By its use of unaccustomed language, art makes the world strange again, so that we can see it with the freshness of a child. *Ostranenie* (defamiliarization), the concept at the center of Shklovsky's poetics, is an inversion of Samuel Johnson's notion that art "approximates the remote and familiarizes the wonderful."

The concept of defamiliarization is central to the formalist project, but the term can be used in different ways at different levels of approach to the literary object. At the most basic level of discourse, the formalists analyzed sentences taken from literary texts to see how they estranged reality as a purely aesthetic end in itself. But at the higher level where discourse becomes social, the formalists saw texts' representations of reality as a technique for defamiliarizing the social ideas of the dominant culture, and thus for challenging our automatic acceptance of these ideas. They would say, for example, that an apparently naive and incoherent narrative voice (like that of Gogol's *The Nose*) functions so as to expose the cruelty and hypocrisy of the social ideas of the time.

At a still higher and more abstract level, the formalists, as Tony Bennett has put it, "were concerned with the formal mechanisms whereby literary works tended to reveal or make strange the systems of coherence imposed on reality by the codes and conventions of other, usually earlier literary forms."[1] For example, Shklovsky's essay on *Tristram Shandy* (1921) distinguishes between *fabula* (or story), that is, the temporal-causal sequence of narrated events that comprise the raw materials of the work, and *sjuzet* (or plot), the way in which these raw materials are formally manipulated, in order to argue that *Tristram Shandy,* as Bennett puts it, "is told in such a way as to limit and reveal the narrative conventions of the time. . . ."

The distinction between *fabula* and *sjuzet* owes a great deal to another nineteenth-century forebear of the formalists, the academic literary historian Alexander Veselovsky. Around 1906, Veselovsky evolved a poetics of "motifs," in which the literary work is dissected into its smallest irreducible components, and plot is seen as a complex cluster of story-motifs, ordered, altered, and rearranged by art; Veselovsky thought that shifting motifs correlated with changes in cultural attitudes.

[1]Tony Bennett, *Formalism and Marxism* (London: Methuen, 1979), p. 23.

The formalists predictably disagreed with his version of historical determinism but adopted Veselovsky's techniques of thematic analysis, as exemplified by Boris Tomashevsky's "Thematics" (1925) and Vladimir Propp's *The Morphology of the Folk-Tale* (1928).

In effect, the formalists viewed literature as a mode of construction. Poetry was defined by its use of poetic language, fiction as the craft of manipulating story materials by narrative technique. What was not a matter of construction, such as the origins and the cultural meaning of a literary work, was not specifically literary, and was therefore dismissed as not a true part of poetics. The difficulty with such a view, as one historian of formalism has suggested, is that "it does not permit us to evaluate" individual texts. "But the OPOYAZ members never introduced the problems of evaluation into their system."[2]

If Shklovsky established the principal issues governing the literary qualities of texts, Roman Jakobson most succinctly defined the poetic in what would today be called semiotic fashion: as a special use of language. Poetry was "an utterance oriented toward the mode of expression"; in poetry "a word is perceived as a word and not merely as a proxy for the denoted object or an outburst of emotion. . . . Words and their arrangement . . . their outward and inward form acquire weight and value of their own."[3]

At the outset, the Russian formalists talked as though it were the emotive quality of poetry that differentiated it from common language, but a *semantic* feature of that sort was bound to seem unsatisfactory in the long run; obviously some expressions of feeling are poetic and some are not, while a great deal of what is clearly poetry is not primarily emotional expression. Besides, emotion was a sort of content, and with such a discriminant, the formalists would have been entrapped in the notion of an external form enclosing a crude content. Jakobson's idea made it possible to drop entirely the notion of a separable content and to view poetic form as that which integrates the raw material of language into a shaped structure. Jakobson's sense of form as a dynamic shaping process thus resembles the Aristotelian *eidos;* as we shall see, it has more in common with the Chicago neo-Aristotelians' notions of form than that of the New Critics.

The work of Vladimir Propp on folklore (represented here by "Fairy Tale Transformations," p. 785) exemplifies this notion of literature as a system. Previous ways of analyzing folktales had operated at the level of the plot as a whole: the classification system of Antti Aarne (begun 1907, codified by Stith Thompson in 1932)[4] was designed to allow folklorists to compare tales from different cultures, to allow us to show the similarities of a "Cinderella" story from China and one told by the Lakota. The defect of the system is that it groups tales together in terms of the whole plot, and the factors by which tales are grouped together or separated can sometimes seem arbitrary. For example, the story most of us know as Bluebeard focuses on a person who marries an ogre, violates a condition the ogre imposes, and is about to

---

[2]Krystyna Pomorska, "Russian Formalism in Retrospect," in *Readings in Russian Poetics,* ed. Ladislaw Matejka and Krystyna Pomorska (Cambridge: MIT Press, 1971), p. 275.

[3]Victor Erlich, *Russian Formalism: History — Doctrine* (The Hague: Mouton, 1963), p. 183.

[4]Antti Aarne, *Vergleichende märchenforschung* (Helsinki, 1907); Stith Thompson, *Motif-index of Folk Literature* (Bloomington IN, 1932–36).

be killed when he or she is saved by a rescuer. Aarne-Thompson classifies the story as Type 312 if the rescuer is male, Type 311 if female, but whether the ogre is male or female does not make any difference.

Trying to bring greater system to the understanding of folklore and fictional plots in general, Propp analyzed a group of 100 fairy tales collected by Afanase'ev, breaking each of them down into individual plot elements, then generalizing those elements. For example, in one tale Baba Jaga (a demonic female figure in Russian folklore) gives Ivan a horse. Within one "function" (Gift), the *donor* is Baba Jaga, the *recipient* is Ivan, and the *gift* is the horse. Propp found 31 functions, usually related to the verbs in his plot element, and 120 other "components," which may correspond to nouns, to adjectives, or to phrases indicating where an action takes place. Propp's system seems protostructuralist; in this we can see how structuralist anthropologists like Claude Lévi-Strauss used Propp in devising their classifications of myth. But Propp is not primarily interested in creating a purely theoretical system with static symmetry; his principal object is to understand how folklore develops historically. Russia was Christianized fairly late in its history, so Propp understands tales where the hero's helpers are apostles and the villain is the devil as more recent than those where the helpers are friendly animals and the villain is a forest demon. Other historical connections may be less clear because they can move in both directions. Normally we think of romances as developing out of pre-existing folk materials, but a romance can be recited and retold in the form of stories that can break down into folktales (as many of us know Greek and Roman "myths" without knowing the specific poems and romances in which they originate).

If the idea of the literary was the founding feature of Russian formalism, literary history rapidly became one of its primary concerns. For the formalists, the older modes of literary history were essentially inadequate because they had never established any strong sense of what made a particular text into literature in a given age. Without any systematic notion of the literary, the only causal mechanisms available were what Boris Eikhenbaum called "the naïve theory of 'inheritance' and 'influence' and hence naïve biographism based on individual psychology."[5] The formalists believed that at any moment a national literature was not just a collection of individual works but a system of genres. This system is hierarchical: one genre is dominant at any given time. And the genres fall into dialectical relations with each other, epic against romance, comedy against tragedy, pastoral poetry against the poetic satire. As cultures change, the literary system changes, but the dominance of genres does not follow in a clear and predictable line of succession. Shklovsky put it this way: "When literary schools change, the succession passes not from father to son, but from uncle to nephew." Applying this to early modern England, epic clearly seems the dominant genre (the *Faerie Queene, Paradise Lost*). In the eighteenth century, the philosophical poem dominates (*Essay on Man*), while epic is a depressed, even despised genre. Narrative poetry resumes its primacy in the early nineteenth century, but its form is personal and autobiographical rather than epic (*The Prelude, Childe Harold's Pilgrimage*).

[5]Boris Mikhailovich Eikhenbaum, "Literature and Literary Life," in *Moi Vramennik* (Leningrad, 1929): 52.

The Russian formalists held that this generic change within literary systems happens primarily by reason of formal exhaustion. A dominant genre attracts lesser talents, becomes less and less creative, more and more imitative, becomes coarse as strong sensations need to be delivered to provide literary impact. Held together by conventions, the genre becomes automatized (the mark of the non-literary, as Shklovsky says), and topples from its position. A new genre takes its place at the top, and the process repeats itself with the new dominant. This motor for literary history stands in compelling contrast with the Marxists' view that literature responds primarily to exterior social and economic change.

THE NEW CRITICISM

The Russian formalists were Underground Men, whose ideas were absent from the critical dialogue of the West until the 1960s. The New Criticism, to the contrary, is one of the more conspicuous success stories of the century, and if the movement is centered somewhat less coherently than the others, that may have been one of the principal reasons for its popularity, because the New Criticism is associated less with a body of theoretical doctrine about the nature of language and poetry than with a method of critical exegesis and explication.

The name "New Criticism" seems to have been bestowed by John Crowe Ransom in a 1941 book of that title, which examines the work of I. A. Richards and William Empson, T. S. Eliot, Yvor Winters, and the philosopher Charles W. Morris. The most important New Critics include this group, Ransom himself, and his fellow Southern "fugitive" writers Allen Tate, Cleanth Brooks, and Robert Penn Warren. Other important theorists associated with the movement include René Wellek, R. P. Blackmur, Robert B. Heilman, Austin Warren, and Murray Krieger. After this point it is hard to tell where to stop, since by the 1950s the New Critical method of poetic explication had come to dominate the teaching of literature in England and America, and most working literary critics had been touched by it in one way or another. One should look to I. A. Richards and T. S. Eliot as the primary founders of this method, the former through his philosophical theories and the latter through his critical practice and tastes.

Like the Russian formalists, Richards was mainly concerned with what differentiated poetry from common language. For him the issue was principally referentiality. Richards held that in common language we make statements that refer to matters of fact, whereas in poetry we make pseudostatements that may appear to be referential but in fact are not. Statements made in poetry cannot be verified; their function is affective rather than cognitive. A poem arouses and allays feelings through the dance of conflicting attitudes stimulated by its complex language. Such an aesthetic moment shakes up the reader's established responses to real life by stimulating the reader's experience of a sense of harmony established among opposing impulses. The form of the poem consists of these stimuli and responses within an ideal reader. (Richards's notion of poetry is at bottom a more behavioristic version of Coleridge, who held that the imagination operates by reconciling opposing qualities into an ideal unity of form.) Richards was primarily a theorist; the critical practice inherent in his ideas was taken over by his student, William Empson. Empson's *Seven Types of Ambiguity* (1930) was an attempt to establish the ways in which texts create, through ambiguity, a multiplicity of meanings, which stimulate the reader to see their harmonious reconciliation. Since it would be possible using any good dictionary to find dozens of possible meanings for the words in a short poem and thousands of possible combinations of these meanings, Empson was attacked for employing a method that, when used mechanically, would produce an inchoate cloud of possible interpretations for any text. Empson was in fact sensitive to the issue of literary intentionality and the question of how the many possible constituents of meaning coalesce into a single complex and moving idea; his epilogue to *Seven Types of Ambiguity* discusses the limits to ambiguity and the relation between audience response and authorial intent.

Two decades later, the most rigorous of the American New Critics, including Ransom and Wimsatt, would reject the reader-oriented formulation of Richards and Empson: The "affective fallacy" would insist that the form of a poem is not to be identified with the psychological process undergone by its audience. (Since this process is likely to differ in various readers, it would leave the form at best indeterminate and at worst under the control of the audience.) But purged of its affective slant, this view of form as an interplay of feelings and attitudes, like the interwoven themes of music, was to prove persuasive and fertile.

T. S. Eliot was also to lend ideas to the New Criticism. In "Tradition and the Individual Talent" Eliot spoke of literature as an "ideal order," a tradition which exists not successively in history but is somehow present simultaneously as it exerts influence upon the newly created work. (See Eliot's essay, p. 537.) This viewpoint had justified the breach between the New Criticism and the historical scholarship that had dominated the academy. In "Hamlet and His Problems," Eliot also presented the "objective correlative," the idea of one-to-one correspondence between the images in a poem and the feelings for which the image is supposed to be the formula. Given this correspondence, poetry could have emotive significance, but its themes could be discussed *objectively* in a more concrete explication of the poem's emotional content. Although these were influential ideas, Eliot was perhaps even more influential in his tastes, which valorized the poets and playwrights of the English Renaissance over the Augustans, Romantics, and Victorians who had dominated the canon, and in his critical practice, which lucidly explicated the poetry of Donne and the plays of Middleton as though they were his contemporaries.

Despite the efforts of René Wellek to give the New Criticism a pedigree in Kantian aesthetics, its development from the late 1930s on was primarily as a critical practice rather than a set of theoretical doctrines. The general theory was simply that literature was a special kind of language and that practical criticism reflects and is constrained by that principle. The most influential ideological statements tended to explain what criticism should not do, rather than what it should. Pride of place should be given to a pair of papers by William K. Wimsatt and Monroe C. Beardsley defending new critical practice against a series of "fallacies": One was "The Affective Fallacy" (1949), which rejected the notion that the poem could be defined in terms of the internal experiences of actual readers (although the New

Critics, without precisely admitting to it, tended to analyze poetry in terms of the response of *ideal* readers).

Even more influential was "The Intentional Fallacy" (1946), which, consistent with Eliot's assertion of the impersonality of poetry in "Tradition and the Individual Talent," attacks the notion of the work of art as the essentially private product of the internal experience of a particular individual. The poem is defined as a public text, and its meaning by what the public norms of language allow it to mean. The text's aesthetic success or failure must be judged in those terms alone. Within its original context, the intentional fallacy was a convincing refutation of Crocean idealism, which would have located the aesthetic object in the author's lyrical intuition, and of the old historicism, which referred the meaning of the text to the circumstances of its genesis and its historical context. The intent of the intentional fallacy was to liberate the reader: Thereafter, the only apparatus one needed to read Chaucer and Shakespeare was a good text and a historical dictionary. But the ultimate effect of anti-intentionalism was to foster the irresponsible interpretation of texts, a search for originality of reading without regard to the creator's probable purposes.

There were other fallacies and heresies: the *fallacy of imitative form* attempted to cut the text off from the world it supposedly represented in order to purify the New Criticism of the mimetic principle, as it had already been purified of the expressive and affective ones. The *fallacy of neoclassic species* was aimed at R. S. Crane and the Chicago critics, whose formal theories located the text within an open system of genres. The *biographical heresy* was aimed at those who would identify the speaker of the poem with its author. In general, these treatises aimed to isolate the text as a "verbal icon" (to use Wimsatt's phrase) whose form was to be found entirely within itself.

As various historians of critical theory have pointed out, the creators of this version of formalism may have had ulterior reasons for purifying the text. Many of the American New Critics were from the South, a depressed region that during and after World War II had been undergoing a social and economic revolution, which had displaced traditional values and culture. As the Marxist Terry Eagleton puts it, the New Criticism "was the ideology of an uprooted, defensive intelligentsia who reinvented in literature what they could not find in reality. Poetry was the new religion, a nostalgic haven from the alienations of industrial capitalism."[6] Poetry was not only viewed as a force opposing the crassness and secularization of modern life, but as the location of the spiritual values these critics held dear. As Cleanth Brooks once confessed, "it is no accident that so many of the [New Critics] have gone on, either to avow an orthodox religious position or else to affirm the possibility and necessity for metaphysics as a science."[7] Brooks's associates at the *Kenyon Review,* including critics like John Crowe Ransom and Allen Tate, felt that "the whole effort of the literary imagination is toward a kind of incarnation of reality in language."[8]

[6]Terry Eagleton, *Literary Criticism: An Introduction* (Minneapolis: University of Minnesota Press, 1983), p. 47.

[7]"Metaphor and the Function of Criticism," in *Spiritual Problems in Contemporary Literature,* ed. S. R. Hooper (New York: Harper Torchbooks, 1957), p. 134.

[8]Allen Tate, quoted in Michael Millgate, "An Interview with Allen Tate," *Shenandoah* 12 (1961): 31.

We can see this quasi-religious impulse in the theories of John Crowe Ransom, who sought in poetry something larger than aesthetic form, something that in *The World's Body* (1941) he had called "ontological": a capturing of the *body* of experience. And in criticism he was seeking a way of helping the reader recapture that essence:

> The poet perpetuates in his poem an order of existence which in actual life is constantly crumbling beneath his touch. . . . For each poem even, ideally, there is distinguishable a logical object or universal, but at the same time a tissue of irrelevance from which it does not really emerge. The critic has to take the poem apart, or analyze it, for the sake of uncovering these features. With all the finesse possible, it is rude and patchy business. . . . But without it there could hardly be much understanding of the value of poetry, or of the natural history behind any adult poem.[9]

For Ransom, poetry is defined by the interplay between structure and texture. Like prose, poetry has a determinate meaning (or logical structure), but in the case of poetry the determinate meaning is deformed by (among other things) the pressure of versification. The necessity of finding rhymes and rhythmic form results in an admixture of what he calls "indeterminate meaning," which may be a mere dross of verbiage that testifies to the human process of creation or may include wonderful, shockingly brilliant novelties that contribute to poetic texture.

Although there was considerable agreement on the principles of art and on the technique of literary explication that was the critic's "job of work," each New Critic developed a slightly different terminology for discussing the issues. For Cleanth Brooks, the terms equivalent to Ransom's structure and texture would be the "paraphraseable content" of a poem (which he equates with its "rational or logical structure") and its "essential structure." In "The Heresy of Paraphrase" (1947) (another heresy!), Brooks insists that the poem not only cannot be equated with its paraphrasable content, but that the content should not be seen as an inner core wrapped about in an exterior form consisting of metrical language. Harking back to Richards, in *The Well Wrought Urn* (1947) Brooks instead defines the "essential structure" of the poem as being like that of

> architecture or painting: it is a pattern of resolved stresses. Or, to move closer still . . . the structure of a poem resembles that of a ballet or musical composition. It is a pattern of resolutions and balances and harmonizations developed through a temporal scheme.[10]

The thematic criticism of the New Critics tended to operate by finding within the texture of the poem oppositions and conflicts that were resolved into a harmonious balance. The principal mediator of this resolution was poetic language, specifically the capacity of language to carry multiple meanings that could disclose hidden conflicts and tensions at the outset of the poem and converge into a harmonious balance at the end. For I. A. Richards's pupil William Empson, the proper term for this

[9]John Crowe Ransom, *The World's Body* (New York: Scribners, 1938): 348–49.
[10]Cleanth Brooks, "The Heresy of Paraphrase" in *The Well Wrought Urn: Studies in the Structure of Poetry* (New York: Harcourt, Brace and World, 1947): p. 203.

polysemic capacity of language was *ambiguity,* of which he distinguished and elaborately discussed seven distinct types. The American New Critics preferred to locate individual master tropes (or figures of speech) that would serve as the center for their discourse. For Cleanth Brooks, the master tropes were *paradox* and *irony*, the latter defined not in its strict sense — saying the opposite of what is intended — but very broadly, as occurring whenever a statement is undercut or qualified by its context. Similarly, for Allen Tate the chief issue in poetry was the "*tension* between two opposing forces." Although the criticism of Robert Penn Warren flirted with irony, his usual master trope, like that of R. P. Blackmur, was the literary *symbol.* For Robert B. Heilman, the principal issue was the *image,* and it was through the conflict of opposing clusters of images that eventual resolution was achieved. For Murray Krieger, as for the Russian formalists, the master trope was *metaphor.* These divergences were more apparent than real, for each of these literary figures of speech and of thought was in practice broadened from its usual definition to potentially include all the others as well.

What may seem strange, especially given the contrary example of the Russian formalists, is that despite the New Critical emphasis on poetic language, none of the major theorists had any interest in contemporary discoveries in linguistics and semiotics; in fact they disdained "professionalism" in the study of language. This disdain may have been held over from the amateur's stance that the New Critics cultivated, a stance opposed to the professionalism of historical scholarship, against which the movement had originally defined itself.

As we have noted, the dominance of the New Critical thematic explication was nearly absolute through the 1960s. Even today the critical practice of many American teachers of literature owes a great deal to Cleanth Brooks and William Empson. But as a theory, the New Criticism has few current defenders, and its vitality has suffered more than one might gather by counting its remaining devotees. Nevertheless, while the New Criticism has been supplanted by a variety of other interpretive modes, these modes have been forced to define themselves against a once-dominant New Critical tradition, and in this negative sense the New Criticism still lives.

Its more important surviving legacy is the cult of the interpretation and reinterpretation of texts that makes up so much of the critic's professional life. John Crowe Ransom had begun by noting that for the poem to capture the world's body, the critic must recapture it for the common reader. The New Criticism redefined the professoriate as the priesthood of twentieth-century humanism, making the verbal icon accessible to the laity. The critic's proper job of work was the decoding of a text whose surface meaning, however evident to the average reader, is seen as insufficient. The journals and little magazines accordingly filled with interpretations, but eventually the very success of the New Critical methods bred failure. By the 1960s it had spawned an insistent hunger for reinterpretation of canonical texts (or at least for the books and articles upon which professional academic success depends). And eventually the New Criticism, within its formal strictures of fallacies and heresies, could provide for this demand only by more farfetched decodings. But if New Critical theory has been jettisoned in favor of readings based on Marxist, feminist, or deconstructionist literary theories, the view of literature as a mystery to which the critic alone has the key survives. The profession has not so readily relinquished the verbal icon.

NEO-ARISTOTELIANISM

Just as the New Criticism arose out of the New South, neo-Aristotelianism grew out of the innovative Hutchins curriculum at the University of Chicago, which replaced the traditional lecture system with a program of the close study of the "Great Books of the Western Tradition." Moved by the general intellectual ferment of the time and galvanized by the philosophical semantics of Richard McKeon, the historical scholar R. S. Crane came out in 1935 against teaching literature to undergraduates through its purely historical origins and in favor of a new approach using textual explication and aesthetics.[11] As chairman of the English department, Crane was able to hire over the next decade a number of humanists who assisted him in developing a critical theory and practice that has become known as neo-Aristotelianism or Chicago criticism; this group included Elder Olson, Norman Maclean, and W. R. Keast, in addition to McKeon and Crane himself.

Though Crane had placed himself on the side of the New Critics on the issue of history versus criticism, he and his group were scornful of New Critical theories of literature, which they considered reductive, simplistic, and a serious distortion of the nature of literature and language. As a result, the 1940s and 1950s saw an acrimonious debate in the pages of scholarly journals and little magazines, intemperate on both sides, between Crane's group and such New Critics as Brooks, Wimsatt, Warren, and Heilman. A sample taste of this rancorous relationship can be found in the Dialogue section on p. 807 where Crane criticizes Cleanth Brooks. By 1960, when the dust had settled, the New Critics held the field, primarily because their critical methods, propagated in successful textbooks like *Understanding Poetry* (1938), had revolutionized undergraduate and even secondary-school training in literature across America. The textual explications of the Chicago school, in contrast, were confined primarily to scholarly books and learned journals. And the neo-Aristotelian method of analyzing literature was a more complex approach, which did not lend itself to popularization. On the other hand, the New Criticism succeeded at the cost of ideological stagnation, while neo-Aristotelianism developed a second generation of critics (including Wayne C. Booth, Sheldon Sacks, Ralph Rader, Robert Marsh, Norman Friedman, Mary Doyle Springer, and Austin Wright) and a third generation (including Don Bialostosky, Brian Corman, Walter Davis, Barbara Foley, Elizabeth Langland, James Phelan, Peter Rabinowitz, and Adena Rosmarin), all of whom are endeavoring to revise, extend, and adapt Crane's ideas to new projects.

Aristotle's concept of *mimesis,* or imitation, is not central to Chicago criticism. The crucial Aristotelian concepts are from the *Metaphysics* rather than the *Poetics;* they

---

[11]R. S. Crane, "History versus Criticism in the Study of Literature" (1935), reprinted in *The Idea of the Humanities* (Chicago: University of Chicago Press, 1967), vol. 2, pp. 3–24.

include the *eidos,* or "shaping form," and the *synolon,* or "concrete whole" of formed matter, found in nature or manufactured by art. The *synolon* is analyzed in terms of its formal, material, efficient, and final causes. Poetic works of art are *synola* in which plot, character, and thought (the formal cause) give shape to language (the material cause) using various techniques or devices of disclosure (the efficient cause) to create an object with the power to affect a reader in various ways (the final cause).

The "concrete whole" is matter shaped by form to be "inherently meaningful and beautiful."[12] The work's power comes from the inferred sense of the whole, not from the parts; in fact our sense of the whole *as a pattern* is what governs the perceived meaning of the parts. Language, however crucial to our perception of the form, does not define poetic form as it did for the New Critics: It is only a means — and not even the most important one — to an end. Not even plot, which was so crucial for Crane's notions of form, is wholly decisive. Although our sense of the whole takes shape through our experience of the parts, we revise our sense of the parts through our growing sense of the whole to which they contribute. And while the powers of some literary works may require temporary or permanent ambiguities, many merely *potential* ambiguities within a text are cleared up by this shaping process.

R. S. Crane viewed Aristotle primarily as the founder of a positivistic and "differential" method (one opposed to Plato's idealistic and synthesizing method). In tragedy the final cause, the *dynamis,* is the catharsis of pity and fear, and Aristotle judges various Attic tragedies by how well their various elements are designed, the ultimate criterion being their capacity to effect the tragic *dynamis.* Crane wanted to extend the systematic approach of the *Poetics* to other genres with different powers, which different structures of plot, character, thought, language, and technique were designed to serve.

While other genre critics (like Northrop Frye) felt the need to map literature as a field, for the Chicago critics, genres had a different purpose. They functioned as multiple models to which the critic might look in creating strong hypotheses about the specific texts under analysis, hypotheses leading to predictions that might (like scientific hypotheses) be verified or falsified by the text itself or by features of its creation or reception. The openness and pluralism of the genre system served to make it less likely that the critic would have to distort the text to make it fit a single procrustean model. The aim was a method similar to that of science, where conjectures are tested and refuted, and false leads eliminated, until the best explanation is found. Indeed, the critical aims of the Chicago school included the attainment of power through the successful search for objective truth. They were displaced scientists, unlike most of the New Critics, whose motivations, by their own accounts, were more like those of disappointed priests seeking in literature for a new Word to replace the one the world had lost.

---

[12]Ralph Rader, "Defoe, Richardson, Joyce, and the Concept of Form in Fiction," in *Autobiography, Biography and the Novel* (Los Angeles: Clark Memorial Library, 1973), p. 29.

Selected Bibliography

Bann, Stephen, and John E. Bowlt, eds. *Russian Formalism: A Collection of Articles and Texts in Translation.* New York: Barnes and Noble, 1973.

Bennett, Tony. *Formalism and Marxism.* London: Methuen, 1979.

Blackmur, R. P. *Language as Gesture.* New York: Harcourt, Brace and World, 1952.

———. *The Lion and the Honeycomb.* New York: Harcourt, Brace and World, 1955.

———. *New Criticism in the United States.* Tokyo: Kenkyusha, 1959.

Booth, Wayne C. *The Rhetoric of Fiction.* Chicago: University of Chicago Press, 1961; 2nd edition, 1983.

———. *A Rhetoric of Irony.* Chicago: University of Chicago Press, 1974.

———. *Critical Understanding: The Powers and Limits of Pluralism.* Chicago: University of Chicago Press, 1979.

———. *The Company We Keep: An Ethics of Fiction.* Berkeley and Los Angeles: University of California Press, 1988.

Brooks, Cleanth, and Robert Penn Warren. *Understanding Poetry.* New York: Henry Holt, 1938.

———. *Modern Poetry and the Tradition.* Chapel Hill: University of North Carolina Press, 1939.

———. *The Well Wrought Urn: Studies in the Structure of Poetry.* New York: Reynal and Hitchcock, 1947.

Crane, Ronald Salmon. *Critics and Criticism: Ancient and Modern.* Chicago: University of Chicago Press, 1952.

———. *The Languages of Criticism and the Structure of Poetry.* Toronto: University of Toronto Press, 1953.

———. *The Idea of the Humanities, and Other Essays.* 2 vols. Chicago: University of Chicago Press, 1967.

Davis, Walter A. *The Act of Interpretation: A Critique of Literary Reason.* Chicago: University of Chicago Press, 1978.

Eikhenbaum, Boris Mikhailovich. *O. Henry and the Theory of the Short Story.* Ann Arbor: Dept. of Slavic Languages and Literatures of the University of Michigan, 1968.

———. *Lermontov: A Study in Literary-Historical Evaluation.* Ann Arbor: Ardis, 1981.

Eliot, Thomas Stearns. *The Sacred Wood: Essays on Poetry and Criticism.* London: Methuen, 1920.

———. *For Lancelot Andrewes.* London: Faber and Gwyer, 1928.

———. *The Use of Poetry and the Use of Criticism.* London: Faber and Faber, 1933.

Empson, William. *Seven Types of Ambiguity.* London: Chatto & Windus, 1930.

Erlich, Victor. *Russian Formalism: History — Doctrine.* The Hague: Mouton, 1955.

Foley, Barbara. *Telling the Truth: The Theory and Practice of Documentary Fiction.* Ithaca: Cornell University Press, 1986.

Friedman, Norman. *Form and Meaning in Fiction.* Athens: University of Georgia Press, 1975.

Gallagher, Catherine. "The History of Literary Criticism." *Dædalus,* 126 (1997): 133–53.

Gorman, David. "A Bibliography of Russian Formalism in English." *Style* 26 (1992): 554–76.

Green, Daniel. "Literature Itself: The New Criticism and Aesthetic Experience." *Philosophy and Literature* 27 (2003): 62–79.

Jakobson, Roman. *Selected Writings.* 7 vols. The Hague: Mouton, 1962.

———. *The Framework of Language.* Ann Arbor: Graduate School of the University of Michigan, 1980.

Jancovich, Mark. *The Cultural Politics of the New Criticism.* Cambridge: Cambridge University Press, 1992.

Lemon, Lee T., and Marion J. Reis, eds. *Russian Formalist Criticism: Four Essays.* Lincoln: University of Nebraska Press, 1965.

Matejka, Ladislav, and Krystyna Pomorska, eds. *Readings in Russian Poetics.* Cambridge: MIT Press, 1971.

Medici, Anthony G. "The Restless Ghost of the New Criticism." *Style* 31 (1997): 760–73.

Olson, Elder. *Tragedy and the Theory of Drama.* Chicago: University of Chicago Press, 1962.

———. *On Value Judgments in the Arts.* Chicago: University of Chicago Press, 1976.

Phelan, James. *Worlds from Words: A Theory of Language in Fiction.* Chicago: University of Chicago Press, 1981.

———. *Reading People, Reading Plots.* Chicago: University of Chicago Press, 1991.

Propp, Vladimir. *Theory and History of Folklore.* Minneapolis: University of Minnesota Press, 1984.

Rader, Ralph. "Defoe, Richardson, Joyce, and the Concept of Form in the Novel." In *Autobiography, Biography and the Novel.* Los Angeles: William Andrews Clark Memorial Library, 1973.

———. "Fact, Theory and Literary Explanation." *Critical Inquiry* 1 (1974): 245–72.

———. "The Dramatic Monologue and Related Lyric Forms." *Critical Inquiry* 3 (1976): 131–51.

———. "The Emergence of the Novel in England: Genre in History vs. History of Genre." *Narrative* 1 (1993): 69–83.

Ransom, John Crowe. *The World's Body.* New York: Scribner's, 1938.

———. *The New Criticism.* Norfolk, CT: New Directions, 1941.

———. *Poems and Essays.* New York: Vintage, 1955.

Richards, I. A. *Principles of Literary Criticism.* New York: Harcourt Brace Jovanovich, 1924.

Richter, David H. *Fable's End: Completeness and Closure in Rhetorical Fiction.* Chicago: University of Chicago Press, 1974.

———. "The Second Flight of the Phoenix: Neo-Aristotelianism Since Crane." *The Eighteenth Century: Theory and Interpretation* 23 (1982): 27–48.

Sacks, Sheldon. *Fiction and the Shape of Belief.* Berkeley: University of California Press, 1964.

———. "Golden Birds and Dying Generations." *Comparative Literature Studies* 6 (1969): 274–91.

———. "*Clarissa* and the Tragic Traditions." In *Studies in Eighteenth-Century Culture,* ed. Harold E. Pagliaro. Cleveland: Case Western Reserve University Press, 1972, pp. 195–221.

Schneider, Anna-Dorothea. *Literaturkritik und Bildungspolitik: R. S. Crane, die Chicago (Neo-Aristotelian) Critics und die University of Chicago.* Heidelberg: 1994.

Shaitanov, Igor. "Aleksandr Veselovskii's Historical Poetics: Genre in Historical Poetics." *New Literary History* 32 (2001): 429–43.

Shklovsky, Victor Borisovich. *Works.* Moscow: Khudozh' Lit'ra, 1973–4.

Spurlin, William J., and Michael Fischer, eds. *The New Criticism and Contemporary Literary Theory: Connections and Continuities.* New York: Garland, 1995.

Steiner, Peter. *Russian Formalism: A Meta-Poetics.* Ithaca: Cornell University Press, 1984.

Striedter, Jurij. *Literary Structure, Evolution, and Value: Russian Formalism and Czech Structuralism Reconsidered.* Cambridge: Harvard University Press, 1989.

Tate, Allen. *Reactionary Essays on Poetry and Ideas.* New York: Scribners, 1936.

———. *Reason in Madness: Critical Essays.* New York: G. P. Putnam, 1941.

Thompson, Ewa Majewska. *Russian Formalism and Anglo-American New Criticism: A Comparative Study.* Hawthorne, NY: Mouton, 1971.

Tynyanov, Yuri. *The Problem of Verse Language.* Ann Arbor: Ardis, 1981.

Vygotsky, L. S. *Mind in Society: The Development of Higher Psychological Processes.* Cambridge: Harvard University Press, 1978.

Warren, Austin. *Rage for Order: Essays in Criticism.* Ann Arbor: University of Michigan Press, 1948.

Wellek, René, and Austin Warren. *Theory of Literature.* New York: Harcourt, Brace and World, 1949.

——. *A History of Modern Criticism 1759–1950.* 6 vols. New Haven: Yale University Press, 1955–87.

——. *Concepts of Criticism.* New Haven: Yale University Press, 1963.

Willingham, John R. "The New Criticism: Then and Now." In *Contemporary Literary Theory,* ed. Douglas Atkins and Janice Morrow. Amherst: University of Massachusetts Press, 1989, pp. 24–41.

Wimsatt, William K. *The Verbal Icon: Studies in the Meaning of Poetry.* Lexington: University Press of Kentucky, 1954.

——. *Hateful Contraries: Studies in Literature and Criticism.* Lexington: University Press of Kentucky, 1965.

——, and Cleanth Brooks. *Literary Criticism: A Short History.* New York: Alfred A. Knopf, 1957.

Wolfson, Susan J. "Reading for Form." *Modern Language Quarterly* 61 (2000) 1–11.

I. A. Richards

1893–1979

A pioneering thinker whose ideas would shape the New Criticism, Ivor Armstrong Richards was born in Sandbach, Cheshire. Educated at Magdalen College, Cambridge University, Richards was a lecturer there in the new discipline of "English" and the moral sciences from 1922 to 1929, years in which he wrote three profoundly influential books: The Meaning of Meaning: A Study of the Influence of Language upon Thought and of the Science of Symbolism *(1923) with C. K. Ogden,* Principles of Literary Criticism *(1924), and* Practical Criticism *(1929). His studies in psychology and semantics contributed to his interest in the "close reading" of a text. During the 1930s, Richards devoted much of his time to developing C. K. Ogden's system of Basic English, a synthetic language of only 850 words that, it was hoped, would become the language of universal human intelligibility — a program he brought to China, where he lived and taught from 1929 to 1936. (Meanwhile, his student William Empson developed Richards's ideas on reading into one variant of the New Criticism.) In 1944 Richards became a professor of English at Harvard University and in 1963 emeritus professor. Among his other works are* Science and Poetry *(1926),* Coleridge on Imagination *(1934),* The Philosophy of Rhetoric *(1936),* Speculative Instruments *(1955), and* Poetries *(1974).*

From *Principles of Literary Criticism*

Chapter XXXIV
The Two Uses of Language

> *The intelligible forms of ancient poets*
> *The fair humanities of old religion . . .*
> *They live no longer in the faith of reason:*
> *But still the heart doth need a language, still*
> *Doth the old instinct bring back the old names.*
> — COLERIDGE, *Piccolomini*

There are two totally distinct uses of language. But because the theory of language is the most neglected of all studies they are in fact hardly ever distinguished. Yet both for the theory of poetry and for the narrower aim of understanding much which is said about poetry a clear comprehension of the differences between these uses is indispensable. For this we must look somewhat closely at the mental processes which accompany them.

It is unfortunate but not surprising that most of the psychological terms which we naturally employ tend to blur the distinction. "Knowledge," "belief," "assertion," "thought," and "understanding," for example, as ordinarily used, are ambiguous in a fashion which disguises and obscures the point which must be brought out. They record distinctions which are oblique to the distinctions required, they are cross-cuts of analysis made in the wrong place and in the wrong direction, useful enough for some purposes no doubt, but for this present purpose very confusing. We shall do well to put them out of mind for a while if possible.

The chief departure made from current conceptions in the sketch of the mind given in Chapter XI lay in the substitution of the *causes*, the *characters*, and the *consequences* of a mental event, for its aspects as *thought*, *feeling*, and *will*. This treatment was introduced with a view to the analysis which now occupies us. Among the causes of most mental events, we urged, two sets may be distinguished. On the one hand there are the present stimuli reaching the mind through the sensory nerves, and, in cooperation with these, the effects of past stimuli associated with them. On the other hand is a set of quite different factors, the state of the organism, its needs, its readiness to respond to this or that kind of stimulus. The impulses which arise take their character and their course from the interaction of these two sets. We must keep them clearly distinguished.

The relative importance of the two sets of factors varies enormously. A sufficiently hungry man will eat almost anything which can be chewed or swallowed. The nature of the substance, within these limits, has very little effect upon his behaviour. A replete person, by contrast, will only eat such things as he expects will taste pleasant, or regards as possessing definite beneficial properties, for example, medicines. His behaviour, in other words, depends almost entirely upon the character of his optical or olfactory stimulation.

So far as an impulse owes its character to its stimulus (or to such effects of past accompanying or connected stimuli as are revived) so far is it a *reference*, to use the term which we introduced in Chapter XI, to stand for the property of mental events which we substitute for thought or cognition.[1] It is plain that the independent internal conditions of the organism usually intervene to distort reference in some degree. But very many of our needs can only be satisfied if the impulses are left undistorted. Bitter experience has taught us to leave some of them alone, to let them reflect or correspond with external states of affairs as much as they can, undisturbed as far as possible by internal states of affairs, our needs and desires.

In all our behaviour can be distinguished stimuli we receive, and the ways in which we use them. What we receive may be any kind of stimulus, but only when the reaction we make to it tallies with its nature and varies with it in quasi-independence of the uses we make of it does reference occur.

---

[1] The reader who is a psychologist will notice many points in this statement at which elaboration and qualifications are required. For example, when we are "introspecting," factors normally belonging to the second set may enter the first. But he will be able, if he grasps the general theory, to supply these complications himself. I did not wish to burden the text with unnecessary intricacies. [Richards]

Those to whom visual images are of service in considering complex matters may find it convenient at this point to imagine a circle or sphere constantly bombarded by minute particles (stimuli). Within the sphere may be pictured complex mechanisms continually changing for reasons having nothing to do with the external stimuli. These mechanisms by opening little gateways select which of the stimuli shall be allowed to come in and take effect. So far as the subsequent convulsions are due to the nature of the impacts and to lingering effects of impacts which have accompanied similar impacts in the past, the convulsions are referential. So far as they are due to the independent motions of the internal mechanisms themselves, reference fails. This diagrammatic image may possibly be of convenience to some. By those who distrust such things it may with advantage be disregarded. It is not introduced as a contribution to neurology, and is in no way a ground for the author's view.

The extent to which reference is interfered with by needs and desires is underestimated even by those who, not having yet forgotten the events of 1914–1918, are most sceptical as to the independence of opinions and desires.[2] Even the most ordinary and familiar objects are perceived as it pleases us to perceive them rather than as they are, whenever error does not directly deprive us of advantages. It is almost impossible for anyone to secure a correct impression of his own personal appearance or of the features of anyone in whom he is personally interested. Nor is it perhaps often desirable that he should.

For the demarcation of the fields where impulse should be as completely as possible dependent upon and correspondent with external situation, those in which reference should take prior place from those in which it may be subordinated to appetencies with advantage, is not a simple matter. On many views of the good and of what should be, themselves results of subordinating reference to emotional satisfactions, there could be no question. Truth, it would be said, has claims prior to all other considerations. Love not

grounded upon knowledge would be described as worthless. We ought not to admire what is not beautiful and if our mistress be not really beautiful when impartially considered we ought, so the doctrine runs, to admire her, if at all, for other reasons. The chief points of interest about such views are the confusions which make them plausible. Beauty as an internal quality of things is usually involved, as well as Good the unanalysable Idea. Both are special twists given to some of our impulses by habits deriving ultimately from desires. They linger in our minds because to think of a thing as Good or Beautiful gives more *immediate* emotional satisfaction than to *refer* to it as satisfying our impulses in one special fashion (cf. Chapter VII) or another (cf. Chapter XXXII).

To think about Good or Beauty is not necessarily to refer to anything. For the term "thinking" covers mental operations in which the impulses are so completely governed by internal factors and so out of control of stimulus that no reference occurs. Most "thinking of" includes reference in some degree, of course, but not all, and similarly much reference would not commonly be described as thinking. When we drop something which is too hot to hold we would not usually be said to have done so through thinking. The two terms overlap, and their definitions, if there be a definition of "thinking" as commonly used, are of different types. This is why "Thought" was on an earlier page described as marking an oblique distinction.

To return, the claims of reference are by no means easy to adjust with other claims. An immense extension of our powers of referring has recently been made. With amazing swiftness Science has opened out field after field of possible reference. Science is simply the organization of references with a view solely to the convenience and facilitation of reference. It has advanced mainly because other claims, typically the claims of our religious desires, have been set aside. For it is no accident that Science and Religion conflict. They are different principles upon which impulses may be organized, and the more closely they are examined the more inevitable is the incompatibility seen to be. Any so-called reconciliation which is ever effected will involve bestowing the name Religion upon something utterly different from any of the systematisations of impulses which it

[2]Richards's implication is that the destruction of World War I would not have occurred if both sides had not distorted the likely outcome based on "needs and desires."

now denotes, for the reason that the belief elements present would have a different character.

Many attempts have been made to reduce Science to a position of subjection to some instinct or emotion or desire, to curiosity for example. A special passion for knowledge for its own sake has even been invented. But in fact all the passions and all the instincts, all human needs and desires may *on occasion* supply the motive force for Science. There is no human activity which may not on occasion require undistorted reference. The essential point, however, is that Science is autonomous. The impulses developed in it are modified only by one another, with a view to the greatest possible completeness and systematisation, and for the facilitation of further references. So far as other considerations distort them they are not yet Science or have fallen out of it.

To declare Science autonomous is very different from subordinating all our activities to it. It is merely to assert that so far as any body of references is undistorted it belongs to Science. It is not in the least to assert that no references may be distorted if advantage can thereby be gained. And just as there are innumerable human activities which require undistorted references if they are to be satisfied, so there are innumerable other human activities not less important which equally require distorted references or, more plainly, *fictions*.

The use of fictions, the imaginative use of them rather, is not a way of hoodwinking ourselves. It is not a process of pretending to ourselves that things are not as they are. It is perfectly compatible with the fullest and grimmest recognition of the exact state of affairs on all occasions. It is no make-believe. But so awkwardly have our references and our attitudes become entangled that such pathetic spectacles as Mr. Yeats trying desperately to believe in fairies or Mr. Lawrence impugning the validity of solar physics, are all too common. To be forced by desire into any unwarrantable belief is a calamity. The state which ensues is often extraordinarily damaging to the mind. But this common misuse of fictions should not blind us to their immense services provided we do not take them for what they are not, degrading the chief means by which

our attitudes to actual life may be adjusted into the material of a long-drawn delirium.[3]

If we knew enough it might be possible that all necessary attitudes could be obtained through scientific references alone. Since we do not know very much yet, we can leave this very remote possibility, once recognized, alone.

Fictions whether aroused by statements or by analogous things in other arts may be used in many ways. They may be used, for example, to deceive. But this is not a characteristic use in poetry. The distinction which needs to be kept clear does not set up fictions in opposition to verifiable truths in the scientific sense. A statement may be used for the sake of the *reference*, true or false, which it causes. This is the *scientific* use of language. But it may also be used for the sake of the effects in emotion and attitude produced by the reference it occasions. This is the *emotive* use of language. The distinction once clearly grasped is simple. We may either use words for the sake of the references they promote, or we may use them for the sake of the attitudes and emotions which ensue. Many arrangements of words evoke attitudes without any reference being required *en route*. They operate like musical phrases. But usually references are involved *as conditions* for, or *stages in*, the ensuing development of attitudes, yet it is still the attitudes not the references which are important. It matters not at all in such cases whether the references are true or false. Their sole function is to bring about and support the attitudes which are the further response. The questioning, verificatory way of handling them is irrelevant, and in a competent reader it is not allowed to interfere. "Better a plausible impossibility than an improbable possibility" said Aristotle very wisely;[4] there is less danger of an inappropriate reaction.

The differences between the mental processes involved in the two cases are very great, though

[3]Revelation Doctrines when once given a foothold tend to interfere everywhere. They serve as a kind of omnipotent major premise justifying any and every conclusion. A specimen: "Since the function of Art is to pierce through the Real World, then it follows that the artist cannot be too definite in his outlines, and that good drawing is the foundation of all good art." — Charles Gardner, *Vision and Vesture*, p. 54. [Richards]

[4]Aristotle, *Poetics*, Ch. 25, p. 78.

easily overlooked. Consider what failure for each use amounts to. For scientific language a difference in the references is itself failure: the end has not been attained. But for emotive language the widest differences in reference are of no importance if the further effects in attitude and emotion are of the required kind.

Further, in the scientific use of language not only must the references be correct for success, but the connections and relations of references to one another must be of the kind which we call logical. They must not get in one another's way, and must be so organised as not to impede further reference. But for emotive purposes logical arrangement is not necessary. It may be and often is an obstacle. For what matters is that the series of attitudes due to the references should have their own proper organisation, their own emotional interconnection, and this often has no dependence upon the logical relations of such references as may be concerned in bringing the attitudes into being.

A few notes of the chief uses of the word "Truth" in Criticism may help to prevent misunderstanding:

1. The scientific sense that, namely, in which references, and derivatively statements symbolising references, are true, need not delay us. A reference is true when the things to which it refers are actually together in the way in which it refers to them. Otherwise it is false. This sense is one very little involved by any of the arts. For the avoidance of confusions it would be well if the term "true" could be reserved for this use. In purely scientific discourse it could and should be, but such discourse is uncommon. In point of fact the emotive power which attaches to the word is far too great for it to be abandoned in general discussion; the temptation to a speaker who needs to stir certain emotions and evoke certain attitudes of approval and acceptance is overwhelming. No matter how various the senses in which it may be used, and even when it is being used in no sense whatever, its effects in promoting attitudes will still make it indispensable; people will still continue to use the word with the same promiscuity as ever.

2. The most usual other sense is that of acceptability. The "Truth" of *Robinson Crusoe* is the acceptability of things we are told, their acceptability in the interests of the effects of the narrative, not their correspondence with any actual facts involving Alexander Selkirk[5] or another. Similarly the falsity of happy endings to *Lear* or to *Don Quixote*, is their failure to be acceptable to those who have fully responded to the rest of the work. It is in this sense that "Truth" is equivalent to "internal necessity" or rightness. That is "true" or "internally necessary" which completes or accords with the rest of the experience, which cooperates to arouse our ordered response, whether the response of Beauty or another. "What the Imagination seizes as Beauty must be Truth," said Keats, using this sense of "Truth," though not without confusion.[6] Sometimes it is held that whatever is redundant or otiose, whatever is not required, although not obstructive or disruptive, is also false. "Surplusage!" said Pater, "the artist will dread that, as the runner on his muscles" himself perhaps in this instance sweating his sentence down too finely.[7] But this is to make excessive demands upon the artist. It is to apply the axe of retrenchment in the wrong place. Superabundance is a common characteristic of great art, much less dangerous than the preciousness that too contrived an economy tends to produce. The essential point is whether what is unnecessary interferes or not with the rest of the response. If it does not, the whole thing is all the better probably for the extra solidity which it thereby gains.

This internal acceptability or "convincingness" needs to be contrasted with other acceptabilities. Thomas Rymer, for example, refused to accept Iago for external reasons: "To entertain the audience with something new and surprising against common sense and nature, he would pass upon us a close, dissembling rascal, instead of an open-hearted, frank, plain-dealing Souldier, a character constantly born by them for some thousands of years in the World." "The truth is," he observes, "this author's head was full of villainous, unnatural images."[8]

[5] The original on whose real-life adventures Defoe based *Robinson Crusoe*.
[6] See Keats, "Letter to Benjamin Bailey," p. 331.
[7] *Essay on Style*, p. 19. [Richards]
[8] *A Short View of Tragedy*. [Richards]

He is remembering no doubt Aristotle's remark that "the artist must preserve the type and yet ennoble it," but interpreting it in his own way. For him the type is fixed simply by convention and his acceptances take no note of internal necessities but are governed merely by accordance with external canons. His is an extreme case, but to avoid his error in subtler matters is in fact sometimes the hardest part of the critic's undertaking. But whether our conception of the type is derived in some such absurd way, or taken, for example, as from a handbook of zoology, is of slight consequence. It is the taking on any *external* canon which is critically dangerous. When in the same connection Rymer objects that there never was a Moorish General in the service of the Venetian Republic, he is applying another external canon, that of historic fact. This mistake is less insidious, but Ruskin used to be particularly fond of the analogous mistake in connection with the "truth" of drawing.

3. Truth may be equivalent to Sincerity. This character of the artist's work we have already touched upon briefly in connection with Tolstoy's theory of communication (Chapter XXIII).[9] It may perhaps be most easily defined from the critic's point of view negatively, as the absence of any apparent attempt on the part of the artist to work effects upon the reader which do not work for himself. Too simple definitions must be avoided. It is well known that Burns in writing "*Ae fond kiss*" was only too anxious to escape Nancy's (Mrs. Maclehose's) attentions, and similar instances could be multiplied indefinitely. Absurdly naïve views upon the matter[10] exemplified by the opinion that Bottomley must have believed himself to be inspired or he would not have moved his audiences, are far too common. At the level at which Bottomley harangued any kind of exaltation in the orator, whether due to pride or to champagne, would make his stuff effective. But at Burns's level a very different situation arises. Here his probity and sincerity *as an artist* are involved; external circumstances are irrelevant, but there is perhaps internal evidence

[9]See Tolstoy, *What Is Art?*, p. 52.
[10]Cf. A. Clutton-Brock, *The Times*, 11 July 1922, p. 13. [Richards] Horatio Bottomley was a demagogic politician.

in the poem of a flaw in its creating impulse. Compare as a closely similar poem in which there is no flaw, Byron's "*When we two parted.*"

Chapter XXXV
Poetry and Beliefs

What I see very well is the wide-spread, infinite harm of putting fancy for knowledge (to speak like Socrates), or rather of living by choice in a twilight of the mind where fancy and knowledge are indiscernible. — *Euripides the Rationalist*

It is evident that the bulk of poetry consists of statements which only the very foolish would think of attempting to verify. They are not the kind of things which can be verified. If we recall what was said in Chapter XVI as to the natural generality or vagueness of reference we shall see another reason why references as they occur in poetry are rarely susceptible of scientific truth or falsity. Only references which are brought into certain highly complex and very special combinations, so as to correspond to the ways in which things actually hang together, can be either true or false, and most references in poetry are not knit together in this way.

But even when they are, on examination, frankly false, this is no defect, unless, indeed, the obviousness of the falsity forces the reader to reactions which are incongruent or disturbing to the poem. And equally, a point more often misunderstood, their truth, when they are true, is no merit.[11] The people who say "How True!" at intervals while reading Shakespeare are misusing his work, and, comparatively speaking, wasting their time. For all that matters in either case is

[11]No merit, that is, *in this connection*. There may be some exceptions to this, cases in which the explicit recognition of the truth of a statement as opposed to the simple acceptance of it, is *necessary* to the full development of the further response. But I believe that such cases will on careful examination be found to be very rare with competent readers. Individual differences, corresponding to the different degrees to which individuals have their belief feelings, their references, and their attitudes entangled, are to be expected. There are, of course, an immense number of scientific beliefs present among the conditions of every attitude. But since acceptances would do equally well in their place they are not *necessary* to it. [Richards]

acceptance, that is to say, the initiation and development of the further response.

Poetry affords the clearest examples of this subordination of reference to attitude. It is the supreme form of *emotive* language. But there can be no doubt that originally all language was emotive; its scientific use is a later development, and most language is still emotive. Yet the late development has come to seem the natural and the normal use, largely because the only people who have reflected upon language were at the moment of reflection using it scientifically.

The emotions and attitudes resulting from a statement used emotively need not be directed towards anything to which the statement refers. This is clearly evident in dramatic poetry, but much more poetry than is usually supposed is dramatic in structure. As a rule a statement in poetry arouses attitudes much more wide and general in direction than the references of the statement. Neglect of this fact makes most verbal analysis of poetry irrelevant. And the same is true of those critical but emotive utterances about poetry which gave rise to this discussion. No one, it is plain, can read poetry successfully without, consciously or unconsciously, observing the distinction between the two uses of words. That does not need to be insisted upon. But further no one can understand such utterances about poetry as that quoted from Dr. Mackail in our third chapter, or Dr. Bradley's cry that "Poetry is a spirit," or Shelley's that "A poem is the very image of life expressed in its eternal truth,"[12] or the passages quoted above from Coleridge, without distinguishing the making of a statement from the incitement or expression of an attitude. But too much inferior poetry has been poured out as criticism, too much sack and too little bread; confusion between the two activities, on the part of writers and readers alike, is what is primarily responsible for the backwardness of critical studies. What other stultifications of human endeavour it is also responsible for we need not linger here to point out. The separation of prose from poetry, if we may so paraphrase the distinction, is no mere academic activity. There is hardly a

[12] See Shelley, "A Defence of Poetry," p. 346.

problem outside mathematics which is not complicated by its neglect, and hardly an emotional response which is not crippled by irrelevant intrusions. No revolution in human affairs would be greater than that which a wide-spread observance of this distinction would bring about.

One perversion in especial needs to be noticed. It is constantly present in critical discussion, and is in fact responsible for Revelation Doctrines. Many attitudes, which arise without dependence upon any reference, merely by the interplay and resolution of impulses otherwise awakened, can be momentarily encouraged by suitable beliefs held as scientific beliefs are held. So far as this encouragement is concerned, the truth or falsity of these beliefs does not matter, the immediate effect is the same in either case. When the attitude is important, the temptation to base it upon some reference which is treated as established scientific truths are treated is very great, and the poet thus easily comes to invite the destruction of his work; Wordsworth puts forward his Pantheism, and other people doctrines of Inspiration, Idealism and Revelation.

The effect is twofold; and appearance of security and stability is given to the attitude, which thus seems to be justified; and at the same time it is no longer so necessary to sustain this attitude by the more difficult means peculiar to the arts, or to pay full attention to form. The reader can be relied upon to do more than his share. That neither effect is desirable is easily seen. The attitude for the sake of which the belief is introduced is thereby made not more but less stable. Remove the belief, once it has affected the attitude; the attitude collapses. It may later be restored by more appropriate means, but that is another matter. And all such beliefs are very likely to be removed; their logical connections with other beliefs scientifically entertained are, to say the least, shaky. In the second place these attitudes, produced not by the appropriate means but, as it were by a short cut, through beliefs, are rarely so healthy, so vigorous and full of life as the others. Unlike attitudes normally produced they usually require an increased stimulus every time that they are reinstated. The belief has to grow more and more fervent, more and more convinced, in order to produce the same attitude. The believer has to pass from one paroxysm of conviction to another, enduring each time a greater strain.

This substitution of an intellectual formula for the poem or work of art is of course most easily observed in the case of religion, where the temptation is greatest. In place of an experience, which is a direct response to a certain selection of the possibilities of stimulation, we have a highly indirect response, made, not to the actual influences of the world upon us, but to a special kind of belief as to some particular state of affairs.[13] There is a suppressed conditional clause implicit in all poetry. If things were such and such then . . . and so the response develops. The amplitude and fineness of the response, its sanction and authority, in other words, depend upon this freedom from actual assertion in all cases in which the belief is questionable on any ground whatsoever. For any such assertion involves suppressions, of indefinite extent, which may be fatal to the wholeness, the *integrity* of the experience. And the assertion is almost always unnecessary; if we look closely we find that the greatest poets, as poets, though frequently not as critics, refrain from assertion. But it is easy, by what seems only a slight change of approach, to make the initial step an act of faith, and to make the whole response dependent upon a belief as to a matter of fact. Even when the belief is true, the damage done to the whole experience may be great, in the case of a person whose reasons for this belief are inadequate, for example, and the increased temporary vivacity which is the cause of perversion is no sufficient compensation. As a convenient example it may be permissible to refer to the Poet Laureate's anthology, *The Spirit of Man*, and I have the less hesitation since the passages there gathered together are chosen with such unerring taste and discrimination. But to turn them into a statement of a philosophy is very noticeably to

[13]In view of a possible misunderstanding at this point, compare Chapter X, especially the final paragraph. If a belief in Retributive Justice, for example, is fatal to *Prometheus Unbound*, so in another way is the belief that the Millennium is at hand. To steer an unperplexed path between these opposite dangers is extremely difficult. The distinctions required are perhaps better left to the reader's reflection than laboured further in the faulty terminology which alone at present is available. [Richards]

degrade them and to restrict and diminish their value. The use of verse quotations as chapter headings is open to the same objection. The experiences which ensue may seem very similar to the experiences of free reading; they feel similar; but all the signs which can be most trusted, after-effects for example, show them to be different. The vast differences in the means by which they are brought about is also good ground for supposing them to be dissimilar, but this difference is obscured through the ambiguities of the term "belief."

There are few terms which are more troublesome in psychology than belief, formidable though this charge may seem. The sense in which we believe a scientific proposition is not the sense in which we believe emotive utterances, whether they are political "We will not sheathe the sword," or critical "The progress of poetry is immortal," or poetic. Both senses of belief are complicated and difficult to define. Yet we commonly appear to assume that they are the same or that they differ only in the kind and degree of evidence available. Scientific belief we may perhaps define as readiness to act as though the reference symbolised by the proposition which is believed were true. Readiness to act in *all* circumstances and in *all* connections into which it can enter. This rough definition would, of course, need elaborating to be complete, but for our present purposes it may suffice. The other element usually included in a definition of belief, namely a feeling or emotion of acceptance, the "This is sooth, accept it!" feeling, is often absent in scientific belief and is not essential.

Emotive belief is very different. Readiness to act as though some references were true is often involved, but the connections and circumstances in which this readiness remains are narrowly restricted. Similarly the extent of the action is ordinarily limited. Consider the acceptances involved in the understanding of a play, for example. They form a system any element of which is believed while the rest are believed and so long as the acceptance of the whole growing system leads to successful response. Some, however, are of the form "Given this then that would follow," general beliefs, that is to say, of the kind which led Aristotle, in the passage quoted above, to describe Poetry as a more philosophical thing than history because chiefly conversant of universal truth.[14] But if we look closely into most instances of such beliefs we see that they are entertained only in the special circumstances of the poetic experience. They are held as conditions for further effects, our attitudes and emotional responses, and not as we hold beliefs in laws of nature, which we expect to find verified on all occasions. If dramatic necessities were actually scientific laws we should know much more psychology than any reasonable person pretends that we do. That these beliefs as to "how any person of a certain character would speak or act, probably or necessarily," upon which so much drama seems to depend, are not scientific, but are held only for the sake of their dramatic effect, is shown clearly by the ease with which we abandon them if the advantage lies the other way. The medical impossibility of Desdemona's last speech is perhaps as good an example as any.

The bulk of the beliefs involved in the arts are of this kind, provisional acceptances, holding only in special circumstances (in the state of mind which is the poem or work of art) acceptances made for the sake of the "imaginative experience" which they make possible. The difference between these emotive beliefs and scientific beliefs is not one of degree but of kind. As feelings they are very similar, but as attitudes their difference in structure has widespread consequences.

There remains to be discussed another set of emotive effects which may also be called beliefs. Instead of occurring part way in, or at the beginning of a response, they come as a rule at the end, and thus are less likely to be confused with scientific beliefs. Very often the whole state of mind in which we are left by a poem, or by music, or, more rarely perhaps, by other forms of art, is of a kind which it is natural to describe as a belief. When all provisional acceptances have lapsed, when the single references and their connections which may have led up to the final response are forgotten, we may still have an attitude and an emotion which has to introspection all the characters of a belief. This belief, which is a

[14]See Aristotle, *Poetics*, Ch. 9, p. 65.

consequence not a cause of the experience, is the chief source of the confusion upon which Revelation Doctrines depend.

If we ask what in such cases it is which is believed, we are likely to receive, and to offer, answers both varied and vague. For strong belief-feelings, as is well known and as is shown by certain doses of alcohol or hashish, and preeminently of nitrous oxide, will readily attach themselves to almost any reference, distorting it to suit their purpose. Few people without experience of the nitrous-oxide revelation have any conception of their capacity for believing or of the extent to which belief-feelings and attitudes are parasitic. Thus when, through reading *Adonais*, for example, we are left in a strong emotional attitude which feels like belief, it is only too easy to think that we are believing in immortality or survival, or in something else capable of statement, and fatally easy also to attribute the value of the poem to the alleged effect, or conversely to regret that it should depend upon such a scientifically doubtful conclusion. Scientific beliefs, as opposed to these emotive beliefs, are beliefs "*that* so and so." They can be stated with greater or less precision, as the case may be, but always in some form. It is for some people difficult to admit beliefs which are objectless, which are not about anything or in anything; beliefs which cannot be stated. Yet most of the beliefs of children and primitive peoples, and of the unscientific generally seem to be of this kind. Their parasitic nature helps to confuse the issue. What we have to distinguish are beliefs which are grounded in fact, i.e., are due to reference, and beliefs which are due to other causes, and merely attach themselves to such references as will support them.

That an objectless belief is a ridiculous or an incomplete thing is a prejudice deriving only from confusion. Such beliefs have, of course, no place in science, but in themselves they are often of the utmost value. Provided always that they do not furnish themselves with illicit objects. It is the objectless belief which is masquerading as a belief in this or that, which is ridiculous; more often than not it is also a serious nuisance. When they are kept from tampering with the development of reference such emotional attitudes may be, as revelation doctrines in such strange forms maintain, among the most important and valuable effects which the arts can produce.

It is often held that recent generations suffer more from nervous strain than some at least of their predecessors, and many reasons for this have been suggested. Certainly the types of nervous disease most prevalent seem to have changed. An explanation not sufficiently noticed perhaps is the break-down of traditional accounts of the universe, and the strain imposed by the vain attempt to orient the mind by belief of the scientific kind alone. In the prescientific era, the devout adherent to the Catholic account of the world, for example, found a sufficient basis for nearly all his main attitudes in what he took to be scientific truth. It would be fairer to say that the difference between ascertained fact and acceptable fiction did not obtrude itself for him. Today this is changed, and if he believes such an account, he does not do so, if intelligent, without considerable difficulty or without a fairly persistent strain. The complete sceptic, of course, is a new phenomenon, dissenters in the past having commonly disbelieved only because they held a different belief of the same kind. These topics have, it is true, been touched upon by psychoanalysts, but not with a very clear understanding of the situation. The Vienna School would merely have us away with antiquated lumber; the Zurich School would hand us a new outfit of superstitions.[15] Actually what is needed is a habit of mind which allows both reference and the development of attitudes their proper independence. This habit of mind is not to be attained at once, or for most people with ease. We try desperately to support our attitudes with beliefs as to facts, verified or accepted as scientifically established, and by so doing we weaken our own emotional backbone. For the justification of any attitude *per se* is its success for the needs of the being. It is not justified by the soundness of the views which may seem to be, and in pathological cases are, its ground and causes. The source of our attitudes should be in experience itself; compare Whitman's praise of the cow which does not worry about its soul. Opinion as to matters of fact, knowledge, belief, are not necessarily involved in

---

[15]The psychoanalytic schools of Sigmund Freud and Carl Jung, respectively.

any of our attitudes to the world in general, or to particular phases of it. If we bring them in, if, by a psychological perversion only too easy to fall into, we make them the basis of our adjustment, we run extreme risks of later disorganisation elsewhere.

Many people find great difficulty in accepting or even in understanding this position. They are so accustomed to regarding "recognised facts" as the natural basis of attitudes, that they cannot conceive how anyone can be otherwise organized. The hard-headed positivist and the convinced adherent of a religion from opposite sides encounter the same difficulty. The first at the best suffers from an insufficient material for the development of his attitudes; the second from intellectual bondage and unconscious insincerity. The one starves himself; the other is like the little pig in the fable who chose to have his house built of cabbages and ate it, and so the grim wolf with privy paw devoured him. For clear and impartial awareness of the nature of the world in which we live and the development of attitudes which will enable us to live in it finely are both necessities, and neither can be subordinated to the other. They are almost independent, such connections as exist in well-organised individuals being adventitious. Those who find this a hard saying may be invited to consider the effect upon them of those works of art which most unmistakably attune them to existence. The central experience of Tragedy and its chief value is an attitude indispensable for a fully developed life. But in the reading of *King Lear* what facts verifiable by science, or accepted and believed in as we accept and believe in ascertained facts, are relevant? None whatever. Still more clearly in the experiences of some music, of some architecture and of some abstract design, attitudes are evoked and developed which are unquestionably independent of all beliefs as to fact, and these are exceptional only in being protected by accident from the most insidious perversion to which the mind is liable. For the intermingling of knowledge and belief is indeed a perversion, through which both activities suffer degradation.

These objectless beliefs, which though merely attitudes seem to be knowledge, are not difficult to explain. Some system of impulses not ordinarily in adjustment within itself or adjusted to the world finds something which orders it or gives it fit exercise. Then follows the peculiar sense of ease, of restfulness, of free, unimpeded activity, and the feeling of acceptance, of something more positive than acquiescence. This feeling is the reason why such states may be called beliefs. They share this feeling with, for example, the state which follows the conclusive answering of a question. Most attitude-adjustments which are successful possess it in some degree, but those which are very regular and familiar, such as sitting down to meat or stretching out in bed, naturally tend to lose it. But when the required attitude has been long needed, where its coming is unforeseen and the manner in which it is brought about complicated and inexplicable, where we know no more than that formerly we were unready and that now we are ready for life in some particular phase, the feeling which results may be intense. Such are the occasions upon which the arts seem to lift away the burden of existence, and we seem ourselves to be looking into the heart of things. To be seeing whatever it is as it really is, to be cleared in vision and to be recipients of a revelation.

We have considered already the detail of these states of consciousness and their conjectural impulse basis. We can now take this feeling of a revealed significance, this attitude of readiness, acceptance and understanding, which has led to so many Revelation Doctrines, not as actually implying knowledge, but for what it is — the conscious accompaniment of our successful adjustment to life. But it is, we must admit, no certain sign by itself that our adjustment is adequate or admirable. Even the most firm adherents to Revelation Doctrines admit that there are bogus revelations, and on our account it is equally important to distinguish between "feelings of significance" which indicate that all is well and those which do not. In a sense all indicate that *something* is going well, otherwise there would be no acceptance, no belief but rejection. The real question is "What is it?" Thus after the queer reshuffling of inhibitions and releases which follows the taking of a dose of alcohol, for example, the sense of revelation is apt to occur with unusual authority. Doubtless this feeling of significance is a sign that as the organism is for the moment, its affairs are for the moment thriving.

But when the momentary special condition of the system has given place to the more usual, more stable and more generally advantageous adjustment, the authority of the vision falls away from it; we find that what we were doing is by no means so wonderful or so desirable as we thought and that our belief was nonsensical. So it is less noticeably with many moments in which the world seems to be showing its real face to us.

The chief difficulty of all Revelation Doctrines has always been to discover what it is which is revealed. If these states of mind are knowledge it should be possible to state what it is that they know. It is often easy enough to find something which we can suppose to be what we know. Belief feelings, we have seen, are *parasitic*, and will attach themselves to all kinds of hosts. In literature it is especially easy to find hosts. But in music, in the nonrepresentative arts of design, in architecture or ceramics, for example, the task of finding something to believe, or to believe in, is not so easy. Yet the "feeling of significance" is as common[16] in these other arts as in literature. Denial of this is usually proof only of an interest limited to literature.

This difficulty has usually been met by asserting that the alleged knowledge given in the revelation is nonintellectual. It refuses to be rationalised, it is said. Well and good; but if so why call it knowledge? Either it is capable of corroborating of or conflicting with the other things we usually call knowledge, such as the laws of thermodynamics, capable of being stated and brought into connection with what else we know; or it is not knowledge, not capable of being stated. We cannot have it both ways, and no sneers at the limitations of logic, the commonest of the resources of the confused, amend the

---

[16]Cf. Gurney, *The Power of Sound*, p. 126. "A splendid melodic phrase seems continually not like an object of sense, but like an *affirmation*; not so much prompting admiring ejaculation as compelling passionate assent." His explanation, through association with speech, seems to me inadequate. He adds that the use of terms such as "*expressiveness* and *significance*, as opposed to meaninglessness and triviality, may be allowed, without the implication of any reference to transcendental views which one may fail to understand, or theories of interpretation which one may entirely repudiate." [Richards]

dilemma. In fact it resembles knowledge only in being an attitude and a feeling very similar to some attitudes and feelings which may and often do accompany knowledge. But "Knowledge" is an immensely potent emotive word engendering reverence towards any state of mind to which it is applied. And these "feelings of significance" are those among our states of mind which most deserve to be revered. That they should be so obstinately described as knowledge even by those who most carefully remove from them all the characteristics of knowledge is not surprising.

Traditionally what is said to be known thus mystically through the arts is Beauty, a remote and divine entity not otherwise to be apprehended, one of the Eternal Absolute Values. And this is doubtless emotively a way of talking which is effective for a while. When its power abates, as the power of such utterances will, there are several developments which may easily be used to revive it. "Beauty is eternal, and we may say that it is already manifest as a heavenly thing — the beauty of Nature is indeed an earnest to us of the ultimate goodness which lies behind the apparent cruelty and moral confusion of organic life. . . . Yet we feel that these three are ultimately one, and human speech bears constant witness to the universal conviction that Goodness is beautiful, that Beauty is good, that Truth is Beauty. We can hardly avoid the use of the word 'trinity,' and if we are theists at all we cannot but say that they are one, because they are the manifestation of one God. If we are not theists there is no explanation."[17]

Human speech is indeed the witness, and to what else does it not witness? It would be strange if in a matter of such moment as this the greatest of all emotive words did not come into play. "In religion we believe that God is Beauty and Life, that God is Truth and Light, that God is Goodness and Love, and that because he is all these they are all one, and the Trinity in Unity and Unity in Trinity is to be worshipped."[18] No one who can interpret emotive language, who can avoid the temptation to illicit belief so constantly presented by it need find such utterances "meaningless." But the wrong approach is easy and far too often pressingly invited by the speakers, labouring themselves under misconceptions. To excite a serious and reverent attitude is one thing. To set forth an explanation is another. To confuse the two and mistake the incitement of an attitude for a statement of fact is a practice which should be discouraged. For intellectual dishonesty is an evil which is the more dangerous the more it is hedged about with emotional sanctities. And after all there *is* another explanation, which would long ago have been quietly established to the world's great good had men been less ready to sacrifice the integrity of their thought and feeling for the sake of a local and limited advantage.

[17]Percy Dearmer, *The Necessity of Art*, p. 180. [Richards]
[18]A. W. Pollard, *ibidem*, p. 135. [Richards]

Victor Shklovsky

1893–1984

The versatile Russian man of letters Victor Shklovsky was born the son of a teacher in Petersburg and studied at the university there. An outspoken founding member of the Russian literary society OPOYAZ, Shklovsky wrote one of the central theoretical statements of the formalist school ("Art as Technique," 1917) and his ideas were singled out for special denunciation by Leon Trotsky. Problems with the Bolsheviks prompted his emigration in 1921, but he returned two years later. Within a few years, after the publication of The Theory of Prose *(1925), he backed away from the politically risky business of theorizing and took up other pursuits, particularly film criticism, screenwriting, and historical fiction. He wrote books on Tolstoy (1928), Mayakovsky (1940), and Dostoevsky (1957), and is also remembered for his autobiographical account of the revolutionary years, A Sentimental Journal: Memoirs 1917–1922 (1923). Ultimately, Shklovsky came to be considered an honored member of the Soviet literary establishment.*

Art as Technique

"Art is thinking in images." This maxim, which even high school students parrot, is nevertheless the starting point for the erudite philologist who is beginning to put together some kind of systematic literary theory. The idea, originated in part by Potebnya, has spread. "Without imagery there is no art, and in particular no poetry," Potebnya writes.[1] And elsewhere, "Poetry, as well as prose, is first and foremost a special way of thinking and knowing."[2]

Poetry is a special way of thinking; it is, precisely, a way of thinking in images, a way which permits what is generally called "economy of mental effort," a way which makes for "a sensation of the relative ease of the process." Aesthetic feeling is the reaction to this economy. This is how the academician Ovsyaniko-Kulikovsky,[3] who undoubtedly read the works of Potebnya attentively, almost certainly understood and faithfully summarized the ideas of his teacher. Potebnya and his numerous disciples consider poetry a special kind of thinking — thinking by means of images; they feel that the purpose of imagery is to help channel various objects and activities into groups and to clarify the unknown by means of the known. Or, as Potebnya wrote:

The relationship of the image to what is being clarified is that: (a) the image is the fixed predicate of that which undergoes change — the unchanging

means of attracting what is perceived as changeable. . . . (b) the image is far clearer and simpler than what it clarifies.[4]

In other words:

Since the purpose of imagery is to remind us, by approximation, of those meanings for which the image stands, and since, apart from this, imagery is unnecessary for thought, we must be more familiar with the image than with what it clarifies.[5]

It would be instructive to try to apply this principle to Tyutchev's comparison of summer lightning to deaf and dumb demons or to Gogol's comparison of the sky to the garment of God.[6]

"Without imagery there is no art" — "Art is thinking in images." These maxims have led to far-fetched interpretations of individual works of art. Attempts have been made to evaluate even music, architecture, and lyric poetry as imagistic thought. After a quarter of a century of such attempts Ovsyaniko-Kulikovsky finally had to assign lyric poetry, architecture, and music to a special category of imageless art and to define them as lyric arts appealing directly to the emotions. And thus he admitted an enormous area of art which is not a mode of thought. A part of this area, lyric poetry (narrowly considered), is quite like the visual arts; it is also verbal. But, much more important, visual art passes quite imperceptibly into nonvisual art; yet our perceptions of both are similar.

Translated by Lee T. Lemon and Marion Reis.

[1] Alexander Potebnya, *Iz zapisok po teorii slovesnosti* [*Notes on the Theory of Language*] (Kharkov, 1905), p. 83. [Shklovsky]

[2] Ibid., p. 97. [Shklovsky]

[3] Dmitry Ovsyaniko-Kulikovsky (1835–1920), a leading Russian scholar, was an early contributor to Marxist periodicals and a literary conservative, antagonistic towards the deliberately meaningless poems of the Futurists. [Tr.]

[4] Potebnya, *Iz zapisok po teorii slovesnosti*, p. 314. [Shklovsky]

[5] Ibid., p. 291. [Shklovsky]

[6] Fyodor Tyutchev (1803–1873), a poet, and Nicholas Gogol (1809–52), a master of prose fiction and satire, are mentioned here because their bold use of imagery cannot be accounted for by Potebnya's theory. Shklovsky is arguing that writers frequently gain their effects by comparing the commonplace to the exceptional rather than vice versa. [Tr.]

Nevertheless, the definition "Art is thinking in images," which means (I omit the usual middle terms of the argument) that art is the making of symbols, has survived the downfall of the theory which supported it. It survives chiefly in the wake of Symbolism, especially among the theorists of the Symbolist movement.

Many still believe, then, that thinking in images — thinking, in specific scenes of "roads and landscape" and "furrows and boundaries"[7] — is the chief characteristic of poetry. Consequently, they should have expected the history of "imagistic art," as they call it, to consist of a history of changes in imagery. But we find that images change little; from century to century, from nation to nation, from poet to poet, they flow on without changing. Images belong to no one: they are "the Lord's." The more you understand an age, the more convinced you become that the images a given poet used and which you thought his own were taken almost unchanged from another poet. The works of poets are classified or grouped according to the new techniques that poets discover and share, and according to their arrangement and development of the resources of language; poets are much more concerned with arranging images than with creating them. Images are given to poets; the ability to remember them is far more important than the ability to create them.

Imagistic thought does not, in any case, include all the aspects of art nor even all the aspects of verbal art. A change in imagery is not essential to the development of poetry. We know that frequently an expression is thought to be poetic, to be created for aesthetic pleasure, although actually it was created without such intent — e.g., Annensky's opinion that the Slavic languages are especially poetic and Andrey Bely's ecstasy over the technique of placing adjectives after nouns, a technique used by eighteenth-century Russian poets. Bely joyfully accepts the technique as something artistic, or more exactly, as intended, if we consider intention as art. Actually, this reversal of the usual adjective-noun order is a peculiarity of the language (which had been influenced by Church Slavonic). Thus a work may be (1) intended as prosaic and accepted as poetic, or (2) intended as poetic and accepted as prosaic. This suggests that the artistry attributed to a given work results from the way we perceive it. By "works of art," in the narrow sense, we mean works created by special techniques designed to make the works as obviously artistic as possible.

Potebnya's conclusion, which can be formulated "poetry equals imagery," gave rise to the whole theory that "imagery equals symbolism," that the image may serve as the invariable predicate of various subjects. (This conclusion, because it expressed ideas similar to the theories of the Symbolists, intrigued some of their leading representatives — Andrey Bely, Merezhkovsky and his "eternal companions" — and, in fact, formed the basis of the theory of Symbolism.) The conclusion stems partly from the fact that Potebnya did not distinguish between the language of poetry and the language of prose. Consequently, he ignored the fact that there are two aspects of imagery: imagery as a practical means of thinking, as a means of placing objects within categories; and imagery as poetic, as a means of reinforcing an impression. I shall clarify with an example. I want to attract the attention of a young child who is eating bread and butter and getting the butter on her fingers. I call, "Hey, butterfingers!" This is a figure of speech, a clearly prosaic trope. Now a different example. The child is playing with my glasses and drops them. I call, "Hey, butterfingers!"[8] This figure of speech is a poetic trope. (In the first example, "butterfingers" is metonymic; in the second, metaphoric — but this is not what I want to stress.)

Poetic imagery is a means of creating the strongest possible impression. As a method it is, depending upon its purpose, neither more nor less effective than other poetic techniques; it is neither more nor less effective than ordinary or negative parallelism, comparison, repetition, balanced structure, hyperbole, the commonly accepted rhetorical figures, and all those methods which

[7]This is an allusion to Vyacheslav Ivanov's *Borozdy i mezhi [Furrows and Boundaries]* (Moscow, 1916), a major statement of Symbolist theory. [Tr.]

[8]The Russian text involves a play on the word for "hat," colloquial for "clod," "duffer," etc. [Tr.]

emphasize the emotional effect of an expression (including words or even articulated sounds).[9] But poetic imagery only externally resembles either the stock imagery of fables and ballads or thinking in images — e.g., the example in Ovsyaniko-Kulikovsky's *Language and Art* in which a little girl calls a ball a little watermelon. Poetic imagery is but one of the devices of poetic language. Prose imagery is a means of abstraction: a little watermelon instead of a lampshade, or a little watermelon instead of a head, is only the abstraction of one of the object's characteristics, that of roundness. It is no different from saying that the head and the melon are both round. This is what is meant, but it has nothing to do with poetry.

The law of the economy of creative effort is also generally accepted. [Herbert] Spencer wrote:

> On seeking for some clue to the law underlying these current maxims, we may see shadowed forth in many of them, the importance of economizing the reader's or the hearer's attention. To so present ideas that they may be apprehended with the least possible mental effort, is the desideratum towards which most of the rules above quoted point. . . . Hence, carrying out the metaphor that language is the vehicle of thought, there seems reason to think that in all cases the friction and inertia of the vehicle deduct from its efficiency; and that in composition, the chief, if not the sole thing to be done, is to reduce this friction and inertia to the smallest possible amount.[10]

And R[ichard] Avenarius:

> If a soul possess inexhaustible strength, then, of course, it would be indifferent to how much might be spent from this inexhaustible source; only the necessarily expended time would be important. But since its forces are limited, one is led to expect that the soul hastens to carry out the apperceptive process as expediently as possible — that is, with

comparatively the least expenditure of energy, and, hence, with comparatively the best result.

Petrazhitsky, with only one reference to the general law of mental effort, rejects [William] James's theory of the physical basis of emotion, a theory which contradicts his own. Even Alexander Veselovsky acknowledged the principle of the economy of creative effort, a theory especially appealing in the study of rhythm, and agreed with Spencer: "A satisfactory style is precisely that style which delivers the greatest amount of thought in the fewest words." And Andrey Bely, despite the fact that in his better pages he gave numerous examples of "roughened" rhythm[11] and (particularly in the examples from Baratynsky) showed the difficulties inherent in poetic epithets, also thought it necessary to speak of the law of the economy of creative effort in his book[12] — a heroic effort to create a theory of art based on unverified facts from antiquated sources, on his vast knowledge of the techniques of poetic creativity, and on Krayevich's high school physics text.

These ideas about the economy of energy, as well as about the law and aim of creativity, are perhaps true in their application to "practical" language; they were, however, extended to poetic language. Hence they do not distinguish properly between the laws of practical language and the laws of poetic language. The fact that Japanese poetry has sounds not found in conversational Japanese was hardly the first factual indication of the differences between poetic and everyday language. Leo Jakubinsky has observed that the law of the dissimilation of liquid sounds does not apply to poetic language.[13] This suggested to him that poetic language tolerated the admission of hard-to-pronounce conglomerations of similar sounds. In his article, one of the first examples of scientific criticism, he indicates inductively, the

[9]Shklovsky is here doing two things of major theoretical importance: (1) he argues that different techniques serve a single function, and that (2) no single technique is all-important. The second permits the formalists to be concerned with any and all literary devices; the first permits them to discuss the devices from a single consistent theoretical position. [Tr.]

[10]Herbert Spencer, *The Philosophy of Style* (Humboldt Library, vol. 34, New York, 1882), pp. 2–3. [Shklovsky] Shklovsky's quoted reference, in Russian, preserves the idea of the original but shortens it. [Tr.]

[11]The Russian *zatrudyonny* means "made difficult." The suggestion is that poems with "easy" or smooth rhythms slip by unnoticed; poems that are difficult or "roughened" force the reader to attend to them. [Tr.]

[12]*Simvolizm*, probably. [Tr.]

[13]Leo Jakubinsky, "O zvukakh poeticheskovo yazyka" ["On the Sounds of Poetic Language"], *Sborniki* I (1916): 38. [Shklovsky]

contrast (I shall say more about this point later) between the laws of poetic language and the laws of practical language.[14]

We must, then, speak about the laws of expenditure and economy in poetic language not on the basis of an analogy with prose, but on the basis of the laws of poetic language.

If we start to examine the general laws of perception, we see that as perception becomes habitual, it becomes automatic. Thus, for example, all of our habits retreat into the area of the unconsciously automatic; if one remembers the sensations of holding a pen or of speaking in a foreign language for the first time and compares that with his feeling at performing the action for the ten thousandth time, he will agree with us. Such habituation explains the principles by which, in ordinary speech, we leave phrases unfinished and words half expressed. In this process, ideally realized in algebra, things are replaced by symbols. Complete words are not expressed in rapid speech; their initial sounds are barely perceived. Alexander Pogodin offers the example of a boy considering the sentence "The Swiss mountains are beautiful" in the form of a series of letters: T, S, m, a, b.[15]

This characteristic of thought not only suggests the method of algebra, but even prompts the choice of symbols (letters, especially initial letters). By this "algebraic" method of thought we apprehend objects only as shapes with imprecise extensions; we do not see them in their entirety but rather recognize them by their main characteristics. We see the object as though it were enveloped in a sack. We know what it is by its configuration, but we see only its silhouette. The object, perceived thus in the manner of prose perception, fades and does not leave even a first impression; ultimately even the essence of what it was is forgotten. Such perception explains why we fail to hear the prose word in its entirety (see

Leo Jakubinsky's article[16]) and, hence, why (along with other slips of the tongue) we fail to pronounce it. The process of "algebrization," the over-automatization of an object, permits the greatest economy of perceptive effort. Either objects are assigned only one proper feature — a number, for example — or else they function as though by formula and do not even appear in cognition:

> I was cleaning a room and, meandering about, approached the divan and couldn't remember whether or not I had dusted it. Since these movements are habitual and unconscious, I could not remember and felt that it was impossible to remember — so that if I had dusted it and forgot — that is, had acted unconsciously, then it was the same as if I had not. If some conscious person had been watching, then the fact could be established. If, however, no one was looking, or looking on unconsciously, if the whole complex lives of many people go on unconsciously, then such lives are as if they had never been.[17]

And so life is reckoned as nothing. Habitualization devours works, clothes, furniture, one's wife, and the fear of war. "If the whole complex lives of many people go on unconsciously, then such lives are as if they had never been." And art exists that one may recover the sensation of life; it exists to make one feel things, to make the stone *stony*. The purpose of art is to impart the sensation of things as they are perceived and not as they are known. The technique of art is to make objects "unfamiliar," to make forms difficult, to increase the difficulty and length of perception because the process of perception is an aesthetic end in itself and must be prolonged. *Art is a way of experiencing the artfulness of an object; the object is not important.*

The range of poetic (artistic) work extends from the sensory to the cognitive, from poetry to prose, from the concrete to the abstract: from Cervantes's Don Quixote — scholastic and poor nobleman, half consciously bearing his humiliation in the court of the duke — to the broad but empty Don

[14]Leo Jakubinsky, "Skopleniye odinakovykh plavnykh v prakticheskom i poeticheskom yazykakh" ["The Accumulation of Identical Liquids in Practical and Poetic Language"], *Sborniki* II (1917): 13–21. [Shklovsky]

[15]Alexander Pogodoin, *Yazyk, kak tvorchestvo [Language as Art]* (Kharkov, 1931), p. 42. [Shklovsky] The original sentence was in French, "*Les montaignes de la Suisse sont belles,*" with the appropriate initials. [Tr.]

[16]Jakubinsky, *Sborniki* I (1916). [Shklovsky]

[17]Leo Tolstoy's *Diary,* entry dated February 29, 1897. [Shklovsky] The date is transcribed incorrectly; it should read March 1, 1897. [Tr.]

Quixote of Turgenev; from Charlemagne to the name "king" [in Russian "Charles" and "king" obviously derive from the same root, *korol*]. The meaning of a work broadens to the extent that artfulness and artistry diminish; thus a fable symbolizes more than a poem, and a proverb more than a fable. Consequently, the least self-contradictory part of Potebnya's theory is his treatment of the fable, which, from his point of view, he investigated thoroughly. But since his theory did not provide for "expressive" works of art, he could not finish his book. As we know, *Notes on the Theory of Literature* was published in 1905, thirteen years after Potebnya's death. Potebnya himself completed only the section on the fable.[18]

After we see an object several times, we begin to recognize it. The object is in front of us and we know about it, but we do not see it[19] — hence we cannot say anything significant about it. Art removes objects from the automatism of perception in several ways. Here I want to illustrate a way used repeatedly by Leo Tolstoy, that writer who, for Merezhkovsky at least, seems to present things as if he himself saw them, saw them in their entirety, and did not alter them.

Tolstoy makes the familiar seem strange by not naming the familiar object. He describes an object as if he were seeing it for the first time, an event as if it were happening for the first time. In describing something he avoids the accepted names of its parts and instead names corresponding parts of other objects. For example, in "Shame" Tolstoy "defamiliarizes" the idea of flogging in this way: "to strip people who have broken the law, to hurl them to the floor, and to rap on their bottoms with switches," and, after a few lines, "to lash about on the naked buttocks." Then he remarks:

Just why precisely this stupid, savage means of causing pain and not any other — why not prick the shoulders or any part of the body with needles, squeeze the hands or the feet in a vise, or anything like that?

[18]Alexander Potebnya, *Iz lektsy po teorii slovesnosti* [Lectures on the Theory of Language] (Kharkov, 1914). [Shklovsky]

[19]Victor Shklovsky, *Voskresheniye slova [The Resurrection of the Word]* (Petersburg, 1914). [Shklovsky]

I apologize for this harsh example, but it is typical of Tolstoy's way of pricking the conscience. The familiar act of flogging is made unfamiliar both by the description and by the proposal to change its form without changing its nature. Tolstoy uses this technique of "defamiliarization" constantly. The narrator of "Kholstomer," for example, is a horse, and it is the horse's point of view (rather than a person's) that makes the content of the story seem unfamiliar. Here is how the horse regards the institution of private property:

I understood well what they said about whipping and Christianity. But then I was absolutely in the dark. What's the meaning of "his own," "his colt"? From these phrases I saw that people thought there was some sort of connection between me and the stable. At the time I simply could not understand the connection. Only much later, when they separated me from the other horses, did I begin to understand. But even then I simply could not see what it meant when they called me "man's property." The words "my horse" referred to me, a living horse, and seemed as strange to me as the words "my land," "my air," "my water."

But the words made a strong impression on me. I thought about them constantly, and only after the most diverse experiences with people did I understand, finally, what they meant. They meant this: In life people are guided by words, not by deeds. It's not so much that they love the possibility of doing or not doing something as it is the possibility of speaking with words, agreed on among themselves, about various topics. Such are the words "my" and "mine," which they apply to different things, creatures, objects, and even to land, people, and horses. They agree that only one may say "mine" about this, that, or the other thing. And the one who says "mine" about the greatest number of things is, according to the game which they've agreed to among themselves, the one they consider the most happy. I don't know the point of all this, but it's true. For a long time I tried to explain it to myself in terms of some kind of real gain, but I had to reject that explanation because it was wrong.

Many of those, for instance, who called me their own never rode on me — although others did. And so with those who fed me. Then again, the coachman, the veterinarians, and the outsiders in general treated me kindly, yet those who called me their own did not. In due time, having widened the scope of my observations, I satisfied myself that the notion "my," not only in relation to us horses, has no other basis than a narrow human instinct which is called a sense of or right to private property. A man says "this house is mine" and never lives in it; he only worries about its construction and upkeep. A merchant says "my shop," "my dry goods shop," for instance, and does not even wear clothes made from the better cloth he keeps in his own shop.

There are people who call a tract of land their own, but they never set eyes on it and never take a stroll on it. There are people who call others their own, yet never see them. And the whole relationship between them is that the so-called "owners" treat the others unjustly.

There are people who call women their own, or their "wives," but their women live with other men. And people strive not for the good in life, but for goods they can call their own.

I am now convinced that this is the essential difference between people and ourselves. And therefore, not even considering the other ways in which we are superior, but considering just this one virtue, we can bravely claim to stand higher than men on the ladder of living creatures. The actions of men, at least those with whom I have had dealings, are guided by *words* — ours, by deeds.

The horse is killed before the end of the story, but the manner of the narrative, its technique, does not change:

Much later they put Serpukhovsky's body, which had experienced the world, which had eaten and drunk, into the ground. They could profitably send neither his hide, nor his flesh, nor his bones anywhere.

But since his dead body, which had gone about in the world for twenty years, was a great burden to everyone, its burial was only a superfluous embarrassment for the people. For a long time no one had needed him; for a long time he had been a burden on all. But nevertheless, the dead who buried the dead found it necessary to dress this bloated body, which immediately began to rot, in a good uniform and good boots; to lay it in a good new coffin with new tassels at the four corners, then to place this new coffin in another of lead and ship it to Moscow; there to exhume ancient bones and at just that spot, to hide this putrefying body, swarming with maggots, in its new uniform and clean boots, and to cover it over completely with dirt.

Thus we see that at the end of the story Tolstoy continues to use the technique even though the motivation for it [the reason for its use] is gone.

In *War and Peace* Tolstoy uses the same technique in describing whole battles as if battles were something new. These descriptions are too long to quote; it would be necessary to extract a considerable part of the four-volume novel. But Tolstoy uses the same method in describing the drawing room and the theater:

The middle of the stage consisted of flat boards; by the sides stood painted pictures representing trees, and at the back a linen cloth was stretched down to the floor boards. Maidens in red bodices and white skirts sat on the middle of the stage. One, very fat, in a white silk dress, sat apart on a narrow bench to which a green pasteboard box was glued from behind. They were all singing something. When they had finished, the maiden in white approached the prompter's box. A man in silk with tight-fitting pants on his fat legs approached her with a plume and began to sing and spread his arms in dismay. The man in the tight pants finished his song alone; then the girl sang. After that both remained silent as the music resounded; and the man, obviously waiting to begin singing his part with her again, began to run his fingers over the hand of the girl in the white dress. They finished their song together, and everyone in the theater began to clap and shout. But the men and women on stage, who represented lovers, start to bow, smiling and raising their hands.

In the second act there were pictures representing monuments and openings in the linen cloth representing the moonlight, and they raised lamp shades on a frame. As the musicians started to play the bass horn and counter-bass, a large number of people in black mantles poured onto the stage from right and left. The people, with something like daggers in their hands, started to wave their arms. Then still more people came running out and began to drag away the maiden who had been wearing a white dress but who now wore one of sky blue. They did not drag her off immediately, but sang with her for a long time before dragging her away. Three times they struck on something metallic behind the side scenes, and everyone got down on his knees and began to chant a prayer. Several times all of this activity was interrupted by enthusiastic shouts from the spectators.

The third act is described:

. . . But suddenly a storm blew up. Chromatic scales and chords of diminished sevenths were heard in the orchestra. Everyone ran about and again they dragged one of the bystanders behind the scenes as the curtain fell.

In the fourth act, "There was some sort of devil who sang, waving his hands, until the boards were moved out from under him and he dropped down."[20]

In *Resurrection* Tolstoy describes the city and the court in the same way; he uses a similar technique in "Kreutzer Sonata" when he describes marriage — "Why, if people have an affinity of souls, must they sleep together?" But he did not defamiliarize only those things he sneered at:

> Pierre stood up from his new comrades and made his way between the campfires to the other side of the road where, it seemed, the captive soldiers were held. He wanted to talk with them. The French sentry stopped him on the road and ordered him to return. Pierre did so, but not to the campfire, not to his comrades, but to an abandoned, unharnessed carriage. On the ground, near the wheel of the carriage, he sat cross-legged in the Turkish fashion, and lowered his head. He sat motionless for a long time, thinking. More than an hour passed. No one disturbed him. Suddenly he burst out laughing with his robust, good natured laugh — so loudly that the men near him looked around, surprised at his conspicuously strange laughter.
>
> "Ha, ha, ha," laughed Pierre. And he began to talk to himself. "The soldier didn't allow me to pass. They caught me, barred me. Me — me — my immortal soul. Ha, ha, ha," he laughed with tears starting in his eyes.
>
> Pierre glanced at the sky, into the depths of the departing, playing stars. "And all this is mine, all this is in me, and all this is I," thought Pierre. "And all this they caught and put in a planked enclosure." He smiled and went off to his comrades to lie down to sleep.[21]

Anyone who knows Tolstoy can find several hundred such passages in his work. His method of seeing things out of their normal context is also apparent in his last works. Tolstoy described the dogmas and rituals he attacked as if they were unfamiliar, substituting everyday meanings for

the customarily religious meanings of the words common in church ritual. Many persons were painfully wounded; they considered it blasphemy to present as strange and monstrous what they accepted as sacred. Their reaction was due chiefly to the technique through which Tolstoy perceived and reported his environment. And after turning to what he had long avoided, Tolstoy found that his perceptions had unsettled his faith.

The technique of defamiliarization is not Tolstoy's alone. I cited Tolstoy because his work is generally known.

Now, having explained the nature of this technique, let us try to determine the approximate limits of its application. I personally feel that defamiliarization is found almost everywhere form is found. In other words, the difference between Potebnya's point of view and ours is this: An image is not a permanent referent for those mutable complexities of life which are revealed through it; its purpose is not to make us perceive meaning, but to create a special perception of the object — *it creates a "vision" of the object instead of serving as a means for knowing it.*

The purpose of imagery in erotic art can be studied even more accurately; an erotic object is usually presented as if it were seen for the first time. Gogol, in "Christmas Eve," provides the following example:

> Here he approached her more closely, coughed, smiled at her, touched her plump, bare arm with his fingers, and expressed himself in a way that showed both his cunning and his conceit.
>
> "And what is this you have, magnificent Solokha?" and having said this, he jumped back a little.
>
> "What? An arm, Osip Nikiforovich!" she answered.
>
> "Hmm, an arm! *He, he, he!*" said the secretary cordially, satisfied with his beginning. He wandered about the room.
>
> "And what is this you have, dearest Solokha?" he said in the same way, having approached her again and grasped her lightly by the neck, and in the very same way he jumped back.
>
> "As if you don't see, Osip Nikiforovich!" answered Solokha, "a neck, and on my neck a necklace."
>
> "Hmm! On the neck a necklace! *He, he, he!*" and the secretary again wandered about the room, rubbing his hands.

[20]The Tolstoy and Gogol translations are ours. The passage occurs in Vol. II, Part 8, Chap. 9 of the edition of *War and Peace* published in Boston by the Dana Estes Co. in 1904–1912. [Tr.]
[21]Leo Tolstoy, *War and Peace*, IV, Part 13. Chap. 14. [Tr.]

"And what is this you have, incomparable Solokha?" . . . It is not known to what the secretary would stretch his longer fingers now.

And Knut Hamsun has the following in *Hunger:* "Two white prodigies appeared from beneath her blouse."

Erotic subjects may also be presented figuratively with the obvious purpose of leading us away from their "recognition." Hence sexual organs are referred to in terms of lock and key,[22] or quilting tools,[23] or bow and arrow, or rings and marlinspikes, as in the legend of Stavyor, in which a married man does not recognize his wife, who is disguised as a warrior. She proposes a riddle:

"Remember, Stavyor, do you recall
How we little ones walked to and fro in the street?
You and I together sometimes played with a
    marlinspike —
You had a silver marlinspike,
But I had a gilded ring?
I found myself at it just now and then,
But you fell in with it ever and always."
Says Stavyor, son of Godinovich,
"What! I didn't play with you at marlinspikes!"
Then Vasilisa Mikulichna: "So he says.
Do you remember, Stavyor, do you recall,
Now must you know, you and I together learned to
    read and write;
Mine was an ink-well of silver,
And yours a pen of gold?
But I just moistened it a little now and then,
And I just moistened it ever and always."[24]

In a different version of the legend we find a key to the riddle:

Here the formidable envoy Vasilyushka
Raised her skirts to the very navel,
And then the young Stavyor, son of Godinovich,
Recognized her gilded ring. . . .[25]

But defamiliarization is not only a technique of the erotic riddle — a technique of euphemism — it is also the basis and point of all riddles. Every riddle pretends to show its subject either by words which specify or describe it but which, during the telling, do not seem applicable (the type: "black and white and 'red' — read — all over") or by means of odd but imitative sounds ("'Twas brillig, and the slithy toves / Did gyre and gimble in the wabe").[26]

Even erotic images not intended as riddles are defamiliarized ("boobies," "tarts," "piece," etc.). In popular imagery there is generally something equivalent to "trampling the grass" and "breaking the guelder-rose." The technique of defamiliarization is absolutely clear in the widespread image — a motif of erotic affectation — in which a bear and other wild beasts (or a devil, with a different reason for nonrecognition) do not recognize a man.[27]

The lack of recognition in the following tale is quite typical:

A peasant was plowing a field with a piebald mare. A bear approached him and asked, "Uncle, what's made this mare piebald for you?"
"I did the piebalding myself."
"But how?"
"Let me, and I'll do the same for you."
The bear agreed. The peasant tied his feet together with a rope, took the ploughshare from the two-wheeled plough, heated it on the fire, and applied it to his flanks. He made the bear piebald by scorching his fur down to the hide with the hot ploughshare. The man untied the bear, which went off and lay down under a tree.
A magpie flew at the peasant to pick at the meat on his shirt. He caught her and broke one of her legs. The magpie flew off to perch in the same tree

[26]We have supplied familiar English examples in place of Shklovsky's word-play. Shklovsky is saying that we create words with no referents or with ambiguous referents in order to force attention to the objects represented by the similar-sounding words. By making the reader go through the extra step of interpreting the nonsense word, the writer prevents an automatic response. A toad is a toad, but "tove" forces one to pause and think about the beast. [Tr.]
[27]E. R. Romanov, "Besstrashny barin" *Velikorusskiye skazki* (Zapiski Imperskovo Russkovo Geograficheskovo Obschestva, XLII, No. 52). Belorussky sbornik, "Spravyadlivy soldat" ["The Intrepid Gentleman," *Great Russian Tales* (Notes of the Imperial Russian Geographical Society, XLII, No. 52). White Russian Anthology, "The Upright Soldier" (1886–1912).] [Shklovsky]

[22][Dmitry] Savodnikov, *Zagadki russkovo naroda* [*Riddles of the Russian People*] (St. Petersburg, 1901), Nos. 102–107. [Shklovsky]
[23]Ibid., Nos. 588–591. [Shklovsky]
[24]A. E. Gruzinsky, ed., *Pesni, sobrannye P[avel] N. Rybnikovym* [*Songs Collected by P. N. Rybnikov*] (Moscow, 1909–1910), No. 30. [Shklovsky]
[25]Ibid., No. 171.

under which the bear was lying. Then, after the magpie, a horsefly landed on the mare, sat down, and began to bite. The peasant caught the fly, took a stick, shoved it up its rear, and let it go. The fly went to the tree where the bear and the magpie were. There all three sat.

The peasant's wife came to bring his dinner to the field. The man and his wife finished their dinner in the fresh air, and he began to wrestle with her on the ground.

The bear saw this and said to the magpie and the fly, "Holy priests! The peasant wants to piebald someone again."

The magpie said, "No, he wants to break someone's legs."

The fly said, "No, he wants to shove a stick up someone's rump."[28]

The similarity of technique here and in Tolstoy's "Kholstomer," is, I think, obvious.

Quite often in literature the sexual act itself is defamiliarized; for example, the *Decameron* refers to "scraping out a barrel," "catching nightingales," "gay wool-beating work" (the last is not developed in the plot). Defamiliarization is often used in describing the sexual organs.

A whole series of plots is based on such a lack of recognition; for example, in Afanasyev's *Intimate Tales* the entire story of "The Shy Mistress" is based on the fact that an object is not called by its proper name — or, in other words, on a game of nonrecognition. So too in Onchukov's "Spotted Petticoats," tale no. 525, and also in "The Bear and the Hare" from *Intimate Tales,* in which the bear and the hare make a "wound."

Such constructions as "the pestle and the mortar," or "Old Nick and the infernal regions" *(Decameron),* are also examples of the technique of defamiliarization. And in my article on plot construction I write about defamiliarization in psychological parallelism. Here, then, I repeat that the perception of disharmony in a harmonious context is important in parallelism. The purpose of parallelism, like the general purpose of imagery, is to transfer the usual perception of an object into the sphere of a new perception — that is, to make a unique semantic modification.

In studying poetic speech in its phonetic and lexical structure as well as in its characteristic distribution of words and in the characteristic thought structures compounded from the words, we find everywhere the artistic trademark — that is, we find material obviously created to remove the automatism of perception; the author's purpose is to create the vision which results from that deautomatized perception. A work is created "artistically" so that its perception is impeded and the greatest possible effect is produced through the slowness of the perception. As a result of this lingering, the object is perceived not in its extension in space, but, so to speak, in its continuity. Thus "poetic language" gives satisfaction. According to Aristotle, poetic language must appear strange and wonderful; and, in fact, it is often actually foreign: the Sumerian used by the Assyrians, the Latin of Europe during the Middle Ages, the Arabisms of the Persians, the Old Bulgarian of Russian literature, or the elevated, almost literary language of folk songs. The common archaisms of poetic language, the intricacy of the sweet new style [*dolce stil nuovo*],[29] the obscure style of the language of Arnaut Daniel with the "roughened" [*harte*] forms *which make pronunciation difficult* — these are used in much the same way. Leo Jakubinsky has demonstrated the principle of phonetic "roughening" of poetic language in the particular case of the repetition of identical sounds. The language of poetry is, then, a difficult, roughened, impeded language. In a few special instances the language of poetry approximates the language of prose, but this does not violate the principle of "roughened" form.

> Her sister was called Tatyana.
> For the first time we shall
> Wilfully brighten the delicate
> Pages of a novel with such a name.[30]

wrote Pushkin. The usual poetic language of Pushkin's contemporaries was the elegant style of Derzhavin; but Pushkin's style, because it seemed trivial then, was unexpectedly difficult for them. We should remember the consternation of

[28]D[mitry] S. Zelenin, *Velikorusskiye skazki Permskoy gubernii [Great Russian Tales of the Permian Province* (St. Petersburg, 1913)], No. 70. [Shklovsky]

[29]Dante, *Purgatorio,* 24:56. Dante refers to the new lyric style of his contemporaries. [Tr.]

[30]Alexander Pushkin, *Eugene Onegin,* I.ii.24.

Pushkin's contemporaries over the vulgarity of his expressions. He used the popular language as a special device for prolonging attention, just as his contemporaries generally used Russian words in their usually French speech (see Tolstoy's examples in *War and Peace*).

Just now a still more characteristic phenomenon is under way. Russian literary language, which was originally foreign to Russia, has so permeated the language of the people that it has blended with their conversation. On the other hand, literature has now begun to show a tendency towards the use of dialects (Remizov, Klyuyev, Essenin, and others,[31] so unequal in talent and so alike in language, are intentionally provincial) and of barbarisms (which gave rise to the Severyanin group[32]). And currently Maxim Gorky is changing his diction from the old literary language to the new literary colloquialism of Leskov.[33] Ordinary speech and literary language have thereby changed places (see the work of Vyacheslav Ivanov and many others). And finally, a strong tendency, led by Khlebnikov, to create a new and properly poetic language has emerged. In the light of these developments we can define poetry as *attenuated, tortuous* speech. Poetic speech is *formed speech*. Prose is ordinary speech — economical, easy, proper; the goddess of prose [*dea prosae*] is a goddess of the accurate, facile type, of the "direct" expression of a child. I shall discuss roughened form and retardation as the general *law* of art at greater length in an article on plot construction.[34]

Nevertheless, the position of those who urge the idea of economy of artistic energy as something which exists in and even distinguishes poetic language seems, at first glance, tenable for the problem of rhythm. Spencer's description of rhythm would seem to be absolutely incontestable:

> Just as the body in receiving a series of varying concussions, must keep the muscles ready to meet the most violent of them, as not knowing when such may come: so, the mind in receiving unarranged articulations, must keep its perspectives active enough to recognize the least easily caught sounds. And as, if the concussions recur in definite order, the body may husband its forces by adjusting the resistance needful for each concussion; so, if the syllables be rhythmically arranged, the mind may economize its energies by anticipating the attention required for each syllable.[35]

This apparently conclusive observation suffers from the common fallacy, the confusion of the laws of poetic and prosaic language. In *The Philosophy of Style* Spencer failed utterly to distinguish between them. But rhythm may have two functions. The rhythm of prose, or of a work song like "Dubinushka," permits the members of the work crew to do their necessary "groaning together" and also eases the work by making it automatic. And, in fact, it is easier to march with music than without it, and to march during an animated conversation is even easier, for the walking is done unconsciously. Thus the rhythm of prose is an important automatizing element; the rhythm of poetry is not. There is "order" in art, yet not a single column of a Greek temple stands exactly in its proper order; poetic rhythm is similarly disordered rhythm. Attempts to systematize the irregularities have been made, and such attempts are part of the current problem in the theory of rhythm. It is obvious that the systematization will not work, for in reality the problem is not one of complicating the rhythm but of disordering the rhythm — a disordering which cannot be predicted. Should the disordering of rhythm become a convention, it would be ineffective as a device for the roughening of language. But I will not discuss rhythm in more detail since I intend to write a book about it.[36]

[31] Alexey Remizov (1877–1957) is best known as a novelist and satirist; Nicholas Klyuyev (1885–1937) and Sergey Essenin (1895–1925) were "peasant poets." All three were noted for their faithful reproduction of Russian dialects and colloquial language. [Tr.]

[32] A group noted for its opulent and sensuous verse style. [Tr.]

[33] Nicholas Leskov (1831–1895), novelist and short story writer, helped popularize the *skaz*, or yarn, and hence, because of the part dialect peculiarities play in the *skaz*, also altered Russian literary language. [Tr.]

[34] Shklovsky is probably referring to his *Razvyortyvaniye syuzheta* [*Plot Development*] (Petrograd, 1291). [Tr.]

[35] Spencer, p. 169. Again the Russian text is shortened from Spencer's original. [Tr.]

[36] We have been unable to discover the book Shklovsky promised. [Tr.]

Vladimir Propp

1895–1970

Vladimir Yakovlevich Propp is the originator of folklore studies in the mode of historical and structural typology. Initially a philologist of Russian and German, Propp in 1918 took his degree at Petersburg, where he taught from the 1930s (when the institution had become known as Leningrad University) until his death. Propp's work, such as the groundbreaking Morphology of the Folktale *(1928), was suppressed because of official suspicion of formalist influence, but Western intellectuals, notably Claude Lévi-Strauss (see Ch. 2) rescued him from obscurity in the 1960s. Among Propp's other studies are those on the origins of the tale of enchantment (1947), the Russian heroic saga (1958), and the poetics of peasant folk songs (1963). The translation of "Fairy Tale Transformations" is from* Readings in Russian Poetics *(1971).*

[Fairy Tale Transformations]

I

The study of the fairy tale may be compared in many respects to that of organic formation in nature. Both the naturalist and the folklorist deal with species and varieties which are essentially the same. The Darwinian problem of the origin of species arises in folklore as well. The similarity of phenomena both in nature and in our field resists any direct explanation which would be both objective and convincing. It is a problem in its own right. Both fields allow two possible points of view: either the internal similarity of two externally dissimilar phenomena does not derive from a common genetic root — the theory of spontaneous generation — or else this morphological similarity does indeed result from a known genetic tie — the theory of differentiation owing to subsequent metamorphoses or transformations of varying cause and occurrence.

In order to resolve this problem, we need a clear understanding of what is meant by similarity in fairy tales. Similarity has so far been invariably defined in terms of a plot and its variants. We find such an approach acceptable only if based upon the idea of the spontaneous generation of species.

Adherents to this method do not compare plots; they feel such comparison to be impossible or, at the very least, erroneous.[1] Without our denying the value of studying individual plots and comparing them solely from the standpoint of their similarity, another method, another basis for comparison may be proposed. Fairy tales can be compared from the standpoint of their composition or structure; their similarity then appears in a new light.[2]

We observe that the actors in the fairy tale perform essentially the same actions as the tale progresses, no matter how different from one another in shape, size, sex, and occupation, in nomenclature and other static attributes. This determines the relationship of the constant factors to the variables. The functions of the actors are constant; everything else is a variable. For example:

1. The king sends Ivan[3] after the princess; Ivan departs.
2. The king sends Ivan after some marvel; Ivan departs.

---

[1] Antti A. Aarne warns against such an "error" in his *Leitfaden der vergleichenden Märchenforschung* (Hamina, 1913). [Propp]

[2] See Propp's *Morphology of the Folktale* (Austin, 1968) [Tr.]

[3] Russian equivalent of "Jack," as the standard name for the hero of a folktale.

Translated by C. H. Severens.

3. The sister sends her brother for medicine; he departs.
4. The stepmother sends her stepdaughter for fire; she departs.
5. The smith sends his apprentice for a cow; he departs.

The dispatch and the departure on a quest are constants. The dispatching and departing actors, the motivations behind the dispatch, and so forth, are variables. In later stages of the quest, obstacles impede the hero's progress; they, too, are essentially the same, but differ in the form of imagery.

The function of the actors may be singled out. Fairy tales exhibit thirty-one functions, not all of which may be found in any one fairy tale; however, the absence of certain functions does not interfere with the order of appearance of the others. This aggregate constitutes one system, one composition. This system has proved to be extremely stable and widespread. The investigator, for example, can determine very accurately that both the ancient Egyptian fairy tale of the two brothers and the tale of the firebird, the tale of *Morozka*, the tale of the fisherman and the fish, as well as a number of myths follow the same general pattern. An analysis of the details bears this out. Thirty-one functions do not exhaust the system. Such a motif as "Baba-Jaga[4] gives Ivan a horse" contains four elements, of which only one represents a function, while the other three are of a static nature.

In all, the fairy tale knows about one hundred and fifty elements or constituents. Each of these elements can be labeled according to its bearing on the sequence of action. Thus, in the above example, Baba-Jaga is a donor, the word "gives" signals the moment of transmittal, Ivan is a recipient, and the horse is the gift. If the labels for all one hundred and fifty fairy tale elements are written down in the order dictated by the tales themselves, then, by definition, all fairy tales will fit such a table. Conversely, any tale which fits such a table is a fairy tale, and any tale which does not fit it belongs in another category. Every rubric is a constituent of the fairy tale, and reading the

table vertically yields a series of basic forms and a series of derived forms.

It is precisely these constituents which are subject to comparison. This would correspond in zoology to a comparison of vertebra with vertebra, of tooth with tooth, etc. But there is a significant difference between organic formations and the fairy tale which makes our task easier. In the first instance, a change in a part or feature brings about a change in another feature, whereas each element of the fairy tale can change independently of the other elements. This has been noted by many investigators, although there have been so far no attempts to infer from it all the conclusions, methodological and otherwise.[5] Thus, Kaarle Krohn, in agreeing with Spiess on the question of constituent interchangeability, still considers it necessary to study the fairy tale in terms of entire structures rather than in terms of constituents. In so doing, Krohn does not (in keeping with the Finnish school) supply much in the way of evidence to support his stand. We conclude from this that the elements of the fairy tale may be studied independently of the plot they constitute. Studying the rubrics vertically reveals norms and types of transformations. What holds true for an isolated element also holds true for entire structures. This is owing to the mechanical manner in which the constituents are joined.

2

The present work does not claim to exhaust the problem. We will only indicate here certain basic

---

[4]In Slavic folktales, a man-eating witch who lives in a hut that stands on chicken legs.

[5]See F. Panzer, *Märchen, Sage und Dichtung* (Munich, 1905.) "Seine Komposition ist eine Mosaikarbeit, die das schildernde Bild aus deutlich abgegrenzten Steinchen gefügt hat. Und diese Steinchen bleiben umso leichter *auswechselbar*, die einzelnen Motive können umso leichter variieren, als auch nirgends für eine Verbindung in die Tiefe gesorgt ist." (His composition is a mosaic that has fashioned the descriptive image out of clearly delineated pieces. And these pieces are more readily *interchangeable*, the individual *motifs* can vary more easily, since at no time is there any provision made for an interconnection in depth.) This is clearly a denial of the theory of stable combinations or permanent ties. The same thought is expressed even more dramatically and in greater detail by K. Spiess in *Das deutsche Volksmärchen* (Leipzig, 1917). See also K. L. Krohn, *Die folkloristische Arbeitsmethode* (Oslo, 1926). [Propp]

guideposts which might subsequently form the basis of a broader theoretical investigation.

Even in a brief presentation, however, it is necessary before examining the transformations themselves to establish the criteria which allow us to distinguish between basic and derived forms. The criteria may be expressed in two ways: in terms of general principles and in terms of special rules.

First, the general principles. In order to establish these principles, the fairy tale has to be approached from a standpoint of its environment, that is, the conditions under which it was created and exists. Life and, in the broad sense of the word, religion are most important for us here. The causes of transformations frequently lie outside the fairy tale, and we will not grasp the evolution of the tale unless we consider the environmental circumstances of the fairy tale.

The basic forms are those connected with the genesis of the fairy tale. Obviously, the tale is born out of life; however, the fairy tale reflects reality only weakly. Everything which derives from reality is of secondary formation. In order to determine the origins of the fairy tale, we must draw upon the broad cultural material of the past.

It turns out that the forms which, for one reason or another, are defined as basic are linked with religious concepts of the remote past. We can formulate the following premise: if the same form occurs both in a religious monument and in a fairy tale, the religious form is primary and the fairy tale form is secondary. This is particularly true of archaic religions. Any archaic religious phenomenon, dead today, is older than its artistic use in a current fairy tale. It is, of course, impossible to prove that here. Indeed, such a dependency in general cannot be *proved*; it can only be *shown* on the basis of a large range of material. Such is the first general principle, which is subject to further development. The second principle may be stated thus: if the same element has two variants, of which one derives from religious forms and the other from daily life, the religious formation is primary and the one drawn from life is secondary.

However, in applying these principles, we must observe reasonable caution. It would be an error to try to trace all basic forms back to religion and all derived ones to reality. To protect ourselves against such errors, we need to shed more light on the methods to be used in comparative studies of the fairy tale and religion and the fairy tale and life.

We can establish several types of relationships between the fairy tale and religion. The first is a direct genetic dependency, which in some cases is patently obvious, but which in other cases requires special historical research. Thus, if a serpent is encountered both in the fairy tale and in religion, it entered the fairy tale by way of religion, not the other way around.

However, the presence of such a link is not obligatory even in the case of very great similarity. Its presence is probable only when we have access to direct cult and *ritual* material. Such ritual material must be distinguished from a combination of religious and *epic* material. In the first case, we can raise the question of a direct kinship along descending lines, analogous to the kinship line of fathers and children; in the second case we can speak only of parallel kinship or, to continue the analogy, the kinship of brothers. Thus the story of Samson and Delilah[6] cannot be considered the prototype of the fairy tale resembling their story: both the fairy tale and the Biblical text may well go back to a common source.

The primacy of cult material should likewise be asserted with a certain degree of caution. Nonetheless, there are instances when this primacy may be asserted with absolute confidence. True, evidence is frequently not found in the document itself but in the concepts which are reflected there and which underlie the fairy tale. But we are often able to form our judgment about the concepts only by means of the documents. For example, the Rig-Veda,[7] little studied by folklorists, belongs to such sources of the fairy tale. If it is true that the fairy tale knows approximately one hundred and fifty constituents, it is noteworthy that the Rig-Veda contains no fewer than sixty. True, their use is lyrical rather than epic, but it should not be forgotten that these are hymns of high priests, not of commoners. It is doubtless

---

[6]Judges 13–16.
[7]Oldest of the collections of Sanskrit hymns and lore (ca. 1000 B.C.E.).

true that in the hands of the people (shepherds and peasants) this lyric took on features of the epic. If the hymn praises Indra as the serpent-slayer (in which case the details sometimes coincide perfectly with those of the fairy tale), the people were able in one form or another to *narrate* precisely how Indra killed the serpent.

Let us check this assertion with a more concrete example. We readily recognize Baba-Jaga and her hut in the following hymn:

> Mistress of the wood, mistress of the wood, whither do you vanish? Why do you not ask of the village? Are you afraid then?

> When the hue and cry of birds bursts forth, the mistress of the wood imagines herself a prince riding forth to the sound of cymbals.

> Cattle seem to be grazing on the edge of the woods. Or is it a hut which stands darkly visible there? In the night is heard a squeaking and creaking as of a heavy cart. It is the mistress of the wood.

> An unseen voice calls to the cattle. An ax rings out in the woods. A voice cries out sharply. So fancies the nocturnal guest of the mistress of the wood.

> The mistress of the wood will do no harm unless alarmed. Feed on sweet fruits and peacefully sleep to full contentment.

> Smelling of spices, fragrant, unsowing but ever having plenty, mother of the wild beasts, I praise the mistress of the wood.

We have certain fairy tale elements here: the hut in the woods, the reproach linked with inquiry (in the fairy tale it is normally couched in the form of direct address), a hospitable night's rest (she provides food, drink and shelter), a suggestion of the mistress of the wood's potential hostility, an indication that she is the mother of the wild beasts (in the fairy tale she calls them together); missing are the chicken legs of her hut as well as any indication of her external appearance, etc. One small detail presents a remarkable coincidence: wood is apparently being chopped for the person spending the night in the forest hut. In Afanas'ev (No. 99)[8] the father, after leaving his

daughter in the hut, straps a boot last to the wheel of his cart. The last clacks loudly, and the girl says: *Se mij baten' ka drovcja rubae* [Me pa be a-choppin' wood].

Furthermore, all of these coincidences are not accidental, for they are not the only ones. These are only a few out of a great many precise parallels between the fairy tale and the Rig-Veda.

The parallel mentioned cannot, of course, be viewed as proof that our Baba-Jaga goes back to the Rig-Veda. One can only stress that on the whole the line proceeds from religion to the fairy tale, not conversely, and that it is essential here to initiate accurate comparative studies.

However, everything said here is true only if religion and the fairy tale lie at a great chronological distance from each other, if, for example, the religion under consideration has already died out, and its origin is obscured by the prehistoric past. It is quite a different matter when we compare a living religion and a living fairy tale belonging to one and the same people. The reverse situation may occur, a dependency which is impossible in the case of a dead religion and a modern fairy tale. Christian elements in the fairy tale (the apostles as helpers, the devil as spoiler) are *younger* than the fairy tale, not older, as in the preceding example. In point of fact, we really ought not to call this relationship the reverse of the one in the preceding case. The fairy tale derives from ancient religions, but modern religions do not derive from the fairy tale. Modern religion does not create the fairy tale but merely *changes* its material. Yet there are probably isolated examples of a truly reversed dependency, that is, instances in which the elements of religion are derived from the fairy tale. A very interesting example is in the Western Church's canonization of the miracle of St. George the Dragon Slayer. This miracle was canonized much later than was St. George himself, and it occurred despite the stubborn resistance of the Church.[9] Because the battle with the serpent is a part of many pagan religions, we have to assume that it derives precisely from them. In the

---

[8]All references to Afanas'ev have been adjusted to the 1957 edition of *Narodnye russkie skazki A. N. Afanas'eva* (Moscow, 1957). [Tr.] Alexander Nikolaievich Afanasyev

(1826–1871) was a historian who in 1860 wrote the first systematic study of Russian folktales.

[9]J. B. Aufhauser, *Das Drachenwunder des heiligen Georg* (Leipzig, 1911). [Propp]

thirteenth century, however, there was no longer a living trace of these religions, only the epic tradition of the people could play the role of transmitter. The popularity of St. George on the one hand and his fight with the dragon on the other caused his image to merge with that of the dragon fight; the Church was forced to acknowledge the completed fusion and to canonize it.

Finally, we may find not only direct genetic dependency of the fairy tale on the religion, not only parallelism and reversed dependency, but also the complete absence of any link despite outward similarity. Identical concepts may arise independently of one another. Thus the magic steed is comparable with the holy steeds of the Teutons and with the fiery horse Agni in the Rig-Veda. The former have nothing in common with Sivka-Burka, while the latter coincides with him in all respects. The analogy may be applied only if it is more or less complete. Heteronymous phenomena, however similar, must be excluded from such comparisons.

Thus the study of *basic* forms necessitates a comparison of the fairy tale with various religions.

Conversely, the study of *derived* forms in the fairy tale shows how it is linked with reality. A number of transformations may be explained as the intrusions of reality into the fairy tale. This forces us to clarify the problem concerning the methods to be used in studying the fairy tale's relationship to life.

In contrast to other types of tales (the anecdote, the novella, the fable, and so on), the fairy tale shows a comparatively sparse sprinkling of elements from real life. The role of daily existence in creating the fairy tale is often overrated. We can resolve the problem of the fairy tale's relationship to life only if we remember that artistic realism and the presence of elements from real life are two different concepts which do not always overlap. Scholars often make the mistake of searching for facts from real life to support a realistic narrative.

Nikolai Lerner, for example, takes the following lines from Pushkin's "Bova":

This is really a golden Council,
No idle chatter here, but deep thought:
A long while the noble lords all thought.
Arzamor, old and experienced,

All but opened his mouth (to give counsel,
Perhaps, was the old greybeard's desire),
His throat he loudly cleared, but thought better
And in silence his tongue did bite
[All the council members keep silent and begin to drowse.]

and comments:

In depicting the council of bearded senility we may presume the poem to be a satire on the governmental forms of old Muscovite Russia. . . . We note that the satire might have been directed not only against Old Russia but against Pushkin's Russia as well. The entire assembly of snoring 'thinkers' could easily have been uncovered by the young genius in the society of his own day.

In actual fact, however, this is strictly a *fairy tale* motif. In Afanas'ev (for example, in No. 140) we find: "He asked once — the boyars were silent; a second time — they did not respond; a third time — not so much as half a word." We have here the customary scene in which the supplicant entreats aid, the entreaty usually occurring three times. It is first directed to the servants, then to the boyars (clerks, ministers), and third to the hero of the story. Each party in this triad may likewise be trebled in its own right. Thus we are not dealing with real life but with the amplification and specification (added names, etc.) of a folklore element. We would be making the same mistake if we were to consider the Homeric image of Penelope and the conduct of her suitors as corresponding to the facts of life in ancient Greece and to Greek connubial customs. Penelope's suitors are *false suitors,* a well-known device in epic poetry throughout the world. We should first isolate whatever is folkloric and only afterward raise the question as to the correspondence between specifically Homeric moments and factual life in ancient Greece.

Thus we see that the problem which deals with the fairy tale's relationship to real life is not a simple one. To draw conclusions about life directly from the fairy tale is inadmissible.

But, as we will see below, the role of real life in the *transformation* of the fairy tale is enormous. Life cannot destroy the overall structure of the fairy tale, but it does produce a wealth of younger material which replaces the old in a wide variety of ways.

3

The following are the principal and more precise criteria for distinguishing the basic form of a fairy tale element from a derived form:

1. A fantastical treatment of a constituent in the fairy tale is older than its rational treatment. Such a case is rather simple and does not require special development. If in one fairy tale Ivan receives a magical gift from Baba-Jaga and in another from an old woman passing by, the former is older than the latter. This viewpoint is theoretically based on the link between the fairy tale and religion. Such a viewpoint, however, may turn out to be invalid with respect to other types of tales (fables, etc.) which on the whole may be older than the fairy tale. The realism of such tales dates from time immemorial and cannot be traced back to religious concepts.

2. Heroic treatment is older than humorous treatment. This is essentially a frequent variant of the preceding case. Thus the idea of entering into mortal combat with a dragon precedes that of beating it in a card game.

3. A form used logically is older than a form used nonsensically.[10]

4. An international form is older than a national form.

Thus, if the dragon is encountered virtually the world over but is replaced in some fairy tales of the North by a bear or, in the South, by a lion, then the basic form is the dragon, while the lion and bear are derived forms.

Here we ought to say a few words concerning the methods of studying the fairy tale on an international scale. The material is so expansive that a single investigator cannot possibly study all the one hundred elements in the fairy tales of the entire world. He must first work through the fairy tales of one people, distinguishing between their basic and their derived forms. He must then repeat the same procedure for a second people, after which he may proceed to a comparative study.

In this connection, the thesis on international forms may be narrowed and stated thus: a broadly national form is older than a regional or provincial form. But, if we once start along this path, we cannot refute the following statement: a wide-spread form predates an isolated form. However, it is theoretically possible that a truly ancient form has survived only in isolated instances and that all other occurrences of it are younger. Therefore great caution must be exercised when applying the quantitative principle (the use of statistics); moreover, *qualitative* considerations of the material under study must be brought into play. An example: in the fairy tale "Pretty Vasilisa" (No. 104 in Afanas'ev) the figure of Baba-Jaga is accompanied by the appearance of three mounted riders who symbolize morning, day, and night. The question spontaneously arises: is this not a fundamental feature peculiar to Baba-Jaga, one which has been lost in the other fairy tales? Yet, after a rigorous examination of special considerations (which do not warrant mention at this point), this opinion must be rejected.

4

By way of example we will go through all the possible changes of a single element — Baba-Jaga's hut. Morphologically, the hut represents the abode of the donor (that is, the actor who furnishes the hero with the magical tool). Consequently, we will direct attention not only to the hut but to the appearance of all the donor's abodes. We consider the basic Russian form of the abode to be the hut on chicken legs; it is in the forest, and it rotates. But since *one* element does not yield all the changes possible in a fairy tale, we will consider other examples as well.

1. *Reduction.* Instead of the full form, we may find the following types of changes:

i. The hut on chicken legs in the forest.
ii. The hut on chicken legs.
iii. The hut in the forest.
iv. The hut.
v. The pine forest (Afanas´ev No. 95).
vi. No mention of the abode.

Here the basic form is truncated. The chicken legs, the rotation, and the forest are omitted, and finally the very hut is dispensed with. Reduction

---

[10]For other examples, see I. V. Karnauxova in *Krest' janskoe iskusstvo SSSR* [Peasant Art in the USSR] (Leningrad, 1927). [Propp]

may be termed an incomplete basic form. It is to be explained by a lapse of memory which in turn has more complex causes. Reduction points to the lack of agreement between the fairy tale and the whole tenor of the life surrounding it; reduction points to the low degree of relevance of the fairy tale to a given environment, to a given epoch, or to the reciter of the fairy tale.

2. *Expansion.* We turn now to the opposite phenomenon, by which the basic form is extended and broadened by the addition of extra detail. Here is an expanded form: The hut on chicken legs in the forest rests on pancakes and is shingled with cookies.

More often than not, expansion is accompanied by reduction. Certain features are omitted, others are added. Expansion may be divided into categories according to origin (as is done below for substitutions). Some expanded forms derive from daily life, others represent an embellished detail from the fairy tale canon. This is illustrated by the preceding example. Examination reveals the donor to be a blend of hostile and hospitable qualities. Ivan is usually welcomed at the donor's abode. The forms this welcome may take are extremely varied. (She gave him food and drink. Ivan addresses the hut with the words: "We'd like to climb up and have a bite to eat." The hero sees in the hut a table laid, he samples all the food or eats his fill; he goes outside and slaughters some of the donor's cattle and chickens, etc.) This quality on the part of the donor is expressed by his very abode. In the German fairy tale *Hansel and Gretel,* this form is used somewhat differently, in conformance with the childlike nature of the story.

3. *Contamination.* In general, the fairy tale is in a state of decline today, and contamination is relatively frequent. Sometimes contaminated forms spread and take root. The idea that Baba-Jaga's hut turns continuously on its axis is an example of contamination. In the course of the action, the hut has a very specific purpose: it is a watchtower; the hero is tested to see whether or not he is worthy of receiving the magical tool. The hut greets Ivan with its closed side, and consequently it is sometimes called the "windowless, doorless hut." Its open side, that is, the side with the door, faces away from Ivan. It would appear that Ivan could very easily go around to the other side of the hut and enter through the door. But this Ivan cannot and in the fairy tale never does do. Instead, he utters the incantation: "Stand with your back to the forest and your front to me," or "Stand, as your mother stood you," and so on. The result was usually: "The hut turned." This "turned" became "spins," and the expression, "when it has to, it turns this way and that" became simply, "It turns this way and that." The expression thus lost its sense but was not deprived of a certain characteristic vividness.

4. *Inversion.* Often the basic form is reversed. Female members of the cast are replaced by males, and vice versa. This procedure may involve the huts as well. Instead of a closed and inaccessible hut, we sometimes get a hut with a wide-open door.

5–6. *Intensification and Attenuation.* These types of transformation only apply to the *actions* of the cast. Identical actions may occur at various degrees of intensity. One example of intensification: the hero is exiled instead of merely being sent on a quest. Dispatch is one of the constant elements of the fairy tale; this element occurs in such a variety of forms that all degrees of dispatch intensity are demonstrable. The dispatch may be initiated in various ways. The hero is often asked to go and fetch some unusual thing. Sometimes the hero is given a task. ("Do me the service.") Often it is an order accompanied by threats, should he fail, and promises, should he succeed. Dispatch may also be a veiled form of exile: an evil sister sends her brother for the milk of a fierce animal in order to get rid of him; the master sends his helper to bring back a cow supposedly lost in the forest; a stepmother sends her stepdaughter to Baba-Jaga for fire. Finally, we have literal exile. These are the basic stages of dispatch, each of which allows a number of variations and transitional forms; they are especially important in examining fairy tales dealing with exiled characters. The order, accompanied by threats and promises, may be regarded as the basic form of dispatch. If the element of promise is omitted, such a reduction may be simultaneously considered an intensification — we are left with a dispatch *and* a threat. Omission of the threat will soften and weaken this form. Further attenuation consists in completely omitting the dispatch. As he prepares to leave, the son asks his parents for their blessing.

The six types of transformations discussed so far may be interpreted as very familiar *changes* in the basic form. There are, however, two other large groups of transformations: substitutions and assimilations. Both of them may be analyzed according to their origin.

7. *Internally Motivated Substitution.* Looking again at their donor's dwelling, we find the following forms:

    i. A palace.
    ii. A mountain alongside a fiery river.

These are not cases of either reduction or expansion, etc. They are not changes but substitutions. The indicated forms, however, are not drawn from without; they are drawn from the fairy tale's own reserves. A dislocation, a rearrangement of forms and material, has taken place. The palace (often of gold) is normally inhabited by a princess. Subsequently this dwelling is ascribed to the donor. Such dislocations in the fairy tale play a very important role. Each element has its own peculiar form. However, this form is not always exclusively bound to the given element. (The princess, for example, usually a sought member of the cast, may play the role of the donor, or that of the helper, etc.) One fairy tale image suppresses another; Baba-Jaga's daughter may appear as the princess. In the latter case, appropriately enough, Baba-Jaga does not live in her hut but in a palace, that is, the abode normally associated with a princess. Linked to this one are the palaces of copper, silver, and gold. The maidens living in such palaces are simultaneously donor and princess. The palaces possibly came about as the result of trebling the golden palace. Possibly they arose in complete independence, having, for example, no connection whatsoever with the idea of the Ages of Gold, Silver, and Iron, etc.

Similarly, the mountain alongside the fiery river is no other than the abode of the dragon, an abode which has been attributed to the donor.

These dislocations play an enormous role in creating transformations. The majority of all transformations are substitutions or dislocations generated from within the fairy tale.

8. *Externally Motivated Substitutions.* If we have the forms:

    i. An inn.
    ii. A two-storied house,

it is apparent that the fantastic hut has been replaced by forms of dwelling normal to real life. The majority of such substitutions may be explained very easily, but there are substitutions which require a special ethnographic exegesis. Elements from life are always immediately obvious, and, more often than not, scholars center their attention upon them.

9. *Confessional Substitutions.* Current religion is also capable of suppressing old forms, replacing them with new ones. Here we are involved with instances in which the devil functions as a winged messenger, or an angel is the donor of the magical tool, or an act of penance replaces the performance of a difficult task (the donor tests the hero). Certain legends are basically fairy tales in which all elements have undergone supporting substitutions. Every people has its own confessional substitutions. Christianity, Islam, and Buddhism are reflected in the fairy tales of the corresponding peoples.

10. *Substitution by Superstition.* Obviously, superstition and local beliefs may likewise suppress the original material of a fairy tale. However, we encounter this type of substitution much more rarely than we might expect at first glance (the errors of the mythological school). Pushkin was mistaken in saying that in the fairy tale:

> Wonders abound, a wood-demon lurks,
> Rusalka sits in the boughs.

If we encounter a wood-demon in the fairy tale, he almost always replaces Baba-Jaga. Water nymphs are met with but a single time in the entire Afanas'ev collection, and then only in an introductory flourish of dubious authenticity. In the collections by Onchukov, Zelinin, the Sokolovs, and others, there is not a single mention of Rusalka. The wood-demon only finds its way into the fairy tale because, as a creature of the forest, it resembles Baba-Jaga. The fairy tale accepts only those elements which can be readily accommodated in its construction.

11. *Archaic Substitutions.* We have already mentioned that the basic forms of the fairy tale go

back to extinct religious concepts. Based on this fact, we can sometimes separate the basic forms from the derived ones. In certain unique instances, however, the basic form (more or less normal in the fairy tale epic) has been replaced by a form no less ancient which can likewise be traced back to a religious source, but whose occurrence is unique. For example, rather than the battle with the dragon in the fairy tale "The Witch and the Sun's Sister" (No. 93 in Afanas'ev), we have the following: the dragon's mate suggests to the prince, "Let Prince Ivan come with me to the scales and we'll see who outweighs whom." The scales toss Ivan sky-high. Here we have traces of psychostasia (the weighing of souls). Where this form — well known in ancient Egypt — came from and how it came to be preserved in the fairy tale are questions which need study.

It is not always easy to distinguish between an archaic substitution and a substitution imposed by superstition. Both have their roots (sometimes) in deep antiquity. But if some item in the fairy tale is also found in a living faith, the substitution may be considered as a relatively new one (the wood-demon). A pagan religion may have two offshoots: one in the fairy tale and the other in a faith or custom. They may well have confronted each other in the course of centuries, and the one may have suppressed the other. Conversely, if a fairy tale element is not attested to in a living faith (the scales), the substitution has its origin in deep antiquity and may be considered archaic.

12. *Literary Substitutions.* Literary material shows the same low degree of likelihood of being accepted by the fairy tale that current superstition does. The fairy tale possesses such resistance that other genres shatter against it; they do not readily blend. If a clash takes place, the fairy tale wins. Of all the various literary genres, that of the fairy tale is the most likely to absorb elements from legend and epic. On rare occasions the novel provides a substitution; but even in such a case, it is only the chivalric romance which plays a certain role. The chivalric romance itself, however, is frequently a product of the fairy tale. The process occurs in stages: fairy tale → romance → fairy tale. Therefore, works such as "Eruslan Lazarevich" are among the "purest" of fairy tales in terms of

construction, despite the bookish nature of individual elements. The *Schwank,* the novella, and other forms of popular prose are more flexible and more receptive to elements from other genres.

13. *Modification.* There are substitutions whose origin is not readily ascertainable. More often than not, these are imaginative substitutions which came into being through the teller's own resourcefulness. Such forms defy ethnographic or historical specification. We should note, however, that these substitutions play a greater role in animal tales and other types of tales than in fairy tales. (The bear is replaced by the wolf, one bird by another, etc.) Of course, they may occur in the fairy tale, too. Thus, as the winged messenger, we find an eagle, a falcon, a raven, geese, and others. As the sought-after marvel, we find a stag with antlers of gold, a steed with a mane of gold, a duck with feathers of gold, a pig with bristles of gold, and so on. Derived, secondary forms are generally those most likely to undergo modification. This may be shown by comparing a number of forms in which the sought wonder is simply a transformation of the sought princess with golden locks. If a comparison of the basic and the derived forms exhibits a certain descending line, a comparison of two derived forms reveals a certain parallelism. There are elements in the fairy tale having a particular variety of forms. One example is the "difficult task." If the task does not have a basic form, it makes little difference to the fairy tale, in terms of the unity of its construction, what kind of task is assigned. This phenomenon is even more apparent when we compare elements which have never belonged to a basic type of fairy tale. Motivation is one such element. But transformations sometimes create the need to motivate a certain act. As a result, we see a wide variety of motivations for one and the same act. Thus the hero's exile (exile is a secondary formation) is motivated by widely varied circumstances. On the other hand, the dragon's abduction of the maidens (a primary form) is hardly ever motivated externally but is motivated from within.

Certain features of the hut are also subject to modification. Instead of a hut on chicken legs, we encounter a hut on goat horns or on sheep legs.

14. *Substitutions of Unknown Origin.* We have been discussing substitutions from the point of

view of their origin, but their origin is not always ascertainable; it does not always appear as a simple modification. Therefore we require a category for substitutions of unknown origin. For example, the little sister of the sun from the fairy tale "Little Sister" (Afanas'ev No. 93) plays the donor's role and may be considered a rudimentary form of the princess. She lives in the "solar rooms." We cannot know whether this reflects a sun cult, or the creative imagination of the narrator, or some suggestion by the collector asking the storyteller whether he knows any fairy tales dealing with a particular subject, or whether thus and so can be found; in such a case, the teller sometimes fabricates something to please the collector.

This places a limitation on substitutions. We could, of course, set up several more varieties which might be applied to a given isolated case. However, there is no need for that now. The substitutions specified here are meaningful throughout the entire breadth of fairy tale material; their application to isolated cases may be easily inferred and demonstrated by employing the transformational types cited.

Let us turn to another class of changes, that of assimilations. By assimilation we understand an incomplete suppression of one form by another, the two forms merging into a single form. Because assimilations follow the same classification scheme as the substitutions, they will be enumerated in brief.

15. *Internally Motivated Assimilations.* An example occurs in the forms:

> i. A hut under a golden roof.
> ii. A hut by a fiery river.

In a fairy tale we often meet with a palace under a golden roof. A hut plus a palace under a golden roof equals a hut under a golden roof. The same is true in the case of the hut by the fiery river.

The fairy tale "Fedor Vodovich and Ivan Vodovich" (Onchukov No. 4) provides a very interesting example. Two such very heterogeneous elements as the miraculous birth of the hero and his pursuit by the dragon's wives (sisters) have been drawn together by assimilation. The wives of the dragon, in pursuing the hero, usually turn into a well, a cloud, or a bed and situate themselves in Ivan's path. If he samples some fruit or takes a drink of water, etc., he is torn to pieces. For the miraculous birth, this motif is used in the following manner: the princess strolls about her father's courtyard, sees a well with a small cup, and by it a bed (the apple tree has been forgotten). She drinks a cupful and lies down on the bed to rest. From this she conceives and gives birth to two sons.

16. *Externally Motivated Assimilations.* Take the form:

> i. A hut on the edge of the village.
> ii. A cave in the woods.

Here we find that the imaginary hut has become a real hut and a real cave, but the solitude of its inhabitant has been preserved. Indeed, in the second instance, the forest element is also preserved. Fairy tale plus reality produces an assimilation which favors real life.

17. *Confessional Assimilations.* This process may be exemplified by the replacement of the dragon by the devil; however, the devil, like the dragon, dwells in a lake. The concept of evil beings of the deep does not necessarily have anything in common with the so-called lower mythology of the peasants; it is often explained as simply one type of transformation.

18. *Assimilation via Superstition.* This is a relatively rare phenomenon. The wood-demon living in a hut on chicken legs is an example.

19–20. *Literary and Archaic Assimilations.* These are encountered even more rarely. Assimilations with the folk epic and legend are of some importance in the Russian fairy tale. Here, however, we are more likely to find suppression rather than the assimilation of one form by another, while the components of the fairy tale are preserved as such. Archaic assimilations require a detailed examination of each occurrence. They do occur, but identifying them is possible only after highly specialized research.

Our survey of the transformation of types can end at this point. It is impossible to assert that absolutely all fairy tale forms will be accommodated by our classificatory scheme, but at any rate a significant number clearly are. It would have been possible to bring in still other types of transformations, such as specification and generalization. In the first case, general phenomena become particularized (instead of the thrice-tenth kingdom, we find the city Khvalinsk); in the latter case, the opposite occurs (the thrice-tenth kingdom becomes simply a "different, other" kingdom, etc.). But almost all types of specification may also be regarded as substitutions, and generalizations, as reductions. This is true, too, for rationalization (a winged steed becomes an earthbound horse) as well as for the conversion of the fairy tale into an anecdote, etc. A correct and consistent application of the types of transformation indicated will give a firmer foundation to the study of the fairy tale in the process of its development.

What is true for the individual elements of the fairy tale is also true for the fairy tale as a whole. If an extra element is added, we have amplification; in the reverse case, we have reduction, etc. Applying these methods to entire fairy tales is important for comparative studies on fairy tale plots.

One very important problem remains. If we write out all the occurrences (or at least a great many of them) of one element, not all the forms of one element can be traced back to some single basis. Let us suppose that we accept Baba-Jaga as the basic form of the donor. Such forms are a witch, Grannie-Behind-the-Door, Grandma-Widow, an old lady, an old man, a shepherd, a wood-demon, an angel, the devil, three maids, the king's daughter, etc. — all may be satisfactorily explained as substitutions and other transformations of Baba-Jaga. But then we encounter a "fingernail-sized peasant with an elbow-length beard." Such a form for the donor does not come from Baba-Jaga. If such a form does occur in a religion, we have a form which has been coordinated with Baba-Jaga; if not, we have a substitution of unknown origin. Each element may have several basic forms, although the number of such parallel, coordinated forms is usually insignificant.

5

Our outline would be incomplete if we did not show a model for applying our observations. We will use more palpable material to exhibit a series of transformations; let us take the forms:

The dragon abducts the king's daughter —
the dragon tortures the king's daughter —
the dragon demands the king's daughter.

From the point of view of the morphology of the fairy tale, we are dealing here with an element which we will call *basic harm*. Such harm usually serves as the start of the plot. In accordance with the principles proposed in this paper, we should compare not only abduction with abduction, etc., but also with all the various types of basic harm as one of the components of the fairy tale.

Caution demands that all three forms be regarded as coordinated forms, but it is possible to suggest that the first is still the basic form. In Egypt we find death conceived of as the abduction of the soul by a dragon. But this concept has been forgotten, whereas the idea that illness is a demon settled within the body lives on today. Finally, the dragon's demand for the princess as tribute reflects a shadowy archaism from real life. It is accompanied by the appearance of an army, which surrounds the city and threatens war. However, we cannot be certain. Be that as it may, all three forms are very old, and each allows a number of transformations.

Let us take the first form:

The dragon abducts the king's daughter.

The dragon is viewed as the embodiment of evil. Confessional influence turns the dragon into a devil:

Devils abduct the king's daughter.

The same influence affects the object of abduction:

The devil abducts the priest's daughter.

The dragon figure has already become foreign to the village. It has been replaced by a dangerous animal that is better known (externally motivated substitution), the animal acquiring fantastic attributes (modifications):

A bear with fur of iron carries off the king's children.

The villain merges with Baba-Jaga. One part of the fairy tale influences another part (internally motivated substitution). Baba-Jaga is the essence of the female sex, and, correspondingly, the person abducted is a male (inversion):

A witch abducts the son of an old couple.

In one of the forms constantly complicating the fairy tale, the hero's brothers carry out a secondary abduction of their brother's prize. The intent to do harm has now been transferred to the hero's kin. This is a canonical form of complicating the action:

His brothers abduct Ivan's bride.

The wicked brothers are replaced by other villainous relatives from reserve members of the fairy tale's cast (internally motivated substitution):

The king (Ivan's father-in-law) abducts Ivan's wife.

The princess herself may take over the same function, and the fairy tale may assume more amusing forms. Here the figure of the villain has been reduced:

The princess flees from her husband.

In all these cases, a human being was abducted, but, by way of example, the light of day may be abducted (an archaic substitution):

The dragon abducts the light of the kingdom.

The dragon is replaced by other monstrous animals (modification); the object of abduction merges with the imagined life of the court:

The mink-beast pilfers animals from the king's menagerie.

Talismans play a significant role in the fairy tale. They are often the only means by which Ivan can attain his goal. Hence it is understandable that they are often the object of abduction. If the action is thus complicated in the middle of the fairy tale, such an abduction is even obligatory as far as fairy tale canon is concerned. This middle moment in the fairy tale may be transferred to the beginning (internally motivated substitution). The abductor of the talisman is often a cheat, or a landowner, and so on (externally motivated substitution):

A shrewd lad abducts Ivan's talisman.
A landowner abducts the peasant's talisman.

The firebird fairy tale represents a transitional stage leading to other forms; here the stolen apples of gold are not talismans (cf. orpine apples). We should add that the theft of the talisman is not possible as a complication at the fairy tale's midpoint unless the talisman has already been acquired. The talisman can be made off with at the beginning only if its possession is properly motivated, however briefly. It is for this reason that the stolen items which appear at the beginning of the tale are not often talismans. The firebird found its way from the middle section of the tale back to the beginning. The bird is one of the basic forms of transporting Ivan to the thrice-tenth kingdom. Golden feathers and similar features are usually attributed to the animal life of the fairy tale:

The firebird steals the king's apples.

In every case the abduction is preserved. The disappearance of a bride, a daughter, a wife, etc., is ascribed to a mythic substratum in the fairy tale. However, this explanation of such a disappearance is alien to modern peasant life, therefore an alien, imported mythology is replaced by sorcery. Disappearance is ascribed to magic spells cast by evil sorcerers and sorceresses. The nature of the villainous deed changes, but its result is still the same: a disappearance entailing a quest (substitution via superstition):

A sorcerer abducts the king's daughter,
Nursie bewitches Ivan's bride and forces her to flee.

Again we see the activity transferred to wicked relatives:

Sisters force the girl's groom to flee.

Turning to the transformations of our second base form (a dragon tortures the king's daughter), we encounter transformations on the same patterns:

The devil tortures the king's daughter, etc.

Here the torture assumes the nature of seizure and vampirism, which can be fully explained ethnographically. Instead of the dragon and the devil, we see again another of the fairy tale's evil beings:

Baba-Jaga tortures the mistress of the knights.

A third variation of the basic form poses the threat of forced marriage:

The dragon demands the king's daughter.

This reveals a number of transformations:

A water sprite demands the king's son, etc.

This same form, morphologically speaking, may lead to a declaration of war without any of the king's offspring being demanded (reduction); a transfer of similar forms to relatives produces:

The sister, a witch, seeks to devour the king's son (her brother).

This case (Afanas'ev No. 93) is of special interest. Here the prince's sister is called a dragoness. Thus we have a classical example of internal assimilation. It points up the need for caution in studying kinship ties in the fairy tale. The marriage of brother and sister and other forms are not necessarily remnants of an old custom; rather, they may be the results of certain transformations, as the above case clearly shows.

The objection may be raised against all of the preceding that anything at all could be fitted into a single phrase having but two components. This is far from true. How would the start of the plot of the fairy tale "Frost, Sun and Wind" and many others fit into such a form? Second, the observed phenomena represent the same constructional element with respect to the overall composition. Although differently stated, they result in identical patterns in the progress of the plot's: a plea for help may be masked as a departure from home, as a meeting with a donor, etc. Not every fairy tale containing a theft produces this construction. If this construction does not follow, subsequent patterns, however similar, cannot be compared, for they are heteronymous. Otherwise, we have to admit that an element from the fairy tale has entered a construction foreign to the tale. Thus we return to the necessity of making juxtapositions on the basis of identical components and not external similarity.

Cleanth Brooks

1906–1994

To many minds, Cleanth Brooks is the archetypal New Critic, the man whose catch phrases, critical studies, and college textbooks epitomized New Critical ideas, practice, and pedagogy. Brooks was born in Kentucky, educated at Vanderbilt, Tulane, and Oxford (where he was a Rhodes scholar), and began his teaching career at Louisiana State University in 1932. From 1935 to 1942, Brooks and the poet Robert Penn Warren edited The Southern Review, *which promulgated the New Critical program; the two later collaborated on* Understanding Poetry *(1938) and* Understanding Fiction *(1943), textbooks which further advanced the New Critical cause. The year 1947 saw the publication of Brooks's classic of criticism,* The Well Wrought Urn, *and the beginning of his career at Yale, where he became a professor emeritus of rhetoric thirteen years later. Brooks's other works include two studies of William Faulkner (1963 and 1978),* Modern Poetry and the Tradition *(1939),* Literary Criticism: A Short History *(1957) with W. K. Wimsatt, and* A Shaping Joy: Studies in the Writer's Craft *(1972). "My Credo" was written in 1952 and published in the* Kenyon Review. *"Irony as a Principle of Structure," from* Literary Opinion in America *(1951), edited by M. D. Zabel, is a revision of an article that first appeared in the February 1948 issue of* College English.

From *My Credo: Formalist Criticism*

Here are some articles of faith I could subscribe to:

That literary criticism is a description and an evaluation of its object.

That the primary concern of criticism is with the problem of unity — the kind of whole which the literary work forms or fails to form, and the relation of the various parts to each other in building up this whole.

That the formal relations in a work of literature may include, but certainly exceed, those of logic.

That in a successful work, form and content cannot be separated.

That form is meaning.

That literature is ultimately metaphorical and symbolic.

That the general and the universal are not seized upon by abstraction, but got at through the concrete and the particular.

That literature is not a surrogate for religion.

That, as Allen Tate[1] says, "specific moral problems" are the subject matter of literature, but that the purpose of literature is not to point a moral.

That the principles of criticism define the area relevant to literary criticism; they do not constitute a method for carrying out the criticism.

Such statements as these would not, however, even though greatly elaborated, serve any useful purpose here. The interested reader already knows the general nature of the critical position adumbrated — or, if he does not, he can find it set forth in writings of mine or of other critics of like sympathy. Moreover, a condensed restatement of the position here would probably beget as many misunderstandings as have past attempts to set it forth. It seems much more profitable to use the present occasion for dealing with some persistent misunderstandings and objections.

In the first place, to make the poem or the novel the central concern of criticism has appeared to mean cutting it loose from its author and from his life as a man, with his own particular hopes, fears, interests, conflicts, etc. A criticism so limited may seem bloodless and hollow. It will seem so to the typical professor of literature in the graduate school, where the study of literature is still primarily a study of the ideas and personality of the author as revealed in his letters, his diaries, and the recorded conversations of his friends. It will certainly seem so to literary gossip columnists who purvey literary chitchat. It may also seem so to the young poet or novelist, beset with his own problems of composition and with his struggles to find a subject and a style and to get a hearing for himself.

In the second place, to emphasize the work seems to involve severing it from those who actually read it, and this severance may seem drastic and therefore disastrous. After all, literature is written to be read. Wordsworth's poet was a man speaking to men.[2] In each Sunday *Times*, Mr. J. Donald Adams[3] points out that the hungry sheep look up and are not fed; and less strenuous moralists than Mr. Adams are bound to feel a proper revulsion against "mere aestheticism." Moreover, if we neglect the audience which reads the work, including that for which it was presumably written, the literary historian is prompt to point out that the kind of audience that Pope had did condition the kind of poetry that he wrote. The poem has its roots in history, past or present. Its place in the historical context simply cannot be ignored.

I have stated these objections as sharply as I can because I am sympathetic with the state of mind which is prone to voice them. Man's experience is indeed a seamless garment, no part of which can be separated from the rest. Yet if we urge this fact of inseparability against the drawing of distinctions, then there is no point in talking about criticism at

---

[1]Poet and fellow New Critic (1899–1979).

[2]See Wordsworth, Preface to *Lyrical Ballads*, p. 306.

[3]Journalist (1891–1968) best known for a weekly column, "Speaking of Books," in the *New York Times Book Review*. The statement attributed to Adams is a line from Milton's "Lycidas," metaphorically speaking about churchgoers who are given insufficient guidance by their ministers.

all. I am assuming that distinctions are necessary and useful and indeed inevitable.

The formalist critic knows as well as anyone that poems and plays and novels are written by men — that they do not somehow happen — and that they are written as expressions of particular personalities and are written from all sorts of motives — for money, from a desire to express oneself, for the sake of a cause, etc. Moreover, the formalist critic knows as well as anyone that literary works are merely potential until they are read — that is, that they are recreated in the minds of actual readers, who vary enormously in their capabilities, their interests, their prejudices, their ideas. But the formalist critic is concerned primarily with the work itself. Speculation on the mental processes of the author takes the critic away from the work into biography and psychology. There is no reason, of course, why he should not turn away into biography and psychology. Such explorations are very much worth making. But they should not be confused with an account of the work. Such studies describe the process of composition, not the structure of the thing composed, and they may be performed quite as validly for the poor work as for the good one. They may be validly performed for any kind of expression — non-literary as well as literary.

Irony as a Principle of Structure

One can sum up modern poetic technique by calling it the rediscovery of metaphor and the full commitment to metaphor. The poet can legitimately step out into the universal only by first going through the narrow door of the particular. The poet does not select an abstract theme and then embellish it with concrete details. On the contrary, he must establish the details, must abide by the details, and through his realization of the details attain to whatever general meaning he can attain. The meaning must issue from the particulars; it must not seem to be arbitrarily forced upon the particulars. Thus, our conventional habits of language have to be reversed when we come to deal with poetry. For here it is the tail that wags the dog. Better still, here it is the tail of the kite — the tail that makes the kite fly — the tail that renders the kite more than a frame of paper blown crazily down the wind.

The tail of the kite, it is true, seems to negate the kite's function: it weights down something made to rise; and in the same way, the concrete particulars with which the poet loads himself seem to deny the universal to which he aspires. The poet wants to "say" something. Why, then, doesn't he say it directly and forthrightly? Why is he willing to say it only through his metaphors? Through his metaphors, he risks saying it partially and obscurely, and risks not saying it at all. But the risk must be taken, for direct statement leads to abstraction and threatens to take us out of poetry altogether.

The commitment to metaphor thus implies, with respect to general theme, a principle of indirection. With respect to particular images and statements, it implies a principle of organic relationship. That is, the poem is not a collection of beautiful or "poetic" images. If there really existed objects which were somehow intrinsically "poetic," still the mere assemblage of these would not give us a poem. For in that case, one might arrange bouquets of these poetic images and thus create poems by formula. But the elements of a poem are related to each other, not as blossoms juxtaposed in a bouquet, but as the blossoms are related to the other parts of a growing plant. The beauty of the poem is the flowering of the whole plant, and needs the stalk, the leaf, and the hidden roots.

If this figure seems somewhat highflown, let us borrow an analogy from another art: the poem is like a little drama. The total effect proceeds from all the elements in the drama, and in a good poem, as in a good drama, there is no waste motion and there are no superfluous parts.

In coming to see that the parts of a poem are related to each other organically, and related to the total theme indirectly, we have come to see the importance of *context*. The memorable verses in poetry — even those which seem somehow intrinsically "poetic" — show on inspection that they derive their poetic quality from their relation to a particular context. We may, it is true, be tempted to say that Shakespeare's "Ripeness is all" is poetic because it is a sublime thought, or because it possesses simple eloquence; but that is to forget the context in which the passage appears. The proof that this is so becomes obvious when we contemplate such unpoetic lines as "vitality is all," "serenity is all," "maturity is all," — statements whose philosophical import in the abstract is about as defensible as that of "ripeness is all." Indeed, the commonplace word "never" repeated five times becomes one of the most poignant lines in *Lear,* but it becomes so because of the supporting context. Even the "meaning" of any particular item is modified by the context. For what is said is said in a particular situation and by a particular dramatic character.

The last instances adduced can be most properly regarded as instances of "loading" from the context. The context endows the particular word or image or statement with significance. Images so charged become symbols; statements so charged become dramatic utterances. But there is another way in which to look at the impact of the context upon the part. The part is modified by the pressure of the context.

Now the *obvious* warping of a statement by the context we characterize as "ironical." To take the simplest instance, we say "this is a fine state of affairs," and in certain contexts the statement means quite the opposite of what it purports to say literally. This is sarcasm, the most obvious kind of irony. Here a complete reversal of meaning is effected: effected by the context, and pointed, probably, by the tone of voice. But the modification can be most important even though it falls far short of sarcastic reversal, and it need not be underlined by the tone of voice at all. The tone of irony can be effected by the skillful disposition of the context. Gray's *Elegy* will furnish an obvious example:

> Can storied urn or animated bust
> Back to its mansion call the fleeting breath?
> Can Honour's voice provoke the silent dust,
> Or Flatt'ry soothe the dull cold ear of death?

In its context, the question is obviously rhetorical. The answer has been implied in the characterization of the breath as fleeting and of the ear of death as dull and cold. The form is that of a question, but the manner in which the question has been asked shows that it is no true question at all.

These are obvious instances of irony, and even on this level, much more poetry is ironical than the reader may be disposed to think. Many of Hardy's poems and nearly all of Housman's, for example, reveal irony quite as definite and overt as this. Lest these examples, however, seem to specialize irony in the direction of the sardonic, the reader ought to be reminded that irony, even in its obvious and conventionally recognized forms, comprises a wide variety of modes: tragic irony, self-irony, playful, arch, mocking, or gentle irony, etc. The body of poetry which may be said to contain irony in the ordinary senses of the term stretches from *Lear,* on the one hand, to "Cupid and Campaspe Played," on the other.

What indeed would be a statement wholly devoid of an ironic potential — a statement that did not show any qualification of the context? One is forced to offer statements like "Two plus two equals four," or "The square on the hypotenuse of a right triangle is equal to the sum of the squares on the two sides." The meaning of these statements is unqualified by any context; if they are true, they are equally true in any possible context.[1] These statements are properly abstract, and their terms are pure denotations. (If "two" or "four" actually happened to have connotations for the fancifully minded, the connotations would be quite irrelevant: they do not participate in the meaningful structure of the statement.)

But connotations are important in poetry and do enter significantly into the structure of

[1]This is not to say, of course, that such statements are not related to a particular "universe of discourse." They are indeed, as are all statements of whatever kind. But I distinguish here between "context" and "universe of discourse." "Two plus two equals four" is not dependent on a special dramatic context in the way in which a "statement" made in a poem is. Compare "two plus two equals four" and the same "statement" as contained in Housman's poem:

> — To think that two and two are four
> And neither five nor three
> The heart of man has long been sore
> And long 'tis like to be.   [Brooks]

meaning which is the poem. Moreover, I should claim also — as a corollary of the foregoing proposition — that poems never contain abstract statements. That is, any "statement" made in the poem bears the pressure of the context and has its meaning modified by the context. In other words, the statements made — including those which appear to be philosophical generalizations — are to be read as if they were speeches in a drama. Their relevance, their propriety, their rhetorical force, even their meaning, cannot be divorced from the context in which they are imbedded.

The principle I state may seem a very obvious one, but I think that it is nonetheless very important. It may throw some light upon the importance of the term *irony* in modern criticism. As one who has certainly tended to overuse the term *irony* and perhaps, on occasion, has abused the term, I am closely concerned here. But I want to make quite clear what that concern is: it is not to justify the term *irony* as such, but rather to indicate why modern critics are so often tempted to use it. We have doubtless stretched the term too much, but it has been almost the only term available by which to point to a general and important aspect of poetry.

Consider this example: The speaker in Matthew Arnold's "Dover Beach" states that the world, "which seems to lie before us like a land of dreams . . . hath really neither joy nor love nor light. . . ." For some readers the statement will seem an obvious truism. (The hero of a typical Hemingway short story or novel, for example, will say this, though of course in a rather different idiom.) For other readers, however, the statement will seem false, or at least highly questionable. In any case, if we try to "prove" the proposition, we shall raise some very perplexing metaphysical questions, and in doing so, we shall certainly also move away from the problems of the poem and, finally, from a justification of the poem. For the lines are to be justified in the poem in terms of the context: the speaker is standing beside his loved one, looking out of the window on the calm sea, listening to the long withdrawing roar of the ebbing tide, and aware of the beautiful delusion of moonlight which "blanches" the whole scene. The "truth" of the statement, and of the poem itself, in which it is imbedded, will be

validated, not by a majority report of the association of sociologists, or a committee of physical scientists, or of a congress of metaphysicians who are willing to stamp the statement as proved. How is the statement to be validated? We shall probably not be able to do better than to apply T. S. Eliot's test: does the statement seem to be that which the mind of the reader can accept as coherent, mature, and founded on the facts of experience? But when we raise such a question, we are driven to consider the poem as drama. We raise such further questions as these: Does the speaker seem carried away with his own emotions? Does he seem to oversimplify the situation? Or does he, on the other hand, seem to have won to a kind of detachment and objectivity? In other words, we are forced to raise the question as to whether the statement grows properly out of a context; whether it acknowledges the pressures of the context; whether it is "ironical" — or merely callow, glib, and sentimental.

I have suggested elsewhere that the poem which meets Eliot's test comes to the same thing as I. A. Richards's "poetry of synthesis" — that is, a poetry which does not leave out what is apparently hostile to its dominant tone, and which, because it is able to fuse the irrelevant and discordant, has come to terms with itself and is invulnerable to irony.[2] Irony, then, in this further sense, is not only an acknowledgment of the pressures of a context. Invulnerability to irony is the stability of a context in which the internal pressures balance and mutually support each other. The stability is like that of the arch: the very forces which are calculated to drag the stones to the ground actually provide the principle of support — a principle in which thrust and counterthrust become the means of stability.

In many poems the pressures of the context emerge in obvious ironies. Marvell's "To His Coy Mistress" or Raleigh's "Nymph's Reply" or even Gray's "Elegy" reveal themselves as ironical, even to readers who use irony strictly in the conventional sense.

But can other poems be subsumed under this general principle, and do they show a comparable

[2]See I. A. Richards, *Principles of Literary Criticism* (New York: Harcourt Brace Jovanovich, 1924), pp. 774ff.

basic structure? The test case would seem to be presented by the lyric, and particularly the simple lyric. Consider, for example, one of Shakespeare's songs:

Who is Silvia: what is she
    That all our swains commend her?
Holy, fair, and wise is she;
    The heavens such grace did lend her,
That she might admired be.

Is she kind as she is fair?
    For beauty lives with kindness.
Love doth to her eyes repair,
    To help him of his blindness,
And, being help'd, inhabits there.

Then to Silvia let us sing,
    That Silvia is excelling;
She excels each mortal thing
    Upon the dull earth dwelling:
To her let us garlands bring.

On one level the song attempts to answer the question "Who is Silvia?" and the answer given makes her something of an angel and something of a goddess. She excels each mortal thing "Upon the dull earth dwelling." Silvia herself, of course, dwells upon that dull earth, though it is presumably her own brightness which makes it dull by comparison. (The dull earth, for example, yields bright garlands which the swains are bringing to her.) Why does she excel each mortal thing? Because of her virtues ("Holy, fair, and wise is she"), and these are a celestial gift. She is heaven's darling ("The heavens such grace did lend her").

Grace, I suppose, refers to grace of movement, and some readers will insist that we leave it at that. But since Silvia's other virtues include holiness and wisdom, and since her grace has been lent from above, I do not think that we can quite shut out the theological overtones. Shakespeare's audience would have found it even more difficult to do so. At any rate, it is interesting to see what happens if we are aware of these overtones. We get a delightful richness, and we also get something very close to irony.

The motive for the bestowal of grace — that she might admired be — is oddly untheological. But what follows is odder still, for the love that "doth to her eyes repair" is not, as we might expect, Christian "charity" but the little pagan god Cupid ("Love doth to her eyes repair, / To

help him of his blindness.") But if Cupid lives in her eyes, then the second line of the stanza takes on another layer of meaning. "For beauty lives with kindness" becomes not merely a kind of charming platitude — actually often denied in human experience. (The Petrarchan lover, for example, as Shakespeare well knew, frequently found a beautiful and *cruel* mistress.) The second line, in this context, means also that the love god lives with the kind Silvia, and indeed has taken these eyes that sparkle with kindness for his own.

Is the mixture of pagan myth and Christian theology, then, an unthinking confusion into which the poet has blundered, or is it something wittily combined? It is certainly not a confusion, and if blundered into unconsciously, it is a happy mistake. But I do not mean to press the issue of the poet's self-consciousness (and with it, the implication of a kind of playful irony). Suffice it to say that the song is charming and delightful, and that the mingling of elements is proper to a poem which is a deft and light-fingered attempt to suggest the quality of divinity with which lovers perennially endow maidens who are finally mortal. The touch is light, there is a lyric grace, but the tone is complex, nonetheless.

I shall be prepared, however, to have this last example thrown out of court since Shakespeare, for all his universality, was a contemporary of the metaphysical poets, and may have incorporated more of their ironic complexity than is necessary or normal. One can draw more innocent and therefore more convincing examples from Wordsworth's Lucy poems.

She dwelt among the untrodden ways
    Beside the springs of Dove,
A maid whom there were none to praise
    And very few to love;

A violet by a mossy stone
    Half hidden from the eye!
Fair as a star, when only one
    Is shining in the sky.

She lived unknown, and few could know
    When Lucy ceased to be;
But she is in her grave, and, oh,
    The difference to me.

Which is Lucy really like — the violet or the star? The context in general seems to support the violet comparison. The violet, beautiful but almost unnoticed, already half hidden from the eye, is now, as the poem ends, completely hidden in its grave, with none but the poet to grieve for its loss. The star comparison may seem only vaguely relevant — a conventional and here a somewhat anomalous compliment. Actually, it is not difficult to justify the star comparison: to her lover's eyes, she is the solitary star. She has no rivals, nor would the idea of rivalry, in her unself-conscious simplicity, occur to her.

The violet and the star thus balance each other and between themselves define the situation: Lucy was, from the viewpoint of the great world, unnoticed, shy, modest, and half hidden from the eye, but from the standpoint of her lover, she is the single star, completely dominating that world, not arrogantly like the sun, but sweetly and modestly, like the star. The implicit contrast is that so often developed ironically by John Donne in his poems where the lovers, who amount to nothing in the eyes of the world, become, in their own eyes, each the other's world — as in "The Good-Morrow," where their love makes "one little room an everywhere," or as in "The Canonization," where the lovers drive into the mirrors of each other's eyes the "towns, countries, courts" — which make up the great world; and thus find that world in themselves. It is easy to imagine how Donne would have exploited the contrast between the violet and the star, accentuating it, developing the irony, showing how the violet was really like its antithesis, the star, etc.

Now one does not want to enter an Act of Uniformity against the poets. Wordsworth is entitled to his method of simple juxtaposition with no underscoring of the ironical contrast. But it is worth noting that the contrast with its ironic potential is there in his poem. It is there in nearly all of Wordsworth's successful lyrics. It is certainly to be found in "A slumber did my spirit seal."

A slumber did my spirit seal;
   I had no human fears:
She seemed a thing that could not feel
   The touch of earthly years.

No motion has she now, no force;
   She neither hears nor sees,

Rolled round in earth's diurnal course,
   With rocks, and stones, and trees.

The lover's insensitivity to the claims of mortality is interpreted as a lethargy of spirit — a strange slumber. Thus the "human fears" that he lacked are apparently the fears normal to human beings. But the phrase has a certain pliability. It could mean fears *for* the loved one as a mortal human being; and the lines that follow tend to warp the phrase in this direction: it does not occur to the lover that he needs to fear for one who cannot be touched by "earthly years." We need not ague that Wordsworth is consciously using a witty device, a purposed ambiguity; nor need we conclude that he is confused. It is enough to see that Wordsworth has developed, quite "normally," let us say, a context calculated to pull "human fears" in opposed directions, and that the slightest pressure of attention on the part of the reader precipitates an ironical effect.

As we move into the second stanza, the potential irony almost becomes overt. If the slumber has sealed the lover's spirit, a slumber, immersed in which he thought it impossible that his loved one could perish, so too a slumber has now definitely sealed *her* spirit: "No motion has she now, no force; / She neither hears nor sees." It is evident that it is her unnatural slumber that has waked him out of his. It is curious to speculate on what Donne or Marvell would have made of this.

Wordsworth, however, still does not choose to exploit the contrast as such. Instead, he attempts to suggest something of the lover's agonized shock at the loved one's present lack of motion — of his response to her utter and horrible inertness. And how shall he suggest this? He chooses to suggest it, not by saying that she lies as quiet as marble or as a lump of clay; on the contrary, he attempts to suggest it by imagining her in violent motion — violent, but imposed motion, the same motion indeed which the very stones share, whirled about as they are in earth's diurnal course. Why does the image convey so powerfully the sense of something inert and helpless? Part of the effect, of course, resides in the fact that a dead lifelessness is suggested more sharply by an object's being whirled about by something else than by an image of the object in repose. But there are other matters which are at work here: the sense of the girl's falling back into the clutter of things, companioned by things chained like a tree to one particular spot, or by things completely inanimate, like rocks and stones. Here, of course, the concluding figure leans upon the suggestion made in the first stanza, that the girl once seemed something not subject to earthly limitations at all. But surely, the image of the whirl itself is important in its suggestion of something meaningless — motion that mechanically repeats itself. And there is one further element: the girl, who to her lover seemed a thing that could not feel the touch of earthly years, is caught up helplessly into the empty whirl of the earth which measures and makes time. She is touched by and held by earthly time in its most powerful and horrible image. The last figure thus seems to me to summarize the poem — to offer to almost every facet of meaning suggested in the earlier lines a concurring and resolving image which meets and accepts and reduces each item to its place in the total unity.

Wordsworth, as we have observed above, does not choose to point up specifically the ironical contrast between the speaker's former slumber and the loved one's present slumber. But there is one ironical contrast which he does stress: this is the contrast between the two senses in which the girl becomes insulated against the "touch of earthly years." In the first stanza, she "could not feel / The touch of earthly years" because she seemed divine and immortal. But in the second stanza, now in her grave, she still does not "feel the touch of earthly years," for, like the rocks and stones, she feels nothing at all. It is true that Wordsworth does not repeat the verb "feels"; instead he writes "She neither *hears* nor *sees*." But the contrast, though not commented upon directly by any device of verbal wit, is there nonetheless, and is bound to make itself felt in any sensitive reading of the poem. The statement of the first stanza has been literally realized in the second, but its meaning has been ironically reversed.

Ought we, then, to apply the term *ironical* to Wordsworth's poem? Not necessarily. I am trying to account for my temptation to call such a poem ironical — not to justify my yielding to the temptation — least of all to insist that others so transgress. Moreover, Wordsworth's poem seems to be admirable, and I entertain no notion that

it might have been more admirable still had John Donne written it rather than William Wordsworth. I shall be content if I can make a much more modest point: namely, that since both Wordsworth and Donne are poets, their work has at basis a similar structure, and that the dynamic structure — the pattern of thrust and counterthrust — which we associate with Donne has its counterpart in Wordsworth. In the work of both men, the relation between part and part is organic, which means that each part modifies and is modified by the whole.

Yet to intimate that there are potential ironies in Wordsworth's lyric may seem to distort it. After all, is it not simple and spontaneous? With these terms we encounter two of the critical catchwords of the nineteenth century, even as *ironical* is in danger of becoming a catchword of our own period. Are the terms *simple* and *ironical* mutually exclusive? What after all do we mean by *simple* or by *spontaneous*? We may mean that the poem came to the poet easily and even spontaneously: very complex poems may — indeed have — come just this way. Or the poem may seem in its effect on the reader a simple and spontaneous utterance: some poems of great complexity possess this quality. What is likely to cause trouble here is the intrusion of a special theory of composition. It is fairly represented as an intrusion since a theory as to how a poem is written is being allowed to dictate to us how the poem is to be read. There is no harm in thinking of Wordsworth's poem as simple and spontaneous unless these terms deny complexities that actually exist in the poem, and unless they justify us in reading the poem with only half our minds. A slumber ought not to seal the *reader's* spirit as he reads this poem, or any other poem.

I have argued that irony, taken as the acknowledgment of the pressures of context, is to be found in poetry of every period and even in simple lyrical poetry. But in the poetry of our own time, this pressure reveals itself strikingly. A great deal of modern poetry does use irony as its special and perhaps its characteristic strategy. For this there are reasons, and compelling reasons. To cite only a few of these reasons: there is the breakdown of a common symbolism; there is the general scepticism as to universals; not least important, there is the depletion and corruption of the very language itself, by advertising and by the mass-produced arts of radio, the moving picture, and pulp fiction. The modern poet has the task of rehabilitating a tired and drained language so that it can convey meanings once more with force and with exactitude. This task of qualifying and modifying language is perennial; but it is imposed on the modern poet as a special burden. Those critics who attribute the use of ironic techniques to the poet's own bloodless sophistication and tired scepticism would be better advised to refer these vices to his potential readers, a public corrupted by Hollywood and the Book of the Month Club. For the modern poet is not addressing simple primitives but a public sophisticated by commercial art.

At any rate, to the honor of the modern poet be it said that he has frequently succeeded in using his ironic techniques to win through to clarity and passion. Randall Jarrell's "Eighth Air Force" represents a success of this sort.

If, in an odd angle of the hutment,
A puppy laps the water from a can
Of flowers, and the drunk sergeant shaving
Whistles *O Paradiso!* — shall I say that man
Is not as men have said: a wolf to man?

The other murderers troop in yawning;
Three of them play Pitch, one sleeps, and one
Lies counting missions, lies there sweating
Till even his heart beats: One; One; One.
O murderers! . . . Still, this is how it's done:

This is a war. . . . But since these play, before they die,
Like puppies with their puppy; since, a man,
I did as these have done, but did not die —
I will content the people as I can
And give up these to them: Behold the man!

I have suffered, in a dream, because of him,
Many things; for this last saviour, man,
I have lied as I lie now. But what is lying?
Men wash their hands, in blood, as best they can:
I find no fault in this just man.

There are no superfluous parts, no dead or empty details. The airmen in their hutment are casual enough and honest enough to be convincing. The raw building is domesticated: there are the flowers in water from which the mascot, a puppy, laps. There is the drunken sergeant, whistling an opera aria as he shaves. These "murderers," as the poet is casually to call the airmen in the next stanza, display a touching regard for the human values. How, then, can one say that man is a wolf to man, since these men "play before they die, like puppies with their puppy." But the casual presence of the puppy in the hutment allows us to take the stanza both ways, for the dog is a kind of tamed and domesticated wolf, and his presence may prove on the contrary that the hutment is the wolf den. After all, the timber wolf plays with its puppies.

The second stanza takes the theme to a perfectly explicit conclusion. If three of the men play pitch, and one is asleep, at least one man is awake and counts himself and his companions murderers. But his unvoiced cry "O murderers" is met, countered, and dismissed with the next two lines: ". . . Still this is how it's done: / This is a war. . . ."

The note of casuistry and cynical apology prepares for a brilliant and rich resolving image, the image of Pontius Pilate, which is announced specifically in the third stanza:

I will content the people as I can
And give up these to them: behold the man!

Yet if Pilate, as he is first presented, is a jesting Pilate, who asks "What is truth?" it is a bitter and grieving Pilate who concludes the poem. It is the integrity of Man himself that is at stake. Is man a cruel animal, a wolf, or is he the last savior, the Christ of our secular religion of humanity?

The Pontius Pilate metaphor, as the poet uses it, becomes a device for tremendous concentration. For the speaker (presumably the young airman who cried "O murderers") is himself the confessed murderer under judgment, and also the Pilate who judges, and, at least as a representative of man, the savior whom the mob would condemn. He is even Pilate's better nature, his wife, for the lines "I have suffered, in a dream, because of him, / Many things" is merely a rearrangement of Matthew 27:19, the speech of Pilate's wife to her husband. But this last item is more than a reminiscence of the scriptural scene. It reinforces the speaker's present dilemma. The modern has had high hopes for man; are the hopes merely a dream? Is man incorrigible, merely a cruel beast? The speaker's present torture springs from that hope and from his reluctance to dismiss it as an empty dream. This Pilate is even harder-pressed than was the Roman magistrate. For he must convince himself of this last savior's innocence. But he has lied for him before. He will lie for him now.

> Men wash their hands in blood, as best they can:
> I find no fault in this just man.

What is the meaning of "Men wash their hands in blood, as best they can"? It can mean: Since my own hands are bloody, I have no right to condemn the rest. It can mean: I know that man can love justice, even though his hands are bloody, for there is blood on mine. It can mean: Men are essentially decent: they try to keep their hands clean even if they have only blood in which to wash them.

None of these meanings cancels out the others. All are relevant, and each meaning contributes to the total meaning. Indeed, there is not a facet of significance which does not receive illumination from the figure.

Some of Jarrell's weaker poems seem weak to me because they lean too heavily upon this concept of the goodness of man. In some of them, his approach to the theme is too direct. But in this poem, the affirmation of man's essential justness by a Pilate who contents the people as he washes his hands in blood seems to me to supply every qualification that is required. The sense of self-guilt, the yearning to believe in man's justness, the knowledge of the difficulty of so believing — all work to render accurately and dramatically the total situation.

It is easy at this point to misapprehend the function of irony. We can say that Jarrell's irony pares his theme down to acceptable dimensions. The theme of man's goodness has here been so qualified that the poet himself does not really believe in it. But this is not what I am trying to say. We do not ask a poet to bring his poem into line with our personal beliefs — still less to flatter our personal beliefs. What we do ask is that the poem dramatize the situation so accurately, so honestly, with such fidelity to the total situation that it is no longer a question of our beliefs, but of our participation in the poetic experience. At his best, Jarrell manages to bring us, by an act of imagination, to the most penetrating insight. Participating in that insight, we doubtless become better citizens. (One of the "uses" of poetry, I should agree, is to make us better citizens.) But poetry is not the eloquent rendition of the citizen's creed. It is not even the accurate rendition of his creed. Poetry must carry us beyond the abstract creed into the very matrix out of which, and from which, our creeds are abstracted. That is what "Eighth Air Force" does. That is what, I am convinced, all good poetry does.

For the theme in a genuine poem does not confront us as abstraction — that is, as one man's generalization from the relevant particulars. Finding its proper symbol, defined and refined by the participating metaphors, the theme becomes a part of the reality in which we live — an insight, rooted in and growing out of concrete experience, many-sided, three-dimensional. Even the resistance to generalization has its part in this process — even the drag of the particulars away from the universal — even the tension of opposing themes — play their parts. The kite properly loaded, tension maintained along the kite string, rises steadily *against* the thrust of the wind.

❖ DIALOGUE WITH CLEANTH BROOKS

R. S. Crane
1886–1967

Ronald Salmon Crane was the leader and moving spirit of the Chicago School of neo-Aristotelian criticism, one of the two major formalist movements in America. Crane was born in Michigan, took his A.B. from the University of Michigan, Ann Arbor (1908), and his doctorate at the University of Pennsylvania (1911). In 1911 he started teaching at Northwestern University in Illinois, then moved on in 1924 to the University of Chicago, where he became full professor in 1925 and head of the English department in 1935. Crane's interest in literary theory and his notion that criticism, rather than historical scholarship, was the preferred mode of teaching literature, began in the 1930s during the implementation of the innovative Hutchins curriculum. Crane's publications are primarily academic articles dense with thought, rather than critical books; the best and farthest reaching of his articles were collected in two volumes as The Idea of the Humanities and Other Essays Critical and Historical *(1967). His only theoretical treatise is* The Languages of Criticism and the Structure of Poetry *(1953). In* Critics and Criticism *(1952), Crane and his colleagues at Chicago presented their neo-Aristotelian system and analyzed the weaknesses of the rival formalism, the New Criticism. In the following selection, Crane takes aim at Cleanth Brooks for impoverishing criticism by reducing poetics to a simplistic analysis of language.*

From *The Critical Monism of Cleanth Brooks*

[W]hereas for Coleridge at least three sciences are necessary for criticism — grammar, logic, and psychology — Brooks finds it possible to get along with only one, namely, grammar; and with only one part of that, namely, its doctrine of qualification. His whole effort can be described not unfairly as an attempt to erect a theory of poetry by extending and analogizing from the simple proposition of grammar that the meaning of one word or group of words is modified by its juxtaposition in discourse with another word or group of words. The paradoxes and ironic oppositions and resolutions of discrepant "attitudes" which, in his system, distinguish poetry sharply from science and other nonpoetical modes of writing are merely the more striking forms which such qualification takes when it is considered, merely qua qualification of meaning by context, apart from, and in contrast with, what he takes to be the self-contained and "abstract" meaning, not dependent on any special context, of predications of fact or universal truth, such as "Two plus two equals four" or "The square on the hypotenuse of a right triangle is equal to the sum of the squares on the other two sides." To talk about the "prose-sense" of poems is to reduce them, or some part of them, to the status of assertions of this kind, and it is for the sake of eradicating this error — the source of "the heresy of paraphrase" — that he insists on finding the essence of poetry in its exclusive reliance on properties of speech which in earlier analyses of language were treated between the consideration of individual words and the consideration of linguistic wholes determined differently by the different ends of logic, dialectic, poetic, and rhetoric, as, for example, in Aristotle's discussions of ambiguity and equivocation; the modes of opposition or contrariety; the different senses of sameness and difference; the kinds of metaphor, including that which involves antithesis; amplification and depreciation in thought and words; the ways of making discourse lively and dramatic; the technique of the unexpected; and so on. Brooks has retained very little of the complexity and precision of this old "grammatical" teaching, and he presents what remains of it as peculiarly relevant to poetry rather than as applicable generally to discourse, and, indeed, as constitutive by itself of the whole of poetic theory. For all his simplification and distortion of the ancient analyses, however, it is clear that the apparatus of terms and distinctions he brings to the study of poetry is a composite of elements that can be traced historically to the prepropositional sections of logic and dialectic, the theory of diction, merely qua diction, of poetic, and the stylistic part of rhetoric.

His key concepts, "paradox" and "irony," reflect unmistakably their grammatical origin. They are terms that designate the mutual "qualification" — and especially one mode of it — that inevitably occurs when the meanings of individual words or sentences or passages are not fixed by prior definition but are determined immediately, in the discourse itself, by the "contexts" in which they stand. "Irony," he says, "is the most general term that we have for the kind of qualification which the various elements in a context receive from the context. This kind of qualification . . . . is of tremendous importance in any poem. Moreover, irony is our most general term for indicating that recognition of incongruities — which, again, pervades all poetry to a degree far beyond what our conventional criticism has been heretofore willing to allow." And "paradox" would seem to differ from "irony" only as it signifies "irony" especially in its narrower sense — not the general phenomenon of contextual qualification (the importance of which, Brooks tells us, we, or at least the "new critics," have at last come to see) but the special kind of qualification, so long neglected, which involves the resolution of opposites: in short, the antithetical metaphor of Aristotle, Johnson's "heterogeneous ideas yoked by violence together," and Coleridge's "imagination."[1]

So much for the manner in which Brooks constitutes the distinctive "language of poetry." His main interest, however, is in its distinctive "structure," and this would seem, on first thought, to be something requiring formulation in different, and even nongrammatical, terms. He tells us indeed, in his recent essay, that the statements made in a poem — including those which look like philosophical generalizations — "are to be read as if they were speeches in a drama," and in *The Well-Wrought Urn* he remarks that "the structure of a poem resembles that of a play." This sounds promising — and the analogy does, in fact, as we shall see, imply one idea which, if Brooks had worked it out, might have led to a more adequate theory than the one he gives us; but the promise is dimmed when we recollect that a "drama" is after all, when considered apart from the specific emotional quality of its plot, merely a grammatical entity, that is, a sequence of speeches with conflicting contexts.

Again, he has much to say about "unity," as when he remarks that the poet "must perforce dramatize the oneness of the experience, even though paying tribute to its diversity," and that the poet gives us "an insight which preserves the unity of experience," his final task being, indeed, "to unify experience." "He must return to us the unity of the experience itself as man knows it in his own experience." But this, too, is disappointing, for it merely attributes to the poet the same necessity for "balancing and harmonizing connotations, attitudes, and meanings" which elsewhere in Brooks — and more typically — is said to follow from the nature of the linguistic instrument the poet uses, as contrasted with the fixed statement-making language of science. It is not, therefore, any special principle of unity derived from the nature of the "experience" or object

---

[1]Aristotle discusses the special power of metaphor when it is combined with antithesis in the *Rhetoric* at 1412b; in a general discussion of the so-called "metaphysical poets" in his Life of Donne, published in *Lives of the Poets* (1783), Samuel Johnson speaks thus of their figures of speech; in his *Biographia Literaria*, ch. 14, Coleridge speaks of the imagination as striving toward "the balance or reconciliation of opposite or discordant qualities" (see p. 329).

represented in a given kind of poem that determines poetical structure; rather it is the presence in poems of poetical structure — i.e., ironical opposition and resolution — that determines, and is the sign of, the unification of experience. And, as Brooks makes abundantly clear, the "structure of poetry" is a structure common to all poems.

Only one alternative remains: to get the "structure" of poems out of their linguistic elements or parts. And this is what Brooks tells us explicitly that he is doing. "The structure obviously is everywhere conditioned by the nature of the material which goes into the poem. The nature of the material sets the problem to be solved, and the solution is the ordering of the material." And again, and most plainly: "What is true of the poet's language in detail is true of the larger wholes of poetry." But what is true of the poet's language in detail, in Brooks's account of it, is that it is a language — "of paradox," as he says — which inevitably organizes itself, when two words are put together, into "organic" relations according to some pattern of ambiguity, metaphor, or ironic contrast. And nothing less, or more, than this can be said about the total organization of parts — that is to say, of lines and passages — in the poem as a whole. Brooks devotes a short paragraph in *The Well-Wrought Urn* to a familiar line of Gray's[2] *Elegy*:

> Grandeur is not to smile at the "short and simple annals of the poor." Properly speaking, of course, the poor do not have "annals." Kingdoms have annals, and so do kings, but the peasantry does not. The choice of the term is ironical, and yet the "short and simple" records of the poor are their "annals" — the important records for them.

Here is poetry, the whole of poetry, so far as its essence as "paradoxical" language is concerned, for here is ironic contrast and its resolution; and the only difference between this one line and the whole *Elegy* is merely a matter of the degree of complexity exhibited by the ironic interrelationships. We may speak, indeed, of partial "contexts" and of total "contexts," the latter being built up, as Brooks suggests in one place, out of the former; but the two are completely homogeneous in their elements and structure, and the relation between them is best described as that of microcosm to macrocosm.

The limiting consequences of this radical reduction of poetics to grammar become apparent as soon as we consider what problems of criticism Brooks's system will not permit us to solve. Thus we cannot, by any legitimate extension of his principles, develop an apparatus for discriminating essentially and not solely in terms of accidents of subject matter or historical style — between poems so obviously different in the special kinds of pleasure they give us as are the *Odyssey* and *The Waste Land,* "Who Is Sylvia?" and "The Canonization," "Westminster Bridge" and Gray's *Elegy, The Rape of the Lock* and "Tears, Idle Tears."[3] What is revealed, if we stay with Brooks, is merely the ironical "structure" which all these, and other, poems have in common as contrasted with nonpoetical works or bad poems. But this is to shut our eyes to a whole range of questions, turning on specific differences in poetic ends and the means suitable for their realization, which are real problems for poets writing poems and hence, one would suppose, important problems for critics. For, literally speaking at any rate, a poet does not write poetry but individual poems. And these are inevitably, as finished wholes, instances of one or another poetic kind, differentiated not by any necessities of the linguistic instrument of poetry but primarily by the nature of the poet's conception, as finally embodied in his poem, of a particular form to be achieved through the representation, in speech used dramatically or otherwise, of some distinctive state of feeling, or moral choice, or action, complete in itself and productive of a certain emotion or complex of emotions in the reader. It is thus only relatively to the form of the poem, as the representation of a particularized

---

[2]Thomas Gray, English poet (1716–1771); his "Elegy Written in a Country Churchyard" (1751) is one of the best-known eighteenth-century poems. The full stanza from which the line is quoted runs:

Let not Ambition mock their useful toil,
Their homely joys, and destiny obscure;
Nor Grandeur hear with a disdainful smile
The short and simple annals of the Poor.

[3]The list, starting with "Who Is Sylvia?" and ending here, consists of texts Brooks analyzes in *The Well-Wrought Urn: Studies in the Structure of Poetry* (1947).

human activity of a given emotional quality, that the poet can know whether his poem is too long or too short, whether the things to be said or left unsaid are properly chosen, whether the parts are rightly ordered and connected, or whether the words, metaphors, and "paradoxes" are appropriate or not to the thought, emotion, character, situation, or general effect. In other words, the principles of the poet's artistic reasoning (however instinctive this may be) are always, and necessarily, ends or effects of some determinate sort to be accomplished in his poem, whether ultimately in the poem as a whole or mediately in some part of it; and the principles will differ, and along with them his decisions as to what must or can be done in constituting his action and its mode of representation, rendering his characters and their thoughts, and fashioning his diction, according as he is writing a simple lyric of feeling or a moral lyric of character, a tragedy or a mock-epic. A sign of the adequacy to its subject of any theory of poetry which aims, as Brooks's theory does, to treat poetry as poetry and not another thing, is surely the extent to which it is able to cope, in specific terms, with problems of this nature. The construction of an adequate theory is not an impossible task, but it requires a basic analysis that will take account, as Brooks never does, of more than one among the several variable "parts" which are combined in different ways in each of the many distinguishable species of poetic works.

W. K. Wimsatt
1907–1975
Monroe C. Beardsley
1915–1985

Of the three important essays on which W. K. Wimsatt and Monroe C. Beardsley collaborated, "The Intentional Fallacy" (1946) is probably the most celebrated. The premier heresy hunter among the New Critics, William Kurtz Wimsatt was born in Washington, D.C., and educated at Georgetown University and at Yale, where he took his Ph.D. in 1939 and taught until his death. Yale published his dissertation, The Prose Style of Samuel Johnson, *in 1941. In addition to other works on Samuel Johnson and Alexander Pope, Wimsatt is also the author of* The Verbal Icon *(1954),* Literary Criticism: A Short History *(with Cleanth Brooks, 1957),* Hateful Contraries *(1965), and* The Day of the Leopards *(1976), a bitter response to contemporary trends in life and letters. Wimsatt argued for a "tensional" criticism that would avoid the intentional, affective, genetic, and stylistic "fallacies." Like Shelley, he found the value of poetry in its mystical incarnation, through metaphor, of relations and connections within reality. The formalist aesthetician Monroe Curtis Beardsley was born in Bridgeport, Connecticut, and educated at Yale (B.A., 1936; Ph.D., 1939). He taught philosophy there before moving on to Mt. Holyoke College (1944–46), Swarthmore College (1947–69), and finally Temple University. Beardsley's books include* Aesthetics from Classical Greece to the Present *(1966),* Aesthetic Inquiry *(1967), and* The Possibility of Criticism *(1970). The text of "The Intentional Fallacy" is taken from the version reprinted in* The Verbal Icon.

The Intentional Fallacy

I

The claim of the author's "intention" upon the critic's judgment has been challenged in a number of recent discussions, notably in the debate entitled *The Personal Heresy*, between Professors Lewis and Tillyard. But it seems doubtful if this claim and most of its romantic corollaries are as yet subject to any widespread questioning. The present writers, in a short article entitled "Intention" for a *Dictionary*[1] of literary criticism, raised the issue but were unable to pursue its implications at any length. We argued that the design or intention of the author is neither available nor desirable as a standard for judging the success of a work of literary art, and it seems to us that this is a principle which goes deep into some differences in the history of critical attitudes. It is a principle which accepted or rejected points to the polar opposites of classical "imitation" and romantic expression. It entails many specific truths about inspiration, authenticity, biography, literary history and scholarship, and about some trends of contemporary poetry, especially its allusiveness. There is hardly a problem of literary criticism in which the critic's approach will not be qualified by his view of "intention."

"Intention," as we shall use the term, corresponds to *what he intended* in a formula which more or less explicitly has had wide acceptance. "In order to judge the poet's performance, we must know *what he intended*." Intention is design or plan in the author's mind. Intention has obvious affinities for the author's attitude toward his work, the way he felt, what made him write.

We begin our discussion with a series of propositions summarized and abstracted to a degree where they seem to us axiomatic.

1. A poem does not come into existence by accident. The words of a poem, as Professor Stoll has remarked, come out of a head, not out of a hat. Yet to insist on the designing intellect as a *cause* of a poem is not to grant the design or intention as a *standard* by which the critic is to judge the worth of the poet's performance.

2. One must ask how a critic expects to get an answer to the question about intention. How is he to find out what the poet tried to do? If the poet succeeded in doing it, then the poem itself shows what he was trying to do. And if the poet did not succeed, then the poem is not adequate evidence, and the critic must go outside the poem — for evidence of an intention that did not become effective in the poem. "Only one *caveat* must be borne in mind," says an eminent intentionalist[2] in a moment when his theory repudiates itself; "the poet's aim must be judged at the moment of the creative act, that is to say, by the art of the poem itself."

3. Judging a poem is like judging a pudding or a machine. One demands that it work. It is only because an artifact works that we infer the intention of an artificer. "A poem should not mean but be."[3] A poem can *be* only through its *meaning* — since its medium is words — yet it *is*, simply *is*, in the sense that we have no excuse for inquiring what part is intended or meant. Poetry is a feat of style by which a complex of meaning is handled all at once. Poetry succeeds because all or most of what is said or implied is relevant; what is irrelevant has been excluded, like lumps from pudding and "bugs" from machinery. In this respect poetry differs from practical messages, which are successful if and only if we correctly infer the intention. They are more abstract than poetry.

4. The meaning of a poem may certainly be a personal one, in the sense that a poem expresses a personality or state of soul rather than a physical object like an apple. But even a short lyric poem is dramatic, the response of a speaker (no matter how abstractly conceived) to a situation (no matter how universalized). We ought to impute the thoughts and attitudes of the poem immediately to the dramatic *speaker*, and if to the author at all, only by an act of biographical inference.

---

[1] *Dictionary of World Literature*, ed. Joseph T. Shipley (New York, 1942), pp. 326–29. [Wimsatt and Beardsley]

[2] J. E. Spingarn, "The New Criticism," in *Criticism in America* (New York, 1924), pp. 24–25. [Wimsatt and Beardsley]

[3] Archibald MacLeish in "Ars Poetica."

5. There is a sense in which an author, by revision, may better achieve his original intention. But it is a very abstract sense. He intended to write a better work, or a better work of a certain kind, and now has done it. But it follows that his former concrete intention was not his intention. "He's the man we were in search of, that's true," says Hardy's rustic constable, "and yet he's not the man we were in search of. For the man we were in search of was not the man we wanted."

"Is not a critic," asks Professor Stoll, "a judge, who does not explore his own consciousness, but determines the author's meaning or intention, as if the poem were a will, a contract, or the constitution? The poem is not the critic's own." He has accurately diagnosed two forms of irresponsibility, one of which he prefers. Our view is yet different. The poem is not the critic's own and not the author's (it is detached from the author at birth and goes about the world beyond his power to intend about it or control it). The poem belongs to the public. It is embodied in language, the peculiar possession of the public, and it is about the human being, an object of public knowledge. What is said about the poem is subject to the same scrutiny as any statement in linguistics or in the general science of psychology.

A critic of our *Dictionary* article, Ananda K. Coomaraswamy, has argued[4] that there are two kinds of inquiry about a work of art: (1) whether the artist achieved his intentions; (2) whether the work of art "ought ever to have been undertaken at all" and so "whether it is worth preserving." Number (2), Coomaraswamy maintains, is not "criticism of any work of art *qua* work of art," but is rather moral criticism; number (1) is artistic criticism. But we maintain that (2) need not be moral criticism: that there is another way of deciding whether works of art are worth preserving and whether, in a sense, they "ought" to have been undertaken, and this is the way of objective criticism of works of art as such, the way which enables us to distinguish between a skillful murder and a skillful poem. A skillful murder is an example which Coomaraswamy uses, and in his system the difference between the murder and the poem is simply a "moral" one, not an "artistic" one, since each if carried out according to plan is "artistically" successful. We maintain that (2) is an inquiry of more worth than (1), and since (2) and not (1) is capable of distinguishing poetry from murder, the name "artistic criticism" is properly given to (2).

II

It is not so much a historical statement as a definition to say that the intentional fallacy is a romantic one. When a rhetorician of the first century A.D. writes: "Sublimity is the echo of a great soul," or when he tells us that "Homer enters into the sublime actions of his heroes" and "shares the full inspiration of the combat," we shall not be surprised to find this rhetorician considered as a distant harbinger of romanticism and greeted in the warmest terms by Saintsbury.[5] One may wish to argue whether Longinus should be called romantic, but there can hardly be a doubt that in one important way he is.

Goethe's three questions for "constructive criticism" are "What did the author set out to do? Was his plan reasonable and sensible, and how far did he succeed in carrying it out?" If one leaves out the middle question, one has in effect the system of Croce — the culmination and crowning philosophic expression of romanticism. The beautiful is the successful intuition-expression, and the ugly is the unsuccessful; the intuition or private part of art is *the* aesthetic fact, and the medium or public part is not the subject of aesthetic at all.

The Madonna of Cimabue is still in the Church of Santa Maria Novella; but does she speak to the visitor of to-day as to the Florentines of the thirteenth century?

Historical interpretation labours . . . to reintegrate in us the psychological conditions which have changed in the course of history. It . . . enables us to see a work of art (a physical object) as its *author saw it* in the moment of production.[6]

[5]The rhetorician is Longinus; see "On the Sublime," p. 97.
[6]It is true that Croce himself in his *Ariosto, Shakespeare and Corneille* (London, 1920), chap. 7, "The Practical Personality and the Poetical Personality," and in his *Defense*

[4]Ananda K. Coomaraswamy, "Intention," in *American Bookman* 1 (1944), pp. 41–48. [Wimsatt and Beardsley]

The first italics are Croce's, the second ours. The upshot of Croce's system is an ambiguous emphasis on history. With such passages as a point of departure a critic may write a nice analysis of the meaning or "spirit" of a play by Shakespeare or Corneille — a process that involves close historical study but remains aesthetic criticism — or he may, with equal plausibility, produce an essay in sociology, biography, or other kinds of nonaesthetic history.

III

> I went to the poets; tragic, dithyrambic, and all sorts. . . . I took them some of the most elaborate passages in their own writings, and asked what was the meaning of them. . . . Will you believe me? . . . there is hardly a person present who would not have talked better about their poetry than they did themselves. Then I knew that not by wisdom do poets write poetry, but by a sort of genius and inspiration.[7]

That reiterated mistrust of the poets which we hear from Socrates may have been part of a rigorously ascetic view in which we hardly wish to participate, yet Plato's Socrates saw a truth about the poetic mind which the world no longer commonly sees — so much criticism, and that the most inspirational and most affectionately remembered, has proceeded from the poets themselves.

Certainly the poets have had something to say that the critic and professor could not say; their message has been more exciting: that poetry should come as naturally as leaves to a tree, that poetry is the lava of the imagination, or that it is emotion recollected in tranquillity. But it is necessary that we realize the character and authority of such testimony. There is only a fine shade of difference between such expressions and a kind of earnest advice that authors often give. Thus Edward Young, Carlyle, Walter Pater:

> I know two golden rules from *ethics,* which are no less golden in *Composition,* than in life. 1. *Know thyself;* 2dly, *Reverence thyself.*

This is the grand secret for finding readers and retaining them: let him who would move and convince others, be first moved and convinced himself. Horace's rule, *Si vis me flere,* is applicable in a wider sense than the literal one. To every poet, to every writer, we might say: Be true, if you would be believed.

Truth! there can be no merit, no craft at all, without that. And further, all beauty is in the long run only *fineness* of truth, or what we call expression, the finer accommodation of speech to that vision within.

And Housman's little handbook to the poetic mind yields this illustration:

> Having drunk a pint of beer at luncheon — beer is a sedative to the brain, and my afternoons are the least intellectual portion of my life — I would go out for a walk of two or three hours. As I went along, thinking of nothing in particular, only looking at things around me and following the progress of the seasons, there would flow into my mind, with sudden and unaccountable emotion, sometimes a line or two of verse, sometimes a whole stanza at once.

This is the logical terminus of the series already quoted. Here is a confession of how poems were written which would do as a definition of poetry just as well as "emotion recollected in tranquillity" — and which the young poet might equally well take to heart as a practical rule. Drink a pint of beer, relax, go walking, think on nothing in particular, look at things, surrender yourself to yourself, search for the truth in your own soul, listen to the sound of your own inside voice, discover and express the *vraie vérité.*[8]

It is probably true that all this is excellent advice for poets. The young imagination fired by Wordsworth and Carlyle is probably closer to the verge of producing a poem than the mind of the student who has been sobered by Aristotle or Richards. The art of inspiring poets, or at least of inciting something like poetry in young persons, has probably gone further in our day than ever before. Books of creative writing such as those issued from the Lincoln School are interesting

---

of Poetry (Oxford, 1933), p. 24, and elsewhere, early and late, has delivered telling attacks on emotive geneticism, but the main drive of the *Aesthetic* is surely toward a kind of cognitive intentionalism. [Wimsatt and Beardsley]

[7]From the *Apology.*

[8]True truth.

evidence of what a child can do.[9] All this, however, would appear to belong to an art separate from criticism — to a psychological discipline, a system of self-development, a yoga, which the young poet perhaps does well to notice, but which is something different from the public art of evaluating poems.

Coleridge and Arnold were better critics than most poets have been, and if the critical tendency dried up the poetry in Arnold and perhaps in Coleridge, it is not inconsistent with our argument, which is that judgment of poems is different from the art of producing them. Coleridge has given us the classic "anodyne" story, and tells what he can about the genesis of a poem which he calls "psychological curiosity," but his definitions of poetry and of the poetic quality "imagination" are to be found elsewhere and in quite other terms.

It would be convenient if the passwords of the intentional school, "sincerity," "fidelity," "spontaneity," "authenticity," "genuineness," "originality," could be equated with the terms such as "integrity," "relevance," "unity," "function," "maturity," "subtlety," "adequacy," and other more precise terms of evaluation — in short, if "expression" always meant aesthetic achievement. But this is not so.

"Aesthetic" art, says Professor Curt Ducasse, an ingenious theorist of expression, is the conscious objectification of feelings, in which an intrinsic part is the critical moment. The artist corrects the objectification when it is not adequate. But this may mean that the earlier attempt was not successful in objectifying the self, or "it may also mean that it was a successful objectification of a self which, when it confronted us clearly, we disowned and repudiated in favor of another."[10] What is the standard by which we disown or accept the self? Professor Ducasse does not say.

---

[9]See Hughes Mearns, *Creative Youth* (Garden City, 1925), esp. pp. 10, 27–29. The technique of inspiring poems has apparently been outdone more recently by the study of inspiration in successful poets and other artists. See, for instance, Rosamond E. M. Harding, *An Anatomy of Inspiration* (Cambridge, 1940); Julius Portnoy, *A Psychology of Art Creation* (Philadelphia, 1942); Rudolf Arnheim and others, *Poets at Work* (New York, 1947); Phyllis Bartlett, *Poems in Process* (New York, 1951); Brewster Ghiselin (ed.), *The Creative Process: A Symposium* (Berkeley and Los Angeles, 1952). [Wimsatt and Beardsley]

[10]Curt Ducasse, *The Philosophy of Art* (New York, 1929), p. 116. [Wimsatt and Beardsley]

Whatever it may be, however, this standard is an element in the definition of art which will not reduce to terms of objectification. The evaluation of the work of art remains public; the work is measured against something outside the author.

IV

There is criticism of poetry and there is author psychology, which when applied to the present or future takes the form of inspirational promotion; but author psychology can be historical, too, and then we have literary biography, a legitimate and attractive study in itself, one approach, as Professor Tillyard would argue, to personality, the poem being only a parallel approach. Certainly it need not be with a derogatory purpose that one points out personal studies, as distinct from poetic studies, in the realm of literary scholarship. Yet there is danger of confusing personal and poetic studies; and there is the fault of writing the personal as if it were poetic.

There is a difference between internal and external evidence for the meaning of a poem. And the paradox is only verbal and superficial that what is (1) internal is also public: it is discovered through the semantics and syntax of a poem, through our habitual knowledge of the language, through grammars, dictionaries, and all the literature which is the source of dictionaries, in general through all that makes a language and culture; while what is (2) external is private or idiosyncratic; not a part of the work as a linguistic fact: it consists of revelations (in journals, for example, or letters or reported conversations) about how or why the poet wrote the poem — to what lady, while sitting on what lawn, or at the death of what friend or brother. There is (3) an intermediate kind of evidence about the character of the author or about private or semiprivate meanings attached to words or topics by an author or by a coterie of which he is a member. The meaning of words is the history of words, and the biography of an author, his use of a word, and the associations which the word had for *him*, are part of the word's history and meaning.[11] But the three types

---

[11]And the history of words *after* a poem is written may contribute meanings which if relevant to the original pattern

of evidence, especially (2) and (3), shade into one another so subtly that it is not always easy to draw a line between examples, and hence arises the difficulty for criticism. The use of biographical evidence need not involve intentionalism, because while it may be evidence of what the author intended, it may also be evidence of the meaning of his words and the dramatic character of his utterance. On the other hand, it may not be all this. And a critic who is concerned with evidence of type (1) and moderately with that of type (3) will in the long run produce a different sort of comment from that of the critic who is concerned with (2) and with (3) where it shades into (2).

The whole glittering parade of Professor Lowes's *Road to Xanadu*, for instance, runs along the border between types (2) and (3) or boldly traverses the romantic region of (2). "'Kubla Khan,'" says Professor Lowes, "is the fabric of a vision, but every image that rose up in its weaving had passed that way before. And it would seem that there is nothing haphazard or fortuitous in their return." This is not quite clear — not even when Professor Lowes explains that there were clusters of associations, like hooked atoms, which were drawn into complex relation with other clusters in the deep well of Coleridge's memory, and which then coalesced and issued forth as poems. If there was nothing "haphazard or fortuitous" in the way the images returned to the surface, that may mean (1) that Coleridge could not produce what he did not have, that he was limited in his creation by what he had read or otherwise experienced, or (2) that having received certain clusters of associations, he was bound to return them in just the way he did, and that the value of the poem may be described in terms of the experiences on which he had to draw. The latter pair of propositions (a sort of Hartleyan associationism which Coleridge himself repudiated in the *Biographia*) may not be assented to. There were certainly other combinations, other poems, worse or better, that might have been written by men who had read Bartram and Purchas and Bruce and Milton. And this will be true no matter how many times we are able to

add to the brilliant complex of Coleridge's reading. In certain flourishes (such as the sentence we have quoted) and in chapter headings like "The Shaping Spirit," "The Magical Synthesis," "Imagination Creatrix," it may be that Professor Lowes pretends to say more about the actual poems than he does. There is a certain deceptive variation in these fancy chapter titles; one expects to pass on to a new stage in the argument, and one finds — more and more sources, more and more about "the streamy nature of association."[12]

"Wohin der Weg?" quotes Professor Lowes for the motto of his book. "Kein Weg! Ins Unbetretene."[13] Precisely because the way is *unbetreten*, we should say, it leads away from the poem. Bartram's *Travels* contains a good deal of the history of certain words and of certain romantic Floridian conceptions that appear in "Kubla Khan." And a good deal of that history has passed and was then passing into the very stuff of our language. Perhaps a person who has read Bartram appreciates the poem more than one who has not. Or, by looking up the vocabulary of "Kubla Khan" in the *Oxford English Dictionary*, or by reading some of the other books there quoted, a person may know the poem better. But it would seem to pertain little to the poem to know that *Coleridge* had read Bartram. There is a gross body of life, of sensory and mental experience, which lies behind and in some sense causes every poem, but can never be and need not be known in the verbal and hence intellectual composition which is the poem. For all the objects of our manifold experience, for every unity, there is an action of the mind which cuts off roots, melts away context — or indeed we should never have objects or ideas or anything to talk about.

It is probable that there is nothing in Professor Lowes's vast book which could detract from anyone's appreciation of either *The Ancient Mariner* or "Kubla Khan." We next present a case where preoccupation with evidence of type (3) has gone so far as to distort a critic's view of a poem (yet a

---

should not be ruled out by a scruple about intention. [Wimsatt and Beardsley.]

[12]Chaps. 8, "The Pattern," and 16, "The Known and Familiar Landscape," will be found of most help to the student of the poem. [Wimsatt and Beardsley]

[13]Goethe: "Whither leads the road? No road! Into the untraveled."

case not so obvious as those that abound in our critical journals).

In a well known poem by John Donne[14] appears this quatrain:

Moving of th' earth brings harmes and feares,
   Men reckon what it did and meant,
But trepidation of the spheares,
   Though greater farre, is innocent.

A recent critic in an elaborate treatment of Donne's learning has written of this quatrain as follows:

He touches the emotional pulse of the situation by a skillful allusion to the new and the old astronomy. . . . Of the new astronomy, the "moving of the earth" is the most radical principle; of the old, the "trepidation of the spheres" is the motion of the greatest complexity. . . . The poet must exhort his love to quietness and calm upon his departure; and for this purpose the figure based upon the latter motion (trepidation), long absorbed into the traditional astronomy, fittingly suggests the tension of the moment without arousing the "harmes and feares" implicit in the figure of the moving earth.[15]

The argument is plausible and rests on a well substantiated thesis that Donne was deeply interested in the new astronomy and its repercussions in the theological realm. In various works Donne shows his familiarity with Kepler's *De Stella Nova*, with Galileo's *Siderius Nuncius*, with William Gilbert's *De Magnete*, and with Clavius's commentary on the *De Sphaera* of Sacrobosco. He refers to the new science in his Sermon at Paul's Cross and in a letter to Sir Henry Goodyer. In *The First Anniversary* he says the "new philosophy calls all in doubt." In the *Elegy on Prince Henry* he says that the "least moving of the center" makes "the world to shake."

It is difficult to answer argument like this, and impossible to answer it with evidence of like nature. There is no reason why Donne might not have written a stanza in which the two kinds of celestial motion stood for two sorts of emotion at parting. And if we become full of astronomical ideas and see Donne only against the background

of the new science, we may believe that he did. But the text itself remains to be dealt with, the analyzable vehicle of a complicated metaphor. And one may observe: (1) that the movement of the earth according to the Copernican theory is a celestial motion, smooth and regular, and while it might cause religious or philosophic fears, it could not be associated with the crudity and earthiness of the kind of commotion which the speaker in the poem wishes to discourage; (2) that there is another moving of the earth, an earthquake, which has just these qualities and is to be associated with the tear-floods and sigh-tempests of the second stanza of the poem; (3) that "trepidation" is an appropriate opposite of earthquake, because each is a shaking or vibratory motion; and "trepidation of the spheres" is "greater far" than an earthquake, but not much greater (if two such motions can be compared as to greatness) than the annual motion of the earth; (4) that reckoning what it "did and meant" shows that the event has passed, like an earthquake, not like the incessant celestial movement of the earth. Perhaps a knowledge of Donne's interest in the new science may add another shade of meaning, an overtone to the stanza in question, though to say even this runs against the words. To make the geocentric and heliocentric antithesis the core of the metaphor is to disregard the English language, to prefer private evidence to public, external to internal.

V

If the distinction between kinds of evidence has implications for the historical critic, it has them no less for the contemporary poet and his critic. Or, since every rule for a poet is but another side of a judgment by a critic, and since the past is the realm of the scholar and critic, and the future and present that of the poet and the critical leaders of taste, we may say that the problems arising in literary scholarship from the intentional fallacy are matched by others which arise in the world of progressive experiment.

The question of "allusiveness," for example, as acutely posed by the poetry of Eliot, is certainly one where a false judgment is likely to involve the intentional fallacy. The frequency and depth of literary allusion in the poetry of Eliot and others has

---

[14]"A Valediction, Forbidding Mourning."
[15]Charles M. Coffin, *John Donne and the New Philosophy* (New York, 1927), pp. 97–98. [Wimsatt and Beardsley]

driven so many in pursuit of full meanings to the *Golden Bough* and the Elizabethan drama that it has become a kind of commonplace to suppose that we do not know what a poet means unless we have traced him in his reading — a supposition redolent with intentional implications. The stand taken by F. O. Matthiessen is a sound one and partially forestalls the difficulty.

> If one reads these lines with an attentive ear and is sensitive to their sudden shifts in movement, the contrast between the actual Thames and the idealized vision of it during an age before it flowed through a megalopolis is sharply conveyed by that movement itself, whether or not one recognizes the refrain to be from Spenser.

Eliot's allusions work when we know them — and to a great extent even when we do not know them, through their suggestive power.

But sometimes we find allusions supported by notes, and it is a nice question whether the notes function more as guides to send us where we may be educated, or more as indications in themselves about the character of the allusions. "Nearly everything of importance . . . that is apposite to an appreciation of 'The Waste Land,'" writes Matthiessen of Miss Weston's book,[16] "has been incorporated into the structure of the poem itself, or into Eliot's Notes." And with such an admission it may begin to appear that it would not much matter if Eliot invented his sources (as Sir Walter Scott invented chapter epigraphs from "old plays" and "anonymous" authors, or as Coleridge wrote marginal glosses for *The Ancient Mariner*). Allusions to Dante, Webster, Marvell, or Baudelaire doubtless gain something because these writers existed, but it is doubtful whether the same can be said for an allusion to an obscure Elizabethan:

> The sound of horns and motors, which shall bring Sweeney to Mrs. Porter in the spring.

"Cf. Day, *Parliament of Bees:*" says Eliot,

> When of a sudden, listening, you shall hear,
> A noise of horns and hunting, which shall bring
> Actaeon to Diana in the spring,
> Where all shall see her naked skin.

[16]Jessie Weston's *From Ritual to Romance* (1920), an influence on *The Waste Land*.

The irony is completed by the quotation itself; had Eliot, as is quite conceivable, composed these lines to furnish his own background, there would be no loss of validity. The conviction may grow as one reads Eliot's next note: "I do not know the origin of the ballad from which these lines are taken: it was reported to me from Sydney, Australia." The important word in this note — on Mrs. Porter and her daughter who washed their feet in soda water — is "ballad." And if one should feel from the lines themselves their "ballad" quality, there would be little need for the note. Ultimately, the inquiry must focus on the integrity of such notes as parts of the poem, for where they constitute special information about the meaning of phrases in the poem, they ought to be subject to the same scrutiny as any of the other words in which it is written. Matthiessen believes that notes were the price Eliot "had to pay in order to avoid what he would have considered muffling the energy of his poem by extended connecting links in the text itself." But it may be questioned whether the notes and the need for them are not equally muffling. F. W. Bateson has plausibly argued that Tennyson's "The Sailor Boy" would be better if half the stanzas were omitted, and the best versions of ballads like "Sir Patrick Spens" owe their power to the very audacity with which the minstrel has taken for granted the story upon which he comments. What then if a poet finds he cannot take so much for granted in a more recondite context and rather than write informatively, supplies notes? It can be said in favor of this plan that at least the notes do not pretend to be dramatic, as they would if written in verse. On the other hand, the notes may look like unassimilated material lying loose beside the poem, necessary for the meaning of the verbal symbol, but not integrated, so that the symbol stands incomplete.

We mean to suggest by the above analysis that whereas notes tend to seem to justify themselves as external indexes to the author's *intention*, yet they ought to be judged like any other parts of a composition (verbal arrangement special to a particular context), and when so judged their reality as parts of the poem, or their imaginative integration with the rest of the poem, may come into question. Matthiessen, for instance, sees that Eliot's titles for poems and his epigraphs are informative apparatus, like the notes. But while he is worried by some of the notes and thinks that Eliot "appears to be mocking himself for writing the note at the same time that he wants to convey something by it," Matthiessen believes that the "device" of epigraphs "is not at all open to the objection of not being sufficiently structural." "The *intention*," he says, "is to enable the poet to secure a condensed expression in the poem itself." "In each case the epigraph is *designed* to form an integral part of the effect of the poem." And Eliot himself, in his notes, has justified his poetic practice in terms of intention.

> The Hanged Man, a member of the traditional pack, fits my purpose in two ways: because he is associated in my mind with the Hanged God of Frazer, and because I associate him with the hooded figure in the passage of the disciples to Emmaus in Part V. . . . The man with Three Staves (an authentic member of the Tarot pack) I associate, quite arbitrarily, with the Fisher King himself.

And perhaps he is to be taken more seriously here, when off guard in a note, than when in his Norton Lectures he comments on the difficulty of saying what a poem means and adds playfully that he thinks of prefixing to a second edition of *Ash Wednesday* some lines from *Don Juan:*

> I don't pretend that I quite understand
> My own meaning when I would be *very* fine;
> But the fact is that I have nothing planned
> Unless it were to be a moment merry.

If Eliot and other contemporary poets have any characteristic fault, it may be in *planning* too much.

Allusiveness in poetry is one of several critical issues by which we have illustrated the more abstract issue of intentionalism, but it may be for today the most important illustration. As a poetic practice allusiveness would appear to be in some recent poems an extreme corollary of the romantic intentionalist assumption, and as a critical issue it challenges and brings to light in a special way the basic premise of intentionalism. The following instance from the poetry of Eliot may serve to epitomize the practical implications of what we have been saying. In Eliot's "Love Song of J. Alfred Prufrock," toward the end, occurs the line: "I have heard the mermaids singing, each to each," and this bears a certain resemblance to a line in a Song by John Donne, "Teach me to heare Mermaides singing," so that for the reader acquainted to a certain degree with Donne's poetry, the critical question arises: Is Eliot's line an allusion to Donne's? Is Prufrock thinking about Donne? Is Eliot thinking about Donne? We suggest that there are two radically different ways of looking for an answer to this question. There is (1) the way of poetic analysis and exegesis, which inquires whether it makes any sense if Eliot-Prufrock *is* thinking about Donne. In an earlier part of the poem, when Prufrock asks, "Would it have been worth while, . . . To have squeezed the universe into a ball," his words take half their sadness and irony from certain energetic and passionate lines of Marvell "To His Coy Mistress." But the exegetical inquirer may wonder whether mermaids considered as "strange sights" (to hear them is in Donne's poem analogous to getting with child a mandrake root) have much to do with Prufrock's mermaids, which seem to be symbols of romance and dynamism, and which incidentally have literary authentication, if they need it, in a line of a sonnet by Gérard de Nerval. This method of inquiry may lead to the conclusion that the given resemblance between Eliot and Donne is without significance and is better not thought of, or the method may have the disadvantage of providing no certain conclusion. Nevertheless, we submit that this is the true and objective way of criticism, as contrasted to what the very uncertainty of exegesis might tempt a second kind of critic to undertake: (2) the way of biographical or genetic inquiry, in which, taking advantage of the fact that Eliot is still alive, and in the spirit of a man who would settle a bet, the critic writes to Eliot and asks what he meant, or if he had Donne in mind. We shall not here weigh the probabilities — whether Eliot would answer that he meant nothing at all, had nothing at all in mind — a sufficiently good answer to such a question — or in an unguarded moment might furnish a clear and, within its limits, irrefutable answer. Our point is that such an answer to such an inquiry would have nothing to do with the poem "Prufrock"; it would not be a critical inquiry. Critical inquiries, unlike bets, are not settled in this way. Critical inquiries are not settled by consulting the oracle.

2

STRUCTURALISM AND DECONSTRUCTION

No one disputes the principle of the arbitrary nature of the sign, but it is often easier to discover a truth than to assign to it its proper place.
— FERDINAND DE SAUSSURE

What requires explanation is not the text itself so much as the possibility of reading and interpreting the text, the possibility of literary effects and literary communication.
— JONATHAN CULLER

The passage beyond philosophy does not consist in turning the page of philosophy (which usually comes down to philosophizing badly), but in continuing to read philosophers in a certain way.
— JACQUES DERRIDA

The author has disappeared. . . . God and man have died a common death.
— MICHEL FOUCAULT

The special insight of the structuralist approach is that, though language may not be everything, practically everything we do that is specifically human is expressed in language. Most obviously we communicate with one another in hundreds of "natural" languages, whose conventions predate any human memory; and in recent decades we have become dependent upon computers, whose functioning is based on the creation of artificial languages for sorting and processing data, and for solving problems.

But most of the other activities of daily life, from the elegant to the homely, are equally dependent upon various codes. The performance of music requires a complex notation, as does the solution of mathematical problems. Our economic life rests upon the exchange of labor and goods for symbols, such as cash, checks, stock certificates, and various other documents that are more or less easily exchangeable for each other and for other people's labor and goods. The language of fashion is one we learn to speak with difficulty, and when we wonder if our tie is too loud or our dress too formal, we are considering whether our friends will be upset by the message our clothes convey. Social life depends on the meaningful gestures and signals of "body language" and revolves around the exchange of small, symbolic favors: drinks, parties, dinners. Family connections in patriarchal culture depend on the exchange — so momentous that it is difficult to think of it as symbolic — of a woman from one family group into another.

Merely noting that everything is language and cataloging the overwhelming variety of ways in which reality is structured in systems of signs and symbols does not get us very far. Structuralism required a method of analyzing systems of symbols, and this was provided by two developments. One was the theory of the nineteenth-century American philosopher Charles Sanders Peirce, which is termed *semiotics*. Peirce analyzed sign systems into three general types: (1) iconic signs, in which the signifier resembles the thing signified (such as the stick figures on washroom doors that signify "Men" or "Women"); (2) indexes, in which the signifier is a reliable indicator of the presence of the signified (like smoke and fire); and (3) true symbols, in which the signifier's relation to the thing signified is completely arbitrary and conventional (just as the sound /kat/ or the written word *cat* are conventional signs for the familiar feline).

The other development was the linguistic theory of Ferdinand de Saussure, who established that the special symbol systems of the natural languages are systems based on differences. In his lecture notes published posthumously as *Cours de linguistique générale* (1916), Saussure established the basic principles of structural linguistics and of structuralism more generally.[1] These principles rest on a number of technical distinctions:

1. *Langue* versus *parole*. A language is a system of constitutive rules — that is, the rules *are* the language in the same way that the rules of chess constitute the game of chess. (If we break the rules of chess by, say, taking two moves at a time, there is no penalty as there is when we break traffic laws or other normative rules; we just aren't playing chess any longer.) But the system of the language (*langue*) appears only in the behavior of its individual speakers, who produce instances of speech (*parole*). Speakers may or may not be aware of the rules of the language, but they usually know whether an individual instance is correct or deviant. The activity of the linguist is to infer the rules of the *langue* from the evidence of *parole*. American linguist Noam Chomsky's distinction between *competence* (ideal language ability) and *performance* (individual activity) is similar to that of *langue* and *parole*.

2. *Synchronic* versus *diachronic*. The system of a *langue* is complete at any one time, but languages, in their sound systems (phonology), their grammatical relationships (syntax), and their lexicons, change over time. In studying a language, one has to distinguish between a synchronic study, which attempts to display the *langue* at one particular time, and a *diachronic* investigation, which studies change.

3. *Paradigmata* and *syntagmata*. The two fundamental relationships of symbols are parataxis and syntaxis. An example of parataxis is the relationship of items in the same category on a menu: In ordering soup, one may choose the beef consommé *or* the lobster bisque *or* the clam chowder. The items are similar enough to belong to

---

[1]"Semiotics" and "structuralism" have been used here as though they were essentially similar terms, and certainly there was a great deal that connected the two movements. But semiotics takes off from Peirce — for whom language is one of numerous sign systems — and structuralism takes off from Saussure, for whom language was the sign system par excellence. As a result, semioticians discuss sign systems generically, while structuralists tend to use linguistic models exclusively — to speak of "the language of fashion" and so forth. A structuralist would compose a grammar of narrative, while a semiotician would analyze the multiple codes that relate expression to content, and so on.

one category (soups) yet different (in their ingredients). In a language, the consonants and vowels are paradigms on the phonological level, nouns and verbs are paradigms on the grammatical level, and so on.

Syntaxis is the relationship of items from different categories in a meaningful structure. Back in the restaurant, when we choose a soup, an appetizer, a main course, and a dessert, we try to select a combination that will "go together" pleasantly. Or we try to pick items of clothing that will harmonize in color, texture, and social tone when worn together. The rules of syntax in a natural language are far more complex than the rules for wearing clothes or for ordering in a restaurant; it takes several years of hard work, from the ages of two to four, to learn the most basic relationships. But when we have succeeded, we comprehend subtle differences in the syntax of sentences, even some that traditional grammar textbooks ignore.

In Noam Chomsky's famous pair of sentences, "John is eager to please" and "John is easy to please," for example, the sentences appear to differ merely in one lexical item: for the third word of each sentence, a different member of the paradigm class of adjectives has been selected. But any native speaker also intuitively knows that the sentences also differ in their syntax. "John" is implicitly the "subject" of *please* in the first sentence and the "object" of *please* in the second, despite the fact that the sentences are apparently cut to the same pattern, and that "John" is by traditional standards the subject of the copula "is" in both.

4. *The basic units, or* emes. To return to paradigm classes, the problem is one of identifying the basic categories in an unfamiliar language, where the categories may not be the same as in one's native tongue. Saussure's basic principle was that distinctions within categories depend on differences; the practical difficulty is figuring out which differences, of all those we can learn to distinguish, really make a difference — which is not a simple matter.

Take the sound system of English. The letter *t* stands for the sound /t/ — but at various positions in words /t/ is not a single sound but several different sounds. The first sound in the word *tip* is not the same as the last sound in the word *pit*. The first *t* is *aspirated* — pronounced with an explosion of air — while the second is not. To complicate things further, the *t* sound in *bottle* is not the same as either of the other two. But in English, these differences *do not* make a difference. If you pronounce *pit* with an aspirated *t,* you have still said *pit;* no one will mistake which word you have pronounced. Aspiration is a feature that does not make a basic difference in English (though it does in Hindi and in several other languages). But voicing does make a difference in English. Words like *tip* and *dip,* or *pit* or *bit,* differ according to whether the initial consonant is *voiced* (pronounced with the vocal cords vibrating) or *unvoiced.* The point is that /t/ in all its various pronunciations (allophones) is a single *phoneme* in English, a basic and minimal unit of the sound system. And the phoneme /t/ differs from the phoneme /d/ because of the feature of voicing, and from all the other phonemes of English because of various other sorts of differences.

If the basic minimal unit of a sound system is the phoneme, the basic minimal unit of grammar is the *morpheme.* One example of a morpheme in English is the plural, which is formed in a number of different ways, usually by adding /s/ or /z/ or /iz/ to the singular noun (as in bat/bats, pin/pins, church/churches, respectively), but sometimes by changing the vowel (mouse/mice), or in other irregular ways. Languages other than English often have similar grammatical categories, but even languages with a common origin employ important variations (verbs in French have many more tenses, nouns in French always show gender). Some languages have grammatical categories and relationships that are totally distinct from those found in European languages. In each case it is important to locate the individual units of meaning as they occur, as spaces within a system made up of *differences*.

The impact of Saussure's general principles for discussing the structure of a language was felt first in linguistics. For several decades after Saussure's death, linguists and anthropologists trained in linguistics traveled to remote corners of the world, recording and analyzing the principles of hundreds of natural languages. But soon after the development of structural linguistics, the basic principles began to be generalized to other sorts of codes and structures, which could be analyzed in analogous fashion in terms of the combinations and permutations of various "emes," or basic elements. The smallest units or building blocks of stories were termed "mythemes" by Claude Lévi-Strauss; Julia Kristeva has called the irreducible atoms of social thought "ideologemes."

As Roland Barthes said in "The Structuralist Activity" (1964), structuralism is not a set of beliefs, but two complementary practices: analysis and synthesis. The structuralist analyzes the products of human making into their smallest significant component parts, then tries to discover the principles of their articulation — how the parts fit together and function.[2] In this very broad sense, the first structuralist was Aristotle, and the *Poetics* the first work of structuralist literary criticism. It would not be odd to consider formalist critics like R. S. Crane and Northrop Frye as structuralists. But today, the term is usually restricted to those whose practice of analysis and synthesis is performed using the tools, techniques, and terminology of linguistics.

Perhaps the chief human vector for the spread of structuralism was Roman Jakobson, one of the great linguists of the century. In his paper on "Linguistics and Poetics" (translated in 1960), Jakobson presented the following model of the act of communication: A *sender,* having made *contact* with a *receiver,* sends a *message* about some external *context* using a *code.* These six factors — sender, contact, receiver, message, context, and code — define the six functions of communication. Most normal communication is *referential:* It emphasizes the context, the content that is to be conveyed. The *emotive* function of communication emphasizes the sender, while the *conative* emphasizes the receiver. The *phatic* function is that of establishing contact, like saying "hello" when we pick up the telephone. The *metalinguistic* function is to investigate the code that sender and receiver are both using to clear up disagreements or ambiguities. Finally, there is the linguistic function that centers on the message qua message. This Jakobson defines as the *poetic* function.

Jakobson began as an ally of the Russian Formalists in the 1920s, migrated to Czechoslovakia, where he joined the Prague Linguistic Circle in the 1930s, and then traveled to New York, where he exerted a wide influence on numerous intellectuals, including the ethnologist Claude Lévi-Strauss. They collaborated on literary essays, including an essay on Baudelaire's sonnet, "The Cats" (1962),[3] but the most important

---

[2]Roland Barthes, "The Structuralist Activity," in *Critical Essays,* trans. Richard Howard (New York: Farrar, Straus and Giroux, 1972).

[3]Roman Jakobson and Claude Lévi-Strauss, "Charles Baudelaire's 'The Cats'" (1962), in *Structuralism: A Reader,* ed. Michael Lane (London: Jonathan Cape, 1970).

product was Lévi-Strauss's integration of linguistics and myth in his book *Structural Anthropology* (1958), which changed the theory and practice of cultural studies around the world.

MYTH AND LANGUAGE

Claude Lévi-Strauss began his career with a dissertation on *The Elementary Structures of Kinship* (1949), which was a synthesis of the available data on the rules by which a vast number of cultures regulated marriage and kinship ties. Lévi-Strauss's method was to use language-data to verify social rules (for example, if a culture has a word for "mother's brother" that is *also* its word for "father-in-law," this correspondence strongly suggests that a boy is supposed to marry his maternal cross-cousin). In the course of his research, Lévi-Strauss developed a general theory of the way in which the exchange and circulation of women between families is used to knit cultures together.

But in the course of that study he recognized that another aspect of culture is used for exchange and circulation: language. As Lévi-Strauss began to theorize about the homologies between languages and kinship systems, it occurred to him that cultures with complex kinship structures, which gave the individual a small number of marital choices, tended to speak languages with complex syntax and a small lexicon, while cultures (like our own) with simple kinship structures, which give the individual a vast number of marital choices, tended to speak languages with simple syntax and a large lexicon.[4] We can see here a key feature of Lévi-Strauss's method: to try to construct revealing analogies between very different aspects of life and society by seeing each as a structural system of symbols. While the surface structure of the symbols might be very different, the way in which they are combined (syntaxis) might point to a similar deep structure.

Given this interest, Lévi-Strauss was attracted to the study of the richest source of symbols in anthropology: mythology. His four volumes of *Mythologiques* (*The Raw and the Cooked* [1964]; *From Honey to Ashes* [1967]; *The Origin of Table Manners* [1968]; and *L'Homme Nu* [1971]) present an elaborate survey of world myths to illustrate his basic thesis about mythic thinking: That myths are the way the "savage mind" — not the minds of savages, but the untamed mind within all of us — gives order to the world.

"The Structural Study of Myth" (1955), reprinted in part here, presents Lévi-Strauss's method in its purest form, as a way of reconstructing the *langue* of myth by the analysis of a particular *parole*. His analysis of the Oedipus myth demonstrates how he breaks down the chronological structure of the story in order to isolate the various elements (or *mythemes*) operating within the text. He next attempts to understand the relation between the mythemes as members of paradigm classes separated from one another by the way they embody concrete differences. He then finds a way

---

[4]Claude Lévi-Strauss, "Language and the Analysis of Social Laws" (1951), in *Structural Anthropology* (New York: Basic Books, 1963), pp. 62–63.

of generalizing the concrete issues of the story as a system of abstract binary terms. Finally, he interprets the interaction of the mythemes as giving order and structure to a significant spiritual conflict. In the case of Oedipus, the myth mediates between conflicting theories: that humanity is born out of the earth (autochthonous) or of the sexual union between man and woman.[5] Lévi-Strauss's point is that as long as the spiritual conflict continues (and if it is a genuine conflict, it can never be fully resolved), the myth will continue to be told, elaborated, varied, and retold in other forms that — structurally, at least — address the same issue.

STRUCTURALIST POETICS

One of the central texts of high structuralism in its most confident phase was the collaborative essay of Roman Jakobson and Lévi-Strauss on Baudelaire's sonnet, "The Cats." Their elaborate analysis of the geometrical symmetry of the grammatical structures within the sonnet showed what structuralism could do. But their conclusion — that the cats symbolize love cleansed of feminine impurity and knowledge cleansed of the sages' austerity — has, despite the seemingly scientific method, not won universal assent. As Michael Riffaterre has said, "the poem has been rebuilt by the two critics into a 'superpoem' inaccessible to the normal reader, and yet the structures described do not explain what establishes contact between poetry and reader. No grammatical analysis of a poem can give us more than the grammar of the poem."[6]

The difficulty is not with grammatical analysis as such (in fact, Riffaterre presents his own grammatical analysis of "Les Chats"). Stylistics, the linguistic analysis of literary effects, is a venerable and useful tool of criticism, but most linguists would begin with an impression of the poem's effect and then seek something in the syntax that might have caused that effect.[7] The problem arises from the hypothesis that, by checking successively into every symmetry of every grammatical category, the critic will stumble onto the secret of the poem. As Jonathan Culler attempted to show in the first half of *Structuralist Poetics* (1975), this hypothesis simply doesn't work: Structural analysis is not an effective discovery procedure. Or rather, it is too effective. Culler demonstrates that the elaborate syntactic symmetries that Jakobson and Lévi-Strauss found in the four strophes of "The Cats" can also be found in the first four prosy sentences of Jakobson's own "Postscriptum" to *Questions de poétique.*

In a long and useful pair of chapters, Culler goes on to discuss the poetics of the lyric poem in terms of the conventions through which we interpret its form and meaning and the operations we perform on the text in order to "naturalize" its language. (In effect, he suggests that to read a poem we have to *undo* the poet's defamiliarization of

[5]Two further examples of the interpretation of myth, dealing with relatively unfamiliar American Indian tales, have been omitted.

[6]Michael Riffaterre, "Describing Poetic Structures: Two Approaches to Baudelaire's *Les Chats,*" in *Structuralism,* ed. Jacques Ehrmann (New York: Doubleday, 1970), pp. 201–02.

[7]As for example in David Richter, "Two Studies in Iconic Syntax: Alfred Lord Tennyson's 'Tears, Idle Tears' and William Carlos Williams's 'The Dance,'" *Language and Style* 18 (1985): 136–51.

the material.) After giving a reading of a minimalist one-line poem by Apollinaire, Culler presents the universal principles underlying his performance:

> Such an interpretation depends upon three general conventions — that a poem should be unified, that it should be thematically significant, and that this significance can take the form of reflection on poetry — and four general interpretive operations: that one should try to establish binary relations of opposition or equivalence, that one should look for and integrate puns and ambiguities, that items may be read as synecdoches (or metaphors, etc.) in order to attain the level of generality required, and that what a poem says can be related to the fact that it is a poem.[8]

When Culler wrote *Structuralist Poetics,* very little of the work of Umberto Eco had been translated from Italian; *The Role of the Reader* did not appear until 1979, although its constituent essays had been printed in various periodicals as early as 1962. The essay reprinted here, "The Myth of Superman" from *The Role of the Reader,* is typical in its combination of wit and intellectual rigor and in its immense range of reference, from revered texts like *Oedipus Rex* and *Finnegans Wake* to ephemera like Superman comics, Nero Wolfe detective stories, and the "Doctor Kildare" television series. Eco's essay takes up only one very limited question within narrative poetics: the way narrative time needs to be handled in fiction that belongs to a series, which must therefore be designed to have an indefinite number of sequels. It has been included as an example of what can be done practically, using a structuralist poetics of narrative. But *The Role of the Reader* as a whole has a much broader program: to understand the levels of discourse that occur within narratives (Eco's complex diagram lists ten such levels) and the interactions among them that give rise to interpretation. The result will be to reveal how each text produces the exact sort of Model Reader it needs to bring out its qualities — how "closed" texts elicit passively credulous and "open" texts actively suspicious readings.[9]

Perhaps the most influential theorist of narrative is Gérard Genette, whose trilogy *Figures* contains a series of arrestingly original and interconnected essays on the art of both fiction and poetry. As the overall title of the three volumes suggests, Genette's interest is in tropes, figures of speech; but he is far from being a naive grammarian, interested only in classifying and regulating the use of tropes. Figures of speech are important because they introduce into the usual system of signification a discontinuity requiring the reader's mediation. When we refer to "twenty sail of the line" instead of "twenty ships" we use the figure of *synecdoche* — the part for the whole. As we interpret the figure, we note the presence of one signifier (sail) and the absence of another (ship). Thus, the working of the figure depends on something it cannot contain: the reader's sense of the absent signifier. Or, as Genette put it, "A figure is a gap in relation to usage, but a gap that is nevertheless a part of usage: that is the paradox of rhetoric."

---

[8]Jonathan Culler, "Poetics of the Lyric," in *Structuralist Poetics* (Ithaca: Cornell University Press, 1975), p. 177.

[9]These are not exhaustive categories. Eco finds a third sort of text, "an exclusive club whose chairman is probably *Tristram Shandy,*" which is neither open nor closed but operates as a trap. It lures the reader into "an excess of cooperation and then punishes him for having overdone it."

THE PASSING OF STRUCTURALISM

Structuralism had slowly grown in influence from just after World War II until the middle of the 1960s, spreading from the anthropological studies of Lévi-Strauss to affect the study of literature, philosophy, history, mathematics, politics, economics — all the human sciences. There was a palpable sense at the time that a new method for the synthesis of knowledge was at hand, a method more powerful than the synthesis provided by Platonic dialectic in the ancient world or by Thomistic logic in the Middle Ages. The notion, barely glimpsed, that by using the tools of semiotics and linguistics, structuralism might manage to reunite the branches of knowledge that post-Renaissance specialization had severed, gave its adherents a messianic sense of mission. But in the late 1960s, as radical politics came and went leaving disillusion in its wake, the confident, broadly humanistic, universalizing mission of structuralism foundered as well.

The primary problem was the irresponsible promise of a synthesis of all human knowledge, a promise that was slow in bearing fruit. Many adherents expounded the principles of structuralism and made claims for what structuralism would surely do for the study of literature, but few produced concrete achievements that justified those claims. The claims may in fact have been implausible. One question we have already raised is whether the enabling assumption of structuralism — that everything is a language — is adequate. As James Phelan has suggested, literature is a *second-order* sign system built upon the *first-order* sign system of language. In effect, structuralism stands or falls on its assumption that a second-order system must reproduce the categories and relations of the first-order system. But we have no evidence that this must be the case, and natural science suggests the contrary: Biology, built on biochemistry, does not imitate its organization; nor does chemistry, built on molecular physics, reproduce its lower-order system.

Structuralism may also have lost momentum because it had shifted the focus of the study of literature from the exegesis of individual texts to the exploration of general conditions of the act of interpretation. Ironically, deconstruction, despite its implicit attack on the traditional values and bases of humanistic study, proceeds according to the techniques of close reading in which literary critics throughout the English-speaking world had already been trained under the dominance of New Criticism. In some ways, therefore, it was easier for American academics to follow deconstructionists such as Jacques Derrida and Paul de Man than to carry on the quest of Jakobson, Genette, and Eco.

But of course, in another sense, structuralism is not dead at all. Though it has had to relinquish its broadest assumptions together with its character as a world-historical movement, most of its original adherents — like Todorov and Eco, Genette and Riffaterre — have continued to pursue the study of systems of signs, and the results of their study have become, under the names semiotics, stylistics, and narratology, essential elements in the current battery of approaches to literature.

DERRIDA AND DECONSTRUCTION

One of the difficulties in reading Derrida is that there is no central document, no single, classic essay, like Sidney's *Apology for Poetry* or Kant's *Critique of Judgment,* that contains and expresses a body of systematic thought. In this, he is like some earlier philosophers, such as Hegel and Nietzsche, for whom no selection can give a sense of the whole. But what is unique to Derrida is that, while his rhetoric circles around the same themes, his terminology changes from essay to essay. (Even his principal term, "deconstruction," is not fully stable. At one point, Derrida wanted to replace it with "de-sedimentation," though that word never quite caught on.) This fluidity is entirely by design. Given his program, Derrida has tried to resist anything that would lead to setting up deconstruction as a *system of thought.*

Although it is risky to state that Derrida has a central issue, we can begin with his notion that all thought is necessarily inscribed in language, and that language itself is fraught with intractable paradoxes. We can repress or ignore these paradoxes, but we cannot escape from them or solve them. This is the burden of Derrida's most difficult work, *Of Grammatology.*

Derrida's basic concern is with how Western philosophy has built its metaphysics on a pervasive but fragile base, one that privileges the activity of *speech* over that of *writing.* Speech is opposed to writing and held to be logically prior as well as chronologically older. The valorization of speech begins in Plato's *Phaedrus,* in which Socrates condemns writing as a bastardized form of communication, separated from the Father (the moment of origin). Writing can easily mislead because the speaker is no longer there to explain what he had in mind. Socrates prefers speech because the speaker seems so immediately present in the voice. Meaning enters into sound, and sound as a real presence enters the listener and becomes meaning once more.

Derrida traces this position from Plato down through the centuries to philosophers such as Edmund Husserl and Martin Heidegger. Here we can discuss one classic example, that of the founder of structuralism. Ferdinand de Saussure treats writing as a means of representing speech; it remains an external accessory, however, a supplement that need not be fully taken into account in any philosophy of language. In fact, Saussure feels that writing is in a sense dangerous because it "disguises" language and "usurps" the role of speech (writing corrupts speech at times, as when people mispronounce words because of the way they are spelled). For all these reasons, writing is a *dangerous* supplement, which threatens the integrity of speech. The notion of the "dangerous supplement" is important to Derrida, for the very idea of a supplement challenges and calls into question the dichotomies and hierarchies on which philosophies are built. Like the appendix to a book, a supplement is part of and not part of the text at the same time: It seems to be adding something to what is already complete in itself, and the addition is thus implicitly a correction, even in a sense a recantation.

In Derrida's analysis of the writings of Jean-Jacques Rousseau, for example, he calls attention to Rousseau's characterization of education as a supplement to nature. As a supplement, education adds to something that is already supposedly complete in itself; at the same time, if education adds to nature, then nature must be somehow incomplete — at least to the extent that one must be educated to know what is natural and what is not. Nature is the prior term, a presence that is there at the start. Yet the "supplement" of education reveals an inherent absence or lack within nature — and also an essential condition of its being.

At another point in the *Confessions,* Rousseau himself speaks of masturbation as a "dangerous supplement" to coital sexuality: a perverse addiction that can substitute for and take the place of heterosexual intercourse. But paradoxically, the fact that masturbation can act as a supplement shows that it shares in the nature of sexuality. Furthermore, what characterizes masturbation — the focus on an imagined sexual object, the impossibility of genuinely possessing what one desires — also characterizes heterosexual intercourse. One could thus turn the dichotomy upside down and claim that heterosexual intercourse is a more generalized version of masturbation.

To generalize Derrida's method from the last example: a dominant entity is defined by a form of presence (heterosexual intercourse) next to its supplement (masturbation), which is defined by a corresponding absence as inferior and marginal. But the distinguishing qualities of the marginal entity are in fact the defining qualities of the dominant. The result is that the rigid hierarchy of the dichotomy dissolves: As we consider the matter, it is no longer clear which is dominant and which marginal.

To come back now to where we began, with Derrida's analysis of the dichotomy of speech and writing, we valorize speech over writing because there, signifier and signified, sound and meaning, seem to be given together, fused for the moment. Form and meaning are simultaneously present. Voice appears as the direct manifestation of thought. In contrast, written words lack this presence; they are physical marks a reader must interpret and animate to supply meanings that do not seem to be *given.*

But in fact, the kind of absence that distinguishes writing from speech is the very condition of the existence of signs in the first place. As we showed above, the structural model of language presupposes absence in the sense that it is an elaborate system of presences and absences that allows signifiers to operate. The letter or phoneme /t/ exists only as part of a system of differences that distinguish it from /d/ or /f/ or any of the other letters or phonemes. The phoneme /t/ differs from /d/ by the quality of voicing (vibration of the vocal cords), which is absent in the former and present in the latter. But /t/ is not a defective /d/; there is only a relational meaning here, not a real presence.

Furthermore, for a token to be a sign, it must be iterable — repeatable. We learn the meaning of a sign by hearing the same sound in similar contexts. The difference between a sign and a mere noise is that one cannot repeat the latter (even if one clap of thunder were exactly like another, it would make no difference). In the case of a language-sign, one must be able to repeat it back, to quote it; but to quote a sign is to produce it as an example, to reproduce it in the absence of the original communicative intention. For a signifier to have value as a sign, therefore, it must be possible to counterfeit it, and when a sign is counterfeited or cited or produced as an example, it is without its original meaning. But this is *always* possible for *any* sign. Therefore the notion that a sign depends upon the presence conferred by voice cannot be maintained, and we cannot hold that speech is logically prior to writing. (Derrida is not denying, of course, that speech preceded writing historically.)

If speech is not prior to writing, then it does not make sense to treat writing as an auxiliary form of speech; indeed, Derrida suggests, we should treat speech as a form of writing — and refer both to an *arché-écriture* (from the Greek and French: "original-writing"). Rather than achieving meaning through the presence of voice, language strives toward meaning through the play of signifiers. This play occurs through the mechanism of what Derrida calls *différance* (a coinage that would be pronounced identically with the usual spelling *différence*, reminding us that there are some things that writing can convey that sound cannot). Derrida's seminal essay of that title, reproduced below, is difficult but rewarding. It's difficult because Derrida is trying to talk about precisely what eludes language, a system that operates (as Saussure showed) via formal differences that lack any content. The verb *différer* in French is ambiguous: it means both "to differ" and "to defer." A word, a letter, or a sound is known not through what it is but through its differences relative to other possibilities — the other possibilities that are not present but absent, existing only through the transient traces they leave on memory. Ultimate meaning, genuine presence, is always deferred — just as looking one word up in a dictionary leads to another and so on indefinitely. Between signifier and signified, therefore, there is not the rigid relation of container and contained. Rather, there is always "freeplay" (*jeu*), which suggests that language can never be pinned down to meaning, that it is always already indeterminate. If in reading through the essay you feel that Derrida is repeating himself, going around the same circles more than once, you would be right. Without marking itself off into separate sections, *"Différance"* runs through the paradoxes inherent to language and its representation of reality at least three times: The first time, Derrida focuses on language itself (using quotations from Saussure), the second time with regard to consciousness and the paradoxes of the subject (using ideas in Freud), and the third with regard to the nature of our knowledge of Being (using the phenomenology of Heidegger). In each case, *différance* is, so to speak, the black hole in the middle of the system of language, the principle of absence that makes things happen.

It is hard to overestimate the furor Derrida's theory of language provoked. He was not merely saying, like the New Critic William Empson, that poetry depends on seven types of ambiguity. He was claiming in effect that everything in the human sciences — history, political philosophy, psychology, and so on — was a species of poetry, invariably based on a terminology that was necessarily as indeterminate as the language in which it was written. But the real target of his notion of language was the structuralist attempt to synthesize all humanistic knowledge by using the tools of linguistics, for if there was freeplay in the signifier-signified relationship, there was no guarantee of even making sense. In the 1920s, the German mathematician Kurt Gödel put an end to the massive Russell-Whitehead project for systematizing mathematics by proving conclusively that any mathematical system complicated enough to be useful had either to contain contradictions or to be incomplete. Derrida's *Grammatology* was in effect the Gödel's proof for the human sciences in the late 1960s. It split the structuralist community down the middle, and even thirty years later, the debate continues between those who accept and those who dispute the validity and the motivation of the deconstructive turn.

But there is more at stake than the apparently abstract question of whether or not there is freeplay between the signifier and the signified. For, in its most general sense, the activity of deconstruction involves the skeptical re-examination, not just of speech and writing, but of *all* the dialectical polarities that have formed the basis of Western culture, a re-examination searching for the point of privilege upon which standard hierarchies rest. We are used to arguing about various other presences and absences: art versus genius, culture versus nature, transcendence versus immanence, soul versus body, divine versus human, human versus animal, man versus woman, being versus becoming, and so on. In each case, the first term denotes the presence and the second the absence of something. Derrida uses the paradoxes involved in the logic of "supplements" in an effort to decenter the first term of each pair, to remove it from its privileged position relative to the second. Against the dominant metaphysics of presence, Derrida sets the countermetaphysics of absence. To the extent that these polarities are at the heart of Western culture, deconstruction attempts to expose the illusions upon which authority in Western culture is established. Where the conservative W. B. Yeats complained that "Things fall apart. The center cannot hold," the anarchistic Derrida calls into question the very concept of a center. This is the argument of Derrida's most famous single essay, "Structure, Sign, and Play in the Discourse of the Human Sciences," reprinted here.

Invited to a conference on structuralism in 1966, Derrida proceeded to question the "whole history of the concept of structure" as the activity of naming and renaming in a succession of metaphors the center of the totality of existence: "the history of metaphysics, like the history of the West, is the history of these metaphors." Derrida then proceeded to deconstruct the concept of the center, beginning with the geometrical paradox that the center *defines* the circle but is not part of the line that *is* the circle. This center is, in effect, a transcendental point of absolute presence. So long as we can believe in a transcendental signified — a point of absolute meaning outside and above the world of discourse that gives significance to the whole — the center holds. But once we cease to have God and have only god-terms, once we accept that everything is a text and falls within the framework of discourse, then the very notion of a center must be challenged. And that, says Derrida, is where we currently stand: after the critiques of metaphysics by Nietzsche and Heidegger, after the critique of consciousness by Freud, the fundamental notions of being, truth, and self cannot be naively "centered" as they have been by the major philosophers from Plato through Hegel.

This brings Derrida to structuralism and its attempts to find a center through the science of signs. Most of "Structure, Sign, and Play" is devoted to a deconstruction of the opposition between nature and culture in the work of the founder of structuralism, Claude Lévi-Strauss. One must work out for oneself the chain of paradoxes, one within another, that Derrida finds in Lévi-Strauss's project in *Mythologiques* — for instance, that it is an empirical study that nevertheless rejects the principle of empiricism. Derrida concludes by exposing the ambivalence, the duality of Lévi-Strauss's attitudes. On the one hand, Lévi-Strauss accepts the presence of freeplay within the structure of myths and embraces the notion that mythography is itself a sort of mythical thinking; on the other hand, there is Lévi-Strauss's "ethic of presence, an ethic of nostalgia for origins, an ethic of archaic and natural innocence, of a purity of presence and self-presence in speech." Lévi-Strauss, and thus the structuralist activity in general, seems to be caught halfway between the old metaphysics, which "dreams of deciphering a truth or an origin," and the new revolutionary philosophy, like his own, that "tries to pass beyond man and humanism."

In his conclusion to "Structure, Sign, and Play," Derrida seems to be disclosing his attitudes toward the great precursors. In particular, he seems to be defining himself in opposition to Hegel and as a disciple of Nietzsche. Derrida circumvents Hegel's historical, progressive uses of dialectic; his oppositions always stay open, undecidable, untranscended. And like Nietzsche's philosophy, Derrida's attitudes toward political and social issues seem to be based on aesthetics rather than ethics; he revels in the sense of intellectual crisis and welcomes the coming transvaluation of all values.[10]

But what is more significant, Derrida's ironic gibe at "the nostalgia for the origin" is a slap directed at the existentialist philosopher Martin Heidegger, who influenced him deeply and against whom he reacted equally intensely. Although Heidegger, like Derrida, was an opponent of metaphysics, he did not go far enough for his disciple. As Christopher Norris has put it, Derrida questioned "Heidegger's own metaphysical motives, his quest for a grounding philosophy which would point the way back toward primordial Being. This nostalgic attachment to a lost or forgotten origin is, according to Derrida, the hallmark of all metaphysics."[11] Metaphysics, the abstract bugbear of twentieth-century philosophers from Wittgenstein onward, is like the "tar-baby" of the Uncle Remus stories: In combating it one inevitably gets involved in it. As Derrida states in "Structure, Sign, and Play," "*there is no sense* in doing without the concepts of metaphysics in order to attack metaphysics. We . . . cannot utter a single destructive proposition which has not already slipped into the form, the logic, and the implicit postulations of precisely what it seeks to contest." Derrida's strategy is to disrupt systematic thought, to wage a guerrilla campaign against it in constantly shifting terms, to stay on the margins of philosophy and avoid its central castle. "The passage beyond philosophy does not consist in turning the page of philosophy . . . but in continuing to read philosophers *in a certain way*."

Exactly what Derrida meant by "in a certain way," becomes apparent in our selection, "The Father of Logos," from his lengthy essay, "Plato's Pharmacy." Taking up the section of Plato's *Phaedrus* in which Socrates recites (or perhaps invents) a myth about the origin of writing, Derrida walks us carefully through that small segment of the dialogue, attentive to the nuances and ambiguous usages of Greek nouns and verbs, searching out Plato's verbal play, his silent gliding between one sense and another. Plato's ostensible purpose here is an argument against mere rhetorical skill, a contention that language can be fashioned to be adequately descriptive of the real world, but by the end of our stroll it has become clear that the operations of Socrates' own rhetoric seem to deny the solidity of either discourse or reality.

---

[10]See the introductions to Hegel (p. 369), Nietzsche (p. 435), and Heidegger (p. 611).
[11]Christopher Norris, *The Deconstructive Turn* (London: Methuen, 1983), p. 24.

BARTHES AND FOUCAULT

As Derrida's message began its guerrilla war on the ends and assumptions of structuralism, a number of structuralism's leading figures became converts, including Roland Barthes, whose shifting aims and ideas are instructive. Barthes's interest, since his 1953 essay "Writing Degree Zero," has been in the immense tacit knowledge the reader must possess, over and above the syntax and basic semantics of a given language, to understand and interpret cultural systems of symbols. Barthes worked in *Mythologies* to demystify the complex languages and cultural systems represented by wrestling matches, striptease shows, advertisements, and other maps of popular culture (see the selection, "Striptease," p. 869). Later he attempted to codify the kind of knowledge structuralist analysis was and was not capable of providing, and how it related to other forms of semiotic analysis. The clearest exposition of this is in "The Structuralist Activity" (p. 871). The apex of Barthes's structuralist project appeared in the 1966 essay, "Introduction to the Structural Analysis of Narratives," a densely written attempt to do complete justice to the *langue* of fiction. Though he is normally a supple and witty stylist, Barthes's tone here was dry and abstract, as though he were somewhat daunted by the complex task of analyzing into their separate components the elements (the *emes*) in the interpretation of narrative, and he characterized his essay, which was based on the previous work of Vladimir Propp, Claude Bremond, A. J. Greimas, and Tzvetan Todorov, as a "tentative effort" rather than a triumphant success.

In *S/Z* (1970), Barthes simplified and reduced these multiple integrative dimensions into a skein of five *codes,* to which the individual bits of text (*lexies*) each make their contribution. Barthes distinguished a *hermeneutic* code of enigmas and their solutions; a *semic* code of characteristics that go into the description of characters and places; a *proairetic* code of actions; a *symbolic* code of themes; and a *referential* code comprising the historical and cultural allusions within the text. The elaborate result was a 220-page commentary on "Sarrasine" (a minor story by Balzac) that — since it remained on the levels of "functions" and "actions" and was incomplete even there — was clearly only a mere sketch toward a full interpretation. *S/Z* was simultaneously the masterpiece and the reductio ad absurdum of Barthes's holistic approach to fiction, because it made clear that any genuinely complete analysis of a fictional text would be so long and complex as to be nearly unreadable. It was widely admired but never imitated, even by Barthes himself.

By the next year, Barthes had produced "From Work to Text," an account of the difference in the way the object of literary study is perceived by formal and structural criticism on the one hand, and by poststructural criticism on the other. The essay is short, terse, informal, almost a set of jottings, but Barthes manages to characterize the stance of the deconstructive critic with lucidity and accuracy. Perhaps the most influential section of "From Work to Text" is the last, in which Barthes contrasts the emotional involvement of the reader before and after the deconstructive turn. The older, passive way of reading produced *plaisir* (pleasure), the consumer's enjoyment in being immersed in another's vision, actions, characters. The new way produces what Barthes terms *jouissance,* a nearly untranslatable word ("bliss" is the usual equivalent) that suggests both the joy and the sense of loss experienced in the sexual climax. Here and in later, more elaborate treatments of the phenomenology of reading, such as *The Pleasure of the Text,* Barthes's central contribution to Derrida's project was in clarifying its emotional as well as its intellectual appeal.

Whereas Barthes was a structuralist turned poststructuralist, Michel Foucault had never accepted the linguistic basis of structuralism. He had instead an independent poststructuralist framework of thought that is presented at greater length later in this book (see the introduction to New Historicism and Cultural Studies, p. 1320, and the introduction to Gender Studies and Queer Theory, p. 1611). Nevertheless, some of his influential essays contributed to the rejection of the structuralist model we have been exploring, and as an analyst of philosophical discourse he was as radical as Derrida. Like Derrida, Foucault was a disciple of the later Nietzsche and saw the will-to-power as dominant over any search for truth — as defining, in fact, the meaning and location of truth. As he puts it in his essay "Truth and Power":

> Truth isn't outside power, or lacking in power: contrary to a myth whose history and functions would repay further study, truth isn't the reward of free spirits, the child of protracted solitude, nor the privilege of those who have succeeded in liberating themselves. Truth is a thing of this world: it is produced only by virtue of multiple forms of constraint. And it induces regular effects of power. Each society has its regime of truth, its "general politics" of truth: that is, the types of discourse which it accepts and makes function as true; the mechanisms and instances which enable one to distinguish true and false statements, the means by which each is sanctioned; the techniques and procedures accorded value in the acquisition of truth, the status of those who are charged with saying what is true.[12]

Today, Foucault goes on, the general politics confers truth on the form of scientific discourse; statements are true if and only if they have been the object of well-financed studies, and capitalism not only creates the studies but devotes other massive institutions (education, the media, and so on) to the diffusion and consumption of this form of truth. But though this might be true today, Foucault, like Derrida, became convinced that Western civilization was moving toward a new moment of crisis, a change in the dominant *epistemé* (as Foucault called the historical modes of power/knowledge). His work is marked by an apocalyptic sense that it is in our interest — and our duty — to prepare the way for a new power and truth.

We can find some of these strains within Foucault's thought in his essay "What Is an Author?" included here. Foucault concentrates on the humanistic version of truth-power: authorship seen as a form of author-ity. Despite the apparent collapse of the Romantic conception of the author as incomprehensible genius and the advent of formalism and structuralism, which have successively substituted the central terms of *work* and of *écriture* (writing) for the romantic god-term of *author,* Foucault claims that authorship still retains its old power within advanced capitalism. While the author has been declared dead by some literary theorists, the author-function remains, "a certain functional principle by which, in our culture, one limits, excludes, and chooses; in

[12]Michel Foucault, "Truth and Power," in *The Foucault Reader,* ed. Paul Rabinow (New York: Pantheon Books, 1984), pp. 72–73.

short, by which one impedes the free circulation, the free manipulation, the free composition, decomposition, and recomposition of fiction. . . . The author is therefore the ideological figure by which one marks the manner in which we fear the proliferation of meaning." As long as literature belongs to the author, it cannot be truly ours. But Foucault looks forward to a moment of change in society when the "author-function will disappear." Foucault has no faith, however, that as author-ity fades, literature will belong to "us." He pessimistically foresees that it will instead be replaced by a new "system of constraint" yet to be understood or experienced. The old order changes, giving way to the new, but for Foucault, order is always a synonym for the prisons and asylums through which society controls thought. For Foucault, only a total breakdown of society could liberate us from the order of discourse.

DECONSTRUCTION AND CRITICISM

Like the structuralism it questions and attempts to supplant, deconstruction is not solely, or even primarily, a mode of literary criticism. As Derrida says in "Structure, Sign, and Play," he only wants "to read philosophers *in a certain way.*" Indeed, deconstructionists like Rodolphe Gasché have suggested that the application of Derrida's methods to literary texts in search of new interpretations is paradoxical, almost perverse, since Derrida's revolutionary contribution was to treat philosophical texts as if they were bound by the same sorts of linguistic ambiguity and fluidity that had long been thought to characterize literature. (In effect Derrida constitutes the ultimate vindication of poetry against Plato's attack. For Derrida it is the poets, celebrating the freeplay of the signifier, who have had the right notion of language, and the philosophers, aiming for precision of terminology, who have been pursuing a will o' the wisp.)

Nevertheless, Derrida has had more impact in departments of English and French than in philosophy, as deconstruction has been applied less to Ayer or Sartre than to Yeats and Proust. To a large extent, the deconstruction of literature was made possible by the previous triumph of the New Criticism, which treated poetry as an especially complex mode of discourse, essentially dependent on tropes like irony or ambiguity, that led to the evocation of a set of propositions or attitudes toward the real world. If the ultimate purpose of poetry was to say something — in however complicated a form — then, like traditional philosophy and the other humane sciences, it was a discourse that sought "a truth and an origin." As such, it could also read *"in a certain way."* Furthermore, scholars trained in the New Criticism could easily adapt their methods to deconstruction; if once they sought paradox and ambiguity in pursuit of the meaning of texts, they could now seek it in the pursuit of the posited void at the center of meaning. In effect, the move from New Criticism to deconstruction principally involved abandoning the search for the balance and resolution that critics like Cleanth Brooks had sought behind the paradoxes and ambiguities of the text.

In America in the 1970s, the prime locus for this new mode of reading was Yale University, which had also become a haven for many of the New Critics in their last years. Professors Harold Bloom, Geoffrey Hartman, and J. Hillis Miller of the Yale

English Department and Paul de Man of the Department of French and Comparative Literature became known collectively as the "Gang of Four," in ironic token of the radicalism of their readings and their coherence as a group. With the death of de Man in 1983 and the departure of Miller for California a few years later, the group broke up, but not before it had succeeded in bringing deconstruction to America.

Actually, Bloom (see Ch. 4, Psychoanalytic Theory and Criticism) was never really a philosophically orthodox deconstructionist, though his notion that all reading was in fact creative misreading was not inconsistent with the Derridean notion of freeplay. With respect to the other three, it seems clear that the intellectual center and prime mover was de Man, whose "Semiology and Rhetoric" is reprinted here.

This essay is not only a defense of deconstruction but a brief and telling demonstration of its powers applied to three short texts, ranging from a trivial joke from the television comedy "All in the Family" to a moving passage from Proust's *Remembrance of Things Past*. The central argument of de Man's essay — that meaning is not a dependable function of syntax — challenges a form of structuralism that had long ceased to be current, but de Man's conclusion — that one does not deconstruct *texts* so much as show the means by which they deconstruct *themselves* — is crucially important. Or to use a metaphor derived from Roland Barthes, the deconstructionist finds the thread dangling from the sweater, pulls on it, and watches as the fabric of the garment unravels into the pile of yarn from which it was made.

If every text can be said to contain its own deconstruction, de Man's essay supplies most of the methods employed in the deconstructive act. What we find most often is not an overt contradiction within a single level of the structure of the text — a paradox of the sort Cleanth Brooks would have appreciated — but a demonstration of the inconsistency between a text's grammar and its rhetoric, between its message and its activity, between what a text means and the way it goes about meaning it. Thus de Man shows how Proust's passage evoking the power of metaphor operates less in terms of metaphor (substitution) than in terms of metonymy (association).

De Man's examples are so brief and schematic that it may not be entirely clear what claims he is making for deconstruction as a mode of reading and how it differs from other modes of literary analysis that take tropes or figures of language as central tools. That is one reason we have included, at the end of this chapter, an essay by Lawrence Lipking, "The Practice of Theory." Taking Yeats's "Sailing to Byzantium" as his starting point, Lipking begins with the historical and biographical significance of the poem for Yeats, presents a formalist reading of the poem that is not quite "new critical," then goes on to show how the poem looks to the disciplines of structuralism and deconstruction. Lipking is decidedly not a card-carrying deconstructionist, and indeed has considerable doubts about the value in the classroom of theory in general and deconstruction in particular. So his essay, both in its transparence of argument and what it argues, serves as a challenge to the other essays in this chapter.

As a mode of literary criticism, deconstruction became extremely influential in the late 1970s and early 1980s, when a second generation of theorist-critics, disciples of de Man and Derrida, such as Barbara Johnson, Cynthia Chase, Timothy

Bahti, and Carol Jacobs, produced their most influential work, rereading important texts by Herman Melville, George Eliot, William Wordsworth, and so on. Despite the inventiveness of these readings, it became clear that regardless of the text analyzed, the usual end product of deconstructive criticism was *aporia:* the intellectual vertigo caused by looking into an apparently endless hall of mirrors. This is an effect that, unfortunately, palls on repetition. Many scholars, initially struck by the power of deconstruction, found that, no matter how inventive the path, each venture led invariably to the same vista. Deconstruction nevertheless continued to be one of the most attractive modes of literary theory in the years following de Man's death from cancer in 1983.

But beginning in the summer of 1987, the news broke slowly over the literary world that Ortwin de Graef, a Belgian graduate student writing a thesis on de Man, had discovered over 100 articles by the critic published between 1940 and 1942 in Belgian newspapers sympathetic to the Nazi occupation, including essays espousing anti-Semitic and pro-Nazi sentiments. Even de Man's closest friends at Yale were clearly astonished to hear of this element from his past. De Man had not only kept silent about this episode but had actively misled acquaintances about where and how he had spent the wartime years. It was clear that de Man's posthumous reputation would be tarnished by his wartime collaboration, but it was not de Man's reputation alone that was at stake, but that of the theories of deconstruction with which he was indelibly associated.

When deconstruction began in France in the late 1960s, it had been associated with the leftist critical journal *Tel Quel,* and the politics of its founder, Jacques Derrida, which insofar as they were intelligible also leaned to the Left. But in the intense rivalry that developed in the 1970s between deconstruction and Marxist or New Historicist criticism, deconstruction was painted into the political right wing as a movement whose obsession with textuality blinded it to the significance of lived experience and historical change. American practitioners of deconstruction, in particular, feared that not only Marxists but liberals who (like the structuralist Tzvetan Todorov) had found de Man's theories antihumanistic might seek to find all deconstructionists guilty by association.

As journalists raked the scandal amid the atmosphere of a witch hunt, former students of de Man's, like Chase, colleagues like Hartman and Miller, and even Derrida himself, wrote elaborate and tormented defenses of de Man and, implicitly, of themselves. This controversy, a Dreyfus case in reverse, is fraught with paradoxes of the sort de Man himself would have approved: that many of de Man's defenders are Jews (including Derrida himself); that the focus of the scandal has been dead for over two decades; and that de Man's offenses around 1942 predated his adoption of deconstruction by over 25 years. It is difficult to make out any strong connection between de Man's collaboration with Nazi sympathizers and his literary theories, but if there is one it is most likely to be negative. De Man's deconstructionist theories seem a more rigorous extension of his attacks in the 1950s on "salvational poetics" — of which Nazi cultural imperialism would be one crude version. If this is so, then de Man's life as a critic and theorist might be viewed as a long atonement for his juvenile sins.

The fate of deconstruction after the de Man scandal has been somewhat similar to the fall of structuralism: While its messianic atmosphere has dissipated, its utility has persisted. The primary use of deconstruction today is as a tool for breaking down binarisms and problematizing fields of discourse with seemingly fixed categories. Gender theorists such as Judith Butler (see Ch. 8, Gender Studies and Queer Theory) for example, value the deconstructive turn as a way of overturning essentialist views on sexual orientation and identity. As a tool of analysis and discursive rhetoric, deconstruction, like semiotics, is very much alive.

Selected Bibliography

Abrams, M. H. "The Deconstructive Angel." *Critical Inquiry* 3 (1977): 425–38.

Angermüller, Johannes. "Derrida, Phenomenology, and Structuralism: Why American Critics Turned Deconstructionists." In *Pioneering North America: Mediators of European Culture and Literature*, ed. Klaus Martens and Andreas Hau. Würzburg, Germany: Königshausen & Neumann, 2000, pp. 163–70.

Arac, Jonathan, Wlad Godzich, and Wallace Martin, eds. *The Yale Critics: Deconstruction in America*. Minneapolis: University of Minnesota Press, 1983.

Bal, Mieke. *Narratology*. Paris: Klincksieck, 1977.

Barthes, Roland. *Writing Degree Zero*. 1953; New York: Beacon, 1970.

——. *Critical Essays*. 1964; Evanston: Northwestern University Press, 1970.

——. *Mythologies*. 1957; New York: Hill and Wang, 1972.

——. *S/Z*. 1970; New York: Hill and Wang, 1974.

——. *The Pleasure of the Text*. New York: Hill and Wang, 1975.

——. *Sade, Fourier, Loyola*. New York: Hill and Wang, 1976.

——. *Image, Music, Text*. New York: Hill and Wang, 1977.

——. *A Barthes Reader*. New York: Hill and Wang, 1982.

——. *The Responsibility of Forms: New Critical Essays on Music, Art and Representation*. New York: Hill and Wang, 1984.

——. *The Rustle of Language*. New York: Hill and Wang, 1986.

Benveniste, Émile. *Problems in General Linguistics*. Coral Gables: University of Miami Press, 1971.

Bloom, Harold, et al. *Deconstruction and Criticism*. New York: Seabury, 1979.

Bové, Paul. *Deconstructive Poetics: Heidegger and Modern American Poetry*. New York: Columbia University Press, 1980.

Cain, William E. "Deconstruction in America: The Recent Literary Criticism of J. Hillis Miller." *College English* 41 (1979): 367–82.

Cassirer, Ernst. "Structuralism in Modern Linguistics." *Word* 1 (1945): 99–120.

——. *Symbol, Myth and Culture*. New Haven: Yale University Press, 1979.

Caws, Peter. *Structuralism: The Art of the Intelligible*. Atlantic Highlands, NJ: Humanities, 1988.

Chase, Cynthia. "The Decomposition of the Elephants: Double-Reading *Daniel Deronda*." *PMLA* 93 (1978): 215–27.

Chatman, Seymour, ed. *Essays on the Language of Literature*. Boston: Houghton Mifflin, 1967.

——. *Story and Discourse: Narrative Structure in Fiction and Film*. Ithaca: Cornell University Press, 1978.

Chomsky, Noam. *Syntactic Structures*. The Hague: Mouton, 1957.

———. *Aspects of the Theory of Syntax.* Cambridge: MIT Press, 1965.

Cohn, Dorrit. *Transparent Minds: Narrative Modes for Presenting Consciousness in Fiction.* Princeton: Princeton University Press, 1978.

Coward, Rosalind, and John Ellis. *Language and Materialism: Developments in Semiology and the Theory of the Subject.* London: Routledge and Kegan Paul, 1977.

Culler, Jonathan. *Structuralist Poetics.* Ithaca: Cornell University Press, 1975.

———. *The Pursuit of Signs: Semiotics, Literature, Deconstruction.* Ithaca: Cornell University Press, 1981.

———. *On Deconstruction: Theory and Criticism after Structuralism.* Ithaca: Cornell University Press, 1982.

———. *Roland Barthes.* New York: Oxford University Press, 1984.

———. *Ferdinand de Saussure.* Ithaca: Cornell University Press, 1986.

de Man, Paul. *Blindness and Insight.* New York: Oxford University Press, 1971.

———. *Allegories of Reading: Figural Language in Rousseau, Nietzsche, Rilke, and Proust.* New Haven: Yale University Press, 1979.

———. *The Rhetoric of Romanticism.* New York: Columbia University Press, 1984.

———. *The Resistance to Theory.* Minneapolis: University of Minnesota Press, 1986.

Derrida, Jacques. *Of Grammatology.* 1967; Baltimore: Johns Hopkins University Press, 1976.

———. *Writing and Difference.* 1967; Chicago: University of Chicago Press, 1978.

———. *Margins of Philosophy.* 1972; Chicago: University of Chicago Press, 1982.

———. *Positions,* trans. Alan Bass. 1972; Chicago: University of Chicago Press, 1981.

———. *Dissemination.* 1972; Chicago: University of Chicago Press, 1982.

———. *Speech and Phenomena, and Other Essays on Husserl's Theory of Signs.* 1973; Evanston: Northwestern University Press, 1978.

———. *Glas.* 1974; Lincoln: University of Nebraska Press, 1986.

———. *The Post Card: From Socrates to Freud and Beyond.* 1980; Chicago: University of Chicago Press, 1987.

———. "Like the Sound of the Sea Deep within a Shell: Paul de Man's War," trans. Peggy Kamuf. In *Responses on Paul de Man's Wartime Journalism,* ed. Werner Hamacher, Neil Hertz, and Thomas Kennan. Lincoln: University of Nebraska Press, 1988, pp. 127–64.

———. "Given Time: The Time of the King," trans. Peggy Kamuf. *Critical Inquiry* 18 (1992): 161–87.

———. "Shibboleth: For Paul Célan," trans. Joshua Wilner. In *Wordtraces: Readings of Paul Celan,* ed. Aris Fioretos. Baltimore: Johns Hopkins University Press, 1994, pp. 3–72.

———. *The Gift of Death.* Chicago: University Chicago Press, 1995.

———. *Acts of Religion.* New York: Routledge, 2001.

———. *On Cosmopolitanism and Forgiveness.* New York: Routledge, 2001.

———. *Negotiations: Interventions and Interviews 1971–2001.* Stanford: Stanford University Press, 2002.

Derrida, Jacques, Pascale-Anne Brault, and Michael Naas. *Adieu to Emmanuel Levinas.* Stanford: Stanford University Press, 1999.

Donoghue, Denis. *Ferocious Alphabets.* Boston: Little, Brown, 1981.

Dreyfus, Hubert L., and Paul Rabinow. *Michel Foucault: Beyond Structuralism and Hermeneutics,* 2nd ed. Chicago: University of Chicago Press, 1983.

Eco, Umberto. *A Theory of Semiotics.* Bloomington: Indiana University Press, 1975.

———. *The Role of the Reader: Explorations in the Semiotics of Texts.* Bloomington: Indiana University Press, 1979.

———. *Semiotics and the Philosophy of Language.* London: Macmillan, 1984.

Edelstein, Dan. "Between Myth and History: Michelet, Lévi-Strauss, Barthes, and the Structural Analysis of Myth." *CLIO* 32 (2003): 397–414.

Foucault, Michel. *The Order of Things: An Archaeology of the Human Sciences.* 1966; London: Tavistock, 1970.

———. *The Archeology of Knowledge.* 1969; New York: Pantheon, 1972.

———. *Language, Counter-Memory, Practice.* Ithaca: Cornell University Press, 1977.

———. *The Foucault Reader.* New York: Pantheon, 1984.

Gasché, Rodolphe. "The Scene of Writing: A Deferred Outset." *Glyph* 1 (1977): 150–71.

———. "Deconstruction as Criticism." *Glyph* 6 (1979): 177–216.

———. *Inventions of Difference: On Jacques Derrida.* Cambridge: Harvard University Press, 1994.

———. *The Wild Card of Reading: On Paul de Man.* Cambridge: Harvard University Press, 1998.

Genette, Gérard. *Narrative Discourse: An Essay in Method.* Ithaca: Cornell University Press, 1980.

———. *Figures of Literary Discourse.* New York: Columbia University Press, 1982.

Girard, René. *Deceit, Desire, and the Novel: The Self and Other in Literary Structure.* Baltimore: Johns Hopkins University Press, 1965.

———. *Violence and the Sacred.* Baltimore: Johns Hopkins University Press, 1977.

Graef, Ortwin de. *Serenity in Crisis: A Preface to Paul de Man 1939–1960.* Lincoln: University of Nebraska Press, 1993.

Greimas, A. J. *Structural Semantics: An Attempt at a Method.* Lincoln: University of Nebraska Press, 1984.

Harari, Josué. *Structuralists and Structuralisms.* Ithaca: Cornell University Press, 1971.

———. ed. *Textual Strategies: Perspectives in Post-Structuralist Criticism.* Ithaca: Cornell University Press, 1979.

Harris, Zellig. *Methods in Structural Linguistics.* Chicago: University of Chicago Press, 1951.

Hartman, Geoffrey H. *Beyond Formalism.* New Haven: Yale University Press, 1970.

———. *The Fate of Reading and Other Essays.* Chicago: University of Chicago Press, 1975.

———. *Criticism in the Wilderness.* New Haven: Yale University Press, 1980.

———. *Saving the Text: Literature/Derrida/Philosophy.* Baltimore: Johns Hopkins University Press, 1981.

Hawkes, Terence. *Structuralism and Semiotics.* Berkeley: University of California Press, 1977.

Herman, Luc, Kris Humbeeck, and Geert Lernout, eds. *(Dis)continuities: Essays on Paul de Man.* Amsterdam: Rodopi, 1989.

Hjelmslev, Louis. *Prolegomena to a Theory of Language.* Madison: University of Wisconsin Press, 1961.

Holland, Norman N. *The Critical I.* New York: Columbia University Press, 1992.

Husserl, Edmund. *The Idea of Phenomenology.* The Hague: Nijhoff, 1964.

Jakobson, Roman. *Selected Writings.* 8 vols. The Hague: Mouton, 1962–.

——— and Lawrence Jones. *Shakespeare's Verbal Art in "Th' Expense of Spirit."* The Hague: Mouton, 1970.

Jameson, Fredric. *The Prison House of Language: A Critical Account of Structuralism and Russian Formalism.* Princeton: Princeton University Press, 1971.

Johnson, Barbara. *The Critical Difference: Essays in the Contemporary Rhetoric of Reading.* Baltimore: Johns Hopkins University Press, 1980.

———. *A World of Difference.* Baltimore: Johns Hopkins University Press, 1987.

Kofman, Sarah. *Nietzsche et la scène philosophique*. Paris Union generale d'editions, 1979.
———. *Lectures de Derrida*. Paris: Editions Galilee, 1984.
Kristeva, Julia. *Essays in Semiotics*. The Hague: Mouton, 1971.
Lane, Michael, ed. *Structuralism: A Reader*. London: Cape, 1970.
Leitch, Vincent. *Deconstructive Criticism: An Advanced Introduction*. New York: Columbia University Press, 1983.
Lévi-Strauss, Claude. *Structural Anthropology*. 1958; New York: Basic Books, 1963.
———. *The Savage Mind*. Chicago: University of Chicago Press, 1966.
———. *The Raw and the Cooked*. 1964; New York: Harper and Row, 1969.
———. *From Honey to Ashes*. 1966; London: Cape, 1973.
Lotman, Yuri. *Analysis of the Poetic Text*. Ann Arbor: Ardis, 1976.
Lyons, John. *Structural Semantics*. Oxford: Blackwell, 1973.
Macksey, Richard, and Eugenio Donato, eds. *The Languages of Criticism and the Sciences of Man*. Baltimore: Johns Hopkins University Press, 1970.
———. *The Structuralist Controversy: The Languages of Criticism and the Sciences of Man*. Baltimore: Johns Hopkins University Press, 1970.
Martin, Bill. *Humanism and Its Aftermath: The Shared Fate of Deconstruction and Politics*. Atlantic Highlands, NJ: Humanities, 1995.
McDonald, Christie V. "Jacques Derrida's Reading of Rousseau." *The Eighteenth Century: Theory and Interpretation* 20 (1970): 82–95.
McQuillan, Martin. *Paul de Man*. London: Routledge, 2001.
Meyer, Michel, and Jacques Derrida. "From Grammatology to Problematology" *Revue Internationale de Philosophie* 52 (1998): 359–65, 497–529.
Miller, J. Hillis. "Ariadne's Thread: Repetition and the Narrative Line." *Critical Inquiry* 3 (1976): 57–78.
———. *Fiction and Repetition: Seven English Novels*. Cambridge: Harvard University Press, 1982.
———. *The Linguistic Moment: From Wordsworth to Stevens*. Princeton: Princeton University Press, 1985.
———. *The Ethics of Reading: Kant, de Man, Eliot, Trollope, James and Benjamin*. New York: Columbia University Press, 1987.
Murfin, Ross C. "Deconstruction and Derrida." In *Bram Stoker, Dracula*, ed. John Paul Riquelme. New York: Palgrave, 2002, pp. 538–59.
Nietzsche, Friedrich. *Complete Works*. 18 vols. Ed. Oscar Levy. New York: Russell and Russell, 1964.
Norris, Christopher. *The Deconstructive Turn: Essays in the Rhetoric of Philosophy*. New York: Methuen, 1984.
———. *The Contest of Faculties: Philosophy and Theory after Deconstruction*. New York: Methuen, 1985.
Patrick, Morag. *Derrida, Responsibility and Politics*. Aldershot, Eng.: Ashgate, 1997.
Piaget, Jean. *Structuralism*. New York: Basic Books, 1970.
Prince, Gerald. "Introduction à l'étude du narrataire." *Poétique* 14 (1963): 178–96.
Ricoeur, Paul. *The Conflict of Interpretations: Essays in Hermeneutics*. Evanston: Northwestern University Press, 1974.
———. *The Rule of Metaphor*. Toronto: University of Toronto Press, 1977.
———. *Time and Narrative*. Chicago: University of Chicago Press, 1984.
Riffaterre, Michael. *Semiotics of Poetry*. Bloomington: Indiana University Press, 1978.
———. *Text Production*. New York: Columbia University Press, 1983.
Robey, David, ed. *Structuralism: An Introduction*. London: Oxford University Press, 1973.

Rorty, Richard. "Philosophy as a Kind of Writing: An Essay on Derrida." *New Literary History* 10 (1978): 1411–60.

Royle, Nicholas. *After Derrida.* Manchester: Manchester University Press, 1995.

Ryan, Michael. *Marxism and Deconstruction.* Baltimore: Johns Hopkins University Press, 1982.

Saper, Craig J., and Laura Kipnis. *Artificial Mythologies: A Guide to Cultural Invention.* Minneapolis: University of Minnesota Press, 1997.

Saussure, Ferdinand de. *Course in General Linguistics.* 1923; New York: Philosophical Library, 1959.

Searle, John. *Speech Acts.* Cambridge: Cambridge University Press, 1969.

———. "Reiterating the Differences: A Reply to Derrida." *Glyph* 1 (1977): 198–208.

Sebeok, Thomas, ed. *Style in Language.* Cambridge: MIT Press, 1964.

———, ed. *Approaches to Semiotics.* The Hague: Mouton, 1964.

Silverman, Hugh J., and Gary E. Aylesworth, eds. *The Textual Sublime: Deconstruction and Its Differences.* Albany: State University of New York Press, 1990.

Smith, Barbara Herrnstein. *On the Margins of Discourse: The Relation of Literature to Language.* Chicago: University of Chicago Press, 1979.

Smith, Robert. *Derrida and Autobiography.* Cambridge: Cambridge University Press, 1995.

Sprinker, Michael. "Textual Politics: Foucault and Derrida." *Boundary* 28 (1980): 75–98.

Todorov, Tzvetan. *The Poetics of Prose.* Ithaca: Cornell University Press, 1977.

———. *Introduction to Poetics.* Minneapolis: University of Minnesota Press, 1981.

———. *Symbolism and Interpretation.* Ithaca: Cornell University Press, 1982.

———. *Theories of the Symbol.* Ithaca: Cornell University Press, 1982.

Ullmann, Stephen. *Language and Style.* Oxford: Blackwell, 1964.

Waters, Lindsay, and Wlad Godzich, eds. *Reading de Man Reading.* Minneapolis: University of Minnesota Press, 1988.

Ferdinand de Saussure

1857–1913

Ferdinand de Saussure was born in Geneva and educated at the University of Geneva and the University of Berlin before taking his Ph.D. at the University of Leipzig in 1880. The linguist and philologist taught at the École Pratique des Hautes Études in Paris before returning to his birthplace and a professorship at the University of Geneva, where he taught from 1891 to 1912. Saussure published specialized monographs in linguistics during his lifetime, such as his Memoir on the Primitive System of Vowels in the Indo-European Languages *(1879). His current fame is based on the course in general linguistics that he gave in Geneva, which was posthumously recreated from lecture notes by his students and published in 1916 as* Cours de linguistique générale (The Course in General Linguistics), *from which the following selections are taken.*

Nature of the Linguistic Sign

I. SIGN, SIGNIFIED, SIGNIFIER

Some people regard language, when reduced to its elements, as a naming-process only — a list of words, each corresponding to the thing that it names. For example:

ARBOR

EQUOS

etc.   etc.

This conception is open to criticism at several points. It assumes that ready-made ideas exist before words; it does not tell us whether a name is vocal or psychological in nature (*arbor,* for instance, can be considered from either viewpoint); finally, it lets us assume that the linking of a name and a thing is a very simple operation — an assumption that is anything but true. But this rather naive approach can bring us near the truth by showing us that the linguistic unit is a double entity, one formed by the associating of two terms.

We have seen in considering the speaking-circuit that both terms involved in the linguistic sign are psychological and are united in the brain by an associative bond. This point must be emphasized.

The linguistic sign unites, not a thing and a name, but a concept and a sound-image.[1] The latter is not the material sound, a purely physical thing, but the psychological imprint of the sound, the impression that it makes on our senses. The sound-image is sensory, and if I happen to call it "material," it is only in that sense, and by way of opposing it to the other term of the association, the concept, which is generally more abstract.

The psychological character of our sound-images becomes apparent when we observe our own speech. Without moving our lips or tongue, we can talk to ourselves or recite mentally a selection of verse. Because we regard the words of our language as sound-images, we must avoid speaking of the "phonemes" that make up the words. This term, which suggests vocal activity, is applicable to the spoken word only, to the realization of the inner image in discourse. We can avoid that misunderstanding by speaking of the *sounds* and *syllables* of a word provided we remember that the names refer to the sound-image.

The linguistic sign is then a two-sided psychological entity that can be represented by the drawing:

The two elements are intimately united, and each recalls the other. Whether we try to find the meaning of the Latin word *arbor* or the word that Latin uses to designate the concept "tree," it is clear that only the associations sanctioned by that language appear to us to conform to reality, and we disregard whatever others might be imagined.

Translated by Wade Baskin.

[1]The term sound-image may seem to be too restricted inasmuch as beside the representation of the sounds of a word there is also that of its articulation, the muscular image of the phonational act. But for F. de Saussure language is essentially a depository, a thing received from without. The sound-image is par excellence the natural representation of the word as a fact of potential language, outside any actual use of it in speaking. The motor side is thus implied or, in any event, occupies only a subordinate role with respect to the sound-image. [Bally and Sèchehaye.] Bally and Sèchehaye redacted the lecture notes of Saussure's students into *Cours de linguistique générale.* [Tr.]

Our definition of the linguistic sign poses an important question of terminology. I call the combination of a concept and a sound-image a *sign,* but in current usage the term generally designates only a sound-image, a word, for example (*arbor,* etc.). One tends to forget that *arbor* is called a sign only because it carries the concept "tree," with the result that the idea of the sensory part implies the idea of the whole.

Ambiguity would disappear if the three notions involved here were designated by three names, each suggesting and opposing the others. I propose to retain the word *sign* [*signe*] to designate the whole and to replace *concept* and *sound-image* respectively by *signified* [*signifié*] and *signifier* [*signifiant*]; the last two terms have the advantage of indicating the opposition that separates them from each other and from the whole of which they are parts. As regards *sign,* if I am satisfied with it, this is simply because I do not know of any word to replace it, the ordinary language suggesting no other.

The linguistic sign, as defined, has two primordial characteristics. In enunciating them I am also positing the basic principles of any study of this type.

2. PRINCIPLE I: THE ARBITRARY NATURE OF THE SIGN

The bond between the signifier and the signified is arbitrary. Since I mean by sign the whole that results from the associating of the signifier with the signified, I can simply say: *the linguistic sign is arbitrary.*

The idea of "sister" is not linked by any inner relationship to the succession of sounds *s-ö-r* which serves as its signifier in French; that it could be represented equally by just any other sequence is proved by differences among languages and by the very existence of different languages: the signified "ox" has as its signifier *b-ö-f* on one side of the border and *o-k-s* (*Ochs*) on the other.

No one disputes the principle of the arbitrary nature of the sign, but it is often easier to discover a truth than to assign to it its proper place. Principle I dominates all the linguistics of language; its consequences are numberless. It is true that not all of them are equally obvious at first glance; only after many detours does one discover them, and with them the primordial importance of the principle.

One remark in passing: when semiology becomes organized as a science, the question will arise whether or not it properly includes modes of expression based on completely natural signs, such as pantomime. Supposing that the new science welcomes them, its main concern will still be the whole group of systems grounded on the arbitrariness of the sign. In fact, every means of expression used in society is based, in principle, on collective behavior or — what amounts to the same thing — on convention. Polite formulas, for instance, though often imbued with a certain natural expressiveness (as in the case of a Chinese who greets his emperor by bowing down to the ground nine times), are nonetheless fixed by rule; it is this rule and not the intrinsic value of the gestures that obliges one to use them. Signs that are wholly arbitrary realize better than the others the ideal of the semiological process; that is why language, the most complex and universal of all systems of expression, is also the most characteristic; in this sense linguistics can become the master-pattern for all branches of semiology although language is only one particular semiological system.

The word *symbol* has been used to designate the linguistic sign, or more specifically, what is here called the signifier. Principle I in particular weighs against the use of this term. One characteristic of the symbol is that it is never wholly arbitrary; it is not empty, for there is the rudiment of a natural bond between the signifier and the signified. The symbol of justice, a pair of scales, could not be replaced by just any other symbol, such as a chariot.

The word *arbitrary* also calls for comment. The term should not imply that the choice of the signifier is left entirely to the speaker (we shall see below that the individual does not have the power to change a sign in any way once it has become established in the linguistic community); I mean that it is unmotivated, i.e. arbitrary in that it actually has no natural connection with the signified.

In concluding let us consider two objections that might be raised to the establishment of Principle I:

1. *Onomatopoeia* might be used to prove that the choice of the signifier is not always arbitrary. But onomatopoeic formations are never organic elements of a linguistic system. Besides, their number is much smaller than is generally supposed. Words like French *fouet* "whip" or *glas* "knell" may strike certain ears with suggestive sonority, but to see that they have not always had this property we need only examine their Latin forms (*fouet* is derived from *fāgus* "beech-tree," *glas* from *classicum* "sound of a trumpet"). The quality of their present sounds, or rather the quality that is attributed to them, is a fortuitous result of phonetic evolution.

As for authentic onomatopoeic words (e.g. *glug-glug, tick-tock,* etc.), not only are they limited in number, but also they are chosen somewhat arbitrarily, for they are only approximate and more or less conventional imitations of certain sounds (cf. English *bow-bow* and French *ouaoua*). In addition, once these words have been introduced into the language, they are to a certain extent subjected to the same evolution — phonetic, morphological, etc. — that other words undergo (cf. *pigeon,* ultimately from Vulgar Latin *pīpiō,* derived in turn from an onomatopoeic formation): obvious proof that they lose something of their original character in order to assume that of the linguistic sign in general, which is unmotivated.

2. *Interjections,* closely related to onomatopoeia, can be attacked on the same grounds and come no closer to refuting our thesis. One is tempted to see in them spontaneous expressions of reality dictated, so to speak, by natural forces. But for most interjections we can show that there is no fixed bond between their signified and their signifier. We need only compare two languages on this point to see how much such expressions differ from one language to the next (e.g. the English equivalent of French *aïe!* is *ouch!*). We know, moreover, that many interjections were once words with specific meanings (cf. French *diable!* "darn!" *mordieu!* "golly!" from *mort Dieu* "God's death," etc.).[2]

Onomatopoeic formations and interjections are of secondary importance, and their symbolic origin is in part open to dispute.

3. PRINCIPLE II: THE LINEAR NATURE OF THE SIGNIFIER

The signifier, being auditory, is unfolded solely in time from which it gets the following characteristics: (a) it represents a span, and (b) the span is measurable in a single dimension; it is a line.

While Principle II is obvious, apparently linguists have always neglected to state it, doubtless because they found it too simple; nevertheless, it is fundamental, and its consequences are incalculable. Its importance equals that of Principle I; the whole mechanism of language depends upon it. In contrast to visual signifiers (nautical signals, etc.) which can offer simultaneous groupings in several dimensions, auditory signifiers have at their command only the dimension of time. Their elements are presented in succession; they form a chain. This feature becomes readily apparent when they are represented in writing and the spatial line of graphic marks is substituted for succession in time.

Sometimes the linear nature of the signifier is not obvious. When I accent a syllable, for instance, it seems that I am concentrating more than one significant element on the same point. But this is an illusion; the syllable and its accent constitute only one phonational act. There is no duality within the act but only different oppositions to what precedes and what follows.

---

[2]Cf. English *goodness!* and *zounds!* (from *God's wounds*). [Tr.]

[Binary Oppositions]

2. Linguistic Value from a Conceptual Viewpoint

When we speak of the value of a word, we generally think first of its property of standing for an idea, and this is in fact one side of linguistic value. But if this is true, how does *value* differ from *signification*? Might the two words be synonyms? I think not, although it is easy to confuse them, since the confusion results not so much from their similarity as from the subtlety of the distinction that they mark.

From a conceptual viewpoint, value is doubtless one element in signification, and it is difficult to see how signification can be dependent upon value and still be distinct from it. But we must clear up the issue or risk reducing language to a simple naming-process.

Let us first take signification as it is generally understood. . . . As the arrows in the drawing show, it is only the counterpart of the sound-image. Everything that occurs concerns only the sound-image and the concept when we look upon the word as independent and self-contained.

But here is the paradox: on the one hand the concept seems to be the counterpart of the sound-image, and on the other hand the sign itself is in turn the counterpart of the other signs of language.

Language is a system of interdependent terms in which the value of each term results solely from the simultaneous presence of the others, as in the diagram:

How, then, can value be confused with signification, i.e. the counterpart of the sound-image? It seems impossible to liken the relations represented here by horizontal arrows to those represented above by vertical arrows. Putting it another way — and again taking up the example of the sheet of paper that is cut in two — it is clear that the observable relation between the different pieces A, B, C, D etc. is distinct from the relation between the front and back of the same piece as in A/A', B/B', etc.

To resolve the issue, let us observe from the outset that even outside language all values are apparently governed by the same paradoxical principle. They are always composed:

(1) of a *dissimilar* thing that can be *exchanged* for the thing of which the value is to be determined; and

(2) of *similar* things that can be *compared* with the thing of which the value is to be determined.

Both factors are necessary for the existence of a value. To determine what a five-franc piece is worth one must therefore know: (1) that it can be exchanged for a fixed quantity of a different thing, e.g., bread; and (2) that it can be compared with a similar value of the same system, e.g., a one-franc piece, or with coins of another system (a dollar, etc.). In the same way a word can be exchanged for something dissimilar, an idea; besides, it can be compared with something of the same nature, another word. Its value is therefore not fixed so long as one simply states that it can be "exchanged" for a given concept, i.e., has this or that signification: one must also compare it with similar values, with other words that stand in opposition to it. Its content is really fixed only by the concurrence of everything that exists outside it. Being part of a system, it is endowed not only with a signification but also and especially with a value, and this is something quite different.

A few examples will show clearly that this is true. Modern French *mouton* can have the same signification as English *sheep* but not the same value, and this for several reasons, particularly because in speaking of a piece of meat ready to be served on the table, English uses *mutton* and not *sheep*. The difference in value between *sheep* and *mouton* is due to the fact that *sheep* has beside it a second term while the French word does not.

Within the same language, all words used to express related ideas limit each other reciprocally; synonyms like French *redouter* "dread," *craindre* "fear," and *avoir peur* "be afraid" have value only through their opposition: if *redouter* did not exist, all its content would go to its competitors. Conversely, some words are enriched through contact with others: e.g. the new element introduced in *décrépit* (un vieillard *décrépit*) results from the coexistence of *décrépi* (un mur *décrépi*). The value of just any term is accordingly determined by its environment; it is impossible to fix even the value of the word signifying "sun" without first considering its surroundings: in some languages it is not possible to say "sit in the *sun*."

Everything said about words applies to any term of language, e.g., to grammatical entities. The value of a French plural does not coincide with that of a Sanskrit plural even though their signification is usually identical; Sanskrit has three numbers instead of two (*my eyes, my ears, my arms, my legs*, etc. are dual);[1] it would be wrong to attribute the same value to the plural in Sanskrit and in French; its value clearly depends on what is outside and around it.

If words stood for pre-existing concepts, they would all have exact equivalents in meaning from one language to the next; but this is not true. French uses *louer* (*une maison*) "let (a house)" indifferently to mean both "pay for" and "receive payment for," whereas German uses two words, *mieten* and *vermieten*; there is obviously no exact correspondence of values. The German verbs *schätzen* and *urteilen* share a number of significations, but that correspondence does not hold at several points.[2]

Inflection offers some particularly striking examples. Distinctions of time, which are so familiar to us, are unknown in certain languages. Hebrew does not recognize even the fundamental distinctions between the past, present, and future.[3] Proto-Germanic has no special form for the future; to say that the future is expressed by the present is wrong, for the value of the present is not the same in Germanic as in languages that have a future along with the present. The Slavic languages regularly single out two aspects of the verb: the perfective represents action as a point, complete in its totality; the imperfective represents it as taking place, and on the line of time. The categories are difficult for a Frenchman to understand, for they are unknown in French; if they were predetermined, this would not be true. Instead of pre-existing ideas then, we find in all the foregoing examples *values* emanating from the system. When they are said to correspond to concepts, it is understood that the concepts are purely differential and defined not by their positive content but negatively by their relations with the other terms of the system. Their most precise characteristic is in being what the others are not.

Now the real interpretation of the diagram of the signal becomes apparent. Thus

means that in French the concept "to judge" is linked to the sound-image *juger;* in short, it symbolizes signification. But it is quite clear that initially the concept is nothing, that is only a value determined by its relations with other similar values, and that without them the signification would not exist. If I state simply that a word signifies something when I have in mind the associating of

<hr />

[1]The use of the comparative form for two and the superlative for more than two in English (e.g., *may the* better *boxer win*: *the* best *boxer in the world*) is probably a remnant of the old distinction between the dual [English has the remnants of a lost dual in archaic words like *eyne*] and the plural number. [Tr.]

[2]*Schätzen* means "to appraise" — to judge something's value; *urteilen* means "to judge generally."

[3]The biblical Hebrew verb has an immensely complicated mode and aspect system, but the tenses themselves are rudimentary, compared with French. In general Saussure's analysis of other languages is Francocentric (languages like German that use auxiliaries rather than inflecting the verb to convey the future tense are said not to have one).

a sound-image with a concept, I am making a statement that may suggest what actually happens, but by no means am I expressing the linguistic fact in its essence and fullness.

3. Linguistic Value from a Material Viewpoint

The conceptual side of value is made up solely of relations and differences with respect to the other terms of language, and the same can be said of its material side. The important thing in the word is not the sound alone but the phonic differences that make it possible to distinguish this word from all others, for differences carry signification.

This may seem surprising, but how indeed could the reverse be possible? Since one vocal image is no better suited than the next for what it is commissioned to express, it is evident, even *a priori*, that a segment of language can never in the final analysis be based on anything except its noncoincidence with the rest. *Arbitrary* and *differential* are two correlative qualities.

The alteration of linguistic signs clearly illustrates this. It is precisely because the terms *a* and *b* as such are radically incapable of reaching the level of consciousness — one is always conscious of only the *a/b* difference — that each term is free to change according to laws that are unrelated to its signifying function. No positive sign characterizes the genitive plural in Czech *žen*; still, the two forms *žena: žen* function as well as the earlier forms *žena: ženb; žen* has value only because it is different.

Here is another example that shows even more clearly the systematic role of phonic differences: in Greek, *éphēn* is an imperfect and *éstēn* an aorist[4] although both words are formed in the same way; the first belongs to the system of the present indicative of *phēmí* "I say," whereas there is no present *stēmi;*[5] now it is precisely the relation

phēmī: éphēn that corresponds to the relation between the present and the imperfect (cf. *deíknūmi: edeíknūn*, etc.). Signs function, then, not through their intrinsic value but through their relative position.

In addition, it is impossible for sound alone, a material element, to belong to language. It is only a secondary thing, substance to be put to use. All our conventional values have the characteristic of not being confused with the tangible element which supports them. For instance, it is not the metal in a piece of money that fixes its value. A coin nominally worth five francs may contain less than half its worth of silver. Its value will vary according to the amount stamped upon it and according to its use inside or outside a political boundary. This is even more true of the linguistic signifier, which is not phonic but incorporeal — constituted not by its material substance but by the differences that separate its sound-image from all others.

The foregoing principle is so basic that it applies to all the material elements of language, including phonemes. Every language forms its words on the basis of a system of sonorous elements, each element being a clearly delimited unit and one of a fixed number of units. Phonemes are characterized not, as one might think, by their own positive quality but simply by the fact that they are distinct. Phonemes are above all else opposing, relative, and negative entities.

Proof of this is the latitude that speakers have between points of convergence in the pronunciation of distinct sounds. In French, for instance, general use of a dorsal *r* does not prevent many speakers from using a tongue-tip trill; language is not in the least disturbed by it; language requires only that the sound be different and not, as one might imagine, that it have an invariable quality. I can even pronounce the French *r* like German *ch* in *Bach, doch*, etc., but in German I could not use *r* instead of *ch*, for German gives recognition to both elements and must keep them apart. Similarly, in Russian there is no latitude for *t* in the direction of *t'* (palatalized[6] *t*), for the result would be the confusing of two sounds differentiated by the language (cf. *govorit'* "speak" and *goverit* "he

[4]The imperfect and the aorist are two aspects of the verb in classical Greek. The aorist denotes a single past action; the imperfect denotes a process in the past. English usually uses the past vs. past + participle to convey the same distinction; e.g., "I ran"/"I was running." But some verbs do not have an imperfect and require an alternate verb to indicate process: e.g., "I saw a nightingale"/"I was looking at a nightingale" — not "I was seeing a nightingale."

[5]The asterisk means that there is no such Greek form; the first person singular present corresponding to *phemi* is *histemi*.

[6]With a bit of "ch" added, as in the "t" in nature.

speaks"), but more freedom may be taken with respect to *th* (aspirated *t*) since this sound does not figure in the Russian system of phonemes.

Since an identical state of affairs is observable in writing, another system of signs, we shall use writing to draw some comparisons that will clarify the whole issue. In fact:

1) The signs used in writing are arbitrary; there is no connection, for example, between the letter *t* and the sound that it designates.

2) The value of letters is purely negative and differential. The same person can write *t*, for instance, in different ways:

$$ t \quad \mathcal{t} \quad t $$

The only requirement is that the sign for *t* not be confused in his script with the signs used for *l*, *d*, etc.

3) Values in writing function only through reciprocal opposition within a fixed system that consists of a set number of letters. This third characteristic, though not identical to the second, is closely related to it, for both depend on the first. Since the graphic sign is arbitrary, its form matters little or rather matters only within the limitations imposed by the system.

4) The means by which the sign is produced is completely unimportant, for it does not affect the system (this also follows from characteristic 1). Whether I make the letters in white or black, raised or engraved, with pen or chisel — all this is of no importance with respect to their signification.

4. The Sign Considered in Its Totality

Everything that has been said up to this point boils down to this: in language there are only differences. Even more important: a difference generally implies positive terms between which the difference is set up; but in language there are only differences *without positive terms*. Whether we take the signified or the signifier, language has neither ideas nor sounds that existed before the linguistic system, but only conceptual and phonic differences that have issued from the system. The idea or phonic substance that a sign contains is of less importance than the other signs that surround it. Proof of this is that the value of a term may be

modified without either its meaning or its sound being affected, solely because a neighboring term has been modified.

But the statement that everything in language is negative is true only if the signified and the signifier are considered separately; when we consider the sign in its totality, we have something that is positive in its own class. A linguistic system is a series of differences of sound combined with a series of differences of ideas; but the pairing of a certain number of acoustical signs with as many cuts made from the mass of thought engenders a system of values; and this system serves as the effective link between the phonic and psychological elements within each sign. Although both the signified and the signifier are purely differential and negative when considered separately, their combination is a positive fact; it is even the sole type of facts that language has, for maintaining the parallelism between the two classes of differences is the distinctive function of the linguistic institution.

Certain diachronic facts are typical in this respect. Take the countless instances where alteration of the signifier occasions a conceptual change and where it is obvious that the sum of the ideas distinguished corresponds in principle to the sum of the distinctive signs. When two words are confused through phonetic alteration (e.g., French *décrépit* from *dēcrepitus* and *décrépi* from *crispus*), the ideas that they express will also tend to become confused if only they have something in common.[7] Or a word may have different forms (cf. *chaise* "chair" and *chaire* "desk"[8]). Any nascent difference will tend invariably to become significant but without always succeeding or being successful on the first trial. Conversely, any conceptual difference perceived by the mind seeks to find expression through a distinct signifier, and two ideas that are no longer distinct in the mind tend to merge into the same signifier.

When we compare signs — positive terms — with each other, we can no longer speak of difference; the expression would not be fitting, for it

[7] Saussure's notion that *décrépi* comes from the Latin *crispus* (curled) is probably fanciful.

[8] *Chaire* is more accurately the pulpit from which a clergyman preaches or the lectern from which a professor lectures. It derives from the Latin *cathedra*.

applies only to the comparing of two sound-images, e.g. *father* and *mother*, or two ideas, e.g. the idea "father" and the idea "mother"; two signs, each having a signified and signifier, are not different but only distinct. Between them there is only *opposition*. The entire mechanism of language, with which we shall be concerned later, is based on oppositions of this kind and on the phonic and conceptual differences that they imply.

What is true of value is true also of the unit. A unit is a segment of the spoken chain that corresponds to a certain concept; both are by nature purely differential.

Applied to units, the principle of differentiation can be stated in this way: *the characteristics of the unit blend with the unit itself.* In language, as in any semiological system, whatever distinguishes one sign from the others constitutes it. Difference makes characters just as it makes value and the unit.

Another rather paradoxical consequence of the same principle is this: in the last analysis what is commonly referred to as a "grammatical fact" fits the definition of the unit, for it always expresses an opposition of terms; it differs only in that the opposition is particularly significant (e.g. the formation of German plurals of the type *Nacht: Nächte*). Each term present in the grammatical fact (the singular without umlaut or final *e* in opposition to the plural with umlaut and *−e*) consists of the interplay of a number of oppositions within the system. When isolated, neither *Nacht* nor *Nächte* is anything: thus everything is opposition. Putting it another way, the *Nacht: Nächte* relation can be expressed by an algebraic formula *a/b* in which *a* and *b* are not simple terms but result from a set of relations. Language, in a manner of speaking, is a type of algebra consisting solely of complex terms. Some of its oppositions are more significant than others; but units and grammatical facts are only different names for designating diverse aspects of the same general fact: the functioning of linguistic oppositions. This statement is so true that we might very well approach the problem of units by starting from grammatical facts. Taking an opposition like *Nacht:Nächte*, we might ask what are the units involved in it. Are they only the two words, the whole series of similar words, *a* and *ä*, or all singulars and plurals, etc.?

Units and grammatical facts would not be confused if linguistic signs were made up of something besides differences. But language being what it is, we shall find nothing simple in it regardless of our approach; everywhere and always there is the same complex equilibrium of terms that mutually condition each other. Putting it another way, *language is a form and not a substance.* This truth could not be overstressed, for all the mistakes in our terminology, all our incorrect ways of naming things that pertain to language, stem from the involuntary supposition that the linguistic phenomenon must have substance.

CHAPTER V: SYNTAGMATIC AND ASSOCIATIVE RELATIONS

1. Definitions

In a language-state everything is based on relations. How do they function?

Relations and differences between linguistic terms fall into two distinct groups, each of which generates a certain class of values. The opposition between the two classes gives a better understanding of the nature of each class. They correspond to two forms of our mental activity, both indispensable to the life of language.

In discourse, on the one hand, words acquire relations based on the linear nature of language because they are chained together. This rules out the possibility of pronouncing two elements simultaneously. The elements are arranged in sequence on the chain of speaking. Combinations supported by linearity are *syntagms*.[9] The syntagm is always composed of two or more consecutive units (e.g., French *re-lire* "re-read," *contre tous* "against everyone," *la vie humaine* "human life," *Dieu est bon* "God is good," *s'il fait beau temps, nous sortirons* "if the weather is nice, we'll go out," etc.). In the syntagm a term acquires its value only because it stands in opposition to everything that precedes or follows it, or to both.

Outside discourse, on the other hand, words acquire relations of a different kind. Those that have something in common are associated in the

[9]It is scarcely necessary to point out that the study of *syntagms* is not to be confused with syntax. Syntax is only one part of the study of syntagms. [Bally and Sèchenaye, eds.]

memory, resulting in groups marked by diverse relations. For instance, the French word *enseignement* "teaching" will unconsciously call to mind a host of other words (*enseigner* "teach," *renseigner* "acquaint," etc.; or *armement* "armament," *changement* "amendment," etc.; or *éducation* "education," *apprentissage* "apprenticeship," etc.). All those words are related in some way.

We see that the co-ordinations formed outside discourse differ strikingly from those formed inside discourse. Those formed outside discourse are not supported by linearity. Their seat is in the brain; they are a part of the inner storehouse that makes up the language of each speaker. They are *associative relations*.

The syntagmatic relation is *in praesentia*. It is based on two or more terms that occur in an effective series. Against this, the associative relation unites terms *in absentia* in a potential mnemonic series.

From the associative and syntagmatic viewpoint a linguistic unit is like a fixed part of a building, e.g. a column. On the one hand, the column has a certain relation to the architrave that it supports; the arrangement of the two units in space suggests the syntagmatic relation. On the other hand, if the column is Doric, it suggests a mental comparison of this style with others (Ionic, Corinthian, etc.) although none of these elements is present in space: the relation is associative.

Each of the two classes of co-ordination calls for some specific remarks.

2. Syntagmatic Relations

The examples on pages [849–50] have already indicated that the notion of syntagm applies not only to words but to groups of words, to complex units of all lengths and types (compounds, derivatives, phrases, whole sentences).

It is not enough to consider the relation that ties together the different parts of syntagms (e.g., French *contre* "against" and *tous* "everyone" in *contre tous*, *contre* and *maître* "master" in *contremaître* "foreman");[10] one must also bear in mind the relation that links the whole to its parts (e.g., *contre tous* in opposition on the one hand to

---

[10]Cf. English *head* and *waiter* in *headwaiter*. [Tr.]

contre and on the other *tous*, or *contremaître* in opposition to *contre* and *maître*).

An objection might be raised at this point. The sentence is the ideal type of syntagm. But it belongs to speaking, not to language. Does it not follow that the syntagm belongs to speaking? I do not think so. Speaking is characterized by freedom of combinations; one must therefore ask whether or not all syntagms are equally free.

It is obvious from the first that many expressions belong to language. These are the pat phrases in which any change is prohibited by usage, even if we can single out their meaningful elements (cf. *à quoi bon?* "what's the use?" *allons donc!* "nonsense!"). The same is true, though to a lesser degree, of expressions like *prendre la mouche* "take offense easily,"[11] *forcer la main à quelqu'un* "force someone's hand," *rompre une lance* "break a lance,"[12] or even *avoir mal (à la tête, etc.)* "have (a headache, etc.)," *à force de (soins, etc.)* "by dint of (care, etc.)," *que vous en semble?* "how do you feel about it?" *pas n'est besoin de . . .* "there's no need for . . .," etc., which are characterized by peculiarities of signification or syntax. These idiomatic twists cannot be improvised; they are furnished by tradition. There are also words which, while lending themselves perfectly to analysis, are characterized by some morphological anomaly that is kept solely by dint of usage (cf. *difficulté* "difficulty" beside *facilité* "facility," etc., and *mourrai* "[I] shall die" beside *dormirai* "[I] shall sleep").[13]

There are further proofs. To language rather than to speaking belong the syntagmatic types that are built upon regular forms. Indeed, since there is nothing abstract in language, the types exist only if language has registered a sufficient number of specimens. When a word like *indécorable* arises in speaking, its appearance supposes a fixed type, and this type is in turn possible only through remembrance of a sufficient number of similar words belonging to language (*impardonable* "unpardonable," *intolérable*

---

[11]Literally "take the fly." Cf. English *take the bull by the horns*. [Tr.]

[12]Cf. English *bury the hatchet*. [Tr.]

[13]The anomaly of the double *r* in the future forms of certain verbs in French may be compared to irregular plurals like *oxen* in English. [Tr.]

"intolerable," *infatigable* "indefatigable," etc.). Exactly the same is true of sentences and groups of words built upon regular patterns. Combinations like *la terre tourne* "the world turns," *que vous dit-il?* "what does he say to you?" etc. correspond to general types that are in turn supported in the language by concrete remembrances.

But we must realize that in the syntagm there is no clear-cut boundary between the language fact, which is a sign of collective usage, and the fact that belongs to speaking and depends on individual freedom. In a great number of instances it is hard to class a combination of units because both forces have combined in producing it, and they have combined in indeterminable proportions.

3. Associative Relations

Mental association creates other groups besides those based on the comparing of terms that have something in common; through its grasp of the nature of the relations that bind the terms together, the mind creates as many associative series as there are diverse relations. For instance, in *enseignement* "teaching," *enseigner* "teach," *enseignons* "(we) teach," etc., one element, the radical, is common to every term; the same word may occur in a different series formed around another common element, the suffix (cf. *enseignement*, *armement*, *changement*, etc.); or the association may spring from the analogy of the concepts signified (*enseignement*, *instruction*, *apprentissage*, *éducation*, etc.); or again, simply from the similarity of the sound-images (e.g., *enseignement* and *justement* "precisely").[14] Thus there is at times a double similarity of meaning and form, at times similarity only of form or of meaning. A word can always evoke everything that can be associated with it in one way or another.

Whereas a syntagm immediately suggests an order of succession and a fixed number of elements, terms in an associative family occur neither in fixed numbers nor in a definite order. If we associate *painful*, *delightful*, *frightful*, etc. we are unable to predict the number of words that the memory will suggest or the order in which they will appear. A particular word is like the center of a constellation; it is the point of convergence of a indefinite number of co-ordinated terms.

But of the two characteristics of the associative series — indeterminate order and indefinite number — only the first can always be verified; the second may fail to meet the test. This happens in the case of inflectional paradigms, which are typical of associative groupings. Latin *dominus*, *dominī*, *dominō*, etc. is obviously an associative group formed around a common element, the noun theme *domin–*, but the series[15]

is not indefinite as in the case of *enseignement, changement*, etc.; the number of cases is definite. Against this, the words have no fixed order of succession, and it is by a purely arbitrary act that the grammarian groups them in one way rather than in another; in the mind of speakers the nominative case is by no means the first one in the declension, and the order in which terms are called depends on circumstances.

[14]The last case is rare and can be classed as abnormal, for the mind naturally discards associations that becloud the intelligibility of discourse. But its existence is proved by a lower category of puns based on the ridiculous confusions that can result from pure and simple homonymy like the French statement "Les musicians produisent les *sons* ["sounds, bran"] et les grainetiers les vendent" "musicians produce *sons* and seedsmen sell them." [Cf. Shakespeare's "Not on thy *sole*, but on thy *soul*." (Tr.)] This is distinct from the case where an association, while fortuitous, is supported by a comparison of ideas (cf. French *ergot* "spur": *ergoter* "wrangle"; German *blau* "blue": *durchblauen* "thrash soundly"); the point is that one member of the pair has a new interpretation. Folk etymologies like these are of interest in the study of semantic evolution, but from the synchronic viewpoint they are in the same category as *enseigner: enseignement*. [Bally and Sèchenaye, eds.]

[15]Cf. English *education* and the corresponding associative series: *educate, educates*, etc.; *internship*, training, etc.; *vocation, devotion*, etc.; and *lotion, fashion*, etc. [Tr.]

Roman Jakobson

1896–1982

Roman Jakobson, the most eminent member of the Prague Circle, is one of this century's foremost linguists. Jakobson became a professor of Russian at the Higher Dramatic School in Moscow, his birthplace, in 1920. In 1929, he and two other members of the Prague school announced a substantive break with the theories of Ferdinand de Saussure, perhaps the most potent influence on their own studies until then. In 1933 Jakobson began his association with Masarykova (later Purkyně) University in Czechoslovakia, becoming professor of Russian philology in 1934 and of Czech medieval literature in 1936. The unsettled politics of the time precipitated his departure from the university; he sojourned briefly at the universities of Copenhagen, Oslo, and Uppsala before finding his way to New York City in 1941. From 1943 to 1947 he taught at Columbia University, and then moved on to Harvard University, where he was a professor of Slavic languages and literature and general linguistics until 1967. Jakobson has written a wealth of speech studies; he is the author, with Morris Halle and C. G. M. Fant, of Preliminaries to Speech Analysis *(1952), and with Halle of* Fundamentals of Language *(1956). More recently he has written on Shakespeare (1970), Yeats (1977), and the grammatical structure of children's speech (1977). Excerpted here, "Linguistics and Poetics" was published in 1960.*

From *Linguistics and Poetics*

I have been asked for summary remarks about poetics in its relation to linguistics. Poetics deals primarily with the question, *What makes a verbal message a work of art?* Because the main subject of poetics is the *differentia specifica* of verbal art in relation to other arts and in relation to other kinds of verbal behavior, poetics is entitled to the leading place in literary studies.

Poetics deals with problems of verbal structure, just as the analysis of painting is concerned with pictorial structure. Since linguistics is the global science of verbal structure, poetics may be regarded as an integral part of linguistics.

Arguments against such a claim must be thoroughly discussed. It is evident that many devices studied by poetics are not confined to verbal art. We can refer to the possibility of transposing *Wuthering Heights* into a motion picture, medieval legends into frescoes and miniatures, or *L'après-midi d'un faune* into music, ballet, and graphic art. However ludicrous the idea of the

Iliad and *Odyssey* in comics may seem, certain structural features of their plot are preserved despite the disappearance of their verbal shape. The question of whether W. B. Yeats was right in affirming Blake was "the one perfectly fit illustrator for the *Inferno* and the *Purgatorio*" is a proof that different arts are comparable.[1] The problems of the baroque or any other historical style transgress the frame of a single art. When handling the surrealistic metaphor, we could hardly pass by Max Ernst's pictures or Luis Buñuel's films, *The Andalusian Dog* and *The*

[1]Jakobson is alluding to various adaptations of one art form to another. William Wyler's 1939 film of the novel *Wuthering Heights*, by Emily Brontë (1847), to Claude Debussy's tone poem, *Afternoon of a Faun* (1894), based on the poem of the same title (1876) by Stephane Mallarmé, 1950's Classics Illustrated comic book versions of Homer's *Iliad* and *Odyssey*, William Blake's 102 watercolor illustrations (1824–27) of Dante's *Divine Comedy*.

Golden Age.[2] In short, many poetic features belong not only to the science of language but to the whole theory of signs, that is, to general semiotics. This statement, however, is valid not only for verbal art but also for all varieties of language, since language shares many properties with certain other systems of signs or even with all of them (pan-semiotic features).

Likewise, a second objection contains nothing that would be specific for literature: the question of relations between the word and the world concerns not only verbal art but actually all kinds of discourse. Linguistics is likely to explore all possible problems of relation between discourse and the "universe of discourse": what of this universe is verbalized by a given discourse and how it is verbalized. The truth values, however, as far as they are — to say with the logicians — "extralinguistic entities," obviously exceed the bounds of poetics and of linguistics in general.

Sometimes we hear that poetics, in contradistinction to linguistics, is concerned with evaluation. This separation of the two fields from each other is based on a current but erroneous interpretation of the contrast between the structure of poetry and other types of verbal structure: the latter are said to be opposed by their "casual," designless nature to the "noncasual," purposeful character of poetic language. In point of fact, any verbal behavior is goal-directed, but the aims are different and the conformity of the means used to the effect aimed at is a problem that evermore preoccupies inquirers into the diverse kinds of verbal communication. There is a close correspondence, much closer than critics believe, between the question of linguistic phenomena expanding in space and time and the spatial and temporal spread of literary models. Even such discontinuous expansion as the resurrection of neglected or forgotten poets — for instance, the posthumous discovery and subsequent canonization of Emily Dickinson (d. 1886) and Gerard

Manley Hopkins (d. 1889), the tardy fame of Lautréamont (d. 1870) among surrealist poets, and the salient influence of the hitherto ignored Cyprian Norwid (d. 1883) on Polish modern poetry — finds a parallel in the history of standard languages that tend to revive outdated models, sometimes long forgotten, as was the case in literary Czech, which toward the beginning of the nineteenth century leaned toward sixteenth-century models.

Unfortunately, the terminological confusion of "literary studies" with "criticism" tempts the student of literature to replace the description of the intrinsic values of a literary work with a subjective, censorious verdict. The label "literary critic" applied to an investigator of literature is as erroneous as "grammatical (or lexical) critic" would be applied to a linguist. Syntactic and morphologic research cannot be supplanted by a normative grammar,[3] and likewise no manifesto, foisting a critic's own tastes and opinions on creative literature, can serve as a substitute for an objective scholarly analysis of verbal art. This statement should not be mistaken for the quietist principle of *laissez faire*; any verbal culture involves programmatic, planning, normative endeavors. Yet why is a clear-cut discrimination made between pure and applied linguistics or between phonetics and orthoëpy,[4] but not between literary studies and criticism?

Literary studies, with poetics as their focal point, consist like linguistics of two sets of problems: synchrony and diachrony. The synchronic description envisages not only the literary production of any given stage but also that part of the literary tradition which for the stage in question has remained vital or has been revived. Thus, for instance, Shakespeare, on the one hand, and Donne, Marvell, Keats, and Emily Dickinson, on the other, are experienced by the present English poetic world, whereas the works of James Thomson and Longfellow, for the time being, do not belong to viable artistic values. The selection

---

[2]Luis Buñuel's film collaborations with Salvador Dali, *Un Chien Andalou* (1929) and *L'Age d'or* (1930). The latter was the occasion of a riot by French fascists at the theater at which the film was shown; ink was thrown at the screen and surrealist paintings by Joan Miro, Yves Tanguy, Man Ray, and Dali himself were slashed.

[3]A normative grammar prescribes how language ought to be used, as opposed to a descriptive grammar, which relates how language is in fact used.
[4]Orthoëpy is the "correct" pronunciation of words, the phonological equivalent of normative grammar.

of classics and their reinterpretation by a novel trend is a substantial problem of synchronic literary studies. Synchronic poetics, like synchronic linguistics, is not to be confused with statics.[5] Any stage discriminates between more conservative and more innovative forms. Any contemporary stage is experienced in its temporal dynamics, and, on the other hand, the historical approach both in poetics and in linguistics is concerned not only with changes, but also with continuous, enduring, static factors. A thoroughly comprehensive historical poetics or history of language is a superstructure to be built on a series of successive synchronic descriptions.

Insistence on keeping poetics apart from linguistics is warranted only when the field of linguistics appears to be illicitly restricted, for example, when the sentence is viewed by some linguists as the highest analyzable construction, or when the scope of linguistics is confined to grammar alone or uniquely to nonsemantic questions of external form or to the inventory of denotative devices with no reference to free variations. Voegelin has clearly pointed out the two most important and related problems that face structural linguistics, namely, a revision of "the monolithic hypothesis about language" and a concern with "the interdependence of diverse structures within one language."[6] No doubt, for any speech community, for any speaker, there exists a unity of language, but this over-all code represents a system of interconnected subcodes; every language encompasses several concurrent patterns, each characterized by different functions.

Obviously we must agree with Sapir that, on the whole, "ideation reigns supreme in language,"[7] but this supremacy does not authorize linguistics to disregard the "secondary factors." The emotive elements of speech, which, as Joos is prone to believe, cannot be described "with a finite number of absolute categories," are classified by him "as nonlinguistic elements of the real world." Hence, "for us they remain vague,

protean, fluctuating phenomena," he concludes, "which we refuse to tolerate in our science."[8] Joos is indeed a brilliant expert in reduction experiments, and his emphatic demand for the "expulsion" of emotive elements "from linguistic science" is a radical experiment in reduction — *reductio ad absurdum.*

Language must be investigated in all the variety of its functions. Before discussing the poetic function we must define its place among the other functions of language. An outline of these functions demands a concise survey of the constitutive factors in any speech event, in any act of verbal communication. The ADDRESSER sends a MESSAGE to the ADDRESSEE. To be operative the message requires a CONTEXT referred to (the "referent" in another, somewhat ambiguous, nomenclature), graspable by the addressee, and either verbal or capable of being verbalized; a CODE fully, or at least partially, common to the addresser and addressee (or in other words, to the encoder and decoder of the message); and, finally, a CONTACT, a physical channel and psychological connection between the addresser and the addressee, enabling both of them to enter and stay in communication. All these factors inalienably involved in verbal communication may be schematized as follows:

$$\begin{array}{c}\text{CONTEXT}\\ \text{ADDRESSER} \qquad \text{MESSAGE} \qquad \text{ADDRESSEE}\\ \text{CONTACT}\\ \text{CODE}\end{array}$$

Each of these six factors determines a different function of language. Although we distinguish six basic aspects of language, we could, however, hardly find verbal messages that would fulfill only one function. The diversity lies not in a monopoly of some one of these several functions but in a different hierarchical order of functions. The verbal structure of a message depends primarily on the predominant function. But even though as set (*Einstellung*)[9] toward the referent, an orientation toward the CONTEXT — briefly, the so-called REFERENTIAL, "denotative," "cognitive"

---

[5] The study of what does not change.

[6] C. F. Voegelin, "Casual and Noncasual Utterances within Unified Structures," in *Style in Language,* ed. by T. A. Sebeok (Cambridge, Mass., 1960), p. 57.

[7] E. Sapir, *Language* (New York, 1921), p. 40.

[8] M. Joos, "Description of Language Design," *Journal of the Acoustical Society of America,* XXII (1950), pp. 701–708.

[9] Orientation.

function — is the leading task of numerous messages, the accessory participation of the other functions in such messages must be taken into account by the observant linguist.

The so-called EMOTIVE or "expressive" function, focused on the ADDRESSER, aims a direct expression of the speaker's attitude toward what he is speaking about. It tends to produce an impression of a certain emotion, whether true or feigned; therefore, the term "emotive," launched and advocated by Marty,[10] has proved to be preferable to "emotional." The purely emotive stratum in language is presented by the interjections. They differ from the means of referential language both by their sound pattern (peculiar sound sequences or even sounds elsewhere unusual) and by their syntactic role (they are not components but equivalents of sentences). *"Tut! Tut!* said McGinty:"* the complete utterance of Conan Doyle's character consists of two suction clicks.[11] The emotive function, laid bare in the interjections, flavors to some extent all our utterances, on their phonic, grammatical, and lexical level. If we analyze language from the standpoint of the information it carries, we cannot restrict the notion of information to the cognitive aspect of language. A man, using expressive features to indicate his angry or ironic attitude, conveys ostensible information, and evidently this verbal behavior cannot be likened to such nonsemiotic, nutritive activities as "eating grapefruit" (despite Chatman's bold simile). The difference between [bɪg] and the emphatic prolongation of the vowel [bɪ:g] is a conventional, coded linguistic feature like the difference between the short and long vowel in such Czech pairs as [vi] "you" and [vi:] "knows," but in the latter pair the differential information is phonemic and in the former emotive. As long as we are interested in phonemic invariants, the English /i/ and /i:/ appear to be mere variants of one and the same phoneme, but if we are concerned with emotive units, the relation between the invariants and variants is reversed: length and shortness are invariants implemented by variable phonemes. Saporta's surmise that emotive difference is a nonlinguistic feature, "attributable to the delivery of the message and not to the message,"[12] arbitrarily reduces the informational capacity of messages.

A former actor of Stanislavskij's Moscow Theater[13] told me how at his audition he was asked by the famous director to make forty different messages from the phrase *Segodnja večerom* "This evening," by diversifying its expressive tint. He made a list of some forty emotional situations, then emitted the given phrase in accordance with each of these situations, which his audience had to recognize only from the changes in the sound shape of the same two words. For our research work in the description and analysis of contemporary Standard Russian (under the auspices of the Rockefeller Foundation) this actor was asked to repeat Stanislavskij's test. He wrote down some fifty situations framing the same elliptic sentence and made of it fifty corresponding messages for a tape recording. Most of the messages were correctly and circumstantially decoded by Moscovite listeners. May I add that all such emotive cues easily undergo linguistic analysis.

Orientation toward the ADDRESSEE, the CONATIVE function, finds its purest grammatical expression in the vocative and imperative, which syntactically, morphologically, and often even phonemically deviate from other nominal and verbal categories. The imperative sentences cardinally differ from declarative sentences: the latter are and the former are not liable to a truth test. When in O'Neill's play *The Fountain*, Nano, "(in a fierce tone of command)," says "Drink!" — the imperative cannot be challenged by the question "is it true or not?" which may be, however, perfectly well asked after such sentences as "one drank," "one will drink," "one would drink." In contradistinction to the imperative sentences, the declarative sentences are convertible into interrogative sentences: "did one drink?" "will one drink?" "would one drink?"

[10]A. Marty, *Untersuchungen zur Grundlegung der allgemeinen Grammatik und Sprachphilosophie*, Vol. I (Halle, 1908).

[11]A sound denoting disapproval, alternately spelled "tsk, tsk." McGinty appears in Doyle's novella *The Valley of Fear* (1915).

[12]S. Saporta, "The Application of Linguistics to the Study of Poetic Language," in *Style in Language*, p. 88.

[13]The Moscow Art Theater was the birthplace of "method acting."

The traditional model of language as elucidated particularly by Bühler[14] was confined to these three functions — emotive, conative, and referential — and the three apexes of this model — the first person of the addresser, the second person of the addressee, and the "third person," properly — someone or something spoken of. Certain additional verbal functions can be easily inferred from this triadic model. Thus the magic, incantatory function is chiefly some kind of conversion of an absent or inanimate "third person" into an addressee of a conative message. "May this sty dry up, *tfu, tfu, tfu, tfu*" (Lithuanian spell[15]). "Water, queen river, daybreak! Send grief beyond the blue sea, to the sea-bottom, like a grey stone never to rise from the sea-bottom, may grief never come to burden the light heart of God's servant, may grief be removed and sink away." (North Russian incantation.[16]) "Sun, stand thou still upon Gibeon; and thou, Moon, in the valley of Aj-a-lon. And the sun stood still, and the moon stayed" (Josh. 10.12). We observe, however, three further constitutive factors of verbal communication and three corresponding functions of language.

There are messages primarily serving to establish, to prolong, or to discontinue communication, to check whether the channel works ("Hello, do you hear me?"), to attract the attention of the interlocutor or to confirm his continued attention ("Are you listening?" or in Shakespearean diction, "Lend me your ears!" — and on the other end of the wire "Umhum!"). This set for CONTACT, or in Malinowski's terms PHATIC function,[17] may be displayed by a profuse exchange of ritualized formulas, by entire dialogues with the mere purport of prolonging communication. Dorothy Parker caught eloquent examples: "'Well!' the young man said. 'Well!' she said. 'Well, here we are,' he said. 'Here we are,' she said, 'Aren't we?' 'I should say we were,' he said, 'Eeyop! Here we are.' 'Well!' she said. 'Well!' he said,

'well.'"[18] The endeavor to start and sustain communication is typical of talking birds; thus the phatic function of language is the only one they share with human beings. It is also the first verbal function acquired by infants; they are prone to communicate before being able to send or receive informative communication.

A distinction has been made in modern logic between two levels of language, "object language" speaking of objects and "metalanguage" speaking of language.[19] But metalanguage is not only a necessary scientific tool utilized by logicians and linguists; it plays also an important role in our everyday language. Like Molière's Jourdain who used prose without knowing it,[20] we practice metalanguage without realizing the metalingual character of our operations. Whenever the addresser and/or the addressee need to check up whether they use the same code, speech is focused on the CODE: it performs a METALINGUAL (i.e., glossing) function. "I don't follow you — what do you mean?" asks the addressee, or in Shakespearean diction, "What is't thou say'st?" And the addresser in anticipation of such recapturing question inquires: "Do you know what I mean?" Imagine such an exasperating dialogue: "The sophomore was plucked." "But what is *plucked*?" "*Plucked* means the same as *flunked*." "And *flunked*?" "*To be flunked* is *to fail an exam*." "And what is *sophomore*?" persists the interrogator innocent of school vocabulary. "A *sophomore* is (or means) a *second-year student*." All these equational sentences convey information merely about the lexical code of English; their function is strictly metalingual. Any process of language learning, in particular child acquisition of the mother tongue, makes wide use of such metalingual operations; and aphasia may often be defined as a loss of ability for metalingual operations.

---

[14]K. Bühler, "Die Axiomatik der Sprachwissenschaft," *Kant-Studien*, XXXVIII (Berlin, 1933), pp. 19–90.

[15]V. J. Mansikka, *Litauische Zaubersprüche = Folklore Fellows Communications*, no. 87 (1929), p. 69.

[16]P. N. Rybnikov, *Pesni*, Vol. 3 (Moscow, 1910), p. 217f.

[17]B. Malinowski, "The Problem of Meaning in Primitive Languages," in C. K. Ogden and I. A. Richards, *The Meaning of Meaning* (New York and London, 1953⁹), pp. 296–336.

[18]From "Here We Are" (1931), a short story by Dorothy Parker (1893–1967).

[19]Term introduced by A. Tarski, *Pojęcie prawdy w językach nauk dedukcyjnych* (Warsaw, 1933) and "Der Wahrheitsbegriff in den formalisierten Sprachen," *Studia Philosophica*, I (1936).

[20]In *Le Bourgeois gentilhomme* (1670), a comedy-ballet by Molière, the wealthy but uneducated M. Jourdain is thrilled to learn from his tutor, the Philosopher, that he has been "speaking prose all my life without knowing it."

We have brought up all the six factors involved in verbal communication except the message itself. The set (*Einstellung*) toward the MESSAGE as such, focus on the message for its own sake, is the POETIC function of language. This function cannot be productively studied out of touch with the general problems of language, and, on the other hand, the scrutiny of language requires a thorough consideration of its poetic function. Any attempt to reduce the sphere of the poetic function to poetry or to confine poetry to the poetic function would be a delusive oversimplification. The poetic function is not the sole function of verbal art but only its dominant, determining function, whereas in all other verbal activities it acts as a subsidiary, accessory constituent. This function, by promoting the palpability of signs, deepens the fundamental dichotomy of signs and objects. Hence, when dealing with the poetic function, linguistics cannot limit itself to the field of poetry.

"Why do you always say *Joan and Margery*, yet never *Margery and Joan*? Do you prefer Joan to her twin sister?" "Not at all, it just sounds smoother." In a sequence of two coordinate names, as far as no problems of rank interfere, the precedence of the shorter name suits the speaker, unaccountably for him, as a well-ordered shape for the message.

A girl used to talk about "the horrible Harry." "Why horrible?" "Because I hate him." "But why not *dreadful, terrible, frightful, disgusting*?" "I don't know why, but *horrible* fits him better." Without realizing it, she clung to the poetic device of paronomasia.

The political slogan "I like Ike" /ay layk ayk/, succinctly structured, consists of three monosyllables and counts three diphthongs /ay/, each of them symmetrically followed by one consonantal phoneme, / . . l . . k . . k/. The makeup of the three words presents a variation: no consonantal phonemes in the first word, two around the diphthong in the second, and one final consonant in the third. A similar dominant nucleus /ay/ was noticed by Hymes in some of the sonnets of Keats.[21] Both cola[22] of the trisyllabic formula "I

---

[21]D. Hymes, "Phonological Aspects of Style: Some English Sonnets," in *Style in Language*, pp. 123–126.
[22]Parts of a sentence.

like / Ike" rhyme with each other, and the second of the two rhyming words is fully included in the first one (echo rhyme), /layk/ — /ayk/, a paronomastic[23] image of a feeling which totally envelops its object. Both cola alliterate with each other, and the first of the two alliterating words is included in the second: /ay/ —/ayk/, a paronomastic image of the loving subject enveloped by the beloved object. The secondary, poetic function of this campaign slogan reinforces its impressiveness and efficacy.

As we said, the linguistic study of the poetic function must overstep the limits of poetry, and, on the other hand, the linguistic scrutiny of poetry cannot limit itself to the poetic function. The particularities of diverse poetic genres imply a differently ranked participation of the other verbal functions along with the dominant poetic function. Epic poetry, focused on the third person, strongly involves the referential function of language; the lyric, oriented toward the first person, is intimately linked with the emotive function; poetry of the second person is imbued with the conative function and is either supplicatory or exhortative, depending on whether the first person is subordinated to the second one or the second to the first.

Now that our cursory description of the six basic functions of verbal communication is more or less complete, we may complement our scheme of the fundamental factors with a corresponding scheme of the functions:

REFERENTIAL

EMOTIVE   POETIC   CONATIVE
PHATIC

METALINGUAL

What is the empirical linguistic criterion of the poetic function? In particular, what is the indispensable feature inherent in any piece of poetry? To answer this question we must recall the two basic modes of arrangement used in verbal behavior, *selection* and *combination*. If "child" is the topic of the message, the speaker

---

[23]Paronomasia is playing on the sounds of words.

selects one among the extant, more or less similar, nouns like child, kid, youngster, tot, all of them equivalent in a certain respect, and then, to comment on this topic, he may select one of the semantically cognate verbs — sleeps, dozes, nods, naps. Both chosen words combine in the speech chain. The selection is produced on the basis of equivalence, similarity and dissimilarity, synonymy and antonymy, while the combination, the build-up of the sequence, is based on contiguity. *The poetic function projects the principle of equivalence from the axis of selection into the axis of combination.* Equivalence is promoted to the constitutive device of the sequence. In poetry one syllable is equalized with any other syllable of the same sequence; word stress is assumed to equal word stress, as unstress equals unstress; prosodic long is matched with long, and short with short; word boundary equals word boundary, no boundary equals no boundary; syntactic pause equals syntactic pause, no pause equals no pause. Syllables are converted into units of measure, and so are morae[24] or stresses.

It may be objected that metalanguage also makes a sequential use of equivalent units when combining synonymic expressions into an equational sentence: $A = A$ ("*Mare is the female of the horse*"). Poetry and metalanguage, however, are in diametrical opposition to each other: in metalanguage the sequence is used to build an equation, whereas in poetry the equation is used to build a sequence.

In poetry, and to a certain extent in latent manifestations of the poetic function, sequences delimited by word boundaries become commensurable whether they are sensed as isochronic or graded. "Joan and Margery" showed us the poetic principle of syllable gradation,[25] the same

principle that in the closes of Serbian folk epics has been raised to a compulsory law.[26] Without its two dactylic words the combination "*innocent by stander*" would hardly have become a hackneyed phrase. The symmetry of three disyllabic verbs with an identical initial consonant and identical final vowel added splendor to the laconic victory message of Caesar: "*Veni, vidi, vici.*"[27]

Measure of sequences is a device that, outside of the poetic function, finds no application in language. Only in poetry with its regular reiteration of equivalent units is the time of the speech flow experienced, as it is — to cite another semiotic pattern — with musical time. Gerard Manley Hopkins, an outstanding searcher in the science of poetic language, defined verse as "speech wholly or partially repeating the same figure of sound."[28] Hopkins's subsequent question, "but is all verse poetry?" can be definitely answered as soon as the poetic function ceases to be arbitrarily confined to the domain of poetry. Mnemonic lines cited by Hopkins (like "Thirty days hath September"), modern advertising jingles, and versified medieval laws, mentioned by Lotz,[29] or finally Sanskrit scientific treatises in verse which in Indic tradition are strictly distinguished from true poetry (*kāvya*) — all these metrical texts make use of the poetic function without, however, assigning to this function the coercing, determining role it carries in poetry. Thus verse actually exceeds the limits of poetry, but at the same time verse always implies the poetic function. And apparently no human culture ignores versemaking, whereas there are many cultural patterns without "applied" verse; and even in such cultures as possess both pure and applied verses, the latter appear to be a secondary, unquestionably derived

---

[24]Units of pronunciation that determine whether a syllable is long or short (in Latin and Greek poetry) or where the stress falls in some languages (e.g., Japanese).

[25]Jakobson's point is that we find it pleasant when the stresses on words come equidistant in time (isochrony), unpleasant when they come too close together or too far apart. Thus "**Joan** and **Mar**-ge-ry," is found pleasant because the two stresses are separated by one syllable, "**Mar**-ge-ry and **Joan**" less pleasant because three unstressed syllables intervene. A poem by I. A. Richards is titled "**Har**vard **Yard** in **Ap**ril, **Ap**ril in **Har**vard **Yard**," which sounds pleasant because the chiasmus turns on the disyllable "April." If we reverse the two cola

("April in **Har**vard **Yard**, **Har**vard **Yard** in **Ap**ril"), the effect is unpleasant, partly because the stresses on **Yard** and **Har** clash as they meet. (The monotony of four stressed broad *a*'s in a row also contributes to the unpleasantness.)

[26]T. Maretić *Metrika narodnih naših pjesama* (Zagreb, 1907), § 81–83.

[27]"I came, I saw, I conquered." According to Suetonius's *Lives of the Twelve Caesars*, this was Julius Caesar's laconic report to Rome after defeating Pharnaces at the Battle of Zela (47 B.C.E.).

[28]G. M. Hopkins, *The Journals and Papers*, ed. by H. House (London, 1959), p. 289.

[29]J. Lotz, "Metric Typology," in *Style in Language*, p. 137.

phenomenon. The adaptation of poetic means for some heterogeneous purpose does not conceal their primary essence, just as elements of emotive language, when utilized in poetry, still maintain their emotive tinge. A filibusterer may recite *Hiawatha* because it is long, yet poeticalness still remains the primary intent of this text itself. Self-evidently, the existence of versified, musical, and pictorial commercials does not separate the questions of verse or of musical and pictorial form from the study of poetry, music, and fine arts.

To sum up, the analysis of verse is entirely within the competence of poetics, and the latter may be defined as that part of linguistics which treats the poetic function in its relationship to the other functions of language. Poetics in the wider sense of the word deals with the poetic function not only in poetry, where this function is superimposed upon the other functions of language, but also outside of poetry, when some other function is superimposed upon the poetic function.

Claude Lévi-Strauss

b. 1908

Claude Lévi-Strauss, one of the major figures of social anthropology and of twentieth-century intellectual life generally, was born in Brussels and took degrees in philosophy and law at the University of Paris (1927–32). From 1934 to 1937, Lévi-Strauss served as a professor of sociology at the University of São Paulo in Brazil; his research among the Brazilian Indians informs the heart of his intellectual autobiography, Tristes tropiques *(1955). From 1941 to 1945 he was a visiting professor at the New School for Social Research in New York, where he came in contact with the ideas of Roman Jakobson. Made director of studies at the École Practique des Haute Études of the University of Paris in 1950, he was appointed in 1959 to the chair of social anthropology at the Collège de France. Lévi-Strauss's works include* The Elementary Structures of Kinship *(1949),* Structural Anthropology *(1958).* The Savage Mind *(1962), and the four volumes of* Mythologiques *(1964–71). "The Structural Study of Myth" first appeared in* Journal of American Folklore *78 (1955); this version is from the 1963 translation of* Structural Anthropology. *His latest books are* The Jealous Potter *(1988),* Regarder écouter lire *(1993),* Saudades do Brasil *(1995), and* The Story of Lynx *(1995).*

The Structural Study of Myth

It would seem that mythological worlds have been built up only to be shattered again, and that new worlds were built from the fragments.

— FRANZ BOAS[1]

Despite some recent attempts to renew them, it seems that during the past twenty years anthropology has increasingly turned from studies in the field of religion. At the same time, and precisely because the interest of professional anthropologists has withdrawn from primitive religion, all kinds of amateurs who claim to belong to other disciplines have seized this opportunity to move in, thereby turning into their private playground what we had left as a wasteland. The prospects for the scientific study of religion have thus been undermined in two ways.

The explanation for this situation lies to some extent in the fact that the anthropological study of religion was started by men like Tylor, Frazer, and Durkheim, who were psychologically oriented although not in a position to keep up with the progress of psychological research and theory. Their interpretations, therefore, soon became vitiated by the outmoded psychological approach which they used as their basis. Although they were undoubtedly right in giving their attention to intellectual processes, the way they handled these remained so crude that it discredited them altogether. This is much to be regretted, since, as Hocart so profoundly noted in his introduction to a posthumous book recently published,[2] psychological interpretations were withdrawn from the intellectual field only to be introduced again in the field of affectivity, thus adding to "the inherent defects of the psychological school . . . the mistake of deriving clear-cut ideas . . . from

vague emotions." Instead of trying to enlarge the framework of our logic to include processes which, whatever their apparent differences, belong to the same kind of intellectual operation, a naïve attempt was made to reduce them to inarticulate emotional drives, which resulted only in hampering our studies.

Of all the chapters of religious anthropology probably none has tarried to the same extent as studies in the field of mythology. From a theoretical point of view the situation remains very much the same as it was fifty years ago, namely, chaotic. Myths are still widely interpreted in conflicting ways: as collective dreams, as the outcome of a kind of esthetic play, or as the basis of ritual. Mythological figures are considered as personified abstractions, divinized heroes, or fallen gods. Whatever the hypothesis, the choice amounts to reducing mythology either to idle play or to a crude kind of philosophic speculation.

In order to understand what a myth really is, must we choose between platitude and sophism? Some claim that human societies merely express, through their mythology, fundamental feelings common to the whole of mankind, such as love, hate, or revenge or that they try to provide some kind of explanations for phenomena which they cannot otherwise understand — astronomical, meteorological, and the like. But why should these societies do it in such elaborate and devious ways, when all of them are also acquainted with empirical explanations? On the other hand, psychoanalysts and many anthropologists have shifted the problems away from the natural or cosmological toward the sociological and psychological fields. But then the interpretation becomes too easy: If a given mythology confers prominence on a certain figure, let us say an evil grandmother, it will be claimed that in such a society grandmothers are actually evil and that mythology reflects the social structure and the social relations; but should the actual data be conflicting, it would be as readily claimed that the purpose of mythology is to provide an outlet for repressed feelings. Whatever the situation, a

Translated by Claire Jacobson and Brooke Grundfest Schoepf.

[1]In Boas's Introduction to James Teit, "Traditions of the Thompson River Indians of British Columbia," *Memoirs of the American Folklore Society,* VI (1898), p. 18. [Lévi-Strauss]

[2]A. M. Hocart, *Social Origins* (London: 1954), p. 7. [Lévi-Strauss]

clever dialectic will always find a way to pretend that a meaning has been found.

Mythology confronts the student with a situation which at first sight appears contradictory. On the one hand it would seem that in the course of a myth anything is likely to happen. There is no logic, no continuity. Any characteristic can be attributed to any subject; every conceivable relation can be found. With myth, everything becomes possible. But on the other hand, this apparent arbitrariness is belied by the astounding similarity between myths collected in widely different regions. Therefore the problem: If the content of a myth is contingent, how are we going to explain the fact that myths throughout the world are so similar?

It is precisely this awareness of a basic antinomy pertaining to the nature of myth that may lead us toward its solution. For the contradiction which we face is very similar to that which in earlier times brought considerable worry to the first philosophers concerned with linguistic problems; linguistics could only begin to evolve as a science after this contradiction had been overcome. Ancient philosophers reasoned about language the way we do about mythology. On the one hand, they did notice that in a given language certain sequences of sounds were associated with definite meanings, and they earnestly aimed at discovering a reason for the linkage between those *sounds* and that *meaning*. Their attempt, however, was thwarted from the very beginning by the fact that the same sounds were equally present in other languages although the meaning they conveyed was entirely different. The contradiction was surmounted only by the discovery that it is the combination of sounds, not the sounds themselves, which provides the significant data.

It is easy to see, moreover, that some of the more recent interpretations of mythological thought originated from the same kind of misconception under which those early linguists were laboring. Let us consider, for instance, Jung's idea that a given mythological pattern — the so-called archetype — possesses a certain meaning. This is comparable to the long-supported error that a sound may possess a certain affinity with a meaning: for instance, the "liquid" semivowels with

water, the open vowels with things that are big, large, loud, or heavy, etc., a theory which still has its supporters.[3] Whatever emendations the original formulation may now call for,[4] everybody will agree that the Saussurean principle of the *arbitrary character of linguistic signs* was a prerequisite for the accession of linguistics to the scientific level.

To invite the mythologist to compare his precarious situation with that of the linguist in the prescientific stage is not enough. As a matter of fact we may thus be led only from one difficulty to another. There is a very good reason why myth cannot simply be treated as language if its specific problems are to be solved; myth *is* language: to be known, myth has to be told; it is a part of human speech. In order to preserve its specificity we must be able to show that it is both the same thing as language, and also something different from it. Here, too, the past experience of linguists may help us. For language itself can be analyzed into things which are at the same time similar and yet different. This is precisely what is expressed in Saussure's distinction between *langue* and *parole,* one being the structural side of language, the other the statistical aspect of it, *langue* belonging to a reversible time, *parole* being nonreversible. If those two levels already exist in language, then a third one can conceivably be isolated.

We have distinguished *langue* and *parole* by the different time referents which they use. Keeping this in mind, we may notice that myth uses a third referent which combines the properties of the first two. On the one hand, a myth always refers to events alleged to have taken place long ago. But what gives the myth an operational value is that the specific pattern described is timeless; it explains the present and the past as well as the future. This can be made clear through a comparison between myth and what appears to have largely replaced it in modern societies, namely, politics.

[3]See, for instance, Sir R. A. Paget, "The Origin of Language," *Journal of World History,* I, No. 2 (UNESCO, 1953). [Lévi-Strauss]
[4]See Émile Benveniste, "Nature du signe linguistique," *Acta Linguistica,* I, No. 1 (1939); and Chapter V in *Structural Anthropology.* [Lévi-Strauss]

When the historian refers to the French Revolution, it is always as a sequence of past happenings, a nonreversible series of events the remote consequences of which may still be felt at present. But to the French politician, as well as to his followers, the French Revolution is both a sequence belonging to the past — as to the historian — and a timeless pattern which can be detected in the contemporary French social structure and which provides a clue for its interpretation, a lead from which to infer future developments. Michelet, for instance, was a politically minded historian. He describes the French Revolution thus: "That day . . . everything was possible. . . . Future became present . . . that is, no more time, a glimpse of eternity."[5] It is that double structure, altogether historical and ahistorical, which explains how myth, while pertaining to the realm of *parole* and calling for an explanation as such, as well as to that of *langue* in which it is expressed, can also be an absolute entity on a third level which, though it remains linguistic by nature, is nevertheless distinct from the other two.

A remark can be introduced at this point which will help to show the originality of myth in relation to other linguistic phenomena. Myth is the part of language where the formula *traduttore, traditore*[6] reaches its lowest truth value. From that point of view it should be placed in the gamut of linguistic expressions at the end opposite to that of poetry, in spite of all the claims which have been made to prove the contrary. Poetry is a kind of speech which cannot be translated except at the cost of serious distortions; whereas the mythical value of the myth is preserved even through the worst translation. Whatever our ignorance of the language and the culture of the people where it originated, a myth is still felt as a myth by any reader anywhere in the world. Its substance does not lie in its style, its original music, or its syntax, but in the *story* which it tells. Myth is language, functioning on an especially high level where meaning succeeds practically at

"taking off" from the linguistic ground on which it keeps on rolling.

To sum up the discussion at this point, we have so far made the following claims: (1) If there is a meaning to be found in mythology, it cannot reside in the isolated elements which enter into the composition of a myth, but only in the way those elements are combined. (2) Although myth belongs to the same category as language, being, as a matter of fact, only part of it, language in myth exhibits specific properties. (3) Those properties are only to be found *above* the ordinary linguistic level, that is, they exhibit more complex features than those which are to be found in any other kind of linguistic expression.

If the above three points are granted, at least as a working hypothesis, two consequences will follow: (1) Myth, like the rest of language, is made up of constituent units. (2) These constituent units presuppose the constituent units present in language when analyzed on other levels — namely, phonemes, morphemes, and sememes — but they, nevertheless, differ from the latter in the same way as the latter differ among themselves; they belong to a higher and more complex order. For this reason, we shall call them *gross constituent units*.

How shall we proceed in order to identify and isolate these gross constituent units or mythemes? We know that they cannot be found among phonemes, morphemes, or sememes, but only on a higher level; otherwise myth would become confused with any other kind of speech. Therefore, we should look for them on the sentence level. The only method we can suggest at this stage is to proceed tentatively, by trial and error, using as a check the principles which serve as a basis for any kind of structural analysis: economy of explanation; unity of solution; and ability to reconstruct the whole from a fragment, as well as later stages from previous ones.

The technique which has been applied so far by this writer consists in analyzing each myth individually, breaking down its story into the shortest possible sentences, and writing each sentence on an index card bearing a number corresponding to the unfolding of the story.

Practically each card will thus show that a certain function is, at a given time, linked to a given

---

[5]Jules Michelet, *Histoire de la Révolution française*, IV, 1. I took this quotation from M. Merleau-Ponty, *Les Aventures de la dialectique* (Paris: 1955), p. 273. [Lévi-Strauss]

[6]To translate is to betray.

subject. Or, to put it otherwise, each gross constituent unit will consist of a *relation*.

However, the above definition remains highly unsatisfactory for two different reasons. First, it is well known to structural linguists that constituent units on all levels are made up of relations, and the true difference between our *gross* units and the others remains unexplained; second, we still find ourselves in the realm of a nonreversible time, since the numbers of the cards correspond to the unfolding of the narrative. Thus the specific character of mythological time, which as we have seen is both reversible and nonreversible, synchronic and diachronic, remains unaccounted for. From this springs a new hypothesis, which constitutes the very core of our argument: The true constituent units of a myth are not the isolated relations but *bundles of such relations,* and it is only as bundles that these relations can be put to use and combined so as to produce a meaning. Relations pertaining to the same bundle may appear diachronically at remote intervals, but when we have succeeded in grouping them together we have reorganized our myth according to a time referent of a new nature, corresponding to the prerequisite of the initial hypothesis, namely a two-dimensional time referent which is simultaneously diachronic and synchronic, and which accordingly integrates the characteristics of *langue* on the one hand, and those of *parole* on the other. To put it in even more linguistic terms, it is as though a phoneme were always made up of all its variants.

Two comparisons may help to explain what we have in mind.

Let us first suppose that archaeologists of the future coming from another planet would one day, when all human life had disappeared from the earth, excavate one of our libraries. Even if they were at first ignorant of our writing, they might succeed in deciphering it — an undertaking which would require, at some early stage, the discovery that the alphabet, as we are in the habit of printing it, should be read from left to right and from top to bottom. However, they would soon discover that a whole category of books did not fit the usual pattern — these would be the orchestra scores on the shelves of the music division. But after trying, without success, to decipher staffs one after the

other, from the upper down to the lower, they would probably notice that the same patterns of notes recurred at intervals, either in full or in part, or that some patterns were strongly reminiscent of earlier ones. Hence the hypothesis: What if patterns showing affinity, instead of being considered in succession, were to be treated as one complex pattern and read as a whole? By getting at what we call *harmony,* they would then see that an orchestra score, to be meaningful, must be read diachronically along one axis — that is, page after page, and from left to right — and synchronically along the other axis, all the notes written vertically making up one gross constituent unit, that is, one bundle of relations.

The other comparison is somewhat different. Let us take an observer ignorant of our playing cards, sitting for a long time with a fortune-teller. He would know something of the visitors: sex, age, physical appearance, social situation, etc., in the same way as we know something of the different cultures whose myths we try to study. He would also listen to the séances and record them so as to be able to go over them and make comparisons — as we do when we listen to myth-telling and record it. Mathematicians to whom I have put the problem agree that if the man is bright and if the material available to him is sufficient, he may be able to reconstruct the nature of the deck of cards being used, that is, fifty-two or thirty-two cards according to the case, made up of four homologous sets consisting of the same units (the individual cards) with only one varying feature, the suit.

Now for a concrete example of the method we propose. We shall use the Oedipus myth, which is well known to everyone. I am well aware that the Oedipus myth has only reached us under late forms and through literary transmutations concerned more with esthetic and moral preoccupations than with religious or ritual ones, whatever these may have been. But we shall not interpret the Oedipus myth in literal terms, much less offer an explanation acceptable to the specialist. We simply wish to illustrate — and without reaching any conclusions with respect to it — a certain technique, whose use is probably not legitimate in this particular instance, owing to the problematic elements indicated above. The "demonstration" should therefore be conceived, not in terms of what the scientist means by this term, but at best in terms of what is meant by the street peddler, whose aim is not to achieve a concrete result, but to explain, as succinctly as possible, the functioning of the mechanical toy which he is trying to sell to the onlookers.

The myth will be treated as an orchestra score would be if it were unwittingly considered as a unilinear series; our task is to re-establish the correct arrangement. Say, for instance, we were confronted with a sequence of the type: 1,2,4,7,8,2,3,4,6,8,1,4,5,7,8,1,2,5,7,3,4,5,6,8 . . . , the assignment being to put all the 1's together, all the 2's, the 3's, etc.; the result is a chart:

1	2		4			7	8
	2	3	4		6		8
1			4	5		7	8
1	2			5		7	
		3	4	5	6		8

Table 1

Cadmos seeks his sister Europa, ravished by Zeus			
	Cadmos kills the dragon		
		The Spartoi kill one another	
			Labdacos (Laios' father) = *lame (?)*
		Oedipus kills his father, Laios	Laios (Oedipus' father) = *left-sided (?)*
	Oedipus kills the Sphinx		
			Oedipus = *swollen-foot (?)*
Oedipus marries his mother, Jocasta			
		Eteocles kills his brother, Polynices	
Antigone buries her brother, Polynices, despite prohibition			

We shall attempt to perform the same kind of operation on the Oedipus myth, trying out several arrangements of the mythemes until we find one which is in harmony with the principles enumerated above. Let us suppose, for the sake of argument, that the best arrangement is as shown in Table 1 (although it might certainly be improved with the help of a specialist in Greek mythology).

We thus find ourselves confronted with four vertical columns, each of which includes several relations belonging to the same bundle. Were we to *tell* the myth, we would disregard the columns and read the rows from left to right and from top to bottom. But if we want to *understand* the myth, then we will have to disregard one half of the diachronic dimension (top to bottom) and read from left to right, column after column, each one being considered as a unit.

All the relations belonging to the same column exhibit one common feature which is our task to discover. For instance, all the events grouped in the first column on the left have something to do with blood relations which are overemphasized, that is, are more intimate than they should be. Let us say, then, that the first column has as its common feature the *overrating of blood relations*. It is obvious that the second column expresses the same thing, but inverted: *underrating of blood relations*. The third column refers to monsters being slain. As to the fourth, a few words of clarification are needed. The remarkable connotation of the surnames in Oedipus' father-line has often been noticed. However, linguists usually disregard it, since to them the only way to define the meaning of a term is to investigate all the contexts in which it appears, and personal names, precisely because they are used as such, are not accompanied by any context. With the method we propose to follow the objection disappears, since the myth itself provides its own context. The significance is no longer to be sought in the eventual meaning of each name, but in the fact that all the names have a common feature: All the hypothetical meanings (which may well remain hypothetical) refer to *difficulties in walking straight and standing upright*.

What then is the relationship between the two columns on the right? Column three refers to monsters. The dragon is a chthonian[7] being which has to be killed in order that mankind be born from the Earth; the Sphinx is a monster unwilling to permit men to live. The last unit reproduces the first one, which has to do with the *autochthonous*[8] *origin* of mankind. Since the monsters are overcome by men, we may thus say that the common feature of the third column is *denial of the autochthonous origin of man.*[9]

This immediately helps us to understand the meaning of the fourth column. In mythology it is a universal characteristic of men born from the Earth that at the moment they emerge from the depth they either cannot walk or they walk clumsily. This is the case of the chthonian beings in the mythology of the Pueblo: Muyingwu, who leads the emergence, and the chthonian Shumaikoli are lame ("bleeding-foot," "sore-foot"). The same happens to the Koskimo of the Kwakiutl after they have been swallowed by the chthonian monster, Tsiakish: When they returned to the surface of the earth "they limped forward or tripped sideways." Thus the common feature of the fourth column is *the persistence of the autochthonous origin of man*. It follows that column four is to column three as column one is to column two. The inability to connect two kinds of relationships

---

[7] Living within or under the earth.

[8] Born or sprung from the earth. Lévi-Strauss uses the term in a sense in opposition to "born from the sexual union of man and woman."

[9] We are not trying to become involved with specialists in an argument; this would be presumptuous and even meaningless on our part. Since the Oedipus myth is taken here merely as an example treated in arbitrary fashion, the chthonian nature ascribed to the Sphinx might seem surprising; we shall refer to the testimony of Marie Delcourt: "In the archaic legends, [she is] certainly born of the Earth itself" (*Oedipe ou la légende du conquérant* [*Liège:* 1944], p. 108). No matter how remote from Delcourt's our method may be (and our conclusions would be,

no doubt, if we were competent to deal with the problem in depth), it sees to us that she has convincingly established the nature of the Sphinx in the archaic tradition, namely, that of a female monster who attacks and rapes young men; in other words, the personification of a female being with an inversion of the sign. This explains why, in the handsome iconography compiled by Delcourt at the end of her work, men and women are always found in an inverted "sky/earth" relationship.

As we shall point out below, we selected the Oedipus myth as our first example because of the striking analogies that seem to exist between certain aspects of archaic Greek thought and that of the Pueblo Indians, from whom we have borrowed the examples that follow. In this respect it should be noted that the figure of the Sphinx, as reconstructed by Delcourt, coincides with two figures of North American mythology (who probably merge into one). We are referring, on the one hand, to "the old hag," a repulsive witch whose physical appearance presents a "problem" to the young hero. If he "solves" this problem — that is, if he responds to the advances of the abject creature — he will find in his bed, upon awakening, a beautiful young woman who will confer power upon him (this is also a Celtic theme). The Sphinx, on the other hand, recalls even more "the child-protruding woman" of the Hopi Indians, that is, a phallic mother par excellence. This young woman was abandoned by her group in the course of a difficult migration, just as she was about to give birth. Henceforth she wanders in the desert as the "Mother of Animals," which she withholds from hunters. He who meets her in her bloody clothes "is so frightened that he has an erection," of which she takes advantage to rape him, after which she rewards him with unfailing success in hunting. See H. R. Voth, "The Oraibi Summer Snake Ceremony," *Field Columbian Museum,* Publication No. 83, Anthropological Series, Vol. III, No. 4 (Chicago: 1903), pp. 352–53 and p. 353, n 1. [Lévi-Strauss] is overcome (or rather replaced) by the assertion that contradictory relationships are identical inasmuch as they are both self-contradictory in a similar way. Although this is still a provisional formulation of the structure of mythical thought, it is sufficient at this stage.

Turning back to the Oedipus myth, we may now see what it means. The myth has to do with the inability, for a culture which holds the belief that mankind is autochthonous (see, for instance, Pausanias, VIII, xxix, 4: plants provide a *model* for humans), to find a satisfactory transition between this theory and the knowledge that human beings are actually born from the union of man and woman. Although the problem obviously cannot be solved, the Oedipus myth provides a kind of logical tool which relates the original problem — born from one or born from two? — to the derivative problem: born from different or born from same? By a correlation of this type, the overrating of blood relations is to the underrating of blood relations as the attempt to escape autochthony is to the impossibility to succeed in it. Although experience contradicts theory, social life validates cosmology by its similarity of structure. Hence cosmology is true.

Two remarks should be made at this stage.

In order to interpret the myth, we left aside a point which has worried the specialists until now, namely, that in the earlier (Homeric) versions of the Oedipus myth, some basic elements are lacking, such as Jocasta killing herself and Oedipus piercing his own eyes. These events do not alter the substance of the myth although they can easily be integrated, the first one as a new case of autodestruction (column three) and the second as another case of crippledness (column four). At the same time there is something significant in these additions, since the shift from foot to head is to be correlated with the shift from autochthonous origin to self-destruction.

Our method thus eliminates a problem which has, so far, been one of the main obstacles to the progress of mythological studies, namely, the quest for the *true* version, or the *earlier* one. On the contrary, we define the myth as consisting of all its versions; or to put it otherwise, a myth remains the same as long as it is felt as such. A striking example is offered by the fact that our interpretation may take into account the Freudian use of the Oedipus myth and is certainly applicable to it. Although the Freudian problem has ceased to be that of autochthony *versus* bisexual reproduction, it is still the problem of understanding how *one* can be born from *two:* How is it that we do not have only one procreator, but a mother plus a father? Therefore, not only Sophocles, but Freud himself, should be included among the recorded versions of the Oedipus myth on a par with earlier or seemingly more "authentic" versions.

An important consequence follows. If a myth is made up of all its variants, structural analysis should take all of them into account. After analyzing all the known variants of the Theban version, we should thus treat the others in the same way: first, the tales about Labdacos' collateral line including Agave, Pentheus, and Jocasta herself; the Theban variant about Lycos with Amphion and Zetos as the city founders; more remote variants concerning Dionysus (Oedipus' matrilateral cousin); and Athenian legends where Cecrops take the place of Cadmos, etc. For each of them a similar chart should be drawn and then compared and reorganized according to the findings: Cecrops killing the serpent with the parallel episode of Cadmos; abandonment of Dionysus with abandonment of Oedipus; "Swollen Foot" with Dionysus' *loxias,* that is, walking obliquely; Europa's quest with Antiope's; the founding of Thebes by the Spartoi or by the brothers Amphion and Zetos; Zeus kidnapping Europa and Antiope and the same with Semele; the Theban Oedipus and the Argian Perseus, etc. We shall then have several two-dimensional charts, each dealing with a variant, to be organized in a three-dimensional order, as shown in Figure 1, so that three different readings become possible: left to right, top to bottom, front to back (or vice versa). All of these charts cannot be expected to be identical; but experience shows that any difference to be observed may be correlated with other differences, so that a logical treatment of the whole will allow simplifications, the final outcome being the structural law of the myth.

At this point the objection may be raised that the task is impossible to perform, since we can only work with known versions. Is it not possible

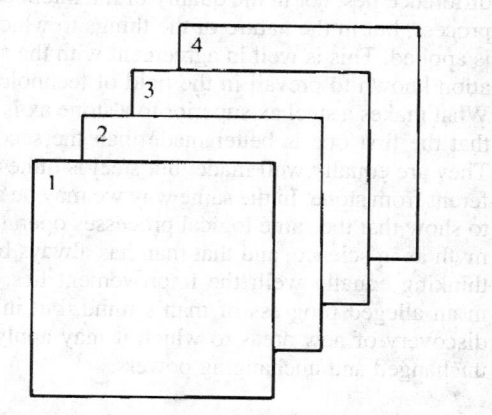

Figure 1

that a new version might alter the picture? This is true enough if only one or two versions are available, but the objection becomes theoretical as soon as a reasonably large number have been recorded. Let us make this point clear by a comparison. If the furniture of a room and its arrangement were known to us only through its reflection in two mirrors placed on opposite walls, we should theoretically dispose of an almost infinite number of mirror images which would provide us with a complete knowledge. However, should the two mirrors be obliquely set, the number of mirror images would become very small; nevertheless, four or five such images would very likely give us, if not complete information, at least a sufficient coverage so that we would feel sure that no large piece of furniture is missing in our description.

On the other hand, it cannot be too strongly emphasized that all available variants should be taken into account. If Freudian comments on the Oedipus complex are a part of the Oedipus myth, then questions such as whether Cushing's version of the Zuni origin myth should be retained or discarded become irrelevant. There is no single "true" version of which all the others are but copies or distortions. Every version belongs to the myth.

The reason for the discouraging results in works on general mythology can finally be understood. They stem from two causes. First, comparative mythologists have selected preferred versions instead of using them all. Second, we have seen that the structural analysis of *one* variant of *one* myth belonging to *one* tribe (in some cases, even *one* village) already requires two dimensions. When we use several variants of the same myth for the same tribe or village, the frame of reference becomes three-dimensional, and as soon as we try to enlarge the comparison, the number of dimensions required increases until it appears quite impossible to handle them intuitively. The confusions and platitudes which are the outcome of comparative mythology can be explained by the fact that multidimensional frames of reference are often ignored or are naïvely replaced by two- or three-dimensional ones. Indeed, progress in comparative mythology depends largely on the cooperation of mathematicians who would undertake to express in symbols multidimensional relations which cannot be handled otherwise.

Three final remarks may serve as conclusion.

First, the question has often been raised why myths, and more generally oral literature, are so much addicted to duplication, triplication, or quadruplication of the same sequence. If our hypotheses are accepted, the answer is obvious: The function of repetition is to render the structure of the myth apparent. For we have seen that the synchronic-diachronic structure of the myth permits us to organize it into diachronic sequences (the rows in our tables) which should be read synchronically (the columns). Thus, a myth exhibits a "slated" structure, which comes to the surface, so to speak, through the process of repetition.

However, the slates are not absolutely identical. And since the purpose of myth is to provide a logical model capable of overcoming a contradiction (an impossible achievement if, as it happens, the contradiction is real), a theoretically infinite number of slates will be generated, each one slightly different from the others. Thus, myth grows spiral-wise until the intellectual impulse which has produced it is exhausted. Its *growth* is a continuous process, whereas its *structure* remains discontinuous. If this is the case, we should assume that it closely corresponds, in the realm of the spoken word, to a crystal in the realm of physical matter. This analogy may help us to better understand the relationship of myth to both *langue* on the one hand and *parole* on the other. Myth is an intermediary entity between a statistical aggregate of molecules and the molecular structure itself.

Prevalent attempts to explain alleged differences between the so-called primitive mind and scientific thought have resorted to qualitative differences between the working processes of the mind in both cases, while assuming that the entities which they were studying remained very much the same. If our interpretation is correct, we are led toward a completely different view — namely, that the kind of logic in mythical thought is as rigorous as that of modern science, and that the

difference lies, not in the quality of the intellectual process, but in the nature of the things to which it is applied. This is well in agreement with the situation known to prevail in the field of technology: What makes a steel ax superior to a stone ax is not that the first one is better made than the second. They are equally well made, but steel is quite different from stone. In the same way we may be able to show that the same logical processes operate in myth as in science, and that man has always been thinking equally well; the improvement lies, not in an alleged progress of man's mind, but in the discovery of new areas to which it may apply its unchanged and unchanging powers.

Roland Barthes
1915–1980

Before his untimely death in a traffic accident, the French critic and man of letters Roland Barthes was a prolific interpreter, disseminator, and reviser of most of the complex theoretical concepts that wound through his country's centers of learning from the 1950s on. Barthes's father, a naval officer, died in battle in the first year of his son's life. Barthes grew up in Bayonne, attended secondary school in Paris, and received degrees in classical letters (1939) and grammar and philosophy (1943) from the University of Paris. He taught French in Bucharest (1948–49) and Alexandria (1949–50). Although Barthes was director of the social sciences at the École Pratique des Hautes Études in Paris from 1960 to 1977, there is the sense that he was more comfortable intellectually on the margins of the academy, carrying on guerrilla conversation with it. (On Racine [1963], for example, caused a furor among institutional classicists because of its nontraditional approach to the canonical playwright.) Barthes was elected to the chair of literary semiology at the Collège de France in 1976 and acknowledged as the leading critic of his generation in 1978. Barthes's works, many of which have been translated since his death, include Writing Degree Zero *(1953),* Mythologies *(1957),* Elements of Semiology *(1964),* Criticism and Truth *(1966),* S/Z *(1970),* Sade/Fourier/Loyola *(1971),* Critical Essays *(1972),* The Pleasure of the Text *(1973),* A Lover's Discourse: Fragments *(1977),* The Grain of the Voice *(1981),* The Responsibilities of Forms *(1982), and* The Rustle of Language *(1984). "Striptease" is from* Mythologies *(1957); it made its first English appearance in 1971. "The Death of the Author" and "From Work to Text" are both from* Image — Music — Text *(1977). "The Structuralist Activity" is from* Critical Essays *(1972).*

Striptease

Striptease — at least Parisian striptease — is based on a contradiction: Woman is desexualized at the very moment when she is stripped naked. We may therefore say that we are dealing in a sense with a spectacle based on fear, or rather on the pretense of fear, as if eroticism here went no further than a sort of delicious terror, whose ritual signs have only to be announced to evoke at once the idea of sex and its conjuration.

It is only the time taken in shedding clothes which makes voyeurs of the public; but here, as in any mystifying spectacle, the decor, the props, and the stereotypes intervene to contradict the initially provocative intention and eventually bury it in insignificance: evil is *advertised* the better to impede and exorcise it. French striptease seems to stem from what I have earlier called "Operation Margarine,"[1] a mystifying device which consists in inoculating the public with a touch of evil, the better to plunge it afterward into a permanently immune Moral Good: a few particles of eroticism, highlighted by the very situation on which the show is based, are in fact absorbed in a reassuring ritual which negates the flesh as surely as the vaccine or the taboo circumscribe and control the illness or the crime.

There will therefore be in striptease a whole series of coverings placed upon the body of the woman in proportion as she pretends to strip it bare. Exoticism is the first of these barriers, for it is always of a petrified kind which transports the body into the world of legend or romance: a Chinese woman equipped with an opium pipe (the indispensable symbol of "Sininess"), an undulating vamp with a gigantic cigarette holder, a Venetian decor complete with gondola, a dress with panniers and a singer of serenades: all aim at establishing the woman *right from the start* as an object in disguise. The end of the striptease is then no longer to drag into the light a hidden depth, but to signify, through the shedding of an incongruous and artificial clothing, nakedness as a *natural* vesture of woman, which amounts in the end to regaining a perfectly chaste state of the flesh.

The classic props of the music hall, which are invariably rounded up here, constantly make the unveiled body more remote, and force it back into the all-pervading ease of a well-known rite: the furs, the fans, the gloves, the feathers, the fish-net stockings, in short, the whole spectrum of adornment, constantly makes the living body return to the category of luxurious objects which surround man with a magical decor. Covered with feathers or gloved, the woman identifies herself here as a stereotyped element of music hall, and to shed objects as ritualistic as these is no longer a part of a further, genuine undressing. Feathers, furs, and gloves go on pervading the woman with their magical virtue even once removed, and give her something like the enveloping memory of a luxurious shell, for it is a self-evident law that the whole of striptease is given in the very nature of the initial garment: if the latter is improbable, as in the case of the Chinese woman or the woman in furs, the nakedness which follows remains itself unreal, smooth, and enclosed like a beautiful slippery object, withdrawn by its very extravagance from human use: this is the underlying significance of the G-string covered with diamonds or sequins which is the very end of striptease. This ultimate triangle, by its pure and geometrical shape, by its hard and shiny material, bars the way to the sexual parts like a sword of purity, and definitively drives the woman back into a mineral world, the (precious) stone being here the irrefutable symbol of the absolute object, that which serves no purpose.

Translated by Annette Lavers.

[1] Elsewhere in *Mythologies*, Barthes discusses the paradoxical way margarine is advertised in France, beginning with a horrified shudder at the very idea of putting such a substance into pastry or desserts, then slowly presenting its advantages, until at the end one feels relieved of one's prejudice.

Contrary to the common prejudice, the dance which accompanies the striptease from beginning to end is in no way an erotic element. It is probably quite the reverse: the faintly rhythmical undulation in this case exorcises the fear of immobility. Not only does it give to the show the alibi of Art (the dances in strip shows are always "artistic"), but above all it constitutes the last barrier, and the most efficient of all: the dance, consisting of ritual gestures which have been seen a thousand times, acts on movements as a cosmetic, it hides nudity, and smothers the spectacle under a glaze of superfluous yet essential gestures, for the act of becoming bare is here relegated to the rank of parasitical operations carried out in an improbable background. Thus we see the professionals of striptease wrap themselves in the miraculous ease which constantly clothes them, makes them remote, gives them the icy indifference of skillful practitioners, haughtily taking refuge in the sureness of their technique: their science clothes them like a garment.

All this, this meticulous exorcism of sex, can be verified *a contrario* in the "popular contests" (*sic*) of amateur striptease: there, "beginners" undress in front of a few hundred spectators without resorting or resorting very clumsily to magic, which unquestionably restores to the spectacle its erotic power. Here we find at the beginning far fewer Chinese or Spanish women, no feathers or furs (sensible suits, ordinary coats), few disguises as a starting point — gauche steps, unsatisfactory dancing, girls constantly threatened by immobility, and above all by a "technical" awkwardness (the resistance of briefs, dress or bra) which gives to the gestures of unveiling an unexpected importance, denying the woman the alibi of art and the refuge of being an object, imprisoning her in a condition of weakness and timorousness.

And yet, at the Moulin Rouge,[2] we see hints of another kind of exorcism, probably typically French, and one which in actual fact tends less to nullify eroticism than to tame it: the compère[3] tries to give striptease a reassuring petit-bourgeois status. To start with, striptease is a *sport*: there is a Striptease Club, which organizes healthy contests whose winners come out crowned and rewarded with edifying prizes (a subscription to physical training lessons), a novel (which can only be Robbe-Grillet's *Voyeur*[4]), or useful prizes (a pair of nylons, five thousand francs). Then, striptease is identified with a *career* (beginners, semi-professionals, professionals), that is, to the honorable practice of a specialization (strippers are skilled workers). One can even give them the magical alibi of work: *vocation*; one girl is, say, "*doing well*" or "*well on the way to fulfilling her promise*," or on the contrary "*taking her first steps*" on the arduous path of striptease. Finally and above all, the competitors are socially situated: one is a salesgirl, another a secretary (there are many secretaries in the Striptease Club). Striptease here is made to rejoin the world of the public, is made familiar and bourgeois, as if the French, unlike the American public (at least according to what one hears), following an irresistible tendency of their social status, could not conceive eroticism except as a household property, sanctioned by the alibi of weekly sport much more than by that of a magical spectacle: and this is how, in France, striptease is nationalized.

[2]Famed Parisian nightclub in Montmartre.
[3]The master of ceremonies.
[4]A complex postmodern novel (1957) about a serial killer.

The Structuralist Activity

What is structuralism? Not a school, nor even a movement (at least, not yet), for most of the authors ordinarily labeled with this word are unaware of being united by any solidarity of doctrine or commitment. Nor is it a vocabulary. *Structure* is already an old word (of anatomical and grammatical provenance), today quite overworked: all the social sciences resort to it abundantly, and the word's use can distinguish no one, except to engage in polemics about the content assigned to it; *functions, forms, signs* and *significations* are scarcely more pertinent: they are, today, words of common usage, from which one asks (and obtains) whatever one wants, notably the camouflage of the old determinist schema of cause and product; we must doubtless go back to pairings like those of *significans/significatum*[1] and *synchronic/diachronic* in order to approach what distinguishes structuralism from other modes of thought: the first because it refers to the linguistic model as originated by Saussure, and because along with economics, linguistics is, in the present state of affairs, the true science of structure, the second, more decisively, because it seems to imply a certain revision of the notion of history, insofar as the notion of the synchronic (although in Saussure this is a preeminently *operational* concept) accredits a certain immobilization of time, and insofar as that of the diachronic tends to represent the historical process as a pure succession of forms. This second pairing is all the more distinctive in that the chief resistance to structuralism today seems to be of Marxist origin and that it focuses on the notion of history (and not of structure); whatever the case, it is probably the serious recourse to the nomenclature of signification (and not to the word itself, which is, paradoxically, not at all distinctive) which we must ultimately take as structuralism's *spoken sign*: watch who uses *signifier* and *signified*, *synchronic* and *diachronic*, and you will know whether the structuralist vision is constituted.

Translated by Richard Howard.
[1] Signifier and signified.

This is valid for the intellectual metalanguage, which explicitly employs methodological concepts. But since structuralism is neither a school nor a movement, there is no reason to reduce it *a priori*, even in a problematical way, to the activity of philosophers; it would be better to try and find its broadest description (if not its definition) on another level than that of reflexive language. We can in fact presume that there exist certain writers, painters, musicians, in whose eyes a certain *exercise* of structure (and not only its thought) represents a distinctive experience, and that both analysts and creators must be placed under the common sign of what we might call *structural man*, defined not by his ideas or his languages, but by his imagination — in other words, by the way in which he mentally experiences structure.

Hence the first thing to be said is that in relation to *all* its users, structuralism is essentially an *activity*, i.e., the controlled succession of a certain number of mental operations: we might speak of structuralist activity as we once spoke of surrealist activity (surrealism, moreover, may well have produced the first experience of structural literature, a possibility which must some day be explored). But before seeing what these operations are, we must say a word about their goal.

The goal of all structuralist activity, whether reflexive or poetic, is to reconstruct an "object" in such a way as to manifest thereby the rules of functioning (the "functions") of this object. Structure is therefore actually a *simulacrum* of the object, but a directed, *interested* simulacrum, since the imitated object makes something appear which remained invisible, or if one prefers, unintelligible in the natural object. Structural man takes the real, decomposes it, then recomposes it; this appears to be little enough (which makes some say that the structuralist enterprise is "meaningless," "uninteresting," "useless," etc.). Yet, from another point of view, this "little enough" is decisive: for between the two objects, or the two tenses, of structuralist activity, there occurs *something new*, and what is new is nothing less than the generally intelligible: the simulacrum is intellect added to object, and this addition has an anthropological value, in that it is man himself, his history, his situation, his freedom and the very resistance which nature offers to his mind.

We see, then, why we must speak of a structuralist *activity:* creation or reflection are not, here, an original "impression" of the world, but a veritable fabrication of a world which resembles the first one, not in order to copy it but to render it intelligible. Hence one might say that structuralism is essentially *an activity of imitation*, which is also why there is, strictly speaking, no *technical* difference between structuralism as an intellectual activity on the one hand and literature in particular, art in general on the other: both derive from a *mimesis*, based not on the analogy of substances (as in so-called realist art), but on the analogy of functions (what Lévi-Strauss calls *homology*). When Troubetskoy reconstructs the phonetic object as a system of variations; when Dumézil elaborates a functional mythology; when Propp constructs a folk tale resulting by structuration from all the Slavic tales he had previously decomposed; when Lévi-Strauss discovers the homologic functioning of the totemic imagination, or Granger the formal rules of economic thought, or Gardin the pertinent features of prehistoric bronzes; when Richard decomposes a poem by Mallarmé into its distinctive vibrations — they are all doing nothing different from what Mondrian, Boulez or Butor are doing when they articulate a certain object — what will be called, precisely, a *composition* — by the controlled manifestation of certain units and certain associations of these units.[2] It is of little consequence

whether the initial object liable to the simulacrum activity is given by the world in an already assembled fashion (in the case of the structural analysis made of a constituted language or society or work) or is still scattered (in the case of the structural "composition"); whether this initial object is drawn from a social reality or an imaginary reality. It is not the nature of the copied object which defines an art (though this is a tenacious prejudice in all realism), it is the fact that man adds to it in reconstructing it: technique is the very being of all creation. It is therefore to the degree that the goals of structuralist activity are indissolubly linked to a certain technique that structuralism exists in a distinctive fashion in relation to other modes of analysis or creation: we recompose the object *in order* to make certain functions appear, and it is, so to speak, the way that makes the work; this is why we must speak of the structuralist activity rather than the structuralist work.

The structuralist activity involves two typical operations: dissection and articulation. To dissect the first object, the one which is given to the simulacrum activity, is to find in it certain mobile fragments whose differential situation engenders a certain meaning; the fragment has no meaning in itself, but it is nonetheless such that the slightest variation wrought in its configuration produces a change in the whole; a *square* by Mondrian, a *series* by Pousseur,[3] a *versicle* of Butor's *Mobile*, the "mytheme" in Lévi-Strauss, the phoneme in the work of the phonologists, the "theme" in certain literary criticism — all these units (whatever their inner structure and their extent, quite different according to cases) have no significant existence except by their frontiers: those which separate them from other actual units of the discourse (but this is a problem of articulation) and also those which distinguish them from other virtual units, with which they form a certain class (which linguistics calls a paradigm); this notion of a paradigm is essential, apparently, if we are to understand the structuralist vision: the paradigm is a group, a reservoir — as limited as

[2]Barthes compares the painter Piet Mondrian, the composer Pierre Boulez, and the novelist Michel Butor to a series of scholars whose work has been either explicitly structuralist or has contributed to structuralism: Prince Nikolai Sergeevich Troubetskoy (1890–1938), author of *Principles of Phonology*, was one of the founders of the Prague School of Linguistics in the 1930s; Georges Dumézil's work *Mythe et epopée* (1968–73) established the analogues between myths of different European and Asian cultures; Jean-Claude Gardin developed an "expert system" for identifying features of prehistoric artifacts; Gilles-Gaston Granger wrote *Methodologie economique*; Jean-Pierre Richard (1922–) wrote *L'Univers imaginaire de Mallarmé*; for Lévi-Strauss and Propp, see pp. 859 and 785.

[3]Henri Pousseur (1929–), a French composer, worked in partnership with postmodern author Michel Butor (1926–), whose *Mobile* (1962) is subtitled *Study for a Representation of the U.S.*

possible — of objects (of units) from which one summons, by an act of citation, the object or unit one wishes to endow with an actual meaning; what characterizes the paradigmatic object is that it is, vis-à-vis other objects of its class, in a certain relation of affinity and dissimilarity: two units of the same paradigm must resemble each other somewhat *in order* that the difference which separates them be indeed evident: *s* and *z* must have both a common feature (dentality) and a distinctive feature (presence or absence of sonority) so that we cannot, in French, attribute the same meaning to *poisson* and *poison*; Mondrian's squares must have both certain affinities by their shape as squares and certain dissimilarities by their proportion and color; the American automobiles (in Butor's *Mobile*) must be constantly regarded in the same way, yet they must differ each time by both their make and color; the episodes of the Oedipus myth (in Lévi-Strauss's analysis) must be both identical and varied — in order that all these languages, these works may be intelligible. The dissection operation thus produces an initial dispersed state of the simulacrum, but the units of the structure are not at all anarchic: before being distributed and fixed in the continuity of the composition, each one forms with its own virtual group or reservoir an intelligent organism, subject to a sovereign motor principle: that of the smallest difference.

Once the units are posited, structural man must discover in them or establish for them certain rules of association: this is the activity of articulation, which succeeds the summoning activity. The syntax of the arts and of discourse is, as we know, extremely varied; but what we discover in every work of structural enterprise is the submission to regular constraints whose formalism, improperly indicted, is much less important than their stability; for what is happening, at this second stage of the simulacrum-activity, is a kind of battle against chance; this is why the constraint of recurrence of the units has an almost demiurgic value: it is by the regular return of the units and of the associations of units that the work appears constructed, i.e., endowed with meaning; linguistics calls these rules of combination forms, and it would be advantageous to retain this rigorous sense of an overtaxed word:

form, it has been said, is what keeps the contiguity of units from appearing as pure effect of chance: the work of art is what man wrests from chance. This perhaps allows us to understand on the one hand why so-called nonfigurative works are nonetheless to the highest degree works of art, human thought being established not on the analogy of copies and models but with the regularity of assemblages; and on the other hand why these same works appear, precisely, fortuitous and thereby useless to those who discern in them no *form:* in front of an abstract painting, Khrushchev[4] was certainly wrong to see only the traces of a donkey's tail whisked across the canvas; at least he knew in his way, though, that art is a certain conquest of chance (he simply forgot that every rule must be learned, whether one wants to apply or interpret it).

The simulacrum, thus constructed, does not render the world as it has found it, and it is here that structuralism is important. First of all, it manifests a new category of the object, which is neither the real nor the rational, but the *functional*, thereby joining a whole scientific complex which is being developed around information theory and research. Subsequently and especially, it highlights the strictly human process by which men give meaning to things. Is this new? To a certain degree, yes; of course the world has never stopped looking for the meaning of what is given it and of what it produces; what is new is a mode of thought (or a "poetics") which seeks less to assign completed meanings to the objects it discovers than to know how meaning is possible, at what cost and by what means. Ultimately, one might say that the object of structuralism is not man endowed with meanings, but man fabricating meanings, as if it could not be the *content* of meanings which exhausted the semantic goals of humanity, but only the act by which these meanings, historical and contingent variables, are produced. *Homo significans*: such would be the new man of structural inquiry.

---

[4] Nikita Khrushchev (1894–1971) was leader of the Soviet Union from 1953 to 1964. Barthes alludes to his comment about a 1962 exhibit of a contemporary painting in Moscow: "It's dog shit! . . . A donkey could smear better than this with his tail."

According to Hegel,[5] the ancient Greek was amazed by the *natural* in nature; he constantly listened to it, questioned the meaning of mountains, springs, forests, storms; without knowing what all these objects were telling him by name, he perceived in the vegetal or cosmic order a tremendous *shudder* of meaning, to which he gave the name of a god: Pan. Subsequently, nature has changed, has become social: everything that is given to man is *already* human, down to the forest and the river which we cross when we travel. But confronted with this social nature, which is quite simply culture, structural man is no different from the ancient Greek: he too listens for the natural in culture, and constantly perceives in it not so much stable, finite, "true" meanings as the shudder of an enormous machine which is humanity tirelessly undertaking to create meaning, without which it would no longer be human. And it is because this fabrication of meaning is more important, to its view, than the meanings themselves, it is because the function is extensive with the works, that structuralism constitutes itself as an activity, and refers the exercise of the work and the work itself to a single identity: a serial composition or an analysis by Lévi-Strauss are not objects except insofar as they have been *made:* their present being *is* their past act: they are *having-been-mades;* the artist, the analyst recreates the course taken by meaning, he need not designate it: his function, to return to Hegel's example, is a *manteia;*[6] like the ancient soothsayer, he *speaks* the locus of meaning but does not name it. And it is because literature, in particular, is a mantic activity that it is both intelligible and interrogating, speaking and silent, engaged in the world by the course of meaning which it remakes with the world, but disengaged from the contingent meanings which the world elaborates: an answer to the man who consumes it yet always a question to nature, an answer which questions and a question which answers.

How then does structural man deal with the accusation of unreality which is sometimes flung at him? Are not forms in the world, are not forms responsible? Was it really his Marxism that was revolutionary in Brecht? Was it not rather the decision to link to Marxism, in the theater, the placing of a spotlight or the deliberate fraying of a costume?[7] Structuralism does not withdraw history from the world: it seeks to link to history not only certain contents (this has been done a thousand times) but also certain forms, not only the material but also the intelligible, not only the ideological but also the aesthetic. And precisely because all thought about the historically intelligible is also a participation in that intelligibility, structural man is scarcely concerned to *last*; he knows that structuralism, too, is a certain *form* of the world, which will change with the world; and just as he experiences his validity (but not his truth) in his power to speak the old languages of the world in a new way, so he knows that it will suffice that a new language rise out of history, a new language which speaks to him in his turn, for his task to be done.

---

[5]In the *Phenomenology of Spirit;* see also p. 369.
[6]Greek for prophet.

[7]Barthes suggests that it is Brecht's formal innovations in the theater rather than his politics that are revolutionary. See also p. 1250.

The Death of the Author

In his story "Sarrasine" Balzac, describing a castrato disguised as a woman, writes the following sentence: "*This was woman herself, with her sudden fears, her irrational whims, her instinctive worries, her impetuous boldness, her fussings, and her delicious sensibility.*" Who is speaking thus? Is it the hero of the story bent on remaining ignorant of the castrato hidden beneath the woman? Is it Balzac the individual, furnished by his personal experience with a philosophy of

Woman? Is it Balzac the author professing "literary" ideas on femininity? Is it universal wisdom? Romantic psychology? We shall never know, for the good reason that writing is the destruction of every voice, of every point of origin. Writing is that neutral, composite, oblique space where our subject slips away, the negative where all identity is lost, starting with the very identity of the body writing.

No doubt it has always been that way. As soon as a fact is *narrated* no longer with a view to acting directly on reality but intransitively, that is to say, finally outside of any function other than that of the very practice of the symbol itself, this disconnection occurs, the voice loses its origin, the author enters into his own death, writing begins. The sense of this phenomenon, however, has varied; in ethnographic societies the responsibility for a narrative is never assumed by a person but by a mediator, shaman, or relator whose "performance" — the mastery of the narrative code — may possibly be admired but never his "genius." The author is a modern figure, a product of our society insofar as, emerging from the Middle Ages with English empiricism, French rationalism and the personal faith of the Reformation, it discovered the prestige of the individual, of, as it is more nobly put, the "human person." It is thus logical that in literature it should be this positivism, the epitome and culmination of capitalist ideology, which has attached the greatest importance to the "person" of the author. The *author* still reigns in histories of literature, biographies of writers, interviews, magazines, as in the very consciousness of men of letters anxious to unite their person and their work through diaries and memoirs. The image of literature to be found in ordinary culture is tyrannically centered on the author, his person, his life, his tastes, his passions, while criticism still consists for the most part in saying that Baudelaire's work is the failure of Baudelaire the man, van Gogh's his madness, Tchaikovsky's his vice. The *explanation* of a work is always sought in the man or woman who produced it, as if it were always in the end, through the more or less transparent allegory of the fiction, the voice of a single person, the *author* "confiding" in us.

Though the sway of the Author remains powerful (the New Criticism has often done no more than consolidate it), it goes without saying that certain writers have long since attempted to loosen it. In France, Mallarmé was doubtless the first to see and to foresee in its full extent the necessity to substitute language itself for the person who until then had been supposed to be its owner. For him, for us too, it is language which speaks, not the author; to write is, through a prerequisite impersonality (not at all to be confused with the castrating objectivity of the realist novelist), to reach that point where only language acts, "performs," and not "me." Mallarmé's entire poetics consists in suppressing the author in the interests of writing (which is, as will be seen, to restore the place of the reader). Valéry, encumbered by a psychology of the Ego, considerably diluted Mallarmé's theory, but his taste for classicism, leading him to turn to the lessons of rhetoric, he never stopped calling into question and deriding the Author; he stressed the linguistic and, as it were, "hazardous" nature of his activity, and throughout his prose works he militated in favor of the essentially verbal condition of literature, in the face of which all recourse to the writer's interiority seemed to him pure superstition. Proust himself, despite the apparently psychological character of what are called his *analyses*, was visibly concerned with the task of inexorably blurring, by an extreme subtilization, the relation between the writer and his characters; by making of the narrator not he who has seen and felt nor even he who is writing, but he who *is going to write* (the young man in the novel — but, in fact, how old is he and who is he? — wants to write but cannot; the novel ends when writing at last becomes possible), Proust gave modern writing its epic. By a radical reversal, instead of putting his life into his novel, as is so often maintained, he made of his very life a work for which his own book was the model; so that it is clear to us that Charlus does not imitate Montesquiou but that Montesquiou — in his anecdotal, historical reality — is no more than a secondary fragment, derived from Charlus.[1] Lastly, to

Translated by Stephen Heath.

[1]Baron de Charlus, a character in Marcel Proust's *Remembrance of Things Past* based largely on the dandy and esthete Comte Robert de Montesquiou.

go no further than this prehistory of modernity, Surrealism, though unable to accord language a supreme place (language being system and the aim of the movement being, romantically, a direct subversion of codes — itself moreover illusory: a code cannot be destroyed, only "played off"), contributed to the desacralization of the image of the Author by ceaselessly recommending the abrupt disappointment of expectations of meaning (the famous surrealist "jolt"), by entrusting the hand with the task of writing as quickly as possible what the head itself is unaware of (automatic writing), by accepting the principle and the experience of several people writing together. Leaving aside literature itself (such distinctions really becoming invalid), linguistics has recently provided the destruction of the Author with a valuable analytical tool by showing that the whole of the enunciation is an empty process, functioning perfectly without there being any need for it to be filled with the person of the interlocutors. Linguistically, the author is never more than the instance writing, just as *I* is nothing other than the instance saying *I*: language knows a "subject," not a "person," and this subject, empty outside of the very enunciation which defines it, suffices to make language "hold together," suffices, that is to say, to exhaust it.

The removal of the Author (one could talk here with Brecht of a veritable "distancing," the Author diminishing like a figurine at the far end of the literary stage),[2] is not merely an historical fact or an act of writing; it utterly transforms the modern text (or — which is the same thing — the text is henceforth made and read in such a way that at all its levels the author is absent). The temporality is different. The Author, when believed in, is always conceived of as the past of his own book: book and author stand automatically on a single line divided into a *before* and an *after*. The Author is thought to *nourish* the book, which is to say that he exists before it, thinks, suffers, lives for it, is in the same relation of antecedence to his work as a father to his child. In complete contrast, the modern scriptor is born simultaneously with the text, is in no way equipped with a being preceding or exceeding the writing, is not the subject with the book as predicate; there is no other time than that of the enunciation and every text is eternally written *here and now*. The fact is (or, it follows) that *writing* can no longer designate an operation of recording, notation, representation, "depiction" (as the classics would say); rather, it designates exactly what linguists, referring to Oxford philosophy, call a performative,[3] a rare verbal form (exclusively given in the first person and in the present tense) in which the enunciation has no other content (contains no other proposition) than the act by which it is uttered — something like the *I declare* of kings or the *I sing* of very ancient poets. Having buried the Author, the modern scriptor can thus no longer believe, as according to the pathetic view of his predecessors, that this hand is too slow for his thought or passion and that consequently, making a law of necessity, he must emphasize this delay and indefinitely "polish" his form. For him, on the contrary, the hand, cut off from any voice, borne by a pure gesture of inscription (and not of expression), traces a field without origin — or which, at least, has no other origin than language itself, language which ceaselessly calls into question all origins.

We know now that a text is not a line of words releasing a single "theological" meaning (the "message" of the Author-God) but a multidimensional space in which a variety of writings, none of them original, blend and clash. The text is a tissue of quotations drawn from the innumerable centers of culture. Similar to Bouvard and Pécuchet,[4] those eternal copyists, at once sublime and comic and whose profound ridiculousness indicates precisely the truth of writing, the writer can only imitate a gesture that is always anterior, never original. His only power is to mix writings, to counter the ones with the others, in such a way as never to rest on any one of them. Did he wish to *express himself*, he ought at least to know that

---

[2]Barthes refers to German playwright Bertolt Brecht's doctrine of *Verfremdung* (or alienation), in which the spectators are emotionally distanced from the events represented on stage.

[3]Barthes refers to the speech-act theory of J. L. Austin, *How to Do Things with Words* (1962), see p. 685.

[4]Two copying clerks, soulmates who meet by chance, the protagonists of Gustave Flaubert's unfinished novel of that name published posthumously in 1881.

the inner "thing" he thinks to "translate" is itself only a ready-formed dictionary, its words only explainable through other words, and so on indefinitely; something experienced in exemplary fashion by the young Thomas De Quincey, he who was so good at Greek that in order to translate absolutely modern ideas and images into that dead language, he had, so Baudelaire tells us (in *Paradis Artificiels*), "created for himself an unfailing dictionary, vastly more extensive and complex than those resulting from the ordinary patience of purely literary themes." Succeeding the Author, the scriptor no longer bears within him passions, humors, feelings, impressions, but rather this immense dictionary from which he draws a writing that can know no halt: life never does more than imitate the book, and the book itself is only a tissue of signs, an imitation that is lost, infinitely deferred.

Once the Author is removed, the claim to decipher a text becomes quite futile. To give a text an Author is to impose a limit on that text, to furnish it with a final signified, to close the writing. Such a conception suits criticism very well, the latter then allotting itself the important task of discovering the Author (or its hypostases: society, history, psyché, liberty) beneath the work: when the Author has been found, the text is "explained" — victory to the critic. Hence there is no surprise in the fact that, historically, the reign of the Author has also been that of the Critic, nor again in the fact that criticism (be it new) is today undermined along with the Author. In the multiplicity of writing, everything is to be *disentangled*, nothing *deciphered*; the structure can be followed, "run" (like the thread of a stocking) at every point and at every level, but there is nothing beneath: the space of writing is to be ranged over, not pierced; writing ceaselessly posits meaning ceaselessly to evaporate it, carrying out a systematic exemption of meaning. In precisely this way literature (it would be better from now on to say *writing*), by refusing to assign a "secret," an ultimate meaning, to the text (and to the world as text), liberates what may be called an antitheological activity, an activity that is truly revolutionary since to refuse to fix meaning is,

in the end, to refuse God and his hypostases — reason, science, law.

Let us come back to the Balzac sentence. No one, no "person," says it: its source, its voice, is not the true place of the writing, which is reading. Another — very precise — example will help to make this clear: recent research (J.-P. Vernant[5]) has demonstrated the constitutively ambiguous nature of Greek tragedy, its texts being woven from words with double meanings that each character understands unilaterally (this perpetual misunderstanding is exactly the "tragic"); there is, however, someone who understands each word in its duplicity and who, in addition, hears the very deafness of the characters speaking in front of him — this someone being precisely the reader (or here, the listener). Thus is revealed the total existence of writing: a text is made of multiple writings, drawn from many cultures and entering into mutual relations to dialogue, parody, contestation, but there is one place where this multiplicity is focused and that place is the reader, not, as was hitherto said, the author. The reader is the space on which all the quotations that make up a writing are inscribed without any of them being lost; a text's unity lies not in its origin but in its destination. Yet this destination cannot any longer be personal: the reader is without history, biography, psychology; he is simply that *someone* who holds together in a single field all the traces by which the written text is constituted. Which is why it is derisory to condemn the new writing in the name of a humanism hypocritically turned champion of the reader's rights. Classic criticism has never paid any attention to the reader; for it, the writer is the only person in literature. We are now beginning to let ourselves be fooled no longer by the arrogant antiphrastical recriminations of good society in favor of the very thing it sets aside, ignores, smothers, or destroys; we know that to give writing its future, it is necessary to overthrow the myth: the birth of the reader must be at the cost of the death of the Author.

[5]Cf. Jean-Pierre Vernant (with Pierre Vidal-Naquet), *Mythe et tragédie en Grèce ancienne*, Paris 1972, esp. pp. 19–40, 99–131. [Barthes]

From Work to Text

It is a fact that over the last few years a certain change has taken place (or is taking place) in our conception of language and, consequently, of the literary work which owes at least its phenomenal existence to this same language. The change is clearly connected with the current development of (amongst other disciplines) linguistics, anthropology, Marxism and psychoanalysis (the term "connection" is used here in a deliberately neutral way: one does not decide a determination, be it multiple and dialectical). What is new and which affects the idea of the work comes not necessarily from the internal recasting of each of these disciplines, but rather from their encounter in relation to an object which traditionally is the province of none of them. It is indeed as though the *interdisciplinarity* which is today held up as a prime value in research cannot be accomplished by the simple confrontation of specialist branches of knowledge. Interdisciplinarity is not the calm of an easy security; it begins *effectively* (as opposed to the mere expression of a pious wish) when the solidarity of the old disciplines breaks down — perhaps even violently, via the jolts of fashion — in the interests of a new object and a new language neither of which has a place in the field of the sciences that were to be brought peacefully together, this unease in classification being precisely the point from which it is possible to diagnose a certain mutation. The mutation in which the idea of the work seems to be gripped must not, however, be over-estimated: it is more in the nature of an epistemological slide than of a real break. The break, as is frequently stressed, is seen to have taken place in the last century with the appearance of Marxism and Freudianism; since then there has been no further break, so that in a way it can be said that for the last hundred years we have been living in repetition. What History, our History, allows us today is merely to slide, to vary, to exceed, to repudiate. Just as Einsteinian science demands that *the relativity of the frames of reference* be included in the object studied, so the combined action of Marxism, Freudianism and structuralism demands, in literature, the relativization of the relations of writer, reader and observer (critic). Over against the traditional notion of the *work,* for long — and still — conceived of in a, so to speak, Newtonian way, there is now the requirement of a new object, obtained by the sliding or overturning of former categories. That object is the *Text.* I know the word is fashionable (I am myself often led to use it) and therefore regarded by some with suspicion, but that is exactly why I should like to remind myself of the principal propositions at the intersection of which I see the Text as standing. The word "proposition" is to be understood more in a grammatical than in a logical sense: the following are not argumentations but enunciations, "touches," approaches that consent to remain metaphorical. Here then are these propositions; they concern method, genres, signs, plurality, filiation, reading and pleasure.

1. The Text is not to be thought of as an object that can be computed. It would be futile to try to separate out materially works from texts. In particular, the tendency must be avoided to say that the work is classic, the text avant-garde; it is not a question of drawing up a crude honours list in the name of modernity and declaring certain literary productions "in" and others "out" by virtue of their chronological situation: there may be "text" in a very ancient work, while many products of contemporary literature are in no way texts. The difference is this: the work is a fragment of substance, occupying a part of the space of books (in a library for example), the Text is a methodological field. The opposition may recall (without at all reproducing term for term) Lacan's distinction between "reality" and "the real": the one is displayed, the other demonstrated; likewise, the work can be seen (in bookshops, in catalogues, in exam syllabi), the text is a process of demonstration, speaks according to certain rules (or against certain rules); the work can be held in the hand, the text is held in language, only exists in the movement of a discourse (or rather, it is Text for the very reason that it knows itself as text); the Text is not the decomposition of the work, it is

Translated by Richard Howard.

the work that is the imaginary tail of the Text; or again, *the Text is experienced only in an activity of production*. It follows that the Text cannot stop (for example on a library shelf); its constitutive movement is that of cutting across (in particular, it can cut across the work, several works).

2. In the same way, the Text does not stop at (good) Literature; it cannot be contained in a hierarchy, even in a simple division of genres. What constitutes the Text is, on the contrary (or precisely), its subversive force in respect of the old classifications. How do you classify a writer like Georges Bataille? Novelist, poet, essayist, economist, philosopher, mystic? The answer is so difficult that the literary manuals generally prefer to forget about Bataille who, in fact, wrote texts, perhaps continuously one single text. If the Text poses problems of classification (which is furthermore one of its "social" functions), this is because it always involves a certain experience of limits (to take up an expression from Philippe Sollers). Thibaudet used already to talk — but in a very restricted sense — of limit-works (such as Chateaubriand's *Vie de Rancé,* which does indeed come through to us today as a "text"); the Text is that which goes to the limit of the rules of enunciation (rationality, readability, etc.). Nor is this a rhetorical idea, resorted to for some "heroic" effect: the Text tries to place itself very exactly *behind* the limit of the *doxa*[1] (is not general opinion — constitutive of our democratic societies and powerfully aided by mass communications — defined by its limits, the energy with which it excludes, its *censorship*?). Taking the word literally, it may be said that the Text is always *paradoxical.*

3. The Text can be approached, experienced, in reaction to the sign. The work closes on a signified. There are two modes of signification which can be attributed to this signified; either it is claimed to be evident and the work is then the object of a literal science, of philology, or else it is considered to be secret, ultimate, something to be sought out, and the work then falls under the scope of a hermeneutics, of an interpretation (Marxist, psychoanalytic, thematic, etc.); in short, the work itself functions as a general sign and it is normal that it should represent an institutional category of

the civilization of the Sign. The Text, on the contrary, practices the infinite deferment of the signified, is dilatory; its field is that of the signifier and the signifier must not be conceived of as "the first stage of meaning," its material vestibule, but, in complete opposition to this, as its *deferred action.* Similarly, the *infinity* of the signifier refers not to some idea of the ineffable (the unnameable signified) but to that of a *playing;* the generation of the perpetual signifier (after the fashion of a perpetual calendar) in the field of the text (better, of which the text is the field) is realized not according to an organic progress of maturation or a hermeneutic course of deepening investigation, but, rather, according to a serial movement of disconnections, overlappings, variations. The logic regulating the Text is not comprehensive (define "what the work means") but metonymic; the activity of associations, contiguities, carryings-over coincides with a liberation of symbolic energy (lacking it, man would die); the work — in the best of cases — is *moderately* symbolic (its symbolic runs out, comes to a halt); the Text is *radically* symbolic: *a work conceived, perceived and received in its integrally symbolic nature is a text.* Thus is the Text restored to language; like language, it is structured but off-centred, without closure (note, in reply to the contemptuous suspicion of the "fashionable" sometimes directed at structuralism, that the epistemological privilege currently accorded to language stems precisely from the discovery there of a paradoxical idea of structure: a system with neither close nor centre).

4. The Text is plural. Which is not simply to say that it has several meanings, but that it accomplishes the very plural of meaning: an *irreducible* (and not merely an acceptable) plural. The Text is not a co-existence of meanings but a passage, an overcrossing; thus it answers not to an interpretation, even a liberal one, but to an explosion, a dissemination. The plural of the Text depends, that is, not on the ambiguity of its contents but on what might be called the *stereographic plurality* of its weave of signifiers (etymologically, the text is a tissue, a woven fabric). The reader of the Text may be compared to someone at a loose end (someone slackened off from any imaginary); this passably empty subject strolls — it is what happened to the author of these lines, then it was that he had a vivid idea of

[1]Opinion.

the Text — on the side of a valley, a *oued*[2] flowing down below (*oued* is there to bear witness to a certain feeling of unfamiliarity); what he perceives is multiple, irreducible, coming from a disconnected, heterogeneous variety of substances and perspectives: lights, colours, vegetation, heat, air, slender explosions of noises, scant cries of birds, children's voices from over on the other side, passages, gestures, clothes of inhabitants near or far away. All these *incidents* are half-identifiable: they come from codes which are known but their combination is unique, founds the stroll in a difference repeatable only as difference. So the Text: it can be it only in its difference (which does not mean its individuality), its reading is semelfactive[3] (this rendering illusory any inductive-deductive science of texts — no "grammar" of the text) and nevertheless woven entirely with citations, references, echoes, cultural languages (what language is not?), antecedent or contemporary, which cut across it through and through in a vast stereophony. The intertextual in which every text is held, it itself being the text-between of another text, is not to be confused with some origin of the text: to try to find the "sources," the "influences" of a work, is to fall in with the myth of filiation;[4] the citations which go to make up a text are anonymous, untraceable, and yet *already read:* they are quotations without inverted commas. The work has nothing disturbing for any monistic philosophy (we know that there are opposing examples of these); for such a philosophy, plural is the Evil. Against the work, therefore, the text could well take as its motto the words of the man possessed by demons (*Mark* 5:9): "My name is Legion: for we are many." The plural of demoniacal texture which opposes text to work can bring with it fundamental changes in reading, and precisely in areas where monologism appears to be the Law: certain of the "texts" of Holy Scripture traditionally recuperated by theological monism (historical or anagogical) will perhaps offer themselves to a diffraction of meanings (finally, that is to say, to a materialist reading), while the Marxist interpretation of works, so far resolutely monistic, will be able to materialize itself more by pluralizing itself (if, however, the Marxist "institutions" allow it).

5. The work is caught up in a process of filiation. Are postulated: a *determination* of the work by the world (by race, then by History), a *consecution* of works amongst themselves, and a *conformity* of the work to the author. The author is reputed the father and the owner of his work: literary science therefore teaches *respect* for the manuscript and the author's declared intentions, while society asserts the legality of the relation of author to work (the *"droit d'auteur"* or "copyright," in fact of recent date since it was only really legalized at the time of the French Revolution). As for the Text, it reads without the inscription of the Father. Here again, the metaphor of the Text separates from that of the work: the latter refers to the image of an *organism* which grows by vital expansion, by "development" (a word which is significantly ambiguous, at once biological and rhetorical); the metaphor of the Text is that of the *network;* if the Text extends itself, it is as a result of a combinatory systematic (an image, moreover, close to current biological conceptions of the living being). Hence no vital "respect" is due to the Text: it can be *broken* (which is just what the Middle Ages did with two nevertheless authoritative texts — Holy Scripture and Aristotle); it can be read without the guarantee of its father, the restitution of the intertext paradoxically abolishing any legacy. It is not that the Author may not "come back" in the Text, in his text, but he then does so as a "guest." If he is a novelist, he is inscribed in the novel like one of his characters, figured in the carpet; no longer privileged, paternal, aletheological,[5] his inscription is ludic.[6] He becomes, as it were, a paper-author: his life is no longer the origin of his fictions but a fiction contributing to his work; there is a reversion of the work on to the life (and no longer the contrary); it is the work of Proust, of Genet which allows their lives to be read as a text. The word "bio-graphy" reacquires a strong, etymological sense, at the same time as the sincerity of the enunciation — veritable "cross" borne by literary morality — becomes a

[2]A North African watercourse; a wadi.
[3]A nonce word made up from the Latin roots "semel" (half) and "factive" (creative).
[4]Descent, derivation.

[5]A portmanteau word composed of *aletheia,* "truth," and *theological.*
[6]Playful.

false problem: the *I* which writes the text, it too, is never more than a paper-*I*.

6. The work is normally the object of a consumption; no demagogy is intended here in referring to the so-called consumer culture but it has to be recognized that today it is the "quality" of the work (which supposes finally an appreciation of "taste") and not the operation of reading itself which can differentiate between books: structurally, there is no difference between "cultured" reading and casual reading in trains. The Text (if only by its frequent "unreadability") decants the work (the work permitting) from its consumption and gathers it up as play, activity, production, practice. This means that the Text requires that one try to abolish (or at the very least to diminish) the distance between writing and reading, in no way by intensifying the projection of the reader into the work but by joining them in a single signifying practice. The distance separating reading from writing is historical. In the times of the greatest social division (before the setting up of democratic cultures), reading and writing were equally privileges of class. Rhetoric, the great literary code of those times, taught one to *write* (even if what was then normally produced were speeches, not texts). Significantly, the coming of democracy reversed the word of command: what the (secondary) School prides itself on is teaching to *read* (well) and no longer to write (consciousness of the deficiency is becoming fashionable again today: the teacher is called upon to teach pupils to "express themselves," which is a little like replacing a form of repression by a misconception). In fact, *reading,* in the sense of consuming, is far from *playing* with the text. "Playing" must be understood here in all its polysemy:[7] the text itself *plays* (like a door, like a machine with "play") and the reader plays twice over, playing the Text as one plays a game, looking for a practice which reproduces it, but, in order that that practice not be reduced to a passive, inner *mimesis* (the Text is precisely that which resists such a reduction), also playing the Text in the musical sense of the term. The history of music (as a practice, not as an "art") does indeed parallel that of the Text fairly closely: there was a period when practicing amateurs were

numerous (at least within the confines of a certain class) and "playing" and "listening" formed a scarcely differentiated activity; then two roles appeared in succession, first that of the performer, the interpreter to whom the bourgeois public (though still itself able to play a little — the whole history of the piano) delegated its playing, then that of the (passive) amateur, who listens to music without being able to play (the gramophone record takes the place of the piano). We know that today post-serial music has radically altered the role of the "interpreter," who is called on to be in some sort the co-author of the score, completing it rather than giving it "expression." The Text is very much a score of this new kind: it asks of the reader a practical collaboration. Which is an important change, for who executes the work? (Mallarmé posed the question, wanting the audience to *produce* the book). Nowadays only the critic executes the work (accepting the play on words). The reduction of reading to a consumption is clearly responsible for the "boredom" experienced by many in the face of the modern ('unreadable') text, the avant-garde film or painting: to be bored means that one cannot produce the text, open it out, *set it going.*

7. This leads us to pose (to propose) a final approach to the Text, that of pleasure. I do not know whether there has ever been a hedonistic aesthetics (eudæmonist philosophies are themselves rare). Certainly there exists a pleasure of the work (of certain works); I can delight in reading and re-reading Proust, Flaubert, Balzac, even — why not? — Alexandre Dumas. But this pleasure, no matter how keen and even when free from all prejudice, remains in part (unless by some exceptional critical effort) a pleasure of consumption; for if I can read these authors, I also know that I cannot *re-write* them (that it is impossible today to write "like that") and this knowledge, depressing enough, suffices to cut me off from the production of these works, in the very moment their remoteness establishes my modernity (is not to be modern to know clearly what cannot be started over again?). As for the Text, it is bound to *jouissance,*[8] that is to a pleasure without separation. Order of the signifier, the

---

[7]Multiplicity of meaning.

[8]Joy, bliss. See the introduction to Structuralism and Deconstruction, p. 819.

Text participates in its own way in a social utopia; before History (supposing the latter does not opt for barbarism), the Text achieves, if not the transparence of social relations, that at least of language relations: the Text is that space where no language has a hold over any other, where languages circulate (keeping the circular sense of the term).

These few propositions, inevitably, do not constitute the articulations of a Theory of the Text and this is not simply the result of the failings of the person here presenting them (who in many respects has anyway done no more than pick up what is being developed round about him). It stems from the fact that a Theory of the Text cannot be satisfied by a metalinguistic exposition: the destruction of metalanguage, or at least (since it may be necessary provisionally to resort to metalanguage) its calling into doubt, is part of the theory itself: the discourse on the Text should itself be nothing other than text, research, textual activity, since the Text is that *social* space which leaves no language safe, outside, nor any subject of the enunciation in position as judge, master, analyst, confessor, decoder. The theory of the Text can coincide only with a practice of writing.

Paul de Man

1919–1983

At once the most suasive and reticent of deconstructive theorists, Paul de Man exerted a powerful influence on a generation of the most elite students of literature in the United States. Born in Antwerp to a prominent Belgian family, de Man studied science and philosophy at the University of Brussels from 1939 to 1942. In 1947 he moved to New York City and from 1949 to 1951 taught at Bard College. Starting in 1952 de Man attended Harvard University, earning a Ph.D. in comparative literature in 1960. From there he moved on to teach at Cornell (1960–67), Johns Hopkins (1967–70), and Yale (1970–83), where he taught until his death. For a theorist of his stature, de Man published little criticism, all of it in the form of essays: Blindness and Insight: Essays in the Rhetoric of Contemporary Criticism *(1971; revised 1983);* Allegories of Reading: Figural Language in Rousseau, Nietzsche, Rilke, and Proust *(1979);* The Rhetoric of Romanticism *(1984);* The Resistance to Theory *(1986; edited by Wlad Godzich). Since his death, de Man's reputation has been tarnished by the revelation that during World War II, when he was a student at the University of Brussels, he wrote anti-Semitic articles for a publication that sympathized with the Nazi regime (these columns and reviews are collected in* Wartime Journalism: 1940–1942, *1988). "Semiology and Rhetoric," originally published in* Diacritics *(1975), is reprinted from* Allegories of Reading.

Semiology and Rhetoric

To judge from various recent publications, the spirit of the times is not blowing in the direction of formalist and intrinsic criticism. We may no longer be hearing very much about relevance, but we do continue to hear a great deal about reference, about the nonverbal "outside" to which language refers, by which it is conditioned, and upon which it acts. The stress falls not so much on the fictional status of literature — a property now perhaps somewhat too easily taken for granted — but on the interplay between these fictions and categories that are said to partake of reality, such as the self, man, society, "the artist, his culture, and the human community," as one critic puts it. Hence the emphasis on hybrid texts considered to be partly literary and partly referential, on popular fictions deliberately aimed toward social and psychological gratification, on literary autobiography as a key to the understanding of the self, and so on. We speak as if, with the problems of literary form resolved once and forever, and with techniques of structural analysis refined to near-perfection, we could now move "beyond formalism" toward the questions that really interest us and reap, at last, the fruits of the ascetic concentration on techniques that prepared us for this decisive step. With the internal law and order of literature well policed, we can now confidently devote ourselves to the foreign affairs, the external politics of literature. Not only do we feel able to do so, but we also think we owe it to ourselves to take this step: our moral conscience would not allow us to do otherwise. Behind the assurance that valid interpretation is possible, behind the recent interest in writing and reading as potentially effective public speech acts, stands a highly respectable moral imperative that strives to reconcile the internal, formal, private structures of literary language with their external, referential, and public effects.

I want, for the moment, to consider briefly this tendency in itself, as an undeniable and recurrent historical fact, without regard for its truth or falseness or for its value as desirable or pernicious. It is a fact that this sort of thing happens again and again in literary studies. On the one hand, literature cannot merely be received as a definite unit of referential meaning that can be decoded without leaving a residue. The code is unusually conspicuous, complex, and enigmatic; it attracts an inordinate amount of attention to itself, and this attention has to acquire the rigor of a method. The structural moment of concentration on the code for its own sake cannot be avoided, and literature necessarily breeds its own formalism. Technical innovations in the methodological study of literature only occur when this kind of attention predominates. It can legitimately be said, for example, that, from a technical point of view, very little has happened in American criticism since the innovative works of the New Criticism. There certainly have been numerous excellent books of criticism since, but in none of them have the techniques of description and interpretation evolved beyond the techniques of close reading established in the forties. Formalism, it seems, is an all-absorbing and tyrannical muse; the hope that one can be at the same time technically original and discursively eloquent is not borne out by the history of literary criticism.

On the other hand — and this is the real mystery — no literary formalism, no matter how accurate and enriching in its analytic powers, is ever allowed to come into being without seeming reductive. When form is considered to be the external trappings of literary meaning or content, it seems superficial and expendable. The development of intrinsic, formalist criticism in the twentieth century has changed this model: form is now a solipsistic category of self-reflection, and the referential meaning is said to be extrinsic. The polarities of inside and outside have been reversed, but they are still the same polarities that are at play: internal meaning has become outside reference, and the outer form has become the intrinsic structure. A new version of reductiveness at once follows this reversal: formalism nowadays is mostly described in an imagery of imprisonment and claustrophobia: the "prison house of language," "the impasse of formalist criticism," and the like. Like the grandmother in Proust's novel, ceaselessly driving the young Marcel out into the garden, away from the unhealthy inwardness of his closeted reading, critics cry out for the fresh air of referential meaning. Thus, with the structure of the code so opaque, but with the meaning so anxious to blot out the obstacle of form, it is no wonder that the reconciliation of form and meaning seems so attractive. The attraction of reconciliation is the elective breeding-ground of false models and metaphors; it accounts for the metaphorical model of literature as a kind of box that separates an inside from an outside, with the reader or critic as the person who opens the lid in order to release into the open what was secreted but inaccessible inside. It matters little whether we call the inside of the box the content or the form and the outside the meaning or the appearance. The recurrent debate opposing intrinsic to extrinsic criticism stands under the aegis of an inside/outside metaphor that has never been seriously questioned.

Metaphors are much more tenacious than facts, and I certainly don't expect to dislodge this age-old model in one short expository essay. I merely wish to speculate on a different set of terms, perhaps less simple in their differential relationship than the strictly polar, binary opposition between inside and outside, and therefore less likely to enter into the easy play of chiasmic reversals. I derive these terms (which are as old as the hills) pragmatically from the observation of developments and debates in recent critical methodology.

One of the most controversial among these developments coincides with a new approach to poetics — or, as it is called in Germany, poetology — as a branch of general semiotics. In France, a semiology of literature was the outcome of the long-deferred but all the more explosive encounter of the nimble French literary mind with the category of form. Semiology, as opposed to semantics, is the science or study of signs as signifiers; it does not ask what words mean but how they mean. Unlike American New Criticism, which derived the internalization of form from the practice of highly self-conscious modern writers, French semiology turned to linguistics for its model and adopted Saussure and Jakobson rather than Valéry or Proust for its masters.[1] By an awareness of the arbitrariness of the sign (Saussure) and of literature as an autotelic statement "focused on the way it is expressed" (Jakobson), the entire question of meaning can be bracketed, thus freeing critical discourse from the debilitating burden of paraphrase. The demystifying power of semiology, within the context of French historical and thematic criticism, has been considerable. It demonstrated that the perception of the literary dimensions of language is largely obscured if one submits uncritically to the authority of reference. It also revealed how tenaciously this authority continues to assert itself in a variety of disguises, ranging from the crudest ideology to the most refined forms of aesthetic and ethical judgment. It especially exploded the myth of semantic correspondence between sign and referent, the wishful hope of having it both ways, of being, to paraphrase Marx, a formalist critic in the morning and a communal moralist in the afternoon, of serving both the technique of form and the substance of meaning. The results, in the practice of French criticism, have been as fruitful as they are irreversible. Perhaps for the first time since the late eighteenth century, French critics can come at least somewhat closer to the kind of linguistic awareness that never ceased to be operative in French poets and novelists, that forced all of them, including Sainte-Beuve, to write their main works "contre Sainte-Beuve."[2] The distance was never so considerable in England and the United States, which does not mean, however, that we may be able, in this country, to dispense with a preventative semiological hygiene altogether.

One of the most striking characteristics of literary semiology as it is practiced today, in France and elsewhere, is the use of grammatical (especially syntactical) structures conjointly with rhetorical structures, without apparent awareness of a possible discrepancy between them. In their literary analyses, Barthes, Genette, Todorov, Greimas, and their disciples all simplify and regress from Jakobson in letting grammar and rhetoric function in perfect continuity, and in passing from grammatical to rhetorical structures without difficulty or interruption. Indeed, as the study of grammatical structures is refined in contemporary theories of generative, transformational, and distributive grammar, the study of tropes and of figures (which is how the term rhetoric is used throughout this essay, not in the derived sense of comment, eloquence, or persuasion) becomes a mere extension of grammatical models, a particular subset of syntactical relations. In the recent *Dictionnaire encyclopédique des sciences du langage,* Ducrot and Todorov write: ." . . rhetoric has always been satisfied with a paradigmatic view over words (word substituting for each other), without questioning their syntagmatic relationship (the contiguity of words to each other). There ought to be another perspective, complementary to the first, in which metaphor, for example, would not be defined as a substitution but as a particular type of combination. Research inspired by linguistics or, more narrowly, by syntactical studies, has begun to reveal this possibility — but it remains to be explored."[3]

[1] See the introduction to this chapter, pp. 820–23.

[2] "Against Sainte-Beuve," the title of a book by Marcel Proust.

[3] From the entry on rhetoric in Ducrot and Todorov, *Dictionnaire encyclopédique des sciences du langage* (Paris, Seuil, 1972), p. 352. [De Man]

Todorov, who calls one of his books a *Grammar of the Decameron*,[4] rightly thinks of his own work and that of his associates as first explorations in the elaboration of a systematic grammar of literary modes, genres, and also literary figures. Perhaps the most perceptive work to come out of this school, Genette's studies of figural modes, can be shown to be assimilations of rhetorical transformations or combinations to syntactical, grammatical patterns. Thus a recent study, now printed in *Figures III* and entitled "Métonymie chez Proust," shows the combined presence, in a wide and astute selection of passages, of paradigmatic, metaphorical figures with syntagmatic, metonymic structures.[5] The combination of both is treated descriptively and nondialectically without suggesting the possibility of logical tensions.

One can ask whether this reduction of figure to grammar is legitimate. The existence of grammatical structures within and beyond the unit of the sentence in literary texts is undeniable, and their description and classification are indispensable. The question remains if and how figures of rhetoric can be included in such a taxonomy. This question is at the core of the debate going on, in a wide variety of apparently unrelated forms, in contemporary poetics; but I do not plan to make clear the connection between this "real" problem and the countless pseudo-problems that agitate literary studies. This historical picture of contemporary criticism is too confused to make the mapping out of such a topography a useful exercise. Not only are these questions mixed in and mixed up within particular groups or local trends, but they are often co-present, without apparent contradiction, within the work of a single author.

Neither is the theory of the question suitable for quick expository treatment. To distinguish the epistemology of grammar from the epistemology of rhetoric is a redoubtable task. On an entirely naive level, we tend to conceive of grammatical systems as tending toward universality and as simply generative, that is, as capable of deriving an infinity of versions from a single model (that may govern transformations as well as derivations) without the intervention of another model that would upset the first. We therefore think of the relationship between grammar and logic, the passage from grammar to propositions, as being relatively unproblematic: no true propositions are conceivable in the absence of grammatical consistency or of controlled deviation from a system of consistency no matter how complex. Grammar and logic stand to each other in a dyadic relationship of unsubverted support. In a logic of acts rather than of statements, as in Austin's theory of speech acts,[6] which has had such a strong influence on recent American work in literary semiology, it is also possible to move between speech acts and grammar without difficulty. The performance of what are called illocutionary acts, such as ordering, questioning, denying, and assuming, within the language is congruent with the grammatical structures of syntax in the corresponding imperative, interrogative, negative, and optative sentences. "The rules of illocutionary acts," writes Richard Ohmann in a recent paper, "determine whether performance of a given act is well-executed, in just the same way as grammatical rules determine whether the product of a locutionary act — a sentence — is well formed. . . . But whereas the rules of grammar concern the relationships among sound, syntax, and meaning, the rules of illocutionary acts concern relationships among people."[7] And since rhetoric is then conceived exclusively as persuasion, as actual action upon others (and not as an intralinguistic figure or trope), the continuity between the illocutionary realm of grammar and the perlocutionary realm of rhetoric is self-evident. It becomes the basis for a new rhetoric that, exactly as is the case for Todorov and Genette, would also be a new grammar.

Without engaging the substance of the question, it can be pointed out, without having to go beyond recent and American examples, and without calling upon the strength of an age-old tradition, that the continuity here assumed between grammar

---

[4]Tzvetan Todorov, *Grammaire du Décaméron* (The Hague: Mouton, 1969).

[5]Gérard Genette, *Figures III* (Paris: Seuil, 1972), pp. 41–63. [De Man]

[6]See J. L. Austin, *How to Do Things with Words*, pp. 685–90.

[7]"Speech, Literature, and the Space in Between," *New Literary History* 4 (1971). [De Man]

and rhetoric is not borne out by theoretical and philosophical speculation. Kenneth Burke mentions *deflection* (which he compares structurally to Freudian displacement), defined as "any slight bias or even unintended error," as the rhetorical basis of language, and deflection is then conceived as a dialectical subversion of the consistent link between sign and meaning that operates within grammatical patterns;[8] hence Burke's well-known insistence on the distinction between grammar and rhetoric. Charles Sanders Peirce, who, with Nietzsche and Saussure, laid the philosophical foundation for modern semiology, stressed the distinction between grammar and rhetoric in his celebrated and so suggestively unfathomable definition of the sign. He insists, as is well known, on the necessary presence of a third element, called the interpretant, within any relationship that the sign entertains with its object. The sign must be interpreted if we are to understand the idea it is to convey, and this is so because the sign is not the thing but a meaning derived from the thing by a process — here called representation — that is not simply generative, that is, dependent on a univocal origin. The interpretation of the sign is not, for Peirce, a meaning but another sign; it is a reading, not a decodage, and this reading has, in its turn, to be interpreted into another sign, and so on, ad infinitum. Peirce calls this process by means of which "one sign gives birth to another" pure rhetoric, as distinguished from pure grammar, which postulates the possibility of unproblematic, dyadic meaning, and pure logic, which postulates the possibility of the universal truth of meanings. Only if the sign engendered meaning in the same way that the object engenders the sign — that is, by representation — would there be no need to distinguish between grammar and rhetoric.[9]

These remarks should indicate at least the existence and the difficulty of the question, a difficulty which puts its concise theoretical exposition beyond my powers. I must retreat therefore into a pragmatic discourse and try to illustrate the tension between grammar and rhetoric in a few specific textual examples. Let me begin by considering what is perhaps the most commonly known instance of an apparent symbiosis between a grammatical and a rhetorical structure, the so-called rhetorical question, in which the figure is conveyed directly by means of a syntactical device. I take the first example from the subliterature of the mass media: asked by his wife whether he wants to have his bowling shoes laced over or laced under, Archie Bunker[10] answers with a question. He asks, "What's the difference?" Being a reader of sublime simplicity, his wife replies by patiently explaining the difference between lacing over and lacing under, whatever this may be, but provokes only ire. "What's the difference?" did not ask for difference but meant instead "I don't give a damn what the difference is." The same grammatical pattern engenders two meanings that are mutually exclusive: the literal meaning asks for the concept (difference) whose existence is denied by the figurative meaning. As long as we are talking about bowling shoes, the consequences are relatively trivial; Archie Bunker, who is a great believer in the authority of origins (as long, of course, as they are the right origins), muddles along in a world where literal and figurative meanings get in each other's way, though not without discomforts. But if a *de*-Bunker rather than a Bunker, a de-bunker of the *arché* (origin), an "Archie DeBunker" such as Nietzsche or Jacques Derrida, asks the question "What is the Difference?" we cannot even tell from his grammar whether he "really" wants to know "what"

[8]Kenneth Burke, "Rhetoric — Old and New," *Journal of General Education* 5 (1951), rpt. in *New Rhetorics,* ed. Martin Steinmann, Jr. (New York: Scribner, 1967), p. 75. [De Man]

[9]See Peirce, *Collected Papers,* ed. Charles Hartshorne and Paul Weiss (Cambridge, Mass.: Harvard University Press, 1960), II, 156–157: ." . . if a sunflower, in turning toward the sun, becomes by that very act fully capable, without further condition, of reproducing a sunflower which turns in precisely corresponding ways toward the sun, and of so doing with the

same reproductive power, the sunflower would become a Representamen [and not a sign] of the sun." It seems, however, that thought-signs, or words, are in this respect precisely not heliotropic. [De Man]

[10]Irascible protagonist of the 1970s television comedy series "All in the Family."

difference is or is merely telling us that we should not even try to find out. Confronted with the question of the difference between grammar and rhetoric, grammar allows us to ask the question, but the sentence by means of which we ask it may deny the very possibility of asking. For what is the use of asking, I ask, when we cannot even authoritatively decide whether a question asks or doesn't ask?

The point is as follows. A perfectly clear syntactical paradigm (the question) engenders a sentence that has at least two meanings, one which asserts and the other which denies its own illocutionary mode. It is not that there are simply two meanings, one literal and the other figural, and that we have to decide which one of these meanings is the right one in this particular situation. The confusion can only be cleared up by the intervention of an extratextual intention, such as Archie Bunker setting his wife straight; but the very anger he displays is indicative of more than impatience: it reveals his despair when confronted with a structure of linguistic meaning that he cannot control and that holds the discouraging prospect of an infinity of similar future confusions, all of them potentially catastrophic in their consequences. Nor is this intervention really a part of the minitext constituted by the figure, which holds our attention only as long as it remains suspended and unresolved. I follow the usage of common speech in calling this semiological enigma "rhetorical." The grammatical model of the question becomes rhetorical not when we have, on the one hand, a literal meaning and, on the other hand, a figural meaning, but when it is impossible to decide by grammatical or other linguistic devices which of the two meanings (that can be entirely contradictory) prevails. Rhetoric radically suspends logic and opens up vertiginous possibilities of referential aberration. And although it would perhaps be somewhat more remote from common usage, I would not hesitate to equate the rhetorical, figural potentiality of language with literature itself. I could point to a great number of antecedents to this equation of literature with figure; the most recent reference would be to Monroe Beardsley's insistence in his contribution to the essays in honor of William Wimsatt that literary language is characterized by being "distinctly above the norm in ratio of implicit (or, I would say rhetorical) to explicit meaning."[11]

Let me pursue the question of the rhetorical question through one more example. Yeats's "Among School Children" ends with the famous line: "How can we know the dancer from the dance?" Although there are some revealing inconsistencies within the commentaries, the line is usually interpreted as stating, with the increased emphasis of a rhetorical device, the potential unity between form and experience, between creator and creation. It could be said that it denies the discrepancy between the sign and the referent from which we started. Many elements in the imagery and the dramatic development of the poem strengthen this traditional reading; without having to look any further than the immediately preceding lines, one finds powerful consecrated images of the continuity from part to whole that makes synecdoche into the most seductive of metaphors: the organic beauty of the tree, stated in the parallel syntax of a similar rhetorical question, or the convergence, in the dance, of erotic desire with musical form:

> O chestnut tree, great-rooted blossomer,
> Are you the leaf, the blossom or the bole?
> O body swayed to music, O brightening glance,
> How can we know the dancer from the dance?

A more extended reading, always assuming that the final line is to be read as a rhetorical question, reveals that the thematic and rhetorical grammar of the poem yields a consistent reading that extends from the first line to the last and that can account for all the details in the text. It is equally possible, however, to read the last line literally rather than figuratively, as asking with some urgency the question asked at the beginning of this essay within the context of contemporary criticism: it is *not* that sign and referent are so exquisitely fitted to each other that all difference between them is at times blotted out; but, rather, since the two essentially different elements, sign and meaning, are so intricately intertwined in the

[11]Frank Brady, John Palmer, and Martin Price, eds., *Literary Theory and Structure: Essays in Honor of William K. Wimsatt* (New Haven: Yale University Press, 1973), p. 37. [De Man]

imagined "presence" which the poem addresses, how can we possibly make the distinctions that would shelter us from the error of identifying what cannot be identified? The clumsiness of the paraphrase reveals that it is not necessarily the literal reading which is simpler than the figurative one, as was the case in my first example; here the figural reading, which assumes the question to be rhetorical, is perhaps naive, whereas the literal reading leads to greater complications of theme and statement. For it turns out that the entire scheme set up by the first reading can be undermined, or deconstructed, in the terms of the second, in which the final line is read literally as meaning that, since the dancer and the dance are not the same, it might be useful, perhaps even desperately necessary — for the question can be given a ring of urgency: "Please tell me, how *can* I know the dancer from the dance?" — to tell them apart. But this will replace the reading of each symbolic detail by a divergent interpretation. The oneness of trunk, leaf, and blossom, for example, that would have appealed to Goethe, would find itself replaced by the much less reassuring Tree of Life from the Mabinogion[12] that appears in the poem "Vacillation," in which the fiery blossom and the earthly leaf are held together, as well as apart, by the crucified and castrated god Attis, of whose body it can hardly be said that it is "not bruised to pleasure soul." This hint should suffice to suggest that two entirely coherent but entirely incompatible readings can be made to hinge on one line whose grammatical structure is devoid of ambiguity but whose rhetorical mode turns the mood as well as the mode of the entire poem upside down. Neither can we say, as was already the case in the first example, that the poem simply has two meanings which exist side by side. The two readings have to engage each other in direct confrontation, for the one reading is precisely the error denounced by the other and has to be undone by it. Nor can we in any way make a valid decision as to which of the readings can be given priority over the other; neither can exist in the other's absence. There can be no dance without a dancer, no

sign without a referent. On the other hand, the authority of the meaning engendered by the grammatical structure is fully obscured by the duplicity of a figure that cries out for the differentiation that it conceals.

Yeats's poem is not explicitly "about" rhetorical questions but about images or metaphors, and about the possibility of convergence between experiences of consciousness such as memory or emotions (what the poem calls passion, piety, and affection) and entities accessible to the senses, such as bodies, persons, or icons. We return to the inside/outside model from which we started and which the poem puts into question by means of a syntactical device (the question) made to operate on a grammatical as well as on a rhetorical level. The couple grammar/rhetoric, certainly not a binary opposition since they in no way exclude each other, disrupts and confuses the neat antithesis of the inside/outside pattern. We can transfer this scheme to the act of reading and interpretation. By reading we get, as we say, inside a text that was first something alien to us and which we now make our own by an act of understanding. But this understanding becomes at once the representation of an extratextual meaning; in Austin's terms, the illocutionary speech act becomes a perlocutionary actual act; in Frege's terms, *Bedeutung* becomes *Sinn.*[13] Our recurrent question is whether this transformation is semantically controlled along grammatical or along rhetorical lines. Does the metaphor of reading really unite outer meaning and inner understanding, action and reflection, into one single totality? The assertion is powerfully and suggestively made in a passage from Proust that describes the experience of reading as such a union. It describes the young Marcel hiding in the closed space of his room in order to read. The example differs from the earlier ones in that we are not dealing with a grammatical structure which also functions rhetorically but have instead the representation, the dramatization, in terms of the experience of a subject, of a rhetorical structure — just as, in many other passages, Proust dramatizes tropes by means of landscapes or descriptions of objects.

---

[12]Welsh Arthurian epic.

[13]Significance becomes meaning.

The figure here dramatized is that of metaphor, an inside/outside correspondence as represented by the act of reading. The reading scene is the culmination of a series of actions taking place in enclosed spaces and leading up to the "dark coolness" of Marcel's room.

I had stretched out on my bed, with a book, in my room which sheltered, tremblingly, its transparent and fragile coolness against the afternoon sun, behind the almost closed blinds through which a glimmer of daylight had nevertheless managed to push its yellow wings, remaining motionless between the wood and the glass, in a corner, poised like a butterfly. It was hardly light enough to read, and the sensation of the light's splendor was given to me only by the noise of Camus . . . hammering dusty crates; resounding in the sonorous atmosphere that is peculiar to hot weather, they seemed to spark off scarlet stars; and also by the flies executing their little concert, the chamber music of summer: evocative not in the manner of a human tune that, heard perchance during the summer, afterwards reminds you of it; it is connected to summer by a more necessary link: born from beautiful days, resurrecting only when they return, containing some of their essence, it does not only awaken their image in our memory; it guarantees their return, their actual, persistent, unmediated presence.

The dark coolness of my room related to the full sunlight of the street as the shadow relates to the ray of light, that is to say it was just as luminous and it gave my imagination the total spectacle of the summer, whereas my senses, if I had been on a walk, could only have enjoyed it by fragments; it matched my repose which (thanks to the adventures told by my book and stirring my tranquility) supported, like the quiet of a motionless hand in the middle of a running brook, the shock and the motion of a torrent of activity.[14]

From the beginning of the passage, inwardness is valorized positively as something desirable that has to protect itself against the intrusion of outside forces, but that nevertheless has to borrow, as it were, some of its constitutive properties from the outside. A chain of binary properties is set up and antithetically differentiated in terms of the inside/outside polarity: properties of coolness, darkness, repose, silence, imagination, and totality, associated with inwardness, contrast with the heat, the light, the activity, the sounds, the senses, and the fragmentation that govern the outside. By the act of reading, these static oppositions are put in motion, thus allowing for the play of substitutions by means of which the claim for totalization can be made. Thus, in a beautifully seductive effort of chiaroscuro,[15] mediated by the metaphor of light as a poised butterfly, the inner room is convincingly said to acquire the amount of light necessary to reading. In the wake of this light, warmth can also enter the room, incarnate in the auditive synaesthesia[16] of the various sounds. According to the narrator, these metaphorical substitutions and reversals render the presence of summer in the room more completely than the actual experience of summer in the outside world could have done. The text achieves this synthesis and comments on it in normative[17] terms, comparable to the manner in which treatises of practical rhetoric recommend the use of one figure in preference to another in a given situation: here it is the substitutive totalization by metaphor which is said to be more effective than the mere contiguity of metonymic association. As opposed to the random contingency of metonymy ("*par hasard*"),[18] the metaphor is linked to its proper meaning by, says Proust, the "necessary link" that leads to perfect synthesis. In the wake of this synthesis, the entire conceptual vocabulary of metaphysics enters the text: a terminology of generation, of transcendental necessity, of totality, of essence, of permanence, and of unmediated presence. The passage acts out and asserts the priority of metaphor over metonymy in terms of the categories of metaphysics and with reference to the act of reading.

The actual test of the truth of the assertion comes in the second paragraph when the absurd ratio set up at the beginning has to be verified by a further substitution. This time, what has to be exchanged are not only the properties of light and

[14]*A la recherche du temps perdu* (Paris: Pléiade, 1954), I, 83. Translation by de Man. [De Man]

[15]Mixture of light and shadow.
[16]Sensual confusion, as when a sound strikes one as like a color.
[17]Evaluative.
[18]By chance.

dark, warm and cool, fragment and totality (part and whole), but the properties of action and repose. The full seduction of the text can come into being only when the formal totalization of light and dark is completed by the transfer from rest to action that represents the extratextual, referential moment. The text asserts the transfer in the concluding sentence: "The dark coolness of my room . . . supported, like the quiet of a motionless hand in the middle of a running brook, the shock and the motion of a torrent of activity." The verb "to support" here carries the full weight of uniting rest and action (*repos et activité*), fiction and reality, as firmly as the base supports the column. The transfer, as is so often the case in Proust, is carried out by the liquid element of the running brook. The natural, representational connotation of the passage is with coolness, so particularly attractive within the predominant summer-mood of the entire *Recherche*. But coolness, it will be remembered, is one of the characteristic properties of the "inside" world. It cannot therefore by itself transfer us into the opposite world of activity. The movement of the water evokes a freshness which in the binary logic of the passage is associated with the inward, imaginary world of reading and fiction. In order to accede to action, it would be necessary to capture one of the properties belonging to the opposite chain, such as warmth. The mere "cool" action of fiction cannot suffice: it is necessary to reconcile the cool immobility of the hand with the heat of action if the claim made by the sentence is to stand up as true. This transfer is carried out, within the same sentence, when it is said that repose supports "a torrent of activity." The expression "torrent d'activité" is not, or is no longer, a metaphor in French: it is a cliché, a dead or sleeping metaphor that has lost the suggestive, connotative values contained in the word "torrent." It simply means "a great deal of activity," the amount of activity that is likely to agitate one to the point of getting hot. Heat is thus surreptitiously smuggled into the passage from a cold source, closing the ring of antithetical properties and allowing for their exchange and substitution: from the moment tranquility can be active and warm without losing its coolness and its distinctive quality of repose, the fragmented experience of reality can become whole without losing its quality of being real.

The transfer is made to seem convincing and seductive by the double play of the cliché "torrent of activity." The proximate, contiguous image of the brook awakens, as it were, the sleeping beauty of the dozing metaphor which, in its common use, had become the metonymic association of two words united by sheer habit and no longer by the inner necessity, the "necessary link," of a transcendental signification. "Torrent" functions in a double semantic register: in its reawakened literal meaning it relays the attribute of coolness that is actually part of the running water, whereas in its figural nonmeaning it designates the quantity of activity connotative of the contrary property of warmth.

The rhetorical structure of this sentence is therefore not simply metaphorical. It is at least doubly metonymic, first because the coupling of words in a cliché is governed not by the necessary link that reveals their potential identity but by the contingent habit of proximity; second, because the reawakening of the metaphorical term "torrent" is carried out by a statement that happens to be in the vicinity, but without there being any necessity for this proximity on the level of the referential meaning. The most striking thing is that this doubly metonymic structure is found in a text that also contains highly seductive and successful metaphors (as in the chiaroscuro effect of the beginning, or in the condensation of light in the butterfly image) and that explicitly asserts the superiority of metaphor over metonymy in terms of metaphysical categories.

That these metaphysical categories do not remain unaffected by such a reading would become clear from an inclusive reading of Proust's novel and would become even more explicit in a language-conscious philosopher such as Nietzsche who, as a philosopher, has to be concerned with the epistemological consequences of the kind of rhetorical seductions exemplified by the Proust passage. It can be shown that the systematic critique of the main categories of metaphysics undertaken by Nietzsche in his late work, the critique of the concepts of causality, of the subject, of identity, of referential and revealed truth, and others, occurs along the same pattern of deconstruction that is operative in Proust's text; and it can also be shown that this pattern exactly corresponds to Nietzsche's description, in texts that precede *The Will to Power* by more than fifteen years, of the structure of the main rhetorical tropes. The key to this critique of metaphysics, which is itself a recurrent gesture throughout the history of thought, is the rhetorical model of the trope or, if one prefers to call it that, literature. It turns out that in these innocent-looking didactic exercises we are in fact playing for very sizable stakes.

It is therefore all the more necessary to know what is linguistically involved in a rhetorically conscious reading of the type here undertaken on a brief fragment from a novel and extended by Nietzsche to the entire text of post-Hellenic thought. Our first examples, which dealt with rhetorical questions, were rhetorizations of grammar, figures generated by syntactical paradigms, whereas the Proust example could be better described as a grammatization of rhetoric. The passage from a paradigmatic structure based on contingent association, such as metonymy, shows the mechanical, repetitive aspect of grammatical forms to be operative in a passage that seems at first sight to celebrate the self-willed and autonomous inventiveness of a subject. Figures are assumed to be inventions, the products of a highly particularized individual talent, whereas no one can claim credit for the programmed pattern of grammar. Yet our reading of the Proust passage shows that precisely when the highest claims are being made for the unifying power of metaphor, these very images rely in fact on the deceptive use of semi-automatic grammatical patterns. The deconstruction of metaphor and of all rhetorical patterns, such as mimesis, paronomasis,[19] or personification, that use resemblance as a way to disguise differences, takes us back to the impersonal precision of grammar and of a semiology derived from grammatical patterns. Such a deconstruction puts into question a whole series of concepts that underlie the value judgments of our critical discourse: the metaphors of primacy, of genetic history, and, most notably, of the autonomous power to will of the self.

[19]Plays on words, puns.

There seems to be a difference, then, between what I called the rhetorization of grammar (as in the rhetorical question) and the grammatization of rhetoric, as in the deconstructive readings of the type sketched in the passage from Proust. The former ends up in indetermination, in a suspended uncertainty that was unable to choose between two modes of reading, whereas the latter seems to reach a truth, albeit by the negative road of exposing an error, a false pretense. After the deconstructive reading of the Proust passage we can no longer believe the assertion made in this passage about the intrinsic, metaphysical superiority of metaphor over metonymy. We seem to end up in a mood of negative assurance that is highly productive of critical discourse. The further text of Proust's novel, for example, responds perfectly to an extended application of this deconstructive pattern: not only can similar gestures be repeated throughout the novel, at all the crucial articulations or all passages where large aesthetic and metaphysical claims are being made (the scenes of involuntary memory, the workshop of Elstir, the septette of Vinteuil, the convergence of author and narrator at the end of the novel), but a vast thematic and semiotic network is revealed, a network that structures the entire narrative and that remains invisible to a reader caught in a naive metaphorical mystification. The whole of literature would respond in similar fashion, although the techniques and the patterns would have to vary considerably, of course, from author to author. But there is absolutely no reason why analyses of the kind here suggested for Proust would not be applicable, with proper modifications of technique, to Milton or to Dante or to Hölderlin. This will in fact be the task of literary criticism in the coming years.

It would seem that we are saying that criticism is the deconstruction of literature, the reduction to the rigors of grammar of rhetorical mystifications. And if we hold up Nietzsche as the philosopher of such a critical deconstruction, then the literary critic would become the philosopher's ally in his struggle with the poets. Criticism and literature would separate around the epistemological axis that distinguishes grammar from rhetoric. It is easy enough to see that this apparent glorification of the critic-philosopher in the name of truth is in fact a glorification of the poet as the primary source of this truth; if truth is the recognition of the systematic character of a certain kind of error, then it would be fully dependent on the prior existence of this error. Philosophers of science like Gaston Bachelard or Wittgenstein are notoriously dependent on the aberrations of the poets. We are back at our unanswered question: does the grammatization of rhetoric end up in the negative certainty, or does it, like the rhetorization of grammar, remain suspended in the ignorance of its own truth or falsehood?

Two concluding remarks should suffice to answer the question. First of all, it is not true that Proust's text can simply be reduced to the mystified assertion — the superiority of metaphor over metonymy — that our reading deconstructs. The reading is not "our" reading, since it uses only the linguistic elements provided by the text itself; the distinction between author and reader is one of the false distinctions that the deconstruction makes evident. The deconstruction is not something we have added to the text; it constituted the text in the first place. A literary text simultaneously asserts and denies the authority of its own rhetorical mode; and, by reading the text as we did, we were only trying to come closer to being as rigorous a reader as the author had to be in order to write the sentence in the first place. Poetic writing is the most advanced and refined mode of deconstruction; it may differ from critical or discursive writing in the economy of its articulation, but it is not different in kind.

But if we recognize the existence of the deconstructive moment as constitutive of all literary language, we have surreptitiously reintroduced the categories that this deconstruction was supposed to eliminate and that have merely been displaced. We have, for example, displaced the question of the self from the referent into the figure of the narrator, who then becomes the *signifié*[20] of the passage. It again becomes possible to ask such naive questions as what Proust's, or Marcel's, motives may have been in thus manipulating language: was he fooling himself, or was he represented as fooling himself and fooling us

into believing that fiction and action are as easy to unite, by reading, as the passage asserts? The pathos of the entire section, which would have been more noticeable if the quotation had been a little more extended, the narrator's constant vacillation between guilt and well-being, invites such questions. They are absurd questions, of course, since the reconciliation of fact and fiction occurs itself as a mere assertion made in a text, and is thus productive of more text at the moment when it asserts its decision to escape from textual confinement. But even if we free ourselves of all false questions of intent and rightfully reduce the narrator to the status of a mere grammatical pronoun, without which the deconstructive narrative could not come into being, this subject remains endowed with a function that is not grammatical but rhetorical, in that it gives voice, so to speak, to a grammatical syntagm.[21] The term "voice," even when we speak of the passive or interrogative voice, is, of course, a metaphor inferring by analogy the intent of the subject from the structure of the predicate. In the case of the deconstructive discourse that we call literary, or rhetorical, or poetic, this creates a distinctive complication illustrated by the Proust passage. The deconstructive reading revealed a first paradox: the passage valorizes metaphor as being the "right" literary figure, but then proceeds to constitute itself by means of the epistemologically incompatible figure of metonymy. The deconstructive critical discourse reveals the presence of this delusion and affirms it as the irreversible mode of its truth. It cannot pause there however. For if we then ask the obvious and simple next question, whether the rhetorical mode of the text in question is that of metaphor or metonymy, it is impossible to give an answer. Individual metaphors, such as the chiaroscuro effect or the butterfly, are shown to be subordinate figures in a general clause whose syntax is metonymic; from this point of view, it seems that the rhetoric is superseded by a grammar that deconstructs it. But this metonymic clause has as its subject a voice whose relationship to this clause is again metaphorical. The narrator who tells us about the impossibility of

---

[20]Signified; the thing represented by a sign.

[21]Linkage.

metaphor is himself, or itself, a metaphor, the metaphor of a grammatical syntagm whose meaning is the denial of metaphor stated, by antiphrasis, as its priority. And this subject-metaphor is, in its turn, open to the kind of deconstruction to the second degree, the rhetorical deconstruction of psycholinguistics, in which the more advanced investigations of literature are presently engaged, against considerable resistance.

We end up, therefore, in the case of the rhetorical grammatization of semiology, just as in the grammatical rhetorization of illocutionary phrases, in the same state of suspended ignorance. Any question about the rhetorical mode of a literary text is always a rhetorical question that

does not even know whether it is really questioning. The resulting pathos is an anxiety (or bliss, depending on one's momentary mood or individual temperament) of ignorance, not an anxiety of reference — as becomes thematically clear in Proust's novel when reading is dramatized, in the relationship between Marcel and Albertine, not as an emotive reaction to what language does, but as an emotive reaction to the impossibility of knowing what it might be up to. Literature as well as criticism — the difference between them being delusive — is condemned (or privileged) to be forever the most rigorous and, consequently, the most unreliable language in terms of which man names and modifies himself.

❖ DIALOGUE WITH PAUL DE MAN

Lawrence Lipking

b. 1934

The son of a prizefighter, eighteenth-century scholar Lawrence Lipking was born in New York City in 1934. He attended Columbia University for two years before transferring to Western Reserve University (now Case Western Reserve University), where he graduated magna cum laude in 1955. He went on to Cornell, where he received an M.A. in 1956 and a Ph.D. in 1962. While at Princeton University, where he was a professor of comparative literature, Lipking published The Ordering of the Arts in Eighteenth-Century England *(1970) and was a co-editor of the* Norton Anthology of English Literature. *Since 1979 he has been professor of English at Northwestern University. In 1982, he published* The Life of the Poet, *and in 1988,* Abandoned Women and Poetic Tradition. *Lipking may be best known today for his 1998 literary biography,* Samuel Johnson: The Life of an Author, *in which he concentrates on the part Johnson self-consciously played in the formation of the figure of the professional author.*

Lipking has long been interested in the problem of meaning in art, to the extent that it can be constructed in an age of deconstruction, and the role of the author in an age of "The Death of the Author." In the following essay, "The Practice of Theory," he discusses, through a pedagogical model, the ways in which deconstruction dismantles the previously dominant model of New Criticism (and any notion of value in the arts beyond the purely aesthetic), but may also be replacing the New Criticism with an equally limiting dominant model of scholarship. Lipking is specifically addressing the sort of close reading de Man has demonstrated in "Semiology and Rhetoric," for example, with Yeats's "Among School Children," among other texts, and practiced by other critics who have adopted his method. But this essay has a broader reach than a reply to de Man, since it questions the adequacy of formalism, structuralism, and deconstruction in their representation of texts that float free, unanchored by biography and history.

"The Practice of Theory" originated as a talk delivered at the 1983 ADE Summer Seminar at Southwest Texas State University. ADE stands for Associated Departments of English, and is an organization for department chairs in English.

The Practice of Theory

I have been asked to talk about poststructuralism in the classroom — the uses of contemporary literary theory in teaching undergraduates, as well as some of its consequences — and that is what I intend to try to do. But I had better admit at once that in some respects this invitation strikes me as comic. To begin with, you have asked the wrong person. Deconstruction is not my game. It is a bit as if a sheep had been commissioned to say something sympathetic about wolves, from a wolf's point of view. Even with the best intentions, he could not help feeling sheepish — especially when the thought of those teeth crossed his mind. Yet there are worse things for a sheep to try to do, of course, than to think like a wolf. It may give him a fresh perspective on life and even, in some situations, make it possible for him to survive. That is what I hope for today.

A more serious objection to my project, however, might be offered by many theorists themselves: Does theory belong in the classroom? One currently fashionable line of argument would insist that it does not. The truth of a difficult idea, such critics maintain, does not depend on its accessibility to undergraduates or its ability to generate plausible "readings." Theory must be judged by its own standards, not by its immediate practical uses, and not everyone is equally qualified to pursue it. Indeed, the pragmatic American tendency to rush every new idea into the classroom, reducing an adventure of thought to a pedagogical exercise, accounts for the weakness of our theory in relation to the Continental mode. Truth stands on a high hill, and salespersons like to take shortcuts. Better to keep our students and theory apart.

This view is of course elitist. That makes it un-American but not necessarily wrong. And

young theorists seem to me entitled to this line of defense, at least up to a point. The excitement of much current intellectual debate about literature has been stirred by the number of questions that remain to be answered. It seems that everything that literary critics once thought they knew about — the author, the reader, the meaning, the structure, the world — is called into question. Nor should one underestimate the sense of possibility that has resulted. At least a dozen times, during the past few years, some bright young person has told me how fortunate she feels to be alive at a moment when literary theory has come to the forefront, when our own field has replaced philosophy, linguistics, history, psychology at the frontier of knowledge. So much is still to be done! Each time I have replied the same way: how lucky for you that you think that! And however ironic, my comment is also sincere. Young theorists must be granted a piece of the future, a chance to work out their ideas without being called instantly to account. They need some time to be muddled, or even to find the truth. And the classroom may not be the best place for that search. Our students do not refute our ideas by failing to understand them — fortunately for us!

But can theory be *kept* from the classroom? Another group of theorists strongly denies it. Even the most naive discussion of a literary work, they would argue, is based on assumptions and presuppositions that determine what can be seen and what can be talked about. Theory surrounds us like the air we breathe. In a recent survey in *New Literary History* (Winter 1983), which asked a wide sample of scholars how theory had affected their teaching, about half the respondents replied that everything they do partakes of theory. "Any study of literature is implicitly or explicitly a theoretical study, even if, and in a sense all the more tellingly when, it denies itself as such" (427). Thus literary historians and critics who consider their work unrelated to theory, on this analysis, are self-deluded; they obey principles all the more dogmatic for never being brought out in the open. And the practice of every classroom reflects the assumptions that teachers and students bring with them. There is no way out of this circle. Consider the depth of the epistemological and psychological problems raised by a reader who says, "I know what I like." Knowing and liking can hardly be taken for granted. From this point of view the classroom necessarily functions as a laboratory where the usefulness of theories is tested as an arena where they fight for supremacy. In literary studies there may be good theories and bad theories; but no sanctuary exists in which there are no theories.

To some extent this disagreement about whether theory belongs in the classroom is more apparent than real. It results from different definitions of theory. The first group tends to regard literary theory as a rigorous and strenuous field of knowledge, related to philosophy and often to science, whose object is to formulate axioms and laws of inquiry that may or may not bear any relation to concrete works of literature or common sense. Adherents of this view often justify it by its future. Literary theory, they may say, does not yet exist; and to ask it to demonstrate its usefulness when its very possibility has yet to be established is clearly a hostile demand. But the second group regards theory more descriptively, as the principles or rules of procedure that motivate what we actually do with texts. Seen this way, theory is not only possible but necessary and inevitable. It is the breath and finer spirit of all practice, practice itself in a self-reflective mood. Hence all teaching departs from and turns back into theory, insofar as the purpose of teaching is to make students conscious of what they are doing. Where instinctive reading was, there theory shall be.

These two positions, distinct as they are in logic, may easily coexist in the same mind. In fact they usually do. However reluctant to prostitute his ideas for the sake of undergraduates, the philosopher who is also a teacher can seldom resist the temptation to tell them the truth. And more than one literary theorist conceives her work as bringing reports from the frontline of the classroom to the command post of *Boundary 2*.[1] Theory and practice mingle in unholy alliance like writing papers and grading them or having a taste for reading and getting a job. We make our livings by juggling the two together. It is only natural, then, for professors to feel that their own most stringent ideas are just what the public needs. Nothing is more common, in contemporary American criticism, than a strange combination of elitism and evangelism. On the one hand the critic insists on the right to follow his ideas to their ultimate, most uncanny consequences, free from the constraints of ordinary language, common readers, authorial intentions, historical conventions, or even "the work." On the other hand he often claims that his own work provides an example from which other readers might profit, a hermeneutic[2] model that might redeem the rest of humanity from its shortsightedness. A particularly heady atmosphere of such elitism and evangelism accounts for much of the Early Christian air around New Haven.[3] I do not want to claim that I am above it. Like most other literary critics, I too both take pride in the uniqueness of my insights and think that everyone else ought to share them. But most of the public refuses to rise to our heights, and before we can convert them we must find some common ground. For professors that ground is usually the classroom.

There is another reason why some of the most refined contemporary literary theory seems adaptable to undergraduate teaching. To a high degree the form of that theory *is* practice. However esoteric, most theorists begin with a text, and they arrive at their generalizations not through direct statement but through teasing them out of that text. Sometimes the text is a philosophical treatise, sometimes a poem, and often, of late, a

[1] A journal of postmodern culture and politics then edited by theorist Paul Bové.
[2] Interpretive.
[3] Lipking alludes to the Christian commitment of the New Critics, some of whom taught at Yale.

chance remark, a piece of marginalia, or a fragment in a notebook ("I have forgotten my umbrella"). But whatever the provenance of the text or the use to which the text is put, the method of theory still tends toward close reading. One way of describing recent developments in criticism would be as an intensification of close reading, New Criticism with a vengeance, in which the reading eventually becomes so close — like a page held a few inches from the eye — that the sentences break into fragments and the words dissolve into syllables. ("Atone" turns into "at one" and "therapist" parts to reveal "the rapist.") Most deconstructionists, to be sure, reject this association with close reading. They prefer to regard their enterprise not as a method but as the subversion of any method, not as close reading but as the detonation, primed from within, of any stable reading. So be it. Yet whatever the intention behind the deconstruction of texts, its surface manifestations often bear a remarkable resemblance to old-fashioned explication. Indeed, in standard professional terms (such as the comments of readers of *PMLA*)[4] the main effect of recent theory has been to lend a new impetus and sense of importance to finer and finer close readings. Most of the practical criticism that teaches the *PMLA* editorial board these days begins and ends with theoretical statements, sometimes quite esoteric. But in between lies the reading. Theory itself requires it. And any teacher who is willing to spend a few days mastering the vocabulary of such explications will find much that can be passed on to his or her own students.

How might this work in practice? Poststructuralists have tended to be quite reticent about the use of their ideas in literature courses (aside from courses in literary theory). But let me provide an example. I take, as my exhibit, a poem that gets taught to a great many undergraduates, "Sailing to Byzantium." The choice of this text seems appropriate for several reasons. First, it is canonical. Many teachers know it by heart and probably feel fairly certain that they understand it. Second, it has served more than one generation of critics as a test case for their methods. For several

of the New Critics it seemed a perfect verbal icon or type of the concrete universal, a timeless artifact whose form and theme alike expressed the fusion of structure and content, or nature and art, that every great poem embodies. Yet other sorts of critics had no trouble adapting it to their own methods of analysis, as when Northrop Frye observed in it all the archetypes of the comic vision: "the city, the tree, the bird, the community of sages, the geometrical gyre and the detachment from the cyclic world."[5] If any theory of poetry works, it ought to be able to account for "Sailing to Byzantium." Yet a third reason for choosing this poem is that for me, and I suspect for some other readers, it has gone a bit dead. We know what to say about it and may be quite skilled at getting our students to say the same things, but its formal perfection often leaves us cold; and students are wonderfully quick at picking up such attitudes, even when they have not been expressed. For those of us in this predicament, a new way of reading "Sailing to Byzantium" would be highly useful.

I

That is no country for old men. The young
In one another's arms, birds in the trees
— Those dying generations — at their song,
The salmon-falls, the mackerel-crowded seas,
Fish, flesh, or fowl, commend all summer long
Whatever is begotten, born, and dies.
Caught in that sensual music all neglect
Monuments of unageing intellect.

II

An aged man is but a paltry thing,
A tattered coat upon a stick, unless
Soul clap its hands and sing, and louder sing
For every tatter in its mortal dress,
Nor is there singing school but studying
Monuments of its own magnificence;
And therefore I have sailed the seas and come
To the holy city of Byzantium.

III

O sages standing in God's holy fire
As in the gold mosaic of a wall,
Come from the holy fire, perne in a gyre,
And be the singing-masters of my soul.
Consume my heart away; sick with desire

---

[4]Publication of the Modern Language Association of America, the journal published by the largest organization of college-level literature teachers.

[5]See p. 691 for more on Frye.

And fastened to a dying animal
It knows not what it is; and gather me
Into the artifice of eternity.

IV

Once out of nature I shall never take
My bodily form from any natural thing.
But such a form as Grecian goldsmiths make
Of hammered gold and gold enamelling
To keep a drowsy Emperor awake;
Or set upon a golden bough to sing
To lords and ladies of Byzantium
Of what is past, or passing, or to come.

I omit the first few stages, which for certain theorists have now become quite problematical. That is, my discussion will have little to say about the texts of the poem, its historical and biographical background, or even the minimal information that some teachers will think necessary to allow students to make basic sense of the poem (where is that country? what is Byzantium? how old was W. B. Yeats?). The Norton Anthology is good enough for me. In fact it is far too good, since it insists on providing interpretations — "The theme of this poem, though not the treatment, is similar to that of Keats's *Ode on a Grecian Urn*" — whereas all I want is a glossary or word-hoard that will supply all the possible meanings of "perne" and "gyre" as well as their etymologies. The rest does not matter, because in this class "Sailing to Byzantium" will not be an illustration of the doctrine in *A Vision*;[6] an autobiographical testament, an example of a poetic genre, a symbol of art, a verbal icon, or anything else except a piece of language. Students who have done homework on the "sources" or "meaning" of the poem will be told to shut up or, more subtly, questioned until it becomes obvious that they do not know what they are talking about. I will give no quizzes here. The language is all that counts. But does "Sailing to Byzantium" make any sense when regarded strictly as a piece of language? That question is exactly what provides the energy for class discussion. "*Does this make sense?*" I ask again and again; and, unlike older critics and teachers, I do not coerce my students by implying that the perfect coherence and correctness of the sense will

become manifest if they work hard enough to decipher it. One of my own teachers used to say, "It is not the poem that is on trial here but you"; in this class, though, the poem is on trial. We notice, for instance, its tendency to contradict itself. When the class is asked why soul should "louder sing / For every tatter in its mortal dress," one student answers that the soul is desperately singing to try to drown out the sound of ripping, and another student thinks that the soul is singing in celebration of those tatters, which bring it closer to freedom; and, after other students have had their say, we do not try to resolve this contradiction or find the proper meaning as it appeared to Yeats. Instead we observe the duplicity of that word "for," which can signify either "in spite of" or "on behalf of" as well as many other things. Thus the line does not make sense, if by sense we understand a single unequivocal meaning or even the Aristotelian logic that asserts that nothing can be both itself and not itself at the same time. Language goes its own way; it does not obey Aristotle or Yeats or Humpty-Dumpty.[7]

Read in this light, a surprising amount of "Sailing to Byzantium" turns out not to make any sense or to make so many senses that no interpretation can make sense of them. I will not rehearse the difficulty of generations of schoolchildren with the syntax of "Nor is there singing school but studying" (probably that was what they asked the old man about when he walked through the long schoolroom questioning). Does it imply that there is, or is not, a singing school? My students will not be forced to choose. Is the artifice of eternity something permanent (an eternal artifice) or something evanescent (an illusion without any substance)? My students will not have to make up their minds. What is the syntax of the opening "That" (which Yeats himself once said was the worst syntax he ever wrote)? In this classroom all answers will be entertained.

Perhaps this sounds like total permissiveness, an extreme version of the situation encouraged by

---

[6]Yeats's explanation of his mystical beliefs (1925).

[7]Lipking alludes to Lewis Carroll's *Through the Looking Glass* (1871): "When *I* use a word," Humpty Dumpty said, in a rather scornful tone, "it means just what I choose it to mean, neither more nor less."

some reader-response theorists in which each student is invited to use the text in order to make up some poem of his or her own, through free association or a homemade personal identity kit. But that is not my scheme. I do not ask my class, "Does this make sense *for you?*" Instead, the more austere form of the question — "Does this make sense?" — directs attention away from personal responses and toward the condition of language that makes variant responses possible or even inevitable. The cacophony of voices in my classroom does not result from rampant individualism. Rather, it reflects the cacophony within the language of the poem — its multiple, uncontrollable meanings. Anything goes, not because I have permitted it, but because language itself, as an arbitrary and unstable system of differences, must be capable of saying anything. Nor does this cacophony stop at the level of the phrase and the sentence. It applies as well to the whole structure of the poem, to the story or allegory of meaning it tries to construct. In my classroom we spend most of our time looking squarely at a "fact" that most other classrooms spend all their time trying to avoid. To put it simply: in strict logical terms most of "Sailing to Byzantium" does not work. The elementary polarities that seem to provide its frame — the dialectic of "that country" and Byzantium, of young and old, of time and timelessness, of body and soul, above all of nature and art — do not hold up under a careful reading. Thus the schematic contrast of "Whatever is begotten, born, and dies" with "what is past, or passing, or to come" does not satisfy my students. They notice that some of the parallelism is false; that "lives," for instance, would match "passing" much better than "born" does and that the relation of "begotten" to "past" is far from obvious. Even the neat contrast between "dies" and "to come," the time-bound state of the living and the eternity of the artifice, does not quite work, since the fact that birds die does not keep their songs too from being repeated eternally by later generations. The poem has deliberately fudged such issues. My students begin to realize that their own confusions respond to something confused or ungraspable in "Sailing to Byzantium" itself.

A similar analysis might be applied to every element of the poem. I will spare you the details.

But one point of internal contradiction is so important and obvious that it is noticed by a great many students, and even some critics. When the speaker claims that "Once out of nature I shall never take/My bodily form from any natural thing," he seems to ignore the blatant fact that every bodily form must be taken from nature, whether the form of a bird or simply the golden form embodied by an artist. In a famous letter, Sturge Moore[8] told Yeats that "Sailing to Byzantium" had let him down in the fourth stanza, "as such a goldsmith's bird is as much nature as a man's body, especially if it only sings like Homer and Shakespeare of what is past or passing or to come to Lords and Ladies"; and Yeats was impressed enough by the point to write "Byzantium," since Moore had showed him "that the idea needed exposition." But neither Moore nor Yeats saw how deep the criticism went. The false opposition between nature and art begins not in the fourth stanza but in the first, where the description of "nature" is thoroughly conditioned by "art." The lushness and prettiness of "that country," where the young are always in one another's arms and the salmon are always running, has a basic artificiality that only a poet could overlook. No student overlooks it. The poem composes a colorful postcard that resembles Ireland no more than a travel brochure. Indeed, the language itself confesses its interest in "sensual music" — not the unmediated country of the senses but the senses patterned by art. Insofar as any form can be "out of nature," the form of the first stanza already achieves that state. Hence the speaker's departure from nature, attained with such seeming difficulty, is actually always already present, contained in the framework or dialectic that allows the poem to begin. It is easy to leave nature if you have never been there in the first place — or impossible if you have been.

Seen in this way, the opposition of nature and art in "Sailing to Byzantium" may be understood for what it is: not a reference to anything existing

[8]Thomas Sturge Moore (1870–1944) wrote poetry, plays, and literary criticism, and was an art critic and a graphic artist in his own right; he designed some of Yeats's book covers and the masks and costumes for some of his plays at the Abbey Theater.

in "the world" but a system of differences in which each term gives meaning to the other. That country and Byzantium are equally unreal; they acquire significance only by being contrasted with each other. Hence a student who has never learned to equate that country with Ireland or Byzantium with what Yeats said about it may well have an advantage in analyzing the poem; no irrelevant images or "facts" will interfere with the self-contained system of language that is all we can know or need to know.

At this point of the discussion my students, if they have been paying attention, have been born into structuralism. But we have not yet accounted for the full extent to which "Sailing to Byzantium" does not work — the unease with which we perceived not only the artificiality of its system of differences but the slippage or instability in the system. It is time to enter the poststructuralist age. Let us read even closer.

We come back to "That." By this time even that somewhat jaundiced engineer in the back row is ready to wave his hand and explain the point of "That": it contrasts with "this," the holy city to which the speaker has sailed, about which we know the one important thing: it is the opposite of "That." But teacher is not so easy to please. Once again I ask my magic question: Does this make sense? How can a "that" be specified so soon, before the system of the poem or of language has established a place for it? Doesn't it seem to propose that "That" might exist prior to a system or syntax, as if a "that" could be there without a "this"? After a long pause, one of the brighter students suggests that the speaker seems to be pointing — pointing toward something outside of language, something we cannot see. The footnote tells us "Ireland." But "Ireland" is also a mere form of language, a word that substitutes for whatever the speaker is pointing at, a word that does not satisfy our search for what the speaker sees. Perhaps later we will know.

But later never comes. The absent referent of "That" will never materialize on the page. Nor is there any evidence that the speaker himself ever knew exactly what he was talking about. By pointing outside the system of language, the poem creates the illusion of a presence somewhere else. But that presence is communicated only through absences and deferrals, the endless strategies through which language tempts us to believe that we will arrive at a meaning. There is never an end to this process. It is not only the poem that does not work but the whole system of language to which it belongs. No matter how long the class stays on after the bell, it will never explain away *that*. No, it does not make sense.

Perhaps I can clarify this point by reading the allegory of "Sailing to Byzantium" once more, as a struggle between the medium of language in which the poet lives and the pure significance he hopes some day to find. At the moment his sense is still entrapped in words. Consider the resonance of a phrase like "Fish, flesh, or fowl." It asks for an analysis that has nothing to do with meaning and everything to do with sounds. The consonants of the first noun are modulated by the "l" introduced in the second, and that "l" then resolves the phrase as a whole. At the same time the vowels gradually open until the initial pinched "i" has lengthened into the diphthong "ow." Reverse the sequence — "fowl, flesh, or fish" — and the phrase would become harsh and constricted; substitute "meat" for "flesh" and it becomes grotesque. What shall we conclude? Clearly the effect depends not on meaning, let alone "unageing intellect"; it would not survive translation to another language, like Byzantine Greek. Rather, it depends on "sensual music," the pleasant way that certain cadences strike the ear. Linguistically, one might say that the emphasis has fallen on the signifier, not the signified, on the words, not their significance. But such music does not seem good enough for the speaker. He wants another artistic world in which the signifier and the signified are one and the music explains itself. Byzantium, as he conceives it, is such a world. There the sages are at once the medium and the message, the artifact and its interpreters. They speak directly to the soul and teach it how to sing without the need for any mediation, in a universal language (there is no indication that Yeats thought his soul would need to learn Greek in order to talk to its masters). In Byzantium the arbitrariness of the sign disappears, and the song itself makes the world of which it sings.

Yet the poem itself does not, of course, arrive there. It is only "sailing" to Byzantium. At best it projects that state of a seamless union between word and meaning, subject and object, signifier and signified, into the future. It does not, it cannot, reach that state. Language does not allow such perfection or such closure. As we have already seen, the poem contains the evidence of its own betrayal, a deconstruction of its own distinctions between nature and art or time and the timeless. "The idea," Yeats thought, "needed exposition"; but that exposition could only be another poem, which leads in turn to another poem in an infinite regress of explanations and resolutions that never quite work. We do not command our own language, and we cannot escape it. Hence the true "meaning" of "Sailing to Byzantium," as revealed by rigorous close reading, is the impossibility of ever arriving at a true meaning. The closer we come to Byzantium, the more we discover that we have never left home. The soul will never stand outside itself and "know what it is." At home and abroad we swim in a sea of language.

At this point the class is still, and I realize that for the past few minutes I have done all the talking. Nothing to say, at such moments, but "Class dismissed." But fellow teachers may want to ask a few more questions. What use has this exercise been? Does it furnish a model of teaching literature that ought to be exported to other classrooms? What are its implications for undergraduate education or for the future of our profession? These are hard questions, and I will not pretend that I have all the answers. But a theory so dedicated to exploring the self-consciousness and inner contradictions of literature can hardly avoid the demand to be self-conscious about its own practice. If poststructuralism turns out not to have been a mere fashion or elite amusement, then its consequences will eventually affect us all. Let me try some tentative comments on where this analysis leads. To begin with, I will admit something that most of you have already suspected: my account of that classroom session was rather too neat. Perhaps it was even phony. For it left out one crucial element that every teacher knows about, the resistance of students. I do not mean only dumb resistance, the silence or apathy of those who have not done the reading or who will never be persuaded, by any means, to pay attention to something as hard and beautiful

and unlike a videogame as a poem by Yeats. I mean also the resistance of the good students, those who genuinely take pleasure in some poetry and want to understand it. Those students are also uneasy. Many of them were intrigued by "Sailing to Byzantium" when they read it — some of them even loved it — and came to class prepared to share their pleasure, to learn more about Yeats and his kind of poetry, to grasp the theme and story better, and to find out how the poem works. They may also have looked forward to praising it or to hearing why Yeats was "great." But some of them now perceive the class as having been a subtle — or not so subtle — attack on "Sailing to Byzantium," an analysis of how the poem does not make sense and does not work. Nor are they consoled to hear, now and in later classes, that all the other poems they like do not work in just the same way. They resisted the teacher while he was asking questions, and now that he has finished they continue to resist him. On the final examination they will ignore the classroom discussion and put down some chestnuts gathered from the Norton Anthology. ("In his old age, the poet repudiates the world of biological change, . . . putting behind him images of breeding and sensuality to turn to 'monuments of unageing intellect,' in a world of art and artifice outside of time.") They will get a B-.

How much notice does a theorist need to take of such resistance? The answer will vary from teacher to teacher. If self-satisfied, he may not notice it at all; if skillful, she may overcome it; if discouraged, he may resolve to give up teaching entirely or to stop mixing theory with practice. But a young teacher might become more self-conscious about her theory. One respondent to the *NLH* survey, a graduate student who had just taught his first course in theory, was honest enough to confess that it did not live up to his expectations: the students "had serious difficulties in the 'application' of theory to literary texts" because of "a marked resistance to the positing of representation as a theoretical problem" (434). I like that graduate student and have hopes for his future. But the problems he faces with undergraduates will not go away.

Let me state them more fully. The power of the poststructuralist reading, even in the sheepish version I have given of it, lies in its relentless questioning of texts. In one respect it can afford to pursue its analysis much further than conventional critical methods can, since it does not consider itself obliged to offer a defense of the value or coherence of the works it questions. The New Critical program included a vision of the uniqueness of literature and, at one extreme, even a kind of political and religious salvation through poetry; I. A. Richards,[9] its distant father, thought that learning how to read better might help people to understand each other better and perhaps save the world. Most poststructuralists consider such ideas crackpot. Since "language speaks, not man" (in Heidegger's[10] celebrated wordplay), our efforts to master ourselves by mastering language are bound to fail. Moreover, the effort to confer a special privilege on literary language by insisting on its ineffable, incarnational superiority to all other writing or on its more immediate contact with "the world's body" seems a basic misunderstanding of the principles of writing, which is not related to any hierarchy of values or to any world except the world of writing. Poststructuralists know better. They know that literary works cannot be traced to any point of origin (no author; no reality) and that literature is just like all other kinds of writing, only more so (the more so is what makes it interesting to study). The methods by which poetry tries to convince us that we are in the presence of someone, some emotion, some immediate experience are interesting precisely because of the manifold ways in which they fail. The answer ends, the questioning goes on.

This line of thought does have power. Anyone who has ever written a poem can testify, if honest, to how much of it escapes control, to how many internal contradictions must be papered over. Language runs away with us. The same thing is true of freshman papers, and the poems of Yeats. And by refusing to deny the fissures and instabilities of writing, even when that writing is endorsed by a brand name like Shakespeare or Yeats, the teacher and student alike can become conscious of the problems they share with every creature who writes. For many young theorists

that consciousness has been liberating. It seems to offer a way not merely of seeing literature but of seeing through it. And it also corresponds to the skepticism about authority, the doubt that the elders knew what they were talking about, that now seems so much a part of American life. If some of the idealistic students in my classroom are disappointed at watching Yeats torn down, a few of the others are delighted that the poem is at last getting what it deserves: a long, hard look that spares nothing. The poet himself, after all, advised us to cast a cold eye.[11] To what extent such skepticism represents a reasoned position, and to what extent it reflects an impatience with learning, a hostility toward the past, or even a general resentment on the part of the young and unemployed toward those whose jobs have given them an interest in preserving civilization is a problem far too difficult for me to solve. But in the more limited arena of literary criticism, the politics of interpretation undoubtedly plays a significant role. For anyone who reads much criticism today, one striking phenomenon is how many essays end with a celebration of indeterminacy and a denunciation of all interpreters who think they can find the key to a piece of writing. My own reading of "Sailing to Byzantium" could easily be adapted to this vein by heaping scorn on earlier critics who thought they had discovered its meaning. These conclusions often puzzle me for two related reasons. First, I am never quite sure who *are* those benighted dogmatists who stir such rage. Most of the conservative literary historians and critics I know are modest people who would never dream of saying that their work had put an end to interpretation once and for all. Second, the denunciation of dogmatism often concluded an example of close reading that seems very sure of itself, very closed to alternative possibilities. Many of you will have noticed that my allegorizing of "Sailing to Byzantium" as a text about the very gap between signifier and signified that it pretends to resolve was advanced with no ifs, ands, or buts. It is always someone else's dogma that seems at issue.

[9]See p. 763 for more on Richards.
[10]See p. 611 for more on Heidegger.

[11]Yeats's epitaph, published in the poem "Under Ben Bulben," is "Cast a cold eye / on life, on death / Horseman, pass by."

I do not accuse such critics of bad faith. The more sophisticated among them would readily admit their own blind spots, on the grounds that writing itself depends on presuppositions and biases, built right into the frame that is the condition of its possibility. But this admission seldom results in much fellow feeling or charity toward the blind spots of others. Many of our best young critics seem to feel oppressed. Traditional methods of reading, and sometimes the prestige of the literary canon itself, hang like a weight on the spirit. I always respect such feelings. While the oppressed may be guilty of injustice to others, they are seldom wrong about their own oppression. But whatever the cause, much of the current practice of poststructuralism bears an overt political message: authority is not to be trusted. In strict political terms, as many have noted, this message can hardly be considered threatening, since it almost never is accompanied by a program or by any agreement about what should be done to change the situation. A refusal to accept Yeats's intention as relevant to "Sailing to Byzantium" does not get us much closer to manning the barricades. Yet a teaching founded on such principles would eventually change our profession. It would force us all to reexamine our language, to build curricula in which theory or the contest of ideas played a major part, to question texts instead of passing them on, and to admit to our students that we do not know whether what we are doing has any value.

I do not think it will happen. One reason, of course, is simply the power and torpor of institutions. There is something comical about the idea that most professors or literary historians might suddenly stop what they were doing, convert from Saul to Paul or Jack to Jacques, begin reading theory, and start to speak in tongues of *paragones or écriture*. Moreover, the political moment seems wrong. Not long ago I heard an eloquent young deconstructionist, trained in the sixties, argue that the old literary faiths seem obsolete to people of his generation, only to be interrupted by a recent Ph.D. who protested that to people of her generation his jargon sounded like nonsense. The times, they are changing — backwards.

But there seem to me two better reasons why poststructuralism, at least in its purest and most rigorous forms, does not have a particularly bright future in American classrooms; and on this sheeplike note I shall end. The first is that, in my own admittedly fallible and tentative opinion, the theoretical arguments of deconstruction do not support the ardent claims on its behalf. Even if we grant its premises, not much seems to follow from them. I urge you not to take my word for this. In the past few months some introductory primers to deconstruction have been pouring out of the presses. They are accessible and, for the most part, clearly written, and they can be read in an evening. Anyone who grumbles about deconstruction without quite knowing what it is should certainly read one. Then, if you like, you too can teach your students how to make sense of a poem — or how not to make it.

But you will not find all the answers in those books; and I do not think you will find them in Derrida either. Specifically, what deconstruction (and its adaptations to literary theory) has not yet achieved is a way of addressing the concerns of those bright, resistant undergraduates whom I spoke of before. Let me put some words in their mouths. Why are we supposed to talk about poems as if they were only pieces of language? Can't we talk about them instead in other ways, as if they were things made in a person's head, or pictures, or feelings, or one person talking to another? Are there some reasons why all these other ways are wrong, something that you're not telling us (you seem very pleased with yourself)? Or is it just that you're afraid that if we talk about those things you won't be able to control the discussion?

Next: Why aren't we allowed to talk about "Sailing to Byzantium," or even about a novel, as if it had something to do with life? You explained to us that novels can give us only a screen of words, not life firsthand, and we see that; but why can't we talk about both, about life and the words? Anyway, would the words mean anything at all if we didn't sense life behind them? You bore us with all your words. We want to know how to live, and that's why we learned how to read in the first place.

Finally: Did you really mean it when you said that writing is never finished and never makes sense, just like our papers? Aren't our papers different from "Sailing to Byzantium"? Don't you honestly think that "Sailing to Byzantium" is a great poem, better than the article that you wrote about it in *Diacritics*?[12] Then why won't you tell us why? Why did you become a teacher in the first place? We think that we'll switch to economics.

Kids can be so cruel.

I do not think that all these questions are completely fair; and some of them you will find answered, more or less ingeniously, in the books I have mentioned. But the present state of deconstruction does not seem comfortable with such questions and tends to answer them quite indifferently. The issues of pluralism, representation, and evaluation have been put in abeyance, at least until someone in Paris rediscovers them. Thus theory decrees that readers must fend for themselves. If a conflict arises between current speculations and the questions raised by students, many poststructuralists would prefer to replace the students rather than the theory. I honor their choice. But it also means that their theories must stop at the doors of the classroom. To a large extent that has happened. Despite the buzz and swarm of theorists in motion and the alarm they set off in many circles, most of the practice of teaching literature to undergraduates still goes on in the same old way. Deconstructionists and their enemies tend to agree that theory is too high a thing to be grounded in adolescents.

Yet a healthier reason for the uncertain state of deconstruction in the classroom may also be put forward: it has too many rivals. Up to this point I have been talking about contemporary literature theory as if it were identical with the term "poststructuralism" and about poststructuralism as if it

---

[12]Journal devoted to theorists' responses to other theorists.

meant the same thing as deconstruction. That was convenient for my argument and made it possible for me to give this talk. But it does not correspond to reality (even that weak form of reality connected with theory). The most prominent feature of the American theoretical scene, as most of us know, is its diversity: semioticians, reader responders, Marxists, psychoanalysts, feminists, phenomenologists, hermeneuts, mythographers, not to mention some unreconstructed New Critics and neo-Aristotelians. There is even one growing school of theorists devoted to the proposition that theory is useless and ought to be discontinued. The number and wealth of these schools may be considered a source of dismay or of pride. A European might conclude that every American concern eventually turns into a supermarket. But to me our republic of theory signifies health.

Indeed, what gives me most hope about our younger theorists, the generation just now emerging, is that so many are frankly eclectic. In strict logical terms, deconstruction may or may not be compatible with feminism, archetypal criticism, Saint Thomas Aquinas, word processing, and what goes on in the classroom; but flexible minds join points even further apart. The practice of theory will be the result of such joining. In the most recent MLA *Job Lists*, a considerable number of entries end with the words "and theory": medieval literature and theory, Victorian poetry and theory, contemporary film and theory, and so on. Those listings may be illogical, but to me they seem just right. For the future of theory in our profession depends on those "and"s: the way that our bright young people test their ideas, not in the purity of a vacuum chamber, but in the cunning corridors of history and the murk of undergraduate minds. I think they will do it well.

Michel Foucault

1926–1984

Michel Foucault, a major intellectual presence in France since the 1960s, was renowned for his writings, which attempted to erase the traditional boundaries between the disciplines of science, history, philosophy, and sociology. Born in Poitiers, the son of a doctor, Foucault was trained as a philosopher, but his earliest work, such as Madness and Civilization *(1961), dealt with history — specifically, the history of attitudes toward mental illness and its treatment. Foucault taught at the University of Clermont-Ferrand between 1960 and 1968, spent two years at the University of Paris-Vincennes, and in 1970 was elevated to a professorship at the Collège de France — the highest position in the French academic system. He was also a visiting professor at a host of universities worldwide. In addition to* Madness and Civilization, *other works that have been translated into English include* The Birth of the Clinic *(1963),* The Order of Things *(1966),* The Archaeology of Knowledge *(1969),* Discipline and Punish *(1975), three volumes of* The History of Sexuality *(1976, 1985, 1986), and* Power/Knowledge *(1980). "What Is an Author?" originally appeared in the* Bulletin de la Société Française de Philosophie *in 1969.*

What Is an Author?

The coming into being of the notion of "author" constitutes the privileged moment of *individualization* in the history of ideas, knowledge, literature, philosophy, and the sciences. Even today, when we reconstruct the history of a concept, literary genre, or school of philosophy, such categories seem relatively weak, secondary, and superimposed scansions in comparison with the solid and fundamental unit of the author and the work.

I shall not offer here a sociohistorical analysis of the author's persona. Certainly it would be worth examining how the author became individualized in a culture like ours, what status he has been given, at what moment studies of authenticity and attribution began, in what kind of system of valorization the author was involved, at what point we began to recount the lives of authors rather than of heroes, and how this fundamental category of "the-man-and-his-work criticism" began. For the moment, however, I want to deal solely with the relationship between text and author and with the manner in which the text points to this "figure" that, at least in appearance, is outside it and antecedes it.

Beckett nicely formulates the theme with which I would like to begin: " 'What does it matter who is speaking,' someone said, 'what does it matter who is speaking.' " In this indifference appears one of the fundamental ethical principles of contemporary writing [*écriture*]. I say "ethical" because this indifference is not really a trait characterizing the manner in which one speaks and writes, but rather a kind of immanent rule, taken up over and over again, never fully applied, not designating writing as something completed, but dominating it as a practice. Since it is too familiar to require a lengthy analysis, this immanent rule can be adequately illustrated here by tracing two of its major themes.

First of all, we can say that today's writing has freed itself from the dimension of expression. Referring only to itself, but without being restricted to the confines of its interiority, writing is identified with its own unfolded exteriority. This means that it is an interplay of signs arranged less according to its signified content

Translated by Josué Harari.

than according to the very nature of the signifier. Writing unfolds like a game [*jeu*] that invariably goes beyond its own rules and transgresses its limits. In writing, the point is not to manifest or exalt the act of writing, nor is it to pin a subject within language; it is rather a question of creating a space into which the writing subject constantly disappears.

The second theme, writing's relationship with death, is even more familiar. This link subverts an old tradition exemplified by the Greek epic, which was intended to perpetuate the immortality of the hero: if he was willing to die young, it was so that his life, consecrated and magnified by death, might pass into immortality; the narrative then redeemed this accepted death. In another way, the motivation, as well as the theme and the pretext of Arabian narratives — such as *The Thousand and One Nights* — was also the eluding of death: one spoke, telling stories into the early morning, in order to forestall death, to postpone the day of reckoning that would silence the narrator. Scheherazade's narrative is an effort, renewed each night, to keep death outside the circle of life.

Our culture has metamorphosed this idea of narrative, or writing, as something designed to ward off death. Writing has become linked to sacrifice, even to the sacrifice of life: it is now a voluntary effacement which does not need to be represented in books, since it is brought about in the writer's very existence. The work, which once had the duty of providing immortality, now possesses the right to kill, to be its author's murderer, as in the cases of Flaubert, Proust, and Kafka. That is not all, however: this relationship between writing and death is also manifested in the effacement of the writing subject's individual characteristics. Using all the contrivances that he sets up between himself and what he writes, the writing subject cancels out the signs of his particular individuality. As a result, the mark of the writer is reduced to nothing more than the singularity of his absence; he must assume the role of the dead man in the game of writing.

None of this is recent; criticism and philosophy took note of the disappearance — or death — of the author some time ago. But the consequences of their discovery of it have not been sufficiently examined, nor has its import been accurately measured. A certain number of notions that are intended to replace the privileged position of the author actually seem to preserve that privilege and suppress the real meaning of his disappearance. I shall examine two of these notions, both of great importance today.

The first is the idea of the work. It is a very familiar thesis that the task of criticism is not to bring out the work's relationships with the author, not to reconstruct through the text a thought or experience, but rather, to analyze the work through its structure, its architecture, its intrinsic form, and the play of its internal relationships. At this point, however, a problem arises: "What is a work? What is this curious unity which we designate as a work? Of what elements is it composed? Is it not what an author has written?" Difficulties appear immediately. If an individual were not an author, could we say that what he wrote, said, left behind in his papers, or what has been collected of his remarks, could be called a "work"? When Sade was not considered an author, what was the status of his papers? Were they simply rolls of paper onto which he ceaselessly uncoiled his fantasies during his imprisonment?

Even when an individual has been accepted as an author, we must still ask whether everything that he wrote, said, or left behind is part of his work. The problem is both theoretical and technical. When undertaking the publication of Nietzsche's works, for example, where should one stop? Surely everything must be published, but what is "everything"? Everything that Nietzsche himself published, certainly. And what about the rough drafts for his works? Obviously. The plans for his aphorisms? Yes. The deleted passages and the notes at the bottom of the page? Yes. What if, within a workbook filled with aphorisms, one finds a reference, the notation of a meeting or of an address, or a laundry list: is it a work, or not? Why not? And so on, ad infinitum. How can one define a work amid the millions of traces left by someone after his death? A theory of the work does not exist, and the empirical task of those who naively undertake the editing of works often suffers in the absence of such a theory.

We could go even further: does *The Thousand and One Nights* constitute a work? What about

Clement of Alexandria's *Miscellanies* or Diogenes Laertius' *Lives*? A multitude of questions arises with regard to this notion of the work. Consequently, it is not enough to declare that we should do without the writer (the author) and study the work in itself. The word "work" and the unity that it designates are probably as problematic as the status of the author's individuality.

Another notion which has hindered us from taking full measure of the author's disappearance, blurring and concealing the moment of this effacement and subtly preserving the author's existence, is the notion of writing [*écriture*]. When rigorously applied, this notion should allow us not only to circumvent references to the author, but also to situate his recent absence. The notion of writing, as currently employed, is concerned with neither the act of writing nor the indication — be it symptom or sign — of a meaning which someone might have wanted to express. We try, with great effort, to imagine the general condition of each text, the condition of both the space in which it is dispersed and the time in which it unfolds.

In current usage, however, the notion of writing seems to transpose the empirical characteristics of the author into a transcendental anonymity. We are content to efface the more visible marks of the author's empiricity by playing off, one against the other, two ways of characterizing writing, namely, the critical and the religious approaches. Giving writing a primal status seems to be a way of retranslating, in transcendental terms, both the theological affirmation of its sacred character and the critical affirmation of its creative character. To admit that writing is, because of the very history that it made possible, subject to the test of oblivion and repression, seems to represent, in transcendental terms, the religious principle of the hidden meaning (which requires interpretation) and the critical principle of implicit significations, silent determinations, and obscured contents (which gives rise to commentary). To imagine writing as absence seems to be a simple repetition, in transcendental terms, of both the religious principle of inalterable and yet never fulfilled tradition, and the aesthetic principle of the work's survival, its perpetuation beyond the author's death, and its enigmatic *excess* in relation to him.

This usage of the notion of writing runs the risk of maintaining the author's privileges under the protection of writing's a priori status: it keeps alive, in the grey light of neutralization, the interplay of those representations that formed a particular image of the author. The author's disappearance, which, since Mallarmé, has been a constantly recurring event, is subject to a series of transcendental barriers. There seems to be an important dividing line between those who believe that they can still locate today's discontinuities [*ruptures*] in the historico-transcendental tradition of the nineteenth century, and those who try to free themselves once and for all from that tradition.[1]

It is not enough, however, to repeat the empty affirmation that the author has disappeared. For the same reason, it is not enough to keep repeating (after Nietzsche) that God and man have died a common death. Instead, we must locate the space left empty by the author's disappearance, follow the distribution of gaps and breaches, and watch for the openings that this disappearance uncovers.

First, we need to clarify briefly the problems arising from the use of the author's name. What is an author's name? How does it function? Far from offering a solution, I shall only indicate some of the difficulties that it presents.

The author's name is a proper name, and therefore it raises the problems common to all proper names. (Here I refer to Searle's analyses, among others.[2]) Obviously, one cannot turn a proper name into a pure and simple reference. It has other than indicative functions: more than an indication, a gesture, a finger pointed at someone, it is the equivalent of a description. When one says "Aristotle," one employs a word that is the equivalent of one, or a series of, definite descriptions, such as "the author of the *Analytics*," "the founder of ontology," and so forth. One cannot stop there, however, because a proper name does

[1]For a discussion of the notions of discontinuity and historical tradition see Foucault's *Les Mots et les choses* (Paris: Gallimard, 1966), translated as *The Order of Things* (New York: Pantheon, 1971). [Tr.]

[2]John Searle, *Speech Acts: An Essay in the Philosophy of Language* (Cambridge: Cambridge University Press, 1969), pp. 162–74. [Tr.]

not have just one signification. When we discover that Rimbaud did not write *La Chasse spirituelle,* we cannot pretend that the meaning of this proper name, or that of the author, has been altered. The proper name and the author's name are situated between the two poles of description and designation: they must have a certain link with what they name, but one that is neither entirely in the mode of designation nor in that of description; it must be a *specific* link. However — and it is here that the particular difficulties of the author's name arise — the links between the proper name and the individual named and between the author's name and what it names are not isomorphic and do not function in the same way. There are several differences.

If, for example, Pierre Dupont does not have blue eyes, or was not born in Paris, or is not a doctor, the name Pierre Dupont will still always refer to the same person; such things do not modify the link of designation. The problems raised by the author's name are much more complex, however. If I discover that Shakespeare was not born in the house that we visit today, that is a modification which, obviously, will not alter the functioning of the author's name. But if we proved that Shakespeare did not write those sonnets which pass for his, that would constitute a significant change and affect the manner in which the author's name functions. If we proved that Shakespeare wrote Bacon's *Organon* by showing that the same author wrote both the works of Bacon and those of Shakespeare, that would be a third type of change which would entirely modify the functioning of the author's name. The author's name is not, therefore, just a proper name like the rest.

Many other facts point out the paradoxical singularity of the author's name. To say that Pierre Dupont does not exist is not at all the same as saying that Homer or Hermes Trismegistus did not exist. In the first case, it means that no one has the name Pierre Dupont; in the second, it means that several people were mixed together under one name, or that the true author had none of the traits traditionally ascribed to the personae of Homer or Hermes. To say that X's real name is actually Jacques Durand instead of Pierre Dupont is not the same as saying that Stendhal's name was Henri Beyle.[3] One could also question the meaning and functioning of propositions like "Bourbaki is so-and-so, so-and-so, etc."[4] and "Victor Eremita, Climacus, Anticlimacus, Frater Taciturnus, Constantine Constantius, all of these are Kierkegaard."

These differences may result from the fact that an author's name is not simply an element in a discourse (capable of being either subject or object, of being replaced by a pronoun, and the like); it performs a certain role with regard to narrative discourse, assuring a classificatory function. Such a name permits one to group together a certain number of texts, define them, differentiate them from and contrast them to others. In addition, it establishes a relationship among the texts. Hermes Trismegistus did not exist, nor did Hippocrates — in the sense that Balzac existed — but the fact that several texts have been placed under the same name indicates that there has been established among them a relationship of homogeneity, filiation,[5] authentification of some texts by the use of others, reciprocal explication, or concomitant utilization. The author's name serves to characterize a certain mode of being of discourse: the fact that the discourse has an author's name, that one can say "this was written by so-and-so" or "so-and-so is its author," shows that this discourse is not ordinary everyday speech that merely comes and goes, not something that is immediately consumable. On the contrary, it is a speech that must be received in a certain mode and that, in a given culture, must receive a certain status.

It would seem that the author's name, unlike other proper names, does not pass from the interior of a discourse to the real and exterior individual who produced it; instead, the name seems always to be present, marking off the edges of the text, revealing, or at least characterizing, its mode of being. The author's name manifests the appearance of a certain discursive set and indicates the status of this discourse within a society and a culture. It has no legal status, nor is it located in the fiction of the work; rather, it is located in the break

---

[3]Marie-Henri Beyle wrote under the name of Stendhal.

[4]Bourbaki was the collective name of a group of French mathematicians.

[5]Descent, derivation.

that founds a certain discursive construct and its very particular mode of being. As a result, we could say that in a civilization like our own there are a certain number of discourses that are endowed with the "author-function," while others are deprived of it. A private letter may well have a signer — it does not have an author; a contract may well have a guarantor — it does not have an author. An anonymous text posted on a wall probably has a writer — but not an author. The author-function is therefore characteristic of the mode of existence, circulation, and functioning of certain discourses within a society.

Let us analyze this "author-function" as we have just described it. In our culture, how does one characterize a discourse containing the author-function? In what way is this discourse different from other discourses? If we limit our remarks to the author of a book or a text, we can isolate four different characteristics.

First of all, discourses are objects of appropriation. The form of ownership from which they spring is of a rather particular type, one that has been codified for many years. We should note that, historically, this type of ownership has always been subsequent to what one might call penal appropriation. Texts, books, and discourses really began to have authors (other than mythical, "sacralized" and "sacralizing" figures) to the extent that authors became subject to punishment, that is, to the extent that discourses could be transgressive. In our culture (and doubtless in many others), discourse was not originally a product, a thing, a kind of goods; it was essentially an act — an act placed in the bipolar field of the sacred and the profane, the licit and the illicit, the religious and the blasphemous. Historically, it was a gesture fraught with risks before becoming goods caught up in a circuit of ownership.

Once a system of ownership for texts came into being, once strict rules concerning author's rights, author-publisher relations, rights of reproduction, and related matters were enacted — at the end of the eighteenth and the beginning of the nineteenth century — the possibility of transgression attached to the act of writing took on, more and more, the form of an imperative peculiar to literature. It is as if the author, beginning with the moment at which he was placed in the system of property that characterizes our society, compensated for the status that he thus acquired by rediscovering the old bipolar field of discourse, systematically practicing transgression and thereby restoring danger to a writing which was now guaranteed the benefits of ownership.

The author-function does not affect all discourses in a universal and constant way, however. This is its second characteristic. In our civilization, it has not always been the same types of texts which have required attribution to an author. There was a time when the texts that we today call "literary" (narratives, stories, epics, tragedies, comedies) were accepted, put into circulation, and valorized without any question about the identity of their author; their anonymity caused no difficulties since their ancientness, whether real or imagined, was regarded as a sufficient guarantee of their status. On the other hand, those texts that we now would call scientific — those dealing with cosmology and the heavens, medicine and illnesses, natural sciences and geography — were accepted in the Middle Ages, and accepted as "true," only when marked with the name of their author. "Hippocrates said," "Pliny recounts," were not really formulas of an argument based on authority; they were the markers inserted in discourses that were supposed to be received as statements of demonstrated truth.

A reversal occurred in the seventeenth or eighteenth century. Scientific discourses began to be received for themselves, in the anonymity of an established or always redemonstrable truth; their membership in a systematic ensemble, and not the reference to the individual who produced them, stood as their guarantee. The author-function faded away, and the inventor's name served only to christen a theorem, proposition, particular effect, property, body, group of elements, or pathological syndrome. By the same token, literary discourses come to be accepted only when endowed with the author-function. We now ask of each poetic or fictional text: from where does it come, who wrote it, when, under what circumstances, or beginning with what design? The meaning ascribed to it and the status or value accorded it depend upon the manner in which we answer these questions. And if a text should be discovered in a state of anonymity — whether as a consequence of an accident or the author's explicit wish — the game becomes one of rediscovering the author. Since literary anonymity is not tolerable, we can accept it only in the guise of an enigma. As a result, the author-function today plays an important role in our view of literary works. (These are obviously generalizations that would have to be refined insofar as recent critical practice is concerned.)

The third characteristic of this author-function is that it does not develop spontaneously as the attribution of a discourse to an individual. It is, rather, the result of a complex operation which constructs a certain rational being that we call "author." Critics doubtless try to give this intelligible being a realistic status, by discerning, in the individual, a "deep" motive, a "creative" power, or a "design," the milieu in which writing originates. Nevertheless, these aspects of an individual which we designate as making him an author are only a projection, in more or less psychologizing terms, of the operations that we force texts to undergo, the connections that we make, the traits that we establish as pertinent, the continuities that we recognize, or the exclusions that we practice. All these operations vary according to periods and types of discourse. We do not construct a "philosophical author" as we do a "poet," just as, in the eighteenth century, one did not construct a novelist as we do today. Still, we can find through the ages certain constants in the rules of author-construction.

It seems, for example, that the manner in which literary criticism once defined the author — or rather constructed the figure of the author beginning with existing texts and discourses — is directly derived from the manner in which Christian tradition authenticated (or rejected) the texts at its disposal. In order to "rediscover" an author in a work, modern criticism uses methods similar to those that Christian exegesis employed when trying to prove the value of a text by its author's saintliness. In *De viris illustribus,* Saint Jerome explains that homonymy is not sufficient to identify legitimately authors of more than one work: different individuals could have had the same name, or one man could have, illegitimately, borrowed another's patronymic. The name as an individual trademark is not enough when one works within a textual tradition.

How then can one attribute several discourses to one and the same author? How can one use the author-function to determine if one is dealing with one or several individuals? Saint Jerome proposes four criteria: (1) if among several books attributed to an author one is inferior to the others, it must be withdrawn from the list of the author's works (the author is therefore defined as a constant level of value); (2) the same should be done if certain texts contradict the doctrine expounded in the author's other works (the author is thus defined as a field of conceptual or theoretical coherence); (3) one must also exclude works that are written in a different style, containing words and expressions not ordinarily found in the writer's production (the author is here conceived as a stylistic unity); (4) finally, passages quoting statements that were made, or mentioning events that occurred after the author's death must be regarded as interpolated texts (the author is here seen as a historical figure at the crossroads of a certain number of events).

Modern literary criticism, even when — as is now customary — it is not concerned with questions of authentification, still defines the author the same way: the author provides the basis for explaining not only the presence of certain events in a work, but also their transformations, distortions, and diverse modifications (through his biography, the determination of his individual perspective, the analysis of his social position, and the revelation of his basic design). The author is also the principle of a certain unity of writing — all differences having to be resolved, at least in part, by the principles of evolution, maturation, or influence. The author also serves to neutralize the contradictions that may emerge in a series of texts: there must be — at a certain level of his thought or desire, of his consciousness or unconscious — a point where contradictions are resolved, where incompatible elements are at last tied together or organized around a fundamental or originating contradiction. Finally, the author is a particular source of expression that, in more or less completed forms, is manifested equally well, and with similar validity, in works, sketches, letters, fragments, and so on. Clearly, Saint

Jerome's four criteria of authenticity (criteria which seem totally insufficient for today's exegetes) do define the four modalities according to which modern criticism brings the author-function into play.

But the author-function is not a pure and simple reconstruction made secondhand from a text given as passive material. The text always contains a certain number of signs referring to the author. These signs, well known to grammarians, are personal pronouns, adverbs of time and place, and verb conjugation. Such elements do not play the same role in discourses provided with the author-function as in those lacking it. In the latter, such "shifters" refer to the real speaker and to the spatio-temporal coordinates of his discourse (although certain modifications can occur, as in the operation of relating discourses in the first person). In the former, however, their role is more complex and variable. Everyone knows that, in a novel narrated in the first person, neither the first person pronoun, nor the present indicative refer exactly either to the writer or to the moment in which he writes, but rather to an alter ego whose distance from the author varies, often changing in the course of the work. It would be just as wrong to equate the author with the real writer as to equate him with the fictitious speaker; the author-function is carried out and operates in the scission itself, in this division and this distance.

One might object that this is a characteristic peculiar to novelistic or poetic discourse, a "game" in which only "quasi-discourses" participate. In fact, however, all discourses endowed with the author-function do possess this plurality of self. The self that speaks in the preface to a treatise on mathematics — and that indicates the circumstances of the treatise's composition — is identical neither in its position nor in its functioning to the self that speaks in the course of a demonstration, and that appears in the form of "I conclude" or "I suppose." In the first case, the "I" refers to an individual without an equivalent who, in a determined place and time, completed a certain task; in the second, the "I" indicates an instance and a level of demonstration which any individual could perform provided that he accept the same system of symbols, play of axioms, and set of previous demonstrations. We could also, in the same treatise, locate a third self, one that speaks to tell the work's meaning, the obstacles encountered, the results obtained, and the remaining problems; this self is situated in the field of already existing or yet-to-appear mathematical discourses. The author-function is not assumed by the first of these selves at the expense of the other two, which would then be nothing more than a fictitious splitting in two of the first one. On the contrary, in these discourses the author-function operates so as to effect the dispersion of these three simultaneous selves.

No doubt analysis could discover still more characteristic traits of the author-function. I will limit myself to these four, however, because they seem both the most visible and the most important. They can be summarized as follows: (1) the author-function is linked to the juridical and institutional system that encompasses, determines, and articulates the universe of discourses; (2) it does not affect all discourses in the same way at all times and in all types of civilization; (3) it is not defined by the spontaneous attribution of a discourse to its producer, but rather by a series of specific and complex operations; (4) it does not refer purely and simply to a real individual, since it can give rise simultaneously to several selves, to several subjects — positions that can be occupied by different classes of individuals.

Up to this point I have unjustifiably limited my subject. Certainly the author-function in painting, music, and other arts should have been discussed, but even supposing that we remain within the world of discourse, as I want to do, I seem to have given the term "author" much too narrow a meaning. I have discussed the author only in the limited sense of a person to whom the production of a text, a book, or a work can be legitimately attributed. It is easy to see that in the sphere of discourse one can be the author of much more than a book — one can be the author of a theory, tradition, or discipline in which other books and authors will in their turn find a place. These authors are in a position which we shall call "transdiscursive." This is a recurring phenomenon — certainly as old as our civilization.

Homer, Aristotle, and the Church Fathers, as well as the first mathematicians and the originators of the Hippocratic tradition, all played this role.

Furthermore, in the course of the nineteenth century, there appeared in Europe another, more uncommon, kind of author, whom one should confuse with neither the "great" literary authors, nor the authors of religious texts, nor the founders of science. In a somewhat arbitrary way we shall call those who belong in this last group "founders of discursivity." They are unique in that they are not just the authors of their own works. They have produced something else: the possibilities and the rules for the formation of other texts. In this sense, they are very different, for example, from a novelist, who is, in fact, nothing more than the author of his own text. Freud is not just the author of *The Interpretation of Dreams* or *Jokes and Their Relation to the Unconscious;* Marx is not just the author of the *Communist Manifesto* or *Capital:* they both have established an endless possibility of discourse.

Obviously, it is easy to object. One might say that it is not true that the author of a novel is only the author of his own text; in a sense, he also, provided that he acquires some "importance," governs and commands more than that. To take a very simple example, one could say that Ann Radcliffe not only wrote *The Castles of Athlin and Dunbayne* and several other novels, but also made possible the appearance of the Gothic horror novel at the beginning of the nineteenth century; in that respect, her author-function exceeds her own work. But I think there is an answer to this objection. These founders of discursivity (I use Marx and Freud as examples, because I believe them to be both the first and the most important cases) make possible something altogether different from what a novelist makes possible. Ann Radcliffe's texts opened the way for a certain number of resemblances and analogies which have their model or principle in her work. The latter contains characteristic signs, figures, relationships, and structures which could be reused by others. In other words, to say that Ann Radcliffe founded the Gothic horror novel means that in the nineteenth-century gothic novel one will find, as in Ann Radcliffe's works, the theme of the heroine caught in the trap of her own innocence, the hidden castle, the character of the black, cursed hero devoted to making the world expiate the evil done to him, and all the rest of it.

On the other hand, when I speak of Marx or Freud as founders of discursivity, I mean that they made possible not only a certain number of analogies, but also (and equally important) a certain number of differences. They have created a possibility for something other than their discourse, yet something belonging to what they founded. To say that Freud founded psychoanalysis does not (simply) mean that we find the concept of the libido or the technique of dream analysis in the works of Karl Abraham or Melanie Klein; it means that Freud made possible a certain number of divergences — with respect to his own texts, concepts, and hypotheses — that all arise from the psychoanalytical discourse itself.

This would seem to present a new difficulty, however: is the above not true, after all, of any founder of a science, or of any author who has introduced some important transformation into a science? After all, Galileo made possible not only those discourses that repeated the laws that he had formulated, but also statements very different from what he himself had said. If Cuvier is the founder of biology or Saussure the founder of linguistics, it is not because they were imitated, nor because people have since taken up again the concept of organism or sign; it is because Cuvier made possible, to a certain extent, a theory of evolution diametrically opposed to his own fixism; it is because Saussure made possible a generative grammar radically different from his structural analyses. Superficially, then, the initiation of discursive practices appears similar to the founding of any scientific endeavor.

Still, there is a difference, and a notable one. In the case of a science, the act that founds it is on an equal footing with its future transformations; this act becomes in some respects part of the set of modifications that it makes possible. Of course, this belonging can take several forms. In the future development of a science, the founding act may appear as little more than a particular instance of a more general phenomenon which unveils itself in the process. It can also turn out to be marred by intuition and empirical bias; one must then reformulate it, making it the object of a certain number of supplementary theoretical operations which establish it more rigorously, etc. Finally, it can seem to be a hasty generalization which must be limited, and whose restricted domain of validity must be retraced. In other words, the founding act of a science can always be reintroduced within the machinery of those transformations that derive from it.

In contrast, the initiation of a discursive practice is heterogeneous to its subsequent transformations. To expand a type of discursivity, such as psychoanalysis as founded by Freud, is not to give it a formal generality that it would not have permitted at the outset, but rather to open it up to a certain number of possible applications. To limit psychoanalysis as a type of discursivity is, in reality, to try to isolate in the founding act an eventually restricted number of propositions or statements to which, alone, one grants a founding value, and in relation to which certain concepts or theories accepted by Freud might be considered as derived, secondary, and accessory. In addition, one does not declare certain propositions in the work of these founders to be false: instead, when trying to seize the act of founding, one sets aside those statements that are not pertinent, either because they are deemed inessential, or because they are considered "prehistoric" and derived from another type of discursivity. In other words, unlike the founding of a science, the initiation of a discursive practice does not participate in its later transformations.

As a result, one defines a proposition's theoretical validity in relation to the work of the founders — while, in the case of Galileo and Newton, it is in relation to what physics or cosmology *is* (in its intrinsic structure and "normativity") that one affirms the validity of any proposition that those men may have put forth. To phrase it very schematically: the work of initiators of discursivity is not situated in the space that science defines; rather, it is the science or the discursivity which refers back to their work as primary coordinates.

In this way we can understand the inevitable necessity, within these fields of discursivity, for a "return to the origin." This return, which is part of the discursive field itself, never stops modifying it. The return is not a historical supplement which would be added to the discursivity, or merely an ornament; on the contrary, it constitutes an effective and necessary task of transforming the discursive practice itself. Re-examination of Galileo's text may well change our knowledge of the history of mechanics, but it will never be able to change mechanics itself. On the other hand, re-examining Freud's texts modifies psychoanalysis itself just as a re-examination of Marx's would modify Marxism.[6]

What I have just outlined regarding the initiation of discursive practices is, of course, very schematic; this is true, in particular, of the opposition that I have tried to draw between discursive initiation and scientific founding. It is not always easy to distinguish between the two; moreover, nothing proves that they are two mutually exclusive procedures. I have attempted the distinction for only one reason: to show that the author-function, which is complex enough when one tries to situate it at the level of a book or a series of texts that carry a given signature, involves still more determining factors when one tries to analyze it in larger units, such as groups of works or entire disciplines.

To conclude, I would like to review the reasons why I attach a certain importance to what I have said.

[6]To define these returns more clearly, one must also emphasize that they tend to reinforce the enigmatic link between an author and his works. A text has an inaugurative value precisely because it is the work of a particular author, and our returns are conditioned by this knowledge. As in the case of Galileo, there is no possibility that the rediscovery of an unknown text by Newton or Cantor will modify classical cosmology or set theory as we know them (at best, such an exhumation might modify our historical knowledge of their genesis). On the other hand, the discovery of a text like Freud's "Project for a Scientific Psychology" — insofar as it is a text by Freud — always threatens to modify not the historical knowledge of psychoanalysis, but its theoretical field, even if only by shifting the accentuation or the center of gravity. Through such returns, which are part of their make-up, these discursive practices maintain a relationship with regard to their "fundamental" and indirect author unlike that which an ordinary text entertains with its immediate author. [Tr.]

First, there are theoretical reasons. On the one hand, an analysis in the direction that I have outlined might provide for an approach to a typology of discourse. It seems to me, at least at first glance, that such a typology cannot be constructed solely from the grammatical features, formal structures, and objects of discourse: more likely there exist properties or relationships peculiar to discourse (not reducible to the rules of grammar and logic), and one must use these to distinguish the major categories of discourse. The relationship (or nonrelationship) with an author, and the different forms this relationship takes, constitutes — in a quite visible manner — one of these discursive properties.

On the other hand, I believe that one could find here an introduction to the historical analysis of discourse. Perhaps it is time to study discourses not only in terms of their expressive value or formal transformations, but according to their modes of existence. The modes of circulation, valorization, attribution, and appropriation of discourses vary with each culture and are modified within each. The manner in which they are articulated according to social relationships can be more readily understood. I believe, in the activity of the author-function and in its modifications, than in the themes or concepts that discourses set in motion.

It would seem that one could also, beginning with analyses of this type, re-examine the privileges of the subject. I realize that in undertaking the internal and architectonic analysis of a work (be it a literary text, philosophical system, or scientific work), in setting aside biographical and psychological references, one has already called back into question the absolute character and founding role of the subject. Still, perhaps one must return to this question, not in order to re-establish the theme of an originating subject, but to grasp the subject's points of insertion, modes of functioning, and system of dependencies. Doing so means overturning the traditional problem, no longer raising the questions "How can a free subject penetrate the substance of things and give it meaning? How can it activate the rules of a language from within and thus give rise to the designs which are properly its own?" Instead, these questions will be raised: "How, under what conditions, and in what forms can something like a subject appear in the order of discourse? What place can it occupy in each type of discourse, what functions can it assume, and by obeying what rules?" In short, it is a matter of depriving the subject (or its substitute) of its role as originator, and of analyzing the subject as a variable and complex function of discourse.

Second, there are reasons dealing with the "ideological" status of the author. The question then becomes: How can one reduce the great peril, the great danger with which fiction threatens our world? The answer is: One can reduce it with the author. The author allows a limitation of the cancerous and dangerous proliferation of significations within a world where one is thrifty not only with one's resources and riches, but also with one's discourses and their significations. The author is the principle of thrift in the proliferation of meaning. As a result, we must entirely reverse the traditional idea of the author. We are accustomed, as we have seen earlier, to saying that the author is the genial creator of a work in which he deposits, with infinite wealth and generosity, an inexhaustible world of significations. We are used to thinking that the author is so different from all other men, and so transcendent with regard to all languages that, as soon as he speaks, meaning begins to proliferate, to proliferate indefinitely.

The truth is quite the contrary: the author is not an indefinite source of significations which fill a work; the author does not precede the works, he is a certain functional principle by which, in our culture, one limits, excludes, and chooses; in short, by which one impedes the free circulation, the free manipulation, the free composition, decomposition, and recomposition of fiction. In fact, if we are accustomed to presenting the author as a genius, as a perpetual surging of invention, it is because, in reality, we make him function in exactly the opposite fashion. One can say that the author is an ideological product, since we represent him as the opposite of his historically real function. (When a historically given function is represented in a figure that inverts it, one has an ideological production.) The author is therefore the ideological figure by which one marks the manner in which we fear the proliferation of meaning.

In saying this, I seem to call for a form of culture in which fiction would not be limited by the figure of the author. It would be pure romanticism, however, to imagine a culture in which the fictive would operate in an absolutely free state, in which fiction would be put at the disposal of everyone and would develop without passing through something like a necessary or constraining figure. Although, since the eighteenth century, the author has played the role of the regulator of the fictive, a role quite characteristic of our era of industrial and bourgeois society, of individualism and private property, still, given the historical modifications that are taking place, it does not seem necessary that the author-function remain constant in form, complexity, and even in existence. I think that, as our society changes, at the very moment when it is in the process of changing, the author-function will disappear, and in such a manner that fiction and its polysemic texts will once again function according to another mode, but still with a system of

constraint — one which will no longer be the author, but which will have to be determined or, perhaps, experienced.

All discourses, whatever their status, form, value, and whatever the treatment to which they will be subjected, would then develop in the anonymity of a murmur. We would no longer hear the questions that have been rehashed for so long: "Who really spoke? Is it really he and not someone else? With what authenticity or originality? And what part of his deepest self did he express in his discourse?" Instead, there would be other questions, like these: "What are the modes of existence of this discourse? Where has it been used, how can it circulate, and who can appropriate it for himself? What are the places in it where there is room for possible subjects? Who can assume these various subject-functions?" And behind all these questions, we would hear hardly anything but the stirring of an indifference: "What difference does it make who is speaking?"

Jacques Derrida

1930–2004

The prime mover of poststructuralism, Jacques Derrida was born in Algiers and educated in France. Trained as a philosopher — early in his career he published a study of Edmund Husserl, the founder of phenomenology — Derrida taught history of philosophy at the École des Hautes Études en Sciences Sociales, and served as visiting professor at a dozen leading American universities. He died of cancer of the pancreas on October 8, 2004. His passing was marked both by glowing tributes (such as that in Le Monde*) and by unusually spiteful obituaries in liberal newspapers such as the* New York Times *and the London* Independent. *Derrida was very much the "bad boy" of the philosophic world, and his fame — or notoriety — in America can be traced to a talk he delivered at a structuralist conference at Johns Hopkins University in 1966. "Structure, Sign, and Play in the Discourse of the Human Sciences" confounded the structuralist enterprise and many of its adherents and precipitated the rise of post-structuralist theories. Derrida's publications were steadily translated into English; among them are* Speech and Phenomena *(1967),* Of Grammatology *(1967),* Writing and Difference *(1967),* Margins of Philosophy *(1972),* Positions *(1972),* Glas *(1974),* The Post Card *(1980),* Limited, Inc. *(1988),* Acts of Literature *(1991),* Cinders *(1991),* Memoirs of the Blind *(1993),* Aporias *(1993),* Specters of Marx *(1994),* On the Name *(1995),* The Gift of Death *(1995), and* Archive Fever: A Freudian Impression *(1996). This translation of "Structure, Sign, and Play in the Discourse of the Human Sciences" is from*

The Structuralist Controversy *(1970), translated by Richard Macksey and Eugenio Donato; another version appears in* Writing and Difference *(1967; translated 1978 by Alan Bass). "Différance" is a key essay, difficult because of its compression, since Derrida has tried to fit his ideas on language, knowledge, and mind into a nutshell. In "The Father of Logos," lighter in texture, Derrida responds to the theory of language inherent in Plato's* Phaedrus *(see p. 46).*

Structure, Sign, and Play in the Discourse of the Human Sciences

Perhaps something has occurred in the history of the concept of structure that could be called an "event," if this loaded word did not entail a meaning which it is precisely the function of structural — or structuralist — thought to reduce or to suspect. But let me use the term "event" anyway, employing it with caution and as if in quotation marks. In this sense, this event will have the exterior form of a *rupture* and a *redoubling.*

It would be easy enough to show that the concept of structure and even the word "structure" itself are as old as the *episteme*[1] — that is to say, as old as western science and western philosophy — and that their roots thrust deep into the soil of ordinary language, into whose deepest recesses the *episteme* plunges to gather them together once more, making them part of itself in a metaphorical displacement. Nevertheless, up until the event which I wish to mark out and define, structure — or rather the structurality of structure — although it has always been involved, has always been neutralized or reduced, and this by a process of giving it a center or referring it to a point of presence, a fixed origin. The function of this center was not only to orient, balance, and organize the structure — one cannot in fact conceive of an unorganized structure — but above all to make sure that the organizing principle of the structure would limit what we might call the *freeplay* of the structure. No doubt that by orienting and organizing the coherence of the system, the center of a structure permits the freeplay of its elements inside the total form. And even today the notion of a structure lacking any center represents the unthinkable itself.

Nevertheless, the center also closes off the freeplay it opens up and makes possible. *Qua* center, it is the point at which the substitution of contents, elements, or terms is no longer possible. At the center, the permutation or the transformation of elements (which may of course be structures enclosed within a structure) is forbidden. At least this permutation has always remained *interdicted*[2] (I use this word deliberately). Thus it has always been thought that the center, which is by definition unique, constituted that very thing within a structure which governs the structure, while escaping structurality. This is why classical thought concerning structure could say that the center is, paradoxically, *within* the structure and *outside* it. The center is at the center of the totality, and yet, since the center does not belong to the totality (is not part of the totality), the totality *has its center elsewhere.* The center is not the center. The concept of centered structure — although it represents coherence itself, the condition of the *episteme* as philosophy or science — is contradictorily coherent. And, as always, coherence in contradiction expresses the force of a desire. The concept of centered structure is in fact the concept of a freeplay based on a fundamental ground, a freeplay which is constituted upon a fundamental

---

Translated by Richard Macksey and Eugenio Donato.
[1] System of thought and knowledge of a culture.

[2] *Interdite:* "forbidden," "disconcerted," "confounded," "speechless." [Tr.]

immobility and a reassuring certitude, which is itself beyond the reach of the freeplay. With this certitude anxiety can be mastered, for anxiety is invariably the result of a certain mode of being implicated in the game, of being caught by the game, of being as it were from the very beginning at stake in the game.[3] From the basis of what we therefore call the center (and which, because it can be either inside or outside, is as readily called the origin as the end, as readily *arché* as *telos*),[4] the repetitions, the substitutions, the transformations, and the permutations are always *taken* from a history of meaning [*sens*] — that is, a history, period — whose origin may always be revealed or whose end may always be anticipated in the form of presence. This is why one could perhaps say that the movement of any archeology, like that of any eschatology,[5] is an accomplice of this reduction of the structurality of structure and always attempts to conceive of structure from the basis of a full presence which is out of play.

If this is so, the whole history of the concept of structure, before the rupture I spoke of, must be thought of as a series of substitutions of center for center, as a linked chain of determinations of the center. Successively, and in a regulated fashion, the center receives different forms or names. The history of metaphysics, like the history of the West, is the history of these metaphors and metonymies. Its matrix — if you will pardon me for demonstrating so little and for being so elliptical in order to bring me more quickly to my principal theme — is the determination of being as *presence* in all the senses of this word. It would be possible to show that all the names related to fundamentals, to principles, or to the center have always designated the constant of a presence — *eidos, arché, telos, energeia, ousia* (essence, existence, substance, subject) *aletheia,*[6] transcendentality, consciousness, or conscience, God, man, and so forth.

The event I called a rupture, the disruption I alluded to at the beginning of this paper, would presumably have come about when the structurality of structure had to begin to be thought, that is to say, repeated, and this is why I said that this disruption was repetition in all of the senses of this word. From then on it became necessary to think the law which governed, as it were, the desire for the center in the constitution of structure and the process of signification prescribing its displacements and its substitutions for this law of the central presence — but a central presence which was never itself, which has always already been transported outside itself in its surrogate. The surrogate does not substitute itself for anything which has somehow pre-existed it. From then on it was probably necessary to begin to think that there was no center, that the center could not be thought in the form of a being-present, that the center had no natural locus, that it was not a fixed locus but a function, a sort of non-locus in which an infinite number of sign-substitutions came into play. This moment was that in which language invaded the universal problematic; that in which, in the absence of a center or origin, everything became discourse — provided we can agree on this word — that is to say, when everything became a system where the central signified, the original or transcendental signified, is never absolutely present outside a system of differences. The absence of the transcendental signified extends the domain and the interplay of signification *ad infinitum*.

Where and how does this decentering, this notion of the structurality of structure, occur? It would be somewhat naïve to refer to an event, a doctrine, or an author in order to designate this occurrence. It is no doubt part of the totality of an era, our own, but still it has already begun to proclaim itself and begun to *work*. Nevertheless, if I wished to give some sort of indication by choosing one or two "names," and by recalling those authors in whose discourses this occurrence has most nearly maintained its most radical formulation, I would probably cite the Nietzschean critique of metaphysics, the critique of the concepts of being and truth, for which were substituted the concepts of play, interpretation, and sign (sign without truth present); the Freudian critique of

[3]" . . . qui naît toujours d'une certaine manière d'être impliqué dans le jeu, d'être pris au jeu, d'être comme être d'entreé de jeu dans le jeu." [Tr.]

[4]Beginning as end. *Telos* means "end" in the sense of "purpose."

[5]Study of last things.

[6]The six preceding Greek terms mean, respectively: form, origin, purpose, energy, being, and truth.

self-presence, that is, the critique of consciousness, of the subject, of self-identity and of self-proximity or self-possession; and, more radically, the Heideggerean destruction of metaphysics, of onto-theology, of the determination of being as presence. But all these destructive discourses and all their analogues are trapped in a sort of circle. This circle is unique. It describes the form of the relationship between the history of metaphysics and the destruction of the history of metaphysics. *There is no sense* in doing without the concepts of metaphysics in order to attack metaphysics. We have no language — no syntax and no lexicon — which is alien to this history; we cannot utter a single destructive proposition which has not already slipped into the form, the logic, and the implicit postulations of precisely what it seeks to contest. To pick out one example from many: the metaphysics of presence is attacked with the help of the concept of the *sign*. But from the moment anyone wishes this to show, as I suggested a moment ago, that there is no transcendental or privileged signified and that the domain or the interplay of signification has, henceforth, no limit, he ought to extend his refusal to the concept and to the word sign itself — which is precisely what cannot be done. For the signification "sign" has always been comprehended and determined, in its sense, as sign-of, signifier referring to a signified, signifier different from its signified. If one erases the radical difference between signifier and signified, it is the word signifier itself which ought to be abandoned as a metaphysical concept. When Lévi-Strauss says in the preface to *The Raw and the Cooked*[7] that he has "sought to transcend the opposition between the sensible and the intelligible by placing [himself] from the very beginning at the level of signs," the necessity, the force, and the legitimacy of his act cannot make us forget that the concept of the sign cannot in itself surpass or bypass this opposition between the sensible and the intelligible. The concept of the sign is determined by this opposition: through and throughout the totality of its history and by its system. But we cannot do without the concept of the sign, we cannot give up this metaphysical complicity without also giving up the critique we

are directing against this complicity, without the risk of erasing difference [altogether] in the self-identity of a signified reducing into itself its signifier, or, what amounts to the same thing, simply expelling it outside itself. For there are two heterogeneous ways of erasing the difference between the signifier and the signified: one, the classic way, consists in reducing or deriving the signifier, that is to say, ultimately in *submitting* the sign to thought; the other, the one we are using here against the first one, consists in putting into question the system in which the preceding reduction functioned: first and foremost, the opposition between the sensible and the intelligible. The *paradox* is that the metaphysical reduction of the sign needed the opposition it was reducing. The opposition is part of the system, along with the reduction. And what I am saying here about the sign can be extended to all the concepts and all the sentences of metaphysics, in particular to the discourse on "structure." But there are many ways of being caught in this circle. They are all more or less naïve, more or less empirical, more or less systematic, more or less close to the formulation or even to the formalization of this circle. It is these differences which explain the multiplicity of destructive discourses and the disagreement between those who make them. It was within concepts inherited from metaphysics that Nietzsche, Freud, and Heidegger worked, for example. Since these concepts are not elements or atoms and since they are taken from a syntax and a system, every particular borrowing drags along with it the whole of metaphysics. This is what allows these destroyers to destroy each other reciprocally — for example, Heidegger considering Nietzsche, with as much lucidity and rigor as bad faith and misconstruction, as the last metaphysician, the last "Platonist." One could do the same for Heidegger himself, for Freud, or for a number of others. And today no exercise is more widespread.

What is the relevance of this formal schema when we turn to what are called the "human sciences"? One of them perhaps occupies a privileged place — ethnology.[8] One can in fact assume that ethnology could have been born as a

[7]*Le Cru et le cuit* (Paris: Plon, 1964). [Tr.]

[8]Cultural anthropology.

science only at the moment when a de-centering had come about: at the moment when European culture — and, in consequence, the history of metaphysics and of its concepts — had been *dislocated,* driven from its locus, and forced to stop considering itself as the culture of reference. This moment is not first and foremost a moment of philosophical or scientific discourse, it is also a moment which is political, economic, technical, and so forth. One can say in total assurance that there is nothing fortuitous about the fact that the critique of ethnocentrism — the very condition of ethnology — should be systematically and historically contemporaneous with the destruction of the history of metaphysics. Both belong to a single and same era.

Ethnology — like any science — comes about within the element of discourse. And it is primarily a European science employing traditional concepts, however much it may struggle against them. Consequently, whether he wants to or not — and this does not depend on a decision on his part — the ethnologist accepts into his discourse the premises of ethnocentrism at the very moment when he is employed in denouncing them. This necessity is irreducible; it is not a historical contingency. We ought to consider very carefully all its implications. But if nobody can escape this necessity, and if no one is therefore responsible for giving in to it, however little, this does not mean that all the ways of giving in to it are of an equal pertinence. The quality and the fecundity of a discourse are perhaps measured by the critical rigor with which this relationship to the history of metaphysics and to inherited concepts is thought. Here it is a question of a critical relationship to the language of the human sciences and a question of a critical responsibility of the discourse. It is a question of putting expressly and systematically the problem of the status of a discourse which borrows from a heritage the resources necessary for the deconstruction of that heritage itself. A problem of *economy* and *strategy.*

If I now go on to employ an examination of the texts of Lévi-Strauss as an example, it is not only because of the privilege accorded to ethnology among the human sciences, nor yet because the thought of Lévi-Strauss weighs heavily on the contemporary theoretical situation. It is above all because a certain choice has made itself evident in the work of Lévi-Strauss and because a certain doctrine has been elaborated there, and precisely in a *more or less explicit manner,* in relation to this critique of language and to this critical language in the human sciences.

In order to follow this movement in the text of Lévi-Strauss, let me choose as one guiding thread among others the opposition between nature and culture. In spite of all its rejuvenations and its disguises, this opposition is congenital to philosophy. It is even older than Plato. It is at least as old as the Sophists. Since the statement of the opposition — *physis/nomos, physis/techne*[9] — it has been passed on to us by a whole historical chain which opposes "nature" to the law, to education, to art, to technics — and also to liberty, to the arbitrary, to history, to society, to the mind, and so on. From the beginnings of his quest and from his first book, *The Elementary Structures of Kinship,*[10] Lévi-Strauss has felt at one and the same time the necessity of utilizing this opposition and the impossibility of *making* it acceptable. In the *Elementary Structures,* he begins from this axiom or definition: that belongs to nature which is *universal* and spontaneous, not depending on any particular culture or on any determinate norm. That belongs to culture, on the other hand, which depends on a system of *norms* regulating society and is therefore capable of *varying* from one social structure to another. These two definitions are of the traditional type. But, in the very first pages of the *Elementary Structures,* Lévi-Strauss, who has begun to give these concepts an acceptable standing, encounters what he calls a *scandal,* that is to say, something which no longer tolerates the nature/culture opposition he has accepted and which seems to require *at one and the same time* the predicates of nature and those of culture. This scandal is the *incest-prohibition.* The incest-prohibition is universal; in this sense one could call it natural. But it is also a prohibition, a system of norms and interdicts; in this sense one could call it cultural.

[9]Nature vs. culture; nature vs. art.
[10]*Les Structures élémentaires de la parenté* (Paris: Presses Universitaires de France, 1949). [Tr.]

Let us assume therefore that everything universal in man derives from the order of nature and is characterized by spontaneity, that everything which is subject to a norm belongs to culture and presents the attributes of the relative and the particular. We then find ourselves confronted by a fact, or rather an ensemble of facts, which, in the light of the preceding definitions, is not far from appearing as a scandal: the prohibition of incest presents without the least equivocation, and indissolubly linked together, the two characteristics in which we recognized the contradictory attributes of two exclusive orders. The prohibition of incest constitutes a rule, but a rule, alone of all the social rules, which possesses at the same time a universal character (p. 9).

Obviously there is no scandal except in the *interior* of a system of concepts sanctioning the difference between nature and culture. In beginning his work with the *factum*[11] of the incest-prohibition, Lévi-Strauss thus puts himself in a position entailing that this difference, which has always been assumed to be self-evident, becomes obliterated or disputed. For, from the moment that the incest-prohibition can no longer be conceived within the nature/culture opposition, it can no longer be said that it is a scandalous fact, a nucleus of opacity within a network of transparent significations. The incest-prohibition is no longer a scandal one meets with or comes up against in the domain of traditional concepts; it is something which escapes these concepts and certainly precedes them — probably as the condition of their possibility. It could perhaps be said that the whole of philosophical conceptualization, systematically relating itself to the nature/culture opposition, is designed to leave in the domain of the unthinkable the very thing that makes this conceptualization possible: the origin of the prohibition of incest.

I have dealt too cursorily with this example, only one among so many others, but the example nevertheless reveals that language bears within itself the necessity of its own critique. This critique may be undertaken along two tracks, in two "manners." Once the limit of nature/culture opposition makes itself felt, one might want to question systematically and rigorously the history of these concepts. This is a first action. Such a systematic and historic questioning would be neither a philological nor a philosophical action in the classic sense of these words. Concerning oneself with the founding concepts of the whole history of philosophy, de-constituting them, is not to undertake the task of the philologist or of the classic historian of philosophy. In spite of appearances, it is probably the most daring way of making the beginnings of a step outside of philosophy. The step "outside philosophy" is much more difficult to conceive than is generally imagined by those who think they made it long ago with cavalier ease, and who are in general swallowed up in metaphysics by the whole body of the discourse that they claim to have disengaged from it.

In order to avoid the possibly sterilizing effect of the first way, the other choice — which I feel corresponds more nearly to the way chosen by Lévi-Strauss — consists in conserving in the field of empirical discovery all these old concepts, while at the same time exposing here and there their limits, treating them as tools which can still be of use. No longer is any truth-value attributed to them; there is a readiness to abandon them if necessary if other instruments should appear more useful. In the meantime, their relative efficacy is exploited, and they are employed to destroy the old machinery to which they belong and of which they themselves are pieces. Thus it is that the language of the human sciences criticizes *itself.* Lévi-Strauss thinks that in this way he can separate *method* from *truth,* the instruments of the method and the objective significations aimed at by it. One could almost say that this is the primary affirmation of Lévi-Strauss; in any event, the first words of the *Elementary Structures* are: "One begins to understand that the distinction between state of nature and state of society (we would be more apt to say today: state of nature and state of culture), while lacking any acceptable historical signification, presents a value which fully justifies its use by modern sociology: its value as a methodological instrument."

Lévi-Strauss will always remain faithful to this double intention: to preserve as an instrument that whose truth-value he criticizes.

On the one hand, he will continue in effect to contest the value of the nature/culture opposition.

[11]Given fact.

More than thirteen years after the *Elementary Structures, The Savage Mind*[12] faithfully echoes the text I have just quoted: "The opposition between nature and culture which I have previously insisted on seems today to offer a value which is above all methodological." And this methodological value is not affected by its "ontological" non-value (as could be said, if this notion were not suspect here): "It would not be enough to have absorbed particular humanities into a general humanity; this first enterprise prepares the way for others . . . which belong to the natural and exact sciences: to reintegrate culture into nature, and finally, to reintegrate life into the totality of its physiochemical conditions" (p. 327).

On the other hand, still in *The Savage Mind,* he presents as what he calls *bricolage*[13] what might be called the discourse of this method. The *bricoleur,* says Lévi-Strauss, is someone who uses "the means at hand," that is, the instruments he finds at his disposition around him, those which are already there, which had not been especially conceived with an eye to the operation for which they are to be used and to which one tries by trial and error to adapt them, not hesitating to change them whenever it appears necessary, or to try several of them at once, even if their form and their origin are heterogeneous — and so forth. There is therefore a critique of language in the form of *bricolage,* and it has even been possible to say that *bricolage* is the critical language itself. I am thinking in particular of the article by G[érard] Genette, "Structuralisme et Critique littéraire," published in homage to Lévi-Strauss in a special issue of *L'Arc* (no. 26, 1965), where it is stated that the analysis of *bricolage* could "be applied almost word for word" to criticism, and especially to "literary criticism."[14]

If one calls *bricolage* the necessity of borrowing one's concept from the text of a heritage which is more or less coherent or ruined, it must be said that every discourse is *bricoleur.* The

engineer, whom Lévi-Strauss opposes to the *bricoleur,* should be one to construct the totality of his language, syntax, and lexicon. In this sense the engineer is a myth. A subject who would supposedly be the absolute origin of his own discourse and would supposedly construct it "out of nothing," "out of whole cloth," would be the creator of the *verbe,* the *verbe* itself. The notion of the engineer who had supposedly broken with all forms of *bricolage* is therefore a theological idea; and since Lévi-Strauss tells us elsewhere that *bricolage* is mythopoetic, the odds are that the engineer is a myth produced by the *bricoleur.* From the moment that we cease to believe in such an engineer and in a discourse breaking with the received historical discourse, as soon as it is admitted that every finite discourse is bound by a certain *bricolage,* and that the engineer and the scientist are also species of *bricoleurs* then the very idea of *bricolage* is menaced and the difference in which it took on its meaning decomposes.

This brings out the second thread which might guide us in what is being unraveled here.

Lévi-Strauss describes *bricolage* not only as an intellectual activity but also as a mythopoetical activity. One reads in *The Savage Mind,* "Like *bricolage* on the technical level, mythical reflection can attain brilliant and unforeseen results on the intellectual level. Reciprocally, the mythopoetical character of *bricolage* has often been noted" (p. 26).

But the remarkable endeavor of Lévi-Strauss is not simply to put forward, notably in the most recent of his investigations, a structural science of knowledge of myths and of mythological activity. His endeavor also appears — I would say almost from the first — in the status which he accords to his own discourse on myths, to what he calls his "mythologicals." It is here that his discourse on the myth reflects on itself and criticizes itself. And this moment, this critical period, is evidently of concern to all the languages which share the field of the human sciences. What does Lévi-Strauss say of his "mythologicals"? It is here that we rediscover the mythopoetical virtue (power) of *bricolage.* In effect, what appears most fascinating in this critical search for a new status of the discourse is the stated abandonment of all reference to a *center,* to a *subject,* to a privileged *reference,* to an origin, or

---

[12]*La Pensée sauvage* (Paris: Plon, 1962). [Tr.]

[13]A *bricoleur* is a jack-of-all-trades, someone who potters about with odds-and-ends, who puts things together out of bits and pieces. [Tr.]

[14]Reprinted in: G. Genette, *Figures* (Paris: Editions du Seuil, 1966), p. 145. [Tr.]

to an absolute *arché*. The theme of this decentering could be followed throughout the "Overture" to his last book, *The Raw and the Cooked.* I shall simply remark on a few key points.

1. From the very start, Lévi-Strauss recognizes that the Bororo myth which he employs in the book as the "reference-myth" does not merit this name and this treatment. The name is specious and the use of the myth improper. This myth deserves no more than any other its referential privilege:

> In fact the Bororo myth which will from now on be designated by the name *reference-myth* is, as I shall try to show, nothing other than a more or less forced transformation of other myths originating either in the same society or in societies more or less far removed. It would therefore have been legitimate to choose as my point of departure any representative of the group whatsoever. From this point of view, the interest of the reference-myth does not depend on its typical character, but rather on its irregular position in the midst of a group (p. 10).

2. There is no unity or absolute source of the myth. The focus or the source of the myth are always shadows and virtualities which are elusive, unactualizable, and nonexistent in the first place. Everything begins with the structure, the configuration, the relationship. The discourse on this acentric structure, the myth, that is, cannot itself have an absolute subject or an absolute center. In order not to shortchange the form and the movement of the myth, that violence which consists in centering a language which is describing an acentric structure must be avoided. In this context, therefore, it is necessary to forego scientific or philosophical discourse, to renounce the *epistemé* which absolutely requires, which is the absolute requirement that we go back to the source, to the center, to the founding basis, to the principle, and so on. In opposition to *epistémic* discourse, structural discourse on myths — *mythological* discourse — must itself be *mythomorphic.* It must have the form of that of which it speaks. This is what Lévi-Strauss says in *The Raw and the Cooked,* from which I would now like to quote a long and remarkable passage:

> In effect the study of myths poses a methodological problem by the fact that it cannot conform to the Cartesian principle of dividing the difficulty into as many parts as are necessary to resolve it. There exists no veritable end or term to mythical analysis, no secret unity which could be grasped at the end of the work of decomposition. The themes duplicate themselves to infinity. When we think we have disentangled them from each other and can hold them separate, it is only to realize that they are joining together again, in response to the attraction of unforeseen affinities. In consequence, the unity of the myth is only tendential and projective; it never reflects a state or a moment of the myth. An imaginary phenomenon implied by the endeavor to interpret, its role is to give a synthetic form to the myth and to impede its dissolution into the confusion of contraries. It could therefore be said that the science or knowledge of myths is an *anaclastic,* taking this ancient term in the widest sense authorized by its etymology, a science which admits into its definition the study of the reflected rays along with that of the broken ones. But, unlike philosophical reflection, which claims to go all the way back to its source, the reflections in question here concern rays without any other than a virtual focus. . . . In wanting to imitate the spontaneous movement of mythical thought, my enterprise, itself too brief and too long, has had to yield to its demands and respect its rhythm. Thus is this book on myths itself and in its own way a myth.

This statement is repeated a little farther on (p. 20): "Since myths themselves rest on second-order codes (the first-order codes being those in which language consists), this book thus offers the rough draft of a third-order code, destined to insure the reciprocal possibility of translation of several myths. This is why it would not be wrong to consider it a myth: the myth of mythology, as it were." It is by this absence of any real and fixed center of the mythical or mythological discourse that the musical model chosen by Lévi-Strauss for the composition of his book is apparently justified. The absence of a center is here the absence of a subject and the absence of an author: "The myth and the musical work thus appear as orchestra conductors whose listeners are the silent performers. If it be asked where the real focus of the work is to be found, it must be replied that its determination is impossible. Music and mythology bring man face to face with virtual objects whose shadow alone is actual. . . . Myths have no authors" (p. 25).

Thus it is at this point that ethnographic *bricolage* deliberately assumes its mythopoetic function. But by the same token, this function makes the philosophical or epistemological requirement of a center appear as mythological, that is to say, as a historical illusion.

Nevertheless, even if one yields to the necessity of what Lévi-Strauss has done, one cannot ignore its risks. If the mythological is mythomorphic, are all discourses on myths equivalent? Shall we have to abandon any epistemological requirement which permits us to distinguish between several qualities of discourse on the myth? A classic question, but inevitable. We cannot reply — and I do not believe Lévi-Strauss replies to it — as long as the problem of the relationships between the philosopheme or the theorem, on the one hand, and the mytheme or the mythopoem(e), on the other, has not been expressly posed. This is no small problem. For lack of expressly posing this problem, we condemn ourselves to transforming the claimed transgression of philosophy into an unperceived fault in the interior of the philosophical field. Empiricism would be the genus of which these faults would always be the species. Trans-philosophical concepts would be transformed into philosophical naïvetés. One could give many examples to demonstrate this risk: the concepts of sign, history, truth, and so forth. What I want to emphasize is simply that the passage beyond philosophy does not consist in turning the page of philosophy (which usually comes down to philosophizing badly), but in continuing to read philosophers *in a certain way*. The risk I am speaking of is always assumed by Lévi-Strauss and it is the very price of his endeavor. I have said that empiricism is the matrix of all the faults menacing a discourse which continues, as with Lévi-Strauss in particular, to elect to be scientific. If we wanted to pose the problem of empiricism and *bricolage* in depth, we would probably end up very quickly with a number of propositions absolutely contradictory in relation to the status of discourse in structural ethnography. On the one hand, structuralism justly claims to be the critique of empiricism.[15] But at the same time there is not a single book or study by Lévi-Strauss which does not offer itself as an empirical essay which can always be completed or invalidated by new information. The structural schemata are always proposed as hypotheses resulting from a finite quantity of information and which are subjected to the proof of experience. Numerous texts could be used to demonstrate this double postulation. Let us turn once again to the "Overture" of *The Raw and the Cooked,* where it seems clear that if this postulation is double, it is because it is a question here of a language on language:

> Critics who might take me to task for not having begun by making an exhaustive inventory of South American myths before analyzing them would be making a serious mistake about the nature and the role of these documents. The totality of the myths of a people is of the order of the discourse. Provided that this people does not become physically or morally extinct, this totality is never closed. Such a criticism would therefore be equivalent to reproaching a linguist with writing the grammar of a language without having recorded the totality of the words which have been uttered since that language came into existence and without knowing the verbal exchanges which will take place as long as the language continues to exist. Experience proves that an absurdly small number of sentences . . . allows the linguist to elaborate a grammar of the language he is studying. And even a partial grammar or an outline of a grammar represents valuable acquisitions in the case of unknown languages. Syntax does not wait until it has been possible to enumerate a theoretically unlimited series of events before becoming manifest, because syntax consists in the body of rules which presides over the generation of these events. And it is precisely a syntax of South American mythology that I wanted to outline. Should new texts appear to enrich the mythical discourse, then this will provide an opportunity to check or modify the way in which certain grammatical laws have been formulated, an opportunity to discard certain of them and an opportunity to discover new ones. But in no instance can the requirement of a total mythical discourse be raised as an objection. For we have just seen that such a requirement has no meaning (pp. 15–16).

---

[15]Because the aim of structuralism is to learn the constitutive rules of an activity, which are implicit in every instance of the activity, so that the massing of large quantities of data is unnecessary.

Totalization is therefore defined at one time as *useless,* at another time as *impossible.* This is no doubt the result of the fact that there are two ways of conceiving the limit of totalization. And I assert once again that these two determinations coexist implicitly in the discourses of Lévi-Strauss. Totalization can be judged impossible in the classical style: one then refers to the empirical endeavor of a subject or of a finite discourse in a vain and breathless quest of an infinite richness which it can never master. There is too much, more than one can say. But nontotalization can also be determined in another way: not from the standpoint of the concept of finitude as assigning us to an empirical view, but from the standpoint of the concept of *freeplay.* If totalization no longer has any meaning, it is not because the infinity of a field cannot be covered by a finite glance or a finite discourse, but because the nature of the field — that is, language and a finite language — excludes totalization. This field is in fact that of *freeplay,* that is to say, a field of infinite substitutions in the closure of a finite ensemble. This field permits these infinite substitutions only because it is finite, that is to say, because instead of being an inexhaustible field, as in the classical hypothesis, instead of being too large, there is something missing from it: a center which arrests and grounds the freeplay of substitutions. One could say — rigorously using that word whose scandalous signification is always obliterated in French — that this movement of the freeplay, permitted by the lack, the absence of a center of origin, is the movement of *supplementarity.* One cannot determine the center, the sign which *supplements*[16] it, which takes its place in its absence — because this sign adds itself, occurs in addition, over and above, comes as a *supplement.*[17] The movement of signification adds something, which results in the fact that there is always more, but this addition is a floating one because it comes to perform a vicarious function, to supplement a lack on the part of the signified. Although Lévi-Strauss in his use of the word supplementary never

emphasizes as I am doing here the two directions of meaning which are so strangely compounded within it, it is not by chance that he uses this word twice in his "Introduction to the Work of Marcel Mauss,"[18] at the point where he is speaking of the "superabundance of signifier, in relation to the signifieds to which this superabundance can refer":

> In his endeavor to understand the world, man therefore always has at his disposition a surplus of signification (which he portions out amongst things according to the laws of symbolic thought — which it is the task of ethnologists and linguists to study). This distribution of a *supplementary* allowance [*ration* supplémentaire] — if it is permissible to put it that way — is absolutely necessary in order that on the whole the available signifier and the signified it aims at may remain in the relationship of complementarity which is the very condition of the use of symbolic thought (p. xlix).

(It could no doubt be demonstrated that this *ration supplémentaire* of signification is the origin of the *ratio* itself.) The word reappears a little farther on, after Lévi-Strauss has mentioned "this floating signifier, which is the servitude of all finite thought":

> In other words — and taking as our guide Mauss's precept that all social phenomena can be assimilated to language — we see in *mana, Wakau, oranda* and other notions of the same type, the conscious expression of a semantic function, whose role it is to permit symbolic thought to operate in spite of the contradiction which is proper to it. In this way are explained the apparently insoluble antinomies attached to this notion. . . . At one and the same time force and action, quality and state, substantive and verb; abstract and concrete, omnipresent and localized — *mana* is in effect all these things. But is it not precisely because it is none of these things that *mana* is a simple form, or more exactly, a symbol in the pure state, and therefore capable of becoming charged with any sort of symbolic content whatever? In the system of symbols constituted by all cosmologies, *mana* would simply be a *valeur symbolique zéro,* that is to say, a

---

[16]The point being that the word, both in English and French, means "to supply a deficiency," on the one hand, and "to supply something additional," on the other. [Tr.] See pp. 826–28, on Derrida's antinomy of the supplement.

[17]". . . ce signe s'ajoute, vient en sus, en *supplément.*" [Tr.]

[18]"Introduction à l'oeuvre de Marcel Mauss," in: Marcel Mauss, *Sociologie et anthropologie* (Paris: Presses Universitaires de France, 1950). [Tr.] Marcel Mauss (1872–1950) was the French social anthropologist who wrote *The Gift* (1925).

sign marking the necessity of a symbolic content *supplementary* [my italics] to that with which the signified is already loaded, but which can take on any value required, provided only that this value still remains part of the available reserve and is not, as phonologists put it, a group-term.

Lévi-Strauss adds the note:

> Linguists have already been led to formulate hypotheses of this type. For example: "A zero phoneme is opposed to all the other phonemes in French in that it entails no differential characters and no constant phonetic value. On the contrary, the proper function of the zero phoneme is to be opposed to phoneme absence." (R. Jakobson and J. Lutz, "Notes on the French Phonemic Pattern," *Word,* vol. 5, no. 2 [August, 1949], p. 155). Similarly, if we schematize the conception I am proposing here, it could almost be said that the function of notions like *mana* is to be opposed to the absence of signification, without entailing by itself any particular signification (p. 1 and note).

The *superabundance* of the signifier, its *supplementary* character, is thus the result of a finitude, that is to say, the result of a lack which must be *supplemented.*

It can now be understood why the concept of freeplay is important in Lévi-Strauss. His references to all sorts of games, notably to roulette, are very frequent, especially in his *Conversations,*[19] in *Race and History,*[20] and in *The Savage Mind.* This reference to the game or free-play is always caught up in a tension.

It is in tension with history, first of all. This is a classical problem, objections to which are now well worn or used up. I shall simply indicate what seems to me the formality of the problem: by reducing history, Lévi-Strauss has treated as it deserves a concept which has always been in complicity with a teleological and eschatological metaphysics, in other words, paradoxically, in complicity with that philosophy of presence to which it was believed history could be opposed. The thematic of historicity, although it seems to be a somewhat late arrival in philosophy, has always been required by the determination of being as presence. With or without etymology, and in spite of the classic antagonism which opposes these significations throughout all of classical thought, it could be shown that the concept of *epistemé* has always called forth that of *historia,* if history is always the unity of a becoming, as tradition of truth or development of science or knowledge oriented toward the appropriation of truth in presence and self-presence, toward knowledge in consciousness-of-self.[21] History has always been conceived as the movement of a resumption of history, a diversion between two presences. But if it is legitimate to suspect this concept of history, there is a risk, if it is reduced without an express statement of the problem I am indicating here, of falling back into an ahistoricism of a classical type, that is to say, in a determinate moment of the history of metaphysics. Such is the algebraic formality of the problem as I see it. More concretely, in the work of Lévi-Strauss it must be recognized that the respect for structurality, for the internal originality of the structure, compels a neutralization of time and history. For example, the appearance of a new structure, of an original system, always comes about — and this is the very condition of its structural specificity — by a rupture with its past, its origin, and its cause. One can therefore describe what is peculiar to the structural organization only by not taking into account, in the very moment of this description, its past conditions: by failing to pose the problem of the passage from one structure to another, by putting history into parentheses. In this "structuralist" moment, the concepts of chance and discontinuity are indispensable. And Lévi-Strauss does in fact often appeal to them as he does, for instance, for that structure of structures, language, of which he says in the "Introduction to the Work of Marcel Mauss" that it "could only have been born in one fell swoop":

> Whatever may have been the moment and the circumstances of its appearance in the scale of animal

---

[19]Presumably: G. Charbonnier, *Entretiens avec Claude Lévi-Strauss* (Paris: Plon-Julliard, 1961). [Tr.]

[20]*Race and History* (Paris: UNESCO Publications, 1958). [Tr.]

[21]." . . l'unité d'un devenir, comme tradition de la vérité dans la présence et la présence à soi, vers le savoir dans la conscience de soi." [Tr.]

life, language could only have been born in one fell swoop. Things could not have set about signifying progressively. Following a transformation the study of which is not the concern of the social sciences, but rather of biology and psychology, a crossing over came about from a stage where nothing had a meaning to another where everything possessed it (p. xlvi).

This standpoint does not prevent Lévi-Strauss from recognizing the slowness, the process of maturing, the continuous toil of factual transformations, history (for example, in *Race and History*). But, in accordance with an act which was also Rousseau's and Husserl's, he must "brush aside all the facts" at the moment when he wishes to recapture the specificity of a structure. Like Rousseau, he must always conceive of the origin of a new structure on the model of catastrophe — an overturning of nature in nature, a natural interruption of the natural sequence, a brushing aside *of* nature.

Besides the tension of freeplay with history, there is also the tension of freeplay with presence. Freeplay is the disruption of presence. The presence of an element is always a signifying and substitutive reference inscribed in a system of differences and the movement of a chin. Freeplay is always an interplay of absence and presence, but if it is to be radically conceived, freeplay must be conceived of before the alternative of presence and absence; being must be conceived of as presence or absence beginning with the possibility of freeplay and not the other way around. If Lévi-Strauss, better than any other, has brought to light the freeplay of repetition and the repetition of freeplay, one no less perceives in his work a sort of ethic presence, an ethic of nostalgia for origins, an ethic of archaic and natural innocence, of a purity of presence and self-presence in speech[22] — an ethic, nostalgia, and even remorse which he often presents as the motivation of the ethnological project when he moves toward archaic societies — exemplary societies in his eyes. These texts are well known.

As a turning toward the presence, lost or impossible, of the absent origin, this structuralist

thematic of broken immediateness is thus the sad, *negative,* nostalgic, guilty, Rousseauist facet of the thinking of freeplay of which the Nietzschean *affirmation* — the joyous affirmation of the freeplay of the world and of the innocence of becoming, the affirmation of a world of signs without fault, without truth, without origin, offered to an active interpretation — would be the other side. *This affirmation then determines the non-center otherwise than as loss of the center.* And it plays the game without security. For there is a *sure* freeplay: that which is limited to the *substitution of given and existing, present,* pieces. In absolute chance, affirmation also surrenders itself to *genetic* indetermination, to the *seminal* adventure of the trace.[23]

There are thus two interpretations of interpretation, of structure, of sign, of freeplay. The one seeks to decipher, dreams of deciphering, a truth or an origin which is free from freeplay and from the order of the sign, and lives like an exile the necessity of interpretation. The other, which is no longer turned toward the origin, affirms freeplay and tries to pass beyond man and humanism, the

---

[22]". . de la présence à soi dans la parole." [Tr.]

[23]"Tournée vers la présence, perdue ou impossible, de l'origine absente, cette thématique structuraliste de l'immédiateté rompue est donc la face triste, *négative,* nostalgique, coupable, rousseauiste, de la pensée du jeu dont *l'affirmation* nietzschéenne, l'affirmation joyeuse du jeu du monde et de l'innocence du devenir, l'affirmation d'un monde de signes sans faute, sans vérité, sans origine, offert à une interprétation active, serait l'autre face. *Cette affirmation détermine alors le* non-centre *autrement que comme perte du centre.* Et elle joue sans sécurité. Car il y a un jeu *sûr:* celui qui se limite à la *substitution* de pièces *données et existantes, présentes.* Dans le hasard absolu, l'affirmation se livre aussi à l'indétermination *génétique,* à l'aventure *séminale* de la trace." [Tr.] Derrida contrasts two methods of freeplay, Lévi-Strauss's and his own. The former is "sad" and "negative" in that it seeks a substitute for the absent center once provided by metaphysics; it is "nostalgic" for origins, "guilty" over European imperialism, "Rousseauist" in propounding a myth of the noble savage and privileging myth over rational thought. Its method of freeplay is "sure" in that its substitutions of one mytheme for another within the system of myths create a closed system. On the contrary, Derrida's system of freeplay, like the philosophy of Nietzsche, is "joyful" in its affirmation of the power of the will to assign and alter all values. For Derrida, the lack of a center betokens freedom, not the loss of security. The Derridean is an adventurer who must abandon certainty for chance in following the "trace" — the chain of signifiers — wherever it leads.

name man being the name of that being who, throughout the history of metaphysics or of ontotheology — in other words, through the history of all of his history — has dreamed of full presence, the reassuring foundation, the origin and the end of the game. The second interpretation of interpretation, to which Nietzsche showed us the way, does not seek in ethnography, as Lévi-Strauss wished, the "inspiration of a new humanism."

There are more than enough indications today to suggest we might perceive that these two interpretations of interpretation — which are absolutely irreconcilable even if we live them simultaneously and reconcile them in an obscure economy — together share the field which we call, in such a problematic fashion, the human sciences.

For my part, although these two interpretations must acknowledge and accentuate their difference and define their irreducibility, I do not believe that today there is any question of *choosing* — in the first place because here we are in a region (let's say, provisionally, a region of historicity) where the category of choice seems particularly trivial; and in the second, because we must first try to conceive of the common ground, and the *différance* of this irreducible difference.[24] Here there is a sort of question, call it historical, of which we are only glimpsing today the *conception, the formation, the gestation, the labor.* I employ these words, I admit, with a glance toward the business of childbearing — but also with a glance toward those who, in a company from which I do not exclude myself, turn their eyes away in the face of the as yet unnameable which is proclaiming itself and which can do so, as is necessary whenever a birth is in the offing, only under the species of the non-species, in the formless, mute, infant, and terrifying form of monstrosity.

[24]From *différer,* in the sense of "to postpone," "put off," "defer." Elsewhere Derrida uses the word as a synonym for the German *Aufschub:* "postponement," and relates it to the central Freudian concepts of *Verspätung, Nachträglichkeit,* and to the *"détours* to death" of *Beyond the Pleasure Principle* by Sigmund Freud (Standard Edition, ed. James Strachey, vol. XIX, London, 1961), Ch. V. [Tr.]

The Father of Logos from *Plato's Pharmacy*

The story begins like this:

Socrates: Very well. I heard, then, that at Naucratis in Egypt there lived one of the old gods of that country, the one whose sacred bird is called the ibis; and the name of the divinity was Theuth. It was he who first invented numbers and calculation, geometry and astronomy, not to speak of draughts and dice, and above all writing (*grammata*). Now the King of all Egypt at that time was Thamus who lived in the great city of the upper region which the Greeks call the Egyptian Thebes; the god himself they call Ammon. Theuth came to him and exhibited his arts and declared that they ought to be imparted to the other Egyptians. And Thamus questioned him

Translated by Barbara Johnson.

about the usefulness of each one; and as Theuth enumerated, the King blamed or praised what he thought were the good or bad points in the explanation. Now Thamus is said to have had a good deal to remark on both sides of the question about every single art (it would take too long to repeat it here); but when it came to writing, Theuth said, "This discipline (*to mathēma*), my King, will make the Egyptians wiser and will improve their memories (*sophōterous kai mnēmonikōterous*): my invention is a recipe (*pharmakon*[1]) for both memory and wisdom." But the King said . . . etc. (274c–e).

[1]Greek word translated variously as *recipe, drug,* and *poison.* Derrida's reading of the *Phaedrus* will depend on this play of language and difference. For more on Plato's *Phaedrus,* see p. 46.

Let us cut the King off here. He is faced with the *pharmakon*. His reply will be incisive.

Let us freeze the scene and the characters and take a look at them. Writing (or, if you will, the *pharmakon*) is thus presented to the King. Presented: like a kind of present offered up in homage by a vassal to his lord (Theuth is a demigod speaking to the king of the gods), but above all as a finished work submitted to his appreciation. And this work is itself an art, a capacity for work, a power of operation. This *artefactum* is an art. But the value of this gift is still uncertain. The value of writing — or of the *pharmakon* — has of course been spelled out to the King, but it is the King who will give it its value, who will set the price of what, in the act of receiving, he constitutes or institutes. The king or god (Thamus represents[2] Ammon, the king of the gods, the king of kings, the god of gods. Theuth says to him: *Ō basileu*) is thus the other name for the origin of value. The value of writing will not be itself, writing will have no value, unless and to the extent that god-the-king approves of it. But god-the-king nonetheless experiences the *pharmakon* as a product, an *ergon*, which is not his own, which comes to him from outside but also from below, and which awaits his condescending judgment in order to be consecrated in its being and value. God the king does not know how to write, but that ignorance or incapacity only testifies to his sovereign independence. He has no need to write. He speaks, he says, he dictates, and his word suffices. Whether a scribe from his secretarial staff then adds the supplement of a transcription or not, that consignment is always in essence secondary.

From this position, without rejecting the homage, the god-king will depreciate it, pointing out not only its uselessness but its menace and its mischief. Another way of not receiving the offering of writing. In so doing, god-the-king-that-speaks is acting like a father. The *pharmakon* is here presented to the father and is by him rejected, belittled, abandoned, disparaged. The father is always suspicious and watchful toward writing.

Even if we did not want to give in here to the easy passage uniting the figures of the king, the god, and the father, it would suffice to pay systematic attention — which to our knowledge has never been done — to the permanence of a Platonic schema that assigns the origin and power of speech, precisely of *logos*,[3] to the paternal position. Not that this happens especially and exclusively in Plato. Everyone knows this or can easily imagine it. But the fact that "Platonism," which sets up the whole of Western metaphysics in its conceptuality, should not escape the generality of this structural constraint, and even illustrates it with incomparable subtlety and force, stands out as all the more significant.

Not that logos *is* the father, either. But the origin of logos is *its father*. One could say anachronously that the "speaking subject" is the *father* of his speech. And one would quickly realize that this is no metaphor, at least not in the sense of any common, conventional effect of rhetoric. *Logos* is a son, then, a son that would be destroyed in his very *presence* without the present *attendance* of his father. His father who answers. His father who speaks for him and answers for him. Without his father, he would be nothing but, in fact, writing. At least that is what is said by the one who says: it is the father's thesis. The specificity of writing would thus be intimately bound to the absence of the father. Such an absence can of course exist along very diverse modalities, distinctly or confusedly, successively or simultaneously: to have lost one's father, through natural or violent death, through random violence or patricide; and then to solicit the aid and attendance, possible or impossible, of the paternal presence, to solicit it directly or to claim to be getting along without it, etc. The reader will have noted Socrates' insistence on the misery, whether pitiful or arrogant, of a *logos* committed to writing: " . . . It

---

[2] For Plato, Thamus is doubtless another name for Ammon, whose figure (that of the sun king and of the father of the gods) we shall sketch out later for its own sake. On this question and the debate to which it has given rise, see Frutiger, *Mythes*, p. 233, n. 2, and notably Eisler, "Platon und das ägyptische Alphabet," *Archiv für Geschichte der Philosophie*, 1922; Pauly-Wissowa, *Real-Encyclopädie der classischen Altertumswissenschaft* (art. Ammon); Roscher, *Lexikon der griechischen und römischen Mythologie* (art. Thamus). [Derrida]

[3] Greek for both *word* (discourse, reason) and *thing*.

always needs its father to attend to it, being quite unable to defend itself or attend to its own needs" (275e).

This misery is ambiguous: it is the distress of the orphan, of course, who needs not only an attending presence but also a presence that will attend to its needs; but in pitying the orphan, one also makes an accusation against him, along with writing, for claiming to do away with the father, for achieving emancipation with complacent self-sufficiency. From the position of the holder of the scepter, the desire of writing is indicated, designated, and denounced as a desire for orphanhood and patricidal subversion. Isn't this *pharmakon* then a criminal thing, a poisoned present?

The status of this orphan, whose welfare cannot be assured by any attendance or assistance, coincides with that of a *graphein*[4] which, being nobody's son at the instant it reaches inscription, scarcely remains a son at all and no longer *recognizes* its origins, whether legally or morally. In contrast to writing, living *logos* is alive in that it has a living father (whereas the orphan is already half dead), a father that is *present, standing* near it, behind it, within it, sustaining it with his rectitude, attending it in person in his own name. Living *logos*, for its part, recognizes its debt, lives off that recognition, and forbids itself, thinks it can forbid itself patricide. But prohibition and patricide, like the relations between speech and writing, are structures surprising enough to require us later on to articulate Plato's text between a patricide prohibited and a patricide proclaimed. The deferred murder of the father and rector.

The *Phaedrus* would already be sufficient to prove that the responsibility for *logos*, for its meaning and effects, goes to those who attend it, to those who are present with the presence of a father. These "metaphors" must be tirelessly questioned. Witness Socrates, addressing Eros: "If in our former speech Phaedrus or I said anything harsh against you, blame Lysias, the father of the subject (*ton tou logou patera*)" (275*b*). *Logos* — "discourse" — has the meaning here of argument, line of reasoning, guiding thread animating the

spoken discussion (the *Logos*). To translate it by "subject" [*sujet*], as Robin[5] does, is not merely anachronistic. The whole intention and the organic unity of signification is destroyed. For only the "living" discourse, only a spoken word (and not a speech's theme, object, or subject) can have a father; and, according to a necessity that will not cease to become clearer to us from now on, the *logoi* are the children. Alive enough to protest on occasion and to let themselves be questioned; capable, too, in contrast to written things, of responding when their father is there. They are their father's responsible presence.

Some of them, for example, descend from Phaedrus, who is sometimes called upon to sustain them. Let us refer again to Robin, who translates *logos* this time not by "subject" but by "argument," and disrupts in a space of ten lines the play on the *tekhnē tō logōn*. (What is in question is the *tekhnē* the sophists and rhetors had or pretended to have at their disposal, which was at once an art and an instrument, a recipe, an occult but transmissible "treatise," etc. Socrates considers the then classical problem in terms of the opposition between persuasion [*peithō*] and truth [alētheia] [260 *a*].)

Socrates: I agree — if, that is, the arguments (*logoi*) that come forward to speak for oratory should give testimony that it is an art (*tekhnē*). Now I seem, as it were, to hear some arguments advancing to give their evidence that it tells lies, that it is not an art at all, but an artless routine. "Without a grip on truth," says the Spartan, "there can be no genuine art of speaking (*tou de legein*) either now or in the future."

Phaedrus: Socrates, we need these arguments (*Toutōn dei tōn logōn, ō Sōkrates*). Bring the witnesses here and let's find out what they have to say and how they'll say it (*ti kai pōs legousin*).

Socrates: Come here, then, noble brood (*gennaia*), and convince Phaedrus, father of such fine children (*kallipaida te Phaidron*), that if he doesn't give enough attention to philosophy, he will never become a competent speaker on any subject. Now let Phaedrus answer (260*e*–261*a*).

---

[4]Greek for *writing*.

[5]Robin Waterfield was the translator of the *Phaedrus* in the Oxford World's Classics edition.

It is again Phaedrus, but this time in the *Symposium*,[6] who must speak first because he is both "head of the table" and "father of our subject" (*patēr tou logou*) (177d).

What we are provisionally and for the sake of convenience continuing to call a metaphor thus in any event belongs to a whole system. If *logos* has a father, if it is a *logos* only when attended by its father, this is because it is always a being (*on*) and even a certain species of being (the *Sophist*, 260a), more precisely a *living* being. *Logos* is a *zōon*. An animal that is born, grows, belongs to the *phusis*.[7] Linguistics, logic, dialectics, and zoology are all in the same camp.

In describing *logos* as a *zōon*, Plato is following certain rhetors and sophists before him who, as a contrast to the cadaverous rigidity of writing, had held up the living spoken word, which infallibly conforms to the necessities of the situation at hand, to the expectations and demands of the interlocutors present, and which sniffs out the spots where it ought to produce itself, feigning to bend and adapt at the moment it is actually achieving maximum persuasiveness and control.[8]

Logos, a living, animate creature, is thus also an organism that has been engendered. An *organism*: a differentiated body *proper*, with a center and extremities, joints, a head, and feet. In order to be "proper," a written discourse *ought* to submit to the laws of life just as a living discourse does. Logographical necessity (*anangkē logographikē*) ought to be analogous to biological, or rather zoological, necessity. Otherwise obviously, it would have neither head nor tail. Both *structure* and *constitution* are in question in the risk run by *logos* of losing through writing both its tail and its head:

> *Socrates*: And what about the rest? Don't you think the different parts of the speech (*ta tou logou*) are tossed in hit or miss? Or is there really a cogent reason for starting his second point in the

second place? And is that the case with the rest of the speech? As for myself, in my ignorance, I thought that the writer boldly set down whatever happened to come into his head. Can you explain his arrangement of the topics in the order he has adopted as the result of some principle of composition, some logographic necessity?
>
> *Phaedrus*: It's very kind of you to think me capable of such an accurate insight into his methods.
>
> *Socrates*: But to this you will surely agree: every discourse (*logon*), like a living creature (*ōsper zōon*), should be so put together (*sunestanai*) that it has its own body and lacks neither head nor foot, middle nor extremities, all composed in such a way that they suit both each other and the whole (264b–c).

The organism thus engendered must be well born, of noble blood: "*gennaia!*" we recall, is what Socrates called the *logoi*, those "noble creatures." This implies that the organism, having been engendered, must have a beginning and an end. Here, Socrates' standards become precise and insistent: a speech must have a beginning and an end, it must begin with the beginning and end with the end: "It certainly seems as though Lysias, at least, was far from satisfying our demands: it's from the end, not the beginning, that he tries to swim (on his back!) upstream through the current of his discourse. He starts out with what the lover ought to say at the very end to his beloved!" (264a). The implications and consequences of such a norm are immense, but they are obvious enough for us not to have to belabor them. It follows that the spoken discourse behaves like someone attended in origin and present in person. *Logos*: "*Sermo tanquam persona ipse loquens,*" as one Platonic Lexicon puts it.[9] Like any person the *logos-zōon* has a father.

But what is a father?

Should we consider this known, and with this term — the known — classify the other term within what one would hasten to classify as a metaphor? One would then say that the origin or cause of *logos* is being compared to what we

---

[6] Plato's dialogue on the nature of love.

[7] Greek for *nature*.

[8] The association *logos-zōon* appears in the discourse of Isocrates *Against the Sophists* and in that of Alcidamas *On the Sophists*. Cf. also W. Süss, who compares these two discourses line by line with the *Phaedrus*, in *Ethos: Studien zur älteren griechischen Rhetorik* (Leipzig, 1910), pp. 34 ff.) and A. Diès, "Philosophie et rhétorique," in *Autour de Platon* (Paris: Gabriel Beauchesne, 1927) I, 103.

[9] Fr. Ast, *Lexique platonicien*. Cf. also. B. Parain, *Essai sur le logos platonicien* (Paris: Gallimard, 1942), p. 211; and P. Louis, *Les Métaphores de Platon* (Paris: Les Belles Lettres, 1945), pp. 43–44.

know to be the cause of a living son, his father. One would understand or imagine the birth and development of *logos* from the standpoint of a domain foreign to it, the transmission of life or the generative relation. But the father is not the generator or procreator in any "real" sense prior to or outside all relation to language. In what way, indeed, is the father/son relation distinguishable from a mere cause/effect or generator/engendered relation, if not by the instance of logos? Only a power of speech can have a father. The father is always father to a speaking/living being. In other words, it is precisely *logos* that enables us to perceive and investigate something like paternity. If there were a simple metaphor in the expression "father of logos," the first word, which seemed the more *familiar*, would nevertheless receive more meaning *from* the second than it would transmit *to* it. The first familiarity is always involved in a relation of cohabitation with *logos*. Living-beings, father and son, are announced to us and related to each other within the household of *logos*. From which one does not escape, in spite of appearances, when one is transported, by "metaphor," to a foreign territory where one meets fathers, sons, living creatures, all sorts of beings that come in handy for explaining to anyone that doesn't know, by comparison, what *logos*, that strange thing, is all about. Even though this hearth is the heart of all metaphoricity, "father of logos" is not a simple metaphor. To have simple metaphoricity, one would have to make the statement that some living creature incapable of language, if anyone still wished to believe in such a thing, has a father. One must thus proceed to undertake a general reversal of all metaphorical directions, no longer asking whether *logos* can have a father but understanding that what the father claims to be the father of cannot go without the essential possibility of *logos*.

A *logos indebted* to a father, what does that mean? At least how can it be read within the stratum of the Platonic text that interests us here?

The figure of the father, of course, is also that of the good (*agathon*). Logos *represents* what it is indebted to: the father who is also chief, capital, and good(s). Or rather *the* chief, *the* capital, *the* good(s). *Patēr* in Greek means all that at once.

Neither translators nor commentators of Plato seem to have accounted for the play of these schemas. It is extremely difficult, we must recognize, to respect this play in a translation, and the fact can at least be explained in that no one has ever raised the question. Thus, at the point in the *Republic* where Socrates backs away from speaking of the good in itself (VI, 506e), he immediately suggests replacing it with its *ekgonos*, its son, its offspring:

> ... let us dismiss for the time being the nature of the good in itself, for to attain to my present surmise of that seems a pitch above the impulse that wings my flight today. But what seems to be the offspring (*ekgonos*) of the good and most nearly made in its likeness I am willing to speak if you too wish it, and otherwise to let the matter drop.
>
> Well, speak on, he said, for you will duly pay me the tale of the parent another time.
>
> I could wish, I said, that I were able to make and you to receive the payment, and not merely as now the interest (*tokous*). But at any rate receive this interest and the offspring of the good (*tokon te kai ekgonon autou tou agathou*).

Tokos, which is here associated with *ekgonos*, signifies production and the product, birth and the child, etc. This word functions with this meaning in the domains of agriculture, of kinship relations, and of fiduciary operations. None of these domains, as we shall see, lies outside the investment and possibility of a *logos*.

As product, the *tokos* is the child, the human or animal brood, as well as the fruits of the seed sown in the field, and the interest on a capital investment: it is a *return* or *revenue*. The distribution of all these meanings can be followed in Plato's text. The meaning of *patēr* is sometimes even inflected in the exclusive sense of financial capital. In the *Republic* itself, and not far from the passage we have just quoted. One of the drawbacks of democracy lies in the role that capital is often allowed to play in it: "But these moneymakers with down-bent heads, pretending not even to see the poor, but inserting the sting of their money into any of the remainder who do not resist, and harvesting from them in interest as it were a manifold progeny of the parent sum (*tou patros ekgonous tokous pollaplasious*), foster the drone and pauper element in the state" (555e).

Now, about this father, this capital, this good, this origin of value and of appearing beings, it is not possible to speak simply or directly. First of all because it is no more possible to look them in the face than to stare at the sun. On the subject of this bedazzlement before the face of the sun, a rereading of the famous passage of the *Republic* (VII, 515*c* ff) is strongly recommended here.

Thus will Socrates evoke only the visible sun, the son that resembles the father, the *analogon* of the intelligible sun: "It was the sun, then, that I meant when I spoke of that offspring of the Good (*ton tou agathou ekgonon*), which the Good has created in its own image (*hon tagathon egennēsen analogon heautōi*), and which stands in the visible world in the same relation to vision and visible things as that which the good itself bears in the intelligible world to intelligence and to intelligible objects" (508*c*).

How does *Logos* intercede in this *analogy* between the father and the son, the *nooumena* and the *horōmena*?[10]

The Good, in the visible-invisible figure of the father, the sun, or capital, is the origin of all *onta*,[11] responsible for their appearing and their coming into *logos*, which both assembles and distinguishes them: "We predicate 'to be' of many beautiful things and many good things, saying of them severally that they *are*, and so define them in our speech (*einai phamen te kai diorizomen tōi logōi*)" (507 *b*).

The good (father, sun, capital) is thus the hidden illuminating, blinding source of *logos*. And since one cannot speak of that which enables one to speak (being forbidden to speak of it or to speak to it face to face), one will speak only of that which speaks and of things that, with a single exception, one is constantly speaking of. And since an account or reason cannot be given of what *logos* (account or reason: *ratio*) is accountable or owing *to*, since the capital cannot be counted nor the chief looked in the eye, it will be necessary, by means of a discriminative, diacritical operation, to count up the plurality of interests, returns, products, and offspring: "Well, speak on

(*lege*), he said, for you will duly pay me the tale of the parent another time — I could wish, I said, that I were able to make and you to receive the payment, and not merely as now the interest. But at any rate receive this interest and the offspring of the good. Have a care, however, lest I deceive you unintentionally with a false reckoning (*ton logon*) of the interest (*tou tokou*)" (507*a*).

From the foregoing passage we should also retain the fact that, along with the account (*logos*) of the supplements (to the father-good-capital-origin, etc.), along with what comes above and beyond the One in the very movement through which it absents itself and becomes invisible, thus requiring that its place be supplied, along with differance and diacriticity, Socrates introduces or discovers the ever open possibility of the *kibdēlon*, that which is falsified, adulterated, mendacious, deceptive, equivocal. Have a care, he says, lest I deceive you with a false reckoning of the interest (*kibdēlon apodidous ton logon tou tokou*). *Kibdēleuma* is fraudulent merchandise. The corresponding verb (*kibdēleuō*) signifies "to tamper with money or merchandise, and, by extension, to be of bad faith."

This recourse to *logos*, from fear of being blinded by any direct intuition of the face of the father, of good, of capital, of the origin of being in itself, of the form of forms, etc., this recourse to logos as that which *protects us from the sun*, protects us under it and from it, is proposed by Socrates elsewhere, in the *analogous* order of the sensible or the visible. We shall quote at length from that text. In addition to its intrinsic interest, the text, in its official Robin translation, manifests a series of slidings, as it were, that are highly significant.[12] The passage in question is the critique, in the *Phaedo*, of "physicalists":

Socrates proceeded: — I thought that as I had failed in the contemplation of true existence (*ta onta*), I ought to be careful that I did not lose the eye of my soul; as people may injure their bodily eye by observing and gazing on the sun during an eclipse, unless they take the precaution of only

---

[10]The *nooumena* and the *horomena* refer to the intelligible and the visible, respectively.

[11]Greek for *beings*.

[12]I am indebted to the friendship and alertness of Francine Markovits for having brought this to my attention. This text should of course be placed alongside those of books VI and VII of the *Republic*. [Derrida]

looking at the image (*eikona*) reflected in the water, or in some analogous medium. So in my own case, I was afraid that my soul might be blinded altogether if I looked at things with my eyes or tried to apprehend them with the help of the senses. And I thought that I had better have recourse to the world of *idea* (*en logois*) and seek there the truth of things. . . . So, basing myself in each case of the idea (*logon*) that I judged to be the strongest . . ." (99*d*–100*a*).

Logos is thus a *resource*. One must *turn* to it, and not merely when the solar source is *present* and risks burning the eyes if stared at; one has also to turn away toward *logos* when the sun seems to withdraw during its eclipse. Dead, extinguished, or hidden, that star is more dangerous than ever.

We will let these yarns of suns and sons spin on for a while. Up to now we have only followed this line so as to move from *logos* to the father, so as to tie speech to the *kurios*,[13] the master, the lord, another name given in the *Republic* to the good-sun-capital-father (508*a*). Later, within the same tissue, within the same texts, we will draw on other filial filaments, pull the same strings once more, and witness the weaving or unraveling of other designs.

[13]The meaning Derrida playfully avoids citing here is the biblical one: *Kurios* is the Greek word used in the Septuagint to translate the Hebrew tetragrammaton, the unpronounced name of God usually translated into English as "the LORD."

Differance[1]

Translated by David B. Allison.

The verb "to differ" [*différer*] seems to differ from itself. On the one hand, it indicates difference as distinction, inequality, or discernibility; on the other, it expresses the interposition of delay, the interval of a *spacing* and *temporalizing* that puts off until "later" what is presently denied, the possible that is presently impossible. Sometimes the *different* and sometimes the *deferred* correspond [in French] to the verb "to differ." This correlation, however, is not simply one between act and object, cause and effect, or primordial and derived.

In the one case "to differ" signifies nonidentity; in the other case it signifies the order of the *same*. Yet there must be a common, although entirely differant[2] [*différante*], root within the sphere that relates the two movements of differing

to one another. We provisionally give the name *differance* to this *sameness* which is not *identical*: by the silent writing of its *a*, it has the desired advantage of referring to differing, *both* as spacing/temporalizing and as the movement that structures every dissociation.

As distinct from difference, differance thus points out the irreducibility of temporalizing (which is also temporalization — in transcendental language which is no longer adequate here, this would be called the constitution of primordial temporality — just as the term "spacing" also includes the constitution of primordial spatiality). Difference is not simply active (any more than it is a subjective accomplishment); it rather indicates the middle voice, it precedes and sets up the opposition between passivity and activity. With its *a*, differance more properly refers to what in classical language would be called the origin or production of differences and the differences between

[1]When this essay was originally delivered, as a lecture, it would have been impossible to distinguish between "*différence*" (the normal spelling) and "*différance*" (Derrida's coinage) because they would have been pronounced identically. An "a" would be introduced in the participle *différant*, meaning either differing or deferring

[2]The reader should bear in mind that "differance," or difference with an a, incorporates two significations : "to differ"

and "to defer." The two meanings of *différer* are distinguishable by French speakers by their transitivity; *différer*, meaning "to defer," requires a direct object, whereas *différer*, meaning "to differ," is intransitive.

differences, the *play* [*jeu*] of differences. Its locus and operation will therefore be seen wherever speech appeals to difference.

Differance is neither a *word* nor a *concept*. In it, however, we shall see the juncture — rather than the summation — of what has been most decisively inscribed in the thought of what is conveniently called our "epoch": the difference of forces in Nietzsche, Saussure's principle of semiological difference, differing as the possibility of [neurone] facilitation,[3] impression and delayed effect in Freud, difference as the irreducibility of the trace of the other in Levinas,[4] and the ontic-ontological difference in Heidegger.

Reflection on this last determination of difference will lead us to consider difference as the *strategic* note or connection — relatively or provisionally *privileged* — which indicates the closure of presence, together with the closure of the conceptual order and denomination, a closure that is effected in the functioning of traces.

I shall speak, then, of a letter — the first one, if we are to believe the alphabet and most of the speculations that have concerned themselves with it.

I shall speak then of the letter *a*, this first letter which it seemed necessary to introduce now and then in writing the word "difference." This seemed necessary in the course of writing about writing, and of writing within a writing whose different strokes all pass, in certain respects, through a gross spelling mistake, through a violation of the rules governing writing, violating the law that governs writing and regulates its conventions of propriety. In fact or theory we can always erase or lessen this spelling mistake, and, in each case, while these are analytically different from one another but for practical purposes the same, find it grave, unseemly, or, indeed, supposing the greatest ingenuousness, amusing. Whether or not we care to quietly overlook this infraction, the attention we give it beforehand will allow us to recognize, as though prescribed by some mute irony, the inaudible but displaced character of this literal permutation. We can always act as though this makes no difference. I must say from the start that my account serves less to justify this silent spelling mistake, or still less to excuse it, than to aggravate its obtrusive character.

On the other hand, I must be excused if I refer, at least implicitly, to one or another of the texts that I have ventured to publish. Precisely what I would like to attempt to some extent (although this is in principle and in its highest degree impossible, due to essential *de jure* reasons) is to bring together an *assemblage* of the different ways I have been able to utilize — or, rather, have allowed to be imposed on me — what I will provisionally call the word or concept of differance in its new spelling. It is literally neither a word nor a concept, as we shall see. I insist on the word "assemblage" here for two reasons: on the one hand, it is not a matter of describing a history, of recounting the steps, text by text, context by context, each time showing which scheme has been able to impose this graphic disorder, although this could have been done as well; rather, we are concerned with the *general system of all these schemata*. On the other hand, the word "assemblage" seems more apt for suggesting that the kind of bringing-together proposed here has the structure of an interlacing, a weaving, or a web, which would allow the different threads and different lines of sense or force to separate again, as well as being ready to bind others together.

[3]For the term "facilitation" (*frayage*) in Freud, cf. "Project for a Scientific Psychology I" in *The Complete Psychological Works of Sigmund Freud*, 24 vols. (New York and London: Macmillan, 1964), 1, 300, note 4 by the translator, James Strachey: "The word 'facilitation' as a rendering of the German '*Bahnung*' seems to have been introduced by Sherrington a few years after the *Project* was written. The German word, however, was already in use." The sense that Derrida draws upon here is stronger in the French or German; that is, the opening-up or clearing-out of a pathway. In the context of the "Project for a Scientific Psychology I," facilitation denotes the conduction capability that results from a difference in resistance levels in the memory and perception circuits of the nervous system. Thus, lowering the resistance threshold of a contact barrier serves to "open up" a nerve pathway and "facilitates" the excitatory process for the circuit. Cf. also J. Derrida, *L'Ecriture et la différence*, Chap. VII, "Freud et la scène de l'écriture" (Paris: Seuil, 1967), esp. pp. 297–305. [Tr.]

[4]Emmanuel Levinas (1906–1995) was a Lithuanian/French philosopher, whose *Totality and Infinity* (1961) strongly influenced Derrida. For Levinas, ethics begins when we confront the face of the absolutely Other (*autrui*) and recognize our responsibility to acknowledge it. Religion, in effect, is a metaphorical extension of that Other face, in that God is the Other of all Others.

In a quite preliminary way, we now recall that this particular graphic intervention was conceived in the writing-up of a question about writing; it was not made simply to shock the reader or grammarian. Now, in point of fact, it happens that this graphic difference (the *a* instead of the *e*), this marked difference between two apparently vocalic notations, between vowels, remains purely graphic: it is written or read, but it is not heard. It cannot be heard, and we shall see in what respects it is also beyond the order of understanding. It is put forward by a silent mark, by a tacit monument, or, one might even say, by a pyramid — keeping in mind not only the capital form of the printed letter but also that passage from Hegel's *Encyclopaedia* where he compares the body of the sign to an Egyptian pyramid. The *a* of differance, therefore, is not heard; it remains silent, secret, and discreet, like a tomb.[5]

It is a tomb that (provided one knows how to decipher its legend) is not far from signaling the death of the king.

It is a tomb that cannot even be made to resonate. For I cannot even let you know, by my talk, now being spoken before the Société Française de Philosophie, which difference I am talking about at the very moment I speak of it. I can only talk about this graphic difference by keeping to a very indirect speech about writing, and on the condition that I specify each time that I am referring to difference with an *e* or differance with an *a*. All of which is not going to simplify matters today, and will give us all a great deal of trouble when we want to understand one another. In any event, when I do specify which difference I mean — when I say "with an *e*" or "with an *a*" — this will refer irreducibly to a *written text*, a text governing my talk, a text that I keep in front of me, that I will read, and toward which I shall have to try to lead your hands and eyes. We cannot refrain here from going by way of a written text, from ordering ourselves by the disorder that is produced therein — and this is what matters to me first of all.

Doubtless this pyramidal silence of the graphic difference between the *e* and the *a* can function only within the system of phonetic writing and within a language or grammar historically tied to phonetic writing and to the whole culture which is inseparable from it. But I will say that it is just this — this silence that functions only within what is called phonetic writing — that points out or reminds us in a very opportune way that, contrary to an enormous prejudice, there is no phonetic writing. There is no purely and strictly phonetic writing. What is called phonetic writing can only function — in principle and *de jure*, and not due to some factual and technical inadequacy — by incorporating nonphonetic "signs" (punctuation, spacing, etc.); but when we examine their structure and necessity, we will quickly see that they are ill described by the concept of signs. Saussure had only to remind us that the play of difference was the functional condition, the condition of possibility, for every sign; and it is itself silent. The difference between two phonemes, which enables them to exist and to operate, is inaudible. The inaudible opens the two present phonemes to hearing, as they present themselves. If, then, there is no purely phonetic writing, it is because there is no purely phonetic phone. The difference that brings out phonemes and lets them be heard and understood [*entendre*] itself remains inaudible.

It will perhaps be objected that, for the same reasons, the graphic difference itself sinks into darkness, that it never constitutes the fullness of a sensible term, but draws out an invisible connection, the mark of an inapparent relation between two spectacles. That is no doubt true. Indeed, since from this point of view the difference between the *e* and the *a* marked in "differance" eludes vision and hearing, this happily suggests that we must here let ourselves be referred to an order that no longer refers to sensibility. But we are not referred to intelligibility either, to an ideality not fortuitously associated with the objectivity of *theōrein* or understanding. We must be referred to an order, then, that resists philosophy's founding opposition between the sensible and the intelligible. The order that resists this opposition, that resists it because it sustains it, is designated in a movement of differance (with an *a*) between

---

[5]On "pyramid" and "tomb" see J. Derrida, "Le Puits et la pyramide" in *Hegel et la pensée moderne* (Paris: Presses Universitaires de France, 1970), esp. pp. 44–45. [Tr.]

two differences or between two letters. This difference belongs neither to the voice nor to writing in the ordinary sense, and it takes place, like the strange space that will assemble us here for the course of an hour, *between* speech and writing and beyond the tranquil familiarity that binds us to one and to the other, reassuring us sometimes in the illusion that they are two separate things.

Now, how am I to speak of the *a* of differance? It is clear that it cannot be *exposed*. We can expose only what, at a certain moment, can become *present*, manifest; what can be shown, presented as a present, a being-present in its truth, the truth of a present or the presence of a present. However, if differance $\boxed{\text{is}}$ (I also cross out the "is") what makes the presentation of being-present possible, it never presents itself as such. It is never given in the present or to anyone. Holding back and not exposing itself, it goes beyond the order of truth on this specific point and in this determined way, yet is not itself concealed, as if it were something, a mysterious being, in the occult zone of a nonknowing. Any exposition would expose it to disappearing as a disappearance. It would risk appearing, thus disappearing.

Thus, the detours, phrases, and syntax that I shall often have to resort to will resemble — will sometimes be practically indiscernible from — those of negative theology. Already we had to note *that* differance *is not*, does not exist, and is not any sort of being-present (*on*). And we will have to point out everything *that* it *is not*, and, consequently, that it has neither existence nor essence. It belongs to no category of being, present or absent. And yet what is thus denoted as differance is not theological, not even in the most negative order of negative theology. The latter, as we know, is always occupied with letting a supraessential reality go beyond the finite categories of essence and existence, that is, of presence, and always hastens to remind us that, if we deny the predicate of existence to God, it is in order to recognize him as a superior, inconceivable, and ineffable mode of being. Here there is no question of such a move, as will be confirmed as we go along. Not only is differance irreducible to every ontological or theological — onto-theological — reappropriation, but it

opens up the very space in which onto-theology — philosophy — produces its system and its history. It thus encompasses and irrevocably surpasses onto-theology or philosophy.

For the same reason, I do not know where *to begin* to mark out this assemblage, this graph, of differance. Precisely what is in question here is the requirement that there be a *de jure* commencement, an absolute point of departure, a responsibility arising from a principle. The problem of writing opens by questioning the *archē*. Thus what I put forth here will not be developed simply as a philosophical discourse that operates on the basis of a principle, of postulates, axioms, and definitions and that moves according to the discursive line of a rational order. In marking out differance, everything is a matter of strategy and risk. It is a question of strategy because no transcendent truth present outside the sphere of writing can theologically command the totality of this field. It is hazardous because this strategy is not simply one in the sense that we say that strategy orients the tactics according to a final aim, a *telos* or the theme of a domination, a mastery or an ultimate reappropriation of movement and field. In the end, it is a strategy without finality. We might call it blind tactics or empirical errance, if the value of empiricism did not itself derive all its meaning from its opposition to philosophical responsibility. If there is a certain errance in the tracing-out of differance, it no longer follows the line of logico-philosophical speech or that of its integral and symmetrical opposite, logico-empirical speech. The concept of *play* [*jeu*] remains beyond this opposition; on the eve and aftermath of philosophy, it designates the unity of chance and necessity in an endless calculus.

By decision and, as it were, by the rules of the game, then, turning this thought around, let us introduce ourselves to the thought of differance by way of the theme of strategy or strategem. By this merely strategic justification, I want to emphasize that the efficacy of this thematics of differance very well may, and even one day must, be sublated, i.e., lend itself, if not to its own replacement, at least to its involvement in a series of events which in fact it never commanded. This also means that it is not a theological thematics.

I will say, first of all, that differance, which is neither a word nor a concept, seemed to me to be strategically the theme most proper to think out, if not master (thought being here, perhaps, held in a certain necessary relation with the structional limits of mastery), in what is most characteristic of our "epoch." I start off, then, strategically, from the place and time in which "we" are, even though my opening is not justifiable in the final account, and though it is always on the basis of differance and its "history" that we can claim to know who and where "we" are and what the limits of an "epoch" can be.

Although "differance" is neither a word nor a concept, let us nonetheless attempt a simple and approximative semantic analysis which will bring us in view of what is at stake [en vue de l'enjeu].

We do know that the verb "to differ" [différer] (the Latin verb differre) has two seemingly quite distinct meanings; in the Littré dictionary, for example, they are the subject of two separate articles. In this sense, the Latin differre is not the simple translation of the Greek diapherein; this fact will not be without consequence for us in tying our discussion to a particular language, one that passes for being less philosophical, less primordially philosophical, than the other. For the distribution of sense in the Greek diapherein does not carry one of the two themes of the Latin differre, namely, the action of postponing until later, of taking into account, the taking-account of time and forces in an operation that implies an economic reckoning, a detour, a respite, a delay, a reserve, a representation — all the concepts that I will sum up here in a word I have never used but which could be added to this series: temporalizing. "To differ" in this sense is to temporalize, to resort, consciously or unconsciously, to the temporal and temporalizing mediation of a detour that suspends the accomplishment or fulfillment of "desire" or "will," or carries desire or will out in a way that annuls or tempers their effect. We shall see, later, in what respects this temporalizing is also a temporalization and spacing, is space's becoming-temporal and time's becoming-spatial, is "primordial constitution" of space and time, as metaphysics or transcendental phenomenology would call it in the language that is here criticized and displaced.

The other sense of "to differ" [différer] is the most common and most identifiable, the sense of not being identical, of being other, of being discernible, etc. And in "differents," whether referring to the alterity of dissimilarity or the alterity of allergy or of polemics,[6] it is necessary that interval, distance, *spacing* occur among the different elements and occur actively, dynamically, and with a certain perseverance in repetition.

But the word "difference" (with an e) could never refer to differing as temporalizing or to difference as *polemos*. It is this loss of sense that the word differance (with an a) will have to schematically compensate for. Differance can refer to the whole complex of its meanings at once, for it is immediately and irreducibly multivalent, something which will be important for the discourse I am trying to develop. It refers to this whole complex of meanings not only when it is supported by a language or interpretive context (like any signification), but it already does so somehow of itself. Or at least it does so more easily by itself than does any other word: here the a comes more immediately from the present participle [différant] and brings us closer to the action of "differing" that is in progress, even before it has produced the effect that is constituted as different or resulted in difference (with an e). Within a conceptual system and in terms of classical requirements, differance could be said to designate the productive and primordial constituting causality, the process of scission and division whose differings and differences would be the constituted products or effects. But while bringing us closer to the infinitive and active core of differing, "differance" with an a neutralizes what the infinitive denotes as simply active, in the same way that "parlance" does not signify the simple fact of speaking, of speaking to or being spoken to. Nor is resonance the act of resonating. Here in the usage of our language we must consider that the ending -ance is undecided between active and passive. And we shall see why what is designated by "differance" is neither

[6] An allergy is a nasty reaction to what is Other (Greek *allos*) to one. Polemics are fierce arguments, but Derrida wants to allude to the Greek root *polemos* (war).

simply active nor simply passive, that it announces or rather recalls something like the middle voice, that it speaks of an operation which is not an operation, which cannot be thought of either as a passion or as an action of a subject upon an object, as starting from an agent or from a patient, or on the basis of, or in view of, any of these *terms*. But philosophy has perhaps commenced by distributing the middle voice, expressing a certain intransitiveness, into the active and the passive voice, and has itself been constituted in this repression.

How are difference as temporalizing and diference as spacing conjoined?

Let us begin with the problem of signs and writing — since we are already in the midst of it. We ordinarily say that a sign is put in place of the thing itself, the present thing — "thing" holding here for the sense as well as the referent. Signs represent the present in its absence; they take the place of the present. When we cannot take hold of or show the thing, let us say the present, the being-present, when the present does not present itself, then we signify, we go through the detour of signs. We take up or give signs; we make signs. The sign would thus be a deferred presence. Whether it is a question of verbal or written signs, monetary signs, electoral delegates, or political representatives, the movement of signs defers the moment of encountering the thing itself, the moment at which we could lay hold of it, consume or expend it, touch it, see it, have a present intuition of it. What I am describing here is the structure of signs as classically determined, in order to define — through a commonplace characterization of its traits — signification as the difference of temporalizing. Now this classical determination presupposes that the sign (which defers presence) is conceivable only *on the basis of* the presence that it defers and *in view of* the deferred presence one intends to reappropriate. Following this classical semiology, the substitution of the sign for the thing itself is both *secondary* and *provisional*: it is second in order after an original and lost presence, a presence from which the sign would be derived. It is provisional with respect to this final and missing presence, in view of which the sign would serve as a movement of mediation.

In attempting to examine these secondary and provisional aspects of the substitute, we shall no doubt catch sight of something like a primordial difference. Yet we could no longer even call it primordial or final, inasmuch as the characteristics of origin, beginning, *telos*, *eschaton*,[7] etc., have always denoted presence — *ousia*, *parousia*,[8] etc. To question the secondary and provisional character of the sign, to oppose it to a "primordial" difference, would thus have the following consequences:

1. Difference can no longer be understood according to the concept of "sign," which has always been taken to mean the representation of a presence and has been constituted in a system (of thought or language) determined on the basis of and in view of presence.

2. In this way we question the authority of presence or its simple symmetrical contrary, absence or lack. We thus interrogate the limit that has always constrained us, that always constrains us — we who inhabit a language and a system of thought — to form the sense of being in general as presence or absence, in the categories of being or beingness (*ousia*). It already appears that the kind of questioning we are thus led back to is, let us say, the Heideggerian kind, and that difference *seems* to lead us back to the ontic-ontological difference. But permit me to postpone this reference. I shall only note that between difference as temporalizing-temporalization (which we can no longer conceive within the horizon of the present) and what Heidegger says about temporalization in *Sein und Zeit* (namely, that as the transcendental horizon of the question of being it must be freed from the traditional and metaphysical domination by the present or the now) — between these two there is a close, if not exhaustive and irreducibly necessary, interconnection.

---

[7]Derrida is playing on two Greek terms that both mean "end" but in different ways, telos meaning "purpose," *eschaton* meaning "last or utmost thing" (and is used in religious contexts for death and what comes after).

[8]*Ousia* means "being"; *parousia* means "presence or arrival" (it is the usual term in the Gospels for the Second Coming). Derrida's plays on words are not innocent — like Levinas he is interested in exploring the relation between ontology (the philosophy of being or absolute existence) and theology.

But first of all, let us remain with the semiological aspects of the problem to see how differance as temporalizing is conjoined with differance as spacing. Most of the semiological or linguistic research currently dominating the field of thought (whether due to the results of its own investigations or due to its role as a generally recognized regulative model) traces its genealogy, rightly or wrongly, to Saussure[9] as its common founder. It was Saussure who first of all set forth the *arbitrariness* of signs and the *differential character* of signs as principles of general semiology and particularly of linguistics. And, as we know, these two themes — the arbitrary and the differential — are in his view inseparable. Arbitrariness can occur only because the system of signs is constituted by the differences between the terms, and not by their fullness. The elements of signification function not by virtue of the compact force of their cores but by the network of oppositions that distinguish them and relate them to one another. "Arbitrary and differential" says Saussure "are two correlative qualities."

As the condition for signification, this principle of difference affects the *whole sign*, that is, both the signified and the signifying aspects. The signified aspect is the concept, the ideal sense. The signifying aspect is what Saussure calls the material or physical (e.g., acoustical) "image." We do not here have to enter into all the problems these definitions pose. Let us only cite Saussure where it interests us:

> The conceptual side of value is made up solely of relations and differences with respect to the other terms of language, and the same can be said of its material side. . . . Everything that has been said up to this point boils down to this: in language there are only differences. Even more important: a difference generally implies positive terms between which the difference is set up; but in language there are only differences *without positive terms.* Whether we take the signified or the signifier, language has neither ideas nor sounds that existed before the linguistic system, but only conceptual and phonic differences that have issued from the system. The idea or phonic substance that a sign

contains is of less importance than the other signs that surround it.[10]

The first consequence to be drawn from this is that the signified concept is never present in itself, in an adequate presence that would refer only to itself. Every concept is necessarily and essentially inscribed in a chain or a system, within which it refers to another and to other concepts, by the systematic play of differences. Such a play, then — differance — is no longer simply a concept, but the possibility of conceptuality, of the conceptual system and process in general. For the same reason, differance, which is not a concept, is not a mere word; that is, it is not what we represent to ourselves as the calm and present self-referential unity of a concept and sound [*phonie*]. We shall later discuss the consequences of this for the notion of a word.

The difference that Saussure speaks about, therefore, is neither itself a concept nor one word among others. We can say this *a fortiori*[11] for differance. Thus we are brought to make the relation between the one and the other explicit.

Within a language, within the *system* of language, there are only differences. A taxonomic operation can accordingly undertake its systematic, statistical, and classificatory inventory. But, on the one hand, these differences *play a role* in language, in speech as well, and in the exchange between language and speech. On the other hand, these differences are themselves *effects*. They have not fallen from the sky ready made; they are no more inscribed in a *topos noētos*[12] than they are prescribed in the wax of the brain. If the word "history" did not carry with it the theme of a final repression of differance, we could say that differences alone could be "historical" through and through and from the start.

What we note as *differance* will thus be the movement of play that "produces" (and not by something that is simply an activity) these

---

[9]See the section on Ferdinand de Saussure, pp. 820–22.

[10]Ferdinand de Saussure, *Cours de linguistique générale*, ed. C. Bally and A. Sèchehaye (Paris: Payot, 1916) [Derrida]; English translation by Wade Baskin, *Course in General Linguistics* (New York: Philosophical Library, 1959), pp. 117–18, 120. [Tr.]

[11]With a stronger reason.

[12]Mental region.

differences, these effects of difference. This does not mean that the differance which produces differences is before them in a simple and in itself unmodified and indifferent present. Differance is the nonfull, nonsimple "origin"; it is the structured and differing origin of differences.

Since language (which Saussure says is a classification) has not fallen from the sky, it is clear that the differences have been produced; they are the effects produced, but effects that do not have as their cause a subject or substance, a thing in general, or a being that is somewhere present and itself escapes the play of difference. If such a presence were implied (quite classically) in the general concept of cause, we would therefore have to talk about an effect without a cause, something that would very quickly lead to no longer talking about effects. I have tried to indicate a way out of the closure imposed by this system, namely, by means of the "trace." No more an effect than a cause, the "trace" cannot of itself, taken outside its context, suffice to bring about the required transgression.

As there is no presence before the semiological difference or outside it, we can extend what Saussure writes about language to signs in general: "Language is necessary in order for speech to be intelligible and to produce all of its effects; but the latter is necessary in order for language to be established; historically, the fact of speech always comes first."[13]

Retaining at least the schema, if not the content, of the demand formulated by Saussure, we shall designate by the term *differance* the movement by which language, or any code, any system of reference in general, becomes "historically" constituted as a fabric of differences. Here, the terms "constituted," "produced," "created," "movement," "historically," etc., with all they imply, are not to be understood only in terms of the language of metaphysics, from which they are taken. It would have to be shown why the concepts of production, like those of constitution and history, remain accessories in this respect to what is here being questioned; this, however, would draw us too far away today, toward the theory of the representation of the "circle" in which we seem to be enclosed. I only use these terms here, like many other concepts, out of strategic convenience and in order to prepare the deconstruction of the system they form at the point which is now most decisive. In any event, we will have understood, by virtue of the very circle we appear to be caught up in, that differance, as it is written here, is no more static than genetic, no more structural than historical. Nor is it any less so. And it is completely to miss the point of this orthographical impropriety to want to object to it on the basis of the oldest of metaphysical oppositions — for example, by opposing some generative point of view to a structuralist-taxonomic point of view, or conversely. These oppositions do not pertain in the least to differance; and this, no doubt, is what makes thinking about it difficult and uncomfortable.

If we now consider the chain to which "differance" gets subjected, according to the context, to a certain number of nonsynonymic substitutions, one will ask why we resorted to such concepts as "reserve," "protowriting," "prototrace," "spacing," indeed to "supplement" or *pharmakon*," and, before long, to "hymen," etc.[14]

Let us begin again. Differance is what makes the movement of signification possible only if each element that is said to be "present," appearing on the stage of presence, is related to something other than itself but retains the mark of a past element and already lets itself be hollowed out by the mark of its relation to a future element.

[13]*Course in General Linguistics*, p. 18. [Tr.]

[14]On "supplement" see above, *Speech and Phenomena*, Chap. 7, pp. 88–104. Cf. also Derrida, *De la grammatologie* (Paris: Editions de Minuit, 1967). On "*pharmakon*" see Derrida, "La Pharmacie de Platon," *Tel Quel*, No. 32 (Winter, 1967), pp. 17–59; No. 33 (Spring 1968), pp. 4–48. On "hymen" see Derrida, "La Double séance," *Tel Quel*, No. 41 (Spring, 1970), pp. 3–43; No. 42 (Summer, 1970), pp. 3–45. "La Pharmacie de Platon" and "La Double séance" have been reprinted in a recent text of Derrida, *La Dissémination* (Paris: Editions du Seuil, 1972). [Tr.] This bibliography should make us understand that Derrida's writings of this period present alternative versions of the language-game that Derrida has been conducting with "differance": the revelation of deep aporias within the nature of language, whether the central term chosen for analysis is "difference" or some alternative.

This trace relates no less to what is called the future than to what is called the past, and it constitutes what is called the present by this very relation to what it is not, to what it absolutely is not; that is, not even to a past or future considered as a modified present. In order for it to be, an interval must separate it from what it is not; but the interval that constitutes it in the present must also, and by the same token, divide the present in itself, thus dividing, along with the present, everything that can be conceived on its basis, that is, every being — in particular, for our metaphysical language, the substance or subject. Constituting itself, dynamically dividing itself, this interval is what could be called *spacing*; time's becoming-spatial or space's becoming-temporal (*temporalizing*). And it is this constitution of the present as a "primordial" and irreducibly nonsimple and, therefore, in the strict sense nonprimordial, synthesis of traces, retentions, and protentions (to reproduce here, analogically and provisionally, a phenomenological and transcendental language that will presently be revealed as inadequate) that I propose to call protowriting, prototrace, or differance. The latter (is) (both) spacing (and) temporalizing.[15]

Given this (active) movement of the (production of) differance without origin, could we not, quite simply and without any neographism, call it *differentiation*? Among other confusions, such a word would suggest some organic unity, some primordial and homogeneous unity, that would eventually come to be divided up and take on difference as an event. Above all, formed on the verb "to differentiate," this word would annul the economic signification of detour, temporalizing delay, "deferring." I owe a remark in passing to a recent reading of one of Koyré's texts entitled "Hegel at Jena."[16] In that text, Koyré[17] cites long passages from the Jena *Logic* in German and gives his own translation. On two occasions in Hegel's text he encounters the expression "*differente Beziehung.*" This word (*different*), whose root is Latin, is extremely rare in German and also, I believe, in Hegel, who instead uses *verschieden* or *ungleich*, calling difference *Unterscheid* and qualitative variety *Verschiedenheit*. In the Jena *Logic*, he uses the word *different* precisely at the point where he deals with time and the present. Before coming to Koyré's valuable remark, here are some passages from Hegel, as rendered by Koyré:

The infinite, in this simplicity is — as a moment opposed to the self-identical — the negative. In its moments, while the infinite presents the totality to (itself) and in itself, (it is) excluding in general, the point or limit; but in this, its own (action of) negating, it relates itself immediately to the other and negates itself. The limit or moment of the present (*der Gegen-wart*), the absolute "this" of time or the now, is an absolutely negative simplicity, absolutely excluding all multiplicity from itself, and by this very fact is absolutely determined; it is not an extended whole or *quantum* within itself (and) which would in itself also have an undetermined aspect or qualitative variety, which of itself would be related, indifferently (*gleichgültig*) or externally to another, but on the contrary, this is an absolutely different relation of the simple.[18]

And Koyré specifies in a striking note: "Different relation: *differente Beziehung.* We could say: differentiating relation." And on the following page, from another text of Hegel, we can read: "*Diese Beziehung ist Gegenwart, als*

---

[15]Derrida often brackets or "crosses out" certain key terms taken from metaphysics and logic, and in doing this, he follows Heidegger's usage in *Zur Seinsfrage*. The terms in question no longer have their full meaning, they no longer have the status of a purely signified content of expression — no longer, that is, after the deconstruction of metaphysics. Generated out of the play of differance, they still retain a vestigial trace of sense, however, a trace that cannot simply be gotten around (*incontourable*). An extensive discussion of all this is to be found in *De la grammatologie*, pp. 31–40. [Tr.]

[16]Alexandre Koyré, "Hegel à Iéna," *Revue d'histoire et de philosophie religieuse*, XIV (1934), 420–58; reprinted in Koyré, *Etudes d'histoire de la pensée philosophique* (Paris: Armand Colin, 1961), pp. 135–73.

[17]Alexandre Koyré (1892–1964), French historian of philosophy and scientific method. Derrida's point in the complex passage that follows is that Hegel needs to grasp at a term other than the normal German words for "difference" when seeking to discuss the relation between infinite time and the present moment.

[18]Koyré, *Etudes d'histoire*, pp. 153–54. The quotation from Hegel (my translation) comes from "Jenenser Logik, Metaphysik, und Naturphilosophie," *Sämtliche Werke* (Leipzig: F. Meiner, 1925), XVIII, 202. Koyré reproduces the original German text on pp. 153–54, note 2. [Tr.]

eine differente Beziehung" (This relation is [the] present, as a different relation). There is another note by Koyré: "The term *'different'* is taken here in an active sense."

Writing "differing" or "differance" (with an *a*) would have had the utility of making it possible to translate Hegel on precisely this point with no further qualifications — and it is a quite decisive point in his text. The translation would be, as it always should be, the transformation of one language by another. Naturally, I maintain that the word "differance" can be used in other ways, too; first of all, because it denotes not only the activity of primordial difference but also the temporalizing detour of deferring. It has, however, an even more important usage. Despite the very profound affinities that differance thus written has with Hegelian speech (as it should be read), it can, at a certain point, not exactly break with it, but rather work a sort of displacement with regard to it. A definite rupture with Hegelian language would make no sense, nor would it be at all likely; but this displacement is both infinitesimal and radical. I have tried to indicate the extent of this displacement elsewhere; it would be difficult to talk about it with any brevity at this point.

Differences are thus "produced" — differed — by differance. But *what* differs, or *who* differs? In other words, *what is* differance? With this question we attain another stage and another source of the problem.

What differs? Who differs? What is differance?

If we answered these questions even before examining them as questions, even before going back over them and questioning their form (even what seems to be most natural and necessary about them), we would fall below the level we have now reached. For if we accepted the form of the question in its own sense and syntax ("What?" "What is?" "Who is?"), we would have to admit that difference is derived, supervenient, controlled, and ordered from the starting point of a being-present, one capable of being something, a force, a state, or power in the world, to which we could give all kinds of names: a *what*, or being-present as a *subject*, a *who*. In the latter case, notably, we would implicitly admit that the being-present (for example, as a self-present being or consciousness) would eventually result in

differing: in delaying or in diverting the fulfillment of a "need" or "desire," or in differing from itself. But in none of these cases would such a being-present be "constituted" by this difference.

Now if we once again refer to the semiological difference, what was it that Saussure in particular reminded us of? That "language [which consists only of differences] is not a function of the speaking subject." This implies that the subject (self-identical or even conscious of self-identity, self-conscious) is inscribed in the language, that he is a "function" of the language. He becomes a *speaking* subject only by conforming his speech — even in the aforesaid "creation," even in the aforesaid "transgression" — to the system of linguistic prescriptions taken as the system of differences, or at least to the general law of differance, by conforming to that law of language which Saussure calls "language without speech." "Language is necessary for the spoken word to be intelligible and so that it can produce all of its effects."[19]

If, by hypothesis, we maintain the strict opposition between speech and language, then differance will be not only the play of differences within the language but the relation of speech to language, the detour by which I must also pass in order to speak, the silent token I must give, which holds just as well for linguistics in the strict sense as it does for general semiology; it dictates all the relations between usage and the formal schema, between the message and the particular code, etc. Elsewhere I have tried to suggest that this differance within language, and in the relation between speech and language, forbids the essential dissociation between speech and writing that Saussure, in keeping with tradition, wanted to draw at another level of his presentation. The use of language or the employment of any code which implies a play of forms — with no determined or invariable substratum — also presupposes a retention and protention of differences, a spacing and temporalizing, a play of traces. This play must be a sort of inscription prior to writing, a protowriting without a present origin, without an

---

[19]De Saussure, *Course in General Linguistics*, p. 37. [Derrida]

archē.[20] From this comes the systematic crossing-out of the *archē* and the transformation of general semiology into a grammatology, the latter performing a critical work upon everything within semiology — right down to its matrical concept of signs — that retains any metaphysical presuppositions incompatible with the theme of differance.

We might be tempted by an objection: to be sure, the subject becomes a *speaking* subject only by dealing with the system of linguistic differences; or again, he becomes a *signifying* subject (generally by speech or other signs) only by entering into the system of differences. In this sense, certainly, the speaking or signifying subject would not be self-present, insofar as he speaks or signifies, except for the play of linguistic or semiological difference. But can we not conceive of a presence and self-presence of the subject before speech or its signs, a subject's self-presence in a silent and intuitive consciousness?

Such a question therefore supposes that prior to signs and outside them, and excluding every trace and differance, something such as consciousness is possible. It supposes, moreover, that, even before the distribution of its signs in space and in the world, consciousness can gather itself up in its own presence. What then is consciousness? What does "consciousness" mean? Most often in the very form of "meaning" ["*vouloir-dire*"], consciousness in all its modifications is conceivable only as self-presence, a self-perception of presence. And what holds for consciousness also holds here for what is called subjective existence in general. Just as the category of subject is not and never has been conceivable without reference to presence as *hypokeimenon*[21] or *ousia*, etc., so the subject as consciousness has never been able to be evinced otherwise than as self-presence. The privilege accorded to consciousness thus means a privilege accorded to the present; and even if the transcendental temporality of consciousness is described in depth, as Husserl described it, the power of synthesis and of the incessant gathering-up of traces is always accorded to the "living present."

This privilege is the ether [22] of metaphysics, the very element of our thought insofar as it is caught up in the language of metaphysics. We can only de-limit such a closure today by evoking this import of presence, which Heidegger has shown to be the onto-theological determination of being. Therefore, in evoking this import of presence, by an examination which would have to be of a quite peculiar nature, we question the absolute privilege of this form or epoch of presence in general, that is, consciousness as meaning [*vouloir-dire*] in self-presence.

We thus come to posit presence — and, in particular, consciousness, the being-next-to-itself of consciousness — no longer as the absolutely matrical[23] form of being but as a "determination" and an "effect." Presence is a determination and effect within a system which is no longer that of presence but that of differance; it no more allows the opposition between activity and passivity than that between cause and effect or in-determination and determination, etc. This system is of such a kind that even to designate consciousness as an effect or determination — for strategic reasons, reasons that can be more or less clearly considered and systematically ascertained — is to continue to operate according to the vocabulary of that very thing to be de-limited.

Before being so radically and expressly Heideggerian, this was also Nietzsche's and Freud's move, both of whom, as we know, and often in a very similar way, questioned the self-assured certitude of consciousness. And is it not remarkable that both of them did this by starting out with the theme of differance?

This theme appears almost literally in their work, at the most crucial places. I shall not expand on this here; I shall only recall that for Nietzsche "the important main activity is unconscious" and

[20]Beginning. Derrida shifts to Greek to allude to the first sentence of the Gospel of John, *en archē ēn ho logos* ("In the beginning was the Word").

[21]In Plato's metaphysics, *hypokeimenon* is the foundation that underlies something or is presupposed by it.

[22]Derrida compares consciousness to the term for the "element" making up empty space, relative to which a star or planet was supposed to move. As Derrida is well aware, the Michaelson-Morley experiment proved that ether was a metaphysical fiction, that bodies move only relative to each other and that there is no absolute motion.

[23]Originary; "referring to origins."

that consciousness is the effect of forces whose essence, ways, and modalities are not peculiar to it. Now force itself is never present; it is only a play of differences and quantities. There would be no force in general without the difference between forces; and here the difference in quantity counts more than the content of quantity, more than the absolute magnitude itself.

> Quantity itself therefore is not separable from the difference in quantity. The difference in quantity is the essence of force, the relation of force with force. To fancy two equal forces, even if we grant them opposing directions, is an approximate and crude illusion, a statistical dream in which life is immersed, but which chemistry dispels.[24]

Is not the whole thought of Nietzsche a critique of philosophy as active indifference to difference, as a system of reduction or adiaphoristic repression? Following the same logic — logic itself — this does not exclude the fact that philosophy lives *in* and *from* differance, that it thereby blinds itself to the *same*, which is not the identical. The same is precisely differance (with an *a*), as the diverted and equivocal passage from one difference to another, from one term of the opposition to the other. We could thus take up all the coupled oppositions on which philosophy is constructed, and from which our language lives, not in order to see opposition vanish but to see the emergence of a necessity such that one of the terms appears as the differance of the other, the other as "differed" within the systematic ordering of the same (e.g., the intelligible as differing from the sensible, as sensible differed; the concept as differed-differing intuition, life as differing-differed matter; mind as differed-differing life; culture as differed-differing nature; and all the terms designating what is other than *physis* — *technē*, *nomos*,[25] society, freedom, history, spirit, etc. — as *physis* differed or *physis* differing:[26] *physis* *in differance*). It is out of the unfolding of this "same" as differance that the sameness of difference and of repetition is presented in the eternal return.

In Nietzsche, there are so many themes that can be related with the kind of symptomatology that always serves to diagnose the evasions and ruses of anything disguised in its differance. Or again, these terms can be related with the entire thematics of active interpretation, which substitutes an incessant deciphering for the disclosure of truth as a presentation of the thing itself in its presence, etc. What results is a cipher without truth, or at least a system of ciphers that is not dominated by truth value, which only then becomes a function that is understood, inscribed, and circumscribed.

We shall therefore call differance this "active" (in movement) discord of the different forces and of the differences between forces which Nietzsche opposes to the entire system of metaphysical grammar, wherever that system controls culture, philosophy, and science.

It is historically significant that this diaphoristics, understood as an energetics or an economy of forces, set up to question the primacy of presence qua consciousness, is also the major theme of Freud's thought; in his work we find another diaphoristics, both in the form of a theory of ciphers or traces and an energetics. The questioning of the authority of consciousness is first and always differential.[27]

The two apparently different meanings of differance are tied together in Freudian theory: differing [*le différer*] as discernibility, distinction, deviation, diastem, *spacing*; and deferring [*le différer*] as detour, delay, relay, reserve, *temporalizing*. I shall recall only that:

1. The concept of trace (*Spur*), of facilitation (*Bahnung*), of forces of facilitation are, as early as the composition of the *Entwurf*,[28] inseparable from the concept of difference. The origin of memory and of the psyche as a memory in general

---

[24]G. Deleuze, *Nietzsche et la philosophie* (Paris: Presses Universitaires de France, 1970), p. 49. [Tr.]

[25]In Greek, "nature — art, law." Derrida is listing the central terms of various philosophers.

[26]*differed or . . . differing*: In using the present and past participles of his key term, Derrida may allude to Spinoza, who distinguished between *natura naturata* and *natura naturans* (passive nature, devoid of consciousness, and active nature, endowed with consciousness).

[27]Derrida suggests that Freud's psychology is also one based on differance, in which consciousness is a by-product of mental activity, not a central principle.

[28]Freud's *Project for a Scientific Psychology* (written 1895, published 1950).

(conscious or unconscious) can only be described by taking into account the difference between the facilitation thresholds, as Freud says explicitly. There is no facilitation [*Bahnung*] without difference and no difference without a trace.

2. All the differences involved in the production of unconscious traces and in the process of inscription (*Niederschrift*) can also be interpreted as moments of differance, in the sense of "placing on reserve." Following a schema that continually guides Freud's thinking, the movement of the trace is described as an effort of life to protect itself *by deferring* the dangerous investment, by constituting a reserve (*Vorrat*). And all the conceptual oppositions that furrow Freudian thought relate each concept to the other like movements of a detour, within the economy of differance. The one is only the other deferred, the one differing from the other. The one is the other in differance, the one is the differance from the other. Every apparently rigorous and irreducible opposition (for example, that between the secondary and primary) is thus said to be, at one time or another, a "theoretical fiction." In this way again, for example (but such an example covers everything or communicates with everything), the difference between the pleasure principle and the reality principle is only differance as detour (*Aufschieben, Aufschub*). In *Beyond the Pleasure Principle*, Freud writes:

> Under the influence of the ego's instincts of self-preservation, the pleasure principle is replaced by the reality principle. This latter principle does not abandon the intention of ultimately obtaining pleasure, but it nevertheless demands and carries into effect the postponement of satisfaction, the abandonment of a number of possibilities of gaining satisfaction and the temporary toleration of unpleasure as a step on the long indirect road (*Aufschub*) to pleasure.[29]

Here we touch on the point of greatest obscurity, on the very enigma of differance, on how the concept we have of it is divided by a strange separation. We must not hasten to make a decision too quickly. How can we conceive of differance as a systematic detour which, within the element of the same, always aims at either finding again the pleasure or

the presence that had been deferred by (conscious or unconscious) calculation, and, *at the same time*, how can we, on the other hand, conceive of differance as the relation to an impossible presence, as an expenditure without reserve, as an irreparable loss of presence, an irreversible wearing-down of energy, or indeed as a death instinct and a relation to the absolutely other that apparently breaks up any economy? It is evident — it is evidence itself — that system and nonsystem, the same and the absolutely other, etc., cannot be conceived *together*.

If differance is this inconceivable factor, must we not perhaps hasten to make it evident, to bring it into the philosophical element of evidence, and thus quickly dissipate its mirage character and illogicality, dissipate it with the infallibility of the calculus we know well — since we have recognized its place, necessity, and function within the structure of differance? What would be accounted for philosophically here has already been taken into account in the system of differance as it is here being calculated. I have tried elsewhere, in a reading of Bataille,[30, 31] to indicate what might be the establishment of a rigorous, and in a new sense "scientific," *relating* of a "restricted economy" — one having nothing to do with an unreserved expenditure, with death, with being exposed to nonsense, etc. — to a "general economy" or system that, so to speak, *takes account of* what is unreserved. It is a relation between a differance that is accounted for and a differance that fails to be accounted for, where the establishment of a pure presence, without loss, is one with the occurrence of absolute loss, with death. By establishing this relation between a restricted and a general system, we shift and recommence the very project of philosophy under the privileged heading of Hegelianism.

The economic character of differance in no way implies that the deferred presence can always be recovered, that it simply amounts to an investment that only temporarily and without loss delays the presentation of presence, that is, the perception of gain or the gain of perception. Contrary to the metaphysical, dialectical, and

[29] Freud, *Complete Psychological Works*, XVIII, 10. [Derrida]

[30] Derrida, *L'Ecriture et la différence*, pp. 369–407. [Tr.]
[31] Georges Bataille (1897–1962), radical French philosopher.

"Hegelian" interpretation of the economic movement of differance, we must admit a game where whoever loses wins and where one wins and loses each time. If the diverted presentation continues to be somehow definitively and irreducibly withheld, this is not because a particular present remains hidden or absent, but because differance holds us in a relation with what exceeds (though we necessarily fail to recognize this) the alternative of presence or absence. A certain alterity — Freud gives it a metaphysical name, the unconscious — is definitively taken away from every process of presentation in which we would demand for it to be shown forth in person. In this context and under this heading, the unconscious is not, as we know, a hidden, virtual, and potential self-presence. It is differed — which no doubt means that it is woven out of differences, but also that it sends out, that it delegates, representatives or proxies; but there is no chance that the mandating subject "exists" somewhere, that it is present or is "itself," and still less chance that it will become conscious. In this sense, contrary to the terms of an old debate, strongly symptomatic of the metaphysical investments it has always assumed, the "unconscious" can no more be classed as a "thing" than as anything else; it is no more of a thing than an implicit or masked consciousness. This radical alterity, removed from every possible mode of presence, is characterized by irreducible aftereffects, by delayed effects. In order to describe them, in order to read the traces of the "unconscious" traces (there are no "conscious" traces), the language of presence or absence, the metaphysical speech of phenomenology, is in principle inadequate.

The structure of delay (*retardement*: *Nachträglichkeit*) that Freud talks about indeed prohibits our taking temporalization (temporalizing) to be a simple dialectical complication of the present; rather, this is the style of transcendental phenomenology. It describes the living present as a primordial and incessant synthesis that is constantly led back upon itself, back upon its assembled and assembling self, by retentional traces and protentional openings. With the alterity of the "unconscious," we have to deal not with the horizons of modified presents — past or future — but with a "past" that has never been nor will ever be present, whose "future" will never be produced or reproduced in the form of presence. The concept of trace is therefore incommensurate with that of retention, that of the becoming-past of what had been present. The trace cannot be conceived — nor, therefore, can differance — on the basis of either the present or the presence of the present.

A past that has never been present: with this formula Emmanuel Levinas designates (in ways that are, to be sure, not those of psychoanalysis) the trace and the enigma of absolute alterity, that is, the Other [*autrui*]. At least within these limits, and from this point of view, the thought of differance implies the whole critique of classical ontology undertaken by Levinas. And the concept of trace, like that of differance, forms — across these different traces and through these differences between traces, as understood by Nietzsche, Freud, and Levinas (these "authors' names" serve only as indications) — the network that sums up and permeates our "epoch" as the de-limitation of ontology (of presence).

The ontology of presence is the ontology of beings and beingness. Everywhere, the dominance of beings is solicited by differance — in the sense that *sollicitare* means, in old Latin, to shake all over, to make the whole tremble. What is questioned by the thought of differance, therefore, is the determination of being in presence, or in beingness. Such a question could not arise and be understood without the difference between Being and beings opening up somewhere. The first consequence of this is that differance is not. It is not a being-present, however excellent, unique, principal, or transcendent one makes it. It commands nothing, rules over nothing, and nowhere does it exercise any authority. It is not marked by a capital letter. Not only is there no realm of differance, but differance is even the subversion of every realm. This is obviously what makes it threatening and necessarily dreaded by everything in us that desires a realm, the past or future presence of a realm. And it is always in the name of a realm that, believing one sees it ascend to the capital letter, one can reproach it for wanting to rule.

Does this mean, then, that differance finds its place within the spread of the ontic-ontological difference, as it is conceived, as the "epoch" conceives itself within it, and particularly "across" the Heideggerian meditation, which cannot be gotten around?

There is no simple answer to such a question.

In one particular respect, differance is, to be sure, but the historical and epochal *deployment* of Being or of the ontological difference. The *a* of differance marks the *movement* of this deployment.

And yet, is not the thought that conceives the *sense* or *truth* of Being, the determination of differance as ontic-ontological difference — difference conceived within the horizon of the question of *Being* — still an intrametaphysical effect of differance? Perhaps the deployment of differance is not only the truth or the epochality of Being. Perhaps we must try to think this *unheard-of* thought, this silent tracing, namely, that the history of Being (the thought of which is committed to the Greco-Western logos), as it is itself produced across the ontological difference, is only one epoch of the *diapherein*.[32] Then we could no longer even call it an "epoch," for the concept of epochality belongs within history understood as the history of Being. Being has always made "sense," has always been conceived or spoken of as such, only by dissimulating itself in beings; thus, in a particular and very strange way, difference (is) "older" than the ontological difference or the truth of Being. In this age it can be called the play of traces. It is a trace that no longer belongs to the horizon of Being but one whose sense of Being is borne and bound by this play; it is a play of traces or differance that has no sense and is not, a play that does not belong. There is no support to be found and no depth to be had for this bottomless chessboard where being is set in play.

It is perhaps in this way that the Heraclitean play of the *hen diapheron heautōi*, of the one differing from itself, of what is in difference with itself, already becomes lost as a trace in determining the *diapherein* as ontological difference.[33]

To think through the ontological difference doubtless remains a difficult task, a task whose statement has remained nearly inaudible. And to prepare ourselves for venturing beyond our own logos, that is, for a difference so violent that it refuses to be stopped and examined as the epochality of Being and ontological difference, is neither to give up this passage through the truth of Being, nor is it in any way to "criticize," "contest," or fail to recognize the incessant necessity for it. On the contrary, we must stay within the difficulty of this passage; we must repeat this passage in a rigorous reading of metaphysics, wherever metaphysics serves as the norm of Western speech, and not only in the texts of "the history of philosophy." Here we must allow the trace of whatever goes beyond the truth of Being to appear/disappear in its fully rigorous way. It is a trace of something that can never present itself; it is itself a trace that can never be presented, that is, can never appear and manifest itself as such in its phenomenon. It is a trace that lies beyond what profoundly ties fundamental ontology to phenomenology. Like differance, the trace is never presented as such. In presenting itself it becomes effaced; in being sounded it dies away, like the writing of the *a*, inscribing its pyramid in differance.

We can always reveal the precursive and secretive traces of this movement in metaphysical speech, especially in the contemporary talk about the closure of ontology, i.e., through the various attempts we have looked at (Nietzsche, Freud, Levinas) — and particularly in Heidegger's work.

The latter provokes us to question the essence of the present, the presence of the present.

What is the present? What is it to conceive the present in its presence?

Let us consider, for example, the 1946 text entitled "Der Spruch des Anaximander." Heidegger there recalls that the forgetting of Being forgets about the difference between Being and beings:

> But the point of Being (*die Sache des Seins*) is to be the Being *of* beings. The linguistic form of this enigmatic and multivalent genitive designates a genesis (*Genesis*), a provenance (*Herkunft*) of the pre*sent* from pre*sence* (*des Anwesenden aus dem Anwesen*). But with the unfolding of these two, the essence (*Wesen*) of this provenance remains hidden

---

[32]Derrida uses the Greek verb *diapherein* as the verb form of differance. His suggestion here is that metaphysics (the study of Being) is an epoch, therefore time-bound, an era coming to an end via the critique that he has traced to Nietzsche, Husserl, Heidegger, Freud, and Levinas.

[33]Derrida cites the pre-Socratic philosopher Heraclitus who viewed the universe as in a state of endless flux and change.

(*verborgen*). Not only is the essence of this provenance not thought out, but neither is the simple relation between pre*sence* and pre*sent* (*Anwesen und Anwesenden*). Since the dawn, it seems that pre*sence* and being-pre*sent* are each separately something. Imperceptibly, pre*sence* becomes itself a pre*sent* . . . . The essence of pre*sence* (*Das Wesen des Anwesens*), and thus the difference between pre*sence* and pre*sent*, is forgotten. *The forgetting of Being is the forgetting of the difference between Being and beings.*[34]

In recalling the difference between Being and beings (the ontological difference) as the difference between presence and present, Heidegger puts forward a proposition, indeed, a group of propositions; it is not our intention here to idly or hastily "criticize" them but rather to convey them with all their provocative force.

Let us then proceed slowly. What Heidegger wants to point out is that the difference between Being and beings, forgotten by metaphysics, has disappeared without leaving a trace. The very trace of differance has sunk from sight. If we admit that differance (is) (itself) something other than presence and absence, if it *traces*, then we are dealing with the forgetting of the difference (between Being and beings), and we now have to talk about a disappearance of the trace's trace. This is certainly what this passage from "Der Spruch des Anaximander" seems to imply:

> The forgetting of Being is a part of the very essence of Being, and is concealed by it. The forgetting belongs so essentially to the destination of Being that the dawn of this destination begins precisely as an unconcealment of the pre*sent* in its pre*sence*. This means: the history of Being begins by the forgetting of Being, in that Being retains its essence, its difference from beings. Difference is wanting; it remains forgotten. Only what is differentiated — the present and presence (*das Anwesende und das Anwesen*) — becomes uncovered, but not *insofar as* it is differentiated. On the contrary, the matinal[35] trace (*die frühe Spur*) of difference effaces itself from the moment that presence appears as a being-present (*das Anwesen wie*

ein Anwesendes erscheint) and finds its provenance in a supreme (being)-present (*in einem höchsten Anwesenden*).[36]

The trace is not a presence but is rather the simulacrum of a presence that dislocates, displaces, and refers beyond itself. The trace has, properly speaking, no place, for effacement belongs to the very structure of the trace. Effacement must always be able to overtake the trace; otherwise it would not be a trace but an indestructible and monumental substance. In addition, and from the start, effacement constitutes it as a trace — effacement establishes the trace in a change of place and makes it disappear in its appearing, makes it issue forth from itself in its very position. The effacing of this early trace (*die frühe Spur*) of difference is therefore "the same" as its tracing within the text of metaphysics. This metaphysical text must have retained a mark of what it lost or put in reserve, set aside. In the language of metaphysics the paradox of such a structure is the inversion of the metaphysical concept which produces the following effect: the present becomes the sign of signs, the trace of traces. It is no longer what every reference refers to in the last instance; it becomes a function in a generalized referential structure. It is a trace, and a trace of the effacement of a trace.

In this way the metaphysical text is *understood*; it is still readable, and remains to be read. It proposes *both* the monument and the mirage of the trace, the trace as simultaneously traced and effaced, simultaneously alive and dead, alive as always to simulate even life in its preserved inscription; it is a pyramid.

Thus we think through, without contradiction, or at least without granting any pertinence to such contradiction, what is perceptible and imperceptible about the trace. The "matinal trace" of difference is lost in an irretrievable invisibility, and yet even its loss is covered, preserved, regarded, and retarded. This happens in a text, in the form of presence.

Having spoken about the effacement of the matinal trace, Heidegger can thus, in this contradiction without contradiction, consign or

---

[34]Martin Heidegger, *Holzwege* (Frankfurt: V. Klostermann, 1957), pp. 335–36. All translations of quotations from *Holzwege* are mine. [Tr.]
[35]Early.

[36]Heidegger, p. 336. [Tr.]

countersign the sealing of the trace. We read on a little further:

> The difference between Being and beings, however, can in turn be experienced as something forgotten only if it is already discovered with the presence of the present (*mit dem Anwesen des Anwesenden*) and if it is thus sealed in a trace (*so eine Spur geprägt hat*) that remains preserved (*gewahrt bleibt*) in the language which Being appropriates.[37]

Further on still, while meditating upon Anaximander's τὸ χρεών, translated as *Brauch* (sustaining use), Heidegger writes the following:

> Dispensing accord and deference (*Fug und Ruch verfügend*), our sustaining use frees the pre*sent* (*das Anwesende*) in its sojourn and sets it free every time for its sojourn. But by the same token the present is equally seen to be exposed to the constant danger of hardening in the insistence (*in das blosse Beharren verhärtet*) out of its sojourning duration. In this way sustaining use (*Brauch*) remains itself and at the same time an abandonment (*Aushändigung*: handing-over) of presence (*des Anwesens*) *in den Un-fug*, to discord (disjointedness). Sustaining use joins together the dis- (*Der Brauch fügt das Un-*).[38]

And it is at the point where Heidegger determines *sustaining use* as *trace* that the question must be asked: can we, and how far can we, think of this trace and the *dis-* of differance as *Wesen des Seins*? Doesn't the *dis* of differance refer us beyond the history of Being, beyond our language as well, and beyond everything that can be named by it? Doesn't it call for — in the language of being — the necessarily violent transformation of this language by an entirely different language?

Let us be more precise here. In order to dislodge the "trace" from its cover (and whoever believes that one tracks down some *thing*? — one tracks down tracks), let us continue reading this passage:

> The translation of τὸ χρεών by "sustaining use" (*Brauch*) does not derive from cogitations of an etymologico-lexical nature. The choice of the word "sustaining use" derives from an antecedent *trans*lation (*Über*setzen) of the thought that

attempts to conceive difference in the deployment of Being (*im Wesen des Seins*) toward the historical beginning of the forgetting of Being. The word "sustaining use" is dictated to thought in the apprehension (*Erfahrung*) of the forgetting of Being. *Tò χρεών* properly names a trace (*Spur*) of what remains to be conceived in the word "sustaining use," a trace that quickly disappears (*alsbald verschwindet*) into the history of Being, in its world-historical unfolding as Western metaphysics.[39]

How do we conceive of the outside of a text? How, for example, do we conceive of what stands opposed to the text of Western metaphysics? To be sure, the "trace that quickly disappears into the history of Being, . . . as Western metaphysics," escapes all the determinations, all the names it might receive in the metaphysical text. The trace is sheltered and thus dissimulated in these names; it does not appear in the text as the trace "itself." But this is because the trace itself could never itself appear as such. Heidegger also says that difference can never appear *as such*: "Lichtung des Unterschiedes kann deshalb auch nicht bedeuten, dass der Unterschied als der Unterschied erscheint."[40] There is no essence of differance; not only can it not allow itself to be taken up into the *as such* of its name or its appearing, but it threatens the authority of the *as such* in general, the thing's presence in its essence. That there is no essence of difference at this point also implies that there is neither Being nor truth to the play of writing, *insofar* as it involves differance.

For us, differance remains a metaphysical name; and all the names that it receives from our language are still, so far as they are names, metaphysical. This is particularly so when they speak of determining differance as the difference between presence and present (*Anwesen/Anwesend*), but already and especially so when, in the most general way, they speak of determining difference as the difference between Being and beings.

---

[37]Ibid. [Tr.]

[38]Ibid., pp. 339–40. [Tr.]

[39]Ibid., p. 340. [Tr.]

[40]A nearly untranslatable sentence from Heidegger: Literally it reads, "Clearing of difference can for that reason not signify either, for difference appears as difference." Clearing (*Lichtung*) for Heidegger is the mysterious process by which through perception Beings come into existence for us, so the point is the same as Derrida's gloss, "there is no essence of differance."

"Older" than Being itself, our language has no name for such a differance. But we "already know" that if it is unnamable, this is not simply provisional; it is not because our language has still not found or received this *name*, or because we would have to look for it in another language, outside the finite system of our language. It is because there is no *name* for this, not even essence or Being — not even the name "differance," which is not a name, which is not a pure nominal unity, and continually breaks up in a chain of different substitutions.

"There is no name for this": we read this as a truism. What is unnamable here is not some ineffable being that cannot be approached by a name; like God, for example. What is unnamable is the play that brings about the nominal effects, the relatively unitary or atomic structures we call names, or chains of substitutions for names. In these, for example, the nominal effect of "differance" is itself involved, carried off, and reinscribed, just as the false beginning or end of a game is still part of the game, a function of the system.

What we do know, what we could know if it were simply a question of knowing, is that there never has been and never will be a unique word, a master name. This is why thinking about the letter *a* of differance is not the primary prescription, nor is it the prophetic announcement of some imminent and still unheard-of designation. There is nothing kerygmatic about this "word" so long as we can perceive its reduction to a lower-case letter.

There will be no unique name, not even the name of Being. It must be conceived without *nostalgia*; that is, it must be conceived outside the myth of the purely maternal or paternal language belonging to the lost fatherland of thought. On the contrary, we must *affirm* it — in the sense that Nietzsche brings affirmation into play — with a certain laughter and with a certain dance.

After this laughter and dance, after this affirmation that is foreign to any dialectic, the question arises as to the other side of nostalgia, which I will call Heideggerian *hope*. I am not unaware that this term may be somewhat shocking. I venture it all the same, without excluding any of its implications, and shall relate it to what seems to me to be retained of metaphysics in "Der Spruch des Anaximander," namely, the quest for the proper word and the unique name. In talking about the "first word of Being" (*das frühe Wort des Seins: τὸ χρεών*), Heidegger writes,

> The relation to the pre*sent*, unfolding its order in the very essence of pre*sence*, is unique (*ist eine einzige*). It is pre-eminently incomparable to any other relation; it belongs to the uniqueness of Being itself (*Sie gehört zur Einzigkeit des Seins selbst*). Thus, in order to name what is deployed in Being (*das Wesende des Seins*), language will have to find a single word, the unique word (*ein einziges, das einzige Wort*). There we see how hazardous is every word of thought (every thoughtful word: *denkende Wort*) that addresses itself to Being (*das dem Sein zugesprochen wird*). What is hazarded here, however, is not something impossible, because Being speaks through every language; everywhere and always.[41]

Such is the question: the marriage between speech and Being in the unique word, in the finally proper name. Such is the question that enters into the affirmation put into play by differance. The question bears (upon) each of the words in this sentence: "Being / speaks / through every language; / everywhere and always /."

[41]Ibid., pp. 337–38. [Tr.]

Umberto Eco

b. 1932

Although his surprise best-selling novel The Name of the Rose *(1980; tr. 1983) made him internationally famous, Umberto Eco has long been recognized in other circles as the leading contemporary theorist of semiotics. Born in Alessandria, Italy, Eco was educated at the University of Turin (Ph.D. 1954) and has taught at the universities of Turin, Florence, Milan, and Bologna, where he has been professor of semiotics since 1975. Eco has also been a visiting professor at universities the world over — in the United States alone he has taught at New York University, Yale, Columbia, and Northwestern. The sheer number of Eco's publications is daunting; those books that deal with semiotics and are available in English include* A Theory of Semiotics *(1975),* The Role of the Reader: Explorations in the Semiotics of Texts *(1979),* Semiotics and the Philosophy of Language *(1984),* The Open Work *(1989),* The Limits of Interpretation *(1990),* Interpretation and Overinterpretation *(1992), and* The Search for the Perfect Language *(1995). In addition, Eco has published two volumes of occasional essays,* Travels in Hyperreality *(1986) and* Apocalypse Postponed *(1994), and two more novels combining suspense with erudition,* Foucault's Pendulum *(1989) and* The Island of the Day Before *(1995). "The Myth of Superman," from* The Role of the Reader, *was first published in English in a 1972 issue of* Diacritics.

The Myth of Superman

The hero equipped with powers superior to those of the common man has been a constant of the popular imagination — from Hercules to Siegfried, from Roland to Pantagruel, all the way to Peter Pan. Often the hero's virtue is humanized, and his powers, rather than being supernatural, are the extreme realization of natural endowments such as astuteness, swiftness, fighting ability, or even the logical faculties and the pure spirit of observation found in Sherlock Holmes. In an industrial society, however, where man becomes a number in the realm of the organization which has usurped his decision-making role, he has no means of production and is thus deprived of his power to decide. Individual strength, if not exerted in sports activities, is left abased when confronted with the strength of machines which determine man's very movements. In such a society the positive hero must embody to an unthinkable degree the power

Translated by Natalie Chilton.

demands that the average citizen nurtures but cannot satisfy.

Superman is not from Earth; he arrived here as a youth from the planet Krypton. Growing up on Earth, Superman finds he is gifted with superhuman powers. His strength is practically unlimited. He can fly through space at the speed of light, and, when he surpasses that speed, he breaks through the time barrier and can transfer himself to other epochs. With no more than the pressure of his hands, he can subject coal to the temperature required to change it into diamond; in a matter of seconds, at supersonic speed, he can fell an entire forest, make lumber from trees, and construct a ship or a town; he can bore through mountains, lift ocean liners, destroy or construct dams; his X-ray vision allows him to see through any object to almost unlimited distances and to melt metal objects at a glance; his superhearing puts him in extremely advantageous situations permitting him to tune in on conversations however far away. He is kind, handsome, modest, and helpful; his life is dedicated to the battle against the forces of evil; and the police find him an untiring collaborator.

Nevertheless, the image of Superman is not entirely beyond the reach of the reader's self-identification. In fact, Superman lives among men disguised as the journalist Clark Kent; as such, he appears fearful, timid, not overintelligent, awkward, nearsighted, and submissive to his matriarchal colleague, Lois Lane, who, in turn, despises him, since she is madly in love with Superman. In terms of narrative, Superman's double identity has a function, since it permits the suspense characteristic of a detective story and great variation in the mode of narrating our hero's adventures, his ambiguities, his histrionics. But, from a mythopoeic point of view, the device is even subtle: in fact, Clark Kent personifies fairly typically the average reader who is harassed by complexes and despised by his fellow men; through an obvious process of self-identification, any accountant in any American city secretly feeds the hope that one day, from the slough of his actual personality, there can spring forth a superman who is capable of redeeming years of mediocre existence.

THE STRUCTURE OF MYTH AND THE "CIVILIZATION" OF THE NOVEL

With the undeniable mythological connotation of our hero established, it is necessary to specify the narrative structure through which the myth is offered daily or weekly to the public. There is, in fact, a fundamental difference between the figure of Superman and the traditional heroic figures of classical and nordic mythology or the figures of Messianic religions.

The traditional figure of religion was a character of human or divine origin, whose image had immutable characteristics and an irreversible destiny. It was possible that a story, as well as a number of traits, backed up the character; but the story followed a line of development already established, and it filled in the character's features in a gradual, but definitive, manner.

In other words, a Greek statue could represent Hercules or a scene of Hercules' labors; in both cases, but more so in the latter, Hercules would be seen as someone who has a story, and this story

would characterize his divine features. The story has taken place and can no longer be denied. Hercules has been made real through a development of temporal events. But once the development ended his image symbolized, along with the character, the story of his development, and it became the substance of the definitive record and judgments about him. Even the account greatly favored by antiquity was almost always the story of something which had already happened and of which the public was aware.

One could recount for the nth time the story of Roland the Paladin, but the public already knew what happened to the hero. New additions and romantic embellishments were not lacking, but neither would they have impaired the substance of the myth being narrated. A similar situation existed in the plastic arts and the paintings of Gothic cathedrals or of Counter-Reformation and Renaissance churches. What had already happened was often narrated in moving and dramatic ways.

The "civilization" of the modern novel offers a story in which the reader's main interest is transferred to the unpredictable nature of *what will happen* and, therefore, to the plot invention which now holds our attention. The event has not happened *before* the story; it happens *while* it is being told, and usually even the author does not know what will take place.

At the time of its origin, the *coup de théâtre*[1] where Oedipus finds himself guilty as a result of Tiresias' revelation "worked" for the public, not because it caught them unaware of the myth, but because the mechanism of the "plot," in accordance with Aristotelian rules, succeeded in making them once more co-participants through pity and terror. The reader is brought to identify both with the situation and with the character. In contrast, there is Julien Sorel shooting Madame de Rênal, or Poe's detective discovering the party guilty of the double crime in Rue de la Morgue, or Javert paying his debt of gratitude to Jean Valjean,[2] where we are spectators to a *coup de*

---

[1] A sudden dramatic event that alters a situation, which Aristotle called a *peripeteia*.

[2] Eco refers to Stendhal's *The Red and the Black*, Poe's "Murders in the Rue Morgue," and Hugo's *Les Misérables*.

théâtre whose unpredictable nature is part of the invention and, as such, takes on aesthetic value. This phenomenon becomes important in direct proportion to the popularity of the novel, and the *feuilleton,*[3] for the masses — the adventures of Rocambole and of Arsène Lupin[4] — have, as craft, no other value than the ingenious invention of unexpected events.

This new dimension of the story sacrifices for the most part the mythic potential of the character. The mythic character embodies a law, or a universal demand, and therefore must be in part *predictable* and cannot hold surprises for us; the character of a novel wants, rather, to be a man like anyone else, and what could befall him is as unforeseeable as what may happen to us. Such a character will take on what we will call an "aesthetic universality," a capacity to serve as a reference point for behavior and feelings which belong to us all. He does not contain the universality of myth, nor does he become an archetype, the emblem of a supernatural reality. He is the result of a universal rendering of a particular and eternal event. The character of a novel is a "historic type." Therefore, to accommodate this character, the aesthetics of the novel must revive an old category particularly necessary when art abandons the territory of myth; this we may term the "typical."

The mythological character of comic strips finds himself in this singular situation: he must be an archetype, the totality of certain collective aspirations, and therefore he must necessarily become immobilized in an emblematic and fixed nature which renders him easily recognizable (this is what happens to Superman); but, since he is marketed in the sphere of a "romantic" production for a public that consumes "romances," he must be subjected to a development which is typical, as we have seen, of novelistic characters.

[3]Light, serialized fiction, such as that contained in those parts of a French newspaper also devoted to reviews and entertaining articles.

[4]*Rocambole, or The Knaves of Hearts and the Companions of Crime:* a romance by Pierre Alexis, Vicomte de Ponson du Terrail (1829–1871). *Arsène Lupin, Gentleman-burglar,* a romance by Maurice Leblanc (1864–1941).

THE PLOT AND THE "CONSUMPTION" OF THE CHARACTER

A tragic plot, according to Aristotle, involves the character in a series of events, reversals, recognitions, pitiful and terrifying cases that culminate in a catastrophe;[5] a novelistic plot, let us add, develops these dramatic units in a continuous and narrated series which, in the popular novel, becomes an end in itself. They must proliferate as much as possible *ad infinitum. The Three Musketeers,* whose adventures continue in *Twenty Years Later* and conclude finally in *The Vicomte de Bragelonne* (but here intervene parasitic narrators who continue to tell us about the adventures of the Musketeers' sons, or the clash between d'Artagnan and Cyrano de Bergerac, and so on), is an example of narrative plot which multiplies like a tapeworm; the greater its capacity to sustain itself through an indefinite series of contrasts, oppositions, crises, and solutions, the more vital it seems.

Superman, by definition the character whom nothing can impede, finds himself in the worrisome narrative situation of being a hero without an adversary and therefore without the possibility of any development. A further difficulty arises because his public, for precise psychological reasons, cannot keep together the various moments of a narrative process over the space of several days. Each story concludes within the limits of a few pages; or, rather, every weekly edition is composed of two or three complete stories in which a particular narrative episode is presented, developed, and resolved. Aesthetically and commercially deprived of the possibility of narrative development, Superman gives serious problems to his scriptwriters. Little by little, varying formulae are offered to provoke and justify a contrast; Superman, for example, does have a weakness. He is rendered almost helpless by the radiation of kryptonite, a metal of meteoric origin, which his adversaries naturally procure at any cost in order to neutralize their avenger. But a creature gifted with superhuman intellectual and physical powers easily finds a means to get out of such scrapes, and that is what Superman

[5]See Aristotle, *Poetics,* p. 46ff.

does. Furthermore, one must consider that as a narrative theme the attempt to weaken him through the employment of kryptonite does not offer a broad range of solutions, and it must be used sparingly.

There is nothing left to do except to put Superman to the test of several obstacles which are intriguing because they are unforeseen but which are, however, surmountable by the hero. In that case two effects are obtained. First, the reader is struck by the strangeness of the obstacles — diabolically conceived inventions, curiously equipped apparitions from outer space, machines that can transmit one through time, teratological results of new experiments, the cunning of evil scientists to overwhelm Superman with kryptonite, the hero's struggles with creatures endowed with powers equal to his, such as Mxyzptlk, the gnome, who comes from the fifth dimension and who can be countered only if Superman manages to make him pronounce his own name backwards (Kltpzyxm), and so on. Second, thanks to the hero's unquestionable superiority, the crisis is rapidly resolved and the account is maintained within the bounds of the short story.

But this resolves nothing. In fact, the obstacle once conquered (and within the space allotted by commercial requirements), Superman has still *accomplished something.* Consequently, the character has made a gesture which is inscribed in his past and which weighs on his future. He has taken a step toward death, he has gotten older, if only by an hour; his storehouse of personal experiences has irreversibly enlarged. *To act,* then, for Superman, as for any other character (or for each of us), means to "consume" himself.

Now, Superman cannot "consume" himself, since a myth is "inconsumable." The hero of the classical myth became "inconsumable" precisely because he was already "consumed" in some exemplary action. Or else he had the possibility of a continuing rebirth or of symbolizing some vegetative cycle — or at least a certain circularity of events or even of life itself. But Superman is myth on condition of being a creature immersed in everyday life, in the present, apparently tied to our own conditions of life and death, even if endowed with superior faculties. An immortal Superman would no longer be a man, but a god,

and the public's identification with his double identity would fall by the wayside.

Superman, then, must remain "inconsumable" and at the same time be "consumed" according to the ways of everyday life. He possesses the characteristics of timeless myth, but is accepted only because his activities take place in our human and everyday world of time. The narrative paradox that Superman's scriptwriters must resolve somehow, even without being aware of it, demands a paradoxical solution with regard to time.

TEMPORALITY AND "CONSUMPTION"

The Aristotelian definition of time is "the amount of movement from before to after," and since antiquity time has implied the idea of *succession;* the Kantian analysis has established unequivocally that this idea must be associated with an idea of *causality:* "It is a necessary law of our sensibility and therefore a condition of all perception that preceding Time necessarily determines what follows."[6] This idea has been maintained even by relativistic physics, not in the study of the transcendental conditions of the perceptions, but in the definition of the nature of time in terms of cosmological objectivity, in such a way that time would appear as the *order of causal chains.* Reverting to these Einsteinian concepts, Reichenbach recently redefined the order of time as the order of causes, the order of open causal chains which we see verified in our universe, and the *direction* of time in terms of *growing entropy*[7] (taking up in terms even of information theory the thermodynamic concept which had recurrently interested philosophers and which they adopted as their own in speaking of the irreversibility of time.[8]

Before causally determines *after,* and the series of these determinations cannot be traced back, at least in our universe (according to the epistemological model that explains the world in which we live), but is irreversible. That other cosmological models can foresee other solutions to

[6]*Critique of Pure Reason,* "Analytic of Principles," Ch. 2, sec. 3. [Eco]
[7]Disorder.
[8]See in particular Hans Reichenbach, *The Direction of Time* (Berkeley and Los Angeles: University of California Press, 1956). [Eco]

this problem is well known; but, in the sphere of our daily understanding of events (and, consequently, in the structural sphere of a narrative character), this concept of time is what permits us to move around and to recognize events and their directions.

Expressing themselves in other words, but always on the basis of the order of *before* and *after* and of the causality of the before on the after (emphasizing variously the determination of the before on the after), existentialism and phenomenology have shifted the problem of time into the sphere of the structures of subjectivity, and discussions about action, possibility, plan, and liberty have been based on time. Time as a *structure of possibility* is, in fact, the problem of our moving toward a future, having behind us a past, whether this past is seen as a block with respect to our freedom to plan (planning which forces us to choose necessarily what we have already been) or is understood as a basis of future possibilities and therefore possibilities of conserving or changing what has been, within certain limits of freedom, yet always within the terms of positive processes.

Sartre says that "the past is the ever-growing totality of the in-itself which we are." When I want to tend toward a possible future, I must be and cannot not be this past. My possibilities of choosing or not choosing a future depend upon acts already accomplished, and they constitute the point of departure for my possible decisions. And as soon as I make another decision, it, in turn, belongs to the past and modifies what I am and offers another platform for successive projects. If it is meaningful to put the problem of freedom and of the responsibility of our decisions in philosophical terms, the basis of the discussion and the point of departure for a phenomenology of these acts is always the structure of temporality.[9]

For Husserl, the "I" is free inasmuch as it is in the past. In effect, the past determines me and therefore also determines my future, but the future, in turn, "frees" the past. My temporality is my freedom, and on my freedom depends my "Being-having-been" which determines me. But, in its continuous synthesis with the future, the content of my "Being-having-been" depends on the future. Now, if the "I" is free because it is already determined together with the "I-that-should-be," there exists within this freedom (so encumbered by conditions, so burdened with what was and is hence irreversible) a "sorrowfulness" (*Schmerzhaftigkeit*) which is none other than "facticity." (Compare with Sartre: "I am my future in the continuous prospective of the possibility of not being it. In this is the suffering which we described before and which gives sense to my present; I am a being whose sense is always problematic.")[10] Each time I plan I notice the tragic nature of the condition in which I find myself, without being able to avoid it. Nevertheless, I plan to oppose the tragic elements with the possibility of something positive, which is a change from that which is and which I put into effect as I direct myself toward the future. Plan, freedom, and condition are articulated while I observe this connection of structures in my actions, according to a dimension of *responsibility*. This is what Husserl observes when he says that, in this "directed" being of the "I" toward possible scopes, an ideal "teleology" is established and that the future as possible "having" with respect to the original futurity in which I already always *am* is the universal prefiguration of the aim of life.

In other words, the subject situated in a temporal dimension is aware of the gravity and difficulty of his decisions, but at the same time he is aware that he must decide, that it is he who must decide, and that this process is linked to an indefinite series of necessary decision making that involves all other men.

A PLOT WHICH DOES NOT "CONSUME" ITSELF

If contemporary discussions which involve man in meditation upon his destiny and his condition are based on this concept of time, the narrative structure of Superman certainly evades it in order to save the situation which we have already discussed. In Superman it is the concept of time that breaks down. The very structure of time falls

[9]For the Sartrian discussion, see *Being and Nothingness*, Ch. 2. [Eco]

[10]Ibid. [Eco]

apart, not in the time *about which,* but, rather, in the time *in which the story is told.*

In Superman stories the time that breaks down is the *time of the story,* that is, the notion of time which ties one episode to another. In the sphere of a story, Superman accomplishes a given job (he routs a band of gangsters); at this point the story ends. In the same comic book, or in the edition of the following week, a new story begins. If it took Superman up again at the point where he left off, he would have taken a step toward death. On the other hand, to begin a story without showing that another had preceded it would manage, momentarily, to remove Superman from the law that leads from life to death through time. In the end (Superman has been around since 1938), the public would realize the comicality of the situation — as happened in the case of Little Orphan Annie, who prolonged her disaster-ridden childhood for decades.

Superman's scriptwriters have devised a solution which is much shrewder and undoubtedly more original. The stories develop in a kind of oneiric climate — of which the reader is not aware at all — where what has happened before and what has happened after appear extremely hazy. The narrator picks up the strand of the event again and again, as if he had forgotten to say something and wanted to add details to what had already been said.

It occurs, then, that along with Superman stories, Superboy stories are told, that is, stories of Superman when he was a boy, or a tiny child under the name of Superbaby. At a certain point, Supergirl appears on the scene. She is Superman's cousin, and she, too, escaped from the destruction of Krypton. All of the events concerning Superman are retold in one way or another in order to account for the presence of this new character (who has hitherto not been mentioned, because, it is explained, she has lived in disguise in a girls' school, awaiting puberty, at which time she could come out into the world; the narrator goes back in time to tell in how many and in which cases she, of whom nothing was said, participated during those many adventures where we saw Superman alone involved). One imagines, using the solution of travel through time, that Supergirl, Superman's contemporary, can

encounter Superboy in the past and be his playmate; and even Superboy, having broken the time barrier by sheer accident, can encounter Superman, his own self of many years later.

But, since such a fact could comprise the character in a series of developments capable of influencing his future actions, the story ends here and insinuates that Superboy has dreamed, and one's approval of what has been said is deferred. Along these lines the most original solution is undoubtedly that of the *Imaginary Tales.* It happens, in fact, that the public will often request delightful new developments of the scriptwriters; for example, why doesn't Superman marry Lois Lane, the journalist, who has loved him for so long? If Superman married Lois Lane, it would of course be another step toward his death, as it would lay down another irreversible premise; nevertheless, it is necessary to find continually new narrative stimuli and to satisfy the "romantic" demands of the public. And so it is told "what would have happened *if* Superman had married Lois." The premise is developed in all of its dramatic implications, and at the end is the warning: Remember, this is an "imaginary" story which in truth has not taken place. (In this respect, note Roberto Giammanco's remarks about the consistently homosexual nature of characters like Superman or Batman — another variation of the theme of "superpowers." This aspect undoubtedly exists, particularly in Batman, and Giammanco offers reasons for it which we refer to later; but, in the specific case of Superman, it seems that we must speak not so much of homosexuality as of "parsifalism."[11] In Superman the element of masculine societies is nearly absent, though it is quite evident in characters like Batman and Robin, Green Arrow and his partner, and so on. Even if he often collaborates with the Legion of Super Heroes of the Future — youngsters gifted with extraordinary powers, usually ephebic but of both sexes — Superman does not neglect working with his cousin, Supergirl, as well, nor can one say that Lois Lane's advances, or those of Lana Lang, an

[11]In Wolfram von Eschenbach's medieval epic, *Parsifal,* the hero, of amazing powers, is a pure but utterly naive and foolish boy.

old schoolmate and rival of Lois, are received by Superman with the disgust of a misogynist. He shows, instead, the bashful embarrassment of an average young man in a matriarchal society. On the other hand, the most perceptive philologists have not overlooked his unhappy love for Lori Lemaris, who, being a mermaid, could offer him only an underwater *ménage*[12] corresponding to a paradisiacal exile which Superman must refuse because of his sense of duty and the indispensable nature of his mission. What characterizes Superman is, instead, the platonic dimension of his affections, the implicit vow of chastity which depends less on his will than on the state of things, and the singularity of his situation. If we have to look for a structural reason for this narrative fact, we cannot but go back to our preceding observations: the "parsifalism" of Superman is one of the conditions that prevents his slowly "consuming" himself, and it protects him from the events, and therefore from the passing of time, connected with erotic ventures.)

The *Imaginary Tales* are numerous, and so are the *Untold Tales* or those stories that concern events already told but in which "something was left out," so they are told again from another point of view, and in the process lateral aspects come to the fore. In this massive bombardment of events which are no longer tied together by any strand of logic, whose interaction is ruled no longer by any necessity, the reader, without realizing it, of course, loses the notion of temporal progression. Superman happens to live in an imaginary universe in which, as opposed to ours, causal chains are not open (A provokes B, B provokes C, C provokes D, and so on, *ad infinitum*), but closed (A provokes B, B provokes C, C provokes D, and D provokes A), and it no longer makes sense to talk about temporal progression on the basis of which we usually describe the happenings of the macrocosm.

One could observe that, apart from the mythopoeic and commercial necessities which together force such a situation, a similar structural assessment of Superman stories reflects, even though at a low level, a series of diffuse

persuasions in our culture about the problem of concepts of causality, temporality, and the irreversibility of events; and, in fact, a great deal of contemporary art, from Joyce to Robbe-Grillet, or a film such as *Last Year at Marienbad,* reflects paradoxical temporal situations, whose models, nevertheless, exist in the epistemological discussions of our times. But it is a fact that, in works such as *Finnegans Wake* or Robbe-Grillet's *In the Labyrinth,* the breakdown of familiar temporal relations happens in a conscious manner, on the part both of the writer and of the one who derives aesthetic satisfaction from the operation. The disintegration of temporality has the function both of quest and of denunciation and tends to furnish the reader with imaginative models capable of making him accept situations of the new science and of reconciling the activity of an imagination accustomed to old schemes with the activity of an intelligence which ventures to hypothesize or to describe universes that are not reducible to an image or a scheme. In consequence, these works (but here another problem opens up) carry out a mythopoeic function, offering the inhabitant of the contemporary world a kind of symbolic suggestion or allegorical diagram of that absolute which science has resolved, not so much in a metaphysical modality of the world, but in a possible way of establishing our relation with the world and, therefore, in a possible way of describing the world.

The adventures of Superman, however, do not have this critical intention, and the temporal paradox on which they are sustained should not be obvious to the reader (just as the authors themselves are probably unaware of it), since a confused notion of time is the only condition which makes the story credible. Superman comes off as a myth only if the reader loses control of the temporal relationships and renounces the need to reason on their basis, thereby giving himself up to the uncontrollable flux of the stories which are accessible to him and, at the same time, holding on to the illusion of a continuous present. Since the myth is not isolated exemplarily in a dimension of eternity, but, in order to be assimilated, must enter into the flux of the story in question, this same story is refuted as flux and seen instead as an immobile present.

[12]Household.

In growing accustomed to the idea of events happening in an ever-continuing present, the reader loses track of the fact that they should develop according to the dictates of time. Losing consciousness of it, he forgets the problems which are at its base, that is, the existence of freedom, the possibility of planning, the necessity of carrying plans out, the sorrow that such planning entails, the responsibility that it implies, and, finally, the existence of an entire human community whose progressiveness is based on making plans.

SUPERMAN AS A MODEL OF "HETERODIRECTION"

The proposed analysis would be greatly abstracted and could appear apocalyptic if the man who reads Superman, and for whom Superman is produced, were not the selfsame man with whom several sociological reports have dealt and who has been defined as "other directed man."

In advertising, as in propaganda, and in the area of human relations, the absence of the dimension of "planning" is essential to establishing a paternalistic pedagogy, which requires the hidden persuasion that the subject is not responsible for his past, nor master of his future, not even subject to the laws of planning according to the three "ecstasies" of temporality (Heidegger). All of this would imply pain and labor, while society is capable of offering to the heterodirected man the results of projects already accomplished. Such are they as to respond to man's desires, which themselves have been introduced in man in order to make him recognize that what he is offered is precisely what he would have planned.

The analysis of temporal structures in Superman has offered us the image of a *way of telling stories* which would seem to be fundamentally tied to pedagogic principles that govern that type of society. Is it possible to establish connections between the two phenomena affirming that Superman is no other than one of the pedagogic instruments of this society and that the destruction of time that it pursues is part of a plan to make obsolete the idea of planning and of personal responsibility?

DEFENSE OF THE ITERATIVE SCHEME

A series of events repeated according to a set scheme (iteratively, in such a way that each event takes up again from a sort of virtual beginning, ignoring where the preceding event left off) is nothing new in popular narrative. In fact, this scheme constitutes one of its more characteristic forms.

The device of iteration is one on which certain escape mechanisms are founded, particularly the types realized in television commercials: one distractedly watches the playing out of a sketch, then focuses one's attention on the punch line that reappears at the end of the episode. It is precisely on this foreseen and awaited reappearance that our modest but irrefutable pleasure is based.

This attitude does not belong only to the television spectator. The reader of detective stories can easily make an honest self-analysis to establish the modalities that explain his "consuming" them. First, from the beginning the reading of a traditional detective story presumes the enjoyment of following a scheme: from the crime to the discovery and the resolution through a chain of deductions. The scheme is so important that the most famous authors have founded their fortune on its very immutability. Nor are we dealing only with a schematism in the order of a "plot," but with a fixed schematism involving the same sentiments and the same psychological attitudes: in Simenon's Maigret or in Agatha Christie's Poirot, there is a recurrent movement of compassion to which the detective is led by his discovery of the facts and which merges into an empathy with the motives of the guilty party, an act of *caritas* which is combined with, if not opposed to, the act of justice that unveils and condemns.

Furthermore, the writer of stories then introduces a continuous series of connotations (for example, the characteristics of the policeman and of his immediate "entourage") to such an extent that their reappearance in each story is an essential condition of its reading pleasure. And so we have the by now historical "tics" of Sherlock Holmes, the punctilious vanity of Hercule Poirot, the pipe and the familiar fixes of Maigret, on up to the daily idiosyncrasies of the most unabashed heroes of postwar detective stories, such as the cologne water and Player's #6 of Peter Cheyney's

Slim Callaghan or the cognac with a glass of cold water of Brett Halliday's Michael Shayne. Vices, gestures, nervous tics permit us to find an old friend in the character portrayed, and they are the principal conditions which allow us to "enter into" the event. Proof of this is when our favorite author writes a story in which the usual character does not appear and we are not even aware that the fundamental scheme of the book is still like the others: we read the book with a certain detachment and are immediately prone to judge it a "minor" work, a momentary phenomenon, or an interlocutory remark.

All this becomes very clear if we take a famous character such as Nero Wolfe, immortalized by Rex Stout. For sheer preterition[13] and by way of caution, in the likelihood of one of our readers' being so "highbrow" as to have never encountered our character, let us briefly recall the elements which combine to form Nero Wolfe's "type" and his environment. Nero Wolfe, from Montenegro, a naturalized American from time immemorial, is outlandishly fat, so much so that his leather easy chair must be expressly designed for him. He is fearfully lazy. In fact, he never leaves the house and depends, for his investigations, on the open-minded Archie Goodwin, with whom he indulges in a continuous relationship of a sharp and tensely polemic nature, tempered somewhat by their mutual sense of humor. Nero Wolfe is an absolute glutton, and his cook, Fritz, is the vestal virgin in the pantry, devoted to the unending care of this highly cultivated palate and equally greedy stomach; but along with the pleasures of the table, Wolfe cultivates an all-absorbing and exclusive passion for orchids; he has a priceless collection of them in the green-house on the top floor of the villa where he lives. Quite possessed by gluttony and flowers, assailed by a series of accessory tics (love of scholarly literature, systematic misogyny, insatiable thirst for money), Nero Wolfe conducts his investigations, masterpieces of psychological penetration, sitting in his office, carefully weighing the information with which the enterprising Archie furnishes him, studying the protagonists of each event who are

<hr>

[13]There is a problem with the translation: preterition means an intentional act of omission.

obliged to visit him in his office, arguing with Inspector Cramer (attention: he always holds a methodically extinguished cigar in his mouth), quarreling with the odious Sergeant Purley Stebbins; and, finally, in a fixed setting from which he never veers, he summons the protagonists of the case to a meeting in his studio, usually in the evening. There, with skillful dialectical subterfuges, almost always before he himself knows the truth, he drives the guilty one into a public demonstration of hysteria and thus into giving himself away.

Those who know Rex Stout's stories know that these details hardly scratch the surface of the repertoire of *topoi,* of recurrent stock situations which animate these stories. The gamut is much more ample: Archie's almost canonic arrest under suspicion of reticence and false testimony; the legal diatribes about the conditions on which Wolfe will take on a client; the hiring of part-time agents like Saul Panzer or Orrie Cather; the painting in the studio behind which Wolfe or Archie can watch, through a peephole, the behavior and reactions of a subject put to the test in the office itself; the scenes with Wolfe and an insincere client — one could go on forever; we realize, at the end, that the list of these *topoi* is such that it could exhaust almost every possibility of the events permitted within the number of pages allowed to each story. Nevertheless, there are infinite variations of the theme; each crime has new psychological and economic motivations, each time the author devises what appears as a new situation. We say "appear"; the fact is that the reader is never brought to verify the extent to which something new is told. The noteworthy moments are those when Wolfe repeats his usual gestures, when he goes up for the nth time to take care of his orchids while the case itself is reaching its dramatic climax, when Inspector Cramer threateningly enters with one foot between the door and the wall, pushing aside Goodwin and warning Wolfe with a shake of his finger that this time things will not go so smoothly. The attraction of the book, the sense of repose, of psychological extension which it is capable of conferring, lies in the fact that, plopped in an easy chair or in the seat of a train compartment, the reader continuously recovers, point by point, what he already knows, what he wants to know again: that is why he has purchased the book. He derives pleasure from the nonstory (if indeed a story is a development of events which should bring us from the point of departure to a point of arrival where we would never have dreamed of arriving); the distraction consists in the refutation of a development of events, in a withdrawal from the tension of past-present-future to the focus of an *instant,* which is loved because it is recurrent.

THE ITERATIVE SCHEME AS A REDUNDANT MESSAGE

It is certain that mechanisms of this kind proliferate more widely in the popular narrative of today than in the eighteenth-century romantic *feuilleton,* where, as we have seen, the event was founded upon a *development* and where the character was required to "consume" himself through to death. Perhaps one of the first inexhaustible characters during the decline of the *feuilleton* and bridging the two centuries at the close of *la belle époque*[14] is Fantomas.[15] (Each episode of *Fantomas* closes with a kind of "unsuccessful catharsis"; Juve and Fandor finally come to get their hands on the elusive one when he, with an unforeseeable move, foils the arrest. Another singular fact: Fantomas — responsible for blackmail and sensational kidnappings — at the beginning of each episode finds himself inexplicably poor and in need of money and, therefore, also of new "action." In this way the cycle can keep going.) With him the epoch ends. It remains to be asked if modern iterative mechanisms do not answer some profound need in contemporary man and, therefore, do not seem more justifiable and better motivated than we are inclined to admit at first glance.

If we examine the iterative scheme from a structural point of view, we realize that we are in the presence of a typical *high-redundance message.* A novel by Souvestre and Allain or by Rex Stout is a message which informs us very little and which, on the contrary, thanks to the use of redundant elements, keeps hammering away at the same meaning which we have peacefully acquired upon reading the first work of the series (in the case in point, the meaning is a certain mechanism of the action, due to the intervention of "topical" characters). The taste for the iterative scheme is presented then as a taste for redundance. The hunger for entertaining narrative based on these mechanisms is a *hunger for redundance.* From this viewpoint, the greater part of popular narrative is a narrative of redundance.

Paradoxically, the same detective story that one is tempted to ascribe to the products that satisfy the taste for the unforeseen or the sensational is, in fact, read for exactly the opposite reason, as an invitation to that which is taken for granted, familiar, expected. Not knowing who the guilty party is becomes an accessory element, almost a pretext; certainly, it is true that in the action detective story (where the iteration of the scheme triumphs as much as in the investigation detective story), the suspense surrounding the guilty one often does not even exist; it is not a matter of discovering who committed the crime, but, rather, of following certain "topical" gestures of "topical" characters whose stock behavior we already love. To explain this "hunger for redundance," extremely subtle hypotheses are not needed. The *feuilleton,* founded on the triumph of information, represented the preferred fare of a society that lived in the midst of messages loaded with redundance; the sense of tradition, the norms of associative living, moral principles, the valid rules of proper comportment in the environment of nineteenth-century bourgeois society, of the typical public which represented the consumers of the *feuilleton* — all this constituted a system of foreseeable communication that the social system provided for its members and which allowed life to flow smoothly without unexpected jolts and without upsets in its value system. In this sphere the "informative" shock of a short story by Poe or the *coup de théâtre* of Ponson du Terrail[16] acquired a precise meaning. In a contemporary industrial society, instead, the alternation of standards, the dissolution of tradition, social mobility,

[14]The turn of the twentieth century.

[15]*Fantomas* (1911–13) was a serialized novel by Marcel Allain (1885–1969) and Pierre Souvestre (1874–1914) about an elusive criminal.

[16]Author of romances like *Rocambole* in n. 4.

the fact that models and principles are "consumable" — everything can be summed up under the sign of a continuous load of information which proceeds by way of massive jolts, implying a continual reassessment of sensibilities, adaptation of psychological assumptions, and requalification of intelligence. Narrative of a redundant nature would appear in this panorama as an indulgent invitation to repose, the only occasion of true relaxation offered to the consumer. Conversely, "superior" art only proposes schemes in evolution, grammars which mutually eliminate each other, and codes of continuous alternations.

Is it not also natural that the cultural person who in moments of intellectual tension seeks a stimulus in an action painting or in a piece of serial music should in moments of relaxation and escape (healthy and indispensable) tend toward triumphant infantile laziness and turn to the consumer product for pacification in an orgy of redundance?

As soon as we consider the problem from this angle, we are tempted to show more indulgence toward escape entertainments (among which is included our myth of Superman), reproving ourselves for having exercised an acid moralism on what is innocuous and perhaps even beneficial.

The problem changes according to the degree to which pleasure in redundance breaks the convulsed rhythm of an intellectual existence based upon the reception of information and becomes the *norm* of every imaginative activity.

The problem is not to ask ourselves if different ideological contents conveyed by the same narrative scheme can elicit different effects. Rather, an iterative scheme becomes and remains that *only* to the extent that the scheme sustains and expresses a world; we realize this even more, once we understand how the world has the same configuration as the structure which expressed it. The case of Superman reconfirms this hypothesis. If we examine the ideological contents of Superman stories, we realize that, on the one hand, that content sustains itself and functions communicatively thanks to the narrative structure; on the other hand, the stories help define their expressive structure as the circular, static conveyance of a pedagogic message which is substantially immobilistic.

CIVIC CONSCIOUSNESS AND POLITICAL CONSCIOUSNESS

Superman stories have a characteristic in common with a series of other adventures that hinge on heroes gifted with *superpowers*. In Superman the real elements blend into a more homogeneous totality, which justifies the fact that we have devoted special attention to him; and it is no accident that Superman is the most popular of the heroes we talk about: he not only represents the forerunner of the group (in 1938), but of all the characters he is still the one who is most carefully sketched, endowed with a recognizable personality, dug out of longstanding anecdote, and so he can be seen as the representative of all his similars. (In any case, the observation that follows can be applied to a whole series of superheroes, from Batman and Robin to Green Arrow, Flash, the Manhunter from Mars, Green Lantern, and Aquaman up to the more recent Fantastic Four, Devil, and Spider Man, where the literary "genre," however, has acquired a more sophisticated form of self-irony.)

Each of these heroes is gifted with such powers that he could actually take over the government, defeat the army, or alter the equilibrium of planetary politics. On the other hand, it is clear that each of these characters is profoundly kind, moral, faithful to human and natural laws, and therefore it is right (and it is nice) that he use his powers only to the end of good. In this sense the pedagogic message of these stories would be, at least on the plane of children's literature, highly acceptable, and the same episodes of violence with which the various stories are interspersed would appear directed toward this final indictment of evil and the triumph of honest people.

The ambiguity of the teaching appears when we ask ourselves, *What is Good?* It is enough to reexamine in depth the situation of Superman, who encompasses the others, at least in their fundamental structure.

Superman is practically omnipotent, as we have said, in his physical, mental, and technological capacities. His operative capacity extends to a cosmic scale. A being gifted with such capacities offered to the good of humanity (let us pose the problem with a maximum of candor and of responsibility, taking everything as probable) would have an enormous field of action in front of him. From a man who could produce work and wealth in astronomic dimensions in a few seconds, one could expect the most bewildering political, economic, and technological upheavals in the world. From the solution of hunger problems to the tilling of uninhabitable regions, from the destruction of inhuman systems (if we read Superman into the "spirit of Dallas," why does he not go to liberate six hundred million Chinese from the yoke of Mao?), Superman could exercise good on a cosmic level, or on a galactic level, and furnish us in the meantime with a definition that through fantastic amplification could clarify precise ethical lines everywhere.

Instead, Superman carries on his activity on the level of the small community where he lives (Smallville as a youth, Metropolis as an adult), and — as in the case of the medieval countryman who could have happened to visit the Sacred Land, but not the closed and separate community which flourished fifty kilometers from the center of his life — if he takes trips to other galaxies with ease, he practically ignores, not exactly the dimension of the "world," but that of the "United States" (only once, but in one of the *Imaginary Tales,* he becomes president of the United States).

In the sphere of his own little town, evil, the only evil to combat, is incarnate in species which adheres to the underworld, that of organized crime. He is busy by preference, not against blackmarket drugs, nor, obviously, against corrupt administrators or politicians, but against bank and mail-truck robbers. In other words, *the only visible form that evil assumes is an attempt on private property.* Outerspace evil is added spice; it is casual, and it always assumes unforeseeable and transitory forms; the underworld is an endemic evil, like some kind of impure stream that pervades the course of human history, clearly divided into zones of Manichaean incontrovertibility — where each authority is fundamentally pure and good and where each wicked man is rotten to the core without hope of redemption.

As others have said, in Superman we have a perfect example of civic consciousness, completely split from political consciousness.

Superman's civic attitude is perfect, but it is exercised and structured in the sphere of a small, closed community (a "brother" of Superman — as a model of absolute fidelity to established values — might appear in someone such as the movie and television hero Dr. Kildare).

It is strange that Superman, devoting himself to good deeds, spends enormous amounts of energy organizing benefit performances in order to collect money for orphans and indigents. The paradoxical waste of means (the same energy could be employed to produce directly riches or to modify radically larger situations) never ceases to astound the reader who sees Superman forever employed in parochial performances. As evil assumes only the form of an offense to private property, *good is represented only as charity.* This simple equivalent is sufficient to characterize Superman's moral world. In fact, we realize that Superman is obliged to continue his activities in the sphere of small and infinitesimal modifications of the immediately visible for the same motives noted in regard to the static nature of his plots: each general modification would draw the world, and Superman with it, toward final consumption.

On the other hand, it would be inexact to say that Superman's judicious and measured virtue depends only on the structure of the plot, that is, on the need to forbid the release of excessive and irretrievable developments. The contrary is also true: the immobilizing metaphysics underlying this kind of conceptual plot is the direct, though not the desired, consequence of a total structural mechanism which seems to be the only one suited to communicate, through the themes discussed, a particular kind of teaching. The plot must be static and must evade any development, because Superman *must* make virtue consist of many little activities on a small scale, never achieving a total awareness. Conversely, virtue must be characterized in the accomplishment of only partial acts, so that the plot can remain static. Again, the discussion does not take on the features of the authors' preferences as much as their adaptation to a concept of "order" which pervades the cultural model in which the authors live and where they construct on a small scale "analogous" models which mirror the larger one.

3

READER-RESPONSE THEORY

The literary work cannot be completely identical with the text, or with the [reader's] realization of the text, but in fact must lie halfway between the two.
— WOLFGANG ISER

Interpretive communities are made up of those who share interpretive strategies not for reading (in the conventional sense) but for writing texts, for constituting their properties and assigning their intentions.
— STANLEY FISH

It is . . . impossible to say from a text alone how people will respond to it. Only after we have understood how some specific individual responds, how the different parts of his individual personality re-create the different details of the text, can we begin to formulate general hypotheses about the way many or all readers respond. Only then — if then.
— NORMAN N. HOLLAND

The critics grouped together here as reader-response theorists share a topic rather than a set of assumptions. They all have in common the conviction that the audience plays a vitally important role in shaping the literary experience and the desire to help to explain that role. But their interpretations of that role and their definitions of the literary experience vary enormously, in ways that dwarf the usual doctrinal distinctions even within diverse movements like formalism or semiotics.

Interest in the role of the reader goes back to the early classical period. Plato's Book X of *Republic* testifies to the philosopher's concern lest the audience be corrupted by texts that imitate falsely or concentrate the attention of the audience on unworthy matters; the *Ion,* while centrally involved with the question of creativity, suggests that the *enthousiasmós* the muse grants to the poet is transmitted, like magnetic force, through the performer to the spectator. In Aristotle's *Poetics,* tragedy is partially defined in terms of the emotional activity of the spectator, and the construction of the text is constantly subject to the question of how the audience will view the completed product. In Horace the audience becomes central. The chief criterion of excellence in *The Art of Poetry* is what will delight and instruct the reader or spectator, and the text is defined in operational terms as something whose language, incidents, and characters are to be judged as part of a literary (and in general, a cultural) scene. The legacy of Horace long endured; the rhetorical principle of criticism, based on an operational mode of thought, dominated Western literary criticism for nearly eighteen hundred years.

The displacement of the audience from the center of critical attention to its periphery is the result of Romanticism, which exalted the genius of the author at the expense of the critic (who might be considered the reader's better-paid persona). Most nineteenth- and early twentieth-century criticism centered on the author, and even the shift toward formalism at midcentury displaced the creator only to focus attention on the text itself. The New Critics may have paid greatest attention to the intentional fallacy, since the tendency of the historical scholars they had displaced was to read for authorial meaning. But Wimsatt and Beardsley also wrote a companion piece, "The Affective Fallacy," to defend the autonomous text against the encroachment of critics (primarily I. A. Richards) who might attempt to define the text in terms of the emotions it aroused in a real audience. The autonomous text of the New Criticism expressed feelings and attitudes to an ideal audience, and no evidence of how actual readers had reacted to it could possibly budge the critics' theory. While the once-controversial and experimental works of high modernism (the fiction of Joyce and Woolf, the poetry of Yeats and Eliot) were becoming canonical texts in the first two decades after World War II, the New Criticism was establishing theoretical strictures valorizing the objective textual surface and cultivating the tactic of ignoring the audience.

During the New Critical ascendancy works of audience-oriented theory, like Louise Rosenblatt's *Literature as Exploration* (1938), led a buried life, valued by the education establishment and used in pedagogy but ignored by literary theorists. But like Plato's banishment of the poets, the exile of the audience could not be enforced for long. The return of the reader to center stage was encouraged by one of the Chicago Aristotelians, Wayne C. Booth, with *The Rhetoric of Fiction* (1961). Booth's innovative ideas fit within the prevailing formalism, but in the following decades, other definably different modes of audience-centered criticism emerged. Within the structuralist movement, the audience became a central focus for theorists like Gerald Prince in addition to critics we have already discussed, like Gérard Genette, Jonathan Culler, and Umberto Eco (Ch. 2). A reader-oriented version of psychological criticism also developed, led by such theorists as David Bleich and Norman Holland. More recently, a phenomenological criticism of literature has arisen, which considers the reader as the performer of the text. And the reader has become a key topic in the feminist criticism of Judith Fetterley and Patrocinio Schweickart.

RHETORICAL CRITICISM

Probably the loosest of these groupings is the rhetorical approach, since it covers any perspective that treats the text as sending signals to the reader for interpretation. From Horace to Samuel Johnson, the principal variants in rhetorical theory have turned on two issues: the *object* communicated and the *character* of the audience addressed. On the first axis some critics, such as Dante, have emphasized the way literature communicates ethical and religious doctrine, while others, such as Horace, have concerned themselves chiefly with the pleasures enjoyed by the reader. On the other axis, critics such as Johnson have been concerned with what will be most generally pleasing to any audience, while others, such as Dryden, have assumed that texts are written to please and instruct a particular national group, or even a class within that group, and that the specific characteristics of the audience will dictate the rhetoric employed in the text. In a sense, the discrepancies in contemporary rhetorical criticism are most strongly marked along the axis of reader participation. The range runs from Wayne Booth, who emphasizes the way texts shape their audience into "proper" readers, through Susan Sontag, whose ideal condition would be the mutual transparency of text and reader, to Stanley Fish, who (in one phase of his work) views the text as being created by the reader's mental experience of it.

Booth's approach is both the most traditionally formalistic of the audience-centered modes and the one that has achieved the most widespread recognition. So thoroughly have its methods been embraced by contemporary practical critics that some textbook writers have taken it for a form of the New Criticism. In fact, Booth, like his mentor R. S. Crane, opposed New Critical doctrine on fiction and wrote *The Rhetoric of Fiction* partly to refute the ideas of New Critics like Allen Tate and Caroline Gordon. The prevailing doctrines, derived from the theory and practice of Henry James, valorized realistic stories told through a "natural," objective narrative technique that avoided authorial commentary and other overt signals of the creator behind the tale. Booth's book made it clear that such "natural" techniques of modernism were no less artificial, no less rhetorical, than the direct address to the reader practiced by Fielding and Sterne.

The real question was not *whether* the novelist should use rhetoric — it was impossible to avoid doing so — but what sort of rhetoric to use. Each of the author's technical decisions would shape in a particular way the reader's evaluation of the characters and the action, making some effects easy and others impossible. The axioms that arise from Booth's theory are less simple than those implicit in the New Criticism. They suggest that a reader's emotional distance from the characters in a narrative depends not only on the characters' values and beliefs but on the distance from the reader at which the narrative technique places them. Even relatively vicious characters can become sympathetic if readers are granted access to their consciousness and distanced from that of their victims.

The impact of *The Rhetoric of Fiction* was immense, not only in the development of theory but also in altering the canon of fiction. The popularity of eighteenth-century novelists like Defoe, Fielding, and Sterne, long muted by the disapproval of the New Critics, recovered, in part owing to Booth's debunking of modernist premises. In addition, Booth's terminology — such as "implied author" for the formal location of authorial values within a text, or "unreliable narrator" for a narrator (either personified or not within the text) whose values (intellectual, aesthetic, or ethical) depart from those of the implied author — has become the standard vocabulary in fiction courses.

Booth's concern with "implied authors" and "unreliable narrators," while presenting a view of literature as ineluctably rhetorical, largely focuses on the ways in which authors make texts that will engage or persuade their audiences: The focus, in other words, remains on the writer more than the reader and largely takes for granted the ways in which readers decode the symbols on the page. Booth's former student, Peter Rabinowitz, has reversed the emphasis. While Rabinowitz still deals with the literary text as a formal object, he focuses on the tacit knowledge the reader must possess to re-create its form.

Rabinowitz's most essential distinction is between the "narrative audience" and the "authorial audience": personifications of the two aspects of reading that all of us perform. As part of the "narrative audience," we follow the events of the narrative as if they were really happening; at the same time, as members of the "authorial audience," we read the text knowing that it is just a story created by an author with some sort of effect in mind.[1] The emotional power of a text depends on the success of the pretense that the events it portrays are real. Our sense of the shape of the narrative, our ability to predict what is going to happen, and our need to sympathize with some characters more than with others depends on our communion with the values and plans of the creating author. Ideally, that is. Actual readers may find it impossible to believe in the reality of a given narrative and may fail to capture an author's signals about the plot and values of a story, either because of the author's lack of artistry or because of conflict with their own ideas, values, and preconceptions. For Rabinowitz both the "narrative audience" and the "authorial audience" are virtual beings, a product of the text and of the rules for reading texts, rules we generally absorb while we are still too young to read on our own.

The first part of Rabinowitz's *Before Reading* (part of which is reprinted in this chapter) consists of an analysis of some of the rules for reading texts that constitute the contemporary interpretive community: "rules of notice," which assign priority to certain kinds of details; "rules of signification," which help us interpret the meaning, symbolic and literal, of what we read; "rules of configuration," which give us a sense of completeness, closure and genre; and "rules of coherence" that allow us to harmonize and naturalize textual gaps or disjunctures. The second part, keyed to the book's subtitle, *Narrative Conventions and the Politics of Interpretation,* is an inquiry into the meaning of rules of reading as social texts, products of the ideology of the current age. Here Rabinowitz questions, for example, why we so often sympathize with irresponsible idealists when they are males (like Jay Gatsby) but find them lacking or contemptible when they are females (like Emma Bovary), and suggests that the rules of reading our society follows are implicitly sexist, racist, and bourgeois rather than working-class in bias. He suggests that the first steps toward the formation of a just society should include understanding the ways in which we have been molded by our culture's implicit rules of reading. In this way, Rabinowitz's rhetorical mode of audience-oriented criticism shows links with some of the Marxists discussed in Chapter 5.

---

[1]For texts with narrators who present facts and values in a way so skewed that we need to allow for their distortions merely to reconstruct what is happening on the level of the text, Rabinowitz also distinguishes an "ideal narrative audience." This would contain the virtual audience for whom Jason Compson in Faulkner's *The Sound and the Fury,* or Whitey the Barber in Ring Lardner's "Haircut" is speaking.

Whereas Booth views readers as being constructed by authors, and Rabinowitz hopes that readers can become aware of the ways in which they are manipulated by their culture's rules of reading, Stanley Fish argues that the text is completely malleable and that the all-powerful reader can interrogate it as he or she wishes. Fish began his career by advocating a method of interpretation that he called "affective stylistics," which could be seen as a special mode of the New Criticism. According to this method, the reader reads the text slowly, word by word, alive at each moment to the shifts in apparent position and direction. Texts that seemed to lead first to one conclusion, then another, Fish termed "self-consuming artifacts." The following passage from Sir Thomas Browne is an example:

> That Judas perished by hanging himself, there is no certainty in Scripture: though in one place it seems to affirm it, and by a doubtful word hath given occasion to translate it; yet in another place, in a more punctual description, it maketh it improbable, and seems to overthrow it.

Fish argues that Browne seems to commit himself to Judas's death by hanging up to the first comma, then gradually and *almost* entirely takes it all back: "The prose is continually opening, but then closing, on the possibility of verification in one direction or another."[2] (In a sense, this a variation on New Critic William Empson's sixth type of ambiguity, ambiguity of syntax.) But gradually Fish moved away from the idea that these features belonged primarily to the text, and insisted on their location within the reader. In effect, the text is not the words on the page but the minutely detailed performance they elicit from the reader.

In his groundbreaking book, *Is There a Text in This Class?*, Fish locates the text within the reader rather than in the words on the page. This is a bold procedure, since each reader is likely to come up with at least a slightly different "text." (Elsewhere, in *Self-Consuming Artifacts,* Fish blocks this objection by his appeal to the "informed reader.") Fish is willing to concede that the text-within-the-reader is unstable, but he attempts to demonstrate, as do Derrida and his followers, that the text-as-author's-words is equally unstable, although he does not base this radical skepticism about meaning on the Derridean metaphysics of absence. Instead, for each posited location of meaning within the so-called hermeneutic circle, Fish casts doubt by pushing the point of anchor back, one step at a time — from the words to the conventions for reading the words to the linguistic rules themselves, and so forth. But Fish does not give the full proof, and his argument assumes that readers either can complete it for themselves or trust it can be done.[3]

---

[2] Stanley Fish, "Literature in the Reader," in *Is There a Text in This Class?* (Cambridge: Harvard University Press, 1980), p. 24.

[3] The "hermeneutic circle" (a vicious circle only when one is trying to think about it) refers to the difficulty of finding a stable point in the ascription of meaning to any text. Since any word has a large finite number of meanings, we are able to give a stable meaning to any word only from context, but the context itself consists of other words, with equally unstable meanings. Attempts to find a stable point by locating it in (for example) the speaker's intention, simply move the circularity elsewhere.

Whether the reader is convinced is not important, however, since Fish finally accounts for the *relative* stability of readers' sense of canonical texts of literature by appealing to the idea of *interpretive communities*. Interpretive communities have tacitly agreed to certain principles of textual interpretation, which authors must recognize as they write their poems or plays or novels. (In legal circles Fish's theory is seen as one way of accounting for the relationship between statute law and the "community" of judges whose profession it is to interpret that law.) In "How to Recognize a Poem When You See One" (reprinted on p. 1023), Stanley Fish demonstrates that we can belong to different communities at the same time, via his story about writing a reading list for a morning class in linguistics on the blackboard:

Jacobs — Rosenbaum
Levin
Thorne
Hayes
Ohman (?)

The reading list was interpreted as a poem by the students in his subsequent class in seventeenth-century religious poetry, which met in the same room. The students had no trouble finding in the list a symbolic structure similar to the texts they had been studying. In "Jacobs" they found Jacob's ladder, traditionally moralized as the Christian's ascent to heaven. "Rosenbaum" — rose-tree in German — would then allude to the means of ascent, here no ladder but a tree (like the tree of life) whose character is given by the Rose (a traditional symbol for the Virgin Mary). And so it went: even the shape of the assignment list was interpreted as being like an altar, since some seventeenth-century poets, like George Herbert, wrote "hieroglyphic" poetry in which the printed lines arranged themselves into angel's wings and other objects. It is easy to claim that Fish's students were reading more into the list than was legitimately there, but the moral of the story, as Fish draws it, is that "reading into" texts is inevitable. Reading is never "just reading"; it is always "reading as." It always involves a "construction" of meaning by the reader in accordance with genre-specific conventions of interpretation established within a community. And it wasn't just the poetry students who were "reading as": Fish's linguistics students had to construct the list of names as an "assignment" (with a different series of conventions) just as his poetry students had constructed it as a "poem."

Fish's arguments that textual genres (like "poem" or "assignment") in effect create texts by highlighting certain features of the words on the page and suppressing others, have won general acceptance, as far as they go here. But is every hypothesis about a text plausible? Fish's denial that texts have any determinate structures independent of the strategies that readers deploy to interpret them has been received with much more skepticism. James Phelan's "Data, Danda, and Disagreement," excerpted below (p. 1031), uses Stephen Pepper's distinction between data and danda (facts independent of, or dependent on, the viewpoint of the observer) to argue that hypotheses about texts can indeed be evaluated in terms of how they account for the textual data, so that while many different hypotheses may be warrantable, it may be possible to determine that some hypotheses are not.

THE STRUCTURALIST READER

The structuralist concern with the role of reader as the decoder of the text has already been discussed. In Chapter 2, Umberto Eco's "The Myth of Superman" presents in theoretical and in practical terms how the central issues of semiotics have been applied to the audience. In *Structuralist Poetics*, Jonathan Culler argued, more generally, that structuralism had been led astray by its long search for syntactic keys to authorial meaning and suggests that the movement would gain momentum if it concentrated its attention on the conventions that readers must learn and the procedures they must follow in interpreting the text. In a sense, this would dictate a search for rules and conventions. Eco's "The Myth of Superman" is a study of how certain of those conventions function in representing time within popular fiction — like comic books that must permit indefinite sequelae.

The most "rhetorical" structuralist analyst of the reader's role is Gerald Prince. In "Introduction to the Study of the Narratee," Prince, taking off from Wayne Booth's differentiation between *real* and *implied* authors, distinguishes between the *reader,* the human being who peruses the text, and the *narratee* (in French, *narrataire*), whom the narrator explicitly or implicitly addresses within the text.[4] The narratee also differs from the *ideal reader* ("one who would understand perfectly and would approve entirely the least of his words, the most subtle of his intentions") and from the *virtual reader,* "a certain type of reader" on whom the author bestows "certain qualities, faculties and inclinations according to his opinion of men in general . . . and according to the obligations he feels should be respected."[5]

Prince's narratee may be a very well-defined individual, like the "you" to whom Jean-Baptiste Clamence speaks in Albert Camus's *The Fall,* who is defined explicitly as a French lawyer on holiday in Amsterdam. Or the narratee may be defined only by class, like the middle-class lady or gentleman reading Balzac's *Père Goriot:* "You who hold this book with a white hand, you who settle back in a well-padded arm-chair." At other times, the narratee is defined by very subtle signals indeed, such as what has to be explained and what does not. (The narratee of Hemingway's *The Sun Also Rises* does not know what sort of drink Pernod is or the order of events in a bullfight.) The narratee's various functions are outlined by Prince:

> He constitutes a relay between the narrator and the reader, he helps establish the narrative framework, he serves to characterize the narrator, he emphasizes certain themes, he contributes to the development of the plot, he becomes the spokesman for the moral of the work.

What links Prince with Genette, Culler, and Eco, and with other semioticians like Michael Riffaterre, is his confidence that the parameters of reading can be specified and codified. But on this point, other structuralists, like Roland Barthes, have been less sure. In his late study, *The Pleasure of the Text* (1975), Barthes distinguishes between "*textes de plaisir,*" those readerly texts whose order can be uncovered, and

[4]In *Poétique*, no. 14 (1973): 177–96.
[5]See also Peter Rabinowitz, "Truth in Fiction: A Re-examination of Audiences," *Critical Inquiry* 4 (1977): 121–41.

"*textes de jouissance*" or texts of bliss, those writerly texts, like the novels of Alain Robbe-Grillet, whose indefinite ambiguity frustrates the structuralist design.

THE PSYCHOLOGY AND SOCIOLOGY OF THE AUDIENCE

In both the formalist-rhetorical and the semiotic-structuralist versions of reader-oriented criticism, the reader considered is generally the reader constructed within the tale: either the posited or implied reader for whom the rhetoric is contrived, or the narratee located explicitly, like a half-realized character, within the narrative framework. The psychological and sociological versions of reader-oriented criticism introduce a different reader, the *actual* reader whom Prince distinguishes from the objects of his concern. Psychoanalytic critics like Norman Holland and social psychologists like David Bleich leave the ideal reader behind in favor of the quivering and unpredictable individual reader and his or her genuine but subjective response. Shared by these theories is a relaxed acceptance of a fact most of us have observed: There are so many idiosyncratic differences between the response of one reader and that of another that, after listening to a group of people discussing a text, we sometimes wonder if they have all read the same words.

One of the earliest of the psychological theorists was Louise Rosenblatt, whose *Literature as Exploration* (1938) pioneered the notion of reading as a *transaction* between text and reader. Rosenblatt conceived of the reading process in this way:

> Through the medium of words, the text brings into the reader's consciousness certain concepts, certain sensuous experiences, certain images of things, people, actions, and scenes. The special meanings and, more particularly, the submerged associations that these words and images have for the individual reader will largely determine what the work communicates to *him*. The reader brings to the work personality traits, memories of past events, present needs and preoccupations, a particular mood of the moment, and a particular physical condition. These and many other elements in a never-to-be-duplicated combination determine his response to the peculiar contribution of the text.[6]

For Rosenblatt, each reading of a given text, even by a single individual, will be different, not because the text is inexhaustible but because each time we read it we are at least slightly different people. Despite this seemingly free-wheeling attitude, Rosenblatt retains the sense that though our response to the work of art is inevitably subjective, some sorts of subjectivity are preferable to others. Minimally, a reader's response should be to what is in the text, not to what is projected onto the text. At one point Rosenblatt warns that "an undistorted vision of the work of art requires a consciousness of one's own preconceptions and prejudices concerning the situations presented in the work, in contrast to the basic attitudes toward life assumed in the text." While it is useful to know what sorts of distortions one is likely to perpetrate on situations in literature and in life (psychologists call this "reality-testing"), the implication of Rosenblatt's warning is that it is possible to achieve an "undistorted" view of a text — something equivalent to an objective interpretation.

[6]Louise Rosenblatt, *Literature as Exploration* (rev. ed.; London: Heinemann, 1968), pp. 30–31.

Rosenblatt presents the reader's subjective response in terms of the common-sense psychology of prejudices and preoccupations; Norman Holland arrived at his reader-oriented criticism by way of orthodox Freudianism (see the introduction to Psychoanalytic Theory, p. 1106). His book *The Dynamics of Literary Response* (1968) presumed that the content of the text essentially determined the reader's response. Holland's text then had a manifest content (the story or poem, its events, its characters, its language, its form) and a latent content of primitive fantasy (oral aggression, anal withholding) hedged about and hidden by defenses (like symbolization or sublimation). In the reading transaction, the audience, in absorbing consciously the manifest content, would also be stimulated, under the table as it were, by the latent content, and the reader's own orality or anality would be gratified by the experience. In effect, the reader's experience would mirror the text's central fantasy and modes of defense.

As Holland explains in his introduction to *5 Readers Reading* — "The Question: Who Reads What How?" — reprinted in this chapter, this model gradually began to seem less and less satisfactory as it became clearer that the actual responses of self-aware individuals differed a great deal more than this approach could explain. In Holland's new model, the text still possesses manifest and latent content, but instead of assuming that all individuals will react to this content in much the same way, Holland suggests not only that different types of readers will react in different ways, but that even people with similar obsessions may react differently according to their individual styles of coping. In "UNITY IDENTITY TEXT SELF," Holland claims that "any individual shapes the materials the literary work offers him . . . to give him what he characteristically both wishes and fears, and . . . he also constructs his characteristic way of achieving what he wishes and defeating what he fears."

As an example, Holland invites us to imagine three readers responding to *Hamlet,* all of whom share a love-hate relationship with authority figures. The one whose characteristic defense against authority figures is to establish "alternatives in response to their demands" might find in the play "dualisms, split characters, the interplay of multiple plots." The one who reacts by "establishing limits and qualifications on authority" might stress "irony and occasional farce, Osric, Polonius, the gravediggers." The one who reacts with total compliance would respond "by seeking out and accepting, totally, uncritically, with a gee-gosh, the authority of its author."[7]

Holland would reject Rosenblatt's notion that an "undistorted" view of a text is possible; for Holland the solid ground upon which interpretation may be based is that of the individual personality itself. Texts may come and go, but the self, the personality style, the *identity theme* that determines the individual's repertoire of fantasies and defense mechanisms remains remarkably constant over time. What Holland suggests is that to the extent that a work of art threatens the reader's identity theme, the reader recomposes the text so that it replicates this theme. In effect, Holland substitutes the unity of the self for the unity of art. He usually speaks of the

---

[7]Norman Holland, "UNITY IDENTITY TEXT SELF," *PMLA* 90 (1975): 817–18.

self as though it were more objectively knowable than texts are. As Holland admits from time to time, however, we can know others' selves only through our own (and thus the issue of counter-transference between the reader of the text and the observer of that reader cannot be evaded). Furthermore, Holland's idea of the self — his notion that one's identity does not change as the result of life experience — is debatable. Whether the defensive reading of the text replicates precisely the self that began to read or whether the self is not at least slightly altered by the experience are questions that cannot be defined out of existence.

David Bleich's theory of reading, as presented in *Readings and Feelings* (1975) and *Subjective Criticism* (1978), is closer to social psychology than to orthodox Freudianism. Bleich places the reading of texts in a social setting — the classroom — where knowledge about art and life is synthesized by a group. For Bleich, the text is a symbolic object upon which readers act, and the reader's initial and private response to a text is totally subjective, including all sorts of idiosyncratic associations and feelings. Within the social setting of the classroom, the private response is "negotiated" into meaningful knowledge via the individual's sense of the group's purposes. In the course of articulating a response to a text under the social pressure of the group, the reader prunes away, or at least brackets off as private or irrelevant, those aspects of the response that may not apply to others or that are inconsistent with the aim of the class. The response to the text is generalized, placed within a context determined by the ideology of the group. Bleich feels that within the pedagogical setting, knowledge does not move from teacher to student but is constructed by students in accord with a sense of the group aim, which may be initially defined and articulated by a teacher. But Bleich's notions of reading apply beyond his posited pedagogical setting, since people often read or experience works of art within a social setting, with friends or family, and try to communicate a sense of the experience to others.

Any study of this process inevitably leads to the sociology of literature, a field in which one might expect the Marxists to have done a great deal of work. In practice, however, Marxist theorists have tended to shy away from empirical studies of the literary marketplace and how individuals and groups within social settings actually read texts. Two fine studies in literary sociology are Jeffrey Sammons's *Literary Sociology and Practical Criticism* (1977) and Janice Radway's *Reading the Romance: Women, Patriarchy, and Popular Literature* (1984). The former is a lucid overview of the major issues of literary sociology; the latter, a practical demonstration of what can be done in the field. Radway examines why women read popular romances, but instead of merely theorizing about the repressed American housewife and her need for escape, she uses interviews and questionnaires to study the responses of a community of romance readers. Radway's study is well grounded in reader-response theory, and her initial chapter presents an overview of literary reception.

A feminist approach to the reading process that is related to the work of both Bleich and Radway is contained in Judith Fetterley's *The Resisting Reader,* the introduction to which is reprinted in this chapter. Fetterley argues that the socialization produced by reading literature carries a special burden for the female reader.

Because most canonical authors are male, their subjects, styles, modes of symbolism, desires, and images for those desires all presume a masculine attitude toward the world, which the female reader is forced to adopt in the course of reception. Just as sexist language (such as the use of "man" to include both men and women) denigrates women by implying that they are not to be taken into account, Fetterley believes the shape of desire in narratives written by men "immasculates" women by forcing them to internalize the values of the other sex.

This is particularly true of American literature, according to Fetterley, who draws on Nina Baym's essay, "Melodramas of Beset Manhood,"[8] which argues that once the westward expansion of the frontier came to be defined as the central experience of American history, the crucial moments of American literature came to be seen as those that showed men encountering Mother Nature at the edge of civilization in the wilderness. Fetterley sharply suggests that if Baym is correct, then "America is female; to be American is to be male; and the quintessential American experience is betrayal by woman." Like Rabinowitz, Fetterley believes that the first step in contesting ideology is to make oneself aware of it, and she suggests that women become "resisting readers" of patriarchal texts, reading not passively with but actively against the grain of the masculine ideology that informs them.

While Fetterley argues cogently for the violence done to the female sensibility by the process of "immasculation," her own readings of male texts are sometimes not merely resistant but deeply obtuse. For example, her analysis reads Sherwood Anderson's "I Want To Know Why" as yet one more quintessential example of "betrayal by woman." In Fetterley's reading, the narrator, an adolescent boy mad for horses, feels the sting of disillusionment when he catches Jerry Tillford, a heroic jockey he idolizes, in the act of kissing a red-headed whore. What is lost in Fetterley's binary fixation on men and women is the polymorphous perversity of Anderson's tale: the way the narrator's libido attaches first to a powerful horse, and then to the rider who can successfully control it; the way the tale's climax speaks less of betrayed ideals than of homosocial desire and sexual jealousy.

THE PHENOMENOLOGISTS

In effect, formalist/structuralist theories have staked out the reader within the text, while psycho/social theories have been based on the actual reader outside the text. To the extent that there can be a middle ground, it is occupied by the phenomenological approaches to literature, which focus on literature as it is experienced by the thinking subject, the "I" in the center of our conscious world. Two traditions occupy this territory — one represented by the French phenomenologists Jean-Paul Sartre and Georges Poulet, the other by the German critics of the school of Constance, Wolfgang Iser and Hans Robert Jauss.

Although the late Jean-Paul Sartre has often been labeled a Marxist critic, his discussion of the role of the reader and the writer in *What Is Literature?* (1966) is thoroughly existentialist — and existentialism, as has often been observed, is the

[8]Nina Baym, "Melodramas of Beset Manhood: How Theories of American Literature Exclude Women Authors." *American Quarterly* 33, no. 2 (1981): 123–39.

ethical and political branch of phenomenology. The reader of "Why Write?" (see p. 662) will find major similarities between it and the theories of Georges Poulet.

Poulet's discussion of the act of reading emphasizes the way reading transforms the book-as-object — the heavy, dead, material thing — into a subject, an intelligence, a mind to which we subordinate our own.

> Whenever I read, I mentally pronounce an *I*, yet the *I* which I pronounce is not myself. This is true even when the hero of a novel is presented in the third person, and even when there is no hero and nothing but reflections or propositions. . . . Another *I*, who has replaced my own, and who will continue to do so as long as I read. . . . A second self takes over, a self which thinks and feels for me.

For Poulet, the purpose of this abdication of the self is, paradoxically, the further realization of the self:

> The annexation of my consciousness by . . . the other which is the work . . . in no way implies that I am the victim of any deprivation of consciousness. Everything happens, on the contrary, as though, from the moment I become a prey to what I read, I begin to share the use of my consciousness with . . . the conscious subject ensconced at the heart of the work.[9]

Poulet's characteristic images are close to those of Plato. The subjective consciousness of the text is *inbreathed* by the reader in a sort of passive inspiration, like the *enthousiasmós* of the *Ion* or the *Phaedrus*. For Iser and Jauss the relationship of author and reader is less like that of the demon and the human being it has possessed than that of the composer and the performer of a piece of music, a metaphor that suggests a new kind of connection between writer and reader. For the formalists and structuralists, the reader is essentially determined by the text. Fish's interpretive communities create the text themselves; the author's words are an indeterminate framework to which the community brings the meaning. Psychological critics like Holland view the text as fantasy material with which the reader copes, as with a disturbing dream. But Iser and Jauss perceive in the text the mutual dependence — the creative collaboration — of composer and performer. Although the composer is clearly the primary genius whose intentions must be respected, without the performer the composer would remain mute. Following the terminology of Roman Ingarden, Iser and Jauss speak of the text as being *concretized* by the reader: The vague and ideal word is in the reading process made flesh. The difference between Iser and Jauss is primarily one of perspective: Iser's interest is in the *act* of reading as it happens for each of us; Jauss's concern has been with the *history* of reading and the contribution a history of reception can make to the broader concerns of literary history.

For Iser, the reader's performative activity is called into play by the gaps that every text contains, since no text can be fully explicit about everything. In the process of reading, for example, we imagine what the hero and heroine look like in

---

[9]Georges Poulet, "Criticism and the Experience of Interiority," in Richard Macksey and Eugenio Donato, *The Structuralist Controversy: The Languages of Criticism and the Sciences of Man* (Baltimore: Johns Hopkins University Press, 1972), p. 56.

ways consistent with the descriptions we are given in the text; nevertheless, two readers' mental pictures of Tom Jones would be vastly different. (This, Iser says, is why film realizations of novels invariably make us say to ourselves, "That's not the way I pictured him.") But beyond filling in descriptions the text leaves indeterminate, the reader also imagines scenes the text leaves tacit, dialogue that is left unspoken, and so on. Furthermore, it is not just a matter of understanding and creating a full sense of illusion out of the words that are directly before the reader's eyes. In a novel, the reading process takes place within the flow of a narrative moving from a beginning through a middle to an end. As we read a given sentence, we may be forced to revise our understanding of what we have already read and processed, or to form expectations of what will happen in the future, expectations that may be fulfilled or shattered. Underlying this process, and guiding it, are "two main structural components within the text: first, a repertoire of familiar literary patterns and recurrent literary themes, together with allusions to familiar social and historical contexts; and second, techniques or strategies used to set the familiar against the unfamiliar." The text in any mature work of art, in other words, depends on the reader's prior understanding of the themes and conventions of story-telling, but it works *against* those conventions as much as it employs them in order to *defamiliarize* the reader, who would otherwise be bored by a predictable text.

During the last two hundred years, according to Iser's *The Implied Reader,* these general principles have been worked out in the English novel in very different ways. The reader in the eighteenth century was "guided — directly or indirectly, through affirmation or through negation — toward a conception of human nature and of reality." The nineteenth-century reader, by contrast, "was not told what part he was to play. Instead he had to discover the fact that society had imposed a part on him, the object being for him eventually to take up a critical attitude toward this imposition." Readers of the Victorian novel, therefore, were nudged into making the correct discoveries for themselves. Both of these modes depend upon the reader's capacity for subscribing to the illusion provoked by the text. The twentieth-century novel, in contrast, insists on rupturing these illusions and calling attention to its own use of technique — all this in order

> to provoke the reader into establishing for himself the connections between perception and thought. . . . In this way he may then be given the chance of discovering himself, both in and through his constant involvement in "home-made" illusions and fictions.[10]

For Iser, the history of the novel is the history of the ways in which writers created gaps for their readers to fill, and to an extent, his ideas are easily assimilated to those of rhetorical critics like Peter Rabinowitz. For Hans Robert Jauss, on the other hand, literary history is as much the history of the reader as of the canonized authors, or to be more accurate, of the relationship between writing and the reading public that consumes and stimulates its production. These ideas are based on the philosophy of Hans-Georg Gadamer (see p. 718), whose theories of interpretation

---

[10]Wolfgang Iser, *The Implied Reader: Patterns of Communication in Prose Fiction from Bunyan to Beckett* (Baltimore: Johns Hopkins University Press, 1974), pp. xiii–xiv.

turn on the positive contributions made by our prejudices. Normally, "prejudice" has a negative connotation when it refers to one cause of our injustice to others, but for Gadamer and his pupils, these prejudices (in German, *Vorurteilungen*) are what allow us to understand the changing world at all. Our preunderstandings give us a settled context, a *horizon of expectations,* against which we can place and evaluate the new. And our horizon of expectations is constantly changing as our life experience adds to and alters our framework of vision.

In literary terms, there is a dialogical relation between the text and the reading public. The public reads the text from within its current horizon of expectations — that set of cultural, ethical, and aesthetic norms current at any given moment — and attempts to bring the work within those horizons. For some works, like popular literature meant for instant consumption, there will be no problem in fitting the text into such a horizon, but other works may challenge the audience's horizon of expectations along one or more fronts. Such works may succeed in changing the preunderstanding of the reading public, or a substantial portion of it, as was the case with Flaubert's *Madame Bovary.* On the other hand, such works may fail to engage the audience entirely and may be forgotten; or, like Melville's *Moby-Dick,* they may be read, but their most individual qualities may be ignored because they cannot be assimilated to the preunderstanding of the day. Forgotten or misread works, however, may be rediscovered by a later audience, when the horizon of expectations has, so to speak, caught up with them. Change in the horizon is produced partly by literary texts themselves, whose success creates a market and stimulates imitation by other authors, and partly by changes in economic, social, and political conditions, which make ideas and relations within texts more or less attractive.

For Jauss the writing of literary history would require that we recreate the horizon of expectations of the reading public for any given period. This we can piece together, partly from the texts themselves, and partly from the public and private responses of various levels of the reading public: other authors, publishers, critics, and private consumers. Creating the materials out of which a literary history might be written would require both synchronic and diachronic studies. One might begin with a synchronic study, in effect taking a "snapshot" of the literary world at a given date (Jauss himself has done a study of the horizon of expectations in France in 1857, the year of *Madame Bovary* and of Baudelaire's *Fleurs du Mal*), and by comparing such "snapshots" at various dates, put together a sense of how these horizons changed over time. In addition, diachronic studies, like histories of the reception of a given text from its publication to the present day, would be a useful supplement to the snapshots.

These "time-lapse photos" would give a stronger sense of how literary opinion shifts over the centuries (Jauss has produced a study over time of the reception of Baudelaire's "Spleen" poems). The end product will take a long time to produce, given the sheer amount of research into the reception of texts the method requires. But the result proposed is a literary history that goes beyond the "scissors-and-paste" histories detailing the lives and works of those authors that are currently valued. The history Jauss envisions would allow us to understand the evolution of textual production in relation to changes in the cultural scene that generated that evolution, including many factors we currently ignore, such as those evanescent productions whose popularity in one age were a passport to obscurity in the next.

As one might expect, the Marxists were most offended by Jauss's insistence that literary history needed to be reformed in order to include the participation of the readers who made up the market for literature. One might have thought them the group most concerned with the influence of the individual in a mass society, yet Jauss's competition with them exposed their neglect of the group they theoretically most favored. In fact, the publication of "Literary History as a Challenge to Literary Theory" provoked a decade of quarreling between the reception theorists of Constance and the Marxists across what was then the border with East Germany. By the 1980s, however, both parties saw that what they had in common dwarfed their area of contention, and indeed, some post-Althusserian Marxists (like the British Tony Bennett) have proposed programs for revamping literary history using methods that closely resemble Jauss's proposals. In addition to these quarrels with the Marxists, Jauss's theories have also provoked a large number of scholars, not just in Germany but in England and North America as well, into undertaking reception studies, which are just beginning to produce the "snapshots" and "time-lapse photos" of the audience that will eventuate in the new literary history Jauss prophesied.

But as Jauss shows in "The Three Horizons of Reading," reprinted below, the process of historical reconstruction operates not just at the macro level but on the micro level each time we read a text and situate ourselves against it. In *Truth and Method*, Jauss's mentor, Hans-Georg Gadamer, described the process of reading as involving three stages that are distinct. Understanding is the basic hermeneutic process of uncovering what the poetic text means; interpretation involves uncovering how the poetic text works on us; application involves understanding the poet and oneself, the reader, in their historical relation to each other. These stages may actually occur simultaneously, and they influence each other, so Jauss is well aware that he is artificially separating them. All of them involve asking questions of a text and receiving answers. In understanding, for example, our immediate response to a text is to mis-understand it because we take the words in senses that are easy and familiar to us, but then as we project where the text is going, we are brought up short when it contradicts our expectations. We revise our sense and try again, and by trial and error arrive at an understanding that is consistent and coherent. The same process of dialogue of reader with text occurs in the other stages, which naturally affect one another: as we understand a text in terms of its era, we foreground verbal meanings that would be implausibly archaic in a contemporary text; as we come to understand a passage as metaphorical, interpretation is given something more to do. And, as Jauss shows, this complex hermeneutic process not only reveals the text, it reveals to us who *we* are as its interpreters.

COGNITIVE THEORY

The most recent of the reader-response approaches is that of cognitive theory. If one wishes, one can trace cognitive theory as far back as Plato, whose dialogues are as much about knowing as about being. But the contemporary discipline — which is about as *inter*disciplinary as such areas can be — probably got its start from Noam Chomsky, who around 1960 conjectured that natural languages are too similar in their deep structures to be the random product of culture, and are learned too quickly to be entirely the behaviorist result of the verbal stimuli children receive and their rewarded responses. Chomsky argued that children are born with a "Language Acquisition Device" hard-wired into their brains.

While his theory is still contested, the controversy sparked widespread investigations into the relationship of mind and brain, by which it became clear that, whether the tracks are hard-wired from birth or laid down by experience, the brain processes language in very specific sites. Neurologists examining patients with aphasias caused by brain lesions had long ago discovered that we store people's names in a different site from common nouns, and that certain lesions prevented people from understanding metaphor and others metonymy. Cognitive theory has progressed through advances in neural science that have enabled us, without creating brain lesions in healthy subjects, to correlate specific thought processes with activity in specific areas of the brain by mapping which sites demand greater blood flow or demonstrate greater electrical conductivity. We now know that we store short-term memories in different places from long-term memories, and it is suspected that the vivid dreams we experience while unconscious may be, *pace* Freud, an artifact of the process of sorting and "dumping" the data of the previous day.

Another accelerant to cognitive theory has been the growth and ubiquity of computer data processing since 1970, since almost all of us use and many of us are able to create programs — sets of instructions with feedback loops — that enable relatively simple machines based on silicon on/off switches to solve difficult mathematical problems or comb with enormous speed through a mass of data for the precise bit of information we want. Our sense of how linear programming works has given us some ideas about how that computer made of meat between our ears operates; it has become reasonably clear that, given the slow speed of conductivity in the neurons of our brain, we cannot possibly be operating by linear programming, that the human brain instead performs more like a multitude of separate simple computers wired together ("parallel processing").

One consequence of the parallel development of neuroscience and cognitive theory is that the relationship between nature and culture has, in some areas, become murkier. We can think of metaphor and metonymy as tropes of purely literary interest to a Longinus or a Paul de Man, but cognitive psychologists view such verbal analogues and connections as deeply enmeshed in the ways human beings learn their world: they are the tools we think with. Telling stories artistically, as Homer and Proust did, is a way to immortality, but basic narratives, telling each other stories about predators or food supplies, seems to have been a major factor in why homo sapiens succeeded in the struggle for existence.

The essays included below, by Elaine Scarry, Mark Turner, and Lisa Zunshine, involve quite different applications of cognitive psychology to literature, but they are similar in the way each of them attempts to get inside the process of reading, to understand how the brain processes literary texts. Most other reader-response theory, whatever its philosophical base, has posited an opaque black box between the literary text, on the one hand, and the response readers are able to verbalize after reflecting on their experience. That is not true here. Mark Turner's essay invites us to understand how we process complex metaphors. Elaine Scarry's is an effort to understand under what circumstances the ekphrastic function of descriptive language — its ability to paint pictures of a virtual world — can become sharp and vivid rather than feeble or impoverished. Lisa Zunshine's demonstration, in line with George Miller's experiments with short-term memory, investigates why and under what circumstances certain kinds of high modernist narrative flirt with the limits of our ability to process them. Cognitive theory, by thinking "outside the box," is able, sometimes with surprising results, to get inside that box.

Interest in the reader is a late development in critical theory. As a topic for investigation, it has attracted each of the major schools of thought, from Marxism through structuralism and feminism to deconstruction. It is likely that, following its neglect in the wake of the "affective fallacy," critical understanding of the audience — in all its various manifestations — has changed more in the past twenty-five years than in the previous two thousand.

Selected Bibliography

Altick, Richard. *The English Common Reader: A Social History of the Mass Reading Public, 1800–1900.* Chicago: University of Chicago Press, 1957.

Barthes, Roland. *The Pleasure of the Text.* New York: Hill and Wang, 1975.

Baym, Nina. "Melodramas of Beset Manhood: How Theories of American Literature Exclude Women Authors." *American Quarterly* 33 (1981): 123–39.

Bleich, David. *Readings and Feelings: An Introduction to Subjective Criticism.* Urbana, IL: National Council of Teachers of English, 1975.

———. *Subjective Criticism.* Baltimore: Johns Hopkins University Press, 1978.

Booth, Wayne C. *The Rhetoric of Fiction.* Chicago: University of Chicago Press, 1961; 2nd ed. 1983.

———. *A Rhetoric of Irony.* Chicago: University of Chicago Press, 1974.

———. *The Company We Keep: Ethical Criticism and the Ethics of Reading.* Berkeley: University of California Press, 1988.

Butte, George. *I Know That You Know That I Know: Narrating Subjects from Moll Flanders to Marnie.* Columbus: Ohio State University Press, 2004.

Carruthers, Peter, and Peter K. Smith, eds. *Theories of Theories of Mind.* Cambridge: Cambridge University Press, 1996.

Cruse, Amy. *The Englishman and His Books in the Early Nineteenth Century.* London: George G. Harrap, 1930.

Eco, Umberto. *The Role of the Reader: Explorations in the Semiotics of Texts.* Bloomington: Indiana University Press, 1979.

Escarpit, Robert. *Sociology of Literature.* Painesville, OH: Lake Erie College Press, 1965.

———. "The Sociology of Literature." *International Encyclopaedia of Social Science.* Vol. 9. New York: Macmillan, 1968, pp. 417–25.

Esrock, Ellen J. *The Reader's Eye: Visual Imaging as Reader Response.* Baltimore: Johns Hopkins University Press, 1994.

Fetterley, Judith. *The Resisting Reader: A Feminist Approach to American Fiction.* Bloomington: Indiana University Press, 1978.

——. "Reading about Reading: 'A Jury of Her Peers,' 'The Murders in the Rue Morgue,' and 'The Yellow Wallpaper.'" In *Gender and Reading: Essays on Readers, Texts, and Contexts,* ed. Elizabeth Flynn and Patrocinio Schweickart. Baltimore: Johns Hopkins University Press, 1986, pp. 147–64.

Fish, Stanley. *Self-Consuming Artifacts: The Experience of Seventeenth-Century Literature.* Berkeley: University of California Press, 1972.

——. *Is There a Text in This Class? The Authority of Interpretive Communities.* Cambridge: Harvard University Press, 1980.

——. *Doing What Comes Naturally: Change, Rhetoric, and the Practice of Theory in Literary and Legal Studies.* Durham: Duke University Press, 1989.

Flynn, Elizabeth A. "Gender and Reading." *College English* 45 (1983): 236–53.

Gadamer, Hans-Georg. *Truth and Method.* London: Sheed and Ward, 1975.

Harris, Paul L. *The Work of Imagination.* Oxford: Blackwell, 2001.

Hohendahl, Peter Uwe. "Introduction to Reception Aesthetics." *New German Critique* 10 (1977): 29–63.

Holland, Norman N. *The Dynamics of Literary Response.* New York: Oxford University Press, 1968.

——. *5 Readers Reading.* New Haven: Yale University Press, 1975.

——. "I-ing Film." *Critical Inquiry* 12 (1986): 654–71.

——. "I-ing Lacan." In *Criticism and Lacan: Essays and Dialogue on Language, Structure, and the Unconscious,* ed. Patrick C. Hogan and Lalita Pandit. Athens: University of Georgia Press, 1990, pp. 97–108.

——. *The Critical I.* New York: Columbia University Press, 1992.

Holub, Robert C. *Reception Theory: A Critical Introduction.* London: Methuen, 1984.

Ingarden, Roman. *The Cognition of the Literary Work of Art.* Evanston, IL: Northwestern University Press, 1973.

Iser, Wolfgang. *The Implied Reader: Patterns of Communication in Prose Fiction from Bunyan to Beckett.* Baltimore: Johns Hopkins University Press, 1974.

——. *The Act of Reading: A Theory of Aesthetic Response.* Baltimore: Johns Hopkins University Press, 1978.

——. "Towards a Literary Anthropology." In *The Future of Literary Theory,* ed. Ralph Cohen. New York: Routledge, 1989, pp. 208–28.

——. "Fictionalizing: The Anthropological Dimension of Literary Fictions." *New Literary History* 21 (1990): 939–55.

Jauss, Hans Robert. *Aesthetic Experience and Literary Hermeneutics.* Minneapolis: University of Minnesota Press, 1982.

——. *Toward an Aesthetics of Reception,* trans. Timothy Bahti. Minneapolis: University of Minnesota Press, 1982.

Johnson, Mark. *The Body in the Mind: The Bodily Basis of Meaning, Imagination and Reason.* Chicago: University of Chicago Press, 1987.

Kavanagh, Thomas M., ed. *The Limits of Theory.* Stanford: Stanford University Press, 1989.

Koelb, Clayton. *The Incredulous Reader: Literature and the Function of Disbelief.* Ithaca: Cornell University Press, 1984.

Leavis, Q. D. *Fiction and the Reading Public.* London: Chatto and Windus, 1932.

Lesser, Simon O. *Fiction and the Unconscious.* Boston: Vintage, 1957.

Mailloux, Steven J. *Interpretive Conventions.* Ithaca: Cornell University Press, 1982.

Miles, David H. "Literary Sociology: Some Introductory Notes." *German Quarterly* 48 (1975): 20–45.

Miller, Owen J. "Reading as a Process of Reconstruction: A Critique of Recent Structuralist Formulations." In *Interpretation of Narrative,* ed. Mario J. Valdès and Owen J. Miller. Toronto: University of Toronto Press, 1978, pp. 19–27.

Naumann, Manfred. "Literary Production and Reception." *New Literary History* 8 (1976): 107–26.

Ortony, Andrew, ed. *Metaphor and Thought.* Cambridge: Cambridge University Press, 1993.

Phelan, James. *Reading People, Reading Plots: Character, Progression, and the Interpretation of Narrative.* Chicago: University of Chicago Press, 1989.

———. *Living to Tell about It: A Rhetoric and Ethics of Character Narration.* Ithaca: Cornell University Press, 2005.

Poulet, Georges. "Criticism and the Experience of Interiority." In *The Structuralist Controversy: The Languages of Criticism and the Sciences of Man,* ed. Richard Macksey and Eugenio Donato. Baltimore: Johns Hopkins University Press, 1972.

Preston, John. *The Created Self: The Reader's Role in Eighteenth-Century Fiction.* New York: Barnes and Noble, 1970.

Prince, Gerald. "Introduction to the Study of the Narratee." *Poétique* 14 (1973): 177–96.

Rabinowitz, Peter. "Truth in Fiction: A Reexamination of Audiences." *Critical Inquiry* 4 (1977): 121–41.

———. *Before Reading.* Ithaca: Cornell University Press, 1987.

———. "Readings of Narrative, 1937–1987." *PMLA* 108 (1993): 410–532.

———. "'Betraying the Sender': The Rhetoric and Ethics of Fragile Texts." *Narrative* 2 (1994): 201–13.

Radway, Janice A. *Reading the Romance: Women, Patriarchy, and Popular Literature.* Chapel Hill: University of North Carolina Press, 1984.

Reichert, John. *Making Sense of Literature.* Chicago: University of Chicago Press, 1977.

Richards, I. A. *Practical Criticism: A Study of Literary Judgment.* New York: Harcourt, Brace, 1935.

Richardson, Alan, and Francis F. Steen, eds. *Literature and the Cognitive Revolution.* A special issue. *Poetics Today* 23 (2002).

Richter, David H. "The Reader as Ironic Victim." *Novel* 14 (1981): 135–51.

———. "The Reception of the Gothic Novel in the 1790's." In *The Idea of the Novel in the Eighteenth Century,* ed. Robert Uphaus. East Lansing, MI: Colleagues Press, 1988.

———. "The Unguarded Prison: Reception Theory, Structural Marxism, and the Structure of Literary History." *The Eighteenth Century: Theory and Interpretation* 30 (1989): 1–17.

Rosenblatt, Louise. *The Reader, the Text, the Poem: The Transactional Theory of the Literary Work.* Carbondale: Southern Illinois University Press, 1978.

———. *Literature as Exploration.* New York: Modern Language Association, 1983.

Sammons, Jeffrey. *Literary Sociology and Practical Criticism.* Bloomington: Indiana University Press, 1977.

Sartre, Jean-Paul. *What Is Literature?* New York: Philosophical Library, 1966.

Scarry, Elaine. *Dreaming by the Book.* New York: Farrar, Straus & Giroux, 1999.

Schücking, L. L. *The Sociology of Literary Taste,* 3rd ed. Chicago: University of Chicago Press, 1966.

Spolsky, Ellen. *Gaps in Nature: Literary Interpretation and the Modular Mind.* Albany: State University of New York Press, 1993.

Stockwell, Peter. *Cognitive Poetics: An Introduction.* London: Routledge, 2002.

Suleiman, Susan, and Inge Crosman, eds. *The Reader in the Text: Essays on Audience and Interpretation.* Princeton: Princeton University Press, 1980.

Turner, Mark. *Death Is the Mother of Beauty: Mind, Metaphors, and Criticism.* Chicago: University of Chicago Press, 1987.

———. *Reading Minds: The Study of English in the Age of Cognitive Science.* Princeton: Princeton University Press, 1991.

———. *The Literary Mind.* New York: Oxford University Press, 1996.

Tompkins, Jane P., ed. *Reader-Response Criticism: From Formalism to Post-Structuralism.* Baltimore: Johns Hopkins University Press, 1980.

Weimann, Robert. "'Reception Aesthetics' and the Crisis of Literary History." *Clio* 5 (1975): 3–33.

Zunshine, Lisa. *Why We Read Fiction: An Explanation from Cognitive Theory.* Columbus: Ohio State University Press, forthcoming 2006.

Hans Robert Jauss

1921–1997

Hans Robert Jauss has been acknowledged the leader and principal theorist of the movement termed "reception aesthetics," which views literary history as formed, at least in part, by the readings and assessments that texts have received throughout the past. Jauss was born in 1921 and served on the Eastern front in the Waffen-SS *throughout World War II. He completed his Ph.D. at the University of Heidelberg and taught there, and at Münster and Giessen, before joining the faculty at Konstanz, where he was professor of Romance languages and literature from 1967 until his death. He held visiting professorships at the Sorbonne, Columbia, Yale, Berkeley, and UCLA. Jauss's prodigious scholarly output (which also comprises over 75 articles, in addition to editions and translations) includes* Erinnerung in Marcel Proust's À la Recherche du temps perdue *(Memory in Marcel Proust's Remembrance of Things Past, 1955);* Untersuchungen zu mittelalterischen Tierdichtung *(Researches into Medieval Beast Literature, 1959);* La génèse de la poésie allegorique française au Moyen-Age *(The Origin of Medieval French Allegory, 1962);* Literaturgeschichte als Provokation der Literaturwissenschaft *(Literary History as a Challenge to Literary Theory, 1967);* Kleine Apologie der ästhetischen Erfahrung *(Short Defense of Aesthetic Experience, 1972);* Alternität und Modernität der mittelalterischen Literatur *(Ancientness and Modernity in Medieval Literature, 1977); and* Ästhetische Erfahrung und literarische Hermeneutik *(Aesthetic Experience and Literary Hermeneutics, 1977). Jauss's major essays have been translated into English and are collected in* Toward an Aesthetics of Reception *(1978),* Aesthetic Experience and Literary Hermeneutics *(1982), and* Question and Answer: Forms of Dialogic Understanding *(1989). "The Three Horizons of Reading" is excerpted from "The Poetic Text within the Change of Horizons of Reading: The Example of Baudelaire's 'Spleen II,'" which in turn appeared in* Toward an Aesthetics of Reception.

[The Three Horizons of Reading] from Toward an Aesthetics of Reception

I. THE DISTINGUISHING OF VARIOUS HORIZONS OF READING AS A PROBLEM FOR LITERARY HERMENEUTICS

The following study has the character of an experiment. I will attempt to distinguish methodologically into three stages of interpretation that which normally remains undistinguished in the interpretive practice of philological commentary as well as textual analysis. If it is the case there that understanding and interpretation as well as immediate reception and reflective exegesis of a literary text are at once blended in the course of interpretation, then here the horizon of a first, aesthetically perceptual reading will be distinguished from that of a second, retrospectively interpretive reading. To this I will add a third, historical reading that begins with the reconstruction of the horizon of expectations in which the poem "Spleen" inscribed itself with the appearance of the *Fleurs du mal*, and that then will follow the history of its reception or "readings" up to the most recent one, that is, my own.

The three steps of my interpretation — no methodological innovation of mine — are grounded in the theory that the hermeneutic process is to be conceived as a unity of the three moments of understanding (*intelligere*), interpretation (*interpretare*), and application (*applicare*).[1] Hans-Georg Gadamer deserves the credit for having brought the significance of this triadic unity of the hermeneutic process back to light.[2] This unity has determined, in a manner more or less one-sidedly realized, all textual interpretation from time immemorial; it was explicitly formulated by pietistic hermeneutics during the Enlightenment as the doctrine of the three *subtilitates*; it became

discredited with the victory of the historicist and positivist ideal of scholarship; and it took center stage in the development of theory with the renewal of theological and juridical hermeneutics.[3] The obvious backwardness of literary hermeneutics is explainable by the facts that here the hermeneutic process reduces to interpretation alone, that no theory of understanding has been developed for texts of an aesthetic character, and that the question of "application" has been relegated to book reviewers' criticism as an unscholarly one. Gadamer's suggestion, "to redefine the hermeneutics of the human studies from the perspective of the hermeneutics of jurisprudence and theology," is thus an opportunity for literary hermeneutics,[4] for the sake of which I ask the question whether and how the hermeneutic unity of all three moments realizes itself in the interpretation of a poetic text.

I direct my hermeneutic experiment at this problem by dividing into three steps the interpretation of a poem that already has a history of reception. The steps might be described phenomenologically as three successive readings. In dividing the hermeneutic process into three steps, the distinction between the three readings must be fabricated to a certain degree; yet only in this manner is it possible to demonstrate what kind of understanding, interpretation, and application might be proper to a text of aesthetic character. If there is to be an autonomous literary hermeneutics, it must prove itself in the fact — as Peter Szondi correctly demanded — "that it does not just consider the aesthetic character of the text to be interpreted in an appreciation that only follows upon the interpretation, but rather that makes the aesthetic character the premise of the interpretation itself."[5] This premise cannot be fulfilled with

Translated by Timothy Bahti.

[1] See pp. 721–37 for an explanation of these Gadamerian distinctions.

[2] *Wahrheit und Methode* (Tübingen, 1960), pp. 290 ff. Available in English as *Truth and Method*, translation edited by Garrett Barden and John Cumming (New York, 1975). [Jauss]

[3] Jauss is reminding us that interpretive method was codified first for the interpretation of the Bible and of legal codes.

[4] Ibid., p. 294. [Jauss]

[5] *Einführung in die literarische Hermeneutik* (Frankfurt, 1975), p. 13. [Jauss]

the methods of traditional stylistics (in the sense of Leo Spitzer's "critique des beautés"),[6] linguistic poetics, and "textual analysis" alone. Whatever may be recognized in the final texture of the text, in the closed whole of its structure, as a verbal function bearing significance or as aesthetic equivalency, always presupposes something provisionally understood. That which the poetic text, thanks to its aesthetic character, provisionally offers to understanding proceeds from its processlike effect; for this reason it cannot be directly deduced from a description of its final structure as "artifact," however comprehensively this might have construed its "levels" and its aesthetic equivalencies. Today, the structural description of texts can and should be grounded hermeneutically in an analysis of the process of reception: the debate between Roman Jakobson and Claude Lévi-Strauss, and Michael Riffaterre teaches as much.[7] The poetic text can be disclosed in its aesthetic function only when the poetic structures that are read out of the finished aesthetic object as its characteristics are retranslated, from out of the objectification of the description, back into the process of the experience of the text that allows the reader to take part in the genesis of the aesthetic object. Put another way, and using the formulation with which Michael Riffaterre in 1962 introduced the turn

from the structural description to the analysis of the reception of the poetic text: the text, which structural poetics described as the endpoint and sum of the devices actualized in it, must from now on be considered as the point of departure for its aesthetic effect; and this must be investigated in the succession of the pregiven elements of the reception that govern the process of aesthetic perception, and thereby also limit the arbitrariness of readings that are supposedly merely subjective.[8]

With the experiment begun here, I go further and in another direction than Riffaterre, who recently developed his structural stylistics into a *Semiotics of Poetry* (1978), which is more interested in the pregiven elements of reception and in the "rules of actualization" than in the aesthetic activity of the reader who takes up or receives the text.[9] I, on the other hand, seek to divide this activity into the two hermeneutic acts, understanding and interpretation, in that I distinguish reflective interpretation as the phase of a second reading from immediate understanding within aesthetic perception as the phase of the first reading. This distinction was necessitated by my interest in making, once and for all, the aesthetic character of the poetic text expressly and demonstrably into the premise of its interpretation. To recognize how the poetic text, thanks to its aesthetic character, allows us to initially perceive and understand something, the analysis cannot begin with the question of the significance of the particular within the achieved form of the whole; rather, it must pursue the significance still left open in the process of perception that the text, like a "score," indicates for the reader. The investigation of the aesthetic character proper to the poetic text, in distinction to the theological, the juridical, or even the philosophical one, must follow the orientation

---

[6]The term *critique des beautés* is from the French critic Chateaubriand (1768–1848), who counseled commentators on literature to discuss the good points of a text rather than (as had been traditional) enumerate its faults. Leo Spitzer (1887–1960), a founder of the post–World War II comparative literature movement, attempted to use the analytic methods of linguistics to isolate moments of stylistic excellence. Jauss's snarky reference to Spitzer suggests his dissatisfaction with locating linguistic structures "out there" in the text rather than in how the text is performed by a reader.

[7]R. Posner drew this conclusion from the debate: "Obviously, neither the prosody nor the semantics of the poem can be revealed through the mere description of the written text — to say nothing of the aesthetic code of the poem that above all makes use of these textual levels. Similarly to how one can get the prosodic indicators right only by beginning with their acoustic realization, one also can only describe the semantics adequately if one begins with a text that is already fully received and understood." See his "Strukturalismus in der Gedichtsinterpretation," *Sprache im technischen Zietalter* 29 (1969), pp. 27–58, esp. p. 47. [Jauss]

[8]Now in *Essais de stylistique structurale* (Paris, 1971), pp. 307 ff.; cf. his "The Reader's Perception of Narrative," in *Interpretation of Narrative* (Toronto, 1978). [Jauss]

[9]Ibid., p. 29: "Instead of only looking for rules regulating narrative structures, I propose that we look for rules regulating actualization of such structures in the text, that is, regulating the very performance of literature as communication." On his "reader-reception modes," see *Semiotics of Poetry* (Bloomington, Indiana, 1978), pp. 115 ff. [Jauss]

given to aesthetic perception through the construction of the text, the suggestion of its rhythm, and the gradual achievement of its form.

In the poetic text, aesthetic understanding is primarily directed at the process of perception; therefore it is hermeneutically related to the horizon of expectations of the first reading — which often, especially with historically distant texts or with hermetic[10] lyrics, can only be made visible in its shaped coherence and its fullness of significance through repeated readings. The explicit interpretation in the second and in each further reading also remains related to the horizon of expectations of the first, i.e., perceptual reading — as long as the interpreter claims to make concrete a specific coherence of significance from out of the horizon of meaning of this text, and would not, for example, exercise the license of allegories to translate the meaning of the text into a foreign context, that is, to give it a significance transcending the horizon of meaning and thereby the intentionality of the text.[11] The interpretation of a poetic text always presupposes aesthetic perception as its pre-understanding; it may only concretize significances that appeared or could have appeared possible to the interpreter within the horizon of his preceding reading.

Gadamer's dictum, "To understand means to understand something as an answer,"[12] must therefore be limited in regard to the poetic text. Here it can only concern the secondary act of *interpretive* understanding insofar as this concretizes a specific significance as an answer to a question; it may not, however, concern the primary act of *perceptual* understanding that introduces and constitutes the aesthetic experience of the poetic text. To be sure, aesthetic perception also always already includes understanding. For as is well known, the poetic text as an aesthetic object makes possible, in contrast to everyday perception that degenerates into a norm, a mode of perception at once more complex and more meaningful, which as aesthetic pleasure is able to rejuvenate cognitive vision or visual recognition (*aisthesis*).[13] Yet this accomplishment of aisthesis, capable of meaningful understanding, is not already in need of interpretation, and thus it also does not necessarily have the character of an answer to an implicit or explicit question. If it should hold for the reception of a poetic text that here — as Gadamer himself, following Husserl, has formulated it — "the eidetic reduction is spontaneously achieved in aesthetic experience,"[14] then the understanding within the act of aesthetic perception may not be assigned to an interpretation that — by the very fact that something is understood as an answer — reduces the surplus of meaning of the poetic text to one of its possible utterances. In the eidetic reduction of aesthetic perception, the reflective reduction on the part of the interpretation that would understand the text as an answer to an implicit question, can for the time being remain suspended, while at the same time an understanding can be at work allowing the reader to experience language in its power and, thereby, the world in its fullness of significance.

The distinguishing of reflective interpretation from the perceptual understanding of a poetic text is thus not as artificial as it might at first have seemed. It is made possible throughout the self-evident horizonal structure of the experience of rereading. Every reader is familiar with the experience that the significance of a poem often discloses itself only on rereading, after returning from the end to the beginning. Here the experience of the first reading becomes the horizon of the second one: what the reader received in the progressive

---

[10]Mystical or private.

[11]Jauss hints here at the temptation to "creatively misread" difficult texts by turning their private symbols into an allegory we manufacture out of whole cloth.

[12]In a still unpublished lecture on literary hermeneutics, Dubrovnik, 1978. [Jauss]

[13]On this, see my *Ästhetische Erfahrung und literarische Hermeneutik* (Munich, 1979), p. 62 and chapter A 6. This book is forthcoming in the English translation of Michael Shaw from the University of Minnesota Press. [Jauss]

[14]The Dubrovnik lecturer (see note [12]). *Wahrheit und Methode*, p. 291, touches on my qualification that in aesthetic perception understanding certainly implies interpretation, but does not at the same time have to articulate it as a theme. "Interpretation is not an act that occasionally and retrospectively attaches to understanding; rather, understanding is always interpretation, and interpretation therefore the explicit form of understanding." [Jauss]

horizon of interpretation. If one adds that the interpretation itself may in turn become the foundation for an application — more precisely, that a text from the past is of interest not only in reference to its primary context, but that it is also interpreted to disclose a possible significance for the contemporary situation — then what comes to light is that the triadic unity of understanding, interpretation, and application (such as it is accomplished in the hermeneutic process) corresponds to the three horizons of relevance — thematic, interpretive, and motivational — the mutual relation of which, according to Alfred Schütz, determines the constitution of the subjective experience of the life-world [*Lebenswelt*].[15]

In executing the experiment of a repeated reading that will seek to identify thematically the three acts of the hermeneutic process, I may take up and develop further notions that Michael Riffaterre, Wolfgang Iser, and Roland Barthes have introduced into the analysis of the processes of reception. Riffaterre analyzes the course of the reception of a poem as the play of anticipation and correction conditioned through the categories of equivalence of tension, surprise, disappointment, irony, and comedy. An "overdetermination" is common to these categories that demands attention through the respective correction of an expectation, thereby steering the reader's course of reception and, consequently, progressively determining the meaning of the text to be interpreted. In my experience, Riffaterre's categories are more appropriate to narrative texts than to lyric ones: the reading of a poem awakens not so much tension regarding its continuation, as the expectation of what I would like to call lyrical consistency — the expectation that the lyrical movement will allow one to grasp verse by verse a coherence at first hidden, and thus allow the spectacle of the world to arise anew from a particular situation. Innovation and recognition become complementary in lyrical aisthesis, so that the positive category of satisfied expectation may be placed alongside Riffaterre's negative categories of surprise and disappointment, in which he speaks of satisfied expectation only

pejoratively, as if it were equivalent to the effect of a cliché.[16,17]

Finally, his model for the reception of a poem presupposes the ideal reader ("superreader") who is not only equipped with the sum total of literary historical knowledge available today, but also is capable of consciously registering every aesthetic impression and referring it back to the text's structure of effect. Thus the interpreting competence overshadows the analysis of the perceptual understanding, even though Riffaterre interprets within the open horizon of the syntagmatic unfolding and correction of the system. To escape this dilemma, I have not fabricated something like a "naive reader," but rather have transposed myself into the role of a reader with the educational horizon of our contemporary present. The role of this historical reader should presuppose that one is experienced in one's associations with lyrics, but that one can initially suspend one's literary historical or linguistic competence, and put in its place the capacity occasionally to wonder during the course of the reading, and to express this wonder in the form of questions. Beside this historical reader from 1979, I have placed a commentator with scholarly competence, who deepens the aesthetic impressions of the reader whose understanding takes the form of pleasure, and who refers back to the text's structures of effect as much as possible. (In what follows, this commentary is indicated through indentation.)

Since I still do not yet suffer from not having become an empiricist, I can calmly put up with the fact that my solution does not yet provide the model for the overdue empirical research into reception. I will probably bring upon myself the reproach of not being typical enough as a reader, and not being sufficiently versed in linguistics or semiotics as an analyst; and yet I hope to have tested practically the theoretical postulate of combining structural and semiotic analysis with phenomenological interpretation and hermeneutic reflection. To find a methodological starting-point

---

[15] *Das Problem der Relevanz* (Frankfurt, 1971). [Jauss]

[16] *Essais de stylistique structurale*, p. 340. [Jauss]

[17] Jauss suggests that the aesthetic appreciation of lyric poetry is heightened when expectations are fulfilled, when things fall into place so that we see a completed design, whereas with narrative the direct fulfillment of expectations usually makes for a dull story.

capable of further development, it was for me above all a matter of separating more sharply than has been done before the levels of aesthetic perception and reflective interpretation in the interpretation of poetic texts. An initial methodological advance may already result from this separation, namely that with the help of the question-answer relationship, the textual signals may now be specified within their syntagmatic coherence as the givens of the course of the reception that establish consistency. The "structures-of-appeal," "offers-of-identification," and "absences of meaning" [*Appellstrukturen, Identifikationsangebote, und Sinnlücken*] that Wolfgang Iser has conceived as categories in his theory of aesthetic effect are most easily made concrete in the course of the reception as inducements toward the constitution of meaning when one describes the effective factors of the poetic text as expectations, and transposes them into questions that the text in such passages either produces, leaves open, or answers.[18] If Iser, in *The Act of Reading* — in contrast to Riffaterre, who views the process of reception under the dominant category of overdetermination and interprets it *nolens volens*[19] — has rehabilitated the aesthetic character of fictional texts under the dominant category of "indeterminacy" (and "redeterminability"), it nonetheless remained to me to describe the course of the reception in the first, perceptual reading as an experience of accumulating evidence that is also aesthetically more convincing, which, in turn, as the pregiven horizon for a second, interpretive reading, at once opens up and delimits the space for possible concretizations.

Accordingly, the change of horizons between the first and the second readings may be described as follows: the reader — who performs the "score" of the text in the course of the reception of verse after verse, and who is led toward the ending in a perceptual act of anticipation, from the particular toward the possible whole of form and meaning — becomes aware of the fulfilled form of the poem, but not yet of its fulfilled significance, let alone of its "whole meaning." Whoever acknowledges the hermeneutic premise that the meaningful whole of a lyric work is no longer to be understood as if substantial, as if its meaning were pregiven and timeless; rather it is to be understood as a meaning to be performed — whoever acknowledges this premise awaits from the reader the recognition that from now on he may, in the act of interpretive understanding, hypostasize one among other possible significations of the poem, the relevance of which for him does not exclude the worth of others for discussion. From now on, the reader will seek and establish the still unfulfilled significance retrospectively, through a new reading from the perspective of the fulfilled form, in a return from the end to the beginning, from the whole to the particular. Whatever initially resisted understanding manifests itself in the questions that the first going-through has left open. In answering them, one may expect that from the particular elements of significance — in various respects still indeterminate — a fulfilled whole may be established on the level of meaning through the labor of interpretation, which whole is every bit as much on the level of meaning as on the level of form. This meaningful whole can be found only through a selective taking of perspectives and cannot be attained through a supposedly objective description — this falls under the hermeneutic premise of partiality. With this, the question of the historical horizon is posed, the horizon that conditioned the genesis and effect of the work and that once again delimits the present reader's interpretation. To investigate it is now the task of a third, historical reading.

This third step, insofar as it concerns the interpretation of a work from the premises of its time and genesis, is the one most familiar to historical-philological hermeneutics. Yet there the historically reconstructive reading is traditionally the first step, to which historicism adds the injunction that the interpreter has to ignore himself and his standpoint to be able to take up ever more purely the "objective meaning" of the text. Under the spell of this scholarly ideal, the objectivistic illusions of which are evident to almost everyone today, the hermeneutics of the classical and modern philologies sought to privilege historical understanding over the aesthetic appreciation, which, for its part, was rarely attempted at all. Such historicism failed to recognize that the aesthetic character of its texts — as a hermeneutic

[18]*Der Akt des Lesens* (Munich, 1976). [Jauss]
[19]Latin for "willy-nilly."

bridge denied to other disciplines — is that which makes possible the historical understanding of art across the distance in time in the first place, and which therefore must be integrated into the execution of the interpretation as a hermeneutic premise. But inversely, aesthetic understanding and interpretation also remain in reference to the controlling function of the historicist-reconstructive reading. It prevents the text from the past from being naively assimilated to the prejudices and expectations of meaning of the present, and thereby — through explicitly distinguishing the past horizon from the present — allows the poetic text to be seen in its alterity. The investigation of the "otherness," the unique distance, within the contemporaneity of the literary text, demands a reconstructive reading that can begin by seeking out the questions (most often inexplicit ones) to which the text was the response in its time. An interpretation of a literary text as a response should include two things: its response to expectations of a formal kind, such as the literary tradition prescribed for it before its appearance; and its response to questions of meaning such as they could have posed themselves within the historical life-world of its first readers.[20] The reconstruction of the original horizon of expectations would nonetheless fall back into historicism if the historical interpretation could not in turn serve to transform the question, "What did the text say?" into the question, "What does the text say to me, and what do I say to it?" If, like theological or juridical hermeneutics, literary hermeneutics is to move from understanding, through interpretation, to application, then application here certainly cannot dissolve into practical action, but rather instead can satisfy the no less legitimate interest of using literary communication with the past to measure and to broaden the horizon of one's own experience vis-à-vis the experience of the other.

The omission of the distinguishing of horizons can have consequences such as may be indicated with the analysis of the reception of a Poe story by Roland Barthes.[21] Its strength lies in the demonstration of how the structuralist description of the narrative principle — which explains the text as a variant of a pregiven model — can be transformed into the textual analysis of "significance" that allows one to understand the text as a process, as an ongoing production of meaning or more precisely, of possibilities of meaning ("the forms, the codes according to which meanings are possible").[22] Its weakness lies in a naive fusing of horizons: according to its own intention, the reading is supposed to be unmediated and ahistorical ("we will take up the text as it is, as it is when we read it"[23]), and yet this reading only comes about through a "superreader" who brings a comprehensive knowledge of the nineteenth century into play and who, in the course of the reception, notes those passages above all where cultural and linguistic codes can be recalled or associated. One cannot speak of a joining of the interpretation to the process of aesthetic perception, for this, as the "code of the 'actants'" in combination with the "symbolic code or field," can itself only be one more code among others (the "scientific, rhetorical, chronological, destinatory code," etc.).[24] Thus, a reading arises that is neither historical nor aesthetic, but rather is as subjective as it is impressionistic, and yet is supposed to ground the theory that each particular text is a tissue of texts — the interminable play of a free-floating intertexuality in "the struggle between man and signs."[25]

Literary hermeneutics, which Barthes not accidentally views as a (for him) "aenigmatic code," is on the contrary surely no longer interested today in interpreting the text as the revelation of the single truth concealed within it.[26] Against the theory of the "plural text," with its notion of

---

[20]In illustration of Jauss's point that literary texts are often responses to other literary texts that are "alive" for the writer, one could point to Pope's *Essay on Man*, which proposes to "vindicate the ways of God to man," clearly situating itself as a response to Milton's *Paradise Lost*. Jauss is arguing also that the issues such texts are raising for their first readers — in this case, about whether the world reflects a benevolent and omniscient God — are ones that the poet's contemporaries are still asking, unsatisfied by the earlier text's answers.

[21]"Analyse textuelle d'un conte d'Edgar Poe," in *Sémiotique narrative et textuelle*, ed. Claude Chabrol (Paris, 1973), pp. 29–54. [Jauss]
[22]Ibid., p. 30. [Jauss]
[23]Ibid., p. 32. [Jauss]
[24]Ibid., p. 51. [Jauss]
[25]Ibid., pp. 30 and 52. [Jauss]
[26]Ibid., p. 30. [Jauss]

"intertextuality" as a limitless and arbitrary production of possibilities of meaning and of no less arbitrary interpretations, literary hermeneutics poses the hypothesis that the concretization of the meaning of literary works progresses historically and follows a certain "logic" that precipitates in the formation and transformation of the aesthetic canon. Furthermore, it postulates that in the change of horizons of the interpretations, one may distinguish absolutely between arbitrary interpretations and those available to a consensus, between those that are merely original and those that are formative of a norm. The fundamental aspect that supports this hypothesis can lie only in the aesthetic character of the texts: as a regulative principle, it allows for there being a series of interpretations, but that are also capable of being reintegrated with respect to the meaning made concrete. Here I may recall the attempt at a pluralistic interpretation of Apollinaire's poem "L'arbre," undertaken at the second colloquium of the *Poetik und Hermeneutik* group. On the one hand, the distance vis-à-vis the poem adopted by each reader itself allowed for a different aesthetic perception to arise, and each specific concretization of the significance necessarily had to ignore other, no less plausible interpretations. And yet, the surprising confirmation that the individual interpretations did not contradict one another despite their differences led to the conclusion that even this "pluralistic text" can provide a unifying aesthetic orientation for perceptual understanding within the horizon of the first reading.[27]

To be sure, one may object that, after Baudelaire, a modern poem cannot furnish the reader with this evidence of a compelling whole after only the first reading, but rather only in rereading. And one may object that, mutatis mutandis,[28] a poem from an older tradition or from another culture often only discloses itself for aesthetic understanding when historicist understanding has removed the obstacles to its reception and rendered possible an aesthetic perception of the formerly unenjoyable text. I am also thoroughly of this opinion,[29] so that I can use these objections for precisely one last point.

The priority of aesthetic perception within the triad of literary hermeneutics has need of the *horizon*, but not the temporal priority, of the first reading; this horizon of aesthetic understanding may also be gained only in the course of rereading or with the help of historicist understanding.[30] Aesthetic perception is no universal code with timeless validity, but rather — like all aesthetic experience — is intertwined with historical experience. Thus, for the interpretation of texts from other cultures, the aesthetic character of poetic texts from the western tradition can only offer heuristic advantages. Literary interpretation must compensate with the three achievements of the hermeneutic process for the fact that aesthetic perception itself is subject to historical exchange. It thereby gains the opportunity of broadening historicist knowledge through aesthetic understanding, and perhaps of constituting, through its unconstrained kind of application, a corrective to other applications that are subject to situational pressures and the compulsions of decision-making.

---

[27] *Immanente Ästhetik — Ästhetische Reflexion: Poetik und Hermeneutik II*, ed. Wolfgang Iser (Munich, 1966), pp. 461–84, esp. pp. 473 and 480: "For a concrete interpretation and for a judgment of the quality of the poem, it is not enough to provide its structural principle and to describe Apollinaire's poetic technique. A series of ambiguities is not yet a compelling whole. If this whole provokes an ever newer interpretation on the basis of the technique in which it is unfolded, then this interpretation is neither accidental in its details nor free from a fundamental orientation that is compellingly provided through the construction of the text. The first reading provides this compulsion through the suggestion of the rhythm. The interpretation must give itself over to this medium in which the poem moves" (Dieter Henrich). This

interpretation is translated as "Group Interpretation of Apollinaire's 'Arbre,'" in *New Perspectives in German Literary Criticism*, ed. Richard E. Amacher and Victor Lange (Princeton, 1979), pp. 182–207. [Jauss]

[28] Latin for "when necessary changes have been made."

[29] On this, see my *Alterität und Modernität der mittelalterlichen Literatur* (Munich, 1977), esp. p. 10 ff. [Jauss]

[30] Jauss's point is that the order of the three horizons of reading is not temporal: readers may not be able to appreciate a text aesthetically till they have grounded themselves in the history of its period.

Wayne C. Booth

b. 1921

His 1971 Quantrell Prize for undergraduate teaching at the University of Chicago is one indication that Wayne Clayson Booth has been the most effective teacher — in the most far-reaching sense — of the neo-Aristotelians. He was born in American Fork, Utah, and educated at Brigham Young University, where he received his B.A. in 1944. After serving in the infantry during World War II, Booth completed his M.A. and Ph.D. at the University of Chicago, where his mentor was R. S. Crane (see Ch. 1). He taught at Haverford and at Earlham College, where he became professor and chairman of the department of English before returning to a named chair at Chicago in 1962. Booth has received fellowships from the Ford Foundation (1952), the Guggenheim Foundation (1956–57 and 1969–70), and the National Endowment for the Humanities (1975–76). He served as dean of the college of the University of Chicago from 1964 to 1969, and as president of the Modern Language Association in 1982. Booth's meteoric success began with the publication of The Rhetoric of Fiction *(1961; second ed., 1983), which shifted from the formalism of Crane to the explicit consideration of the audience and the ways in which texts make the readers they require. Other works have included* A Rhetoric of Irony *(1974),* Modern Dogma and the Rhetoric of Assent *(1974), and his most ambitious work, a pluralistic guide to the variety of pluralisms,* Critical Understanding *(1979). The* Company We Keep: Ethical Criticism and the Ethics of Reading *(1988) is a long-considered effort to clarify some of the controversy excited by Booth's hint, in* The Rhetoric of Fiction, *at the potentially injurious effect of narratives by Céline and Nabokov. Booth's most recent books include* For the Love of It: Amateuring and Its Rivals *(1999), a meditation on amateur musicianship and the healing and enrichment it has brought to his life, and a manifesto,* The Rhetoric of Rhetoric: The Quest for Effective Communication *(2004).*

Control of Distance in Jane Austen's Emma

Jane Austen was instinctive and charming. . . . For signal examples of what composition, distribution, arrangement can do, of how they intensify the life of a work of art, we have to go elsewhere.
— HENRY JAMES

A heroine whom no one but myself will much like.
— JANE AUSTEN describing Emma

SYMPATHY AND JUDGMENT IN "EMMA"

Henry James once described Jane Austen as an instinctive novelist whose effects, some of which are admittedly fine, can best be explained as "part of her unconsciousness." It is as if she "fell-a-musing" over her work-basket, he said, lapsed into "wool-gathering," and afterward picked up "her dropped stitches" as "little masterstrokes of

imagination."[1] The amiable accusation has been repeated in various forms, most recently as a claim that Jane Austen creates characters toward whom we cannot react as she consciously intends.[2]

[1] "The Lesson of Balzac," *The Question of Our Speech* (Cambridge, 1905), p. 63. A fuller quotation can be found in R. W. Chapman's indispensable *Jane Austen: A Critical Bibliography* (Oxford, 1955). Some important Austen items published too late to be included by Chapman are: (1) Ian Watt, *The Rise of the Novel* (Berkeley, Calif., 1957); (2) Stuart M. Tave, review of Marvin Mudrick's *Jane Austen: Irony as Defense and Discovery* (Princeton, N.J., 1952) in *Philological Quarterly* 32 (July 1953): 256–57; (3) Andrew H. Wright, *Jane Austen's Novels: A Study in Structure* (London, 1953), pp. 36–82; (4) Christopher Gillie, *"Sense and Sensibility:* An Assessment," *Essays in Criticism* 9 (January 1959): 1–9, esp. 5–6; (5) Edgar F. Shannon, Jr., *"Emma:* Character and Construction," *PMLA* 71 (September 1956); 637–50. [Booth]

[2] See, for example, Mudrick, pp. 91, 165; Frank O'Connor, *The Mirror in the Roadway* (London, 1957), p. 30. [Booth]

Although we cannot hope to decide whether Jane Austen was entirely conscious of her own artistry, a careful look at the technique of any of her novels reveals a rather different picture from that of the unconscious spinster with her knitting needles. In *Emma* especially, where the chances for technical failure are great indeed, we find at work one of the unquestionable masters of the rhetoric of narration.

At the beginning of *Emma*, the young heroine has every requirement for deserved happiness but one. She has intelligence, wit, beauty, wealth, and position, and she has the love of those around her. Indeed, she thinks herself completely happy. The only threat to her happiness, a threat of which she is unaware, is herself: charming as she is, she can neither see her own excessive pride honestly nor resist imposing herself on the lives of others. She is deficient both in generosity and in self-knowledge. She discovers and corrects her faults only after she has almost ruined herself and her closest friends. But with the reform in her character, she is ready for marriage with the man she loves, the man who throughout the book has stood in the reader's mind for what she lacks.

It is clear that with a general plot of this kind Jane Austen gave herself difficulties of high order. Though Emma's faults are comic, they constantly threaten to produce serious harm. Yet she must remain sympathetic or the reader will not wish for and delight sufficiently in her reform.

Obviously, the problem with a plot like this is to find some way to allow the reader to laugh at the mistakes committed by the heroine and at her punishment, without reducing the desire to see her reform and thus earn happiness. In *Tom Jones* this double attitude is achieved . . . partly through the invention of episodes producing sympathy and relieving any serious anxiety we might have, and partly through the direct and sympathetic commentary. In *Emma*, since most of the episodes must illustrate the heroine's faults and thus increase either our emotional distance or our anxiety, a different method is required. If we fail to see Emma's faults as revealed in the ironic texture from line to line, we cannot savor to the full the comedy as it is prepared for us. On the other hand, if we fail to love her, as Jane Austen herself predicted we would[3] — if we fail to love her more and more as the book progresses — we can neither hope for the conclusion, a happy and deserved marriage with Knightley following upon her reform, nor accept it as an honest one when it comes.[4] Any attempt to solve the problem by reducing either the love or the clear view of her faults would have been fatal.

SYMPATHY THROUGH CONTROL OF INSIDE VIEWS

The solution to the problem of maintaining sympathy despite almost crippling faults was primarily to use the heroine herself as a kind of narrator, though in third person, reporting on her own experience. So far as we know, Jane Austen never formulated any theory to cover her own practice; she invented no term like James's "central intelligence" or "lucid reflector" to describe her method of viewing the world of the book primarily through Emma's own eyes. We can thus never know for sure to what extent James's accusation of "unconsciousness" was right. But whether she was inclined to speculate about her method scarcely matters; her solution was clearly a brilliant one. By showing most of the story through Emma's eyes, the author insures that we shall travel with Emma rather than stand against her. It is not simply that Emma provides, in the unimpeachable evidence of her own conscience, proof that she has many redeeming qualities that do not appear on the surface; such evidence could be given with authorial commentary, though perhaps

---

[3] "A heroine whom no one but myself will much like" (James Edward Austen-Leigh, *Memoir of His Aunt* [London, 1870; Oxford, 1926], p. 157). [Booth]

[4] The best discussion of this problem is Reginald Farrer's "Jane Austen," *Quarterly Review* 228 (July 1917): 1–30; reprinted in William Heath's *Discussion of Jane Austen* (Boston, 1961). For one critic the book fails because the problem was never recognized by Jane Austen herself: Mr. E. N. Hayes, in what may well be the least sympathetic discussion of *Emma* yet written, explains the whole book as the author's failure to see Emma's faults. "Evidently Jane Austen wished to protect Emma . . . The author is therefore in the ambiguous position of both loving and scorning the heroine" ("'Emma': A Dissenting Opinion," *Nineteenth-Century Fiction* 4 [June 1949]: 18, 19. [Booth]

not with such force and conviction. Much more important, the sustained inside view leads the reader to hope for good fortune for the character with whom he travels, quite independently of the qualities revealed.

Seen from the outside, Emma would be an unpleasant person, unless, like Mr. Woodhouse and Knightley, we knew her well enough to infer her true worth. Though we might easily be led to laugh at her, we could never be made to laugh sympathetically. While the final unmasking of her faults and her humiliation would make artistic sense to an unsympathetic reader, her marriage with Knightley would become irrelevant if not meaningless. Unless we desire Emma's happiness and her reform which alone can make that happiness possible, a good third of this book will seem irredeemably dull.

Yet sympathetic laughter is never easily achieved. It is much easier to set up a separate fool for comic effects and to preserve your heroine for finer things. Sympathetic laughter is especially difficult with characters whose faults do not spring from sympathetic virtues. The grasping but witty Volpone can keep us on his side so long as his victims are more grasping and less witty than he, but as soon as the innocent victims, Celia and Bonario, come on stage, the quality of the humor changes; we no longer delight unambiguously in his triumphs. In contrast to this, the great sympathetic comic heroes often are comic largely because their faults, like Uncle Toby's sentimentality, spring from an excess of some virtue. Don Quixote's madness is partly caused by an excess of idealism, an excess of loving concern for the unfortunate. Every crazy gesture he makes gives further reason for loving the well-meaning old fool, and we can thus laugh at him in somewhat the same spirit in which we laugh at our own faults — in a benign, forgiving spirit. We may be contemptible for doing so; to persons without a sense of humor such laughter often seems a wicked escape. But self-love being what it is, we laugh at ourselves in a thoroughly forgiving way, and we laugh in the same way at Don Quixote: we are convinced that his heart, like ours, is in the right place.

Nothing in Emma's comic misunderstandings can serve for the same effect. Her faults are not excesses of virtue. She attempts to manipulate Harriet not from an excess of kindness but from a desire for power and admiration. She flirts with Frank Churchill out of vanity and irresponsibility. She mistreats Jane Fairfax because of Jane's *good* qualities. She abuses Miss Bates because of her own essential lack of "tenderness" and "good will."

We have only to think of what Emma's story would be if seen through Jane Fairfax's or Mrs. Elton's or Robert Martin's eyes to recognize how little our sympathy springs from any natural view, and to see how inescapable is the decision to use Emma's mind as a reflector of events — however beclouded her vision must be. To Jane Fairfax, who embodies throughout the book most of the values which Emma discovers only at the end, the early Emma is intolerable.

But Jane Austen never lets us forget that Emma is not what she might appear to be. For every section devoted to her misdeeds — and even they are seen for the most part through her own eyes — there is a section devoted to her self-reproach. We see her rudeness to poor foolish Miss Bates, and we see it vividly. But her remorse and act of penance in visiting Miss Bates after Knightley's rebuke are experienced even more vividly. We see her successive attempts to mislead Harriet, but we see at great length and in high color her self-castigation (Chs. 16, 17, 48). We see her boasting proudly that she does not need marriage, boasting almost as blatantly of her "resources" as does Mrs. Elton (Ch. 10). But we know her too intimately to take her conscious thoughts at face value. And we see her, thirty-eight chapters later, chastened to an admission of what we have known all along to be her true human need for love. "If all took place that might take place among the circle of her friends, Hartfield must be comparatively deserted; and she left to cheer her father with the spirits only of ruined happiness. The child to be born at Randalls must be a tie there even dearer than herself; and Mrs. Weston's heart and time would be occupied by it. . . . All that were good would be withdrawn" (Ch. 48).

Perhaps the most delightful effects from our sustained inside view of a very confused and very charming young woman come from her frequent thoughts about Knightley. She is basically right all along about his pre-eminent wisdom and virtue, and she is our chief authority for taking *his* authority so seriously. And yet in every thought about him she is misled. Knightley rebukes her; the reader knows that Knightley is in the right. But Emma?

> Emma made no answer, and tried to look cheerfully unconcerned, but was really feeling uncomfortable, and wanting him very much to be gone. She did not repeat what she had done; she still thought herself a better judge of such a point of female right and refinement than he could be; but yet she had a sort of habitual respect for his judgment in general, which made her dislike having it so loudly against her; and to have him sitting just opposite to her in an angry state, was very disagreeable [Ch. 8].

Even more striking is the lack of self-knowledge shown when Mrs. Weston suggests that Knightley might marry Jane Fairfax.

> Her objections to Mr. Knightley's marrying did not in the least subside. She could see nothing but evil in it. It would be a great disappointment to Mr. John Knightley [Knightley's brother]; consequently to Isabella. A real injury to the children — a most mortifying change, and material loss to them all; — a very great deduction from her father's daily comfort — and, as to herself, she could not at all endure the idea of Jane Fairfax at Donwell Abbey. A Mrs. Knightley for them all to give way to! — No, Mr. Knightley must never marry. Little Henry must remain the heir of Donwell [Ch. 26].

Self-deception could hardly be carried further, at least in a person of high intelligence and sensitivity.

Yet the effect of all this is what our tolerance for our own faults produces in our own lives. While only immature readers ever really identify with any character, losing all sense of distance and hence all chance of an artistic experience, our emotional reaction to every event concerning Emma tends to become like her own. When she feels anxiety or shame, we feel analogous emotions. Our modern awareness that such "feelings" are not identical with those we feel in our own lives in similar circumstances has tended to blind us to the fact that aesthetic form can be built out of patterned emotions as well as out of other materials. It is absurd to pretend that because our emotions and desires in responding to fiction are

in a very real sense disinterested, they do not or should not exist. Jane Austen, in developing the sustained use of a sympathetic inside view, has mastered one of the most successful of all devices for including a parallel emotional response between the deficient heroine and the reader.

Sympathy for Emma can be heightened by withholding inside views of others as well as by granting them of her. The author knew, for example, that it would be fatal to grant any extended inside view of Jane Fairfax. The inadequacies of impressionistic criticism are nowhere revealed more clearly than in the suggestion often made about such minor characters that their authors would have liked to make them vivid but didn't know how.[5] Jane Austen knew perfectly well how to make such a character vivid; Anne in *Persuasion* is a kind of Jane Fairfax turned into heroine. But in *Emma*, Emma must shine supreme. It is not only that the slightest glance inside Jane's mind would be fatal to all of the author's plans for mystification about Frank Churchill, though this is important. The major problem is that any extended view of her would reveal her as a more sympathetic person than Emma herself. Jane is superior to Emma in most respects except the stroke of good fortune that made Emma the heroine of the book. In matters of taste and ability, of head and of heart, she is Emma's superior, and Jane Austen, always in danger of losing our sympathy for Emma, cannot risk any degree of distraction. Jane could, it is true, be granted fewer virtues, and then made more vivid. But to do so would greatly weaken the force of Emma's mistakes of heart and head in her treatment of the almost faultless Jane.

CONTROL OF JUDGMENT

But the very effectiveness of the rhetoric designed to produce sympathy might in itself lead

[5] A. C. Bradley, for example, once argued that Jane Austen intended Jane Fairfax to be as interesting throughout as she becomes at the end, but "the moralist in Jane Austen stood for once in her way. The secret engagement is, for her, so serious an offence, that she is afraid to win our hearts for Jane until it has led to great unhappiness" ("Jane Austen," in *Essays and Studies, by Members of the English Association*, II [Oxford, 1911], p. 23). [Booth]

to a serious misreading of the book. In reducing the emotional distance, the natural tendency is to reduce — willy-nilly — moral and intellectual distance as well. In reacting to Emma's faults from the inside out, as if they were our own, we may very well not only forgive them but overlook them.[6]

There is, of course, no danger that readers who persist to the end will overlook Emma's serious mistakes; since she sees and reports those mistakes herself, everything becomes crystal clear at the end. The real danger inherent in the experiment is that readers will overlook the mistakes as they are committed and thus miss much of the comedy that depends on Emma's distorted view from page to page. If readers who dislike Emma cannot enjoy the preparation for the marriage to Knightley, readers who do not recognize her faults with absolute precision cannot enjoy the details of the preparation for the comic abasement which must precede that marriage.

It might be argued that there is no real problem, since the conventions of her time allowed for reliable commentary whenever it was needed to place Emma's faults precisely. But Jane Austen is not operating according to the conventions, most of which she had long since parodied and outgrown; her technique is determined by the needs of the novel she is writing. We can see this clearly by contrasting the manner of *Emma* with that of

[6]I know of only one full-scale attempt to deal with the "tension between sympathy and judgment" in modern literature, Robert Langbaum's *The Poetry of Experience* (London, 1957). Langbaum argues that in the dramatic monologue, with which he is primarily concerned, the sympathy engendered by the direct portrayal of internal experience leads the reader to suspend his moral judgment. Thus, in reading Browning's portraits of moral degeneration — e.g., the duke in "My Last Duchess" or the monk in "Soliloquy of a Spanish Cloister" — our moral judgment is overwhelmed "because we prefer to participate in the duke's power and freedom, in his hard core of character fiercely loyal to itself. Moral judgment is in fact important as the thing to be suspended, as a measure of the price we pay for the privilege of appreciating to the full this extraordinary man" (p. 83). While I think that Langbaum seriously underplays the extent to which moral judgment remains even after psychological vividness has done its work, and while he perhaps defines "morality" too narrowly when he excludes from it such things as power and freedom and fierce loyalty to one's own character, his book is a stimulating introduction to the problems raised by the internal portraiture of flawed characters. [Booth]

Persuasion, the next and last-completed work. In *Emma* there are many breaks in the point of view, because Emma's beclouded mind cannot do the whole job. In *Persuasion*, where the heroine's viewpoint is faulty only in her ignorance of Captain Wentworth's love, there are very few. Anne Elliot's consciousness is sufficient, as Emma's is not, for most of the needs of the novel which she dominates. Once the ethical and intellectual framework has been established by the narrator's introduction, we enter Anne's consciousness and remain bound to it much more rigorously than we are bound to Emma's. It is still true that whenever something must be shown that Anne's consciousness cannot show, we move to another center; but since her consciousness can do much more for us than Emma's, there need be few departures from it.

The most notable shift for rhetorical purposes in *Persuasion* comes fairly early. When Anne first meets Captain Wentworth after their years of separation that follow her refusal to marry him, she is convinced that he is indifferent. The major movement of *Persuasion* is toward her final discovery that he still loves her; *her* suspense is thus strong and inevitable from the beginning. The reader, however, is likely to believe that Wentworth is still interested. All the conventions of art favor such a belief: the emphasis is clearly on Anne and her unhappiness; the lover has returned; we have only to wait, perhaps with some tedium, for the inevitable outcome. Anne learns (Ch. 7) that he has spoken of her as so altered "he should not have known her again!" "These were words which could not but dwell with her. Yet she soon began to rejoice that she had heard them. They were of sobering tendency; they allayed agitation; they composed, and consequently must make her happier." And suddenly we enter Wentworth's mind for one time only: "Frederick Wentworth had used such words, or something like them, but without an idea that they would be carried round to her. He had thought her wretchedly altered, and, in the first moment of appeal, had spoken as he felt. He had not forgiven Anne Elliot. She had used him ill" — and so he goes on, for five more paragraphs. The necessary point, the fact that Frederick believes himself to be indifferent, has been made, and it could not have been made without some kind of shift from Anne's consciousness.

At the end of the novel, we learn that Wentworth was himself deceived in this momentary inside view: "He had meant to forget her, and believed it to be done. He had imagined himself indifferent, when he had only been angry." We may want to protest against the earlier suppression as unfair, but we can hardly believe it to be what Miss Lascelles calls "an oversight."[7] It is deliberate manipulation of inside views in order to destroy our conventional security. We are thus made ready to go along with Anne in her long and painful road to the discovery that Frederick loves her after all.

The only other important breaks in the angle of vision of *Persuasion* come at the beginning and at the end. Chapter one is an excellent example of how a skillful novelist can, by the use of his own direct voice, accomplish in a few pages what even the best novelist must take chapters to do if he uses nothing but dramatized action. Again at the conclusion the author enters with a resounding reaffirmation that the Wentworth-Elliot marriage is as good a thing as we have felt it to be from the beginning.

> Who can be in doubt of what followed? When any two young people take it into their heads to marry, they are pretty sure by perseverance to carry their point, be they ever so poor, or ever so imprudent, or ever so little likely to be necessary to each other's ultimate comfort. This may be bad morality to conclude with, but I believe it to be truth; and if such parties succeed, how should a Captain Wentworth and an Anne Elliot, with the advantage of maturity of mind, consciousness of right, and one independent fortune between them, fail of bearing down every opposition?[8]

[7]*Jane Austen and Her Art* (Oxford, 1939), p. 204. [Booth]
[8]It seems to be difficult for some modern critics, accustomed to ferreting values out from an impersonal or ironic context without the aid of the author's voice, to make use of reliable commentary like this when it is provided. Even a highly perceptive reader like Mark Schorer, for example, finds himself doing unnecessary acrobatics with the question of style, and particularly metaphor, as clues to the norms against which the author judges her characters. In reading *Persuasion*, he finds these clues among the metaphors "from commerce and property, the counting house and the inherited estate" with which it abounds ("Fiction and the Matrix of Analogy,"

Except for these few intrusions and one in Chapter 19, Anne's own mind is sufficient in *Persuasion*, but we can never rely completely on Emma. It is hardly surprising that Jane Austen has provided many correctives to insure our placing her errors with precision.

The chief corrective is Knightley. His commentary on Emma's errors is a natural expression of his love; he can tell the reader and Emma at the same time precisely how she is mistaken. Thus, nothing Knightley says can be beside the point. Each affirmation of a value, each accusation of error is in itself an action in the plot. When he rebukes Emma for manipulating Harriet, when he attacks her for being "insolent" and "unfeeling" in her treatment of Miss Bates, we have Jane Austen's judgment on Emma, rendered dramatically. But it has come from someone who is essentially sympathetic toward Emma, so that his judgments against her are presumed to be temporary. His sympathy reinforces ours even as he criticizes, and her respect for his opinion, shown in her self-abasement after he has criticized, is one of our main reasons for expecting her to reform.

If Henry James had tried to write a novel about Emma, and had cogitated at length on the problem of getting her story told dramatically, he could not have done better than this. It is possible, of course, to think of *Emma* without Knightley as

Kenyon Review [Autumn 1949]: 540). No one would deny that the novel is packed with such metaphors, although Schorer is somewhat overingenious in marshaling to his cause certain dead metaphors that Austen could not have avoided without awkward circumlocution (esp. p. 542). But the crucial question surely is: What precisely are these metaphors of the countinghouse doing in the novel? Whose values are they supposed to reveal? Accustomed to reading modern fiction in which the novelist very likely provides no direct assistance in answering this question, Schorer leaves it really unanswered; at times he seems almost to imply that Jane Austen is unconsciously giving herself away in her use of them (e.g., p. 543).

But the novel is really very clear about it all. The introduction, coming directly from the wholly reliable narrator, establishes unequivocally and without "analogy" the conflict between the world of the Elliots, depending for its values on selfishness, stupidity, and pride — and the world of Anne, a world where "elegance of mind and sweetness of character" are the supreme values. The commercial values stressed by Schorer are only a selection from what is actually a rich group of evils. And Anne's own expressed views again and again provide direct guidance to the reader. [Booth] *raisonneur*, just as it is possible to think of *The Golden Bowl*, say, without the Assinghams as *ficelles* to reflect something not seen by the Prince or Princess. But Knightley, though he receives less independent space than the Assinghams and is almost never seen in an inside view, is clearly more useful for Jane Austen's purposes than any realistically limited *ficelle* could possibly be. By combining the role of commentator with the role of hero, Jane Austen has worked more economically than James, and though economy is as dangerous as any other criterion when applied universally, even James might have profited from a closer study of the economies that a character like Knightley can be made to achieve. It is as if James had dared to make one of the four main characters, say the Prince, into a thoroughly good, wise, perceptive man, a thoroughly clear rather than a partly confused "reflector."

Since Knightley is established early as completely reliable, we need no views of his secret thoughts. He has no secret thoughts, except for the unacknowledged depths of his love for Emma and his jealousy of Frank Churchill. The other main characters have more to hide, and Jane Austen moves in and out of minds with great freedom, choosing for her own purposes what to reveal and what to withhold. Always the seeming violation of consistency is in the consistent service of the particular needs of Emma's story. Sometimes a shift is made simply to direct our suspense, as when Mrs. Weston suggests a possible union of Emma and Frank Churchill, at the end of her conversation with Knightley about the harmful effects of Emma's friendship with Harriet (Ch. 5). "Part of her meaning was to conceal some favourite thoughts of her own and Mr. Weston's on the subject, as much as possible. There were wishes at Randalls respecting Emma's destiny, but it was not desirable to have them suspected."

One objection to this selective dipping into whatever mind best serves our immediate purposes is that it suggests mere trickery and inevitably spoils the illusion of reality. If Jane Austen can tell us what Mrs. Weston is thinking, why not what Frank Churchill and Jane Fairfax are thinking? Obviously, because she chooses to build a mystery, and to do so she must refuse,

arbitrarily and obtrusively, to grant the privilege of an inside view to characters whose minds would reveal too much. But is not the mystery purchased at the price of shaking the reader's faith in Jane Austen's integrity? If she simply withholds until later what she might as well relate now — if her procedure is not dictated by the very nature of her materials — why should we take her seriously?

If a natural surface were required in all fiction, then this objection would hold. But if we want to read *Emma* in its own terms, the real question about these shifts cannot be answered by an easy appeal to general principles. Every author withholds until later what he "might as well" relate now. The question is always one of desired effects, and the choice of any one effect always bans innumerable other effects. There is, indeed, a question to be raised about the use of mystery in *Emma*, but the conflict is not between an abstract end that Jane Austen never worried about and a shoddy mystification that she allowed to betray her. The conflict is between two effects both of which she cares about a good deal. On the one hand she cares about maintaining some sense of mystery as long as she can. On the other, she works at all points to heighten the reader's sense of dramatic irony, usually in the form of a contrast between what Emma knows and what the reader knows.

As in most novels, whatever steps are taken to mystify inevitably decrease the dramatic irony, and, whenever dramatic irony is increased by telling the reader secrets the characters have not yet suspected, mystery is inevitably destroyed. The longer we are in doubt about Frank Churchill, the weaker our sense of ironic contrast between Emma's views and the truth. The sooner we see through Frank Churchill's secret plot, the greater our pleasure in observing Emma's innumerable misreadings of his behavior and the less interest we have in the mere mystery of the situation. And we all find that on second reading we discover new intensities of dramatic irony resulting from the complete loss of mystery; knowing what abysses of error Emma is preparing for herself, even those of us who may on first reading have deciphered nearly all the details of the Churchill mystery find additional ironies.

But it is obvious that these ironies could have been offered even on a first reading, if Austen had been willing to sacrifice her mystery. A single phrase in her own name — "his secret engagement to Jane Fairfax" — or a short inside view of either of the lovers could have made us aware of every ironic touch.

The author must, then, choose whether to purchase mystery at the expense of irony. For many of us Jane Austen's choice here is perhaps the weakest aspect of this novel. It is a commonplace of our criticism that significant literature arouses suspense not about the "what" but about the "how." Mere mystification has been mastered by so many second-rate writers that her efforts at mystification seem second-rate.

But again we must ask whether criticism can be conducted effectively by balancing one abstract quality against another. Is there a norm of dramatic irony for all works, or even for all works of a given kind? Has anyone ever formulated a "law of first and second readings" that will tell us just how many of our pleasures on page one should depend on our knowledge of what happens on page the last? We quite properly ask that the books we call great be able to stand up under repeated reading, but we need not ask that they yield identical pleasures on each reading. The modern works whose authors pride themselves on the fact that they can never be read but only re-read may be very good indeed, but they are not made good by the fact that their secret pleasures can only be wrested from them by repeated readings.

In any case, even if one accepted the criticism of Jane Austen's efforts at mystification, the larger service of the inside views is clear: the crosslights thrown by other minds prevent our being blinded by Emma's radiance.

THE RELIABLE NARRATOR AND THE NORMS OF "EMMA"

If mere intellectual clarity about Emma were the goal in this work, we should be forced to say that the manipulation of inside views and the extensive commentary of the reliable Knightley are more than is necessary. But for maximum intensity of the comedy and romance, even these are not enough. The "author herself" — not necessarily the real Jane Austen but an implied author, represented in this book by a reliable narrator — heightens the effects by directing our intellectual, moral, and emotional progress. She performs, of course, most of the functions described in Chapter 7. But her most important role is to reinforce both aspects of the double vision that operates throughout the book: our inside view of Emma's worth and our objective view of her great faults.

The narrator opens *Emma* with a masterful simultaneous presentation of Emma and of the values against which she must be judged: "Emma Woodhouse, handsome, clever, and rich, with a comfortable home and happy disposition, seemed to unite some of the best blessings of existence; and had lived nearly twenty-one years in the world with very little to distress or vex her." This "seemed" is immediately reinforced by more directly stated reservations. "The real evils of Emma's situation were the power of having rather too much her own way, and a disposition to think a little too well of herself; these were the disadvantages which threatened alloy to her many enjoyments. The danger, however, was at present so unperceived, that they did not by any means rank as misfortunes with her."

None of this could have been said by Emma, and if shown through her consciousness, it could not be accepted, as it must be, without question. Like most of the first three chapters, it is non-dramatic summary, building up, through the ostensible business of getting the characters introduced, to Emma's initial blunder with Harriet and Mr. Elton. Throughout these chapters, we learn much of what we must know from the narrator, but she turns over more and more of the job of summary to Emma as she feels more and more sure of our seeing precisely to what degree Emma is to be trusted. Whenever we leave the "real evils" we have been warned against in Emma, the narrator's and Emma's views coincide: we cannot tell which of them, for example, offers the judgment on Mr. Woodhouse that "his talents could not have recommended him at any time," or the judgment on Mr. Knightley that he is "a sensible man," "always welcome" at Hartfield, or even that "Mr. Knightley, in fact, was one of the few people who could see faults in Emma Woodhouse, and the only one who ever told her of them."

But there are times when Emma and her author are far apart, and the author's direct guidance aids the reader in his own break with Emma. The beautiful irony of the first description of Harriet, given through Emma's eyes (Ch. 3) could no doubt be grasped intellectually by many readers without all of the preliminary commentary. But even for the most perceptive its effect is heightened, surely, by the sense of standing with the author and observing with her precisely how Emma's judgment is going astray. Perhaps more important, we ordinary, less perceptive readers have by now been raised to a level suited to grasp the ironies. Certainly, most readers would overlook some of the barbs directed against Emma if the novel began, as a serious modern novelist might well begin it, with this description:

> [Emma] was not struck by any thing remarkably clever in Miss Smith's conversation, but she found her altogether very engaging — not inconveniently shy, not unwilling to talk — and yet so far from pushing, shewing so proper and becoming a deference, seeming so pleasantly grateful for being admitted to Hartfield, and so artlessly impressed by the appearance of every thing in so superior a style to what she had been used to, that she must have good sense and deserve encouragement. Encouragement should be given. Those soft blue eyes . . . should not be wasted on the inferior society of Highbury. . . .

And so Emma goes on, giving herself away with every word, pouring out her sense of her own beneficence and general value. Harriet's past friends, "though very good sort of people, must be doing her harm." Without knowing them, Emma knows that they "must be coarse and unpolished, and very unfit to be the intimates of a girl who wanted only a little more knowledge and elegance to be quite perfect." And she concludes with a beautiful burst of egotism: "She would notice her; she would improve her; she would detach her from her bad acquaintance, and introduce her into good society; she would form her opinions and her manners. It would be an interesting, and certainly a very kind undertaking; highly becoming her own situation in life, her leisure, and powers." Even the most skillful reader might not easily plot an absolutely true course through these ironies without the prior direct assistance we have been given. Emma's views are not so outlandish that they could never have been held by a female novelist writing in her time. They cannot serve effectively as signs of her character unless they are clearly disavowed as signs of Jane Austen's views. Emma's unconscious catalogue of her egotistical uses for Harriet, given under the pretense of listing the services she will perform, is thus given its full force by being framed explicitly in a world of values which Emma herself cannot discover until the conclusion of the book.

The full importance of the author's direct imposition of an elaborate scale of norms can be seen by considering that conclusion. The sequence of events is a simple one: Emma's faults and mistakes are brought home to her in a rapid and humiliating chain of rebukes from Knightley and blows from hard fact. These blows to her self-esteem produce at last a genuine reform (for example, she brings herself to apologize to Miss Bates, something she could never have done earlier in the novel). The change in her character removes the only obstacle in the way of Knightley's proposal, and the marriage follows. "The wishes, the hopes, the confidence, the predictions of the small band of true friends who witnessed the ceremony, were fully answered in the perfect happiness of the union."

It may be that if we look at Emma and Knightley as real people, this ending will seem false. G. B. Stern laments, in *Speaking of Jane Austen*, "Oh, Miss Austen, it was not a good solution; it was a bad solution, an unhappy ending, could we see beyond the last pages of the book." Edmund Wilson predicts that Emma will find a new protégée like Harriet, since she has not been cured of her inclination to "infatuations with women." Marvin Mudrick even more emphatically rejects Jane Austen's explicit rhetoric; he believes that Emma is still a "confirmed exploiter," and for him the ending must be read as ironic.[9]

[9]The first two quotations are from Wilson's "A Long Talk about Jane Austen," *A Literary Chronicle: 1920–1950* (New York, 1952). The third is from Mudrick, *Jane Austen*, p. 206. [Booth]

But it is precisely because this ending is neither life itself nor a simple bit of literary irony that it can serve so well to heighten our sense of a complete and indeed perfect resolution to all that has gone before. If we look at the values that have been realized in this marriage and compare them with those realized in conventional marriage plots, we see that Jane Austen means what she says: this will be a happy marriage because there is simply nothing left to make it anything less than perfectly happy. It fulfills every value embodied in the world of the book — with the possible exception that Emma may never learn to apply herself as she ought to her reading and her piano! It is a union of intelligence: of "reason," of "sense," of "judgment." It is a union of virtue: of "good will," of generosity, of unselfishness. It is a union of feeling: of "taste," "tenderness," "love," "beauty."[10]

In a general way, then, this plot offers us an experience superficially like that offered by most tragicomedy as well as by much of the cheapest popular art: we are made to desire certain good things for certain good characters, and then our desires are gratified. If we depended on general criteria derived from our justified boredom with such works, we should reject this one. But the critical difference lies in the precise quality of the values appealed to and the precise quality of the characters who violate or realize them. All of the cheap marriage plots in the world should not lead us to be embarrassed about our pleasure in Emma and Knightley's marriage. It is more than just the marriage: it is the *rightness* of *this* marriage, as a conclusion to all of the comic wrongness that has gone before. The good for Emma includes both her necessary reform and the resulting marriage.

[10]It has lately been fashionable to underplay the value of tenderness and good will in Jane Austen, in reaction to an earlier generation that overdid the picture of "gentle Jane." The trend seems to have begun in earnest with D. W. Harding's "Regulated Hatred: An Aspect of the Work of Jane Austen," *Scrutiny* 8 (March 1940): 346–62. While I do not feel as strongly aroused against this school of readers as does R. W. Chapman (see his *A Critical Bibliography*, p. 52, and his review of Mudrick's work in the *T. L. S.* [September 19, 1952]), it seems to me that another swing of the pendulum is called for: when Jane Austen praises the "relenting heart," she means that praise, though she is the same author who can lash the unrelenting heart with "regulated hatred." [Booth]

Marriage to an intelligent, amiable, good, and attractive man is the best thing that can happen to this heroine, and the readers who do not experience it as such are, I am convinced, far from knowing what Jane Austen is about — whatever they may say about the "bitter spinster's" attitude toward marriage.

Our modern sensibilities are likely to be rasped by any such formulation. We do not ordinarily like to encounter perfect endings in our novels — even in the sense of "perfectedness" or completion, the sense obviously intended by Jane Austen. We refuse to accept it when we see it: witness the many attempts to deny Dostoevski's success with Alyosha and Father Zossima in *The Brothers Karamazov*. Many of us find it embarrassing to talk of emotions based on moral judgment at all, particularly when the emotions have any kind of affirmative cast. Emma herself is something of a "modern" in this regard throughout most of the book. Her self-deception about marriage is as great as about most other important matters. Emma boasts to Harriet of her indifference to marriage, at the same time unconsciously betraying her totally inadequate view of the sources of human happiness.

> If I know myself, Harriet, mine is an active, busy mind, with a great many independent resources; and I do not perceive why I should be more in want of employment at forty or fifty than one-and-twenty. Women's usual occupations of eye and hand and mind will be as open to me then, as they are now; or with no important variation. If I draw less, I shall read more; if I give up music, I shall take to carpet-work.

Emma at carpet-work! If she knows herself indeed.

> And as for objects of interest, objects for the affections, which is, in truth, the great point of inferiority, the want of which is really the great evil to be avoided in *not* marrying [a magnificent concession, this] I shall be very well off, with all the children of a sister I love so much, to care about. There will be enough of them, in all probability, to supply every sort of sensation that declining life can need. There will be enough for every hope and every fear; and though my attachment to none can equal that of a parent, it suits my ideas of comfort better than what is warmer and blinder. My nephews and nieces! — I shall often have a niece with me [Ch. 10].

Without growing solemn about it — it is wonderfully comic — we can recognize that the humor springs here from very deep sources indeed. It can be fully enjoyed, in fact, only by the reader who has attained to a vision of human felicity far more profound than Emma's "comfort" and "want" and "need." It is a vision that includes not simply marriage, but a kind of loving converse not based, as is Emma's here, on whether the "loved" person will serve one's irreducible needs.

The comic effect of this repudiation of marriage is considerably increased by the fact that Emma always thinks of marriage for others as *their* highest good, and in fact unconsciously encourages her friend Harriet to fall in love with the very man she herself loves without knowing it. The delightful denouement is thus what we want not only because it is a supremely good thing for Emma, but because it is a supremely comic outcome of Emma's profound misunderstanding of herself and of the human condition. In the schematic language of Chapter 5, it satisfies both our practical desire for Emma's well-being and our appetite for the qualities proper to these artistic materials. It is thus a more resounding resolution than either of these elements separately could provide. The other major resolution of the work — Harriet's marriage with her farmer — reinforces this interpretation. Emma's sin against Harriet has been something far worse than the mere meddling of a busy-body. To destroy Harriet's chances for happiness — chances that depend entirely on her marriage — is as close to viciousness as any author could dare to take a heroine designed to be loved. We can laugh with Emma at this mistake (Ch. 54) only because Harriet's chance for happiness is restored.

Other values, like money, blood, and "consequence," are real enough in *Emma,* but only as they contribute to or are mastered by good taste, good judgment, and good morality. Money alone can make a Mrs. Churchill, but a man or woman "is silly to marry without it." Consequence untouched by sense can make a very inconsequential Mr. Woodhouse; untouched by sense or virtue it can make the much more contemptible Mr. and Miss Elliot of *Persuasion.* But it is a pleasant thing to have, and it does no harm unless, like the early Emma, one takes it too seriously. Charm and elegance without sufficient moral force can make a Frank Churchill; unschooled by morality it can lead to the baseness of Henry Crawford in *Mansfield Park* or Wickham in *Pride and Prejudice.* Even the supreme virtues are inadequate in isolation: good will alone will make a comic Miss Bates or a Mr. Weston, judgment with insufficient good will a comic Mr. John Knightley, and so on.

I am willing to risk the commonplace in such a listing because it is only thus that the full force of Jane Austen's comprehensive view can be seen. There is clearly at work here a much more detailed ordering of values than any conventional public philosophy of her time could provide. Obviously, few readers in her own time, and far fewer in our own, have ever approached this novel in full and detailed agreement with the author's norms. But they were led to join her as they read, and so are we.

EXPLICIT JUDGMENTS ON EMMA WOODHOUSE

We have said in passing almost enough of the other side of the coin — the judgment of particular actions as they relate to the general norms. But something must be said of the detailed "placing" of Emma, by direct commentary, in the hierarchy of values established by the novel. I must be convinced, for example, not only that tenderness for other people's feelings is an important trait but also that Emma's particular behavior violates the true standards of tenderness, if I am to savor to the full the episode of Emma's insult to Miss Bates and Knightley's reproach which follow. If I refuse to blame Emma, I may discover a kind of intellectual enjoyment in the episode, and I will probably think that any critic who talks of "belief" in tenderness as operating in such a context is taking things too seriously. But I can never enjoy the episode in its full intensity or grasp its formal coherence. Similarly, I must agree not only that to be dreadfully boring is a minor fault compared with the major virtue of "good will," but also that Miss Bates's exemplification of this fault and of this virtue entitle her to the respect which Emma denies. If I do not — while yet being able to laugh at Miss Bates — I can hardly understand, let alone enjoy, Emma's mistreatment of her.

But these negative judgments must be counteracted by a larger approval, and, as we would expect, the novel is full of direct apologies for Emma. Her chief fault, lack of good will or tenderness, must be read not only in relationship to the code of values provided by the book as a whole — a code which judges her as seriously deficient; it must also be judged in relationship to the harsh facts of the world around her, a world made up of human beings ranging in degree of selfishness and egotism from Knightley, who lapses from perfection when he tries to judge Frank Churchill, his rival, down to Mrs. Elton, who has most of Emma's faults and none of her virtues. In such a setting, Emma is easily forgiven. When she insults Miss Bates, for example, we remember that Miss Bates lives in a world where many others are insensitive and cruel. "Miss Bates, neither young, handsome, rich, nor married, stood in the very worst predicament in the world for having much of the public favour; and she had no intellectual superiority to make atonement to herself, or frighten those who might hate her, into outward respect." While it would be a mistake to see only this "regulated hatred" in Jane Austen's world, overlooking the tenderness and generosity, the hatred of viciousness is there, and there is enough vice in evidence to make Emma almost shine by comparison.

Often, Jane Austen makes this apology-by-comparison explicit. When Emma lies to Knightley about Harriet, very close to the end of the book, she is excused with a generalization about human nature: "Seldom, very seldom, does complete truth belong to any human disclosure; seldom can it happen that something is not a little disguised, or a little mistaken; but where, as in this case, though the conduct is mistaken, the feelings are not, it may not be very material. — Mr. Knightley could not impute to Emma a more relenting heart than she possessed, or a heart more disposed to accept of his."

THE IMPLIED AUTHOR AS FRIEND AND GUIDE

With all of this said about the masterful use of the narrator in *Emma*, there remain some "intrusions" unaccounted for by strict service to the story itself. "What did she say?" the narrator asks, at the crucial moment in the major love scene. "Just what she ought, of course. A lady always does. — She said enough to show there need not be despair — and to invite him to say more himself." To some readers this has seemed to demonstrate the author's inability to write a love scene, since it sacrifices "the illusion of reality."[11] But who has ever read this far in *Emma* under the delusion that he is reading a realistic portrayal which is suddenly shattered by the unnatural appearance of the narrator? If the narrator's superabundant wit is destructive of the kind of illusion proper to this work, the novel has been ruined long before.

But we should now be in a position to see precisely why the narrator's wit is not in the least out of place at the emotional climax of the novel. We have seen how the inside views of the characters and the author's commentary have been used from the beginning to get the values straight and to keep them straight and to help direct our reactions to Emma. But we also see here a beautiful case of the dramatized author as friend and guide. "Jane Austen," like "Henry Fielding," is a paragon of wit, wisdom, and virtue. She does not talk about her qualities; unlike Fielding she does not in *Emma* call direct attention to her artistic skill. But we are seldom allowed to forget about her for all that. When we read this novel we accept her as representing everything we admire most. She is as generous and wise as Knightley; in fact, she is a shade more penetrating in her judgment. She is as subtle and witty as Emma would like to think herself. Without being sentimental she is in favor of tenderness. She is able to put an adequate but not excessive value on wealth and rank. She recognizes a fool when she sees one, but unlike Emma she knows that it is both immoral and foolish to be rude to fools. She is, in short, a perfect human being, within the concept of perfection established by the book she writes; she even recognizes that human perfection of the kind *she* exemplifies is not quite attainable in real life. The process of her domination is of course circular; her character establishes the values for us according to which her character is then found

[11]Edd Winfield Parks, "Exegesis in Austen's Novels," *The South Atlantic Quarterly* 2. (January 1952): 117. [Booth]

to be perfect. But this circularity does not affect the success of her endeavor; in fact it insures it.

Her "omniscience" is thus a much more remarkable thing than is ordinarily implied by the term. All good novelists know all about their characters — all that they need to know. And the question of how their narrators are to find out all that *they* need to know, the question of "authority," is a relatively simple one. The real choice is much more profound than this would imply. It is a choice of the moral, not merely the technical, angle of vision from which the story is to be told.

Unlike the central intelligences of James and his successors, "Jane Austen" has learned nothing at the end of the novel that she did not know at the beginning. She needed to learn nothing. She knew everything of importance already. We have been privileged to watch with her as she observes her favorite character climb from a considerably lower platform to join the exalted company of Knightley, "Jane Austen," and those of us readers who are wise enough, good enough, and perceptive enough to belong up there too. As Katherine Mansfield says, "the truth is that every true admirer of the novels cherishes the happy thought that he alone — reading between the lines — has become the secret friend of their author."[12] Those who love "gentle Jane" as a secret friend may undervalue the irony and with those who see her in effect as the greatest of Shaw's heroines, flashing about her with the weapons of irony, may undervalue the emphasis on tenderness and good will. But only a very few can resist her.

The dramatic illusion of her presence as a character is thus fully as important as any other element in the story. When she intrudes, the illusion is not shattered. The only illusion we care about, the illusion of traveling intimately with a hardy little band of readers whose heads are screwed on tight and whose hearts are in the right place, is actually strengthened when we are refused the romantic love scenes. Like the author herself, we don't care about the love scenes. We can find love scenes in almost any novelist's works, but only here can we find a mind and heart that can give us clarity without oversimplification, sympathy and romance without sentimentality, and biting irony without cynicism.

[12] *Novels and Novelists*, ed. J. Middleton Murry (London, 1930), p. 304. [Booth]

Wolfgang Iser

b. 1926

Partly because his method involves critical analysis rather than historical scholarship and partly because he works on well-known British fiction, Wolfgang Iser is more familiar to North American critics than his phenomenologist colleague, Hans Robert Jauss. Iser was born in Marienberg, Germany, in 1926, and received his Ph.D. from the University of Heidelberg in 1957. His published books include Die Weltanschauungs Henry Fieldings (Henry Fielding's World View, 1952), Walter Pater — Die Autonomie des Ästhetischen *(1960; translated as* Walter Pater: The Aesthetic Moment), Die Appelstruktur der Texte (The Affective Structure of the Text, 1970), *and* Spensers Arkadien: Fiktion und Geschichte in der Englische Renaissance (Spenser's Arcadia: Fiction and History in the English Renaissance, 1970). *In North America, his most influential works are the two theoretical treatises based on the hermeneutics of Hans-Georg Gadamer and Roman Ingarden,* Der Implizite Leser *(1972; translated as* The Implied Reader*) and* Der Akte des Lesens *(1976; translated as* The Act of Reading*). Starting in the mid-1980s, Iser's work turned from purely phenomenological research to* *what he called "literary anthropology," a study of the cultural uses of literature. His recent work along that line is contained in* Prospecting: From Reader Response to Literary Anthropology *(1989);* The Fictive and the Imaginary: Charting Literary Anthropology *(1993); and* Staging Politics: The Lasting Impact of Shakespeare's Historical Plays *(1993). Iser is professor of English literature at the University of Konstanz in Germany and permanent visiting professor at the University of California at Irvine. Iser's Wellek Library lecture series,* The Range of Interpretation, *was published in 2000; his latest book is* How to Do Theory *(Blackwell, 2005).*

The Reading Process:
A Phenomenological Approach

I

The phenomenological theory of art lays full stress on the idea that, in considering a literary work, one must take into account not only the actual text but also, and in equal measure, the actions involved in responding to that text. Thus Roman Ingarden confronts the structure of the literary text with the ways in which it can be *konkretisiert* (realized).[1] The text as such offers different "schematised views"[2] through which the subject matter of the work can come to light, but the actual bringing to light is an action of *Konkretisation*. If this is so, then the literary work has two poles, which we might call the artistic and the esthetic: the artistic refers to the text created by the author, and the esthetic to the realization accomplished by the reader. From this polarity it follows that the literary work cannot be completely identical with the text, or with the realization of the text, but in fact must lie halfway between the two. The work is more than the text, for the text only takes on life when it is realized, and furthermore the realization is by no means independent of the individual disposition of the reader — though this in turn is acted upon by the different patterns of the text. The convergence of text and reader brings the literary work into existence, and this convergence can never be precisely pinpointed, but must always remain virtual, as it is not to be identified either with the reality of the text or with the individual disposition of the reader.

It is the virtuality of the work that gives rise to its dynamic nature, and this in turn is the precondition for the effects that the work calls forth. As the reader uses the various perspectives offered him by the text in order to relate the patterns and the "schematised views" to one another, he sets the work in motion, and this very process results ultimately in the awakening of responses within himself. Thus, reading causes the literary work to unfold its inherently dynamic character. That this is no new discovery is apparent from references made even in the early days of the novel. Laurence Sterne remarks in *Tristram Shandy:* ". . . no author, who understands the just boundaries of decorum and good-breeding, would presume to think all: The truest respect which you can pay to the reader's understanding, is to halve this matter amicably, and leave him something to imagine, in his turn, as well as yourself. For my own part, I am eternally paying him compliments of this kind, and do all that lies in my power to keep his imagination as busy as my own."[3] Sterne's conception of a literary text is that it is something like an arena in which reader and author participate in a game of the imagination. If the reader were given the whole story, and there were nothing left for him to do, then his imagination would never enter the field, the result would

[1]Cf. Roman Ingarden, *Vom Erkennen des literarischen Kuntstwerks* (Tübingen, 1968), pp. 49 ff. [Iser]

[2]For a detailed discussion of this term see Roman Ingarden, *Das literarische Kunstwerk* (Tübingen, 1960), pp. 270 ff. [Iser]

[3]Laurence Sterne, *Tristram Shandy* (London, 1956), II, 11: 79. [Iser]

be the boredom which inevitably arises when everything is laid out cut and dried before us. A literary text must therefore be conceived in such a way that it will engage the reader's imagination in the task of working things out for himself, for reading is only a pleasure when it is active and creative. In this process of creativity, the text may either not go far enough, or may go too far, so we may say that boredom and overstrain form the boundaries beyond which the reader will leave the field of play.

The extent to which the "unwritten" part of a text stimulates the reader's creative participation is brought out by an observation of Virginia Woolf's in her study of Jane Austen:

> Jane Austen is thus a mistress of much deeper emotion than appears upon the surface. She stimulates us to supply what is not there. What she offers is, apparently, a trifle, yet is composed of something that expands in the reader's mind and endows with the most enduring form of life scenes which are outwardly trivial. Always the stress is laid upon character. . . . The turns and twists of the dialogue keep us on the tenterhooks of suspense. Our attention is half upon the present moment, half upon the future. . . . Here, indeed, in this unfinished and in the main inferior story, are all the elements of Jane Austen's greatness.[4]

The unwritten aspects of apparently trivial scenes and the unspoken dialogue within the "turns and twists" not only draw the reader into the action but also lead him to shade in the many outlines suggested by the given situations, so that these take on a reality of their own. But as the reader's imagination animates these "outlines," they in turn will influence the effect of the written part of the text. Thus begins a whole dynamic process: the written text imposes certain limits on its unwritten implications in order to prevent these from becoming too blurred and hazy, but at the same time these implications, worked out by the reader's imagination, set the given situation against a background which endows it with far greater significance than it might have seemed to possess on its own. In this way, trivial scenes suddenly take on the shape of an "enduring form of life." What constitutes this form is never named, let alone explained in the text, although in fact it is the end product of the interaction between text and reader.

II

The question now arises as to how far such a process can be adequately described. For this purpose a phenomenological analysis recommends itself, especially since the somewhat sparse observations hitherto made of the psychology of reading tend mainly to be psychoanalytical, and so are restricted to the illustration of predetermined ideas concerning the unconscious. We shall, however, take a closer look later at some worthwhile psychological observations.

As a starting point for a phenomenological analysis we might examine the way in which sequent sentences act upon one another. This is of especial importance in literary texts in view of the fact that they do not correspond to any objective reality outside themselves. The world presented by literary texts is constructed out of what Ingarden has called *intentionale Satzkorrelate* (intentional sentence correlatives):

> Sentences link up in different ways to form more complex units of meaning that reveal a very varied structure giving rise to such entities as a short story, a novel, a dialogue, a drama, a scientific theory. . . . In the final analysis, there arises a particular world, with component parts determined in this way or that, and with all the variations that may occur within these parts — all this as a purely intentional correlative of a complex of sentences. If this complex finally forms a literary work, I call the whole sum of sequent intentional sentence correlatives the "world presented" in the work.[5]

This world, however, does not pass before the reader's eyes like a film. The sentences are "component parts" insofar as they make statements, claims, or observations, or convey information, and so establish various perspectives in the text. But they remain only "component parts" — they are not the sum total of the text itself. For the intentional correlatives disclose subtle connections

---

[4]Virginia Woolf, *The Common Reader*, First Series (London, 1957), p. 174. [Iser]

[5]Ingarden, *Vom Erkennen des literarischen Kunstwerks*, p. 29. [Iser]

which individually are less concrete than the statements, claims, and observations, even though these only take on their real meaningfulness through the interaction of their correlatives.

How is one to conceive the connection between the correlatives? It marks those points at which the reader is able to "climb aboard" the text. He has to accept certain given perspectives, but in doing so he inevitably causes them to interact. When Ingarden speaks of intentional sentence correlatives in literature, the statements made or information conveyed in the sentence is already in a certain sense qualified: the sentence does not consist solely of a statement — which, after all, would be absurd, as one can only make statements about things that exist — but aims at something beyond what it actually says. This is true of all sentences in literary works, and it is through the interaction of these sentences that their common aim is fulfilled. This is what gives them their own special quality in literary texts. In their capacity as statements, observations, purveyors of information, etc., they are always indications of something that is to come, the structure of which is foreshadowed by their specific content.

They set in motion a process out of which emerges the actual content of the text itself. In describing man's inner consciousness of time, Husserl once remarked: "Every originally constructive process is inspired by pre-intentions, which construct and collect the seed of what is to come, as such, and bring it to fruition."[6] For this bringing to fruition, the literary text needs the reader's imagination, which gives shape to the interaction of correlatives foreshadowed in structure by the sequence of the sentences. Husserl's observation draws our attention to a point that plays a not insignificant part in the process of reading. The individual sentences not only work together to shade in what is to come; they also form an expectation in this regard. Husserl calls this expectation "preintentions." As this structure is characteristic of *all* sentence correlatives, the interaction of these correlatives will not be a fulfillment of the expectation so much as a continual modification of it.

[6]Edmund Husserl, *Zur Phänomenologie des inneren Zeitbewusstseins, Gesammelte Werke* (The Hague, 1966), 10:52. [Iser]

For this reason, expectations are scarcely ever fulfilled in truly literary texts. If they were, then such texts would be confined to the individualization of a given expectation, and one would inevitably ask what such an intention was supposed to achieve. Strangely enough, we feel that any confirmative effect — such as we implicitly demand of expository texts, as we refer to the objects they are meant to present — is a defect in a literary text. For the more a text individualizes or confirms an expectation it has initially aroused, the more aware we become of its didactic purpose, so that at best we can only accept or reject the thesis forced upon us. More often than not, the very clarity of such texts will make us want to free ourselves from their clutches. But generally the sentence correlatives of literary texts do not develop in this rigid way, for the expectations they evoke tend to encroach on one another in such a manner that they are continually modified as one reads. One might simplify by saying that each intentional sentence correlative opens up a particular horizon, which is modified, if not completely changed, by succeeding sentences. While these expectations arouse interest in what is to come, the subsequent modification of them will also have a retrospective effect on what has already been read. This may now take on a different significance from that which it had at the moment of reading.

Whatever we have read sinks into our memory and is foreshortened. It may later be evoked again and set against a different background with the result that the reader is enabled to develop hitherto unforeseeable connections. The memory evoked, however, can never reassume its original shape, for this would mean that memory and perception were identical, which is manifestly not so. The new background brings to light new aspects of what we had committed to memory; conversely these, in turn, shed their light on the new background, thus arousing more complex anticipations. Thus, the reader, in establishing these interrelationships between past, present and future, actually causes the text to reveal its potential multiplicity of connections. These connections are the product of the reader's mind working on the raw material of the text, though they are not the text itself — for this consists just of sentences, statements, information, etc.

This is why the reader often feels involved in events which, at the time of reading, seem real to him, even though in fact they are very far from his own reality. The fact that completely different readers can be differently affected by the "reality" of a particular text is ample evidence of the degree to which literary texts transform reading into a creative process that is far above mere perception of what is written. The literary text activates our own faculties, enabling us to recreate the world it presents. The product of this creative activity is what we might call the virtual dimension of the text, which endows it with its reality. This virtual dimension is not the text itself, nor is it the imagination of the reader: it is the coming together of text and imagination.

As we have seen, the activity of reading can be characterized as a sort of kaleidoscope of perspectives, preintentions, recollections. Every sentence contains a preview of the next and forms a kind of viewfinder for what is to come; and this in turn changes the "preview" and so becomes a "viewfinder" for what has been read. This whole process represents the fulfillment of the potential, unexpressed reality of the text, but it is to be seen only as a framework for a great variety of means by which the virtual dimension may be brought into being. The process of anticipation and retrospection itself does not by any means develop in a smooth flow. Ingarden has already drawn attention to this fact and ascribes a quite remarkable significance to it:

> Once we are immersed in the flow of *Satzdenken* (sentence-thought), we are ready, after completing the thought of one sentence, to think out the "continuation," also in the form of a sentence — and that is, in the form of a sentence that connects up with the sentence we have just thought through. In this way the process of reading goes effortlessly forward. But if by chance the following sentence has no tangible connection whatever with the sentence we have just thought through, there then comes a blockage in the stream of thought. This hiatus is linked with a more or less active surprise, or with indignation. This blockage must be overcome if the reading is to flow once more.[7]

[7]Ingarden, *Vom Erkennen des literarischen Kunstwerks*, p. 32. [Iser]

The hiatus that blocks the flow of sentences is, in Ingarden's eyes, the product of chance, and is to be regarded as a flaw; this is typical of his adherence to the classical idea of art. If one regards the sentence sequence as a continual flow, this implies that the anticipation aroused by one sentence will generally be realized by the next, and the frustration of one's expectations will arouse feelings of exasperation. And yet literary texts are full of unexpected twists and turns, and frustration of expectations. Even in the simplest story there is bound to be some kind of blockage, if only because no tale can ever be told in its entirety. Indeed, it is only through inevitable omissions that a story gains its dynamism. Thus whenever the flow is interrupted and we are led off in unexpected directions, the opportunity is given to us to bring into play our own faculty for establishing connections — for filling in the gaps left by the text itself.[8]

These gaps have a different effect on the process of anticipation and retrospection, and thus on the "gestalt" of the virtual dimension, for they may be filled in different ways. For this reason, one text is potentially capable of several different realizations, and no reading can ever exhaust the full potential, for each individual reader will fill in the gaps in his own way, thereby excluding the various other possibilities; as he reads, he will make his own decision as to how the gap is to be filled. In this very act the dynamics of reading are revealed. By making his decision he implicitly acknowledges the inexhaustibility of the text; at the same time it is this very inexhaustibility that forces him to make his decision. With "traditional" texts this process was more or less unconscious, but modern texts frequently exploit it quite deliberately. They are often so fragmentary that one's attention is almost exclusively occupied with the search for connections between the fragments; the object of this is not to complicate the "spectrum" of connections, so much as to make us aware of the

[8]For a more detailed discussion of the function of "gaps" in literary texts see Wolfgang Iser, "Indeterminacy and the Reader's Response in Prose Fiction," *Aspects of Narrative* (English Institute Essays), ed. J. Hillis Miller (New York, 1971), pp. 1–45. [Iser]

nature of our own capacity for providing links. In such cases, the text refers back directly to our own preconceptions — which are revealed by the act of interpretation that is a basic element of the reading process. With all literary texts, then, we may say that the reading process is selective, and the potential text is infinitely richer than any of its individual realizations. This is borne out by the fact that a second reading of a piece of literature often produces a different impression from the first. The reasons for this may lie in the reader's own change of circumstances, still, the text must be such as to allow this variation. On a second reading familiar occurrences now tend to appear in a new light and seem to be at times corrected, at times enriched.

In every text there is a potential time sequence which the reader must inevitably realize, as it is impossible to absorb even a short text in a single moment. Thus the reading process always involves viewing the text through a perspective that is continually on the move, linking up the different phases, and so constructing what we have called the virtual dimension. This dimension, of course, varies all the time we are reading. However, when we have finished the text, and read it again, clearly our extra knowledge will result in a different time sequence; we shall tend to establish connections by referring to our awareness of what is to come, and so certain aspects of the text will assume a significance we did not attach to them on a first reading, while others will recede into the background. It is a common enough experience for a person to say that on a second reading he noticed things he had missed when he read the book for the first time, but this is scarcely surprising in view of the fact that the second time he is looking at the text from a different perspective. The time sequence that he realized on his first reading cannot possibly be repeated on a second reading, and this unrepeatability is bound to result in modifications of his reading experience. This is not to say that the second reading is "truer" than the first — they are, quite simply, different: the reader establishes the virtual dimension of the text by realizing a new time sequence. Thus even on repeated viewings a text allows and, indeed, induces innovative reading.

In whatever way, and under whatever circumstances the reader may link the different phases of the text together, it will always be the process of anticipation and retrospection that leads to the formation of the virtual dimension, which in turn transforms the text into an experience for the reader. The way in which this experience comes about through a process of continual modification is closely akin to the way in which we gather experience in life. And thus the "reality" of the reading experience can illuminate basic patterns of real experience:

> We have the experience of a world, not understood as a system of relations which wholly determine each event, but as an open totality the synthesis of which is inexhaustible. . . . From the moment that experience — that is, the opening on to our *de facto* world — is recognized as the beginning of knowledge, there is no longer any way of distinguishing a level of *a priori* truths and one of factual ones, what the world must necessarily be and what it actually is.[9]

The manner in which the reader experiences the text will reflect his own disposition, and in this respect the literary text acts as a kind of mirror; but at the same time, the reality which this process helps to create is one that will be *different* from his own (since, normally, we tend to be bored by texts that present us with things we already know perfectly well ourselves). Thus we have the apparently paradoxical situation in which the reader is forced to reveal aspects of himself in order to experience a reality which is different from his own. The impact this reality makes on him will depend largely on the extent to which he himself actively provides the unwritten part of the text, and yet in supplying all the missing links, he must think in terms of experiences different from his own; indeed, it is only by leaving behind the familiar world of his own experience that the reader can truly participate in the adventure the literary text offers him.

III

We have seen that, during the process of reading, there is an active interweaving of anticipation and retrospection, which on a second reading may

[9]M. Merleau-Ponty, *Phenomenology of Perception*, trans. Colin Smith (New York, 1962), pp. 219, 221. [Iser]

turn into a kind of advance retrospection. The impressions that arise as a result of this process will vary from individual to individual, but only within the limits imposed by the written as opposed to the unwritten text. In the same way, two people gazing at the night sky may both be looking at the same collection of stars, but one will see the image of a plough, and the other will make out a dipper. The "stars" in a literary text are fixed; the lines that join them are variable. The author of the text may, of course, exert plenty of influence on the reader's imagination — he has the whole panoply of narrative techniques at his disposal — but no author worth his salt will ever attempt to set the *whole* picture before his reader's eyes. If he does, he will very quickly lose his reader, for it is only by activating the reader's imagination that the author can hope to involve him and so realize the intentions of his text.

Gilbert Ryle, in his analysis of imagination, asks: "How can a person fancy that he sees something, without realizing that he is not seeing it?" He answers as follows:

> Seeing Helvellyn [the name of a mountain] in one's mind's eye does not entail, what seeing Helvellyn and seeing snapshots of Helvellyn entail, the having of visual sensations. It does involve the thought of having a view of Helvellyn and it is therefore a more sophisticated operation than that of having a view of Helvellyn. It is one utilization among others of the knowledge of how Helvellyn should look, or, in one sense of the verb, it is thinking how it should look. The expectations which are fulfilled in the recognition at sight of Helvellyn are not indeed fulfilled in picturing it, but the picturing of it is something like a rehearsal of getting them fulfilled. So far from picturing involving the having of faint sensations, or wraiths of sensations, it involves missing just what one would be due to get, if one were seeing the mountain.[10]

If one sees the mountain, then of course one can no longer imagine it, and so the act of picturing the mountain presupposes its absence. Similarly, with a literary text we can only picture things which are not there; the written part of the text gives us the knowledge, but it is the unwritten part that gives us the opportunity to picture things; indeed without the elements of indeterminacy, the gaps in the text, we should not be able to use our imagination.[11]

The truth of this observation is borne out by the experience many people have on seeing, for instance, the film of a novel. While reading *Tom Jones*, they may never have had a clear conception of what the hero actually looks like, but on seeing the film, some may say, "That's not how I imagined him." The point here is that the reader of *Tom Jones* is able to visualize the hero virtually for himself, and so his imagination senses the vast number of possibilities; the moment these possibilities are narrowed down to one complete and immutable picture, the imagination is put out of action, and we feel we have somehow been cheated. This may perhaps be an oversimplification of the process, but it does illustrate plainly the vital richness of potential that arises out of the fact that the hero in the novel must be pictured and cannot be seen. With the novel the reader must use his imagination to synthesize the information given him, and so his perception is simultaneously richer and more private; with the film he is confined merely to physical perception, and so whatever he remembers of the world he had pictured is brutally cancelled out.

IV

The "picturing" that is done by our imagination is only one of the activities through which we form the "gestalt" of a literary text. We have already discussed the process of anticipation and retrospection, and to this we must add the process of grouping together all the different aspects of a text to form the consistency that the reader will always be in search of. While expectations may be continually modified, and images continually expanded, the reader will still strive, even if unconsciously, to fit everything together in a consistent pattern. "In the reading of images, as in the hearing of speech, it is always hard to distinguish what is given to us from what we supplement in the process of projection which is triggered off by recognition . . . it is the guess of the beholder that tests the medley of forms and colours for

[10]Gilbert Ryle, *The Concept of Mind* (Harmondsworth, 1968), p. 255. [Iser]

[11]Cf. Iser, "Indeterminacy," pp. 11 ff., 42 ff. [Iser]

coherent meaning, crystallizing it into shape when a consistent interpretation has been found."[12] By grouping together the written parts of the text, we enable them to interact, we observe the direction in which they are leading us, and we project onto them the consistency which we, as readers, require. This "gestalt" must inevitably be colored by our own characteristic selection process. For it is not given by the text itself; it arises from the meeting between the written text and the individual mind of the reader with its own particular history of experience, its own consciousness, its own outlook. The "gestalt" is not the true meaning of the text; at best it is a configurative meaning; " . . . comprehension is an individual act of seeing-things-together, and only that."[13] With a literary text such comprehension is inseparable from the reader's expectations, and where we have expectations, there too we have one of the most potent weapons in the writer's armory — illusion.

Whenever "consistent reading suggests itself . . . illusion takes over."[14] Illusion, says Northrop Frye, is "fixed or definable, and reality is best understood as its negation."[15] The "gestalt" of a text normally takes on (or, rather, is given) this fixed or definable outline, as this is essential to our own understanding, but on the other hand, if reading were to consist of nothing but an uninterrupted building up of illusions, it would be a suspect, if not downright dangerous, process: instead of bringing us into contact with reality, it would wean us away from realities. Of course, there is an element of "escapism" in all literature, resulting from this very creation of illusion, but there are some texts which offer nothing but a harmonious world, purified of all contradiction and deliberately excluding anything that might disturb the illusion once established, and these are the texts that we generally do not like to classify as literary. Women's magazines and the brasher forms of the detective story might be cited as examples.

However, even if an overdose of illusion may lead to triviality, this does not mean that the process of illusion-building should ideally be dispensed with altogether. On the contrary, even in texts that appear to resist the formation of illusion, thus drawing our attention to the cause of this resistance, we still need the abiding illusion that the resistance itself is the consistent pattern underlying the text. This is especially true of modern texts, in which it is the very precision of the written details which increases the proportion of indeterminacy; one detail appears to contradict another, and so simultaneously stimulates and frustrates our desire to "picture," thus continually causing our imposed "gestalt" of the test to disintegrate. Without the formation of illusions, the unfamiliar world of the text would remain unfamiliar; through the illusions, the experience offered by the text becomes accessible to us, for it is only the illusion, on its different levels of consistency, that makes the experience "readable." If we cannot find (or impose) this consistency, sooner or later we will put the text down. The process is virtually hermeneutic. The text provokes certain expectations which in turn we project onto the text in such a way that we reduce the polysemantic possibilities to a single interpretation in keeping with the expectations aroused, thus extracting an individual, configurative meaning. The polysemantic nature of the text and the illusion-making of the reader are opposed factors. If the illusion were complete, the polysemantic nature would vanish; if the polysemantic nature were all-powerful, the illusion would be totally destroyed. Both extremes are conceivable, but in the individual literary text we always find some form of balance between the two conflicting tendencies. The formation of illusions, therefore, can never be total, but it is this very incompleteness that in fact gives it its productive value.

With regard to the experience of reading, Walter Pater once observed: "For to the grave reader words too are grave; and the ornamental word, the figure, the accessory form or colour or reference, is rarely content to die to thought precisely at the right moment, but will inevitably linger awhile, stirring a long 'brainwave' behind

[12]E. H. Gombrich, *Art and Illusion* (London, 1962), p. 204. [Iser]

[13]Louis O. Mink, "History and Fiction as Modes of Comprehension," *New Literary History* I (1970): 553. [Iser]

[14]Gombrich, *Art and Illusion*, p. 278. [Iser.]

[15]Northrop Frye, *Anatomy of Criticism* (New York, 1967), pp. 169 f. [Iser]

it of perhaps quite alien associations."[16] Even while the reader is seeking a consistent pattern in the text, he is also uncovering other impulses which cannot be immediately integrated or will even resist final integration. Thus the semantic possibilities of the text will always remain far richer than any configurative meaning formed while reading. But this impression is, of course, only to be gained through reading the text. Thus the configurative meaning can be nothing but a *pars pro toto*[17] fulfillment of the text, and yet this fulfillment gives rise to the very richness which it seeks to restrict, and indeed in some modern texts, our awareness of this richness takes precedence over any configurative meaning.

This fact has several consequences which, for the purpose of analysis, may be dealt with separately, though in the reading process they will all be working together. As we have seen, a consistent, configurative meaning is essential for the apprehension of an unfamiliar experience, which through the process of illusion-building we can incorporate in our own imaginative world. At the same time, this consistency conflicts with the many other possibilities of fulfillment it seeks to exclude, with the result that the configurative meaning is always accompanied by "alien associations" that do not fit in with the illusions formed. The first consequence, then, is the fact that in forming our illusions, we also produce at the same time a latent disturbance of these illusions. Strangely enough, this also applies to texts in which our expectations are actually fulfilled — though one would have thought that the fulfillment of expectations would help to complete the illusion. "Illusion wears off once the expectation is stepped up; we take it for granted and want more."[18]

The experiments in gestalt psychology referred to by Gombrich in *Art and Illusion* make one thing clear: ". . . though we may be intellectually aware of the fact that any given experience *must* be an illusion, we cannot, strictly speaking, watch ourselves having an illusion."[19] Now, if illusion were not a transitory state, this would mean that we could be, as it were, permanently caught up in it. And if reading were exclusively a matter of producing illusion — necessary though this is for the understanding of an unfamiliar experience — we should run the risk of falling victim to a gross deception. But it is precisely during our reading that the transitory nature of the illusion is revealed to the full.

As the formation of illusions is constantly accompanied by "alien associations" which cannot be made consistent with the illusions, the reader constantly has to lift the restrictions he places on the "meaning" of the text. Since it is he who builds the illusions, he oscillates between involvement in and observation of those illusions; he opens himself to the unfamiliar world without being imprisoned in it. Through this process the reader moves into the presence of the fictional world and so experiences the realities of the text as they happen.

In the oscillation between consistency and "alien associations," between involvement in and observation of the illusion, the reader is bound to conduct his own balancing operation, and it is this that forms the esthetic experience offered by the literary text. However, if the reader were to achieve a balance, obviously he would then no longer be engaged in the process of establishing and disrupting consistency. And since it is this very process that gives rise to the balancing operation, we may say that the inherent nonachievement of balance is a prerequisite for the very dynamism of the operation. In seeking the balance we inevitably have to start out with certain expectations, the shattering of which is integral to the esthetic experience.

Furthermore, to say merely that "our expectations are satisfied" is to be guilty of another serious ambiguity. At first sight such a statement seems to deny the obvious fact that much of our enjoyment is derived from surprises, from betrayals of our expectations. The solution to this paradox is to find some ground for a distinction between "surprise" and "frustration." Roughly, the distinction can be made in terms of the effects which the two kinds of experiences have upon us. Frustration blocks or checks activity. It necessitates new orientation for our activity, if we are to escape the *cul de sac*. Consequently, we abandon the frustrating object and

[16]Walter Pater, *Appreciations* (London, 1920), p. 18. [Iser]
[17]Partial.
[18]Gombrich, *Art and Illusion*, p. 54. [Iser]
[19]Ibid., p. 5. [Iser]

return to blind impulse activity. On the other hand, surprise merely causes a temporary cessation of the exploratory phase of the experience, and a recourse to intense contemplation and scrutiny. In the latter phase the surprising elements are seen in their connection with what has gone before, with the whole drift of the experience, and the enjoyment of these values is then extremely intense. Finally, it appears that there must always be some degree of novelty or surprise in all these values if there is to be a progressive specification of the direction of the total act . . . and any aesthetic experience tends to exhibit a continuous interplay between "deductive" and "inductive" operations.[20]

It is this interplay between "deduction" and "induction" that gives rise to the configurative meaning of the text, and not the individual expectations, surprises, or frustrations arising from the different perspectives. Since this interplay obviously does not take place in the text itself, but can only come into being through the process of reading, we may conclude that this process formulates something that is unformulated in the text and yet represents its "intention." Thus, by reading we uncover the unformulated part of the text, and this very indeterminacy is the force that drives us to work out a configurative meaning while at the same time giving us the necessary degree of freedom to do so.

As we work out a consistent pattern in the text, we will find our "interpretation" threatened, as it were, by the presence of other possibilities of "interpretation," and so there arise new areas of indeterminacy (though we may only be dimly aware of them, if at all, as we are continually making "decisions" which will exclude them). In the course of a novel, for instance, we sometimes find that characters, events, and backgrounds seem to change their significance; what really happens is that the other "possibilities" begin to emerge more strongly, so that we become more directly aware of them. Indeed, it is this very shifting of perspectives that makes us feel that a novel is much more "true-to-life." Since it is we ourselves who establish the levels of interpretation and switch from one to another as we conduct our balancing operation, we ourselves impart to the text the dynamic lifelikeness which, in turn, enables us to absorb an unfamiliar experience into our personal world.

As we read, we oscillate to a greater or lesser degree between the building and the breaking of illusions. In a process of trial and error, we organize and reorganize the various data offered us by the text. These are the given factors, the fixed points on which we base our "interpretation," trying to fit them together in the way we think the author meant them to be fitted. "For to perceive, a beholder must *create* his own experience. And his creation must include relations comparable to those which the original producer underwent. They are not the same in any literal sense. But with the perceiver, as with the artist, there must be an ordering of the elements of the whole that is in form, although not in details, the same as the process of organization the creator of the work consciously experienced. Without an act of recreation the object is not perceived as a work of art."[21]

The act of recreation is not a smooth or continuous process, but one which, in its essence, relies on *interruptions* of the flow to render it efficacious. We look forward, we look back, we decide, we change our decisions, we form expectations, we are shocked by their nonfulfillment, we question, we muse, we accept, we reject; this is the dynamic process of recreation. This process is steered by two main structural components within the text: first, a repertoire of familiar literary patterns and recurrent literary themes, together with allusions to familiar social and historical contexts; second, techniques or strategies used to set the familiar against the unfamiliar. Elements of the repertoire are continually backgrounded or foregrounded with a resultant strategic overmagnification, trivialization, or even annihilation of the allusion. This defamiliarization of what the reader thought he recognized is bound to create a tension that will intensify his expectations as well as his distrust of those expectations. Similarly, we may be confronted by narrative techniques that establish links between things we find difficult to connect, so that we are

---

[20]B. Ritchie, "The Formal Structure of the Aesthetic Object," in *The Problems of Aesthetics*, ed. Eliseo Vivas and Murray Krieger (New York, 1965), pp. 230 f. [Iser]

[21]John Dewey, *Art as Experience* (New York, 1958), p. 54. [Iser]

forced to reconsider data we at first held to be perfectly straightforward. One need only mention the very simple trick, so often employed by novelists, whereby the author himself takes part in the narrative, thus establishing perspectives which would not have arisen out of the mere narration of the events described. Wayne Booth once called this the technique of the "unreliable narrator,"[22] to show the extent to which a literary device can counter expectations arising out of the literary text. The figure of the narrator may act in permanent opposition to the impressions we might otherwise form. The question then arises as to whether this strategy, opposing the formation of illusions, may be integrated into a consistent pattern, lying, as it were, a level deeper than our original impressions. We may find that our narrator, by opposing us, in fact turns us against him and thereby strengthens the illusion he appears to be out to destroy; alternatively, we may be so much in doubt that we begin to question all the processes that lead us to make interpretative decisions. Whatever the cause may be, we will find ourselves subjected to this same interplay of illusion-forming and illusion-breaking that makes reading essentially a recreative process.

We might take, as a simple illustration of this complex process, the incident in Joyce's *Ulysses* in which Bloom's cigar alludes to Ulysses's spear. The context (Bloom's cigar) summons up a particular element of the repertoire (Ulysses's spear); the narrative technique relates them to one another as if they were identical. How are we to "organize" these divergent elements, which, through the very fact that they are put together, separate one element so clearly from the other? What are the prospects here for a consistent pattern? We might say that it is ironic — at least that is how many renowned Joyce readers have understood it.[23] In this case, irony would be the form of organization that integrates the material. But if this is so, what is the object of the irony? Ulysses's spear, or Bloom's cigar? The uncertainty surrounding this simple question already puts a strain on the consistency we have established and, indeed, begins to puncture it, especially when other problems make themselves felt as regards the remarkable conjunction of spear and cigar. Various alternatives come to mind, but the variety alone is sufficient to leave one with the impression that the consistent pattern has been shattered. And even if, after all, one can still believe that irony holds the key to the mystery, this irony must be of a very strange nature; for the formulated text does not merely mean the opposite of what has been formulated. It may even mean something that cannot be formulated at all. The moment we try to impose a consistent pattern on the text, discrepancies are bound to arise. These are, as it were, the reverse side of the interpretative coin, an involuntary product of the process that creates discrepancies by trying to avoid them. And it is their very presence that draws us into the text, compelling us to conduct a creative examination not only of the text but also of ourselves.

This entanglement of the reader is, of course, vital to any kind of text, but in the literary text we have the strange situation that the reader cannot know what his participation actually entails. We know that we share in certain experiences, but we do not know what happens to us in the course of this process. This is why, when we have been particularly impressed by a book, we feel the need to talk about it; we do not want to get away from it by talking about it — we simply want to understand more clearly what it is in which we have been entangled. We have undergone an experience, and now we want to know consciously *what* we have experienced. Perhaps this is the prime usefulness of literary criticism — it helps to make conscious those aspects of the text which would otherwise remain concealed in the subconscious; it satisfies (or helps to satisfy) our desire to talk about what we have read.

The efficacy of a literary text is brought about by the apparent evocation and subsequent negation of the familiar. What at first seemed to be an affirmation of our assumptions leads to our own rejection of them, thus tending to prepare us for a re-orientation. And it is only when we have outstripped our preconceptions and left the shelter of the familiar that we are in a position to gather new

[22]Cf. Wayne C. Booth, *The Rhetoric of Fiction* (Chicago, 1961), pp. 211 ff., 339 ff. [Iser]

[23]Richard Ellmann, "Ulysses: The Divine Nobody," in *Twelve Original Essays on Great English Novels,* ed. Charles Shapiro (Detroit, 1960), p. 247, classified this particular allusion as "mock-heroic." [Iser]

experiences. As the literary text involves the reader in the formation of illusion and the simultaneous formation of the means whereby the illusion is punctured, reading reflects the process by which we gain experience. Once the reader is entangled, his own preconceptions are continually overtaken, so that the text becomes his "present" while his own ideas fade into the "past"; as soon as this happens he is open to the immediate experience of the text, which was impossible so long as his preconceptions were his "present."

V

In our analysis of the reading process so far, we have observed three important aspects that form the basis of the relationship between reader and text: the process of anticipation and retrospection, the consequent unfolding of the text as a living event, and the resultant impression of lifelikeness.

Any "living event" must, to a greater or lesser degree, remain open. In reading, this obliges the reader to seek continually for consistency, because only then can he close up situations and comprehend the unfamiliar. But consistency-building is itself a living process in which one is constantly forced to make selective decisions — and these decisions in their turn give a reality to the possibilities which they exclude, insofar as they may take effect as a latent disturbance of the consistency established. This is what causes the reader to be entangled in the text-"gestalt" that he himself has produced.

Through this entanglement the reader is bound to open himself up to the workings of the text and so leave behind his own preconceptions. This gives him the chance to have an experience in the way George Bernard Shaw once described it: "You have learnt something. That always feels at first as if you had lost something."[24] Reading reflects the structure of experience to the extent that we must suspend the ideas and attitudes that shape our own personality before we can experience the unfamiliar world of the literary text. But during this process, something happens to us.

This "something" needs to be looked at in detail, especially as the incorporation of the unfamiliar into our own range of experience has been to a certain extent obscured by an idea very common in literary discussion: namely, that the process of absorbing the unfamiliar is labeled as the *identification* of the reader with what he reads. Often the term "identification" is used as if it were an explanation, whereas in actual fact it is nothing more than a description. What is normally meant by "identification" is the establishment of affinities between oneself and someone outside oneself — a familiar ground on which we are able to experience the unfamiliar. The author's aim, though, is to convey the experience and, above all, an attitude toward that experience. Consequently, "identification" is not an end in itself, but a stratagem by means of which the author stimulates attitudes in the reader.

This of course is not to deny that there does arise a form of participation as one reads; one is certainly drawn into the text in such a way that one has the feeling that there is no distance between oneself and the events described. This involvement is well summed up by the reaction of a critic to reading Charlotte Brontë's *Jane Eyre:* "We took up *Jane Eyre* one writer's evening, somewhat piqued at the extravagant commendations we had heard, and sternly resolved to be as critical as Croker. But as we read on we forgot both commendations and criticism, identified ourselves with Jane in all her troubles, and finally married Mr. Rochester about four in the morning."[25] The question is how and why did the critic identify himself with Jane?

In order to understand this "experience," it is well worth considering Georges Poulet's observations on the reading process. He says that books only take on their full existence in the reader.[26] It is true that they consist of ideas thought out by someone else, but in reading the reader becomes the subject that does the thinking. Thus there disappears the subject-object division that otherwise

[24]G. B. Shaw, *Major Barbara* (London, 1964), p. 316. [Iser]

[25]William George Clark, *Fraser's* (December, 1849): 692, quoted by Kathleen Tillotson, *Novels of the Eighteen-Forties* (Oxford, 1961), p. 19 f. [Iser]
[26]Cf. Georges Poulet, "Phenomenology of Reading," *New Literary History* I (1969): 54. [Iser]

is a prerequisite for all knowledge and all observation, and the removal of this division puts reading in an apparently unique position as regards the possible absorption of new experiences. This may well be the reason why relations with the world of the literary text have so often been misinterpreted as identification. From the idea that in reading we must think the thoughts of someone else, Poulet draws the following conclusion: "Whatever I think is a part of *my* mental world. And yet here I am thinking a thought which manifestly belongs to another mental world, which is being thought in me just as though I did not exist. Already the notion is inconceivable and seems even more so if I reflect that, since every thought must have a subject to think it, this *thought* which is alien to me and yet in me, must also have in me a *subject* which is alien to me. . . . Whenever I read, I mentally pronounce an *I,* and yet the *I* which I pronounce is not myself."[27]

But for Poulet this idea is only part of the story. The strange subject that thinks the strange thought in the reader indicates the potential presence of the author, whose ideas can be "internalized" by the reader: "Such is the characteristic condition of every work which I summon back into existence by placing my consciousness at its disposal. I give it not only existence, but awareness of existence."[28] This would mean that consciousness forms the point at which author and reader converge, and at the same time it would result in the cessation of the temporary self-alienation that occurs to the reader when his consciousness brings to life the ideas formulated by the author. This process gives rise to a form of communication which, however, according to Poulet, is dependent on two conditions: the life-story of the author must be shut out of the work and the individual disposition of the reader must be shut out of the act of reading. Only then can the thoughts of the author take place subjectively in the reader, who thinks what he is not. It follows that the work itself must be thought of as a consciousness, because only in this way is there an adequate basis for the author-reader relationship — a relationship that can only come about through the negation of the author's own life-story and the reader's own disposition. This conclusion is actually drawn by Poulet when he describes the work as the self-presentation or materialization of consciousness: "And so I ought not to hesitate to recognize that so long as it is animated by this vital inbreathing inspired by the act of reading, a work of literature becomes (at the expense of the reader whose own life it suspends) a sort of human being, that it is a mind conscious of itself and constituting itself in me as the subject of its own objects."[29] Even though it is difficult to follow such a substantialist conception of the consciousness that constitutes itself in the literary work, there are, nevertheless, certain points in Poulet's argument that are worth holding onto. But they should be developed along somewhat different lines.

If reading removes the subject-object division that constitutes all perception, it follows that the reader will be "occupied" by the thoughts of the author, and these in turn will cause the drawing of new "boundaries." Text and reader no longer confront each other as object and subject, but instead the "division" takes place within the reader himself. In thinking the thoughts of another, his own individuality temporarily recedes into the background, since it is supplanted by these alien thoughts, which now become the theme on which his attention is focused. As we read, there occurs an artificial division of our personality, because we take as a theme for ourselves something that we are not. Consequently when reading we operate on different levels. For although we may be thinking the thoughts of someone else, what we are will not disappear completely — it will merely remain a more or less powerful virtual force. Thus, in reading there are these two levels — the alien "me" and the real, virtual "me" — which are never completely cut off from each other. Indeed, we can only make someone else's thoughts into an absorbing theme for ourselves, provided the virtual background of our own personality can adapt to it. Every text we read draws a different boundary within our personality, so that the virtual background (the real "me") will take on a different form, according to the theme of the text concerned. This is inevitable, if

[27]Ibid., p. 56. [Iser]
[28]Ibid., p. 59. [Iser]

[29]Ibid. [Iser]

only for the fact that the relationship between alien theme and virtual background is what makes it possible for the unfamiliar to be understood.

In this context there is a revealing remark made by D. W. Harding, arguing against the idea of identification with what is read: "What is sometimes called wish-fulfilment in novels and plays can . . . more plausibly be described as wish-formulation or the definition of desires. The cultural levels at which it works may vary widely; the process is the same. . . . It seems nearer the truth . . . to say that fictions contribute to defining the reader's or spectator's values, and perhaps stimulating his desires, rather than to suppose that they gratify desire by some mechanism of vicarious experience."[30] In the act of reading, having to think something that we have not yet experienced does not mean only being in a position to conceive or even understand it; it also means that such acts of conception are possible and successful to the degree that they lead to something being

[30]D. W. Harding, "Psychological Processes in the Reading of Fiction," in *Aesthetics in the Modern World,* ed. Harold Osborne (London, 1968), p. 313 f. [Iser]

formulated in us. For someone else's thoughts can only take a form in our consciousness if, in the process, our unformulated faculty for deciphering those thoughts is brought into play — a faculty which, in the act of deciphering, also formulates itself. Now since this formulation is carried out on terms set by someone else, whose thoughts are the theme of our reading, it follows that the formulation of our faculty for deciphering cannot be along our own lines of orientation.

Herein lies the dialectical structure of reading. The need to decipher gives us the chance to formulate our own deciphering capacity — i.e., we bring to the fore an element of our being of which we are not directly conscious. The production of the meaning of literary texts — which we discussed in connection with forming the "gestalt" of the text — does not merely entail the discovery of the unformulated, which can then be taken over by the active imagination of the reader; it also entails the possibility that we may formulate ourselves and so discover what had previously seemed to elude our consciousness. These are the ways in which reading literature gives us the chance to formulate the unformulated.

Norman N. Holland

b. 1927

An orthodox New Critic in his first book on Restoration comedy, Norman Holland is best known for his contributions to psychoanalytical and reader-response criticism. Holland was born in New York City and educated at the Massachusetts Institute of Technology (B.S., 1947) and at Harvard, where he received an LL.B. in 1950 and a Ph.D. in English in 1956. During the next ten years, Holland taught English at MIT while undergoing psychoanalytic training at the Boston Psychoanalytic Institute. One result of this dual endeavor was Psychoanalysis and Shakespeare *(1966). In 1966 Holland moved to the State University of New York at Buffalo as professor and chairman of the English department. There he analyzed the theory underlying the literary techniques of his Shakespeare book in writing* The Dynamics of Literary Response *(1968), which claims that meaning is produced in a transaction between text and reader: The text manages the reader's defensive transformation of its informing fantasy. In 1970 Holland founded the Center for the Psychological Study of the Arts and served as director until 1979. During that decade, Holland's interests shifted from the text to the reader, influenced by Heinz Lichtenstein's notion of the "identity theme" by which the individual ego styles its response to threatening stimuli. Holland's reader-response criticism appears in works such as* Poems in

Persons *(1973)*, 5 Readers Reading *(1975)*, Laughing *(1982)*, The I *(1985)*, The Brain of Robert Frost: A Cognitive Approach to Literature *(1988)*, *and* The Critical I *(1991)*. *Since 1983, Holland has been Millbauer Eminent Scholar and professor of English at the University of Florida, Gainesville. "The Question: Who Reads What How?" is from* 5 *Readers Reading. His recent published essays include "The Neurosciences and the Arts"* (2001) *and "Psychoanalysis as a Science"* (2004).

The Question: Who Reads What How?

The story was William Faulkner's "A Rose for Emily," and its one description of Miss Emily as a young girl was as clear as a description could be. The narrator, apparently one of the townspeople, says: "We had long thought of them as a tableau, Miss Emily a slender figure in white in the background, her father a spraddled silhouette in the foreground, his back to her and clutching a horsewhip, the two of them framed by the back-flung front door." Faulkner has pictured the Griersons as exactly as a photographer would, but that precision quite disappears when the description passes over into the mind of a reader. It disappears even if the reader is as well trained and fairly experienced as the five students of English literature who are the subjects of this book. Sam, Saul, Shep, Sebastian, and Sandra (as I shall call them) all spoke about this "tableau."

Good-natured, easygoing, dapper Sam singled it out as virtually the first thing he wanted to talk about in the story: "The father was very domineering. One of the most striking [*sic*] images in the book is that of the townsfolk looking through the door as her father stands there with a horsewhip in his hands, feet spread apart and between or through him you see a picture of Emily standing in the background, and that pretty much sums up exactly the kind of relationship they had." Sam was stressing the father's dominance and, in doing so, was positioning the townspeople so that they could see Emily between her father's legs.

This was part of what he found highly romantic in the story. "The frailty and femininity that that evokes!" he sighed. "Just that one frail, 'slender figure in white,' just those words there really show us the Emily that was and the Emily that might have been." Yet, almost at the same moment he was responding to this lacy, feminine Emily, he could say, "The word 'tableau' is important. While they [the townspeople] may be envious and while they may be angry at the way that these people act, they yet need it, it seems, they in a way like to have it, much as one is terrified at the power of a god and yet needing him so much and, you know, sidling up to him and paying homage to him and in the same way I think Emily comes to function as this god symbol." A curious turnabout from frailty and femininity.

By contrast, Saul, a scholarly type, was circumspect. Sam, in his expansive way, trusted his memory, but Saul, when I asked him about that image, took out his copy of the story and read it over carefully to himself. "Ummm. I had remembered the word 'tableau,' and I had forgotten the rest of it. 'Horsewhip' there — rings — 'spraddled silhouette.' That seems right to me. That summarizes the relationship, I think. She's in the back in white, of course, I think of these white gowns in the plantation balls. The father a 'spraddled silhouette.' He's no longer stern and erect. He's spraddled across the door." Saul was seeing Emily's father exactly the opposite way from Sam, as a weakened, sprawled figure, at least until he read over to himself the sentence with the horsewhip in it again. "A horsewhip suggesting all sorts of nasty, sexual, sadistic overtones," but then he blurred that image. "Do they mean the horsewhip rather than his own stern demeanor? Or just the normal embodiment of his traditions suggests the decline like 'spraddled' does? And then 'framed by the back-flung front door' just completes the tableau. It's a nice device. Faulkner makes that one work, too. That's a nice emblem." Well, maybe so, but Saul had so divided it up and dissolved it into questions and alternatives as to leave me quite puzzled about what he thought the thrust of the image finally was.

Shep presented himself as a rebel and radical, but his reading of the tableau seemed to me no more original or idiosyncratic than Saul's or Sam's. I read the passage to him, and he commented simply. "O.K. Protective image. That he's defending Southern womanhood, perhaps, and defending it in that same sort of mindless way that says, 'Well, now, we've got to defend it.'" He went on to decide that Southern womanhood might well have defended itself and then to make a suggestion quite opposite to "protective image." "You could, I suppose, as an alternative interpretation say that the horsewhip is something which he's also adept with indoors as well as outdoors, but I don't think so. Maybe there's overtones that Daddy is sadistic enough — horsewhips being pretty sadistic things to carry around when you're greeting people, you know — that Daddy is sadistic enough where he wouldn't mind taking a belt at Emily once in a while, but I don't think they're much more than overtones." In talking about the tableau as such, he talked only about Emily's father, and in this curiously alternative or opposed way. Earlier he had recalled Emily as a young woman (and the tableau is the only place she is so described): "I can see her as a very good-looking, dark-haired girl who had a penchant for wearing dark clothes." Again, I sense in his substituting dark for white a will opposing the text, although at the same time, Shep said he liked this story very much.

Sophisticated, sardonic, somewhat cynical, a lapsed Catholic with aspirations toward aristocracy, Sebastian did not discuss the tableau as such, although he clearly remembered it in typing Emily as "the aristocrat of the Southern town, whose father is the original superego with a horsewhip, beating off suitors." "He's denying her access to suitable sexual partners." Often, Sebastian tended to distance and type the characters this way and to flirt with the actual, physical details. Here he saw Miss Emily as "the aristocrat," her father as "the original superego," but converted the "suitors" to "sexual partners."

Sandra, the fifth reader, was a tall, very attractive woman, gentle and subdued in her manner. She liked the story intensely, had read it several times, and had even, in her freshman year, written a term paper on it. Yet she recalled the tableau oddly: "They said they always had this picture of him standing, you know, sitting in the door with a whip in his hand." As for Emily, "I see her as very young and dressed in white and standing up, I guess she's supposed to be standing up behind her father, who would probably be looking *very* cross, say, if someone had come to call on her. No doubt, she would have a certain amount — Possibly fearful, but probably more regretful because she's being, they even say, robbed of something at that point. . . . There would be a great amount of strain on her face because of her inability to do anything except just watch." Sandra saw the emotional overtones in the tableau in a more subtle, emphatic way than the four male readers did, so that she, too, had her own version of the image.

Indeed, one can say that each of the readers had a different version of Emily and her father. He was standing, sitting; erect, sprawled; domineering, weakened; sadistic, protective, and so on — sometimes even to the same reader. Emily was dressed in white, as for a plantation ball, or black; frail, but godlike; fearful, but "the aristocrat." Some of these differences involve outright misreadings, but most do not. Conceivably, one could "teach" or coerce these five readers into consensus, but even so, whatever in each person's character originally colored his perception of the tableau would go on coloring his perception of every other element in the story. What is that something, that ineffable effect of personality on perception? That is the issue this book explores.

As the late Stanley Edgar Hyman once said, "Each reader poems his own poem." Yet we know very little — practically nothing — about such "poeming," about the way a reader recreates the literary experience in himself. Today's literary critics are expert in pointing out an essence for any literary work. Today's psychologists — particularly the psychoanalytic psychologists — are equally adept at conceptualizing the essential dynamics of individuals. Yet we do not know how literature and readers interact.

We can find out, if you and I apply to what Sam and the other readers said, a combination of the close reading literary critics have so skillfully developed in the last decades and psychological methods of reading from language to personality.

We shall move slowly — sometimes we shall seem to go word by word — but once we have put psychoanalytic interpretation together with the literary critic's, we shall have established four principles that account for the way readers read to fit their personalities.

As for now, however, in the words of a recent book on the problem of literary response, "We know almost nothing about the process of reading and the interaction of man and book."[1] In a manner all too common in the world of belles-lettres, however, the "almost nothing" we know tends to become complexity piled upon complexity, language explained by more language, authorities resting on other authorities — a splendid disguise of abstractions much like the emperor's new clothes. "Scholars and critics," Walter Slatoff writes, "who would distinguish carefully between various sorts of Neo-Platonism, or examine in minute detail the structure of a chapter or the transmutations of a prevailing metaphor, or trace the full nuances of a topical allusion, will settle happily for mere labels like distance, involvement, identification,"[2] labels that not only suffer from vagueness but deceive, creating the illusion that they refer to some real reaction people in fact shared and the critic in fact observed.

This tradition — assuming a uniform response on the part of readers and audiences that the critic somehow knows and understands — goes back to Aristotle's concept of catharsis, and his notions about people's apparently fixed responses to details of wording. Or this tradition might even have originated in Plato's assertion that poetry debilitates. Although the Greeks observed the phenomena that they ascribed to audiences better than later theorists, the tradition flourished after them, reaching a peak with the "rules" of the lesser neoclassical critics. Early psychoanalytic writers on literature followed, rather uncritically, this collectivist view from the litterateurs. Thus we find Otto Rank defending his oedipal interpretations of myths because, "The people imagine the hero in this manner, investing him

with their own infantile fantasies."[3] Freud himself assumed a collective response to *Oedipus Rex* in the letter of October 15, 1897, in which he reported to his confidant Fliess, "I have found love of the mother and jealousy of the father in my own case too, and now believe it to be a general phenomenon of early childhood." "If that is the case, the gripping power of *Oedipus Rex,* in spite of all the rational objections to the inexorable fate that the story presupposes, becomes intelligible." "Every member of the audience was once a budding Oedipus in phantasy, and this dream-fulfillment played out in reality causes everyone to recoil in horror, with the full measure of repression which separates his infantile from his present state."[4]

Everyone recoils? Freud himself avoided this fallacy when he studied jokes as a kind of mini-literature; they have a "frame" and a text with especially sensitive formal balances and a response. What would one think of a theory of jokes that always concluded, "and so you laugh" or "and so you don't laugh," regardless of whether you did nor didn't in fact laugh? After all, someone might have heard the joke before; someone else might be depressed; a third person might have no sense of humor, and so on. Indeed, responses to jokes are so various that, for a time, researchers (at Yale) were exploring a "mirth response test," trying to sort personality types by observing which cartoons they found funny.[5] Should we then postulate that responses to tragedy, something so infinitely more subtle than a cartoon, are fixed? No, and for some decades now we have, in fact, known the contrary.

It was in the 1920s that I. A. Richards asked his Cambridge undergraduates for the protocols that led to his ground-breaking *Practical Criticism.*[6] He

[1]Walter J. Slatoff, *With Respect to Readers: Dimensions of Literary Response* (Ithaca and London: Cornell University Press, 1970), p. 188. [Holland]

[2]Ibid., p. 35. [Holland]

[3]Otto Rank, *The Myth of the Birth of the Hero* (1914) (New York: Vintage Books, 1959), Chapter 3, p. 89n. [Holland]

[4]Marie Bonaparte, Anna Freud, Ernst Kris, eds., *The Origins of Psychoanalysis,* trans. Eric Mosbacher and James Strachey (New York: Basic Books, 1954), letter of October 15, 1897. [Holland]

[5]Jacob Levine, "Response to Humor," *Scientific American* 194 (1956): 31–35. [Holland]

[6]I. A. Richards, *Practical Criticism: A Study of Literary Judgment* (New York: Harcourt, Brace, 1951). [Holland]

asked his students "to comment freely in writing on" a series of poems, their authorship undisclosed. Richards found that these supposedly well-educated young Englishmen were evaluating very strangely indeed, misreading the plain sense of the poems, imposing cranky sets of preconceptions, responding in terms of stock sentimentalities, cynicisms, and other doctrines, as well as (perhaps) irrelevant memories. Richards, let us notice, was exploring his readers' conscious, verbalized responses to literature. Interested in education, he tended to concentrate on those parts of literary response that could be taught, and indeed, his analysis of misreadings helped to reform, root and branch, the teaching of literature over the next four decades. Today, even among schoolchildren, one finds more sophisticated reading than Richards found among his jazz-age Cantabrigians.[7]

One would expect the giant entertainment corporations, with millions riding on each reel of celluloid, to have studied response far more carefully than impoverished English teachers could. But the published research in this field remains rather elementary.[8] There are many studies of effect, but they move casually back and forth between the transfer of information, the fulfillment of individuals' needs (for example, to escape), the impact on morality (typically delinquency), and immediate reactions of "like" and "dislike." Indeed, the industry has developed machines — the Lazarsfeld-Stanton program analyzer, the Cirlin Reactograph — with which an audience can indicate its fluctuating likes, dislikes, and indifferences. Of course, such a device cannot sort out variables — one cannot tell, for example, whether a member of the audience is disliking the whole movie or just the "bad guy" in it. In general, this one-dimensional quality carries over to the analysis of the content of films. The most sophisticated scheme I have seen only gets to issues like "Main story type," that is, "Is it a Western or a gangster movie?" "Marital status and changes of leads A, B, and C," "Sports (type and prominence)," or "Importance of part and characterization of unskilled labor." I understand that much research in this field is kept secret because of its commercial value. If what has been published is an accurate sample, there would seem to be little reason to do so.

Such simple categories show that a study of audience response demands at least one thing: some sensibly subtle way of analyzing the texts, both the text the artist creates and the text of what the audience says. I. A. Richards had that, with his marvelous sense of language, but his experience showed a second tool one must have to understand audiences. Without a psychology adequate to explain individual responses, one does not know what to do with them except pass judgment on them. "We rarely concern ourselves, for example," says Walter Slatoff, surveying the post-Richards critical scene, "with the problem of individual differences among readers. . . . On the few occasions we do entertain such questions we speak as though they were settled by reducing response to two categories — appropriate and inappropriate."[9] Thus, although Richards avowed a concern to maintain differences of opinion, he shifted the problem of evaluating poems to a much harsher dogmatism: passing judgment on "the relative values of different states of mind, about varying forms, and degrees, of order in the personality."[10]

Had Richards had a usable psychology of individuals, he would have been able, presumably, to see how his protocols were reflecting personality at all levels, not just the teachable surface of consciousness. Indeed, David Bleich has recently done just that: shown how some of Richard's protocols reveal the unconscious themes his Cantabrigians were projecting into the texts as

---

[7]James R. Squire, *The Responses of Adolescents While Reading Four Short Stories*, NCTE Research Report No. 2, 1964. James R. Wilson, *Responses of College Freshmen to Three Novels*, NCTE Research Report No. 7, 1966. Alan C. Purves with Victoria Rippere, *Elements of Writing about a Literary Work: A Study of Response to Literature*, NCTE Research Report No. 9, 1968. All published by National Council of Teachers of English, 508 South Sixth Street, Champaign, Illinois 61820. [Holland]

[8]Leo A. Handel, *Hollywood Looks at Its Audience: A Report of Film Audience Research* (Urbana: University of Illinois Press, 1950), particularly Chapters 11 and 12, provides an accurate sample of what is being published currently, although the work is twenty years old. [Holland]

[9]Slatoff, *With Respect to Readers*, pp. 13–14. [Holland]
[10]Richards, *Practical Criticism*, pp. 347–49. [Holland]

part of their response.[11] "It has become a matter of course that any item of human behavior shows a continuum of dynamic meaning, reaching from the surface through many layers of crust to the 'core'" — thus, Erik Erikson,[12] articulating with his customary eloquence one of the most basic and widely confirmed of psychoanalytic discoveries. Freud's earliest case histories showed it and so did this morning's experience in hundreds of clinics and consulting-rooms. I know, for example, how the style and subject and method of this book stem from very early experiences of my own and my whole present character, including various half-conscious wishes and fears. Although these unconscious and infantile sources are by no means the only ones, if so conscious an act as writing an experimental and theoretical book has strong buried components, I find it hard to believe that responding to a play, a movie, or a poem does not. And, of course, it does.

As the remainder of this book will show, readers respond to literature in terms of their own "lifestyle" (or "character" or "personality" or "identity"). By such terms, psychoanalytic writers mean an individual's characteristic way of dealing with the demands of outer and inner reality. Such a style will have grown through time from earliest infancy. It will also be what the individual brings with him to any new experience, including the experience of literature. Each new experience develops the style, while the pre-existing style shapes each new experience. And this style can be described quite accurately (but not, of course, impersonally).

In short, psychoanalysis offers a powerful theory of individual responses to literature, and it has done so ever since Freud's 1905 study of jokes. (Interestingly, in that very early study, he also showed how social and economic factors would affect the pattern of inhibitions an individual brought to a joke and so affect his responses, but *indirectly,* as they filtered through his personality.)

Other writers have extended this first psychoanalytic aesthetics, Freud's theory of jokes, to other genres and to literature generally.[13]

For the most part, however, psychoanalytic students of literature, like conventional literary critics, have looked not at the actual individual reading but at the text, the words-on-the-page. Then they have posited a response on the basis of the text. Thus, paradoxically, the psychology that more than any other deals closely and intensely with individuals — psychoanalytic psychology — has in this instance retreated from the living human being, the spirit, if you will, to the letter.

By contrast, conventional psychological literature offers hundreds of studies that deal with actual readers but that suffer from a lack of theory.[14] For example, physiological studies tell how heart rate, the electrical resistance of the palm of the hand, or its sweat pattern, vary as subjects watch a movie. Indeed, an Italian experiment even investigated the differing ways identical and fraternal twins fidgeted![15] But I find it hard to believe a single variable such as pulse rate or fidget frequency could

[11]David Bleich, "The Determination of Literary Value," *Literature and Psychology* 17 (1967): 19–30. [Holland]

[12]Erik H. Erikson, "The Dream Specimen of Psychoanalysis," in Robert P. Knight and Cyrus R. Friedman, eds., *Psychoanalytic Psychiatry and Psychology,* Clinical and Theoretical Papers of the Austen Riggs Center, Vol. 1 (New York: Hallmark-Hubner Press, 1954), p. 140. [Holland]

[13]Norman N. Holland, *The Dynamics of Literary Response* (New York: Oxford University Press, 1968). Robert Waelder, *Psychoanalytic Avenues to Art* (New York: International Universities Press, 1965). Ernst Kris, *Psychoanalytic Explorations in Art* (New York: International Universities Press, 1952). Simon O. Lesser, *Fiction and the Unconscious* (Boston: Beacon Press, 1957). Philip Weissman, *Creativity in the Theater: A Psychoanalytic Study* (New York: Dell Publishing Co., 1965). In addition to Freud's essays on *Jokes* (1905) and "The 'Uncanny'" (1919), see my attempt at a synthesis: "Freud on the Response," in Holland, *Psychoanalysis and Shakespeare* (New York: McGraw-Hill Book Co., 1966). [Holland]

[14]I am exceedingly grateful to Ms. Betty Jane Saik, Ms. Mary Z. Bartlett, and Mr. Stephen Gormey for assembling and helping me punch-card as complete an index of studies of response to the arts as *Psychological Abstracts* affords. It was after our own work, in 1972, that an excellent survey appeared by Alan C. Purves and Richard Beach, *Literature and the Reader: Research in Response to Literature, Reading Interests, and the Teaching of Literature* (University of Illinois at Urbana-Champaign: National Council of Teachers of English, 1972). It supports our general conclusion that results are many but unsystematic. [Holland]

[15]When I am not using these studies substantively, I shall simply list them by author and *Psychological Abstracts (PA)* reference. Edward Opton, Jr., *PA* (1967): 5663. Jack Block, *PA* (1963): 7682. Richard C. Pillard et al., *PA* (1967): 6610. Luigi Gedda et al., *PA* (1956): 443. [Holland]

represent a complex, multivariant transaction like a response to a film.

Other studies resort to personality tests, but I think it is not much of an improvement over the physiological approach to be able to say that reading gruesome passages from Edgar Allan Poe increases the anxious and aggressive responses to inkblots. Much closer to the method of this book is the study in which judges were able to match viewers' open-ended comments on a movie to their Rorschach responses. Again, however, the experiment merely shows the correlation; it does not suggest an underlying mechanism, only that "individual differences in the perception of a motion picture are a function of global aspects of personality as elicited by the Rorschach."[16] Different personality tests lead to similarly vague conclusions: "Movie attendance is related in some instances to the central aspects of personality." A child's choices among stories "cohere with other observable characteristics of his personality."[17] Other studies claim to have shown that men watch the men in movies more than women do; that boys prefer adventure stories, while girls prefer stories about love, private life, and glamour; that children who are already pretty aggressive identify with different characters in a Western according to the degree of their pre-existing aggression, their sex, and the ending of the film.[18] No doubt, these studies (and hundreds more like them) follow out admirably the canons of experimental rigor. As a continuing line of research, however, they end most inconclusively, to judge, if nothing else, by the number of experimenters who turn to the same old issues over and over again. Instead of coherent research, one finds random observations. What these studies may have gained in rigor they certainly lack in theory.

One returns then to literary and psychoanalytic studies, weak in experiment but strong on theory.

Not always, of course. I do not feel that my understanding of the differences in readers' responses is advanced by a literary critic's introducing an "*informed* reader" with (also italicized) "*literary* competence" or even a more generalized "reading self," who (or that) is roughly the critic's age, shares his ethnic background, "has experienced war, marriage, and the responsibility of children," and so on.[19] Some statements about response by literary and psychoanalytic folk do add more rigor and theory than sense; some do suggest pervasive links between, on the one hand, the reader's personality (in depth) and his conscious reading skill and, on the other, his response. I am thinking of Morse Peckham's explanation of the effect of one's past aesthetic experiences on response, a theory supported by very detailed analyses from a variety of arts and corresponding to psychoanalytic notions of the role of the ego in art.[20] Similarly, child therapists like Lilli Peller and Kate Friedlaender have shown how children's stories reflect at a conscious level the child's unconscious fantasies, and therefore how the age appropriate to the fantasy determines the age at which a child will like the story. They, too, are showing a theoretical basis for combining the detailed analysis of a story with the depth analysis of the response.[21]

Such studies, in effect, deal with classes of readers. Psychoanalysis, however, is par excellence the science of human individuality (if there can be a "science" of uniqueness), and we would

[16]Lutz von Rosenstiel, *PA* (1967): 4630. Marvin Spiegelman, "Effect of Personality on the Perception of a Motion Picture," *Journal of Projective Techniques* 19 (1955): 461–464. [Holland]

[17]E. M. Scott, *PA* (1958): 4129. G. Foulds, *PA* (1943): 994. [Holland]

[18]Eleanor E. Maccoby et al., *PA* (1960): 4080. Paul I. Lyness, *PA* (1952): 7218. Robert S. Albert, *PA* (1959): 4603. [Holland]

[19]Stanley E. Fish, *Self-Consuming Artifacts: The Experience of Seventeenth-Century Literature* (Berkeley: University of California Press, 1972), p. 406. Slatoff, *With Respect to Readers*, pp. 55–56. [Holland]

[20]Morse Peckham, *Man's Rage for Chaos: Biology, Behavior, and the Arts* (New York: Chilton Books, 1965). See also my review article, "Psychoanalytic Criticism and Perceptual Psychology," *Literature and Psychology* 16 (1966): 81–92. [Holland]

[21]Lilli E. Peller, "Libidinal Phases, Ego Development, and Play," *The Psychoanalytic Study of the Child* 9 (1954): 178–98; "Reading and Daydreams in Latency; Boy-Girl Differences," *Journal of the American Psychoanalytic Association* 6 (1958): 57–70; "Daydreams and Children's Favorite Books: Psychoanalytic Comments," *The Psychoanalytic Study of the Child* 14 (1959): 414–33. Kate Friedlaender, "Children's Books and Their Function in Latency and Pre-puberty," *American Imago* 3 (1942): 129–50. [Holland]

expect it to be most interesting about literary response when it speaks about individuals. However, it must then necessarily give up repeatable experiments. For example, a group of experimenters, in projecting films for hospitalized psychiatric patients, found that the viewers interposed their individual defensive patterns between themselves and the film to keep the affect something they could tolerate. Hence, one could not assume that any given film would necessarily arouse certain feelings. Similarly, in an example of "poetry therapy," David V. Forrest showed how disturbed patients responded to the well-known lyric, "Western wind, when wilt thou blow," in terms of their several personality types, paranoid, schizoid, hysteric, and so on.[22] These papers suggest structures relating personality to response (through defense mechanisms or diagnostic categories that combine defense and level of fixation). They do not, however, take the further step: going beyond types and categories to examine the work of art, the response, and the responder in detail.

One often finds analyses of the individual (but not the work) in case histories. Avery Weisman, for example, describes a rigid, obsessional man who could not face a sea captain's loss of authority in a movie and left the theater before the film's end. The whole setting — other patrons, streets, bodily sensations — seemed unreal to him: he had dealt with his guilt and anxiety by separating his intellectual processes of reality-testing from his conventional, pleasurable attachment to the dream world of the film. Edith Buxbaum, in a famous case, tells of a boy compulsively driven to read detective stories almost to the exclusion of any other activity. He was satisfying his aggressive wishes toward his mother by allying himself with the murderer. At the same time, he assuaged his guilt by feeling like the victim and also the detective. Thus his symptom

served both defense and the gratification of instincts, and he became locked into it. Still more tragic was the patient of Gilbert J. Rose who committed suicide after witnessing a performance of Duerrenmatt's *The Visit:* he, like the hero of the play, felt himself the victim of a fantastically powerful bitch-goddess.[23]

Caroline Shrodes, however, has studied individual students' responses to particular literary works on the assumption that literary experience matches the therapeutic process: from identification and interaction with the work, to emotional catharsis, to insight into one's particular conflicts and relationships.[24] Less clinically, David Bleich in a growing series of moving and perceptive essays has analyzed the responses of ordinary readers, students usually, in order to elicit the unconscious themes of the text. In other words, he reverses the usual assumption of critics, that by analyzing the text one can understand the response; rather, he argues, by analyzing what readers find in it, one comes to understand the text.[25] And he is right to do so. To analyze the text in formal isolation as so many "words-on-a-page" (in the old formula of the New Criticism) is a highly artificial procedure. A literary text, after all, in an objective sense consists only of a certain configuration of specks of carbon black on dried wood pulp. When these marks become words, when those words become images or metaphors or characters or events, they do so because the reader plays the part of a prince to the sleeping

[22]Gordon Globus and Roy Shulman, "Considerations on Affective Response to Motion Pictures" (unpublished paper, Department of Psychiatry, Boston University School of Medicine); also cited in Holland, *Dynamics* (see note 13), pp. 94–95. David V. Forrest, "The Patient's Sense of the Poem: Affinities and Ambiguities," in Jack J. Leedy, ed., *Poetry Therapy: The Use of Poetry in the Treatment of Emotional Disorders* (Philadelphia: J. B. Lippincott Co., 1969), Chapter 20, pp. 231–59. [Holland]

[23]Avery D. Weisman, "Reality Sense and Reality Testing," *Behavioral Science* 3 (1958): 228–61. Edith Buxbaum, "The Role of Detective Stories in a Child Analysis," *Psychoanalytic Quarterly* 10 (1941): 373–81. Gilbert J. Rose, "Creative Imagination in Terms of Ego 'Core' and Boundaries," *International Journal of Psycho-Analysis* 45 (1964): 75–85. [Holland]

[24]Caroline Shrodes, "Bibliotherapy: An Application of Psychoanalytic Theory," *American Imago* 17 (1960): 311–19; "The Dynamics of Reading: Implications for Bibliotherapy," *ETC.: A Review of General Semantics* 18 (1961): 21–33. Both articles are based on her "Bibliotherapy: A Theoretical and Clinical Experimental Study" (Ph.D. dissertation, University of California, Berkeley, 1949). [Holland]

[25]David Bleich, "The Determination of Literary Value," *Literature and Psychology* 17 (1967): 19–30; "Emotional Origins of Literary Meaning," *College English* 31 (1969): 30–40; "Psychological Bases of Learning from Literature," *College English* 33 (1971): 32–45. [Holland]

beauty. He gives them life out of his own desires. When he does so, he brings his lifestyle to bear on the work. He mingles his unconscious loves and fears and adaptations with the words and images he synthesizes at a conscious level.

It is, therefore, quite impossible to say from a text alone how people will respond to it. Only after we have understood how some specific individual responds, how the different parts of his individual personality recreate the different details of the text, can we begin to formulate general hypotheses about the way many or all readers respond. Only then — if then.

At the same time, however, the reader is surely responding to *something*. The literary text may be only so many marks on a page — at most a matrix of psychological possibilities for its readers. Nevertheless only some possibilities, we would say, truly fit the matrix. One would not say, for example, that a reader of that sentence from "A Rose for Emily" who thought the "tableau" described an Eskimo was really responding to the story at all — only pursuing some mysterious inner exploration. In the basic question of this book, "Who reads what how?" there must be a "what," and our next task is to find out what it is.

Stanley Fish

b. 1938

The agent provocateur of contemporary literary theory, Stanley Fish was born in Providence, Rhode Island, and raised in Philadelphia. He received his A.B. at Penn (1959) and his A.M. and Ph.D. (1962) at Yale, which published his dissertation on John Skelton. Fish taught at Berkeley, becoming a full professor in 1974. In that year, Fish moved to Johns Hopkins as Kenan professor, and in 1986, as both professor of law and as chairman of the English department, to Duke University, where he has attracted a stellar group of theorists, including Fredric Jameson (Ch. 5) and Barbara Herrnstein Smith (Part One). Fish left Duke to become Dean of Arts and Sciences at the University of Illinois at Chicago, and in 2005 became Dandson-Kahn Distinguished Professor of Humanities and Law at Florida International University. In his most recent metatheoretical work, Fish has attacked theory as pointless, impotent to constrain the will-to-power of interpretation, whereas formerly, he had restricted his rhetorical assaults to individual theorists like Wolfgang Iser or to fields like linguistics and stylistics. Fish's career as a gadfly began with his second book, Surprised by Sin: The Reader in Paradise Lost *(1967), which transgressed with both feet the "affective fallacy" by which the New Criticism had eliminated the study of the audience. The object of Fish's concern has shifted from the implied reader immanent within the text in* Self-Consuming Artifacts: The Experience of Seventeenth-Century Literature *(1972), to the experience of actual readers and interpretive communities of readers in* Is There a Text in This Class? *(1980). Most recently, Fish has generalized his pragmatic approach to rhetoric and the reader beyond literary concerns; his social and political essays appear in* Doing What Comes Naturally: Change, Rhetoric, and the Practice of Theory in Literary and Legal Studies *(1989),* There's No Such Thing As Free Speech: And It's a Good Thing, Too *(1994),* Professional Correctness: Literary Studies and Political Change *(1995), and* The Trouble with Principle *(1999). Fish has also revisited and revised his* Paradise Lost *interpretation in* How Milton Works *(2001). "How to Recognize a Poem When You See One" first appeared in* Is There a Text in This Class? *(1980).*

How to Recognize a Poem When You See One

Last time I sketched out an argument by which meanings are the property neither of fixed and stable texts nor of free and independent readers but of interpretive communities that are responsible both for the shape of a reader's activities and for the texts those activities produce. In this lecture I propose to extend that argument so as to account not only for the meanings a poem might be said to have but for the fact of its being recognized as a poem in the first place. And once again I would like to begin with an anecdote.

In the summer of 1971 I was teaching two courses under the joint auspices of the Linguistic Institute of America and the English Department of the State University of New York at Buffalo. I taught these courses in the morning and in the same room. At 9:30 I would meet a group of students who were interested in the relationship between linguistics and literary criticism. Our nominal subject was stylistics but our concerns were finally theoretical and extended to the presuppositions and assumptions which underlie both linguistic and literary practice. At 11:00 these students were replaced by another group whose concerns were exclusively literary and were in fact confined to English religious poetry of the seventeenth century. These students had been learning how to identify Christian symbols and how to recognize typological patterns and how to move from the observation of these symbols and patterns to the specification of the poetic intention that was usually didactic or homiletic. On the day I am thinking about, the only connection between the two classes was an assignment given to the first which was still on the blackboard at the beginning of the second. It read:

Jacobs — Rosenbaum
Levin
Thorne
Hayes
Ohman (?)

I am sure that many of you will already have recognized the names on this list, but for the sake of the record, allow me to identify them. Roderick Jacobs and Peter Rosenbaum are two linguists who have coauthored a number of textbooks and coedited a number of anthologies. Samuel Levin is a linguist who was one of the first to apply the operations of transformational grammar to literary texts. J. P. Thorne is a linguist at Edinburgh who, like Levin, was attempting to extend the rules of transformational grammar to the notorious irregularities of poetic language. Curtis Hayes is a linguist who was then using transformational grammar in order to establish an objective basis for his intuitive impression that the language of Gibbon's *Decline and Fall of the Roman Empire* is more complex than the language of Hemingway's novels. And Richard Ohmann is the literary critic who, more than any other, was responsible for introducing the vocabulary of transformational grammar to the literary community. Ohmann's name was spelled as you see it here because I could not remember whether it contained one or two *n*'s. In other words, the question mark in parenthesis signified nothing more than a faulty memory and desire on my part to appear scrupulous. The fact that the names appeared in a list that was arranged vertically, and that Levin, Thorne, and Hayes formed a column that was more or less centered in relation to the paired names of Jacobs and Rosenbaum, was similarly accidental and was evidence only of a certain compulsiveness if, indeed, it was evidence of anything at all.

In the time between the two classes I made only one change. I drew a frame around the assignment and wrote on the top of that frame "p. 43." When the members of the second class filed in I told them that what they saw on the blackboard was a religious poem of the kind they had been studying and I asked them to interpret it. Immediately they began to perform in a manner that, for reasons which will become clear, was more or less pre-dictable. The first student to speak pointed out that the poem was probably a hieroglyph,[1] although he was not sure whether it was in the shape of a cross or an altar. This question was set aside as the other students, following his lead, began to concentrate on individual words, interrupting each other with suggestions that came so quickly that they seemed spontaneous. The first line of the poem (the very order of events assumed the already constituted status of the object) received the most attention: Jacobs was explicated as a reference to Jacob's ladder, traditionally allegorized as a figure for the Christian ascent to heaven. In this poem, however, or so my students told me, the means of ascent is not a ladder but a tree, a rose tree or rosenbaum. This was seen to be an obvious reference to the Virgin Mary who was often characterized as a rose without thorns, itself an emblem of the immaculate conception. At this point the poem appeared to the students to be operating in the familiar manner of an iconographic riddle. It at once posed the question, "How is it that a man can climb to heaven by means of a rose tree?" and directed the reader to the inevitable answer: by the fruit of that tree, the fruit of Mary's womb, Jesus. Once this interpretation was established it received support from, and conferred significance on, the word "thorne," which could only be an allusion to the crown of thorns, a symbol of the trial suffered by Jesus and of the price he paid to save us all. It was only a short step (really no step at all) from this insight to the recognition of Levin as a double reference, first to the tribe of Levi, of whose priestly function Christ was the fulfillment, and second to the unleavened bread carried by the children of Israel on their exodus from Egypt, the place of sin, and in response to the call of Moses, perhaps the most familiar of the old testament types of Christ. The final word of the poem was given at least three complementary readings: it could be "omen," especially since so much of the poem is concerned with foreshadowing and prophecy; it could be Oh Man, since it is man's story as it intersects with the divine plan that is the

[1]A poem whose shape on the printed page carries symbolic meaning, such as George Herbert's "Easter Wings." Older texts of this sort are often called *emblems*, modern ones, *concrete poetry*.

poem's subject; and it could, of course, be simply "amen," the proper conclusion to a poem celebrating the love and mercy shown by a God who gave his only begotten son so that we may live.

In addition to specifying significances for the words of the poem and relating those significances to one another, the students began to discern larger structural patterns. It was noted that of the six names in the poem three — Jacobs, Rosenbaum, and Levin — are Hebrew, two — Thorne and Hayes — are Christian, and one — Ohman — is ambiguous, the ambiguity being marked in the poem itself (as the phrase goes) by the question mark in parenthesis. This division was seen as a reflection of the basic distinction between the old dispensation and the new, the law of sin and the law of love. That distinction, however, is blurred and finally dissolved by the typological perspective which invests the old testament events and heroes with new testament meanings. The structure of the poem, my students concluded, is therefore a double one, establishing and undermining its basic pattern (Hebrew vs. Christian) at the same time. In this context there is finally no pressure to resolve the ambiguity of Ohman since the two possible readings — the name is Hebrew, the name is Christian — are both authorized by the reconciling presence in the poem of Jesus Christ. Finally, I must report that one student took to counting letters and found, to no one's surprise, that the most prominent letters in the poem were S, O, N.

Some of you will have noticed that I have not yet said anything about Hayes. This is because of all the words in the poem it proved the most recalcitrant to interpretation, a fact not without consequence, but one which I will set aside for the moment since I am less interested in the details of the exercise than in the ability of my students to perform it. What is the source of that ability? How is it that they were able to do what they did? What is it that they did? These questions are important because they bear directly on a question often asked in literary theory. What are the distinguishing features of literary language? Or, to put the matter more colloquially, How do you recognize a poem when you see one? The commonsense answer, to which many literary critics and linguists are committed, is that the act of recognition is triggered by the observable presence of distinguishing features. That is, you know a poem when you see one because its language displays the characteristics that you know to be proper to poems. This, however, is a model that quite obviously does not fit the present example. My students did not proceed from the noting of distinguishing features to the recognition that they were confronted by a poem; rather, it was the act of recognition that came first — they knew in advance that they were dealing with a poem — and the distinguishing features then followed.

In other words, acts of recognition, rather than being triggered by formal characteristics, are their source. It is not that the presence of poetic qualities compels a certain kind of attention but that the paying of a certain kind of attention results in the emergence of poetic qualities. As soon as my students were aware that it was poetry they were seeing, they began to look with poetry-seeing eyes, that is, with eyes that saw everything in relation to the properties they knew poems to possess. They knew, for example (because they were told by their teachers), that poems are (or are supposed to be) more densely and intricately organized than ordinary communications; and that knowledge translated itself into a willingness — one might even say a determination — to see connections between one word and another and between every word and the poem's central insight. Moreover, the assumption that there *is* a central insight is itself poetry-specific, and presided over its own realization. Having assumed that the collection of words before them was unified by an informing purpose (because unifying purposes are what poems have), my students proceeded to find one and to formulate it. It was in the light of that purpose (now assumed) that significances for the individual words began to suggest themselves, significances which then fleshed out the assumption that had generated them in the first place. Thus the meanings of the words and the interpretation in which those words were seen to be embedded emerged together, as a consequence of the operations my students began to perform once they were told that this was a poem.

It was almost as if they were following a recipe — if it's a poem do this, if it's a poem, see it that way — and indeed definitions of poetry *are*

recipes, for by directing readers as to what to look for in a poem, they instruct them in ways of looking that will produce what they expect to see. If your definition of poetry tells you that the language of poetry is complex, you will scrutinize the language of something identified as a poem in such a way as to bring out the complexity you know to be "there." You will, for example, be on the look-out for latent ambiguities; you will attend to the presence of alliterative and consonantal patterns (there will always be some), and you will try to make something of them (you will always succeed); you will search for meanings that subvert, or exist in a tension with the meanings that first present themselves; and if these operations fail to produce the anticipated complexity, you will even propose a significance for the words that are *not* there, because, as everyone knows, everything about a poem, including its omissions, is significant. Nor, as you do these things, will you have any sense of performing in a willful manner, for you will only be doing what you learned to do in the course of becoming a skilled reader of poetry. Skilled reading is usually thought to be a matter of discerning what is there, but if the example of my students can be generalized, it is a matter of knowing how to *produce* what can thereafter be said to be there. Interpretation is not the art of construing but the art of constructing. Interpreters do not decode poems; they make them.

To many, this will be a distressing conclusion, and there are a number of arguments that could be mounted in order to forestall it. One might point out that the circumstances of my students' performance were special. After all, they had been concerned exclusively with religious poetry for some weeks, and therefore would be uniquely vulnerable to the deception I had practiced on them and uniquely equipped to impose religious themes and patterns on words innocent of either. I must report, however, that I have duplicated this experiment any number of times at nine or ten universities in three countries, and the results are always the same, even when the participants know from the beginning that what they are looking at was originally an assignment. Of course this very fact could itself be turned into an objection: doesn't the reproducibility of the exercise prove that there is something about these words that leads everyone to perform in the same way? Isn't it just a happy accident that names like Thorne and Jacobs have counterparts or near counterparts in biblical names and symbols? And wouldn't my students have been unable to do what they did if the assignment I gave to the first class had been made up of different names? The answer to all of these questions is no. Given a firm belief that they were confronted by a religious poem, my students would have been able to turn any list of names into the kind of poem we have before us now, because they would have read the names within the assumption that they were informed with Christian significance. (This is nothing more than a literary analogue to Augustine's rule of faith.[2]) You can test this assertion by replacing Jacobs-Rosenbaum, Levin, Thorne, Hayes, and Ohman with names drawn from the faculty of Kenyon College — Temple, Jordan, Seymour, Daniels, Star, Church. I will not exhaust my time or your patience by performing a full-dress analysis, which would involve, of course, the relation between those who saw the River Jordan and those who saw *more* by seeing the Star of Bethlehem, thus fulfilling the prophecy by which the temple of Jerusalem was replaced by the inner temple or church built up in the heart of every Christian. Suffice it to say that it could easily be done (you can take the poem home and do it yourself) and that the shape of its doing would be constrained not by the names but by the interpretive assumptions that gave them a significance even before they were seen. This would be true even if there were no names on the list, if the paper or blackboard were blank; the blankness would present no problem to the interpreter, who would immediately see in it the void out of which God created the earth, or the abyss into which unregenerate sinners fall, or, in the best of all possible poems, both.

Even so, one might reply, all you've done is demonstrate how an interpretation, if it is prosecuted with sufficient vigor, can impose itself on material which has its own proper shape. Basically, at the ground level, in the first place,

when all is said and done, "Jacobs-Rosenbaum Levin Thorne Hayes Ohman (?)" is an assignment, it is only a trick that allows you to transform it into poem, and when the effects to the trick have worn off, it will return to its natural form and be seen as an assignment once again. This is a powerful argument because it seems at once to give interpretation its due (as an act of the will) and to maintain the independence of that on which interpretation works. It allows us, in short, to preserve our commonsense intuition that interpretation must be interpretation of *something*. Unfortunately, the argument will not hold because the assignment we all see is no less the product of interpretation than the poem into which it was turned. That is, it requires just as much work, and work of the same kind, to see this as an assignment as it does to see it as a poem. If this seems counterintuitive, it is only because the work required to see it as an assignment is work we have already done, in the course of acquiring the huge amount of background knowledge that enables you and me to function in the academic world. In order to know what an assignment is, that is, in order to know what to do with something identified as an assignment, you must first know what a class is (know that it isn't an economic grouping) and know that classes meet at specified times for so many weeks, and that one's performance in a class is largely a matter of performing between classes.

Think for a moment of how you would explain this last to someone who did not already know it. "Well," you might say, "a class is a group situation in which a number of people are instructed by an informed person in a particular subject." (Of course the notion of "subject" will itself require explication.) "An assignment is something you do when you're not in class." "Oh, I see," your interlocutor might respond, "an assignment is something you do to take your mind off what you've been doing in class." "No, an assignment is a part of a class." "But how can that be if you only do it when the class is not meeting?" Now it would be possible, finally, to answer that question, but only by enlarging the horizons of your explanation to include the very concept of a university, what it is one might be doing there, why one might be doing it instead of doing a thousand other things, and so

[2]A reference to *Confessions* 6:4, in which St. Augustine recommends reading the less edifying biblical narratives from the Old Testament as sacred allegory, a practice extended by Aquinas and Dante to secular literature as well.

on. For most of us these matters do not require explanation, and indeed, it is hard for us to imagine someone for whom they do; but that is because our tacit knowledge of what it means to move around in academic life was acquired so gradually and so long ago that it doesn't seem like knowledge at all (and therefore something someone else might *not* know) but a part of the world. You might think that when you're on campus (a phrase that itself requires volumes) that you are simply walking around on the two legs God gave you; but your walking is informed by an internalized awareness of institutional goals and practices, of norms of behavior, of lists of do's and don't's, of invisible lines and the dangers of crossing them; and, as a result, you see everything as *already* organized in relation to those same goals and practices. It would never occur to you, for example, to wonder if the people pouring out of that building are fleeing from a fire; you *know* that they are exiting from a class (what could be more obvious?) and you know that because your perception of their action occurs within a knowledge of what people in a university could possibly be doing and the reasons they could have for doing it (going to the next class, going back to the dorm, meeting someone in the student union). It is within that same knowledge that an assignment becomes intelligible so that it appears to you immediately as an obligation, as a set of directions, as something with parts, some of which may be more significant than others. That is, it is a proper question to ask of an assignment whether some of its parts might be omitted or slighted, whereas readers of poetry know that no part of a poem can be slighted (the rule is "everything counts") and they do not rest until every part has been given a significance.

In a way this amounts to no more than saying what everyone already knows: poems and assignments are different, but my point is that the differences are a result of the different interpretive operations we perform and not of something inherent in one or the other. An assignment no more compels its own recognition than does a poem; rather, as in the case of a poem, the shape of an assignment emerges when someone looks at something identified as one with assignment-seeing eyes, that is, with eyes which are capable of seeing the words as already embedded within the institutional structure that makes it possible for assignments to have a sense. The ability to see, and therefore to make, an assignment is no less a learned ability than the ability to see, and therefore to make, a poem. Both are constructed artifacts, the products and not the producers of interpretation, and while the differences between them are real, they are interpretive and do not have their source in some bedrock level of objectivity.

Of course one might want to argue that there is a bedrock level at which these names constitute neither an assignment nor a poem but are merely a list. But that argument too fails because a list is no more a natural object — one that wears its meaning on its face and can be recognized by anyone — than an assignment or a poem. In order to see a list, one must already be equipped with the concepts of seriality, hierarchy, subordination, and so on, and while these are by no means esoteric concepts and seem available to almost everyone, they are nonetheless learned, and if there were someone who had not learned them, he or she would not be able to see a list. The next recourse is to descend still lower (in the direction of atoms) and to claim objectivity for letters, paper, graphite, black marks on white spaces, and so on; but these entities too have palpability and shape only because of the assumption of some or other system of intelligibility, and they are therefore just as available to a deconstructive dissolution as are poems, assignments, and lists.

The conclusion, therefore, is that all objects are made and not found, and that they are made by the interpretive strategies we set in motion. This does not, however, commit me to subjectivity because the means by which they are made are social and conventional. That is, the "you" who does the interpretative work that puts poems and assignments and lists into the world is a communal you and not an isolated individual. No one of us wakes up in the morning and (in French fashion) reinvents poetry or thinks up a new educational system or decides to reject seriality in favor of some other, wholly original, form of organization. We do not do these things because we could not do them, because the mental operations we can perform are limited by the institutions in which we are *already* embedded. These institutions precede us, and it is only by inhabiting them, or being inhabited by them, that we have access to the public and conventional senses they make. Thus while it is true to say that we create poetry (and assignments and lists), we create it through interpretive strategies that are finally not our own but have their source in a publicly available system of intelligibility. Insofar as the system (in this case a literary system) constrains us, it also fashions us, furnishing us with categories of understanding, with which we in turn fashion the entities to which we can then point. In short, to the list of made or constructed objects we must add ourselves, for we no less than the poems and assignments we see are the products of social and cultural patterns of thought.

To put the matter in this way is to see that the opposition between objectivity and subjectivity is a false one because neither exists in the pure form that would give the opposition its point. This is precisely illustrated by my anecdote in which we do *not* have free-standing readers in a relationship of perceptual adequacy or inadequacy to an equally free-standing text. Rather, we have readers whose consciousnesses are constituted by a set of conventional notions which when put into operation constitute in turn a conventional, and conventionally seen, object. My students could do what they did, and do it in unison, because as members of a literary community they knew what a poem was (their knowledge was public), and that knowledge led them to look in such a way as to populate the landscape with what they knew to be poems.

Of course poems are not the only objects that are constituted in unison by shared ways of seeing. Every object or event that becomes available within an institutional setting can be so characterized. I am thinking, for example, of something that happened in my classroom just the other day. While I was in the course of vigorously making a point, one of my students, William Newlin by name, was just as vigorously waving his hand. When I asked the other members of the class what it was that Mr. Newlin was doing, they all answered that he was seeking permission to speak. I then asked them how they knew that. The immediate reply was that it was obvious; what else could he be thought to be doing? The meaning of his gesture, in other words, was right there

on its surface, available for reading by anyone who had eyes to see. That meaning, however, would not have been available to someone without any knowledge of what was involved in being a student. Such a person might have thought that Mr. Newlin was pointing to the fluorescent lights hanging from the ceiling, or calling our attention to some subject that was about to fall ("the sky is falling," "the sky is falling"). And if the someone in question were a child of elementary or middle-school age, Mr. Newlin might well have been seen as seeking permission not to speak but to go to the bathroom, an interpretation or reading that would never occur to a student at Johns Hopkins or any other institution of "higher learning" (and how would we explain to the uninitiated the meaning of *that* phrase).

The point is the one I have made so many times before: it is neither the case that the significance of Mr. Newlin's gesture is imprinted on its surface where it need only be read off, or that the construction put on the gesture by everyone in the room was individual and idiosyncratic. Rather, the source of our interpretive unanimity was a structure of interests and understood goals, a structure whose categories so filled our individual consciousnesses that they were rendered as one, immediately investing phenomena with the significance they *must* have, given the already-in-place assumption about what someone could possibly be intending (by word or gesture) in a classroom. By seeing Mr. Newlin's raised hand with a single shaping eye, we were demonstrating what Harvey Sacks has characterized as "the fine power of a culture. It does not, so to speak, merely fill brains in roughly the same way, it fills them so that they are alike in fine detail."[3] The occasion of Sacks's observation was the ability of his hearers to understand a sequence of two sentences — "The baby cried. The mommy picked it up." — exactly as he did (assuming, for example that "the 'mommy' who picks up the 'baby' is the mommy of that baby"), despite the fact that alternative ways of understanding were demonstrably possible. That is, the mommy of the second sentence could well have been the

[3]"On the Analysability of Stories by Children," in *Ethnomethodology*, ed. Roy Turner (Baltimore: Penguin, 1974), p. 218. [Fish]

mommy of the some other baby, and it need not even have been a baby that this "floating" mommy was picking up. One is tempted to say that in the absence of a specific context we are authorized to take the words literally, which is what Sacks's hearers do; but as Sacks's observes, it is within the assumption of a context — one so deeply assumed that we are unaware of it — that the words acquire what seems to be their literal meaning. There is nothing *in the words* that tells Sacks and his hearers how to relate the mommy and the baby of this story, just as there is nothing *in the form* of Mr. Newlin's gesture that tells his fellow students how to determine its significance. In both cases the determination (of relation and significance) is the work of categories of organization — the family, being a student — that are from the very first giving shape and value to what is heard and seen.

Indeed, these categories are the very shape of seeing itself, in that we are not to imagine a perceptual ground more basic than the one they afford. That is, we are not to imagine a moment when my students "simply see" a physical configuration of atoms and *then* assign the configuration a significance, according to the situation they happen to be in. To be in the situation (this or any other) is to "see" with the eyes of its interests, its goals, its understood practices, values, and norms, and so to be conferring significance *by* seeing, not after it. The categories of my students' vision are the categories by which they understand themselves to be functioning as students (what Sacks might term "doing studenting"), and objects will appear to them in forms related to that way of functioning rather than in some objective or preinterpretive form. (This is true even when an object is seen as not related, since nonrelation is not a pure but a differential category — the specification of something by enumerating what it is not; in short, nonrelation is merely one form of relation, and its perception is always situation-specific.)

Of course, if someone who was not functioning as a student was to walk into my classroom, he might very well see Mr. Newlin's raised hand (and "raised hand" is already an interpretation-laden description) in some other way, as evidence of a disease, as the salute of a political follower, as a muscle-improving exercise, as an attempt to kill flies, but he would always see it in *some* way, and

never as purely physical data waiting for his interpretation. And, moreover, the way of seeing, whatever it was, would never be individual or idiosyncratic, since its source would always be the institutional structure of which the "see-er" was an extending agent. This is what Sacks means when he says that a culture fills brains "so that they are alike in fine detail"; it fills them so that no one's interpretive acts are exclusively his own but fall to him by virtue of his position in some socially organized environment and are therefore always shared and public. It follows, then, that the fear of solipsism, of the imposition by the unconstrained self of its own prejudices, is unfounded because the self does not exist apart from the communal or conventional categories of thought that enable its operations (of thinking, seeing, reading). Once one realizes that the conceptions that fill consciousness, including any conception of its own status, are culturally derived, the very notion of an unconstrained self, of a consciousness wholly and dangerously free, becomes incomprehensible.

But without the notion of the unconstrained self, the arguments of Hirsch, Abrams, and the other proponents of objective interpretation are deprived of their urgency. They are afraid that in the absence of the controls afforded by a normative system of meanings, the self will simply substitute its own meanings for the meanings (usually identified with the intentions of the author) that texts bring with them, the meanings that texts *"have"*; however, if the self is conceived of not as an independent entity but as a social construct whose operations are delimited by the systems of intelligibility that inform it, then the meanings it confers on texts are not its own but have their source in the interpretive community (or communities) of which it is a function. Moreover, these meanings will be neither subjective nor objective, at least in the terms assumed by those who argue within the traditional framework: they will not be objective because they will always have been the product of a point of view rather than having been simply "read off"; and they will not be subjective because that point of view will always be social or institutional. Or by the same reasoning one could say that they are *both* subjective and objective: they are subjective because they inhere in a particular point of view and are therefore not universal; and they are objective because the point of view that delivers them is public and conventional rather than individual or unique.

To put the matter in either way is to see how unhelpful the terms "subjective" and "objective" finally are. Rather than facilitating inquiry, they close it down, by deciding in advance what shape inquiry can possibly take. Specifically, they assume, without being aware that it is an assumption and therefore open to challenge, the very distinction I have been putting into question, the distinction between interpreters and the objects they interpret. That distinction in turn assumes that interpreters and their objects are two different kinds of *a*contextual entities, and within these twin assumptions the issue can only be one of control: will texts be allowed to constrain their own interpretation or will irresponsible interpreters be allowed to obscure and overwhelm texts. In the spectacle that ensues, the spectacle of Anglo-American critical controversy, texts and selves fight it out in the persons of their respective champions, Abrams, Hirsch, Reichert, Graff on the one hand, Holland, Bleich, Slatoff, and (in some characterizations of him) Barthes on the other. But if selves are constituted by the ways of thinking and seeing that inhere in social organizations, and if these constituted selves in turn constitute texts according to these same ways, then there can be no adversary relationship between text and self because they are the necessarily related products of the same cognitive possibilities. A text cannot be overwhelmed by an irresponsible reader and one need not worry about protecting the purity of a text from a reader's idiosyncrasies. It is only the distinction between subject and object that gives rise to these urgencies, and once the distinction is blurred they simply fall away. One can respond with a cheerful yes to the question "Do readers make meanings?" and commit oneself to very little because it would be equally true to say that meanings, in the form of culturally derived interpretive categories, make readers.

Indeed, many things look rather different once the subject-object dichotomy is eliminated as the assumed framework within which critical discussion occurs. Problems disappear, not because they have been solved but because they are shown never to have been problems in the first place. Abrams, for example, wonders how, in the absence of a normative system of stable meanings, two people could ever agree on the interpretation of a work or even of a sentence; but the difficulty is only a difficulty if the two (or more) people are thought of as isolated individuals whose agreement must be compelled by something external to them. (There is something of the police state in Abrams's vision, complete with posted rules and boundaries, watchdogs to enforce them, procedures for identifying their violators as criminals.) But if the understandings of the people in question are informed by the same notions of what counts as a fact, of what is central, peripheral, and worthy of being noticed — in short, by the same interpretive principles — then agreement between them will be assured, and its source will not be a text that enforces its own perception but a way of perceiving that results in the emergence to those who share it (or those whom it shares) of the same text. That text might be a poem, as it was in the case of those who first "saw" "Jacobs-Rosenbaum Levin Hayes Thorne Ohman (?)," or a hand, as it is every day in a thousand classrooms; but whatever it is, the shape and meaning it appears immediately to have will be the "ongoing accomplishment"[4] of those who agree to produce it.

[4] A phrase used by the ethnomethodologists to characterize the interpretive activities that create and maintain the features of everyday life. See, for example, Don H. Zimmerman, "Fact as a Practical Accomplishment," in *Ethnomethodology*, pp. 128–143. [Fish]

James Phelan

b. 1951

James Phelan was born in Flushing, New York, in 1951, and educated at Boston College and at the University of Chicago, where he completed his doctorate in English in 1977. Since that year he has taught in the English department at Ohio State University, where he is currently Humanities Distinguished Professor. Rather than working in only one historical period, Phelan gravitates toward theoretical issues or problems, most often connected with the genre of narrative, and pursues them in texts from different periods. His recent work, however, has focused primarily on twentieth-century British and American narrative, and he now claims the twentieth century as a specialty. He has written about style in Worlds from Words *(1981), about character and narrative progression in* Reading People, Reading Plots *(1989), about technique, ethics, and audiences in* Narrative as Rhetoric *(1996), and, most recently, about character narration in* Living to Tell about It *(2004). He has also published the autobiographical journal* Beyond the Tenure Track *(1991) and has edited, with Peter J. Rabinowitz,* Understanding Narrative *(1994), and the Blackwell* Companion to Narrative Theory *(2005). The following selection is taken from his essay in* Diacritics, *"Data, Danda, and Disagreement."*

Phelan's response to "How to Know a Poem When You See One" digs into the underlying logic of Stanley Fish's argument. Fish contends that texts are what they are because of the way readers frame them, since the hypotheses readers choose determine what data they will discover. Phelan's wedge into this nearly impregnable argument involves Stephen Pepper's distinction between facts that all observers will report (data) and facts that exist only by virtue of a prior hypothesis (danda). After reading Phelan, you may wonder whether he has exploded Fish's notion that how we understand what we read depends on our prior assumptions, or whether the crucial data/danda distinction is just one more prior assumption.

From *Data, Danda,*[1] *and Disagreement*

Fish's project in *Is There a Text in This Class?* is to repudiate the notion of the text as a self-sufficient object while also maintaining that interpretation is not therefore a subjective and solipsistic enterprise. Fish explains that his early attempts to formulate an interpretive model — his "affective stylistics" — did not succeed because he had to equivocate about the nature of the text. When he argued that literature was in the reader, that the reader's activity of processing a text was

---

[1] A term coined by Stephen C. Pepper (1891–1972), American philosopher; literally in Latin it means "what must be given." Pepper distinguished between *data* (information that will be found by all observers, regardless of their interpretive frame) and *danda* (information that will be found by observers only if they share a particular world-hypothesis or interpretive frame). For example, observers will agree that Hamlet does not kill Claudius in Act III, scene ii, and that Hamlet claims his inaction is because he does not wish to slay him while he is praying; these matters are data. A Freudian critic might argue that Hamlet's inaction stems from an unresolved Oedipus complex (that Hamlet identifies with Claudius, who killed his father as he, Hamlet, in the Oedipal phase, wished to do); that would be danda.

equivalent to the text's meaning, he did succeed in destroying the text's self-sufficiency. However, when he strove to avoid subjectivity by arguing that all informed readers would process a text the same way, he reestablished the text at the center of interpretive activity: although readers' acts constituted meaning, readers performed those acts at the bidding of the text.

In order to eliminate this equivocation, Fish moved from a reader-centered theory of meaning to a community-centered one. Through his analyses of other critics, and even of his own early work, Fish concluded that our critical assumptions created rather than followed from the properties of a text. With this move, Fish repudiated the notion of the self-sufficient text by maintaining that texts took on different stable shapes as interpreters brought different interpretive assumptions and strategies to them. Moreover, he eliminated subjectivity by maintaining that readers always must acquire their assumptions from the communities to which they belong. What is more radical about this position is that it denies the existence of any facts independent of our assumptions. Any one interpretation, in other words, rests not on independent and universally recognizable data but only on other interpretations (about how to arrange evidence, about what an interpretation should do, and so on). To interpret a work is to create it; that is, to interpret a work is to take a formless mass and mold it into one of several possible shapes.

In elaborating and defending this position, Fish tries to establish that his position can do all the things his likely opponents would want a theory of interpretation to do. Fish explains that his position is able to rule out many readings because it maintains that the largest community of readers sanctions only a limited number of interpretive strategies at any one time. But Fish also maintains that the nature of those accepted strategies can and does change and he supports this contention by analyzing both how individual critics change their minds and how new interpretations become accepted. Critics change their minds because not all assumptions exist at the same level. For example, a critic might assume that a newly discovered manuscript in which Jane Austen stated that she had no ironic intentions would count as sufficient evidence against his prior assumptions. Other critics, of course, might not weigh such new evidence as heavily, and so the two groups of critics would enter into an interpretive dispute. This dispute could be resolved only if there were some third more basic assumption both sides would be willing to accept, e.g., that the purpose of Austen criticism is to demonstrate her greatness as a novelist, and if one reading or the other could be shown to be at odds with that assumption.

This account of how critics change their minds helps explain how interpretations come to be accepted. New interpretations are never complete breaks with the old; they must always rely on some more widely accepted assumptions about what will count as relevant evidence. Furthermore, new interpretations define themselves in some oppositional relationship to the old, and the community of readers also sanctions what those relationships can be.

Fish's final major point is also one that further emphasizes his differences from the pluralists: his position does not mean that any of us should give up the certainty he now has about any text. We do not have to give up our certainty, indeed could not give it up, because we can never exist in a neutral state and freely choose which assumptions we shall accept. Since we are always operating with some assumptions, we shall always find some interpretations more compelling than others. And the experience of changing our minds will not weaken our certainty because we change our minds only if we are convinced of the power of the new assumptions. Again Fish's point is that interpretation is all we have; consequently, we should all do what he has done: "stop worrying and learn to love interpretation."

FISH AND HYPOTHESIS TESTING: NOTES ON THE CONSTRAINTS OF DATA

Fish's insistence that we are always in the grip of some assumptions completes his exposition of his theory so well that the theory seems to become invulnerable to objections. Once he says that we are never free of assumptions, he can treat any objections as themselves the product of other assumptions. Consequently, any objection itself becomes evidence that Fish's position is correct. Heads he wins, tails everybody else loses. But let us look harder at the logic of Fish's position to see whether his coin can land on its edge.

In order for Fish's theory to be as compelling as possible he must be able to show that hypothesis testing, and especially hypothesis disconfirmation, are controlled not by appeals to independent evidence but by appeals to other assumptions. If Fish cannot explain disconfirmation this way, then his view of interpretation is not an account of the way things must be but only a description of what unrigorous interpreters do. One of Fish's own example texts indicates that he is mistaking what critics often do for what they must do.

While teaching a class in stylistics one summer, Fish wrote the following assignment on the board (the names of course denote prominent stylistic critics):

> Jacobs-Rosenbaum
> Levin
> Thorne
> Hayes
> Ohman (?)

Drawing a frame around it and adding "p. 43" at the top, Fish left it on the board for his next class, a group studying seventeenth-century religious poetry, told them it was a religious poem and asked them to interpret it. They were able to do so with only a little trouble. "Jacobs" becomes a reference to Jacob's ladder, "Rosenbaum" (rose-tree) a reference to the Virgin Mary, "who was often characterized as a rose without thorns, itself an emblem of the immaculate conception." After a few more interpretive swoops, the text becomes an iconographic riddle asking the question, "How is that a man can climb to heaven by means of a rose tree?" and answering, "by the fruit of that tree, the fruit of Mary's womb, Jesus." Fish cites the example to persuade us that poems, like assignments, are not things independent of interpreters but things created by them.

The example is instructive first because it indicates the usefulness of Pepper's distinction between data and danda and second because it suggests conclusions about the relation between data and hypotheses different from the ones Fish draws. To declare it as "fact" that "Jacobs" refers to linguist Roderick Jacobs or to Jacob, son of Isaac, is actually an interpretation that follows from one's assumption that the text is an assignment or a poem; thus, the meaning of "Jacobs" is a dandum. What both modes recognize, of course, is the existence of the datum, the word "Jacobs" itself. Pepper's distinction sheds light on Fish's conclusions once we notice that his report of the students' religious interpretation gives no account of the function of "Hayes" and that he admits that of all the words in the poem it "proved most recalcitrant to interpretation." Because of this failure, Fish's example does not demonstrate that there are no facts independent of assumptions but rather that there are no danda independent of assumptions (and that, of course, is a tautological demonstration).

The example also demonstrates that the easiest part of hypothesis testing is hypothesis confirmation. Fish in effect asks his students whether *it is possible* to interpret the data of the text as a religious poem, and given the nature of that data — a series of single words with no strong explicit syntactic connections, plus the frame and the "p. 43" — it is not surprising that the answer is yes. But asking whether an interpretive hypothesis is possible is very different from asking which one of two or more alternative hypotheses is better or best; once we ask that second question we are more likely to uncover negative evidence for any one hypothesis and thus be able to judge the adequacy of each hypothesis for the data it seeks to explain. When we apply the test of adequacy here, we are of course able to recognize the assignment hypothesis as superior.

The example also damages Fish's case because it takes away one of his characteristic argumentative moves, the declaration that appealing to the text itself cannot resolve interpretive disagreements because the text is only the product of our assumptions. Since "Hayes" is a datum, something that all communities would acknowledge as part of the text, this avenue of appeal is blocked. Fish, then, would probably reply to my objections by saying that to judge the assignment-hypothesis as superior is to make another interpretation, one based on the more fundamental assumption that hypotheses offering greater adequacy and correspondence are to be judged superior to those offering less. Why not decide, as some critics have done, including Fish himself at one stage of his career, that ingenuity should be the criterion for choosing among interpretations? In this case, we would prefer the religious reading of Fish's text. But this move will not save Fish's case for two reasons. First, shifting the grounds of preference does not shift the relation between data and hypotheses. Although we would now prefer the poem-interpretation, we would still recognize that it does not account for "Hayes," and would thus also recognize that the hypothesis does not create the data. Second, the notion of ingenuity itself presupposes the independence of that which the hypothesis is ingenious about. Thus, while this shift in criteria would make it more likely for Fish's students to find a function for "Hayes," we would still acknowledge that the data of this text prove somewhat "recalcitrant" to the poem-interpretation, recalcitrance being one measure of the interpretation's ingenuity.

Although the existence of independent data places constraints on hypotheses, these data rarely point directly to what Fish frequently calls "obvious and inescapable" interpretations. Instead, as the critical history of any work shows, the same data seem to conform to numerous different interpretations. Nevertheless, when two critics offer different answers to the same question about a text, data can often be appealed to as a way of disconfirming one of their answers. This process of disconfirmation is generally more involved than in the case of Fish's example and thus too lengthy to illustrate fully here with a traditional text,[2] but I can sketch a few preliminary steps. Cleanth Brooks reads Wordsworth's "She dwelt among the untrodden ways" as a poem structured by the ironic tension between the images of the second stanza ("A violet by a mossy stone / Half hidden from the eye / Fair as a star when only one / Is shining in the sky"). Brooks asks, "Which is Lucy really like — the violet or the star?" and answers that she is a violet to the world and a star to her love ["Irony as a Principle of Structure," in *Literary Opinion in America*, ed. Morton Dauwen Zabel (New York: Harper and Row, 1962), p. 735]. When another critic suggests that the poem is not structured by an ironic tension and points out that the grammatical data of stanza two do not precisely correspond to the interpretation that the images are equivalent, he has taken one step toward disconfirming Brooks's hypothesis. To take a different and more recent example, Sandra Gilbert and Susan Gubar assert that in *Persuasion* Anne Elliot "could have become most of the women in the novel" [*The Madwoman in the Attic: The Woman Writer and the Nineteenth Century Literary Imagination* (New York: Yale Univ. Press, 1979), p. 177]. This hypothesis encounters serious difficulty when we match it with the datum that the authorial voice introduces Anne as a woman "with an elegance of mind and a sweetness of character" (Chapter 1) even while she lives in her own oppressive household. This characterization seems to preclude the possibility that Anne could ever become the vulgar Mrs. Clay or the feckless and hypochondriacal Mary. In sum, although hypotheses exert a powerful influence on the way critics perceive and order data, those data are still available independently and thus can often disconfirm interpretive hypotheses.

[2]I have elsewhere made an extended attempt at disconfirmation using the by now standard example of "A slumber did my spirit seal" ["Validity *Redux*: The Relation between Author, Reader, and Text in the Act of Interpretation," *Papers in Comparative Studies* 1 (1982), 80–111]. [Phelan]

Judith Fetterley

b. 1938

Judith Fetterley was born in New York City but was raised in Toronto until the age of ten, when her family moved to Franklin, Indiana. Fetterley's special interest and slant on U.S. culture comes from this complex position as both insider and outsider. Fetterley took her A.B. from Swarthmore in 1960, then worked for the Harvard Business School and the American Friends Service Committee before returning to graduate school at Indiana University, where she received her Ph.D. in 1969. Fetterley taught at the University of Pennsylvania from 1967 to 1973, then moved to the State University of New York at Albany, where she is currently professor of English and women's studies. Fetterley's scholarly and theoretical work includes The Resisting Reader: A Feminist Approach to American Fiction *(1978) along with numerous articles on nineteenth- and twentieth-century American writers. She also founded and is general editor for the Rutgers University Press American Women Writers reprint series. Fetterley has edited* Provisions: A Reader from Nineteenth-Century American Women Writers *(1985) and (with Marjorie Pryse) the* Norton Anthology of American Women Regionalists, 1850–1910 *(1995). Currently she is at work on a new book on nineteenth-century American women writers and the politics of recovery.*

Introduction to
The Resisting Reader

I

Literature is political. It is painful to have to insist on this fact, but the necessity of such insistence indicates the dimensions of the problem. John Keats once objected to poetry "that has a palpable design upon us."[1] The major works of American fiction constitute a series of designs on the female reader, all the more potent in their effect because they are "impalpable." One of the main things that keeps the design of our literature unavailable to the consciousness of the woman reader, and hence impalpable, is the very posture of the apolitical, the pretense that literature speaks universal truths through forms from which all the merely personal, the purely subjective, has been burned away or at least transformed through the medium of art into the representative. When only one reality is

encouraged, legitimized, and transmitted and when that limited vision endlessly insists on its comprehensiveness, then we have the conditions necessary for that confusion of consciousness in which impalpability flourishes. it is the purpose of this book to give voice to a different reality and different vision, to bring a different subjectivity to bear on the old "universality." To examine American fictions in light of how attitudes toward women shape their form and content is to make available to consciousness that which has been largely left unconscious and thus to change our understanding of these fictions, our relation to them, and their effect on us. It is to make palpable their designs.

American literature is male. To read the canon of what is currently considered classic American literature is perforce to identify as male. Though exceptions to this generalization can be found here and there — a Dickinson poem, a Wharton novel — these exceptions usually function to obscure the argument and confuse the issue: American literature is male. Our literature neither

[1]From Keats's letter to John Hamilton Reynolds of February 3, 1818. Keats goes on to say that "Poetry should be great & unobtrusive, a thing which enters into one's soul, and does not startle or amaze it with itself but with its subject."

leaves women alone nor allows them to participate. It insists on its universality at the same time that it defines that universality in specifically male terms. "Rip Van Winkle" is paradigmatic of this phenomenon. While the desire to avoid work, escape authority, and sleep through the major decisions of one's life is obviously applicable to both men and women, in Irving's story this "universal" desire is made specifically male. Work, authority, and decision-making are symbolized by Dame Van Winkle, and the longing for flight is defined against her. She is what one must escape from, and the "one" is necessarily male. In Mailer's *An American Dream,* the fantasy of eliminating all one's ills through the ritual of scapegoating is equally male: the sacrificial scapegoat is the woman/wife and the cleansed survivor is the husband/male. In such fictions the female reader is co-opted into participation in an experience from which she is explicitly excluded; she is asked to identify with a selfhood that defines itself in opposition to her; she is required to identify against herself.

The woman reader's relation to American literature is made even more problematic by the fact that our literature is frequently dedicated to defining what is peculiarly American about experience and identity. Given the pervasive male bias of this literature, it is not surprising that in it the experience of being American is equated with the experience of being male. In Fitzgerald's *The Great Gatsby,* the background for the experience of disillusionment and betrayal revealed in the novel is the discovery of America, and Daisy's failure of Gatsby is symbolic of the failure of America to live up to the expectations in the imagination of the men who "discovered" it. America is female; to be American is male; and the quintessential American experience is betrayal by woman. Henry James certainly defined our literature, if not our culture, when he picked the situation of women as the subject of *The Bostonians,* his very American tale.

Power is the issue in the politics of literature, as it is in the politics of anything else. To be excluded from a literature that claims to define one's identity is to experience a peculiar form of powerlessness — not simply the powerlessness which derives from not seeing one's experience articulated, clarified, and legitimized in art, but more significantly the powerlessness which results from the endless division of self against self, the consequence of the invocation to identify as male while being reminded that to be male — to be universal, to be American — is to be *not female.* Not only does powerlessness characterize woman's experience of reading, it also describes the content of what is read. Each of the works chosen for this study presents a version and an enactment of the drama of men's power over women. The final irony, and indignity, of the woman reader's relation to American literature, then, is that she is required to dissociate herself from the very experience the literature engenders. Powerlessness is the subject and powerlessness the experience, and the design insists that Rip Van Winkle/Frederic Henry/Nick Carraway/Stephen Rojack speak for us all.

The drama of power in our literature is often disguised. In "Rip Van Winkle," Rip poses as powerless, the hen-pecked husband cowering before his termagant Dame. Yet, when Rip returns from the mountains, armed by the drama of female deposition witnessed there, to discover that his wife is dead and he is free to enjoy what he has always wanted, the "Shucks, Ma'am, I don't mean no harm" posture dissolves. In Sherwood Anderson's "I Want to Know Why," the issue of power is refracted through the trauma of a young boy's discovery of what it means to be male in a culture that gives white men power over women, horses, and niggers. More sympathetic and honest than "Rip," Anderson's story nevertheless exposes both the imaginative limits of our literature and the reasons for those limits. Storytelling and art can do no more than lament the inevitable — boys must grow up to be men; it can provide no alternative vision of being male. Bathed in nostalgia, "I Want to Know Why" is infused with the perspective it abhors, because finally to disavow that perspective would be to relinquish power. The lament is self-indulgent; it offers the luxury of feeling bad without the responsibility of change. And it is completely male-centered, registering the tragedy of sexism through its cost to men. At the end we cry for the boy and not for the whores he will eventually make use of.

In Hawthorne's "The Birthmark," the subject of power is more explicit. The fact of men's power over women and the full implications of that fact are the crux of the story. Aylmer is free to experiment on Georgiana, to the point of death, because she is both woman and wife. Hawthorne indicates the attractiveness of the power that marriage puts in the hands of men through his description of Aylmer's reluctance to leave his laboratory and through his portrayal of Aylmer's inherent discomfort with women and sex. And why does Aylmer want this power badly enough to overcome his initial reluctance and resistance? Hitherto Aylmer has failed in all his efforts to achieve a power equal to that of "Mother" nature. Georgiana provides an opportunity for him to outdo nature by remaking her creation. And if he fails, he still will have won because he will have destroyed the earthly embodiment and representative of his adversary. Hawthorne intends his character to be seen as duplicitous, and he maneuvers Aylmer through the poses of lover, husband, and scientist to show us how Aylmer attempts to gain power and to use that power to salve his sense of inadequacy. But even so, Hawthorne, like Anderson, is unwilling to do more with the sickness than call it sick. He obscures the issue of sexual politics behind a haze of "universals" and clothes the murder of wife by husband in the language of idealism.

Though the grotesque may serve Faulkner as a disguise in the same way that the ideal serves Hawthorne, "A Rose for Emily" goes farther than "The Birthmark" in making the power of men over women an overt subject. Emily's life is shaped by her father's absolute control over her; her murder of Homer Barron is *re*action, not action. Though Emily exercises the power the myths of sexism make available to her, that power is minimal; her retaliation is no alternative to the patriarchy which oppresses her. Yet Faulkner, like Anderson and Hawthorne, ultimately protects himself and short-circuits the implications of his analysis, not simply through the use of the grotesque, which makes Emily eccentric rather than central, but also through his choice of her victim. In having Emily murder Homer Barron, a northern day-laborer, rather than Judge Stevens, the southern patriarch,

Faulkner indicates how far he is willing to go in imagining even the minimal reversal of power involved in retaliation. The elimination of Homer Barron is no real threat to the system Judge Stevens represents. Indeed, a few day-laborers may have to be sacrificed here and there to keep that system going.

In *A Farewell to Arms,* the issue of power is thoroughly obscured by the mythology, language, and structure of romantic love and by the invocation of an abstract, though spiteful, "they" whose goal it is to break the good, the beautiful, and the brave. Yet the brave who is broken is Catherine; at the end of the novel Catherine is dead, Frederic is alive, and the resemblance to "Rip Van Winkle" and "The Birthmark" is unmistakable. Though the scene in the hospital is reminiscent of Aylmer's last visit to Georgiana in her chambers, Hemingway, unlike Hawthorne, separates his protagonist from the source of his heroine's death, locating the agency of Catherine's demise not simply in "them" but in her biology. Frederic survives several years of war, massive injuries, the dangers of a desperate retreat, and the threat of execution by his own army; Catherine dies in her first pregnancy. Clearly, biology is destiny. Yet, Catherine is as much a scapegoat as Dame Van Winkle, Georgiana, Daisy Fay, and Deborah Rojack. For Frederic to survive, free of the intolerable burdens of marriage, family, and fatherhood, yet with his vision of himself as the heroic victim of cosmic antagonism intact, Catherine must die. Frederic's necessities determine Catherine's fate. He is, indeed, the agent of her death.

In its passionate attraction to the phenomenon of wealth, *The Great Gatsby* reveals its author's consuming interest in the issue of power. In the quintessentially male drama of poor boy's becoming rich boy, ownership of women is invoked as the index of power: he who possesses Daisy Fay is the most powerful boy. But when the rich boy, fearing finally for his territory, repossesses the girl and, by asking "Who is he," strips the poor boy of his presumed power, the resultant animus is directed not against the rich boy but against the girl, whose rejection of him exposes the poor boy's powerlessness. The struggle for power between men is deflected into safer and more certain channels, and the consequence is the familiar demonstration of male power over women. This demonstration, however, is not simply the result of a greater safety in directing anger at women than at men. It derives as well from the fact that even the poorest male gains something from a system in which all women are at some level his subjects. Rather than attack the men who represent and manifest that system, he identifies with them and acquires his sense of power through superiority to women. It is not surprising, therefore, that the drama of *The Great Gatsby* involves an attack on Daisy, whose systematic reduction from the glamorous object of Gatsby's romantic longings to the casual killer of Myrtle Wilson provides an accurate measure of the power available to the most "powerless" male.

By his choice of scene, context, and situation, Henry James in *The Bostonians* directly confronts the hostile nature of the relations between men and women and sees in that war the defining characteristics of American culture. His honesty provides the opportunity for a clarification rather than a confusion of consciousness and offers a welcome relief from the deceptions of other writers. Yet the drama, while correctly labeled, is still the same. *The Bostonians* is an unrelenting demonstration of the extent, and an incisive analysis of the sources, of the power of men as a class over women as a class. Yet, though James laments women's oppression, and laments it because of its effects *on women,* he nevertheless sees it as inevitable. *The Bostonians* represents a kind of end point in the literary exploration of sex/class power; it would be impossible to see more clearly and feel more deeply and still remain convinced that patriarchy is inevitable. Indeed, there is revolution latent in James's novel, and, while he would be articulating and romanticizing the tragic elements in women's powerlessness, *The Bostonians* provides the material for that analysis of American social reality which is the beginning of change.

Norman Mailer's *An American Dream* represents another kind of end point. Mailer is thoroughly enthralled by the possibility of power that sexism makes available to men, absolutely convinced that he is in danger of losing it, and completely dedicated to maintaining it, at whatever cost. It is impossible to imagine a more frenzied commitment to the maintenance of male power than Mailer's. In *An American Dream* all content has been reduced to the enactment of men's power over women, and to the development and legitimization of that act Mailer brings every strategy he can muster the least of which is an extended elaboration of the mythology of female power. In Mailer's work the effort to obscure the issue, disguise reality, and confuse consciousness is so frantic that the antitheses he provides to protect his thesis become in fact his message and his confusions shed a lurid illumination. If *The Bostonians* induces one to rearrange James's conceptual framework and so to make evitable his inevitable, *An American Dream* induces a desire to eliminate Mailer's conceptual framework altogether and start over. Beyond his frenzy is only utter nausea and weariness of spirit and a profound willingness to give up an exhausted, sick, and sickening struggle. In Mailer, the drama of power comes full circle; at once the most sexist writer, he is also the most freeing, and out of him it may be possible to create anew.

II

But what have I to say of *Sexual Politics* itself? Millett has undertaken a task which I find particularly worthwhile: the consideration of certain events or works of literature from an unexpected, even startling point of view. Millett never suggests that hers is a sufficient analysis of any of the works she discusses. Her aim is to wrench the reader from the vantage point he has long occupied, and force him to look at life and letters from a new coign.[2] Hers is not meant to be the last word on any writer, but a wholly new word, little heard before and strange. For the first time we have been asked to look at literature as women; we, men, women and Ph.D.'s, have always read it as men. Who cannot point to a certain over-emphasis in the way Millett reads Lawrence or Stalin or Euripides. What matter? We are rooted in our vantage points and require transplanting which, always dangerous, involves violence and the possibility of death.

— CAROLYN HEILBRUN[3]

---

[2]Vantage point.
[3]Carolyn Heilbrun, "Millett's *Sexual Politics:* A Year Later," *Aphra* 2 (Summer 1971), 39. [Fetterley]

The method that is required is not one of correlation but of *liberation*. Even the term "method" must be reinterpreted and in fact wrenched out of its usual semantic field, for the emerging creativity in women is by no means a merely cerebral process. In order to understand the implications of this process it is necessary to grasp the fundamental fact that women have had the power of *naming* stolen from us. We have not been free to use our own power to name ourselves, the world, or God. The old naming was not the product of dialogue — a fact inadvertently admitted in the Genesis story of Adam's naming the animals and the woman. Women are now realizing that the universal imposing of names by men has been false because partial. That is, inadequate words have been taken as adequate. — MARY DALY[4]

Re-vision — the act of looking back, of seeing with fresh eyes, of entering an old text from a new critical direction — is for us more than a chapter in cultural history: it is an act of survival. Until we can understand the assumptions in which we are drenched we cannot know ourselves. And this drive to self-knowledge, for woman, is more than a search for identity: it is part of her refusal of the self-destructiveness of male-dominated society. A radical critique of literature, feminist in its impulse, would take the work first of all as a clue to how we live, how we have been living, how we have been led to imagine ourselves, how our language has trapped as well as liberated us; and how we can begin to see — and therefore live — afresh. — ADRIENNE RICH[5]

A culture which does not allow itself to look clearly at the obvious through the universal accessibility of art is a culture of tragic delusion, hardly viable. — CYNTHIA OZICK[6]

When a system of power is thoroughly in command, it has scarcely need to speak itself aloud; when its workings are exposed and questioned, it

becomes not only subject to discussion, but even to change. — KATE MILLETT[7]

Consciousness is power. To create a new understanding of our literature is to make possible a new effect of that literature on us. And to make possible a new effect is in turn to provide the conditions for changing the culture that the literature reflects. To expose and question that complex of ideas and mythologies about women and men which exist in our society and are confirmed in our literature is to make the system of power embodied in the literature open not only to discussion but even to change. Such questioning and exposure can, of course, be carried on only by a consciousness radically different from the one that informs the literature. Such a closed system cannot be opened up from within but only from without. It must be entered into from a point of view which questions its values and assumptions and which has its investment in making available to consciousness precisely that which the literature wishes to keep hidden. Feminist criticism provides that point of view and embodies that consciousness.

In "A Woman's Map of Lyric Poetry," Elizabeth Hampsten, after quoting in full Thomas Campion's "My Sweetest Lesbia," asks, "And Lesbia, what's in it for her?"[8] The answer to this question is the subject of Hampsten's essay and the answer is, of course, nothing. But implicit in her question is another answer — a great deal, for someone. As Lillian Robinson reminds us, "and, always, *cui bono* — who profits?"[9] The questions of who profits, and how, are crucial because the attempt to answer them leads directly to an understanding of the function of literary sexual politics. Function is often best known by effect. Though one of the most persistent of literary stereotypes is the castrating bitch, the cultural reality is not the emasculation of men by women but the *immasculation* of women by men. As readers and

[4]Mary Daly, *Beyond God the Father: Toward a Philosophy of Women's Liberation* (Boston: Beacon, 1973), p. 8. [Fetterley]
[5]Adrienne Rich, "When We Dead Awaken: Writing as Re-Vision," *College English* 34 (1972), 18. [Fetterley]
[6]Cynthia Ozick, "Women and Creativity: The Demise of the Dancing Dog," *Motive* 29 (1969); reprinted in *Woman in Sexist Society*, eds. Vivian Gornick and Barbara Moran (New York: Signet-New American Library, 1972), p. 450. [Fetterley]

[7]Kate Millett, *Sexual Politics* (Garden City: Doubleday, 1970), p. 58. [Fetterley]
[8]*College English* 34 (1973), 1075. [Fetterley]
[9]"Dwelling in Decencies: Radical Criticism and the Feminist Perspective," *College English* 32 (1971), 887; reprinted in *Sex, Class, and Culture* (Bloomington: Indiana University Press, 1978), p. 16. [Fetterley]

teachers and scholars, women are taught to think as men, to identify with a male point of view, and to accept as normal and legitimate a male system of values, one of whose central principles is misogyny.

One of the earliest statements of the phenomenon of immasculation, serving indeed as a position paper, is Elaine Showalter's "Women and the Literary Curriculum." In the opening part of her article, Showalter imaginatively recreates the literary curriculum the average young woman entering college confronts:

> In her freshman year she would probably study literature and composition, and the texts in her course would be selected for their timeliness, or their relevance, or their power to involve the reader, rather than for their absolute standing in the literary canon. Thus she might be assigned any one of the texts which have recently been advertised for Freshman English: an anthology of essays, perhaps such as *The Responsible Man*, "for the student who wants literature relevant to the world in which he lives," or *Conditions of Men*, or *Man in Crisis: Perspectives on The Individual and His World*, or again, *Representative Men: Cult Heroes of Our Time*, in which thirty-three men represent such categories of heroism as the writer, the poet, the dramatist, the artist, and the guru, and the only two women included are the Actress Elizabeth Taylor and The Existential Heroine Jacqueline Onassis. . . . By the end of her freshman year, a woman student would have learned something about intellectual neutrality; she would be learning, in fact, how to think like a man.[10]

Showalter's analysis of the process of immasculation raises a central question: "What are the effects of this long apprenticeship in negative capability[11] on the self-image and the self-confidence of women students?" And the answer is self-hatred and self-doubt: "Women are estranged from their own experience and unable to perceive its shape and authenticity. . . . they are expected to identify as readers with a masculine experience and perspective, which is presented as the human one. . . . Since they have no faith in the validity of their own perceptions and experiences, rarely seeing them

confirmed in literature, or accepted in criticism, can we wonder that women students are so often timid, cautious, and insecure when we exhort them to 'think for themselves'?"[12]

The experience of immasculation is also the focus of Lee Edwards' article, "Women, Energy, and *Middlemarch*." Summarizing her experience, Edwards concludes:

> Thus, like most women, I have gone through my entire education — as both student and teacher — as a schizophrenic, and I do not use this term lightly, for madness is the bizarre but logical conclusion of our education. Imagining myself male, I attempted to create myself male. Although I knew the case was otherwise, it seemed I could do nothing to make this other critically real.

Edwards extends her analysis by linking this condition to the effects of the stereotypical presentation of women in literature:

> I said simply, and for the most part silently that, since neither those women nor any women whose acquaintances I had made in fiction had much to do with the life I led or wanted to lead, I was not female. Alien from the women I saw most frequently imagined, I mentally arranged them in rows labeled respectively insipid heroines, sexy survivors, and demonic destroyers. As organizer I stood somewhere else, alone perhaps, but hopefully above them.[13]

Intellectually male, sexually female, one is in effect no one, nowhere, immasculated.

Clearly, then, the first act of the feminist critic must be to become a resisting rather than an assenting reader and, by this refusal to assent, to begin the process of exorcizing the male mind that has been implanted in us. The consequence of this exorcism is the capacity for what Adrienne Rich describes as re-vision — "the act of looking back, of seeing with fresh eyes, of entering an old text from a new critical direction." And the consequence, in turn, of this re-vision is that books will no longer be read as they have been read and thus will lose their power to bind us unknowingly to their designs. While women obviously cannot rewrite literary works so that they become ours by virtue of reflecting our reality, we can accurately

---

[10]*College English* 32 (1971), 855. [Fetterley]
[11]Showalter means something like "self-abnegation," not the prelude to creativity postulated by Keats; cf. p. 330.

[12]Ibid., 856–57. [Fetterley]
[13]*Massachusetts Review* 13 (1972), 226, 227. [Fetterley]

name the reality they do reflect and so change literary criticism from a closed conversation to an active dialogue.

In making available to women this power of naming reality, feminist criticism is revolutionary. The significance of such power is evident if one considers the strength of the taboos against it:

> I permit no woman to teach ... she is to keep silent.
> — ST. PAUL

> By Talmudic law a man could divorce a wife whose voice could be heard next door. From there to Shakespeare: "Her voice was ever soft, / Gentle, and low — an excellent thing in woman." And to Yeats: "The women that I picked spoke sweet and low / And yet gave tongue." And to Samuel Beckett, guessing at the last torture, The Worst: "a woman's voice perhaps, I hadn't thought of that, they might engage a soprano."
> — MARY ELLMANN[14]

> The experience of the class in which I voiced my discontent still haunts my nightmares. Until my face froze and my brain congealed, I was called prude and, worse yet, insensitive, since I willfully misread the play in the interest of proving a point false both to the work and in itself.
> — LEE EDWARDS[15]

The experience Edwards describes of attempting to communicate her reading of the character of Shakespeare's Cleopatra is a common memory for most of us who have become feminist critics. Many of us never spoke; those of us who did speak were usually quickly silenced. The need to keep certain things from being thought and said reveals to us their importance. Feminist criticism represents the discovery/recovery of a voice, a unique and uniquely powerful voice capable of canceling out those other voices, so movingly described in Sylvia Plath's *The Bell Jar,* which spoke about us and to us and at us but never for us.

III

The eight works analyzed in this book were chosen for their individual significance, their representative value, and their collective potential. They are interconnected in the ways that they comment on and illuminate each other, and they form a dramatic whole whose meaning transcends the mere sum of the parts. These eight are meant to stand for a much larger body of literature; their individual and collective designs can be found elsewhere repeatedly.

The four short stories form a unit, as do the four novels. These units are subdivided into pairs. "Rip Van Winkle" and "I Want to Know Why" are companion pieces whose focus is the fear of and resistance to growing up. The value of Anderson's story lies mainly in the light it sheds on Irving's, making explicit the fear of sexuality only implied in "Rip" and focusing attention on the strategy of deflecting hostility away from men and onto women. "The Birthmark" and "A Rose for Emily" are richly related studies of the consequences of growing up and, by implication, of the reasons for the resistance to it. In both stories sexual desire leads to death. More significantly, they are brilliant companion analyses of that sex/class hostility that is the essence of patriarchal culture and that underlies the adult identity Anderson's boy recoils from assuming. "The Birthmark" is the story of how to murder your wife and get away with it; "A Rose for Emily" is the story of how the system which allows you to murder your wife makes it possible for your wife to murder you.

Both *A Farewell to Arms* and *The Great Gatsby* are love stories; together they demonstrate the multiple uses of the mythology of romantic love in the maintenance of male power. In addition they elaborate on the function of scapegoating evident in "Rip Van Winkle" and "The Birthmark." In its more obvious connection of the themes of love and power, *The Great Gatsby* brings closer to consciousness the hostility which *A Farewell to Arms* seeks to disguise and bury. *The Bostonians* and *An American Dream* form the most unlikely and perhaps the most fascinating of the pairs. In both, the obfuscation of romantic love has been cleared away and the issue of power directly joined. James's novel describes a social reality — male power, female powerlessness — which Mailer's denies by creating a social mythology — female power, male powerlessness — that inverts that reality.

---

[14]*Thinking About Women* (New York: Harcourt Brace Jovanovich, 1968), pp. 149–50. [Fetterley]

[15]Edwards, p. 230. [Fetterley]

Yet finally, the intention of Mailer's mythology is to maintain the reality it denies. *The Bostonians* forces the strategies of *An American Dream* into the open by its massive documentation of women's oppression, and *An American Dream* provides the political answer to *The Bostonians'* inevitability by its massive, though unintended, demonstration of the fact that women's oppression grows not out of biology but out of men's need to oppress.

The sequence of both the stories and the novels is generated by a scale of increasing complexity, increasing consciousness, and increasing "feminist" sympathy and insight. Thus, the movement of the stories is from the black and white of "Rip Van Winkle," with its postulation of good guy and villain and its formulation in terms of innocent fable, to the complexity of "A Rose for Emily," whose action forces sexual violence into consciousness and demands understanding for the erstwhile villain. The movement of the novels is similar. *A Farewell to Arms* is as simplistic and disguised and hostile as "Rip Van Winkle"; indeed, the two have many affinities, not the least of which is the similarity of their sleep-centered protagonists who believe that women are a bad dream that will go away if you just stay in bed long enough. The sympathy and complexity of consciousness in *The Bostonians* is even larger than that in "A Rose for Emily," and is exceeded only by the imagination of *An American Dream,* which is "feminist" not by design but by default. Yet the decision to end with *An American Dream* comes not simply from its position on the incremental scale. *An American Dream* is "Rip Van Winkle" one hundred and fifty years later, intensified to be sure, but *exactly the same story.* Thus, the complete trajectory of the immasculating imagination of American literature is described by the movement from "Rip Van Winkle" to *An American Dream,* and that movement is finally circular. This juxtaposition of beginning and end provides the sharpest possible exposure of that circular quality in the design of our literature, apparent in the movements within and between works, which defines its imaginative limits. Like the race horse so loved by Anderson's boy, the imagination which informs our "classic" American literature runs endlessly round a single track, unable because unwilling to get out of the race.

Peter Rabinowitz

b. 1944

Peter Rabinowitz was born and raised in New Rochelle, New York, and educated at the University of Chicago where he earned his doctorate in comparative literature. Since his undergraduate years, Rabinowitz has negotiated divided loyalties to music and literature, and to educational politics as well. In the summer of 1964 he taught at a Freedom School in Meridian, Mississippi. His next academic appointment was at Kirkland, an experimental women's college, where he and his wife, the former Nancy Sorkin, were one of the first couples in the country to share a single tenure-track job. When Kirkland merged with Hamilton College, the Rabinowitzes helped create the comparative literature program at the new institution, where they teach and where Peter is currently chair. Rabinowitz is the author of Before Reading: Narrative Conventions and the Politics of Interpretation *(1987) and academic articles on detective fiction, forgotten novels, theory, and the music of Mahler, Gottschalk, and Scott Joplin. He is the co-editor, with James Phelan, of* Understanding Narrative *(1994), and has co-authored a book,* Resistance and Respect in the Teaching of Literature *(1997), with education professor Michael W. Smith. Rabinowitz's current project is a book, with composer Jay Reise, on the act of listening. The following selection is taken from the first chapter of* Before Reading.

From *Before Reading*

WHO IS READING?

There can be no reading without a reader — but the term *reader* is slippery, not only because all individual readers read differently, but also because for almost all of them, there are several different ways of appropriating a text. This fact has been recognized, at least implicitly, by the large number of critics whose models of reading are multitiered. Usually, a two-leveled opposition is posited, although different critics use different terms. For Hirsch, it is "significance" and "meaning." For Wayne Booth, it is "understanding" and "overstanding." For Tzvetan Todorov, there are three terms: "interpretation," "description," and "reading."[1] Many other critics, despite the recent arguments of Fish, remain wedded, in one form or another, to the distinction between literal meaning and interpretation.

These distinctions all discriminate among activities that a reader can engage in under different circumstances or for different purposes. I would like to start with a different kind of distinction, one that discriminates among *simultaneous* roles that the audience of a text can play. There are three of these roles that will be central to my argument, but I will reserve the third for Chapter 3 and will only outline the first two here. First, there is the *actual audience*. This consists of the flesh-and-blood people who read the book. This is the audience that booksellers are most concerned with — but it happens to be the audience over which an author has no guaranteed control. Each member of the actual audience is different, and each reads in his or her own way, with a distance from other readers depending upon such variables as class, gender, race, personality, training, culture, and historical situation.

This difference among readers has always posed a problem for writers, one that has grown with increased literacy and the correspondingly increased heterogeneity of the reading public. An author has, in most cases, no firm knowledge of the actual readers who will pick up his or her book. Yet he or she cannot begin to fill up a blank page without making assumptions about the readers' beliefs, knowledge, and familiarity with conventions. As a result, authors are forced to guess; they design their books rhetorically for some more or less specific *hypothetical* audience, which I call the *authorial audience.* Artistic choices are based upon these assumptions — conscious or unconscious — about readers, and to a certain extent, artistic success depends on their shrewdness, on the degree to which actual and authorial audience overlap. Some assumptions are quite specific. William Demby's *Catacombs,* for instance, takes place in the early 1960s, and it achieves its sense of impending doom only if the reader already knows that John F. Kennedy will be assassinated when the events of the novel reach November 22, 1963. One of the Encyclopedia Brown mysteries is soluble only by the reader who knows that skydivers always wear two parachutes. Other assumptions are more general: "Rip van Winkle" assumes readers who know that during the Revolution, the American colonies became independent of England. Some assumptions are historical: Flaubert assumes considerable knowledge of the revolution of 1848 in *Sentimental Education.* Some are sociological: at least one critic has argued convincingly that *The Turn of the Screw* makes proper sense only to a reader who knows something about the conduct deemed proper to governesses in the nineteenth century.[2] Some authors rely on our precise knowledge of cultural fads (Peter Cameron, in "Fear of Math," assumes that his audience will draw the proper conclusions about a character when he tells us that she eats a "tabbouleh-and-pita bread sandwich"),[3] others on our knowledge of more widespread cultural conventions (in Nabokov's *Lolita,* the refusal of the

[1]E. D. Hirsch, Jr., *Validity in Interpretation* (New Haven: Yale University Press, 1967), esp. p. 8; Wayne C. Booth, *Critical Understanding* (Chicago: University of Chicago Press, 1979) passim; Tzvetan Todorov, *Poetics of Prose,* trans. Richard Howard (Ithaca: Cornell University Press, 1977), pp. 238–46. [Rabinowitz]

[2]Elliott M. Schrero, "Exposure in *The Turn of the Screw,*" *Modern Philology* 78 (February 1981): 261–74. [Rabinowitz]
[3]*New Yorker,* March 11, 1985, 42. [Rabinowitz]

Enchanted Hunters to accept Humbert Humbert as a guest when he first shows up makes sense only if readers recognize both that they have garbled his name so that it sounds Jewish, and that the phrase in their advertising, "Near Churches," is a code phrase for "No Jews").[4] Some authors presume that we have a knowledge of specific previous texts (Stoppard assumes that his readers know *Hamlet* before reading *Rosencrantz and Guildenstern Are Dead*). Sometimes authors assume that our higher motives will triumph (Dostoyevsky assumes that we are capable of sympathy for the sufferings of Raskolnikov in *Crime and Punishment* even though he is a murderer). Sometimes authors — even the same authors — assume that we will be influenced by our baser prejudices (in *The Idiot* we are expected to be distrustful of Ganya because his teeth are "altogether too dazzling and even").[5] The potential range of assumptions an author can make, in other words, is infinite.

The notion of the authorial audience is clearly tied to authorial intention, but it gets around some of the problems that have traditionally hampered the discussion of intention by treating it as a matter of social convention rather than of individual psychology. In other words, my perspective allows us to treat the reader's attempt to read as the author intended, not as a search for the author's private psyche, but rather as the joining of a particular social/interpretive community; that is, the acceptance of the author's invitation to read in a particular socially constituted way that is shared by the author and his or her expected readers. Indeed, authorial reading is not only a way of reading but, perhaps equally important, a way of talking about how you read — that is, the result of a community agreement that allows discussion of a certain sort to take place by treating meanings in a particular way (as found rather

than made). In this sense, what Susan R. Suleiman says about the notions of the implied author and the implied reader which are themselves only variant formulations of the notion of authorial intention) applies to the authorial audience as well: they are, she says, "necessary fictions, guaranteeing the consistency of a specific reading without guaranteeing its validity in any absolute sense."[6] But it is crucial to note that this is not just an arbitrary convention invented by academics for their own convenience — it is a broader social usage, one that is shared by authors as well as their readers, including their nonprofessional readers. My position here is thus very close to that of Foley, who rightly sees fiction "as a contract designed by an intending author who invites his or her audience to adopt certain paradigms for understanding reality."[7] In other words, as Terry Eagleton argues, intention is best seen not in terms of "essentially private 'mental acts,'" but rather in terms of social practice.[8]

[6]Susan R. Suleiman, "Introduction," in *The Reader in the Text,* ed. Susan R. Suleiman and Inge Crossman (Princeton: Princeton University Press, 1980), p. 11. [Rabinowitz]

[7]Barbara Foley, *Telling the Truth* (Ithaca: Cornell University Press, 1986), p. 43. [Rabinowitz]

[8]Terry Eagleton, *Literary Theory* (Minneapolis: University of Minnesota Press, 1983), p. 114. See also Patrocinio P. Schweickart's claim that validity is not "a property inherent in an interpretation, but rather ... a *claim* implicit in the *act* of propounding an interpretation" — that is, that validity is "contingent on the agreement of others" ("Reading Ourselves," in *Gender and Reading,* ed. Elizabeth A. Flynn and Patrocinio P. Schweickart [Baltimore: Johns Hopkins University Press, 1986], p. 56). Fish argues similarly that authorial intention "is not private but a form of conventional behavior" ("Working on the Chain Gang," *Critical Inquiry* 9 [September 1982]: 213); Hirsch, with less enthusiasm, notes that "we can circumvent the whole question of author psychology by adopting a semiotic account of interpretation. Instead of referring an interpretation back to an original author, we could ... refer it back to an original code or convention system" ("Politics of Theories of Interpretation," *Critical Inquiry* 9 [September 1982]: 239). Hirsch insists that this would not really be an adequate account, but I suspect it is as adequate as any that relies on actual psychology. It is worth remembering that this is not simply a matter of arbitrary definitions; as Mailloux's arguments in "Rhetorical Hermeneutics" (*Critical Inquiry* 11 [June 1985]: 620–41) make clear, the very act of treating readings in this way has serious effects on the ways in which people subsequently *do* read — on what counts as evidence, for instance. [Rabinowitz]

[4]Although I have taught this novel several times, none of my students — coming as they do from a cultural context quite different from that of the authorial audience — has caught this, or any of the other references to anti-Semitism in the novel. [Rabinowitz]

[5]Fyodor Dostoyevsky, *The Idiot,* trans. David Magarshack (Baltimore: Penguin, 1955), p. 48 (pt. 1, chap. 2). In Dickens' *Dombey and Son,* we are expected to distrust Carker for the same reason. [Rabinowitz]

By thinking in terms of the authorial audience rather than private intention, furthermore, we are reminded of the constraints within which writers write. For despite the theoretically infinite number of potential authorial audiences, it does not follow that authors have total control over the act of writing, any more than that readers have total control over the act of interpretation. In a trivial sense, of course, they do: authors can put down whatever marks they wish on the page; readers can construe them however they wish. But once authors and readers accept the communal nature of writing and reading, they give up some of that freedom. Specifically, once he or she has made certain initial decisions, any writer who wishes to communicate — even if he or she wishes to communicate ambiguity — has limited the range of subsequent choices.

Some of those limitations spring from what might be called brute facts. Writers of realistic historical novels, for instance, shackle themselves to events that are independent of their imaginations. As Suleiman has argued:

> The most obvious . . . difference between fictional and historical characters in a novel is that the latter impose greater constraints on the novelist who wants to be a "painter of his time." He cannot make Napoleon die — or win the battle — at Waterloo, just as he cannot make Hugo the court poet of Napoleon III. . . . And if the novelist chooses to place in the foreground events as well-known and public as the Boulanger affair or the Panama scandal, then he will have to bend to similar constraints even as far as the activities of the *fictional* characters are concerned.[9]

Thus, once Margaret Mitchell chose to write *Gone with the Wind* as a historical novel about the Civil War, she relinquished control over certain areas of her text. She could have saved Melanie had she wished, or killed off Rhett, but there was no way to give victory to the South or to preserve Atlanta from the flames.

More central to my argument, though, are *conventional* limitations on choice. There are no brute facts preventing an author from writing a religious parable in which a cross represented Judaism, but it would not communicate successfully. As Mary Pratt puts it, "Although the fictional discourse in a work of literature may in theory take any form at all, readers have certain expectations about what form it will take, and *they can be expected to decode the work according to those assumptions unless they are overtly invited or required to do otherwise*" (italics in original).[10] The writer who wishes to be understood — even to be understood by a small group of readers — has to work within such conventional restraints.

Despite these limitations, however, there are still an incalculable number of possible authorial audiences; and since the structure of a work is designed with the authorial audience in mind, actual readers must come to share its characteristics as they read if they are to experience the text as the author wished.[11] Reading as authorial audience therefore involves a kind of distancing from the actual audience, from one's own immediate needs and interests. This distancing, however, must be distinguished sharply from the apparently similar kind of objectivity, represented in its baldest form by Dr. Blimber, in Dickens' *Dombey and Son,* who claimed "that all the fancies of the poets, and lessons of the sages, were a mere collection of words and grammar, and had no other meaning in the world."[12] Of course, few critics

[10]Mary Louise Pratt, *Toward a Speech Act Theory of Literary Discourse* (Bloomington: Indiana University Press, 1977), p. 204. Pratt's own strong critique of speech-act theory (including her own work) can be found in "The Ideology of Speech-Act Theory," *Centrum,* n.s. 1 (Spring 1981): 5–18. I think that my definition of fictionality (Chapter 3) solves some of the questions that Pratt raises; while my book tends to focus on a type of reading that includes an attempt at author-reader cooperation, I have accepted many of the arguments on which her critique is based, and have tried not to "normalize" this particular kind of reading, nor to define others as "deviant" (see "The Value[s] of Authorial Reading" below). Even if one accepts her new position, though, much of Pratt's earlier work remains useful as a description of certain kinds of reading. [Rabinowitz]

[11]See Booth's discussion of this process in *Rhetoric of Fiction,* 2nd ed. (Chicago: University of Chicago Press), pp. 138–41. [Rabinowitz]

[12]Charles Dickens, *Dombey and Son* (New York: Dutton/Everyman's Library, 1907), pp. 134–35 (chap. 11). [Rabinowitz]

[9]Susan Robin Suleiman, *Authoritarian Fictions* (New York: Columbia University Press, 1983), p. 120. [Rabinowitz]

subscribe to Blimberism in its purest form, yet many critical windows are draped with remnants from Blimber's school. Northrop Frye insists that "the fundamental act of criticism is a disinterested response to a work of literature in which all one's beliefs, engagements, commitments, prejudices, stampedings of pity and terror, are ordered to be quiet."[13] Similarly, the reader postulated by Stanley Fish's once-popular "Affective Stylistics" is psychologically blank and politically unaware, an automaton who approaches each new sentence with the same anesthetized mind.[14] In a radically different critical tradition, Gerald Prince's degree-zero narratee — whom he assumes to be the addressee of the text except where "an indication to the contrary is supplied in the narration intended for him" — has no "personality or social characteristics," and although he (apparently, the degree-zero narratee is male) knows grammar and the denotations of words, he knows neither connotations nor conventions. He is, in other words, capable of reading a text without any distorting presuppositions; neither his "character" nor his "position in society . . . colors his perception of the events described to him."[15]

Authorial reading, however, is quite different. It does *not* escape "distorting presuppositions." Rather, it recognizes that distorting presuppositions lie at the heart of the reading process. To read as authorial audience is to read in an impersonal way, but only in a special and limited sense.

The authorial audience has knowledge and beliefs that may well be *extra*personal — that is, not shared by the actual individual reader (I, for instance, do not personally share the racist perspective of the authorial audience of Ian Fleming's *Live and Let Die*). The authorial audience's knowledge and beliefs may even be extra-communal — that is, not shared by any community (and we all belong to several) of which the actual reader is a member at the historical moment of reading (what current community shares the belief in Zeus characteristic of the authorial audience of the *Odyssey*?). But these authorial audiences, whatever their distance from actual readers, certainly have their own engagements and prejudices. To join the authorial audience, then, you should not ask what a *pure* reading of a given text would be. Rather, you need to ask what sort of *corrupted* reader this particular author wrote for: what were that reader's beliefs, engagements, commitments, prejudices, and stampedings of pity and terror?

The reader, in other words, can read as the author intended only by being in the right place to begin with — and that can come about only through an intuitive mix of experience and faith, knowledge and hunch — plus a certain amount of luck. There is consequently no ideal point of departure that will work for any and all books. And since each point of departure involves its own corruptions, commitments, and prejudices, every authorial reading has significant ideological strands. As I suggested earlier, my primary concern here is with a particular aspect of the authorial audience's corruptions: the literary conventions that it applies to the text in order to transform it. As such critics as Culler are now making clearer, reading (especially the reading of literature) is not only not a natural activity — it is not even a logical consequence of knowledge of the linguistic system and its written signs. It is, rather, a separately learned, *conventional* activity.

In other words, literary conventions are not in the text waiting to be uncovered, but in fact *precede* the text and make discovery possible in the first place.[16] Note, however, that I speak here of

---

[13]Northrop Frye, *Well-Tempered Critic* (Bloomington: Indiana University Press, 1963), p. 140. Frye backs off a bit from the implications of this statement by distinguishing later between the pure disinterested critical act and the act of ordinary reading. [Rabinowitz]

[14]Stanley Fish, "Literature in the Reader: Affective Stylistics," in *Is There a Text in This Class?* (Cambridge: Harvard University Press, 1980), pp. 21–67. Indeed, as Culler has pointed out, he or she does not even learn from reading; see *Pursuit of Signs* (Ithaca: Cornell University Press, 1982), p. 130. [Rabinowitz]

[15]Gerald Prince, "Introduction," trans. Francis Mariner. In *Reader-Response Criticism,* ed. Jane Tompkins (Baltimore: Johns Hopkins University Press, 1980), pp. 10–11. But see also his claim, "There may frequently be points in my reading where . . . I have to rely not only on my linguistic knowledge and the textual information supplied but also on my mastery of logical operations, my familiarity with interpretive conventions and my knowledge of the world" (*Narratology* [Berlin: Mouton, 1982], p. 128). [Rabinowitz]

[16]As Culler argues, "The implication that the ideal reader is a *tabula rasa* on which the text inscribes itself not only

discovery, not creation. The notion of reading as authorial audience is closer to what Steven Mailloux calls "textual realism" (the belief that "meaning-full texts exist independent of interpretation") than to what he calls "readerly idealism" (the belief that "meaning is made, not found," since "textual facts are never prior to or independent of the hermeneutic activity of readers and critics").[17] True, I share the idealists' belief that texts are incomplete when we get them and must be put together according to the principles of the reader's interpretive community, but in the case of successful authorial reading, the author and readers are members of the same community, so while the reader does in fact engage in an act of production, he or she makes what the author intended to be found. Of course, as I will discuss in more detail in Chapters 6 and 7, not all attempts at authorial reading are successful. Even readers who try to find out what an author intends may thus in fact *make* something the author never expected; in such cases, though, the readers will still act as if they have in fact *found* the meaning of the text.

I am not arguing that we do not use logic to interpret literary texts. Given that Edna Losser is

twenty in 1900 when Margaret Ayer Barnes' *Edna His Wife* opens, we can reasonably infer — as the author intended us to — that she is in her fifties when the novel ends, in the early 1930s. But such inferences are not sufficient for a complete authorial reading. Nor am I arguing that one cannot describe the features of literary artifacts or the rules that govern reading according to "logical" categories. Thus, for instance, Gerald Prince is quite correct when he claims, "Should an event A precede an event B in time, the two may be temporally adjacent, or proximate, or distant."[18] Similarly, we can claim, with some precision, that in any book, the rule that we should eliminate likely suspects either applies or does not apply. But providing a logical classification of all possibilities is quite different from providing a logical system that explains which of those possibilities will be actualized in a given novel. A reader who picks up Ellery Queen's *Tragedy of X* for the first time knows to eliminate obvious suspects, not because of some *systematic* understanding of possible literary types, but rather because it is the *conventional* thing to do in that kind of book. For this reason, discussions of the actual conventions of reading will always appear arbitrary and ad hoc compared to the classifications of structuralists.[19]

Knowledge of these conventions is a major part of what Culler calls "literary competence."[20]

---

makes nonsense of the whole process of literary education and conceals the conventions and norms which make possible the production of meaning but also insures the bankruptcy of literary theory, whose speculations on the properties of literary texts become ancillary and *ex post facto* generalizations which are explicitly denied any role in the activity of reading" (*Pursuit of Signs* [Ithaca: Cornell University Press, 1981], p. 121). See also Mailloux's claim that "a reader's understanding of authorial intention always depends on shared communicative conventions, but the success of the intention to achieve certain perlocutionary effects is not guaranteed by those conventions, only made possible by them" (*Interpretive Conventions* [Ithaca: Cornell University Press, 1982], p. 106). This notion of reading is confirmed by research into cognitive psychology. See, for instance, Mary Crawford and Roger Chaffin's claim that "understanding is a product of both the text and the prior knowledge and viewpoint that the reader brings to it" ("Reader's Construction of Meaning," in *Gender and Reading,* ed. Elizabeth A. Flynn and Patrocinio P. Schweickart [Baltimore: Johns Hopkins University Press, 1986], p. 3). [Rabinowitz]

[17]Steven Mailloux, "Rhetorical Hermeneutics," *Critical Inquiry* 11 (June 1985): 622. Mailloux attacks both schools and argues against doing "Theory" at all. Although I do not follow this path, I find his alternative, — a study of the *institutional* politics of interpretation — a profitable one as well. [Rabinowitz]

[18]Gerald Prince, *Narratology* (Berlin: Mouton, 1982), p. 64. [Rabinowitz]

[19]For a different perspective, see Todorov's discussion of the difference between logical ("theoretical") and historical genres (*The Fantastic,* trans. Richard Howard [Ithaca: Cornell University Press, 1975], chap. 1). [Rabinowitz]

[20]Jonathan Culler, *Structuralist Poetics* (Ithaca: Cornell University Press, 1975), esp. chap. 6. Conventions are also one aspect of Hans Robert Jauss' notion of "horizon of expectations." See, for instance, *Toward an Aesthetic of Reception,* trans. Timothy Bahti (Minneapolis: University of Minnesota Press, 1982). For a strong critique of Culler's notion of competence, see Pratt, "Interpretive Strategies/Strategic Interpretations," *Boundary2* 11 (Fall–Winter 1981/82), esp. pp. 215–21. Pratt points out that, as Culler uses the concept, literary competence can end up as a theoretical justification for the mainstream practices of academic criticism. Literary competence, however, need not be restricted to what the academy believes it to be; as I hope will be clear in Chapters 6 and 7, my own stress on actual authorial intention, rather than on received opinion about the "right" way to read "good" books, helps avoid this problem. [Rabinowitz]

It is not simply that we need to know conventions in order to read Joyce; even the simplest literary artifact (say, a comic strip) calls nonlinguistic conventions (such as the left-to-right spatial representation of the passage of time) into play.[21] As Janice Radway puts it, "Comprehension is . . . a process of sign production where the reader actively attributes significance to signifiers on the basis of previously learned cultural codes."[22]

As I will demonstrate, the reliance of reading on conventions that precede the text has enormous consequences for the processes of interpretation and evaluation, in many ways the central activities of the academic literary community.

THE VALUE(S) OF AUTHORIAL READING

In this book, I will focus primarily on authorial reading. In so doing, I am not claiming that this is either the only or even the best way to read. I do not agree with Steven Knapp and Walter Benn Michaels that "the meaning of a text is simply identical to the author's intended meaning" or that "authorial intention is the necessary object of interpretation."[23] And I do not agree with Wayne Booth and E. D. Hirsch, Jr., who often suggest that there is a moral imperative to read as the author intended.[24] At the same time, I would argue that authorial reading is more than just

another among a large set of equally valid and equally important ways of approaching a text. Authorial reading has a special status for at least two reasons.

First, while Knapp and Michaels are wrong that "the object of *all* reading is *always* the historical author's intention" (italics added),[25] it is true that most people actually do read — or attempt to read — this way most of the time. Of course, different individuals may disagree about what the author's intention is, just as they may react differently to it once they think they have found it. Nonetheless, the initial question most commonly asked of a literary text in our culture is, What is the author saying? The critical revolutions of the 1970s and 1980s may have deluded us, but the millions of readers of Len Deighton's *SS-GB* or Judith Krantz's *Scruples* were interested neither in deconstructing texts nor in discovering their underlying semiotic codes. In fact, even among the most jaded readers — academics — the majority still attempts to read as authorial audience. Authorial reading continues to provide the basis for most academic articles and papers — and, even more, for classroom teaching.

Second, and perhaps more important for critical theory, reading as authorial audience provides the foundation for many other types of reading. True, some approaches to texts skip over the authorial audience entirely: certain kinds of structuralist or stylistic studies, for instance, or the kind of subjective reading proposed by David Bleich in *Readings and Feelings*.[26] But then again, many types of reading depend for their power on a prior understanding of the authorial meaning.[27] The manifest/latent distinction of certain Freudian studies, for instance, collapses if we don't have a

[21]For a good unpacking of the conventions of the comic strip, see Seymour Chatman, *Story and Discourse* (Ithaca: Cornell University Press, 1978), pp. 37–41. [Rabinowitz]

[22]Janice Radway, *Reading the Romance* (Chapel Hill: University of North Carolina Press, 1984), p. 7. Radway sees this as a process of "making" meaning, but as I have argued, reading as authorial audience at least attempts to "find" a meaning that is in some sense already there. [Rabinowitz]

[23]Steven Knapp and Walter Benn Michaels, "Against Theory," *Critical Inquiry* 8 (Summer 1982): 724, and "A Reply to Our Critics," *Critical Inquiry* 9 (Summer 1983): 796. For a series of incisive responses to Knapp and Michaels, see *Critical Inquiry* 9 (June 1983): 725–89. [Rabinowitz]

[24]See Booth: "It is simply self-maiming to pretend that any blissful improvisation on [Henry James'] words, sentences, or themes . . . can equal the value of his making" (*Critical Understanding*, p. 284). See also E. D. Hirsch, Jr., *The Aims of Interpretation* (Chicago: University of Chicago Press, 1976). For positions that oppose Booth's, see, for instance, Barbara Herrnstein Smith, *On the Margins of Discourse* (Chicago: University of Chicago Press, 1978), esp. chap. 6;

and "English 692" [Joanna Brent, Rita Conley, et al.], "Poem Opening: An Invitation to Transactive Criticism," *College English* 40 (September 1978): 2–16. [Rabinowitz]

[25]Knapp and Michaels, "A Reply to Our Critics," p. 798. [Rabinowitz]

[26]Urbana, IL: National Council of Teachers of English, 1975, esp. pp. 80–95. For a further development of Bleich's ideas, see also his *Subjective Criticism* (Baltimore: Johns Hopkins University Press, 1978). [Rabinowitz]

[27]Booth has called such readings "parasitical" ("M. H. Abrams," *Critical Inquiry* 2 [Spring 1976]: 441). See J. Hillis Miller's response, "Critic as Host," *Critical Inquiry* 3 (Spring 1977): 439–47. [Rabinowitz]

manifest meaning to begin with. Georg Lukács' Marxist analysis of Balzac depends on the distinction between what Balzac wanted to see and what he really did see.[28] Most important — if importance has any connection to the power of a critical movement to make us recognize the world with new eyes — we see the same dependence on authorial intention in much feminist criticism. Judith Fetterley's "resisting reader" can come into being only if there is something to resist.[29]

Two examples may clarify how certain kinds of political criticism can be strengthened if they are built on a foundation of authorial reading. Imagine a critic who wanted to uncover Natasha's victimization in *War and Peace* — to show how Russian society restricts the development of her natural talents, how it curbs and punishes her spirit and individuality. Such a critic could well point out Natasha's unjust fate — even explain its social, psychological, and historical causes — without any reference to authorial intention. But if — and only if — the critic works through an authorial reading of the text, the scope of this political analysis can be enlarged to explore the *contradiction* between the authorial audience and the critic. For only by starting with an authorial reading could the critic analyze the social, historical, and biographical implications of the fact that from Tolstoy's point of view (and from the point of view of the authorial audience, as well as of millions of actual readers), Natasha does not suffer in the end. Indeed, her victimization is worse than invisible — it is construed as a

reward.[30] Without this grounding in an authorial reading, Tolstoy's misogynist text is indistinguishable from feminist irony.

Similarly, reading *Jane Eyre* in the context of Jean Rhys' *Wide Sargasso Sea* — and Mary Wollstonecraft's *Maria* — provides a useful perspective that underscores the inhumanity of Rochester's — and Jane's — treatment of Bertha and suggests that we look behind her function as a convenient Gothic plot device to consider her as a significant character who has been driven mad by her social and economic conditions. But again, with authorial reading one can go further to explore the extent to which Brontë was herself unable to see the oppression behind that convention.[31]

Thus, in arguing for the importance of reading as authorial audience, I am not suggesting that it is either the final reading or the most important. Were I teaching either Tolstoy or Brontë, I would be disappointed in a student who could produce an authorial reading but who could not, in Terry Eagleton's phrase, "show the text as it cannot know itself"[32] — that is, move beyond that reading to look at the work critically from some perspective other than the one called for by the author. But while authorial reading without further critique is often incomplete, so is a critical reading without an understanding of the authorial audience as its base.

So far, I have argued the importance of authorial reading on the grounds that many readers try to engage in it, and that it is a necessary precondition for many other kinds of reading. But it does not logically follow that it is actually possible. Indeed, I would argue that in a sense it is not. I am not referring here to the problems of interpretation that arise because authors simply fail at the

---

[28]Lukács claims, for instance, that Balzac was faced with a contradiction between the torments of "the transition to the capitalist system of production" and his awareness that this "transformation was not only socially inevitable, but at the same time progressive. This contradiction in his experience Balzac *attempted* to force into a system based on a Catholic legitimism and tricked out with Utopian conceptions of English Toryism. But this system was contradicted all the time by the social realities of his day and the Balzacian vision which mirrored them" (*Studies in European Realism* [New York: Grossett and Dunlap, 1964], pp. 12–13, emphasis added). [Rabinowitz]

[29]See also Mailloux's claim that "every feminist and non-feminist approach must posit some kind of reading experience upon which to base its interpretation. Only after a reader-response description is completed or assumed can a feminist critique begin" (*Interpretive Conventions* [Ithaca: Cornell University Press, 1982], p. 89). [Rabinowitz]

[30]See, in this regard, Eve Kosofsky Sedgwick's discussion of the " 'happy ending' " of *Our Mutual Friend* and what it really means for Lizzie (*Between Men: English Literature and Male Homosocial Desire* [New York: Columbia University Press, 1985], p. 178). [Rabinowitz]

[31]For a different perspective on this problem, considered in the context of European imperialism, see Gayatri Chakravorty Spivak, "Three Women's Texts and a Critique of Imperialism," *Critical Inquiry* 12 (Autumn 1985): 243–61. [Rabinowitz]

[32]Terry Eagleton, *Criticism and Ideology* (London: New Left Books, 1976), p. 43. [Rabinowitz]

act of writing, or because, when editors are allowed to muddle with finished texts, authors, as Hershel Parker puts it, "very often lose authority, with the result that familiar literary texts at some points have no meaning, only partially authorial meaning, or quite adventitious meaning unintended by the author or anyone else."[33] Even beyond this, even among the most polished and accurately edited of texts, there are many (perhaps all) where neither scholarship nor imagination is sufficient to allow us to recover the text in the sense of experiencing the full response that the author intended us to have as we read. This impossibility stems directly from the actual/authorial split. These audiences differ in, among other things, the knowledge and belief they bring to a text. To the extent that the knowledge distinguishing the authorial from the actual audience is positive or additive (that is, to the extent that the authorial audience knows something that the actual audience does not), the gap can often be bridged through education. The reader of *The Catacombs* who does not know the date of Kennedy's assassination can be informed. But knowledge can also be negative. That is, sometimes actual readers can respond to a text as authorial audience only by *not* knowing something that they in fact know — not knowing, as they read John Steinbeck's *In Dubious Battle,* the actual (often unidealistic) course that the American labor movement would eventually follow; not knowing, as they read *U.S.A.,* that Dos Passos would later shift his political views. As for beliefs — they are usually neither additive nor negative, but substitutive: it was difficult for some college-age readers in the late 1960s to accept the passion with which Clarissa protected her virginity.[34]

The problems of recovery caused by the actual/authorial split have a musical equivalent: what I call the authentic-performance paradox. Many performing groups assume that by recreating the physical sounds that a composer had available, they come closer to recreating the intended musical experiences. But do contemporary listeners really move closer to Beethoven's intended experiences when they listen to his sonatas on a Conrad Graf fortepiano? In at least one way, they take a significant step *away* from Beethoven. I am not convinced by those structuralists who argue that binary oppositions underlie all of our perceptions of the world, but structuralists are surely right that we see things not in themselves but rather in terms of their relations, and specifically in terms of oppositions determined largely by culturally imposed categories that may change radically over time. Thus, when *I* hear Beethoven on an early-nineteenth-century fortepiano (and I think this experience is shared by many contemporary listeners), I hear it first and foremost *against* modern sounds. That is, the sound is defined by me (and hence experienced by me) partly in terms of its being not-that-of-a-modern-piano. That component of the listening experience was obviously not envisioned by Beethoven. Similarly, the range of choices that Mozart faced now seems restricted in ways that it did not in 1790, since we now know what Beethoven, Wagner, Schoenberg, and Jay Reise have added to available harmonic and formal vocabulary.[35]

In other words, we live in a world with a history and with traditions, and it is impossible to experience what an author wanted us to because it is impossible to forget all that has happened between the time when a text was written and the time when it is read. What reasonably educated member of our culture can read *Hamlet* — even

---

[33]Hershel Parker, *Flawed Texts and Verbal Icons* (Evanston, IL: Northwestern University Press, 1984), p. 4. [Rabinowitz]

[34]John Steinbeck's novel *In Dubious Battle* (1936) concerns a strike of California fruit-pickers in violent conflict with labor goons; by the 1950s, some unions on both coasts were enmeshed with organized crime. John Dos Passos's trilogy *U.S.A.* (*The 42nd Parallel* [1930], *1919* [1932], and *The Big Money* [1936]) contained biting satire on American capitalism and patriotic hypocrisies, which made the author a darling of the Left, although he never joined the Communist

Party. In Spain during the Civil War in 1938, Dos Passos became disenchanted with the Soviet Union and its supporters, and his later work reflected a sharp political turn to the Right. Samuel Richardson's *Clarissa, or the History of a Young Lady* (1747–48) concerns a young heiress who is raped after resisting repeated attempts at seduction.

[35]For a fuller discussion of this problem, see my "Circumstantial Evidence: Music Analysis and Theories of Reading," *Mosaic* 18 (Fall 1985): 159–73. [Rabinowitz]

for the first time — without being influenced by the traditions of interpretation encrusted on it? Of course, tradition is a factor in authorial reading as well; the tradition of literature out of which *Hamlet* grew is, to some extent, part of Shakespeare's assumed starting point. But the traditions coming *afterward* are assuredly not, and modern readers are more likely to be familiar with the latter (which cannot be erased) than with the former.

Thus, while books do sometimes have the power to take readers out of themselves, that power is limited. Nor is that limitation necessarily to be lamented. Despite romantic notions about the beneficial consequences of great art, books are in fact capable of moving readers in immoral as well as in moral directions. In the climactic chapter of Thomas Dixon, Jr.'s once-popular *The Leopard's Spots,* for instance, our hero, entering a chaotic Democratic convention, makes a stunning speech that unites the party, gains him the nomination for the governorship, provides the first step toward the routing of the Republicans — and, happily, wins over the father of the woman he loves. Few of the readers who pick up this text have trouble recognizing that, for the authorial audience, this is an inspiring moment — especially since Dixon gives clear signals as to how we should react:

> Two thousand men went mad. With one common impulse they sprang to their feet, screaming, shouting, cheering, shaking each other's hands, crying and laughing. With the sullen roar of crashing thunder another whirlwind of cheers swept the crowd, shook the earth, and pierced the sky with its challenge. Wave after wave of applause swept the building and flung their rumbling echoes among the stars.[36]

But should the actual reader respond emotionally, as the author intended, to the *content* of the speech?

> "Shall we longer tolerate negro inspectors of white schools, and negroes in charge of white institutions?

> Shall we longer tolerate the arrest of white women by negro officers and their trial before negro magistrates?

> "Let the manhood of the Aryan race with its four thousand years of authentic history answer that question!" [436]

"The African has held one fourth of this globe for 3000 years. He has never taken one step in progress or rescued one jungle from the ape and the adder, except as the slave of a superior race . . . and he has not produced one man who has added a feather's weight to the progress of humanity." [437]

The ability to "forget" the viciousness of this passage is not an ability to be nourished, even if it increases our aesthetic enjoyment of this text. And New Critical dogma to the contrary, it is not simply in works of lesser aesthetic quality that this problem emerges.[37] The ability to forget the ways that women have been abused is not a moral asset either, even if it increases our enjoyment of the way Don Giovanni makes a laughingstock of Donna Elvira, or our pleasure in Rochester's final release from the burden of a mad wife.

But while it is neither always possible nor always desirable to experience a text as an author intended, it does not follow that all interpretation need be subjective or idiosyncratic. We can, after all, describe what we cannot experience — and we can often determine what the authorial audience's response is without sharing it fully. A reader can, for instance, know that the authorial audience of *The Leopard's Spots* finds the speech gratifying, or that the authorial audience of *Jane Eyre* finds Bertha unsympathetic — even if, as actual audience, the gratification or the lack of sympathy are problematic. This is important because, as I have argued, authorial reading has a special status against which other readings can be

---

[36]Thomas Dixon, Jr., *The Leopard's Spots: A Romance of the White Man's Burden, 1865–1900* (New York: Doubleday, Page, 1902), p. 443 (bk. 3, chap. 13). Further references to this edition are made in the text. [Rabinowitz]

[37]Thus, for instance, Brooks and Warren admit that there are some works that "offend us at too deep a level" for us to accept them. "But always we should be careful that we have made the imaginative effort to understand what values may be there, and what common ground might, with more effort, be found." It is significant, though, that they hasten to add, "Furthermore, in the end, we may find that we have rejected the story not because of its theme as such, but because we have found the story unconvincing" (*Understanding Fiction,* 2nd ed. [New York: Appleton-Century-Crofts, 1959], p. 276). [Rabinowitz]

measured (although not necessarily negatively); it is a kind of norm (although not necessarily a positive value), in that it serves as a point of orientation (although not necessarily as an ultimate destination). In short, authorial reading — in the sense of *understanding* the values of the authorial audience — has its own kind of validity, even if, in the end, actual readers share neither the experiences nor the values presumed by the author.

THE DIFFICULTIES OF AUTHORIAL READING

Any discussion of reading must eventually come to grips with a fundamental fact: texts are often ambiguous. This claim of ambiguity, of course, is itself ambiguous, for it means several different things. It means, for instance, that readers from different interpretive communities — readers who are using the text for different ends — may well find different things in it, and may well call on different kinds of evidence to support their claims: Marxists and Freudians may well see *The Trial* as different texts that are both contained within the same marks on the page. It also means, as many deconstructionist readings have made clear, that the nature of our linguistic system is such that actual readers may find meanings in a text that subvert the meaning apparently intended by the author. It means, in addition, that authors often attempt to communicate ambiguity itself — thus, even readers in the same interpretive community may well see different things in *The Trial*, since Kafka was consciously trying to confuse.

The actual/authorial distinction, however, suggests yet another type of ambiguity. Even among readers attempting to read as authorial audience (whatever they may call it) — that is, even among readers who share ties to the same critical methodologies — there are bound to be disagreements that literary theory can explain but never erase. For even within a given interpretive community, interpretation depends radically on the reader's starting point, which will influence (although not necessarily determine) his or her reading experience. And the proper starting point is always, as I have suggested, presupposed by the text, not contained within it.

To be sure, it is often claimed that texts provide their own rules for unlocking their meanings. "What attitude are we to take toward Walter Mitty?" ask Brooks and Warren. "The reader will need no special help in deciding how to 'take' this story . . . The action of the story serves to suggest the proper blend of sympathy and amusement."[38] And it is true that we often apply rules of interpretation with so little thought that the act of literary perception appears to be automatic; furthermore, texts do, to some extent, give directions for their own decoding. But the phrase "give directions" is revealing. Every literary theoretician these days needs a governing metaphor about texts: text as seduction, text as fabric, text as abyss, text as system. I suppose that my metaphor would have to be text as unassembled swing set. It's a concrete thing that, when completed, offers opportunities (more or less restricted depending on the particular swing set involved) for free play, but you have to assemble it first. It comes with rudimentary directions, but you have to know what directions *are,* as well as how to perform basic tasks.[39] It comes with its own materials, but you must have certain tools of

[38] Ibid., p. 63. [Rabinowitz]

[39] See Gerald Graff's comment that "the reason most students are baffled by what we ask them to do is that they do not know what kind of thing it is that they are supposed to *say* about literary works, and they can't infer those kinds of things from the literary works themselves, because literary works themselves don't tell one what it is one is supposed to say about them" ("The Joys of Not Reading," presented at the Conference on Narrative Poetics, Ohio State University, April 1986). See also Eagleton's remark, "The competent reader is the one who can apply to the text certain rules; but what are the rules for applying rules?" (*Literary Theory* [Minneapolis: University of Minnesota Press, 1983], p. 125). Wolfgang Iser also relies heavily on the notion of giving directions; see, in particular, *The Act of Reading* (Baltimore: Johns Hopkins University Press, 1978). Iser, however, stresses what the text offers, rather than what the reader is presumed to bring; that is, he starts with a reader who already incorporates all the rules I am discussing here. And by suggesting that all worthwhile texts develop their own codes (see, for instance, p. 21), he smudges the line between the text's directions and the readerly presuppositions that allow those directions to work. He thus minimizes the different types of presuppositions required by different texts. Despite his theoretical insistence that "the reader's role can be fulfilled in different ways, according to historical or individual circumstances" (p. 37), he rarely discusses different possible approaches to a text (for an exception, see his pp. 201–02). As a consequence, his analyses, and especially his view of the canon, differ radically from mine. [Rabinowitz]

your own at hand. Most important, the instructions are virtually meaningless unless you know, beforehand, what sort of an object you are aiming at. If you have never seen a swing set before, your chances of riding on the trapeze without cracking open your head are slight.

The same is true of reading. You must be somewhere to begin with. Even when a text gives some fairly explicit guidance, you need to know how to recognize it and how to apply it. The moment I pick up Vanessa James' Harlequin romance, *The Fire and the Ice,* and find a story that begins with an erotically charged confrontation between a journalist heroine and her new boss (a wealthy playboy she had attacked in print two years earlier), I know a great deal about what to expect — but that is only because I have met the genre and its conventions before. One can well appreciate the kind of insensitive reading that led such critics as I. A. Richards to launch an attack on stock responses — but the fact remains that without some stock responses to begin with, reading is impossible.[40]

Now suppose you are given something to assemble and a set of directions. If you make a mistake in construction, you may eventually find yourself in a self-contradictory position, one where you cannot go further — where following the directions is made impossible by the material reality ("attach the dowel to the holes in posts A and B" — where the posts are six inches further apart than the dowel is long). At this point, you have to reconsider your whole "interpretation," often starting over again from scratch. So it is with reading. The reader of *Crime and Punishment* who assumed that the rule of the least likely suspect applied and that, as in Agatha Christie's *A.B.C. Murders,* our protagonist had been framed — such a reader would eventually reach an interpretive dead end. And unless the reader were exceptionally dull witted or strong willed, he or she would eventually have to rethink what had been done so far.[41]

But sometimes erroneous assembly produces something internally consistent: the swing set holds up, but the swings are three inches closer to the ground than the manufacturer had in mind. And that can happen in reading as well. That is, there is a significant number of texts (perhaps all texts) where two or more starting points can result in conflicting, but equally coherent and consistent, *meanings* — using the word broadly to include the step-by-step experience of tension and relaxation, surprise, confusion, and euphoria. Jane Austen fans will remember the scene in *Emma* where Emma and Harriet have a conversation in which neither understands the other — although both *think* they are communicating — because they are beginning with different assumptions about the referent of the pronoun "he." This kind of misunderstanding comes up in our conversations with authors, too — more often than we may believe.[42] An example may show more specifically what I mean.

On the surface, Agatha Christie's *Mystery of the Blue Train* is a commonplace member of the genre "classical British detective story." It has a murder; it has an adequate collection of readily identifiable cardboard characters, most with plausible motives and questionable alibis; it has trains and timetables, jewels and false jewels, accusations and false accusations, disguises and discrepancies; and, of course, it has an eccentric detective. A reader experienced in the genre will know fairly quickly what to fasten on to. Of particular importance will be such details as who has

---

[40]See, for instance, Richards, *Practical Criticism: A Study of Literary Judgment* (New York: Harcourt, Brace, and World/Harvest, 1964), pp. 223–40, esp. p. 232. See also Rosenblatt, *Literature as Exploration* (New York: Appleton-Century, 1938), pp. 113–23. [Rabinowitz]

[41]For an amusing exploration of this issue, see James Thurber's story about an attempt to read *Macbeth* as if it were

a classical detective story: "The Macbeth Murder Mystery," in *The Thurber Carnival* (New York: Modern Library, 1957), pp. 60–63. [Rabinowitz]

[42]I thus disagree with Monroe C. Beardsley's claim that "the more complicated a text, the more difficult it becomes (in general) to devise two disparate and incompatible readings that are equally faithful to it" ("Textual Meaning and Authorial Meaning," *Genre* 1 [1968]: 171). One problem with Beardsley's position is that he does not take sufficient account of the differing conceptions of what it means to be "faithful" to a given text. In this regard, see Thomas S. Kuhn's observation that when philosophers and historians read the same texts, they read them differently. "Undoubtedly the two had looked at the same signs, but they had been trained (programmed if you will) to process them differently" (*The Essential Tension: Selected Studies in Scientific Tradition and Change* [Chicago: University of Chicago Press, 1977], p. 6). [Rabinowitz]

seen the victim after the train has left the Gare de Lyon. Such a reader, from his or her experience with other similar novels, will also know that in detective stories, "there must be no love interest."[43] He or she will therefore rightfully dismiss as window dressing the romantic story of the pure and simple Katherine Grey, who has just inherited a fortune from the crotchety old woman to whom she was a companion.

Read in this way, the book works well. As we expect, some of the apparent clues turn out to be important, others to be red herrings, and there is the expected unexpected twist so that the average reader will, at the end, experience that very special emotion that only a good classical English detective story can offer: the rush of "Oh! I should have caught that!" I have taught the novel several times as a model of the genre, and most students have enjoyed it and been both surprised and pleased by the ending.

I had two students, however, who used a different point of departure. The rule that love interest is secondary, after all, is not *in* the text. Nor, for that matter, is it an article of faith of any regularly constituted interpretive community. Rather, it is brought to bear *on* the text from the outside. And without a prior decision to apply that rule, there is no textually imposed reason not to pay more attention to Katherine Grey, especially since her actions are given considerable prominence, as is her perspective on the events. In fact, it is possible to treat the novel as a kind of romance. From this standpoint, the timing of the trains becomes a secondary consideration, and a different stock pattern emerges: a sympathetic and lovely young woman is wooed by two apparently suitable suitors. From our knowledge of such texts as *Sense and Sensibility* and *War and Peace,* we expect that one of them will be eliminated. But we wouldn't be satisfied if one were simply bumped off (like Tolstoy's Andrei) or one were simply rejected, for we like them both, and this is not the sort of novel in which the tragedy of life or even the sadness of having to make difficult decisions seems a major

theme. The best solution, therefore, is to have one of them lose our respect, like Austen's Willoughby; he must turn out to be a scoundrel beneath the surface. Given the subject matter of the story, the most appropriate resolution would be to have one of the suitors turn out to be the killer. The author, in fact, fulfills the expectations raised by this pattern; indeed, so that we can maintain our love and respect for Katherine, Christie goes so far as to assure us that she has known the truth for some time. When Knighton turns out to be the villain, then, the reader starting off from this romance premise experiences something quite different from the surprise that the detective reader experiences: a satisfying, Austenesque confirmation of expectations.

These two readings of the book — and given the radically different effects they produce, they have to be considered two distinct readings — do not stem from differences in critical methodology. And for this reason, they are (in contrast, say, to Freudian and Marxist readings of *The Trial*) irreconcilable. The argument that Joseph K.'s experiences represent his inner psychodrama does not necessarily contradict the claim that they reflect the irrationality of modern-day society; one can well believe both simultaneously. But one cannot simultaneously be surprised and not surprised by the ending of *The Mystery of the Blue Train.* Each reading confers a different meaning on the text, and each is consistent and coherent in itself.

How can we explain this double-barreled detective story? We could, perhaps, conclude that all texts are open, that they are all susceptible to multiple (even infinite) equally correct readings. Alternatively, we could claim that this novel plays on the conflict between knowledge and ignorance, and that it thus either speaks the truth through paradox or artfully deconstructs the genres to which it appears to belong. We might also conclude that it is a poor text. But there is another perfectly reasonable claim one could make: that it is a detective story that does not provide enough *internal* evidence for the actual reader to determine correctly the nature of the authorial audience. This does not make it any less of a mystery story — but to read it correctly (in the sense of successfully joining the authorial

---

[43]S. S. Van Dine, "Twenty Rules for Writing Detective Stories," in *The Art of the Mystery Story: A Collection of Critical Essays,* ed. Howard Haycraft (New York: Grossett and Dunlap/Universal Library, 1947), p. 189. [Rabinowitz]

audience), you have to know what its genre is *before* you read it. In other words, it is a text that readily opens itself up to misreadings — a term that I use to refer not to readings that simply skirt the authorial audience, but rather to readings that *attempt* to incorporate the strategies of the authorial audience, but fail to do so. In this regard, as we shall see, it is far from an unusual case.

In Chapters 6 and 7, I have a great deal to say about the implications of such misreadings, especially about the ways in which they interact with ideology. But before doing so, I need to look more closely at the kinds of conversations on which competing authorial readings are apt to be based.

RULES OF READING

The term *convention* may appear, at first, somewhat restricted — for many people, when they think of literary conventions, think of formulas of plot and character. Conventions, however, inform our reading in far more complex ways. There are any number of ways of classifying them, and I would like to suggest now a four-part system. Let me make it clear from the outset that this framework is neither exhaustive nor privileged. That is, I intend neither to provide a complete taxonomy of interpretive conventions nor to oust other systems that have been offered (my scheme, for instance, complements, rather than replaces, the typology suggested by Steven Mailloux).[44] Rather, I am offering what I hope will be a useful if rough sorting out of an extremely thorny area — a system that is not only convenient for organizing the ways that we can think about narrative conventions, but that also serves to illuminate some of the relationships between them. Specifically, the

system sets out four types of rules. These rules govern operations or activities that, from the author's perspective, it is appropriate for the reader to perform when transforming texts — and indeed, that it is even necessary for the reader to perform if he or she is to end up with the expected meaning. And they are, from the other end, what readers implicitly call upon when they argue for or against a particular paraphrase of a text. The rules, in other words, serve as a kind of assumed contract between author and reader — they specify the grounds on which the intended reading should take place. They are, of course, socially constructed — and they can vary with genre, culture, history, and text. And readers do not always apply them as authors hope they will — even if they are trying to do so, which they sometimes are not.[45] Indeed, as I will argue in Chapter 7, canonization is, in large part, a matter of misapplication. But even when readers do not apply the *specific* rules the author had in mind, in our culture virtually *all* readers apply *some* rules in each of the four categories whenever they approach a text.

First, there are what I call rules of notice. Despite repeated claims by critics that everything counts in literature (especially poetry), we know from experience that there are always more details in a text — particularly a novel — than we can ever hope to keep track of, much less account for. We have learned to tame this multiplicity with a number of implicit rules, shared by readers and writers alike, that give priority to certain kinds of details, and that thus help us sort out figures from ground by making a hierarchy of importance. Some rules of notice cover a wide spectrum of texts: for instance, there is the simple rule that titles are privileged. This may seem trivial, but it is a tremendous help for the first-time viewer of *Hamlet*. In the opening scenes, there

[44]See, for instance, the distinction Mailloux proposes among traditional, regulative, and constitutive conventions, as well as among social, linguistic, literary, and authorial conventions and conventions within individual works (*Interpretive Conventions* [Ithaca: Cornell University Press, 1982], esp. chap. 5). See also the distinction among linguistic, pragmatic, and literary conventions in Ellen Schauber and Ellen Spolsky, "Reader, Language, and Character," in *Theories of Reading, Looking, and Listening*, ed. Henry Garvin (Lewisburg, PA: Bucknell University Press, 1981); and the classification of codes in Barthes, *S/Z*, trans. Richard Miller (New York: Hill and Wang, 1974). [Rabinowitz]

[45]See, for instance, Umberto Eco's claim that "we must keep in mind a principle, characteristic of any examination of mass communication media . . . : the message which has been evolved by an educated elite (in a cultural group or a kind of communications headquarters, which takes its lead from the political or economic group in power) is expressed at the outset in terms of a fixed code, but it is caught by diverse groups of receivers and deciphered on the basis of other codes" (*Role of the Reader* [Bloomington: Indiana University Press, 1979], p. 141). [Rabinowitz]

are so many characters that he or she would not know where to focus attention without some cue. Similarly, the first and last sentences of most texts are privileged; that is, any interpretation of a text that cannot account for those sentences is generally deemed more defective than a reading that cannot account for some random sentence in the middle. Other rules of notice are specific to smaller groups of texts. For instance, when we are given some apparently obscure detail about a character's grandmother in a novel by Faulkner, we are supposed to pay more attention to it than we would in one by Dostoyevsky.

Second, there are rules of signification. These are the rules that tell us how to recast or symbolize or draw the significance from the elements that the first set of rules has brought to our attention. Included here are rules for determining symbolic meaning (the rules that tell us when to invoke the religious connotations of words, for instance); rules for distinguishing degrees of realism in fiction (the rules that allow us to discriminate, for instance, among the degrees and types of realism in the various representations of Napoleon in *War and Peace*, Anthony Burgess' *Napoleon Symphony*, and Woody Allen's *Love and Death*); the rule that allows us, in fiction, to assume that post hoc *is* propter hoc;[46] rules that permit us to assume that characters have psychologies and to draw conclusions about those psychologies from their actions.

Third, there are rules of configuration. Certain clumps of literary features tend to occur together; because of our familiarity with such groupings, we know how to assemble disparate elements in order to make patterns emerge. We can thus both develop expectations and experience a sense of completion. Our ability to perceive form — in Kenneth Burke's sense of the creation and satisfaction of appetites ("Psychology and Form") — involves applying rules of configuration. As Barbara Herrnstein Smith's *Poetic Closure* demonstrates, so does our ability to experience closure. And so does our recognition of the plot patterns and formulas so often illuminated in traditional genre studies. One need not get much further than the opening scenes of Philip Barry's

Holiday to know how it is going to end. But that is not because it signals its own unique form; rather, it is because we know how to put together a few elements — a charming man, a rigid fiancée, an attractively zany fiancée's sister — and see an emerging pattern.[47]

Finally, there are rules of coherence. The most general rule here, familiar in part through such critics as Wayne Booth and Mary Louise Pratt,[48] states that we should read a text in such a way that it becomes the best text possible. Of course, as Pratt notes, "this is not to say . . . that we do or should assume all literary works to be somehow perfect. It means only that in literary works . . . the range of deviations which will be construed as intentional is much larger" than in "many other speech contexts."[49] From this follow more specific rules that deal with textual disjunctures, permitting us to repair apparent inconsistencies by transforming them into metaphors, subtleties, and ironies. Even deconstructive readings, which widen rather than bridge textual gaps, often find some overarching theme or philosophical point in terms of which the discontinuities make sense.[50]

---

[46]After this . . . because of this.

[47]In the film version, there is an added signal, since we assume that the characters played by Cary Grant and Katharine Hepburn will be the ones who get romantically entangled. [Rabinowitz]

[48]See, for instance, Booth, *Critical Understanding*, esp. chap. 7; Pratt, *Toward a Speech Act Theory of Literary Discourse* (Bloomington: Indiana University Press, 1977), esp. chap. 5. [Rabinowitz]

[49]Pratt, *Toward a Speech Act Theory of Literary Discourse*, p. 170. See also Ronald Dworkin's rather more extravagant claim that "an interpretation of a piece of literature attempts to show which way of reading (or speaking or directing or acting) the text reveals it as the best work of art. Different theories or schools or traditions of interpretation disagree . . . because they assume significantly different normative theories about what literature is and what it is for and about what makes one work of literature better than another" ("Law as Interpretation," *Critical Inquiry* 9 [September 1982]: 183). In subsuming *all* interpretation under rules of coherence, Dworkin is not the only critic to privilege this category of rules. [Rabinowitz]

[50]Thus, it is not surprising that Serge Doubrovsky, writing in 1966 of what was then "the new criticism" in France — and what now appears to have been the initial stage of what eventually grew into post-structuralism — argues as follows: "Unity, totality, coherence: I believe that to be a motto common to all the new critics or, if you prefer, their common postulate" (*New Criticism in France*, trans. Derek Coltman [Chicago: University of Chicago Press, 1973], p. 119). [Rabinowitz]

Now while there is a certain logical order to these rules, I am not suggesting that we read a text by applying them one after another. Reading is a more complex holistic process in which various rules interact with one another in ways that we may never understand, even though we seem to have little difficulty putting them into practice intuitively. Thus, for instance, rules of notice would seem to precede rules of configuration, since we cannot perceive a pattern until we notice the elements out of which it is formed. But one of the ways elements become visible is that they form parts of a recognizable pattern. Thus, when Lisa is stabbed in the breast near the end of D. H. Thomas' *White Hotel,* the authorial audience notices that it is the left rather than the right breast in part because her left breast has been mentioned so many times in the novel (repetition is one of the basic means of attracting attention). But it is noticeable for another reason as well: the reference fills out a basic configurational pattern in the novel centering around the theme of clairvoyance.

In addition, a given convention may well be capable of reformulation so that it fits into more than one of the four categories. Take, for instance, the way we are expected to respond to the conventional use of literary parallels. It involves a rule of notice (it is appropriate to pay attention to textual elements that parallel one another), but it is also a rule of signification (parallel forms suggest parallel meanings), a rule of configuration (given an element A, there is a good chance that there will be an element A′ parallel to it), and a rule of coherence (given elements A and B, their mutual presence can be explained to the extent that we are able to interpret them as parallel to one another). The division of conventions into these four types, therefore, is intended neither as a descriptive model of the way the human mind actually reads nor as an absolute and exhaustive classification. It is, rather, a practical analytic device, of value to the extent that it is useful for answering particular questions.

Elaine Scarry
b. 1946

The contemporary critic who has made the strongest claims for both the value of beauty and the faculty of imagination was born in 1946 in Summit, New Jersey. Elaine Margaret Scarry graduated from Chatham College and went on to a doctorate in English at the University of Connecticut in 1974. While teaching at the University of Pennsylvania she published the groundbreaking The Body in Pain *(1985), in which Scarry theorized about imagination, as the faculty through which we connect with others and make the world we live in, and about its enemy, extreme pain, brought by illness, war, or torture, as a force that acts destructively upon the individual, unmaking both the subject and his or her world. Nominated for a National Book Award,* The Body in Pain *was instantly felt to be an important book, as much for the intensity and engagement of its style as for its argument. Scarry left Penn for Harvard, but continued to work on the mind and the way it makes its world.* Resisting Representation *(1994) considered other areas of experience besides pain that resist representation and challenge the capacity of language. In* On Beauty and Being Just *(1999), Scarry took on Plato and Tolstoy directly, defending beauty from the charge that it is inherently corrupting, and showing how beauty inspires goodness and justice rather than promoting suffering and evil.* Dreaming by the Book *(1999) has been Scarry's strongest contribution to the ancient field of aesthetics, using cognitive theory to attempt to understand in detail how the mind takes in and appreciates the experience of the beautiful. In recent days, Scarry has shifted to politics, questioning the role of the armed services: articles published in*

2000 argued that unexplained passenger plane crashes had been the inadvertent result of electromagnetic interference from navy ships and air force jets, while in "Who Defended the Country?" (2003) she suggested that the passengers on Flight 93, who brought down their own plane on September 11, 2001, had been more effective in defending America than the military. The following essay, "On Vivacity," originally appeared in the journal Representations *in the fall of 1995.*

On Vivacity: The Difference between Daydreaming and Imagining-Under-Authorial-Instruction

When we speak in everyday conversation about the imagination, we often attribute to it powers that are greater than ordinary sensation. But when we are asked to perform the concrete experiment of comparing an imagined object with a perceptual one — that is, of actually stopping, closing our eyes, concentrating on the imagined face or the imagined room, then opening our eyes and comparing its attributes to whatever greets us when we return to the sensory world — we at once reach the opposite conclusion: the imagined object lacks the vitality and vivacity of the perceived; it is in fact these very attributes of vitality and vivacity that enable us to differentiate the actual world present to our senses from the one that we introduce through the exercise of the imagination. Even if, as Jean-Paul Sartre observes, the object we select to imagine in this experiment is the face of a beloved friend, one we know in intricate detail (as Sartre knew the faces of Annie and Pierre), it will be, by comparison with an actually present face, "thin," "dry," "two-dimensional," and "inert."[1]

In November 1992, I gave the Avenali Lectures in the Humanities at the University of California, Berkeley. The lectures were collectively entitled "On the Senses" and the first of them (the essay that follows) was called "The Problem of Vivacity." The members of the Berkeley community were, as always, incomparable in their intellectual generosity and I am grateful to have been subjected to their inspiration, challenges, and demands. [Scarry]

[1] Jean-Paul Sartre gives an extended account of the imagined image in "The Imaginary Life," in *The Psychology of Imagination* (New York, 1991), pp. 177–212. [Scarry]

It seems that we tend to notice this phenomenon only when we are especially keen on seeing a face, only when we desperately care to have it present in the mind with clarity and force. We then notice the deficiency and, like Proust's Marcel,[2] who berates himself for his inability to picture the face of Albertine or the face of his grandmother, we conclude that the vacuity of our imagining is somehow peculiar to our feeling about this particular person and that there must be a hidden defect in our affection. In fact the vacuity is general, and all that is peculiar or particular to such cases is the intensity of "wishing to imagine" that makes us confront, with more than usual honesty, the fact that we cannot do so. It is when we are soaked with the longing to imagine that we notice, as John Keats confessed, "the fancy cannot cheat so well / As she is fam'd to do."[3] By means of the vividness of perceptions, we remain at all moments capable of recovering, of "recognizing" the material world and distinguishing it from our imaginary world, even as we lapse into and out of our gray and ghostly daydreams. Aristotle refers to this grayness as "the feebleness" of images. Sartre calls it their "essential poverty."

Of course, insofar as the imagination is enfeebled and impoverished, it is so only on sensory grounds. To complain that the imagined object

[2] Protagonist of autobiographical novel by Marcel Proust (1871–1922), also known as *In Search of Lost Time*; Albertine is Marcel's mistress.
[3] John Keats, "Ode to a Nightingale," In *John Keats: Complete Poems*, ed. Jack Stillinger (Cambridge, Mass., 1982), p. 281. [Scarry]

lacks vivacity and vitality is only to complain that it is not a perceptual object, since vivacity and vitality are the very heart of perception. We should not be surprised to learn that the sensory realm surpasses the imaginary realm on sensory ground; we should only be surprised that this does not always strike us with the force of tautology. Phrased another way, only by decoupling "vividness" from "the imaginary" (where we unreflectingly and inaccurately place it in many everyday conversations about aesthetics) and attaching it to its proper moorings in perception, can we then even recognize, first, that the imagined object is not ordinarily vivid; and second, that its not being vivid is tautologically bound up with its being imaginary.

Now it is a remarkable fact that this ordinary enfeeblement of images has a striking exception in the verbal arts where images somehow *do* acquire the vivacity of perceptual objects, and it is the purpose of this essay to trace some of the ways this comes about. The verbal arts are of particular concern here because they — unlike painting, music, sculpture, theater, and film — are almost wholly devoid of *actual* sensory content. There is nothing mysterious about the fact that a painting approximates or exceeds the vivacity of the visible world, since it is itself a piece of the visible world. A painting by Henri Matisse or one of the great Florentine colorists,[4] for example, saturates our eyes with actual sensory experience. The airy yellow and ochre stripes of *Interior at Nice*[5] set off an unceasing succession of retinal arabesques that — carrying us out across the white shimmer of curtain, or back into the golden sheen held cuplike in the olive green taffeta chair — are, whatever else they are, starkly perceptual acts. The same is true of music (why should it not share the vividness of the audible world when it is itself audible?), of sculpture (which inhabits, hence participates in, the vividness of the tactile and visual realms), and of theater and film (brimming with auditory and visual commitments). But verbal art, especially

narrative, is almost bereft of any sensuous content.[6] Its visual features, as has often been observed, consist of monotonous small black marks on a white page. It has *no* acoustical features. Its tactile features are limited to the weight of its pages, their smooth surfaces, and their exquisitely thin edges. The attributes it has that are directly apprehensible by perception are, then, meager in number. More important, these attributes are utterly irrelevant, sometimes even antagonistic, to the mental images the work seeks to produce (steam rising across a window pane, the sound of a stone dropped in a pool, the feel of dry August grass underfoot), the ones whose vivacity is under investigation here.

To be clear, it might be useful to distinguish three phenomena. First, *immediate sensory content*: the light-filled surface of Matisse's *Interior at Nice*, the sweet fleeting notes of "Honeysuckle Rose" on Fats Waller's[7] piano recording, or indeed the particular room one, at this moment, inhabits while reading. Second, *delayed sensory content* or what can be called "instructions for the production of actual sensory content." A musical score has no immediate acoustical content (only the immediate visual content of lines and dots and the immediate tactile content of the smooth, thin-edged pages) but it does directly specify a sequence of actions that, if followed, produce actually audible content. In the third case, in contradistinction to the first two, there is *no* actual sensory content, whether immediate or delayed. There is instead only *mimetic content*, the figural rooms and faces and weather that we mimetically

---

[4]Scarry probably refers to the fresco painters who worked in Florence in the fifteenth century, such as Masaccio, Ghirlandaio, Fra Angelico, and Fra Filippo Lippi.
[5]Sometimes this painting is entitled *My Room at the Beau-Rivage* (1917–18). [Scarry]

[6]I find (fifteen months after completing this essay) that the same observation has been made by the nineteenth-century Russian aesthetician N. G. Chernishevsky, who, in *Life and Aesthetics* (1853), writes, "All other arts, like live reality, act directly on our senses; poetry acts on the imagination." Chernishevsky, however, assumes that the imagination, in the act of reading, accomplishes only the impoverished image-making of daydreaming; for he writes, "It is evident . . . that the images of poetry are weak, anemic, indefinite, as compared with the corresponding images in life," and he concludes that the beauty of life is much greater than the beauty of art, whose strength resides in "its generalities" (conclusion to *Life and Aesthetics*, reprinted in *Documents of Modern Literary Realism*, ed. George J. Becker [Princeton, 1962], pp. 48, 49, 61). [Scarry]
[7]Thomas Waller (1904–1943), jazz pianist and composer.

see, touch, and hear, though in no case do we actually do so.

It probably makes sense in this third case, as in the second, to use the word "instructions" (a word I will return to at much greater length later). When we say "Emily Brontë describes Catherine's face," we might also say "Brontë gives us a set of instructions for how to imagine or construct Catherine's face." This reformulation is cumbersome but also accurate in that it shifts the site of mimesis from the objects to the mental act. We habitually say of images in novels that they "represent" or "are mimetic of" the real world. But the mimesis is perhaps less in them than in our seeing of them. In imagining Catherine's face, we perform a mimesis of actually seeing a face; in imagining the sweep of the wind across the moors, we perform a mimesis of actually hearing the wind. Imagining is an act of perceptual mimesis, whether undertaken in our own daydreams or under the instruction of great writers. And the question is: how does it come about that this perceptual mimesis, which, when undertaken on one's own is ordinarily so feeble and impoverished, sometimes when under authorial instruction so closely approximates actual perception. In the poem "Birthplace," Seamus Heaney[8] describes a young boy named Seamus Heaney staying up all night to read for the first time a novel (Thomas Hardy's *Return of the Native*) and at dawn not knowing whether the newborn sounds of bird and rooster and dog were coming to him from the surface of the field or from the surface of the page. We say that Hardy, Seamus Heaney himself, Proust, and Keats are sensory writers, but the question is, by what miracle could there even be such a thing as a sensory writer, a writer able to incite us to the bringing forth of mental images that resemble in their quality not our own daydreaming but our own (much more freely practiced) perceptual acts?[9]

Each of the arts incites us to the practice of all three acts: immediate perception, delayed perception, and mimetic perception. But painting, sculpture, music, film, and theater are weighted toward the first, or (perhaps more accurately) they bring about the second and the third by means of their elaborate commitments to the first; whereas the verbal arts take place almost exclusively in the third. Within the verbal, a further distinction must be made. Both narrative and poetry devote themselves centrally to mimetic perception, but poetry, unlike narrative, retains a strong engagement with the second category, delayed perception: like the musical score, its sequence of printed signs contains a set of instructions for the production of actual sound; the page does not itself sing but exists forever on the verge of song. Poetry — again unlike narrative — even has immediate sensory content, since the visual disposition of the lines and stanzas provide an at once apprehensible visual rhythm that is a prelude to, or rehearsal for, or promise of, the beautiful regulation of sound to come.

William Wordsworth describes two fish imprisoned in a glass bowl that, though they lack the song of larks and bees, produce in their "glittering motions" (their "golden flash and silver gleam") a type of sun-writing:

> How beautiful! — Yet none knows why
> This ever graceful change,
> Renewed — renewed incessantly —
> Within your quiet range.[10]

Is this beautiful display closer to the scattering of light in the yellow stripes of Matisse's *Interior at Nice* (or for that matter, his many paintings of goldfish), or is it instead like the scattering of light in the silver flash and gleam of the sword dance in *Far from the Madding Crowd*, and again the lightning dance of Gabriel Oak[11] when, "sensitive of every ray," he secures the hayricks in a midnight

---

[8]Poet, born in Belfast in 1939. "The Birthplace" is from his collection *Fieldwork* (1979).

[9]I am not making a distinction here between artist and layperson. I assume that the daydreams of artists are every bit as gray as those of nonartists. This is why Seamus Heaney, when under the sway of Hardy, experiences what we do when under Hardy's sway, and why he is as amazed by it as we are.

As I will argue later, being "under the sway" of another person is critical to the production of vivacity. [Scarry]

[10]William Wordsworth, "Gold and Silver Fishes in a Vase," in *Wordsworth: Poetical Works*, ed. Thomas Hutchinson and Ernest de Selincourt (London, 1936), p. 412. [Scarry]

[11]Protagonist of Thomas Hardy's early novel *Far from the Madding Crowd* (1874).

storm. Although its tone and content overlap with Matisse's, there can be no question that in terms of the categories posed here, Wordsworth's sun-writing and Hardy's light-writing are the same. Matisse's "colors bright" and pigment "sensitive of every ray" are physically present and engage us in a starkly actual perceptual act, whereas Wordsworth and Hardy produce in our minds sudden radiant ignitions that are vividly mimetic of actually seen light but are not themselves actually seen. Yet because of the sound of the poem, the palpable touch of the interior parts of the mouth glancing across one another even in silent reading, and because of the visual scanning of the lines, the material surface of the poem is closer to the material surface of Matisse's painting than is Hardy's prose: that is, while Wordsworth is much closer to Hardy than he is to Matisse, he is a little closer to Matisse than Hardy is. Everything that I wish to say in what follows is as true of poetry as of prose, but it is harder to say clear sentences about the subject because one has to stop and qualify. Both narrative and poem take place in the realm of the nonactual, but the poem is a few inches to the left of the narrative since it has its metrical feet in the material world. Therefore, in looking at how vivacity is achieved in the imagination, I will stay with prose. Prose requires of us neither form or actual perception (neither immediate perception nor delayed perception); it instead requires nonactual or mimetic perception.

We will find that imaginary vivacity comes about by producing the deep structure of perception. On one level this is wholly unsurprising: if imagining is a mimesis of perception, then successful imagining will of course come about through the accuracy or acuity of the mimesis. What is perhaps less self-evident is the fact that what in perception is imitated is not only the sensory outcome[12] (the way something looks or sounds or feels beneath the hands) but the actual structure of production that gave rise to the perception, that is, the material conditions that made it

look, sound, or feel the way it did.[13] I will illustrate this phenomenon with a very specific example before turning back to more global features of narrative that illustrate the same phenomenon.

FROM THE GENERAL PROBLEM OF VIVACITY TO THE SPECIFIC PROBLEM OF SOLIDITY

Up until now, the question of vivacity has been framed in a way that is equally applicable to imaginary seeing, imaginary hearing, imaginary touch, imaginary taste, and imaginary smell. Here, in contrast, it will be framed in a way uniquely relevant to touch.

A primary example of the mimesis of touch is the way that the "solidity" of an imagined object is achieved. To bring this about is key since solidity is ordinarily a main feature distinguishing perceptual objects from their gauzy counterparts in our imagination where they are, to return to Sartre, lacking in density, thin, two-dimensional. The imagined object is not incidentally two-dimensional. Its two-dimensionality is what it is: Aristotle says in De Anima that "images are like sensuous content except in that they contain no matter"[14]; Ashbery describes in "Tapestry" the way the inner eye "Draws an outline, or a blueprint, / Of what was just there: dead on the line."[15] The perceptible world, in contrast, is not just incidentally but essentially solid. John Locke urged that "there is no idea we receive more constantly

[13]Accounts of mental picture-making are often circular: they answer the question of how pictures get produced in the mind by re-asserting that pictures do get produced in the mind. ("What is the 'ut' in 'ut pictura poesis'?" asks Allen Grossman of both Horace and Ludwig Wittgenstein [personal conversation, August 1992].) My argument — that the imagination produces a mimesis of sensation by miming the deep structure that brings the sensation about — may sound equally circular. But if we measure the strength of the argument by its ability to produce practical outcomes, then we will see that it (at least partially) succeeds. That is, if I can identify steps that, if followed, enable daydreamers to see the faces of their friends more clearly, then I will take it that the account has validity. [Scarry]

[14]Aristotle, On the Soul (De Anima), 3.8.431A, in Complete Works of Aristotle, ed. Jonathan Barnes, Revised Oxford Translation (Princeton, 1984), 1:687. [Scarry]

[15]John Ashbery, "Tapestry," in As We Know (New York, 1979), p. 90.

[12]For a review of the research in cognitive psychology suggesting that in making mental images we draw on the very neural mechanisms that we use in perceiving, see Stephen M. Kosslyn, Image and Brain: The Resolution of the Imagery Debate (Cambridge, Mass., 1994), pp. 295, 301, 325. [Scarry]

from sensation than solidity,"[16] and to his observation we may add the counterpart that there is probably no idea we receive less constantly in the ordinary exercise of the imagination.

How, then, does a writer create a solid surface: a wall, for example, or the four walls that will make up a room? In his description of his childhood room at Combray at the opening of *Swann's Way*,[17] Proust describes the way the bright images from a magic lantern[18] would play across the walls, overlaying the wall's opaqueness with their own "impalpable iridescence" the figure of Golo,[19] now moving in a jerky trot, now stopping quizzically, his form adaptable to any part of the wall:

> And nothing could arrest his slow progress. If the lantern were moved I could still distinguish Golo's horse advancing across the window-curtains, swelling out with their curves and diving into their folds. The body of Golo himself, being of the same supernatural substance as his steeds, overcame every material obstacle — everything that seemed to bar his way — by taking it as an ossature[20] and embodying it in himself: even the door-handle, for instance, over which, adapting itself at once, would float irresistibly his red cloak or his pale face, which never lost its nobility or its melancholy, never betrayed the least concern at this transvertebration.[21]

The room at Combray occasions, quite famously, Marcel's meditations on habit: "The mere change of lighting," he writes, "was enough to destroy the familiar impression I had of my room" (*Remembrance*, 1:10); "the anaesthetic effect of habit [was] destroyed" (1:11). But far more fundamental than Proust's philosophic speculation on the regulation of the familiar and the unfamiliar is the prior perceptual mimesis of the solidity

of the room produced by the "impalpable iridescence" of Golo fleeting across its surfaces. It is not that we need attend to the solidity of the walls — in fact quite the reverse: we simply assume them and, unimpressed by our miraculous hold on their solidity, go on to the seemingly more philosophic and psychologically complex issue of habit. Taken in isolation, the walls, the curtains, the doorknob are for the reader (as opposed to Marcel inside the book) certainly as thin and impalpable as the bright colored images issuing from the magic lantern. Yet precisely by instructing us to move the one across the surface of the other, the transparency of one works to verify the density of the other.

I have argued that while Proust drenches the magic lantern passage in the philosophic issue of habit, what is actually occurring is the slow coaxing into solidity of the Combray wall; and in fact, I am willing to say that the issue of habit in this passage, however fascinating in its own right, is an excuse for lingering on the walls precisely so that there will be time for their materialization to take place. Our own belief in the solidity of these walls permits a phenomenon analogous to what takes place in the perceptible world. Locke says that in the ordinary operations of perception, the idea of solidity "hinders our further sinking downwards" (*Essay*, 151); it establishes the floor beneath us that, even as we are unmindful of it, makes us cavalier about venturing out. The same is, I believe, true of the fictional walls. The idea of the solid wall prevents not our further sinking downward but our further *sinking inward*. It provides the *vertical floor* of all subsequent imaginings that lets us perform, without vertigo or alarm, the projective act, and thereby lifts the inhibitions on mental vivacity ordinarily in place as protections.

But why should it be the case that the mental image of a wall can be coaxed into solidity by the passing of a transparent surface over it? The instruction for this reproduces the way solidity is visually inferred in the perceptible world. The movement of Golo across window drapes, wall, and door conflates two different phenomena that J. J. Gibson identifies in his classic study of perception. The first is called "kinetic occlusion." If one surface passes in front of another surface — a

---

[16]John Locke, *An Essay Concerning Human Understanding*, ed. Alexander Campbell Fraser (New York, 1959), 1:151. All subsequent references are to chap. 4 ("The Idea of Solidity"). [Scarry]

[17]First published segment (1913) of Proust's *In Search of Lost Time*.

[18]An early form of slide projector.

[19]In French legend, Golo is the evil steward who threatens the chastity and the life of Genevieve de Brabant.

[20]The metal framework that supports a sculpture.

[21]Marcel Proust, *Remembrance of Things Past*, trans. C. K. Scott Moncrieff and Terence Kilmartin (New York, 1982), 1:10. [Scarry]

picture dropping from a wall (Gibson's example), or more simply, my hand passing over my face — the movement of the object "progressively covers and uncovers the physical texture of [the object] behind it." There occurs at the front edge of the moving object what Gibson calls a "wiping-out" or "shearing-away" of what lies behind, followed by its restoration: the "wiping-out and shearing-across of texture in the array specify depth at an edge in the world."[22] Furthermore, they specify durability, "the continued existence of a hidden surface." Proust's instructions to us in the Combray passage combine the assertion of depth and duration through kinetic occlusion with a second phenomenon, since the moving Golo (unlike the falling picture or my moving hand) is transparent and therefore provides only partial wiping out, only incomplete occlusion of the surface over which he passes. Analyzing the information that lies in "the structure of ambient light," Gibson describes the nature of "the shadow," which "does not occlude the texture of the background as the object does, nor wipe it out when it moves. Hence a shadow is usually distinguishable from [a solid] object and also from a stain on the background" (*Senses*, 214). Drapes and walls, even the doorknob, are visibly ingested into Golo's body. Their ongoing recoverability certifies that Golo is only a shadow, as in turn and more importantly, his shadowiness continually confirms the solidity, the grabability, of the doorknob beneath. The difference here between the soft objects over which Golo passes (like the drapes) and hard objects (like the walls and doorknob) does not matter since, as Locke observes, solidity requires only "repletion" and hence is distinct from the attributes of hardness and softness: a solid object may be either hard or soft; hardness and softness, Locke writes, are merely judgments that express the relation of the thing "to the constitutions of our own bodies" (*Essay*, 154).

Because I will be concentrating for quite some time on this minute inflection of film passing over wall, let me rehearse the overall architecture of the argument. First, solidity — if we may trust Locke in consultation with our own aliveness — is the key experience for percipient creatures; solidity relies on touch to provide access not just to material surfaces but to deep haptic[23] experience as well. Second, solidity is difficult to reproduce in the imagination because it entails touch, the sense whose operation is most remote to us in imagining: Thomas Hobbes argued that the imaginary is exclusively visual; and certainly vision and audition are, by almost every theorist, credited as the main sensory candidates for the mimetic operations of imagining. Third, the very *difficulty* of achieving in the imaginary realm tactilely or haptically confirmed solidity is matched by the *importance* of doing so. Doing so is crucial because it is impossible to create imaginary persons if one has not created a space for them. Speaking of the perceptible world, Locke says that "space in itself seems to be nothing but *a capacity or possibility for extended beings, or bodies, to exist*"; space is "only the consideration of a bare possibility of body to exist."[24] When in the late pages of *Remembrance of Things Past*, Marcel is deserted by Albertine, he confesses that it is only the specification of the setting, the room, that permits him to imagine her and to suffer in imagining, with acuity: "How I repeated to myself these words, shed, passage, drawing-room, renewing the shock at will. . . . No, I had not imagined it at all, except as a vague dwelling. I had suffered first of all when the place where Albertine was had acquired a geographical identity" (*Remembrance*, 3:480, 481). The operations of this principle are evident in the fact that the most vivid writers are almost always simultaneously the writers most associated with place: Hardy and Wessex, Proust and Combray, Seamus Heaney and the bogs. Fourth and finally, even more important than the provision of an inhabitable space for (or "solid" wall behind) imaginary persons is the creation for the reader of a fiction's *vertical floor* that, by promising to stop our inward fall, permits us to enter capaciously into the projective space with fearlessness and with the lifting of inhibitions on vivacity that permits.

[22]J. J. Gibson, *The Senses Considered as Perceptual Systems* (Boston, 1966), pp. 203, 204. [Scarry]

[23]Having to do with the sense of touch.

[24]John Locke, *Miscellaneous Papers*, cited in Locke, *Essay Concerning Human Understanding*, pp. 155–56 n. 4. [Scarry]

The passing of a filmy surface over another (by comparison, dense) surface is by no means the only way of solidifying walls. But it is a key way and it not only recurs in writers universally saluted for their vividness but also occurs in these writers precisely at the moment where the new-born fictional world is most fragile and at risk because that fictional world is only now in the midst of coming into being. Proust, for example, constructs the room at Balbec in precisely the same way: by laying forth a transparent layer of glass two feet out from the wall, then gliding over that glacine surface the moving reflections from the changing sea. Proust introduces the passage by citing its sensory difference from the room at Combray. Yet the underlying instructions to us on how to construct it mentally are identical:

Among the rooms which used most commonly to take shape in my mind during my long nights of sleeplessness, there was none that differed more utterly from the rooms at Combray. . . than my room in the Grand Hôtel de la Plage, at Balbec, the ripolin-painted[25] walls of which enclosed, like the polished sides of a bathing-pool in which the water glows blue, a finer air, pure, azure-tinted, saline. . . . [The room] which I found myself occupying had set against the walls, on three sides of it, a series of low book-cases with glass fronts, in which, according to where they stood, by a law of nature which [the designer] had not perhaps foreseen, was reflected this or that section of the ever-changing view of the sea, so that the walls were lined with a frieze of sea-scapes, interrupted only by the polished mahogany of the actual shelves. (1:416, 417)

As at Combray, here at Balbec a film passes over and hence coaxes into solidity the walls behind it. As at Combray, where Proust engaged us in speculations about habit and defamiliarization (rather than conscious issues of solidity, transparency, complete and incomplete kinetic occlusion), so here at Balbec Proust engages us in speculation about the difference between unreal oceans in the glassy mobile reflections and the real oceans somewhere outside, unseen. Yet precisely through that lengthy speculation, Proust requires us to keep steadily available to our inner mind the glassy reflections and the wall behind, thereby engaging us (through complete and incomplete kinetic occlusion) in the production of solid walls: "The walls were lined with a frieze of sea-scapes, interrupted only by the polished mahogany of the actual shelves."

I want to argue that the Combray-Balbec passages make it possible to recognize three key solutions to the mystery of how the verbal arts enlist our own imaginations in mental actions that in their vivacity more closely resemble sensing than daydreaming. Each of the three will let us move from the local instance of solidity to the more generalizable features of narrative. The first, as I have been suggesting all along, is the specification of the material antecedents of the perception to be produced. Second, while this mimesis entails a coaxing of the imagination into outcomes that move it beyond its ordinary Aristotelian enfeeblement, this is most strikingly accomplished when that very enfeeblement can successfully be enlisted into the process. Third, by the peculiar gravitational rules of the imagination, two or more images that are each independently weightless can nevertheless confer weight on one another; just as by the geometry of the imagination two or more images, each independently two-dimensional, can nevertheless confer three-dimensionality on one another. A fourth observation specifies a rule that regulates the preceding three. It is simply this: that these methods of construction, so liberally present in these writings, are flatly withheld from the characters in those writings when they are trying to imagine absent persons or places. That is, when poets and novelists get us to imagine imagining, they almost never permit the exposure of the rules they are themselves liberally using.

I want to elaborate each of these four. But I do not want to suggest wrongly here that what we are looking at is a specifically Proustian solution, and, in order to avoid that, let me quickly set out a range of examples that turn on this same phenomenon of conflating kinetic occlusion with transparency. The visually brilliant Japanese cartoon, Hayao Miyazaki's *The Castle of Cagliostro*,[26] is, unlike verbal narrative, actually

[25]Ripolin is a French brand synonymous with enamel paint.

[26]Hayao Miyazaki, *Castle of Cagliostro*, trans. Carl Macec (Tokyo, 1980), film. [Scarry] The most famous of the Studio

sensorially present.[27] Yet because the cartoon as a genre luxuriates in its own self-announcing unreality, its operations are often deeply sympathetic with mental imagining; it has to have very rigorous procedures for making itself believable since it has disavowed from the outset the strategy of realistic texture; it aspires to be mistaken for the real but disdains the ordinary features that would make that aspiration relatively easy to fulfill. A cartoon is like something done on a dare: BELIEVE THIS IF YOU CAN, EVEN AS I ASSURE YOU THAT IT CANNOT BE THE CASE! The twelve-minute opening of this film, about to unfold its story, consists of almost nothing but a spectacular, tour de force rapid-fire catalogue of eight or eighteen or thirty-eight instances of the glide of the transparent over the assertedly solid: clouds move rapidly over the sky — cut; the shadow of the clouds then moves rapidly over the ground — cut; rain falls over the windshield of the car — cut; and so forth. As though satisfied that the solidity of its own self-announcingly two-dimensional surfaces has been established, the cartoon then abruptly stops this procedure, jealously reserving it for the long climactic passage in the story where our hero manages to invade the castle by being carried through the long slide of gliding waters running through the shafts and surfaces of an underground aqueduct (the "ripolin-painted walls of which," we might say with Proust, "enclosed, like the polished sides of a bathing-pool in which the water glows blue, a finer air, pure, azure-tinted, saline").

Ghibli animators, Miyazaki (1941–) is probably best known for *Princess Mononoke* (1997) and *Spirited Away* (2001).

[27]Both cartoons and paintings have actual visual content, but both lack actual touch. They have instead, only visually inferred touch. It is perhaps therefore not surprising to discover many instances of transparent substances passing over walls, especially in a cartoon or in a painting that has a flattened or derealized surface. The principle, for example, is at work in Henri Matisse's entire oeuvre of the Nice period: *My Room at the Beau-Rivage* (1917–18), *Interior with a Violin Case* (1918), *La Fenêtre fermée* (1918–19), *Woman on a Sofa* (1921), *Interior with Phonograph, Interior à Etretat, le 14 Juillet* (1920), *Interieur: Fleurs et perruches* (1924), *Anemones in an Earthenware Vase* (1924). This principle is present not only in the interior content of films but also in their framing event: a film's most essential feature is its projection of an insubstantial moving image on a wall. [Scarry]

More familiar, and certainly more relevant to the mystery of how sensory mimesis can come about in the total absence of any actual sensory assistance (that is, how it can come about in verbal narrative or poetry), is the writer that Seamus Heaney stayed up all night to read. Thomas Hardy's reliance on the visual glide of the transparent over the solid occurs, as it does in Proust, precisely at the moment when a new world is about to come into being. This is true even within the brief compass of the lyric, as in the very early "Student's Love-Song" of the 1870s that describes the moving shadows of his paper, his bed, and an apple tree across his bookcase at sunset:

> Once more the cauldron of the sun
> Smears the bookcase with winy red,
> And here my page is, and there my bed,
> And the apple-tree shadows travel along.
> Soon their intangible track will be run.[28]

The same glaze of the iridescent on the persistent recurs in the most remembered line of the 1912 elegies describing Hardy's unawareness that his wife was in the next room dying "while I / Saw morning harden upon the wall."[29] But the room or wall that stands in something of the same relation to Hardy that Combray and Balbec do to Proust is the milking wall at Talbothays Dairy that gradually comes to form the vast center of *Tess of the d'Urbervilles*. At the moment when Tess — having walked from Blackmoor Valley through "the uplands and lowlands of Egdon" — arrives in the Froom Valley dairy, we suddenly pass through a set of objects that might themselves be taken as models of Gibson's many species of "optical array," exposing the structure of the material world. We are told to imagine that Tess passes "vivid green moss" and "wooden posts rubbed to a glossy smoothness by the flanks of infinite cows," and that the pure white of those flanks "reflected the sunshine in dazzling brilliancy, and the polished brass knobs on their

[28]Thomas Hardy, "The Sun on the Bookcase (Student's Love-Song: 1870)," in *Complete Poems of Thomas Hardy*, ed. James Gibson (New York, 1982), p. 311. [Scarry]

[29]Thomas Hardy, "The Going," in *Complete Poems*, p. 338. [Scarry]

horns glittered." Then we are instructed "to see" the cows standing beside the dairy wall itself:

> The sun, lowering itself behind this patient row, threw their shadows accurately inwards upon the wall. Thus it threw shadows of these obscure and homely figures every evening with as much care over each contour as if it had been the profile of a Court beauty on a palace wall; copied them as diligently as it had copied Olympian shapes on marble *façades* long ago, or the outline of Alexander, Caesar, and the Pharaohs.[30]

We are instructed to construct an image of animal shadows cast on a wall and, importantly, to sustain that image long enough to contemplate the precision of their outlines and their similarity to the casting of other shadows on other walls. Just as Proust's contemplation of "habit" at Combray (which we *do* overtly attend to) enables him to enlist us into the successful construction of Combray's solidity (which we *do not* overtly attend to), and again just as Proust's conspicuous contemplation of real and reflected oceans at Balbec enables him to enlist us inconspicuously into the labor of constructing Balbec's solidity, so Hardy engages us in speculation about continental, Greek, Roman, and Egyptian civilizations as all present in this dairy precisely so that the dairy wall itself has time to come solidly into being. Agreeing or not agreeing to that asserted analogy with Egypt or Greece is much less important than the mental making it (in either case) commits us to. The shadows confirm the solidity of the wall as well as the solidity of the cows, which cast shadows precisely because light cannot pass through their thick bodies. Shadows on the floor of this world assure us that that floor can support these heavy creatures — Hardy tells us, in the heat of high summer, they "followed the shadow of the smallest tree as it moved around the stem" (*Tess*, 208) — and that it can support our weight as well, hindering our own inward fall.

Though it requires restraint to refrain from entering into a description of Hardy's many brilliant variations on the principles at work in the Talbothays passage, it will be more useful to return to the principles themselves, the first of which is the specification of the material antecedents of the perception. Admittedly, it seems odd to argue that this is the case; we seem to be saying that in order to produce a vivid image of lightning, we must first specify the humidity. It is as though perceptual mimesis requires a running start, or as though we must directly participate in a mimesis of material production in order to elicit a mimesis of perceptual outcome. But it may well be that a coherent explanation does exist. For example, it may be the case, as Gibson's writing everywhere implies, that perceptual acuity exists precisely in order to ensure that we can infer the structure of material reality (and thereby make our way safely through it). Hence, a mimesis of that same perceptual acuity cannot take place unaccompanied by that antecedent structure, by, in other words, the very object that perception exists to serve.

To this can be added a second explanation, that the display of the material antecedents provides the imagination with a sequence of coherent steps for constructing the image. It is certainly the case that writers known for their sensory vivacity actually build objects within their pages (with the result that we are shown a very discrete path along which to build them in our own minds). J.-K. Huysman's *Against Nature* opens not with a description of Des Esseintes's new house but with a record of his deliberations on precisely how to construct the house. It will surprise no one to be reminded that the main objects of attention are the four walls of the room Des Esseintes will ordinarily occupy, his study, and that when he completes his elaborate deliberations on paint color — choosing orange walls and deep indigo blue trim — he is careful to specify a sheen of light on the surface of each, resulting from the "glazed" Cape skins in the case of the orange, and from the "lacquer" substance of the indigo blue. Huysmans's goal is to make palpable the impalpable iridescence of the Proustian film. Des Esseintes arranges for a large object, a giant tortoise, to be permanently moving across the floor; but he discovers that its dull brown hue cannot achieve the effect of moving light he had hoped to achieve, and so he arranges to have the shell of the turtle "encrusted" with flashing jewels,

---

[30]Thomas Hardy, *Tess of the d'Urbervilles* (New York, 1985), p. 160. [Scarry]

inserted according to a pattern that he specifies at length to the craftsman, as well as to us.[31] Similarly, it is noticeable how often the literary works singled out as exemplars of *enargeia*[32] in the *ut pictura poesis*[33] tradition happen to be passages specifying step-by-step construction: the shield of Achilles in book eighteen of the *Iliad* is taken as the inaugural text, and other great exemplars include the lyrics of Anacreon, that, as Jean Hagstrum writes, "consist merely of the poet's addressing Hephaestus or some human artisan and requesting him to create an art object [a cup, a bowl] according to the specifications laid down by the poet in his poem.[34]

Quite apart from the merit of such explanations, it simply *is* the case that the great sensory writers reproduce antecedent material causes. One may even test this by noticing how it alters the outcome of the thought experiments Sartre recommends. For example, Sartre complains that the image of the person in his daydreaming mind is extremely difficult to move. And in fact, most of us will probably discover — if we try Sartre's experiment — that what he says is more or less true. But if we now put a sheet of ice under the image, it becomes much easier to move the man around: indeed, even if the figure is seated in a chair, he can be moved about with startling ease.

The glide of the transparent over the surface of something else is, as was acknowledged earlier, only one way of achieving solidity but so key a way that Proust and Hardy (and Hayao Miyazaki) rely

on it at moments when the fiction is very fragile. What makes it especially potent can be seen by noticing a second feature at work in the Combray-Balbec-Talbothays passages, one that depends on the filminess of the gliding layer. As was clear in the discussion of the kinetic occlusion (Gibson's picture falling in front of a wall or my hand passing in front of my face), the moving layer can itself be a solid. The moving picture (itself solid) confirms the "continued existence of [the] hidden surface" (*Senses*, 204) of the wall; the moving hand (itself solid) confirms the "continued existence of [the] hidden surface" of my face. If, in the childhood room at Combray, Marcel's grandmother paused in her reading and walked about the room, causing the doorknob to disappear then reappear, eclipsing then re-exposing the curtains would it not be as successful as Golo? The answer seems to be no. Why the filmy Golo rather than the solid grandmother should produce the most vivid mimesis carries us into a second much larger phenomenon. If we try to picture two objects in our minds — first a piece of airy gauze; then, starting over, an object such as a chair or a wall — it will be the case that our imagined gauze more closely approximates actually perceived gauze than our imagined wall resembles an actually perceived wall. In other words, the attributes of any image (gauze, wall, chair, a friend's face) have the Sartrean features of thinness and transparency. But as it happens, in the perceptual world gauze itself is (in comparison with faces, walls and chairs) transparent and without density. Some physical objects have features that more closely approximate the phenomenology of imaginary objects than do others. In fact so true is this that we often speak of actual mist, actual gauze, filmy curtains, fog, and blurry rain as dreamlike. Gibson, in fact, explicitly notices that the four key ways in which light ordinarily exposes the structure of the material world — slant, reflectance, intrinsic color, illumination — are absent or "indeterminate" in fog (215); and thus we may say that in fog the physical universe approaches the condition of imagination.

Now if in the exercise of the imagination we — rather than picturing in succession first the gauze, then starting over the wall — instead pass the first over the second, the wall has much more solidity than in the earlier phase. And this, as has been

---

[31]J.-K. Huysmans, *Against Nature*, trans. Robert Baldick (New York, 1959), pp. 28–31, 53, 54. [Scarry]

[32]Term coined by Jean Hagstrum for the power of language to create a vivid sense of presence.

[33]Latin for "a poem is like a picture," from Horace, *Art of Poetry*, (see p. 82).

[34]Jean H. Hagstrum, *The Sister Arts: The Tradition of Literary Pictorialism and English Poetry from Dryden to Gray* (Chicago, 1958), p. 25. Hagstrum does not himself single out the construction process as important to the poem's vividness and explicitly faults Gotthold Lessing for his emphasis on the construction process in the account of the making of Achilles' shield (19). Nevertheless the reappearance of instances of construction in the very passages Hagstrum has singled out to illustrate *enargeia*, in combination with instances such as those in Huysmans, make this conclusion inescapable. (I follow Hagstrum's spelling here for *enargeia*, a term he distinguishes from *energeia*.) [Scarry]

restated quite a few times here, reproduces one of the ways touch can be visually inferred in the material world. But unlike other instances of visually inferred solidity, such as a solid passing over a solid (my hand passing over my face), this one has the secondary feature that it draws on the imagination's own properties; it precisely capitalizes on, rather than disavows, the ordinary feebleness of the imagination. The transparent objects in the Combray-Balbec-Talbothays passages (the filmy body of Golo and his steeds, the ever changing frieze of seascapes, the row of shadows cast from the cows) are, like gauzy curtains and mist and fog, objects that, even when they exist in the actual world, are immediately recognizable as imaginary-like; indeed, quite explicitly in all three passages, Proust and Hardy have made them precursors of art (hence Hardy's invocation of cameos from Egypt and Greece). But their primary function is not to introduce art but rather to duplicate the phenomenology of perception, and to do so by taking what the imagination is best at (dry, thin, two-dimensionality) and enlisting it into the operation.

This same principle underlies the entire genre of the ghost story. Why, when the lights go out and the storytelling begins, is the most compelling tale (or most convincing, most believable) a ghost story? Since most of us have no experience of ghosts in the material world, this should be the tale least easily believed. The answer is that the story instructs its hearers to create an image whose own properties are second nature to the imagination: it instructs its hearers to depict in the mind something thin, dry, filmy, two-dimensional, and without solidity. Hence the imaginers' conviction: we at once recognize, perhaps with amazement, that we are picturing, if not with vivacity, then with exquisite correctness, precisely the thing described. It is not hard to successfully imagine a ghost. What is hard is successfully imagining an object, any object, that does *not* look like a ghost.

Of the two actions I have described here, it is crucial to emphasize that typically the verbal arts engage us in one of the two, but not in both simultaneously. The passing of a solid over a solid (Marcel's grandmother in front of the curtains) reproduces the material antecedents of persistence but does not enlist the imagination's special expertise in two-dimensional, fading objects. Conversely, a ghost reproduces the imagination's expertise in fading objects but has no counterpart in the material world, either in its surface texture or in its deep structure of production. But the paper shadows and apple-tree shadows on Hardy's sun soaked bookshelf do the work of both grandmother and ghost simultaneously, as does this same phenomenon at work throughout the Combray-Balbec-Talbothays passages. To this triad of solid-walled rooms belongs a fourth, the Gateshead Red Room of the ten-year-old Jane Eyre:

> Shaking my hair from my eyes, I lifted my head and tried to look boldly round the dark room. At this moment a light gleamed on the wall. Was it, I asked myself, a ray from the moon penetrating some aperture in the blind? No; moonlight was still, and this stirred; while I gazed, it glided up to the ceiling and quivered over my head. I can now conjecture readily that this streak of light was, in all likelihood, a gleam from a lantern, carried by some one across the lawn: but then, prepared as my mind was for horror, shaken as my nerves were by agitation, I thought the swift-darting beam was a herald of some coming vision from another world.[35]

The passing of this luminous, ghostly film over solid walls has here again occurred at a moment when the fiction is especially fragile: the story is still in its very early pages. These same two principles are also at work in our mental construction of the space in which Flaubert's Charles Bovary first courts Emma: here the filmy substance, which "glimmers," "quivers," and "drifts" across the great stone walls and floors of the farm kitchen at Les Bertaux, consists of light, dust, and ash.[36]

---

[35]Charlotte Brontë, *Jane Eyre: An Authoritative Text, Backgrounds, Criticism*, ed. Richard J. Dunn (New York, 1971), p. 14. [Scarry]

[36]In Charles Bovary's first visit to Les Bertaux, the stone walls in the farm kitchen are covered with metal utensils, which are in turn covered by the play of "glimmering" light from the hearth fire and the breaking of dawn through the window. In Charles Bovary's return visits, the light "quiver[s]" across the ceiling and "pattern[s]" the stone floor over whose surface there also "drift[s]" a thin film of dust and in whose fireplace there is a film of blue ash lit by morning light coming down the chimney. Ceiling and floor thus acquire the

The third key feature of these passages is shared by many fictional passages. The people on the inside of the fiction report to us on the sensory qualities in there that we ourselves cannot reach or test. The person inside "Ode to a Nightingale" tells us when the bird is sensorially present to him and when it has ceased to be sensorially present to him, even though for us the bird is sensorially present in *neither* case. The same is true in Proust. For us, all fictionally asserted objects are equally airy: the bedroom wall, considered in isolation, is no more solid, no more something that will bear our weight or impede our actual movement, than is the spectral Golo; nor are the imaginary azure blue walls and mahogany wood more substantial than the shimmering glaze of seascapes playing over the glass. But for Marcel inside the fiction, the walls are certainly more substantial, and his own reports that this is so become very influential. We stand in relation to Marcel in somewhat the same way that an earth station stands to persons inside a space ship: those on the ground have some forms of sensory experience that are close to being there (seeing visual images on a screen, hearing the astronauts' voices) and others for which, because we have no access, we must rely on the astronauts' reports. We might ask them to perform weight experiments, for example, as we watch them lift certain objects and visually infer their gravity from the difficulty of the action of lifting that we can see on the screen. Or we might ask them to touch two surfaces, to see if their hands pass through the object or are impeded. When we are in the position of reading, as when

we are on the ground station, we cannot use touch. Now Locke says that the sense of touch, the immediate sensation of impenetrability, is key to the formation of the sense of solidity: "If any one asks me, *What this solidity is*, I send him to his senses to inform him. Let him put a flint or a football between his hands, and then endeavour to join them, and he will know" (*Essay*, 156, 157). Some philosophers take Locke to mean, "apart from data of the sense of touch, we could not put meaning into the term 'solidity,'"[37] though we have seen that partial judgments can be visually inferred. It is precisely touch that Marcel reports back to us on. Not surprisingly, Proust has Marcel contemplate the feel of the doorknob in his hand: as it happens, the doorknob is so familiar and congenial that it seems to turn on its own; but crucial is the fact that Marcel has been placed in the position of grasping it, as he does not, for example, reach out to shake Golo's hand. Golo has entered Marcel's visual world; Golo has even entered Marcel's auditory world (since the grandmother is reading aloud and at one moment Golo turns to her quizzically as though anxious to hear the next turn in his own story). But Golo does not enter the realm of touch. Nor does the spectral light in the Red Room enter the realm of Jane Eyre's touch; it instead impels her to seize, then shake, the door and lock; once outside the solid walls, her act of sensory verification continues, for she reports, "I had now got hold of Bessie's hand, and she did not snatch it from me" (*Jane Eyre*, 14).

This is also the cause of the peculiar blend of merriment and sadness in the incident at Talbothays when the other milkmaids — Miriam, Izz, and Retty Priddle — stand by their bedroom window, "undressing in the orange light of the vanished sun," guessing and confessing the love they all feel for Angel Clare, who is (as we learn from their quiet exclamations) during those moments coming in and out of view on the ground below and whom they have also just seen during the late afternoon work in the dairy. They

---

solidity of the walls (Gustave Flaubert, *Madame Bovary*, trans. Francis Steegmuller [New York, 1991], pp. 16, 17, 25).

Though in invoking Proust, Hardy, Brontë, and Flaubert I am staying within one tradition, the same phenomenology is at work elsewhere. Robert Pinsky observes that Dante's *Inferno* may be "a supreme example of one kind of surface passing over another, one made more solid or opaque by the sliding." Invoking Cantos 12 and 6 of *Inferno* and Canto 21 of *Purgatorio*, Pinsky calls attention to the many passages in which the ability of a physical body to displace material stones or ground is contrasted with the inability of a shade to do so. "Hell itself (and its inhabitants) is one great scrim passing over a more solid reality. Or the reverse, apparent material reality is really a scrim of transparent illusion passing over the more solid moral reality underneath" (Robert Pinsky, personal correspondence, 22 November 1994). [Scarry]

[37]Alexander Campbell Fraser drawing on Locke's *Third Letter* to Stillingfleet in *Essay Concerning Human Understanding*, p. 156 n. 2. [Scarry]

act as astronaut reporters both for Tess (who listens to their conversation as she lies in bed) and for us:

> "You needn't say anything, Izz," answered Retty. For I zid you kissing his shade. . . . Why — he was standing over the whey-tub to let off the whey, and the shade of his face came upon the wall behind, close to Izz, who was standing there filling a vat. She put her mouth against the wall and kissed the shade of his mouth; I zid her, though he didn't."
> (*Tess*, 192)

The kissing of a shaded image on a wall recurs in Hardy's poem, "The White-washed Wall," where the act again works as a "report" back to us about the non-solidity of the shadow and the solidity of the wall. The same is true at Balbec. Were Marcel the perfect astronaut agent he might attempt to touch both the shifting seascapes and the wall in order to display the difference. But he does something almost equally helpful. In the midst of the Balbec passage, he recalls Françoise's warnings to him about the solidity of walls: "stormy days, when the wind was so strong that Françoise, as she took me to the Champs-Elysées, would advise me not to walk too close to the walls or I might have my head knocked off by a falling slate" (*Remembrance*, 1:416).

Now it is a remarkable fact that the boy Marcel performing these experiments for us has no more substance than the very Golos, sea shimmers, and walls about which he is issuing his reports. Marcel and Tess and Jane and the person inside "Ode to a Nightingale" have, through long familiarity, a reality that can obscure how startling these outcomes are. It is therefore helpful to restate them using new images. Place, then, in the mind a man, a book, and leaf. Each is a weightless image. Each is lighter than a piece of fluff. But then have the man place the leaf on his fingertip. Then, removing the leaf, put the book on his outstretched hand. Then put the leaf in one hand, and the book in the other, and have him raise and lower each arm an inch in turn, looking from one to the other. The mimesis of weight is soon achieved, even though one piece of fluff, the man, is somehow verifying another piece of fluff's weight, the book's as well as his own. The verbal arts are full of such weight experiments, as

when Huysmans, in *Against Nature*, gives us an account of Des Esseintes's shaky hands: "He could keep them steady enough when he was gripping a heavy object, but they trembled uncontrollably when holding something light such as a wineglass" (23). We ordinarily think of fictional persons as having a wide range of reporting abilities from the reliable to the unreliable to the out-and-out liars. But this variation tends to occur in the sphere of psychological judgments. Fictional persons almost never misreport to us the tactile qualities of their fictional worlds.

We have seen, then, in the Combray-Balbec-Talbothays-Gateshead passages, first, the mimesis of the material antecedents of perception; second, the purposeful enlisting of the imagination's own habitually thin image-making; and third, the use of one in-itself-weightless image to calibrate and confirm the weightedness of a second in-itself-weightless image, either by verbal report or by the tactile brush of one of the images across the surface of the other. The fourth rule regulates the preceding three. Although these others are elaborately present in great sensory writings (writings that bring about acute mimesis of perception), they are almost never given to fictional persons within those texts who are themselves struggling to imagine another person or place. When Jane Eyre begins drawing lessons, she does draw walls, but Charlotte Brontë does not permit her to coax the walls into solidity by moving over their surface a roving light: "[I] sketched," Jane tells us, "my first cottage (whose walls, by-the-by, outrivalled in slope those of the leaning tower of Pisa)" (*Jane Eyre*, 65). When Angel Clare deserts Tess to farm in Brazil, Tess places a ribboned ring next to her heart, then on her finger, in order to make Angel sensorially present, "to fortify herself in the sensation" of her connection to him (*Tess*, 312). We are instructed to brush our mental image of the ring against our mental image of Tess's breast and hand, and this light brush of image upon image inside the mind helps materialize both woman and ring in our imaginations. The reader can imagine Tess more vividly than Tess can imagine Angel, for Hardy does not permit Tess to use the procedures for achieving mental vivacity that he has given the reader (and she is, of course, greatly imperiled by her inability to make Angel continually present in her mind). Hardy could let her, for example, place Angel's absent face in her mind, then brush an imagined flower against it. Hardy could let her picture Angel Clare in a room in Brazil where the shadow of trees and orchids plays upon his shirt and the wall behind him. She is instead limited to the slender resources of the sensorially present ring. The same holds true for Proust. Deserted by Albertine, Marcel is not permitted to coax her into reality by the procedures the author himself elsewhere so liberally uses. The specification of the setting she inhabits that suddenly pushes Marcel into the vivid production of images (a passage I cited earlier) is one that has been introduced by another person wholly accidentally, rather than one generated by the conscious exercise of Marcel's own mind; and he can ignite the room's vivacity only by reciting its name, not by materially reconstructing it. Similarly, what I have earlier referred to as the astronaut principle either does not come about at all, or comes about by sightings of (sensory reports about) the missing person given by another actual person (actual within the fictional frame) rather than by imaginary emissaries.[38] Marcel can act as an astronaut for us, but he himself is not usually empowered to produce in his mind the picture of an astronaut who will report to him on the tactile properties of the absent worlds he is trying to see. The astronaut-reporter is therefore never exposed as a strategy of imaginative recovery. This conscious

withholding from fictional persons of the conditions of their own invention means that whenever the verbal arts seem to ask us to imagine imagining (to picture the mental process of picture-making), it is only the enfeebled condition of daydreaming that we see (rather than the mechanisms of vivid imagining we are at that very moment ourselves practicing). This is especially striking in Hardy because the great philosophic issue underlying all his writings is the failure of persons to be able to imagine other persons in their full weight and solidity.

THE PLACE OF INSTRUCTION IN ACHIEVING IMAGINARY VIVACITY

I have been looking here at the way the verbal arts achieve the vivacity of perception by attending to the specific instance of solidity, the putting into place of the vertical floor that bears our weight and stops our inward fall into the risky projective space of the narrative. I want to suggest, as rapidly as possible in the small space that remains, that in order for the verbal arts to achieve the "vivacity" of the material world, they must somehow also imitate its "persistence" and, most crucially, its quality of "givenness." It seems almost certainly the case that it is the "instructional" character of the verbal arts that fulfills this mimetic requirement for "givenness." Through its mimesis of givenness, the instruction brings about the radical change we see from daydreaming to vivid image-making. Our freely practiced imaginative acts bear less resemblance to our freely practiced perceptual acts than do our constrained imaginative acts, those occurring under authorial direction.

It would be an easy, but also a serious, intellectual error to think that this element of direction comes about as the result of authoritarian motives, either a poet's wish to dominate, or a reader's wish to be dominated, though these phenomena may inevitably become secondary or tertiary entailments and hence heighten the need for contractual entry into this process of directed image-making. It results instead from the need to suppress our own awareness of the voluntary, which interferes with the mimesis of perception. Artists themselves provide strong evidence that

[38]One exceptional place where wholly mental images of Albertine *do* undergo sensory testing by another wholly mentally imaged person is in Marcel's jealous lesbian fantasies. Jealousy works to vivify the beloved precisely because it entails brushing one mental image (Albertine) against another mental image (lesbian lover). It is probably to solidify missing persons that the psychological state of jealousy is so often voluntarily introduced by both real life and fictional daydreamers. Because jealousy intensifies our mental picture of the beloved, people often conclude (wrongly, I think) that we only begin to sense the reality of the other person when we have already begun to lose the person to a rival. But once jealousy is placed within the framework of imagining, we see that it accidentally occasions a strategy of vivification that could, if we only recognized it, be just as easily reproduced by less painful forms of tactile contact between images (such as brushing an imaginary shadow across an imaginary wall in back of the chair in which the imagined friend is sitting). [Scarry]

successful image-making entails suppressing the awareness of volition, since they have, over many centuries, reported the ease of writing under the dictation, the direction, or the instruction of a muse: "Having formed these beings," says Charlotte Brontë of Emily Brontë's Catherine and Heathcliff, "she did not know what she had done"; and Elizabeth Gaskell says of Charlotte Brontë, "Sometimes weeks or even months elapsed before she felt that she had anything to add to that portion of her story which was already written. Then, some morning, she would waken up, and the progress of her tale lay clear and bright before her, in distinct vision."[39] This same visionary ease belonged to William Blake, who persistently describes himself as a "Secretary" taking "dictation" from some external source.[40] In contrast, writers' accounts of creation when the muse is absent (Yeats's "Adam's Curse," for example) stress levels of labor and effort familiar to us in daydreaming.

We know that daydreaming actually originates in the volitional. Indeed it would be hard to see — given its fadedness and other failings — why we would devote ourselves to this ghostly practice if it did not have the virtue of the voluntary. Sartre's opening account of imagining stresses this attribute (and elsewhere throughout his writings Sartre identifies freedom as the imagination's great endowment to us):

> [The act of the imagination] is an incantation destined to produce the object of one's thought, the thing one desires, in a manner that one can take possession of it. In that act there is always something of the imperious and the infantile, a refusal to take distance or difficulties into account. Thus, the very young child acts upon the world from his bed by orders and entreaties. The objects obey these orders of consciousness: they appear. (*Psychology*, 177)

Sartre returns to this attribute continually. We will the images into being; we will the images out of being. "Thus I can stop [he says] the existence of the unreal object at any moment, I am not dragged along despite myself to the specification of its qualities: it exists only while I know it and want it" (190). We start it. We stop it. It never takes us "by surprise" (187).[41] But of course it is here that Sartre's description is wholly falsified by the verbal arts, for the verbal arts at every moment precisely *do* take us by surprise, one of many indications *not* that we have stopped voluntarily producing images but that our awareness of the role of our volition has been suppressed.

The importance of suppressing that awareness can be inferred from the fact that most of Sartre's complaints about the failings of imagining are simply translations or rephrasings of its virtue of being volitional. Daydreamed images, for example, are "inert": they do not generate other images; if you put a picture in your mind, he complains, it does not on its own go on to sponsor other images (187, 191). But this simply means that each frame of the picture, each change of the picture, even each second-by-second iteration of a static picture must be individually willed. In the physical, perceptible world, in contrast, the image both persists and undergoes changes even without our intervention. If one looks at the surface on which this book is held — perhaps your hands, or a lamp-lit table, one will find that now . . . seven seconds later . . . the thing still sustains itself. If one instead imagines a lamp-lit table in some distant room, it is probably now . . . seven seconds later . . . already beginning to become lost to you, and can be held onto only by a palpable labor of sustaining it. (It is possible that my voice interferes with it and robs it of its vibrancy, but my speaking does nothing to dissolve or jeopardize the actual surface on which the book now rests). The givenness or receptivity of perception does not mean that we exercise no control over it. Philosophers of perception and psychologists of perception — J. J. Gibson most strikingly — give

[39]Elizabeth Gaskell, *The Life of Charlotte Brontë* (London, 1985), pp. 333, 306. [Scarry]

[40]William Blake's verbal and visual accounts of the phenomenon of dictation (including his occasional resistance to it) are described by Leopold Damrosch Jr., *Symbol and Truth in Blake's Myth* (Princeton, 1980), pp. 302–7. [Scarry]

[41]We might assume that in aberrant image-making states — such as obsession and madness — the person has lost his or her freedom over the production of images. It is interesting that even here Sartre continues to insist on the exercise of the voluntary: in obsession, "consciousness resists itself"; in madness, he writes drawing on Pierre Janet, "the mind forces itself to produce the object in which it stands in fear" (*Psychology*, pp. 178, 192). [Scarry]

elaborate accounts of the way sensory perception allows us to "lay hold of" the world, as in a library reading room one may direct attention now to the lights, now to a neighbor's whispered comments, now to a noise from the courtyard outside, and one may leave the room and so at once eliminate all the perceptible attributes. But were one to look back at the reading desk, it would be there,[42] it would be there for the taking, and it is this "there for the taking" quality that is key.

This sense of "givenness," the sense of something "received" and simultaneously "there for the taking," is descriptive not only of perceptual objects but of imaginary-objects-specified-by-instruction and hence arriving, as it were, from some outside source. Just as Anacreon's lyrics give Hephaestus or another craftsman a set of directions on the object to be produced, and just as Huysmans's Des Esseintes issues elaborate specifications to the craftsmen of his walls and floors, so the verbal arts at every moment address the reader as a Hephaestus who is to undertake an explicit work of construction. In a novel by Hardy, for example, every patch of prose that is twenty-five lines long contains a set (depending on how one counts) of between thirty and fifty instructions for the production of pictures. The fact that it is, at least in part, the instructional character of the verbal arts that is responsible for the increased suppleness and capaciousness of our power to imagine, is suggested by the fact that two other spheres where imagemaking takes place under explicit direction — experiments in cognitive psychology and the practice of hypnosis — demonstrate the same increased

vivacity; and other than instruction, these other two spheres do not have a great deal in common with the verbal arts.

Under the conditions of daydreaming, for example, Sartre, as well as Henri Bergson and Gilbert Ryle,[43] all say that it is difficult to move or to animate the image, that the image cannot be easily turned upside down, and that the image (of a face, for example) inhabits a generalized posture and cannot be shifted through an array of

---

[42]Like vivacity, persistence and continuity are the main features that enable us to sort out our sixteen hours of waking life from our eight hours of sleep life. It is persistence, Proust says, that gives the perceptible world its superiority: he writes that though in sleep "fragments of wisdom float there luminously . . . the waking state remains none the less superior to the extent that it is possible to continue it every morning, but not to continue the dream life every night" (*Remembrance*, 3:118). Were sleep life to continue where it left off the night before, its reality would begin to rival perceptible reality. This is perhaps why a continually repeating dream — even if free of sinister content — becomes troubling: its sheer persistence (even if it merely starts over rather than picking up where the night before left off) itself seems to contain a claim of reality. [Scarry]

[43]Gilbert Ryle, however, argues that there is no mental image, and he takes our difficulty in turning mental pictures upside down as evidence of the nonexistence of mental pictures (*The Concept of Mind* [London, 1949], p. 255). Ryle contrasts his own view with David Hume's (249–50). In both philosophy and cognitive psychology, people can be divided into those who believe we produce mental images and those who believe no such images exist in the mind (in cognitive psychology the two are called "pictorialists" and "descriptionists," respectively).

The same division reappears among literary critics, as has recently been illustrated by Ellen Esrock's fascinating interviews with people such as Geoffrey Hartman and Northrop Frye (*The Reader's Eye: Visual Imaging as Reader Response* [Baltimore, 1994], p. 183). Esrock argues that literary theory celebrated the image up until about 1920, then from 1920 to 1960 erased it altogether, not only in schools of literary theory such as New Criticism, but even in phenomenology where one might have guessed its presence would be key (1, 3, 21–38).

From my point of view as a believer in the mental image, those who do not credit the existence of the image only confirm the fact that those images are normally faded, so faded that some people are (wrongly) tempted to doubt their existence. Stephen Kosslyn, a leading researcher on images in cognitive psychology, reports that people who at first describe themselves as having no mental images will often, when asked a specific question — such as, "Which is darker green peas or a Christmas tree?" — suddenly agree that they *do* have images that they simply had not noticed before (personal conversation, January 1995). There may really be, of course, two different species of imaginers, some who have images, some who do not; just as within the group that has images there is substantial variation in the forms of imaging they can undertake (on the latter, see Kosslyn's chapter entitled "People Are Different," in *Ghosts in the Mind's Machine: Creating and Using Images in the Brain* [New York, 1983], pp. 193–204).

There are, then, three possibilities: 1) Everyone has images but not everyone recognizes, or describes herself as having, those images; or 2) No one has images but a large part of the population for some reason believes themselves to have them; or 3) There exist two populations, one of which has mental images and the other of which does not. In the first and second cases, people differ in how they describe mental life; in the third, people differ in mental life itself. [Scarry] angles as would occur in perceptual reality. Yet the verbal arts continually engage us in moving images about, brushing one image across the surface of a second image, rotating the figure perhaps from an upright posture to the ground. When Hardy describes Car Darch[44] walking with her companions across a meadow at night, he instructs us first to move the image of the woman away from us across the field; then to move a stream of treacle down her neck, back, and waist; then he instructs us to suddenly turn her vertical image horizontally onto the ground; then to move the image back and forth across the image of the ground as she tries to remove the treacle. Experiments in cognitive psychology, similarly, routinely engage the imaginer in rotating geometric figures in the air, moving the image closer or further away.[45] A third area is hypnosis, where subjects, far from being unable to move the image, precisely differentiate real persons from their hallucinated counterparts by their own ability to move the hallucinated person's arm but not the arm of the real person.[46]

Motion is introduced here only as a sample of vivid image-making under the instruction of authors, cognitive experimenters, and hypnotists. The instructional idiom is more immediately recognizable in the second and third practices than in the first because literature consists of a steady stream of erased imperatives. The mental act of picturing that a person is asked to carry out during an experiment on cognition usually takes place in the form of sentences that are overt instructions —

> Looking from one window, you see the Statue of Liberty; from a window in another wall you see a harp.[47]

> Focus your attention steadily at the center of this imaged line on the [imaged] disk and try to maintain this image . . . till I ask you to stop imaging.[48]

> Image the scenes *exactly* as they are described . . . imagine the scenes exactly as described.[49]

— as is also true of the pictures people are asked to make under hypnosis:

> *Look carefully now* and tell me whether you can see the mask and maybe some of the robber's face through his mask. *Look carefully now* and tell me when you can see him standing there with the mask over his face. . . . *Look carefully now* and tell me when you hear him being aggressive. *Hear him* swearing. *Tell me* when you hear him swearing a lot, so I'll know you're right back there, seeing and hearing him.[50]

---

[44]Character in Hardy's *Tess of the D'Urbervilles.*

[45]On rotation, see, for example, Roger Brown and Richard J. Herrnstein, "Icons and Images," in *Imagery*, ed. Ned Block (Cambridge, Mass., 1981), pp. 33–49; Roger Shepard and Jacqueline Metzler, "Mental Rotation of Three-Dimensional Objects," *Science* 171 (19 February 1971): 701–03; and Roger Shepard and Christine Feng, "A Chronometric Study of Mental Paper Folding," *Cognitive Psychology* 3 (April 1972): 228–43. On instruction, see John Jonides et al., "Imagery Instructions Improve Memory in Blind Subjects," *Bulletin of the Psychonomic Society* 5, no. 5 (May 1975): 424; George Singer and P.W. Sheehan, "The Effect of Demand Characteristics on the Figural After-Effect with Real and Imaged Inducing Figures," *American Journal of Psychology* 78, no. 1 (March 1965): 96–102; and Peter Sheehan and Ulric Neisser, "Some Variables Affecting the Vividness of Imagery in Recall," *British Journal of Psychology* 60 (1969): 71–80. [Scarry]

[46]F. J. Evan describes the mobility and immobility of arms in his article on "Hypnosis," in *Encyclopedia of Psychology*, ed. Raymond J. Corsini (New York, 1984), 2:173. [Scarry]

[47]Janice M. Keenan and Robert E. Moore, "Memory for Images of Concealed Objects: A Reexamination of Neisser and Kerr," *Journal of Experimental Psychology: Human Learning and Memory* 5, no. 4 (1979): 376. [Scarry]

[48]Singer and Sheehan, "The Effect of Demand Characteristics," 99. [Scarry]

[49] Keenan and Moore, "Memory for Images of Concealed Objects," 378. [Scarry]

[50]Peter W. Sheehan, Dixie Statham, and Graham A. Jamieson, "Pseudomemory Effects and Their Relationship to Level of Susceptibility to Hypnosis and State Instruction," *Journal of Personality and Social Psychology* 60, no. 1 (1991): 132, italics added. The scholarly literature on hypnosis sometimes directly uses the word "instruction" in summarizing its own procedures: "Subjects were *instructed* to relive the half-hour before going to bed and were then taken through a staged reliving of the evening . . . by hourly steps, until around 2 o'clock. . . . Subjects . . . were *instructed to look* at the [imaginary] clock and check the time" (Terry McCann and Peter W. Sheehan, "Hypnotically Induced Pseudomemories — Sampling Their Conditions Among Hypnotizable Subjects," *Journal of Personality and Social Psychology* 54, no. 2 [1988]: 341, italics added). [Scarry]

Even when the idiom of instruction takes place in the optative voice ("I wish you to picture . . . Let your mind drift back two years to your grandfather's house"), it is only slightly less overtly instructional than the more direct imperatives of sensory mimesis, "picture . . . look closely . . . hear." In turn, it might be said that each of the descriptive sentences in a novel or poem is implicitly preceded by these erased imperatives (and that erasure no doubt magnifies our sense of the object's "givenness"). The opening paragraph of *Tess of the d'Urbervilles* might read:

On an evening in the latter part of May [*picture this*] a middle-aged man was walking homeward from Shaston to the village of Marlott, in the adjoining Vale of [*hear the names*] Blakemore or Blackmoor. [*Look closely at the walker's legs.*] The pair of legs that carried him were rickety, and there was a bias in his gait which inclined him somewhat to the left of a straight line. [*Let your eyes drift up to his face now.*] He occasionally gave a smart nod, as if in confirmation of some opinion, [*drift now to the region of his skull*] though he was not thinking of anything in particular. [*Look, now, at his arm: tell us what you see so we know you are actually looking directly at his arm.*] An empty egg-basket was slung upon his arm. [*Picture a second person.*] Presently he was met by an elderly parson [*look closely at his legs*] astride on a [*look closely at the color*] gray mare, who, as he rode, [*hear the sounds coming now*] hummed a wandering tune. [*Hear a voice saying*] 'Good night t'ee,' [*and look to see who it comes from*] said the man with the basket. (*Tess*, 43)

The speed with which we perform the act of construction is astonishing, especially since any one of these sentences — the second, for example — is actually composed of an intricate array of small instructions:

[*Look closely at the walker's legs.*] The pair of legs [*now picture their work of weight bearing*] that carried him [*assess how well they hold that weight*] were rickety, [*and how that affects his motion*] and there was a bias in his gait [*watch which way the load leans*] which inclined him [*superimpose a geometric figure into the midst of this representational picture*] somewhat to the left of a straight line.

Reading entails an immense labor of imaginative construction.

Perhaps the best test of the features I have attempted to describe is not only whether they occur in great sensory writers but whether they can, if followed, alter the condition of our own ordinary daydreaming. So someday try this. Imagine the face of a friend. Then on a separate occasion imagine the face of the same friend. But this time place the person at a table by the window where the shadows of an apple tree play across the person's face and shirt. And look at the precise pattern of the shadows. A leaf floats in the window. Let the friend put the leaf in one hand and a book in the other. Perhaps add a second book to the already weighted hand. Even better, have an actually present friend verbally specify the sequencing and variations of these images as you produce them. See if it isn't the case that your imagined friend's face now appears more specified, vibrant, dense, mobile, and animate than when you had imagined it before. When I try this, the friend even starts laughing.

I have been arguing throughout this paper that though we think of the imagination and the verbal arts as continuous, they are instead discontinuous. The verbal arts are at once counterfactual and counterfictional. Like the daydream, the verbal arts are counterfactual: both the daydream and the poem bring into being things not previously existing in the world. But the verbal arts are also counterfictional, displacing the ordinary attributes of imagining — its faintness, two-dimensionality, fleetingness, and dependence on volitional labor — with the vivacity, solidity, persistence, and givenness of the perceptible world. I have shown that this comes about because we are given procedures for reproducing the deep structure of perception, and because the procedures themselves have an instructional character that duplicates the "givenness" of perception. I alternate between believing that long centuries of analysis have been devoted to solving the mystery of how vivid image-making comes about, and believing instead that we have not yet even begun to provide an answer for this question. It is the problem, says Allen Grossman, that one wakes up each morning worrying about but then forgets to return to later in the day.[51] There ought to be something written about this subject, says John Ashbery; and it is with Ashbery's words that I will end:

> Something
> Ought to be written about how this affects
> You when you write poetry:
> The extreme austerity of an almost empty mind

Colliding with the lush, Rousseau-like foliage of
    its desire to communicate
Something between breaths, if only for the sake
Of others and their desire to understand you and
    desert you
For other centers of communication, so that under-
    standing
May begin, and in doing so be undone.[52]

---

[51]Allen Grossman in conversation (August 1992), responding to my description of this essay. [Scarry]

[52]John Ashbery, "And *Ut Pictura Poesis* Is Her Name," in *Selected Poems* (New York, 1985), p. 235. [Scarry]

Mark Turner

b. 1954

If, as he has claimed with pardonable exaggeration, we live in an age that is about to witness the discovery of the human mind, the responsibility partly lies with the doyen of cognitive theory, Mark Turner. Turner's uniquely interdisciplinary approach to language and cognition brings together the humanities, the social sciences, and the natural sciences in an effort to understand higher-order cognitive operations in human beings. Turner was educated at the University of California, Berkeley, where he did bachelor's and master's degrees in both English and mathematics before completing his doctorate in English in 1983. His teaching career has taken him from the University of Chicago to the University of Maryland to Case Western Reserve, where he is currently dean of arts and sciences. Since 1987 he has been the sole author of four books, and has collaborated on four others. His solo flights include Death Is the Mother of Beauty: Mind, Metaphor, Criticism *(1987);* Reading Minds: The Study of English in the Age of Cognitive Science *(1991); and* The Literary Mind: The Origins of Language and Thought *(1996). Equally significant are his co-authored books, such as* More than Cool Reason: A Field Guide to Poetic Metaphor *(with George Lakoff, 1989) and* The Way We Think: Conceptual Blending and the Mind's Hidden Complexities *(with Gilles Fauconnier, 2002). The following essay, "Poetry: Metaphor and the Conceptual Context of Invention," was originally printed in* Poetics Today *in the fall of 1990.*

Poetry: Metaphor and the Conceptual Context of Invention

Poetic invention is an amorphous subject, not much discussed in contemporary criticism. Invention seems to be either precritical or beyond analysis, yet our practice of making critical distinctions about invention, as when we judge a poet to be strikingly inventive, implies that poetic invention should be susceptible of analysis. What do classic and successful inventions tell us about particular formal and public acts of literary representation and the tacit and private preliterary way we understand our selves and our experience?

Invention is not originality. Only since the Romantics have these two cognitive phenomena been typically confused. The structure of invention, and of particular classic and successful literary inventions, may be wholly unoriginal or may have a dominant unoriginal aspect that serves as the ground upon which contingent originality plays. We are vigilant for the new and the variable and concentrate on it. Consequently, our consciousness is blind to the unoriginal, which we take to be merely background.

Of course, the unoriginal is not background, at least not in the sense usually conveyed by that description. The unoriginal is normally the dominant active matrix in any original achievement. Originality is no more than the exploitation of what is unoriginal. Originality, far from being autonomous, is contingent at every point upon the unoriginal structures that inform it. When we step into a room, or into a poem, we do not have to think consciously "this is a room" or "this is a poem." The automatic nature of our interactions with the unoriginal leads us to think of the unoriginal as simple in itself and too simple for analysis, but this apparent simplicity is false. Relative to the complexity of the unoriginal conceptual context of invention, it is the original in invention that is simple. The concept of a "room" or a "poem" is immeasurably more complex than the original aspects of any one room or any one poem. Explaining the structure of an original moment is relatively easy, once we can explain the underbrush of unoriginal structures it exploits, but that is hard. This essay, for example, will consider one small, automatic constraint on invention. This constraint is a profoundly unoriginal component of invention and is routinely exploited to achieve originality. But, far from being obvious, this constraint seems to have gone unnoticed in poetic theory. Far from being simple, it shows a complexity that I can do no more than indicate here.

The purpose of calling attention to an unoriginal aspect of invention in poetic expression is not to homogenize nonliterary and literary practice. It is rather to tease out what belongs to the poet, against the background of what belongs to poetry, against the background of what belongs to language. The imagination must operate in a known space; it must work with unoriginal structures of invention. These are the conditions that the imagination must meet in order to be intelligible. Originality is just a step away from pedestrian thought, and pedestrian thought accounts for most of the invention in any poem. A room is more pedestrian than the Sistine Chapel, but the invention of the "room,"[1] which belongs to no individual, is beyond the original inventive range of any individual architect, even Brunelleschi or Michelangelo. This unoriginal concept informs

I would like to thank Frank Thomas for assistance with this essay, Mark Johnson for developing in his publications the theory of image-schemas which I use here, and Gilles Fauconnier, Ronald Langacker, Kathy Harris, Jeff Elman, Liz Bates, David McNeill, John Goldsmith, Jim McCawley, Nancy Dray, Peter Dembowski, and David Palermo for conversations about this essay. The rudiments of the constraint I give in this essay are implicit but not analyzed in Lakoff and Turner (1989) and Turner (1987).

[1] One room can differ from another in an almost unlimited number of unoriginal and pedestrian ways, all of which we know without need of reflection. This is an indication of the complexity in a full knowledge of the concept "room." [Turner]

every exceptional room, as it does every pedestrian room.

Let us begin a demonstration of these propositions by turning to John Bunyan's *Pilgrim's Progress*.[2] In one component of its literary invention, *Pilgrim's Progress* is unswervingly unoriginal: it is structured by a conventional metaphoric understanding of life as a journey. That conventional and wholly unoriginal metaphoric understanding is constrained in certain ways which are derived from a general constraint, one that, I claim, applies to all metaphor, original and unoriginal. *Pilgrim's Progress* never requires of itself or its readers any work to meet those constraints. The conventional metaphoric understanding of life as a journey already conforms to those constraints, and *Pilgrim's Progress* simply inherits those prefabricated and quite unoriginal satisfactions.[3]

Let us look at a few of these unoriginal satisfactions. A metaphor is a mapping of a source conceptual schema[4] (such as our conceptual schema for journey) onto a target[5] conceptual schema (such as our conceptual schema for life). For example, in the conceptual metaphoric understanding of life as a journey, components of the schema for journey are mapped onto components of the schema for life: The person leading a life is a traveler; his purposes are destinations; the means for achieving purposes are routes; difficulties in life are impediments to travel; counselors are guides; progress is the distance traveled; and so on. The target schema, life, is understood in terms of the source schema, journey.

In any such conceptual metaphor, the mapping is constrained to be one-to-one: two distinct senses in the source are not mapped onto one sense in the target, for that would destroy the identity of that one sense in the target. In the conventional metaphoric understanding of life as a journey, this constraint against violating identity in the target is automatically satisfied by a fixed mapping. For example, in the source schema, the traveler is distinct from the destination; in the target schema, the person leading the life is distinct from a goal; and the conventional metaphor maps those two distinct senses in the source onto those two distinct senses in the target. *Pilgrim's Progress* simply inherits this prefabricated and

---

[2]Allegorical narrative (1678) by John Bunyan (1628–1688), depicting the journey of Christian and Faithful on the way to the Celestial City.

[3]*Pilgrim's Progress* fleshes out this conventional metaphor elaborately, and exploits in concert with it many other conventional metaphors, such as THE MIND IS A BODY, STATES ARE LOCATIONS, and GENERIC IS SPECIFIC. (For a discussion of these metaphors, see Lakoff and Turner [1989].) Many of the allegorical moments in *Pilgrim's Progress* do not appear to be extensions of any conventionalized metaphor. See, for example, the Interpreter's presentation of a parlor as the heart of a man never sanctified by the grace of the gospel, the dust in the parlor as his original sin and inward corruptions, the man who sweeps the dust as the law, water as grace, and the damsel that sprinkles water on the dust as gospel. The effect of law on sin in the heart is to be understood in terms of the effect of the sweeper on dust in the house: he merely stirs it up to worse effect, unless water is first sprinkled upon it. Since neither Christian nor the reader possesses a conventionalized conceptual metaphor with this set of mappings, both must rely upon the Interpreter to indicate it to them, or hazard what they know to be guesses at the significance of the sweeping scene. [Turner]

[4]The notion of a schema will be used throughout this article. Schemata are skeletal organizations of conceptual knowledge. They have variables, can embed, and can represent knowledge at all levels. For a history of the development of the idea of a schema, see Rumelhart (1980). Rumelhart discusses the history of the concept of a schema, from its original sense in Kant (1787) through its use in psychology by Head (1920) and Bartlett (1932). The idea of a schema, or

frame, will for most readers be familiar from a range of now-classic books and articles from the 1960s and 1970s. See, for example, Fillmore (1968); Minsky (1975); Rumelhart and Ortony (1977); and Schank and Abelson (1977). See also Goffman (1974) and Goodman (1976 [1968]). The idea of a schema or frame or script is now a commonplace in work on cognition. See Fauconnier (1985); Fillmore (1985); and Rumelhart, McClelland, and the PDP Research Group (1986: 20–22). [Turner]

[5]"Source" and "target" are commonly used technical terms in discussions of metaphor. See, for example, the entry on "metaphor" in the *Oxford International Encyclopedia of Linguistics* (forthcoming), in which the terminology is explained. The target conceptual domain is the domain to be understood metaphorically. The source conceptual domain is the domain in terms of which the target is to be understood metaphorically. A conceptual metaphor consists of a target, a source, and a mapping between them. Conventional metaphoric expressions draw their vocabulary from the source but are taken to refer to the target, as when we take "I'm getting nowhere" — whose vocabulary is drawn from the source schema for journeys — to refer to the state of someone's life, which is the target. [Turner] The "source" and "target" are the equivalent of the "vehicle" and "tenor" of a metaphor.

quite unoriginal satisfaction of the constraint against violating identity in the target.

If we look at an extension of the conventional metaphoric understanding of life as a journey, we find that the constraint against violating identity in the target still applies. For example, if we say, "I am a traveler in life and I am the destination," then we find ourselves constrained to take the first and second "I" as pointing to two different senses (such as the knowing self and the self to be known) so that two different senses in the source (traveler and destination) do not map onto one sense in the target.

Now let us consider not the identity of senses in the target but rather order relations in the target. Here, too, we will find our metaphoric invention constrained. First, let us consider some order relations in the target and in the source. We conventionally conceive of the moments of life as being temporally ordered:[6] for any two moments in life, one must precede the other; no moment precedes itself; and precedence is transitive. We also conventionally conceive of the points on a path, such as the path of a journey, as spatially ordered: for any two spatial points on the path, one must precede the other; no point precedes itself; and precedence is transitive. And we conventionally conceive of a traveler on a journey as encountering the spatial points on the path in the order of their physical succession. Now let us consider what happens when we try to map ordered components of the source onto ordered components of the target.

When we understand life metaphorically as a journey, we are constrained not to violate the order of moments in our concept of life. We cannot without provoking remark say, for example, "First I was getting somewhere in life and then I got off to a good start," because we take this as asking us to violate the original temporal order of two moments in the target: the prior moment in the target ("First I was") is forced to correspond to the later moment in the source ("getting somewhere"), and the later moment in the target ("and then I") is forced to correspond to the prior moment in source ("got off to a good start"). This reverses the order of moments in our schema of life — which is the target — and disturbs us badly.

The conventional metaphoric understanding of life as a journey automatically and fixedly satisfies this constraint by mapping spatial priority in the source onto temporal priority in the target, and *Pilgrim's Progress* inherits and deploys this prefabricated and unoriginal satisfaction of the constraint against violating order in the target.

But there are texts that ask for originality in satisfying these unoriginal constraints. The Farewell Discourse (chapters thirteen through seventeen) in the Fourth Gospel is a locus classicus[7] whose exceptionally rich history of commentary wrestles with many of these demands. Before we turn to this text, it will be helpful to pause to make some framing and theoretical remarks.

First, we must remark that it is worthy of wonder that any such constraints even exist upon metaphoric invention, original or unoriginal. These constraints, once stated, may seem obvious, but that is only because their automatic transmission fools us into thinking that they are inevitable and require no explanation. There is nothing inevitable about them, or rather, we have no explanation as yet of how they could be inevitable. They are constraints concerned with preventing the violation of the target, but notice that they apply only to particular parts of the target; other parts of the target can be violated with impunity. Why are some parts of the target protected while others are not? That requires an explanation, and the shape of the explanation is neither obvious nor simple. Metaphoric thought is notoriously cavalier, and metaphoric language is notoriously slippery: When we understand some target concept metaphorically, we frequently violate or discard indispensable parts of it. Through metaphor, inanimate objects can become people ("My car refused to start this morning"), moods can become colors ("I'm feeling blue"), thoughts can become physical objects while minds become bodies ("I cannot grasp this

[6]Technically, a relation < on a set *A* is called an order relation (or a simple order, or a linear order) if it has the properties of comparability (for every *x* and *y* in *A* for which *x* does not equal *y*, either $x<y$ or $y<x$), nonreflexivity (for no *x* in *A* does the relation $x<x$ hold), and transitivity (if $x<y$ and $y<z$, then $x<z$). [Turner]

[7]Latin for "place of the highest class," usually denotes a passage cited as an illustration of something.

notion"). The wide latitude of metaphor in thought and language often makes it seem unconstrained in its operation, a species of pure free play. Consider, for example, "Trees climb the hills toward the Golan and descend to test their resolve near the desert." Here, a static configuration appears to be understood metaphorically as a dynamic movement, and the agentless event of dynamic movement appears to be understood metaphorically as an action by an intentional agent. We are not bothered that dynamism is mapped onto stasis, that an action is mapped onto an event, or that intentional animate agents are mapped onto plants. Why then are we bothered when, as in the case we previously considered, the ordering of a sequence is violated?

Aristotle originally noticed that a metaphor is constrained not to violate various things in the target. He expressed this by saying that the source must fit the target in certain ways, including what appear to be conceptual ways.[8] Considering that the problem of fitness was raised by Aristotle, and that metaphor theory has in many ways been a series of responses to and development of Aristotle's few comments on metaphor, it is odd how little inquiry has been made into the actual details of what makes a metaphor conceptually fit. This topic has been overshadowed by others in the theory of metaphor. There has been voluminous work on what constitutes metaphor and how metaphoric language is demarked from other forms of language, on how it is that a metaphor can mean, and on whether or not metaphor can

have truth-value, but relatively little work on the conceptual details of metaphor.[9]

To be sure, there have been blanket, general characterizations of the conceptual process of metaphor, such as Aristotle's apparent characterization of the invention of metaphor as the perception of similarity in dissimilar things (*Poetics*: 1459a), Max Black's characterization of metaphor as the interaction of two different, entire systems of implications,[10] Nelson Goodman's characterization of metaphor as "a transfer of a schema" (1976 [1968]: 73) or as concerned with "withdrawing a term or rather a schema of terms from an initial literal application and applying it in a new way to effect a new sorting either of the same or of a different realm" (1979: 178), and Paul Ricoeur's (1977) elaborate

[8]Aristotle writes in *The Rhetoric* (1405a), "Metaphors, like epithets, must be fitting, which means that they must fairly correspond to the thing signified: failing this, their inappropriateness will be conspicuous: the want of harmony between two things is emphasized by their being placed side by side."

There are many grounds on which a metaphor might be judged fitting or unfitting. As Wayne Booth points out (1979: 47–70), any rhetoric text from Aristotle's to Whately's would comment that a metaphor might be judged appropriate or inappropriate in its grandeur or triviality to what is being presented, in its contribution to the ethos the speaker desires to establish, in its level of difficulty or interest for the audience, in the style of its expression, and so on. I am concerned not with these forms of fitness but rather with the conceptual fitness of a metaphor. [Turner]

[9]For a survey of such work, see Cooper (1987). Recent work on the conceptual details of metaphor includes most prominently Dedre Gentner's (1983, 1986) work on structure-mapping, which I will discuss in footnote 13. Older work on the conceptual details of metaphor centers on the chestnut that metaphors are conceptually constrained not to be "mixed," but this claim is in general false; often, mixed metaphors do not bother us, and often, different metaphors can cohere (see Lakoff and Turner 1989: "Composing": 70–71, and "Coherence among Metaphors": 86–89). Wayne Booth (1979: 50) gives the following example of a "mixed" metaphor that does not disturb us at all, and that may be all the stronger for being mixed. A lawyer expresses the struggle between a large utility company and a small utility company in a figure: "So now we see what it is. They [the large utility company] got us [the small utility company] where they want us. They holding us up with one hand, their good sharp fishin' knife in the other, and they sayin', 'you *jes* set still, little catfish, we're jes going to *gut* ya.'" Booth observes later in the article that consistency would require that the catfish be told to "hang still" rather than "set still," but that this conceptual inconsistency does not bother us. I suspect that we would be rather bothered indeed if the metaphor were instead: "You jes vanish, little catfish, we're jes going to gut ya"; or "You jes jump back in the water, little catfish, we're jes going to gut ya," or "You jes digest, little catfish, we're jes going to gut ya"; or "You jes grow older, little catfish, we're jes going to gut ya," although these metaphors are not mixed, and that we would be equally bothered if the metaphor were: "You jes hold a board meeting, little catfish, we're jes going to gut ya," which is mixed. In all these cases, we hear the conceptual gears of the metaphor grind. We feel that something at the conceptual level does not fit, that something at the conceptual level has gone awry. [Turner]

[10]Black (1979: 28): "The metaphorical utterance works by 'projecting upon' the primary subject a set of 'associated implications,' comprised in the implicative complex, that are predicable of the secondary subject." [Turner]

characterization of metaphor, quite difficult to summarize, as novel attribution that creates semantic tension (because of its deviance from the literal) that results in new meaning (all at various levels, from the word to the sentence to the text).

At the opposite pole, there have been multitudinous specific analyses of how specific linguistic metaphors can be read.[11] Literary criticism, particularly criticism of poetry, frequently presents thick descriptions of the workings of a specific poetic metaphor in a specific poem. New Critical approaches promoted this activity to a central place in the criticism of poems. Deconstructive approaches have done the same thing, though with the ambition of finding incoherence and instability, rather than coherence and stability, in texts.

But there has been very little work at a level between these blanket characterizations and these self-contained case studies. There has been little midlevel work that would tell us about the general constraints on conceptual fit between source domain and target domain in a conceptual metaphor.[12]

Let us turn to a famous passage in the Fourth Gospel to demonstrate how an original aspect of invention can be constituted as an exploitation of an unoriginal constraint in metaphoric invention. Jesus speaks to the Apostles:

"Set your troubled hearts at rest. Trust in God always; trust also in me. There are many dwelling-places in my Father's house; if it were not so I should have told you; for I am going on purpose to prepare a place for you. And if I go and prepare a place for you, I shall come again and receive you to myself, so that where I am you may be also; and my way there is known to you." Thomas said, "Lord, we do not know where you are going, so how can we know the way?" Jesus replied, "I am the way; I am the truth and I am the life; no one comes to the Father except by me." (John 13:36–14:6, *New English Bible*)

The subject of this passage is trust. Jesus will take a journey and then return, he implies, to take the Apostles on the same journey to the same destination. This may be read literally or metaphorically or both. The metaphoric reading calls upon the conventional metaphoric understanding of life as a journey and upon its conventional extension to the metaphoric understanding of death as a departure (see further Lakoff and Turner [1989]). To this point, there is no felt violation of the target. The metaphoric reading simply inherits prefabricated satisfactions of constraints from conventionalized metaphoric understandings, as we have seen before in the case of *Pilgrim's Progress*.

At this point Thomas asks a perfectly sensible question that makes sense either literally or metaphorically. It concerns the state of knowledge of the person being told about the journey. The first reading of his question is literal: How can we know the physical path to a destination whose location is unknown to us? The second reading is metaphoric: How can we know the "way" that will lead us to a goal when the goal is unknown to us? This is a question about conceptual structure and applies equally to the literal and the metaphoric readings.

---

[11]There have been before now random observations that specific metaphoric mappings are unacceptable because they go awry in some way. For example, Eva Kittay and Adrienne Lehrer (1981) note that when we attempt to make sense of Donne's "The Bait," in which courtship is presented metaphorically in terms of fishing, there is one mapping that we might try out but find unacceptable because it "does not work. The 'beloved' cannot at once be the prey and herself the means of catching the prey." That observation is true, even obviously true, but no account is given of why that specific metaphoric mapping is constrained in that way, and no general constraint is given (see Kittay 1987: 273; Kittay and Lehrer 1981: 47). [Turner]

[12]Nelson Goodman implies that such constraints exist, but gives only hints about what they might be, as in, "A schema may be transported almost anywhere. The choice of territory for invasion is arbitrary: but the operation within that territory is almost never completely so. We may at will apply temperature-predicates to sounds or hues or personalities or to degrees of nearness to a correct answer; but *which* elements in the chosen realm are warm, or are warmer than others, is then very largely determinate. Even where a schema is imposed upon a most unlikely and uncongenial realm, antecedent practice channels the application of the labels. When a label has not only literal but prior metaphorical uses, these too may serve as part of the precedent for a later metaphorical application; perhaps, for instance the way we apply 'high' to sounds was guided by the earlier metaphorical application to numbers (via number of vibrations per second) rather than directly by the literal application according to altitude" (1976 [1968]: 74–75). What is missing from this enticing passage is any account of why certain choices are determinate, how antecedent practice channels the application of labels, or how prior uses serve as part of the precedent for later metaphorical application. [Turner]

When Jesus answers that he is the way, both the literal and the metaphoric readings fall apart. Literally, his statement violates our schema of a journey because a person cannot be a way, much less both a traveler and a way. Metaphorically, his statement asks us to map two senses in the source, namely, both the traveler and the way, onto one sense in the target, Jesus. We feel this construal to be a flagrant violation of protected structure in the target.

It is this dissonance that signals to us that we must perform some original work to arrive at a different construal that satisfies constraints. One strategy is to attribute to the passage a double reading: Jesus is taking one journey, whether literal or metaphoric, in which he is the literal or metaphoric traveler; and we, or the Apostles, are to take another journey, a metaphoric journey, in which we, or the Apostles, are the metaphoric travelers and Jesus is the metaphoric way or conduit to a state of being that is metaphorically both a location and the destination of this particular journey.

There are other ways to attempt to satisfy constraints. We might observe that divinity in the Fourth Gospel is marked not by iconographic attributes or miracle stories but rather by discourse that violates what we take to be reliable conceptions. In this text, divinity talks like this. The divine, unlike the mortal or the everyday, can be a traveler and a way, an agent and a path. The divine can violate identity, as when, in Trinitarian doctrine, we are told that three are one.[13]

It is not just that the divine can violate constraints, but that the divine frequently is signaled exactly through such violation. The constraint on preserving identity is violated, and its violation is a carrier not just of some significance, but of a particular significance. We would not recognize the attribution of divinity in this passage in the absence of knowing constraints.

We have seen a few specific manifestations of what may be a general constraint on metaphor

and demonstrations of the unoriginal and original exploitations of that general constraint in literary invention. Let us now try to express that general constraint. This constraint has to do with the forms of our experience and how these forms structure our thoughts. We experience images in various modalities: a visual image of a road, an auditory image of a scream, a kinesthetic image of a pinch, an olfactory image of the smell of roses, and so on. No rich image is wholly unique; rather, it shares skeletal structure with other images. We have a skeletal image of a scream that inheres within our rich images of particular screams. We have a skeletal image of a flat, bounded planar space that inheres within our rich images of individual tables, individual floors, individual plateaus. We have a skeletal image of verticality that inheres within our rich images of individual trees, individual buildings, individual people. Following Mark Johnson, I will use the technical term "image-schema" for such skeletal forms that structure our images.[14]

As I conceive of them, image-schemas are extremely skeletal images which we use in cognitive operations. We have many such image-schemas: of bounded space, of a path, of contact, and of such orientations as up/down, front/back, and center/periphery. We have many image-schemas of part/whole relational structure. We

[13]We have what I will call in a moment an "image-schema" for *one* and a different "image-schema" for *three*. In quotidian experience and in our metaphoric conception of a target, three cannot be one. The divine is marked as transcending such constraints. [Turner]

[14]An "image-schema," according to Johnson, "is a recurring, dynamic pattern of our perceptual interactions and motor programs that gives coherence and structure to our experience. The VERTICALITY schema, for instance, emerges from our tendency to employ an UP/DOWN orientation in picking out meaningful structures of our experience. We grasp this structure of verticality repeatedly in thousands of perceptions and activities we experience every day, such as perceiving a tree, our felt sense of standing upright, the activity of climbing stairs, forming a mental image of a flagpole, measuring our children's heights, and experiencing the level of water rising in the bathtub" (Johnson 1987: xiv). The notion that we use image-schemas to structure our perceptions and conceptions is implicit in Palermo (1987, 1988a, 1988b). Langacker (1987, 1988a, 1988b) has been articulating since 1974 the ways in which semantic structure is based on what he calls "images," which resemble Johnson's image-schemata. Technically, Langacker views Johnson's "image-schemata" as a subset of Langacker's "images" (personal communication). [Turner]

also have dynamic image-schemas, such as the image-schema for a rising motion, or a dip, or an expansion, and so on. When we understand a scene, we naturally structure it in terms of such elementary image-schemas.

Let us turn now to a first approximation of the general constraint on metaphor by taking up just images. It appears to be the case that when we map one image metaphorically onto another, we are constrained not to violate the schematic structure of the target image. For example, a verticality schema in the target cannot without provoking remark have mapped onto it its inverse; a bounded interior in the target cannot have mapped onto it both bits of an interior and bits of an exterior; and so on.

Consider, for example, Auden's lines from "1929":

But thinking so I came at once
Where solitary man sat weeping on a bench,
Hanging his head down, with his mouth distorted
Helpless and ugly as an embryo chicken.
(1976: 50,11.9–12)

The hanging head of the solitary man is a bounded interior, with an exterior; it has an internal up/down structure (for example, the top of the head and the bottom of the head); its direction is roughly downward (looking down); its open mouth is a concavity in the boundary; its parts (mouth, eyes, top of head, and so on) have relational structure, such as adjacency. Although our rich image of the hanging head may include all sorts of detail, that detail is structured by these image-schemas. I refer to this structure as the "image-schematic structure" of the target image. We are constrained not to violate it when we map the image of the embryo chicken onto it: the interior of the chicken head maps to the interior of the human head, the boundary to the boundary, the verticality to the verticality, and so on. A similar example might be Blake's personification of a sunflower,[15] in which the image of a human body is mapped onto the image of a sunflower, preserving the part/whole relations and the orientation of the sunflower. The schematic structure of the target image is not violated.

The next consideration to bring to bear in formulating this constraint is that many things other than images appear to be structured by image-schemas. Our concepts of time, of events in time, and of causal relations seem to be structured by these image-schemas. We like to think of time, which has no shape, as having a shape such as linear or circular, and of that shape as having skeletal structure. We like to think of events in time, which have no shape, as having shape such as continuity, extension, discreteness, completion, open-endedness, circularity, part/whole relations, and so on. We like to think of causal relations as having such skeletal shapes as links and paths. These shapes, these image-schemas, need not be static. We have a dynamic image-schema of one thing coming out of another, and we use it to structure one of our concepts of causation.

With this addition we can reformulate the general unoriginal constraint on metaphoric invention thus: *In metaphor, we are constrained not to violate the image-schematic structure of the target; this entails that we are constrained not to violate whatever image-schematic structure may be possessed by nonimage components of the target.* The formulation of this constraint requires many clarifications and comments.

First, the constraint says nothing about what can or cannot, or should or should not, be mapped from the source to the target, nothing about what components of the target can or should be involved in the metaphoric invention, and nothing whatever about strategies of mapping or of reconception that might be used in the service of satisfying the constraint.

---

[15]Turner is alluding to Blake's "Ah Sun-flower" from *Songs of Experience* (1794). In its entirety the poem goes:

Ah Sun-flower! weary of time,
Who countest the steps of the Sun;
Seeking after that sweet golden clime
Where the travelers journey is done;

Where the Youth pined away with desire,
And the pale Virgin shrouded in snow;
Arise from their graves, and aspire
Where my Sun-flower wishes to go.

Second, the constraint is not inviolable; however, if it is violated, the violation is to be taken as a carrier of significance. Usually, we assume that violations are to be avoided as we construct a meaning for the utterance. The constraint thus guides our understanding by blocking certain possibilities. But when we conclude that the utterance is to be taken as violating the constraint, then we must look for some significance in the violation. For example, we might take the violation as an aggressive and intentional request that we change our conception of the target in exactly the way indicated by the violation. We then take the violation as urging us to form some different conception of the target, that is, one not violated by the utterance. To put the same point differently, one drastic way to satisfy the constraint is to build a new conception of the target. But we assume that a violation of the constraint is never insignificant. If ultimately we find no significance in the violation, we will find the metaphoric invention either faulty or beyond our powers.

Third, this formulation is summary, and does no more than hint at the complexity of the subject. I have nothing approaching a definition or taxonomy of image-schemas, a theory of how they arise and work, or an explanation of their role in structuring concepts. My formulation of this constraint does offer a challenge to anyone who thinks that what is automatic and unoriginal in invention is simple in itself and too simple to need analysis. It is manifest that our unoriginal understanding is informed by something like image-schemas, that metaphoric invention is constrained in ways having to do with image-schemas, and that originality in metaphoric invention can be constituted as exploitations of these constraints.[16] Yet finding a fair characterization of these phenomena would require a theory of image-schemas, of their relation to images, of their origin, of their relation across modalities (as when we talk of a "screaming red" or a "sharp tartness"), of their use in structuring concepts, and, beyond all this, a larger

[16]The image-schematic constraint hypothesized here bears a complicated relationship to Dedre Gentner's structure-mapping theory of analogy. See Gentner (1983, 1986). Gentner writes:

> The central idea in structure-mapping is that an analogy is a mapping of knowledge from one domain (the base) into another (the target) which conveys that a system of relations that holds among the base objects also holds among the target objects. Thus an analogy is a way of focusing on relational commonalities independently of the objects in which those relations are embedded. In interpreting an analogy, people seek to put the objects of the base in one-to-one correspondence with the objects in the target so as to obtain the maximum structural match. Objects are placed in correspondence by virtue of their like roles in the common relational structure; there does not need to be any resemblance between the target objects and their corresponding base objects. Central to the mapping process is the principle of systematicity: people prefer to map connected *systems of relations* governed by higher-order relations with inferential import, rather than isolated predicates. (1986: 3–4)

Gentner here hypothesizes a heuristic used in analogical understanding. It bears the following relationship to the image-schematic constraint on metaphor that I propose.

If relational structure is image-schematic, as it would seem to be, then the image-schematic constraint I propose entails that we are constrained not to violate the relational structure of the target. This relational corollary to the image-schematic constraint is compatible with Gentner's heuristic just in those cases of metaphor where the relational structure of the target is not violated and is also maximally involved in the mapping: such a case satisfies both the image-schematic constraint and Gentner's heuristic. In one way, the relational corollary to the image-schematic constraint on metaphor is stronger than Gentner's heuristic because Gentner's heuristic of seeking maximal structural match does not imply a constraint against violating relational structure in the target; indeed, Gentner's heuristic apparently would allow us to violate some relational structure in the target if doing so enabled us to involve more of the relational structure in an analogical match than would otherwise be possible. Violating some relational structure in the target should be welcomed, according to Gentner's heuristic, if it permits greater final structural match. In another way, the relational corollary to the image-schematic constraint on metaphor is weaker than Gentner's heuristic because it is merely a constraint against violating image-schematic structure in the target and says nothing about what should be involved in the mapping, whereas Gentner's heuristic concerns exactly that. Although the image-schematic constraint and Gentner's heuristic can in some cases be compatible, the image-schematic constraint concerns many aspects of metaphor that Gentner's heuristic apparently does not. The full image-schematic constraint itself concerns all image-schematic structure, including many things (like *slowness* as part of an event shape) that are crucial to metaphor but that do not appear to fall under what Gentner would describe as relational structure (see further Turner [1988]). [Turner] theory that could account for why they seem to have privilege in metaphoric invention.[17]

Let us return for just a moment to the lines we briefly inspected earlier, "Trees climb the hills toward the Golan and descend to test their resolve near the desert." We asked earlier why we are not bothered by the violations in this poetic metaphor, and now we can answer. We can understand the form of the line of trees[18] as the trace of a movement (or "summary scan," to use Langacker's [1987] term): The trace of a climb that crests and then descends has the same image-schematic structure as the line of the trees. Consequently, when one is mapped onto the other, there is no violation of the image-schematic structure of the target. So much for the images. Now consider the events and actions in this passage. The target is an event that involves the trees and the desert: the trees occupy a position (a literal position) and are opposed in their occupation of it by desert forces that may dislodge them from that position. The source for understanding this target event metaphorically is an action: testing one's resolve. Such testing has an event shape: we occupy a position (metaphoric or literal) and are opposed in that occupation by some force that would (metaphorically or literally) dislodge us; if we abandon that position, we say our resolve failed. The event shape of the source corresponds to the event shape of the target. Both are structured as a positioned entity that has been moved to that position by one force exerted upon it, and that encounters in that position a countervailing force. The outcome is either the stasis or movement of that entity, and this outcome is determined by the size of the vector forces. Again, the image-schematic structure of the target (here, the image-schematic structure of the event shape) is not violated. So much for the events and actions. Finally, consider

[17]The rudiments of the image-schematic constraint conjectured here are presented implicitly but not analyzed in Lakoff and Turner (1989). It began as the hypothesis that conceptual metaphor preserves image-schematic structure and was called "The Invariance Hypothesis." But this strong version of the Invariance Hypothesis was an overstatement in two ways. The first way is trivial: Many components of image-schematic structure in the source are simply not involved in the mapping. For example, when we understand our boss as a crab, the image of the crab, and consequently its image-schematic structure, are simply not part of the mapping. Accordingly, that image-schematic structure in the source is not preserved by the mapping; it is not carried over to the target. (Lakoff and I implicitly explain this in chapter 4 when we discuss how the Maxim of Quantity guides us to exclude various components of the source and target from the mapping.) The second way in which the strong version is too strong is substantive: Components of the source that are indeed involved in the mapping often have image-schematic structure that is not mapped onto the target. Consider LIFE IS A JOURNEY. There is a path in the source domain, and it is mapped onto the target. That path in the source has image-schematic structure. But much of this image-schematic structure is simply not mapped onto the target. For example, it is part of the image-schematic structure of the path to be fixed, to be independent of our traversal of it. Traversing the path neither creates nor destroys it. Consequently, we can meet a fork in the path, choose one fork, take a step, change our mind, step back, and take the other fork. Metaphorically, meeting a fork corresponds to coming upon alternatives. But the fixity of the fork does not map onto the fixity of the alternatives. Many of our decisions are irrevocable: Shall we boil this egg or scramble it? Shall we marry Tom or Harry? In these cases, the rejected alternative disappears the moment we engage in the chosen alternative. If we boil the egg, we cannot then scramble it, and if we scramble it, we cannot then decide to boil it. Metaphorically, one of the forks is destroyed the moment we step down the other. We cannot take a step back and be again at the metaphoric fork in the road because the fork doesn't exist anymore. The metaphoric path, unlike the source path, changes as a result of being traversed. The fixity of the path in the source, its independence of our traversal, is not mapped onto the target. The reason it cannot be so mapped in these cases is that to do so would violate the image-schematic structure of the target. In the source, there is preservation, which is image-schematic structure. In the target, there is destruction, which is image-schematic structure. To map the source preservation onto the target destruction would be to violate the image-schematic structure of the target, and so we do not map that part of the image-schematic structure of the source. We see from this example that the strongest version of the constraint and the one I present here are incompatible for a range of cases. For these cases, obeying the strong version of the constraint violates the weaker version, and obeying the weaker version of the constraint violates the stronger version. It appears that the strongest compromise version of the constraint for which there are no clear counterexamples would be: *In metaphoric mapping, for those components of the source and target domains determined to be involved in the mapping, preserve the image-schematic structure of the target, and import as much image-schematic structure from the source as is consistent with that preservation.* [Turner]

[18]Ambiguity allows us to imagine the image of the trees in various ways. Here, for the sake of discussion, I assume that an unbroken line of trees first climbs, then crests, then descends. Alternatively, one arm of a forest might climb in one direction while another arm descends in a different direction. In any case, we are constrained not to violate the schematic structure of the target image. [Turner]

the causal structure of the target: there is a causal link between the desert and the stasis or recession of the endpoint of the line of trees in the target. In the source, there is a causal link between the desert and the intentional holding or abandoning of the occupied literal or metaphoric position. Mapping one onto the other does not violate the causal structure of the target: a link is mapped onto a link. It is important to observe that many things in the target have been violated, such as intentionality, but *not* image-schematic structure.

Let us take up, as a last example, a poem that draws upon the same conventional metaphoric understanding of life as a journey that we saw in *Pilgrim's Progress* and the Fourth Gospel, but one that is more difficult than either of them. *Pilgrim's Progress* simply inherited the conventional and unoriginal satisfaction of the image-scheme constraint from the conventional metaphoric understanding of life as a journey. The passage from the Fourth Gospel, however, asked us to do some original work in order to satisfy that unoriginal constraint. "At North Farm" by John Ashbery moves further out along that gradient:

> Somewhere someone is traveling furiously toward
>   you,
> At incredible speed, traveling day and night,
> Through blizzards and desert heat, across torrents,
>   through narrow passes.
> But will he know where to find you,
> Recognize you when he sees you,
> Give you the thing he has for you?
>
> Hardly anything grows here,
> Yet the granaries are bursting with meal,
> The sacks of meal piled to the rafters.
> The streams run with sweetness, fattening fish;
> Birds darken the sky. Is it enough
> That the dish of milk is set out at night,
> That we think of him sometimes,
> Sometimes and always, with mixed feelings?
>
> (1984: 1)

Pilgrim's Progress virtually compels the reader with multiple linguistic cues to understand it as structured by the conventional metaphoric understanding of life as a journey and inherits from that conventional metaphoric understanding a prefabricated and unoriginal satisfaction of the image-schematic constraint. The passage from the Fourth Gospel virtually compels the reader to understand it as structured by the conventional metaphoric understanding of life as a journey, but requires of the reader (and apparently of the Apostle Thomas) some original conceptual work in order to satisfy that constraint. The violation of the constraint is indeed the spur to perform that work, which we take as having been accomplished exactly when the constraint has been respected.

"At North Farm," by contrast, only suggests that we take parts of it as structured by the metaphor of life as a journey, and leaves quite widely open to us the range of possible metaphoric construals if we choose to do so. Yet as we go about those construals, we are guided by the expectation that they are to respect that unoriginal image-schematic constraint.

In "At North Farm," there are no or few overt indications that the expressions must be understood metaphorically. The entire second stanza, for example, can be taken as a literal description. The questions of the first stanza can be equally literal. Only the first sentence, with its description of incredible speeds and travel without rest through extreme conditions, offers extravagances that seem unlikely to be literal. If we do bring our capacities for metaphoric construal to bear on this first sentence, and, in the interests of consistency and richness, extend them to the rest of the poem, we find ample warrant to take the schema of travel and journeying as the source: in the expressions "somewhere someone is traveling," "toward," "speed," "traveling day and night," "Through blizzards and desert heat," and so on, we can find unproblematic expression of our conventional metaphoric understanding of life experience as journeys, especially of progress toward goals as journeys toward destinations, where impediments and hardships in the journey correspond metaphorically to difficulties in reaching the goal.

Beyond that, the possibilities for metaphoric construal open in many directions. Some of the possible metaphoric correspondences might be the correspondence of apparent physical capacities of the traveler to personal capacities of the person with the goal (specifically, physical stamina may correspond to psychological stamina); the correspondence of physical relentlessness of the traveler to the psychological or social relentlessness of the person with the goal; and the correspondence of reaching the physical location of the person addressed ("you") to beginning a psychological and social interaction with that person.

To take a complex example, one reminiscent of the passage from the Fourth Gospel, consider that there appears to be doubt about whether the traveler knows the location of the person addressed ("you"). This location constitutes the traveler's destination, but how can the traveler know the path to that destination without knowing where it is? As the Apostle Thomas said, "Lord, we do not know where you are going, so how can we know the way?" Moreover, there is doubt about whether the traveler can even recognize the person sought. We can take this first as just referring to the source domain of travel: We may construe these doubts as indicating that the traveler knows or hopes that the person sought exists, but is not certain where, and consequently does not know the path, but is exploring possible avenues. The traveler may not even recognize the person sought. Alternatively, given the ambiguity of "will he . . . recognize [and] give," we may construe that even if the traveler finds the person sought, the traveler may decline to recognize that person socially and give whatever he has to give. To what might these construals correspond metaphorically? Being ignorant of the physical path to the location may correspond metaphorically to being ignorant of how to engage "you."

These are only a few of the possible metaphoric construals, and I will not pursue others but simply observe that as we go about these construals, we are guided and empowered by the unoriginal constraint that we not violate the image-schematic structure of the target. For example, we are not to destroy the image-schematic "one-ness" of a sense in the target by mapping onto it two different senses in the source. Nor are we to destroy the order of temporal moments in the target. Nor can a path in the source that may be a dead-end be mapped onto an interaction in the target that certainly achieves the goal, for that would violate the image-schematic relation of "leading to": if in the target the interaction certainly leads to the goal, but in the source the path does *not* certainly lead to the destination, then mapping the destination onto the goal and the path onto the interaction would violate the

image-schema of "leading to" in the target, and we are constrained against doing that. In all cases, we are guided by an image-schematic constraint which applies, I claim, to the myriad complex, inventive, and original possible metaphoric construals that I do not consider here.

There is a system to imagination. Though infinitely variable and unpredictable, imagination is grounded in structures of invention either wholly unoriginal or with an originality that consists of exploitation within a known and unoriginal space. Were imagination free, we would take its products to be unintelligible, meritless caprices rather than significant, valuable achievements. Metaphoric imagination, including metaphoric imagination in those poems we regard as most original, suggestive, and demanding, appears to be guided by an utterly unoriginal constraint so unrecognized in criticism and so daunting in its complexity that it cannot yet be truly formulated but must be gestured toward, with a heavy reliance upon the reader's intuitive sense of what it means: the image-schematic structure of the target is not to be violated.

It is predictable and unobjectionable that literary criticism would attend in the main to those aspects of imagination that might be expected to vary from age to age, or country to country, or author to author, or even passage to passage. We are vigilant for the new and the variable. But attending to what varies and not to what abides means that we see only a contingent aspect, when we believe ourselves to be seeing the whole. In one respect, to understand the sophisticated ways in which the Ashbery poem can work we must understand the unoriginal structure of invention it shares with both *Pilgrim's Progress* and the Farewell Discourse from the Fourth Gospel. To understand its originality is in one respect to understand its movement to satisfy an abiding unoriginal constraint on metaphor that *Pilgrim's Progress* satisfies in a prefabricated way and the Farewell Discourse satisfies in its own original way, a constraint that governs, guides, and empowers all these poems. It is not possible to understand such a novel and arresting poem as "At North Farm" without considering those unoriginal structures of invention that are the known space in which imagination moves, and whose constrained exploitation *is* poetic originality.

Works Cited

Aristotle [384–322 B.C.]. 1984. [1954] *The Rhetoric and the Poetics of Aristotle*, introduction by Edward P. J. Corbett (New York: Modern Library).

Ashbery, John. 1984. *A Wave* (New York: Penguin).

Auden, W. H. 1976. *Collected Poems*, edited by Edward Mendelson (New York: Random House).

Black, Max. 1979. "More About Metaphor," in *Metaphor and Thought*, edited by A. Ortony, 19–43 (Cambridge: Cambridge University Press).

Booth, Wayne. 1979. "Metaphor as Rhetoric," in *On Metaphor*, edited by S. Sacks, 47–70 (Chicago: University of Chicago Press).

Cooper, D. 1987. *Metaphor* (Oxford: Blackwell).

Fauconnier, Gilles. 1985. *Mental Spaces: Aspects of Meaning Construction in Natural Language* (Cambridge, MA: Bradford Books/MIT Press).

Fillmore, Charles. 1968. "The Case for Case," in *Universals in Linguistic Theory*, edited by E. Bach and R. Harms, 1–90 (New York: Holt, Rinehart and Winston).

———. 1985 "Frames and the Semantics of Understanding." *Quaderni di Semantica* 6 (2): 222–53.

Gentner, Dedre. 1983. "Structure-Mapping: A Theoretical Framework for Analogy," *Cognitive Science* 7 (2): 155–70.

———. 1986. "The Mechanisms of Analogical Learning." Paper presented at the ARI Conference on Analogical Similarity, to appear in *Similarity and Analogical Reasoning*, edited by S. Vosniadou et al. (London: Cambridge University Press).

Goffman, Erving. 1974. *Frame Analysis* (New York: Harper and Row).

Goodman, Nelson. 1976. [1968]. *Languages of Art* (Indianapolis: Hackett).

———. 1979. "Metaphor as Moonlighting," in *On Metaphor*, edited by S. Sacks, 175–80 (Chicago: University of Chicago Press).

Johnson, Mark. 1987. *The Body in the Mind* (Chicago: University of Chicago Press).

Kittay, Eva. 1987. *Metaphor: Its Cognitive Force and Linguistic Structure* (Oxford: Clarendon).

Kittay, Eva, and Adrienne Lehrer. 1981. "Semantic Fields and the Structure of Metaphor," *Studies in Language* 5: 31–63.

Lakoff, George, and Mark Turner. 1989. *More than Cool Reason: A Field Guide to Poetic Metaphor* (Chicago: University of Chicago Press).

Langacker, Ronald. 1987. *Foundations of Cognitive Grammar*. Vol. 1, *Theoretical Prerequisites* (Stanford: Stanford University Press).

———. 1988a. "An Overview of Cognitive Grammar," in Rudzka-Ostyn 1988: 3–48.

———. 1988b. "A View of Linguistic Semantics," in Rudzka-Ostyn 1988: 49–90.

Minsky, Marvin. 1975. "A Framework for Representing Knowledge," in *The Psychology of Computer Vision*, edited by P. H. Winston, 211–77 (New York: McGraw-Hill).

Palermo, David. 1987. "The Transfer Dilemma: From Cross-Modal Perception to Metaphor." Paper presented at the Third International Conference on Thinking, Honolulu, Hawaii.

———. 1988a. "Metaphor: A Portal for Viewing the Child's Mind," in *Essays and Experiments in Honor of Charles C. Spiker*, edited by L. P. Lipsitt et al., 111–36 (Hillsdale, NJ: Lawrence Erlbaum Associates).

———. 1988b. "Knowledge and the Child's Developing Theory of the World." in *Advances in Child Development and Behavior*, Vol. 22, edited by H. W. Reese, 269–95 (New York: Academic Press).

Ricoeur, Paul. 1977. *The Rule of Metaphor: Multi-Disciplinary Studies of the Creation of Meaning in Language*. Translated by Robert Czerny (Toronto: University of Toronto Press).

Rudzka-Ostyn, Brygida. 1988. *Topics in Cognitive Linguistics* (Amsterdam/Philadelphia: John Benjamins).

Rumelhart, David E. 1980. "Schemata: The Building Blocks of Cognition," in *Theoretical Issues in Reading Comprehension: Perspectives from Cognitive Psychology, Linguistics, Artificial Intelligence, and Education*, edited by Rand J. Spiro et al. (Hillsdale, NJ: Lawrence Erlbaum Associates).

Rumelhart, D. E., J. L. McClelland, and the PDP Research Group. 1986. *Parallel Distributed Processing: Explorations in the Microstructure of Cognition*. Vol. 2, *Psychological and Biological Models* (Cambridge, MA: Bradford Books/ MIT Press).

Rumelhart, David, and Andrew Ortony. 1977. "The Representation of Knowledge in Memory," in *Schooling and the Acquisition of Knowledge*, edited by R. C. Anderson et al., 99–135 (Hillsdale, NJ: Lawrence Erlbaum Associates).

Schank, Robert, and Robert Abelson. 1977. *Scripts, Plans, Goals, and Understanding* (Hillsdale, NJ: Lawrence Erlbaum Associates).

Turner, Mark. 1987. *Death is the Mother of Beauty: Mind, Metaphor, Criticism* (Chicago: University of Chicago Press).

———. 1988. "Categories and Analogies," in *Analogical Reasoning: Perspectives of Artificial Intelligence, Cognitive Science, and Philosophy*, edited by David H. Helman, 3–24 (Dordrecht: Kluwer).

Lisa Zunshine

b. 1968

Lisa Zunshine was born in 1968 in what was then Soviet Russia and came to the United States as a refugee in 1990. In 2000, she received a Ph.D. in eighteenth-century British Literature at the University of California and was hired as an assistant professor at the University of Kentucky. Her books include Bastards and Foundlings: Illegitimacy in Eighteenth-Century Britain *(2005) and* Why We Read Fiction: An Explanation from Cognitive Theory *(2006), as well as edited volumes:* Nabokov at the Limits: Redrawing Critical Boundaries *(1999),* Philanthropy and Fiction in Eighteenth-Century England *(2006), and* Approaches to Teaching the Novels of Samuel Richardson *(2006, co-edited with Jocelyn Harris). Her essays have appeared in* Narrative, Poetics Today, Philosophy and Literature, Modern Philology, The Eighteenth-Century: Theory and Interpretation, Eighteenth-Century Life, The Eighteenth-Century Novel, *and a variety of edited collections. The following essay appeared in slightly different form in* Narrative *(2003).*

Theory of Mind and Experimental Representations of Fictional Consciousness

Let me begin with a seemingly nonsensical question. When Peter Walsh unexpectedly comes to see Clarissa Dalloway "at eleven o'clock on the morning of the day she [is] giving a party," and, "positively trembling," asks her how she is, "taking both her hands; kissing both her hands," thinking that "she's grown older," and deciding that he "shan't tell her anything about it . . . for she's grown older" (40), how do we know that his "trembling" is to be accounted for by his excitement at seeing his Clarissa again after all these years, and not, for instance, by his progressing Parkinson's disease?

Assuming that you are a particularly good-natured reader of *Mrs. Dalloway*, you could patiently explain to me that if Walsh's trembling were occasioned by an illness, Woolf would tell us so. She wouldn't leave us long under the impression that Walsh's body language betrays his agitation, his joy, and his embarrassment, and that the meeting has instantaneously and miraculously brought back the old days when Clarissa and Peter

had "this queer power of communicating without words" because, reflecting Walsh's "trembling," Clarissa herself is "so surprised, . . . so glad, so shy, so utterly taken aback to have [him] come to her unexpectedly in the morning!" (40). Too much, you would point out, hinges on our getting the emotional undertones of the scene right for Woolf to withhold from us a crucial piece of information about Walsh's health.

I then would ask you why it is that were Walsh's trembling caused by an illness, Woolf would have to explicitly tell us so, but as it is not, she can simply take for granted that we will interpret it as being caused by his emotions. In other words, what allows Woolf to assume that we will automatically read a character's body language as indicative of his thoughts and feelings?

She assumes this because of our collective past history as readers, you perhaps would say. Writers have been using descriptions of their characters' behaviors to inform us about their feelings since time immemorial, and we expect authors to do so when we open the book. We all learn, whether consciously or not, that the default interpretation of behavior reflects the character's state of mind, and every fictional story that we read reinforces our tendency to make that kind of interpretation first.[1]

Had this imaginary conversation about readers' automatic assumptions taken place twenty years ago, it would have ended here. Or it would have never happened — not even in this hypothetical form — because the answers to my naïve questions would have seemed so obvious. Today, however, this conversation has to go on because recent research in cognitive psychology and anthropology has shown that not *every* reader can learn that the default meaning of a character's behavior lies with the character's mental state. To understand what enables most of us to constrain the range of possible interpretations, we may have to go beyond the explanation that evokes our personal reading histories and admit some evidence from our evolutionary history.

In what follows, then, I attempt to make a broader case for introducing the recent findings of cognitive scientists into literary studies by showing how their research into our ability to explain behavior in terms of the underlying states of mind — or our *mind-reading* ability — can furnish us with a series of surprising insights into our interaction with literary texts. I begin by discussing the research on autism that alerted cognitive psychologists to the existence of the cognitive capacity that enables us to narrow the range of interpretations of people's behavior down to their mental states, and that makes literature, as we know it, possible. I then consider the potentially controversial issue of the "effortlessness" with which we thus read other people's — including literary characters' — minds. To explore one specific aspect of the role played by such mind-reading in fictional representations of consciousness, I then return to *Mrs. Dalloway*. Here I describe a series of recent experiments

exploring our capacity for imagining serially embedded representations of mental states (that is, "representations of representations of representations" of mental states)[2] and suggest that Woolf's prose pushes this particular capacity beyond its everyday "zone of comfort," a realization that may account partially for the trepidation that Woolf's writing tends to provoke in some of her readers. I conclude by addressing two issues concerning the interdisciplinary potential of the new field of cognitive approaches to literature. First, I discuss the relationship between cognitive analysis and the more traditional literary-historical analysis of Woolf. Second, I suggest that literary critics should take a more proactive stand toward cognitive scientists' increasing tendency to use literature in their study of human cognition.

I. THEORY OF MIND AND AUTISM

Mind-reading is a term used by cognitive psychologists to describe our ability to explain people's behavior in terms of their thoughts, feelings, beliefs, and desires; for example, "Lucy *reached* for the chocolate because she *wanted* something sweet," or "Peter Walsh was *trembling* because he was *excited* to see Clarissa again." They also call this ability our Theory of Mind (ToM), and I will use the two terms interchangeably throughout this essay.

This proliferation of fancy terminology adds extra urgency to the question of why we need this newfangled concept of mind-reading or ToM to explain what appears so obvious. Our ability to interpret the behavior of real-life people — *and, by extension*, of literary characters[3] — in terms of their underlying states of mind seems to be such

[1] Like Hermione Lee, we could ground it in Woolf's position as a "pioneer of reader-response theory." Woolf, she writes, "was extremely interested in the two-way dialogue between readers and writers. Books change their readers; they teach you how to read them. But readers also change books. 'Undoubtedly,' Woolf herself had written, 'all writers are immensely influenced by the people who read them'" ("Virginia Woolf's Essays" 91). [Zunshine]

[2] For a related analysis of "representations of representations" or "metarepresentations," see Zunshine, "Eighteenth-Century Print Culture." [Zunshine]

[3] An important tenet of a cognitive approach to literature is that, as Paul Hernadi puts it, "there is no clear division between literary and nonliterary signification. . . . Literary experience is not triggered in a cognitive or emotive vacuum: modern readers, listeners, and spectators mentally process the virtual comings and goings of imagined characters as if they were analogous to remembered actual events" (60, 62). For a related discussion, see Mark Turner, *The Literary Mind.* [Zunshine]

an integral part of being human that we could be understandably reluctant to dignify it with a fancy term and elevate it into a separate object of study. Indeed, the main reason that ToM has received the sustained attention of cognitive psychologists over the last twenty years is that they had come across people whose ability to "see bodies as animated by minds" (Brook and Ross 81) was drastically impaired — people with autism. By studying autism and a related constellation of cognitive deficits (such as Asperger syndrome),[4] cognitive scientists and philosophers of mind began to appreciate our mind-reading ability as a special cognitive endowment, structuring in suggestive ways our everyday communication and cultural representations.

Most scholars working with ToM agree that this adaptation must have developed during the "massive neurocognitive evolution" which took place during the Pleistocene, when our brain increased threefold in size. The determining factor behind the increase in brain size was the social nature of our species (which we share with other primates).[5] The emergence of a ToM "module" was evolution's answer to the "staggeringly complex" challenge faced by our ancestors, who needed to make sense of the behavior of other people in their group, which could include up to two hundred individuals. In his influential 1995 study, *Mindblindness: An Essay on Autism and a Theory of Mind*, Simon Baron-Cohen points out that "attributing mental states to a complex system (such as a human being) is by far the easiest way of understanding it," that is, of "coming up with an explanation of the complex system's behavior and predicting what it will do next" (21).[6] Thus our tendency to explain observed

behavior in terms of underlying mental states seems to be so effortless and automatic because our evolved cognitive architecture "prods" us toward learning and practicing mind-reading daily, from the beginning of awareness. (This is not to say, however, that our actual interpretations of other people's mental states are always correct — far from it!)

Baron-Cohen describes autism as the "most severe of all childhood psychiatric conditions," one that affects between approximately four to fifteen children per ten thousand and that "occurs in every country in which it has been looked for and across social classes" (60). Although "mind-reading is not an all-or-none affair [since] . . . [p]eople with autism lack the ability to a greater or lesser degree" (Origgi and Sperber 163), and although the condition may be somewhat alleviated if the child receives a range of "educational and therapeutic interventions," autism presently remains "a lifelong disorder" (Baron-Cohen 60). Autism is highly heritable,[7] and its key symptoms, which manifest themselves in the first years of life, include the profound impairment of social and communicative development and the "lack of the usual flexibility, imagination, and pretence" (Baron-Cohen 60). It is also characterized — crucially for our present discussion — by a lack of interest in fiction and storytelling, differing in degree, though not in kind, across the wide spectrum of autism cases.

In his book *An Anthropologist on Mars*, Oliver Sacks describes one remarkable case of autism, remarkable because the afflicted woman, Temple Grandin, has been able to overcome her handicap to some degree. She has a doctorate in agricultural science, teaches at the University of Arizona, and can speak about her perceptions, thus giving us a unique insight into what it means not to be able to

[4]Discovered by Hans Asperger in 1944, Asperger syndrome is a mild form of autism (victims often have high intelligence and language skills) characterized by lack of empathy, avoidance of eye contact, inability to take social cues, and physical clumsiness.

[5]On the social intelligence of nonhuman primates, see Byrne and Whiten, *Machiavellian Intelligence* and "The Emergence of Metarepresentation"; Gomez, "Visual Behavior"; Premack and Dasser, "Perceptual Origins." [Zunshine]

[6]For a discussion of alternatives to the Theory of Mind approach, see Dennett, *The Intentional Stance*. [Zunshine]

[7]Leo Kanner first described autism in 1943. For more than twenty years after that, autism was "mistakenly thought to be caused by a cold family environment." In 1977, however, "a landmark twin study showed that the incidence of autism is strongly influenced by genetic factors," and, since then, "numerous other investigations have since confirmed that autism is a highly heritable disorder" (Hughes and Plomin 48). For the "pre-history" of the term autism, particularly as introduced by Eugen Bleuler in 1911 and developed by Piaget in 1923, see Harris 3. [Zunshine]

read other people's minds. Sacks reports Grandin's school experience: "Something was going on between the other kids, something swift, subtle, constantly changing — an exchange of meanings, a negotiation, a swiftness of understanding so remarkable that sometimes she wondered if they were all telepathic. She is now aware of the existence of those social signals. She can infer them, she says, but she herself cannot perceive them, cannot participate in this magical communication directly, or conceive of the many-leveled, kaleidoscopic states of mind behind it" (272).

Predictably, Grandin comments on having a difficult time understanding fictional narratives. She remembers being "bewildered by *Romeo and Juliet*: 'I never knew what they were up to'" (259). Fiction presents a challenge to people with autism because in many ways it calls for the same kind of mind-reading as is necessary in regular human communication — that is, the inference of the mental state from the behavior.

To compensate for her inability to interpret facial expressions, which at first left her a "target of tricks and exploitation," Grandin has built up over the years something resembling a "library of videotapes, which she could play in her mind and inspect at any time — 'videos' of how people behaved in different circumstances. She would play these over and over again, and learn, by degrees, to correlate what she saw, so that she could then predict how people in similar circumstances might act" (259–60). This account of Grandin's "library" suggests that we do not just "learn" how to communicate with people and read their emotions (or how to read the minds of fictional characters based on their behavior) — Grandin, after all, has had as many opportunities to "learn" these things as you and me — but that we also have evolved cognitive architecture that makes this particular kind of learning possible. If this architecture is damaged, as in the case of autism, a wealth of experience would never fully make up for the damage.

Whereas the correlation between the impaired ToM and the lack of interest in fiction and storytelling is highly suggestive, the jury is still out on the exact nature of the connection between the two. It could be argued, for example, that the cognitive mechanisms that evolved to process information about human thoughts and feelings are constantly on the alert, checking out their environment for cues that fit their input conditions.[8] On some level, then, works of fiction manage to "cheat" these mechanisms into "believing" that they are in the presence of material that they were "designed" to process, i.e., that they are in the presence of agents endowed with a potential for a rich array of intentional stances. Literature pervasively capitalizes on and stimulates ToM mechanisms that evolved to deal with real people, even as readers remain aware on some level that fictive characters are not real people at all.[9]

Thus one preliminary implication of applying what we know about ToM to our study of fiction is that ToM makes literature as we know it possible. The very process of making sense of what we read appears to be grounded in our ability to invest the flimsy verbal constructions that we generously call "characters" with a potential for a variety of thoughts, feelings, and desires, and then to look for the "cues" that allow us to guess at their feelings and thus to predict their actions.[10] (The illusion is complete: like Erich Auerbach, we are convinced that "the people whose story the author is telling experience much more than [the author] can ever hope to tell" [549].)

II. "EFFORTLESS" MIND-READING

As we discuss mind-reading as an evolved cognitive capacity enabling both our interaction with each other and our ability to make sense of fiction, we have to be aware of the definitional differences

---

[8]By using the word "mechanism," I am not trying to smuggle the outdated "body as a machine" metaphor into literary studies. Tainted as this word is by its previous history, it can still function as a convenient shorthand designation for extremely complex cognitive processes. [Zunshine]

[9]For a discussion, see Leslie 120–25; Carruthers, "Autism as Mind-Blindness" 262–63; Hernadi 58; and Spolsky, "Why and How." [Zunshine]

[10]The scale of such investment emerges as truly staggering if we attempt to spell out the host of unspoken assumptions that make it possible (for a discussion, see Zunshine, "Richardson's *Clarissa*"). This realization lends new support to what theorists of narrative view as the essential underdetermination or "undertelling" of fiction, its "interior nonrepresentation" (Sternberg 119). [Zunshine]

between the terminology used by cognitive scientists and literary critics. Cognitive psychologists and philosophers of mind investigating our ToM ask such questions as: what is the evolutionary history of this adaptation, i.e., in response to what environmental challenges did it evolve? At what age and in what forms does it begin to manifest itself? What are its neurological foundations? They focus on the ways "in which mind-reading [plays] an essential part in *successful* communication" (Baron-Cohen 29, emphasis mine). When cognitive scientists turn to literary (or, as in the case below, cinematic) examples to illustrate our ability for investing fictional characters with minds of their own and reading those minds, they stress the "effortlessness" with which we do so. As Dennett observes, "watching a film with a highly original and unstereotyped plot, we see the hero smile at the villain and we all swiftly and effortlessly arrive at the same complex theoretical diagnosis: 'Aha!' we conclude (but perhaps not consciously), 'He wants her to think he doesn't know she intends to defraud her brother!'" (48). Readers outside the cognitive science community may find this emphasis on "effortlessness" and "success" unhelpful. Literary critics, in particular, know that the process of attributing thoughts, beliefs, and desires to other people may lead to *misinterpreting* those thoughts, beliefs, and desires. Thus, they would rightly resist any notion that we could effortlessly — that is, correctly and unambiguously, nearly telepathically — figure out what the person whose behavior we are trying to explain is thinking. It is important to underscore here that cognitive scientists and lay readers (here including literary critics) bring very different frames of reference to measuring the relative "success" of mind-reading. For the lay reader, the example of a glaring failure in mind-reading and communication might be a person's interpreting her friend's tears of joy as tears of grief and reacting accordingly. For a cognitive psychologist, a glaring failure in mind-reading would be a person's not even knowing that the water coursing down her friend's face is supposed to be somehow indicative of his feelings at that moment. If you find the latter possibility absurd, recall that this is how (many) people with autism experience the world, perhaps because of neurological deficits

that prevent their cognitive architecture from narrowing the range of interpretive possibilities and restricting them, in this particular case, to the domain of emotions.

Consequently, one of the crucial insights offered by cognitive psychologists is that by thus parsing the world and narrowing the scope of relevant interpretations of a given phenomenon, our cognitive adaptations enable us to contemplate an infinitely rich array of interpretations *within* that scope. As Nancy Easterlin puts it, "without the inborn tendency to organize information in specific ways, we would not be able to experience choice in our responses" ("Making Knowledge" 137).[11] "Constraints," N. Katherine Hayles observes in a different context, "operate constructively by restricting the sphere of possibilities" (145).[12] In other words, our ToM allows us to connect Peter Walsh's trembling to his emotional state (in the absence of any additional information that could account for his body language in a different way), thus usefully constraining our interpretive domain and enabling us to start considering endlessly nuanced choices *within that domain*. The context of the episode would then constrain our interpretation even further; we could decide, for instance, that it is unlikely that Peter is trembling because of a barely concealed hatred and begin to explore the complicated gamut of his bittersweet feelings. Any additional information that we would bring to bear upon our reading of the passage — biographical, sociohistorical, literary-historical — would alert us to new shades in its meaning, and could, in principle, lead us to some startling conjectures about Walsh's state of mind. Note too, that the description of Walsh's "trembling" may connect to something in my personal experience that will induce me to give significantly more weight to one detail of the text and to ignore others, which means that you and I may wind up with wildly different readings of Peter's and Clarissa's emotions "at eleven o'clock on the morning of the day she [is] giving a party." None of this can happen, however, before

[11]For a qualification of the term "inborn" in relation to the processing of incoming data, see Spolsky, *Satisfying Skepticism* 164. [Zunshine]

[12]For an important recent discussion of "constraints," see Spolsky, "Cognitive Literary Historicism." [Zunshine]

we have first eliminated a whole range of other explanations, such as explanations evoking various physical forces (for instance, a disease) acting upon the body, and have focused instead solely on the mind of the character.

This elimination of irrelevant interpretations can happen so fast as to be practically imperceptible. Consider an example from Stanley Fish's famous essay, "How to Recognize a Poem."[13] To demonstrate his point that our mental operations are "limited by institutions in which we are already embedded," Fish reports the following classroom experiment:

> While I was in the course of vigorously making a point, one of my students, William Newlin by name, was just as vigorously waving his hand. When I asked the other members of the class what it was that [he] was doing, they all answered that he was seeking permission to speak. I then asked them how they knew that. The immediate reply was that it was obvious; what else could he be thought of doing? The meaning of his gesture, in other words, was right there on its surface, available for reading by anyone who had the eyes to see. That meaning, however, would not have been available to someone without any knowledge of what was involved in being a student. Such a person might have thought that Mr. Newlin was pointing to the fluorescent lights hanging from the ceiling, or calling our attention to some object that was about to fall ("the sky is falling," "the sky is falling"). And if the someone in question were a child of elementary or middle-school age, Mr. Newlin might well have been seen as seeking permission not to speak but to go to the bathroom, an interpretation or reading that would never have occurred to a student at Johns Hopkins or any other institution of "higher learning." (110–11)

Fish's point that "it is only by inhabiting . . . the institutions [that] precede us [here, the college setting] that we have access to the public and conventional senses they make [here, the raised hand means the person seeks permission to speak]" (110) is well taken. Yet note that all of his patently "wrong" explanations (e.g., Mr. Newlin thought that the sky was falling; he wanted to go to the bathroom, etc.) are "correct" in the sense that they call on a ToM; that is, they explain the student's behavior in terms of his underlying thoughts, beliefs, and desires. As Fish puts it, "what else could he be *thought* of doing?" (emphasis mine). Nobody ventured to suggest, for example, that there was a thin, practically invisible string threaded through the loop in the classroom's ceiling, one end of which was attached to Mr. Newlin's sleeve and another held by a person sitting behind him who could pull the string any time and produce the corresponding movement of Mr. Newlin's hand. Absurd, we should say, especially since nobody could observe any string hovering over Mr. Newlin's head. Is it not equally absurd, however, to explain a behavior in terms of a mental state that is completely unobservable? Yet we do it automatically, and the only reason that no "normal" (i.e., non-autistic) person would think of a "mechanistic" explanation (such as the string pulling on the sleeve) is that we have cognitive adaptations that prompt us to "see bodies as animated by minds."

But then, by the very logic of Fish's essay, which urges us not to take for granted our complex *institutional* embedment that allows us to make sense of the world, shouldn't we inquire with equal vigor into our *cognitive* embedment that — as I hope I have demonstrated in the example above — profoundly informs the institutional one? Given the suggestively constrained range of the "wrong" interpretations offered by Fish (that is, all his interpretations connect the behavior to a mental state), shouldn't we qualify his assertion that unless we read Mr. Newlin's raised hand in the context of his being a student, "there is nothing *in the form* of [his] gesture that tells his fellow students how to determine its significance" (112)? Surely the *form* of the gesture — staying with the word that Fish himself has emphasized — is quite informative because its very deliberateness seems to delimit the range of possible "wrong" interpretations. That is, had Mr. Newlin unexpectedly jerked his hand instead of "waving" it "vigorously," some mechanical explanation such as a physiological spasm or someone pushing his elbow, perhaps even a wire attached to his sleeve, would seem far less absurd.

To return, then, to the potentially problematic issue of the effortlessness with which we "read" minds: a flagrantly "wrong," from lay readers' perspective, interpretation, such as taking tears of

[13]See pp. 1022–30.

grief for tears of joy or thinking that Mr. Newlin raises his hand to point out that the sky is falling, is still "effortless" from the point of view of cognitive psychologists because of the ease with which we correlate tears with an emotional state or the raised hand with a certain underlying desire/intention. Mind-reading is thus effortless in the sense that we "intuitively" connect people's behavior to their mental states — as in the example involving Walsh's "trembling" — although our subsequent description of their mental states could run a broad gamut of mistaken or disputed meanings. For any description is, as Fish reminds us on a different occasion, "always and already interpretation," a "text," a story reflecting the personal history, biases, and desires of the reader.[14]

III. CAN COGNITIVE SCIENCE TELL US WHY WE ARE AFRAID OF MRS. DALLOWAY?

How much prompting do we need to begin to attribute a mind of her own to a fictional character? Very little, it seems, since any indication that we are dealing with a self-propelled entity (e.g., "Peter Walsh has come back") leads us to assume that this entity possesses thoughts, feelings, and desires, at least some of which we could intuit, interpret, and, frequently, misinterpret. Writers exploit our constant readiness to posit a mind whenever we observe behavior when they experiment with the amount and kind of interpretation of the characters' mental states that they supply themselves and that they expect their readers to supply. When Woolf shows Clarissa observing Peter's body language (Clarissa notices that he is "positively trembling"), she has an option of providing us with a representation of either Clarissa's mind that would make sense of Peter's physical action (something to the effect of "how excited must he be to see her again!") or of Peter's own mind (as in "so excited was he to see his Clarissa again!"). Instead she tells us, first, that Peter is thinking that Clarissa has grown

older and, second, that Clarissa is thinking that Peter looks "exactly the same; . . . the same queer look; the same check suit" (40). Peter's "trembling" still feels like an integral part of this scene, but make no mistake: we, the readers, are called on to supply the missing bit of information (such as "he must be excited to see her again") that makes the narrative emotionally cohesive.

Hemingway famously made it his trademark to underrepresent his protagonists' feelings by forcing the majority of his characters' physical actions to stand in for mental states (for example, as in the ending of A Farewell to Arms: "After a while I went out and left the hospital and walked back to the hotel in the rain" [314]). Hemingway could afford such a deliberate, and in its own way highly elaborate, undertelling for the same reason that Woolf could afford to let Peter's trembling "speak for itself": our evolved cognitive tendency to assume that there *must be* a mental stance behind each physical action and our striving to represent to ourselves that possible mental stance even when the author has left us with the absolute minimum of necessary cues for constructing such a representation.

It is thus when we start to inquire into how writers of fiction *experiment* with our mind-reading ability, and perhaps even push it further, that the insights offered by cognitive scientists become particularly pertinent. Although cognitive scientists' investigation of ToM is very much a project-in-progress, literary scholars have enough carefully documented research already available to them to begin asking such questions as: is it possible that literary narrative trains our capacity for mind-reading and also tests its limits? How do different cultural-historical milieus encourage different literary explorations of this capacity? How do different genres? Speculative and tentative as the answers to these questions could only be at this point, they mark the possibility of a genuine interaction between cognitive psychology and literary studies, with both fields having much to offer to each other.

This section's tongue-in-cheek title refers to my attempt to apply a series of recent experiments conducted by cognitive psychologists studying ToM to *Mrs. Dalloway*. I find the results of such an application both exciting and unnerving. On

[14]For a discussion, see Fish, *Is There a Text in this Class?* [Zunshine]

the one hand, I can argue now with a reasonable degree of confidence that certain aspects of Woolf's prose do place extraordinarily high demands on our mind-reading ability and that this could account, *at least in part*, for the fact that many readers feel challenged by that novel. On the other hand, I have come to be "afraid" of *Mrs. Dalloway* — and, indeed, other novels — in a different fashion, realizing that any initial inquiry into the ways fiction teases our ToM immediately raises more questions about ToM and fiction than we are currently able to answer. My ambivalence, in other words, stems from the realization that ToM underlies our interaction with literary texts in such profound and complex ways that any endeavor to isolate one particular aspect of such an interaction feels like carving the text at joints that are fundamentally, paradigmatically absent.

This proviso should be kept in mind as we turn to the experiments investigating one particular aspect of ToM, namely, our ability to navigate multiple levels of intentionality present in a narrative. Although ToM is formally defined as a second-order intentionality, as in the statements "I believe that you desire X" or "Peter Walsh thinks that Clarissa 'would think [him] a failure'" (43), the levels of intentionality can "recurse" further back, for example, to the fourth level, as in a statement like "I believe that you think that she believes that he thinks that X." Dennett, who first discussed this recursiveness of the levels of intentionality in 1983, thought it could be, in principle, infinite. A recent series of striking experiments reported by Robin Dunbar and his colleagues have suggested, however, that our cognitive architecture may discourage the proliferation of cultural narratives that involve "infinite" levels of intentionality.

In those experiments, subjects were given two types of stories — one that involved a "simple account of a sequence of events in which 'A gave rise to B, which resulted in C, which in turn caused D, etc.'" and another that introduced "short vignettes on everyday experiences (someone wanting to date another person, someone wanting to persuade her boss to award a pay raise), . . . [all of which] contained between three and five levels of embedded intentionality." Subjects were then asked to complete a "series of

questions graded by the levels of intentionality present in the story," including some factual questions "designed to check that any failures of intentionality questions were not simply due to failure to remember the material facts of the story." The results of the study were revealing: "Subjects had little problem with the factual causal reasoning story: error rates were approximately 5% across six levels of causal sequencing. Error rates on the mind-reading tasks were similar (5–10%) up to and including fourth-level intentionality, but rose dramatically to nearly 60% on fifth-order tasks." Cognitive scientists knew that this "failure on the mind-reading tasks [was] not simply a consequence of forgetting what happened, because subjects performed well on the memory-for-facts tasks embedded into the mind-reading questions" (Dunbar 241). The results thus suggest that people have marked difficulties processing stories that involve mind-reading above the fourth level.

An important point that should not be lost in the discussion of these experiments is that it is the *content* of the information in question that makes the navigation of multiply-embedded data either relatively easy or difficult. Cognitive evolutionary psychologists suggest the following reason for the relative ease with which we can process long sequences such as "A gave rise to B, which resulted in C, which in turn caused D, which led to E, which made possible F, which eventually brought about G, etc.," as opposed to similarly long sequences that require attribution of states of mind, such as "A wants B to believe that C thinks that D wanted E to consider F's feelings about G." It is likely that cognitive adaptations that underwrite the attribution of states of mind differ in functionally important ways from the adaptations that underwrite reasoning that does not involve such an attribution, a difference possibly predicated on the respective evolutionary histories of both types of adaptations.[15] A representation of a mind as represented by a mind as

[15]For a discussion, see Carey and Spelke and Cosmides and Tooby on domain specificity. For a recent application of the theory of domain specificity to the study of literature, see Zunshine, "Rhetoric, Cognition, and Ideology." [Zunshine]

represented by yet another mind will thus be supported by cognitive processes distinct (to a degree which remains a subject of debate) from cognitive processes supporting a mental representation, for example, of events related to each other as a series of causes and effects or of a representation of a Russian doll nested within another doll nested within another doll. The cognitive process of representing depends crucially on *what* is being represented.

Consider now a randomly selected passage roughly halfway into Woolf's *Mrs. Dalloway*, in which Richard Dalloway and Hugh Whitbread come to Lady Bruton to write a letter to the *Times*, and in which, to understand what is going on, we have to confront a series of multiply embedded states of mind:

> And Miss Brush went out, came back; laid papers on the table; and Hugh produced his fountain pen; his silver fountain pen, which had done twenty years' service, he said, unscrewing the cap. It was still in perfect order; he had shown it to the makers; there was no reason, they said, why it should ever wear out; which was somehow to Hugh's credit, and to the credit of the sentiments which his pen expressed (so Richard Dalloway felt) as Hugh began carefully writing capital letters with rings round them in the margin, and thus marvelously reduced Lady Bruton's tangles to sense, to grammar such as the editor of the *Times*, Lady Bruton felt, watching the marvelous transformation, must respect. (110)

What is going on in this passage? We are seemingly invited to deduce the excellence of Millicent Bruton's civic ideas — put on paper by Hugh — first from the resilience of the pen that he uses, and then from the beauty of his "capital letters with rings around them on the margins." Of course, this reduction of lofty sentiments and superior analytic skills to mere artifacts, such as writing utensils and calligraphy, achieves just the opposite effect. By the end of the paragraph, we are ready to accept Richard Dalloway's view of the resulting epistle as "all stuffing and bunkum," but a harmless bunkum at that. Its inoffensiveness and futility are underscored by the tongue-in-cheek phallic description of the silver pen (should "silver" bring to our mind "gray"?) that has served Hugh for twenty years but that is still "in

perfect order" — or so Hugh thinks — once he's done "unscrewing the cap."

There are several ways to map this passage out in terms of the nested levels of intentionality. I will start by listing the smallest irreducible units of embedded intentionality and gradually move up to those that capture as much of the whole narrative gestalt of the described scene as possible:

1. The makers of the pen *think* that it will never wear out. (First level)
2. Hugh *says* that the makers of the pen *think* it will never wear out. (Second level)
3. Lady Bruton *wants* the editor of the *Times* to *respect* and publish her ideas. (Second level)
4. Hugh *wants* Lady Bruton and Richard to *believe* that because the makers of the pen *think* that it will never wear out, the editor of the *Times* will *respect* and publish the ideas recorded by this pen. (Fourth level)
5. Richard *is aware* that Hugh *wants* Lady Bruton and Richard Dalloway to *believe* that because the makers of the pen *think* that it will never wear out, the editor of the *Times* will *respect* and publish the ideas recorded by this pen. (Fifth level)
6. Richard *suspects* that Lady Bruton indeed *believes* that because, as Hugh *says*, the makers of the pen *think* that it will never wear out, the editor of the *Times* will *respect* and publish the ideas recorded by this pen. (Fifth level)
7. By inserting a parenthetical observation ("so Richard Dalloway felt"), Woolf *intends us to recognize* that Richard *is aware* that Hugh *wants* Lady Bruton and Richard to *think* that because the makers of the pen *believe* that it will never wear out, the editor of the *Times* will *respect* and publish the ideas recorded by this pen. (Sixth level)

It could be argued, of course, that in the process of reading we automatically cut through Woolf's stylistic pyrotechnics to come up with a series of more comprehensible, first-, second-, and third-level attributions of states of mind, such as "Richard does not particularly like Hugh"; "Lady Bruton thinks that Hugh is writing a marvelous letter"; "Richard feels that Lady Bruton thinks that Hugh is writing a marvelous letter, but he is skeptical about the whole enterprise"; and so on. Such abbreviated attributions may seem destructive since the effect that they have on Woolf's prose is equivalent to the effect of paraphrasing on poetry, but they do, in fact, convey some general sense of what is going on in the paragraph. The main problem with them, however, is that to arrive at such simplified descriptions of Richard's and Lady Bruton's states of mind, we have to grasp the full meaning of this passage, and to do that, we first have to process several sequences that embed at least five levels of intentionality. Moreover, we have to do it on the spot, unaided by pen and paper and not forewarned that the number of levels of intentionality that we are about to encounter is considered by cognitive scientists to create "a very significant load on most people's cognitive abilities" (Dunbar 240).

Note that in this particular passage, Woolf not only "demands" that we process a string of fifth- and sixth-level intentionalities but she also introduces such embedded intentionalities through descriptions of body language that in some ways approach those of Hemingway in their emotional blandness. No more telling "trembling," as in the earlier scene featuring Peter and Clarissa. Instead, we get Richard watching Lady Bruton watching Hugh producing his pen, unscrewing the cap, and beginning to write. True, Woolf offers us two emotionally colored words ("carefully" and "marvelously"), but what they signal is that Hugh cares a great deal about his writing and that Lady Bruton admires the letter that he produces — two snapshots of the states of mind that only skim the surface of the complex affective undertow of this episode.

Because Woolf has depicted physical actions relatively lacking in immediate emotional content, here, in striking contrast to the scene in Clarissa's drawing-room, she hastens to provide an authoritative interpretation of each character's mental state. We are told what Lady Bruton feels as she watches Hugh (she feels that the editor of the *Times* will respect so beautifully written a letter); we are told what Hugh thinks as he unscrews the cap (he thinks that the pen will never wear out and that its longevity contributes to the worth of the sentiments it produces); we are told what Richard feels as he watches Hugh, his capital letters, and Lady Bruton (he is amused both by Hugh's exalted view of himself and by Lady Bruton's readiness to take Hugh's self-importance at its face value). The apparently unswerving linear hierarchy of the scene — Richard can represent the minds of both Hugh and Lady Bruton, but Hugh and Lady Bruton cannot represent Richard's representations of their minds — seems to enforce the impression that each mind is represented fully and correctly.

Of course, Woolf is able to imply that her representations of Hugh's, Lady Bruton's, and Richard's minds are exhaustive and correct because, creatures with a ToM that we are, we *just know* that there *must be* mental states behind the emotionally opaque body language of the protagonists. The paucity of textual cues that could allow us to imagine those mental states ourselves leaves us no choice but to accept the representations provided by the author. We have to work hard for them, of course, for sifting through all those levels of embedded intentionality tends to push the boundaries of our mind-reading ability to its furthest limits.

When we try to articulate our perception of the cognitive challenge induced by this task of processing fifth- and sixth-level intentionality, we may say that Woolf's writing is difficult or even refuse to continue reading her novels. The personal aesthetics of individual readers thus could be grounded *at least in part* in the nuances of their individual mind-reading capacities. By saying this I do not mean to imply that if somebody "loves" or "hates" Woolf, it should tell us something about that person's general mind-reading "sophistication" — a cognitive literary analysis does not support such misguided value judgments. The nuances of each person's mind-reading profile are unique to that person, just as, for example, we all have the capacity for developing memories (unless that capacity has been clinically impaired), but each individual's actual memories are unique.

My combination of memories serves me, and it would be meaningless to claim that it somehow serves me "better" than my friend's combination of memories serves her. At the same time, I see no particular value in celebrating the person's dislike of Woolf as the manifestation of his or her individual cognitive make-up. My teaching experience has shown that if we alert our students to the fact that Woolf tends to play this particular kind of cognitive "mind game" with her readers, it significantly eases their anxiety about "not getting" her prose and actually helps them to start enjoying her style.[16]

IV. COGNITIVE LITERARY ANALYSIS OF MRS. DALLOWAY

It is now time to return to the imaginary conversation that opened my essay. Some versions of that exchange did take place at several scholarly forums where I have presented my research on ToM and literature. Once, for instance, after I described the immediate pedagogical payoffs of counting the levels of intentionality in *Mrs. Dalloway* with my undergraduates, I was asked if I could foresee the time when such a cognitive reading would supersede and render redundant the majority of other, more traditional approaches to Woolf.[17] My immediate answer was, and still remains, an unqualified no, but since then I have had the opportunity to consider several of that question's implications that are important for those of us wishing cognitive approaches to literature to thrive.

First of all, counting the levels of intentionality in *Mrs. Dalloway* does not constitute *the* cognitive approach to Woolf. It merely begins to explore one particular way — among numerous others — in which Woolf builds on and experiments with our ToM, and — to cast the net broader — in which fiction builds on and experiments with our cognitive propensities.[18] Many of these propensities, I feel safe saying in spite of remarkable advances in the cognitive sciences during the last two decades, still remain unknown to us.

However, the current state of cognitive approaches to literature already testifies to the spectacular diversity of venues offered by the parent fields of cognitive neuroscience, artificial intelligence, philosophy of mind, cognitive linguistics, evolutionary biology, cognitive psychology, and cognitive anthropology. Literary critics have begun to investigate the ways in which recent research in these areas opens new avenues in gender studies (F. Elizabeth Hart); feminism (Elizabeth Grosz); cultural materialism (Mary Thomas Crane, Alan Richardson); deconstruction (Ellen Spolsky); literary aesthetics (Elaine Scarry, Gabrielle Starr); history of moral philosophy (Blakey Vermeule); ecocriticism (Nancy Easterlin); and narrative theory (Porter Abbott, David Herman, Paul Hernadi). What these scholars' publications show is that far from displacing the traditional approaches or rendering them redundant, a cognitive approach ensures their viability as it builds on, strengthens, and develops their insights.

Second, the ongoing dialogue with, for instance, cultural historicism or feminism is not simply a matter of choice for scholars of literature interested in cognitive approaches. There is no such thing as a cognitive ability, such as ToM, free-floating "out there" in isolation from its human embodiment and its historically and culturally concrete expression. Evolved cognitive predispositions, to borrow Patrick Colm Hogan's characterization of literary universals, "are

---

[16]Thus bringing the findings of cognitive scientists to bear upon the literary text does not diminish its aesthetic value. As Scarry has argued in response to the fear that science would "unweave the rainbow" of artistic creation, "the fact of the matter is that when we actually look at the nature of artistic creation and composition, understanding it does not mean doing it less well. To become a dancer, for example, one must do the small steps again and again and understand them, if one is to achieve virtuosity. Right now we need virtuosity, not only within each discipline, but across the disciplines as well" ("Panel Discussion" 253). [Zunshine]

[17]For a discussion, see Easterlin, "Voyages in the Verbal Universe." [Zunshine]

[18]As a friend working with cognitive/evolutionary approaches to fiction observed recently, "literature-fiction-writing is so powerful because it eats theories for breakfast, including cognitive/evolutionary approaches" (Blakey Vermeule, personal communication, 20 November 2002). [Zunshine]

instantiated variously, particularized in specific circumstances" (226).[19] *Everything* that we learn about Woolf's life and about the literary, cultural, and sociohistorical contexts of *Mrs. Dalloway* is thus potentially crucial for understanding why this particular woman, at this particular historical juncture, seeing herself as working both within and against a particular set of literary traditions, began to push beyond the boundaries of her readers' cognitive "zone of comfort" (that is, beyond the fourth level of intentionality).

At the same time, to paraphrase David Herman ("Regrounding"), the particular combination of these personal, literary, and historical contexts, in all their untold complexity, is a "necessary though not a sufficient condition" for understanding why Woolf wrote the way she did. No matter how much we learn about the writer herself and her multiple environments, and no matter how much we find out about the cognitive endowments of our species that, "particularized in specific circumstances," make fictional narratives possible, we can only go so far in our cause-and-effect analysis. As George Butte puts it, "accounts of material circumstances can describe changes in gender systems and economic privileges, but they cannot explain why *this* bankrupt merchant wrote *Moll Flanders*, or why *this* genteelly-impoverished clergyman's daughter wrote *Jane Eyre*." There will always remain a gap between our ever-increasing store of knowledge and the phenomenon of Woolf's prose — or, for that matter, Defoe's, Austen's, Brontë's, and Hemingway's prose.

Yet to consider just one example of how crucial our "other" knowledges are for our cognitive inquiry into *Mrs. Dalloway*, let us situate Woolf's experimentation with multiple levels of intentionality within the history of the evolution of the means of textual reproduction. It appears that a written culture is, on the whole, more able than an oral culture to support elaborately nested intentionality simply because a paragraph with six levels of intentional embedment does not yield itself easily to memorization and subsequent oral transmission.

It is thus highly unlikely that we would find many (or any) passages that require us to go beyond the fourth level of intentionality in oral epics such as *Gilgamesh* or *The Iliad*. Walter Benjamin captures the broad point of this difference when he observes that the "listener's naïve relationship to the storyteller is controlled by his interest in retaining what he is told. The cardinal point for the unaffected listener is to assure himself of the possibility of reproducing the story" (97). The availability of the means of written transmission, such as print, enables the writer "to carry the incommensurable to extremes in representations of human life,"[20] and by so doing, to explore (or shall we actually say "develop," thus drawing upon Paul Hernadi's recent argument about the evolutionary origins of literature?)[21] the hitherto quiescent cognitive spaces.

Of course, for a variety of aesthetic, personal, and financial reasons, not every author writing under the conditions of print will venture into such cognitive unknown. Even a cursory look through the best-selling mainstream fiction, from Belva Plain to Danielle Steel, confirms the continuous broad popular appeal of narratives dwelling under the fourth level of intentional embedment. It is, then, the personal histories of individuals (here, individual writers and their audiences) that insure that, as Alan Richardson and Francis Steen observe, the history of cognitive structures "is neither identical to nor separate from the culture they make possible" (3).

In the case of Woolf, scholars agree that severing ties with the Duckworth — the press that had brought forth her first two novels and was geared toward an audience that was "Victorian,

---

[19]For a discussion of embodied cognition, see also Hart. [Zunshine]

[20]For a related discussion, see Hogan 242–43. [Zunshine]

[21]Hernadi argues that "literature, whether encountered in live performance or in textual and electronic recording, can challenge and thus enhance our brains' vital capacities for expression, communication, representation, and signification." He further connects the fictional text's capacity for developing our minds to the evolutionary history of the literary endeavor. He points out that, "the protoliterary experiences of some early humans could, other things being equal, enable them to outdo their less imaginative rivals in the biological competition for becoming the ancestors of later men and women" (56). [Zunshine]

conventional, anti-experimentation" (*Diary* 1:261) — "liberated [her] experimentalism" (Whitworth 150). Having her own publishing house, the Hogarth Press, meant that she was "able to do what" she "like[d] — no editors, or publishers, and only people to read who more or less like that sort of thing" (*Letters* 167). Another factor possibly informing the cognitive extremes of *Mrs. Dalloway* was Woolf's acute awareness of the passing of time: "my theory is that at 40 one either increases the pace or slows down" (*Diary* 2:259). Woolf wanted to *increase* the pace of her explorations, to be able to "embody, at last," as she would write several years later, "the exact shapes my brain holds" (*Diary* 4:53). Having struggled in her previous novels with the narrator "chocked with observations" (*Jacob's Room* 67), she discovered in the process of working on *Mrs. Dalloway* how to "dig out beautiful caves behind [her] characters; . . . The idea is that the caves shall connect, and each comes to daylight at the present moment" (*Diary* 2:263). Embodying the "exact shapes" of Woolf's brain thus meant, among other things, shifting "the focus from the mind of the narrator to the minds of the characters" and "from the external world to the minds of the characters perceiving it" (Dick 51, 52), a technique that would eventually prompt Auerbach to inquire in exasperation, "Who is speaking in this paragraph?" (531).[22]

Woolf's meditations on her writing remind us of yet another reason that simply counting levels of intentionality in *Mrs. Dalloway* will never supersede other forms of critical inquiry into the novel. When Woolf explains that she wants to construct a "present moment" as a delicate "connection" among the "caves" dug behind each character, the emerging image overlaps suggestively with Dennett's image of the infinitely recursive levels of intentionality. ("Aha," concludes the delighted cognitive literary critic, "Woolf had some sort of proto-theory of recursive mind-reading!") But with her vivid description of the catacomb-like subjectivity of the

shared present moment,[23] Woolf also manages to do something else — and that "something else" proceeds to quietly burrow into our (and her) cognitive theorizing.

This brings us to a seemingly counterintuitive but important point underlying cognitive literary analysis. Even as I map the passage featuring Richard Dalloway and Hugh Whitbread at Lady Bruton's as a linear series of embedded intentionalities, I expect that something else present in that passage will complicate that linearity and re-pose Auerbach's question, albeit with a difference. Will it be the phallic overtones of the description of Hugh's pen? Or the intrusion of rhetoric of economic exchange — "credit," "makers," "produce," "capital," "margin"? Or the vexed gender contexts of the "ventriloquism" implied by the image of Millicent Bruton spouting political platitudes in Hugh's voice?[24] Or the equally vexed social class contexts of the "seating arrangements" that hierarchize the mind-reading that goes on in the passage? (After all, Woolf must have "seated" Lady Bruton's secretary, Miss Brush, too far from the desk to be able to see the shape of Hugh's letters so as not to add yet another level of mental embedment by having Miss Brush watch Richard watching Lady Bruton watching Hugh.) Cognitive *literary* analysis thus

[22]Strictly speaking, Auerbach's question refers to *To the Lighthouse*, but it is equally pertinent for our discussion of *Mrs. Dalloway*. [Zunshine]

[23]A remarkable new study by George Butte, *I Know That You Know That I Know: Narrating Subjects from* Moll Flanders *to* Marnie, offers a fascinating perspective on a writer's interest in constructing a "present moment" as a delicate "connection" among the characters' subjectivities. Applying Maurice Merleau-Ponty's analysis of interlocking consciousnesses (*Phenomenology of Perception*) to a broad selection of eighteenth- and nineteenth-century novels, as well as to the films of Hitchcock, Hawks, and Woody Allen, Butte argues compellingly that something had changed in the narrative representation of consciousness at the time of Jane Austen: writers became able to represent the "deep intersubjectivity" of their characters, portraying them as aware of each other's perceptions of themselves and as responding to such perceptions with body language observable by their interlocutors, which generated a further series of mutual perceptions and reactions. Although Butte does not refer in his work to cognitive science or the Theory of Mind, his argument is in many respects compatible with the literary criticism that does. [Zunshine]

[24]On Woolf's definition of narrative ventriloquism, see DiBattista 132. [Zunshine]

continues beyond the line drawn by cognitive scientists — with the reintroduction of something else, a "noise," if you will, that is usually carefully controlled for and excised, whenever possible, from the laboratory settings.

V. WOOLF, PINKER, AND THE PROJECT OF INTERDISCIPLINARITY

Challenging as it is, Woolf's prose is still so fundamentally rooted in our cognitive capacities that I am compelled to qualify an argument advanced recently by Steven Pinker in his remarkable and provocative *Blank Slate*. Pinker sees Woolf as having inaugurated an aesthetic movement whose "philosophy did not acknowledge the ways in which it was appealing to human pleasure" (413). Although he admits that "modernism comprises many styles and artists, . . . not [all of which] rejected beauty and other human sensibilities" and that modernist "fiction and poetry offered invigorating intellectual workouts," here is what he has to say about modernism as a whole and Woolf in particular:

> The giveaway [explanation for the current crisis in the arts and humanities] may be found in a famous statement from Virginia Woolf: "[On] or about December 1910, human [character] changed." She was referring to the new philosophy of modernism that would dominate the elite arts and criticism for much of the twentieth century, and whose denial of human nature was carried over with a vengeance to postmodernism, which seized control in its later decades. . . . Modernism certainly proceeded *as if* human nature had changed. All the tricks that artists had used for millennia to please the human palate were cast aside. . . . In literature, omniscient narration, structured plots, the orderly introduction of characters, and general readability were replaced by a stream of consciousness, events presented out of order, baffling characters and causal sequences, subjective and disjointed narration, and difficult prose. (409–10)[25]

As literary critics, we have several ways of responding to Pinker's claims about Woolf. We can hope that not "many students, teachers, theorists, and critics of literature will take [him] seriously as an authority on literature or the aesthetics more generally, especially since he misrepresents both Woolf and modernism."[26] At first sight, this is a comfortable stance. It assumes a certain cultural detachment of literary studies and implies that cognitive scientists should just leave literature alone, acknowledging it as an exclusive playing field for properly trained professionals — us. The problem with this view is that it disregards two facts: first, that more people read Pinker (who "misrepresents" Woolf) rather than, say, *PMLA* (which could set the matter straight), and, second, that as a very special, richly concentrated cognitive artifact, literature already is fair game for scientists, including Pinker, Daniel Dennett, Paul Harris, Robin Dunbar, and others, and it will become even more so as cognitive inquiry spreads further across cultural domains.

I suggest that instead of simply ignoring Pinker's assertion that the modernist writers' generally "difficult" prose cannot, by and large, "please the human palate," we should engage his argument, incorporating both the insights from our own field and those offered by cognitive scientists. By taking seriously the idea that our cognitive evolutionary heritage structures the ways in which we make sense of fictional narrative, we can gain a better understanding of why and how different "human palates" in different historical milieus can be "pleased" by quite different literary fare. Furthermore, we can show that it is by paying attention to the elite, to the exceptional, to the cognitively challenging, such as Woolf's experimentation with the levels of intentional embedment, that we can develop, for instance, a more sophisticated perspective on the workings of our ToM. As James Phelan observes, would not Pinker himself and "those in his audience who view modernist literature as he does be more likely to be persuaded to change their dismissive view of it, if literary critics show that [Woolf's]

[25]Pinker actually misquotes Woolf in his book to make his point stronger. According to Pinker, Woolf wrote that "In or about December 1910, human nature changed." [Zunshine]

[26]I quote here an anonymous reader for *PMLA*. [Zunshine]

representations of consciousness, though initially challenging to a reader, are highly intelligible because they capture in their own ways insights that Pinker and other cognitive scientists have been offering (and popularizing)?"[27] And what exactly are the epistemological and ethical grounds on which we stand when we mock Pinker's claim to being an "authority on literature" if we have not yet made this kind of good-faith effort to meet Pinker halfway and offer our literary-historical expertise to develop a more sophisticated cognitive perspective on modernist representations of fictional consciousness?

Consider again the above-discussed insights of Robin Dunbar and his colleagues. As I hope to have demonstrated in this essay, Dunbar's research into our processing of stories that involve mind-reading above the fourth level can have far-reaching consequences for literary analysis. Yet there is no reason why, based on our knowledge of literary history, we should not ask him to qualify some of his arguments (and, indeed, would not Dunbar himself appreciate precisely this kind of response?), even if at this point, given how new the whole field is, we may have to settle for less-than-definitive answers to our criticism.

For example, Dunbar offers a fascinating speculation about the significance of his findings for our understanding of why there are generally more good readers than good writers:

> The fact that people seem to experience considerable difficulty with fifth-order intentional statements, but not fourth-order ones, may explain why writing fiction is much harder than reading it, and may thus in part explain why good writers are [much] less common than good readers. . . . A novelist writing about relationship between three people has to "*intend* that the reader *think* that character A *supposes* that character B *wants* character C to *believe* that . . ." — five orders of intentionality. The reader, in contrast, has a much easier task: he or she merely has to "*think* that A *supposes* that B *wants* C to *believe* that . . ." — four orders of intentionality. (241)

Dunbar's argument has interesting implications for our theorizing the figure of the unreliable narrator as well as the relationship between the author and the narrator. For instance, our frequently ambivalent reaction to a suddenly perceived split of the narratorial presence — we may react to it by feeling excited, intrigued, and yet unsettled — could be related, among other things, to our semiconscious realization that we must factor in yet another level of intentionality, thus adding to the cognitive challenge already presented by the text. At the same time, as Phelan notes, Dunbar's speculation that the difficulty that we have with processing fifth-order intentional statements may provide insight into why good writers are less common than good readers is "unpersuasive" because it "would predict that until we get to fictions with five or more levels of intentionality" — which happened relatively recently in our literary history and was predicated on, among other things, the evolution of the means of textual reproduction — "the number of good writers and good readers should be approximately the same." Since the latter is clearly not the case, and since the marked paucity of literary texts going beyond the fourth level of embedded intentionality, say, in the Middle Ages, would not lead us to assume that the number of good writers and good readers in that period was approximately the same, Dunbar may want to consider how this historical dimension complicates his provocative argument.

These examples support my claim that there is now the possibility of a genuine interaction between cognitive science and literary studies, one that does not just pay obligatory lip service to interdisciplinarity while quietly assuming the superiority of science. Paradoxically, it is only while we refuse to "take seriously" the research of cognitive scientists who dare to pronounce "on literature or . . . aesthetics more generally," that we can be made to feel that our contribution to this interdisciplinary exchange would represent little or nothing of value. Once we enter the conversation and engage with respect the arguments of Dunbar, Pinker, Dennett, and others, we realize that because of their ever-increasing — and well-warranted — interest in how the human mind processes literary narratives, our expertise could make a crucial difference for the future shape of the whole field of cognitive science.

[27]The quotations of Phelan are from a personal communication from 17 April 2003. [Zunshine]

Works Cited

Abbott, Porter. "Humanists, Scientists and Cultural Surplus." *Substance* 94/95: 30 (2001): 203–17.

Auerbach, Erich. *Mimesis.* Princeton: Princeton Univ. Press, 1991.

Baron-Cohen, Simon. *Mindblindness: An Essay on Autism and Theory of Mind.* Cambridge: MIT Press, 1995.

Benjamin, Walter. *Illuminations.* New York: Harcourt, Brace & World, 1955.

Brook, Andrew, and Don Ross. *Daniel Dennett.* Cambridge: Cambridge Univ. Press, 2002.

Butte, George. *I Know That You Know That I Know: Narrating Subjects from* Moll Flanders *to* Marnie. Columbus: The Ohio State Univ. Press, 2004.

Byrne, Richard W., and Andrew Whiten. "The Emergence of Metarepresentation in Human Ontogeny and Primate Phylogeny." In *Natural Theories of Mind: Evolution, Development, and Simulation of Everyday Mindreading,* edited by Andrew Whiten, 267–82. Oxford: Basil Blackwell, 1991.

——— . *Machiavellian Intelligence: Social Expertise and the Evolution of Intellect in Monkeys, Apes, and Humans.* Oxford: Oxford Univ. Press, 1988.

Carey, Susan, and Elizabeth Spelke. "Domain-Specific Knowledge and Conceptual Change." In *Mapping the Mind: Domain Specificity in Cognition and Culture,* edited by Lawrence A. Hirschfeld and Susan A. Gelman, 169–200. New York: Cambridge Univ. Press, 1994.

Carruthers, Peter. "Autism as Mind-Blindness: An Elaboration and Partial Defense." In *Theories of Theories of Mind,* edited by Peter Carruthers and Peter K. Smith, 257–73. Cambridge: Cambridge Univ. Press, 1996.

Cosmides, Leda, and John Tooby. "Origins of Domain Specificity: The Evolution of Functional Organization." In *Mapping the Mind: Domain Specificity in Cognition and Culture,* edited by Lawrence A. Hirschfeld and Susan A. Gelman, 85–116. New York: Cambridge Univ. Press, 1994.

Crane, Mary Thomas. *Shakespeare's Brain: Reading with Cognitive Theory.* Princeton: Princeton Univ. Press, 2001.

Dennett, Daniel. *The Intentional Stance.* Cambridge: MIT Press, 1987.

DiBattista, Maria. "Virginia Woolf and the Language of Authorship." In *The Cambridge Companion to Virginia Woolf,* edited by Sue Roe and Susan Sellers, 127–45. Cambridge: Cambridge Univ. Press, 2000.

Dick, Susan. "Literary Realism in *Mrs. Dalloway, To the Lighthouse, Orlando* and *The Waves.*" In *The Cambridge Companion to Virginia Woolf,* edited by Sue Roe and Susan Sellers, 50–71. Cambridge: Cambridge Univ. Press, 2000.

Dunbar, Robin. "On the Origin of the Human Mind." In *Evolution and the Human Mind: Modularity, Language, and Meta-Cognition,* edited by Peter Carruthers and Andrew Chamberlain, 238–53. Cambridge: Cambridge Univ. Press, 2000.

Easterlin, Nancy. "Making Knowledge: Bioepistemology and the Foundations of Literary Theory." *Mosaic* 32 (1999): 131–47.

——— . "Voyages in the Verbal Universe: The Role of Speculation in Darwinian Literary Criticism." *Interdisciplinary Literary Studies: A Journal of Criticism and Theory* 2, no. 2 (Spring 2001): 59–73.

Fish, Stanley. "How to Recognize a Poem When You See One." In *American Criticism in the Poststructuralist Age,* edited by Ira Konigsberg, 102–15. Ann Arbor: Univ. of Michigan Press, 1981.

——— . *Is There a Text in This Class?* Cambridge: Cambridge Univ. Press, 1980.

Gomez, Juan C. "Visual Behavior as a Window for Reading the Mind of Others in Primates." In *Natural Theories of Mind: Evolution, Development, and Simulation of Everyday Mindreading,* edited by Andrew Whiten, 195–208. Oxford: Basil Blackwell, 1991.

Grosz, Elizabeth. "Feminist Futures?" *Tulsa Studies in Women's Literature* 21, no. 1 (Spring 2002): 13–20.

Harris, Paul L. *The Work of Imagination.* Oxford: Blackwell Publishers, 2001.

Hart, F. Elizabeth. "The Epistemology of Cognitive Literary Studies." *Philosophy and Literature* 25 (2002): 314–34.

Hayles, N. Katherine. "Desiring Agency: Limiting Metaphors and Enabling Constraints in Dawkins and Deleuze/Guattari." *Substance* 94/95: 30 (2001): 144–59.

Hemingway, Ernest. *A Farewell to Arms.* New York: Charles Scribner's Sons, 1929.

Herman, David. "Regrounding Narratology: The Study of Narratively Organized Systems for Thinking." In *What Is Narratology?* edited by Jan-Christoph Meister, Tom Kindt, and Hans-Harald Müller. Berlin: de Gruyter, 2003.

——— . "Scripts, Sequences, and Stories: Elements of a Postclassical Narratology." *PMLA* 112 (1997): 1046–59.

Hernadi, Paul. "Literature and Evolution." *Substance* 94/95: 30 (2001): 55–71.

Hogan, Patrick Colm. "Literary Universals." *Poetics Today* 18 (1997): 223–49.

Hughes, Claire, and Robert Plomin. "Individual Differences in Early Understanding of Mind: Genes, Non-Shared Environment and Modularity." In *Evolution and the Human Mind: Modularity, Language, and Meta-Cognition*, edited by Peter Carruthers and Andrew Chamberlain, 47–61. Cambridge: Cambridge Univ. Press, 2000.

Kanner, Leo. "Autistic Disturbances of Affective Contact." *Nervous Children* 2 (1943): 217–50.

Lee, Hermione. *Virginia Woolf*. New York: Alfred A. Knopf, 1997.

——— . "Virginia Woolf's Essays." In *The Cambridge Companion to Virginia Woolf*, edited by Sue Roe and Susan Sellers, 91–108. Cambridge: Cambridge Univ. Press, 2000.

Leslie, Alan. "ToMM, ToBY, and Agency: Core Architecture and Domain Specificity." In *Mapping the Mind: Domain Specificity in Cognition and Culture*, edited by Lawrence Hirschfeld and Susan Gelman, 119–48. New York: Cambridge Univ. Press, 1994.

Origgi, Gloria, and Dan Sperber. "Evolution, Communication and the Proper Function of Language." In *Evolution and the Human Mind: Modularity, Language, and Meta-Cognition*, edited by Peter Carruthers and Andrew Chamberlain, 140–69. Cambridge: Cambridge Univ. Press, 2000.

Pinker, Steven. *The Blank Slate: The Modern Denial of Human Nature*. New York: Viking, 2002.

Premack, David, and Verena Dasser. "Perceptual Origins and Conceptual Evidence for Theory of Mind in Apes and Children." In *Natural Theories of Mind: Evolution, Development, and Simulation of Everyday Mindreading*, edited by Andrew Whiten, 253–66. Oxford: Basil Blackwell, 1991.

Richardson, Alan. *British Romanticism and the Science of Mind*. Cambridge: Cambridge Univ. Press, 2001.

Richardson, Alan, and Francis Steen. "Literature and the Cognitive Revolution: An Introduction." *Poetics Today* 23 (2002): 1–8.

Sacks, Oliver. *An Anthropologist on Mars*. New York: Alfred A. Knopf, 1995.

Scarry, Elaine. *Dreaming by the Book*. New York: Farrar, Straus, Giroux, 1999.

——— . "Panel Discussion: Science, Culture, Meaning Values." In *Unity of Knowledge: The Convergence of Natural and Human Science*, 233–57. New York: The New York Academy of Sciences, 2001.

Spolsky, Ellen. "Cognitive Literary Historicism: A Response to Adler and Gross." *Poetics Today*, forthcoming.

——— . *Satisfying Skepticism: Embodied Knowledge in the Early Modern World*. Aldershot: Ashgate, 2001.

——— . "Why and How to Take the Wheat and Leave the Chaff." *Substance* 94/95: 30, nos. 1–2 (2001): 178–98.

Starr, Gabrielle G. "Ethics, Meaning, and the Work of Beauty." *Eighteenth-Century Studies* 35 (2002): 361–78.

Sternberg, Meir. "How Narrativity Makes a Difference." *Narrative* 9 (2001): 115–22.

Turner, Mark. *The Literary Mind*. New York: Oxford Univ. Press, 1996.

Vermeule, Blakey. *The Party of Humanity: Writing Moral Psychology in Eighteenth-Century Britain*. Baltimore: The Johns Hopkins Univ. Press, 2000.

Whitworth, Michael. "Virginia Woolf and Modernism." In *The Cambridge Companion to Virginia Woolf*, edited by Sue Roe and Susan Sellers, 146–63. Cambridge: Cambridge Univ. Press, 2000.

Woolf, Virginia. *The Diary of Virginia Woolf*. 5 vols. Edited by Anne Olivier Bell. London: Penguin, 1977–84.

——— . *Jacob's Room*. London: Hogarth, 1976.

——— . *The Letters of Virginia Woolf*. Vol. 2. Edited by Nigel Nicholson. London: Hogarth Press, 1975–80.

——— . *Mrs. Dalloway*. San Diego: Harcourt Brace, 1981.

Zunshine, Lisa. "Eighteenth-Century Print Culture and the 'Truth' of Fictional Narrative." *Philosophy and Literature* 25 (2001): 215–32.

——— . "Rhetoric, Cognition, and Ideology in Anna Laetitia Barbauld's 1781 *Hymns in Prose for Children*." *Poetics Today* 23 (2001): 231–59.

——— . "Richardson's *Clarissa* and a Theory of Mind." In *The Work of Fiction: Cognition, Culture, and Complexity*, edited by Ellen Spolsky and Alan Richardson. Aldershot: Ashgate Press, 2004.

4

PSYCHOANALYTIC THEORY AND CRITICISM

The Unconscious is structured like a language. — JACQUES LACAN

Oedipus, blind, was on the path to oracular godhood, and the strong poets have followed him by transforming their blindness towards their precursors into the revisionary insights of their own work. — HAROLD BLOOM

The analyst . . . accepts the text and puts all his effort and desire, his passion and personal virtuosity, into reciting it, while remaining indifferent to the events that he enacts. This "indifference," called "benevolent neutrality," is the modest toga with which we cover our interpretive desire. Yet by shedding it, by implicating ourselves, we bring to life, to meaning, the dead discourses . . . which summon us. — JULIA KRISTEVA

Because Sigmund Freud once acknowledged that most of his discoveries about the unconscious mind had been anticipated by the poets and artists of the past, it should not be surprising that the light of depth psychology has long been trained upon literature in an effort to explain its origins, character, and effects. While Freud's own reflections on literature are included in Part One of this book, this chapter contains essays by followers of Freud who, like Peter Brooks, have discovered new ways of using Freudian theory to understand the psychological significance of literary form, or who, like Harold Bloom, have used Freud's doctrines as an enabling metaphor for building a new theory of literature. It also contains essays by Jacques Lacan, the French psychoanalyst whose recasting of Freud's ideas in a new semiotic form has done so much to revitalize our thinking about language and the mind, and by followers and revisers of Lacan, like Laura Mulvey, Slavoj Žižek, and Julia Kristeva who can help us to understand both the powers of Lacan's thought and its limitations.

Freud's ideas originated not in the ivory tower of theory but in his Vienna consulting room, where he practiced as a neurologist specializing in the treatment of hysteria. Only after experimenting with various physical cures did Freud come to believe that many of his patients' symptoms were caused by something less tangible.

At first he hypothesized that hysteria was always a delayed psychosomatic reaction to a real trauma, like childhood rape or incest; eventually, however, he concluded that the cause was the patient's own incestuous desires, desires so unacceptable that they could not be admitted to consciousness but were instead repressed and held in the unconscious, emerging as symptoms in later life.

In Freud's original scheme, the unconscious was part of a system consisting of (1) the conscious mind; (2) the preconscious mind, which included anything on which attention was not currently focused, including forgotten memories and thoughts that could with effort be brought back up into consciousness; and (3) the unconscious itself, whose workings were not directly available to consciousness. The evidence for the existence of the unconscious, as well as the sense of its contents, comes from dreams and fantasies and from *parapraxes* (meaningful mistakes) — slips of the tongue, pen, or memory — that also reveal repressed desires and fears. In the original formulation, the unconscious was a realm of energies, generated by the instincts or drives, focusing and binding onto objects *(cathexis),* and being diverted from their goals. Two major drives function in the unconscious: the sexual drive *(libido),* which aims at pleasure, and the aggressive drive, which aims at destruction. These drives are generally fused, and often the term *libido* is used for both.

In the course of infancy and childhood, the libido is focused on different parts of the body *(erogenous zones),* starting with the mouth in early infancy and shifting to include the anus around the second year and the genitals in the third year. These are the oral, anal, and phallic phases of what is termed *infantile sexuality,* and whether or not it feels appropriate to use the term *sexual* for the pleasure infants get from sucking on their thumbs (or adults from smoking), it is clearly a drive, and one that has to do with pleasure rather than with nourishment or any other obviously physiological mechanism.

As Freud elaborated his notion of a mind within the mind, the unconscious was transformed from a simple, dark cave of repression into a complex transactional world. In his later, "topographical" formulation of the unconscious (1923), Freud theorized a polity inhabited in earliest infancy only by the *id* (the location of the drives). As the infant becomes socialized, however, the direct satisfaction of the drives is no longer possible. Most of us gradually learn to eat and eliminate wastes at socially appropriate times and to refrain from grabbing the man or woman we want and forcibly eliminating our rivals. Thus the unconscious develops as the battleground between the pleasure principle — the desire to gratify impulses immediately — and the reality principle, which controls these impulses for the sake of higher social values.

Part of this learning takes the form of the suppression or redirection of our unconscious drives: The libido is opposed by alternative energies or shifted to a more appropriate object or aim or occasion. These shiftings of the libido are called *defenses,* and their operation is the function of a differentiated part of the unconscious, the *ego.* One of the major defenses against the power of the drives is *repression,* which Freud discovered in his patients, but there are many others as well. Among those most often occurring in literature are *projection* (ascribing an impulse of one's own to someone else) and *symbolization* (shifting the object of a drive to something else that can stand as a metaphorical or metonymic substitute for it).

Freud used the term "primary process" to refer to the direct work of libido-energy within the unconscious — primary because it is how psychic energy functions before the development of the ego. It is characterized by the instantaneous gratification of impulses or their rapid rechanneling into other, similar activities. The person who cannot express anger at work but shouts at his or her spouse at home is engaging in "primary process thinking." The term "secondary process" denotes the working of the mature ego, which might channel the energy of inexpressible anger at the boss into doing a better job at work — or finding a more satisfying career.

The third part of the unconscious is called the *superego*, which begins to form during childhood as a result of the Oedipus complex, one of the most powerfully determinative elements in the growth of the child. The Oedipus complex begins in a late phase of infantile sexuality, between the child's third and sixth year, and it takes a different form in males than it does in females. Boys and girls together begin life relating more powerfully to the mother than to the father, and both sexes wish to possess the mother exclusively. They also begin to sense that their claim to exclusive attention is thwarted by the mother's attention to the father, and, already in the phallic stage in which the genitals have become an erogenous zone, they connect that attention to the sexual activities that mother and father participate in and from which they are excluded. The result is a murderous rage against the father (and any other siblings who may be potential competitors) and a desire to possess the mother. (There is also a rage against the mother for permitting the primacy of the father.) Many things keep this rage from being acted out, including feelings of love for the father, dependency on him, and fear of loss of approval or retaliation for aggressive behavior.

Where the Oedipus complex differs in boys and girls is in the functioning of the related *castration complex*. Boys know from observing their own bodies and those of their fathers that they have a penis but that some people (including their mother) do not. Freud theorized that during the Oedipal rivalry, boys fantasize that punishment for their rage will take the form of the loss of the penis. Fear of this leads the boy to repress his rage and desire. In a successful Oedipal outcome, the boy learns to identify with the father in the hope of someday possessing a woman like his mother. In girls, the castration complex does not take the form of *anxiety,* because their lack of a penis suggests that the dreaded castration has already occurred, as it has to the desired mother as well. The result is a frustrated rage in which the girl shifts her sexual desire from the mother to the father (who possesses the penis she wants), and then, when her sexual advances to the father are opposed, begins to identify with the mother in order eventually to possess another man like the father.

The process, as Freud theorized it, is like so many love affairs, long and painful; it involves not only frustration and repression of desires but the turning of desire against itself in the form of self-criticism, self-punishment, and even self-hatred. The conflict generates the moralist of the unconscious, the superego, which is itself divided into the ego-ideal, the repository of images of perfection against which the child (and later the adult) will unhappily compare him- or herself, and the conscience, where approval and disapproval of one's actions are registered. It must be remembered, of course, that Freud's conscience is part of the unconscious, and its work of judgment and self-punishment takes the form of irrational feelings of guilt and unworthiness, and neurotic behavior against which the ego must make defenses as surely as it does against the id.

The final topographical configuration of the unconscious as id, superego, and ego may seem rather like Plato's tripartite soul, mythologized in the *Phaedrus* as Evil Horse, Good Horse, and Charioteer, which may reflect Plato's intuitive sense of the unconscious as well as Freud's own classical education.

STYLES OF FREUDIAN CRITICISM

Traditionally, there have been three stages at which psychoanalysis may enter the study of the literary work: We can examine the mind of the author, the minds of the author's characters, and our own minds as we read the text. Though Freud concludes his essay on "Creative Writers and Daydreaming" (see p. 509) with the suggestion that artistic works allow the audience to revel in their own forbidden fantasies, his focus is primarily on the text as the fantasy-construct of the artist. And there is a long tradition of Freudian criticism that seeks in the text for the buried motives and hidden neurotic conflicts that generated the writer's art. One widely admired study of this sort is Frederick C. Crews's *The Sins of the Fathers: Hawthorne's Psychological Themes* (1966), which examines the tales of the 1840s for the different ways in which they embody the unresolved Oedipus complex suggested by what we know of Hawthorne's youth and manhood. Hawthorne provided a great deal of material for such a study in his private diaries, and biographers began their work soon after his death. The hazards of doing psychoanalytic criticism in this mode are inversely proportional to the amount of material available on the author's life and private thoughts. It is never completely safe to guess at the psychic significance of a work of art, even that of a candid living author, and for some major writers (like Chaucer and Shakespeare), we have only the most minimal sense of what their private lives may have been like, so that psychoanalytic criticism in this mode must be mere speculation.

After the author, we can analyze the characters. This has also been a popular mode of criticism, beginning with *Hamlet and Oedipus* by Freud's disciple and biographer, Ernest Jones, who interpreted Hamlet's problematic hesitation to slay Claudius as stemming from an identification with his uncle, since Hamlet, too, wished to kill the elder Hamlet and marry Gertrude. It is tempting to analyze characters whom we see rendered with telling truth both internally and externally, but, in fact, the hazards of speculation about characters are even greater than about authors. Although Hamlet's actions and language reveal a great deal about him, all we will ever know is contained in the four thousand lines of Shakespeare's play.

Another problem stems from the fact that characters are both more and less than real persons. While some aspects of characters have a *mimetic* function (the representation of human action and motivation), others have primarily *textual* functions (the revelation — or concealment — of information to an audience), which has no precise parallel in life.[1] The contradictions in Hamlet's character may result from the

[1]One should remember that though literary characters are not the same as real persons, real persons in the masks they present to the world often resemble literary characters.

psychic complexities Shakespeare imagined, but they also result from the fact that Hamlet is an agent in a tragic drama with a highly developed system of conventions. An additional problem of psychoanalytic interpretation is whether a character's degree of self-awareness is to be seen as a psychological "fact" or an unintended consequence of the character's textual function. One might raise this question about James Bryan's discussion of J. D. Salinger's *The Catcher in the Rye* (1974), in which Holden Caulfield's maladjustment is ascribed to his repressed incestuous desires for his prepubescent sister Phoebe. The material on which Bryan bases his interpretation comes directly from Holden, whose only mildly embarrassed awareness of his sister's sexiness argues against rather than for Bryan's diagnosis of neurotic repression.[2]

It is tempting to seek in psychoanalysis the secret of a text, but it can be more illuminating to reverse the explanation and to look to literature, as Freud himself did, for clarifications of psychology. Such an approach is exemplified in Samuel Alexander's discussion (1939) of the *Henry IV* plays, which claims that they portray the growth of the ego (Prince Hal), resisting the id's blandishments of immediate gratification (Falstaff), rejecting also the superego's repression (the Chief Justice), mastering phallic desire (Hotspur), and reconciling his rivalry with the father (King Henry) before assuming the crown of adulthood.

Since authors may not provide much material for the would-be analyst and, since characters are not real persons, it would seem that the safest form of psychoanalytic criticism is the analysis of the audience. The readers' gaze into their own unconscious responses to literature is limited only by their insight into their own psychic processes. In the hands of Norman Holland and David Bleich this has produced a reader-response mode of analytic criticism (see the introduction to Reader-Response Theory, p. 962). The questions that tend to be raised about methods like those of Holland and Bleich have less to do with the tact and accuracy of their findings than with their subjectivity. If readers find anal imagery in a poem, are they revealing its author's fixations or only their own? Two possible answers result, depending on whether the analytic critic believes in the objective existence of a "text" to be analyzed. Those who do believe, like David Bleich or Norman Holland in his early phase, have replied that in the first place, *all* criticism is necessarily subjective, and the personal character of analytic criticism is only more honestly and explicitly so; and that in the second place, idiosyncratic readings can be identified and corrected by the usual forms of reality-testing, through self-examination and self-analysis and through exposure to debate with others. Those who do not, like Holland in his later phase (*5 Readers Reading* [1975] and thereafter), would reply that the question, in the form in which it was posed, is meaningless. The text has no meaning before it is read, and there can be no distinction between what is "in" the text and what is "in" the reader.

Author, character, and audience usually exhaust the spectrum of Freudian criticism. A fourth alternative has been proposed by Peter Brooks in *Reading for the Plot*

---

[2]James Bryan, "The Psychological Structure of *The Catcher in the Rye*," *PMLA* 89 (1974): 1065–74.

(1984). In its central chapter, "Freud's Masterplot" reprinted in this chapter, Brooks discusses *Beyond the Pleasure Principle* (1920), that ambiguous late treatise in which Freud examines the *repetition-compulsion,* a neurotic form of behavior that substitutes repetition for remembrance when a memory is too distressing for repression to overcome. Freud finds that he cannot account for the excruciating manifestations of the repetition-compulsion on the basis of the pleasure principle. He is forced to theorize that it is the product of a death-drive, which balances the life-drive of libido. For Brooks, the repetition-compulsion is the central motif of literature. Repetition not only sets the conditions of narrative (one thinks of fairy tales, in which the same situation recurs three times), but it is also basic, through rhyme, refrains, and thematic devices, to poetry. Brooks reads *Beyond the Pleasure Principle* "as a text about textuality" in which "plot mediates meanings within the contradictory human world of the eternal and the mortal. Freud's masterplot speaks of the temporality of desire, and speaks to our very desire for fictional plots."

A more metaphorical variety of Freudian criticism is that of Harold Bloom, who begins with the notion that literary influence is analogous to paternity. Weak poets may merely copy their forebears, but for strong poets of the post-Romantic era, Bloom expects an Oedipal rivalry between the younger "ephebe" and the earlier strong poet he has chosen as his artistic "father." The "son" needs metaphorically to kill or castrate the "father" to make room for his own adult life, and he does so by creatively *misreading* his predecessor in ways that necessitate his own corrective labors. Bloom's theory is not simple, and he posits a vast repertoire of ways in which the younger "ephebe" can perform this liberating act of misprision. Bloom's work has not only proved influential in itself, it has also inspired imitation and challenge. In *The Madwoman in the Attic* (1979), Sandra Gilbert and Susan Gubar have appropriated Bloom's method for their feminist purposes. In effect, they discuss how Bloom's question must be adapted when talking of *women* writers and the Fathers who would seem to exclude them from the succession by reason of their sex, and the special anxiety of authorship women suffer, which can be overcome, at least in part, by participation in the powerful sisterhood of the female literary tradition (see Feminist Criticism, p. 1502).

LACAN

The revisions to Freudian theory of Jacques Lacan, the French psychoanalyst whose thought has had such a broad influence on literary theory since the 1960s through seminars attended by Parisian intellectuals — including Louis Althusser, Michel Foucault, Paul Ricoeur, Roland Barthes, and Julia Kristeva — can only be discussed briefly. His ideas are still unfamiliar to many practicing American psychoanalysts, perhaps because Lacan largely jettisoned the therapeutic model of psychoanalysis leading to the cure of symptoms, considering it a branch more of philosophy than of medicine. Of course, while Lacan deviated from the mainstream of psychoanalytic thought and was expelled from the International Psychoanalytic Association, he believed himself to be returning to Freud rather than departing from him.

Where Freud views the mechanisms of the unconscious as generated by libido (sexual energy) in a transactional system resembling that of thermodynamics, Lacan centers the theory of the unconscious on the sense within us of something *absent*.[3] The sense of absence can take the form of mere lack *(manque)* or need *(besoin)*, which force the psyche to make demands, or it can take the higher form of desire *(désir)*. It is in the true desire — for an object that is itself conscious and can desire us in return — that the higher forms of self-consciousness arise. (This dialectic of desire Lacan took not from Freud but from Hegel's *Phenomenology of Spirit,* 1807.) Lacan's term for the universal symbol, or signifier of desire is the *Phallus.* It is important not to confuse the Phallus in this sense with the male sexual organ, the penis. *Both* sexes experience the absence of and desire for the Phallus — which may be one reason Lacan's restructuring of Freud has appealed to feminists like Hélène Cixous and Luce Irigaray.

This revision of Freud shifts the description of mental processes from a purely biological model to a semiotic one. Freud, for instance, discusses the first phase of childhood as the oral phase, in which the child's pleasure come largely from suckling; the anal phase follows, when the child learns to control and to enjoy controlling the elimination of feces. In Lacan, the analogue of the oral phase is the Mirror-Stage, from six to eighteen months, in which the child's image of its bodily self changes from mere formlessness and fragmentation to a jubilant identification with the unified shape it can see in the mirror. During this development, the child experiences itself as "le Désir de la Mère," the desire of the mother in both senses. The baby not only knows it needs its mother but also feels itself to be what completes and fulfills the mother (the Phallus). Within this phase of development there is no unconscious, because there is nothing to repress and no way to repress it. From this phase Lacan derives the psychic field of the Imaginary, which continues into adult life, where the sense of reality is grasped purely as images and fantasies of the fulfillment of desire.

Repression and the unconscious arrive together with the insertion of the child into language, around eighteen months, when Freud's anal stage begins. As the child learns the names of things, its desires are no longer met automatically; the child finds that it must ask for what it wants and that it can no longer ask for things that do not have names. As the child learns to ask for a signified by pronouncing a signifier, it learns that one thing can symbolize another. As Muller and Richardson have put it, "from this point on the child's desire, like an endless quest for a lost paradise, must be channelled like an underground river through the subterranean passageways of the symbolic order, which make it possible that things be present in their absence in some ways through words."[4] Now desires can be repressed, and the child can ask for something that metaphorically or metonymically replaces the desired object. Lacan punningly called this stage of development "le Nom-du-Père": "the Name-of-the-Father," which, in French, is pronounced like "the no-of-the-Father"; for language

[3]Like the deconstructionist Jacques Derrida and the Marxist Louis Althusser, whom he influenced, Lacan subscribes to a metaphysic based on *absence* rather than one based on *presence.*

[4]John P. Muller and William J. Richardson, *Lacan and Language: A Reader's Guide to Écrits* (New York: International Universities Press, 1982), p. 23.

is only the first of the negations and subjections to law that will now begin to affect the child. The child has entered what Lacan calls the field of the Symbolic.

A third Lacanian field, less discussed in his writings than the others, is that of the Real. By this Lacan seems to mean those incomprehensible aspects of experience that exist beyond the grasp of images and symbols through which we think and constitute our reality. The Real functions rather like the noumena in Kant (see pp. 320–21). Lacan recognizes that adult humans are always inscribed within language, but he does not suggest that language must thereby constitute the ultimate reality.

Since in Lacan's dialectic of desire one object may symbolize another, which is a substitute for still another, Lacan has said that "the unconscious is structured like a language." Lacan derives his ideas of language and the unconscious not from Freud but from one of the fathers of semiotics, Ferdinand de Saussure, as he was interpreted by the structuralist anthropologist Claude Lévi-Strauss. Lévi-Strauss considered the unconscious not as "the repository of a unique history which makes each of us an irreplaceable being" but rather as "reducible to a function — the symbolic function," which in turn was merely "the aggregate of the laws" of language.[5]

The primary laws of language in structural linguistics are those of the selection and combination of primary basic elements.[6] Metaphor is a mode of symbolization in which one thing is signified by another that is like it, that is part of the same paradigmatic class. And Lacan saw metaphor as equivalent to the Freudian defense of condensation (in which one symbol becomes the substitute for a whole series of associations). Metonymy is a mode of symbolization in which one thing is signified by another that is associated with it but not of the same class — a syntagmatic relationship — which Lacan regarded as equivalent to Freudian displacement. Because most of the Freudian defenses could be read as versions either of condensation or displacement, it appears that unconscious psychic mechanisms operate like linguistic tropes. On the other hand, we should not look within Lacan's linguistic psychology for anything like the hierarchical structure imposed on the elements of language by a syntax.[7]

If the unconscious is like a language, it is one characterized as a foreign tongue: "the discourse of the Other." What Lacan means by this is not clear or simple. Since in Lacan's thought the original Other is the father, the unconscious is Other in its origins — in the *Nom-du-Père*. But the unconscious is also the residence of alterity and alienation within ourselves, the Other to whom we must speak and whom we hear speaking in our internal dialogue. In treating the unconscious as a language rather

<hr>

[5]Claude Lévi-Strauss, "The Effectiveness of Symbols," in *Structural Anthropology* (New York: Anchor Books, 1967), p. 198.

[6]Technically these are called paradigmatic and syntagmatic relationships and are discussed at greater length in the introduction to Chapter 2, Structuralism, Semiotics, and Deconstruction.

[7]This gap may betoken a blind spot in Lacan's use of linguistics. Much of the French theory that is ultimately based on Saussure (Lacan, Derrida, Althusser), seems trapped in the limitations of structural linguistics, a rigid schema of polarized differences that was better able to explain the phonology and morphology of words than the hierarchical reorderings of grammar. If Lacan regretted that Freud's conception of language had been impoverished by the state of linguistics in his time, we may regret that Lacan was not exposed to the revolution in syntactic theory that began with Zellig Harris and Noam Chomsky.

than a polity, Lacan eliminates the notion of the ego as a homunculus inside our-selves, constantly defending itself against the depredations of the id. What he leaves in its place is far less solid and reified. The ego is an Imaginary construct, a false image of identity and wholeness; but the ego is less important to Lacan than the sub-ject, and the subject is simply the fluid position from which an "I" speaks and the signification of desire takes place. The subject is not entirely effaced, but it is decen-tered from a privileged spot to that of a function of language.

Like Freud, Lacan approached literature primarily as material that, properly interpreted, illustrated the major concepts of his psychology. He gave seminars on "Desire and the Interpretation of Desire in *Hamlet*"[8]; and the somewhat more acces-sible "Seminar on 'The Purloined Letter.' "[9] The latter essay takes off from a strictly Freudian account of Poe's "The Purloined Letter" by the analyst Marie Bonaparte, who, noting the resemblances between the detective Dupin and his quarry, the Minister D., suggested that the latter was a father figure and analyzed the story as an Oedipal triangle in which Dupin succeeds in destroying the father/minister for the sake of the mother/queen. Lacan finds that the resemblances and repetitions, once he starts to look, go much further than this, and involve the author — and the reader — in the Lacanian dialectic of desire.

Lacan's indirect influence on criticism has been considerable, primarily because his psychology has affected the philosophy and literary theory of the many French intellectuals who attended his seminars (and at a further remove, British and American scholars influenced by the French, as Fredric Jameson has been influenced by Althusser). But a strain of direct Lacanian criticism also began to appear in the 1980s, in separate essays and in collections such as those edited by Shoshana Felman (1981) and Robert Con Davis (1983). Many of these works have taken the form of interpenetrative readings of Lacan and a literary text, which inevitably find the basic themes of Lacan's psychology within the text. Perhaps this is a workable compromise while Lacan's ideas are still relatively unfamiliar, but one suspects that, like Lacanian analysis itself, Lacanian criticism will be centered intensively on the Word and the chains of association that are developed within the text.

Three complete selections from Lacan are reprinted in this chapter. "The Mirror Stage," already alluded to above, presents Lacan's meditations on the epoch-making moment when the developing child experiences the Aha! moment, recognizing that whole, complete individual in the mirror as itself. More occurs than the inception of the Imaginary realm of psychic experience. For without that moment, Lacan sug-gests, we would tumble into the terrifying world of psychasthenia, where psychotics who have lost their ontological anchors, who do not know who or where they are, experience physical space as a devouring threat. On the other side, however, Lacan would have us recollect that this recognition is, like so many developmental moves, a *méconnaissance*, a misrecognition. For the truth is that, despite the wholeness that

[8]Published 1977 in *Yale French Studies* 55/56, and reprinted in Shoshana Felman's *Literature and Psychoanalysis: The Question of Reading: Otherwise* (Baltimore: Johns Hopkins University Press, 1981).
[9]Published in the French edition of *Écrits* and translated by Jeffrey Mehlman in *Yale French Studies* 47/48 (1966).

the mirror promises, we are not unitary selves, nor are we conscious of everything going on in our interior lives. "The Mirror Stage" thus concludes with a series of swipes at Jean-Paul Sartre, and other existentialists, whose arguments about the *Pour-Soi* and the *En-Soi* (see p. 659) presume that human selves are Real rather than Imaginary constructs.

The second selection is "The Agency of the Letter in the Unconscious or Reason since Freud." If "The Mirror Stage" is about the inception of the Imaginary, this selection is about the transactional workings of the Symbolic realm, particularly Lacan's analysis of metaphor and metonymy as tropes for the ego defenses Freud called displacement and condensation. Freud was well aware of this connection (see p. 498), for he had made it himself. Lacan here draws further consequences, as he presents the way language constructs the subject as a decentered focus of consciousness in dialogue with the unconscious as the voice of the Other. This is one of Lacan's most central essays, first presented as a lecture to students of literature at the Sorbonne, rather than to a conclave of psychoanalysts — as was the case with "The Mirror Stage" — and it is no accident that it has become one of the most influential for Lacanian literary critics. And while nothing Lacan wrote could be called easy reading, this is one of his most difficult pieces, owing partly to Lacan's bizarrely dissociative style, partly to his semiotic terminology, and partly, particularly in this essay, to his use of "algorithms," pseudo-mathematical formulas that express complicated psychoanalytic relationships using algebraic symbols. It helps to read this essay more than once, the first time quickly to get the basic thrust, the second time slower and with greater care, to get a sense of the trees as well as the forest. Unusually extensive gloss notes have been provided where the reader is in serious danger of being led astray.

The third selection is "The Meaning of the Phallus," which is Lacan's attempt to straighten out the confusion he feels has been caused by a grotesquely overliteral misreading of Freud's view of the castration complex. This, more than anything else, along with the notion of "penis envy," led feminists to dismiss Freud as insulting to women. Indeed, it may seem insulting to both sexes to argue that children catch sight of their nude mother and come to the conclusion that she has been castrated. In the first place, Lacan clearly differentiates here between the penis, which men but not women possess, and which functions within the order of the Real, and the Phallus, which functions within the Symbolic order as the signifier of Desire, a unique transcendental signifier lacking any corresponding signified. In the first stage of the castration complex, children of both sexes respond in the same way to the realization that the Mother is incomplete in herself, that she does not possess the Phallus, since she is the subject of Desire as well as the object of the child's desires. In the second stage, however, sexual differentiation occurs, as the male child, through another *méconnaissance* (mistaken recognition), mistakes his penis for the Phallus. Realizing, however, that he only appears to possess the Phallus but does not, his sexual desire will take the form of an intense desire to recuperate his loss, to *have* the Phallus. In the female child, by contrast, the dialectic of Desire is shaped by disappointment and Lack, into a desire to *be* the Phallus. The distinction between having and being, as Lacan demonstrates, leads to an understanding of the differences between male and female sexuality, their characteristic responses to inadequacy and *aphanisis* (loss of sexual pleasure), as well of the different origins of male and female homosexuality. As we shall see in later chapters, feminism has been deeply ambivalent about Lacan and his reformulation of Freud's explanations of the Oedipus complex. Some have found the elimination of the anatomical basis of development enormously appealing, since anatomy, while not entirely eliminated as a factor, certainly is not destiny. Others have argued that Lacan's "phallologocentrism," with its valorization of the Phallus as transcendental signifier, along with its association of masculinity with reason and discourse and femininity with imagination, is as deeply flawed in the same old way as Freud.

LACAN WITH A DIFFERENCE

One feminist revision of Lacan is that of Julia Kristeva. Kristeva, born in Bulgaria, moved to Paris during the cultural thaw of 1966, where she was mentored by Roland Barthes. Kristeva's doctoral thesis, *La Révolution du langage poétique* (1974; about one third of the original was translated into English as *Revolution in Poetic Language*, 1984), marks a turning point between pure linguistics and psychoanalysis, for the book is an application of psychoanalytic theory to language and literature. Kristeva takes off from Lacan's notion of field of the Imaginary; in Lacan's terms, the Imaginary is the realm of the wordless image, informed by desire (*le désir de la mère*), and thus characterized by Lacan as feminine; whereas the field of the Symbolic, the realm of the word informed by the *nom-du-père*, is characterized as masculine, although both are obviously operative in individuals of both sexes. Nevertheless, for Lacanians literature as a Symbolic product is implicitly marked as a masculine domain.

Kristeva's feminist revision of Lacan involves substituting what she calls the Semiotic for the Imaginary. She posits that prior to its insertion into language, the infant is the site of drives (pulsions) and primary processes: "discrete quantities of energy move through the body of the subject who is not yet constituted as such."[10] These quanta of energy operate according to regulated bodily rhythms whose articulations are, like language, a signifying process, though they do not constitute a symbol system. Kristeva calls the "nonexpressive totality formed by the drives and their stases" the *chora*, after Plato's term for "an invisible and formless being which receives all things and mysteriously participates in the intelligible, and which is most incomprehensible."[11] For the child to learn language at all, the chora must be repressed. But as Terry Eagleton has put it, "the repression . . . is not total: for the semiotic can still be discerned as a kind of pulsional pressure within language itself, in tone, rhythm, the bodily and material qualities of language, but also in contradiction, meaninglessness, disruption, silence and absence."[12]

[10]Julia Kristeva, *Revolution in Poetic Language* (New York: Columbia University Press, 1984), p. 25.

[11]Plato, *Timaeus* 51 a-b (Cornford translation), in *Plato: Collected Dialogues*, ed. Edith Hamilton and Huntington Cairns (New York: Pantheon Books, 1961), p. 1178.

[12]Terry Eagleton, *Literary Theory: An Introduction* (Minneapolis: University of Minnesota Press, 1983), p. 188.

In all language, but particularly within poetic language (with its emphasis on sonority and on tropes), one may discern the irruption of the chora: Like all productions of the subject, poetic discourse is split between the pre-Oedipal Semiotic and the Oedipal Symbolic: "The very practice of art necessitates reinvesting the maternal chora so that it transgresses the symbolic order."[13] The "revolution" to which Kristeva's title refers has to do with this "transgression": The semiotic always subverts the symbolic and sometimes, especially in poetic discourse, the semiotic manages to overrun the symbolic and to rule the signifying process.

The key difference is that where Lacan conceives of the Imaginary and the Symbolic as gendered binaries, the former non-linguistic and feminine, the latter linguistic and masculine, Kristeva's terms are not stark dichotomies. Her Semiotic field is not mute image but rather operates as a continual pressure upon language; nor is it gendered exclusively as feminine either. As Toril Moi puts it, the image of the pre-Oedipal mother, with whom Kristeva locates the semiotic field, "looms as large for baby boys as for baby girls" and thus "cannot be reduced to an example of 'femininity' for the simple reason that the opposition between feminine and masculine does not exist in pre-Oedipality."[14] Indeed, Kristeva's applications of her theory about the literary operations of the "semiotic" in *La Révolution du langage poétique* were texts by male poets, such as Lautréamont, Mallarmé, and Artaud.

Kristeva's later study, *Pouvoirs de l'horreur* (1980; translated as *Powers of Horror: An Essay on Abjection*, 1982), centers on the concept of abjection, an affect that includes physical disgust, spiritual repulsion, and religious renunciation. For Kristeva, the origin of abjection is coterminous with the origin of the self when the infant separates as an individual from the pre-Oedipal mother. It is the obverse side of the pleasure the infant takes in fusion with the mother's body; in this moment of abjection Kristeva discovers the sources of fetish and taboo, and, more generally, of language and culture. She explores the social ramifications of abjection in Eastern and Western societies, but her primary interest is the place of women — as objects of disgust and of religious taboo. Kristeva's psychoanalytic approach — Lacanian with a difference—also informs her feminist theory, such as the essay "Women's Time," which appears in full in Chapter 7.

GENDERING THE GAZE

But it is possible to write Lacanian criticism that is feminist without necessarily revising Lacan. One feminist critic who uses Lacanian psychoanalysis to expose the patriarchal basis of Hollywood cinema is Laura Mulvey, whose famous essay "Visual Pleasure and Narrative Cinema" (1975), reprinted here, has inspired not only an entire school of film theory, but an approach to literature in which narrative point of view, the seeing eye of the text and its reader, is substituted for the gaze of

[13]Kristeva, *Revolution in Poetic Language*, p. 102.
[14]Toril Moi, *Sexual/Textual Politics* (New York: Methuen, 1985), p. 165.

the camera and the spectator. In a sense the issues raised by such reader-oriented feminists as Judith Fetterley and Patrocinio Schweickart connect with Mulvey's analysis of the psychology of the reader as split between identification with the (usually female) object of the gaze of desire and identification with the (usually male) subject who functions as the protagonist of the narrative.[15]

Mulvey believes that the split psychodynamics between the male subject and female object is intractable within narrative film, whose drive from beginning through middle to end must turn on an erotics of desire and frustration.[16] She recommends as the only envisageable feminist solution the rejection of narrative itself. Her feminist heroes, like Chantal Akerman, are independent filmmakers who follow an aesthetic — pioneered by Bertolt Brecht in the theater and Jean-Luc Godard in film — of breaking the spectator's engagement with protagonists within plots and making discovery rather than pleasure the object of the film experience. Such an asceticism inevitably leads to a division between the commercial movies that define contemporary culture and an avant-garde cinema of ideas whose major audience, ironically, comprises the academics and intellectuals already converted to those ideas. Teresa de Lauretis, in *Alice Doesn't* (1984), rejects the hopelessness of Mulvey's conclusion, and explicates how women might "construct the terms of reference of another measure of desire and the conditions of visibility for another social subject" (155). Mulvey, too, has had second thoughts about the use being made of her work.

One also wonders, with a distance of more than twenty years from Mulvey's groundbreaking essay, whether her distinction between male as subject and female as passive object of the gaze may have been based too exclusively on the "classic cinema" of directors like Hitchcock and von Sternberg, who were notoriously obsessed with their leading ladies. The blockbuster films of the 1990s continue to show objects of voyeurism, but our gaze is often focused on male actors such as Arnold Schwartzenegger and Bruce Willis rather than on female icons comparable to Marlene Dietrich and Kim Novak. Have the postfeminist nineties created a new female-oriented cinema, where the erotic gaze of desire has shifted to sweaty leading men? Or has popular culture merely found new female objects of the gaze such as the supermodel, who can inspire desire without narrative? Minimally, it would seem that the classic split between the male subject and female object of the gaze

---

[15]Judith Fetterley has given the name "immasculation" to the process whereby female readers are forced to identify with male authors and characters, and thus with patriarchal ideology; she suggests that one answer is to become a "resisting reader": to read against the grain of the text when it asks one to reject one's own femininity (see pp. 1040–41). Patrocinio Schweickart in "Reading Ourselves" gives some support to this strategy but argues that it may go too far, since at least some androcentric texts contain what Fredric Jameson calls a "utopian moment" that can be recuperated for women by (mentally) reversing the sexes, giving the role of Subject to the female. See "Reading Ourselves: Toward a Feminist Theory of Reading," in *Gender and Reading: Essays on Readers Texts and Contexts,* ed. Elizabeth Flynn and Patrocinio P. Schweickart (Baltimore: Johns Hopkins University Press, 1986), pp. 1–62.

[16]For a fuller explanation of this erotics of plot, see Peter Brooks's "Freud's Masterplot," p. 1161.

has broken down within contemporary popular film, and that now *either* a Demi Moore *or* a Bruce Willis can be either the *subject* or the *object* of the gaze. The Oedipal agon continues to be the basic fantasy underlying film plots, but the male version of the conflict is featured less exclusively than it used to be, and where it is present, it can often operate unencumbered by obsessive heterosexual erotics.[17]

ŽIŽEK: LACAN MEETS LENIN

Perhaps the most approachable, certainly the most enjoyable, practitioner of the Lacanian approach to literature and culture is Slavoj Žižek, a Slovenian theorist who writes all his books (and he has written dozens, at this point) in a racy colloquial English, and who has a genuine gift for explaining difficult psychoanalytical concepts by finding a startling and illuminating metaphor from ordinary experience. He illustrates the Lacanian *objet petit a*, for example, by comparing it with the little toy inside those chocolate eggs one buys for children, and imagining the child saying to the egg: "I love you, but inexplicably I love something inside of you more than you, and therefore I destroy you." Žižek's books tend to be readings of texts rather than philosophical tomes, and the texts are usually films and popular literature, including the Sherlock Holmes detective stories, although he knows the canon of world literature as well as anyone else writing today, and his readings are genuinely filled with surprises, like those chocolate eggs.

A democratic liberal, with an anarchistic streak, Žižek finds himself deeply depressed by the universal triumph of global capitalism because it has robbed humanity, all over the world, of any sense that political progress and change is possible. When offered a government post just after Slovenia became an independent state, Žižek refused to be minister of culture or education, but offered, perhaps seriously, to become head of the secret police. This is because Žižek combines Lacanian theory with his own brand of Marxism, one that includes a certain nostalgia for the totalitarian state. For Žižek, a repressive government focuses people's lives and gives them hope, even if it is only the hope of overthrowing it. With the downfall of the Soviet state and the decay of Marxist governments worldwide, Žižek, a lifelong atheist, has turned in the direction of Christianity, which interests him as yet another vision demanding absolute obedience. For Žižek, any belief system that provides mankind with a Sublime Object of Ideology is better than none.

---

[17]More is going on here than the traditional split between subject and object of the gaze. The close relationships between oddly matched "buddies" in contemporary action films (such as Bruce Willis and Samuel L. Jackson in *Die Hard with a Vengeance* or Sean Connery and Nicolas Cage in *The Rock*) are often triangulated through their mutual concern about one or both men's relationships with a woman (wife, girlfriend, daughter) who is either kept offscreen or relegated to a bit part. Eve Kosofsky Sedgwick's discussion of male homosocial desire and how it can be handled so as to defuse its erotic potential clearly applies to more than the nineteenth-century narratives she treats in *Between Men*. See the discussion of Sedgwick, p. 1620.

Selected Bibliography

Bersani, Leo. *The Freudian Body: Psychoanalysis and Art*. New York: Columbia University Press, 1985.

Bloom, Harold. *The Anxiety of Influence*. New York: Oxford University Press, 1975.

———. *A Map of Misreading*. Oxford and New York: Oxford University Press, 1980.

———. *Agon: Toward a Theory of Revisionism*. Oxford and New York: Oxford University Press, 1982.

Bonaparte, Marie. *The Life and Works of Edgar Allan Poe*. 1933; London: Imago, 1949.

Boothby, Richard. *Death and Desire: Psychoanalytic Theory in Lacan's Return to Freud*. New York: Routledge, 1991.

Bowie, Malcolm. *Freud, Proust, and Lacan: Theory as Fiction*. New York: Cambridge University Press, 1987.

———. *Lacan*. Cambridge: Harvard University Press, 1991.

Brennan, Teresa. *History after Lacan*. New York: Routledge, 1991.

———. *The Interpretation of the Flesh: Freud and Femininity*. New York: Routledge, 1994.

Brenner, Charles. *An Elementary Textbook of Psychoanalysis*. New York: Anchor Books, 1974.

Brooks, Peter. *Reading for the Plot*. New York: Knopf, 1984.

Burgoyne, Bernard. *The Klein-Lacan Dialogue*. New York: Other Press, 1999.

Clément, Catherine. *The Lives and Legends of Jacques Lacan*. New York: Columbia University Press, 1983.

Crews, Frederick. *The Sins of the Fathers: Hawthorne's Psychological Themes*. New York: Oxford University Press, 1966.

———. *Out of My System: Psychology, Ideology and Critical Method*. New York: Oxford University Press, 1976.

Davis, Robert Con, ed. *Lacan and Narration: The Psychoanalytic Difference in Narrative Theory*. Baltimore: Johns Hopkins University Press, 1983.

Deleuze, Gilles, and Félix Guattari. *Anti-Oedipus: Capitalism and Schizophrenia*, trans. Robert Hurley, Mark Seem, and Helen R. Lane. Preface by Michel Foucault. Minneapolis: University of Minnesota Press, 1983.

———. *Kafka: Towards a Minor Literature*. Minneapolis: University of Minnesota Press, 1985.

Derrida, Jacques. "The Purveyor of Truth." *Yale French Studies* 52 (1975): 31–113.

Elliott, Anthony, and Stephen Frosh, eds. *Psychoanalysis in Contexts: Paths between Theory and Modern Culture*. New York: Routledge, 1995.

Felman, Shoshana. "Turning the Screw of Interpretation." *Yale French Studies* 55/56 (1977): 94–207.

———, ed. *Literature and Psychoanalysis: The Question of Reading: Otherwise*. Baltimore: Johns Hopkins University Press, 1981.

———. "Rereading Femininity." *Yale French Studies* 62 (1981): 19–44.

Freud, Anna. *The Ego and the Mechanisms of Defense*. 1936; New York: International Universities Press, 1966.

Freud, Sigmund. *The Standard Edition of the Complete Psychological Works*. 24 vols. 1940–68; London: Hogarth Press and the Institute of Psychoanalysis, 1953.

Gallop, Jane. *The Daughter's Seduction: Feminism and Psychoanalysis*. Ithaca: Cornell University Press, 1982.

———. *Reading Lacan*. Ithaca: Cornell University Press, 1984.

Gilman, Sander L., ed. *Introducing Psychoanalytic Theory*. New York: Brunner/Mazel, 1982.

Grosz, Elizabeth. *Jacques Lacan: A Feminist Introduction*. New York: Routledge, 1990.

Hartman, Geoffrey H., ed. *Psychoanalysis and the Question of the Text: Selected Papers from the English Institute.* Baltimore: Johns Hopkins University Press, 1979.

Holland, Norman N. *The Dynamics of Literary Response.* New York: Oxford University Press, 1968.

———. *Poems in Persons.* New York: Norton, 1975.

———. *5 Readers Reading.* New Haven: Yale University Press, 1975.

Johnson, Barbara. "The Frame of Reference: Poe, Lacan, Derrida." *Yale French Studies* 55/56 (1977): 457–505.

Jones, Ernest. *Hamlet and Oedipus.* New York: Doubleday, 1949.

Jung, Carl Gustav. *Complete Works.* 17 vols. Ed. Herbert Read, Michael Fordham, and Gerhard Adler. New York: Pantheon, 1953–.

Kris, Ernst. *Psychoanalytic Explorations in Art.* 1952; New York: Schocken Books, 1964.

Kristeva, Julia. *Desire in Language.* New York: Columbia University Press, 1980.

Kurzweil, Edith, and William Phillips, eds. *Literature and Psychoanalysis.* New York: Columbia University Press, 1983.

Lacan, Jacques. "The Seminar on 'The Purloined Letter.' " *Yale French Studies* 48 (1972): 39–72.

———. *Écrits: A Selection.* New York: Norton, 1977.

———. *The Seminar of Jacques Lacan,* ed. Jacques-Alain Miller. *Book I: Freud's Papers on Technique 1953–1954,* trans. John Forrester. New York and London: Norton, 1988.

———. *The Seminar of Jacques Lacan,* ed. Jacques-Alain Miller. *Book II: The Ego in Freud's Theory and in the Technique of Psychoanalysis 1954–1955,* trans. Sylvana Tomaselli. New York and London: Norton, 1988.

———. *The Seminar of Jacques Lacan,* ed. Jacques-Alain Miller. *Book III: The Psychoses 1955–1956,* trans. Russell Grigg. New York and London: Norton, 1993.

Laplanche, Jean, and Jean-Baptiste Pontalis. *The Language of Psychoanalysis.* London: Hogarth Press, 1973.

Lawrence, D. H. *Studies in Classical American Literature.* New York: Penguin, 1977.

Leader, Darian, and Judy Groves. *Introducing Lacan.* London: Icon Books, 2000.

Lesser, Simon O. *Fiction and the Unconscious.* Chicago: University of Chicago Press, 1957.

MacCannell, Juliet Flower. *Figuring Lacan: Criticism and the Cultural Unconscious.* Beckenham: Croon Helm, 1986.

Muller, John P., and William J. Richardson. *Lacan and Language: A Reader's Guide to Écrits.* New York: International Universities Press, 1982.

Mulvery, Laura. *Visual and Other Pleasures.* Basingstoke, Eng.: Macmillan, 1989.

——— *Fetishism and Curiosity.* Bloomington: Indiana University Press, 1996.

Nancy, J.-L., and P. Lacoue-Labarthe (1973). *The Title of the Letter: A Reading of Lacan,* trans. F. Raffoul and D. Pettigrew. Albany: State University of New York Press, 1992.

Rabaté, Jean-Michel, ed. *The Cambridge Companion to Lacan.* Cambridge: Cambridge University Press, 2003.

Roudinesco, Elisabeth, and Barbara Bray. *Jacques Lacan: Outline of a life, History of a System of Thought.* New York: Columbia University Press, 1997.

Shamdasani, Sonu, and Michael Munchow, eds. *Speculations after Freud: Psychoanalysis, Philosophy and Culture.* New York: Routledge, 1994.

Skura, Meredith Anne. *The Literary Use of the Psychoanalytic Process.* New Haven: Yale University Press, 1981.

Smith, Joseph H., and William Kerrigan, eds. *Interpreting Lacan.* New Haven and London: Yale University Press, 1983.

Trilling, Lionel. "Art and Neurosis" and "Freud and Literature." *The Liberal Imagination.* New York: Doubleday, 1947.

Turkle, Sherry. *Psychoanalytic Politics: Freud's French Revolution.* New York: Basic Books, 1978.

Wilden, Anthony. *The Language of the Self: The Function of Language in Psychoanalysis.* New York: Dell, 1968.

Wright, Elizabeth. *Psychoanalytic Criticism: Theory in Practice.* New York and London: Methuen, 1984.

Žižek, Slavoj. *The Sublime Object of Ideology.* New York: Verso, 1989.

———. *Looking Awry: An Introduction to Jacques Lacan through Popular Culture.* Cambridge: MIT Press, 1991.

———. *Enjoy Your Symptom! Jacques Lacan in Hollywood and Out.* New York: Routledge, 1992.

———. *The Metastases of Enjoyment.* New York: Verso, 1994.

———. *The Ticklish Subject: The Absent Center of Political Ontology.* London: Verso, 1999.

———. *The Puppet and the Dwarf: The Perverse Core of Christianity.* Cambridge: MIT Press, 2003.

Zupancic, Alenka. *Kant and Lacan: Ethics of the Real.* London: Verso, 2000.

Jacques Lacan

1901–1981

Probably the most controversial figure in French psychiatry, Jacques Marie Émile Lacan dedicated himself to getting strictly back to Freud by way of structural linguistics. An admirer of the surrealists, Lacan published his doctoral thesis on paranoid psychosis (1932). Expelled in 1953 from the International Psychoanalytic Association for unorthodox analytical practices, Lacan with Daniel Lagache, another analyst, created the Société Française de Psychoanalyse. As his theoretical positions continued to develop, Lacan and his followers went on to found the École Freudienne in Paris in 1964. The publication of his Écrits *(1966) gained Lacan international attention. Leading intellectuals flocked to his seminars, and he exercised a cryptic but powerful influence on the French cultural scene of the 1970s. Concerned that the École was losing its integrity, Lacan unilaterally dissolved it in 1980. His intention to begin a new one was unfulfilled at the time of his death from cancer the next year. Editions of Lacan available in English include selections from* Écrits *(1977);* The Language of the Self *(1968, translated and with a commentary by Anthony Wilden);* The Four Fundamental Concepts of Psychoanalysis *(1977);* Feminine Sexuality *(1982); and three volumes of* The Seminar of Jacques Lacan, *edited by Jacques-Alain Miller:* Freud's Writings on Technique 1953–1954 *(1988),* The Ego in Freud's Theory and in the Technique of Psychoanalysis 1954–55 *(1988), and* The Psychoses 1955–1956 *(1993). "The Mirror Stage as Formative of the Function of the I as Revealed in Psychoanalytic Experience," translated by Alan Sheridan, is from* Écrits: A Selection; *it was originally delivered as a lecture on July 17, 1949, to the 16th International Congress of Psychoanalysis. "The Agency of the Letter in the Unconscious, or Reason since Freud," translated by Alan Sheridan, is also* from Écrits: A Selection; an earlier version of this piece was delivered as a lecture at the Sorbonne on May 9, 1957. "The Meaning of the Phallus," translated by Jacqueline Rose, is from Feminine Sexuality: Jacques Lacan and the École Freudienne; it was originally delivered as a lecture, in German, at the Max Planck Institute in Munich in 1958.

The Mirror Stage as Formative of the Function of the I as Revealed in Psychoanalytic Experience

The conception of the mirror stage that I introduced at our last congress, thirteen years ago, has since become more or less established in the practice of the French group. However, I think it worthwhile to bring it again to your attention, especially today, for the light it sheds on the formation of the I[1] as we experience it in psychoanalysis. It is an experience that leads us to oppose any philosophy directly issuing from the *Cogito*.[2]

Some of you may recall that this conception originated in a feature of human behavior illuminated by a fact of comparative psychology. The child, at an age when he is for a time, however short, outdone by the chimpanzee in instrumental intelligence, can nevertheless already recognize as such his own image in a mirror. This recognition is indicated in the illuminative mimicry of the *Aha-Erlebnis*,[3] which Köhler sees as the expression of situational apperception, an essential stage of the act of intelligence.

This act, far from exhausting itself, as in the case of the monkey, once the image has been mastered and found empty, immediately rebounds in the case of the child in a series of gestures in which he experiences in play the relation between the movements assumed in the image and the reflected environment, and between this virtual complex and the reality it reduplicates — the child's own body, and the persons and things, around him.

This event can take place, as we have known since Baldwin, from the age of six months, and its repetition has often made me reflect upon the startling spectacle of the infant in front of the mirror. Unable as yet to walk, or even to stand up, and held tightly as he is by some support, human or artificial (what, in France, we call a "*trotte-bébé*"[4]), he nevertheless overcomes, in a flutter of jubilant activity, the obstructions of his support and, fixing his attitude in a slightly leaning-forward position, in order to hold it in his gaze, brings back an instantaneous aspect of the image.

For me, this activity retains the meaning I have given it up to the age of eighteen months. This meaning discloses a libidinal dynamism,[5] which has hitherto remained problematic, as well as an ontological structure of the human world that accords with my reflections on paranoiac knowledge.

Translated by Alan Sheridan.

[1] Standard Freudian translations usually Latinize Freud's German terms (*der Ich, das Es*, literally "the I" and "the It") into "the ego" and "the id." Lacan prefers to peel off this distancing artifact of translation.

[2] Shorthand for "cogito ergo sum," Latin for "I think, therefore I am," French philosopher René Descartes's phrase summing up his position that we have absolute knowledge of our own identity because thinking implies a thinker. Lacan's essay interrogates this relation between thinking and being.

[3] German for "aha! experience." Term used by the psychologist Wolfgang Kohler (1887–1967), known for his experiments with dogs and monkeys on animal intelligence, for the moment of insight when the mind bridges a cognitive gap.

[4] A walker.

[5] An operation of the pleasure principle.

We have only to understand the mirror stage *as an identification*,[6] in the full sense that analysis gives to the term: namely, the transformation that takes place in the subject when he assumes an image — whose predestination to this phase-effect is sufficiently indicated by the use, in analytic theory, of the ancient term *imago*.[7]

This jubilant assumption of his specular image by the child at the *infans*[8] stage, still sunk in his motor incapacity and nursling dependence, would seem to exhibit in an exemplary situation the symbolic matrix in which the *I* is precipitated in a primordial form, before it is objectified in the dialectic of identification with the other, and before language restores to it, in the universal, its function as subject.

This form would have to be called the Ideal-I,[9] if we wished to incorporate it into our usual register, in the sense that it will also be the source of secondary identifications, under which term I would place the functions of libidinal normalization. But the important point is that this form situates the agency of the ego, before its social determination, in a fictional direction, which will always remain irreducible for the individual alone, or rather, which will only rejoin the coming-into-being (*le devenir*) of the subject asymptotically,[10] whatever the success of the dialectical syntheses by which he must resolve as *I* his discordance with his own reality.

The fact is that the total form of the body by which the subject anticipates in a mirage the maturation of his power is given to him only as *Gestalt*,[11] that is to say, in an exteriority in which this form is certainly more constituent than constituted, but in which it appears to him above all in a contrasting size (*un relief de stature*) that fixes it and in a symmetry that inverts it, in contrast with the turbulent movements that the subject feels are animating him. Thus, this *Gestalt* — whose pregnancy should be regarded as bound up with the species, though its motor style remains scarcely recognizable — by these two aspects of its appearance, symbolizes the mental permanence of the *I*, at the same time as it prefigures its alienating destination; it is still pregnant with the correspondences that unite the *I* with the statue in which man projects himself, with the phantoms that dominate him, or with the automaton in which, in an ambiguous relation, the world of his own making tends to find completion.

Indeed, for the *imagos* — whose veiled faces it is our privilege to see in outline in our daily experience and in the penumbra of symbolic efficacity[12] — the mirror-image would seem to be the threshold of the visible world, if we go by the mirror disposition that the *imago of one's own body* presents in hallucinations or dreams, whether it concerns its individual features, or even its infirmities, or its object-projections; or if we observe the role of the mirror apparatus in the appearances of the *double*, in which psychical realities, however heterogeneous, are manifested.

That a *Gestalt* should be capable of formative effects in the organism is attested by a piece of biological experimentation that is itself so alien to the idea of psychical causality that it cannot bring itself to formulate its results in these terms. It nevertheless recognizes that it is a necessary

---

[6]Normally this term is used for an ego-defense, in which one identifies with someone other than oneself, but Lacan is using it for a stage in the formation of the self.

[7]Freud uses the term *imago* (Latin for image or statue) for the mental picture of a beloved parent that becomes the pattern on which the individual's loving object relations are based ("On the Universal Tendency to Debasement in the Sphere of Love"). Jung uses the term to refer to internal archetypes (such as the Anima) with whom the individual identifies. As before, Lacan applies the term to the image of the self.

[8]The Latin word means "unable to speak." Lacan is pointing to the fact that this occurs before the development of language.

[9]Throughout this article I leave in its peculiarity the translation I have adopted for Freud's *Ideal-Ich* [i.e., "je-idéal"], without further comment, other than to say that I have not maintained it since. [Lacan] The usual English term is "Ego Ideal," which in Freudian terminology forms part of the Superego.

[10]In mathematics an asymptote is a line that a curve approaches but never touches. Lacan's point is that the Imaginary sense of self created in the Mirror Stage approximates but is never identical with the Ego that is formed later through the Oedipal struggle, alluded to later in the same sentence.

[11]German for pattern.

[12]Cf. Claude Lévi-Strauss, *Structural Anthropology*, Chapter X. [Lacan] Lacan refers to the chapter ("The Effectiveness of Symbols") in which Lévi-Strauss explicitly compares psychoanalysis with the way in which a shaman, inducing a patient to re-experience the cause of her illness, cures her of it.

condition for the maturation of the gonad of the female pigeon that it should see another member of its species, of either sex; so sufficient in itself is this condition that the desired effect may be obtained merely by placing the individual within reach of the field of reflection of a mirror. Similarly, in the case of the migratory locust, the transition within a generation from the solitary to the gregarious form can be obtained by exposing the individual, at a certain stage, to the exclusively visual action of a similar image, provided it is animated by movements of a style sufficiently close to that characteristic of the species. Such facts are inscribed in an order of homeomorphic[13] identification that would itself fall within the larger question of the meaning of beauty as both formative and erogenic.[14]

But the facts of mimicry are no less instructive when conceived as cases of heteromorphic identification, in as much as they raise the problem of the signification of space for the living organism — psychological concepts hardly seem less appropriate for shedding light on these matters than ridiculous attempts to reduce them to the supposedly supreme law of adaptation. We have only to recall how Roger Caillois (who was then very young, and still fresh from his breach with the sociological school[15] in which he was trained) illuminated the subject by using the term "*legendary psychasthenia*"[16] to classify

morphological mimicry as an obsession with space in its derealizing effect.

I have myself shown in the social dialectic that structures human knowledge as paranoiac[17] why human knowledge has greater autonomy than animal knowledge in relation to the field of force of desire, but also why human knowledge is determined in that "little reality" (*ce peu de réalité*), which the Surrealists, in their restless way, saw as its limitation. These reflections lead me to recognize in the spatial captation manifested in the mirror-stage, even before the social dialectic, the effect in man of an organic insufficiency in his natural reality — in so far as any meaning can be given to the word "nature."

I am led, therefore, to regard the function of the mirror-stage as a particular case of the function of the *imago*, which is to establish a relation between the organism and its reality — or, as they say, between the *Innenwelt* and the *Umwelt*.[18]

In man, however, this relation to nature is altered by a certain dehiscence[19] at the heart of the organism, a primordial Discord betrayed by the signs of uneasiness and motor uncoordination of the neo-natal months. The objective notion of the anatomical incompleteness of the pyramidal system[20] and likewise the presence of

---

[13]Of the same form, opposed to "heteromorphic," of different form.

[14]Giving rise to sexual desire.

[15]The "sociological school" Caillois broke with was that of the Surrealists, led by André Breton, whose ultimate goal was resistance to Fascism through the liberation of the mind which would be achieved via the externalization of images from the individual unconscious.

[16]The issue Lacan is referring to here is that some psychological disturbances take the symptomatic form of a terrifying sense of dislocation, not knowing where one is, because one has disappeared into one's surroundings, like animals (e.g., chameleons, octopi) who can alter their appearance for camouflage. In "Mimicry and Legendary Psychasthenia" (*Minatoure* 7 [1935]), anthropologist Roger Caillois (1913–1978) wrote: "from the moment when it can no longer be a process of defense, mimicry can be nothing else but [a disturbance in the perception of space]. . . . There can be no doubt that the perception of space is a complex phenomenon. . . . The feeling of personality, considered as the organism's feeling of distinction from its surroundings, of the connection between

consciousness and a particular point in space, cannot fail under these conditions to be seriously undermined; one then enters into the psychology of psychasthenia, and more specifically of legendary psychasthenia, if we agree to use this name for the disturbance in the above relations between personality and space. . . . [Schizophrenics are] dispossessed souls [for whom] space seems to be a devouring force. Space pursues them, encircles them, digests them. . . . It ends by replacing them. . . . He tries to look at himself from any point whatever in space. He feels himself becoming space, dark space where things cannot be put. . . . All these expressions shed light on a single process: depersonalization by assimilation to space, i.e., what mimicry achieves morphologically in certain animal species. The magical hold (one can truly call it so without doing violence to the language) of night and obscurity, the fear of the dark, probably also has its roots in the peril in which it puts the opposition between the organism and the milieu."

[17]Cf. "Aggressivity in Psychoanalysis," p. 8 and *Écrits*, p. 180. [Lacan]

[18]*Innenwelt* is German for inner world; *Umwelt* means outer world.

[19]Natural splitting.

[20]Part of the central nervous system involved in voluntary movement.

certain humoral residues of the maternal organism confirm the view I have formulated as the fact of a real *specific prematurity of birth* in man.

It is worth noting, incidentally, that this is a fact recognized as such by embryologists, by the term *foetalization*, which determines the prevalence of the so-called superior apparatus of the neurax,[21] and especially of the cortex, which psycho-surgical operations lead us to regard as the intra-organic mirror.[22]

This development is experienced as a temporal dialectic that decisively projects the formation of the individual into history. The *mirror stage* is a drama whose internal thrust is precipitated from insufficiency to anticipation — and which manufactures for the subject, caught up in the lure of spatial identification, the succession of fantasies that extends from a fragmented body-image to a form of its totality that I shall call orthopedic[23] — and, lastly, to the assumption of the armor of an alienating identity, which will mark with its rigid structure the subject's entire mental development. Thus, to break out of the circle of the *Innenwelt* into the *Umwelt* generates the inexhaustible quadrature of the ego's verifications.[24]

This fragmented body — which term I have also introduced into our system of theoretical references — usually manifests itself in dreams when the movement of the analysis encounters a certain level of aggressive disintegration in the individual. It then appears in the form of disjointed limbs, or of those organs represented in exoscopy,[25] growing wings and taking up arms for intestinal persecutions — the very same that the visionary Hieronymus Bosch[26] has fixed, for all time, in painting, in their ascent from the fifteenth century to the imaginary zenith of modern man. But this form is even tangibly revealed at the organic level, in the lines of "fragilization" that define the anatomy of fantasy, as exhibited in the schizoid and spasmodic symptoms of hysteria.

Correlatively, the formation of the *I* is symbolized in dreams by a fortress, or a stadium — its inner arena and enclosure, surrounded by marshes and rubbish-tips, dividing it into two opposed fields of contest where the subject flounders in quest of the lofty, remote inner castle whose form (sometimes juxtaposed in the same scenario) symbolizes the id in a quite startling way. Similarly, on the mental plane, we find realized the structures of fortified works, the metaphor of which arises spontaneously, as if issuing from the symptoms themselves, to designate the mechanisms of obsessional neurosis — inversion, isolation, reduplication, cancellation and displacement.[27]

But if we were to build on these subjective givens alone — however little we free them from the condition of experience that makes us see them as partaking of the nature of a linguistic technique — our theoretical attempts would remain exposed to the charge of projecting themselves into the unthinkable of an absolute subject. This is why I have sought in the present hypothesis, grounded in a conjunction of objective data, the guiding grid for a *method of symbolic reduction*.

It establishes in the *defences of the ego* a genetic order, in accordance with the wish formulated by Miss Anna Freud, in the first part of her great work,[28] and situates (as against a frequently expressed prejudice) hysterical repression and its returns at a more archaic stage than obsessional inversion and its isolating processes, and the latter in turn as preliminary to paranoid alienation, which dates from the deflection of the specular *I* into the social *I*.

This moment in which the mirror-stage comes to an end inaugurates, by the identification with the

---

[21]Nervous system.

[22]Lacan refers to surgical experiments that allowed neurologists to "map" areas of the cerebral cortex corresponding to the different parts of the physical human body.

[23]From Greek roots meaning "straight" and "child"; Lacan is suggesting that the mirror stage enables the child to develop properly.

[24]Lacan's point is that the "reality testing" by which the ego attempts to ascertain what is appropriate relative to what is "out there," involves an impossible feat (quadrature = squaring the circle), because the mind can never actually get outside itself.

[25]Viewed from outside.

[26]Flemish painter, born Jeroen van Aken (1450–1516), whose work, like the "Hell" panel from *The Garden of Earthly Delights*, includes surrealistic imagery including animated body parts, such as Lacan has alluded to.

[27]Lacan is listing ego defenses, for which see the discussion of Freud, p. 1108.

[28]*The Ego and the Mechanisms of Defense* (1935) by Anna Freud (1895–1982).

imago of the counterpart and the drama of primordial jealousy (so well brought out by the school of Charlotte Bühler in the phenomenon of infantile *transitivism*[29]), the dialectic that will henceforth link the *I* to socially elaborated situations.

It is this moment that decisively tips the whole of human knowledge into mediatization through the desire of the other, constitutes its objects in an abstract equivalence by the co-operation of others, and turns the *I* into that apparatus for which every instinctual thrust constitutes a danger, even though it should correspond to a natural maturation — the very normalization of this maturation being henceforth dependent, in man, on a cultural mediation as exemplified, in the case of the sexual object, by the Oedipus complex.[30]

In the light of this conception, the term primary narcissism,[31] by which analytic doctrine designates the libidinal investment characteristic of that moment, reveals in those who invented it the most profound awareness of semantic latencies. But it also throws light on the dynamic opposition between this libido and the sexual libido, which the first analysts tried to define when they invoked destructive and, indeed, death instincts, in order to explain the evident connection between the narcissistic libido and the alienating function of the *I*, the aggressivity it releases in any relation to the other, even in a relation involving the most Samaritan of aid.[32]

In fact, they were encountering that existential negativity whose reality is so vigorously proclaimed by the contemporary philosophy of being and nothingness.[33]

But unfortunately that philosophy grasps negativity only within the limits of a self-sufficiency of consciousness, which, as one of its premises, links to the *méconnaissances*[34] that constitute the ego, the illusion of autonomy to which it entrusts itself. This flight of fancy, for all that it draws, to an unusual extent, on borrowings from psychoanalytic experience, culminates in the pretension of providing an existential psychoanalysis.

At the culmination of the historical effort of a society to refuse to recognize that it has any function other than the utilitarian one, and in the anxiety of the individual confronting the "concentrational"[35] form of the social bond that seems to arise to crown this effort, existentialism must be judged by the explanations it gives of the subjective impasses that have indeed resulted from it; a freedom that is never more authentic than when it is within the walls of a prison; a demand for commitment, expressing the impotence of a pure consciousness to master any situation; a voyeuristic–sadistic idealization of the sexual relation; a personality that realizes itself only in suicide; a consciousness of the other that can be satisfied only by Hegelian murder.[36]

These propositions are opposed by all our experience, in so far as it teaches us not to regard

---

[29]Psychologist Charlotte Bühler (1893–1974) observed and called by this name a behavior whereby a child does not distinguish between its own experience and that of another (e.g., crying when another child has been hurt).

[30]Lacan's point is that the "I" formed by the mirror stage is always already an Other (seen as a specular whole from the outside), and all the other Others through normal development, including the specular Father and Mother of the Oedipal struggle, take their shape by virtue of this formation.

[31]Freud's term for the exclusive investment of a small child in its own pleasures and needs. Primary narcissism is healthy, but those who do not outgrow it (in the narcissistic character disorder) direct libido exclusively toward representations of themselves.

[32]Alluding to the parable of the Good Samaritan (Luke 10:30–37), in which the Samaritan aids someone Other, an Israelite, Lacan suggests that the motive for altruism is narcissistic, in the sense that it promotes an aggrandized sense of self.

[33]Citing the title of Jean-Paul Sartre's *L'Être et le néant*, Lacan goes on to critique existentialist philosophy, which posits a self that is always present to itself, always self-aware. (Lacan, to the contrary, has all along been suggesting that the monadic "self" we are aware of is an Imaginary product of the Mirror Stage.)

[34]Mistaken recognitions (here, of the image in the mirror with the "self").

[35]"*Concentrationnaire*," an adjective coined after World War II (this article was written in 1949) to describe the life of the concentration camp. In the hands of certain writers it became, by extension, applicable to many aspects of "modern" life. [Tr.]

[36]This paragraph arranges a series of critiques of existentialism, alluding successively to Jean-Paul Sartre's story "Le Mur," his novel *La Nausée*, to *L'Age de raison*, the first volume of his trilogy *Les Chemins de la liberté*, and to Albert Camus's *L'Etranger* (in which the protagonist murders an Arab to assert his existential freedom).

the ego as centered on the *perception–conscious-ness system*,[37] or as organized by the "reality principle" — a principle that is the expression of a scientific prejudice most hostile to the dialectic of knowledge. Our experience shows that we should start instead from the *function of méconnaissance* that characterizes the ego in all its structures, so markedly articulated by Miss Anna Freud. For, if the *Verneinung*[38] represents the patent form of that function, its effects will, for the most part, remain latent, so long as they are not illuminated by some light reflected on to the level of fatality, which is where the id manifests itself.

We can thus understand the inertia characteristic of the formations of the *I*, and find there the most extensive definition of neurosis — just as the captation[39] of the subject by the situation gives us the most general formula for madness, not only the madness that lies behind the walls of asylums, but also the madness that deafens the world with its sound and fury.

[37]Freud's phrase for the conscious mind, which was only a part, and not the most important one for psychic functioning.

[38]German for denial (one of Freud's ego defenses).

[39]Literally "seizure." The captation of the "subject by the situation" suggests the fragility of the "I" — as with the schizophrenic in Caillois's description, who fades into the surroundings. But Lacan means to imply that societies too can become psychotic in this way, murdering others through a "deadening of the passions."

The sufferings of neurosis and psychosis are for us a schooling in the passions of the soul, just as the beam of the psychoanalytic scales, when we calculate the tilt of its threat to entire communities, provides us with an indication of the deadening of the passions in society.

At this junction of nature and culture, so persistently examined by modern anthropology,[40] psychoanalysis alone recognizes this knot of imaginary servitude that love must always undo again, or sever.

For such a task, we place no trust in altruistic feeling, we who lay bare the aggressivity that underlies the activity of the philanthropist, the idealist, the pedagogue, and even the reformer.

In the recourse of subject to subject that we preserve, psychoanalysis may accompany the patient to the ecstatic limit of the "*Thou art that*,"[41] in which is revealed to him the cipher of his mortal destiny, but it is not in our mere power as practitioners to bring him to that point where the real journey begins.

[40]Anthropologist Claude Lévi-Strauss had posited that the incest taboo (and hence the Oedipal struggle) lies at the boundary of nature and culture (see p. 824).

[41]The knowledge of one's own mortality. Lacan alludes to the skull often in the foreground of paintings of idyllic pastoral beauty; "thou art that" is what the skull says to the viewer.

The Agency of the Letter in the Unconscious or Reason since Freud[1]

Of Children in Swaddling Clothes

O cities of the sea, I behold in you your citizens,
women as well as men tightly bound with stout
bonds around their arms and legs by folk who will
not understand your language; and you will only be
able to give vent to your griefs and sense of loss of
liberty by making tearful complaints, and sighs, and
lamentations one to another; for those who bind
you will not understand your language nor will you
understand them.

— LEONARDO DA VINCI[2]

Although the nature of this contribution was
determined by the theme of the third volume of
La Psychanalyse,[3] I owe to what will be found
there to insert it at a point somewhere between
writing (*l'écrit*) and speech — it will be half-way
between the two.

Writing is distinguished by a prevalence of the
text in the sense that this factor of discourse will
assume in this essay a factor that makes possible
the kind of tightening up that I like in order to
leave the reader no other way out than the way in,
which I prefer to be difficult. In that sense, then,
this will not be writing.

Because I always try to provide my seminars
each time with something new, I have refrained
so far from giving such a text, with one exception,
which is not particularly outstanding in the context of the series, and which I refer to at all only
for the general level of its argument.

For the urgency that I now take as a pretext for
leaving aside such an aim only masks the difficulty that, in trying to maintain it at the level at
which I ought to present my teaching here, I

might push it too far from speech, whose very different techniques are essential to the formative
effect I seek.

That is why I have taken the expedient offered
me by the invitation to lecture to the philosophy
group of the Fédération des étudiants ès lettres[4] to
produce an adaptation suitable to what I have to
say: its necessary generality matches the exceptional character of the audience, but its sole object
encounters the collusion of their common training, a literary one, to which my title pays homage.

Indeed, how could we forget that to the end of
his days Freud constantly maintained that such a
training was the prime requisite in the formation
of analysts, and that he designated the eternal *uni-*
versitas litterarum as the ideal place for its institution.[5]

Thus my recourse (in rewriting) to the movement of the (spoken) discourse, restored to its
vitality, by showing whom I meant it for, marks
even more clearly those for whom it is not
intended.

I mean that it is not intended for those who, for
any reason whatever, in psychoanalysis, allow
their discipline to avail itself of some false identity — a fault of habit, but its effect on the mind
is such that the true identity may appear as simply
one alibi among others, a sort of refined reduplication whose implications will not be lost on the
most subtle minds.

So one observes with a certain curiosity the
beginnings of a new direction concerning symbolization and language in the *International*
Journal of Psychoanalysis, with a great many
sticky fingers leafing through the pages of Sapir

Translated by Alan Sheridan.

[1] Even the translation of Lacan's title is controversial. The
French word "instance," here translated "agency," also means
"urgency," "insistence," and "authority."

[2] *Codice Atlantico* 145. [Lacan]

[3] *Psychanalyse et sciences de l'homme.* [Lacan]

[4] The lecture took place on 9 May, 1957, in the
Amphithéâtre Descartes of the Sorbonne, and the discussion
was continued afterwards over drinks. [Lacan] The audience
was the "Federation of Students of Language and Literature."

[5] *Die Frage der Laienanalyse, G.W.,* XIV: 281–83. [Lacan]

and Jespersen.[6] These exercises are still some-what unpracticed, but it is above all the tone that is lacking. A certain "seriousness" as one enters the domain of veracity cannot fail to raise a smile.

And how could a psychoanalyst of today not realize that speech is the key to that truth, when his whole experience must find in speech alone its instrument, its context, its material, and even the background noise of its uncertainties.

I. THE MEANING OF THE LETTER

As my title suggests, beyond this "speech," what the psychoanalytic experience discovers in the unconscious is the whole structure of language. Thus from the outset I have alerted informed minds to the extent to which the notion that the unconscious is merely the seat of the instincts will have to be rethought.

But how are we to take this "letter" here? Quite simply, literally.[7]

By "letter" I designate that material support that concrete discourse borrows from language.

This simple definition assumes that language is not to be confused with the various psychical and somatic functions that serve it in the speaking subject — primarily because language and its structure exist prior to the moment at which each subject at a certain point in his mental development makes his entry into it.

Let us note, then, that aphasias, although caused by purely anatomical lesions in the cerebral apparatus that supplies the mental center for these functions, prove, on the whole, to distribute their deficits between the two sides of the signifying effect of what we call here "the letter" in the creation of signification.[8] A point that will be clarified later.

Thus the subject, too, if he can appear to be the slave of language is all the more so of a discourse in the universal movement in which his place is already inscribed at birth, if only by virtue of his proper name.

Reference to the experience of the community, or to the substance of this discourse, settles nothing. For this experience assumes its essential dimension in the tradition that this discourse itself establishes. This tradition, long before the drama of history is inscribed in it, lays down the elementary structures of culture. And these very structures reveal an ordering of possible exchanges which, even if unconscious, is inconceivable outside the permutations authorized by language.

With the result that the ethnographic duality of nature and culture is giving way to a ternary conception of the human condition — nature, society, and culture — the last term of which could well be reduced to language, or that which essentially distinguishes human society from natural societies.

But I shall not make of this distinction either a point or a point of departure, leaving to its own obscurity the question of the original relations between the signifier and labor. I shall be content, for my little jab at the general function of *praxis* in the genesis of history, to point out that the very society that wished to restore, along with the privileges of the producer, the causal hierarchy of the relations between production and the ideological superstructure to their full political rights, has none the less failed to give birth to an esperanto in which the relations of language to socialist realities would have rendered any literary formalism radically impossible.[9]

---

[6]Edward Sapir and Otto Jespersen are well-known traditional linguists.

[7]"À la lettre." [Tr.]

[8]This aspect of aphasia, so useful in overthrowing the concept of "psychological function," which only obscures every aspect of the question, becomes quite clear in the purely linguistic analysis of the two major forms of aphasia worked out by one of the leaders of modern linguistics, Roman Jakobson. See the most accessible of his works, the *Fundamentals of Language* (with Morris Halle), (Mouton: 1956), Gravenhage,

part II, Chapters 1 to 4. [Lacan] Lacan's point is that while language pre-exists any individual, certain aspects of language are imprinted on the physical structure of the brain, as is shown by Jakobson's discovery that certain brain lesions make it impossible for an individual to understand the trope of metaphor, while others make it impossible to understand the trope of metonymy.

[9]We may recall that the discussion of the need for a new language in communist society did in fact take place, and Stalin, much to the relief of those who adhered to his philosophy, put an end to it with the following formulation: language is not a superstructure. [Lacan]

For my part, I shall trust only those assumptions that have already proven their value by virtue of the fact that language through them has attained the status of an object of scientific investigation.

For it is by virtue of this fact that linguistics[10] is seen to occupy the key position in this domain, and the reclassification of the sciences and a regrouping of them around it signals, as is usually the case, a revolution in knowledge; only the necessities of communication made me inscribe it at the head of this volume under the title "the sciences of man" — despite the confusion that is thereby covered over.[11]

To pinpoint the emergence of linguistic science we may say that, as in the case of all sciences in the modern sense, it is contained in the constitutive moment of an algorithm that is its foundation. This algorithm is the following:

$$\frac{S}{s}$$

which is read as: the signifier over the signified, "over" corresponding to the bar separating the two stages.

This sign should be attributed to Ferdinand de Saussure although it is not found in exactly this form in any of the numerous schemas, which none the less express it, to be found in the printed version of his lectures of the years 1906–7, 1908–9, and 1910–11, which the piety of a group of his disciples caused to be published under the title, *Cours de linguistique générale,* a work of prime importance for the transmission of a teaching worthy of the name, that is, that one can come to terms with only in its own terms.[12]

[10]By "linguistics" I mean the study of existing languages *(langues)* in their structure and in the laws revealed therein; this excludes any theory of abstract codes sometimes included under the heading of communication theory, as well as the theory, originating in the physical sciences, called information theory, or any semiology more or less hypothetically generalized. [Lacan]

[11]*Psychanalyse et sciences de l'homme.* [Lacan]

[12]As the reader will see from the selection in Ch. 2 (see p. 842–46), Saussure writes the signifier/signified relationship differently than Lacan: in Saussure's version the signified is placed over the signifier rather than under it and the *s/S* relation is circled, indicating its stability, with arrows moving up and down, indicating the move that can be made from word to thing and from thing to word.

That is why it is legitimate for us to give him credit for the formulation S/*s* by which, in spite of the differences among schools, the beginning of modern linguistics can be recognized.

The thematics of this science is henceforth suspended, in effect, at the primordial position of the signifier and the signified as being distinct orders separated initially by a barrier resisting signification. And that is what was to make possible an exact study of the connections proper to the signifier, and of the extent of their function in the genesis of the signified.

For this primordial distinction goes well beyond the discussion concerning the arbitrariness of the sign, as it has been elaborated since the earliest reflections of the ancients, and even beyond the impasse which, through the same period, has been encountered in every discussion of the bi-univocal correspondence between the word and the thing, if only in the mere act of naming. All this, of course, is quite contrary to the appearances suggested by the importance often imputed to the role of the index finger pointing to an object in the learning process of the *infans* subject learning his mother tongue, or the use in foreign language teaching of so-called "concrete" methods.

One cannot go further along this line of thought than to demonstrate that no signification can be sustained other than by reference to another signification:[13] in its extreme form this amounts to the proposition that there is no language *(langue)* in existence for which there is any question of its inability to cover the whole field of the signified, it being an effect of its existence as a language *(langue)* that it necessarily answers all needs. If we try to grasp in language the constitution of the object, we cannot fail to notice that this constitution is to be found only at the level of concept, a very different thing from a simple nominative, and that the *thing,* when reduced to the noun, breaks up into the double, divergent beam of the "cause" *(causa)* in which it has taken shelter in the French word *chose,* and the nothing *(rien)* to which it has abandoned its Latin dress *(rem).*

[13]Cf. the *De Magistro* of St. Augustine, especially the chapter "De significatione locutionis" which I analyzed in my seminar of 23 June, 1954. [Lacan]

These considerations, important as their existence is for the philosopher, turn us away from the locus in which language questions us as to its very nature. And we will fail to pursue the question further as long as we cling to the illusion that the signifier answers to the function of representing the signified, or better, that the signifier has to answer for its existence in the name of any signification whatever.

For even reduced to this latter formulation, the heresy is the same — the heresy that leads logical positivism in search of the "meaning of meaning,"[14] as its objective is called in the language of its devotees. As a result, we can observe that even a text highly charged with meaning can be reduced, through this sort of analysis, to insignificant bagatelles, all that survives being mathematical algorithms that are, of course, without any meaning.[15]

To return to our formula S/s: if we could infer nothing from it but the notion of the parallelism of its upper and lower terms, each one taken in its globality, it would remain the enigmatic sign of a total mystery. Which of course is not the case.

In order to grasp its function I shall begin by reproducing the classic, yet faulty illustration (see top of next column) by which its usage is normally introduced, and one can see how it opens the way to the kind of error referred to above.

[14]English in the original. [Tr.] *The Meaning of Meaning* is the title of a 1923 book by I. A. Richards and C. K. Ogden on the relationship between language and thought.

[15]So, Mr. I. A. Richards, author of a work precisely in accord with such an objective, has in another work shown us its application. He took for his purposes a page from Mongtse (Mencius, to the Jesuits) and called the piece, *Mencius on the Mind*. The guarantees of the purity of the experiment are nothing to the luxury of the approaches. And our expert on the traditional Canon that contains the text is found right on the spot in Peking where our demonstration-model mangle has been transported regardless of cost.

But we shall be no less transported, if less expensively, to see a bronze that gives out bell-tones at the slightest contact with thought, transformed into a rag to wipe the blackboard of the most dismaying British psychologism. And not without eventually being identified with the meninx of the author himself — all that remains of him or his object after having exhausted the meaning of the latter and the good sense of the former. [Lacan]

TREE

In my lecture, I replaced this illustration with another, which has no greater claim to correctness than that it has been transplanted into that incongruous dimension that the psychoanalyst has not yet altogether renounced because of his quite justified feeling that his conformism takes its value entirely from it. Here is the other diagram:

LADIES   GENTLEMEN

where we see that, without greatly extending the scope of the signifier concerned in the experiment, that is, by doubling a noun through the mere juxtaposition of two terms whose complementary meanings ought apparently to reinforce each other, a surprise is produced by an unexpected precipitation of an unexpected meaning: the image of twin doors symbolizing, through the solitary confinement offered Western Man for the satisfaction of his natural needs away from home, the imperative that he seems to share with the great majority of primitive communities by which his public life is subjected to the laws of urinary segregation.

It is not only with the idea of silencing the nominalist debate with a low blow that I use this example, but rather to show how in fact the signifier enters the signified, namely, in a form which, not being immaterial, raises the question of its place in reality. For the blinking gaze of a short sighted person might be justified in wondering whether this was indeed the signifier as he peered closely at the little enamel signs that bore it, a signifier whose signified would in this call receive its final honors from the double and solemn procession from the upper nave.[16]

But no contrived example can be as telling as the actual experience of truth. So I am happy to have invented the above, since it awoke in the person whose word I most trust a memory of childhood, which having thus happily come to my attention is best placed here.

A train arrives at a station. A little boy and a little girl, brother and sister, are seated in a compartment face to face next to the window through which the buildings along the station platform can be seen passing as the train pulls to a stop. "Look," says the brother, "we're at Ladies!"; "Idiot!" replies his sister, "Can't you see we're at Gentlemen."

Besides the fact that the rails in this story materialize the bar in the Saussurian algorithm (and in a form designed to suggest that its resistance may be other than dialectical), we should add that only someone who didn't have his eyes in front of the holes (it's the appropriate image here) could possibly confuse the place of the signifier and the signified in this story, or not see from what radiating center the signifier sends forth its light into the shadow of incomplete significations.

For this signifier will now carry a purely animal Dissension, destined for the usual oblivion of natural mists, to the unbridled power of ideological warfare, relentless for families, a torment to the Gods. For these children, Ladies and Gentlemen will be henceforth two countries towards which each of their souls will strive on divergent wings, and between which a truce will be the more impossible since they are actually the same country and neither can compromise on its own superiority without detracting from the glory of the other.

But enough. It is beginning to sound like the history of France. Which it is more human, as it ought to be, to evoke here than that of England, destined to tumble from the Large to the Small End of Dean Swift's egg.[17]

It remains to be conceived what steps, what corridor, the S of the signifier, visible here in the plurals[18] in which it focuses its welcome beyond the window, must take in order to rest its elbows on the ventilators through which, like warm and cold air, indignation and scorn come hissing out below.

One thing is certain: if the algorithm S/s with its bar is appropriate, access from one to the other cannot in any case have a signification. For in so far as it is itself only pure function of the signifier, the algorithm can reveal only the structure of a signifier in this transfer.

Now the structure of the signifier is, as it is commonly said of language itself, that it should be articulated.

This means that no matter where one starts to designate their reciprocal encroachments and increasing inclusions, these units are subjected to the double condition of being reducible to ultimate differential elements and of combining them according to the laws of a closed order.[19]

These elements, one of the decisive discoveries of linguistics, are *phonemes;* but we must not expect to find any *phonetic* constancy in the modulatory variability to which this term applies, but rather the synchronic system of differential couplings necessary for the discernment of sounds in a given language. Through this, one sees that an essential element of the spoken word itself was predestined to flow into the mobile characters which, in a jumble of lower-case Didots or Garamonds,[20] render validly present what we call the "letter," namely, the essentially localized structure of the signifier.

With the second property of the signifier, that of combining according to the laws of a closed order, is affirmed the necessity of the topological substratum of which the term I ordinarily use, namely, the signifying chain, gives an approximate idea: rings of a necklace that is a ring in another necklace made of rings.

---

[16]Lacan's point is that the bar dividing the signifier from the signified cannot really separate the two here, since the two signifieds are apparently the same, except for the different signifiers that appropriate them as women's and men's toilets.

[17]In *Gulliver's Travels,* Book I, Swift symbolized the strife between Catholics and Protestants as that between the natives of Blefuscu, who break their eggs at the Big End, and those of Lilliput, who break them at the Small End.

[18]Not, unfortunately, the case in the English here — the plural of "gentleman" being indicated other than by the addition of an "s." [Tr.]

[19]Lacan alludes to the principles of structural linguistics; see the introduction to Structuralism and Deconstruction, p. 819.

[20]Names of different type-faces. [Tr.]

Such are the structural conditions that define grammar as the order of constitutive encroachments of the signifier up to the level of the unit immediately superior to the sentence, and lexicology as the order of constitutive inclusions of the signifier to the level of the verbal locution.

In examining the limits by which these two exercises in the understanding of linguistic usage are determined, it is easy to see that only the correlations between signifier and signifier provide the standard for all research into signification, as is indicated by the notion of "usage" of a taxeme or semanteme which in fact refers to the context just above that of the units concerned.[21]

But it is not because the undertakings of grammar and lexicology are exhausted within certain limits that we must think that beyond those limits signification reigns supreme. That would be an error.

For the signifier, by its very nature, always anticipates meaning by unfolding its dimension before it. As is seen at the level of the sentence when it is interrupted before the significant term: "I shall never . . . ," "All the same it is . . . ," "And yet there may be . . ." Such sentences are not without meaning, a meaning all the more oppressive in that it is content to make us wait for it.[22]

But the phenomenon is no different which by the mere recoil of a "but" brings to the light, comely as the Shulamite, honest as the dew, the negress adorned for the wedding and the poor woman ready for the auction-block.[23]

From which we can say that it is in the chain of the signifier that the meaning "insists" but that none of its elements "consists" in the signification of which it is at the moment capable.

We are forced, then, to accept the notion of an incessant sliding of the signified under the signifier[24] which Ferdinand de Saussure illustrates with an image resembling the wavy lines of the upper and lower Waters in miniatures from manuscripts of *Genesis;* a double flux marked by fine streaks of rain, vertical dotted lines supposedly confining segments of correspondence.

All our experience runs counter to this linearity, which made me speak once, in one of my seminars on psychosis, of something more like "anchoring points" (*"points de capiton"*) as a schema for taking into account the dominance of the letter in the dramatic transformation that dialogue can effect in the subject.[25]

The linearity that Saussure holds to be constitutive of the chain of discourse, in conformity with its emission by a single voice and with its horizontal position in our writing — if this linearity is necessary, in fact, it is not sufficient. It applies to the chain of discourse only in the direction in which it is orientated in time, being taken as a signifying factor in all languages in which 'Peter hits Paul' reverses its time when the terms are inverted.

But one has only to listen to poetry, which Saussure was no doubt in the habit of doing,[26] for a polyphony to be heard, for it to become clear that all discourse is aligned along the several staves of a score.

There is in effect no signifying chain that does not have, as if attached to the punctuation of each

---

[21]Lacan's point is that the organization of most basic elements into a structure operates at the phonological level of the word (where the units are phonemes), the syntactic level of the sentence (where the units are words, or morphemes at least), and the semantic level of the utterance. "Taxeme" and "semanteme" signify atomistic units of grammar and meaning.

[22]To which verbal hallucination, when it takes this form, opens a communicating door with the Freudian structure of psychosis — a door until now unnoticed (cf. "On a Question Preliminary to any Possible Treatment of Psychosis," pp. 179–225). [Lacan]

[23]The allusions are to the "I am black, but comely . . ." of the *Song of Solomon,* and to the nineteenth-century cliché of the "poor, but honest" woman. [Tr.]

[24]Compare Jacques Derrida's (somewhat later) notion of *jeu,* the free play between the signifier and the signified; see the introduction to Structuralism and Deconstruction, p. 819.

[25]I spoke in my seminar of 6 June, 1956, of the first scene of *Athalie,* incited by an allusion — tossed off by a highbrow critic in the *New Statesman and Nation* — to the "high whoredom" of Racine's heroines, to renounce reference to the savage dramas of Shakespeare, which have become compulsional in analytic circles where they play the role of status-symbol for the Philistines. [Lacan]

[26]The publication by Jean Starobinski, in *Le Mercure de France* (February 1964) of Saussure's notes on anagrams and their hypogrammatical use, from the Saturnine verses to the writings of Cicero, provide the corroboration that I then lacked (note 1966). [Lacan]

of its units, a whole articulation of relevant contexts suspended "vertically," as it were, from that point.

Let us take our word "tree" again, this time not as an isolated noun, but at the point of one of these punctuations, and see how it crosses the bar of the Saussurian algorithm. (The anagram of *"arbre"* and *"barre"* should be noted.)[27]

For even broken down into the double specter of its vowels and consonants, it can still call up with the robur and the plane tree the significations it takes on, in the context of our flora, of strength and majesty. Drawing on all the symbolic contexts suggested in the Hebrew of the Bible, it erects on a barren hill the shadow of the cross. Then reduces to the capital Y, the sign of dichotomy which, except for the illustration used by heraldry, would owe nothing to the tree however genealogical we may think it. Circulatory tree, tree of life of the cerebellum, tree of Saturn, tree of Diana, crystals formed in a tree by lightning, is it your figure that traces our destiny for us in the tortoise-shell cracked by the fire, or your lightning that causes that slow shift in the axis of being to surge up from an unnamable night into the ˋˋ*Εν*π*άν*τ*α*[28] of language:

No! says the Tree, it says No! in the shower of
    sparks
    Of its superb head

lines that require the harmonics of the tree just as much as their continuation:

Which the storm treats as universally
    As it does a blade of grass.[29]

For this modern verse is ordered according to the same law of the parallelism of the signifier that creates the harmony governing the primitive Slavic epic or the most refined Chinese poetry.

As is seen in the fact that the tree and the blade of grass are chosen from the same mode of the existent in order for the signs of contradiction — saying "No!" and "treat as" — to affect them, and also so as to bring about, through the categorical contrast of the particularity of "superb" with the "universally" that reduces it, in the condensation of the "head" *(tête)* and the "storm" *(tempête)*, the indiscernible shower of sparks of the eternal instant.

But this whole signifier can only operate, it may be said, if it is present in the subject. It is this objection that I answer by supposing that it has passed over to the level of the signified.

For what is important is not that the subject know anything whatsoever. (If LADIES and GENTLEMEN were written in a language unknown to the little boy and girl, their quarrel would simply be the more exclusively a quarrel over words, but no less ready to take on signification.)

What this structure of the signifying chain discloses is the possibility I have, precisely in so far as I have this language in common with other subjects, that is to say, in so far as it exists as a language, to use it in order to signify *something quite other* than what it says. This function of speech is more worth pointing out than that of "disguising the thought" (more often than not indefinable) of the subject; it is no less than the function of indicating the place of this subject in the search for the true.

I have only to plant my tree in a locution; climb the tree, even project on to it the cunning illumination a descriptive context gives to a word; raise it *(arborer)* so as not to let myself be imprisoned in some sort of *communiqué* of the facts, however official, and if I know the truth, make it heard, in spite of all the *between-the-lines* censures by the only signifier my acrobatics through the branches of the tree can constitute, provocative to the point of burlesque, or perceptible only to the practiced eye, according to whether I wish to be heard by the mob or by the few.

---

[27]The anagram works only in French, and Saussure had used the Latin signifier for tree, *"arbor,"* which is not an anagram for anything.
[28]Greek for "all-in-one." Here Lacan delineates what Derrida later calls the "trace": the way signifiers build up layers of meaning from the different ways they are used.
[29]
  "Non! dit l'Arbre, il dit: Non! dans l'étincellement
    De sa tête superbe
  Que la tempête traite universellement
    Comme elle fait une herbe."
(Paul Valéry, "Au Platane," *Les Charmes*) [Lacan]

The properly signifying function thus depicted in language has a name. We learned this name in some grammar of our childhood, on the last page, where the shade of Quintilian, relegated to some phantom chapter concerning "final considerations on style," seemed suddenly to speed up his voice in an attempt to get in all he had to say before the end.

It is among the figures of style, or tropes — from which the verb "to find" (trouver) comes to us — that this name is found. This name is *metonymy*.

I shall refer only to the example given there: "thirty sails." For the disquietude I felt over the fact that the word "ship," concealed in this expression, seemed, by taking on its figurative sense, through the endless repetition of the same old example, only to increase its presence, obscured (voilait) not so much those illustrious sails (voiles) as the definition they were supposed to illustrate.

The part taken for the whole, we said to ourselves, and if the thing is to be taken seriously, we are left with very little idea of the importance of this fleet, which "thirty sails" is precisely supposed to give us: for each ship to have just one sail is in fact the least likely possibility.

By which we see that the connection between ship and sail is nowhere but in the signifier, and that it is in the *word-to-word* connection that metonymy is based.[30]

I shall designate as metonymy, then, the one side (versant) of the effective field constituted by the signifier, so that meaning can emerge there.

The other side is *metaphor*. Let us immediately find an illustration; Quillet's dictionary seemed an appropriate place to find a sample that would not seem to be chosen for my own purposes, and I didn't have to go any further than the well known line of Victor Hugo:

His sheaf was neither miserly nor spiteful . . .[31]

under which aspect I presented metaphor in my seminar on the psychoses.

It should be said that modern poetry and especially the Surrealist school have taken us a long way in this direction by showing that any conjunction of two signifiers would be equally sufficient to constitute a metaphor, except for the additional requirement of the greatest possible disparity of the images signified, needed for the production of the poetic spark, or in other words for metaphoric creation to take place.

It is true this radical position is based on the experiment known as automatic writing, which would not have been attempted if its pioneers had not been reassured by the Freudian discovery. But it remains a confused position because the doctrine behind it is false.

The creative spark of the metaphor does not spring from the presentation of two images, that is, of two signifiers equally actualized. It flashes between two signifiers one of which has taken the

---

[30]I pay homage here to the works of Roman Jakobson — to which I owe much of this formulation; works to which a psychoanalyst can constantly refer in order to structure his own experience, and which render superfluous the "personal communications" of which I could boast as much as the next fellow.

Indeed, one recognizes in this oblique form of allegiance the style of that immortal couple, Rosencrantz and Guildenstern, who are virtually indistinguishable, even in the imperfection of their destiny, for it survives by the same method as Jeannot's knife, and for the same reason for which Goethe praised Shakespeare for presenting the character in double form: they represent, in themselves alone, the whole *Gesellschaft*, the Association itself (*Wilhelm Meisters Lehrjahre*, ed. Trunz, Christian Wegner Verlag, Hamburg, V (5): 299) — I mean the International Psychoanalytical Association.

We should savour the passage from Goethe as a whole: "*Dieses leise Auftreten dieses Schmiegen und Biegen, dies*

Jasagen, Streicheln und Schmeicheln, dieses Behendigkeit, dies Schwänzein, diese Allheit und Leerheit, diese rechtliche Schurkerei, diese Unfähigkeit, wie kann sie durch einen Menschen ausgedrückt werden? Es sollten ihrer wenigstens ein Dutzend sein, wenn man sie haben könnte; denn sie bloss in Gesellschaft etwas, sie sind die Gesellschaft . . ."

Let us thank also, in this context, the author R. M. Loewenstein of "Some Remarks on the Role of Speech in Psychoanalytic Technique" (*I.J.P.*, Nov.–Dec., 1956, XXXVII (6): 467) for taking the trouble to point out that his remarks are "based on" work dating from 1952. This is no doubt the explanation for the fact that he has learned nothing from work done since then, yet which he is not ignorant of, as he cites me as their "editor" (sic). [Lacan]

[31]"Sa gerbe n'était pas avare ni haineuse," a line from "Booz endormi." [Tr.]

place of the other in the signifying chain, the occulted signifier remaining present through its (metonymic) connection with the rest of the chain.

One word for another: that is the formula for the metaphor and if you are a poet you will produce for your own delight a continuous stream, a dazzling tissue of metaphors. If the result is the sort of intoxication of the dialogue that Jean Tardieu wrote under this title, that is only because he was giving us a demonstration of the radical superfluousness of all signification in a perfectly convincing representation of a bourgeois comedy.

It is obvious that in the line of Hugo cited above, not the slightest spark of light springs from the proposition that the sheaf was neither miserly nor spiteful, for the reason that there is no question of the sheaf's having either the merit or demerit of these attributes, since the attributes, like the sheaf, belong to Booz, who exercises the former in disposing of the latter and without informing the latter of his sentiments in the case.

If, however, his sheaf does refer us to Booz, and this is indeed the case, it is because it has replaced him in the signifying chain at the very place where he was to be exalted by the sweeping away of greed and spite. But now Booz himself has been swept away by the sheaf, and hurled into the outer darkness where greed and spite harbor him in the hollow of their negation.

But once *his* sheaf has thus usurped his place, Booz can no longer return there; the slender thread of the little word *his* that binds him to it is only one more obstacle to his return in that it links him to the notion of possession that retains him at the heart of greed and spite. So *his* generosity, affirmed in the passage, is yet reduced to *less than nothing* by the munificence of the sheaf which, coming from nature, knows neither our reserve nor our rejections, and even in its accumulation remains prodigal by our standards.

But if in this profusion the giver has disappeared along with his gift, it is only in order to rise again in what surrounds the figure of speech in which he was annihilated. For it is the figure of the burgeoning of fecundity, and it is this that announces the surprise that the poem celebrates, namely, the promise that the old man will receive in the sacred context of his accession to paternity.

So, it is between the signifier in the form of the proper name of a man and the signifier that metaphorically abolishes him that the poetic spark is produced, and it is in this case all the more effective in realizing the signification of paternity in that it reproduces the mythical event in terms of which Freud reconstructed the progress, in the unconscious of all men, of the paternal mystery.

Modern metaphor has the same structure. So the line *Love is a pebble laughing in the sunlight*, recreates love in a dimension that seems to me most tenable in the face of its imminent lapse into the mirage of narcissistic altruism.

We see, then that, metaphor occurs at the precise point at which sense emerges from non-sense, that is, at that frontier which, as Freud discovered, when crossed the other way produces the word that in French is *the* word *par excellence,* the word that is simply the signifier *"esprit"*;[32] it is at this frontier that we realize that man defies his very destiny when he derides the signifier.

But to come back to our subject, what does man find in metonymy if not the power to circumvent the obstacles of social censure? Does not this form, which gives its field to truth in its very oppression, manifest a certain servitude inherent in its presentation?

One may read with profit a book by Leo Strauss, from the land that traditionally offers asylum to those who choose freedom, in which the author reflects on the relation between the art of writing and persecution.[33] By pushing to its

---

[32] *"Mot,"* in the broad sense means, "word." In the narrower sense, however, it means "a witticism." The French *"esprit"* is translated, in this context, as "wit," the equivalent of Freud's *Witz.* [Tr.]

"Esprit" is certainly the equivalent of the German *Witz* with which Freud marked the approach of his third fundamental work on the unconscious. The much greater difficulty of finding this equivalent in English is instructive: "wit," burdened with all the discussion of which it was the object from Davenant and Hobbes to Pope and Addison, abandoned its essential virtues to "humor," which is something else. There only remains the "pun," but this word is too narrow in its connotation. [Lacan] The other meaning for *"esprit"* is "spirit" — the mind or soul.

[33] Leo Strauss, *Persecution and the Art of Writing,* The Free Press, Glencoe, Illinois. [Lacan]

limits the sort of connaturality that links this art to that condition, he lets us glimpse a certain something which in this matter imposes its form, in the effect of truth on desire.

But haven't we felt for some time now that, having followed the ways of the letter in search of Freudian truth, we are getting very warm indeed, that it is burning all about us?

Of course, as it is said, the letter killeth while the spirit giveth life. We can't help but agree, having had to pay homage elsewhere to a noble victim of the error of seeking the spirit in the letter; but we should also like to know how the spirit could live without the letter. Even so, the pretensions of the spirit would remain unassailable if the letter had not shown us that it produces all the effects of truth in man without involving the spirit at all.

It is none other than Freud who had this revelation, and he called his discovery the unconscious.

II. THE LETTER IN THE UNCONSCIOUS

In the complete works of Freud, one out of every three pages is devoted to philological references, one out of every two pages to logical inferences, everywhere a dialectical apprehension of experience, the proportion of analysis of language increasing to the extent that the unconscious is directly concerned.

Thus in "The Interpretation of Dreams" every page deals with what I call the letter of the discourse, in its texture, its usage, its immanence in the matter in question. For it is with this work that the work of Freud begins to open the royal road to the unconscious. And Freud gave us notice of this; his confidence at the time of launching this book in the early days of this century[34] only confirms what he continued to proclaim to the end: that he had staked the whole of his discovery on this essential expression of his message.

The first sentence of the opening chapter announces what for the sake of the exposition could not be postponed: that the dream is a rebus. And Freud goes on to stipulate what I have said from the start, that it must be understood quite literally. This

derives from the agency in the dream of that same literal (or phonematic) structure in which the signifier is articulated and analyzed in discourse. So the unnatural images of the boat on the roof, or the man with a comma for a head, which are specifically mentioned by Freud, are examples of dream-images that are to be taken only for their value as signifiers, that is to say, in so far as they allow us to spell out the "proverb" presented by the rebus of the dream. The linguistic structure that enables us to read dreams is the very principle of the "significance of the dream," the *Traumdeutung*.

Freud shows us in every possible way that the value of the image as signifier has nothing whatever to do with its signification, giving as an example Egyptian hieroglyphics in which it would be sheer buffoonery to pretend that in a given text the frequency of a vulture, which is an *aleph,* or of a chick, which is a *vau,* indicating a form of the verb "to be" or a plural, prove that the text has anything at all to do with these ornithological specimens. Freud finds in this writing certain uses of the signifier that are lost in ours, such as the use of determinatives, where a categorical figure is added to the literal figuration of a verbal term; but this is only to show us that even in this writing, the so-called "ideogram" is a letter.

But it does not require the current confusion on this last term for there to prevail in the minds of psychoanalysts lacking linguistic training the prejudice in favor of a symbolism deriving from natural analogy, or even of the image as appropriate to the instinct. And to such an extent that, outside the French school, which has been alerted, a distinction must be drawn between reading coffee grounds and reading hieroglyphics, by recalling to its own principles a technique that could not be justified were it not directed towards the unconscious.

It must be said that this is admitted only with difficulty and that the mental vice denounced above enjoys such favor that today's psychoanalyst can be expected to say that he decodes before he will come around to taking the necessary tour with Freud (turn at the statute of Champollion,[35]

---

[34]Cf. the correspondence, namely letters 107 and 109. [Lacan]

[35]Jean-François Champollion (1790–1832), the first scholar to decipher the Ancient Egyptian hieroglyphics. [Tr.]

says the guide) that will make him understand that what he does is decipher; the distinction is that a cryptogram takes on its full dimension only when it is in a lost language.

Taking the tour is simply continuing in the *Traumdeutung.*

Entstellung, translated as "distortion" or "transposition," is what Freud shows to be the general precondition for the functioning of the dream, and it is what I designated above, following Saussure, as the sliding of the signified under the signifier, which is always active in discourse (its action, let us note, is unconscious).

But what we call the two "sides" of the effect of the signifier on the signified are also found here.

Verdichtung, or "condensation," is the structure of the superimposition of the signifiers, which metaphor takes as its field, and whose name, condensing in itself the word *Dichtung,*[36] shows how the mechanism is connatural with poetry to the point that it envelops the traditional function proper to poetry.

In the case of *Verschiebung,* "displacement," the German term is closer to the idea of that veering off of signification that we see in metonymy, and which from its first appearance in Freud is represented as the most appropriate means used by the unconscious to foil censorship.

What distinguishes these two mechanisms, which play such a privileged role in the dream-work (*Traumarbeit*), from their homologous function in discourse? Nothing, except a condition imposed upon the signifying material, called *Rücksicht auf Darstellbarkeit,* which must be translated by "consideration of the means of representation." (The translation by "role of the possibility of figurative expression" being too approximative here.) But this condition constitutes a limitation operating *within* the system of writing; this is a long way from dissolving the system into a figurative semiology on a level with phenomena of natural expression. This fact could perhaps shed light on the problems involved in certain modes of pictography which, simply

because they have been abandoned in writing as imperfect, are not therefore to be regarded as mere evolutionary stages. Let us say, then, that the dream is like the parlor-game in which one is supposed to get the spectators to guess some well known saying or variant of it solely by dumb-show. That the dream uses speech makes no difference since for the unconscious it is only one among several elements of the representation. It is precisely the fact that both the game and the dream run up against a lack of taxematic material for the representation of such logical articulations as causality, contradiction, hypothesis, etc., that proves they are a form of writing rather than of mime. The subtle processes that the dream is seen to use to represent these logical articulations, in a much less artificial way than games usually employ, are the object of a special study in Freud in which we see once more confirmed that the dream-work follows the laws of the signifier.

The rest of the dream-elaboration is designated as secondary by Freud, the nature of which indicates its value: they are fantasies or daydreams (*Tagtraum*) to use the term Freud prefers in order to emphasize their function of wish-fulfillment (*Wunscherfüllung*). Given the fact that these fantasies may remain unconscious, their distinctive feature is in this case their signification. Now, concerning these fantasies, Freud tells us that their place in the dream is either to be taken up and used as signifying elements for the statement of the unconscious thoughts (*Traumgedanke*), or to be used in the secondary elaboration just mentioned, that is to say, in a function not to be distinguished from our waking thought (*von unserem wachen Denken nicht zu unterschieden*). No better idea of the effects of this function can be given than by comparing it to areas of color which, when applied here and there to a stencil-plate, can make the stencilled figures, rather forbidding in themselves, more reminiscent of hieroglyphics or of a rebus, look like a figurative painting.

Forgive me if I seem to have to spell out Freud's text; I do so not only to show how much is to be gained by not cutting it about, but also in order to situate the development of psychoanalysis according to its first guide-lines, which were fundamental and never revoked.

[36]German for "literature," or more specifically "poetry."

Yet from the beginning there was a general *méconnaissance*[37] of the constitutive role of the signifier in the status that Freud from the first assigned to the unconscious and in the most precise formal manner.

There are two reasons for this, of which the least obvious, of course, is that this formalization was not sufficient in itself to bring about a recognition of the agency of the signifier because the *Traumdeutung* appeared long before the formalizations of linguistics for which one could no doubt show that it paved the way by the sheer weight of its truth.

The second reason, which is after all only the reverse side of the first, is that if psychoanalysts were fascinated exclusively by the significations revealed in the unconscious, it is because these significations derived their secret attraction from the dialectic that seemed to be immanent in them.

I have shown in my seminars that it is the need to counteract the continuously accelerating effects of this bias that alone explains the apparent changes of direction or rather changes of tack, which Freud, through his primary concern to preserve for posterity both his discovery and the fundamental revisions it effected in our knowledge, felt it necessary to apply to his doctrine.

For, I repeat, in the situation in which he found himself, having nothing that corresponded to the object of his discovery that was at the same level of scientific development — in this situation, at least he never failed to maintain this object on the level of its ontological dignity.

The rest was the work of the gods and took such a course that analysis today takes its bearings in those imaginary forms that I have just shown to be drawn "resist-style" *(en reserve)* on the text they mutilate — and the analyst tries to accommodate his direction to them, confusing them, in the interpretation of the dream, with the visionary liberation of the hieroglyphic aviary, and seeking generally the control of the exhaustion of the analysis in a sort of "scanning"[38] of

these forms whenever they appear, in the idea that they are witnesses of the exhaustion of the regressions and of the remodelling of the object relation from which the subject is supposed to derive his "character-type."[39]

The technique that is based on such positions can be fertile in its various effects, and under the aegis of therapy, difficult to criticize. But an internal criticism must none the less arise from the flagrant disparity between the mode of operation by which the technique is justified — namely the analytic rule, all the instruments of which, beginning with "free association," depend on the conception of the unconscious of its inventor — and, on the other hand, the general *méconnaissance* that reigns regarding this conception of the unconscious. The most ardent adherents of this technique believe themselves to be freed of any need to reconcile the two by the merest pirouette: the analytic rule (they say) must be all the more religiously observed since it is only the result of a lucky accident. In other words, Freud never knew what he was doing.

A return to Freud's text shows on the contrary the absolute coherence between his technique and his discovery, and at the same time this coherence allows us to put all his procedures in their proper place.

That is why any rectification of psychoanalysis must inevitably involve a return to the truth of that discovery, which, taken in its original moment, is impossible to obscure.

For in the analysis of dreams, Freud intends only to give us the laws of the unconscious in their most general extension. One of the reasons why dreams were most propitious for this demonstration is exactly, Freud tells us, that they reveal the same laws whether in the normal person or in the neurotic.

But in either case, the efficacy of the unconscious does not cease in the waking state. The psychoanalytic experience does nothing other than establish that the unconscious leaves none of

[37]French for "misunderstanding" or "failure of recognition."
[38]That is the process by which the results of a piece of research are assured through a mechanical exploration of the entire extent of the field of its object. [Lacan]

[39]By referring only to the development of the organism, the typology fails to recognize *(méconnaît)* the structure in which the subject is caught up respectively in fantasy, in drive, in sublimation. I am at present developing the theory of this structure (note 1966). [Lacan]

our actions outside its field. The presence of the unconscious in the psychological order, in other words in the relation-functions of the individual, should, however, be more precisely defined: it is not coextensive with that order, for we know that if unconscious motivation is manifest in conscious psychical effects, as well as in unconscious ones, conversely it is only elementary to recall to mind that a large number of psychical effects that are quite legitimately designated as unconscious, in the sense of excluding the characteristic of consciousness, are nonetheless without any relation whatever to the unconscious in the Freudian sense. So it is only by an abuse of the term that unconscious in that sense is confused with psychical, and that one may thus designate as psychical what is in fact an effect of the unconscious, as on the somatic for instance.

It is a matter, therefore, of defining the topography of this unconscious. I say that it is the very topography defined by the algorithm:

$$\frac{S}{s}$$

What we have been able to develop concerning the effects of the signifier on the signified suggests its transformation into:[40]

$$f(S)\frac{1}{s}$$

We have shown the effects not only of the elements of the horizontal signifying chain, but also of its vertical dependencies in the signified, divided into two fundamental structures called metonymy and metaphor. We can symbolize them by, first:[41]

$$f(S \ldots S')S \cong S(-)s$$

that is to say, the metonymic structure, indicating that it is the connection between signifier and

signifier that permits the elision in which the signifier installs the lack-of-being in the object relation, using the value of "reference back" possessed by signification in order to invest it with the desire aimed at the very lack it supports. The sign – placed between () represents here the maintenance of the bar — which, in the original algorithm, marked the irreducibility in which, in the relations between signifier and signified, the resistance of signification is constituted.[42]

Secondly,

$$f\left(\frac{S'}{S}\right)S \cong S(+)s$$

the metaphoric structure indicating that it is in the substitution of signifier for signifier that an effect of signification is produced that is creative or poetic, in other words, which is the advent of the signification in question.[43] The sign + between () represents here the crossing of the bar — and the constitutive value of this crossing for the emergence of signification.

This crossing expresses the condition of passage of the signifier into the signified that I pointed out above, although provisionally confusing it with the place of the subject.

It is the function of the subject, thus introduced, that we must now turn to since it lies at the crucial point of our problem.

"I think, therefore I am" (cogito ergo sum) is not merely the formula in which is constituted, with the historical high point of reflection on the conditions of science, the link between the transparency of the transcendental subject and his existential affirmation.

Perhaps I am only object and mechanism (and so nothing more than phenomenon), but assuredly in so far as I think so, I am — absolutely. No doubt philosophers have brought important corrections to this formulation, notably that in that which thinks (cogitans), I can never constitute

[40]Perhaps to be read: "The function of the signifier in the unconscious as related to the signified meaning."
[41]Perhaps to be read: "The function of a chain of signifiers connected with a particular signifier is congruent to the signifier's relation to its signified." The metonymic chain, in other words, is to its signifier what the signifier is to its signified.

[42]The sign $\cong$ here designates congruence. [Lacan]
[43]S' designating here the term productive of the signifying effect (or significance); one can see that the term is latent in metonymy, patent in metaphor. [Lacan]

myself as anything but object (*cogitatum*). Nonetheless it remains true that by way of this extreme purification of the transcendental subject, my existential link to its project seems irrefutable, at least in its present form, and that: "*cogito ergo sum*" *ubi cogito, ibi sum,*[44] overcomes this objection.

Of course, this limits me to being there in my being only in so far as I think that I am in my thought; just how far I actually think this concerns only myself and if I say it, interests no one.[45]

Yet to elude this problem on the pretext of its philosophical pretensions is simply to admit one's inhibition. For the notion of subject is indispensable even to the operation of a science such as strategy (in the modern sense) whose calculations exclude all "subjectivism."

It is also to deny oneself access to what might be called the Freudian universe — in the way that we speak of the Copernican universe. It was in fact the so-called Copernican revolution to which Freud himself compared his discovery, emphasizing that it was once again a question of the place man assigns to himself at the center of a universe.

Is the place that I occupy as the subject of a signifier concentric or excentric, in relation to the place I occupy as subject of the signified? — that is the question.

It is not a question of knowing whether I speak of myself in a way that conforms to what I am, but rather of knowing whether I am the same as that of which I speak. And it is not at all inappropriate to use the word "thought" here. For Freud uses the term to designate the elements involved in the unconscious, that is the signifying mechanisms that we now recognize as being there.

It is nonetheless true that the philosophical *cogito* is at the center of the mirage that renders modern man so sure of being himself even in his uncertainties about himself, and even in the mistrust he has learned to practice against the traps of self-love.

Furthermore, if, turning the weapon of metonymy against the nostalgia that it serves, I refuse to seek any meaning beyond tautology, if in the name of "war is war" and "a penny's a penny" I decide to be only what I am, how even here can I elude the obvious fact that I am in that very act?

And it is no less true if I take myself to the other, metaphoric pole of the signifying quest, and if I dedicate myself to becoming what I am, to coming into being, I cannot doubt that even if I lose myself in the process, I am in that process.

Now it is on these very points, where evidence will be subverted by the empirical, that the trick of the Freudian conversion lies.

This signifying game between metonymy and metaphor, up to and including the active edge that splits my desire between a refusal of the signifier and a lack of being, and links my fate to the question of my destiny, this game, in all its inexorable subtlety, is played until the match is called, there where I am not, because I cannot situate myself there.

That is to say, what is needed is more than these words with which, for a brief moment I disconcerted my audience: I think where I am not, therefore I am where I do not think. Words that render sensible to an ear properly attuned with what elusive ambiguity[46] the ring of meaning flees from our grasp along the verbal thread.

What one ought to say is: I am not wherever I am the plaything of my thought; I think of what I am where I do not think to think.

This two-sided mystery is linked to the fact that the truth can be evoked only in that dimension of alibi in which all "realism" in creative works takes its virtue from metonymy; it is likewise linked to this other fact that we accede to meaning only through the double twist of metaphor when we have the one and only key: the S and the *s* of the Saussurian algorithm are not on the same level, and man only deludes himself when he believes his true place is at their axis, which is nowhere.

---

[44]"Wherever I think 'I think therefore I am,' there I am."

[45]It is quite otherwise if by posing a question such as "Why philosophers?" I become more candid than nature, for then I am asking not only the question that philosophers have been asking themselves for all time, but also the one in which they are perhaps most interested. [Lacan]

[46]"*Ambiguité de furet*" — literally, "ferret-like ambiguity." This is one of a number of references in Lacan to the game "hunt-the-slipper" (*jeu du furet*). [Tr.]

Was nowhere, that is, until Freud discovered it; for if what Freud discovered isn't that, it isn't anything.

The contents of the unconscious with all their disappointing ambiguities give us no reality in the subject more consistent than the immediate; their virtue derives from the truth and in the dimension of being: *Kern unseres Wesen*[47] are Freud's own terms.

The double-triggered mechanism of metaphor is the very mechanism by which the symptom, in the analytic sense, is determined. Between the enigmatic signifier of the sexual trauma and the term that is substituted for it in an actual signifying chain there passes the spark that fixes in a symptom the signification inaccessible to the conscious subject in which that symptom may be resolved — a symptom being a metaphor in which flesh or function is taken as a signifying element.

And the enigmas that desire seems to pose for a "natural philosophy" — its frenzy mocking the abyss of the infinite, the secret collusion with which it envelops the pleasure of knowing and of dominating with *jouissance,* these amount to no other derangement of instinct than that of being caught in the rails — eternally stretching forth towards the *desire for something else* — of metonymy. Hence its "perverse" fixation at the very suspension-point of the signifying chain where the memory-screen is immobilized and the fascinating image of the fetish is petrified.

There is no other way of conceiving the indestructibility of unconscious desire — in the absence of a need which, when forbidden satisfaction, does not sicken and die, even if it means the destruction of the organism itself. It is in a memory, comparable to what is called by that name in our modern thinking-machines (which are in turn based on an electronic realization of the composition of signification), it is in this sort of memory that is found the chain that *insists* on reproducing itself in the transference, and which is the chain of dead desire.

It is the truth of what this desire has been in his history that the patient cries out through his symptom, as Christ said that the stones themselves would have cried out if the children of Israel had not lent them their voice.

And that is why only psychoanalysis allows us to differentiate within memory the function of recollection. Rooted in the signifier, it resolves the Platonic aporias of reminiscence through the ascendancy of history in man.

One has only to read the "Three Essays on Sexuality" to observe, in spite of the pseudobiological glosses with which it is decked out for popular consumption, that Freud there derives all accession to the object from a dialectic of return.

Starting from Hölderlin's νοστος,[48] Freud arrives less than twenty years later at Kierkegaard's repetition; that is, in submitting his thought solely to the humble but inflexible consequences of the "talking cure,"[49] he was unable ever to escape the living servitudes that led him from the sovereign principle of the Logos to re-thinking the Empedoclean antinomies of death.[50]

And how else are we to conceive the recourse of a man of science to a *Deus ex machina* than on that "other scene" he speaks of as the locus of the dream, a *Deus ex machina* only less derisory for the fact that it is revealed to the spectator that the machine directs the director? How else can we imagine that a scientist of the nineteenth century, unless we realize that he had to bow before the force of evidence that went well beyond his prejudices, valued more highly than all his other works his *Totem and Taboo,* with its obscene, ferocious figure of the primordial father, not to be exhausted in the expiation of Oedipus' blindness, and before which the ethnologists of today bow as before the growth of an authentic myth?[51]

[48]Greek for "return (to the homeland)." See the introduction to Heidegger, p. 611.

[49]English in the original. [Tr.]

[50]Empedocles denied the human experience of death: "When I am, Death is not; when Death is, I am not."

[51]In *Totem and Taboo,* Freud posits that the incest taboo arose in reaction to a primordial family struggle, in which the Father takes all the women for himself until the Sons, rising against him, kill him and eat his flesh. Lacan ironically alludes to the anthropologists who have taken Freud's fantasy as "authentic myth."

[47]"The nucleus of our being." [Tr.]

So that imperious proliferation of particular symbolic creations, such as what are called the sexual theories of the child, which supply the motivation down to the smallest detail of neurotic compulsions, these reply to the same necessities as do myths.

Thus, to speak of the precise point we are treating in my seminars on Freud, little Hans, left in the lurch at the age of five by his symbolic environment, and suddenly forced to face the enigma of his sex and his existence, developed, under the direction of Freud and of his father, Freud's disciple, in mythic form, around the signifying crystal of his phobia, all the permutations possible on a limited number of signifiers.

The operation shows that even on the individual level the solution of the impossible is brought within man's reach by the exhaustion of all possible forms of the impossibilities encountered in solution by recourse to the signifying equation. It is a striking demonstration that illuminates the labyrinth of a case which so far has only been used as a source of demolished fragments. We should be struck, too, by the fact that it is in the coextensivity of the development of the symptom and of its curative resolution that the nature of the neurosis is revealed: whether phobic, hysterical, or obsessive, the neurosis is a question that being poses for the subject "from where it was before the subject came into the world" (Freud's phrase, which he used in explaining the Oedipal complex to little Hans).

The "being" referred to is that which appears in a lightning moment in the void of the verb "to be" and I said that it poses its question for the subject. What does that mean? It does not pose it *before* the subject, since the subject cannot come to the place where it is posed, but it poses it *in place* of the subject, that is to say, in that place it poses the question *with* the subject, as one poses a problem *with* a pen, or as Aristotle's man thought *with* his soul.

Thus Freud introduced the ego into his doctrine,[52] by defining it according to the resistances that are proper to it. What I have tried to convey is that these resistances are of an imaginary nature much in the same sense as those coaptative lures that the ethology of animal behavior shows us in display or combat, and that these lures are reduced in man to the narcissistic relation introduced by Freud, which I have elaborated in my essay on the mirror stage. I have tried to show that by situating in this ego the synthesis of the perceptual functions in which the sensori-motor selections are integrated, Freud seems to abound in that delegation that is traditionally supposed to represent reality for the ego, and that this reality is all the more included in the suspension of the ego.

For this ego, which is notable in the first instance for the imaginary inertias that it concentrates against the message of the unconscious, operates solely with a view to covering the displacement constituted by the subject with a resistance that is essential to the discourse as such.

That is why an exhaustion of the mechanisms of defense, which Fenichel the practitioner shows us so well in his studies of analytic technique (while his whole reduction on the theoretical level of neuroses and psychoses to genetic anomalies in libidinal development is pure platitude), manifests itself, without Fenichel's accounting for it or realizing it himself, as simply the reverse side of the mechanisms of the unconscious. Periphrasis, hyperbaton, ellipsis, suspension, anticipation, retraction, negation, digression, irony, these are the figures of style (Quintilian's *figurae sententiarum*); as catachresis, litotes, antonomasia, hypotyposis are the tropes, whose terms suggest themselves as the most proper for the labeling of these mechanisms. Can one really see these as mere figures of speech when it is the figures themselves that are the active principle of the rhetoric of the discourse that the analysand in fact utters?[53]

By persisting in describing the nature of resistance as a permanent emotional state, thus making it alien to the discourse, today's psychoanalysts

---

[52]This and the next paragraph were rewritten solely with a view to greater clarity of expression (note 1968). [Lacan]

[53]Lacan lists some of Quintilian's obscurer figures of speech and thought as equivalents to the ego-defenses of repression, reversal, undoing, and so on, just as metaphor and metonymy have already been viewed as the symbolic equivalents of displacement and condensation.

have simply shown that they have fallen under the blow of one of the fundamental truths that Freud rediscovered through psychoanalysis. One is never happy making way for a new truth, for it always means making our way into it: the truth is always disturbing. We cannot even manage to get used to it. We are used to the real. The truth we repress.

Now it is quite specially necessary to the scientist, to the seer, even to the quack, that he should be the only one to *know*. The idea that deep in the simplest (and even sickest) of souls there is something ready to blossom is bad enough! But if someone seems to know as much as they about what we ought to make of it . . . then the categories of primitive, prelogical, archaic, or even magical thought, so easy to impute to others, rush to our aid! It is not right that these nonentities keep us breathless with enigmas that prove to be only too unreliable.

To interpret the unconscious as Freud did, one would have to be as he was, an encyclopedia of the arts and muses, as well as an assiduous reader of the *Fliegende Blätter*.[54] And the task is made no easier by the fact that we are at the mercy of a thread woven with allusions, quotations, puns, and equivocations. And is that our profession, to be antidotes to trifles?

Yet that is what we must resign ourselves to. The unconscious is neither primordial nor instinctual; what it knows about the elementary is no more than the elements of the signifier.

The three books that one might call canonical with regard to the unconscious — "The Interpretation of Dreams," "The Psychopathology of Everyday Life," and "Jokes and Their Relation to the Unconscious" — are simply a web of examples whose development is inscribed in the formulas of connection and substitution (though carried to the tenth degree by their particular complexity — diagrams of them are sometimes provided by Freud by way of illustration); these are the formulas we give to the signifier in its *transference*-function. For in "The Interpretation of Dreams" it is in the sense of such a function that the term *Übertragung*, or

transference, is introduced, which later gave its name to the mainspring of the intersubjective link between analyst and analysand.

Such diagrams are not only constitutive of each of the symptoms in a neurosis, but they alone make possible the understanding of the thematic of its course and resolution. The great case-histories provided by Freud demonstrate this admirably.

To fall back on a more limited incident, but one more likely to provide us with the final seal on our proposition, let me cite the article on fetishism of 1927,[55] and the case Freud reports there of a patient who, to achieve sexual satisfaction, needed a certain shine on the nose (*Glanz auf der Nase*); analysis showed that his early, English-speaking years had seen the displacement of the burning curiosity that he felt for the phallus of his mother, that is to say, for that eminent *manque-à-être*, for that want-to-be, whose privileged signifier Freud revealed to us, into a *glance at the nose*[56] in the forgotten language of his childhood, rather than a *shine on the nose*.[57]

It is the abyss opened up at the thought that a thought should make itself heard in the abyss that provoked resistance to psychoanalysis from the outset. And not, as is commonly said, the emphasis on man's sexuality. This latter has after all been the dominant object in literature throughout the ages. And in fact the more recent evolution of psychoanalysis has succeeded by a bit of comical legerdemain in turning it into a quite moral affair, the cradle and trysting-place of oblativity and attraction. The Platonic setting of the soul, blessed and illuminated, rises straight to paradise.

The intolerable scandal in the time before Freudian sexuality was sanctified was that it was so "intellectual." It was precisely in that that it showed itself to be the worthy ally of all those terrorists whose plottings were going to ruin society.

At a time when psychoanalysts are busy remodeling psychoanalysis into a right-thinking movement whose crowning expression is the

---

[54]A German comic newspaper of the late nineteenth and early twentieth centuries. [Tr.]

[55]*Fetischismus, G.W.* XIV: 311; "Fetishism," *Collected Papers,* V: 198; *Standard Edition* XXI: 149. [Lacan.]
[56]English in the original. [Tr.]
[57]English in the original. [Tr.]

sociological poem of the *autonomous ego,* I would like to say, to all those who are listening to me, how they can recognize bad psychoanalysts; this is by the word they use to deprecate all technical or theoretical research that carries forward the Freudian experience along its authentic lines. That word is *"intellectualization"* — execrable to all those who, living in fear of being tried and found wanting by the wine of truth, spit on the bread of men, although their slaver can no longer have any effect other than that of leavening.

III. THE LETTER, BEING AND THE OTHER[58]

Is what thinks in my place, then, another I? Does Freud's discovery represent the confirmation, on the level of psychological experience, of Manicheism?[59]

In fact, there is no confusion on this point: what Freud's researches led us to is not a few more or less curious cases of split personality. Even at the heroic epoch I have been describing, when, like the animals in fairy stories, sexuality talked, the demonic atmosphere that such an orientation might have given rise to never materialized.[60]

The end that Freud's discovery proposes for man was defined by him at the apex of his thought in these moving terms: *Wo es war, soll Ich werden.* I must come to the place where that was.[61]

This is one of reintegration and harmony, I could even say of reconciliation *(Versöhnung).*

But if we ignore the self's radical ex-centricity to itself with which man is confronted, in other words, the truth discovered by Freud, we shall falsify both the order and methods of psychoanalytic mediation; we shall make of it nothing more than the compromise operation that it has, in effect, become, namely, just what the letter as well as the spirit of Freud's work most repudiates. For since he constantly invoked the notion of compromise as supporting all the miseries that his analysis is supposed to assuage, we can say that any recourse to compromise, explicit or implicit, will necessarily disorient psychoanalytic action and plunge it into darkness.

But neither does it suffice to associate oneself with the moralistic tartufferies of our time or to be forever spouting something about the "total personality" in order to have said anything articulate about the possibility of mediation.

The radical heteronomy that Freud's discovery shows gaping within man can never again be covered over without whatever is used to hide it being profoundly dishonest.

Who, then, is this other to whom I am more attached than to myself, since, at the heart of my assent to my own identity it is still he who agitates me?

His presence can be understood only as a second degree of otherness, which already places him in the position of mediating between me and the double of myself, as it were with my counterpart.

If I have said that the unconscious is the discourse of the Other (with a capital O), it is in order to indicate the beyond in which the recognition of desire is bound up with the desire for recognition.

In other words this other is the Other that even my lie invokes as a guarantor of the truth in which it subsists.

By which we can also see that it is with the appearance of language that the dimension of truth emerges.

Prior to this point, we can recognize in the psychological relation, which can be easily isolated in the observation of animal behavior, the existence of subjects, not by means of some projective mirage, the phantom of which a certain type of psychologist delights in hacking to pieces, but simply on account of the manifested presence

---

[58]*La lettre, l'être et l'autre.* [Lacan]

[59]One of my colleagues went so far in this direction as to wonder if the id *(Es)* of the last phase wasn't in fact the "bad ego." (It should now be obvious whom I am referring to — 1966.) [Lacan]

[60]Note, nonetheless, the tone with which one spoke in that period of the "elfin pranks" of the unconscious; a work of Silberer's is called *Der Zufall und die Koboldstreiche des Unbewussten* (Chance and the Elfin Tricks of the Unconscious) — completely anachronistic in the context of our present soul-managers. [Lacan]

[61]"Where Id was, there shall Ego be," is the usual English translation, suggesting the triumph of the autonomous ego in analytic ideology. But since "ego" and "id" are Latin for "I" and "it" (Freud had used the common German pronouns "ich" and "es"), Lacan's "I must come to the place where that was" is equally correct and holds very different connotations.

of intersubjectivity. In the animal hidden in his lookout, in the well-laid trap of certain others, in the feint by which an apparent straggler leads a predator away from the flock, something more emerges than in the fascinating display of mating or combat ritual. Yet there is nothing even there that transcends the function of lure in the service of a need, or which affirms a presence in that beyond-the-veil where the whole of Nature can be questioned about its design.

For there even to be a question (and we know that it is one Freud himself posed in "Beyond the Pleasure Principle"), there must be language.

For I can lure my adversary by means of a movement contrary to my actual plan of battle, and this movement will have its deceiving effect only in so far as I produce it in reality and for my adversary.

But in the propositions with which I open peace negotiations with him, what my negotiations propose to him is situated in a third locus which is neither my speech nor my interlocutor.

This locus is none other than the locus of signifying convention, of the sort revealed in the comedy of the sad plaint of the Jew to his crony: "Why do you tell me you are going to Cracow so I'll believe you are going to Lvov, when you really are going to Cracow?"[62]

Of course the flock-movement I just spoke of could be understood in the conventional context of game-strategy, where it is a rule that I deceive my adversary, but in that case my success is evaluated within the connotation of betrayal, that is to say, in relation to the Other who is the guarantor of Good Faith.

Here the problems are of an order the heteronomy of which is completely misconstrued (méconnue) if reduced to an "awareness of others," or whatever we choose to call it. For the "existence of the other" having once upon a time reached the ears of the Midas of psychoanalysis through the partition that separates him from the secret meetings of the phenomenologists, the news is now being whispered through the reeds: "Midas, King Midas, is the other of his patient. He himself has said it."

What sort of breakthrough is that? The other, what other?

The young André Gide, defying the landlady to whom his mother had confided him to treat him as a responsible person, opening with a key (false only in that it opened all locks of the same make) the lock that this lady took to be a worthy signifier of her educational intentions, and doing it quite obviously for her benefit — what "other" was he aiming at? She who was supposed to intervene and to whom he would then say: "Do you think my obedience can be secured with a ridiculous lock?" But by remaining out of sight and holding her peace until that evening in order, after primly greeting his return, to lecture him like a child, she showed him not just another with the face of anger, but another André Gide who is no longer sure, either then or later in thinking back on it, of just what he really meant to do — whose own truth has been changed by the doubt thrown on his good faith.

Perhaps it would be worth our while pausing a moment over this empire of confusion which is none other than that in which the whole human opera-buffa plays itself out, in order to understand the ways in which analysis can proceed not just to restore an order but to found the conditions for the possibility of its restoration.

Kern unseres Wesen, the nucleus of our being, but it is not so much that Freud commands us to seek it as so many others before him have with the empty adage "Know thyself" — as to reconsider the ways that lead to it, and which he shows us.

Or rather that which he proposes for us to attain is not that which can be the object of knowledge, but that (doesn't he tell us as much?) which creates our being and about which he teaches us that we bear witness to it as much and more in our whims, our aberrations, our phobias and fetishes, as in our more or less civilized personalities.

Madness, you are no longer the object of the ambiguous praise with which the sage decorated the impregnable burrow of his fear; and if after all he finds himself tolerably at home there, it is only

---

[62]Freud analyzes this feeble wheeze in *Jokes and Their Relation to the Unconscious.* His point, there, is the way the truth of the speaker (who says, rightly, that he is going to Cracow) is the lie of the listener (who assumes that the speaker's words are going to misdirect him, and so is *actually* misdirected by the truth).

because the supreme agent forever at work digging its tunnels is none other than reason, the very Logos that he serves.

So how do you imagine that a scholar with so little talent for the "commitments" that solicited him in his age (as they do in all ages), that a scholar such as Erasmus held such an eminent place in the revolution of a Reformation in which man has as much of a stake in each man as in all men?

The answer is that the slightest alteration in the relation between man and the signifier, in this case in the procedures of exegesis, changes the whole course of history by modifying the moorings that anchor his being.

It is precisely in this that Freudianism, however misunderstood it has been, and however confused its consequences have been, to anyone capable of perceiving the changes we have lived through in our own lives, is seen to have founded an intangible but radical revolution. There is no point in collecting witnesses to the fact:[63] everything involving not just the human sciences, but the destiny of man, politics, metaphysics, literature, the arts, advertising, propaganda, and through these even economics, everything has been affected.

Is all this anything more than the discordant effects of an immense truth in which Freud traced for us a clear path? What must be said, however, is that any technique that bases its claim on the mere psychological categorization of its object is not following this path, and this is the case of psychoanalysis today except in so far as we return to the Freudian discovery.

Furthermore, the vulgarity of the concepts by which it recommends itself to us, the embroidery of pseudo-Freudianism (frofreudisme) which is no longer anything but decoration, as well as the

bad repute in which it seems to prosper, all bear witness to its fundamental betrayal of its founder.

By his discovery, Freud brought within the circle of science the boundary between the object and being that seemed to mark its outer limit.

That this is the symptom and the prelude of a re-examination of the situation of man in the existent such as has been assumed up to the present by all our postulates of knowledge — don't be content, I beg of you, to write this off as another case of Heideggerianism, even prefixed by a neo- that adds nothing to the dustbin style in which currently, by the use of his ready-made mental jetsam, one excuses oneself from any real thought.

When I speak of Heidegger, or rather when I translate him, I at least make the effort to leave the speech he proffers us its sovereign significance.

If I speak of being and the letter, if I distinguish the other and the Other,[64] it is because Freud shows me that they are the terms to which must be referred the effects of resistance and transference against which, in the twenty years I have engaged in what we all call after him the impossible practice of psychoanalysis, I have done unequal battle. And it is also because I must help others not to lose their way there.

It is to prevent the field of which they are the inheritors from becoming barren, and for that reason to make it understood that if the symptom is a metaphor, it is not a metaphor to say so, any more than to say that man's desire is a metonymy. For the symptom is a metaphor whether one likes it or not, as desire is a metonymy, however funny people may find the idea.

Finally, if I am to rouse you to indignation over the fact that, after so many centuries of religious hypocrisy and philosophical bravado, nothing has yet been validly articulated as to what links metaphor to the question of being and metonymy to its lack, there must be an object there to answer to that indignation both as its instigator and its victim: that object is humanistic man and the credit, hopelessly affirmed, which he has drawn over his intentions.

[63]To pick the most recent in date, François Mauriac, in the *Figaro Littéraire* of 25 May, apologizes for refusing "to tell the story of his life." If no one these days can undertake to do that with the old enthusiasm, the reason is that, "a half century since, Freud, whatever we think of him" has already passed that way. And after being briefly tempted by the old saw that this is only the "history of our body," Mauriac returns to the truth that his sensitivity as a writer makes him face: to write the history of oneself is to write the confession of the deepest part of our neighbors' souls as well. [Lacan]

[64]The "other" (*objet petit a*) is the "object" with which the ego interacts, any object of desire or its fetishistic equivalents; the "Other" is the unconscious, the decentered location of the subject that is brought into being by the fall into language.

The Meaning of the Phallus

What follows is the unaltered text of a paper delivered in German on 9 May 1958, at the Max Planck Institute of Munich where Professor Paul Matussek had invited me to speak.

The vaguest idea of the state of mind then prevailing in circles, not for the most part uninformed, will give some measure of the impact of terms such as "the other scene," to take one example used here, which I was the first to extract from Freud's work.

If "deferred action" (*Nachtrag*), to rescue another such term from its current affectation, makes this effort unfeasible, it should be realized that they were unheard of at that time.

We know that the unconscious castration complex[1] has the function of a knot:

1. in the dynamic structuring of symptoms in the analytic sense of the term, meaning that which can be analyzed in neuroses, perversions and psychoses;

2. as the regulator of development giving its *ratio*[2] to this first role: that is, by installing in the subject an unconscious position without which he would be unable to identify with the ideal type of his sex, or to respond without grave risk to the needs of his partner in the sexual relation, or even to receive adequately the needs of the child thus procreated.

What we are dealing with is an antinomy internal to the assumption by man (*Mensch*)[3] of his sex: why must he take up its attributes only by means of a threat, or even in the guise of a privation? As we know, in *Civilization and Its Discontents*, Freud went so far as to suggest not a contingent, but an essential disturbance of human sexuality, and one of his last articles[4] turns on the irreducibility for any finite (*endliche*) analysis of the effects following from the castration complex in

the masculine unconscious and from *penisneid* [penis envy] in the unconscious of the woman.

This is not the only point of uncertainty, but it is the first that the Freudian experience and its resulting metapsychology introduced into our experience of man. It cannot be solved by any reduction to biological factors, as the mere necessity of the myth underlying the structuring of the Oedipus complex makes sufficiently clear.

Any recourse to an hereditary amnesic given would in this instance be mere artifice, not only because such a factor is in itself disputable, but because it leaves the problem untouched, namely, the link between the murder of the father and the pact of the primordial law, given that it is included in that law that castration should be the punishment for incest.

Only on the basis of the clinical facts can there be any fruitful discussion. These facts go to show that the relation of the subject to the phallus is set up regardless of the anatomical difference between the sexes, which is what makes its interpretation particularly intractable in the case of the woman and in relationship to her, specifically on the four following counts:

1. as to why the little girl herself considers, if only for a moment, that she is castrated, in the sense of being deprived of the phallus, at the hand of someone who is in the first instance her mother, an important point, and who then becomes her father, but in such a way that we must recognize in this transition a transference in the analytic sense of the term;

2. as to why, at a more primordial level, the mother is for both sexes considered as provided with a phallus, that is, as a phallic mother;

3. as to why, correlatively, the meaning of castration only acquires its full (clinically manifest) weight as regards symptom formation when it is discovered as castration of the mother;

4. these three problems culminate in the question of the reason for the phallic phase[5] in development. We know that Freud used this term to

Translated by Jacqueline Rose.
[1] See Freud, p. 497.
[2] Reason, rationale.
[3] In German a neuter term for a person of either sex.
[4] Lacan is referring to Freud's *Analysis Terminable and Interminable* (1937).

[5] See Freud, p. 497.

specify the earliest genital maturation — as on the one hand characterized by the imaginary predominance of the phallic attribute and masturbatory pleasure, and on the other by a localizing of this pleasure for the woman in the clitoris, which is thereby raised to the function of the phallus. This would seem to rule out for both sexes, until the end of this phase, that is, until the dissolution of the Oedipus complex, any instinctual awareness of the vagina as the place of genital penetration.

This ignorance smacks of mis-recognition [méconnaissance] in the technical sense of the term, especially as it is on occasions disproved. All it agrees with, surely, is Longus's fable in which he depicts the initiation of Daphnis and Chloë as dependent on the revelations of an old woman.[6]

It is for this reason that certain authors have been led to regard the phallic phase as an effect of repression, and the function assumed in it by the phallic object as a symptom. The difficulty starts when we need to know *which* symptom? Phobia, according to one, perversion according to another — or, indeed, to the same one. In this last case, it's not worth speculating: not that interesting transmutations of the object from phobia into fetish do not occur, but their interest resides precisely in the different place which they occupy in the structure. There would be no point in asking these authors to formulate this difference from the perspective of object relations which is currently in favor. This being for lack of any reference on the matter other than the loose notion of the part object,[7] uncriticized since Karl Abraham[8] first introduced it, which is more the pity in view of the easy option which it provides today.

The fact remains that, if one goes back to the surviving texts of the years 1928–32, the now abandoned debate on the phallic phase is a refreshing example of a passion for doctrine, which has been given an additional note of nostalgia by the degradation of psychoanalysis consequent on its American transplantation.[9]

A mere summary of the debate could only distort the genuine diversity of the positions taken by figures such as Helene Deutsch, Karen Horney and Ernest Jones, to mention only the most eminent.

The series of three articles which Jones devoted to the subject is especially suggestive: if only for the starting premise on which he constructs his argument, signalled by the term *aphanisis*,[10] which he himself coined. For by correctly posing the problem of the relationship between castration and desire, he reveals such a proximity to what he cannot quite grasp that the term which will later provide us with the key to the problem seems to emerge out of his very failure.

The amusing thing is the way he manages, on the authority of the very letter of Freud's text, to formulate a position which is directly opposed to it: a true model in a difficult genre.

The problem, however, refuses to go away, seeming to subvert Jones's own case for a re-establishment of the equality of natural rights (which surely gets the better of him in the Biblical "Man and woman God created them" with which he concludes). What does he actually gain by normalizing the function of the phallus as part object if he has to invoke its presence in the mother's body as internal object, a term which is a function of the fantasies uncovered by Melanie Klein,[11] and if he cannot therefore separate himself from her doctrine which sees these fantasies as a recurrence of the Oedipal formation which is located right back in earliest infancy.

---

[6]In *Daphnis and Chloë*, a pastoral romance in Greek by Longus (probably early third century C.E.), the titular characters do not know how to consummate their love until it is explained to Daphnis by Lycanion, an old woman.

[7]Fetishistic feelings that attach not to an entire person but to a single body part (e.g., the mother's breast).

[8]Karl Abraham (1877–1925) was one of Freud's early disciples, known principally for having set up the institution of analytic training which gives practitioners of psychoanalysis their credential of expertise.

[9]This and the next four paragraphs involve Lacan's attack on American psychoanalysts (Deutsch, Horney, and Jones) whom he accuses of distorting Freud's doctrines, muddle-headedly evading the key issue of the castration complex.

[10]Jones's term for loss of sexual desire.

[11]English psychoanalyst (1882–1960) who disagreed with Freud's notion that the superego develops as a result of the Oedipal struggle (among many other things); for Klein it occurs at the age of two or three. Lacan assumes that any American psychoanalyst who bases his theories on Klein must be at best misguided.

We will not go far wrong if we re-open the question by asking what could have imposed on Freud the obvious paradox of his position. For one has to allow that he was better guided than anyone else in his recognition of the order of unconscious phenomena, which order he had discovered, and that for want of an adequate articulation of the nature of these phenomena his followers were bound to go more or less astray.

It is on the basis of such a wager — laid down by me as the principle of a commentary of Freud's work which I have been pursuing for seven years — that I have been led to certain conclusions: above all, to argue, as necessary to any articulation of analytic phenomena, for the notion of the signifier, in the sense in which it is opposed to that of the signified in modern linguistic analysis.[12] The latter, born since Freud, could not be taken into account by him, but it is my contention that Freud's discovery stands out precisely for having had to anticipate its formulas, even while setting out from a domain in which one could hardly expect to recognize its sway. Conversely, it is Freud's discovery that gives to the opposition of signifier to signified the full weight which it should imply: namely, that the signifier has an active function in determining the effects in which the signifiable appears as submitting to its mark, becoming through that passion the signified.

This passion of the signifier then becomes a new dimension of the human condition, in that it is not only man who speaks, but in man and through man that it [ça] speaks,[13] that his nature is woven by effects in which we can find the structure of language, whose material he becomes, and that consequently there resounds in him, beyond anything ever conceived of by the psychology of ideas, the relation of speech.

It is in this sense that one can say that the consequences of the discovery of the unconscious have not been so much as glimpsed in the theory, although its repercussions have been felt in the praxis to a much greater extent than we are as yet aware of, even if only translated into effects of retreat.

Let me make clear that to argue for man's relation to the signifier as such has nothing to do with a "culturalist" position in the ordinary sense of the term, such as that which Karen Horney found herself anticipating in the dispute over the phallus and which Freud himself characterized as feminist.[14] The issue is not man's relation to language as a social phenomenon, since the question does not even arise of anything resembling that all too familiar ideological psychogenesis, not superseded by a peremptory recourse to the entirely metaphysical notion, underlying the mandatory appeal to the concrete, which is so pathetically conveyed by the term "affect."

It is a question of rediscovering in the laws governing that other scene (*eine andere Schauplatz*) which Freud designated, in relation to dreams, as that of the unconscious, the effects discovered at the level of the materially unstable elements which constitute the chain of language: effects determined by the double play of combination and substitution in the signifier, along the two axes of metaphor and metonymy which generate the signified; effects which are determinant in the institution of the subject. What emerges from this attempt is a topology in the mathematical sense of the term,[15] without which, as soon becomes clear, it is impossible even to register the structure of a symptom in the analytic sense of the term.

It speaks in the Other,[16] I say, designating by this Other the very place called upon by a recourse to speech in any relation where it intervenes. If it speaks in the Other, whether or not the subject hears it with his own ears, it is because it

---

[14]Karen Horney (1885–1952) disputed the universality of penis envy among females and suggested that males feel "womb envy." Lacan intends for his explanation of the phallus as a signifier to cut through the "culturalist" issues of patriarchy and feminism.

[15]In the "mathematical sense," topology is the study of what properties of geometrical objects remain constant under deformation.

[16]Phrases like "It speaks in the Other," which recur for the next few pages, need to be translated into the Lacanian terminology those attending his seminar would already have internalized. Here "It" is the Freudian id, the site of the drives, and the Other is the Symbolic realm of language-signs ("the very place called on by a recourse to speech").

[12]See the Introduction to Structuralism and Deconstruction, p. 811.

[13]"It" here means the Freudian *id*.

is there that the subject, according to a logic prior to any awakening of the signified, finds his signifying place. The discovery of what he articulates in that place, that is, in the unconscious, enables us to grasp the price of the division (*Spaltung*)[17] through which he is thus constituted.

The phallus is elucidated in its function here. In Freudian doctrine, the phallus is not a fantasy, if what is understood by that is an imaginary effect. Nor is it as such an object (part, internal, good, bad, etc. . . .) in so far as this term tends to accentuate the reality involved in a relationship. It is even less the organ, penis or clitoris, which it symbolizes. And it is not incidental that Freud took his reference for it from the simulacrum which it represented for the Ancients.

For the phallus is a signifier, a signifier whose function in the intrasubjective economy of analysis might lift the veil from that which it served in the mysteries. For it is to this signified that it is given to designate as a whole the effect of there being a signified, inasmuch as it conditions any such effect by its presence as signifier.

Let us examine, then, the effects of this presence. First they follow from the deviations of man's needs by the fact that he speaks, in the sense that as long as his needs are subjected to demand they return to him alienated. This is not the effect of his real dependency (one should not expect to find here the parasitic conception represented by the notion of dependency in the theory of neuroses) but precisely of the putting into signifying form as such and of the fact that it is from the place of the Other that his message is emitted.[18]

<hr>

[17]German for cleavage or splitting. Freud used this term for those who simultaneously know something and refuse to acknowledge it.

[18]Lacan is demonstrating, here and in what follows, the distortions (or knots) that follow from the expression of need in language. To demand something in a love relationship is implicitly to imply that the other person has power over one and that one is not getting what one has demanded, or that one is getting it, but only as a result of having asked, which devalues the gift. The Hegelian dialectic of desire (see the Introduction to this chapter) also leads to knots here, where what one wants is to be what the other person most desires, but whatever is given can no longer be desired (since one can desire only what one lacks).

What is thus alienated in needs constitutes an *Urverdrängung* (primal repression) because it cannot, by definition, be articulated in demand. But it reappears in a residue which then presents itself in man as desire (*das Begehren*). The phenomenology which emerges from analytic experience is certainly such as to demonstrate the paradoxical, deviant, erratic, eccentric and even scandalous character by which desire is distinguished from need. A fact too strongly attested not to have always won the recognition of moralists worthy of the name. It does seem that early Freudianism had to give this fact its due status. Yet paradoxically psychoanalysis finds itself at the head of an age-old obscurantism, all the more wearisome for its denial of the fact through the ideal of a theoretical and practical reduction of desire to need.

Hence the necessity for us to articulate that status here, starting with demand whose proper characteristics are eluded in the notion of frustration (which was never employed by Freud).

Demand in itself bears on something other than the satisfactions which it calls for. It is demand for a presence or an absence. This is manifest in the primordial relation to the mother, pregnant as it is with that Other to be situated *some way short of* any needs which it might gratify. Demand constitutes this Other as already possessing the "privilege" of satisfying needs, that is, the power to deprive them of the one thing by which they are satisfied. This privilege of the Other thus sketches out the radical form of the gift of something which it does not have, namely, what is called its love.

Hence it is that demand cancels out (*aufhebt*) the particularity of anything which might be granted by transmuting it into a proof of love, and the very satisfactions of need which it obtains are degraded (*sich erniedrigt*) as being no more than a crushing of the demand for love (all of which is palpable in the psychology of early child-care to which our nurse-analysts are so dedicated).

There is, then, a necessity for the particularity thus abolished to reappear *beyond* demand. Where it does indeed reappear, but preserving the structure harboring within the unconditional character of the demand for love. In a reversal which is not a simple negation of negation, the force of pure loss arises from the relic of an obliteration. In place of the unconditional aspect of demand, desire substitutes the "absolute" condition: in effect this condition releases that part of the proof of love which is resistant to the satisfaction of a need. Thus desire is neither the appetite for satisfaction, nor the demand for love, but the difference resulting from the subtraction of the first from the second, the very phenomenon of their splitting (*Spaltung*).

One can see how the sexual relation occupies this closed field of desire in which it will come to play out its fate. For this field is constituted so as to produce the enigma which this relation provokes in the subject, by "signifying" it to him twice over: as a return of the demand it arouses in the form of a demand made on the subject of need, and as an ambiguity cast onto the Other who is involved, in the proof of love demanded. The gap in this enigma betrays what determines it, conveyed at its simplest in this formula: that for each partner in the relation, the subject and the Other, it is not enough to be the subjects of need, nor objects of love, but they must stand as the cause of desire.

This truth is at the heart of all the mishaps of sexual life which belong in the field of psychoanalysis.

It is also the precondition in analysis for the subject's happiness: and to disguise this gap by relying on the virtue of the "genital" to resolve it through the maturation of tenderness (that is by a recourse to the Other solely as reality), however piously intended, is none the less a fraud. Admittedly it was French psychoanalysts with their hypocritical notion of genital oblativity[19] who started up the moralizing trend which, to the tune of Salvationist choirs, is now followed everywhere.

In any case man cannot aim at being whole (the "total personality" being another premise where modern psychotherapy goes off course) once the play of displacement and condensation, to which he is committed in the exercise of his functions, marks his relation as subject to the signifier.

The phallus is the privileged signifier of that mark where the share of the logos is wedded to

the advent of desire. One might say that this signifier is chosen as what stands out as most easily seized upon in the real of sexual copulation, and also as the most symbolic in the literal (typographical) sense of the term, since it is the equivalent in that relation of the (logical) copula. One might also say that by virtue of its turgidity, it is the image of the vital flow as it is transmitted in generation.

All these propositions merely veil over the fact that the phallus can only play its role as veiled, that is, as in itself the sign of the latency with which everything signifiable is struck as soon as it is raised (*aufgehoben*) to the function of signifier.

The phallus is the signifier of this *Aufhebung* itself which it inaugurates (initiates) by its own disappearance. This is why the demon of Αἰδώς [*Scham*, shame] in the ancient mysteries rises up exactly at the moment when the phallus is unveiled (cf. the famous painting of the Villa of Pompei).[20]

It then becomes the bar which, at the hands of this demon, strikes the signified, branding it as the bastard offspring of its signifying concatenation.

In this way a condition of complementarity is produced by the signifier in the founding of the subject: which explains his *Spaltung* as well as the intervening movement through which this is effected.
Namely:

1. that the subject designates his being only by crossing through everything which it signifies, as can be seen in the fact that he wishes to be loved for himself, a mirage not dispelled merely by being denounced as grammatical (since it abolishes discourse);

2. that the living part of that being in the *urverdrängt* [primary repressed] finds its signifier by receiving the mark of the *Verdrängung* [repression] of the phallus (whereby the unconscious is language).

The phallus as signifier gives the ratio of desire (in the musical sense of the term as the "mean and extreme" ratio of harmonic division).

---

[19]Self-sacrifice.

[20]At the House of the Vettii in Pompeii is a mural depicting the god Priapus weighing his enormous penis in a pair of scales against a sack of gold.

It is, therefore, as an algorithm that I am going to use it now, relying — necessarily if I am to avoid drawing out my account indefinitely — on the echoes of the experience which unites us to give you the sense of this usage.

If the phallus is a signifier then it is in the place of the Other that the subject gains access to it. But in that the signifier is only there veiled and as the ratio of the Other's desire, so it is this desire of the Other as such which the subject has to recognize, meaning, the Other as itself a subject divided by the signifying *Spaltung*.

What can be seen to emerge in psychological genesis confirms this signifying function of the phallus.

Thus, to begin with, we can formulate more correctly the Kleinian fact that the child apprehends from the outset that the mother "contains" the phallus.

But it is the dialectic of the demand for love and the test of desire which dictates the order of development.

The demand for love can only suffer from a desire whose signifier is alien to it. If the desire of the mother *is* the phallus, then the child wishes to be the phallus so as to satisfy this desire. Thus the division immanent to desire already makes itself felt in the desire of the Other, since it stops the subject from being satisfied with presenting to the Other anything real it might *have* which corresponds to this phallus — what he has being worth no more than what he does not have as far as his demand for love is concerned, which requires that he *be* the phallus.

Clinical practice demonstrates that this test of the desire of the Other is not decisive in the sense that the subject learns from it whether or not he has a real phallus, but inasmuch as he learns that the mother does not.[21] This is the moment of

experience without which no symptomatic or structural consequence (that is, phobia or *penis-neid*) referring to the castration complex can take effect. It is here that the conjunction is signed between desire, in so far as the phallic signifier is its mark, and the threat or the nostalgia of lack-in-having.

It is, of course, the law introduced into this sequence by the father which will decide its future.

But simply by keeping to the function of the phallus, we can pinpoint the structures which will govern the relations between the sexes.

Let us say that these relations will revolve around a being and a having which, because they refer to a signifier, the phallus, have the contradictory effect of on the one hand lending reality to the subject in that signifier, and on the other making unreal the relations to be signified.

This follows from the intervention of an "appearing" which gets substituted for the "having" so as to protect it on one side and to mask its lack on the other, with the effect that the ideal or typical manifestations of behavior in both sexes, up to and including the act of sexual copulation, are entirely propelled into comedy.

These ideals gain new strength from the demand which it is in their power to satisfy, which is always the demand for love,[22] with its complement of reducing desire to demand.

Paradoxical as this formulation might seem, I would say that it is in order to be the phallus, that is to say, the signifier of the desire of the Other, that the woman will reject an essential part of her femininity, notably all its attributes through masquerade. It is for what she is not that she expects to be desired as well as loved. But she finds the signifier of her own desire in the body of the one to whom she addresses her demand for love. Certainly we should not forget that the organ actually invested with this signifying function takes on the value of a fetish. But for the woman the result is still a convergence onto the same object of an experience of love which as such (cf. above) ideally deprives her of that which it gives, and a desire which finds in

[21]Lacan has arrived at the point where the Freudian castration complex is restated in its symbolic meaning. It isn't that little boys and girls think their mother has been castrated in any physical sense, it is that they have worked out that, since they as children are *le désir de la mère*, the object of maternal desire, and since the phallus is the signifier of desire and since one cannot desire what one already has, the mother must lack the phallus. (The "phallic mother" of early object relations is the imago of the spectrally powerful figure before the child works that out.)

[22]The sexes differ over the issue of being and having, and Lacan's paradoxical formulation is that women want to *be* the phallus, whereas men want to *have* the phallus.

that same experience its signifier. Which is why it can be observed that the lack of satisfaction proper to sexual need, in other words, frigidity, is relatively well tolerated in women, whereas the *Verdrängung* inherent to desire is lesser in her case than in the case of the man.

In men, on the other hand, the dialectic of demand and desire gives rise to effects, whose exact point of connection Freud situated with a sureness which we must once again admire, under the rubric of a specific depreciation (*Erniedrigung*) of love.[23]

If it is the case that the man manages to satisfy his demand for love in his relationship to the woman to the extent that the signifier of the phallus constitutes her precisely as giving in love what she does not have — conversely, his own desire for the phallus will throw up its signifier in the form of a persistent divergence towards "another woman" who can signify this phallus under various guises, whether as a virgin or a prostitute. The result is a centrifugal tendency of the genital drive in the sexual life of the man which makes impotence much harder for him to bear, at the same time as the *Verdrängung* inherent to desire is greater.

[23]Lacan alludes to the Groucho Marx paradox, that one wouldn't want to join a club that would be willing to have one as a member. Once a woman becomes, in the realm of the signifier, the phallus the man wants, he ceases to want it, and is drawn to other women. Similarly, though, for the woman, the gift of the phallus deprives the man of what he has, and thereby diminishes her desire. One sees why Lacan refers to the relations between the sexes as a comedy...

We should not, however, think that the type of infidelity which then appears to be constitutive of the masculine function is exclusive to the man. For if one looks more closely, the same redoubling is to be found in the woman, except that in her case, the Other of love as such, that is to say, the Other as deprived of that which he gives, is hard to perceive in the withdrawal whereby it is substituted for the being of the man whose attributes she cherishes.

One might add here that masculine homosexuality, in accordance with the phallic mark which constitutes desire, is constituted on its axis, whereas the orientation of feminine homosexuality, as observation shows, follows from a disappointment which reinforces the side of the demand for love. These remarks should be qualified by going back to the function of the mask inasmuch as this function dominates the identifications through which refusals of love are resolved.

The fact that femininity takes refuge in this mask, because of the *Verdrängung* inherent to the phallic mark of desire, has the strange consequence that, in the human being, virile display itself appears as feminine.

Correlatively, one can glimpse the reason for a feature which has never been elucidated and which again gives a measure of the depth of Freud's intuition: namely, why he advances the view that there is only one libido, his text clearly indicating that he conceives of it as masculine in nature. The function of the signifier here touches on its most profound relation: by way of which the Ancients embodied in it both the Νοῦς [*Nous*, sense] and the Λογὸς [*Logos*, reason].

Harold Bloom

b. 1930

Harold Bloom's theories of poetic misprision and anxiety have changed how critics think about literary tradition. Bloom was born in New York City, took his B.A. at Cornell, and received his Ph.D. from Yale in 1955. He has been a member of the Yale faculty since then and is at present Sterling Professor of English and the Humanities. Bloom's brilliance is fabled; he possesses an eidetic memory and is said to have read English before he spoke it. In 1985 he received one of the so-called genius awards from the MacArthur Foundation. His studies of Romantic poets include Shelley's Mythmaking *(1959),*

The Visionary Company (*1961*), Blake's Apocalypse (*1963*), *and* The Ringers in the Tower (*1971*). *His theories about creative misreading in the poetic tradition have unfolded recursively through several books, including* The Anxiety of Influence (*1973*) *excerpted here,* A Map of Misreading (*1975*), Kabbalah and Criticism (*1975*), Poetry and Repression (*1976*), *and* Agon: Towards a Theory of Revisionism (*1982*). *After shaking up traditional notions of literary history in his "revision" books, Bloom defended the objects of traditional history in* The Western Canon: The Books and School of the Ages (*1994*), *and did a how-to book in* How to Read and Why (*2000*). *He seems to have turned for a long-term project, however, to the Bible and religion. In* The Book of J (*1990*), *Bloom identifies the author of the J-text, the oldest strand of narrative in Genesis, Exodus, and Numbers, as a woman, specifically a princess of the line of David writing in the reigns of Solomon and Rehoboam; the book has sold millions of copies but has been scorned by biblical scholars, less for its wild speculations than for its defective understanding of the Hebrew text. Bloom's latest pronouncements on religion are contained in* The American Religion: The Emergence of the Post-Christian Nation (*1992*), Omens of Millenium: The Gnosis of Angels, Dreams, and Resurrection (*1996*), *and* Where Shall Wisdom Be Found? (*2004*).

A Meditation upon Priority

This short book offers a theory of poetry by way of a description of poetic influence, or the story of intrapoetic relationships. One aim of this theory is corrective: to deidealize our accepted accounts of how one poet helps to form another. Another aim, also corrective, is to try to provide a poetics that will foster a more adequate practical criticism.

Poetic history, in this book's argument, is held to be indistinguishable from poetic influence, since strong poets make that history by misreading one another, so as to clear imaginative space for themselves.

My concern is only with strong poets, major figures with the persistence to wrestle with their strong precursors, even to the death. Weaker talents idealize; figures of capable imagination appropriate for themselves. But nothing is got for nothing, and self-appropriation involves the immense anxieties of indebtedness, for what strong maker desires the realization that he has failed to create himself? Oscar Wilde, who knew he had failed as a poet because he lacked strength to overcome his anxiety of influence, knew also the darker truths concerning influence. *The Ballad of Reading Gaol* becomes an embarrassment to read, directly one recognizes that every lustre it exhibits is reflected from *The Rime of the Ancient Mariner;* and Wilde's lyrics

anthologize the whole of English High Romanticism. Knowing this, and armed with his customary intelligence, Wilde bitterly remarks in *The Portrait of Mr. W. H.* that: "Influence is simply a transference of personality, a mode of giving away what is most precious to one's self, and its exercise produces a sense, and, it may be, a reality of loss. Every disciple takes away something from his master." This is the anxiety of influencing, yet no reversal in this area is a true reversal. Two years later, Wilde refined this bitterness in one of Lord Henry Wotton's elegant observations in *The Picture of Dorian Gray,* where he tells Dorian that all influence is immoral:

> Because to influence a person is to give him one's own soul. He does not think his natural thoughts, or burn with his natural passions. His virtues are not real to him. His sins, if there are such things as sins, are borrowed. He becomes an echo of someone else's music, an actor of a part that has not been written for him.

To apply Lord Henry's insight to Wilde, we need only read Wilde's review of Pater's *Appreciations,* with its splendidly self-deceptive closing observation that Pater "has escaped disciples." Every major aesthetic consciousness seems peculiarly more gifted at denying obligation as the hungry generations go on treading one another down. Stevens, a stronger heir of Pater than even Wilde was, is revealingly vehement in his letters:

> While, of course, I come down from the past, the past is my own and not something marked Coleridge, Wordsworth, etc. I know of no one who has been particularly important to me. My reality-imagination complex is entirely my own even though I see it in others.

He might have said: "particularly because I see it in others," but poetic influence was hardly a subject where Stevens's insights could center. Towards the end, his denials became rather violent, and oddly humored. Writing to the poet Richard Eberhart, he extends a sympathy all the stronger for being self-sympathy:

> I sympathize with your denial of any influence on my part. This sort of thing always jars me because, in my own case, I am not conscious of having been influenced by anybody and have purposely held off from reading highly mannered people like Eliot and Pound so that I should not absorb anything, even unconsciously. But there is a kind of critic who spends his time dissecting what he reads for echoes, imitations, influences, as if no one was ever simply himself but is always compounded of a lot of other people. As for W. Blake, I think that this means Wilhelm Blake.

This view, that poetic influence scarcely exists, except in furiously active pedants, is itself an illustration of one way in which poetic influence is a variety of melancholy or an anxiety-principle. Stevens was, as he insisted, a highly individual poet, as much an American original as Whitman or Dickinson, or his own contemporaries: Pound, Williams, Moore. But poetic influence need not make poets less original; as often it makes them more original, though not therefore necessarily better. The profundities of poetic influence cannot be reduced to source-study, to the history of ideas, to the patterning of images. Poetic influence, or as I shall more frequently term it, poetic misprision, is necessarily the study of the life-cycle of the poet-as-poet. When such study considers the context in which that life-cycle is enacted, it will be compelled to examine simultaneously the relations between poets as cases akin to what Freud called the family romance, and as chapters in the history of modern revisionism, "modern" meaning here post-Enlightenment. The modern poet, as W. J. Bate shows in *The Burden of the Past and the English Poet,* is the inheritor of a melancholy engendered in the mind of the Enlightenment by its skepticism of its own double heritage of imaginative wealth, from the ancients and from the Renaissance masters. In this book I largely neglect the area Bate has explored with great skill, in order to center upon intrapoetic relationships as parallels of family romance. Though I employ these parallels, I do so as a deliberate revisionist of some of the Freudian emphases.

Nietzsche and Freud are, so far as I can tell, the prime influences upon the theory of influence presented in this book. Nietzsche is the prophet of the antithetical, and his *Genealogy of Morals* is the profoundest study available to me of the revisionary and ascetic strains in the aesthetic temperament. Freud's investigations of the mechanisms of defense and their ambivalent functionings provide the clearest analogues I have found for the revisionary ratios that govern intrapoetic relations. Yet, the theory of influence expounded here is un-Nietzschean in its deliberate literalism, and in its Viconian insistence that priority in divination is crucial for every strong poet, lest he dwindle merely into a latecomer. My theory rejects also the qualified Freudian optimism that happy substitution is possible, that a second chance can save us from the repetitive quest for our earliest attachments. Poets as poets cannot accept substitutions, and fight to the end to have their initial chance alone. Both Nietzsche and Freud underestimated poets and poetry, yet each yielded more power to phantasmagoria than it truly possesses. They too, despite their moral realism, overidealized the imagination. Nietzsche's disciple, Yeats, and Freud's disciple, Otto Rank, show a greater awareness of the artist's fight against art, and of the relation of this struggle to the artist's antithetical battle against nature.

Freud recognized sublimation as the highest human achievement, a recognition that allies him to Plato and to the entire moral traditions of both Judaism and Christianity. If Wordsworth's

Ode: Intimations of Immortality from Recollections of Early Childhood possessed only the wisdom found also in Freud, then we could cease calling it "the Great Ode." Wordsworth too saw repetition or second chance as essential for development, and his ode admits that we can redirect our needs by substitution or sublimation. But the ode plangently also awakens into failure, and into the creative mind's protest against time's tyranny. A Wordsworthian critic, even one as loyal to Wordsworth as Geoffrey Hartman, can insist upon clearly distinguishing between *priority,* as a concept from the natural order, and *authority,* from the spiritual order, but Wordsworth's ode declines to make this distinction. "By seeking to overcome priority," Hartman wisely says, "art fights nature on nature's own ground, and is bound to lose." The argument of this book is that strong poets are condemned to just this unwisdom; Wordsworth's Great Ode fights nature on nature's own ground, and suffers a great defeat, even as it retains its greater dream. That dream, in Wordsworth's ode, is shadowed by the anxiety of influence, due to the greatness of the precursor-poem, Milton's *Lycidas,* where the human refusal wholly to sublimate is even more rugged, despite the ostensible yielding to Christian teachings of sublimation.

For every poet begins (however "unconsciously") by rebelling more strongly against the consciousness of death's necessity than all other men and women do. The young citizen of poetry, or ephebe as Athens would have called him, is already the antinatural or antithetical man, and from his start as a poet he quests for an impossible object, as his precursor quested before him. That this quest encompasses necessarily the diminishment of poetry seems to me an inevitable realization, one that accurate literary history must sustain. The great poets of the English Renaissance are not matched by their Enlightened descendants, and the whole tradition of the post-Enlightenment, which is Romanticism, shows a further decline in its Modernist and post-Modernist heirs. The death of poetry will not be hastened by any reader's broodings, yet it seems just to assume that poetry in our tradition, when it dies, will be self-slain, murdered by its own past strength. An implied anguish throughout this book is that Romanticism, for all its glories, may have been a vast visionary tragedy, the self-baffled enterprise not of Prometheus but of blinded Oedipus, who did not know that the Sphinx was his Muse.

Oedipus, blind, was on the path to oracular godhood, and the strong poets have followed him by transforming their blindness towards their precursors into the revisionary insights of their own work. The six revisionary movements that I will trace in the strong poet's life-cycle could as well be more, and could take quite different names than those I have employed. I have kept them to six, because these seem to be minimal and essential to my understanding of how one poet deviates from another. The names, though arbitrary, carry on from various traditions that have been central in Western imaginative life, and I hope can be useful.

The greatest poet in our language is excluded from the argument of this book for several reasons. One is necessarily historical; Shakespeare belongs to the giant age before the flood, before the anxiety of influence became central to poetic consciousness. Another has to do with the contrast between dramatic and lyric form. As poetry has become more subjective, the shadow cast by the precursors has become more dominant. The main cause, though, is that Shakespeare's prime precursor was Marlowe, a poet very much smaller than his inheritor. Milton, with all his strength, yet had to struggle, subtly and crucially, with a major precursor in Spenser, and this struggle both formed and malformed Milton. Coleridge, ephebe of Milton and later of Wordsworth, would have been glad to find his Marlowe in Cowper (or in the much weaker Bowles), but influence cannot be willed. Shakespeare is the largest instance in the language of a phenomenon that stands outside the concern of this book: the absolute absorption of the precursor. Battle between strong equals, father and son as mighty opposites, Laius and Oedipus at the crossroads; only this is my subject here, though some of the fathers, as will be seen, are composite figures. That even the strongest poets are subject to influences not poetical is obvious even to me, but again my concern is only with *the poet in a poet,* or the aboriginal poetic self.

A change like the one I propose in our ideas of influence should help us read more accurately any group of past poets who were contemporary with one another. To give one example, as misinterpreters of Keats, *in their poems,* the Victorian disciples of Keats most notably include Tennyson, Arnold, Hopkins, and Rossetti. That Tennyson triumphed in his long, hidden contest with Keats, no one can assert absolutely, but his clear superiority over Arnold, Hopkins, and Rossetti is due to his relative victory or at least holding of his own in contrast to their partial defeats. Arnold's elegiac poetry uneasily blends Keatsian style with anti-Romantic sentiment, while Hopkins's strained intensities and convolutions of diction and Rossetti's densely inlaid art are also at variance with the burdens they seek to alleviate in their own poetic selves. Similarly, in our time we need to look again at Pound's unending match with Browning, as at Stevens's long and largely hidden civil war with the major poets of English and American Romanticism — Wordsworth, Keats, Shelley, Emerson, and Whitman. As with the Victorian Keatsians, these are instances among many, if a more accurate story is to be told about poetic history.

This book's main purpose is necessarily to present one reader's critical vision, in the context both of the criticism and poetry of his own generation, where their current crises most touch him, and in the context of his own anxieties of influence. In the contemporary poems that most move me, like the *Corsons Inlet* and *Saliences* of A. R. Ammons and the *Fragment* and *Soonest Mended* of John Ashbery, I can recognize a strength that battles against the death of poetry, yet also the exhaustions of being a latecomer. Similarly, in the contemporary criticism that clarifies for me my own evasions, in books like *Allegory* by Angus Fletcher, *Beyond Formalism* by Geoffrey Hartman, and *Blindness and Insight* by Paul de Man, I am made aware of the mind's effort to overcome the impasse of Formalist criticism, the barren moralizing that Archetypal criticism has come to be, and the antihumanistic plain dreariness of all those developments in European criticism that have yet to demonstrate that they can aid in reading any one poem by any poet whatsoever. My Interchapter, proposing a more antithetical

practical criticism than any we now have, is my response in this area of the contemporary.

A theory of poetry that presents itself as a severe poem, reliant upon aphorism, apothegm, and a quite personal (though thoroughly traditional) mythic pattern, still may be judged, and may ask to be judged, as argument. Everything that makes up this book — parables, definitions, the working-through of the revisionary ratios as mechanisms of defense — intends to be part of a unified meditation on the melancholy of the creative mind's desperate insistence upon priority. Vico,[1] who read all creation as a severe poem, understood that priority in the natural order and authority in the spiritual order had been one and had to remain one, *for poets,* because only this harshness constituted Poetic Wisdom. Vico reduced both natural priority and spiritual authority to property, a Hermetic reduction that I recognize as the *Ananke,* the dreadful necessity still governing the Western imagination.

Valentinus,[2] second-century Gnostic speculator, came out of Alexandria to teach the Pleroma, the Fullness of thirty Aeons, manifold of Divinity: "It was a great marvel that they were in the Father without knowing Him." To search for where you already are is the most benighted of quests, and the most fated. Each strong poet's Muse, his Sophia, leaps as far out and down as can be, in a solipsistic passion of quest. Valentinus posited a Limit, at which quest ends, but no quest ends, if its context is Unconditioned Mind, the cosmos of the greatest post-Miltonic poets. The Sophia of Valentinus recovered, wed again within the Pleroma, and only her Passion or Dark Intention was separated out into our world, beyond the Limit. Into this Passion, the Dark Intention that Valentinus called "strengthless and female fruit," the ephebe must fall. If he emerges from it, however crippled and blinded, he will be among the strong poets.

---

[1]Giambattista Vico (1668–1744), author of the *Scienza Nuova* (1725).
[2]Second-century Egyptian religious philosopher, founder of the Roman and Alexandrian Gnostics, author of *The Gospel of Truth.*

SYNOPSIS: SIX REVISIONARY RATIOS

1. *Clinamen,* which is poetic misreading or misprision proper; I take the word from Lucretius,[3] where it means a "swerve" of the atoms so as to make change possible in the universe. A poet swerves away from his precursor, by so reading his precursor's poem as to execute a *clinamen* in relation to it. This appears as a corrective movement in his own poem, which implies that the precursor poem went accurately up to a certain point, but then should have swerved, precisely in the direction that the new poem moves.

2. *Tessera,* which is completion and antithesis; I take the word not from mosaic-making, where it is still used, but from the ancient mystery cults, where it meant a token of recognition, the fragment say of a small pot which with the other fragments would reconstitute the vessel. A poet antithetically "completes" his precursor, by so reading the parent-poem as to retain its terms but to mean them in another sense, as though the precursor had failed to go far enough.

3. *Kenosis,* which is a breaking-device similar to the defense mechanisms our psyches employ against repetition compulsions; *kenosis* then is a movement towards discontinuity with the precursor. I take the word from St. Paul, where it means the humbling or emptying-out of Jesus by himself, when he accepts reduction from divine to human status. The later poet, apparently emptying himself of his own afflatus, his imaginative godhood, seems to humble himself as though he were ceasing to be a poet, but this ebbing is so performed in relation to a precursor's poem-of-ebbing that the precursor is emptied out also, and so the later poem of deflation is not as absolute as it seems.

[3] In his cosmogony, *De rerum natura.*

4. *Daemonization,* or a movement towards a personalized Counter-Sublime, in reaction to the precursor's Sublime; I take the term from general Neo-Platonic usage, where an intermediary being, neither divine nor human, enters into the adept to aid him. The later poet opens himself to what he believes to be a power in the parent-poem that does not belong to the parent proper, but to a range of being just beyond that precursor. He does this, in his poem, by so stationing its relation to the parent-poem as to generalize away the uniqueness of the earlier work.

5. *Askesis,* or a movement of self-purgation which intends the attainment of a state of solitude; I take the term, general as it is, particularly from the practice of pre-Socratic shamans like Empedocles. The later poet does not, as in *kenosis,* undergo a revisionary movement of emptying, but of curtailing; he yields up part of his own human and imaginative endowment, so as to separate himself from others, including the precursor, and he does this in his poem by so stationing it in regard to the parent-poem as to make that poem undergo an *askesis* too; the precursor's endowment is also truncated.

6. *Apophrades,* or the return of the dead; I take the word from the Athenian dismal or unlucky days upon which the dead returned to reinhabit the houses in which they had lived. The later poet, in his own final phase, already burdened by an imaginative solitude that is almost a solipsism, holds his own poem so open again to the precursor's work that at first we might believe the wheel has come full circle, and that we are back in the later poet's flooded apprenticeship, before his strength began to assert itself in the revisionary ratios. But the poem is now *held* open to the precursor, where once it *was* open, and the uncanny effect is that the new poem's achievement makes it seem to us, not as though the precursor were writing it, but as though the later poet himself had written the precursor's characteristic work.

Peter Brooks

b. 1938

Peter Preston Brooks was born in New York City and educated at Harvard University, where he received his Ph.D. in French in 1965. He taught French and comparative literature at Yale and is now University Professor of English at the University of Virginia. His publications include The Novel of Worldliness *(1969),* The Child's Part *(1972), and* The Melodramatic Imagination *(1975). Recent essays have analyzed works by Balzac, Flaubert, Maupassant, Zola, and Henry James. His most influential book, a classic manifesto on the relationship between literature and modern French psychoanalysis, is* Reading for the Plot: Design and Intention in Narrative *(1984; second edition, 1990), from which the following selection is excerpted. His most recent books are* Body Work: Objects of Desire in Modern Narrative *(1993),* Psychoanalysis and Storytelling *(1994),* Law's Stories: Narrative and Rhetoric in the Law *(1996), and* Troubling Confessions: Speaking Guilt in Law and Literature *(2000). Brooks has also written a novel,* World Elsewhere *(1999).*

Freud's Masterplot

> *As if they would confine th' Interminable,*
> *And tie him to his own prescript.*[1]

In one of his best essays in "narratology," where he is working toward a greater formalization of principles advanced by Vladimir Propp and Viktor Shklovsky,[2] Tzvetan Todorov elaborates a model of narrative transformation whereby narrative plot *(le récit)* is constituted in the tension of two formal categories, difference and resemblance.[3] Transformation — a change in a predicate term common to beginning and end — represents a synthesis of difference and resemblance; it is, we might say, the same-but-different. Now "the same-but-different" is a common (and if inadequate, not altogether false) definition of metaphor. If

Aristotle affirmed that the master of metaphor must have an eye for resemblances,[4] modern treatments of the subject have affirmed equally the importance of difference included within the operation of resemblance, the chief value of the metaphor residing in its "tension." Narrative operates as metaphor in its affirmation of resemblance, in that it brings into relation different actions, combines them through perceived similarities (Todorov's common predicate term), appropriates them to a common plot, which implies the rejection of merely contingent (or unassimilable) incident or action. The plotting of meaning cannot do without metaphor, for meaning in plot is the structure of action in closed and legible wholes. Metaphor is in this sense totalizing. Yet it is equally apparent that the key figure of narrative must in some sense be not metaphor but

---

I wish at the outset of this essay to express my debt to two colleagues whose thinking has helped to clarify my own: Andrea Bertolini and David A. Miller. It is to the latter that I owe the term "the narratable." [Brooks]

[1] From Milton, *Samson Agonistes*, lines 307–08.

[2] See the introduction to Formalism, p. 749.

[3] Tzvetan Todorov, "Les Transformations narratives," in *Poétique de la prose* (Paris: Seuil, 1971), p. 240. Todorov's

terms *récit* and *histoire* correspond to the Russian Formalist distinction between *sjužet* and *fabula*. In English, we might use with the same sense of distinctions: narrative *plot* and *story*. [Brooks]

[4] See Aristotle, *Poetics*, p. 59.

metonymy: the figure of contiguity and combination, the figure of syntagmatic relations.[5] The description of narrative needs metonymy as the figure of movement, of linkage in the signifying chain, of the slippage of the signified under the signifier. That Jacques Lacan has equated metonymy and desire[6] is of the utmost pertinence, since desire must be considered the very motor of narrative, its dynamic principle.

The problem with "the same-but-different" as a definition of narrative would be the implication of simultaneity and stasis in the formulation. The postulation of a static model indeed is the central deficiency of most formalist and structuralist work on narrative, which has sought to make manifest the structures of narrative in spatial and atemporal terms, as versions of Lévi-Strauss's "atemporal matrix structure."[7] Todorov is an exception in that, faithful to Propp, he recognizes the need to consider sequence and succession as well as the paradigmatic matrix. He supplements his definition with the remark: "Rather than a 'coin with two faces,' [transformation] is an operation in two directions: it affirms at once resemblance and difference; it puts time into motion and suspends it, in a single movement; it allows discourse to acquire a meaning without this meaning becoming pure information; in a word, it makes narrative possible and reveals its

very definition."[8] The image of a double operation upon time has the value of returning us to the evident but frequently eluded fact that narrative meanings are developed in time, that any narrative partakes more or less of what Proust called "un jeu formidable . . . avec le Temps," and that this game of time is not merely in the world of reference (or in the *fabula*) but as well in the narrative, in the *sjužet,* be it only that the meanings developed by narrative *take time:* the time of reading.[9] If at the end of a narrative we can suspend time in a moment where past and present hold together in a metaphor which may be the very recognition which, said Aristotle, every good plot should bring,[10] that moment does not abolish the movement, the slidings, the errors and partial recognitions of the middle. As Roland Barthes points out, in what so far must be counted our most satisfactory dynamic analysis of plot, the proairetic and hermeneutic codes — code of actions, code of enigmas and answers — are irreversible: their interpretation is determined linearly, in sequence, in one direction.[11]

Ultimately — Barthes writes elsewhere — the passion that animates us as readers of narrative is the passion for (of) meaning.[12] Since for Barthes meaning (in the "classical" or "readable" text) resides in full predication, completion of the codes in a "plenitude" of signification, this passion appears to be finally a desire for the end. It is at the end — for Barthes as for Aristotle — that recognition brings its illumination, which then can shed retrospective light. The function of the end, whether considered syntactically (as in Todorov and Barthes) or ethically (as in Aristotle) or as formal or cosmological closure

[5]See Roman Jakobson, "Two Types of Language and Two Types of Aphasic Disturbances," in Jakobson and Halle, *Fundamentals of Language* (The Hague: Mouton, 1956). Todorov in a later article adds to "transformation" the term "succession," and sees the pair as definitional of narrative. He discusses the possible equation of these terms with Jakobson's "metaphor" and "metonymy," to conclude that "the connection is possible but does not seem necessary." (Todorov, "The Two Principles of Narrative," *Diacritics,* Fall, 1971, p. 42.) But there seem to be good reasons to maintain Jakobson's terms as "master tropes" referring to two aspects of virtually any text. [Brooks]
[6]See Jacques Lacan, "The Mirror Stage, as Formative of the Function of the I as Revealed in Psychoanalytic Experience" (1977). See p. 1123.
[7]See Claude Lévi-Strauss, "La Structure et la forme," *Cahiers de l'Institut de science économique appliquée,* 99, série M, no. 7 (1960), p. 29. This term is cited with approval by A. J. Greimas in *Sémantique structurale* (Paris: Larousse, 1966) and Roland Barthes, in "Introduction à l'analyse structurale des récits," *Communications* 8 (1966). [Brooks]

[8]Todorov, "Les Transformations narratives," *Poétique de la prose,* p. 240. Translations from the French, here and elsewhere, are my own. [Brooks]
[9]Proust's phrase is cited by Gérard Genette in "Discours du récit," *Figures III* (Paris: Seuil, 1972), p. 182. Whereas Barthes maintains in "Introduction à l'analyse structurale des récits" that time belongs only to the referent of narrative, Genette gives attention to the time of reading and its necessary linearity. See pp. 77–78. [Brooks]
[10]See Aristotle, *Poetics,* p. 59.
[11]See Roland Barthes, *S/Z* (Paris: Seuil, 1970), p. 37. [Brooks]
[12]"Introduction à l'analyse structurale des récits," p. 27. [Brooks]

(as in Barbara H. Smith or Frank Kermode)[13] continues to fascinate and to baffle. One of the strongest statements of its determinative position in narrative plots comes in a passage from Sartre's *La Nausée* which bears quotation once again. Roquentin is reflecting on the meaning of "adventure" and the difference between living and narrating. When you narrate, you appear to start with a beginning. You say, "It was a fine autumn evening in 1922. I was a notary's clerk in Marommes." But, says Roquentin:

> In reality you have started at the end. It was there, invisible and present, it is what gives these few words the pomp and value of a beginning. "I was out walking, I had left the town without realizing it, I was thinking about my money troubles." This sentence, taken simply for what it is, means that the man was absorbed, morose, a hundred miles from an adventure, exactly in a mood to let things happen without noticing them. But the end is there, transforming everything. For us, the man is already the hero of the story. His moroseness, his money troubles are much more precious than ours, they are all gilded by the light of future passions. And the story goes on in the reverse: instants have stopped piling themselves up in a haphazard way one on another, they are caught up by the end of the story which draws them and each one in its turn draws the instant preceding it: "It was night, the street was deserted." The sentence is thrown out negligently, it seems superfluous; but we don't let ourselves be duped, we put it aside: this is a piece of information whose value we will understand later on. And we feel that the hero has lived all the details of this night as annunciations, as promises, or even that he has lived only those that were promises, blind and deaf to all that did not herald adventure. We forget that the future wasn't yet there; the man was walking in a night without premonitions, which offered him in disorderly fashion its monotonous riches, and he did not choose.[14]

The beginning in fact presupposes the end. The very possibility of meaning plotted through time depends on the anticipated structuring force of the ending: the interminable would be the meaningless. We read the incidents of narration as "promises and annunciations" of final coherence: the metaphor reached through the chain of metonymies. As Roquentin further suggests, we read only those incidents and signs which can be construed as promise and annunciation, enchained toward a construction of significance — those signs which, as in the detective story, appear to be *clues* to the underlying intentionality of event.

The sense of beginning, then, is determined by the sense of an ending. And if we inquire further into the nature of the ending, we no doubt find that it eventually has to do with the human end, with death. In *Les Mots,* Sartre pushes further his reflection on ends. He describes how in order to escape contingency and the sense of being unjustified he had to imagine himself as one of the children in *L'Enfance des hommes illustrés,* determined, as promise and annunciation, by what he would become for posterity. He began to live his life retrospectively, in terms of the death that alone would confer meaning and necessity on existence. As he succinctly puts it, "I became my own obituary."[15] All narration is obituary in that life acquires definable meaning only at, and through, death. In an independent but convergent argument, Walter Benjamin has claimed that life assumes transmissible form only at the moment of death. For Benjamin, this death is the very "authority" of narrative: we seek in fictions the knowledge of death, which in our own lives is denied to us. Death — which may be figural but in the classic instances of the genre is so often literal — quickens meaning: it is the "flame," says Benjamin, at which we warm our "shivering" lives.[16]

We need to know more about this deathlike ending which is nonetheless animating of meaning in relation to initiatory desire, and about how the interrelationship of the two determines, shapes, necessitates the middle — Barthes's "dilatory space" of retard, postponement — and the

[13]Barbara Herrnstein Smith's *Poetic Closure* (1968) analyzed "formal closure"; Frank Kermode's *The Sense of an Ending* (1967) invoked the concept of cosmological closure.
[14]Jean-Paul Sartre, *La Nausée* (Paris: Livre de Poche, 1957), pp. 62–63. [Brooks]

[15]Sartre, *Les Mots* (Paris: Gallimard, 1968), p. 171. [Brooks]
[16]Walter Benjamin, "The Storyteller," in *Illuminations,* translated by Harry Zohn (New York: Schocken Books, 1969), p. 101. [Brooks]

kinds of vacillation between illumination and blindness that we find there. If the end is recognition which retrospectively illuminates beginning and middle, it is not the exclusive truth of the text, which must include the processes along the way — the processes of "transformation" — in their metonymical complexity. If beginning is desire, and is ultimately desire for the end, between lies a process we feel to be necessary (plots, Aristotle tells us, must be of "a certain length")[17] but whose relation to originating desire and to end remains problematic. It is here that Freud's most ambitious investigation of ends in relation to beginnings may be of help — and may suggest a contribution to a properly dynamic model of plot.

We undertake, then, to read *Beyond the Pleasure Principle* as an essay about the dynamic interrelationship of ends and beginnings, and the kind of processes that constitute the middle. The enterprise may find a general sort of legitimation in the fact that *Beyond the Pleasure Principle* is in some sense Freud's own masterplot, the text in which he most fully lays out a total scheme of how life proceeds from beginning to end, and how each individual life in its own way repeats the masterplot. Of Freud's various intentions in this text, the boldest — and most mysterious — may be to provide a theory of comprehension of the dynamic of the life-span, its necessary duration and its necessary end, hence, implicitly, a theory of the very narratability of life. In his pursuit of his "beyond," Freud is forced to follow the implications of argument — "to throw oneself into a line of thought and follow it wherever it leads," as he says late in the essay — to ends that he had not originally or consciously conceived.[18] *Beyond the Pleasure Principle* shows the very plotting of a masterplot made necessary by the structural demands of Freud's thought, and it is in this sense that we shall attempt to read it as a model for narrative plot.

Narrative always makes the implicit claim to be in a state of repetition, as a going over again of a ground already covered: a *sjužet* repeating the *fabula*, as the detective retraces the tracks of the criminal.[19] This claim to an act of repetition — "I sing," "I tell" — appears to be initiatory of narrative. It is equally initiatory of *Beyond the Pleasure Principle*; it is the first problem and clue that Freud confronts. Evidence of a "beyond" that does not fit neatly into the functioning of the pleasure principle comes first in the dreams of patients suffering from war neuroses, or from the traumatic neuroses of peace: dreams which return to the moment of trauma, to relive its pain in apparent contradiction of the wish-fulfillment theory of dreams. This "dark and dismal" example is superseded by an example from "normal" life, and we have the celebrated moment of child's play: the toy thrown away, the reel on the string thrown out of the crib and pulled back, to the alternate exclamation of *fort* and *da*.[20] When he has established the equivalence between making the toy disappear and the child's mother's disappearance, Freud is faced with a set of possible interpretations. Why does the child repeat an unpleasurable experience? It may be answered that by staging his mother's disappearance and return, the child is compensating for his instinctual renunciation. Yet the child has also staged disappearance alone, without reappearance, as a game. This may make one want to argue that the essential experience involved is the movement from a passive to an active role in regard to his mother's disappearance, claiming mastery in a situation which he has been compelled to submit to.

Repetition as the movement from passivity to mastery reminds us of "The Theme of the Three Caskets," where Freud, considering Bassanio's choice of the lead casket in *The Merchant of Venice* — the correct choice in the suit of Portia — decides that the choice of the right maiden in

---

[17]See Aristotle, *Poetics*, p. 65.
[18]Sigmund Freud, "Beyond the Pleasure Principle" (1920), in *The Standard Edition of the Complete Psychological Works of Sigmund Freud*, ed. James Strachey (London: Hogarth Press, 1955), 18, 59. Subsequent page references will be given between parentheses in the text. [Brooks]

[19]J. Hillis Miller, in "Ariadne's Web" (unpublished manuscript), notes that the term *diegesis* suggests that narrative is a retracing of a journey already made. On the detective story, see Tzvetan Todorov, "Typologie du roman policier," *Poétique de la prose*, pp. 58–59. [Brooks]
[20]"Gone" and "here."

man's literary play is also the choice of death; by this choice, he asserts an active mastery of what he must in fact endure. "Choice stands in the place of necessity, of destiny. In this way man overcomes death, which he has recognized intellectually."[21] If repetition is mastery, movement from the passive to the active; and if mastery is an assertion of control over what man must in fact submit to — choice, we might say, of an imposed end — we have already a suggestive comment on the grammar of plot, where repetition, taking us back again over the same ground, could have to do with the choice of ends.

But other possibilities suggest themselves to Freud at this point. The repetition of unpleasant experience — the mother's disappearance — might be explained by the motive of revenge, which would yield its own pleasure. The uncertainty which Freud faces here is whether repetition can be considered a primary event, independent of the pleasure principle, or whether there is always some direct yield of pleasure of another sort involved. The pursuit of this doubt takes Freud into the analytic experience, to his discovery of patients' need to repeat, rather than simply remember, repressed material: the need to reproduce and to "work through" painful material from the past as if it were present. The analyst can detect a "compulsion to repeat," ascribed to the unconscious repressed, particularly discernible in the transference, where it can take "ingenious" forms. The compulsion to repeat gives patients a sense of being fatefully subject to a "perpetual recurrence of the same thing"; it suggests to them pursuit by a daemonic power. We know also, from Freud's essay on "The Uncanny," that this feeling of the daemonic, arising from involuntary repetition, is a particular attribute of the literature of the uncanny.[22]

Thus in analytic work (as also in literary texts) there is slim but real evidence of a compulsion to repeat which can override the pleasure principle, and which seems "more primitive, more elementary, more instinctual than the pleasure principle

which it overrides" (23). We might note at this point that the transference itself is a metaphor, a substitutive relationship for the patient's infantile experiences, and thus approximates the status of a text. Now repetition is so basic to our experience of literary texts that one is simultaneously tempted to say all and to say nothing on the subject. To state the matter baldly: rhyme, alliteration, assonance, meter, refrain, all the mnemonic elements of fictions and indeed most of its tropes are in some manner repetitions which take us back in the text, which allow the ear, the eye, the mind to make connections between different textual moments, to see past and present as related and as establishing a future which will be noticeable as some variation in the pattern. Todorov's "same but different" depends on repetition. If we think of the trebling characteristic of the folk tale, and of all formulaic literature, we may consider that the repetition by three constitutes the minimal repetition to the perception of series, which would make it the minimal intentional structure of action, the minimum plot. Narrative must ever present itself as a repetition of events that have already happened, and within this postulate of a generalized repetition it must make use of specific, perceptible repetitions in order to create plot, that is, to show us a significant interconnection of events. Event gains meaning by repeating (with variation) other events. Repetition is a *return* in the text, a doubling back. We cannot say whether this return is a return *to* or a return *of*: for instance, a return to origins or a return of the repressed. Repetition through this ambiguity appears to suspend temporal process, or rather, to subject it to an indeterminate shuttling or oscillation which binds different moments together as a middle which might turn forward or back. This inescapable middle is suggestive of the daemonic. The relation of narrative plot to story may indeed appear to partake of the daemonic, as a kind of tantalizing play with the primitive and the instinctual, the magic and the curse of reproduction or "representation." But in order to know more precisely the operations of repetition, we need to read further in Freud's text.

"What follows is speculation" (24). With this gesture, Freud, in the manner of Rousseau's dismissal of the facts in the *Discourse on the Origins of Inequality,* begins the fourth chapter

[21]Freud, "The Theme of the Three Caskets" (1913), *Standard Edition*, 12, 299. [Brooks]
[22]See Freud, "The Uncanny" (*Das Unheimliche*) (1919), in *Standard Edition*, 17, 219–52. [Brooks]. Or see p. 514 in this volume.

and his sketch of the economic and energetic model of the mental apparatus: the system Pcpt-Cs and Ucs,[23] the role of the outer layer as shield against excitations, and the definition of trauma as the breaching of the shield, producing a flood of stimuli which knocks the pleasure principle out of operation. Given this situation, the repetition of traumatic experiences in the dreams of neurotics can be seen to have the function of seeking retrospectively to master the flood of stimuli, to perform a mastery or binding of mobile energy through developing the anxiety whose omission was the cause of the traumatic neurosis. Thus the repetition compulsion is carrying out a task that must be accomplished *before* the dominance of the pleasure principle can begin. Repetition is hence a primary event, independent of the pleasure principle and more primitive. Freud now moves into an exploration of the theory of the instincts.[24] The instinctual is the realm of freely mobile, "unbound" energy: the "primary process," where energy seeks immediate discharge, where no postponement of gratification is tolerated. It appears that it must be "the task of the higher strata of the mental apparatus to bind the instinctual excitation reaching the primary process" before the pleasure principle can assert its dominance over the psychic economy (34–35). We may say that at this point in the essay we have moved from a postulate of repetition as the assertion of mastery (as in the passage from passivity to activity in the child's game) to a conception whereby repetition works as a process of *binding* toward the creation of an energetic constant-state situation which will permit the emergence of mastery, and the possibility of postponement.

That Freud at this point evokes once again the daemonic and the uncanny nature of repetition, and refers us not only to children's play but as

---

[23]Standard abbreviations for "perceptual-conscious" and "unconscious."

[24]I shall use the term "instinct" since it is the translation of *Trieb* given throughout the Standard Edition. But we should realize that "instinct" is inadequate and somewhat misleading, since it loses the sense of "drive" associated with the word *Trieb*. The currently accepted French translation, *pulsion*, is more to our purposes: the model that interests me here might indeed be called "pulsional." [Brooks]

well to their demand for exact repetition in story-telling, points our way back to literature. Repetition in all its literary manifestations may in fact work as a "binding," a binding of textual energies that allows them to be mastered by putting them into serviceable form within the energetic economy of the narrative. Serviceable form must in this case mean perceptible form: repetition, repeat, recall, symmetry, all these journeys back in the text, returns to and returns of, that allow us to bind one textual moment to another in terms of similarity or substitution rather than mere contiguity. Textual energy, all that is aroused into expectancy and possibility in a text — the term will need more definition, but corresponds well enough to our experience of reading — can become usable by plot only when it has been bound or formalized. It cannot otherwise be plotted in a course to significant discharge, which is what the pleasure principle is charged with doing. To speak of "binding" in a literary text is thus to speak of any of the formalizations (which, like binding, may be painful, retarding) that force us to recognize sameness within difference, or the very emergence of a *sjužet* from the material of *fabula*.

We need at present to follow Freud into his closer inquiry concerning the relation between the compulsion to repeat and the instinctual. The answer lies in "a universal attribute of instincts and perhaps of organic life in general," that *"an instinct is an urge inherent in organic life to restore an earlier state of things"* (36). Instincts, which we tend to think of as a drive toward change, may rather be an expression of "the conservative nature of living things." The organism has no wish to change; if its conditions remained the same, it would constantly repeat the very same course of life. Modifications are the effect of external stimuli, and these modifications are in turn stored up for further repetition, so that, while the instincts may give the appearance of tending toward change, they "are merely seeking to reach an ancient goal by paths alike old and new" (38). Hence Freud is able to proffer, with a certain bravado, the formulation: *"the aim of all life is death."* We are given an evolutionary image of the organism in which the tension created by external influences has forced living substance to "diverge ever more widely from its original course of life and to make ever more complicated *détours* before reaching its aim of death" (38–39). In this view, the self-preservative instincts function to assure that the organism shall follow its own path to death, to ward off any ways of returning to the inorganic which are not immanent to the organism itself. In other words, "the organism wishes to die only in its own fashion." It must struggle against events (dangers) which would help it to achieve its goal too rapidly — by a kind of short-circuit.

We are here somewhere near the heart of Freud's masterplot for organic life, and it generates a certain analytic force in its superimposition on fictional plots. What operates in the text through repetition is the death instinct, the drive toward the end. Beyond and under the domination of the pleasure principle is this baseline of plot, its basic "pulsation," sensible or audible through the repetitions which take us back in the text. Repetition can take us both backwards and forwards because these terms have become reversible: the end is a time before the beginning. Between these two moments of quiescence, plot itself stands as a kind of divergence or deviance, a postponement in the discharge which leads back to the inanimate. For plot starts (must give the illusion of starting) from that moment at which story, or "life," is stimulated from quiescence into a state of narratability, into a tension, a kind of irritation, which demands narration. Any reflection on novelistic beginnings shows the beginning as an awakening, an arousal, the birth of an appetency, ambition, desire or intention.[25] To say this is of course to say — perhaps more pertinently — that beginnings are the arousal of an intention in reading, stimulation into a tension. (The specifically erotic nature of the tension of writing and its rehearsal in reading could be demonstrated through a number of exemplary texts, notably Rousseau's account, in *The Confessions,* of how his novel *La Nouvelle*

Héloïse was born of a masturbatory reverie and its necessary fictions, or the very similar opening of Jean Genet's *Notre-Dame des fleurs;* but of course the sublimated forms of the tension are just as pertinent.) The ensuing narrative — the Aristotelean "middle" — is maintained in a state of tension, as a prolonged deviance from the quiescence of the "normal" — which is to say, the unnarratable — until it reaches the terminal quiescence of the end. The development of a narrative shows that the tension is maintained as an ever more complicated postponement or *détour* leading back to the goal of quiescence. As Sartre and Benjamin compellingly argued, the narrative must tend toward its end, seek illumination in its own death. Yet this must be the right death, the correct end. The complication of the *détour* is related to the danger of short-circuit: the danger of reaching the end too quickly, of achieving the improper death. The improper end indeed lurks throughout narrative, frequently as the wrong choice: choice of the wrong casket, misapprehension of the magical agent, false erotic object-choice. The development of the subplot in the classical novel usually suggests (as William Empson has intimated) a different solution to the problems worked through by the main plot, and often illustrates the danger of short-circuit.[26] The subplot stands as one means of warding off the danger of short-circuit, assuring that the main plot will continue through to the right end. The desire of the text (the desire of reading) is hence desire for the end, but desire for the end reached only through the at least minimally complicated *détour,* the intentional deviance, in tension, which is the plot of narrative.

Deviance, *détour,* an intention which is irritation: these are characteristics of the narratable, of "life" as it is the material of narrative, of *fabula* become *sjužet.* Plot is a kind of arabesque or squiggle toward the end. It is like Corporal Trim's arabesque with his stick, in *Tristram Shandy,* retraced by Balzac at the start of *La Peau de chagrin* to indicate the arbitrary, transgressive,

[25]On the beginning as intention, see Edward Said, *Beginnings: Intention and Method* (New York: Basic Books, 1975). It occurs to me that the exemplary narrative beginning might be that of Kafka's *Metamorphosis:* waking up to find oneself transformed into a monstrous vermin. [Brooks]

[26]See William Empson, "Double Plots," in *Some Versions of Pastoral* (New York: New Directions, 1960), pp. 25–84. [Brooks]

gratuitous line of narrative, its deviance from the straight line, the shortest distance between beginning and end — which would be the collapse of one into the other, of life into immediate death. Freud's text will in a moment take us closer to understanding of the formal organization of this deviance toward the end. But it also at this point offers further suggestions about the beginning. For when he has identified both the death instincts and the life (sexual) instincts as conservative, tending toward the restoration of an earlier state of things, Freud feels obliged to deconstruct the will to believe in a human drive toward perfection, an impulsion forward and upward: a force which — he here quotes *Faust* as the classic text of man's forward striving — "*ungebändigt immer vorwärts dringt.*"[27] The illusion of the striving toward perfection is to be explained by instinctual repression and the persisting tension of the repressed instinct, and the resulting difference between the pleasure of satisfaction *demanded* and that which is *achieved,* a difference which "provides the driving factor which will permit of no halting at any position attained" (36). This process of subtraction reappears in modified form in the work of Lacan, where it is the difference between *need* (the infant's need for the breast) and *demand* (which is always demand for recognition) that gives as its result *desire,* which is precisely the driving power, of plot certainly, since desire for Lacan is a metonymy, the forward movement of the signifying chain. If Roman Jakobson is able, in his celebrated essay, to associate the metonymic pole with prose fiction (particularly the nineteenth-century novel) — as the metaphoric pole is associated with lyric poetry — it would seem to be because the meanings peculiar to narrative inhere (or, as Lacan would say, "insist") in the metonymic chain, in the drive of desire toward meaning in time.[28]

The next-to-last chapter of *Beyond the Pleasure Principle* cannot here be rehearsed in

detail. In brief, it leads Freud twice into the findings of biology, first on the track of the origins of death, to find out whether it is a necessary or merely a contingent alternative to interminability, then in pursuit of the origins of sexuality, to see whether it satisfies the description of the instinctual as conservative. Biology can offer no sure answer to either investigation, but it offers at least metaphorical confirmation of the necessary dualism of Freud's thought, and encouragement to reformulate his earlier opposition of ego instincts to sexual instincts as one between life instincts and death instincts, a shift in the grouping of oppositional forces which then allows him to reformulate the libidinal instincts themselves as the Eros "of the poets and philosophers" which holds all living things together, and which seeks to combine things in ever greater living wholes. Desire would then seem to be totalizing in intent, a process tending toward combination in new unities: metonymy in the search to become metaphor. But for the symmetry of Freud's opposition to be complete, he needs to be able to ascribe to Eros, as to the death instinct, the characteristic of a need to restore an earlier state of things. Since biology will not answer, Freud, in a remarkable gesture, turns toward myth, to come up with Plato's Androgyne, which precisely ascribes Eros to a search to recover a lost primal unity which was split asunder.[29] Freud's apologetic tone in this last twist to his argument is partly disingenuous, for we detect a contentment to have formulated the forces of the human masterplot as "philosopher and poet." The apology is coupled with a reflection that much of the obscurity of the processes Freud has been considering "is merely due to our being obliged to operate with the scientific terms, that is to say with the figurative language, peculiar to psychology" (60). *Beyond the Pleasure Principle,* we are to understand, is not merely metapsychology, it is also mythopoesis, necessarily resembling "an equation with two unknown quantities" (57), or, we

[27]"Unhampered always moves forwards."

[28]See Jakobson, "Two Types of Language . . .." See, in Lacan's work, especially "Le Stade du miroir" and "L'Instance de la lettre dans l'inconscient," in *Écrits* (Paris: Seuil, 1966). [Brooks] For Lacan's essays, see pp. 1123 and 1129.

[29]In Plato's *Symposium,* Aristophanes explains the nature of love in the form of a fable. Humanity was originally designed to be androgynous, but a mischievous demiurge split the double-sexed creature in half. The result is that we are all incomplete, seeking in Eros for our missing halves.

might say, a formal dynamic the terms of which are not substantial but purely relational. We perceive that *Beyond the Pleasure Principle* is itself a plot which has formulated that dynamic necessary to its own *détour*.

The last chapter of Freud's text recapitulates, but not without difference. He returns to the problem of the relationship between the instinctual processes of repetition and the dominance of the pleasure principle. One of the earliest and most important functions of the mental apparatus is to bind the instinctual impulses which impinge upon it, to convert freely mobile energy into a quiescent cathexis. This is a preparatory act on behalf of the pleasure principle, which permits its dominance. Sharpening his distinction between a *function* and a *tendency,* Freud argues that the pleasure principle is a "tendency operating in the service of a function whose business it is to free mental apparatus from excitation or to keep the amount of excitation in it constant or to keep it as low as possible" (62). This function is concerned "with the most universal endeavour of all living substance — namely to return to the quiescence of the inorganic world." Hence one can consider "binding" to be a preliminary function which prepares the excitation for its final elimination in the pleasure of discharge. In this manner, we could say that the repetition compulsion and the death instinct serve the pleasure principle; in a larger sense, the pleasure principle, keeping watch on the invasion of stimuli from without and especially from within, seeking their discharge, serves the death instinct, making sure that the organism is permitted to return to quiescence. The whole evolution of the mental apparatus appears as a taming of the instincts so that the pleasure principle — itself tamed, displaced — can appear to dominate in the complicated *détour* called life which leads back to death. In fact, Freud seems here at the very end to imply that the two antagonistic instincts serve one another in a dynamic interaction which is a perfect and self-regulatory economy which makes both end and *détour* perfectly necessary and interdependent. The organism must live in order to die in the proper manner, to die the right death. We must have the arabesque of plot in order to reach the end. We must have metonymy in order to reach metaphor.

We emerge from reading *Beyond the Pleasure Principle* with a dynamic model which effectively structures ends (death, quiescence, non-narratability) against beginnings (Eros, stimulation into tension, the desire of narrative) in a manner that necessitates the middle as *détour,* as struggle toward the end under the compulsion of imposed delay, as arabesque in the dilatory space of the text. We detect some illumination of the necessary distance between beginning and end, the drives which connect them but which prevent the one collapsing back into the other: the way in which metonymy and metaphor serve one another, the necessary temporality of the same-but-different which to Todorov constitutes the narrative transformation. The model suggests further that along the way of the path from beginning to end — in the middle — we have repetitions serving to bind the energy of the text in order to make its final discharge more effective. In fictional plots, these bindings are a system of repetitions which are returns to and returns of, confounding the movement forward to the end with a movement back to origins, reversing meaning within forward-moving time, serving to formalize the system of textual energies, offering the possibility (or the illusion) of "meaning" wrested from "life."

As a dynamic-energetic model of narrative plot, then, *Beyond the Pleasure Principle* gives an image of how "life," or the *fabula,* is stimulated into the condition of narrative, becomes *sjužet:* enters into a state of deviance and *détour* (ambition, quest, the pose of a mask) in which it is maintained for a certain time, through an at least minimally complex extravagance, before returning to the quiescence of the non-narratable. The energy generated by deviance, extravagance, excess — an energy which belongs to the textual hero's career and to the reader's expectation, his desire of and for the text — maintains the plot in its movement through the vacillating play of the middle, where repetition as binding works toward the generation of significance, toward recognition and the retrospective illumination which will allow us to grasp the text as total metaphor, but not therefore to discount the metonymies that have led to it. The desire of the text is ultimately the desire for the end, for that recognition which is the moment of the death of the reader in the text. Yet recognition cannot abolish textuality, does not annul the middle which, in its oscillation between blindness and recognition, between origin and endings, is the truth of the narrative text.

It is characteristic of textual energy in narrative that it should always be on the verge of premature discharge, of short-circuit. The reader experiences the fear — and excitation — of the improper end, which is symmetrical to — but far more immediate and present than — the fear of endlessness. The possibility of short-circuit can of course be represented in all manner of threats to the protagonist or to any of the functional logics which demand completion; it most commonly takes the form of temptation to the mistaken erotic object choice, who may be of the "Belle Dame sans merci" variety, or may be the too-perfect and hence annihilatory bride. Throughout the Romantic tradition, it is perhaps most notably the image of incest (of the fraternal-sororal variety) which hovers as the sign of a passion interdicted because its fulfillment would be too perfect, a discharge indistinguishable from death, the very cessation of narrative movement. Narrative is in a state of temptation to oversameness, and where we have no literal threat of incest (as in Chateaubriand, or Faulkner), lovers choose to turn the beloved into a soul-sister so that possession will be either impossible or mortal: Werther and Lotte, for instance, or, at the inception of the tradition, Rousseau's *La Nouvelle Héloïse,* where Saint-Preux's letter to Julie following their night of love begins: "Mourons, ô ma douce amie." Incest is only the exemplary version of a temptation of short-circuit from which the protagonist and the text must be led away, into *détour,* into the cure which prolongs narrative.

It may finally be in the logic of our argument that repetition speaks in the text of a return which ultimately subverts the very notion of beginning and end, suggesting that the idea of beginning presupposes the end, that the end is a time before the beginning, and hence that the interminable never can be finally bound in a plot. Analysis, Freud would eventually discover, is inherently interminable, since the dynamics of resistance and the transference can always generate new beginnings in relation to any possible end.[30] It is the role of fictional plots to impose an end which yet suggests a return, a new beginning: a rereading. A narrative, that is, wants at its end to refer us back to its middle, to the web of the text: to recapture us in its doomed energies.

One ought at this point to make a new beginning, and to sketch the possible operation of the model in the study of the plot of a fiction. One could, for instance, take Dickens's *Great Expectations.* One would have to show how the energy released in the text by its liminary "primal scene" — Pip's terrifying meeting with Magwitch in the graveyard — is subsequently bound in a number of desired but unsatisfactory ways (including Pip's "being bound" as apprentice, the "dream" plot of Satis House, the apparent intent of the "expectations"), and simultaneously in censored but ultimately more satisfying ways (through all the returns of the repressed identification of Pip and his convict). The most salient device of this novel's "middle" is literally the journey back — from London to Pip's home town — a repeated return to apparent origins which is also a return of the repressed, of what Pip calls "that old spell of my childhood." It would be interesting to demonstrate that each of Pip's choices in the novel, while consciously life-furthering, forward oriented, in fact leads back, to the insoluble question of origins, to the palindrome of his name, so that the end of the narrative — its "discharge" — appears as the image of a "life" cured of "plot," as celibate clerk for Clarrikers.

Pip's story, while ostensibly the search for progress, ascension, and metamorphosis, may after all be the narrative of an attempted homecoming: of the effort to reach an assertion of origin through ending, to find the same in the different, the time before in the time after. Most of the great nineteenth-century novels tell this same tale. Georg Lukács has called the novel "the literary form of the transcendent homelessness of the idea," and argued that it is in the discrepancy between idea and the organic that time, the

---

[30] See Freud, "Analysis Terminable and Interminable" (1937), in *Standard Edition,* 23, 216–53. [Brooks]

process of duration, becomes constitutive of the novel as of no other genre:

> Only in the novel, whose very matter is seeking and failing to find the essence, is time posited together with the form: time is the resistance of the organic — which possesses a mere semblance of life — to the present meaning, the will of life to remain within its own completely enclosed immanence.... In the novel, meaning is separated from life, and hence the essential from the temporal; we might almost say that the entire inner action of the novel is nothing but a struggle against the power of time.[31]

The understanding of time, says Lukács, the transformation of the struggle against time into a process full of interest, is the work of memory — or more precisely, we could say with Freud, of "remembering, repeating, working through." Repetition, remembering, reenactment are the ways in which we replay time, so that it may not be lost. We are thus always trying to work back through time to that transcendent home, knowing of course that we cannot. All we can do is subvert or, perhaps better, pervert time: which is what narrative does.[32]

To forgo any true demonstration on a novel, and to bring a semblance of conclusion, we may return to the assertion, by Barthes and Todorov, that narrative is essentially the articulation of a set of verbs. These verbs are no doubt ultimately all versions of desire. Desire is the wish for the end, for fulfillment, but fulfillment delayed so

that we can understand it in relation to origin, and to desire itself. The story of Scheherezade is doubtless the story of stories. This suggests that the tale as read is inhabited by the reader's desire, and that further analysis should be directed to that desire, not (in the manner of Norman Holland) his individual desire and its origins in his own personality,[33] but his transindividual and intertextually determined desire as a reader. Because it concerns ends in relation to beginnings and the forces that animate the middle in between, Freud's model is suggestive of what a reader engages when he responds to plot. It images that engagement as essentially dynamic, an interaction with a system of energy which the reader activates. This in turn suggests why we can read *Beyond the Pleasure Principle* as a text concerning textuality, and conceive that there can be psychoanalytic criticism of the text itself that does not become — as has usually been the case — a study of the psychogenesis of the text (the author's unconscious), the dynamics of literary response (the reader's unconscious), or the occult motivations of the characters (postulating an "unconscious" for them). It is rather the superimposition of the model of the functioning of the mental apparatus on the functioning of the text that offers the possibility of a psychoanalytic criticism. And here the superimposition of Freud's psychic masterplot on the plots of fiction seems a valid and useful maneuver. Plot mediates meanings with the contradictory human world of the eternal and the mortal. Freud's masterplot speaks of the temporality of desire, and speaks to our very desire for fictional plots.

---

[31]Georg Lukács, *The Theory of the Novel*, trans. Anna Bostock (Cambridge, Mass.: MIT Press, 1971), p. 122. [Brooks]

[32]Genette discusses Proust's "perversion" of time in "Discours du récit," p. 182. "Remembering, Repeating, and Working Through" *(Erinnern, Wiederholen und Durcharbeiten,* 1914) is the subject of one of Freud's papers on technique. See *Standard Edition*, 12, 145–56. [Brooks]

[33]See Holland, "The Question: Who Reads What How?" in Ch. 3 (p. 1015).

Laura Mulvey

b. 1941

Laura Mulvey was born in Oxford, England, and studied history at St. Hilda's College, Oxford, before embarking on a dual career as a film director and a film theorist. Her films, co-directed with her husband Peter Wollen, include Penthesilea *(1974),* Riddles of the Sphinx *(1978),* Amyl *(1980),* Crystal Gazing *(1981), and* The Bad Sister *(1983). Her most recent film, a solo project, was* Disgraced Monuments *(1996). Her books on the gaze in cinema and photography include* Visual and Other Pleasures *(1989),* Citizen Kane *(1993), and* Mary Kelly *(1998). She currently teaches film and media studies at Birkbeck College, University of London. "Visual Pleasure and Narrative Cinema" written in 1973, was published in* Screen *in 1975. In a piece entitled "Afterthoughts on Visual Pleasure and Narrative Cinema," published in* Framework *in 1981, Mulvey reflects on her famous essay.*

Visual Pleasure and Narrative Cinema

I. INTRODUCTION

(a) A Political Use of Psychoanalysis

This paper intends to use psychoanalysis to discover where and how the fascination of film is reinforced by pre-existing patterns of fascination already at work within the individual subject and the social formations that have moulded him. It takes as its starting-point the way film reflects, reveals and even plays on the straight, socially established interpretation of sexual difference which controls images, erotic ways of looking and spectacle. It is helpful to understand what the cinema has been, how its magic has worked in the past, while attempting a theory and a practice which will challenge this cinema of the past. Psychoanalytic theory is thus appropriated here as a political weapon, demonstrating the way the unconscious of patriarchal society has structured film form.

The paradox of phallocentrism[1] in all its manifestations is that it depends on the image of the castrated woman to give order and meaning to its

world. An idea of woman stands as linchpin to the system: it is her lack that produces the phallus as a symbolic presence, it is her desire to make good the lack that the phallus signifies. Recent writing in *Screen* about psychoanalysis and the cinema has not sufficiently brought out the importance of the representation of the female form in a symbolic order in which, in the last resort, it speaks castration and nothing else. To summarise briefly: the function of woman in forming the patriarchal unconscious is twofold: she firstly symbolises the castration threat by her real lack of a penis and secondly thereby raises her child into the symbolic. Once this has been achieved, her meaning in the process is at an end. It does not last into the world of law and language except as a memory, which oscillates between memory of maternal plentitude and memory of lack. Both are posited on nature (or on anatomy in Freud's famous phrase).[2] Woman's desire is subjugated to her

---

(see introduction to Gender Studies, pp. 613–14.) Mulvey's terminology here — the *phallus* as the signifier of desire, the *imaginary* and *symbolic* orders as the sites of image and word, the dialectical relation between *lack, need,* and *desire* — derives from Jacques Lacan; see the introduction to Psychoanalytic Theory, p. 1106.

[1]*Phallocentrism* refers to the organization of the symbolic order, specifically, the binary opposition in which the phallus represents the positive principle of presence as a masculine entity, as opposed to a "castrated" feminine entity

[2]Freud's famous phrase is "Anatomy is destiny."

image as bearer of the bleeding wound; she can exist only in relation to castration and cannot transcend it. She turns her child into the signifier of her own desire to possess a penis (the condition, she imagines, of entry into the symbolic). Either she must gracefully give way to the word, the name of the father and the law, or else struggle to keep her child down with her in the half-light of the imaginary. Woman then stands in patriarchal culture as a signifier for the male other, bound by a symbolic order in which man can live out his fantasies and obsessions through linguistic command by imposing them on the silent image of woman still tied to her place as bearer, not maker, of meaning.

There is an obvious interest in this analysis for feminists, a beauty in its exact rendering of the frustration experienced under the phallocentric order. It gets us nearer to the roots of our oppression, it brings closer an articulation of the problem, it faces us with the ultimate challenge: how to fight the unconscious structured like a language (formed critically at the moment of arrival of language) while still caught within the language of the patriarchy? There is no way in which we can produce an alternative out of the blue, but we can begin to make a break by examining patriarchy with the tools it provides, of which psychoanalysis is not the only but an important one. We are still separated by a great gap from important issues for the female unconscious which are scarcely relevant to phallocentric theory: the sexing of the female infant and her relationship to the symbolic, the sexually mature woman as non-mother, maternity outside the signification of the phallus, the vagina. But, at this point, psychoanalytic theory as it now stands can at least advance our understanding of the *status quo,* of the patriarchal order in which we are caught.

(b) Destruction of Pleasure as a Radical Weapon

As an advanced representation system, the cinema poses questions about the ways the unconscious (formed by the dominant order) structures ways of seeing and pleasure in looking. Cinema has changed over the last few decades. It is no longer the monolithic system based on large capital investment exemplified at its best by Hollywood in the 1930s, 1940s and 1950s. Technological advances (16mm and so on) have changed the economic conditions of cinematic production, which can now be artisanal as well as capitalist.[3] Thus it has been possible for an alternative cinema to develop. However self-conscious and ironic Hollywood managed to be, it always restricted itself to a formal *mise en scène*[4] reflecting the dominant ideological concept of the cinema. The alternative cinema provides a space for the birth of a cinema which is radical in both a political and an aesthetic sense and challenges the basic assumptions of the mainstream film. This is not to reject the latter moralistically, but to highlight the ways in which its formal preoccupations reflect the psychical obsessions of the society which produced it and, further, to stress that the alternative cinema must start specifically by reacting against these obsessions and assumptions. A politically and aesthetically avant-garde cinema is now possible, but it can still only exist as a counterpoint.

The magic of the Hollywood style at its best (and of all the cinema which fell within its sphere of influence) arose, not exclusively, but in one important aspect, from its skilled and satisfying manipulation of visual pleasure. Unchallenged, mainstream film coded the erotic into the language of the dominant patriarchal order. In the highly developed Hollywood cinema it was only through these codes that the alienated subject, torn in his imaginary memory by a sense of loss, by the terror of potential lack in fantasy, came near to finding a glimpse of satisfaction: through its formal beauty and its play on his own formative obsessions. This article will discuss the interweaving of that erotic pleasure in film, its meaning and, in particular, the central place of the image of woman. It is said that analysing pleasure, or beauty, destroys it. That is the intention of this article. The satisfaction and reinforcement of the ego that represent the high point of film history hitherto must be attacked. Not in

[3]The 35mm film used by Hollywood was too expensive to permit very extensive use by those outside the studios; the advent of 16mm film in the 1960s allowed an alternative cinema to develop and proliferate.

[4]Staging.

favour of a reconstructed new pleasure, which cannot exist in the abstract, nor of intellectualised unpleasure, but to make way for a total negation of the ease and plenitude of the narrative fiction film. The alternative is the thrill that comes from leaving the past behind without simply rejecting it, transcending outworn or oppressive forms, and daring to break with normal pleasurable expectations in order to conceive a new language of desire.

II. PLEASURE IN LOOKING/ FASCINATION WITH THE HUMAN FORM

A. The cinema offers a number of possible pleasures. One is scopophilia (pleasure in looking). There are circumstances in which looking itself is a source of pleasure, just as, in the reverse formation, there is pleasure in being looked at. Originally, in his *Three Essays on Sexuality,*[5] Freud isolated scopophilia as one of the component instincts of sexuality which exist as drives quite independently of the erotogenic zones. At this point he associated scopophilia with taking other people as objects, subjecting them to a controlling and curious gaze. His particular examples centre on the voyeuristic activities of children, their desire to see and make sure of the private and forbidden (curiosity about other people's genital and bodily functions, about the presence or absence of the penis and, retrospectively, about the primal scene). In this analysis scopophilia is essentially active. (Later, in "Instincts and Their Vicissitudes," Freud developed his theory of scopophilia further, attaching it initially to pregenital auto-eroticism, after which, by analogy, the pleasure of the look is transferred to others. There is a close working here of the relationship between the active instinct and its further development in a narcissistic form.) Although the instinct is modified by other factors, in particular the constitution of the ego, it continues to exist as the erotic basis for pleasure in looking at another person as object. At the extreme, it can become

fixated into a perversion, producing obsessive voyeurs and Peeping Toms whose only sexual satisfaction can come from watching, in an active controlling sense, an objectified other.

At first glance, the cinema would seem to be remote from the undercover world of the surreptitious observation of an unknowing and unwilling victim. What is seen on the screen is so manifestly shown. But the mass of mainstream film, and the conventions within which it has consciously evolved, portray a hermetically sealed world which unwinds magically, indifferent to the presence of the audience, producing for them a sense of separation and playing on their voyeuristic fantasy. Moreover the extreme contrast between the darkness in the auditorium (which also isolates the spectators from one another) and the brilliance of the shifting patterns of light and shade on the screen helps to promote the illusion of voyeuristic separation. Although the film is really being shown, is there to be seen, conditions of screening and narrative conventions give the spectator an illusion of looking in on a private world. Among other things, the position of the spectators in the cinema is blatantly one of repression of their exhibitionism and projection of the repressed desire onto the performer.

B. The cinema satisfies a primordial wish for pleasurable looking, but it also goes further, developing scopophilia in its narcissistic aspect. The conventions of mainstream film focus attention on the human form. Scale, space, stories are all anthropomorphic. Here, curiosity and the wish to look intermingle with a fascination with likeness and recognition: the human face, the human body, the relationship between the human form and its surroundings, the visible presence of the person in the world. Jacques Lacan has described how the moment when a child recognises its own image in the mirror is crucial for the constitution of the ego. Several aspects of this analysis are relevant here. The mirror phase occurs at a time when children's physical ambitions outstrip their motor capacity, with the result that their recognition of themselves is joyous in that they imagine their mirror image to be more complete, more perfect than they experience in their own body. Recognition is thus overlaid with misrecognition: the

---

[5]Sigmund Freud published *Three Essays on the Theory of Sexuality* in 1905, "Instincts and Their Vicissitudes" in 1915.

image recognised is conceived as the reflected body of the self, but its misrecognition as superior projects this body outside itself as an ideal ego, the alienated subject which, reintrojected as an ego ideal, prepares the way for identification with others in the future. This mirror moment predates language for the child.[6]

Important for this article is the fact that it is an image that constitutes the matrix of the imaginary, of recognition/misrecognition and identification, and hence of the first articulation of the I, of subjectivity. This is a moment when an older fascination with looking (at the mother's face, for an obvious example) collides with the initial inklings of self-awareness. Hence it is the birth of the long love affair/despair between image and self-image which has found such intensity of expression in film and such joyous recognition in the cinema audience. Quite apart from the extraneous similarities between screen and mirror (the framing of the human form in its surroundings, for instance), the cinema has structures of fascination strong enough to allow temporary loss of ego while simultaneously reinforcing it. The sense of forgetting the world as the ego has come to perceive it (I forgot who I am and where I was) is nostalgically reminiscent of that pre-subjective moment of image recognition. While at the same time, the cinema has distinguished itself in the production of ego ideals, through the star system for instance. Stars provide a focus or centre both to screen space and screen story where they act out a complex process of likeness and difference (the glamorous impersonates the ordinary).

C. Sections A and B have set out two contradictory aspects of the pleasurable structures of looking in the conventional cinematic situation. The first, scopophilic, arises from pleasure in using another person as an object of sexual stimulation through sight. The second, developed through narcissism and the constitution of the ego, comes from identification with the image seen. Thus, in film terms, one implies a separation of the erotic identity of the subject from the object on the screen (active scopophilia), the other demands identification of the ego with the object on the screen through the spectator's fascination with and recognition of his like. The first is a function of the sexual instincts, the second of ego libido. This dichotomy was crucial for Freud. Although he saw the two as interacting and overlaying each other, the tension between instinctual drives and self-preservation polarises in terms of pleasure. But both are formative structures, mechanisms without intrinsic meaning. In themselves they have no signification, unless attached to an idealisation. Both pursue aims in indifference to perceptual reality, and motivate eroticised phantasmagoria that affect the subject's perception of the world to make a mockery of empirical objectivity.

During its history, the cinema seems to have evolved a particular illusion of reality in which this contradiction between libido and ego has found a beautifully complementary fantasy world. In *reality* the fantasy world of the screen is subject to the law which produces it. Sexual instincts and identification processes have a meaning within the symbolic order which articulates desire. Desire, born with language, allows the possibility of transcending the instinctual and the imaginary, but its point of reference continually returns to the traumatic moment of its birth: the castration complex. Hence the look, pleasurable in form, can be threatening in content, and it is woman as representation/image that crystallises this paradox.

III. WOMAN AS IMAGE, MAN AS BEARER OF THE LOOK

A. In a world ordered by sexual imbalance, pleasure in looking has been split between active/male and passive/female. The determining male gaze projects its fantasy onto the female figure, which is styled accordingly. In their traditional exhibitionist role women are simultaneously looked at and displayed, with their appearance coded for strong visual and erotic impact so that they can be said to connote *to-be-looked-at-ness.* Woman displayed as sexual object is the *leitmotif*[7] of erotic spectacle: from pin-ups to strip-tease,

[6]See Jacques Lacan, "The Mirror Stage as Formative of the Function of the I as Revealed in Psychoanalytic Experience," p. 1123.

[7]Recurring theme.

from Ziegfeld to Busby Berkeley,[8] she holds the look, and plays to and signifies male desire. Mainstream film neatly combines spectacle and narrative. (Note, however, how, in the musical, song-and-dance numbers interrupt the flow of the diegesis.[9]) The presence of woman is an indispensable element of spectacle in normal narrative film, yet her visual presence tends to work against the development of a story-line, to freeze the flow of action in moments of erotic contemplation. This alien presence then has to be integrated into cohesion with the narrative. As Budd Boetticher has put it:

> What counts is what the heroine provokes, or rather what she represents. She is the one, or rather the love or fear she inspires in the hero, or else the concern he feels for her, who makes him act the way he does. In herself the woman has not the slightest importance.

(A recent tendency in narrative film has been to dispense with this problem altogether; hence the development of what Molly Haskell has called the "buddy movie," in which the active homosexual eroticism of the central male figures can carry the story without distraction.) Traditionally, the woman displayed has functioned on two levels: as erotic object for the characters within the screen story, and as erotic object for the spectator within the auditorium, with a shifting tension between the looks on either side of the screen. For instance, the device of the show-girl allows the two looks to be unified technically without any apparent break in the diegesis. A woman performs within the narrative; the gaze of the spectator and that of the male characters in the film are neatly combined without breaking narrative verisimilitude. For a moment the sexual impact of the performing woman takes the film into a no man's land outside its own time and space. Thus Marilyn Monroe's first appearance in *The River of No Return* and Lauren Bacall's songs in *To Have and Have Not*. Similarly, conventional close-ups of legs (Dietrich, for instance) or a face (Garbo) integrate into the narrative a different mode of eroticism. One part of a fragmented body destroys the Renaissance space, the illusion of depth demanded by the narrative; it gives flatness, the quality of a cut-out or icon, rather than verisimilitude, to the screen.

B. An active/passive heterosexual division of labour has similarly controlled narrative structure. According to the principles of the ruling ideology and the psychical structures that back it up, the male figure cannot bear the burden of sexual objectification. Man is reluctant to gaze at his exhibitionist like. Hence the split between spectacle and narrative supports the man's role as the active one of advancing the story, making things happen. The man controls the film fantasy and also emerges as the representative of power in a further sense: as the bearer of the look of the spectator, transferring it behind the screen to neutralise the extradiegetic tendencies represented by woman as spectacle. This is made possible through the processes set in motion by structuring the film around a main controlling figure with whom the spectator can identify. As the spectator identifies with the main male protagonist, he projects his look onto that of his like, his screen surrogate, so that the power of the male protagonist as he controls events coincides with the active power of the erotic look, both giving a satisfying sense of omnipotence. A male movie star's glamorous characteristics are thus not those of the erotic object of the gaze, but those of the more perfect, more complete, more powerful ideal ego conceived in the original moment of recognition in front of the mirror. The character in the story can make things happen and control events better than the subjects/spectator, just as the image in the mirror was more in control of motor co-ordination.

In contrast to woman as icon, the active male figure (the ego ideal of the identification process) demands a three-dimensional space corresponding to that of the mirror recognition, in which the alienated subject internalised his own representation of

---

[8]Florenz Ziegfeld (1867–1932) was the producer, from 1907, of the *Ziegfeld Follies,* an annual musical revue staged in New York, featuring beautiful, often scantily clad, chorus girls. Busby Berkeley (1895–1976) was the director and choreographer of numerous films, beginning with *42nd Street* (1933); he created geometrically elaborate dance numbers featuring hundreds of nearly identical starlets.

[9]The act of telling a story (as opposed to the story that is told).

his imaginary existence. He is a figure in a landscape. Here the function of film is to reproduce as accurately as possible the so-called natural conditions of human perception. Camera technology (as exemplified by deep focus in particular) and camera movements (determined by the action of the protagonist), combined with invisible editing (demanded by realism), all tend to blur the limits of screen space. The male protagonist is free to command the stage, a stage of spatial illusion in which he articulates the look and creates the action. (There are films with a woman as main protagonist, of course. To analyse this phenomenon seriously here would take me too far afield. Pam Cook and Claire Johnston's study of *The Revolt of Mamie Stover* in Phil Hardy [ed.], *Raoul Walsh* [Edinburgh, 1974], shows in a striking case how the strength of this female protagonist is more apparent than real.)

CI. Sections III A and B have set out a tension between a mode of representation of woman in film and conventions surrounding the diegesis. Each is associated with a look: that of the spectator in direct scopophilic contact with the female form displayed for his enjoyment (connoting male fantasy) and that of the spectator fascinated with the image of his like set in an illusion of natural space, and through him gaining control and possession of the woman within the diegesis. (This tension and the shift from one pole to the other can structure a single text. Thus both in *Only Angels Have Wings* and in *To Have and Have Not,* the film opens with the woman as object of the combined gaze of spectator and all the male protagonists in the film. She is isolated, glamorous, on display, sexualised. But as the narrative progresses she falls in love with the main male protagonist and becomes his property, losing her outward glamorous characteristics, her generalised sexuality, her show-girl connotations; her eroticism is subjected to the male star alone. By means of identification with him, through participation in his power, the spectator can indirectly possess her too.)

But in psychoanalytic terms, the female figure poses a deeper problem. She also connotes something that the look continually circles around but disavows: her lack of a penis, implying a threat of castration and hence unpleasure. Ultimately, the meaning of woman is sexual difference, the visually ascertainable absence of the penis, the material evidence on which is based the castration complex essential for the organisation of entrance to the symbolic order and the law of the father. Thus the woman as icon, displayed for the gaze and enjoyment of men, the active controllers of the look, always threatens to evoke the anxiety it originally signified. The male unconscious has two avenues of escape from this castration anxiety: preoccupation with the re-enactment of the original trauma (investigating the woman, demystifying her mystery), counterbalanced by the devaluation, punishment or saving of the guilty object (an avenue typified by the concerns of the *film noir*[10]); or else complete disavowal of castration by the substitution of a fetish object or turning the represented figure itself into a fetish so that it becomes reassuring rather than dangerous (hence overvaluation, the cult of the female star).

This second avenue, fetishistic scopophilia, builds up the physical beauty of the object, transforming it into something satisfying in itself. The first avenue, voyeurism, on the contrary, has associations with sadism: pleasure lies in ascertaining guilt (immediately associated with castration), asserting control and subjugating the guilty person through punishment or forgiveness. This sadistic side fits in well with narrative. Sadism demands a story, depends on making something happen, forcing a change in another person, a battle of will and strength, victory/defeat, all occurring in a linear time with a beginning and an end. Fetishistic scopophilia, on the other hand, can exist outside linear time as the erotic instinct is focused on the look alone. These contradictions and ambiguities can be illustrated more simply by using works by Hitchcock and Sternberg, both of whom take the look almost as the content or subject matter of many of their films. Hitchcock is the more complex, as he uses both mechanisms. Sternberg's work, on the other hand, provides many pure examples of fetishistic scopophilia.

[10]The term *film noir*, literally "black cinema," refers to genre movies of the 1940s and early 1950s portraying the underside of a corrupt society with seductive female villains and cynical heroes. Well-known examples include Michael Curtiz's *Casablanca*, Howard Hawks's *The Big Sleep,* and Billy Wilder's *Sunset Boulevard.*

C2. Sternberg once said he would welcome his films being projected upside-down so that the story and character involvement would not interfere with the spectator's undiluted appreciation of the screen image. This statement is revealing but ingenuous: ingenuous in that his films do demand that the figure of the woman (Dietrich, in the cycle of films with her, as the ultimate example) should be identifiable; but revealing in that it emphasises the fact that for him the pictorial space enclosed by the frame is paramount, rather than narrative or identification processes. While Hitchcock goes into the investigative side of voyeurism, Sternberg produces the ultimate fetish, taking it to the point where the powerful look of the male protagonist (characteristic of traditional narrative film) is broken in favour of the image in direct erotic rapport with the spectator. The beauty of the woman as object and the screen space coalesce; she is no longer the bearer of guilt but a perfect product, whose body, stylised and fragmented by close-ups, is the content of the film and the direct recipient of the spectator's look.

Sternberg plays down the illusion of screen depth; his screen tends to be one-dimensional, as light and shade, lace, steam, foliage, net, streamers and so on reduce the visual field. There is little or no mediation of the look through the eyes of the main male protagonist. On the contrary, shadowy presences like La Bessière in *Morocco* act as surrogates for the director, detached as they are from audience identification. Despite Sternberg's insistence that his stories are irrelevant, it is significant that they are concerned with situation, not suspense, and cyclical rather than linear time, while plot complications revolve around misunderstanding rather than conflict. The most important absence is that of the controlling male gaze within the screen scene. The high point of emotional drama in the most typical Dietrich films, her supreme moments of erotic meaning, take place in the absence of the man she loves in the fiction. There are other witnesses, other spectators watching her on the screen, their gaze is one with, not standing in for, that of the audience. At the end of *Morocco,* Tom Brown has already disappeared into the desert when Amy Jolly kicks off her gold sandals and walks after him. At the end of *Dishonoured,* Kranau is indifferent to the fate of Magda.

In both cases, the erotic impact, sanctified by death, is displayed as a spectacle for the audience. The male hero misunderstands and, above all, does not see.

In Hitchcock, by contrast, the male hero does see precisely what the audience sees. However, although fascination with an image through scopophilic eroticism can be the subject of the film, it is the role of the hero to portray the contradictions and tensions experienced by the spectator. In *Vertigo* in particular, but also in *Marnie* and *Rear Window,* the look is central to the plot, oscillating between voyeurism and fetishistic fascination. Hitchcock has never concealed his interest in voyeurism, cinematic and non-cinematic. His heroes are exemplary of the symbolic order and the law — a policeman *(Vertigo),* a dominant male possessing money and power *(Marnie)* — but their erotic drives lead them into compromised situations. The power to subject another person to the will sadistically or to the gaze voyeuristically is turned onto the woman as the object of both. Power is backed by a certainty of legal right and the established guilt of the woman (evoking castration, psychoanalytically speaking). True perversion is barely concealed under a shallow mask of ideological correctness — the man is on the right side of the law, the woman on the wrong. Hitchcock's skilful use of identification processes and liberal use of subjective camera from the point of view of the male protagonist draw the spectators deeply into his position, making them share his uneasy gaze. The spectator is absorbed into a voyeuristic situation within the screen scene and diegesis, which parodies his own in the cinema.

In an analysis of *Rear Window,* Douchet takes the film as a metaphor for the cinema. Jeffries is the audience, the events in the apartment block opposite correspond to the screen. As he watches, an erotic dimension is added to his look, a central image to the drama. His girlfriend Lisa had been of little sexual interest to him, more or less a drag, so long as she remained on the spectator side. When she crosses the barrier between his room and the block opposite, their relationship is reborn erotically. He does not merely watch her through his lens, as a distant meaningful image, he also sees her as a guilty intruder exposed by a dangerous man threatening her with punishment, and thus finally giving him the opportunity to save her. Lisa's exhibitionism has already been established by her obsessive interest in dress and style, in being a passive image of visual perfection; Jeffries's voyeurism and activity have also been established through his work as a photo-journalist, a maker of stories and captor of images. However, his enforced inactivity,[11] binding him to his seat as a spectator, puts him squarely in the fantasy position of the cinema audience.

In *Vertigo,* subjective camera predominates. Apart from one flashback from Judy's point of view, the narrative is woven around what Scottie sees or fails to see. The audience follows the growth of his erotic obsession and subsequent despair precisely from his point of view. Scottie's voyeurism is blatant: he falls in love with a woman he follows and spies on without speaking to. Its sadistic side is equally blatant: he has chosen (and freely chosen, for he had been a successful lawyer) to be a policeman, with all the attendant possibilities of pursuit and investigation. As a result, he follows, watches and falls in love with a perfect image of female beauty and mystery. Once he actually confronts her, his erotic drive is to break her down and force her *to tell* by persistent cross-questioning.

In the second part of the film, he re-enacts his obsessive involvement with the image he loved to watch secretly. He reconstructs Judy as Madeleine, forces her to conform in every detail to the actual physical appearance of his fetish. Her exhibitionism, her masochism, make her an ideal passive counterpart to Scottie's active sadistic voyeurism. She knows her part is to perform, and only by playing it through and then replaying it can she keep Scottie's erotic interest. But in the repetition he does break her down and succeeds in exposing her guilt. His curiosity wins through; she is punished.

Thus, in *Vertigo,* erotic involvement with the look boomerangs: the spectator's own fascination is revealed as illicit voyeurism as the narrative content enacts the processes and pleasures that he is himself exercising and enjoying. The Hitchcock hero here is firmly placed within the symbolic order, in narrative terms. He has all the attributes of the patriarchal superego. Hence the spectator, lulled into a false sense of security by the apparent legality of his surrogate, sees through his look and finds himself exposed as complicit, caught in the moral ambiguity of looking. Far from being simply an aside on the perversion of the police, *Vertigo* focuses on the implications of the active/looking, passive/looked-at split in terms of sexual difference and the power of the male symbolic encapsulated in the hero. Marnie, too, performs for Mark Rutland's gaze and masquerades as the perfect to-be-looked-at image. He, too, is on the side of the law until, drawn in by obsession with her guilt, her secret, he longs to see her in the act of committing a crime, make her confess and thus save her. So he, too, becomes complicit as he acts out the implications of his power. He controls money and words; he can have his cake and eat it.

IV. SUMMARY

The psychoanalytic background that has been discussed in this article is relevant to the pleasure and unpleasure offered by traditional narrative film. The scopophilic instinct (pleasure in looking at another person as an erotic object) and, in contradistinction, ego libido (forming identification processes) act as formations, mechanisms, which mould this cinema's formal attributes. The actual image of woman as (passive) raw material for the (active) gaze of man takes the argument a step further into the content and structure of representation, adding a further layer of ideological significance demanded by the patriarchal order in its favourite cinematic form — illusionistic narrative film. The argument must return again to the psychoanalytic background: women in representation can signify castration, and activate voyeuristic or fetishistic mechanisms to circumvent this threat. Although none of these interacting layers is intrinsic to film, it is only in the film form that they can reach a perfect and beautiful contradiction, thanks to the possibility in the cinema of shifting the emphasis of the look. The place of the look defines cinema, the possibility of varying it and exposing it. This is what makes cinema quite different in its voyeuristic potential from, say, strip-tease, theatre, shows and so on. Going far beyond highlighting a woman's to-be-looked-at-ness, cinema builds the

---

[11]The hero of *Rear Window* is housebound with a broken leg as the story begins.

way she is to be looked at into the spectacle itself. Playing on the tension between film as controlling the dimension of time (editing, narrative) and film as controlling the dimension of space (changes in distance, editing), cinematic codes create a gaze, a world and an object, thereby producing an illusion cut to the measure of desire. It is these cinematic codes and their relationship to formative external structures that must be broken down before mainstream film and the pleasure it provides can be challenged.

To begin with (as an ending), the voyeuristic — scopophilic look that is a crucial part of traditional filmic pleasure can itself be broken down. There are three different looks associated with cinema: that of the camera as it records the pro-filmic event, that of the audience as it watches the final product, and that of the characters at each other within the screen illusion. The conventions of narrative film deny the first two and subordinate them to the third, the conscious aim being always to eliminate intrusive camera presence and prevent a distancing awareness in the audience. Without these two absences (the material existence of the recording process, the critical reading of the spectator), fictional drama cannot achieve reality, obviousness and truth. Nevertheless, as this article has argued, the structure of looking in narrative fiction film contains a contradiction in its own premises: the female image as a castration threat constantly endangers the unity of the diegesis and bursts through the world of illusion as an intrusive, static, one-dimensional fetish. Thus the two

looks materially present in time and space are obsessively subordinated to the neurotic needs of the male ego. The camera becomes the mechanism for producing an illusion of Renaissance space, flowing movements compatible with the human eye, an ideology of representation that revolves around the perception of the subject; the camera's look is disavowed in order to create a convincing world in which the spectator's surrogate can perform with verisimilitude. Simultaneously, the look of the audience is denied an intrinsic force: as soon as fetishistic representation of the female image threatens to break the spell of illusion, and the erotic image on the screen appears directly (without mediation) to the spectator, the fact of fetishisation, concealing as it does castration fear, freezes the look, fixates the spectator and prevents him from achieving any distance from the image in front of him.

This complex interaction of looks is specific to film. The first blow against the monolithic accumulation of traditional film conventions (already undertaken by radical film-makers) is to free the look of the camera into its materiality in time and space and the look of the audience into dialectics and passionate detachment. There is no doubt that this destroys the satisfaction, pleasure and privilege of the "invisible guest," and highlights the way film has depended on voyeuristic active/passive mechanisms. Women, whose image has continually been stolen and used for this end, cannot view the decline of the traditional film form with anything much more than sentimental regret.

Slavoj Žižek
b. 1949

Slavoj Žižek was born in Ljubljana, Slovenia, where he has remained to this day, aside from having lectured at dozens of universities around the world. He received his B.A., M.A., and D.A. in philosophy at the University of Ljubljana, where he is currently a professor. He also received a D.A. in psychoanalysis at the Université Paris-VIII in 1985. Žižek was analyzed by Jacques-Alain Miller, Jacques Lacan's son-in-law, and is deeply invested in a post-Lacanian view of politics and popular culture, but is also influenced by Schelling and Hegel. Žižek analyzes the various metaphors of contemporary culture, representing everything from gender and religion to film and popular music, in order to extrapolate conclusions about the nature of symbols themselves as representations of the impossible, which he sees as fundamental to desire. Žižek's political interests are more than just scholarly; he ran for president of the Republic of Slovenia in 1990 in the nation's first multiparty election. Žižek is known for the mischievous nature of his scholarship, which includes a highly polemical proposal to re-actualize Leninist communism, in "Repeating Lenin" (1997), and the text for a recent Abercrombie & Fitch catalog, a commercial periodical known for its transgressive, idealized representations of teenage sexuality. His first book, The Sublime Object of Ideology *(1989), has been followed by too many to list here. They include* Looking Awry: An Introduction to Jacques Lacan through Popular Culture *(1991),* Enjoy Your Symptom! Jacques Lacan In Hollywood and Out *(1992),* Everything You Always Wanted to Know about Lacan (But Were Afraid to Ask Hitchcock) *(1992),* The Ticklish Subject: The Absent Centre of Political Ontology *(1999),* The Fragile Absolute: Or Why the Christian Legacy Is Worth Fighting For *(2000),* Did Someone Say Totalitarianism?: Four Interventions in the Misuse of a Notion *(2001),* Organs without Bodies *(2003),* The Puppet and the Dwarf *(2003), and, most recently,* Iraq: The Borrowed Kettle *(2004). This essay, "Courtly Love, or, Woman as Thing," was originally printed in* The Metastases of Enjoyment: Six Essays on Woman and Causality *(1994).*

Courtly Love, or, Woman as Thing

Why talk about courtly love [*l'amour courtois*] today, in an age of permissiveness when the sexual encounter is often nothing more than a "quickie" in some dark corner of an office? The impression that courtly love is out of date, long superseded by modern manners, is a lure blinding us to how the logic of courtly love still defines the parameters within which the two sexes relate to each other. This claim, however, in no way implies an evolutionary model through which courtly love would provide the elementary matrix out of which we generate its later, more complex variations. Our thesis is, instead, that history has to be read retroactively: the anatomy of man offers the key to the anatomy of the ape, as Marx put it. It is only with the emergence of masochism, of the masochist couple, towards the end of the last century that we can now grasp the libidinal economy of courtly love.

THE MASOCHISTIC THEATER OF COURTLY LOVE

The first trap to be avoided apropos of courtly love is the erroneous notion of the Lady as the sublime object[1]: as a rule, one evokes here the process of spiritualization, the shift from raw sensual coveting to elevated spiritual longing. The Lady is thus perceived as a kind of spiritual guide into the higher sphere of religious ecstasy, in the sense of Dante's Beatrice.[2] In contrast to this

[1]The aesthetics of the sublime are discussed in Longinus and in Kant; see pp. 95 and 247, respectively. Kant in particular is interested in the terror invested in the sublime object. Elsewhere, Žižek writes about Madeleine, the central female character in Hitchcock's *Vertigo*, as a "sublime object."

[2]Based on the real Beatrice Portinari, whom Dante Alighieri glimpsed in the streets of Florence as a boy of twelve, Beatrice is the saint who takes over from Virgil and guides the pilgrim Dante through Paradise.

notion, Lacan emphasizes a series of features which belie such a spiritualization: true, the Lady in courtly love loses concrete features and is addressed as an abstract ideal, so that "writers have noted that all the poets seem to be addressing the same person. . . . In this poetic field the feminine object is emptied of all real substance."[3] However, this abstract character of the Lady has nothing to do with spiritual purification; rather, it points towards the abstraction that pertains to a cold, distanced, inhuman partner — the Lady is by no means a warm, compassionate, understanding fellow-creature:

> By means of a form of sublimation specific to art, poetic creation consists in positing an object I can only describe as terrifying, an inhuman partner.
>
> The Lady is never characterized for any of her real, concrete virtues, for her wisdom, her prudence, or even her competence. If she is described as wise it is only because she embodies an immaterial wisdom or because she represents its functions more than she exercises them. On the contrary, she is as arbitrary as possible in the tests she imposes on her servant.[4]

The knight's relationship to the Lady is thus the relationship of the subject-bondsman, vassal, to his feudal Master-Sovereign who subjects him to senseless, outrageous, impossible, arbitrary, capricious ordeals. It is precisely in order to emphasize the non-spiritual nature of these ordeals that Lacan quotes a poem about a Lady who demanded that her servant literally lick her arse: the poem consists of the poet's complaints about the bad smells that await him down there (one knows the sad state of personal hygiene in the Middle Ages), about the imminent danger that, as he is fulfilling his duty, the Lady will urinate on his head. . . . The Lady is thus as far as possible from any kind of purified spirituality: she functions as an inhuman partner in the sense of a radical Otherness which is wholly incommensurable with our needs and desires; as such, she is simultaneously a kind of automaton, a machine which utters meaningless demands at random.

This coincidence of absolute, inscrutable Otherness and pure machine is what confers on the Lady her uncanny, monstrous character — the Lady is the Other which is not our "fellow creature"; that is to say, she is someone with whom no relationship of empathy is possible. This traumatic Otherness is what Lacan designates by means of the Freudian term *das Ding*,[5] the Thing — the Real that "always returns to its place,"[6] the hard kernel that resists symbolization. The idealization of the Lady, her elevation to a spiritual, ethereal Ideal, is therefore to be conceived of as a strictly secondary phenomenon: it is a narcissistic projection whose function is to render her traumatic dimension invisible. In this precise and limited sense, Lacan concedes that "the element of idealizing exaltation that is expressly sought out in the ideology of courtly love has certainly been demonstrated; it is fundamentally narcissistic in character."[7] Deprived of every real substance, the Lady functions as a mirror on to which the subject projects his narcissistic ideal. In other words — those of Christina Rossetti, whose sonnet "In an Artist's Studio" speaks of Dante Gabriel

---

[3]Jacques Lacan, *The Ethics of Psychoanalysis* (London: Routledge, 1992), p. 149. [Žižek]

[4]Ibid., p. 150; translation modified. [Žižek]

[5]Literally "the thing." Freud's term for the originary lost object against which all other losses are measured. Lacan elsewhere notes that there are two German words for "thing," *Ding* and *Sache*, and that Freud uses *Sache* for things that can be symbolized, reserving *Ding* for the missing object that can be neither imagined nor spoken of, which lives in Lacan's realm of the Real — for which see the introduction to Psychoanalytic Theory and Criticism, p. 1106. See also Lacan's "The Freudian Thing" in *Ecrits: A Selection*, p. 114.

[6]Is not Lacan's definition of the Real as that which always returns to its place "pre-Einsteinian" and, as such, de-valorized by the relativization of space with regard to the observer's point of view — that is, by the cancellation of the notion of absolute space and time? However, the theory of relativity involves its own absolute constant; the space-time interval between two events is an absolute that never varies. Space–time interval is defined as the hypotenuse of a right-angled triangle whose legs are the time and space distance between the two events. One observer may be in a state of motion such that for him there is a time and a distance involved between the two events; another may be in a state of motion such that his measuring devices indicate a different distance and a different time between the events, but the space-time interval between them does not vary. *This* constant is the Lacanian Real that "remains the same in all possible universes." [Žižek]

[7]Lacan, *The Ethics of Psychoanalysis*, p. 151. [Žižek]

Rossetti's relationship to Elizabeth Siddal,[8] his Lady — the Lady appears "not as she is, but as she fills his dream."[9] For Lacan, however, the crucial accent lies elsewhere:

> The mirror may on occasion imply the mechanisms of narcissism, and especially the dimension of destruction or aggression that we will encounter subsequently. But it also fulfills another role, a role as limit. It is that which cannot be crossed. And the only organization in which it participates is that of the inaccessibility of the object.[10]

Thus, before we embrace the commonplaces about how the Lady in courtly love has nothing to do with actual women, how she stands for the man's narcissistic projection which involves the mortification of the flesh-and-blood woman, we have to answer this question: where does that empty surface come from, that cold, neutral screen which opens up the space for possible projections? That is to say, if men are to project on to the mirror their narcissistic ideal, the mute mirror-surface must already be there. This surface functions as a kind of "black hole" in reality, as a limit whose Beyond is inaccessible.

The next crucial feature of courtly love is that it is thoroughly a matter of courtesy and etiquette; it has nothing to do with some elementary passion overflowing all barriers, immune to all social rules. We are dealing with a strict fictional formula, with a social game of "as if," where a man pretends that his sweetheart is the inaccessible Lady. And it is precisely this feature which enables us to establish a link between courtly love and a phenomenon which, at first, seems to have nothing whatsoever to do with it: namely, masochism, as a specific form of perversion articulated for the first time in the middle of the last century in the literary works and life-practice of Sacher-Masoch.[11] In his celebrated study of masochism,[12] Gilles Deleuze demonstrates that masochism is not to be conceived of as a simple symmetrical inversion of sadism. The sadist and his victim never form a complementary "sado-masochist" couple. Among those features evoked by Deleuze to prove the asymmetry between sadism and masochism, the crucial one is the opposition of the modalities of negation. In sadism we encounter direct negation, violent destruction and tormenting, whereas in masochism negation assumes the form of disavowal — that is, of feigning, of an "as if" which suspends reality.

Closely depending on this first opposition is the opposition of institution and contract. Sadism follows the logic of institution, of institutional power tormenting its victim and taking pleasure in the victim's helpless resistance. More precisely, sadism is at work in the obscene, superego underside that necessarily redoubles and accompanies, as its shadow, the "public" law. Masochism, on the contrary, is made to the measure of the victim: it is the victim (the servant in the masochistic relationship) who initiates a contract with the Master (woman), authorizing her to humiliate him in any way she considers appropriate (within the terms defined by the contract) and binding himself to act "according to the whims of the sovereign Lady," as Sacher-Masoch put it. It is the servant, therefore, who writes the screenplay — that is, who

---

[8] Lizzie Siddal (1829–1862) was a model of working-class English origins who posed for most of the important pre-Raphaelite painters, including Millais and Holman Hunt, as well as Dante Gabriel Rossetti, who married her in 1860, and who painted her as Dante's Beatrice both before and after her death from an overdose of laudanum.

[9] It is clear, therefore, that it would be a fateful mistake to identify the Lady in courtly love, this unconditional Ideal of the Woman, with woman in so far as she is not submitted to phallic enjoyment: the opposition of everyday, "tamed" woman, with whom sexual relationship may appear possible, and the Lady *qua* "inhuman partner," has nothing whatsoever to do with the opposition of woman submitted to phallic signifier and woman *qua* bearer of the Other enjoyment. The Lady is the projection of man's narcissistic Ideal; her figure emerges as the result of the masochistic pact by way of which woman accepts the role of *dominatrix* in the theater staged by man. For that reason, Rossetti's *Beata Beatrix*, for example, is not to be perceived as the figuration of the Other enjoyment: as with Isolde's love death in Wagner's *Tristan*, we are dealing with *man's* fantasy. [Žižek]

[10] Lacan, *The Ethics of Psychoanalysis*, p. 151. [Žižek]

[11] Lepold von Sacher-Masoch (1836–1895), author of *Venus in Furs* (1869), a novel consisting of fantasies of domination. The eponym "masochism" was coined by Richard von Krafft-Ebing in *Psychopathia Sexualis* (1886).

[12] Gilles Deleuze, "Coldness and Cruelty," in *Masochism* (New York: Zone Press, 1991.) [Žižek] For more on Deleuze, see p. 1777.

actually pulls the strings and dictates the activity of the woman [*dominatrix*]: he stages his own servitude.[13] One further differential feature is that masochism, in contrast to sadism, is inherently theatrical: violence is for the most part feigned, and even when it is "real," it functions as a component of a scene, as a part of a theatrical performance. Furthermore, violence is never carried out, brought to its conclusion; it always remains suspended, as the endless repeating of an interrupted gesture.

It is precisely this logic of disavowal which enables us to grasp the fundamental paradox of the masochistic attitude. That is to say, how does the typical masochistic scene look? The man-servant establishes in a cold, businesslike way the terms of the contract of the woman-master: what she is to do to him, what scene is to be rehearsed endlessly, what dress she is to wear, how far she is to go in the direction of the real, physical torture (how severely she is to whip him, in what precise way she is to enchain him, where she is to stamp him with the tips of her high heels, etc.). When they finally pass over to the masochistic game proper, the masochist constantly maintains a kind of reflective distance; he never really gives way to his feelings or fully abandons himself to the game; in the midst of the game, he can suddenly assume the stance of a stage director, giving precise instructions (put more pressure on that point, repeat that movement . . .), *without thereby in the least "destroying the illusion."* Once the game is over, the masochist again adopts the attitude of a respectful bourgeois and starts to talk with the Sovereign Lady in a matter-of-fact, businesslike way: "Thank you for your favor. Same time next week?" and so on. What is of crucial importance here is the total self-externalization of the masochist's most intimate passion: the most intimate desires become objects of contract and composed negotiation. The nature of the masochistic theater is therefore thoroughly "non-psychological": the surrealistic passionate masochistic game,

which suspends social reality, none the less fits easily into that everyday reality.[14]

For this reason, the phenomenon of masochism exemplifies in its purest form what Lacan had in mind when he insisted again and again that psychoanalysis is not psychology. Masochism confronts us with the paradox of the symbolic order *qua* the order of "fictions": there is more truth in the mask we wear, in the game we play, in the "fiction" we obey and follow, than in what is concealed beneath the mask. The very kernel of the masochist's being is externalized in the staged game towards which he maintains his constant distance. And the Real of violence breaks out precisely when the masochist is hystericized — when the subject refuses the role of an object-instrument of the enjoyment of his Other, when he is horrified at the prospect of being reduced in the eyes of the Other to *objet a*;[15] in order to escape this deadlock, he resorts to *passage à l'acte*,[16] to the "irrational" violence aimed at the other. Towards the end of P. D. James's *A Taste for Death*, the murderer describes the circumstances of the crime, and lets it be known that the factor which resolved his indecision and pushed him towards the act (the murder) was the attitude of the victim (Sir Paul Berowne):

> He wanted to die, God rot him, he wanted it! He practically asked for it. He could have tried to stop me, pleaded, argued, put up a fight. He could have begged for mercy, "No, please don't do it. Please!" That's all I wanted from him. Just that one

[13]For that reason lesbian sadomasochism is far more subversive than the usual "soft" lesbianism, which elevates tender relationships between women in contrast to aggressive-phallic male penetration: although the content of lesbian sadomasochism imitates "aggressive" phallic heterosexuality, this content is subverted by the very contractual form. [Žižek]

[14]Here the logic is the same as in the "non-psychological" universe of *Twin Peaks*, in which we encounter two main types of people: "normal," everyday people (based on soap-opera clichés) and "crazy" eccentrics (the lady with a log, etc); the uncanny quality of the *Twin Peaks* universe hinges on the fact that the relationship between these two groups follows the rules of "normal" communication: "normal" people are not at all amazed or outraged by the strange behavior of the eccentrics; they accept them as part of their daily routine. [Žižek]

[15]Also "*objet petit a*" where *a* stands for *autre* [other] to distinguish it from the capitalized Other/Autre. In Lacan's system, it may apply to any individual loved object, but is frequently used in a more limited sense, as a sexual fetish.

[16]In French law, the term denotes a stage, often involving psychological dissociation, between a criminal's departure from ordinary behavior and the violent act itself.

word. . . . He looked at me with such contempt. . . . He knew then. Of course he knew. And I wouldn't have done it, not if he'd spoken to me as if I were even half-human.[17]

He didn't even look surprised. He was supposed to be terrified. He was supposed to prevent it from happening. . . . He just looked at me as if he were saying "So it's you. How strange that it has to be you." As if I had no choice. Just an instrument. Mindless. But I did have a choice. And so did he. Christ, he could have stopped me. Why didn't he stop me?[18]

Several days before his death, Sir Paul Berowne experienced an "inner breakdown" resembling symbolic death: he stepped down as a government Minister and cut all his principal "human ties," assuming thereby the "excremental" position of a saint, of *objet petit a*, which precludes any intersubjective relationship of empathy. This attitude was what the murderer found unbearable: he approached his victim as $, a split subject — that is to say, he wanted to kill him, yet he was simultaneously waiting for a sign of fear, of resistance, from the victim, a sign which would prevent the murderer from accomplishing the act. The victim, however, did not give any such sign, which would have subjectivized the murderer, acknowledging him as a (divided) subject. Sir Paul's attitude of non-resistance, of indifferent provocation, objectivized the murderer, reducing him to an instrument of the Other's will, and so left him with no choice. In short, what compelled the murderer to act was the experience of having his desire to kill the victim coincide with the victim's death drive.

This coincidence recalls the way a male hysterical "sadist" justifies his beating of a woman: "Why does she make me do it? She really wants me to hurt her, she compels me to beat her so that she can enjoy it — *so I'll beat her black and blue and teach her what it really means to provoke me!*" What we encounter here is a kind of loop in which the (mis)perceived effect of the brutal act upon the victim retroactively legitimizes the act: I set out to beat a woman and when, at the very

point where I think that I thoroughly dominate her, I notice that I am actually her slave — since she wants the beating and provoked me to deliver it — I get really mad and beat her. . . .[19]

THE COURTLY "IMP OF THE PERVERSE"

How, on closer examination, are we to conceptualize the inaccessibility of the Lady-Object in courtly love? The principal mistake to avoid is reducing this inaccessibility to the simple dialectic of desire and prohibition according to which we covet the forbidden fruit precisely in so far as it is forbidden — or, to quote Freud's classic formulation:

> . . . the psychical value of erotic needs is reduced as soon as their satisfaction becomes easy. An obstacle is required in order to heighten libido; and where natural resistances to satisfaction have not

[19] An exemplary case of the inverse constellation — of the gaze *qua objet a* hystericizing the other — is provided by Robert Montgomery's *Lady in the Lake*, a film whose interest consists in its very failure. The point of view of the hard-boiled detective to which we are confined via a continuous subjective camera in no way arouses in us, the spectators, the impression that we are actually watching the events through the eyes of the person shown by the camera in the prologue or the epilogue (the only "objective shots" in the film) or when it confronts a mirror. Even when Marlowe "sees himself in the mirror," the spectator does not accept that the face he sees, the eyes on it, is the point of view of the camera. When the camera drags on in its clumsy, slow way it seems, rather, that the point of view is that of a living dead from Romero's *Night of the Living Dead* (the same association is further encouraged by the Christmas choral music, very unusual for a *film noir*). More precisely, it is as if the camera is positioned next to or closely behind Marlowe and somehow looks over his back, imitating the virtual gaze of his shadow, of his "undead" sublime double. There is no double to be seen next to Marlowe, since this double, what is in Marlowe "more than himself," is the gaze itself as the Lacanian *objet petit a* that does not have a specular image. (The voice that runs a commentary on the story belongs to this gaze, not to Marlowe *qua* diegetic person.) This object-gaze is the cause of the desire of women who, all the time, turn towards it (i.e. look into the camera): it lays them bare in an obscene way — or, in other words, it hystericizes them by simultaneously attracting and repelling them. It is on account of this objectivization of the gaze that *The Lady in the Lake* is not a *film noir*: the essential feature of a *film noir* proper is that the point of view of the narration is that of a *subject*. [Žižek]

[17] P. D. James, *A Taste for Death* (London and Boston, MA: Faber & Faber 1986) p. 439. [Žižek]

[18] Ibid., p. 440. [Žižek]

been sufficient men have at all times erected conventional ones so as to be able to enjoy love.[20]

Within this perspective, courtly love appears as simply the most radical strategy for elevating the value of the object by putting up conventional obstacles to its attainability. When, in his seminar *Encore*, Lacan provides the most succinct formulation of the paradox of courtly love, he says something that is apparently similar, yet fundamentally different: "A very refined manner to supplant the absence of the sexual relationship is by feigning that it is us who put the obstacle in its way."[21] The point, therefore, is not simply that we set up additional conventional hindrances in order to heighten the value of the object: *external hindrances that thwart our access to the object are there precisely to create the illusion that without them, the object would be directly accessible* — what such hindrances thereby conceal is the inherent impossibility of attaining the object. The place of the Lady-Thing is originally empty: she functions as a kind of "black hole" around which the subject's desire is structured. The space of desire is bent like space in the theory of relativity; the only way to reach the Object-Lady is indirectly, in a devious, meandering way — proceeding straight on ensures that we miss the target. This is what Lacan has in mind when, apropos of courtly love, he evokes "the meaning we must attribute to the negotiation of the detour in the psychic economy":

> The detour in the psyche isn't always designed to regulate the commerce between whatever is organized in the domain of the pleasure principle and whatever presents itself as the structure of reality. There are also detours and obstacles which are organized so as to make the domain of the vacuole stand out as such. . . . The techniques involved in courtly love — and they are precise enough to allow us to perceive what might on occasion

become fact, what is properly speaking of the sexual order in the inspiration of this eroticism — are techniques of holding back, of suspension, of *amor interruptus*. The stages courtly love lays down previous to what is mysteriously referred to as *le don de merci*, "the gift of mercy" — although we don't know exactly what it meant — are expressed more or less in terms that Freud uses in his *Three Essays* as belonging to the sphere of foreplay.[22]

For that reason, Lacan accentuates the motif of anamorphosis[23] (in his Seminar on the Ethics of Psychoanalysis, the title of the chapter on courtly love is "Courtly Love as Anamorphosis"): the Object can be perceived only when it is viewed from the side, in a partial, distorted form, as its own shadow — if we cast a direct glance at it we see nothing, a mere void. In a homologous way, we could speak of temporal anamorphosis: the Object is attainable only by way of an incessant postponement, as its absent point of reference. The Object, therefore, is literally something that is created — whose place is encircled — through a network of detours, approximations and near-misses. It is here that *sublimation* sets in — sublimation in the Lacanian sense of the elevation of an object into the dignity of the Thing: "sublimation" occurs when an object, part of everyday reality, finds itself at the place of the impossible Thing. Herein resides the function of those artificial obstacles that suddenly hinder our access to some ordinary object: they elevate the object into a stand-in for the Thing. This is how the impossible changes into the prohibited: by way of the short circuit between the Thing and some positive object rendered inaccessible through artificial obstacles.

The tradition of Lady as the inaccessible object is alive and well in our century — in surrealism, for example. Suffice it to recall Luis Buñuel's *That Obscure Object of Desire*, in

---

[20]Sigmund Freud, "On the Universal Tendency to Debasement in the Sphere of Love" (1912), in James Strachey, ed., *The Standard Edition of the Complete Psychological Works of Sigmund Freud*, vol. 11 (London: Hogarth Press, 1986) p. 187. [Žižek]

[21]Jacques Lacan, *Le séminaire, livre XX: Encore* (Paris: Éditions du Seuil, 1975) p. 65. [Žižek]

[22]Lacan, *The Ethics of Psychoanalysis*, p. 152. [Žižek]

[23]An image distorted in such a way that it looks "normal" from a particular viewing angle; one example is Hans Holbein's painting *The Ambassadors,* in the National Gallery, London, which includes an anamorphic skull in the foreground that pops out at the viewer who encounters the painting from below and to the right (coming upstairs, for example).

which a woman, through a series of absurd tricks, postpones again and again the final moment of sexual re-union with her aged lover (when, for example, the man finally gets her into bed, he discovers beneath her nightgown an old-fashioned corset with numerous buckles which are impossible to undo . . .). The charm of the film lies in this very nonsensical short circuit between the fundamental, metaphysical Limit and some trivial empirical impediment. Here we find the logic of courtly love and of sublimation at its purest: some common, everyday object or act becomes inaccessible or impossible to accomplish once it finds itself in the position of the Thing — although the thing should be easily within reach, the entire universe has somehow been adjusted to produce, again and again, an unfathomable contingency blocking access to the object. Buñuel himself was quite aware of this paradoxical logic: in his autobiography he speaks of "the non-explainable impossibility of the fulfillment of a simple desire," and a whole series of films offers variations on this motif: in *The Criminal Life of Archibaldo de la Cruz* the hero wants to accomplish a simple murder, but all his attempts fail; in *The Exterminating Angel,* after a party, a group of rich people cannot cross the threshold and leave the house; in *The Discreet Charm of the Bourgeoisie* two couples want to dine together, but unexpected complications always prevent the fulfillment of this simple wish . . .

It should be clear, now, what determines the difference with regard to the usual dialectic of desire and prohibition: the aim of the prohibition is not to "raise the price" of an object by rendering access to it more difficult, but to raise this object itself to the level of the Thing, of the "black hole," around which desire is organized. For that reason, Lacan is quite justified in inverting the usual formula of sublimation, which involves shifting the libido from an object that satisfies some concrete, material need to an object that has no apparent connection to this need: for example, destructive literary criticism becomes sublimated aggressivity, scientific research into the human body becomes sublimated voyeurism, and so on. What Lacan means by sublimation, on the contrary, is shifting the libido from the void of the "unserviceable" Thing to some concrete, material object of need that assumes a sublime quality the moment it occupies the place of Thing.[24]

What the paradox of the Lady in courtly love ultimately amounts to is thus the paradox of *detour:* our "official" desire is that we want to sleep with the Lady; whereas in truth, there is nothing we fear more than a Lady who might generously yield to this wish of ours — what we truly expect and want from the Lady is simply yet another new ordeal, yet one more postponement. In his *Critique of Practical Reason,* Kant offers a parable about a libertine who claims that he cannot resist the temptation to gratify his illicit sexual desire, yet when he is informed that the gallows now await him as the price to be paid for his adultery, he suddenly discovers that he can resist the temptation after all (proof, for Kant, of the pathological nature of sexual desire — Lacan opposes Kant by claiming that a man of true amorous passion would be even more aroused by the prospect of the gallows . . .). But for the faithful servant of a Lady the choice is structured in a totally different way: perhaps he would even prefer the gallows to an immediate gratification of his desire for the Lady. The Lady therefore functions as a unique short circuit in which *the Object of desire itself coincides with the force that prevents its attainment* — in a way, the object "is" its own withdrawal, its own retraction.

It is against this background that one must conceive of the often mentioned, yet no less often misunderstood, "phallic" value of the woman in Lacan — his equation Woman = Phallus. That is to say, precisely the same paradox characterizes the phallic signifier *qua* signifier of castration. "Castration means that *jouissance* must be refused, so that it can be reached on the inverted

24"... [P]ar une inversion de l'usage du terme de sublimation, j'ai le droit de dire que nous voyons ici la déviation quant au but se faire en sens inverse de l'objet d'un besoin" (Jacques Lacan, *Le séminaire, livre VIII: Le transfert* [Paris: Éditions du Seuil, 1991] p. 250). The same goes for every object which functions as a sign of love: its use is suspended, it changes into a means of the articulation of the demand for love. [Žižek] ladder of the Law of desire."[25] How is this "economic paradox" feasible, how can the machinery of desire be "set in motion" — that is to say, how can the subject be made to renounce enjoyment not for another, higher Cause but simply in order to gain access to it? Or — to quote Hegel's formulation of the same paradox — how is it that we can attain identity only by losing it? There is only one solution to this problem: the phallus, the signifier of enjoyment, had simultaneously to be the signifier of "castration," that is to say, *one and the same signifier had to signify enjoyment as well as its loss.* In this way, it becomes possible that the

very agency which entices us to search for enjoyment induces us to renounce it.[26]

Back to the Lady: are we, therefore, justified in conceiving of the Lady as the personification of the Western metaphysical passion, as an exorbitant, almost parodical example of metaphysical *hubris,* of the elevation of a particular entity or feature into the Ground of all being? On closer examination, what constitutes this metaphysical or simply philosophical *hubris?* Let us take what might appear to be a surprising example. In Marx, the specifically *philosophical* dimension is at work when he points out that production, one of the four moments of the totality of production, distribution, exchange and consumption, is simultaneously the encompassing totality of the four moments, conferring its specific color on that totality. (Hegel made the same point in asserting that every genus has two species, itself and its species — that is to say, the genus is always one of its own species.) The "philosophical" or "metaphysical" is this very "absolutization," this elevation of a particular moment of the totality into its Ground, this *hubris* which "disrupts" the harmony of a balanced Whole.

Let us mention two approaches to language: that of John L. Austin[27] and that of Oswald Ducrot.[28] Why is it legitimate to treat their work as "philosophy"? Austin's division of all verbs into performatives and constatives is not yet philosophy proper: we enter the domain of philosophy with his "unbalanced," "excessive" hypothesis

[25]Jacques Lacan, *Écrits: A Selection* (New York: Norton, 1977) p. 324. The first to formulate this "economic paradox of castration" in the domain of philosophy was Kant. One of the standard reproaches to Kant is that he was a contradictory thinker who got stuck halfway: on the one hand *already* within the new universe of democratic rights (*égaliberté,* to use Étienne Balibar's term), on the other hand *still* caught in the paradigm of man's subordination to some superior Law (imperative). However, Lacan's formula of fetishism (a fraction with *a* above minus phi of castration) enables us to grasp the co-dependence of these two allegedly opposed aspects. The crucial feature that distinguishes the democratic field of *égaliberté* from the pre-bourgeois field of traditional authority is the potential *infinity* of rights: rights are never fully realized or even explicitly formulated, since we are dealing with an unending process of continually articulating new rights. On that account, the status of rights in the modern democratic universe is that of *objet petit a,* of an evasive object-cause of desire. Where does this feature come from? Only one consistent answer is possible: *rights are (potentially) infinite because the renunciation upon which they are based is also infinite.* The notion of a radical, "infinite" renunciation as the price the individual must pay for his entry into the social-symbolic universe — that is to say, the notion of a "discontent in civilization," of an irreducible antagonism between man's "true nature" and the social order — emerged only with the modern democratic universe. Previously, within the field of traditional authority, "sociability," a propensity for subordination to authority and for aligning oneself with some community, was conceived of as an integral part of the very "nature" of man *qua zōon politikon.* (This, of course, does not mean that this renunciation — "symbolic castration," in psychoanalytic terms — was not, implicitly, at work from the very beginning: we are dealing here with the logic of retroactivity where things "become what they always-already were": the modern bourgeois universe of Rights made visible a renunciation that was *always-already* there.) And the infinite domain of rights arises precisely as a kind of "compensation": it is what we *get in exchange* for the infinite renunciation as the price we had to pay for our entry into society. [Žižek]

[26]This paradox of castration also offers the key to the function of perversion, to its constitutive loop: the pervert is a subject who directly assumes the paradox of desire and inflicts pain in order to enable enjoyment, who introduces schism in order to enable reunion, and so on. And, incidentally, theology resorts to obscure talk about the "inscrutable divine mystery" precisely at the point where it would otherwise be compelled to acknowledge the perverse nature of God: "the ways of the Lord are mysterious," which usually means that when misfortune pursues us everywhere, we must presuppose that He plunged us into misery in order to force us to take the opportunity to achieve spiritual salvation. . . . [Žižek]

[27]For more on J. L. Austin, see p. 679.

[28]Perhaps best known as the editor, with Tzvetan Todorov, of the *Encyclopedic Dictionary of the Sciences of Language,* Oswald Ducrot is a French linguist who teaches at EHESS (École des Hautes Étudessen Sciences Sociales).

that every proposition, including a constative, *already is a performative* — that the performative, as one of the two moments of the Whole, simultaneously *is* the Whole. The same goes for Oswald Ducrot's thesis that every predicate possesses, over and above its informative value, an argumentative value. We remain within the domain of positive science as long as we simply endeavor to discern in each predicate the level of information and the level of argumentation — that is, the specific modality of how certain information "fits" some argumentative attitude. We enter philosophy with the "excessive" hypothesis that *the predicate as such, including its informative content, is nothing but a condensed argumentative attitude,* so that we can never "distil" from it its "pure" informative content, untainted by some argumentative attitude. Here, of course, we encounter the paradox of "non-all": the fact that "no aspect of a predicate's content remains unaffected by some argumentative attitude" does not authorize us to draw the seemingly obvious universal conclusion that "the entire content of a predicate is argumentative" — the elusive surplus that persists, although it cannot be pinned down anywhere, is the Lacanian Real.

This, perhaps, offers another way of considering Heidegger's "ontological difference": as the distance that always yawns between the (specific feature, elevated into the) Ground of the totality and the Real which eludes this Ground, which itself cannot be "Grounded" in it. That is to say, "non-metaphysical" is not a "balanced" totality devoid of any *hubris,* a totality (or, in more Heideggerian terms: the Whole of entities) in which no particular aspect or entity is elevated into its Ground. The domain of entities gains its consistency from its sup-posited Ground, so that "non-metaphysics" can only be an insight into the difference between Ground and the elusive Real which — although its positive content ("reality") is grounded in the Ground — none the less eludes and undermines the reign of the Ground.

And now, back to the Lady again: this is why the Lady is *not* another name for the metaphysical Ground but, on the contrary, one of the names for the self-retracting Real which, in a way, grounds the Ground itself. And in so far as one of the names for the metaphysical Ground of all entities is "supreme Good," the Lady *qua* Thing can also be designated as the embodiment of radical Evil, of the Evil that Edgar Allan Poe, in two of his stories, "The Black Cat" and "The Imp of the Perverse," called the "spirit of perverseness":

> Of this spirit philosophy takes no account. Yet I am not more sure that my soul lives, than I am that perverseness is one of the primitive impulses of the human heart. . . . Who has not, a hundred times, found himself committing a vile or a stupid action, for no other reason than because he knows he should *not?* Have we not a perpetual inclination, in the teeth of our best judgment, to violate that which is *Law,* merely because we understand it to be such? ("The Black Cat")

> . . . it is, in fact, a *mobile* without motive, a motive not *motiviert.* Through its promptings we act without comprehensible object; or, if this shall be understood as a contradiction in terms, we may so far modify the proposition as to say, that through its promptings we act, for the reason that we should *not.* In theory, no reason can be more unreasonable; but, in fact, there is none more strong. . . . I am not more certain that I breathe, than that the assurance of the wrong or error of any action is often the one unconquerable *force* which impels us, and alone impels us to its prosecution. Nor will this overwhelming tendency to do wrong for the wrong's sake, admit of analysis, or resolution into ulterior elements. It is a radical, a primitive impulse — elementary. ("The Imp of the Perverse")

The affinity of crime as an unmotivated *acte gratuit* to art is a standard topic of Romantic theory (the Romantic cult of the artist comprises the notion of the artist *qua* criminal): it is deeply significant that Poe's formulas ("a *mobile* without motive, a motive not *motiviert*") immediately recall Kant's determinations of the aesthetic experience ("purposefulness without purpose," etc.). What we must not overlook here is the crucial fact that this command — "You must because you are not allowed to!" that is to say, a purely negative grounding of an act accomplished only because it is prohibited — is possible only within the differential symbolic order in which negative determination as such has a positive reach — in which the very *absence* of a feature functions as a *positive feature.* Poe's "imp of the perverse" therefore marks the point at which the motivation of an act, as it were, cuts off its external link to empirical objects and grounds itself solely in the immanent circle of self-reference — in short, Poe's "imp" corresponds to the point of freedom in the strict Kantian sense.

This reference to Kant is far from accidental. According to Kant, the faculty of desiring does not possess a transcendental status, since it is wholly dependent upon pathological objects and motivations. Lacan, on the contrary, aims to demonstrate the transcendental status of this faculty — that is, the possibility of formulating a motivation for our desire that is totally independent of pathology (such a non-pathological object-cause of desire is the Lacanian *objet petit a*). Poe's "imp of the perverse" offers us an immediate example of such a pure motivation: when I accomplish an act "only because it is prohibited," I remain within the universal-symbolic domain, without reference to any empirical-contingent object — that is to say, I accomplish what is *stricto sensu* a non-pathological act. Here, then, Kant miscalculated his wager: by cleansing the domain of ethics of pathological motivations, he wanted to extirpate the very possibility of doing Evil in the guise of Good; what he actually did was to open up a new domain of Evil far more uncanny than the usual "pathological" Evil.

EXEMPLIFICATIONS

From the thirteenth century to modern times, we encounter numerous variations on this matrix of courtly love. In *Les Liaisons dangereuses*,[29] for example, the relationship between the Marquise de Montreuil and Valmont is clearly the relationship between a capricious Lady and her servant. The paradox here turns on the nature of the task the servant must perform in order to earn the promised gesture of Mercy: he must seduce other ladies. His Ordeal requires that, even at the height of passion, he maintain a cold distance towards his victims: in the very moment of triumph, he must humiliate them by abandoning them without reason, thereby proving his fidelity to the Lady. Things get complicated when Valmont falls in

love with one of his victims (Présidente de Tourvel) and thereby "betrays his Duty": the Marquise is quite justified in dismissing his excuse (the famous "'c'est pas ma faute" : it's beyond my control, it's the way things are . . .) as beneath Valmont's dignity, as a miserable recourse to a "pathological" state of things (in the Kantian sense of the term).

The Marquise's reaction to Valmont's "betrayal" is thus strictly ethical: Valmont's excuse is exactly the same as the excuse invoked by moral weaklings when they fail to perform their duty — "I just couldn't help it, such is my nature, I'm simply not strong enough. . . ." Her message to Valmont recalls Kant's motto "Du kannst, denn du sollst! [You can, because you must!]." For that reason, the punishment imposed by the Marquise on Valmont is quite appropriate: in renouncing the Présidente de Tourvel, he must have recourse to exactly the same words — that is, he must compose a letter to her, explaining to her that "it's not his fault" if his passion for her has expired, it's simply the way things are. . . .

Another variation on the matrix of courtly love emerges in the story of Cyrano de Bergerac[30] and Roxane. Ashamed of his obscene natural deformity (his too-long nose), Cyrano has not dared to confess his love to the beautiful Roxane; so he interposes between himself and her a good-looking young soldier, conferring on him the role of proxy through whom he expresses his desire. As befits a capricious Lady, Roxane demands that her lover articulate his love in elegant poetic terms; the unfortunate simple-minded young soldier is not up to the task, so Cyrano hastens to his assistance, writing passionate love letters for the soldier from the battlefield. The dénouement takes place in two stages, tragic and melodramatic. Roxane tells the soldier that she does not love his beautiful body alone; she loves his refined soul even more: she is so deeply moved by his letters that she would continue to love him even if his body were to become mutilated and ugly. The soldier shudders at these words: he realizes that Roxane does not love him as he really is but as the author of his

---

[29]Epistolary novel (1782) by Pierre Choderlos de Laclos (1741–1803), filmed by Stephen Frears in 1988.

[30]Žižek refers to the Romantic drama (1897) by Edmond Rostand (1869–1918). It was filmed by Jean-Paul Rappeneau in 1993.

letters — in other words, she unknowingly loves Cyrano. Unable to endure this humiliation, he rushes suicidally into an attack and dies. Roxane enters a cloister, where she has regular visits from Cyrano, who keeps her informed about the social life of Paris. During one of these visits Roxane asks him to read aloud the last letter of her dead lover. The melodramatic moment now sets in: Roxane suddenly notices that Cyrano does not read the letter, he recites it — thereby proving that he is its true author. Deeply shaken, she recognizes in this crippled merrymaker her true love. But it is already too late: Cyrano has come to this meeting mortally wounded. . . .

One of the most painful and troubling scenes from David Lynch's *Wild at Heart*[31] is also comprehensible only against the matrix of the logic of suspension that characterizes courtly love. In a lonely motel room, Willem Dafoe exerts a rude pressure on Laura Dern: he touches and squeezes her, invading the space of her intimacy and repeating in a threatening way "Say fuck me!" that is, extorting from her a word that would signal her consent to a sexual act. The ugly, unpleasant scene drags itself on, and when, finally, the exhausted Laura Dern utters a barely audible "Fuck me!" Dafoe abruptly steps away, assumes a nice, friendly smile and cheerfully retorts: "No thanks, I don't have time today; but on another occasion I would do it gladly. . . ." He has attained what he really wanted: not the act itself, just her consent to it, her symbolic humiliation. What intervenes here is the function of the big Other, the trans-subjective symbolic order: by means of his intrusive pressure, Dafoe wants to extort the inscription, the "registration," of her consent in the field of the big Other.

The reverse variation on the same motif is at work in a short love scene from Truffaut's *La Nuit américaine*[32] (*Day for Night*). When, on the drive from the hotel to the studio, a car tire blows, the assistant cameraman and the script-girl find themselves alone on a lake shore. The assistant, who has pursued the girl for a long time, seizes the opportunity and bursts into a pathetic speech about how much he desires her and how much it would mean to him if, now that they are alone, she were to consent to a quick sexual encounter; the girl simply says "Yes, why not?" and starts to unbutton her trousers. . . . This non-sublime gesture, of course, totally bewilders the seducer, who conceived of her as the unattainable Lady: he can only stammer "How do you mean? Just like that?" What this scene has in common with the scene from *Wild at Heart* (and what sets it within the matrix of courtly love) is the unexpected gesture of refusal: the man's response to the woman's "Yes!" obtained by long, arduous effort, is to refuse the act.

We encounter a more refined variation on the matrix of courtly love in Eric Rohmer's *Ma nuit chez Maud*:[33] courtly love provides the only logic that can account for the hero's lie at the end. The central part of the film depicts the night that the hero and his friend Maud spend together; they talk long into the small hours and even sleep in the same bed, but the sexual act does not take place, owing to the hero's indecision — he is unable to seize the opportunity, obsessed as he is by the mysterious blonde woman whom he saw the evening before in a church. Although he does not yet know who she is, he has already decided to marry her (i.e. the blonde is his Lady). The final scene takes place several years later. The hero, now happily married to the blonde, encounters Maud on a beach; when his wife asks him who this unknown woman is, the hero tells a lie — apparently to his detriment; he informs his wife that Maud was his last love adventure before marriage. Why this lie? Because the truth could have aroused the suspicion that Maud also occupied the place of the Lady, with whom a brief, noncommittal sexual encounter is not possible — precisely by telling a lie to his wife, by claiming that he did have sex with Maud, he assures her that Maud was not his Lady, but just a passing friend.

[31]Released in 1990, based on a novel of the same title by Barry Gifford.
[32]Released in 1973, based on a screenplay by Suzanne Schiffman.
[33]The film (*My Night at Maud's*, 1969) is the fourth in Rohmer's series *Six contes moraux* (*Six Moral Tales*).

The definitive version of courtly love in recent decades, of course, arrives in the figure of the *femme fatale* in *film noir*:[34] the traumatic Woman-Thing who, through her greedy and capricious demands, brings ruin to the *hard-boiled* hero. The key role is played here by the third person (as a rule the gangster boss) to whom the *femme fatale* "legally" belongs: his presence renders her inaccessible and thus confers on the hero's relationship with her the mark of transgression. By means of his involvement with her, the hero betrays the paternal figure who is also his boss (in *The Glass Key, The Killers, Criss-Cross, Out of the Past*,[35] etc.).

This link between the courtly Lady and the *femme fatale* from the *noir* universe may appear surprising: is not the *femme fatale* in *film noir* the very opposite of the noble sovereign Lady to whom the knight vows service? Is not the hard-boiled hero ashamed of the attraction he feels for her; doesn't he hate her (and himself) for loving her; doesn't he experience his love for her as a betrayal of his true self? However, if we bear in mind the original traumatic impact of the Lady, not its secondary idealization, the connection is clear: like the Lady, the *femme fatale* is an "inhuman partner," a traumatic Object with whom no relationship is possible, an apathetic void imposing senseless, arbitrary ordeals.[36]

FROM THE COURTLY GAME TO *THE CRYING GAME*[37]

The key to the extraordinary and unexpected success of Neil Jordan's *The Crying Game* is perhaps the ultimate variation that it delivers on the motif of courtly love. Let us recall the outlines of the story: Fergus, a member of the IRA guarding a captured black British soldier, develops friendly links with him; the soldier asks him, in the event of his liquidation, to pay a visit to his girlfriend, Dil, a hairdresser in a London suburb, and to give her his last regards. After the death of the soldier, Fergus withdraws from the IRA, moves to London, finds a job as a bricklayer and pays a visit to the soldier's love, a beautiful black woman. He falls in love with her, but Dil maintains an ambiguous ironic, sovereign distance towards him. Finally, she gives way to his advances; but before they go to bed together she leaves for a brief moment, returning in a transparent nightgown; while casting a covetous glance at her body, Fergus suddenly perceives her penis — "she" is a transvestite. Sickened, he crudely pushes her away. Shaken and wet with tears, Dil tells him that she thought he knew all the time how things stood (in his obsession with her, the hero — as well as the public — did not notice a host of telltale details, including the fact that the bar where they usually met was a meeting-place for transvestites). This scene of the failed sexual encounter is structured as the exact inversion of the scene referred to by Freud as the primordial trauma of fetishism: the child's gaze, sliding down the naked female body towards the sexual organ, is shocked to find nothing where one expects to see something (a penis) — in the case of *The Crying Game*, the shock is caused when the eye finds *something* where it expected *nothing*.

After this painful revelation, the relationship between the two is reversed: now it turns out that

[34]A movie genre so named by French film critics Raymond Borde and Étienne Chaumeton in 1946. Popular during and just after World War II (and successfully revived recently), the genre features a disillusioned, alienated protagonist, a seductress whose charms are often fatal both to the protagonist and to herself, and a film technique that emphasizes night shots and strange angles. Recent examples of film noir are Lawrence Kasdan's *Body Heat*, Alex Proyas's *Dark City*, Andy and Larry Wachowski's *Bound,* and John Dahl's *The Last Seduction.*

[35]There were two versions of *The Glass Key* made within a few years of each other from the same Dashiell Hammett novel of 1931, but probably Žižek is referring to the more familiar Stuart Heisler version (1942) starring Alan Ladd, rather than the Frank Tuttle version (1935) starring George Raft. The film noir version of *The Killers* is by Robert Siodmak (1946) from Hemingway's 1927 short story. Siodmak also made *Criss-Cross* (1949); both films starred Burt Lancaster. *Out of the Past* (1947) by Jacques Tourneur, from a Daniel Mainwaring novel, starred Robert Mitchum.

[36]Films that transpose the *noir* matrix into another genre (science fiction, musical comedy, etc.) often exhibit some

crucial ingredient of the *noir* universe more patently than the *noir* proper. When, for example, in *Who Framed Roger Rabbit?*, Jessica Rabbit, a cartoon character, answers the reproach of her corruption with "I'm not bad, I was just drawn that way!," she thereby displays the truth about *femme fatale* as a male fantasy — that is, as a creature whose contours are drawn by man. [Žižek]

[37]Released in 1992, original screenplay by Neil Jordan.

Dil is passionately in love with Fergus, although she knows her love is impossible. From a capricious and ironic sovereign Lady she changes into the pathetic figure of a delicate, sensitive boy who is desperately in love. It is only at this point that true love emerges, love as a metaphor in the precise Lacanian sense:[38] we witness the sublime moment when *eromenos* (the loved one) changes into *erastes* (the loving one) by stretching out her hand and "returning love." This moment designates the "miracle" of love, the moment of the "answer of the Real"; as such, it perhaps enables us to grasp what Lacan has in mind when he insists that the subject itself has the status of an "answer of the Real." That is to say, up to this reversal the loved one has the status of an object: he is loved on account of something that is "in him more than himself" and that he is unaware of — I can never answer the question "What am I as an object for the other? What does the other see in me that causes his love?." We thus confront an asymmetry — not only the asymmetry between subject and object, but asymmetry in a far more radical sense of a discord between what the lover sees in the loved one and what the loved one knows himself to be.

Here we find the inescapable deadlock that defines the position of the loved one: the other sees something in me and wants something from me, but I cannot give him what I do not possess — or, as Lacan puts it, there is no relationship between what the loved one possesses and what the loving one lacks. The only way for the loved one to escape this deadlock is to stretch out his hand towards the loving one and to "return love" — that is, to exchange, in a metaphorical gesture, his status as the loved one for the status of the loving one. This reversal designates the point of subjectivization: the object of love changes into the subject the moment it answers the call of love. And it is only by way of this reversal that a genuine love emerges: I am truly in love not when I am simply fascinated by the *agalma*[39] in the other, but when I experience the other, the object of love,

as frail and lost, as lacking "it," and my love none the less survives this loss.

We must be especially attentive here so that we do not miss the point of this reversal: although we now have two loving subjects instead of the initial duality of the loving one and the loved one, the asymmetry persists, since it was the object itself that, as it were, confessed to its lack by means of its subjectivization. Something deeply embarrassing and truly scandalous abides in this reversal by means of which the mysterious, fascinating, elusive object of love discloses its deadlock, and thus acquires the status of another subject.

We encounter the same reversal in horror stories: is not the most sublime moment in Mary Shelley's *Frankenstein* the moment of the monster's subjectivization — the moment when the monster-object (who has been continually described as a ruthless killing machine) starts talking in the first person, revealing his miserable, pitiful existence? It is deeply symptomatic that all the films based on Shelley's *Frankenstein* have avoided this gesture of subjectivization. And perhaps, in courtly love itself, the long-awaited moment of highest fulfilment, when the Lady renders *Gnade*, mercy, to her servant, is not the Lady's surrender, her consent to the sexual act, nor some mysterious rite of initiation, but simply a sign of love on the part of the Lady, the "miracle" that the Object answered, stretching its hand out towards the supplicant.[40]

---

[38]See Chapters 3 and 4 of Lacan, *Le séminaire, livre VIII; Le transfert* (1960–61). [Žižek]

[39]Greek for votive offering, Lacan used the term in Seminar VIII to denote the mystical, supremely beautiful thing in the Other that provokes one's desire. (Lacan also uses it to signify the treasure that is pursued by means of psychoanalysis.)

[40]This moment when the object of fascination subjectivizes itself and stretches out its hand is the magical moment of crossing the frontier that separates the fantasy-space from "ordinary" reality: it is as if, at this moment, the object that otherwise belongs to another, sublime space intervenes in "ordinary" reality. Suffice it to recall a scene from *Possessed*, Clarence Brown's early Hollywood melodrama with Joan Crawford. Crawford, a poor small-town girl, stares amazed at the luxurious private train that slowly passes in front of her at the local railway station; through the windows of the carriages she sees the rich life going on in the illuminated inside — dancing couples, cooks preparing dinner, and so on. The crucial feature of the scene is that we, the spectators, together with Crawford, perceive the train as a magic, immaterial apparition from another world. When the last carriage passes by, the train comes to a halt and we see on the observation deck a good-natured drunkard with a glass of champagne in his hand, which stretches over the railing towards Crawford — as if, for a brief moment, the fantasy-space intervened in reality. . . . [Žižek]

So, back to *The Crying Game*: Dil is now ready to do anything for Fergus, and he is more and more moved and fascinated by the absolute, unconditional character of her love for him, so that he overcomes his aversion and continues to console her. At the end, when the IRA again tries to involve him in a terrorist act, he even sacrifices himself for Dil and assumes responsibility for a killing she committed. The last scene of the film takes place in the prison where she visits him, again dressed up as a provocatively seductive woman, so that every man in the visiting room is aroused by her looks. Although Fergus has to endure more than four thousand days of prison — they count them up together — she cheerfully pledges to wait for him and visit him regularly. . . . The external impediment — the glass-partition in the prison preventing any physical contact — is here the exact equivalent to the obstacle in courtly love that renders the object inaccessible; it thereby accounts for the absolute, unconditional character of this love in spite of its inherent impossibility — that is, in spite of the fact that their love will never be consummated, since he is a "straight" heterosexual and she is a homosexual transvestite. In his Introduction to the published screenplay, Jordan points out that

> the story ended with a kind of happiness. I say a kind of happiness, because it involved the separation of a prison cell and other more profound separations, of racial, national, and sexual identity. But for the lovers, it was the irony of what divided them that allowed them to smile. So perhaps there is hope for our divisions yet.[41]

Is not the division — the unsurmountable barrier — that allows for a smile the most concise mechanism of courtly love? What we have here is an "impossible" love which will never be consummated, which can be realized only as a feigned spectacle intended to fascinate the gaze of the spectators present, or as an endlessly postponed expectation; this love is absolute precisely in so far as it transgresses not only the barriers of class, religion and race, but also the ultimate barrier of sexual orientation, of sexual identification. Herein resides the film's paradox and, at the same time, its irresistible charm: far from denouncing heterosexual love as a product of male repression, it renders the precise circumstances in which this love can today retain its absolute, unconditional character.

THE CRYING GAME GOES EAST

This reading of *The Crying Game* immediately brings to mind one of the standard reproaches to Lacanian theory: in all his talk about feminine inconsistency, and so on, Lacan speaks about woman only as she appears or is mirrored in male discourse, about her distorted reflection in a medium that is foreign to her, never about woman as she is in herself: to Lacan, as earlier to Freud, feminine sexuality remains a "dark continent." In answer to this reproach, we must emphatically assert that if the fundamental Hegelian paradox of reflexivity remains in force anywhere, it is here: the remove, the step back, from woman-in-herself to how woman *qua* absent Cause distorts male discourse brings us much closer to the "feminine essence" than a direct approach. That is to say, is not "woman" ultimately just the name for a distortion or inflection of the male discourse? Is not the specter of "woman-in-herself," far from being the active cause of this distortion, rather its reified-fetishized effect.

All these questions are implicitly addressed by *M. Butterfly* (directed by David Cronenberg, script by David Henry Hwang from his own play), a film whose subtitle could well have been "*The Crying Game*" *Goes to China*. The first feature of this film that strikes the eye is the utter "improbability" of its narrative: without the information (given in the credits) that the story is based on true events, nobody would take it seriously.[42] During

[41]*A Neil Jordan Reader* (New York: Vintage Books, 1993), pp. xii–xiii. The question to be raised here is also that of inserting *The Crying Game* into the series of Jordan's other films: are not the earlier *Mona Lisa* and *Miracle* variations on the same motif? In all three cases, the relationship between the hero and the enigmatic woman he is obsessed with is doomed to fail — because she is a lesbian, because she is the hero's mother, because she is not a "she" at all but a transvestite. Jordan thus provides a veritable matrix of the impossibilities of sexual relationship. [Žižek]

[42]Bernard Boursicot (b. 1944), a French diplomat stationed in Beijing, met Shi Peipu (b. 1940), a composer and former

the Great Cultural Revolution, a minor French diplomat in Beijing (Jeremy Irons) falls in love with a Chinese opera singer who sings some Puccini arias at a reception for foreigners (John Lone). His courting leads to a lasting love relationship; the singer, who is to him the fatal love object (with reference to Puccini's opera, he affectionately calls her "my butterfly"), apparently becomes pregnant, and produces a child. While their affair is going on she induces him to spy for China, claiming that this is the only way the Chinese authorities will tolerate their association. After a professional failure the diplomat is transferred to Paris, where he is assigned to the minor post of diplomatic courier. Soon afterwards, his love joins him there and tells him that if he will carry on spying for China, the Chinese authorities will allow "their" child to join them. When, finally, French security discovers his spying activities and they are both arrested, it turns out that "she" is not a woman at all, but a man — in his Eurocentric ignorance, the hero did not know that in Chinese opera, female roles are sung by men.

It is here that the story stretches the limits of our credulity: how was it that the hero, in their long years of consummated love, did not see that he was dealing with a man? The singer incessantly evoked the Chinese sense of shame, s/he never undressed, they had (unbeknownst to him, anal) sex discreetly, s/he sitting on his lap. . . in short, what he mistook for the shyness of the Oriental woman was, on "her" side, a deft manipulation destined to conceal the fact that "she" was not a woman at all. The choice of the music that obsesses the hero is crucial here: the famous aria "Un bel di, vedremo" from

Beijing opera star, in 1964. In real life Boursicot met Shi in male attire but Boursicot got the idea that Shi was actually a woman who had been raised as a boy because of his family's fixation on male heirs. (Shi denies having misled Boursicot.) They became lovers, Boursicot unaware of Shi's sex, and in 1965 Shi claimed to be pregnant and produced, months later, a son, whom they named Bertrand. During the Cultural Revolution, Boursicot passed documents to China, purportedly in order to keep Shi and Bertrand out of prison, and in 1982 got them out of China. In 1983, in France, both Shi and Boursicot were arrested for espionage, and Shi's sex was revealed to Boursicot, who attempted, unsuccessfully, to commit suicide by cutting his throat. Both went to prison in 1986.

Madama Butterfly, perhaps the most expressive example of Puccini's gesture that is the very opposite of bashful self-concealment — the obscenely candid self-exposure of the (feminine) subject that always borders upon *kitsch*. The subject pathetically professes what she is and what she wants, she lays bare her most intimate and frail dreams — a confession which, of course, reaches its apogee in the desire to die (in "Un bel di, vedremo," Madama Butterfly imagines the scene of Pinkerton's return: at first, she will not answer his call, "in part for fun and in part not to die at the first encounter [*per non morir al primo incontro*]").

From what we have just said, it may seem that the hero's tragic blunder consists in projecting his fantasy-image on to an inadequate object — that is to say, in mistaking a real person for his fantasy-image of the love object, the Oriental woman of the Madama Butterfly type. However, things are definitely more complex. The key scene of the film occurs after the trial, when the hero and his Chinese partner, now in an Ordinary man's suit, find themselves alone in the closed compartment of a police car on their way to prison. The Chinese takes off his clothes and offers himself naked to the hero, desperately proclaiming his availability: "Here I am, your butterfly!" He proposes himself as what he is outside the hero's fantasy-frame of a mysterious Oriental woman. At this crucial moment, the hero retracts: he avoids his lover's eyes and rejects the offer. It is here that he gives up his desire and is thereby marked by an indelible guilt: he betrays the true love that aims at the real kernel of the object beneath the phantasmic layers. That is to say, the paradox resides in the fact that although he loved the Chinese without any underhand thoughts, while the Chinese manipulated his love on behalf of the Chinese secret service, it now becomes obvious that the Chinese's love was in some sense purer and far more authentic. Or, as John le Carré put it in *A Perfect Spy*: "Love is whatever you can still betray."

As every reader of "true" spy adventures knows very well, a large number of cases in which a woman has seduced a man out of duty, in order to extract from him some vital piece of information (or vice versa) end with a happy marriage — far from dispelling the mirage of love, the disclosure of the deceitful manipulation that brought the lovers together only strengthened their bond. To put it in Deleuzian terms: we are dealing here with a split between the "depth" of reality, the intermixture of bodies in which the other is the instrument I mercilessly exploit, in which love itself and sexuality are reduced to means manipulated for politico-military purposes, and the level of love *qua* pure surface event. Manipulation at the level of bodily reality renders all the more manifest love *qua* surface event, *qua* effect irreducible to its bodily support.[43]

The painful final scene of the film conveys the hero's full recognition of his guilt.[44] In prison, the hero stages a performance for his vulgar and noisy fellow-prisoners: dressed as Madama Butterfly (a Japanese kimono, heavily made-up face) and accompanied by excerpts from Puccini's opera, he retells his story; at the very climax of "Un bel di, vedremo," he cuts his throat with a razor and collapses dead. This scene of a man performing public suicide dressed as a woman has a long and respectable history: suffice it to mention Hitchcock's *Murder* (1930), in which the murderer Handel Fane, dressed as a female trapeze artist, hangs himself in front of a packed house after finishing his number. In *M. Butterfly*, as in *Murder*, this act is of a strictly ethical nature: in both cases the hero stages a psychotic identification with his love object, with his *sinthome* (synthetic formation of the nonexistent woman, "Butterfly") — that is, he "regresses" from the object-choice to an immediate identification with the object; the only way out of the insoluble deadlock of this identification is suicide *qua* the ultimate *passage à l'acte*. By his suicidal act the hero makes up for his guilt, for his rejection of the object when the object was offered to him outside the fantasy-frame.

Here, of course, the old objection again awaits us: ultimately, does not *M. Butterfly* offer a tragicomic confused bundle of male fantasies about women, not a true relationship with a woman? The entire action of the film takes place among men. Does not the grotesque incredibility of the plot simultaneously mask and point towards the fact that what we are dealing with is a case of homosexual love for the transvestite? The film is simply dishonest, and refuses to acknowledge this obvious fact. This "elucidation," however, fails to address the true enigma of *M. Butterfly* (and of *The Crying Game*): how can a hopeless love between the hero and his partner, a man dressed up as a woman, realize the notion of heterosexual love far more "authentically" than a "normal" relationship with a woman?

How, then, are we to interpret this perseverance of the matrix of courtly love? It bears witness to a certain deadlock in contemporary feminism. True, the courtly image of man serving his Lady is a semblance that conceals the actuality of male domination; true, the masochist's theater is a private *mise en scène* designed to recompense the guilt contracted by man's social domination; true, the elevation of woman to the sublime object of love equals her debasement into the passive stuff or screen for the narcissistic projection of the male ego-ideal, and so on. Lacan himself points out how, in the very epoch of courtly love, the actual social standing of women as objects of exchange in male power-plays was probably at its lowest. However, this very semblance of man serving his Lady provides women with the fantasy-substance of their identity whose effects are real: it provides them with all the features that constitute so-called "femininity" and define woman not as she is in her *jouissance féminine*, but as she refers to herself with regard to her (potential) relationship to man, as an object of his desire. From this fantasy-structure springs the near-panic reaction — not only of men, but also of many a woman — to a feminism that wants to deprive woman of her very "femininity." By opposing "patriarchal domination," women simultaneously undermine the fantasy-support of their own "feminine" identity.

The problem is that once the relationship between the two sexes is conceived of as a symmetrical, reciprocal, voluntary partnership or

[43]As for this Deleuzian opposition of surface event and bodily depth, see Chapter 5 below. [Žižek]

[44]At this point the film differs from "reality": the "true" hero is still alive and rotting in a French prison. [Žižek] Boursicot and Shi actually served only one year, and were released in 1987. The most recent information available is that Shi is living in Paris with the "son" Bertrand (a.k.a. Shi Dudu), and that Boursicot has come "out of the closet" and is living with a partner.

contract, the fantasy matrix which first emerged in courtly love remains in power. Why? In so far as sexual difference is a Real that resists symbolization, the sexual relationship is condemned to remain an asymmetrical non-relationship in which the Other, our partner, prior to being a subject, is a Thing, an "inhuman partner"; as such, the sexual relationship cannot be transposed into a symmetrical relationship between pure subjects. The bourgeois principle of contract between equal subjects can be applied to sexuality only in the form of the *perverse* — masochistic — contract in which, paradoxically, the very form of balanced contract serves to establish a relationship of domination. It is no accident that in the so-called alternative sexual practices ("sadomasochistic" lesbian and gay couples) the Master-and-Slave relationship re-emerges with a vengeance, including all the ingredients of the masochistic theater. In other words, we are far from inventing a new "formula" capable of replacing the matrix of courtly love.

For that reason, it is misleading to read *The Crying Game* as an anti-political tale of escape into privacy — that is to say, as a variation on the theme of a revolutionary who, disillusioned by the cruelty of the political power-play, discovers sexual love as the sole field of personal realization, of authentic existential fulfilment. Politically, the film remains faithful to the Irish cause, which functions as its inherent background. The paradox is that in the very sphere of privacy where the hero hoped to find a safe haven, he is compelled to accomplish an even more vertiginous revolution in his most intimate personal attitudes. Thus *The Crying Game* eludes the usual ideological dilemma of "privacy as the island of authenticity, exempt from political power-play" versus "sexuality as yet another domain of political activity": it renders visible the *antagonistic* complicity between public political activity and personal sexual subversion, the antagonism that is already at work in Sade, who demanded a sexual revolution as the ultimate accomplishment of the political revolution. In short, the subtitle of *The Crying Game* could have been "Irishmen, yet another effort, if you want to become republicans!"

5

MARXIST CRITICISM

Not least among the tasks now confronting thought is that of placing all the reactionary arguments against Western culture in the service of progressive enlightenment.
— THEODOR W. ADORNO

It is the view of the world, the ideology or weltanschauung *underlying a writer's work, that counts. And it is the writer's attempt to reproduce this view of the world which constitutes his "intention" and is the formative principle underlying the style of a given piece of writing.*
— GEORG LUKÁCS

The socialist critic does not see literature in terms of ideology and class-struggle because they happen to be his or her political interests, arbitrarily projected onto literary works. Such matters are the very stuff of history, and in so far as literature is a historical phenomenon, they are the very stuff of literature too.
— TERRY EAGLETON

Always historicize!

— FREDRIC JAMESON

Like Sigmund Freud, Karl Marx not only created an immense, subtle, and complex body of research but inspired an entire discourse written by his followers, a world of diverse social theory that speaks for itself but speaks, at the same time, in Marx's name. American philosophy and literary criticism have only recently become leavened by Marxist social theory, for reasons that have to do with the gyrations of twentieth-century history and politics. For American workers in the 1920s and 1930s, Marx was a hero who had proclaimed a new world of equality and meaningful work, whose followers set up schools to educate the proletariat of the future. But for many of those who grew up in the 1950s and 1960s, an era dominated by a Cold War between the Marxist-Leninist Soviet Union and the capitalist United States, Marxism carried a whiff of sulphur with it, as a dangerous and unpatriotic credo, a philosophy of the Other. After the purges and show trials of the 1930s, after the Hitler-Stalin pact, after the revelations of the Gulag, Marx became the "God that failed" even to many former socialists who had believed. It is no accident that so many of the important works of British and American historical scholarship written from the 1940s to the 1970s (with notable exceptions, like Christopher Hill's *Milton and the English Revolution*) proceeded in deliberate disregard of Marx and his theories of history and culture. During the 1960s European Marxists like Herbert Marcuse were read and discussed widely, at least within the counterculture. Today, with the Soviet Union no longer standing as a grim parody of the workers' state Marx had envisioned, it is possible for those of all political stripes to view Marx and the richly complex European traditions that he spawned as the key tools for viewing literature as a social text and as the product of history.

Marx's historicism was a product of the later Enlightenment, when historical change first began to be viewed as a source of explanation of changing social and cultural moves. While Philip Sidney viewed history as a source of ethical exempla, Samuel Johnson's criticism marks the beginnings of literature seen as a social text; he treated Shakespeare and the major English authors of the seventeenth century as men who must be judged (where morals were not concerned) by the standards of their own day rather than by those of his. Johnson's friend, Thomas Warton, was to write the first *History of English Poetry* (1774–81), operating on the then-novel assumption that an appreciation of the classics of one's own language had to be mediated by an understanding of the manners and concerns of earlier times. Their Scottish contemporary Adam Smith authored not only the great apologia for capitalism, *The Wealth of Nations* (1776), but a treatise on moral philosophy that presented human societies as advancing unevenly through successive stages of social and political development driven by the motor of economic change. Walter Scott, who absorbed Smith's lessons at the University of Edinburgh, used them to construct in *Waverley* (1814) and *Old Mortality* (1816) fables of the Jacobite risings where a still feudal Scotland, savage and hierarchical, bravely confronts at a hopeless disadvantage the more advanced commercial nation of England. And Marx may have derived his sense of how history works in practice as much from Scott, the novelist he most loved, as from his teacher, the philosopher Hegel.

Marx's social theories are more fully explicated in the introduction to Marx (see p. 397), and they are reviewed in Raymond Williams's discussion of "Base and Superstructure" (see p. 1272). Briefly, however, Marx was a dialectical materialist. He was a materialist in the sense that he believed, unlike Hegel, that what drives historical change are the material realities of the economic base of society *(Grundlage)*, rather than the ideological superstructure *(Überbau)* of politics, law, philosophy, religion, and art that is built upon that economic base. Like Hegel, Marx believed that change comes about through dialectical oppositions within a given state of society. Apparently stable societies develop sites of resistance: contradictions built into the social system that ultimately lead to social revolution and the development of a new society upon the ruins of the old. These contradictions are resolved by the structural shift to a new level of operation that in turn generates other contradictions, new tensions, further revolutions.

Beyond these basic assumptions, however, Marxist theory and the application of Marxist theory to literature have taken a dizzying variety of forms, depending, among other things, on how the literary text is positioned relative to material reality and to ideology.[1] Wide discrepancies were inevitable in part because Marxism is primarily a political and economic philosophy rather than a guide to the explication of literary texts. The few comments Marx and Engels addressed to matters of art and literature left many of the most important questions of method open. Differences also arise because Marxism is, as we have hinted, not only a philosophy but a movement with a conflicted history of its own where ideas, including ideas about art, have had fateful political consequences. For example, Georg Lukács's attack on naturalism was also a covert attack on Soviet Realist art, which used naturalist premises, and therefore on its political sponsor, Joseph Stalin. Because of this conflicted history, there are many Marxist critics but no single Marxist school of criticism in the usual sense, and we will have to mention many more representatives of the tradition Marx began than we can include in this chapter.

THE AMERICAN LIBERALS

Largely because of the long-standing fear of the Soviet Union, there has been no strong American tradition of socialism since the Bolshevik revolution, and only the briefest of periods — in the mid-1930s — when the Communist party attracted any share of intellectuals. To the extent that American criticism was touched directly by this movement (as in the writings of Granville Hicks), it was of a form usually termed (not without reason) "vulgar Marxism," which featured the adulation of the proletariat: works written by proletarians themselves and works celebrating proletarian characters, denouncing capitalism, and forecasting the revolution. Leon Trotsky had himself written with contempt (in *Literature and Revolution,* 1923) of such efforts to force literature to serve politics directly. Yet Raymond Williams has

---

[1]The Marxist term "ideology" is an essentially contested concept. The notion of ideology presented in the introduction to Marx (see p. 397), as "a culture's collective consciousness of its own being," is one of several currently used in Marxist circles, but there are many others, often in direct contradiction to it. My definition is close to a sense in which Marx uses the term in the following famous passage from *A Contribution to a Critique of Political Economy* (1859): "A distinction should always be made between the material transformation of the economic conditions of production . . . and the legal, political, religious, aesthetic, or philosophic — in short, ideological — forms in which men become conscious of this conflict and fight it out" (see p. 410). But if here "ideology" means any representation of consciousness, the most common use of "ideology" in Marx and Engels is the pejorative one of "false consciousness," a set of illusions fostered by the dominant class in order to assure social stability — and its own continued dominance (Letter to Mehring, 1893). Ideology in this sense is expected to wither away and vanish in the Marxist utopia of the dictatorship of the proletariat. Louis Althusser's often quoted dictum, "Ideology has no history," would seem to contradict this view, since it implies that ideology will retain a function forever — and thus even in the workers' state. But Althusser's definition of ideology ("the 'lived' relation between men and their world, or a reflected form of this unconscious relation") is closer to the unpejorative usage of Marx in the *Critique of Political Economy.* See Raymond Williams, *Keywords: A Vocabulary of Culture and Society* (London: Oxford University Press, 1976), pp. 126–30; and Louis Althusser, *For Marx* (New York: Pantheon, 1969), p. 252.

Another worrisome ambiguity lurking in the word *ideology* arises from the relative concreteness with which it is represented to the consciousness. While most Marxist thinkers view "ideology" as something explicit and official, like a body of laws, a political doctrine, or a philosophy, other Marxists (or the same ones, in other circumstances) use the term to denote something more vague and implicit, even unconscious: a way of understanding, a worldview.

conceded that, although such a position is "crude and reductionist . . . no Marxist . . . can wholly give it up without abandoning the Marxist tradition."[2]

"Vulgar Marxism" as such did not become an important American tradition, but a group of New York intellectuals, associated with the Left magazine *Partisan Review,* had flirted with Communism during the Spanish Civil War and had become disillusioned with Stalinist Russia but not with the utopian ideals that Marxism represented. The most broadly learned among them was Edmund Wilson (see p. 622), whose journalistic essays and books introduced European writers and ideas to what even in the 1930s and 1940s was a largely provincial America. Their leading literary critic, Lionel Trilling, was instrumental in turning the college of Columbia University into a training camp for ideas on culture and society. Important followers and contemporaries included Philip Rahv, Alfred Kazin, and Irving Howe. Neither Wilson nor Trilling should be credited with fashioning a significant critical methodology or a doctrinally pure way of reading Marx. Indeed, it may be going too far to call them Marxists, since both were influenced almost as heavily by Freud, and they avoided using most conventional Marxist terminology. They wrote, instead, in an Arnoldian tradition of cultural commentary, committed to literature as an expression of culture, and concerned primarily with expressing in their writings both the tension within their own responses to literature and the broadest and most complex views of life.

REFLECTION THEORIES: TROTSKY, LUKÁCS AND BRECHT

At least two major theories derive from the notion that literature consists of an imitation of social reality. The first, which can be traced to Marx but is best expressed by Leon Trotsky, Georgii Plekhanov, and other writers of the Third International (an organization founded in Moscow in 1919 to support the Bolshevik revolution), equates mimesis with a pure "slice of life" and considers it unimportant that writers take a radical stance toward the reality they portray. The royalist reactionary Balzac is thus a more valuable writer in his accurate portraits of society than a less perceptive writer of doctrinally correct (i.e., socialist) tendencies.

A second, more complex version of reflection theory is found in the criticism of Georg Lukács. Lukács held that writers must do more than reflect the mere surface features of their society: They must also portray the various forces acting on that society that eventuate in social change. Lukács despised the naturalists (like Émile Zola and Theodore Dreiser) who were satisfied to present characters typical of the social order. In "The Ideology of Modernism" (1956), reprinted here, Lukács pours equal scorn on the modernists' exaltation of the subjective and the psychological at the expense of any portrayal of the dynamic movements underlying social change. To either naturalism or modernism, Lukács prefers the realism — less sophisticated though it be — of Walter Scott. Scott's Edward Waverley is not the typical English

---

[2]Raymond Williams, "Marxism, Structuralism, and Literary Analysis" in *New Left Review* 129 (1981): 51–66.

gentleman of his time, nor is he invested with much psychological depth; nevertheless, in Waverley, whose relationships and loyalties position him between the mercantile English and the still feudal Highland Scots on the eve of the 1745 rebellion, Scott created a character who embodies the social and political conflicts of his epoch.

A third version of Marxist reflection aesthetics is to be found in Bertolt Brecht's essays on the theater, from which "The Popular and the Realistic" is reprinted here. Like Lukács, Brecht had little sympathy for aesthetic regimes enforced by commissars, like the Socialist Realism approved by Stalin's hand-picked minister of culture, Andrei Zhdanov. He envisioned the masses as intelligent and aggressive, too feisty to be satisfied with naturalistic texts that depict circumstances as overwhelming to the individual or collective will, and with minds too nimble to be satisfied by derivative or hackneyed stories or plays. German workers of 1930 responded, he found, to his *Threepenny Opera*, despite its being set in eighteenth-century London among beggars and thieves: They were able to abstract the social truth it embodied as long as the story avoided the narcotic of cheap feelings, as long as it was presented with wit and humor, in a way that made them think. Realism, for Brecht, is a question of the social truth embodied within and beneath the surface representation; the latter can be as abstract or concrete, as familiar or deeply alien, as the dramatist wishes, so long as it does not lull the audience into a slumber where thought becomes impossible.

FORMS OF MEDIATION THEORY: BENJAMIN AND ADORNO

Just as there have been various forms of Marxian "reflection" so have there also been different versions of the principle of "mediation" — the notion that ideology establishes relationships between the two levels of Marxist dialectic, between the base and the superstructure, between the relations of production and the work of art. These versions arose in part because of the aesthetic inadequacy of the concept of reflection. "Reflection" was a useful term for discussing the novel, but most other modes of literature and art could not incorporate, as a novel could, a view of an entire society. At times the term "mediation" has been used merely to denote the more subtle versions of mimesis — like that of Lukács — but it more properly describes theories like Walter Benjamin's notion of correspondences.

One would not say that, for example, the poetry of Baudelaire reflects his society, in the sense that it depicts an image of it. But as Benjamin noted, industrialization had produced changes in the city and its crowds that resulted in a new version of both the individual and the individual's attitude toward himself, which connected with aspects of Baudelaire's poetry. Benjamin describes Baudelaire's notion of the *correspondance* as "an experience which seeks to establish itself in crisis-proof form." It is the artist's reaction to the impermanence of post-industrial urban life, typified in the shock and abrasion of the crowded streets. Benjamin viewed Baudelaire as nostalgic about the decline of that mystical quality of art Benjamin called "aura" — that spiritual quality, a relic of the human attachment to ritual and magic, which gives a work of art an almost animate sensibility: "To perceive the aura of an object means to invest it with the ability to look at us in return."

In "The Work of Art in the Age of Mechanical Reproduction" (1936), reprinted below, Benjamin examines the central fact of industrialism's relation to art in the twentieth century: that, for the first time, a painting or sculpture can be infinitely replicated. On the one hand there is the genuine possibility of art for the masses, not simply because anyone can possess a copy of Botticelli's *Birth of Venus* but also because of the evolution of film, a medium intended for mass audiences. On the other hand, the mystical aura, the cult value of the art object, is simultaneously beginning to disappear. As a socialist, Benjamin ought to be applauding this trend, but the essay is caught up in emotional ambiguity because of his own nostalgia for the cult of memory. Although the preface bravely declares that his theses "brush aside a number of outmoded concepts, such as creativity and genius, eternal value and mystery," the tone of the later sections seems at odds with this intent. When Benjamin contrasts the stage actor, engaged both in acting as an art and in a particular role, with the alienated film actor, who is at best an "exile" and at worst a "stage prop," or when he notes that aura survives in film in the obscene adulation paid to film stars, or when he observes that film is the art uniquely suited to the "distracted" and "absent-minded" spectator, a reader may infer that the proletarianization of art progressively dehumanizes both participants and spectators. Reading Benjamin, one may feel trapped within his ironies, but perhaps Benjamin was trapped in them himself. Although he knew well that socialism meant industrialization, mechanical reproduction, and the death of the cult value of art, he nevertheless felt intensely the loss of that value.

Benjamin was willing to allow for Baudelairean correspondences, for the mediation of ideology, at the level of content. Other members of the so-called Frankfurt school, like Theodor W. Adorno, were not so willing. For Adorno, the Frankfurt school's principal aesthetician, the relationship between art and society operated on the formal level and could easily be located even in nonreferential art such as music. Thus, in *Philosophy of Modern Music* (1949), Adorno suggested that the rootless chaos and tragic ambiguity of Arnold Schönberg's musical harmonies, together with his drive to mechanize and systematize composition, served as a correspondence with the dominant ideology of the early twentieth century. (Adorno judged Schönberg to be a more authentic artist than Igor Stravinsky, whose shifting formal allegiances — from neoclassicism to primitivism — were either ideologically reactionary or attempts to evade history altogether.)

As one might expect, Adorno took the opposite position from Lukács on the issue of modernism in literature and defended the bleak vision of novelists like Kafka. While Adorno agrees with Lukács that modern fiction is morbidly subjective and obsessed with the torture of the individual consciousness, he claimed that the modern novel took "a critical posture towards social reality by means of its style . . . not by its 'content' or view of the world."[3] In a sense, modernist fiction exemplifies "negative dialectic" — Adorno's term for criticism that operates without reproducing the conceptual features of what it criticizes — a necessary feature in capitalist society, where, according to Adorno, concepts distort and mask social realities.

---

[3]Gillian Rose, *The "Melancholy Science": An Introduction to the Thought of Theodor W. Adorno* (London: Macmillan, 1978), p. 124.

The way modern mass culture distorts its representation of social reality — the opposite side of the "negative dialectic" — can be seen in "The Culture Industry: Enlightenment as Mass Deception," by Adorno in collaboration with his Frankfurt School colleague, Max Horkheimer. In this chapter from *Dialectic of Enlightenment* (1944), a selection from which is reprinted below, Horkheimer and Adorno portray with the steely logic of a nightmare Benjamin's vision of a postindustrial culture. Benjamin had been ambivalent about mechanical reproduction, partly because of the lure of cultural aura, partly because of his fear that mass culture could be used to support Fascism. But Horkheimer and Adorno, writing at a time when European Fascism had, to all intents and purposes, been defeated, view contemporary popular culture as a political tool of American capitalism. The workers have been subjugated by technology, but resistance is impossible because the technology that enslaves them also keeps them entertained, at a shallow level, with cheap films and nearly free music from the radio; every moment of their leisure time is occupied, because so long as the people are fed mindless pleasures they cannot think, cannot relate to one another, cannot form any sense of the system they serve.

People differ, of course, in the kinds of entertainments they find absorbing, but the culture industry caters to differences: for the more refined soul there are symphony programs and higher-toned dramatic films; for the less educated there is pseudo jazz and cowboy movies. What is important is that no one be left out, so that no one is left to question the system of domination. The fact that most of the film actors and musicians lack any real talent allows the audience to have fantasies of social mobility, because they feel that they too, had they been chosen, could have been movie stars or teen idols. The product of the culture industry, in other words, is ideology in the sense of "false consciousness." The films and the music provoke a phony sense of community, since the community one belongs to is that of the passive consumer of culture: the audience can talk to one another about a particular film star or musical performer, but they lack any real sense of solidarity. Most of all, however the audience talks, the system never allows anyone to talk back. Horkheimer and Adorno are writing in the days before television network broadcasting — during the brief interval between the invention of the technology and its exploitation — but they were well aware that the ultimate medium of ideology was about to be rolled out for an ever more passive mass audience. Their idea that the mass media were creating a pseudo public sphere that was being used to legitimate political decisions made by the power of money was equally prophetic — and inspired, as we shall see, their disciple Jürgen Habermas.

Reading "The Culture Industry" today, one may feel that its authors had chosen a cushy spot — sunny California — from which to critique the vast wasteland of American culture, at a time — 1944 — when their fellow socialists lay dead in German concentration camps or on the battlefields of the Eastern Front. One needs to remember that Horkheimer and Adorno had seen their own liberal society, that of the Weimar Republic, turn quickly into a Fascist regime that used culture for ideological purposes, and that, as European socialists, they discovered in the Roosevelt New Deal a mere travesty of the just society of which they dreamed.

GENETIC STRUCTURALISM:
LUCIEN GOLDMANN AND RAYMOND WILLIAMS

Between the mediation theories of the Frankfurt school and the structural Marxism of the Althusserians, there are transitional modes of Marxist criticism. One of the most important was that practiced by Lucien Goldmann, who called himself a "genetic" structuralist because the structures he was concerned about were derived from the work's genesis in the ideology of its times. Like Adorno, Goldmann believed that the correspondences between a work and an age would be correspondences of form rather than content. But unlike most Marxist critics, who would claim that the ideology of an age is invariably present in all of its products, Goldmann felt that only the greatest works of an age contain its deepest consciousness.

Goldmann's analysis of seventeenth-century France in *The Hidden God* (1955) presents *homologies* — analogies of function rather than content — between literary and ideological structures, which during that period take the form of tragic dilemmas. The seventeenth-century Jansenists were torn between obedience to a silent God and participation in the new rationalism; the "nobility of the robe" (the gentry deriving from the legal profession) were torn between the authority of the king and the new spirit of commercial enterprise. Similarly, in the plays of Racine, who was both a Jansenist and a scion of the *noblesse de robe,* the protagonists (such as Hippolytus and Andromache) must choose between service to a hidden God and the pleasures and duties of the world — and are damned no matter which they choose.

The most distinguished English practitioner of genetic structuralism was probably Raymond Williams. The son of working-class parents from the border country of Wales, Williams brought to his readings of literature a proletarian background highly unusual in a Marxist critic, few of whom have had any close acquaintance with hard manual labor. Instead of Benjamin's more abstract and aestheticized term "correspondences," Williams spoke of the "complex forms of feeling" within which literature and ideology find common ground. In Williams's *The Country and the City* (1973), for example, his thought about the industrial revolution is filtered through his personal sense of what alienation from the countryside might have meant to the poets of the eighteenth and early nineteenth centuries. As with Goldmann, the structures of feeling Williams found in poetry exhibit homologies with elements in the nonaesthetic segments of the superstructure or the relations of production in the base.

In fact, Williams talks of seeking "structures of feeling" in art instead of "ideology" as such; the novel phrase differentiates the concrete, lived experience represented in art ("social experiences *in solution*" as he calls it) from the "precipitated" manner in which social relationships are likely to be characterized in an expository text, a treatise, or a newspaper article.

It would be misleading to characterize Williams as merely a follower of Goldmann, however. Williams was a rather protean social and historical critic whose work shifted rapidly through a number of phases. He began his career rejecting the revolutionary doctrines of Marxism, particularly its concept of the masses, and went through a left-Leavisite phase of cultural criticism that kept what Williams himself termed "a certain conscious distance" from Marxism. After *Culture and Society* (1958), however, Williams converged with Marxist thought. Following his "genetic structuralist" phase, Williams became what he called a "cultural materialist," influenced primarily by the Italian Marxist Antonio Gramsci and his concept of *hegemony*.

To Gramsci, power is expressed partly through the direct means of control (*dominio:* rule) and partly through something at once less formal and conscious and yet more total (*egemonia:* hegemony). As Williams says in *Marxism and Literature* (1977), from which the selection in this chapter is taken:

> Hegemony is . . . a lived system of meanings and values — constitutive and constitut-ing — which, as they are experienced as practices appear as reciprocally confirming. It thus constitutes a sense of reality for most people in the society . . . beyond which it is very difficult for most members of the society to move. . . . It is . . . in the strongest sense a "culture" but a culture which has also to be seen as the lived dominance and subordina-tion of particular classes. (See p. 1278)

Williams finds this conception attractive because it allows for the notion of *alternative* hegemonies centered in the working class and for revolutionary activity in the shape of cultural rather than political action. The implication is that hegemonies may be relatively successful, but they are never complete. Instead of a single ruling class, there are interpenetrating hegemonic groups; and instead of a single cata-strophic revolution, there are dominant, emergent, and residual elements of culture belonging to classes whose power has peaked or is increasing or declining. This concept of hegemony modifies the rigid base/superstructure formula of Marxist thought, a modification Williams had already sought in the homologies of Gold-mann. In general, Williams seems to have sought a more fluid and responsive Marx-ism — also an aim of Louis Althusser.

LOUIS ALTHUSSER AND STRUCTURAL MARXISM

The newest development of Marxist thought — post-Althusserian Marxism — orig-inates in the structural thought of the mature Marx as interpreted by Louis Althusser and in the theories of the signifier developed by Jacques Lacan (see Ch. 4), which were later to influence Jacques Derrida (Ch. 2). In *Reading Capital,* Althusser ques-tions the traditional portrait of Marx as a Hegelian humanist; for Althusser there were two Marxes, a young Marx (up to the year 1845), whose ideas roughly corre-sponded with the usual view of dialectical materialism, and a mature Marx (from 1857 onward), whose way of thinking was radically different. For Althusser, the older Marx, author of *Capital,* had evolved a form of dialectic that was different from Hegel's — not just an inversion of it — and no longer held to the simple deter-ministic relation of base and superstructure. Economics is determinative but only *"in the last instance."*[4] But Althusser's most important shift is in his vision of history. Earlier writers on Marx had assumed that history is a real force, concrete, univocal,

---

[4]Louis Althusser, "Contradiction and Overdetermination," in *For Marx,* trans. Ben Brewster (New York: Pantheon, 1969), pp. 84–114.

and ineluctable. In Althusser's reading of Marx, history has become a myth, or perhaps more properly, a text, in that it is a symbolic structure, produced by discourse. We cannot evade history any more than we can think without our faculty for symbolization, but neither can we view history from outside that subjective faculty.

In Althusser's interpretation, Marx becomes a canny reader of his own chosen texts, those of his predecessors, the classical economists; in quoting Marx, Althusser presents him as aware of their oversights, their subtle shifts in point of view. Althusser's point is that these writers' areas of blindness are as significant as their areas of insight, for the gaps and incoherencies that a critical reading of the texts reveals are the signs of what the writers are unconsciously hiding from themselves. This is not the personal, Freudian repression of individuals, but blind spots left by what the ideology of their age is unable to talk about.

Pierre Macherey's *A Theory of Literary Production* (1966) presents a literary-critical version of these ideas. In "Jules Verne: The Faulty Narrative," Macherey shows how Verne's plans for his novels went awry. *The Mysterious Island,* for example, originated in Verne's wish to rewrite *Robinson Crusoe* more rigorously. Unlike Defoe, who had provided Crusoe with a shipload of modern equipment and tools, Verne would demonstrate how castaways with a knowledge of science manage to recreate modern technology out of nothing on an empty island. The novel begins thus, but halfway along Verne reveals that the castaways are not alone on the island; he introduces Captain Nemo and his crew, who give the castaways a crate of tools. Most readers would interpret this as a mere lapse on Verne's part, a melodramatic corruption of his plan. For Macherey, there are no mistakes, and Verne's introduction of Nemo betokens his attempt to *evade* what he knows: That science cannot be pure knowledge, as he would wish, but relies on the technological capacity of a capitalistic society to bring it into being. Furthermore, Verne's book implicitly acknowledges that there are no empty lands, only those whose aborigines are rendered invisible by imperialist ideology, just as technology cannot arise purely from scientific knowledge but must in fact emerge from a technological social organization. Macherey argues that the rifts in Verne's plot are there because of preexisting rifts in the ideology of bourgeois capitalism and that the novel itself, as an aesthetic practice whose raw materials are ideology, tends to widen these rifts as it foregrounds them, making them visible to the reader.

By reifying the flat notions of ideology in the roundness of a narrative, the artist unwittingly exposes their incoherencies to the view of a critical reader. This version of Marxism is practiced by Raymond Williams's disciple, Terry Eagleton, and by Althusser's most important American disciple, Fredric Jameson. Jameson's highly acclaimed *The Political Unconscious* (1981) presents a theory of interpretation in which Althusser's politics and Lacan's theory of the unconscious intersect.

EAGLETON

Terry Eagleton did not begin as a post-Althusserian Marxist but as a Christian humanist of working-class origins, studying literature at Cambridge under Raymond Williams. His post-Althusserian phase began in the mid-1970s, when he broke decisively with the humanist-socialist position he had inherited from Williams, just as Williams himself was refashioning a rigorous and dialectical Marxism based on the ideas of the Italian thinker Antonio Gramsci. In *Marxism and Literary Criticism* (1976), Eagleton surveys Marxist aesthetics from Marx's and Engels's own essays and letters to the continental neo-Marxists of the 1960s, portraying this history as a long decline from the insights of the original master until its post-Althusserian renaissance in his own day. He attacked not only the antiartistic repressions of Stalin and Zhdanov but also the British Marxists of the 1930s, like Christopher Caudwell and Arnold Kettle, and contrasted the broad world-historical issues favored by Georg Lukács (for Eagleton a "stiff-necked Stalinist") with the more subtle questions about the social determinants of art which post-Althusserian Marxists like Pierre Macherey were able to ask.

Eagleton went on in *Criticism and Ideology* (1976) to provide a fuller explanation of post-Althusserian literary theory as well as some practical criticism based on that theory. This work contains Eagleton's declaration of independence from Raymond Williams, whose shifting allegiances Eagleton subjects to the same sort of sharp but ultimately generous scrutiny that many well-adjusted post-adolescents apply to their fathers. For readers trying to learn how to read or write neo-Marxist criticism, the most important sections, however, are the second and third chapters. Here Eagleton presents the literary work as determined not solely by the "economic base," as in classical Marxism, but by a large number of interrelated factors, including the "literary mode of production" — whether the text is transmitted orally, through handwritten manuscripts, printed books, periodicals, etc. —, the "general ideology," the "aesthetic ideology" of the time, and the "authorial ideology" — the writer's particular slant on the social conflicts of his or her day. In addition, Eagleton presents the Althusserian thesis that ideology, far from being a coherent and unified mode of social consciousness (as Lukács, for example, had conceived of it), is actually fragmented and inconsistent. The artistic work, as a production of ideology, foregrounds such incoherencies and makes them visible to the reader. Thus, art can have revolutionary effects, regardless of the social views of the artist.

Ultimately, Eagleton came to see his attempt to create a "science of the text" as too sterile. During the Thatcher years, when the gains of the workers under the Labour Party quickly evaporated, this working-class theorist decided that criticism would have to do more than analyze literature. He espoused what he called a "revolutionary criticism," for which he claimed practical as well as intellectual aims:

> What seemed important when I wrote [*Criticism and Ideology*], at a time when "Marxist criticism" had little anchorage in Britain, was to examine its prehistory and to systematize the categories essential for a "science of the text." [This] is perhaps no longer the focal concern of Marxist cultural studies. Partly under the pressure of global capitalist crisis, partly under the influence of new themes and forces within socialism, the centre of such studies is shifting from narrowly textual or conceptual analysis to problems of cultural production and the political use of artefacts. . . . This shift in direction was in turn obscurely related to certain deep-seated changes in my own personal and political life. . . .[5]

[5]Terry Eagleton, *Walter Benjamin, or Towards a Revolutionary Criticism* (London: Verso, 1981), p. xii.

One index to these "deep-seated changes" may be Eagleton's dedication of his book on Walter Benjamin to the poststructuralist feminist critic Toril Moi, whose intellectual influence he gratefully acknowledges. Moi's influence may be seen in Eagleton's vision of a "revolutionary criticism" based primarily on the "paradigm" of "feminist criticism." Like those contemporary feminist critics who attempt to make patriarchy visible in order to dismantle it, Eagleton proposes to "dismantle the ruling concepts of 'literature,' reinserting 'literary' texts into the whole field of cultural practices." He proposes further to "deconstruct the received hierarchies of 'literature,'" to reevaluate the canon, and to reveal the role of literature "in the ideological construction of the subject."[6] In effect, Eagleton is calling for a new political criticism that would apply to class issues the lessons that feminists have learned in their approach to gender. His books on subjects from Shakespeare to Richardson to Brontë to Wilde have come out at a rate of nearly one per year, but it remains an open question whether Eagleton has succeeded in fulfilling the promise of his theoretical manifesto.

JAMESON AND THE POLITICAL UNCONSCIOUS

Fredric Jameson came to Marxism through his dissertation on Sartre, and his position as the foremost American Marxist critic solidified after the publication of *Marxism and Form* (1971). Like Eagleton, Jameson was at pains to jettison the tedious and tendentious forms of Russian Marxism, and he championed the more Hegelian Marxism of Lukács, Benjamin, and Adorno. What was most original in *Marxism and Form* was Jameson's final chapter, "Towards Dialectical Criticism," in which he sets forth his own ideas of what a genuine dialectical-materialist criticism would be like. The most important of these is his notion of criticism as "metacommentary" that must always "include a commentary on its own intellectual instruments as part of its own working structure."[7] Jameson would argue that while for a formalist like Wayne Booth the concept of "point of view" is a neutral tool of analysis without historical content — after all, any narrative, whenever written, must be told from some point of view — in fact, the notion of "point of view" is not timeless at all; it reflects the specific historical situation of Henry James (who invented the term) and the "lived experience" of the middle class in the late nineteenth century: "seeing life from the relatively restricted vision of our own monad."[8] For Jameson, a genuinely dialectical criticism would be self-conscious about the terms and structures that it assumes and would attempt to understand these tools in their historical contexts.

The last part of "Towards Dialectical Criticism" presents a complex "allegorical" vision of literary interpretation based on Jameson's notion of the interconvertibility of form and content. For Jameson, in addition to the usual "form" and "content" of any literary text, there is the "form of the content" and the "content of the form." Jameson claims that the "content" of a literary work "never really is initially

---

[6]Ibid., p. 98.
[7]Fredric Jameson, *Marxism and Form: Twentieth-Century Dialectical Theories of Literature* (Princeton, NJ: Princeton University Press, 1971), p. 336.
[8]Ibid., p. 355.

formless . . . but is rather already meaningful from the outset, being . . . the very components of our concrete social life itself: words, thoughts, objects, desires, people, places, activities."[9] It is the lived experience of the social world. On the other side "form" itself has its "content": styles and plots encode ideas about the material world. One obvious example would be the love sonnet of the Renaissance, whose importance underscores the dynastic or commercial character of the marital bond in that era. (In our own era, men and women who can marry for love as a matter of course do not need to create such formal objectifications of feeling.) Sometimes the "content of the form" operates in surprising ways. For example, Jameson views the surface violence and anxiety of science fiction movies of the 1950s not merely as a covert reference to the terror of nuclear annihilation during a period of escalation in the Cold War, but as also encoding a collective wish-fulfillment fantasy on the part of postwar society, a utopian fantasy about genuinely gratifying work that is personified in the ubiquitous scientist hero whose activity — empowering, untrammeled by routine, rewarded by deep self-satisfactions rather than by cash — suggests "a return to older modes of work organization, the more personal and psychologically satisfying world of the guilds."[10] In *Marxism and Form* Jameson presents his vision of a new dialectical criticism that would interpret literature in such a way as to penetrate to the repressed collective political desires of the society in which it was produced: He would show that criticism in action ten years later in *The Political Unconscious* (1981).

The title of *The Political Unconscious* refers to the ideas of Althusser and Macherey discussed previously: that society represses its internal contradictions by means of ideology but that by carefully reading literary texts we are often able to witness the "return of the repressed," the surfacing of the fissures in the ideology of a society. For Jameson, literary texts are allegorical, encoding both the "false consciousness" of their age and its "utopian" dreams. This encoding takes place within the three "concentric frameworks" of *politics* (the plotting of particular events), *society* (the tensions operating between groups), and *history* (the succession of social formations within the larger vision of social change). For Jameson, these three frameworks point also to three moments in the act of interpretation that he calls the three "horizons" of the text. In the first horizon, it is within the boundaries of the text itself that the symbolic tensions of the political unconscious are set forth; in the second, the text is seen as an ideological utterance within a system of discourse, an example of *parole* within a *langue*. Finally the text is viewed as a field of force within which artifacts deriving from sign-systems dominant in successive social formations can be simultaneously viewed. Jameson aligns these three horizons with "phases" in Northrop Frye's *Anatomy of Criticism* that themselves derive roughly from the literal, the allegorical, and the anagogical modes of medieval interpretation.

In addition, Jameson employs two other methodological tropes. One is the "rectangle" of the structural linguist A. J. Greimas, which structures the themes of a narrative

---

[9]Ibid., pp. 402–03.
[10]Ibid., p. 405.

text into a synchronic system through various modes of equivalence and opposition. The other is what he calls the "molecular" and "molar" aspects of the allegorical representation of ideology in narrative. Generally, Marxist critics have dealt with the large-scale features of a text, its plot and themes, to the exclusion of its fine structure. Jameson calls this the "molar" level (in chemistry, a "mole" is 6.2×10^{19} molecules of a substance). But Jameson believes that the political thematics of narratives can also be found at the "molecular" level of the structure of individual sentences, and demonstrates, in passages from Balzac's "La Vieille Fille," Dreiser's *Sister Carrie,* and Conrad's *Lord Jim* and *Nostromo,* how the political unconscious operates at the stylistic level of the text.

It was *The Political Unconscious* that made Jameson one of the critics most frequently quoted in literary circles. However, some Marxists were less enthusiastic about this text. Terry Eagleton, already in his "revolutionary" phase, suggested that Jameson's subtle analyses of the "utopian moment" in various nineteenth-century texts, while transcending the tendentious arguments of "vulgar Marxism," seemed also to have transcended its revolutionary spirit and its identification with the oppressed: "The question irresistibly raised for the Marxist reader of Jameson is simply this: how is a Marxist-Structuralist critique of a minor novel of Balzac to help shake the foundations of capitalism?"[11]

It is hard to know whether or not Jameson was stung by Eagleton's imputation of right-wing deviationism, but in the years since the publication of *The Political Unconscious,* Jameson has become more a cultural than a literary critic, and the "texts" upon which he works are much more likely to be films or buildings than novels or stories. His magisterial book on postmodernism depicts our contemporary world as suffering from a continuous and unresolved crisis in which our cultural representations parody and subvert themselves. The ultimate cause of these cultural and psychological phenomena is what Jameson calls "late capitalism," with its unfathomable bureaucratic web and fragmented social system. The individual today is even more alienated from any vision of supportive community and rewarding work than the nineteenth-century wage-slave of the industrial revolution. In the post-industrial West, factories themselves have often been moved by multinational corporations to developing countries, where wages are low, leaving behind the service industries and the large-scale corporate activities of finance and marketing. At the same time, the traditional Marxist distinction between economic base and cultural superstructure begins to dissolve in late capitalism, as the primary business of the developed world becomes the creation of culture for everyone, via designs for manufactured objects, architectural planning, media programming, and the computer and information systems. In general, Jameson's cultural criticism has continued to explore the political unconscious of artistic representations: the truth behind the false consciousness of ideology that is allegorically expressed in these fictions, and their utopian fantasy rooted in eternal human desire.

[11]Terry Eagleton, "The Idealism of American Criticism." Review of *The Political Unconscious,* by Fredric Jameson. *New Left Review* 127 (1981): 65.

JÜRGEN HABERMAS AND PUBLIC DISCOURSE

Unlike Eagleton and Jameson, but like Marx himself, Jürgen Habermas is primarily a social philosopher rather than a literary and cultural critic. He is usually considered the premier thinker of the second generation of the Frankfurt school, whose first generation included Herbert Marcuse, Walter Benjamin, Max Horkheimer, and Habermas's teacher and chief influence, Theodor W. Adorno. Like any good Marxist, however, Habermas's goal has been not merely to extend the cultural critique of the Frankfurt school but to transcend it.

The Frankfurt school had itself been a continuation and transcendence of Marx's philosophy. Whereas Marx had embraced scientific rationalism as an antidote to the religious idealism of Hegel and his followers, by the 1930s capitalism had advanced to the point where science and technology appeared to be simultaneously the means of creating a just society and a major obstacle to social equality. The bureaucratic organizations that needed to produce scientific knowledge and use it for practical ends were producing a society organized from the top down, destructive of all dialogue, while the cult of scientific fact and the notion of a split between "hard" facts and "soft" values stifled any communal discussion of social justice. The Frankfurt school rejected the scientistic Marxism coming out of the Soviet Union in favor of an analysis of the social formation and mentalities produced by capitalism, eventuating in, as one can see in the work of Adorno, a grimly pessimistic critique in which artists like Kafka and Schönberg were seen as protesting — by means of literary or musical form — the inhuman societies developing around them.

Habermas saw Adorno's critique of culture as a blind alley leading only to alienation and quietism. He framed the need to heal the split between socioeconomic study and cultural critique, between fact and value, as a problem of the breakdown of public discourse, seeking a way to recuperate the Enlightenment ideal of a just and rational society within the context of late capitalism. For Habermas, the aim of society must be "the end of coercion and the attainment of autonomy through reason, the end of alienation through a consensual harmony of interests, and the end of injustice and poverty through the rational administration of justice."[12] As one might expect given his historical position as a philosopher, writing at a time when rhetoric and discourse are seen as the constituents of reality rather than as verbal veils of deeper material or spiritual truths, Habermas envisions progress as coming not just from material and organizational reform, but from a purification of public discourse.

Habermas's analysis of discourse owes a great deal to Wittgenstein, to Gadamer, and to the speech-act theorists,[13] whose ideas he adopted and against whom he

---

[12]Jane Braaten, *Habermas's Critical Theory of Society* (Albany: State University of New York Press, 1991), p. 111.

[13]Speech-act theory relates to the branch of linguistics called "pragmatics," which operates above the level of the sentence to analyze the ways sentences are construed as part of a social situation. One pioneering volume is that of philosopher of language J. L. Austin (1921–1960), whose *How to Do Things with Words* (Cambridge: Harvard University Press, 1962) contrasts "constative" language, which states facts (e.g., "The distance between New York and Chicago is 713 miles"), with "performative" language by which people promise, or threaten, or perform other acts (e.g., "I sentence you to be hanged by the neck until you are dead"). Austin suggests that "felicity conditions" need to be observed for performatives:

reacted. His theory presumes that social dialogue occurs within a framework that makes certain idealizing assumptions (he calls them "validity claims") about real-life utterances: that what we say is understandable, that its objective propositional content is true, that the speaker is sincere, and that it is appropriate for the speaker to be performing the speech-act. Obviously these assumptions do not hold for all, or even most, real-life utterances, so that we often need to problematize one or another of these validity claims, questioning the speaker's truth or sincerity, say, and rising to a meta-level of discourse in our critique. Nonetheless, conversation and dialogue and the attainment of any consensus needed for action depend on these validity claims.[14] Genuine consensus can be built provided all the participants in a dialogue have a fair share in the discourse, are allowed freely to assert or question any claim that is made, and are able to express attitudes, feelings, and intentions, without being dominated, materially or ideologically, by another speaker. In such a dialogue people attempt to persuade one another not by authority or by false claims of scientific rationality but by the force of the better argument. Habermas knows that such a situation is counterfactual, that contemporary society throws up hundreds of barriers to the production of what he calls "legitimate" consensus, but he holds up the ideal of a society in which the actors attempt to persuade each other on rational grounds. The conditions he envisions as a prerequisite for the attainment of such a consensus of intersubjective truth are the conditions of the just society of which Marx and Adorno dreamed.

Given his melioristic general program for social discourse and social organization, it is clear that neither postmodernism nor poststructural thought has any positive place in Habermas's thought. The fragmented bricolage of postmodernism implicitly presumes that what successive generations each in turn called the "modern" project of progress and enlightenment is over, that the fragmentation of an instrumentalist social system has left modern humanity in an alienation beyond remedy. And the anarchistic rhetoric of Jacques Derrida and Michel Foucault, derived from Heidegger and the later Nietzsche, is equally poisonous to Habermas's project, as it denies both the "validity claims" needed for communicative competence and the possibility of the social conditions needed for legitimate consensus. Habermas argues that the poststructuralist versions of rhetoric held by Richard Rorty and Derrida essentially cheat, in that they employ logic and reason against the values of logic and reason, use the terms of metaphysics in order to destroy metaphysics, and require our consent to reasoned argument without recuperating any new mode of consensus discourse at some meta-level of reason. In a later chapter of the book, Habermas explores equally basic contradictions within the thought of

---

The last example will not "work" as a performative unless the speaker is a judge, the recipient of the utterance is a person who has been found guilty of a capital crime, the scene is a courtroom, and so on. Ultimately Austin was dissatisfied with the distinction between constatives and performatives, and speech-act theory gradually shifted to distinguishing between "locutionary," "illocutionary," and "perlocutionary" speech-acts (in the first one would "say" something; in the second "argue" something to someone; in the third "convince" someone of something). See also John R. Searle, *Speech Acts* (Cambridge, Cambridge University Press, 1969).

[14]Thomas McCarthy, Translator's Introduction to Jürgen Habermas, *Legitimation Crisis* (Boston: Beacon, 1975), p. xiv.

Foucault, a philosopher whose empirical investigations of madness, disease, and criminal behavior operate within a system that denies empiricism, whose rebarbative truths operate within a system that portrays truth as merely a function of power. Habermas's ultimate point is that "the radical critique of reason exacts a high price for taking leave of modernity."[15] It leaves us with a hopeless solipsism, when what is needed for taking on the alienating conditions of late capitalism and the power of the interventionist state is a discourse that can build toward legitimate consensus, not to "pass beyond man and humanism" as Derrida put it (see p. 925), but to redeem the as-yet unrealized ideal of a liberal society. Like post structuralism, postmodernism strikes Habermas as a premature revolutionary movement, one that would give back the gains of the enlightenment before they had been fully realized—but this is a topic that must wait for the debate on postmodernism that will be explored in Chapter 10.

[15]Jürgen Habermas, *The Philosophical Discourse of Modernity: Twelve Lectures*, trans. Frederick G. Lawrence (Cambridge: MIT Press, 1990), p. 336.

Selected Bibliography

Adorno, Theodor. *Prisms: Cultural Criticism and Society.* 1955; London: Neville Spearman, 1967.

———. *Minima Moralia: Reflections from Damaged Life,* trans. E. F. Jephcott. New York: Norton, 1985.

———. *Notes to Literature,* trans. Shierry W. Nicholsen. New York: Columbia University Press, 1991.

———. *Aesthetic Theory,* trans. Rolf Tiedemann. Minneapolis: University of Minnesota Press, 1996.

Althusser, Louis. *For Marx.* New York: Pantheon, 1969.

———. *Lenin and Philosophy and Other Essays.* London: New Left Books, 1971.

Althusser, Louis, and Etienne Balibar. *Reading Capital.* New York: Pantheon, 1970.

Aronson, Ronald, *After Marxism.* New York: Guilford Press, 1995.

Bakhtin, Mikhail. *Between Phenomenology and Marxism.* New York: Cambridge University Press, 1995.

Barker, Francis, Peter Hulme, and Margaret Iverson, eds. *The Uses of History: Marxism, Postmodernism and the Renaissance.* New York: St. Martin's Press, 1991.

Benjamin, Walter. *Illuminations.* New York: Harcourt Brace & World, 1968.

———. *Charles Baudelaire: A Lyric Poet in the Era of High Capitalism.* London: New Left Books, 1973.

———. *Reflections: Essays, Aphorisms, Autobiographical Writings,* ed. Peter Demetz. New York: Harcourt Brace Jovanovich, 1978.

———. *Correspondence of Walter Benjamin.* Chicago: University of Chicago Press, 1994.

Bennett, Tony. *Formalism and Marxism.* London: Methuen, 1979.

Benton, Ted, ed. *The Greening of Marxism.* New York: Guilford Press, 1996.

Brecht, Bertolt. *Brecht on Theatre: The Development of an Aesthetic*, ed. and trans. John Willett. New York: Hill and Wang, 1978.

Caudwell, Christopher. *Illusion and Reality: A Study of the Sources of Poetry.* New York: International Publishers, 1963.

Cohen, Naomi. *Feminism and Marxism in the Nineties: A Revolutionary Women's Agenda.* New York: World View Forum, 1993.

Cook, Deborah. *The Culture Industry Revisited: Theodor W. Adorno on Mass Culture.* Lanham, MD: Rowman & Littlefield, 1996.

Coward, Rosemary, and John Ellis. *Language and Materialism: Developments in Semiology and the Theory of the Subject.* London: Routledge and Kegan Paul, 1977.

Demetz, Peter. *Marx, Engels and the Poets: Origins of Marxist Literary Criticism.* Chicago: University of Chicago Press, 1967.

Dowling, William. *Jameson, Althusser, Marx: An Introduction to the Political Unconscious.* Ithaca: Cornell University Press, 1984.

Eagleton, Terry. *Criticism and Ideology: A Study in Marxist Literary Theory.* London: New Left Books, 1976.

———. *Marxism and Literary Criticism.* Berkeley: University of California Press, 1976.

———. *Criticism and Ideology: A Study in Marxist Theory.* New York: Norton, 1978.

———. *Saint Oscar.* London: Faber and Faber, 1990.

———. *The Ideology of the Aesthetic.* London: Blackwell, 1994.

———. *Ideology.* White Plains: Longman Publishing Group, 1995.

———. *Heathcliff and the Great Hunger.* New York: Norton, 1995.

———. *The Illusions of Postmodernism.* London: Blackwell, 1996.

———. *The Idea of Culture.* Oxford: Blackwell, 2000.

———. *After Theory.* New York: Basic Books, 2003.

Eagleton, Terry, and Drew Milne, eds. *Marxist Literary Theory: A Reader.* Oxford: Blackwell, 1996.

Fekete, John. *The Critical Twilight.* Boston: Routledge and Kegan Paul, 1976.

Fokkema, Douwe W., and Elrud Ibsch. *Theories of Literature in the Twentieth Century: Structuralism, Marxism, Aesthetics of Reception, Semiotics,* 2nd ed. New York: St. Martin's Press, 1995.

Foley, Barbara. *Telling the Truth: The Theory and Practice of Documentary Fiction.* Ithaca: Cornell University Press, 1986.

Freedman, Carl Howard. *The Incomplete Projects: Marxism, Modernity, and the Politics of Culture.* Middletown: Wesleyan University Press, 2002.

Frow, John. *Marxism and Literary History.* Ithaca: Cornell University Press, 1986.

Goldmann, Lucien. *The Hidden God: A Study of the Tragic Vision in the Pensées of Pascal and the Tragedies of Racine.* 1955; London: Routledge and Kegan Paul, 1964.

———. "Marxist Criticism." In *The Philosophy of the Enlightenment.* Cambridge: MIT Press, 1973, pp. 86–97.

Gramsci, Antonio. *The Modern Prince and Other Writings.* London: Lawrence and Wishart, 1957.

———. *Selections from the Prison Notebooks.* London: Lawrence and Wishart, 1971.

Habermas, Jürgen. *The Philosophical Discourse of Modernity: Twelve Lectures,* trans. Frederick G. Lawrence. Cambridge: MIT Press, 1990.

———. *Jürgen Habermas on Society and Politics: A Reader,* trans. Steven Seidman. Boston: Beacon Press, 1989.

———. *The Structural Transformation of the Public Sphere: An Inquiry into a Category of Bourgeois Society.* Cambridge: MIT Press, 1989.

———. *The Theory of Communicative Action, Vol. I: Reason and the Rationalization of Society,* trans. Thomas McCarthy. Boston: Beacon Press, 1985.

———. *The Theory of Communicative Action, Vol. II: Lifeworld and System: A Critique of Functionalist Reason,* trans. Thomas McCarthy. Boston: Beacon Press, 1989.

———. *The Future of Human Nature.* Malden, MA: Blackwell, 2003.

———. *Truth and Justification,* ed. and trans. Barbara Fultner. Cambridge: MIT Press, 2003.

Hartley, George. *The Abyss of Representation: Marxism and the Postmodern Sublime.* Durham: Duke University Press, 2003.

Hawthorn, Jeremy. *Cunning Passages: New Historicism, Cultural Materialism, and Marxism in the Contemporary Literary Debate.* New York: Routledge, 1996.

Hicks, Granville. *The Great Tradition: An Interpretation of American Literature Since the Civil War.* 1933; Chicago: Quadrangle Books, 1969.

Hohendahl, Peter Uwe. "Prolegomena to a History of Literary Criticism." *New German Critique* 11 (1977): 151–63.

Horkheimer, Max. *Eclipse of Reason.* New York: Continuum, 1992.

Horkheimer, Max, and Theodor W. Adorno. *Dialectic of Enlightenment*, trans. John Cumming. New York: Continuum, 1998.

Jameson, Fredric. *Marxism and Form: Twentieth Century Dialectical Theories of Literature.* Princeton: Princeton University Press, 1971.

———. *The Prison-House of Language: A Critical Account of Structuralism and Russian Formalism.* Princeton: Princeton University Press, 1972.

———. *The Political Unconscious: Studies in the Ideology of Form.* Ithaca: Cornell University Press, 1981.

———. *Late Marxism: Adorno or the Persistence of the Dialectic.* New York: Norton, 1990.

———. *Postmodernism, or, the Cultural Logic of Late Capitalism.* Durham: Duke University Press, 1991.

———. *The Seeds of Time.* New York: Columbia University Press, 1996.

———. *Brecht and Method.* London: Verso, 1998.

———. *A Singular Modernity.* London: Verso, 2002.

Kellner, Douglas. *Critical Theory, Marxism, and Modernity.* Baltimore: Johns Hopkins University Press, 1989.

Kettle, Arnold. *Introduction to the English Novel.* 2 vols. 1951; New York: Harper and Row, 1960.

Lifshitz, Mikail. *The Philosophy of Art of Karl Marx.* 1933; London: Pluto Press, 1973.

Lukács, Georg. *Realism in Our Time: Literature and the Class Struggle.* 1957; New York: Harper and Row, 1964.

———. *The Historical Novel.* London: Merlin Press, 1962.

———. *The Theory of the Novel: A Historico-Philosophical Essay on the Forms of Great Epic Literature.* 1920; London: Merlin Press, 1971.

Macherey, Pierre. *A Theory of Literary Production.* 1966; Boston: Routledge and Kegan Paul, 1978.

Marcuse, Herbert. *The Aesthetic Dimension: Toward a Critique of Marxist Aesthetics.* Boston: Beacon Press, 1978.

Marx, Karl, and Friedrich Engels. *Marx and Engels on Literature and Art.* St. Louis: Telos Press, 1973.

Morris, William. *On Art and Socialism.* London: Lehmann, 1947.

Ohmann, Richard. *English in America: A Radical View of the Profession.* New York: Oxford University Press, 1976.

Orwell, George. *Critical Essays.* London: Secker and Warberg, 1946.

Robinson, Lillian S. *Sex, Class, and Culture.* Bloomington: Indiana University Press, 1978.

Rose, Gillian. *The "Melancholy Science": An Introduction to the Thought of Theodor W. Adorno.* London: Macmillan, 1978.

Sartre, Jean-Paul. *What Is Literature?* New York: Harper and Row, 1965.

———. *Between Existentialism and Marxism.* New York: Pantheon, 1974.

Sherman, Howard J. *Reinventing Marxism.* Baltimore: Johns Hopkins University Press, 1995.

Smith, Steven B. *Reading Althusser*. Ithaca: Cornell University Press, 1984.

Trotsky, Leon. *Literature and Revolution*. 1924; Ann Arbor: University of Michigan Press, 1960.

Weimann, Robert. *Structure and Society in Literary History*. Charlottesville: University Press of Virginia, 1976.

Williams, Raymond. *Culture and Society, 1780–1950*. London: Chatto and Windus, 1958.

———. *The Country and the City*. New York: Oxford University Press, 1973.

———. *Marxism and Literature*. New York: Oxford University Press, 1977.

———. *The Sociology of Culture*. Chicago: University of Chicago Press, 1995.

———. *The Politics of Modernism: Against the New Conformists*. London: Verso, 1996.

Wilson, Edmund. *Axel's Castle*. 1931; New York: Scribner's, 1961.

———. *The Triple Thinkers*. 1938; New York: Oxford University Press, 1948.

Wood, Ellen Meiksins, and John Bellamy Foster, eds. *In Defense of History: Marxism and the Postmodern Agenda*. New York: Monthly Review Press, 1997.

Georg Lukács

1885–1971

The most influential Marxist aesthetician of the first half of this century, Georg Lukács was the son of a wealthy Hungarian family. He attended the University of Heidelberg and the University of Berlin, and received a Ph.D. from the University of Budapest in 1906. Lukács wrote several essays on aesthetic and literary theory (including Soul and Form *[1910],* Aesthetic Culture *[1913], and his influential* Theory of the Novel *[written 1916, published 1920]) in a Hegelian phase before joining the Hungarian Communist party in 1918. In 1919 he began a stint as commissar for culture and education in the regime of Bela Kun, an appointment that ended with the fall of Kun. Lukács left Hungary and settled in Vienna, where he produced* History and Class Consciousness *(1923), his most influential work of political theory. Driven by waves of political controversy, Lukács spent 1929–31 in Moscow, then moved to Berlin. When the Nazis came to power in 1933, he returned to Moscow, taking a post at the Soviet Academy of Sciences (1933–44). He managed, as a great many Central European intellectuals did not, to survive the Stalinist purges of 1937–38; it was in this dark time that he wrote* The Historical Novel *(published in English in 1962). Lukács did not return to Hungary until the more receptive political climate of 1945, when he was made a parliamentary minister and professor of aesthetics and cultural philosophy at the University of Budapest. In 1956, the year he wrote "The Ideology of Modernism," Lukács was again unseated by a political uprising. Deported in 1956 to Romania, Lukács worked on two major theoretical tomes, neither of which was complete at his death; neither has yet been translated:* Die Eigenart des Ästhetischen *("The Particularity of the Aesthetic," 1963), and the two-volume* Zur Ontologie der gesellschaftlisches Seins *("Toward an Ontology of Social Being," 1973).*

The Ideology of Modernism

It is in no way surprising that the most influential contemporary school of writing should still be committed to the dogmas of "modernist" antirealism. It is here that we must begin our investigation if we are to chart the possibilities of a bourgeois realism. We must compare the two main trends in contemporary bourgeois literature, and look at the answers they give to the major ideological and artistic questions of our time.

We shall concentrate on the underlying ideological basis of these trends (ideological in the above-defined, not in the strictly philosophical, sense). What must be avoided at all costs is the approach generally adopted by bourgeois-modernist critics themselves: that exaggerated concern with formal criteria, with questions of style and literary technique. This approach may appear to distinguish sharply between "modern" and "traditional" writing (i.e., contemporary writers who adhere to the styles of the last century). In fact, it fails to locate the decisive formal problems and turns a blind eye to their inherent dialectic. We are presented with a false polarization which, by exaggerating the importance of stylistic differences, conceals the opposing principles actually underlying and determining contrasting styles.

To take an example: the *monologue intérieur.* Compare, for instance, Bloom's monologue in the lavatory or Molly's monologue in bed, at the beginning and at the end of *Ulysses,* with Goethe's early-morning monologue as conceived by Thomas Mann in his *Lotte in Weimar.* Plainly, the same stylistic technique is being employed. And certain of Thomas Mann's remarks about Joyce and his methods would appear to confirm this.

Yet it is not easy to think of any two novels more basically dissimilar than *Ulysses* and *Lotte in Weimar.* This is true even of the superficially rather similar scenes I have indicated. I am not referring to the — to my mind — striking difference in intellectual quality. I refer to the fact that

Translated by John and Necke Mander.

with Joyce the stream-of-consciousness technique is no mere stylistic device; it is itself the formative principle governing the narrative pattern and the presentation of character. Technique here is something absolute; it is part and parcel of the aesthetic ambition informing *Ulysses.* With Thomas Mann, on the other hand, the *monologue intérieur* is simply a technical device, allowing the author to explore aspects of Goethe's world which would not have been otherwise available. Goethe's experience is not presented as confined to momentary sense-impressions. The artist reaches down to the core of Goethe's personality, to the complexity of his relations with his own past, present, and even future experience. The stream of association is only apparently free. The monologue is composed with the utmost artistic rigor: it is a carefully plotted sequence gradually piercing to the core of Goethe's personality. Every person or event, emerging momentarily from the stream and vanishing again, is given a specific weight, a definite position, in the pattern of the whole. However unconventional the presentation, the compositional principle is that of the traditional epic; in the way the pace is controlled, and the transitions and climaxes are organized, the ancient rules of epic narration are faithfully observed.

It would be absurd, in view of Joyce's artistic ambitions and his manifest abilities, to qualify the exaggerated attention he gives to the detailed recording of sense-data, and his comparative neglect of ideas and emotions, as artistic failure. All this was in conformity with Joyce's artistic intentions; and, by use of such techniques, he may be said to have achieved them satisfactorily. But between Joyce's intentions and those of Thomas Mann there is a total opposition. The perpetually oscillating patterns of sense- and memory-data, their powerfully charged — but aimless and directionless — fields of force, give rise to an epic structure which is *static,* reflecting a belief in the basically static character of events.

These opposed views of the world — dynamic and developmental on the one hand, static and sensational on the other — are of crucial importance in examining the two schools of literature I have mentioned. I shall return to the opposition later. Here, I want only to point out that an exclusive emphasis on formal matters can lead to serious misunderstanding of the character of an artist's work.

What determines the style of a given work of art? How does the intention determine the form? (We are concerned here, of course, with the intention realized in the work; it need not coincide with the writer's conscious intention.) The distinctions that concern us are not those between stylistic "techniques" in the formalistic sense. It is the view of the world, the ideology or *weltanschauung*[1] underlying a writer's work, that counts. And it is the writer's attempt to reproduce this view of the world which constitutes his "intention" and is the formative principle underlying the style of a given piece of writing. Looked at in this way, style ceases to be a formalistic category. Rather, it is rooted in content; it is the specific form of a specific content.

Content determines form. But there is no content of which Man himself is not the focal point. However various the *données*[2] of literature (a particular experience, a didactic purpose), the basic question is, and will remain: what is Man?

Here is a point of division: if we put the question in abstract, philosophical terms, leaving aside all formal considerations, we arrive — for the realist school — at the traditional Aristotelian dictum (which was also reached by other than purely aesthetic considerations): Man is *zoon politikon,* a social animal. The Aristotelian dictum is applicable to all great realistic literature. Achilles and Werther, Oedipus and Tom Jones, Antigone, and Anna Karenina: their individual existence — their *Sein an sich,*[3] in the Hegelian terminology; their "ontological being," as a more fashionable terminology has it — cannot be distinguished from their social and historical environment. Their human significance, their specific individuality cannot be separated from the context in which they were created.

The ontological view governing the image of man in the work of leading modernist writers is the exact opposite of this. Man, for these writers, is by nature solitary, asocial, unable to enter into relationships with other human beings. Thomas Wolfe once wrote: "My view of the world is based on the firm conviction that solitariness is by no means a rare condition, something peculiar to myself or to a few specially solitary human beings, but the inescapable, central fact of human existence." Man, thus imagined, may establish contact with other individuals, but only in a superficial, accidental manner; only, ontologically speaking, by retrospective reflection. For "the others," too, are basically solitary, beyond significant human relationship.

This basic solitariness of man must not be confused with that individual solitariness to be found in the literature of traditional realism. In the latter case, we are dealing with a particular situation in which a human being may be placed, due either to his character or to the circumstances of his life. Solitariness may be objectively conditioned, as with Sophocles' Philoctetes, put ashore on the bleak island of Lemnos. Or it may be subjective, the product of inner necessity, as with Tolstoy's Ivan Ilych or Flaubert's Frédéric Moreau in the *Education Sentimentale.* But it is always merely a fragment, a phase, a climax, or anticlimax, in the life of the community as a whole. The fate of such individuals is characteristic of certain human types in specific social or historical circumstances. Beside and beyond their solitariness, the common life, the strife and togetherness of other human beings, goes on as before. In a word, their solitariness is a specific social fate, not a universal *condition humaine.*

The latter, of course, is characteristic of the theory and practice of modernism. I would like, in the present study, to spare the reader tedious excursions into philosophy. But I cannot refrain from drawing the reader's attention to Heidegger's description of human existence as a "thrownness-into-being" *(Geworfenheit ins Dasein).* A more graphic evocation of the ontological solitariness of the individual would be hard to imagine. Man is "thrown-into-being." This implies, not merely that man is constitutionally unable to establish relationships with things

---

[1]World-picture.
[2]What is given: the subject matter chosen by the author.
[3]Being in itself.

or persons outside himself; but also that it is impossible to determine theoretically the origin and goal of human existence.

Man, thus conceived, is an ahistorical being. (The fact that Heidegger does admit a form of "authentic" historicity in his system is not really relevant. I have shown elsewhere that Heidegger tends to belittle historicity as "vulgar"; and his "authentic" historicity is not distinguishable from ahistoricity). This negation of history takes two different forms in modernist literature. First, the hero is strictly confined within the limits of his own experience. There is not for him — and apparently not for his creator — any preexistent reality beyond his own self, acting upon him or being acted upon by him. Secondly, the hero himself is without personal history. He is "thrown-into-the-world": meaninglessly, unfathomably. He does not develop through contact with the world; he neither forms nor is formed by it. The only "development" in this literature is the gradual revelation of the human condition. Man is now what he has always been and always will be. The narrator, the examining subject, is in motion; the examined reality is static.

Of course, dogmas of this kind are only really viable in philosophical abstraction, and then only with a measure of sophistry. A gifted writer, however extreme his theoretical modernism, will in practice have to compromise with the demands of historicity and of social environment. Joyce uses Dublin, Kafka and Musil the Hapsburg Monarchy, as the locus of their masterpieces.[4] But the locus they lovingly depict is little more than a backcloth; it is not basic to their artistic intention.

This view of human existence has specific literary consequences. Particularly in one category, of primary theoretical and practical importance, to which we must now give our attention: that of *potentiality*. Philosophy distinguishes between *abstract* and *concrete* (in Hegel, "real") *potentiality*. These two categories, their interrelation and opposition, are rooted in life itself. *Potentiality* — seen abstractly or subjectively — is richer than actual life. Innumerable possibilities for man's

development are imaginable, only a small percentage of which will be realized. Modern subjectivism, taking these imagined possibilities for actual complexity of life, oscillates between melancholy and fascination. When the world declines to realize these possibilities, this melancholy becomes tinged with contempt. Hofmannsthal's Sobeide expressed the reaction of the generation first exposed to this experience:

> The burden of those endlessly pored-over
> And now forever perished possibilities . . .[5]

How far were those possibilities even concrete or "real"? Plainly, they existed only in the imagination of the subject, as dreams or daydreams. Faulkner, in whose work this subjective potentiality plays an important part, was evidently aware that reality must thereby be subjectivized and made to appear arbitrary. Consider this comment of his: "They were all talking simultaneously, getting flushed and excited, quarrelling, making the unreal into a possibility, then into a probability, then into an irrefutable fact, as human beings do when they put their wishes into words." The possibilities in a man's mind, the particular pattern, intensity and suggestiveness they assume, will of course be characteristic of that individual. In practice, their number will border on the infinite, even with the most unimaginative individual. It is thus a hopeless undertaking to define the contours of individuality, let alone to come to grips with a man's actual fate, by means of potentiality. The *abstract* character of potentiality is clear from the fact that it cannot determine development — subjective mental states, however permanent or profound, cannot here be decisive. Rather, the development of personality is determined by inherited gifts and qualities; by the factors, external or internal, which further or inhibit their growth.

But in life potentiality can, of course, become reality. Situations arise in which a man is confronted with a choice; and in the act of choice a man's character may reveal itself in a light that surprises even himself. In literature — and particularly in dramatic literature — the denouement often consists in the realization of just such a

---

[4]*Ulysses, The Castle,* and *The Man without Qualities,* respectively.

[5]*Die Hochzeit von Sobeide* (1899), a drama by Hugo von Hofmannsthal (1874–1929).

potentiality, which circumstances have kept from coming to the fore. These potentialities are, then, "real" or concrete potentialities. The fate of the character depends upon the potentiality in question, even if it should condemn him to a tragic end. In advance, while still a subjective potentiality in the character's mind, there is no way of distinguishing it from the innumerable abstract potentialities in his mind. It may even be buried away so completely that, before the moment of decision, it has never entered his mind even as an abstract potentiality. The subject, after taking his decision, may be unconscious of his own motives. Thus Richard Dudgeon, Shaw's Devil's Disciple, having sacrificed himself as Pastor Anderson, confesses: "I have often asked myself for the motive, but I find no good reason to explain why I acted as I did."

Yet it is a decision which has altered the direction of his life. Of course, this is an extreme case. But the qualitative leap of the denouement, cancelling and at the same time renewing the continuity of individual consciousness, can never be predicted. The concrete potentiality cannot be isolated from the myriad abstract potentialities. Only actual decision reveals the distinction.

The literature of realism, aiming at a truthful reflection of reality, must demonstrate both the concrete and abstract potentialities of human beings in extreme situations of this kind. A character's concrete potentiality once revealed, his abstract potentialities will appear essentially inauthentic. Moravia, for instance, in his novel *The Indifferent Ones,* describes the young son of a decadent bourgeois family, Michel, who makes up his mind to kill his sister's seducer. While Michel, having made his decision, is planning the murder, a large number of abstract — but highly suggestive — possibilities are laid before us. Unfortunately for Michel the murder is actually carried out; and, from the sordid details of the action, Michel's character emerges as what it is — representative of that background from which, in subjective fantasy, he had imagined he could escape.

Abstract potentiality belongs wholly to the realm of subjectivity; whereas concrete potentiality is concerned with the dialectic between the individual's subjectivity and objective reality.

The literary presentation of the latter thus implies a description of actual persons inhabiting a palpable, identifiable world. Only in the interaction of character and environment can the concrete potentiality of a particular individual be singled out from the "bad infinity" of purely abstract potentialities, and emerge as the determining potentiality of just this individual at just this phase of his development. This principle alone enables the artist to distinguish concrete potentiality from a myriad abstractions.

But the ontology on which the image of man in modernist literature is based invalidates this principle. If the "human condition" — man as a solitary being, incapable of meaningful relationships — is identified with reality itself, the distinction between abstract and concrete potentiality becomes null and void. The categories tend to merge. Thus Cesare Pavese notes with John Dos Passos, and his German contemporary, Alfred Döblin, a sharp oscillation between "superficial *verisme*"[6] and "abstract Expressionist schematism." Criticizing Dos Passos, Pavese writes that fictional characters "ought to be created by deliberate selection and description of individual features" — implying that Dos Passos's characterizations are transferable from one individual to another. He describes the artistic consequences: by exalting man's subjectivity, at the expense of the objective reality of his environment, man's subjectivity itself is impoverished.

The problem, once again, is ideological. This is not to say that the ideology underlying modernist writings is identical in all cases. On the contrary: the ideology exists in extremely various, even contradictory forms. The rejection of narrative objectivity, the surrender to subjectivity, may take the form of Joyce's stream of consciousness, or of Musil's "active passivity," his "existence without quality," or of Gide's *"action gratuite,"*[7] where abstract potentiality achieves pseudo-realization. As individual character manifests itself in life's moments of decision, so too in literature. If the distinction between abstract and

---

[6]A crudely realistic style akin to newspaper reportage.
[7]Gratuitous act: a crime committed to prove one's freedom.

concrete potentiality vanishes, if man's inwardness is identified with an abstract subjectivity, human personality must necessarily disintegrate.

T. S. Eliot described this phenomenon, this mode of portraying human personality, as

> Shape without form, shade without colour,
> Paralysed force, gesture without motion.[8]

The disintegration of personality is matched by a disintegration of the outer world. In one sense, this is simply a further consequence of our argument. For the identification of abstract and concrete human potentiality rests on the assumption that the objective world is inherently inexplicable. Certain leading modernist writers, attempting a theoretical apology, have admitted this quite frankly. Often this theoretical impossibility of understanding reality is the point of departure, rather than the exaltation of subjectivity. But in any case the connection between the two is plain. The German poet Gottfried Benn, for instance, informs us that "there is no outer reality, there is only human consciousness, constantly building, modifying, rebuilding new worlds out of its own creativity." Musil, as always, gives a moral twist to this line of thought. Ulrich, the hero of his *The Man without Qualities,* when asked what he would do if he were in God's place, replies: "I should be compelled to abolish reality." Subjective existence "without qualities" is the complement of the negation of outward reality.

The negation of outward reality is not always demanded with such theoretical rigor. But it is present in almost all modernist literature. In conversation, Musil once gave as the period of his great novel, "between 1912 and 1914." But he was quick to modify this statement by adding: "I have not, I must insist, written a historical novel. I am not concerned with actual events. . . . Events, anyhow, are interchangeable. I am interested in what is typical, in what one might call the ghostly aspect of reality." The word "ghostly" is interesting. It points to a major tendency in modernist literature: the attenuation of actuality. In Kafka, the descriptive detail is of an extraordinary immediacy and authenticity. But Kafka's artistic ingenuity is really directed towards substituting his *angst*-ridden vision of the world for objective reality. The realistic detail is the expression of a ghostly un-reality, of a nightmare world, whose function is to evoke *angst.* The same phenomenon can be seen in writers who attempt to combine Kafka's techniques with a critique of society — like the German writer, Wolfgang Koeppen, in his satirical novel about Bonn, *Das Treibhaus.* A similar attenuation of reality underlies Joyce's stream of consciousness. It is, of course, intensified where the stream of consciousness is itself the medium through which reality is presented. And it is carried *ad absurdum* where the stream of consciousness is that of an abnormal subject or of an idiot — consider the first part of Faulkner's *Sound and Fury* or, a still more extreme case, Beckett's *Molloy.*

Attentuation of reality and dissolution of personality are thus interdependent: the stronger the one, the stronger the other. Underlying both is the lack of a consistent view of human nature. Man is reduced to a sequence of unrelated experiential fragments; he is as inexplicable to others as to himself. In Eliot's *Cocktail Party* the psychiatrist, who voices the opinions of the author, describes the phenomenon:

> Ah, but we die to each other daily
> What we know of other people
> Is only our memory of the moments
> During which we knew them. And they have
>   changed since then.
> To pretend that they and we are the same
> Is a useful and convenient social convention
> Which must sometimes be broken. We must also
>   remember
> That at every meeting we are meeting a stranger.

The dissolution of personality, originally the unconscious product of the identification of concrete and abstract potentiality, is elevated to a deliberate principle in the light of consciousness. It is no accident that Gottfried Benn called one of his theoretical tracts *"Doppelleben."*[9] For Benn, this dissolution of personality took the form of a schizophrenic dichotomy. According to him, there was in man's personality no coherent pattern of motivation or behavior. Man's animal nature is opposed to his denaturized, sublimated

---

[8]"The Hollow Men" (1925).

[9]Double life.

thought processes. The unity of thought and action is "backwoods philosophy"; thought and being are "quite separate entities." Man must be either a moral or a thinking being — he cannot be both at once.

These are not, I think, purely private, eccentric speculations. Of course, they are derived from Benn's specific experience. But there is an inner connection between these ideas and a certain tradition of bourgeois thought. It is more than a hundred years since Kierkegaard first attacked the Hegelian view that the inner and outer world form an objective dialectical unity, that they are indissolubly married in spite of their apparent opposition. Kierkegaard denied any such unity. According to Kierkegaard, the individual exists within an opaque, impenetrable "incognito."

This philosophy attained remarkable popularity after the Second World War — proof that even the most abstruse theories may reflect social reality. Men like Martin Heidegger, Ernst Jünger, the lawyer Carl Schmitt, Gottfried Benn and others passionately embraced this doctrine of the eternal incognito which implies that a man's external deeds are no guide to his motives. In this case, the deeds obscured behind the mysterious incognito were, needless to say, these intellectuals' participation in Nazism: Heidegger, as Rector of Freiburg University, had glorified Hitler's seizure of power at his Inauguration; Carl Schmitt had put his great legal gifts at Hitler's disposal. The facts were too well known to be simply denied. But, if this impenetrable incognito were the true *"condition humaine,"*[10] might not — concealed within their incognito — Heidegger or Schmitt have been secret opponents of Hitler all the time, only supporting him in the world of appearances? Ernst von Salomon's cynical frankness about his opportunism in *The Questionnaire* (keeping his reservations to himself or declaring them only in the presence of intimate friends) may be read as an ironic commentary on this ideology of the incognito as we find it, say, in the writings of Ernst Jünger.

This digression may serve to show, taking an extreme example, what the social implications of such an ontology may be. In the literary field, this particular ideology was of cardinal importance; by destroying the complex tissue of man's relations with his environment, it furthered the dissolution of personality. For it is just the opposition between a man and his environment that determines the development of his personality. There is no great hero of fiction — from Homer's Achilles to Mann's Adrian Leverkühn or Sholochov's Grigory Melyekov[11] — whose personality is not the product of such an opposition. I have shown how disastrous the denial of the distinction between abstract and concrete potentiality must be for the presentation of character. The destruction of the complex tissue of man's interaction with his environment likewise saps the vitality of this opposition. Certainly, some writers who adhere to this ideology have attempted, not unsuccessfully, to portray this opposition in concrete terms. But the underlying ideology deprives these contradictions of their dynamic, developmental significance. The contradictions coexist, unresolved, contributing to the further dissolution of the personality in question.

It is to the credit of Robert Musil that he was quite conscious of the implications of his method. Of his hero Ulrich he remarked: "One is faced with a simple choice: either one must run with the pack (when in Rome, do as the Romans do); or one becomes a neurotic." Musil here introduces the problem, central to all modernist literature, of the significance of psychopathology.

This problem was first widely discussed in the Naturalist period. More than fifty years ago, that doyen of Berlin dramatic critics, Alfred Kerr, was writing: "Morbidity is the legitimate poetry of Naturalism. For what is poetic in everyday life? Neurotic aberration, escape from life's dreary routine. Only in this way can a character be translated to a rarer clime and yet retain an air of reality." Interesting, here, is the notion that the poetic necessity of the pathological derives from the prosaic quality of life under capitalism. I would maintain — we shall return to this point — that in

[10]Human condition. Lukács's use of the French alludes to the Marxist novel about opposition to Fascism, *La Condition Humaine (Man's Fate)* by André Malraux.

[11]Heroes of the *Iliad, Doctor Faustus,* and *Quiet Flows the Don.*

modern writing there is a continuity from Naturalism to the Modernism of our day — a continuity restricted, admittedly, to underlying ideological principles. What at first was no more than dim anticipation of approaching catastrophe developed, after 1914, into an all-pervading obsession. And I would suggest that the ever-increasing part played by psychopathology was one of the main features of the continuity. At each period — depending on the prevailing social and historical conditions — psychopathology was given a new emphasis, a different significance and artistic function. Kerr's description suggests that in naturalism the interest in psychopathology sprang from an aesthetic need; it was an attempt to escape from the dreariness of life under capitalism. The quotation from Musil shows that some years later the opposition acquired a moral slant. The obsession with morbidity had ceased to have a merely decorative function, bringing color into the greyness of reality, and become a moral protest against capitalism.

With Musil — and with many other modernist writers — psychopathology became the goal, the *terminus ad quem*,[12] of their artistic intention. But there is a double difficulty inherent in their intention, which follows from its underlying ideology. There is, first, a lack of definition. The protest expressed by this flight into psychopathology is an abstract gesture; its rejection of reality is wholesale and summary, containing no concrete criticism. It is a gesture, moreover, that is destined to lead nowhere; it is an escape into nothingness. Thus the propagators of this ideology are mistaken in thinking that such a protest could ever be fruitful in literature. In any protest against particular social conditions, these conditions themselves must have the central place. The bourgeois protest against feudal society, the proletarian against bourgeois society, made their point of departure a criticism of the old order. In both cases the protest — reaching out beyond the point of departure — was based on a concrete *terminus ad quem:* the establishment of a new order. However indefinite the structure and content of this new order, the will towards its more exact definition was not lacking.

How different the protest of writers like Musil! The *terminus a quo*[13] (the corrupt society of our time) is inevitably the main source of energy, since the *terminus ad quem* (the escape into psychopathology) is a mere abstraction. The rejection of modern reality is purely subjective. Considered in terms of man's relation with his environment, it lacks both content and direction. And this lack is exaggerated still further by the character of the *terminus ad quem*. For the protest is an empty gesture, expressing nausea, or discomfort, or longing. Its content — or rather lack of content — derives from the fact that such a view of life cannot impact a sense of direction. These writers are not wholly wrong in believing that psychopathology is their surest refuge; it is the ideological complement of their historical position.

This obsession with the pathological is not only to be found in literature. Freudian psychoanalysis is its most obvious expression. The treatment of the subject is only superficially different from that in modern literature. As everybody knows, Freud's starting point was "everyday life." In order to explain "slips" and daydreams, however, he had to have recourse to psychopathology. In his lectures, speaking of resistance and repression, he says: "Our interest in the general psychology of symptom-formation increases as we understand to what extent the study of pathological conditions can shed light on the workings of the normal mind." Freud believed he had found the key to the understanding of the normal personality in the psychology of the abnormal. This belief is still more evident in the typology of Kretschmer, which also assumes that psychological abnormalities can explain normal psychology. It is only when we compare Freud's psychology with that of Pavlov, who takes the Hippocratic view that mental abnormality is a deviation from a norm, that we see it in its true light.

Clearly, this is not strictly a scientific or literary-critical problem. It is an ideological problem, deriving from the ontological dogma of the solitariness of man. The literature of realism, based on the Aristotelian concept of man as *zoon politikon*,[14] is entitled to develop a new typology

[13]Starting point.
[14]Political animal.

[12]End point.

for each new phase in the evolution of a society. It displays the contradictions within society and within the individual in the context of a dialectical unity. Here, individuals embodying violent and extraordinary passions are still within the range of a socially normal typology (Shakespeare, Balzac, Stendhal). For, in this literature, the average man is simply a dimmer reflection of the contradictions always existing in man and society; eccentricity is a socially-conditioned distortion. Obviously, the passions of the great heroes must not be confused with "eccentricity" in the colloquial sense: Christian Buddenbrook is an "eccentric"; Adrian Leverkühn is not.

The ontology of *Geworfenheit* makes a true typology impossible; it is replaced by an abstract polarity of the eccentric and the socially average. We have seen why this polarity — which in traditional realism serves to increase our understanding of social normality — leads in modernism to a fascination with morbid eccentricity. Eccentricity becomes the necessary complement of the average; and this polarity is held to exhaust human potentiality. The implications of this ideology are shown in another remark of Musil's: "If humanity dreamt collectively, it would dream Moosbrugger." Moosbrugger, you will remember, was a mentally retarded sexual pervert with homicidal tendencies.

What served, with Musil, as the ideological basis of a new typology — escape into neurosis as a protest against the evils of society — becomes with other modernist writers an immutable *condition humaine*. Musil's statement loses its conditional "if" and becomes a simple description of reality. Lack of objectivity in the description of the outer world finds its complement in the reduction of reality to a nightmare. Beckett's *Molloy* is perhaps the *ne plus ultra*[15] of this development, although Joyce's vision of reality as an incoherent stream of consciousness had already assumed in Faulkner a nightmare quality. In Beckett's novel we have the same vision twice over. He presents us with an image of the utmost human degradation — an idiot's vegetative existence. Then, as help is imminent from a mysterious unspecified source, the rescuer himself sinks into idiocy. The story is told through the parallel streams of consciousness of the idiot and of his rescuer.

Along with the adoption of perversity and idiocy as types of the *condition humaine,* we find what amounts to frank glorification. Take Montherlant's *Pasiphae,* where sexual perversity — the heroine's infatuation with a bull — is presented as a triumphant return to nature, as the liberation of impulse from the slavery of convention. The chorus — i.e., the author — puts the following question (which, though rhetorical, clearly expects an affirmative reply): "Si l'absence de pensée et l'absence de morale ne contribuent pas beaucoup à la dignité des bêtes, des plantes et des eaux . . . ?"[16] Montherlant expresses as plainly as Musil, though with different moral and emotional emphasis, the hidden — one might say repressed — social character of the protest underlying this obsession with psychopathology, its perverted Rousseauism,[17] its anarchism. There are many illustrations of this in modernist writing. A poem of Benn's will serve to make the point:

> O that we were our primal ancestors,
> Small lumps of plasma in hot, sultry swamps;
> Life, death, conception, parturition
> Emerging from those juices soundlessly.
>
> A frond of seaweed or a dune of sand,
> Formed by the wind and heavy at the base;
> A dragonfly or gull's wing — already, these
> Would signify excessive suffering.

This is not overtly perverse in the manner of Beckett or Montherlant. Yet, in his primitivism, Benn is at one with them. The opposition of man as animal to man as social being (for instance, Heidegger's devaluation of the social as *"das Man,"*[18] Klages's assertion of the incompatibility of *Geist* and *Seele,*[19] or Rosenberg's racial mythology)[20] leads straight to a glorification

---

[15]Ultimate point.

[16]"If the absence of thought and the absence of morality do not contribute a good deal to the dignity of animals, plants, and bodies of water. . . ."

[17]Here, adulation of the primitive as noble.

[18]An untranslatable phrase signifying vague personhood. The German word *man* is the indefinite pronoun equivalent to the English "one."

[19]Spirit and soul.

[20]Alfred Rosenberg (1893–1946), a Nazi ideologist of anti-Semitism, author of *The Myth of the Twentieth Century* (1934).

of the abnormal and to an undisguised antihumanism.

A typology limited in this way to the *homme moyen sensuel* and the idiot also opens the door to "experimental" stylistic distortion. Distortion becomes as inseparable a part of the portrayal of reality as the recourse to the pathological. But literature must have a concept of the normal if it is to "place" distortion correctly; that is to say, to see it *as* distortion. With such a typology this placing is impossible, since the normal is no longer a proper object of literary interest. Life under capitalism is, often rightly, presented as a distortion (a petrification or paralysis) of the human substance. But to present psychopathology as a way of escape from this distortion is itself a distortion. We are invited to measure one type of distortion against another and arrive, necessarily, at universal distortion. There is no principle to set against the general pattern, no standard by which the petty-bourgeois and the pathological can be seen in their social context. And these tendencies, far from being relativized with time, become ever more absolute. Distortion becomes the normal condition of human existence; the proper study, the formative principle, of art and literature.

I have demonstrated some of the literary implications of this ideology. Let us now pursue the argument further. It is clear, I think, that modernism must deprive literature of a sense of *perspective*. This would not be surprising; rigorous modernists such as Kafka, Benn, and Musil have always indignantly refused to provide their readers with any such thing. I will return to the ideological implications of the idea of perspective later. Let me say here that, in any work of art, perspective is of overriding importance. It determines the course and content; it draws together the threads of the narration; it enables the artist to choose between the important and the superficial, the crucial and the episodic. The direction in which characters develop is determined by perspective, only those features being described which are material to their development. The more lucid the perspective — as in Molière or the Greeks — the more economical and striking the selection.

Modernism drops this selective principle. It asserts that it can dispense with it, or can replace it with its dogma of the *condition humaine*. A naturalistic style is bound to be the result. This state of affairs — which to my mind characterizes all modernist art of the past fifty years — is disguised by critics who systematically glorify the modernist movement. By concentrating on formal criteria, by isolating technique from content and exaggerating its importance, these critics refrain from judgment on the social or artistic significance of subject matter. They are unable, in consequence, to make the aesthetic distinction between *realism* and *naturalism*. This distinction depends on the presence or absence in a work of art of "hierarchy of significance" in the situations and characters presented. Compared with this, formal categories are of secondary importance. That is why it is possible to speak of the basically *naturalistic* character of modernist literature — and to see here the literary expression of an ideological continuity. This is not to deny that variations in style reflect changes in society. But the particular form this principle of naturalistic arbitrariness, this lack of hierarchic structure, may take is not decisive. We encounter it in the all-determining "social conditions" of Naturalism, in Symbolism's impressionist methods and its cultivation of the exotic, in the fragmentation of objective reality in Futurism and Constructivism and the German *Neue Sachlichkeit*,[21] or, again, in Surrealism's stream of consciousness.

These schools have in common a basically static approach to reality. This is closely related to their lack of perspective. Characteristically, Gottfried Benn actually incorporated this in his artistic program. One of his volumes bears the title, *Static Poems*. The denial of history, of development, and thus of perspective, becomes the mark of true insight into the nature of reality.

> The wise man is ignorant
> of change and development
> his children and children's children
> are no part of his world.

The rejection of any concept of the future is for Benn the criterion of wisdom. But even those modernist writers who are less extreme in their

---

[21]New objectivity or impersonality.

rejection of history tend to present social and historical phenomena as static. It is, then, of small importance whether this condition is "eternal," or only a transitional stage punctuated by sudden catastrophes (even in early Naturalism the static presentation was often broken up by these catastrophes, without altering its basic character). Musil, for instance, writes in his essay, *The Writer in our Age:* "One knows just as little about the present. Partly, this is because we are, as always, too close to the present. But it is also because the present into which we were plunged some two decades ago is of a particularly all-embracing and inescapable character." Whether or not Musil knew of Heidegger's philosophy, the idea of *Geworfenheit* is clearly at work here. And the following reveals plainly how, for Musil, this static state was upset by the catastrophe of 1914: "All of a sudden, the world was full of violence. . . . In European civilization, there was a sudden rift. . . ." In short: this static apprehension of reality in modernist literature is no passing fashion; it is rooted in the ideology of modernism.

To establish the basic distinction between modernism and that realism which, from Homer to Thomas Mann and Gorky, has assumed change and development to be the proper subject of literature, we must go deeper into the underlying ideological problem. In *The House of the Dead* Dostoevsky gave an interesting account of the convict's attitude to work. He described how the prisoners, in spite of brutal discipline, loafed about, working badly or merely going through the motions of work until a new overseer arrived and allotted them a new project, after which they were allowed to go home. "The work was hard," Dostoevsky continues, "but, Christ, with what energy they threw themselves into it! Gone was all their former indolence and pretended incompetence." Later in the book Dostoevsky sums up his experiences: "If a man loses hope and has no aim in view, sheer boredom can turn him into a beast. . . ." I have said that the problem of perspective in literature is directly related to the principle of selection. Let me go further: underlying the problem is a profound ethical complex, reflected in the composition of the work itself. Every human action is based on a presupposition of its inherent meaningfulness, at least to the subject. Absence of meaning makes a mockery of action and reduces art to naturalistic description.

Clearly, there can be no literature without at least the appearance of change or development. This conclusion should not be interpreted in a narrowly metaphysical sense. We have already diagnosed the obsession with psychopathology in modernist literature as a desire to escape from the reality of capitalism. But this implies the absolute primacy of the *terminus a quo,* the condition from which it is desired to escape. Any movement towards a *terminus ad quem* is condemned to impotence. As the ideology of most modernist writers asserts the unalterability of outward reality (even if this is reduced to a mere state of consciousness) human activity is, *a priori,* rendered impotent and robbed of meaning.

The apprehension of reality to which this leads is most consistently and convincingly realized in the work of Kafka. Kafka remarks of Josef K., as he is being led to execution: "He thought of flies, their tiny limbs breaking as they struggle away from the fly-paper." This mood of total impotence, of paralysis in the face of the unintelligible power of circumstances, informs all his work. Though the action of *The Castle* takes a different, even an opposite, direction to that of *The Trial,* this view of the world, from the perspective of a trapped and struggling fly, is all-pervasive. This experience, this vision of a world dominated by *angst* and of man at the mercy of incomprehensible terrors, makes Kafka's work the very type of modernist art. Techniques, elsewhere of merely formal significance, are used here to evoke a primitive awe in the presence of an utterly strange and hostile reality. Kafka's *angst* is the experience *par excellence* of modernism.

Two instances from musical criticism — which can afford to be both franker and more theoretical than literary criticism — show that it is indeed a universal experience with which we are dealing. The composer, Hanns Eisler, says of Schönberg: "Long before the invention of the bomber, he expressed what people were to feel in the air raid shelters." Even more characteristic — though seen from a modernist point of view — is Theodor W. Adorno's analysis (in *The Aging of Modern Music*) of symptoms of decadence in modernist music: "The sounds are still the same.

But the experience of *angst,* which made their originals great, has vanished." Modernist music, he continues, has lost touch with the truth that was its *raison d'être.* Composers are no longer equal to the emotional presuppositions of their modernism. And that is why modernist music has failed. The diminution of the original *angst*-obsessed vision of life (whether due, as Adorno thinks, to inability to respond to the magnitude of the horror or, as I believe, to the fact that this obsession with *angst* among bourgeois intellectuals has already begun to recede) has brought about a loss of substance in modern music, and destroyed its authenticity as a modernist art form.

This is a shrewd analysis of the paradoxical situation of the modernist artist, particularly where he is trying to express deep and genuine experience. The deeper the experience, the greater the damage to the artistic whole. But this tendency towards disintegration, this loss of artistic unity, cannot be written off as a mere fashion, the product of experimental gimmicks. Modern philosophy, after all, encountered these problems long before modern literature, painting or music. A case in point is the problem of *time.* Subjective Idealism had already separated time, abstractly conceived, from historical change and particularity of place. As if this separation were insufficient for the new age of imperialism, Bergson widened it further. Experienced time, subjective time, now became identical with real time; the rift between this time and that of the objective world was complete. Bergson and other philosophers, who took up and varied this theme claimed that their concept of time alone afforded insight into authentic, i.e., subjective, reality. The same tendency soon made its appearance in literature.

The German left-wing critic and essayist of the twenties, Walter Benjamin, has well described Proust's vision and the techniques he uses to present it in his great novel: "We all know that Proust does not describe a man's life as it actually happens, but as it is remembered by a man who has lived through it. Yet this puts it far too crudely. For it is not actual experience that is important, but the texture of reminiscence, the Penelope's tapestry of a man's memory." The connection with Bergson's theories of time is obvious. But whereas with Bergson, in the abstraction of philosophy, the unity of perception is preserved, Benjamin shows that with Proust, as a result of the radical disintegration of the time sequence, objectivity is eliminated: "A lived event is finite, concluded at least on the level of experience. But a remembered event is infinite, a possible key to everything that preceded it and to everything that will follow it."

It is the distinction between a philosophical and an artistic vision of the world. However hard philosophy, under the influence of Idealism, tries to liberate the concepts of space and time from temporal and spatial particularity, literature continues to assume their unity. The fact that, nevertheless, the concept of subjective time cropped up in literature only shows how deeply subjectivism is rooted in the experience of the modern bourgeois intellectual. The individual, retreating into himself in despair at the cruelty of the age, may experience an intoxicated fascination with his forlorn condition. But then a new horror breaks through. If reality cannot be understood (or no effort is made to understand it), then the individual's subjectivity — alone in the universe, reflecting only itself — takes on an equally incomprehensible and horrific character. Hugo von Hofmannsthal was to experience this condition very early in his poetic career:

> It is a thing that no man cares to think on,
> And far too terrible for mere complaint,
> That all things slip from us and pass away,
>
> And that my ego, bound by no outward force —
> Once a small child's before it became mine —
> Should now be strange to me, like a strange dog.

By separating time from the outer world of objective reality, the inner world of the subject is transformed into a sinister, inexplicable flux and acquires — paradoxically, as it may seem — a static character.

On literature this tendency towards disintegration, of course, will have an even greater impact than on philosophy. When time is isolated in this way, the artist's world disintegrates into a multiplicity of partial worlds. The static view of the world, now combined with diminished objectivity, here rules unchallenged. The world of man — the only subject matter of literature — is shattered if a single component is removed. I have shown the consequences of isolating time and reducing it to a subjective category. But time is by no means the only component whose removal can lead to such disintegration. Here, again, Hofmannsthal anticipated later developments. His imaginary "Lord Chandos" reflects: "I have lost the ability to concentrate my thoughts or set them out coherently." The result is a condition of apathy, punctuated by manic fits. The development towards a definitely pathological protest is here anticipated — admittedly in glamorous, romantic guise. But it is the same disintegration that is at work.

Previous realistic literature, however violent its criticism of reality, had always assumed the unity of the world it described and seen it as a living whole inseparable from man himself. But the major realists of our time deliberately introduce elements of disintegration into their work — for instance, the subjectivizing of time — and use them to portray the contemporary world more exactly. In this way, the once natural unity becomes a conscious, constructed unity (I have shown elsewhere that the device of the two temporal planes in Thomas Mann's *Doctor Faustus* serves to emphasize its historicity). But in modernist literature the disintegration of the world of man — and consequently the disintegration of personality — coincides with the ideological intention. Thus *angst,* this basic modern experience, this by-product of *Geworfenheit,* has its emotional origin in the experience of a disintegrating society. But it attains its effects by evoking the disintegration of the world of man.

To complete our examination of modernist literature, we must consider for a moment the question of allegory. Allegory is that aesthetic genre which lends itself *par excellence* to a description of man's alienation from objective reality. Allegory is a problematic genre because it rejects that assumption of an immanent meaning to human existence which — however unconscious, however combined with religious concepts of transcendence — is the basis of traditional art. Thus in medieval art we observe a new secularity (in spite of the continued use of religious subjects) triumphing more and more, from the time of Giotto, over the allegorizing of an earlier period.

Certain reservations should be made at this point. First, we must distinguish between literature and the visual arts. In the latter, the limitations of allegory can be the more easily overcome in that transcendental, allegorical subjects can be clothed in an aesthetic immanence (even if of a merely decorative kind) and the rift in reality in some sense be eliminated — we have only to think of Byzantine mosaic art. This decorative element has no real equivalent in literature; it exists only in a figurative sense, and then only as a secondary component. Allegorical art of the quality of Byzantine mosaic is only rarely possible in literature. Secondly, we must bear in mind in examining allegory — and this is of great importance for our argument — a historical distinction: does the concept of transcendence in question contain within itself tendencies towards immanence (as in Byzantine art or Giotto), or is it the product precisely of a rejection of these tendencies?

Allegory, in modernist literature, is clearly of the latter kind. Transcendence implies here, more or less consciously, the negation of any meaning immanent in the world or the life of man. We have already examined the underlying ideological basis of this view and its stylistic consequences. To conclude our analysis, and to establish the allegorical character of modernist literature, I must refer again to the work of one of the finest theoreticians of modernism — to Walter Benjamin. Benjamin's examination of allegory was a product of his researches into German Baroque drama. Benjamin made his analysis of these relatively minor plays the occasion for a general discussion of the aesthetics of allegory. He was asking, in effect, why it is that transcendence, which is the essence of allegory, cannot but destroy aesthetics itself.

Benjamin gives a very contemporary definition of allegory. He does not labor the analogies between modern art and the Baroque (such analogies are tenuous at best, and were much overdone by the fashionable criticism of the time). Rather, he uses the Baroque drama to criticize modernism, imputing the characteristics of the latter to the former. In so doing, Benjamin became the first critic to attempt a philosophical analysis of the aesthetic paradox underlying modernist art. He writes:

In Allegory, the *facies hippocratica* of history looks to the observer like a petrified primeval landscape.

History, all the suffering and failure it contains, finds expression in the human face — or, rather, in the human skull. No sense of freedom, no classical proportion, no human emotion lives in its features — not only human existence in general, but the fate of every individual human being is symbolized in this most palpable token of mortality. This is the core of the allegorical vision, of the Baroque idea of history as the passion of the world; History is significant only in the stations of its corruption. Significance is a function of mortality — because it is death that marks the passage from corruptibility to meaningfulness.

Benjamin returns again and again to this link between allegory and the annihilation of history:

> In the light of this vision history appears, not as the gradual realization of the eternal, but as a process of inevitable decay. Allegory thus goes beyond beauty. What ruins are in the physical world, allegories are in the world of the mind.

Benjamin points here to the aesthetic consequences of modernism — though projected into the Baroque drama — more shrewdly and consistently than any of his contemporaries. He sees that the notion of objective time is essential to any understanding of history, and that the notion of subjective time is a product of a period of decline. "A thorough knowledge of the problematic nature of art" thus becomes for him — correctly, from his point of view — one of the hallmarks of allegory in Baroque drama. It is problematic, on the one hand, because it is an art intent on expressing absolute transcendence that fails to do so because of the means at its disposal. It is also problematic because it is an art reflecting the corruption of the world and bringing about its own dissolution in the process. Benjamin discovers "an immense, anti-aesthetic subjectivity" in Baroque literature, associated with "a theologically-determined subjectivity." (We shall presently show — a point I have discussed elsewhere in relation to Heidegger's philosophy — how in literature a "religious atheism" of this kind can acquire a theological character.) Romantic — and, on a higher plane, Baroque — writers were well aware of this problem, and gave their understanding, not only theoretical, but artistic — that is to say allegorical — expression. "The image," Benjamin remarks, "becomes a rune in the sphere of allegorical intuition. When touched by the light of theology, its symbolic beauty is gone. The false appearance of totality vanishes. The image dies; the parable no longer holds true; the world it once contained disappears."

The consequences for art are far-reaching, and Benjamin does not hesitate to point them out: "Every person, every object, every relationship can stand for something else. This transferability constitutes a devastating, though just, judgment on the profane world — which is thereby branded as a world where such things are of small importance." Benjamin knows, of course, that although details are "transferable," and thus insignificant, they are not banished from art altogether. On the contrary. Precisely in modern art, with which he is ultimately concerned, descriptive detail is often of an extraordinary sensuous, suggestive power — we think again of Kafka. But this, as we showed in the case of Musil (a writer who does not consciously aim at allegory) does not prevent the materiality of the world from undergoing permanent alteration, from becoming transferable and arbitrary. Just this, modernist writers maintain, is typical of their own apprehension of reality. Yet presented in this way, the world becomes, as Benjamin puts it, "exalted and depreciated at the same time." For the conviction that phenomena are *not* ultimately transferable is rooted in a belief in the world's rationality and in man's ability to penetrate its secrets. In realistic literature each descriptive detail is both *individual* and *typical*. Modern allegory, and modernist ideology, however, deny the *typical*. By destroying the coherence of the world, they reduce detail to the level of mere particularity (once again, the connection between modernism and naturalism is plain). Detail, in its allegorical transferability, though brought into a direct, if paradoxical connection with transcendence, becomes an abstract function of the transcendence to which it points. Modernist literature thus replaces concrete typicality with abstract particularity.

We are here applying Benjamin's paradox directly to aesthetics and criticism, and particularly to the aesthetics of modernism. And, though we have reversed his scale of values, we have not deviated from the course of his argument. Elsewhere, he speaks out even more plainly — as though the Baroque mask had fallen, revealing the modernist skull underneath:

> Allegory is left empty-handed. The forces of evil, lurking in its depths, owe their very existence to allegory. Evil is, precisely, the non-existence of that which allegory purports to represent.

The paradox Benjamin arrives at — his investigation of the aesthetics of Baroque tragedy has culminated in a negation of aesthetics — sheds a good deal of light on modernist literature, and particularly on Kafka. In interpreting his writings allegorically I am not, of course, following Max Brod, who finds a specifically religious allegory in Kafka's works. Kafka refuted any such interpretation in a remark he is said to have made to Brod himself: "We are nihilistic figments, all of us; suicidal notions forming in God's mind." Kafka rejected, too, the gnostic concept of God as an evil demiurge: "The world is a cruel whim of God, an evil day's work." When Brod attempted to give this an optimistic slant, Kafka shrugged off the attempt ironically: "Oh, hope enough, hope without end — but not, alas, for us." These remarks, quoted by Benjamin in his brilliant essay on Kafka, point to the general spiritual climate of his work: "His profoundest experience is of the hopelessness, the utter meaninglessness of man's world, and particularly that of present day bourgeois man." Kafka, whether he says so openly or not, is an atheist. An atheist, though, of that modern species who regard God's removal from the scene not as a liberation — as did Epicurus and the Encyclopedists — but as a token of the "God-forsakenness" of the world, its utter desolation of futility. Jacobsen's *Niels Lyhne* was the first novel to describe this state of mind of the atheistic bourgeois intelligentsia. Modern religious atheism is characterized, on the one hand, by the fact that unbelief has lost its revolutionary *élan* — the empty heavens are the projection of a world beyond hope of redemption. On the other hand, religious atheism shows that the desire for salvation lives on with undiminished force in a world without God, worshipping the voice created by God's absence.

The supreme judges in *The Trial,* the castle administration in *The Castle,* represent transcendence in Kafka's allegories: the transcendence of Nothingness. Everything points to them, and they could give meaning to everything. Everybody believes in their existence and omnipotence; but nobody knows them, nobody knows how they can be reached. If there is a God here, it can only be the God of religious atheism: *atheos absconditus.*[22] We become acquainted with a repellent host of subordinate authorities; brutal, corrupt, pedantic — and, at the same time, unreliable and irresponsible. It is a portrait of the bourgeois society Kafka knew, with a dash of Prague local coloring. But it is also allegorical in that the doings of this bureaucracy and of those dependent on it, its impotent victims, are not concrete and realistic, but a reflection of that Nothingness which governs existence. The hidden, nonexistent God of Kafka's world derives his spectral character from the fact that his own non-existence is the ground of all existence; and the portrayed reality, uncannily accurate as it is, is spectral in the shadow of that dependence. The only purpose of transcendence — the intangible *nichtendes Nichts*[23] — is to reveal the *facies hippocratica*[24] of the world.

That abstract particularity which we saw to be the aesthetic consequence of allegory reaches its high mark in Kafka. He is a marvelous observer; the spectral character of reality affects him so deeply that the simplest episodes have an oppressive, nightmarish immediacy. As an artist, he is not content to evoke the surface of life. He is aware that individual detail must point to general significance. But how does he go about the business of abstraction? He has emptied everyday life of meaning by using the allegorical method; he has allowed detail to be annihilated by his transcendental Nothingness. This allegorical transcendence bars Kafka's way to realism, prevents him from investing observed detail with typical significance. Kafka is not able, in spite of his extraordinary evocative power, in spite of his unique sensibility, to achieve that fusion of the particular and the general which is the essence of realistic art. His aim is to raise the individual detail in its immediate particularity (without generalizing its content) to the level of abstraction. Kafka's method is typical,

[22]The departed no-God.
[23]Annihilating nothingness.
[24]Skull beneath the skin.

here, of modernism's allegorical approach. Specific subject matter and stylistic variation do not matter; what matters is the basic ideological determination of form and content. The particularity we find in Beckett and Joyce, in Musil and Benn, various as the treatment of it may be, is essentially of the same kind.

If we combine what we have up to now discussed separately we arrive at a consistent pattern. We see that modernism leads not only to the destruction of traditional literary forms; it leads to the destruction of literature as such. And this is true not only of Joyce, or of the literature of Expressionism and Surrealism. It was not André Gide's ambition, for instance, to bring about a revolution in literary style; it was his philosophy that compelled him to abandon conventional forms. He planned his *Faux-Monnayeurs*[25] as a novel. But its structure suffered from a characteristically modernist schizophrenia: it was supposed to be written by the man who was also the hero of the novel. And, in practice, Gide was forced to admit that no novel, no work of literature could be constructed in that way. We have here a practical demonstration that — as Benjamin showed in another context — modernism means not the enrichment, but the negation of art.

[25]André Gide, *The Counterfeiters* (1949).

Walter Benjamin
1892–1940

It is said that Walter Benjamin, one of the most influential cultural theorists in the Marxist tradition, did not look into Marx's writings until the final decade of his tragically abbreviated life. Benjamin was born in Berlin to a wealthy Jewish family. His studies at Freiburg, Munich, Berlin, and Berne resulted in a doctorate in 1919, but his dissertation on German tragic drama — a brilliant but unorthodox performance completed when he was thirty-three — was rejected by the University of Frankfurt. With a university career closed to him, Benjamin appears to have turned to journalism. From 1925 to 1933 Benjamin made his living mainly with his pen and became friendly with a number of left-wing intellectuals, including Bertolt Brecht. His visit to Moscow in the winter of 1926–27 affirmed his sympathy with the Soviet state, although he never joined the Communist party. When the Nazi seizure of power drove him from Berlin — he emigrated to Paris in 1933 — commissions from the Frankfurt Institute for Social Research enabled him to eke out a living. During these years of exile, he wrote some of his most admired work, including "The Work of Art in the Age of Mechanical Reproduction" (1936). In 1940, Benjamin committed suicide in Port Bou, Spain, in the mistaken belief that his plan to emigrate to America had been thwarted and that he would have to return to Nazi-occupied France. The translation of "The Work of Art in the Age of Mechanical Reproduction" is from the collection Illuminations (1969).

The Work of Art in the Age of Mechanical Reproduction

Our fine arts were developed, their types and uses were established, in times very different from the present, by men whose power of action upon things was insignificant in comparison with ours. But the amazing growth of our techniques, the adaptability and precision they have attained, the ideas and habits they are creating, make it a certainty that profound changes are impending in the ancient craft of the Beautiful. In all the arts there is a physical component which can no longer be considered or treated as it used to be, which cannot remain unaffected by our modern knowledge and power. For the last twenty years neither matter nor space nor time has been what it was from time immemorial. We must expect great innovations to transform the entire technique of the arts, thereby affecting artistic invention itself and perhaps even bringing about an amazing change in our very notion of art.[1]

— PAUL VALÉRY, *Pièces sur l'art*, "La Conquète de l'ubiquité," Paris

PREFACE

When Marx undertook his critique of the capitalistic mode of production, this mode was in its infancy. Marx directed his efforts in such a way as to give them prognostic value. He went back to the basic conditions underlying capitalistic production and through his presentation showed what could be expected of capitalism in the future. The result was that one could expect it not only to exploit the proletariat with increasing intensity, but ultimately to create conditions which would make it possible to abolish capitalism itself.

The transformation of the superstructure, which takes place far more slowly than that of the substructure, has taken more than half a century to manifest in all areas of culture the change in the conditions of production. Only today can it be indicated what form this has taken. Certain prognostic requirements should be met by these statements.

Translated by Harry Zohn.
[1] Quoted from Paul Valéry, "The Conquest of Ubiquity," *Aesthetics,* trans. Ralph Manheim (New York: Pantheon Books, Bollingen Series, 1964), p. 225. [Tr.]

However, theses about the art of the proletariat after its assumption of power or about the art of a classless society would have less bearing on these demands than theses about the developmental tendencies of art under present conditions of production. Their dialectic is no less noticeable in the superstructure than in the economy. It would therefore be wrong to underestimate the value of such theses as a weapon. They brush aside a number of outmoded concepts, such as creativity and genius, eternal value and mystery — concepts whose uncontrolled (and at present almost uncontrollable) application would lead to a processing of data in the Fascist sense. The concepts which are introduced into the theory of art in what follows differ from the more familiar terms in that they are completely useless for the purposes of Fascism. They are, on the other hand, useful for the formulation of revolutionary demands in the politics of art.

I

In principle a work of art has always been reproducible. Manmade artifacts could always be imitated by men. Replicas were made by pupils in practice of their craft, by masters for diffusing their works, and, finally, by third parties in the pursuit of gain. Mechanical reproduction of a work of art, however, represents something new. Historically, it advanced intermittently and in leaps at long intervals, but with accelerated intensity. The Greeks knew only two procedures of technically reproducing works of art: founding and stamping. Bronzes, terra cottas, and coins were the only art works which they could produce in quantity. All others were unique and could not be mechanically reproduced. With the woodcut, graphic art became mechanically reproducible for the first time, long before script became reproducible by print. The enormous changes which printing, the mechanical reproduction of writing, has brought about in literature are a familiar story. However, within the phenomenon which we are here examining from the perspective of world history, print is merely a special, though particularly important, case. During the Middle Ages engraving and etching were added to the woodcut; at the beginning of the nineteenth century lithography made its appearance.

With lithography the technique of reproduction reached an essentially new stage. This much more direct process was distinguished by the tracing of the design of a stone rather than its incision on a block of wood or its etching on a copperplate and permitted graphic art for the first time to put its products on the market, not only in large numbers as hitherto, but also in daily changing forms. Lithography enabled graphic art to illustrate everyday life, and it began to keep pace with printing. But only a few decades after its invention, lithography was surpassed by photography. For the first time in the process of pictorial reproduction, photography freed the hand of the most important artistic functions which henceforth devolved only upon the eye looking into a lens. Since the eye perceives more swiftly than the hand can draw, the process of pictorial reproduction was accelerated so enormously that it could keep pace with speech. A film operator shooting a scene in the studio captures the images at the speed of an actor's speech. Just as lithography virtually implied the illustrated newspaper, so did photography foreshadow the sound film. The technical reproduction of sound was tackled at the end of the last century. These convergent endeavors made predictable a situation which Paul Valéry pointed up in this sentence: "Just as water, gas, and electricity are brought into our houses from far off to satisfy our needs in response to a minimal effort, so we shall be supplied with visual or auditory images, which will appear and disappear at a simple movement of the hand, hardly more than a sign." Around 1900 technical reproduction had reached a standard that not only permitted it to reproduce all transmitted works of art and thus to cause the most profound change in their impact upon the public; it also had captured a place of its own among the artistic processes. For the study of this standard nothing is more revealing than the nature of the repercussions that these two different manifestations — the reproduction of works of art and the

art of the film — have had on art in its traditional form.

II

Even the most perfect reproduction of a work of art is lacking in one element: its presence in time and space, its unique existence at the place where it happens to be. This unique existence of the work of art determined the history to which it was subject throughout the time of its existence. This includes the changes which it may have suffered in physical condition over the years as well as the various changes in its ownership.[2] The traces of the first can be revealed only by chemical or physical analyses which it is impossible to perform on a reproduction; changes of ownership are subject to a tradition which must be traced from the situation of the original.

The presence of the original is the prerequisite of the concept of authenticity. Chemical analyses of the patina of a bronze can help to establish this, as does the proof that a given manuscript of the Middle Ages stems from an archive of the fifteenth century. The whole sphere of authenticity is outside technical — and, of course, not only technical — reproducibility.[3] Confronted with its manual reproduction, which was usually branded as a forgery, the original preserved all its authority; not so vis à vis technical reproduction. The reason is twofold. First, process reproduction is more independent of the original than manual reproduction. For example, in photography, process reproduction can bring out those aspects

[2]Of course, the history of a work of art encompasses more than this. The history of the Mona Lisa, for instance, encompasses the kind and number of its copies made in the seventeenth, eighteenth, and nineteenth centuries. [Benjamin]

[3]Precisely because authenticity is not reproducible, the intensive penetration of certain (mechanical) processes of reproduction was instrumental in differentiating and grading authenticity. To develop such differentiations was an important function to the trade in works of art. The invention of the woodcut may be said to have struck at the root of the quality of authenticity even before its late flowering. To be sure, at the time of its origin a medieval picture of the Madonna could not yet be said to be "authentic." It became "authentic" only during the succeeding centuries and perhaps most strikingly so during the last one. [Benjamin]

of the original that are unattainable to the naked eye yet accessible to the lens, which is adjustable and chooses its angle at will. And photographic reproduction, with the aid of certain processes, such as enlargement or slow motion, can capture images which escape natural vision. Secondly, technical reproduction can put the copy of the original into situations which would be out of reach for the original itself. Above all, it enables the original to meet the beholder halfway, be it in the form of a photograph or a phonograph record. The cathedral leaves its locale to be received in the studio of a lover of art; the choral production, performed in an auditorium or in the open air, resounds in the drawing room.

The situations into which the product of mechanical reproduction can be brought may not touch the actual work of art, yet the quality of its presence is always depreciated. This holds not only for the art work but also, for instance, for a landscape which passes in review before the spectator in a movie. In the case of the art object, a most sensitive nucleus — namely, its authenticity — is interfered with whereas no natural object is vulnerable on that score. The authenticity of a thing is the essence of all that is transmissible from its beginning, ranging from its substantive duration to its testimony to the history which it has experienced. Since the historical testimony rests on the authenticity, the former too, is jeopardized by reproduction when substantive duration ceases to matter. And what is really jeopardized when the historical testimony is affected is the authority of the object.[4]

One might subsume the eliminated element in the term "aura" and go on to say: that which withers in the age of mechanical reproduction is the aura of the work of art. This is a symptomatic process whose significance points beyond the realm of art. One might generalize by saying: the technique of reproduction detaches the reproduced object from the domain of tradition. By making many reproductions it substitutes a plurality of copies for a unique existence. And in permitting the reproduction to meet the beholder or listener in his own particular situation, it reactivates the object reproduced. These two processes lead to a tremendous shattering of tradition which is the obverse of the contemporary crisis and renewal of mankind. Both processes are intimately connected with the contemporary mass movements. Their most powerful agent is the film. Its social significance, particularly in its most positive form, is inconceivable without its destructive, cathartic aspect, that is, the liquidation of the traditional value of the cultural heritage. This phenomenon is most palpable in the great historical films. It extends to ever new positions. In 1927 Abel Gance exclaimed enthusiastically: "Shakespeare, Rembrandt, Beethoven will make films . . . all legends, all mythologies and all myths, all founders of religion, and the very religions . . . await their exposed resurrection, and the heroes crowd each other at the gate."[5] Presumably without intending it, he issued an invitation to a far-reaching liquidation.

III

During long periods of history, the mode of human sense perception changes with humanity's entire mode of existence. The manner in which human sense perception is organized, the medium in which it is accomplished, is determined not only by nature but by historical circumstances as well. The fifth century, with its great shifts of population, saw the birth of the late Roman art industry and the Vienna Genesis, and there developed not only an art different from that of antiquity but also a new kind of perception. The scholars of the Viennese school, Riegl and Wickhoff, who resisted the weight of classical tradition under which these later art forms had been buried, were the first to draw conclusions from them concerning the organization of perception at the time. However far-reaching their insight, these scholars limited themselves to showing the significant, formal

[4]The poorest provincial staging of *Faust* is superior to a Faust film in that, ideally, it competes with the first performance at Weimar. Before the screen it is unprofitable to remember traditional contents which might come to mind before the stage — for instance, that Goethe's friend Johann Heinrich Merck is hidden in Mephisto, and the like. [Benjamin]

[5]Abel Gance, "Le Temps de l'image est venu," *L'Art Cinématographique* 2 (Paris, 1927): 94–95. [Tr.] Gance was the director of the epic film *Napoleon* (1927).

hallmark which characterized perception in late Roman times. They did not attempt — and, perhaps, saw no way — to show the social transformations expressed by these changes of perception. The conditions for an analogous insight are more favorable in the present. And if changes in the medium of contemporary perception can be comprehended as decay of the aura, it is possible to show its social causes.

The concept of aura which was proposed above with reference to historical objects may usefully be illustrated with reference to the aura of natural ones. We define the aura of the latter as the unique phenomenon of a distance, however close it may be. If, while resting on a summer afternoon, you follow with your eyes a mountain range on the horizon or a branch which casts its shadows over you, you experience the aura of those mountains, of that branch. This image makes it easy to comprehend the social bases of the contemporary decay of the aura. It rests on two circumstances, both of which are related to the increasing significance of the masses in contemporary life. Namely, the desire of contemporary masses to bring things "closer" spatially and humanly, which is just as ardent as their bent toward overcoming the uniqueness of every reality by accepting its reproduction.[6] Every day the urge grows stronger to get hold of an object at very close range by way of its likeness, its reproduction. Unmistakably, reproduction as offered by picture magazines and newsreels differs from the image seen by the unarmed eye. Uniqueness and permanence are as closely linked in the latter as are transitoriness and reproducibility in the former. To pry an object from its shell, to destroy its aura, is the mark of a perception whose "sense of the universal equality of things" has increased to such a degree that it extracts it even from a unique object by means of reproduction. Thus is manifested in the field of perception what in the

theoretical sphere is noticeable in the increasing importance of statistics. The adjustment of reality to the masses and of the masses to reality is a process of unlimited scope, as much for thinking as for perception.

IV

The uniqueness of a work of art is inseparable from its being imbedded in the fabric of tradition. This tradition itself is thoroughly alive and extremely changeable. An ancient statue of Venus, for example, stood in a different traditional context with the Greeks, who made it an object of veneration, than with the clerics of the Middle Ages, who viewed it as an ominous idol. Both of them, however, were equally confronted with its uniqueness, that is, its aura. Originally the contextual integration of art in tradition found its expression in the cult. We know that the earliest art works originated in the service of a ritual — first the magical, then the religious kind. It is significant that the existence of the work of art with reference to its aura is never entirely separated from its ritual function.[7] In other words, the unique value of the "authentic" work of art has its basis in ritual, the location of its original use value. This ritualistic basis, however remote, is still recognizable as secularized ritual even in the most profane forms of the cult of beauty.[8] The secular cult of beauty, developed during the

[6]To satisfy the human interest of the masses may mean to have one's social function removed from the field of vision. Nothing guarantees that a portraitist of today, when painting a famous surgeon at the breakfast table in the midst of his family, depicts his social function more precisely than a painter of the seventeenth century who portrayed his medical doctors as representing this profession, like Rembrandt in his *Anatomy Lesson*. [Benjamin]

[7]The definition of the aura as a "unique phenomenon of a distance however close it may be" represents nothing but the formulation of the cult value of the work of art in categories of space and time perception. Distance is the opposite of closeness. The essentially distant object is the unapproachable one. Unapproachability is indeed a major quality of the cult image. True to its nature, it remains "distant, however close it may be." The closeness which one may gain from its subject matter does not impair the distance which it retains in its appearance. [Benjamin]

[8]To the extent to which the cult value of the painting is secularized, the ideas of its fundamental uniqueness lose distinctness. In the imagination of the beholder the uniqueness of the phenomena which hold sway in the cult image is more and more displaced by the empirical uniqueness of the creator or of his creative achievement. To be sure, never completely so; the concept of authenticity always transcends mere genuineness. (This is particularly apparent in the collector who always retains some traces of the fetishist and who, by owning the work of art, shares in its ritual power.) Nevertheless, the function of the concept of authenticity remains determinate in the

Renaissance and prevailing for three centuries, clearly showed that ritualistic basis in its decline and the first deep crisis which befell it. With the advent of the first truly revolutionary means of reproduction, photography, simultaneously with the rise of socialism, art sensed the approaching crisis which has become evident a century later. At the time, art reacted with the doctrine of *l'art pour l'art*,[9] that is, with a theology of art. This gave rise to what might be called a negative theology in the form of the idea of "pure" art, which not only denied any social function of art but also any categorizing by subject matter. (In poetry, Mallarmé was the first to take this position.)

An analysis of art in the age of mechanical reproduction must do justice to these relationships, for they lead us to an all-important insight: for the first time in world history, mechanical reproduction emancipates the work of art from its parasitical dependence on ritual. To an ever greater degree the work of art reproduced becomes the work of art designed for reproducibility.[10] From a photographic

evaluation of art; with the secularization of art, authenticity displaces the cult value of the work. [Benjamin]

[9]Art for art's sake.

[10]In the case of films, mechanical reproduction is not, as with literature and painting, an external condition for mass distribution. Mechanical reproduction is inherent in the very technique of film production. This technique not only permits in the most direct way but virtually causes mass distribution. It enforces distribution because the production of a film is so expensive that an individual who, for instance, might afford to buy a painting no longer can afford to buy a film. In 1927 it was calculated that a major film, in order to pay its way, had to reach an audience of nine million. With the sound film, to be sure, a setback in its international distribution occurred at first: audiences became limited by language barriers. This coincided with the Fascist emphasis on national interests. It is more important to focus on this connection with Fascism than on this setback, which was soon minimized by synchronization. The simultaneity of both phenomena is attributable to the depression. The same disturbances which, on a larger scale, led to an attempt to maintain the existing property structure by sheer force led the endangered film capital to speed up the development of the sound film. The introduction of the sound film brought about a temporary relief, not only because it again brought the masses into the theaters but also because it merged new capital from the electrical industry with that of the film industry. Thus, viewed from the outside, the sound film promoted national interests, but seen from the inside it helped to internationalize film production even more than previously. [Benjamin]

negative, for example, one can make any number of prints; to ask for the "authentic" print makes no sense. But the instant the criterion of authenticity ceases to be applicable to artistic production, the total function of art is reversed. Instead of being based on ritual, it begins to be based on another practice — politics.

V

Works of art are received and valued on different planes. Two polar types stand out: with one, the accent is on the cult value; with the other, on the exhibition value of the work.[11] Artistic production

[11]This polarity cannot come into its own in the aesthetics of Idealism. Its idea of beauty comprises these polar opposites without differentiating between them and consequently excludes their polarity. Yet in Hegel this polarity announces itself as clearly as possible within the limits of Idealism. We quote from his *Philosophy of History:*

> Images were known of old. Piety at an early time required them for worship, but it could do without *beautiful* images. These might even be disturbing. In every beautiful painting there is also something nonspiritual, merely external, but its spirit speaks to man through its beauty. Worshipping, conversely, is concerned with the work as an object, for it is but a spiritless stupor of the soul. . . . Fine art has arisen . . . in the church . . . , although it has already gone beyond its principle as art.

Likewise, the following passage from *The Philosophy of Fine Art* indicates that Hegel sensed a problem here.

> We are beyond the stage of reverence for works of art as divine and objects deserving our worship. The impression they produce is one of a more reflective kind, and the emotions they arouse require a higher test. . . . — G. W. F. Hegel, *The Philosophy of Fine Arts,* trans., with notes, by F. P. B. Osmaston, vol. 1 (London, 1920), p. 12.

The transition from the first kind of artistic reception to the second characterizes the history of artistic reception in general. Apart from that, a certain oscillation between these two polar modes of reception can be demonstrated for each work of art. Take the Sistine Madonna. Since Hubert Grimme's research it has been known that the Madonna originally was painted for the purpose of exhibition. Grimme's research was inspired by the question: What is the purpose of the molding in the foreground of the painting which the two cupids lean upon? How, Grimme asked further, did Raphael come to furnish the sky with two draperies? Research proved that the Madonna had been commissioned for the public lying-in-state of Pope Sixtus. The Popes lay in state in a certain side chapel of St. Peter's. On that occasion Raphael's picture had been fastened in a nichelike background of the begins with ceremonial objects destined to serve in a cult. One may assume that what mattered was their existence, not their being on view. The elk portrayed by the man of the Stone Age on the walls of his cave was an instrument of magic. He did expose it to his fellow men, but in the main it was meant for the spirits. Today the cult value would seem to demand that the work of art remain hidden. Certain statues of gods are accessible only to the priest in the cella;[12] certain Madonnas remain covered nearly all year round; certain sculptures on medieval cathedrals are invisible to the spectator on ground level. With the emancipation of the various art practices from ritual go increasing opportunities for the exhibition of their products. It is easier to exhibit a portrait bust that can be sent here and there than to exhibit the statue of divinity that has its fixed place in the interior of a temple. The same holds for the painting as against the mosaic or fresco that preceded it. And even though the public presentability of a mass originally may have been just as great as that of a symphony, the latter originated at the moment when its public presentability promised to surpass that of the mass.

With the different methods of technical reproduction of a work of art, its fitness for exhibition increased to such an extent that the quantitative shift between its two poles turned into a qualitative transformation of its nature. This is comparable to the situation of the work of art in prehistoric times when, by the absolute emphasis on its cult value, it was, first and foremost, an instrument of magic. Only later did it come to be recognized as a work of art. In the same way today, by the absolute emphasis on its exhibition value the work of art becomes a creation with entirely new functions, among which the one we are conscious of, the artistic function, later may be recognized as incidental.[13] This much is certain: today photography and the film are the most serviceable exemplifications of this new function.

VI

In photography, exhibition value begins to displace cult value all along the line. But cult value does not give way without resistance. It retires into an ultimate retrenchment: the human countenance. It is no accident that the portrait was the focal point of early photography. The cult of remembrance of loved ones, absent or dead, offers a last refuge for the cult value of the picture. For the last time the aura emanates from the early photographs in the fleeting expression of a human face. This is what constitutes their melancholy, incomparable beauty. But as man withdraws from the photographic image, the exhibition value for the first time shows its superiority to the ritual value. To have pinpointed this new stage constitutes the incomparable significance of Atget,[14] who, around 1900, took photographs of deserted Paris streets. It has quite justly been said of him that he photographed them like scenes of crime. The scene of a crime, too, is deserted; it is photographed for the purpose of establishing evidence. With Atget, photographs become standard evidence for historical occurrences, and acquire

---

chapel, supported by the coffin. In this picture Raphael portrays the Madonna approaching the papal coffin in clouds from the background of the niche, which was demarcated by green drapes. At the obsequies of Sixtus a preeminent exhibition value of Raphael's picture was taken advantage of. Some time later it was placed on the high altar in the church of the Black Friars at Piacenza. The reason for this exile is to be found in the Roman rites which forbid the use of paintings exhibited at obsequies as cult objects on the high altar. This regulation devalued Raphael's picture to some degree. In order to obtain an adequate price nevertheless, the Papal See resolved to add to the bargain the tacit toleration of the picture above the high altar. To avoid attention the picture was given to the monks of the far-off provincial town. [Benjamin]

[12]Cell (prison or monastic).

[13]Bertolt Brecht, on a different level, engaged in analogous reflections: "If the concept of 'work of art' can no longer be applied to the thing that emerges once the work is transformed into a commodity, we have to eliminate this concept with cautious care but without fear, lest we liquidate the function of the very thing as well. For it has to go through this phase without mental reservation, and not as noncommittal deviation from the straight path; rather, what happens here with the work of art will change it fundamentally and erase its past to such an extent that should the old concept be taken up again — and it will, why not? — it will no longer stir any memory of the thing it once designated." [Benjamin]

[14]Jean-Eugène-August Atget (1857–1927), Parisian photographer.

a hidden political significance. They demand a specific kind of approach; free-floating contemplation is not appropriate to them. They stir the viewer; he feels challenged by them in a new way. At the same time picture magazines begin to put up signposts for him, right ones or wrong ones, no matter. For the first time, captions have become obligatory. And it is clear that they have an altogether different character than the title of a painting. The directives which the captions give to those looking at pictures in illustrated magazines soon become even more explicit and more imperative in the film where the meaning of each single picture appears to be prescribed by the sequence of all preceding ones.

VII

The nineteenth-century dispute as to the artistic value of painting versus photography today seems devious and confused. This does not diminish its importance, however; if anything, it underlines it. The dispute was, in fact, the symptom of a historical transformation the universal impact of which was not realized by either of the rivals. When the age of mechanical reproduction separated art from its basis in cult, the semblance of its autonomy disappeared forever. The resulting change in the function of art transcended the perspective of the century; for a long time it even escaped that of the twentieth century, which experienced the development of the film.

Earlier much futile thought had been devoted to the question of whether photography is an art. The primary question — whether the very invention of photograph had not transformed the entire nature of art — was not raised. Soon the film theoreticians asked the same ill-considered question with regard to the film. But the difficulties which photography caused traditional aesthetics were mere child's play as compared to those raised by the film. Whence the insensitive and forced character of early theories of the film. Abel Gance, for instance, compares the film with hieroglyphs: "Here, by a remarkable regression, we have come back to the level of expression of the Egyptians. . . . Pictorial language has not yet matured because our eyes have not yet adjusted to it. There is as yet insufficient respect for,

insufficient cult of, what it expresses."[15] Or, in the words of Séverin-Mars: "What art has been granted a dream more poetical and more real at the same time! Approached in this fashion the film might represent an incomparable means of expression. Only the most high-minded persons, in the most perfect and mysterious moments of their lives, should be allowed to enter its ambience."[16] Alexandre Arnoux concludes his fantasy about the silent film with the question: "Do not all the bold descriptions we have given amount to the definition of prayer?"[17] It is instructive to note how their desire to class the film among the "arts" forces these theoreticians to read ritual elements into it — with a striking lack of discretion. Yet when these speculations were published, films like *L'Opinion publique* and *The Gold Rush* had already appeared. This, however, did not keep Abel Gance from adducing hieroglyphs for purposes of comparison, nor Séverin-Mars from speaking of the film as one might speak of paintings by Fra Angelico. Characteristically, even today ultrareactionary authors give the film a similar contextual significance — if not an outright sacred one, then at least a supernatural one. Commenting on Max Reinhardt's film version of *A Midsummer Night's Dream,* Werfel states that undoubtedly it was the sterile copying of the exterior world with its streets, interiors, railroad stations, restaurants, motorcars, and beaches which until now had obstructed the elevation of the film to the realm of art. "The film has not yet realized its true meaning, its real possibilities . . . these consist in its unique faculty to express by natural means and with incomparable persuasiveness all that is fairylike, marvelous, supernatural."[18]

VIII

The artistic performance of a stage actor is definitely presented to the public by the actor in person; that of the screen actor, however, is

[15] Abel Gance, pp. 100–101. [Tr.]
[16] Séverin-Mars, quoted by Abel Gance, p. 100. [Tr.]
[17] Alexandre Arnoux, *Cinéma pris* (1929), p. 28. [Tr.]
[18] Franz Werfel, "Einsommersnachtstraum, Ein Film von Shakespeare und Reinhardt," *Neues Wiener Journal,* cited in *Lu* (November 1935). [Tr.]

presented by a camera, with a twofold consequence. The camera that presents the performance of the film actor to the public need not respect the performance as an integral whole. Guided by the cameraman, the camera continually changes its position with respect to the performance. The sequence of positional views which the editor composes from the material supplied him constitutes the completed film. It comprises certain factors of movement which are in reality those of the camera, not to mention special camera angles, close-ups, etc. Hence, the performance of the actor is subjected to a series of optical tests. This is the first consequence of the fact that the actor's performance is presented by means of a camera. Also, the film actor lacks the opportunity of the stage actor to adjust to the audience during his performance, since he does not present his performance to the audience in person. This permits the audience to take the position of a critic, without experiencing any personal contact with the actor. The audience's identification with the actor is really an identification with the camera. Consequently the audience takes the position of the camera; its approach is that of testing.[19] This is not the approach to which cult values may be exposed.

IX

For the film, what matters primarily is that the actor represents himself to the public before the camera, rather than representing someone else.

[19]"The film ... provides — or could provide — useful insight into the details of human actions.... Character is never used as a source of motivation; the inner life of the persons never supplies the principal cause of the plot and seldom is its main result." (Bertolt Brecht, "Der Dreigroschenprozess," *Versuche*, p. 268.) The expansion of the field of the testable which mechanical equipment brings about for the actor corresponds to the extraordinary expansion of the field of the testable brought about for the individual through economic conditions. Thus, vocational aptitude tests become constantly more important. What matters in these tests are segmental performances of the individual. The film shot and the vocational aptitude test are taken before a committee of experts. The camera director in the studio occupies a place identical with that of the examiner during aptitude tests. [Benjamin]

One of the first to sense the actor's metamorphosis by this form of testing was Pirandello. Though his remarks on the subject in his novel *Si Gira* were limited to the negative aspects of the question and to the silent film only, this hardly impairs their validity. For in this respect, the sound film did not change anything essential. What matters is that the part is acted not for an audience but for a mechanical contrivance — in the case of the sound film, for two of them. "The film actor," wrote Pirandello, "feels as if in exile — exiled not only from the stage but also from himself. With a vague sense of discomfort he feels inexplicable emptiness: his body loses its corporeality, it evaporates, it is deprived of reality, life, voice, and the noises caused by his moving about, in order to be changed into a mute image, flickering an instant on the screen, then vanishing into silence.... The projector will play with his shadow before the public, and he himself must be content to play before the camera."[20] This situation might also be characterized as follows: for the first time — and this is the effect of the film — man has to operate with his whole living person, yet forgoing its aura. For aura is tied to his presence; there can be no replica of it. The aura which, on the stage, emanates from Macbeth, cannot be separated for the spectators from that of the actor. However, the singularity of the shot in the studio is that the camera is substituted for the public. Consequently, the aura that envelops the actor vanishes, and with it the aura of the figure he portrays.

It is not surprising that it should be a dramatist such as Pirandello who, in characterizing the film, inadvertently touches on the very crisis in which we see the theater. Any thorough study proves that there is indeed no greater contrast than that of the stage play to a work of art that is completely subject to or, like the film, founded in, mechanical reproduction. Experts have long recognized that in the film "the greatest effects are almost always obtained by 'acting' as little as possible...." In 1932 Rudolf Arnheim saw "the

[20]Luigi Pirandello, *Si Gira*, quoted by Léon Pierre-Quint, "Signification du cinéma," *L'Art cinématographique*, pp. 14–15. [Tr.]

latest trend . . . in treating the actor as a stage prop chosen for its characteristics and . . . inserted at the proper place."[21] With this idea something else is closely connected. The stage actor identifies himself with the character of his role. The film actor very often is denied this opportunity. His creation is by no means all of a piece; it is composed of many separate performances. Besides certain fortuitous considerations, such as cost of studio, availability of fellow players, décor, etc., there are elementary necessities of equipment that split the actor's work into a series of mountable episodes. In particular, lighting and its installation require the presentation of an event that, on the screen, unfolds as a rapid and unified scene, in a sequence of separate shootings which may take hours at the studio; not to mention more obvious montage. Thus a jump from the window can be shot in the studio as a jump from a scaffold, and the ensuing flight, if need be, can be shot weeks later when outdoor scenes are taken. Far more

[21]Rudolf Arnheim, *Film als Kunst* (Berlin, 1932), pp. 176 f. In this context certain seemingly unimportant details in which the film director deviates from stage practices gain in interest. Such is the attempt to let the actor play without makeup, as made among others by Dreyer in his *Jeanne d'Arc*. Dreyer spent months seeking the forty actors who constitute the Inquisitors' tribunal. The search for these actors resembled that for stage properties that are hard to come by. Dreyer made every effort to avoid resemblances of age, build, and physiognomy. If the actor thus becomes a stage property, this latter, on the other hand, frequently functions as actor. At least it is not unusual for the film to assign a role to the stage property. Instead of choosing at random from a great wealth of examples, let us concentrate on a particularly convincing one. A clock that is working will always be a disturbance on the stage. There it cannot be permitted its function of measuring time. Even in a naturalistic play, astronomical time would clash with theatrical time. Under these circumstances, it is highly revealing that the film can, whenever appropriate, use time as measured by a clock. From this more than from many other touches it may clearly be recognized that under certain circumstances each and every prop in a film may assume important functions. From here it is but one step to Pudovkin's statement that "the playing of an actor which is connected with an object and is built around it . . . is always one of the strongest methods of cinematic construction." (W. Pudovkin, *Filmregie und Filmmanuskript* [Berlin, 1928], p. 126.) The film is the first art form capable of demonstrating how matter plays tricks on man. Hence, films can be an excellent means of materialistic representation. [Benjamin]

paradoxical cases can easily be construed. Let us assume that an actor is supposed to be startled by a knock at the door. If his reaction is not satisfactory, the director can resort to an expedient: when the actor happens to be at the studio again he has a shot fired behind him without his being forewarned of it. The frightened reaction can be shot now and be cut into the screen version. Nothing more strikingly shows that art has left the realm of the "beautiful semblance" which, so far, had been taken to be the only sphere where art could thrive.

X

The feeling of strangeness that overcomes the actor before the camera, as Pirandello describes it, is basically of the same kind as the estrangement felt before one's own image in the mirror. But now the reflected image has become separable, transportable. And where is it transported? Before the public.[22] Never for a moment does the screen actor cease to be conscious of this fact. While facing the camera he knows that ultimately he will face the public, the consumers who constitute the market. This market, where he offers not only his labor but also his whole self, his heart and soul, is beyond his reach. During the shooting he has as little contact with it as any article made

[22]The change noted here in the method of exhibition caused by mechanical reproduction applies to politics as well. The present crisis of the bourgeois democracies comprises a crisis of the conditions which determine the public presentation of the rulers. Democracies exhibit a member of government directly and personally before the nation's representatives. Parliament is his public. Since the innovations of camera and recording equipment make it possible for the orator to become audible and visible to an unlimited number of persons, the presentation of the man of politics before camera and recording equipment becomes paramount. Parliaments, as much as theaters, are deserted. Radio and film not only affect the function of the professional actor but likewise the function of those who also exhibit themselves before this mechanical equipment, those who govern. Though their tasks may be different, the change affects equally the actor and the ruler. The trend is toward establishing controllable and transferrable skills under certain social conditions. This results in a new selection, a selection before the equipment from which the star and the dictator emerge victorious. [Benjamin]

in a factory. This may contribute to that oppression, that new anxiety which, according to Pirandello, grips the actor before the camera. The film responds to the shriveling of the aura with an artificial build-up of the "personality" outside the studio. The cult of the movie star, fostered by the money of the film industry, preserves not the unique aura of the person but the "spell of the personality," the phony spell of a commodity. So long as the movie-makers' capital sets the fashion, as a rule no other revolutionary merit can be accredited to today's film than the promotion of a revolutionary criticism of traditional concepts of art. We do not deny that in some cases today's films can also promote revolutionary criticism of social conditions, even of the distribution of property. However, our present study is no more specifically concerned with this than is the film production of Western Europe.

It is inherent in the technique of the film as well as that of sports that everybody who witnesses its accomplishments is somewhat of an expert. This is obvious to anyone listening to a group of newspaper boys leaning on their bicycles and discussing the outcome of a bicycle race. It is not for nothing that newspaper publishers arrange races for their delivery boys. These arouse great interest among the participants, for the victor has an opportunity to rise from delivery boy to professional racer. Similarly, the newsreel offers everyone the opportunity to rise from passer-by to movie extra. In this way any man might even find himself part of a work of art, as witness Vertoff's *Three Songs About Lenin* or Ivens's *Borinage*. Any man today can lay claim to being filmed. This claim can best be elucidated by a comparative look at the historical situation of contemporary literature.

For centuries a small number of writers were confronted by many thousands of readers. This changed toward the end of the last century. With the increasing extension of the press, which kept placing new political, religious, scientific, professional, and local organs before the readers, an increasing number of readers became writers — at first, occasional ones. It began with the daily press opening to its readers space for "letters to the editor." And today there is hardly a gainfully employed European who could not, in principle, find an opportunity to publish somewhere or other comments on his work, grievances, documentary reports, or that sort of thing. Thus, the distinction between author and public is about to lose its basic character. The difference becomes merely functional; it may vary from case to case. At any moment the reader is ready to turn into a writer. As expert, which he had to become willy-nilly in an extremely specialized work process, even if only in some minor respect, the reader gains access to authorship. In the Soviet Union work itself is given a voice. To present it verbally is part of a man's ability to perform the work. Literary license is now founded on polytechnic rather than specialized training and thus becomes common property.[23]

[23]The privileged character of the respective techniques is lost. Aldous Huxley writes:

Advances in technology have led ... to vulgarity.... Process reproduction and the rotary press have made possible the indefinite multiplication of writing and pictures. Universal education and relatively high wages have created an enormous public who know how to read and can afford to buy reading and pictorial matter. A great industry has been called into existence in order to supply these commodities. Now, artistic talent is a very rare phenomenon; whence it follows ... that, at every epoch and in all countries, most art has been bad. But the proportion of trash in the total artistic output is greater now than at any other period. That it must be so is a matter of simple arithmetic. The population of Western Europe has a little more than doubled during the last century. But the amount of reading — and seeing — matter has increased, I should imagine, at least twenty and possibly fifty or even a hundred times. If there were n men of talent in a population of x millions, there will presumably be 2n men of talent among 2x millions. The situation may be summed up thus. For every page of print and pictures published a century ago, twenty or perhaps even a hundred pages are published today. But for every man of talent then living, there are now only two men of talent. It may be of course that, thanks to universal education, many potential talents which in the past would have been stillborn are now enabled to realize themselves. Let us assume, then, that there are now three or even four men of talent to every one of earlier times. It still remains true to say that the consumption of reading — and seeing—matter has far outstripped the natural production of gifted writers and draughtsmen. It is the same with hearing-matter. Prosperity, the gramophone and the radio have created an audience of hearers who consume an amount of hearing-matter that has increased out of all proportion to the increase of population and the consequent natural increase of talented musicians. It follows from all this that in all

All this can easily be applied to the film, where transitions that in literature took centuries have come about in a decade. In cinematic practice, particularly in Russia, this changeover has partially become established reality. Some of the players whom we meet in Russian films are not actors in our sense but people who portray *themselves* — and primarily in their own work process. In Western Europe the capitalistic exploitation of the film denies consideration to modern man's legitimate claim to being reproduced. Under these circumstances the film industry is trying hard to spur the interest of the masses through illusion-promoting spectacles and dubious speculations.

XI

The shooting of a film, especially of a sound film, affords a spectacle unimaginable anywhere at any time before this. It presents as process in which it is impossible to assign to a spectator a viewpoint which would exclude from the actual scene such extraneous accessories as camera equipment, lighting machinery, staff assistants, etc. — unless his eye were on a line parallel with the lens. This circumstance, more than any other, renders superficial and insignificant any possible similarity between a scene in the studio and one on the stage. In the theater one is well aware of the place from which the play cannot immediately be detected as illusionary. There is no such place for the movie scene that is being shot. Its illusionary nature is that of the second degree, the result of cutting. That is to say, in the studio the mechanical equipment has penetrated so deeply into reality that its pure aspect freed from the foreign substance of equipment is the result of a special procedure, namely, the shooting by the specially adjusted camera and the mounting of the shot

together with other similar ones. The equipment-free aspect of reality here has become the height of artifice; the sight of immediate reality has become an orchid in the land of technology.

Even more revealing is the comparison of these circumstances, which differ so much from those of the theater, with the situation in painting. Here the question is: How does the cameraman compare with the painter? To answer this we take recourse to an analogy with a surgical operation. The surgeon represents the polar opposite of the magician. The magician heals a sick person by the laying on of hands; the surgeon cuts into the patient's body. The magician maintains the natural distance between the patient and himself; though he reduces it very slightly by the laying on of hands, he greatly increases it by virtue of his authority. The surgeon does exactly the reverse; he greatly diminishes the distance between himself and the patient by penetrating into the patient's body, and increases it but little by the caution with which his hand moves among the organs. In short, in contrast to the magician — who is still hidden in the medical practitioner — the surgeon at the decisive moment abstains from facing the patient man to man; rather, it is through the operation that he penetrates into him.

Magician and surgeon compare to painter and cameraman. The painter maintains in his work a natural distance from reality, the cameraman penetrates deeply into its web.[24] There is a tremendous difference between the pictures they obtain. That of the painter is a total one, that of the cameraman consists of multiple fragments which are

---

the arts the output of trash is both absolutely and relatively greater than it was in the past; and that it must remain greater for just so long as the world continues to consume the present inordinate quantities of reading-matter, seeing-matter, and hearing-matter. — Aldous Huxley, *Beyond the Mexique Bay. A Traveller's Journal* (London, 1949), pp. 274 ff. First published in 1934.

This mode of observation is obviously not progressive. [Benjamin]

[24]The boldness of the cameraman is indeed comparable to that of the surgeon. Luc Durtain lists among specific technical sleights of hand those "which are required in surgery in the case of certain difficult operations. I choose as an example a case from oto-rhino-laryngology; . . . the so-called endonasal perspective procedure; or I refer to the acrobatic tricks of larynx surgery which have to be performed following the reversed picture in the laryngoscope. I might also speak of ear surgery which suggests the precision work of watchmakers. What range of the most subtle muscular acrobatics is required from the man who wants to repair or save the human body! We have only to think of the couching of a cataract where there is virtually a debate of steel with nearly fluid tissue, or of the major abdominal operations (laparotomy)." — Luc Durtain. [Benjamin]

assembled under a new law. Thus, for contemporary man the representation of reality by the film is incomparably more significant than that of the painter, since it offers, precisely because of the thoroughgoing permeation of reality with mechanical equipment, as aspect of reality which is free of all equipment. And that is what one is entitled to ask from a work of art.

XII

Mechanical reproduction of art changes the reaction of the masses toward art. The reactionary attitude toward a Picasso painting changes into the progressive reaction toward a Chaplin movie. The progressive reaction is characterized by the direct, intimate fusion of visual and emotional enjoyment with the orientation of the expert. Such fusion is of great social significance. The greater the decrease in the social significance of an art form, the sharper the distinction between criticism and enjoyment by the public. The conventional is uncritically enjoyed, and the truly new is criticized with aversion. With regard to the screen, the critical and the receptive attitudes of the public coincide. The decisive reason for this is that individual reactions are predetermined by the mass audience response they are about to produce, and this is nowhere more pronounced than in the film. The moment these responses become manifest they control each other. Again, the comparison with painting is fruitful. A painting has always had an excellent chance to be viewed by one person or by a few. The simultaneous contemplation of paintings by a large public, such as developed in the nineteenth century, is an early symptom of the crisis of painting, a crisis which was by no means occasioned exclusively by photography but rather in a relatively independent manner by the appeal of art works to the masses.

Painting simply is in no position to present an object for simultaneous collective experience, as it was possible for architecture at all times, for the epic poem in the past, and for the movie today. Although this circumstance in itself should not lead one to conclusions about the social role of painting, it does constitute a serious threat as soon as painting, under special conditions and, as it were, against its nature, is confronted directly by the masses. In the churches and monasteries of the Middle Ages and at the princely courts up to the end of the eighteenth century, a collective reception of paintings did not occur simultaneously, but by graduated and hierarchized mediation. The change that has come about is an expression of the particular conflict in which painting was implicated by the mechanical reproducibility of paintings. Although paintings began to be publicly exhibited in galleries and salons, there was no way for the masses to organize and control themselves in their reception.[25] Thus the same public which responds in a progressive manner toward a grotesque film is bound to respond in a reactionary manner to surrealism.

XIII

The characteristics of the film lie not only in the manner in which man presents himself to mechanical equipment but also in the manner in which, by means of this apparatus, man can represent his environment. A glance at occupational psychology illustrates the testing capacity of the equipment. Psychoanalysis illustrates it in a different perspective. The film has enriched our field of perception with methods which can be illustrated by those of Freudian theory. Fifty years ago, a slip of the tongue passed more or less unnoticed. Only exceptionally may such a slip have revealed dimensions of depth in a conversation which had seemed to be taking its course on the surface. Since the *Psychopathology of Everyday Life* things have changed. This book isolated and made analyzable things which had heretofore floated along unnoticed in the broad stream of perception. For the entire spectrum of optical, and now also acoustical, perception the film has brought about a similar deepening of apperception. It is only an obverse of this fact that behavior items shown in a movie can be analyzed

[25]This mode of observation may seem crude, but as the great theoretician Leonardo has shown, crude modes of observation may at times be usefully adduced. Leonardo compares painting and music as follows: "Painting is superior to music because, unlike unfortunate music, it does not have to die as soon as it is born. . . . Music which is consumed in the very act of its birth is inferior to painting which the use of varnish has rendered eternal." (Trattato I, 29.) [Benjamin]

much more precisely and from more points of view than those presented on paintings or on the stage. As compared with painting, filmed behavior lends itself more readily to analysis because of its incomparably more precise statements of the situation. In comparison with the stage scene, the filmed behavior item lends itself more readily to analysis because it can be isolated more easily. This circumstance derives its chief importance from its tendency to promote the mutual penetration of art and science. Actually, of a screened behavior item which is neatly brought out in a certain situation, like a muscle of a body, it is difficult to say which is more fascinating, its artistic value or its value for science. To demonstrate the identity of the artistic and scientific uses of photography which heretofore usually were separated will be one of the revolutionary functions of the film.[26]

By close-ups of the things around us, by focusing on hidden details of familiar objects, by exploring commonplace milieus under the ingenious guidance of the camera, the film, on the one hand, extends our comprehension of the necessities which rule our lives; on the other hand, it manages to assure us of an immense and unexpected field of action. Our taverns and our metropolitan streets, our offices and furnished rooms, our railroad stations and our factories appeared to have us locked up hopelessly. Then came the film and burst this prison-world asunder by the dynamite of the tenth of a second, so that now, in the midst of its far-flung ruins and debris, we calmly and adventurously go traveling. With the close-up, space expands; with slow motion, movement is extended. The enlargement of a snapshot does not simply render more precise what in any case was visible, though unclear: it reveals entirely new structural formations of the subject. So, too, slow motion not only presents familiar qualities of movement but reveals in them entirely unknown ones "which, far from looking like retarded rapid movements, give the effect of singularly gliding, floating, supernatural motions."[27] Evidently a different nature opens itself to the camera than opens to the naked eye — if only because an unconsciously penetrated space is substituted for a space consciously explored by man. Even if one has a general knowledge of the way people walk, one knows nothing of a person's posture during the fractional second of a stride. The act of reaching for a lighter or a spoon is familiar routine, yet we hardly know what really goes on between hand and metal, not to mention how this fluctuates with our moods. Here the camera intervenes with the resources of its lowerings and liftings, its interruptions and isolations, its extensions and accelerations, its enlargements and reductions. The camera introduces us to unconscious optics as does psychoanalysis to unconscious impulses.

XIV

One of the foremost tasks of art has always been the creation of a demand which could be fully satisfied only later.[28] The history of every art form

[26]Renaissance painting offers a revealing analogy to this situation. The incomparable development of this art and its significance rested not least on the integration of a number of new sciences, or at least of new scientific data. Renaissance painting made use of anatomy and perspective, of mathematics, meteorology, and chromatology. Valéry writes: "What could be further from us than the strange claim of a Leonardo to whom painting was a supreme goal and the ultimate demonstration of knowledge? Leonardo was convinced that painting demanded universal knowledge, and he did not even shrink from a theoretical analysis which to us is stunning because of its very depth and precision. . . ." — Paul Valéry, "Autour de Corot," *Pièces sur l'art* (Paris), p. 191. [Benjamin]

[27]Rudolf Arnheim, p. 138. [Tr.]

[28]"The work of art," says André Breton, "is valuable only insofar as it is vibrated by the reflexes of the future." Indeed, every developed art form intersects three lines of development. Technology works toward a certain form of art. Before the advent of the film there were photo booklets with pictures which flitted by the onlooker upon pressure of the thumb, thus portraying a boxing bout or a tennis match. Then there were the slot machines in bazaars; their picture sequences were produced by the turning of a crank.

Secondly, the traditional art forms in certain phases of their development strenuously work toward effects which later are effortlessly attained by the new ones. Before the rise of the movie the Dadaists' performances tried to create an audience reaction which Chaplin later evoked in a more natural way.

Thirdly, unspectacular social changes often promote a change in receptivity which will benefit the new art form. Before the movie had begun to create its public, pictures that were no longer immobile captivated an assembled audience in shows critical epochs in which a certain art form aspires to effects which could be fully obtained only with a changed technical standard, that is to say, in a new art form. The extravagances and crudities of art which thus appear, particularly in the so-called decadent epochs, actually arise from the nucleus of its richest historical energies. In recent years, such barbarisms were abundant in Dadaism.[29] It is only now that its impulse becomes discernible: Dadaism attempted to create by pictorial — and literary — means the effects which the public today seeks in the film.

Every fundamentally new, pioneering creation of demands will carry beyond its goal. Dadaism did so to the extent that it sacrificed the market values which are so characteristic of the film in favor of higher ambitions — though of course it was not conscious of such intentions as here described. The Dadaists attached much less importance to the sales value of their work than to its uselessness for contemplative immersion. The studied degradation of their material was not the least of their means to achieve this uselessness. Their poems are "word salad" containing obscenities and every imaginable waste product of language. The same is true of their paintings, on which they mounted buttons and tickets. What they intended and achieved was a relentless destruction of the aura of their creations, which they branded as reproductions with the very

means of production. Before a painting of Arp's or a poem by August Stramm it is impossible to take time for contemplation and evaluation as one would like before a canvas of Derain's or a poem by Rilke. In the decline of middle-class society, contemplation became a school for asocial behavior; it was countered by distraction as a variant of social conduct.[30] Dadaistic activities actually assured a rather vehement distraction by making works of art the center of scandal. One requirement was foremost: to outrage the public.

From an alluring appearance or persuasive structure of sound the work of art of the Dadaists became an instrument of ballistics. It hit the spectator like a bullet, it happened to him, thus acquiring a tactile quality. It promoted a demand for the film, the distracting element of which is also primarily tactile, being based on changes of place and focus which periodically assail the spectator. Let us compare the screen on which a film unfolds with the canvas of a painting. The painting invites the spectator to contemplation; before it the spectator can abandon himself to his associations. Before the movie frame he cannot do so. No sooner has his eye grasped a scene than it is already changed. It cannot be arrested. Duhamel, who detests the film and knows nothing of its significance, though something of its structure, notes this circumstance as follows: "I can no longer think what I want to think. My thoughts have been replaced by moving images."[31] The spectator's process of association in view of these images is indeed interrupted by their constant, sudden change. This constitutes the shock effect of the film, which, like all shocks, should be cushioned by heightened presence of mind.[32] By

---

the so-called *Kaiserpanorama*. Here the public assembled before a screen into which stereoscopes were mounted, one to each beholder. By a mechanical process individual pictures appeared briefly before the stereoscopes, then made way for others. Edison still had to use similar devices in presenting the first movie strip before the film screen and projection were known. This strip was presented to a small public which stared into the apparatus in which the succession of pictures was reeling off. Incidentally, the institution of the *Kaiserpanorama* shows very clearly a dialectic of the development. Shortly before the movie turned the reception of pictures into a collective one, the individual viewing of pictures in these swiftly outmoded establishments came into play once more with an intensity comparable to that of the ancient priest beholding the statue of a divinity in the cella. [Benjamin]

[29]Movement in the 1920s in both poetry and graphic art characterized by a parodistic treatment of mechanized society and an outrageous assault on the viewer. Major works of Dada include the Buñuel-Dali film *Un Chien Andalou* and Alfred Jarry's play *Ubu roi;* its principal theorist was André Breton.

[30]The theological archetype of this contemplation is the awareness of being alone with one's God. Such awareness, in the heyday of the bourgeoisie, went to strengthen the freedom to shake off clerical tutelage. During the decline of the bourgeoisie this awareness had to take into account the hidden tendency to withdraw from public affairs those forces which the individual draws upon in his communion with God. [Benjamin]

[31]Georges Duhamel, *Scènes de la vie future* (Paris, 1930), p. 52. [Tr.]

[32]The film is the art form that is in keeping with the increased threat to his life which modern man has to face. Man's need to expose himself to shock effects is his adjustment

means of its technical structure, the film has taken the physical shock effect out of the wrappers in which Dadaism had, as it were, kept it inside the moral shock effect.[33]

XV

The mass is a matrix from which all traditional behavior toward works of art issues today in a new form. Quantity has been transmuted into quality. The greatly increased mass of participants has produced a change in the mode of participation. The fact that the new mode of participation first appeared in a disreputable form must not confuse the spectator. Yet some people have launched spirited attacks against precisely this superficial aspect. Among these, Duhamel has expressed himself in the most radical manner. What he objects to most is the kind of participation which the movie elicits from the masses. Duhamel calls the movie "a pastime for helots,[34] a diversion for uneducated, wretched, worn-out creatures who are consumed by their worries . . . , a spectacle which requires no concentration and presupposes no intelligence . . . , which kindles no light in the heart and awakens no hope other than the ridiculous one of somebody becoming a 'star' in Los Angeles."[35] Clearly, this is at bottom the same ancient lament that the masses seek distraction whereas art demands concentration from the spectator. That is a commonplace. The question remains whether it provides a platform for the

analysis of the film. A closer look is needed here. Distraction and concentration form polar opposites which may be stated as follows: A man who concentrates before a work of art is absorbed by it. He enters into this work of art the way legend tells of the Chinese painter when he viewed his finished painting. In contrast, the distracted mass absorbs the work of art. This is most obvious with regard to buildings. Architecture has always represented the prototype of a work of art the reception of which is consummated by a collectivity in a state of distraction. The laws of its reception are most instructive.

Buildings have been man's companions since primeval times. Many art forms have developed and perished. Tragedy begins with the Greeks, is extinguished with them, and after centuries its "rules" only are revived. The epic poem, which had its origin in the youth of nations, expires in Europe at the end of the Renaissance. Panel painting is a creation of the Middle Ages, and nothing guarantees its uninterrupted existence. But the human need for shelter is lasting. Architecture has never been idle. Its history is more ancient than that of any other art, and its claim to being a living force has significance in every attempt to comprehend the relationship of the masses to art. Buildings are appropriated in a twofold manner: by use and by perception — or rather, by touch and sight. Such appropriation cannot be understood in terms of the attentive concentration of a tourist before a famous building. On the tactile side there is no counterpart to contemplation on the optical side. Tactile appropriation is accomplished not so much by attention as by habit. As regards architecture, habit determines to a large extent even optical reception. The latter, too, occurs much less through rapt attention than by noticing the object in incidental fashion. This mode of appropriation, developed with reference to architecture, in certain circumstances acquires canonical value. For the tasks which face the human apparatus of perception at the turning points of history cannot be solved by optical means, that is, by contemplation, alone. They are mastered gradually by habit, under the guidance of tactile appropriation.

The distracted person, too, can form habits. More, the ability to master certain tasks in a state

---

to the dangers threatening him. The film corresponds to profound changes in the apperceptive apparatus — changes that are experienced on an individual scale by the man in the street in big-city traffic, on a historical scale by every present-day citizen. [Benjamin]

[33]As for Dadaism, insights important for Cubism and Futurism are to be gained from the movie. Both appear as deficient attempts of art to accommodate the pervasion of reality by the apparatus. In contrast to the film, these schools did not try to use the apparatus as such for the artistic presentation of reality, but aimed at some sort of alloy in the joint presentation of reality and apparatus. In Cubism, the premonition that this apparatus will be structurally based on optics plays a dominant part; in Futurism, it is the premonition of the effects of this apparatus which are brought out by the rapid sequence of the film strip. [Benjamin]

[34]Slaves.

[35]Duhamel, p. 58. [Tr.]

of distraction proves that their solution has become a matter of habit. Distraction as provided by art presents a covert control of the extent to which new tasks have become soluble by apperception. Since, moreover, individuals are tempted to avoid such tasks, art will tackle the most difficult and most important ones where it is able to mobilize the masses. Today it does so in the film. Reception in a state of distraction, which is increasing noticeably in all fields of art and is symptomatic of profound changes in apperception, finds in the film its true means of exercise. The film with its shock effect meets this mode of reception halfway. The film makes the cult value recede into the background not only by putting the public in the position of the critic, but also by the fact that at the movies this position requires no attention. The public is an examiner, but an absent-minded one.

EPILOGUE

The growing proletarianization of modern man and the increasing formation of masses are two aspects of the same process. Fascism attempts to organize the newly created proletarian masses without affecting the property structure which the masses strive to eliminate. Fascism sees its salvation in giving these masses not their right, but instead a chance to express themselves.[36] The masses have a right to change property relations; Fascism seeks to give them an expression while

[36]One technical feature is significant here, especially with regard to newsreels, the propagandist importance of which can hardly be overestimated. Mass reproduction is aided especially by the reproduction of masses. In big parades and monster rallies, in sports events, and in war, all of which nowadays are captured by camera and sound recording, the masses are brought face to face with themselves. This process, whose significance need not be stressed, is intimately connected with the development of the techniques of reproduction and photography. Mass movements are usually discerned more clearly by a camera than by the naked eye. A bird's-eye view best captures gatherings of hundreds of thousands. And even though such a view may be as accessible to the human eye as it is to the camera, the image received by the eye cannot be enlarged the way a negative is enlarged. This means that mass movements, including war, constitute a form of human behavior which particularly favors mechanical equipment. [Benjamin]

preserving property. The logical result of Fascism is the introduction of aesthetics into political life. The violation of the masses, whom Fascism, with its *Führer* cult, forces to their knees, has its counterpart in the violation of an apparatus which is pressed into the production of ritual values.

All efforts to render politics aesthetic culminate in one thing: war. War and war only can set a goal for mass movements on the largest scale while respecting the traditional property system. This is the political formula for the situation. The technological formula may be stated as follows: Only war makes it possible to mobilize all of today's technical resources while maintaining the property system. It goes without saying that the Fascist apotheosis of war does not employ such arguments. Still, Marinetti[37] says in his manifesto on the Ethiopian colonial war: "For twenty-seven years we Futurists have rebelled against the branding of war as antiaesthetic. . . . Accordingly we state: . . . War is beautiful because it establishes man's dominion over the subjugated machinery by means of gas masks, terrifying megaphones, flame throwers, and small tanks. War is beautiful because it initiates the dreamt-of metalization of the human body. War is beautiful because it enriches a flowering meadow with the fiery orchids of machine guns. War is beautiful because it combines the gunfire, the cannonades, the cease-fire, the scents, and the stench of putrefaction into a symphony. War is beautiful because it creates new architecture, like that of the big tanks, the geometrical formation flights, the smoke spirals from burning villages, and many others. . . . Poets and artists of Futurism! . . . remember these principles of an aesthetics of war so that your struggle for a new literature and a new graphic art . . . may be illumined by them!"

This manifesto has the virtue of clarity. Its formulations deserve to be accepted by dialecticians. To the latter, the aesthetics of today's war appears as follows: If the natural utilization of productive forces is impeded by the property system, the increase in technical devices, in speed, and in the sources of energy will press for an unnatural

[37]Italian-French futurist writer and enthusiastic backer of Mussolini (1876–1944), author of *Guerra sola igiene del mundo* (War — Sole Hygiene of the World, 1915).

utilization, and this is found in war. The destructiveness of war furnishes proof that society has been mature enough to incorporate technology as its organ, that technology has not been sufficiently developed to cope with the elemental forces of society. The horrible features of imperialistic warfare are attributable to the discrepancy between the tremendous means of production and their inadequate utilization in the process of production — in other words, to unemployment and the lack of markets. Imperialistic war is a rebellion of technology which collects, in the form of "human material," the claims to which society has denied its natural material. Instead of draining rivers, society directs a human stream into a bed of trenches; instead of dropping seeds from airplanes, it drops incendiary bombs over cities; and through gas warfare the aura is abolished in a new way.

"*Fiat ars — pereat mundus,*"[38] says Fascism, and, as Marinetti admits, expect war to supply the artistic gratification of a sense perception that has been changed by technology. This is evidently the consummation of *"l'art pour l'art."* Mankind, which in Homer's time was an object of contemplation for the Olympian gods, now is one for itself. Its self-alienation has reached such a degree that it can experience its own destruction as an aesthetic pleasure of the first order. This is the situation of politics which Fascism is rendering aesthetic. Communism responds by politicizing art.

[38]Let art exist, let the world perish.

Bertolt Brecht
1898–1956

Bertolt Brecht was born in 1898 in Augsburg, Germany, to good bourgeois parents — a paper mill manager and the daughter of a civil servant. He showed a prodigious literary talent as a young man, publishing his first poems at the age of sixteen. While a medical student at Munich University, he wrote his first play, Baal *(1918), and began to work as dramaturge for the Deutches Theater in 1920. The following year, he abandoned his studies to devote his time to writing for the stage. He came to prominence as a playwright with* Drums in the Night *(1922). Although he did not join the Communist party until 1929, even his early plays demonstrate the theme of a worker or soldier whose search for happiness is obstructed by the pressures of a violent and avaricious society. Brecht began a fertile partnership with composer Kurt Weill, collaborating on music dramas like* The Threepenny Opera *(1928),* Happy End *(1929),* Rise and Fall of the City of Mahagonny *(1930), and* The Seven Deadly Sins *(1933). With the rise of Hitler in 1933, Brecht's published works were burned and his life was in danger. Together with his wife, the actress Helene Weigel, and their children, Brecht left Germany first for Zurich, then for Denmark, where he began work on some of his greatest plays:* Galileo *(1938),* The Good Person of Setzuan *(1940), and* Mother Courage *(1941). As war began, the Brechts trekked eastward, to Finland, then across Russia, and by sea to California, settling near Hollywood, where a German colony of exiles was gathered, including Adorno and Horkheimer. While working on screenplays for Fritz Lang, Brecht also wrote plays, including* The Caucasian Chalk Circle *(1943), and an adaptation, with W. H. Auden, of* The Duchess of Malfi *(1944). After the war, when Soviet Russia had become an adversary rather than an ally, Brecht was investigated by the House Committee on Un-American Activities in 1947; after one day of interrogation he fled to Switzerland, then settled in what had become East Berlin. There he founded the Berliner Ensemble, and staged or restaged the works he had written while on the run. East Berlin was a safer place for Brecht than Los Angeles, and ironically, it was safer than Moscow as well. Brecht's artistic practices ran well wide of the Stalinist party line that dictated naive realism in representation. Brecht's own theory of art rejected realism for an "estrangement-effect" (Verfremdungseffekt), which denied audiences easy sympathy with his characters, insisting that his viewers think rather than feel. After the 1953 death of Stalin, however, fame and honors came to Brecht all at once: A 1955 Paris production of* Mother Courage *starring Helene Weigel established his international reputation, his* Collected Works *began to emerge from the most prestigious West and East German presses, and he was awarded the Stalin Prize for Peace. The following year he suffered a heart attack; he died in Berlin in 1956. One of Brecht's artistic manifestos is the following essay, "The Popular and the Realistic," which was published in 1937.*

The Popular and the Realistic

When considering what slogans to set up for German literature today one must remember that anything with a claim to be considered as literature is printed exclusively abroad, and with few exceptions can only be read there. This gives a peculiar twist to the slogan of *Volkstümlichkeit* [or *Popularity*] *in literature.*

The writer is supposed to write for a people without living among it. When one comes to look closer, however, the gap between the writer and the people has not grown so wide as might be thought. All the same, it would be wrong, i.e. unrealistic, to see this growth as purely "external." Certainly a special effort is needed today in order to write in a popular way. But at the same time it has become easier: easier and more urgent. The people has clearly separated from its top layer; its oppressors and exploiters have parted company with it and become involved in a bloody war against it which can no longer be overlooked. It has become easier to take sides. Open warfare has, as it were, broken out among the "audience."

Nor can the demand for a realist way of writing any longer be so easily overlooked. It has become more or less self-evident. The ruling strata are using lies more openly than before, and the lies are bigger. Telling the truth seems increasingly urgent. The sufferings are greater and the number of sufferers has grown. Compared with the vast sufferings of the masses it seems trivial and even

despicable to worry about petty difficulties and the difficulties of petty groups.

There is only one ally against the growth of barbarism: the people on whom it imposes these sufferings. Only the people offer any prospects. Thus it is natural to turn to them, and more necessary than ever to speak their language.

The words *Popularity* and *Realism* therefore are natural companions. It is in the interest of the people, the broad working masses, that literature should give them truthful representations of life; and truthful representations of life are in fact only of use to the broad working masses, the people; so that they have to be suggestive and intelligible to them, i.e. popular. None the less these conceptions need a thorough clean-up before being thrown into sentences where they will get smelted and put to use. It would be a mistake to treat them as fully explained, unsullied, unambiguous and without a past. ("We all know what's meant by that, no need for hairsplitting.") The German word for "popular," *Volkstümlich*, is itself none too popular. It is unrealistic to imagine that it is. A whole series of words ending in *tum* need handling with care. One has only to think of *Brauchtum, Königstum, Heiligtum,*[1] and it is well known that *Volkstum* too has a quite specific

---

[1] Brecht is gesturing toward words that developed a certain ideological quality under the National Socialist regime then in power in Germany and during the Hohenzollern monarchy that preceded it. *Brauchtum*, derived from *brauchen*, "to need or require" and usually meaning "customs," meant "folklore";

Translated by John Willett.

ceremonious, sacramental and dubious ring which we cannot by any means overlook. We cannot overlook it, because we definitely need the conception of popularity or *Volkstümlichkeit*.

It is part of that supposedly poetic way of wording, by which the "Volk" — more folk than people — is presented as particularly superstitious, or rather as an object of superstition. In this the folk or people appears with its immutable characteristics, its time-honored traditions, forms of art, customs and habits, its religiosity, its hereditary enemies, its unconquerable strength and all the rest. A peculiar unity is conjured up of tormentor and tormented, exploiter and exploited, liar and victim; nor is it by any means a simple matter of the many, "little" working people as against those on top.

The history of all the falsifications that have been operated with this conception of *Volkstum* is a long and complex story which is part of the history of the class war. We shall not embark on it but shall simply keep in mind the fact of such forgery whenever we speak of our need for popular art, meaning art for the broad masses of the people, for the many oppressed by the few, "the people proper," the mass of producers that has so long been the object of politics and now has to become its subject. We shall remind ourselves that powerful institutions have long prevented this "folk" from developing fully, that it has been artificially or forcibly tied down by conventions, and that the conception *Volkstümlich* has been stamped as a static one, without background or development. With this version of the conception we shall have no dealings, or rather we shall have to fight it. Our conception of "popular" refers to the people who are not only fully involved in the process of development but are actually taking it over, forcing it, deciding it. We have in mind a people that is making history and altering the world and itself. We have in mind a fighting people and also a fighting conception of "popularity."

"Popular" means intelligible to the broad masses, taking over their own forms of expression and enriching them / adopting and consolidating their standpoint / representing the most progressive

section of the people in such a way that it can take over the leadership: thus intelligible to other sections too / linking with tradition and carrying it further / handing on the achievements of the section now leading to the section of the people that is struggling for the lead.

We now come to the concept of "Realism." It is an old concept which has been much used by many men and for many purposes, and before it can be applied we must spring-clean it too. This is necessary because when the people takes over its inheritance there has to be a process of expropriation. Literary works cannot be taken over like factories, or literary forms of expression like industrial methods. Realist writing, of which history offers many widely varying examples, is likewise conditioned by the question of how, when and for what class it is made use of: conditioned down to the last small detail. As we have in mind a fighting people that is changing the real world we must not cling to "well-tried" rules for telling a story, worthy models set up by literary history, eternal aesthetic laws. We must not abstract the one and only realism from certain given works, but shall make a lively use of all means, old and new, tried and untried, deriving from art and deriving from other sources, in order to put living reality in the hands of living people in such a way that it can be mastered. We shall take care not to ascribe realism to a particular historical form of novel belonging to a particular period, Balzac's or Tolstoy's, for instance, so as to set up purely formal and literary criteria of realism. We shall not restrict ourselves to speaking of realism in cases where one can (e.g.) smell, look, feel whatever is depicted, where "atmosphere" is created and stories develop in such a way that the characters are psychologically stripped down. Our conception of *realism* needs to be broad and political, free from aesthetic restrictions and independent of convention. *Realist*[2] means: laying bare society's causal network / showing up the dominant

Königtum, from *könig*, "king" meant "monarchical principle"; *Heiligtum* from *heilig*, "holy" meant "shrine" or "sanctuary."

[2]To G. Lukács in particular *Das Wort* owes some most notable essays, which shed light on the concept of realism even if, in my opinion, they define it rather too narrowly. [Brecht] Brecht is responding to Lukács's *Studies in European Realism* (1932), which celebrated both Balzac and Tolstoy as realists.

viewpoint as the viewpoint of the dominators / writing from the standpoint of the class which has prepared the broadest solutions for the most pressing problems afflicting human society / emphasizing the dynamics of development / concrete and so as to encourage abstraction.

It is a tall order, and it can be made taller. And we shall let the artist apply all his imagination, all his originality, his sense of humor and power of invention to its fulfillment. We will not stick to unduly detailed literary models or force the artist to follow over-precise rules for telling a story.

We shall establish that so-called sensuous writing (in which everything can be smelt, tasted, felt) is not to be identified automatically with realist writing, for we shall see that there are sensuously written works which are not realist, and realist works which are not sensuously written. We shall have to go carefully into the question whether the story is best developed by aiming at an eventual psychological stripping-down of characters. Our readers may quite well feel that they have not been given the key to what is happening if they are simply induced by a combination of arts to take part in the inner emotions of our books' heroes. By taking over the forms of Balzac and Tolstoy without a thorough inspection we might perhaps exhaust our readers, the people, just as these writers often do. Realism is not a pure question of form. Copying the methods of these realists, we should cease to be realists ourselves.

For time flows on, and if it did not it would be a poor look-out for those who have no golden tables to sit at. Methods wear out, stimuli fail. New problems loom up and demand new techniques. Reality alters; to represent it the means of representation must alter too. Nothing arises from nothing; the new springs from the old, but that is just what makes it new.

The oppressors do not always appear in the same mask. The masks cannot always be stripped off in the same way. There are so many tricks for dodging the mirror that is held out. Their military roads are termed motor roads. Their tanks are painted to look like Macduff's bushes.[3] Their

agents can show horny hands as if they were workers. Yes: it takes ingenuity to change the hunter into the quarry. What was popular yesterday is no longer so today, for the people of yesterday were not the people as it is today.

Anybody who is not bound by formal prejudices knows that there are many ways of suppressing truth and many ways of stating it: that indignation at inhuman conditions can be stimulated in many ways, by direct description of a pathetic or matter-of-fact kind, by narrating stories and parables, by jokes, by over- and understatement. In the theater reality can be represented in a factual or a fantastic form. The actors can do without (or with the minimum of) makeup, appearing "natural," and the whole thing can be a fake; they can wear grotesque masks and represent the truth. There is not much to argue about here: the means must be asked what the end is. The people know how to ask this. Piscator's[4] great experiments in the theater (and my own), which repeatedly involved the exploding of conventional forms, found their chief support in the most progressive cadres of the working class. The workers judged everything by the amount of truth contained in it; they welcomed any innovation which helped the representation of truth, of the real mechanism of society; they rejected whatever seemed like playing, like machinery working for its own sake, i.e. no longer, or not yet, fulfilling a purpose. The workers' arguments were never literary or purely theatrical. "You can't mix theater and film": that sort of thing was never said. If the film was not properly used the most one heard was: "that bit of film is unnecessary, it's distracting." Workers' choruses spoke intricate rhythmical verse parts ("if it rhymed it'd all slip down like butter, and nothing would stick") and sang difficult (unaccustomed) compositions by Eisler[5] ("it's got some guts in it"). But we had to alter particular lines whose sense was wrong or hard to arrive at. When there were certain subtleties (irregularities, complexities) in

---

[3]In Shakespeare's *Macbeth*, the soldiers of Macduff's army carry tree branches for camouflage.

[4]German theater director Erwin Piscator (1893–1966), whose innovative productions often involved free adaptation of bourgeois plays to reveal their social truth to the proletariat.

[5]Hanns Eisler (1898–1962), Jewish Austrian composer who collaborated with Brecht in theatrical pieces until they were both forced to leave Germany.

marching songs which had rhymes to make them easier to learn and simple rhythms to "put them across" better, then they said: "that's amusing, there was a sort of twist in that." They had no use for anything played out, trivial, so ordinary that one doesn't need to think ("there's nothing in it"). If an aesthetic was needed, here it was. I shall never forget how one worker looked at me when I answered his request to include something extra in a song about the USSR ("It must go in — what's the point otherwise?") by saying that it would wreck the artistic form: he put his head on one side and smiled. At this polite smile a whole section of aesthetic collapsed. The workers were not afraid to teach us, nor were they afraid to learn.

I speak from experience when I say that one need never be frightened of putting bold and unaccustomed things before the proletariat, so long as they have to do with reality. There will always be educated persons, connoisseurs of the arts, who will step in with a "The people won't understand that." But the people impatiently shoves them aside and comes to terms directly with the artist. There is highly cultured stuff made for minorities, designed to form minorities: the two thousandth transformation of some old hat, the spicing-up of a venerable and now decomposing piece of meat. The proletariat rejects it ("they've got something to worry about") with an incredulous, somewhat reflective shake of the head. It is not the spice that is being rejected, but the meat; not the two thousandth form, but the old hat. When they themselves took to writing and acting they were compellingly original. What was known as "agit-prop"[6] art, which a number of second-rate noses were turned up at, was a mine of novel artistic techniques and ways of expression. Magnificent and long-forgotten elements from periods of truly popular art cropped up there, boldly adapted to the new social ends. Daring cuts and compositions, beautiful simplifications (alongside misconceived ones): in all this there was often an astonishing economy and elegance and a fearless eye for complexity. A lot of it may have been primitive, but it was never primitive

with the kind of primitivity that affected the supposedly varied psychological portrayals of bourgeois art. It is very wrong to make a few misconceived stylizations a pretext for rejecting a style of representation which attempts (so often successfully) to bring out the essential and to encourage abstraction. The sharp eyes of the workers saw through naturalism's superficial representation of reality. When they said in *Fuhrmann Henschel*,[7] "that's more than we want to know about it" they were in fact wishing they could get a more exact representation of the real social forces operating under the immediately visible surface. To quote from my own experience: they were not put off by the fantastic costumes and the apparently unreal setting of *The Threepenny Opera*. They were not narrow; they hated narrowness (their living quarters were narrow). They were generous; their employers were stingy. They thought it possible to dispense with some things that the artists felt to be essential, but they were amiable enough about it; they were not against superfluity: they were against certain superfluous people. They did not muzzle the threshing ox, though they saw to it that he threshed.[8] "The universally-applicable creative method": they didn't believe in that sort of thing. They knew that they needed many different methods in order to reach their objective. If you want an aesthetic, there you are.

So the criteria for the popular and the realistic need to be chosen not only with great care but also with an open mind. They must not be deduced from existing realist works and existing popular works, as is often the case. Such an approach would lead to purely formalistic criteria, and questions of popularity and realism would be decided by form.[9]

One cannot decide if a work is realist or not by finding out whether it resembles existing, reputedly realist works which must be counted realist for their time. In each individual case the picture

<hr>

[7]1898 play by Gerhart Hauptmann (1862–1946) about a wagoner driven to suicide.

[8]An allusion to Deuteronomy 25:4 ("Thou shalt not muzzle the ox that threshes the corn").

[9]Brecht is alluding to the "social realism" prescribed in Stalin's regime, which would ban any expressionistic effects.

[6]Short for agitation propaganda, texts designed to stimulate the masses to revolution.

given of life must be compared, not with another picture, but with the actual life portrayed. And likewise where popularity is concerned there is a wholly formalistic procedure that has to be guarded against. The intelligibility of a work of literature is not ensured exclusively by its being written in exactly the same way as other works which people have understood. These other works too were not invariably written just like the works before them. Something was done towards their understanding. In the same way we must do something for the understanding of the new works. Besides *being popular* there is such a thing as *becoming popular*.

If we want a truly popular literature, alive and fighting, completely gripped by reality and completely gripping reality, then we must keep pace with reality's headlong development. The great working masses of the people are on the move. The activity and brutality of their enemies proves it.

Max Horkheimer
1895–1977

Max Horkheimer was born in 1895 in Stuttgart to assimilated Jewish parents. His family pressured him not to pursue academics, but to leave school at sixteen to work in his father's factory. After World War I, he finally began his studies in philosophy and psychology at Munich. When he moved to Frankfurt am Main to study under Hans Cornelius, he met Theodor Adorno, who would become his great friend and collaborator in forming the Frankfurt School of critical theory. In 1930, just five years after receiving his Ph.D., Horkheimer was named the director of the Institute for Social Research. As its first openly Marxist director, he worked with Herbert Marcuse, Erich Fromm, Walter Benjamin, and Adorno. The Institute was active and fruitful until the Nazi government closed it in 1933. Exiled first to Switzerland, Horkheimer was invited to bring the Institute to Columbia University, where the Institute's journal could continue to be published. During this time, he published his first major work, Authority and the Family *(1936). In 1940 Horkheimer became a U.S. citizen and moved to Berkeley, where he and Adorno would publish* Dialectic of Enlightenment *(1947), from which the following essay, "The Culture Industry: Enlightenment as Mass Deception," is excerpted. In this work, Adorno and Horkheimer argued that society's uncritical reception of scientific rationality would lead to the perversion of "reason" that had occurred under the Nazis in Germany. Although Adorno was a much more prolific writer, Horkheimer did continue to publish other works, such as 1967's* Eclipse of Reason. *Influenced by Schopenhauer, Horkheimer became increasingly pessimistic about the erosion of Enlightenment ideals under twentieth-century capitalism. In 1949 Horkheimer moved the Institute back to Frankfurt, where he became Rector of the University. After a five-year stint at the University of Chicago (1954–59), Horkheimer retired from university life, though he continued to write and publish. He died in Nuremberg in 1977.*

Theodor W. Adorno

1903–1969

Theodor Wiesengrund Adorno was born to middle-class parents in Frankfurt, Germany, where he studied psychology, sociology, and music, and took his Ph.D. in philosophy in 1924. He went to Vienna to study composition with the serial composer Alban Berg in 1925, then came back to Frankfurt for postdoctoral study in 1928. Strongly influenced by the Hegelian Marxism of Georg Lukács, he founded with Max Horkheimer the Institute for Social Research that was the nucleus of what became known as the Frankfurt school, a group that also included Herbert Marcuse, Walter Benjamin, and, in the next generation, Jürgen Habermas. In the waning days of the Weimar Republic, Adorno left for England, then spent the war years in America. In 1949 he returned to the University of Frankfurt, where he served as professor of sociology and philosophy, and where he became assistant director of the Institute in 1949, and sole director from 1958 until his death. Adorno's works include The Dialectic of Enlightenment *(1944, with Max Horkheimer; translated 1972);* The Philosophy of Modern Music *(1949; translated 1973);* Minima Moralia: Reflections from Damaged Life *(1951; translated 1974);* Prisms *(1955; translated 1967);* Introduction to the Sociology of Music *(1962; translated 1976);* Negative Dialectics *(1966; translated 1973); and the posthumous* Aesthetic Theory *(1970; translated 1996).*

From *The Culture Industry: Enlightenment as Mass Deception*

The sociological theory that the loss of the support of objectively established religion, the dissolution of the last remnants of precapitalism, together with technological and social differentiation or specialization, have led to cultural chaos is disproved every day; for culture now impresses the same stamp on everything. Films, radio and magazines make up a system which is uniform as a whole and in every part. Even the aesthetic activities of political opposites are one in their enthusiastic obedience to the rhythm of the iron system. The decorative industrial management buildings and exhibition centers in authoritarian countries are much the same as anywhere else. The huge gleaming towers that shoot up everywhere are outward signs of the ingenious planning of international concerns, toward which the unleashed entrepreneurial system (whose monuments are a mass of gloomy houses and business premises in grimy, spiritless cities) was already hastening. Even now the older houses just outside the concrete city centers look like slums, and the new bungalows on the outskirts are at one with the flimsy structures of world fairs in their praise of technical progress and their built-in demand to be discarded after a short while like empty food cans. Yet the city housing projects designed to perpetuate the individual as a supposedly independent unit in a small hygienic

Translated by John Cumming.

dwelling make him all the more subservient to his adversary — the absolute power of capitalism. Because the inhabitants, as producers and as consumers, are drawn into the center in search of work and pleasure, all the living units crystallize into well-organized complexes. The striking unity of microcosm and macrocosm presents men with a model of their culture: the false identity of the general and the particular. Under monopoly all mass culture is identical, and the lines of its artificial framework begin to show through. The people at the top are no longer so interested in concealing monopoly: as its violence becomes more open, so its power grows. Movies and radio need no longer pretend to be art. The truth that they are just business is made into an ideology in order to justify the rubbish they deliberately produce. They call themselves industries; and when their directors' incomes are published, any doubt about the social utility of the finished products is removed.

Interested parties explain the culture industry in technological terms. It is alleged that because millions participate in it, certain reproduction processes are necessary that inevitably require identical needs in innumerable places to be satisfied with identical goods. The technical contrast between the few production centers and the large number of widely dispersed consumption points is said to demand organization and planning by management. Furthermore, it is claimed that standards were based in the first place on consumers' needs, and for that reason were accepted with so little resistance. The result is the circle of manipulation and retroactive need in which the unity of the system grows ever stronger. No mention is made of the fact that the basis on which technology acquires power over society is the power of those whose economic hold over society is greatest. A technological rationale is the rationale of domination itself. It is the coercive nature of society alienated from itself. Automobiles, bombs, and movies keep the whole thing together until their leveling element shows its strength in the very wrong which it furthered. It has made the technology of the culture industry no more than the achievement of standardization and mass production, sacrificing whatever involved a distinction between the logic of the work and that of the social system. This is the result not of a law of movement in technology as such but of its function in today's economy. The need which might resist central control has already been suppressed by the control of the individual consciousness. The step from the telephone to the radio has clearly distinguished the roles. The former still allowed the subscriber to play the role of subject, and was liberal. The latter is democratic: it turns all participants into listeners and authoritatively subjects them to broadcast programs which are all exactly the same. No machinery of rejoinder has been devised, and private broadcasters are denied any freedom. They are confined to the apocryphal field of the "amateur," and also have to accept organization from above. But any trace of spontaneity from the public in official broadcasting is controlled and absorbed by talent scouts, studio competitions and official programs of every kind selected by professionals. Talented performers belong to the industry long before it displays them; otherwise they would not be so eager to fit in. The attitude of the public, which ostensibly and actually favors the system of the culture industry, is a part of the system and not an excuse for it. If one branch of art follows the same formula as one with a very different medium and content; if the dramatic intrigue of broadcast soap operas becomes no more than useful material for showing how to master technical problems at both ends of the scale of musical experience — real jazz or a cheap imitation; or if a movement from a Beethoven symphony is crudely "adapted" for a film soundtrack in the same way as a Tolstoy novel is garbled in a film script: then the claim that this is done to satisfy the spontaneous wishes of the public is no more than hot air. We are closer to the facts if we explain these phenomena as inherent in the technical and personnel apparatus which, down to its last cog, itself forms part of the economic mechanism of selection. In addition there is the agreement — or at least the determination — of all executive authorities not to produce or sanction anything that in any way differs from their own rules, their own ideas about consumers, or above all themselves.

In our age the objective social tendency is incarnate in the hidden subjective purposes of company directors, the foremost among whom are in the most powerful sectors of industry — steel, petroleum, electricity, and chemicals. Culture monopolies are weak and dependent in comparison. They cannot afford to neglect their appeasement of the real holders of power if their sphere of activity in mass society (a sphere producing a specific type of commodity which anyhow is still too closely bound up with easygoing liberalism and Jewish intellectuals) is not to undergo a series of purges. The dependence of the most powerful broadcasting company on the electrical industry, or of the motion picture industry on the banks, is characteristic of the whole sphere, whose individual branches are themselves economically interwoven. All are in such close contact that the extreme concentration of mental forces allows demarcation lines between different firms and technical branches to be ignored. The ruthless unity in the culture industry is evidence of what will happen in politics. Marked differentiations such as those of A and B films,[1] or of stories in magazines in different price ranges, depend not so much on subject matter as on classifying, organizing, and labeling consumers. Something is provided for all so that none may escape; the distinctions are emphasized and extended. The public is catered for with a hierarchical range of mass-produced products of varying quality, thus advancing the rule of complete quantification. Everybody must behave (as if spontaneously) in accordance with his previously determined and indexed level, and choose the category of mass product turned out for his type. Consumers appear as statistics on research organization charts, and are divided by income groups into red, green, and blue areas; the technique is that used for any type of propaganda.

How formalized the procedure is can be seen when the mechanically differentiated products prove to be all alike in the end. That the difference between the Chrysler range and General Motors products is basically illusory strikes every child with a keen interest in varieties. What connoisseurs discuss as good or bad points serve only to perpetuate the semblance of competition and range of choice. The same applies to the Warner Brothers and Metro Goldwyn Mayer productions. But even the differences between the more expensive and cheaper models put out by the same firm steadily diminish: for automobiles, there are such differences as the number of cylinders, cubic capacity, details of patented gadgets; and for films there are the number of stars, the extravagant use of technology, labor, and equipment, and the introduction of the latest psychological formulas. The universal criterion of merit is the amount of "conspicuous production," of blatant cash investment. The varying budgets in the culture industry do not bear the slightest relation to factual values, to the meaning of the products themselves. Even the technical media are relentlessly forced into uniformity. Television aims at a synthesis of radio and film, and is held up only because the interested parties have not yet reached agreement, but its consequences will be quite enormous and promise to intensify the impoverishment of aesthetic matter so drastically, that by tomorrow the thinly veiled identity of all industrial culture products can come triumphantly out into the open, derisively fulfilling the Wagnerian dream of the *Gesamtkunstwerk* — the fusion of all the arts in one work.[2] The alliance of word, image, and music is all the more perfect then in *Tristan* because the sensuous elements which all approvingly reflect the surface of social reality are in principle embodied in the same technical process, the unity of which becomes its distinctive content. This process integrates all the elements of the production, from the novel (shaped with an eye to the film) to the last sound effect. It is the triumph of invested capital, whose title as absolute master is etched deep into the hearts of the dispossessed in the employment line; it is the meaningful content of every film, whatever plot the production team may have selected.

---

[1]During the 1930s, as the Depression took hold, movie attendance diminished and film studios responded by directing the movie theaters they owned and operated to show double features, consisting of an "A" movie (with important film stars and better scripts) and a "B" movie (often a genre film about gangsters or cowboys, with lesser actors). In 1948 a Supreme Court decision required studios to divest themselves of their theaters, and both the A/B system and the double feature slowly but eventually came to an end.

[2]Composer Richard Wagner (1813–1883), in *The Artwork of the Future* (1849) held up as the ideal the work of art that would combine music, poetry, and scenic beauty to appeal to all the senses at once. His opera *Tristan und Isolde* (produced 1865) is mentioned in the next sentence as an example.

The man with leisure has to accept what the culture manufacturers offer him. Kant's formalism still expected a contribution from the individual, who was thought to relate the varied experiences of the senses to fundamental concepts; but industry robs the individual of his function. Its prime service to the customer is to do his schematizing for him. Kant said that there was a secret mechanism in the soul which prepared direct intuitions in such a way that they could be fitted into the system of pure reason.[3] But today that secret has been deciphered. While the mechanism is to all appearances planned by those who serve up the data of experience, that is, by the culture industry, it is in fact forced upon the latter by the power of society, which remains irrational, however we may try to rationalize it; and this inescapable force is processed by commercial agencies so that they give an artificial impression of being in command. There is nothing left for the consumer to classify. Producers have done it for him. Art for the masses has destroyed the dream but still conforms to the tenets of that dreaming idealism which critical idealism balked at. Everything derives from consciousness: for Malebranche and Berkeley,[4] from the consciousness of God; in mass art, from the consciousness of the production team. Not only are the hit songs, stars, and soap operas cyclically recurrent and rigidly invariable types, but the specific content of the entertainment itself is derived from them and only appears to change. The details are interchangeable. The short interval sequence which was effective in a hit song, the hero's momentary fall from grace (which he accepts as good sport), the rough treatment which the beloved gets from the male star, the latter's rugged defiance of the spoilt heiress, are, like all the other details, ready-made clichés to be slotted in anywhere; they never do anything more than fulfill the purpose allotted them in the overall plan. Their whole *raison d'être* is to confirm it by being its constituent parts. As soon as the film begins, it is quite clear how it will end, and who will be rewarded, punished, or forgotten. In light music, once the trained ear has heard the first notes of the hit song, it can guess what is coming and feel flattered when it does come. The average length of the short story has to be rigidly adhered to. Even gags, effects, and jokes are calculated like the setting in which they are placed. They are the responsibility of special experts and their narrow range makes it easy for them to be apportioned in the office. The development of the culture industry has led to the predominance of the effect, the obvious touch, and the technical detail over the work itself — which once expressed an idea, but was liquidated together with the idea. When the detail won its freedom, it became rebellious and, in the period from Romanticism to Expressionism, asserted itself as free expression, as a vehicle of protest against the organization. In music the single harmonic effect obliterated the awareness of form as a whole; in painting the individual color was stressed at the expense of pictorial composition; and in the novel psychology became more important than structure.[5] The totality of the culture industry has put an end to this. Though concerned exclusively with effects, it crushes their insubordination and makes them subserve the formula, which replaces the work. The same fate is inflicted on whole and parts alike. The whole inevitably bears no relation to the details — just like the career of a successful man into which everything is made to fit as an illustration or a proof, whereas it is nothing more than the sum of all those idiotic events. The so-called dominant idea is like a file which ensures order but not coherence. The whole and the parts are alike; there is no antithesis and no connection. Their prearranged harmony is a mockery of what had to be striven after in the great bourgeois works of art. In Germany the graveyard stillness of the dictatorship already hung over the gayest films of the democratic era.

[3]Kant argued that the process of perception involved an active synthesis of sense data on the part of the perceiver; see above, pp. 319–20.

[4]Nicholas Malebranche (1638–1715) argued that our knowledge of external reality comes from seeing "everything" within God. George Berkeley (1685–1753) argued that being requires perception, but that material things continue to exist even when unobserved by humans because they are always perceived by the mind of God.

[5]Here the authors bring up salient features of modernism in music, painting, and prose fiction.

The whole world is made to pass through the filter of the culture industry. The old experience of the moviegoer, who sees the world outside as an extension of the film he has just left (because the latter is intent upon reproducing the world of everyday perceptions), is now the producer's guideline. The more intensely and flawlessly his techniques duplicate empirical objects, the easier it is today for the illusion to prevail that the outside world is the straightforward continuation of that presented on the screen. This purpose has been furthered by mechanical reproduction since the lightning takeover by the sound film.

Real life is becoming indistinguishable from the movies. The sound film, far surpassing the theater of illusion, leaves no room for imagination or reflection on the part of the audience, who is unable to respond within the structure of the film, yet deviate from its precise detail without losing the thread of the story; hence the film forces its victims to equate it directly with reality. The stunting of the mass-media consumer's powers of imagination and spontaneity does not have to be traced back to any psychological mechanisms; he must ascribe the loss of those attributes to the objective nature of the products themselves, especially to the most characteristic of them, the sound film. They are so designed that quickness, powers of observation, and experience are undeniably needed to apprehend them at all; yet sustained thought is out of the question if the spectator is not to miss the relentless rush of facts. Even though the effort required for his response is semi-automatic, no scope is left for the imagination. Those who are so absorbed by the world of the movie — by its images, gestures, and words — that they are unable to supply what really makes it a world, do not have to dwell on particular points of its mechanics during a screening. All the other films and products of the entertainment industry which they have seen have taught them what to expect; they react automatically. The might of industrial society is lodged in men's minds. The entertainments manufacturers know that their products will be consumed with alertness even when the customer is distraught, for each of them is a model of the huge economic machinery which has always sustained the masses, whether at work or at leisure — which is akin to work. From every sound film and every broadcast program the social effect can be inferred which is exclusive to none but is shared by all alike. The culture industry as a whole has molded men as a type unfailingly reproduced in every product. All the agents of this process, from the producer to the women's clubs, take good care that the simple reproduction of this mental state is not nuanced or extended in any way.

The art historians and guardians of culture who complain of the extinction in the West of a basic style-determining power are wrong. The stereotyped appropriation of everything, even the inchoate, for the purposes of mechanical reproduction surpasses the rigor and general currency of any "real style," in the sense in which cultural cognoscenti celebrate the organic precapitalist past.[6] No Palestrina[7] could be more of a purist in eliminating every unprepared and unresolved discord than the jazz arranger in suppressing any development which does not conform to the jargon. When jazzing up Mozart he changes him not only when he is too serious or too difficult but when he harmonizes the melody in a different way, perhaps more simply, than is customary now. No medieval builder can have scrutinized the subjects for church windows and sculptures more suspiciously than the studio hierarchy scrutinizes a work by Balzac or Hugo before finally approving it. No medieval theologian could have determined the degree of the torment to be suffered by the damned in accordance with the ordo of divine love[8] more meticulously than the

[6]Adorno in particular had seen the progression of styles in painting, music, and literature as obeying a historical law. But after the triumphant modernism of the 1920s and 1930s, the progression seemed to come to a halt. Here the authors explain that halt in terms of the ownership of the culture industry and the intention of the owners.

[7]Giovanni Perluigi di Palestrina (1525–1594), Renaissance composer of liturgical music. The authors' suggestion of censorship may refer to a legend that the Council of Trent had threatened to ban polyphonic music, on the ground that the liturgical text became incomprehensible, but that Palestrina composed a mass, the *Missa Papae Marcelli*, that reconciled the authorities to this style.

[8]*Ordo* is Latin for "order." The allusion is to Dante's *Divine Comedy*, where Dante finds written on the gates of Hell that they were built by "divina potestate / la somma sapienza e il primo Amore" — divine power, the highest wisdom, and primal love.

producers of shoddy epics calculate the torture to be undergone by the hero or the exact point to which the leading lady's hemline shall be raised. The explicit and implicit, exoteric and esoteric catalog of the forbidden and tolerated is so extensive that it not only defines the area of freedom but is all-powerful inside it. Everything down to the last detail is shaped accordingly. . . .

Whenever Orson Welles[9] offends against the tricks of the trade, he is forgiven because his departures from the norm are regarded as calculated mutations which serve all the more strongly to confirm the validity of the system. The constraint of the technically-conditioned idiom which stars and directors have to produce as "nature" so that the people can appropriate it, extends to such fine nuances that they almost attain the subtlety of the devices of an avant-garde work as against those of truth. The rare capacity minutely to fulfill the obligations of the natural idiom in all branches of the culture industry becomes the criterion of efficiency. What and how they say it must be measurable by everyday language, as in logical positivism. The producers are experts. The idiom demands an astounding productive power, which it absorbs and squanders. In a diabolical way it has overreached the culturally conservative distinction between genuine and artificial style. A style might be called artificial which is imposed from without on the refractory impulses of a form. But in the culture industry every element of the subject matter has its origin in the same apparatus as that jargon whose stamp it bears. The quarrels in which the artistic experts become involved with sponsor and censor about a lie going beyond the bounds of credibility are evidence not so much of an inner aesthetic tension as of a divergence of interests. The reputation of the specialist, in which a last remnant of objective independence sometimes finds refuge, conflicts with the business politics of the Church, or the concern which is manufacturing the cultural commodity. But the thing itself has been essentially objectified and made viable before the established authorities began to argue about it. Even before Zanuck acquired her, Saint Bernadette was regarded by her latter-day hagiographer as brilliant propaganda for all interested parties.[10] That is what became of the emotions of the character. Hence the style of the culture industry, which no longer has to test itself against any refractory material, is also the negation of style. The reconciliation of the general and particular, of the rule and the specific demands of the subject matter, the achievement of which alone gives essential, meaningful content to style, is futile because there has ceased to be the slightest tension between opposite poles: these concordant extremes are dismally identical; the general can replace the particular, and vice versa.

Nevertheless, this caricature of style does not amount to something beyond the genuine style of the past. In the culture industry the notion of genuine style is seen to be the aesthetic equivalent of domination. Style considered as mere aesthetic regularity is a romantic dream of the past. The unity of style not only of the Christian Middle Ages but of the Renaissance expresses in each case the different structure of social power, and not the obscure experience of the oppressed in which the general was enclosed. The great artists were never those who embodied a wholly flawless and perfect style, but those who used style as a way of hardening themselves against the chaotic expression of suffering, as a negative truth. The style of their works gave what was expressed that force without which life flows away unheard. Those very art forms which are known as classical, such as Mozart's music, contain objective trends which represent something different to the style which they incarnate. As late as Schönberg and Picasso, the great artists have retained a mistrust of style, and at crucial points have subordinated it to the logic of the matter. What Dadaists and Expressionists called the untruth of style as such triumphs today in the sung jargon of a

---

[9]Orson Welles (1915–1985), maverick Hollywood director of *Citizen Kane* (1941).

[10]Darryl F. Zanuck was the studio head of Twentieth-Century Fox, which made *The Song of Bernadette* (1943), a film that won four Oscars and was nominated for eight others, based on the play by the authors' compatriot and fellow exile Franz Werfel.

crooner, in the carefully contrived elegance of a film star, and even in the admirable expertise of a photograph of a peasant's squalid hut. Style represents a promise in every work of art. That which is expressed is subsumed through style into the dominant forms of generality, into the language of music, painting, or words, in the hope that it will be reconciled thus with the idea of true generality. This promise held out by the work of art that it will create truth by lending new shape to the conventional social forms is as necessary as it is hypocritical. It unconditionally posits the real forms of life as it is by suggesting that fulfillment lies in their aesthetic derivatives. To this extent the claim of art is always ideology too. However, only in this confrontation with tradition of which style is the record can art express suffering. That factor in a work of art which enables it to transcend reality certainly cannot be detached from style; but it does not consist of the harmony actually realized, of any doubtful unity of form and content, within and without, of individual and society; it is to be found in those features in which discrepancy appears: in the necessary failure of the passionate striving for identity. Instead of exposing itself to this failure in which the style of the great work of art has always achieved self-negation, the inferior work has always relied on its similarity with others — on a surrogate identity.

In the culture industry this imitation finally becomes absolute. Having ceased to be anything but style, it reveals the latter's secret: obedience to the social hierarchy. Today aesthetic barbarity completes what has threatened the creations of the spirit since they were gathered together as culture and neutralized. To speak of culture was always contrary to culture. Culture as a common denominator already contains in embryo that schematization and process of cataloguing and classification which bring culture within the sphere of administration. And it is precisely the industrialized, the consequent, subsumption which entirely accords with this notion of culture. By subordinating in the same way and to the same end all areas of intellectual creation, by occupying men's senses from the time they leave the factory in the evening to the time they clock in again the next morning with matter that bears the impress of the labor process they themselves have to sustain throughout the day, this subsumption mockingly satisfies the concept of a unified culture which the philosophers of personality contrasted with mass culture.

And so the culture industry, the most rigid of all styles, proves to be the goal of liberalism, which is reproached for its lack of style. Not only do its categories and contents derive from liberalism — domesticated naturalism as well as operetta and revue — but the modern culture monopolies form the economic area in which, together with the corresponding entrepreneurial types, for the time being some part of its sphere of operation survives, despite the process of disintegration elsewhere. It is still possible to make one's way in entertainment, if one is not too obstinate about one's own concerns, and proves appropriately pliable. Anyone who resists can only survive by fitting in. Once his particular brand of deviation from the norm has been noted by the industry, he belongs to it as does the land-reformer to capitalism. Realistic dissidence is the trademark of anyone who has a new idea in business. In the public voice of modern society accusations are seldom audible; if they are, the perceptive can already detect signs that the dissident will soon be reconciled. The more immeasurable the gap between chorus and leaders, the more certainly there is room at the top for everybody who demonstrates his superiority by well-planned originality. Hence, in the culture industry, too, the liberal tendency to give full scope to its able men survives. To do this for the efficient today is still the function of the market, which is otherwise proficiently controlled; as for the market's freedom, in the high period of art as elsewhere, it was freedom for the stupid to starve. Significantly, the system of the culture industry comes from the more liberal industrial nations, and all its characteristic media, such as movies, radio, jazz, and magazines, flourish there. Its progress, to be sure, had its origin in the general laws of capital. Gaumont and Pathé, Ullstein and Hugenberg[11] followed the international trend with some success; Europe's economic dependence on the United States after war and inflation was a contributory factor. The

[11]French and German film studios.

belief that the barbarity of the culture industry is a result of "cultural lag," of the fact that the American consciousness did not keep up with the growth of technology, is quite wrong. It was pre-Fascist Europe which did not keep up with the trend toward the culture monopoly. But it was this very lag which left intellect and creativity some degree of independence and enabled its last representatives to exist — however dismally. In Germany[12] the failure of democratic control to permeate life had led to a paradoxical situation. Many things were exempt from the market mechanism which had invaded the Western countries. The German educational system, universities, theaters with artistic standards, great orchestras, and museums enjoyed protection. The political powers, state and municipalities, which had inherited such institutions from absolutism, had left them with a measure of the freedom from the forces of power which dominates the market, just as princes and feudal lords had done up to the nineteenth century. This strengthened art in this late phase against the verdict of supply and demand, and increased its resistance far beyond the actual degree of protection. In the market itself the tribute of a quality for which no use had been found was turned into purchasing power; in this way, respectable literary and music publishers could help authors who yielded little more in the way of profit than the respect of the connoisseur. But what completely fettered the artist was the pressure (and the accompanying drastic threats), always to fit into business life as an aesthetic expert. Formerly, like Kant and Hume, they signed their letters "Your most humble and obedient servant," and underlined the foundations of throne and altar. Today they address heads of government by their first names, yet in every artistic activity they are subject to their illiterate masters. The analysis Tocqueville[13] offered a century ago has in the meantime proved wholly accurate. Under the private culture monopoly it is a fact that "tyranny leaves the body free and directs its attack at the soul. The ruler no longer says: You must think as I do or die. He says: You are free not to think as I do; your life, your property, everything shall remain yours, but from this day on you are a stranger among us." Not to conform means to be rendered powerless, economically and therefore spiritually — to be "self-employed." When the outsider is excluded from the concern, he can only too easily be accused of incompetence. Whereas today in material production the mechanism of supply and demand is disintegrating,[14] in the superstructure it still operates as a check in the rulers' favor. The consumers are the workers and employees, the farmers and lower middle class. Capitalist production so confines them, body and soul, that they fall helpless victims to what is offered them. As naturally as the ruled always took the morality imposed upon them more seriously than did the rulers themselves, the deceived masses are today captivated by the myth of success even more than the successful are. Immovably, they insist on the very ideology which enslaves them. The misplaced love of the common people for the wrong which is done them is a greater force than the cunning of the authorities. It is stronger even than the rigorism of the Hays Office,[15] just as in certain great times in history it has inflamed greater forces that were turned against it, namely, the terror of the tribunals. It calls for Mickey Rooney in preference to the tragic Garbo, for Donald Duck instead of Betty Boop.[16] The industry submits to the vote which it has itself inspired. What is a loss for the firm which cannot fully exploit a contract with a declining star is a legitimate expense for the

[12]The authors are speaking of the Weimar Republic — "pre-Fascist" post-Imperial Germany between 1918 and 1933.

[13]Alexis de Tocqueville (1805–1859) wrote *De la Democracie en Amerique (Democracy in America)*, a sociological analysis of the United States in 1835–40, which stressed that the tyranny of the majority had supplanted the tyranny of nobility.

[14]This was written during World War II, when the authors were aware of the fact that many Americans not fighting overseas had plenty of money but no consumer goods to buy, whereas the government bought its needs (military equipment) at dictated prices.

[15]A censorship board set up by the film studios in 1934 under Will Hays, the postmaster general, which for twenty years dictated strictly what could not be said or shown in studio films.

[16]Sexy female cartoon character created by Max and Dave Fleischer in 1932; the Hays Production Code forced the "flapper" to wear longer skirts and hide her cleavage, and the character was retired in 1939 (aside from recent nostalgic revivals).

system as a whole. By craftily sanctioning the demand for rubbish it inaugurates total harmony. The connoisseur and the expert are despised for their pretentious claim to know better than the others, even though culture is democratic and distributes its privileges to all. In view of the ideological truce, the conformism of the buyers and the effrontery of the producers who supply them prevail. The result is a constant reproduction of the same thing. A constant sameness governs the relationship to the past as well. What is new about the phase of mass culture compared with the late liberal stage is the exclusion of the new. The machine rotates on the same spot. While determining consumption it excludes the untried as a risk. The movie-makers distrust any manuscript which is not reassuringly backed by a bestseller. Yet for this very reason there is never-ending talk of ideas, novelty, and surprise, of what is taken for granted but has never existed. Tempo and dynamics serve this trend. Nothing remains as of old; everything has to run incessantly, to keep moving. For only the universal triumph of the rhythm of mechanical production and reproduction

promises that nothing changes, and nothing unsuitable will appear. Any additions to the well-proven culture inventory are too much of a speculation. The ossified forms — such as the sketch, short story, problem film, or hit song — are the standardized average of late liberal taste, dictated with threats from above. The people at the top in the culture agencies, who work in harmony as only one manager can with another, whether he comes from the rag trade[17] or from college, have long since reorganized and rationalized the objective spirit. One might think that an omnipresent authority had sifted the material and drawn up an official catalog of cultural commodities to provide a smooth supply of available mass-produced lines. The ideas are written in the cultural firmament where they had already been numbered by Plato — and were indeed numbers, incapable of increase and immutable.

[17]Garment manufacture. The authors may be alluding to the studio head of MGM, Sam Goldwyn (1882–1974), who had succeeded in the garment industry before moving on to movies.

Louis Althusser

1918–1990

The controversial French Marxist Louis Althusser was born in 1918 in Birmandreis, Algeria, and educated at a lycée in Lyons. While awaiting placement into the higher education system in 1939, he was drafted into the French army; he spent five years as a prisoner of the Third Reich. In 1945 Althusser began attending the prestigious École Normale Superieure in Paris, where he completed his doctorate, and where he taught philosophy for the rest of his active career. He is best known for the two books he published in 1965, For Marx *and* Reading "Capital," *in which he re-interprets Marxist theory in a way similar to the way Lacan re-interpreted Freud, arguing that he was recovering Marx's original meaning. And just as Lacan viewed the "self" as an imaginary construct produced by the child's observation of himself in a mirror, Althusser viewed the individual subject as an equally imaginary construct, produced by ideology, which "interpellates" or addresses us as occupying a particular position. In* Lenin and Philosophy *(1969), Althusser argued that one class rules another not through repressive measures but rather through its hegemony over "ideological state apparatuses," like the church or school system. Such institutions not only mold beliefs but reproduce their ruling cadres, as loyal laymen become priests, or loyal students become teachers. Althusser also claimed that philosophy should not be considered a science, as it has no object and no history, but should be viewed as "the class struggle within theory." While some have accused Althusser of mystification, and of distorting Marx by reading him selectively, Fredric Jameson has praised his work for battling the tradition of empiricism, Pierre Macherey has transferred Althusser's concept of "symptomal reading" to the field of literary criticism, and Maurice Godelier has found his social theories applicable to anthropological studies of the development of capitalist societies. Louis Althusser suffered from manic depression throughout most of his life, and in 1976 he married sociologist Hélène Legotier, who thereafter served as his private nurse. In November 1980, he strangled her to death. Due to his well-documented mental instability, he was judged unfit for trial, and locked up in the Centre Hospitalier Sainte Anne, a psychiatric hospital in Paris, for three years. He died in 1990. The selection below, taken from "Ideology and Ideological State Apparatuses," was published in* Lenin and Philosophy.

From *Ideology and Ideological State Apparatuses*

IDEOLOGY IS A "REPRESENTATION" OF THE IMAGINARY RELATIONSHIP OF INDIVIDUALS TO THEIR REAL CONDITIONS OF EXISTENCE

In order to approach my central thesis on the structure and functioning of ideology, I shall first present two theses, one negative, the other positive. The first concerns the object which is "represented" in the imaginary form of ideology, the second concerns the materiality of ideology.

THESIS I: Ideology represents the imaginary relationship of individuals to their real conditions of existence.

We commonly call religious ideology, ethical ideology, legal ideology, political ideology, etc., so many "world outlooks." Of course, assuming that we do not live one of these ideologies as the truth (e.g. "believe" in God, Duty, Justice, etc. . . .), we admit that the ideology we are discussing from a critical point of view, examining it as the ethnologist examines the myths of a "primitive society," that these "world outlooks" are largely imaginary, i.e. do not "correspond to reality."

However, while admitting that they do not correspond to reality, i.e. that they constitute an illusion, we admit that they do make allusion to reality, and that they need only be "interpreted" to discover the reality of the world behind their imaginary representation of that world (ideology = *illusion/allusion*).

There are different types of interpretation, the most famous of which are the *mechanistic* type, current in the eighteenth century (God is the imaginary representation of the real King), and the *"hermeneutic"* interpretation, inaugurated by the earliest Church Fathers, and revived by Feuerbach[1] and the theologico-philosophical school which descends from him, e.g. the theologian Barth[2] (to Feuerbach, for example, God is the essence of real Man). The essential point is that on condition that we interpret the imaginary transposition (and inversion) of ideology we arrive at the conclusion that in ideology "men represent their real conditions of existence to themselves in an imaginary form."

Unfortunately, this interpretation leaves one small problem unsettled: why do men "need" this imaginary transposition of their real conditions of existence in order to "represent to themselves" their real conditions of existence?

The first answer (that of the eighteenth century) proposes a simple solution: Priests or Despots are responsible. They "forged" the Beautiful Lies so that, in the belief that they were obeying God, men would in fact obey the Priests and Despots, who are usually in alliance in their imposture, the Priests acting in the interests of the Despots or *vice versa*, according to the political positions of the "theoreticians" concerned. There

[1]Ludwig Feuerbach (1804–1872), philosopher and theologian, to whose materialist interpretation of religion Marx responded in 1845.
[2]Karl Barth (1886–1968), theologian.

Translated by Ben Brewster.

is therefore a cause for the imaginary transposition of the real conditions of existence: that cause is the existence of a small number of cynical men who base their domination and exploitation of the "people" on a falsified representation of the world which they have imagined in order to enslave other minds by dominating their imaginations.

The second answer (that of Feuerbach, taken over word for word by Marx in his Early Works) is more "profound," i.e. just as false. It, too, seeks and finds a cause for the imaginary transposition and distortion of men's real conditions of existence, in short, for the alienation in the imaginary of the representation of men's conditions of existence. This cause is no longer Priests or Despots, nor their active imagination and the passive imagination of their victims. This cause is the material alienation which reigns in the conditions of existence of men themselves. This is how, in *The Jewish Question* and elsewhere, Marx defends the Feuerbachian idea that men make themselves an alienated (= imaginary) representation of their conditions of existence because these conditions of existence are themselves alienating (in the *1844 Manuscripts*: because these conditions are dominated by the essence of alienated society — "*alienated labor*").[3]

All these interpretations thus take literally the thesis which they presuppose, and on which they depend, i.e. that what is reflected in the imaginary representation of the world found in an ideology is the conditions of existence of men, i.e. their real world.

Now I can return to a thesis which I have already advanced: it is not their real conditions of existence, their real world, that "men" "represent to themselves" in ideology, but above all it is their relation to those conditions of existence which is represented to them there. It is this relation which is at the center of every ideological, i.e. imaginary, representation of the real world. It is this relation that contains the "cause" which has to explain the imaginary distortion of the ideological representation of the real world. Or rather, to leave aside the language of causality it is necessary to advance the thesis that it is the *imaginary nature of this relation* which underlies all the imaginary distortion that we can observe (if we do not live in its truth) in all ideology.

To speak in a Marxist language, if it is true that the representation of the real conditions of existence of the individuals occupying the posts of agents of production, exploitation, repression, ideologization and scientific practice, does in the last analysis arise from the relations of production, and from relations deriving from the relations of production, we can say the following: all ideology represents in its necessarily imaginary distortion not the existing relations of production (and the other relations that derive from them), but above all the (imaginary) relationship of individuals to the relations of production and the relations that derive from them. What is represented in ideology is therefore not the system of the real relations which govern the existence of individuals, but the imaginary relation of those individuals to the real relations in which they live.

If this is the case, the question of the "cause" of the imaginary distortion of the real relations in ideology disappears and must be replaced by a different question: why is the representation given to individuals of their (individual) relation to the social relations which govern their conditions of existence and their collective and individual life necessarily an imaginary relation? And what is the nature of this imaginariness? Posed in this way, the question explodes the solution by a "clique,"[4] by a group of individuals (Priests or Despots) who are the authors of the great ideological mystification, just as it explodes the solution by the alienated character of the real world. We shall see why later in my exposition. For the moment I shall go no further.

THESIS II: Ideology has a material existence.

I have already touched on this thesis by saying that the "ideas" or "representations," etc., which seem to make up ideology do not have an ideal (*idéale* or *idéelle*)[5] or spiritual existence, but a

---

[3] See Marx, . . . *The Alienation of Labor*, p. 400.

[4] I use this very modern term deliberately. For even in Communist circles, unfortunately, it is a commonplace to "explain" some political deviation (left or right opportunism) by the action of a "clique." [Althusser]

[5] *Idéale* means "ideal"; *idéelle* means "ideational," the production or generation of ideas.

material existence. I even suggested that the ideal (*idéale*, *idéelle*) and spiritual existence of "ideas" arises exclusively in an ideology of the "idea" and of ideology, and let me add, in an ideology of what seems to have "founded" this conception since the emergence of the sciences, i.e. what the practicians of the sciences represent to themselves in their spontaneous ideology as "ideas," true or false. Of course, presented in affirmative form, this thesis is unproven. I simply ask that the reader be favorably disposed towards it, say, in the name of materialism. A long series of arguments would be necessary to prove it.

This hypothetical thesis of the not spiritual but material existence of "ideas" or other "representations" is indeed necessary if we are to advance in our analysis of the nature of ideology. Or rather, it is merely useful to us in order the better to reveal what every at all serious analysis of any ideology will immediately and empirically show to every observer, however critical.

While discussing the ideological State apparatuses and their practices, I said that each of them was the realization of an ideology (the unity of these different regional ideologies — religious, ethical, legal, political, aesthetic, etc. — being assured by their subjection to the ruling ideology). I now return to this thesis: an ideology always exists in an apparatus, and its practice, or practices. This existence is material.

Of course, the material existence of the ideology in an apparatus and its practices does not have the same modality as the material existence of a paving-stone or a rifle. But, at the risk of being taken for a Neo-Aristotelian[6] (NB Marx had a very high regard for Aristotle), I shall say that "matter is discussed in many senses," or rather that it exists in different modalities, all rooted in the last instance in "physical" matter.

Having said this, let me move straight on and see what happens to the "individuals" who live in ideology, i.e. in a determinate (religious, ethical, etc.) representation of the world whose imaginary distortion depends on their imaginary relation to their conditions of existence, in other words, in the last instance, to the relations of production and to class relations (ideology = an imaginary relation to real relations). I shall say that this imaginary relation is itself endowed with a material existence.

Now I observe the following.

An individual believes in God, or Duty, or Justice, etc. This belief derives (for everyone, i.e. for all those who live in an ideological representation of ideology, which reduces ideology to ideas endowed by definition with a spiritual existence) from the ideas of the individual concerned, i.e. from him as a subject with a consciousness which contains the ideas of his belief. In this way, i.e. by means of the absolutely ideological "conceptual" device (*dispositif*) thus set up (a subject endowed with a consciousness in which he freely forms or freely recognizes ideas in which he believes), the (material) attitude of the subject concerned naturally follows.

The individual in question behaves in such and such a way, adopts such and such a practical attitude, and, what is more, participates in certain regular practices which are those of the ideological apparatus on which "depend" the ideas which he has in all consciousness freely chosen as a subject. If he believes in God, he goes to Church to attend Mass, kneels, prays, confesses, does penance (once it was material in the ordinary sense of the term) and naturally repents and so on. If he believes in Duty, he will have the corresponding attitudes, inscribed in ritual practices "according to the correct principles." If he believes in Justice, he will submit unconditionally to the rules of the Law, and may even protest when they are violated, sign petitions, take part in a demonstration, etc.

Throughout this schema we observe that the ideological representation of ideology is itself forced to recognize that every "subject" endowed with a "consciousness" and believing in the "ideas" that his "consciousness" inspires in him and freely accepts, must "*act according to his ideas*," must therefore inscribe his own ideas as a free subject in the actions of his material practice. If he does not do so, "that is wicked."

Indeed, if he does not do what he ought to do as a function of what he believes, it is because he

---

[6]Not in the literary-critical sense (e.g., a follower of R. S. Crane), but a materialist in the sense that Aristotle was, excluding ideal essences, but seeing reality as embodied in actions, processes, practices, and habits. See Introduction to Aristotle, p. 55.

does something else, which, still as a function of the same idealist scheme, implies that he has other ideas in his head as well as those he proclaims, and that he acts according to these other ideas, as a man who is either "inconsistent" ("no one is willingly evil") or cynical, or perverse.

In every case, the ideology of ideology thus recognizes, despite its imaginary distortion, that the "ideas" of a human subject exist in his actions, or ought to exist in his actions, and if that is not the case, it lends him other ideas corresponding to the actions (however perverse) that he does perform. This ideology talks of actions: I shall talk of actions inserted into *practices. And* I shall point out that these practices are governed by the *rituals* in which these practices are inscribed, within the *material existence of an ideological apparatus*, be it only a small part of that apparatus: a small mass in a small church, a funeral, a minor match at a sports club, a school day, a political party meeting, etc.

Besides, we are indebted to Pascal's defensive "dialectic" for the wonderful formula which will enable us to invert the order of the notional schema of ideology. Pascal says more or less: "Kneel down, move your lips in prayer, and you will believe." He thus scandalously inverts the order of things, bringing, like Christ, not peace but strife, and in addition something hardly Christian (for woe to him who brings scandal into the world!) — scandal itself. A fortunate scandal which makes him stick with Jansenist defiance to a language that directly names the reality.[7]

I will be allowed to leave Pascal to the arguments of his ideological struggle with the religious ideological State apparatus of his day. And I shall be expected to use a more directly Marxist vocabulary, if that is possible, for we are advancing in still poorly explored domains.

I shall therefore say that, where only a single subject (such and such an individual) is concerned,

the existence of the ideas of his belief is material in that *his ideas are his material actions inserted into material practices governed by material rituals which are themselves defined by the material ideological apparatus from which derive the ideas of that subject.* Naturally, the four inscriptions of the adjective "material" in my proposition must be affected by different modalities: the materialities of a displacement for going to mass, of kneeling down, of the gesture of the sign of the cross, or of the *mea culpa*, of a sentence, of a prayer, of an act of contrition, of a penitence, of a gaze, of a handshake, of an external verbal discourse or an "internal" verbal discourse (consciousness), are not one and the same materiality. I shall leave on one side the problem of a theory of the differences between the modalities of materiality.

It remains that in this inverted presentation of things, we are not dealing with an "inversion" at all, since it is clear that certain notions have purely and simply disappeared from our presentation, whereas others on the contrary survive, and new terms appear.

Disappeared: the term *ideas.*

Survive: the terms *subject, consciousness, belief, actions.*

Appear: the terms *practices, rituals, ideological apparatus.*

It is therefore not an inversion or overturning (except in the sense in which one might say a government or a glass is overturned), but a reshuffle (of a non-ministerial type), a rather strange reshuffle, since we obtain the following result.

Ideas have disappeared as such (insofar as they are endowed with an ideal or spiritual existence), to the precise extent that it has emerged that their existence is inscribed in the actions of practices governed by rituals defined in the last instance by an ideological apparatus. It therefore appears that the subject acts insofar as he is acted by the following system (set out in the order of its real determination): ideology existing in a material ideological apparatus, prescribing material practices governed by a material ritual, which practices exist in the material actions of a subject acting in all consciousness according to his belief.

But this very presentation reveals that we have retained the following notions: subject, consciousness, belief, actions. From this series I shall

---

[7]Althusser is comparing his view, that actions within social practices shape the subject of ideology, to the advice of Blaise Pascal (1623–1662) that the Christian should go through the motions of prayer in order to bring about faith. Pascal was one of the most notable Jansenists (i.e., a follower of Cornelius Jansen [1585–1638], whose view of grace and predestination was declared heretical by the Catholic Church).

immediately extract the decisive central term on which everything else depends: the notion of the *subject*.

And I shall immediately set down two conjoint theses:

1. there is no practice except by and in an ideology;

2. there is no ideology except by the subject and for subjects.

I can now come to my central thesis.

IDEOLOGY INTERPELLATES[8] INDIVIDUALS AS SUBJECTS

This thesis is simply a matter of making my last proposition explicit: there is no ideology except by the subject and for subjects. Meaning, there is no ideology except for concrete subjects, and this destination for ideology is only made possible by the subject: meaning, *by the category of the subject* and its functioning.

By this I mean that, even if it only appears under this name (the subject) with the rise of bourgeois ideology, above all with the rise of legal ideology,[9] the category of the subject (which may function under other names: e.g., as the soul in Plato, as God, etc.) is the constitutive category of all ideology, whatever its determination (regional or class) and whatever its historical date — since ideology has no history.

I say: the category of the subject is constitutive of all ideology, but at the same time and immediately I add that *the category of the subject is only constitutive of all ideology insofar as all ideology has the function (which defines it) of "constituting" concrete individuals as subjects*. In the interaction of this double constitution exists the functioning of all ideology, ideology being nothing but its functioning in the material forms of existence of that functioning.

In order to grasp what follows, it is essential to realize that both he who is writing these lines and the reader who reads them are themselves subjects,

[8]To interpellate is to hail someone in a way that defines one's identity.

[9]Which borrowed the legal category of "subject in law" to make an ideological notion: man is by nature a subject. [Althusser]

and therefore ideological subjects (a tautological proposition), i.e. that the author and the reader of these lines both live "spontaneously" or "naturally" in ideology in the sense in which I have said that "man is an ideological animal by nature."

That the author, insofar as he writes the lines of a discourse which claims to be scientific, is completely absent as a "subject" from "his" scientific discourse (for all scientific discourse is by definition a subject-less discourse, there is no "subject of science" except in an ideology of science) is a different question which I shall leave on one side for the moment.

As St. Paul admirably put it, it is in the "Logos," meaning in ideology, that we "live, move and have our being." It follows that, for you and for me, the category of the subject is a primary "obviousness" (obviousnesses are always primary): it is clear that you and I are subjects (free, ethical, etc. . . .). Like all obviousnesses, including those that make a word "name a thing" or "have a meaning" (therefore including the obviousness of the "transparency" of language), the "obviousness" that you and I are subjects — and that that does not cause any problems — is an ideological effect, the elementary ideological effect.[10] It is indeed a peculiarity of ideology that it imposes (without appearing to do so, since these are "obviousnesses") obviousnesses as obviousnesses, which we cannot *fail to recognize* and before which we have the inevitable and natural reaction of crying out (aloud or in the "still, small voice of conscience"): "That's obvious! That's right! That's true!"

At work in this reaction is the ideological *recognition* function which is one of the two functions of ideology as such (its inverse being the function of *misrecognition — méconnaissance*).[11]

[10]Linguists and those who appeal to linguistics for various purposes often run up against difficulties which arise because they ignore the action of the ideological effects in all discourses — including even scientific discourses. [Althusser]

[11]Althusser uses Lacan's term (mis-recognition) here, because his notion of how the subject is constituted by ideology, as an imaginary relation of the individual to his material circumstances, is parallel to Lacan's Mirror Stage, in which the Imaginary self-image of the individual as a coherent totality is formed by the same process of *méconnaissance*.

To take a highly "concrete" example, we all have friends who, when they knock on our door and we ask, through the door, the question "Who's there?" answer (since "it's obvious") "It's me." And we recognize that "it is him," or "her." We open the door, and "it's true, it really was she who was there." To take another example, when we recognize somebody of our (previous) acquaintance ((*re*)-*connaissance*) in the street, we show him that we have recognized him (and have recognized that he has recognized us) by saying to him "Hello, my friend," and shaking his hand (a material ritual practice of ideological recognition in everyday life — in France, at least; elsewhere, there are other rituals).

In this preliminary remark and these concrete illustrations, I only wish to point out that you and I are *always already* subjects, and as such constantly practice the rituals of ideological recognition, which guarantee for us that we are indeed concrete, individual, distinguishable and (naturally) irreplaceable subjects. The writing I am currently executing and the reading you are currently[12] performing are also in this respect rituals of ideological recognition, including the "obviousness" with which the "truth" or "error" of my reflections may impose itself on you.

But to recognize that we are subjects and that we function in the practical rituals of the most elementary everyday life (the hand-shake, the fact of calling you by your name, the fact of knowing, even if I do not know what it is, that you "have" a name of your own, which means that you are recognized as a unique subject, etc.) — this recognition only gives us the "consciousness" of our incessant (eternal) practice of ideological recognition — its consciousness, i.e. its *recognition* — but in no sense does it give us the (scientific) *knowledge* of the mechanism of this recognition. Now it is this knowledge that we have to reach, if you will, while speaking in ideology, and from within ideology we have to outline a discourse which tries to break with ideology, in order to dare to be the beginning of a scientific (i.e. subjectless) discourse on ideology.

Thus in order to represent why the category of the "subject" is constitutive of ideology, which only exists by constituting concrete subjects as subjects, I shall employ a special mode of exposition: "concrete" enough to be recognized, but abstract enough to be thinkable and thought, giving rise to a knowledge.

As a first formulation I shall say: *all ideology hails or interpellates concrete individuals as concrete subjects*, by the functioning of the category of the subject.

This is a proposition which entails that we distinguish for the moment between concrete individuals on the one hand and concrete subjects on the other, although at this level concrete subjects only exist insofar as they are supported by a concrete individual.

I shall then suggest that ideology "acts" or "functions" in such a way that it "recruits" subjects among the individuals (it recruits them all), or "transforms" the individuals into subjects (it transforms them all) by that very precise operation which I have called *interpellation* or hailing, and which can be imagined along the lines of the most commonplace everyday police (or other) hailing: "Hey, you there!"[13]

Assuming that the theoretical scene I have imagined takes place in the street, the hailed individual will turn round. By this mere one-hundred-and-eighty-degree physical conversion, he becomes a *subject*. Why? Because he has recognized that the hail was "really" addressed to him, and that "it was *really him* who was hailed" (and not someone else). Experience shows that the practical telecommunication of hailings is such that they hardly ever miss their man: verbal call or whistle, the one hailed always recognizes that it is really him who is being hailed. And yet it is a strange phenomenon, and one which cannot be explained solely by "guilt feelings," despite the large numbers who "have something on their consciences."

Naturally for the convenience and clarity of my little theoretical theater I have had to present things

---

[12]NB: this double "currently" is one more proof of the fact that ideology is eternal, since these two "currentlys" are separated by an indefinite interval; I am writing these lines on 6 April 1969, you may read them at any subsequent time. [Althusser]

[13]Hailing as an everyday practice subject to a precise ritual takes a quite "special" form in the policeman's practice of "hailing" which concerns the hailing of "suspects." [Althusser]

in the form of a sequence, with a before and an after, and thus in the form of a temporal succession. There are individuals walking along. Somewhere (usually behind them) the hail rings out: "Hey, you there!" One individual (nine times out of ten it is the right one) turns round, believing/suspecting/knowing that it is for him, i.e. recognizing that "it really is he" who is meant by the hailing. But in reality these things happen without any succession. The existence of ideology and the hailing or interpellation of individuals as subjects are one and the same thing.

I might add: what thus seems to take place outside ideology (to be precise, in the street), in reality takes place in ideology. What really takes place in ideology seems therefore to take place outside it. That is why those who are in ideology believe themselves by definition outside ideology: one of the effects of ideology is the practical *denegation* of the ideological character of ideology by ideology: ideology never says, "I am ideological." It is necessary to be outside ideology, i.e. in scientific knowledge, to be able to say: I am in ideology (a quite exceptional case) or (the general case): I was in ideology. As is well known, the accusation of being in ideology only applies to others, never to oneself (unless one is really a Spinozist or a Marxist, which, in this matter, is to be exactly the same thing). Which amounts to saying that ideology *has no outside* (for itself), but at the same time *that it is nothing but outside* (for science and reality).

Spinoza explained this completely two centuries before Marx, who practiced it but without explaining it in detail. But let us leave this point, although it is heavy with consequences, consequences which are not just theoretical, but also directly political, since, for example, the whole theory of criticism and self-criticism, the golden rule of the Marxist-Leninist practice of the class struggle, depends on it.

Thus ideology hails or interpellates individuals as subjects. As ideology is eternal, I must now suppress the temporal form in which I have presented the functioning of ideology, and say: ideology has always-already interpellated individuals as subjects, which amounts to making it clear that individuals are always-already interpellated by ideology as subjects, which necessarily leads us to one last

proposition: *individuals are always-already subjects*. Hence individuals are "abstract" with respect to the subjects which they always-already are. This proposition might seem paradoxical.

That an individual is always-already a subject, even before he is born, is nevertheless the plain reality, accessible to everyone and not a paradox at all. Freud shows that individuals are always "abstract" with respect to the subjects they always-already are, simply by noting the ideological ritual that surrounds the expectation of a "birth," that "happy event." Everyone knows how much and in what way an unborn child is expected. Which amounts to saying, very prosaically, if we agree to drop the "sentiments," i.e. the forms of family ideology (paternal/maternal/conjugal/fraternal) in which the unborn child is expected: it is certain in advance that it will bear its Father's Name, and will therefore have an identity and be irreplaceable. Before its birth, the child is therefore always-already a subject, appointed as a subject in and by the specific familial ideological configuration in which it is "expected" once it has been conceived. I hardly need add that this familial ideological configuration is, in its uniqueness, highly structured, and that it is in this implacable and more or less "pathological" (presupposing that any meaning can be assigned to that term) structure that the former subject-to-be will have to "find" "its" place, i.e. "become" the sexual subject (boy or girl) which it already is in advance. It is clear that this ideological constraint and pre-appointment, and all the rituals of rearing and then education in the family, have some relationship with what Freud studied in the forms of the pre-genital and genital "stages" of sexuality, i.e. in the "grip" of what Freud registered by its effects as being the unconscious. But let us leave this point, too, on one side.

Let me go one step further. What I shall now turn my attention to is the way the "actors" in this *mise en scène* of interpellation, and their respective roles, are reflected in the very structure of all ideology.

AN EXAMPLE: THE CHRISTIAN RELIGIOUS IDEOLOGY

As the formal structure of all ideology is always the same, I shall restrict my analysis to a single example, one accessible to everyone, that of religious ideology, with the proviso that the same demonstration can be produced for ethical, legal, political, aesthetic ideology, etc.

Let us therefore consider the Christian religious ideology. I shall use a rhetorical figure and "make it speak," i.e. collect into a fictional discourse what it "says" not only in its two Testaments, its Theologians, Sermons, but also in its practices, its rituals, its ceremonies and its sacraments. The Christian religious ideology says something like this:

It says: I address myself to you, a human individual called Peter (every individual is called by his name, in the passive sense, it is never he who provides his own name), in order to tell you that God exists and that you are answerable to Him. It adds: God addresses himself to you through my voice (Scripture having collected the Word of God, Tradition having transmitted it, Papal Infallibility fixing it for ever on "nice" points). It says: this is who you are: you are Peter! This is your origin, you were created by God for all eternity, although you were born in the 1920th year of Our Lord! This is your place in the world! This is what you must do! By these means, if you observe the "law of love" you will be saved, you, Peter, and will become part of the Glorious Body of Christ! Etc. . . . .

Now this is quite a familiar and banal discourse, but at the same time quite a surprising one. . . .

Let me summarize what we have discovered about ideology in general.

The duplicate mirror-structure of ideology ensures simultaneously:

1. the interpellation of "individuals" as subjects;
2. their subjection to the Subject;
3. the mutual recognition of subjects and Subject, the subjects' recognition of each other, and finally the subject's recognition of himself;[14]

4. the absolute guarantee that everything really is so, and that on condition that the subjects recognize what they are and behave accordingly, everything will be all right: Amen — "So be it."

Result: caught in this quadruple system of interpellation as subjects, of subjection to the Subject, of universal recognition and of absolute guarantee, the subjects "work," they "work by themselves" in the vast majority of cases, with the exception of the "bad subjects" who on occasion provoke the intervention of one of the detachments of the (repressive) State apparatus. But the vast majority of (good) subjects work all right "all by themselves," i.e. by ideology (whose concrete forms are realized in the Ideological State Apparatuses). They are inserted into practices governed by the rituals of the ISAs. They "recognize" the existing state of affairs (*das Bestehende*), that "it really is true that it is so and not otherwise," and that they must be obedient to God, to their conscience, to the priest, to de Gaulle,[15] to the boss, to the engineer, that thou shalt "love thy neighbor as thyself," etc. Their concrete, material behavior is simply the inscription in life of the admirable words of the prayer: "*Amen — So be it.*"

Yes, the subjects "work by themselves." The whole mystery of this effect lies in the first two moments of the quadruple system I have just discussed, or, if you prefer, in the ambiguity of the term *subject*. In the ordinary use of the term, subject in fact means: (1) a free subjectivity, a center of initiatives, author of and responsible for its actions; (2) a subjected being, who submits to a higher authority, and is therefore stripped of all freedom except that of freely accepting his submission. This last note gives us the meaning of this ambiguity, which is merely a reflection of the effect which produces it: the individual *is interpellated as a (free) subject in order that he shall submit freely to the commandments of the Subject, i.e. in order that he shall (freely) accept his subjection*, i.e. in order that he shall make the gestures and actions of his subjection "all by

---

[14]Hegel is (unknowingly) an admirable "theoretician" of ideology insofar as he is a "theoretician" of Universal Recognition who unfortunately ends up in the ideology of Absolute Knowledge. Feuerbach is an astonishing "theoretician" of the mirror connection, who unfortunately ends up in the ideology of the Human Essence. To find the material with which to construct a theory of the guarantee, we must turn to Spinoza. [Althusser]

[15]Charles de Gaulle (1890–1970), President of France at the time this essay was written.

---

himself." *There are no subjects except by and for their subjection.* That is why they "work all by themselves."

"*So be it!. . .*" This phrase which registers the effect to be obtained proves that it is not "naturally" so ("naturally": outside the prayer, i.e. outside the ideological intervention). This phrase proves that it *has* to be so if things are to be what they must be, and let us let the words slip: if the reproduction of the relations of production is to be assured, even in the processes of production and circulation, every day, in the "consciousness," i.e. in the attitudes of the individual-subjects occupying the posts which the socio-technical division of labor assigns to them in production, exploitation, repression, ideologization, scientific practice, etc. Indeed, what is really in question in this mechanism of the mirror recognition of the Subject and of the individuals interpellated as subjects, and of the guarantee given by the Subject to the subjects if they freely accept their subjection to the Subject's "commandments"? The reality in question in this mechanism, the reality which is necessarily *ignored* (*méconnue*) in the very forms of recognition (ideology = misrecognition/ignorance) is indeed, in the last resort, the reproduction of the relations of production and of the relations deriving from them.

Raymond Williams

1921–1988

The following selection is from Williams's primer on Marxist concepts, Marxism and Literature *(1977). (For biographical information on Williams, see the introduction on p. 364.)*

From *Marxism and Literature*

1. BASE AND SUPERSTRUCTURE

Any modern approach to a Marxist theory of culture must begin by considering the proposition of a determining base and a determined superstructure. From a strictly theoretical point of view this is not, in fact, where we might choose to begin. It would be in many ways preferable if we could begin from a proposition which originally was equally central, equally authentic: namely the proposition that social being determines consciousness. It is not that the two propositions necessarily deny each other or are in contradiction. But the proposition of base and superstructure, with its figurative element and with its suggestion of a fixed and definite spatial relationship, constitutes, at least in certain hands, a very specialized and at times unacceptable version of the other proposition. Yet in the transition from Marx to Marxism, and in the development of mainstream Marxism itself, the proposition of the determining base and the determined superstructure has been commonly held to be the key to Marxist cultural analysis.

The source of this proposition is commonly taken to be a well-known passage in Marx's 1859 Preface to *A Contribution to the Critique of Political Economy:*

In the social production of their life, men enter into definite relations that are indispensable and independent of their will, relations of production which correspond to a definite stage of development of their material productive forces. The sum total of these relations of production constitutes the economic structure of society, the real foundation, on which rises a legal and political superstructure and to which correspond definite forms of social consciousness. The mode of production of material life conditions the social, political and intellectual life process in general. It is not the consciousness of men that determines their being, but, on the contrary, their social being that determines their consciousness. At a certain stage of their development, the material productive forces of society come in conflict with the existing relations of production or — what is but a legal expression for the same thing — with the property relations within which they have been at work hitherto. From forms of development of the productive forces these relations turn into their fetters. Then begins an epoch of social revolution. With the change of the economic foundation the entire immense superstructure is more or less rapidly transformed. In considering such transformations a distinction should always be made between the material transformation of the economic conditions of production, which can be determined with the precision of natural science, and the legal, political, religious, aesthetic or philosophic — in short, ideological — forms in which men become conscious of this conflict and fight it out.[1]

This is hardly an obvious starting-point for any cultural theory. It is part of an exposition of historical materialist method in the understanding of legal relations and forms of state. The first use of the term "superstructure" is explicitly qualified as "legal and political." (It should incidentally be noted that the English translation in most common use has a plural — "legal and political superstructures" — for Marx's singular "juristicher und politischer Überbau.") "Definite forms of social consciousness" are further said to "correspond" to it (entsprechen). Transformation of the "entire immense superstructure," in the social revolution which begins from the altered relations of productive forces and relations of production, is a process in which "men become conscious of this conflict and fight it out" in "ideological forms" which now include the "religious, aesthetic, or philosophic" as well as the legal and political. Much has been deduced from this formulation, but the real context is inevitably limited. Thus it would be possible, simply from this passage, to define "cultural" ("religious, aesthetic or philosophic") forms in which "men become conscious of this conflict," without necessarily supposing that these specific forms are the whole of "cultural" activity.

There is at least one earlier use, by Marx, of the term "superstructure." It is in *The Eighteenth Brumaire of Louis Napoleon*, 1851–2:

Upon the several forms of property, upon the social conditions of existence, a whole superstructure is reared of various and peculiarly shaped feelings *(empfindungen)*, illusions, habits of thought and conceptions of life. The whole class produces and shapes these out of its material foundation and out of the corresponding social conditions. The individual unit to whom they flow through tradition and education may fancy that they constitute the true reasons for and premises of his conduct.[2]

This is an evidently different use. The "superstructure" is here the whole "ideology" of the class: its "form of consciousness"; its constitutive ways of seeing itself in the world. It would be possible, from this and the later use, to see three senses of "superstructure" emerging: (a) legal and political forms which express existing real relations of production; (b) forms of consciousness which express a particular class view of the world; (c) a process in which, over a whole range of activities, men become conscious of a fundamental economic conflict and fight it out. These three senses would direct our attention, respectively, to (a) institutions; (b) forms of consciousness; (c) political and cultural practices.

It is clear that these three areas are related and must, in analysis, be interrelated. But on just this crucial question of interrelation the term itself is of little assistance, just because it is variably applied to each area in turn. Nor is this at all surprising, since the use is not primarily conceptual, in any precise way, but metaphorical. What it primarily expresses is the important sense of a visible and formal "superstructure" which might be analysed on its own but which cannot be understood without seeing that it rests on a "foundation." The same point must be made of the corresponding metaphorical term. In the use of 1851–2 it is absent, and the origins of a particular form of class consciousness are specified as "forms of property" and "social conditions of existence." In the use of 1859 it appears in almost conscious metaphor: "the economic structure of

[1] Karl Marx and Friedrich Engels, *Selected Works*, vol. 1 (London, 1962), pp. 362–64. (See also Marx, p. 397.)

[2] Ibid., pp. 272–73.

society — the real foundation *(die reale Basis)*, on which rises *(erhebt)* a legal and political superstructure *(Überbau).*" It is replaced, later in the argument, by "the economic foundation" *(ökonomische Grundlage).* The continuity of meaning is relatively clear, but the variation of terms for one part of the relationship ("forms of property, social conditions of existence"; "economic structure of society"; "real basis"; "real foundation"; *Basis; Grundlage)* is not matched by explicit variation of the other term of the relationship, though the actual signification of this term *(Überbau;* superstructure) is, as we have seen, variable. It is part of the complexity of the subsequent argument that the term rendered in English explication (probably first by Engels) as "base" is rendered in other languages in significant variations (in French usually as *infrastructure,* in Italian as *struttura,* and so on, with some complicating effects on the substance of the argument).

In the transition from Marx to Marxism, and then in the development of expository and didactic formulations, the words used in the original arguments were projected, first, as if they were precise concepts, and second, as if they were descriptive terms for observable "areas" of social life. The main sense of the words in the original arguments had been relational, but the popularity of the terms tended to indicate either (a) relatively enclosed categories or (b) relatively enclosed areas of activity. These were then correlated either temporally (first material production, then consciousness, then politics and culture), or in effect, forcing the metaphor, spatially (visible and distinguishable "levels" or "layers" — politics and culture, then forms of consciousness, and so on down to "the base"). The serious practical problems of method, which the original words had indicated, were then usually in effect bypassed by methods derived from a confidence, rooted in the popularity of the terms, in the relative enclosure of categories or areas expressed as "the base," "the superstructure."

It is then ironic to remember that the force of Marx's original criticism had been mainly directed against the *separation* of "areas" of thought and activity (as in the separation of consciousness from material production) and against

the related evacuation of specific content — real human activities — by the imposition of abstract categories. The common abstraction of "the base" and "the superstructure" is thus a radical persistence of the modes of thought which he attacked. That in the course of other arguments he gave some warrant for this, within the intrinsic difficulties of any such formulation, is certainly true. But it is significant that when he came to any sustained analysis, or to a realization of the need for such analysis, he was at once specific and flexible in his use of his own terms. He had already observed, in the formulation of 1859, a distinction between analysing "the economic conditions of production, which can be determined with the precision of natural science" and the analysis of "ideological forms," for which methods were evidently less precise. In 1857 he had noted:

> As regards art, it is well known that some of its peaks by no means correspond to the general development of society; nor do they therefore to the material substructure, the skeleton as it were of its organization.

His solution of the problem he then discusses, that of Greek art, is hardly convincing, but the "by no means correspond" is a characteristic practical recognition of the complexity of real relations. Engels, in his essay *Feuerbach and the End of Classical German Philosophy,* still argued specifically, showing how the "economic basis" of a political struggle could be dulled in consciousness or altogether lost sight of, and how a legal system could be projected as independent of its economic content, in the course of its professional development. Then:

> Still higher ideologies, that is, such as are still further removed from the material, economic basis, take the form of philosophy and religion. Hence the interconnection between conceptions and their material conditions of existence becomes more and more complicated, more and more obscured by intermediate links. But the interconnection exists.

This relational emphasis, including not only complexity but recognition of the ways in which some connections are lost to consciousness, is of course very far from the abstract categories (though it supports the implication of separate areas) of "superstructure" and "base."

In all serious Marxist analysis the categories are of course not used abstractly. But they may have their effect none the less. It is significant that the first phase of the recognition of practical complexities stressed what are really *quantitative* relations. By the end of the nineteenth century it was common to recognize what can best be described as disturbances, or special difficulties, of an otherwise regular relationship. This is true of the idea of "lags" in time, which had been developed from Marx's observation that some of the "peaks" of art "by no means correspond to the general development of society." This could be expressed (though Marx's own "solution" to this problem had not been of this kind) as a matter of *temporal* "delay" or "unevenness." The same basic model is evident in Engels's notion of the relative *distance* ("still further removed") of the "higher ideologies." Or consider Engels's letter to Bloch of September 1890:

> According to the materialist conception of history, the *ultimately* determining element in history is the production and reproduction of real life. More than this neither Marx nor I have ever asserted. Hence if somebody twists this into saying that the economic element is the *only* determining one, he transforms that proposition into a meaningless, abstract, senseless phrase. The economic situation is the basis, but the various elements of the superstructure — political forms of the class struggle and its results, to wit: constitutions established by the victorious class after a successful battle, etc., juridical forms, and even the reflexes of all these actual struggles in the brains of the participants, political, juristic, philosophical theories, religious views and their further development into systems of dogma — also exercise their influence upon the course of the historical struggles and in many cases preponderate in determining their *form*. There is an interaction of all these elements in which, amid all the endless host of accidents (that is, of things and events whose inner interconnection is so remote or so impossible of proof that we can regard it as non-existent, as negligible), the economic movement finally asserts itself as necessary. Otherwise the application of the theory to any period of history would be easier than the solution of a simple equation of the first degree.

This is a vital acknowledgement of real and methodological complexities. It is particularly relevant to the idea of "determination," which will be separately discussed, and to the decisive problem of consciousness as "reflexes" or "reflection." But within the vigour of his contrast between real history and a "meaningless, abstract, senseless phrase," and alongside his recognition of a new (and theoretically significant) exception — "the endless host of accidents" — Engels does not so much revise the enclosed categories — "the basis" ("the economic element," "the economic situation," "the economic movement") and "the various elements" (political, juridical, theoretical) of "the superstructure" — as reiterate the categories and instance certain exceptions, indirectnesses, and irregularities which obscure their otherwise regular relation. What is fundamentally lacking, in the theoretical formulations of this important period, is any adequate recognition of the indissoluble connections between material production, political and cultural institutions and activity, and consciousness. The classic summary of "the relationship between the base and the superstructure" is Plekhanov's[3] distinction of "five sequential elements: (i) the state of productive forces; (ii) the economic conditions; (iii) the socio-political regime; (iv) the psyche of social man; (v) various ideologies reflecting the properties of this psyche" (*Fundamental Problems of Marxism*, Moscow, 1922, 76). This is better than the bare projection of "a base" and "a superstructure," which has been so common. But what is wrong with it is its description of these "elements" as "sequential," when they are in practice indissoluble: not in the sense that they cannot be distinguished for purposes of analysis, but in the decisive sense that these are not separate "areas" or "elements" but the whole, specific activities and products of real men. That is to say, the analytic categories, as so often in idealist thought, have, almost unnoticed, become substantive descriptions, which then take habitual priority over the whole social process to which, as analytic categories, they are attempting to speak. Orthodox analysts began to think of "the base" and "the superstructure" as if they were separable concrete entities. In doing so they lost sight of the very

[3]Gyorgi Valentinovich Plekhanov (1857–1918), Russian revolutionary and political philosopher.

processes — not abstract relations but constitutive processes — which it should have been the special function of historical materialism to emphasize. I shall be discussing later the major theoretical response to this loss: the attempt to reconstitute such processes by the idea of "mediation."

A persistent dissatisfaction, within Marxism, about the proposition of "base and superstructure," has been most often expressed by an attempted refinement and revaluation of "the superstructure." Apologists have emphasized its complexity, substance, and "autonomy" or autonomous value. Yet most of the difficulty still lies in the original extension of metaphorical terms for a relationship into abstract categories or concrete areas *between* which connections are looked for and complexities or relative autonomies emphasized. It is actually more important to observe the character of this extension in the case of "the base" than in the case of the always more varied and variable "superstructure." By extension and by habit, "the base" has come to be considered virtually as an object (a particular and reductive version of "material existence"). Or, in specification, "the base" is given very general and apparently uniform properties. "The base" is the real social existence of man. "The base" is the real relations of production corresponding to a stage of the development of material productive forces. "The base" is a mode of production at a particular stage of its development. Of course these are, in practice, different propositions. Yet each is also very different from Marx's central emphasis on productive *activities*. He had himself made the point against reduction of "the base" to a category:

> In order to study the connexion between intellectual and material production it is above all essential to conceive the latter in its determined historical form and not as a general category. For example, there corresponds to the capitalist mode of production a type of intellectual production quite different from that which corresponded to the medieval mode of production. Unless material production itself is understood in its specific historical form, it is impossible to grasp the characteristics of the intellectual production which corresponds to it or the reciprocal action between the two. (*Theorien über den Mehrwert*, cit. Bottomore and Rubel, 96–97.)

We can add that while a particular stage of "real social existence," or of "relations of production," or of a "mode of production," can be discovered and made precise by analysis, it is never, as a body of activities, either uniform or static. It is one of the central propositions of Marx's sense of history, for example, that in actual development there are deep contradictions in the relationships of production and in the consequent social relationships. There is therefore the continual possibility of the dynamic variation of these forces. The "variations" of the superstructure might be deduced from this fact alone, were it not that the "objective" implications of "the base" reduce all such variations to secondary consequences. It is only when we realize that "the base," to which it is habitual to *refer* variations, is itself a dynamic and internally contradictory process — the specific activities and modes of activity, over a range from association to antagonism, of real men and classes of men — that we can begin to free ourselves from the notion of an "area" or a "category" with certain fixed properties for deduction to the variable processes of a "superstructure." The physical fixity of the terms exerts a constant pressure against just this realization.

Thus, contrary to a development in Marxism, it is not "the base" and "the superstructure" that need to be studied, but specific and indissoluble real processes, within which the decisive relationship, from a Marxist point of view, is that expressed by the complex idea of "determination."

6. HEGEMONY

The traditional definition of "hegemony" is political rule or domination, especially in relations between states. Marxism extended the definition of rule or domination to relations between social classes, and especially to definitions of a *ruling class*. "Hegemony" then acquired a further significant sense in the work of Antonio Gramsci, carried out under great difficulties in a Fascist prison between 1927 and 1935. Much is still uncertain in Gramsci's use of the concept, but his work is one of the major turning-points in Marxist cultural theory.

Gramsci made a distinction between "rule" (*dominio*) and "hegemony." "Rule" is expressed in directly political forms and in times of crisis by direct or effective coercion. But the more normal situation is a complex interlocking of political, social, and cultural forces, and "hegemony," according to different interpretations, is either this or the active social and cultural forces which are its necessary elements. Whatever the implications of the concept for Marxist political theory (which has still to recognize many kinds of direct political control, social class control, and economic control, as well as this more general formation), the effects on cultural theory are immediate. For "hegemony" is a concept which at once includes and goes beyond two powerful earlier concepts: that of "culture" as a "whole social process," in which men define and shape their whole lives; and that of "ideology," in any of its Marxist senses, in which a system of meanings and values is the expression or projection of a particular class interest.

"Hegemony" goes beyond "culture," as previously defined, in its insistence on relating the "whole social process" to specific distributions of power and influence. To say that "men" define and shape their whole lives is true only in abstraction. In any actual society there are specific inequalities in means and therefore in capacity to realize this process. In a class society these are primarily inequalities between classes. Gramsci therefore introduced the necessary recognition of dominance and subordination in what has still, however, to be recognized as a whole process.

It is in just this recognition of the *wholeness* of the process that the concept of "hegemony" goes beyond "ideology." What is decisive is not only the conscious system of ideas and beliefs, but the whole lived social process as practically organized by specific and dominant meanings and values. Ideology, in its normal senses, is a relatively formal and articulated system of meanings, values, and beliefs, of a kind that can be abstracted as a "world-view" or a "class outlook." This explains its popularity as a concept in retrospective analysis (in base–superstructure models or in homology), since a *system* of ideas can be abstracted from that once living social process and represented, usually by the selection of "leading" or typical "ideologists" or "ideological features," as the decisive form in which consciousness was

at once expressed and controlled (or, as in Althusser, was in effect unconscious, as an imposed structure). The relatively mixed, confused, incomplete, or inarticulate consciousness of actual men in that period and society is thus overridden in the name of this decisive generalized system, and indeed in structural homology is procedurally excluded as peripheral or ephemeral. It is the fully articulate and systematic forms which are recognizable as ideology, and there is a corresponding tendency in the analysis of art to look only for similarly fully articulate and systematic expressions of this ideology in the content (base–superstructure) or form (homology) of actual works. In less selective procedures, less dependent on the inherent classicism of the definition of form as fully articulate and systematic, the tendency is to consider works as variants of, or as variably affected by, the decisive abstracted ideology.

More generally, this sense of "an ideology" is applied in abstract ways to the actual consciousness of both dominant and subordinated classes. A dominant class "has" this ideology in relatively pure and simple forms. A subordinate class has, in one version, *nothing but* this ideology as its consciousness (since the production of all ideas is, by axiomatic definition, in the hands of those who control the primary means of production) or, in another version, has this ideology imposed on its otherwise different consciousness, which it must struggle to sustain or develop against "ruling-class ideology."

The concept of hegemony often, in practice, resembles these definitions, but it is distinct in its refusal to equate consciousness with the articulate formal system which can be and ordinarily is abstracted as "ideology." It of course does not exclude the articulate and formal meanings, values and beliefs which a dominant class develops and propagates. But it does not equate these with consciousness, or rather it does not reduce consciousness to them. Instead it sees the relations of domination and subordination, in their forms as practical consciousness, as in effect a saturation of the whole process of living — not only of political and economic activity, nor only of manifest social activity, but of the whole substance of lived identities and relationships, to such a depth that the pressures and limits of what can ultimately be seen as a specific economic, political, and cultural system seem to most of us the pressures and limits of simple experience and common sense. Hegemony is then not only the articulate upper level of "ideology," nor are its forms of control only those ordinarily seen as "manipulation" or "indoctrination." It is a whole body of practices and expectations, over the whole of living: our senses and assignments of energy, our shaping perceptions of ourselves and our world. It is a lived system of meanings and values — constitutive and constituting — which as they are experienced as practices appear as reciprocally confirming. It thus constitutes a sense of reality for most people in the society, a sense of absolute because experienced reality beyond which it is very difficult for most members of the society to move, in most areas of their lives. It is, that is to say, in the strongest sense a "culture," but a culture which has also to be seen as the lived dominance and subordination of particular classes.

There are two immediate advantages in this concept of hegemony. First, its forms of domination and subordination correspond much more closely to the normal processes of social organization and control in developed societies than the more familiar projections from the idea of a ruling class, which are usually based on much earlier and simpler historical phases. It can speak, for example, to the realities of electoral democracy, and to the significant modern areas of "leisure" and "private life," more specifically and more actively than older ideas of domination, with their trivializing explanations of simple "manipulation," "corruption," and "betrayal." If the pressures and limits of a given form of domination are to this extent experienced *and in practice internalized,* the whole question of class rule, and of opposition to it, is transformed. Gramsci's emphasis on the creation of an alternative hegemony, by the practical connection of many different forms of struggle, including those not easily recognizable as and indeed not primarily "political" and "economic," thus leads to a much more profound and more active sense of revolutionary activity in a highly developed society than the persistently abstract models derived from very different historical situations. The sources of any alternative hegemony are indeed difficult to define. For Gramsci they spring from the working class, but not this class as an ideal or abstract construction. What he sees, rather, is a working people which has, precisely, to become a class, and a potentially hegemonic class, against the pressures and limits of an existing and powerful hegemony.

Second, and more immediately in this context, there is a whole different way of seeing cultural activity, both as tradition and as practice. Cultural work and activity are not now, in any ordinary sense, a superstructure: not only because of the depth and thoroughness at which any cultural hegemony is lived, but because cultural tradition and practice are seen as much more than superstructural expressions — reflections, mediations, or typifications — of a formed social and economic structure. On the contrary, they are among the basic processes of the formation itself and, further, related to a much wider area of reality than the abstractions of "social" and "economic" experience. People seeing themselves and each other in directly personal relationships; people seeing the natural world and themselves in it; people using their physical and material resources for what one kind of society specializes to "leisure" and "entertainment" and "art": all these active experiences and practices, which make up so much of the reality of a culture and its cultural production can be seen as they are, without reduction to other categories of content, and without the characteristic straining to fit them (directly as reflection, indirectly as mediation or typification or analogy) to other and determining manifest economic and political relationships. Yet they can still be seen as elements of a hegemony: an inclusive social and cultural formation which indeed to be effective has to extend to and include, indeed to form and be formed from, this whole area of lived experience.

Many difficulties then arise, both theoretically and practically, but it is important to recognize how many blind alleys we may now be saved from entering. If any lived culture is necessarily so extensive, the problems of domination and subordination on the one hand, and of the extraordinary complexity of any actual cultural tradition and practice on the other, can at last be directly approached.

There is of course the difficulty that domination and subordination, as effective descriptions of cultural formation, will, by many, be refused; that the alternative language of co-operative shaping, of common contribution, which the traditional concept of "culture" so notably expressed, will be found preferable. In this fundamental choice there is no alternative, from any socialist position, to recognition and emphasis of the massive historical and immediate experience of class domination and subordination, in all their different forms. This becomes, very quickly, a matter of specific experience and argument. But there is a closely related problem within the concept of "hegemony" itself. In some uses, though not I think in Gramsci, the totalizing tendency of the concept, which is significant and indeed crucial, is converted into an abstract totalization, and in this form it is readily compatible with sophisticated senses of "the superstructure" or even "ideology." The hegemony, that is, can be seen as more uniform, more static, and more abstract than in practice, if it is really understood, it can ever actually be. Like any other Marxist concept it is particularly susceptible to epochal as distinct from historical definition, and to categorical as distinct from substantial description. Any isolation of its "organizing principles," or of its "determining features," which have indeed to be grasped in experience and by analysis, can lead very quickly to a totalizing abstraction. And then the problems of the reality of domination and subordination, and of their relations to co-operative shaping and common contribution, can be quite falsely posed.

A lived hegemony is always a process. It is not, except analytically, a system or a structure. It is a realized complex of experiences, relationships, and activities, with specific and changing pressures and limits. In practice, that is, hegemony can never be singular. Its internal structures are highly complex, as can readily be seen in any concrete analysis. Moreover (and this is crucial, reminding us of the necessary thrust of the concept), it does not just passively exist as a form of dominance. It has continually to be renewed, recreated, defended, and modified. It is also continually resisted, limited, altered, challenged by pressures not at all its own. We have then to add to the concept of hegemony the concepts of counter-hegemony and alternative hegemony, which are real and persistent elements of practice.

One way of expressing the necessary distinction between practical and abstract senses within the concept is to speak of "the hegemonic" rather than the "hegemony," and of "the dominant" rather than simple "domination." The reality of any hegemony, in the extended political and cultural sense, is that, while by definition it is always dominant, it is never either total or exclusive. At any time, forms of alternative or directly oppositional politics and culture exist as significant elements in the society. We shall need to explore their conditions and their limits, but their active presence is decisive, not only because they have to be included in any historical (as distinct from epochal) analysis, but as forms which have had significant effect on the hegemonic process itself. That is to say, alternative political and cultural emphases, and the many forms of opposition and struggle, are important not only in themselves but as indicative features of what the hegemonic process has in practice had to work to control. A static hegemony, of the kind which is indicated by abstract totalizing definitions of a dominant "ideology" or "world-view," can ignore or isolate such alternatives and opposition, but to the extent that they are significant the decisive hegemonic function is to control or transform or even incorporate them. In this active process the hegemonic has to be seen as more than the simple transmission of an (unchanging) dominance. On the contrary, any hegemonic process must be especially alert and responsible to the alternatives and opposition which question or threaten its dominance. The reality of cultural process must then always include the efforts and contributions of those who are in one way or another outside or at the edge of the terms of the specific hegemony.

Thus it is misleading, as a general method, to reduce all political and cultural initiatives and contributions to the terms of the hegemony. That is the reductive consequence of the radically different concept of "superstructure." The specific functions of "the hegemonic," "the dominant," have always to be stressed, but not in ways which suggest any *a priori* totality. The most interesting and difficult part of any cultural analysis, in complex societies, is that which seeks to grasp the hegemonic in its active and formative but also its transformational processes. Works of art, by their substantial and general character, are often especially important as sources of this complex evidence.

The major theoretical problem, with immediate effect on methods of analysis, is to distinguish between alternative and oppositional initiatives and contributions which are made within or against a specific hegemony (which then sets certain limits to them or which can succeed in neutralizing, changing or actually incorporating them) and other kinds of initiative and contribution which are irreducible to the terms of the original or the adaptive hegemony, and are in that sense independent. It can be persuasively argued that all or nearly all initiatives and contributions, even when they take on manifestly alternative or oppositional forms, are in practice tied to the hegemonic: that the dominant culture, so to say, at once produces and limits its own forms of counter-culture. There is more evidence for this view (for example in the case of the Romantic critique of industrial civilization) than we usually admit. But there is evident variation in specific kinds of social order and in the character of the consequent alternative and oppositional formations. It would be wrong to overlook the importance of works and ideas which, while clearly affected by hegemonic limits and pressures, are at least in part significant breaks beyond them, which may again in part be neutralized, reduced, or incorporated, but which in their most active elements nevertheless come through as independent and original.

Thus cultural process must not be assumed to be merely adaptive, extensive, and incorporative. Authentic breaks within and beyond it, in specific social conditions which can vary from extreme isolation to pre-revolutionary breakdowns and actual revolutionary activity, have often in fact occurred. And we are better able to see this, alongside more general recognition of the insistent pressures and limits of the hegemonic, if we develop modes of analysis which instead of reducing works to finished products, and activities to fixed positions, are capable of discerning, in good faith, the finite but significant openness of many actual initiatives and contributions. The finite but significant openness of many works of art, as signifying forms making possible but also requiring persistent and variable signifying responses, is then especially relevant.

7. TRADITIONS, INSTITUTIONS, AND FORMATIONS

Hegemony is always an active process, but this does not mean that it is simply a complex of dominant features and elements. On the contrary, it is always a more or less adequate organization and interconnection of otherwise separated and even disparate meanings, values, and practices, which it specifically incorporates in a significant culture and an effective social order. These are themselves living resolutions — in the broadest sense, political resolutions — of specific economic realities. This process of incorporation is of major cultural importance. To understand it, but also to understand the material on which it must work, we need to distinguish three aspects of any cultural process, which we can call traditions, institutions, and formations.

The concept of tradition has been radically neglected in Marxist cultural thought. It is usually seen as at best a secondary factor, which may at most modify other and more decisive historical processes. This is not only because it is ordinarily diagnosed as superstructure, but also because "tradition" has been commonly understood as a relatively inert, historicized segment of a social structure: tradition as the surviving past. But this version of tradition is weak at the very point where the incorporating sense of tradition is strong: where it is seen, in fact, as an actively shaping force. For tradition is in practice the most evident expression of the dominant and hegemonic pressures and limits. It is always more than an inert historicized segment; indeed it is the most powerful practical means of incorporation. What we have to see is not just "a tradition" but a *selective tradition*: an intentionally selective version of a shaping past and pre-shaped present, which is then powerfully operative in the process of social and cultural definition and identification.

It is usually not difficult to show this empirically. Most versions of "tradition" can be quickly shown to be radically selective. From a whole possible area of past and present, in a particular culture, certain meanings and practices are selected for emphasis and certain other meanings and practices are neglected or excluded. Yet, within a particular hegemony, and as one of its decisive processes, this selection is presented and usually successfully passed off as "the tradition," "the significant past." What has then to be said about any tradition is that it is in this sense an aspect of *contemporary* social and cultural organization, in the interest of the dominance of a specific class. It is a version of the past which is intended to connect with and ratify the present. What it offers in practice is a sense of *predisposed continuity.*

There are, it is true, weaker senses of "tradition," in explicit contrast to "innovation" and "the contemporary." These are often points of retreat for groups in the society which have been left stranded by some particular hegemonic development. All that is now left to them is the retrospective affirmation of "traditional values." Or, from an opposite position, "traditional habits" are isolated, by some current hegemonic development, as elements of the past which have now to be discarded. Much of the overt argument about tradition is conducted between representatives of these two positions. But at a deeper level the hegemonic sense of tradition is always the most active: a deliberately selective and connecting process which offers a historical and cultural ratification of a contemporary order.

It is a very powerful process, since it is tied to many practical continuities — families, places, institutions, a language — which are indeed directly experienced. It is also, at any time, a vulnerable process, since it has in practice to discard whole areas of significance, or reinterpret or dilute them, or convert them into forms which support or at least do not contradict the really important elements of the current hegemony. It is significant that much of the most accessible and influential work of the counter-hegemony is historical: the recovery of discarded areas, or the redress of selective and reductive interpretations. But this in turn has little effect unless the lines to the present, in the actual process of the selective tradition, are clearly and actively traced. Otherwise any recovery can be simply residual or marginal. It is at the vital points of *connection,* where a version of the past is used to ratify the present and to indicate directions for the future, that a selective tradition is at once powerful and vulnerable. Powerful because it is so skilled in making active selective connections, dismissing those it does not want as "out of date" or "nostalgic," attacking those it cannot incorporate as "unprecedented" or "alien." Vulnerable because the real record is effectively recoverable, and many of the alternative or opposing practical continuities are still available. Vulnerable also because the selective version of "a living tradition" is always tied, though often in complex and hidden ways, to explicit contemporary pressures and limits. Its practical inclusions and exclusions are selectively encouraged or discouraged, often so effectively that the deliberate selection is made to verify itself in practice. Yet its selective privileges and interests, material in substance but often ideal in form, including complex elements of style and tone and of basic method, can still be recognized, demonstrated, and broken. This struggle for and against selective traditions is understandably a major part of all contemporary cultural activity.

It is true that the effective establishment of a selective tradition can be said to depend on identifiable institutions. But it is an underestimate of the process to suppose that it depends on institutions alone. The relations between cultural, political, and economic institutions are themselves very complex, and the substance of these relations is a direct indication of the character of the culture in the wider sense. But it is never only a question of formally identifiable institutions. It is also a question of *formations;* those effective movements and tendencies, in intellectual and artistic life, which have significant and sometimes decisive influence on the active development of a culture, and which have a variable and often oblique relation to formal institutions.

Formal institutions, evidently, have a profound influence on the active social process. What is abstracted in orthodox sociology as "socialization" is in practice, in any actual society, a specific kind of incorporation. Its description as "socialization," the universal abstract process on which all human beings can be said to depend, is a way of avoiding or hiding this specific content and intention. Any process of socialization of course includes things that all human beings have to learn, but any specific process ties this necessary learning to a selected range of meanings, values, and practices which, in the very closeness of their association with necessary learning, constitute the real foundations of the hegemonic. In a family children are cared for and taught to care for themselves, but within this necessary process fundamental and selective attitudes to self, to others, to a social order, and to the material world are both consciously and unconsciously taught. Education transmits necessary knowledge and skills, but always by a particular selection from the whole available range, and with intrinsic attitudes, both to learning and social relations, which are in practice virtually inextricable. Institutions such as churches are explicitly incorporative. Specific communities and specific places of work, exerting powerful and immediate pressures on the conditions of living and of making a living, teach, confirm, and in most cases finally enforce selected meanings, values, and activities. To describe the effect of all institutions of these kinds is to arrive at an important but still incomplete understanding of incorporation. In modern societies we have to add the major communications systems. These materialize selected news and opinion, and a wide range of selected perceptions and attitudes.

Yet it can still not be supposed that the sum of all these institutions is an organic hegemony. On the contrary, just because it is not "socialization" but a specific and complex hegemonic process, it is in practice full of contradictions and of unresolved conflicts. This is why it must not be reduced to the activities of an "ideological state apparatus." Such apparatus exists, although variably, but the whole process is much wider, and is in some important respects self-generating. By selection it is possible to identify common features in family, school, community, work, and communications, and these are important. But just because they are specific processes, with variable particular purposes, and with variable but always effective relations with what must in any case, in the short term, be done, the practical consequence is as often confusion and conflict between what are experienced as different purposes and different values, as it is crude incorporation of a theoretical kind. An effective incorporation is usually in practice achieved; indeed to establish and maintain a class society it must be achieved. But no mere training or pressure is truly hegemonic. The true condition of hegemony is effective *self-identification* with the hegemonic forms: a specific and internalized "socialization" which is expected to be positive but which, if that is not possible, will rest on a (resigned) recognition of the inevitable and the necessary. An effective culture, in this sense, is always more than the sum of its institutions: not only because these can be seen, in analysis, to derive much of their character from it, but mainly because it is at the level of a whole culture that the crucial *interrelations,* including confusions and conflicts, are really negotiated.

This is why, in any analysis, we have also to include *formations.* These are most recognizable as conscious movements and tendencies (literary, artistic, philosophical or scientific) which can usually be readily discerned after their formative productions. Often, when we look further, we find that these are articulations of much wider effective formations, which can by no means be wholly identified with formal institutions, or their formal meanings and values, and which can sometimes even be positively contrasted with them. This factor is of the greatest importance for the understanding of what is habitually specialized as intellectual and artistic life. In this fundamental relation between the institutions and formations of a culture there is great historical variability, but it is generally characteristic of developed complex societies that formations, as distinct from institutions, play an increasingly important role. Moreover, since such formations relate, inevitably, to real social structures, and yet have highly variable and often oblique relations with formally discernible social institutions, any social and cultural analysis of them requires procedures radically different from those developed for institutions. What is really being analysed, in each case, is a mode of specialized practice. Moreover, within an apparent hegemony, which can be readily described in generalizing ways, there are not only alternative and oppositional formations (some of them, at certain historical stages, having become or in the process of becoming alternative and oppositional institutions) but, within what can be recognized as the dominant, effectively varying formations which resist any simple reduction to some generalized hegemonic function.

It is at this point, normally, that many of those in real contact with such formations and their work retreat to an indifferent emphasis on the complexity of cultural activity. Others altogether deny (even theoretically) the relation of such formations and such work to the social process and especially the material social process. Others again, when the historical reality of the formations is grasped, render this back to ideal constructions — national traditions, literary and artistic traditions, histories of ideas, psychological types, spiritual archetypes — which indeed acknowledge and define formations, often much more substantially than the usual generalizing accounts of explicit social derivation or superstructural function, but only by radically displacing them from the immediate cultural process. As a result of this displacement, the formations and their work are not seen as the active social and cultural substance that they quite invariably are. In our own culture, this form of displacement, made temporarily or comparatively convincing by the failures of derivative and superstructural interpretation, is itself, and quite centrally, hegemonic.

8. DOMINANT, RESIDUAL, AND EMERGENT

The complexity of a culture is to be found not only in its variable processes and their social definitions — traditions, institutions, and formations — but also in the dynamic interrelations, at every point in the process, of historically varied and variable elements. In what I have called "epochal" analysis, a cultural process is seized as a cultural system, with determinate dominant features: feudal culture or bourgeois culture or a transition from one to the other. This emphasis on dominant and definitive lineaments and features is important and often, in practice, effective. But it then often happens that its methodology is preserved for the very different function of historical analysis, in which a sense of movement within what is ordinarily abstracted as a system is crucially necessary, especially if it is to connect with the future as well as with the past. In authentic historical analysis it is necessary at every point to recognize the complex interrelations between movements and tendencies both within and beyond a specific and effective dominance. It is necessary to examine how these relate to the whole cultural process rather than only to the selected and abstracted dominant system. Thus "bourgeois culture" is a significant generalizing description and hypothesis, expressed within epochal analysis by fundamental comparisons with "feudal culture" or "socialist culture." However, as a description of cultural process, over four or five centuries and in scores of different societies, it requires immediate historical and internally comparative differentiation. Moreover, even if this is acknowledged or practically carried out, the "epochal" definition can exert its pressure as a static type against which all real cultural process is measured, either to show "stages" or "variations" of the type (which is still historical analysis) or, at its worst, to select supporting and exclude "marginal" or "incidental" or "secondary" evidence.

Such errors are avoidable if, while retaining the epochal hypothesis, we can find terms which recognize not only "stages" and "variations" but the internal dynamic relations of any actual process. We have certainly still to speak of the "dominant" and the "effective," and in these senses of the hegemonic. But we find that we have also to speak, and indeed with further differentiation of each, of the "residual" and the "emergent," which in any real process, and at any moment in the process, are significant both in themselves and in what they reveal of the characteristics of the "dominant."

By "residual" I mean something different from the "archaic," though in practice these are often very difficult to distinguish. Any culture includes available elements of its past, but their place in the contemporary cultural process is profoundly variable. I would call the "archaic" that which is wholly recognized as an element of the past, to be observed, to be examined, or even on occasion to be consciously "revived," in a deliberately specializing way. What I mean by the "residual" is very different. The residual, by definition, has been effectively formed in the past, but it is still active in the cultural process, not only and often not at all as an element of the past, but as an effective element of the present. Thus certain experiences, meanings, and values which cannot be expressed or substantially verified in terms of the dominant culture, are nevertheless lived and practised on the basis of the residue — cultural as well as social — of some previous social and cultural institution or formation. It is crucial to distinguish this aspect of the residual, which may have an alternative or even oppositional relation to the dominant culture, from that active manifestation of the residual (this being its distinction from the archaic) which has been wholly or largely incorporated into the dominant culture. In three characteristic cases in contemporary English culture this distinction can become a precise term of analysis. Thus organized religion is predominantly residual, but within this there is a significant difference between some practically alternative and oppositional meanings and values (absolute brotherhood, service to others without reward) and a larger body of incorporated meanings and values (official morality, or the social order of which the other-worldly is a separated neutralizing or ratifying component). Again, the idea of rural community is predominantly residual, but is in some limited respects alternative or oppositional to urban industrial capitalism, though for the most part it is incorporated, as idealization or fantasy, or as an exotic — residential or escape — leisure function of the dominant order itself. Again, in monarchy, there is virtually nothing that is actively residual (alternative or oppositional), but, with a heavy and deliberate additional use of the archaic, a residual function has been wholly incorporated as a specific political and cultural function — marking the limits as well as the methods — of a form of capitalist democracy.

A residual cultural element is usually at some distance from the effective dominant culture, but some part of it, some version of it — and especially if the residue is from some major area of the past — will in most cases have had to be incorporated if the effective dominant culture is to make sense in these areas. Moreover, at certain points the dominant culture cannot allow too much residual experience and practice outside itself, at least without risk. It is in the incorporation of the actively residual — by reinterpretation, dilution, projection, discriminating inclusion and exclusion — that the work of the selective tradition is especially evident. This is very notable in the case of versions of "the literary tradition," passing through selective versions of the character of literature to connecting and incorporated definitions of what literature now is and should be. This is one among several crucial areas, since it is in some alternative or even oppositional versions of what literature is (has been) and what literary experience (and in one common derivation, other significant experience) is and must be, that, against the pressures of incorporation, actively residual meanings and values are sustained.

By "emergent" I mean, first, that new meanings and values, new practices, new relationships and kinds of relationship are continually being created. But it is exceptionally difficult to distinguish between those which are really elements of some new phase of the dominant culture (and in this sense "species-specific") and those which are substantially alternative or oppositional to it: emergent in the strict sense, rather than merely novel. Since we are always considering relations within a cultural process, definitions of the emergent, as of the residual, can be made only in relation to a full sense of the dominant. Yet the social location of the residual is always easier to understand, since a large part of it (though not all) relates to earlier social formations and phases of the cultural process, in which certain real meanings and values were generated. In the subsequent default of a particular phase of a dominant culture there is then a reaching back to those meanings and values which were created in actual societies and actual situations in the past, and which still seem to have significance because they represent areas of human experience, aspiration, and achievement which the dominant culture neglects, undervalues, opposes, represses, or even cannot recognize.

The case of the emergent is radically different. It is true that in the structure of any actual society, and especially in its class structure, there is always a social basis for elements of the cultural process that are alternative or oppositional to the dominant elements. One kind of basis has been valuably described in the central body of Marxist theory: the formation of a new class, the coming to consciousness of a new class, and within this, in actual process, the (often uneven) emergence of elements of a new cultural formation. Thus the emergence of the working class as a class was immediately evident (for example, in nineteenth-century England) in the cultural process. But there was extreme unevenness of contribution in different parts of the process. The making of new social values and institutions far outpaced the making of strictly cultural institutions, while specific cultural contributions, though significant, were less vigorous and autonomous than either general or institutional innovation. A new class is always a source of emergent cultural practice, but while it is still, as a class, relatively subordinate, this is always likely to be uneven and is certain to be incomplete. For new practice is not, of course, an isolated process. To the degree that it emerges, and especially to the degree that it is oppositional rather than alternative, the process of attempted incorporation significantly begins. This can be seen, in the same period in England, in the emergence and then the effective incorporation of a radical popular press. It can be seen in the emergence and incorporation of working-class writing, where the fundamental problem of emergence is clearly revealed, since the basis of incorporation, in such cases, is the effective predominance of received literary forms — an incorporation, so to say, which already conditions and limits the emergence. But the development is always uneven. Straight incorporation is most directly attempted against the visibly alternative and oppositional class elements: trade unions, working-class political parties, working-class life styles (as incorporated into "popular" journalism, advertising, and commercial entertainment). The process of emergence, in such conditions, is then a constantly repeated, an always renewable, move beyond a phase of practical incorporation: usually made much more difficult by the fact that much incorporation looks like recognition, acknowledgement, and thus a form of *acceptance*. In this complex process there is indeed regular confusion between the locally residual (as a form of resistance to incorporation) and the generally emergent.

Cultural emergence in relation to the emergence and growing strength of a class is then always of major importance, and always complex. But we have also to see that it is not the only kind of emergence. This recognition is very difficult, theoretically, though the practical evidence is abundant. What has really to be said, as a way of defining important elements of both the residual and the emergent, and as a way of understanding the character of the dominant, is that *no mode of production and therefore no dominant social order and therefore no dominant culture ever in reality includes or exhausts all human practice, human energy, and human intention.* This is not merely a negative proposition, allowing us to account for significant things which happen outside or against the dominant mode. On the contrary it is a fact about the modes of domination, that they select from and consequently exclude the full range of human practice. What they exclude may often be seen as the personal or the private, or as the natural or even the metaphysical. Indeed it is usually in one or other of these terms that the excluded area is expressed, since what the dominant has effectively seized is indeed the ruling definition of the social.

It is this seizure that has especially to be resisted. For there is always, though in varying degrees, practical consciousness, in specific relationships, specific skills, specific perceptions, that is unquestionably social and that a specifically dominant social order neglects, excludes, represses, or simply fails to recognize. A distinctive and comparative feature of any dominant social order is how far it reaches into the whole range of practices and experiences in an attempt at incorporation. There can be areas of experience it is willing to ignore or dispense with: to assign as private or to specialize as aesthetic or to generalize as natural. Moreover, as a social order changes, in terms of its own developing needs, these relations are variable. Thus in advanced capitalism, because of changes in the social character of labour, in the social character of communications, and in the social character of decision-making, the dominant culture reaches much further than ever before in capitalist society into hitherto "reserved" or "resigned" areas of experience and practice and meaning. The area of effective penetration of the dominant order into the whole social and cultural process is thus now significantly greater. This in turn makes the problem of emergence especially acute, and narrows the gap between alternative and oppositional elements. The alternative, especially in areas that impinge on significant areas of the dominant, is often seen as oppositional and, by pressure, often converted into it. Yet even here there can be spheres of practice and meaning which, almost by definition from its own limited character, or in its profound deformation, the dominant culture is unable in any real terms to recognize. Elements of emergence may indeed be incorporated, but just as often the incorporated forms are merely facsimiles of the genuinely emergent cultural practice. Any significant emergence, beyond or against a dominant mode, is very difficult under these conditions; in itself and in its repeated confusion with the facsimiles and novelties of the incorporated phase. Yet, in our own period as in others, the fact of emergent cultural practice is still undeniable, and together with the fact of actively residual practice is a necessary complication of the would-be dominant culture.

This complex process can still in part be described in class terms. But there is always other social being and consciousness which is neglected and excluded: alternative perceptions of others, in immediate relationships; new perceptions and practices of the material world. In practice these are different in quality from the developing and articulated interests of a rising class. The relations between these two sources of the emergent — the class and the excluded social (human) area — are by no means necessarily contradictory. At times they can be very close and on the relations between them much in political practice depends. But culturally and as a matter of theory the areas can be seen as distinct.

What matters, finally, in understanding emergent culture, as distinct from both the dominant and the residual, is that it is never only a matter of immediate practice; indeed it depends crucially on finding new forms or adaptations of form. Again and again what we have to observe is in effect a *pre-emergence,* active and pressing but not yet fully articulated, rather than the evident emergence which could be more confidently named. It is to understand more closely this condition of pre-emergence, as well as the more evident forms of the emergent, the residual, and the dominant, that we need to explore the concept of structures of feeling.

9. STRUCTURES OF FEELING

In most description and analysis, culture and society are expressed in an habitual past tense. The strongest barrier to the recognition of human cultural activity is this immediate and regular conversion of experience into finished products. What is defensible as a procedure in conscious history, where on certain assumptions many actions can be definitively taken as having ended, is habitually projected, not only into the always moving substance of the past, but into contemporary life, in which relationships, institutions and formations in which we are still actively involved are converted, by this procedural mode, into formed wholes rather than forming and formative processes. Analysis is then centred on relations between these produced institutions, formations, and experiences, so that now, as in that produced past, only the fixed explicit forms exist, and living presence is always, by definition, receding.

When we begin to grasp the dominance of this procedure, to look into its centre and if possible past its edges, we can understand, in new ways, that separation of the social from the personal which is so powerful and directive a cultural mode. If the social is always past, in the sense that it is always formed, we have indeed to find other terms for the undeniable experience of the present: not only the temporal present, the realization of this and this instant, but the specificity of present being, the inalienably physical, within which we may indeed discern and acknowledge institutions, formations, positions, but not always as fixed products, defining products. And then if the social is the fixed and explicit — the known relationships, institutions, formations, positions — all that is present and moving, all that escapes or seems to escape from the fixed and the explicit and the known, is grasped and defined as the personal: this, here, now, alive, active, "subjective."

There is another related distinction. As thought is described, in the same habitual past tense, it is indeed so different, in its explicit and finished forms, from much or even anything that we can presently recognize as thinking, that we set against it more active, more flexible, less singular terms — consciousness, experience, feeling — and then watch even these drawn towards fixed, finite, receding forms. The point is especially relevant to works of art, which really are, in one sense, explicit and finished forms — actual objects in the visual arts, objectified conventions and notations (semantic figures) in literature. But it is not only that, to complete their inherent process, we have to make them present, in specifically active "readings." It is also that the making of art is never itself in the past tense. It is always a formative process, within a specific present. At different moments in history, and significantly different ways, the reality and even the primacy of such presences and such processes, such diverse and yet specific actualities, have been powerfully asserted and reclaimed, as in practice of course they are all the time lived. But they are then often asserted as forms themselves, in contention with other known forms: the subjective as distinct from the objective; experience from belief; feeling from thought; the immediate from the general; the personal from the social. The undeniable power of two great modern ideological systems — the "aesthetic" and the "psychological" — is, ironically, systematically derived from these senses of instance and process, where experience, immediate feeling, and then subjectivity and personality are newly generalized and assembled. Against these "personal" forms, the ideological systems of fixed social generality, of categorical products, of absolute formations, are relatively powerless, within their specific dimension. Of one dominant strain in Marxism, with its habitual abuse of the "subjective" and the "personal," this is especially true.

Yet it is the reduction of the social to fixed forms that remains the basic error. Marx often said this, and some Marxists quote him, in fixed ways, before returning to fixed forms. The mistake, as so often, is in taking terms of analysis as terms of substance. Thus we speak of a world-view or of a prevailing ideology or of a class outlook, often with adequate evidence, but in this regular slide towards a past tense and a fixed form suppose, or even do not know that we have to suppose, that these exist and are lived specifically and definitively, in singular and developing forms. Perhaps the dead can be reduced to fixed forms, though their surviving records are against it. But the living will not be reduced, at least in the first person; living third persons may be different. All the known complexities, the experienced tensions, shifts, and uncertainties, the intricate forms of unevenness and confusion, are against the terms of the reduction and soon, by extension, against social analysis itself. Social forms are then often admitted for generalities but debarred, contemptuously, from any possible relevance to this immediate and actual significance of being. And from the abstractions formed in their turn by this act of debarring — the "human imagination," the "human psyche," the "unconscious," with their "functions" in art and in myth and in dream — new and displaced forms of social analysis and categorization, overriding all specific social conditions, are then more or less rapidly developed.

Social forms are evidently more recognizable when they are articulate and explicit. We have seen this in the range from institutions to formations and traditions. We can see it again in the range from dominant systems of belief and education to influential systems of explanation and argument. All these have effective presence. Many are formed and deliberate, and some are quite fixed. But when they have all been identified they are not a whole inventory even of social consciousness in its simplest sense. For they become social consciousness only when they are lived, actively, in real relationships, and moreover in relationships which are more than systematic exchanges between fixed units. Indeed just because all consciousness is social, its processes occur not only between but within the relationship and the related. And this practical consciousness is always more than a handling of fixed forms and units. There is frequent tension between the received interpretation and practical experience. Where this tension can be made direct and explicit, or where some alternative interpretation is available, we are still within a dimension of relatively fixed forms. But the tension is as often an unease, a stress, a displacement, a latency: the moment of conscious comparison not yet come, often not even coming. And comparison is by no means the only process, though it is powerful and important. There are the experiences to which the fixed forms do not speak at all, which indeed they do not recognize. There are important mixed experiences, where the available meaning would convert part to all, or all to part. And even where form and response can be found to agree, without apparent difficulty, there can be qualifications, reservations, indications elsewhere: what the agreement seemed to settle but still sounding elsewhere. Practical consciousness is almost always different from official consciousness, and this is not only a matter of relative freedom or control. For practical consciousness is what is actually being lived, and not only what it is thought is being lived. Yet the actual alternative to the received and produced fixed forms is not silence: not the absence, the unconscious, which bourgeois culture has mythicized. It is a kind of feeling and thinking which is indeed social and material, but each in an embryonic phase before it can become fully articulate and defined exchange. Its relations with the already articulate and defined are then exceptionally complex.

This process can be directly observed in the history of a language. In spite of substantial and at some levels decisive continuities in grammar and vocabulary, no generation speaks quite the same language as its predecessors. The difference can be defined in terms of additions, deletions, and modifications, but these do not exhaust it. What really changes is something quite general, over a wide range, and the description that often fits the change best is the literary term "style." It is a general change, rather than a set of deliberate choices, yet choices can be deduced from it, as well as effects. Similar kinds of change can be observed in manners, dress, building, and other similar forms of social life. It is an open question — that is to say, a set of specific historical questions — whether in any of these changes this or that group has been dominant or influential, or whether they are the result of much more general interaction. For what we are defining is a particular quality of social experience and relationship, historically distinct from other particular qualities, which gives the sense of a generation or of a period. The relations between this quality and the other specifying historical marks of changing institutions, formations, and beliefs, and beyond these the changing social and economic relations between and within classes, are again an open question: that is to say, a set of specific historical questions. The methodological consequence of such a definition, however, is that the specific qualitative changes are not *assumed* to be epiphenomena of changed institutions, formations, and beliefs, or merely secondary evidence of changed social and economic relations between and within classes. At the same time they are from the beginning taken as *social* experience, rather than as "personal" experience or as the merely superficial or incidental "small change" of society. They are social in two ways that distinguish them from reduced senses of the social as the institutional and the formal: first, in that they are *changes of presence* (while they are being lived this is obvious; when they have been lived it is still their substantial characteristic); second, in that although they are emergent or pre-emergent, they do not have to await definition, classification, or rationalization before they exert palpable pressures and set effective limits on experience and on action.

Such changes can be defined as changes in *structures of feeling*. The term is difficult, but "feeling" is chosen to emphasize a distinction from more formal concepts of "world-view" or "ideology." It is not only that we must go beyond formally held and systematic beliefs, though of course we have always to include them. It is that we are concerned with meanings and values as they are actively lived and felt, and the relations between these and formal or systematic beliefs are in practice variable (including historically variable), over a range from formal assent with private dissent to the more nuanced interaction between selected and interpreted beliefs and acted and justified experiences. An alternative definition would be structures of *experience:* in one sense the better and wider word, but with the difficulty that one of its senses has that past tense which is the most important obstacle to recognition of the area of social experience which is being defined. We are talking about characteristic elements of impulse, restraint, and tone; specifically affective elements of consciousness and relationships: not feeling against thought, but thought as felt and feeling as thought: practical consciousness of a present kind, in a living and interrelating continuity. We are then defining these elements as a "structure": as a set, with specific internal relations, at once interlocking and in tension. Yet we are also defining a social experience which is still *in process,* often indeed not yet recognized as social but taken to be private, idiosyncratic, and even isolating, but which in analysis (though rarely otherwise) has its emergent, connecting, and dominant characteristics, indeed its specific hierarchies. These are often more recognizable at a later stage, when they have been (as often happens) formalized, classified, and in many cases built into institutions and formations. By that time the case is different; a new structure of feeling will usually already have begun to form, in the true social present.

Methodologically, then, a "structure of feeling" is a cultural hypothesis, actually derived from attempts to understand such elements and their connections in a generation or period, and needing always to be returned, interactively, to such evidence. It is initially less simple than more formally structured hypotheses of the social, but it is more adequate to the actual range of cultural evidence: historically certainly, but even more (where it matters more) in our present cultural process. The hypothesis has a special relevance to art and literature, where the true social content is in a significant number of cases of this present and affective kind, which cannot without loss be reduced to belief-systems, institutions, or explicit general relationships, though it may include all these as lived and experienced, with or without tension, as it also evidently includes elements of social and material (physical or natural) experience which may lie beyond, or be uncovered or imperfectly covered by, the elsewhere recognizable systematic elements. The unmistakable presence of certain elements in art which are not covered by (though in one mode they may be reduced to) other formal systems is the true source of the specializing categories of "the aesthetic," "the arts," and "imaginative literature."

We need, on the one hand, to acknowledge (and welcome) the specificity of these elements — specific feelings, specific rhythms — and yet to find ways of recognizing their specific kinds of sociality, thus preventing that extraction from social experience which is conceivable only when social experience itself has been categorically (and at root historically) reduced. We are then not only concerned with the restoration of social content in its full sense, that of a generative immediacy. The idea of a structure of feeling can be specifically related to the evidence of forms and conventions — semantic figures — which, in art and literature, are often among the very first indications that such a new structure is forming. These relations will be discussed in more detail in subsequent chapters, but as a matter of cultural theory this is a way of defining forms and conventions in art and literature as inalienable elements of a social material process: not by derivation from other social forms and pre-forms, but as social formation of a specific kind which may in turn be seen as the articulation (often the only fully available articulation) of structures of feeling which as living processes are much more widely experienced.

For structures of feeling can be defined as social experiences *in solution,* as distinct from other social semantic formations which have been *precipitated* and are more evidently and more immediately available. Not all art, by any means, relates to a contemporary structure of feeling. The effective formations of most actual art relate to already manifest social formations, dominant or residual, and it is primarily to emergent formations (though often in the form of modification or disturbance in older forms) that the structure of feeling, *as solution,* relates. Yet this specific solution is never mere flux. It is a structured formation which, because it is at the very edge of semantic availability, has many of the characteristics of a pre-formation, until specific articulations — new semantic figures — are discovered in material practice: often, as it happens, in relatively isolated ways, which are only later seen to compose a significant (often in fact minority) generation; this often, in turn, the generation that substantially connects to its successors. It is thus a specific structure of particular linkages, particular emphases and suppressions, and, in what are often its most recognizable forms, particular deep starting-points and conclusions. Early Victorian ideology, for example, specified the exposure caused by poverty or by debt or by illegitimacy as social failure or deviation; the contemporary structure of feeling, meanwhile, in the new semantic figures of Dickens, of Emily Brontë, and others, specified exposure and isolation as a *general* condition, and poverty, debt, or illegitimacy as its connecting instances. An alternative ideology, relating such exposure to the nature of the social order, was only later generally formed: offering explanations but now at a reduced tension: the social explanation fully admitted, the intensity of experienced fear and shame now dispersed and generalized.

The example reminds us, finally, of the complex relation of differentiated structures of feeling to differentiated classes. This is historically very variable. In England between 1660 and 1690, for example, two structures of feeling (among the defeated Puritans and in the restored Court) can be readily distinguished, though neither, in its literature and elsewhere, is reducible to the ideologies of these groups or to their formal (in fact complex) class relations. At times the emergence of a new structure of feeling is best related to the rise of a class (England, 1700–60); at other times to contradiction, fracture, or mutation within a class (England, 1780–1830 or 1890–1930), when a formation appears to break away from its class norms, though it retains its substantial affiliation, and the tension is at once lived and articulated in radically new semantic figures. Any of these examples requires detailed substantiation, but what is now in question, theoretically, is the hypothesis of a mode of social formation, explicit and recognizable in specific kinds of art, which is distinguishable from other social and semantic formations by its articulation of *presence*.

Fredric Jameson

b. 1934

Without doubt the foremost Marxist literary critic in America today, Fredric R. Jameson was born in Cleveland, Ohio, raised in New Jersey, and educated at Haverford College and Yale University, where he received his Ph.D. in 1960. He has taught at Harvard University (1959–67), the University of California at San Diego (1967–76), Yale University (1976–83), and the University of California at Santa Cruz (1983–85), and since 1986 he has been Lane Professor of Comparative Literature at Duke University. In addition to studies of Jean-Paul Sartre (1961) and Wyndham Lewis (1979), his major works include Marxism and Form: Twentieth Century Dialectical Theories of Literature *(1971),* The Prison-House of Language: A Critical Account of Russian Formalism and Structuralism *(1972), and* The Political Unconscious: Narrative as a Socially Symbolic Act *(1981); two volumes of collected essays entitled* The Ideologies of Theory *(1988) and* Modernism and Imperialism *(1988); a book of film criticism entitled* Signatures of the Visible *(1990); and* Late Marxism: Adorno or the Persistence of the Dialectic *(1990),* Postmodernism, or, The Cultural Logic of Late Capitalism *(1991),* The Geopolitical Aesthetic: Cinema and Space in the World System *(1992), and the Wellek lecture series published as* The Seeds of Time *(1994). His most recent works are* The Geopolitical Aesthetic: Cinema and Space in the World System *(1996);* The Cultures of Globalization *(1998);* The Cultural Turn: Selected Writings on the Postmodern 1983–1998 *(1998);* Brecht and Method *(1998); and* A Singular Modernity: Notes on the Ontology of the Present *(2002). Two books,* Archeologies of the Future *and* Valences of Dialectic, *are forthcoming. The following selection is from the introductory chapter of* The Political Unconscious.

From *The Political Unconscious*

III

At this point it might seem appropriate to juxtapose a Marxist method of literary and cultural interpretation with those just outlined,[1] and to document its claims to greater adequacy and validity. For better or for worse, however, as I warned in the Preface, this obvious next step is not the strategy projected by the present book, which rather seeks to argue the perspectives of Marxism as necessary preconditions for adequate literary comprehension. Marxist critical insights will therefore here be defended as something like an ultimate *semantic* precondition for the intelligibility of literary and cultural texts. Even this argument, however, needs a certain specification: in particular we will suggest that such semantic enrichment and enlargement of the inert givens and materials of a particular text must take place within three concentric frameworks, which mark a widening out of the sense of the social ground of a text through the notions, first, of political history, in the narrow sense of punctual event and a chroniclelike sequence of happenings in time; then of society, in the now already less diachronic and time-bound sense of a constitutive tension and struggle between social classes; and, ultimately, of history now conceived in its vastest sense of the sequence of modes of production and the succession and destiny of the various human social formations, from prehistoric life to whatever far future history has in store for us.[2]

These distinct semantic horizons are, to be sure, also distinct moments of the process of interpretation, and may in that sense be understood as dialectical equivalents of what Frye has called the successive "phases" in our reinterpretation — our rereading and rewriting — of the literary text. What we must also note, however, is that each phase or horizon governs a distinct reconstruction of its object, and construes the very structure of what can now only in a general sense be called "the text" in a different way.

Thus, within the narrower limits of our first, narrowly political or historical, horizon, the "text," the object of study, is still more or less construed as coinciding with the individual literary work or utterance. The difference between the perspective enforced and enabled by this horizon, however, and that of ordinary *explication de texte,* or individual exegesis, is that here the individual work is grasped essentially as a *symbolic act.*

When we pass into the second phase, and find that the semantic horizon within which we grasp a cultural object has widened to include the social order, we will find that the very object of our analysis has itself been thereby dialectically transformed, and that it is no longer construed as an individual "text" or work in the narrow sense, but has been reconstituted in the form of the great collective and class discourses of which a text is little more than an individual *parole* or utterance. Within this new horizon, then, our object of study

---

[1]Jameson has just discussed psychoanalytic criticism and the myth criticism of Northrop Frye (see p. 691).

[2]A useful discussion of the phenomenological concept of "horizon" may be found in Hans-Georg Gadamer, *Truth and Method,* trans. G. Barden and J. Cumming (New York: Seabury, 1975), pp. 216–20, 267–74. It will become clear in the course of my subsequent discussion that a Marxian conception of our relationship to the past requires a sense of our radical difference from earlier cultures which is not adequately allowed for in Gadamer's influential notion of *Horizontverschmelzung* (fusion of horizons). This is perhaps also the moment to add that from the perspective of Marxism as an "absolute historicism," the stark antithesis proposed by E. D. Hirsch, Jr., between Gadamer's historicist "relativism"

and Hirsch's own conception of a more absolute interpretive validity, will no longer seem particularly irreconcilable. Hirsch's distinction between *Sinn* and *Bedeutung,* between the scientific analysis of a text's intrinsic "meaning" and what he is pleased to call our "ethical" evaluation of its "significance" for us (see, for example, *The Aims of Interpretation* [Chicago: University of Chicago Press, 1976]), corresponds to the traditional Marxist distinction between science and ideology, particularly as it has been retheorized by the Althusserians. It is surely a useful working distinction, although in the light of current revisions of the idea of science one should probably make no larger theoretical claims for it than this operative one. [Jameson] See the introduction to Gadamer, p. 718.

will prove to be the *ideologeme,* that is, the smallest intelligible unit of the essentially antagonistic collective discourses of social classes.

When finally, even the passions and values of a particular social formation find themselves placed in a new and seemingly relativized perspective by the ultimate horizon of human history as a whole, and by their respective positions in the whole complex sequence of the modes of production, both the individual text and its ideologemes know a final transformation, and must be read in terms of what I will call the *ideology of form,* that is, the symbolic messages transmitted to us by the coexistence of various sign systems which are themselves traces or anticipations of modes of production.

The general movement through these three progressively wider horizons will largely coincide with the shifts in focus of the final chapters in this book, and will be felt, although not narrowly and programmatically underscored, in the methodological transformations determined by the historical transformations of their textual objects, from Balzac to Gissing to Conrad.[3]

We must now briefly characterize each of these semantic or interpretive horizons. We have suggested that it is only in the first narrowly political horizon — in which history is reduced to a series of punctual events and crises in time, to the diachronic agitation of the year-to-year, the chroniclelike annals of the rise and fall of political regimes and social fashions, and the passionate immediacy of struggles between historical individuals — that the "text" or object of study will tend to coincide with the individual literary work or cultural artifact. Yet to specify this individual text as a symbolic act is already fundamentally to transform the categories with which traditional *explication de texte* (whether narrative or poetic) operated and largely still operates.

The model for such an interpretive operation remains the readings of myth and aesthetic structure of Claude Lévi-Strauss as they are codified in his fundamental essay "The Structural Study of Myth."[4] These suggestive, often sheerly occasional, readings and speculative glosses immediately impose a basic analytical or interpretive principle: the individual narrative, or the individual formal structure is to be grasped as the imaginary resolution of a real contradiction. Thus, to take only the most dramatic of Lévi-Strauss's analyses — the "interpretation" of the unique facial decorations of the Caduveo Indians — the starting point will be an immanent description of the formal and structural peculiarities of this body art; yet it must be a description already pre-prepared and oriented toward transcending the purely formalistic, a movement which is achieved not by abandoning the formal level for something extrinsic to it — such as some inertly social "content" — but rather immanently, by construing purely formal patterns as a symbolic enactment of the social within the formal and the aesthetic. Such symbolic functions are, however, rarely found by an aimless enumeration of random formal and stylistic features; our discovery of a text's symbolic efficacity must be oriented by a formal description which seeks to grasp it as a determinate structure of still properly formal *contradictions.* Thus, Lévi-Strauss orients his still purely visual analysis of Caduveo facial decorations toward this climactic account of their contradictory dynamic: "the use of a design which is symmetrical but yet lies across an oblique axis . . . a complicated situation based upon two contradictory forms of duality, and resulting in a compromise brought about by a secondary opposition between the ideal axis of the object itself [the human face] and the ideal axis of the figure which it represents."[5] Already on the

[3]In later chapters of *The Political Unconscious,* Jameson analyzes texts by these three authors, viewed as typical of realist, naturalist, and modernist eras in fiction.

[4]Claude Lévi-Strauss, *Structural Anthropology,* trans. C. Jacobson and B. G. Schoepf (New York: Basic, 1963), pp. 206–31. The later four-volume *Mythologiques* reverses the perspective of this analysis: where the earlier essay focused on the individual mythic *parole* or utterance, the later series models the entire system or *langue* in terms of which the various individual myths are related to each other. *Mythologiques* should therefore rather be used as suggestive material on the historical difference between the narrative mode of production of primitive societies and that of our own: in this sense, the later work would find its place in the third and final horizon of interpretation. [Jameson] See p. 859.

[5]Claude Lévi-Strauss, *Tristes Tropiques,* trans. John Russell (New York: Atheneum, 1971), p. 176. [Jameson]

purely formal level, then, this visual text has been grasped as a contradiction by way of the curiously provisional and asymmetrical resolution it proposes for that contradiction.

Lévi-Strauss's "interpretation" of this formal phenomenon may now, perhaps overhastily, be specified. Caduveo are a hierarchical society, organized in three endogamous groups or castes. In their social development, as in that of their neighbors, this nascent hierarchy is already the place of the emergence, if not of political power in the strict sense, then at least of relations of domination: the inferior status of women, the subordination of youth to elders, and the development of a hereditary aristocracy. Yet whereas this latent power structure is, among the neighboring Guana and Bororo, masked by a division into moieties which cuts across the three castes, and whose exogamous exchange appears to function in a nonhierarchical, essentially egalitarian way, it is openly present in Caduveo life, as surface inequality and conflict. The social institutions of the Guana and Bororo, on the other hand, provide a realm of appearance, in which real hierarchy and inequality are dissimulated by the reciprocity of the moieties, and in which, therefore, "asymmetry of class is balanced . . . by symmetry of 'moieties.'"

As for the Caduveo,

they were never lucky enough to resolve their contradictions, or to disguise them with the help of institutions artfully devised for that purpose. On the social level, the remedy was lacking . . . but it was never completely out of their grasp. It was within them, never objectively formulated, but present as a source of confusion and disquiet. Yet since they were unable to conceptualize or to live this solution directly, they began to dream it, to project it into the imaginary. . . . We must therefore interpret the graphic art of Caduveo women, and explain its mysterious charm as well as its apparently gratuitous complication, as the fantasy production of a society seeking passionately to give symbolic expression to the institutions it might have had in reality, had not interest and superstition stood in the way.[6]

In this fashion, then, the visual text of Caduveo facial art constitutes a symbolic act, whereby real social contradictions, insurmountable in their own terms, find a purely formal resolution in the aesthetic realm.

This interpretive model thus allows us a first specification of the relationship between ideology and cultural texts or artifacts: a specification still conditioned by the limits of the first, narrowly historical or political horizon in which it is made. We may suggest that from this perspective, ideology is not something which informs or invests symbolic production; rather the aesthetic act is itself ideological, and the production of aesthetic or narrative form is to be seen as an ideological act in its own right, with the function of inventing imaginary or formal "solutions" to unresolvable social contradictions.

Lévi-Strauss's work also suggests a more general defense of the proposition of a political unconscious than we have hitherto been able to present, insofar as it offers the spectacle of so-called primitive peoples perplexed enough by the dynamics and contradictions of their still relatively simple forms of tribal organization to project decorative or mythic resolutions of issues that they are unable to articulate conceptually. But if this is the case for precapitalist and even pre-political societies, then how much more must it be true for the citizen of the modern *Gesellschaft*,[7] faced with the great constitutional options of the revolutionary period, and with the corrosive and tradition-annihilating effects of the spread of a money and market economy, with the changing cast of collective characters which oppose the bourgeoisie, now to an embattled aristocracy, now to an urban proletariat, with the great fantasms of the various nationalisms, now themselves virtual "subjects of history" of a rather different kind, with the social homogenization and psychic constriction of the rise of the industrial city and its "masses," the sudden appearance of the great transnational forces of communism and fascism, followed by the advent of the superstates and the onset of that great ideological rivalry between capitalism and communism, which, no less passionate and obsessive than that which, at the dawn of modern times, seethed through the wars of religion, marks the

---

[6]Ibid., pp. 179–80. [Jameson]

[7]Community.

final tension of our now global village? It does not, indeed, seem particularly farfetched to suggest that these texts of history, with their fantasmatic collective "actants," their narrative organization, and their immense charge of anxiety and libidinal investment, are lived by the contemporary subject as a genuine politico-historical *pensée sauvage*[8] which necessarily informs all of our cultural artifacts, from the literary institutions of high modernism all the way to the products of mass culture. Under these circumstances, Lévi-Strauss's work suggests that the proposition whereby all cultural artifacts are to be read as symbolic resolutions of real political and social contradictions deserves serious exploration and systematic experimental verification. It will become clear in later chapters of this book that the most readily accessible formal articulation of the operations of a political *pensée sauvage* of this kind will be found in what we will call the structure of a properly political *allegory,* as it develops from networks of topical allusion in Spenser or Milton or Swift to the symbolic narratives of class representatives or "types" in novels like those of Balzac. With political allegory, then, a sometimes repressed ur-narrative[9] or master fantasy about the interaction of collective subjects, we have moved to the very borders of our second horizon, in which what we formerly regarded as individual texts are grasped as "utterances" in an essentially collective or class discourse.

We cannot cross those borders, however, without some final account of the critical operations involved in our first interpretive phase. We have implied that in order to be consequent, the will to read literary or cultural texts as symbolic acts must necessarily grasp them as resolutions of determinate contradictions; and it is clear that the notion of contradiction is central to any Marxist cultural analysis, just as it will remain central in our two subsequent horizons, although it will there take rather different forms. The methodological requirement to articulate a text's fundamental contradiction may then be seen as a test of the completeness of the analysis: this is why, for

example, the conventional sociology of literature or culture, which modestly limits itself to the identification of class motifs or values in a given text, and feels that its work is done when it shows how a given artifact "reflects" its social background, is utterly unacceptable. Meanwhile, Kenneth Burke's play of emphases, in which a symbolic act is on the one hand affirmed as a genuine *act,* albeit on the symbolic level, while on the other it is registered as an act which is "merely" symbolic, its resolutions imaginary ones that leave the real untouched, suitably dramatizes the ambiguous status of art and culture.[10]

Still, we need to say a little more about the status of this external reality, of which it will otherwise be thought that it is little more than the traditional notion of "context" familiar in older social or historical criticism. The type of interpretation here proposed is more satisfactorily grasped as the rewriting of the literary text in such a way that the latter may itself be seen as the rewriting or restructuration of a prior historical or ideological *subtext,* it being always understood that that "subtext" is not immediately present as such, not some common-sense external reality, nor even the conventional narratives of history manuals, but rather must itself always be (re)constructed after the fact. The literary or aesthetic act therefore always entertains some active relationship with the Real;[11] yet in order to do so, it cannot simply allow "reality" to persevere inertly in its own being, outside the text and at distance. It must rather draw the Real into its own texture, and the ultimate paradoxes and false problems of linguistics, and most notably of semantics, are to be traced back to this process, whereby language manages to carry the Real within itself as its own intrinsic or immanent subtext. Insofar, in other words, as symbolic action — what Burke will map as "dream," "prayer," or "chart"[12] — is a way

[10]See the introduction to Burke, p. 633.
[11]Jameson is alluding to the Lacanian field of the Real; see the introduction to Psychoanalytic Theory, p. 1113.
[12]Kenneth Burke, *The Philosophy of Literary Form* (Berkeley: University of California Press, 1973), pp. 5–6; and see also my "Symbolic Inference; or Kenneth Burke and Ideological Analysis," *Critical Inquiry,* 4 (Spring, 1978), 507–23. [Jameson]

[8]Literally "savage mind"; Lévi-Strauss's term for the part of the mind that thinks using myth.
[9]Original narrative.

of doing something to the world, to that degree what we are calling "world" must inhere within it, as the content it has to take up into itself in order to submit it to the transformations of form. The symbolic act therefore begins by generating and producing its own context in the same moment of emergence in which it steps back from it, taking its measure with a view toward its own projects of transformation. The whole paradox of what we have here called the subtext may be summed up in this, that the literary work or cultural object, as though for the first time, brings into being that very situation to which it is also, at one and the same time, a reaction. It articulates its own situation and textualizes it, thereby encouraging and perpetuating the illusion that the situation itself did not exist before it, that there is nothing but a text, that there never was any extra- or con-textual reality before the text itself generated it in the form of a mirage. One does not have to argue the reality of history: necessity, like Dr. Johnson's stone, does that for us.[13] That history — Althusser's "absent cause," Lacan's "Real" — is *not* a text, for it is fundamentally non-narrative and nonrepresentational; what can be added, however, is the proviso that history is inaccessible to us except in textual form, or in other words, that it can be approached only by way of prior (re)textualization. Thus, to insist on either of the two inseparable yet incommensurable dimensions of the symbolic act without the other: to overemphasize the active way in which the text reorganizes its subtext (in order, presumably, to reach the triumphant conclusion that the "referent" does not exist); or on the other hand to stress the imaginary status of the symbolic act so completely as to reify its social ground, now no longer understood as a subtext but merely as some inert given that the text passively or fantasmatically "reflects" — to overstress either of these functions of the symbolic act at the expense of the other is surely to produce sheer ideology, whether it be, as in the first alternative, the ideology of structuralism, or, in the second, that of vulgar materialism.

Still, this view of the place of the "referent" will be neither complete nor methodologically usable unless we specify a supplementary distinction between several types of subtext to be (re)constructed. We have implied, indeed, that the social contradiction addressed and "resolved" by the formal prestidigitation of narrative must, however reconstructed, remain an absent cause, which cannot be directly or immediately conceptualized by the text. It seems useful, therefore, to distinguish, from this ultimate subtext which is the place of social *contradiction,* a secondary one, which is more properly the place of ideology, and which takes the form of the *aporia* or the *antinomy:* what can in the former be resolved only through the intervention of praxis here comes before the purely contemplative mind as logical scandal or double bind, the unthinkable and the conceptually paradoxical, that which cannot be unknotted by the operation of pure thought, and which must therefore generate a whole more properly narrative apparatus — the text itself — to square its circles and to dispel, through narrative movement, its intolerable closure. Such a distinction, positing a system of antinomies as the symptomatic expression and conceptual reflex of something quite different, namely a social contradiction, will now allow us to reformulate that coordination between a semiotic and a dialectical method, which was evoked in the preceding section. The operational validity of semiotic analysis, and in particular of the Greimassian semiotic rectangle,[14] derives, as was

---

[13]Samuel Johnson, when told that Bishop George Berkeley denied the existence of corporeal reality, kicked a stone, saying, "Thus I refute Berkeley."

[14]Jameson explains later that Greimas's "semiotic rectangle . . . is the representation of a binary opposition of two contraries (S and –S) along with the simple negations or contradictories of both terms (the so-called subcontraries –S̄ and S̄): significant slots are constituted by the various possible combinations of these terms, most notably the 'complex' term (or ideal synthesis of the two contraries) and the 'neutral' term (or ideal synthesis of the two subcontraries). See A. J. Greimas and François Rastier, 'The Interaction of Semiotic Constraints,' *Yale French Studies* No. 41 (1968), pp. 86–105" (*The Political Unconscious,* p. 166). For Jameson, the fascination of the "semiotic rectangle" is that a "static analytical scheme" can work in his dialectical criticism "as the very locus and model of ideological closure" (p. 47).

For example, Jameson analyzes the ideology of the "character system" of Conrad's *Lord Jim* in terms of the expansion of a binary opposition between activity and value.

suggested there, not from its adequacy to nature or being, nor even from its capacity to map all forms of thinking or language, but rather from its vocation specifically to model ideological closure and to articulate the workings of binary oppositions, here the privileged form of what we have called the antinomy. A dialectical reevaluation of the findings of semiotics intervenes, however, at the moment in which this entire system of ideological closure is taken as the symptomatic projection of something quite different, namely of social contradiction.

We may now leave this first textual or interpretive model behind, and pass over into the second horizon, that of the social. The latter becomes visible, and individual phenomena are revealed as social facts and institutions, only at the moment in which the organizing categories of analysis become those of social class. I have in another place described the dynamics of ideology in its constituted form as a function of social class:[15] suffice it only to recall here that for Marxism classes must always be apprehended relationally, and that the ultimate (or ideal) form of class relationship and class struggle is always dichotomous. The constitutive form of class relationships is always that between a dominant and a laboring class: and it is only in terms of this axis that class fractions (for example, the petty bourgeoisie) or ec-centric or dependent classes (such as the peasantry) are positioned. To define class in this way

is sharply to differentiate the Marxian model of classes from the conventional sociological analysis of society into strata, subgroups, professional elites and the like, each of which can presumably be studied in isolation from one another in such a way that the analysis of their "values" or their "cultural space" folds back into separate and independent *Weltanschauungen*,[16] each of which inertly reflects its particular "stratum." For Marxism, however, the very content of a class ideology is relational, in the sense that its "values" are always actively in situation with respect to the opposing class, and defined against the latter: normally, a ruling class ideology will explore various strategies of the *legitimation* of its own power position, while an oppositional culture or ideology will, often in covert and disguised strategies, seek to contest and to undermine the dominant "value system."

This is the sense in which we will say, following Mikhail Bakhtin, that within this horizon class discourse — the categories in terms of which individual texts and cultural phenomena are now rewritten — is essentially *dialogical* in its structure.[17] As Bakhtin's (and Voloshinov's) own work in this field is relatively specialized, focusing primarily on the heterogeneous and explosive pluralism of moments of carnival or festival (moments, for example, such as the immense resurfacing of the whole spectrum of the religious or political sects in the English 1640s or the Soviet 1920s) it will be necessary to add the qualification that the normal form of the dialogical is essentially an *antagonistic* one, and that the dialogue of class struggle is one in which two opposing discourses fight it out within the general unity of a shared code. Thus, for instance, the shared master code of religion becomes in the

---

The "semiotic rectangle" presents four points (activity, value, not-activity, not-value) which then define the position of the various agents. Lord Jim himself represents the synthesis of activity and value; Gentleman Brown, of activity and not-value; the pilgrims on the Patna, of value and not-activity; the "desk-chair sailors" of not-value and not-activity (p. 256). This arrangement, for Jameson, represents the deep structure of the ideological work Conrad's novel was expected to perform.

[15]*Marxism and Form*, pp. 376–82; and see below, pp. 288–91. The most authoritative contemporary Marxist statement of this view of social class is to be found in E. P. Thompson, *The Making of the English Working Classes* (New York: Vintage, 1966), pp. 9–11; in *The Poverty of Theory*, Thompson has argued that his view of classes is incompatible with "structural" Marxism, for which classes are not "subjects" but rather "positions" within the social totality (see, for the Althusserian position, Nicos Poulantzas, *Political Power and Social Classes*). [Jameson]

[16]World-pictures.
[17]Mikhail Bakhtin, *Problems of Dostoyevsky's Poetics*, trans. R. W. Rotsel (Ann Arbor: Ardis, 1973), pp. 153–69. See also Bakhtin's important book on linguistics, written under the name of V. N. Voloshinov, *Marxism and the Philosophy of Language*, trans. L. Matejka and I. R. Titunik (New York: Seminar Press, 1973), pp. 83–98; and Bakhtin's posthumous collection, *Esthétique et théorie du roman*, trans. Daria Olivier (Paris: Gallimard, 1978), esp. pp. 152–82. [Jameson] See the introduction to Bakhtin, p. 575.

1640s in England the place in which the dominant formulations of a hegemonic theology are reappropriated and polemically modified.[18]

Within this new horizon, then, the basic formal requirement of dialectical analysis is maintained, and its elements are still restructured in terms of *contradiction* (this is essentially, as we have said, what distinguishes the relationality of a Marxist class analysis from static analysis of the sociological type). Where the contradiction of the earlier horizon was univocal, however, and limited to the situation of the individual text, to the place of a purely individual symbolic resolution, contradiction here appears in the form of the dialogical as the irreconcilable demands and positions of antagonistic classes. Here again, then, the requirement to prolong interpretation to the point at which this ultimate contradiction begins to appear offers a criterion for the completeness or insufficiency of the analysis.

Yet to rewrite the individual text, the individual cultural artifact, in terms of the antagonistic dialogue of class voices is to perform a rather different operation from the one we have ascribed to our first horizon. Now the individual text will be refocused as a *parole,* or individual utterance, of that vaster system, or *langue,* of class discourse. The individual text retains its formal structure as a symbolic act: yet the value and character of such symbolic action are now significantly modified and enlarged. On this rewriting, the individual utterance or text is grasped as a symbolic move in an essentially polemic and strategic ideological confrontation between the classes, and to describe it in these terms (or to reveal it in this form) demands a whole set of different instruments.

For one thing, the illusion or appearance of isolation or autonomy which a printed text projects must now be systematically undermined. Indeed, since by definition the cultural monuments and masterworks that have survived tend necessarily to perpetuate only a single voice in this class dialogue, the voice of a hegemonic class, they cannot be properly assigned their relational place in a dialogical system without the restoration or artificial reconstruction of the voice to which they were initially opposed, a voice for the most part stifled and reduced to silence, marginalized, its own utterances scattered to the winds, or reappropriated in their turn by the hegemonic culture.

This is the framework in which the reconstruction of so-called popular cultures must properly take place — most notably, from the fragments of essentially peasant cultures: folk songs, fairy tales, popular festivals, occult or oppositional systems of belief such as magic and witchcraft. Such reconstruction is of a piece with the reaffirmation of the existence of marginalized or oppositional cultures in our own time, and the reaudition of the oppositional voices of black or ethnic cultures, women's and gay literature, "naive" or marginalized folk art, and the like. But once again, the affirmation of such nonhegemonic cultural voices remains ineffective if it is limited to the merely "sociological" perspective of the pluralistic rediscovery of other isolated social groups: only an ultimate rewriting of these utterances in terms of their essentially polemic and subversive strategies restores them to their proper place in the dialogical system of the social classes. Thus, for instance, Bloch's reading of the fairy tale, with its magical wish-fulfillments and its Utopian fantasies of plenty and the *pays de Cocagne,*[19] restores the dialogical and antagonistic content of this "form" by exhibiting it as a systematic deconstruction and undermining of the hegemonic aristocratic form of the epic, with its somber ideology of heroism and baleful destiny; thus also the work of Eugene Genovese on black religion restores the vitality of these utterances by reading them, not as the replication of imposed beliefs, but rather as a process whereby the hegemonic Christianity of the slave-owners is appropriated, secretly emptied of its content and subverted to the transmission of quite different oppositional and coded messages.[20]

---

[18]See Christopher Hill, *The World Turned Upside Down* (London: Temple Smith, 1972). [Jameson]

[19]Ernst Bloch, "Zerstörung, Rettung des Mythos durch Licht," in *Verfremdungen* I (Frankfurt: Suhrkamp, 1963), pp. 152–62. [Jameson]

[20]Eugene Genovese, *Roll Jordan Roll* (New York: Vintage, 1976), pp. 161–284. [Jameson]

Moreover, the stress on the dialogical then allows us to reread or rewrite the hegemonic forms themselves; they also can be grasped as a process of the reappropriation and neutralization, the cooptation and class transformation, the cultural universalization, of forms which originally expressed the situation of "popular," subordinate, or dominated groups. So the slave religion of Christianity is transformed into the hegemonic ideological apparatus of the medieval system; while folk music and peasant dance find themselves transmuted into the forms of aristocratic or court festivity and into the cultural visions of the pastoral; and popular narrative from time immemorial — romance, adventure story, melodrama, and the like — is ceaselessly drawn on to restore vitality to an enfeebled and asphyxiating "high culture." Just so, in our own time, the vernacular and its still vital sources of production (as in black language) are reappropriated by the exhausted and media-standardized speech of a hegemonic middle class. In the aesthetic realm, indeed, the process of cultural "universalization" (which implies the repression of the oppositional voice, and the illusion that there is only one genuine "culture") is the specific form taken by what can be called the process of legitimation in the realm of ideology and conceptual systems.

Still, this operation of rewriting and of the restoration of an essentially dialogical or class horizon will not be complete until we specify the "units" of this larger system. The linguistic metaphor (rewriting texts in terms of the opposition of a *parole* to a *langue*) cannot, in other words, be particularly fruitful until we are able to convey something of the dynamics proper to a class *langue* itself, which is evidently, in Saussure's sense, something like an ideal construct that is never wholly visible and never fully present in any one of its individual utterances. This larger class discourse can be said to be organized around minimal "units" which we will call *ideologemes*. The advantage of this formulation lies in its capacity to mediate between conceptions of ideology as abstract opinion, class value, and the like, and the narrative materials with which we will be working here. The ideologeme is an amphibious formation, whose essential structural characteristic may be described as its possibility to manifest itself either as a pseudoidea — a conceptual or belief system, an abstract value, an opinion or prejudice — or as a protonarrative, a kind of ultimate class fantasy about the "collective characters" which are the classes in opposition. This duality means that the basic requirement for the full description of the ideologeme is already given in advance: as a construct it must be susceptible to both a conceptual description and a narrative manifestation all at once. The ideologeme can of course be elaborated in either of these directions, taking on the finished appearance of a philosophical system on the one hand, or that of a cultural text on the other; but the ideological analysis of these finished cultural products requires us to demonstrate each one as a complex work of transformation on that ultimate raw material which is the ideologeme in question. The analyst's work is thus first that of the identification of the ideologeme, and, in many cases, of its initial naming in instances where for whatever reason it had not yet been registered as such. The immense preparatory task of identifying and inventorying such ideologemes has scarcely even begun, and to it the present book will make but the most modest contribution: most notably in its isolation of that fundamental nineteenth-century ideologeme which is the "theory" of *ressentiment*,[21] and in its "unmasking" of ethics and the ethical binary opposition of good and evil as one of the fundamental forms of ideological thought in Western culture. However, our stress here and throughout on the fundamentally narrative character of such ideologemes (even where they seem to be articulated only as abstract conceptual beliefs or values) will offer the advantage of restoring the complexity of the transactions between opinion and protonarrative or libidinal fantasy. Thus we will observe, in the case of Balzac, the generation of an overt and constituted ideological and political "value system" out of the operation of an essentially narrative and fantasy dynamic; the chapter on Gissing, on the other hand, will show how an already constituted "narrative paradigm" emits an ideological

[21]Literally, rancor; Nietzsche's term for the hatred felt by the weak for the strong.

message in its own right without the mediation of authorial intervention.

This focus or horizon, that of class struggle and its antagonistic discourses, is, as we have already suggested, not the ultimate form a Marxist analysis of culture can take. The example just alluded to — that of the seventeenth-century English revolution, in which the various classes and class fractions found themselves obliged to articulate their ideological struggles through the shared medium of a religious master code — can serve to dramatize the shift whereby these objects of study are reconstituted into a structurally distinct "text" specific to this final enlargement of the analytical frame. For the possibility of a displacement in emphasis is already given in this example: we have suggested that within the apparent unity of the theological code, the fundamental difference of antagonistic class positions can be made to emerge. In that case, the inverse move is also possible, and such concrete semantic differences can on the contrary be focused in such a way that what emerges is rather the all-embracing unity of a single code which they must share and which thus characterizes the larger unity of the social system. This new object — code, sign system, or system of the production of signs and codes — thus becomes an index of an entity of study which greatly transcends those earlier ones of the narrowly political (the symbolic act), and the social (class discourse and the ideologeme), and which we have proposed to term the historical in the larger sense of this word. Here the organizing unity will be what the Marxian tradition designates as a *mode of production*.

I have already observed that the "problematic" of modes of production is the most vital new area of Marxist theory in all the disciplines today; not paradoxically, it is also one of the most traditional, and we must therefore, in a brief preliminary way, sketch in the "sequence" of modes of production as classical Marxism, from Marx and Engels to Stalin, tended to enumerate them.[22] These modes, or "stages" of human society, have traditionally

included the following: primitive communism or tribal society (the horde), the *gens* or hierarchical kinship societies (neolithic society), the Asiatic mode of production (so-called Oriental despotism), the *polis* or an oligarchical slaveholding society (the ancient mode of production), feudalism, capitalism, and communism (with a good deal of debate as to whether the "transitional" stage between these last — sometimes called "socialism" — is a genuine mode of production in its own right or not). What is more significant in the present context is that even this schematic or mechanical conception of historical "stages" (what the Althusserians have systematically criticized under the term "historicism") includes the notion of a cultural dominant or form of ideological coding specific to each mode of production. Following the same order these have generally been conceived as magic and mythic narrative, kinship, religion or the sacred, "politics" according to the narrower category of citizenship in the ancient city state, relations of personal domination, commodity reification, and (presumably) original and as yet nowhere fully developed forms of collective or communal association.

Before we can determine the cultural "text" or object of study specific to the horizon of modes of production, however, we must make two preliminary remarks about the methodological problems it raises. The first will bear on whether the concept of "mode of production" is a synchronic one, while the second will address the temptation to use the various modes of production for a classifying or typologizing operation, in which cultural texts are simply dropped into so many separate compartments.

---

[22]The "classical" texts on modes of production, besides Lewis Henry Morgan's *Ancient Society* (1877), are Karl Marx, *Pre-Capitalist Economic Formations,* a section of the *Grundrisse* (1857–58) published separately by Eric Hobsbawm (New York: International, 1965), and Friedrich Engels, *The Family, Private Property, and the State* (1884). Important recent contributions to the mode of production "debate" include Etienne Balibar's contribution to Althusser's collective volume, *Reading Capital;* Emmanuel Terray, *Marxism and "Primitive" Societies,* trans. M. Klopper (New York: Monthly Review, 1972); Maurice Godelier, *Horizon: trajets marxistes en anthropologie* (Paris: Maspéro, 1973); J. Chesneaux, ed., *Sur le "mode de production asiatique"* (Paris: Editions Sociales, 1969); and Barry Hindess and Paul Hirst, *Pre-Capitalist Modes of Production* (London: Routledge & Kegan Paul, 1975). [Jameson]

Indeed, a number of theorists have been disturbed by the apparent convergence between the properly Marxian notion of an all-embracing and all-structuring mode of production (which assigns everything within itself — culture, ideological production, class articulation, technology — a specific and unique place), and non-Marxist visions of a "total system" in which the various elements or levels of social life are programmed in some increasingly constricting way. Weber's dramatic notion of the "iron cage" of an increasingly bureaucratic society,[23] Foucault's image of the gridwork of an ever more pervasive "political technology of the body,"[24] but also more traditional "synchronic" accounts of the cultural programming of a given historical "moment," such as those that have variously been proposed from Vico and Hegel to Spengler and Deleuze — all such monolithic models of the cultural unity of a given historical period have tended to confirm the suspicions of a dialectical tradition about the dangers of an emergent "synchronic" thought, in which change and development are relegated to the marginalized category of the merely "diachronic," the contingent or the rigorously nonmeaningful (and this, even where, as with Althusser, such models of cultural unity are attacked as forms of a more properly Hegelian and idealistic "expressive causality"). This theoretical foreboding about the limits of synchronic thought can perhaps be most immediately grasped in the political area, where the model of

the "total system" would seem slowly and inexorably to eliminate any possibility of the *negative* as such, and to reintegrate the place of an oppositional or even merely "critical" practice and resistance back into the system as the latter's mere inversion. In particular, everything about class struggle that was anticipatory in the older dialectical framework, and seen as an emergent space for radically new social relations, would seem, in the synchronic model, to reduce itself to practices that in fact tend to reinforce the very system that foresaw and dictated their specific limits. This is the sense in which Jean Baudrillard has suggested that the "total-system" view of contemporary society reduces the options of resistance to anarchist gestures, to the sole remaining ultimate protests of the wildcat strike, terrorism, and death. Meanwhile, in the framework of the analysis of culture also, the latter's integration into a synchronic model would seem to empty cultural production of all its antisystemic capacities, and to "unmask" even the works of an overtly oppositional or political stance as instruments ultimately programmed by the system itself.

It is, however, precisely the notion of a series of enlarging theoretical horizons proposed here that can assign these disturbing synchronic frameworks their appropriate analytical places and dictate their proper use. This notion projects a long view of history which is inconsistent with concrete political action and class struggle only if the specificity of the horizons is not respected; thus, even if the concept of a mode of production is to be considered a synchronic one (and we will see in a moment that things are somewhat more complicated than this), at the level of historical abstraction at which such a concept is properly to be used, the lesson of the "vision" of a total system is for the short run one of the structural limits imposed on praxis rather than the latter's impossibility.

The theoretical problem with the synchronic systems enumerated above lies elsewhere, and less in their analytical framework than in what in a Marxist perspective might be called their infrastructural regrounding. Historically, such systems have tended to fall into two general groups, which one might term respectively the hard and soft visions of the total system. The first group projects a fantasy future of a "totalitarian" type in

[23]"The Puritan wanted to work in a calling; we are forced to do so. For when asceticism was carried out of monastic cells into everyday life, and began to dominate worldly morality, it did its part in building the tremendous cosmos of the modern economic order. This order is now bound to the technical and economic conditions of machine production which today determine the lives of all the individuals who are born into this mechanism, not only those directly concerned with economic acquisition, with irresistible force. Perhaps it will so determine them until the last ton of fossilized coal is burnt. In Baxter's view the care for external goods should only lie on the shoulders of the saint 'like a light cloak, which can be thrown aside at any moment,' But fate decreed that the cloak should become an iron cage." *The Protestant Ethic and the Spirit of Capitalism,* trans. T. Parsons (New York: Scribners, 1958), p. 181. [Jameson]

[24]Michel Foucault, *Surveiller et punir* (Paris: Gallimard, 1975), pp. 27–28 and passim. [Jameson]

which the mechanisms of domination — whether these are understood as part of the more general process of bureaucratization, or on the other hand derive more immediately from the deployment of physical and ideological force — are grasped as irrevocable and increasingly pervasive tendencies whose mission is to colonize the last remnants and survivals of human freedom — to occupy and organize, in other words, what still persists of Nature objectively and subjectively (very schematically, the Third World and the Unconscious).

This group of theories can perhaps hastily be associated with the central names of Weber and Foucault; the second group may then be associated with names such as those of Jean Baudrillard and the American theorists of a "post-industrial society."[25] For this second group, the characteristics of the total system of contemporary world society are less those of political domination than those of cultural programming and penetration: not the iron cage, but rather the *société de consommation*[26] with its consumption of images and simulacra, its free-floating signifiers and its effacement of the older structures of social class and traditional ideological hegemony. For both groups, world capitalism is in evolution toward a system which is not socialist in any classical sense, on the one hand the nightmare of total control and on the other the polymorphous or schizophrenic intensities of some ultimate counterculture (which may be no less disturbing for some than the overtly threatening characteristics of the first vision). What one must add is that neither kind of analysis respects the Marxian injunction of the "ultimately determining instance" of economic organization and tendencies: for both, indeed, economics (or political economy) of that type is in the new total system of the contemporary world at an end, and the economic finds itself in

both reassigned to a secondary and nondeterminant position beneath the new dominant of political power or of cultural production, respectively.

There exist, however, within Marxism itself precise equivalents to these two non-Marxian visions of the contemporary total system: rewritings, if one likes, of both in specifically Marxian and "economic" terms. These are the analyses of late capitalism in terms of *capitalogic*[27] and of *disaccumulation,*[28] respectively; and while this book is clearly not the place to discuss such theories at any length, it must be observed here that both, seeing the originality of the contemporary situation in terms of systemic tendencies *within* capitalism, reassert the theoretical priority of the organizing concept of the mode of production which we have been concerned to argue.

We must therefore now turn to the second related problem about this third and ultimate horizon, and deal briefly with the objection that cultural analysis pursued within it will tend toward a purely typological or classificatory operation, in which we are called upon to "decide" such issues

[25]Jean Baudrillard, *Le Système des objets* (Paris: Gallimard, 1968); *La Société de consommation* (Paris: Denöel, 1970); *Pour une économie politique du signe* (Paris: Gallimard, 1972). The most influential statement of the American version of this "end of ideology"/consumer society position is, of course, that of Daniel Bell: see his *Coming of Post-Industrial Society* (New York: Basic, 1973) and *The Cultural Contradictions of Capitalism* (New York: Basic, 1976). [Jameson]

[26]Consumer society typical of late capitalism.

[27]See, for a review and critique of the basic literature, Stanley Aronowitz, "Marx, Braverman, and the Logic of Capital," *Insurgent Sociologist*, VIII, No. 2/3 (Fall, 1978), pp. 126–46; and see also Hans-George Backhaus, "Zur Dialektik der Wertform," in A. Schmidt, ed., *Beiträge zur marxistischen Erkenntnistheorie* (Frankfurt: Suhrkamp, 1969), pp. 128–52; and Helmut Reichelt, *Zur logischen Struktur des Kapitalbegriffs bei Karl Marx* (Frankfurt: Europäische Verlagsanstalt, 1970). For the Capitalogicians, the "materialist kernel" of Hegel is revealed by grasping the concrete or objective reality of Absolute Spirit (the Notion in-and-for-itself) as none other than capital (Reichelt, pp. 77–78). This tends, however, to force them into the post-Marxist position for which the dialectic is seen as the thought-mode proper only to capitalism (Backhaus, pp. 140–41): in that case, of course, the dialectic would become unnecessary and anachronistic in a society that had abolished the commodity form. [Jameson]

[28]The basic texts on "disaccumulation theory" are Martin J. Sklar, "On the Proletarian Revolution and the End of Political-Economic Society," *Radical America,* III, No. 3 (May–June, 1969), pp. 1–41; Jim O'Connor, "Productive and Unproductive Labor," *Politics and Society,* 5 (1975), pp. 297–336; Fred Block and Larry Hirschhorn, "New Productive Forces and the Contradictions of Contemporary Capitalism," *Theory and Society,* 7 (1979), 363–95; and Stanley Aronowitz, "The End of Political Economy," *Social Text,* No. 2 (1980), pp. 3–52. [Jameson]

as whether Milton is to be read within a "precapitalist" or a nascent capitalist context, and so forth. I have insisted elsewhere on the sterility of such classificatory procedures, which may always, it seems to me, be taken as symptoms and indices of the repression of a more genuinely dialectical or historical practice of cultural analysis. This diagnosis may now be expanded to cover all three horizons at issue here, where the practice of homology, that of a merely "sociological" search for some social or class equivalent, and that, finally, of the use of some typology of social and cultural systems, respectively, may stand as examples of the misuse of these three frameworks. Furthermore, just as in our discussion of the first two we have stressed the centrality of the category of contradiction for any Marxist analysis (seen, within the first horizon, as that which the cultural and ideological artifact tries to "resolve," and in the second as the nature of the social and class conflict within which a given work is one act or gesture), so too here we can effectively validate the horizon of the mode of production by showing the form contradiction takes on this level, and the relationship of the cultural object to it.

Before we do so, we must take note of more recent objections to the very concept of the mode of production. The traditional schema of the various modes of production as so many historical "stages" has generally been felt to be unsatisfactory, not least because it encourages the kind of typologizing criticized above, in political quite as much as in cultural analysis. (The form taken in political analysis is evidently the procedure which consists in "deciding" whether a given conjuncture is to be assigned to a moment within feudalism — the result being a demand for bourgeois and parliamentary rights — or within capitalism — with the accompanying "reformist" strategy — or, on the contrary, a genuine "revolutionary" moment — in which case the appropriate revolutionary strategy is then deduced.)

On the other hand, it has become increasingly clear to a number of contemporary theorists that such classification of "empirical" materials within this or that abstract category is impermissible in large part because of the level of abstraction of the concept of a mode of production: no historical society has ever "embodied" a mode of production in any pure state (nor is *Capital* the description of a historical society, but rather the construction of the abstract concept of capitalism). This has led certain contemporary theorists, most notably Nicos Poulantzas,[29] to insist on the distinction between a "mode of production" as a purely theoretical construction and a "social formation" that would involve the description of some historical society at a certain moment of its development. This distinction seems inadequate and even misleading, to the degree that it encourages the very empirical thinking which it was concerned to denounce, in other words, subsuming a particular or an empirical "fact" under this or that corresponding "abstraction." Yet one feature of Poulantzas' discussion of the "social formation" may be retained: his suggestion that every social formation or historically existing society has in fact consisted in the overlay and structural coexistence of *several* modes of production all at once, including vestiges and survivals of older modes of production, now relegated to structurally dependent positions within the new, as well as anticipatory tendencies which are potentially inconsistent with the existing system but have not yet generated an autonomous space of their own.

But if this suggestion is valid, then the problems of the "synchronic" system and of the typological temptation are both solved at one stroke. What is synchronic is the "concept" of the mode of production; the moment of the historical coexistence of several modes of production is not synchronic in this sense, but open to history in a dialectical way. The temptation to classify texts according to the appropriate mode of production is thereby removed, since the texts emerge in a space in which we may expect them to be crisscrossed and intersected by a variety of impulses from contradictory modes of cultural production all at once.

Yet we have still not characterized the specific object of study which is constructed by this new and final horizon. It cannot, as we have shown,

[29]Poulantzas, *Political Power and Social Classes*, pp. 13–16. [Jameson]

consist in the concept of an individual mode of production (any more than, in our second horizon, the specific object of study could consist in a particular social class in isolation from the others). We will therefore suggest that this new and ultimate object may be designated, drawing on recent historical experience, as *cultural revolution,* that moment in which the coexistence of various modes of production becomes visibly antagonistic, their contradictions moving to the very center of political, social, and historical life. The incomplete Chinese experiment with a "proletarian" cultural revolution may be invoked in support of the proposition that previous history has known a whole range of equivalents for similar processes to which the term may legitimately be extended. So the Western Enlightenment may be grasped as part of a properly bourgeois cultural revolution, in which the values and the discourses, the habits and the daily space, of the *ancien régime* were systematically dismantled so that in their place could be set the new conceptualities, habits and life forms, and value systems of a capitalist market society. This process clearly involved a vaster historical rhythm than such punctual historical events as the French Revolution or the Industrial Revolution, and includes in its *longue durée* such phenomena as those described by Weber in *The Protestant Ethic and the Spirit of Capitalism* — a work that can now in its turn be read as a contribution to the study of the bourgeois cultural revolution, just as the corpus of work on romanticism is now repositioned as the study of a significant and ambiguous moment in the resistance to this particular "great transformation," alongside the more specifically "popular" (precapitalist as well as working-class) forms of cultural resistance.

But if this is the case, then we must go further and suggest that all previous modes of production have been accompanied by cultural revolutions specific to them of which the neolithic "cultural revolution," say, the triumph of patriarchy over the older matriarchal or tribal forms, or the victory of Hellenic "justice" and the new legality of the *polis* over the vendetta system are only the most dramatic manifestations. The concept of cultural revolution, then — or more precisely, the reconstruction of the materials of cultural and literary history in the form of this new "text" or object of study which is cultural revolution — may be expected to project a whole new framework for the humanities, in which the study of culture in the widest sense could be placed on a materialist basis.

This description is, however, misleading to the degree to which it suggests that "cultural revolution" is a phenomenon limited to so-called "transitional" periods, during which social formations dominated by one mode of production undergo a radical restructuration in the course of which a different "dominant" emerges. The problem of such "transitions" is a traditional crux of the Marxian problematic of modes of production, nor can it be said that any of the solutions proposed, from Marx's own fragmentary discussions to the recent model of Etienne Balibar, are altogether satisfactory, since in all of them the inconsistency between a "synchronic" description of a given system and a "diachronic" account of the passage from one system to another seems to return with undiminished intensity. But our own discussion began with the idea that a given social formation consisted in the coexistence of various synchronic systems or modes of production, each with its own dynamic or time scheme — a kind of metasynchronicity, if one likes — while we have now shifted to a description of cultural revolution which has been couched in the more diachronic language of systemic transformation. I will therefore suggest that these two apparently inconsistent accounts are simply the twin perspectives which our thinking (and our presentation or *Darstellung* of that thinking) can take on this same vast historical object. Just as overt revolution is no punctual event either, but brings to the surface the innumerable daily struggles and forms of class polarization which are at work in the whole course of social life that precedes it, and which are therefore latent and implicit in "prerevolutionary" social experience, made visible as the latter's deep structure only in such "moments of truth" — so also the overtly "transitional" moments of cultural revolution are themselves but the passage to the surface of a permanent process in human societies, of a permanent struggle between the various coexisting modes of production. The triumphant moment in which a new systemic dominant gains ascendency is therefore only the diachronic manifestation of a constant struggle for the perpetuation and reproduction of its dominance, a struggle which must continue throughout its life course, accompanied at all moments by the systemic or structural antagonism of those older and newer modes of production that resist assimilation or seek deliverance from it. The task of cultural and social analysis thus construed within this final horizon will then clearly be the rewriting of its materials in such a way that this perpetual cultural revolution can be apprehended and read as the deeper and more permanent constitutive structure in which the empirical textual objects know intelligibility.

Cultural revolution thus conceived may be said to be beyond the opposition between synchrony and diachrony, and to correspond roughly to what Ernst Bloch has called the *Ungleichzeitigkeit* (or "nonsynchronous development") of cultural and social life.[30] Such a view imposes a new use of

[30]Ernst Bloch, "Nonsynchronism and Dialectics," *New German Critique*, No. 11 (Spring, 1977), pp. 22–38; or *Erbschaft dieser Zeit* (Frankfurt: Suhrkamp, 1973). The "nonsynchronous" use of the concept of mode of production outlined above is in my opinion the only way to fulfill Marx's well-known program for dialectical knowledge "of rising from the abstract to the concrete" (1857 Introduction, *Grundrisse*, p. 101). Marx there distinguished three stages of knowledge: (1) the notation of the particular (this would correspond to something like empirical history, the collection of data and descriptive materials on the variety of human societies); (2) the conquest of abstraction, the coming into being of a properly "bourgeois" science or of what Hegel called the categories of the Understanding (this moment, that of the construction of a static and purely classificatory concept of "modes of production," is what Hindess and Hirst quite properly criticize in *Precapitalist Modes of Production*); (3) the transcendence of abstraction by the dialectic, the "rise to the concrete," the setting in motion of hitherto static and typologizing categories by their reinsertion in a concrete historical situation (in the present context, this is achieved by moving from a classificatory use of the categories of modes of production to a perception of their dynamic and contradictory coexistence in a given cultural moment). Althusser's own epistemology, incidentally — Generalities I, II, and III (*Pour Marx* [Paris: Maspéro, 1965], pp. 187–90) — is a gloss on this same fundamental passage of the 1857 Introduction, but one which succeeds only too well in eliminating its dialectical spirit. [Jameson]

concepts of periodization, and in particular of that older schema of the "linear" stages which is here preserved and canceled all at once. We will deal more fully with the specific problems of periodization in the next chapter: suffice it to say at this point that such categories are produced within an initial diachronic or narrative framework, but become usable only when that initial framework has been annulled, allowing us now to coordinate or articulate categories of diachronic origin (the various distinct modes of production) in what is now a synchronic or metasynchronic way.

We have, however, not yet specified the nature of the textual object which is constructed by this third horizon of cultural revolution, and which would be the equivalent within this dialectically new framework of the objects of our first two horizons — the symbolic act, and the ideologeme or dialogical organization of class discourse. I will suggest that within this final horizon the individual text or cultural artifact (with its appearance of autonomy which was dissolved in specific and original ways within the first two horizons as well) is here restructured as a field of force in which the dynamics of sign systems of several distinct modes of production can be registered and apprehended. These dynamics — the newly constituted "text" of our third horizon — make up what can be termed *the ideology of form,* that is, the determinate contradiction of the specific messages emitted by the varied sign systems which coexist in a given artistic process as well as in its general social formation.

What must now be stressed is that at this level "form" is apprehended as content. The study of the ideology of form is no doubt grounded on a technical and formalistic analysis in the narrower sense, even though, unlike much traditional formal analysis, it seeks to reveal the active presence within the text of a number of discontinuous and heterogeneous formal processes. But at the level of analysis in question here, a dialectical reversal has taken place in which it has become possible to grasp such formal processes as sedimented content in their own right, as carrying ideological messages of their own, distinct from the ostensible or manifest content of the works; it has become possible, in other words, to display such formal operations from the standpoint of what Louis

Hjelmslev[31] will call the "content of form" rather than the latter's "expression," which is generally the object of the various more narrowly formalizing approaches. The simplest and most accessible demonstration of this reversal may be found in the area of literary genre. Our next chapter, indeed, will model the process whereby generic specification and description can, in a given historical text, be transformed into the detection of a host of distinct generic messages — some of them objectified survivals from older modes of cultural production, some anticipatory, but all together projecting a formal conjuncture through which the "conjuncture" of coexisting modes of production at a given historical moment can be detected and allegorically articulated.

Meanwhile, that what we have called the ideology of form is something other than a retreat from social and historical questions into the more narrowly formal may be suggested by the relevance of this final perspective to more overtly political and theoretical concerns; we may take the much debated relation of Marxism to feminism as a particularly revealing illustration. The notion of overlapping modes of production outlined above has indeed the advantage of allowing us to short-circuit the false problem of the priority of the economic over the sexual, or of sexual oppression over that of social class. In our present perspective, it becomes clear that sexism and the patriarchal are to be grasped as the sedimentation and the virulent survival of forms of alienation specific to the oldest mode of production of human history, with its division of labor between men and women, and its division of power between youth and elder. The analysis of the ideology of form, properly completed, should reveal the formal persistence of such archaic structures of alienation — and the sign systems specific to them — beneath the overlay of all the more recent and historically original types of alienation — such as political domination and commodity reification — which have become the dominants of that most complex of all cultural revolutions, late capitalism, in which all the earlier modes of production in one way or another structurally coexist. The affirmation of radical feminism, therefore, that to annul the patriarchal is the most *radical* political act — insofar as it includes and subsumes more partial demands, such as the liberation from the commodity form — is thus perfectly consistent with an expanded Marxian framework, for which the transformation of our own dominant mode of production must be accompanied and completed by an equally radical restructuration of all the more archaic modes of production with which it structurally coexists.

With this final horizon, then, we emerge into a space in which History itself becomes the ultimate ground as well as the untranscendable limit of our understanding in general and our textual interpretations in particular. This is, of course, also the moment in which the whole problem of interpretive priorities returns with a vengeance, and in which the practitioners of alternate or rival interpretive codes — far from having been persuaded that History is an interpretive code that includes and transcends all the others — will again assert "History" as simply one more code among others, with no particularly privileged status. This is most succinctly achieved when the critics of Marxist interpretation, borrowing its own traditional terminology, suggest that the Marxian interpretive operation involves a thematization and a reification of "History" which is not markedly different from the process whereby the other interpretive codes produce their own forms of thematic closure and offer themselves as absolute methods.

It should by now be clear that nothing is to be gained by opposing one reified theme — History — by another — Language — in a polemic debate as to ultimate priority of one over the other. The influential forms this debate has taken in recent years — as in Jürgen Habermas' attempt to subsume the "Marxist" model of production beneath a more all-embracing model of "communication" or intersubjectivity,[32] or in Umberto Eco's assertion of the priority of the Symbolic in general over the technological and productive systems which it must organize as *signs* before

---

[31]Danish linguist, author of *Prolegomena to a Theory of Language* (Ann Arbor: University of Wisconsin Press, 1961).

[32]See Jürgen Habermas, *Knowledge and Human Interests,* trans, J. Shapiro (Boston: Beacon, 1971), esp. Part I. [Jameson]

they can be used as *tools*[33] — are based on the misconception that the Marxian category of a "mode of production" is a form of technological or "productionist" determinism.

It would seem therefore more useful to ask ourselves, in conclusion, how History as a ground and as an absent cause can be conceived in such a way as to resist such thematization or reification, such transformation back into one optional code among others. We may suggest such a possibility obliquely by attention to what the Aristotelians would call the generic satisfaction specific to the form of the great monuments of historiography, or what the semioticians might call the "history-effect" of such narrative texts. Whatever the raw material on which historiographic form works (and we will here only touch on that most widespread type of material which is the sheer chronology of fact as it is produced by the rote-drill of the history manual), the "emotion" of great historiographic form can then always be seen as the radical restructuration of that inert material, in this instance the powerful reorganization of otherwise inert chronological and "linear" data in the form of Necessity: why what happened (at first received as "empirical" fact) had to happen the way it did. From this perspective, then, causality is only one of the possible tropes by which this formal restructuration can be achieved, although it has obviously been a privileged and historically significant one. Meanwhile, should it be objected that Marxism is rather a "comic" or "romance" paradigm, one which sees history in the salvational perspective of some ultimate liberation, we must observe that the most powerful realizations of a Marxist historiography — from Marx's own narratives of the 1848 revolution through the rich and varied canonical studies of the dynamics of the Revolution of 1789 all the way to Charles Bettelheim's study of the Soviet revolutionary experience — remain visions of historical Necessity in the sense evoked above. But Necessity is here represented in the form of the inexorable logic involved in the determinate failure of all the revolutions that have taken place in human history: the ultimate Marxian presupposition — that socialist revolution can only be a total and worldwide process (and that this in turn presupposes the completion of the capitalist "revolution" and of the process of commodification on a global scale) — is the perspective in which the failure or the blockage, the contradictory reversal or functional inversion, of this or that local revolutionary process is grasped as "inevitable," and as the operation of objective limits.

History is therefore the experience of Necessity, and it is this alone which can forestall its thematization or reification as a mere object of representation or as one master code among many others. Necessity is not in that sense a type of content, but rather the inexorable *form* of events; it is therefore a narrative category in the enlarged sense of some properly narrative political unconscious which has been argued here, a retextualization of History which does not propose the latter as some new representation or "vision," some new content, but as the formal effects of what Althusser, following Spinoza, calls an "absent cause." Conceived in this sense, History is what hurts, it is what refuses desire and sets inexorable limits to individual as well as collective praxis, which its "ruses" turn into grisly and ironic reversals of their overt intention. But this History can be apprehended only through its effects, and never directly as some reified force. This is indeed the ultimate sense in which History as ground and untranscendable horizon needs no particular theoretical justification: we may be sure that its alienating necessities will not forget us, however much we might prefer to ignore them.

[33]Umberto Eco, *A Theory of Semiotics* (Bloomington: Indiana University Press, 1976), pp. 21–26. [Jameson]

Terry Eagleton

b. 1943

Terence Francis Eagleton was born in 1943 in Salford, England, and educated at Trinity College, Cambridge, where he became the student and disciple of Marxist literary critic Raymond Williams, who, like Eagleton, came from a rural working-class family of Celtic origin. Eagleton took his doctoral degree at Trinity and became a fellow of Jesus College, Cambridge, at the age of 21. In 1969, Eagleton moved as fellow to Wadham College, Oxford, where he taught for many years. He is now Professor of Cultural Theory and John Rylands Fellow in the Department of English at the University of Manchester. Since the death of Williams in 1988, Eagleton has been regarded as the premier British Marxist literary critic. Eagleton's Marxism has gone through three distinct phases. In the first phase (1966–70), Eagleton wrote four books, including Shakespeare and Society: Critical Studies in Shakespearean Drama *(1967) and* Exiles and Emigres: Studies in Modern Literature *(1970). In these works Eagleton seems to be trying to reconcile Williams's humanist Marxism with the values of his own Roman Catholic upbringing. After a five-year hiatus, Eagleton rapidly published three books that rejected the humanist Marxism of Williams in favor of a post-Althusserian "science of the text":* Myths of Power: A Marxist Study of the Brontës *(1975);* Marxism and Literary Criticism *(1976); and* Criticism and Ideology: A Study in Marxist Literary Theory *(1976). After another five year hiatus (1976–81), Eagleton's position shifted once more. Though he has not explicitly repudiated the "scientific" theorizing of* Criticism and Ideology, *his books since* Walter Benjamin *(1981) have called for a "revolutionary criticism" that explicitly seeks practical social goals as the end of literary study rather than mere knowledge of the text. His latest works include* The Rape of Clarissa: Writing, Sexuality, and Class Struggle in Richardson *(1982),* Literary Theory: An Introduction *(1983; second edition 1997),* The Function of Criticism: From the Spectator to Post-Structuralism *(1984),* William Shakespeare *(1986),* Against the Grain: Selected Essays 1975–85 *(1986),* The Ideology of the Aesthetic *(1990),* Ideology: An Introduction *(1991),* The Significance of Theory *(1990), and* Heathcliff and the Great Hunger *(1995).* The Illusions of Postmodernism *(1998),* The Idea of Culture *(2000),* Sweet Violence: The Idea of the Tragic *(2003); and* After Theory *(2003). He has also published a novel,* Saints and Scholars *(1987), and a memoir,* The Gatekeeper *(2002). The following selection is the second chapter of* Criticism and Ideology.

Categories for a Materialist Criticism

Every work is the work of many things besides an author.
　　　　　　　　　　　　　　　　— VALÉRY

The work of Raymond Williams, flawed as it has been by "humanism" and idealism, represents one of the most significant sources from which a materialist aesthetics might be derived. Refusing that pervasive form of critical idealism which would repress the whole material infrastructure of artistic production, Williams has properly insisted on the reality of art as "material practice." Yet it is not only that his conception of art as "practice" retains strong residual elements of humanism; it is also that, to date at least, the constituent structures of that practice have received little systematic analysis in his work. It is necessary, then, to develop a method whereby those structures can be rigorously specified, and their precise articulations examined.

It is possible to set out in schematic form the major constituents of a Marxist theory of literature. They can be listed as follows:

   (i)   General Mode of Production (GMP)
  (ii)   Literary Mode of Production (LMP)
 (iii)   General Ideology (GI)
 (iv)   Authorial Ideology (AuI)
  (v)   Aesthetic Ideology (AI)
 (vi)   Text

The text, strictly speaking, is hardly a *constituent* of literary theory; it is, rather, its object. But in so far as it must be examined in its relations with the other elements set out, it can be regarded methodologically as a particular "level." The task of criticism is to analyse the complex historical *articulations* of these structures which produce the text.

(i) GENERAL MODE OF PRODUCTION (GMP)

A mode of production may be characterised as a unity of certain forces and social relations of material production. Each social formation is characterised by a combination of such modes of production, one of which will normally be dominant. By "General Mode of Production" I designate that dominant mode; I use the term "general," not because economic production is ever anything other than historically specific, but to distinguish economic production from:

(ii) LITERARY MODE OF PRODUCTION (LMP)

A unity of certain forces and social relations of literary production in a particular social formation. In any literate society there will normally exist a number of distinct modes of literary production, one of which will normally be dominant. These distinct LMPs will be mutually articulated in varying relations of homology, conflict and contradiction: they will constitute an "asymmetrical" totality, since the dominance of a particular LMP will force other modes into positions of subordination and partial exclusion. Structurally conflictal LMPs may thus coexist within a particular social formation: if it is possible in Western societies to produce fiction for the capitalist market, it is also possible to distribute one's handwritten poetry on the streets. Coexistent LMPs, however, need not be historically synchronous with one another. An LMP produced by an historically previous social formation may survive within and interpenetrate later modes: the co-presence of the "patronage" system and capitalist literary production in eighteenth-century England, the persistence of "artisanal" literary production within the capitalist LMP.[1] A classical instance of such survivals is typically to be found in the

---

[1] In the eighteenth century, most authors lived by making bargains with "booksellers" (publishers), selling outright for a fixed fee the copyright to their work. This mode of production Eagleton refers to as "artisanal," like that of other skilled craftsmen, such as cabinet-makers, rugweavers, musical instrument makers, and so on, who sell their work, rather than their time. Only a very few authors were capitalists who, like the novelist Samuel Richardson, were successful publishers of their own work. Meanwhile some writers still attempted, as authors had since the Middle Ages, to subsist on the payments

historical mutation from "oral" to "written" LMPs, where the social relations and kinds of literary product appropriate to the "oral" LMP normally persist as significant constituents of the "written" LMP itself, both interactive with and relatively autonomous of it. In medieval England, for example, "reading" continues to mean, almost invariably, reading aloud in public; and much of the "written" LMP consists in committing to manuscript form products of the "oral" mode. Conversely, the emergence of the "written" LMP perpetuates certain more complex and extensive oral products, developing that LMP as it is itself developed by it. With the development of a "written" LMP in sixth-century Ireland, the druidic "oral" mode, nurtured by the powerful intellectual caste of the *filí*,[2] continues its own separate existence independent of (although not uninfluenced by) written literary production. The Irish "oral" LMP is thus for some considerable time peculiarly unsubordinated to the written mode, even though in passing into that mode it undergoes certain mutations as a literary product, modified in such predominantly oral traits as alliteration and repetition. The significant moment in the mutual articulation of two such distinct LMPs occurs when the act of composition and writing become more or less simultaneous — when the "written" LMP assumes a certain autonomy of the "oral" rather than consigning its products to manuscript. This unity of writing and composition is exemplified by a number of early Irish texts which recreate the oral tradition — a *genre* closely associated with the scribal activities of the early monastic schools, who as "amateur" producers synthesising native and Latin literary elements (and so producing new literary *forms*) emerge in seventh-century Ireland as a distinct LMP in conflict with the dominant LMP of the

professional, legally privileged, ideologically hegemonic *filí*.

The disjunction between historically coexistent LMPs, then, may be synchronic — determined by the structural distribution of possible modes of literary production enabled by the social formation — or diachronic (determined by historical survivals). There is also the case of diachronic disjunction which arises not from survival but from "prefiguration": LMPs which enter into contradiction with the dominant LMP by "anticipating" the productive forms and social relations of a future social formation (the revolutionary artists' commune, "epic theatre"[3] and so on). A particular LMP, then, may combine elements or structures of other past, contemporary or "future" modes. The "little magazine,"[4] for example, characteristically combines structures of the dominant capitalist LMP with elements of collaborative production, "informal" distribution mechanisms and "consumer-participation" untypical of the dominant productive mode. An LMP may constitute a complex unity in itself, as well as forming a complex contradictory unity with other LMPs; its internal complexity will be a function of its modes of articulation with those other LMPs.

Every LMP is constituted by structures of production, distribution, exchange and consumption. Production presupposes a producer or set of producers, materials, instruments and techniques of production, and the product itself. In developed social formations, an initial private stage of production may be transmuted by a subsequent social mode of production (printing and publishing) to convert the original product ("manuscript") into a new one ("book"). The forces of literary production consist in the application of labour-power organised in certain "relations of

---

of wealthy noblemen awarded for faithful attendance and flattery. In the 1740s, Samuel Johnson unsuccessfully attempted to court the patronage of Philip Dormer Stanhope, Lord Chesterfield, to finance the long labor on his dictionary. Johnson eventually was awarded a royal pension, another form of patronage enjoyed by politically well-connected authors.

[2]The *filí* or *fileadh* was an ancient Irish order of poets.

[3]Drama, strictly speaking, belongs to a distinct mode of production from literature, characterised by its own relatively autonomous forces and relations. Dramatic *texts* may belong to the LMP, depending upon the historical character of the theatrical mode of production; but the assimilation of drama to literature is an ideologically significant appropriation. [Eagleton]

[4]Any periodical devoted to serious artistic or literary interests.

production" (scribes, collaborative producers, printing and publishing organisations) to certain materials of production by means of certain determinate productive instruments. These forces of literary production determine and are overdetermined by the modes of literary distribution, exchange and consumption. The handwritten manuscript can only be distributed and consumed on a hand-to-hand basis, within, let us say, a courtly caste; the multiply dictated work (one copied simultaneously by several scribes) is able to achieve wider social consumption; the ballads peddled by a chapman may be consumed by an even wider audience; the "yellowback" railway novel[5] is available to a mass public.

Unified with these productive forces, then, are specific social relations of literary production. The tribal bard professionally authorised to produce for his king or chieftain; the "amateur" medieval poet presenting to his patron a personally requested product for private remuneration; the peripatetic minstrel housed and fed by his peasant audience; the ecclesiastically or royally patronised producer, or the author who sells his product to an aristocratic patron for a dedication fee; the "independent" author who sells his commodity to a bookseller-publisher or to a capitalist publishing firm; the state-patronised producer: all of these forms are familiar enough to the "sociology of literature." The point is to analyse the complex articulations of these various LMPs with the "general" mode of production of a social formation.

Before considering that question, however, it is important to note that the character of an LMP is a significant constituent of the literary product itself. We are not merely concerned here with the sociological outworks of the text; we are concerned rather with how the text comes to be what it is because of the specific determinations of its mode of production. If LMPs are historically extrinsic to particular texts, they are equally internal to them: the literary text bears the impress of its historical mode of production as surely as any product secretes in its form and materials the fashion of its making. The product of an "oral"

[5]Paperback novels sold in railway stations in the 1870s as light reading while traveling.

LMP is typically more socially stylised, "anonymous," shorn of idiosyncratic introspectiveness than the product of a private printing press; the ecclesiastically patronised work is characteristically more devout and didactic than the fiction produced for the markets of monopoly capitalism. The work which survives solely by word of mouth from region to region is constrained to deploy conventions of "impersonality" inimical to the confessional forms of a producer whose relatively "privatised" LMP is under severe pressure from more public modes which threaten to dislodge it. A poet whose professional function is to recount heroic, mythological tales of military victory before kings and noblemen preparing for war will perpetuate *genres* superfluous to an author whose LMP constrains him to woo a Whig aristocrat dedicated to international capitalist "peace." One might add, too, that every literary text in some sense internalises its social relations of production — that every text intimates by its very conventions the way it is to be consumed, encodes within itself its own ideology of how, by whom and for whom it was produced. Every text obliquely posits a putative reader, defining its producibility in terms of a certain capacity for consumption. These, however, are questions of ideology which are properly postponable to a later point; it is enough to assert for the moment that the character of an LMP is an internal constituent rather than merely an extrinsic limit of the character of the text.

(iii) RELATIONS OF LMP AND GMP

The forces of production of the LMP are naturally provided by the GMP itself, of which the LMP is a particular substructure. In the case of literary production, the materials and instruments employed normally perform a common function within the GMP itself. This is less true of certain other modes of artistic production, many of whose materials and instruments, though of course produced by the GMP, perform no significant function within it. (Trombones and greasepaint play no world-historical part within general production.) The relations between LMP and GMP, however, are dialectical, in that new productive forces developed for purposes specific to the LMP may enter into the field of general production. The extent to which the LMP contributes to the expansion of general production is historically variable. The role of pre-printing LMPs within general production is historically negligible; in such situations, the LMP operates with a high degree of autonomy of the GMP from the viewpoint of its contribution to the development of the productive forces. With the growth of printing, however, extensive speculative book production and marketing finally integrate the dominant LMP into the GMP as a specific branch of general commodity production. (This integration, in which literature becomes merely another aspect of commodity production, is typically coupled with significant mutations within the aesthetic region of ideology, and a subordination of that region within the dominant ideological formation.) In developed capitalist social formations, then, the most significant relation of LMP to GMP is that of the LMP's function in the reproduction and expansion of the GMP.

The LMP represents a specific division of labour determined by the character and stage of development of the GMP, becoming more specialised and diverse as the GMP develops. Only with a certain stage of development of the GMP is the relatively autonomous existence of an LMP possible. Literary production and consumption presuppose certain levels of literacy, physical and mental well-being, leisure and material affluence: the material conditions for writing and reading include economic resources, shelter, lighting, and privacy. The capitalist mode of production develops its dominant LMP by increasing the population, concentrating it in urban centres where it is within reach of the mechanisms of literary distribution, and permitting it limited degrees of literacy, affluence, leisure, shelter and privacy. At the same time it increasingly specialises and extends its modes of literary production and distribution to sell literary commodities on this market, and produces the material and cultural conditions essential for professional literary production within it. In such phenomena as poverty, physical and mental debility consequent on prolonged and intensive labour, illiteracy or partial literacy, lack of sufficient shelter, privacy and lighting (Charles

Dickens described the window-tax as "a tax upon knowledge"), the GMP bears upon the LMP to exclude or partially exclude certain social groups and classes from literary production and consumption — a factor which, as we shall see, is also of ideological significance.

The social relations of the LMP are in general determined by the social relations of the GMP. The literary producer stands in a certain social relation to his consumers which is mediated by his social relations to the patrons, publishers and distributors of his product. These social relations are themselves materially embodied in the character of the product itself. The *filí* of early Ireland may again provide a convenient example. Before the emergence of a "written" LMP, the *filí* caste formed the dominant group of a *mélange* of literary entertainers, musicians, lampooners and others (generically categorised as "bards"), controlling the ideological apparatuses of learning and literature as advisers to kings, preservers of oral literary traditions and composers of heroic, panegyric and elegiac verse. They were social functionaries occupying a legally enshrined, privileged status within the social formation, exercising extensive ideological influence over it, and handsomely remunerated by their patrons. These social relations embodied themselves in the character of their literary products: as a secular, traditionalist caste, the *filí* preserved the Gaelic despised for its "pagan" elements by the higher, Latin-oriented clergy; the poetic *genres* they worked were the "privileged," heroic, genealogical and mythological modes of the literature of the Gaelic aristocracy. In this case, then, a peculiarly visible homology between the social relations of LMP and GMP is to be observed: the *filí's* function as literary producers is effectively coterminous with their function within the social relations of Irish society as a whole. By contrast, the individual class-position of a literary producer in certain other LMPs may be in contradiction with his mode of insertion into the class-structure *as an author*. A producer who is himself a member of the dominant social class may, as occasionally in Elizabethan England, be selected for literary patronage in preference to one from a subordinate social class; yet the aristocratic poet or haut-bourgeois novelist becomes, within the capitalist

LMP, a petty-bourgeois producer.[6] (This, indeed, is a contradiction which may enter into "aesthetic ideology" itself, as in the case of bourgeois Romanticism.) The social relations of the LMP, then, while in general determined by the social relations of the GMP, are not necessarily homologous with them. In developed capitalist social formations, the dominant LMP of large-scale capitalist printing, publishing and distributing reproduces the dominant GMP, but incorporates as a crucial constituent a *subordinate* mode of production: the artisanal mode of the literary producer himself, who typically sells his product (manuscript) rather than his labour-power to the publisher in exchange for a fee.

The social classes into which the productive agents of a social formation are distributed may also exert a determination on the character of the LMPs. Coexistent LMPs may be mutually "disjunct" because each stands in distinct and particular relation to a specific social class. Thus, a dominant courtly class may operate an LMP constituted by the "amateur" production of texts for "informal," "coterie" distribution and consumption; an LMP based upon the professional producer and the capitalist mode of production, distribution, exchange and consumption (into which such "amateur" texts may enter) may simultaneously exist to supply literary commodities to a wider, aristocratic and bourgeois readership, while a complex combination of "oral" LMPs may persist within the most subordinate social classes. Such a schema naturally elides the degree of interdetermination which one would expect concretely to exist between such class-structured LMPs. In medieval England, for example, publicly-performed vernacular literature was consumed by all social classes, and the text produced by the "amateur" author at the request of his patron might be gradually disseminated until a stationer would undertake simultaneous duplication of the original, privately-owned manuscript for

profit. Granted such interdeterminations, however, the class-determinations of literary consumption are a significant constituent of an LMP. In developed capitalist formations, for example, the distribution of income and high price of literary products determined by the GMP produces the social relation of "borrowing" rather than exchange between the mass of proletarian and petty-bourgeois consumers and the LMP; the purchase of books is increasingly confined to members of the dominant classes. Indeed the growth of the circulating libraries in nineteenth-century England is a classic instance of a major mutation in the dominant LMP, a radical reconstitution of the structures of production, distribution and consumption. The privileged status of the "three-decker" (three-volume) novel within the aesthetic ideology of Victorian England is a function of the economic power within the LMP of the circulating libraries, for whom such commodities were especially profitable since three subscribers could thus read a novel simultaneously. The libraries and publishers cartelised to keep the market price of such commodities prohibitively high, hence establishing the libraries as effectively the sole structure of literary distribution and consumption. The dominant social relation of consumption in the dominant LMP of Victorian England was the three guineas subscription of a consumer to Mudie's circulating library of New Oxford Street.[7] The libraries, moreover, reconstituted the structures of literary production: they were powerful determinants in the *selection* of producers (if an author failed to get into Mudie's advertising list, he or she was effectively finished), of the *pace* of literary production (an author would need to produce one three-decker a year to scrape a modest living), and of the literary *product* itself. The multiple complicated plots, elaborate digressions and gratuitous interludes of

---

[6] Eagleton's point is that even novelists from the landed aristocracy or from the "haut-bourgeoisie," the class of financiers and rentier capitalists, would *as novelists* become petty-bourgeois producers because their income from fiction depended, like any shopkeeper's, on the volume of their trade and the demand for their goods.

[7] The point of the three-decker novel as far as Mudie's circulating library was concerned was not to allow three subscribers to read the book simultaneously. It was rather to necessitate the purchase of three one-guinea subscriptions by the reader who wished to obtain all three volumes of the novel at once, so as not to have to wait for missing volumes to come in. Because the publication of novels in one volume threatened this way of mulcting the clientele, Mudie's Library boycotted such "subversive" literature.

such works were the effect of producers ingeniously elongating their material to meet the requirements of the form. Parallel modifications were produced in the printing process itself, where margins were widened and type enlarged to achieve the prerequisite bulk. Coupled with these material and textual factors was the hegemony exercised by the libraries in the region of aesthetic ideology: what was produced and consumed was regulated by their severely censorious owners in accordance with the demands of "general" ideology. In the Victorian circulating libraries, then, we observe at work a peculiarly close, complex conjuncture of GMP, LMP, "general" and "aesthetic" ideology, and text. The struggle of a producer like Thomas Hardy against elements of Victorian bourgeois ideology is intimately related to his scathing assaults on this particular LMP.

The extent to which the social relations of literary production reproduce the social relations of "general" production, then, is historically variable and determinate. In the case of the tribal bardic system, the two sets of relations are identical: the literary social relations between chief or king, bard and listeners are themselves "general" social relations, the bard himself is professional ideologue of the social formation. The literary social relations of the medieval era preserve elements of this structure: the medieval author is typically a cleric, part of an ideological apparatus. But his literary production is an aspect of this function rather than identical with it, a voluntary and "amateur" mode of exercising his priesthood; literary relations assume a certain relative autonomy of "general" ones. The same is true of the patronised medieval producer, whose literary relations to his patron and consumers is a specific articulation of the "general" social relations which hold between them. Capitalist formations differ from all of these modes. The specificity of the articulation between "general" and literary social relations in capitalist formations is to be found in the fact that although the literary social relations in general reproduce the social relations of the GMP, they do not necessarily reproduce these social relations as they hold between the *particular individual agents of the literary productive process.* In both tribalist and feudalist formations, the social relations in which the agents

of literary production (patrons, authors, consumers, etc.) stand are determined by or effectively identical with the social relations in which these individual agents stand outside the LMP, in relation to the GMP. The individual functions within "general" social relations fulfilled by the LMP agents in capitalism, however, are autonomous of the functions they fulfil within the social relations of literary production. An aristocratic novelist may be consumed by proletarian readers, or *vice versa,* but these "general" social relations of the particular agents are "cancelled" by the market relations of literary commodity production. It is this unique and peculiar feature of the capitalist LMP which differentiates it markedly from other LMPs whose social relations depend upon certain "general" relations between the particular agents — relations which pre-exist the act of literary production. The capitalist LMP produces its own social relations between the particular agents independently of their pre-existent social functions — social relations which in general reproduce the "general" social relations appropriate to general commodity production.

(iv) GENERAL IDEOLOGY (GI)

As well as giving rise at a certain historical stage to a series of LMPs, a GMP also always produces a dominant ideological formation — a formation I provisionally term "general" to distinguish it from that specific region within it known as the aesthetic region, or, more summarily, as "aesthetic ideology." A dominant ideological formation is constituted by a relatively coherent set of "discourses" of values, representations and beliefs which, realised in certain material apparatuses and related to the structures of material production, so reflect the experiential relations of individual subjects to their social conditions as to guarantee those misperceptions of the "real" which contribute to the reproduction of the dominant social relations.

It is important to stress here that GI denotes, not some abstraction or "ideal type" or "ideology in general," but that particular dominated ensemble of ideologies to be found in any social formation. In speaking of the "relations" or conjunctures between GI and aesthetic or authorial ideologies, then, one is speaking not of certain extrinsically related "sets," but of the mode of insertion of authorial and aesthetic formations into the hegemonic ideology as a whole. I stress this point to avoid that hypostatisation of GI, AI and AuI which might follow from designating them thus for the purposes of analysis.

(v) RELATIONS OF GI AND LMP

GI typically contains certain general elements or structures, all or some of which may at a particular historical stage bear significantly on the character of the LMP. These general structures can be distinguished in the main as the linguistic, the political, and the "cultural." A set of complex interdeterminations will normally hold between them, which demand historical specification.

A literary text is related to GI not only by how it deploys language but by the particular language it deploys. Language, that most innocent and spontaneous of common currencies, is in reality a terrain scarred, fissured and divided by the cataclysms of political history, strewn with the relics of imperialist, nationalist, regionalist and class combat. The linguistic is always at base the *politico*-linguistic,[8] a sphere within which the struggles of imperial conqueror with subjugated state, nation-state with nation-state, region with nation, class with class are fought out. Literature is an agent as well as effect of such struggles, a crucial mechanism by which the language and ideology of an imperialist class establishes its hegemony, or by which a subordinated state, class or region preserves and perpetuates at the ideological level an historical identity shattered or eroded at the political. It is also a zone in which such struggles achieve stabilisation — in which the contradictory political unity of imperial

and indigenous, dominant and subordinate social classes is articulated and reproduced in the contradictory unity of a "common language" itself. The moment of consolidation of the "nation-state" is of paradigmatic significance here — a moment in which the hegemony of a "national" class reflects itself in the linguistic coherence essential to its integrative, centralising state apparatuses. The history of the genesis of English as a "national" language is the history of imperialism and its aftermath — the linguistic class-division between Norman French and English, the development of Anglo-Norman French after the loss of Normandy, the mutations of Old English under Norman French influence, the gradual development from these sources of a distinctive English language legally recognised in 1362, the selection of the old East Midland dialect (embracing the political and ideological power-centres of London, Oxford and Cambridge) as the basis of the hegemonic language. Parallel interactions between the LMP and the linguistic, ideological and political structures of state power can be found by turning once more to the instance of Ireland. Towards the end of the twelfth century in Ireland there arose a cultural apparatus based upon the hereditary custody of native learning and literature by certain families within the hegemonic class — an apparatus which is shattered by the English subjugation of Ireland in the seventeenth century. Bereft of social institutions within which to perpetuate itself, indigenous literary culture passes from the possession of the extirpated native ruling class and is forced down to the level of the Gaelic-speaking peasantry, with resultant changes in aesthetic form and developments in dialectal and provincial literary production. The traditional LMP based on tales of the *Fíanna*[9] recounted by peripatetic or home-based bards is also effectively destroyed by English imperialism: few such tales pass over into the alien language of the imperial class.

The interdeterminations of the linguistic and the political, and their effect on the constitution of an LMP and the character of its products, are thus

---

[8]I do not mean to imply that language is merely "superstructural." Without language, there could be no material production in the sense characteristic of the human animal. Language is first of all a physical, material reality, and as such is part of the forces of material production. The specific historical forms of this general human reality are then constituted at the social, political and ideological levels. [Eagleton]

[9]An Irish band of warriors, soldiers of the legendary Fionn Mac Cumhail.

of central significance to a materialist criticism. No more graphic example of this conjuncture in English literary history can be found than in John Milton's decision to write *Paradise Lost* in his native tongue.[10] Milton's decision was a radically political act — an assertion of bourgeois Protestant nationalism over classical and aristocratic culture, or rather an assertive appropriation of those classical modes for historically progressive ends. The very forms and textures of his poem are a product of this linguistic, political and religious conjuncture within ideology. All literary production, in fact, belongs to that ideological apparatus which can be provisionally termed the "cultural." What is in question is not simply the process of production and consumption of literary texts, but the function of such production within the cultural ideological apparatus. That apparatus includes the specific institutions of literary production and distribution (publishing houses, bookshops, libraries and so on), but it also encompasses a range of "secondary," supportive institutions whose function is more directly ideological, concerned with the definition and dissemination of literary "standards" and assumptions. Among these are literary academies, societies and book-clubs, associations of literary producers, distributors and consumers, censoring bodies, and literary journals and reviews. In developed social formations, the literary substructure of the cultural apparatus interacts more or less intensively with the ideological apparatus of "communications"; but its real power lies in its articulation with the *educational* apparatus. It is within this apparatus that the ideological function of literature — its function, that is to say, in reproducing the social relations of the mode of production — is most apparent. From the infant school to the University faculty, literature is a vital instrument for the insertion of individuals into the perceptual and symbolic forms of the dominant ideological formation, able to accomplish this function with a "naturalness," spontaneity and experiential immediacy possible to no other ideological practice. But it is not only a question of the ideological use

of particular literary works; it is, more fundamentally, a question of the ideological significance of the cultural and academic institutionalisation of literature as such. What is finally at stake is not literary texts but Literature — the ideological significance of that process whereby certain historical texts are severed from their social formations, defined as "literary," bound and ranked together to constitute a series of "literary traditions" and interrogated to yield a set of ideologically presupposed responses. The precise ideological function of this process is historically variable. It is determined in general by the internal structures of the educational apparatus, which are themselves determined in the last instance by the GMP; but it may present itself ideologically in the form of a conservative academicism, related to GI in its literary *positivism,* or (say) in the form of a liberal humanism which preserves a besieged enclave of idealist values supposedly incarnate in Literature from the invasions of a real history now moving beyond its liberal humanist phase. In any case, it is important to emphasise that the cultural ideological apparatus contains a dual set of literary institutions: "primary" institutions of production such as publishing houses, which exist both as elements of the GMP and as parts of the ideological apparatus of "culture," and "secondary" institutions, including the educational ones with which the cultural apparatus interacts, whose relation to the GMP is the more indirect one of contributing to its reproduction by aiding in the reproduction of its social relations through ideology.

A discussion of the specific relations between GI and the literary text belongs to the next chapter; but since the text is, after all, the product of the LMP, it is worth noting here one or two incidental points about the GI–LMP relation as it affects the literary text. The first point is that different LMPs may, in terms of the ideological character of their textual products, reproduce the same ideological formation. There is no necessary homology between GI and LMP: a serialised and directly published Victorian novel, despite belonging to alternative modes of production, may inhibit the same ideology. Conversely, the same LMP may reproduce mutually antagonistic ideological formations: the fiction of Defoe and Fielding. An LMP which reproduces the social

[10]In 1627 Milton seems to have contemplated writing a biblical epic in Latin.

relations of the GMP may conflict with some of its dominant ideological modes: the Romantic dissent from bourgeois values and relations is in part determined by the very integration of the LMP into general commodity production. Conversely, an LMP in conflict with GMP social relations may nevertheless reproduce its dominant ideological forms.

The second point concerns that direct bearing of GI on the literary text which is censorship. Such modes of direct ideological control over the text may take the form of simple repression at the point of production, distribution or consumption, or may be effected more obliquely: licensing, politically select patronage and so on. The most efficient form of censorship is, of course, the perpetuation of mass illiteracy. The factor of literacy represents a peculiarly complex conjuncture of GMP, LMP, GI and aesthetic ideology. The degree and social distribution of literacy are determined in the last instance by the GMP, but literacy is clearly in turn a significant determinant of the LMP, affecting the size and social composition not only of readers but of producers. The degree of literacy of producers and consumers may also influence the character of the literary product — whether, for instance, it is distributed orally, as well as its length and elaborateness (for there is a limit to the memorising capacity of the non- or semi-literate producer). Illiteracy may be effected by the exclusion of certain social groups and classes from the educational apparatus for political reasons; but there is a possibility of conflict here between those reasons and competing ideological imperatives. In nineteenth-century England, for example, there were sound political reasons why the proletariat should be excluded from literacy, but sound religious reasons why it should not be. Literacy is also determined by aesthetic ideology, which in ratifying (in conjuncture with GI) certain languages (French, Latin), or certain uses of language as appropriate to literature, determines the degree of its general availability. There is a practical, as well as theoretical, literacy.

(vi) AUTHORIAL IDEOLOGY (AuI)

I mean by "authorial ideology" the effect of the author's specific mode of biographical insertion into GI, a mode of insertion overdetermined by a series of distinct factors: social class, sex, nationality, religion, geographical region and so on. This formation is never to be treated in isolation from GI, but must be studied in its articulation with it. Between the two formations of GI and AuI, relations of effective homology, partial disjunction and severe contradiction are possible. The producer's biographical (as opposed to "aesthetic" or "textual") ideology may be effectively homologous with the dominant ideology of his or her historical moment, but not necessarily because the producer lives the social conditions of *class* most appropriate for such harmonious insertion into it. The producer may in terms of (say) class-position inhabit an ideological subensemble with conflictual relations to the dominant ideology, but by an overdetermination of other biographical factors (sex, religion, region) may be rendered homologous with it. The converse situation is equally possible. The degree of conjuncture or disjunction between AuI and GI may also be "diachronically" determined: an author may relate to his or her contemporary GI by virtue of "belonging" to an historically previous GI, or (as with the case of the revolutionary author) to a putatively future one.[11] As GI mutates, an AuI which was at one point homologous with it may enter into conflict with it, and *vice versa*. It is not, in short, always a simple matter to specify the historical period to which a writer belongs; nor does a writer necessarily belong only to one "history." It is significant in this respect that the two generally acknowledged major authors of Restoration England — John Milton and John Bunyan — do not in fact "belong" to "Restoration ideology" at all.[12] It is

[11]There is also the case of the insertion of an author into the GI of *another* society, whether contemporaneous or not: the problem of "cosmopolitanism." Such insertion is always in the last instance a question of the determination of the "native" GI. [Eagleton]

[12]Both Milton and Bunyan were Puritans whose political and religious ideas jibed better with the commonwealth period than with the secular, royalist era when their major works (*Paradise Lost*, 1667; *Pilgrim's Progress*, 1678) were published.

equally true, however, that their modes of ideological disinheritance from their contemporary historical moment are determined, in the last instance, by the nature of that moment itself.

AuI is not to be conflated with GI; nor is it to be identified with the "ideology of the text." The ideology of the text is not an "expression" of authorial ideology: it is the product of an aesthetic working of "general" ideology as that ideology is itself worked and "produced" by an overdetermination of authorial-biographical factors. AuI, then, is always GI as lived, worked and represented from a particular overdetermined standpoint within it. There is no question here of "centring" the literary text on the individual subject who produces it; but neither is it a matter of liquidating that subject into "general" aesthetic and ideological forms. It is a question of specifying the ideological determinations of the text — determinations which include the effect of the author's mode of insertion into GI.

(vii) AESTHETIC IDEOLOGY (AI)

I denote by this the specific aesthetic region of GI, articulated with other such regions — the ethical, religious, etc. — in relations of dominance and subordination determined in the last instance by the GMP. AI is an internally complex formation, including a number of sub-sectors, of which the *literary* is one. This literary sub-sector is itself internally complex, constituted by a number of "levels": theories of literature, critical practices, literary traditions, *genres,* conventions, devices and discourses. AI also includes what may be termed an "ideology of the aesthetic" — a signification of the function, meaning and value of the aesthetic itself within a particular social formation, which is in turn part of an "ideology of culture" included within GI.

(viii) RELATIONS OF AI, GI AND LMP

A GMP produces a GI which contributes to reproducing it; it also produces a (dominant) LMP which in general reproduces and is reproduced by the GMP, but which also reproduces and is reproduced by the GI. We may speak of the "ideology of the LMP" to designate the mutually reproductive relation which holds between GI and LMP — a relation which produces within the LMP an ideology of producer, product and consumer, as well as of the activities of production, exchange and consumption. This ideology is itself encoded within AI; more precisely, it is the effect of a conjuncture between AI and GI. The literary producer may be viewed as the privileged servant of a social order symbolised by his royal, ecclesial or aristocratic patron, as the inspired articulator of the collective values of his community, as an "independent" producer freely offering his private product to an amenable audience, as the prophetic or bohemian rebel dissidently marginal to "conventional" society, as a "worker" or "engineer" on a fraternal footing with his readership, and so on. Literary production itself may be ideologically encoded as revelation, inspiration, labour, play, reflection, fantasy, reproduction; the literary product as process, practice, medium, symbol, object, epiphany, gesture; literary consumption as magical influence, arcane ritual, participatory dialogue, passive reception, didactic instruction, spiritual encounter. Each of these ideologies will be determined by a specific conjuncture of LMP/GI/AI, on the basis of the final determination of the GMP. There is, however, no question of a necessarily *symmetrical* relation here between the various formations involved. Each of these formations is internally complex, and a series of internally and mutually conflictual relations may hold between them. An LMP which is itself an amalgam of historically disparate elements may thus combine in contradictory unity disparate ideological elements of both GI and AI. A double-articulation GMP/GI– GI/AI/LMP is, for example, possible, whereby a GI category, when transformed by AI into an ideological component of an LMP, may then enter into conflict with the GMP social relations it exists to reproduce. The bourgeois-Romantic category of the producer as "individual creator," for example, reproduces but also conflicts with the bourgeois conception of the human subject as nuclear individual. Or again, the Romantic and symbolist ideology of the literary product as mysteriously autotelic object at once reproduces and represses its real status as commodity. Similarly, the ideology of "instant" or "disposable" literary art reproduces the consumer ideologies of advanced capitalism at the same time as it conflicts with certain imperatives of deferred fulfilment integral to that ideological formation.

The forces and relations of literary production, on the basis of their determination by the GMP, produce the possibility of certain distinct literary *genres*. The novel, for example, can be produced only at a certain stage of development of an LMP; but whether this potential is historically activated is determined not by the LMP alone, but by its conjuncture with GI and AI. What forms and *genres* are actually selected for development may be dictated by what exists already — dictated, that is, by AI on the basis of GI. Conversely, the concept of and "need for" a new form may develop relatively autonomously within aesthetic ideology, and an LMP modified or transformed to produce it. GI may occasionally impress itself directly upon the LMP to produce a particular form (say, "socialist realism") which is then encoded and elaborated by AI; but such unilateral action is historically untypical. GI more usually appears within the LMP in its particular aesthetic articulation; literary practices are typically the product of a complex conjuncture of LMP/GI/AI, with one or another of these elements assuming dominance.

GI and AI determine not only the process of production but also the process of consumption. The literary text is a text (as opposed to "book") because it is read; with it as with any other social product, the act of consumption is itself constitutive of its existence. Reading is an ideological decipherment of an ideological product; and the history of literary criticism is the history of the possible conjunctures between the ideologies of the text's productive and consumptive moments. Between those two ideological moments there will be relations of effective homology, conflict or contradiction, determined in part by the history of ideological receptions of the text which has intervened between them. The text is consumed within an aesthetic ideology constituted in part by a set of conjunctures between GI and AI which is the history of the text's production and consumption as constructed by the GI/AI conjuncture of the particular moment of consumption. GI may act as a dominant element within the ideology of consumption (witness the eccentric instance of the considerable increase in Trollope readers during the period of the Second World War),[13] but more commonly operates in the high degree of relative autonomy it ascribes to the aesthetic region. As well as an ideology of particular consumption, there will also be one of general consumption within which the former operates — an ideology of *the act of reading itself,* which may be encoded as religious ceremony, socially privileged compact, moral instruction and so on. Any particular act of reading is conducted within a general set of assumptions as to the ideological signification of reading itself within a social formation — assumptions which, as part of AI, belong also to the general "ideology of culture" of GI.

(ix) RELATIONS OF GI, AI AND AuI

The complexity of relations between GI and AI as constitutive of the literary text is properly the subject of the next chapter. It is enough to say here that as an aesthetic product the text is a multiply articulated structure, determined only in the last instance by the moment of its contemporary GI. Its various aesthetic elements may be the product of distinct ideological formations, may belong to disparate "histories," so that it is not necessarily identical, ideologically speaking, with itself. Nor need the "ideology of the text" be consonant with the historical progressiveness or obsolecence of the LMP within which it is produced. An author may produce progressive texts using outmoded forms within an obsolescent or partly obsolescent LMP (William Morris), or may produce ideologically conservative texts within an historically progressive LMP (Henry

---

[13]The Victorian novels of Anthony Trollope collectively present a portrait of England as by far the most prosperous and most powerful nation on earth; Eagleton seems to be suggesting that British men and women eagerly consumed these novels as comfortable "false consciousness" at a time when England had been nearly defeated by Germany and was being overshadowed by the United States, when its overseas empire was clearly about to crumble, and when it was strictly rationing food and all other consumer goods.

Fielding). It is a question in each case of specifying the precise relations between LMP, "ideology of LMP," GI and AI.

Authorial ideology may be an important determinant of both the type of LMP and the aesthetic ideology within which an author works. As with Alexander Pope's "choice" of satire, elegy and the mock-heroic, a certain AuI will exclude certain modes of literary production and license others. At certain levels of production, AuI may be so subordinated to AI that the question of differential relations between them does not arise. In such a situation, to be a literary producer at all is inevitably to work within a particular set of ideological representations of the character and significance of literary production. The relations between AuI and GI may be transformed by their mediation in terms of AI: within the text itself (Balzac is the classical example), the production of GI by means of certain aesthetic forms may "cancel" and contradict that production of GI which is authorial ideology. The methodological significance of AuI in the analysis of the text is therefore variable: it may be effectively homologous with GI/AI, or it may be "cancelled" as a specific factor by their distinct or conjoint effects. In either of these cases, AuI as a particular "level" effectively disappears.

(x) TEXT

The literary text is the product of a specific overdetermined conjuncture of the elements or formations set out schematically above. It is not, however, a merely passive product. The text is so constituted by this conjuncture as to actively determine its own determinants — an activity which is most apparent in its relations to ideology. It is those relations which we must now go on to examine.

6

NEW HISTORICISM
AND CULTURAL STUDIES

*To understand the practices of writers and artists, and not least their products, entails under-
standing that they are the result of the meeting of two histories: the history of the positions
they occupy and the history of their dispositions.*
                                                                    — PIERRE BOURDIEU

*As in more familiar exercises in close reading, one can start anywhere in a culture's reper-
toire of forms and end up anywhere else. . . . But whatever the level at which one operates,
and however intricately, the guiding principle is the same: societies, like lives, contain their
own interpretations. One has only to learn how to gain access to them.*
                                                                    — CLIFFORD GEERTZ

*Modern thought and experience have taught us to be sensitive to what is involved in repre-
sentation, in studying the Other, in racial thinking, in unthinking and uncritical acceptance
of authority and authoritative ideas, in the sociopolitical role of intellectuals, in the great
value of a skeptical critical consciousness. Perhaps if we remember that the study of human
experience usually has an ethical, to say nothing of a political, consequence . . . we will not
be indifferent to what we do as scholars.*
                                                                    — EDWARD W. SAID

THE NEW HISTORICISM:
THEORIES AND PRACTICES

Born around 1982, the New Historicism quickly became one of the most vital modes
of literary study in the 1980s. The name the brilliant young Renaissance scholar
Stephen Greenblatt gave to the approach he pioneered was conferred in haste. Asked
for a title for a special issue of the journal *Genre* in which his own essays and those
of colleagues were appearing, Greenblatt carelessly threw out the title "New
Historicism." Greenblatt has tried ever since to rename what he does "cultural poetics," in order to avoid the connotations of historical inevitability implicit in the word
historicism and to more clearly label his practice as a literary version of cultural
anthropology. But, alas, in vain: The name has stuck fast.

Greenblatt correctly insists that New Historicism is not a theory or a set of doc-trines but a practice.[1] However, it is a practice that has developed out of contempo-rary theory, particularly the structuralist realization that all human systems are symbolic and subject to the rules of language, and the deconstructive realization that there is no way of positioning oneself as an observer outside the closed circle of tex-tuality. What sort of practice New Historicism is and what its motives are is sug-gested by Michael Warner's fast-and-dirty positioning of it in relation to other critical practices current in the mid-1980s:

> New Historicism is a label that historians don't like much because they understand some-thing different by historicism. But nobody's asking historians; the people the New His-toricists are reacting against are the New Critics, and historicism seems an important term for that purpose because it emphasizes that meaning is established in concrete historical situations. . . . If the "Historicism" in the New Historicism is to distinguish it from the New Critics and their idea that a text means what it means regardless of what your cul-tural situation is, the "New" in New Historicism is to distinguish it from the somewhat dreary and encyclopedic historical work that the philologists used to do. . . . While critics have realized on the one hand that language and the symbolic are never essential and timeless but always contingent on cultural politics, on the other hand they have realized that cultural politics is always symbolic. New Historicism has a motto: "The text is histor-ical, and history is textual." The first part means that meaning does not transcend context but is produced within it; the second part means that human actions and institutions and relations, while certainly hard facts, are not hard facts as distinguished from language. They are themselves symbolic representations, though this is not to say, as so many old historicists might conclude, that they are not real.[2]

Warner's characterization seems reasonably fair to the New Critics, who were deeply uncomfortable with the notion that the author's and reader's ways of con-struing a text might diverge with the passage of time. It is less fair to the philolo-gists and historians, whose "dreary" labors give us whatever picture we possess of past ages, and who were far less naive about the way language is used in writing history than Warner suggests. The philosopher of history R. G. Collingwood made it clear several decades before the advent of the New Historicism that historians are politically and culturally implicated in the history they write, that their work tells us as much about them as the period they investigate and explore.[3]

What is new about the New Historicism might be seen in Stephen Greenblatt's "*King Lear* and Harsnett's 'Devil-Fiction,'" reprinted below. Samuel Harsnett's *Declaration of Egregious Popish Impostures* (printed in 1603), exposes the impos-tures of Catholic exorcists, who would pretend to drive out devils from "possessed" individuals, shills of theirs, as a way of demonstrating their power and that of the Roman Catholic Church. Greenblatt did not discover Harsnett's text, which had long

---

[1]See Stephen Greenblatt, "Toward a Poetics of Culture," in *The New Historicism*, ed. H. Aram Veeser (New York: Routledge, 1989), p. 1.
[2]Michael Warner, "Literary Studies and the History of the Book," *The Book* 12 (1987): 5.
[3]See, for example, Collingwood's *Essays in the Philosophy of History*, ed. William Debbins (New York and London: Garland, 1985).

been recognized as one of the books Shakespeare must have read while composing *King Lear* since it contains names of the devils Edgar cites in the "Poor Tom" scenes on the heath. However, Greenblatt's essay is not a conventional source study; his take on the two texts is to compare the unlicensed, forbidden theatrical performances of the Catholic exorcists in Protestant England with the licensed, permitted theatrical performances conducted on the stage of Shakespeare's Globe, in order to view Shakespeare's play as "a secular version of the ritual of exorcism" and to show how the state benefits from a transgression that can be represented but contained within the wooden "O" of the theater.

While the New Historicists are not, by and large, theorists, their work grew out of three or four advances in theory in radically disconnected fields. From Michel Foucault, the historical philosopher, the New Historicists developed the notion that texts within a particular period are linked by a broad totalizing cultural formation (the *épistème*), in which the workings of power and knowledge and their interrelationships can be defined. From Clifford Geertz, the cultural anthropologist, they absorbed a sense of how both primitive and advanced cultures operate through symbolic representation and ritual enactment of conflict, and they incorporated Geertz's ideal of the "thick description" of a culture that can come only from genuine immersion in its ways. From Hayden White, the philosopher of history, they took the notion that figural relationships — the tropes, or figures of speech used by a writer — can be clues to the way historians think and the way their representations of the past are filtered and shifted through the language of history. Finally, from French philosophical sociologists like Pierre Bourdieu and Michel de Certeau, new historical practice appropriated theories of intellectual practice aimed at understanding how the structure of learned professions alters the way knowledge and the power associated with it are originated and distributed.

CULTURAL STUDIES: THE WORLD AS SOCIAL TEXT

All five of the theorists just mentioned have been appropriated equally by the allied practice of cultural studies.[4] Cultural studies, though, is much harder to pin down than the New Historicism. It is not even clear whether cultural studies is older as a practice than the New Historicism or younger, since it depends on what one wants to count as examples of cultural studies. Books addressing cultural studies by name did not begin to appear until the early 1990s. Nevertheless, Simon During, the British editor of *The Cultural Studies Reader* (1993), views the key player as Richard Hoggart, who began

---

[4]There is no consensus concerning the intellectual substructures of New Historicism and cultural studies. Other historians of criticism have portrayed New Historicism as being influenced by the work of Karl Marx, Raymond Williams, the Italian Marxist Antonio Gramsci, Mikhail Bakhtin, philosopher of science Thomas Kuhn, Walter Benjamin, and dozens of others, including American Marxists such as Fredric Jameson and Frank Lentricchia who have ferociously attacked the New Historicists. The variety of influence on cultural studies is literally unbounded, given the wide range of subject matter analyzed. My principle for choosing exemplars in this chapter has been to avoid duplication while focusing on those influences that seem widest and most significant.

the Center for Cultural Studies at the University of Birmingham in the 1950s, and who inspired, along with Raymond Williams, the media studies work of Stuart Hall.[5] In addition to the cultural materialism of British working-class Marxism, During locates an alternate, "structuralist" side to cultural studies arising from Althusserian Marxism and Lacanian psychoanalysis (for a description of these schools see the introductions to Chs. 5 and 4, respectively). The story is probably even more complicated than this, however. Many contemporary scholars would agree that continental criticism such as Theodor Adorno's *Philosophy of Modern Music* (1949), which compares the compositional practices of Schönberg and Stravinsky in terms of their responses to modernity, and Roland Barthes's essays on fashion, restaurant menus, and wrestling matches in *Mythologies* (1957) were engaged in practices not much different from Meaghan Morris's brilliant study of shopping centers reprinted below, or Ien Ang's approach to watching television, which date from the late 1980s and early 1990s.[6] Given its inchoate nature, trying to date cultural studies precisely is impossible, but it would be fair to claim that its origins long preceded its current vogue, which started in the late 1980s.

Stuart Hall's "Cultural Studies: Two Paradigms" (1980) is a careful tracing of the ideological affiliations of the Birmingham group begun by Richard Hoggart in the twin directions of British Marxism and French structuralism. Hall's British Marxist forebears are Raymond Williams and E. P. Thompson, who were not dialecticians so much as students of the culture of the English past. Williams, in fact, was a historian of "forms of feeling," which he is reluctant to ascribe to anything so doctrinaire as ideology, until he was stimulated by Thompson's questioning to take on a harder line, and accept the historical motor for change provided by materialist dialectic. The other structuralist side, for Hall, is represented by Claude Lévi-Strauss, whom Hall locates in the tradition of Emile Durkheim and Marcel Mauss. Hall chronicles the nebulous attachments Lévi-Strauss made with Marxism, although he finds clearer connections between the two paradigms with Louis Althusser and Lucien Goldmann. For Hall the virtue of structuralism is its ability to view the human condition as determined, indeed overdetermined, by symbolic networks operating at different levels, and its comprehension of the lived relationships of society as a totality.

Hall concludes with a paean to Michel Foucault and Antonio Gramsci, who he claims "between them account for most of the most productive work on *concrete analysis* now being undertaken in the field." Of course Gramsci was a somewhat unorthodox Marxist and Foucault was never a believer in the structuralist synthesis of knowledge, and the two are strangely matched, Gramsci's concept of hegemony (see p. 1206) granting the oppressed classes areas of autonomy that Foucault's disciplinary systems would rigorously deny. Indeed, from a different point of view, Marxism and structuralism might be seen as an oddly matched couple, the former

---

[5]See *The Cultural Studies Reader*, ed. Simon During (London: Routledge, 1993); Richard Hoggart, *The Uses of Literacy* (London: Penguin, 1957); and Stuart Hall and Paddy Whannel, *The Popular Arts* (London: Hutchinson, 1964).

[6]See Ien Ang, *Watching Television* (London: Routledge, 1991).

insisting on a dialectical framework for thought, with progress emerging from conflict, the latter an operational schema, reducing every object of analysis to its smallest functional parts, understanding totalities as syntactic structures built out of these atoms.

The two specimens of concrete analysis reprinted here within the mode of cultural studies are in tune with Stuart Hall's general vision, but the theorists that inspired Meaghan Morris and Laura Kipnis were Certeau and Bakhtin rather than Gramsci and Foucault. Meaghan Morris has written on motels, towers, and beach scenes, on *Mad Max* and *Crocodile Dundee* as documents of Australian national identity. Her early essay, "Things to Do with Shopping Centres," takes the Australian version of the suburban mall as her topic, discovering that this is a field which, however well she knows it, she needs to approach with a certain caution. To "read" the mall is to read the instructions of its planners and architects, who, theorists in their own ways, have been envisioning the women who will shop there, who will be its engaged audience. Those women thus exist as one imaginary construction inside another, and, to avoid patronizing the actual women thus inscribed in theory, Morris ultimately restricts her human subjects to the fraction she knows best, herself, and the malls to the three at which she regularly shops. Like Certeau's "Walking in the City," which informs her perspective, Morris understands modern life as a continual struggle to operate against the grain of the disciplines that structure our waking lives; here she looks into the history of the development of these malls, the attempt to give some kind of spatial identity to what is constructed in the vacant spaces outside the modern metropolis and in the ruined spaces within. But in the long run — taking up the "Garden of Eden" metaphor used by a professional shopping mall planner — the loudest voice she hears is that of the serpent: its financiers, its designers, its builders all seem to be beckoning to women to find versions of happiness, knowledge, and power in "a fluffy pink top and a sweet floral skirt."

Laura Kipnis, in "Reading *Hustler*," is a feminist with the opposite problem from Meaghan Morris's: for her there is no danger of identifying all too easily with an institution that interpellates her as a contemporary woman; on the contrary, she finds Larry Flynt's pornographic magazine not merely outrageously offensive but disgusting. Its images do not merely objectify women, they are degrading, gruesome, physically nauseating, capped by a cover of a woman being fed head first into a meat grinder. Kipnis has to control her disgust and bracket her usual social feminism in order to get a handle on what *Hustler* is actually all about. Her analysis, which makes use of Mikhail Bakhtin's contrast between the "classical body" on view in *Playboy* and *Penthouse*, and the "grotesque body" served up in *Hustler*, ultimately finds a disturbingly comprehensive worldview based on class resentment. The white blue-collar reader interpellated by *Hustler* does not see himself as an upwardly mobile dreamer, aspiring to a lifestyle of refined sensual pleasures, but rather as the victim of an elaborate skein of hustles. He sees himself as exploited by bosses who overwork him and dock his pay for trifles, and cheated by a government that assists the wealthy, the middle classes, impoverished minorities, everyone but him. Worst of all he feels despised by educated, petty-bourgeois, feminist women, whom he desires but who do not desire him in return. The photos and cartoons take his revenge. Kipnis's analysis suggests that viewing *Hustler* as an expression of masculine power over women misses the real point: the rancor and class hostility at the core of its vision.

Cultural studies involves viewing and analyzing practically any recorded phenomenon, present or past, as a social text. The "texts" analyzed include such evanescent events as music videos, comic books, letters from summer camp, and radio talk shows: Madonna Studies at one point threatened to become a major subfield. In addition, they include phenomena that are not usually thought of as texts at all, such as government regulations, embroidery, surgical operations, meatpacking, and mapmaking. Since canonical literary works and their formal elements are also viewed as social texts, one could in theory write "cultural studies" about Alexander Pope's pastorals. But, in practice, the tendency has been to seek out subjects disdained by the traditional hierarchies of aesthetic value, or ones that in their exoticism stand outside the older canon.

To some extent, the New Historicism has also focused on nonliterary texts. For example, Richard McCoy has written about the ritual order and physical arrangements of Elizabeth Tudor's coronation, which, as he demonstrates, were composed with as assiduous an eye to metaphor and symbol as any epic poem; he has also studied Henrician and Elizabethan tournaments as performance art, as ritual, and as political act.[7] But McCoy also discusses Sidney and Spenser in the light of the rituals of chivalry, so, in his work, there is certainly nothing like the absolute breach with literary texts and the literary canon that one finds in much of cultural studies.[8]

Like the New Historicism, cultural studies is not a theory as such or even a combination of theories; it is not even a single coherent practice, but rather a disparate set of related practices. Some practitioners of cultural studies relate easily to Gramscian or Althusserian Marxism, while others like Michel Foucault himself and his numerous fellow travelers are loath to situate cultural power principally as a by-product of economics. Even if they do not present a single, consistent social philosophy,[9] essays in cultural studies must situate themselves in relation to *some* literary and social theory to make the questions they raise, the texts they choose, and the methods they follow comprehensible. More eclectic even than New Historicism, cultural

[7]See Richard McCoy, *The Rites of Knighthood: The Literature and Politics of Elizabethan Chivalry* (New York: Cambridge University Press, 1989).

[8]I am not sure precisely how to characterize my own work in progress, which includes a reading of the idea of "identity" (the concept of a sense of self that might be discarded, refashioned, stolen, or feigned) as a cultural phenomenon of England in the 1860s. This *mentalité* was stimulated by Wilkie Collins's sensational novel *The Woman in White* (1860), which sensitized English readers to the idea that one's identity might be stolen by a clever criminal, and clearly had taken hold ten years later, as is shown by the real-life case of the Titchborne claimant, an Australian rogue falsely claiming to be an English baronet, whose struggle in court to get his "rights" absorbed aristocrat and commoner alike for several years. Is the analysis of how England developed a fixation on identity a form of New Historicism or cultural studies? The reviewers will have to tell me. See *Crimes of the Century: The Ideology of True Crime Fiction,* forthcoming.

[9]It is probably a safe guess that most practitioners of both the New Historicism and cultural studies would locate themselves well to the left of both the Labour Party of British Prime Minister Tony Blair and the Democratic Party of former U.S. President Bill Clinton.

studies draws on structuralism, deconstruction, Lacanian psychology, post-Althusserian Marxism, reception theory, feminism, and gender studies; to fully understand its intellectual basis would require reading virtually this entire book. The placement of cultural studies in the same chapter as the New Historicism marks the fact that they share many key influences, including Foucault's social and sexual theories, Geertz's ideal of "thick description," and Bourdieu's analysis of cultural power and capital.

FOUCAULT: ARCHAEOLOGIES AND GENEALOGIES, POWER AND KNOWLEDGE

It is hard to know how to characterize Foucault. He refused to be termed a philosopher, though for a time he held the chair in philosophy at the Collège de France. He was certainly not a literary critic. Most of his works are in the field of social history. *Folie et déraison: Histoire de la folie à l'âge classique* (1961; translated as *Madness and Civilization*, 1973) is a history of the forms of treatment for insanity since the Renaissance. *Surveillir et punir: Naissance de la prison* (1975; translated as *Discipline and Punish*, 1977) deals with the treatment of crime and delinquency over the same period. *The History of Sexuality* (1976), a projected six-volume treatise left unfinished at Foucault's death in 1984, examines moral attitudes toward sexual desire beginning with the ancient Greeks (see the introduction to Gender Studies and Queer Theory, p. 1611). Nevertheless, Foucault stood aloof from the social historians of the *Annales* school (including Fernand Braudel, Phillipe Ariès, and Emmanuel Leroi-Ladurie) who were working on the sort of "local knowledge" prized by Clifford Geertz, and Foucault was pilloried by social historians both in France and abroad for his cavalier use of facts and documents, and for his tendency to create universal generalizations based on slim and sometimes unrepresentative bits of evidence.

It was as a philosopher of history that Foucault was most influential, both on the New Historicists and on the larger and more diverse group of cultural studies scholars. But he was a philosopher of history who preached the obsolescence of history as it had been practiced. For Foucault, history was certainly not the working out of a single plotted idea, as it was for Hegel or Marx. Foucault believed that not only are there no ideas governing reality but that we cannot even know the reality of the past, as we have access only to representations purporting to map the real. Nor is there a unitary self doing this mapping, only a subject constituted by society as an effect of its repressive social and economic structures.

Furthermore, in addition to viewing history as a mode of knowledge that is obsolescent, tied to the modern *épistème* that he felt was on its way out, Foucault believed history constitutes a method of repression. For Foucault, history embodies

the various . . . aspects of the will to knowledge [*vouloir-savoir*]: instinct, passion, the inquisitor's devotion, cruel subtlety, and malice. It discovers the violence of a position that sides with those who are happy in their ignorance, against the effective illusions by which humanity protects itself, a position that encourages the dangers of research and delights in disturbing discoveries. The historical analysis of the rancorous will to knowledge reveals that all knowledge rests upon injustice (that there is no right, not even in the act of knowing, to truth or a foundation for truth) and that the instinct for knowledge is malicious.[10]

For obsolescent history, Foucault wishes to substitute "genealogy" in Nietzsche's sense of a study of "emergences" that "rejects the metahistorical deployment of ideal significations and indefinite teleologies," that "opposes itself to the search for 'origins'" (140).

The key text for Foucault's vision of history is *Les mots et les choses* (1966; translated as *The Order of Things: An Archaeology of the Human Sciences*, 1970). The initial chapter of this work, in which Foucault treats Velázquez's masterpiece, *Las Meninas*, as a text of history, is reprinted below. Though Foucault is a philosophical nominalist, no Platonist could be more rigidly totalizing in his periodization. The four epochs into which Foucault divides Western history — conventionally called the Renaissance, the Enlightenment, the modern age, and the postmodern future — are each separated by what he refers to as a *coupure*, or rupture, that forces a complete break with the mode of thought of the past. For Foucault, these epochs are entirely discontinuous, like an archeological dig in which the culture of one era is separated by fault lines from what precedes and follows it. Each band of culture is integrated by what Foucault calls an *épistème*, a mode of power/knowledge with its own discursive practices: methods of expression that are also methods of oppression.

In the Renaissance, the connections between facts, their ordering and hierarchies, were expressed in terms of similitudes and sympathies, natural metaphors and metonymies that anyone could read in God's creation. In the Enlightenment, such connections were based on classifications, types and their tokens, ordered like grammars or taxonomies. In the modern age, history itself, with its emphasis on the narrative, has become the master mode of organization. For example Marx presents his ideas about economics and the social and political relations that emerge from economics not in the form of charts and tables but as a master narrative of humanity's history from the Bronze Age through the Industrial Revolution that culminates in his prophecy of the decline and violent overthrow of capitalism and the creation of a worker's state. Similarly, Freud presents his idea of the drives and defenses that make people so complex in terms of a developmental narrative in which the individual passes through oral, anal, and phallic phases of pregenital sexuality and emerges from the Oedipal crisis of adolescence before attaining adulthood. To argue against Marx and Freud, one has to attack not just their principles but their narratives — as their revisers have in fact done. This mode of argumentation belongs to the modern age, which in Foucault's view is passing with the coming of postmodernism, which will engender some new *épistème*, or way of organizing knowledge, that will make the historical, or narrative mode obsolete.

Foucault's "archaeological" method, as presented in *The Order of Things*, is essentially synchronic, presenting history as a series of sedimentary layers separated

---

[10]Michel Foucault, "Nietzsche, Genealogy, History," in *Language, Counter-memory, Practice* (Oxford: Basil Blackwell, 1977), pp. 162–63.

by fault lines. In contrast, his separate studies of madness, illness, crime, and sex are "genealogical," diachronic studies that link various discursive practices with one another — often through similitudes and catachreses — "in order to establish those diverse converging, and sometimes divergent, but never autonomous series that enable us to circumscribe the 'locus' of an event, the limits to its fluidity and the conditions of its emergence."[11] Within each of Foucault's genealogies — his stories of the emergence of new methods of punishment, new modes of treatment for mental illness, or new attitudes toward the body and sexuality — his treatment of historical change is more or less coherent.

A self-contradiction appears, however, when one places the various genealogies against one another. Then it becomes evident that although changes in each of the discursive formations are supposed to occur within a *coupure*, a fissure between *épistèmes*, the changes in one area of social regulation do not occur simultaneously with changes in other areas, as one would think they should. The beginning of the regulation of the lives of imprisoned criminals by timetables and rules, for example, starts about a century after one might expect, given Foucault's general vision of the Enlightenment with its fascination with types and taxonomies. Foucault does not attempt to disguise this fact. As he says in *The Archaeology of Knowledge,* "We must not imagine that rupture is a sort of great drift that carries with it all discursive formations at once. . . . The idea of a single break suddenly, at a given moment, dividing all discursive formations, interrupting them in a single moment and reconstituting them in accordance with the same rules — such an idea cannot be sustained. The contemporaneity of several transformations does not mean their exact chronological coincidence: each transformation may have its own particular index of temporal 'viscosity' " (175). But if discursive formations may linger for more than a century because of their "temporal viscosity," the notion of an *épistème* as a coherent historical formation begins to seem empty.

Another hollowness is Foucault's notion of causality. Unlike most social historians, Foucault has no interest in what made things happen, in baring the nexus of conditionality and contingency, of what is necessary and what sufficient for one state of affairs to transmute itself into another. As he says,

> The old questions of the traditional analysis (What link should be made between disparate events? How can a causal succession be established between them? What continuity or overall significance do they possess? Is it possible to define a totality, or must one be content with reconstitution of connexions?) are now being replaced by questions of another type: which strata should be isolated from others? What types of series should be established? What system of relations . . . may be established between them? What series of series may be established? And in what large-scale chronological table may distinct series of events be determined?[12]

For many a historian, such questions represent an evasion of history rather than its fulfillment. Nevertheless, Foucault's notions of historical periodization and of discursive

---

[11]Michel Foucault, "The Discourse on Language," in *The Archaeology of Knowledge and the Discourse on Language* (New York: Pantheon, 1971), p. 230.
[12]Ibid., pp. 3–4.

practices of power/knowledge have been highly influential both on New Historicists and practitioners of cultural studies.

For example, Stephen Greenblatt's discussion of the relationship between the bounded (and thereby licensed) representation of transgression within the theater of the English Renaissance and the remorseless persecution of similar transgressors (Catholics, witches, transvestites) in the society at large derives straight from Foucault, who uses it, among other places, in his *History of Sexuality*. Greenblatt also explicitly rejects the notion of causality as a principal focus of genealogical investigation. In the course of relating Shakespeare's theatrical representations of women who dress up as boys (like Viola in *Twelfth Night*) to a story of cross-dressing by Marin le Marcis in Montaigne's *Travel Journal*, to Jacques Duval's story of a woman married to a hermaphrodite (*De Hermaphroditis*, 1603), and to Galen's and Paré's various misconceptions about the male and female sexual organs (ca. 130 and 1510–90, respectively), Greenblatt hastens to assure us that he realizes that it is unlikely that Shakespeare had studied Galen and Paré, and almost inconceivable that he had heard about the cases of cross-dressing and hermaphroditism mentioned by Montaigne and Duval. These are not sources but intertexts. "The relation I wish to establish between medical and theatrical practice is not one of cause and effect or source and literary realization. We are dealing rather with a shared code, a set of interlocking tropes and similitudes that function not only as the objects but as the conditions of the representation."[13] There is nothing dishonest at all going on here, but Greenblatt appears less defensive when the cultural text against which he reads Shakespeare is, like Samuel Harsnett's *Declaration of Egregious Popish Impostures*, a book Shakespeare is likely to have read while writing *King Lear*, or like William Strachey's account of storm and shipwreck near Bermuda, a text Shakespeare probably saw in manuscript while working on *The Tempest*. Other issues linked to the New Historicism's connection with Foucault are raised and thoroughly aired on Frank Lentricchia's counterblast against Greenblatt from *Ariel and the Police*, reprinted in the dialogue piece below.

GENDER AND THEORY

What Foucault shares with the practitioners of the *Annales* school in France and the various "history from the bottom up" movements in English-speaking countries is a central focus on social history rather than political history: history "without the king," centering on institutions like the family, the trades, and professions, as well as the ways in which societies deal with individuals and groups that are transgressive (heretics, criminals, sexual deviates) or "other" in less obvious ways, such as infants and the aged. Ironically, one charge leveled against the New Historicism in the late 1980s was that it had ignored issues of sex and gender. Judith Lowder

[13]Stephen Greenblatt, *Shakespearean Negotiations: The Circulation of Social Energy in Renaissance England* (Oxford: Clarendon Press, 1988), p. 86.

Newton complained in "History as Usual? Feminism and the 'New Historicism'" (1988) that while the king had been gotten rid of, the patriarch seemed to hold full sway. Newton argued that while many of her female colleagues were engaged with the New Historicism, histories of the critical practice tended to ignore their work on changing gender roles. In particular, she wanted these histories to take account of such feminist scholarship as Catherine Gallagher's *The Industrial Reformation of English Fiction: Social Discourse and Narrative Form, 1832–1867* (1985), Mary Poovey's *Uneven Developments: The Ideological Work of Gender in Mid-Victorian England* (1988), and Nancy Armstrong's *Desire and Domestic Fiction: A Political History of the Novel* (1987).

Armstrong, influenced by the cultural materialism of Raymond Williams as well as by Foucault, has researched the ways in which institutions like the domestic household were created and reshaped by texts of domesticity — courtesy manuals, cookery books, and the domestic novel — written about and often by women with a conscious eye toward the changing structure of the family. Armstrong's notions that changes in society and the role of women are not on the fringes of politics but at its center, expressed in "Some Call It Fiction: On the Politics of Domesticity" (reprinted here), would find an echo in other feminist thinkers and gender theorists. Her placement in this chapter reminds us that both the New Historicism and cultural studies have begun to move gender roles and the changes they have undergone to the center of the agenda.

WHITE: HISTORY AS DISCOURSE

Greenblatt's sense that common "tropes and similitudes" of representation are key indications of historical linkage is indebted to Foucault but also to Hayden White's study of historiography. White's first book, *Metahistory* (1974), was in effect an inside-out version of New Historicism, a demonstration of the textuality of history centering on the ways in which various Enlightenment and post-Romantic historians (including Gibbon, Macaulay, and Burkhardt) were "literary" in the strongest sense of the word. White argued that these historians' imaginative conceptions of the Roman Empire, or the Glorious Revolution, or the Civilization of the Renaissance in Italy were shaped in accordance with the four primary literary genres (tragedy, comedy, romance, and satire) and conveyed their visions of truth through language mediated by the four "master tropes" of metaphor (analogy), metonymy (association), synecdoche (the part for the whole), and irony (reversal).

In analyzing the rhetoric of a particular historian, White sometimes finds that a sequence of tropes works to signify the development of consciousness. In his analysis of E. P. Thompson's classic history, *The Making of the English Working Class* (1963), White argues that Thompson's rhetoric presents the "awakening" of working-class consciousness in the eighteenth century in an analogical, or "metaphorical" mode of thought. White categorizes Thompson's later account of labor in the early nineteenth century as "metonymic," because Thompson emphasizes the ways in which working-class consciousness became defined in terms of the "distinctive kinds" of work into which labor was transformed. White views Thompson's description of laborers after the Peterloo Massacre of 1819 as "synecdochic," since Thompson presents the workers as viewing themselves as parts of one whole. Finally, White argues that Thompson's presentation of the class-consciousness of the workers as developing, around 1835, into a form of *self*-consciousness falls into the mode of irony, from which we would correctly predict "the fatal fracturing of the working-class movement itself."[14]

In "The Historical Text as Literary Artifact" (1974), reprinted here, White theorizes the basis of his project for making history textual, locating his vision of history in relation to predecessors like Robin Collingwood, Northrop Frye, and, on the distant horizon, Aristotle. In each case, White performs an act of misprision, misreading his predecessors in order to create space for his sense of historical writing. Collingwood, an idealist philosopher in the tradition of Croce, had seen the historian's task as forming a constructive intuition, a sense of the shaping form of the human events of his chronicle. White takes this conception of the historian's task, but redefines it in terms of his requirement that the intuition take shape in terms of the tropes of literary language and in the form of a literary genre. The genres themselves are wrested from Northrop Frye's myths of spring, summer, autumn, and winter (see pp. 698–99), although Frye himself did not view historical writing as a form of literature. And finally White defines his poetics of historiography in contrast with Aristotle's poetics, although any historical text written in accord with White's literary vision would have easily qualified with Aristotle as a form of poetry. Within this fascinating essay White makes what may at the time have seemed a strange detour, a long paragraph relating the historian's task of decoding and recoding the past to what happens in psychoanalysis, as a process in which the patient discards the old story about himself he has internalized and re-assembles the fragments of his past into a new and different narrative. It seems no coincidence that in the last three decades an entirely new field of psychoanalysis has sprung up, narrative psychotherapy, based on ideas strikingly similar to White's.

GEERTZ: LOCAL KNOWLEDGE AND THICK DESCRIPTION

Clifford Geertz is no more a literary critic than Foucault or White; he is a cultural anthropologist, and his immense influence on both the New Historicism and cultural studies stems from his "semiotic" view of culture. Like Claude Lévi-Strauss, Geertz reads cultures as systems of signs in which relationships in one social arena stand in for others, but unlike Lévi-Strauss, who argues that kinship patterns within a culture can always be extracted from the interrelationships of myth, Geertz carries no metaphysical baggage and has no preconceived sense of the way in which cultures are constructed. He stands in the central tradition of the field anthropologists who, from the time of Bronislaw Malinowski (1884–1942), went out to see exotic peoples for themselves. However, in contrast to the positivistic ethos of classical anthropology,

---

[14]Hayden White, *Tropics of Discourse: Essays in Cultural Criticism* (Baltimore: Johns Hopkins University Press, 1978), pp. 16–20.

Geertz displays the postmodern sense that the observer cannot be detached from what is observed.

In the opening chapter of *The Interpretation of Cultures,* reprinted here, Geertz insists that, to understand a society, one cannot stand aloof from it, observing behaviors and gleaning information from informants; instead, one needs to be immersed in a culture's relationships to bring out a credible report of what events mean to their participants. Such a credible report Geertz calls a "thick description," borrowing a term from the English philosopher Gilbert Ryle, who contrasted "thin" descriptions of external behavior (which are unable to distinguish a wink from a facial tic) with the "thick" descriptions that include the significance of events. A tic is an involuntary behavior, whereas a wink is a message, one that, as Geertz puts it, communicates "(1) deliberately, (2) to someone in particular, (3) to impart a particular message, (4) according to a socially established code, (5) without the cognizance of the rest of the company."[15] And of course things can get even more complicated: Winks can be feigned, or parodied, or performed to show how one winks.

Different observers of a culture will bring back different reports, of course, particularly because of their individual preconceptions and partly because of the different ways in which each individual will relate to an exotic culture (and will be related to the culture's members). This means that anthropology cannot be a precise science, any more than history can, because the meaning found in cultural activities is ultimately constructed by the anthropologist. The inevitable contradictions between anthropologists' reports cannot be mediated by any "objective" observer (since no observer can be objective), and in the last analysis the proof of an anthropologist's account rests on the conviction that the rhetoric of "thick description" can convey.

Geertz provides in this chapter an interpretive "reading" of an episode of sheep-stealing, murder, and revenge in the Maghreb, but, Geertz's theoretical coda modestly insists that no "close reading" of the sort he has performed can reveal more than a single facet of a complete culture. But if "the culture of a people is an ensemble of texts," then each "reading" of social semiotics brings us closer to an understanding of a society. Cultural theorists have read our own contemporary society through the semiotics of the texts of television series and the layout of shopping centers, just as New Historicists have produced "readings" of Henrician and Elizabethan jousting scorecards, and enriched our sense of the literature as well as the life of the times.

CERTEAU AND BOURDIEU:
CULTURAL FREEDOM, CULTURAL POWER

A fourth major influence on both New Historicism and cultural studies has been French sociology, the Lacan-inflected sociology of Michel de Certeau, and the Marxian sociology of Pierre Bourdieu.

---

[15]Clifford Geertz, "Local Knowledge," in *The Interpretation of Cultures* (New York: Basic Books, 1973), p. 6.

Certeau turned the lens of linguistic analysis on to ordinary human behavior, looking for the underlying rules by which ordinary people go about their everyday rituals of shopping, cooking, going to work, negotiating the spaces of the city and the transportation networks. By looking at practices, he hoped to discover the laws by which we live. As Certeau put it in his introduction, "An investigation analogous to Chomsky's study of the oral uses of language must seek to restore to everyday practices their logical and cultural legitimacy, at least in the sectors—still very limited — in which we have at our disposal the instruments necessary to account for them. This kind of research is complicated by the fact that these practices themselves alternately exacerbate and disrupt our logics. Its regrets are like those of the poet, and like him, it struggles against oblivion." The dark specter lurking behind the thought of Certeau is the Foucault of *Discipline and Punish*, ever seeking in the grid of the city a way for the eye of power to see and exert control over everyone. Certeau is moved by this vision to oppose it; he does not deny the possibility of totalitarian control but seeks to elude it by an inquiry "analogous and contrary" to Foucault's: "If it is true that the grid of 'discipline' is everywhere becoming clearer and more extensive, it is all the more urgent to discover how an entire society resists being reduced to it, what popular procedures (also 'minuscule' and quotidian) manipulate the mechanisms of discipline and conform to them only in order to evade them, and finally, what 'ways of operating' form the counterpart, on the consumer's . . . side, of the mute processes that organize the establishment of socioeconomic order." Again and again Certeau relies on the concept of *bricolage* (improvisational engineering, patching things together with whatever materials are at hand) as a metaphor for the unpredictable ways people operate in asserting their freedom.

One perhaps needs to warn readers that "Walking in the City," the selection from *The Practice of Everyday Life* reprinted here, begins by taking them to a vantage point they can no longer actually occupy, the 110th floor observation deck of the World Trade Center. Certeau himself died before either of the attacks that destroyed it, but the vision of power inherent in the view from the top, which made the building figural for global Western capitalism, and therefore a target for terrorism, was something that Certeau understood all too well.

Pierre Bourdieu, beginning in the early 1970s, had his own original way of looking at practices and power relationships. First of all, he divided society into a series of fields (such as the economic, the political, the cultural, and the educational) within which relationships occur. Although he did not want to reinstate the romantic notion of the "self," Bourdieu also rejected the poststructuralist "subject position," with its vision of actions without agents. Instead, he put forward the notion of a "habitus," which he defined as a "system of dispositions," the social equivalent of "linguistic competence" (Noam Chomsky's term for the sum of all the tacit knowledge one has to possess to speak a language with native fluency; see p. 977). Randal Johnson defines "habitus" not as a set of rules but rather as "the feel for the game" that one possesses for life, that one passes on to other players in the course of playing.[16]

[16]Randal Johnson, "Introduction" to Pierre Bourdieu, *The Field of Cultural Production* (New York: Columbia University Press, 1993), p. 6.

Bourdieu viewed "habitus" as class related: Persons of the same class were likely, he found, to adopt a similar habitus across different social fields.

For the New Historicism and cultural studies, the main contribution of Bourdieu has been his provision of a way of thinking about culture that complicates the Marxist notion of superstructure (see the introduction to Marx, p. 397). For Bourdieu the field of cultural production depends in part on the fields of political power and large-scale economic production, but it also obeys rules of its own that are dictated by its relation to other fields such as education. "The Market in Symbolic Goods" (1971) starts out with the notion that what Bourdieu calls "goods of restricted production" (objects of art and highly skilled craft) were for much of human history financed by the patronage of the aristocracy and the church. A shift toward relative autonomy occurred with the development of mercantile capitalism during the Renaissance, as cultural production came to be regulated primarily by the market, as opposed to the patronage system. The cultural market operates not only on goods being produced at any given moment (contemporary paintings, music, literature, fine porcelains, and such) but on the goods of the past which are simultaneously in circulation. Bourdieu points out that the social value of such symbolic goods, their worth in the cultural field, rests not merely in their rarity (as with gold and gemstones) but in the cultural "capital" derived from the education that needs to be invested to appreciate them. What this means is that the popular art of one era (Elizabethan drama, for example) may subsequently become the highly valued masterpiece of another.

In *Distinction* (1979), Bourdieu applied his theory of habitus and cultural capital to aesthetic taste, arguing — against the aesthetic theory of Kant — that tastes and predispositions, both in matters of bodily taste and art of various kinds, not only are far from universal, but are one of the chief means whereby social distinctions are enforced in a capitalist economy that makes money easier to come by than class. Bourdieu did not merely theorize about taste, he took elaborate surveys of preferences, both in provincial Lille and in Paris, using subjects from different social backgrounds, economic ranges, and educational achievements. He discovered that education and income goes some distance to overcome the disadvantages of working-class origins, particularly in areas covered in the educational curriculum. One might learn that way to prefer a fugue from Bach's "Well-Tempered Clavier" to Strauss's "Blue Danube Waltz." But educational background would be less likely to help one to make the approved aristocratic choice in extracurricular matters like popular music or cinema, where those of good family would be likely to choose a song by Leo Ferré[17] over a ballad by Petula Clark, or a genre film like The *Big Sleep* by Howard Hawks over a middlebrow drama like *Mrs. Miniver*. Bourdieu's argument is that two centuries after the Revolution, the court of Versailles still holds sway, insubstantially, in the way those who truly belong show that they do by subtle choices in the art on their walls, the music coming out of their speakers, what they read, eat, and drink.

[17]Anarchist poet/singer (1911–1993) revered in France but relatively unknown in the English-speaking world — one needs to imagine a Bob Dylan who was fifty-two rather than twenty-seven in 1968.

GUILLORY AND CULTURAL CAPITAL

One application of Pierre Bourdieu's post-Marxist analysis of culture and class is John Guillory's *Cultural Capital: The Problem of Literary Canon Formation* (1993), reprinted in part below. Guillory insists, in the first place, that the function of the school as institution is not peripheral but central to the class structure of capitalist society. Schools not only train the young in the specific information and skills they need to operate in a utilitarian society under capitalism, they also reproduce the structure of that society by creating young heirs to take their places within the social hierarchy. The class basis of culture requires the reproduction of cultural capital: from one generation to the next, in a society based on inequalities, the distribution of such capital must be unequal. Some people must get more than others. The acquisition of a certain quantity of cultural capital is needed to produce the vision and discourse of a member of the ruling class and to distinguish him or her from social inferiors. There is no rule that allows one to predict precisely which forms of cultural capital will be valued in a particular time and place: The mandarins of the Ming Dynasty were required to know literary classics from the previous millennium; the aristocrats of the Enlightenment were required to be able to compose Latin and Greek verses; and the upper bourgeoisie of the nineteenth century were required to know and revere the classics of Western literature from Homer and Virgil through the early modern period. Needless to say, things are different now. Guillory writes that

> At the present moment, the nation-state still requires a relatively homogeneous language to administer its citizenry, but it no longer requires that a distinctive practice of that language identify a culturally homogeneous bourgeoisie. That class has long since been replaced by a culturally heterogeneous New Class, which has in turn been fully integrated into mass culture, a media culture mediating the desires of every class and group. In this new phase of civilization, the historical function of the literary curriculum — to produce at the lower levels of the educational system a practice of Standard English and at the higher levels a more refined bourgeois language, a *literary* English — is no longer important to the social order. (263)

The "crisis of the humanities," which is the name journalism has given to the flight of young men and women in the universities away from specializing in literature, history, and other traditional liberal arts subjects, is thus a purely utilitarian reaction. Students' future employers will want them to calculate market shares and perform multiple regressions, so the less time they spend developing an expertise in the liberal arts, the better. Professors of literature experience themselves as powerless, Guillory argues, precisely because they have become functionless. The allusive literary language that was once the possession of every successful businessman and bureaucrat is no longer a prerequisite for success. The one thing English departments do that still has genuine value for contemporary capitalism is training the university's students in composition and rhetoric. The art of incisive expository writing with "proper" diction and syntax, almost universally neglected at the primary and secondary levels of schooling, is still a necessary component of the education of the professional-managerial elite, one that in fact differentiates those who will rise to executive management positions from those who will stay at the lower sales and technical levels of the corporate structure. One irony is that, in the last two decades, composition training has itself become a specialization within the English faculty, rather than a natural and unspoken part of the expertise of any teacher of literature. Another is that most of the composition training at universities since the 1990s is done by underpaid graduate assistants serving apprenticeships to become professors of literature, who hope, if they are successful in their pursuit, to do less and less of what their society actually values.

The warfare over the canon represents, for Guillory, the thrashing about of a profession whose central preoccupation, literature, no longer has the significance for society it once did. The humanities faculty imagines that it could reclaim its usefulness within the educational system if it could only redefine the canon, or replace it with other objects of study. But the problem, Guillory argues, is that the noncanonical texts that multiculturalists want to substitute for the Western canon do not in fact constitute a different form of cultural capital.

Meanwhile the revolution in the social order has made theory itself, rather than the canon, the center of the study of the humanities. Literary study, in order to be viewed as equivalent in value to the scientific and economic studies that are actually useful within the technical and bureaucratic culture of the current ruling class, had to be made more difficult and technical than heretofore, more rigorous, less a matter of genteel improvisation than the close readings that characterized the New Criticism. Just as the discipline of economics has become ever more pervasively mathematical, providing a factitious precision to its descriptions of the workings of society, literary studies has become wed to the technical rigor of rhetoric and philosophy. At the same time, theory itself has been routinized. As Guillory notes in *Cultural Capital*,

> Those authors or texts designated as theoretical are now increasingly capable of being introduced to students in traditional routinized forms, even by anthologies. It is difficult to imagine how graduate education could proceed at the present moment without recourse to a relatively standardized set of theoretical texts, which are employed not only in the context of application to works of literature but also in the seminar on theory. (260)

The logic of the structural shift of the ruling class in capitalism has driven the task of the humanities from the comprehension and reproduction of the canon of Western literature to the understanding and reproduction of the canon of literary theory, of what one might call the critical tradition. The book you hold in your hands is evidence of this sea-change in the structure of the class system, the school, and the humanities, and we are all, I am afraid — students and teachers alike — in on this together.

CULTURE MEETS NATURE: ECOCRITICISM

The skein of influences on New Historicism and cultural studies extends, by no means strangely, to one of the newer movements within theory, ecocriticism, which we could call "nature studies" by way of distinction, except that it is culture that determines our view of nature.

Cheryll Glotfelty and Harold Fromm, editors of *The Ecocriticism Reader,* argue that the "world" posited by theorists is generally confined to the social world, and needs to be opened out to ask questions about the earth and the rest of the physical universe — but naturally the primary issues they raise are about how nature is represented within cultural frameworks, including traditional literary texts. The questions Glotfelty and Fromm present include:

How is nature represented in this sonnet? . . . Are the values expressed in this play consistent with ecological wisdom? How do our metaphors of the land influence the way we treat it? How can we characterize nature writing as a genre? In addition to race, class, and gender, should *place* become a new critical category? Do men write about nature differently than women do? In what ways has literacy itself affected humankind's relationship to the natural world? How has the concept of wilderness changed over time? In what ways and to what effect is the environmental crisis seeping into contemporary literature and popular culture? What view of nature informs U.S. Government reports, corporate advertising, and televised nature documentaries, and to what rhetorical effect? What bearing might the science of ecology have on literary studies? . . . What cross-fertilization is possible between literary studies and environmental discourse in related disciplines such as history, philosophy, psychology, art history, and ethics? (xviii –xix.)

These questions are not open-ended; they are, as Lawrence Buell puts it, "issue-driven," framed by a sense of "environmental crisis," created by a conspiracy between American government, industry, and a public that refuses to be fully aware of the price that will ultimately be exacted for its selfish wastefulness. The conspiracy to despoil nature has been going on for a long time: the protest against it in literature goes back to Fenimore Cooper, back to Goldsmith certainly, perhaps back to Chaucer. And Buell's "insurgency" is united only in opposition to its enemy: their multifarious critical methods and ideological allegiances, other than to the environment, defy easy identification. Buell's essay in classification, reprinted here, is designed to give a sense of the range and importance of this new area of cultural studies.

THE INEVITABILITY OF CULTURAL STUDIES

Cultural studies is the "hegemonic" critical discourse at the moment, one that contains the humanities and social sciences' collective response to what we might call the Era of Grand Theory, the two decades beginning with the structuralist revolution in the 1960s. The Era of Grand Theory produced a vital set of competing ideas about literature, society, and the mind but failed to coalesce in any single new rationale for textual and literary study. The New Criticism had been displaced and decentered, but nothing had taken its place. In its enormous variety and eclecticism, cultural studies is not a new paradigm of knowledge so much as a way of making do temporarily without a paradigm. Or as Vincent Leitch puts it, cultural studies "aspired to be a new discipline but served as an unstable meeting point for various interdisciplinary feminists, Marxists, literary and media critics, postmodern theorists, social semioticians, rhetoricians, fine arts specialists, and sociologists and historians of culture."[18]

[18]See Vincent Leitch, "Cultural Studies," in *The Johns Hopkins Guide to Literary Criticism and Theory,* ed. Michael Grodin and Michael Kreiswirth (Baltimore: Johns Hopkins University Press, 1994), p. 188.

The eclecticism of Leitch's list is not an anomaly. As of this writing, the "Cultural Studies" page of the Internet "Voice of the Shuttle" resource file describes itself as including "resources in cultural criticism and theory, Marxist and later Marxist critique, popular culture studies, post-colonial theory, and sociology." It also includes resources on select special topics in the field such as "body theory, censorship, culture/canon wars, the Sokal controversy."[19] Other topics with separate pages of their own not listed in the summary include "cyberculture," "generation studies," "Millennial Studies (the Year 2000 Fetish)," and "post-industrial business theory."

Besides its eclecticism, what is most obvious about this list of topics is its topicality: Cultural studies is about whatever is happening at the moment, rather than about a body of texts created in the past. "Happening" topics, generally speaking, are the mass media themselves, which, in a postmodern culture, dominate the cultural lives of its inhabitants, or topics that have been valorized by the mass media. One of the great virtues of cultural studies is in fact its relentlessly critical attitude toward journalism, publishing, cinema, television, and other forms of mass media, whose seemingly transparent windows through which we view "reality" probably constitute the most blatant and pervasive mode of false consciousness of our era. But though some cultural critics would deny it, their bias toward what is "happening" tends to valorize mass culture at the expense of the more local, private, and reclusive formations whose study would require the rigorous methods of field anthropology. In a sense this is as much a bias toward an easier object of study as was the restriction of literary "history," in the era before the New Historicism, to the relations among a small body of canonical texts.

Cultural studies is willing to question the cultural significance of the canon wars in the sense of analyzing what might be at stake for partisans on both sides. However, rather than entering the fray, it has questioned all attempts at canon formation, particularly attempts to valorize the classic Western canon. This negative bias of cultural studies toward canonical literature can be seen as an inevitable result of what Pierre Bourdieu calls the devaluation of canonical literature as part of the cultural capital needed for membership in the ruling class of late capitalist society. Investment bankers were once expected to read Jane Austen and be able to quote Shakespeare; today's managers of mutual funds need only know whether revenues from Kenneth Branagh's *Hamlet* surpassed Mel Gibson's at the box office. Writing still holds a key to power, but not critically acclaimed writing. Even those who still

---

[19]Much ink was lavished on the "Sokal Affair," which began with the publication in the Spring/Summer 1996 issue of the journal *Social Text* of an essay by New York University physicist Alan Sokal claiming that poststructuralist theory had forced scientists to recognize the fact that there was no external world beyond their construction of it. Sokal stated that, given different societies' mathematics and ways of measuring, pi (the ratio between the circumference and diameter of a circle) should be viewed as a social construct rather than a mathematical constant. The essay was a hoax attempting to demonstrate that the most prestigious journal in cultural studies would publish something patently absurd because the views expressed were those the editors wanted to hear.

aspire to write canonical literature, to become the next Faulkner, are aware that writing the Great American Novel can guarantee one a living only if the novel gets optioned as the basis for a movie or turned into a successful television series.[20] Young theorists are trained in the doctrine that everything is some sort of text, analyzable through the structuralist principles that underlie most contemporary theory. It isn't strange that they should find it hard to resist the urge to study the objects and practices contemporary culture actually values rather than those it merely enshrines. The oppositional stance of cultural studies toward the methods and products of contemporary corporate America thus veils what might otherwise be taken as worship of its success. Madonna Studies, anyone?

Selected Bibliography

Ang, Ien. *Watching Television.* New York: Routledge, 1991.

Armstrong, Nancy. *Desire and Domestic Fiction.* New York: Oxford University Press, 1987.

Ashcroft, Bill, Gareth Griffiths, and Helen Tiffin, eds. *The Post-Colonial Studies Reader.* New York: Routledge, 1995.

Barthes, Roland. *Mythologies.* 1957; New York: Farrar, Straus and Giroux, 1972.

Belsey, Catherine. *Critical Practice.* New York: Methuen, 1980.

Berubé, Michael, ed. *Aesthetics and Cultural Studies.* Malden: Blackwell, 2004.

Bourdieu, Pierre. *Outline of a Theory of Practice.* Cambridge: Cambridge University Press, 1977.

———. *Distinction: A Social Critique of the Judgment of Taste.* Cambridge: Harvard University Press, 1984.

———. *Homo Academicus.* 1984; Stanford: Stanford University Press, 1988.

———. *The Field of Cultural Production.* New York: Columbia University Press, 1993.

———. *Practical Reason: On the Theory of Action.* Stanford: Stanford University Press, 1998.

———. *Masculine Domination.* Stanford: Stanford University Press, 2001.

Branch, Michael P., ed. *The ISLE Reader: Ecocriticism 1993–2003.* Athens: University of Georgia Press, 2003.

Brannigan, John. *New Historicism and Cultural Materialism.* New York: St. Martin's Press, 1998.

Brantlinger, Patrick. *Crusoe's Footprints: Cultural Studies in Britain and America.* New York: Routledge, 1990.

Buell, Lawrence. *Writing for an Endangered World.* Cambridge: Harvard University Press, 2001.

Certeau, Michel de. *The Practice of Everyday Life.* Berkeley: University of California Press, 1984.

———. *The Writing of History.* New York: Columbia University Press, 1988.

———. *Culture in the Plural.* Minneapolis: University of Minnesota Press, 1997.

[20]Even half a century ago, Faulkner wrote screenplays in Hollywood for projects like *Land of the Pharaohs* to finance the whiskey he needed to write *Absalom, Absalom!*

Clifford, James. *The Predicament of Culture*. Cambridge: Harvard University Press, 1988.

Dollimore, Jonathan. *Radical Tragedy: Religion, Ideology and Power in the Drama of Shakespeare and His Contemporaries*. Brighton, Eng.: Harvester, 1984.

During, Simon, ed. *The Cultural Studies Reader*. New York: Routledge, 1993.

———. *The Cultural Studies Reader*. 2nd edition. New York: Routledge, 1999.

Foucault, Michel. *Madness and Civilization: A History of Insanity in the Age of Reason*. 1961; New York: Pantheon, 1973.

———. *The Birth of the Clinic: An Archaeology of Medical Perception*. 1963; New York: Pantheon, 1973.

———. *The Order of Things: An Archaeology of the Human Sciences*. 1966; New York: Vintage, 1973.

———. *The Archaeology of Knowledge and the Discourse on Language*. 1969; New York: Pantheon, 1972.

———. *Discipline and Punish: The Birth of the Prison*. 1975; New York: Pantheon, 1977.

———. *Language, Counter-Memory, Practice*. Ithaca: Cornell University Press, 1977.

———. *The Foucault Reader*. New York: Pantheon, 1984.

Fuery, Patrick, and Nick Mansfield. *Cultural Studies and the New Humanities*. New York: Oxford University Press, 1997.

Gallagher, Catherine. *The Industrial Reformation of English Fiction: Social Discourse and Narrative Form, 1832–1867*. Chicago: University of Chicago Press, 1985.

Gallagher, Catherine, and Stephen Greenblatt. *Practicing New Historicism*. Chicago: University of Chicago Press, 2000.

Garrard, Greg. *Ecocriticism*. New York: Routledge, 2004.

Geertz, Clifford. *The Interpretation of Cultures: Selected Essays*. New York: Basic Books, 1973.

———. *Local Knowledge*. New York: Basic Books, 1985.

———. *Works and Lives: The Anthropologist as Author*. Stanford: Stanford University Press, 1988.

———. *Available Light*. Princeton: Princeton University Press, 2000.

Goldberg, Jonathan. *James I and the Politics of Literature*. Baltimore: Johns Hopkins University Press, 1983.

Gramsci, Antonio. *Selections from Cultural Writings*. London: Lawrence and Wishart, 1985.

Greenblatt, Stephen. *Renaissance Self-Fashioning: From More to Shakespeare*. Chicago: University of Chicago Press, 1980.

———. *Shakespearean Negotiations*. Berkeley: University of California Press, 1988.

———. *Will in the World: How Shakespeare Became Shakespeare*. New York: Norton, 2004.

Greenblatt, Stephen, ed. *Representing the English Renaissance*. Berkeley: University of California Press, 1988.

Grossberg, Lawrence, Cary Nelson, and Paula Treichler, eds. *Cultural Studies*. New York: Routledge, 1992.

Guillory, John. *Cultural Capital*. Chicago: University of Chicago Press, 1993.

Hall, Stuart, and Paddy Whannel. *The Popular Arts*. London: Hutchinson, 1964.

Hall, Stuart, ed. *Representation: Cultural Representations and Signifying Practices*. London: Sage, 1997.

Hartley, John. *A Short History of Cultural Studies*. London: Sage, 2003.

Hebdige, Dick. *Subculture: The Meaning of Style*. London: Methuen, 1979.

Hoggart, Richard. *The Uses of Literacy: Changing Patterns in English Mass Culture*. Harmondsworth, Eng.: Penguin, 1957.

Howard, Jean E., and Marion F. O'Connor, eds. *Shakespeare Reproduced: The Text in History and Ideology*. New York: Methuen, 1987.

Hutcheon, Linda. *The Politics of Postmodernism*. London: Routledge, 1989.

JanMohammed, Abdul, and David Lloyd. "Introduction: Toward a Theory of Minority Discourse." *Cultural Critique* 6 (1987): 5–12.

Kipnis, Laura. *Bound and Gagged: Pornography and the Politics of Fantasy in America*. New York: Grove, 1996.

LaCapra, Dominick. *History and Criticism*. Ithaca: Cornell University Press, 1985.

Laclau, Ernesto, and Chantal Mouffe. "Postmarxism without Apologies." *New Left Review* 166 (1987): 79–106.

Lentricchia, Frank. *Ariel and the Police*. Madison: University of Wisconsin Press, 1988.

Lindenberger, Herbert. *Historical Drama: The Relation of Literature and Reality*. Chicago: University of Chicago Press, 1975.

Lindenberger, Herbert, ed. *History in Literature: On Value, Genre, Institutions*. New York: Columbia University Press, 1990.

Lyotard, Jean-François. *The Post-Modern Condition: A Report on Knowledge*. Minneapolis: University of Minnesota Press, 1984.

McCoy, Richard. *The Rites of Knighthood: The Literature and Politics of Elizabethan Chivalry*. Berkeley: University of California Press, 1989.

McGann, Jerome. *The Beauty of Inflections: Literary Investigations in Historical Method and Theory*. Oxford: Clarendon Press, 1985.

McGann, Jerome, ed. *Historical Studies and Literary Criticism*. Madison: University of Wisconsin Press, 1985.

Michaels, Walter Benn. *The Gold Standard and the Logic of Naturalism*. Berkeley: University of California Press, 1987.

Montrose, Louis. "Renaissance Literary Studies and the Subject of History." *English Literary Renaissance* 16 (1986): 3–21.

Morris, Meaghan. "Things to Do with Shopping Centres." In *Grafts: Feminist Cultural Criticism*, ed. Susan Sheridan. London: Verso, 1988.

———. *Too Soon Too Late: History in Popular Culture*. Bloomington: Indiana University Press, 1998.

Newton, Judith. "History as Usual?: Feminism and the 'New Historicism.'" *Cultural Critique* 8 (1988): 87–121.

Poovey, Mary. *Uneven Developments: The Ideological Work of Gender in Mid-Victorian England*. Chicago: University of Chicago Press, 1988.

Richter, David H. *The Progress of Romance: Literary Historiography and the Gothic Novel*. Columbus: Ohio State University Press, 1996.

Ricoeur, Paul. *Time and Narrative*. Chicago: University of Chicago Press, 1984.

Rosendale, Steven. *The Greening of Literary Scholarship*. Iowa City: University of Iowa Press, 2002.

Ryan, Kiernan, ed. *New Historicism and Cultural Materialism: A Reader*. New York: St. Martin's Press, 1996.

Storey, John. *Cultural Studies and the Study of Popular Culture*. Athens: University of Georgia Press, 2003.

Storey, John, ed. *What Is Cultural Studies?* New York: St. Martin's Press, 1996.

Tennenhouse, Leonard. *Power on Display: The Politics of Shakespeare's Genres*. New York: Methuen, 1986.

Thomas, Brook. *The New Historicism and Other Old-Fashioned Topics*. Princeton: Princeton University Press, 1991.

Veeser, H. Aram., ed. *The New Historicism*. New York: Routledge, 1989.
———. *The New Historicism Reader*. New York: Routledge, 1994.
White, Hayden. *Metahistory: The Historical Imagination in Nineteenth-Century Europe*. Baltimore: Johns Hopkins University Press, 1974.
———. *Tropics of Discourse: Essays in Cultural Criticism*. Baltimore: Johns Hopkins University Press, 1978.
———. *The Content of the Form*. Baltimore: Johns Hopkins University Press, 1988.
Williams, Raymond. *The Country and the City*. New York: Oxford University Press, 1973.

Michel de Certeau

1925–1986

Considered the pre-eminent theorist of the ordinary, Michel de Certeau pursued his doctoral degree at the Sorbonne, where he studied the origins of the Jesuit order and mysticism in the seventeenth century. These studies led to an interest in the experience of culture and society in contemporary life. The Practice of Everyday Life, *originally published in French in 1974, was translated into English just two years before Certeau's death, causing a widespread interest in the American academy in the implications of this remarkably interdisciplinary work. Concentrating on the experience of the recipients of texts and power, rather than the producers, Certeau argues for an inclusive understanding of the experience of Western culture. He argues, for example, that workers necessarily seize agency over certain aspects of work environment and time in order to verify their solidarity with co-workers and family. Certeau emphasizes that every writer who describes history and culture is necessarily caught up in the myths and power relations described, and that all historiography should take the writer's subject position into account. Certeau was one of the founders, with Jacques Lacan, of the École Freudienne in Paris, taught at the École des Hautes Études en Sciences Sociales in Paris and at the University of California, San Diego. His other books include* Culture in the Plural *(1974),* The Writing of History *(1975),* The Mystic Fable, Vol. 1: The Sixteenth and Seventeenth Centuries *(1982), and* Heterologies: Discourses on the Other *(1986). The following essay, "Walking in the City," is from* The Practice of Everyday Life.

Walking in the City

Seeing Manhattan from the 110th floor of the World Trade Center. Beneath the haze stirred up by the winds, the urban island, a sea in the middle of the sea, lifts up the skyscrapers over Wall Street, sinks down at Greenwich, then rises again to the crests of Midtown, quietly passes over Central Park and finally undulates off into the distance beyond Harlem. A wave of verticals. Its agitation is momentarily arrested by vision. The gigantic mass is immobilized before the eyes. It is transformed into a texturology in which extremes coincide — extremes of ambition and degradation, brutal oppositions of races and styles, contrasts between yesterday's buildings, already transformed into trash cans, and today's urban irruptions that block out its space. Unlike Rome, New York has never learned the art of growing old by playing on all its pasts. Its present invents itself, from hour to hour, in the act of throwing away its previous accomplishments and challenging the future. A city composed of paroxysmal places in monumental reliefs. The spectator can read in it a universe that is constantly exploding. In it are inscribed the architectural figures of the *coincidatio oppositorum* formerly drawn in miniatures and mystical textures. On this stage of concrete, steel and glass, cut out between two oceans (the Atlantic and the American) by a frigid body of water, the tallest letters in the world compose a gigantic rhetoric of excess in both expenditure and production.[1]

VOYEURS OR WALKERS

To what erotics of knowledge does the ecstasy of reading such a cosmos belong? Having taken a voluptuous pleasure in it, I wonder what is the source of this pleasure of "seeing the whole," of looking down on, totalizing the most immoderate of human texts.

To be lifted to the summit of the World Trade Center is to be lifted out of the city's grasp. One's body is no longer clasped by the streets that turn and return it according to an anonymous law; nor is it possessed, whether as player or played, by the rumble of so many differences and by the nervousness of New York traffic. When one goes up there, he leaves behind the mass that carries off and mixes up in itself any identity of authors or spectators. An Icarus flying above these waters, he can ignore the devices of Daedalus in mobile and endless labyrinths far below.[2] His elevation transfigures him into a voyeur. It puts him at a distance. It transforms the bewitching world by which one was "possessed" into a text that lies before one's eyes. It allows one to read it, to be a solar Eye, looking down like a god. The exaltation of a scopic and gnostic drive: the fiction of knowledge is related to this lust to be a viewpoint and nothing more.

Must one finally fall back into the dark space where crowds move back and forth, crowds that, though visible from on high, are themselves unable to see down below? An Icarian fall. On the 110th floor, a poster, sphinx-like, addresses an enigmatic message to the pedestrian who is for an instant transformed into a visionary: *It's hard to be down when you're up.*

The desire to see the city preceded the means of satisfying it. Medieval or Renaissance painters represented the city as seen in a perspective that no eye had yet enjoyed.[3] This fiction already made the medieval spectator into a celestial eye. It created gods. Have things changed since technical procedures have organized an "all-seeing

---

Translated by Steven Randall.

[1] See Alain Médam's admirable "New York City," *Les Temps modernes*, August–September 1976, 15–33; and the same author's *New York Terminal* (Paris: Galilée, 1977). [Certeau]

[2] In Greek mythology, Daedalus constructed the labyrinth for King Minos of Crete, who then imprisoned him within it. To get away, he invented wings for himself and for his son Icarus. When Icarus flew too near the sun, the wax holding his wings together melted, and he fell headlong into the sea.

[3] See H. Lavedan, *Les Représentations des villes dans l'art du Moyen Age* (Paris: Van Oest, 1942); R. Wittkower, *Architectural Principles in the Age of Humanism* (New York: Norton, 1962); L. Marin, *Utopiques: Jeux d'espaces* (Paris: Minuit, 1973); etc. [Certeau]

power"?[4] The totalizing eye imagined by the painters of earlier times lives on in our achievements. The same scopic drive haunts users of architectural productions by materializing today the utopia that yesterday was only painted. The 1370 foot high tower that serves as a prow for Manhattan continues to construct the fiction that creates readers, makes the complexity of the city readable, and immobilizes its opaque mobility in a transparent text.

Is the immense texturology spread out before one's eyes anything more than a representation, an optical artifact? It is the analogue of the facsimile produced, through a projection that is a way of keeping aloof, by the space planner urbanist, city planner or cartographer. The panorama-city is a "theoretical" (that is, visual) simulacrum, in short a picture, whose condition of possibility is an oblivion and a misunderstanding of practices. The voyeur-god created by this fiction, who, like Schreber's God, knows only cadavers,[5] must disentangle himself from the murky intertwining daily behaviors and make himself alien to them.

The ordinary practitioners of the city live "down below," below the thresholds at which visibility begins. They walk — an elementary form of this experience of the city; they are walkers, *Wandersmänner*,[6] whose bodies follow the thicks and thins of an urban "text" they write without being able to read it. These practitioners make use of spaces that cannot be seen; their knowledge of them is as blind as that of lovers in each other's arms. The paths that correspond in this intertwining, unrecognized poems in which each body is an element signed by many others, elude legibility. It is as though the practices organizing a bustling city were characterized by their blindness.[7] The networks of these moving, intersecting writings compose a manifold story that has neither author nor spectator, shaped out of fragments of trajectories and alterations of spaces: in relation to representations, it remains daily and indefinitely other.

Escaping the imaginary totalizations produced by the eye, the everyday has a certain strangeness that does not surface, or whose surface is only its upper limit, outlining itself against the visible. Within this ensemble, I shall try to locate the practices that are foreign to the "geometrical" or "geographical" space of visual, panoptic, or theoretical constructions. These practices of space refer to a specific form of *operations* ("ways of operating"), to "another spatiality"[8] (an "anthropological," poetic and mythic experience of space), and to an *opaque and blind* mobility characteristic of the bustling city. A *migrational*, or metaphorical, city thus slips into the clear text of the planned and readable city.

1. FROM THE CONCEPT OF THE CITY TO URBAN PRACTICES

The World Trade Center is only the most monumental figure of Western urban development. The atopia-utopia[9] of optical knowledge has long had the ambition of surmounting and articulating the contradictions arising from urban agglomeration. It is a question of managing a growth of human agglomeration or accumulation. "The city is a huge monastery," said Erasmus. Perspective vision and prospective vision constitute the twofold projection of an opaque past and an uncertain future onto a surface that can be dealt with. They inaugurate (in the sixteenth century?)

---

[4]M. Foucault, "L'Oeil du pouvoir," in J. Bentham, *Le Panoptique* (Paris: Belfond, 1977), p. 16. [Certeau] The title is French for "the eye of power." The reference is to nineteenth-century philosopher Jeremy Bentham's Panopticon, a prison designed so that one guard could see into the cells of all the prisoners simultaneously.

[5]D. P. Schreber, *Mémoires d'un névropathe* (Paris: Seuil, 1975), pp. 41, 60, etc. [Certeau] Daniel Paul Schreber was a Dresden high court judge who suffered from paranoid schizophrenia and who believed that rays from God were turning him into a woman. He published *Memoirs of My Nervous Illness* in 1903. Freud wrote up his case history using the autobiography as evidence, since Schreber was never his patient.

[6]German for wayfarers.

[7]Descartes, in his *Regulae,* had already made the blind man the guarantor of the knowledge of things and places against the illusions and deceptions of vision. [Certeau]

[8]M. Merleau-Ponty, *Phénoménologie de la perception* (Paris: Gallimard Tel, 1976), pp. 332–333. [Certeau]

[9]Both words in Greek mean literally "nowhere" although "utopia" has (via Thomas More's 1520 narrative) come to mean "perfect place."

the transformation of the urban *fact* into the *concept* of a city. Long before the concept itself gives rise to a particular figure of history, it assumes that this fact can be dealt with as a unity determined by an urbanistic *ratio*. Linking the city to the concept never makes them identical, but it plays on their progressive symbiosis: to plan a city is both to *think the very plurality* of the real and to make that way of thinking the plural *effective;* it is to know how to articulate it and be able to do it.

An Operational Concept?

The "city" founded by utopian and urbanistic discourse[10] is defined by the possibility of a three-fold operation:

1. The production of its *own* space (*un espace propre*[11])*:* rational organization must thus repress all the physical, mental and political pollutions that would compromise it;

2. the substitution of a nowhen, or of a synchronic system, for the indeterminable and stubborn resistances offered by traditions; univocal scientific strategies, made possible by the flattening out of all the data in a plane projection, must replace the tactics of users who take advantage of "opportunities" and who, through these trap-events, these lapses in visibility, reproduce the opacities of history everywhere;

3. finally, the creation of a *universal* and anonymous *subject* which is the city itself: it gradually becomes possible to attribute to it, as to its political model, Hobbes' State,[12] all the functions and predicates that were previously scattered and assigned to many different real subjects — groups, associations, or individuals. "The city," like a proper name, thus provides a way of conceiving and constructing space on the basis of a finite number of stable, isolatable, and interconnected properties.

[10]See F. Choay, "Figures d'un discours inconnu," *Critique*, April 1973, 293–317. [Certeau]

[11]The word in French means "clean" as well as "own" and Certeau is playing on both meanings.

[12]In Hobbes's *Leviathan* (1650), the commonwealth, created to avoid the war of each against all in the state of nature, is a new artificial person (named after the monster in the book of Job) with the combined power and capacity of all its citizens.

Administration is combined with a process of elimination in this place organized by "speculative" and classificatory operations.[13] On the one hand, there is a differentiation and redistribution of the parts and functions of the city, as a result of inversions, displacements, accumulations, etc.; on the other there is a rejection of everything that is not capable of being dealt with in this way and so constitutes the "waste products" of a functionalist administration (abnormality, deviance, illness, death, etc.). To be sure, progress allows an increasing number of these waste products to be reintroduced into administrative circuits and transforms even deficiencies (in health, security, etc.) into ways of making the networks of order denser. But in reality, it repeatedly produces effects contrary to those at which it aims: the profit system generates a loss which, in the multiple forms of wretchedness and poverty outside the system and of waste inside it, constantly turns production into "expenditure." Moreover, the rationalization of the city leads to its mythification in strategic discourses, which are calculations based on the hypothesis or the necessity of its destruction in order to arrive at a final decision.[14] Finally, the functionalist organization, by privileging progress (i.e., time), causes the condition of its own possibility — space itself — to be forgotten; space thus becomes the blind spot in a scientific and political technology. This is the way in which the Concept-city functions; a place of transformations and appropriations, the object of various kinds of interference but also a subject that is constantly enriched by new attributes, it is simultaneously the machinery and the hero of modernity.

[13]Urbanistic techniques, which classify things spatially, can be related to the tradition of the "art of memory": see Frances A. Yates, *The Art of Memory* (London: Routledge and Kegan Paul, 1966). The ability to produce a spatial organization of knowledge (with "places" assigned to each type of "figure" or "function") develops its procedures on the basis of this "art." It determines utopias and can be recognized even in Bentham's *Panopticon*. Such a form remains stable in spite of the diversity of its contents (past, future, present) and its projects (conserving or creating) relative to changes in the status of knowledge. [Certeau]

[14]See André Glucksmann, "Le Totalitarisme en effet," *Traverses*, No. 9, 1977, 34–40. [Certeau]

Today, whatever the avatars of this concept may have been, we have to acknowledge that if in discourse the city serves as a totalizing and almost mythical landmark for socioeconomic and political strategies, urban life increasingly permits the re-emergence of the element that the urbanistic project excluded. The language of power is in itself "urbanizing," but the city is left prey to contradictory movements that counterbalance and combine themselves outside the reach of panoptic power. The city becomes the dominant theme in political legends, but it is no longer a field of programmed and regulated operations. Beneath the discourses that ideologize the city, the ruses and combinations of powers that have no readable identity proliferate; without points where one can take hold of them, without rational transparency, they are impossible to administer.

The Return of Practices

The Concept-city is decaying. Does that mean that the illness afflicting both the rationality that founded it and its professionals afflicts the urban populations as well? Perhaps cities are deteriorating along with the procedures that organized them. But we must be careful here. The ministers of knowledge have always assumed that the whole universe was threatened by the very changes that affected their ideologies and their positions. They transmute the misfortune of their theories into theories of misfortune. When they transform their bewilderment into "catastrophes," when they seek to enclose the people in the "panic" of their discourses, are they once more necessarily right?

Rather than remaining within the field of a discourse that upholds its privilege by inverting its content (speaking of catastrophe and no longer of progress), one can try another path: one can analyze the microbe-like, singular and plural practices which an urbanistic system was supposed to administer or suppress, but which have outlived its decay; one can follow the swarming activity of these procedures that, far from being regulated or eliminated by panoptic administration, have reinforced themselves in a proliferating illegitimacy, developed and

insinuated themselves into the networks of surveillance, and combined in accord with unreadable but stable tactics to the point of constituting everyday regulations and surreptitious creativities that are merely concealed by the frantic mechanisms and discourses of the observational organization.

This pathway could be inscribed as a consequence, but also as the reciprocal, of Foucault's analysis of the structures of power. He moved it in the direction of mechanisms and technical procedures, "minor instrumentalities" capable, merely by their organization of "details," of transforming a human multiplicity into a "disciplinary" society and of managing, differentiating, classifying, and hierarchizing all deviances concerning apprenticeship, health, justice, the army, or work.[15] "These often minuscule ruses of discipline," these "minor but flawless" mechanisms, draw their efficacy from a relationship between procedures and the space that they redistribute in order to make an "operator" out of it. But what *spatial practices* correspond, in the area where discipline is manipulated, to these apparatuses that produce a disciplinary space? In the present conjuncture, which is marked by a contradiction between the collective mode of administration and an individual mode of reappropriation, this question is no less important, if one admits that spatial practices in fact secretly structure the determining conditions of social life. I would like to follow out a few of these multiform, resistance, tricky and stubborn procedures that elude discipline without being outside the field in which it is exercised, and which should lead us to a theory of everyday practices, of lived space, of the disquieting familiarity of the city.

2. THE CHORUS OF IDLE FOOTSTEPS

"The goddess[16] can be recognized by her step"
— VIRGIL, *Aeneid, I*, 405

Their story begins on ground level, with footsteps. They are myriad, but do not compose a series. They

---

[15]M. Foucault, *Surveiller et punir* (Paris: Gallimard, 1975); *Discipline and Punish*, trans. A. Sheridan (New York: Pantheon, 1977). [Certeau]
[16]Venus.

cannot be counted because each unit has a qualitative character: a style of tactile apprehension and kinesthetic appropriation. Their swarming mass is an innumerable collection of singularities. Their intertwined paths give their shape to spaces. They weave places together. In that respect, pedestrian movements form one of these "real systems whose existence in fact makes up the city."[17] They are not localized; it is rather they that spatialize. They are no more inserted within a container than those Chinese characters speakers sketch out on their hands with their fingertips.

It is true that the operations of walking on can be traced on city maps in such a way as to transcribe their paths (here well-trodden, there very faint) and their trajectories (going this way and not that). But these thick or thin curves only refer, like words, to the absence of what has passed by. Surveys of routes miss what was: the act itself of passing by. The operation of walking, wandering, or "window shopping," that is, the activity of passers-by, is transformed into points that draw a totalizing and reversible line on the map. They allow us to grasp only a relic set in the nowhen of a surface of projection. Itself visible, it has the effect of making invisible the operation that made it possible. These fixations constitute procedures for forgetting. The trace left behind is substituted for the practice. It exhibits the (voracious) property that the geographical system has of being able to transform action into legibility, but in doing so it causes a way of being in the world to be forgotten.

Pedestrian Speech Acts

A comparison with the speech act will allow us to go further[18] and not limit ourselves to the critique of graphic representations alone, looking from the shores of legibility toward an inaccessible beyond. The act of walking is to the urban system what the speech act is to language or to the statements uttered.[19] At the most elementary level, it has a triple "enunciative" function: it is a process of *appropriation* of the topographical system on the part of the pedestrian (just as the speaker appropriates and takes on the language); it is a spatial acting-out of the place (just as the speech act is an acoustic acting-out of language); and it implies *relations* among differentiated positions, that is, among pragmatic "contracts" in the form of movements (just as verbal enunciation is an "allocution," "posits another opposite" the speaker and puts contracts between interlocutors into action).[20] It thus seems possible to give a preliminary definition of walking as a space of enunciation.

We could moreover extend this problematic to the relations between the act of writing and the written text, and even transpose it to the relationships between the "hand" (the touch and the tale of the paintbrush [*le et la geste du pinceau*]) and the finished painting (forms, colors, etc.). At first isolated in the area of verbal communication, the speech act turns out to find only one of its applications there, and its linguistic modality is merely the first determination of a much more general distinction between the *forms used* in a system and the *ways of using* this system (i.e., *rules*), that is, between two "different worlds," since "the same things" are considered from two opposite formal viewpoints.

Considered from this angle, the pedestrian speech act has three characteristics which distinguish it at the outset from the spatial system: the present, the discrete, the "phatic."[21]

First, if it is true that a spatial order organizes an ensemble of possibilities (e.g., by a place in which one can move) and interdictions (e.g., by a wall that prevents one from going further), then the walker actualizes some of these possibilities. In that way, he makes them exist as well as emerge. But he also moves them about and he

[17]Ch. Alexander, "La Cité semi-treillis, mais non arbre," *Architecture, Mouvement, Continuité*, 1967. [Certeau]

[18]See R. Barthes's remarks in *Architecture d'aujourd'hui*, No. 153, December 1970–January 1971, 11–13: "We speak our city . . . merely by inhabiting it, walking through it, looking at it." Cf. C. Soucy, *L'Image du centre dans quatre romans contemporains* (Paris: CSU, 1971), 6–15. [Certeau]

[19]See the numerous studies devoted to the subject since J. Searle's "What Is a Speech Act?" in *Philosophy in America*, ed. Max Black (London: Allen & Unwin; Ithaca, N.Y.: Cornell University Press, 1965), pp. 221–239. [Certeau]

[20]E. Benveniste, *Problèmes de linguistique générale* (Paris: Gallimard, 1974), 11, pp. 79–88, etc. [Certeau]

[21]The use of language to establish the fact of communication, like saying "Hello" when one picks up the ringing telephone.

invents others, since the crossing, drifting away, or improvisation of walking privilege, transform or abandon spatial elements. Thus Charlie Chaplin multiplies the possibilities of his cane: he does other things with the same thing and he goes beyond the limits that the determinants of the object set on its utilization. In the same way, the walker transforms each spatial signifier into something else. And if on the one hand he actualizes only a few of the possibilities fixed by the constructed order (he goes only here and not there), on the other he increases the number of possibilities (for example, by creating shortcuts and detours) and prohibitions (for example, he forbids himself to take paths generally considered accessible or even obligatory). He thus makes a selection. "The user of a city picks out certain fragments of the statement in order to actualize them in secret."[22]

He thus creates a discreteness, whether by making choices among the signifiers of the spatial "language" or by displacing them through the use he makes of them. He condemns certain places to inertia or disappearance and composes with others spatial "turns of phrase" that are "rare," "accidental" or illegitimate. But that already leads into a rhetoric of walking.

In the framework of enunciation, the walker constitutes, in relation to his position, both a near and a far, a *here* and a *there*. To the fact that the adverbs *here* and *there* are the indicators of the locutionary seat in verbal communication[23] — a coincidence that reinforces the parallelism between linguistic and pedestrian enunciation — we must add that this location (*here — there*) (necessarily implied by walking and indicative of a present appropriation of space by an "I") also has the function of introducing an other in relation to this "I" and of thus establishing a conjunctive and disjunctive articulation of places. I would stress particularly the "phatic" aspect, by which I mean the function, isolated by Malinowski and Jakobson, of terms that initiate, maintain, or interrupt contact, such as "hello," "well, well," etc.[24] Walking, which alternately follows a path and has followers, creates a mobile organicity in the environment, a sequence of phatic *topoi*.[25] And if it is true that the phatic function, which is an effort to ensure communication, is already characteristic of the language of talking birds, just as it constitutes the "first verbal function acquired by children," it is not surprising that it also gambols, goes on all fours, dances, and walks about, with a light or heavy step, like a series of "hellos" in an echoing labyrinth, anterior or parallel to informative speech.

The modalities of pedestrian enunciation which a plane representation on a map brings out could be analyzed. They include the kinds of relationships this enunciation entertains with particular paths (or "statements") by according them a truth value ("alethic" modalities of the necessary, the impossible, the possible, or the contingent), an epistemological value ("epistemic" modalities of the certain, the excluded, the plausible, or the questionable) or finally an ethical or legal value ("deontic" modalities of the obligatory, the forbidden, the permitted, or the optional).[26] Walking affirms, suspects, tries out, transgresses, respects, etc., the trajectories it "speaks." All the modalities sign a part in this chorus, changing from step to step, stepping in through proportions, sequences, and intensities which vary according to the time, the path taken and the walker. These enunciatory operations are of an unlimited diversity. They therefore cannot be reduced to their graphic trail.

Walking Rhetorics

The walking of passers-by offers a series of turns (*tours*) and detours that can be compared to "turns of phrase" or "stylistic figures." There is a

[22]R. Barthes, quoted in C. Soucy, *L'Image du centre*, 10. [Certeau]

[23]"*Here* and *now* delimit the spatial and temporal instance coextensive and contemporary with the present instance of discourse containing I": E. Benveniste, *Problèmes de linguistique générale* (Paris: Gallimard, 1966), I, p. 253. [Certeau]

[24]R. Jakobson, *Essais de linguistique générale* (Paris: Seuil Points, 1970), p. 217. [Certeau]

[25]Greek for "commonplaces."

[26]On modalities, see H. Parret, *La Pragmatique des modalités* (Urbino: Centro di Semiotica, 1975); A. R. White, *Modal Thinking* (Ithaca, N.Y.: Cornell University Press, 1975). [Certeau]

rhetoric of walking. The art of "turning" phrases finds an equivalent in an art of composing a path (*tourner un parcours*). Like ordinary language,[27] this art implies and combines styles and uses. *Style* specifies "a linguistic structure that manifests on the symbolic level . . . an individual's fundamental way of being in the world";[28] it connotes a singular. Use defines the social phenomenon through which a system of communication manifests itself in actual fact; it refers to a norm. Style and use both have to do with a "way of operating" (of speaking, walking, etc.), but style involves a peculiar processing of the symbolic, while use refers to elements of a code. They intersect to form a style of use, a way of being and a way of operating.[29]

In introducing the notion of a "residing rhetoric" ("*rhétorique habitante*"), the fertile pathway opened up by A. Médam[30] and systematized by S. Ostrowetsky[31] and J.-F. Augoyard,[32] we assume that the "tropes"[33] catalogued by rhetoric furnish models and hypotheses for the analysis of ways of appropriating places. Two postulates seem to me to underlie the validity of this application: 1) it is assumed that practices of space also correspond to manipulations of the basic elements of a constructed order; 2) it is assumed that they are, like the tropes in rhetoric, deviations relative to a sort of "literal meaning" defined by the urbanistic system. There would thus be a homology between verbal figures and the figures of walking (a stylized selection among the latter is already found in the figures of dancing) insofar as both consist in "treatments" or operations bearing on isolatable units,[34] and in "ambiguous dispositions" that divert and displace meaning in the direction of equivocalness[35] in the way a tremulous image confuses and multiplies the photographed object. In these two modes, the analogy can be accepted. I would add that the geometrical space of urbanists and architects seems to have the status of the "proper meaning" constructed by grammarians and linguists in order to have a normal and normative level to which they can compare the drifting of "figurative" language. In reality, this faceless "proper" meaning (*ce "propre" sans figure*) cannot be found in current use, whether verbal or pedestrian; it is merely the fiction produced by a use that is also particular, the metalinguistic use of science that distinguishes itself by that very distinction.[36]

The long poem of walking manipulates spatial organizations, no matter how panoptic they may be: it is neither foreign to them (it can take place only within them) nor in conformity with them (it does not receive its identity from them). It creates shadows and ambiguities within them. It inserts its multitudinous references and citations into them (social models, cultural mores, personal factors). Within them it is itself the effect of successive encounters and occasions that constantly alter it and make it the other's blazon: in other words, it is like a peddler, carrying something surprising, transverse or attractive compared with

[27] See Paul Lemaire's analyses, *Les Signes sauvages: Une Philosophie du langage ordinaire* (Ottawa: Université d'Ottawa et Université Saint-Paul, 1981), in particular the introduction. [Certeau]

[28] A. J. Greimas, "Linguistique statistique et linguistique structurale," *Le Français moderne*, October 1962, 245. [Certeau]

[29] In a neighboring field, rhetoric and poetics in the gestural language of mute people, I am grateful to E. S. Klima of the University of California, San Diego and U. Bellugi, "Poetry and Song in a Language without Sound," an unpublished paper; see also Klima, "The Linguistic Symbol with and without Sound," in *The Role of Speech in Language*, ed. J. Kavanagh and J. E. Cuttings (Cambridge, Mass.: MIT, 1975). [Certeau]

[30] *Conscience de la ville* (Paris: Anthropos, 1977). [Certeau]

[31] See Ostrowetsky, "Logiques du lieu," in *Sémiotique de l'espace* (Paris: Denoël-Gonthier Médiations, 1979), pp. 155–173. [Certeau]

[32] *Pas à pas. Essai sur le cheminement quotidien en milieu urbain* (Paris: Seuil, 1979). [Certeau]

[33] Figures of speech, but in Greek the word literally means "turns."

[34] In his analysis of culinary practices, P. Bourdieu regards as decisive not the ingredients but the way in which they are prepared and used: "Le Sens pratique," *Actes de la recherche en sciences sociales*, February 1976, 77. [Certeau]

[35] J. Sumpf, *Introduction à la stylistique du français* (Paris: Larousse, 1971), p. 87. [Certeau]

[36] On the "theory of the proper," see J. Derrida, *Marges de la philosophie* (Paris: Minuit, 1972), pp. 247–324; *Margins of Philosophy*, trans. A. Bass (Chicago: University of Chicago Press, 1982). [Certeau]

the usual choice. These diverse aspects provide the basis of a rhetoric. They can even be said to define it.

By analyzing this "modern art of everyday expression" as it appears in accounts of spatial practices,[37] J.-F. Augoyard discerns in it two especially fundamental stylistic figures: synecdoche and asyndeton. The predominance of these two figures seems to me to indicate, in relation to two complementary poles, a formal structure of these practices. *Synecdoche* consists in "using a word in a sense which is part of another meaning of the same word."[38] In essence, it names a part instead of the whole which includes it. Thus "sail" is taken for "ship" in the expression "a fleet of fifty sails"; in the same way, a brick shelter or a hill is taken for the park in the narration of a trajectory. *Asyndeton* is the suppression of linking words such as conjunctions and adverbs, either within a sentence or between sentences. In the same way, in walking it selects and fragments the space traversed; it skips over links and whole parts that it omits. From this point of view, every walk constantly leaps, or skips like a child, hopping on one foot. It practices the ellipsis of conjunctive *loci*.

In reality, these two pedestrian figures are related. Synecdoche expands a spatial element in order to make it play the role of a "more" (a totality) and take its place (the bicycle or the piece of furniture in a store window stands for a whole street or neighborhood). Asyndeton, by elision, creates a "less," opens gaps in the spatial continuum, and retains only selected parts of it that amount almost to relics. Synecdoche replaces totalities by fragments (a *less* in the place of a *more*); asyndeton disconnects them by eliminating the conjunctive or the consecutive (nothing in place of something). Synecdoche makes more dense: it amplifies the detail and miniaturizes the whole. Asyndeton cuts out: it undoes continuity and undercuts its plausibility. A space treated in this way and shaped by practices is transformed into enlarged singularities and separate islands.[39] Through these swellings, shrinkings, and fragmentations, that is, through these rhetorical operations a spatial phrasing of an analogical (composed of juxtaposed citations) and elliptical (made of gaps, lapses, and allusions) type is created. For the technological system of a coherent and totalizing space that is "linked" and simultaneous, the figures of pedestrian rhetoric substitute trajectories that have a mythical structure, at least if one understands by "myth" a discourse relative to the place/nowhere (or origin) of concrete existence, a story jerry-built out of elements taken from common sayings, an allusive and fragmentary story whose gaps mesh with the social practices it symbolizes.

Figures are the acts of this stylistic metamorphosis of space. Or rather, as Rilke puts it, they are moving "trees of gestures." They move even the rigid and contrived territories of the medico-pedagogical institute in which retarded children find a place to play and dance their "spatial stories."[40] These "trees of gestures" are in movement everywhere. Their forests walk through the streets. They transform the scene, but they cannot be fixed in a certain place by images. If in spite of that an illustration were required, we could mention the fleeting images, yellowish-green and metallic blue calligraphies that howl without raising their voices and emblazon themselves on the subterranean passages of the city, "embroideries" composed of letters and numbers, perfect gestures of violence painted with a pistol, Shivas[41] made of written characters, dancing graphics whose fleeting apparitions are accompanied by the rumble of subway trains: New York graffiti.

If it is true that *forests of gestures* are manifest in the streets, their movement cannot be captured in a picture, nor can the meaning of their movements be circumscribed in a text. Their rhetorical

[37] Augoyard, *Pas à pas*. [Certeau]

[38] T. Todorov, "Synecdoques," *Communications*, No. 16 (1970), 30. See also P. Fontanier, *Les Figures du discours* (Paris: Flammarion, 1968), 87–97; J. Dubois et al., *Rhétorique générale* (Paris: Larousse, 1970), 102–112. [Certeau]

[39] On this space that practices organize into "islands," see P. Bourdieu, *Esquisse d'une théorie de la pratique* (Genève: Droz, 1972), 215, etc.; "Le Sens pratique," 51–52. [Certeau]

[40] See Anne Baldassari and Michel Joubert, *Pratiques relationnelles des enfants à l'espace et institution* (Paris: Cre-Cele-Cordes, 1976); and by the same authors, "Ce qui se trame," *Parallèles*, No. 1, June 1976. [Certeau]

[41] Shiva is the Destroyer God of Hindu mythology.

transplantation carries away and displaces the analytical, coherent proper meanings of urbanism; it constitutes a "wandering of the semantic"[42] produced by masses that make some parts of the city disappear and exaggerate others, distorting it, fragmenting it, and diverting it from its immobile order.

3. MYTHS: WHAT "MAKES THINGS GO"

The figures of these movements (synecdoches, ellipses, etc.) characterize both a "symbolic order of the unconscious" and "certain typical processes of subjectivity manifested in discourse."[43] The similarity between "discourse"[44] and dreams[45] has to do with their use of the same "stylistic procedures"; it therefore includes pedestrian practices as well. The "ancient catalog of tropes" that from Freud to Benveniste has furnished an appropriate inventory for the rhetoric of the first two registers of expression is equally valid for the third. If there is a parallelism, it is not only because enunciation is dominant in these three areas, but also because its discursive (verbalized, dreamed, or walked) development is organized as a relation between the *place* from which it proceeds (an origin) and the nowhere it produces (a way of "going by").

From this point of view, after having compared pedestrian processes to linguistic formations, we can bring them back down in the direction of oneiric figuration,[46] or at least discover on that other side what, in a spatial practice, is inseparable from the dreamed place. To walk is to lack a place. It is the indefinite process of being absent and in search of a proper. The moving about that the city multiplies and concentrates makes the city itself an immense social experience of lacking a place — an experience that is, to be sure, broken up into countless tiny deportations (displacements and walks), compensated for by the relationships and intersections of these exoduses that intertwine and create an urban fabric, and placed under the sign of what ought to be, ultimately, the place but is only a name, the City. The identity furnished by this place is all the more symbolic (named) because, in spite of the inequality of its citizens' positions and profits, there is only a pullulation of passers-by, a network of residences temporarily appropriated by pedestrian traffic, a shuffling among pretense of the proper, a universe of rented spaces haunted by a nowhere or by dreamed-of places.

Names and Symbols

An indication of the relationship that spatial practices entertain with that absence is furnished precisely by their manipulations of and with "proper" names. The relationships between the direction of a walk (*le sens de la marche*) and the meaning of words (*le sens des mots*) situate two sorts of apparently contrary movements, one extrovert (to walk is to go outside), the other introvert (a mobility under the stability of the signifier). Walking is in fact determined by semantic tropisms; it is attracted and repelled by nominations whose meaning is not clear, whereas the city, for its part, is transformed for many people into a "desert" in which the meaningless, indeed the terrifying, no longer takes the form of shadows but becomes, as in Genet's plays, an implacable light that produces this urban text without obscurities, which is created by a technocratic power everywhere and which puts the city-dweller under control (under the control of what? No one knows): "The city keeps us under its gaze, which one cannot bear without feeling dizzy," says a resident of Rouen.[47] In the spaces brutally lit by an alien reason, proper names carve out pockets of hidden and familiar meanings. They

[42]Derrida, *Marges*, 287, on metaphor. [Certeau]
[43]Benveniste, *Problèmes*, 1, 86–87. [Certeau]
[44]For Benveniste, "discourse is language considered as assumed by the person who is speaking and in the condition of intersubjectivity" (ibid., 266). [Certeau]
[45]See for example S. Freud, *The Interpretation of Dreams*, trans. J. Strachey (New York: Basic Books, 1955), Chapter VI, § 1–4, on condensation and displacement, "processes of figuration" that are proper to "dreamwork." [Certeau] See Freud, above, p. 500.
[46]Dream symbolism.

[47]Ph. Dard, F. Desbons et al., *La Ville, symbolique en souffrance* (Paris: CEP, 1975), 200. [Certeau]

"make sense"; in other words, they are the impetus of movements, like vocations and calls that turn or divert an itinerary by giving it a meaning (or a direction) (*sens*) that was previously unforeseen. These names create a nowhere in places; they change them into passages.

A friend who lives in the city of Sèvres drifts, when he is in Paris, toward the rue des Saints-*Pères* and the rue de *Sèvres*, even though he is going to see his mother in another part of town: these names articulate a sentence that his steps compose without his knowing it. Numbered streets and street numbers (112th St., or 9 rue Saint-Charles) orient the magnetic field of trajectories just as they can haunt dreams. Another friend unconsciously represses the streets which have names and, by this fact, transmit her — orders or identities in the same way as summonses and classifications; she goes instead along paths that have no name or signature. But her walking is thus still controlled negatively by proper names.

What is it then that they spell out? Disposed in constellations that hierarchize and semantically order the surface of the city, operating chronological arrangements and historical justifications, these words (*Borrégo, Botzaris, Bougain-ville*[48] . . .) slowly lose, like worn coins, the value engraved on them, but their ability to signify outlives its first definition. *Saints-Pères, Corentin Celton, Red Square*[49]. . . . these names make themselves

available to the diverse meanings given them by passers-by; they detach themselves from the places they were supposed to define and serve as imaginary meeting-points on itineraries which, as metaphors, they determine for reasons that are foreign to their original value but may be recognized or not by passers-by. A strange toponymy that is detached from actual places and flies high over the city like a foggy geography of "meanings" held in suspension, directing the physical deambulations below: *Place de l'Étoile, Concorde, Poissonnière.* . . .[50] These constellations of names provide traffic patterns: they are stars directing itineraries. "The Place de la Concorde does not exist," Malaparte said, "it is an idea."[51] It is much more than an "idea." A whole series of comparisons would be necessary to account for the magical powers proper names enjoy. They seem to be carried as emblems by the travelers they direct and simultaneously decorate.

Linking acts and footsteps, opening meanings and directions, these words operate in the name of an emptying-out and wearing-away of their primary role. They become liberated spaces that can be occupied. A rich indetermination gives them, by means of a semantic rarefaction, the function of articulating a second, poetic geography on top of the geography of the literal, forbidden or permitted meaning. They insinuate other routes into the functionalist and historical order of movement. Walking follows them: "I fill this great empty space with a beautiful name."[52] People are put in motion by the remaining relics of meaning,

[48]Paris street or Metro station names. The Rue du Borrégo was the site of one of the final massacres by the soldiers of the French government in its suppression of the Paris Commune; on May 26, 1871, hundreds of "hostages" were stood up against a wall in that street and shot, their bodies dumped into a common grave. Marco Botzaris (1788–1823) was a leader killed in the war of Greek independence; Louis-Antoine de Bougainville (1729–1811) explored Polynesia in the South Pacific and brought back reports of their paradisal qualities.

[49]The Rue des Saints-Pères is named after the "Holy Fathers" of the Church, but is today known for the Faculty of Medicine at No. 45; Corentin Celton was a leader of the French Resistance during World War II, shot in December 1943, whose name is immortalized in a hospital building and a Metro station; Red Square in Moscow (Krasnaya Ploschad) was called "red" (or "beautiful" — the word *krasnaya* is ambiguous) because of the presence of the Cathedral of St. Basil, but became the site of the Kremlin from which the leaders of the Communist party (red in the other sense) ruled the Soviet Union.

[50]The Place de l'Étoile (officially renamed the Place Charles de Gaulle but no one uses that name) is the vast intersection where twelve avenues come together and where the Arc de Triomphe stands. The Place de la Concorde, another great intersection, stands at the other end of the Champs Elysées; earlier named the Place de la Révolution, it was the site of the guillotine where Louis XVI, Marie Antoinette, and thousands of others were executed. The Boulevard Poissonnière runs between the 2e and 9e arrondisements north of the Louvre (and I have no idea why it's listed here by Certeau).

[51]See also, for example, the epigraph in Patrick Modiano, *Place de l'Étoile* (Paris: Gallimard, 1968). [Certeau]

[52]Joachim du Bellay, *Regrets*, 189. [Certeau] Joachim du Bellay (1522?–1560) French lyric poet, leader of La Pleiade.

and sometimes by their waste products, the inverted remainders of great ambitions.[53] Things that amount to nothing, or almost nothing, symbolize and orient walkers' steps: names that have ceased precisely to be "proper."

In these symbolizing kernels three distinct (but connected) functions of the relations between spatial and signifying practices are indicated (and perhaps founded): the *believable*, the *memorable*, and the *primitive*. They designate what "authorizes" (or makes possible or credible) spatial appropriations, what is repeated in them (or is recalled in them) from a silent and withdrawn memory, and what is structured in them and continues to be signed by an in-fantile (*in-fans*)[54] origin. These three symbolic mechanisms organize the topoi of a discourse on/of the city (legend, memory, and dream) in a way that also eludes urbanistic systematicity. They can already be recognized in the functions of proper names: they make habitable or believable the place that they clothe with a word (by emptying themselves of their classifying power, they acquire that of "permitting" something else); they recall or suggest phantoms (the dead who are supposed to have disappeared) that still move about, concealed in gestures and in bodies in motion; and, by naming, that is, by imposing an injunction proceeding from the other (a story) and by altering functionalist identity by detaching themselves from it, they create in the place itself that erosion or nowhere that the law of the other carves out within it.

Credible Things and Memorable Things: Habitability

By a paradox that is only apparent, the discourse that makes people believe is the one that takes away what it urges them to believe in, or never delivers what it promises. Far from expressing a void or describing a lack, it creates such. It makes room for a void. In that way, it opens up clearings; it "allows" a certain play within a system of defined places. It "authorizes" the production of an area of free play (*Spielraum*) on a checkerboard that analyzes and classifies identities. It makes places habitable. On these grounds, I call such discourse a "local authority." It is a crack in the system that saturates places with signification and indeed so reduces them to this signification that it is "impossible to breathe in them." It is a symptomatic tendency of functionalist totalitarianism (including its programming of games and celebrations) that it seeks precisely to eliminate these local authorities, because they compromise the univocity of the system. Totalitarianism attacks what it quite correctly calls *superstitions*: supererogatory semantic overlays that insert themselves "over and above" and "in excess,"[55] and annex to a past or poetic realm a part of the land the promoters of technical rationalities and financial profitabilities had reserved for themselves.

Ultimately, since proper names are already "local authorities" or "superstitions," they are replaced by numbers: on the telephone, one no longer dials *Opera*, but 073.[56] The same is true of the stories and legends that haunt urban space like superfluous or additional inhabitants. They are the object of a witch-hunt, by the very logic of the techno-structure. But their extermination (like the extermination of trees, forests, and hidden places in which such legends live)[57] makes the city a "suspended symbolic order."[58] The habitable city is thereby annulled. Thus, as a woman from Rouen put it, no, here "there isn't any place special, except for my own home, that's all. . . . . There isn't anything." Nothing "special": nothing

---

[55]*Superstare:* "to be above," as something in addition or superfluous. [Certeau]

[56]Many New Yorkers also mourn the passing of the old exchange names, Plaza 2, Butterfield 8, and so on.

[57]See F. Lugassy, *Contribution à une psychosociologie de l'espace urbain. L'Habitat et la forêt* (Paris: Recherche urbaine, 1970). [Certeau]

[58]Dard, Desbons et al., *La Ville, symbolique en souffrance.* [Certeau]

---

[53]For example, *Sarcelles*, the name of a great urbanistic ambition (near Paris), has taken on a symbolic value for the inhabitants of the town by becoming in the eyes of France as a whole the example of a total failure. This extreme avatar provides its citizens with the "prestige" of an exceptional identity. [Certeau]

[54]Latin for "unable to speak."

that is marked, opened up by a memory or a story, signed by something or someone else. Only the cave of the home remains believable, still open for a certain time to legends, still full of shadows. Except for that, according to another city-dweller, there are only "places in which one can no longer believe in anything."[59]

It is through the opportunity they offer to store up rich silences and wordless stories, or rather through their capacity to create cellars and garrets everywhere, that local legends (*legenda*: what is *to be read*, but also what *can be read*) permit exits, ways of going out and coming back in, and thus habitable spaces. Certainly walking about and traveling substitute for exits, for going away and coming back, which were formerly made available by a body of legends that places nowadays lack. Physical moving about has the itinerant function of yesterday's or today's "superstitions." Travel (like walking) is a substitute for the legends that used to open up space to something different. What does travel ultimately produce if it is not, by a sort of reversal, "an exploration of the deserted places of my memory," the return to nearby exoticism by way of a detour through distant places, and the "discovery" of relics and legends: "fleeting visions of the French countryside," "fragments of music and poetry,"[60] in short, something like an "uprooting in one's origins" (Heidegger)? What this walking exile produces is precisely the body of legends that is currently lacking in one's own vicinity; it is a fiction, which moreover has the double characteristic, like dreams or pedestrian rhetoric, of being the effect of displacements and condensations.[61] As a corollary, one can measure the importance of these signifying practices (to tell oneself legends) as practices that invent spaces.

From this point of view, their contents remain revelatory, and still more so is the principle that organizes them. Stories about places are makeshift things. They are composed with the world's debris. Even if the literary form and the actantial schema of "superstitions" correspond to stable models whose structures and combinations have often been analyzed over the past thirty years, the materials (all the rhetorical details of their "manifestation") are furnished by the leftovers from nominations, taxonomies, heroic or comic predicates, etc., that is, by fragments of scattered semantic places. These heterogeneous and even contrary elements fill the homogeneous form of the story. Things *extra* and *other* (details and excesses coming from elsewhere) insert themselves into the accepted framework, the imposed order. One thus has the very relationship between spatial practices and the constructed order. The surface of this order is everywhere punched and torn open by ellipses, drifts, and leaks of meaning: it is a sieve-order.

The verbal relics of which the story is composed, being tied to lost stories and opaque acts, are juxtaposed in a collage where their relations are not thought, and for this reason they form a symbolic whole.[62] They are articulated by lacunae. Within the structured space of the text, they thus produce anti-texts, effects of dissimulation and escape, possibilities of moving into other landscapes, like cellars and bushes: "*ô massifs, ô pluriels.*"[63] Because of the process of dissemination that they open up,

[62]Terms whose relationships are not thought but postulated as necessary can be said to be symbolic. On this definition of symbolism as a cognitive mechanism characterized by a "deficit" of thinking, see Dan Sperber, *Le symbolisme en général* (Paris: Hermann, 1974); *Rethinking Symbolism*, trans. A. L. Morton (Cambridge: Cambridge University Press, 1975). [Certeau]

[63]F. Ponge, *La Promenade dans nos serres* (Paris: Gallimard, 1967). [Certeau] Francis Ponge (1899–1988) wrote the poem quoted here in 1919 while recuperating from diphtheria at the home of Henri Bataille. Ponge is talking about words, specifically nouns, which in French (and English) are either "mass nouns" that don't generally take a plural (like "butter") or count nouns (like "egg") that take a plural. His prose poem takes us through an antique garden, where various bits of language have arranged themselves into a classical landscape: "*ô draperie de mots, assemblage de l'art littéraire, ô massifs, ô pluriels, parterre de voyelles colorées, décors des lignes, ombres de la muette, boucles superbes des consonnes, architecture, fioriture des points et des signes brefs. . . .*" So the literal translation is "o mass nouns, o count nouns."

[59]Ibid., 174, 206. [Certeau]

[60]C. Lévi-Strauss, *Tristes tropiques* (Paris: Plon, 1955), pp. 434–436; *Tristes tropiques*, trans. J. Russell (New York: Criterion, 1962). [Certeau]

[61]One could say the same about the photos brought back from trips, substituted for and turned into legends about the starting place. [Certeau]

stories differ from *rumors* in that the latter are always injunctions, initiators and results of a leveling of space, creators of common movements that reinforce an order by adding an activity of making people believe things to that of making people do things. Stories diversify, rumors totalize. If there is still a certain oscillation between them, it seems that today there is rather a stratification: stories are becoming private and sink into the secluded places in neighborhoods, families, or individuals, while the rumors propagated by the media cover everything and, gathered under the figure of the City, the masterword of an anonymous law, the substitute for all proper names, they wipe out or combat any superstitions guilty of still resisting the figure.

The dispersion of stories points to the dispersion of the memorable as well. And in fact memory is a sort of anti-museum: it is not localizable. Fragments of it come out in legends. Objects and words also have hollow places in which a past sleeps, as in the everyday acts of walking, eating, going to bed, in which ancient revolutions slumber. A memory is only a Prince Charming who stays just long enough to awaken the Sleeping Beauties of our wordless stories. "*Here,* there used to be a bakery." "*That's* where old lady Dupuis used to live." It is striking here that the places people live in are like the presences of diverse absences. What can be seen designates what is no longer there: "you *see,* here there used to be . . . ," but it can no longer be seen. Demonstratives indicate the invisible identities of the visible: it is the very definition of a place, in fact, that it is composed by these series of displacements and effects among the fragmented strata that form it and that it plays on these moving layers.

"Memories tie us to that place. . . . It's personal, not interesting to anyone else, but after all that's what gives a neighborhood its character."[64] There is no place that is not haunted by many different spirits hidden there in silence, spirits one can "invoke" or not. Haunted places are the only ones people can live in — and this inverts the schema of the *Panopticon*. But like the gothic sculptures of kings and queens that once adorned Notre-Dame and have been buried for two centuries in the basement of a building in the rue de la Chausée-d'Antin,[65] these "spirits," themselves broken into pieces in like manner, do not *speak* any more than they *see.* This is a sort of knowledge that remains silent. Only hints of what is known but unrevealed are passed on "just between you and me."

Places are fragmentary and inward-turning histories, pasts that others are not allowed to read, accumulated times that can be unfolded but like stories held in reserve, remaining in an enigmatic state, symbolizations encysted in the pain or pleasure of the body. "I feel good here":[66] the well-being under-expressed in the language it appears in like a fleeting glimmer is a spatial practice.

Childhood and Metaphors of Places

*Metaphor consists in giving the thing
a name that belongs to something
else.* — ARISTOTLE, *Poetics* 1457b

The memorable is that which can be dreamed about a place. In this place that is a palimpsest, subjectivity is already linked to the absence that structures it as existence and makes it "be there," *Dasein*. But as we have seen, this being-there acts only in spatial practices, that is, in *ways of moving into something different* (*manières de passer à l'autre*).[67] It must ultimately be seen as the repetition, in diverse metaphors, of a decisive and originary experience, that of the child's differentiation from the mother's body. It is through that experience that the possibility of space and of a localization (a "not everything") of the subject is inaugurated. We need not return to the famous analysis Freud made of this matrix-experience by

[64]A woman living in the Croix-Rousse quarter in Lyon (interview by Pierre Mayol): see *L'Invention du quotidian*, II, *Habiter, cuisiner* (Paris, UGE 10/18, 1980). [Certeau]

[65]See *Le Monde* for May 4, 1997. [Certeau] The sculpted heads may be of kings of France or kings of Judea; in either case they were removed during the French revolution, when Notre Dame was turned into the Temple of Reason; they were stored in a basement nearby, and rediscovered in 1973.
[66]See note [64].
[67]This can also mean "pass for something else."

following the game played by his eighteen-month-old grandson, who threw a reel away from himself, crying *oh-oh-oh* in pleasure, *fort!* (i.e., "over there," "gone," or "no more") and then pulled it back with the piece of string attached to it with a delighted *da!* (i.e., "here," "back again");[68] it suffices here to remember this (perilous and satisfied) process of detachment from indifferentiation in the mother's body, whose substitute is the spool: this departure of the mother (sometimes she disappears by herself, sometimes the child makes her disappear) constitutes localization and exteriority against the background of an absence. There is a joyful manipulation that can make the maternal object "go away" and make *oneself* disappear (insofar as one considers oneself identical with that object), making it possible to be *there* (because) *without* the other but in a necessary relation to what has disappeared; this manipulation is an "original spatial structure."

No doubt one could trace this differentiation further back, as far as the naming that separates the fetus identified as masculine from his mother — but how about the female fetus, who is from this very moment introduced into another relationship to space? In the initiatory game, just as in the "joyful activity" of the child who, standing before a mirror, sees itself as *one* (it is *she* or *he*, seen as a whole) but *another* (*that*, an image with which the child identifies itself),[69] what counts is the process of this "spatial captation" that inscribes the passage toward the other as the law of being and the law of place. To practice space is thus to repeat the joyful and silent experience of childhood; it is, in a place, *to be other and to move toward the other.*

Thus begins the walk that Freud compares to the trampling underfoot of the mother-land.[70] This relationship of oneself to oneself governs the internal alterations of the place (the relations among its strata) or the pedestrian unfolding of the stories accumulated in a place (moving about the city and traveling). The childhood experience that determines spatial practices later develops its effects, proliferates, floods private and public spaces, undoes their readable surfaces, and creates within the planned city a "metaphorical" or mobile city, like the one Kandinsky dreamed of: "a great city built according to all the rules of architecture and then suddenly shaken by a force that defies all calculation."[71]

[68]See the two analyses provided by Freud in *The Interpretation of Dreams* and *Beyond the Pleasure Principle*, trans. J. Strachey (New York: Liveright, 1980); and also Sami-Ali, *L'Espace imaginaire* (Paris: Gallimard, 1974), 42–64. [Certeau] Little Hans's *fort/da* game is the basis of the repetition compulsion discussed in the introduction to Psychoanalytic Theory and Criticism p. 1106, in Brooks, p. 797, and in Lacan, p. 1122.

[69]J. Lacan, "Le Stade du miroir," *Écrits* (Paris: Seuil, 1966), 93–100; "The Mirror Stage," in *Écrits: A Selection*, trans. A. Sheridan (New York: Norton, 1977). [Certeau] See Lacan, p. 1123.
[70]S. Freud, *Inhibitions, Symptoms and Anxiety* (New York: Norton, 1977).
[71]V. Kandinsky, *Du spirituel dans l'art* (Paris: Denoël, 1969), p. 57.

Michel Foucault

1926–1984

The following selection is the initial chapter of Foucault's Les mots et les choses *(1966; translated as* The Order of Things: An Archaeology of the Human Sciences, *1970).* Las Meninas *("The Maids of Honor") is the title of the Spanish painter Velázquez's 1656 masterpiece (see p. 1358). (For biographical information on Foucault, see the introduction on p. 904.)*

Las Meninas

I

The painter is standing a little back from his canvas. He is glancing at his model; perhaps he is considering whether to add some finishing touch, though it is also possible that the first stroke has not yet been made. The arm holding the brush is bent to the left, towards the palette; it is motionless, for an instant, between canvas and paints. The skilled hand is suspended in mid-air, arrested in rapt attention on the painter's gaze; and the gaze, in return, waits upon the arrested gesture. Between the fine point of the brush and the steely gaze, the scene is about to yield up its volume.

But not without a subtle system of feints. By standing back a little, the painter has placed himself to one side of the painting on which he is working. That is, for the spectator at present observing him he is to the right of his canvas, while the latter, the canvas, takes up the whole of the extreme left. And the canvas has its back turned to that spectator: he can see nothing of it but the reverse side, together with the huge frame on which it is stretched. The painter, on the other hand, is perfectly visible in his full height; or at any rate, he is not masked by the tall canvas which may soon absorb him, when, taking a step towards it again, he returns to his task; he has no doubt just appeared, at this very instant, before the eyes of the spectator, emerging from what is virtually a sort of vast cage projected backwards by the surface he is painting. Now he can be seen, caught in a moment of stillness, at the neutral center of this oscillation. His dark torso and bright face are half-way between the visible and the invisible: emerging from that canvas beyond our view, he moves into our gaze; but when, in a moment, he makes a step to the right, removing himself from our gaze, he will be standing exactly in front of the canvas he is painting; he will enter that region where his painting, neglected for an instant, will, for him, become visible once more, free of shadow and free of reticence. As though the painter could not at the same time be seen on the picture where he is represented and also see that upon which he is representing something. He rules at the threshold of those two incompatible visibilities.

The painter is looking, his face turned slightly and his head leaning towards one shoulder. He is staring at a point to which, even though it is invisible, we, the spectators, can easily assign an object, since it is we, ourselves, who are that point: our bodies, our faces, our eyes. The spectacle he is observing is thus doubly invisible: first, because it is not represented within the space of the painting, and, second, because it is situated precisely in that blind point, in that essential hiding-place into which our gaze disappears from ourselves at the moment of our actual looking. And yet, how could we fail to see that invisibility, there in front of our eyes, since it has its own perceptible equivalent, its sealed-in figure, in the painting itself? We could, in effect, guess what it is the painter is looking at if it were possible for us to glance for a moment at the canvas he is working on; but all we can see of that canvas is its texture, the horizontal and vertical bars of the

Diego Rodriguez Velázquez, *Las Meninas,* 1656. Museo del Prado, Madrid, Spain. Erich Lessing/Art Resources, N. Y.

stretcher, and the obliquely rising foot of the easel. The tall, monotonous rectangle occupying the whole left portion of the real picture, and representing the back of the canvas within the picture, reconstitutes in the form of a surface the invisibility in depth of what the artist is observing: that space in which we are, and which we are. From the eyes of the painter to what he is observing there runs a compelling line that we, the onlookers, have no power of evading: it runs through the real picture and emerges from its surface to join the place from which we see the painter observing us; this dotted line reaches out to us ineluctably, and links us to the representation of the picture.

In appearance, this locus is a simple one; a matter of pure reciprocity: we are looking at a picture in which the painter is in turn looking out at us. A mere confrontation, eyes catching one another's glance, direct looks superimposing themselves upon one another as they cross. And yet this slender line of reciprocal visibility embraces a whole complex network of uncertainties, exchanges, and feints. The painter is turning his eyes towards us only in so far as we happen to occupy the same position as his subject. We, the spectators, are an additional factor. Though greeted by that gaze, we are also dismissed by it, replaced by that which was always there before we were: the model itself. But, inversely, the painter's gaze, addressed to the void confronting him outside the picture, accepts as many models as there are spectators; in this precise but neutral place, the observer and the observed take part in a ceaseless exchange. No gaze is stable, or rather, in the neutral furrow of the gaze piercing at a right angle through the canvas, subject and object, the spectator and the model, reverse their roles to infinity. And here the great canvas with its back to us on the extreme left of the picture exercises its second function: stubbornly invisible, it prevents the relation of these gazes from ever being discoverable or definitely established. The opaque fixity that it establishes on one side renders forever unstable the play of metamorphoses established in the center between spectator and model. Because we can see only that reverse side, we do not know who we are, or what we are doing. Seen or seeing? The painter is observing a place which, from moment to moment, never ceases to change its content, its form, its face, its identity. But the attentive immobility of his eyes refers us back to another direction which they have often followed already, and which soon, there can be no doubt, they will take again: that of the motionless canvas upon which is being traced, has already been traced perhaps, for a long time and forever, a portrait that will never again be erased. So that the painter's sovereign gaze commands a virtual triangle whose outline defines this picture of a picture: at the top — the only visible corner — the painter's eyes; at one of the base angles, the invisible place occupied by the model; at the other base angle, the figure probably sketched out on the invisible surface of the canvas.

As soon as they place the spectator in the field of their gaze, the painter's eyes seize hold of him, force him to enter the picture, assign him a place at once privileged and inescapable, levy their luminous and visible tribute from him, and project it upon the inaccessible surface of the canvas within the picture. He sees his invisibility made visible to the painter and transposed into an image forever invisible to himself. A shock that is augmented and made more inevitable still by a marginal trap. At the extreme right, the picture is lit by a window represented in very sharp perspective; so sharp that we can see scarcely more than the embrasure; so that the flood of light streaming through it bathes at the same time, and with equal generosity, two neighbouring spaces, overlapping but irreducible: the surface of the painting, together with the volume it represents (which is to say, the painter's studio, or the salon in which his easel is now set up), and, in front of that surface, the real volume occupied by the spectator (or again, the unreal site of the model). And as it passes through the room from right to left, this vast flood of golden light carries both the spectator towards the painter and the model towards the canvas; it is this light too, which, washing over the painter, makes him visible to the spectator and turns into golden lines, in the model's eyes, the frame of that enigmatic canvas on which his image, once transported there, is to be imprisoned. This extreme, partial, scarcely indicated window frees a whole flow of daylight which serves as the common locus of the representation. It balances the invisible canvas on the other side of the picture: just as that canvas, by turning its back to the spectators, folds itself in against the picture representing it, and forms, by the superimposition of its reverse and visible side upon the surface of the picture depicting it, the ground, inaccessible to us, on which there shimmers the Image *par excellence,* so does the window, a pure aperture, establish a space as manifest as the other is hidden; as much the common ground of painter, figures, models, and spectators, as the other is solitary (for no one is looking at it, not even the painter). From the right, there streams in through an invisible window the pure volume of a light that renders all representation visible; to the left extends the surface that conceals, on the other side of its all too visible woven texture, the representation it bears. The light, by flooding the scene (I mean the room as well as the canvas, the room represented on the canvas, and the room in which the canvas stands), envelops the figures and the spectators and carries them with it, under the painter's gaze, towards the place where his brush will represent them. But that place is concealed from us. We are observing ourselves being observed by the painter, and made visible to his eyes by the same light that enables us to see him. And just as we are about to apprehend ourselves, transcribed by his hand as though in a mirror, we find that we can in fact apprehend nothing of that mirror but its lusterless back. The other side of a psyche.

Now, as it happens, exactly opposite the spectators — ourselves — on the wall forming the far end of the room, Velázquez has represented a series of pictures; and we see that among all those hanging canvases there is one that shines with particular brightness. Its frame is wider and darker than those of the others; yet there is a fine white line around its inner edge diffusing over its whole surface a light whose source is not easy to determine; for it comes from nowhere, unless it be from a space within itself. In this strange light, two silhouettes are apparent, while above them, and a little behind them, is a heavy purple curtain. The other pictures reveal little more than a few paler patches buried in a darkness without depth. This particular one, on the other hand, opens onto a perspective of space in which recognizable forms recede from us in a light that belongs only to itself. Among all these elements intended to provide representations, while impeding them, hiding them, concealing them because of their position or their distance from us, this is the only one that fulfills its function in all honesty and enables us to see what it is supposed to show. Despite its distance from us, despite the shadows all around it. But it isn't a picture: it is a mirror. It offers us at last that enchantment of the double that until now has been denied us, not only by the distant paintings but also by the light in the foreground with its ironic canvas.

Of all the representations represented in the picture this is the only one visible; but no one is looking at it. Upright beside his canvas, his attention entirely taken up by his model, the painter is unable to see this looking-glass shining so softly behind him. The other figures in the picture are also, for the most part, turned to face what must be taking place in front — towards the bright invisibility bordering the canvas, towards that balcony of light where their eyes can gaze at those who are gazing back at them, and not towards that dark recess which marks the far end of the room in which they are represented. There are, it is true, some heads turned away from us in profile: but not one of them is turned far enough to see, at the back of the room, that solitary mirror, that tiny glowing rectangle which is nothing other than visibility, yet without any gaze able to grasp it, to render it actual, and to enjoy the suddenly ripe fruit of the spectacle it offers.

It must be admitted that this indifference is equaled only by the mirror's own. It is reflecting nothing, in fact, of all that is there in the same space as itself: neither the painter with his back to it, nor the figures in the center of the room. It is not the visible it reflects, in those bright depths. In Dutch painting it was traditional for mirrors to play a duplicating role: they repeated the original contents of the picture, only inside an unreal, modified, contracted, concave space. One saw in them the same things as one saw in the first instance in the painting, but decomposed and recomposed according to a different law. Here, the mirror is saying nothing that has already been said before. Yet its position is more or less completely central: its upper edge is exactly on an imaginary line running half-way between the top and the bottom of the painting, its hands right in the middle of the far wall (or at least in the middle of the portion we can see); it ought, therefore, to be governed by the same lines of perspective as the picture itself; we might well expect the same studio, the same painter, the same canvas to be arranged within it according to an identical space: it could be the perfect duplication.

In fact, it shows us nothing of what is represented in the picture itself. Its motionless gaze extends out in front of the picture, into that necessarily invisible region which forms its exterior face, to apprehend the figures arranged in that space. Instead of surrounding visible objects, this mirror cuts straight through the whole field of the representation, ignoring all it might apprehend within that field, and restores visibility to that which resides outside all view. But the invisibility that it overcomes in this way is not the invisibility of what is hidden: it does not make its way around any obstacle, it is not distorting any perspective, it is addressing itself to what is invisible both because of the picture's structure and because of its existence as painting. What it is reflecting is that which all the figures within the painting are looking at so fixedly, or at least those who are looking straight ahead; it is therefore what the spectator would be able to see if the painting extended further forward, if its bottom edge were brought lower until it included the figures the painter is using as models. But it is also, since the picture does stop there, displaying only the painter and his studio, what is exterior to the picture, in so far as it is a picture — in other words, a rectangular fragment of lines and colors intended to represent something to the eyes of any possible spectator. At the far end of the room, ignored by all, the unexpected mirror holds in its glow the figures that the painter is looking at (the painter in his represented, objective reality, the reality of the painter at his work); but also the figures that are looking at the painter (in that material reality which the lines and the colors have laid out upon the canvas). These two groups of figures are both equally inaccessible, but in different ways: the first because of an effect of composition peculiar to the painting; the second because of the law that presides over the very existence of all pictures in general. Here, the action of representation consists in bringing one of these two forms of invisibility into the place of the other, in an unstable superimposition — and in rendering them both, at the same moment, at the other extremity of the picture — at that pole which is the very height of its representation: that of a reflected depth in the far recess of the painting's depth. The mirror provides a metathesis of visibility that affects both the space represented in the picture and its nature as representation; it allows us to see, in the center of the canvas, what in the painting is of necessity doubly invisible.

A strangely literal, though inverted, application of the advice given, so it is said, to his pupil by the old Pacheco[1] when the former was working in his studio in Seville: "The image should stand out from the frame."

[1] Francesco Pacheco (1564–1644), minor painter of Seville, Velázquez's teacher and later his father-in-law, author of *Arte de la pintura* (1649).

II

But perhaps it is time to give a name at last to that image which appears in the depths of the mirror, and which the painter is contemplating in front of the picture. Perhaps it would be better, once and for all, to determine the identities of all the figures presented or indicated here, so as to avoid embroiling ourselves forever in those vague, rather abstract designations, so constantly prone to misunderstanding and duplication, "the painter," "the characters," "the models," "the spectators," "the images." Rather than pursue to infinity a language inevitably inadequate to the visible fact, it would be better to say that Velázquez composed a picture; that in this picture he represented himself, in his studio or in a room of the Escurial,[2] in the act of painting two figures whom the Infanta Margarita[3] has come there to watch, together with an entourage of duennas, maids of honor, courtiers, and dwarfs; that we can attribute names to this group of people with great precision: tradition recognizes that here we have Doña Maria Augustina Sarmiento, over there Nieto, in the foreground Nicolaso Pertusato, an Italian jester.[4] We could then add that the two personages serving as models to the painter are not visible, at least directly; but that we can see them in a mirror; and that they are, without any doubt, King Philip IV and his wife, Mariana.[5]

These proper names would form useful landmarks and avoid ambiguous designations; they would tell us in any case what the painter is looking at, and the majority of the characters in the picture along with him. But the relation of language to painting is an infinite relation. It is not that words are imperfect, or that, when confronted

[2] Royal palace in Madrid.
[3] "Infanta" designates the crown princess, eldest daughter of the king of Spain. Margherita was the daughter of Philip IV's first wife, Isabella of Bourbon.
[4] Doña Maria was one of the royal maids of honor, on the left of the Infanta. Don José Nieto is the back-lit gentleman standing on the staircase in the background. Pertusato is the youth prodding the royal mastiff.
[5] Philip IV (1605–1665) ruled Spain from 1621 to 65. Mariana, Archduchess of Austria, became his second wife in 1649.

by the visible, they prove insuperably inadequate. Neither can be reduced to the other's terms: it is in vain that we say what we see; what we see never resides in what we say. And it is in vain that we attempt to show, by the use of images, metaphors, or similes, what we are saying; the space where they achieve their splendour is not that deployed by our eyes but that defined by the sequential elements of syntax. And the proper name, in this particular context, is merely an artifice: it gives us a finger to point with, in other words, to pass surreptitiously from the space where one speaks to the space where one looks; in other words, to fold one over the other as though they were equivalents. But if one wishes to keep the relation of language to vision open, if one wishes to treat their incompatibility as a starting-point for speech instead of as an obstacle to be avoided, so as to stay as close as possible to both, then one must erase those proper names and preserve the infinity of the task. It is perhaps through the medium of this grey, anonymous language, always overmeticulous and repetitive because too broad, that the painting may, little by little, release its illuminations.

We must therefore pretend not to know who is to be reflected in the depths of that mirror, and interrogate that reflection in its own terms.

First, it is the reverse of the great canvas represented on the left. The reverse, or rather the right side, since it displays in full face what the canvas, by its position, is hiding from us. Furthermore, it is both in opposition to the window and a reinforcement of it. Like the window, it provides a ground which is common to the painting and to what lies outside it. But the window operates by the continuous movement of an effusion which, flowing from right to left, unites the attentive figures, the painter, and the canvas, with the spectacle they are observing; whereas the mirror, on the other hand, by means of a violent, instantaneous movement, a movement of pure surprise, leaps out from the picture in order to reach that which is observed yet invisible in front of it, and then, at the far end of its fictitious depth, to render it visible yet indifferent to every gaze. The compelling tracer line, joining the reflection to that which it is reflecting, cuts perpendicularly through the lateral flood of light.

Lastly — and this is the mirror's third function — it stands adjacent to a doorway which forms an opening, like the mirror itself, in the far wall of the room. This doorway too forms a bright and sharply defined rectangle whose soft light does not shine through into the room. It would be nothing but a gilded panel if it were not recessed out from the room by means of one leaf of a carved door, the curve of a curtain, and the shadows of several steps. Beyond the steps, a corridor begins; but instead of losing itself in obscurity, it is dissipated in a yellow dazzle where the light, without coming in, whirls around on itself in dynamic repose. Against this background, at once near and limitless, a man stands out in full-length silhouette; he is seen in profile; with one hand he is holding back the weight of a curtain; his feet are placed on different steps; one knee is bent. He may be about to enter the room; or he may be merely observing what is going on inside it, content to surprise those within without being seen himself. Like the mirror, his eyes are directed towards the other side of the scene; nor is anyone paying any more attention to him than to the mirror. We do not know where he has come from: it could be that by following uncertain corridors he has just made his way around the outside of the room in which these characters are collected and the painter is at work; perhaps he too, a short while ago, was there in the forefront of the scene, in the invisible region still being contemplated by all those eyes in the picture. Like the images perceived in the looking-glass, it is possible that he too is an emissary from that evident yet hidden space. Even so, there is a difference: he is there in flesh and blood; he has appeared from the outside, on the threshold of the area represented; he is indubitable — not a probable reflection but an irruption. The mirror, by making visible, beyond even the walls of the studio itself, what is happening in front of the picture, creates in its sagittal[6] dimension, an oscillation between the interior and the exterior. One foot only on the lower step, his body entirely in profile, the ambiguous visitor is coming in and going out at the same time, like

[6]In optics, "sagittal" designates a plane intersecting the rays from an off-center light source.

a pendulum caught at the bottom of its swing. He repeats on the spot, but in the dark reality of his body, the instantaneous movement of those images flashing across the room, plunging into the mirror, being reflected there, and springing out from it again like visible, new, and identical species. Pale, minuscule, those silhouetted figures in the mirror are challenged by the tall, solid stature of the man appearing in the doorway.

But we must move down again from the back of the picture towards the front of the stage; we must leave that periphery whose volute[7] we have just been following. Starting from the painter's gaze, which constitutes an off-center center to the left, we perceive first of all the back of the canvas, then the paintings hung on the wall, with the mirror in their center, then the open doorway, then more pictures, of which, because of the sharpness of the perspective, we can see no more than the edges of the frames, and finally, at the extreme right, the window, or rather the groove in the wall from which the light is pouring. This spiral shell presents us with the entire cycle of representation: the gaze, the palette and brush, the canvas innocent of signs (these are the material tools of representation), the paintings, the reflections, the real man (the completed representation, but as it were freed from its illusory or truthful contents, which are juxtaposed to it); then the representation dissolves again: we can see only the frames, and the light that is flooding the pictures from outside, but that they, in return, must reconstitute in their own kind, as though it were coming from elsewhere, passing through their dark wooden frames. And we do, in fact, see this light on the painting, apparently welling out from the crack of the frame; and from there it moves over to touch the brow, the cheekbones, the eyes, the gaze of the painter, who is holding a palette in one hand and in the other a fine brush . . . And so the spiral is closed, or rather, by means of that light, is opened.

This opening is not, like the one in the back wall, made by pulling back a door; it is the whole breadth of the picture itself, and the looks that pass across it are not those of a distant visitor. The frieze that occupies the foreground and the middle ground of the picture represents — if we include the painter — eight characters. Five of these, their heads more or less bent, turned or inclined, are looking straight out at right angles to the surface of the picture. The center of the group is occupied by the little Infanta, with her flared pink and grey dress. The princess is turning her head towards the right side of the picture, while her torso and the big panniers of her dress slant away slightly towards the left; but her gaze is directed absolutely straight towards the spectator standing in front of the painting. A vertical line dividing the canvas into two equal halves would pass between the child's eyes. Her face is a third of the total height of the picture above the lower frame. So that here, beyond all question, resides the principal theme of the composition; this is the very object of this painting. As though to prove this and to emphasize it even more, Velázquez has made use of a traditional visual device: beside the principal figure he has placed a secondary one, kneeling and looking in towards the central one. Like a donor in prayer, like an angel greeting the Virgin, a maid of honor on her knees is stretching out her hands towards the princess. Her face stands out in perfect profile against the background. It is at the same height as that of the child. This attendant is looking at the princess and only at the princess. A little to the right, there stands another maid of honor, also turned towards the Infanta, leaning slightly over her, but with her eyes clearly directed towards the front, towards the same spot already being gazed at by the painter and the princess. Lastly, two other groups made up of two figures each: one of these groups is further away; the other, made up of the two dwarfs, is right in the foreground. One character in each of these pairs is looking straight out, the other to the left or the right. Because of their positions and their size, these two groups correspond and themselves form a pair: behind, the courtiers (the woman, to the left, looks to the right); in front, the dwarfs (the boy, who is at the extreme right, looks in towards the center of the picture). This group of characters, arranged in this manner, can be taken to constitute, according to the way one looks at the picture and the center of reference chosen, two different figures. The first would be a large X: the top left-hand point of this

[7]Spiral.

X would be the painter's eyes; the top right-hand one, the male courtier's eyes; at the bottom left-hand corner there is the corner of the canvas represented with its back towards us (or, more exactly, the foot of the easel); at the bottom right-hand corner, the dwarf (his foot on the dog's back). Where these two lines intersect, at the center of the X, are the eyes of the Infanta. The second figure would be more that of a vast curve, its two ends determined by the painter on the left and the male courtier on the right — both these extremities occurring high up in the picture and set back from its surface; the center of the curve, much nearer to us, would coincide with the princess's face and the look her maid of honor is directing towards her. This curve describes a shallow hollow across the center of the picture which at once contains and sets off the position of the mirror at the back.

There are thus two centers around which the picture may be organized, according to whether the fluttering attention of the spectator decides to settle in this place or in that. The princess is standing upright in the center of a St. Andrew's cross,[8] which is revolving around her with its eddies of courtiers, maids of honor, animals, and fools. But this pivoting movement is frozen. Frozen by a spectacle that would be absolutely invisible if those same characters, suddenly motionless, were not offering us, as though in the hollow of a goblet, the possibility of seeing in the depths of a mirror the unforeseen double of what they are observing. In depth, it is the princess who is superimposed on the mirror; vertically, it is the reflection that is superimposed on the face. But, because of the perspective, they are very close to one another. Moreover, from each of them there springs an ineluctable line: the line issuing from the mirror crosses the whole of the depth represented (and even more, since the mirror forms a hole in the back wall and brings a further space into being behind it); the other line is shorter: it comes from the child's eyes and crosses only the foreground. These two sagittal lines converge at a very sharp angle, and the point where they meet, springing out from the painted surface, occurs in front of the picture, more or less exactly at the

[8]A St. Andrew's Cross is an X.

spot from which we are observing it. It is an uncertain point because we cannot see it; yet it is an inevitable and perfectly defined point too, since it is determined by those two dominating figures and confirmed further by other, adjacent dotted lines which also have their origin inside the picture and emerge from it in a similar fashion.

What is there, then, we ask at last, in that place which is completely inaccessible because it is exterior to the picture, yet is prescribed by all the lines of its composition? What is the spectacle, what are the faces that are reflected first of all in the depths of the Infanta's eyes, then in the courtiers' and the painter's, and finally in the distant glow of the mirror? But the question immediately becomes a double one: the face reflected in the mirror is also the face that is contemplating it; what all the figures in the picture are looking at are the two figures to whose eyes they too present a scene to be observed. The entire picture is looking out at a scene for which it is itself a scene. A condition of pure reciprocity manifested by the observing and observed mirror, the two stages of which are uncoupled at the two lower corners of the picture: on the left the canvas with its back to us, by means of which the exterior point is made into pure spectacle; to the right the dog lying on the floor, the only element in the picture that is neither looking at anything nor moving, because it is not intended, with its deep reliefs and the light playing on its silky hair, to be anything but an object to be seen.

Our first glance at the painting told us what it is that creates this spectacle-as-observation. It is the two sovereigns. One can sense their presence already in the respectful gaze of the figures in the picture, in the astonishment of the child and the dwarfs. We recognize them, at the far end of the picture, in the two tiny silhouettes gleaming out from the looking-glass. In the midst of all those attentive faces, all those richly dressed bodies, they are the palest, the most unreal, the most compromised of all the painting's images: a movement, a little light, would be sufficient to eclipse them. Of all these figures represented before us, they are also the most ignored, since no one is paying the slightest attention to that reflection which has slipped into the room behind them all, silently occupying its unsuspected space; in so far as they are visible, they are the frailest and the most distant form of all reality. Inversely, in so far as they stand outside the picture and are therefore withdrawn from it in an essential invisibility, they provide the center around which the entire representation is ordered: it is they who are being faced, it is towards them that everyone is turned, it is to their eyes that the princess is being presented in her holiday clothes; from the canvas with its back to us to the Infanta, and from the Infanta to the dwarf playing on the extreme right, there runs a curve (or again, the lower fork of the X opens) that orders the whole arrangement of the picture to their gaze and thus makes apparent the true center of the composition, to which the Infanta's gaze and the image in the mirror are both finally subject.

In the realm of the anecdote, this center is symbolically sovereign, since it is occupied by King Philip IV and his wife. But it is so above all because of the triple function it fulfills in relation to the picture. For in it there occurs an exact superimposition of the model's gaze as it is being painted, of the spectator's as he contemplates the painting, and of the painter's as he is composing his picture (not the one represented, but the one in front of us which we are discussing). These three "observing" functions come together in a point exterior to the picture: that is, an ideal point in relation to what is represented, but a perfectly real one too, since it is also the starting-point that makes the representation possible. Within that reality itself, it cannot not be invisible. And yet, that reality is projected within the picture — projected and diffracted in three forms which correspond to the three functions of that ideal and real point. They are: on the left, the painter with his palette in his hand (a self-portrait of Velázquez); to the right, the visitor, one foot on the step, ready to enter the room; he is taking in the scene from the back, but he can see the royal couple, who are the spectacle itself, from the front; and lastly, in the center, the reflection of the king and queen, richly dressed, motionless, in the attitude of patient models.

A reflection that shows us quite simply, and in shadow, what all those in the foreground are looking at. It restores, as if by magic, what is lacking in every gaze: in the painter's, the model, which his represented double is duplicating over there in the picture; in the king's, his portrait, which is being finished off on that slope of the canvas that he cannot perceive from where he stands; in that of the spectator, the real center of the scene, whose place he himself has taken as though by usurpation. But perhaps this generosity on the part of the mirror is feigned; perhaps it is hiding as much as and even more than it reveals. That space where the king and his wife hold sway belongs equally well to the artist and to the spectator: in the depths of the mirror there could also appear — there ought to appear — the anonymous face of the passer-by and that of Velázquez. For the function of that reflection is to draw into the interior of the picture what is intimately foreign to it: the gaze which has organized it and the gaze for which it is displayed. But because they are present within the picture, to the right and to the left, the artist and the visitor cannot be given a place in the mirror: just as the king appears in the depths of the looking-glass precisely because he does not belong to the picture.

In the great volute that runs around the perimeter of the studio, from the gaze of the painter, with his motionless hand and palette, right around to the finished paintings, representation came into being, reached completion, only to dissolve once more into the light; the cycle was complete. The lines that run through the depth of the picture, on the other hand, are not complete; they all lack a segment of their trajectories. This gap is caused by the absence of the king — an absence that is an artifice on the part of the painter. But this artifice both conceals and indicates another vacancy which is, on the contrary, immediate: that of the painter and the spectator when they are looking at or composing the picture. It may be that, in this picture, as in all the representations of which it is, as it were, the manifest essence, the profound invisibility of what one sees is inseparable from the invisibility of the person seeing — despite all mirrors, reflections, imitations, and portraits. Around the scene are arranged all the signs and successive forms of representation; but the double relation of the representation to its model and to its sovereign, to its author as well as to the person to whom it is being offered, this relation is necessarily interrupted. It can never be present without some residuum, even in a representation that offers itself as a spectacle. In the depth that traverses the picture, hollowing it into a fictitious recess and projecting it forward in front of itself, it is not possible for the pure felicity of the image ever to present in a full light both the master who is representing and the sovereign who is being represented.

Perhaps there exists, in this painting by Velázquez, the representation as it were, of Classical[9] representation, and the definition of the space it opens up to us. And, indeed, representation undertakes to represent itself here in all its elements, with its images, the eyes to which it is offered, the faces it makes visible, the gestures that call it into being. But there, in the midst of this dispersion which it is simultaneously grouping together and spreading out before us, indicated compellingly from every side, is an essential void: the necessary disappearance of that which is its foundation — of the person it resembles and the person in whose eyes it is only a resemblance. This very subject — which is the same — has been elided. And representation, freed finally from the relation that was impeding it, can offer itself as representation in its pure form.

[9]*Classical* is Foucault's term for the *épistème* associated with the Enlightenment era (1650–1800).

Clifford Geertz

b. 1923

The notion that culture is a language that can be learned by studying social practices with the same attention to nuance, motif, and transformational tropes that literary critics apply to difficult poetry is one which seems familiar today, owing to Clifford Geertz's many years of labor combating the once dominant "functionalist" approach. Geertz was born in San Francisco and served in the navy during World War II before resuming his education at Antioch College. He took his Ph.D. at Harvard University in 1956. Geertz combined field work in Bali and Morocco with academic appointments at Harvard, MIT, Stanford, and Berkeley, becoming professor of anthropology at the University of Chicago in 1964. In 1972 he moved to Princeton University, where he spent the rest of his career as a professor of social science at the Institute for Advanced Study, where he is now Professor Emeritus. His voluminous publications include Islam Observed: Religious Development in Morocco and Indonesia *(1968),* The Interpretation of Cultures *(1973),* Myth, Symbol and Culture *(1974),* Local Knowledge *(1983),* Works and Lives *(1988),* After the Fact: Two Countries, Four Decades, One Anthropologist *(1995) and* Available Light: Anthropological Reflections on Philosophical Topics *(2001). Geertz tends to avoid the abstract: his essays are, as he says, "empirical studies" because he grows "uncomfortable when I get too far away from the immediacy of social life." The essay reproduced below, "Thick Description," written especially as the introduction to* The Interpretation of Cultures, *is no exception: Its theoretical points emerge as Geertz recounts a real-life episode involving sheep stealing, murder, and revenge in Morocco.*

Thick Description: Toward an Interpretive Theory of Culture

I

In her book, *Philosophy in a New Key*, Susanne Langer[1] remarks that certain ideas burst upon the intellectual landscape with a tremendous force. They resolve so many fundamental problems at once that they seem also to promise that they will resolve all fundamental problems, clarify all obscure issues. Everyone snaps them up as the open sesame of some new positive science, the conceptual center-point around which a comprehensive system of analysis can be built. The sudden vogue of such a *grande idée*, crowding out almost everything else for a while, is due, she says, "to the fact that all sensitive and active minds turn at once to exploiting it. We try it in every connection, for every purpose, experiment with possible stretches of its strict meaning, with generalizations and derivatives."

After we have become familiar with the new idea, however, after it has become part of our general stock of theoretical concepts, our expectations are brought more into balance with its actual uses, and its excessive popularity is ended. A few zealots persist in the old key-to-the-universe view of it; but less driven thinkers settle down after a while to the problems the idea has really generated. They try to apply it and extend it where it applies and where it is capable of extension; and they desist where it does not apply or cannot be extended. It becomes, if it was, in truth, a seminal idea in the first place, a permanent and enduring part of our intellectual armory. But it no longer has the grandiose, all-promising scope, the infinite versatility of apparent application, it once had. The second law of thermodynamics, or the principle of natural selection, or the notion of unconscious motivation, or the organization of the means of production does not explain everything, not even everything human, but it still explains something; and our attention shifts to isolating just what that something is, to disentangling ourselves from a lot of pseudoscience to which, in the first flush of its celebrity, it has also given rise.

Whether or not this is, in fact, the way all centrally important scientific concepts develop, I don't know. But certainly this pattern fits the concept of culture, around which the whole discipline of anthropology arose, and whose domination that discipline has been increasingly concerned to limit, specify, focus, and contain. It is to this cutting of the culture concept down to size, therefore actually insuring its continued importance rather than undermining it, that the essays below are all, in their several ways and from their several directions, dedicated. They all argue, sometimes explicitly, more often merely through the particular analysis they develop, for a narrowed, specialized, and, so I imagine, theoretically more powerful concept of culture to replace E. B. Tylor's[2] famous "most complex whole," which, its originative power not denied, seems to me to have reached the point where it obscures a good deal more than it reveals.

The conceptual morass into which the Tylorean kind of *pot-au-feu*[3] theorizing about culture can lead is evident in what is still one of the better general introductions to anthropology, Clyde Kluckhohn's[4] *Mirror for Man*. In some twenty-seven pages of his chapter on the concept, Kluckhohn managed to define culture in turn as: (1) "the total way of life of a people"; (2) "the social legacy the individual acquires from his group"; (3) "a way of thinking, feeling, and believing";

[1] American philosopher (1895–1986) who studied ways of understanding art and culture as forms of knowledge comparable to scientific knowledge.

[2] Sir Edward Burnett Tylor (1832–1917), pioneer anthropologist at Oxford University.

[3] A French beef and chicken stew with everything but the kitchen sink included.

[4] American anthropologist (1905–1960) who studied the Navaho.

(4) "an abstraction from behavior"; (5) a theory on the part of the anthropologist about the way in which a group of people in fact behave; (6) a "storehouse of pooled learning"; (7) "a set of standardized orientations to recurrent problems"; (8) "learned behavior"; (9) a mechanism for the normative regulation of behavior; (10) "a set of techniques for adjusting both to the external environment and to other men"; (11) "a precipitate of history"; and turning, perhaps in desperation, to similes, as a map, as a sieve, and as a matrix. In the face of this sort of theoretical diffusion, even a somewhat constricted and not entirely standard concept of culture, which is at least internally coherent and, more important, which has a definable argument to make is (as, to be fair, Kluckhohn himself keenly realized) an improvement. Eclecticism is self-defeating not because there is only one direction in which it is useful to move, but because there are so many: it is necessary to choose.

The concept of culture I espouse, and whose utility the essays below attempt to demonstrate, is essentially a semiotic one. Believing, with Max Weber,[5] that man is an animal suspended in webs of significance he himself has spun, I take culture to be those webs, and the analysis of it to be therefore not an experimental science in search of law but an interpretive one in search of meaning. It is explication I am after, construing social expressions on their surface enigmatical. But this pronouncement, a doctrine in a clause, demands itself some explication.

II

Operationalism as a methodological dogma never made much sense so far as the social sciences are concerned, and except for a few rather too well-swept corners — Skinnerian behaviorism,[6] intelligence testing, and so on — it is largely dead now. But it had, for all that, an important point to make, which, however we may feel about trying to define charisma or alienation in terms of operations, retains a certain force: if you want to understand what a science is, you should look in the first instance not at its theories or its findings, and certainly not at what its apologists say about it; you should look at what the practitioners of it do.

In anthropology, or anyway social anthropology, what the practitioners do is ethnography. And it is in understanding what ethnography is, or more exactly *what doing ethnography is*, that a start can be made toward grasping what anthropological analysis amounts to as a form of knowledge. This, it must immediately be said, is not a matter of methods. From one point of view, that of the textbook, doing ethnography is establishing rapport, selecting informants, transcribing texts, taking genealogies, mapping fields, keeping a diary, and so on. But it is not these things, techniques and received procedures, that define the enterprise. What defines it is the kind of intellectual effort it is: an elaborate venture in, to borrow a notion from Gilbert Ryle,[7] "thick description."

Ryle's discussion of "thick description" appears in two recent essays of his (now reprinted in the second volume of his *Collected Papers*) addressed to the general question of what, as he puts it, "*Le Penseur*" is doing: "Thinking and Reflecting" and "The Thinking of Thoughts." Consider, he says, two boys rapidly contracting the eyelids of their right eyes. In one, this is an involuntary twitch; in the other, a conspiratorial signal to a friend. The two movements are, as movements, identical; from an I-am-a-camera, "phenomenalistic" observation of them alone, one could not tell which was twitch and which was wink, or indeed whether both or either was twitch or wink. Yet the difference, however unphotographable, between a twitch and a wink is vast; as anyone unfortunate enough to have had the first taken for the second knows. The winker is communicating, and indeed communicating in a quite precise and special way: (1) deliberately, (2) to someone in particular, (3) to impart a particular message, (4) according to a socially established code, and (5) without cognizance of the

[5]German philosopher and sociologist (1864–1920) best known for *The Protestant Ethic and the Spirit of Capitalism* (1905).
[6]Psychologist B. F. Skinner (1904–1990) attempted to understand human behavior entirely in terms of conditioned response.

[7]Gilbert Ryle, English "ordinary language" philosopher (1900–1976).

rest of the company. As Ryle points out, the winker has not done two things, contracted his eyelids and winked, while the twitcher has done only one, contracted his eyelids. Contracting your eyelids on purpose when there exists a public code in which so doing counts as a conspiratorial signal *is* winking. That's all there is to it; a speck of behavior, a fleck of culture, and — *voilà!* — a gesture.

That, however, is just the beginning. Suppose, he continues, there is a third boy, who, "to give malicious amusement to his cronies," parodies the first boy's wink, as amateurish, clumsy, obvious, and so on. He, of course, does this in the same way the second boy winked and the first twitched: by contracting his right eyelids. Only this boy is neither winking nor twitching, he is parodying someone else's, as he takes it, laughable, attempt at winking. Here, too, a socially established code exists (he will "wink" laboriously, overobviously, perhaps adding a grimace — the artifices of the clown); and so also does a message. Only now it is not conspiracy but ridicule that is in the air. If the others think he is actually winking, his whole project misfires as completely, though with somewhat different results, as if they think he is twitching. One can go further: uncertain of his mimicking abilities, the would-be satirist may practice at home before the mirror, in which case he is not twitching, winking, or parodying, but rehearsing; though so far as what a camera, a radical behaviorist, or a believer in protocol sentences would record he is just rapidly contracting his right eyelids like all the others. Complexities are possible, if not practically without end, at least logically so. The original winker might, for example, actually have been fake-winking, say, to mislead outsiders into imagining there was a conspiracy afoot when there in fact was not, in which case our descriptions of what the parodist is parodying and the rehearser rehearsing of course shift accordingly. But the point is that between what Ryle calls the "thin description" of what the rehearser (parodist, winker, twitcher . . .) is doing ("rapidly contracting his right eyelids") and the "thick description" of what he is doing ("practicing a burlesque of a friend faking a wink to deceive an innocent into thinking a conspiracy is in motion") lies the object of ethnography: a

stratified hierarchy of meaningful structures in terms of which twitches, winks, fake-winks, parodies, rehearsals of parodies are produced, perceived, and interpreted, and without which they would not (not even the zero-form twitches, which, *as a cultural category*, are as much nonwinks as winks are nontwitches) in fact exist, no matter what anyone did or didn't do with his eyelids.

Like so many of the little stories Oxford philosophers like to make up for themselves, all this winking, fake-winking, burlesque-fake-winking, rehearsed-burlesque-fake-winking, may seem a bit artificial. In way of adding a more empirical note, let me give, deliberately unpreceded by any prior explanatory comment at all, a not untypical excerpt from my own field journal to demonstrate that, however evened off for didactic purposes, Ryle's example presents an image only too exact of the sort of piled-up structures of inference and implication through which an ethnographer is continually trying to pick his way:

> The French [the informant said] had only just arrived. They set up twenty or so small forts between here, the town, and the Marmusha area up in the middle of the mountains, placing them on promontories so they could survey the countryside. But for all this they couldn't guarantee safety, especially at night, so although the *mezrag*, trade-pact, system was supposed to be legally abolished it in fact continued as before.
>
> One night, when Cohen (who speaks fluent Berber), was up there, at Marmusha, two other Jews who were traders to a neighboring tribe came by to purchase some goods from him. Some Berbers, from yet another neighboring tribe, tried to break into Cohen's place, but he fired his rifle in the air, (Traditionally, Jews were not allowed to carry weapons; but at this period things were so unsettled many did so anyway.) This attracted the attention of the French and the marauders fled.
>
> The next night, however, they came back, one of them disguised as a woman who knocked on the door with some sort of a story. Cohen was suspicious and didn't want to let "her" in, but the other Jews said, "oh, it's all right, it's only a woman." So they opened the door and the whole lot came pouring in. They killed the two visiting Jews, but Cohen managed to barricade himself in an adjoining room. He heard the robbers planning to burn him alive in the shop after they removed his goods, and so he opened the door and, laying about him wildly with a club, managed to escape through a window.

He went up to the fort, then, to have his wounds dressed, and complained to the local commandant, one Captain Dumari, saying he wanted his 'ar — i.e., four or five times the value of the merchandise stolen from him. The robbers were from a tribe which had not yet submitted to French authority and were in open rebellion against it, and he wanted authorization to go with his *mezrag*-holder, the Marmusha tribal *sheikh*, to collect the indemnity that, under traditional rules, he had coming to him. Captain Dumari couldn't officially give him permission to do this, because of the French prohibition of the *mezrag* relationship, but he gave him verbal authorization, saying, "If you get killed, it's your problem."

So the *sheikh*, the Jew, and a small company of armed Marmushans went off ten or fifteen kilometers up into the rebellious area, where there were of course no French, and, sneaking up, captured the thief-tribe's shepherd and stole its herds. The other tribe soon came riding out on horses after them, armed with rifles and ready to attack. But when they saw who the "sheep thieves" were, they thought better of it and said, "all right, we'll talk." They couldn't really deny what had happened — that some of their men had robbed Cohen and killed the two visitors — and they weren't prepared to start the serious feud with the Marmusha a scuffle with the invading party would bring on. So the two groups talked, and talked, and talked, there on the plain amid the thousands of sheep, and decided finally on five-hundred-sheep damages. The two armed Berber groups then lined up on their horses at opposite ends of the plain, with the sheep herded between them, and Cohen, in his black gown, pillbox hat, and flapping slippers, went out alone among the sheep, picking out, one by one and at his own good speed, the best ones for his payment.

So Cohen got his sheep and drove them back to Marmusha. The French, up in their fort, heard them coming from some distance ("Ba, ba, ba" said Cohen, happily, recalling the image) and said, "what the hell is that?" And Cohen said, "That is my 'ar." The French couldn't believe he had actually done what he said he had done, and accused him of being a spy for the rebellious Berbers, put him in prison, and took his sheep. In the town, his family, not having heard from him in so long a time, thought he was dead. But after a while the French released him and he came back home, but without his sheep. He then went to the Colonel in the town, the Frenchman in charge of the whole region, to complain. But the Colonel said, "I can't do anything about the matter. It's not my problem."

Quoted raw, a note in a bottle, this passage conveys, as any similar one similarly presented would do, a fair sense of how much goes into ethnographic description of even the most elemental sort — how extraordinarily "thick" it is. In finished anthropological writings, including those collected here, this fact — that what we call our data are really our own constructions of other people's constructions of what they and their compatriots are up to — is obscured because most of what we need to comprehend a particular event, ritual, custom, idea, or whatever is insinuated as background information before the thing itself is directly examined. (Even to reveal that this little drama took place in the highlands of central Morocco in 1912 — and was recounted there in 1968 — is to determine much of our understanding of it.) There is nothing particularly wrong with this, and it is in any case inevitable. But it does lead to a view of anthropological research as rather more of an observational and rather less of an interpretive activity than it really is. Right down at the factual base, the hard rock, insofar as there is any, of the whole enterprise, we are already explicating: and worse, explicating explications. Winks upon winks upon winks.

Analysis, then, is sorting out the structures of signification — what Ryle called established codes, a somewhat misleading expression, for it makes the enterprise sound too much like that of the cipher clerk when it is much more like that of the literary critic — and determining their social ground and import. Here, in our text, such sorting would begin with distinguishing the three unlike frames of interpretation ingredient in the situation, Jewish, Berber, and French, and would then move on to show how (and why) at that time, in that place, their copresence produced a situation in which systematic misunderstanding reduced traditional form to social farce. What tripped Cohen up, and with him the whole, ancient pattern of social and economic relationships within which he functioned, was a confusion of tongues.

I shall come back to this too-compacted aphorism later, as well as to the details of the text itself. The point for now is only that ethnography is thick description. What the ethnographer is in fact faced with — except when (as, of course, he must do) he is pursuing the more automatized routines of data collection — is a multiplicity of complex conceptual structures, many of them superimposed upon or knotted into one another, which are at once strange, irregular, and inexplicit, and which he must contrive somehow first to grasp and then to render. And this is true at the most down-to-earth, jungle field work levels of his activity: interviewing informants, observing rituals, eliciting kin terms, tracing property lines, censusing households . . . writing his journal. Doing ethnography is like trying to read (in the sense of "construct a reading of") a manuscript — foreign, faded, full of ellipses, incoherencies, suspicious emendations, and tendentious commentaries, but written not in conventionalized graphs of sound but in transient examples of shaped behavior.

III

Culture, this acted document, thus is public, like a burlesqued wink or a mock sheep raid. Though ideational, it does not exist in someone's head; though unphysical, it is not an occult entity. The interminable, because unterminable, debate within anthropology as to whether culture is "subjective" or "objective," together with the mutual exchange of intellectual insults ("idealist!" — "materialist!"; "mentalist!" — "behaviorist!"; "impressionist!" — "positivist!") which accompanies it, is wholly misconceived. Once human behavior is seen as (most of the time; there *are* true twitches) symbolic action — action which, like phonation in speech, pigment in painting, line in writing, or sonance in music, signifies — the question as to whether culture is patterned conduct or a frame of mind, or even the two somehow mixed together, loses sense. The thing to ask about a burlesqued wink or a mock sheep raid is not what their ontological status is. It is the same as that of rocks on the one hand and dreams on the other — they are things of this world. The thing to ask is what their import is: what it is, ridicule or challenge, irony or anger, snobbery or pride, that, in their occurrence and through their agency, is getting said.

This may seem like an obvious truth, but there are a number of ways to obscure it. One is to imagine that culture is a self-contained "super-organic"

reality with forces and purposes of its own; that is, to reify it. Another is to claim that it consists in the brute pattern of behavioral events we observe in fact to occur in some identifiable community or other; that is, to reduce it. But though both these confusions still exist, and doubtless will be always with us, the main source of theoretical muddlement in contemporary anthropology is a view which developed in reaction to them and is right now very widely held — namely, that, to quote Ward Goodenough, perhaps its leading proponent, "culture [is located] in the minds and hearts of men."

Variously called ethnoscience, componential analysis, or cognitive anthropology (a terminological wavering which reflects a deeper uncertainty), this school of thought holds that culture is composed of psychological structures by means of which individuals or groups of individuals guide their behavior. "A society's culture," to quote Goodenough again, this time in a passage which has become the *locus classicus*[8] of the whole movement, "consists of whatever it is one has to know or believe in order to operate in a manner acceptable to its members." And from this view of what culture is follows a view, equally assured, of what describing it is — the writing out of systematic rules, an ethnographic algorithm, which, if followed, would make it possible so to operate, to pass (physical appearance aside) for a native. In such a way, extreme subjectivism is married to extreme formalism, with the expected result: an explosion of debate as to whether particular analyses (which come in the form of taxonomies, paradigms, tables, trees, and other ingenuities) reflect what the natives "really" think or are merely clever simulations, logically equivalent but substantively different, of what they think.

As, on first glance, this approach may look close enough to the one being developed here to be mistaken for it, it is useful to be explicit as to what divides them. If, leaving our winks and sheep behind for the moment, we take, say, a Beethoven quartet as an admittedly rather special but, for these purposes, nicely illustrative, sample of culture, no one would, I think, identify it with

[8] A short passage that sums up an entire way of thinking.

its score, with the skills and knowledge needed to play it, with the understanding of it possessed by its performers or auditors, nor, to take care, *en passant*,[9] of the reductionists and reifiers, with a particular performance of it or with some mysterious entity transcending material existence. The "no one" is perhaps too strong here, for there are always incorrigibles. But that a Beethoven quartet is a temporally developed tonal structure, a coherent sequence of modeled sound — in a word, music — and not anybody's knowledge of or belief about anything, including how to play it, is a proposition to which most people are, upon reflection, likely to assent.

To play the violin it is necessary to possess certain habits, skills, knowledge, and talents, to be in the mood to play, and (as the old joke goes) to have a violin. But violin playing is neither the habits, skills, knowledge, and so on, nor the mood, nor (the notion believers in "material culture" apparently embrace) the violin. To make a trade pact in Morocco, you have to do certain things in certain ways (among others, cut, while chanting Quranic Arabic,[10] the throat of a lamb before the assembled, undeformed, adult male members of your tribe) and to be possessed of certain psychological characteristics (among others, a desire for distant things). But a trade pact is neither the throat cutting nor the desire, though it is real enough, as seven kinsmen of our Marmusha sheikh discovered when, on an earlier occasion, they were executed by him following the theft of one mangy, essentially valueless sheepskin from Cohen.

Culture is public because meaning is. You can't wink (or burlesque one) without knowing what counts as winking or how, physically, to contract your eyelids, and you can't conduct a sheep raid (or mimic one) without knowing what it is to steal a sheep and how practically to go about it. But to draw from such truths the conclusion that knowing how to wink is winking and knowing how to steal a sheep is sheep raiding is to betray as deep a confusion as, taking thin descriptions for thick, to identify winking with eyelid contractions or sheep raiding with chasing woolly animals out of pastures. The cognitivist fallacy — that culture consists (to quote another spokesman for the movement, Stephen Tyler) of "mental phenomena which can [he means "should"] be analyzed by formal methods similar to those of mathematics and logic" — is as destructive of an effective use of the concept as are the behaviorist and idealist fallacies to which it is a misdrawn correction. Perhaps, as its errors are more sophisticated and its distortions subtler, it is even more so.

The generalized attack on privacy theories of meaning is, since early Husserl and late Wittgenstein, so much a part of modern thought that it need not be developed once more here. What is necessary is to see to it that the news of it reaches anthropology; and in particular that it is made clear that to say that culture consists of socially established structures of meaning in terms of which people do such things as signal conspiracies and join them or perceive insults and answer them, is no more to say that it is a psychological phenomenon, a characteristic of someone's mind, personality, cognitive structure, or whatever, than to say that Tantrism,[11] genetics, the progressive form of the verb, the classification of wines, the Common Law, or the notion of "a conditional curse" (as Westermarck[12] defined the concept of *'ar* in terms of which Cohen pressed his claim to damages) is. What, in a place like Morocco, most prevents those of us who grew up winking other winks or attending other sheep from grasping what people are up to is not ignorance as to how cognition works (though, especially as, one assumes, it works the same among them as it does among us, it would greatly help to have less of that too) as a lack of familiarity with the imaginative universe within which their acts are signs. As Wittgenstein has been invoked, he may as well be quoted:[13]

We . . . say of some people that they are transparent to us. It is, however, important as regards this observation that one human being can be a complete

9French for "along the way."
10Classical Arabic of the Koran.

11An esoteric form of yoga.
12Edvard Westermarck (1862–1939) was a Finnish sociologist.
13The quotation is from *Philosophical Investigations* (1953).

enigma to another. We learn this when we come into a strange country with entirely strange traditions; and, what is more, even given a mastery of the country's language. We do not *understand* the people. (And not because of not knowing what they are saying to themselves.) We cannot find our feet with them.

IV

Finding our feet, an unnerving business which never more than distantly succeeds, is what ethnographic research consists of as a personal experience; trying to formulate the basis on which one imagines, always excessively, one has found them is what anthropological writing consists of as a scientific endeavor. We are not, or at least I am not, seeking either to become natives (a compromised word in any case) or to mimic them. Only romantics or spies would seem to find point in that. We are seeking, in the widened sense of the term in which it encompasses very much more than talk, to converse with them, a matter a great deal more difficult, and not only with strangers, than is commonly recognized. "If speaking *for* someone else seems to be a mysterious process," Stanley Cavell[14] has remarked, "that may be because speaking *to* someone does not seem mysterious enough."

Looked at in this way, the aim of anthropology is the enlargement of the universe of human discourse. That is not, of course, its only aim — instruction, amusement, practical counsel, moral advance, and the discovery of natural order in human behavior are others; nor is anthropology the only discipline which pursues it. But it is an aim to which a semiotic concept of culture is peculiarly well adapted. As interworked systems of construable signs (what, ignoring provincial usages, I would call symbols), culture is not a power, something to which social events, behaviors, institutions, or processes can be causally attributed; it is a context, something within which they can be intelligibly — that is, thickly — described.

The famous anthropological absorption with the (to us) exotic — Berber horsemen, Jewish peddlers, French Legionnaires — is, thus, essentially a device for displacing the dulling sense of familiarity with which the mysteriousness of our own ability to relate perceptively to one another is concealed from us. Looking at the ordinary in places where it takes unaccustomed forms brings out not, as has so often been claimed, the arbitrariness of human behavior (there is nothing especially arbitrary about taking sheep theft for insolence in Morocco), but the degree to which its meaning varies according to the pattern of life by which it is informed. Understanding a people's culture exposes their normalness without reducing their particularity. (The more I manage to follow what the Moroccans are up to, the more logical, and the more singular, they seem.) It renders them accessible: setting them in the frame of their own banalities, it dissolves their opacity.

It is this maneuver, usually too casually referred to as "seeing things from the actor's point of view," too bookishly as "the *verstehen*[15] approach," or too technically as "emic[16] analysis," that so often leads to the notion that anthropology is a variety of either long-distance mind reading or cannibal-isle fantasizing, and which, for someone anxious to navigate past the wrecks of a dozen sunken philosophies, must therefore be executed with a great deal of care. Nothing is more necessary to comprehending what anthropological interpretation is, and the degree to which it *is* interpretation, than an exact understanding of what it means — and what it does not mean — to say that our formulations of other peoples' symbol systems must be actor-oriented.[17]

What it means is that descriptions of Berber, Jewish, or French culture must be cast in terms of the constructions we imagine Berbers, Jews, or Frenchmen to place upon what they live through,

[14]American philosopher (b. 1926).

[15]German for "understanding."
[16]Breaking a complex system down into its minimal components ("emes").
[17]Not only other peoples': anthropology *can* be trained on the culture of which it is itself a part, and it increasingly is; a fact of profound importance, but which, as it raises a few tricky and rather special second order problems, I shall put to the side for the moment. [Geertz]

the formulae they use to define what happens to them. What it does not mean is that such descriptions are themselves Berber, Jewish, or French — that is, part of the reality they are ostensibly describing; they are anthropological — that is, part of a developing system of scientific analysis. They must be cast in terms of the interpretations to which persons of a particular denomination subject their experience, because that is what they profess to be descriptions of; they are anthropological because it is, in fact, anthropologists who profess them. Normally, it is not necessary to point out quite so laboriously that the object of study is one thing and the study of it another. It is clear enough that the physical world is not physical and *A Skeleton Key to Finnegans Wake*[18] not *Finnegans Wake*. But, as, in the study of culture, analysis penetrates into the very body of the object — that is, *we begin with our own interpretations of what our informants are up to, or think they are up to, and then systematize those* — the line between (Moroccan) culture as a natural fact and (Moroccan) culture as a theoretical entity tends to get blurred. All the more so, as the latter is presented in the form of an actor's-eye description of (Moroccan) conceptions of everything from violence, honor, divinity, and justice, to tribe, property, patronage, and chiefship.

In short, anthropological writings are themselves interpretations, and second and third order ones to boot. (By definition, only a "native" makes first order ones: it's *his* culture.)[19] They are, thus, fictions; fictions, in the sense that they are "something made," "something fashioned" — the original meaning of *fictiō* — not that they are false, unfactual, or merely "as if" thought experiments. To construct actor-oriented descriptions of the involvements of a Berber chieftain, a Jewish merchant, and a French soldier with one another in 1912 Morocco is clearly an imaginative act, not all that different from constructing similar descriptions of, say, the involvements with one another of a provincial French doctor, his silly, adulterous wife, and her feckless lover in nineteenth century France.[20] In the latter case, the actors are represented as not having existed and the events as not having happened, while in the former they are represented as actual, or as having been so. This is a difference of no mean importance; indeed, precisely the one Madame Bovary had difficulty grasping. But the importance does not lie in the fact that her story was created while Cohen's was only noted. The conditions of their creation, and the point of it (to say nothing of the manner and the quality) differ. But the one is as much a *fictiō* — "a making" — as the other.

Anthropologists have not always been as aware as they might be of this fact: that although culture exists in the trading post, the hill fort, or the sheep run, anthropology exists in the book, the article, the lecture, the museum display, or, sometimes nowadays, the film. To become aware of it is to realize that the line between mode of representation and substantive content is as undrawable in cultural analysis as it is in painting; and that fact in turn seems to threaten the objective status of anthropological knowledge by suggesting that its source is not social reality but scholarly artifice.

It does threaten it, but the threat is hollow. The claim to attention of an ethnographic account does not rest on its author's ability to capture primitive facts in faraway places and carry them home like a mask or a carving, but on the degree to which he is able to clarify what goes on in such places, to reduce the puzzlement — what manner of men are these? — to which unfamiliar acts emerging out of unknown backgrounds naturally

[18]*Finnegans Wake* is James Joyce's esoteric last novel (1939); the *Skeleton Key*, a guide to its interpretation, was written by mythology expert Joseph Campbell and popular writer Henry Morton Robinson (1961).

[19]The order problem is, again, complex. Anthropological works based on other anthropological works (Lévi-Strauss', for example) may, of course, be fourth order or higher, and informants frequently, even habitually, make second order interpretations — what have come to be known as "native models." In literate cultures, where "native" interpretation can proceed to higher levels — in connection with the Maghreb, one has only to think of Ibn Khaldun; with the United States, Margaret Mead — these matters becomes intricate indeed. [Geertz]

[20]Geertz has just summarized the plot of Gustave Flaubert's novel, *Madame Bovary* (1857), a tragedy that turns on the heroine's confusion between the romances she read as an adolescent and the humdrum provincial life in which she is immersed.

give rise. This raises some serious problems of verification, all right — or, if "verification" is too strong a word for so soft a science (I, myself, would prefer "appraisal"), of how you can tell a better account from a worse one. But that is precisely the virtue of it. If ethnography is thick description and ethnographers those who are doing the describing, then the determining question for any given example of it, whether a field journal squib or a Malinowski-sized monograph, is whether it sorts winks from twitches and real winks from mimicked ones. It is not against a body of uninterpreted data, radically thinned descriptions, that we must measure the cogency of our explications, but against the power of the scientific imagination to bring us into touch with the lives of strangers. It is not worth it, as Thoreau said, to go round the world to count the cats in Zanzibar.

V

Now, this proposition, that it is not in our interest to bleach human behavior of the very properties that interest us before we begin to examine it, has sometimes been escalated into a larger claim: namely, that as it is only those properties that interest us, we need not attend, save cursorily, to behavior at all. Culture is most effectively treated, the argument goes, purely as a symbolic system (the catch phrase is, "in its own terms"), by isolating its elements, specifying the internal relationships among those elements, and then characterizing the whole system in some general way — according to the core symbols around which it is organized, the underlying structures of which it is a surface expression, or the ideological principles upon which it is based. Though a distinct improvement over "learned behavior" and "mental phenomena" notions of what culture is, and the source of some of the most powerful theoretical ideas in contemporary anthropology, this hermetical approach to things seems to me to run the danger (and increasingly to have been overtaken by it) of locking cultural analysis away from its proper object, the informal logic of actual life. There is little profit in extricating a concept from the defects of psychologism only to plunge it immediately into those of schematicism.

Behavior must be attended to, and with some exactness, because it is through the flow of behavior — or, more precisely, social action — that cultural forms find articulation. They find it as well, of course, in various sorts of artifacts, and various states of consciousness; but these draw their meaning from the role they play (Wittgenstein would say their "use") in an ongoing pattern of life, not from any intrinsic relationships they bear to one another. It is what Cohen, the sheikh, and "Captain Dumari" were doing when they tripped over one another's purposes — pursuing trade, defending honor, establishing dominance — that created our pastoral drama, and that is what the drama is, therefore, "about." Whatever, or wherever, symbol systems "in their own terms" may be, we gain empirical access to them by inspecting events, not by arranging abstracted entities into unified patterns.

A further implication of this is that coherence cannot be the major test of validity for a cultural description. Cultural systems must have a minimal degree of coherence, else we would not call them systems; and, by observation, they normally have a great deal more. But there is nothing so coherent as a paranoid's delusion or a swindler's story. The force of our interpretations cannot rest, as they are now so often made to do, on the tightness with which they hold together, or the assurance with which they are argued. Nothing has done more, I think, to discredit cultural analysis than the construction of impeccable depictions of formal order in whose actual existence nobody can quite believe.

If anthropological interpretation is constructing a reading of what happens, then to divorce it from what happens — from what, in this time or that place, specific people say, what they do, what is done to them, from the whole vast business of the world — is to divorce it from its applications and render it vacant. A good interpretation of anything — a poem, a person, a history, a ritual, an institution, a society — takes us into the heart of that of which it is the interpretation. When it does not do that, but leads us instead somewhere else — into an admiration of its own elegance, of its author's cleverness, or of the beauties of Euclidean order — it may have its intrinsic charms; but it is something else than what the task at hand — figuring out what all that rigamarole with the sheep is about — calls for.

The rigamarole with the sheep — the sham theft of them, the reparative transfer of them, the political confiscation of them — is (or was) essentially a social discourse, even if, as I suggested earlier, one conducted in multiple tongues and as much in action as in words.

Claiming his ʿar, Cohen invoked the trade pact, recognizing the claim, the sheikh challenged the offenders' tribe; accepting responsibility, the offenders' tribe paid the indemnity; anxious to make clear to sheikhs and peddlers alike who was now in charge here, the French showed the imperial hand. As in any discourse, code does not determine conduct, and what was actually said need not have been. Cohen might not have, given its illegitimacy in Protectorate eyes, chosen to press his claim. The sheikh might, for similar reasons, have rejected it. The offenders' tribe, still resisting French authority, might have decided to regard the raid as "real" and fight rather than negotiate. The French were they more *habile* and less *dur* (as, under Mareschal Lyautey's seigniorial tutelage, they later in fact became), might have permitted Cohen to keep his sheep, winking — as we say — at the continuance of the trade pattern and its limitation to their authority. And there are other possibilities: the Marmushans might have regarded the French action too great an insult to bear and gone into dissidence themselves; the French might have attempted not just to clamp down on Cohen but to bring the sheikh himself more closely to heel; and Cohen might have concluded that between renegade Berbers and Beau Geste soldiers,[21] driving trade in the Atlas highlands was no longer worth the candle and retired to the better-governed confines of the town. This, indeed, is more or less what happened, somewhat further along, as the Protectorate moved toward genuine sovereignty. But the point here is not to describe what did or did not take place in Morocco. (From this simple incident one can widen out into enormous complexities of social experience.) It is to demonstrate what a piece of anthropological interpretation consists in: tracing the curve of a social discourse; fixing it into an inspectable form.

The ethnographer "inscribes" social discourse; *he writes it down*. In so doing, he turns it from a passing event, which exists only in its own moment of occurrence, into an account, which exists in its inscriptions and can be reconsulted. The sheikh is long dead, killed in the process of being, as the French called it, "pacified"; "Captain Dumari," his pacifier, lives, retired to his souvenirs, in the south of France; and Cohen went last year, part refugee, part pilgrim, part dying patriarch, "home" to Israel. But what they, in my extended sense, "said" to one another on an Atlas plateau sixty years ago is — very far from perfectly — preserved for study. "What," Paul Ricoeur, from whom this whole idea of the inscription of action is borrowed and somewhat twisted, asks, "what does writing fix?"

> Not the event of speaking, but the "said" of speaking, where we understand by the "said" of speaking that intentional exteriorization constitutive of the aim of discourse thanks to which the *sagen* — the saying — wants to become *Aus-sage* — the enunciation, the enunciated. In short, what we write is the *noema* ["thought," "content," "gist"] of the speaking. It is the meaning of the speech event, not the event as event.[22]

This is not itself so very "said" — if Oxford philosophers run to little stories, phenomenological ones run to large sentences; but it brings us anyway to a more precise answer to our generative question, "what does the ethnographer do?" — he writes.[23] This, too, may seem a less than startling discovery, and to someone familiar with the current "literature," an implausible one. But as the

---

[21]The brave but high-handed soldiers of the French Foreign Legion, as portrayed in the many films of that title, all based on the 1924 novel by P. C. Wren.

[22]The quotation is from Paul Ricoeur, *From Text to Action* (1988).

[23]Or, again, more exactly, "inscribes." Most ethnography is in fact to be found in books and articles, rather than in films, records, museum displays, or whatever; but even in them there are, of course, photographs, drawings, diagrams, tables, and so on. Self-consciousness about modes of representation (not to speak of experiments with them) has been very lacking in anthropology. [Geertz]

standard answer to our question has been, "He observes, he records, he analyzes" — a kind of *veni, vidi, vici* conception of the matter — it may have more deep-going consequences than are at first apparent, not the least of which is that distinguishing these three phases of knowledge-seeking may not, as a matter of fact, normally be possible; and, indeed, as autonomous "operations" they may not in fact exist.

The situation is even more delicate, because, as already noted, what we inscribe (or try to) is not raw social discourse, to which, because, save very marginally or very specially, we are not actors, we do not have direct access, but only that small part of it which our informants can lead us into understanding.[24] This is not as fatal as it sounds, for, in fact, not all Cretans are liars,[25] and it is not necessary to know everything in order to understand something. But it does make the view of anthropological analysis as the conceptual manipulation of discovered facts, a logical reconstruction of a mere reality, seem rather lame. To set forth symmetrical crystals of significance, purified of the material complexity in which they were located, and then attribute their existence to autogenous principles of order, universal properties of the human mind, or vast, a priori *weltanschauungen*,[26] is to pretend a science that does not exist and imagine a reality that cannot be found. Cultural analysis is (or should be) guessing at meanings, assessing the guesses, and drawing explanatory conclusions from the best guesses, not discovering the Continent of Meaning and mapping out its bodiless landscape.

VI

So, there are three characteristics of ethnographic description: it is interpretive; what it is interpretive of is the flow of social discourse; and the interpreting involved consists in trying to rescue the "said" of such discourse from its perishing occasions and fix it in perusable terms. The *kula*[27] is gone or altered; but, for better or worse, *The Argonauts of the Western Pacific* remains. But there is, in addition, a fourth characteristic of such description, at least as I practice it: it is microscopic.

This is not to say that there are no large-scale anthropological interpretations of whole societies, civilizations, world events, and so on. Indeed, it is such extension of our analyses to wider contexts that, along with their theoretical implications, recommends them to general attention and justifies our constructing them. No one really cares anymore, not even Cohen (well . . . maybe, Cohen), about those sheep as such. History may have its unobtrusive turning points, "great noises in a little room"; but this little go-round was surely not one of them.

It is merely to say that the anthropologist characteristically approaches such broader interpretations and more abstract analyses from the direction of exceedingly extended acquaintances with extremely small matters. He confronts the same grand realities that others — historians, economists, political scientists, sociologists — confront in more fateful settings: Power, Change, Faith, Oppression, Work, Passion, Authority, Beauty, Violence, Love, Prestige; but he confronts them in contexts obscure enough — places like Marmusha and lives like Cohen's — to take the capital letters off them. These all-too-human constancies, "those big words that make us all afraid," take a homely form in such homely contexts. But

---

[24]So far as it has reinforced the anthropologist's impulse to engage himself with his informants as persons rather than as objects, the notion of "participant observation" has been a valuable one. But, to the degree it has led the anthropologist to block from his view the very special, culturally bracketed nature of his own role and to imagine himself something more than an interested (in both senses of that word) sojourner, it has been our most powerful source of bad faith. [Geertz]

[25][Geertz] refers to the Epimenides paradox: Epimenides (ca. 600 B.C.E.) of Knossos (on Crete) reportedly said Κρῆτες αει ψευσται ("Cretans, always liars"); if what Epimenides said is true, then it must be false that Cretans always lie, and if it is false that Cretans always lie, that contradicts the statement Epimenides made. His point is not philosophical, though, but practical: that the hermeneutics of culture are not a vicious circle because we can piece together subsets of the meaning of a culture without needing to understand it in its entirety.

[26]German for "worldviews."

[27]Elaborate trading relationships among the Trobriand Islanders as described in cultural anthropologist Bronislaw Malinowski's *Argonauts of the Western Pacific* (1922).

that is exactly the advantage. There are enough profundities in the world already.

Yet, the problem of how to get from a collection of ethnographic miniatures on the order of our sheep story — an assortment of remarks and anecdotes — to wall-sized culturescapes of the nation, the epoch, the continent, or the civilization is not so easily passed over with vague allusions to the virtues of concreteness and the down-to-earth mind. For a science born in Indian tribes, Pacific islands, and African lineages and subsequently seized with grander ambitions, this has come to be a major methodological problem, and for the most part a badly handled one. The models that anthropologists have themselves worked out to justify their moving from local truths to general visions have been, in fact, as responsible for undermining the effort as anything their critics — sociologists obsessed with sample sizes, psychologists with measures, or economists with aggregates — have been able to devise against them.

Of these, the two main ones have been: the Jonesville-is-the-USA "microcosmic" model; and the Easter-Island-is-a-testing-case "natural experiment" model. Either heaven in a grain of sand,[28] or the farther shores of possibility.

The Jonesville-is-America writ small (or America-is-Jonesville writ large) fallacy is so obviously one that the only thing that needs explanation is how people have managed to believe it and expected others to believe it. The notion that one can find the essence of national societies, civilizations, great religions, or whatever summed up and simplified in so-called "typical" small towns and villages is palpable nonsense. What one finds in small towns and villages is (alas) small-town or village life. If localized, microscopic studies were really dependent for their greater relevance upon such a premise — that they captured the great world in the little — they wouldn't have any relevance.

But, of course, they are not. The locus of study is not the object of study. Anthropologists don't study villages (tribes, towns, neighborhoods . . .);

they study *in* villages. You can study different things in different places, and some things — for example, what colonial domination does to established frames of moral expectation — you can best study in confined localities. But that doesn't make the place what it is you are studying. In the remoter provinces of Morocco and Indonesia I have wrestled with the same questions other social scientists have wrestled with in more central locations — for example, how comes it that men's most importunate claims to humanity are cast in the accents of group pride? — and with about the same conclusiveness. One can add a dimension — one much needed in the present climate of size-up-and-solve social science; but that is all. There is a certain value, if you are going to run on about the exploitation of the masses in having seen a Javanese sharecropper turning earth in a tropical downpour or a Moroccan tailor embroidering kaftans by the light of a twenty-watt bulb. But the notion that this gives you the thing entire (and elevates you to some moral vantage ground from which you can look down upon the ethically less privileged) is an idea which only someone too long in the bush could possibly entertain.

The "natural laboratory" notion has been equally pernicious, not only because the analogy is false — what kind of a laboratory is it where *none* of the parameters are manipulable? — but because it leads to a notion that the data derived from ethnographic studies are purer, or more fundamental, or more solid, or less conditioned (the most favored word is "elementary") than those derived from other sorts of social inquiry. The great natural variation of cultural forms is, of course, not only anthropology's great (and wasting) resource, but the ground of its deepest theoretical dilemma: how is such variation to be squared with the biological unity of the human species? But it is not, even metaphorically, experimental variation, because the context in which it occurs varies along with it, and it is not possible (though there are those who try) to isolate the *y*'s from *x*'s to write a proper function.

The famous studies purporting to show that the Oedipus complex was backwards in the Trobriands, sex roles were upside down in Tchambuli, and the Pueblo Indians lacked aggression (it is characteristic that they were all

<hr>

[28]Geertz is misquoting William Blake's "Auguries of Innocence" (1803): "To See a World in a Grain of Sand / And a Heaven in a Wild Flower."

negative — "but not in the South"), are, whatever their empirical validity may or may not be, not "scientifically tested and approved" hypotheses.[29] They are interpretations, or misinterpretations, like any others, arrived at in the same way as any others, and as inherently inconclusive as any others, and the attempt to invest them with the authority of physical experimentation is but methodological sleight of hand. Ethnographic findings are not privileged, just particular: another country heard from. To regard them as anything more (*or anything less*) than that distorts both them and their implications, which are far profounder than mere primitivity, for social theory.

Another country heard from: the reason that protracted descriptions of distant sheep raids (and a really good ethnographer would have gone into what kind of sheep they were) have general relevance is that they present the sociological mind with bodied stuff on which to feed. The important thing about the anthropologist's findings is their complex specificness, their circumstantiality. It is with the kind of material produced by long-term, mainly (though not exclusively) qualitative, highly participative, and almost obsessively fine-comb field study in confined contexts that the mega-concepts with which contemporary social science is afflicted — legitimacy, modernization, integration, conflict, charisma, structure, . . . meaning — can be given the sort of sensible actuality that makes it possible to think not only realistically and concretely *about* them, but, what is more important, creatively and imaginatively *with* them.

The methodological problem which the microscopic nature of ethnography presents is both real and critical. But it is not to be resolved by regarding a remote locality as a world in a teacup or as the sociological equivalent of a cloud chamber. It is to be resolved — or, anyway, decently kept at bay — by realizing that social actions are comments on more than themselves; that where an interpretation comes from does not determine where it can be impelled to go. Small facts speak to large issues, winks to epistemology, or sheep raids to revolution, because they are made to.

VII

Which brings us, finally, to theory. The besetting sin of interpretive approaches to anything — literature, dreams, symptoms, culture — is that they tend to resist, or to be permitted to resist, conceptual articulation and thus to escape systematic modes of assessment. You either grasp an interpretation or you do not, see the point of it or you do not, accept it or you do not. Imprisoned in the immediacy of its own detail, it is presented as self-validating, or, worse, as validated by the supposedly developed sensitivities of the person who presents it; any attempt to cast what it says in terms other than its own is regarded as a travesty — as, the anthropologist's severest term of moral abuse, ethnocentric.

For a field of study which, however timidly (though I, myself, am not timid about the matter at all), asserts itself to be a science, this just will not do. There is no reason why the conceptual structure of a cultural interpretation should be any less formulable, and thus less susceptible to explicit canons of appraisal, than that of, say, a biological observation or a physical experiment — no reason except that the terms in which such formulations can be cast are, if not wholly nonexistent, very nearly so. We are reduced to insinuating theories because we lack the power to state them.

At the same time, it must be admitted that there are a number of characteristics of cultural interpretation which make the theoretical development of it more than usually difficult. The first is the need for theory to stay rather closer to the ground than tends to be the case in sciences more able to give themselves over to imaginative abstraction. Only short flights of ratiocination tend to be effective in anthropology; longer ones tend to drift off into logical dreams, academic bemusements with formal symmetry. The whole point of a semiotic approach to culture is, as I

[29]Geertz refers to Bronislaw Malinowski (in *Crime and Custom in Savage Society*), who argued that there was no Oedipus complex in the Trobriand Islands, Margaret Mead (in *Sex and Temperament*) who argued that sex roles were reversed in Tchambuli, and Ruth Benedict (in *Patterns of Culture*) who argued that the culture of the Zuni of New Mexico made them unaggressive. All these hypotheses have been, shall we say, stringently questioned; see his argument in note 30, that it is harder to get falsified hypotheses out of the anthropology textbooks than to get more plausible ones in.

have said, to aid us in gaining access to the conceptual world in which our subjects live so that we can, in some extended sense of the term, converse with them. The tension between the pull of this need to penetrate an unfamiliar universe of symbolic action and the requirements of technical advance in the theory of culture, between the need to grasp and the need to analyze, is, as a result, both necessarily great and essentially irremovable. Indeed, the further theoretical development goes, the deeper the tension gets. This is the first condition for cultural theory: it is not its own master. As it is unseverable from the immediacies thick description presents, its freedom to shape itself in terms of its internal logic is rather limited. What generality it contrives to achieve grows out of the delicacy of its distinctions, not the sweep of its abstractions.

And from this follows a peculiarity in the way, as a simple matter of empirical fact, our knowledge of culture . . . cultures . . . a culture . . . grows: in spurts. Rather than following a rising curve of cumulative findings, cultural analysis breaks up into a disconnected yet coherent sequence of bolder and bolder sorties. Studies do build on other studies, not in the sense that they take up where the others leave off, but in the sense that, better informed and better conceptualized, they plunge more deeply into the same things. Every serious cultural analysis starts from a sheer beginning and ends where it manages to get before exhausting its intellectual impulse. Previously discovered facts are mobilized, previously developed concepts used, previously formulated hypotheses tried out; but the movement is not from already proven theorems to newly proven ones, it is from an awkward fumbling for the most elementary understanding to a supported claim that one has achieved that and surpassed it. A study is an advance if it is more incisive — whatever that may mean — than those that preceded it; but it less stands on their shoulders than, challenged and challenging, runs by their side.

It is for this reason, among others, that the essay, whether of thirty pages or three hundred, has seemed the natural genre in which to present cultural interpretations and the theories sustaining them, and why, if one looks for systematic treatises in the field, one is so soon disappointed, the more so if one finds any. Even inventory articles are rare here, and anyway of hardly more than bibliographical interest. The major theoretical contributions not only lie in specific studies — that is true in almost any field — but they are very difficult to abstract from such studies and integrate into anything one might call "culture theory" as such. Theoretical formulations hover so low over the interpretations they govern that they don't make much sense or hold much interest apart from them. This is so, not because they are not general (if they are not general, they are not theoretical), but because, stated independently of their applications, they seem either commonplace or vacant. One can, and this in fact is how the field progresses conceptually, take a line of theoretical attack developed in connection with one exercise in ethnographic interpretation and employ it in another, pushing it forward to greater precision and broader relevance; but one cannot write a "General Theory of Cultural Interpretation." Or, rather, one can, but there appears to be little profit in it, because the essential task of theory building here is not to codify abstract regularities but to make thick description possible, not to generalize across cases but to generalize within them.

To generalize within cases is usually called, at least in medicine and depth psychology, clinical inference. Rather than beginning with a set of observations and attempting to subsume them under a governing law, such inference begins with a set of (presumptive) signifiers and attempts to place them within an intelligible frame. Measures are matched to theoretical predictions, but symptoms (even when they are measured) are scanned for theoretical peculiarities — that is, they are diagnosed. In the study of culture the signifiers are not symptoms or clusters of symptoms, but symbolic acts or clusters of symbolic acts, and the aim is not therapy but the analysis of social discourse. But the way in which theory is used — to ferret out the unapparent import of things — is the same.

Thus we are led to the second condition of cultural theory: it is not, at least in the strict meaning of the term, predictive. The diagnostician doesn't predict measles; he decides that someone has them, or at the very most *anticipates* that someone is rather likely shortly to get them. But this limitation, which is real enough, has commonly been both misunderstood and exaggerated, because it has been taken to mean that cultural interpretation is merely post facto: that, like the peasant in the old story, we first shoot the holes in the fence and then paint the bull's-eyes around them. It is hardly to be denied that there is a good deal of that sort of thing around, some of it in prominent places. It is to be denied, however, that it is the inevitable outcome of a clinical approach to the use of theory.

It is true that in the clinical style of theoretical formulation, conceptualization is directed toward the task of generating interpretations of matters already in hand, not toward projecting outcomes of experimental manipulations or deducing future states of a determined system. But that does not mean that theory has only to fit (or, more carefully, to generate cogent interpretations of) realities past; it has also to survive — intellectually survive — realities to come. Although we formulate our interpretation of an outburst of winking or an instance of sheep-raiding after its occurrence, sometimes long after, the theoretical framework in terms of which such an interpretation is made must be capable of continuing to yield defensible interpretations as new social phenomena swim into view. Although one starts any effort at thick description, beyond the obvious and superficial, from a state of general bewilderment as to what the devil is going on — trying to find one's feet — one does not start (or ought not) intellectually empty-handed. Theoretical ideas are not created wholly anew in each study; as I have said, they are adopted from other, related studies, and, refined in the process, applied to new interpretive problems. If they cease being useful with respect to such problems, they tend to stop being used and are more or less abandoned. If they continue being useful, throwing up new understandings, they are further elaborated and go on being used.[30]

Such a view of how theory functions in an interpretive science suggests that the distinction, relative in any case, that appears in the experimental or observational sciences between "description" and "explanation" appears here as one, even more relative, between "inscription" ("thick description") and "specification" ("diagnosis") — between setting down the meaning particular social actions have for the actors whose actions they are, and stating, as explicitly as we can manage, what the knowledge thus attained demonstrates about the society in which it is found and, beyond that, about social life as such. Our double task is to uncover the conceptual structures that inform our subjects' acts, the "said" of social discourse, and to construct a system of analysis in whose terms what is generic to those structures, what belongs to them because they are what they are, will stand out against the other determinants of human behavior. In ethnography, the office of theory is to provide a vocabulary in which what symbolic action has to say about itself — that is, about the role of culture in human life — can be expressed.

Aside from a couple of orienting pieces concerned with more foundational matters, it is in such a manner that theory operates in the essays collected here. A repertoire of very general, made-in-the-academy concepts and systems of concepts — "integration," "rationalization," "symbol," "ideology," "ethos," "revolution," "identity," "metaphor," "structure," "ritual," "world view," "actor," "function," "sacred," and, of course, "culture" itself — is woven into the body of thick-description ethnography in the hope of rendering mere occurrences scientifically

[30]Admittedly, this is something of an idealization. Because theories are seldom if ever decisively disproved in clinical use but merely grow increasingly awkward, unproductive, strained, or vacuous, they often persist long after all but a handful of people (though *they* are often most passionate) have lost much interest in them. Indeed, so far as anthropology is concerned, it is almost more of a problem to get exhausted ideas out of the literature than it is to get productive ones in, and so a great deal more of theoretical discussion than one would prefer is critical rather than constructive, and whole careers have been devoted to hastening the demise of moribund notions. As the field advances one would hope that this sort of intellectual weed control would become a less prominent part of our activities. But, for the moment, it remains true that old theories tend less to die than to go into second editions. [Geertz]

eloquent.[31] The aim is to draw large conclusions from small, but very densely textured facts; to support broad assertions about the role of culture in the construction of collective life by engaging them exactly with complex specifics.

Thus it is not only interpretation that goes all the way down to the most immediate observational level: the theory upon which such interpretation conceptually depends does so also. My interest in Cohen's story, like Ryle's in winks, grew out of some very general notions indeed. The "confusion of tongues" model — the view that social conflict is not something that happens when, out of weakness, indefiniteness, obsolescence, or neglect, cultural forms cease to operate, but rather something which happens when, like burlesqued winks, such forms are pressed by unusual situations or unusual intentions to operate in unusual ways — is not an idea I got from Cohen's story. It is one, instructed by colleagues, students, and predecessors, I brought to it.

Our innocent-looking "note in a bottle" is more than a portrayal of the frames of meaning of Jewish peddlers, Berber warriors, and French proconsuls, or even of their mutual interference. It is an argument that to rework the pattern of social relationships is to rearrange the coordinates of the experienced world. Society's forms are culture's substance.

VIII

There is an Indian story — at least I heard it as an Indian story — about an Englishman who, having been told that the world rested on a platform which rested on the back of an elephant which rested in turn on the back of a turtle, asked (perhaps he was an ethnographer; it is the way they behave), what did the turtle rest on? Another turtle. And that turtle? "Ah, Sahib, after that it is turtles all the way down."

Such, indeed, is the condition of things. I do not know how long it would be profitable to meditate on the encounter of Cohen, the sheikh, and "Dumari" (the period has perhaps already been exceeded); but I do know that however long I did so I would not get anywhere near to the bottom of it. Nor have I ever gotten anywhere near to the bottom of anything I have ever written about, either in the essays below or elsewhere. Cultural analysis is intrinsically incomplete. And, worse than that, the more deeply it goes the less complete it is. It is a strange science whose most telling assertions are its most tremulously based, in which to get somewhere with the matter at hand is to intensify the suspicion, both your own and that of others, that you are not quite getting it right. But that, along with plaguing subtle people with obtuse questions, is what being an ethnographer is like.

There are a number of ways to escape this — turning culture into folklore and collecting it, turning it into traits and counting it, turning it into institutions and classifying it, turning it into structures and toying with it. But they *are* escapes. The fact is that to commit oneself to a semiotic concept of culture and an interpretive approach to the study of it is to commit oneself to a view of ethnographic assertion as, to borrow W. B. Gallie's by now famous phrase, "essentially contestable."[32] Anthropology, or at least interpretive anthropology, is a science whose progress is marked less by a perfection of consensus than by a refinement of debate. What gets better is the precision with which we vex each other.

This is very difficult to see when one's attention is being monopolized by a single party to the argument. Monologues are of little value here,

[31]The overwhelming bulk of the following chapters concerns Indonesia rather than Morocco, for I have just begun to face up to the demands of my North African material which, for the most part, was gathered more recently. Field work in Indonesia was carried out in 1952–1954, 1957–1958, and 1971; in Morocco in 1964, 1965–1966, 1968–1969, and 1972. [Geertz]

[32]The phrase coined by British philosopher W. B. Gallie was "essentially contested concepts," which he defines as "concepts the proper use of which inevitably involves endless disputes about their proper uses on the part of their users" because each user "continues to maintain that the special functions which the term . . . fulfils on its behalf or in its interpretation, is the correct or proper or primary, or the only important function which the term in question can plainly be said to fulfill." See "Essentially Contested Concepts," *Proceedings of the Aristotelian Society* n.s. 56 (1955–56): 168.

because there are no conclusions to be reported; there is merely a discussion to be sustained. Insofar as the essays here collected have any importance, it is less in what they say than what they are witness to: an enormous increase in interest, not only in anthropology, but in social studies generally, in the role of symbolic forms in human life. Meaning, that elusive and ill-defined pseudoentity we were once more than content to leave philosophers and literary critics to fumble with, has now come back into the heart of our discipline. Even Marxists are quoting Cassirer; even positivists, Kenneth Burke.

My own position in the midst of all this has been to try to resist subjectivism on the one hand and cabbalism on the other, to try to keep the analysis of symbolic forms as closely tied as I could to concrete social events and occasions, the public world of common life, and to organize it in such a way that the connections between theoretical formulations and descriptive interpretations were unobscured by appeals to dark sciences. I have never been impressed by the argument that, as complete objectivity is impossible in these matters (as, of course, it is), one might as well let one's sentiments run loose. As Robert Solow[33] has remarked, that is like saying that as a perfectly aseptic environment is impossible, one might as well conduct surgery in a sewer. Nor, on the other hand, have I been impressed with claims that structural linguistics, computer engineering, or some other advanced form of thought is going to enable us to understand men without knowing them. Nothing will discredit a semiotic approach to culture more quickly than allowing it to drift into a combination of intuitionism and alchemy, no matter how elegantly the intuitions are expressed or how modern the alchemy is made to look.

The danger that cultural analysis, in search of all-too-deep-lying turtles, will lose touch with the hard surfaces of life — with the political, economic, stratificatory realities within which men are everywhere contained — and with the biological and physical necessities on which those surfaces rest, is an ever-present one. The only defense against it, and against, thus, turning cultural analysis into a kind of sociological aestheticism, is to train such analysis on such realities and such necessities in the first place. It is thus that I have written about nationalism, about violence, about identity, about human nature, about legitimacy, about revolution, about ethnicity, about urbanization, about status, about death, about time, and most of all about particular attempts by particular peoples to place these things in some sort of comprehensible, meaningful frame.

To look at the symbolic dimensions of social action — art, religion, ideology, science, law, morality, common sense — is not to turn away from the existential dilemmas of life for some empyrean realm of de-emotionalized forms; it is to plunge into the midst of them. The essential vocation of interpretive anthropology is not to answer our deepest questions, but to make available to us answers that others, guarding other sheep in other valleys, have given, and thus to include them in the consultable record of what man has said.

[33]Robert Merton Solow (b.1924), American economist who taught at Columbia and MIT, winner of the 1987 Nobel Prize in Economics.

Hayden White

b. 1928

While many of us had long suspected that our history books were fiction, it took Hayden White to demonstrate that they were actually poetry, imbued with metaphor, metonymy, and irony. White was born in Martin, Tennessee, and attended Wayne State University before taking his masters and doctoral degrees at the University of Michigan. He began teaching at Wayne State but soon moved to the

University of Rochester, where he rose to full professor and chair of the department. From 1973 to 1977 he directed the Center for the Humanities at Wesleyan University and from 1976–78 was Kenan Professor of History there. In 1978 he moved to the University of California at Santa Cruz, where he became Professor of the History of Consciousness. He is now Professor Emeritus at the University of California at Santa Cruz (History of Consciousness Program) and Professor of Comparative Literature at Stanford University. White has published almost a dozen books, but it was Metahistory: The Historical Imagination in Nineteenth-Century Europe (1973) that established his indispensability to the New Historicism, with its readings of history as both rhetoric and poetry. His other major books are Tropics of Discourse: Essays in Cultural Criticism (1978), The Content of the Form: Narrative Discourse and Historical Representation (1987), and Figural Realism: Studies in the Mimesis Effect (1999). "The Historical Text as Literary Artifact" was originally a lecture given at Yale in 1974; it first appeared in print in Clio 3, no. 3 (June 1974): 277–303. The present version is taken from Tropics of Discourse (1978).

The Historical Text as Literary Artifact[1]

One of the ways that a scholarly field takes stock of itself is by considering its history. Yet it is difficult to get an objective history of a scholarly discipline, because if the historian is himself a

[1]This essay is a revised version of a lecture given before the Comparative Literature Colloquium of Yale University on 24 January, 1974. In it I have tried to elaborate some of the themes that I originally discussed in an article, "The Structure of Historical Narrative," CLIO I (1972): 5–20. I have also drawn upon the materials of my book *Metahistory: The Historical Imagination in Nineteenth-Century Europe* (Baltimore, 1973), especially the introduction, entitled "The Poetics of History." The essay profited from conversations with Michael Holquist and Geoffrey Hartman, both of Yale University and both experts in the theory of narrative. The quotations from Claude Lévi-Strauss are taken from his *Savage Mind* (London, 1966) and "Overture to *Le Cru et le cuit*," in *Structuralism*, ed. Jacques Ehrmann (New York, 1966). The remarks on the iconic nature of metaphor draw upon Paul Henle, *Language, Thought, and Culture* (Ann Arbor, 1966). Jakobson's notions of the tropological nature of style are in "Linguistics and Poetics," in *Style and Language*, ed. Thomas A. Sebeok (New York and London, 1960). In addition to Northrop Frye's *Anatomy of Criticism* (Princeton, 1957), see also his essay on philosophy of history, "New Directions from Old," in *Fables of Identity* (New York, 1963). On story and plot in historical narrative in R. G. Collingwood's thought, see, of course, *The Idea of History* (Oxford, 1956). [White]

practitioner of it, he is likely to be a devotee of one or another of its sects and hence biased; and if he is not a practitioner, he is unlikely to have the expertise necessary to distinguish between the significant and the insignificant events of the field's development. One might think that these difficulties would not arise in the field of history itself, but they do and not only for the reasons mentioned above. In order to write the history of any given scholarly discipline or even of a science, one must be prepared to ask questions *about* it of a sort that do not have to be asked in the practice *of* it. One must try to get behind or beneath the presuppositions which sustain a given type of inquiry and ask the questions that can be begged in its practice in the interest of determining why this type of inquiry has been designed to solve the problems it characteristically tries to solve. This is what metahistory seeks to do. It addresses itself to such questions as, What is the structure of a peculiarly *historical* consciousness? What is the epistemological status of historical *explanations*, as compared with other kinds of explanations that might be offered to account for the materials with which historians ordinarily deal? What are the possible *forms* of historical representation and what are their bases? What authority can historical accounts claim as contributions to a secured knowledge of reality in general and to the human sciences in particular?

Now, many of these questions have been dealt with quite competently over the last quarter-century by philosophers concerned to define history's relationships to other disciplines, especially the physical and social sciences, and by historians interested in assessing the success of their discipline in mapping the past and determining the relationship of that past to the present. But there is one problem that neither philosophers nor historians have looked at very seriously and to which literary theorists have given only passing attention. This question has to do with the status of the historical narrative, considered purely as a verbal artifact purporting to be a model of structures and processes long past and therefore not subject to either experimental or observational controls. This is not to say that historians and philosophers of history have failed to take notice of the essentially provisional and contingent nature of historical representations and of their susceptibility to infinite revision in the light of new evidence or more sophisticated conceptualization of problems. One of the marks of a good professional historian is the consistency with which he reminds his readers of the purely provisional nature of his characterizations of events, agents, and agencies found in the always incomplete historical record. Nor is it to say that literary theorists have *never* studied the structure of historical narratives. But in general there has been a reluctance to consider historical narratives as what they most manifestly are: verbal fictions, the contents of which are as much *invented* as *found* and the forms of which have more in common with their counterparts in literature than they have with those in the sciences.[2]

[2]White's observation is anticipated by Catherine Morland, the heroine of Austen's *Northanger Abbey* (1817), who thinks it "odd that [history] should be so dull, for a great deal of it must be invention. The speeches that are put into the heroes' mouths, their thoughts and designs — the chief of all this must be invention, and invention is what delights me in other books" (Chapter 14).

Now, it is obvious that this conflation of mythic and historical consciousness will offend some historians and disturb those literary theorists whose conception of literature presupposes a radical opposition of history to fiction or of fact to fancy. As Northrop Frye has remarked, "In a sense the historical is the opposite of the mythical, and to tell the historian that what gives shape to his book is a myth would sound to him vaguely insulting."[3] Yet Frye himself grants that "when a historian's scheme gets to a certain point of comprehensiveness it becomes mythical in shape, and so approaches the poetic in its structure." He even speaks of different kinds of historical myths: Romantic myths "based on a quest or pilgrimage to a City of God of classless society"; Comic "myths of progress through evolution or revolution"; Tragic myths of "decline and fall, like the works of Gibbon and Spengler";[4] and Ironic "myths of recurrence or casual catastrophe." But Frye appears to believe that these myths are operative only in such victims of what might be called the "poetic fallacy" as Hegel, Marx, Nietzsche, Spengler, Toynbee, and Sartre — historians whose fascination with the "constructive" capacity of human thought has deadened their responsibility to the "found" data. "The historian works inductively," he says, "collecting his facts and trying to avoid any informing patterns except those he sees, or is honestly convinced he sees, in the facts themselves." He does not work "from" a "unifying form," as the poet does, but "toward" it; and it therefore follows that the historian, like any writer of discursive prose, is to be judged "by the truth of what he says, or by the adequacy of his verbal reproduction of his external model," whether that external model be the actions of past men or the historian's own thought about such actions.

What Frye says is true enough as a statement of the *ideal* that has inspired historical writing since the time of the Greeks, but that ideal presupposes an opposition between myth and history

[3]From Northrop Frye, *Anatomy of Criticism* (1957); see Frye, p. 691.

[4]*The Decline and Fall of the Roman Empire* by British historian Edward Gibbon (1737–1794) began to appear in 1776; German historian Oswald Spengler (1880–1936) wrote *The Decline of the West* (1918).

that is as problematical as it is venerable. It serves Frye's purposes very well, since it permits him to locate the specifically "fictive" in the space between the two concepts of the "mythic" and the "historical." As readers of Frye's *Anatomy of Criticism* will remember, Frye conceives fictions to consist in part of sublimates of archetypal myth-structures. These structures have been displaced to the interior of verbal artifacts in such a way as to serve as their latent meanings. The fundamental meanings of all fictions, their thematic content, consist, in Frye's view, of the "pre-generic plot-structures" or *mythoi* derived from the corpora of Classical and Judaeo-Christian religious literature. According to this theory, we understand *why* a particular story has "turned out" as it has when we have identified the archetypal myth, or pregeneric plot structure, of which the story is an exemplification. And we see the "point" of a story when we have identified its theme (Frye's translation of *dianoia*),[5] which makes of it a "parable or illustrative fable." "Every work of literature," Frye insists, "has both a fictional and a thematic aspect," but as we move from "fictional projection" toward the overt articulation of theme, the writing tends to take on the aspect of "direct address, or straight discursive writing and cease[s] to be literature." And in Frye's view, as we have seen, history (or at least "proper history") belongs to the category of "discursive writing," so that when the fictional element — or mythic plot structure — is *obviously* present in it, it ceases to be history altogether and becomes a bastard genre, product of an unholy, though not unnatural, union between history and poetry.

Yet, I would argue, histories gain part of their explanatory effect by their success in making stories out of *mere* chronicles; and stories in turn are made out of chronicles by an operation which I have elsewhere called "emplotment." And by emplotment I mean simply the encodation of the facts contained in the chronicle as components of specific *kinds* of plot structures, in precisely the way that Frye has suggested is the case with "fictions" in general.

The late R. G. Collingwood[6] insisted that the historian was above all a story teller and suggested that historical sensibility was manifested in the capacity to make a plausible story out of a congeries of "facts" which, in their unprocessed form, made no sense at all. In their efforts to make sense of the historical record, which is fragmentary and always incomplete, historians have to make use of what Collingwood called "the constructive imagination," which told the historian — as it tells the competent detective — what "must have been the case" given the available evidence and the formal properties it displayed to the consciousness capable of putting the right question to it. This constructive imagination functions in much the same way that Kant supposed the *a priori* imagination functions when it tells us that even though we cannot perceive both sides of a tabletop simultaneously, we can be certain it has *two* sides if it has one, because the very concept of *one side* entails at least *one other*. Collingwood suggested that historians come to their evidence endowed with a sense of the *possible* forms that different kinds of recognizably human situations *can* take. He called this sense the nose for the "story" contained in the evidence or for the "true" story that was buried in or hidden behind the "apparent" story. And he concluded that historians provide plausible explanations for bodies of historical evidence when they succeed in discovering the story or complex of stories implicitly contained within them.

What Collingwood failed to see was that no given set of casually recorded historical events can in itself constitute a story;[7] the most it might offer to the historian are story *elements*. The events are *made* into a story by the suppression or subordination of certain of them and the highlighting of others, by characterization, motific repetition, variation of tone and point of view,

[5] The usual translation would be "thought."

[6] Robin George Collingwood (1889–1943), British philosopher of history.

[7] Collingwood was not quite as dim as White suggests. As an idealist philosopher, he saw the constructive act in the historian's intuition of the shape of events, not in the practical act of turning that intuition into a written text.

alternative descriptive strategies, and the like — in short, all of the techniques that we would normally expect to find in the emplotment of a novel or a play. For example, no historical event is *intrinsically tragic*; it can only be conceived as such from a particular point of view or from within the context of a structured set of events of which it is an element enjoying a privileged place. For in history what is tragic from one perspective is comic from another, just as in society what appears to be tragic from the standpoint of one class may be, as Marx purported to show of the 18th Brumaire of Louis Buonaparte, only a farce from that of another class.[8] Considered as potential elements of a story, historical events are value-neutral. Whether they find their place finally in a story that is tragic, comic, romantic or ironic—to use Frye's categories—depends upon the historian's decision to *con*figure them according to the imperatives of one plot structure or *mythos* rather than another. The same set of events can serve as components of a story that is tragic *or* comic, as the case may be, depending on the historian's choice of the plot structure that he considers most appropriate for ordering events of that kind so as to make them into a comprehensible story.

This suggests that what the historian brings to his consideration of the historical record is a notion of the *types* of configurations of events that can be recognized as stories by the audience for which he is writing. True, he can misfire. I do not suppose that anyone would accept the emplotment of the life of President Kennedy as comedy, but whether it ought to be emplotted romantically, tragically, or satirically is an open question. The important point is that most historical sequences can be emplotted in a number of different ways, so as to provide different interpretations of those events and to endow them with different meanings. Thus, for example, what Michelet in his great history of the French Revolution construed as a drama of Romantic

transcendence, his contemporary Tocqueville emplotted as an ironic Tragedy.[9] Neither can be said to have had more knowledge of the "facts" contained in the record; they simply had different notions of the kind of story that best fitted the facts they knew. Nor should it be thought that they told different stories of the Revolution because they had discovered different *kinds* of facts, political on the one hand, social on the other. They sought out different kinds of facts because they had different kinds of stories to tell. But why did these alternative, not to say mutually exclusive, representations of what was substantially the same set of events appear equally plausible to their respective audiences? Simply because the historians shared with their audiences certain preconceptions about how the Revolution might be emplotted, in response to imperatives that were generally extra historical, ideological, aesthetic, or mythical.

Collingwood once remarked that you could never explicate a tragedy to anyone who was not already acquainted with the kinds of situations that are regarded as "tragic" in our culture. Anyone who has taught or taken one of those omnibus courses usually entitled Western Civilization or Introduction to the Classics of Western Literature will know what Collingwood had in mind. Unless you have some idea of the generic attributes of tragic, comic, romantic, or ironic situations, you will be unable to recognize them as such when you come upon them in a literary text. But historical situations do not have built into them intrinsic meanings in the way that literary texts do. Historical situations are not *inherently* tragic, comic or romantic. They may all be inherently ironic, but they need not be emplotted that way. All the historian needs to do to transform a tragic into a comic situation is to shift his point of view or change the scope of his perceptions. Anyway, we only think of situations as tragic or comic because these concepts are part of our generally cultural and specifically literary heritage. *How* a given historical situation is to be

<hr>

[8]White alludes to Marx's notorious remark in *The Eighteenth Brumaire of Louis Napoleon* (1852) that history always repeats itself, "the first time as tragedy, the second time as farce."

[9]Jules Michelet's *History of the French Revolution* came out 1847–53; Alexis de Tocqueville's *The Old Regime and the French Revolution* in 1856.

configured depends on the historian's subtlety in matching up a specific plot structure with the set of historical events that he wishes to endow with a meaning of a particular kind. This is essentially a literary, that is to say fiction-making, operation. And to call it that in no way detracts from the status of historical narratives as providing a kind of knowledge. For not only are the pregeneric plot structures by which sets of events can be constituted as stories of a particular kind limited in number, as Frye and other archetypal critics suggest; but the encodation of events in terms of such plot structures is one of the ways that a culture has of making sense of both personal and public pasts.

We can make sense of sets of events in a number of different ways. One of the ways is to subsume the events under the causal laws which may have governed their concatenation in order to produce the particular configuration that the events appear to assume when considered as "effects" of mechanical forces. This is the way of scientific explanation. Another way we make sense of a set of events which appears strange, enigmatic, or mysterious in its immediate manifestations is to encode the set in terms of culturally provided categories, such as metaphysical concepts, religious beliefs, or story forms. The effect of such encodations is to familiarize the unfamiliar; and in general this is the way of historiography, whose "data" are always immediately strange, not to say exotic, simply by virtue of their distance from us in time and their origin in a way of life different from our own.

The historian shares with his audience *general notions* of the *forms* that significant human situations *must* take by virtue of his participation in the specific processes of sense-making which identify him as a member of one cultural endowment rather than another. In the process of studying a given complex of events, he begins to perceive the *possible* story form that such events *may* figure. In his narrative account of how this set of events took on the shape which he perceives to inhere within it, he emplots his account as a story of a particular kind. The reader, in the process of following the historian's account of those events, gradually comes to realize that the story he is reading is of one kind rather than another:

romance, tragedy, comedy, satire, epic, or what have you. And when he has perceived the class or type to which the story that he is reading belongs, he experiences the effect of having the events in the story explained to him. He has at this point not only successfully *followed* the story; he has grasped the point of it, *understood* it as well. The original strangeness, mystery, or exoticism of the events is dispelled, and they take on a familiar aspect, not in their details, but in their functions as elements of a familiar kind of configuration. They are rendered comprehensible by being subsumed under the categories of the plot structure in which they are encoded as a story of a particular kind. They are familiarized, not only because the reader now has more *information* about the events, but also because he has been shown how the data conform to an *icon* of a comprehensible finished process, a plot structure with which he is familiar as a part of his cultural endowment.

This is not unlike what happens, or is supposed to happen, in psychotherapy. The sets of events in the patient's past which are the presumed cause of his distress, manifested in the neurotic syndrome, have been defamiliarized, rendered strange, mysterious, and threatening and have assumed a meaning that he can neither accept nor effectively reject. It is not that the patient does not *know* what those events were, does not know the facts; for if he did not in some sense know the facts, he would be unable to recognize them and repress them whenever they arise in his consciousness. On the contrary, he knows them all too well. He knows them so well, in fact, that he lives with them constantly and in such a way as to make it impossible for him to see any other facts except through the coloration that the set of events in question gives to his perception of the world. We might say that, according to the theory of psychoanalysis, the patient has overemplotted these events, has charged them with a meaning so intense that, whether real or merely imagined, they continue to shape both his perceptions and his responses to the world long after they should have become "past history." The therapist's problem, then, is not to hold up before the patient the "real facts" of the matter, the "truth" as against the "fantasy" that obsesses him. Nor is it to give him a short course in psychoanalytical theory by which to enlighten him as to the true nature of his distress by cataloguing it as a manifestation of some "complex." This is what the analyst might do in relating the patient's case to a third party, and especially to another analyst. But psychoanalytic theory recognizes that the patient will resist both of these tactics in the same way that he resists the intrusion into consciousness of the traumatized memory traces in the *form* that he obsessively remembers them. The problem is to get the patient to "reemplot" his whole life history in such a way as to change the *meaning* of those events for him and their *significance* for the economy of the whole set of events that make up his life. As thus envisaged, the therapeutic process is an exercise in the refamiliarization of events that have been defamiliarized, rendered alienated from the patient's life-history, by virtue of their overdetermination as causal forces. And we might say that the events are detraumatized by being removed from the plot structure in which they have a dominant place and inserted in another in which they have a subordinate or simply ordinary function as elements of a life shared with all other men.[10]

Now, I am not interested in forcing the analogy between psychotherapy and historiography; I use the example merely to illustrate a point about the fictive component in historical narratives. Historians seek to refamiliarize us with events which have been forgotten through either accident, neglect, or repression. Moreover, the greatest historians have always dealt with those events in the histories of their cultures which are "traumatic" in nature and the meaning of which is either problematical or overdetermined in the significance that they still have for current life, events such as revolutions, civil wars, large-scale processes such as industrialization and urbanization, or institutions which have lost their original function in a society but continue to play an important role on the current social scene. In looking at the ways in which such structures took shape or evolved, historians *refamiliarize* them, not only by providing more information about them, but also by showing how their developments conformed to one or another of the story types that we conventionally invoke to make sense of our own life-histories.

Now, if any of this is plausible as a characterization of the explanatory effect of historical narrative, it tells us something important about the *mimetic* aspect of historical narratives. It is generally maintained — as Frye said — that a history is a verbal model of a set of events external to the mind of the historian. But it is wrong to think of a history as a model similar to a scale model of an airplane or ship, a map, or a photograph. For we can check the adequacy of this latter kind of model by going and looking at the original and, by applying the necessary rules of translation, seeing in what respect the model has actually succeeded in reproducing aspects of the original. But historical structures and processes are not like these originals, we cannot go and look at them in order to see if the historian has adequately reproduced them in his narrative. Nor should we want to, even if we could, for after all it was the very strangeness of the original as it appeared in the documents that inspired the historian's efforts to make a model of it in the first place. If the historian only did that for us, we should be in the same situation as the patient whose analyst merely told him, on the basis of interviews with his parents, siblings, and childhood friends, what the "true facts" of the patient's early life were. We would have no reason to think that anything at all had been *explained* to us.

This is what leads me to think that historical narratives are not only models of past events and processes, but also metaphorical statements which suggest a relation of similitude between such events and processes and the story types that we conventionally use to endow the events of our lives with culturally sanctioned meanings. Viewed in a purely formal way, a historical narrative is not only a *reproduction* of the events reported in it, but also a *complex of symbols* which gives us directions for finding an *icon* of the structure of those events in our literary tradition.

[10]White's explanation here correlates with the ideas of Donald Spence, *Narrative Truth and Historical Truth: Meaning and Interpretation in Psychoanalysis* (1982), and Roy Schafer, *A New Language for Psychoanalysis* (1976); an entire field of narrative psychotherapy has since grown up dedicated to changing the way individuals emplot their personal stories.

I am here, of course, invoking the distinctions between sign, symbol, and icon which C. S. Peirce developed in his philosophy of language.[11] I think that these distinctions will help us to understand what is fictive in all putatively realistic representations of the world and what is realistic in all manifestly fictive ones. They help us, in short, to answer the question, What are historical representations *representations of*? It seems to me that we must say of histories what Frye seems to think is true only of poetry or philosophies of history, namely that, considered as a system of signs, the historical narrative points in two directions simultaneously: *toward* the events described in the narrative and *toward* the story type or mythos which the historian has chosen to serve as the icon of the structure of the events. The narrative itself is not the icon; what it does is *describe* events in the historical record in such a ways as to inform the reader *what to take as an icon* of the events so as to render them "familiar" to him. The historical narrative thus mediates between the events reported in it on the one side and pregeneric plot structures conventionally used in our culture to endow unfamiliar events and situations with meanings, on the other.

The evasion of the implications of the fictive nature of historical narrative is in part a consequence of the utility of the concept "history" for the definition of other types of discourse. "History" can be set over against "science" by virtue of its want of conceptual rigor and failure to produce the kinds of universal laws that the sciences characteristically seek to produce. Similarly, "history" can be set over against "literature" by virtue of its interest in the "actual" rather than the "possible," which is supposedly the object of representation of "literary" works. Thus, within a long and distinguished critical tradition that has sought to determine what is "real" and what is "imagined" in the novel, history has served as a kind of archetype of the "realistic" pole of representation. I am thinking of Frye,

Auerbach, Booth, Scholes and Kellogg, and others.[12] Nor is it unusual for literary theorists, when they are speaking about the "context" of a literary work, to suppose that this context — the "historical milieu" — has a concreteness and an accessibility that the work itself can never have, as if it were easier to perceive the reality of a past world put together from a thousand historical documents than it is to probe the depths of a single literary work that is present to the critic studying it. But the presumed concreteness and accessibility of historical milieux, these contexts of the texts that literary scholars study, are themselves products of the fictive capability of the historians who have studied those contexts. The historical documents are not less opaque than the texts studied by the literary critic. Nor is the world those documents figure more accessible. The one is no more "given" than the other. In fact, the opaqueness of the world figured in historical documents is, if anything, increased by the production of historical narratives. Each new historical work only adds to the number of possible texts that have to be interpreted if a full and accurate picture of a given historical milieu is to be faithfully drawn. The relationship between the past to be analyzed and historical works produced by analysis of the documents is paradoxical; the *more* we know about the past, the more difficult it is to generalize about it.

But if the increase in our knowledge of the past makes it more difficult to generalize about it, it should make it easier for us to generalize about the forms in which that knowledge is transmitted to us. Our knowledge of the past may increase incrementally, but our understanding of it does not. Nor does our understanding of the past progress by the kind of revolutionary breakthroughs that we associate with the development of the physical sciences. Like literature, history progresses by the production of classics, the nature of which is such that they cannot be disconfirmed or negated, in the way that the principal conceptual schemata of the sciences are. And

[11]For Peirce's distinctions among icons, indexes, and symbols, see the introduction to Structuralism to Deconstruction, p. 819.

[12]White is listing narrative theorists. For Frye, see p. 691; for Auerbach, see p. 702; for Booth, see p. 989. Robert Scholes and Robert Kellogg were co-authors of *The Nature of Narrative* (1966).

it is their nondisconfirmability that testifies to the essentially *literary* nature of historical classics. There is something in a historical masterpiece that cannot be negated, and this nonnegatable element is its form, the form which is its fiction.

It is frequently forgotten or, when remembered, denied that no given set of events attested by the historical record comprises a *story* manifestly finished and complete. This is as true as the events that comprise the life of an individual as it is of an institution, a nation, or a whole people. We do not *live* stories, even if we give our lives meaning by retrospectively casting them in the form of stories. And so too with nations or whole cultures. In an essay on the "mythical" nature of historiography, Lévi-Strauss remarks on the astonishment that a visitor from another planet would feel if confronted by the thousands of histories written about the French Revolution. For in those works, the "authors do not always make use of the same incidents; when they do, the incidents are revealed in different lights. And yet these are variations which have to do with the same country, the same period, and the same events — events whose reality is scattered across every level of a multilayered structure." He goes on to suggest that the criterion of validity by which historical accounts might be assessed cannot depend on their elements" — that is to say — their putative factual content. On the contrary, he notes, "pursued in isolation, each element shows itself to be beyond grasp. But certain of them derive consistency from the fact that they can be integrated into a system whose terms are more or less credible when set against the overall coherence of the series."[13] But his "coherence of the series" cannot be the coherence of the *chronological* series, that sequence of "facts" organized into the temporal order of their original occurrence. For the "chronicle" of events, out of which the historian fashions his story of "what really happened," already comes preencoded. There are "hot" and "cold" chronologies, chronologies in which more or fewer dates appear to demand inclusion in a full chronicle of what happened. Moreover, the dates themselves come to us already grouped into classes of dates, classes which are constitutive of putative domains of the historical field, domains which appear as problems for the historian to solve if he is to give a full and culturally responsible account of the past.

All this suggests to Lévi-Strauss that, when it is a matter of working up a comprehensive account of the various domains of the historical record in the form of a story, the "alleged historical continuities" that the historian purports to find in the record are "secured only by dint of fraudulent outlines" imposed by the historian on the record. These "fraudulent outlines" are, in his view, a product of "abstraction" and a means of escape from the "threat of an infinite regress" that always lurks at the interior of every complex set of historical "facts." We can construct a comprehensible story of the past, Lévi-Strauss insists, only by a decision to "give up" one or more of the domains of facts offering themselves for inclusion in our accounts. Our *explanations* of historical structures and processes are thus determined more by what we leave out of our representations than by what we put in. For it is in this brutal capacity to exclude certain facts in the interest of constituting others as components of comprehensible stories that the historian displays his tact as well as his understanding. The "overall coherence" of any given "series" of historical facts is the coherence of story, but this coherence is achieved only by a tailoring of the "facts" to the requirements of the story form. And thus Lévi-Strauss concludes: "In spite of worthy and indispensable efforts to bring another moment in history alive and to possess it, a clairvoyant history should admit that it never completely escapes from the nature of myth."

It is this mediative function that permits us to speak of a historical narrative as an extended metaphor. As a symbolic structure, the historical narrative does not *reproduce* the events it describes; it tells us in what direction to think about the events and charges our thought about the events with different emotional valences. The historical narrative does not *image* the things it indicates; it *calls to mind* images of the things it indicates, in the same way that a metaphor does. When a given concourse of events is emplotted as

[13]As in Levi-Strauss's spatial reinterpretation of the Oedipus myth, p. 860. The specific sources of White's quotations can be found in note 1.

a "tragedy," this simply means that the historian has so described the events as to *remind us* of that form of fiction which we associate with the concept "tragic." Properly understood, histories ought never to be read as unambiguous signs of the events they report, but rather as symbolic structures, extended metaphors, that "liken" the events reported in them to some form with which we have already become familiar in our literary culture.

Perhaps I should indicate briefly what is meant by the *symbolic* and *iconic* aspects of a metaphor. The hackneyed phrase "My love, a rose" is not, obviously, intended to be understood as suggesting that the loved one is *actually* a rose. It is not even meant to suggest that the loved one has the specific attributes of a rose — that is to say, that the loved one is red, yellow, orange, or black, is a plant, has thorns, needs sunlight, should be sprayed regularly with insecticides, and so on. It is meant to be understood as indicating that the beloved shares the *qualities* which the rose has come to *symbolize* in the customary linguistic usages of Western culture. That is to say, considered as a message, the metaphor gives directions for finding an entity that will evoke the images associated *with loved ones and roses alike* in our culture. The metaphor does not *image* the thing it seeks to characterize, *it gives directions* for finding the set of images that are intended to be associated with that thing. It functions as a symbol, rather than as a sign: which is to say that it does not give us either a *description* or an *icon* of the thing it represents, but *tells us* what images to look for in our culturally encoded experience in order to determine how we *should feel* about the thing represented.

So too for historical narratives. They succeed in endowing sets of past events with meanings, over and above whatever comprehension they provide by appeal to putative causal laws, by exploiting the metaphorical similarities between sets of real events and the conventional structures of our fictions. By the very constitution of a set of events in such a way as to make a comprehensible story out of them, the historian charges those events with the symbolic significance of a comprehensible plot structure. Historians may not like to think of their works as translations of fact into fictions; but this is one of the effects of their

works. By suggesting alternative emplotments of a given sequence of historical events, historians provide historical events with all of the possible meanings with which the literary art of their culture is capable of endowing them. The real dispute between the proper historian and the philosopher of history has to do with the latter's insistence that events can be emplotted in one and only one story form. History-writing thrives on the discovery of all the possible plot structures that might be invoked to endow sets of events with different meanings. And our understanding of the past increases precisely in the degree to which we succeed in determining how far that past conforms to the strategies of sense-making that are contained in their purest forms in literary art.

Conceiving historical narratives in this way may give us some insight into the crisis in historical thinking which has been under way since the beginning of our century. Let us imagine that the problem of the historian is to make sense of a hypothetical *set* of events by arranging them in a *series* that is at once chronologically *and* syntactically structured, in the way that any discourse from a sentence all the way up to a novel is structured. We can see immediately that the imperatives of chronological arrangement of the events constituting the set must exist in tension with the imperatives of the syntactical strategies alluded to, whether the latter are conceived as those of logic (the syllogism) or those of narrative (the plot structure).

Thus, we have a set of events

1. $a, b, c, d, e, \ldots\ldots, n,$

ordered chronologically but requiring description and characterization as elements of plot or argument by which to give them meaning. Now, the series can be emplotted in a number of different ways and thereby endowed with different meanings without violating the imperatives of the chronological arrangement at all. We may briefly characterize some of these emplotments in the following ways:

2. $A, b, c, d, e, \ldots\ldots, n$
3. $a, B, c, d, e, \ldots\ldots, n$
4. $a, b, C, d, e, \ldots\ldots, n$
5. $a, b, c, D, e, \ldots\ldots, n$

And so on.

The capitalized letters indicate the privileged status given to certain events or sets of events in the series by which they are endowed with explanatory force, either as causes explaining the structure of the whole series or as symbols of the plot structure of the series considered as a story of a specific kind. We might say that any history which endows any putatively original event (a) with the status of a decisive factor (A) in the structuration of the whole series of events following after it is "deterministic." The emplotments of the history of "society" by Rousseau in his *Second Discourse*, Marx in the *Manifesto*, and Freud in *Totem and Taboo* would fall into this category. So too, any history which endows the last event in the series (e), whether real or only speculatively projected, with the force of full explanatory power (E) is of the type of all eschatological or apocalyptical histories. St. Augustine's *City of God* and the various versions of the Joachite[14] notion of the advent of a millennium, Hegel's *Philosophy of History*, and, in general, all Idealist histories are of this sort. In between we would have the various forms of historiography which appeal to plot structures of a distinctively "fictional" sort (Romance, Comedy, Tragedy, and Satire) by which to endow the series with a perceivable form and a conceivable "meaning."

If the series were simply recorded in the order in which the events originally occurred, under the assumption that the ordering of the events in their temporal sequence itself provided a kind of explanation of why they occurred when and where they did, we would have the pure form of the *chronicle*. This would be a "naive" form of chronicle, however, inasmuch as the categories of time and space alone served as the informing interpretative principles. Over against the naive form of chronicle we could postulate as a logical possibility its "sentimental" counterpart,[15] the

ironic denial that historical series have any kind of larger significance or describe any imaginable plot structure or indeed can even be construed as a story with a discernible beginning, middle, and end. We could conceive such accounts of history as intending to serve as antidotes to their false or overemplotted counterparts (nos. 2, 3, 4, and 5 above) and could represent them as an ironic return to mere chronicle as constituting the only sense which any cognitively responsible history could take. We could characterize such histories thus:

6.   "$a, b, c, d, e . . . . , n$"

with the quotation marks indicating the conscious interpretation of the events as having nothing other than seriality as their meaning.

This schema is of course highly abstract and does not do justice to the possible mixtures of and variations within the types that it is meant to distinguish. But it helps us, I think, to conceive how events might be emplotted in different ways without violating the imperatives of the chronological order of the events (however they are construed) so as to yield alternative, mutually exclusive, and yet, equally plausible interpretations of the set. I have tried to show in *Metahistory* how such mixtures and variations occur in the writings of the master historians of the nineteenth century; and I have suggested in that book that classic historical accounts always represent attempts both to emplot the historical series adequately and implicitly to come to terms with other plausible emplotments. It is this dialectical tension between two or more possible emplotments that signals the element of critical self-consciousness present in any historian of recognizably classical stature.

Histories, then, are not only about events but also about the possible sets of relationships that those events can be demonstrated to figure. These sets of relationships are not, however, immanent in the events themselves; they exist only in the mind of the historian reflecting on them. Here they are present as the modes of relationships conceptualized in the myth, fable, and folklore, scientific knowledge, religion, and literary art, of the historian's own culture. But more importantly, they are, I suggest, immanent in the very language which the historian must use to *describe* events prior to a scientific analysis of them or a

---

[14]Referring to the followers of Gioacchino da Fiore (1135–1202), who believed that the world would have three ages, an age of the Father (corresponding to the Old Testament period), an age of the Son (beginning with the birth of Jesus and ending around 1260), and an age of the Holy Spirit (which would quickly lead to the end of Time and the beginning of Eternity).

[15]See Friedrich Schiller, "On Naïve and Sentimental Poetry," p. 300.

fictional emplotment of them. For if the historian's aim is to familiarize us with the unfamiliar, he must use figurative, rather than technical, language. Technical languages are familiarizing only *to* those who have been indoctrinated in their uses and only *of* those sets of events which the practitioners of a discipline have agreed to describe in a uniform terminology. History possesses no such generally accepted technical specific subject matter. The historian's characteristic instrument of encodation, communication, and exchange is ordinary educated speech. This implies that the only instrument that he has for endowing his data with meaning, of rendering the strange familiar, and of rendering the mysterious past comprehensible, are the techniques of *figurative* language. All historical narratives presuppose figurative characterizations of the events they purport to represent and explain. And this means that historical narratives, considered purely as verbal artifacts, can be characterized by the mode of figurative discourse in which they are cast.

If this is the case, then it may well be that the kind of emplotment that the historian decides to use to give meaning to a set of historical events is dictated by the dominant figurative mode to the language he has used to *describe* the elements of his account *prior* to his composition of a narrative. Geoffrey Hartman once remarked in my hearing, at a conference on literary history, that he was not sure that he knew what historians of literature might want to do, but he did know that to write a history meant to place an event within a context, by relating it as a part to some conceivable whole. He went on to suggest that as far as he knew, there were only two ways of relating parts to wholes, by metonymy and by synecdoche.[16] Having been engaged for some time in the study of the thought of Giambattista Vico,[17] I was much taken with this thought, because it conformed to Vico's notion that the "logic" of all "poetic wisdom" was contained in

[16]Synecdoche (a figure of speech where the part is used for the whole, or the species for the genus) is usually thought of as a specific form of metonymy (where one word is used for another associated word).

[17]Italian rhetorician and philosopher (1668–1744), author of *La Scienza nuova* (1725, 1744), which contains a vision of successive stages through which nations pass. The notion influenced both Peacock and Shelley.

the relationships which language itself provided in the four principal modes of figurative representation: metaphor, metonymy, synecdoche, and irony. My own hunch — and it is a hunch which I find confirmed in Hegel's reflections on the nature of nonscientific discourse — is that in any field of study which, like history, has not yet become disciplined to the point of constructing a formal terminological system for describing its objects, in the way that physics and chemistry have, it is the types of figurative discourse that dictate the fundamental forms of the data to be studied. This means that the *shape* of the *relationships* which will appear to be inherent in the objects inhabiting the field will in reality have been imposed on the field by the investigator in the very *act of identifying and describing* the objects that he finds there. The implication is that historians *constitute* their subjects as possible objects of narrative representation by the very language they use to *describe* them. And if this is the case, it means that the different kinds of historical interpretations that we have of the same set of events, such as the French Revolution as interpreted by Michelet, Tocqueville, Taine, and others, are little more than projections of the linguistic protocols that these historians used to *pre*figure that set of events prior to writing their narratives of it. It is only a hypothesis, but it seems possible that the conviction of the historian that he has "found" the form of his narrative in the events themselves, rather than imposed it upon them, in the way the poet does, is a result of a certain lack of linguistic self-consciousness which obscures the extent to which descriptions of events *already* constitute interpretations of their nature. As thus envisaged, the difference between Michelet's and Tocqueville's accounts of the Revolution does not reside only in the fact that the former emplotted his story in the modality of a Romance and the latter his in the modality of Tragedy; it resides as well in the tropological mode — metaphorical and metonymic, respectively — with each brought to his apprehension of the facts as they appeared in the documents.

I do not have the space to try to demonstrate the plausibility of this hypothesis, which is the informing principle of my book *Metahistory*. But I hope that this essay may serve to suggest an approach to the study of such discursive prose forms as historiography, an approach that is as old as the study of rhetoric and as new as modern linguistics. Such a study would proceed along the lines laid out by Roman Jakobson in a paper entitled "Linguistics and Poetics,"[18] in which he characterized the difference between Romantic poetry and the various forms of nineteenth-century Realistic prose as residing in the essentially metaphorical nature of the former and the essentially metonymical nature of the latter. I think that this characterization of the difference between poetry and prose is too narrow, because it presupposes that complex macrostructural narratives such as the novel are little more than projections of the "selective" (i.e., phonemic) axis of all speech acts. Poetry, and especially Romantic poetry, is then characterized by Jakobson as a projection of the "combinatory" (i.e., morphemic) axis of language. Such a binary theory pushes the analyst toward a dualistic opposition between poetry and prose which appears to rule out the possibility of a metonymical poetry and a metaphorical prose. But the fruitfulness of Jakobson's theory lies in its suggestion that the various forms of both poetry and prose, all of which have their counterparts in narrative in general and therefore in historiography too, can be characterized in terms of the dominant trope which serves as the paradigm, provided by language itself, of all significant relationships conceived to exist in the world by anyone wishing to represent those relationships in language.

Narrative, or the syntagmatic dispersion of events across a temporal series presented as a prose discourse, in such a way as to display their progressive elaboration as a comprehensible form, would represent the "inward turn" that discourse takes when it tries to *show* the reader the true form of things existing behind a merely apparent formlessness. Narrative *style*, in history as well as in the novel, would then be construed as the modality of the movement from a representation of some original state of affairs to some subsequent state. The primary *meaning* of a narrative would then consist of the destructuration of a set of events (real or imagined) originally encoded in one tropological mode and the progressive restructuration of the set

in another tropological mode. As thus envisaged, narrative would be a process of decodation and recodation in which an original perception is clarified by being cast in a figurative mode different from that in which it has come encoded by convention, authority, or custom. And the explanatory force of the narrative would then depend on the contrast between the original encodation and the later one.

For example, let us suppose that a set of experiences comes to us as a grotesque, i.e., as unclassified and unclassifiable. Our problem is to identify the modality of the relationships that bind the discernible elements of the formless totality together in such a way as to make of it a whole of some sort. If we stress the similarities among the elements, we are working in the mode of metaphor; if we stress the differences among them, we are working in the mode of metonymy. Of course, in order to make sense of any set of experiences, we must obviously identify both the parts of a thing that appear to make it up and the nature of the shared aspects of the parts that make them identifiable as a totality. This implies that all original characterizations of anything must utilize *both* metaphor and metonymy in order to "fix" it as something about which we can meaningfully discourse.

In the case of historiography, the attempts of commentators to make sense of the French Revolution are instructive. Burke decodes the events of the Revolution which his contemporaries experience as a grotesque by recoding it in the mode of irony;[19] Michelet recodes these events in the mode of synecdoche; Tocqueville recodes them in the mode of metonymy. In each case, however, the movement from code to recode is narratively described, i.e., laid out on a time-line in such a way as to make the interpretation of the events that made up the "Revolution" a kind of drama that we can recognize as Satirical, Romantic, and Tragic, respectively. This drama can be followed by the reader of the narrative in such a way as to be experienced as a progressive revelation of what the *true* nature of

[18]See Jakobson, p. 852.

[19]White is referring to *Reflections on the Revolution in France* (1791) by Edmund Burke (1729–1797), Irish literary figure and parliamentarian.

the events consists of. The revelation is not experienced, however, as a restructuring of perceptions so much as an illumination of a field of occurrence. But actually what has happened is that a set of events originally encoded in one way is simply being decoded by being recoded in another. The events themselves are not substantially changed from one account to another. That is to say, the data that are to be analyzed are not significantly different in the different accounts. What is different are the modalities of their relationships. These modalities, in turn, although they *may* appear to the reader to be based on different theories of the nature of society, politics, and history, ultimately have their origin in the figurative characterizations of the whole set of events as representing wholes of fundamentally different sorts. It is for this reason that, when it is a matter of setting different interpretations of the same set of historical phenomena over against one another in an attempt to decide which is the best or most convincing, we are often driven to confusion or ambiguity. This is not to say that we cannot distinguish between good and bad historiography, since we can always fall back on such criteria as responsibility to the rules of evidence, the relative fullness of narrative detail, logical consistency, and the like to determine this issue. But it is to say that the effort to distinguish between good and bad interpretations of a historical event such as the Revolution is not as easy as it might at first appear when it is a matter of dealing with alternative interpretations produced by historians of relatively equal learning and conceptual sophistication. After all, a great historical classic cannot be disconfirmed or nullified either by the discovery of some new datum that might call a specific explanation of some element of the whole account into question or by the generation of new methods of analysis which permit us to deal with questions that earlier historians might not have taken under consideration. And it is precisely because great historical classics, such as works by Gibbon, Michelet, Thucydides, Mommsen, Ranke, Burckhardt, Bancroft, and so on, cannot be definitely disconfirmed that we must look to the specifically literary aspects of their work as crucial, and not merely subsidiary, elements in their historiographical technique.

What all this points to is the necessity of revising the distinction conventionally drawn between poetic and prose discourse in discussion of such narrative forms as historiography and recognizing that the distinction, as old as Aristotle,[20] between history and poetry obscures as much as it illuminates about both. If there is an element of the historical in all poetry, there is an element of poetry in every historical account of the world. And this because in our account of the historical world we are dependent, in ways perhaps that we are not in the natural sciences, on the techniques of *figurative language* both for our *characterization* of the objects of our narrative representations and for the *strategies* by which to constitute narrative accounts of the transformations of those objects in time. And this because history has no stipulatable subject matter uniquely its own; it is always written as part of a contest between contending poetic figurations of what the past *might* consist of.

The older distinction between fiction and history, in which fiction is conceived as the representation of the imaginable and history as the representation of the actual, must give place to the recognition that we can only know the *actual* by contrasting it with or likening it to the *imaginable*. As thus conceived, historical narratives are complex structures in which a world of experience is imagined to exist under at least two modes, one of which is encoded as "real," the other of which is "revealed" to have been illusory in the course of the narrative. Of course, it is a fiction of the historian that the various states of affairs which he constitutes as the beginning, the middle, and the end of a course of development are all "actual" or "real" and that he has merely recorded "what happened" in the transition from the inaugural to the terminal phase. But both the beginning state of affairs and the ending one are inevitably poetic constructions, and as such, dependent upon the modality of the figurative

[20]See Aristotle, *Poetics*, chapter 9, p. 59. Since the kind of history White is considering limits itself to discussing events that are "necessary or probable" with respect to the historian's literary schema, this form of history would certainly be poetry in Aristotle's sense.

language used to give them the aspect of coherence. This implies that all narrative is not simply a recording of "what happened" in the transition from one state of affairs to another, but a progressive *redescription* of sets of events in such a way as to dismantle a structure encoded in one verbal mode in the beginning so as to justify a recoding of it in another mode at the end. This is what the "middle" of all narratives consists of.

All of this is highly schematic, and I know that this insistence on the fictive element in all historical narratives is certain to arouse the ire of historians who believe that they are doing something fundamentally different from the novelist, by virtue of the fact that they deal with "real," while the novelist deals with "imagined," events. But neither the form nor the explanatory power of narrative derives from the different contents it is presumed to be able to accommodate. In point of fact, history — the real world as it evolves in time — is made sense of in the same way that the poet or novelist tries to make sense of it, i.e., by endowing what originally appears to be problematical and mysterious with the aspect of a recognizable, because it is a familiar, form. It does not matter whether the world is conceived to be real or only imagined; the manner of making sense of it is the same.

So too, to say that we make sense of the real world by imposing upon it the formal coherency that we customarily associate with the products of writers of fiction in no way detracts from the status as knowledge which we ascribe to historiography. It would only detract from it if we were to believe that literature did not teach us anything about reality, but was a product of an imagination which was not of this world but of some other, inhuman one. In my view, we experience the "fictionalization" of history as an "explanation" for the same reason that we experience great fiction as an illumination of a world that we inhabit along with the author. In both we recognize the forms by which consciousness both constitutes and colonizes the world it seeks to inhabit comfortably.

Finally, it may be observed that if historians were to recognize the fictive element in their narratives, this would not mean the degradation of historiography to the status of ideology or propaganda. In fact, the recognition would serve as a potent antidote to the tendency of historians to become captive of ideological preconceptions which they do not recognize as such but honor as the "correct" perception of "the way things *really* are."[21] By drawing historiography nearer to its origins in literary sensibility, we should be able to identify the ideological, because it is the fictive, element in our own discourse. We are always able to see the fictive element in those historians with whose interpretations of a given set of events we disagree; we seldom perceive that element in our own prose. So, too, if we recognized the literary or fictive element in every historical account, we would be able to move the teaching of historiography onto a higher level of self-consciousness than it currently occupies.

What teacher has not lamented his inability to give instruction to apprentices in the *writing* of history? What graduate student of history has not despaired at trying to comprehend and imitate the model which his instructors *appear* to honor but the principles of which remain uncharted? If we recognize that there is a fictive element in all historical narrative, we would find in the theory of language and narrative itself the basis for a more subtle presentation of what historiography consists of than that which simply tells the student to go and "find out the facts" and write them up in such a way as to tell "what really happened."

In my view, history as a discipline is in bad shape today because it has lost sight of its origins in the literary imagination. In the interest of *appearing* scientific and objective, it has repressed and denied to itself its own greatest source of strength and renewal. By drawing historiography back once more to an intimate connection with its literary basis, we should not only be putting ourselves on guard against *merely* ideological distortions; we should be by way of arriving at that "theory" of history without which it cannot pass for a "discipline" at all.

---

[21]White alludes to the famous statement by historian Leopold von Ranke (1795–1886) in "The Purpose of a Historian": The purpose, he said, was to show "wie es eigentlich gewesen" — how things really happened.

Pierre Bourdieu

1930–2002

It is no surprise that academics should find interesting the man who attempted to demystify their own mysterious behaviors and affiliations, applying a mordant Marxist sociology to the culture of culture. Pierre Bourdieu was born in Denguin, France, and educated at the elite École Normale Superieure where he took his Agrégé in philosophy in 1954. Bourdieu taught philosophy in the provincial lycée at Moulins, then accepted a position at the University of Algiers in the closing days of French colonial possession. He moved back to Paris in 1960, becoming director of studies at the École des Hautes Études in 1964 and professor of sociology at the Collège de France in 1982. Bourdieu's many works include Outline of a Theory of Practice *(1977),* Reproduction in Education, Society and Culture *(1977; revised 1990),* Distinction: A Social Critique of the Judgment of Taste *(1987),* Homo Academicus *(1988),* The Logic of Practice *(1990),* Language and Symbolic Power *(1991),* The Field of Cultural Production: Essays on Art and Literature *(1993),* Free Exchange *(1995),* The Rules of Art: Genesis and Structure of the Literary Field *(1995),* The State Nobility: Elite Schools and the Field of Power *(1996),* On Television *(1998),* Practical Reason: On the Theory of Action *(1998),* The Weight of the World: Social Suffering in Contemporary Society *(1999, with Alain Accardo),* Masculine Domination *(2001),* The Social Structures of the Economy *(2003), and* The Science of Science and Reflexivity *(2004). Bourdieu has himself been analyzed in* Bourdieu: Critical Perspectives, *edited by Craig Calhoun, Edward LiPuma, and Moishe Postone (1993). The selection reprinted is the introduction to* Distinction: A Social Critique of the Judgment of Taste, *translated by Richard Nice.*

From *Distinction: A Social Critique of the Judgment of Taste*

INTRODUCTION

You said it, my good knight! There ought to be laws to protect the body of acquired knowledge.

Take one of our good pupils, for example: modest and diligent, from his earliest grammar classes he's kept a little notebook full of phrases.

After hanging on the lips of his teachers for twenty years, he's managed to build up an intellectual stock in trade; doesn't it belong to him as if it were a house, or money? — PAUL CLAUDEL, *Le soulier de satin*, DAY III, SCENE II[1]

Translated by Richard Nice.
[1]*The Satin Slipper* (1930) is a lengthy play (running time of 11 hours at its revival at the 2004 Edinburgh Festival) by religious poet and dramatist Paul Claudel (1868–1955).

There is an economy of cultural goods, but it has a specific logic. Sociology endeavors to establish the conditions in which the consumers of cultural goods, and their taste for them, are produced, and at the same time to describe the different ways of appropriating such of these objects as are regarded at a particular moment as works of art, and the social conditions of the constitution of the mode of appropriation that is considered legitimate. But one cannot fully understand cultural practices unless "culture," in the restricted, normative sense of ordinary usage, is brought back into "culture" in the anthropological sense, and the elaborated taste for the most refined objects is reconnected with the elementary taste for the flavors of food.

Whereas the ideology of charisma regards taste in legitimate culture as a gift of nature, scientific observation shows that cultural needs are the product of upbringing and education: surveys establish that all cultural practices (museum visits, concert-going, reading etc.), and preferences in literature, painting or music, are closely linked to educational level (measured by qualifications or length of schooling) and secondarily to social origin.[2] The relative weight of home background and of formal education (the effectiveness and duration of which are closely dependent on social origin) varies according to the extent to which the different cultural practices are recognized and taught by the educational system, and the influence of social origin is strongest — other things being equal — in "extra-curricular" and avant-garde culture. To the socially recognized hierarchy of the arts, and within each of them, of genres, schools or periods, corresponds a social hierarchy of the consumers. This predisposes tastes to function as markers of "class." The manner in which culture has been acquired lives on in the manner of using it: the importance attached to manners can be understood once it is seen that it is these imponderables of practice which distinguish the different — and ranked — modes of culture acquisition, early or late, domestic or scholastic, and the classes of individuals which they characterize (such as "pedants" and *mondains*).[3] Culture also has its titles of nobility — awarded by the educational system — and its pedigrees, measured by seniority in admission to the nobility.

The definition of cultural nobility is the stake in a struggle which has gone on unceasingly, from the seventeenth century to the present day, between groups differing in their ideas of culture and of the legitimate relation to culture and to works of art, and therefore differing in the conditions of acquisition of which these dispositions are the product.[4] Even in the classroom, the dominant definition of the legitimate way of appropriating culture and works of art favors those who have had early access to legitimate culture, in a cultured household, outside of scholastic disciplines, since even within the educational system it devalues scholarly knowledge and interpretation as "scholastic" or even "pedantic" in favor of direct experience and simple delight.

The logic of what is sometimes called, in typically "pedantic" language, the "reading" of a work of art, offers an objective basis for this opposition. Consumption is, in this case, a stage in a process of communication, that is, an act of deciphering, decoding, which presupposes practical or explicit mastery of a cipher or code. In a sense, one can say that the capacity to see (*voir*) is a function of the knowledge (*savoir*), or concepts, that is, the words, that are available to name visible things, and which are, as it were, programs for perception. A work of art has meaning and interest only for someone who possesses the cultural competence, that is, the code, into which it is encoded. The conscious or unconscious implementation of explicit or implicit schemes of perception and appreciation which constitutes pictorial or musical culture is the hidden condition for recognizing the styles characteristic of a period, a school or an author, and, more generally, for the familiarity with the internal logic of works that aesthetic enjoyment presupposes. A beholder who lacks the specific code feels lost in a chaos of sounds and rhythms, colors and lines, without rhyme or reason. Not having learnt to adopt the adequate disposition,

[4]The word *disposition* seems particularly suited to express what is covered by the concept of habitus (defined as a system of dispositions) — used later in this chapter. It expresses first the *result of an organizing action*, with a meaning close to that of words such as structure; it also designates a way of being, a habitual state (especially of the body) and, in particular, a *predisposition, tendency, propensity* or *inclination*. [The semantic cluster of "disposition" is rather wider in French than in English, but as this note—translated literally—shows, the equivalence is adequate. Translator.] P. Bourdieu, *Outline of a Theory of Practice* (Cambridge: Cambridge University Press, 1977), p. 214, n. 1. [Bourdieu]

[2]Bourdieu et al., *Un art moyen: essai sur les usages sociaux de la photographie* (Paris: Ed. de Minuit, 1965); P. Bourdieu and A. Darbel, *L'Amour de l'art: les musées et leur public* (Paris, Ed. de Minuit, 1966). [Bourdieu]

[3]Worldly, sophisticated people.

he stops short at what Erwin Panofsky calls the "sensible properties," perceiving a skin as downy or lace-work as delicate, or at the emotional resonances aroused by these properties, referring to "austere" colors or a "joyful" melody. He cannot move from the "primary stratum of the meaning we can grasp on the basis of our ordinary experience" to the "stratum of secondary meanings," i.e., the "level of the meaning of what is signified," unless he possesses the concepts which go beyond the sensible properties and which identify the specifically stylistic properties of the work.[5] Thus the encounter with a work of art is not "love at first sight" as is generally supposed, and the act of empathy, *Einfühlung*, which is the art-lover's pleasure, presupposes an act of cognition, a decoding operation, which implies the implementation of a cognitive acquirement, a cultural code.[6]

This typically intellectualist theory of artistic perception directly contradicts the experience of the art-lovers closest to the legitimate definition; acquisition of legitimate culture by insensible familiarization within the family circle tends to favor an enchanted experience of culture which implies forgetting the acquisition.[7] The "eye" is a product of history reproduced by education. This is true of the mode of artistic perception now accepted as legitimate, that is, the aesthetic disposition, the capacity to consider in and for themselves, as form rather than function, not only the works designated for such apprehension, i.e., legitimate works of art, but everything in the world, including cultural objects which are not yet consecrated — such as, at one time, primitive arts, or, nowadays, popular photography or kitsch[8] — and natural objects. The "pure" gaze is a historical invention linked to the emergence of an autonomous field of artistic production, that is, a field capable of imposing its own norms on both the production and the consumption of its products.[9] An art which, like all Post-Impressionist painting, is the product of an artistic intention which asserts the primacy of the mode of representation over the object of representation demands categorically an attention to form which previous art only demanded conditionally.

The pure intention of the artist is that of a producer who aims to be autonomous, that is, entirely the master of his product, who tends to reject not only the "programs" imposed a priori by scholars and scribes, but also—following the

[5]E. Panofsky, "Iconography and Iconology: An Introduction to the Study of Renaissance Art," *Meaning in the Visual Arts* (New York: Doubleday, 1955), p. 28. [Bourdieu]

[6]It will be seen that this internalized code called culture functions as cultural capital owing to the fact that, being unequally distributed, it secures profits of distinction. [Bourdieu]

[7]The sense of familiarity in no way excludes the ethnocentric misunderstanding which results from applying the wrong code. Thus, Michael Baxandall's work in historical ethnology enables us to measure all that separates the perceptual schemes that now tend to be applied to Quattrocento paintings and those which their immediate addressees applied. The "moral and spiritual eye" of Quattrocento man, that is, the set of cognitive and evaluative dispositions which were the basis of his perception of the world and his perception of pictorial representation of the world, differs radically from the "pure" gaze (purified, first of all, of reference to economic value) with which the modern cultivated spectator looks at works of art. As the contracts show, the clients of Filippo Lippi, Domenico Ghirlandaio or Piero della Francesca were concerned to get "value for money." They approached works of art with the mercantile dispositions of a businessman who can calculate quantities and prices at a glance, and they applied some surprising criteria of appreciation, such as the expense of the colors, which sets gold and ultramarine at the top of the hierarchy. The artists, who shared this world view, were led to include arithmetical and geometrical devices in their compositions so as to flatter this taste for measurement and calculation; and they tended to exhibit the technical virtuosity which, in this context, is the most visible evidence of the quantity and quality of the labor provided; M. Baxandall, *Painting and Experience in Fifteenth-Century Italy: A Primer in the Social History of Pictorial Style* (Oxford: Oxford University Press, 1972). [Bourdieu] Quattrocento is Italian for fifteenth century. The three mentioned painters were all of this era.

[8]Art that is pretentiously worthless.

[9]See P. Bourdieu, "Le marché des biens symboliques," *L'Année Sociologique*, 22 (1973), 49–126; and "Outline of a Sociological Theory of Art Perception," *International Social Science Journal*, 20 (Winter 1968), 589–612. [Bourdieu]

old hierarchy of doing and saying — the interpretations superimposed a posteriori on his work. The production of an "open work," intrinsically and deliberately polysemic, can thus be understood as the final stage in the conquest of artistic autonomy by poets and, following in their footsteps, by painters, who had long been reliant on writers and their work of "showing" and "illustrating." To assert the autonomy of production is to give primacy to that of which the artist is master, i.e., form, manner, style, rather than the "subject," the external referent, which involves subordination to functions — even if only the most elementary one, that of representing, signifying, saying something. It also means a refusal to recognize any necessity other than that inscribed in the specific tradition of the artistic discipline in question: the shift from an art which imitates nature to an art which imitates art, deriving from its own history the exclusive source of its experiments and even of its breaks with tradition. An art which ever increasingly contains reference to its own history demands to be perceived historically; it asks to be referred not to an external referent, the represented or designated "reality," but to the universe of past and present works of art. Like artistic production, in that it is generated in a field, aesthetic perception is necessarily historical, inasmuch as it is differential, relational, attentive to the deviations (écarts) which make styles. Like the so-called naive painter who, operating outside the field and its specific traditions, remains external to the history of the art, the "naive" spectator cannot attain a specific grasp of works of art which only have meaning — or value — in relation to the specific history of an artistic tradition. The aesthetic disposition demanded by the products of a highly autonomous field of production is inseparable from a specific cultural competence. This historical culture functions as a principle of pertinence which enables one to identify, among the elements offered to the gaze, all the distinctive features and only these, by referring them, consciously or unconsciously, to the universe of possible alternatives. This mastery is, for the most part, acquired simply by contact with works of art — that is, through an implicit learning analogous to that which makes it possible to recognize familiar faces without explicit rules or criteria — and it generally remains at a practical level; it is what makes it possible to identify styles, i.e., modes of expression characteristic of a period, a civilization or a school, without having to distinguish clearly, or state explicitly, the features which constitute their originality. Everything seems to suggest that even among professional valuers, the criteria which define the stylistic properties of the "typical works" on which all their judgements are based usually remain implicit.

The pure gaze implies a break with the ordinary attitude towards the world, which, given the conditions in which it is performed, is also a social separation. Ortega y Gasset[10] can be believed when he attributes to modern art a systematic refusal of all that is "human," i.e., generic, common — as opposed to distinctive, or distinguished — namely, the passions, emotions and feelings which "ordinary" people invest in their "ordinary" lives. It is as if the "popular aesthetic" (the quotation marks are there to indicate that this is an aesthetic "in itself" not "for itself")[11] were based on the affirmation of the continuity between art and life, which implies the subordination of form to function. This is seen clearly in the case of the novel and especially the theater, where the working-class audience refuses any sort of formal experimentation and all the effects which, by introducing a distance from the accepted conventions (as regards scenery, plot etc.), tend to distance the spectator, preventing him from getting involved and fully identifying with the characters (I am thinking of Brechtian "alienation"[12] or the disruption of plot in the

[10]José Ortega y Gasset (1883–1955), Spanish philosopher.
[11]Bourdieu alludes ironically to the existential philosophy of Jean-Paul Sartre, where the "en soi" characterizes material things, the "pour soi" transcendent consciousness.
[12]See headnote to Brecht, p. 1249.

nouveau roman).[13] In contrast to the detachment and disinterestedness which aesthetic theory regards as the only way of recognizing the work of art for what it is, i.e., autonomous, *selbständig*, the "popular aesthetic" ignores or refuses the refusal of "facile" involvement and "vulgar" enjoyment, a refusal which is the basis of the taste for formal experiment. And popular judgements of paintings or photographs spring from an "aesthetic" (in fact it is an ethos) which is the exact opposite of the Kantian aesthetic. Whereas, in order to grasp the specificity of the aesthetic judgement, Kant strove to distinguish that which pleases from that which gratifies and, more generally, to distinguish disinterestedness, the sole guarantor of the specifically aesthetic quality of contemplation,[14] from the interest of reason which defines the Good, working-class people expect every image to explicitly perform a function, if only that of a sign, and their judgements make reference, often explicitly, to the norms of morality or agreeableness. Whether rejecting or praising, their appreciation always has an ethical basis.

Popular taste applies the schemes of the ethos, which pertain in the ordinary circumstances of life, to legitimate works of art, and so performs a systematic reduction of the things of art to the things of life. The very seriousness (or naivety) which this taste invests in fictions and representations demonstrates a contrario that pure taste performs a suspension of "naive" involvement which is one dimension of a "quasi-ludic" relationship with the necessities of the world. Intellectuals could be said to believe in the representation — literature, theater, painting — more than in the things represented, whereas the people chiefly expect representations and the conventions which govern them to allow them to believe "naively" in the things represented. The pure aesthetic is rooted in an ethic, or rather, an ethos of elective distance from the necessities of the natural and social world, which may take the form of moral agnosticism (visible when ethical transgression becomes an artistic *parti pris*)[15] or of an aestheticism which presents the aesthetic disposition as a universally valid principle and takes the bourgeois denial of the social world to its limit. The detachment of the pure gaze cannot be dissociated from a general disposition towards the world which is the paradoxical product of conditioning by negative economic necessities — a life of ease — that tends to induce an active distance from necessity.

Although art obviously offers the greatest scope to the aesthetic disposition, there is no area of practice in which the aim of purifying, refining and sublimating primary needs and impulses cannot assert itself, no area in which the stylization of life, that is, the primacy of forms over function, of manner over matter, does not produce the same effects. And nothing is more distinctive, more distinguished, than the capacity to confer aesthetic status on objects that are banal or even "common" (because the "common" people make them their own, especially for aesthetic purposes), or the ability to apply the principles of a "pure" aesthetic to the most everyday choices of everyday life, e.g., in cooking, clothing or decoration, completely reversing the popular disposition which annexes aesthetics to ethics.

In fact, through the economic and social conditions which they presuppose, the different ways of relating to realities and fictions, of believing in fictions and the realities they simulate, with more or less distance and detachment, are very closely linked to the different possible positions in social space and, consequently, bound up with the systems of dispositions (habitus) characteristic of the different classes and class fractions. Taste classifies, and it classifies the classifier. Social subjects, classified by their classifications, distinguish themselves by the distinctions they make, between the beautiful and the ugly, the distinguished and the vulgar, in which their position in the objective classifications is expressed or

---

[13]Postmodern fiction by Alain Robbe-Grillet, Michel Butor, and others.

[14]See Kant, p. 247.

[15]Inclination, disposition.

betrayed. And statistical analysis does indeed show that oppositions similar in structure to those found in cultural practices also appear in eating habits. The antithesis between quantity and quality, substance and form, corresponds to the opposition — linked to different distances from necessity — between the taste of necessity, which favors the most "filling" and most economical foods, and the taste of liberty — or luxury — which shifts the emphasis to the manner (of presenting, serving, eating etc.) and tends to use stylized forms to deny function.

The science of taste and of cultural consumption begins with a transgression that is in no way aesthetic: it has to abolish the sacred frontier which makes legitimate culture a separate universe, in order to discover the intelligible relations which unite apparently incommensurable "choices," such as preferences in music and food, painting and sport, literature and hairstyle. This barbarous reintegration of aesthetic consumption into the world of ordinary consumption abolishes the opposition, which has been the basis of high aesthetics since Kant, between the "taste of sense" and the "taste of reflection," and between facile pleasure, pleasure reduced to a pleasure of the senses, and pure pleasure, pleasure purified of pleasure, which is predisposed to become a symbol of moral excellence and a measure of the capacity for sublimation which defines the truly human man. The culture which results from this magical division is sacred. Cultural consecration does indeed confer on the objects, persons and situations it touches, a sort of ontological promotion akin to a transubstantiation. Proof enough of this is found in the two following quotations, which might almost have been written for the delight of the sociologist:

"What struck me most is this: nothing could be obscene on the stage of our premier theater, and the ballerinas of the Opera, even as naked dancers, sylphs, sprites or Bacchae, retain an inviolable purity."[16]

"There are obscene postures: the simulated intercourse which offends the eye. Clearly, it is impossible to approve, although the interpolation of such gestures in dance routines does give them a symbolic and aesthetic quality which is absent from the intimate scenes the cinema daily flaunts before its spectators' eyes. . . . As for the nude scene, what can one say, except that it is brief and theatrically not very effective? I will not say it is chaste or innocent, for nothing commercial can be so described. Let us say it is not shocking, and that the chief objection is that it serves as a box-office gimmick. . . . In *Hair*, the nakedness fails to be symbolic."[17]

The denial of lower, coarse, vulgar, venal, servile — in a word, natural — enjoyment, which constitutes the sacred sphere of culture, implies an affirmation of the superiority of those who can be satisfied with the sublimated, refined, disinterested, gratuitous, distinguished pleasures forever closed to the profane. That is why art and cultural consumption are predisposed, consciously and deliberately or not, to fulfil a social function of legitimating social differences.

[16]O. Merlin, "Mlle. Thibon dans la vision de Marguerite," *Le Monde*, 9 December 1965. [Bourdieu]
[17]F. Chenique, *"Hair* est-il immoral?" *Le Monde*, 28 January 1970. [Bourdieu]

Stuart Hall

b. 1932

One of the most important figures in the development of contemporary cultural studies as a discipline, Stuart Hall was born in Kingston, Jamaica, in 1932. He moved to Bristol with his mother at age nineteen and became a Rhodes scholar at Oxford University. He received his M.A. from Merton College. With E. P. Thompson, Raphael Samuel, Ralph Miliband, and Raymond Williams, Hall launched two radical leftist journals, The New Reasoner *and* New Left Review, *where he would publish many innovative essays that helped to guide the future of British cultural studies. In 1964, he co-authored* The Popular Arts, *a work that attracted the attention of Richard Hoggart, who invited Hall to direct the Centre for Contemporary Cultural Studies at the University of Birmingham. During this fruitful period, he wrote* Situating Marx: Evaluations and Departures *(1972),* Encoding and Decoding in the Television Discourse *(1973),* Reading of Marx's 1857 Introduction to the Grundrisse *(1973) and* Policing the Crisis *(1978). A post-Gramscian cultural theorist, Hall was a developer of reception theory, which views the audience of a text as complicit in interpretation, rather than a passive recipient. Although Hall agrees with other cultural theorists that mass media's signification system most often reflects the ideologies of the ruling class, he argues that it is also important to study the active, interpretive responses of the people who receive these media. In 1979, Hall became a professor of sociology at the Open University, where he remained until his retirement in 1997. His later works include* The Hard Road to Renewal *(1988),* Resistance Through Rituals *(1989),* Modernity and Its Future *(1992),* The Formation of Modernity *(1992),* Questions of Cultural Identity *(1996),* Cultural Representations and Signifying Practices *(1997), and* Visual Cultural *(1999). Hall currently sits on the Runnymede Trust's commission on the future of multiethnic Britain. The following article, "Cultural Studies: Two Paradigms" was originally published in the journal* Media, Culture, and Society *in 1980.*

Cultural Studies: Two Paradigms

In serious, critical intellectual work, there are no "absolute beginnings" and few unbroken continuities. Neither the endless unwinding of "tradition," so beloved in the History of Ideas, nor the absolutism of the "epistemological rupture," punctuating Thought into its "false" and "correct" parts, once favored by the Althussereans,[1] will do. What we find, instead, is an untidy but characteristic unevenness of development. What is important are the significant *breaks* — where old lines of thought are disrupted, older constellations displaced, and elements, old and new, are regrouped around a different set of premises and themes. Changes in a problematic[2] do significantly transform the nature of the questions asked, the forms in which they are proposed, and the manner in which they can be adequately answered. Such shifts in perspective reflect not only the results of an internal intellectual labor, but the manner in which real historical developments and transformations are appropriated in thought, and provide Thought, not with its guarantee of "correctness" but with its fundamental orientations, its conditions of existence. It is because of this complex articulation between thinking and historical reality, reflected in the social categories of thought, and the continuous dialectic between "knowledge" and "power," that the breaks are worth recording.

Cultural Studies, as a distinctive problematic, emerges from one such moment, in the mid-1950s. It was certainly not the first time that its characteristic questions had been put on the table.

[1]See p. 1263.
[2]Here (and elsewhere) this word is an anglicization of the French noun *problematique*, which means "the complex of issues associated with a topic, considered collectively."

Quite the contrary. The two books which helped to stake out the new terrain — [Richard] Hoggart's *Uses of Literacy* [1957] and [Raymond] Williams's *Culture and Society* [1958] — were both, in different ways, works (in part) of recovery. Hoggart's book took its reference from the "cultural debate," long sustained in the arguments around "mass society" and in the tradition of work identified with [F. R.] Leavis and *Scrutiny. Culture and Society* reconstructed a long tradition which Williams defined as consisting, in sum, of "a record of a number of important and continuing reactions to . . . changes in our social, economic and political life" and offering "a special kind of map by means of which the nature of the changes can be explored" (p.16). The books looked, at first, simply like updating of these earlier concerns, with reference to the postwar world. Retrospectively, their "breaks" with the traditions of thinking in which they were situated seem as important, if not more so, than their continuity with them. The *Uses of Literacy* did set out — much in the spirit of "practical criticism" — to "read" working-class culture for the values and meanings embodied in its patterns and arrangements: as if they were certain kinds of "texts." But the application of this method to a living culture, and the rejection of the terms of the "cultural debate" (polarized around the high/low culture distinction) was a thoroughgoing departure. *Culture and Society* — in one and the same movement — constituted a tradition (*the* "culture-and-society" tradition), defined its "unity" (not in terms of common positions but in its characteristic concerns and the idiom of its inquiry), itself made a distinctive modern contribution to it — *and* wrote its epitaph. The Williams book which succeeded it — *The Long Revolution* — clearly indicated that the "culture-and-society" mode of reflection could only be completed and developed by moving somewhere else — to a significantly different kind of analysis. The very difficulty of some of the writing in *The Long Revolution* — with its attempt to "theorize" on the back of a tradition resolutely empirical and particularist in its idiom of thought, the experiential "thickness" of its concepts, and the generalizing movement of argument in it — stems, in part, from this determination to *move on* (Williams's work, right through to the most recent *Politics and Letters*, is exemplary precisely in its sustained developmentalism). The "good" and the "bad" parts of *The Long Revolution* both arise from its status as a work "of the break." The same could be said of E. P. Thompson's *Making of the English Working Class*, which belongs decisively to this "moment," even though, chronologically, it appeared somewhat later [1963]. It, too, had been "thought" within certain distinctive historical traditions: English Marxist historiography, economic and "labor" history. But in its foregrounding of the questions of culture consciousness and experience, and its accent on agency, it also made a decisive break: with a certain kind of technological evolutionism, with a reductive economism and an organizational determinism. Between them, these three books constituted the caesura out of which — among other things — "Cultural Studies" emerged.

They were, of course, seminal and formative texts. They were not, in any sense, "textbooks" for the founding of a new academic subdiscipline: nothing could have been further from their intrinsic impulse. Whether historical or contemporary in focus, they were, themselves, focused *by*, organized through and constituted responses to, the immediate pressures of the time and society in which they were written. They not only took "culture" seriously — as a dimension without which historical transformations, past and present, simply could not adequately be thought. They were, themselves, "cultural" in the *Culture and Society* sense. They forced on their readers' attention the proposition that "concentrated in the word *culture* are questions directly raised by the great historical changes which the changes in industry, democracy, and class, in their own way, represent, and to which the changes in art are a closely related response" (p. 16). This was a question for the 1960s and 70s as well as the 1860s and 70s. And this is perhaps the point to note that this line of thinking was roughly coterminous with what has been called the "agenda" of the early New Left, to which these writers, in one sense or another, belonged, and whose texts these were. This connection placed the "politics of intellectual work" squarely at the center of Cultural Studies from the beginning — a concern from which, fortunately, it has never been, and can never be, freed. In a deep sense, the "settling of accounts" in *Culture and Society*, the first part of *The Long Revolution*, Hoggart's densely particular, concrete study of some aspects of working-class culture and Thompson's historical reconstruction of the formation of a class culture and popular traditions in the 1790–1830 period formed, between them, the break, and defined the space from which a new area of study and practice opened. In terms of intellectual bearings and emphases, this was — if ever such a thing can be found — Cultural Studies' moment of "re-founding." The institutionalization of Cultural Studies — first, in the Centre at Birmingham, and then in courses and publications from a variety of sources and places — with its characteristic gains and losses, belongs to the 1960s and later.

"Culture" was the site of the convergence. But what definitions of this core concept emerged from this body of work? And, since this line of thinking has decisively shaped Cultural Studies, and represents the most formative *indigenous* or "native" tradition, around what space were its concerns and concepts unified? The fact is that no single, unproblematic definition of "culture" is to be found here. The concept remains a complex one — a site of convergent interests, rather than a logically or conceptually clarified idea. This "richness" is an area of continuing tension and difficulty in the field. It might be useful, therefore, briefly to resume the characteristic stresses and emphases through which the concept has arrived at its present state of (in)-determinacy. (The characterizations which follow are, necessarily crude and over-simplified, synthesizing rather than carefully analytic.) Two main problematics only are discussed. Two rather different ways of conceptualizing "culture" can be drawn out of the many suggestive formulations in Raymond Williams's *Long Revolution*. The first relates "culture" to the sum of the available descriptions through which societies make sense of and reflect their common experiences. This definition takes up the earlier stress on "ideas," but subjects it to a thorough reworking. The conception of "culture" is itself democratized and socialized. It no longer consists of the sum of the "best that has been thought and said," regarded as the summits of an achieved civilization — that ideal of perfection to which, in earlier usage, all

aspired. Even "art" — assigned in the earlier framework a privileged position, as touchstone of the highest values of civilization — is now redefined as only one, special form of a general social process: the giving and taking of meanings, and the slow development of "common" meanings — a common culture: "culture," in this special sense, "is ordinary" (to borrow the title of one of Williams's earlier attempts to make his general position more widely accessible). If even the highest, most refined of descriptions offered in works of literature are also "part of the general process which creates conventions and institutions, through which the meanings that are valued by the community are shared and made active" (p. 55), then there is no way in which this process can be hived off or distinguished or set apart from the other practices of the historical process: "Since our way of seeing things is literally our way of living, the process of communication is in fact the process of community: the sharing of common meanings, and thence common activities and purposes; the offering, reception and comparison of new meanings, leading to tensions and achievements of growth and change" (p. 55). Accordingly, there is no way in which the communication of descriptions, understood in this way, can be set aside and compared externally with other things. "If the art is part of society, there is no solid whole, outside it, to which, by the form of our question, we concede priority. The art is there, as an activity, with the production, the trading, the politics, the raising of families. To study the relations adequately we must study them actively, seeing all activities as particular and contemporary forms of human energy."

If this first emphasis takes up and reworks the connotation of the term "culture" with the domain of "ideas," the second emphasis is more deliberately anthropological, and emphasizes that aspect of "culture" which refers to social *practices*. It is from this second emphasis that the somewhat simplified definition — "culture is a whole way of life" — has been rather too neatly abstracted. Williams did relate this aspect of the concept to the more "documentary" — that is, descriptive, even ethnographic — usage of the term. But the earlier definition seems to me the more central one, into which "way of life" is integrated. The important point in the argument rests on the active and indissoluble relationships between elements or social practices normally separated out. It is in *this* context that the "theory of culture" is defined as "the study of relationships between elements in a whole way of life." "Culture" is not *a* practice; nor is it simply the descriptive sum of the "mores and folkways" of societies — as it tended to become in certain kinds of anthropology. It is threaded through *all* social practices, and is the sum of their interrelationship. The question of what, then, is studied, and how, resolves itself. The "culture" is those patterns of organization, those characteristic forms of human energy which can be discovered as revealing themselves — in "unexpected identities and correspondence" as well as in "discontinuities of an unexpected kind" (p. 63) — within or underlying *all* social practices. The analysis of culture is, then, "the attempt to discover the nature of the organization which is the complex of these relationships." It begins with "the discovery of patterns of a characteristic kind." One will discover them, not in the art, production, trading, politics, the raising of families, treated as separate activities, but through "studying a general organization in a particular example" (p. 61). Analytically, one must study "the relationships between these patterns." The purpose of the analysis is to grasp how the interactions between all these practices and patterns are lived and experienced as a whole, in any particular period. This is its "structure of feeling."

It is easier to see what Williams was getting at, and why he was pushed along this path, if we understand what were the problems he addressed, and what pitfalls he was trying to avoid. This is particularly necessary because *The Long Revolution* (like much of Williams's work) carries on a submerged, almost "silent" dialogue with alternative positions, which are not always as clearly identified as one would wish. There is a clear engagement with the "idealist" and "civilizing" definitions of culture — both the equation of "culture" with *ideas*, in the idealist tradition; and the assimilation of culture to an *ideal*, prevalent in the elitist terms of the "cultural debate." But there is also a more extended engagement with certain kinds of Marxism, against which Williams's definitions are consciously pitched.

He is arguing against the literal operations of the base-superstructure metaphor, which in classical Marxism ascribed the domain of ideas and of meanings to the "superstructures," themselves conceived as merely reflective of and determined in some simple fashion by "the base," without a social effectivity of their own. That is to say, his argument is constructed against a vulgar materialism and an economic determinism. He offers, instead, a radical interactionism: in effect, the interaction of all practices in and with one another, skirting the problem of determinacy. The distinction between practices is overcome by seeing them all as variant forms of *praxis* — of a general human activity and energy. The underlying patterns which distinguish the complex of practices in any specific society at any specific time are the characteristic "forms of its organization" which underlie them all, and which can therefore be traced in each.

There have been several, radical revisions of this early position: and each has contributed much to the redefinition of what Cultural Studies is and should be. We have acknowledged already the exemplary nature of Williams's project, in constantly rethinking and revising older arguments — in going on thinking. Nevertheless, one is struck by a marked line of continuity through these seminal revisions. One such moment is the occasion of his recognition of Lucien Goldmann's work,[3] and through him, of the array of Marxist thinkers who had given particular attention to superstructural forms and whose work began, for the first time, to appear in English translation in the mid-1960s. The contrast between the alternative Marxist traditions which sustained writers like Goldmann and Lukács, as compared with Williams's isolated position and the impoverished Marxist tradition he had to draw on, is sharply delineated. But the points of convergence — both what they are against, and what they are about — are identified in ways which are not altogether out of line with his earlier arguments. Here is the negative, which he sees as linking his work to Goldmann's: "I came to believe that I had to give up, or at least to

[3]See the introduction to Marxist Criticism where "genetic structuralism" is discussed, p. 1205.

leave aside, what I knew as the Marxist tradition: to attempt to develop a theory of social totality; to see the study of culture as the study of relations between elements in a whole way of life; to find ways of studying structure . . . which could stay in touch with and illuminate particular artworks and forms, but also forms and relations of more general social life; to replace the formula of base and superstructure with the more active idea of a field of mutually if also unevenly determining forces" (*NLR* [*New Left Review*] 67, May–June 1971). And here is the positive — the point where the convergence is marked between Williams's "structure of feeling" and Goldmann's "genetic structuralism": "I found in my own work that I had to develop the idea of a structure of feeling. . . . But then I found Goldmann beginning . . . from a concept of structure which contained, in itself, a relation between social and literary facts. This relation, he insisted, was not a matter of content, but of mental structures: 'categories which simultaneously organize the empirical consciousness of a particular social group, and the imaginative world created by the writer.' By definition, these structures are not individually but collectively created." The stress there on the interactivity of practices and on the underlying totalities, and the homologies between them, is characteristic and significant. "A correspondence of content between a writer and his world is less significant than this correspondence of organization, of structure."

A second such "moment" is the point where Williams really takes on board E. P. Thompson's critique of *The Long Revolution* (cf. the review in *NLR* 9 and 10) — that no "whole way of life" is without its dimension of struggle and confrontation between opposed *ways* of life — and attempts to rethink the key issues of determination and domination via Gramsci's concept of "hegemony." This essay ("Base and Superstructure," *NLR* 82 1973) is a seminal one, especially in its elaboration of dominant, residual and emergent cultural practices, and its return to the problematic of determinacy as "limits and pressures."[4] Nonetheless, the earlier emphases recur, with force: "we cannot separate literature and art from other kinds of social practice, in such a way as to make them

[4]See Raymond Williams, p. 1272.

subject to quite special and distinct laws." And, "no mode of production, and therefore no dominant society or order of society, and therefore no dominant culture, in reality exhausts human practice, human energy, human intention." And this note is carried forward — indeed, it is radically accented — in Williams's most sustained and succinct recent statement of his position: the masterly condensations of *Marxism and Literature*. Against the structuralist emphasis on the specificity and "autonomy" of practices, and their analytic separation of societies into their discrete instances, Williams's stress is on "constitutive activity" in general, on "sensuous human activity, as practice," from Marx's first "thesis" on Feuerbach; on different practices conceived as a "whole indissoluble practice"; on totality.[5] "Thus, contrary to one development in Marxism, it is not 'the base' and 'the superstructure' that need to be studied, but specific and indissoluble real processes, within which the decisive relationship, from a Marxist point of view, is that expressed by the complex idea of 'determination'"(*M & L*, pp. 30–31, 82).

At one level, Williams's and Thompson's work can only be said to converge around the terms of the same problematic through the operation of a violent and schematically dichotomous theorization. The organizing terrain of Thompson's work — classes as relations, popular struggle, and historical forms of consciousness, class cultures in their historical particularity — is foreign to the more reflective and "generalizing" mode in which Williams typically works. And the dialogue between them begins with a very sharp encounter. The review of *The Long Revolution*, which Thompson undertook, took Williams sharply to task for the evolutionary way in which culture as a "whole way of life" had been conceptualized; for his tendency to absorb conflicts between class cultures into the terms of an extended

[5]Marx's first "Thesis on Feuerbach" (1845) runs, in part: "The chief defect of all hitherto existing materialism (that of Feuerbach included) is that the thing, reality, sensuousness, is conceived only in the form of the object or of contemplation, but not as sensuous human activity, practice, not subjectively. Hence, in contradistinction to materialism, the active side was developed abstractly by idealism — which, of course, does not know real, sensuous activity as such."

"conversation"; for his impersonal tone — above the contending classes, as it were; and for the imperializing sweep of his concept of "culture" (which, heterogeneously, swept everything into its orbit because it was the study of the interrelationships between the forms of energy and organization underlying *all* practices. But wasn't this — Thompson asked — where History came in?). Progressively, we can see how Williams has persistently rethought the terms of his original paradigm to take these criticisms into account — though this is accomplished (as it so frequently is in Williams) obliquely: via a particular appropriation of Gramsci, rather than in a more direct modification.

Thompson also operates with a more "classical" distinction than Williams, between "social being" and "social consciousness" (the terms he infinitely prefers, from Marx, to the more fashionable "base and superstructure"). Thus, where Williams insists on the absorption of all practices into the totality of "real, indissoluble practice," Thompson does deploy an older distinction between what is "culture" and what is "not culture." "Any theory of culture must include the concept of the dialectical interaction between culture and something that is *not* culture." Yet the definition of culture is not, after all, so far removed from Williams's: "We must suppose the raw material of life experience to be at one pole, and all the infinitely complex human disciplines and systems, articulate and inarticulate, formalized in institutions or dispersed in the least formal ways, which 'handle,' transmit or distort this raw material to be at the other." Similarly, with respect to the commonality of "practice" which underlies all the distinct practices: "It is the active process — which is at the same time the process through which men make their history — that I am insisting upon" (*NLR* 9, p. 33, 1961). And the two positions come close together around — again — certain distinctive negatives and positives. Negatively, against the "base/superstructure" metaphor, and a reductionist or "economistic" definition of determinacy. On the first: "The dialectical intercourse between social being and social consciousness — or between 'culture' and intercourse between social being and social consciousness — or between 'culture' and '*not*

culture' — is at the heart of any comprehension of the historical process within the Marxist tradition. . . . The tradition inherits a dialectic that is right, but the particular mechanical metaphor through which it is expressed is wrong. This metaphor from constructional engineering . . . must in any case be inadequate to describe the flux of conflict, the dialectic of a changing social process. . . . All the metaphors which are commonly offered have a tendency to lead the mind into schematic modes and away from the interaction of being-consciousness." And on "reductionism": "Reductionism is a lapse in historical logic by which political or cultural events are 'explained' in terms of the class affiliations of the actors. . . . But the mediation between 'interest' and 'belief' was not through Nairn's 'complex of superstructures' but through the people themselves" ("Peculiarities of the English," *Social Register*, 1965, pp. 351–352). And, more positively — a simple statement which may be taken as defining virtually the whole of Thompson's historical work, from *The Making* to *Whigs and Hunters*, *The Poverty of Theory* and beyond — "capitalist society was founded upon forms of exploitation which are simultaneously economic, moral and cultural. Take up the essential defining productive relationship . . . and turn it round, and it reveals itself now in one aspect (wage-labor), now in another (an acquisitive ethos), and now in another (the alienation of such intellectual faculties as are not required by the worker in his productive role)" (ibid., p. 356).

Here, then, despite the many significant differences, is the outline of one significant line of thinking in Cultural Studies — some would say, *the* dominant paradigm. It stands opposed to the residual and merely reflective role assigned to "the cultural." In its different ways, it conceptualizes culture as interwoven with all social practices; and those practices, in turn, as a common form of human activity: sensuous human praxis, the activity through which men and women make history. It is opposed to the base-superstructure way of formulating the relationship between ideal and material forces, especially where the "base" is defined as the determination by "the economic" in any simple sense. It prefers the wider formulation — the dialectic between social being and social consciousness: neither separable into its distinct poles (in some alternative formulations, the dialectic between "culture" and "non-culture"). It defines "culture" as *both* the meanings and values which arise amongst distinctive social groups and classes, on the basis of their given historical conditions and relationships, through which they "handle" and respond to the conditions of existence; *and* as the lived traditions and practices through which those "understandings" are expressed and in which they are embodied. Williams brings together these two aspects — definitions and ways of life — around the concept of "culture" itself. Thompson brings the two elements — consciousness and conditions — around the concept of "experience." Both positions entail certain difficult fluctuations around these key terms. Williams so totally absorbs "definitions of experience" into our "ways of living," and both into an indissoluble real material practice-in-general, as to obviate any distinction between "culture" and "not-culture." Thompson sometimes uses "experience" in the more usual sense of consciousness, as the collective ways in which men "handle, transmit or distort" their given conditions, the raw materials of life; sometimes as the domain of the "lived," the mid-term *between* "conditions" and "culture"; and sometimes as the objective conditions themselves — against which particular modes of consciousness are counterposed. But, whatever the terms, both positions tend to read structures of relations in terms of how they are "lived" and "experienced." Williams's "structure of feeling" — with its deliberate condensation of apparently incompatible elements — is characteristic. But the same is true of Thompson, despite his far fuller historical grasp of the "given-ness" or structured-ness of the relations and conditions into which men and women necessarily and involuntarily enter, and his clearer attention to the determinacy of productive and exploitative relations under capitalism. This is a consequence of giving culture-consciousness and experience so pivotal a place in analysis. The *experiential pull* in this paradigm, and the emphasis on the creative and on historical agency, constitute the two key elements in the *humanism* of the position outlined. Each consequently accords "experience" an authenticating position in any cultural analysis. It is, ultimately, where and how people experience their conditions of life, define them and respond to them, which, for Thompson defines why every mode of production is also a culture, and every struggle between classes is always also a struggle between cultural modalities; and which, for Williams, is what a "cultural analysis," in the final instance, should deliver. In "experience," all the different practices intersect; within "culture" the different practices interact — even if on an uneven and mutually determining basis. This sense of cultural totality — of *the whole* historical process — overrides any effort to keep the instances and elements distinct. Their real interconnection, under given historical conditions, must be matched by a totalizing movement "in thought," in the analysis. It establishes for both the strongest protocols against any form of analytic abstraction which distinguishes practices, or which sets out to test the "actual historical movement" in all its intertwined complexity and particularity by any more sustained logical or analytical operation. These positions, especially in their more concrete historical rendering (*The Making, The Country and the City*) are the very opposite of a Hegelian search for underlying Essences. Yet, in their tendency to reduce practices to *praxis* and to find common and homologous "forms" underlying the most apparently differentiated areas, their movement is "essentializing." They have a particular way of understanding the totality — though it is with a small "t," concrete and historically determinate, uneven in its correspondences. They understand it "expressively." And since they constantly inflect the more traditional analysis towards the experiential level, or read the other structures and relations downwards from the vantage point of how they are "lived," they are properly (even if not adequately or fully) characterized as "culturalist" in their emphasis: even when all the caveats and qualifications against a too rapid "dichotomous theorizing" have been entered. (Cf. for "culturalism," Richard Johnson's two seminal articles on the operation of the paradigm: in "Histories of Culture/Theories of Ideology," *Ideology and Cultural Production*, eds. M. Barrett, P. Corrigan et al., Croom Helm, 1979; and "Three Problematics" in

Working Class Culture, Clarke, Critcher and Johnson, Hutchinsons and CCCS, 1979. For the dangers in "dichotomous theorizing," cf. the Introduction, "Representaion and Cultural Production," to Barrett, Corrigan et al.)

The "culturalist" strand in Cultural Studies was interrupted by the arrival on the intellectual scene of the "structuralisms." These, possibly more varied than the "culturalisms," nevertheless shared certain positions and orientations in common which makes their designation under a single title not altogether misleading. It has been remarked that whereas the "culturalist" paradigm can be defined without requiring a conceptual reference to the term "ideology" (the *word*, of course, does appear: but it is not a key concept), the "structuralist" interventions have been largely articulated around the concept of "ideology": in keeping with its more impeccably Marxist lineage, "culture" does not figure so prominently. Whilst this may be true of the Marxist structuralists, it is at best less than half the truth about the structuralist enterprise as such. But it is now a common error to condense the latter exclusively around the impact of Althusser and all that has followed in the wake of his interventions — where "ideology" has played a seminal, but modulated role: and to omit the significance of Lévi-Strauss.[6] Yet, in strict historical terms, it was Lévi-Strauss, and the early semiotics, which made the first break. And though the Marxist structuralisms have superseded the latter, they owed, and continue to owe, an immense theoretical debt (often fended off or downgraded into footnotes, in the search for a retrospective orthodoxy) to his work. It was Lévi-Strauss's structuralism which, in its appropriation of the linguistic paradigm, after Saussure, offered the promise to the "human sciences of culture" of a paradigm capable of rendering them scientific and rigorous in a thoroughly new way. And when, in Althusser's work, the more classical Marxist themes were recovered, it remained the case that Marx was "read" — and reconstituted — through the terms of the linguistic paradigm. In *Reading Capital*, for example, the case is made that the mode of production — to coin a phrase — could best be understood as if

"structured like a language" (through the selective combination of invariant elements).[7] The a-historical and synchronic stress, against the historical emphases of "culturalism," derived from a similar source. So did a preoccupation with "the social, *sui generis*" — used not adjectivally but substantively: a usage Lévi-Strauss derived, not from Marx, but from Durkheim (the Durkheim who analyzed the social categories of thought — e.g. in *Primitive Classification* — rather than the Durkheim of *The Division of Labour*, who became the founding father of American structural-functionalism).[8]

Lévi-Strauss did, on occasion, toy with certain Marxist formulations. Thus, "Marxism, if not Marx himself, has too commonly reasoned as though practices followed directly from praxis. Without questioning the undoubted primacy of infrastructures, I believe that there is always a mediator between praxis and practices, namely, the conceptual scheme by the operation of which matter and form, neither with any independent existence, are realized as structures, that is as entities which are both empirical and intelligible." But this — to coin another phrase — was largely "gestural." This structuralism shared with culturalism a radical break with the terms of the base/superstructure metaphor, as derived from the simpler parts of the *German Ideology*.[9] And, though "It is to this theory of the superstructures, scarcely touched on by Marx" to which Lévi-Strauss aspired to contribute, his contribution was such as to break in a radical way with [all its] terms of reference, as finally and irrevocably as the "culturalists" did. Here — and we must include Althusser in this characterization — culturalists and structuralists alike ascribed to the

[7] Hall's "structured like a language" is a quotation from Jacques Lacan; his point is that the structural Marxist Louis Althusser in effect reads Marx through Lacan. See the introduction to Psychoanalytic Theory, p. 1106, and the introduction to Marxist Criticism, p. 1198.

[8] Emile Durkheim (1858-1917) was a French philosopher, not an American, and is usually spoken of as the father of sociology as a discipline. *Primitive Classification* is a collaborative work with Marcel Mausss, "De quelques formes primitives de classification: contribution à l'étude des représentations collectives." *Année sociologique* 6 (1903): 1–72. *The Division of Labor in Society* was published in 1893.

[9] See Marx, p. 397.

[6] See the introduction to Structuralism, p 819.

domains hitherto defined as "superstructural" a specificity and effectivity, a constitutive primacy, which pushed them beyond the terms of reference of "base" and "superstructure." Lévi-Strauss and Althusser, too, were anti-reductionist and anti-economist in their very cast of thought, and critically attacked that transitive causality which, for so long, had passed itself off as "classical Marxism."

Lévi-Strauss worked consistently with the term "culture." He regarded "ideologies" as of much lesser importance; mere "secondary rationalization." Like Williams and Goldmann, he worked, not at the level of correspondences between the *content* of a practice, but at the level of their forms and structures. But the manner in which these were conceptualized was altogether at variance with either the "culturalism" of Williams or Goldmann's "genetic structuralism." This divergence can be identified in three distinct ways. First, he conceptualized "culture" as the categories and frameworks in thought and language through which different societies classified out their conditions of existence — above all (since Lévi-Strauss was an anthropologist), the relations between the human and the natural worlds. Second, he thought of the manner and practice through which these categories and mental frameworks were produced and transformed, largely on an analogy with the ways in which language itself — the principal medium of "culture" — operated. He identified what was specific to them and their operation as the "production of meaning": they were, above all, *signifying* practices. Third, after some early flirtations with Durkheim and Mauss's social categories of thought, he largely gave up the question of the relation *between* signifying and non-signifying practices — between "culture" and "not-culture," to use other terms — for the sake of concentration on the *internal* relations within signifying practices by means of which the categories of meaning were produced. This left the question of determinacy, of totality, largely in abeyance. This causal logic of determinacy was abandoned in favor of a structuralist causality — a logic of *arrangement*, of internal relations, of articulation of parts within a structure. Each of these aspects is also positively present in Althusser's work and that of the Marxist structuralists, even when the terms of reference

had been regrounded in Marx's "immense theoretical revolution." In one of Althusser's seminal formulations about ideology — defined as the themes, concepts and representations through which men and women "live," in an imaginary relation, their relation to their real conditions of existence — we can see the skeleton outline of Lévi-Strauss's "conceptual schemes between praxis and practices." "Ideologies" are here being conceptualized, not as the contents and surface forms of ideas, but as the unconscious categories through which conditions are represented and lived. We have already commented on the active presence in Althusser's thinking of the linguistic paradigm — the second element identified above. And though, in the concept of "over-determination" — one of his most seminal and fruitful contributions — Althusser did return to the problems of the relations *between* practices and the question of determinacy (proposing, incidentally, a thoroughly novel and highly suggestive reformulation, which has received far too little subsequent attention), he did tend to reinforce the "relative autonomy" of different practices, and their internal specificities, conditions and effects at the expense of an "expressive" conception of the totality, with its typical homologies and correspondences.

Aside from the wholly distinct intellectual and conceptual universes within which these alternative paradigms developed, there were certain points where, despite their apparent overlaps, culturalism and structuralism were starkly counterposed. We can identify this counterposition at one of its sharpest points precisely around the concept of "experience," and the role the term played in each perspective. Whereas, in "culturalism," experience was the ground — the terrain of "the lived" — where consciousness and conditions intersected, structuralism insisted that "experience" could not, by definition, be the ground of anything, since one could only "live" and experience one's conditions *in and through* the categories, classifications and frameworks of the culture. These categories, however, did not arise from or in experience: rather, experience was their "effect." The culturalists had defined the forms of consciousness and culture as collective. But they had stopped far short of the radical proposition that, in culture and in language, the subject was "spoken by" the categories of culture in which he/she thought, rather than individual productions: they were *unconscious* structures. That is why, though Lévi-Strauss spoke only of "Culture," his concept provided the basis for an easy translation, by Althusser, into the conceptual framework of ideology: "Ideology is indeed a system of 'representations,' but in the majority of these cases these representations have nothing to do with 'consciousness': . . . it is above all as structures that they impose on the vast majority of men, not via their 'consciousness' . . . it is within this ideological unconsciousness that men succeed in altering the 'lived' relation between them and the world and acquiring that new form of specific unconsciousness called 'consciousness'" (*For Marx*, p. 233). It was, in this sense, that "experience" was conceived, not as an authenticating source but as an effect: not as a reflection of the real but as an "imaginary relation." It was only a short step — the one which separates *For Marx* from the "Ideological State Apparatuses" essay — to the development of an account of how this "imaginary relation" served, not simply the dominance of a ruling class over a dominated one, but (through the reproduction of the relations of production, and the constitution of labor-power in a form fit for capitalist exploitation) the expanded reproduction of the mode of production itself. Many of the other lines of divergence between the two paradigms flow from this point: the conception of "men" as bearers of the structures that speak and place them, rather than as active agents in the making of their own history; the emphasis on a structural rather than a historical "logic"; the preoccupation with the constitution — in "theory" — of a nonideological, scientific discourse; and hence the privileging of conceptual work and of Theory as guaranteed; the recasting of history as a march of the structures (cf. passim, *The Poverty of Theory*[10]): the structuralist "machine. . . ."

There is no space in which to follow through the many ramifications which have followed from the development of one or [an]other of these "master paradigms" in Cultural Studies. Though they by no means account for all, or even nearly

[10]Book by E. P. Thompson (1978).

all, of the many strategies adopted, it is fair to say that, between them, they have defined the principal lines of development in the field. The seminal debates have been polarized around their thematics; some of the best concrete work has flowed from the efforts to set one or [an]other of these paradigms to work on particular problems and materials. Characteristically — the sectarian and self-righteous climate of critical intellectual work in England being what it is, and its dependency being so marked — the arguments and debates have most frequently been over-polarized into their extremes. At these extremities, they frequently appear only as mirror-reflections or inversions of one another. Here, the broad typologies we have been working with — for the sake of convenient exposition — become the prison-house of thought.

Without suggesting that there can be any easy synthesis between them, it might usefully be said at this point that neither "culturalism" nor "structuralism" is, in its present manifestation, adequate to the task of constructing the study of culture as a conceptually clarified and theoretically informed domain of study. Nevertheless, something fundamental to it emerges from a rough comparison of their respective strengths and limitations.

The great strength of the structuralisms is their stress on "determinate conditions." They remind us that, unless the dialectic really can be held, in any particular analysis, between both halves of the proposition — that "men make history . . . on the basis of conditions which are not of their making" — the result will inevitably be a naive humanism, with its necessary consequence: a voluntarist and populist political practice. The fact that "men" can become conscious of their conditions, organize to struggle against them and in fact transform them — without which no active politics can even be conceived, let alone practiced — must not be allowed to override the awareness of the fact that, in capitalist relations, men and women are placed and positioned in relations which constitute them as agents. "Pessimism of the intellect, optimism of the will" is a better starting point than a simple heroic affirmation. Structuralism does enable us to begin to think — as Marx insisted — of the *relations* of a structure on the basis of something other than their reduction to relationships between "people." This was Marx's privileged level of abstraction: that which enabled him to break with the obvious but incorrect starting point of "political economy" — bare individuals.

But this connects with a second strength: the recognition by structuralism not only of the necessity of abstraction as the instrument of thought through which "real relations" are appropriated, but also of the presence, in Marx's work, of a continuous and complex movement *between different levels of abstraction*. It is, of course, the case — as "culturalism" argues — that, in historical reality, practices do not appear neatly distinguished out into their respective instances. However, to think about or to analyze the complexity of the real, the act or practice of thinking is required; and this necessitates the use of the power of abstraction and analysis, the formation of concepts with which to cut into the complexity of the real, in order precisely to reveal and bring to light relationships and structures which cannot be visible to the naive naked eye, and which can neither present nor authenticate themselves: "In the analysis of economic forms, neither microscopes nor chemical reagents are of assistance. The power of abstraction must replace both." Of course, structuralism has frequently taken this proposition to its extreme. Because thought is impossible without "the power of abstraction," it has confused this with giving an absolute primacy to the level of the formation of concepts — and at the highest, most abstract level of abstraction only: Theory with a capital "T" then becomes judge and jury. But this is precisely to lose the insight just won from Marx's own practice. For it is clear in, for example, *Capital*, that the *method* — whilst, of course, taking place "in thought" (as Marx asked in the 1857 Introduction, where else?) — rests, not on the simple exercise of abstraction but on the movement and relations which the argument is constantly establishing between *different levels* of abstraction: at each, the premises in play must be distinguished from those which — for the sake of the argument — have to be held constant. The movement to another level of magnification (to deploy the microscope metaphor) requires the specifying of further conditions of existence not supplied at a previous, more abstract level: in this way, by successive abstractions of different magnitudes, to *move towards* the constitution, the *reproduction*, of "the concrete in thought" as an effect of a certain kind of thinking. This method is adequately represented in *neither* the absolutism of Theoretical Practice, in structuralism, nor in the anti-abstraction "Poverty of Theory" position into which, in reaction, culturalism appears to have been driven or driven itself. Nevertheless it is intrinsically *theoretical*, and must be. Here, structuralism's insistence that thought does not reflect reality, but is articulated on and appropriates it, is a necessary starting point. An adequate *working through* of the consequences of this argument might begin to produce a method which takes us outside the permanent oscillations between abstraction/anti-abstraction and the false dichotomies of Theoreticism *vs.* Empiricism which have both marked and disfigured the structuralism-culturalism encounter to date.

Stucturalism has another strength, in its conception of "the whole." There is a sense in which, though culturalism constantly insists on the radical particularity of its practices, its mode of conceptualizing the "totality" has something of the complex simplicity of an expressive totality behind it. Its complexity is constituted by the fluidity with which practices move into and out of one another: but this complexity is reducible, conceptually, to the "simplicity" of praxis — human activity, as such — in which the same contradictions constantly appear, homologously reflected in each. Structuralism goes too far in erecting the machine of a "Structure," with its self-generating propensities (a "Spinozean eternity," whose function is only the sum of its effects: a truly structural*ist* deviation), equipped with its distinctive instances. Yet it represents an advance over culturalism in the conception it has of the necessary *complexity* of the unity of a structure (over-determination being a more successful way of thinking this complexity than the combinatory invariance of structuralist causality). Moreover, it has the conceptual ability to think of a unity which is constructed through the *differences* between, rather than the homology of, practices. Here, again, it has won a critical insight about Marx's method: one thinks of the complex passages of the 1857 Introduction to the *Grundrisse* where Marx demonstrates how it is possible to think of the "unity" of a social formation as constructed, not out of identity but out of *difference*.[11] Of course, the stress on difference can — and has — led the structuralisms into a fundamental conceptual heterogeneity, in which all sense of structure and totality is lost. Foucault and other post-Althusserans have taken this devious path into the absolute, not the relative, autonomy of practices, via their necessary heterogeneity and "necessary non-correspondence." But the emphasis on unity-in-difference, on complex unity — Marx's concrete as the "unity of many determinations" — can be worked in another, and ultimately more fruitful, direction: towards the problematic of relative autonomy and "over-determination," and the study of *articulation*. Again, articulation contains the danger of a high formalism. But it also has the considerable advantage of enabling us to think of how specific practices (articulated around contradictions which do not all arise in the same way, at the same point, in the same moment), can nevertheless be thought *together*. The structuralist paradigm thus does — if properly developed — enable us to begin really to *conceptualize* the specificity of different practices (analytically distinguished, abstracted out), without losing its grip on the ensemble which they constitute. Culturalism constantly affirms the specificity of different practices — "culture" must not be absorbed into "the economic": but it lacks an adequate way of establishing this specificity theoretically.

The third strength which structuralism exhibits lies in its decentering of "experience" and its seminal work in elaborating the neglected category of "ideology." It is difficult to conceive of a Cultural Studies thought within a Marxist paradigm which is innocent of the category of "ideology." Of course, culturalism constantly makes reference to this concept: but it does not in fact lie at the center of its conceptual universe. The authenticating power and reference of "experience" imposes a barrier between culturalism and a proper conception of "ideology." Yet, without it, the effectivity of "culture" for the reproduction of a particular mode of production cannot be grasped. It is true that there is a marked tendency in the more recent structuralist conceptualizations of "ideology" to give it a functionalist reading — as the necessary cement of the social formation. From this position, it is indeed impossible — as culturalism would correctly argue — to conceive either of ideologies which are not, by definition, "dominant": or of the concept of struggle (the latter's appearance in Althusser's famous ISA's[12] article being — to coin yet another phrase — largely "gestural"). Nevertheless, work is already being done which suggests ways in which the field of ideology may be adequately conceptualized as a terrain of struggle (through the work of Gramsci, and more recently, of Laclau),[13] and these have structuralist rather than culturalist bearings.

Culturalism's strengths can almost be derived from the weaknesses of the structuralism position already noted, and from the latter's strategic absences and silences. It has insisted, correctly, on the affirmative moment of the development of conscious struggle and organization as a necessary element in the analysis of history, ideology and consciousness: against its persistent downgrading in the structuralist paradigm. Here, again, it is largely Gramsci who has provided us with a set of more refined terms through which to link the largely "unconscious" and given cultural categories of "common sense" with the formation of more active and organic ideologies, which have the capacity to intervene in the ground of common sense and popular traditions and, through such interventions, to organize masses of men and women. In this sense, culturalism *properly* restores the dialectic between the unconsciousness of cultural categories and the moment of conscious organization: even if, in its characteristic movement, it has tended to match structuralism's over-emphasis on "conditions" with an altogether too-inclusive emphasis on "consciousness." It

[11]Hall may be thinking of this sentence from the *Grundrisse*: "The conclusion we reach is not that production, distribution, exchange and consumption are identical, but that they all form the members of a totality, distinctions within a unity."

[12]Hall refers to Althusser's article, "Ideology and Ideological State Apparatuses"; see p. 1263.
[13]Ernesto Laclau, Argentine political theorist, author of *Politics and Ideology in Marxist Theory* (1977), well-known today for his collaborative work with Chantal Mouffe.

therefore not only recovers — as the necessary moment of any analysis — the process by means of which classes-in-themselves, defined primarily by the way in which economic relations position "men" as agents — become active historical and political forces — for themselves: it also — against its own anti-theoretical good sense — *requires* that, when properly developed, each moment must be understood in terms of the level of abstraction at which the analysis is operating. Again, Gramsci has begun to point a way through this false polarization in his discussion of "the passage between the structure and the sphere of the complex superstructures," and its distinct forms and moments.

We have concentrated in this argument largely on a characterization of what seem to us to be the two seminal paradigms at work in Cultural Studies. Of course, they are by no means the only active ones. New developments and lines of thinking are by no means adequately netted with reference to them. Nevertheless, these paradigms can, in a sense, be deployed to measure what appear to us to be the radical weaknesses or inadequacies of those which offer themselves as alternative rallying-points. Here, briefly, we identify three.

The first is that which follows on from Lévi-Strauss, early semiotics and the terms of the linguistic paradigm, and the centering on "signifying practices," moving by way of psychoanalytic concepts and Lacan to a radical recentering of virtually the whole terrain of Cultural Studies around the terms "discourse" and "the subject." One way of understanding this line of thinking is to see it as an attempt to fill that empty space in early structuralism (of both the Marxist and non-Marxist varieties) where, in earlier discourses, "the subject" and subjectivity might have been expected to appear but did not. This is, of course, precisely one of the key points where culturalism brings its pointed criticisms to bear on structuralism's "process without a subject." The difference is that, whereas culturalism would correct for the hyper-structuralism of earlier models by restoring the unified subject (collective or individual) of consciousness at the center of "the Structure," discourse theory, by way of the Freudian concepts of the unconscious and the Lacanian concepts of how subjects are constituted in language (through the entry into the Symbolic and the Law of Culture), restores the *decentered* subject, the contradictory subject, as a set of positions in language and knowledge, from which culture can appear to be enunciated. This approach clearly identifies a gap, not only in structuralism but in Marxism itself. The problem is that the manner in which this "subject" of culture is conceptualized is of a transhistorical and "universal" character: it addresses the subject-in-general, not historically determinate social subjects, or socially determinate particular languages. Thus it is incapable, so far, of moving its in-general propositions to the level of concrete historical analysis. The second difficulty is that the processes of contradiction and struggle — lodged by early structuralism wholly at the level of "the structure" — are now, by one of those persistent mirror-inversions, lodged exclusively at the level of the unconscious processes of the subject. It may be, as culturalism often argues, that the "subjective" is a necessary moment of any such analysis. But this is a very different proposition from dismantling the whole of the social processes of particular modes of production and social formations, and reconstituting them exclusively at the level of unconscious psychoanalytic processes. Though important work has been done, both within this paradigm and to define and develop it, its claims to have replaced *all* the terms of the earlier paradigms with a more adequate set of concepts seems wildly over-ambitious. Its claims to have integrated Marxism into a more adequate materialism is, largely, a semantic rather than a conceptual claim.

A second development is the attempt to return to the terms of a moral classical "political economy" of culture. This position argues that the concentration on the cultural and ideological aspects has been wildly overdone. It would restore the older terms of "base/superstructure," finding, in the last-instance determination of the cultural-ideological by the economic, that hierarchy of determinations which both alternatives appear to lack. This position insists that the economic processes and structures of cultural production are more significant than their cultural-ideological aspect; and that these are quite adequately caught in the more classical terminology of profit, exploitation, surplus-value and the analysis of culture as commodity. It retains a notion of ideology as "false consciousness."

There is, of course, some strength to the claim that both structuralism and culturalism, in their different ways, have neglected the economic analysis of cultural and ideological production. All the same, with the return to this more "classical" terrain, many of the problems which originally beset it also reappear. The specificity of the effect of the cultural and ideological dimension once more tends to disappear. It tends to conceive the economic level as not only a "necessary" but a "sufficient" explanation of cultural and ideological effects. Its focus on the analysis of the commodity form, similarly, blurs all the carefully established distinctions between different practices, since it is the most *generic* aspects of the commodity-form which attract attention. Its deductions are therefore, largely, confined to an epochal level of abstraction: the generalizations about the commodity-form hold true throughout the capitalist epoch as a whole. Very little by way of concrete and conjunctural analysis can be derived at this high-level "logic of capital" form of abstraction. It also tends to its own kind of functionalism — a functionalism of "logic" rather than of "structure" or history. This approach, too, has insights which are well worth following through. But it sacrifices too much of what has been painfully secured, without a compensating gain in explanatory power.

The third position is closely related to the structuralist enterprise, but has followed the path of "difference" through into a radical heterogeneity. Foucault's work — currently enjoying another of those uncritical periods of discipleship through which British intellectuals reproduce today their dependency on yesterday's French ideas — has had an exceedingly positive effect: above all because in suspending the nearly-insoluble problems of determination Foucault has made possible a welcome return to the concrete analysis of particular ideological and discursive formations, and the sites of their elaboration. Foucault and Gramsci between them account for much of the most productive work on *concrete analysis* now being undertaken in the field: thereby reinforcing and — paradoxically — supporting the sense of the concrete historical instance which has always been one of culturalism's principal strengths. But, again, Foucault's example is positive only if his general epistemological position is not swallowed whole. For in fact Foucault so resolutely suspends judgment, and adopts so thoroughgoing a skepticism about any determinacy or relationship between practices, other than the largely contingent, that we are entitled to see him, not as an agnostic on these questions but as deeply committed to the necessary non-correspondence of all practices to one another. From such a position neither a social formation, nor the State can be adequately thought. And indeed Foucault is constantly falling into the pit which he has dug for himself. For when — against his well-defended epistemological positions — he stumbles across certain "correspondences" (for example, the simple fact that all the major moments of transition he has traced in each of his studies — on the prison, sexuality, medicine, the asylum, language and political economy — all appear to converge around exactly that point where industrial capitalism and the bourgeoisie make their fateful, historical rendezvous), he lapses into a vulgar reductionism, which thoroughly belies the sophisticated positions he has elsewhere advanced.[14]

I have said enough to indicate that, in my view, the line in Cultural Studies which has attempted to *think forward* from the best elements in the structuralist and culturalist enterprises, by way of some of the concepts elaborated in Gramsci's work, comes closest to meeting the requirements of the field of study. And the reason for that should by now also be obvious. Though neither structuralism nor culturalism will do, as self-sufficient paradigms of study, they have a centrality to the field which all the other contenders lack because, between them (in their divergences as well as their convergences) they address what must be the *core problem* of Cultural Studies. They constantly return us to the terrain marked out by those strongly coupled but not mutually exclusive concepts culture/ideology. They pose, together, the problems consequent on trying to think *both* the specificity of different

---

[14]He is quite capable of wheeling in through the back door the classes he recently expelled from the front. [Hall]

practices and the forms of the articulated unity they constitute. They make a constant, if flawed return to the base/superstructure metaphor. They are correct in insisting that this question — which resumes all the problems of a nonreductive determinacy — is the heart of the matter: and that, on the solution of this problem will turn the capacity of Cultural Studies to supersede the endless oscillations between idealism and reductionism they confront — even if in radically opposed ways — the dialectic between conditions and consciousness. At another level, they pose the question of the relation between the logic of thinking and the "logic" of historical process. They continue to hold out the promise of a properly materialist theory of culture. In their sustained and mutually reinforcing antagonisms they hold out no promise of an easy synthesis. But, between them, they define where, if at all, is the space, and what are the limits, within which such a synthesis might be constituted. In Cultural Studies, theirs are the "names of the game."

Nancy Armstrong

b. 1938

The American scholar who has perhaps done the most to breach the barrier between feminism and cultural studies, Nancy Armstrong attended Wellesley College for two years, had three children in rapid succession, completed her B.A. at the State University of New York at Buffalo, and left, children in tow, for the Ph.D. program at the University of Wisconsin–Madison in 1967. Before receiving her doctorate in 1977, she taught on a Fulbright Fellowship in Portugal at the University of Coimbra, where she tries to return every two or three years. Since then, she has taught at Wayne State University, the State University of New York at Buffalo, the University of Minnesota, and Yale, Wesleyan, and Brown Universities. She is currently Nancy Duke Lewis Professor of Comparative Literature, Modern Culture and Media, English, and Women's Studies and chair of the English Department at Brown. Her books include two collections of essays edited with Leonard Tennenhouse: The Ideology of Conduct: Essays on Literature and the History of Sexuality *(1986) and* The Violence of Representation *(1989);* Desire and Domestic Fiction: A Political History of the Novel *(1987),* The Imaginary Puritan: Literature, Intellectual Labor, and the Origins of Personal Life *(with Leonard Tennenhouse, 1992);* Fiction in the Age of Photography *(1997) and* How Novels Think: The Limits of British Individualism 1719–1900 *(forthcoming). "Some Call It Fiction" was originally presented to the Focused Research Program in Gender and Women's Studies at the University of California at Irvine during 1985–88, before being published in Juliet Flower MacCannell's collection of papers from that program,* The Other Perspective in Gender and Culture *(1990).*

Some Call It Fiction:
On the Politics of Domesticity

*It is queer how out of touch with truth women are.
They live in a world of their own, and there has
never been anything like it, and never can be.*
— JOSEPH CONRAD, *Heart of Darkness*

For some years now, American scholars have been puzzling out the relationship between literature and history. Apparently the right connections were not made when literary histories were first compiled. Yet in turning to the question of how some of the most famous British novelists were linked to their moment in time, I have found I must begin at step one, with extremely powerful conventions of representation. Though old and utterly familiar, nothing new has taken their place. Their potency has not diminished in this country despite the theory revolution and the calls for a new literary history that came in its wake. The conventions to which I refer are many and various indeed, but all reinforce the assumption that history consists of economic or political events, as if these were essentially different from other cultural events. Some of us — a distinct minority, to be sure — feel that to proceed on this assumption is to brush aside most of the activities composing everyday life and so shrink the category of "the political" down to a very limited set of cultural practices. And then, having classified most of our symbolic activities as "personal," "social," or "cultural" (it is all much the same), traditional histories would have us place them in a secondary relationship either to the economy or to the official institutions of state. This essay is written in opposition to models of history that confine political practices to activities directly concerned with the marketplace, the official institutions of the state, or else resistance to these. I write as one who feels that such models have not provided an adequate basis for understanding the formation of a modern bureaucratic culture or for our place, as intellectuals, within it. More than that, I regard any model that places personal life in a separate sphere and that grants literature a secondary and passive role in political history as unconsciously sexist. I believe such models necessarily fail to account for the formation of a modern bureaucratic culture because they fail to account for the place of women within it.

Some of our best theorizers of fiction's relationship to history — Raymond Williams in England and Edward Said[1] in the United States — have done much to tear down the barrier between culture and state. They demonstrate that the middle-class hegemony succeeded in part because it constructed separate historical narratives for self and society, family and factory, literature and history. They suggest that by maintaining these divisions within culture, liberal intellectuals continue to sanitize certain areas of culture — namely, the personal, domestic, and literary. The practices that go by these names consequently appear to be benignly progressive, in their analyses, to provide a place of escape from the political world, and even to offer forms of resistance. Still, I would argue, such efforts as those of Williams and Said will be only partially successful so long as they continue to ignore *the sexual division of labor* that underwrites and naturalizes the difference between culture and politics.

THE LIMITS OF POLITICAL HISTORY

To put some life into all these abstractions, let me now turn to domestic fiction and the difficulties that scholars encounter when they try to place writing of this kind in history. Ian Watt convincingly describes the socioeconomic character of the new readership for whom Defoe, Richardson, and Fielding wrote, a readership whose rise in turn gave rise to the novel. But Watt has no similar explanation for Austen. Her popularity he ascribes to her talent, and her talent, to nature. And so he concludes that nature must have given

[1] See Williams, p. 1272, and Said, p. 1801.

Austen a good eye for details.[2] Although Williams moves well beyond such reflection theories in his ground-breaking account of the information revolution, his model of history ultimately serves us no better than Watt's when it comes to explaining domestic fiction. His *Long Revolution* regards intellectual labor as a political force in its own right without which capitalism could not have unfolded as smoothly and completely as it appears to have done. But however much power Williams grants this domain, it belongs to culture and, as such, exists in a secondary relationship with political history. To historicize writing, he feels compelled to give it a source in events outside of and prior to writing. He does not entertain the possibility that the classic unfolding of capitalism was predicated on writing, much less on writing by women or writing that appealed to the interests of a female readership.[3] For Williams as for Watt, historical events take place in the official institutions of state or else through resistance to these institutions, and both forms of power are exercised primarily through men.

I have found Watt and Williams especially helpful for establishing links between the history of fiction and the rise of the new middle classes in England. At the same time, I am perplexed to find that, in establishing a relationship between writing and political history, these otherwise conscientious scholars completely neglect to account for the most obvious fact of all, namely, that sometime during the eighteenth century, in the words of Virginia Woolf, "the middle class

woman began to write."[4] If, as Watt and Williams say, the rise of the novel was directly related to the rise of the new middle classes, then some of our best literary evidence suggests that the rise of the novel was related to the emergence of women's writing as well. In drawing this equation, of course, I have doubled the difficulties entailed in historicizing fiction, for I have suggested that to historicize fiction we must politicize not only intellectual labor but female labor as well. Much of British fiction exists at the intersection of these two definitively modern subsets of culture and is thereby twice removed from the mainstream of political history.

The writing I call domestic fiction is gender-inflected writing. Unlike the work of earlier women of letters, it comes to us as women's writing. In designating certain forms of writing as feminine, it designates other writing as masculine. The enclosure that marks a Jane Austen novel does not simply distinguish her "world" from that of a Shakespeare, a Blake, a Dickens, or a Yeats. The boundaries it constructs between inside and outside are personal in a far more wide-reaching and historically significant way. They mark the difference between the world over which women novelists have authority — the domain of the personal — and that which is ruled by men and their politics. In doing this, Austen makes Richardson the father of the novel, for, like him, she identifies the work of the novelist with the

---

[2]Ian Watt, *The Rise of the Novel* (Berkeley: University of California Press, 1957), p. 57. [Armstrong]

[3]In *The Long Revolution* (New York: Columbia University Press, 1961), Williams sets out to show how the "creative" or cultural dimension of social experience opposed existing forms of political authority during the seventeenth and eighteenth centuries and won. Part one of his book indeed gives culture priority over the official institutions of state (as it must during the eighteenth century), claiming that cultural history "is more than a department, a special area of change. In this creative area the changes and conflicts of the whole way of life are necessarily involved" (p. 122). But latent in this promise to extend the category of "the political" broadly to include "the whole way of life" is the contradictory suggestion that political practices are also a special category of "the whole." The second notion of politics emerges in part

two, where Williams describes such historical processes as the growth of the reading public, of the popular press, and of standard English through which the new middle classes converted the power of language into economic power. Here the narrow definition of political events, as those which take place in the houses of government, the courts, and the marketplace, assumes control over the "creative" cultural dimension of social experience. For example, Williams writes, "as 1688 is a significant political date, so 1695 is significant in the history of the press. For in that year Parliament declined to renew the 1662 Licensing Act, and the stage for expansion was now fully set" (p. 180). Had Williams actually gathered data that would compose the record of "the whole" of life, he might have broken out of this circle. But, in producing cultural histories, he invariably bows to tradition and stops before entering into the female domain. [Armstrong]

[4]Virginia Woolf, *A Room of One's Own* (New York: Harcourt, Brace and World, 1975), p. 69. [Armstrong] See Woolf in this text, p. 596.

writing of women as well as with other forms of labor that are suitably feminine.[5] To move beyond the impasse that prevents us from situating this work in history, we have, it seems to me, to toss out the idea that the gendering of vast areas of culture was a consequence of political events over which men had control. To consider gender itself as a political formation over which modern cultures gave women authority, we will have to invert these priorities. Having done so, one comes face to face with the possibility that a revolution in the home preceded the spread of the factory system and all that hinged upon its becoming the means of distributing the wealth of the nation.[6]

[5]For an account of the early eighteenth-century tradition that links the novel to criminal culture, see Lennard Davis, *Factual Fictions: The Origins of the English Novel* (New York: Columbia University Press, 1983), pp. 123–37. For the objection to novels because of their quasi-erotic appeal, see John Richetti, *Popular Fiction Before Richardson's Narrative Patterns, 1700–1734* (Oxford: Clarendon, 1969). In an issue of Addison's *Spectator*, for example, Mr. Spectator warns readers about the perils of May, advising that women "be in a particular Manner how they meddle with Romances, Chocolates, Novels, and the like inflamers, which I look upon to be very dangerous to be made use of during this great Carnival of Nature," quoted in *Four Before Richardson: Selected English Novels, 1720–1727*, William H. McBurney, ed. (Lincoln: University of Nebraska Press, 1963), p. ix. Toward the end of the eighteenth century, however, one discovers a good number of pedagogical treatises echo Austen's *Northanger Abbey* in advocating certain works of fiction as the fitting way to occupy leisure time. The fiction that was supposed to have a salutary effect on young women was either produced by lady novelists that gained currency during the age of Burney and the other lady novelists or else by earlier novelists who celebrated the same domestic virtues and saw the same form of domestic happiness as the ultimate reward for demonstrating these virtues. It was during this time, as Homer O. Brown explains, that certain novels were published under the editorship of Scott and Barbauld and marked as polite reading, and on the basis of this limited and anomalous body of works, a history of the novel was constructed backward in time (from his book in progress, *Institutions of the English Novel in the Eighteenth Century*). [Armstrong.] See Homer Obed Brown, *Institutions of the English Novel from Defoe to Scott* (Philadelphia: University of Pennsylvania Press, 1997).

[6]A number of social historians have suggested that the factory system, and with it the economic domination of the new middle classes, was stalled until the beginning of the nineteenth century. In *The Making of the English Working Class* (New York: Random House, 1966) p. 198, E. P. Thompson suggests that fear of Jacobinism produced a

To deal with this possibility, I begin with the proposition Marx put forth in *The German Ideology* and Gramsci[7] later developed into the concept of "hegemony" in his essays on the formation of intellectuals and the organization of culture and education: no political revolution is complete without a cultural revolution. To dominate, the dominant group must offer to one and all a view that makes their form of domination seem true and necessary if not desirable and right. Gramsci developed the contradiction inherent in Marx's notion of labor — that labor was not only a commodity, but also a social practice — into a theory that stressed the double-sidedness of middle-class power: it controlled not only the physical dimension of production but also the social dimension. During the twentieth century, moreover, Gramsci could see that a form of power that worked through spatial location, supervision, and individuals' relationship with machines was giving way to something more ubiquitous — bureaucratic control that divided and hierarchized individuals so as to place their labor on separate social planes. And indeed, as the wage was generalized to include members of this and other bureaucracies, those who performed productive labor shrank in number and importance.

More recently, therefore, a number of us who work in the humanities and social sciences have begun to feel theories of resistance which depend upon an essentialized class or, for that matter, any

new alignment between landowners and industrialists that divided the traditional resistance to industrialization. In *The Machinery Question and the Making of Political Economy* (Cambridge: Cambridge University Press, 1980), Maxine Berg explains how the development of political economy as a problem-solving logic at the end of the eighteenth century helped to make industrialization seem like an answer rather than a problem to be avoided at all costs. It was under such conditions that various authors first saw how many people had economic interests in common with the industrialists and described them as a class. In *Desire and Domestic Fiction: A Political History of the Novel* (New York: Oxford University Press, 1987), I carry this argument further by suggesting that well before they felt they had economic interests in common, numerous social groups ranging between the lower gentry and skilled workers were persuaded, in large part by authors unknown to us today, to buy into a single notion of personal life that centered around the kind of woman one desired to marry and the sort of happiness she would provide (pp. 59–95). [Armstrong]

[7]See the introduction to Marxist Criticism, p. 1198.

other essentialized group will no longer do. Once taken up by theory, such essentialisms quickly cease to represent the possibility of power coalescing outside a pluralistic society. Rather, they identify contradictory positions within that system and, in so doing, only supply more differences in a differential system that exists on an abstract plane of ideas. The system to which I refer is no system in the abstract, however, but the disciplinary institution itself. Slouching by way of homology from one cultural site to another, it has achieved the status of a paradigm. In its atomizing structure, political issues get lost. Everything matters. All truths are equivalent — only some are more complex and, in this respect alone, more satisfying than others. In the maze of differences, the difference between positive and negative has all but disappeared, and the paradise of liberalism seems near at hand.[8]

[8]In discussing Feuerbach, Marx not only stresses that the "ruling ideas" of an epoch are the ideas of a ruling class who "regulate the production and distribution of ideas of their age" (p. 64). He also speculates that during the modern epoch, the production and distribution of ideas (i.e., the production of consciousness) will become increasingly important to the preservation of the bourgeois "state" and to its eventual disintegration or overthrow, *The German Ideology,* Part One, C. J. Arthur, ed. (New York: International Publishers, 1985). Without sliding back into the idealist philosophy from which Marx sought to rescue "the production of ideas," Gramsci applies the contradiction inherent in Marx's notion of labor to intellectual labor. The intellectual does not necessarily identify with the ruling class by reproducing the ideas inherited from the past but at certain moments may expand their political horizon by lending unity and coherence to the view of an emergent group, *The Modern Prince and Other Writings* (New York: International Publishers, 1957). In *Hegemony and Socialist Strategy,* Winston Moore and Paul Cammack, trs. (London: Verso, 1985), Ernesto Laclau and Chantal Mouffe update this principle for a postmodern society by broadening Gramsci's notions of both power and resistance. Where the difference between production in the traditional sense and the production of information has virtually disappeared, the antagonism between worker and owner is likewise dispersed. Where such polarities could once be taken for granted, then, it becomes extremely difficult to create polarities along political lines. Laclau and Mouffe find it necessary to depart from Gramsci's reliance on the emergence of labor in conflict with capital and to turn instead to the intellectual labor of negativities and positivities out of the contemporary swamp of equivalences. For another important analysis of power in post-modern society, see Bonaventura de Sousa Santos, "Law and Community: The Changing Nature of State Power in Late Capitalism," *International Journal of the Sociology of the Law* (1980), 8: 379–97. [Armstrong]

So perceiving *her* historical moment, one can consider in a radically materialist light the Foucauldian propositions that the modern state was called into being in writing, exists mainly as a state of mind, and perpetuates itself through the well orchestrated collection, regulation, and dissemination of information. The idea of order that Foucault sometimes calls "discourse" or "power" and at other times names "sexuality" or "discipline" is indeed a ruling idea. But in a world that is ruled more surely by ideas than by physical or economic means, one has to be especially careful not to hypothesize some corresponding "reality" as their source. We cannot grant these ideas the autonomy, universality, and mystic interconnection that they have achieved, but neither can we seek out some more primary truth behind or below them. Rather, we must understand them, as Foucault suggests, as the self-conception of a class that has achieved hegemony. And hegemony in the case of modern post-industrial societies, depends on self-conceptions capable of swallowing up all opposition in a single system of micro-differences.

The power of the system depends upon the production of a particular form of consciousness that is at once unique and standardizing. In place of what he calls the "repressive hypothesis," the assumption that culture either "suppresses" or "imposes itself on" the individual's desire, Foucault offers a productive hypothesis that turns this commonplace on its ear. The first volume of *The History of Sexuality* argues that the very forms of subjectivity we consider most essential to ourselves as selves had no existence prior to their symbolization, that the deepest and most private recesses of our being are culturally produced.[9] His *Discipline and Punish* mounts a detailed historical argument to show that the truth of the modern individual existed first as writing, before she or he was transformed successively into speech, thought, and unconscious desire.[10] Thus Foucault

[9]Michel Foucault, *The History of Sexuality,* vol. 1, *An Introduction,* Robert Hurley, tr. (New York: Pantheon, 1978). [Armstrong] See Foucault in this text, p. 1627.

[10]*Discipline and Punish: The Birth of the Prison.* Alan Sheridan, tr. (New York: Vintage, 1979). All citations are to this edition. [Armstrong]

enables us to see the European Enlightenment as a revolution in words, which gave writing a new and awesome power over the world of objects as it shaped the individuals who established a relationship with that world through reading. In England, I would like to suggest, this cultural revolution was the only kind of revolution to occur during the eighteenth century, because in England the revolution in words took a form that prevented popular revolution.[11]

Having torn down the conceptual barrier between writing and political history, we have cleared the way to see the intellectual labor of women as part of the mainstream of political events. Foucault will not help us achieve this particular step, however. His *History of Sexuality* is not concerned with the history of gender. Nor does it deal with the role that writing for, by, and about women played in the history of sexuality. For this reason, his procedures cannot identify the decisive events that detached family life from politics, and these are the very events that tie the formation of a domestic domain to the development of an institutional culture in England. Foucault's *Discipline and Punish* overlooks the fact that the modern household served as the groundbreaking prototype of modern institutions. His *History of Sexuality* neglects to theorize the power of that prototype as it spills over from this account of modern personal life into his account of institutional power to saturate and make intelligible the theory of discipline. Despite the anti-Cartesian thrust of his work, Foucault does not finally break through the barrier that separates his position as

theorizer of the sexual subject in *The History of Sexuality* from the one he takes up in order to theorize the political subject in *Discipline and Punish*. Yet not only does he use the same figure to think out the two; he also gives the strategies producing the sexual subject (those organizing the home) priority in his thinking over the strategies that subject the individual to the state (those of disciplinary institutions).

Central to the central chapter on "Panopticism" in *Discipline and Punish* is Foucault's figure of the city under plague. In contrast with leprosy, which calls for exclusionary strategies more consistent with the aristocratic imagination of power, the plague, as he plays with the figure, seems to require inclusion and enclosure as preconditions for a modern system of surveillance. The division of the population into progressively smaller subdivisions of which the household is the basic module, is followed by the ritual purification of each and every household:

> Five or six days after the beginning of the quarantine, the process of purifying the houses one by one is begun. All the inhabitants are made to leave; in each room "the furniture and goods" are raised from the ground or suspended from the air; perfume is poured around the room; after carefully sealing the windows, doors and even the keyholes with wax, the perfume is set alight. Finally, the entire house is closed while the perfume is consumed; those who have carried out the work are searched, as they were on entry, "in the presence of the residents of the house, to see that they did not have something on their persons as they left that they did not have on entering." Four hours later, the residents are allowed to re-enter their homes. (p. 197)

[11]In *The Imaginary Puritan: Literature and the Origins of Personal Life* (forthcoming), Leonard Tennenhouse and I explain at length how the English Revolution failed to produce the base transformations that mark political revolution. We argue for a more adequate definition of the political, showing that while political change, in the narrow sense of the term, failed to occur, cultural change was profound and lasting. Before the modern middle classes gained economic control, and well before they gained control of the Houses of Parliament, a new class of intellectuals gained hegemony over aristocratic culture as it translated puritanism into the secular practices composing modern domesticity and personal life. [Armstrong] See *The Imaginary Puritan: Literature, Intellectual Labor, and the Origins of Personal Life* (Berkeley: University of California Press, 1992).

Such enclosure and purification of the house produces a new household free from the taint of any unregulated intercourse with the world, its membrane permeable only to certain kinds of information. Reading this account of the plague, I am struck by the difference between its place in the modern imagination and its use by Boccaccio, who imagined a small aristocratic community safely ensconced in the country to pass the time free from the infection of the city.[12] In this early modern world, those who remain in the city are to be

[12]In the *Decameron* (1353).

regarded as a different social body altogether, behaving much like the riotous and grotesquely permeable body celebrated by Bakhtin.[13] How significant, then, that Foucault, in contrast with Bakhtin, imagines a city purified from the inside out by the production of hygienically pure domestic spaces within the body politic! In this attempt to fantasize the present from the position of the past, households serve as magical spaces where people go to die in order that they may be reborn as modern individuals — enclosed and self-regulating.

Having pursued the internal logic of his figure thus far, Foucault extends it outward from the newly enclosed domestic world — as from a new source of power — into the cultural and political domains, and from there into history. First, he notes how a "whole literary fiction of the festival grew up around the plague: suspended laws, lifted prohibitions, the frenzy of passing time, bodies mingling together without respect, individuals unmasked, abandoning their statutory identity and the figure under which they had been recognized, allowing a quite different truth to appear. But," he continues, "there was also a political dream of the plague, which was exactly its reverse: not the collective festival, but strict divisions; not laws transgressed, but the penetration of regulation into even the smallest details of everyday life . . . ; not masks that were put on and taken off, but the assignment to each individual of his 'true' name, his 'true' place, his 'true' disease" (pp. 197–198). On the metaphor of the city under plague thus rests Foucault's entire theory of the development of modern institutions: "If it is true that the leper gave rise to rituals of exclusion, which to a certain extent provided the model for and general form of the Great Confinement, then the plague gave rise to disciplinary projects" (p. 198). Metaphorical use of disease allows him to declare the eighteenth-century hospital with its anatomy theater as the historical prototype for the modern prison.

And to be sure, I *like* Foucault for transgressing the boundary between the therapeutic and the punitive to demonstrate how much they have in common. But this, to my mind, is also a way of avoiding the full implications of his chosen

metaphor, the city under plague, implications that would destroy the differences between sexual subject and political subject, and between these and the subject's material body, all of which rest upon preserving the line that divvies up cultural information according to gender. This is the line between inside and outside that is implanted in his metaphor from the beginning to distinguish personal from political life. This is the first division of the conceptual zygote, the line without which the fantasy of an entire political world cannot develop its inexorable symmetry, a symmetry that cuts beneath and through particular features that culture manifests at one site rather than another. While he opens the category of political power considerably by including institutions other than those officially charged to distribute wealth and power, Foucault extends the cultural scope of discipline only so far as institutions that, in becoming institutions, came to be dominated by men. Thus if power does not originate in the minds of individual men or in the bodies of men collectively, it arises from the cultural patterns that make men think of themselves as certain kinds of men and exercise power accordingly.

But if one pursues the implications of Foucault's chosen metaphor for modern power, his city under plague, in contrast with a Boccaccian remedy, contains a certain form of household that is the perfect and obvious answer to the indiscriminate mingling of bodies spreading the infection. When we expand our concept of the political further even than Foucault's, we discover grounds on which to argue that the modern household rather than the clinic provided the proto-institutional setting where government through relentless supervision first appeared, and appeared in its most benevolent guise. Foucault never takes note of these continuities between home and state even though they are as plain as the words on his page. More curious still is his failure to acknowledge the fact that a home espoused by various subgroups aspiring for the status of "respectability," a home overseen by a woman, actually preceded the formation of other social institutions by at least fifty years. There is little to suggest this household took root in practice much before the beginning of the nineteenth century, even though it frequently appeared in the

[13]In *Rabelais and His World* (1965).

literature and political argumentation of the previous century. From writing, it can be argued, the new family passed into the realm of common sense, where it came to justify the distribution of national wealth through wages paid to men. Indeed, it remains extremely powerful to this day as both metaphor and metonymy, the unacknowledged model and source of middle-class power.[14]

THE POWER OF DOMESTICITY

It is at this point in my argument that a feminist perspective must be invoked, but it cannot be a feminism that sinks comfortably into the rhetoric of victimization. It has to be thoroughly politicized. By this I mean we must be willing to accept the idea that, as middle-class women, we are empowered, although we are not empowered in traditionally masculine ways. We have to acknowledge that as middle-class intellectuals we are not critical mirrors of a separate and more primary process orchestrated by others — be they politicians, bureaucrats, captains of industry, or simply men. As women intellectuals we are doubly implicated in the process of reproducing the state of mind upon which other openly and avowedly political institutions depend. It is on this basis that I reject the notion that women's writing exists in a domain of experience outside of political history. I can no longer accept what conventional histories assume — that such writing occupies the secondary status of a "reflection" or "consequence" of changes within more primary social institutions — the army, hospital, prison, or factory. To the contrary, my evidence reveals domestic fiction actively disentangled the language of sexual relations from that of political economy. The rhetoric of this fiction (in Wayne Booth's sense of the term[15]) laid out a new cultural logic that would eventually become common sense, sensibility, and public opinion. In this way, female knowledge successfully combatted one kind of power, based on title, wealth, and physical force, with another, based on the control of literacy. By equating good reading with what was good for women readers, a new standard for reading laid down the semantic ground for common sense and established the narrative conventions structuring public opinion. The new standard of literacy helped to bring a new class of people into existence. This class laid claim to the right to privacy on behalf of each individual. Yet this class set in motion the systematic invasion of private life by surveillance, observation, evaluation, and remediation. In a word, it ruled, still rules, through countless microtechniques of socialization, all of which may be lumped together under the heading of education.[16] During the second half of the nineteenth century, institutions were created to perform these operations upon masses of people in much the same way as domestic fiction did upon characters.

Those of us who have grown up within an institutional culture consequently carry around a voice much like that of a fictional narrator in his or her head. Sensitive to the least sign of disorder — a foul word, a piece of clothing undone, some food sliding off one's fork, or, worse still, some loss of control over bodily functions — the presence of this voice, now nearly two hundred years old, more surely keeps us in line than fear of the police or the military. For the unofficial forms of power have a terrible advantage over those which are openly and avowedly regulatory. They make us afraid of ourselves. They operate on the supposition that we harbor desires dangerous to the general good. Believing in the presence of a self that is essentially subversive, we keep watch over ourselves — in mirrors, on clocks, on scales, through medical exams, and by means of any number of other such

[14]I have argued this at length in *Desire and Domestic Fiction*. This essay began as an early version of the introduction and later developed into a theoretical investigation of my argument with literature, history, and academic feminism. I refer readers to the book for evidence supporting the necessarily brief outline of the events in the history of modern sexuality which composes part of this essay. [Armstrong]

[15]See the introduction to Reader-Response Theory, p. 962.

[16]In "'The Mother Made Conscious': The Historical Development of a Primary School Pedagogy," *History Workshop* (1985), vol. 20, Carolyn Steedman has researched the rationale and analyzed the process by which the techniques of mothering were extended beyond the household and, through the establishment of a national educational system, became the gentle but unyielding girders of a new institutional culture. [Armstrong]

practices. Thus we internalize a state that is founded on the conflict between self and state interests, and we feel perfectly justified in enacting its power — which is, after all, only good for oneself — upon others.

Convinced that power exerted in and through the female domain is at least as powerful as the more conventional forms of power associated with the male, I want to sketch out the relationship between the two during the modern period. I will suggest that modern institutional cultures depend upon the separation of "the political" from "the personal" and that they produce and maintain this separation on the basis of gender — the formation of masculine and feminine domains of culture. For, I will argue, even as certain forms of cultural information were separated into these two opposing fields, they were brought together as an intricate set of pressures that operated on the subject's body and mind to induce self-regulation. We can observe this peculiarly effective collaboration of the official and unofficial forms of power perhaps most clearly in the formation of a national education system during the Victorian period and in the whole constellation of efforts that went on simultaneously to appropriate leisure time.[17] British fiction participates in both efforts and therefore demonstrates the modes of collaboration between them.

To introduce their highly influential *Practical Education* in 1801, Maria Edgeworth and her father announce their break with the curriculum that reinforced traditional political distinctions: "On religion and politics we have been silent because we have no ambition to gain partisans, or to make proselytes, and because we do not address ourselves to any sect or party."[18] In virtually the same breath, they assure readers, "With respect to what is commonly called the education of the heart, we have endeavored to suggest the easiest means of inducing useful and agreeable habits, well regulated sympathy and benevolent affections" (p. viii). Their program substitutes abstract terms of emotion and behavior for those of one's specific socioeconomic identity. Rooting identity in the very subjective qualities that earlier curricula had sought to inculcate in young women alone, the Edgeworths' program gives priority to the schoolroom and parlor over the church and courts for purposes of regulating human behavior. In doing this, their educational program promises to suppress the political signs of human identity (which is of course a powerful political gesture in its own right). Perfectly aware of the power to be exercised through education, the Edgeworths justify their curriculum for cultivating the heart on grounds that it offered a new and more effective method of policing. In their words, "It is the business of education to prevent crimes, and to prevent all those habitual propensities which necessarily lead to their commission" (p. 354).

To accomplish their ambitious political goal, the Edgeworths invoke an economy of pleasure which cannot in fact be understood apart from the novel and the criticism that was produced both to censor and to foster it. First, the Edgeworths accept the view prevailing during the eighteenth century which said that fiction was sure to mislead female desire:

> With respect to sentimental stories, and books of mere entertainment, we must remark, that they should be sparingly used, especially in the education of girls. This species of reading cultivates what is called the heart prematurely, lowers the tone of the mind, and induces indifference for those common pleasures and occupations which . . . constitute by far the greatest portion of our daily happiness. (p. 105)

But the same turn of mind could as easily recognize the practical value of pleasure when it is harnessed and aimed at the right goals. Convinced that "the pleasures of literature" acted upon the reader in much the same way as a child's "taste for sugar-plums" (p. 80), forward-thinking educators began to endorse the reading of fiction, so long as it was governed by principles that made conformity seem desirable.

[17]See, for example, Peter Stallybrass and Allon White, *The Politics and Poetics of Transgression* (London: Methuen, 1986); Peter Clark, *The English Alehouse: A Social History, 1200–1830* (London: Longman, 1983); Thomas Walter Laqueur, *Religion and Respectability: Sunday Schools and Working Class Culture, 1780–1850* (New Haven: Yale University Press, 1976). [Armstrong]

[18]Maria Edgeworth and Robert L. Edgeworth, *Practical Education* (London, 1801), 2: ix. Citations in the text are to this edition. [Armstrong]

In formulating a theory of mass education in which fiction had a deceptively marginal role to play, the Edgeworths and their colleagues were adopting a rhetoric which earlier reformers had used to level charges of violence and corruption against the old aristocracy. They placed themselves in the tradition of radical Protestant dissent going back to the sixteenth century, a tradition which had always argued that political authority should be based on moral superiority. Sexual relations so often provided the terms for making this claim that no representation of the household could be considered politically neutral. To contest that notion of the state which depended upon inherited power, puritan treatises on marriage and household governance represented the family as a self-enclosed social unit into whose affairs the state had no right to intervene. Against genealogy they posited domesticity. But in claiming sovereignty for the natural father over his household, these treatises were not proposing a new distribution of political power. They were simply trying to limit the monarch's power. To understand the social transformation that was achieved by the English Revolution (according to Christopher Hill, not achieved until more than a century later), we have to turn away from what we consider to be the political themes of the puritan argument and consider instead what happens to gender.[19]

According to Kathleen M. Davis, the puritan doctrine of equality insisted upon the difference of sexual roles, in which the female was certainly subordinate to the male, and not upon the equality of the woman in kind. "The result of this partnership," she explains, "was a definition of mutual and complementary duties and characteristics." Gender was so clearly understood in these oppositional terms that it could be graphically represented:[20]

Husband	Wife
Get goods	Gather them together and save them
Travel, seek a living	Keep the house
Get money and provisions	Do not vainly spend it
Deal with many men	Talk with few
Be "entertaining"	Be solitary and withdrawn
Be skillful in talk	Boast of silence
Be a giver	Be a saver
Apparel yourself as you may	Apparel yourself as it becomes you
Dispatch all things outdoors	Oversee and give order within

In so representing the household as the opposition of complementary genders, the authors of countless puritan tracts asked readers to imagine the household as a self-enclosed social unit. But if these authors wanted to define the family as an independent source of authority, their moment did not arrive. The puritan household consisted of a male and a female who were structurally identical, positive and negative versions of the same thing. The authority of the housewife described above could not yet be imagined as a positive thing in its own right. Until she took up her vigil and began to order personal life, a single understanding of power reigned, and men fought to determine the balance among its various parts.

Unlike the authors of seventeenth-century marriage manuals and domestic economies, the educational reformers of nineteenth-century England could look back on a substantial body of writing whose main purpose was to produce a historically new woman. During the centuries between the English Revolution and the present day, this woman was inscribed with values which appealed

[19]For a discussion of the paternalism that emerged in opposition to patriarchy in seventeenth-century puritan writing, see Leonard Tennenhouse, *Power on Display: The Politics of Shakespeare's Genres* (New York: Methuen, 1986), especially the chapter entitled "Family Rites." In describing the alternative to patriarchy that arose at the end of the seventeenth and beginning of the eighteenth century in aristocratic families, Randolph Trumbach opposes the term "patriarchal" to the term "domesticity," by which he refers to the modern household. This social formation is authorized by internal relations of gender and generation rather than by way of analogy to external power relations between monarch and subject or between God and man, *The Rise of the Egalitarian Family* (New York: Academic Press, 1978), pp. 119–63. [Armstrong]

[20]Kathleen M. Davis, "The Sacred Condition of Equality — How Original Were Puritan Doctrines of Marriage?" *Social History* (1977), 5: 570. Davis quotes this list from John Dod and Robert Cleaver, *A Godly Forme of Householde Gouernment* (London, 1614). [Armstrong]

to a whole range of competing interest groups, and, through her, these groups seized authority over domestic relations and personal life. In this way, I believe, they created a need for the kind of surveillance which modern institutions provide. Indeed, the last two decades of the seventeenth century saw an explosion of writing aimed at educating the daughters of the numerous aspiring social groups. The new curriculum promised to educate these women in such a way as to make them more desirable than women who had only their own rank and fortune to recommend them. This curriculum exalted a woman whose value resided chiefly in her femaleness rather than in the traditional signs of status, a woman who possessed emotional depth rather than a physically stimulating surface, one who, in other words, excelled in the very qualities that differentiated her from the male. As gender was redefined in these terms, the woman exalted by an aristocratic tradition of letters ceased to appear so desirable. In becoming the other side of this new sexual coin, she represented surface rather than depth, embodied material as opposed to moral value, and displayed idle sensuality instead of unflagging concern for the well-being of others. So conceived, the aristocratic woman no longer defined what was truly and most desirably female.

But it was not until the mid-nineteenth century that the project of defining people on the basis of gender began to acquire some of the immense political influence it still exercises today. Around the 1830s, one can see the discourse of sexuality relax its critical gaze on the aristocracy as the newly forming working classes became a more obvious target of moral reform. Authors suddenly took notice of social elements who had hardly mattered before. These reformers and men of letters discovered that rebellious artisans and urban laborers, for example, lacked the kind of motivation that supposedly characterized normal individuals. Numerous writers sought out the source of poverty, illiteracy, and demographic change in these underdeveloped individuals, whose behavior was generally found to be not only promiscuous but also ambiguously gendered. Once they succeeded in translating an overwhelming economic problem into a sexual scandal, middle-class intellectuals could step forward and offer

themselves, their technology, their supervisory skills, and their institutions of education and social welfare as the appropriate remedy for growing political resistance.

In all fairness, as Foucault notes, the middle classes rarely applied institutional procedures to others without first trying them out on themselves. When putting together a national curriculum, the government officials and educators in charge adopted one modeled on the educational theory that grew up around the Edgeworths and their intellectual circle, the heirs of the dissenting tradition.[21] This was basically the same as the curriculum proposed by eighteenth-century pedagogues and reformers as the best way of producing a marriageable daughter. By the end of the eighteenth century, the Edgeworths were among those who had already determined that the program aimed at producing the ideal woman could be applied to boys just as well as to girls. And by the mid-nineteenth century, one can see the government figuring out how to administer much the same program on a mass basis. In providing the conceptual foundation for a national curriculum, a particular idea of the self thus became commonplace, and as gendered forms of identity determined how people thought of themselves as well as others, that self became the dominant social reality.

Such an abbreviated history cannot do justice to the fierce controversies punctuating the institution of a national education system in England. I simply call attention to this material as a site where political history obviously converged with the history of sexuality as well as with that of the novel to produce a specific kind of individual. I do this to suggest the political implications of representing these as separate narratives. As it began to deny its political and religious bias and to present itself instead as a moral and psychological truth, the rhetoric of reform obviously severed its ties with an aristocratic past and took up a new role in history. It no longer constituted a form of resistance but enclosed a specialized domain of culture apart from political relations where apolitical truths

[21] See Brian Simon, *Studies in the History of Education, 1780–1870* (London: Lawrence and Wishart, 1960), pp. 1–62. [Armstrong]

could be told. The novel's literary status hinged upon this event. Henceforth fiction would deny the political basis for its meaning and refer instead to the private regions of the self or to the specialized world of art but never to the use of words that created and still maintains these distinctions so basic to our culture. Favored among kinds of fiction were novels that best performed the rhetorical operations of division and self-containment and thus turned existing political information into the discourse of sexuality. These works of fiction gave novels a good name, a name free of politics, and often the name of a woman such as Pamela, Evelina, Emma, or Jane Eyre.[22] Then, with the translation of human identity into sexual identity came widespread repression of the political literacy characterizing an earlier culture, and with it, too, mass forgetting that there was a history of sexuality to tell.

THE POLITICS OF DOMESTIC FICTION

Let me offer a detailed example of the exchange between reader and literary text to provide a sense of how the power of domesticity works through such an exchange. Charlotte Brontë flaunted this very power in writing her novel *Shirley*.[23] The novel contains an otherwise gratuitous scene where Shakespeare's *Coriolanus* is read aloud and critiqued, as if to give the reader precise rules for reading, rules that should fascinate literary historians. They are not Brontë's own but rules developed during the preceding century by countless authors of ladies' conduct books and educational treatises. These authors proposed the first curriculum to include native British literature. Around the time Brontë sat down to write *Shirley*, a new generation of writers had taken up the question of how to distinguish good reading from bad. Their efforts swelled the growing number of Victorian magazines. Whether or not girls should read novels was the concern that shaped the debates over a curriculum for women during the eighteenth century, then nineteenth-century pedagogical theory developed around the question of how to make fiction useful for teaching foreigners and working-class people as well as women and children. Rules for reading developed along with the national standard curriculum that extended a curriculum originally meant only for girls of the literate classes to young Englishmen and women at various levels and their counterparts throughout the colonies. It is much the same theory of education that informs our educational system today. By using this example from *Shirley* to illustrate the rationale and procedures by which Victorian intellectuals extended what had been regarded as a female form of literacy to male education, I also want to mark an important difference between Charlotte Brontë's understanding of this process and our own. She was, I believe, far more aware of the politics of literary interpretation than we are.

One of her least colorful heroines, Carolyn Helstone, uses Shakespeare to while away an evening of leisure with her beloved cousin and future husband Robert Moore, a surly manufacturer, whose authoritarian way of dealing with factory hands is earning him threats of Luddite[24] reprisals. During this, their one intimate moment together until the end of the novel, they reject all the pastimes available to lovers in an Austen novel in favor of reading Shakespeare's *Coriolanus*. Far more detailed than any such exchange in earlier fiction, this act of reading spells out the procedures by which reading literature was thought to produce a form of knowledge that was also a form of social control. Robert Moore is half Belgian, half English. It is through reading Shakespeare that, according to Carolyn, he "shall be entirely English."[25] For, as she patiently explains to him, "Your French forefathers don't speak so sweetly, not so solemnly, nor so impressively as your English ancestors,

[22]Eponymous heroines of novels by Samuel Richardson (1740), Fanny Burney (1778), Jane Austen (1816), and Charlotte Brontë (1847).

[23]Published in 1849.

[24]Named after the semilegendary Ned Lud, who in a fit had smashed stocking frames in 1779, the Luddites were organized groups of laborers who destroyed industrial machinery in the British midlands and northern counties during the years 1811–16.

[25]Charlotte Brontë, *Shirley*, Andrew and Judith Hock, eds. (Harmondsworth: Penguin, 1974), p. 114. Citations of the text are to this edition. [Armstrong]

Robert." But being English does not identify a set of political affiliations — as it would in Shakespeare's time. It refers instead to essential qualities of human mind. Carolyn has selected a part for Robert to read aloud that, in her words, "is toned with something in you. It shall waken your nature, fill your mind with music, it shall pass like a skillful hand over your heart. . . . Let glorious William come near and touch it; you will see how he will draw the English power and melody out of its chords."

I have called this relationship between reader and text an exchange in order to stress the fact that writing cannot be turned to the task of constituting readers without giving up old features and acquiring new ones of its own; to dwell on the reader is to explain but one half of the transformational logic of this exchange. Just as Robert, the rude Belgian, becomes a gentle Englishman by reading Shakespeare, so, too, the Jacobean playwright is transformed by the domestic setting in which he is read. Carolyn urges Robert to receive the English of another historical moment as the voice of an ancestor speaking to him across time and cultural boundaries. To no one's surprise, the written Shakespeare, thus resurrected, has acquired the yearnings and anxieties of an early nineteenth-century factory owner. And as we observe the Bard becoming the nineteenth-century man, we also witness an early version of our own literary training. Here, extending through the educated middle-class female to the male and, through him, acquiring universal application, we can see how voices that speak from positions vastly different in social space and time quickly translate into aspects of modern consciousness.

Thus Shakespeare becomes the means of reproducing specifically modern states of mind within the reader. Reading Shakespeare is supposed "to stir you," Carolyn explains, "to give you new sensations. It is to make you feel your life strongly, not only your virtues, but your vicious, perverse points. Discover by the feeling the reading will give you at once how high and how low you are" (p. 115). If Shakespeare loses the very turns of mind that would identify him with his moment in history, then Robert loses features of a similar kind in Brontë's representation of the scene of reading. And this, of course, is the point. Reading Shakespeare translates Robert's political attitudes into essential features of mind. It simultaneously objectifies those features and subjects them to evaluation. The "English power" that Robert acquires by reading literature is simply the power of observing himself through the lens of liberal humanism — as a self flushed with the grandiosity of an ordinariness that has been totally liberated from historical bias and political commitment. For it is through this lens that the novel has us perceive the transformations that come over Robert as he reads *Coriolanus* under the gentle tutelage of Carolyn Helstone: "stepping out of the narrow line of private prejudices, he began to revel in the large picture of human nature, to feel the reality stamped upon the characters who were speaking from that page before him" (p. 116).

Her tutoring induces Robert to renounce one mode of power — which Carolyn associates with the imperiously patriarchal nature of *Coriolanus* — and to adopt another — which she identifies as a benevolent form of paternalism. As it is administered by a woman and used to mediate a sexual exchange, *Coriolanus* becomes the means for effecting historical change: *Coriolanus* becomes Carolyn. Performed as writing and reading, that is, the play becomes the means of internalizing a form of authority identified with the female. The political implications of feminizing the reader are clear as Carolyn gives Robert a moral to "tack to the play: . . . you must not be proud to your workpeople; you must not neglect chances of soothing them, and you must not be of an inflexible nature, uttering a request as austerely as if it were a command" (p. 114). Brontë is less than subtle in dramatizing the process by which reading rids Robert of the foreign devil. She seems to know exactly what political objective is fulfilled as he fills the mold of the Englishman and benevolent father. Brontë also puts the woman in charge of this process even though she gives her heroine the less imperious passages to read. Retiring, feminine, and thoroughly benign, Carolyn's power is hardly visible as such. Yet she is clearly the one who declares that reading has the power "to stir you; to give you new sensations. It is to make you feel your life strongly, not only your virtues, but your vicious, perverse points" (p. 115). And when Robert has finished reading, she is the one to ask, "Now, have you felt Shakespeare?" (p. 117). She suppresses all that belongs to the past as so much noise in her effort to being under examination the grand currents of emotion that run straight from Shakespeare to the modern day reader, a reader who is thoroughly English. In thus guiding his reading with her smiles and admonitions, Carolyn executes a set of delicate procedures capable of translating any and all cultural information into shades of modern middle-class consciousness and the substance of a literary text. Although its setting — during the Luddite rebellions — makes *Shirley* anachronistic by about thirty years, the solution it proposes for the problem of political resistance, through the production of a new ruling-class mentality, marks this novel as utterly Victorian — perhaps even ahead of its time.

As similar textualizing strategies were deployed here and elsewhere throughout Victorian culture, an intricate system of psychological differences completely triumphed over a long-standing tradition of overtly political signs to usher in a new form of state power. This power — the power of representation over the thing represented — wrested authority from the old aristocracy on grounds that a government was morally obliged to rehabilitate deviant individuals rather than subdue them by force. The Peterloo Massacre of 1819 made it clear that the state's capacity for violence had become a source of embarrassment to the state. Overt displays of force worked against legitimate authority just as they did against subversive factions.[26] If acts of open rebellion had justified intervention in areas of society that government had not had to deal with before, then the government's use of force gave credence to the workers' charges of government oppression. The power of surveillance came into dominance at precisely this moment in

English history, displacing traditional displays of violence. Remarkably like the form of vigilance that insured an orderly household, this power did not create equality so much as trivialize the material signs of difference by translating all such signs into differences in the quality, intensity, direction, and self-regulatory capability of an individual's desire.

In saying this, I am not suggesting that we should use British fiction to identify forms of repression or to perform acts of liberation, although my project has a definite political goal. I simply want to represent the discourse of sexuality as deeply implicated in — if not directly responsible for — the shape of the novel, and to show the novel's implication, at the same time, in producing a subject who knew herself and saw that self in relation to others according to the same feminizing strategies that had shaped fiction. I regard fiction, in other words, both as a document and as an agency of cultural history. I believe it helped to formulate the ordered space we now recognize as the household, that it made that space totally functional and used it as the context for representing normal behavior. In doing all this, fiction contested alternative bases for human relationships. As the history of this female domain is figured into political history, then, it will outline boldly the telling cultural move upon which, I believe, the supremacy of middle-class culture ultimately hinged. That is, it will reenact the moment when writing invaded, revised, and contained the household according to strategies that distinguished private from social life and thus detached sexuality from political history.

Where others have isolated rhetorical strategies that naturalize the subordination of female to male, no one has thoroughly examined the figure that differentiates the sexes as it links them together by sexual desire. And if no one asks why, how, and when gender differentiation became the root of human identity, no degree of theoretical sophistication can help us understand the totalizing power of this figure and the very real interests such power inevitably serves. So basic are the terms "male" and "female" to the semiotics of modern life that no one can use them without to some degree performing the very reifying gesture whose operations we need to

[26]E. P. Thompson, pp. 680–85. [Armstrong] What became known as the "Peterloo Massacre" was the Fifteenth Hussars' attack on a peaceful and well-organized demonstration of over sixty thousand workers massed at St. Peter's Fields outside Manchester, England, in 1819; they had been protesting against the Corn Laws and in favor of Parliamentary reform. Eleven workers were killed and many hundreds seriously injured by sabre cuts and flying hooves.

understand and whose power we want to historicize. Whenever we cast our political lot in the dyadic formation of gender, we place ourselves in a classic double bind, which confines us to alternatives that are not really alternatives at all. That is to say, any political position founded primarily on sexual identity ultimately confirms the limited choices offered by such a dyadic model. Once one thinks within such a structure, sexual relationships appear as the model for all power relationships. This makes it possible to see the female as representative of all subjection and to use her subjectivity as if it were a form of resistance. Having inscribed social conflict within a domestic configuration, however, one loses sight of all the various and contrary political affiliations for which any given individual provides the site. This power of sexuality to appropriate the voice of the victim works as surely through inversion, of course, as by strict adherence to the internal organization of the model.

Still, there is a way in which I owe everything to the very academic feminism I seem to critique, for unless it were now acceptable to read women's texts as women's texts, there would be no call to historicize this area of culture. In view of the fact that women writers have been taken up by the Norton Anthology as part of the standard survey of British literature and also as a collection all of their own, and in view of the fact that we now have male feminists straining to hop on the bandwagon, I feel it is simply time to take stock. It is time to consider why literary criticism presently feels so comfortable with a kind of criticism that began as a critique both of the traditional canon and of the interpretive procedures the canon called forth. This should tell us that by carving out a separate domain for women within literary criticism, feminist criticism has yet to destabilize the reigning metaphysics of sexuality. Literary historians continue to remain aloof from but still firmly anchored in a narrow masculinist notion of politics as more and more areas within literary studies have given ground to the thematics of sexuality promoted by academic feminism. Indeed, a sexual division of labor threatens to reproduce itself within the academy whereby women scholars interpret literature as the expression of the sexual subject while male scholars attend to matters of history and politics. To subvert this process, I believe we must read fiction not as literature but as the history of gender differences and a means by which we have reproduced a class and culture specific form of consciousness.

Lawrence Buell

b. 1939

Born in Bryn Mawr, Pennsylvania, Lawrence Buell attended Princeton University for his B.A. and Cornell University for his M.A. and Ph.D., which he received in 1966. While finishing his doctorate, Buell instructed in English at Tunghai University in Taichung, Taiwan, before he became a professor at Oberlin College. The author of Literary Transcendentalism *(1973),* New England Literary Culture *(1986),* The Environmental Imagination: Thoreau, Nature Writing, and the Formation of American Culture *(1995),* Writing for an Endangered World: Literature, Culture, and Environment in the United States and Beyond *(2001), and* Emerson *(2003), Buell is interested in the connections between environment (and environmentalism) and the formation of national identity in the United States, particularly during the nineteenth century. Buell is currently professor of American literature, language, and culture at Harvard University. The following essay, "The Ecocritical Insurgency," was originally printed in* New Literary History *in the summer of 1999.*

The Ecocritical Insurgency

"Ecocriticism" is a new movement, of the '90s really, still at an early state of unfolding. Although the term was coined twenty years ago, although critical readings of literary texts and movements in relation to ideas of nature, wilderness, natural science, and spatial environments of all sorts have been pursued for the better part of a century, only in the last decade has the study of literature in relation to environment begun, quite suddenly, to assume the look of a major critical insurgency. The "Who's listening?" question that nagged me when I began such work in the late 1980s has given way to "How can I keep up with all that's coming out?" and "Can I even keep track of, let alone stay in touch with, all the players?"

Will this burgeoning of literature-and-environment studies continue? Almost surely so, for at least two reasons. First, the field of application for environmentally-valenced critical inquiry is immense in duration and range. Given that human beings are inescapably biohistorical creatures who construct themselves, at least partially, through encounter with physical environments they cannot not inhabit, any artifact of imagination may be expected to bear traces of that. From this it follows that the scope of the inquiry extends in principle from the oldest surviving literary texts, such as the Sumerian epic *Gilgamesh*, to the literature of the present moment — as is borne out by the sweep of such critical books as Robert Pogue Harrison's *Forests: The Shadows of Civilization* and Louise Westling's *The Green Breast of the New World,* both of which start with *Gilgamesh.*[1] Second, as human civilizations enter the *fin de siècle,*[2] "the environment" looms up as a more pressing, multifarious problem than ever before. If, as W. E. B. Du Bois famously remarked, the key problem of the twentieth century has been the problem of the color line,[3] it is not at all unlikely that the twenty-first century's most pressing problem will be the sustainability of earth's environment — and that the responsibility for addressing this problem, or constellation of problems, will increasingly be seen as the responsibility of *all* the human sciences, not just of specialized disciplinary enclaves like ecology or law or public policy.

So literature-and-environment studies are here to stay, no doubt about it. But what has ecocriticism achieved thus far? Where has it succeeded, where fallen short? What new directions might it be expected to take? What directions does it need to take in order to fulfill its potential? At different points, the nine essays in this special issue address all those questions, and so will I — in the form of a review of the movement's history, emphases, internal disagreements, and future prospects, with special but not exclusive reference to the essays in the present issue.

COHERENCE VS. DISSENSUS: IN THE MOVEMENT, IN THESE ESSAYS

As their heterogeneity attests, to the extent that contemporary literature-and-environment studies can in fact be rightly called "a movement," so far it looks less like, say, New Critical formalism, structuralism, deconstructionism, and New Historicism than like feminist and ethnic revisionism or Gay Studies; for it is on the whole more issue-driven than methodology-driven.[4] Ecocriticism so far

---

[1] Robert Pogue Harrison, *Forests: The Shadows of Civilization* (Chicago, 1992); Louise Westling, *The Green Breast of the New World* (University, Miss., 1996). [Buell]

[2] French for "end of the century," usually, but not here, referring to the end of the nineteenth century.

[3] The quotation is from the "Forethought" to *The Souls of Black Folk* (1903); for Du Bois, see p. 567.

[4] Ecocriticism also differs from the latter kind of insurgency in that the question of its imbrication with identitarian considerations is (even) more complicated. For one thing, the question of what my "environmental identity" is and how that relates, or does not relate, to my standing to speak *qua* scholar about environmental issues and their relation to human interests is even more problematic — albeit less volatile, since the environment can not talk back — than the question of how, for example, my racial identity does or does not bear on my unpacking of issues of racial representation. For another, and

lacks the kind of field-defining statement that was supplied for more methodologically-focused insurgencies by, for example, Wellek and Warren's *Theory of Literature* for New Critical formalism and Edward Said's *Orientalism* for colonial discourse studies.[5]

To be sure, it is possible to locate the inception point of the contemporary movement rather precisely: organizationally, as a ferment within the Western Literature Association that put the term "ecocriticism" into circulation, that gave birth to the Association for the Study of Literature and Environment, its periodical *ISLE*, and a series of major conferences of increasingly international scope;[6] and substantively, as an inquiry focused especially in the first instance on Anglophone and particularly U.S. nonfiction and poetry about the natural world,[7] an inquiry that, as one can see

from the notes of the contributions to this issue, has begun to generate a sizeable secondary literature and with it, perhaps, the beginning of something like an ecocritical canon, upon or against which current work often builds.[8]

Yet the mutual divergence of archives and approaches here is on the whole more striking than the convergences.[9] Jonathan Bate reconceives the represented cultural-environmental life-worlds of

---

by the same token, if only because literary discourse is so manifestly a product of human agents focused largely on the realm of human affairs and directed exclusively toward human audiences, no matter how salient "the problem of the environment" becomes in the contemporary world, we may expect ecocriticism to experience more extratribal skepticism and intratribal malaise (vehement assertions of its import contending with doubts as to its impertinence or peripherality) relative to critical inquiry directed at aspects of identity located more squarely within the human body and/or the realm of human affairs: gender, race, class, and sexuality. [Buell]

[5] René Wellek was a former member of the Prague School of Linguistics who in the 1950s became an apologist for the New Criticism; for the connections between formalist schools, see the introduction to Formalisms, p. 749. For Said, see p. 1801.

[6] *ISLE* (Interdisciplinary Studies in Literature and Environment) features a mix of literary-critical and creative work focused on environmental issues, as do (for example) *Terra Nova, Trumpeter,* and *Orion.* Less scholarly in flavor than *ISLE,* however, these journals illustrate more markedly the bridges that many academic ecocritics have tried from the first to form with lay reading communities. Meanwhile, a number of more specifically academic journals in various fields have been hospitable to ecocritical contributions: *Studies in Romanticism, American Literary History, Environmental History, Environmental Ethics,* and so on. This in turn testifies to the exceptionally wide interdisciplinary range of interest shown by ecocritics as a group, from medicine, public health, and engineering sciences to religion, music, and sculpture. [Buell]

[7] This is still too true. Part of the problem is that ecocriticism has not yet discovered how to conceptualize metropolis, on which more below. Part of the problem is that it has not yet become sufficiently cross-national. So far ecocriticism is being practiced most vigorously in the United States, the United Kingdom, Japan, and Australia; but not sufficiently in

a comparatist spirit, with honorable exceptions like Patrick Murphy (through critical articles and editorial projects) and Scott Slovic (through international symposia he has helped to organize). The untapped opportunities are still much greater than the achievement thus far. For example, India offers distinguished traditions of environmental historiography, ecological science, and environmentalist thought as well as a rich literary archive that engages environmental issues; but ecocriticism has not, so far, tapped very deeply into it. [Buell]

[8] *The Ecocriticism Reader: Landmarks in Literary Ecology,* ed. Cheryll Glotfelty and Harold Fromm (Athens, Ga., 1996), pp. 393–402, provides a selected bibliography of recommended books, articles, and journals, including an annotated booklist of "top fifteen choices," a large majority dating from the 1980s or thereafter. Three of our nine essays are by "top-fifteen" authors (Bate, Elder, Harrison), and the *Ecocriticism Reader* also includes essays by Howarth, Love, and Phillips. [Buell]

[9] By my quick count, no one critical book of humanistic scholarship having to do with environmental representation or history is cited by a two-thirds majority of our nine contributors. The dozen mentioned at least twice (though often in cursory base-touching ways), are (in order of publication): Leo Marx, *The Machine in the Garden: Technology and the Pastoral Ideal in America* (New York, 1964) (Howarth, Love); Donald Worster, *Nature's Economy: A History of Ecological Ideas* (Cambridge, 1977) (Howarth, Phillips); Gillian Beer, *Darwin's Plots* (London, 1983) (Bate, Howarth); *Deep Ecology,* ed. Michael Tobias (San Diego, 1985) (Hayles, Hitt); Jonathan Bate, *Romantic Ecology: Wordsworth and the Environmental Tradition* (London, 1991) (Bate, Hitt); Max Oelschlaeger, *The Idea of Wilderness* (New Haven, 1991) (Hitt, Howarth); Karl Kroeber, *Ecological Literary Criticism: Romantic Imagining and the Biology of Mind* (New York, 1994) (Hitt, Rowlett); Lawrence Buell, *The Environmental Imagination* (Cambridge, Mass., 1995) (Elder, Hitt, Howarth, Love, Phillips); *Uncommon Ground: Toward Reinventing Nature,* ed. William Cronon (New York, 1995) (Harrison, Hayles, Hitt); Joseph Carroll, *Evolution and Literary Theory* (Columbia, Mo., 1995) (Love, Rowlett); and *The Ecocriticism Reader* (Howarth, Love, Phillips). Among these, six are among the *Ecocriticism Reader*'s top fifteen (Marx, Worster, Elder, Bate, Oelschlaeger, Buell). In short, the degree of convergence of critical genealogies represented here is certainly not negligible, but neither is it particularly conspicuous. [Buell]

Jane Austen and Thomas Hardy as a barometer of nineteenth-century social change that attests to the persistence of an environmentally-aware sense of Englishness based on country life; this essay represents a green-revisionary turn within British traditions of literary-cultural critique that run back from Raymond Williams through F. R. Leavis to ancient roots in Matthew Arnold.[10] More than any other literary scholar, Bate has influenced the rise of British ecocriticism, through his *Romantic Ecology* (1991), but it and his later work owe very little to American literary studies. Quite the opposite is true for John Elder, author of one of the influential early contributions of the American phase of the movement (*Imagining the Earth* [1985], recently republished by the University of Georgia Press). Though Elder's interest in reconciling the categories of "nature" and "culture" constitutes an important ground of affinity to Bate's, Elder's long interest in the life and writings of Robert Frost and of American nature poetry more generally, together with his commitment to coordinating formal literary study with the life-practices of environmental immersion and education (always envisaged, as here, in an upcountry New England context), not only give his work a distinctively American turn but also identify him much more closely than Bate with the distinctively anti-institutional thrust of a sizeable number of American ecocriticism's first fomenters and practitioners: the desire to bring academic writing closer to creative nature writing, as well as to environmental(ist) life-praxis, by taking literary study outdoors, *in situ*. Elder aims to discover the basis of Frostian aesthetics in the internalization and reminiscence of agrarian work-rhythms that the ecocritic is to discover not just through vicarious identification or scholastic investigation but also, indeed even more crucially, by reenacting them.

Robert Pogue Harrison, on the other hand, is an American scholar who approaches the poetry of Wallace Stevens in the first instance not as an Americanist but by way of a specialization in comparative literature. Harrison is less an insider to the ecocritical movement than Bate or Elder, or

than the author of the one extended treatment of Stevens's environmental thought Harrison cites.[11] Indeed the way Harrison positions himself in an Americanist context is calculated to cause uneasiness among the considerable subset of ecocritics strongly attached to a "deep ecology" model of understanding the bond between nature and the human self in terms of some kind of shared spiritual and/or biophiliac identity. For Harrison cautiously but explicitly distances himself from myths of the primordialism of American wilderness and the correlative assumption in American romantic thinking of an "innermost self" that is primordial nature's "aboriginal correlate."[12] In this respect his essay aligns itself with the thrust of William Cronon's interdisciplinary anthology *Uncommon Ground* (to which Harrison contributed), which makes ancillary use of poststructuralist theory to underscore an argument that Cronon and the other environmental historians whose work is most extensively featured in that volume have been making on empirical grounds: that the "pristine" nature encountered by North American settlers was subject to anthropogenic modification long before the Columbian arrival.

On the other hand, most seasoned ecocritical practitioners are likely to take more or less in stride Harrison's critique (and his representation of Stevens's own critique) of primordialist false consciousness or the illusion of an essential "ecological self," both of which Bate and Elder for example would surely recognize as culture-produced myths, although they would probably differ from Harrison in wanting to envisage these myths as potentially more enabling than disabling. The fourth essay, however, by another contributor to *Uncommon Ground*, is written from a critical standpoint that not only differs far more sharply from Elder's and Bate's but from Harrison's as well: consideration of technologies of virtual ecology and of fictions that erase the distinction between physical world and simulacrum as sites of reflection on human perception, negotiation,

[10]For Williams on the Romantic reaction to nature, see p. 364. For Leavis and Arnold, see pp. 650 and 412.

[11]Gyorgi Voros, *Notations of the Wild: Ecology in the Poetry of Wallace Stevens* (Iowa City, 1997). [Buell]
[12]Robert Pogue Harrison, "Not Ideas about the Thing but the Thing Itself," in this issue of *NLH*, p. 670. [Buell]

and manipulation of physical environment. N. Katherine Hayles's conceptual base of operation is the conversation between literary studies and science studies (Hayles holds degrees in both literature and chemistry), from which vantage point it makes sense to start from a presentist[13] view of "the virtual and the natural as aligned," rather than to rotate around the history of their disjunction or the project of recuperating nature in an increasingly virtualized postmodern world order. In this view, "ecology" refers not to the biota but to the systematization of life-regimes by increasingly informatics-driven cultural regimes; and the task of critical reflection is to appraise in light of this awareness "the profound interconnections that bind us all together, human actors and non-human life forms, intelligent machines and intelligent people."[14]

Hayles's departure from Bate's, Elder's, and Harrison's emphasis on landscape-based primary texts against the background of a strong interest in the history of (perceptions of) physical environment cannot but intensify the question as to whether the category of "ecocriticism" is either infinitely ductile or else so porous as to amount to nothing more than an empty signifier. I myself am not at all confident that Harrison and especially Hayles would be so willing to accept classification as ecocritic as the other seven contributors might (not that anyone likes to be stuck in a pigeonhole); but even if their two essays were subtracted from this symposium its internal diversity would still be great enough to warrant a more concerted attempt to specify just what, if any, the movement's internal coherence and outer boundaries might be.

To the question of what ecocriticism "at bottom" means or should mean, at one level there is no avoiding a Humpty Dumpty answer: ecocriticism means what its self-identified and imputed practitioners say it does. Inclusivist definitions

have, moreover, often been urged by the movement's most visible proponents. For example, Cheryll Glotfelty's Introduction to the *Ecocriticism Reader* offers a many-mansions definition of ecocriticism as "the study of the relationship between literature and the physical environment" in any and all ways that these two terms can be brought into relation.[15] Yet it would not be accurate to characterize the movement as nothing more than an infinitely-expanding menu of noncompetitive, happily-coexistent possibilities, nor to suppose that all who have become associated with it (whether by choice or by ascription) feel equally content to let pluralism take precedence over the quest for consensus.

For one thing, a number of the essays in this gathering display strongly normative dispositions. Their perspectives are heterogeneous in the aggregate, but in the individual case they often express a strong sense of conviction about the right way to frame the inquiry. Elder deeply believes that ecocritical education must involve environmental education at the experiential level. This seems at least partially at odds with Harrison's and particularly Hayles's disbelief in the myth of individual rapport with the natural world. Dana Phillips believes so deeply in the disjunction of literary texts from physical worlds that the prospect of a revival of even a qualified version of literary representation as extratextual mimesis seems to him wrongheaded.[16] On the other hand, William Howarth deeply believes that ecocriticism and literary scholarship generally must rest on a better-informed understanding of

---

[13]"Presentism" (usually pejorative though not here) involves viewing the problems of the past in present-day terms, rather than attempting to understand why people in the past, from their own perspective, did what they did.

[14]N. Katherine Hayles, "The Illusion of Autonomy and the Fact of Recursivity: Virtual Ecologies, Entertainment, and *Infinite Jest*," in this issue of *NLH*, p. 696. [Buell]

[15]Glotfelty, "Introduction," *Ecocriticism Reader*, p. xviii. [Buell]

[16]Since Phillips's chief target of attack is chapter 4 of my *The Environmental Imagination*, it would be evasive to refrain from providing some reply to it, but an unfair exploitation of my advantaged position as commentator to make more than this summary response: namely that since Phillips's often incisive micro-level observations come (or so I think) at the cost of reducing book to chapter, chapter to monolithic claim, and "realism" to monolithic formation, the essay's main value seems to me rather as further evidence of the nonmonolithic character of the ecocritical community and as symptomatic of a theory-anxiety surrounding discussion of certain particular issues, especially the issue of the referential dimension of literary texts — on which more below. [Buell]

---

landscape history and the contributing natural sciences, a position that seems to presuppose some sort of mimetic link between environmentally-valenced literary text and physical landscape.

SOME DISTINCTIVE ECOCRITICAL EMPHASES

1.

In different ways, Elder, Hayles, Howarth, Glen A. Love, Phillips, and John Rowlett all proceed from a conviction that informed knowledge of the natural world and/or natural science(s) ought to matter for the practitioner of environmentally-valenced literary studies. This has certainly been one of the major preoccupations within the ecocritical movement, albeit not universally shared or advanced in the same way. Love's essay is perhaps the most instructive formulation of this view in that it is the most comprehensive in scope, positioning itself most self-consciously within an unfolding tradition of ecocritical thought; and since it argues most explicitly for a kind of unified field theory of ecocritical discourse: namely, that ecocriticism should base itself on the model of evolutionary biology, more specifically upon the kind of pan-disciplinary, sociobiological syntheses conceived by figures like Edward O. Wilson and Jared Diamond. Love hopefully identifies a counterpart trajectory of literary-critical synthesis from the book most often taken by ecocritical insiders to be contemporary ecocriticism's first major statement,[17] Joseph

Meeker's recently-republished *The Comedy of Survival* (1974) — an imaginative and venturesome attempt to theorize comedy as an ecological as well as a literary mode, to Joseph Carroll's *Evolution and Literary Theory* (1995), a recent argument on behalf of conceiving evolutionary biology as a model for literary inquiry. Love's standing as himself an inspirational figure in one of the academic departments in the U.S. so far most committed to a strong ecocritical presence (the University of Oregon — the other two being the University of California at Davis and the University of Nevada at Reno) adds weight to his account.

Although the vision of a new synthesis of literary and environmental studies that would somehow bridge the two cultures has been one of ecocriticism's major projects, it is by no means the only project; nor is the kind of synthetic conceptualization Love favors the only path that the subset of science-oriented ecocritics have favored. Nor do they necessarily privilege the same modes of scientific inquiry. Howarth seems rather to favor bringing humanities and science together in the context of study of specific landscapes and regions; and for him the history of geology is at least as important as that of the life sciences. Rowlett is scrupulous in wanting to preserve due historical and substantive distinctions between the field of ornithology and the disciplines of poesis and criticism, even as he seeks to bring the two domains closer together and gently chides Leonard Lutwack's *Birds in Literature* for failing to draw fully enough upon the author's expertise as a birder when doing literary criticism. Hayles begins from a vision of how contemporary literary texts are interpenetrated by technological discourses and how criticism rests on the premise of a very different kind of scientistic approach to the understanding of the production of thought and expression. Thus her commitment to the premise that the natural world, as well as representations thereof, is for all practical purposes produced by technology — now if not always already — is vastly different from Love's premise, shared in different measure also by Howarth and Rowlett, of scientific knowledge as a means for ecocriticism to achieve a more informed recuperation of the natural world.

[17]Every concerned party will wish to propose his or her own genealogy, of course. To my mind, the most seminal precontemporary critical texts are, for U.S. literary studies, Marx's *The Machine in the Garden* (which Love mentions but criticizes for its argument — which Marx has since revised — that pastoral exhausted itself in the early twentieth century) and, for British literary studies, Raymond Williams, *The Country and the City* (New York, 1973). It is intriguing, *vis-à-vis* what I have to say above and below about ecocritical treatments of mimeticism, that although both Marx and Williams mainly approach their central binaries (nature/technology for Marx, country/city for Williams) as ideological formations, they differ on the issue of whether literary representations should be read primarily as symbolic configurations (Marx) or also as attempted representations of historical landscapes (Williams). [Buell]

2.

Another facet of this contrast I have just drawn is that Hayles's approach, broadly speaking, leads to a critical discourse wholly congruent with and indeed likely influenced by poststructuralist models of inquiry, which for Love and to some extent also for Howarth seems rather a roadblock to the project of acquiring the scientific understanding needed to redirect critical attention toward literature's engagement with the physical environment. Hence in part the popular association of the ecocritical movement with resistance to theory — an association justifiable up to a point in light of the impetus in some quarters of the movement to emphasize environmental education as the key underpinning of critical practice (either at the experiential level, as in Elder, or at the level of formal learning, as in Howarth, Love, and Rowlett), and/or to montage critical practice with nature writing and other forms of poesis.[18] Yet no less typical of the way the movement has unfolded, indeed increasingly so as time goes on, has been an anxiety to achieve a constructive engagement with poststructuralist thinking and ensuing strands of literary and cultural theory. Thus for example Jhan Hochman's *Green Cultural Studies* develops an environmentalist hermeneutic on the basis of a revisionary cultural constructionist model, and Verena Andermatt Conley's *Ecopolitics* rereads the archive of French poststructuralism as a narrative in which green concerns figured to a much greater extent than has been realized.[19] In the present collection, Christopher Hitt returns to a centerpiece of deconstructionist and New Historicist romantic theory, the conception of the sublime as an armature for the will to linguistic and/or imperial dominance. Hitt gives the formation an ecocentric turn by fixing upon the pivotal moment of blockage or frustration in the face of encounter with nature's alien power that traditional revisionist theory can see only as that which must be repressed or overcome.

Both the endeavor to rebut or contain the antimimeticism of linguistic and cultural constructionist versions of critical practice and more theoretically-driven attempts to turn these models to advantage evince a certain predictable anxiety about the referential properties of literary texts. To me this comes out in an especially telling way (though here I may exaggerate out of personal interest in being the subject of remark) in the resistance expressed cautiously by Hitt and truculently by Phillips to my argument for the importance of a post-poststructuralist account of environmental mimesis: for a critical practice that operates from a premise of bidirectionality, imagining texts as gesturing outward toward the material world notwithstanding their constitution as linguistic, ideological, cultural artifacts that inevitably filter and even in some respects grotesquify their renditions of the extratextual. How hard it is in the present climate of critical opinion to think "mimesis" without going to one extreme or another! — whether it be to want to overprotect ecocriticism against textuality or social construction theory by exaggerating literature's capacity to render factical environments or environmental phenomena, or whether it be to warn us off from trying to reopen such an unfashionable subject, or whether it be to want to play down or finesse the issue as Hayles does by placing primary emphasis on artifact, culture, environment as the product of simultaneously interpenetrating technologies. That questions of mimesis, reference, and extratextuality have produced such intense contrary reactions persuades me that even in today's age of "remediation," as Jay David Bolter and Richard Grusin wittily call it,[20] this age in which (as Hayles perceives) technologies of simulation interlock the realms of

---

[18] David Robertson's *Real Matter* (Salt Lake City, 1997) and Elder's *Reading the Mountains of Home* (Cambridge, Mass., 1998) are good examples of such montaging, as are a number of critical texts by practitioners known chiefly as creative writers rather than as scholars though they do or have taught within universities, such as Gary Snyder's *The Practice of the Wild* (San Francisco, 1990) (another of the *Ecocriticism Reader*'s top fifteen) and several of the essays in Leslie Silko's *Yellow Woman and a Beauty of the Spirit* (New York, 1996). [Buell]

[19] Jhan Hochman, *Green Cultural Studies* (Moscow, Idaho, 1998); Verena Andermatt Conley, *Ecopolitics* (London, 1997). [Buell]

[20] Jay David Bolter and Richard Grusin, *Remediation* (Cambridge, Mass., 1999). [Buell]

minds, texts, matter *via* their multiply replicative simulacra, even now — indeed perhaps especially now — the ancient question of the mimetic status of literary texts, the relation of image to world, will doubtless remain very much alive within the literature and environment movement. This indeed I should identify as a second major focus of ecocritical work, partially related to yet also in considerable measure distinct from the first, the question of the pertinence of scientific models of inquiry to literary study.[21]

By now it will have become obvious that my preferred approach to sizing up the contemporary ecocritical scene is to create in essay-meditation form a counterpart of the special-issue-symposium genre: that is, to map it as a concourse of interlocking but semi-autonomous projects. So far I have named two. In the interest of conciseness I must now become more briskly schematic.

3. Understanding Landscapes, Regions, Place.

Howarth's essay on (re)imagining wetlands is a luminous and erudite case study of a particular landscape form, considered both ecologically and phenomenologically, all the more valuable on account of the neglect of swamplands as a literary-critical topic, despite the manifest importance of such marginal lands not only in ecological research and environmental historiography but also, as Howarth begins to suggest, in literature as well (Hemingway's "Big Two-Hearted River," Faulkner's "The Bear," Zora Neale Hurston's *Their Eyes Were Watching God*, A. R. Ammons's "Corson's Inlet," and so on). Ecocritical study of other landscape types favored by literary discourse is in a flourishing state: for example, mountains, rivers and watersheds, forests, and deserts. Harrison's *Forests* is an exemplary case, and worth setting beside Howarth as instancing the obverse approach of starting with symbolic/ideological topoi rather than with forest ecology or history.

So far ecocriticism has focused overwhelmingly on nonmetropolitan landscapes (as do virtually all the contributors here), but there is no inherent reason why it should continue to do so. On the contrary, the movement can never be expected to reach full critical maturity until it has figured out how, as it were, to envisage John Muir and Jane Addams as part of the same narrative. Until this is done, the ecocritical movement will surely remain much more tied than it should to the Euroamerican bourgeois imaginary (nature writing and to a lesser extent nature poetry being to a large extent written by white middle-class authors and consumed by white middle-class readers).

One project of this kind, which Hayles's treatment of *Infinite Jest* illustrates in part, is engagement with post–Rachel Carson literature of toxic anxiety and resistance, which puts greater emphasis than ever before upon the interpenetration of "country" and "city," and dramatizes the presence within the history of urbanization and industrialization of forms of environmentalism that most ecocritics have so far overlooked. Love seems to me absolutely right in suggesting that environmental degradation may prove a key incentive to the growth of a less parochial, more environmentally-informed literary criticism.[22]

This and other landscape-oriented ecocritical work would in the long run promise to give a far richer account than we now have of the placial

[21]In addition to my own work and the critique of it by Hitt and Phillips, see for example, Leonard M. Scigaj's post-poststructuralist ecocritical rehabilitation of reference in "Contemporary Ecological and Environmental Poetry: *Différance or Référance?*" *ISLE*, 3 (1996), 1–27, a revised version of which will appear in Scigaj's *Sustainable Poetry* (University Press of Kentucky, 1999); and Elisa New's argument, against "magisterial gaze" theory, on behalf of eye/mind/literature's capacity to receive and render the material world, in her *The Line's Eye* (Cambridge, Mass., 1999). [Buell]

[22]The archive of eco-degradation literature cutting across town-country landscapes has lately been growing fast: Don DeLillo's *White Noise* and *Underworld*; Terry Tempest Williams's *Refuge*; A. R. Ammons's *Garbage*; Richard Powers's *Gain*; Percival Everett's *Watershed*. For critical treatments, see for example Cynthia Deitering, "The Postnatural Novel: Toxic Consciousness in Fiction of the 1980s," *Ecocriticism Reader*, 196–203; Kamala Platt, "Ecological Chicana Literature: Ana Castillo's 'Virtual Realism,'" *ISLE*, 3 (1996), 67–96; Lawrence Buell, "Toxic Discourse," *Critical Inquiry*, 24 (1998), 639–65; and (in the field of social discourse studies) Barbara Adam, *Timescapes of Modernity* (London, 1998). [Buell]

basis of human and social experience, conceiving "place" not simply in the light of an imagined descriptive or symbolic structure, not simply as social construction, not simply as an ecology, but all of these three simultaneously. Indeed, we are now, I believe, in the midst of a time of intense interest in place theory, to which the ecocritical movement has begun to make important contributions and surely will make more.[23]

4. Questioning Anthropo-Normativity.

As Love hints in his allusion to a colleague's revisionist reading of *Moby-Dick* on the basis of "the Whaleness of the Whale,"[24] ecocriticism has begun, but only begun, to revisit the archive of literary history with a view to appraising its status both as reinscription and as critique of anthropocentricism. Both Howarth and Rowlett, by the very fact of concentrating as they do on the fascinations of contemplation and mimesis of birds and of wetlands ecology, raise the environmental-ethical question, without greatly developing it theoretically, of the extent to which ecocritical exegesis should take up the issue of literature's sensitivity — or insensitivity — to the history and phenomenon of human dominance of the nonhuman world; and should look for symptoms of autocritique, troubled uncertainty, alternative environmental-ethical models of thinking.

Perhaps the most substantial work of this kind to date, both in ecocriticism *per se* and in such contiguous fields as environmental ethics and cultural studies, has had to do with how human representations of animals, and of human relations with animals, unsettle anthropocentric norms.[25] In this critical studies has followed the lead of such prominent nature writers as Barry Lopez ("Renegotiating the Contracts," *Of Wolves and Men, Arctic Dreams*), as well as the (sometimes quite contrasting) work in various genres by Native American intellectuals.[26] Often critical discussions have linked human (mis)treatment of animals and the rest of the natural world to androcentrism, racism, and classicism, sometimes in critiques whose emphasis on humanitarian feeling directed at animals as evasion of social responsibility puts the work altogether outside the pale of what might reasonably be called *ecocriticism*,[27] sometimes with a view to diagnosing dominationism as a pathology working across species lines such that, for example, women and animals become conceived coordinately, as analogous vulnerable targets of patriarchal victimage.

A particularly rich vein of ecocritical inquiry has been feminist study of the symptomatics and history of how (mostly male) observers imaged women as "natural" and nature as gendered female, and of how women's imaging treatment of the nonhuman world has differed, historically and across cultures, from men's. It is no coincidence that two of the *Ecocriticism Reader's* top fifteen recommendations are influential works of

[23]In addition to the essays in this volume by Bate and Elder, see for example *The Desert Is No Lady: Southwestern Landscapes in Women's Writing and Art*, ed. Vera Norwood and Janice Monk (New Haven, 1987); Kent Ryden, *Mapping the Invisible Landscape* (Iowa City, 1993); Gary Snyder, *A Place in Space: Ethics, Aesthetics, and Watersheds* (Washington, D.C., 1995). Phenomenologists Edward Casey and David Abram, anthropologist Keith Basso, architectural historian Delores Hayden, social theorists Henri Lefebvre and Doreen Massey, social geographers David Harvey and John Agnew, and humanistic geographers Yi-fu Tuan and Robert David Sack are some of the scholars in other fields who have done particularly important work on place theory upon which environmentally-valenced literary scholarship has been drawing. Sack's *Homo Geographicus* (Baltimore, 1997) is perhaps the most ambitious attempt thus far to formulate "place" with the requisite tripartite balance and amplitude, sketchy and schematic though it is in a number of spots. As this range of models suggests, self-identified ecocritics by no means have a monopoly on place theory; their work exists in an uneasy dialogue with literary scholarship of a more thoroughgoingly social constructionist persuasion, such as *The Geography of Identity*, ed. Patricia Yaeger (Ann Arbor, 1996). [Buell]
[24]Glen A. Love, "Ecocriticism and Science: Toward Consilience?" of *NLH* 30: 3 (1999), p. 573. [Buell]

[25]See for example Marian Scholtmeijer, *Animal Victims in Modern Fiction* (Toronto, 1993). [Buell]
[26]For example, Linda Hogan's recent novel *Power* (New York, 1998), about a Native American prosecuted for hunting an endangered species, differs from the (predominantly Anglo) nature-writing norm by setting species-protectionist and first-peoples-antidiscrimination commitments at odds. [Buell]
[27]For example, James Turner's *Reckoning with the Beast: Animals, Pain, and Humanity in the Victorian Mind* (Baltimore, 1980). [Buell]

this kind (Carolyn Merchant's intellectual/cultural history *The Death of Nature* and Annette Kolodny's *The Lay of the Land*, an exposé of androcentric patterns of representation in early American male writers). It is regrettable and misleading that the present collection includes no such work, includes indeed the work of only one woman scholar. For not only was ecofeminism[28] a key influence behind the early phases of the movement — key in directing attention both to gender issues and, more broadly, to all kinds of pathologies in anthropo-normative thinking — it is also the case that important new work continues to be produced that builds more elegantly on earlier findings that had been expressed in too sketchy or tractarian form (for example, Westling's *Green Breast of the New World)* and/or questions and complicates previous binaries (for example, Vera Norwood's *Made from This Earth: American Women and Nature* [Chapel Hill, 1993]). Today the impression seems to be gaining ground in some quarters that feminist scholarship is in retreat. In literature-and-environment studies, however, it is being practiced just as vigorously as ever, and with increasing sophistication.

5. Environmental(ist) Rhetoric.

For the most part, the contributors to this symposium choose for demonstration purposes primary texts from the repertoire of what other literary scholars would immediately classify as imaginative literature: prose fiction, poetry, nonfiction nature writing. But as Howarth's essay especially suggests, the literature and environment movement has by no means bound itself to this archive but has in fact interested itself in unpacking modes of articulacy across every expressive genre. This is still another way it has sometimes brought together science and literature, as in M. Jimmie Killingsworth and Jacqueline S. Palmer's *Ecospeak: Rhetoric and Environmental Politics in America*, a study of conventions of environmental advocacy in both popular and academic genres across the human sciences; and Carl G. Herndl and Stuart C. Brown's collection *Green Culture: Environmental Rhetoric in Contemporary America*, which presents a series of studies focusing largely on particular interest groups and activist projects.[29]

At this point we perhaps seem to have reached, indeed transgressed, the very border of the "literary," and again the nagging question arises of whether, if there is no limit to what might count as "ecocriticism," the term can be said to denote anything substantive. But that would be a shortsighted response. Rather, the foregoing studies of green rhetoric should be seen as testifying crucially (a) to the interdisciplinarity of vision that is or at least always should be at some level present in ecocritical thought even when it is trained exclusively on poems or novels, (b) to the importance for many ecocritical practitioners of the link between literary representations of environment and the realms of social affairs, as well as the realms of science, and (c) to the transferability and pertinence of eco*critical* expertise — the exegetical and conceptual tools requisite to textual analysis — to virtually all aspects of environmental inquiry, whether scientists and public policy experts recognize it or not. That does not mean we should expect Al Gore to sit down and read the last dozen exegeses of the representation of seasonality in Thoreau's *Walden* or Annie Dillard's *Pilgrim at Tinker Creek*. But it does mean that ecocritics have every right to believe that if they do their jobs right — not, of course to be taken for granted — they will not only be able

[28]"Ecofeminism," be it noted, has been made to cover a variety of possibilities, such that many scholars whom some might so categorize would wish to disclaim the label: the critique of patriarchal representation of nature as female, revisionist rehabilitation of the importance of women's roles in the history of natural history, scientific research, writing about nature; the advocacy of an "ethics of care" toward nature as against an ethics of extraction or exploitation; and the recuperation of an alleged mystical affinity (biological or spiritual) between woman and nature. [Buell]

[29]M. Jimmie Killingsworth and Jacqueline S. Palmer, *Ecospeak: Rhetoric and Environmental Politics in America* (Carbondale, 1992); *Green Culture: Environmental Rhetoric in Contemporary America,* ed. Carl G. Heindl and Stuart C. Brown (Madison, 1995). [Buell]

to reveal to fellow literature department colleagues some hidden things about even the most
familiar and classic works but also have a basis to
consider themselves participants in a pandiscipli-
nary inquiry of the first order of historical significance. From the multiple epicenters of this
inquiry — through a mixture of collaboration,
solitary concentration, and sheer luck — not just
new regulatory codes, pharmaceuticals, engineering marvels and the like may ensue but new

insights, new revaluations of the physical world
and humanity's relation to it, that will make a difference in the way others live their lives.
Admittedly nothing is more shocking for many
humanists than to find their ideas taken seriously.
But it might just happen in this case. That self-
identified ecocritics tend to be folk who seriously
entertain that possibility is one reason why the
best ecocritical work is so strange, timely, and
intriguing.

Stephen Greenblatt

b. 1943

*Renaissance scholar Stephen Jay Greenblatt is in the vanguard of academics responsible for the rise
of New Historicist studies in the United States. Greenblatt was born in Cambridge, Massachusetts; he
took a B.A. (1964), an M.Phil. (1968), and a Ph.D. (1969) in English at Yale, and an A.B. (1966) and
M.A. (1968) at Pembroke College, Cambridge University. Starting in 1969 Greenblatt taught at the
University of California at Berkeley, becoming a full professor in 1980. Since 1997 Greenblatt has
taught at Harvard University, where he is now John Cogan University Professor of the Humanities.
Among Greenblatt's honors are a Fulbright scholarship (1964–66), a Guggenheim fellowship (1975),
and a visiting professorship at the University of Peking (1982). His books include* Sir Walter Raleigh:
The Renaissance Man and His Roles *(1973),* Allegory and Representation *(1979),* Renaissance Self-
Fashioning: From More to Shakespeare *(1980),* Representing the English Renaissance *(1988),*
Shakespearean Negotiations: The Circulation of Social Energy in Renaissance England *(1988),*
Learning to Curse: Essays in Early Modern Culture *(1990),* Marvelous Possessions: The Wonder of
the New World *(1991),* Re-Drawing the Boundaries: The Transformation of English and American
Literary Studies *(1992, ed., with Giles Gunn),* New World Encounters *(1992),* Practicing New
Historicism *(1999, with Catherine Gallagher),* Hamlet in Purgatory *(2001), and his best-selling biog-
raphy of Shakespeare,* Will in the World *(2004). Greenblatt is also the editor of* Representations, *a
Berkeley-based journal in which New Historicist articles regularly appear. The selections here are
from a special issue of* Genre *(Spring/Summer 1982), titled* The Power of Forms in the English
Renaissance. *In the Introduction, Greenblatt makes reference to some of the other essays in the volume but not to his own "King Lear and Harsnett's 'Devil-Fiction.'"*

Introduction to *The Power of Forms in the English Renaissance*

"I am Richard II. Know ye not that?" exclaimed Queen Elizabeth on August 4, 1601, in the wake of the abortive Essex rising. On the day before the rising, someone had paid the Lord Chamberlain's Men forty shillings to revive their old play about the deposing and killing of Richard II. As far as we know, the play — almost certainly Shakespeare's — was performed only once at the Globe, but in Elizabeth's bitter recollection the performance has metastasized: "this tragedy was played 40tie times in open streets and houses."[1]

The Queen enjoyed and protected the theater; against moralists who charged that it was a corrupting and seditious force, she evidently sided with those who replied that it released social tensions, inculcated valuable moral lessons, and occupied with harmless diversion those who might otherwise conspire against legitimate authority. But there were some in the Essex faction who saw in the theater the power to subvert, or rather the power to wrest legitimation from the established ruler and confer it on another. This power, notwithstanding royal protection, censorship, and the players' professions of unswerving loyalty, could be purchased for forty shillings.

The story of Richard II was obviously a highly charged one in a society where political discussion was conducted, as in parts of the world today, with Aesopian indirection. Clearly it is not the text alone — over which the censor had some control — that bears the full significance of Shakespeare's play, or of any version of the story. It is rather the story's full situation — the genre it is thought to embody, the circumstances of its performance, the imaginings of its audience — that governs its shifting meanings. "40tie times in open streets and houses": for the Queen the repeatability of the tragedy, and hence the numbers of people who have been exposed to its infection, is part of the danger, along with the fact (or rather her conviction) that the play had broken out of the boundaries of the playhouse, where such stories are clearly marked as powerful illusions, and moved into the more volatile zone — the zone she calls "open" — of the streets. In the streets the story begins to lose the conventional containment of the playhouse, where audiences are kept at a safe distance both from the action on stage and from the world beyond the walls. And in the wake of this subversive deregulation, the terms that mark the distinction between the lucid and the real become themselves problematic: are the "houses" to which Elizabeth refers public theaters or private dwellings where her enemies plot her overthrow? can "tragedy" be a strictly literary term when the Queen's own life is endangered by the play?[2]

Modern historical scholarship has assured Elizabeth that she had nothing to worry about: *Richard II* is not at all subversive but rather a hymn to Tudor order. The play, far from encouraging thoughts of rebellion, regards the deposition of the legitimate king as a "sacrilegious" act that drags the country down into "the abyss of chaos"; "that Shakespeare and his audience regarded Bolingbroke as a usurper," declares J. Dover Wilson, "is incontestable."[3] But in 1601 neither Queen Elizabeth nor the Earl of Essex were so sure: after all, someone on the eve of a rebellion

---

[1] Elizabeth was speaking to William Lambarde the antiquary; see the Arden edition of Shakespeare's *King Richard II*, ed. Peter Ure (Cambridge: Harvard University Press, 1956), pp. lvii–lxii. [Greenblatt]

[2] The ambiguity is intensified by the Queen's preceding comment, according to Lambarde: "*Her Majestie.* 'He that will forget God, will also forget his benefactors; this tragedy was played 40tie times in open streets and houses'" (Ure, p. lix). [Greenblatt]

[3] John Dover Wilson, "The Political Background of Shakespeare's *Richard II* and *Henry IV*," *Shakespeare-Jahrbuch*, 75 (1939), 47. The condemnation of Bolingbroke is "evident," we are told, "from the whole tone and emphasis of *Richard II*" (p. 48). I am grateful to Patricia Allen for the reference to this essay. [Greenblatt]

thought the play sufficiently seditious to warrant squandering two pounds on the players, and the Queen understood the performance as a threat. Moreover, even before the Essex rising, the actual deposition scene (IV.i.154–318 in the Arden edition) was carefully omitted from the first three quartos of Shakespeare's play and appears for the first time only after Elizabeth's death.

How can we account for the discrepancy between Dover Wilson's historical reconstruction and the anxious response of the figures whose history he purports to have accurately reconstructed? The answer lies at least in part in the difference between a conception of art that has no respect whatsoever for the integrity of the text ("I am Richard II. Know ye not that?") and one that hopes to find, through historical research, a stable core of meaning within the text, a core that united disparate and even contradictory parts into an organic whole. That whole may provide a perfectly orthodox celebration of legitimacy and order, as measured by homilies, royal pronouncements, and official propaganda, but the Queen is clearly responding to something else: to the presence of *any* representation of deposition, whether regarded as sacrilegious or not; to the choice of this particular story at this particular time; to the place of the performance; to her own identity as it is present in the public sphere and as it fuses with the figure of the murdered king. Dover Wilson is not a New Critic: he does not conceive of the text as an iconic object whose meaning is perfectly contained within its own formal structure. Yet for him historical research has the effect of conferring autonomy and fixity upon the text, and it is precisely this fixity that is denied by Elizabeth's response.

Dover Wilson's work is a distinguished example of the characteristic assumptions and methods of the mainstream literary history practiced in the first half of our century, and a further glance at these may help us to bring into focus the distinctive assumptions and methods exemplified in the essays collected in this volume. To be sure, these essays are quite diverse in their concerns and represent no single critical practice; a comparative glance, for example, at the brilliant pieces by Franco Moretti and John Traugott will suggest at once how various this work is. Yet diverse as they are, many of the present essays give voice, I think, to what we may call the new historicism, set apart from both the dominant historical scholarship of the past and the formalist criticism that partially displaced this scholarship in the decades after World War Two. The earlier historicism tends to be monological; that is, it is concerned with discovering a single political vision, usually identical to that said to be held by the entire literate class or indeed the entire population ("In the eyes of the later middle ages," writes Dover Wilson, Richard II "represented the type and exemplar of royal martyrdom" [p. 50]). This vision, most often presumed to be internally coherent and consistent, though occasionally analyzed as the fusion of two or more elements, has the status of an historical fact. It is not thought to be the product of the historian's interpretation, nor even of the particular interests of a given social group in conflict with other groups. Protected then from interpretation and conflict, this vision can serve as a stable point of reference, beyond contingency, to which literary interpretation can securely refer. Literature is conceived to mirror the period's beliefs, but to mirror them, as it were, from a safe distance.

The new historicism erodes the firm ground of both criticism and literature. It tends to ask questions about its own methodological assumptions and those of others: in the present case, for example, it might encourage us to examine the ideological situation not only of *Richard II* but of Dover Wilson on *Richard II*. The lecture from which I have quoted — "The Political Background of Shakespeare's *Richard II* and *Henry IV*" — was delivered before the German Shakespearean Society, at Weimar, in 1939. We might, in a full discussion of the critical issues at stake here, look closely at the relation between Dover Wilson's reading of *Richard II* — a reading that discovers Shakespeare's fears of chaos and his consequent support for legitimate if weak authority over the claims of ruthless usurpers — and the eerie occasion of his lecture ("these plays," he concludes, "should be of particular interest to German students at this moment of that everlasting adventure which we call history" [p. 51]).

Moreover, recent criticism has been less concerned to establish the organic unity of literary works and more open to such works as fields of force, places of dissension and shifting interests, occasions for the jostling of orthodox and subversive impulses. "The Elizabeth playhouse, playwright, and player," writes Louis Adrian Montrose in a brilliant recent essay, "exemplify the contradictions of Elizabethan society and make those contradictions their subject. If the world is a theatre and the theatre is an image of the world, then by reflecting upon its own artifice, the drama is holding the mirror up to nature."[4] As the problematizing of the mirror metaphor suggests, Renaissance literary works are no longer regarded either as a fixed set of texts that are set apart from all other forms of expression and that

[4]"The Purpose of Playing: Reflections on a Shakespearean Anthropology," *Helios,* n.s. 7 (1980), 57. [Greenblatt]

contain their own determinate meanings or as a stable set of reflections of historical facts that lie beyond them. The critical practice represented in [*The Power of Forms in the English Renaissance*] challenges the assumptions that guarantee a secure distinction between "literary foreground" and "political background" or, more generally, between artistic production and other kinds of social production. Such distinctions do in fact exist, but they are not intrinsic to the texts; rather they are made up and constantly redrawn by artists, audiences, and readers. These collective social constructions on the one hand define the range of aesthetic possibilities within a given representational mode and, on the other, link that mode to the complex network of institutions, practices, and beliefs that constitute the culture as a whole. In this light, the study of genre is an exploration of the poetics of culture.

King Lear *and* Harsnett's "Devil-Fiction"

Modern critics tend to assume that Shakespearean self-consciousness and irony lead to a radical transcendence of the network of social conditions, paradigms, and practices in the plays. I would submit, by contrast, that Renaissance theatrical representation itself is fully implicated in this network and that Shakespeare's self-consciousness is in significant ways bound up with the institutions and the symbology of power it anatomizes.

To grasp this we might consider *King Lear.* We happen to know one of the books that Shakespeare had been reading and seems indeed to have had open before him as he revised the old play of *King Leir.* The book, printed in 1603, is by Samuel Harsnett, then chaplain to the Bishop of London, and is entitled *A Declaration of Egregious Popish Impostures, to with-draw the harts of her Majesties Subjects from their allegeance, and from the truth of Christian*

Religion professed in England, under the pretense of casting out devils. Practised by Edmunds, alias Weston a Jesuit, and divers Romish Priests his wicked associates. Whereunto are annexed the Copies of the Confessions and Examinations of the parties themselves, which were pretended to be possessed, and dispossessed, taken upon oath before her Majesties Commissioners for Causes Ecclesiasticall.[1] From

[1]On Harsnett, see D. P. Walker, *Unclean Spirits: Possession and Exorcism in France and England in the Late Sixteenth and Early Seventeenth Centuries* (Philadelphia: University of Pennsylvania Press, 1981), pp. 43–49; Keith Thomas, *Religion and the Decline of Magic* (London: Weidenfeld and Nicolson, 1971), pp. 477–92. On Harsnett and *Lear,* see Kenneth Muir, "Samuel Harsnett and *King Lear,*" *RES,* New Series 2 (1951), 11–21; William Elton, *King Lear and the Gods* (San Marino, CA: Huntington Library, 1966). [Greenblatt]

this remarkable book — a scathing account of a series of spectacular exorcisms conducted between the spring of 1585 and the summer of 1586 principally in the house of a recusant gentleman, Sir George Peckham of Denham, Buckinghamshire — Shakespeare took many small details, especially for the demonology Edgar exhibits in his disguise as the possessed Poor Tom. My interest here is not in these details which have been noted since the eighteenth century, but in the broader institutional implications of Harsnett's text and of the uses to which Shakespeare puts it.

The *Declaration* is a semi-official attack on exorcism as practiced by Jesuits secretly residing in England (and under constant threat of capture and execution), but the charges are not limited to Catholicism, since Harsnett had earlier written against the Puritan exorcist John Darrell. Like other spokesmen for the Anglican establishment, Harsnett concedes that at some distant time exorcism was a legitimate practice (as, of course, it is in the Bible), but miracles have ceased and corporeal possession by demons is no longer possible. What has taken its place, he writes, is fraud, and, more precisely, theater: exorcisms are stage plays written by cunning clerical dramatists and performed by skilled actors. To be sure, not all the participants are professionals, but the priests, as Harsnett depicts them, run what is in effect an acting school. They begin by talking about the way successful exorcisms abroad had taken place and describe in lurid detail the precise symptoms of the possessed; then the young "schollers," as Harsnett calls those whom the priests have chosen to manipulate, "*frame* themselves jumpe and fit unto the Priests humors, to mop, mow, jest, raile, rave, roare, commend & discommend, and as the priest would have them, upon fitting occasions (according to the difference of times, places, and commers in) in all things to play the devils accordinglie" (p. 38).

Harsnett's *Declaration* then is a massive document of disenchantment; the solemn ceremony of exorcism is, as the attack on Darrell puts it, "now discovered to be but a pure play," and the reverence and fear that the performance inspires are nothing but "miserable shiftes to helpe [the exorcist] off the stage, that he might not be hissed at of all the world."[2] The Jesuits and their retinue are not a holy band driven by religious persecution to move from place to place but closely resemble "vagabond players, that coast from Towne to Towne with a trusse and a cast of fiddles, to carry in theyr consort, broken queanes, and *Ganimedes,* as well for their night pleasance, as their dayes pastime" (p. 149). The power this sleazy crew possesses is the power of the theater. If the end of a comedy, Harsnett notes, is applause for the author and actors, while the end of a tragedy is the "moving of affection, and passion in the spectators," our "*Daemonopoiia,* or devil-fiction, is *Tragico-commaedia,*" for it elicits both exclamations of admiration — "*O that all the Protestans* (sic) *in England did see the power of the Catholick Church*" — and tears (p. 50).

The spectators, of course, do not know that they are merely responding to an effective if tawdry play; they believe that they are celebrants at a moving and sanctified communal ritual. "The devil speakes treason . . . so aptly, distinctly, and elegantly on the stage, that it enchaunted the harts, and affections of the poore bewitched people, and chained them to the Pope" (p. 154); the lowest estimate of the conversions achieved "by this well acted tragedie" is five hundred, and Harsnett states that "devil-tragedians" themselves claim four to five thousand converts. To impress these large crowds, the exorcists, led by Father Edmunds, invoke the vast forces of heaven and hell, call forth by name whole legions of devils, and drive them from the bodies of the possessed by means of powerful amulets and charms. The performance is spectacular, with the writhing demoniac bound in a chair and tortured until the devils are compelled to depart. But the devils, says Harsnett, are tattered figures from the old Church plays, their names grotesque forgeries, and the hallowed vestments and holy objects contemptible stage properties. As for the possessed themselves, they are either histrionic scoundrels like Robert Maynie or servant girls like the sisters

---

[2]Samuel Harsnett, *A Discovery of the Fraudulent Practices of John Darrel* (London, 1599), p. A3ʳ. [Greenblatt]

Sara and Friswood Williams, whose position of social dependency made them susceptible to the powers of suggestion, intimidation, and torture.

Harsnett's detailed identification of exorcism as theater, a conception that is elaborated through almost three hundred pages, is more than a satirical analogy; it is a polemical institutional analysis whose purpose is not only to expose the fraudulence of exorcism but to link that practice to the pervasive theatricality of the Catholic Church (or, as Harsnett elsewhere terms it, "the Pope's playhouse").[3] Priests do not actually believe in their "charmes, and consecrate attire," but only "act, fashion, and play them" in order to gull the ignorant (p. 88); the Mass itself is nothing but "a pageant of moppes, mowes, elevations, crouches, and ridiculous gesticulations" (p. 158). Theatricality here is not so much the consequence of the Church's deviation from the truth as the very essence of that deviation and hence the explanatory key to the entire institution: Catholicism is a "Mimick superstition (it being the onely religion to catch fooles, children, and women, by reason it is naught else, save a conceited pageant of Puppits, and gaudes" (p. 20).

Now *King Lear* at once stages a version of these disenchanted perceptions — most notably in the representation of Edgar's histrionic and fraudulent demonic possession, complete with names drawn directly from the *Declaration* — and insinuates itself paradoxically into the place made vacant by Harsnett's attack: that is, where

[3]Harsnett, *Discovery*, p. A3ʳ. [Greenblatt]

Harsnett had condemned exorcism as a stage play, Shakespeare's play is itself a secular version of the ritual of exorcism. What exactly is being exorcised? Harsnett would say, in effect, that the question is misguided: what matters is the theatrical experience, the power of the performance to persuade the audience that it has heard the voices of radical evil and witnessed the violent expulsion of the agents of Darkness.

The ritual in this staged form is acceptable because the institution it serves is not a theatrical church but a public, state-supervised theater, and the on-lookers are induced to pay homage (and the price of admission) not to a competing religious authority but to professional entertainers safely circumscribed by the wooden walls of the playhouse. Within these walls, the force of Shakespeare's theatrical improvisation is to appropriate the power of the traditional, quasi-magical practice and of the newer, rationalized analysis and then, with this convergent power, to raise questions about the production of the enabling distinctions between supernatural and secular evil, real and theatrical ritual, authority and madness, belief and illusion. Such disturbing questions are at once licensed and contained by the aesthetic, economic, and physical demarcation of playing companies in a play space. Hence the ideological and historical situation of *King Lear* produces the oscillation, the simultaneous affirmation and negation, the constant undermining of its own assertions and questioning of its own practices — in short, the supreme aesthetic self-consciousness — that lead us to celebrate its universality, its literariness, and its transcendence of all ideology.

Frank Lentricchia Jr.

b. 1940

Frank Lentricchia Jr., Katherine Everett Gilbert Professor of Literature, grew up the child of hard-working Italian immigrants in Utica, New York. He majored in math at Utica College until he discovered literature, going on for graduate work in English at Duke University, and receiving his doctorate in 1966. "I'm an aesthete," Lentricchia said in an interview, "but I suspect that my strong ties with my family and background, grandparents, the life they had, the work they did, always has made me feel that a literary criticism that cannot see the roots of literature in our culture, in our every-day existence, is for me . . . a betrayal of my background." Lentricchia published his first book, The Gaiety of Language, *on Yeats and Stevens, in 1968. Since then, Lentricchia has written primarily on twentieth-century American fiction and poetry, aiming always to understand literature as a social text without being deaf to its music. His works include* Robert Frost: Modern Poetics and the Landscapes of the Self *(1975),* Introducing Don DeLillo *(1991), and* Modernist Lyric in the Culture of Capital *(2002). Lentricchia's other academic interest is the history and theory of literary criticism itself, where he has often argued against attempts to confine literature to a separate sphere, and during which he has sought, found, and sometimes discarded heroic exemplars, such as Kenneth Burke and Michel Foucault. His theoretical work includes* After the New Criticism *(1980),* Criticism and Social Change *(1983),* Ariel and the Police *(1988), the best-selling* Critical Terms for Literary Study *(1990), and* Close Reading: The Reader *(2002). In the following excerpt from his chapter on New Historicism in* Ariel and the Police, *Lentricchia assaults Stephen Greenblatt's New Historicism for a series of predictable theoretical moves that conceal, he argues, how little is really going on.*

From *Ariel and the Police*

FROM *FOUCAULT'S LEGACY — A NEW HISTORICISM?*

A strong feature of new-historicist rhetoric and substance is on display in the typical beginnings of Greenblatt's essays, where he would violate the traditional literary sensibility with lengthy citations of bizarre, apparently off-center materials: an account, roughly contemporary with Shakespeare — thickly, arcanely detailed — of a social practice (say, exorcism) far removed from the high literary practice of the Renaissance. With that gambit Greenblatt would shock his traditional reader into the awareness that here, at last, is no literary business as usual. Greenblatt's beginnings seem to promise what, in theory, new historicism, so hermeneutically savvy, isn't supposed to promise — direct access to history's gritty ground-level texture. In that very moment, while doing that sort of rhetorical work in the arena of contemporary critical maneuvering,

Greenblatt initiates his reader to a central new-historicist perspective on culture that recalls the debt of new historicism not only to Foucault but also to the *Annales* school[1] and Geertz's[2] functional anthropology — a strange mix of voices ultimately dominated by Foucauldian tone: the feeling, usually just evoked, almost never argued through, that all social life is organized and controlled down to its oddest and smallest details.

Old historicists are politically innocent — issues of ideology and class conflict rarely touch their literary work. Greenblatt more or less tells us that they needed to open their Marx. New historicists not only have reopened their Marx; they have embraced Michel Foucault (the deeper theoretical influence on their work), and the effect of this (I think, uncritical) acceptance is traced everywhere in new historicism in the coded term "power." The odd theoretical identity of new historicism is constituted by its unlikely marriage of Marx and Foucault, with Foucault as dominant partner.[3] Greenblatt describes his intention as an attempt to "achieve a concrete apprehension of the consequences for human expression — for the 'I' — of a specific form of power, power at once localized in particular institutions — the court, the church, the colonial administration, the patriarchal family — and diffused in ideological structures of meaning, characteristic modes of expression, recurrent narrative patterns."[4] In the context of the specific analyses he produces in his landmark book, *Renaissance Self-Fashioning* (1980),

Greenblatt's statement on power in his introduction rings with all the paranoid resonances sounded in Foucault's account of the death of the "I" in *Discipline and Punish*. The liberal disposition (Greenblatt's and ours) to read "self-fashioning" as free, expressive self-making is repeatedly and wickedly subverted in *Renaissance Self-Fashioning*. Greenblatt's title announces to liberal optimists (we see this with hindsight) Foucault's depressing message, and his description of power endorses Foucault's theory of power, preserving not only the master's repeated insistence on the concrete institutional character of power, its palpability, as it were, but also his glide into a conception of a power that is elusively and literally undefinable — not finitely anchored but diffused from nowhere to everywhere, and saturating all social relations to the point that all conflicts and "jostlings" among social groups become a mere show of political dissension, a prearranged theater of struggle set upon the substratum of a monolithic agency which produces "opposition" as one of its delusive political effects. Greenblatt's account of the "I," like Foucault's, will dramatize its entrapment in a totalitarian narrative coincidental with the emergence of the modern world as dystopian fruition.

To summon the specter of totalitarianism is to summon determinism once again, not in Taine's positivistic manner[5] but in the political style of *1984*.[6] New historicists are officially on record as critics both of determinism and its sentimental alternative (Greenblatt says that "Renaissance English theater in general functioned neither as a simple extension of constituted religious or political authority nor as a counterchurch or subversive assault upon that authority").[7] Moreover, new historicists typically strike more than pro forma attitudes on the issue; Greenblatt is capable of spectacular acrobatic efforts in the analysis of the relationship of literary texts and history in order to

[1]Group of French socioeconomics historians headed by Marc Bloch (1886–1944) and Lucien Febvre (1878–1956) who, working from provincial archives, uncovered long-lost features of medieval and early modern societies.

[2]See p. 1366 for more on Clifford Geertz.

[3]Though Foucault inhabits *Renaissance Self-Fashioning* mainly in Greenblatt's notes, my point is that Foucault's key obsessions and terms shape Greenblatt's argument, particularly in its "Marxist" moments, more than does the work of Clifford Geertz which appears to be more central to Greenblatt than it is. In any event, Geertz's descriptive and apolitical account of culture enhances Greenblatt's Foucauldian legacy of "political grid-lock" (a phrase I steal from a conversation with Lee Patterson, who invented it). [Lentricchia]

[4]Greenblatt, *Renaissance Self-Fashioning*, p. 6. [Lentricchia]

[5]Hippolyte Taine (1828–1893), French historian, preached a deterministic view of literary history as determined by the various writers' race, environment, and times.

[6]Greenblatt's dissertation was partly on Orwell. [Lentricchia]

[7]Stephen Greenblatt, "Loundun and London," *Critical Inquiry* 12 (Winter 1986): 343. [Lentricchia]

avoid determinist schemas of understanding. But the new historicism nevertheless does have a concept of determination; and far from making it worthless, this concept — which just might be the typically anxious expression of post-Watergate American humanist intellectuals — makes new historicism what it is.

Toward the end of a highly detailed and fascinating essay on the relations among theater, the practice of exorcism, and religious and political authority in the Renaissance in France and England — his most recent study of the relations of literature to its contexts — Greenblatt pulls back from his empirical work for a pause of theoretical reflection that may not refresh. He persuades us that English theater is not a reflex of constituted political authority, but in the process of making that point against old-historicist determinism, he may have instituted a profounder version of it. Consider these remarks:

1. It is no accident, I think, that one of Harsnett's tasks as Bishop [of London] Bancroft's assistant was to license plays for publication: this licensing is an element in the fashioning of social categories — the process of demarcation — that confers upon the public theater the cultural meaning that Harsnett wishes to exploit. The official church dismantles and cedes to the players the powerful mechanisms of an unwanted and dangerous charisma: in return, the players confirm the charge that those mechanisms are theater and hence illusory. . . . They therefore do the state some service.[8]

2. Elizabethan theater does not simply reflect the official policy toward the demoniac; it is in part constituted by it and it contributes in its turn to the concrete shaping of spiritual and political discourse upon which it drew.[9]

With those statements that sit at the heart of his theoretical reflections Greenblatt affirms both ends of the spectrum of Marxist literary criticism, from the legendary vulgarity of reflectionist modes (and the artist as pawn and lackey) to the sophistication of the culturally sensitive Western (modernist-bent) Marxism (which grants literature formative power). Elizabethan theater shapes political discourse and at the same time is constituted by an official policy, which is executed by villainous agents whom Greenblatt can name (Bancroft, Harsnett), who exploit the theater by granting it a little freedom in return for which the players "do the state some service." But there is always something else in Greenblatt — the Foucauldian transposition of an apparent Marxist perspective. He tells us that in order to grasp the pattern of the relations of artistic and other social practices "we must be particularly sensitive to similitudes for in the Renaissance similitudes are the most well-travelled pathways of exchange, the great trade route along which cultural power is circulated." There are various social practices, like those of theater and exorcism (whose similitude is said to be "coercive"), there are — to cite *Renaissance Self-Fashioning* again — institutions, like those of the patriarchal family, church, and colonial administration, and there are characteristic modes of expression, from everyday communication to high literary narrative. The ground of grounds for understanding these practices and institutions is either "similitude" itself — the great Renaissance idea — or cultural power which is indistinguishable from political power and which "circulates" (Greenblatt's master trope for the action of power). In the first instance Greenblatt retrieves Taine and Lovejoy:[10] similitude is the invisible expressive center, a "world view" which functions as the principle of making sense of all things, causing (in this particular instance) all things to be visible and coherent in a relation of similarity. In the second instance he summons up Foucault by suggesting that the ground of all practice — cultural and political power — is not itself either an "idea" or a practice: "circulating" power — the master agency located in, and motivated by, no specific agent — fashions and demarcates all social categories, causes all relations of similitude and enhances and flows through all practices and human agents, is not itself a subject but

[8]Greenblatt alludes to Othello's line, "I have done the state some service and they know't" (V.ii).

[9]Stephen Greenblatt, "Loundun and London," *Critical Inquiry* 12 (Winter 1986): 341, 342. [Lentricchia]

[10]Arthur O. Lovejoy (1873–1962), German-born American philosopher and historian of ideas, author of *The Great Chain of Being* (1936).

sweeps up all subjects, even Bishop Bancroft and his personal operative, his intellectual, Harsnett.[11]

Bancroft and Harsnett are triggering or channeling agents only, nothing more. Not free agents. The anonymous power for which they are the medium has the obvious advantage that conspiratorial versions of history in the name of Marx do not have. The "circulating" activity of this power in all social and cultural spaces gives new and shocking meaning to the notion that nothing is outside politics. But the curious (or is it the predictable?) thing about this concept of a power that coerces all practices is that it gives rise in Foucault and (as we'll see) in Greenblatt to the desire to get outside politics — strange new-historicist desire! — and it has no way of explaining (with its but casual interests in class and economics) why some distinctively not marginal types enjoy staying inside, not only feel powerful but act accordingly.

Greenblatt's recuperation, under the mask of power, of Hegelian expressive unity of culture (a monological vision), is one but not the most interesting theoretical anomaly of new historicism. The most interesting anomaly is generated by Foucault's insistence that historians cannot objectively represent the past because they cannot know and therefore put distance between themselves and the circumstances which produced and disciplined them as social beings enmeshed in the practice of a historical *discipline*. At one level a lurking Hegelianism subverts the Foucauldian new-historicist desire to move beyond mainstream historicist practice and guarantees, in advance, the unity of the culture under historical question. At another, deeper level, mainstream historicist desire, under the very mask of its new-historicist negation, resurfaces in Greenblatt's modest statement of limitation. Greenblatt gives voice to Foucault's project of introducing the forbidden concepts of rupture and discontinuity as antidotes to traditional reliance on the grand humanist assumptions of the narrative unity of history; then (in the same breath) he puts Foucault's theoretical program at bay when he speaks of the "impossibility of fully reconstructing and reentering the culture of the sixteenth century, of leaving behind

one's own situation: it is everywhere evident in this book that the questions I ask of my material and indeed the very nature of this material are shaped by the questions I ask of myself. I do not shrink from these impurities — they are the price and perhaps the virtue of this approach — but I have tried to compensate for the indeterminacy and incompleteness they generate by constantly returning to particular lives and particular situations." This apology for his limitation as a historian (it is an unwanted echo of an earlier one made by Taine) remarks ruefully on the price of new historicism — we can't help but note the implication in Greenblatt's tone that objectivity, determinacy, and completeness in historical interpretation are values reluctantly being bid elegiac farewell — yet oddly this apology shifts into a subtle claim to virtue. What is called an "impurity" is embraced as the enabling weapon of a new historicism. Forbidden traditional desires for objectivity and a unified narrative of past and present are replaced by open deployment of self-concerns; the supposed discontinuity of present and past (a Foucauldian axiom) is mapped as a continuous narrative whose source and end is "myself."[12]

The question then is, when Greenblatt says "myself," who exactly is he talking about? When he says that he seizes upon a "handful of arresting figures who seem to contain within themselves much of what we need," just who is the "we" in "need" and what is the nature of this need? Greenblatt's "myself" is representative, it finds its home in "we," and "we" is nothing other than the community of disappointed liberal middle-class literary intellectuals — and how many of us really stand outside this class? — whose basic need is to believe in the autonomy of self-fashioning and who find this need dramatized in certain standard writers of the sixteenth century, who find, therefore, the Renaissance to be peculiarly modern, a theme of traditional Renaissance theory with this twist: this need for autonomy is thought to be set up and stimulated in the emerging bourgeois world and then wholly and cruelly denied. New historicism is another expression of the bitter and well-grounded first-world suspicion that modern history

[11]Stepen Greenblatt, "Loundun and London," *Critical Inquiry* 12 (Winter 1986): 341, 343. [Lentricchia]

[12]Greenblatt, *Renaissance Self-Fashioning*, pp. 5, 6. [Lentricchia]

is the betrayal of liberalism. The Renaissance turns out to be "modern" not only in a sense not intended by Jacob Burckhardt[13] but in one which would have horrified his liberal confidence: the Renaissance is *our* culture because it is the origin of our disciplinary society. That, I take it, is the final, if unintended, significance of Greenblatt's remark that we study the Renaissance "by analogy to ourselves." The personal story that he tells in the epilogue of his book functions as a cautionary tale of the archetypal political awakening of

liberal man to the realities of power. His advice is to imaginatively interiorize the dream of self-fashioning because, only by so doing will we keep ourselves from being swept away in history's narrative of repression, in the inevitable movement to the carceral[14] nightmare as the daylight world of everyday life. Greenblatt tells us at the end that the human subject which he (and we) wanted to be autonomous and believed to be so "begins to seem remarkably unfree, the ideological product of the relations of power in a particular society."[15]

---

[13]Swiss cultural historian (1818–1897), whose *Civilization of the Renaissance in Italy* sees modernity, individualism, and the secular state emerging out of medieval culture around 1400.

[14]Having to do with prisons.
[15]Greenblatt, *Renaissance Self-Fashioning*, p. 256. [Lentricchia]

Meaghan Morris
b. 1950

Meaghan Morris, a key feminist voice in Australian cultural studies, was born in Tenterfield, New South Wales, and went to Maitland Girls High before attending the University of Sydney, where she took an honors B.A. She did a Maîtrise ès lettres at the radical Vincennes campus of the University of Paris, and returned to Sydney to do her doctorate at the University of Technology. Morris has taught in art schools and been a film critic; she also taught cultural studies in Australia and as a visiting professor at the University of Wisconsin, the University of Illinois, and Duke University. Her books include The Pirate's Fiancée: Feminism, Reading, Postmodernism *(1988);* Ecstasy and Economics *(1993); and* Too Soon, Too Late: History in Popular Culture *(1998). Together with John Frow, she has edited* Australian Cultural Studies: A Reader. *Currently Morris is Chair Professor at Lingnan University in Hong Kong. "Things to Do with Shopping Centres" originally appeared in Susan Sheridan's collection,* Grafts: Feminist Cultural Criticism *(1988).*

Things to Do with Shopping Centres

The first thing I want to do is to cite a definition of modernity. It comes not from recent debates in feminist theory or aesthetics or cultural studies, but from a paper called "Development in the Retail Scene" given in Perth in 1981 by John

Lennen of Myer Shopping Centres. To begin his talk (to a seminar organized by the Australian Institute of Urban Studies), Lennen told this fable: "As Adam and Eve were leaving the Garden of Eden, Adam turned to Eve and said,

'Do not be distressed, my dear, we live in times of change.'[1] After quoting Adam, Lennen went on to say, "Cities live in times of change. We must not be discouraged by change, but rather we must learn to manage change." He meant that the role of shopping centres was changing from what it had been in the 1970s, and that retailers left struggling with the consequences (planning restrictions, post-boom economic conditions, new forms of competition) should not be discouraged, but should change their practices accordingly.

I want to discuss some issues for feminist criticism that emerge from a study I'm doing of the management of change in certain sites of "cultural production" involving practices regularly, if by no means exclusively, carried out by women — shopping, driving, the organization of leisure, holiday and/or unemployment activities. By "sites," I mean shopping centres, cars, highways, "homes" and motels. It's a large project, and this essay is a kind of preface to one or two of its problems. The essay has a framing theme, however — the "Edenic" allegories of consumerism in general, and of shopping centres in particular, that one can find elaborated in a number of different discourses, (and cultural "sites"). It also has an argument, which will take the form of a rambling response to three questions that I've often been asked by women with whom I've discussed the project.

One of these is very general: "what's feminist about it?" I can't answer that in any direct or immediate way, since obviously "feminism" is not a set of approved concerns and methods, a kind of planning code, against which one can measure one's own interests and aspirations. To be frank, it's a question that I find almost unintelligible. While I do understand the polemical, and sometimes theoretical, value of arguing that something is *not* feminist, to demand a definition of positive feminist identity seems to me to require so many final decisions to be taken, and to assume so much about shared and settled values, that it makes the very concept of a "project" — undecided and unsettled — impossible. So I shall take this question here as an invitation to make up answers as I go, and the essay will be the response. (That's a way of saying that for me, the answer to "what's feminist about it?" should be "I don't know yet.")

The other two questions are more specific, and relate particularly to shopping centres.[2]

The first question is asked almost invariably by women with whom I've discussed the topic of shopping. They say: "Yes, you do semiotics . . . are you looking at how shopping centres are all the same everywhere? — laid out systematically, everyone can read them?" They don't ask about shopping centres and change, or about a semiotics of the management of change.

In fact, my emphasis is rather the opposite. It's true that at one level of analysis (and of our "practice" of shopping centres), layout and design principles ensure that all centres are minimally readable to anyone literate in their use — that is, to almost if not quite everybody in the Western suburban culture I'm concerned with here. This "readability" may be minimal indeed: many centres operate a strategy of alternating surprise and confusion with familiarity and harmony; and in different parts of any one centre, clarity and opacity will occur in different degrees of intensity for different "users." To a newcomer, for example, the major supermarket in an unfamiliar centre is usually more difficult to read than the spatial relations between the specialty food shops and the boutiques. Nevertheless, there are always some basic rules of contiguity and association at work to assist you to make a selection (of shops, as well as products).

However, I am more interested in a study that differentiates particular shopping centres. Differentiating shopping centres means, among other things, looking at how particular centres produce and maintain what the architectural writer

---

[1] Australian Institute of Urban Studies, *Shopping for a Retail Policy* (Canberra: A.I.U.S. Publication 99, 1982). [Morris]

[2] In this paper I normally use the term "shopping centre" as the most common Australian synonym for what is elsewhere called a "shopping mall." "Mall" is in one way less ambiguous, because it is less easily confused with the central "shopping district" or "downtown" (usually called in Australia, "town" or "the city"). However while "mall" in Australia may be used in this sense, it more usually refers to a shopping street — mostly in "town" — which is now closed to traffic. [Morris]

Neville Quarry calls (in an appreciation of one particular effort) "a unique sense of place"[3] — in other terms, a myth of identity. I see this as a "feminist" project because it requires the predication of a more complex and localized affective relation to shopping spaces (and to the links between those spaces and other sites of domestic and familial labour) than does the scenario of the cruising grammarian reading similarity from place to place. In one way, all shoppers may be cruising grammarians. I do not need to deny this, however, in order to choose to concentrate instead on the ways that particular centres strive to become "special," for better or for worse, in the everyday lives of women in local communities. Men, of course, may have this relation to *a* shopping centre, too. So my "feminism" at this stage is defined in non-polemical and non-exclusive (that is, non-self-identical) terms.

Obviously, shopping centres produce a sense of place for economic, "come-*hither*" reasons, and sometimes because the architects and planners involved may be committed, these days, to an aesthetics or even a politics of the local. But we cannot derive commentary on their function, people's responses to them, or their own cultural production of "place" in and around them, from this economic rationale. Besides, shopping-centre identities aren't fixed, consistent or permanent. Shopping centres do get facelifts, and change their image — increasingly so as the great classic structures in any region begin to age, fade and date.

But the cost of renovating them (especially the larger ones) means that the identity effect produced by any one centre's spatial play in time is not only complex, highly nuanced and variable in detail, but also simple, massive and relatively enduring overall, and over time, in space. At every possible "level" of analysis — and there are very many indeed with such a complex, continuous social event — shopping centres are overwhelmingly and constitutively paradoxical. This is one of the things that makes it very hard to differentiate them. On the one hand, they seem so monolithically present — solid, monumental, rigidly and indisputably on the landscape, and in our lives. On the other hand, when you try to dispute with them, they dissolve at any one point into a fluidity and indeterminacy that might suit any philosopher's delirium of an abstract femininity — partly because the shopping centre "experience" at any one point includes the experience of crowds of people (or of their relative absence), and so of all the varied responses and uses that the centre provokes and contains.

To complicate matters, this *dual* quality is very much a part of shopping centre strategies of appeal, their "seductiveness," and also of their management of change. The stirring tension between the massive stability of the structure, and the continually shifting, ceaseless spectacle within and around the "centre," is one of the things that people who like shopping centres really love about shopping centres. At the same time, shopping-centre management methods (and contracts) are very much directed towards organizing and unifying — at the level of administrative control, if not of achieved aesthetic effect — as much of this spectacle as possible by regulating tenant mix, signing and advertising styles, common space decor, festivities, and so on. This does not mean, however, that they succeed in "managing" either the total spectacle (which includes what people do with what they provide) or the responses it provokes (and may include).

So the task of analyzing shopping centres partly involves on the one hand exploring common sensations, perceptions and emotional states aroused by them (which can be negative, of course, as well as delirious), and on the other hand, battling against those perceptions and states in order to make a place from which to speak other than that of fascinated describer — either standing "outside" the spectacle qua ethnographer, or (in a pose which seems to me to amount to much the same thing) ostentatiously absorbed in her own absorption in it, qua celebrant of "popular culture."

If the former mode of description may be found in much sociology of consumerism, or "leisure," the latter mode is the more common

<hr>

[3] Review of The Jam Factory in "A Shopping Guide," unpublished paper. A different section of this paper is published as "Knox City Shopping Centre: A Review," *Architecture Australia*, November 1978, vol. 67, no. 5, p. 68. [Morris]

today in cultural studies — and it has its persuasive defenders. Iain Chambers, for example, has argued strongly that to appreciate the democratic "potential" of the way that people live through (not "alongside") culture — appropriating and transforming everyday life — we must first pursue the "wide-eyed presentation of actualities" that Adorno disapproved of in some of Benjamin's work on Baudelaire.[4,5] It's difficult to disagree with this as a general orientation, and I don't. But if we look more closely at the terms of Adorno's objection (and leave aside here the vexed question of its pertinence to Benjamin's work), it's possible to read in them now a description of shopping-centre mystique: "your study is located at the crossroads of magic and positivism. That spot is bewitched."[6] With a confidence that feminist philosophers have taught us to question, Adorno continues that "Only theory could break the spell . . ." (although in context, he means Benjamin's own theoretical practice, not a force of theory-in-general).

In my view, neither a strategy of "wide-eyed presentation" nor a faith in theory as the exorcist is adequate to dealing with the critical problems posed by feminism in the analysis of "everyday life." If we locate our own study at that "crossroads of magic and positivism" to be found in the grand central court of any large regional mall, then social experiences more complex than wide-eyed bewitchment are certain to occur — and to elicit, for a feminist, a more critical response than "presentation" requires. If it is today fairly easy to reject the rationalist and gynophobic prejudice implied by Adorno's scenario (theory breaking the witch's spell), and if it is also easy to refuse the old critiques of "consumption" as false consciousness (bewitchment by the mall), then it is perhaps not so easy at the moment *also* to question

the "wide-eyed" pose of critical amazement at the performance of the everyday.

There's a great deal to be said about that, but my one point here must be that at the very least, a feminist analysis of shopping centres will insist initially upon ambivalence about its objects rather than a simple astonishment "before" them. Ambivalence allows a thinking of relations between contradictory states: it is also a "pose," no doubt, but one that is probably more appropriate to an everyday practice of using the same shopping centres often, for different reasons (rather than visiting several occasionally, just in order to see the sights). Above all, it does not eliminate the moment of everyday discontent — of anger, frustration, sorrow, irritation, hatred, boredom, fatigue. Feminism is minimally a movement of discontent with "the everyday" and with wide-eyed definitions of the everyday as "the way things are." While feminism too may proceed by "staring hard at the realities of the contemporary world we all inhabit," as Chambers puts it, feminism also allows the possibility of rejecting what we see and refusing to take it as "given." Like effective shopping, feminist criticism includes moments of sharpened focus, narrowed gaze — of sceptical, if not paranoid, assessment. (This is a more polemical sense in which I shall consider this project to be "feminist" in the context of cultural studies.)

Recent feminist theory in a number of academic domains has provided a great many tools for any critical study of myths of identity and difference, and the rhetoric of "place" in everyday life. But in using them in shopping centres, I strike another difficulty: a rhetorical one this time, with resonances of interdisciplinary conflict. It's the difficulty of what can seem to be a lack, or lapse, of appropriateness between my discourse as feminist intellectual and my objects of study.

To put it bluntly: isn't there something really "off" about mobilizing the weapons (and I use that violent metaphor deliberately) of an elite, possibly still fashionable but definitively *un*popular theoretical discourse against a major element in the lived culture of "ordinary women" to whom that discourse might be as irrelevant as a stray copy of a book by Roland Barthes chosen to decorate a simulated yuppy apartment on display at Canberra's

---

[4]Iain Chambers, *Popular Culture: The Metropolitan Experience,* New York and London 1986, p. 13. [Morris]

[5]Morris is referring to Benjamin's analysis of the *flâneur,* the strolling gent in the nineteenth-century city, as a type of the modern, a text that haunts not only her essay but Certeau's "Walking in the City."

[6]Theodor Adorno, "Letters to Walter Benjamin," in *Aesthetics and Politics* (translation editor Ronald Taylor, afterword by Fredric Jameson), London 1977, p. 129. [Morris]

FREEDOM furniture showroom? And wouldn't using that discourse, and its weapons, be "off" in a way that it isn't off to use them to reread Gertrude Stein, or other women modernists, or indeed to rewrite devalued and non-modernist writings by women so that they may be used to revise existing concepts of the literary canon?

Of course, these are not questions that any academic, even feminist, is obliged to ask or to answer. One can simply define one's "object" strategically, in the limited way most appropriate to a determined disciplinary, and institutional, context. They are also questions that it's impossible to answer without challenging their terms — by pointing out, for example, that a politics of "relevance," and "appropriateness" (in so far as it can be calculated at all) depends as much on the "from where" and the "to whom" of any discourse as it does on its relations to an "about." For example, the reason that I referred to "interdisciplinary conflict" above is that during my research, I have found the pertinence or even the "good taste" of using a theoretical vocabulary derived from semiotics to discuss "ordinary women's lives" questioned more severely by sociologists or historians (for whom the question becomes more urgent, perhaps, as so-called "theory" becomes respectable) than by non-academic (I do not say "ordinary") women — who have been variously curious, indifferent, or amused.

Nevertheless, these are questions that feminist intellectuals do ask each other; and we will no doubt continue to do so as long as we retain some sense of a wider social (as well as "interdisciplinary") context and political import for our work. So I want to suggest the beginnings of an answer, one "appropriate" to a cross-disciplinary gathering of feminist intellectuals, by questioning the function of the "ordinary woman" as a figure in our polemics. As a feminist, I cannot and do not wish the image, or the reality, of other women away. As a semiotician, however, I must notice that "images" of other women, even those which I've just constructed in mentioning "them" as a problem ("sociologists and historians" for me, rather than "ordinary women") — are, in fact, images.

Take a visual image of the unnamed "ordinary woman" walking through a shopping centre. Some image like this is perhaps what we have in mind if we talk about the gap between a feminist intellectual's discourse on shopping centres and her "objects of study." But this particular image was originally published in an Australian government report on The Shopping Centre As a Community Leisure Resource.[7] It was in fact taken, without its subject's knowledge or consent, by a sociological surveillance camera at Sydney's Blacktown Westpoint shopping centre in 1977 or 1978. Framed as a still image, it proclaims its realist status: the candid-camera effect of capturing an iconic moment of spontaneity and joy is reinforced by bits of accessory reality protruding casually into the frame (stroller, vertical section of a "companion"). These details help us to imagine that we know what is happening here: a young mother is strolling in the mall, enjoying herself enormously in its ambience, and sharing her pleasure with a friend. She becomes "representative" of the leisure-resource potential of "the shopping centre" for working-class women. ("The shopping centre," too, is abstracted as representative, since all we see of it is the speckled floor found in any downmarket centre anywhere.) But of course, we only know what is happening in the image. We don't know what she is laughing at, how she felt about her companion — or her child — at that instant, what her expression was like two seconds before and after the moment she passed the camera, or what her ideas about shopping centres, or Blacktown Westpoint in particular, might have been.

This image of an ordinary woman, then, is not a glimpse of her reality, but a polemical declaration about reality mobilized between the authors (or better, the authority) of a governmental report and its readership. I can deduce very little about that woman at Blacktown, let alone about "women" in "shopping centres," from it. Nor can I adopt the pretence (as some sociologists still might) that my discourse, my camera or even my "questionnaire," if I really had the real women here to talk to now, would give me unmediated access to or true knowledge of her thoughts and

[7]Department of Environment, Housing and Community Development, The Shopping Centre as a Community Leisure Resource, Australian Government Publishing Service, Canberra 1978. [Morris]

feelings. Even her thoughts and feelings about shopping at Blacktown Westpoint now, or ten years ago. Above all, I cannot try to look through this image of a woman to my imaginary Real Woman and ask of her *what does shopping-woman want?*".

So one possible step away from being "off" is to construct my initial object of study as neither "that woman," nor even her image, but the image of shopping-woman framed as illustration to the sociological *text*.

The study of shopping centres today is necessarily involved in a history of the positioning of women as objects of knowledge, indeed as targets for the manoeuvres of retailers, planners, developers, sociologists, market researchers and so on. There's a lot of feminist research available now on precisely that, especially in relation to fashion and the history of department stores — research which also takes the further necessary step of writing histories of how the target *moves*, how the object *evades*: this is the study of women's resistance, action, creativity, or if you like, of cultural production, understood as the transformation of initially imposed constraints.[8]

But I would need then to take a second step away from being off, and also away from trying to be on target with/about women (as the Blacktown Westpoint image attempts to be), by challenging my initial question about the gap between my theoretical speech and its object. For having said that the text-image relation could be my object, the gap narrows too easily to a purely professional dispute (a critique of sociological constructions, for example). My difficulty in the

shopping-centre project will thus be not simply my relation as intellectual to the culture I'm speaking "about," but to whom I will imagine that I will be speaking. So if, in a first instance, the task of differentiating shopping centres involves a struggle with fascinated description — consuming and consumerist list-making, attempts to freeze and fix a spectacular reality — my second problem will be to produce a mode of address that will "evade" the fascinated or mirroring relationship to both the institutional discourses "about" women that I'm contesting, and the imaginary figure of Everywoman that those discourses — along with many feminist arguments — keep on throwing up.

However in making that argument, I also evaded the problem of "other" (rather than "ordinary") women. I slid from restating the now conventional case that an image of a woman shopping is not a "real" (or really representative) woman shopping to talking as though that difference absolved me from thinking about other women's ideas about their experience in shopping centres, as "users" and as workers there. This is a problem of method, to which I'd like to return. First, I want to make a detour to consider the second enquiry I've had from "other" women: "What's the point of differentiating shopping centres? So what if they're *not* all the same?"

Here I want to make two points about method. The first is that if this project on "Things to Do with Shopping Centres" could have a subtitle, it would be *"Pedestrian Notes on Modernity."* I agree with Alice Jardine's argument in her book *Gynesis* that feminist criticism has much to gain from studying recent debates about "modernity" in thought (that is, "modernity" in the general European sense of life after industrialization — a sense which includes but is broader than the American aesthetic term "postmodernity"). Those debates are important, not only because of the history of "women" as an object of power-knowledge in the terms I described above, but because of the function of images of "Woman" to signify the *problem* of (power) knowledge. I also agree with Jardine that as well as looking at how "woman" or "femininity" came to function as a fulcrum metaphor in those debates, especially in the 1970s, we need now to make a history of

[8]A few examples are Rosalind Coward, *Female Desire*, London 1984; Angela McRobbie and Mica Nava, eds, *Gender and Generation*, London 1984 (especially the essay by Erica Carter, "Alice in the Consumer Wonderland: West German Case Studies in Gender and Consumer Culture," pp. 185–214); Judith Williamson, *Consuming Passions: The Dynamics of Popular Culture*, London and New York 1986; Elizabeth Wilson, *Adorned in Dreams: Fashion and Modernity*, London 1985. For an essay with less emphasis on consumer evasiveness, see David Chaney, "The Department Store as a Cultural Form," *Theory, Culture and Society*, vol. 1, no. 3, 1983, pp. 22–31. A more recent account of the debate about consumer "productivity" is Mica Nava, "Consumerism and Its Contradictions," *Cultural Studies*, vol. 1, no. 2, 1987, pp. 204–10. [Morris]

women modernists — instead of only and continually talking about mainly male philosophers (give or take a few female feminists) and the masculine avant gardes of nearly a century ago. However I don't think I do quite agree with Jardine that there's a risk of women becoming, as she puts it, "that profoundly archaic silhouette — poet and madwoman — who finally took a peek at modernity and then quickly closed the door."[9]

I think that if the broad impact of modernization in culture is seen as what's beyond the door, not just aesthetic and philosophical modern*ism* (a distinction which Jardine herself is careful to make), then women have had to go through that door en masse a long time ago; or, if we consider that the home has been one of the major experimental sites of modernization,[10] then "modernity" has rather come through our doors whether we wished it so or not: and that if any archaic silhouette is peeking and hovering at a door, it's perhaps that of the theorist (feminist or otherwise) looking back, longingly, at aesthetic and philosophical dilemmas you can find made redundant on television, or on remainder at shoppingtown, any old day of the week. That's one sense in which I'd claim the word "pedestrian." Studying shopping centres should be (like studying women modernists) one way to contest the idea that you can find, for example, at moments in the work of Julia Kristeva, that the cultural production of "actual women" has historically fallen short of a modernity understood as, or in terms derived from, the critical construction of modern*ism*.[11] In this project, I prefer to study instead the everyday, the so-called banal, the supposedly un- or non-experimental, asking not, "why does it fall short of modernism?" but "how do classical theories of modernism fall short of women's modernity?"

Secondly, the figure of the pedestrian gives me a way of imaging a critical method for analysing shopping centres that doesn't succumb unequivocally to the lure of using the classical images of the Imaginary, in the psychoanalytic sense, as a mirror to the Shoppingtown spectacle. Such images are very common now in the literature about shopping centres: especially about big, enclosed, enveloping, "spectacular" centres like one of those I'm studying, Indooroopilly Shoppingtown. Like department stores before them (and which they now usually contain), they are described as palaces of dreams, halls of mirrors, galleries of illusion . . . and the fascinated analyst becomes identified as a theatre critic, reviewing the spectacle, herself in the spectacle, and the spectacle in herself. This rhetoric is closely related, of course, to the vision of shoppingtown as Eden, or paradise: the shopping centre is figured as, if not exactly u-topian,[12] then a mirror to utopian desire, the desire of fallen creatures nostalgic for the primal garden, yet aware that their paradise is now an illusion.

The pedestrian, or the woman walker, doesn't escape this dreamy ambivalence. Indeed, sociological studies suggest that women who don't come in cars to shopping centres spend much more time in them than those that do. The slow, evaluative, appreciatively critical relation is not enjoyed to the same extent by women who hit the carpark, grab the goods, and head on out as fast as possible. Obviously, different women do both at different times. But if walking around for a long time in one centre creates engagement with and absorption in the spectacle, then one sure way at least to begin from a sharply defined sense of critical estrangement is to arrive at a drive-in centre on foot — and have to find a way to walk in. (Most women non-drivers, of course, don't arrive on foot — especially with children — but by public transport: which can, in Australia, produce an acutely estranging effect.)

[9]Alice Jardine, *Gynesis: Configurations of Woman and Modernity*, Ithaca and London 1985, p. 49. [Morris]

[10]See Stuart Ewen, *Captains of Consciousness: Advertising and the Social Roots of the Consumer Culture*, New York 1976; Stuart and Elizabeth Ewen, *Channels of Desire: Mass Images and the Shaping of American Consciousness*, New York 1982; Kerreen M. Reiger, *The Disenchantment of The Home: Modernizing the Australian Family 1880–1940*, Oxford 1985. [Morris]

[11]See for example the interview with Françoise van Rossum-Guyon, "Questions à Julia Kristeva — A partir de Polylogue," *Revue des sciences humaines*, 168 (*Ecriture, féminité, féminisme*), 1977, pp. 495–501. [Morris]

[12]British (and Australian) writers sometimes use the abbreviation "U" to mean "upper-class" in social tone. The U-non-U distinction was made in a 1956 book by Nancy Mitford called *Noblesse Oblige: An Enquiry into the Identifiable Characteristics of the British Aristocracy*.

I have to insert a qualification here about the danger of constructing exemplary allegorical figures (even that of the "woman walker") if they're taken to refer to some model of the "empirical social user" of shopping centres. It's a fairly futile exercise to try to make generalizations, beyond statistical averaging, about the users of shopping centres at any particular time — even in terms of class, race, age or gender. It's true that where you find a centre in a socially homogenized area (very common in some suburban regions of most Australian cities), you do find a high incidence of regular use by specific social groups (which may contribute strongly to the centre's identity effect). At a lot of centres, nevertheless, that's not the case. And even where it is, such generalizations remain abstractions, for concrete reasons: cars, public transport, visiting and tourist practices (since shopping centres can be used for sightseeing), and day-out patterns of movement, all mean that centres do not automatically "reflect" the composition of their immediate social environment. Also, there are different practices of use in one centre on any one day: some people may be there for the one and only time in their lives: there are occasional users choosing that centre rather than this on that day for particular, or quite arbitrary reasons; people may shop at one centre and go to another to socialize or hang around. The use of centres as meeting places (and sometimes for free warmth and shelter) by young people, pensioners, the unemployed and the homeless is a familiar part of their social function — often planned for, now, by centre management (distribution of benches, video games, security guards). And many of a centre's habitual users may not always live in its vicinity.

Shopping centres illustrate very well, I think, the argument that you can't treat a public at a cultural event as directly expressive of social groups and classes, or their supposed sensibility.[13] Publics aren't stable, homogeneous entities — and polemical claims assuming that they are tell us little beyond the display of political position and identification being made by the speaker. These displays may be interesting in themselves, but they don't necessarily say much about the wider social realities such polemics often invoke.

Shopping-centre designers know this very well, in fact — and some recent retailing theory talks quite explicitly about the marketing need to break down the old standardized predication of a "vast monolithic middle-class market" for shopping-centre product, that characterized the strategy of the 1970s.[14] The prevailing marketing philosophy for the 1980s (especially in the United States, but visible also in parts of Australia) has been rather to develop spectacles of "diversity and market segmentation." That is, to produce images of class, ethnic, age and gender *differentiation* in particular centres — not because a Vietnamized centre, for example, would better "express" the target culture and better serve Vietnamese (though it may well do so, particularly since retail theorists seem to have pinched the idea partly from the forms of community politics), but because the display of difference will today increase a centre's "tourist" appeal to everyone else from elsewhere.[15]

This is a response, of course, to the disintegration of the postwar "middle class," and the ever-growing disparity in the developed nations between rich and poor. This change is quite menacing to the suburban shopping centres, however structurally complicit the companies that profit from them may have been in bringing the change about; and what's interesting is the attempt to "manage" the change in terms of a differential thematization of "shoppers" — and thus of the centres to serve them. Three years ago, one theorist imagined the future thus: "Centres will be designed specifically to meet demands of the *economic* shopper, the *recreational* shopper, or

[13]See John Frow, "Accounting for Tastes: Some Problems in Bourdieu's Sociology of Culture," *Cultural Studies*, vol. 1, no. 1, 1987, pp. 59–73. [Morris]

[14]George Sternlieb and James W. Hughes, "Introduction: The Uncertain Future of Shopping Centres," in Sternlieb and Hughes, eds, *Shopping Centres, U.S.A*, New Jersey 1981, p. 3. [Morris]

[15]For an excellent early study of the relationship between tourism and "social structural differentiation," see Dean MacCannell, *The Tourist: A New Theory of the Leisure Class*, New York 1975. [Morris]

the *pragmatic* shopper, and so on."[16] His scenario is already being realized, although once again this does not mean that as "shoppers" we do in fact conform to, let alone become, the proffered image of our "demands."

That said, I want to make one more point about pedestrian leisureliness and critical time. One thing that it's important to do with particular centres is to write them a (differential) history. This can be surprisingly difficult and time-consuming. The shopping centre "form" itself — a form often described as "one of the few new building types created in our time"[17] — certainly has had its histories written, mostly in heroic and expansive terms. But I've found empirically that while some local residents are able to tell stories of a particular development and its effects on their lives, the people who manage centres in Australia are often disconcerted at the suggestion that *their* centre could have a history. There are several obvious reasons for that — short-term employment patterns, employee and even managerial indifference to the workplace, ideologies about what counts as proper history, the consecration of shopping centres to the perpetual present of consumption ("now-ness"), suspicion of "media enquiries" (that is, of me) in centres hostile to publicity they don't control, and also the feeling that in many cases, the history is best forgotten. For example, the building of Indooroopilly Shoppingtown required the blitzing of a huge chunk of old residential Indooroopilly.

But there's a parallel avoidance of local shopping-centre histories in much of the critical writing on centres — except for those which (like Southdale Mall or Faneuil Hall Marketplace in the United States, and Roselands in Australia) figure as pioneers in the history of development. Leaving aside for the moment the material produced by commercial interests (which tends to be dominated, as one might expect, by complex economic and futuristic speculation developed, in relation to particular centres, along interventionist lines), I'd argue that an odd gap usually appears between, on the one hand, critical writing where the shopping place becomes the metaphorical site for a practice of personal reminiscence (autobiography, the production of a written self), and on the other, the purely formal description of existing structures found in architectural criticism.[18] Walter Benjamin's *A Berlin Chronicle* (for older market forms) and Donald Horne's memoir of the site of Miranda Fair in *Money Made Us* are examples of the first practice, and the article by Neville Quarry that I've mentioned an example of the second.[19]

The gap between these two genres (reminiscence and formal description) may in turn correspond to one produced by so-called "Man-Environment" studies. For example, Amos Rapoport's influential book *The Meaning of the Built Environment* depends entirely on the humanist distinction between "users' meanings" (the personal) and "designers' meanings" (the professional).[20] I think that a feminist study of shopping centres should *occupy* this user/designer, memory/aesthetics gap, not, of course, to "close" or to "bridge" it, but to dislocate the relationship between the poles that create it, and so dissolve

[16]John A. Dawson. *Shopping Centre Development*, London and New York 1983, chapter 7. [Morris]

[17]Victor Gruen and Larry Smith, *Shopping Towns U.S.A.*, New York 1960, p. 11. Victor Gruen is widely regarded as the inventor of the modern enclosed mall, and his book was influential on subsequent accounts. See for example, Nadine Beddington, *Design for Shopping Centres*, London 1982, p. 22. [Morris]

[18]This essay was written before I had an opportunity to read William Severini Kowinski's wonderful "odyssey" of shopping-centre life in the USA, *The Malling of America: An Inside Look at the Great Consumer Paradise*, New York 1985. [Morris]

[19]The Neville Quarry article is nowhere cited; Quarry (1933–2004) was an Australian architect of pronounced views. Walter Benjamin's *Berliner Chronik* was published posthumously, edited by Gershom Sholem (1970); Donald Horne's *Money Made Us* (1976) is a book about the way economic values have shaped Australian society.

[20]For Rapoport, "meanings are in people, not in objects or things. However *things do elicit meanings* . . . Put differently, the question is how (and, of course, whether) meanings can be encoded in things in such a way that they can be decoded by intended users." (*The Meaning of the Built Environment; A Nonverbal Communication Approach*, Beverly Hills 1982, p. 19.) [Morris]

In this approach, "meaning" is treated as a sort of independently existing substance exchanged, or channelled, between complete, autonomous subjects. In spite of Rapoport's stress on "nonverbal communication," his concept of "meaning" corresponds to the perfectly conventional humanist model of verbal communication — precisely because it is a *communication* model rather than a theory of discourses. [Morris] their imaginary autonomy. Of course, any vaguely anti-humanist critique would want to say as much. What is of particular interest to me as a feminist is to make relations between on the one hand those competing practices of "place" (which Michel de Certeau calls "spatial stories")[21, 22] that by investing sites with meaning make them sites of social conflict, and on the other, women's discourses of memory and local history.

A shopping centre is a "place" combining an extreme project of general "planning" competence (efforts at total unification, total management) with an intense degree of aberrance and diversity in local performance. It is also a "place" consecrated to timelessness and stasis (no clocks, perfect weather . . .) yet lived and celebrated, lived and loathed, in intimately historic terms: for some, as ruptural event[23] (catastrophic or Edenic) in the social experience of a community, for others, as the enduring scene (as the cinema once was, and the home still may be) of all the changes, fluctuations, and repetitions of the passing of everyday life. For both of these reasons, a shopping centre seems to me to be a good place to begin to consider women's "cultural production" of modernity.

This is also why I suggested that it can be important to write a history of particular shopping centres. It is one way in which the clash of conflicting programmes for the management of change, and for resisting, refusing or evading 'management,' can better be understood.

Such a history can be useful in other ways. It helps to denaturalize the myths of spectacular identity-in-place that centres produce in order to compete with each other, by analysing how these myths, those spectacles, are constructed for particular spaces over time. The qualification 'particular' is crucial, I think, because like many critics now I have my doubts that polemical

demonstrations of the fact that such "myth-making" takes place have much to offer a contemporary cultural politics. Like revelations of essentialism or, indeed, "naturalism" in other people's arguments, simple demythologization all too often retrieves, at the end of the process, its own untransformed basic premises now masked as surprising conclusions. I also think that the project itself is anachronistic: commercial culture today proclaims and advertises, rather than "naturalizes," its powers of artifice, myth invention, simulation.[24] In researching the history of myth-making in a particular place, however, one is obliged to consider how it works in concrete social circumstances that inflect, in turn, its workings — and one is obliged to learn from that place, make discoveries, change the drift of one's analysis, rather than use it as a site of theoretical self-justification.

Secondly, such a history must assume that centres and their myths are actively transformed by their "users" (although in very ambiguous ways) and that the history itself would count as one such transformation by a user. In my study this will mean, in practice, that I'm only going to analyse shopping centres that I know personally.

I'm not going to use them to tell my life story, but I am going to refuse the discursive position of externalized visitor/observer, or ethnographer/celebrant, by setting up as my objects only those centres where I have, or have had, some practice other than that of analyst — places I've lived near or used as consumer, window-shopper, tourist, or as escapee from a passing mood (since refuge, or R&R, is one of the social functions of shopping centres, though women who just hate them may find that hard to accept). As the sociologist John Carroll reports with the cheerfulness of the true conservative, "The Promotions Manager of one of the Shopping World chains in Australia has speculated that these centres

---

[21]Michel de Certeau, *The Practice of Everyday Life*, Berkeley and London 1984, pp. 115–31. I have tried to develop this notion further in my essay "At *Henry Parkes Motel*," *Cultural Studies*, vol. 2, no.1, 1988, pp. 1–16, 29–47. [Morris]

[22]See p. 1342.

[23]Morris alludes to Foucault's notion of the *coupure*, the event that causes paradigms to shift. See p. 1328.

[24]I have argued this in more detail via a critique of Roland Barthes's *Mythologies* in "Sydney Tower," *Island Magazine*, 9/10, March 1982, pp. 53–66. Barthes's own well-known critique of his early work is "Change the Object Itself," in Roland Barthes, *Image-Music-Text* (translated by Stephen Heath), Glasgow, 1977, pp.165–9; also available as "Mythology Today," Roland Barthes, *The Rustle of Language*, trans. Richard Howard, Oxford 1986, pp. 65–8. [Morris]

may replace Valium."[25,26] Carroll doesn't add anything about their role in creating needs for Valium, or in selling it, but only if you combine all three functions do you get a sense, I think, of Shopping World's lived ambiguity.

And here I return to the question of "other women" and my relation to their relation to these shopping centres. I've argued quite clearly, I hope, my objections in the present context to procedures of sampling "representative" shoppers, framing exemplary figures, targeting empirical "user groups," and so on. That doesn't mean that I think there's anything "wrong" with those methods, that I wouldn't use them in another context or borrow, in this context, from studies which have used them. Nor does it mean that I think there's no way to produce knowledge of shopping centres except from "personal experience" (which would preclude me, for example, from considering what it's like to work in one for years).

However I'm interested in something a little more fugitive — or pedestrian — than either a professionally based informatics, or a narcissistically enclosed reverie, can give me. I'm interested in impromptu shopping-centre encounters: chit-chat, with women I meet in and around and because of these centres that I know personally (ranging from close family friends at some to total strangers at others). Collecting chit-chat in situ is, of course, a pedestrian professional practice ("journalism"). But I also want to analyse it in terms of the theoretical concerns I've outlined (rather than as "evidence" of how others really feel) as a means of doubting and revising, rather than confirming, my own "planning" programme.

In order to pass on to a few comments about one shopping centre "history," I'd like first to describe the set of three to which it belongs in my project. I chose this set initially for quite personal reasons: three favourite shopping centres, one of which my family used, and two of which I had often used as a tourist; two of which I loved, and one of which I hated. But I discovered subsequently that this "set"

also conforms to a system of formal distinctions conventionally used by the people who build and manage shopping centres. These are planners' terms, "designers' meanings."[27] But most of us are familiar in practice with these distinctions, and some whole cities (like Canberra) are built around them.

Until recently, there has been a more or less universally accepted classification system based on three main types of centre: the "neighbourhood" centre, the "community" centre, and the "regional" centre. Some writers add extra categories, like the "super-regional," a huge and now mostly uneconomic dinosaur (rare in Australia, but common in more populous countries) with four to six full-line department stores. With the ageing of the classic suburban form and the burgeoning of rival retail formats better adapted to current economic conditions (discount chains, hypermarkets, neo-arcades, ethnic and other "theme" environments, history-zones, specialty malls,[28] multi-use centres and urban megastructures), the basic schema is losing some of its reality-productive power. But it remains operative (and, in Australia, dominant) for those classic and still active structures of suburban life that I'm discussing.

The basic triad — neighbourhood/community/regional — is defined not in terms of catchment-area size, or type of public attracted, or acreage occupied. It depends instead on the type of major store that a centre offers to "anchor" its specialty shops. (As an anchor, it is usually placed at the end of the central strip.) Neighbourhood stores have only a supermarket, while community centres have a supermarket and either a discount house or a chain store (Big W, Target). Regional centres have both of these, plus at least one full department store. The anchor store is also called the magnet: it is considered to regulate the flows of attraction, circulation and expulsion of people, commodities and cars.

[25]John Carroll, "Shopping World: An Afternoon in the Palace of Modern Consumption," *Quadrant*, August 1979, p. 15. [Morris]
[26]A tranquillizing drug.

[27]A standard definitional text is the Urban Land Institute's *Shopping Centre Development Handbook,* Washington DC, 1977. [Morris]
[28]This is an interesting development whereby an old shopping centre can be renovated (as well as new centres built) to provide 150 shoe shops, or 50 hardware stores, rather than the old total lifestyle mix. [Morris]

For example, Indooroopilly Shoppingtown in Brisbane is a canonical example of the classical postwar regional shopping centre. It's also an aristocrat — a "Westfield." As Australia's leading shopping-centre developer, now achieving the ultimate goal of operating in the United States[29] and buying into the movie business, Westfield celebrates its own norm-setting status in an art corridor at Sydney's Miranda Fair,[30] where you can visit glorious full-colour photographs of all the other major Westfields in Australia, including Indooroopilly.[31] Indooroopilly Shoppingtown itself is a place with a postcard — a site unto itself from which people can state their whereabouts in writing. It's an instance of the model form celebrated in the general histories I mentioned above. These are expansionist histories of postwar centrifugal movements of cars and people away from old city centres — because of urban congestion in American and Australian cases, and congestion or war damage or both in European towns and cities.[32]

Ideally these centres, according to the histories, are so-called "greenfield" developments on the edge of or outside towns — on that ever-receding transformation zone where the country becomes the city as suburbia. Of course, they have often in fact been the product of suburb-blitzing, not suburb-creating processes — though the blitzing of one may help to create another on the city's periphery. So strong has been the force of the centrifugal imaginary, however, that in the case of the Brisbane *Courier-Mail's* coverage of the building of Indooroopilly Shoppingtown, the houses being moved to make way for it were represented as flying off happily like pioneers out to the far frontiers of the city.[33] The postwar regional centre, then, is traditionally represented as the "revolutionary," explosive suburban form.

At the opposite end of the spectrum, Fortitude Valley Plaza, again in Brisbane, is an example of a neighbourhood centre. The term "neighbourhood" may conjure up cosy, friendly images of intimacy, but this centre is actually at a major urban transit point, over a railway station, in a high density area and on one of the most polluted roads in Australia. It's also an early example neither of greenfield nor blitzing development, but of the recently very popular practice of "infill" (or "twilight zone") development. "Infill" has been filling in the central shopping districts of many country towns and old suburbs over the past few years. It means that bits of shopping centre and arcade snake around to swallow the gaps between existing structures. This practice has been important in the downtown revivals that succeeded (along with the energy crisis) the heroic age of the regional shopping centre.

Again, the *Courier-Mail's* coverage was metaphorically apt. Because there had been an old open railway line on the site, the Valley Plaza was seen to be resourcefully filling in the "previous useless airspace" wasted by the earlier structure.[34] It was promoted as a thrifty, perhaps even ecologically sound, solution to a problem of resources. The Valley Plaza is also an example of a centre that has undergone an identity change.

[29]Westfield as of 2002 had over sixty American properties under development. [Morris]

[30]Westfield shopping center in Miranda, a suburb of Sydney; once the largest in Australia, Miranda Fair is now the eighth largest. [Morris]

[31]An upmarket suburb of Brisbane. [Morris]

[32]Of course, these are usually histories of a white and upwardly mobile middle class. As well as the references already given, it is interesting to consult the older works on suburban shopping-centre development to see this class and race specific history being written. For example: G. Baker and B. Funaro, *Shopping Centres, Design and Operation,* New York 1951; Wilfred Burns, *British Shopping Centres,* London 1959; James Hornbeck, *Stores and Shopping Centres,* New York 1962; Colin S. Jones, *Regional Shopping Centres,* London 1969; Louis G. Redstone, *New Dimensions in Shopping Centres and Stores,* New York 1973. See also J. M. Freeland, *Architecture in Australia: A History,* Harmondsworth 1972 (Cheshire, 1968), chapter 14. [Morris]

[33]See "From Dust to Shops," *Courier-Mail* 26 February 1969; "Mini-city to open — July 8," *Courier-Mail,* 7 April 1970; and a *Courier-Mail* story on 6 March 1980, in which the then alderman Sallyanne Atkinson, "a campaigner for the preservation of Queensland buildings," claimed that the mobility of Queensland houses was one of their special virtues ("Many weatherboard homes in Queensland are unique because they can be moved," she said. "Many occupy prime real estate sites that are tremendously valuable.") Ms. Atkinson eventually located her office in Indooroopilly Shoppingtown and became mayor of Brisbane. [Morris]

[34]*Courier-Mail,* 2 July 1968. [Morris]

When I first studied it in 1983, it was a bit dank and dated — vintage pop futurist in style, with plenty of original but pollution-blackened 1960s orange and once-zappy geometrical trimmings. Now it's light green, and Chinatownified (with Chinese characters replacing the op-art effects), to blend in with the ethnic repackaging of Fortitude Valley as a whole.

Finally, Green Hills is an example of the mediating category, a "community" centre in East Maitland, a town near the industrial city of Newcastle in New South Wales. It's a Woolworths centre, with a supermarket and a Big W Discount House. Unlike the other two it is a mostly open mall, and it is very difficult to photograph in snapshot fashion, not just because it's both very long and rather careless of external display (though it has a coherent inner form as a simulated village square), but because the centre is also rather blurry and hard to see from a passing car. It's badly signed and bordered, and in fact it's mostly hidden from view in relation to the major highway (the New England) that runs right alongside. Whatever the original considerations and/or accidents behind this design, its effect now is in fact a very appropriate paranoid country town, insiders-only identity. Like much country town cultural production, you have to know where it is to find it.

Yet it was, for many years, very successful. Generically a community centre, it has none the less had a regional function — with its Big W Discount magnet pulling in people from all over the Hunter Valley who might once have gone on through to Newcastle. People didn't just come to Maitland — they went to Green Hills. So if, in this particular triad, Indooroopilly is explosive and the Valley Plaza is thrifty in the local rhetorics of space, Green Hills was represented in terms of a go-ahead conservatism — extending and renewing the old town of Maitland, while acting to help maintain the town's traditional economic and cultural independence.

I want to examine the representation of Green Hills in more detail, and one reason for looking at the triad of formal distinctions has been to provide a context for doing so. In the short history of Green Hills that I've been able to construct, it's clear that allusions to the other shopping centre forms, and especially to the suburban-explosive model, played a very complex role firstly in Woolworths' strategic presentation of the project to build Green Hills, and secondly, once it was built, in the promotional rhetoric used to specify an ideal public to whom the centre would appeal (something like "the loyal citizens" of Maitland).

In presenting a couple of elements of that history now, I must make two strong qualifications about what sort of history it is (in the context of this paper), and why. First, it is primarily derived from coverage in the local newspaper, the *Maitland Mercury*. Other sources generate other stories. This version is specifically concerned with the rhetorical collusion between the local media and the interests of Woolworths; and also with the ways that this relationship cut across two preexisting but at this point contradictory collusions of interest between the media and the council on the one hand, and the media and local small business interests on the other. (Small business, of course, was understandably most alarmed about the prospect of the Green Hills development.) Close relations between these parties — council, media, small business — are very common in nearly all country newspapers now, which tend to define the town's interests very much in terms of the doings of civic fathers on the one hand, and those of local enterprise on the other. Sport and the cycle of family life are two major sites on which those doings are played out. In that sense, country newspapers are unashamedly one long advertorial.[35] But in the building of Green Hills, civic fathers and local business were opposed in a conflict that took the form of a debate about the meaning of "local community." To describe this conflict briefly, I shall give it the form of an over-coherent, paranoid story.

Second, as my choice of sources suggests, this version could be criticized as lopsidedly restricted to "designers' meanings," planners' programmes. I don't mind too much about that, for two reasons. One is that as a long-term if irregular "user" of Green Hills, I was more interested in pursuing what I didn't already know about it, or hadn't noticed when it was happening. This "place" had simply

[35] Advertisement in the guise of news.

appeared where once there had been a border-zone that in the 1960s had signified the joys of driving out of town and the ambivalence of returning, and was, in earlier decades, the field of the illicit outside town (the forbidden picnic-ground).

The other reason is that I actually have no clear idea of what follows from the espousal of an emphasis on "users' meanings" (or as anti-humanists might say, "practices of consumption") — except, perhaps, for more celebrant sociology, and/or a reinvigorated local history. It is clear why such an emphasis should now be emerging: if many of Adorno's most paranoid theses about the administered society now seem to have come to pass, from little Green Hills to urban shopping-world megastructures (with banking, residential, computer, entertainment and governmental facili-ties, laterally linked to homes, offices, and indus-tries and departments of state elsewhere), then new modes of resistance have also begun to develop in response to their spectacular inefficiencies, failures and vulnerabilities (as well as to the pleasures they provide). To stress the latter rather than the former is not only realistic, but cheering and encouraging. It makes better political sense.

Yet in recent years there has been a proliferation of articles calling for studies of "consumption" not derived from "production," and a strange paucity of arguments which begin from that assumption, rather than repeatedly demonstrating its necessity. There has also been much recycling of exemplary inaugural stories (punk always seems to come to mind) that unvaryingly reiterate basic principles of cultural action — bricolage, cut-up, appropriation, assemblage and so on. As time passes in shopping-town, however, it's tempting to wonder how much longer (and for whom) those stories can do the rounds. Both of these developments suggest to me that apart from resuming the established twin prac-tices of empirical micro-studies of groups and the-oretical manifesto writing (neither of which in practice actually challenges, let alone changes, the production/consumption dichotomy, stressing rather a redistribution of emphasis within it), it's really quite hard to imagine exactly (apart from autobiography) what to do next.

Part of the problem, perhaps, is the common substitution I performed above between "users'

meanings" and "practices of consumption." It's an easy slide: from user to consumer to consump-tion, from persons to structures and processes. A whole essay could be written about what's wrong with making this and the parallel slide from notions of individual and group "creativity" to cultural "production" to political "resistance" — which can lead to the kind of criticism that a friend once parodied as "the discovery that wash-ing your car on Sunday is a revolutionary event."[36]

All I want to say here is that if the produc-tion/consumption opposition is not just a "designer/user" relation writ large (because rela-tions of production cannot be trivialized to "peo-ple planning things"), then it doesn't follow that representations of a shopping centre design proj-ect circulated by local media and consumed (cre-atively or otherwise) by some of its readership can be slotted away as production history. Indeed, I'm not sure that media practices can usefully be "placed" on either "side" of such a dichotomy. I think that the dichotomy itself needs to be reex-amined, especially since it now floats free of its old anchorage in theories of social totality; and the assumption that production and consumption can be read somehow as parallel or diverging realities depends on another assumption (becom-ing more dubious with every chip of change in technology) that we know enough now about pro-duction and can move to the other side. As though production, somehow, stays put.

The story of Green Hills is in a way an allegory about a politics of staying put, and it begins, para-noiacally, not with the first obvious appearance of a sign staking out a site, but behind the scenes — with an article in the [New South Wales] State Planning Authority journal SPAN in January 1969 and a report about it published in the *Newcastle Morning Herald* (24 January 1969). The *Herald's* story had the provocative title "Will Maitland Retain Its Entity or Become a Newcastle Suburb?"

[36]Thanks to Paul Willemen. This part of my article is a response to a theme which came up so insistently in discus-sion of the original conference paper that it seemed to require comment. [Morris]

Several general problems were facing Maitland, and many other country towns in Eastern Australia, at this time: population drift, shrinking local employment prospects, declining or anachronistic community facilities, the "nothing to do" syndrome. Maitland also had regional problems as a former rural service centre and coalfields capital en route to becoming a dormitory suburb, menaced by residential creep towards Newcastle — then about twenty miles away and getting closer. Maitland in particular suffered as well from physical fragmentation after ruinous floods in 1949 and 1955 (newsreel footage of which may be seen in Phillip Noyce's film *Newsfront*). The 1955 flood devastated the old commercial centre and the inner residential area: houses were shifted out and away in response to a "natural" blitzing.

So the threat of suburbanization and annexation uttered by the *Herald* produced an outraged response in that afternoon's *Maitland Mercury* from the Maitland mayor who, in spurning these "dismal prophecies," mentioned the "hope" that Woolworths would soon name the day for a development at East Maitland. From this moment on, and during all the conflicts that followed, Woolworths never figured in the council discourse as a national chain just setting up a store in a likely spot, but as a gallant and caring saviour come to make Maitland whole again — to stop the gap, to restore definition, to contain the creeping and seeping and to save Our Town's "Entity." In actual fact, of course, and following a well-known law of development, Green Hills was built on the town fringe nearest Newcastle, and the ensuing growth around it took the town kilometers closer to Newcastle and helped to fragment further the old city centre.

Four months after the SPAN and *Herald* incidents, the *Mercury* published a photo of an anonymous man staring at a mystery sign behind wire in the bush, saying "This site has been selected for another all Australian development by Woolworths" (*Maitland Mercury*, 16 May 1969). The site was at that time still a ragged border wasteland, across the hill from a notorious old "slum" called Eastville. The *Mercury* photo initiated a long-running mystery story about the conversion of the indefinite bush-border into a "site,"

the site into a place, the place into a suburb, in a process of territorialization that I'll call the fabrication of a place name.

To summarize the episodes briefly: first, the mystery sign turned out to be not just a bait to initiate interest, but a legal loophole that allowed Woolworths to claim, when challenged by local business firms, that it had fulfilled the terms of a 1965 agreement to develop the site by a certain date (*Maitland Mercury*, 25 June 1969). The sign itself could count as a developmental structure, and it had appeared just in time. Second, the first sign was replaced by another: a board at first adorned only by the letter "G." Maitland "citizens" were to participate in a guessing competition to find the name of the place, and a new letter was added each week until the full place-name, and the name of a lucky winner, emerged. This happened on 22 October 1969; and on the following Remembrance Day, 11 November, the city council abolished the name of the slum across the highway, Eastville. Eastville's name was to be forgotten, said the *Mercury*, in order to "unify the area with East Maitland" ("Eastville To Go West," *Maitland Mercury* 12 November 1969).

The basic Green Hills complex — at this stage a neighbourhood centre with a supermarket only — was opened in February 1972. The ceremony included ritual displays of crowd hysteria, with frenzied women fainting and making off with five thousand pairs of 8-cent pantyhose in the first five minutes (*Maitland Mercury*, 10 February 1972). This rite of baptism, or of public consent to the place-name, was repeated even more fervently in November 1977 when the Big W Discount House was added to make Green Hills a community centre. This time, women came wearing signs of Green Hills identity: said the *Mercury*, "A sea of green mums flooded in. . . . The mums dressed in sea green, celery green, grass green, olive green, green florals — every green imaginable — to take advantage of a 2NX[37] offer of free dinner tickets for women dressed in that colour" (*Maitland Mercury*, 14 November 1977).

That wasn't the end of it. The process now known as "metro-nucleation" had begun. In 1972,

[37]Newcastle, Australia, radio station.

a company associated with Woolworths began a hundred-home subdivision behind the centre. The area then acquired more parking, a pub, a motel, light industry, an old peoples' home, more specialty shops at the centre itself in 1980, and then, in 1983, a community health centre. This centre, said the *Mercury* — forgetting that the forgetting of Eastville had been to unify East Maitland — would serve "to service people living in the Berefield, Maitland, Bolwarra, East Maitland *and* Green Hills areas" (*Maitland Mercury* 14 November 1983). Maitland's "entity" at this stage was still a dubious mess, but Green Hills' identity was established, its status as a place-name secure. Presented rhetorically as a gesture of community unification, it had been, in effect, suburban-explosive in function.

The story continues, of course: I shan't follow it further, except to note that after this decade of expansion (a decade of acute economic distress for Maitland, and the Hunter Valley coal towns in general) Green Hills went into a certain decline. Woolworths got into trouble nationally and their Big W discount stores failed to keep pace with newer retail styles. Green Hills in particular faced stiff competition when a few blocks of the old city centre were torn down for a Coles-Myer Super K semi-hypermarket,[38] and when rapid infill development brought the twilight zone to town. Even residents hostile to these changes transferred their interest to them: one said, "It's awesome how many places they think we can use just to buy our few pounds of mince."[39]

I want to conclude with a few general points about things to do with this story. First, there are obviously a number of standardized elements in it that would appear in any such story set anywhere. For example, oceanic and hysterical crowd behaviour, in which the crowd itself becomes a decorative feature of the shopping centre's performance, is a traditional motif (and the *Mercury* in the late 1960s ran news features on how people

behaved at shopping centres in Sydney and the United States[40]). More generally, the process of development itself was impeccably normal.

Yet in looking at local instances of these general models, the well-known things that shopping centres do, one is also studying the practical inflections, or rewritings, of those models that can account for, and found, a regional politics. In the Green Hills case, I think that the Woolworths success story was written by the media very much in terms of a specific response to pre-existing discourses about Maitland's "very own" problems of identity and unity. In this sense, Woolworths' "success" was precisely to efface the similarity between what was happening in Maitland and what was going on elsewhere. That's the kind of problem I'd like to consider further: the ways in which the exploitation of the sense of "difference" in contemporary culture can be quite as complex as, and necessarily related to, the construction and deconstruction of imaginary identities.

Second, I'd like to use the Green Hills study to question some recent accounts in cultural studies of so-called "commodity semiosis" — the processes whereby commodities become signs, and signs become commodities — and the tendency to feminize (for example, through a theme of seduction) the terms in which that semiosis is discussed.

In a interesting critique of the work of Jean Baudrillard,[41] Andrew Wernick writes:

> The sales aim of commodity semiosis is to differentiate the product as a valid, or at least resonant, social totem, and this would be impossible without being able to appeal to taken-for-granted systems of cultural reference.[42]

While it is inappropriate (if consonant with marketspeak) simply to equate a whole shopping

[38]Anglicization of *hypermarché*, French term for supermarket, applied to massive supermarkets like Carrefour in France where one can buy clothing, automobile tires, groceries, including gourmet items like live lobsters and fresh truffles, all under one roof.

[39]Hamburger meat.

[40]See the *Maitland Mercury*, 18 April 1969, on Sydney's Roselands ("it could be Japan, but it's not . . .") and 23 October 1969, on American children being taken sixteen miles to a 24-hour Foodland "in the middle of the night," wearing pyjamas. [Morris]

[41]See p. 1945.

[42]Andrew Wernick, "Sign and Commodity: Aspects of the Cultural Dynamic of Advanced Capitalism," *Canadian Journal of Political and Social Theory*, vol. VIII, nos. 1–2. p. 31. [Morris] For Baudrillard, see p. 1945.

centre with "the product" in Wernick's sense, I could say that in the Green Hills case, Woolworths' strategy in selling the centre to the town was to appeal to that taken-for-granted cultural reference system of "booster" discourse deployed by ideologues of Australian country towns — towns which have long been losing their old reasons for being, and so their sense of the meaning and aim of their "history," Donald Horne has defined the elements of "booster" discourse in Australia as (1) getting bigger and (2) making it last[43] — aims which we might rephrase in combination here as "keeping it up."

If space today in some feminist theories, and theories of the feminine, is often thematized as feminine (in the ways which Alice Jardine has studied in *Gynesis*), and if commodity "appeal" is frequently theorized as feminine (as in Baudrillard's *De la séduction*, for example), I think that feminists might well keep looking at rhetorics of space and commerce that are — as systems of cultural reference — decidedly masculine. To borrow a phrase again from *Gynesis*, the booster reference system to which the Green Hills campaign appealed could equally be called "male paranoia." For Jardine,

> Male paranoia involves, fundamentally, the fear of the loss either of all boundaries or of those boundaries becoming too painfully constricting. And this encounter with boundaries is almost always described by men as an encounter with what is called "God" — that being who has no boundaries.[44]

She's talking about President Schreber.[45] But to make her statement refer to manoeuvres in Maitland, I need only name the God who has no boundaries as the spirit of Development: in booster discourse it is Development that is seen paradoxically — and wrongly — to protect against both

loss of entity and the painfully constricting condition that town councils still call (well into the era of "limits") "lack of growth."

I am not suggesting here that capital imperatives (development/growth/accumulation) are the same as or reducible to some psychology of "masculinity."[46] I simply want to claim firstly, that the rhetoric of maleness can provide certain projects with a reference-system vital, in the propaganda phase, to securing its means of realization (the discourses of economic rationalism provide an obvious example with their reifications of the "tough," the "hard" decisions, admitting no dispute that the "decisions" in question must be made); and secondly, that this rhetoric is in many domains of our lives still active, effective, destructive and seemingly impervious to the crisis of reason said (in the name of the feminine) to be engulfing it.

However my rewriting of "male paranoia" might nonetheless be merely a smart joke unless I add two more comments on the Green Hills story. One is that part of Woolworths' campaign against local small business was precisely to claim that the town might be saved from suburbanization by Newscastle (that is, from loss of boundaries) only if Maitland could further suburbanize itself internally — burst its outside borders, diversify, and come to "rival" Newcastle. The claim to rivalry was usually mediated by explicit comparisons between an ideal of what Green Hills would become and Newcastle's proud and historic Jesmond Big W — a structure in fact quite unlike Green Hills, but quite like Indooroopilly Shoppingtown. In a cruel twist, therefore, the local business interests were positioned not only as losers, but as unpatriotic for even trying to win — traitors to (imaginary) hometown desires, which could better be satisfied by Woolworths.

The other comment is that male paranoia's claim to rivalry was materialized at Green Hills in

---

[43]Donald Horne, *Money Made Us*, Harmondsworth 1976, chapter 8. [Morris]

[44]Jardine, *Gynesis*, p. 98. [Morris]

[45]Daniel Paul Schreber (1842–1911) was the Dresden appeals court judge (*Senatespräsident* was his German title, hence "president" Schreber) who was hospitalized for paranoid schizophrenia. In the asylum, he wrote *Memoirs of My Nervous Illness* (1903), which was read by Sigmund Freud, who analyzed his delusions in *Three Case Histories* (1909).

[46]My thanks to Louise Johnson for pointing out to me the possibility of this interpretation, and for other criticisms that helped me revise this paper. [Morris]

the achievement of a suburbanizing decor which gave it that hallucinatory resemblance to shoppingtowns everywhere else, plus a little frisson of distinction, that shivery edge of identity. I can say practically nothing here about the inner workings of Green Hills: but one thing that a feminist critique of commodity semiosis might notice there is that among the taken-for-granted cultural reference systems appealed to by suburban shopping centres is a garden furniture aesthetic that not only makes all centres seem the same, but, through a play of echoing spatial analogy, makes shopping centres seem like a range of other sites consecrated to the performance of family life, to women's work, to women's work in leisure: shoppingtown, beer garden, picnic spot, used-car yard (with bunting), scenic lookout, town garden, public park, suburban backyard.

The brightly coloured benches of Green Hills — along with coloured rubbish cones,[47] rustic borders, foliage, planters, mulch and well-spaced saplings — are all direct descendents of what in 1960 Robin Boyd called, in *The Australian Ugliness*, the "desperately picturesque accoutrements" then just bursting out brightly as "features" at Australian beauty-spots.[48] There's nothing desperate about their picturesqueness now, although they may mean desperation to some of their users (as well as cheer and comfort to others, especially those who remember the unforgiving discomforts of seatless, as well as featureless, Australian country town streets). Today, I think, they work to produce a sense of "setting" that defines an imaginary coherence of public space in Australia — or more precisely, of a "lifestyle" space declaring the dissolution of boundaries between public and private space, between public domains of work and private spheres of leisure.

Janet Wolff has argued that the emergence of the distinction between public and private spheres in the nineteenth century made impossible a female *flâneur* — a female strolling heroine

"botanizing on the asphalt" as Walter Benjamin put it in his study of Baudelaire.[49] I want to argue that it is precisely the proclaimed dissolution of public and private on the botanized asphalt of shoppingtown today that makes possible, not a *flâneuse,* since that term becomes anachronistic, but a practice of modernity by women for which it is most important not to begin by identifying heroines and victims (even of conflicts with male paranoia), but a profound ambivalence about shifting roles.

Yet here again, I want to differentiate. At places "like" Green Hills, the given function of hallucinatory spatial resemblance and recall is not, as it might be in an urban road-romance, a thinning out of significance through space so that one place ends up like any other in its drab indifference. Nor is it, as it might be in a big city, a move in a competitive game where one space says of its nearby rivals, "We Do All the Same Things Better." Green Hills appeals instead to a dream of plenitude and of a paradoxically absolute yet expansive self-sufficiency: a country town (if not "male") paranoia seeking reassurance that nothing is lacking in this one spot. It's the motherland dream of staying home, staying put: and as an uncle said to me on a stray visit to Green Hills, made simply to be sociable, waving round at the mulch and the benches and the glass facade of Big W — "Why go elsewhere when you've got it all here?" The centre itself, in his imagination, was not a fallen land of fragmented modernity, but the Garden of Eden itself. (Two years later, however, he sent me by myself to buy him cut-price T-shirts from Super-K in town — now the place where everyone wants to shop but no one cares to visit.)

Having arrived at last at the irresistible Big W magnet, I'd like to conclude with a comment on a text which seems to me to be a "radical" culture-criticism equivalent of the Garden of Eden fable by Myer's John Lennen with which I began.

[47]Garbage cans.
[48]Robin Boyd, *The Australian Ugliness.* (Victoria 1963 and Melbourne 1960), p. 105. [Morris]

[49]Janet Wolff, "The Invisible Flâneuse: Women and the Literature of Modernity," *Theory Culture & Society,* vol. 2, no. 3, 1985, pp. 37–46. [Morris]

It's a passage from Terry Eagleton's book *Walter Benjamin, or Towards a Revolutionary Criticism;* and it is also, although obliquely, a parable of modernity that depends on figuring consumption as a seductively fallen state. Paraphrasing and developing Benjamin's study of the *flâneur*, Eagleton writes:

> the commodity disports itself with all comers without its halo slipping, promises permanent possession to everyone in the market without abandoning its secretive isolation. Serializing its consumers, it nevertheless makes intimate *ad hominem* address to each.[50]

Now if this is not, as in Lennen's paper, a figure of Adam comforting Eve with a note on the postmodern condition, it's certainly Adam comforting himself with a certain ambivalent fantasy about Eve. It's a luscious, self-seducingly *risqué* fantasy that Adam has, a commodity thought, rather like the exquisite bottle of perfume or the pure wool jumper in the import shop, nestling deep in an upmarket neo-arcade, its ambience aglow with *Miami Vice* pastels or (since that's now been a little overdone) cooled by marbloid Italianate tiling.

But its pertinence to retailing, commodity semiosis, and shopping practices today is questionable not least because the development of forms like the neo-arcade (or the fantastically revamped prewar elegance of certain city department stores) is a response to the shopping-centre forms I've been discussing: a response which works by offering signs of old-fashioned commodity fetishism precisely because suburban shopping centres don't do so. Part of my argument has been that in suburban shopping practices it isn't necessarily or always the objects consumed that count in the act of consumption, but rather that unique sense of place. Beyond that, however, I think that the Benjamin-Eagleton style of boudoir-talk about commodities can be doubly misleading.

[50]Terry Eagleton, *Walter Benjamin, or Towards a Revolutionary Criticism*, London 1981, p. 27. [Morris]

First, one might ask, what is the sound of an intimate *ad hominem* address from a raincoat at Big W? Where is the secretive isolation of the thongs in a pile at Super-K? The commodities in a discount house boast no halo, no aura. On the contrary, they promote a lived aesthetic of the serial, the machinic, the mass-reproduced: as one pair of thongs wears out, it is replaced by an identical pair, the same sweatshirt is bought in four different colours, or two different and two the same; a macramé planter defies all middle-class whole-earth naturalness connotations in its dyes of lurid chemical mustard and killer neon pink. Second, commodity boudoir-talk gathers up into the single and class-specific image of the elite courtesan a number of different relations women and men may invent both to actual commodities, the activity of combining them and, above all, to the changing discursive frames (like shopping centres) that invest the practices of buying, trafficking with, and using commodities with their variable local meanings.

So one of the things I'd like to do with shopping centres is to make it more difficult for "radical" culture critics to fall back quite so comfortably on the classic image of European bourgeois luxury to articulate theories of sexual and economic exchange. If I were, for the sake of argument, to make up a fable of Adam and Eve and the fall into modernity, I wouldn't have my image of Eve taking comfort from modernist explanation (as she does from Lennen's Adam), and I wouldn't have her flattering him as she does for Eagleton's "comers." I'd have an image of her as a pedestrian, laughing at both of them, walking on past saying, "Boys, you sound just like the snake."

But of course, that's not good enough. It's the Eden story that's the problem, the fable of the management of change that's wrong — with its images of the garden, the snake, the couple, the Fall, and the terms that the story imposes, no matter how or by whom it's rewritten. To deny that shopping centres, and consumption, provide allegories of modernity as a fallen state is to claim that for feminism, some stories may be beyond salvage.

A film about these matters (and about elite courtesans) shown at the Feminist Criticism and

Cultural Production Conference — *Seduction* — *The Cruel Woman* by Elfi Mikesch and Monika Treut — interested me in its luxuriant difference from an imaginary text I've often wanted to write about country town familial sado-masochism, called "Maitland S&M."

This text is about the orchestration of modes of domestic repetition, the going back again and again over the same stories, the same terrains, the same sore spots, which I think a centre like Green Hills has successfully incorporated and mobilized in its fabrication of a myth of staying put at home. In case this sounds like feminist paranoia about, once again, planners, designers and producers, I should stress that one of the things that is fascinating about Big W aesthetics is the way that the store provides little more than a set of managerial props for the performance of inventive scenarios in a drama that circulates endlessly between home and the pub and the carpark and Green Hills and back again to home. One can emerge for a good session of ritualized pain and sorrow (as well as, of course, more pedestrian experiences) dressed in nothing more ferocious or costly than a fluffy pink top and a sweet floral skirt.

My main point, however, is that in so far as I have myself used the story of Green Hills as an allegory, it has been to argue that while it's clearly crucial, and fun, for feminist criticism to keep on rewriting the given stories of culture, to keep on revising and transforming their meanings, we must also remember that with some stories in some places, we do become cruelly bound by repetition, confined by the reiteration of the terms we're contesting. Otherwise, in an act of voluntary if painful servitude, feminist criticism ties its own hands and finds itself, again and again, at Green Hills, bound back home — to the same old story.

John Guillory

b. 1952

Born in New Orleans, Louisiana, Guillory was educated first at Tulane and then at Yale University, where he received his Ph.D. in 1979. He taught at Yale until 1989, then at Johns Hopkins and Harvard, and since 1999 has been Julius Silver Professor of English at New York University, where he is currently department chair. His first book, Poetic Authority: Spenser, Milton, and Literary History, *was published in 1983. His second book,* Cultural Capital: The Problem of Literary Canon Formation, *was published by the University of Chicago Press in 1993 and won the René Wellek Prize of the American Comparative Literature Association. Guillory has two books in progress: one in Renaissance studies entitled* Things of Heaven and Earth: The Figure of Philosophy in Renaissance Writing; *the other,* Literary Study in the Age of Professionalism, *an attempt to understand the history and future of departments of literature in the context of the emergence of the modern constellation of disciplines. The following selection is from* Cultural Capital.

From *Cultural Capital:* The Problem of Literary Canon Formation

MULTICULTURAL INTERLUDE: THE QUESTION OF A CORE CURRICULUM

Every relationship of "hegemony" is an educational relationship. — GRAMSCI, *Prison Notebooks*

While the debate over the canon concerns what texts should be taught in the schools, what remains invisible within this debate — too large to be seen at all — is the school itself. The absence of reflection on the school as an institution is the condition for the most deluded assumption of the debate, that the school is the vehicle of transmission for something like a national culture. What is transmitted by the school is, to be sure, a kind of culture; but it is the *culture of the school.* School culture does not unify the nation culturally so much as it projects out of a curriculum of artifact-based knowledge an imaginary cultural unity never actually coincident with the culture of the nation-state. In this way the left hand of the educational system — the dissemination of a supposedly national culture — remains ignorant of what the right hand is doing — the differential tracking of students according to class or the possession of cultural capital. If the structure of the system, its multiple levels and its division between public and private institutions, divides the population in this way, the culture the *university* produces (as opposed to other kinds or levels of school), can only be "national" for that plurality which acquires this level of education. What this group may learn to think of as a national culture is always a specific *relation* to the knowledge defined by the university curriculum.[1]

The extraordinary effects of confusing school culture with national culture are most conspicuous when the national culture is made to swallow whole the even larger fish called "Western culture," and in such a way as to produce an image of the American nation as the telos[2] of Western cultural evolution. Here we may adduce William Bennett's complacent version of this narrative in "To Reclaim a Legacy":

> We are a part and a product of Western civilization. That our society was founded upon such principles as justice, liberty, government with the consent of the governed, and equality under the law is the result of ideas descended directly from great epochs of Western civilization — Enlightenment England and France, Renaissance Florence, and Periclean Athens. These ideas, so revolutionary in their times yet so taken for granted now, are the glue that binds together our pluralistic nation. The fact that we as Americans — whether black or white, Asian or Hispanic, rich or poor — share these beliefs aligns us with other cultures of the Western tradition.[3]

The interesting point about this argument is not the typically American chauvinism Bennett immediately denies ("It is not ethnocentric or chauvinistic to acknowledge this"), or the dubious assimilation of Western thinkers to democratic political principles many or even most of them would not in fact have endorsed. What remains interesting and consequential in Bennett's statement is a confusion which, as we shall see, characterizes both Bennett and his opponents in the canon debate: the slippage between *culture* and *civilization.* The semantic burden of the latter term obliquely recognizes what the concept of the national culture denies — the necessity of defining that culture largely by reference to the High Cultural artifacts to which access is provided in the schools. Bennett admits as much, without

[1] Bourdieu makes this point in his essay "Systems of Education and Systems of Thought," *International Social Science Journal* 19 (1967), 349: "An individual's contact with his culture depends basically on the circumstances in which he has acquired it, among other things because the act whereby culture is communicated is, as such, the exemplary expression of a certain type of relation to the culture." [Guillory] See Bourdieu, p. 1398.

[2] End product.
[3] William Bennett, "To Reclaim a Legacy," 21. [Guillory]

drawing any adverse conclusion from this point: "No student of our civilization should be denied access to the best that tradition has to offer." Is "our civilization," then, the same as "our culture"? One may reasonably question what necessary *cultural* relation a university-trained suburban manager or technocrat has to Plato or Homer by virtue of his or her American citizenship — no more, in fact, than an educationally disadvantaged dweller in the most impoverished urban ghetto. The suburban technocrat and the ghetto dweller on the other hand have very much more in common culturally with each other than either of them ever need have with the great writers of Western civilization. If "Western" civilization — defined by a collection of cultural artifacts — can imaginarily displace the real cultural continuities that obtain at the national level, such an exemplary expression of the social imaginary is the effect of a crucial ambiguity in the concept of culture itself, an ambiguity familiar enough in the history of the concept as the distinction between culture in the sense of refinement — in this case, familiarity with the great works of "civilization" — and in the ethnographic sense of common beliefs, behaviors, attitudes — what a "national culture" would really have to mean.[4] The attempt to make the first sense of culture *stand for* the second names a certain project for the university, but one which it seems less well suited to undertake than ever (for reasons I will consider presently). The apparent failure of the university's cultural project of constituting a national culture elicits from the New Right the clamorous demand for a return to what was after all the *bourgeois* school, the institution enabling the old bourgeoisie to identify itself culturally by acquiring the cultural capital formerly restricted to the aristocratic or clerical estates. This capital consisted of nothing other than the "great works" of Western civilization.

If the national cultural project of the school is no longer a real possibility (it was always a class project anyway), the canon debate has nevertheless decisively problematized the notion of culture in its controversial language. The absence, however, of any concept of a specific *school* culture in the debate has meant that the perceived monolith of Western culture has had to be contested by the assertion of an antithetical "multiculturalism" as the basis of a politically progressive curriculum. Multiculturalism defines Western culture as its political antagonist, and vice versa. Yet the rather too neat polarization of these terms elides the question of what school culture really is, that is, what *relation to culture* is produced by the formal study of cultural artifacts. Whatever other effects the introduction of multicultural curricula may have, the *theory* of multiculturalism perpetuates the confusion of culture as the study of preserved artifacts with the sense of culture as common beliefs, behaviors, attitudes. It is by no means the case that the study of cultural works simply operates as the agency of cultural transmission in the second sense — although school culture, as Bourdieu has shown, does its part to install a *class* habitus[5] in the subjects of its pedagogy. This habitus is defined not by the content of cultural works (Plato is not really part of "our culture"), but by the relation to culture inculcated by the school, the relation named precisely by Bennett's "legacy" — a relation of *ownership*. It is not the ideas expressed in the great works that account for their status in arguments such as Bennett's, but the fact that these works are appropriated as the cultural capital of a dominant fraction. That appropriation is in turn justified by representing the ideational content of the great works as an expression of the same ideas which are realized in the current social order, with its current distribution of cultural goods.

---

[4] See the entry for "culture" in Raymond Williams's *Keywords: A Vocabulary of Culture and Society*, revised edition (New York: Oxford University Press, 1976, 1983), 87–93, for a lucid account of what is at stake in the different meanings of "culture" historically. We might sum up the difference between our national culture and our school culture by acknowledging that for national culture "Nike" is the name of an athletic shoe, for school culture a Greek goddess. [Guillory]

[5] Bourdieu defines *habitus* as a "system of dispositions," the social equivalent of "linguistic competence" (Noam Chomsky's term for the sum of all the tacit knowledge one has to possess to speak a natural language), or the feel a skilled player has for a game. Bourdieu viewed *habitus* as class-related: Persons of the same class were likely, he found, to adopt a similar habitus across different social fields.

In order to accomplish the cultural task of appropriation, however, the school must traverse the heavily mined terrain of a certain alienation produced by the formal study of cultural works. We should not forget that the effects of this alienation are sometimes permanent, and that it is precisely "one's own" culture which sometimes fails to survive the culture of the school (that is to say, the school sometimes produces, despite its acculturative function, dissident intellectuals). Similarly the formal study of cultural works produced within minority cultures is not a means of reproducing minority culture (in the ethnographic sense). If the formal study of Latin-American novels in the university does not really transmit or reproduce Latino culture, it follows that the relation of even Latino students to these artifacts will not be entirely unlike the relation of "American" students to the works of "Western" (American or European) culture. The question is what this relation is, or what it should be.

One conclusion to be drawn immediately from this argument is that there is no ground of commensuration between Western cultural artifacts on the one hand, if examples of these are the *Odyssey* or the Parthenon; and Latino culture on the other, if the latter means the totality of a living culture, and not just its artifacts. Insofar as it is only the *works* of Western or Latino culture to which one has direct access in the school, these works will ultimately be constructed and legitimated as objects of study *in the same way,* by a process of deracination from the actual cultural circumstances of their production and consumption.[6] If

works by Afro-American, Latin-American, or postcolonial writers are read now in formal programs of university study, this fact may be the immediate result of a political project of inclusion, or the affirmation of cultural diversity. But the survival of these works in future school curricula will be seen otherwise, as a consequence of their status as interesting and important cultural works that no intellectually responsible program of study can ignore. The current project of affirming *cultures themselves* through the legitimation of cultural works in university curricula is enabled by the very conflation between the senses of culture to which I have drawn attention. The very intensity of our "symbolic struggle" reduces cultural conditions of extreme complexity to an allegorical conflict between a Western cultural Goliath and its Davidic multicultural antagonists. Hence it is never really Greek culture, or French culture, or Roman culture, that is compared with Latino culture or Afro-American culture, but always "Western" culture. Multiculturalism finds itself in the position of having to credit both the reality and the homogeneity of that fictional cultural entity, which achieves its spurious self-identity only by consisting of *nothing but* cultural artifacts.[7]

If the fiction of the cultural homogeneity of the West is nevertheless a very powerful one (because it is ideological), perhaps the better

---

[6]Bourdieu, "Systems of Education and Systems of Thought," *International Social Science Journal* 19 (1967), 351, points to an analogous confusion when the concept of culture is made to refer indifferently both to popular culture and to school culture: "Just as Basil Bernstein contrasts the 'public language' of the working classes, employing descriptive rather than analytical concepts, with a more complex 'formal language,' more conducive to verbal elaboration and abstract thought, we might contrast an academic culture, confined to those who have been long subjected to the disciplines of the school, with a 'popular' culture, peculiar to those who have been excluded from it, were it not that, by using the same concept of culture in both cases, we should be in danger of concealing that these two systems of patterns of perception, language, thought, action and appreciation are separated by an essential difference. This is that only the system of patterns

cultivated by the school, i.e. academic culture (in the subjective sense of personal cultivation or *Bildung* in German), is organized primarily by reference to a system of works embodying that culture, by which it is both supported and expressed." [Guillory]

[7]This argument should not be taken to deny the fact that the "West" is a real politico-economic entity, even though its cultural homogeneity lags far behind the unity of its politico-economic system. The *image* of that cultural unity remains the ideological support for the real unity of the West in its imperial relations with the Third World, or in its militarist competition with what was formerly the Eastern Bloc. The collapse of the Soviet Union as a result of that competition, and the consolidation of a Western alliance in the Persian Gulf War are sufficient evidence of what was and is at stake in maintaining the fiction of the cultural unity of the West. Finally, do we need to be reminded that it is Coca-Cola and not Plato which signifies Western culture in the realm of what Immanuel Wallerstein calls "geo-culture"? On this subject, see John Tomlinson, *Cultural Imperialism: A Critical Introduction* (Baltimore: Johns Hopkins University Press, 1991). [Guillory]

strategy for resisting its domination-effect may be to expose the relation between the "culture" it pretends to embody and the institution which is its support in reality. It is just by suppressing culture in the ethnographic sense — or reserving that sense of culture for non-"Western" artifacts — that the traditional curriculum can appropriate the "great works" of Western civilization for the purpose of constituting an imaginary cultural unity such as Bennett or Hirsch[8] envisions. The deracination of the text tradition thus forces us to define the intertextual relation, say, between Aquinas and Aristotle as evidence of the continuity of Western culture, but it allows us to set aside the fact that Aristotle and Aquinas have almost nothing in common *culturally*. It should be remarked here also that the construction of Western culture depends more upon a body of philosophical than literary texts. If the canon debate originated in university literature departments, the defenders of the canon extended the debate to the question of the humanities curriculum as a whole — the "core" curriculum — by resurrecting the philosophical text tradition as the basis for that core curriculum. This text tradition can be invoked more easily than national vernacular literatures to maintain the fiction of a profound evolution or destiny of Western thought extending from the pre-Socratics to the present.[9] Yet the fact remains

that this continuity was always the historical support for *nationalist* agendas. The schools in the early modern nation-states provided an instrument by means of which the state could dissolve the residually feudal bonds of local sovereignty and reattach personal loyalty to itself. Nationalism is, as we have seen, entirely on the surface in Bennett's document. In the early modern period, the great vernacular literary works of the nation-states were taught in such a way as to constitute retroactively a pre-national "West" (usually classical rather than medieval), a continuity intended to cover over the traumatic break of early modern societies with traditional feudal cultures. The "West" was always the creation of nationalism, and that is why one observes that the assertion of the continuity of Western tradition exactly corresponds in its intensity to the assertion of nationalism itself.[10]

The homogenizing textual effects of deracination are even more obvious when we consider the fact that, for us, Plato and Aristotle, Virgil and Dante, are great works of literature *in English*. The translation of the "classics" into one's own vernacular is a powerful institutional buttress of imaginary cultural continuities; it confirms the nationalist agenda by permitting the easy appropriation of texts in foreign languages. Yet the device of translation should not be regarded as extraordinary or atypical of school culture, for translation is only a more explicit version of the same technique of deracination by which all cultural works are constructed as objects of study. This point may clarify the otherwise confusing status of "oral literature," which has become a favored site for the contestation of Western culture's hegemony. It is not a mere contingency that oral works must become "written" in order to be brought into the arena of curricular conflict as "noncanonical" works, excluded or devalued by the Western text tradition. In fact, oral works *cannot* otherwise enter the institutional field, since

[8]Eric Donald Hirsch (b. 1928), formerly professor of English at the University of Virginia, argued in his best-selling book, *Cultural Literacy: What Every American Needs to Know* (1987), that the deficiencies of American primary and secondary education were owing partly to the systematic neglect of geographical, historical, and scientific facts, without which students were unable to make sense of political and cultural ideas. Hirsch's book concluded with a list of facts with which he thought every citizen ought to be familiar. While Guillory admits that Hirsch's agenda is not quite so simplistic as those of right-wing pundits like Bennett, he argues elsewhere that the "handy finiteness" of Hirsch's list of significant facts conferring cultural literacy "is the ideological denial of the heterogeneity" of Western culture (p. 354).

[9]This is the argument of Joan Shelley Rubin, *The Making of Middlebrow Culture* (Chapel Hill: University of North Carolina Press, 1992). Discussing John Erskine's original idea for a "great books" program at Columbia University, Rubin notes: "[B]y contending that 'great books' portrayed timeless, universal human situations [Erskine] permitted the conclusion that the classics of Western literature *were* the American heritage" (173). [Guillory]

[10]The example of Heidegger almost goes without saying, but not quite. Heidegger's belief in the deep affinity between the Greek and German languages, supposedly the only truly philosophical languages, forces us to recall that the text tradition which is the support of the notion of the West is itself supported in modern European thought both by philological and racial concepts of continuity. [Guillory]

orality as a cultural condition can only be studied at all ethnographically, as the "writing of culture." When the condition of oral production is on the other hand ignored in the context of interpreting or evaluating these works (by treating oral works as though they were other written works), the real difference between school culture and the culture which gives rise to works disappears from view. By suppressing the context of a cultural work's production and consumption, the school produces the illusion that "our" culture (or the culture of the "other") is transmitted simply by contact with the works themselves. But a text tradition is not sufficient in itself either to constitute or to transmit a culture, and thus school culture can never be more than a part of a total process of acculturation which, for societies with schools, is always complex and has many other institutional sites.

The function imposed upon schools of acculturating students in "our" culture often thus requires that texts be read "out of context," as signs of cultural continuity, or cultural unity. We need not deny that the text tradition can sustain intertextual dialogue over centuries and millennia, however, in order to insist that what is revealed by the historical context of this dialogue is cultural discontinuity and heterogeneity.[11] A rather different pedagogy, one that emphasizes

historical contextualization, would at the very least inhibit the assimilation of cultural works to the agenda of constituting a national culture, or the Western culture which is its ideological support.[12] For the very same reason, only the simplest countercultural pedagogy can make the works of the multicultural curriculum stand in a "subversive" relation to Western culture. The historicization of these works too will have to confront the mutual influence and interrelation between dominant Western and dominated non-Western cultures (in the case of postcolonial works, for example, the fact that "Western culture" appears as a cultural unity *only* through the lens of the colonial educational system, and that postcolonial literatures are in constant dialogue with the works taught in that system). While there exists a multiplicity of sites of cultural production, then, this multiplicity can never really be equated with the multiplicity of cultures, as though every cultural work were only the organic expression of a discrete and autonomous culture.[13] The fact that we now expect the curriculum to reflect as a principle of its organization the very distinctness of cultures, Western or non-Western, canonical or noncanonical, points to a

---

[11]Bourdieu, "Systems of Education and Systems of Thought": "Because of its own inertia, the school carries along categories and patterns of thought belonging to different ages. In the observance of the rules of the dissertation in three points, for example, French schoolchildren are still contemporaries of Saint Thomas. The feeling of the 'unity of European culture' is probably due to the fact that the school brings together and reconciles — as it must for the purposes of teaching — types of thought belonging to very different periods" (352). What I have been calling a "text tradition" is obviously the site of critical judgment, in the sense that the entire domain of intertextuality, or response to earlier by later writers, is a powerful agency for the preservation of these writers. Nevertheless I have consistently argued for locating the site of canon formation in the school, for the reason implied by Bourdieu in the passage just quoted. The point of the sociological argument, for both Bourdieu and myself, is that authors learn whom to read and how to judge in the schools, and that even the judgment of recent but uncanonized work must eventually be validated in the passage of writers into school curricula in order for one to speak of canonicity. One should not forget that literary history is filled with the names

of writers whose high standing with other, more famous authors was still insufficient to insure their canonicity. [Guillory]

[12]Schools do not always have to acknowledge the fact of deracination, nor do they necessarily have to employ historicizing strategies of recontextualization in classroom practice. Precisely to the extent that they deny the former and decline the latter, they can realize the objective of merely reproducing culture as dogma, as in the case of religious schools. The operation of culture as dogma will be taken up in Chapter 3, Ideology and Canonical Form. [Guillory]

[13]This point has been eloquently argued by Kwame Anthony Appiah in the context of the production and consumption of African cultural works: "If there is a lesson in the broad shape of this circulation of cultures, it is surely that we are all already contaminated by each other, that there is no longer a fully autochthonous *echt*-African culture awaiting salvage by our artists (just as there is, of course, no American culture without African roots). And there is a clear sense in some postcolonial writing that the postulation of a unitary Africa over against a monolithic West — the binarism of Self and Other — is the last of the shibboleths of the modernizers that we must learn to live without." "Is the Post- in Postmodernism the Post- in Postcolonial?" *Critical Inquiry* 17 (1991), 354. [Guillory]

certain insistent error of culturalist politics, its elision of the difference the school itself makes in the supposed transmission of culture.

From the perspective of long-term developments in the educational system, the canon debate itself may seem oddly beside the point. Bennett and his associates already acknowledged in their 1984 document that the "crisis of the humanities" refers to the fact that fewer undergraduates choose to major in traditional humanities than in the past. One has the impression in surveying the musings of the right-wing pundits that this fact is the result of nothing less than abdication by the professors of their duty to teach the traditional texts.[14] Nothing could be further from the truth — these texts still constitute the vastly greater part of the humanities curriculum — and in that sense the complaint of the New Right is simply fraudulent. A welcome reality check is provided by Patrick Brantlinger in his analysis of the "crisis":

> Tradition gives the humanities an importance that current funding and research priorities belie. At giant public "multiversities" like the Big Ten schools, humanities courses are taken by many students only as requirements — a sort of force-feeding in writing skills, history, great books, and appropriate "values" before they select the chutes labeled "pre-professional" — pre-med, pre-law, and so forth. . . . Clearly, one doesn't need to blame the radical sixties for the current marginalization and sense of irrelevance that pervades the humanities today.[15]

The crisis of the humanities is the result not of university professors' unwillingness to teach great works (the idea is an insult especially to those teachers and graduate students who could not find employment in the recessions of the 70s and 80s) but of the decisions students themselves make in the face of economic realities. Granted the fact that the crisis is not the result of curricular decisions by humanities teachers, why is the content of the curriculum the site of such

controversy? The canon debate will not go away, and it is likely to intensify as the positions of the right and of the multiculturalists are further polarized. The very strength of the reactionary backlash, its success in acquiring access to the national media and funding for its agitprop, suggests that the symptomatic importance of the debate is related in some as yet obscurely discerned way to the failure of the contestants to give an account of the general decline in the significance of the humanities in the educational system. It has proven to be much easier to quarrel about the content of the curriculum than to confront the implications of a fully emergent professional-managerial class which no longer requires the cultural capital of the old bourgeoisie. The decline of the humanities was never the result of newer noncanonical courses or texts, but of a large-scale "capital flight" in the domain of culture. The debate over what amounts to the supplementation (or modernization) of the traditional curriculum is thus a misplaced response to that capital flight, and as such the debate has been conducted largely in the realm of the pedagogic imaginary. I would propose, then, that the division now characterizing the humanities syllabus — between Western and multicultural, canonical and noncanonical, hegemonic and nonhegemonic works — is the symptom of a more historically significant split between two kinds of cultural capital, one of which is "traditional," the other organic to the constitution of the professional-managerial class.

In this larger socioeconomic context, the polarization of the debate into a conflict between Western culture and multiculturalism has proven to be a political misstep for the left. For both the reactionary scapegoating of the noncanonical syllabus as the cause of the crisis of the humanities, and multiculturalism's reduction of canonical works to the ideology of a monolithic Western culture fail to recognize the real relations between the humanities curriculum and the social forces which operate on it. If the debate is ever to acknowledge the presence of these forces, it will have to move beyond the curricular distinction between the canonical and the noncanonical; it will have to raise the much larger question of what is at stake in the relation between the kinds

---

[14] See Allan Bloom, *The Closing of the American Mind* (New York: Simon and Schuster, 1987), p. 352. [Guillory]

[15] Patrick Brantlinger, *Crusoe's Footprints: Cultural Studies in Britain and America* (New York: Routledge, 1990), p. 7. [Guillory]

of cultural capital. Since both canonical and non-canonical works constitute at base, despite their apparent conflict, the same *kind* of cultural capital, the social forces displacing this kind of capital will sooner or later strand the participants in the canon debate on an ever shrinking island within the university itself.

What needs urgently to be recognized now is that the polarization of the curriculum into canonical and noncanonical works is very much more in the interest of the right than of the left. The investment of the right in the great works of Western civilization — a "core" curriculum — is in extreme bad faith. For Bennett has already decided that what Bloom calls the "big questions" have been given definitive answers in the American social and political system, which rests on the unshakeable foundation of the *free market*. Yet it is the market itself which produces the effect of cultural capital flight. The professional-managerial class has made the correct assessment that, so far as its future profit is concerned, the reading of great works is not worth the investment of very much time or money. The perceived devaluation of the humanities curriculum is in reality a decline in its *market* value. If the liberal arts curriculum still survives as the preferred course of study in some elite institutions, this fact has everything to do with the class constituency of these institutions. With few exceptions, it is only those students who belong to the financially secure upper classes who do not feel compelled to acquire professional or technical knowledge as undergraduates. The professional-managerial class, on the other hand, many of whose members have only recently attained to middle and upper middle-class status, depends entirely on the acquisition of technical knowledge in order to maintain its status, or to become upwardly mobile. The challenge posed to a class analysis of culture by the professional-managerial class has been well described by Gouldner in his *The Future of Intellectuals and the Rise of the New Class*: "What is needed for the systematic analysis of the old and new class is a *general theory of capital* in which moneyed capital is seen as part of the whole, as a special case of capital. Conversely, what is required for the understanding of culture as capital is nothing less than a political economy of culture."[16] Whether such a political economy of culture has been successfully elaborated in the work of Gouldner or Bourdieu, it is entirely indicative of the conceptual limits of the curriculum debate that it could be carried on for over a decade virtually without reference to either figure.

In this context the right-wing design of purging noncanonical works from the curriculum has as one of its evident objectives the revaluation of the cultural capital of canonical works by associating them with currently popular nationalist and xenophobic sentiments. Mary Louise Pratt is surely correct in identifying the aim of this polemic as the creation of "a narrowly specific cultural capital that will be the normative *referent* for everyone, but will remain the *property* of a small and powerful caste that is linguistically and ethnically unified."[17] The crucial question, however, is not how "narrowly specific" this cultural capital is to be, but how it is to produce the effect of unifying a "caste." Because this unity is not preexistent in American society — capital itself is dispersed now among a number of ethnicities, genders, and even linguistic groups — it must be constituted in the university *after the fact,* as a new project for that institution. This circumstance explains why the right's agenda for the university always makes room for *some* members of minority groups,

[16] Alvin W. Gouldner, *The Future of Intellectuals and the Rise of the New Class* (New York: Oxford University Press, 1979), p. 21. Gouldner argues persuasively that "An investment in education is not simply a consumable. Something is left over, which produces a subsequent flow of income. It is *cultural capital,* the economic basis of the New Class" (27). On the other hand, I am not convinced that the problem-solving orientation of the New Class constitutes what Gouldner calls a "culture of critical discourse." This is not to say that the professional-managerial class has not produced some forms of social criticism — it has — but that this criticism is seldom systemic (it is usually anti-state but not anti-capital). I am also aware that arguments *against* systemic critique have been made on certain "post-Marxist" grounds. Foucault's concept of the "specific intellectual" might in this context be compared to Gouldner's concept of the New Class intellectual. My own argument follows Bourdieu, however, in his version of systemic critique. [Guillory]

[17] Pratt, "Humanities for the Future: Reflections on the Western Culture Debate at Stanford," *South Atlantic Quarterly* 89 (1990): 9. [Guillory]

because the right believes these self-made individuals can be assimilated to the "caste" of all those with an interest in preserving the rights and privileges of their acquired capital. Such assimilation will leave (and has left) the grossly inequitable social structure more or less unchallenged. It is not quite the case, then, that the New Right wishes to purge the university of all linguistic or ethnic others, but that it sets the university the project of unifying the new possessors of cultural capital by cultural means, by means of a "common" curriculum which will identify them as (justly) privileged. In this way Bennett's "legacy" can be reclaimed for its proper inheritors, those who leave the university possessed of capital, of whatever kind. The cultural legacy so probated will present an image to a somewhat more ethnically heterogeneous propertied class of its unified cultural identity as the inheritors of cultural capital.

If this analysis is correct it does not seem the most effective strategy for the left to cede to the right the *definition* of cultural capital; but this is exactly what a multiculturalism does when it yields canonical works to the right, when it accepts the right's characterization of the canonical syllabus as constitutive of a unified and monolithic Western culture. Basing its agenda upon such assumptions, a left politics of representation seems to have no other choice than to institutionalize alternative syllabi as representative images of non-Western or "counter"-cultures. This is finally why the project of legitimizing noncanonical works in the university produces an irresolvable contradiction between the presentation of these works as equal in cultural value to canonical works, and at the same time as the embodiment of countercultural values which by their very definition are intended to delegitimize the cultural values embodied in canonical works. The polarization of the debate into Western culturalism versus multiculturalism must then be seen not as a simple conflict between regressive and progressive pedagogies but as the symptom of the transformation of cultural capital in response to social conditions not yet recognized as the real and ultimately determining context of the canon debate. Both the right-wing attempt to shore up the cultural capital of the "great works" by advocating a return to a core curriculum, and the pluralist advocacy of multiculturalism respond to the same demographic circumstances, the heterogeneous constituency of the university. But neither version of culturalist politics responds to the heterogenous constitution of cultural capital, and hence both movements are condemned to register this condition symptomatically, as a false perception of the mutual (cultural) exclusivity of canonical and noncanonical works.

It is chastening to recall that a leftist analysis of the heterogeneity of cultural capital was available long before Bourdieu or Gouldner, in the work of Antonio Gramsci. In his prescient notes on the subject of education, Gramsci recognized that the displacement of the classical curriculum by professional and technical knowledge would have the effect of precipitating the "humanist" curriculum into what seems to be a permanent state of crisis:

> The basic division of schools into classical (i.e. grammar) and trade schools was a rational scheme: trade schools for the instrumental classes, classical schools for the ruling classes and intellectuals. The development of the industrial base in both town and country led to a growing need for a new type of urban intellectual: alongside the classical school there developed the technical school (professional but not manual), and this brought into question the very principle of the concrete orientation of general culture based on the Greco-Roman tradition. This orientation, once brought into question was in fact doomed, since its formative capacity was largely based on the general and traditionally indisputable prestige of a particular form of civilization.[18]

Gramsci expresses in his notes what may seem to the present liberal academy a surprising conservatism on curricular issues. Without arguing for the retention of the classical curriculum — Gramsci allows that it had to be replaced — he was concerned to point out the paradoxical social effects of the "new type of school" which, while it "appears and is advocated as being democratic" is actually "destined not merely to perpetuate social differences but to crystallize them in

[18]Antonio Gramsci, *The Modern Prince and Other Writings* (New York: International Publishers, 1957), 126. [Guillory]

Chinese complexities."[19] The apparently conservative tenor of his remarks should not be confused, then, with the usual complaint about "specialization," which expresses nostalgia for the even less democratic educational system of the past (Gramsci insists that the older system was always "intended for the new generation of the ruling class"). The question is not whether technical or professional knowledges will or should be taught, but whether there exists a body of knowledge to which *everyone* should have access in the schools. Gramsci's solution to the emergence of a "crisis of the humanities" was to propose the formation of a "single, humanistic, formative, primary school of general culture which will correctly balance the development of ability for manual (technical, industrial) work with the development of ability for intellectual work."[20] Gramsci's proposal may seem, at this date, uncritical of the content of such a curriculum, since he did not have to consider his own society as in our sense "pluralist"; but we should remember that his sense of a politically strategic educational practice is supported by what is perhaps the most powerful theory of intellectual labor in the Marxist tradition, as well as by the very concept of hegemony that is invoked in virtually all forms of current cultural criticism. For these reasons a serious consideration of Gramsci's analysis may be in order.

What Gramsci called the "unitary school" was supposed to "break [the] pattern" of the traditional educational system, in which "each group has its own type of school, intended to perpetuate a specific traditional function, ruling or subordinate."[21] The new technical and professional schools reinstated the division of society "into juridically fixed and crystallized estates rather than moving towards the transcendence of class divisions." The issue here is not only class division but the conditions of possibility for democratic self-government, since Gramsci rightly sees the schools as providing the means for participating in government: "But democracy, by definition, cannot mean merely that an unskilled worker can become skilled. It must mean that every 'citizen' can 'govern' and that society places him, even if only abstractly, in a general condition to achieve this" (318). This is of course an old theme, but the simultaneous and not unrelated decline of both public education and participatory democracy in the United States should confirm its continued pertinence. For reasons too obvious to belabor, Gramsci's "unitary school" was never a goal in this country; but since our concern is with the American educational system, we can at least note that the very limited "democratization" of that system has been accompanied by the gradual displacement upwards to the university level of the curriculum Gramsci conceived as the basis of a "unitary school." This arrangement accomplishes the effect of class fractioning by tracking most students into the work force at the end of their primary or secondary schooling (an effect reinforced also by the distinction between public and private schools). Given the social pressure to enforce vocational tracking at the lower levels of the educational system, and to dispense more highly valued professional and technical knowledge at the university level, the slot into which the humanities curriculum is confined is very small — as we know, the first two years of college study. In the absence of a "unitary school" at the primary or secondary levels, the possibility of installing a core curriculum of philosophical or literary works exists only during this brief period. Many colleges, of course, have always had some form of a core curriculum, but the important point is that the formal study of a set list of "great works" is condemned to have something of a remedial status for those students who have not read literary or philosophical works, either historical or contemporary, at the lower levels of the system, and who will not continue to study them after their sophomore year. It is only by first recognizing the remedial status of the first two years of college study that we can then pose the question of what Gramsci's analysis may have to offer the present debate.

It will first be necessary to exit the social imaginary by acknowledging that there is no question of producing a *national* culture by

[19]Antonio Gramsci, *The Antonio Gramsci Reader: Selected Writings 1916–1935,* ed. David Forgacs (New York: Schocken Books, 1988), 317. [Guillory]

[20]Gramsci, *The Modern Prince,* 127. [Guillory]

[21]Gramsci, *The Antonio Gramsci Reader,* 318. [Guillory]

means of a *university* curriculum. Or conversely of producing a national multiculturalist ethos by the same means. The question is rather what social effects are produced by the knowledges disseminated in the university, and by the manner of their dissemination. It should not be the business of the university to produce a "common culture" even if the educational system inevitably produces a school culture, a specific relation to knowledge among its subjects. The objective of political integration is not to be confused with the altogether questionable objective of cultural assimilation. Gramsci's analysis suggests that a necessary social condition of democracy is the general exercise of a certain kind of intellectual labor, and that a specific body of knowledge (by which is meant neither *information* in Hirsch's sense, nor *culture* in Bennett's) is the necessary medium in the schools for the exercise of this intellectual labor. The point of the unitary school is that it is a school for everyone; by definition it is not the university. A necessary objective of a Gramscian reconsideration of the curriculum debate would thus be the rearticulation of that debate in the context of the educational system *as* a system. In this context, we can recognize that the constraints upon the university curriculum at its present moment and in its present form account for the fact that the project of a core curriculum is so easily annexed to a socially regressive agenda. Time is one such constraint, since it intensifies the effect of deracination to the point of reducing the study of "great works" to a shallow rehearsal of contextless ideas; such "ideas" turn out unsurprisingly to be nothing more than the clichés of right-wing ideology.[22] It has been all too easy as a consequence for the left/liberal professoriate to identify the only respectable adversarial stance with opposition to a core curriculum. The institutionalization of the distinction between canonical and noncanonical works thus emerges as the necessary response to any attempt to reinstitute an exclusively traditional curriculum. As an expression of the same culturalist politics which confuses school culture with culture in general, this adversarial position unfortunately also deprives the teaching of canonical works of an adequate progressive rationale.

It is perhaps time for progressive teachers to take back the humanities curriculum — all of it — as an integrated program of study. Such a program will be severely limited by the narrow stratum of the educational system which it is forced to inhabit, but until we can begin to think and speak about education as a system of interrelated levels, these limits will continue to function subliminally, beyond analysis or intervention. In the meantime, we can imagine that an integrated curriculum would supersede the distinction between canonical and noncanonical works in the recognition that a syllabus of study always enacts a negotiation between *historical* works and *modern* works. There is no question now, nor has there even been, of the inevitability of curricular change: the latter-day curriculum is the archaeological evidence of its own sedimented history. When we read Plato or Homer or Virgil in a humanities course, then, we are reading what *remains* of the classical curriculum after the vernacular revolutions of the

---

[22]There is reason to believe that the inevitable brevity and shallowness of the great-books tour are not so undesirable to the New Right. For they are less interested finally in inquiring closely into historical complexities or discursive ambiguities than in making sure that students come away from their experience of reading great works with the *right ideas*. This objective is quite openly acknowledged by the classicist Donald Kagan, who has been celebrated in the right-wing media for using his position as the dean of Yale College as a bully pulpit for what he calls "common studies." Mindful of the liberal persuasion of many of his faculty, however, the dean has expressed some doubt about their suitability to teach these works in the *right way:* "Consider what a core constructed by the current faculty would look like, and the consequences that would ensue if they also had the responsibility of teaching it." See Donald Kagan, "Yale University: Testing the Limits," *Academic Questions* 4 (1991), 33. On the historical origins of the idea of "great books" in American society, and the tendency toward the "superficial" assimilation of the books, see Rubin, *The Making of Middlebrow Culture,* 192ff. Rubin demonstrates persuasively that Mortimer Adler's transformation of John Erskine's notion of a great-books program into the Encyclopaedia Britannica's *Great Books of the Western World* produced nothing less than a monument of middlebrow culture. The almost exclusive emphasis on philosophical rather than literary works in the Britannica project called forth the famous "Syntopicon" of "Great Ideas," which virtually assured that no one would ever have to read the books themselves. [Guillory]

early modern period. The fact that we no longer read these works in Greek or Latin, or that we read far fewer classical Greek or Latin works than students of premodern school systems, represents a real loss; but this loss must be reckoned as the price of the *integration* of these works into a modern curriculum. The inevitable loss of older works in any humanities curriculum, even one hypothetically much larger than current programs tend to be, is the result, as we have observed, of the *absolute* accumulation of cultural works. The reactionary defense of the traditional "canon" thus betrays itself as ignorant of the cultural history sedimented in the very syllabus it desires to fix. On the other hand it should no longer be necessary to present certain other works, "noncanonical" works, as intrinsically opposed to a hegemonic principle of canonicity, as this is likewise to forget the history sedimented in any syllabus of study.

An alternative theoretical formulation of the curriculum problem will thus have to repudiate the practice of fetishizing the curriculum, of locating the politics of pedagogy in the anxious drawing up of a list of representative names. The *particular* names matter even less at the university level, since the number of historical and modern works worth studying is vastly greater than any (remedial) course of study could begin to consider. The syllabus should rather be conceived as the means of providing *access* to cultural works, both historical and modern (the contrary assumption — that works not on the syllabus will never be read — is an entirely disreputable assumption for teachers to make). Since noncanonical works are in every case either historical works (the objects of research or revaluation) or modern works (the objects of legitimation for the first time as cultural capital), they are in fact what all canonical works once were. To contend otherwise is to commit oneself to the notion that some works are intrinsically canonical, simply expressive of the dominant ideology, and other works intrinsically noncanonical, utterly unassimilable to hegemonic culture. If that were true, what would the struggle to legitimize new works as objects of study be *for*? Hegemony, in Gramsci's sense, is to be fought for; it is something that is continually won and lost by struggles which take place at the specific sites of social practice.

What difference would such a reformulation of terms make? First, that current research programs such as women's studies, or Afro-American studies be recognized as such, as research programs and not as the institution of separate curricula for separate constituencies. But even more important, the humanities curriculum should be presented as an integrated program of study in which the written works studied constitute a certain kind of cultural capital, and in which works therefore cannot be allegorized as intrinsically canonical or intrinsically noncanonical, intrinsically hegemonic or intrinsically antihegemonic. No cultural work of any interest at all is simple enough to be credibly allegorized in this way, because any cultural work will *objectify* in its very form and content the same social conflicts that the canon debate allegorizes by means of a divided curriculum. Further, a conception of an integrated curriculum would make it impossible to forget that what one internalizes in the school is not one's own culture but the culture of the school (which has in turn a certain relation, but not a relation of identity, to culture in the ethnographic sense). The school produces a culture, then, neither unambiguously good or bad, but it does not simply reproduce a given culture, hegemonic or antihegemonic, through the *content* of the curriculum. If it is a defensible objective of the school to disseminate knowledge about the "multicultural" diversity of the nation (defensible because the nation *is* so diverse), it follows from this very objective that it is just as important for majority students to study the cultural products of minority cultures as it is for minority students to be able to study the cultural works of their own cultures. Hence when works by minority writers are legitimized as cultural capital by becoming objects of study in the university, it will follow that everyone will have a right of access to them.

Especially in the wake of a reactionary backlash which indicts the liberal critique of the canon for the abandonment of all standards of judgment, it is no longer politically strategic to argue for the necessity of teaching certain "noncanonical" works solely on the grounds that these works represent social minorities. It is on the contrary much more strategic to argue that the school has the social obligation of providing access to these works, *because they are important and significant cultural works*. In this way we will disabuse ourselves and our students of the idea that canonical or noncanonical syllabi have natural constituencies, the members of dominant or subordinate cultures respectively. The latter notion operates tacitly in the canon debate as the illegitimate displacement of liberal concepts of representation to a site — the school — where democratic objectives are better served by the modestly coercive structure of (in Gramsci's terms) a "unitary" curriculum. Extrapolating from Gramsci's analysis of the relation between the school and democracy, we can predict that different curricula for different constituencies will produce the same effects of social stratification as different schools for different classes. There is not, and should not be, one national culture, but there is, and there should be, one educational system.

But here we return to the fundamental point: pluralism has been able to affirm different cultures but not the fact that cultures are inescapably interdependent both at the moment of a cultural work's production and at that of its consumption. The question is whether or not the school is to acknowledge this "postmodern" condition. It is certainly acknowledged in the domain of mass culture, where cultural products are very often produced for particular constituencies, but where their circulation "interculturally" is virtually assured by the restless promiscuity of commodity exchange. These conditions need not be denied in the university but rather made the occasion of what Christopher Miller, in responding to Hirsch's notion of a national culture, has called "intercultural literacy": "Intercultural literacy would consist of a mode of inquiry that respects the accumulation of shared symbols (thus the term *literacy*) but also invites research into the processes by which cultures are formed and particularly encourages analysis of how cultures constitute themselves *by reference to each other*."[23]

An integrated curriculum would imply a second, pragmatic assumption: It is just as important for both minority and nonminority students to study historical works as it is for both groups to study modern works. The study of historical works need not be justified as an apotropaic[24] exercise — because these works are supposed to embody hegemonic values — but because they *are* historical works. The cultures which give rise to them are as other to all of us as minority cultures are to some of us. Here we can take leave of another fetish of the canon debate, namely, the exclusive emphasis on cultural artifacts as representative of cultures, in the absence of real knowledge about the history of these cultures. The relative lack of reference to history in the curriculum debate is symptomatic of how the concept of culture is deformed in the mirror of the pedagogic imaginary, all the more so since this deformation fails to account for the immanent historicity of even the most recent works. No program of multiculturalism will succeed in producing more than a kind of favorable media-image of minority cultures if it is not supported at every point by an understanding of the historical relations between cultures. At the same time one must insist that it is no longer intellectually defensible to equate historical knowledge with "Western history." It has always been the case (if not always acknowledged) that Western history is the history of the *global* relations of Western states, societies, and cultures; and even more that it is only as a consequence of its global relations that the "West" could conceive or write its own history. If the curriculum is to produce intercultural literacy, in recognition of the imbricated[25] sites of cultural production, we must assume that the context of cultural production is nothing *less* than global.

Were the left/liberal academy to reappropriate the "humanities," that is, to take back the authority to define the cultural capital embodied in its curriculum of study, it would have to devise a rationale for an integrated curriculum of textual/historical study exceeding the laudable

[23]Christopher L. Miller, "Literary Studies and African Literature: The Challenge of Intercultural Literacy," in *Africa and the Disciplines: Contributions of Research in Africa to the Social Sciences and Humanities,* ed. Robert H. Bates et al. (Chicago: University of Chicago Press, 1983). [Guillory]

[24]Intended to avert evil.
[25]Composed of overlapping parts.

objective of affirming cultural diversity. A left rationale for an integrated curriculum would have to present all of the cultural works in that curriculum, whatever their provenance, as a species of cultural capital constitutively different from the capital embodied in technical and professional knowledge. This difference can be defined by the proposition that *everyone* has a right of access to cultural works, to the means of both their production and their consumption. The dissemination of these means produces at every level of the educational system a form of "literacy," or what we would otherwise recognize as the practices of *reading* and *writing*. It would make an immense social difference if the knowledge designated by the latter terms were the property of everyone; but we are speaking here of what may be called "socialized" education, that is, of something that does not exist in this country. If the current educational institution does indeed (like every other social institution) reproduce social inequities, it achieves this effect by the unequal distribution of cultural capital, or by presenting cultural works in the classroom as the organic expression of the dominant classes' entitlement to those works. This effect cannot be undone by changing the university curriculum alone, because it is an effect of the educational *system,* of which the university is only a part. Does this mean that curricular reform is pointless, or that it has no social consequences? On the contrary, the university curriculum is at this moment a privileged site for raising questions about the educational system as a whole, just because it is the site at which a "crisis" of cultural capital (or the "humanities") has occurred. The claim of the present argument is that an analysis of this crisis in terms of the distribution of cultural capital will produce a more strategic theory of curricular reform than will a pluralist critique.

If progressive teachers have a considerable stake in disseminating the kind of knowledge (the study of cultural works as a practice of reading and writing) that is the vehicle for critical thinking, this knowledge is nevertheless only the vehicle for critical thought, not its realization. As cultural capital it is always also the object of appropriation by the dominant classes. The pluralist strategy of institutionalizing the category of the noncanonical is incapable of grasping this essential ambiguity of the school as an institution. For the same reason that a syllabus of canonical works cannot reproduce a culture of the dominant outside a certain total structuration of the educational system, no syllabus of noncanonical works can function ipso facto as the embodiment of that system's critique. To demand that critical thinking be institutionalized entails an obvious contradiction, but the desire for the institutionalization of a pluralist critique is what drives the current form of curricular revision. We can at most, however, institutionalize the *conditions* of critical thought, in this case a curriculum that makes possible the maximum dissemination of the practices of reading and writing. Inasmuch as the study of cultural works in historical context constitutes a good condition for these practices, no curricular intervention which does not *reaffirm* the cultural capital of these works can ensure the viability of that condition. In the present regime of capital distribution, the school will remain both the agency for the reproduction of unequal social relations and a necessary site for the critique of that system.

Laura Kipnis
b. 1956

A native of Chicago, Laura Kipnis dropped out of college and drove a cab for a year before moving to California to attend the San Francisco Art Institute. After a year in the Whitney Museum Independent Study Program as a video artist, she pursued her M.F.A. at the Nova Scotia College of

Art. A self-taught cultural theorist, Kipnis transitioned from making confrontational video art to writing about confrontational art and social experience while working as a fellow at the University of Michigan. She is now professor of radio, television, and film studies at Northwestern University. Her writing is concerned with the intersections of politics, aesthetics, and pornography, read through Marx and Freud. In her own words, Kipnis's perspective is "anti-pro-feminist," seeking to rescue maligned aspects of culture and social relations from the taboo, and to examine the aesthetic nature of offensive subjects. Her most recent book, Against Love: A Polemic *(2003), argues for an open-minded approach to adultery, aware of the widespread dissatisfaction with romance that it may indicate. Her first book,* Ecstasy Unlimited: On Sex, Capital, Gender, and Aesthetics, *appeared in 1993, followed by* Bound and Gagged: Pornography and the Politics of Fantasy in America *in 1996. The following essay, "(Male) Desire and (Female) Disgust: Reading* Hustler," *was originally published in the 1992 volume* Cultural Studies.

(Male) Desire and (Female) Disgust: Reading Hustler

Let's begin with two images. The first is of feminist author-poet Robin Morgan as she appears in the anti-pornography documentary *Not a Love Story.* Posed in her large book-lined living room, poet-husband Kenneth Pitchford at her side, she inveighs against a number of sexualities and sexual practices: masturbation — on the grounds that it promotes political quietism — as well as "superficial sex, kinky sex, appurtenances and [sex] toys" for benumbing "normal human sensuality." She then breaks into tears as she describes the experience of living in a society where pornographic media thrives.[1] The second image is the one conjured by a recent letter to *Hustler* magazine from E.C., a reader who introduces an account of an erotic experience involving a cruel-eyed, high-heeled dominatrix with this vivid vocational self-description: "One night, trudging home from work — I gut chickens, put their guts in a plastic bag and stuff them back in the chicken's asshole — I varied my routine by stopping at a small pub. . . ."[2] Let's say that these two images, however hyperbolically (the insistent tears, the insistent vulgarity), however inadvertently, offer a route toward a consideration of the relation between discourses on sexuality and the social division of labor, between sexual representation and class. On one side we have Morgan, laboring for the filmmakers and audience as a feminist intellectual, who constructs, from a particular social locus, a normative theory of sexuality. And while "feminist intellectual" is not necessarily the highest paying job category, it is a markedly different class location — and one definitively up the social hierarchy — from that of E.C., whose work is of a character which tends

[1]For an interesting and far more extensive analysis of the politics of *Not a Love Story* see B. Ruby Rich, "Anti-Porn: Soft Issue, Hard World" in *Films For Women,* ed. Charlotte Brunsdon, [London BFI], 1986, pp. 31–43. [Kipnis]

[2]Several writers who have visited the *Hustler* offices testify that to their surprise these letters *are* sent by actual readers, and *Hustler* receives well over 1,000 letters a month. As to whether this particular letter is genuine in its authorship I have no way of knowing, but I'm happy enough to simply consider it as part of the overall discourse of *Hustler.* [Kipnis]

to be relegated to the lower rungs within a social division of labor that categorizes jobs dealing with things that smell, or that for other reasons we prefer to hide from view — garbage, sewerage, dirt, animal corpses — as of low status, both monetarily and socially. E. C.'s letter, carefully (certainly more carefully than Morgan) framing his sexuality in relation to his material circumstances and to actual conditions of production, is fairly typical of the discourse of *Hustler* — in its vulgarity, its explicitness about "kinky" sex, and in its imbrication[3] of sexuality and class. So as opposed to the set of norms Morgan attempts to put into circulation (a "normal human sensuality" far removed from E. C.'s night of bliss with his Mistress, who incidentally, "mans" herself with just the kind of appurtenances Morgan seems to be referring to), *Hustler* also offers a theory of sexuality — a "low theory." Like Morgan's radical feminism, it too offers an explicitly political and counter-hegemonic analysis of power and the body; unlike Morgan it is also explicit about its own class location.

The feminist anti-porn movement has achieved at least temporary hegemony over the terms in which debates on pornography take place: current discourses on porn on the left and within feminism are faced with the task of framing themselves in relation to a set of arguments now firmly established as discursive landmarks: pornography is defined as a discourse about male domination, is theorized as the determining instance in gender oppression — if not a direct cause of rape — and its pleasures, to the extent that pleasure is not simply conflated with misogyny, are confined to the male sphere of activity. "Pro-sex" feminists have developed arguments against these positions on a number of grounds, but invariably in response to the terms set by their opponents: those classed by the discourse as sexual deviants (or worse, as "not feminists") — S/M lesbians, women who enjoy porn — have countered on the basis of experience, often in first person, asserting both that women *do* "look" and arguing the compatibility of feminism and alternative sexual practices — while condemning anti-porn forces for their universalizing abandon in claiming to speak for all women.

[3]Interconnection.

There have been numerous arguments about the use and misuse of data from media effects research by the anti-porn movement and charges of misinterpretation and misrepresentation of data made by pro-porn feminists (as well as some of the researchers). On the gendered pleasure front, psychoanalytic feminists have argued that identification and pleasure don't necessarily immediately follow assigned gender: for instance, straight women may get turned on by gay male porn or may identify with the male in a heterosexual coupling. Others have protested the abrogation of hard-won sexual liberties implicit in any restrictions on sexual expression, further questioning the politics of the alliance of the anti-porn movement and the radical right.[4] Gayle Rubin (1984)[5] has come closest to undermining the terms of the anti-porn discourse itself: she points out, heretically, that feminism, a discourse whose object is the organization of gendered oppression, may in fact not be the most appropriate or adequate discourse to analyze sexuality, in relation to which it becomes "irrelevant and often misleading." Rubin paves the way for a re-examination of received truths about porn: is pornography, in fact, so obviously and so simply a discourse about gender? Has feminism, in arrogating porn as its own privileged object, foreclosed on other questions? If feminism, as Rubin goes on, "lacks angles of vision which can encompass the social organization of sexuality," it seems clear that at least one of these angles of vision is a theory of class, which has been routinely undertheorized and undetermined within the anti-porn movement in favor of a totalizing theory of misogyny. While class stratification, and the

[4]Central anti-anti-porn texts are *Pleasure and Danger*, ed. Carole S. Vance (Boston: Routledge, 1984); *Caught Looking: Feminism, Pornography and Censorship*, ed. Kate Ellis, et al. (Seattle: Real Comet Press, 1988); *Powers of Desire: The Politics of Sexuality*, ed. Ann Snitow, Christine Stansell, and Sharon Thompson (New York: Monthly Review Press, 1983), especially section VI on "Current Controversies." Also see Linda Williams, *Hard Core: Power, Pleasure and Die Frenzy of the Visible* (Berkeley: U California P, 1989) and Andrew Ross, "The Popularity of Pornography" in *No Respect: Intellectuals and Popular Culture* (London: Routledge, 1989). See pp. 171–208 for a thorough summation of anti-pornography arguments. [Kipnis]

[5]"Thinking Sex: Notes for a Radical Theory of the Politics of Sexuality" from Carol S. Vance, ed., *Pleasure and Danger*. [Kipnis]

economic and profit motives of those in the porn industry have been exhaustively covered, we have no theory of how class plays itself out in nuances of representation.

The extent of misogyny is certainly monumental, so monumental as to be not only tragic, but banal in its everyday omnipresence. If it appears as superficially more evident in the heightened and exaggerated realms of fantasy, pleasure, and projection — the world of pornography — then this is certainly only a localized appearance, and an appearance which may be operating under other codes than those of gender alone. So if the question of misogyny is momentarily displaced here to allow consideration of questions of class, it isn't because one supersedes the other but because bringing issues of class into the porn debates may offer a way of breaking down the theoretical monolith of misogyny — and in a manner that doesn't involve jumping on the reassuring bandwagon of repression and policing the image world or the false catharsis of taking symptoms for causes. The recent tradition of cultural studies work on the body might pose some difficult questions for feminism (and thus might contribute to the kind of revamped critical discourse on sexuality that Rubin calls for): questions such as whether anti-porn feminists, in abjuring questions of class in analyzing representation, are constructing (and attempting to enforce) a theory and politics of the body on the wrong side of struggles against bourgeois hegemony, and ultimately complicit in its enforcement. But at the same time, in taking on porn as an object, U.S. cultural studies — or at least that tendency to locate resistance, agency, and micro-political struggle just about everywhere in mass cultural reception — might have difficulty finding good news as it takes on the fixity of sexuality and power.

Hustler is certainly the most reviled instance of mass circulation porn, and at the same time probably one of the most explicitly class-antagonistic mass circulation periodicals of any genre. Although it's been the tendency among writers on porn to lump it together into an unholy triad with *Penthouse* and *Playboy*, the other two top circulating men's magazines, *Hustler* is a different beast in any number of respects, even in conventional men's magazine terms. *Hustler* set itself apart from its inception through its explicitness, and its crusade *for* explicitness, accusing *Playboy* and *Penthouse* of hypocrisy, veiling the body, and basically not delivering the goods. The strategy paid off — *Hustler* captured a third of the men's market with its entree into the field in 1974 by being the first to reveal pubic hair — with *Penthouse* swiftly following suit (in response to which a *Hustler* pictorial presented its model shaved),[6] then upping the explicitness ante and creating a publishing scandal by displaying a glimpse of pubic hair on its cover in July 1976 (this a typically *Hustler* commemoration of the Bicentennial: the model wore stars and stripes, although not enough of them). Throughout these early years *Hustler*'s pictorials persisted in showing more and more of the forbidden zone (the "pink" in *Hustler*-speak) with *Penthouse* struggling to keep up and *Playboy* — whose focus was always above the waist anyway — keeping a discreet distance. *Hustler* then introduced penises, first limp ones, currently hefty erect-appearing ones, a sight verboten in traditional men's magazines where the strict prohibition on the erect male sexual organ impels the question of what traumas it might provoke in the male viewer. *Hustler*, from its inception, made it its mission to disturb and unsettle its readers, both psychosexually and socio-sexually, interrogating, as it were, the typical men's magazine codes and conventions of sexual representation: *Hustler*'s early pictorials included pregnant women, middle-aged women (horrified news commentaries referred to "geriatric pictorials"), overweight women, hermaphrodites, amputees, and in a moment of true frisson for your typical heterosexual male, a photo spread of a pre-operative transsexual, doubly well-endowed. *Hustler* continued to provoke reader outrage with a 1975 interracial pictorial (black male, white female) which according to *Hustler* was protested by both the KKK and the NAACP. It's been known to picture explicit photo spreads on the consequences of venereal

[6]This corresponds to Linda Williams's analysis of pornography as a "machine of the visible" devoted to intensifying the visibility of all aspects of sexuality, but most particularly, to conducting detailed investigations of female bodies. Williams, pp. 34–57. [Kipnis]

disease, the most graphic war carnage . . . None of these your typical, unproblematic turn-on.

And even more so than in its explicitness, *Hustler*'s difference from *Playboy* and *Penthouse* is in the sort of body it produces. Its pictorials, far more than other magazines, emphasize gaping orifices, as well as a consistent sharp focus on *other* orifices. *Hustler* sexuality is far from normative. It speaks openly of sexual preferences as "fetishes" and its letters and columns are full of the most specific and wide-ranging practices and sexualities, which don't appear to be hierarchized, and many of which have little to do with the standard heterosexual telos of penetration. (Male-male sexuality is sometimes raised as a possibility as well, along with the men's magazine standard woman-woman scenario.) The *Hustler* body is an unromanticized body — no vaselined lenses or soft focus: this is neither the airbrushed top-heavy fantasy body of *Playboy*, nor the ersatz opulence, the lingeried and sensitive crotch shots of *Penthouse*, transforming female genitals into *objets d'art*. It's a body, not a surface or a suntan: insistently material, defiantly vulgar, corporeal. In fact, the *Hustler* body is often a gaseous, fluid-emitting, *embarrassing* body, one continually defying the strictures of bourgeois manners and mores and instead governed by its lower intestinal tract — a body threatening to erupt at any moment. *Hustler*'s favorite joke is someone accidentally defecating in church.

Particularly in its cartoons, but also in its editorials and political humor, *Hustler* devotes itself to what tends to be called "grossness": an obsessive focus on the lower stratum, humor animated by a downward movement, representational techniques of exaggeration and inversion. *Hustler*'s bodily topography is straight out of Rabelais, as even a partial inventory of the subjects it finds of interest indicates: fat women, assholes, monstrous and gigantic sexual organs, body odors (the notorious Scratch and Sniff centerfold, which due to "the limits of the technology," publisher Larry Flynt apologized, smelled definitively of lilacs); and anything that exudes from the body: piss, shit, semen, menstrual blood, particularly when it sullies a sanitary or public site: and most especially, farts: farting in public, farting loudly, Barbara Bush farting, priests and nuns farting, politicians farting, the professional classes farting, the rich farting . . . (see Bakhtin, *Rabelais and His World* [Bloomington: Indiana UP, 1984]. Certainly a far remove from your sleek, overlaminated *Playboy/Penthouse* body. As *Newsweek* complained, "The contents of an average issue read like something Krafft-Ebing[7] might have whispered to the Marquis de Sade . . . *Hustler* is into erotic fantasies involving excrement, dismemberment, and the sexual longings of rodents . . . where other skin slicks are merely kinky, *Hustler* can be downright frightful . . . The net effect is to transform the erotic into the emetic."[8]

It's not clear if what sets *Newsweek* to crabbing is that *Hustler* transgresses bourgeois mores of the proper or that *Hustler* violates men's magazine conventions of sexuality. On both fronts its discourse is transgressive — in fact on *every* front *Hustler* devotes itself to producing generalized transgression. Given that control over the body has long been associated with the bourgeois political project, with both the "ability and the right to control and dominate others,"[9] *Hustler*'s insistent and repetitive return to the iconography of the body out of control, rampantly transgressing bourgeois norms and sullying bourgeois property and proprieties, raises certain political questions. On the politics of such social transgressions, for example, Peter Stallybrass and Allon White,[10] following Bakhtin, write of a transcoding between bodily and social topography, a transcoding which sets up an homology between the lower bodily stratum and the lower social classes — the reference to the body being invariably a reference to the social.

Here perhaps is a clue to *Newsweek*'s pique, as well as a way to think about why it is that the repressive apparatuses of the dominant social order return so invariably to the body and to somatic symbols. (And I should say that I write this

[7]Richard, Freiherr von Krafft-Ebing (1840–1902), German psychiatrist, author of *Psychopathia Sexualis* (1886), a catalogue of fetishes and perversions.

[8]*Newsweek* (February 16, 1976), p. 69. [Kipnis]

[9]Lenore Davidoff, "Class and Gender in Victorian England," *Feminist Studies* 5, 1997, p. 97. [Kipnis]

[10]Peter Stallybrass and Allon White, *The Politics and Poetics of Transgression* (Ithaca: Cornell UP, 1986). [Kipnis]

during the Cincinnati Mapplethorpe obscenity trial,[11] so this tactic is excessively visible at this particular conjuncture.) It's not only because these bodily symbols "are the ultimate elements of social classification itself" but because the transcoding between the body and the social sets up the mechanisms through which the body is a privileged political trope of lower social classes, and through which bodily grossness operates as a critique of dominant ideology. The power of grossness is predicated on its opposition from *and to* high discourses, themselves prophylactic against the debasements of the low (the lower classes, vernacular discourses, low culture, shit . . .). And it is dominant ideology itself that works to enforce and reproduce this opposition — whether in producing class differences, somatic symbols, or culture. The very highness of high culture is structured through the obsessive banishment of the low, and through the labor of suppressing the grotesque body (which is, in fact, simply the material body, gross as that can be) in favor of what Bakhtin refers to as "the classical body." This classical body — a refined, orifice-less, laminated surface — is homologous to the forms of official high culture which legitimate their authority by reference to the values — the highness — inherent in this classical body. According to low-theoretician Larry Flynt: "Tastelessness is a necessary tool in challenging preconceived notions in an uptight world where people are afraid to discuss their attitudes, prejudices and misconceptions." This is not so far from Bakhtin on Rabelais:

> Things are tested and reevaluated in the dimensions of laughter, which has defeated fear and all gloomy seriousness. This is why the material bodily lower stratum is needed, for it gaily and simultaneously materializes and unburdens. It liberates objects from the snares of false seriousness, from illusions and sublimations inspired by fear.

So in mapping social topography against bodily topography, it becomes apparent how the unsettling effects of grossness and erupting bodies condense all the unsettling effects (to those in power) of a class hierarchy tenuously held in place through symbolic (and less symbolic) policing of the threats posed by bodies, by lower classes, by angry mobs.

Bakhtin and others have noted that the invention of the classical body and the formation of this new bodily canon have their inception in the sixteenth-century rise of individualism and the attendant formation and consolidation of bourgeois subjectivity and bourgeois political hegemony, setting off, at the representational level, the struggle of grotesque and classical concepts.[12] A similar historical argument is made by Norbert Elias[13] in his study *The History of Manners*, which traces the effects of this social process on the structure of individual affect. The invention of Bakhtin's classical body entails and is part of a social transformation within which thresholds of sensitivity and refinement in the individual psyche become heightened. Initially this reform of affect takes place in the upper classes, within whom increasingly refined manners and habits — initially a mechanism of class distinction — are progressively restructuring standards of privacy, disgust, shame, and embarrassment. These affect-reforms are gradually, although incompletely, disseminated downward through the social hierarchy (and finally to other nations whose lack of "civilization" might reasonably necessitate colonial etiquette lessons). These new standards of delicacy and refinement become the very substance of bourgeois subjectivity: constraints that were originally socially generated gradually become reproduced in individuals as habits, reflexes, as the structure of the modern psyche. And as Elias reminds us, the foundational Freudian distinction between id and ego corresponds to historically specific demands placed on public behavior in which certain instinctual behaviors and impulses — primarily bodily ones like sex and elimination — are relegated to the private

[11]The exhibition of Robert Mapplethorpe's photography show, *The Perfect Moment*, at Cincinnati's Contemporary Art Center in April of 1990 was closed by the police hours after it opened, and both the museum and its director, Dennis Barrie, indicted for pandering obscenity — the show included homoerotic photographs. A jury acquitted both Barrie and the museum in October of the same year.

[12]Bakhtin, p. 320; Frances Barker, *The Tremulous Private Body* (New York: Methuen, 1984). [Kipnis]
[13]Norbert Elias, *The History of Manners* (New York: Urizen, 1978). [Kipnis]

sphere, behind closed doors, or in the case of the most shameful and most socially prohibited drives and desires, warehoused as the contents of the unconscious.

So we can see, returning to our two opening images, how Morgan's tears, her sentiment, might be constructed *against* E. C.'s vulgarity, how her desire to distance herself from and if possible banish from existence the cause of her distress — the sexual expression of people unlike herself — has a sort of structural imperative: as Stallybrass and White (1986) put it, the bourgeois subject has "continuously defined and redefined itself through the exclusion of what it marked out as low — as dirty, repulsive, noisy, contaminating . . . [the] very act of exclusion was constitutive of its identity." So disgust has a long and complicated history, the context within which should be placed the increasingly strong tendency of the bourgeois to want to remove the distasteful from the sight of society (including, of course, dead animals, which might interest E. C. — as "people in the course of the civilizing process seek to suppress in themselves every characteristic they feel to be animal . . ." [Elias, 1978, p. 120]). These gestures of disgust are crucial in the production of the bourgeois body, now so rigidly split into higher and lower stratum that tears will become the only publicly permissible display of bodily fluid. So the bodies and bodily effluences start to stack up into neat oppositions: on the one side upper bodily productions, a heightened sense of delicacy, and the project of removing the distasteful from sight (and sight, of course, at the top of the hierarchization of the senses central to bourgeois identity and rationality); and on the other hand, the lower body and *its* productions, the insistence on vulgarity and violations of the bourgeois body. To the extent that, in Morgan's project, discourse and tears are devoted to concealing the counter-bourgeois body from view by regulating its representation and reforming its pleasures into ones more consequent with refined sensibilities, they can be understood, at least in part, as the product of a centuries-long socio-historical process, a process that has been a primary mechanism of class distinction, and one that has played an important role as an ongoing tool in class hegemony. So perhaps it becomes a bit more difficult to see feminist disgust in isolation, and disgust at pornography as strictly a gender issue, for any gesture of disgust is not without a history and not without a class character. And whatever else we may say about feminist arguments about the proper or improper representation of women's bodies — and I don't intend to imply that my discussion is exhaustive of the issue — bourgeois disgust, even as mobilized against a sense of violation and violence to the female body, is not without a function in relation to class hegemony, and more than problematic in the context of what purports to be a radical social movement.

Perhaps this is the moment to say that a large part of what impels me to write this essay is my own disgust in reading *Hustler*. In fact, I have wanted to write this essay for several years, but every time I trudge out and buy the latest issue, open it and begin to try to bring analytical powers to bear upon it, I'm just so disgusted that I give up, never quite sure whether this almost automatic response is one of feminist disgust or bourgeois disgust. Of course, whether as feminist, bourgeois, or academic, I and most likely you are what could be called *Hustler*'s implied target, rather than its implied reader. The discourse of *Hustler* is quite specifically *constructed against* — not only the classical body, a bourgeois hold-over of the aristocracy, but against all the paraphernalia of petit-bourgeoisiehood as well. At the most manifest level *Hustler* is simply against any form of social or intellectual pretension: it is against the pretensions (and the social power) of the professional classes — doctors, optometrists, dentists are favored targets; it is against liberals, and particularly cruel to academics who are invariably prissy and uptight. (An academic to his wife: "Eat your pussy? You forget Gladys, I have a Ph.D.") It is against the power of government — which is by definition corrupt, as are elected officials, the permanent government, even foreign governments. Of course, it is against the rich, particularly rich women, down on the Chicago Cubs, and devotes many pages to the hypocrisy of organized religion — with a multiplication of jokes on the sexual instincts of the clergy, the sexual possibilities of the crucifixion, the scam of the virgin birth — and, as mentioned previously, the plethora of jokes involving farting/shitting/fucking in church and the bodily functions of nuns, priests, and ministers. In *Hustler* any form of social power is fundamentally crooked and illegitimate.

These are just *Hustler*'s more manifest targets. Reading a bit deeper, its offenses provide a detailed road map of a cultural psyche. Its favored tactic is to zero in on a subject, an issue, which the bourgeois imagination prefers to be unknowing about, which a culture has founded itself upon suppressing, and prohibits irreverent speech about. Things we would call "tasteless" at best, or might even become physically revulsed by: the materiality of aborted fetuses,[14] where homeless people go to the bathroom, cancer, the proximity of sexual organs to those of elimination — any aspect of the material body, in fact. A case in point, one which again subjected *Hustler* to national outrage: its two cartoons about Betty Ford's mastectomy.[15] If one can distance oneself from one's automatic indignation for a moment, *Hustler* might be seen as posing, through the strategy of transgression, an interesting metadiscursive question: which are the subjects that are taboo ones for even sick humor? Consider for a moment that while, for example, it was not uncommon, following the Challenger explosion,[16] to hear the sickest jokes about scattered body parts, while jokes about amputees and paraplegics are not entirely unknown even on broadcast TV (and, of course, abound on the pages of *Hustler*), while jokes about blindness are considered so benign that one involving Ray Charles features in a current "blind taste test" soda pop commercial, mastectomy is one subject that appears to be completely off limits as a humorous

topic. But back to amputees for a moment, perhaps a better comparison: apparently a man without a limb is considered less tragic by the culture at large, less mutilated, and less of a cultural problem it seems, than a woman without a breast. A mastectomy more of a tragedy than the deaths of the seven astronauts. This, as I say, provides some clues into the deep structure of a cultural psyche — as does our outrage. After all, what *is* a woman without a breast in a culture that measures breasts as the measure of the woman? Not a fit subject for comment. It's a subject so veiled that it's not even available to the "working through" of the joke. (And again a case where *Hustler* seems to be deconstructing the codes of the men's magazine: where *Playboy* creates a fetish of the breast, and whose *raison d'être* is, in fact, very much the cultural obsession with them, *Hustler* perversely points out that they are, after all, materially, merely tissue — another limb.)[17]

Hustler's uncanny knack for finding and attacking the jugular of a culture's sensitivity might more aptly be regarded as intellectual work on the order of the classic anthropological studies which translate a culture into a set of structural oppositions (obsession with the breast/prohibition of mastectomy jokes), laying bare the structure of its taboos and arcane superstitions. (Or do only "primitive" cultures have irrational taboos?) *Hustler*, in fact, performs a similar cultural mapping to that of anthropologist Mary Douglas, whose study *Purity and Danger*[18] produces a very similar social blueprint. The vast majority of *Hustler* humor seems to be animated by the desire to violate what Douglas describes as "pollution" taboos and rituals — these being a society's set of

---

[14]And there are ongoing attempts to regulate this sort of imagery. In the current NEA controversies, a Republican representative plans to introduce amendments that would prohibit funding of art that depicts aborted fetuses, the *New York Times* reports (October 10, 1990, p. B6). This would seem to be something of a shortsighted strategy for anti-abortion forces, as the aborted fetus has been the favored incendiary image of anti-abortion forces, including anti-abortion artists. See Laura Kipnis (1986), "Refunctioning Reconsidered: Toward a Left Popular Culture," *High Culture/Low Theory*, ed. Cohin MacCabe, (New York: St. Martin's, 1986), pp. 29-31. [Kipnis]

[15]Shortly after her husband Gerald Ford succeeded Richard Nixon on his resignation from the presidency in 1974, Betty Ford underwent surgery for breast cancer.

[16]On January 28, 1986, the space shuttle Challenger exploded on takeoff, with the loss of all seven in the crew.

[17]Of course, the counter-argument could be made that such a cartoon really indicates the murderous male desire to see a woman mutilated, and that the cartoon thus stands in for the actual male desire to do violence to women. This was, of course, a widespread interpretation of the infamous *Hustler* "woman in the meat grinder" cover, about which more later. This sort of interpretation would hinge on essentializing the male imagination and male sexuality as, a priori, violent and murderous, and on a fairly literal view of humor and representation, one that envisions a straight leap from the image to the social practice rather than the series of mediations between the two I'm describing here. [Kipnis]

[18]*Purity and Danger: An Analysis of Concepts of Pollution and Taboo* (London: Routledge, 1966). [Kipnis]

beliefs, rituals, and practices having to do with dirt, order, and hygiene (and by extension, the pornographic). As to the pleasure produced by such cultural violations as *Hustler*'s, Douglas cheerily informs us, "It is not always an unpleasant experience to confront ambiguity," and while it is clearly more tolerable in some areas than in others, "there is a whole gradient on which laughter, revulsion and shock belong at different points and intensities."

The sense of both pleasure and danger that violation of pollution taboos can invoke is clearly dependent on the existence of symbolic codes, codes that are for the most part only semi-conscious. Defilement can't be an isolated event, it can only engage our interest or provoke our anxiety to the extent that our ideas about such things are systematically ordered, and that this ordering matters deeply — in our culture, in our subjectivity. As Freud[19] notes, "Only jokes that have a purpose run the risk of meeting with people who do not want to listen to them."

Of course, a confrontation with ambiguity and violation can be profoundly displeasurable as well, as the many opponents of *Hustler* might attest. And for Freud this displeasure has to do with both gender and class.[20] One of the most interesting things about Freud's discussion of jokes is the theory of humor and gender he elaborates in the course of his discussion of them, with class almost inadvertently intervening as a third term. He first endeavors to produce a typology of jokes according to their gender effects. For example, in regard to excremental jokes (a staple of *Hustler* humor) Freud tells us that this is material *common to both sexes*, as both experience a common sense of shame surrounding bodily functions. And it's true that *Hustler*'s numerous jokes on the proximity of the sexual organs to elimination functions, the confusion of assholes and vaginas, turds and penises, shit and sex — i.e., a couple

[19]Sigmund Freud, *Jokes and Their Relation to the Unconscious* (New York: Norton, 1963). [Kipnis]

[20]Freud's observations on jokes, particularly on obscene humor, might be extended to the entirety of *Hustler* as so much of its discourse, even aside from its cartoons and humor, is couched in the joke form. [Kipnis]

fucking in a hospital room while someone in the next bed is getting an enema, all get covered with shit — can't really be said to have a gender basis or target (unless, that is, we women put ourselves, more so than men, in the position of upholders of "good taste").

But obscene humor, whose purpose is to expose sexual facts and relations verbally, is, for Freud, a consequence of male and female sexual incommensurability, and the dirty joke is something like a seduction gone awry. The motive for (men's) dirty jokes is "in reality nothing more than women's incapacity to tolerate undisguised sexuality, an incapacity correspondingly increased with a rise in the educational and social level." Whereas both men and women are subject to sexual inhibition or repression, apparently upper-class women are the more seriously afflicted in the Freudian world, and dirty jokes thus function as a sign for both sexual difference ("smut is like an exposure of the sexually different person to whom it is directed . . . it compels the person who is assailed to imagine the part of the body or the procedure in question"), and class difference. So apparently, if it weren't for women's lack of sexual willingness and class refinement the joke would be not a joke, but a proposition: "If the woman's readiness emerges quickly the obscene speech has a short life; it yields at once to a sexual action," hypothesizes Freud. While there are some fairly crude gender and class stereotypes in circulation here — the figure of the lusty barmaid standing in for the lower-class woman — it's also true that obscene jokes and pornographic images *are* perceived by *some* women as an act of aggression against women. But these images and jokes are aggressive only insofar as they're capable of causing the woman discomfort, and they're capable of causing discomfort *only* insofar as there *are* differing levels of sexual inhibition between at least some men and some women. So Freud's view would seem to hold out: the obscene joke is directed originally toward women; it presupposes not only the presence of a woman, but that women are sexually constituted differently than men; and upper classness or upper-class identification — as Morgan's discourse also indicates — exacerbates this difference.

But if there are differing levels of inhibition, displeasure, or interest between some men and some women (although *Hustler*'s readership is primarily male, it's not exclusively male), the origins of this pleasure/displeasure disjunction are also a site of controversy in the porn debates. For Freud it's part of the process of *differentiation* between the sexes, not originative — little girls are just as "interested" as little boys. Anti-porn forces tend to reject a constructionist argument such as Freud's in favor of a description of female sexuality as inborn and biologically based — something akin to the "normal human sensuality" Morgan refers to.[21] Women's discomfiture at the dirty joke, from this vantage point, would appear to be twofold. There is the discomfort at the intended violation — at being assailed "with the part of the body or the procedure in question." But there is the further discomfort at being addressed as a subject of repression — as a subject with a history — and the rejection of porn can be seen as a defense erected against representations which mean to unsettle her in her subjectivity. In other words, there is a violation of the *idea* of the "naturalness" of female sexuality and subjectivity, which is exacerbated by the social fact that not all women *do* experience male pornography in the same way. That "pro-sex" feminists, who tend to follow some version of a constructionist position on female sexuality, seem to feel less violated by porn is some indication that these questions of subjectivity are central to porn's address, misaddress, and violations. To the extent that pornography's discourse engages in setting up disturbances around questions of subjectivity and sexual difference — after all, what does *Hustler*-variety porn consist of but the male fantasy of women whose sexual desires are in concert with men's — and that this fantasy of undifferentiation is perceived as doing violence to female subjectivity by some women but not others, the perception of this violence is an issue of difference between women.[22] But the violence

here is that of misaddress, of having one's desire misfigured as the male's desire. It is the violence of being absent from the scene. The differentiation between female spectators as to how this address or misaddress is perceived appears to be bound up with the degree to which a certain version of female sexuality is hypostatized as natural, versus a sense of mobility of sexuality, at least at the level of fantasy. But hypostatizing female sexuality and assigning it to all women involves universalizing an historically specific class position as well, not as something acquired and constructed through difference, privilege, and hierarchy, but as also somehow inborn — as identical to this natural female sexuality. Insisting that all women are violated by pornography insists that class or class identification doesn't figure as a difference between women, that "normal human sensuality" erases all difference between women.

For Freud, even the form of the joke is classed, with a focus on joke technique associated with higher social classes and education levels. In this light it's interesting to note how little *Hustler* actually engages in the technique of the joke — even to find a pun is rare. But then as far as obscene humor, we're subject to glaring errors of judgment about the "goodness" of jokes insofar as we judge them on formal terms, according to Freud — the technique of these jokes is often "quite wretched, but they have immense success in provoking laughter." Particularly in regard to obscene jokes, we aren't "in a position to distinguish by our feelings what part of the pleasure arises from the sources of their technique and what part from those of their purpose. Thus, strictly speaking, we do not know what we are laughing at." And so too with displeasure — it would seem we can't be

---

[21] For an interesting deconstruction of the essentialist/anti-essentialism debate see Diana Fuss (1989a), *Essentially Speaking: Feminism, Nature and Difference*. (New York: Routledge 1989). [Kipnis]

[22] By violence here I mean specifically violence to subjectivity. On the issue of representations of actual physical violence to women's bodies that is represented as non-consensual — as opposed to the sort of tame consensual S/M occasionally found

in *Hustler* — my view is that this sort of representation should be analyzed as a subgenre of mainstream violent imagery, not only in relation to pornography. I find the continual conflation of sexual pornography and violence a deliberate roadblock to thinking through issues of porn — only abetted by a theorist like Andrea Dworkin for whom *all* heterosexuality is violence. The vast majority of porn represents sex, not physical violence, and while sexuality generally undoubtedly contains elements of aggression and violence, it's important to make these distinctions. [Kipnis] entirely sure what we're *not* laughing at either, and this would be particularly true of both the bourgeois and the anti-pornography feminist, to the extent that both seem likely to displace or disavow pleasure or interest in smut, one in favor of technique — like disgust, a mechanism of class distinction — and the other against perceived violations against female subjectivity. So for both, the act of rejection takes on far more significance than the terrains of pleasure; for both, the nuances and micrologics of *displeasure* are defining practices.

Yet at the same time, there does seem to be an awful lot of interest in porn among both, albeit a negative sort of interest. It's something of a Freudian cliche that shame, disgust, and morality are reaction-formations to an original interest in what is not "clean." One defining characteristic of a classic reaction-formation is that the subject actually comes close to "satisfying the demands of the opposing instinct while actually engaged in the pursuit of the virtue which he affects," the classic example being the housewife obsessed with cleanliness who ends up "concentrating her whole existence on dust and dirt."[23] And it does seem to be the case that a crusader against porn will end up making pornography the center of her existence. Theorizing it as central to women's oppression means, in practical terms, devoting one's time to reading it, thinking about it, and talking about it. It also means simultaneously conferring this *interest*, this subject-effect, onto others — predicting tragic consequences arising from such dirty pursuits, unvaryingly dire and uniform effects, as if the will and individuality of consumers of porn are suddenly seized by some (projected) all-controlling force, a force which becomes — or already is — the substance of a monotonic male sexuality. Thusly summing up male sexuality, Andrea Dworkin (1987) writes: "Any violation of a woman's body can become sex for men; this is the essential truth of pornography."

The belief in these sorts of essential truths seem close to what Mary Douglas (1966) calls "danger-beliefs" —

[A] strong language of mutual exhortation. At this level the laws of nature are dragged in to sanction the moral code: this kind of disease is caused by adultery, that by incest . . . the whole universe is harnessed to men's attempts to force one another into good citizenship. Thus we find that certain moral values are upheld and certain social rules defined by beliefs in dangerous contagion. (p. 3)

And Douglas, like Freud, also speaks directly about the relation of gender to the "gradient" where laughter, revulsion, and shock collide: her discussion of danger beliefs also opens onto questions of class and hierarchy as well. For her, gender is something of a trope in the realm of purity rituals and pollution violations: it functions as a displacement from issues of social hierarchy.

I believe that some pollutions are used as analogies for expressing a general view of the social order. For example, there are beliefs that each sex is a danger to the other . . . Such patterns of sexual danger can be seen to express symmetry or hierarchy. It is implausible to interpret them as expressing something about the actual relation of the sexes. I suggest that many ideas about sexual dangers are better interpreted as symbols of the relation between parts of society, as mirroring designs of hierarchy or symmetry which apply in the larger social system. (p. 3)[24]

To put a feminist spin on Douglas's pre-feminist passage, while men do certainly pose

[24]The passage in the ellipsis reads "For example, there are beliefs that each sex is a danger to the other through contact with sexual fluids." Compare Douglas to this passage by Andrea Dworkin, ". . . in literary pornography, to ejaculate is to *pollute* the woman" [her emphasis]. Dworkin goes on to discuss, in a lengthy excursus on semen, the collaboration of women-hating women's magazines, which "sometimes recommend spreading semen on the face to enhance the complexion" and pornography, where ejaculation often occurs on the woman's body or face [see Linda Williams, pp. 93–119, on another reading of the "money shot"], to accept semen and eroticize it. Her point seems to be that men prefer that semen be a violation of the woman by the man, as if the only way they can get sexual pleasure is through violation. Thus semen is "driven into [the woman] to dirty her or make her more dirty or make her dirty by him." But at the same time semen has to be eroticized to get the woman to comply in her own violation. Andrea Dworkin, (*Intercourse* [New York: Macmillan, 1987], p. 187). In any case, that Dworkin sees contact with male "sexual fluids" as harmful to women seems clear, as does the relation of this pollution (Dworkin's word) danger to Douglas's analysis. [Kipnis]

[23]Jean Laplanche and Jean Bertrand Pontalis, *The Language of Psychoanalysis* (New York : Norton, 1973). [Kipnis]

actual sexual danger to women, the content of pollution beliefs expresses that danger symbolically at best: it would be implausible to take the content of these beliefs literally. So while, for Douglas, gender is a trope for social hierarchy, a feminist might interpret the above passage to mean that *danger* is a trope for gender hierarchy. Douglas's observations on the series of displacements between defilement, danger, gender, and class puts an interesting cast on female displeasure in pornography in relation to class hierarchies and "the larger social system" — in relation to *Hustler*'s low-class tendentiousness and its production of bourgeois displeasure, and why it might happen that the feminist response to pornography ends up reinscribing the feminist into the position of enforcer of class distinctions.

But historically, female reformism aimed at bettering the position of women has often had an unfortunately conservative social thrust, as in the case of the temperance movement. The local interests of women in reforming male behavior can easily dovetail with the interests of capital in producing and reproducing an orderly, obedient, and sober workforce. In social history terms we might note that *Hustler* galumphs onto the social stage at the height of the feminist second wave, and while the usual way to phrase this relation would be the term "backlash," it can also be seen as a retort — even a political response — to feminist calls for reform of the male imagination. There's no doubt that *Hustler* sees itself as doing battle with feminists: ur-feminist Gloria Steinem makes frequent appearances in the pages of the magazine as an uptight, and predictably, upper-class, bitch. It's fairly clear that from *Hustler*'s point of view, feminism is a class-based discourse. So *Hustler*'s production of sexual differences is also the production of a form of class consciousness — to accede to feminist reforms would be to identify upward on the social hierarchy.

But any automatic assumptions about *Hustler*-variety porn aiding and abetting the entrenchment of male power might be put into question by actually reading the magazine. Whereas Freud's observations on dirty jokes are phallocentric in the precise sense of the word — phallic sexuality is made central — *Hustler* itself seems much less certain about the place of the phallus, much more wry and often troubled about male and female sexual incommensurability. On the one hand it offers the standard men's magazine fantasy babe — always ready, always horny, willing to do anything, and who finds the *Hustler* male inexplicably irresistible. But just as often there is her flip side: the woman who is disgusted by the *Hustler* male's desires and sexuality, a superior, rejecting, often upper-class woman. It becomes clear how class resentment is modulated through resentment of what is seen as the power of women to humiliate and reject: "Beauty isn't everything, except to the bitch who's got it. You see her stalking the aisles of Cartier, stuffing her perfect face at exorbitant cuisineries, tooling her Jag along private-access coastline roads. . . ." Doesn't this reek of a sense of disenfranchisement rather than any sort of certainty about male power over women? The fantasy life here is animated by cultural disempowerment in relation to a sexual caste system and a social class system. This magazine is tinged with frustrated desire and rejection: *Hustler* gives vent to a vision of sex in which sex is an arena for failure and humiliation rather than domination and power. There are numerous ads addressed to male anxieties and sense of inadequacy: various sorts of penis enlargers ("Here is your chance to overcome the problems and insecurities of a penis that is too small. Gain self-confidence and your ability to satisfy women will sky rocket" reads a typical ad), penis extenders, and erection aids (Stay-Up, Stay-Hard . . .).[25] One of the problems with most porn from even a pro-porn feminist point of view is that men seize the power and privilege to have public fantasies about women's bodies, to imagine and represent women's bodies without any risk, without any concomitant problematization of the male body — which is invariably produced as powerful and inviolable. But *Hustler* does put the male body at

[25] *Hustler*'s advertising consists almost entirely of ads for sex toys, sex aids, porn movies, and phone sex services, as the automobile makers, liquor companies and manufacturers of other upscale items that comprise the financial backbone of *Playboy* and *Penthouse* refuse to hawk their wares in the pages of *Hustler*. In order to survive financially, *Hustler* began, among other enterprises, a successful and extensive magazine distribution company which distributes, among other periodicals, the *New York Review of Books*. [Kipnis]

risk, representing and never completely alleviating male anxiety (and for what it's worth, there is a surprising amount of castration humor in *Hustler* as well). Rejecting the sort of compensatory fantasy life mobilized by *Playboy* and *Penthouse* in which all women are willing and all men are studs — as long as its readers fantasize and identify upward, with money, power, good looks, and consumer durables — *Hustler* pulls the window dressing off the market/exchange nature of sexual romance: the market in attractiveness, the exchange basis of male-female relations in patriarchy. Sexual exchange is a frequent subject of humor: women students are coerced into having sex with professors for grades, women are fooled into having sex by various ruses, lies, or barters usually engineered by males in power positions: bosses, doctors, and the like. All this is probably truer than not true, but problematic from the standpoint of male fantasy: power, money, and prestige are represented as essential to sexual success, but the magazine works to disparage and counter identification with these sorts of class attributes on every other front. The intersections of sex, gender, class, and power here are complex, contradictory, and political.

Much of *Hustler*'s humor *is*, in fact, manifestly political, and much of it would even get a warm welcome in left-leaning circles, although its strategies of conveying those sentiments might give some of the flock pause. A 1989 satirical photo feature titled "Farewell to Reagan: Ronnie's Last Bash" demonstrates how the magazine's standard repertoire of aesthetic techniques — nudity, grossness, and offensiveness — can be directly translated into scathingly effective political language. It further shows how the pornographic idiom can work as a form of political speech that refuses to buy into the pompously serious and highminded language in which official culture conducts its political discourse: *Hustler* refuses the language of high culture along with its political forms. The photospread, laid out like a series of black and white surveillance photos, begins with this no-words-minced introduction:

It's been a great eight years — for the power elite, that is. You can bet Nancy planned long and hard how to celebrate Ron Reagan's successful term of filling special-interest coffers while fucking John Q. Citizen right up the yazoo. A radical tax plan that more than halved taxes for the rich while doubling the working man's load; detaxation of industries, who trickled down their windfalls into mergers, takeovers, and investments in foreign lands; crooked deals with enemies of U.S. allies in return for dirty money for right wing killers to reclaim former U.S. business territories overseas; more than 100 appointees who resigned in disgrace over ethics or outright criminal charges . . . are all the legacies of the Reagan years . . . , and we'll still get whiffs of bullyboy Ed Meese's sexual intimidation policies for years to come, particularly with conservative whores posing as Supreme Court justices.

The photos that follow are of an elaborately staged orgiastic White House farewell party as imagined by the *Hustler* editors, with the appropriate motley faces of the political elite photomontaged onto naked and semi-naked bodies doing fairly obscene and polymorphously perverse things to each other. (The warning "Parody: Not to be taken seriously. Celebrity heads stripped onto our model's bodies," accompanies each and every photo — more about *Hustler*'s legal travails further on.) That more of the naked bodies are female and that many are in what could be described as a service relation to male bodies clearly opens up the possibility of a reading limited to its misogynistic tendencies. But what becomes problematic for such a singular reading is that within these parodic representations, this staging of the rituals of male hegemony also works in favor of an overtly counter-hegemonic political treatise. The style is something like a *Mad* magazine cartoon come to life with a multiplication of detail in every shot (the Ted Kennedy dartboard in one corner, in another stickers that exhort "Invest in South Africa," the plaque over Reagan's bed announcing "Joseph McCarthy slept here"). The main room of the party: various half-naked women cavort, Edwin Meese is glimpsed filching a candelabra, Reagan greets a hooded Ku Klux Klanner at the door, and a helpful caption translates the action: "Ron tells an embarrassed Jesse Helms it wasn't a come-as-you-are party," while in the background the corpse of Bill Casey watches benignly over the proceedings (his gaping mouth doubles as an ashtray), as does former press secretary James

Brady — the victim of John Hinkley's attempted assassination and Reagan's no-gun control policy — who, propped in a wheelchair, wears a sign bluntly announcing "Vegetable Dip" around his neck. In the next room Ollie North as a well-built male stripper gyrates on top of a table while a fawning Poindexter, Secord, and Weinberger gathered at his feet stuff dollar bills into his holster/g-string in homoerotic reverie. In the next room Jerry Falwell's masturbating to a copy of *Hustler* concealed in the Bible, a bottle of Campari at his bedside and an "I love Mom" button pinned to his jacket (this a triumphant *Hustler* pouring salt on the wound — more on the Falwell Supreme Court case further on). In another room "former Democrat and supreme skagbait Jeanne Kirkpatrick demonstrates why she switched to the Republican Party," as, grinning and topless, we find her on the verge of anally penetrating a bespectacled George Bush with the dildo attached to her ammunition belt. A whiny Elliott Abrams, pants around his ankles and dick in hand, tries unsuccessfully to pay off a prostitute who won't have him; and a naked Pat Robertson, doggie style on the bed, is being disciplined by a naked angel with a cat-o-nine-tails. And on the last page the invoice to the American Citizens: $283,000,000.[26]

While the anti-establishment politics of the photospread are fairly clear, *Hustler* can also be maddeningly incoherent, all over what we usually think of as the political spectrum. Its incoherence as well as its low-rent tendentiousness can be laid at the door of publisher Larry Flynt as much as

anywhere, as Flynt, in the early days of the magazine, maintained such iron control over the day-to-day operations that he had to approve even the pull quotes. Flynt is a man apparently both determined and destined to play out the content of his obsessions as psychodrama on our public stage; if he weren't so widely considered such a disgusting pariah, his life could probably supply the material for many epic dramas. The very public nature of Flynt's blazing trail through the civil and criminal justice system and his one-man campaign for the first amendment justify a brief descent into the murkiness of the biographical, not to make a case for singular authorship, but because Flynt himself has had a decisive historical and political impact in the realpolitik of state power. In the end it has been porn king Larry Flynt — not the left, not the avantgarde — who has decisively expanded the perimeters of political speech.

Larry Flynt is very much of the class he appears to address — his story is like a pornographic Horatio Alger. He was born in Magoffin County, Kentucky, in the Appalachians — the poorest county in America. The son of a pipe welder, he quit school in the eighth grade, joined the Navy at fourteen with a forged birth certificate, got out, worked in a G.M. auto assembly plant, and turned $1,500 in savings into a chain of go-go bars in Ohio named the Hustler Clubs. The magazine originated as a 2-page newsletter for the bars, and the rest was rags to riches: Flynt's income was as high as $30 million a year when *Hustler* was at its peak circulation of over 2 million (he then built himself a scale replica of the cabin he grew up in in the basement of his mansion to, he says, remind him where he came from, one replete with chickenwire and hay, and a three-foot lifelike statue of the chicken he claims to have lost his virginity to at age eight).

Since the magazine's inception Flynt has spent much of his time in and out of the nation's courtrooms on various obscenity and libel charges as well as an array of contempt charges and other bizarre legal entanglements — notably his somehow becoming entangled in the government's prosecution of automaker John DeLorean. All proceeded as normal (for Flynt) until his well-publicized 1978 conversion to evangelical

[26]Most of those referred to were cabinet and subcabinet level officials in the Reagan administration. These include Elliot Abrams (assistant secretary of state); George Bush (vice president); Bill Casey (director of the Central Intelligence Agency [he died in 1987]); Jeanne Kirkpatrick (ambassador to the United Nations); Edwin Meese (attorney general); Oliver North (counter-terrorism co-ordinator for the National Security Council); John Poindexter (national security advisor); Caspar Weinberger (secretary of defense). Jesse Helms was senior senator from North Carolina and head of the Foreign Relations committee. Jerry Falwell and Pat Robertson were fundamentalist Christian leaders, respectively, of "Moral Majority" and "Christian Coalition." Richard V. Secord was an arms trader used as a go-between by North and Poindexter to sell arms to Nicaraguan death squads in the Iran-Contra scandal.

Christianity at the hands of presidential sister Ruth Carter Stapleton. The two were pictured chastely hand in hand as Flynt announced plans to turn *Hustler* into a *religious* skin magazine and told a Pentecostal congregation in Houston (where he was attending the National Women's Conference) "I owe every woman in America an apology." Ironically, it was this religious conversion that led to the notorious *Hustler* cover of a woman being ground up in a meat grinder, which was, in fact, another sheepish and flat-footed attempt at apologia by Flynt. "We will no longer hang women up as pieces of meat," was actually the widely ignored caption to the photo. (Recall here Freud's observation on the sophistication of the joke form as a class trait.)[27]

In 1978, shortly after the religious conversion, during another of his obscenity trials in Lawrenceville, Georgia, Flynt was shot three times by an unknown assassin with a 44 magnum. His spinal nerves were severed, leaving him paralyzed from the waist down and in constant pain. He became a recluse, barricading himself in his Bel Air mansion, surrounded by bodyguards. His wife Althea, then 27, a former go-go dancer in the Hustler clubs, took over control of the corporation and the magazine, and returned the magazine to its former focus. Flynt became addicted to morphine and Dilaudid, finally detoxing to methadone. (He repudiated the religious conversion after the shooting.) Now confined to a wheelchair, he continued to be hauled into court by the government for obscenity and in various civil suits. He was sued by *Penthouse* publisher Bob Guccione and a female *Penthouse* executive who claimed *Hustler* had libeled her by printing that she had contracted VD from Guccione. He was sued by author Jackie Collins after the magazine published nude photos it incorrectly identified as the nude author. He was fined $10,000 a day — increased to $20,000 a day — when he refused to turn over to the feds tapes he claimed he possessed documenting a government frame of DeLorean. Flynt's public behavior was becoming increasingly bizarre. He appeared in court wearing an American flag as a diaper and was arrested. At another 1984 Los Angeles trial, described by a local paper as "legal surrealism," his own attorney asked for permission to gag his client and after an "obscene outburst" Flynt, like Black Panther Bobby Seale, was bound and gagged at his own trial.

The same year the FCC was forced to issue an opinion on Flynt's threat to force television stations to show his X-rated presidential campaign commercials. Flynt, whose compulsion it was to find loopholes in the nation's obscenity laws, vowed to use his presidential campaign(!) to test those laws by insisting that TV stations show his campaign commercials featuring hard core sex acts. (The equal time provision of the Federal Communications Act prohibits censorship of any ad in which a candidate's voice or picture appears — while the U.S. Criminal Code prohibited dissemination of obscene material.) He had begun to make it his one-man mission to exploit every loophole in the first amendment as well. In 1986 a federal judge ruled that the U.S. Postal Service could not constitutionally prohibit *Hustler* and Flynt from sending free copies of the magazine to members of Congress, a ruling stemming from Flynt's decision to mail free copies of *Hustler* to members of Congress, so they could be "well informed on all social issues and trends." Flynt's next appearance, ensconced in a gold-plated wheelchair, was at the $45 million federal libel suit brought by the Reverend Jerry Falwell over the notorious Campari ad parody, in which the head of the Moral Majority describes his "first time" as having occurred with his mother behind an outhouse. A Virginia jury dismissed the libel charge but awarded Falwell $200,000 for intentional infliction of emotional distress. A federal district court upheld the verdict, but when it landed in the Rehnquist Supreme Court the judgment was reversed by a unanimous Rehnquist-written decision that the Falwell parody was not reasonably believable, and thus fell into the category of satire — an art form often "slashing and one-sided." This Supreme Court decision

[27]The story of the cover was related by Paul Krassner ["Is This the Real Message of Pornography?" *Harper's* (November 1984) p. 35] who worked for *Hustler* in 1978. Recall also that this cover was instrumental in the founding the following year of Women Against Pornography. The meat grinder joke seems to encapsulate many of the aforementioned issues of class, humor, vulgarity, and gender. [Kipnis]

significantly extended the freedom of the press won in the 1964 *New York Times* vs. Sullivan ruling (which mandated that libel could only be founded in cases of "reckless disregard"), and "handed the press one of its most significant legal triumphs in recent years," was "an endorsement of robust political debate," and ended the influx of "pseudo-libel suits" by celebrities with hurt feelings, crowed the grateful national press, amidst stories generally concluding that the existence of excrescences like *Hustler* are the price of freedom of the press.

Flynt and wife Althea had over the years elaborated various charges and conspiracy theories about the shooting, including charges of a CIA-sponsored plot (Flynt claimed to have been about to publish the names of JFK's assassins — conspiracy theories being another repeating feature of the *Hustler mentalité*).[28] Further speculation about the shooting focused on the mob, magazine distribution wars, and even various disgruntled family members. The shooting was finally acknowledged by white supremacist Joseph Paul Franklin, currently serving two life sentences for racially motivated killings. No charges were ever brought in the Flynt shooting. That Flynt, who has been regularly accused of racism, should be shot by a white supremacist is only one of the many ironies of his story. In another — one which would seem absurd in the most hackneyed morality tale — this man who made millions on the fantasy of endlessly available fucking is now left impotent. And in 1982, after four years of constant and reportedly unbearable pain, the nerves leading to his legs were cauterized to stop all sensation — Flynt, who built an empire on offending bourgeois sensibilities with their horror of errant bodily functions, is now left with no bowel or urinary control.

Flynt, in his obsessional one-man war against state power's viselike grip on the body of its citizenry, seized as his *matériel* the very pornographic idioms from which he had constructed his *Hustler* empire. The exhibitionism, the desire to shock, the deployment of the body — these are the very affronts that have made him the personification of evil to both the state and anti-porn feminists. Yet willingly or not, Flynt's own

[28]French for a set of shared attitudes, beliefs, and practices.

body has been very much on the line as well — the pornographer's body has borne the violence of the political and private enforcement of the norms of the bourgeois body. If *Hustler*'s development of the pornographic idiom as a political form seems — as with other new cultural political forms — politically incoherent to traditional political readings based on traditional political alliances and political oppositions — right-left, misogynist-feminist — then it is those very political meanings that *Hustler* throws into question. It is *Hustler*'s very political incoherence — in conventional political terms — that makes it so available to counter-hegemonic readings, to opening up new political alliances and strategies. And this is where I want to return to the question of *Hustler*'s misogyny, another political category *Hustler* puts into question. Do I feel assaulted and affronted by *Hustler*'s images, as do so many other women? Yes. Is that a necessary and sufficient condition on which to base the charge of its misogyny? Given my own gender and class position I'm not sure that I'm exactly in a position to trust my immediate response.

Take, for example, *Hustler*'s clearly political use of nudity. It's unmistakable from the "Reagan's Farewell Party" photospread that *Hustler* uses nudity as a leveling device, a deflating technique following in a long tradition of political satire. And perhaps this is the subversive force behind another of *Hustler*'s scandals (or publishing coups from its point of view), its notorious nude photospread of Jackie Onassis, captured sunbathing on her Greek island, Skorpios. Was this simply another case of misogyny? The strategic uses of nudity we've seen elsewhere in the magazine might provoke a conceptual transition in thinking through the Onassis photos: from Onassis as unwilling sexual object to Onassis as political target. Given that nudity is used throughout the magazine as an offensive against the rich and powerful — Reagan, North, Falwell, Abrams, as well as Kirkpatrick, and in another feature, Thatcher, all, unfortunately for the squeamish, through the magic of photomontage, nude — it would be difficult to argue that the nudity of Onassis functions strictly in relation to her sex, exploiting women's vulnerability as a class, or that its message can be reduced to a genericizing one like "you may be rich but you're just a cunt like any other cunt." Onassis's appearance on the pages of *Hustler* does raise questions of sex and gender insofar as we're willing to recognize what might be referred to as a sexual caste system, and the ways in which the imbrication of sex and caste make it difficult to come to any easy moral conclusions about *Hustler*'s violation of Onassis and her right to control and restrict how her body is portrayed. As recent pulp biographies inform us, the Bouvier sisters, Jacqueline and Princess Lee,[29] were more or less bred to take up positions as consorts of rich and powerful men, to, one could put it bluntly, professionally deploy their femininity. This is not so entirely dissimilar from *Hustler*'s quotidian and consenting models, who while engaged in a similar activity are confined to very different social sites. Such social sites as those pictured in a regular *Hustler* feature, "The Beaver Hunt," a photo gallery of snapshots of non-professional models sent in by readers.[30] Posed in paneled rec rooms, on plaid Sears sofas or chenille bedspreads, amidst the kind of matching bedroom suites seen on late night easy credit furniture ads, nude or in polyester lingerie, they are identified as secretaries, waitresses, housewives, nurses, bank tellers, cosmetology students, cashiers, factory workers, saleswomen, data processors, nurse's aides. . . . Without generalizing from this insufficiency of data about any kind of *typical* class-based notions about the body and its appropriate display,[31] we can simply ask, where are the

doctors, lawyers, corporate execs, and college professors? Or moving up the hierarchy, where are the socialites, the jet-setters, the wives of the chairmen of the board? Absent because of their fervent feminism? Or merely because they've struck a better deal? Simply placing the snapshots of Onassis in the place of the cashier, the secretary, the waitress, violates the rigid social distinctions of place and hardened spatial boundaries (boundaries most often purchased precisely as protection from the hordes) intrinsic to class hierarchy. These are precisely the distinctions that would make us code differently the deployment of femininity that achieves marriage to a billionaire shipping magnate from those that land you a spot in this month's Beaver Hunt. These political implications of the Onassis photospread indicate, I believe, the necessity of a more nuanced theory of misogyny than those currently in circulation. If any symbolic exposure or violation of *any* woman's body is automatically aggregated to the transhistorical misogyny machine that is the male imagination, it overlooks the fact that *all* women, simply by virtue of being women, are not necessarily political allies, that women can both symbolize and exercise class power and privilege, not to mention oppressive political power.

Feminist anti-pornography arguments, attempting to reify the feminine as an a priori privileged vantage point against pornographic male desires work on two fronts: apotropaic[32] against the reality

[29]Bouvier was Jackie Onassis's maiden name. Her sister, Princess Lee, was Caroline Lee Bouvier Canfield Radziwill Ross (1933), whose second husband was an exiled Polish prince.

[30]Recently *Hustler*, after yet another legal entanglement, began threatening in its model release form to prosecute anyone who sent in a photo without the model's release. They now demand photocopies of two forms of ID for both age and identity purposes; they also stopped paying the photographer and began paying only the model (currently $250 and the promise of consideration for higher paying photospreads). [Kipnis]

[31]Throughout this essay, my intent has not been to associate a particular class with particular or typical standards of the body, but rather to discuss how *Hustler* opposes hegemonic, historically bourgeois, conceptions of the body. Whether the *Hustler* bodily idiom represents a particular class or class fraction is not readily ascertainable without extensive audience studies of the sort difficult to carry out with a privatized forum like porn magazines. The demographics that are available aren't

current (because the magazine doesn't subsist on advertising, its demographics aren't made public, and *Hustler* is notoriously unwilling to release even circulation figures). The only readership demographics I've been able to find were published in *Mother Jones* magazine in 1976, and were made available to them because publisher Larry Flynt desired, for some reason, to add *Mother Jones* to his distribution roster. Jeffrey Klein [in "Born against Porn," *Mother Jones* (February-March 1978), p.35] writes: "Originally it was thought that *Hustler* appealed to a blue collar audience yet . . . demographics indicate that except for their gender (85 percent male), *Hustler* readers can't be so easily categorized. About 40 percent attended college; 23 percent are professionals; 59 percent have household incomes of $15,000 or more a year [about $29,000 in 1989 dollars], which is above the national mean, given the median reader age of 30." His analysis of these figures is: "Probably it's more accurate to say that *Hustler* appeals to what people would like to label a blue-collar urge, an urge most American men seem to share." [Kipnis]

[32]Attempts to ward off an evil influence.

of male violence they simultaneously work to construct a singular version of (a politically correct) femininity against other "unreconstructed" versions. Their reification of femininity defends against any position that might suggest that femininity is not an inherent virtue, an inborn condition, or in itself a moral position from which to speak — positions such as those held by pro-sex feminists, psychoanalytic theory, and the discourse of pornography itself. But among the myriad theoretical problems which the reification of femininity gives rise to,[30] there are the contradictions of utilizing class disgust as a vehicle of the truly feminine. A theory of representation that automatically conflates bodily representations with real women's bodies, and symbolic or staged sex or violence as equivalent to real sex or violence, clearly acts to restrict political expression and narrow the forms of political struggle by ignoring differences between women — and the class nature of feminist reformism. The fact that real violence against women is so pervasive as to be almost unlocalizable may lead us to want to localize it within something so easily at hand as representation; but the political consequences for feminism — to reduce it to another variety of bourgeois reformism — make this not a sufficient tactic.

However, having said this, I must add that *Hustler* is certainly not politically unproblematic. If *Hustler* is counter-hegemonic in its refusal of bourgeois proprieties, its transgressiveness has real limits. It is often only incoherent and banal where it means to be alarming and confrontational. Its banality can be seen in its politics of race, an area where its refusal of polite speech has little countercultural force. *Hustler* has been frequently accused of racism, but *Hustler* basically just wants to offend — anyone, of any race, any ethnic group. Not content merely to offend the right, it makes doubly sure to offend liberal and left sensibilities too, not content merely to taunt

whites, it hectors blacks. Its favored tactic in regard to race is to simply reproduce the stupidest stereotype it can think of — the subject of any *Hustler* cartoon featuring blacks will invariably be huge sexual organs which every women lusts after, or alternately, black watermelon-eating lawbreakers. *Hustler*'s letter columns carry out a raging debate on the subject of race, with black readers writing both that they find *Hustler*'s irreverence funny or resent its stereotypes, whites both applauding and protesting. It should also be noted that in the area of ugly stereotypes *Hustler* is hardly alone these days. The most explicitly political forms of popular culture recently are ones which also refuse to have proper representations — as any number of examples from the world of rap, which has also been widely accused of misogyny, as well as anti-Semitism, would attest. What this seems to imply is that there is no guarantee that counter-hegemonic or even specifically anti-bourgeois cultural forms are necessarily also going to be progressive. And as one of the suppositions in recent American cultural studies seems to have been that there is something hopeful to find in popular culture this might demand some rethinking.[31] *Hustler* is against government, against authority, against the bourgeoisie, diffident on male power — but its anti-liberalism, anti-feminism, anti-communism, and anti-progressivism leave little space for envisioning any alternative kind of political organization.

Hustler does powerfully articulate class resentment, and to the extent that anti-porn feminism lapses into bourgeois reformism, and that we devote ourselves to sanitizing representation, we are legitimately a target of that resentment. Leninism is on the wane around the world. The model of a vanguard party who will lead the rest of us to true consciousness holds little appeal these days. The policing of popular representation seems like only a path to more domination, and I despair for the future of a feminist politics that seems dedicated to following other vanguard parties into dogma and domination.

[30]For an analysis of the structuring contradictions in the discourse of Catharine MacKinnon, who along with Dworkin, is the leading theorist of the anti-pornography movement, see William Beatty Warner (1989), "Treating Me Like an Object: Reading Catharine MacKinnon's Feminism," in Linda Kauffman, ed., *Feminism and Institutions: Dialogues on Feminist Theory* (Cambridge: Basil Blackwell, 1989). [Kipnis]

[31]For a critique of this tendency see Mike Budd, Robert M. Entman, and Clay Steinman, "The Affirmative Character of U.S. Cultural Studies" [*Critical Studies in Mass Communications* (1990): pp. 169–184]. [Kipnis]

7

FEMINIST LITERARY CRITICISM

The madwoman in literature by women is not, as she might be in male literature, an antagonist or foil to the heroine. Rather she is usually in some sense the author's double, an image of her own anxiety and rage.
— SANDRA GILBERT AND SUSAN GUBAR

To write chapters decrying the sexual stereotyping of women in our literature while closing our eyes to the sexual harassment of our women students and colleagues . . . destroys both the spirit and meaning of what we are about.
— ANNETTE KOLODNY

The existence of a feminist movement was an essential precondition to the growth of feminist literature. . . . The fact that a parallel Black feminist movement has been much slower in evolving cannot help but have impact upon the situation of Black women writers and artists and explains in part why . . . we have been so ignored.
— BARBARA SMITH

Feminist criticism is currently so appealing to male theorists that some feminists are beginning to regard the development with some suspicion.
— ELAINE SHOWALTER

What is feminist criticism and what is not? To begin, feminist criticism does not include all literary criticism written by women, since some commentators on literature, from Anna Laetitia Barbauld to Camille Paglia, do not seem to meet their own era's definition of feminism or ours. Nor does it include all criticism written by feminists. Eve Kosofsky Sedgwick considers herself a feminist, but her book on male homosocial desire, *Between Men,* whose introduction forms part of Chapter 8, explores a subject whose relation to feminism is tangential. The characteristic common to the essays grouped here is their concern for how being a woman affects both reading and writing: How men write about women; how women read both men's and women's writing; how the sexes differ in their use of language and the roots of their creativity.

This chapter primarily explores a particular tradition of Anglo-American feminist literary criticism, a particular set of stages in the evolution of thinking about sex and writing. Chronicles presenting a history of feminist criticism, such as those of K. K. Ruthven and Toril Moi, or in Elaine Showalter's essay "Toward a Feminist Poetics," usually present a standard evolutionary sequence. It begins with a critique of patriarchal culture. In the field of literary criticism, this critique strives to expose the explicit and implicit misogyny in male writing about women. This phase would also include, as a corrective, a presentation of the very different ways in which women read male writers — and each other. The second phase might be characterized by a concern about the place of female writers within a canon largely shaped by male publishers, reviewers, and academic critics. The third phase (which Showalter calls "gynocritics" as a translation of the French *gynocritique*) consists of a search for the conditions of women's language and creativity, for modes of textuality based in gender.

This is the evolutionary history, or a part of it, of feminist literary criticism in England and America in the 1970s and 1980s. It should be remembered, however, that each of the phases continues to inspire significant work: none of the successive stages of feminist criticism has been ousted from its evolutionary niche by its successors. But both the evolutionary history and the issues of concern to successive stages of feminist criticism look somewhat different when one turns to France, where patriarchy has taken a different form than in Anglophone cultures. In "Women's Time" (1979), reprinted below, Julia Kristeva distinguishes between three "generations" of feminists. The first, which she identifies with women who came to feminism before the radicalizing moment of May 1968 (when students and workers united in a strike intended to bring on a new French revolution), was concerned to reform patriarchy and to achieve liberal political goals—abortion, contraception, equal pay, professional recognition, etc. This process of reform, Kristeva states, is transforming the world, but does not represent a revolution in values, for women are only attempting to appropriate the things men had formerly kept for themselves. The second, post-1968 generation, that of Hélène Cixous, proposes a radical shift in values: the valorization of "feminine" over "masculine" characteristics, a revaluation that Kristeva rejects as a mere inversion of the dialectic of patriarchy. Like René Girard, Kristeva reads patriarchy as a political institution that channels sacred violence against scapegoats for the sake of social order. If women have been throughout recorded time the usual symbolic sacrifices, as they have, Kristeva sees no improvement to the social order if they change places with men. The third generation, according to Kristeva, in the process of formation in the late 1970s, was a generation for whom "the very dichotomy man/woman as an opposition between two rival entities" is coming to be understood as "belonging to metaphysics." In effect Kristeva heralds the deconstruction of the premises of both patriarchy and feminism in a move that today might be called "post-feminism." In a different sense, Kristeva also prophecies the work of Judith Butler and other gender theorists we shall meet in Chapter 8, Gender Studies and Queer Theory.

Patriarchal misogyny, the canon, and women's writing are key issues for the critics represented in this chapter, but it is important to note that the feminist criticism of the 1970s and 1980s had important forebears whose representatives appear in Part One of this book. Christine de Pisan in the Middle Ages and Aphra Behn in the Restoration were concerned to counter misogyny and the claim that women could not be effective and creative writers. Germaine de Staël in eighteenth-century France had a strong sense of what literary tasks women writers could perform more effectively than men. Simone de Beauvoir explicated the ways in which Woman becomes the site of Alterity for men — always an Object, never allowed to attain the status of Subject on her own. And many of the concerns addressed in this chapter were raised as long ago as 1929 in Virginia Woolf's *A Room of One's Own*. Woolf's ironic commentary, set in the British Museum and one of the new women's colleges at Oxford, on how women have been traditionally denigrated by male scholars and teachers, long predates the work of both de Beauvoir and images-of-women critics such as Kate Millett and Mary Ellmann. Woolf's analysis of the women novelists of the nineteenth century — how Austen succeeded in devising a "feminine" sentence that allowed her to say just what she needed to, while the adoption of a "masculine" prose by Charlotte Brontë and George Eliot hampered their expressiveness — anticipates more recent research on women's language and writing. And Woolf's emphatic endorsement of Coleridge's claim that a great mind is naturally androgynous takes a stand on an issue that moves us beyond the concerns of the current chapter into those of the next.

WOMEN READING MEN READING WOMEN

Woolf's groundbreaking exploration of the major issues precipitated no immediate outpouring of feminist studies. Feminist criticism is a cultural outgrowth of the women's movement in general, and the 1930s and 1940s, owing to the Depression, the rise of fascism, and World War II, were not favorable times for feminist politics. After the war, however, feminist criticism revived and focused on the ways in which male authors present women — distorted by their own masculine prejudices and needs. The precursor text here is Simone de Beauvoir's *The Second Sex* (1949), in which de Beauvoir analyzes sexism in most of its cultural forms (see p. 673 for a detailed discussion). De Beauvoir recognizes that even the greatest poets and writers, and even those who were most favorably disposed toward women, like Stendhal, created Women either subtly or grossly as the Other they required.

Although *The Second Sex* was published in North America in 1953, Beauvoir did not become an iconic figure here until the 1970s, when the American feminist movement began to gather steam. By that time, two other important American works, Mary Ellmann's *Thinking about Women* (1968) and Kate Millett's *Sexual Politics* (1970), had launched the feminist critique of male writing. Ellmann's *Thinking about Women* is an ironic work, concerned less about the way male writers talk about women than about the way male reviewers talk about women *writers;* the result is a "phallic criticism" that emphasizes the writers' figurative "bust, waist, and hip measurements" rather than their literary qualities. Kate Millett's book proclaimed the general thesis that, if the century from 1830 to 1930 had been one of sexual revolution, the succeeding three decades had been years of counterrevolution. In the earlier period, women gained the right to education, the right to work, and the right to vote, and generally achieved the capacity for political existence independent of men; in the more recent period, ideologies from Freudian psychology to Marxism to fascism had conspired to keep women in their place. In literary terms, Millett's critique of the new patriarchy operates through readings of Henry Miller, Norman

Mailer, and D. H. Lawrence. By the standards of today's feminist writers, Millett's readings of texts can often seem simplistic and reductive; her passages for analysis, however, are aptly chosen for the polemical points she makes.

WOMEN READING

In the 1960s Millett and Ellmann were primarily concerned with how men read women; in the 1970s women began to read men — and each other — in new and theoretically interesting ways. Perhaps the most sophisticated of the reader-response feminist critics is Annette Kolodny, whose "Some Notes on Defining a 'Feminist Literary Criticism'" (1975), explored problems of methodology, aiming to prove to prejudiced males that feminist questions required serious thought. Kolodny's position was empiricist. While women's experience in the past and present differed from men's, it would be unsafe to claim that women's literature was distinctive until this could be demonstrated directly. Kolodny appears to be skeptical about contemporary claims, like those of Showalter, for a distinctively female kind of writing. The case she makes out is that women read differently from men; they read both life and literature from the perspective of a disparate personal experience.[1] Kolodny's "A Map for Rereading" (1980) discusses two issues: how the differing interpretive modes of men and women appear *within* two stories (Charlotte Perkins Gilman's "The Yellow Wallpaper" and Susan Keating Glaspell's "A Jury of Her Peers"); and how the discrepancy between male and female ways of apprehending the world was mirrored in the fate of these two stories in the male-dominated literary marketplace. Kolodny has been more concerned than most feminist critics with finding a rhetoric to counter male opposition to feminism. In "Dancing Through the Minefield" (reprinted in this chapter), Kolodny presents her feminist theses so "that current hostilities might be transformed into a true dialogue with our critics."

Kolodny's theoretical perspective on the differences between male and female ways of reading the codes of literature and life is echoed in the practical criticism of Judith Fetterley. Fetterley's book, *The Resisting Reader* (1978; see p. 1035), begins by dismantling the assumption that texts — in her case, the primary texts of American fiction — are written for a universal audience. In fact, Fetterley states, "to read the canon of what is currently considered classic American literature is perforce to identify as male. . . . It insists on its universality at the same time that it defines that universality in specifically male terms" (p. xii). Traditionally, women have allowed themselves to be "immasculated" — inscribed within masculinity — in reading these texts, but they do so at the heavy price of internalizing self-hatred or at least self-doubt. Today, that price is too high: "The first act of the feminist critic must be to become a resisting rather than an assenting reader, to begin the process of exorcising the male mind that has been implanted in us" (p. xxii).

Jonathan Culler's "Reading as a Woman," reprinted below, takes a somewhat different slant on the issue of feminist reading. It would be easy to mistake Culler's

[1]"Some Notes on Defining a 'Feminist Literary Criticism,'" *Critical Inquiry* 2 (1975): 75–92.

analysis of the different ways women read men, and each other, for a careful exposition of theorists discussed elsewhere in this introduction (Ellmann, Millett, and Showalter) or discussed in other chapters (such as Judith Fetterley, discussed in Chapter 3 as a reader-response critic, or Luce Irigaray, discussed in Chapter 8). It is only after presenting three modes or moments of feminist reading that Culler's own ideas come to the fore:

> From these varied writings, a general structure emerges. In the first moment or mode, where woman's experience is treated as a firm ground for interpretation, one swiftly discovers that this experience is not the sequence of thoughts present to the reader's consciousness as she moves through the text but a reading or interpretation of "woman's experience" — her own and others' — which can be set in a vital and productive relation to the text. In the second mode, the problem is how to make it possible to read as a woman: the possibility of this fundamental experience induces an attempt to produce it. In the third mode, the appeal to experience is veiled but still there, as a reference to maternal rather than paternal relations or to woman's situation and experience of marginality, which may give rise to an altered mode of reading. The appeal to the experience of the reader provides leverage for displacing or undoing the system of concepts or procedures of male criticism, but "experience" always has this divided, duplicitous character: it has always already occurred and yet is still to be produced — an indispensable point of reference, yet never simply there. . . . For a woman to read as a woman is not to repeat an identity or an experience but to play a role she constructs with reference to her identity as a woman, which is also a construct, so that the series can continue: a woman reading as a woman reading as a woman. . . .

Culler is in effect deconstructing the idea of "woman's experience" in terms of the role it plays in feminist reading, always receding from the point of reference it is given. When it is appealed to as a natural fact, that only uncovers its cultural construction; appealed to as a cultural construct, we come to wonder how a phallocentric culture can construct something as foreign to it as "woman's experience." Woman must know who she is in order to read as she does, but only learns who she is in the course of reading. This is not by any means a vicious circle, but it gives one much to ponder.

WOMEN TALKING

One of the more intriguing questions feminist criticism has broached is whether there is a special "women's language" that is different from that spoken by men. One would expect that inscription within patriarchy would have its effects on the way women speak, and this notion has been firmly endorsed by the pioneering studies of linguist Robin Lakoff in *Language and Woman's Place* (1975). Lakoff suggests that more is involved in "talking like a lady" than mere vocabulary (e.g., the use of adjectives like "adorable" or "divine" and of color-words like "mauve"; the avoidance of scatological terms). Lakoff considers some syntactic constructions as typically female, like the "tag-question," which seeks agreement rather than aggressively taking a stand (e.g., "Mozart is a wonderful composer, isn't he?"). She suggests that women's traditional powerlessness is reflected in their greater use of indirect utterances but that such usages also reinforce current sex roles.

While Lakoff was developing the concept of "genderlect" — dialectical differences owing to gender — she tended to believe that sexist usages were unalterably fixed in language. She doubted that it was possible to dislodge the generic use of "man" to include women or of "he" as the neutral pronoun; but she was equally uncertain that these forms were seriously sexist and was inclined to consider them innocuous asymmetries. But are they innocuous? In an empirical study (1980), Jeanette Silveira found that respondents often did not understand that females were included in the generic "man" or "he," and that this was true of female as well as male subjects.[2] On the issue of change, Lakoff's conservatism seemed justified at the time by the long and futile history — going back to 1850 — of attempts at pronoun reform (the use of constructed neuter pronouns like "thon" or "hiser"). But since 1975 an effective series of guidelines for using sex-neutral language has been adopted by most publishers. Not only has the generic masculine been dropped but also phrases suggesting that certain jobs are gender-oriented, either by direct implication ("fireman" or "policeman") or by marking the less-common gender (e.g., "lady lawyer" or "male nurse"). Another sexist practice noted by Lakoff, that of referring to a female author by both first and last names (Jane Austen, Emily Dickinson) but to a male author by last name alone (Dickens, Lawrence), seems to be passing. Similarly "Ms." as the marriage-neutral form of address for women has become common if not universal. In effect, Lakoff's work has dated because society has become sensitive to sexist language and has made some significant attempts at reform.

Lakoff's work has dated in another sense, too: Some of its assertions have been questioned by later empirical studies. For example, her claim that women use tag questions more often than men do was supported by two experiments and refuted by three others. It now appears that social setting may be more important than gender in determining whether speakers produce tag questions; even powerful males tend to use many tag questions when they are running meetings. In general, theories of "genderlect" are less popular than they were in the 1970s, as researchers recognize that the variations in speech patterns *within* each gender are greater than the differences *between* genders.

Feminist linguists have focused instead on sociolinguistic issues, such as the frequency with which women are addressed in familiar terms ("dear" or "honey") by people they do not know, the relative frequency with which women and men interrupt each other and allow themselves to be interrupted,[3] the large number of pejorative terms for women as opposed to those for men,[4] and the unexamined assumptions that women will take their father's name at birth and their husband's name upon marriage. (Feminist linguists sensitive to this issue have changed or

---

[2] Jeanette Silveira, "Generic Masculine Words and Thinking," in *The Voices and Words of Women and Men,* ed. Cheris Kramarae (Oxford: Pergamon Press, 1980), pp. 165–78.

[3] Candice West and Don H. Zimmerman, "Small Insults: A Study of Interruptions in Cross-sex Conversations between Unacquainted Persons," in *Language, Gender, and Society,* ed. Barrie Thorne et al. (Rowley, MA: Newbury House, 1983), pp. 103–18.

[4] Julia Penelope Stanley found 220 terms for a sexually promiscuous woman, only 22 for a man. See "Paradigmatic Woman: The Prostitute," in *Papers in Language Variation,* ed. David Shores (Birmingham: University of Alabama Press, 1977).

reinvented their names: e.g., Cheris Kramarae previously published as Chris Kramer, Julia Penelope Stanley is now Julia Penelope.)

More recently, the work of Deborah Tannen, another sociolinguist and a former collaborator of Robin Lakoff, has enjoyed extraordinary popular success. Tannen's *You Just Don't Understand: Women and Men in Conversation* (1990) explicates the mutual misprisions of men and women in terms of the differences between their customary purposes of dialogue: Males make "report talk" presenting facts evaluable with hierarchal logic, while females make "rapport talk" to create alliances and cement relationships. Whether these generalizations are any more defensible than Lakoff's, the success of *You Just Don't Understand,* which stayed on the *New York Times* bestseller list for over four years, was immense, partly because the book was interpreted as an important tool for corporate management techniques. Tannen has followed up *You Just Don't Understand* with further discussions of gender styles, including *That's Not What I Meant* (1992) and *Talking Nine to Five: Men and Women in the Workplace: Language Sex and Power* (1995). Her earlier scholarly articles on such psycholinguistic issues as interruption, origination of topics, and ethnic styles of conversation are collected in *Gender and Discourse* (1994).

WOMEN WRITING

Perhaps the least controversial aspect of recent feminist studies has been its attempt to locate and expand a female tradition of writing. Some authors (from Christine de Pisan to Kate Chopin) have been exhumed from near-oblivion and raised to the status of classics; others (like Anne Bradstreet and Mary Shelley), never really lost to sight, have been reinterpreted as central to the literary canon rather than as marginal, if well-known, figures. As in all efforts to expand the canon, more candidates will inevitably be proposed than will eventually find a place within. And if some writers now receiving general attention are those like Charlotte Perkins Gilman, who enrich and deepen feminists' sense of their own history, others, like Mary Shelley and Anna Laetitia Barbauld, espoused conservative attitudes toward "woman's place," which their present-day readers would be loath to adopt.

If the criterion is whether literature by women is taught in colleges and universities, the effort to expand the canon has been successful. But much of this success has occurred within special "women's studies" programs and in special courses within traditional programs, so that one may wonder whether women have truly been included within the traditional canon or whether a counter-canon of literature by women has been advanced to parallel the former canon defined primarily by men. And feminist critics like Nina Baym have questioned whether the canon has been created in a gender-neutral fashion or whether the books have been cooked.

Nina Baym's historical research, in "Melodramas of Beset Manhood" (1981), reprinted below, reveals that women authors such as Susannah Rowson dominated the American fiction market in the decades before 1800, and that many women including Harriet Beecher Stowe and Emma D. E. N. Southworth, were among the most widely read novelists in the nineteenth century. How did it happen, Baym asks, that by 1977 the canon "did not contain any women novelists"? Bracketing the simplistic hypotheses that women wrote nothing but sensational trash and that American literary historians were simply misogynistic bigots hostile to women's writing, Baym explores the way the formation of an American canon was influenced by an emerging Idea of America. Texts were not evaluated according to an ostensibly pure aesthetic: Instead, the best American literature was believed to be that which most clearly reflected the current consensus as to what was quintessentially American. Various formulations of the essence of American culture were in competition in the early years of the twentieth century, but eventually a consensus formed around the myth "that in this new land, untrammeled by history and social accident, a person will be able to achieve complete self-definition. . . . Society exerts an unmitigatedly destructive pressure on individuality. . . . Thus . . . the essential quality of America comes to reside in its unsettled wilderness and the opportunities that such a wilderness offers to the individual as the medium on which he may inscribe, unhindered, his own destiny and his own nature."

One likely foundation for this vision of the essence of American culture is Frederick Jackson Turner's enormously influential historical study, *The Frontier in American History* (1920), with its nostalgic vision of the uniqueness of the American experiment until the closing of the Western frontier at the end of the nineteenth century. Although Baym does not specifically mention Turner's book, it was republished in 1947, and all of the books she accuses of peddling the American myth of the individual versus society (by Lionel Trilling, Henry Nash Smith, Charles Feidelson, R. W. B. Lewis, Richard Chase, and Daniel Hoffman) appeared within the following decade. Whether the origin of the myth is Turner or, as Baym thinks, Trilling, is immaterial: The result was that works in touch with this myth, like James Fenimore Cooper's *Leatherstocking Tales* (1823–41) and Nathaniel Hawthorne's *The Scarlet Letter* (1850), or ones that operated in some ironic relation to it, like Mark Twain's *Huckleberry Finn* (1885) and F. Scott Fitzgerald's *The Great Gatsby* (1925), were canonized at the expense of works, many of them by women, that centered on the discontents of civilization rather than the romance of the wilderness. In a sense, the issue is not purely a feminist one, since Baym argues that writers like William Dean Howells and Henry James also posed a "continual challenge to the masculinist bias of American critical theory."

One question that remains is how to understand the body of literature by women, and whether it forms a tradition on its own that can be understood apart from the body of literature by men. Most critics are likely to identify the three major texts of the second phase of feminist criticism, the analysis of women's writing, as Ellen Moers's *Literary Women* (1976), Elaine Showalter's *A Literature of Their Own* (1977), and Sandra Gilbert and Susan Gubar's *The Madwoman in the Attic* (1979). As Toril Moi's survey of feminist criticism puts it, "Taken together, these three books represent the coming-of-age of Anglo-American feminist criticism."[5]

Moers's *Literary Women* is subtitled *"The Great Writers,"* as if to establish its relationship to F. R. Leavis's *The Great Tradition* (1948; see p. 650), and there is

[5]Toril Moi, *Sexual/Textual Politics: Feminist Literary Theory* (New York: Methuen, 1985), p. 52.

indeed something Leavisite about its socially oriented survey of centuries of female creativity. Moers focuses on those aspects of women writers that derive from the central fact of their being women and ignores the rest as far as possible. Thus, Moers interprets Mary Shelley's *Frankenstein* as a myth of birth, in which the newborn is "at once monstrous agent of destruction and piteous victim of parental abandonment," a myth she sees as the product of Shelley's personal history — as an unwed mother at the time of its writing and as an infant whose birth occasioned her mother's death. Moers's method, if it can be called that, is impressionistic and biographical; in calling up her most admired heroine, George Sand, she asks the reader to picture "her typical country evening at Nohant. At the center sits Madame Sand with the needle work she loved in her hands, surrounded by a houseful of friends, children, lovers, guests, neighbors. Nohant was a messy household, full of laughter and games and theatricals and family arguments and good intellectual talk and tobacco smoke and music — just like yours and mine." Later critics were to avoid her chattiness and decry her insistence on biographical explanations, but feminist criticism was advanced by her wide-ranging discussion of the canon of women's literature and the central place of women's experience in forming that canon.

Elaine Showalter's book, *A Literature of Their Own,* has been more influential than Moers's. In addition to establishing a complex relationship to Woolf's *A Room of One's Own,* Showalter's title alludes ironically to John Stuart Mill, who in *The Subjection of Women* (1869) stated that "if women lived in a different country from men and had never read any of their writings, they would have a literature of their own." As things stood, Mill thought, they did not: "[A] much longer time is necessary ... before [women's literature] can emancipate itself from the influence of accepted models, and guide itself by its own impulses." Showalter would not claim that the body of texts produced by women has the coherent character of a national literature that can be studied entirely apart from the texts produced by men, and she suspects that the hypothesis of a distinctive "female imagination" will encourage the stereotyped images of women that feminists have been so eager to dispel. Nevertheless, Showalter claims that women, as a subculture within English society, have produced something definable as a "female literary tradition" in the English novel from the generation of the Brontës to the present.

Showalter's analysis of nineteenth-century English fiction by women presents an evolutionary theory of the development of women's writing, which she argues ran parallel to that by blacks, Jews, and other groups outside the white Christian male power elite:

> In looking at literary subcultures ... we can see that they all go through three major phases. First, there is a prolonged phase of *imitation* of the prevailing modes of the dominant tradition, and *internalization* of its standards of art and its views on social roles. Second, there is a phase of *protest* against these standards and values, and *advocacy* of minority rights and values, including a demand for autonomy. Finally, there is a phase of *self-discovery,* a turning inward freed from some of the dependency of opposition, a search for identity. An appropriate terminology for women writers is to call these stages *Feminine, Feminist,* and *Female.* These are obviously not rigid categories. ... The phases overlap. ... One might ... find all three phases in the career of a single novelist. Nonetheless, it seems useful to point to periods of crisis when a shift of literary values

occurred. In this book I identify the Feminine phase as the period from the appearance of the male pseudonym in the 1840s to the death of George Eliot in 1880; the Feminist phase as 1880 to 1920, or the winning of the vote; and the Female phase as 1920 to the present, but entering a new stage of self-awareness about 1960 (p. 13).

Obviously in Showalter's program there is some danger of overestimating the extent to which the female tradition and the male tradition are separable and (as Kenneth Ruthven has put it) of feminist critics "repeating exactly the same mistake for which they take male critics to task, namely an exclusive preoccupation with the writings of one sex."[6] This is a problem, however, of which Showalter is well aware. What seems less guarded is her bias against that version of feminism represented by Virginia Woolf — a foremother whom she attacks with what may seem an Electra's fury. Showalter considers Woolf's idealization of androgyny a mere flight from any genuine femininity and terms her vision of womanhood "as deadly as it is disembodied" (p. 289). Showalter's arguments against an androgynous ideal seem *ad feminam* (so to speak), and she does not understand the appeal of androgyny even to women (like Mary Shelley) who loved men and were devoted to their children.

Whatever the controversies surrounding Showalter's attitudes toward nineteenth- and twentieth-century fiction by women, her methodology is simple and straightforward. *The Madwoman in the Attic,* by Sandra Gilbert and Susan Gubar, brought to the female tradition some less traditional ways of reading, similar to those we associate with Yale (which eventually published their study). In particular, Gilbert and Gubar take off from the poetics of Harold Bloom's *Anxiety of Influence* (see Ch. 4). But where Bloom was concerned with the Oedipal relation between the "strong" poet and the forebear he has chosen as his ghostly "father," whose works he must misread to make room for his own, Gilbert and Gubar are concerned with the female half of the equation, with the woman writer who, defined always by men, is uncomfortable defining herself, who, lacking a pen/penis, is anxious about whether she can create at all. Whatever women's lesser disabilities today, women writers in the nineteenth century eventually "overcame their 'anxiety of authorship,' repudiated debilitating patriarchal prescriptions, and recovered or remembered the lost foremothers who could help them find their distinctive female power" (p. 59).

But within a patriarchy, women's writing cannot fully express itself; as a result, women writers (consciously or unconsciously) revised their own meanings to make them acceptable to their culture. "Women from Jane Austen and Mary Shelley to Emily Brontë and Emily Dickinson produced literary works . . . whose surface designs conceal or obscure deeper, less accessible (and less socially acceptable) levels of meaning" (p. 73). Women authors used a "cover story" — coded messages disguising their intent. They often created villainesses, in Gilbert and Gubar's readings of the novels, who speak powerfully for the values they were forced to repress. Under the surface, Bertha Mason Rochester, the titular Madwoman in the Attic, is the true heroine of *Jane Eyre*. Her frank impulsiveness and sensuality underlie what the reader values in Jane herself.

---

[6]K. K. Ruthven, *Feminist Literary Studies: An Introduction* (Cambridge: Cambridge University Press, 1984), p. 125.

The Madwoman in the Attic gave an enormous new impetus to feminist criticism, yet there were skeptics, largely among Gilbert and Gubar's fellow feminists. In her review of *Madwoman* in *Signs*, Mary Jacobus attacked the book's "unstated complicity with the autobiographical 'phallacy,' whereby male critics hold that women's writing is somehow closer to their own experience than men's, that the female text *is* the author."[7] Toril Moi has a different problem with *The Madwoman in the Attic*, in fact she has, as one can see from the selection from *Sexual/Textual Politics* reprinted below as a "Dialogue" with Gilbert and Gubar, an interlocking set of problems.[8] Moi is a poststructuralist theorist whose allegiances, like Kristeva's, reach out to both Marx and Freud as reinterpreted by contemporary theory. As a neo-Marxist, Moi sees patriarchy as a production of ideology, but rejects the way Gilbert and Gubar characterize it as a relentless and all-pervasive force. If it were that, Moi asks, how did women manage to write at all? Moi suggests that Gilbert and Gubar need to think about ideology the way Althusser does, as fragmentary and contradictory, and not as irresistibly coherent. Moi is critical as well of Gilbert and Gubar's suggestion that women have been "fragmented" by patriarchy and long to become whole and complete. Wholeness and completeness of the self, for a psychoanalytic thinker like Moi, is an illusion, an obsession that belongs to the Lacanian Imaginary, as a product of the "mirror stage" (see p. 1114). Gilbert and Gubar should be deconstructing this sort of "phallic" thinking, which Moi argues underlies patriarchy, rather than reproducing it with feminist overtones.

WOMEN ON THE MARGINS

In *A Literature of Their Own,* Elaine Showalter's attempt to describe female writing as a variant of the experience of minority cultures searching for a place within the mainstream implicitly suggests that women's writing belongs to the white, male, Protestant, and British or American traditions with one exception: that of gender. While this was true of the British writers Showalter discussed, obviously some women may be multiply marginalized, not only women but as African Americans, Chicanos, Asian Americans, Caribbean Islanders, or as lesbians on the margin of the heterosexual majority.

The marginalization of the African American female writer has become a significant issue as writers such as Phillis Wheatley and Zora Neale Hurston, Alice Walker and Toni Morrison, Gwendolyn Brooks and Nikki Giovanni are entering the canon, either in courses in American literature or through their success as popular best-sellers. In a number of ways, the issues of black feminist criticism overlap with those of white feminism. But African American women have long felt excluded from white feminist politics, and some of the central texts of women's studies ignore women who are not white. In her manifesto, "Toward a Black Feminist Criticism," Barbara Smith expresses outrage at this failure to recognize that "Black and female identity ever coexist, specifically in a group of Black women writers." Smith attacks as "barely disguised cultural imperialism"

[7]*Signs* 6 (1981): 520.
[8]Moi, pp. 57–69.

Showalter's proposal to build a feminist scholarship on the model of "black American novelists." Smith also notes that most studies of women writers written by white women tend to ignore African Americans and other minorities — Moers's *Literary Women* "includes the names of four Black and one Puertoriqueña writer in her seventy pages of bibliographical notes" — and that other feminist writers show a "suspiciously selective" ignorance of the existence of black women writers. The feminists are not the only target here, however, for Smith sees both black and white male scholars of black writing as even more distortive of the creative achievements of black women. The essay by Deborah McDowell, "New Directions for Black Feminist Criticism," while entirely sympathetic to the sense of marginality against which earlier black feminists reacted, seeks to escape the divisiveness of black versus white, women vs. men, lesbian vs. heterosexual, that organizes Smith's manifesto. For McDowell black feminist criticism is less a cause than a task, for which one must go beyond politics and slogans. Whereas earlier black feminists had simply equated their race and sex with a special use of language, McDowell calls instead for concrete investigations into the content of black female poetics using contemporary methodologies. Like Kolodny, McDowell considers the walls of separation between male and female, black and white, at best a mixed blessing. She quotes the Nigerian playwright Wole Soyinka on the creative asphyxiation that accompanies too exclusive an attention to ideology, fearing that a separatist black feminist criticism could become a narrower and less vital enterprise than it has the potential to be.

Lesbian feminist literary criticism centers on a different sort of marginality. Just as black women writers and critics have felt excluded from white feminist studies, so lesbian writers and critics have been excluded by feminist attempts to seek a specifically heterosexual female identity. Bonnie Zimmerman points out the homophobia of both Moers's *Literary Women* and Patricia Meyer Spacks's *The Female Imagination:* "Spacks claims that Gertrude Stein, 'whose life lack[ed] real attachments' (a surprise to Alice B. Toklas) also 'denied whatever is special to women' (which lesbianism is not?)"[9] Lesbian feminist criticism confronts some of the same difficulties as heterosexual feminism, such as whether lesbian writing has a historical continuity apart from the writing of women and, indeed, of men, and whether it encounters unique difficulties of its own. For example, establishing the canon of lesbian writers involves first establishing writers' sexual orientation, which may be ambiguous or simply indecipherable owing to lack of evidence. Lesbian literature itself is difficult to define: Adrienne Rich defines lesbianism so inclusively as to embrace all female bonding and most female creativity, yet the lesbian canon might also be restricted to texts by exclusively homosexual women.

The expansion of the feminist dialogue to take into account various groups previously marginalized within the women's movement is only one version, perhaps, of the tendency of women's studies to expand its boundaries and to address areas traditionally dominated by men. It is impossible to do justice to the breadth of the movement here, but no study of feminist criticism can be complete without at least

---

[9]Bonnie Zimmerman, "What Has Never Been: An Overview of Lesbian Feminist Literary Criticism," in *The New Feminist Criticism,* ed. Elaine Showalter (New York: Pantheon, 1985), p. 203.

mentioning the connections between feminism and psychoanalysis (drawn by writers such as Jane Gallop and Mary Jacobus), between feminism and deconstruction (Peggy Kamuf and Nancy K. Miller), and between feminism and Marxism (Juliet Mitchell and Michèle Barrett).

Like Marxism, feminism was a social and political movement long before it was a mode of literary criticism, but, also like Marxism, the cultural wing of the ideology has naturally attracted many of the brightest and most energetic minds. This poses a problem to the movement as a whole. Just as Terry Eagleton scoffed at the idea that Jameson's analyses of Balzac were going to shake the foundations of capitalism, so some feminists have wondered how analyzing Charlotte Brontë would alter the fact that women's pay is only seventy-one percent of men's.

It is obviously necessary for women to understand their past and the accomplishments that their forebears have achieved against heavy odds. But there is at least a slight edge of irony about the success of feminist criticism as an academic career choice. Lillian Robinson has been concerned that feminist critics be feminists first and critics second. "Some people are trying to make an honest woman out of the feminist critic, to claim that every 'worthwhile' department should stock one. I am not terribly interested in whether feminism becomes a respectable part of academic criticism. I am very much concerned that feminist critics become a useful part of the women's movement. . . . Marx's note about philosophers may apply to cultural critics as well: that up to now they have interpreted the world and the real point is to change it."[10]

MEN ON THE MARGINS OF FEMINISM

Up to this point all but one of the feminist writers cited in this chapter have been women,[11] and the question might be raised whether feminist criticism is a closed shop or an equal opportunity employer, or, more generally, the place of men in feminism? Jonathan Culler's "Reading as a Woman," reprinted below, is a somewhat ambivalent specimen of what happens when men write feminist criticism: Culler stations himself at a "meta" level above the projects of the female theorists he discusses, analyzing how they relate to "women's experience" and to each other, much as I have been doing myself in this introduction. The "dialogue" piece we have included in response to Culler, by Elaine Showalter, is one that assesses the powers and limitations of men in feminism. Like Culler, men can write as feminists, but they cannot write as women; socially constructed as "reading as a woman" may be, it is not a role that may be taken up by just anyone who wishes. Showalter applauds Culler's restraint, but her toleration for men in feminism has limits, and they are tested when men attempt to demonstrate that they can be more effectively feminist than any woman, as she suspects Terry Eagleton of doing in his book *The Rape of Clarissa*. We have also included Eagleton's response to Showalter, and Showalter's

---

[10]Lillian S. Robinson, *Sex, Class, and Culture* (Bloomington: Indiana University Press, 1978), pp. 19–20.

[11]It is worth mentioning perhaps that Kenneth Knowles Ruthven, cited on p. 1511, published his 1984 book *Feminist Literary Studies* as K. K. Ruthven.

brief reply, as an example of a different sort of dialogue, a dialogue of the deaf, that is not uncommon within the critical tradition. Both pieces, short as they are, reward close analysis for what is said, and not said, within them.

THE FATE OF ANGLO-AMERICAN FEMINISM

Most scholars would agree that the essays reproduced in this chapter represent a particular phase of Anglo-American feminism, one whose theoretical constitution was essentially complete before 1985. This does not mean that the movement has died out or even lost its steam. On the contrary, all the projects promoted by that constitution are continuing with great vigor. For example, Showalter's argument, elaborated in *A Literature of Their Own*, that there was a long and healthy tradition of women's writing all through the nineteenth century, has been extended backwards by many other hands, and extraordinary efforts are under way to rediscover women's writing from all periods and to make it available to readers. The advent of computers and the internet has assisted enormously in this endeavor, because poetry and fiction by women that commercial publishers might deem too marginal in popular interest to warrant republication in book form can now be circulated as text files or hard copy to interested readers using electronic media. Thus the Women's Collective at Brown University, to take only one example, has made available to scholars literally hundreds of seventeenth- and eighteenth-century British novels by women that would otherwise have to be sought in rare book collections.[12] While scholars of my generation merely learned of the existence of popular women novelists at the time of Defoe, such as Eliza Haywood and Delariviere Manley, scholars today can read their works and come directly to terms with their concerns and those of their readership. Similar efforts are under way to unearth unsung and underappreciated American women writers, and, as Deborah McDowell predicted, women writers of color are reaping gains as well. Where a dozen years ago college reading lists were incomplete without Kate Chopin's *The Awakening* (1899), today the most assigned novels by women writers are probably Toni Morrison's *Beloved* (1987) and Zora Neale Hurston's *Their Eyes Were Watching God* (1937). And while Judith Fetterley recommended "resistant reading" to women threatened with "immasculation" by canonical male texts (see p. 1035), a good deal of interesting research has gone on, in ways hinted at by Annette Kolodny in "Dancing Through the Minefield," into how women actually read. Both Susan Snaider Lanser and Peter Rabinowitz have suggested that women may be decoding texts in ways that men would not.[13]

[12]When I was a young scholar, for example, the major poetical romance by Lady Mary Wroth, *The Countess of Montgomery's Urania* (1621), was an obscure work mentioned in literary histories and available only in one of the rare copies held at the North Library of the British Museum. About a decade ago, with the rapid growth of Wroth's reputation as one of the major poets of the seventeenth century, it became possible to read the *Urania* using the computer text version made available by the Women's Collective. Today it is possible to consult a hardbound scholarly edition edited by the late Josephine Roberts.

[13]See Susan Snaider Lanser, *Fictions of Authority: Women Writers and Narrative Voice* (Ithaca: Cornell University Press, 1992); and Peter Rabinowitz, "End Sinister: Neat Closure as Disruptive Force," in *Reading Narrative: Form, Ethics, Ideology* (Columbus: Ohio State University Press, 1989).

But while the projects of Anglo-American feminism continue, the 1980s saw the development of a rift in American feminist criticism between adherents of the Anglo-American tradition and a new generation of feminist theorists interested both in considering the implications of deconstructivist, psychoanalytic, Marxist, and New Historical theory for their studies of gender difference and in opening up such originally androcentric movements to a consideration of gender.[14] There was a reluctance on the part of some of the most important Anglo-American feminists to problematize the concept of gender and to theorize about the relationship between femaleness and femininity. Showalter's edited collection, *The New Feminist Criticism,* published in 1985, was designed to showcase the best that had been known and thought in the feminist world, but it pointedly sidelined the theorizing about gender that had been going on in France for at least a decade. A single short and rather lukewarm essay by Ann Rosalind Jones, positioned at the end of the volume, briefly summarized some of the positions of Julia Kristeva, Hélène Cixous, Luce Irigaray, and Monique Wittig, without presenting the Lacanian psychoanalytic theory that would have allowed the reader to make sense of them.[15] Showalter's own treatment of the French feminists in her introduction was less than lukewarm, dourly arguing that "Anglo-American feminist poetics must insist on an analysis of specific cultural contexts rather than merely relying on an idealized and abstract view of the feminine" (p. 15).

It is not clear exactly what motivated the refusal to admit theorizing about gender into the big tent of Anglo-American feminism, but the reason may have been academic politics. The world of literary scholarship was deeply split in the early 1980s between traditional scholars who could make no sense of the theoretical revolution that had been building for at least a decade and theorists who were using the new Marxism, psychoanalysis, semiotics, and deconstruction to produce radically new work, who saw no sense at all in continuing the old practices. Showalter's stand in favor of "specific cultural contexts" may have been a way of stationing feminism as a mode of traditional criticism that should be supported by old-style scholars for its conservative methodology as well as by radical theorists taken with its political program. But the genie of gender theory was already out of the bottle, and the ideas and movements that are currently reshaping our understanding of the relationship between sex, gender, and literature are considered in Chapter 8.

Selected Bibliography

Abel, Elizabeth, ed. *Writing and Sexual Difference.* Chicago: University of Chicago Press, 1982.

Auerbach, Nina. *Woman and the Demon: The Life of a Victorian Myth.* Cambridge: Harvard University Press, 1982.

[14]See, for example, the work of Nancy Armstrong, p. 1418.

[15]Ann Rosalind Jones, "Writing the Body: Toward an Understanding of *l'Écriture Féminine*," in *The New Feminist Criticism: Women, Literature, Theory,* ed. Elaine Showalter (New York: Pantheon, 1985), pp. 361–77. Showalter's volume also sidelines reader-response feminist theory, presenting the central strand as what she calls "gynocritics," the analysis of female creativity.

Baym, Nina. *Woman's Fiction: A Guide to Novels by and about Women in America*. Ithaca: Cornell University Press, 1978.

——. *Feminism and American Literary History*. New Brunswick: Rutgers University Press, 1992.

Beauvoir, Simone de. *Le Deuxième sexe*. Paris: Gallimard, 1949. Trans. H. M. Parshley as *The Second Sex*. New York: Knopf, 1972.

Belsey, Catherine. *Critical Practice*. London: Methuen, 1980.

Blau Duplessis, Rachel. *Writing Beyond the Ending: Narrative Strategies of Twentieth-Century Women Writers*. Bloomington: Indiana University Press, 1985.

Brownstein, Rachel. *Becoming a Heroine: Reading about Women in Novels*. New York: Viking, 1982.

Cameron, Deborah. *Feminism in Linguistic Theory*. London: Macmillan, 1992.

Chodorow, Nancy. *The Reproduction of Mothering: Psychoanalysis and the Sociology of Gender*. Berkeley: University of California Press, 1978.

——. *Feminism and Psychoanalytic Theory*. New Haven: Yale University Press, 1989.

De Lauretis, Teresa. *Alice Doesn't: Feminism, Semiotics, Cinema*. Bloomington: Indiana University Press, 1984.

Delany, Sheila. *Writing Women: Women Writers and Women in Literature, Medieval to Modern*. New York: Schocken, 1984.

Donovan, Josephine, ed. *Feminist Literary Criticism: Explorations in Theory*. Lexington: University Press of Kentucky, 1975.

Douglas, Ann. *The Feminization of American Culture*. New York: Knopf, 1978.

Ellmann, Mary. *Thinking about Women*. New York: Harcourt Brace Jovanovich, 1968.

Felman, Shoshana. "Rereading Femininity." *Yale French Studies* 62 (1981): 19–44.

Fetterley, Judith. *The Resisting Reader: A Feminist Approach to American Fiction*. Bloomington: Indiana University Press, 1978.

Firestone, Shulamith. *The Dialectic of Sex: The Case for Feminist Revolution*. London: Women's Press, 1979.

Flynn, Elizabeth A., and Patrocinio P. Schweickart. *Gender and Reading: Essays on Readers, Texts and Contexts*. Baltimore: Johns Hopkins University Press, 1986.

Gallop, Jane. *The Daughter's Seduction: Feminism and Psychoanalysis*. Ithaca: Cornell University Press, 1982.

Gates, Henry Louis, Jr., ed. *Reading Black, Reading Feminist: A Critical Anthology*. New York: Meridian, 1990.

Gilbert, Sandra M., and Susan Gubar. *The Madwoman in the Attic: The Woman Writer and the Nineteenth-Century Literary Imagination*. New Haven: Yale University Press, 1979.

Greer, Germaine. *The Female Eunuch*. London: McGibbon and Kee, 1970.

hooks, bell [Gloria Watkins]. *Ain't I a Woman? Black Women and Feminism*. Boston: South End Press, 1981.

Jacobus, Mary. *Women's Writing and Writing about Women*. New York: Barnes and Noble, 1979.

Jehlen, Myra. "Archimedes and the Paradox of Feminist Criticism." *Signs* 6 (1981): 575–601.

Kahn, Coppélia, and Gayle Greene, eds. *Making a Difference: Feminist Literary Criticism*. New York: Methuen, 1985.

Kamuf, Peggy. "Replacing Feminist Criticism." *Diacritics* 12 (1982): 42–47.

Kolodny, Annette. "Some Notes on Defining a 'Feminist Literary Criticism.'" *Critical Inquiry* 2 (1975): 75–92.

——. "Dancing Through the Minefield: Some Observations on the Theory, Practice and Politics of a Feminist Literary Criticism." *Feminist Studies* 6 (1980): 1–25.

———. *The Land Before Her: Fantasy and Experience of the American Frontiers, 1630–1860.* Chapel Hill: University of North Carolina Press, 1984.

Kowaleski-Wallace, Elizabeth, ed. *Encyclopedia of Feminist Literary Theory.* New York: Garland, 1997.

Kramarae, Cheris. *Women and Men Speaking: Frameworks for Analysis.* Rowley, MA: Newbury House, 1981.

Kristeva, Julia. *About Chinese Women.* New York: Urizen Books, 1977.

———. "Women's Time." *Signs* 7 (1981): 13–35.

Lakoff, Robin. *Language and Women's Place.* New York: Harper and Row, 1975.

Leavy, Barbara. *In Search of the Swan Maiden: A Narrative on Folklore and Gender.* New York: New York University Press, 1994.

Looser, Devoney, and E. Ann Kaplan, eds. *Generations: Academic Feminists in Dialogue.* Minneapolis: University of Minnesota Press, 1995.

McConnell-Ginet, Sally, Ruth Borker, and Nelly Furman, eds. *Women and Language in Literature and Society.* New York: Praeger, 1980.

Marks, Elaine, and Isabelle de Courtrivon, eds. *New French Feminisms: An Anthology.* Amherst: University of Massachusetts Press, 1980.

Martin, Wendy. *An American Triptych: Anne Bradstreet, Emily Dickinson, and Adrienne Rich.* Chapel Hill: University of North Carolina Press, 1984.

Miller, Nancy K. "The Text's Heroine: A Feminist Critic and Her Fictions." *Diacritics* 12 (1982): 48–53.

Millett, Kate. *Sexual Politics.* New York: Avon Books, 1970.

Mitchell, Juliet. *Psychoanalysis and Feminism.* New York: Pantheon, 1974.

———. *Women's Estate.* New York: Vintage Books, 1971.

———. *The Longest Revolution.* New York: Pantheon, 1984.

Moers, Ellen. *Literary Women.* New York: Doubleday, 1976.

Moi, Toril. *Sexual/Textual Politics: Feminist Literary Theory.* New York: Methuen, 1985.

Newton, Judith Lowder. *Women, Power, and Subversion: Social Strategies in British Fiction, 1778–1860.* Athens: University of Georgia Press, 1981.

———, and Deborah Rosenfelt, eds. *Feminist Criticism and Social Change.* New York: Methuen, 1985.

Nicholson, Linda, ed. *The Second Wave: A Reader in Feminist Theory.* New York: Routledge, 1997.

Poovey, Mary. *The Proper Lady and the Woman Writer: Ideology as Style in the Works of Mary Wollstonecraft, Mary Shelley, and Jane Austen.* Chicago: University of Chicago Press, 1984.

Rich, Adrienne. *On Lies, Secrets and Silence.* New York: Norton, 1979.

Robinson, Lillian. *Sex, Class and Culture.* Bloomington: Indiana University Press, 1978.

Rogers, Katherine M. *The Troublesome Helpmate: A History of Misogyny in Literature.* Seattle: University of Washington Press, 1966.

Ruthven, Kenneth K. *Feminist Literary Studies: An Introduction.* Cambridge: Cambridge University Press, 1984.

Showalter, Elaine. *A Literature of Their Own: British Women Novelists from Brontë to Lessing.* Princeton: Princeton University Press, 1977.

———, ed. *The New Feminist Criticism: Essays on Women, Literature, Theory.* New York: Pantheon, 1985.

————. *Sexual Anarchy: Gender and Culture at the Fin de Siècle*. New York: Viking, 1990.

Spacks, Patricia Meyer. *The Female Imagination*. New York: Knopf, 1975.

Spender, Dale. *Man Made Language*. London: Routledge and Kegan Paul, 1980.

Spivak, Gayatri Chakravorty. *In Other Worlds: Essays in Cultural Politics*. New York: Methuen, 1987.

Thorne, Barrie, Cheris Kramarae, and Nancy Henley, eds. *Language, Gender, and Society*. Rowley, MA: Newbury House, 1983.

Walker, Alice. *In Search of Our Mother's Gardens*. New York: Harcourt Brace Jovanovich, 1983.

Warhol, Robyn R., and Diane Price Herndl. *Feminisms: An Anthology of Literary Theory and Criticism*, 2nd ed. New York: Routledge, 1997.

Washington, Mary Helen. *Midnight Birds: Stories of Contemporary Black Women Writers*. Garden City, NY: Anchor Books, 1980.

Whelehan, Imelda, ed. *Modern Feminist Thought*. New York: NYU Press, 1995.

Zimmerman, Bonnie. "What Has Never Been: An Overview of Lesbian Feminist Literary Criticism." *Feminist Studies* 7 (1981): 451–75.

Nina Baym

b. 1936

Nina Baym's work has been instrumental in bringing about academic recognition of women's studies across the United States. Born in Princeton, New Jersey, Baym received her B.A. from Cornell University (1957) and her M.A. (1958) and Ph.D. (1963) in English from Harvard University. After receiving her doctorate, Baym taught English and American literature at the University of Illinois at Urbana-Champaign, where she became a full professor in 1972 and Director of the School of Humanities in 1976. Retired, she is now professor emerita at the University of Illinois at Urbana-Champaign. Baym has been a Guggenheim fellow (1975–76) and a fellow of the National Endowment for the Humanities (1982–83). She has served on the editorial boards of several major journals, including American Quarterly, New England Quarterly, *and* American Literature, *and is an editor of* The Norton Anthology of American Literature. *Her publications include* The Shape of Hawthorne's Career *(1976),* Woman's Fiction: A Guide to Novels by and about Women in America (1820–1870) *(1978),* Nathaniel Hawthorne and His Mother *(1982),* Novels, Readers, and Reviewers: Responses to Fiction in Antebellum America *(1984),* Feminism and American Literary History *(1992), and* American Women of Letters and the Nineteenth-Century Sciences *(2002). "Melodramas of Beset Manhood" is reprinted from* American Quarterly *33 (1981).*

Melodramas of Beset Manhood

How Theories of American Fiction Exclude Women Authors

This paper is about American literary criticism rather than American literature. It proceeds from the assumption that we never read American literature directly or freely, but always through the perspective allowed by theories. Theories account for the inclusion and exclusion of texts in anthologies, and theories account for the way we read them. My concern is with the fact that the theories controlling our reading of American literature have led to the exclusion of women authors from the canon.

Let me use my own practice as a case in point. In 1977 there was published a collection of essays on images of women in major British and American literature, to which I contributed.[1] The American field was divided chronologically among six critics, with four essays covering literature written prior to World War II. Taking seriously the charge that we were to focus only on the major figures, the four of us — working quite independently of each other — selected altogether only four women writers. Three of these were from the earliest period, a period which predates the novel: the poet Anne Bradstreet and the two diarists Mary Rowlandson and Sarah Kemble Knight. The fourth was Emily Dickinson. For the period between 1865 and 1940 no women were cited at all. The message that we — who were taking women as our subject — conveyed was clear: there have been almost no major women writers in America; the major novelists have all been men.

Now, when we wrote our essays we were not undertaking to reread all American literature and make our own decisions as to who the major authors were. That is the point: we accepted the going canon of major authors. As late as 1977, that canon did not include any women novelists. Yet, the critic who goes beyond what is accepted and tries to look at the totality of literary production in America quickly discovers that women authors have been active since the earliest days of settlement. Commercially and numerically they have probably dominated American literature since the middle of the nineteenth century. As long ago as 1854, Nathaniel Hawthorne complained to his publisher about the "damned mob of scribbling women" whose writings — he fondly imagined — were diverting the public from his own.

Names and figures help make this dominance clear. In the years between 1774 and 1799 — from the calling of the First Continental Congress to the close of the eighteenth century — a total of thirty-eight original works of fiction were published in this country.[2] Nine of these, appearing pseudonymously or anonymously, have not yet been attributed to any author. The remaining twenty-nine are the work of eighteen individuals, of whom four are women. One of these women, Susannah Rowson, wrote six of them, or more than a fifth of the total. Her most popular work, *Charlotte* (also known as *Charlotte Temple*), was printed three times in the decade it was published, nineteen times between 1800 and 1810, and eighty times by the middle of the nineteenth century. A novel by a second of the four women, Hannah Foster, was called *The Coquette* and had thirty editions by mid-nineteenth century. *Uncle Tom's Cabin*, by a woman, is probably the all-time biggest seller in American history. A woman, Mrs. E.D.E.N. Southworth, was probably the most widely read novelist in the nineteenth century. How is it possible for a critic or historian of American literature to leave these books, and these authors, out of the picture?

[1] Marlene Springer, ed., *What Manner of Woman: Essays on English and American Life and Literature* (New York: New York University Press, 1977). [Baym]

[2] See Lyle H. Wright, *American Fiction: A Contribution Towards a Bibliography*, vol. 1, *1774–1850*, 2d ed. (San Marino, Calif.: Huntington Library Press, 1969). [Baym]

I see three partial explanations for the critical invisibility of the many active women authors in America. The first is simple bias. The critic does not like the idea of women as writers, does not believe that women can be writers, and hence does not see them even when they are right before his eyes. His theory or his standards may well be nonsexist but his practice is not. Certainly, an *a priori* resistance to recognizing women authors as serious writers has functioned powerfully in the mind-set of a number of influential critics. One can amusingly demonstrate the inconsistencies between standard and practice in such critics, show how their minds slip out of gear when they are confronted with a woman author. But this is only a partial explanation.

A second possibility is that, in fact, women have not written the kind of work that we call "excellent," for reasons that are connected with their gender although separable from it. This is a serious possibility. For example, suppose we required a dense texture of classical allusion in all works that we called excellent. Then, the restriction of a formal classical education to men would have the effect of restricting authorship of excellent literature to men. Women would not have written excellent literature because social conditions hindered them. The reason, though gender-connected, would not be gender per se.

The point here is that the notion of the artist, or of excellence, has efficacy in a given time and reflects social realities. The idea of "good" literature is not only a personal preference, it is also a cultural preference. We can all think of species of women's literature that do not aim in any way to achieve literary excellence as society defines it: for example, the "Harlequin Romances." Until recently, only a tiny proportion of literary women aspired to artistry and literary excellence in the terms defined by their own culture. There tended to be a sort of immediacy in the ambitions of literary women leading them to professionalism rather than artistry, by choice as well as by social pressure and opportunity. The gender-related restrictions were really operative, and the responsible critic cannot ignore them. But again, these restrictions are only partly explanatory.

There are, finally, I believe, gender-related restrictions that do not arise out of cultural realities contemporary with the writing woman, but out of later critical theories. These theories may follow naturally from cultural realities pertinent to their own time, but they impose their concerns anachronistically, after the fact, on an earlier period. If one accepts current theories of American literature, one accepts as a consequence — perhaps not deliberately but nevertheless inevitably — a literature that is essentially male. This is the partial explanation that I shall now develop.

Let us begin where the earliest theories of American literature begin, with the hypothesis that American literature is to be judged less by its form than by its content. Traditionally, one ascertains literary excellence by comparing a writer's work with standards of performance that have been established by earlier authors, where formal mastery and innovation are paramount. But from its historical beginnings, American literary criticism has assumed that literature produced in this nation would have to be ground-breaking, equal to the challenge of the new nation, and completely original. Therefore, it could not be judged by referring it back to earlier achievements. The earliest American literary critics began to talk about the "most American" work rather than the "best" work because they knew no way to find out the best other than by comparing American with British writing. Such a criticism struck them as both unfair and unpatriotic. We had thrown off the political shackles of England; it would not do for us to be servile in our literature. Until a tradition of American literature developed its own inherent forms, the early critic looked for a standard of Americanness rather than a standard of excellence. Inevitably, perhaps, it came to seem that the quality of "Americanness," whatever it might be, *constituted* literary excellence for American authors. Beginning as a nationalistic enterprise, American literary criticism and theory has retained a nationalist orientation to this day.

Of course, the idea of Americanness is even more vulnerable to subjectivity than the idea of the best. When they speak of "most American," critics seldom mean the statistically most representative or most typical, the most read or the most sold. They have some qualitative essence in mind, and frequently their work develops as an explanation of this idea of "American" rather than a description and evaluation of selected authors. The predictable recurrence of the term "America" or "American" in works of literary criticism treating a dozen or fewer authors indicates that the critic has chosen his authors on the basis of their conformity to his idea of what is truly American. For examples: *American Renaissance, The Romance in America, Symbolism and American Literature, Form and Fable in American Fiction, The American Adam, The American Novel and Its Tradition, The Place of Style in American Literature* (a subtitle), *The Poetics of American Fiction* (another subtitle). But an idea of what is American is no more than an idea, needing demonstration. The critic all too frequently ends up using his chosen authors as demonstrations of Americanness, arguing through them to his definition.

So Marius Bewley explains in *The Eccentric Design* that "for the American artist there was no social surface responsive to his touch. The scene was crude, even beyond successful satire," but later, in a concluding chapter titled "The Americanness of the American Novel," he agrees that "this 'tradition' as I have set it up here has no room for the so-called realists and naturalists."[3] F. O. Matthiessen, whose *American Renaissance* enshrines five authors, explains that "the one common denominator of my five writers, uniting even Hawthorne and Whitman, was their devotion to the possibilities of democracy."[4] The jointly written *Literary History of the United States* proclaims in its "address to the reader" that American literary history "will be a history of the books of the great and the near-great writers in a literature which is most revealing when studied as a by-product of American experience."[5] And Joel Porte announces confidently in *The Romance in America* that "students of American literature . . . have provided a solid theoretical basis for establishing that the rise and growth of fiction in this country is dominated by our authors' conscious adherence to a tradition of non-realistic romance sharply at variance with the broadly novelistic mainstream of English writing. When there has been disagreement among recent critics as to the contours of American fiction, it has usually disputed, not the existence per se of a romance tradition, but rather the question of which authors, themes, and stylistic strategies *deserve* to be placed with certainty at the heart of that tradition" (emphasis added).[6]

Before he is through, the critic has had to insist that some works in America are much more American than others, and he is as busy excluding certain writers as "un-American" as he is including others. Such a proceeding in the political arena would be extremely suspect, but in criticism it has been the method of choice. Its final result goes far beyond the conclusion that only a handful of American works are very good. *That* statement is one we could agree with, since very good work is rare in any field. But it is odd indeed to argue that only a handful of American works are really American.[7]

Despite the theoretical room for an infinite number of definitions of Americanness, critics have generally agreed on it — although the shifting canon suggests that agreement may be a matter of fad rather than fixed objective qualities.[8] First, America as a nation must be the ultimate subject of the work. The author must be writing about aspects of experience and character that are American only, setting Americans off from other people and the country from other nations. The author must be writing his story specifically to display these aspects, to meditate on them, and to derive from them some generalizations and conclusions about "the" American experience. To Matthiessen the topic is the possibilities of

---

[3]Marius Bewley, *The Eccentric Design: Form in the Classic American Novel* (New York: Columbia University Press, 1963), pp. 15, 291. [Baym]

[4]F. O. Matthiessen, *American Renaissance* (New York: Oxford University Press, 1941), p. ix. [Baym]

[5]Robert E. Spiller et al., eds., *Literary History of the United States* (New York: Macmillan, 1959), p. xix. [Baym]

[6]Joel Porte, *The Romance in America: Studies in Cooper, Poe, Hawthorne, Melville, and James* (Middletown, Conn.: Wesleyan University Press, 1969), p. ix. [Baym]

[7]A good essay on this topic is William C. Spengemann's "What Is American Literature?" *Centennial Review* 22 (Spring 1978): 119–38. [Baym]

[8]See Jay B. Hubbell, *Who Are the Major American Authors?* (Durham, N.C.: Duke University Press, 1972). [Baym]

democracy; Sacvan Bercovitch (in *The Puritan Origins of the American Self*) finds it in American identity. Such content excludes, at one extreme, stories about universals, aspects of experience common to people in a variety of times and places — mutability, mortality, love, childhood, family, betrayal, loss. Innocence versus experience is an admissible theme *only* if innocence is the essence of the American character, for example.

But at the other extreme, the call for an overview of America means that detailed, circumstantial portrayals of some aspect of American life are also, peculiarly, inappropriate: stories of wealthy New Yorkers, Yugoslavian immigrants, Southern rustics. Jay B. Hubbell rather ingratiatingly admits as much when he writes, "in both my teaching and my research I had a special interest in literature as a reflection of American life and thought. This circumstance may explain in part why I found it difficult to appreciate the merits of the expatriates and why I was slow in doing justice to some of the New Critics. I was repelled by the sordid subject matter found in some of the novels written by Dreiser, Dos Passos, Faulkner, and some others."[9] Richard Poirier writes that "the books which in my view constitute a distinctive American tradition ... resist within their pages forces of environment that otherwise dominate the world," and he distinguishes this kind from "the fiction of Mrs. Wharton, Dreiser, or Howells."[10] The *Literary History of the United States* explains that "historically, [Edith Wharton] is likely to survive as the memorialist of a dying aristocracy."[11] And so on. These exclusions abound in all the works which form the stable core of American literary criticism at this time.

Along with Matthiessen, the most influential exponent of this exclusive Americanness is Lionel Trilling, and his work has particular applicability because it concentrates on the novel form. Here is a famous passage from his 1940 essay, "Reality in America," in which Trilling is criticizing Vernon Parrington's selection of authors in *Main Currents in American Thought:*

> A culture is not a flow, nor even a confluence: the form of its existence is struggle — or at least debate — it is nothing if not a dialectic. And in any culture there are likely to be certain artists who contain a large part of the dialectic within themselves, their meaning and power lying in their contradictions: they contain within themselves, it may be said, the very essence of the culture. To throw out Poe because he cannot be conveniently fitted into a theory of American culture ... to find his gloom to be merely personal and eccentric ... as Hawthorne's was ... to judge Melville's response to American life to be less noble than that of Bryant or of Greeley, to speak of Henry James as an escapist ... this is not merely to be mistaken in aesthetic judgment. Rather it is to examine without attention and from the point of view of a limited and essentially arrogant conception of reality the documents which are in some respects the most suggestive testimony to what America was and is, and of course to get no answer from them.[12]

Trilling's immediate purpose is to exclude Greeley and Bryant from the list of major authors and to include Poe, Melville, Hawthorne, and James. We probably share Trilling's aesthetic judgment. But note that he does not base his judgment on aesthetic grounds; indeed, he dismisses aesthetic judgment with the word "merely." He argues that Parrington has picked the wrong artists because he doesn't understand the culture. Culture is his real concern.

But what makes Trilling's notion of culture more valid than Parrington's? Trilling really has no argument; he resorts to such value-laden rhetoric as "a limited and essentially arrogant conception of reality" precisely because he cannot objectively establish his version of culture over Parrington's. For the moment, there are two significant conclusions to draw from this quotation. First, the disagreement is over the nature of our culture. Second, there is no disagreement

---

[9]Ibid., pp. 335–36. [Baym]

[10]Richard Poirier, *A World Elsewhere: The Place of Style in American Literature* (New York: Oxford University Press, 1966), p. 5. [Baym]

[11]Spiller et al., *Literary History of the United States*, p. 1211. [Baym]

[12]Lionel Trilling, *The Liberal Imagination* (Garden City, N.Y.: Anchor Books, 1950), pp. 7–9. [Baym]

over the value of literature — it is valued as a set of "documents" which provide "suggestive testimony to what America was and is."

One might think that an approach like this which is subjective, circular, and in some sense nonliterary or even antiliterary would not have had much effect. But clearly Trilling was simply carrying on a longstanding tradition of searching for cultural essence, and his essays gave the search a decided and influential direction toward the notion of cultural essence as some sort of tension. Trilling succeeded in getting rid of Bryant and Greeley, and his choice of authors is still dominant. They all turn out — and not by accident — to be white, middle-class, male, of Anglo-Saxon derivation or at least from an ancestry which had settled in this country before the big waves of immigration which began around the middle of the nineteenth century. In every case, however, the decision made by these men to become professional authors pushed them slightly to one side of the group to which they belonged. This slight alienation permitted them to belong, and yet not to belong, to the so-called "mainstream." These two aspects of their situation — their membership in the dominant middle-class white Anglo-Saxon group, and their modest alienation from it — defined their boundaries, enabling them to "contain within themselves" the "contradictions" that, in Trilling's view, constitute the "very essence of the culture." I will call the literature they produced, which Trilling assesses so highly, a "consensus criticism of the consensus."

This idea plainly excludes many groups but it might not seem necessarily to exclude women. In fact, nineteenth-century women authors were overwhelmingly white, middle-class, and Anglo-Saxon in origin. Something more than what is overtly stated by Trilling (and others cited below) is added to exclude them. What critics have done is to assume, for reasons shortly to be expounded, that the women writers invariably represented the consensus, rather than the criticism of it; to assume that their gender made them part of the consensus in a way that prevented them from partaking in the criticism. The presence of these women and their works is acknowledged in literary theory and history as an impediment and

obstacle, that which the essential American literature had to criticize as its chief task.

So, in his lively and influential book of 1960, *Love and Death in the American Novel*, Leslie Fiedler describes women authors as creators of the "flagrantly bad best-seller" against which "our best fictionists" — all male — have had to struggle for "their integrity and their livelihoods."[13] And, in a 1978 reader's introduction to an edition of Charles Brockden Brown's *Wieland*, Sydney J. Krause and S. W. Reid write as follows:

> What it meant for Brown personally, and belles lettres in America historically, that he should have decided to write professionally is a story unto itself. Americans simply had no great appetite for serious literature in the early decades of the Republic — certainly nothing of the sort with which they devoured ... the ubiquitous melodramas of beset womanhood, "tales of truth," like Susanna Rowson's *Charlotte Temple* and Hannah Foster's *The Coquette*.[14]

There you see what has happened to the woman writer. She has entered literary history as the enemy. The phrase "tales of truth" is put in quotes by the critics, as though to cast doubt on the very notion that a "melodrama of beset womanhood" could be either true or important. At the same time, ironically, they are proposing for our serious consideration, as a candidate for intellectually engaging literature, a highly melodramatic novel with an improbable plot, inconsistent characterizations, and excesses of style that have posed tremendous problems for all students of Charles Brockden Brown. But by this strategy it becomes possible to begin major American fiction historically with male rather than female authors. The certainty here that stories about women could not contain the essence of American culture means that the matter of American experience is inherently male. And this makes it highly unlikely that American women would write fiction encompassing such experience. I would suggest that the theoretical model of a

[13]Leslie Fiedler, *Love and Death in the American Novel* (New York: Criterion Books, 1960), p. 93. [Baym]
[14]Charles Brockden Brown, *Wieland*, ed. Sydney J. Krause and S. W. Reid (Kent, Ohio: Kent State University Press, 1978), p. xii. [Baym]

story which may become the vehicle of cultural essence is: "a melodrama of beset manhood." This melodrama is presented in a fiction which, as we will later see, can be taken as representative of the author's literary experience, his struggle for integrity and livelihood against flagrantly bad best-sellers written by women. Personally beset in a way that epitomizes the tensions of our culture, the male author produces his melodramatic testimony to our culture's essence — so the theory goes.

Remember that the search for cultural essence demands a relatively uncircumstantial kind of fiction, one which concentrates on national universals (if I may be pardoned the paradox). This search has identified a sort of nonrealistic narrative, a romance, a story free to catch an essential, idealized American character, to intensify his essence and convey his experience in a way that ignores details of an actual social milieu. This nonrealistic or antisocial aspect of American fiction is noted — as a fault — by Trilling in a 1947 essay, "Manners, Morals, and the Novel." Curiously, Trilling here attacks the same group of writers he had rescued from Parrington in "Reality in America." But, never doubting that his selection represents "the" American authors, he goes ahead with the task that really interests him — criticizing the culture through its representative authors:

> The novel in America diverges from its classic [i.e., British] intention which . . . is the investigation of the problem of reality beginning in the social field. The fact is that American writers of genius have not turned their minds to society. Poe and Melville were quite apart from it; the reality they sought was only tangential to society. Hawthorne was acute when he insisted that he did not write novels but romances — he thus expressed his awareness of the lack of social texture in his work. . . . In America in the nineteenth century, Henry James was alone in knowing that to scale the moral and aesthetic heights in the novel one had to use the ladder of social observation.[15]

Within a few years after publication of Trilling's essay, a group of Americanists took its rather disapproving description of American novelists and found in this nonrealism or romanticism

[15]Trilling, *The Liberal Imagination*, p. 206. [Baym]

the essentially American quality they had been seeking. The idea of essential Americanness then developed in such influential works of criticism as *Virgin Land* by Henry Nash Smith (1950), *Symbolism and American Literature* by Charles Feidelson (1953), *The American Adam* by R. W. B. Lewis (1955), *The American Novel and Its Tradition* by Richard Chase (1957), and *Form and Fable in American Fiction* by Daniel G. Hoffman (1961). These works, and others like them, were of sufficiently high critical quality, and sufficiently like each other, to compel assent to the picture of American literature that they presented. They used sophisticated New Critical close-reading techniques to identify a myth of America which had nothing to do with the classical fictionist's task of chronicling probable people in recognizable social situations.

The myth narrates a confrontation of the American individual, the pure American self divorced from specific social circumstances, with the promise offered by the idea of America. This promise is the deeply romantic one that in this new land, untrammeled by history and social accident, a person will be able to achieve complete self-definition. Behind this promise is the assurance that individuals come before society, that they exist in some meaningful sense prior to, and apart from, societies in which they happen to find themselves. The myth also holds that, as something artificial and secondary to human nature, society exerts an unmitigatedly destructive pressure on individuality. To depict it at any length would be a waste of artistic time; and there is only one way to relate it to the individual — as an adversary.

One may believe all this and yet look in vain for a way to tell a believable story that could free the protagonist from society or offer the promise of such freedom, because nowhere on earth do individuals live apart from social groups. But in America, given the original reality of large tracts of wilderness, the idea seems less a fantasy, more possible in reality or at least more believable in literary treatment. Thus it is that the essential quality of America comes to reside in its unsettled wilderness and the opportunities that such a wilderness offers to the individual as the medium on which he may inscribe, unhindered, his own destiny and his own nature.

As the nineteenth century wore on, and settlements spread across the wilderness, the struggle of the individual against society became more and more central to the myth; where, let's say, Thoreau could leave in chapter I of *Walden,* Huckleberry Finn has still not made his break by the end of chapter 42 (the conclusion) of the book that bears his name. Yet one finds a struggle against society as early as the earliest Leatherstocking tale (*The Pioneers,* 1823). In a sense, this supposed promise of America has always been known to be delusory. Certainly by the twentieth century the myth has been transmuted into an avowedly hopeless quest for unencumbered space *(On the Road),* or the evocation of flight for its own sake (*Rabbit, Run* and *Henderson the Rain King*), or as pathetic acknowledgment of loss — for example, the close of *The Great Gatsby* where the narrator Nick Carraway summons up "the old island here that flowered once for Dutch sailors' eyes — a fresh, green breast of the new world . . . the last and greatest of all human dreams" where man is "face to face for the last time in history with something commensurate to his capacity for wonder."

We are all very familiar with this myth of America in its various fashionings, and owing to the selective vision that has presented this myth to us as the whole story, many of us are unaware of how much besides it has been created by literary Americans. Keeping our eyes on this myth, we need to ask whether anything about it puts it outside women's reach. In one sense, and on one level, the answer is no. The subject of this myth is supposed to stand for human nature, and if men and women share a common human nature, then all can respond to its values, its promises, and its frustrations. And in fact, as a teacher I find women students responsive to the myth insofar as its protagonist is concerned. It is true, of course, that in order to represent some kind of believable flight into the wilderness, one must select a protagonist with a certain believable mobility, and mobility has until recently been a male prerogative in our society. Nevertheless, relatively few men are actually mobile to the extent demanded by the story, and hence the story is really not much more vicarious, in this regard, for women than for men. The problem is thus not to be located in the protagonist or his gender per se; the problem is with the other participants in his story — the entrammeling society and the promising landscape. For both of these are depicted in unmistakably feminine terms, and this gives a sexual character to the protagonist's story which does, indeed, limit its applicability to women. And this sexual definition has melodramatic, misogynist implications.

In these stories, the encroaching, constricting, destroying society is represented with particular urgency in the figure of one or more women. There are several possible reasons why this might be so. It seems to be a fact of life that we all — women and men alike — experience social conventions and responsibilities and obligations first in the persons of women, since women are entrusted by society with the task of rearing young children. Not until he reaches mid-adolescence does the male connect up with other males whose primary task is socialization; but at about this time — if he is heterosexual — his lovers and spouses become the agents of a permanent socialization and domestication. Thus, although women are not the source of social power, they are experienced as such. And although not all women are engaged in socializing the young, the young do not encounter women who are not. So from the point of view of the young man, the only kind of women who exist are entrappers and domesticators.

For heterosexual man, these socializing women are also the locus of powerful attraction. First, because everybody has social and conventional instincts: second, because his deepest emotional attachments are to women. This attraction gives urgency and depth to the protagonist's rejection of society. To do it, he must project onto the woman those attractions that he feels, and cast her in the melodramatic role of temptress, antagonist, obstacle — a character whose mission in life seems to be to ensnare him and deflect him from life's important purposes of self-discovery and self-assertion. (A Puritan would have said: from communion with Divinity.) As Richard Chase writes in *The American Novel and Its Tradition,* "The myth requires celibacy." It is partly against his own sexual urges that the male must struggle, and so he perceives the socializing and domesticating woman as a doubly powerful threat; for this reason, Chase goes on to state, neither Cooper nor "any other American novelist until the age of James and Edith Wharton" could imagine "a fully developed woman of sexual age."[16] Yet in making this statement, Chase is talking about his myth rather than Cooper's. (One should add that, for a homosexual male, the demands of society that he link himself for life to a woman make for a particularly misogynist version of this aspect of the American myth, for the hero is propelled not by a rejected attraction but by true revulsion.) Both heterosexual and homosexual versions of the myth cooperate with the hero's perceptions and validate the notion of woman as threat.

Such a portrayal of women is likely to be uncongenial, if not basically incomprehensible, to a woman. It is not likely that women will write books in which women play this part; and it is by no means the case that most novels by American men reproduce such a scheme. Even major male authors prominent in the canon have other ways of depicting women: for example, Cooper's *Pathfinder* and *The Pioneers*, Hemingway's *For Whom the Bell Tolls*, Fitzgerald's *The Beautiful and Damned*. The novels of Henry James and William Dean Howells pose a continual challenge to the masculinist bias of American critical theory. And in one work — *The Scarlet Letter* — a "fully developed woman of sexual age" who is the novel's protagonist has been admitted into the canon, but only by virtue of strenuous critical revisions of the text that remove Hester Prynne from the center of the novel and make her subordinate to Arthur Dimmesdale.

So Leslie Fiedler, in *Love and Death in the American Novel*, writes this of *The Scarlet Letter*:

It is certainly true, in terms of the plot, that Chillingworth drives the minister toward confession and penance, while Hester would have lured him to evasion and flight. But this means, for all of Hawthorne's equivocations, that the eternal feminine does not draw us on toward grace, rather that

the woman promises only madness and damnation. . . . [Hester] is the female temptress of Puritan mythology, but also, though sullied, the secular madonna of sentimental Protestantism.[17]

In the rhetorical "us" Fiedler presumes that all readers are men, that the novel is an act of communication among and about males. His characterization of Hester as one or another myth or image makes it impossible for the novel to be in any way about Hester as a human being. Giving the novel so highly specific a gender reference, Fiedler makes it inaccessible to women and limits its reference to men in comparison to the issues that Hawthorne was treating in the story. Not the least of these issues was, precisely, the human reference of a woman's tale.

Amusingly, then, since he has produced this warped reading, Fiedler goes on to condemn the novel for its sexual immaturity. *The Scarlet Letter* is integrated into Fiedler's general exposure of the inadequacies of the American male — inadequacies which, as his treatment of Hester shows, he holds women responsible for. The melodrama here is not Hawthorne's but Fiedler's — the American critic's melodrama of beset manhood. Of course, women authors as major writers are notable and inevitably absent from Fiedler's chronicle.

In fact, many books by women — including such major authors as Edith Wharton, Ellen Glasgow, and Willa Cather — project a version of the particular myth we are speaking of but cast the main character as a woman. When a woman takes the central role, it follows naturally that the socializer and domesticator will be a man. This is the situation in *The Scarlet Letter*. Hester is beset by the male reigning oligarchy and by Dimmesdale, who passively tempts her and is responsible for fathering her child. Thereafter, Hester (as the myth requires) elects celibacy, as do many heroines in versions of this myth by women: Thea in Cather's *The Song of the Lark*, Dorinda in Glasgow's *Barren Ground*, Anna Leath in Wharton's *The Reef*. But what is written

---

[16]Richard Chase, *The American Novel and Its Tradition* (Garden City, N.Y.: Anchor Books, 1957), pp. 55, 64. [Baym]

[17]Fiedler, *Love and Death in the American Novel*, p. 236. [Baym]

in the criticism about these celibate women? They are said to be untrue to the imperatives of their gender, which require marriage, childbearing, domesticity. Instead of being read as a woman's version of the myth, such novels are read as stories of the frustration of female nature. Stories of female frustration are not perceived as commenting on, or containing, the essence of our culture, and so we do not find them in the canon.

So the role of entrapper and impediment in the melodrama of beset manhood is reserved for women. Also, the role of the beckoning wilderness, the attractive landscape, is given a deeply feminine quality. Landscape is deeply imbued with female qualities, as society is; but where society is menacing and destructive, landscape is compliant and supportive. It has the attributes simultaneously of a virginal bride and a non-threatening mother; its female qualities are articulated with respect to a male angle of vision: what can nature do for me, asks the hero, what can it give me?

Of course, nature has been feminine and maternal from time immemorial, and Henry Nash Smith's *Virgin Land* picks up a timeless archetype in its title. The basic nature of the image leads one to forget about its potential for imbuing with sexual meanings any story in which it is used, and the gender implications of a female landscape have only recently begun to be studied. Recently, Annette Kolodny has studied the traditional canon from this approach.[18] She theorizes that the hero, fleeing a society that has been imagined as feminine, then imposes on nature some ideas of women which, no longer subject to the correcting influence of real-life experience, become more and more fantastic. The fantasies are infantile, concerned with power, mastery, and total gratification: the all-nurturing mother, the all-passive bride. Whether one accepts all the Freudian or Jungian implications of her argument, one cannot deny the way in which heroes of American myth turn to nature as sweetheart and nurture, anticipating the satisfaction of all desires

through her and including among these the desires for mastery and power. A familiar passage that captures these ideas is one already quoted: Carraway's evocation of the "fresh green breast" of the New World. The fresh greenness is the virginity that offers itself to the sailors, but the breast promises maternal solace and delight. *The Great Gatsby* contains our two images of women: while Carraway evokes the impossible dream of a maternal landscape, he blames a nonmaternal woman, the socialite Daisy, for her failure to satisfy Gatsby's desires. The true adversary, of course, is Tom Buchanan, but he is hidden, as it were, behind Daisy's skirts.

I have said that women are not likely to cast themselves as antagonists in a man's story; they are even less likely, I suggest, to cast themselves as virgin land. The lack of fit between their own experience and the fictional role assigned to them is even greater in the second instance than in the first. If women portray themselves as brides or mothers it will not be in terms of the mythic landscape. If a woman puts a female construction on nature — as she certainly must from time to time, given the archetypal female resonance of the image — she is likely to write of it as more active, or to stress its destruction or violation. On the other hand, she might adjust the heroic myth to her own psyche by making nature out to be male — as, for example, Willa Cather seems to do in *O Pioneers!* But a violated landscape or a male nature does not fit the essential American pattern as critics have defined it, and hence these literary images occur in an obscurity that criticism cannot see. Thus, one has an almost classic example of the double bind. When the woman writer creates a story that conforms to the expected myth, it is not recognized for what it is because of a superfluous sexual specialization in the myth as it is entertained in the critics' minds. (Needless to say, many male novelists also entertain this version of the myth, and do not find the masculinist bias with which they imbue it to be superfluous. It is possible that some of these novelists, especially those who write in an era in which literary criticism is a powerful influence, have formed their ideas from their reading in criticism.) But if she does not conform to the myth, she is understood to be writing minor or trivial literature.

[18]Annette Kolodny, *The Lay of the Land: Metaphor As Experience and History in American Life and Letters* (Chapel Hill: University of North Carolina Press, 1975). [Baym]

Two remaining points can be treated much more briefly. The description of the artist and of the act of writing which emerges when the critic uses the basic American story as his starting point contains many attributes of the basic story itself. This description raises the exclusion of women to a more abstract, theoretical — and perhaps more pernicious — level. Fundamentally, the idea is that the artist writing a story of this essential American kind is engaging in a task very much like the one performed by his mythic hero. In effect, the artist writing his narrative is imitating the mythic encounter of hero and possibility in the safe confines of his study; or, reversing the temporal order, one might see the mythic encounter of hero and possibility as a projection of the artist's situation.

Although this idea is greatly in vogue at the moment, it has a history. Here, for example, is Richard Chase representing the activity of writing in metaphors of discovery and exploration, as though the writer were a hero in the landscape: "The American novel has usually seemed content to explore . . . the remarkable and in some ways unexampled territories of life in the New World and to reflect its anomalies and dilemmas. It has . . . wanted . . . to discover a new place and a new state of mind."[19] Richard Poirier takes the idea further:

> The most interesting American books are an image of the creation of America itself. . . . They carry the metaphoric burden of a great dream of freedom — of the expansion of national consciousness into the vast spaces of a continent and the absorption of those spaces into ourselves. . . . The classic American writers try through style temporarily to free the hero (and the reader) from systems, to free them from the pressures of time, biology, economics, and from the social forces which are ultimately the undoing of American heroes and quite often of their creators. . . . The strangeness of American fiction has . . . to do . . . with the environment [the novelist] tries to create for his hero, usually his surrogate.[20]

The implicit union of creator and protagonist is made specific and overt at the end of Poirier's passage here. The ideas of Poirier and Chase, and others like them, are summed up in an anthology called *Theories of American Literature*, edited by Donald M. Kartiganer and Malcolm A. Griffith. The editors write, "It is as if with each new work our writers feel they must invent again the complete world of a literary form." (Yet, the true subject is not what the writers feel, but what the critics think they feel.) "Such a condition of nearly absolute freedom to create has appeared to our authors both as possibility and liability, an utter openness suggesting limitless opportunity for the imagination, or an enormous vacancy in which they create from nothing. For some it has meant an opportunity to play Adam, to assume the role of an original namer of experience.[21] One can see in this passage the transference of the American myth from the Adamic hero *in* the story to the Adamic creator *of* the story, and the reinterpretation of the American myth as a metaphor for the American artist's situation.

This myth of artistic creation, assimilating the act of writing novels to the Adamic myth, imposes on artistic creation all the gender-based restrictions that we have already examined in that myth. The key to identifying an "Adamic writer" is the formal appearance, or, more precisely, the *informal* appearance, of his novel. The unconventionality is interpreted as a direct representation of the open-ended experience of exploring and taming the wilderness, as well as a rejection of "society" as it is incorporated in conventional literary forms. There is no place for a woman author in this scheme. Her roles in the drama of creation are those allotted to her in a male melodrama: either she is to be silent, like nature, or she is the creator of conventional works, the spokesperson of society. What she might do as an innovator in her own right is not to be perceived.

In recent years, some refinements of critical theory coming from the Yale and Johns Hopkins and Columbia schools have added a new variant to the idea of creation as a male province. I quote from a 1979 book entitled *Home as Found* by

---

[19]Chase, *American Novel*, p. 5. [Baym]
[20]Poirier, *A World Elsewhere*, pp. 3, 5, 9. [Baym]

[21]Donald M. Kartiganer and Malcolm A. Griffith, eds., *Theories of American Literature: The Critical Perspective* (New York: Macmillan, 1962), pp. 4–5. [Baym]

Eric Sundquist. The author takes the idea that in writing a novel the artist is really writing a narrative about himself and proposes this addition:

> Writing a narrative about oneself may represent an extremity of Oedipal usurpation or identification, a bizarre act of self fathering. . . . American authors have been particularly obsessed with *fathering* a tradition of their own, with becoming their "own sires." . . . The struggle . . . is central to the crisis of representation, and hence of style, that allows American authors to find in their own fantasies those of a nation and to make of those fantasies a compelling and instructive literature.[22]

These remarks derive clearly from the work of such critics as Harold Bloom, as any reader of recent critical theory will note. The point for our purpose is the facile translation of the verb "to author" into the verb "to father," with the profound gender restrictions of that translation unacknowledged. According to this formulation, insofar as the author writes about a character who is his surrogate — which, apparently, he always does — he is trying to become his own father.

We can scarcely deny that men think a good deal about, and are profoundly affected by, relations with their fathers. The theme of fathers and sons is perennial in world literature. Somewhat more spaciously, we recognize that intergenerational conflict, usually perceived from the point of view of the young, is a recurrent literary theme, especially in egalitarian cultures. Certainly, this idea involves the question of authority, and "authority" is a notion related to that of "the author." And there is some gender-specific significance involved since authority in most cultures that we know tends to be invested in adult males. But the theory has built from these useful and true observations to a restriction of literary creation to a sort of therapeutic act that can only be performed by men. If literature is the attempt to *father* oneself by the author, then every act of

writing by a woman is both perverse and absurd. And, of course, it is bound to fail.

Since this particular theory of the act of writing is drawn from psychological assumptions that are not specific to American literature, it may be argued that there is no need to confine it to American authors. In fact, Harold Bloom's *Anxiety of Influence,* defining literature as a struggle between fathers and sons, or the struggle of sons to escape from their fathers, is about British literature.[23] And so is Edward Said's book *Beginnings,* which chronicles the history of the nineteenth-century British novel as exemplification of what he calls "filiation." His discussion omits Jane Austen, George Eliot, all three Brontë sisters, Mrs. Gaskell, Mrs. Humphrey Ward — not a sign of a woman author is found in his treatment of Victorian fiction. The result is a revisionist approach to British fiction that recasts it in the accepted image of the American myth. Ironically, just at the time that feminist critics are discovering more and more important women, the critical theorists have seized upon a theory that allows the women less and less presence. This observation points up just how significantly the critic is engaged in the act of *creating* literature.

Ironically, then, one concludes that in pushing the theory of American fiction to this extreme, critics have "deconstructed" it by creating a tool with no particular American reference. In pursuit of the uniquely American, they have arrived at a place where Americanness has vanished into the depths of what is alleged to be the universal male psyche. The theory of American fiction has boiled down to the phrase in my title: a melodrama of beset manhood. What a reduction this is of the enormous variety of fiction written in this country, by both women and men! And, ironically, nothing could be further removed from Trilling's idea of the artist as embodiment of a culture. As in the working out of all theories, its weakest link has found it out and broken the chain.

---

[22]Eric J. Sundquist, *Home as Found: Authority and Genealogy in Nineteenth-Century American Literature* (Baltimore: Johns Hopkins University Press, 1979), pp. xviii–xix. [Baym]

[23]See Bloom, p. 1155.

Sandra M. Gilbert

b. 1936

Susan Gubar

b. 1944

Sandra M. Gilbert and Susan Gubar are best known for their collaborative explorations of women's literary tradition. They have co-authored The Madwoman in the Attic: The Woman Writer and the Nineteenth-Century Literary Imagination *(1979) and have extended their tracing of the special characteristics of women's writing into the twentieth century in a three-volume sequel collectively entitled* No Man's Land, *the volumes of which are separately titled* The War of the Words *(1988),* Sexchanges *(1991), and* Letters from the Front *(1994). They have also coedited* Shakespeare's Sisters: Feminist Essays on Women Poets *(1979) and* The Norton Anthology of Literature by Women, *second edition (1996), which provides canonical treatment of literature by women in English for college courses and have coauthored* Masterpiece Theatre: An Academic Melodrama *(1995). Both Gilbert and Gubar were born in New York City. Sandra Mortola Gilbert took a B.A. at Cornell (1957), an M.A. at New York University (1961), and a Ph.D. at Columbia (1968). After appointments at Indiana University and Princeton, she is now professor of English at the University of California at Davis. Throughout her career Gilbert has written poetry of her own; her most recent volumes are* Ghost Volcano *(1995),* Kissing the Bread *(2000), and* Inventions of Farewell *(2001). Susan David Gubar, Distinguished Professor of English at Indiana University at Bloomington, received her B.A. from City College of New York (1965), her M.A. from the University of Michigan (1968), and her Ph.D. from the University of Iowa (1972). Gubar's career includes a Guggenheim fellowship (1983–84) and teaching at the University of Illinois and at Tufts. Gubar has written numerous essays on eighteenth-century literature, science fiction and fantasy, and contemporary women's writing. Gubar's recent solo books have been* Racechanges: White Skin Black Face in American Culture *(1997),* Critical Condition: Feminism at the Turn of the Century *(2000), and* Poetry after Auschwitz *(2003). "Infection in the Sentence" is the second chapter of* The Madwoman in the Attic.

From *Infection in the Sentence: The Woman Writer and the Anxiety of Authorship*

*The man who does not know sick women does not
know women.* — S. WEIR MITCHELL

*I try to describe this long limitation, hoping that
with such power as is now mine, and such use of
language as is within that power, this will convince
any one who cares about it that this "living" of
mine had been done under a heavy handicap. . . .*
— CHARLOTTE PERKINS GILMAN

A Word dropped careless on a Page
May stimulate an eye
When folded in perpetual seam
The Wrinkled Maker lie

Infection in the sentence breeds
We may inhale Despair
At distances of Centuries
From the Malaria — — EMILY DICKINSON

I stand in the ring
in the dead city
and tie on the red shoes
. . . .

They are not mine,
they are my mother's,
her mother's before,
handed down like an heirloom
but hidden like shameful letters.

— ANNE SEXTON

What does it mean to be a woman writer in a culture whose fundamental definitions of literary
authority are, as we have seen, both overtly and
covertly patriarchal? If the vexed and vexing
polarities of angel and monster, sweet dumb
Snow White and fierce mad Queen, are major
images literary tradition offers women, how
does such imagery influence the ways in which
women attempt the pen? If the Queen's
looking glass speaks with the King's voice, how
do its perpetual kingly admonitions affect the
Queen's own voice? Since his is the chief voice
she hears, does the Queen try to sound like the
King, imitating his tone, his inflections, his phrasing, his point of view? Or does she "talk back" to

him in her own vocabulary, her own timbre, insisting on her own viewpoint? We believe these are
basic questions feminist literary criticism — both
theoretical and practical — must answer, and consequently they are questions to which we shall
turn again and again, not only in this chapter but
in all our readings of nineteenth-century literature
by women.

Dis-eased and infected by the sentences of patriarchy, yet unable to deny the urgency of that
"poet-fire"[1] she felt within herself, what strategies
did the woman writer develop for overcoming her
anxiety of authorship? How did she dance out of
the looking glass of the male text into a tradition
that enabled her to create her own authority?
Denied the economic, social, and psychological
status ordinarily essential to creativity; denied the
right, skill, and education to tell their own stories
with confidence, women who did not retreat into
angelic silence seem at first to have had very limited opinions. On the one hand, they could accept
the "parsley wreath"[2] of self-denial, writing in
"lesser" genres — children's books, letters,
diaries — or limiting their readership to "mere"
women like themselves and producing what
George Eliot called "Silly Novels by Lady
Novelists."[3] On the other hand, they could
become males *manqués,* mimics who disguised
their identities and, denying themselves, produced most frequently a literature of bad faith and
inauthenticity. Given such weak solutions to what
appears to have been an overwhelming problem,

---

[1]Gilbert and Gubar allude to Elizabeth Barrett Browning's
sonnet to George Sand.

[2]As opposed to the laurel wreath traditionally given to
(male) poets of distinction.

[3]See George Eliot, "Silly Novels by Lady Novelists,"
Westminster Review 64 (1856): 442–61. [Gilbert and Gubar]

how could there be a great tradition of literature by women? Yet, as we shall show, there is just such a tradition, a tradition especially encompassing the works of nineteenth-century women writers who found viable ways of circumventing the problematic strategies we have just outlined.

Inappropriate as male-devised genres must always have seemed, some women have always managed to work seriously in them. Indeed, when we examine the great works written by nineteenth-century women poets and novelists, we soon notice two striking facts. First, an extraordinary number of literary women either eschewed or grew beyond both female "modesty" and male mimicry. From Austen to Dickinson, these female artists all dealt with central female experiences from a specifically female perspective. But this distinctively feminine aspect of their art has been generally ignored by critics because the most successful women writers often seem to have channeled their female concerns into secret or at least obscure corners. In effect, such women have created submerged meanings, meanings hidden within or behind the more accessible, "public" content of their works, so that their literature could be read and appreciated even when its vital concern with female dispossession and disease was ignored. Second, the writing of these women often seems "odd" in relation to the predominantly male literary history defined by the standards of what we have called patriarchal poetics. Neither Augustans nor Romantics, neither Victorian sages nor Pre-Raphaelite sensualists, many of the most distinguished late eighteenth-century and nineteenth-century English and American women writers do not seem to "fit" into any of those categories to which our literary historians have accustomed us. Indeed, to many critics and scholars, some of these literary women look like isolated eccentrics.

We may legitimately wonder, however, if the second striking fact about nineteenth-century literature by women may not in some sense be a function of the first. Could the "oddity" of this work be associated with women's secret but insistent struggle to transcend their anxiety of authorship? Could the "isolation" and apparent "eccentricity" of these women really represent their common female struggle to solve the problem of what Anne Finch[4] called the literary woman's "fall," as well as their common female search for an aesthetic that would yield a healthy space in an overwhelmingly male "Palace of Art"? Certainly when we consider the "oddity" of women's writing in relation to its submerged content, it begins to seem that when women did not turn into male mimics or accept the "parsley wreath" they may have attempted to transcend their anxiety of authorship by *revising* male genres, using them to record their own dreams and their own stories *in disguise*. Such writers, therefore, both participated in and — to use one of Harold Bloom's key terms[5] — "swerved" from the central sequences of male literary history, enacting a uniquely female process of revision and redefinition that necessarily caused them to seem "odd." At the same time, while they achieved essential authority by telling their own stories, these writers allayed their distinctively female anxieties of authorship by following Emily Dickinson's famous (and characteristically female) advice to "Tell all the Truth but tell it slant — ."[6] In short, like the twentieth-century American poet H. D., who declared her aesthetic strategy by entitling one of her novels *Palimpsest,*[7] women from Jane Austen and Mary Shelley to Emily Brontë and Emily Dickinson produced literary works that are in some sense palimpsestic, works whose surface designs conceal or obscure deeper, less accessible (and less socially acceptable) levels of meaning. Thus these authors managed the difficult task of achieving true female literary authority by simultaneously conforming to and subverting patriarchal literary standards.

Of course, as the allegorical figure of Duessa[8] suggests, men have always accused women of the

---

[4]The Countess of Winchilsea (1661–1720), a poet whose *Miscellanies* was published in 1713.

[5]See Bloom, p. 1155.

[6]J. 1129, *The Complete Poems of Emily Dickinson,* 3 vols., ed. Thomas H. Johnson (Cambridge, MA: The Belknap Press of Harvard University Press, 1955). [Gilbert and Gubar]

[7]A palimpsest is a manuscript that has been erased and written over.

[8]In Spenser's *Faerie Queene,* Duessa is the daughter of Falsehood and Shame.

duplicity that is essential to the literary strategies we are describing here. In part, at least, such accusations are well founded, both in life and in art. As in the white-black relationship, the dominant group in the male-female relationship rightly fears and suspects that the docility of the subordinate caste masks rebellious passions. Moreover, just as blacks did in the master-slave relationships of the American South, women in patriarchy have traditionally cultivated accents of acquiescence in order to gain freedom to live their lives on their own terms, if only in the privacy of their own thoughts. Interestingly, indeed, several feminist critics have recently used Frantz Fanon's model of colonialism to describe the relationship between male (parent) culture and female (colonized) literature.[9] But with only one language at their disposal, women writers in England and America had to be even more adept at doubletalk than their colonized counterparts. We shall see, therefore, that in publicly presenting acceptable facades for private and dangerous visions women writers have long used a wide range of tactics to obscure but not obliterate their most subversive impulses. Along with the twentieth-century American painter Judy Chicago, any one of these artists might have noted that "formal issues" were often "something that my content had to be hidden behind in order for my work to be taken seriously." And with Judy Chicago, too, any one of these women might have confessed that "Because of this duplicity, there always appeared to be something 'not quite right' about my pieces according to the prevailing aesthetic."[10]

To be sure, male writers also "swerve" from their predecessors, and they too produce literary texts whose revolutionary messages are concealed behind stylized facades. The most original male writers, moreover, sometimes seem "not quite right" to those readers we have recently come to call "establishment" critics. As Bloom's theory of the anxiety of influence implies, however, and as our analysis of the metaphor of literary paternity also suggests, there are powerful paradigms of male intellectual struggle which enable the male writer to explain his rebelliousness, his "swerving," and his "originality" both to himself and to the world, no matter how many readers think him "not quite right." In a sense, therefore, he conceals his revolutionary energies only so that he may more powerfully reveal them, and swerves or rebels so that he may triumph by founding a new order, since his struggle against his precursor is a "battle of strong equals."

For the woman writer, however, concealment is not a military gesture but a strategy born of fear and dis-ease. Similarly, a literary "swerve" is not a motion by which the writer prepares for a victorious accession to power but a necessary evasion. Locked into structures created by and for men, eighteenth- and nineteenth-century women writers did not so much rebel against the prevailing aesthetic as feel guilty about their inability to conform to it. With little sense of a viable female culture, such women were plainly much troubled by the fact that they needed to communicate truths which other (i.e. male) writers apparently never felt or expressed. Conditioned to doubt their own authority anyway, women writers who wanted to describe what, in Dickinson's phrase, is "not brayed of tongue"[11] would find it easier to doubt themselves than the censorious voices of society. The evasions and concealments of their art are therefore far more elaborate than those of most male writers. For, given the patriarchal biases of nineteenth-century literary culture, the literary woman did have something crucial to hide.

Because so many of the lost or concealed truths of female culture have recently been retrieved by feminist scholars, women readers in particular have lately become aware that nineteenth-century literary women felt they had things to hide. Many feminist critics, therefore, have begun to write about these phenomena of evasion and concealment in women's writing. In *The Female Imagination,* for instance, Patricia Meyer Spacks repeatedly describes the ways in

[9]See, for instance, Barbara Charlesworth Gelpi, "A Common Language: The American Woman Poet," in *Shakespeare's Sisters,* ed. Gilbert and Gubar, pp. 269–79. [Gilbert and Gubar]

[10]Judy Chicago, *Through the Flower: My Struggle as a Woman Artist* (New York: Doubleday, 1977), p. 40. [Gilbert and Gubar]

[11]Dickinson, *Poems,* J. 512 ("The Soul has Bandaged moments —"). [Gilbert and Gubar]

which women's novels are marked by "subterranean challenges" to truths that the writers of such works appear on the surface to accept. Similarly, Carolyn Heilbrun and Catharine Stimpson discuss "the presence of absence" in literature by women, the "hollows, centers, caverns within the work — places where activity that one might expect is missing . . . or deceptively coded." Perhaps most trenchantly, Elaine Showalter has recently pointed out that feminist criticism, with its emphasis on the woman writer's inevitable consciousness of her own gender, has allowed us to "see meaning in what has previously been empty space. The orthodox plot recedes, and another plot, hitherto submerged in the anonymity of the background, stands out in bold relief like a thumbprint."[12]

But what is this other plot? Is there any *one* other plot? What is the secret message of literature by women, if there is a single secret message? What, in other words, have women got to hide? Most obviously, of course, if we return to the angelic figure of Makarie[13] — that ideal of "contemplative purity" who no doubt had headaches precisely because her author inflicted upon her a life that seemed to have "no story" — what literary women have hidden or disguised is what each writer knows is in some sense her own story. Because, as Simone de Beauvoir puts it, women "still dream through the dreams of men," internalizing the strictures that the Queen's looking glass utters in its kingly voice, the message or story that has been hidden is "merely," in Carolyn Kizer's bitter words, "the private lives of one half of humanity."[14] More specifically, however, the one plot that seems to be concealed in most of the nineteenth-century literature by women which will concern us here is in some sense a story of the woman writer's quest for her own story; it is the story, in other words, of the woman's quest for self-definition. Like the speaker of Mary Elizabeth Coleridge's[15] "The Other Side of a Mirror," the literary woman frequently finds herself staring with horror at a fearful image of herself that has been mysteriously inscribed on the surface of the glass, and she tries to guess the truth that cannot be uttered by the wounded and bleeding mouth, the truth behind the "leaping fire / Of jealousy and fierce revenge," the truth "of hard unsanctified distress." Uneasily aware that, like Sylvia Plath, she is "inhabited by a cry," she secretly seeks to unify herself by coming to terms with her own fragmentation. Yet even though, with Mary Elizabeth Coleridge, she strives to "set the crystal surface" of the mirror free from frightful images, she continually feels, as May Sarton puts it, that she has been "broken in two / By sheer definition."[16] The story "no man may guess," therefore, is the story of her attempt to make herself whole by healing her own infections and diseases.

[12]Patricia Meyer Spacks, *The Female Imagination* (New York: Knopf, 1975), p. 317; Carolyn Heilbrun and Catharine Stimpson, "Theories of Feminist Criticism: A Dialogue," in Josephine Donovan, ed., *Feminist Literary Criticism* (Lexington: The University Press of Kentucky, 1975), p. 62; Elaine Showalter, "Review Essay," *Signs* 1, no. 2 (Winter 1975): 435. See also Annis V. Pratt, "The New Feminist Criticism: Exploring the History of the New Space," in *Beyond Intellectual Sexism: A New Woman, A New Reality,* ed. Joan I. Roberts (New York: David McKay, 1976). On p. 183 Pratt describes what she calls her "drowning theory," which "comes from a phenomenon in black culture: You have a little black church back in the marsh and you're going to sing 'Go Down Moses' [but] Every now and then the members of the congregation want to break loose and sing 'Oh Freedom' . . . Whenever they sing that, they've got this big old black pot in the vestibule, and as they sing they pound the pot. That way, no white folks are going to hear. The drowning effect, this banging on the pot to drown out what they are actually saying about feminism, came in with the first woman's novel and hasn't gone out yet. Many women novelists have even succeeded in hiding the covert or implicit feminism in their books from themselves. . . . As a result we get explicit cultural norms superimposed upon an authentic creative mind in the form of all kinds of feints, ploys, masks and disguises embedded in the plot structure and characterization." [Gilbert and Gubar]

[13]Makarie is a character in *Wilhelm Meisters Wanderjahre* (1821–29) by Johann Wolfgang von Goethe (1749–1832).

[14]De Beauvoir, *The Second Sex* (New York: Knopf, 1973), p. 132; Kizer, "Three," from "Pro Femina," in *No More Masks!,* ed. Florence Howe and Ellen Bass (New York: Doubleday, 1973), p. 175. [Gilbert and Gubar]

[15]English poet (1861–1907), author of *Fancy's Following* (1896) and *Fancy's Guerdon* (1897).

[16]Plath, "Elm," *Ariel* (New York: Harper & Row, 1966), p. 16; Sarton, "Birthday on the Acropolis," *A Private Mythology* (New York: Norton, 1966), p. 48. [Gilbert and Gubar]

To heal herself, however, the woman writer must exorcise the sentences which bred her infection in the first place; she must overtly or covertly free herself of the despair she inhaled from some "Wrinkled Maker," and she can only do this by revising the Maker's texts. Or, to put the matter in terms of a different metaphor, to "set the crystal surface free" a literary woman must shatter the mirror that has so long reflected what every woman was supposed to be. For these reasons, then, women writers in England and America, throughout the nineteenth century and on into the twentieth, have been especially concerned with assaulting and revising, deconstructing and reconstructing those images of women inherited from male literature, especially, as we noted in our discussion of the Queen's looking glass, the paradigmatic polarities of angel and monster. Examining and attacking such images, however, literary women have inevitably had consciously or unconsciously to reject the values and assumptions of the society that created these fearsome paradigms. Thus, even when they do not overtly criticize patriarchal institutions or conventions (and most of the nineteenth-century women we shall be studying do *not* overtly do so), these writers almost obsessively create characters who enact their own, covert authorial anger. With Charlotte Brontë, they may feel that there are "evils" of which it is advisable "not too often to think." With George Eliot, they may declare that the "woman question" seems "to overhang abysses, of which even prostitution is not the worst."[17] But over and over again they project what seems to be the energy of their own despair into passionate, even melodramatic characters who act out the subversive impulses every woman inevitably feels when she contemplates the "deep-rooted" evils of patriarchy.

It is significant, then, that when the speaker of "The Other Side of a Mirror" looks into her glass the woman that she sees is a madwoman, "wild / With more than womanly despair," the monster that she fears she really is rather than the angel she has pretended to be. What the heroine of

George Eliot's verse-drama *Armgart* calls "basely feigned content, the placid mask / Of woman's misery" *is* merely a mask, and Mary Elizabeth Coleridge, like so many of her contemporaries, records the emergence from behind the mask of a figure whose rage "once no man on earth could guess."[18] Repudiating "basely feigned content," this figure arises like a bad dream, bloody, envious, enraged, as if the very process of writing had itself liberated a madwoman, a crazy and angry woman, from a silence in which neither she nor her author can continue to acquiesce. Thus although Coleridge's mirrored madwoman is an emblem of "speechless woe" because she has "no voice to speak her dread," the poet ultimately speaks *for* her when she whispers "I am she!" More, she speaks for her in writing the poem that narrates her emergence from behind the placid mask, "the aspects glad and gay, / That erst were found reflected there."

As we explore nineteenth-century literature, we will find that this madwoman emerges over and over again from the mirrors women writers hold up both to their own natures and to their own visions of nature. Even the most apparently conservative and decorous women writers obsessively create fiercely independent characters who seek to destroy all the patriarchal structures which both their authors and their authors' submissive heroines seem to accept as inevitable. Of course, by projecting their rebellious impulses not into their heroines but into mad or monstrous women (who are suitably punished in the course of the novel or poem), female authors dramatize their own self-division, their desire both to accept the strictures of patriarchal society and to reject them. What this means, however, is that the madwoman in literature by women is not merely, as she might be in male literature, an antagonist or foil to the heroine. Rather, she is usually in some sense the *author's* double, an image of her own anxiety and rage. Indeed, much of the poetry and fiction written by women conjures up this mad creature so that female authors can come to terms with their own uniquely female feelings of fragmentation, their

[17]*The George Eliot Letters,* 7 vols., ed. Gordon S. Haight (New Haven: Yale University Press, 1954–55), 5:58. [Gilbert and Gubar]

[18]Eliot, *Poems,* 2 vols. (New York: Croscup, 1896), p. 124. [Gilbert and Gubar]

own keen sense of the discrepancies between what they are and what they are supposed to be.

We shall see, then, that the mad double is as crucial to the aggressively sane novels of Jane Austen and George Eliot as she is in the more obviously rebellious stories told by Charlotte and Emily Brontë. Both gothic and anti-gothic writers represent themselves as split like Emily Dickinson between the elected nun and the damned witch, or like Mary Shelley between the noble, censorious scientist and his enraged, childish monster. In fact, so important is this female schizophrenia of authorship that, as we hope to show, it links these nineteenth-century writers with such twentieth-century descendants as Virginia Woolf (who projects herself into both ladylike Mrs. Dalloway and crazed Septimus Warren Smith), Doris Lessing (who divides herself between sane Martha Hesse and mad Lynda Coldridge), and Sylvia Plath (who sees herself as both a plaster saint and a dangerous "old yellow" monster).

To be sure, in the works of all these artists — both nineteenth- and twentieth-century — the mad character is sometimes created only to be destroyed: Septimus Warren Smith and Bertha Mason Rochester are both good examples of such characters, as is Victor Frankenstein's monster. Yet even when a figure of rage seems to function only as a monitory image, her (or his) fury must be acknowledged not only by the angelic protagonist to whom s/he is opposed, but, significantly, *by the reader as well.* With his usual perceptiveness, Geoffrey Chaucer anticipated the dynamics of this situation in the *Canterbury Tales.* When he gave the Wife of Bath a tale of her own, he portrayed her projecting her subversive vision of patriarchal institutions into the story of a furious hag who demands supreme power over her own life and that of her husband: only when she gains his complete acceptance of her authority does this witch transform herself into a modest and docile beauty. Five centuries later, the threat of the hag, the monster, the witch, the madwoman, still lurks behind the compliant paragon of women's stories.

To mention witches, however, is to be reminded once again of the traditional (patriarchally defined) association between creative women and monsters. In projecting their anger and dis-ease into dreadful figures, creating dark doubles for themselves and their heroines, women writers are both identifying with and revising the self-definitions patriarchal culture has imposed on them. All the nineteenth- and twentieth-century literary women who evoke the female monster in their novels and poems alter her meaning by virtue of their own identification with her. For it is usually because she is in some sense imbued with interiority that the witch-monster-madwoman becomes so crucial an avatar of the writer's own self. From a male point of view, women who reject the submissive silences of domesticity have been seen as terrible objects — Gorgons, Sirens, Scyllas, serpent-Lamias, Mothers of Death or Goddesses of Night. But from a female point of view the monster woman is simply a woman who seeks the power of self-articulation, and therefore, like Mary Shelley giving the first-person story of a monster who seemed to his creator to be merely a "filthy mass that moves and talks," she presents this figure for the first time from the inside out. Such a radical misreading of patriarchal poetics frees the woman artist to imply her criticism of the literary conventions she has inherited even as it allows her to express her ambiguous relationship to a culture that has not only defined her gender but shaped her mind. In a sense, as a famous poem by Muriel Rukeyser implies, all these women ultimately embrace the role of that most mythic of female monsters, the Sphinx, whose indecipherable message is the key to existence, because they know that the secret wisdom so long hidden from men is precisely *their* point of view.[19]

There is a sense, then, in which the female literary tradition we have been defining participates on all levels in the same duality or duplicity that necessitates the generation of such doubles as monster characters who shadow angelic authors and mad anti-heroines who complicate the lives of sane heroines. Parody, for instance, is another one of the key strategies through which this female duplicity reveals itself. As we have noted, nineteenth-century women writers frequently both use and misuse (or subvert) a common male tradition or genre. Consequently, we shall see over and over again that a "complex vibration"

[19]Rukeyser, "Myth," *Breaking Open* (New York: Random House, 1973), p. 20. [Gilbert and Gubar]

occurs between stylized generic gestures and unexpected deviations from such obvious gestures, a vibration that undercuts and ridicules the genre being employed. Some of the best-known recent poetry by women openly uses such parody in the cause of feminism: traditional figures of patriarchal mythology like Circe, Leda, Cassandra, Medusa, Helen, and Persephone have all lately been reinvented in the images of their female creators, and each poem devoted to one of these figures is a reading that reinvents her original story.[20] But though nineteenth-century women did not employ this kind of parody so openly and angrily, they too deployed it to give contextual force to their revisionary attempts at self-definition. Jane Austen's novels of sense and sensibility, for instance, suggest a revolt against both those standards of female excellence. Similarly, Charlotte Brontë's critical revision of *Pilgrim's Progress* questions the patriarchal ideal of female submissiveness by substituting a questing Everywoman for Bunyan's questing Christian. In addition, as we shall show in detail in later chapters, Mary Shelley, Emily Brontë, and George Eliot covertly reappraise and repudiate the misogyny implicit in Milton's mythology by misreading and revising Milton's story of woman's fall. Parodic, duplicitous, extraordinarily sophisticated, all this female writing is both revisionary and revolutionary, even when it is produced by writers we usually think of as models of angelic resignation.

To summarize this point, it is helpful to examine a work by the woman who seems to be the most modest and gentle of the three Brontë sisters. Anne Brontë's *The Tenant of Wildfell Hall* (1848) is generally considered conservative in its espousal of Christian values, but it tells what is in fact a story of woman's liberation. Specifically, it describes a woman's escape from the prisonhouse of a bad marriage, and her subsequent attempts to

achieve independence by establishing herself in a career as an artist. Since Helen Graham, the novel's protagonist, must remain incognito in order to elude her husband, she signs with false initials the landscapes she produces when she becomes a professional artist, and she titles the works in such a way as to hide her whereabouts. In short, she uses her art both to express and to camouflage herself. But this functionally ambiguous aesthetic is not merely a result of her flight from home and husband. For even earlier in the novel, when we encounter Helen before her marriage, her use of art is duplicitous. Her painting and drawing seem at first simply to be genteel social accomplishments, but when she shows one of her paintings to her future husband, he discovers a pencil sketch of his own face on the back of the canvas. Helen has been using the reverse side of her paintings to express her secret desires, and although she has remembered to rub out all the other sketches, this one remains, eventually calling his attention to the dim traces on the backs of all the others.

In the figure of Helen Graham, Anne Brontë has given us a wonderfully useful paradigm of the female artist. Whether Helen covertly uses a supposedly modest young lady's "accomplishments" for unladylike self-expression or publicly flaunts her professionalism and independence, she must in some sense deny or conceal her own art, or at least deny the self-assertion implicit in her art. In other words, there is an essential ambiguity involved in her career as an artist. When, as a girl, she draws on the backs of her paintings, she must make the paintings themselves work as public masks to hide her private dreams, and only behind such masks does she feel free to choose her own subjects. Thus she produces a public art which she herself rejects as inadequate but which she secretly uses to discover a new aesthetic space for herself. In addition, she subverts her genteelly "feminine" works with personal representations which endure only in tracings, since her guilt about the impropriety of self-expression has caused her to efface her private drawings just as it has led her to efface herself.

It is significant, moreover, that the sketch on the other side of Helen's canvas depicts the face of the Byronically brooding, sensual Arthur

[20]For "complex vibration," see Elaine Showalter, "Review Essay," p. 435. For reinventions of mythology, see Mona Van Duyn, "Leda" and "Leda Reconsidered," in *No More Masks!,* pp. 129–32, and Margaret Atwood, "Circe/Mud Poems," in *You Are Happy* (New York: Harper & Row, 1974), pp. 71–94. A poet like H. D. continually reinvents Persephone, Medusa, and Helen in her uniquely female epics, for example in *Helen in Egypt* (New York: New Directions, 1961). [Gilbert and Gubar]

Huntingdon, the man she finally decides to marry. Fatally attracted by the energy and freedom that she desires as an escape from the constraints of her own life, Helen pays for her initial attraction by watching her husband metamorphose from a fallen angel into a fiend, as he relentlessly and self-destructively pursues a diabolical career of gaming, whoring, and drinking. In this respect, too, Helen is prototypical, since we shall see that women artists are repeatedly attracted to the Satanic/Byronic hero even while they try to resist the sexual submission exacted by this oppressive younger son who seems, at first, so like a brother or a double. From Jane Austen, who almost obsessively rejected this figure, to Mary Shelley, the Brontës, and George Eliot, all of whom identified with his fierce presumption, women writers develop a subversive tradition that has a unique relationship to the Romantic ethos of revolt.

What distinguishes Helen Graham (and all the women authors who resemble her) from male Romantics, however, is precisely her anxiety about her own artistry, together with the duplicity that anxiety necessitates. Even when she becomes a professional artist, Helen continues to fear the social implications of her vocation. Associating female creativity with freedom from male domination, and dreading the misogynistic censure of her community, she produces art that at least partly hides her experience of her actual place in the world. Because her audience potentially includes the man from whom she is trying to escape, she must balance her need to paint her own condition against her need to circumvent detection. Her strained relationship to her art is thus determined almost entirely by her gender, so that from both her anxieties and her strategies for overcoming them we can extrapolate a number of the crucial ways in which women's art has been radically qualified by their femaleness.

As we shall see, Anne Brontë's sister Charlotte depicts similar anxieties and similar strategies for overcoming anxiety in the careers of all the female artists who appear in her novels. From timid Frances Henri to demure Jane Eyre, from mysterious Lucia to flamboyant Vashti, Brontë's women artists withdraw behind their art even while they assert themselves through it, as if deliberately adopting Helen Graham's duplicitous techniques

of self-expression. For the great women writers of the past two centuries are linked by the ingenuity with which all, while no one was really looking, danced out of the debilitating looking glass of the male text into the health of female authority. Tracing subversive pictures behind socially acceptable facades, they managed to appear to dissociate themselves from their own revolutionary impulses even while passionately enacting such impulses. Articulating the "private lives of one half of humanity," their fiction and poetry both records and transcends the struggle of what Marge Piercy has called "Unlearning to not speak."[21]

We must not forget, however, that to hide behind the facade of art, even for so crucial a process as "Unlearning to not speak," is still to be hidden, to be confined: to be secret is to be secreted. In a poignant and perceptive poem to Emily Dickinson, Adrienne Rich has noted that in her "half-cracked way" Dickinson chose "silence for entertainment, / chose to have it out at last / on [her] own premises."[22] This is what Jane Austen, too, chose to do when she ironically defined her work-space as two inches of ivory, what Emily Brontë chose to do when she hid her poems in kitchen cabinets (and perhaps destroyed her Gondal stories), what Christina Rossetti chose when she elected an art that glorified the religious constrictions of the "convent threshold." Rich's crucial pun on the word *premises* returns us, therefore, to the confinement of these women, a confinement that was inescapable for them even at their moments of greatest triumph, a confinement that was implicit in their secretness. This confinement was both literal and figurative. Literally, women like Dickinson, Brontë, and Rossetti were imprisoned in their homes, their father's houses; indeed, almost all nineteenth-century women were in some sense imprisoned in men's houses. Figuratively, such women were, as we have seen, locked into male texts, texts from which they

[21]Marge Piercy, "Unlearning to not speak," *To Be Of Use* (New York: Doubleday, 1973), p. 38. [Gilbert and Gubar]
[22]"I am in danger — sir — ," *Adrienne Rich's Poetry,* ed. Barbara Charlesworth Gelpi and Albert Gelpi (New York: Norton, 1975), pp. 30–31. [Gilbert and Gubar]

could escape only through ingenuity and indirection. It is not surprising, then, that spatial imagery of enclosure and escape, elaborated with what frequently becomes obsessive intensity, characterizes much of their writing.

In fact, anxieties about space sometimes seem to dominate the literature of both nineteenth-century women and their twentieth-century descendants. In the genre Ellen Moers has recently called "female Gothic,"[23] for instance, heroines who characteristically inhabit mysteriously intricate or uncomfortably stifling houses are often seen as captured, fettered, trapped, even buried alive. But other kinds of works by women — novels of manners, domestic tales, lyric poems — also show the same concern with spatial constrictions. From Ann Radcliffe's melodramatic dungeons to Jane Austen's mirrored parlors, from Charlotte Brontë's haunted garrets to Emily Brontë's coffin-shaped beds, imagery of enclosure reflects the woman writer's own discomfort, her sense of powerlessness, her fear that she inhabits alien and incomprehensible places. Indeed, it reflects her growing suspicion that what the nineteenth century called "woman's place" is itself irrational and strange. Moreover, from Emily Dickinson's haunted chambers to H. D.'s tightly shut sea-shells and Sylvia Plath's grave-caves, imagery of entrapment expresses the woman writer's sense that she has been dispossessed precisely because she is so thoroughly possessed — and possessed in every sense of the word.

The opening stanzas of Charlotte Perkins Gilman's punningly titled "In Duty Bound" show how inevitable it was for a female artist to translate into spatial terms her despair at the spiritual constrictions of what Gilman ironically called "home comfort."

In duty bound, a life hemmed in,
   Whichever way the spirit turns to look;
No chance of breaking out, except by sin;
   Not even room to shirk —
   Simply to live, and work.

An obligation preimposed, unsought,
   Yet binding with the force of natural law;
The pressure of antagonistic thought;
   Aching within, each hour,
   A sense of wasting power.

A house with roof so darkly low
   The heavy rafters shut the sunlight out;
One cannot stand erect without a blow;
   Until the soul inside
   Cries for a grave — more wide.[24]

Literally confined to the house, figuratively confined to a single "place," enclosed in parlors and encased in texts, imprisoned in kitchens and enshrined in stanzas, women artists naturally found themselves describing dark interiors and confusing their sense that they were house-bound with their rebellion against being duty bound. The same connections Gilman's poem made in the nineteenth century had after all been made by Anne Finch in the eighteenth, when she complained that women who wanted to write poetry were scornfully told that "the dull mannage of a servile house" was their "outmost art and use." Inevitably, then, since they were trapped in so many ways in the architecture — both the houses and the institutions — of patriarchy, women expressed their anxiety of authorship by comparing their "presumptuous" literary ambitions with the domestic accomplishments that had been prescribed for them. Inevitably, too, they expressed their claustrophobic rage by enacting rebellious escapes.

Dramatizations of imprisonment and escape are so all-pervasive in nineteenth-century literature by women that we believe they represent a uniquely female tradition in this period. Interestingly, though works in this tradition generally begin by using houses as primary symbols of female imprisonment, they also use much of the other paraphernalia of "woman's place" to enact their central symbolic drama of enclosure and escape. Ladylike veils and costumes, mirrors, paintings, statues, locked cabinets, drawers, trunks, strongboxes, and other domestic furnishings appear and reappear in female novels and poems throughout the nineteenth century and on

---

[23]Ellen Moers, *Literary Women* (New York: Doubleday, 1976), pp. 90–112. [Gilbert and Gubar]

[24]*The Living of Charlotte Perkins Gilman* (1935; New York: Harper & Row, 1975), p. 77. [Gilbert and Gubar]

into the twentieth to signify the woman writer's sense that, as Emily Dickinson put it, her "life" has been "shaven and fitted to a frame," a confinement she can only tolerate by believing that "the soul has moments of escape / When bursting all the doors / She dances like a bomb abroad."[25] Significantly, too, the explosive violence of these "moments of escape" that women writers continually imagine for themselves returns us to the phenomenon of the mad double so many of these women have projected into their works. For it is, after all, through the violence of the double that the female author enacts her own raging desire to escape male houses and male texts, while at the same time it is through the double's violence that this anxious author articulates for herself the costly destructiveness of anger repressed until it can no longer be contained.

As we shall see, therefore, infection continually breeds in the sentences of women whose writing obsessively enacts this drama of enclosure and escape. Specifically, what we have called the distinctively female diseases of anorexia and agoraphobia are closely associated with this dramatic/thematic pattern. Defining themselves as prisoners of their own gender, for instance, women frequently create characters who attempt to escape, if only into nothingness, through the suicidal self-starvation of anorexia. Similarly, in a metaphorical elaboration of bulimia, the disease of overeating which is anorexia's complement and mirror-image (as Marlene Boskind-Lodahl has recently shown),[26] women writers often envision an "outbreak" that transforms their characters into huge and powerful monsters. More obviously, agoraphobia and its complementary opposite, claustrophobia, are by definition associated with the spatial imagery through which these poets and novelists express their feelings of social confinement and their yearning for spiritual escape. The paradigmatic female story, therefore — the story such angels in the house of literature as Goethe's Makarie and Patmore's Honoria[27] were in effect "forbidden" to tell — is frequently an arrangement of the elements most readers will readily remember from Charlotte Brontë's *Jane Eyre*. Examining the psychosocial implications of a "haunted" ancestral mansion, such a tale explores the tension between parlor and attic, the psychic split between the lady who submits to male dicta and the lunatic who rebels. But in examining these matters the paradigmatic female story inevitably considers also the equally uncomfortable spatial options of expulsion into the cold outside or suffocation in the hot indoors, and in addition it often embodies an obsessive anxiety both about starvation to the point of disappearance and about monstrous inhabitation.

Many nineteenth-century male writers also, of course, used imagery of enclosure and escape to make deeply felt points about the relationship of the individual and society. Dickens and Poe, for instance, on opposite sides of the Atlantic, wrote of prisons, cages, tombs, and cellars in similar ways and for similar reasons. Still, the male writer is so much more comfortable with his literary role that he can usually elaborate upon his visionary theme more consciously and objectively than the female writer can. The distinction between male and female images of imprisonment is — and always has been — a distinction between, on the one hand, that which is both metaphysical and metaphorical, and on the other hand, that which is social and actual. Sleeping in his coffin, the seventeenth-century poet John Donne was piously rehearsing the constraints of the grave in advance, but the nineteenth-century poet Emily Dickinson, in purdah in her white dress, was anxiously living those constraints in the present. Imagining himself buried alive in tombs and cellars, Edgar Allan Poe was letting his mind poetically wander into the deepest recesses of his own psyche, but Dickinson, reporting that "I do not cross my Father's ground to any house in town," was recording a real, self-willed, self-burial. Similarly, when Byron's Prisoner of Chillon notes that "my very

---

[25]Dickinson, *Poems*, J. 512 ("The Soul has Bandaged moments — "). [Gilbert and Gubar]

[26]Boskind-Lodahl, "Cinderella's Step-Sisters: A Feminist Perspective on Anorexia Nervosa and Bulimia," *Signs* 2, no. 2 (1976): 342–56. [Gilbert and Gubar]

[27]*The Angel in the House* (1854–63) was the lyric sequence by Coventry Patmore (1823–90) extolling his own marriage.

chains and I grew friends," the poet himself is making an epistemological point about the nature of the human mind, as well as a political point about the tyranny of the state. But when Rose Yorke in *Shirley* describes Caroline Helstone as living the life of a toad enclosed in a block of marble, Charlotte Brontë is speaking through her about her own deprived and constricted life, and its real conditions.[28]

Thus, though most male metaphors of imprisonment have obvious implications in common (and many can be traced back to traditional images used by, say, Shakespeare and Plato), such metaphors may have very different aesthetic functions and philosophical messages in different male literary works. Wordsworth's prison-house in the "Intimations" ode serves a purpose quite unlike that served by the jails in Dickens's novels. Coleridge's twice-five miles of visionary greenery ought not to be confused with Keats's vale of soul-making, and the escape of Tennyson's Art from her Palace should not be identified with the resurrection of Poe's Ligeia. Women authors, however, reflect the literal reality of their own confinement in the constraints they depict, and so all at least begin with the same unconscious or conscious purpose in employing such spatial imagery. Recording their own distinctively female experience, they are secretly working through and within the conventions of literary texts to define their own lives.

While some male authors also use such imagery for implicitly or explicitly confessional projects, women seem forced to live more intimately with the metaphors they have created to solve the "problem" of their fall. At least one critic does deal not only with such images but with their psychological meaning as they accrue around houses. Noting in *The Poetics of Space* that "the house image would appear to have become the topography of our inmost being," Gaston Bachelard shows the ways in which houses, nests, shells, and wardrobes are in us as much as we are in them.[29] What is significant from our point of view, however, is the extraordinary discrepancy between the almost consistently "felicitous space" he discusses and the negative space we have found. Clearly, for Bachelard the protective asylum of the house is closely associated with its maternal features, and to this extent he is following the work done on dream symbolism by Freud and on female inner space by Erikson. It seems clear too, however, that such symbolism must inevitably have very different implications for male critics and for female authors.

Women themselves have often, of course, been described or imagined as houses. Most recently Erik Erikson advanced his controversial theory of female "inner space" in an effort to account for little girls' interest in domestic enclosures. But in medieval times, as if to anticipate Erikson, statues of the Madonna were made to open up and reveal the holy family hidden in the Virgin's inner space. The female womb has certainly, always and everywhere, been a child's first and most satisfying house, a source of food and dark security, and therefore a mythic paradise imaged over and over again in sacred caves, secret shrines, consecrated huts. Yet for many a woman writer these ancient associations of house and self seem mainly to have strengthened the anxiety about enclosure which she projected into her art. Disturbed by the real physiological prospect of enclosing an unknown part of herself that is somehow also not herself, the female artist may, like Mary Shelley, conflate anxieties about maternity with anxieties about literary creativity. Alternatively, troubled by the anatomical "emptiness" of spinsterhood, she may, like Emily Dickinson, fear the inhabitations of nothingness and death, the transformation of womb into tomb. Moreover, conditioned to believe that as a house she is herself owned (and ought to be inhabited) by a man, she may once again but for yet another reason see herself as inescapably an object. In other words, even if she does not experience her womb as a kind of tomb or perceive her child's occupation of her house/body as depersonalizing,

[28]Dickinson, *The Letters of Emily Dickinson,* 3 vols., ed. Thomas H. Johnson (Cambridge, MA: The Belknap Press of Harvard University Press, 1958), 2:460; Byron, "The Prisoner of Chillon," lines 389–92; Brontë, *Shirley* (New York: Dutton, 1970), p. 316; see also Brontë to W. S. Williams, 26 July 1849. [Gilbert and Gubar]

[29]Gaston Bachelard, *The Poetics of Space,* trans. Maria Jolas (Boston: Beacon, 1970), p. xxxii. [Gilbert and Gubar]

she may recognize that in an essential way she has been defined simply by her purely biological usefulness to her species.

To become literally a house, after all, is to be denied the hope of that spiritual transcendence of the body which, as Simone de Beauvoir has argued, is what makes humanity distinctively human. Thus, to be confined in childbirth (and significantly "confinement" was the key nineteenth-century term for what we would now, just as significantly, call "delivery") is in a way just as problematical as to be confined in a house or prison. Indeed, it might well seem to the literary woman that, just as ontogeny may be said to recapitulate phylogeny, the confinement of pregnancy replicates the confinement of society. For even if she is only metaphorically denied transcendence, the woman writer who perceives the implications of the house/body equation must unconsciously realize that such a trope does not just "place" her in a glass coffin, it transforms her into a version of the glass coffin herself. There is a sense, therefore, in which, confined in such a network of metaphors, what Adrienne Rich has called a "thinking woman" might inevitably feel that now she has been imprisoned within her own alien and loathsome body.[30] Once again, in other words, she has become not only a prisoner but a monster.

As if to comment on the unity of all these points — on, that is, the anxiety-inducing connections between what women writers tend to see as their parallel confinements in texts, houses, and maternal female bodies — Charlotte Perkins Gilman brought them all together in 1890 in a striking story of female confinement and escape, a paradigmatic tale which (like *Jane Eyre*) seems to tell *the* story that all literary women would tell if they could speak their "speechless woe." "The Yellow Wallpaper," which Gilman herself called "a description of a case of nervous breakdown," recounts in the first person the experiences of a woman who is evidently suffering from a severe postpartum psychosis.[31] Her husband, a censorious and paternalistic physician, is treating her according to methods by which S. Weir Mitchell, a famous "nerve specialist," treated Gilman herself for a similar problem. He has confined her to a large garret room in an "ancestral hall" he has rented, and he has forbidden her to touch pen to paper until she is well again, for he feels, says the narrator, "that with my imaginative power and habit of story-making, a nervous weakness like mine is sure to lead to all manner of excited fancies, and that I ought to use my will and good sense to check the tendency" (15–16).

The cure, of course, is worse than the disease, for the sick woman's mental condition deteriorates rapidly. "I think sometimes that if I were only well enough to write a little it would relieve the press of ideas and rest me," she remarks, but literally confined in a room she thinks is a one-time nursery because it has "rings and things" in the walls, she is literally locked away from creativity. The "rings and things," although reminiscent of children's gymnastic equipment, are really the paraphernalia of confinement, like the gate at the head of the stairs, instruments that definitively indicate her imprisonment. Even more tormenting, however, is the room's wallpaper: a sulphurous yellow paper, torn off in spots, and patterned with "lame uncertain curves" that "plunge off at outrageous angles" and "destroy themselves in unheard of contradictions." Ancient, smoldering, "unclean" as the oppressive structures of the society in which she finds herself, this paper surrounds the narrator like an inexplicable text, censorious and overwhelming as her physician husband, haunting as the "hereditary estate" in which she is trying to survive. Inevitably she studies its suicidal implications — and inevitably, because of her "imaginative power and habit of story-making," she revises it, projecting her own passion for escape into its otherwise incomprehensible hieroglyphics. "This wallpaper," she decides, at a key point in her story,

has a kind of sub-pattern in a different shade, a particularly irritating one, for you can only see it in certain lights, and not clearly then.

But in the places where it isn't faded and where the sun is just so — I can see a strange, provoking, formless sort of figure, that seems to skulk about behind that silly and conspicuous front design. [18]

[30]*Adrienne Rich's Poetry*, p. 12: "A thinking woman sleeps with monsters. / The beak that grips her, she becomes" ("Snapshots of a Daughter-in-Law," #3). [Gilbert and Gubar]
[31]Charlotte Perkins Gilman, *The Yellow Wallpaper* (Old Westbury: The Feminist Press, 1973). All references in the text will be to page numbers in this edition. [Gilbert and Gubar]

As time passes, this figure concealed behind what corresponds (in terms of what we have been discussing) to the facade of the patriarchal text becomes clearer and clearer. By moonlight the pattern of the wallpaper "becomes bars! The outside pattern I mean, and the woman behind it is as plain as can be." And eventually, as the narrator sinks more deeply into what the world calls madness, the terrifying implications of both the paper and the figure imprisoned behind the paper begin to permeate — that is, to *haunt* — the rented ancestral mansion in which she and her husband are immured. The "yellow smell" of the paper "creeps all over the house," drenching every room in its subtle aroma of decay. And the woman creeps too — through the house, in the house, and out of the house, in the garden and "on that long road under the trees." Sometimes, indeed, the narrator confesses, "I think there are a great many women" both behind the paper and creeping in the garden,

> and sometimes only one, and she crawls around fast, and her crawling shakes [the paper] all over.... And she is all the time trying to climb through. But nobody could climb through that pattern — it strangles so; I think that is why it has so many heads. [30]

Eventually it becomes obvious to both reader and narrator that the figure creeping through and behind the wallpaper is both the narrator and the narrator's double. By the end of the story, moreover, the narrator has enabled this double to escape from her textual/architectural confinement: "I pulled and she shook, I shook and she pulled, and before morning we had peeled off yards of that paper." Is the message of the tale's conclusion mere madness? Certainly the righteous Doctor John — whose name links him to the anti-hero of Charlotte Brontë's *Villette*[32] — has been temporarily defeated, or at least momentarily stunned. "Now why should that man have fainted?" the narrator ironically asks as she creeps around her attic. But John's unmasculine swoon of surprise is the least of the triumphs Gilman imagines for her madwoman. More significant are the madwoman's own imaginings and creations, mirages of health and freedom with which her author endows her like a fairy godmother showering gold on a sleeping heroine. The woman from behind the wallpaper creeps away, for instance, creeps fast and far on the long road, in broad daylight. "I have watched her sometimes away off in the open country," says the narrator, "creeping as fast as a cloud shadow in a high wind."

Indistinct and yet rapid, barely perceptible but inexorable, the progress of that cloud shadow is not unlike the progress of nineteenth-century literary women out of the texts defined by patriarchal poetics into the open spaces of their own authority. That such an escape from the numb world behind the patterned walls of the text was a flight from dis-ease into health was quite clear to Gilman herself. When "The Yellow Wallpaper" was published she sent it to Weir Mitchell, whose strictures had kept her from attempting the pen during her own breakdown, thereby aggravating her illness, and she was delighted to learn, years later, that "he had changed his treatment of nervous prostration since reading" her story. "If that is a fact," she declared, "I have not lived in vain."[33] Because she was a rebellious feminist besides being a medical iconoclast, we can be sure that Gilman did not think of this triumph of hers in narrowly therapeutic terms. Because she knew, with Emily Dickinson, that "Infection in the sentence breeds," she knew that the cure for female despair must be spiritual as well as physical, aesthetic as well as social. What "The Yellow Wallpaper" shows she knew, too, is that even when a supposedly "mad" woman has been sentenced to imprisonment in the "infected" house of her own body, she may discover that, as Sylvia Plath was to put it seventy years later, she has "a self to recover, a queen."[34]

[32]John Bretton is the doctor for the school where Lucy Snowe works in Charlotte Brontë's *Villette*.

[33]*The Living of Charlotte Perkins Gilman*, p. 121. [Gilbert and Gubar]

[34]"Stings," *Ariel*, p. 62. [Gilbert and Gubar]

❖ DIALOGUE WITH SANDRA M. GILBERT AND SUSAN GUBAR

Toril Moi

b. 1953

Toril Moi was born in Norway and educated at the University of Bergen. She is the author of Sexual/Textual Politics *(1985),* Simone de Beauvoir: The Making of an Intellectual Woman *(1993), and* "What Is a Woman?" and Other Essays *(1999). She has also edited* The Kristeva Reader *(1986) and* French Feminist Thought *(1987). Her current research focuses on sex, gender, sexuality, and the body, on the one hand, and on modernity, modernism, theatricality, and the ordinary, on the other. Moi is the James B. Duke Professor of Literature and Romance Studies at Duke University, having taught there since 1989.*

Moi's Sexual/Textual Politics: Feminist Literary Theory *was a groundbreaking study of feminist theory comparing the Anglo-American empirical approach to feminism with the French poststructuralist écriture féminine. Beginning with Virginia Woolf, Moi analyzed the history of twentieth-century feminism, analyzing gaps and exposing the hidden ideology within the writing of "empirical" theorists such as Elaine Showalter, Kate Millett, and Sandra Gilbert and Susan Gubar. The following consideration is taken from Moi's analysis of* The Madwoman in the Attic.

From *Sexual/Textual Politics*

Gilbert and Gubar are theoretically aware. Their own brand of feminist critical theory is seductively sophisticated, particularly when contrasted with the general level of theoretical debate among Anglo-American feminist critics. But what kind of theory are they really advocating? And what are the political implications of their theses? The first troubling aspect of their approach is their insistence on the identity of author and character. Like Kate Millett[1] before them, Gilbert and Gubar repeatedly claim that the character (particularly the madwoman) is the *author's* double,

"an image of her own anxiety and rage" (78), maintaining that it is

> through the violence of the double that the female author enacts her own raging desire to escape male houses and male texts, while at the same time it is through the double's violence that this anxious author articulates for herself the costly destructiveness of anger repressed until it can no longer be contained. (85)

Their critical approach postulates a *real* woman hidden behind the patriarchal textual facade, and the feminist critic's task is to uncover her truth. In an incisive review of *The Madwoman in the Attic*, Mary Jacobus rightly criticizes the authors' "unstated complicity with the autobiographical 'phallacy,'" whereby male critics hold

---

[1]Author of *Sexual Politics* (London: Virago, 1977), whom Moi faults for equating the (male) author of a text with its narrator or protagonist.

that women's writing is somehow closer to their experience than men's, that the female text *is* the author, or at any rate a dramatic extension of her unconscious" (520).[2] Though the two critics avoid oversimplistic conclusions, they nevertheless end up at times in a dangerously reductionist position: under the manifest text, which is nothing but a "surface design" which "conceals or obscures deeper, less accessible . . . levels of meaning" (73), lies the *real* truth of the texts.

This is reminiscent of reductionist varieties of psychoanalytic or Marxist criticism, though it is no longer the author's Oedipus complex or relation to the class struggle that counts as the only truth of the text, but her constant, never-changing *feminist rage*. This position, which in less sophisticated guises is perhaps the most recurrent theme of Anglo-American feminist criticism, manages to transform *all* texts written by women into feminist texts, because they may always and without exception be held to embody somehow and somewhere the author's "female rage" against patriarchal oppression. Thus Gilbert and Gubar's readings of Jane Austen lack the force of their readings of Charlotte Brontë precisely because they persist in defining anger as the *only* positive signal of a feminist consciousness. Austen's gentle irony is lost on them, whereas the explicit rage and moodiness of Charlotte Brontë's texts furnish them with superb grounds for stimulating exegesis.

Quite apart from the reductive aspects of this approach, the insistence on the female author as the instance that provides the only true meaning of the text (that meaning being, in general, the author's anger) actually undermines Gilbert and Gubar's anti-patriarchal stance. Having quoted Edward Said's *Beginnings* with its "miniature meditation on the word *authority*" (4) as a description of "both the author and the authority of any literary text" (5), they quote Said's claim that "the unity or integrity of the text is maintained by a series of genealogical connections: author-text, beginning-middle-end, text-meaning, reader-interpretation, and so on. *Underneath all these is the imagery of succession, of paternity, of*

hierarchy" (5).[3] But it seems inconsistent, to say the least, to accept with Said that the traditional view of the relationship between author and text is hierarchical and authoritarian, only to proceed to write a book of over 700 pages that never once questions the authority of the *female* author. For if we are truly to reject the model of the author as God the Father of the text, it is surely not enough to reject the patriarchal ideology implied in the paternal metaphor. It is equally necessary to reject the *critical practice* it leads to, a critical practice that relies on the author as the transcendental signified of his or her text. For the patriarchal critic, the author is the source, origin and meaning of the text. If we are to undo this patriarchal practice of *authority*, we must take one further step and proclaim with Roland Barthes the death of the author. (See pp. 874–77.) Barthes's comments on the role of the author are well worth quoting in this context:

> Once the Author is removed, the claim to decipher a text becomes quite futile. To give a text an Author is to impose a limit on that text, to furnish it with a final signified, to close the writing. Such a conception suits criticism very well, the latter then allotting itself the important task of discovering the Author (or its hypostases: society, history, psyché, liberty) beneath the work: when the Author has been found, the text is "explained" — victory to the critic. ("The Death of the Author," 147)

The relevance of Barthes's critique of the author(ity)-centred critic for *The Madwoman in the Attic* should be clear. But what then is the alternative? According to Barthes, it is to accept the *multiplicity* of writing where "everything is to be *disentangled*, nothing *deciphered*" ("The Death of the Author," 147):

> The space of writing is to be ranged over, not pierced; writing ceaselessly posits meaning ceaselessly to evaporate it, carrying out a systematic exemption of meaning. In precisely this way literature (it would be better from now on to say *writing*), by refusing to assign a "secret," an ultimate meaning, to the text (and to the world as text), liberates what may be called an anti-theological

[2]Mary Jacobs, "Review of *The Madwoman in the Attic*," Signs 6.3 (1981): 517–23. [Moi]

[3]Gilbert and Gubar's italics. They are quoting Said, 162. Edward Said, *Beginnings: Intention and Method*. New York: Basic, 1975. [Moi]

activity, an activity that is truly revolutionary since to refuse to fix meaning is, in the end, to refuse God and his hypostases — reason, science, law. ("The Death of the Author," 147)

Gilbert and Gubar's belief in the true female authorial voice as the essence of all texts written by women masks the problems raised by their theory of patriarchal ideology. For them, as for Kate Millett, ideology becomes a monolithic unified totality that knows no contradictions; against this a miraculously intact "femaleness" may pit its strength. If patriarchy generates its own all-pervasive ideological structures, it is difficult to see how women in the nineteenth century could manage to develop or maintain a feminist consciousness untainted by the dominant patriarchal structures. As Mary Jacobus has pointed out, Gilbert and Gubar's emphasis on the deceitful strategies of the woman writer makes her "evasive at the cost of a freedom which twentieth-century women poets have eagerly sought: the freedom of being read as more than exceptionally articulate victims of a patriarchally engendered plot" ("Review of *The Madwoman in the Attic*," 522).

In other words: how did women manage to write at all, given the relentless patriarchal indoctrination that surrounded them from the moment they were born? Gilbert and Gubar avoid this question, blandly stating as the conclusion of their first chapter that "Despite the obstacles presented by those twin images of angel and monster, despite the fears of sterility and the anxieties of authorship from which women have suffered, generations of texts *have* been possible for female writers" (44). Indeed, but why? Only a more sophisticated account of the contradictory, fragmentary nature of patriarchal ideology would help Gilbert and Gubar to answer this question. In this context, Cora Kaplan's[4] arguments against Kate Millett are still relevant.[5]

[4]Writer who argued that Kate Millett's *Sexual Politics* treats patriarchal ideology as a set of false beliefs deployed against women by a well-organized male conspiracy. Kaplan suggested that male misogyny may be unconscious and that women themselves often internalize patriarchal values. ("Radical Feminism and Literature: Rethinking Millett's *Sexual Politics*." *Red Letters* 9 [1979]: 4–16.)
[5]See chapter 1 of *The Madwoman in the Attic*, pp. 26–9. [Moi]

Feminists must be able to account for the paradoxically productive aspects of patriarchal ideology (the moments in which the ideology backfires on itself, as it were) as well as for its obvious oppressive implications if they are to answer the tricky question of how it is that some women manage to counter patriarchal strategies despite the odds stacked against them. In the nineteenth century, for instance, it would seem true to say that bourgeois patriarchy's predilection for liberal humanism as a "legitimizing ideology" lent ammunition and arguments to the growing bourgeois feminist movement. If one held that the rights of the individual were sacred, it became increasingly difficult to argue that women's rights somehow were not. Just as Mary Wollstonecraft's essay on the rights of woman[6] was made possible by the emancipatory if bourgeois-patriarchal ideas of *liberté*, *égalité* and *fraternité*, so John Stuart Mill's essay on the subjection of women was the product of patriarchal liberal humanism. Gilbert and Gubar overlook these points, referring to Mill only twice *en passant*, and both times as a parallel to Mary Wollstonecraft. Their theory of covert and inexpressed rage as the essence of century "femaleness" cannot comfortably cope with a "male" text that *openly* tackles the problem of women's oppression.

This *impasse* in Gilbert and Gubar's work is both accentuated and compounded by their persistent use of the epithet "female." It has long been an established practice among most feminists to use "feminine" (and "masculine") to represent *social constructs* (patterns of sexuality and behavior imposed by cultural and social norms), and to reserve "female" and "male" for the purely biological aspects of sexual difference. Thus "feminine" represents nurture and "female" nature in this usage. "Femininity" is a cultural construct: one isn't born a woman, one becomes one, as Simone de Beauvoir puts it.[7] Seen in this perspective, patriarchal oppression consists of imposing certain social standards of femininity on all biological women, in order precisely to

[6]*A Vindication of the Rights of Woman*; see pp. 277–84.
[7]*The Second Sex*, see p. 679.

make us believe that the chosen standards for "femininity" *are natural*. Thus a woman who refuses to conform can be labeled both *unfeminine* and *unnatural*. It is in the patriarchal interest that these two terms (femininity and femaleness) stay thoroughly confused. Femininists, on the contrary, have to disentangle this confusion, and must therefore always insist that though women undoubtedly are *female*, this in no way guarantees that they will be *feminine*. This is equally true whether one defines femininity in the old patriarchal ways or in a new feminist way.

Gilbert and Gubar's refusal to admit a separation between nature and nurture at the lexical level renders their whole argument obscure. For what *is* this "female creativity" they are studying? Is it a natural, essential, inborn quality in all women? Is it "feminine" creativity in the sense of a creativity conforming to certain social standards of female behavior, or is it a creativity typical of a feminine subject position in the psychoanalytical sense? Gilbert and Gubar seem to hold the first hypothesis, though in a slightly more historicized form: in a given patriarchal society all women (because they are biologically female) will adopt certain strategies to counter patriarchal oppression. These strategies will be "female" since they will be the same for all women submitted to such conditions. Such an argument relies heavily on the assumption that patriarchal ideology is homogeneous and all-encompassing in its effects. It also gives little scope for an understanding of how genuinely difficult it is for women to achieve anything like "full femininity," or of the ways in which women can come to take up a masculine subject position — that is to say, become solid defenders of the patriarchal *status quo*.

In the last chapter of their theoretical preamble ("The Parables of the Cave"), Gilbert and Gubar discuss Mary Shelley's "Author's Introduction" to *The Last Man* (1826) where the author tells us how she found the scattered leaves of the Sibyl's messages during a visit to her cave.[8] Mary Shelley then decides to spend her life deciphering

and transmitting the message of these fragments in a more coherent form. Gilbert and Gubar use this story as a parable of their understanding of the situation of the woman writer under patriarchy:

> This last parable is the story of the woman artist who enters the cavern of her own mind and finds there the scattered leaves not only of her own power but of the tradition which might have generated that power. The body of her precursor's art, and thus the body of her own art lies in pieces around her, dismembered, dis-remembered, disintegrated. How can she remember it and become a member of it, join it and rejoin it, integrate it and in doing so achieve her own integrity, her own selfhood? (98)

This parable is also a statement of Gilbert and Gubar's feminist aesthetics. The emphasis here is on wholeness — on the *gathering* of the Sibyl's leaves (but nobody asks why the Sibyl of the myth chose to *scatter* her wisdom in the first place): women's writing can only come into existence as a structured and objectified whole. Parallel to the wholeness of the text is the wholeness of the woman's self; the integrated humanist individual is the essence of all creativity. A fragmented conception of self or consciousness would seem to Gilbert and Gubar the same as a sick or dis-eased self. The good text is an organic whole, in spite of the sophisticated apparatus the authors of *The Madwoman in the Attic* bring to bear on the works they study.

But this emphasis on integrity and totality as an ideal for women's writing can be criticized precisely as a patriarchal or — more accurately — a phallic construct. As Luce Irigaray and Jacques Derrida have argued, patriarchal thought models its criteria for what counts as "positive" values on the central assumption of the Phallus and the Logos as transcendental signifiers of Western culture. The implications of this are often astonishingly simplistic: anything conceived of as analogous to the so-called "positive" values of the Phallus counts as good, true or beautiful; anything that is *not* shaped on the pattern of the Phallus is defined as chaotic, fragmented, negative or nonexistent. The Phallus is often conceived of as a whole, unitary and simple form, as opposed to the terrifying chaos of the female genitals. Now it can

---

[8]For a different account of Mary Shelley's attitude towards femininity see Jacobus, "Is There a Woman in This Text?" *New Literary History* 14.1 (1982): 117–41. [Moi]

be argued that Gilbert and Gubar's belief in unitary wholes plays directly into the hands of such phallic aesthetic criteria. As we have seen in the case of the feminist reception of Virginia Woolf, a certain feminist preference for realism over modernism can be interpreted in the same way. To this extent, some Anglo-American feminism — and Gilbert and Gubar are no exceptions — is still laboring under the traditional patriarchal aesthetic values of New Criticism.

Gilbert and Gubar's final hope that their book will contribute to recreate a lost "female" unity bears out this assumption:

> There is a sense in which, for us, this book is a dream of the rising of Christina Rossetti's "mother country." And there is a sense in which it is an attempt at reconstructing the Sibyl's leaves, leaves which haunt us with the possibility that if we can piece together their fragments the parts will form a whole that tells the story of the career of a single woman artist, a "mother of us all," as Gertrude Stein would put it, a woman whom patriarchal poetics dismembered and whom we have tried to remember. (101)

The passage continues with a rough outline of the story of this single woman artist from Jane Austen and Maria Edgeworth to George Eliot and Emily Dickinson. The concern with wholeness, with the woman writer as the *meaning* of the texts studied, is here pressed to its logical conclusion: the desire to write the narrative of a mighty "Ur-woman."

From one viewpoint this is a laudable project, since feminists obviously wish to make women speak; but from another viewpoint it carries some dubious political and aesthetic implications. For one thing it is not an unproblematic project to try to speak *for* the other woman, since this is precisely what the ventriloquism of patriarchy has always done: men have constantly spoken *for* women, or in the name of women. Is it right that women now should take up precisely that masculine position in relation to other women? We might argue, in other words, that Gilbert and Gubar arrogate to themselves the same authorial authority they bestow on all women writers. As for "telling a story," this can in itself be constructed as an autocratic gesture. As we have

seen, Gilbert and Gubar quote Edward Said approvingly when he writes that underneath "beginning-middle-end" is the "imagery of succession, of paternity, of hierarchy" (5). But a *story* is precisely that which ever since Aristotle has been the very model of a beginning, a middle and an end. Perhaps it isn't such a good feminist idea to start telling the whole, integrated and unified story of the Great Mother-Writer after all?

> This enormously energetic, often witty, shrewd and resourceful book is, it seems to me, limited in the end precisely by its preoccupation with plot; though its arts are not the traditionally female ones of the wicked Queen, they risk in their own way being as reductive. They become a form of tight lacing which immobilizes the play of meaning in the texts whose hidden plots they uncover. What they find there, again and again, is not just "plot" but "author," the madwoman in the attic of their title. . . . Like the story of Snow White, this is a plot doomed to repetition; their book (ample partly because it can only repeat) reenacts endlessly the revisionary struggle, unlocking the secrets of the female text again and again with the same key. ("Review of *The Madwoman in the Attic*," 518–19)

In the end, Jacobus argues, this eternal return to the "original and originating 'story' of women's repression by patriarchy" occurs at the cost of ignoring precisely the political implications of the critics' own stance: "If culture, writing, and language are inherently repressive, as they may be argued to be, so is interpretation itself; and the question which arises for the feminist critic is, How are they specifically repressive for the woman writer?" ("Review," 520). Jacobus concludes that "the story between the lines may be feminist criticism's problematic relation to the patriarchal criticism it sets out to revise" ("Review," 522). At this point, surely, we should ask ourselves if it is not time to revise a feminist aesthetics that seems in these particular respects to lead to the same patriarchal and authoritarian dead end. In other words, it is time for us to confront the fact that the main problem in Anglo-American feminist criticism lies in the radical contradiction it presents between feminist politics and patriarchal aesthetics.

Annette Kolodny

b. 1941

Annette Kolodny's career is an exemplary combination of feminist scholarship and political activism. Born in New York City, Kolodny was briefly on the editorial staff of Newsweek *before attending the University of California at Berkeley, where she received her M.A. and Ph.D. In 1969–70, she taught at Yale before moving to Canada with her husband, who had been denied conscientious objector status and faced conscription into the military. At the University of British Columbia in 1970–74, Kolodny designed Western Canada's first accredited, multidisciplinary women's studies program. On her return to the United States in 1974, Kolodny organized a women's studies program at the University of New Hampshire. Her first book,* The Lay of the Land, *appeared in 1975. When Kolodny was denied promotion and tenure, she filed an anti-Semitism and sexism suit against the university and in 1980 was awarded a landmark out-of-court settlement, a portion of which she used to set up a legal fund and a task force against discrimination. Kolodny stayed in New Hampshire to complete* The Land Before Her *(1984) before joining the faculty at Rensselaer Polytechnic Institute. She is currently the College of Humanities Professor of American Literature and Culture at the University of Arizona, where she previously served as dean of the College of Humanities. Her experiences as a feminist in higher education administration are detailed in* Failing the Future: A Dean Looks at Higher Education in the Twenty-first Century *(1998). The following selection is excerpted from her prize-winning article of the same title, which was originally published in* Feminist Studies 6 *(1980).*

Dancing through the Minefield: Some Observations on the Theory, Practice, and Politics of a Feminist Literary Criticism

Had anyone the prescience, ten years ago, to pose the question of defining a "feminist" literary criticism, she might have been told, in the wake of Mary Ellmann's *Thinking About Women,*[1] that it involved exposing the sexual stereotyping of women in both our literature and our literary criticism and, as well, demonstrating the inadequacy of established critical schools and methods to deal fairly or sensitively with works written by women.

In broad outline, such a prediction would have stood well the test of time, and, in fact, Ellmann's book continues to be widely read and to point us in useful directions. What could not have been anticipated in 1969, however, was the catalyzing force of an ideology that, for many of us, helped to bridge the gap between the world as we found it and the world as we wanted it to be. For those of us who studied literature, a previously unspoken sense of exclusion from authorship, and a painfully personal distress at discovering whores, bitches, muses, and heroines dead in childbirth where we

[1]Mary Ellmann, *Thinking About Women* (New York: Harcourt Brace Jovanovich, Harvest, 1968). [Kolodny]

had once hoped to discover ourselves, could — for the first time — begin to be understood as more than "a set of disconnected, unrealized private emotions."[2] With a renewed courage to make public our otherwise private discontents, what had once been "felt individually as personal insecurity" came at last to be "viewed collectively as structural inconsistency"[3] within the very disciplines we studied. Following unflinchingly the full implications of Ellmann's percipient observations, and emboldened by the liberating energy of feminist ideology — in all its various forms and guises — feminist criticism very quickly moved beyond merely "expos[ing] sexism in one work of literature after another,"[4] and promised, instead, that we might at last "begin to record new choices in a new literary history."[5] So powerful was that impulse that we experienced it, along with Adrienne Rich, as much "more than a chapter in cultural history": it became, rather, "an act of survival."[6] What was at stake was not so much literature or criticism as such, but the historical, social, and ethical consequences of women's participation in, or exclusion from, either enterprise.

The pace of inquiry these last ten years has been fast and furious — especially after Kate Millett's 1970 analysis of the sexual politics of literature[7] added a note of urgency to what had earlier been Ellmann's sardonic anger — while the diversity of that inquiry easily outstripped all efforts to define feminist literary criticism as either a coherent system or a unified set of methodologies. Under its wide umbrella, everything has been thrown into question: our established canons, our aesthetic criteria, our interpretative strategies, our reading habits, and, most of all, ourselves as critics and as teachers. To delineate its full scope would require nothing less than a book — a book that would be outdated even as it was being composed.

To have attempted so many difficult questions and to have accomplished so much — even acknowledging the inevitable false starts, overlapping, and repetition — in so short a time, should certainly have secured feminist literary criticism an honored berth on that ongoing intellectual journey which we loosely term in academia, "critical analysis." Instead of being welcomed onto the train, however, we've been forced to negotiate a minefield. The very energy and diversity of our enterprise have rendered us vulnerable to attack on the grounds that we lack both definition and coherence; while our particular attentiveness to the ways in which literature encodes and disseminates cultural value systems calls down upon us imprecations echoing those heaped upon the Marxist critics of an earlier generation. If we are scholars dedicated to rediscovering a lost body of writings by women, then our finds are questioned on aesthetic grounds. And if we are critics, determined to practice revisionist readings, it is claimed that our focus is too narrow, and our results are only distortions or, worse still, polemical misreadings.

The very vehemence of the outcry, coupled with our total dismissal in some quarters,[8] suggests not our deficiencies, however, but the potential magnitude of our challenge. For what we are asking be scrutinized are nothing less than

---

[2]See Clifford Geertz, "Ideology as a Cultural System," in his *The Interpretation of Cultures: Selected Essays* (New York: Basic Books, 1973), p. 232. [Kolodny]

[3]Ibid., p. 204. [Kolodny]

[4]Lillian S. Robinson, "Cultural Criticism and the *Horror Vacui*," *College English* 33, no. 1 (1972); reprinted as "The Critical Task" in her *Sex, Class, and Culture* (Bloomington: Indiana University Press, 1978), p. 51. [Kolodny]

[5]Elaine Showalter, *A Literature of Their Own: British Women Novelists from Brontë to Lessing* (Princeton: Princeton University Press, 1977), p. 36. [Kolodny]

[6]Adrienne Rich, "When We Dead Awaken: Writing as Re-Vision," *College English* 34, no. 1 (October 1972); reprinted in *Adrienne Rich's Poetry,* ed. Barbara Charlesworth Gelpi and Albert Gelpi (New York: W. W. Norton Co., 1975), p. 90. [Kolodny]

[7]Kate Millett, *Sexual Politics* (Garden City, N.Y.: Doubleday and Co., 1970). [Kolodny]

[8]Consider, for example, Robert Boyers's reductive and inaccurate generalization that "what distinguishes ordinary books and articles about women from feminist writing is the feminist insistence on asking the same questions of every work and demanding ideologically satisfactory answers to those questions as a means of evaluating it," in his "A Case Against Feminist Criticism," *Partisan Review* 43, no. 4 (1976): 602. It is partly as a result of such misconceptions, that we have the paucity of feminist critics who are granted a place in English departments which otherwise pride themselves on the variety of their critical orientations. [Kolodny]

shared cultural assumptions so deeply rooted and so long ingrained that, for the most part, our critical colleagues have ceased to recognize them as such. In other words, what is really being bewailed in the claims that we distort texts or threaten the disappearance of the great Western literary tradition itself[9] is not so much the disappearance of either text or tradition but, instead, the eclipse of that particular *form* of the text, and that particular *shape* of the canon, which previously reified male readers' sense of power and significance in the world. Analogously, by asking whether, as readers, we ought to be "really satisfied by the marriage of Dorothea Brooke to Will Ladislaw? of Shirley Keeldar to Louis Moore?"[10] or whether, as Jean Kennard suggests, we must reckon with the ways in which "the qualities we have been invited to admire in these heroines [have] been sacrificed to structural neatness,"[11] is to raise difficult and profoundly perplexing questions about the ethical implications of our otherwise unquestioned aesthetic pleasures. It is, after all, an imposition of high order to ask the viewer to attend to Ophelia's sufferings in a scene where, before, he'd always so comfortably kept his eye fixed firmly on Hamlet. To understand all this, then, as the real nature of the challenge we have offered and, in consequence, as the motivation for the often overt hostility we've aroused, should help us learn to negotiate the minefield, if not with grace, then with at least a clearer comprehension of its underlying patterns.

[9]Ambivalent though he is about the literary continuity that begins with Homer, Harold Bloom nonetheless somewhat ominously prophesies "that the first true break . . . will be brought about in generations to come, if the burgeoning religion of Liberated Woman spreads from its clusters of enthusiasts to dominate the West," in his *A Map of Misreading* (New York: Oxford University Press, 1975), p. 33. On p. 36, he acknowledges that while something "as violent [as] a quarrel would ensue if I expressed my judgment" on Robert Lowell and Norman Mailer, "it would lead to something more intense than quarrels if I expressed my judgment upon . . . the 'literature of Women's Liberation.'" [Kolodny]

[10]Dorothea Brooke and Will Ladislaw marry in the denouement of George Eliot's novel, *Middlemarch* (1871–72), Shirley Keeldar and Louis Moore in that of Charlotte Brontë's *Shirley* (1849). [Kolodny]

[11]Jean E. Kennard, *Victims of Convention* (Hamden, Conn.: Archon Books, 1978), p. 14. [Kolodny]

The ways in which objections to our work are usually posed, of course, serve to obscure their deeper motivations. But this may, in part, be due to our own reticence at taking full responsibility for the truly radicalizing premises that lie at the theoretical core of all we have so far accomplished. It may be time, therefore, to redirect discussion, forcing our adversaries to deal with the substantive issues and pushing ourselves into a clearer articulation of what, in fact, we are about. Up until now, I fear, we have only piecemeal dealt with the difficulties inherent in challenging the authority of established canons and then justifying the excellence of women's traditions, sometimes in accord with standards to which they have no intrinsic relation.

At the very point at which we must perforce enter the discourse — that is, claiming excellence or importance for our "finds" — all discussion has already, we discover, long ago been closed. "If Kate Chopin were *really* worth reading," an Oxford-trained colleague once assured me, "she'd have lasted — like Shakespeare"; and he then proceeded to vote against the English department's crediting a women's studies seminar I was offering in American women writers. The canon, for him, conferred excellence; Chopin's exclusion demonstrated only her lesser worth. As far as he was concerned, I could no more justify giving the English department credit for the study of Chopin than I could dare publicly to question Shakespeare's genius. Through hindsight, I've now come to view that discussion as not only having posed fruitless oppositions, but also as having entirely evaded the much more profound problem lurking just beneath the surface of our disagreement. That is, that the fact of canonization puts any work beyond questions of establishing its merit and, instead, invites students to offer only increasingly more ingenious readings and interpretations, the purpose of which is to validate the greatness already imputed by canonization.

Had I only understood it for what it was then, into this circular and self-serving set of assumptions I might have interjected some statement of my right to question why *any* text is revered and my need to know what it tells us about "how we live, how we have been living, how we have been led to imagine ourselves, [and] how our language has trapped as well as liberated us."[12] The very fact of our critical training within the strictures imposed by an established canon of major works and authors, however, repeatedly deflects us from such questions. Instead, we find ourselves endlessly responding to the *riposte* that the overwhelmingly male presence among canonical authors was only an accident of history — and never intentionally sexist — coupled with claims to the "obvious" aesthetic merit of those canonized texts. It is, as I say, a fruitless exchange, serving more to obscure than to expose the territory being protected and dragging us, again and again, through the minefield.

It is my contention that current hostilities might be transformed into a true dialogue with our critics if we at last make explicit what appear, to this observer, to constitute the three crucial propositions to which our special interests inevitably give rise. They are, moreover, propositions which, if handled with care and intelligence, could breathe new life into now moribund areas of our profession: (1) Literary history (and, with that, the historicity of literature) is a fiction; (2) insofar as we are taught how to read, what we engage are not texts but paradigms; and, finally, (3) that since the grounds upon which we assign aesthetic value to texts are never infallible, unchangeable, or universal, we must reexamine not only our aesthetics but, as well, the inherent biases and assumptions informing the critical methods which (in part) shape our aesthetic responses. For the sake of brevity, I won't attempt to offer the full arguments for each but, rather, only sufficient elaboration to demonstrate what I see as their intrinsic relation to the potential scope of and present challenge implied by feminist literary study.

1. *Literary history (and, with that, the historicity of literature) is a fiction.* To begin with, an established canon functions as a model by which to chart the continuities and discontinuities, as well as the influences upon and the interconnections between works, genres, and authors. That model we tend to forget, however, is of our own making.

[12]Rich, "When We Dead Awaken," p. 90. [Kolodny]

It will take a very different shape, and explain its inclusions and exclusions in very different ways, if the reigning critical ideology believes that new literary forms result from some kind of ongoing internal dialectic within preexisting styles and traditions or if, by contrast, the ideology declares that literary change is dependent upon societal development and thereby determined by upheavals in the social and economic organization of the culture at large.[13] Indeed, whenever in the previous century of English and American literary scholarship one alternative replaced the other, we saw dramatic alterations in canonical "wisdom."

This suggests, then, that our sense of a "literary history" and, by extension, our confidence in a "historical" canon, is rooted not so much in any definitive understanding of the past, as it is in our need to call up and utilize the past on behalf of a better understanding of the present. Thus, to paraphrase David Couzens Hoy, it becomes "necessary to point out that the understanding of art and literature is such an essential aspect of the present's self-understanding that this self-understanding conditions what even gets taken" as comprising that artistic and literary past. To quote Hoy fully, "this continual reinterpretation of the past goes hand in hand with the continual reinterpretation by the present of itself."[14] In our own time, uncertain as to which, if any, model truly accounts for our canonical choices or accurately explains literary history, and pressured further by the feminists' call for some justification of the criteria by which women's writings were largely excluded from both that canon and history, we suffer what Harold Bloom has called "a remarkable dimming" of "our mutual sense of canonical standards."[15]

Into this apparent impasse, feminist literary theorists implicitly introduce the observation that our choices and evaluations of current literature

[13]The first is a proposition currently expressed by some structuralists and formalist critics; the best statement of the second probably appears in Georg Lukács, *Writer and Critic* (New York: Grosset and Dunlap, 1970), p. 119. [Kolodny]

[14]David Couzens Hoy, "Hermeneutic Circularity, Indeterminacy, and Incommensurability," *New Literary History* 10, no. 1 (Autumn 1978): 166–67. [Kolodny]

[15]Bloom, *Map of Misreading*, p. 36. [Kolodny]

have the effect either of solidifying or of reshaping our sense of the past. The authority of any established canon, after all, is reified by our perception that current work seems to grow, almost inevitably, out of it (even in opposition or rebellion), and is called into question when what we read appears to have little or no relation to what we recognize as coming before. So, were the larger critical community to begin to seriously attend to the recent outpouring of fine literature by women, this would surely be accompanied by a concomitant researching of the past, by literary historians, in order to account for the present phenomenon. In that process, literary history would itself be altered: works by seventeenth-, eighteenth-, or nineteenth-century women, to which we had not previously attended, might be given new importance as "precursors" or as prior influences upon present-day authors; while selected male writers might also be granted new prominence as figures whom the women today, or even yesterday, needed to reject. I am arguing, in other words, that the choices we make in the present inevitably alter our sense of the past that led to them.

Related to this is the feminist challenge to that patently mendacious critical fallacy that we read the "classics" in order to reconstruct the past "the way it really was," and that we read Shakespeare and Milton in order to apprehend the meanings that they intended. Short of time machines or miraculous resurrections, there is simply no way to know, precisely or surely, what "really was," what Homer intended when he sang, or Milton when he dictated. Critics more acute than I have already pointed out the impossibility of grounding a reading in the imputation of authorial intention because the further removed the author is from us, so too must be her or his systems of knowledge and belief, points of view, and structures of vision (artistic and otherwise).[16] (I omit here the difficulty of finally either proving or disproving the imputation of intentionality because, inescapably, the only appropriate authority is unavailable: deceased.) What we have really come to mean when we speak of competence in reading historical texts, therefore, is the ability to recognize literary conventions which have survived through time — so as to remain operational in the mind of the reader — and, where these are lacking, the ability to translate (or perhaps transform?) the text's ciphers into more current and recognizable shapes. But we never really reconstruct the past in its own terms. What we gain when we read the "classics," then, is neither Homer's Greece nor George Eliot's England *as they knew it* but, rather, an approximation of an already fictively imputed past made available, through our interpretive strategies, for present concerns. Only by understanding this can we put to rest that recurrent delusion that the "continuing relevance" of the classics serves as "testimony to perennial features of human experience."[17] The only "perennial feature" to which our ability to read and reread texts written in previous centuries testifies is our inventiveness — in the sense that all of literary history is a fiction which we daily recreate as we reread it. What distinguishes feminists in this regard is their desire to alter and extend what we take as historically relevant from out of that vast storehouse of our literary inheritance and, further, feminists' recognition of the storehouse for what it really is: a resource for remodeling our literary history, past, present, and future.

2. *Insofar as we are taught how to read, what we engage are not texts but paradigms.* To pursue the logical consequences of the first proposition leads, however uncomfortably, to the conclusion that we appropriate meaning from a text according

---

[16]John Dewey offered precisely this argument in 1934 when he insisted that a work of art "is recreated every time it is esthetically experienced. . . . It is absurd to ask what an artist 'really' meant by his product: he himself would find different meanings in it at different days and hours and in different stages of his own development." Further, he explained, "It is simply an impossibility that any one today should experience the Parthenon as the devout Athenian contemporary citizen experienced it, any more than the religious statuary of the twelfth century can mean, esthetically, even to a good Catholic today just what it meant to the worshipers of the old period," in *Art as Experience* (New York: Capricorn Books, 1958), pp. 108–09. [Kolodny]

[17]Charles Altieri, "The Hermeneutics of Literary Indeterminacy: A Dissent from the New Orthodoxy," *New Literary History* 10, no. 1 (Autumn 1978): 90. [Kolodny]

to what we need (or desire) or, in other words, according to the critical assumptions or predispositions (conscious or not) that we bring to it. And we appropriate different meanings, or report different gleanings, at different times — even from the same text — according to our changed assumptions, circumstances, and requirements. This, in essence, constitutes the heart of the second proposition. For insofar as literature is itself a social institution, so, too, reading is a highly socialized — or learned — activity. What makes it so exciting, of course, is that it can be constantly relearned and refined, so as to provide either an individual or an entire reading community, over time, with infinite variations of the same text. It *can* provide that, but, I must add, too often it does not. Frequently our reading habits become fixed, so that each successive reading experience functions, in effect, normatively, with one particular kind of novel stylizing our expectations of those to follow, the stylistic devices of any favorite author (or group of authors) alerting us to the presence or absence of those devices in the works of others, and so on. "Once one has read his first poem," Murray Krieger has observed, "he turns to his second and to the others that will follow thereafter with an increasing series of preconceptions about the sort of activity in which he is indulging. In matters of literary experience, as in other experiences," Krieger concludes, "one is a virgin but once."[18]

For most readers, this is a fairly unconscious process, and not unnaturally, what we are taught to read well and with pleasure, when we are young, predisposes us to certain specific kinds of adult reading tastes. For the professional literary critic, the process may be no different, but it is at least more conscious. Graduate schools, at their best, are training grounds for competing interpretive paradigms or reading techniques: affective stylistics, structuralism, and semiotic analysis, to name only a few of the more recent entries. The delight we learn to take in the mastery of these interpretive strategies is then often mistakenly construed as our delight in reading specific texts, especially in the case of works that would otherwise be unavailable or even offensive to us. In my own graduate career, for example, with superb teachers to guide me, I learned to take great pleasure in *Paradise Lost,* even though as both a Jew and a feminist, I can subscribe neither to its theology nor to its hierarchy of sexual valuation. If, within its own terms (as I have been taught to understand them), the text manipulates my sensibilities and moves me to pleasure — as I will affirm it does — then, at least in part, that must be because, in spite of my real-world alienation from many of its basic tenets, I have been able to enter that text through interpretive strategies which allow me to displace less comfortable observations with others to which I have been taught pleasurably to attend. Though some of my teachers may have called this process "learning to read the text properly," I have now come to see it as learning to effectively manipulate the critical strategies which they taught me so well. Knowing, for example, the poem's debt to epic conventions, I am able to discover in it echoes and reworkings of both lines and situations from Virgil and Homer; placing it within the ongoing Christian debate between Good and Evil, I comprehend both the philosophic and the stylistic significance of Satan's ornate rhetoric as compared to God's majestic simplicity in Book III. But, in each case, an interpretative model, already assumed, had guided my discovery of the evidence for it.[19]

When we consider the implications of these observations for the processes of canon formation and for the assignment of aesthetic value, we find ourselves locked in a chicken-and-egg dilemma, unable easily to distinguish as primary the importance of *what* we read as opposed to *how* we have learned to read it. For, simply put, we read well, and with pleasure, what we already know how to read; and what we know how to read is to a large extent dependent upon what we have already read (works from which we've developed our expectations and learned our interpretive strategies).

---

[18]Murray Krieger, *Theory of Criticism: A Tradition and Its System* (Baltimore: The Johns Hopkins University Press, 1976), p. 6. [Kolodny]

[19]See Stanley E. Fish, "Normal Circumstances, Literal Language, Direct Speech Acts, the Ordinary, the Everyday, the Obvious, What Goes without Saying, and Other Special Cases," *Critical Inquiry* 4, no. 4 (Summer 1978): 627–28. [Kolodny]

What we then choose to read — and, by extension, teach and thereby "canonize" — usually follows upon our previous reading. Radical breaks are tiring, demanding, uncomfortable, and sometimes wholly beyond our comprehension.

Though the argument is not usually couched in precisely these terms, a considerable segment of the most recent feminist rereadings of women writers allows the conclusion that, where those authors have dropped out of sight, the reason may be due not to any lack of merit in the work but, instead, to an incapacity of predominantly male readers to properly interpret and appreciate women's texts — due, in large part, to a lack of prior acquaintance. The fictions which women compose about the worlds they inhabit may owe a debt to prior, influential works by other women or, simply enough, to the daily experience of the writer herself or, more usually, to some combination of the two. The reader coming upon such fiction, with knowledge of neither its informing literary traditions nor its real-world contexts, will thereby find himself hard-pressed, though he may recognize the words on the page, to competently decipher its intended meanings. And this is what makes the recent studies by Patricia Meyer Spacks, Ellen Moers, Elaine Showalter, Sandra Gilbert and Susan Gubar, and others so crucial. For, by attempting to delineate the connections and interrelations that make for a female literary tradition, they provide us invaluable aids for recognizing and understanding the unique literary traditions and sex-related contexts out of which women write.

The (usually male) reader who, both by experience and by reading, has never made acquaintance with those contexts — historically, the lying-in room, the parlor, the nursery, the kitchen, the laundry, and so on — will necessarily lack the capacity to fully interpret the dialogue or action embedded therein; for, as every good novelist knows, the meaning of any character's action or statement is inescapably a function of the specific situation in which it is embedded.[20] Virginia Woolf therefore quite properly anticipated the male reader's disposition to write off what he

could not understand, abandoning women's writings as offering "not merely a difference of view, but a view that is weak, or trivial, or sentimental because it differs from his own." In her 1929 essay, "Women and Fiction," Woolf grappled most obviously with the ways in which male writers and male subject matter had already preempted the language of literature. Yet she was also tacitly commenting on the problem of (male) audience and conventional reading expectations when she speculated that the woman writer might well "find that she is perpetually wishing to alter the established values [in literature] — to make serious what appears insignificant to a man, and trivial what is to him important."[21] "The 'competence' necessary for understanding [a] literary message . . . depends upon a great number of codices," after all; as Cesare Segre has pointed out, to be competent, a reader must either share or at least be familiar with, "in addition to the code language . . . the codes of custom, of society, and of conceptions of the world"[22] (what Woolf meant by "values"). Males ignorant of women's "values" or conceptions of the world will necessarily, thereby, be poor readers of works that in any sense recapitulate their codes.

The problem is further exacerbated when the language of the literary text is largely dependent upon figuration. For it can be argued, as Ted Cohen has shown, that while "in general, and with some obvious qualifications . . . all literal use of language is accessible to all whose language it is . . . figurative use can be inaccessible to all but those who share information about one another's knowledge, beliefs, intentions, and attitudes."[23] There was nothing fortuitous, for example, in Charlotte Perkins Gilman's decision to situate the progressive mental breakdown and increasing incapacity of the protagonist of *The Yellow Wallpaper* in an upstairs room that had once served as a nursery (with barred windows, no less). But the reader unacquainted with the

[20]Ibid., p. 643. [Kolodny]

[21]Virginia Woolf, "Women and Fiction," *Granite and Rainbow: Essays* (London: Hogarth, 1958), p. 81. [Kolodny]

[22]Cesare Segre, "Narrative Structures and Literary History," *Critical Inquiry* 3, no. 2 (Winter 1976): 272–73. [Kolodny]

[23]Ted Cohen, "Metaphor and the Cultivation of Intimacy," *Critical Inquiry* 5, no. 1 (Autumn 1978): 9. [Kolodny]

ways in which women traditionally inhabited a household might not have taken the initial description of the setting as semantically relevant; and the progressive infantilization of the adult protagonist would thereby lose some of its symbolic implications. Analogously, the contemporary poet who declares, along with Adrienne Rich, the need for "a whole new poetry beginning here" is acknowledging that the materials available for symbolization and figuration from women's contexts will necessarily differ from those that men have traditionally utilized:

> Vision begins to happen in such a life
> as if a woman quietly walked away
> from the argument and jargon in a room
> and sitting down in the kitchen, began turning in
>   her lap
> bits of yarn, calico and velvet scraps,
> . . . .
> pulling the tenets of a life together
> with no mere will to mastery,
> only care for the many-lived, unending
> forms in which she finds herself.[24]

What, then, is the fate of the woman writer whose competent reading community is composed only of members of her own sex? And what, then, the response of the male critic who, on first looking into Virginia Woolf or Doris Lessing, finds all of the interpretative strategies at his command inadequate to a full and pleasurable deciphering of their pages? Historically, the result has been the diminished status of women's products and their consequent absence from major canons. Nowadays, however, by pointing out that the act of "interpreting language is no more sexually neutral than language use or the language system itself," feminist students of language, like Nelly Furman, help us better understand the crucial linkage between our gender and our interpretive, or reading, strategies. Insisting upon "the contribution of the . . . reader [in] the active attribution of significance to formal signifiers,"[25]

Furman and others promise to shake us all — female and male alike — out of our canonized and conventional aesthetic assumptions.

3. *Since the grounds upon which we assign aesthetic value to texts are never infallible, unchangeable, or universal, we must reexamine not only our aesthetics but, as well, the inherent biases and assumptions informing the critical methods which (in part) shape our aesthetic responses.* I am, on the one hand, arguing that men will be better readers, or appreciators, of women's books when they have read more of them (as women have always been taught to become astute readers of men's texts). On the other hand, it will be noted, the emphasis of my remarks shifts the act of critical judgment from assigning aesthetic valuations to texts and directs it, instead, to ascertaining the adequacy of any interpretive paradigm to a full reading of both female and male writing. My third proposition — and, I admit, perhaps the most controversial — thus calls into question that recurrent tendency in criticism to establish norms for the evaluation of literary works when we might better serve the cause of literature by developing standards for evaluating the adequacy of our critical methods.[26] This does not mean that I wish to discard aesthetic valuation. The choice, as I see it, is not between retaining or discarding aesthetic values; rather, the choice is between having some awareness of what constitutes (at least in part) the bases of our aesthetic responses and going without such an awareness. For it is my view that insofar as aesthetic responsiveness continues to be an integral aspect of our human response system — in part spontaneous, in part learned and educated — we will inevitably develop theories to help explain, formalize, or even initiate those responses.

In challenging the adequacy of received critical opinion or the imputed excellence of established canons, feminist literary critics are essentially seeking to discover how aesthetic value is assigned in the first place, where it resides (in the text or in the reader), and, most importantly, what

[24]From Adrienne Rich's "Transcendental Etude" in her *The Dream of a Common Language: Poems 1974–1977* (New York: W. W. Norton and Co., 1978), pp. 76–77. [Kolodny]

[25]Furman, "The Study of Women and Language, Nelly: Comment on Vol. 3, no. 3" in *Signs* 4, no. 1 (Autumn 1978), p. 184. [Kolodny]

[26]"A recurrent tendency in criticism is the establishment of false norms for the evaluation of literary works," notes Robert Scholes in his *Structuralism in Literature: An Introduction* (New Haven: Yale University Press, 1974), p. 131. [Kolodny]

validity may really be claimed by our aesthetic "judgments." What ends do those judgments serve, the feminist asks; and what conceptions of the world or ideological stances do they (even if unwittingly) help to perpetuate? In so doing, she points out, among other things, that any response labeled "aesthetic" may as easily designate some immediately experienced moment or event as it may designate a species of nostalgia, a yearning for the components of a simpler past, when the world seemed known or at least understandable. Thus the value accorded an opera or a Shakespeare play may well reside in the viewer's immediate viewing pleasure, or it may reside in the play's nostalgic evocation of a once-comprehensible and ordered world. At the same time, the feminist confronts, for example, the reader who simply cannot entertain the possibility that women's worlds are symbolically rich, the reader who, like the male characters in Susan Glaspell's 1917 short story, "A Jury of Her Peers," has already assumed the innate "insignificance of kitchen things."[27] Such a reader, she knows, will prove himself unable to assign significance to fictions that attend to "kitchen things" and will, instead, judge such fictions as trivial and as aesthetically wanting. For her to take useful issue with such a reader, she must make clear that what appears to be a dispute about aesthetic merit is, in reality, a dispute about the *contexts of judgment;* and what is at issue, then, is the adequacy of the prior assumptions and reading habits brought to bear on the text. To put it bluntly: we have had enough pronouncements of aesthetic valuation for a time; it is now our task to evaluate the imputed norms and normative reading patterns that, in part, led to those pronouncements.

By and large, I think I've made my point. Only to clarify it do I add this coda: when feminists turn their attention to the works of male authors which have traditionally been accorded high aesthetic value and, where warranted, follow Tillie Olsen's advice that we assert our "right to say: this is surface, this falsifies reality, this degrades,"[28] such statements do not necessarily mean that we will end up with a diminished canon. To question the source of the aesthetic pleasures we've gained from reading Spenser, Shakespeare, Milton, and so on, does not imply that we must deny those pleasures. It means only that aesthetic response is once more invested with epistemological, ethical, and moral concerns. It means, in other words, that readings of *Paradise Lost* which analyze its complex hierarchal structures but fail to note the implications of gender within that hierarchy; or which insist upon the inherent (or even inspired) perfection of Milton's figurative language but fail to note the consequences, for Eve, of her specifically gender-marked weakness, which, like the flowers to which she attends, requires "propping up"; or which concentrate on the poem's thematic reworking of classical notions of martial and epic prowess into Christian (moral) heroism but fail to note that Eve is stylistically edited out of that process — all such readings, however useful, will no longer be deemed wholly adequate. The pleasures we had earlier learned to take in the poem will not be diminished thereby, but they will become part of an altered reading attentiveness.

These three propositions I believe to be at the theoretical core of most current feminist literary criticism, whether acknowledged as such or not. If I am correct in this, then that criticism represents more than a profoundly skeptical stance toward all other preexisting and contemporaneous schools and methods, and more than an impassioned demand that the variety and variability of women's literary expression be taken into full account, rather than written off as caprice and exception, the irregularity in an otherwise regular design. It represents that locus in literary study where, in unceasing effort, female self-consciousness turns in upon itself, attempting to grasp the deepest conditions of its own unique

[27]For a full discussion of the Glaspell short story which takes this problem into account, please see my "A Map for Re-Reading: Or, Gender and the Interpretation of Literary Texts," forthcoming in a Special Issue on Narrative, *New Literary History* (1980). [Kolodny]

[28]Tillie Olsen, *Silences* (New York: Delacorte Press/Seymour Lawrence, 1978), p. 45. [Kolodny]

and multiplicitous realities, in the hope, eventually, of altering the very forms through which the culture perceives, expresses, and knows itself. For, if what the larger women's movement looks for in the future is a transformation of the structures of primarily male power which now order our society, then the feminist literary critic demands that we understand the ways in which those structures have been — and continue to be — reified by our literature and by our literary criticism. Thus, along with other "radical" critics and critical schools, though our focus remains the power of the word to both structure and mirror human experience, our overriding commitment is to a radical alteration — an improvement, we hope — in the nature of that experience.

What distinguishes our work from those similarly oriented "social consciousness" critiques, it is said, is its lack of systematic coherence. Pitted against, for example, psychoanalytic or Marxist readings, which owe a decisive share of their persuasiveness to their apparent internal consistency as a system, the aggregate of feminist literary criticism appears woefully deficient in system, and painfully lacking in program. It is, in fact, from all quarters, the most telling defect alleged against us, the most explosive threat in the minefield. And my own earlier observation that, as of 1976, feminist literary criticism appeared "more like a set of interchangeable strategies than any coherent school or shared goal orientation," has been taken by some as an indictment, by others as a statement of impatience. Neither was intended. I felt then, as I do now, that this would "prove both its strength *and* its weakness,"[29] in the sense that the apparent disarray would leave us vulnerable to the kind of objection I've just alluded to; while the fact of our diversity would finally place us securely where, all along, we should have been: camped out, on the far side of the minefield, with the other pluralists and pluralisms.

In our heart of hearts, of course, most critics are really structuralists (whether or not they accept the label) because what we are seeking are patterns (or structures) that can order and explain the otherwise inchoate; thus, we invent, or believe we discover, relational patternings in the texts we read which promise transcendence from difficulty and perplexity to clarity and coherence. But, as I've tried to argue in these pages, to the imputed "truth" or "accuracy" of these findings, the feminist must oppose the painfully obvious truism that what is attended to in a literary work, and hence what is reported about it, is often determined not so much by the work itself as by the critical technique or aesthetic criteria through which it is filtered or, rather, read and decoded. All the feminist is asserting, then, is her own equivalent right to liberate new (and perhaps different) significances from these same texts; and, at the same time, her right to choose which features of a text she takes as relevant because she is, after all, asking new and different questions of it. In the process, she claims neither definitiveness nor structural completeness for her different readings and reading systems, but only their usefulness in recognizing the particular achievements of woman-as-author and their applicability in conscientiously decoding woman-as-sign.

That these alternate foci of critical attentiveness will result in alternate readings or interpretations of the same text — even among feminists — should be no cause for alarm. Such developments illustrate only the pluralist contention that, "in approaching a text of any complexity . . . the reader must choose to emphasize certain aspects which seem to him crucial" and that, "in fact, the variety of readings which we have for many works is a function of the selection of crucial aspects made by the variety of readers." Robert Scholes, from whom I've been quoting, goes so far as to assert that "there is no single 'right' reading for any complex literary work," and, following the Russian formalist school, he observes that "we do not speak of readings that are simply true or false, but of readings that are more or less rich, strategies that are more or less appropriate."[30] Because those who share the term "feminist" nonetheless practice a diversity of critical strategies, leading, in some cases, to quite different readings, we must

[29]Annette Kolodny, "Literary Criticism," Review Essay in *Signs* 2, no. 2 (Winter 1976): 420. [Kolodny]

[30]Scholes, *Structuralism in Literature*, pp. 144–45. These comments appear within his explication of Tzvetan Todorov's theory of reading. [Kolodny]

acknowledge among ourselves that sister critics, "having chosen to tell a different story, may in their interpretation identify different aspects of the meanings conveyed by the same passage."[31]

Adopting a "pluralist" label does not mean, however, that we cease to disagree; it means only that we entertain the possibility that different readings, even of the same text, may be differently useful, even illuminating, within different contexts of inquiry. It means, in effect, that we enter a dialectical process of examining, testing, even trying out the contexts — be they prior critical assumptions or explicitly stated ideological stances (or some combination of the two) — that led to the disparate readings. Not all will be equally acceptable to every one of us, of course, and even those prior assumptions or ideologies that are acceptable may call for further refinement and/or clarification. But, at the very least, because we will have grappled with the assumptions that led to it, we will be better able to articulate *why* we find a particular reading or interpretation adequate or inadequate. This kind of dialectical process, moreover, not only makes us more fully aware of what criticism is, and how it functions; it also gives us access to its future possibilities, making us conscious, as R. P. Blackmur put it, "of what we have done," "of what can be done next, or done again,"[32] or, I would add, of what can be done differently. To put it still another way: just because we will no longer tolerate the specifically sexist omissions and oversights of earlier critical schools and methods does not mean that, in their stead, we must establish our own "party line."

In my view, our purpose is not and should not be the formulation of any single reading method or potentially procrustean set of critical procedures nor, even less, the generation of prescriptive categories for some dreamed-of nonsexist literary canon.[33] Instead, as I see it, our task is to initiate nothing less than a playful pluralism, responsive to the possibilities of multiple critical schools and methods, but captive of none, recognizing that the many tools needed for our analysis will necessarily be largely inherited and only partly of our own making. Only by employing a plurality of methods will we protect ourselves from the temptation of so oversimplifying any text — and especially those particularly offensive to us — that we render ourselves unresponsive to what Scholes has called "its various systems of meaning and their interaction."[34] Any text we deem worthy of our critical attention is usually, after all, a locus of many and varied kinds of (personal, thematic, stylistic, structural, rhetorical, etc.) relationships. So, whether we tend to treat a text as a *mimesis,* in which words are taken to be recreating or representing viable worlds; or whether we prefer to treat a text as a kind of equation of communication, in which decipherable messages are passed from writers to readers; and whether we locate meaning as inherent in the text, the act of reading, or in some collaboration between reader and text — whatever our predilection, let us not generate from it a straitjacket that limits the scope of possible analysis. Rather, let us generate an ongoing dialogue of competing potential possibilities — among feminists and, as well, between feminist and nonfeminist critics.

The difficulty of what I describe does not escape me. The very idea of pluralism seems to threaten a kind of chaos for the future of literary inquiry while, at the same time, it seems to deny the hope of establishing some basic conceptual model which can organize all data — the hope which always begins any analytical exercise. My effort here, however, has been to demonstrate the

[31] I borrow this concise phrasing of pluralistic modesty from M. H. Abrams's "The Deconstructive Angel," *Critical Inquiry* 3, no. 3 (Spring 1977): 427. Indications of the pluralism that was to mark feminist inquiry were to be found in the diversity of essays collected by Susan Koppelman Cornillon for her early and ground-breaking anthology, *Images of Women in Fiction: Feminist Perspectives* (Bowling Green, Ohio: Bowling Green University Popular Press, 1972). [Kolodny]

[32] R. P. Blackmur, "A Burden for Critics," *The Hudson Review* 1 (1948): 171. Blackmur, of course, was referring to the way in which criticism makes us unconscious of how art functions; I use his wording here because I am arguing that that same awareness must also be focused on the critical act itself. "Consciousness," he avers, "is the way we feel the critic's burden." [Kolodny]

[33] I have earlier elaborated my objection to prescriptive categories for literature in "The Feminist as Literary Critic," Critical Response in *Critical Inquiry* 2, no. 4 (Summer 1976): 827–28. [Kolodny]

[34] Scholes, *Structuralism in Literature,* pp. 151–52. [Kolodny]

essential delusions that inform such objections: If literary inquiry has historically escaped chaos by establishing canons, then it has only substituted one mode of arbitrary action for another — and, in this case, at the expense of half the population. And if feminists openly acknowledge ourselves as pluralists, then we do not give up the search for patterns of opposition and connection — probably the basis of thinking itself; what we give up is simply the arrogance of claiming that our work is either exhaustive or definitive. (It is, after all, the identical arrogance we are asking our nonfeminist colleagues to abandon.) If this kind of pluralism appears to threaten both the present coherence of and the inherited aesthetic criteria for a canon of "greats," then, as I have earlier argued, it is precisely that threat which, alone, can free us from the prejudices, the strictures, and the blind spots of the past. In feminist hands, I would add, it is less a threat than a promise.

What unites and repeatedly invigorates feminist literary criticism, then, is neither dogma nor method but, as I have indicated earlier, an acute and impassioned *attentiveness* to the ways in which primarily male structures of power are inscribed (or encoded) within our literary inheritance; the consequences of that encoding for women — as characters, as readers, and as writers; and, with that, a shared analytic *concern* for the implications of that encoding not only for a better understanding of the past, but also for an improved reordering of the present and future as well. If that *concern* identifies feminist literary criticism as one of the many academic arms of the larger women's movement, then that *attentiveness,* within the halls of academe, poses no less a challenge for change, generating, as it does, the three propositions explored here. The critical pluralism that inevitably follows upon those three propositions, however, bears little resemblance to what Lillian Robinson has called "the greatest bourgeois theme of all, the myth of pluralism, with its consequent rejection of ideological commitment as 'too simple' to embrace the (necessarily complex) truth."[35]

Only ideological commitment could have gotten us to enter the minefield, putting in jeopardy our careers and our livelihood. Only the power of ideology to transform our conceptual worlds, and the inspiration of that ideology to liberate long-suppressed energies and emotions, can account for our willingness to take on critical tasks that, in an earlier decade, would have been "abandoned in despair or apathy."[36] The fact of differences among us proves only that, despite our shared commitments, we have nonetheless refused to shy away from complexity, preferring rather to openly disagree than to give up either intellectual honesty or hard-won insights.

Finally, I would argue, pluralism informs feminist literary inquiry not simply as a description of what already exists but, more importantly, as the only critical stance consistent with the current status of the larger women's movement. Segmented and variously focused, the different women's organizations neither espouse any single system of analysis nor, as a result, express any wholly shared, consistently articulated ideology. The ensuing loss in effective organization and political clout is a serious one, but it has not been paralyzing; in spite of our differences, we have united to *act* in areas of clear mutual concern (the push for the Equal Rights Amendment is probably the most obvious example). The trade-off, as I see it, has made possible an ongoing and educative dialectic of analysis and proffered solutions, protecting us thereby from the inviting traps of reductionism and dogma. And so long as this dialogue remains active, both our politics and our criticism will be free of dogma — but never, I hope, of feminist ideology, in all its variety. For, "whatever else ideologies may be — projections of unacknowledged fears, disguises for ulterior motives, phatic expressions of group solidarity" (and the women's movement, to date, has certainly been all of these, and more) — whatever ideologies express, they are, as Clifford Geertz astutely observes, "most distinctively, maps of problematic social reality and matrices for the

[35]Lillian Robinson, "Dwelling in Decencies: Radical Criticism and the Feminist Perspective," *College English* 32, no. 8 (May 1971); reprinted in *Sex, Class, and Culture*, p. 11. [Kolodny]

[36]"Ideology bridges the emotional gap between things as they are and as one would have them be, thus insuring the performance of roles that might otherwise be abandoned in despair or apathy," comments Geertz in "Ideology as a Cultural System," p. 205. [Kolodny]

creation of collective conscience." And despite the fact that "ideological advocates . . . tend as much to obscure as to clarify the true nature of the problems involved," as Geertz notes, "they at least call attention to their existence and, by polarizing issues, make continued neglect more difficult. Without Marxist attack, there would have been no labor reform; without Black Nationalists, no deliberate speed."[37] Without Seneca Falls, I would add, no enfranchisement of women, and without "consciousness raising," no feminist literary criticism nor, even less, women's studies.

Ideology, however, only truly manifests its power by ordering the *sum* of our actions.[38] If feminist criticism calls anything into question, it must be that dog-eared myth of intellectual neutrality. For, what I take to be the underlying spirit, or message, of any consciously ideologically premised criticism — that is, that ideas are important *because* they determine the ways we live, or want to live, in the world — is vitiated by confining those ideas to the study, the classroom, or the pages of our books.

[37]Ibid., pp. 220, 205. [Kolodny]

[38]I here follow Fredric Jameson's view in *The Prison-House of Language: A Critical Account of Structuralism and Russian Formalism* (Princeton: Princeton University Press, 1974), p. 107, that: "Ideology would seem to be that grillwork of form, convention, and belief which orders our actions." [Kolodny]

To write chapters decrying the sexual stereotyping of women in our literature, while closing our eyes to the sexual harassment of our women students and colleagues; to display Katherine Hepburn and Rosalind Russell in our courses on "The Image of the Independent Career Women in Film," while managing not to notice the paucity of female administrators on our own campus; to study the women who helped make universal enfranchisement a political reality, while keeping silent about our activist colleagues who are denied promotion or tenure; to include segments on "Women in the Labor Movement" in our American studies or women's studies courses, while remaining willfully ignorant of the department secretary fired for her efforts to organize a clerical workers' union; to glory in the delusions of "merit," "privilege," and "status" which accompany campus life in order to insulate ourselves from the millions of women who labor in poverty — all this is not merely hypocritical; it destroys both the spirit and the meaning of what we are about. It puts us, however unwittingly, in the service of those who laid the minefield in the first place. In my view, it is a fine thing for many of us, individually, to have traversed the minefield; but that happy circumstance will only prove of lasting importance if, together, we expose it for what it is (the male fear of sharing power and significance with women) and deactivate its components, so that others, after us, may literally dance through the minefield.

Julia Kristeva

b. 1941

Born in Bulgaria, Julia Kristeva took a degree from the Literary Institute of Sofia before going to Paris in 1966 and submitting a troisième cycle *doctoral thesis and then a thesis for the* Doctorat d'État. *A tenured professor at the University of Paris, she was an early contributor to the influential avant-garde journal* Tel Quel, *an officer of the International Association of Semiotics, and an editor of the review* Sémiotica. *She is also a "Lacanian" psychoanalyst, which is not to suggest that Kristeva is merely an epigone or follower of Jacques Lacan or of the other imposing figures she has studied under, such as Lucien Goldmann and Claude Lévi-Strauss. Rather, Kristeva has persistently contributed to the development of structuralist and poststructuralist thought, at once helping shape emerging ideas and incorporating them as they emerge into her own eclectic, ever-evolving body of thought. Her* Σημειωτιχὴ *(1969), for example, is a critique of structuralism that pointed in the direction of the notion of "semanalysis" — a semiotic/psychoanalytical approach to texts for which Kristeva is perhaps best known. Her other works include* The Text of the Novel *(1970),* About Chinese Women *(1974),* Revolution in Poetic Language *(1974),* Powers of Horror: An Essay on Abjection *(1980),* Desire in Language: A Semiotic Approach to Literature and Art *(1980),* In the Beginning Was Love: Psychoanalysis and Faith *(1985),* Black Sun: Depression and Melancholia *(1987),* Language: The Unknown *(1989),* Nations without Nationalism *(1993),* Proust and the Sense of Time *(1993),* Time and Sense: Proust and the Experience of Literature *(1996),* Hannah Arendt *(2001),* Intimate Revolt *(2002),* Colette *(2004), and the as yet untranslated* Le Plaisir des formes *(2003). She has also published four novels. "Women's Time" was originally published as "Le Temps des femmes" in* Cahiers de recherche de sciences des textes et documents, *no. 5 (Winter 1979), and is reprinted from its first English translation, by Alice Jardine and Harry Blake, in* Signs *(1981).*

Women's Time

The nation — dream and reality of the nineteenth century — seems to have reached both its apogee and its limits when the 1929 crash and the National-Socialist apocalypse demolished the pillars that, according to Marx, were its essence: economic homogeneity, historical tradition, and linguistic unity.[1] It could indeed be demonstrated that World War II, though fought in the name of national values (in the above sense of the term), brought an end to the nation as a reality: It was turned into a mere illusion which, from that point forward, would be preserved only for ideological or strictly political purposes, its social and philosophical coherence having collapsed. To move quickly toward the specific problematic that will occupy us in this article, let us say that the chimera of economic *homogeneity* gave way to *interdependence* (when not submission to the economic superpowers), while *historical* tradition and *linguistic* unity were recast as a broader and deeper determinant: what might be called a *symbolic denominator*, defined as the cultural and religious memory forged by the interweaving of history and geography. The variants of this memory produce social territories which then redistribute the cutting up into political parties which is still in use but losing strength. At the same

Translated by Alice Jardine and Harry Blake.

[1] The following discussion emphasizes Europe in a way which may seem superfluous to some American readers given the overall emphasis on deterritorialization. It is, however, essential to the movement of an article that is above all devoted to the necessity of paying attention to the place from which we speak. [Tr.]

time, this memory or symbolic denominator, common to them all, reveals beyond economic globalization and/or uniformization certain characteristics transcending the nation that sometimes embrace an entire continent. A new social ensemble superior to the nation has thus been constituted,[2] within which the nation, far from losing its own traits, rediscovers and accentuates them in a strange temporality, in a kind of "future perfect," where the most deeply repressed past gives a distinctive character to a logical and sociological distribution of the most modern type. For this memory or symbolic common denominator concerns the response that human groupings, united in space and time, have given not to the problems of the *production* of material goods (i.e., the domain of the economy and of the human relationships it implies, politics, etc.) but, rather, to those of *reproduction*, survival of the species, life and death, the body, sex, and symbol. If it is true, for example, that Europe is representative of such a sociocultural ensemble, it seems to me that its existence is based more on this "symbolic denominator," which its art, philosophy, and religions manifest, than on its economic profile, which is certainly interwoven with collective memory but whose traits change rather rapidly under pressure from its partners.

It is clear that a social ensemble thus constituted possesses both a *solidity* rooted in a particular mode of reproduction and its representations through which the biological species is connected to its humanity, which is a tributary of time; as well as a certain *fragility* as a result of the fact that, through its universality, the symbolic common denominator is necessarily echoed in the corresponding symbolic denominator of another sociocultural ensemble. Thus, barely constituted as such, Europe finds itself being asked to compare itself with, or even to recognize itself in, the cultural, artistic, philosophical, and religious constructions belonging to other supranational sociocultural ensembles. This seems natural when the entities involved were linked by history (e.g., Europe and North America, or Europe and Latin America), but the phenomenon also occurs when the universality of this denominator we have called symbolic juxtaposes modes of production and reproduction apparently opposed in both the past and the present (e.g., Europe and India, or Europe and China). In short, with sociocultural ensembles of the European type, we are constantly faced with a double problematic: that of their *identity* constituted by historical sedimentation, and that of their *loss of identity* which is produced by this connection of memories which escape from history only to encounter anthropology. In other words, we confront two temporal dimensions: the time of linear history, or *cursive time* (as Nietzsche called it),[3] and the time of another history, thus another time, *monumental time* (again according to Nietzsche), which englobes these supranational, sociocultural ensembles within even larger entities.

I should like to draw attention to certain formations which seem to me to summarize the dynamics of a sociocultural organism of this type. The question is one of sociocultural groups, that is, groups defined according to their place in production, but especially according to their role in the mode of reproduction and its representations, which, while bearing the specific sociocultural traits of the formation in question, are *diagonal* to it and connect it to other sociocultural formations. I am thinking in particular of sociocultural groups which are usually defined as age groups (e.g., "young people in Europe"), as sexual divisions (e.g., "European women"), and so forth. While it is obvious that "young people" or "women" in Europe have their own particularity, it is nonetheless just as obvious that what defines them as "young people" or as "women" places them in a diagonal relationship to their European "origin"

---

[2]Kristeva is perhaps gesturing, in her discussion of nationalism becoming transcendentally absorbed into something larger, toward the European Union; the first direct elections for the European Parliament were held in the year she wrote this (1979).

[3]Nietzsche discusses "monumental history" and its alternatives (antiquarian history, critical history) in the essay "On the Use and Abuse of History for Life" published in *Untimely Meditations* (1874); in section VII, he contrasts what he considers culturally unhealthy attempts at objectivity, on the part of "monumental" historians, with what he envisions, a new form of history written as narrative art.

and links them to similar categories in North America or in China, among others. That is, insofar as they also belong to "monumental history," they will not be only European "young people" or "women" of Europe but will echo in a most specific way the universal traits of their structural place in reproduction and its representations.

Consequently, the reader will find in the following pages, first, an attempt to situate the problematic of women in Europe within an inquiry on time: that time which the feminist movement both inherits and modifies. Second, I will attempt to distinguish two phases or two generations of women which, while immediately universalist and cosmopolitan in their demands, can nonetheless be differentiated by the fact that the first generation is more determined by the implications of a national problematic (in the sense suggested above), while the second, more determined by its place within the "symbolic denominator," is European *and* trans-European. Finally, I will try, both through the problems approached and through the type of analysis I propose, to present what I consider a viable stance for a European — or at least a European woman — within a domain which is henceforth worldwide in scope.

WHICH TIME?

"Father's time, mother's species," as Joyce put it;[4] and, indeed, when evoking the name and destiny of women, one thinks more of the *space* generating and forming the human species than of *time*, becoming, or history. The modern sciences of subjectivity, of its genealogy and accidents, confirm in their own way this intuition, which is perhaps itself the result of a sociohistorical conjuncture. Freud, listening to the dreams and fantasies of his patients, thought that "hysteria was linked to place."[5] Subsequent studies on the acquisition of the symbolic function by children show that the permanence and quality of maternal love condition the appearance of the first spatial references

which induce the child's laugh and then induce the entire range of symbolic manifestations which lead eventually to sign and syntax.[6] Moreover, antipsychiatry and psychoanalysis as applied to the treatment of psychoses, before attributing the capacity for transference and communication to the patient, proceed to the arrangement of new places, gratifying substitutes that repair old deficiencies in the maternal space. I could go on giving examples. But they all converge on the problematic of space, which innumerable religions of matriarchal (re)appearance attribute to "woman," and which Plato, recapitulating in his own system the atomists of antiquity, designated by the aporia of the *chora*,[7] matrix space, nourishing, unnameable, anterior to the One, to God and, consequently, defying metaphysics.[8]

As for time, female[9] subjectivity would seem to provide a specific measure that essentially retains *repetition* and *eternity* from among the multiple modalities of time known through the history of civilizations. On the one hand, there are cycles, gestation, the eternal recurrence of a biological rhythm which conforms to that of nature and imposes a temporality whose stereotyping may shock, but whose regularity and unison with what is experienced as extrasubjective time, cosmic time, occasion vertiginous visions and

---

[4]In *Finnegans Wake* (1939); Kristeva will continue to juxtapose time and space against the paternal and maternal principles.

[5]Sigmund Freud and Carl G. Jung, *Correspondance* (Paris: Gallimard, 1975), 1:87. [Kristeva]

[6]R. Spitz, *La Première année de la vie de l'enfant* [First year of life: a psychoanalytic study of normal and deviant development of object relations] (Paris: PUF, 1958); D. Winnicott, *Jeu et réalité* [Playing and Reality] (Paris: Gallimard, 1975); Julia Kristeva, "Noms de lieu" in *Polylogue* (Paris: Editions du Seuil, 1977), translated as "Place Names" in Julia Kristeva, *Desire in Language: A Semiotic Approach to Literature and Art,* ed. Leon S. Roudiez, trans. Thomas Gora, Alice Jardine, and Leon Roudiez (New York: Columbia University Press, 1980) (hereafter cited as *Desire in Language*). [Kristeva]

[7]For Kristeva's revision of Lacan, see the introduction to Psychoanalytic Theory, p. 1116.

[8]Plato *Timeus* 52: "Indefinitely a place; it cannot be destroyed, but provides a ground for all that can come into being; itself being perceptible, outside of all sensation, by means of a sort of bastard reasoning; barely assuming credibility, it is precisely that which makes us dream when we perceive it, and affirm that all that exists must be somewhere, in a determined place . . ." (author's translation). [Kristeva]

[9]As most readers of recent French theory in translation know, *le féminin* does not have the same pejorative connotations it has come to have in English. It is a term used to speak

unnameable *jouissance*.[10] On the other hand, and perhaps as a consequence, there is the massive presence of a monumental temporality, without cleavage or escape, which has so little to do with linear time (which passes) that the very word "temporality" hardly fits: All-encompassing and infinite like imaginary space, this temporality reminds one of Kronos in Hesiod's mythology, the incestuous son whose massive presence covered all of Gea in order to separate her from Ouranos, the father.[11] Or one is reminded of the various myths of resurrection which, in all religious beliefs, perpetuate the vestige of an anterior or concomitant maternal cult, right up to its most recent elaboration, Christianity, in which the body of the Virgin Mother does not die but moves from one spatiality to another within the same time via dormition (according to the Orthodox faith) or via assumption (the Catholic faith).[12]

The fact that these two types of temporality (cyclical and monumental) are traditionally linked to female subjectivity insofar as the latter is thought of as necessarily maternal should not make us forget that this repetition and this eternity are found to be the fundamental, if not the sole, conceptions of time in numerous civilizations and experiences, particularly mystical ones.[13] The fact that certain currents of modern feminism recognize themselves here does not

render them fundamentally incompatible with "masculine" values.

In return, female subjectivity as it gives itself up to intuition becomes a problem with respect to a certain conception of time: time as project, teleology, linear and prospective unfolding; time as departure, progression, and arrival — in other words, the time of history.[14] It has already been abundantly demonstrated that this kind of temporality is inherent in the logical and ontological values of any given civilization, that this temporality renders explicit a rupture, an expectation, or an anguish which other temporalities work to conceal. It might also be added that this linear time is that of language considered as the enunciation of sentences (noun + verb; topic-comment; beginning-ending), and that this time rests on its own stumbling block, which is also the stumbling block of that enunciation — death. A psychoanalyst would call this "obsessional time," recognizing in the mastery of time the true structure of the slave. The hysteric (either male or female) who suffers from reminiscences would, rather, recognize his or her self in the anterior temporal modalities: cyclical or monumental. This antinomy, one perhaps embedded in psychic structures, becomes, nonetheless, within a given civilization, an antinomy among social groups and ideologies in which the radical positions of certain feminists would rejoin the discourse of marginal groups of spiritual or mystical inspiration and, strangely enough, rejoin recent scientific preoccupations. Is it not true that the problematic of a time indissociable from space, of a space-time in infinite expansion, or rhythmed by accidents or catastrophes, preoccupies both space science and genetics?[15] And, at another level, is it not true that the contemporary media revolution,[16] which is

---

about women in general, but, as used most often in this article, it probably comes closest to our "female" as defined by Elaine Showalter in *A Literature of Their Own* (Princeton, N.J.: Princeton University Press, 1977). I have therefore used either "women" or "female" according to the context (cf. also n. 9 in "Introduction to Julia Kristeva's 'Women's Time'" [this issue; hereafter cited as "Introduction"]). "Subjectivity" here refers to the state of being "a thinking, speaking, acting, doing or writing agent" and never, e.g., as opposed to "objectivity" (see the glossary in *Desire in Language*). [Tr.]

[10]I have retained *jouissance* — that word for pleasure which defies translation — as it is rapidly becoming a "believable neologism" in English (see the glossary in *Desire in Language*). [Tr.]

[11]This particular mythology has important implications — equal only to those of the oedipal myth — for current French thought. [Tr.]

[12]See Julia Kristeva, "Hérétique de l'amour," *Tel quel*, no. 74 (1977), pp. 30–49. [Kristeva]

[13]See H. C. Puech, *La Gnose et la temps* (Paris: Gallimard, 1977). [Kristeva]

[14]See "Introduction." [Tr.]

[15]Kristeva gestures toward the conflict among astronomers between the "steady state" and "big bang" theories explaining the expansion of the universe and the conflict among biologists between the "gradualist" and "punctuated equilibrium" theories of evolution.

[16]Kristeva gestures toward the centralization of information on digital computers, which at the date of writing were still large institutional machines controlled and programmed by specialists.

manifest in the storage and reproduction of information, implies an idea of time as frozen or exploding according to the vagaries of demand, returning to its source but uncontrollable, utterly bypassing its subject and leaving only two preoccupations to those who approve of it: Who is to have power over the origin (the programming) and over the end (the use)?

It is for two precise reasons, within the framework of this article, that I have allowed myself this rapid excursion into a problematic of unheard of complexity. The reader will undoubtedly have been struck by a fluctuation in the term of reference: mother, woman, hysteric. . . . I think that the apparent coherence which the term "woman" assumes in contemporary ideology, apart from its "mass" or "shock" effect for activist purposes, essentially has the negative effect of effacing the differences among the diverse functions or structures which operate beneath this word. Indeed, the time has perhaps come to emphasize the multiplicity of female expressions and preoccupations so that from the intersection of these differences there might arise, more precisely, less commercially, and more truthfully, the real *fundamental difference* between the two sexes: a difference that feminism has had the enormous merit of rendering painful, that is, productive of surprises and of symbolic life in a civilization which, outside the stock exchange and wars, is bored to death.

It is obvious, moreover, that one cannot speak of Europe or of "women in Europe" without suggesting the time in which this sociocultural distribution is situated. If it is true that a female sensibility emerged a century ago, the chances are great that by introducing *its own* notion of time, this sensibility is not in agreement with the idea of an "eternal Europe" and perhaps not even with that of a "modern Europe." Rather, through and with the European past and present, as through and with the ensemble of "Europe," which is the repository of memory, this sensibility seeks its own trans-European temporality. There are, in any case, three attitudes on the part of European feminist movements toward this conception of linear temporality, which is readily labeled masculine and which is at once both civilizational and obsessional.

TWO GENERATIONS

In its beginnings, the women's movement, as the struggle of suffragists and of existential feminists, aspired to gain a place in linear time as the time of project and history. In this sense, the movement, while immediately universalist, is also deeply rooted in the sociopolitical life of nations. The political demands of women; the struggles for equal pay for equal work, for taking power in social institutions on an equal footing with men; the rejection, when necessary, of the attributes traditionally considered feminine or maternal insofar as they are deemed incompatible with insertion in that history — all are part of the *logic of identification*[17] with certain values: not with the ideological (these are combated, and rightly so, as reactionary) but, rather, with the logical and ontological values of a rationality dominant in the nation-state. Here it is unnecessary to enumerate the benefits which this logic of identification and the ensuing struggle have achieved and continue to achieve for women (abortion, contraception, equal pay, professional recognition, etc.); these have already had or will soon have effects even more important than those of the Industrial Revolution. Universalist in its approach, this current in feminism *globalizes* the problems of women of different milieux, ages, civilizations, or simply of varying psychic structures, under the label "Universal Woman." A consideration of *generations* of women can only be conceived of in this global way as a succession, as a progression in the accomplishment of the initial program mapped out by its founders.

[17]The term "identification" belongs to a wide semantic field ranging from everyday language to philosophy and psychoanalysis. While Kristeva is certainly referring in principle to its elaboration in Freudian and Lacanian psychoanalysis, it can be understood here, as a logic, in its most general sense (see the entry on "identification" in Jean LaPlanche and J. B. Pontalis, *Vocabulaire de la psychanalyse* [The language of psychoanalysis] [Paris: Presses Universitaires de France, 1967; rev. ed., 1976]). [Tr.] It is also possible that Kristeva may be referring to the projective ego defense of "identification with the aggressor" (as Freud characterizes the mechanism operating in masochistic women attracted to narcissistic men). In the first phase of feminism, women want to become identical to men, by getting what men already have.

In a second phase, linked, on the one hand, to the younger women who came to feminism after May 1968 and, on the other, to women who had an aesthetic of psychoanalytic experience, linear temporality has been almost totally refused, and as a consequence there has arisen an exacerbated distrust of the entire political dimension. If it is true that this more recent current of feminism refers to its predecessors and that the struggle for sociocultural recognition of women is necessarily its main concern, this current seems to think of itself as belonging to another generation — qualitatively different from the first one — in its conception of its own identity and, consequently, of temporality as such. Essentially interested in the specificity of female psychology and its symbolic realizations, these women seek to give a language to the intrasubjective and corporeal experiences left mute by culture in the past. Either as artists or writers, they have undertaken a veritable exploration of the *dynamic of signs*, an exploration which relates this tendency, at least at the level of its aspirations, to all major projects of aesthetic and religious upheaval. Ascribing this experience to a new generation does not only mean that other, more subtle problems have been added to the demands for sociopolitical identification made in the beginning. It also means that, by demanding recognition of an irreducible identity, without equal in the opposite sex and, as such, exploded, plural, fluid, in a certain way nonidentical, this feminism situates itself outside the linear time of identities which communicate through projection and revindication. Such a feminism rejoins, on the one hand, the archaic (mythical) memory and, on the other, the cyclical or monumental temporality of marginal movements. It is certainly not by chance that the European and trans-European problematic has been posited as such at the same time as this new phase of feminism.

Finally, it is the mixture of the two attitudes — *insertion* into history and the radical *refusal* of the subjective limitations imposed by this history's time on an experiment carried out in the name of the irreducible difference — that seems to have broken loose over the past few years in European feminist movements, particularly in France and in Italy.

If we accept this meaning of the expression "a new generation of women," two kinds of questions might then be posed. What sociopolitical processes or events have provoked this mutation? What are its problems: its contributions as well as dangers?

SOCIALISM AND FREUDIANISM

One could hypothesize that if this new generation of women shows itself to be more diffuse and perhaps less conscious in the United States and more massive in Western Europe, this is because of a veritable split in social relations and mentalities, a split produced by socialism and Freudianism. I mean by *socialism* that egalitarian doctrine which is increasingly broadly disseminated and accepted as based on common sense, as well as that social practice adopted by governments and political parties in democratic regimes which are forced to extend the zone of egalitarianism to include the distribution of goods as well as access to culture. By *Freudianism* I mean that lever, inside this egalitarian and socializing field, which once again poses the question of sexual difference and of the difference among subjects who themselves are not reducible one to the other.

Western socialism, shaken in its very beginnings by the egalitarian or differential demands of its women (e.g., Flora Tristan[18]), quickly got rid of those women who aspired to recognition of a specificity of the female role in society and culture, only retaining from them, in the egalitarian and universalistic spirit of Enlightenment Humanism, the idea of a necessary identification between the two sexes as the only and unique means for liberating the "second sex." I shall not develop here the fact that this "ideal" is far from being applied in practice by these socialist-inspired movements and parties and that it was in part from the revolt against this situation that the new generation of women in Western Europe was born after May 1968. Let us just say that in theory, and as put into practice in Eastern Europe,

[18]Flora Tristan (Flore-Celestine-Therèse-Henriette Tristan-Moscoso, 1803–1844) was a socialist writer and activist whose ideas bore fruit only after her death, in the revolutions of 1848.

socialist ideology, based on a conception of the human being as determined by its place in *production* and the *relations of production*, did not take into consideration this same human being according to its place in *reproduction*, on the one hand, or in the *symbolic order*, on the other. Consequently, the specific character of women could only appear as nonessential or even nonexistent to the totalizing and even totalitarian spirit of this ideology.[19] We begin to see that this same egalitarian and in fact censuring treatment has been imposed, from Enlightenment Humanism through socialism, on religious specificities and, in particular, on Jews.[20]

What has been achieved by this attitude remains nonetheless of capital importance for women, and I shall take as an example the change in the destiny of women in the socialist countries of Eastern Europe. It could be said, with only slight exaggeration, that the demands of the suffragists and existential feminists have, to a great extent, been met in these countries, since three of the main egalitarian demands of early feminism have been or are now being implemented despite vagaries and blunders: economic, political, and professional equality. The fourth, sexual equality, which implies permissiveness in sexual relations (including homosexual relations), abortion, and contraception, remains stricken by taboo in Marxian ethics as well as for reasons of state. It is, then, this fourth equality which is the problem and which therefore appears *essential* in the struggle of a new generation. But simultaneously and as a consequence of these socialist accomplishments — which are in fact a total deception[21] — the struggle is no longer concerned with the quest for equality but, rather, with difference and specificity. It is precisely at this point that the new generation encounters what

might be called the *symbolic* question.[22] Sexual difference — which is at once biological, physiological, and relative to reproduction — is translated by and translates a difference in the relationship of subjects to the symbolic contract which *is* the social contract: a difference, then, in the relationship to power, language, and meaning. The sharpest and most subtle point of feminist subversion brought about by the new generation will henceforth be situated on the terrain of the inseparable conjunction of the sexual and the symbolic, in order to try to discover, first, the specificity of the female, and then, in the end, that of each individual woman.

A certain saturation of socialist ideology, a certain exhaustion of its potential as a program for a new social contract (it is obvious that the effective realization of this program is far from being accomplished, and I am here treating only its system of thought) makes way for . . . Freudianism. I am, of course, aware that this term and this practice are somewhat shocking to the American intellectual consciousness (which rightly reacts to a muddled and normatizing form of psychoanalysis) and, above all, to the feminist consciousness. To restrict my remarks to the latter: Is it not true that Freud has been seen only as a denigrator or even an exploiter of women? as an irritating phallocrat in a Vienna which was at once Puritan and decadent — a man who fantasized women as sub-men, castrated men?

CASTRATED AND/OR SUBJECT TO LANGUAGE

Before going beyond Freud to propose a more just or more modern vision of women, let us try, first, to understand his notion of castration. It is, first of all, a question of an *anguish* or *fear* of castration, or of correlative penis *envy*; a question, therefore, of *imaginary* formations readily perceivable in the *discourse* of neurotics of both sexes, men and

[19]See D. Desanti, "L'Autre Sexe des bolcheviks," *Tel quel*, no. 76 (1978); Julia Kristeva, *Des Chinoises* (Paris: Editions des femmes, 1975), translated as *On Chinese Women*, trans. Anita Barrows (New York: Urizen Press, 1977). [Kristeva]

[20]See Arthur Hertzberg, *The French Enlightenment and the Jews* (New York: Columbia University Press, 1968); *Les Juifs et la révolution française*, ed. B. Blumenkranz and A. Seboul (Paris: Edition Privat, 1976). [Kristeva]

[21]The French word *deception* can also be translated "disappointment."

[22]Here, "symbolic" is being more strictly used in terms of that function defined by Kristeva in opposition to the semiotic: "it involves the thetic phase, the identification of subject and its distinction from objects, and the establishment of a sign system" (see the glossary in *Desire in Language*, and Alice Jardine, "Theories of the Feminine: Kristeva," *Enclitic*, in press). [Tr.]

women. But, above all, a careful reading of Freud, going beyond his biologism and his mechanism, both characteristic of his time, brings out two things. First, as presupposition for the "primal scene," the castration fantasy and its correlative (penis envy) are hypotheses, a priori suppositions intrinsic to the theory itself, in the sense that these are not the ideological fantasies of their inventor but, rather, logical necessities to be placed at the "origin" in order to explain what unceasingly functions in neurotic discourse. In other words, neurotic discourse, in man and woman, can only be understood in terms of its own logic when its fundamental causes are admitted as the fantasies of the primal scene and castration, even if (as may be the case) nothing renders them present in reality itself. Stated in still other terms, the reality of castration is no more real than the hypothesis of an explosion which, according to modern astrophysics, is at the origin of the universe: Nothing proves it, in a sense it is an article of faith, the only difference being that numerous phenomena of life in this "big-bang" universe are explicable only through this initial hypothesis. But one is infinitely more jolted when this kind of intellectual method concerns inanimate matter than when it is applied to our own subjectivity and thus, perhaps, to the fundamental mechanism of our epistemophilic thought.

Moreover, certain texts written by Freud (*The Interpretation of Dreams*, but especially those of the second topic, in particular the *Metapsychology*) and their recent extensions (notably by Lacan),[23] imply that castration is, in sum, the imaginary construction of a radical operation which constitutes the symbolic field and all beings inscribed therein. This operation constitutes signs and syntax; that is, language, as a *separation* from a presumed state of nature, of pleasure fused with nature so that the introduction of an articulated network of differences, which refers to objects henceforth and only in this way separated from a subject, may constitute *meaning*. This logical operation of separation (confirmed by all psycholinguistic and child

psychology) which preconditions the binding of language which is already syntactical, is therefore the common destiny of the two sexes, men and women. That certain biofamilial conditions and relationships cause women (and notably hysterics) to deny this separation and the language which ensues from it, whereas men (notably obsessionals) magnify both and, terrified, attempt to master them — this is what Freud's discovery has to tell us on this issue.[24]

The analytic situation indeed shows that it is the penis which, becoming the major referent in this operation of separation, gives full meaning to the *lack* or to the *desire* which constitutes the subject during his or her insertion into the order of language. I should only like to indicate here that, in order for this operation constitutive of the symbolic and the social to appear in its full truth and for it to be understood by both sexes, it would be just to emphasize its extension to all that is privation of fulfillment and of totality; exclusion of a pleasing, natural, and sound state: in short, the break indispensable to the advent of the symbolic.

It can now be seen how women, starting with this theoretical apparatus, might try to understand their sexual and symbolic difference in the framework of social, cultural, and professional realization, in order to try, by seeing their position therein, either to fulfill their own experience to a maximum or — but always starting from this point — to go further and call into question the very apparatus itself.

LIVING THE SACRIFICE

In any case, and for women in Europe today, whether or not they are conscious of the various mutations (socialist and Freudian) which have produced or simply accompanied their coming into their own, the urgent question on our agenda might be formulated as follows: *What can be our place in the symbolic contract?* If the social contract, far from being that of equal men, is based on an essentially sacrificial relationship of separation and

---

[23]See, in general, Jacques Lacan, *Ecrits* (Paris: Editions du Seuil, 1966) and, in particular, Jacques Lacan, *Le Séminaire XX: Encore* (Paris: Editions du Seuil, 1975). [Tr.]

[24]Kristeva's rapid summary of Lacan's revision of Freud's theory of the castration complex; for an expanded version, see p. 1149–55.

articulation of differences which in this way produces communicable meaning, what is our place in this order of sacrifice and/or of language? No longer wishing to be excluded or no longer content with the function which has always been demanded of us (to maintain, arrange, and perpetuate this sociosymbolic contract as mothers, wives, nurses, doctors, teachers . . .), how can we reveal our place, first as it is bequeathed to us by tradition, and then as we want to transform it?

It is difficult to evaluate what in the relationship of women to the symbolic as it reveals itself now arises from a sociohistorical conjuncture (patriarchal ideology, whether Christian, humanist, socialist or so forth), and what arises from a structure. We can speak only about a structure observed in a sociohistorical context, which is that of Christian, Western civilization and its lay ramifications. In this sense of psychosymbolic structure, women, "we" (is it necessary to recall the warnings we issued at the beginning of this article concerning the totalizing use of this plural?) seem to feel that they are the casualties, that they have been left out of the sociosymbolic contract, of language as the fundamental social bond. They find no affect there, no more than they find the fluid and infinitesimal significations of their relationships with the nature of their own bodies, that of the child, another woman, or a man. This frustration, which to a certain extent belongs to men also, is being voiced today principally by women, to the point of becoming the essence of the new feminist ideology. A therefore difficult, if not impossible, identification with the sacrificial logic of separation and syntactical sequence at the foundation of language and the social code leads to the rejection of the symbolic — lived as the rejection of the paternal function and ultimately generating psychoses.

But this limit, rarely reached as such, produces two types of counterinvestment of what we have termed the sociosymbolic contract. On the one hand, there are attempts to take hold of this contract, to possess it in order to enjoy it as such or to subvert it. How? The answer remains difficult to formulate (since, precisely, any formulation is deemed frustrating, mutilating, sacrificial) or else is in fact formulated using stereotypes taken from extremist and often deadly ideologies. On the other hand, another attitude is more lucid from the beginning, more self-analytical which — without refusing or sidestepping this sociosymbolic order — consists in trying to explore the constitution and functioning of this contract, starting less from the knowledge accumulated about it (anthropology, psychoanalysis, linguistics) than from the very personal affect experienced when facing it as subject and as a woman. This leads to the active research,[25] still rare, undoubtedly hesitant but always dissident, being carried out by women in the human sciences; particularly those attempts, in the wake of contemporary art, to break the code, to shatter language, to find a specific discourse closer to the body and emotions, to the unnameable repressed by the social contract. I am not speaking here of a "woman's language," whose (at least syntactical) existence is highly problematical and whose apparent lexical specificity is perhaps more the product of a social marginality than of a sexual-symbolic difference.[26]

Nor am I speaking of the aesthetic quality of productions by women, most of which — with a

[25]This work is periodically published in various academic women's journals, one of the most prestigious being *Signs: Journal of Women in Culture and Society*, University of Chicago Press. Also of note are the special issues: "Ecriture, féminité, féminisme," *La Revue des sciences humaines* (Lille III), no. 4 (1977); and "Les Femmes et la philosophie," *Le Doctrinal de sapience* (Editions Solin), no. 3 (1977). [Kristeva]

[26]See linguistic research on "female language": Robin Lakoff, *Language and Women's Place* (New York: Harper & Row, 1974); Mary R. Key, *Male/Female Language* (Metuchen, N.J.: Scarecrow Press, 1973); A. M. Houdebine, "Les Femmes et la langue," *Tel quel*, no. 74 (1977), pp. 84–95. The contrast between these "empirical" investigations of women's "speech acts" and much of the research in France on the conceptual bases for a "female language" must be emphasized here. It is somewhat helpful, if ultimately inaccurate, to think of the former as an "external" study of language and the latter as an "internal" exploration of the process of signification. For further contrast, see, e.g., "Part II: Contemporary Feminist Thought in France: Translating Difference" in *The Future of Difference*, ed. Hester Eisenstein and Alice Jardine (Boston: G. K. Hall & Co., 1980); the "Introductions" to *New French Feminisms*, ed. Elaine Marks and Isabelle de Courtivron (Amherst: University of Massachusetts Press, 1980); and for a very helpful overview of the problem of "difference and language" in France, see Stephen Heath, "Difference" in *Screen* 19 no. 3 (Autumn 1978): 51–112. [Tr.]

few exceptions (but has this not always been the case with both sexes?) — are a reiteration of a more or less euphoric or depressed romanticism and always an explosion of an ego lacking narcissistic gratification.[27] What I should like to retain, nonetheless, as a mark of collective aspiration, as an undoubtedly vague and unimplemented intention, but one which is intense and which has been deeply revealing these past few years, is this: The new generation of women is showing that its major social concern has become the sociosymbolic contract as a sacrificial contract. If anthropologists and psychologists, for at least a century, have not stopped insisting on this in their attention to "savage thought," wars, the discourse of dreams, or writers, women are today affirming — and we consequently face a mass phenomenon — that they are forced to experience this sacrificial contract against their will.[28] Based on this, they are attempting a revolt which they see as a resurrection but which society as a whole understands as murder. This attempt can lead us to a not less and sometimes more deadly violence. Or to a cultural innovation. Probably to both at once. But that is precisely where the stakes are, and they are of epochal significance.

THE TERROR OF POWER OR THE POWER OF TERRORISM

First in socialist countries (such as the USSR and China) and increasingly in Western democracies, under pressure from feminist movements, women are being promoted to leadership positions in government, industry, and culture. Inequalities, devalorizations, underestimations, even persecution of women at this level continue to hold sway in vain. The struggle against them is a struggle against archaisms. The cause has nonetheless been understood, the principle has been accepted.[29] What remains is to break down the resistance to change. In this sense, this struggle, while still one of the main concerns of the new generation, is not, strictly speaking, *its* problem. In relationship to *power*, its problem might rather be summarized as follows: What happens when women come into power and identify with it? What happens when, on the contrary, they refuse power and create a parallel society, a counterpower which then takes on aspects ranging from a club of ideas to a group of terrorist commandos?[30]

The assumption by women of executive, industrial, and cultural power has not, up to the present time, radically changed the nature of this power. This can be clearly seen in the East, where women promoted to decision-making positions suddenly obtain the economic as well as the narcissistic advantages refused them for thousands of years and become the pillars of the existing governments, guardians of the status quo, the most zealous protectors of the established order.[31] This identification by women with the very power structures previously considered as frustrating, oppressive, or inaccessible has often been used in modern times by totalitarian regimes: the German National-Socialists and the Chilean junta are examples of this.[32] The fact that this is a paranoid type of counterinvestment in an initially denied

[27]This is one of the more explicit references to the mass marketing of "écriture féminine" in Paris over the last ten years. [Tr.]

[28]The expression *à leur corps défendant* translates as "against their will," but here the emphasis is on women's bodies: literally, "against their bodies." I have retained the former expression in English, partly because of its obvious intertextuality with Susan Brownmiller's *Against Our Will* (New York: Simon & Schuster, 1975). Women are increasingly describing their experience of the violence of the symbolic contract as a form of rape. [Tr.]

[29]Many women in the West who are once again finding all doors closed to them above a certain level of employment, especially in the current economic chaos, may find this statement, even qualified, troubling, to say the least. It is accurate, however, *in principle*: whether that of infinite capitalist recuperation or increasing socialist expansion — within both economies, our integration functions as a kind of *operative illusion*. [Tr.]

[30]The very real existence and autonomous activities of both of these versions of women's groups in Europe may seem a less urgent problem in the United States where feminist groups are often absorbed by the academy and/or are forced to remain financially dependent on para-academic/government agencies. [Tr.]

[31]See *Des Chinoises*. [Kristeva]

[32]See M.A. Macciocchi, *Elements pour une analyse du fascisme* (Paris: 10/18, 1976); Michèle Mattelart, "Le Coup d'état au féminin," *Les Temps modernes* (January 1975). [Kristeva]

symbolic order can perhaps explain this troubling phenomenon; but an explanation does not prevent its massive propagation around the globe, perhaps in less dramatic forms than the totalitarian ones mentioned above, but all moving toward leveling, stabilization, conformism, at the cost of crushing exceptions, experiments, chance occurrences.

Some will regret that the rise of a libertarian movement such as feminism ends, in some of its aspects, in the consolidation of conformism; others will rejoice and profit from this fact. Electoral campaigns, the very life of political parties, continue to bet on this latter tendency. Experience proves that too quickly even the protest or innovative initiatives on the part of women inhaled by power systems (when they do not submit to them right off) are soon credited to the system's account; and that the long-awaited democratization of institutions as a result of the entry of women most often comes down to fabricating a few "chiefs" among them. The difficulty presented by this logic of integrating the second sex into a value system experienced as foreign and therefore counterinvested is how to avoid the centralization of power, how to detach women from it, and how then to proceed, through their critical, differential, and autonomous interventions, to render decision-making institutions more flexible.

Then there are the more radical feminist currents which, refusing homologation to any role of identification with existing power no matter what the power may be, make of the second sex a *countersociety*. A "female society" is then constituted as a sort of alter ego of the official society, in which all real or fantasized possibilities for *jouissance* take refuge. Against the sociosymbolic contract, both sacrificial and frustrating, this countersociety is imagined as harmonious, without prohibitions, free and fulfilling. In our modern societies which have no hereafter or, at least, which are caught up in a transcendency either reduced to this side of the world (Protestantism) or crumbling (Catholicism and its current challenges), the countersociety remains the only refuge for fulfillment since it is precisely an a-topia, a place outside the law, utopia's floodgate.

As with any society, the countersociety is based on the expulsion of an excluded element, a scapegoat charged with the evil of which the community duly constituted can then purge itself;[33] a purge which will finally exonerate that community of any future criticism. Modern protest movements have often reiterated this logic, locating the guilty one — in order to fend off criticism — in the foreign, in capital alone, in the other religion, in the other sex. Does not feminism become a kind of inverted sexism when this logic is followed to its conclusion? The various forms of marginalism — according to sex, age, religion, or ideology — represent in the modern world this refuge for *jouissance*, a sort of laicized transcendence. But with women, and insofar as the number of those feeling concerned by this problem has increased, although in less spectacular forms than a few years ago, the problem of the countersociety is becoming massive: It occupies no more and no less than "half of the sky."

It has, therefore, become clear, because of the particular radicalization of the second generation, that these protest movements, including feminism, are not "initially libertarian" movements which only later, through internal deviations or external chance manipulations, fall back into the old ruts of the initially combated archetypes. Rather, the very logic of counterpower and of countersociety necessarily generates, by its very structure, its essence as a simulacrum of the combated society or of power. In this sense and from a viewpoint undoubtedly too Hegelian, modern feminism has only been but a moment in the interminable process of coming to consciousness about the implacable violence (separation, castration, etc.) which constitutes any symbolic contract.

[33]The principles of a "sacrificial anthropology" are developed by René Girard in *La Violence et le sacré* [Violence and the sacred] (Paris: Grasset, 1972) and esp. in *Des choses cachées depuis la fondation du monde* (Paris: Grasset, 1978). [Kristeva] There Girard argues, on the basis of the myths of various nations, that human societies all over the world channeled impulses that might otherwise break out into a general violence of each against all into a ritual sacrifice of surrogate victims. Even when human sacrifice is no longer practiced, societies create scapegoats to give the rest of the society cohesion. Kristeva's allusion to Girard is by way of critique of second-generation feminists who in valorizing the feminine are scapegoating the masculine, and thus buying into the "sacrificial economy" she (and Girard) hope humanity can transcend.

Thus the identification with power in order to consolidate it or the constitution of a fetishist counterpower — restorer of the crises of the self and provider of a *jouissance* which is always already a transgression — seem to be the two social forms which the face-off between the new generation of women and the social contract can take. That one also finds the problem of terrorism there is structurally related.

The large number of women in terrorist groups (Palestinian commandos, the Baader-Meinhoff Gang, Red Brigades, etc.[34]) has already been pointed out, either violently or prudently according to the source of information. The exploitation of women is still too great and the traditional prejudices against them too violent for one to be able to envision this phenomenon with sufficient distance. It can, however, be said from now on that this is the inevitable product of what we have called a denial of the sociosymbolic contract and its counterinvestment as the only means of self-defense in the struggle to safeguard an identity. This paranoid-type mechanism is at the base of any political involvement. It may produce different civilizing attitudes in the sense that these attitudes allow a more or less flexible reabsorption of violence and death. But when a subject is too brutally excluded from this sociosymbolic stratum; when, for example, a woman feels her affective life as a woman or her condition as a social being too brutally ignored by existing discourse or power (from her family to social institutions); she may, by counterinvesting the violence she has endured, make of herself a "possessed" agent of this violence in order to combat what was experienced as frustration — with arms which may

seem disproportional, but which are not so in comparison with the subjective or more precisely narcissistic suffering from which they originate. Necessarily opposed to the bourgeois democratic regimes in power, this terrorist violence offers as a program of liberation an order which is even more oppressive, more sacrificial than those it combats. Strangely enough, it is not against totalitarian regimes that these terrorist groups with women participants unleash themselves but, rather, against liberal systems, whose essence is, of course, exploitative, but whose expanding democratic legality guarantees relative tolerance. Each time, the mobilization takes place in the name of a nation, of an oppressed group, of a human essence imagined as good and sound; in the name, then, of a kind of fantasy of archaic fulfillment which an arbitrary, abstract, and thus even bad and ultimately discriminatory order has come to disrupt. While that order is accused of being oppressive, is it not actually being reproached with being too weak, with not measuring up to this pure and good, but henceforth lost, substance? Anthropology has shown that the social order is sacrificial, but sacrifice orders violence, binds it, tames it. Refusal of the social order exposes one to the risk that the so-called good substance, once it is unchained, will explode, without curbs, without law or right, to become an absolute arbitrariness.

Following the crisis of monotheism, the revolutions of the past two centuries, and more recently fascism and Stalinism, have tragically set in action this logic of the oppressed goodwill which leads to massacres. Are women more apt than other social categories, notably the exploited classes, to invest in this implacable machine of terrorism? No categorical response, either positive or negative, can currently be given to this question. It must be pointed out, however, that since the dawn of feminism, and certainly before, the political activity of exceptional women, and thus in a certain sense of liberated women, has taken the form of murder, conspiracy, and crime. Finally, there is also the connivance of the young girl with her mother, her greater difficulty than the boy in detaching herself from the mother in order to accede to the order of signs as invested by the absence and separation constitutive of the paternal function. A girl will

[34]The Baader-Meinhoff Gang was a terrorist group based in Germany that began by firebombing a Frankfurt department store in 1968. It was led by Andreas Baader and his lover Gudrun Ensslin; another leader was Ulrike Meinhof, a journalist who helped Baader escape from custody. By 1977 the key members of the group were all dead, primarily by suicide while in prison. The "Red Brigades" are Italian terrorist groups who, beginning around 1972, assassinated government and business leaders, financing their operations through kidnappings. They were responsible for the kidnap/murder of former Italian prime minister Aldo Moro in 1978; in the wake of this crime they were repressed with ferocity by the Italian police, although remnants of these groups reportedly still exist.

never be able to reestablish this contact with her mother — a contact which the boy may possibly rediscover through his relationship with the opposite sex — except by becoming a mother herself, through a child, or through a homosexuality which is in itself extremely difficult and judged as suspect by society; and, what is more, why and in the name of what dubious symbolic benefit would she want to make this detachment so as to conform to a symbolic system which remains foreign to her? In sum, all of these considerations — her eternal debt to the woman-mother — make a woman more vulnerable within the symbolic order, more fragile when she suffers within it, more virulent when she protects herself from it. If the archetype of the belief in a good and pure substance, that of utopias, is the belief in the omnipotence of an archaic, full, total, englobing mother with no frustration, no separation, with no break-producing symbolism (with no castration, in other words), then it becomes evident that we will never be able to defuse the violences mobilized through the counterinvestment necessary to carrying out this phantasm, unless one challenges precisely this myth of the archaic mother. It is in this way that we can understand the warnings against the recent invasion of the women's movements by paranoia,[35] as in Lacan's scandalous sentence "There is no such thing as Woman."[36] Indeed, she does *not* exist with a capital "W," possessor of some mythical unity — a supreme power, on which is based the terror of power and terrorism as the desire for power. But what an unbelievable force for subversion in the modern world! And, at the same time, what playing with fire!

CREATURES AND CREATRESSES

The desire to be a mother, considered alienating and even reactionary by the preceding generation of feminists, has obviously not become a standard for the present generation. But we have seen in the past few years an increasing number of women who not only consider their maternity compatible with their professional life or their feminist involvement (certain improvements in the quality of life are also at the origin of this: an increase in the number of day-care centers and nursery schools, more active participation of men in child care and domestic life, etc.) but also find it indispensable to their discovery, not of the plenitude, but of the complexity of the female experience, with all that this complexity comprises in joy and pain. This tendency has its extreme: in the refusal of the paternal function by lesbian and single mothers can be seen one of the most violent forms taken by the rejection of the symbolic outlined above, as well as one of the most fervent divinizations of maternal power — all of which cannot help but trouble an entire legal and moral order without, however, proposing an alternative to it. Let us remember here that Hegel distinguished between female right (familial and religious) and male law (civil and political). If our societies know well the uses and abuses of male law, it must also be recognized that female right is designated, for the moment, by a blank. And if these practices of maternity, among others, were to be generalized, women themselves would be responsible for elaborating the appropriate legislation to check the violence to which, otherwise, both their children and men would be subject. But are they capable of doing so? This is one of the important questions that the new generation of women encounters, especially when the members of this new generation refuse to ask those questions, seized by the same rage with which the dominant order originally victimized them.

Faced with this situation, it seems obvious — and feminist groups become more aware of this when they attempt to broaden their audience — that the refusal of maternity cannot be a mass policy and that the majority of women today see the possibility for fulfillment, if not entirely at least to a large degree, in bringing a child into the world. What does this desire for motherhood correspond to? This is one of the new questions for the new generation, a question the preceding generation had foreclosed. For want of an answer to this question, feminist ideology leaves the door open to the

[35]Cf. Micheline Enriquez, "Fantasmes paronoiaques: différences des sexes, homosexualité, loi du père," *Topiques*, no. 13 (1974). [Kristeva]

[36]See Jacques Lacan, "Dieu et la jouissance de la femme" in *Encore* (Paris: Editions du Seuil, 1975), pp. 61–71, esp. p. 68. This seminar has remained a primary critical and polemical focus for multiple tendencies in the French women's movement. For a brief discussion of the seminar in English, see Heath (n. 26 above). [Tr.]

return of religion, whose discourse, tried and proved over thousands of years, provides the necessary ingredients for satisfying the anguish, the suffering, and the hopes of mothers. If Freud's affirmation — that the desire for a child is the desire for a penis and, in this sense, a substitute for phallic and symbolic dominion — can be only partially accepted, what modern women have to say about this experience should nonetheless be listened to attentively. Pregnancy seems to be experienced as the radical ordeal of the splitting of the subject:[37] redoubling up of the body, separation and coexistence of the self and of an other, of nature and consciousness, of physiology and speech. This fundamental challenge to identity is then accompanied by a fantasy of totality — narcissistic completeness — a sort of instituted, socialized, natural psychosis. The arrival of the child, on the other hand, leads the mother into the labyrinths of an experience that, without the child, she would only rarely encounter: love for an other. Not for herself, nor for an identical being, and still less for another person with whom "I" fuse (love or sexual passion). But the slow, difficult, and delightful apprenticeship in attentiveness, gentleness, forgetting oneself. The ability to succeed in this path without masochism and without annihilating one's affective, intellectual, and professional personality — such would seem to be the stakes to be won through guiltless maternity. It then becomes a creation in the strong sense of the term. For this moment, utopian?

On the other hand, it is in the aspiration toward artistic and, in particular, literary creation that woman's desire for affirmation now manifests itself. Why literature?

Is it because, faced with social norms, literature reveals a certain knowledge and sometimes the truth itself about an otherwise repressed, nocturnal, secret, and unconscious universe? Because it thus redoubles the social contract by exposing the unsaid, the uncanny? And because it makes a game, a space of fantasy and pleasure, out of the abstract and frustrating order of social signs, the words of everyday communication? Flaubert said, "Madame Bovary, c'est moi." Today many women imagine, "Flaubert, c'est moi." This identification with the potency of the imaginary is not only an identification, an imaginary potency (a fetish, a belief in the maternal penis maintained at all costs), as a far too normative view of the social and symbolic relationship would have it. This identification also bears witness to women's desire to lift the weight of what is sacrificial in the social contract from their shoulders, to nourish our societies with a more flexible and free discourse, one able to name what has thus far never been an object of circulation in the community: the enigmas of the body, the dreams, secret joys, shames, hatreds of the second sex.

It is understandable from this that women's writing has lately attracted the maximum attention of both "specialists" and the media.[38] The pitfalls encountered along the way, however, are not to be minimized: For example, does one not read there a relentless belittling of male writers whose books, nevertheless, often serve as "models" for countless productions by women? Thanks to the feminist label, does one not sell numerous works whose naive whining or market-place romanticism would otherwise have been rejected as anachronistic? And does one not find the pen of many a female writer being devoted to phantasmic attacks against Language and Sign as the ultimate supports of phallocratic power, in the name of a semi-aphonic corporality whose truth can only be found in that which is "gestural" or "tonal"?

And yet, no matter how dubious the results of these recent productions by women, the symptom is there — women are writing, and the air is heavy with expectation: What will they write that is new?

IN THE NAME OF THE FATHER, THE SON . . . AND THE WOMAN?

These few elements of the manifestations by the new generation of women in Europe seem to me

---

[37]The "split subject" (from *Spaltung* as both "splitting" and "cleavage"), as used in Freudian psychoanalysis, here refers directly to Kristeva's "subject in process / in question / on trial" as opposed to the unity of the transcendental ego (see n. 14 in "Introduction"). [Tr.]

[38]Again a reference to *écriture féminine* as generically labeled in France over the past few years and not to women's writing in general. [Tr.]

to demonstrate that, beyond the sociopolitical level where it is generally inscribed (or inscribes itself), the women's movement — in its present stage, less aggressive but more artful — is situated within the very framework of the religious crisis of our civilization.

I call "religion" this phantasmic necessity on the part of speaking beings to provide themselves with a *representation* (animal, female, male, parental, etc.) in place of what constitutes them as such, in other words, symbolization — the double articulation and syntactic sequence of language, as well as its preconditions or substitutes (thoughts, affects, etc.). The elements of the current practice of feminism that we have just brought to light seem precisely to constitute such a representation which makes up for the frustrations imposed on women by the anterior code (Christianity or its lay humanist variant). The fact that this new ideology has affinities, often revindicated by its creators, with so-called matriarchal beliefs (in other words, those beliefs characterizing matrilinear societies) should not overshadow its radical novelty. This ideology seems to me to be part of the broader antisacrificial current which is animating our culture and which, in its protest against the constraints of the sociosymbolic contract, is no less exposed to the risks of violence and terrorism. At this level of radicalism, it is the very principle of sociality which is challenged.

Certain contemporary thinkers consider, as is well known, that modernity is characterized as the first epoch in human history in which human beings attempt to live without religion. In its present form, is not feminism in the process of becoming one?

Or is it, on the contrary and as avant-grade feminists hope, that having started with the idea of difference, feminism will be able to break free of its belief in Woman, Her power, Her writing, so as to channel this demand for difference into each and every element of the female whole, and, finally, to bring out the singularity of each woman, and beyond this, her multiplicities, her plural languages, beyond the horizon, beyond sight, beyond faith itself?

A factor for ultimate mobilization? Or a factor for analysis?

Imaginary support in a technocratic era where all narcissism is frustrated? Or instruments fitted to these times in which the cosmos, atoms, and cells — our true contemporaries — call for the constitution of a fluid and free subjectivity?

The question has been posed. Is to pose it already to answer it?

ANOTHER GENERATION IS ANOTHER SPACE

If the preceding can be *said* — the question whether all this is *true* belongs to a different register — it is undoubtedly because it is now possible to gain some distance on these two preceding generations of women. This implies, of course, that a *third* generation is now forming, at least in Europe. I am not speaking of a new group of young women (though its importance should not be underestimated) or of another "mass feminist movement" taking the torch passed on from the second generation. My usage of the word "generation" implies less a chronology than a *signifying space*, a both corporeal and desiring mental space. So it can be argued that as of now a third attitude is possible, thus a third generation, which does not exclude — quite to the contrary — the *parallel* existence of all three in the same historical time, or even that they be interwoven one with the other.

In this third attitude, which I strongly advocate — which I imagine? — the very dichotomy man/woman as an opposition between two rival entities may be understood as belonging to *metaphysics*.[39] What can "identity," even "sexual identity," mean in a new theoretical and scientific space where the very notion of identity is challenged?[40] I am not simply suggesting a very hypothetical bisexuality which, even if it existed, would only, in fact, be the aspiration toward the totality of one of the sexes and thus an effacing of difference. What I mean is, first of all, the demassification of the problematic of *difference*, which would imply, in a first phase, an apparent de-dramatization of the

[39]By this point in theoretical discourse, to say that a distinction belongs to metaphysics is implicitly to deconstruct it; see Derrida, p. 917.

[40]See Seminar on *Identity* directed by Lévi-Strauss (Paris: Grasset & Fasquelle, 1977). [Kristeva]

"fight to the death" between rival groups and thus between the sexes. And this not in the name of some reconciliation — feminism has at least had the merit of showing what is irreducible and even deadly in the social contract — but in order that the struggle, the implacable difference, the violence be conceived in the very place where it operates with the maximum intransigence, in other words, in personal and sexual identity itself, so as to make it disintegrate in its very nucleus.

It necessarily follows that this involves risks not only for what we understand today as "personal equilibrium" but also for social equilibrium itself, made up as it now is of the counterbalancing of aggressive and murderous forces massed in social, national, religious, and political groups. But is it not the insupportable situation of tension and explosive risk that the existing "equilibrium" presupposes which leads some of those who suffer from it to divest it of its economy, to detach themselves from it, and to seek another means of regulating difference?

To restrict myself here to a personal level, as related to the question of women, I see arising, under the cover of a relative indifference toward the militance of the first and second generations, an attitude of retreat from sexism (male as well as female) and, gradually, from any kind of anthropomorphism. The fact that this might quickly become another form of spiritualism turning its back on social problems, or else a form of repression[41] ready to support all status quos, should not hide the radicalness of the process. This process could be summarized as an *interiorization of the founding separation of the sociosymbolic contract*, as an introduction of its cutting edge into the very interior of every identity whether subjective, sexual, ideological, or so forth. This in such a way that the habitual and increasingly explicit attempt to fabricate a scapegoat victim as foundress of a society or a countersociety may be replaced by the analysis of the potentialities of *victim/executioner* which characterize each identity, each subject, each sex.

What discourse, if not that of a religion, would be able to support this adventure which surfaces as

a real possibility, after both the achievements and the impasses of the present ideological reworkings, in which feminism has participated? It seems to me that the role of what is usually called "aesthetic practices" must increase not only to counterbalance the storage and uniformity of information by present-day mass media, data-bank systems, and, in particular, modern communications technology, but also to demystify the identity of the symbolic bond itself, to demystify, therefore, the *community* of language as a universal and unifying tool, one which totalizes and equalizes. In order to bring out — along with the *singularity* of each person and, even more, along with the multiplicity of every person's possible identifications (with atoms, e.g., stretching from the family to the stars) — the *relativity of his/her symbolic as well as biological existence*, according to the variation in his/her specific symbolic capacities. And in order to emphasize the *responsibility* which all will immediately face of putting this fluidity into play against the threats of death which are unavoidable whenever an inside and an outside, a self and an other, one group and another, are constituted. At this level of interiorization with its social as well as individual stakes, what I have called "aesthetic practices" are undoubtedly nothing other than the modern reply to the eternal question of morality. At least, this is how we might understand an ethics which, conscious of the fact that its order is sacrificial, reserves part of the burden for each of its adherents, therefore declaring them guilty while immediately affording them the possibility for *jouissance*, for various productions, for a life made up of both challenges and differences.

Spinoza's question can be taken up again here: Are women subject to ethics? If not to that ethics defined by classical philosophy — in relationship to which the ups and downs of feminist generations seem dangerously precarious — are women not already participating in the rapid dismantling that our age is experiencing at various levels (from wars to drugs to artificial insemination) and which poses the *demand* for a new ethics? The answer to Spinoza's question can be affirmative only at the cost of considering feminism as but a *moment* in the thought of that anthropomorphic identity which currently blocks the horizon of the discursive and scientific adventure of our species.

[41]Repression (*le refoulement* or *Verdrangung*) as distinguished from the foreclosure (*la foreclusion* or *Verwerfung*) evoked earlier in the article (see LaPlanche and Pontalis). [Tr.]

Jonathan Culler

b. 1944

To the extent that structuralism and poststructuralism have been well received in North America, much of the credit should be given to Jonathan Dwight Culler, whose lucid distillations of structuralist, semiotic, and deconstructivist theories have reached a wide audience. Culler was born in Cleveland, Ohio, but moved with his family to New Haven, Connecticut, in 1946, when his father, A. Dwight Culler, accepted a position as professor of Victorian literature at Yale. Culler received a B.A. in history and literature (1966) at Harvard and a Rhodes scholarship to St. John's College at Oxford (1966–69), where he took a B.Phil. in comparative literature (1968) and a D.Phil. in modern languages (1972). Culler was a fellow of Selwyn College, Cambridge (1969–74), and of Brasenose College, Oxford (1974–77), and since 1977 he has been a professor of English and comparative literature at Cornell University. His list of publications is extensive — his books include Flaubert: The Uses of Uncertainty *(1974),* Saussure *(1976, 1977; revised 1986),* The Pursuit of Signs *(1981),* On Deconstruction *(1983), and* Framing the Sign: Criticism and Its Institutions *(1988). Most recently he has edited, with Kevin Lamb,* Just Being Difficult: Academic Writing in the Public Arena *(2003). "Reading as a Woman," reproduced below, is a section from Culler's* On Deconstruction *(1983).*

Reading as a Woman

Suppose the informed reader of a work of literature is a woman. Might this not make a difference, for example, to "the reader's experience" of the opening chapter of *The Mayor of Casterbridge*, where the drunken Michael Henchard sells his wife and infant daughter to a sailor for five guineas at a country fair? Citing this example, Elaine Showalter quotes Irving Howe's celebration of Hardy's opening:

> To shake loose from one's wife; to discard that drooping rag of a woman, with her mute complaints and maddening passivity; to escape not by slinking abandonment but through the public sale of her body to a stranger, as horses are sold at a fair; and thus to wrest, through sheer amoral wilfulness, a second chance out of life — it is with this stroke, so insidiously attractive to male fantasy, that *The Mayor of Casterbridge* begins.

The male fantasy that finds this scene attractive may also be at work transforming Susan Henchard into a "drooping rag," passive and complaining — a portrait scarcely sustained by the text. Howe goes on to argue that in appealing to "the depths of common fantasy," the scene draws us into complicity with Henchard. Showalter comments:

> In speaking of "our common fantasies," he quietly transforms the novel into a male document. A woman's experience of this scene must be very different; indeed, there were many sensation novels of the 1870s and 1880s which presented the sale of women into marriage from the point of view of the bought wife. In Howe's reading, Hardy's novel becomes a kind of sensation-fiction, playing on the suppressed longings of its male audience, evoking sympathy for Henchard because of his crime, not in spite of it. ["The Unmanning of the Mayor of Casterbridge," pp. 102–3]

Howe is certainly not alone in assuming that "the reader" is male. "Much reading," writes Geoffrey Hartman in *The Fate of Reading*, "is indeed like girl-watching, a simple expense of spirit" (p. 248). The experience of reading seems to be that of a man (a heart-man?) for whom girl-watching is the model of an expense of spirit in a waste of shame.[1] When we posit a woman reader,

[1]This alerts one to the remarkable scenario of Hartman's recent criticism. *The Fate of Reading* offers this prognostic:

the result is an analogous appeal to experience: not to the experience of girl-watching but to the experience of being watched, seen as a "girl," restricted, marginalized. A recent anthology that stresses the continuity between women's experience and the experience of women reading is appropriately entitled *The Authority of Experience: Essays in Feminist Criticism.* One contributor, Maurianne Adams, explains:

> Now that the burden of trying to pretend to a totally objective and value-free perspective has finally been lifted from our shoulders, we can all admit, in the simplest possible terms, that our literary insights and perceptions come, in part at least, from our sensitivity to the nuances of our own lives and our observations of other people's lives. Every time we rethink and reassimilate *Jane Eyre,* we bring to it a new orientation. For women critics, this orientation is likely not to focus particular attention upon the dilemmas of the male, to whom male critics have already shown themselves understandably sensitive, but rather on Jane herself and her particular circumstances. ["*Jane Eyre*: Woman's Estate," pp. 140–41]

"Rereading *Jane Eyre,*" she notes, "I am led inevitably to feminist issues, by which I mean the status and economics of female dependence in marriage, the limited options available to Jane as an outlet for her education and energies, her need to love and to be loved, to be of service and to be needed. These aspirations, the ambivalence expressed by the narrator toward them, and the conflicts among them, are all issues raised by the novel itself" (p. 140).

An unusual version of this appeal to women's experience is an essay in the same collection by Dawn Lander that explores the literary commonplace that "the frontier is no place for a woman," that women hate the primitive conditions, the absence of civilization, but must stoically endure them. Lander reports that her own experience as a woman living in the desert made her question this

---

most reading is like girl-watching, doubtless "perjur'd, murderous, bloody, full of blame." The cure is a period of *Criticism in the Wilderness,* after which, chastened and purified, criticism can turn to *Saving the Text* — saving it, it turns out, from a frivolous, seductive, and "self-involved" deconstruction that ignores the sacred. [Culler] The quotation in the note, and the last eight words of the sentences to which it is appended, are from Shakespeare's Sonnet 116.

cliché and seek out what frontier women had written about their lives, only to discover that her "own feelings about the wilderness were duplicated in the experience of historic and contemporary women" ("Eve among the Indians," p. 197). Appealing to the authority first of her own experience and then of others' experiences, she reads the myth of women's hatred of the frontier as an attempt by men to make the frontier an escape from everything women represent to them: an escape from renunciation to a paradise of male camaraderie where sexuality can be an aggressive, forbidden commerce with nonwhite women. Here the experience of women provides leverage for exposing this literary topos as a self-serving male view of the female view.

Women's experience, many feminist critics claim, will lead them to value works differently from their male counterparts, who may regard the problems women characteristically encounter as of limited interest. An eminent male critic, commenting on *The Bostonians,* observes that "the doctrinaire demand for equality of the sexes may well seem to promise but a wry and constricted story, a tale of mere eccentricity" (Lionel Trilling, *The Opposing Self,* p. 109). This is no doubt what Virginia Woolf calls "the difference of view, the difference of standard" (*Collected Essays,* vol. 1, p. 204). Responding to a male critic who had patronizingly reproached her for trying to "aggrandize [Charlotte] Gilman's interesting but minor story" of incarceration and madness, "The Yellow Wallpaper," by comparing it with Poe's "The Pit and the Pendulum," Annette Kolodny notes that while she finds it as skillfully crafted and tightly composed as anything in Poe, other considerations doubtless take precedence when judging whether it is "minor" or not: "what may be entering into *my* responses is the fact that, as a female reader, I find the story a chillingly symbolic evocation of realities which women daily encounter even in our own time" ("Reply to Commentaries," p. 589). Conviction that their experience as women is a source of authority for their responses as readers has encouraged feminist critics in their revaluation of celebrated and neglected works.

In this first moment of feminist criticism, the concept of a woman reader leads to the assertion of continuity between women's experience of social and familial structures and their experience as readers. Criticism founded on this postulate of continuity takes considerable interest in the situations and psychology of female characters, investigating attitudes to women or the "images of women" in the works of an author, a genre, or a period. In attending to female characters in Shakespeare, the editors of a critical anthology observe, feminist critics are "compensating for the bias in a critical tradition that has tended to emphasize male characters, male themes, and male fantasies" and drawing attention instead to the complexity of women characters and their place in the order of male values represented in the plays (Lenz et al., *The Woman's Part*, p. 4). Such criticism is resolutely thematic — focused on woman as a theme in literary works — and resolute too in its appeal to the literary and non-literary experience of readers.

> Feminist criticism of Shakespeare begins with an individual reader, usually, although not necessarily, a female reader — a student, teacher, actor — who brings to the plays her own experience, concerns, questions. Such readers trust their responses to Shakespeare even when they raise questions that challenge prevailing critical assumptions. Conclusions derived from these questions are then tested rigorously against the text, its myriad contexts, and the explorations of other critics. [p. 3]

Criticism based on the presumption of continuity between the reader's experience and a woman's experience and on a concern with images of women is likely to become most forceful as a critique of the phallocentric assumptions that govern literary works. This feminist critique is by now a familiar genre, authoritatively established by such works as Simone de Beauvoir's *The Second Sex*, which, while indicating familiar ways of thinking about women, provides readings of the myths of women in Montherlant, Lawrence, Claudel, Breton, and Stendhal.[2] A similar enterprise, in which a woman reader responds critically to the visions embodied in the literature celebrated by her culture, is Kate Millett's *Sexual Politics*, which analyzes the sexual visions or ideologies of

Lawrence, Miller, Mailer, and Genet. If these discussions seem exaggerated or crude, as they have seemed to male critics who find it hard to defend the sexual politics of the writers they may have admired, it is because by posing the question of the relation between sex and power and assembling relevant passages from Lawrence, Miller, and Mailer, one displays in all their crudity the aggressive phallic visions of three "counterrevolutionary sexual politicians" (p. 233). (Genet, by contrast, subjects the code of male and female roles to withering scrutiny.)

Millett's strategy in reading as a woman is "to take an author's ideas seriously when, like the novelists covered in this study, they wish to be taken seriously," and to confront them directly. "Critics who disagree with Lawrence, for example, about any issue are fond of saying that his prose is awkward . . . . It strikes me as better to make a radical investigation which can demonstrate why Lawrence's analysis of a situation is inadequate, or biased, or his influence pernicious, without ever needing to imply that he is less than a great and original artist" (p. xii).

Instead of playing down, as critics are wont to do, those works whose sexual vision is most elaborately developed, Millett pursues Lawrence's sexual religion to an apotheosis where sexuality is separated from sex: the priests of "The Woman Who Rode Away" are "supernatural males, who are 'beyond sex' in a pious fervor of male supremacy that disdains any genital contact with woman, preferring instead to deal with her by means of a knife." This pure or ultimate maleness is, Lawrence says, "something primevally male and cruel" (p. 290). Miller's sexual ethos is much more conventional: "his most original contribution to sexual attitudes is confined to giving the first full expression to an ancient sentiment of contempt": he has "given voice to certain sentiments which masculine culture had long experienced but always rather carefully suppressed" (pp. 309, 313). As for Mailer, his defense of Miller against Millett's critique confirms Millett's analysis of Mailer himself, as "a prisoner of the virility cult" "whose powerful intellectual comprehension of what is most dangerous in the masculine sensibility is exceeded only by his attachment to the malaise" (p. 314). Here is

[2]See de Beauvoir, p. 673.

Mailer restating, in Miller's defense, their male ideology:

> For he captured something in the sexuality of men as it had never been seen before, precisely that it was man's sense of awe before woman, his dread of her position one step closer to eternity (for in that step were her powers) which made men detest women, revile them, humiliate them, defecate symbolically on them, do everything to reduce them so one might dare to enter them and take pleasure of them. . . . Men look to destroy every quality in a woman which will give her the powers of a male, for she is in their eyes already armed with the power that she brought them forth, and that is a power beyond measure — the earliest etchings of memory go back to that woman between whose legs they were conceived, nurtured, and near strangled in the hours of birth. [*The Prisoner of Sex*, p. 116]

How does a woman read such authors? A feminist criticism confronts the problem of women as the consumer of male-produced literature.

Millett also offers, in an earlier chapter, brief discussions of other works: *Jude the Obscure, The Egoist, Villette,* and Wilde's *Salomé.* Analyzing these reactions to the sexual revolution of the nineteenth century, she establishes a feminist response that has served as a point of departure for debates within feminist criticism — disagreements about whether, for example, despite his sensitive portrait of Sue Bridehead, Hardy is ultimately "troubled and confused" when it comes to the sexual revolution.[3] But the possibility of quarreling with Millett to develop more subtle feminist readings should not obscure the main point. As Carolyn Heilbrun puts it,

> Millett has undertaken a task which I find particularly worthwhile: the consideration of certain events or works of literature from an unexpected, even startling point of view. . . . Her aim is to wrench the reader from the vantage point he has long occupied, and force him to look at life and letters from a new coign. Hers is not meant to be the last word on any writer, but a wholly new word, little heard before

and strange. For the first time we have been asked to look at literature as women: we, men, women and Ph.D's, have always read it as men. Who cannot point to a certain overemphasis in the way Millett reads Lawrence or Stalin or Euripides. What matter? We are rooted in our vantage point and require transplanting. ["Millett's *Sexual Politics*: A Year Later," p. 39]

As Heilbrun suggests, reading as a woman is not necessarily what occurs when a woman reads: women can read, and have read, as men. Feminist readings are not produced by recording what happens in the mental life of a female reader as she encounters the words of *The Mayor of Casterbridge,* though they do rely heavily on the notion of the experience of the woman reader. Shoshana Felman asks, "Is it enough to be a woman in order to speak as a woman? Is 'speaking as a woman' determined by some biological condition or by a strategic, theoretical position, by anatomy or by culture?" ("Women and Madness: The Critical Phallacy," p. 3). The same question applies to "reading as a woman."

To ask a woman to read as a woman is in fact a double or divided request. It appeals to the condition of being a woman as if it were a given and simultaneously urges that this condition be created or achieved. Reading as a woman is not simply, as Felman's disjunctions might seem to imply, a theoretical position, for it appeals to a sexual identity defined as essential and privileges experiences associated with that identity. Even the most sophisticated theorists make this appeal — to a condition or experience deemed more basic than the theoretical position it is used to justify. "As a female reader, I am haunted rather by another question," writes Gayatri Spivak, adducing her sex as the ground for a question ("Finding Feminist Readings," p. 82). Even the most radical French theorists, who would deny any positive or distinctive identity to woman and see *le feminin* as any force that disrupts the symbolic structures of Western thought, always have moments, in developing a theoretical position, when they speak as women, when they rely on the fact that they *are* women. Feminist critics are fond of quoting Virginia Woolf's remark that women's "inheritance," what they are given, is "the difference of view, the difference of standard"; but the question

---

[3]See, for example, an early rejoinder by Mary Jacobus, who argues that what Millett calls Hardy's "confusion" is in fact "careful non-alignment": "through Sue's obscurity he probes the relationship between character and idea in such a way as to leave one's mind engaged with her as it is engaged with few women in fiction" ("Sue the Obscure," pp. 305, 325). [Culler]

then becomes, what is the difference? It is never given as such but must be produced. Difference is produced by differing. Despite the decisive and necessary appeal to the authority of women's experience and of a female reader's experience, feminist criticism is in fact concerned, as Elaine Showalter astutely puts it, "with the way in which the *hypothesis* of a female reader changes our apprehension of a given text, awakening us to the significance of its sexual codes" ("Towards a Feminist Poetics," p. 25, my italics).[4]

Showalter's notion of the *hypothesis* of a female reader marks the double or divided structure of "experience" in reader-oriented criticism. Much male response criticism conceals this structure — in which experience is posited as a given yet deferred as something to be achieved — by asserting that readers simply do in fact have a certain experience. This structure emerges explicitly in a good deal of feminist criticism which takes up the problem that women do not always read or have not always read as women: they have been alienated from an experience appropriate to their condition as women.[5] With the shift to the hypothesis of a female reader, we move to a second moment or level of feminist criticism's dealings with the reader. In the first moment, criticism appeals to

experience as a given that can ground or justify a reading. At the second level the problem is precisely that women have not been reading as women. "What is crucial here," writes Kolodny, "is that reading is a *learned* activity which, like many other learned interpretive strategies in our society, is inevitably sex-coded and gender-inflected" ("Reply to Commentaries," p. 588). Women "are expected to identify," writes Showalter, "with a masculine experience and perspective, which is presented as the human one" ("Women and the Literary Curriculum," p. 856). They have been constituted as subjects by discourses that have not identified or promoted the possibility of reading "as a woman." In its second moment, feminist criticism undertakes, through the postulate of a woman reader, to bring about a new experience of reading and to make readers — men and women — question the literary and political assumptions on which their reading has been based.

In feminist criticism of the first sort, women readers identify with the concerns of women characters; in the second case, the problem is precisely that women are led to identify with male characters, against their own interests as women. Judith Fetterley,[6] in a book on the woman reader and American fiction, argues that "the major works of American fiction constitute a series of designs upon the female reader." Most of this literature "insists on its universality at the same time that it defines that universality in specifically male terms" (*The Resisting Reader,* p. xii). One of the founding works of American literature, for instance, is "The Legend of Sleepy Hollow." The figure of Rip Van Winkle, writes Leslie Fiedler, "presides over the birth of the American imagination; and it is fitting that our first successful homegrown legend should memorialize, however playfully, the flight of the dreamer from the shrew" (*Love and Death in the American Novel,*

---

[4]Feminist criticism is, of course, concerned with other issues as well, particularly the distinctiveness of women's writing and the achievements of women writers. The problems of reading as a woman and of writing as a woman are in many respects similar, but concentration on the latter leads feminist criticism into areas that do not concern me here, such as the establishment of a criticism focused on women writers that parallels criticism focused on male writers. Gynocriticism, says Showalter, who has been one of the principal advocates of this activity, is concerned "with woman as the producer of textual meaning, with the history, themes, genres, and structures of literature by women. Its subjects include the psychodynamics of female creativity; linguistics and the problem of a female language; the trajectory of the individual or collective female literary career; literary history; and, of course, studies of particular writers and works" ("Towards a Feminist Poetics," p. 25). For work of this kind, see Sandra Gilbert and Susan Gubar, *The Madwoman in the Attic,* and the collection edited by Sally McConnell-Ginet, Ruth Borker, and Nelly Furman, *Women and Language in Literature and Society* (New York: Praeger, 1980). [Culler]

[5]The analogy with social class is instructive: progressive political writing appeals to the proletariat's experience of

oppression, but usually the problem for a political movement is precisely that the members of a class do not have the experience their situation would warrant. The most insidious oppression alienates a group from its own interests as a group and encourages it to identify with the interests of the oppressors, so that political struggles must first awaken a group to its interests and its "experience." [Culler]

[6]See Fetterley, p. 1035.

p. xx). It is fitting because, ever since then, novels seen as archetypally American — investigating or articulating a distinctively American experience — have rung the changes on this basic schema, in which the protagonist struggles against constricting, civilizing, oppressive forces embodied by woman. The typical protagonist, continues Fiedler, the protagonist seen as embodying the universal American dream, has been "a man on the run, harried into the forest and out to sea, down the river or into combat — anywhere to avoid 'civilization,' which is to say, the confrontation of a man and a woman which leads to the fall to sex, marriage, and responsibility."

Confronting such plots, the woman reader, like other readers, is powerfully impelled by the structure of the novel to identify with a hero who makes woman the enemy. In "The Legend of Sleepy Hollow," where Dame Van Winkle represents everything one might wish to escape and Rip the success of a fantasy, Fetterley argues that "what is essentially a simple act of identification when the reader of the story is male becomes a tangle of contradictions when the reader is female" (*The Resisting Reader*, p. 9). "In such fictions the female reader is co-opted into participation in an experience from which she is explicitly excluded; she is asked to identify with a selfhood that defines itself in opposition to her; she is required to identify against herself" (p. xii).

One should emphasize that Fetterley is not objecting to unflattering literary representations of women but to the way in which the dramatic structure of these stories induces women to participate in a vision of woman as the obstacle to freedom. Catherine in *A Farewell to Arms* is an appealing character, but her role is clear: her death prevents Frederic Henry from coming to feel the burdens she fears she imposes, while consolidating his investment in an idyllic love and in his vision of himself as a "victim of cosmic antagonism" (p. xvi). "If we weep at the end of the book," Fetterley concludes, "it is not for Catherine but for Frederic Henry. All our tears are ultimately for men, because in the world of *A Farewell to Arms* male life is what counts. And the message to women reading this classic love story and experiencing its image of the female ideal is clear and simple: the only good woman is

a dead one, and even then there are questions" (p. 71). Whether or not the message is quite this simple, it is certainly true that the reader must adopt the perspective of Frederic Henry to enjoy the pathos of the ending.

Fetterley's account of the predicament of the woman reader — seduced and betrayed by devious male texts — is an attempt to change reading: "Feminist criticism is a political act whose aim is not simply to interpret the world but to change it by changing the consciousness of those who read and their relation to what they read" (p. viii). The first act of a feminist critic is "to become a resisting rather than an assenting reader and, by this refusal to assent, to begin the process of exorcizing the male mind that has been implanted in us" (p. xxii).

This is part of a broader struggle. Fetterley's account of the woman reader's predicament is powerfully confirmed by Dorothy Dinnerstein's analysis of the effects, on women as well as men, of human nurturing arrangements. "Woman, who introduced us to the human situation and who at the beginning seemed to us responsible for every drawback of that situation, carries for all of us a pre-rational onus of ultimately culpable responsibility forever after" (*The Mermaid and the Minotaur*, p. 234). Babies of both sexes are generally nurtured at first by the mother, on whom they are completely dependent. "The initial experience of dependence on a largely uncontrollable outside source of good is focused on a woman, and so is the earliest experience of vulnerability to disappointment and pain" (p. 28). The result is a powerful resentment of this dependency and a compensatory tendency to identify with male figures, who are perceived as distinct and independent. "Even to the daughter, the mother may never come to seem so completely an 'I' as the father, who was an 'I' when first encountered" (p. 107). This perception of the mother affects her perception of all women, including herself, and encourages her "to preserve her 'I' ness by thinking of men, not women, as her real fellow creatures" — and to become engaged as a reader in plots of escape from women and domination of women (p. 107). What feminists ignore or deny at their peril, warns Dinnerstein, "is that women share men's anti-female feelings — usually in a mitigated form, but deeply nevertheless. This fact stems partly, to be sure, from causes that other writers have already quite adequately spelled out: that we have been steeped in self-derogatory societal stereotypes, pitted against each other for the favors of the reigning sex, and so on. But it stems largely from another cause, whose effects are much harder to undo: that we, like men, had female mothers" (p. 90). Without a change in nurturing arrangements, fear and loathing of women will not disappear, but some measure of progress might come with an understanding of what women want: "What women want is to stop serving as scapegoats (their own scapegoats as well as men's and children's scapegoats) for human resentment of the human condition. They want this so painfully, and so pervasively, and until quite recently it was such a hopeless thing to want, that they have not yet been able to say out loud that they want it" (p. 234).

This passage illustrates the structure at work in the second moment of feminist criticism and shows something of its power and necessity. This persuasive writing appeals to a fundamental desire or experience of women — what women want, what women feel — but an experience posited to displace the self-mutilating experiences Dinnerstein has described. The experience appealed to is nowhere present as indubitable evidence or *point d'appui*,[7] but the appeal to it is not factitious: what more fundamental appeal could there be than to such a possibility? This postulate empowers an attempt to alter conditions so that women will not be led to cooperate in making women scapegoats for the problems of the human condition.

The most impressive works in this struggle are doubtless books like Dinnerstein's, which analyzes our predicament in terms that make comprehensible a whole range of phenomena, from the self-estrangement of women readers to the particular cast of Mailer's sexism. In literary criticism, a powerful strategy is to produce readings that identify and situate male misreading. Though it is difficult to work out in positive, independent terms what it might mean to read as a woman, one may confidently propose a purely differential definition: to read as a woman is to avoid reading as a man, to identify the specific defenses and distortions of male readings and provide correctives.

By these lights, feminist criticism is a critique of what Mary Ellmann, in her witty and erudite *Thinking about Women,* calls "phallic criticism." Fetterley's most impressive and effective chapter, for example, may well be her discussion of *The Bostonians*,[8] where she documents the striking tendency of male critics to band together and take the part of Basil Ransom in his determination to win Verena away from her feminist friend, Olive Chancellor. Treating the relation between the women as perverse and unnatural, critics identify with Ransom's fear that female solidarity threatens male dominance and the male character: "The whole generation is womanized; the masculine tone is passing out of the world; . . . The masculine character . . . that is what I want to preserve, or rather, as I may say, to recover; and I must tell you that I don't in the least care what becomes of you ladies while I make the attempt."

Rescuing Verena from Olive is part of this project, for which the critics show considerable enthusiasm. Some recognize Ransom's failings and James's precise delineation of them (others regard this complexity as an artistic error on James's part), but all seem to agree that when Ransom carries Verena off, this is a consummation devoutly to be wished. The narrator tells us in the concluding sentence of the book that Verena will have cause to shed more tears: "It is to be feared that with the union, so far from brilliant, into which she was about to enter, these were not to be the last she was destined to shed." But critics generally regard this, as one of them observes, as "a small price to pay for achieving a normal relationship." Faced with a threat to what they regard as normalcy, male critics become caught up in Ransom's crusade and outdo one another in finding reasons to disparage Olive, the character in whom James shows the greatest interest, as well as the feminist movements James criticizes. The result is a male chorus. "The criticism of *The Bostonians* is remarkable for its relentless sameness, its reliance on values outside the novel, and its cavalier dismissal of the need for textual support" (*The Resisting Reader,* p. 113).

---

[7]Rallying point.

[8]Novel (1886) by Henry James.

The hypothesis of a female reader is an attempt to rectify this situation: by providing a different point of departure it brings into focus the identification of male critics with one character and permits the analysis of male misreadings. But what it does above all is to reverse the usual situation in which the perspective of a male critic is assumed to be sexually neutral, while a feminist reading is seen as a case of special pleading and an attempt to force the text into a predetermined mold. By confronting male readings with the elements of the text they neglect and showing them to be a continuation of Ransom's position rather than judicious commentary on the novel as a whole, feminist criticism puts itself in the position that phallic criticism usually attempts to occupy. The more convincing its critique of phallic criticism, the more feminist criticism comes to provide the broad and comprehensive vision, analyzing and situating the limited and interested interpretations of male critics. Indeed, at this level one can say that feminist criticism is the name that should be applied to all criticism alert to the critical ramifications of sexual oppression, just as in politics "women's issues" is the name now applied to many fundamental questions of personal freedom and social justice.

A different way of going beyond phallic criticism is Jane Tompkins's discussion of *Uncle Tom's Cabin,* a novel relegated to the trash heap of literary history by male critics and fellow travelers such as Ann Douglas, in her influential book *The Feminization of American Culture.* "The attitude Douglas expresses toward the vast quantity of literature written by women in this country between 1820 and 1870 is the one that the male-dominated scholarly tradition has always expressed — contempt. The query one hears behind every page of her indictment of feminization is: why can't a woman be more like a man?" ("*Sentimental Power,*" p. 81). Though in some respects the most important book of the century, *Uncle Tom's Cabin* is placed in a genre — the sentimental novel — written by, about, and for women, and therefore seen as trash, or at least as unworthy of serious critical consideration. If one does take this book seriously, one discovers, Tompkins argues, that it displays in exemplary fashion the features of a major American genre defined by Sacvan

Bercovitch, "the American Jeremiad":[9] "a mode of public exhortation . . . designed to join social criticism to spiritual renewal, public to private identity, the shifting 'signs of the times' to certain traditional metaphors, themes, and symbols," especially those of typological narratives (p. 93). Bercovitch's book, notes Tompkins, "provides a striking instance of how totally academic criticism has foreclosed on sentimental fiction; since, even when a sentimental novel fulfills a man's theory to perfection, he cannot see it. For him the work doesn't even exist. Despite the fact that his study takes no note of the most obvious and compelling instance of the jeremiad since the Great Awakening,[10] Bercovitch's description in fact provides an excellent account of the combination of elements that made Stowe's novel work" (p. 93). Rewriting the Bible as the story of a Negro slave, "*Uncle Tom's Cabin* retells the culture's central myth — the story of the crucifixion — in terms of the nation's greatest political conflict — slavery — and of its most cherished social beliefs — the sanctity of motherhood and the family" (p. 89).

Here the hypothesis of a woman reader helps to identify male exclusions that forestall serious analysis, but once that analysis is undertaken it becomes possible to argue

> that the popular domestic novel of the nineteenth century represents a monumental effort to reorganize culture from the woman's point of view, that this body of work is remarkable for its intellectual complexity, ambition, and resourcefulness, and that, in certain cases, it offers a critique of American society far more devastating than any delivered by better-known critics such as Hawthorne and Melville. . . . Out of the ideological materials they had at their disposal, the sentimental novelists elaborated a myth that gave women the central position of power and authority in the culture; and of these efforts *Uncle Tom's Cabin* is the most dazzling exemplar. [pp. 81–82]

In addition to the devastating attack on slavery, reputed to have "changed the hearts" of many of its readers, the novel attempts to bring on,

[9]*American Jeremiad* (1980) is Bercovitch's book on Puritanism and the American literary renaissance of the 1840s.
[10]The American religious revival of the early eighteenth century associated with Jonathan Edwards.

through the same sort of change of heart, a new social order. In the new society, envisioned in a chapter called "The Quaker Settlement," man-made institutions fade into irrelevance, and the home guided by the Christian woman becomes, not a refuge from the real order of the world, but the center of meaningful activity (p. 95). "The removal of the male from the center to the periphery of the human sphere is the most radical component of this millenarian scheme which is rooted so solidly in the most traditional values — religion, motherhood, home, and family. [In the details of this chapter,] Stowe reconceives the role of men in human history: while Negroes, children, mothers, and grandmothers do the world's primary work, men groom themselves contentedly in a corner" (p. 98).

In this sort of analysis, feminist criticism does not rely on the experience of the woman reader as it does at the first level but employs the hypothesis of a woman reader to provide leverage for displacing the dominant male critical vision and revealing its misprisions. "By 'feminist,' " suggests Peggy Kamuf, "one understands a way of reading texts that points to the masks of truth with which phallocentrism hides its fiction" ("Writing like a Woman," p. 286). The task at this level is not to establish a woman's reading that would parallel a male reading but rather, through argument and an attempt to account for textual evidence, to produce a comprehensive perspective, a compelling reading. The conclusions reached in feminist criticism of this sort are not specific to women in the sense that one can sympathize, comprehend, and agree only if one has had certain experiences which are women's. On the contrary, these readings demonstrate the limitations of male critical interpretations in terms that male critics would purport to accept, and they seek, like all ambitious acts of criticism, to attain a generally convincing understanding — an understanding that is feminist because it is a critique of male chauvinism.

In this second moment of feminist criticism there is an appeal to the potential experience of a woman reader (which would escape the limitations of male readings) and then the attempt to make such an experience possible by developing questions and perspectives that would enable a woman to read as a woman — that is, not "as a man." Men have aligned the opposition male/female with rational/emotional, serious/frivolous, or reflective/spontaneous; and feminist criticism of the second moment works to prove itself more rational, serious, and reflective than male readings that omit and distort. But there is a third moment in which, instead of contesting the association of the male with the rational, feminist theory investigates the way our notions of the rational are tied to or in complicity with the interests of the male. One of the most striking analyses of this kind is Luce Irigaray's *Speculum*,[11] *de l'autre femme*, which takes Plato's parable of the cave, with its contrast between a maternal womb and a divine paternal *logos*, as the point of departure for a demonstration that philosophical categories have been developed to relegate the feminine to a position of subordination and to reduce the radical Otherness of woman to a specular relation: woman is either ignored or seen as man's opposite. Rather than attempt to reproduce Irigaray's complex argument, one might take a single striking example adduced by Dorothy Dinnerstein, Peggy Kamuf, and others: the connection between patriarchy and the privileging of the rational, the abstract, or the intellectual.

In *Moses and Monotheism*, Freud establishes a relation between three "processes of the same character": the Mosaic prohibition against making a sensible image of God (thus, "the compulsion to worship a God whom one cannot see"), the development of speech ("the new realm of intellectuality was opened up, in which ideas, memories, and inferences became decisive in contrast to the lower psychical activity which had direct perceptions by the sense-organs as its content") and, finally, the replacement of a matriarchal social order by a patriarchal one. The last involves more than a change in juridical conventions. "This turning from the mother to the father points in addition to a victory of intellectuality over sensuality — that is, an advance of civilization, since maternity is proved by the evidence of the senses while paternity is a hypothesis, based on an inference and a premiss. Taking sides in this way with a thought-process in preference to a sense perception has proved to be a momentous step" (vol. 23, pp. 113–14). Several pages further on, Freud explains the common character of these processes:

[11]Latin for "mirror."

An advance in intellectuality consists in deciding against direct sense-perception in favour of what are known as the higher intellectual processes — that is, memories, reflections, and inferences. It consists, for instance, in deciding that paternity is more important than maternity, although it cannot, like the latter, be established by the evidence of the senses, and that for that reason the child should bear his father's name and be his heir. Or it declares that our God is the greatest and mightiest, although he is invisible like a gale of wind or like the soul. [pp. 117–18]

Freud appears to suggest that the establishment of patriarchal power is merely an instance of the general advance of intellectuality and that the preference for an invisible God is another effect of the same cause. But when we consider that the invisible, omnipotent God is God the Father, not to say God of the Patriarchs, we may well wonder whether, on the contrary, the promotion of the invisible over the visible and of thought and inference over sense perception is not a consequence or effect of the establishment of paternal authority: a consequence of the fact that the paternal relation is invisible.

If one wished to argue that the promotion of the intelligible over the sensible, meaning over form, and the invisible over the visible was an elevation of the paternal principle and paternal power over the maternal, one could draw support from the character of Freud's arguments elsewhere, since he shows that numerous enterprises are determined by unconscious interests of a sexual character. Dorothy Dinnerstein's discussions would also support the view that the intangibility and uncertainty of the paternal relation have considerable consequences. She notes that fathers, because of their lack of direct physical connection with babies, have a powerful urge to assert a relation, giving the child their name to establish genealogical links, engaging in various "initiation rites through which they symbolically and passionately affirm that it is they who have themselves created human beings, as compared with the mere flesh spawned by woman. Think also of the anxious concern that men have so widely shown for immortality through heirs, and their efforts to control the sexual life of women to make sure that the children they sponsor really do come from their own seed: the tenuousness of their physical tie to the young clearly pains men in a way that it could not pain bulls or stallions" (*The Mermaid and the Minotaur*, p. 80).

Men's powerful "impulse to affirm and tighten by cultural inventions their unsatisfactorily loose mammalian connection with children" leads them to value highly cultural inventions of a symbolic nature (pp. 80–81). One might predict an inclination to value what are generally termed metaphorical relations — relations of resemblance between separate items that can be substituted for one another, such as obtain between the father and the miniature replica with the same name, the child — over metonymical, maternal relationships based on contiguity.

Indeed, if one tried to imagine the literary criticism of a patriarchal culture, one might predict several likely concerns: (1) that the role of the author would be conceived as a paternal one and any maternal functions deemed valuable would be assimilated to paternity; [12] (2) that much would be invested in paternal authors, to whose credit everything in their textual progeny would redound; (3) that there would be great concern about which meanings were legitimate and which illegitimate (since the paternal author's role in the generation of meanings can only be inferred); and that criticism would expend great efforts to develop principles for, on the one hand, determining which meanings were truly the author's own progeny, and on the other hand, controlling intercourse with texts so as to prevent the proliferation of illegitimate interpretations. Numerous aspects of criticism, including the preference for metaphor over metonymy, the conception of the author, and the concern to distinguish legitimate from illegitimate meanings, can be seen as part of the promotion of the paternal. Phallogocentrism unites an interest in patriarchal authority, unity of meaning, and certainty of origin.

The task of feminist criticism in this third moment is to investigate whether the procedures,

[12]See Gilbert and Gubar, *The Madwoman in the Attic*, pp. 3–92. Feminist critics have shown considerable interest in Harold Bloom's model of poetic creation because it makes explicit the sexual connotations of authorship and authority. This oedipal scenario, in which one becomes a poet by struggling with a poetic father for possession of the muse, indicates the problematical situation of a woman who would be a poet. What relation can she have to the tradition? [Culler]

assumptions, and goals of current criticism are in complicity with the preservation of male authority, and to explore alternatives. It is not a question of rejecting the rational in favor of the irrational, of concentrating on metonymical relations to the exclusion of the metaphorical, or on the signifier to the exclusion of the signified, but of attempting to develop critical modes in which the concepts that are products of male authority are inscribed within a larger textual system. Feminists will try various strategies — in recent French writing "woman" has come to stand for any radical force that subverts the concepts, assumptions, and structures of traditional male discourse.[13] One might suspect, however, that attempts to produce a new feminine language will prove less effective at this stage than critiques of phallocentric criticism, which are by no means limited to the strategies of feminist criticism's second moment. There, feminist readings identify male bias by using concepts and categories that male critics purport to accept. In this third moment or mode, many of these concepts and theoretical categories — notions of realism, of rationality, of mastery, of explanation — are themselves shown to belong to phallocentric criticism.

Consider, for instance, Shoshana Felman's discussion of the text and readings of Balzac's short story "Adieu," a tale of a woman's madness, its origin in an episode of the Napoleonic wars, and her former lover's attempt to cure it. Feminist perspectives of the first and second moment bring out what was previously ignored or taken for granted, as male critics set aside women and madness to praise the "realism" of Balzac's description of war. Felman shows that critics' dealings with the text repeat the male protagonist's dealings with his former mistress, Stéphanie. "It is quite striking to observe to what extent the logic of the unsuspecting 'realistic' critic can reproduce, one after the

other, all of Philippe's delusions" ("Women and Madness: The Critical Phallacy," p. 10).

Philippe thinks he can cure Stéphanie by making her recognize and name him. To restore her reason is to obliterate her otherness, which he finds so unacceptable that he is willing to kill both her and himself if he should fail in his cure. She must recognize him and recognize herself as "his Stéphanie" again. When she finally does so, as a result of Philippe's elaborate realistic reconstruction of the scene of wartime suffering where she lost her reason, she dies. The drama played out in the story reflects back on the attempt by male critics to make the story a recognizable instance of realism, and thus questions their notions of "realism" or reality, of reason, and of interpretive mastery, as instances of a male passion analogous to Philippe's. "On the critical as well as on the literary stage, the same attempt is played out to appropriate the signifier and to reduce its differential repetition; we see the same endeavor to do away with difference, the same policing of identities, the same design of mastery, of *sense-control.* . . . Along with the illusions of Philippe, the realistic critic thus repeats, in turn, his allegorical act of murder, his obliteration of the Other: the critic also, in his own way, *kills the woman*, while killing, at the same time, the question of the text and the text as question" (p. 10).

Balzac's story helps to identify notions critics have employed with the male stratagems of its protagonist and thus to make possible a feminist reading that situates these concepts and describes their limitations. Insofar as the structure and details of Balzac's story provide a critical description of its male critics, exploration and exploitation of its textuality is a feminist way of reading, but a way of reading that poses rather than solves the question of how to get around or to go beyond the concepts and categories of male criticism. Felman concludes, "from this confrontation in which Balzac's text itself seems to be an ironic reading of its own future reading, the question arises: how *should* we read?" (p. 10).

This is also the question posed in feminist criticism's second moment — how should we read? what kind of reading experience can we imagine or produce? what would it be to read "as a woman"? Felman's critical mode thus leads back to the second level at which political choices are

[13]The articles in Elaine Marks and Isabelle de Courtivron's *New French Feminisms* provide an excellent conspectus of recent strategies. See also the discussions in *Yale French Studies* 62 (1981), "Feminist Readings: French Texts/ American Contexts." The relation between feminism and deconstruction is a complicated question. For some brief indications, see Chapter Two, section 4, below. Derrida's *Eperons*, on Nietzsche and the concept of woman, is a relevant but in many ways unsatisfying document in this case. [Culler]

debated and where notions of what one wants animate critical practice. In this sense, the third level, which questions the framework of choice and the affiliations of critical and theoretical categories, is not more radical than the second; nor does it escape the question of "experience."

From these varied writings, a general structure emerges. In the first moment or mode, where woman's experience is treated as a firm ground for interpretation, one swiftly discovers that this experience is not the sequence of thoughts present to the reader's consciousness as she moves through the text but a reading or interpretation of "woman's experience" — her own and others' — which can be set in a vital and productive relation to the text. In the second mode, the problem is how to make it possible to read as a woman: the possibility of this fundamental experience induces an attempt to produce it. In the third mode, the appeal to experience is veiled but still there, as a reference to maternal rather than paternal relations or to woman's situation and experience of marginality, which may give rise to an altered mode of reading. The appeal to the experience of the reader provides leverage for displacing or undoing the system of concepts or procedures of male criticism, but "experience" always has this divided, duplicitous character: it has always already occurred and yet is still to be produced — an indispensable point of reference, yet never simply there.

Peggy Kamuf provides a vivid way of understanding this situation of deferral if we transpose what she says about writing as a woman to reading as a woman:

> — "a woman [reading] as a woman" — the repetition of the "identical" term splits that identity, making room for a slight shift, spacing out the differential meaning which has always been at work in the single term. And the repetition has no reason to stop there, no finite number of times it can be repeated until it closes itself off logically, with the original identity recuperated in a final term. Likewise, one can find only arbitrary beginnings for the series, and no term which is not already a repetition: ". . . a woman [reading] as a woman [reading] as a . . ." ["Writing like a Woman," p. 298]

For a woman to read as a woman is not to repeat an identity or an experience that is given but to play a role she constructs with reference to her identity as woman, which is also a construct, so that the series can continue: a woman reading as a woman reading as a woman. The noncoincidence reveals an interval, a division within woman or within any reading subject and the "experience" of that subject.

Works Cited

Adams, Maurianne. "*Jane* Eyre: Woman's Estate." In *The Authority of Experience: Essays in Feminist Criticism*. Eds. Lee Edwards and Arlyn Diamond. Amherst: University of Massachusetts Press, 1977, pp. 137–59.

Dinnerstein, Dorothy. *The Mermaid and the Minotaur: Sexual Arrangements and Human Malaise*. New York: Harper, 1976.

Douglas, Ann. *The Feminization of American Culture*. New York: Knopf, 1977.

Ellman, Mary. *Thinking about Women*. New York: Harcourt Brace, 1968.

Felman, Shoshana. "Women and Madness: The Critical Phallacy." *Diacritics* 5:4, 1975, pp. 2–10.

Fetterley, Judith. *The Resisting Reader: A Feminist Approach to American Fiction*. Bloomington: Indiana University Press, 1978.

Fiedler, Leslie. *Love and Death in the American Novel*. New York: Criterion, 1960.

Freud, Sigmund. *Complete Psychological Works*. Ed. James Strachey. London: Hogarth, 1953–74. 24 vols.

Hartman, Geoffrey H. *The Fate of Reading and Other Essays*. Chicago: University of Chicago Press, 1975.

Heilbrun, Carolyn. "Millett's *Sexual Politics*: A Year Later." *Aphra*, 2 (1971), 38–47.

Irigaray, Luce. *Speculum, de l'autre femme*. Paris: Minuit, 1974.

Kamuf, Peggy. "Writing Like a Woman." In *Women and Language in Literature and Society*. Ed. S. McConnell-Ginet et al. New York: Praeger, 1980, pp. 284–99.

Kolodny, Annette. "Reply to Commentaries: Women Writers, Literary Historians, and Martian Readers." *New Literary History*, 11 (1980), 587–92.

Lander, Dawn. "Eve Among the Indians." In *The Authority of Experience: Essays in Feminist Criticism*. Eds. Lee Edwards and Arlyn Diamond. Amherst: University of Massachusetts Press, 1977, pp. 194–211.

Lenz, Carolyn, et. al., *The Woman's Part: Feminist Criticism of Shakespeare*. Urbana: University of Illinois Press, 1980.

Mailer, Norman. *The Prisoner of Sex*. Boston: Little, Brown, 1971.

Millett, Kate. *Sexual Politics*. New York: Doubleday, 1970.

Showalter, Elaine. "Towards a Feminist Poetics." In *Women Writing and Writing About Women*. Ed. M. Jacobus. London: Croom Helm, 1979, pp. 22–41.

——— "Women and the Literary Curriculum." *College English*, 32 (1971), 855–62.

Spivak, Gayatri. "Finding Feminist Readings: Dante-Yeats." *Social Text*, 3 (1980), 73–87.

Tompkins, Jane. "Sentimental Power: *Uncle Tom's Cabin* and the Politics of Literary History." *Glyph*, 8 (1981), 79–102.

Trilling, Lionel. *The Opposing Self*. New York: Viking, 1955.

Woolf, Virginia. *Collected Essays*. London: Hogarth, 1966. 4 vols.

❖ DIALOGUE BETWEEN ELAINE SHOWALTER AND TERRY EAGLETON

Elaine Showalter

b. 1941

A founder of feminist criticism in the United States, Elaine Showalter remains one of its most creative and influential proponents. Showalter developed the concept and practice of gynocriticism. Showalter was born Elaine Cottler in Cambridge, Massachusetts. Against the wishes of her parents, she pursued an intellectual career, taking degrees in English at Bryn Mawr College (B.A., 1962), at Brandeis University (M.A., 1964), and at the University of California at Davis (Ph.D., 1970). She has taught at Davis, at the University of Delaware, at the Douglass College of Rutgers University, and she is now professor emerita at Princeton University. Her academic honors include a Guggenheim fellowship (1977–78) and a Rockefeller Humanities fellowship (1981–82). Author of the pioneering A Literature of Their Own: British Women Novelists from Brontë to Lessing *(1977), Showalter has also published* The Female Malady: Women, Madness, and English Culture (1830–1980) *(1986). She has written dozens of articles and essays on feminist topics and has edited* Women's Liberation and Literature *(1971), the first textbook on women in literature;* These Modern Women: Autobiographies of American Women in the 1920s *(1978); and* The New Feminist Criticism *(1985). Showalter's recent work includes* Sexual Anarchy: Gender and Culture at the Fin de Siècle *(1990),* Sister's Choice: Traditions and Change in American Women's Writing *(1991),* Daughters of Decadence: Women Writers of the Fin-de-Siècle *(1993),* Hystories: Hysterical Epidemics and Modern Culture *(1997); and* Inventing Herself: Claiming a Feminist Intellectual Heritage *(2001).*

Showalter's "Critical Cross-Dressing: Male Feminists and the Woman of the Year," reproduced in part below, was originally published in Raritan *in 1983. Showalter begins topically with a consideration of* Tootsie, *a film nominated for ten Academy Awards that very year. The theme of* Tootsie *is feminism, and much of its comedy is about exposing blatant and subtle male chauvinism in the workplace, but what Showalter finds rebarbative is that the liberated eccentric who makes things happen is "Dorothy Michaels," played by Dustin Hoffman in drag. When male theorists get into feminism, playing the* Tootsie *role, Showalter suggests that they have a tendency to take over, or at least imply that feminism would be a more effective operation if only men were put in charge of it. Showalter takes on Jonathan Culler's deconstruction of the performance of "reading as a woman" somewhat gingerly, aware that Culler's sharp arguments are double-edged, but has less mercy on Terry Eagleton's materialist approach to rape in* The Rape of Clarissa. *His reply to Showalter takes the form of a parable about his own reaction at Cambridge to interlopers, upper-class twits playing at leftist politics, implicitly asking Showalter whether social movements should include only those who would be most directly benefited by them, and whether feminism has too many friends and too much power to need or want male support. Eagleton's headnote is at Chapter 5, p. 1307, and won't be repeated here.*

ELAINE SHOWALTER

From *Critical Cross-Dressing:*
Male Feminists and the Woman of the Year

It's better to be a woman in our day. With us is all the joy of advance, the glory of conquering . . . Thank heaven we are women!
— from GEORGE GISSING, The Odd Women (1893)

READING AS A WOMAN: JONATHAN CULLER AND THE DECONSTRUCTION OF FEMINIST CRITICISM

It's a quantum leap from the flamboyant self-promotion of *Tootsie* to Jonathan Culler's account of the theoretical issues of women's reading in *On Deconstruction.* If the seriousness of a book is in inverse relation to the figuration of the cover, the white jacket of *On Deconstruction,* adorned only with the title, and three small lines, is the peak of minimalist prestige. Scrupulous, lucid, and tough-minded, *On Deconstruction* not only clarifies debates within feminist criticism, but moves the arguments a step ahead. Culler takes feminism seriously as a political ideology and a critical practice, describing it as "one of the most powerful forms of renovation in contemporary criticism." He takes to task "self-styled historians of criticism and critical theory" who have left feminist criticism out of history; and he is one of the few critics under discussion here who gives detailed and knowledgeable reference to feminist texts, instead of vague well-meaning gestures in the direction of *Signs.*

The alliance of feminism and deconstruction is not new; male theorists such as Derrida and Lacan have for some time used woman as the wild card, the joker in the pack who upsets the logocentric and phallocentric stack of appellations, and a number of brilliant young feminist critics, including Jane Gallop, Nancy Miller, Peggy Kamuf, Gayatri Spivak, and Margaret Homans, have made common cause with deconstructionist theory. But Culler's analysis cuts two ways. First he uses deconstructive techniques to demonstrate some difficulties in the feminist appeal to the woman

reader's experience, an experience and an identity which is always constructed rather than given. Second, he uses feminist criticism to give deconstruction a body, to link its philosophical abstractions to specific literary and political choices. Feminist critics confront, on immediately practical terms, many of the issues deconstruction defines. Where Derrida insists that hierarchical oppositions (such as man/woman) must be deconstructed through reversal rather than denial, feminist critics must put this principle into action, must choose whether to ally themselves with the reformist position of sexual equality, which denies difference, or with the radical position, which asserts the difference, the power and the superiority of the feminine. Their position on the specificity of women's writing, their critical style and voice, will be determined by this choice. Culler recognizes that both positions are valid, although as a Derridean he prefers the rhetorical reversal. Most feminist critics, in fact, play both ends against the middle, advocating social, academic, institutional equality, but textual difference. These positions are not oppositional, but responsive to women's different roles as citizens or as writers.

Feminist criticism also poses in dramatic and concrete terms the poststructuralist concern with the reader's experience as constitutive of the text. While reader-response criticism in general proposes a reading self or an informed reader who produces textual meaning, it prefers not to discuss the nature of the reader in specifically human terms.[1] But as Culler observes, feminist criticism "has a considerable stake in the question of the relation of the reading self and the experience of the reader to other moments of the self and other aspects of experience." The question of the *woman* reader brings this relation forward, and "issues

---

[1]For the variety of readers posited by different theorists, see the Introduction to Reader-Response Theory, p. 962.

often swept under the carpet by male stories of reading are brought into the open in the debates and divisions of feminist criticsm."

In tracing out feminist approaches to "reading as a woman," Culler sees three modes or stages. In the first, the critic appeals to female experience as a source of authority on female characters, on values, and on phallocentric assumptions. Yet, he points out, the "nature" of woman is a social construct, so "to ask of woman to read as a woman is in fact a double or divided request. It appeals to the condition of being a woman as if it were a given and simultaneously urges that this condition be created or achieved." In its second phase, feminist criticism confronts the reasons why women often read as men do, given their indoctrination by male literary and critical values. While identification with male experience may, as Dorothy Dinnerstein has argued in *The Mermaid and the Minotaur*, be the widespread result of nurturing arrangements which lead both sexes to reject and resent the female mother on whom they are initially dependent, it is reinforced and intensified in the case of academic women by their professional training and their prolonged immersion in patriarchal institutions. Reading as a woman thus becomes a willed project of unlearning, a resistance to what Judith Fetterley has called "immasculation." In this mode, the hypothesis of a woman reader, rather than a call upon female experience, serves to expose the misreadings, distortions and omissions of phallic criticism.

Culler sees the third mode of feminist criticism as the investigation of the "ways our notions of the rational are tied to or are in complicity with the interests of the male." This investigation includes the French feminist attack upon phallogocentrism and the interrogation of current critical assumptions. Its task is to "develop critical modes in which the concepts that are products of male authority are inscribed within a larger textual system." More theoretical than the other two, this third phase is still nevertheless linked to female experience, Culler argues, through its stress on maternal thematics and marginality. He concludes that "reading as a woman" is always a paradoxical act, in that the identity as "Woman" must always be deferred: "For a woman to read as a woman is not to repeat an identity or an experience that is given but to play a role she constructs with reference to her identity as a woman, which is also a construct, so that the series can continue: a woman reading as a woman reading as a woman."

But can a *man* read as a woman? Culler does not ask what might happen when a man attempts to produce a feminist reading, a situation in which the construction of the reader's gender identity is fore-grounded. He does not present himself as a feminist critic, but rather as an analyst of feminist critical work. For the most part, Culler places himself outside of, although sympathetic to, feminist reading. Yet in two instances, he does offer his own feminist reading of texts, and these raise interesting questions as to whether a male feminist is in fact a man reading as a woman reading as a woman.

Near the beginning of the section on feminist criticism, Culler comments on Geoffrey Hartman's observation in *The Fate of Reading* that "much reading is indeed like girl-watching, a simple expense of spirit," explaining that "the experience of reading seems to be that of a man (a heart-man?) for whom girl-watching is the model of an expense of spirit in a waste of shame. When we posit a woman reader, the result is an analogous appeal to experience; not to the experience of girl-watching, but to the experience of being watched, seen as a 'girl,' restricted, marginalized." Here Culler invokes the woman reader as a preamble to his inversion of Hartman's text.

By the end of his excursus on "Reading as a Woman," Culler has abandoned the hypothesis of a woman reader and produces his own rhetorically unmediated reading of Freud's *Moses and Monotheism*. Freud, he points out, links the development of speech, the Mosaic prohibition of material images of God and the turn from a matriarchal to a patriarchal social order, and treats the results as an advance to a more symbolic and thus higher stage of intellectuality. In doing this, says Culler, Freud is really promoting the elevation of the paternal principle which values the invisibility and the symbolic nature of its own relation with the child. Culler proceeds from this argument to speculate on the relation between the "promotion of the paternal" and the likely concerns of literary criticism in a patriarchal culture: (1) the conception of the author's role as paternal and the assimilation of any valued maternal functional to paternity; (2) the investment in paternal authors; (3) the obsession with the legitimacy of meaning and with the prevention of illegitimate interpretations.

I would argue that what Culler has done here is to read consciously from his own gender experience, with an ironic sense of its own ideological bounds. That is to say that he has not read as a *woman*, but as a man and a feminist. Indeed, Culler's deconstructionist priorities lead him to overstate the essentialist dilemma of defining the *woman* reader, when in most cases what is intended and implied is a *feminist* reader. Reading as a feminist, I hasten to add, is not unproblematic; but it has the important aspect of offering male readers a way to produce feminist criticism that avoids female impersonation. The way into feminist criticism, for the male theorist, must involve a confrontation with what might be implied by reading as a man and with a questioning or a surrender of paternal privileges.

WRITING AS A WOMAN: TERRY EAGLETON AND THE RAPE OF FEMINIST THEORY

But when male theorists borrow the language of feminist criticism without a willingness to explore the masculinist bias of their own reading system, we get a phallic "feminist" criticism that competes with women instead of breaking out of patriarchal bounds. Terry Eagleton's *The Rape of Clarissa: Writing, Sexuality, and Class Struggle in Samuel Richardson* (1982) brings together three "revolutionary" reading strategies: feminist criticism, historical materialism, and poststructuralist textualism. Although Eagleton refuses to give priority to any of these methods (indeed the copyright page of the American edition states that "The University of Minnesota Press is an equal opportunity educator and employer," as if to guarantee the constitutional equality of ideas as well), the aggressive title and the erotic cover of *The Rape of Clarissa* (Fragonard's *Le Verrou*)[2]

[2]Jean Honoré Fragonard's 1778 painting portrays a man sliding the bolt of a bedchamber door shut with one hand while struggling with a resisting young woman with the other; a lonely apple on a side table symbolically suggests the idea of the Fall.

certainly foreground the sexual issues. Eagleton also acknowledges the centrality of the feminist revolution in his text when he declares that "if Richardson may once again become readable, it will be in large measure because of the women's movement."

Eagleton presents the book as a bold incursion into several alien territories and it is meant to have the dash and daring of a highwayman's attack. First, it is a foray into psychoanalysis, a "terrain," he notes, "which the English have always found a little unnerving," Second, it is an invasion of the eighteenth century, "long the preserve of literary conservatism, rarely penetrated by Marxist criticism." And finally, it is a raid of feminist criticism, in order to claim overdue recognition for *Clarissa* as "the major feminist text of the language." Richardson, according to Eagleton, was the most "gifted and popular ideologue" of the eighteenth-century exaltation of the "feminine," and *Clarissa* is "the true history of women's oppression at the hands of eighteenth-century patriarchy." Like his "eighteenth century," Eagleton's "feminist criticism" is another well-barricaded preserve to be penetrated by the daring Marxist Macheath. Obviously more is at stake than the recuperation of Richardson.

Clues to precisely what *is* at stake may be deciphered in the textual strategies Eagleton employs, the "hermeneutic violence" he deploys in the name of revolutionary criticism. He is very good at exposing the sexism of those critics who have been of Lovelace's party: Dorothy Van Ghent, V. S. Pritchett, and especially William Beatty Warner, who reads the rape as Lovelace's clever way of deconstructing Clarissa. But Eagleton's own reading sees Clarissa, in her apparently infinite accessibility to interpretation, as the Lacanian "transcendental signifier" — the phallus itself. It is her phallic power that the anxiety-ridden Lovelace really craves: "Lovelace must possess Clarissa so that he may reunite himself with the lost phallus, and unmask her as reassuringly 'castrated.'"

What then, we ask, is Lovelace so anxious about? In part, Eagleton suggests, he is anxious about writing, about the appropriation of a womanly, or at any rate, an unmanly act. "What is worrying about Lovelace," according to Eagleton, "is that for a man he spends too much time writing." If the letter, in the eighteenth-century context, is associated with the feminine entrance into literature, and, more generally, with the expression of those concerns for the individual and for the emotional that Eagleton also describes as part of the bourgeois "feminization of discourse," then the scribbling Lovelace may be less than virile. And on a different level, the written word in fiction seems to share the metaphoric properties of the feminine. As Eagleton asserts, "The problem of writing is in this sense the problem of the woman: how is she to be at once decorous and spontaneous, translucently candid yet subdued to social pressure? Writing, like woman, marks a frontier between public and private, at once agonized outpouring and prudent stratagem."

The allegory here of "writing as a woman" seems forced, especially when we recognize that what is being described is neither female anxiety of authorship, such as Sandra Gilbert and Susan Gubar analyze in *The Madwoman in the Attic*,[3] nor the dilemma of Clarissa herself as correspondent and narrator. Instead it is the male gender anxiety of the character, the novelist, and ultimately the Marxist critic, who fears that his writing (rather than revolutionary action) is effeminate. By possessing feminist criticism, so to speak, Eagleton effectively recuperates for himself its "phallic" signifying power. In his synthesis of feminism, Marxism and poststructuralism, Eagleton also intermingles (or ignores) critics, so that there is no sense of a background of feminist readings of *Clarissa* against which his reading defines itself. This may be the inadvertent result of haste, or an aspect of English critical style, but it also suggests a disconcerting insensitivity to the politics of acknowledgment.

What happens if we contrast Terry Eagleton's reading of *Clarissa* to another feminist reading by a woman? Like Eagleton, Terry Castle,[4] in *Clarissa's Ciphers,* locates her reading in an intersection of feminism, deconstruction, and politics. Like him too she deplores the Lovelacean bias of Warner and Van Ghent, and sees Lovelace as infantile and banal. But unlike Eagleton, Castle sees Clarissa as the *victim* of "hermeneutic violence" practiced against women. Interrupted, "shut up," censored, silenced, violated, Clarissa's powers of expression, her access to language and to literary modes of production are severely constrained, while her oppressors' rights to language go unquestioned. Despite her eloquence, Clarissa's rhetoric is powerless because it is not grounded in the political authority and force that backs up the patriarchal discourse of Lovelace and the Harlowes. In the "black transaction" of the rape, *Clarissa* as novel inevitably tends to polarize its male and female readers, encouraging us to "examine the ways in which the gender of the reader (along with the resulting differences in socialization and *power*) may condition the meanings he or she finds in the text." In particular, Castle argues, the female/feminist reader responds to the silences in *Clarissa* and these correspond to the silences in the cultural history of women. The rape is the ultimate silencing, and a form of "hermeneutic intimidation" for Clarissa's efforts to define her own nature.

Terry Eagleton describes *Sir Charles Grandison* as Richardson's effort to appreciate the "tide of feminization" for patriarchy, to produce a new kind of hero who would combine Clarissa's feminine virtues — tenderness, feeling, goodness, chastity — with masculine power and effectiveness. The effort failed, however, because without the reality of female powerlessness and dependency behind it, goodness seemed priggish, chastity pointless, and tenderness merely effeminate. Thus Grandison's unreality indicates "a genuine ideological dilemma." If Eagleton had gone one step further, to consider his own ideological dilemma, *The Rape of Clarissa* would have been a more important book for feminist critics. Energetic, entertaining, and inventive though it be, Eagleton's phallic feminism seems like another raid on the resources of the feminine in order to modernize male dominance. We are led back to the politics of *Tootsie* — the appropriation of the tide of feminist feeling in the interests of patriarchy, the production of a new kind of (critical) hero. Whereas Terry Castle, breaking hermeneutic silence by reading and writing as a woman, testifies to the increased power of women to define their own nature, and builds her case on the work of such feminist critics of *Clarissa* as Nancy Miller, Janet Todd, Rachel Brownstein,

[3]See Gilbert and Gubar, p. 1531.
[4]Readers should be clear that Terry Castle, professor of English at Stanford, is female, and that Terry Eagleton is male.

Judith Wilt, and Margaret Doody, the effect of Eagleton's text is to silence or marginalize feminist criticism by speaking for it, and to use feminist language to reinforce the continued dominance of a male literary canon.

As Eagleton points out with reference to Sir *Charles Grandison*, the "genuinely progressive drive to generalize the discourse of femininity to men, exposes, in the very thinness of the text, an insurmountable sexual difference." In critical terms, as Larry Lipking disarmingly concedes in his essay "Aristotle's Sisters," sexual difference begins with "a fact that few male theorists have ever had to confront: the possibility of never having been empowered to speak." As women understand it, the problem of writing as a woman is initially one of overcoming fear. Eagleton notices that the people around Clarissa would prefer her *not* to write, that Mrs. Harlowe, for example, would prefer her daughter to read — that is, "to conform herself to another's text rather than to produce her own meanings." Like other kinds of criticism, feminist criticism is both reading and writing, both the interpretation of a text and the independent production of meaning. It is through the autonomous act of writing, and the confrontation with the anxiety that it generates, that feminist critics have developed theories of women's writing, theories proved on our own pulses. What I chiefly miss in *The Rape of Clarissa* is any sign from Eagleton that there is something equivocal and personal in his own polemic, some anxiety of authorship that is related to his own cultural position.

It has to be added, nevertheless, that in his latest book, *Literary Theory: An Introduction*, where he is no longer scolding feminist criticism for its separatist tendencies and lack of theoretical rigor (as he does in his book on Benjamin), or speaking for it (as he does in *The Rape of Clarissa*) for his own interpretative ends, Eagleton is persuasive, pungent and self-aware. At his best — and *Literary Theory* is his best — Eagleton is a persuasive analyst of literary culture, and his clear-headed account of the mutual goals — yet mutual independence — of socialist and feminist criticism makes this book immensely valuable. If in *The Rape of Clarissa* Eagleton's use of feminist criticism is self-interested, here he accords it a full measure of autonomy and respect. One senses in this book that feminist ideas have penetrated Eagleton's reading system everywhere, and that, along with Marxist aesthetics, they inform his entire account of the development of contemporary critical discourse.

LOOKING FOR THE WOMAN: DEMONS, DIACRITICS, AND THE WOMAN OF THE YEAR

Mercedes Kellogg, at table with Raquel Welch, who wore a bow tie, wing collar and tuxedo: "What does it mean when the 'Woman of the Year' dresses like a man?"
— JOHN DUKA, *New York Times,* December 1982

To a considerable degree, recent debates within feminist criticism about the importance of gender in the production of the feminist text have made space for male theorists like Eagleton, Culler, Booth, and Scholes to enter the field. Nina Auerbach's *Woman and the Demon: The Life of a Victorian Myth* challenges the feminist critical commonplace that literary stereotypes of women (such as the angel in the house, the victim, the queen, the witch, the old maid, and the fallen woman) are male mystifications, reducing and dehumanizing women. Properly understood, she argues, these figures are paradigms, or better, myths of ascendant womanhood. George MacDonald's malevolent Lilith, Rossetti's monumental "stunners," Dickens's expiring angels, all testify to female grandeur and to the woman-worship of an age losing its religious faith. In textual terms, then, male writers and artists inscribed "subversive paradigms of a divine and demonic female power at the cultural center of Victorian patriarchy and chivalry." Auerbach's analysis turns conventional interpretation on its head: although she does not exactly claim that Dickens, Rossetti, and Thackeray are feminist writers, she explains that their work is part of a Victorian "feminism" so "pervasive — in the broad power of this many-faceted myth of a mobile presiding woman — that the word has lost its meaning." Certainly, for Auerbach's purposes, there is no point in distinguishing between male and female purveyors of the myth.

Within French/deconstructionist feminist criticism, these issues take a different and even more enabling form for male critics. First of all, after the decentering of the human subject, and the alleged disappearance or death of the author, "the question of whether a 'man' or a 'woman' wrote a text," as Alice Jardine explains, "becomes non-sensical." Second, for French theorists, "*l'écriture féminine*," or women's writing, stands for a style, not a signature. Writing is feminine when it is open-ended, playful, avant-garde, audacious, nonlinear; *l'écriture féminine* can as well be signed by a man as by a woman.

In recent years, in fact, it has been necessary for American feminist critics to argue in behalf of our special commitment to women's writing as a historical and social category. The material conditions and contexts of women's writing have to be repeatedly stressed, because the patriarchal literary canon has a centripetal force and a social power that pulls discussion towards its center; women's writing gets left out unless feminist criticism insists that historically speaking, the question of whether a man or woman wrote a text is of primary importance. Reviewing the first wave of male feminist criticism, one notes that it nearly all "happens" to be about texts signed by men: Rabelais, Richardson, Hemingway, Lawrence. As Culler predicts, patriarchal criticism tends to disclose whatever it values in the maternal by assimilating it to the paternal function. Unless male feminist critics become more aware of the ways they too have been constituted as readers and writers by gender systems, their books may continue to be written for men and in behalf of male literary traditions.

Without closing the door on male feminists, I think that Franco-American theory has gone much too far in discounting the importance of signature and gender in authorship. The male author occupies a different literary place; the author of an *écriture féministe* needs to consider his or her own cultural circumstance. The movement away from the historical specificity of gender is hinted in the cover of the *Diacritics* special issue of summer 1982, titled "Cherchez La Femme: Feminist Critique/Feminine Text." On a white background is a figure in a black tuxedo and high heels, resting one knee on a bentwood chair à la Marlene Dietrich. The figure has no head or hands. On the back cover, a dress, hat, gloves, and shoes arrange themselves in a graceful bodiless tableau in space. No "vulgar" feminist, the chic Diacritical covergirl hints at the ephemera of gender indentities, of gender signatures.

There is an interview with Derrida in this issue of *Diacritics,* but all the other contributors are women, as are the editors. Yet I am haunted by the ambiguity of that cover. Sometimes I have a dream of the feminist literary conference of the future. The demonic woman rises to speak, but she mutates before our eyes into a mermaid, a vampire, a column of fire. The diacritical woman rises to speak, but she has no head. Holding out the empty sleeves of her fashionable jacket, she beckons to the third panelist. He rises swiftly and commands the podium. He is forceful; he is articulate; he is talking about Heidegger or Derrida or Lévi-Strauss or Brecht. He is wearing a dress.

TERRY EAGLETON
A Response to Elaine Showalter

In seeking to address these issues not in the first place abstractly or theoretically (thus risking one form of appropriation), but in terms of my own experience, I shall inevitably appropriate the issues into that experience by way of an — unavoidably falsifying — allegory, one which if it succeeds in its task of cautiously elucidating a

certain partial parallelism will do so only at the expense of suppressing a certain difference, a move which may well render the entire piece redundant, which may be no bad thing.

In the early 1960s I went from a working-class North-of-England background to Cambridge, at a time when the university was even more male-and upper class-dominated than it is today. I found myself one of a dismally minuscule group of proletarian students, besieged by gun-toting aristocrats like some exotic endangered species. My roommate, a Cockney,[5] was hauled in by his tutor and asked why he dressed like a garage mechanic. All the young men around us (there were hardly any young women) seemed chinless, well over six foot, and brayed rather than spoke. They all seemed to be called Jeremy or Alisdair, stamped their feet in cinemas and elbowed the Cambridge townspeople off the narrow pavements. We plebeians clung defensively together, cracking bitter jokes about the arrogance of the English ruling class and flamboyantly drinking the most socially disreputable beer we could find.

The group we *really* couldn't stand, however, were the English public school socialists. With Conservatives you knew where you were; what really spooked us was to discover a minority of chinless braying Jeremies who actually spoke our own political language, quoted *Capital* in languid tones and ran the university Labour club. None of them had ever clapped eyes on a row of back-to-back houses,[6] but they were genuine in their socialist views and interested in learning about our own very different social experience. We spent a lot of time huddled in pubs venting our spleen upon them. Who the bloody hell did they think they were, claiming our cause for themselves? They didn't have any *experience* of being working class: they were just full of a lot of highfalutin phrases they had picked up in books along side their public school Virgil,[7] oedipally on the run from their city director[8] fathers. We mocked their Brideshead[9] accents in private and were severe with them in public, scrutinizing their socialist credentials for the least flicker of ideological impurity. We made them feel bungling, inept, wet behind the ears,

second-class socialists. We spent most of our time working out our justifiable aggression on them, not on the real enemy. They needed us, so as to be able to boast back home of working-class friends; but we needed them too, to be gloriously reinforced in our unsullied proletarian essence.

Most of my Cambridge working-class friends are now Tories,[10] social democrats,[11] or political cynics. Because their politics were so closely bound to an intense, bitter personal experience, they couldn't survive the changes brought about by later middle-class affluence. Most of the public-school Marxists, by contrast, are still on the Left, some of them doing substantial radical work. Their politics were also of course bound by inversion to personal experience: they weren't just being altruistic. But the connections were more complex and oblique, and in certain ways, though not in others, there had never been much in it personally for them to become socialists. On the whole their commitment came through in later life, surviving our adolescent jeers.

Looking back on this gloomy experience, I now think I can see what was most wrong about our sectarianism. It wasn't only its tedious self-righteousness — its unreflective fear of the troublingly uncategorizable other/ally. It was the bland assumption that we could ever really afford to be that choosy. It was the unexamined belief that in a world groaning in agony, where radicals of any sort are hardly thick on the ground, we had time, leisure, and allies enough to sit comfortably loose to[12] the bungling, well-intentioned Alisdairs. We watched them setting their faltering feet on the lowest rungs of the ladder, making all the inevitable mistakes of tone and style; and having climbed that ladder securely ourselves, we turned round and kicked it casually away.

The history of the Labour Party in Britain is littered with smooth-talking ambitious men who

[5]Working-class Londoner.

[6]Working-class housing development in Northern industrial England, in which rows of small houses are separated by a yard with a common outdoor lavatory.

[7]Dante's guide through Hell in the Inferno.

[8]Member of the board of directors of a corporation in London's financial center, the City.

[9]Archetypal aristocratic country house, in Evelyn Waugh's novel, *Brideshead Revisited* (1945).

[10]Members of the Conservative Party.

[11]Formerly, a British party somewhat more liberal than the Conservatives, now merged with the Liberal Party as the centrist Lib-Dems. The left party in Great Britain (not very far left by Eagleton's standard) is Labour.

[12]"Sit loose to" is a North British colloquialism meaning "relinquish" or "get rid of."

climbed to power on the backs of working men and women, took over their language, claimed empathy with their sufferings, and then proceeded to sell them out. The recurrent mistake of working people was to be generous-hearted enough to trust these opportunists — allow them to speak in their name, be grateful for allies from elsewhere, believe that support from any quarter was better than none. Working people were advised to drop their sectarian prejudices, sink their differences in some fetish of unity and recognise that left-talking middle-class politicians were really on their side.

With impressive good will, the working class listened to this advice and allowed itself to be hijacked by a bunch of patronizing well-wishers who mouthed socialist sentiments while running country houses and buying an expensive private education for their children. When the heat was on, these men (along with a few women) turned the judiciary, and occasionally the troops, on the working men and women who had trusted them as allies.

I still think that we were wrong to have been so self-righteous. Yet of course we were not.

ELAINE SHOWALTER
In Reply

I'll trade a story with Terry Eagleton. In a recent study of male-female interaction in conversation, Pamela Fishman discovered that men dominated, both by ignoring topics introduced by the women, and by developing topics that they had initiated themselves. As Fishman comments: "We have seen that, at least among intimates in their homes, women raise many more topics than men. They do so because their topics often fail. They fail because the men don't work interactionally to develop them, whereas the women usually do work at developing topics raised by men. Thus the definition of what are appropriate or inapproriate topics for a conversation is the man's choice. . . . Men control topics as much, if not more, by veto as by a positive effort."

Could this possibly have any bearings on the question of men and feminist discourse? Terry Eagleton's "response" invites two possible interpretations:

1) He has not read "Critical Cross-Dressing" and has produced an all-purpose response to what he imagines feminist critics feel about male feminism.

2) He has read "Critical Cross-Dressing" and has decided not to respond to any of the topics it introduces, but rather to change the grounds of discussion by initiating a narrative of his own.

In either case, I don't see the point of continuing a one-sided dialog, and I will leave the story of Terry and Jeremy for others to consider.

Barbara Smith

b. 1946

For at least twenty years, Barbara Smith has been a writer, a teacher, and a black feminist leader. Born in Cleveland, Smith was educated at Mount Holyoke College and at the University of Pittsburgh. She has taught English and women's studies at the University of Massachusetts, Barnard College, and New York University, and has been a visiting professor at the University of Minnesota and at Hobart and William Smith colleges. In 1974, she was co-founder of the Combahee River Collective, a black feminist group in Boston, which she helped direct until 1980. In 1982 she co-edited All the Women Are White, All the Blacks Are Men, but Some of Us Are Brave, *the title of which reflects Smith's feeling that black women have frequently been excluded from both feminist and African American studies. In 1983 Smith edited* Home Girls, *a black feminist anthology highlighting the relationships between race, gender, sexual orientation, and class that became a major influence on the current renaissance of African American women writers. Her latest book is* The Truth That Never Hurts: Writings on Race, Gender, and Freedom *(1998). A short story writer as well as a feminist theorist, Smith has been artist-in-residence at the Hambridge Center for the Arts, the Millay Colony, Yaddo, and the Blue Mountain Center. As a result of her many activities, Smith was presented with the Outstanding Woman of Color award for 1982 and the Women Educator's Curriculum Award for 1983. She is currently the publisher of the Kitchen Table/Women of Color Press. The following piece was published as a pamphlet in 1977, and reprinted in* Some of Us Are Brave.

Toward a Black Feminist Criticism

For all my sisters, especially Beverly and Demita

I do not know where to begin. Long before I tried to write this I realized that I was attempting something unprecedented, something dangerous merely by writing about Black women writers from a feminist perspective and about Black lesbian writers from any perspective at all. These things have not been done. Not by white male critics, expectedly. Not by Black male critics. Not by white women critics who think of themselves as feminists. And most crucially not by Black women critics who, although they pay the most attention to Black women writers as a group, seldom use a consistent feminist analysis or write about Black lesbian literature. All segments of the literary world — whether establishment, progressive, Black, female, or lesbian — do not know, or at least act as if they do not know, that Black women writers and Black lesbian writers exist.

For whites, this specialized lack of knowledge is inextricably connected to their not knowing in any concrete or politically transforming way that Black women of any description dwell in this place. Black women's existence, experience, and culture and the brutally complex systems of oppression which shape these are in the "real world" of white and/or male consciousness beneath consideration, invisible, unknown.

This invisibility, which goes beyond anything that either Black men or white women experience and tell about in their writing, is one reason it is so difficult for me to know where to start. It seems overwhelming to break such a massive silence. Even more numbing, however, is the realization that so many of the women who will read this have not yet noticed us missing either from their reading matter, their politics, or their lives. It is galling that ostensible feminists and acknowledged lesbians have been so blinded to the implications of any womanhood that is not white womanhood and that they have yet to struggle with the deep racism in themselves that is at the source of this blindness.

I think of the thousands and thousands of books, magazines, and articles which have been devoted, by this time, to the subject of women's writing and I am filled with rage at the fraction of those pages that mention Black and other Third World women. I finally do not know how to begin because in 1977 I want to be writing this for a Black feminist publication, for Black women who know and love these writers as I do and who, if they do not yet know their names, have at least profoundly felt the pain of their absence.

The conditions that coalesce into the impossibilities of this essay have as much to do with politics as with the practice of literature. Any discussion of Afro-American writers can rightfully begin with the fact that for most of the time we have been in this country we have been categorically denied not only literacy, but the most minimal possibility of a decent human life. In her landmark essay, "In Search of Our Mothers' Gardens," Alice Walker discloses how the political, economic, and social restrictions of slavery and racism have historically stunted the creative lives of Black women.[1]

At the present time I feel that the politics of feminism have a direct relationship to the state of Black women's literature. A viable, autonomous Black feminist movement in this country would open up the space needed for the exploration of Black women's lives and the creation of consciously Black woman-identified art. At the same time a redefinition of the goals and strategies of the white feminist movement would lead to much needed change in the focus and content of what is now generally accepted as women's culture.

I want to make in this essay some connections between the politics of Black women's lives, what we write about, and our situation as artists. In order to do this I will look at how Black women have been viewed critically by outsiders, demonstrate the necessity for Black feminist criticism,

and try to understand what the existence or nonexistence of Black lesbian writing reveals about the state of Black women's culture and the intensity of *all* Black women's oppression.

The role that criticism plays in making a body of literature recognizable and real hardly needs to be explained here. The necessity for nonhostile and perceptive analysis of works written by persons outside the "mainstream" of white/male cultural rule has been proven by the Black cultural resurgence of the 1960s and '70s and by the even more recent growth of feminist literary scholarship. For books to be read and remembered they have to be talked about. For books to be understood they must be examined in such a way that the basic intentions of the writers are at least considered. Because of racism Black literature has usually been viewed as a discrete subcategory of American literature and there have been Black critics of Black literature who did much to keep it alive long before it caught the attention of whites. Before the advent of specifically feminist criticism in this decade, books by white women, on the other hand, were not clearly perceived as the cultural manifestation of an oppressed people. It took the surfacing of the second wave of the North American feminist movement to expose the fact that these works contain a stunningly accurate record of the impact of patriarchal values and practice upon the lives of women and more significantly that literature by women provides essential insights into female experience.

In speaking about the current situation of Black women writers, it is important to remember that the existence of a feminist movement was an essential precondition to the growth of feminist literature, criticism, and women's studies, which focused at the beginning almost entirely upon investigations of literature. The fact that a parallel Black feminist movement has been much slower in evolving cannot help but have impact upon the situation of Black women writers and artists and explains in part why during this very same period we have been so ignored.

There is no political movement to give power or support to those who want to examine Black women's experience through studying our history, literature, and culture. There is no political presence that demands a minimal level of consciousness and respect from those who write

---

[1] Alice Walker, "In Search of Our Mothers' Gardens," in *Ms.* (May 1974) and in *Southern Exposure* 4: 4, *Generations: Women in the South* (Winter 1977): 60–64. [Smith]

or talk about our lives. Finally, there is not a developed body of Black feminist political theory whose assumptions could be used in the study of Black women's art. When Black women's books are dealt with at all, it is usually in the context of Black literature which largely ignores the implications of sexual politics. When white women look at Black women's works they are of course ill-equipped to deal with the subtleties of racial politics. A Black feminist approach to literature that embodies the realization that the politics of sex as well as the politics of race and class are crucially interlocking factors in the works of Black women writers is an absolute necessity. Until a Black feminist criticism exists we will not even know what these writers mean. The citations from a variety of critics which follow prove that without a Black feminist critical perspective not only are books by Black women misunderstood, they are destroyed in the process.

Jerry H. Bryant, the *Nation's* white male reviewer of Alice Walker's *In Love & Trouble: Stories of Black Women,* wrote in 1973:

> The subtitle of the collection, "Stories of Black Women," is probably an attempt by the publisher to exploit not only black subjects but feminine ones. There is nothing feminist but these stories, however.[2]

Blackness and feminism are to his mind mutually exclusive and peripheral to the act of writing fiction. Bryant of course does not consider that Walker might have titled the work herself, nor did he apparently read the book which unequivocally reveals the author's feminist consciousness.

In *The Negro Novel in America,* a book that Black critics recognize as one of the worst examples of white racist pseudoscholarship, Robert Bone cavalierly dismisses Ann Petry's classic, *The Street.* He perceives it to be ". . . a superficial social analysis" of how slums victimize their Black inhabitants.[3] He further objects that:

> It is an attempt to interpret slum life in terms of *Negro* experience, when a larger frame of reference is required. As Alain Locke has observed, "*Knock*

on Any Door is superior to *The Street* because it designates class and environment, rather than mere race and environment, as its antagonist."[4]

Neither Robert Bone nor Alain Locke, the Black male critic he cites, can recognize that *The Street* is one of the best delineations in literature of how sex, race, *and* class interact to oppress Black women.

In her review of Toni Morrison's *Sula* for *The New York Times Book Review* in 1973, putative feminist Sara Blackburn makes similarly racist comments. She writes:

> . . . Toni Morrison is far too talented to remain only a marvelous recorder of the black side of provincial American life. If she is to maintain the large and serious audience she deserves, she is going to have to address a riskier contemporary reality than this beautiful but nevertheless distanced novel. *And if she does this, it seems to me that she might easily transcend that early and unintentionally limiting classification "black woman writer" and take her place among the most serious, important and talented American novelists now working.*[5] [Italics mine.]

Recognizing Morrison's exquisite gift, Blackburn unashamedly asserts that Morrison is "too talented" to deal with mere Black folk, particularly those double nonentities, Black women. In order to be accepted as "serious," "important," "talented," and "American," she must obviously focus her efforts upon chronicling the doings of white men.

The mishandling of Black women writers by whites is paralleled more often by their not being handled at all, particularly in feminist criticism. Although Elaine Showalter in her review essay on literary criticism for *Signs* states that: "The best work being produced today [in feminist criticism] is exacting and cosmopolitan," her essay is neither.[6] If it were, she would not have failed to mention a single Black or Third World woman writer, whether "major" or "minor," to cite her questionable categories. That she also does not even hint that lesbian writers of any color exist renders her purported overview virtually

---

[2]Jerry H. Bryant, "The Outskirts of a New City," in the *Nation* 12 (November 1973): 502. [Smith]

[3]Robert Bone, *The Negro Novel in America* (New Haven: Yale University Press, 1958), p. 180. [Smith]

[4]Idem. (*Knock on Any Door* is a novel by Black writer Willard Motley.) [Smith]

[5]Sara Blackburn, "You Still Can't Go Home Again," in *The New York Times Book Review,* 30 December 1973, p. 3. [Smith]

[6]Elaine Showalter, "Review Essay: Literary Criticism," *Signs* 2 (Winter 1975): 460. [Smith]

meaningless. Showalter obviously thinks that the identities of being Black and female are mutually exclusive, as this statement illustrates:

> Furthermore, there are other literary subcultures (black American novelists, for example) whose history offers a precedent for feminist scholarship to use.[7]

The idea of critics like Showalter *using* Black literature is chilling, a case of barely disguised cultural imperialism. The final insult is that she footnotes the preceding remark by pointing readers to works on Black literature by white males Robert Bone and Roger Rosenblatt!

Two recent works by white women, Ellen Moers's *Literary Women: The Great Writers* and Patricia Meyer Spacks's *The Female Imagination*, evidence the same racist flaw.[8] Moers includes the names of four Black and one Puertorriqueña writer in her seventy pages of bibliographical notes and does not deal at all with Third World women in the body of her book. Spacks refers to a comparison between Negroes (sic) and women in Mary Ellmann's *Thinking About Women* under the index entry, "blacks, women and." "*Black Boy* (Wright)" is the preceding entry. Nothing follows. Again there is absolutely no recognition that Black and female identity ever coexist, specifically in a group of Black women writers. Perhaps one can assume that these women do not know who Black women writers are, that they have little opportunity like most Americans to learn about them. Perhaps. Their ignorance seems suspiciously selective, however, particularly in the light of the dozens of truly obscure white women writers they are able to unearth. Spacks was herself employed at Wellesley College at the same time that Alice Walker was there teaching one of the first courses on Black women writers in the country.

I am not trying to encourage racist criticism of Black women writers like that of Sara Blackburn, to cite only one example. As a beginning I would at least like to see in print white women's acknowledgment of the contradictions of who and what are being left out of their research and writing.[9]

Black male critics can also *act* as if they do not know that Black women writers exist and are, of course, hampered by an inability to comprehend Black women's experience in sexual as well as racial terms. Unfortunately there are also those who are as virulently sexist in their treatment of Black women writers as their white male counterparts. Darwin Turner's discussion of Zora Neale Hurston in his *In a Minor Chord: Three Afro-American Writers and Their Search for Identity* is a frightening example of the near assassination of a great Black woman writer.[10] His descriptions of her and her work as "artful," "coy," "irrational," "superficial," and "shallow" bear no relationship to the actual quality of her achievements. Turner is completely insensitive to the sexual political dynamics of Hurston's life and writing.

In a recent interview the notoriously misogynist writer, Ishmael Reed, comments in this way upon the low sales of his newest novel:

> . . . but the book only sold 8000 copies. I don't mind giving out the figure: 8000. Maybe if I was one of those young *female* Afro-American writers that are so hot now, I'd sell more. You know, fill my books with ghetto women who can *do no wrong*. . . . But come on, I think I could have sold 8000 copies by myself.[11]

The politics of the situation of Black women are glaringly illuminated by this statement. Neither Reed nor his white male interviewer has the slightest compunction about attacking Black women in print. They need not fear widespread public denunciation since Reed's statement is in perfect agreement with the values of a society that hates Black people, women, and Black women. Finally the two of them feel free to base

[7] Ibid., p. 445. [Smith]

[8] Ellen Moers, *Literary Women: The Great Writers* (Garden City, N.Y.: Anchor Books, 1977); Patricia Meyer Spacks, *The Female Imagination* (New York: Avon Books, 1976). [Smith]

[9] An article by Nancy Hoffman, "White Women, Black Women: Inventing an Adequate Pedagogy," in the *Women's Studies Newsletter* 5: 1 & 2 (Spring 1977): 21–24, gives valuable insights into how white women can approach the writing of Black women. [Smith]

[10] Darwin T. Turner, *In a Minor Chord: Three Afro-American Writers and Their Search for Identity* (Carbondale and Edwardsville: Southern Illinois University Press, 1971). [Smith]

[11] John Domini, "Roots and Racism: An Interview with Ishmael Reed," in *The Boston Phoenix*, 5 April 1977, p. 20. [Smith]

their actions on the premise that Black women are powerless to alter either their political or cultural oppression.

In her introduction to "A Bibliography of Works Written by American Black Women" Ora Williams quotes some of the reactions of her colleagues toward her efforts to do research on Black women. She writes:

> Others have reacted negatively with such statements as, "I really don't think you are going to find very much written," "Have 'they' written anything that is any good?" and, "I wouldn't go overboard with this woman's lib thing." When discussions touched on the possibility of teaching a course in which emphasis would be on the literature by Black women, one response was, "Ha, ha. That will certainly be the most nothing course ever offered!"[12]

A remark by Alice Walker capsulizes what all the preceding examples indicate about the position of Black women writers and the reasons for the damaging criticism about them. She responds to her interviewer's question, "Why do you think that the black woman writer has been so ignored in America? Does she have even more difficulty than the black male writer, who perhaps has just begun to gain recognition?" Walker replies:

> There are two reasons why the black woman writer is not taken as seriously as the black male writer. One is that she's a woman. Critics seem unusually ill-equipped to intelligently discuss and analyze the works of black women. Generally, they do not even make the attempt; they prefer, rather, to talk about the lives of black women writers, not about what they write. And, since black women writers are not — it would seem — very likable — until recently they were the least willing worshippers of male supremacy — comments about them tend to be cruel.[13]

A convincing case for Black feminist criticism can obviously be built solely upon the basis of the negativity of what already exists. It is far more gratifying, however, to demonstrate its necessity by showing how it can serve to reveal for the first time the profound subtleties of this particular body of literature.

Before suggesting how a Black feminist approach might be used to examine a specific work I will outline some of the principles that I think a Black feminist critic could use. Beginning with a primary commitment to exploring how both sexual and racial politics and Black and female identity are inextricable elements in Black women's writings, she would also work from the assumption that Black women writers constitute an identifiable literary tradition. The breadth of her familiarity with these writers would have shown her that not only is theirs a verifiable historical tradition that parallels in time the tradition of Black men and white women writing in this country, but that thematically, stylistically, aesthetically, and conceptually Black women writers manifest common approaches to the act of creating literature as a direct result of the specific political, social, and economic experience they have been obliged to share. The way, for example, that Zora Neale Hurston, Margaret Walker, Toni Morrison, and Alice Walker incorporate the traditional Black female activities of rootworking, herbal medicine, conjure, and midwifery into the fabric of their stories is not mere coincidence, nor is their use of specifically Black female language to express their own and their characters' thoughts accidental. The use of Black women's language and cultural experience in books *by* Black women *about* Black women results in a miraculously rich coalescing of form and content and also takes their writing far beyond the confines of white/male literary structures. The Black feminist critic would find innumerable commonalities in works by Black women.

Another principle which grows out of the concept of a tradition and which would also help to strengthen this tradition would be for the critic to look first for precedents and insights in interpretation within the works of other Black women. In other words she would think and write out of her own identity and not try to graft the ideas or methodology of white/male literary thought upon the precious materials of Black women's art.

[12]Ora Williams, "A Bibliography of Works Written by American Black Women," in *College Language Association Journal* 15:3 (March 1972): 355. There is an expanded book-length version of this bibliography: *American Black Women in the Arts and Social Sciences: A Bibliographic Survey* (Metuchen, N.J.: The Scarecrow Press, 1973; rev. and expanded ed., 1978). [Smith]

[13]John O'Brien, ed., *Interviews with Black Writers* (New York: Liveright, 1973), p. 201. [Smith]

Black feminist criticism would by definition be highly innovative, embodying the daring spirit of the works themselves. The Black feminist critic would be constantly aware of the political implications of her work and would assert the connections between it and the political situation of all Black women. Logically developed, Black feminist criticism would owe its existence to a Black feminist movement while at the same time contributing ideas that women in the movement could use.

Black feminist criticism applied to a particular work can overturn previous assumptions about it and expose for the first time its actual dimensions. At the "Lesbians and Literature" discussion at the 1976 Modern Language Association convention Bertha Harris suggested that if in a woman writer's work a sentence refuses to do what it is supposed to do, if there are strong images of women and if there is a refusal to be linear, the result is innately lesbian literature. As usual, I wanted to see if these ideas might be applied to the Black women writers that I know and quickly realized that many of their works were, in Harris's sense, lesbian. Not because women are "lovers," but because they are the central figures, are positively portrayed and have pivotal relationships with one another. The form and language of these works are also nothing like what white patriarchal culture requires or expects.

I was particularly struck by the way in which Toni Morrison's novels *The Bluest Eye* and *Sula* could be explored from this new perspective.[14] In both works the relationships between girls and women are essential, yet at the same time physical sexuality is overtly expressed only between men and women. Despite the apparent heterosexuality of the female characters I discovered in rereading *Sula* that it works as a lesbian novel not only because of the passionate friendship between Sula and Nel, but because of Morrison's consistently critical stance toward the heterosexual institutions of male/female relationships, marriage, and the family. Consciously or not,

[14]Toni Morrison, *The Bluest Eye* (New York: Pocket Books, 1972, 1976, orig. 1970) and *Sula* (New York: Alfred A. Knopf, 1974). All subsequent references to this work will be designated in the text. [Smith]

Morrison's work poses both lesbian and feminist questions about Black women's autonomy and their impact upon each other's lives.

Sula and Nel find each other in 1922 when each of them is twelve, on the brink of puberty and the discovery of boys. Even as awakening sexuality "clotted their dreams," each girl desires "a someone" obviously female with whom to share her feelings. Morrison writes:

> . . . for it was in dreams that the two girls had met. Long before Edna Finch's Mellow House opened, even before they marched through the chocolate halls of Garfield Primary School . . . they had already made each other's acquaintance in the delirium of their noon dreams. They were solitary little girls whose loneliness was so profound it intoxicated them and sent them stumbling into Technicolored visions that always included a presence, a someone who, quite like the dreamer, shared the delight of the dream. When Nel, an only child, sat on the steps of her back porch surrounded by the high silence of her mother's incredibly orderly house, feeling the neatness pointing at her back, she studied the poplars and fell easily into a picture of herself lying on a flower bed, tangled in her own hair, waiting for some fiery prince. He approached but never quite arrived. But always, watching the dream along with her, were some smiling sympathetic eyes. Someone as interested as she herself in the flow of her imagined hair, the thickness of the mattress of flowers, the voile sleeves that closed below her elbows in gold-threaded cuffs.
>
> Similarly, Sula, also an only child, but wedged into a household of throbbing disorder constantly awry with things, people, voices and the slamming of doors, spent hours in the attic behind a roll of linoleum galloping through her own mind on a gray-and-white horse tasting sugar and smelling roses in full view of someone who shared both the taste and the speed.
>
> So when they met, first in those chocolate halls and next through the ropes of the swing, they felt the ease and comfort of old friends.0 Because each had discovered years before that they were neither white nor male, and that all freedom and triumph was forbidden to them, they had set about creating something else to be. Their meeting was fortunate, for it let them use each other to grow on. Daughters of distant mothers and incomprehensible fathers (Sula's because he was dead; Nel's because he wasn't), they found in each other's eyes the intimacy they were looking for. (51–52)

As this beautiful passage shows, their relationship, from the very beginning, is suffused with an erotic romanticism. The dreams in which they are initially drawn to each other are actually complementary aspects of the same sensuous fairytale. Nel imagines a "fiery prince" who never quite arrives while Sula gallops like a prince "on a gray-and-white horse."[15] The "real world" of patriarchy requires, however, that they channel this energy away from each other to the opposite sex. Lorraine Bethel explains this dynamic in her essay "Conversations With Ourselves: Black Female Relationships in Toni Cade Bambara's *Gorilla, My Love* and Toni Morrison's *Sula*." She writes:

> I am not suggesting that Sula and Nel are being consciously sexual, or that their relationship has an overt lesbian nature. I am suggesting, however, that there is a certain sensuality in their interactions that is reinforced by the mirror-like nature of their relationship. Sexual exploration and coming of age is a natural part of adolescence. Sula and Nel discover men together, and though their flirtations with males are an important part of their sexual exploration, the sensuality that they experience in each other's company is equally important.[16]

Sula and Nel must also struggle with the constrictions of racism upon their lives. The knowledge that "they were neither white nor male" is the inherent explanation of their need for each other. Morrison depicts in literature the necessary bonding that has always taken place between Black women for the sake of barest survival. Together the two girls can find the courage to create themselves.

Their relationship is severed only when Nel marries Jude, an unexceptional young man who thinks of her as "the hem — the tuck and fold that hid his raveling edges" (83). Sula's inventive wildness cannot overcome social pressure or the influence of Nel's parents who "had succeeded in rubbing down to a dull glow any sparkle or splutter she had" (83). Nel falls prey to convention

while Sula escapes it. Yet at the wedding which ends the first phase of their relationship, Nel's final action is to look past her husband toward Sula:

> . . . a slim figure in blue, gliding, with just a hint of a strut, down the path towards the road. . . . Even from the rear Nel could tell that it was Sula and that she was smiling; that something deep down in that litheness was amused. (85)

When Sula returns ten years later, her rebelliousness full-blown, a major source of the town's suspicions stems from the fact that although she is almost thirty, she is still unmarried. Sula's grandmother, Eva, does not hesitate to bring up the matter as soon as she arrives. She asks:

> "When you gone to get married? You need to have some babies. It'll settle you. . . . Ain't no woman got no business floatin' around without no man." (92)

Sula replies: "I don't want to make somebody else. I want to make myself" (92). Self-definition is a dangerous activity for any woman to engage in, especially a Black one, and it expectedly earns Sula pariah status in Medallion.

Morrison clearly points out that it is the fact that Sula has not been tamed or broken by the exigencies of heterosexual family life which most galls the others. She writes:

> Among the weighty evidence piling up was the fact that Sula did not look her age. She was near thirty and, unlike them, had lost no teeth, suffered no bruises, developed no ring of fat at the waist or pocket at the back of her neck. (115)

In other words she is not a domestic serf, a woman run down by obligatory childbearing or a victim of battering. Sula also sleeps with the husbands of the town once and then discards them, needing them even less than her own mother did, for sexual gratification and affection. The town reacts to her disavowal of patriarchal values by becoming fanatically serious about their own family obligations, as if in this way they might counteract Sula's radical criticism of their lives.

Sula's presence in her community functions much like the presence of lesbians everywhere to expose the contradictions of supposedly "normal" life. The opening paragraph of the essay "Woman Identified Woman" has amazing relevance as an

---

[15]My sister, Beverly Smith, pointed out this connection to me. [Smith]

[16]Lorraine Bethel, "Conversations With Ourselves: Black Female Relationships in Toni Cade Bambara's *Gorilla, My Love* and Toni Morrison's *Sula*," unpublished paper written at Yale, 1976, 47 pp. (Bethel has worked from a premise similar to mine in a much more developed treatment of the novel.) [Smith]

explanation of Sula's position and character in the novel. It asks:

> What is a lesbian? A lesbian is the rage of all women condensed to the point of explosion. She is the woman who, often beginning at an extremely early age, acts in accordance with her inner compulsion to be a more complete and freer human being than her society — perhaps then, but certainly later — cares to allow her. These needs and actions, over a period of years, bring her into painful conflict with people, situations, the accepted ways of thinking, feeling and behaving, until she is in a state of continual war with everything around her, and usually with herself. She may not be fully conscious of the political implications of what for her began as personal necessity, but on some level she has not been able to accept the limitations and oppression laid on her by the most basic role of her society — the female role.[17]

The limitations of the *Black* female role are even greater in a racist and sexist society as is the amount of courage it takes to challenge them. It is no wonder that the townspeople see Sula's independence as imminently dangerous.

Morrison is also careful to show the reader that despite their years of separation and their opposing paths, Nel and Sula's relationship retains its primacy for each of them. Nell feels transformed when Sula returns and thinks:

> It was like getting the use of an eye back, having a cataract removed. Her old friend had come home. Sula. Who made her laugh, who made her see old things with new eyes, in whose presence she felt clever, gentle and a little raunchy. (95)

Laughing together in the familiar "rib-scraping" way, Nel feels "new, soft and new" (98). Morrison uses here the visual imagery which symbolizes the women's closeness throughout the novel.

Sula fractures this closeness, however, by sleeping with Nel's husband, an act of little import according to her system of values. Nel, of course, cannot understand. Sula thinks ruefully:

> Nel was the one person who had wanted nothing from her, who had accepted all aspects of her.

Now she wanted everything, and all because of *that*. Nel was the first person who had been real to her, whose name she knew, who had seen as she had the slant of life that made it possible to stretch it to its limits. Now Nel was one of *them*. (119–20)

Sula also thinks at the realization of losing Nel about how unsatisfactory her relationships with men have been and admits:

> She had been looking all along for a friend, and it took her a while to discover that a lover was not a comrade and could never be — for a woman. (121)

The nearest that Sula comes to actually loving a man is in a brief affair with Ajax and what she values most about him is the intellectual companionship he provides, the brilliance he "allows" her to show.

Sula's feelings about sex with men are also consistent with a lesbian interpretation of the novel. Morrison writes:

> She went to bed with men as frequently as she could. It was the only place where she could find what she was looking for: *misery and the ability to feel deep sorrow.* . . . During the lovemaking she found and needed to find the cutting edge. When she left off cooperating with her body and began to assert herself in the act, particles of strength gathered in her like steel shavings drawn to a spacious magnetic center, forming a tight cluster that nothing, it seemed, could break. *And there was utmost irony and outrage in lying under someone, in a position of surrender, feeling her own abiding strength and limitless power.* . . . When her partner disengaged himself, she looked up at him in wonder trying to recall his name. . . . waiting impatiently for him to turn away. . . . *leaving her to the postcoital privateness in which she met herself, welcomed herself, and joined herself in matchless harmony.* (122–23) [Italics mine.]

Sula uses men for sex which results not in communion with them, but in her further delving into self.

Ultimately the deepest communion and communication in the novel occurs between two women who love each other. After their last painful meeting, which does not bring reconciliation, Sula thinks as Nel leaves her:

> "So she will walk on down that road, her back so straight in that old green coat . . . thinking how much I have cost her and never remember the days

---

[17]New York Radicalesbians, "Woman Identified Woman," in *Lesbians Speak Out* (Oakland: Women's Press Collective, 1974), p. 87. [Smith]

when we were two throats and one eye and we had no price." (147)

It is difficult to imagine a more evocative metaphor for what women can be to each other, the "pricelessness" they achieve in refusing to sell themselves for male approval, the total worth that they can only find in each other's eyes.

Decades later the novel concludes with Nel's final comprehension of the source of the grief that has plagued her from the time her husband walked out. Morrison writes:

> "All that time, all that time, I thought I was missing Jude." And the loss pressed down on her chest and came up into her throat. "We was girls together," she said as though explaining something. "O Lord, Sula," she cried, "girl, girl, girlgirlgirl."
> It was a fine cry — loud and long — but it had no bottom and it had no top, just circles and circles of sorrow. (174)

Again Morrison exquisitely conveys what women, Black women, mean to each other. This final passage verifies the depth of Sula and Nel's relationship and its centrality to an accurate interpretation of the work.

Sula is an exceedingly lesbian novel in the emotions expressed, in the definition of female character, and in the way that the politics of heterosexuality are portrayed. The very meaning of lesbianism is being expanded in literature, just as it is being redefined through politics. The confusion that many readers have felt about *Sula* may well have a lesbian explanation. If one sees Sula's inexplicable "evil" and nonconformity as the evil of not being male-identified, many elements in the novel become clear. The work might be clearer still if Morrison had approached her subject with the consciousness that a lesbian relationship was at least a possibility for her characters. Obviously Morrison did not *intend* the reader to perceive Sula and Nel's relationship as inherently lesbian. However, this lack of intention only shows the way in which heterosexist assumptions can veil what may logically be expected to occur in a work. What I have tried to do here is not to prove that Morrison wrote something that she did not, but to point out how a Black feminist critical perspective at least allows consideration of this level of the novel's meaning.

In her interview in *Conditions: One* Adrienne Rich talks about unconsummated relationships and the need to re-evaluate the meaning of intense yet supposedly non-erotic connections between women. She asserts:

> We need a lot more documentation about what actually happened: I think we can also imagine it, because we know it happened — we know it out of our own lives.[18]

Black women are still in the position of having to "imagine," discover, and verify Black lesbian literature because so little has been written from an avowedly lesbian perspective. The near nonexistence of Black lesbian literature which other Black lesbians and I so deeply feel has everything to do with the politics of our lives, the total suppression of identity that all Black women, lesbian or not, must face. This literary silence is again intensified by the unavailability of an autonomous Black feminist movement through which we could fight our oppression and also begin to name ourselves.

In a speech, "The Autonomy of Black Lesbian Women," Wilmette Brown comments upon the connection between our political reality and the literature we must invent:

> Because the isolation of Black lesbian women, given that we are superfreaks, given that our lesbianism defies both the sexual identity that capital gives us and the racial identity that capital gives us, the isolation of Black lesbian women from heterosexual Black women is very profound. Very profound. I have searched throughout Black history, Black literature, whatever, looking for some women that I could see were somehow lesbian. Now I know that in a certain sense they were all lesbian. But that was a very painful search.[19]

Heterosexual privilege is usually the only privilege that Black women have. None of us have racial or sexual privilege, almost none of us have class privilege, maintaining "straightness" is our last resort. Being out, particularly out in print, is

---

[18]Elly Bulkin, "An Interview With Adrienne Rich: Part I," in *Conditions: One,* Vol. 1, no. 1 (April 1977), p. 62. [Smith]
[19]Wilmette Brown, "The Autonomy of Black Lesbian Women," ms. of speech delivered July 24, 1976, Toronto, Canada, p. 7. [Smith]

the final renunciation of any claim to the crumbs of "tolerance" that nonthreatening "ladylike" Black women are sometimes fed. I am convinced that it is our lack of privilege and power in every other sphere that allows so few Black women to make the leap that many white women, particularly writers, have been able to make in this decade, not merely because they are white or have economic leverage, but because they have had the strength and support of a movement behind them.

As Black lesbians we must be out not only in white society, but in the Black community as well, which is at least as homophobic. That the sanctions against Black lesbians are extremely high is well illustrated in this comment by Black male writer Ishmael Reed. Speaking about the inroads that whites make into Black culture, he asserts:

> In Manhattan you find people actively trying to impede intellectual debate among Afro-Americans. The powerful "liberal/radical/existentialist" influences of the Manhattan literary and drama establishment speak through tokens, like for example that ancient notion of the *one* black ideologue (who's usually a Communist), the *one* black poetess (who's usually a feminist lesbian).[20]

To Reed, "feminist" and "lesbian" are the most pejorative terms he can hurl at a Black woman and totally invalidate anything she might say, regardless of her actual politics or sexual identity. Such accusations are quite effective for keeping Black women writers who are writing with integrity and strength from any conceivable perspective in line, but especially ones who are actually feminist and lesbian. Unfortunately Reed's reactionary attitude is all too typical. A community which has not confronted sexism, because a widespread Black feminist movement has not required it to, has likewise not been challenged to examine its heterosexism. Even at this moment I am not convinced that one can write explicitly as a Black lesbian and live to tell about it.

Yet there are a handful of Black women who have risked everything for truth. Audre Lorde, Pat Parker, and Ann Allen Shockley have at least broken ground in the vast wilderness of works that do not exist.[21] Black feminist criticism will again have an essential role not only in creating a climate in which Black lesbian writers can survive, but in undertaking the total reassessment of Black literature and literary history needed to reveal the Black woman-identified-women that Wilmette Brown and so many of us are looking for.

Although I have concentrated here upon what does not exist and what needs to be done, a few Black feminist critics have already begun this work. Gloria T. Hull at the University of Delaware has discovered in her research on Black women poets of the Harlem Renaissance that many of the women who are considered "minor" writers of the period were in constant contact with each other and provided both intellectual stimulation and psychological support for each other's work. At least one of these writers, Angelina Weld Grimké, wrote many unpublished love poems to women. Lorraine Bethel, a recent graduate of Yale College, has done substantial work on Black women writers, particularly in her senior essay. "This Infinity of Conscious Pain: Blues Lyricism and Hurston's Black Female Folk Aesthetic and Cultural Sensibility in *Their Eyes Were Watching God*," in which she brilliantly defines and uses the principles of Black feminist criticism. Elaine Scott at the State University of New York at Old Westbury is also involved in highly creative and politically resonant research on Hurston and other writers.

The fact that these critics are young and, except for Hull, unpublished merely indicates the impediments we face. Undoubtedly there are other women working and writing whom I do not

---

[20]Domini, op. cit., p. 18. [Smith]

[21]Audre Lorde, *New York Head Shop and Museum* (Detroit: Broadside, 1974); *Coal* (New York: W. W. Norton, 1976); *Between Our Selves* (Point Reyes, Calif.: Eidolon Editions, 1976); *The Black Unicorn* (New York: W. W. Norton, 1978). Pat Parker, *Child of Myself* (Oakland: Women's Press Collective, 1972 and 1974); *Pit Stop* (Oakland: Women's Press Collective, 1973); *Womanslaughter* (Oakland: Diana Press, 1978); *Movement in Black* (Oakland: Diana Press, 1978). Ann Allen Shockley, *Loving Her* (Indianapolis: Bobbs-Merrill, 1974).[Smith]

There is at least one Black lesbian writers' collective, Jemima, in New York. They do public readings and have available a collection of their poems. They can be contacted c/o Boyce, 41–11 Parsons Blvd., Flushing, NY 11355. [Smith]

even know, simply because there is no place to read them. As Michele Wallace states in her article, "A Black Feminist's Search for Sisterhood":

> We exist as women who are Black who are feminists, each stranded for the moment, working independently because there is not yet an environment in this society remotely congenial to our struggle — [or our thoughts].[22]

I only hope that this essay is one way of breaking our silence and our isolation, of helping us to know each other.

Just as I did not know where to start I am not sure how to end. I feel that I have tried to say too much and at the same time have left too much unsaid. What I want this essay to do is lead everyone who reads it to examine *everything* that they have ever thought and believed about feminist culture and to ask themselves how their thoughts connect to the reality of Black women's writing and lives. I want to encourage in white women, as a first step, a sane accountability to all the women who write and live on this soil. I want most of all for Black women and Black lesbians somehow not to be so alone. This last will require the most expansive of revolutions as well as many new words to tell us how to make this revolution real. I finally want to express how much easier both my waking and my sleeping hours would be if there were one book in existence that would tell me something specific about my life. One book based in Black feminist and Black lesbian experience, fiction or nonfiction. Just one work to reflect the reality that I and the Black women whom I love are trying to create. When such a book exists then each of us will not only know better how to live, but how to dream.

[22]Michele Wallace, "A Black Feminist's Search for Sisterhood," in *The Village Voice*, 28 July 1975, p. 7. [Smith]

8

GENDER STUDIES
AND QUEER THEORY[1]

It is the nature of power — particularly the kind of power that operates in our society — to be repressive, and to be especially careful in repressing useless energies, the intensity of pleasures, and irregular modes of behavior.
— MICHEL FOUCAULT

Woman . . . is only a more or less complacent facilitator for the working out of man's fantasies. It is possible, and even certain, that she experiences vicarious pleasure there, but this pleasure is above all a masochistic prostitution of her body to a desire that is not her own. . . .
— LUCE IRIGARAY

Gender is not a performance that a prior subject elects to do, but gender is performative. *. . . It is a* compulsory *performance in the sense that acting out of line with heterosexual norms brings with it ostracism, punishment, and violence, not to mention the transgressive pleasures produced by those very prohibitions.*
— JUDITH BUTLER

GENDER STUDIES AND FEMINISM

From the words themselves one might expect that "feminism" is a political movement and "gender studies" a research project. There is some truth to this, but in a more important sense it was the ease with which certain forms of feminism within the academy had become co-opted politically into a series of research projects in

[1]The term *queer theory* was popularized by Teresa de Lauretis in a special "Queer Theory" issue of the journal *Differences* (vol. 3, no. 2, 1992). One of de Lauretis's motives was to link up the theoretical activities of academics with the activist politics of the gay and lesbian rights group Queer Nation. The "in your face" quality of the term *queer* appeals to such groups because it forces straight people using or hearing the term to confront their own feelings about homosexuals and homosexuality. De Lauretis's other motive was to distinguish the theorists presented in her special issue, who were questioning and problematizing issues of gender identity and sexual orientation, from other researchers in gay and lesbian studies who were happy with the notion of stable gender identity. In the years since the publication of the "Queer Theory" issue of *Differences,* that distinction has muddied. While some gay and lesbian gender theorists may still resist the term *queer theory,* most on both sides of the gender identity issue have embraced it because of its defiant political implications.

women's studies, with the usual rewards for the top players, that gave rise to the new field of gender studies. Much of the most praised feminist research in the 1980s took the form of new editions of women writers, proposals to add such writers to the existing literary canon, and analyses of the work of patriarchy in keeping males in the front ranks. Effective as this work was in changing what teachers taught and what students read, there was a sense on the part of some feminist critics that though the expansion team was successfully playing the game, it was still the old game that was being played, when what was needed was a new game entirely. The argument posed was that in order to counter patriarchy, it was necessary not merely to think about new texts, but to think about them in radically new ways.

The problem was not that male chauvinists held the named chairs at Princeton — feminists of stature would in their turn be appointed to those professorships — or that males got most of the pages in the Norton Anthologies, but that academic discourse about gender and the gender system was being conducted within a language and a logic, a discursive system, that had been fashioned by male supremacy and reproduced that unconscious ideology at every step. Contemporary feminists might note the prevalence of that ideology in my own figure of speech in the previous paragraph, where male team sports (only the all-male professional leagues have expansion teams) are used as a metaphor for gender politics. But how does one change a discursive system from within, when we can only speak with words that have already been tainted by ideology?

The first step is to recognize the need for a change. The work of Gilbert and Gubar, in revising for the female tradition Bloom's crypto-Freudian analysis of the male poet's impetus to originality, had obviously not gone far enough. Freud viewed women as inherently lacking, warped by the sense that they had already been castrated. In representing this metaphoric wound as the site of female creativity and resistance, Gilbert and Gubar had in effect reinforced Freud's demeaning psychological discourse. For the pioneers of what has come to be known as gender studies, a way to avoid this double bind was to recuperate Freud with a difference, to find a way of reading psychology that could turn the tables on patriarchy. The key to doing this was the work of French psychologist Jacques Lacan.[2] Lacan's postmodern reading of Freud replaced the Viennese doctor's thermodynamic metaphors (about energies, drives, and transferences) with linguistic metaphors: The unconscious was structured not like an infernal machine but like a language. Although Lacan was often given to misogynistic remarks, his recasting of Freud's conception of the physical penis (a fleshly organ for women to envy) into the privileged signifier of the Phallus, a symbol with which both sexes identify as *le désir de la Mère* and from which both sexes feel alienated after the fall into language, was a major step toward feminist revisions of Freud.

THE FEMALE (AS) TEXT: IRIGARAY AND CIXOUS

One of the most influential of the French theorists, Luce Irigaray, is a disciple of Lacan. Irigaray's difficult, learned, ironically allusive thesis, *Speculum of the Other*

---

[2]See Lacan in the introduction to Psychoanalytic Theory, p. 1111, and Lacan readings, pp. 1123, 1129, and 1149.

Woman (1974), undertakes a re-examination of Plato, Freud, and a dozen thinkers in between. Like Simone de Beauvoir, Irigaray is outraged about the way women have been seen as an Other by men, spoken about and spoken for, but never allowed to speak themselves.[3] Her critique of Freud is largely of his theories of sexual differences (like the notions of penis envy and the castration complex), theories that falter, according to Irigaray, on Freud's failure to perceive that men and women actually *are* different, rather than more or less adequate versions of the same (male) norm. Quoting Freud against himself, Irigaray demonstrates the incoherence of his theories of femininity.

Despite Irigaray's training as a Lacanian psychoanalyst, her own version of femininity seems to have a biological basis that harks back to the source of the errors she exposes in Freud. In her most famous essay, "This Sex Which Is Not One" (1977), she characterizes both males and females as essentially like their primary genitalia: men, like the phallus, are single (-minded), hard, simple, direct; women, like the two lips of the vulva and their sensations, are multiple, diffuse, soft, indirect. Similarly, Irigaray's notion of women's writing takes off from this genital analogy of the labia, which always touch each other:

> This "style" or "writing" of women tends to put the torch to fetish words, proper terms, well-constructed forms. This "style" does not privilege sight; instead, it takes each figure back to its source, which is among other things *tactile*. It comes back in touch with itself in that origin without ever constituting in it, constituting itself in it, as some sort of unity. *Simultaneity* is its "proper" aspect — a proper(ty) that is never fixed in the possible identity-to-self of some form or other. It is always *fluid,* without neglecting the characteristics of fluids that are difficult to idealize: those rubbings between two infinitely near neighbors that create a dynamics. Its "style" resists and explodes every firmly established form, figure, idea, or concept. Which does not mean that it lacks style . . . but its "style" cannot be upheld as a thesis, cannot be the object of a position.[4]

Despite the abstract tenor of this characterization, the general traits Irigaray posits for women's discourse — inconsistency, fluidity, incoherence, tactility — are the very ones men have used to denigrate the female intellect. Irigaray's position seems a jumping-off point for a separatist feminism that renounces for women whatever has been tainted by masculinity — logic, coherence, power.

Hélène Cixous is a more difficult writer than Irigaray, but the problems of reading her are somewhat different. Where Irigaray is learned, detached, abstract, and so ambiguously ironical that her meaning is often in danger of being misunderstood, Cixous speaks primarily through images and metaphors. The intense poetic quality of her prose is part of what has caused her essay "The Laugh of the Medusa" to become the central manifesto of French feminism. Cixous's difficulty is intentional and programmatic: Feeling that the major modes of conceptual analysis themselves are anti-female, she writes in a way that resists dialectic. To show this, Cixous (following Derrida in *Of Grammatology*) sets up a series of binary oppositions

---

[3]See de Beauvoir, p. 673.
[4]Luce Irigaray, "The Power of Discourse," in *This Sex Which Is Not One* (Ithaca: Cornell University Press, 1985), p. 79.

(active/passive, sun/moon, culture/nature, day/night, father/mother, logos/pathos). Each pair can be analyzed as a hierarchy in which the former term represents the positive and masculine and the latter the negative and feminine principle. Nor can the terms live in harmony: Cixous suggests that, in each case, the masculine term is forced to "kill" the feminine one. This for her is the deadly "phallocentric" principle that she derives from Derrida's critique of logocentrism. Cixous rejects the idea of "feminine writing," as "a dangerous and stylish expression full of traps. . . . My work in fact aims at getting rid of words like 'feminine and masculine,' even 'man' and 'woman.'. . ."[5]

One might think Cixous, like Virginia Woolf, would be an exponent of androgyny; in fact Cixous attacks androgyny as an annulment of differences, and supports instead what she calls "the *other bisexuality*," which involves the "multiplication of the effects of the inscription of desire, over all parts of my body and the other body, indeed, this *other bisexuality* doesn't annul differences, but stirs them up, pursues them, increases them" ("The Laugh of the Medusa"). For Cixous, woman is bisexual; man, unwilling to give up the phallus, is monosexual. This is the point at which the binary polarities, having been kicked out the door, creep back in through the window, and they return upside down, with the female terms on top. At one point Cixous speaks "of a decipherable libidinal femininity which can be read in a writing produced by a male or a female." But as she later explains "libidinal femininity," she ends up attributing it almost exclusively to biological females. She finds its essential, moist, life-giving properties, for example, in the work of women writers like Clarice Lispector, while the work of a male writer like Maurice Blanchot is "a text that goes toward the drying up." (She finds a feminine sensibility in one male writer, Heinrich von Kleist, but that, as she says, is "highly exceptional.") Female sexuality is "giving," where the male is retentive, avaricious; female sexuality achieves full genitality, while male sexuality is fixated in oral dominance or anal "exchange."[6] Where Derrida presented the standard polarities of Western culture in order to dismantle and discredit dialectical thinking, it seems that Cixous has adopted Derridean terminology for a philosophically different program that simply inverts the standard pairings.

BORN A WOMAN

For other gender theorists, Lacan is not the answer. Instead one can attempt to analyze the system of gender down to its roots, to see where it comes from and how it is implicated in the material and familial relationships of our society. One of the key texts in that analysis is Gayle Rubin's "The Traffic in Women," reproduced in part below. Like Monique Wittig, Rubin takes her approach from Simone de Beauvoir's line "One is not born a woman." One is indeed born female, Rubin admits, but the oppression of women is something that happens because of the way society is constituted. Rubin begins by analyzing patriarchy within capitalist society using Marxist

---

[5]Interview with Cixous in Verena Andermatt Conley, *Hélène Cixous: Writing the Feminine* (Lincoln and London: University of Nebraska Press, 1984), p. 129.

[6]Conley, 129–33.

terminology to understand relationships that Marx and Engels tended to avoid. If capitalism works by extracting as much surplus value from the worker as possible, there are limits to the exploitation: the worker may be a wage slave, but after working all day he needs to show up at the job site in shape to do his next day's work. To keep the system going, women who are not a direct part of the wage system themselves must become in effect the slaves of the slaves, subordinates employed to prepare food and do other forms of housework (including raising the next generation of wage slaves and houseworkers).

If this were all, gender oppression would disappear after a socialist revolution. But Rubin, a trained anthropologist, is well aware that Western capitalism is only one economic system among many, and that patriarchy — the current term for a sex/gender system that generates gender oppression under capitalism[7] — is only the most recent and developed of a great variety of such systems. Rubin investigates the different systems in primitive societies as described by Evans-Pritchard and Lévi-Strauss, most of which involve the acquisition of power through alliances that depend on the exchange of women between men. This exchange, in turn, depends on compulsory heterosexuality and on women being sexually passive. When women are pawns in relationships between men, it helps if "the woman in question did not have too many ideas of her own about whom she might want to sleep with."

The material position of women is only half of the problem with the sex/gender system; psychology accounts for the rest. As presented in the introduction to Freud and to psychoanalytical theory (Chapter 4), gender takes shape in the Oedipal crisis. Before the crisis, both boys and girls relate primarily to their mothers, whom they love and with whom they identify. Girls are feminized when they realize that their anatomy is like their mother's but that this anatomy is defective: the person she loves, her heterosexual mother, is attracted, not to another woman, someone who looks like her, but rather the father, who has a different anatomy. In a "successful" resolution of the castration complex, the girl continues to identify with her mother but devalues her (and also herself) as she shifts her desire to someone with the penis she lacks. Boys have it considerably easier: they need to shift their identification from the mother to the father, but can continue to desire their mother. This puts them in conflict with their father, but only temporarily, since in the long run, as Rubin puts it, "the social contract guarantees their rights to a woman of their own." Rubin presents our sex/gender system, whereby heterosexual parents reproduce themselves as heterosexual children, and where women are mere pawns in a system of alliances between men, as having a mutually reinforcing stability. That suggests that only a very radical change of society could produce a semblance of equality between the sexes: one where heterosexuality is not compulsory and where childrearing is shared (so that children of both sexes identify with both parents).

What Rubin presents through elaborate analysis — that the sex/gender system cannot be made just, that it would need to be utterly uprooted or destroyed — is

---

[7]Rubin is unhappy with *patriarchy* as a term for the current sex/gender system because its biblical origin (the "patriarchs" are Abraham, Isaac, and Jacob) suggests its relationship between a pastoral and nomadic, rather than urban and capitalistic social system.

presupposed in Monique Wittig's refreshingly brutal essay, "One Is Not Born a Woman," reprinted here. To be a lesbian, and to form a lesbian society, is the only possible form of liberation from a gender system in which a woman is, by her defined position within the social system, a slave to men. "Lesbians are not women," was in fact the triumphant conclusion of her MLA presentation later published as "The Straight Mind." Because lesbians, as opposed to women, do not define themselves vis-à-vis men, they have liberated themselves; they can consequently work outside the system for a revolution that will liberate females as an oppressed class, a revolution that will destroy "woman" as a category. Indeed, women's liberation — the program of Anglo-American feminism — is to Wittig a contradiction in terms, and even the androgynous vision of Cixous strikes Wittig as a mediocre half measure, an accommodation with the enemy. Wittig's forte is her ability to imagine a society wiped clean of the sex/gender system: in her novels, such as *Les Guérrillères*, even the gender inherent in the French language (where normally every noun or pronoun is inflected as masculine or feminine) has been jettisoned.

BINARIES AND TALK ABOUT BINARIES

It is difficult to talk about "heterosexuality" without raising the question of its binary opposite, "homosexuality." And just as the impulse of gender theory began with an effort to destabilize the customary boundaries of "masculinity" and "femininity," to clear the way for a different sort of discourse that could subvert the entrenched language of patriarchy, the next stage for gender theory was to take on the issues of sexual orientation and sexual identity.

While our society portrays binary oppositions like "masculine" and "feminine" or "straight" and "gay" as elementary "natural" categories, the rules have little to do with nature and everything to do with culture. The word *homosexual* has an astonishingly short history, dating from the last quarter of the nineteenth century, and *heterosexual* is an even newer term, apparently coined in opposition to "homosexual." It is not clear that "sexual identity" had the binary structure it does today much before the coining of these terms, and even today many people perform sexual acts that do not accord with the label they would apply to themselves. Precisely which sexual acts are "normal" and accepted and for whom depends upon the society in which one lives. For example, among the upper classes in Periclean Athens, it was considered normal for mature men to play the active sexual role with women, with both male and female slaves, and with male adolescents of their own class; and it was normal for male adolescents to take the passive sexual role with an adult mentor. But Athenian society thought it abnormal for men to continue to prefer the passive sexual role after coming to mature years and shameful to be the slave of sexual desire at any age.

Nor do the various binary oppositions hold their shape under close inspection. "Homosexuality" and "heterosexuality" cover not two but many forms of identity and map an enormous range of overlapping behaviors. The readers of Dr. Alfred Kinsey's pioneering surveys of sexual behavior in American men and women (1948 and 1953) were shocked to learn that men and women who considered themselves heterosexual had, more often than not, a history of experimentation with homosexual activities, and that it was unusual for homosexuals not to have tried heterosexual acts. Today we are no longer shocked: Indeed, we tend to think that every man, however masculine, has his feminine side (and vice versa), and that being too "manly" to stay in touch with one's inner woman is a defect rather than a virtue. In this sense we are all bisexual, to one degree or another: Our "sexual orientation" is merely a bias to one side or the other. Adrienne Rich speaks of the "lesbian continuum" as a way of suggesting the range of activities by which women bond to each other, not confined to "consciously desired genital sexual experience with another woman," activities including "the sharing of a rich inner life, the bonding against male tyranny, the giving and receiving of practical and political support."[8]

Similarly, the distinction between "masculine" and "feminine" activities and behaviors is constantly changing, so that women who wear baseball caps and fatigues, pump iron, and smoke cigars (at the appropriate times and seasons) can be perceived as more piquantly sexy by some heterosexual men than those women who wear white frocks and gloves and look down demurely. (Needless to say, the sexual orientation of the observer makes a difference: What most lesbians find appealing in a woman may differ from what attracts most heterosexual men.) One needs to question, too, whether such change simply involves crossing borders: Is the drag queen appropriating onto his male body the signifiers of feminine gender (makeup, wigs, gowns, high heels), or does the drag queen represent a separate form of sexuality? Even the physical dualism of sexual genetic structures and bodily parts breaks down when one considers those instances — the XXY syndromes, natural sexual bimorphisms, as well as surgical transsexuals — that defy attempts at binary classification. However, the real question for all the theorists represented in this chapter is not about the physical signifiers of sexuality but about its psychology and its discourse.

SEX AND POLITICS

If none of this is late-breaking news, much of the credit goes to contemporary gender theorists, who have been researching the historical parameters of sex and gender for the past twenty years. But while theirs is a research project, mostly financed by the universities, it is a politically committed research project, more an Arnoldian "criticism of life" than a disinterested investigation of literary texts. Toward the end of his essay "Homographesis," Lee Edelman becomes momentarily defensive about drawing conclusions that could be seen as leading merely to newer and more subtle readings of literary texts, and feels compelled to insist that his analysis of the rhetoric of gender is not "an apolitical formalism" but the grounding of an effective political critique of the patriarchal, homophobic ideology of gender.

The political movement, comparable to suffragist feminism, that aims to overturn the homophobic constructions of contemporary American discourse and the legal penalties gay men and lesbians endure was given a powerful impetus nearly thirty

[8]Adrienne Rich, "Compulsory Heterosexuality" (1980), in *The Lesbian and Gay Studies Reader*, ed. Henry Abelove et al. (New York: Routledge, 1993), p. 227.

years ago with the legendary Stonewall rebellion of 1969 in New York City, which occurred in reaction to an illegal police raid on a gay bar. A more militant "gay liberation" program has been the unspoken motivation of much of gender studies since that time. The force, even stridency, of such political critique has much to do with conditions in contemporary America, where gays and lesbians are among the few minorities still suffering under *legal* discrimination, discrimination that is not merely a threat to dignity and peace of mind but which can have serious, even lethal, consequences.

While European countries have long decriminalized all sexual activities between consenting adults, it was not until 2003, in *Lawrence v. Texas*, that the Supreme Court invalidated "sodomy" laws in thirteen American states. Although many gays have served with conspicuous bravery in the U.S. military, admitting one's homosexual orientation constitutes sufficient grounds for dishonorable discharge from the armed services. For more than a decade, AIDS research was limited and underfinanced, at least partly because almost all of those dying at the outset were gay males. (AIDS was popularly called "the gay plague," as though the viral disease were a punishment from Jehovah.) Homosexuality is often considered just grounds for denying a parent custody and visitation rights, and millions of gay men and women have children they love dearly. One's estate descends without a will and untaxed to one's spouse of the opposite sex but not to a long-term companion of the same sex, and few employers extend the fringe benefits of employment — insurance, medical coverage, and so on — to anyone except a husband or wife.

Those who are outraged that Jews, women, and blacks still often suffer from illegal discrimination should find even more unspeakable the *legal* burdens under which gays and lesbians live. It is no wonder that so many are reluctant to come "out of the closet" and announce their preference for fear of the hundreds of legal penalties and the thousands of extralegal modes of retaliation. Homophobic prejudices are all the more irrational since homosexuality is neither a disease nor a life-style decision one intentionally makes. Recent biological research has begun to suggest that attraction to one's own or the opposite sex is governed, at least in part, by complex genetic codes. However, gay liberationists are not entirely happy about the prospect of isolating a "gay gene." While it might help dissolve some people's prejudices to think of homosexuality as a genetically determined trait, it could also encourage homophobic parents to abort fetuses carrying the gene and would allow societies more repressive than ours to discover gays in even the darkest closet. More important to the issues raised by the theorists collected here, the notion of biological determinism reifies and essentializes homosexuality as a genetic outcome rather than encouraging us to understand it as a social practice or a discourse.

FOUCAULT AND THE HISTORICIZATION OF SEXUALITY

That homosexuality should be thought of preeminently as a "discourse" rather than as an action that can be studied by positivistic scientific method, or thoughts and feelings that can be analyzed by the polls of social science, is a sign of the pervasive influence on gay studies of Michel Foucault.[9] When it appeared in 1976, Foucault's *Le Volonté de savoir* (*The Will to Knowledge*), Volume I of *The History of Sexuality,* seemed to promise an appropriate sequel to his historical studies of madhouses (*Folie et Deraison* [*Madness and Civilization*], 1961), hospitals (*Le Naissance du Clinique* [*The Birth of the Clinic*], 1963), and prisons (*Surveillir et Punir* [*Discipline and Punish*], 1975) as the sites in which society isolates and punishes deviation.

While the popular view of the Victorian era is that it was a unique period of sexual repression preceded and followed by eras of greater personal liberty and sexual candor, Foucault suggests that in fact a variety of different forms of repression had succeeded one another in the centuries before, during, and after the nineteenth century. Though Foucault was gay, the gay male is not the sole or even the principal focus of *The History of Sexuality,* but only one of four categories he suggests as sites of study. (The others are the hysterical female, the masturbating child, and the Malthusian couple.) Foucault planned to analyze the transformations of power and knowledge from the early modern era to the present in relation to each of these categories.

Foucault's first volume is an extended meditation, without very much in the way of specific data, on the way he intends to approach sexuality as a site of what he had come to call *pouvoir/savoir* ("power/knowledge"). For Foucault, knowledge confers power, just as having power allows one to define what counts as knowledge. But, for Foucault, power is not necessarily the centralized power of the monarch or the ruling class; it is not a system imposed from above, like the juridical system of law; Foucault conceives of power as a field of forces operating in all directions in private as well as public life. Foucault uses this conception of power to analyze the different ways in which the human body, conceived as a type of machine from the seventeenth century onward, was "improved" in its operation by what he calls a "technology" of sex that was directed by experts of various sorts — priests, lawyers, doctors, scientists, educators, therapists — and operated both through and outside the family structure. The specific forms of repression, prohibition, and blockage of sexual desires operate differently in different areas and at different times (genuine liberation for the individual being a hopeless ideal beyond the reach of any social system Foucault is capable of envisioning). In the early twentieth century, for example, an unhappy and rebellious adolescent might have been diagnosed by educators as suffering from excessive masturbation, which was presumed to cause insanity; today, however, he or she might be treated by therapists who would interview the parents about their own sexual problems, which would be presumed to be responsible for those of their children.

Foucault had apparently prepared to spend the rest of what promised to be a long life researching the changing social practices and discourses of various forms of sexuality. But during a stay at the University of California at Berkeley, he decided to shift his project from exterior questions concerning the impact of power and knowledge on the individual to the more psychological issue of how individuals come

---

[9]For more on Foucault, see the introductions to Structuralism and Deconstruction and New Historicism and Cultural Studies, pp. 819 and 1320, respectively, and the Foucault texts in those chapters.

"to recognize themselves as subjects of a 'sexuality'" through the "hermeneutics of desire" (*Uses of Pleasure,* 4–6). Foucault, in other words, shifted his study toward the production of a history of sexual identity rather than a history of sexual practices. The second volume of the *History of Sexuality, The Uses of Pleasure* (1984; translated 1985), which takes up the place of sexuality and desire in ancient Greece, and the third volume, *The Care of the Self* (1984; translated 1986), which covers the first two centuries of the Roman empire, bear the marks of this shift in Foucault's program. These volumes, obviously meant to be continued, were also written under the pressure of time, as Foucault was diagnosed with AIDS in the early 1980s. Both volumes were published after Foucault's death in 1984.

QUEER THEORY AND HOMOSEXUAL PANIC

The history of sexuality has continued to be a subject of theorizing and research since Foucault, and perhaps the most celebrated American contributor to this field has been Eve Kosofsky Sedgwick. Her groundbreaking *Between Men: English Literature and Male Homosocial Desire* (1985) theorized that the strong and close personal relationships between men needed for success in nineteenth-century Britain placed Victorian males in a state of continual homosexual panic, a panic that was often assuaged by triangulating the relationship through a woman. David Copperfield's relation to Steerforth via Little Em'ly is an obvious fictional representation of this, but such triangulated relationships also appear, as one might expect, in literary biography and other non-fiction narratives of the age. One recalls, for example, that Arthur Henry Hallam was not only Tennyson's closest friend at the time of his death, but had become his sister's fiancé. Sedgwick's *Epistemology of the Closet* (1990) advances her study to the end of World War I, with discussions of Melville, Wilde, James, and Proust. It also makes explicit the antihomophobic politics on which it is founded. Indeed, Sedgwick insists that homosexuality is everyone's issue, as heterosexual males define their own identity in opposition to — and thus in terms of — that of the gay Other, and maneuver in significant ways to obscure their own objects of desire.

The issue of gay identity as such dominates the work of Judith Butler. Butler's book *Gender Trouble* (1990) uses a deconstructive rhetoric to subvert the binarisms of male/female, masculine/feminine, and gay/straight. While many gay liberationists have attempted to construct positive models of gay identity as a way of resisting a homophobic society, to Butler the entire issue of gender identity is political poison. The essentialization of categories like "gay" and "straight" or "female" and "male," is inherently restrictive. Just as the 1970s feminist project of creating a positive image of Woman implicitly defined an ideal for every woman to live up to, depriving each individual of the right to be whoever and whatever she was, the creation of fixed images of gay and lesbian identity can result in the "regulatory imperative" to be a "proper" gay or lesbian individual.

In "Imitation and Gender Insubordination" (1991), Butler confesses that she "suffered for a long time from being told that what I 'am' is a copy, an imitation, a derivative example, a shadow of the real." For those who essentialize sexuality, biological sex defines one's gender, and gender defines one's sexual orientation. Heterosexuals define themselves by oppressing those who transgress, whose signifiers don't line up. And just as the notion of a platonic ideal of Woman has been used to oppress lesbians, the image of the Ideal Lesbian can be used to oppress those who do not come up to whatever mark the politics of the group has set forth. In good Derridean fashion, Butler deconstructs the binary of original versus copy, questioning not merely which is the real and which the imitation, but whether our entire concept of gender is not in fact based on imitations for which no real essences exist. Both homosexuals and heterosexuals seem to want to buy into this destructive mythic logic, in which gender is "an imitation that performatively constitutes itself as the original." But to perform something is to play at something; to play at something is not *to be* that something. Just as Derrida insisted on recognizing language as a freeplay of signifiers lacking a stable center, Butler suggests that we would spare ourselves a great deal of misery by recognizing that there are no fixed sexual identities that shape our actions and thoughts, that gender is something we "put on" or perform. What we do, our performances from moment to moment, driven by strong inner imperatives, are all we are or can be.

In dialogue with Judith Butler is Martha Nussbaum, also by training a philosopher, whose central interest is ethics as it can be taught by the experience of imaginative literature. To Nussbaum, the error of essentializing sexual preferences is comparatively trivial by comparison with the distance that Butler opens up between what oppressors can do and what the oppressed can do about it. To view gender as an "insubordinate" performative act that deconstructs and parodies the cultural clichés that underlie sexism or homophobia is implicitly to suggest that there is nothing concrete that can be done about them. Nussbaum suggests that in following Foucault's logic, Butler finds herself in a position where she cannot recommend social action because she is incapable of imagining a favorable outcome, a change whose structure of power would leave us more free and happy than we were before. How far this invalidates Butler's argument, and indeed whether Nussbaum has actually understood Butler in the first place, is something readers can decide for themselves.

GAY LIVES, GAY TEXTS

The 1998 essays by Judith Halberstam, "An Introduction to Female Masculinity," and by Lauren Berlant and Michael Warner, "Sex in Public," are primarily about gay identities and practices and their relation to the heterosexual world within which those identities take shape, and both are informed, inevitably, by the theories of Foucault, Sedgwick, and Butler. In terms of the varieties of sexual preferences outlined by Sedgwick in *Epistemology of the Closet*, Judith Halberstam (also known as "Jack") is a transgendered female. Her sexual identity is masculine — she desires women — but her body is female and, unlike transsexuals, she has no plan or wish to acquire a male anatomy. The history of gender theory has, to an extent, orphaned those in her category. From the beginning, vastly more attention has been paid to the question of what femininity is all about than to the multiple forms of masculinity. The varieties of masculinity, particularly as they are inflected by race and ethnicity, have only recently begun to be studied, but in a sense transgendered females like Halberstam offer an opportunity to study masculinity in an especially pure form, in the absence of maleness.

Halberstam likes to stress the asymetrical aspects of gender identification. As she stated in an interview, "Since femininity signifies in general as the effect of artifice, as the essence of 'performativity' . . . , we have an easier time understanding it as transferable, mobile, fluid. But masculinity has an altogether different relation to performance, the real and the natural, and it appears to be far more difficult to pry masculinity and maleness apart than femininity and femaleness."[10] Alluding to Butler's view of performativity here, Halberstam suggests that performing masculinity involves not performing, or at least not appearing to perform: it is the impassivity of male icons like Clint Eastwood that conveys their masculinity. Halberstam would argue that the dominance of male over female in Western culture has made masculinity the "default" position. It takes far more effort for a man to cross-dress and look feminine than for a woman to cross-dress and look masculine. Social mores arrange other asymmetries, such as those of the public toilet. A masculine woman may well be tempted to use the "wrong" toilet in the airport, because in the Ladies' Room she is likely to be noticed and to have to explain her presence, or even demonstrate her femaleness to a security guard. She would be less likely to arouse suspicion in a Men's Room, where men are, or pretend to be, oblivious of each other's appearance and of the fact that others are present for private functions. On the other hand, there might be violent consequences to being caught.[11] Given Halberstam's concern with the details of performing gender, one has little sense that she considers her gender something she merely acts out. She seems to consider her identity as a masculine woman as something innate. She was a tomboy who — unlike Frankie Adams, in *The Member of the Wedding* — refused at adolescence to conform herself to the standard of enacted femininity demanded of females by her society.

That standard is just one part of "heteronormativity" which is the central topic of Berlant and Warner's "Sex in Public," reproduced here. At stake are "the radical aspirations of queer culture building" — and "radical" is the key word. As the authors define it, heteronormativity is the "institutions, structures of understanding, and practical orientations that make heterosexuality seem not only coherent . . . but privileged." A very small part of their issue is that heterosexuality itself is the presumed or "unmarked" position: people who are gay have to make that clear to the people getting to know them, whereas people who are straight don't have to do anything. And attitudes held by heterosexuals are considered the norm for everyone. For example, while it is certainly considered heteronormal to date and experiment widely at the outset of sexual activity, it is presumed that variety loses its spice, and that an optimum life history will involve episodes of lengthy intimacy, marriage, and

[10] "Masculinity without Men," *Genders* 29 (1999).
[11] Halberstam does not mention in her book the case of Brandon Teena, the female-to-male transgender from Falls River, Nebraska, who was raped and then murdered in 1993 by two young men who had discovered her secret. Teena was the subject of a documentary film in 1998 and the 1999 feature film *Boys Don't Cry*, for which Hilary Swank won her first Academy Award.

the cares of raising a family. Gays who "settle down" into long-term partnerships, whether or not they choose to have or adopt children, have in effect been co-opted into this aspect of heteronormativity.[12] Berlant and Warner argue that "queer social practices like sex and theory" should "try to unsettle" the hegemonic force of heteronormativity. The "outlaw" aspects of queer sex, of which sex toys and leather bars are only two examples, have a value to Berlant and Warner, not merely in themselves, but in the way they serve to destabilize the deadening culture that accepts "difference" in the abstract but doesn't really want to be challenged by it. That the heterosexual population — in the liberal cities at least — has come to accept most elements of the gay lifestyle as desirable or indifferent aspects of urban life is a sign of how far and how quickly the center of the culture has moved from the standard homophobia of my own childhood fifty years ago. Have we arrived here at a post–queer theory, where the key danger to gay and lesbian culture is what Herbert Marcuse once called "repressive tolerance"?[13] Maybe not quite yet: Berlant and Warner seem to relish the "queer outlaw" role in theory, but are also upset that an anti-pornography zoning statute might banish gay sex clubs with live performances to lonely streets near the New York City waterfront, where patrons would have a greater likelihood of being mugged than their former locations in the better patrolled parts of Greenwich Village. Perhaps homoradicalism can be as incoherent an ideology as heteronormativity.

"Claiming the Pardoner," the 1993 essay by Steven Kruger, reproduced here, is more in the tradition of Foucault than of Butler and Sedgwick. At the center of Kruger's task is both philosophical and historical inquiry, to attempt to get inside the medieval culture of sexual differences, and to understand what Chaucer thought he was doing when he created the most stunningly realized of the Canterbury pilgrims, who tells what is by consensus the most artistically rendered of the tales. But of course as "a gay man living in 1992" Kruger cannot be a disinterested party analyzing a historical topic out of pure curiosity: there is something at stake for him personally. Kruger attempts to "navigate between Chaucer's text, a historical understanding of the late medieval construction of male homosexuality and of homophobia, and [his] own . . . political stances and needs. Those needs include . . . a rediscovered or reconstructed gay history, and the ultimate question at issue for [him] here is what role Chaucer's Pardoner might play in the writing of that history." As can be the case with African Americans reading Twain's *Huckleberry Finn* or

---

[12]The wedge issue of gay marriage shows that "heteronormativity" is not always coherent. Religious conservatives are appalled by the possibility of what they would consider a parody of the sacred institution, which they define as taking place between one man and one woman. Liberal heterosexuals are likely to favor gay marriage because it would help bring queer culture into line with heteronormativity. Berlant and Warner might well find both positions repugnant since, for both conservative and liberal heterosexuals, gay marriage would be "about" their own views on life rather than those of the people most directly concerned.

[13]See "Repressive Tolerance" (1965) in Robert Paul Wolff, Barrington Moore, Jr., and Herbert Marcuse, *A Critique of Pure Tolerance* (Boston: Beacon Press, 1969), 95–137. Marcuse, a former member of the Frankfurt School with Horkheimer and Adorno, argued that the liberal ideology of toleration of dissent makes it more difficult to radically reform the capitalist world.

Jews reading Shakespeare's *The Merchant of Venice*, Kruger's reading of Chaucer's Pardoner is freighted with the ambivalence with which a reader claims kinship with a representation tinged with contempt for the Other, whether racism, anti-Semitism, or in this case homophobia.

RESISTING THE FREUDIAN MATRIX

Butler and Sedgwick are engaged in one side of the theoretical task of gay liberation, that of liberating the movement from its recapitulation of the same binarism and exclusionary politics that characterize patriarchal ideology, and that, as we have seen, continue to characterize some schools of feminist thought. The other side of the theoretical task is that of accomplishing for gays what Cixous and Irigaray achieved for women in their rereadings of Freud and Lacan: the recuperation of the psychoanalytical discourse of gender as a language that heals rather than wounds the spirit. This is not an easy task, as Freud's view of homosexuality was that it stems from a wrong turning, a regression to an earlier stage of development caused by failure to make a necessary leap. According to Freud, the individual progresses through a series of stages, from early infantile sexuality, an autoeroticism that seeks pleasure purely in the self, to a primary narcissism in which one loves oneself in undifferentiated unity with the parent, to the conflicts of the Oedipal crisis, in which genuine object relations develop that lead to desire for the opposite sex. In the case of the homosexual, Freud argues that some crushing of the self-image occurs in the course of development that leads the child to choose as a sexual object a figure of the same sex, embodying the ideal elements the child feels to be missing from himself.

In his response to Freud, *Homosexual Desire*, reprinted in part below, Guy Hocquenghem may have become the first of the queer theorists, since his 1972 essay appeared in French four years before *La Volonté de savoir*, the first volume of Foucault's *History of Sexuality*. Foucault may in fact have been responding to Hocquenghem, since they knew each other and since Hocquenghem was certainly responding to the early Foucault of *Madness and Civilization*, with its vision of medical science creating classes of people who, for the sake of decency, had to be locked up:

> Homosexuality is a manufactured product of the normal world. . . . What is manufactured is a psychologically repressive category, "homosexuality": an abstract division of desire which allows even those who escape to be dominated, inscribing within the law what is outside the law. The category under discussion, as well as the term indicating it, is a fairly recent invention. The growing imperialism of a society seeking to attribute a social status to everything, even to the unclassifiable, created this particular form of disequilibrium: up to the end of the eighteenth century, people who denied the existence of God, who could not speak, or who practised sodomy, were locked up in the same prisons. Just as the advent of psychiatry and mental hospitals demonstrates society's ability to invent specific means for classifying the unclassifiable (see Foucault's *Histoire de la folie à l'âge classique*), so modern thought creates a new disease, homosexuality. According to Havelock Ellis, the word "homosexual" was invented in 1869 by a German doctor. Dividing in order to rule, psychiatry's modern pseudo-scientific thought has turned barbarous intolerance into civilised intolerance. (50–51)

In "The 'Third Sex' and 'Masculine-Feminine,'" reproduced below, Hocquenghem's analysis of the medical regime, unless I am mistaking its tone, takes the form of brisk satire. It brushes aside any explanation of homosexuality, such as Hirschfeld's "third sex" theory, that might make sense to real people who have experienced homosexual desire. Hocquenghem lavishes his analysis instead on the theories of Freud and his disciple Sandor Ferenczi, showing how they continually turn each category into a set of binaries that mimic and thus map onto the basic binary of male and female. There must be object-homosexuals and subject-homosexuals, perverts and inverts, masochists and sadists. Homosexual desire as such cannot exist because it would create a third entity, or, even worse, dissolve the entire system of binaries by suggesting that sexual desire, homo, hetero, whatever, is a single indivisible force. That was precisely what Hocquenghem believed: "Homosexual desire: the expression is meaningless. There is no subdivision of desire . . ." (49). To counterbalance the binary gymnastics of the psychoanalysts, Hocquenghem opposes the imaginative truth of Robert Musil's novella, *Young Törless*, whose confused protagonist knows more about desire than his sophisticated friends or his schoolmasters.

While queer theory and gender studies have become areas of theory that are distinct from feminist criticism and women's studies, it would be misleading to ignore the connections among these schools. Gender studies became possible as a result of the projects of feminist criticism, and queer theory has drawn both energies and insights from feminist thinkers. In their first books, both Butler and Sedgwick defined their work as feminist, and Butler, especially, is still very sensitive to the connections between gender theory and feminism. Which is more important: likeness or difference? The contradictions inherent in identity politics inevitably generate dual impulses to split off and to merge, as gay males, lesbians, bisexuals, and cross-dressers sense how different their cultural situations and concerns are from those of "mainstream" feminists but simultaneously understand the political consequences of isolation and the advantages of a combined resistance to normative patriarchy.

Selected Bibliography

Abelove, Henry, Michèle Aina Barale, and David M. Halperin, eds. *The Lesbian and Gay Studies Reader*. New York: Routledge, 1993.

Belsey, Catherine. *Critical Practice*. New York: Methuen, 1980.

Bersani, Leo. "Is the Rectum a Grave?" *October* 43 (1987): 197–222.

Boone, Joseph Allen. *Tradition Counter Tradition: Love and the Form of Fiction*. Chicago: University of Chicago Press, 1987.

Boone, Joseph Allen, and Michael Caddon, eds. *Engendering Men: The Question of Male Feminist Criticism*. New York: Routledge, 1990.

Boswell, John. *Christianity, Social Tolerance, and Homosexuality: Gay People in Western Europe from the Beginning of the Christian Era to the Fourteenth Century*. Chicago: University of Chicago Press, 1980.

Bray, Alan. *Homosexuality in Renaissance England*. London: Gay Men's Press, 1982.

Burger, Glenn, and Steven F. Kruger, eds. *Queering the Middle Ages*. Minneapolis: University of Minnesota Press, 2001.

Butler, Judith. *Gender Trouble: Feminism and the Subversion of Identity.* New York and London: Routledge, 1990.

Butters, Ronald R., John M. Clum, and Michael Mood, eds. *Displacing Homophobia: Gay Male Perspectives in Literature and Culture.* Durham: Duke University Press, 1989.

Castle, Terry. *The Apparitional Lesbian: Female Homosexuality and Modern Culture.* New York: Columbia University Press, 1993.

Cixous, Hélène. "Le Rire de la Méduse." *L'Arc* 61 (1975): 39–54. Trans. Keith and Paula Cohen as "The Laugh of the Medusa," *Signs* I (1976): 875–99.

——. *La Jeune née* (with Catherine Clément). Paris: UGE Press, 1975. Trans. Betsy Wing as *The Newly Born Woman.* Minneapolis: University of Minnesota Press, 1986.

De Lauretis, Teresa. *Alice Doesn't: Feminism, Semiotics, Cinema.* Bloomington: Indiana University Press, 1984.

——, ed. *The Practice of Love: Lesbian Sexualities and Perverse Desire.* Bloomington: Indiana University Press, 1994.

Edelman, Lee. *Homographesis: Essays in Gay Literary and Cultural Theory.* New York and London: Routledge, 1994.

Foucault, Michel. *The History of Sexuality,* Volume I: *The Will to Knowledge,* trans. Robert Hurley. New York: Random House, 1980.

——. Volume II: *The Uses of Pleasure,* trans. Robert Hurley. New York: Pantheon, 1985.

——. Volume III: *The Care of the Self,* trans. Robert Hurley. New York: Pantheon, 1986.

Fuss, Diana, ed. *Inside/Out: Lesbian Theories, Gay Theories.* New York: Routledge, 1991.

Garber, Marjorie. *Vested Interests: Cross-dressing and Cultural Anxiety.* New York: Routledge, 1991.

Goldberg, Jonathan, ed. *Queering the Renaissance.* Durham: Duke University Press, 1994.

Haggerty, George E., and Bonnie Zimmerman. *Professions of Desire: Lesbian and Gay Studies in Literature.* New York: MLA Press, 1995.

Halperin, David. *One Hundred Years of Homosexuality and Other Essays on Greek Love.* New York: Routledge, 1990.

Hocquenghem, Guy. *Homosexual Desire* (1972), trans. Daniella Dangoor. London: Allison and Busby, 1978.

Irigaray, Luce. *Spéculum de l'autre femme.* Paris: Minuit, 1974. Trans. Gillian C. Gill as *The Speculum of the Other Woman.* Ithaca: Cornell University Press, 1985.

——. *Ce sexe qui n'en est pas un.* Paris: Minuit, 1977. Trans. Catharine Porter with Carolyn Burke as *This Sex Which Is Not One.* Ithaca: Cornell University Press, 1985.

Jagose, Annamarie. *Queer Theory.* Victoria: Melbourne University Press, 1996.

Jardine, Alice. *Gynesis: Configurations of Woman and Modernity.* Ithaca: Cornell University Press, 1985.

Jay, Karla, and Allen Young, eds. *Out of the Closets: Voices of Gay Liberation* (1972). New York: NYU Press, 1992.

Kauffman, Linda, ed. *Gender and Theory: Dialogues on Feminist Criticism.* New York: Blackwell, 1985.

Keohane, Nannerl, Michelle Z. Rosaldo, and Barbara C. Gelpi, eds. *Feminist Theory: A Critique of Ideology.* Chicago: University of Chicago Press, 1982.

Koestenbaum, Wayne. *The Queen's Throat: Opera, Homosexuality and the Mystery of Desire.* New York: Poseidon Press, 1993.

Kruger, Steven. *AIDS Narratives.* New York: Garland, 1996.

Marks, Elaine, and Isabelle de Courtivron, eds. *New French Feminisms: An Anthology.* Amherst: University of Massachusetts Press, 1980.

Miller, D. A. *The Novel and the Police.* Berkeley: University of California Press, 1988.

Miller, Nancy K., ed. *The Poetics of Gender.* New York: Columbia University Press, 1986.

Mulvey, Laura. *Visual and Other Pleasures.* Basingstoke, Eng.: Macmillan, 1989.

Norton, Rictor. *The Myth of the Modern Homosexual: Queer History and the Search for Cultural Unity.* London: Cassell, 1997.

Reid-Pharr, Robert. *Black Gay Man.* New York: NYU Press, 2001.

Rich, Adrienne. "Compulsory Heterosexuality and Lesbian Existence." In *Women, Sex and Sexuality,* ed. Catharine Stimpson and Ethel Spector Person. Chicago: University of Chicago Press, 1980, pp. 62–91.

Rosario, Vernon A., ed. *Science and Homosexualities.* New York: Routledge, 1997.

Rubin, Gayle. "Thinking Sex: Notes for a Radical Theory of the Politics of Sexuality." In *Pleasure and Danger: Exploring Female Sexuality,* ed. Carol A. Vance. New York: Routledge, 1984, pp. 267–319.

Sedgwick, Eve Kosofsky. *Between Men: English Literature and Male Homosocial Desire.* New York: Columbia University Press, 1985.

———. *Epistemology of the Closet.* Berkeley: University of California Press, 1990.

Seidman, Steven. *Queer Theory/Sociology.* Cambridge: Blackwell, 1996.

Warner, Michael, ed. *Fear of a Queer Planet: Queer Politics and Social Theory.* Minneapolis: University of Minnesota Press, 1993.

Watney, Simon. *Policing Desire: Pornography, AIDS and the Media.* Minneapolis: University of Minnesota Press, 1987.

Weeks, Jeffrey. *Sex, Politics and Society: The Regulation of Sexuality Since 1800.* New York: Longman, 1981.

———. *Sexuality and Its Discontents: Meanings, Myths and Modern Sexualities.* London: Routledge, 1985.

Wittig, Monique. *The Straight Mind.* Boston: Beacon, 1992.

Michel Foucault

1926–1984

The following selection is taken from Robert Hurley's translation of Le Volonté de savoir *(The Will to Knowledge), Volume I of Foucault's* History of Sexuality *(1980). (For biographical information, see the introduction to Foucault, p. 904.)*

From *The History of Sexuality*

1. OBJECTIVE

... This history of sexuality, or rather this series of studies concerning the historical relationships of power and the discourse on sex, is, I realize, a circular project in the sense that it involves two

Translated by Robert Hurley.

endeavors that refer back to one another. We shall try to rid ourselves of a juridical and negative representation of power, and cease to conceive of it in terms of law, prohibition, liberty, and sovereignty. But how then do we analyze what has occurred in recent history with regard to this thing — seemingly one of the most forbidden areas of our lives and bodies — that is sex? How, if not by way of prohibition and blockage, does power gain access to it? Through which mechanisms, or tactics, or devices? But let us assume in turn that a somewhat careful scrutiny will show that power in modern societies has not in fact governed sexuality through law and sovereignty; let us suppose that historical analysis has revealed the presence of a veritable "technology" of sex, one that is much more complex and above all much more positive than the mere effect of a "defense" could be; this being the case, does this example — which can only be considered a privileged one, since power seemed in this instance, more than anywhere else, to function as prohibition — not compel one to discover principles for analyzing power which do not derive from the system of right and the form of law? Hence it is a question of forming a different grid of historical decipherment by starting from a different theory of power; and, at the same time, of advancing little by little toward a different conception of power through a closer examination of an entire historical material. We must at the same time conceive of sex without the law, and power without the king.

2. METHOD

Hence the objective is to analyze a certain form of knowledge regarding sex, not in terms of repression or law, but in terms of power. But the word *power* is apt to lead to a number of misunderstandings — misunderstandings with respect to its nature, its form, and its unity. By power, I do not mean "Power" as a group of institutions and mechanisms that ensure the subservience of the citizens of a given state. By power, I do not mean, either, a mode of subjugation which, in contrast to violence, has the form of the rule. Finally, I do not have in mind a general system of domination exerted by one group over another, a system whose effects, through successive derivations, pervade the entire social body. The analysis, made in terms of power, must not assume that the sovereignty of the state, the form of the law, or the over-all unity of a domination are given at the outset; rather, these are only the terminal forms power takes. It seems to me that power must be understood in the first instance as the multiplicity of force relations immanent in the sphere in which they operate and which constitute their own organization; as the process which, through ceaseless struggles and confrontations, transforms, strengthens, or reverses them; as the support which these force relations find in one another, thus forming a chain or a system, or on the contrary, the disjunctions and contradictions which isolate them from one another; and lastly, as the strategies in which they take effect, whose general design or institutional crystallization is embodied in the state apparatus, in the formulation of the law, in the various social hegemonies. Power's condition of possibility, or in any case the viewpoint which permits one to understand its exercise, even in its more "peripheral" effects, and which also makes it possible to use its mechanisms as a grid of intelligibility of the social order, must not be sought in the primary existence of a central point, in a unique source of sovereignty from which secondary and descendent forms would emanate; it is the moving substrate of force relations which, by virtue of their inequality, constantly engender states of power, but the latter are always local and unstable. The omnipresence of power: not because it has the privilege of consolidating everything under its invincible unity, but because it is produced from one moment to the next, at every point, or rather in every relation from one point to another. Power is everywhere; not because it embraces everything, but because it comes from everywhere. And "Power," insofar as it is permanent, repetitious, inert, and self-reproducing, is simply the over-all effect that emerges from all these mobilities, the concatenation that rests on each of them and seeks in turn to arrest their movement. One needs to be nominalistic, no doubt: power is not an institution, and not a structure; neither is it a certain strength we are endowed with; it is the name that one attributes to a complex strategical situation in a particular society.

Should we turn the expression around, then, and say that politics is war pursued by other means?[1] If we still wish to maintain a separation

---

[1]Foucault is alluding to the famous definition of Prussian General Karl von Clausewitz (1780–1831) in *On War* (1832): "War is the continuation of politics by other means."

between war and politics, perhaps we should postulate rather that this multiplicity of force relations can be coded — in part but never totally — either in the form of "war," or in the form of "politics"; this would imply two different strategies (but the one always liable to switch into the other) for integrating these unbalanced, heterogeneous, unstable, and tense force relations.

Continuing this line of discussion, we can advance a certain number of propositions:

Power is not something that is acquired, seized, or shared, something that one holds on to or allows to slip away; power is exercised from innumerable points, in the inter-play of nonegalitarian and mobile relations.

Relations of power are not in a position of exteriority with respect to other types of relationships (economic processes, knowledge relationships, sexual relations), but are immanent in the latter; they are the immediate effects of the divisions, inequalities, and disequilibriums which occur in the latter, and conversely they are the internal conditions of these differentiations; relations of power are not in the superstructural[2] positions, with merely a role of prohibition or accompaniment; they have a directly productive role, wherever they come into play.

Power comes from below; that is, there is no binary and all-encompassing opposition between rulers and ruled at the root of power relations, and serving as a general matrix — no such duality extending from the top down and reacting on more and more limited groups to the very depths of the social body. One must suppose rather that the manifold relationships of force that take shape and come into play in the machinery of production, in families, limited groups, and institutions, are the basis for wide-ranging effects of cleavage

[2]Although no Marxist, Foucault is here making use of Marx's distinction between base and superstructure. In the two paragraphs following this one, he refers to Gramsci's notion of hegemony and Althusser's notion of "ideological state apparatuses." See the introduction to Marxist Criticism, p. 1198.

that run through the social body as a whole. These then form a general line of force that traverses the local oppositions and links them together; to be sure, they also bring about redistributions, realignments, homogenizations, serial arrangements, and convergences of the force relations. Major dominations are the hegemonic effects that are sustained by all these confrontations.

Power relations are both intentional and non-subjective. If in fact they are intelligible, this is not because they are the effect of another instance that "explains" them, but rather because they are imbued, through and through, with calculation: there is no power that is exercised without a series of aims and objectives. But this does not mean that it results from the choice or decision of an individual subject; let us not look for the headquarters that presides over its rationality; neither the caste which governs, nor the groups which control the state apparatus, nor those who make the most important economic decisions direct the entire network of power that functions in a society (and makes *it* function); the rationality of power is characterized by tactics that are often quite explicit at the restricted level where they are inscribed (the local cynicism of power), tactics which, becoming connected to one another, attracting and propagating one another, but finding their base of support and their condition elsewhere, end by forming comprehensive systems: the logic is perfectly clear, the aims decipherable, and yet it is often the case that no one is there to have invented them, and few who can be said to have formulated them: an implicit characteristic of the great anonymous, almost unspoken strategies which coordinate the loquacious tactics whose "inventors" or decisionmakers are often without hypocrisy.

Where there is power, there is resistance, and yet, or rather consequently, this resistance is never in a position of exteriority in relation to power. Should it be said that one is always "inside" power, there is no "escaping" it, there is no absolute outside where it is concerned, because one is subject to the law in any case? Or that, history being the ruse of reason, power is the ruse of history, always emerging the winner? This would be to misunderstand the strictly relational character of power relationships. Their existence depends on a multiplicity of points of resistance: these play the role of adversary, target, support, or handle in power relations. These points of resistance are present everywhere in the power network. Hence there is no single locus of great Refusal, no soul of revolt, source of all rebellions, or pure law of the revolutionary. Instead there is a plurality of resistances, each of them a special case: resistances that are possible, necessary, improbable; others that are spontaneous, savage, solitary, concerted, rampant, or violent; still others that are quick to compromise, interested, or sacrificial; by definition, they can only exist in the strategic field of power relations. But this does not mean that they are only a reaction or rebound, forming with respect to the basic domination an underside that is in the end always passive, doomed to perpetual defeat. Resistances do not derive from a few heterogeneous principles; but neither are they a lure or a promise that is of necessity betrayed. They are the odd term in relations of power; they are inscribed in the latter as an irreducible opposite. Hence they too are distributed in irregular fashion: the points, knots, or focuses of resistance are spread over time and space at varying densities, at times mobilizing groups or individuals in a definitive way, inflaming certain points of the body, certain moments in life, certain types of behavior. Are there no great radical ruptures, massive binary divisions, then? Occasionally, yes. But more often one is dealing with mobile and transitory points of resistance, producing cleavages in a society that shift about, fracturing unities and effecting regroupings, furrowing across individuals themselves, cutting them up and remolding them, marking off irreducible regions in them, in their bodies and minds. Just as the network of power relations ends by forming a dense web that passes through apparatuses and institutions, without being exactly localized in them, so too the swarm of points of resistance traverses social stratifications and individual unities. And it is doubtless the strategic codification of these points of resistance that makes a revolution possible, somewhat similar to the way in which the state relies on the institutional integration of power relationships.

It is in this sphere of force relations that we must try to analyze the mechanisms of power. In this way we will escape from the system of Law-and-Sovereign which has captivated political thought for such a long time. And if it is true that Machiavelli was among the few — and this no doubt was the scandal of his "cynicism" — who conceived the power of the Prince in terms of force relationships, perhaps we need to go one step further, do without the persona of the Prince, and decipher power mechanisms on the basis of a strategy that is immanent in force relationships.

To return to sex and the discourses of truth that have taken charge of it, the question that we must address, then, is not: Given a specific state structure, how and why is it that power needs to establish a knowledge of sex? Neither is the question: What over-all domination was served by the concern, evidenced since the eighteenth century, to produce true discourses on sex? Nor is it: What law presided over both the regularity of sexual behavior and the conformity of what was said about it? It is rather: In a specific type of discourse on sex, in a specific form of extortion of truth, appearing historically and in specific places (around the child's body, apropos of women's sex, in connection with practices restricting births, and so on), what were the most immediate, the most local power relations at work? How did they make possible these kinds of discourses, and conversely, how were these discourses used to support power relations? How was the action of these power relations modified by their very exercise, entailing a strengthening of some terms and a weakening of others, with effects of resistance and counterinvestments, so that there has never existed one type of stable subjugation, given once and for all? How were these power relations linked to one another according to the logic of a great strategy, which in retrospect takes on the aspect of a unitary and voluntarist politics of sex? In general terms: rather than referring all the infinitesimal violences that are exerted on sex, all the anxious gazes that are directed at it, and all the hiding places whose discovery is made into an impossible task, to the unique form of a great Power, we must immerse the expanding production of discourses on sex in the field of multiple and mobile power relations.

Which leads us to advance, in a preliminary way, four rules to follow. But these are not intended as methodological imperatives; at most they are cautionary prescriptions.

1. *Rule of Immanence*

One must not suppose that there exists a certain sphere of sexuality that would be the legitimate concern of a free and disinterested scientific inquiry were it not the object of mechanisms of prohibition brought to bear by the economic or ideological requirements of power. If sexuality was constituted as an area of investigation, this was only because relations of power had established it as a possible object; and conversely, if power was able to take it as a target, this was because techniques of knowledge and procedures of discourse were capable of investing it. Between techniques of knowledge and strategies of power, there is no exteriority, even if they have specific roles and are linked together on the basis of their difference. We will start, therefore, from what might be called "local centers" of power-knowledge: for example, the relations that obtain between penitents and confessors, or the faithful and their directors of conscience. Here, guided by the theme of the "flesh" that must be mastered, different forms of discourse — self-examination, questionings, admissions, interpretations, interviews — were the vehicle of a kind of incessant back-and-forth movement of forms of subjugation and schemas of knowledge. Similarly, the body of the child, under surveillance, surrounded in his cradle, his bed, or his room by an entire watch-crew of parents, nurses, servants, educators, and doctors, all attentive to the least manifestations of his sex, has constituted, particularly since the eighteenth century, another "local center" of power-knowledge.

2. *Rules of Continual Variations*

We must not look for who has the power in the order of sexuality (men, adults, parents, doctors) and who is deprived of it (women, adolescents, children, patients); nor for who has the right to know and who is forced to remain ignorant. We must seek rather the pattern of the modifications which the relationships of force imply by the very nature of their process. The "distributions of power" and the "appropriations of knowledge" never represent only instantaneous slices taken from processes involving, for example, a cumulative reinforcement of the strongest factor, or a reversal of relationship, or again, a simultaneous increase of two terms. Relations of power-knowledge are not static forms of distribution, they are "matrices of transformations." The nineteenth-century grouping made up of the father, the mother, the educator, and the doctor, around the child and his sex, was subjected to constant modifications, continual shifts. One of the more spectacular results of the latter was a strange reversal: whereas to begin with the child's sexuality had been problematized within the relationship established between doctor and parents (in the form of advice, or recommendations to keep the child under observation, or warnings of future dangers), ultimately it was in the relationship of the psychiatrist to the child that the sexuality of adults themselves was called into question.

3. *Rule of Double Conditioning*

No "local center," no "pattern of transformation" could function if, through a series of sequences, it did not eventually enter into an over-all strategy. And inversely, no strategy could achieve comprehensive effects if it did not gain support from precise and tenuous relations serving, not as its point of application or final outcome, but as its prop and anchor point. There is no discontinuity between them, as if one were dealing with two different levels (one microscopic and the other macroscopic); but neither is there homogeneity (as if the one were only the enlarged projection or the miniaturization of the other); rather, one must conceive of the double conditioning of a strategy by the specificity of possible tactics, and of tactics by the strategic envelope that makes them work. Thus the father in the family is not the "representative" of the sovereign or the state; and the latter are not projections of the father on a different scale. The family does not duplicate society, just as society does not imitate the family. But the family organization, precisely to the extent that it was insular and heteromorphous with respect to the other power mechanisms, was used to support the great "maneuvers" employed for the Malthusian control of the birthrate,[3] for the populationist incitements, for the medicalization of sex and the psychiatrization of its nongenital forms.

4. Rule of the Tactical Polyvalence of Discourses

What is said about sex must not be analyzed simply as the surface of projection of these power mechanisms. Indeed, it is in discourse that power and knowledge are joined together. And for this very reason, we must conceive discourse as a series of discontinuous segments whose tactical function is neither uniform nor stable. To be more precise, we must not imagine a world of discourse divided between accepted discourse and excluded discourse, or between the dominant discourse and the dominated one; but as a multiplicity of discursive elements that can come into play in various strategies. It is this distribution that we must reconstruct, with the things said and those concealed, the enunciations required and those forbidden, that it comprises; with the variants and different effects — according to who is speaking, his position of power, the institutional context in which he happens to be situated — that it implies; and with the shifts and reutilizations of identical formulas for contrary objectives that it also includes. Discourses are not once and for all subservient to power or raised up against it, any more than silences are. We must make allowance for the complex and unstable process whereby discourse can be both an instrument and an effect of power, but also a hindrance, a stumbling-block, a point of resistance and a starting point for an opposing strategy. Discourse transmits and produces power; it reinforces it, but also undermines and exposes it, renders it fragile and makes it possible to thwart it. In like manner, silence and

secrecy are a shelter for power, anchoring its prohibitions; but they also loosen its holds and provide for relatively obscure areas of tolerance. Consider for example the history of what was once "the" great sin against nature. The extreme discretion of the texts dealing with sodomy — that utterly confused category — and the nearly universal reticence in talking about it made possible a twofold operation: on the one hand, there was an extreme severity (punishment by fire was meted out well into the eighteenth century, without there being any substantial protest expressed before the middle of the century), and on the other hand, a tolerance that must have been widespread (which one can deduce indirectly from the infrequency of judicial sentences, and which one glimpses more directly through certain statements concerning societies of men that were thought to exist in the army or in the courts). There is no question that the appearance in nineteenth-century psychiatry, jurisprudence, and literature of a whole series of discourses on the species and subspecies of homosexuality, inversion, pederasty, and "psychic hermaphrodism" made possible a strong advance of social controls into this area of "perversity"; but it also made possible the formation of a "reverse" discourse: homosexuality began to speak in its own behalf, to demand that its legitimacy or "naturality" be acknowledged, often in the same vocabulary, using the same categories by which it was medically disqualified. There is not, on the one side, a discourse of power, and opposite it, another discourse that runs counter to it. Discourses are tactical elements or blocks operating in the field of force relations; there can exist different and even contradictory discourses within the same strategy; they can, on the contrary, circulate without changing their form from one strategy to another, opposing strategy. We must not expect the discourses on sex to tell us, above all, what strategy they derive from, or what moral divisions they accompany, or what ideology — dominant or dominated — they represent; rather we must question them on the two levels of their tactical productivity (what reciprocal effects of power and knowledge they ensure) and their strategical integration (what conjunction and what force relationship make their utilization necessary in a

[3]In *An Essay on the Principle of Population* (1798), British economist Thomas Robert Malthus (1766–1834), observing that population increased geometrically while consumer goods increased arithmetically, recommended sexual restraint as an alternative to the otherwise inevitable consequences of poverty and starvation.

given episode of the various confrontations that occur).

In short, it is a question of orienting ourselves to a conception of power which replaces the privilege of the law with the viewpoint of the objective, the privilege of prohibition with the viewpoint of tactical efficacy, the privilege of sovereignty with the analysis of a multiple and mobile field of force relations, wherein far-reaching, but never completely stable, effects of domination are produced. The strategical model, rather than the model based on law. And this, not out of a speculative choice or theoretical preference, but because in fact it is one of the essential traits of Western societies that the force relationships which for a long time had found expression in war, in every form of warfare, gradually became invested in the order of political power.

3. DOMAIN

Sexuality must not be described as a stubborn drive, by nature alien and of necessity disobedient to a power which exhausts itself trying to subdue it and often fails to control it entirely. It appears rather as an especially dense transfer point for relations of power: between men and women, young people and old people, parents and offspring, teachers and students, priests and laity, an administration and a population. Sexuality is not the most intractable element in power relations, but rather one of those endowed with the greatest instrumentality: useful for the greatest number of maneuvers and capable of serving as a point of support, as a linchpin, for the most varied strategies.

There is no single, all-encompassing strategy, valid for all of society and uniformly bearing on all the manifestations of sex. For example, the idea that there have been repeated attempts, by various means, to reduce all of sex to its reproductive function, its heterosexual and adult form, and its matrimonial legitimacy fails to take into account the manifold objectives aimed for, the manifold means employed in the different sexual politics concerned with the two sexes, the different age groups and social classes.

In a first approach to the problem, it seems that we can distinguish four great strategic unities which, beginning in the eighteenth century, formed specific mechanisms of knowledge and power centering on sex. These did not come into being fully developed at that time; but it was then that they took on a consistency and gained an effectiveness in the order of power, as well as a productivity in the order of knowledge, so that it is possible to describe them in their relative autonomy.

1. *A hysterization of women's bodies:* a threefold process whereby the feminine body was analyzed — qualified and disqualified — as being thoroughly saturated with sexuality; whereby it was integrated into the sphere of medical practices, by reason of a pathology intrinsic to it; whereby, finally, it was placed in organic communication with the social body (whose regulated fecundity it was supposed to ensure), the family space (of which it had to be a substantial and functional element), and the life of children (which it produced and had to guarantee, by virtue of a biologico-moral responsibility lasting through the entire period of the children's education): the Mother, with her negative image of "nervous woman," constituted the most visible form of this hysterization.

2. *A pedagogization of children's sex:* a double assertion that practically all children indulge or are prone to indulge in sexual activity; and that, being unwarranted, at the same time "natural" and "contrary to nature," this sexual activity posed physical and moral, individual and collective dangers; children were defined as "preliminary" sexual beings, on this side of sex, yet within it, astride a dangerous dividing line. Parents, families, educators, doctors, and eventually psychologists would have to take charge, in a continuous way, of this precious and perilous, dangerous and endangered sexual potential: this pedagogization was especially evident in the war against onanism, which in the West lasted nearly two centuries.

3. *A socialization of procreative behavior:* an economic socialization via all the incitements and restrictions, the "social" and fiscal measures brought to bear on the fertility of couples; a political socialization achieved through the "responsibilization" of couples with regard to the social body as a whole (which had to be limited or on the contrary reinvigorated), and a medical socialization carried out by attributing a pathogenic

value — for the individual and the species — to birth-control practices.

4. *A psychiatrization of perverse pleasure:* the sexual instinct was isolated as a separate biological and psychical instinct; a clinical analysis was made of all the forms of anomalies by which it could be afflicted; it was assigned a role of normalization or pathologization with respect to all behavior; and finally, a corrective technology was sought for these anomalies.

Four figures emerged from this preoccupation with sex, which mounted throughout the nineteenth century — four privileged objects of knowledge, which were also targets and anchorage points for the ventures of knowledge: the hysterical woman, the masturbating child, the Malthusian couple, and the perverse adult. Each of them corresponded to one of these strategies which, each in its own way, invested and made use of the sex of women, children, and men.

What was at issue in these strategies? A struggle against sexuality? Or were they part of an effort to gain control of it? An attempt to regulate it more effectively and mask its more indiscreet, conspicuous, and intractable aspects? A way of formulating only that measure of knowledge about it that was acceptable or useful? In actual fact, what was involved, rather, was the very production of sexuality. Sexuality must not be thought of as a kind of natural given which power tries to hold in check, or as an obscure domain which knowledge tries gradually to uncover. It is the name that can be given to a historical construct: not a furtive reality that is difficult to grasp, but a great surface network in which the stimulation of bodies, the intensification of pleasures, the incitement to discourse, the formation of special knowledges, the strengthening of controls and resistances, are linked to one another, in accordance with a few major strategies of knowledge and power.

It will be granted no doubt that relations of sex gave rise, in every society, to a *deployment of alliance:* a system of marriage, of fixation and development of kinship ties, of transmission of names and possessions. This deployment of alliance, with the mechanisms of constraint that ensured its existence and the complex knowledge it often required, lost some of its importance as economic processes and political structures could no longer rely on it as an adequate instrument or sufficient support. Particularly from the eighteenth century onward, Western societies created and deployed a new apparatus which was superimposed on the previous one, and which, without completely supplanting the latter, helped to reduce its importance. I am speaking of the *deployment of sexuality:* like the *deployment of alliance,* it connects up with the circuit of sexual partners, but in a completely different way. The two systems can be contrasted term by term. The deployment of alliance is built around a system of rules defining the permitted and the forbidden, the licit and the illicit, whereas the deployment of sexuality operates according to mobile, polymorphous, and contingent techniques of power. The deployment of alliance has as one of its chief objectives to reproduce the interplay of relations and maintain the law that governs them; the deployment of sexuality, on the other hand, engenders a continual extension of areas and forms of control. For the first, what is pertinent is the link between partners and definite statutes; the second is concerned with the sensations of the body, the quality of pleasures, and the nature of impressions, however tenuous or imperceptible these may be. Lastly, if the deployment of alliance is firmly tied to the economy due to the role it can play in the transmission or circulation of wealth, the deployment of sexuality is linked to the economy through numerous and subtle relays, the main one of which, however, is the body — the body that produces and consumes. In a word, the deployment of alliance is attuned to a homeostasis of the social body, which it has the function of maintaining; whence its privileged link with the law; whence too the fact that the important phase for it is "reproduction." The deployment of sexuality has its reason for being, not in reproducing itself, but in proliferating, innovating, annexing, creating, and penetrating bodies in an increasingly detailed way, and in controlling populations in an increasingly comprehensive way. We are compelled, then, to accept three or four hypotheses which run counter to the one on which the theme of a sexuality repressed by the modern forms of society is based: sexuality is tied to recent devices of power; it has been expanding at an increasing rate since the seventeenth century; the arrangement that has sustained it is not governed by reproduction; it has been linked from the outset with an intensification of the body — with its exploitation as an object of knowledge and an element in relations of power.

It is not exact to say that the deployment of sexuality supplanted the deployment of alliance. One can imagine that one day it will have replaced it. But as things stand at present, while it does tend to cover up the deployment of alliance, it has neither obliterated the latter nor rendered it useless. Moreover, historically it was around and on the basis of the deployment of alliance that the deployment of sexuality was constructed. First the practice of penance, then that of the examination of conscience and spiritual direction, was the formative nucleus: as we have seen, what was at issue to begin with at the tribunal of penance was sex insofar as it was the basis of relations; the questions posed had to do with the commerce allowed or forbidden (adultery, extramarital relations, relations with a person prohibited by blood or statute, the legitimate or illegitimate character of the act of sexual congress); then, coinciding with the new pastoral[4] and its application in seminaries, secondary schools, and convents, there was a gradual progression away from the problematic of relations toward a problematic of the "flesh," that is, of the body, sensation, the nature of pleasure, the more secret forms of enjoyment or acquiescence. "Sexuality" was taking shape, born of a technology of power that was originally focused on alliance. Since then, it has not ceased to operate in conjunction with a system of alliance on which it has depended for support. The family cell, in the form in which it came to be valued in the course of the eighteenth century, made it possible for the main elements of the deployment of sexuality (the feminine body, infantile precocity, the regulation of births, and to a lesser extent no doubt, the specification of the perverted) to develop along its two primary dimensions: the husband-wife axis and the parents-children axis. The family, in its contemporary form, must not be understood as a social, economic, and political structure of alliance that excludes or at least restrains sexuality, that diminishes it as much as possible, preserving only its useful functions. On the contrary, its role is to anchor sexuality and provide it with a permanent support. It ensures the production of a sexuality that is not homogeneous with the privileges of alliance, while making it possible for the systems of alliance to be imbued with a new tactic of power which they would otherwise be impervious to. The family is the interchange of sexuality and alliance: it conveys the law and the juridical dimension in the deployment of sexuality; and it conveys the economy of pleasure and the intensity of sensations in the regime of alliance.

This interpenetration of the deployment of alliance and that of sexuality in the form of the family allows us to understand a number of facts: that since the eighteenth century the family has become an obligatory locus of affects, feelings, love; that sexuality has its privileged point of development in the family; that for this reason sexuality is "incestuous" from the start. It may be that in societies where the mechanisms of alliance predominate, prohibition of incest is a functionally indispensable rule. But in a society such as ours, where the family is the most active site of sexuality, and where it is doubtless the exigencies of the latter which maintain and prolong its existence, incest — for different reasons altogether and in a completely different way — occupies a central place; it is constantly being solicited and refused; it is an object of obsession and attraction, a dreadful secret and an indispensable pivot. It is manifested as a thing that is strictly forbidden in the family insofar as the latter functions as a deployment of alliance; but it is also a thing that is continuously demanded in order for the family to be a hotbed of constant sexual incitement. If for more than a century the West has displayed such a strong interest in the prohibition of incest, if more or less by common accord it has been seen as a social universal and one of the points through which every society is obliged to pass on the way to becoming a culture, perhaps this is because it was found to be a means of self-defense, not against an incestuous desire, but against the

[4]Pastoral refers to the duties of priests.

expansion and the implications of this deployment of sexuality which had been set up, but which, among its many benefits, had the disadvantage of ignoring the laws and juridical forms of alliance. By asserting that all societies without exception, and consequently our own, were subject to this rule of rules, one guaranteed that this deployment of sexuality, whose strange effects were beginning to be felt — among them, the affective intensification of the family space — would not be able to escape from the grand and ancient system of alliance.[5] Thus the law would be secure, even in the new mechanics of power. For this is the paradox of a society which, from the eighteenth century to the present, has created so many technologies of power that are foreign to the concept of law: it fears the effects and proliferations of those technologies and attempts to recode them in forms of law. If one considers the threshold of all culture to be prohibited incest, then sexuality has been, from the dawn of time, under the sway of law and right. By devoting so much effort to an endless reworking of the transcultural theory of the incest taboo, anthropology has proved worthy of the whole modern deployment of sexuality and the theoretical discourses it generates.

What has taken place since the seventeenth century can be interpreted in the following manner: the deployment of sexuality which first developed on the fringes of familial institutions (in the direction of conscience and pedagogy, for example) gradually became focused on the family: the alien, irreducible, and even perilous effects it held in store for the deployment of alliance (an awareness of this danger was evidenced in the criticism often directed at the indiscretion of the directors, and in the entire controversy, which occurred somewhat later, over the private or public, institutional or familial education of children[6]) were

absorbed by the family, a family that was reorganized, restricted no doubt, and in any case intensified in comparison with the functions it formerly exercised in the deployment of alliance. In the family, parents and relatives became the chief agents of a deployment of sexuality which drew its outside support from doctors, educators, and later psychiatrists, and which began by competing with the relations of alliance but soon "psychologized" or "psychiatrized" the latter. Then these new personages made their appearance: the nervous woman, the frigid wife, the indifferent mother — or worse, the mother beset by murderous obsessions — the impotent, sadistic, perverse husband, the hysterical or neurasthenic girl, the precocious and already exhausted child, and the young homosexual who rejects marriage or neglects his wife. These were the combined figures of an alliance gone bad and an abnormal sexuality; they were the means by which the disturbing factors of the latter were brought into the former; and yet they also provided an opportunity for the alliance system to assert its prerogatives in the order of sexuality. Then a pressing demand emanated from the family: a plea for help in reconciling these unfortunate conflicts between sexuality and alliance; and, caught in the grip of this deployment of sexuality which had invested it from without, contributing to its solidification into its modern form, the family broadcast the long complaint of its sexual suffering to doctors, educators, psychiatrists, priests, and pastors, to all the "experts" who would listen. It was as if it had suddenly discovered the dreadful secret of what had always been hinted at and inculcated in it: the family, the keystone of alliance, was the germ of all the misfortunes of sex. And lo and behold, from the mid-nineteenth century onward, the family engaged in searching out the slightest traces of sexuality in its midst, wrenching from itself the most difficult confessions, soliciting an audience with everyone who might know something about the matter, and opening itself unreservedly to endless examination. The family was the crystal in the deployment of sexuality: it seemed to be the source of a sexuality which it actually only reflected and diffracted. By virtue of its permeability, and through that process of reflections to the outside, it became one of the most valuable tactical components of the deployment.

[5]Foucault refers to the theory of anthropologist Claude Lévi-Strauss that the incest-taboo is universal within human cultures, indeed defines human culture. See Lévi-Strauss, p. 859.
[6]Molière's *Tartuffe* and Jakob Michael Lenz's *Tutor*, separated by more than a century, both depict the interference of the deployment of sexuality in the family organization, apropos of spiritual direction in *Tartuffe* and education in *The Tutor*. [Foucault]

Monique Wittig

1935–2003

Born in Dannemarie in southern Alsace, the daughter of the poet Henri Dubois, Monique attended the Sorbonne at the University Paris, earning a degree in Oriental languages. She was one of the founders of the Mouvement de Liberation Féminine, and like many of her generation, her revolutionary politics were formed by the utopian dreams of May 1968 (when students and workers united in a strike intended to bring on a new French revolution). Wittig began by writing experimental novels, such as The Opoponax *(1964),* Les Guérillères *(1969),* The Lesbian Body *(1975), and* Across the Acheron *(1987). In each of these works, the grammar and syntax of narrative is broken down and reconstructed in ways that reflect the sexual and social reconstructions performed by the characters. Each text depicts a patriarchal society whose norms are violently rejected by female characters, who re-create society so that the power and language infrastructures allow for feminine/homosexual participation. Wittig received her Ph.D. from the École des Hautes Études en Sciences Sociales in Paris, where she studied under Gérard Genette. After publishing* Lesbian Peoples: Material for a Dictionary *(with her partner, Sande Zeig, 1976), Wittig emigrated to the United States, where she lectured at many universities, including Berkeley, Duke, New York University, and Vassar, until she took her final position in 1990 as a professor of French and Women's Studies at the University of Arizona. She died of a sudden heart attack in January 2003. The following essay, "One Is Not Born a Woman," takes its title from Simone de Beauvoir (with whom Wittig collaborated on the periodical* Questions Féministes*), and was originally published in* Feminist Issues *1, no. 2 (1981).*

One Is Not Born a Woman

A materialist feminist[1] approach to women's oppression destroys the idea that women are a "natural group": "a racial group of a special kind, a group perceived *as natural*, a group of men considered as materially specific in their bodies."[2] What the analysis accomplishes on the level of ideas, practice makes actual at the level of facts: by its very existence, lesbian society destroys the artificial (social) fact constituting women as a "natural group." A lesbian society[3] pragmatically reveals that the division from men of which women have been the object is a political one and shows that we have been ideologically rebuilt into a "natural group." In the case of women, ideology goes far since our bodies as well as our minds are the product of this manipulation. We have been compelled in our bodies and in our minds to correspond, feature by feature, with the *idea* of nature that has been established for us. Distorted to such an extent that our deformed body is what they call "natural," what is supposed

[1] Christine Delphy, "Pour un féminisme matérialiste," *L'Arc* 61 (1975). Translated as "For a Materialist Feminism," *Feminist Issues* 1, no. 2 (Winter 1981). [Wittig]

[2] Colette Guillaumin, "Race et nature: système des marques, idée de groupe naturel et rapports sociaux," *Pluriel* 11 (1977). Translated as "Race and Nature: The System of Marks: The Idea of a Natural Group and Social Relationships," *Feminist Issues* 8, no. 2 (Fall 1988). [Wittig]

[3] I use the word *society* with an extended anthropological meaning: strictly speaking, it does not refer to societies, in that lesbian societies do not exist completely autonomously from heterosexual social systems. [Wittig]

to exist as such before oppression. Distorted to such an extent that in the end oppression seems to be a consequence of this "nature" within ourselves (a nature which is only an *idea*). What a materialist analysis does by reasoning, a lesbian society accomplishes practically: not only is there no natural group "women" (we lesbians are living proof of it), but as individuals as well we question "woman," which for us, as for Simone de Beauvoir, is only a myth. She said: "One is not born, but becomes a woman. No biological, psychological, or economic fate determines the figure that the human female presents in society: it is civilization as a whole that produces this creature, intermediate between male and eunuch, which is described as feminine."[4]

However, most of the feminists and lesbian-feminists in America and elsewhere still believe that the basis of women's oppression *is biological as well as* historical. Some of them even claim to find their sources in Simone de Beauvoir.[5] The belief in mother right and in a "prehistory" when women created civilization (because of a biological predisposition) while the coarse and brutal men hunted (because of a biological predisposition) is symmetrical with the biologizing interpretation of history produced up to now by the class of men. It is still the same method of finding in women and men a biological explanation of their division, outside of social facts. For me this could never constitute a lesbian approach to women's oppression, since it assumes that the basis of society or the beginning of society lies in heterosexuality. Matriarchy is no less heterosexual than patriarchy: it is only the sex of the oppressor that changes. Furthermore, not only is this conception still imprisoned in the categories of sex (woman and man), but it holds onto the idea that the capacity to give birth (biology) is what defines a woman. Although practical facts and ways of living contradict this theory in lesbian society, there are lesbians who affirm that "women and men are different species or races

(the words are used interchangeably): men are biologically inferior to women; male violence is a biological inevitability . . ."[6] By doing this, by admitting that there is a "natural" division between women and men, we naturalize history, we assume that "men" and "women" have always existed and will always exist. Not only do we naturalize history, but also consequently we naturalize the social phenomena which express our oppression, making change impossible. For example, instead of seeing giving birth as a forced production, we see it as a "natural," "biological" process, forgetting that in our societies births are planned (demography), forgetting that we ourselves are programmed to produce children, while this is the only social activity "short of war"[7] that presents such a great danger of death. Thus, as long as we will be "unable to abandon by will or impulse a lifelong and centuries-old commitment to childbearing as *the* female creative act,"[8] gaining control of the production of children will mean much more than the mere control of the material means of this production: women will have to abstract themselves from the definition "woman" which is imposed upon them.

A materialist feminist approach shows that what we take for the cause or origin of oppression is in fact only the *mark*[9] imposed by the oppressor: the "myth of woman,"[10] plus its material effects and manifestations in the appropriated consciousness and bodies of women. Thus, this mark does not predate oppression: Colette Guillaumin has shown that before the socioeconomic reality of black slavery, the concept of race did not exist, at least not in its modern meaning, since it was applied to the lineage of families. However, now, race, exactly like sex, is taken as an "immediate

---

[4]Simone de Beauvoir, *The Second Sex* (New York: Bantam, 1952): 249. [Wittig] See de Beauvoir, p. 673.

[5][Kathie Sarahchild, ed.] *Feminist Revolution: Redstockings of the Women's Liberation Movement* (New York: Random House, 1978): 18. [Wittig]

[6]Andrea Dworkin, "Biological Superiority: The World's Most Dangerous and Deadly Idea," *Heresies* 6 (1989): 46. [Wittig]

[7]Ti-Grace Atkinson, *Amazon Odyssey* (New York: Links, 1974): 15. [Wittig]

[8]Dworkin, op. cit. [Wittig]

[9]Guillaumin, op. cit. [Wittig]

[10]Beauvoir, op. cit. [Wittig]

given," a "sensible given," "physical features," belonging to a natural order. But what we believe to be a physical and direct perception is only a sophisticated and mythic construction, an "imaginary formation,"[11] which reinterprets physical features (in themselves as neutral as any others but marked by the social system) through the network of relationships in which they are perceived. (They are seen as *black*, therefore they *are* black; they are seen as *women*, therefore, they *are* women. But before being *seen* that way, they first had to be *made* that way.) Lesbians should always remember and acknowledge how "unnatural," compelling, totally oppressive, and destructive being "woman" was for us in the old days before the women's liberation movement. It was a political constraint, and those who resisted it were accused of not being "real" women. But then we were proud of it, since in the accusation there was already something like a shadow of victory: the avowal by the oppressor that "woman" is not something that goes without saying, since to be one, one has to be a "real" one. We were at the same time accused of wanting to be men. Today this double accusation has been taken up again with enthusiasm in the context of the women's liberation movement by some feminists and also, alas, by some lesbians whose political goal seems somehow to be becoming more and more "feminine." To refuse to be a woman, however, does not mean that one has to become a man. Besides, if we take as an example the perfect "butch," the classic example which provokes the most horror, whom Proust would have called a woman/man, how is her alienation different from that of someone who wants to become a woman? Tweedledum and Tweedledee.[12] At least for a woman, wanting to become a man proves that she has escaped her initial programming. But even if she would like to, with all her strength, she cannot become a man. For becoming a man would demand from a woman not only a man's external appearance but his consciousness as well, that is, the consciousness of

one who disposes by right of at least two "natural" slaves during his life span. This is impossible, and one feature of lesbian oppression consists precisely of making women out of reach for us, since women belong to men. Thus a lesbian *has to* be something else, a not-woman, a not-man, a product of society, not a product of nature, for there is no nature in society.

The refusal to become (or to remain) heterosexual always meant to refuse to become a man or a woman, consciously or not. For a lesbian this goes further than the refusal of the *role* "woman." It is the refusal of the economic, ideological, and political power of a man. This, we lesbians, and nonlesbians as well, knew before the beginning of the lesbian and feminist movement. However, as Andrea Dworkin emphasizes, many lesbians recently "have increasingly tried to transform the very ideology that has enslaved us into a dynamic, religious, psychologically compelling celebration of female biological potential."[13] Thus, some avenues of the feminist and lesbian movement lead us back to the myth of woman which was created by men especially for us, and with it we sink back into a natural group. Having stood up to fight for a sexless society,[14] we now find ourselves entrapped in the familiar deadlock of "woman is wonderful." Simone de Beauvoir underlined particularly the false consciousness which consists of selecting among the features of the myth (that women are different from men) those which look good and using them as a definition for women. What the concept "woman is wonderful" accomplishes is that it retains for defining women the best features (best according to whom?) which oppression has granted us, and it does not radically question the categories "man" and "woman," which are political categories and not natural givens. It puts us in a position of fighting within the class "women" not as the other classes do, for the disappearance of our class, but for the defense of "women" and its reenforcement. It leads us to develop with complacency

---

[11]Guillaumin, op. cit. [Wittig]
[12]Identical twins in Lewis Carroll's *Through the Looking Glass* (1872).

[13]Dworkin, op. cit. [Wittig]
[14]Atkinson, p. 6: "If feminism has any logic at all, it must be working for a sexless society." [Wittig]

"new" theories about our specificity: thus, we call our passivity "nonviolence," when the main and emergent point for us is to fight our passivity (our fear, rather, a justified one). The ambiguity of the term "feminist" sums up the whole situation. What does "feminist" mean? Feminist is formed with the word "femme," "woman," and means: someone who fights for women. For many of us it means someone who fights for women as a class and for the disappearance of this class. For many others it means someone who fights for woman and her defense — for the myth, then, and its reenforcement. But why was the word "feminist" chosen if it retains the least ambiguity? We chose to call ourselves "feminists" ten years ago, not in order to support or reenforce the myth of woman, nor to identify ourselves with the oppressor's definition of us, but rather to affirm that our movement had a history and to emphasize the political link with the old feminist movement.

It is, then, this movement that we can put in question for the meaning that it gave to feminism. It so happens that feminism in the last century could never resolve its contradictions on the subject of nature/culture, woman/society. Women started to fight for themselves as a group and rightly considered that they shared common features as a result of oppression. But for them these features were natural and biological rather than social. They went so far as to adopt the Darwinist theory of evolution. They did not believe like Darwin, however, "that women were less evolved than men, but they did believe that male and female natures had diverged in the course of evolutionary development and that society at large reflected this polarization."[15] "The failure of early feminism was that it only attacked the Darwinist charge of female inferiority, while accepting the foundations of this charge — namely, the view of woman as 'unique.'"[16] And finally it was women scholars — and not feminists — who scientifically destroyed this theory. But the early feminists had failed to regard history as a dynamic process which develops from conflicts of interests.

Furthermore, they still believed as men do that the cause (origin) of their oppression lay within themselves. And therefore after some astonishing victories the feminists of this first front found themselves at an impasse out of a lack of reasons to fight. They upheld the illogical principle of "equality in difference," an idea now being born again. They fell back into the trap which threatens us once again: the myth of woman.

Thus it is our historical task, and only ours, to define what we call oppression in materialist terms, to make it evident that women are a class, which is to say that the category "woman" as well as the category "man" are political and economic categories not eternal ones. Our fight aims to suppress men as a class, not through a genocidal, but a political struggle. Once the class "men" disappears, "women" as a class will disappear as well, for there are no slaves without masters. Our first task, it seems, is to always thoroughly dissociate "women" (the class within which we fight) and "woman," the myth. For "woman" does not exist for us: it is only an imaginary formation,[17] while "women" is the product of a social relationship. We felt this strongly when everywhere we refused to be called a "*woman's* liberation movement." Furthermore, we have to destroy the myth inside and outside ourselves. "Woman" is not each one of us, but the political and ideological formation which negates "women" (the product of a relation of exploitation). "Woman" is there to confuse us, to hide the reality "women." In order to be aware of being a class and to become a class we first have to kill the myth of "woman" including its most seductive aspects (I think about Virginia Woolf when she said the first task of a woman writer is to kill "the angel in the house").[18] But to become a class we do not have to suppress our individual selves, and since no individual can be reduced to her/his oppression

[15]Rosalind Rosenberg, "In Search of Women's Nature," *Feminist Studies* 3, nos. 1–2 (1975): 144. [Wittig]
[16]Rosenberg, 146. [Wittig]

[17]Wittig suggests that "woman" as a concept or myth is like the unitary "self" in Lacan's "mirror stage," a wish-fulfilling product of the field of the Imaginary. See Lacan, p. 1122.
[18]"The angel in the house" is a personification of Victorian womanhood, as in the 1854 poem of the same name by Coventry Patmore (1823– 1896); Woolf's attack on the concept appears in her essay "Professions for Women" (1942).

we are also confronted with the historical necessity of constituting ourselves as the individual subjects of our history as well. I believe this is the reason why all these attempts at "new" definitions of woman are blossoming now. What is at stake (and of course not only for women) is an individual definition as well as a class definition. For once one has acknowledged oppression, one needs to know and experience the fact that one can constitute oneself as a subject (as opposed to an object of oppression), that one can become *someone* in spite of oppression, that one has one's own identity. There is no possible fight for someone deprived of an identity, no internal motivation for fighting, since, although I can fight only with others, first I fight for myself.

The question of the individual subject is historically a difficult one for everybody. Marxism, the last avatar of materialism, the science which has politically formed us, does not want to hear anything about a "subject." Marxism has rejected the transcendental subject, the subject as constitutive of knowledge, the "pure" consciousness. All that thinks per se, before all experience, has ended up in the garbage can of history, because it claimed to exist outside matter, prior to matter, and needed God, spirit, or soul to exist in such a way. This is what is called "idealism." As for individuals, they are only the product of social relations, therefore their consciousness can only be "alienated." (Marx, in *The German Ideology*,[19] says precisely that individuals of the dominating class are also alienated, although they are the direct producers of the ideas that alienate the classes oppressed by them. But since they draw visible advantages from their own alienation they can bear it without too much suffering.) There exists such a thing as class consciousness, but a consciousness which does not refer to a particular subject, except as participating in general conditions of exploitation at the same time as the other subjects of their class, all sharing the same consciousness. As for the practical class problem — outside of the class problems as traditionally defined — that one could encounter (for example, sexual problems), they

were considered "bourgeois" problems that would disappear with the final victory of the class struggle. "Individualistic," "subjectivist," "petit bourgeois," these were the labels given to any person who had shown problems which could not be reduced to the "class struggle" itself.

Thus Marxism has denied the members of oppressed classes the attribute of being a subject. In doing this, Marxism, because of the ideological and political power this "revolutionary science" immediately exercised upon the workers' movement and all other political groups, has prevented all categories of oppressed peoples from constituting themselves historically as subjects (subjects of their struggle, for example). This means that the "masses" did not fight for themselves but for *the* party or its organizations. And when an economic transformation took place (end of private property, constitution of the socialist state), no revolutionary change took place within the new society, because the people themselves did not change.

For women, Marxism had two results. It prevented them from being aware that they are a class and therefore from constituting themselves as a class for a very long time, by leaving the relation "women/men" outside of the social order, by turning it into a natural relation, doubtless for Marxists the only one, along with the relation of mothers to children, to be seen this way, and by hiding the class conflict between men and women behind a natural division of labor (*The German Ideology*). This concerns the theoretical (ideological) level. On the practical level, Lenin, *the* party, all the communist parties up to now, including all the most radical political groups, have always reacted to any attempt on the part of women to reflect and form groups based on their own class problem with an accusation of divisiveness. By uniting, we women are dividing the strength of the people. This means that for the Marxists women *belong* either to the bourgeois class or to the proletariat class, in other words, to the men of these classes. In addition, Marxist theory does not allow women any more than other classes of oppressed people to constitute themselves as historical subjects, because Marxism does not take into account the fact that a class also consists of individuals one by one. Class consciousness is not enough. We must

[19]See Marx, p. 397.

try to understand philosophically (politically) these concepts of "subject" and "class consciousness" and how they work in relation to our history. When we discover that women are the objects of oppression and appropriation, at the very moment that we become able to perceive this, we become subjects in the sense of cognitive subjects, through an operation of abstraction. Consciousness of oppression is not only a reaction to (fight against) oppression. It is also the whole conceptual reevaluation of the social world, its whole reorganization with new concepts, from the point of view of oppression. It is what I would call the science of oppression created by the oppressed. This operation of understanding reality has to be undertaken by every one of us: call it a subjective, cognitive practice. The movement back and forth between the levels of reality (the conceptual reality and the material reality of oppression, which are both social realities) is accomplished through language.

It is we who historically must undertake the task of defining the individual subject in materialist terms. This certainly seems to be an impossibility since materialism and subjectivity have always been mutually exclusive. Nevertheless, and rather than despairing of ever understanding, we must recognize the *need* to reach subjectivity in the abandonment by many of us to the myth "woman" (the myth of woman being only a snare that holds us up). This real necessity for everyone to exist as an individual, as well as a member of a class, is perhaps the first condition for the accomplishment of a revolution, without which there can be no real fight or transformation. But the opposite is also true; without class and class consciousness there are no real subjects, only alienated individuals. For women to answer the question of the individual subject in materialist terms is first to show, as the lesbians and feminists did, that supposedly "subjective," "individual," "private" problems are in fact social problems, class problems; that sexuality is not for women an individual and subjective expression, but a social institution of violence. But once we have shown that all so-called personal problems are in fact class problems, we will still be left with the question of the subject of each singular woman — not the myth, but each one of us.

At this point, let us say that a new personal and subjective definition for all humankind can only be found beyond the categories of sex (woman and man) and that the advent of individual subjects demands first destroying the categories of sex, ending the use of them, and rejecting all sciences which still use these categories as their fundamentals (practically all social sciences).

To destroy "woman" does not mean that we aim, short of physical destruction, to destroy lesbianism simultaneously with the categories of sex, because lesbianism provides for the moment the only social form in which we can live freely. Lesbian is the only concept I know of which is beyond the categories of sex (woman and man), because the designated subject (lesbian) is *not* a woman, either economically, or politically, or ideologically. For what makes a woman is a specific social relation to a man, a relation that we have previously called servitude,[20] a relation which implies personal and physical obligation as well as economic obligation ("forced residence,"[21] domestic corvée,[22] conjugal duties, unlimited production of children, etc.), a relation which lesbians escape by refusing to become or to stay heterosexual. We are escapees from our class in the same way as the American runaway slaves were when escaping slavery and becoming free. For us this is an absolute necessity; our survival demands that we contribute all our strength to the destruction of the class of women within which men appropriate women. This can be accomplished only by the destruction of heterosexuality as a social system which is based on the oppression of women by men and which produces the doctrine of the difference between the sexes to justify this oppression.

[20]In an article published in *L'Idiot international* (May 1970), whose original title was "Pour un mouvement de libération des femmes." [Wittig]
[21]Christiane Rochefort, *Les Stances à Sophie* (Paris: Grasset, 1963). [Wittig]
[22]A tax under the French monarchy exacted in terms of forced labor on public works.

Hélène Cixous

b. 1937

Hélène Cixous, one of the most versatile and radical voices in contemporary French feminism, was born in Oran, Algeria. A brilliant student, she received her agrégation *in English in 1959 and her* Docteur en lettres *in 1968, the year that also saw her participation in the May student uprisings. Cixous taught at the University of Bordeaux (1962), the Sorbonne (1965–67), Nanterre (1967), and the University of Paris VIII-Vincennes (now at Saint-Denis), where she is a professor of English literature. In 1970 with Gérard Genette and Tzvetan Todorov she founded the structuralist journal* Poétique, *and in 1974 established a center for women's studies at the University of Paris VIII. The work of Shakespeare and James Joyce (about whom she wrote her doctoral thesis), Heinrich von Kleist and Franz Kafka, Arthur Rimbaud and the Brazilian writer Clarice Lispector, Jacques Derrida and Jacques Lacan, has been particularly important to her. Cixous has written short stories (Le Prénom de Dieu, 1966), novels (Dédans, 1969, which won the Prix Médicis), and a great deal of literary and cultural criticism. Some of her other writings are* Portrait of Dora *(1976),* The Newly Born Woman *(1975; with Catherine Clément), and* La Venue à l'écriture *(1977; with Annie LeClerc and Madeleine Gagnon). Her most recent fiction includes* La Jour oú je n'étais pas là *(2000),* Benjamin à Montaigne: il ne faut pas le dire *(2001),* Rêve je te dis *(2003), and* Neuter *(2004). Her most recent criticism and theory in English include* Writing Differences: Readings from the Seminar of Hélène Cixous *(1988),* Readings: The Poetics of Blanchot, Joyce, Kafka, Kleist, Lispector and Tsvetayeva *(1991),* Coming to Writing and Other Essays *(1991),* The Hélène Cixous Reader *(1994),* Manna *(1994),* Stigmata: Escaping Texts *(1998), and* Portrait of Jacques Derrida as a Young, Jewish Saint *(2004). "The Laugh of the Medusa," first published in* L'Arc *in 1975, was translated for the first volume of the feminist journal* Signs *(1976).*

The Laugh of the Medusa

I shall speak about women's writing: about *what it will do.* Woman must write her self: must write about women and bring women to writing, from which they have been driven away as violently as from their bodies — for the same reasons, by the same law, with the same fatal goal. Woman must put herself into the text — as into the world and into history — by her own movement.

The future must no longer be determined by the past. I do not deny that the effects of the past are still with us. But I refuse to strengthen them by repeating them, to confer upon them an irremovability the equivalent of destiny, to confuse the biological and the cultural. Anticipation is imperative.

Since these reflections are taking shape in an area just on the point of being discovered, they necessarily bear the mark of our time — a time during which the new breaks away from the old, and, more precisely, the (feminine) new from the old (*la nouvelle de l'ancien*). Thus, as there are no grounds for establishing a discourse, but rather an arid millennial ground to break, what I say has at least two sides and two aims: to break up, to destroy; and to foresee the unforeseeable, to project.

Translated by Keith Cohen and Paula Cohen. The essay's title alludes to Freud's speculation about the head of Medusa, p. 533.

I write this as a woman, toward women. When I say "woman," I'm speaking of woman in her inevitable struggle against conventional man; and of a universal woman subject who must bring women to their senses and to their meaning in history. But first it must be said that in spite of the enormity of the repression that has kept them in the "dark" — that dark which people have been trying to make them accept as their attribute — there is, at this time, no general woman, no one typical woman. What they have *in common* I will say. But what strikes me is the infinite richness of their individual constitutions: you can't talk about *a* female sexuality, uniform, homogeneous, classifiable into codes — any more than you can talk about one unconscious resembling another. Women's imaginary[1] is inexhaustible, like music, painting, writing: their stream of phantasms is incredible.

I have been amazed more than once by a description a woman gave me of a world all her own which she had been secretly haunting since early childhood. A world of searching, the elaboration of a knowledge, on the basis of a systematic experimentation with the bodily functions, a passionate and precise interrogation of her erotogeneity. This practice, extraordinarily rich and inventive, in particular as concerns masturbation, is prolonged or accompanied by a production of forms, a veritable aesthetic activity, each stage of rapture inscribing a resonant vision, a composition, something beautiful. Beauty will no longer be forbidden.

I wished that that woman would write and proclaim this unique empire so that other women, other unacknowledged sovereigns, might exclaim: I, too, overflow; my desires have invented new desires, my body knows unheard-of songs. Time and again, I, too, have felt so full of luminous torrents that I could burst — burst with forms much more beautiful than those which are put up in frames and sold for a stinking fortune. And I, too,

said nothing, showed nothing; I didn't open my mouth, I didn't repaint my half of the world. I was ashamed. I was afraid, and I swallowed my shame and my fear. I said to myself: You are mad! What's the meaning of these waves, these floods, these outbursts? Where is the ebullient, infinite woman who, immersed as she was in her naiveté, kept in the dark about herself, led into self-disdain by the great arm of parental-conjugal phallocentrism, hasn't been ashamed of her strength? Who, surprised and horrified by the fantastic tumult of her drives (for she was made to believe that a well-adjusted normal woman has a . . . divine composure), hasn't accused herself of being a monster? Who, feeling a funny desire stirring inside her (to sing, to write, to dare to speak, in short, to bring out something new), hasn't thought she was sick? Well, her shameful sickness is that she resists death, that she makes trouble.

And why don't you write? Write! Writing is for you, you are for you; your body is yours, take it. I know why you haven't written. (And why I didn't write before the age of twenty-seven.) Because writing is at once too high, too great for you, it's reserved for the great — that is, for "great men"; and it's "silly." Besides, you've written a little, but in secret. And it wasn't good, because it was in secret, and because you punished yourself for writing, because you didn't go all the way; or because you wrote, irresistibly, as when we would masturbate in secret, not to go further, but to attenuate the tension a bit, just enough to take the edge off. And then as soon as we come, we go and make ourselves feel guilty — so as to be forgiven; or to forget, to bury it until the next time.

Write, let no one hold you back, let nothing stop you; not man; not the imbecilic capitalist machinery, in which publishing houses are the crafty, obsequious relayers of imperatives handed down by an economy that works against us and off our backs; and not *yourself*. Smug-faced readers, managing editors, and big bosses don't like the true texts of women — female-sexed texts. That kind scares them.

I write woman: woman must write woman. And man, man. So only an oblique consideration will be found here of man; it's up to him to say where his masculinity and femininity are at: this

---

[1]The imaginary is a "field" in the psychology of Jacques Lacan. Cixous refers later to the other Lacanian field, the symbolic, and to Lack (*manque*), the sense of absence that is the basis of unconscious desire. See the introduction to Psychoanalytic Theory, p. 1106.

will concern us once men have opened their eyes and seen themselves clearly.[2]

Now women return from afar, from always: from "without," from the heath where witches are kept alive; from below, from beyond "culture"; from their childhood which men have been trying desperately to make them forget, condemning it to "eternal rest." The little girls and their "ill-mannered" bodies immured, well-preserved, intact unto themselves, in the mirror. Frigidified. But are they ever seething underneath! What an effort it takes — there's no end to it — for the sex cops to bar their threatening return. Such a display of forces on both sides that the struggle has for centuries been immobilized in the trembling equilibrium of a deadlock.

Here they are, returning, arriving over and again, because the unconscious is impregnable. They have wandered around in circles, confined to the narrow room in which they've been given a deadly brainwashing. You can incarcerate them, slow them down, get away with the old Apartheid routine, but for a time only. As soon as they begin to speak, at the same time as they're taught their name, they can be taught that their territory is black: because you are Africa, you are black. Your continent is dark. Dark is dangerous. You can't see anything in the dark, you're afraid. Don't move, you might fall. Most of all, don't go into the forest. And so we have internalized this horror of the dark.

[2]Men still have everything to say about their sexuality, and everything to write. For what they have said so far, for the most part, stems from the opposition activity/passivity, from the power relation between a fantasized obligatory virility meant to invade, to colonize, and the consequential phantasm of woman as a "dark continent" to penetrate and to "pacify." (We know what "pacify" means in terms of scotomizing the other and misrecognizing the self.) Conquering her, they've made haste to depart from her borders, to get out of sight, out of body. The way man has of getting out of himself and into her whom he takes not for the other but for his own, deprives him, he knows, of his own bodily territory. One can understand how man, confusing himself with his penis and rushing in for the attack, might feel resentment and fear of being "taken" by the woman, of being lost in her, absorbed, or alone. [Cixous]

Men have committed the greatest crime against women. Insidiously, violently, they have led them to hate women, to be their own enemies, to mobilize their immense strength against themselves, to be the executants of their virile needs. They have made for women an antinarcissism! A narcissism which loves itself only to be loved for what women haven't got! They have constructed the infamous logic of antilove.

We the precocious, we the repressed of culture, our lovely mouths gagged with pollen, our wind knocked out of us, we the labyrinths, the ladders, the trampled spaces, the bevies — we are black and we are beautiful.

We're stormy, and that which is ours breaks loose from us without our fearing any debilitation. Our glances, our smiles, are spent; laughs exude from all our mouths; our blood flows and we extend ourselves without ever reaching an end; we never hold back our thoughts, our signs, our writing; and we're not afraid of lacking.

What happiness for us who are omitted, brushed aside at the scene of inheritances; we inspire ourselves and we expire without running out of breath, we are everywhere!

From now on, who, if we say so, can say no to us? We've come back from always.

It is time to liberate the New Woman from the Old by coming to know her — by loving her for getting by, for getting beyond the Old without delay, by going out ahead of what the New Woman will be, as an arrow quits the bow with a movement that gathers and separates the vibrations musically, in order to be more than her self.

I say that we must, for, with a few rare exceptions, there has not yet been any writing that inscribes femininity; exceptions so rare, in fact, that, after plowing through literature across languages, cultures, and ages,[3] one can only be startled at this vain scouting mission. It is well known that the number of women writers (while having increased very slightly from the nineteenth century on) has always been ridiculously small. This is a useless and deceptive fact unless from their

[3]I am speaking here only of the place "reserved" for women by the Western world. [Cixous]

species of female writers we do not first deduct the immense majority whose workmanship is in no way different from male writing, and which either obscures women or reproduces the classic representations of women (as sensitive — intuitive — dreamy, etc.).[4]

Let me insert here a parenthetical remark. I mean it when I speak of male writing. I maintain unequivocally that there is such a thing as *marked* writing; that, until now, far more extensively and repressively than is ever suspected or admitted, writing has been run by a libidinal and cultural — hence political, typically masculine — economy; that this is a locus where the repression of women has been perpetuated, over and over, more or less consciously, and in a manner that's frightening since it's often hidden or adorned with the mystifying charms of fiction; that this locus has grossly exaggerated all the signs of sexual opposition (and not sexual difference), where woman has never *her* turn to speak — this being all the more serious and unpardonable in that writing is precisely *the very possibility of change*, the space that can serve as a springboard for subversive thought, the precursory movement of a transformation of social and cultural structures.

Nearly the entire history of writing is confounded with the history of reason, of which it is at once the effect, the support, and one of the privileged alibis. It has been one with the phallocentric tradition. It is indeed that same self-admiring, self-stimulating, self-congratulatory phallocentrism.

With some exceptions, for there have been failures — and if it weren't for them, I wouldn't be writing (I-woman, escapee) — in that enormous machine that has been operating and turning out its "truth" for centuries. There have been poets who would go to any lengths to slip something by at odds with tradition — men capable of loving love and hence capable of loving others and of wanting them, of imagining the woman who would hold out against oppression and constitute herself as a superb, equal, hence "impossible" subject, untenable in a real social framework. Such a woman the poet could desire only by breaking the codes that negate her. Her appearance would necessarily bring on, if not revolution — for the bastion was supposed to be immutable — at least harrowing explosions. At times it is in the fissure caused by an earthquake, through that radical mutation of things brought on by a material upheaval when every structure is for a moment thrown off balance and an ephemeral wildness sweeps order away, that the poet slips something by, for a brief span, of woman. Thus did Kleist expend himself in his yearning for the existence of sister-lovers, maternal daughters, mother-sisters, who never hung their heads in shame. Once the palace of magistrates is restored, it's time to pay: immediate bloody death to the uncontrollable elements.

But only the poets — not the novelists, allies of representationalism. Because poetry involves gaining strength through the unconscious and because the unconscious, that other limitless country, is the place where the repressed manage to survive: women, or as Hoffmann would say, fairies.

She must write her self, because this is the invention of a *new insurgent* writing which, when the moment of her liberation has come, will allow her to carry out the indispensable ruptures and transformations in her history, first at two levels that cannot be separated.

1. Individually. By writing her self, woman will return to the body which has been more than confiscated from her, which has been turned into the uncanny stranger on display — the ailing or dead figure, which so often turns out to be the nasty companion, the cause and location of inhibitions. Censor the body and you censor breath and speech at the same time.

Write your self. Your body must be heard. Only then will the immense resources of the unconscious spring forth. Our naphtha will

[4]Which works, then, might be called feminine? I'll just point out some examples: one would have to give them full readings to bring out what is pervasively feminine in their significance. Which I shall do elsewhere. In France (have you noted our infinite poverty in this field? — the Anglo-Saxon countries have shown resources of distinctly greater consequence), leafing through what's come out of the twentieth-century — and it's not much — the only inscriptions of femininity that I have seen were by Colette, Marguerite Duras, . . . and Jean Genêt. [Cixous]

spread, throughout the world, without dollars — black or gold — nonassessed values that will change the rules of the old game.

To write. An act which will not only "realize" the decensored relation of woman to her sexuality, to her womanly being, giving her access to her native strength; it will give her back her goods, her pleasures, her organs, her immense bodily territories which have been kept under seal; it will tear her away from the superegoized structure in which she has always occupied the place reserved for the guilty (guilty of everything, guilty at every turn: for having desires, for not having any; for being frigid, for being "too hot"; for not being both at once; for being too motherly and not enough; for having children and for not having any; for nursing and for not nursing . . .) — tear her away by means of this research, this job of analysis and illumination, this emancipation of the marvelous text of her self that she must urgently learn to speak. A woman without a body, dumb, blind, can't possibly be a good fighter. She is reduced to being the servant of the militant male, his shadow. We must kill the false woman who is preventing the live one from breathing. Inscribe the breath of the whole woman.

2. An act that will also be marked by woman's *seizing* the occasion to *speak*, hence her shattering entry into history, which has always been based *on her suppression*. To write and thus to forge for herself the antilogos weapon. To become *at will* the taker and initiator, for her own right, in every symbolic system, in every political process.

It is time for women to start scoring their feats in written and oral language.

Every woman has known the torment of getting up to speak. Her heart racing, at times entirely lost for words, ground and language slipping away — that's how daring a feat, how great a transgression it is for a woman to speak — even just open her mouth — in public. A double distress, for even if she transgresses, her words fall almost always upon the deaf male ear, which hears in language only that which speaks in the masculine.

It is by writing, from and toward women, and by taking up the challenge of speech which has been governed by the phallus, that women will confirm women in a place other than that which is reserved in and by the symbolic, that is, in a place other than silence. Women should break out of the snare of silence. They shouldn't be conned into accepting a domain which is the margin or the harem.

Listen to a woman speak at a public gathering (if she hasn't painfully lost her wind). She doesn't "speak," she throws her trembling body forward; she lets go of herself, she flies; all of her passes into her voice, and it's with her body that she vitally supports the "logic" of her speech. Her flesh speaks true. She lays herself bare. In fact, she physically materializes what she's thinking; she signifies it with her body. In a certain way she *inscribes* what she's saying, because she doesn't deny her drives the intractable and impassioned part they have in speaking. Her speech, even when "theoretical" or political, is never simple or linear or "objectified," generalized: she draws her story into history.

There is not that scission, that division made by the common man between the logic of oral speech and the logic of the text, bound as he is by his antiquated relation — servile, calculating — to mastery. From which proceeds the niggardly lip service which engages only the tiniest part of the body, plus the mask.

In women's speech, as in their writing, that element which never stops resonating, which, once we've been permeated by it, profoundly and imperceptibly touched by it, retains the power of moving us — that element is the song: first music from the first voice of love which is alive in every woman. Why this privileged relationship with the voice? Because no woman stockpiles as many defenses for countering the drives as does a man. You don't build walls around yourself, you don't forego pleasure as "wisely" as he. Even if phallic mystification has generally contaminated good relationships, a woman is never far from "mother" (I mean outside her role functions: the "mother" as nonname and as source of goods). There is always within her at least a little of that good mother's milk. She writes in white ink.

Woman for women. — There always remains in woman that force which produces/is produced by the other — in particular, the other woman. *In* her, matrix, cradler; herself giver as her mother and child; she is her own sister-daughter. You might object, "What about she who is the hysterical offspring of a bad mother?" Everything will be changed once woman gives woman to the other woman. There is hidden and always ready in woman the source; the locus for the other. The mother, too, is a metaphor. It is necessary and sufficient that the best of herself be given to woman by another woman for her to be able to love herself and return in love the body that was "born" to her. Touch me, caress me, you the living no-name, give me my self as myself. The relation to the "mother," in terms of intense pleasure and violence, is curtailed no more than the relation to childhood (the child that she was, that she is, that she makes, remakes, undoes, there at the point where, the same, she others herself). Text: my body — shot through with streams of song; I don't mean the overbearing, clutchy "mother" but, rather, what touches you, the equivoice that affects you, fills your breast with an urge to come to language and launches your force; the rhythm that laughs you; the intimate recipient who makes all metaphors possible and desirable; body (body? bodies?), no more describable than god, the soul, or the Other; that part of you that leaves a space between yourself and urges you to inscribe in language your woman's style. In women there is always more or less of the mother who makes everything all right, who nourishes, and who stands up against separation; a force that will not be cut off but will knock the wind out of the codes. We will rethink womankind beginning with every form and every period of her body. The Americans remind us, "We are all Lesbians"; that is, don't denigrate woman, don't make of her what men have made of you.

Because the "economy" of her drives is prodigious, she cannot fail, in seizing the occasion to speak, to transform directly and indirectly *all* systems of exchange based on masculine thrift. Her libido will produce far more radical effects of political and social change than some might like to think.

Because she arrives, vibrant, over and again, we are at the beginning of a new history, or rather of a process of becoming in which several histories intersect with one another. As subject for history, woman always occurs simultaneously in several places. Woman un-thinks[5] the unifying, regulating history that homogenizes and channels forces, herding contradictions into a single battlefield. In woman, personal history blends together with the history of all women, as well as national and world history. As a militant, she is an integral part of all liberations. She must be farsighted, not limited to a blow-by-blow interaction. She foresees that her liberation will do more than modify power relations or toss the ball over to the other camp; she will bring about a mutation in human relations, in thought, in all praxis: hers is not simply a class struggle, which she carries forward into a much vaster movement. Not that in order to be a woman-in-struggle(s) you have to leave the class struggle or repudiate it; but you have to split it open, spread it out, push it forward, fill it with the fundamental struggle so as to prevent the class struggle, or any other struggle for the liberation of a class or people, from operating as a form of repression, pretext for postponing the inevitable, the staggering alteration in power relations and in the production of individualities. This alteration is already upon us — in the United States, for example, where millions of night crawlers are in the process of undermining the family and disintegrating the whole of American sociality.

The new history is coming; it's not a dream, though it does extend beyond men's imagination, and for good reason. It's going to deprive them of their conceptual orthopedics, beginning with the destruction of their enticement machine.

It is impossible to *define* a feminine practice of writing, and this is an impossibility that will remain, for this practice can never be theorized, enclosed, coded — which doesn't mean that it doesn't exist. But it will always surpass the discourse that regulates the phallocentric system; it does and will take place in areas other than those subordinated to philosophico-theoretical domination. It will be conceived of only by subjects who are breakers of automatisms, by peripheral figures that no authority can ever subjugate.

---

[5] "*Dé-pense*," a neologism formed on the verb *penser*, hence "unthinks," but also "spends" (from *dépenser*). [Tr.]

Hence the necessity to affirm the flourishes of this writing, to give form to its movement, its near and distant byways. Bear in mind to begin with (1) that sexual opposition, which has always worked for man's profit to the point of reducing writing, too, to his laws, is only a historico-cultural limit. There is, there will be more and more rapidly pervasive now, a fiction that produces irreducible effects of femininity. (2) That it is through ignorance that most readers, critics, and writers of both sexes hesitate to admit or deny outright the possibility or the pertinence of a distinction between feminine and masculine writing. It will usually be said, thus disposing of sexual difference: either that all writing, to the extent that it materializes, is feminine; or, inversely — but it comes to the same thing — that the act of writing is equivalent to masculine masturbation (and so the woman who writes cuts herself out a paper penis); or that writing is bisexual, hence neuter, which again does away with differentiation. To admit that writing is precisely working (in) the in-between, inspecting the process of the same and of the other without which nothing can live, undoing the work of death — to admit this is first to want the two, as well as both, the ensemble of the one and the other, not fixed in sequences of struggle and expulsion or some other form of death but infinitely dynamized by an incessant process of exchange from one subject to another. A process of different subjects knowing one another and beginning one another anew only from the living boundaries of the other: a multiple and inexhaustible course with millions of encounters and transformations of the same into the other and into the in-between, from which woman takes her forms (and man, in his turn; but that's his other history).

In saying "bisexual, hence neuter," I am referring to the classic conception of bisexuality, which, squashed under the emblem of castration fear and along with the fantasy of a "total" being (though composed of two halves), would do away with the difference experienced as an operation incurring loss, as the mark of dreaded sectility.

To this self-effacing, merger-type bisexuality, which would conjure away castration (the writer who puts up his sign: "bisexual written here, come and see," when the odds are good that it's neither one nor the other), I oppose the *other bisexuality* on which every subject not enclosed in the false theater of phallocentric representationalism has founded his/her erotic universe. Bisexuality: that is, each one's location in self (*repérage en soi*) of the presence — variously manifest and insistent according to each person, male or female — of both sexes, nonexclusion either of the difference or of one sex, and, from this "self-permission," multiplication of the effects of the inscription of desire, over all parts of my body and the other body.

Now it happens that at present, for historico-cultural reasons, it is women who are opening up to and benefiting from this vatic bisexuality which doesn't annul differences but stirs them up, pursues them, increases their number. In a certain way, "woman is bisexual"; man — it's a secret to no one — being poised to keep glorious phallic monosexuality in view. By virtue of affirming the primacy of the phallus and of bringing it into play, phallocratic ideology has claimed more than one victim. As a woman, I've been clouded over by the great shadow of the scepter and been told: idolize it, that which you cannot brandish. But at the same time, man has been handed that grotesque and scarcely enviable destiny (just imagine) of being reduced to a single idol with clay balls. And consumed, as Freud and his followers note, by a fear of being a woman! For, if psychoanalysis was constituted from woman, to repress femininity (and not so successful a repression at that — men have made it clear), its account of masculine sexuality is now hardly refutable; as with all the "human" sciences, it reproduces the masculine view, of which it is one of the effects.

Here we encounter the inevitable man-with-rock, standing erect in his old Freudian realm, in the way that, to take the figure back to the point where linguistics is conceptualizing it "anew," Lacan preserves it in the sanctuary of the phallos (φ) "sheltered" from *castration's lack!* Their "symbolic" exists, it holds power — we, the sowers of disorder, know it only too well. But we are in no way obliged to deposit our lives in their banks of lack, to consider the constitution of the subject in terms of a drama manglingly restaged, to reinstate again and again the religion of the father. Because we don't want that. We don't fawn around the supreme hole. We have no womanly reason to pledge allegiance to the negative. The feminine (as the poets suspected) affirms: ". . . And yes," says Molly, carrying *Ulysses* off beyond any book and toward the new writing; "I said yes, I will Yes."

The Dark Continent is neither dark nor unexplorable. — It is still unexplored only because we've been made to believe that it was too dark to be explorable. And because they want to make us believe that what interests us is the white continent, with its monuments to Lack. And we believed. They riveted us between two horrifying myths: between the Medusa and the abyss. That would be enough to set half the world laughing, except that it's still going on. For the phallologocentric sublation[6] is with us, and it's militant, regenerating the old patterns, anchored in the dogma of castration. They haven't changed a thing: they've theorized their desire for reality! Let the priests tremble, we're going to show them our sexts!

Too bad for them if they fall apart upon discovering that women aren't men, or that the mother doesn't have one. But isn't this fear convenient for them? Wouldn't the worst be, isn't the worst, in truth, that women aren't castrated, that they have only to stop listening to the Sirens (for the Sirens were men) for history to change its meaning? You only have to look at the Medusa straight on to see her. And she's not deadly. She's beautiful and she's laughing.

Men say that there are two unrepresentable things: death and the feminine sex. That's because they need femininity to be associated with death; it's the jitters that gives them a hard-on! for themselves! They need to be afraid of us. Look at the trembling Perseuses moving backward toward us, clad in apotropes.[7] What lovely backs! Not another minute to lose. Let's get out of here.

Let's hurry: the continent is not impenetrably dark. I've been there often. I was overjoyed one day to run into Jean Genêt. It was in *Pompes funèbres*.[8] He had come there led by his Jean.

There are some men (all too few) who aren't afraid of femininity.

Almost everything is yet to be written by women about femininity: about their sexuality, that is, its infinite and mobile complexity, about their eroticization, sudden turn-ons of a certain minuscule-immense area of their bodies; not about destiny, but about the adventure of such and such a drive, about trips, crossings, trudges, abrupt and gradual awakenings, discoveries of a zone at one time timorous and soon to be forthright. A woman's body, with its thousand and one thresholds of ardor — once, by smashing yokes and censors, she lets it articulate the profusion of meanings that run through it in every direction — will make the old single-grooved mother tongue reverberate with more than one language.

We've been turned away from our bodies, shamefully taught to ignore them, to strike them with that stupid sexual modesty; we've been made victims of the old fool's game: each one will love the other sex. I'll give you your body and you'll give me mine. But who are the men who give women the body that women blindly yield to them? Why so few texts? Because so few women have as yet won back their body. Women must write through their bodies, they must invent the impregnable language that will wreck partitions, classes, and rhetorics, regulations and codes, they must submerge, cut through, get beyond the ultimate reserve-discourse, including the one that laughs at the very idea of pronouncing the word "silence," the one that, aiming for the impossible, stops short before the word "impossible" and writes it as "the end."

Such is the strength of women that, sweeping away syntax, breaking that famous thread (just a tiny little thread, they say) which acts for men as a surrogate umbilical cord, assuring them — otherwise they couldn't come — that the old lady is always right behind them, watching them make phallus, women will go right up to the impossible.

When the "repressed" of their culture and their society returns, it's an explosive, *utterly* destructive, staggering return, with a force never yet unleashed and equal to the most forbidding of suppressions. For when the Phallic period comes to an end, women will have been either annihilated

---

[6]Standard English term for the Hegelian *Aufhebung*, the French *la relève*. [Tr.]

[7]A coinage from two Greek roots meaning "to turn away."

[8]Jean Genêt, *Pompes funèbres* (Paris, 1948), p. 185. [Cixous]

or borne up to the highest and most violent incandescence. Muffled throughout their history, they have lived in dreams, in bodies (though muted), in silences, in aphonic revolts.

And with such force in their fragility; a fragility, a vulnerability, equal to their incomparable intensity. Fortunately, they haven't sublimated; they've saved their skin, their energy. They haven't worked at liquidating the impasse of lives without futures. They have furiously inhabited these sumptuous bodies: admirable hysterics who made Freud succumb to many voluptuous moments impossible to confess, bombarding his Mosaic statue with their carnal and passionate body words, haunting him with their unaudible and thundering denunciations, dazzling, more than naked underneath the seven veils of modesty. Those who, with a single word of the body, have inscribed the vertiginous immensity of a history which is sprung like an arrow from the whole history of men and from biblico-capitalist society, are the women, the supplicants of yesterday, who come as forebears of the new women, after whom no intersubjective relation will ever be the same. You, Dora,[9] you the indomitable, the poetic body, you are the true "mistress" of the Signifier. Before long your efficacity will be seen at work when your speech is no longer suppressed, its point turned in against your breast, but written out over against the other.

In body. — More so than men who are coaxed toward social success, toward sublimation, women are body. More body, hence more writing. For a long time it has been in body that women have responded to persecution, to the familial-conjugal enterprise of domestication, to the repeated attempts at castrating them. Those who have turned their tongues 10,000 times seven times before not speaking are either dead from it or more familiar with their tongues and their mouths than anyone else. Now, I-woman am going to blow up the Law: an explosion henceforth possible and ineluctable; let it be done, right now, *in* language.

Let us not be trapped by an analysis still encumbered with the old automatisms. It's not to be feared that language conceals an invincible adversary, because it's the language of men and their grammar. We mustn't leave them a single place that's any more theirs alone than we are.

If woman has always functioned "within" the discourse of man, a signifier that has always referred back to the opposite signifier which annihilates its specific energy and diminishes or stifles its very different sounds, it is time for her to dislocate this "within," to explode it, turn it around, and seize it; to make it hers, containing it, taking it in her own mouth, biting that tongue with her very own teeth to invent for herself a language to get inside of. And you'll see with what ease she will spring forth from that "within" — the "within" where once she so drowsily crouched — to overflow at the lips she will cover the foam.

Nor is the point to appropriate their instruments, their concepts, their places, or to begrudge them their position of mastery. Just because there's a risk of identification doesn't mean that we'll succumb. Let's leave it to the worriers, to masculine anxiety and its obsession with how to dominate the way things work — knowing "how it works" in order to "make it work." For us the point is not to take possession in order to internalize or manipulate, but rather to dash through and to "fly."[10]

Flying is woman's gesture — flying in language and making it fly. We have all learned the art of flying and its numerous techniques; for centuries we've been able to possess anything only by flying; we've lived in flight, stealing away, finding, when desired, narrow passageways, hidden crossovers. It's no accident that *voler* has a double meaning, that it plays on each of them and thus throws off the agents of sense. It's no accident: women take after birds and robbers just as robbers take after women and birds. They *(illes)*[11] go by, fly the coop, take pleasure in jumbling the order of space, in disorienting it, in changing

---

[10]Also, "to steal." Both meanings of the verb *voler* are played on, as the text itself explains in the following paragraph. [Tr.]

[11]*Illes* is a fusion of the masculine pronoun *ils*, which refers back to birds and robbers, with the feminine pronoun *elles*, which refers to women. [Tr.]

[9]The female subject of Freud's first case study in hysteria.

around the furniture, dislocating things and values, breaking them all up, emptying structures, and turning propriety upside down.

What woman hasn't flown/stolen? Who hasn't felt, dreamt, performed the gesture that jams sociality? Who hasn't crumbled, held up to ridicule, the bar of separation? Who hasn't inscribed with her body the differential, punctured the system of couples and opposition? Who, by some act of transgression, hasn't overthrown successiveness, connection, the wall of circumfusion?

A feminine text cannot fail to be more than subversive. It is volcanic; as it is written it brings about an upheaval of the old property crust, carrier of masculine investments; there's no other way. There's no room for her if she's not a he. If she's a her-she, it's in order to smash everything, to shatter the framework of institutions, to blow up the law, to break up the "truth" with laughter.

For once she blazes *her* trail in the symbolic, she cannot fail to make of it the chaosmos of the "personal" — in her pronouns, her nouns, and her clique of referents. And for good reason. There will have been the long history of gynocide. This is known by the colonized peoples of yesterday, the workers, the nations, the species off whose backs the history of men has made its gold; those who have known the ignominy of persecution derive from it an obstinate future desire for grandeur; those who are locked up know better than their jailers the taste of free air. Thanks to their history, women today know (how to do and want) what men will be able to conceive of only much later. I say woman overturns the "personal," for if, by means of laws, lies, blackmail, and marriage, her right to herself has been extorted at the same time as her name, she has been able, through the very movement of mortal alienation, to see more closely the inanity of "propriety," the reductive stinginess of the masculine-conjugal subjective economy, which she doubly resists. On the one hand she has constituted herself necessarily as that "person" capable of losing a part of herself without losing her integrity. But secretly, silently, deep down inside, she grows and multiplies, for, on the other hand, she knows far more about living and about the relation between the economy of the drives and the management of the ego than any man. Unlike man,

who holds so dearly to his title and his titles, his pouches of value, his cap, crown, and everything connected with his head, woman couldn't care less about the fear of decapitation (or castration), adventuring, without the masculine temerity, into anonymity, which she can merge with without annihilating herself: because she's a giver.

I shall have a great deal to say about the whole deceptive problematic of the gift. Woman is obviously not that woman Nietzsche dreamed of who gives only in order to.[12] Who could ever think of the gift as a gift-that-takes? Who else but man, precisely the one who would like to take everything?

If there is a "propriety of woman," it is paradoxically her capacity to depropriate unselfishly: body without end, without appendage, without principal "parts." If she is a whole, it's a whole composed of parts that are wholes, not simple partial objects but a moving, limitlessly changing ensemble, a cosmos tirelessly traversed by Eros, an immense astral space not organized around any one sun that's any more of a star than the others.

This doesn't mean that she's an undifferentiated magma, but that she doesn't lord it over her body or her desire. Though masculine sexuality gravitates around the penis, engendering that centralized body (in political anatomy) under the dictatorship of its parts, woman does not bring about the same regionalization which serves the couple head/genitals and which is inscribed only within boundaries. Her libido is cosmic, just as her unconscious is worldwide. Her writing can only keep going, without ever inscribing or discerning contours, daring to make these vertiginous crossing of the other(s) ephemeral and passionate sojourns in him, her, them, whom she inhabits long enough to look at from the point closest to their unconscious from the moment they awaken, to love them at the point closest to their drives; and then further,

[12]Reread Derrida's text, "Le Style de la femme," in *Nietzsche aujourd'hui* (Paris: Union Générale d'Editions, Coll. 10/18), where the philosopher can be seen operating an *Aufhebung* of all philosophy in its systematic reducing of woman to the place of seduction: she appears as the one who is taken for; the bait in person, all veils unfurled, the one who doesn't give but who gives only in order to (take). [Cixous]

impregnated through and through with these brief, identificatory embraces, she goes and passes into infinity. She alone dares and wishes to know from within, where she, the outcast, has never ceased to hear the resonance of fore-language. She lets the other language speak — the language of 1,000 tongues which knows neither enclosure nor death. To life she refuses nothing. Her language does not contain, it carries; it does not hold back, it makes possible. When id is ambiguously uttered — the wonder of being several — she doesn't defend herself against these unknown women whom she's surprised at becoming, but derives pleasure from this gift of alterability. I am spacious, singing flesh, on which is grafted no one knows which I, more or less human, but alive because of transformation.

Write! and your self-seeking text will know itself better than flesh and blood, rising, insurrectionary dough kneading itself, with sonorous, perfumed ingredients, a lively combination of flying colors, leaves, and rivers plunging into the sea we feed. "Ah, there's her sea," he will say as he holds out to me a basin full of water from the little phallic mother from whom he's inseparable. But look, our seas are what we make of them, full of fish or not, opaque or transparent, red or black, high or smooth, narrow or bankless; and we are ourselves sea, sand, coral, seaweed, beaches, tides, swimmers, children, waves. . . . More or less wavily sea, earth, sky — what matter would rebuff us? We know how to speak them all.

Heterogeneous, yes. For her joyous benefit she is erogenous; she is the erotogeneity of the heterogeneous: airborne swimmer, in flight, she does not cling to herself; she is dispersible, prodigious, stunning, desirous and capable of others, of the other woman that she will be, of the other woman she isn't, of him, of you.

Woman be unafraid of any other place, of any same, or any other. My eyes, my tongue, my ears, my nose, my skin, my mouth, my body-for-(the)-other — not that I long for it in order to fill up a hole, to provide against some defect of mine, or because, as fate would have it, I'm spurred on by feminine "jealousy"; not because I've been dragged into the whole chain of substitutions that brings that which is substituted back to its ultimate object. That sort of thing you would expect to come straight out of "Tom Thumb," out of the *Penisneid*[13] whispered to us by old grandmother ogresses, servants to their father-sons. If they believe, in order to muster up some self-importance, if they really need to believe that we're dying of desire, that we are this hole fringed with desire for their penis — that's their immemorial business. Undeniably (we verify it at our own expense — but also to our amusement), it's their business to let us know they're getting a hard-on, so that we'll assure them (we the maternal mistresses of their little pocket signifier) that they still can, that it's still there — that men structure themselves only by being fitted with a feather. In the child it's not the penis that the woman desires, it's not that famous bit of skin around which every man gravitates. Pregnancy cannot be traced back, except within the historical limits of the ancients, to some form of fate, to those mechanical substitutions brought about by the unconscious of some eternal "jealous woman"; not to penis envies; and not to narcissism or to some sort of homosexuality linked to the everpresent mother! Begetting a child doesn't mean that the woman or the man must fall ineluctably into patterns or must recharge the circuit of reproduction. If there's a risk there's not an inevitable trap: may women be spared the pressure, under the guise of consciousness-raising, of a supplement of interdictions. Either you want a kid or you don't — *that's your business*. Let nobody threaten you; in satisfying your desire, let not the fear of becoming the accomplice to a sociality succeed the old-time fear of being "taken." And man, are you still going to bank on everyone's blindness and passivity, afraid lest the child make a father and, consequently, that in having a kid the woman land herself more than one bad deal by engendering all at once child — mother — father — family? No; it's up to you to break the old circuits. It will be up to man and woman to render obsolete the former relationship and all its consequences, to consider the launching of a brand-new subject, alive, with defamilialization. Let us demater-paternalize rather than deny woman, in an effort to avoid the co-optation of procreation, a thrilling era of the body. Let us defetishize. Let's get away from the dialectic

[13]Penis-envy.

which has it that the only good father is a dead one, or that the child is the death of his parents. The child is the other, but the other without violence, bypassing loss, struggle. We're fed up with the reuniting of bonds forever to be severed, with the litany of castration that's handed down and genealogized. We won't advance backward anymore; we're not going to repress something so simple as the desire for life. Oral drive, anal drive, vocal drive — all these drives are our strengths, and among them is the gestation drive — just like the desire to write: a desire to live self from within, a desire for the swollen belly, for language, for blood. We are not going to refuse, if it should happen to strike our fancy, the unsurpassed pleasures of pregnancy which have actually been always exaggerated or conjured away — or cursed — in the classic texts. For if there's one thing that's been repressed here's just the place to find it: in the taboo of the pregnant woman. This says a lot about the power she seems invested with at the time, because it has always been suspected, that, when pregnant, the woman not only doubles her market value, but — what's more important — takes on intrinsic value as a woman in her own eyes and, undeniably, acquires body and sex.

There are thousands of ways of living one's pregnancy; to have or not to have with that still invisible other a relationship of another intensity. And if you don't have that particular yearning, it doesn't mean that you're in any way lacking. Each body distributes in its own special way, without model or norm, the nonfinite and changing totality of its desires. Decide for yourself on your position in the arena of contradictions, where pleasure and reality embrace. Bring the other to life. Women know how to live detachment; giving birth is neither losing nor increasing. It's adding to life an other. Am I dreaming? Am I mis-recognizing? You, the defenders of "theory," the sacrosanct yes-men of Concept, enthroners of the phallus (but not of the penis):

Once more you'll say that all this smacks of "idealism," or what's worse, you'll splutter that I'm a "mystic."

And what about the libido? Haven't I read the "Signification of the Phallus"? And what about separation, what about that bit of self for which, to be born, you undergo an ablation — an ablation, so they say, to be forever commemorated by your desire?

Besides, isn't it evident that the penis gets around in my texts, that I give it a place and appeal? Of course I do. I want all. I want all of me with all of him. Why should I deprive myself of a part of us? I want all of us. Woman of course has a desire for a "loving desire" and not a jealous one. But not because she is gelded; not because she's deprived and needs to be filled out, like some wounded person who wants to console herself or seek vengeance: I don't want a penis to decorate my body with. But I do desire the other for the other, whole and entire, male or female; because living means wanting everything that is, everything that lives, and wanting it alive. Castration? Let others toy with it. What's a desire originating from a lack? A pretty meager desire.

The woman who still allows herself to be threatened by the big dick, who's still impressed by the commotion of the phallic stance, who still leads a loyal master to the beat of the drum: that's the woman of yesterday. They still exist, easy and numerous victims of the oldest of farces: either they're cast in the original silent version in which, as titanesses lying under the mountains they make with their quivering, they never see erected that theoretic monument to the golden phallus looming, in the old manner, over their bodies. Or, coming today out of their *infans*[14] period and into the second, "enlightened" version of their virtuous debasement, they see themselves suddenly assaulted by the builders of the analytic empire and, as soon as they've begun to formulate the new desire, naked, nameless, so happy at making an appearance, they're taken in their bath by the new old men, and then, whoops! Luring them with flashy signifiers, the demon of interpretation — oblique, decked out in modernity — sells them the same old handcuffs, baubles, and chains. Which castration do you prefer? Whose degrading do you like better, the father's or the mother's? Oh, what pwetty eyes, you pwetty little girl. Here, buy my glasses and you'll see the Truth-Me-Myself tell you everything you should know. Put them on your nose and take a fetishist's look (you are me, the other analyst — that's what I'm telling you) at

[14]Mute.

your body and the body of the other. You see? No? Wait, you'll have everything explained to you, and you'll know at last which sort of neurosis you're related to. Hold still, we're going to do your portrait, so that you can begin looking like it right away.

Yes, the naives to the first and second degree are still legion. If the New Women, arriving now, dare to create outside the theoretical, they're called in by the cops of the signifier, fingerprinted, remonstrated, and brought into the line of order that they are supposed to know; assigned by force of trickery to a precise place in the chain that's always formed for the benefit of a privileged signifier. We are pieced back to the string which leads back, if not to the Name-of-the-Father, then, for a new twist, to the place of the phallic-mother.

Beware, my friend, of the signifier that would take you back to the authority of a signified! Beware of diagnoses that would reduce your generative powers. "Common" nouns are also proper nouns that disparage your singularity by classifying it into species. Break out of the circles; don't remain within the psychoanalytic closure. Take a look around, then cut through!

And if we are legion, it's because the war of liberation has only made as yet a tiny breakthrough. But women are thronging to it. I've seen them, those who will be neither dupe nor domestic, those who will not fear the risk of being a woman; will not fear any risk, any desire, any space still explored in themselves, among themselves and others or anywhere else. They do not fetishize, they do not deny, they do not hate. They observe, they approach, they try to see the other woman, the child, the lover — not to strengthen their own narcissism or verify the solidity or weakness of the master, but to make love better, to invent.

Other love. — In the beginning are our differences. The new love dares for the other, wants the other, makes dizzying, precipitous flights between knowledge and invention. The woman arriving over and over again does not stand still; she's everywhere, she exchanges, she is the desire-that-gives. (Not enclosed in the paradox of the gift that takes nor under the illusion of unitary fusion. We're past that.) She comes in, comes-in-between herself me and you, between the other me where one is always infinitely more than one and more than me, without the fear of ever reaching a limit; she thrills in our becoming. And we'll keep on becoming! She cuts through defensive loves, motherages, and devourations: beyond selfish narcissism, in the moving, open, transitional space, she runs her risks. Beyond the struggle-to-the-death that's been removed to the bed, beyond the love-battle that claims to represent exchange, she scorns at an Eros dynamic that would be fed by hatred. Hatred: a heritage, again, a remainder, a duping subservience to the phallus. To love, to watch-think-seek the other in the other, to despecularize, to unhoard. Does this seem difficult? It's not impossible, and this is what nourishes life — a love that has no commerce with the apprehensive desire that provides against the lack and stultifies the strange; a love that rejoices in the exchange that multiplies. Wherever history still unfolds as the history of death, she does not tread. Opposition, hierarchizing exchange, the struggle for mastery which can end only in at least one death (one master — one slave, or two nonmasters ≠ two dead) — all that comes from a period in time governed by phallocentric values. The fact that this period extends into the present doesn't prevent woman from starting the history of life somewhere else. Elsewhere, she gives. She doesn't "know" what she's giving, she doesn't measure it; she gives, though, neither a counterfeit impression nor something she hasn't got. She gives more, with no assurance that she'll get back even some unexpected profit from what she puts out. She gives that there may be life, thought, transformation. This is an "economy" that can no longer be put in economic terms. Wherever she loves, all the old concepts of management are left behind. At the end of a more or less conscious computation, she finds not her sum but her differences. I am for you what you want me to be at the moment you look at me in a way you've never seen me before: at every instant. When I write, it's everything that we don't know we can be that is written out of me, without exclusions, without stipulation, and everything we will be calls us to the unflagging, intoxicating, unappeasable search for love. In one another we will never be lacking.

Guy Hocquenghem

1946–1988

Raised in the Paris suburbs and educated at the École Normale Supérieure, Guy Hocquenghem joined the student rebellion in France of 1968, forming an alliance with the Communist Party, from which he would later be expelled on account of his open homosexuality. Hocquenghem became known as the radical activist leader of the Front Homosexuel d'Action Revolutionnaire (FHAR), combining a gay rights movement with radical leftist politics. For Hocquenghem, French bourgeois insularity was equally to blame for racism, sexual discrimination, and class oppression. Sexuality in particular, he writes, must be understood in the innumerable possibilities provided by bodies seeking pleasure. Hocquenghem's work is only beginning to be translated: only his first theoretical work, Homosexual Desire *(1972), and his first novel,* Love in Relief *(1982), have appeared in English. His other works include* L'Après-Mai des faunes: volutions *(1974);* La Dérive homosexuelle *(1977); an essay collection titled* La beauté du métis: réflexions d'un francophobe *(1979);* Le Gay voyage *(1980), a cruising guide to world capitals; and a posthumous memoir,* L'Amphithéâtre des morts *(1994). There are also half a dozen celebrated novels in which Hocquenghem explores sexual possibilities through science fiction. Hocquenghem died of AIDS-related causes in Paris.*

From *Homosexual Desire*

THE "THIRD SEX" AND "MASCULINE-FEMININE"

The world is divided into subject and object, male and female. Man desires woman, the woman's desire is of no consequence. In order to classify the homosexual, we must pass through the system of the similar or the different, i.e. the similar *and* the different. The homosexual is both different (the third sex) and similar (he subdivides into male and female). The discourse on homosexuality is locked permanently inside the cage of these two possibilities.

The homosexual *ought* to be different, otherwise every one would be homosexual. And despite Freud's struggle against the third sex theory, it keeps reappearing in various forms. "Congenital homosexuality" hasn't lost its appeal: the chromosome theory, for example, reconciles the similar

and the different by differentiating between a small minority of people who are "racially" homosexual (because they possess one chromosome too many) and a majority of homosexuals who are such "by culture," which can be explained by the individual's psychological history. The difference must be reduced to a similarity, because no normal individual would admit to being a homosexual; but homosexuals must not take advantage of this by thinking they can be free of phallic and Oedipal predominance. This is why Hirschfeld's attempt to organize the liberation of homosexuals on the basis of the innate and irrepressible nature of their tastes was doomed to failure.[1]

Such a theory certainly has the advantage of allowing the dominant ideology to cast the male

[1] Magnus Hirschfeld (1868–1935), author of *The Homosexuality of Men and Women* (1914), was a pioneering psychoanalytic theorist, arguing that homosexuals were by nature a third sex.

Translated by Daniella Dangoor

homosexual in a role which safeguards the discriminating value of the penis, without which one could simply cast him as a woman. But short of putting all homosexuals into concentration camps, it arouses the danger of letting more than two sexes coexist side by side, of giving up the simple binary system. If there are three sexes, why not more? When it is not totally fascist, the third sex theory is dangerous. Freud fought against this theory in the interests of homosexuals themselves. Everyone is more or less homosexual; there is no reason to see homosexuals as a separate category. But beneath this universalization of homosexuality in fact lurks the universalization of the Oedipus complex. Oedipal imperialism finds it particularly useful to show that beneath the difference lies the similarity; it is particularly reassuring to normal sexuality for the same categories to appear in both homosexuals and heterosexuals, thus stressing the undeniable universality of the phallic signifier. It is, therefore, useful both for the homosexual to be different and for his difference to be reduced to a similarity; it is essential that he be different yet subject to the same rules.

Criticising the third sex theory, Freud wrote that "[this group of] perverts . . . seeks to achieve very much the same ends with the objects of their desires as normal people do with theirs."[2] Homosexuals have simply chosen the wrong object. We can then subdivide them into males and females, and reassert in their terms the universality of the law which binds the sexual drive to its object, a law which they caricature. We can call this the heterosexual conception of the homosexual world: in repressing the other drives, the heterosexual drive channels them through its own order of things. How do people of the same sex practice a sexuality which is defined by the relation between two different sexes? By a simple game of substitution, in which the fundamental law of heterosexuality reappears.

However homosexuality could upset the clarity of this kind of functional subdivision between subject and object, male and female.

The whole issue of the debate regularly raised by psychiatrists as to whether homosexuality is a perversion or, on the contrary, several different phenomena arbitrarily grouped together under this heading, becomes clear in the light of this double need to divide and rule by maintaining the perverse difference. Ferenczi elevated this combinatorial faculty of the sexes as applied to homosexuality to its highest degree. In "The Nosology[3] of Male Homosexuality (Homo-Erotism)," he made a now classic division of homosexuality into masculine and feminine:

> It seemed to me from the beginning that the designation "homosexuality" was nowadays applied to dissimilar and unrelated psychical abnormalities. Sexual relations with members of one's own sex are only a symptom . . .[4]

Freud had written:

> What we have thrown together, for reasons of convenience, under the name of homosexuality may derive from a diversity of processes of psychosexual inhibition and the process which we have uncovered may only be one among many others, and related to one given type of homosexuality.[5]

Homosexuals were alas unable to enjoy their acknowledged diversity for long, for it led to a new classification. Ferenczi insisted on a sharp distinction between "subject homo-erotism" and "object homo-erotism":

> A man who in intercourse with men feels himself to be a woman is inverted in respect to his own ego (homo-erotism through subject-inversion, or, more shortly, "subject homo-erotism"); he feels himself to be a woman, and this not only in genital intercourse, but in all relations of life.[6]

[2]Freud, *Introductory Lectures on Psychoanalysis*, London, 1922, p. 256. [Hocquenghem]

[3]Nosology is the classification of diseases. Sandor Ferenczi (1873–1933) was a Hungarian disciple of Freud.

[4]Sandor Ferenczi, "The Nosology of Male Homosexuality" etc., in *First Contribution to Psychoanalysis*, pp. 298–9. [Hocquenghem]

[5]Freud, "Three Essays" etc., in *op. cit.*, vol. 7, p. 146. [Hocquenghem]

[6]Sandor Ferenczi, "The Nosology of Male Homosexuality" etc., in *op. cit.*, pp. 299–300. [Hocquenghem]

In contrast to this passive homosexual there must obviously be a masculine, active homosexual:

> He feels himself a man in every respect, is as a rule very energetic and active, and there is nothing effeminate to be discovered in his bodily or mental organization. The object of his inclination alone is unchanged, so that one might call him a homo-erotic through exchange of love-object, or, more shortly, an object homo-erotic.[7]

The characterology thus firmly binds the sexual drive to its object: the subject homo-erotic is attracted to masculine and mature men, the object homo-erotic to delicate young boys. Krafft-Ebing[8] had already postulated the existence of two nervous centers in the individual, one male, the other female. The common definition of the homosexual as "a feminine brain in a masculine body"[9] is complemented here by a detailed characterology. Ferenczi indicated that he was aware that the qualifying adjectives of "feminine" and "masculine" which he applied to the invert and to the homo-erotic were purely ideological. But he filled in the picture in these terms:

> It may be . . . indicated here that by *maleness* I understand *activity* (aggressivity) of the sexual hunger, highly developed object-love with overestimation of the object, a polygamy that is in only apparent contrast with the latter trait, and, as a distant derivative of the activity, intellectual talent; by *femaleness* I understand *passivity* (tendency to repression), narcissism and intuitiveness. The physical attributes of sex are, of course, mingled in every individual — although in unequal proportion.[10]

In other words, it is all just a matter of the dosage — but the general characteristics are permanent. We have here one of the best descriptions of the dominant sexual ideology and of the values attached to it, and chance has it that it was written about homosexuality.

Sartre's book *Saint-Genêt* is at times the faithful reflection of this discourse:

> The priority, in the subject itself, of the object over the subject can lead to passivity in love and this, when it affects a male, can incline him towards homosexuality.[11]

The invert or subject homo-erotic embodies the incurable pervert, upon whom classical psychiatry in particular heaps abuse and shame. Ferenczi stated that "the true invert is hardly ever impelled to seek medical advice, he feels at complete ease in the passive role."[12] He is completely different from men, and resembles women. The masculine or object homo-erotic, on the other hand, is described as follows:

> [He] is uncommonly tormented by the consciousness of his abnormality: sexual intercourse never completely satisfies him, he is tortured by qualms of conscience, and over-estimates his sexual object to the uttermost. That he is plagued with conflicts and never comes to terms with his condition is shown by his repeated attempts to obtain medical help for his trouble."[13]

The object homo-erotic is perfectly similar to men, a curable pervert who is conscious of his guilt. The third sex and the necessary similarity combine: the invert is, according to Ferenczi, "a veritable sexual intermediate, a pure anomaly of development. On the other hand, the object homo-erotic is a neurotic, an obsession neurotic." Inversion is incurable, object homo-erotism curable. The parallel is only an apparent one; if anything, we should speak of complementarity.

Homosexuals are then thus subdivided functionally: either they are different from normal people in respect of the object of their desire and similar as subjects, or they are different as subjects but similar in respect of the object. Both the similar and the different therefore operate effectively among them. In *Three Essays on the Theory of Sexuality*, Freud distinguishes between a complete inversion which can be related to the

---

[7]Ibid., p. 300. [Hocquenghem]
[8]The internal reference is to Richard von Krafft-Ebing in *Psychopathia Sexualis* (1886).
[9]See Freud, "Three Essays" etc., in *op. cit.*, vol. 7, p. 142. [Hocquenghem]
[10]Sandor Ferenczi, "The Nosology of Male Homosexuality" etc., in *op. cit.*, p. 302. [Hocquenghem]

[11]Jean-Paul Sartre, *op. cit.*, p. 596. [Hocquenghem]
[12]Sandor Ferenczi, "The Nosology of Male Homosexuality" etc., in *op. cit.*, p. 300. [Hocquenghem]
[13]Ibid., p.309. [Hocquenghem]

subject homo-erotic, in which the man feels like a woman, and an amphigenic inversion or psychosexual hermaphroditism in which some male functions are preserved.[14] All these subdivisions of homosexuality lead in any case to the restoration, amidst the homosexual confusion, of the subject-object and male-female principles.

The complementarity of the two types of homosexual as analyzed by Ferenczi ensures the existence of a microcosmic homosexual world which luckily can be compared point by point with the heterosexual one, is metaphorically related to it as one entity parallel to another, and is cursed with being but a perverse caricature of normality: the males who represent its consciousness are in fact merely neurotics. Ferenczi writes as follows:

> It may happen that two homo-erotics of different types unite to form a pair. The invert finds in the object homo-erotic a quite suitable lover, who adores him, supports him in material affairs, and is imposing and energetic; the man of the objective type, on the other hand, may find pleasure in just the mixture of masculine and feminine traits present in the invert.[15]

The situation thus becomes socially stable, in all its neurotic instability. The homosexual microcosm is a closed one, yet at the same time is incapable of existing on its own; it is threatened with a permanent imbalance in the form of the male's neurosis. Ferenczi hastens to add the following correction:

> I also know homo-erotics, by the way, who exclusively desire non-inverted youths, and only content themselves with inverts in the absence of the former.[16]

We have here the converse of Proust's description. Proust thinks that homosexuals are perpetually in search of true males, and actually deal with false males only because they agree to make love with other men; the object homo-erotic, however, associates with false young boys — he desires the impossible, a young male who will agree to be female for him. This conception of the homosexual world merely reflects the coherence of the heterosexual world by a game of substitution which compounds its neurosis.

We could even go so far as to imagine a mirror of the mirror, according to Ferenczi:

> It must be further remarked that many inverts are by no means quite insusceptible to the endearments of the female sex. It is through intercourse with women (i.e. their like) that they dispose of what may be called the homosexual component of their sexuality.[17]

It would be far simpler, however, to see this as a breakdown of the functional division, as a result of the basic lack of differentiation of desire. Simpler — but of course less effective in the construction of an imaginary where men, women and homosexuals all have their place. Similarly, Ferenczi notes that the dreams of object homo-erotics are "very rich in reversals":

> The symptomatic action of making a slip of the tongue or pen in the use of the gender of articles is common. One patient even made up a bisexual number: the number 101 signified, as the context showed, that for him backwards and forwards were the same.[18]

This patient testified to the indifference of desire to functional divisions, if only through symbols. The differentiation between the object and the subject, and between the drive and what it points to (following the rule that "differences become similar, similarities become different"), accounts for the contradictory phenomena which produce a logic of exclusion. Freud notes that the invert is generally almost as attracted to masculinity as he appears to be towards femininity (a taste for make-up etc.). Freud's remark doesn't make sense in a system which reserves femininity for the object and masculinity for the subject, and vice-versa in the case of the invert. It begins to make sense when we question the notion of difference between object and subject.

[14]See Freud, "Three Essays" etc., in *op. cit.*, vol. 7, p. 136. [Hocquenghem]
[15]Sandor Ferenczi, "The Nosology of Male Homosexuality" etc., in *op. cit.*, pp. 301–2. [Hocquenghem]
[16]Ibid., p.302. [Hocquenghem]

[17]Ibid., p.306. [Hocquenghem]
[18]Ibid., p.309. [Hocquenghem]

Musil speaks of Törless's discovery in the following terms:

> For although Törless did debase himself with Basini, his desire was never satisfied by him; on the contrary, it went growing out beyond Basini, growing out into some new and aimless craving.[19]

And when the headmaster questions Törless in order to put a name to what his behavior or drive might be, the boy answers, "I can't help its not being all these things you suggested."[20]

MASOCHISM AND HOMOSEXUALITY

The active-passive division, as an anthropomorphic conception of sexuality, brings us naturally to the subject of masochism. To be sure, in classical psychoanalysis the status of masochism differs from that of homosexuality: in a chapter entitled "Masochism in Male Homosexuality," Sacha Nacht's book[21] says that "it may seem surprising to couple a perversion with a masochistic neurosis" — surprising, because all psychoanalysis begins with a preliminary bow to the Freudian dictum that "perversion is the negative of neurosis." But we know from experience that whatever the precautions taken by the language of analysis, perversion inevitably assumes the character of a neurosis, from the moment it enters the psychiatrist's explanatory discourse. Thus, for Nacht, the same mechanism leads both to a passive homosexuality and to a moral masochism — the fear of man as the father image, the passive feminine identification with the mother:

> At first the boy who is inclined towards the inversion has made an effort to resist. . . . However, that first aggressive instinct stifled, it will turn into

masochism. . . . This masochistic disposition is strengthened when the subject puts into practice his homosexual inversion.[22]

Here we have another confirmation of the inevitable transformation of the notion of homosexual perversion in its forced Oedipalization; however contradictory it may appear, the association between masochism and professed inversion (and not between disorders caused by the repression of homosexuality) works well.

Inversion is entangled with masochism because perversion is inevitably entangled with neurosis.

So-called "moral" masochism is an Oedipal concentrate; it contains, unadulterated, the sense of guilt which pervades homosexuality. Masochistic Oedipalization gives sexuality both a clear and a guilty conscience in inversion: pleasure in guilt, the guilt of pleasure and, lastly the pleasure of guilt, reign supreme. Freud writes in *Three Essays* that clinical analysis of cases of masochistic perversion shows that they are the result of a "primary passive sexual attitude,"[23] bound of course to the castration complex, which is formative of the sense of guilt. The analysis of masochism adds one more link to the chain which binds passivity-narcissism-homosexuality-guilt through fear of castration, fear of the outside world and fear of phallus-bearing men and phallus-less women. Thus, according to Sartre, Genêt is playing a game of "loser wins" when he accepts a submissive and consenting humiliation, as someone who allows himself to be sodomized. According to Sartre there is no satisfaction for the person sodomized (for Divine, who goes to masturbate in the toilet after offering himself to his man), because there is no orgasm but the genital one: only shame and pain are anal. The masochist is an invert in terms of pain, enjoying pain as pleasure by reversing the master's imaginary in every detail.

What is interesting here is the process by which psychoanalysis perfects its little juggling act and inevitably strikes down all manifestations of anal erotism with constitutional guilt.

---

[19]Robert Musil, *Young Törless*, translated by Eithne Wilkins and Ernst Kaiser, London, 1971, p. 147. [Hocquenghem]

[20]Ibid., p. 184. [Hocquenghem]: Hocquenghem refers to *The Confusions of Young Törless* (1906) by Austrian author Robert Musil; in the psychological novel, set in a boarding school, Törless is drawn by his amoral classmates Beineberg and Reiting into a conspiracy to sexually abuse a beautiful youth named Basini.

[21]Sacha Nacht, *op. cit.* [Hocquenghem]

[22]Ibid. [Hocquenghem]

[23]Freud, "Three Essays" etc., in *op. cit.*, p. 158. [Hocquenghem]

The active-passive categories generally associated with the homosexual, the bugger and the buggered, are correlated with the analytical categories of sadism and masochism. This correlation is made possible by the fact that sadism as defined by Freud permits the establishment of a differentiation, preceding the masculine-feminine one, between active and passive. If we look at the polarity (which appears at the anal stage), "from the point of view of the genital phase . . . trends with a passive aim are attached to the erotogenic zone of the anal orifice."[24] The transformation of sadism into masochism — sadism turned upon the subject's own self — is part of "the destiny of repression"[25] triggered by the formation of the ego as such; it taints with guilt everything concerned with anal (passive) satisfaction. If masochistic pleasure, experienced through the partner's aggression or at the partner's pleasure, is inevitably a guilty pleasure, then according to Freud, that is because it presupposes an "unconscious sense of guilt."[26] This implies that anality, because of the original passive role assigned to it, follows the same destiny as masochism: everything related to the anal is guilty. The buggered person is a masochist, even in spite of himself. He may enjoy himself — but, according to the book, not only has he no right to do so, he *cannot*.

The narcissistic stage is the knot of the differentiation between subject and object, while the anal-erotic stage is the knot of the differentiation between active and passive. Libidinal production enters the Oedipal arena.

The active role of moral masochism in instigating homosexual guilt is made quite clear by Törless's perplexities. At first, Törless is unable to choose between sadism and masochism, not because sadism would be primary and masochism secondary, but because the differentiation requires a vigilant superego whose formation will only take place in the small group itself, through the play of the imaginary among the four students. Törless "pays no attention" to Beineberg's flow of fascistic metaphysics: he cannot situate his desire in relation to a discourse which appears to him to have no direct connection with what is happening. But he will soon understand what it is all about; the sadism which he practices with the other two on Basini stimulates his discovery of the game of shame: "He was ashamed at having delivered up his idea to the others."[27] And Basini's confession, which comes at a time when Törless is wondering with good reason whether he himself is not in turn going to become the masochistic object of his two fellows, puts together the system of the imaginary and of guilt-inducement:

He says, if he didn't beat me, he wouldn't be able to help thinking I was a man, and then he couldn't let himself be so soft and affectionate to me.[28]

It is Basini who narrates Reiting's comments to a hesitating Törless, justificatory comments in which Basini himself sees how he is placed: the subdivision of homosexual activity into pleasure and suffering (to beat or be beaten) constructs the pleasure of guilt (the pleasure of pain, the wish to be beaten). It is only through the projection of the imaginary on to the partner that such a system can be constructed. Masochism is no more secondary than sadism is primary. Törless's sadism is more a questioning of sadism, a secondary sadism to his primary masochism. He anxiously questions Basini on his feelings when he is beaten:

That's not what I'm after. . . . When I drive all that into you like knives, what goes on in you? . . . Tell me![29]

Törless is unable to deal with all the notions which are put to him and whose meaning his desire is ignorant of. His perplexities are those of a polymorphous desire baffled by the signs of the guilt-inducing imaginary. He would like to experience what Basini experiences, but at the same time he feels the disquieting presence of Beineberg's and Reiting's fascinating superegos.

[24]Freud, *Introductory Lectures*, p. 370. [Hocquenghem]
[25]See Freud, "Instincts and Their Vicissitudes," in *The Complete Psychological Works of Sigmund Freud*, vol. 14. [Hocquenghem]
[26]See Freud, "The Economic Problem of Masochism," in *op. cit.*, vol. 19. [Hocquenghem]

[27]Robert Musil, *op. cit.*, p. 115. [Hocquenghem]
[28]Ibid., p. 135. [Hocquenghem]
[29]Ibid., p. 137. [Hocquenghem]

He would be Basini, if being Basini did not presuppose the existence of the other two; just as he would be a masochist if that did not imply the existence of sadism, and homosexual if it did not imply the existence of heterosexuality.

THE PICK-UP MACHINE

When Basini stands naked in front of him, Törless experiences a brutal assault of desire, from which he recoils in anguish: "It's a man, damn it!" he whispers to himself. To encounter desire is first of all to forget the difference in the sexes. Similarly Aschenbach[30] comes under the assault of beauty, and he is only able to withstand it by means of a meditation on art: "Aschenbach . . . was astonished anew, yes, startled at the godlike beauty of the young mortal."[31] All metaphors on the miraculous nature of the homosexual encounter boil down to one thing: when desire strikes, there is no room for the imaginary. By comparing the encounter between Jupien and Charlus[32] with the meeting of the bumble-bee and the flower, Proust is able to express the immediate plugging-in which is so alien to the social order; simply entering a drawing-room, on the other hand, represents for the young Proust himself an extreme case of social anxiety, in the form of the imaginary question, "What are they going to think of me?" Hearing the usher roar out his name for the first time at the entrance to the Guermantes' drawing-room, he experiences the unbounded social anxiety of someone who is always afraid that he is the object of a hoax. And is it really by accident that Proust comes immediately after the Duke of Châtellerault, who recognizes his lover of the night before in the usher (to whom, of course, he had not then given his real name)?[33] Everything

that happens between Charlus and Jupien likewise has no name. Even Tadzio's name is an arbitrary reconstruction on Aschenbach's part.[34] In truth, the pick-up machine is not concerned with names or sexes. The drift where all encounters become possible is the moment in which desire produces and feels no guilt. Anyone who has witnessed the strange balletic quality of a regular homosexual pick-up haunt will be deeply attuned to Proust's description of the innocence of flowers.

It is generally assumed that what we may call homosexual "scattering" — the fact that homosexuals have a multitude of love affairs, each of which may last only a moment — expresses the fundamental instability of the homosexual condition, the search for a dream partner through a series of brief, unsatisfactory affairs. The homosexual pick-up scene may well be experienced in such a way, at least at the level of what "queers" tell each other or what they have found out about themselves. But instead of translating this scattering of love-energy as the inability to find a center, we could see it as a system in action, the system in which polyvocal desire is plugged in on a non-exclusive basis. Aschenbach's drift around Venice is connected with a guilty sexuality because it is identified with a single object, the principle being "you lose one person and the world becomes empty." The homosexual condition is experienced as unhappy because its mechanical scattering is translated as absence and substitution. We could say that on the contrary homosexual love is immensely superior, precisely because everything is possible at any moment: organs look for each other and plug in, unaware of the law of exclusive disjunction. Homosexual encounters do not take place in the seclusion of a domestic setting but outside, in the open air, in forests and on beaches. The cruising homosexual, on the look-out for anything that might come and plug in to his own desire, is reminiscent of the "voyaging schizophrenic"

---

[30]Protagonist of Thomas Mann's novella *Death in Venice* (1913), a famous middle-aged author who falls in love with a youth named Tadzio.

[31]Thomas Mann, *op. cit.*, p. 66. [Hocquenghem]

[32]Jupien is a young tailor who becomes the lover and "secretary" to the aristocratic Baron de Charlus in Proust's *Sodom and Gomorrah*. Châtellerault is, like Charlus, a passive homosexual.

[33]Proust, *Sodom and Gomorrah*, p. 51. [Hocquenghem]

[34]Aschenbach hears the youth called "Adgiu" by his playmates and surmises that the name is actually "Tadzio," short for "Tadeusz" (the Polish equivalent of Thaddeus), which becomes "Tadziu" when used in direct address.

described in *L'Anti-Oedipe*.[35] If the homosexual pick-up machine, which is infinitely more direct and less guilt-induced than the complex system of "civilized loves" (to use Fourier's phrase), were to take off the Oedipal cloak of morality under which it is forced to hide, we would see that its mechanical scattering corresponds to the mode of existence of desire itself.[36]

[35]In this book of social psychology, Gilles Deleuze and Félix Guattari depict the normal psyche as a "desiring machine."

[36]Charles Fourier (1772–1837), French utopian socialist, argued against the standard monogamous forms of European sexuality and proposed ideal societies (phalanges) in which different pairings and groupings would lead to a system of universal love.

References

Ferenczi, Sandor. "The Nosology of Male Homosexuality." *First Contributions to Psychoanalysis*. London, 1952.

Freud, Sigmund. "Three Essays on the Theory of Sexuality." *The Standard Edition of the Complete Psychological Works of Sigmund Freud*, vol. 7. London, 1953.

Mann, Thomas. *Death in Venice*. Translated by H. T. Lowe-Porter. London, 1955.

Nacht, Sacha. *Le masochisme*. Paris, 1948.

Proust, Marcel. *Sodom and Gomorrah*. Translated by C. Scott Moncrieff as *Cities of the Plain*. New York, 1927.

Sartre, Jean-Paul. *Saint-Genêt, Actor and Martyr*. London, 1964.

Gayle Rubin

b. 1949

Gayle Rubin grew up in a small, segregated Southern town in one of the few local pro-integration families. When she began college at the University of Michigan in 1966, she saw a similar kind of unequal segregation between male and female students and led a student revolt against the sexist rules about dress and personal freedoms. Interested in the connections between gender and politics, Rubin helped to start the university's women's studies program. In 1971, while a graduate student in anthropology in Ann Arbor, Rubin gathered a coalition of activists that became the Radicalesbians group. She is now professor of anthropology and comparative literature at the University of Michigan, where she received her Ph.D. in 1994 for her groundbreaking dissertation, "The Valley of the Kings: Leathermen in San Francisco, 1960–1990." From 1996 to 1998, Rubin served as a visiting lecturer of women's studies at the University of California, Santa Cruz. Using the methods of Claude Lévi-Strauss, her work continues to explore the most marginalized sexual practices, especially in urban centers where communities arise to assist members in determining their sexual roles. Following Foucault's arguments about the constructed nature of gender and its source in the infrastructure of power, Rubin theorizes that the prohibition of certain sexual practices is a method of political control, and that all sex, especially that viewed as "deviant," is inherently a declaration of political dissent. The following article, "The Traffic in Women: Notes on the 'Political Economy' of Sex," was originally printed in the 1975 volume, Toward an Anthropology of Women.

From *The Traffic in Women:*
Notes on the "Political Economy" of Sex

The literature on women — both feminist and anti-feminist — is a long rumination on the question of the nature and genesis of women's oppression and social subordination. The question is not a trivial one, since the answers given it determine our visions of the future, and our evaluation of whether or not it is realistic to hope for a sexually egalitarian society. More importantly, the analysis of the causes of women's oppression forms the basis for any assessment of just what would have to be changed in order to achieve a society without gender hierarchy. Thus, if innate male aggression and dominance are at the root of female oppression, then the feminist program would logically require either the extermination of the offending sex, or else a eugenics project to modify its character. If sexism is a by-product of capitalism's relentless appetite for profit, then sexism would wither away in the advent of a successful socialist revolution. If the world historical defeat of women occurred at the hands of an armed patriarchal revolt, then it is time for Amazon guerrillas to start training in the Adirondacks.

It lies outside the scope of this paper to conduct a sustained critique of some of the currently popular explanations of the genesis of sexual inequality — theories such as the popular evolution

exemplified by *The Imperial Animal*,[1] the alleged overthrow of prehistoric matriarchies, or the attempt to extract all of the phenomena of social subordination from the first volume of *Capital*.[2] Instead, I want to sketch some elements of an alternate explanation of the problem.

Marx once asked: "What is a Negro slave? A man of the black race. The one explanation is as good as the other. A Negro is a Negro. He only becomes a slave in certain relations. A cotton spinning jenny is a machine for spinning cotton. It becomes *capital* only in certain relations. Torn from these relationships it is no more capital than gold in itself is money or sugar is the price of sugar" (Marx, 28).* One might paraphrase: What is a domesticated woman? A female of the species. The one explanation is as good as the other. A woman is a woman. She only becomes a domestic, a wife, a chattel, a playboy bunny, a prostitute, or a human dictaphone[3] in certain relations. Torn from these relationships, she is no more the helpmate of man than gold in itself is money . . . etc. What then are these relationships by which a female becomes an oppressed woman? The place to begin to unravel the system of relationships by which women become the prey of men is in the overlapping works of Claude Lévi-Strauss and Sigmund Freud.[4] The domestication of women, under other names, is discussed at length in both of their *oeuvres*. In reading through these works, one begins to have a sense of a systematic social apparatus which takes up females as raw materials and fashions

Acknowledgements are an inadequate expression of how much this paper, like most, is the product of many minds. They are also necessary to free others of the responsibility for what is ultimately a personal vision of a collective conversation. I want to free and thank the following persons: Tom Anderson and Arlene Gorelick, with whom I co-authored the paper from which this one evolved; Rayna Reiter, Larry Shields, Ray Kelly, Peggy White, Norma Diamond, Randy Reiter, Frederick Wyatt, Anne Locksley, Juliet Mitchell, and Susan Harding, for countless conversations and ideas; Marshall Sahlins, for the revelation of anthropology; Lynn Eden, for sardonic editing; the members of Women's Studies 340/004, for my initiation into teaching; Sally Brenner, for heroic typing; Susan Lowes, for incredible patience; and Emma Goldman, for the title. [Rubin]

[1]Book by sociobiologists Lionel Tiger and Robin Fox (1971) based on studies of baboons and macaques, arguing that hierarchical male-dominant social systems are natural to primates (including man).

[2]See the introduction to Marx, p. 397.

*Karl Marx, *Wage-Labor and Capital*. New York: International, 1971.

[3]Business machine like a tape recorder once used by secretaries to type letters dictated by their employers.

[4]For Lévi-Strauss, see p. 859; for Freud, see p. 497.

domesticated women as products. Neither Freud nor Lévi-Strauss sees his work in this light, and certainly neither turns a critical glance upon the processes he describes. Their analyses and descriptions must be read, therefore, in something like the way in which Marx read the classical political economists who preceded him. Freud and Lévi-Strauss are in some sense analogous to Ricardo and Smith:[5] They see neither the implications of what they are saying, nor the implicit critique which their work can generate when subjected to a feminist eye. Nevertheless, they provide conceptual tools with which one can build descriptions of the part of social life which is the locus of the oppression of women, of sexual minorities, and of certain aspects of human personality within individuals. I call that part of social life the "sex/gender system," for lack of a more elegant term. As a preliminary definition, a "sex/gender system" is the set of arrangements by which a society transforms biological sexuality into products of human activity, and in which these transformed sexual needs are satisfied.

The purpose of this essay is to arrive at a more fully developed definition of the sex/gender system, by way of a somewhat idiosyncratic and exegetical reading of Lévi-Strauss and Freud. I use the word "exegetical" deliberately. The dictionary defines "exegesis" as a "critical explanation or analysis; especially, interpretation of the Scriptures." At times, my reading of Lévi-Strauss and Freud is freely interpretive, moving from the explicit content of a text to its presuppositions and implications. My reading of certain psychoanalytic texts is filtered through a lens provided by Jacques Lacan, whose own interpretation of the Freudian scripture has been heavily influenced by Lévi-Strauss.[6]

I will return later to a refinement of the definition of a sex/gender system. First, however, I will try to demonstrate the need for such a concept by discussing the failure of classical Marxism to fully express or conceptualize sex oppression. This failure results from the fact that Marxism, as a theory of social life, is relatively unconcerned with sex. In Marx's map of the social world, human beings are workers, peasants, or capitalists; that they are also men and women is not seen as very significant. By contrast, in the maps of social reality drawn by Freud and Lévi-Strauss, there is a deep recognition of the place of sexuality in society, and of the profound differences between the social experience of men and women.

MARX

There is no theory which accounts for the oppression of women — in its endless variety and monotonous similarity, cross-culturally and throughout history — with anything like the explanatory power of the Marxist theory of class oppression. Therefore, it is not surprising that there have been numerous attempts to apply Marxist analysis to the question of women. There are many ways of doing this. It has been argued that women are a reserve labor force for capitalism, that women's generally lower wages provide extra surplus to a capitalist employer, that women serve the ends of capitalist consumerism in their roles as administrators of family consumption, and so forth.

However, a number of articles have tried to do something much more ambitious — to locate the oppression of women in the heart of the capitalist dynamic by pointing to the relationship between housework and the reproduction of labor. To do this is to place women squarely in the definition of capitalism, the process in which capital is produced by the extraction of surplus value from labor by capital.

---

[5]David Ricardo (1772–1823), author of *Principles of Political Economy and Taxation* (1817), and Adam Smith (1723–1790), author of *The Wealth of Nations* (1776), are the classical economists of whose work Marx's *Capital* is an "implicit critique."

[6]Moving between Marxism, structuralism, and psychoanalysis produces a certain clash of epistemologies. In particular, structuralism is a can from which worms crawl out all over the epistemological map. Rather than trying to cope with this problem, I have more or less ignored the fact that Lacan and Lévi-Strauss are among the foremost living ancestors of the contemporary French intellectual revolution (see Foucault, *The Order of Things.* New York: Pantheon, 1970). It would be fun, interesting, and, if this were France, essential, to start my argument from the center of the structuralist maze and work my way out from there, along the lines of a "dialectical theory of signifying practices" (see Hefner "The *Tel Quel* Order of Things," *SubStance* 8 [1974], 127–38). [Rubin]

Briefly, Marx argued that capitalism is distinguished from all other modes of production by its unique aim: the creation and expansion of capital. Whereas other modes of production might find their purpose in making useful things to satisfy human needs, or in producing a surplus for a ruling nobility, or in producing to insure sufficient sacrifice for the edification of the gods, capitalism produces capital. Capitalism is a set of social relations — forms of property, and so forth — in which production takes the form of turning money, things, and people into capital. And capital is a quantity of goods or money which, when exchanged for labor, reproduces and augments itself by extracting unpaid labor, or surplus value, from labor and into itself.

> The result of the capitalist production process is neither a mere product (use-value) nor a *commodity*, that is, a use-value which has exchange value. Its result, its product, is the creation of *surplus-value* for capital, and consequently the actual *transformation* of money or commodity into capital. . . ." (Marx, 399; italics in the original)*

The exchange between capital and labor which produces surplus value, and hence capital, is highly specific. The worker gets a wage; the capitalist gets the things the worker has made during his or her time of employment. If the total value of the things the worker has made exceeds the value of his or her wage, the aim of capitalism has been achieved. The capitalist gets back the cost of the wage, plus an increment — surplus value. This can occur because the wage is determined not by the value of what the laborer makes, but by the value of what it takes to keep him or her going — to reproduce him or her from day to day, and to reproduce the entire work force from one generation to the next. Thus, surplus value is the difference between what the laboring class produces as a whole, and the amount of that total which is recycled into maintaining the laboring class.

> The capital given in exchange for labour power is converted into necessaries, by the consumption of which the muscles, nerves, bones, and brains of existing labourers are reproduced, and new labourers

are begotten . . . the individual consumption of the labourer, whether it proceed within the workshop or outside it, whether it be part of the process of production or not, forms therefore a factor of the production and reproduction of capital; just as cleaning machinery does. . . . (Marx, 572)**

> Given the individual, the production of labour-power consists in his reproduction of himself or his maintenance. For his maintenance he requires a given quantity of the means of subsistence. . . . Labour-power sets itself in action only by working. But thereby a definite quantity of human muscle, brain, nerve, etc., is wasted, and these require to be restored. . . . (Ibid.:171)

The amount of the difference between the reproduction of labor power and its products depends, therefore, on the determination of what it takes to reproduce that labor power. Marx tends to make that determination on the basis of the quantity of commodities — food, clothing, housing, fuel — which would be necessary to maintain the health, life, and strength of a worker. But these commodities must be consumed before they can be sustenance, and they are not immediately in consumable form when they are purchased by the wage. Additional labor must be performed upon these things before they can be turned into people. Food must be cooked, clothes cleaned, beds made, wood chopped, etc. Housework is therefore a key element in the process of the reproduction of the laborer from whom surplus value is taken. Since it is usually women who do housework, it has been observed that it is through the reproduction of labor power that women are articulated into the surplus value nexus which is the *sine qua non*[7] of capitalism.[8] It can be further argued that since no wage is paid for housework, the labor of women in the home contributes to the ultimate quantity of

---

*Karl Marx, *Theories of Surplus Value.* Moscow: Progress, 1969.

**Karl Marx, *Capital.* New York: International, 1972.

[7]Necessary element.

[8]A lot of the debate on women and housework has centered around the question of whether or not housework is "productive" labor. Strictly speaking, housework is not ordinarily "productive" in the technical sense of the term (Ian Gough, "Marx and Reproductive Labour," *New Left Review* 76 [1972]: 47–72; Marx, *Theories of Surplus Value,* 387–413). But this distinction is irrelevant to the main line of the argument. Housework may not be "productive," in the sense of directly producing surplus value and capital, and yet be a crucial element in the production of surplus value and capital.[Rubin]

surplus value realized by the capitalist. But to explain women's usefulness to capitalism is one thing. To argue that this usefulness explains the genesis of the oppression of women is quite another. It is precisely at this point that the analysis of capitalism ceases to explain very much about women and the oppression of women.

Women are oppressed in societies which can by no stretch of the imagination be described as capitalist. In the Amazon valley and the New Guinea highlands, women are frequently kept in their place by gang rape when the ordinary mechanisms of masculine intimidation prove insufficient. "We tame our women with the banana," said one Mundurucu man (Murphy, 195).* The ethnographic record is littered with practices whose effect is to keep women "in their place" — men's cults, secret initiations, arcane male knowledge, etc. And pre-capitalist, feudal Europe was hardly a society in which there was no sexism. Capitalism has taken over, and rewired, notions of male and female which predate it by centuries. No analysis of the reproduction of labor power under capitalism can explain foot-binding, chastity belts, or any of the incredible array of Byzantine, fetishized indignities, let alone the more ordinary ones, which have been inflicted upon women in various times and places. The analysis of the reproduction of labor power does not even explain why it is usually women who do domestic work in the home, rather than men.

In this light it is interesting to return to Marx's discussion of the reproduction of labor. What is necessary to reproduce the worker is determined in part by the biological needs of the human organism, in part by the physical conditions of the place in which it lives, and in part by cultural tradition. Marx observed that beer is necessary for the reproduction of the English working class, and wine necessary for the French.

> . . . the number and extent of his [the worker's] so-called necessary wants, as also the modes of satisfying them, are themselves the product of historical development, and depend therefore to great extent on the degree of civilization of a country, more

particularly on the conditions under which, and consequently on the habits and degree of comfort in which, the class of free labourers has been formed. In contradistinction therefore to the case of other commodities, there enters into the determination of the value of labour-power a historical and moral element. . . . (Marx, Capital, 171, my italics)

It is precisely this "historical and moral element" which determines that a "wife" is among the necessities of a worker, that women rather than men do housework, and that capitalism is heir to a long tradition in which women do not inherit, in which women do not lead, and in which women do not talk to god. It is this "historical and moral element" which presented capitalism with a cultural heritage of forms of masculinity and femininity. It is within this "historical and moral element" that the entire domain of sex, sexuality, and sex oppression is subsumed. And the briefness of Marx's comment only serves to emphasize the vast area of social life which it covers and leaves unexamined. Only by subjecting this "historical and moral element" to analysis can the structure of sex oppression be delineated.

ENGELS

In The Origin of the Family, Private Property, and the State (1884), Engels sees sex oppression as part of capitalism's heritage from prior social forms. Moreover, Engels integrates sex and sexuality into his theory of society. Origin is a frustrating book. Like the nineteenth-century tomes on the history of marriage and the family which it echoes, the state of the evidence in Origin renders it quaint to a reader familiar with more recent developments in anthropology. Nevertheless, it is a book whose considerable insight should not be overshadowed by its limitations. The idea that the "relations of sexuality" can and should be distinguished from the "relations of production" is not the least of Engels' intuitions:

> According to the materialistic conception, the determining factor in history is, in the final instance, the production and reproduction of immediate life. This again, is of a twofold character: on the one hand, the production of the means of existence, of food, clothing, and shelter and the tools necessary

*Robert Murphy, "Social Structure and Sex Antagonism," Southwestern Journal of Anthropology 15.1 (1959): 81–96.

for that production; on the other side, the production of human beings themselves, the propagation of the species. The social organization under which the people of a particular historical epoch and a particular country live is determined by both kinds of production: by the stage of development of labor on the one hand, and of the family on the other . . . (Engels, 71–72; my italics)*

This passage indicates an important recognition — that a human group must do more than apply its activity to reshaping the natural world in order to clothe, feed, and warm itself. We usually call the system by which elements of the natural world are transformed into objects of human consumption the "economy." But the needs which are satisfied by economic activity even in the richest, Marxian sense, do not exhaust fundamental human requirements. A human group must also reproduce itself from generation to generation. The needs of sexuality and procreation must be satisfied as much as the need to eat, and one of the most obvious deductions which can be made from the data of anthropology is that these needs are hardly ever satisfied in any "natural" form, any more than are the needs for food. Hunger is hunger, but what counts as food is culturally determined and obtained. Every society has some form of organized economic activity. Sex is sex, but what counts as sex is equally culturally determined and obtained. Every society also has a sex/gender system — a set of arrangements by which the biological raw material of human sex and procreation is shaped by human, social intervention and satisfied in a conventional manner, no matter how bizarre some of the conventions may be.[9]

*Friedrich Engels, *The Origin of the Family, Private Property, and the State*. Ed. Eleanor Leacock. New York: International, 1972.

[9]That some of them are pretty bizarre, from our point of view, only demonstrates the point that sexuality is expressed through the intervention of culture (see Ford and Beach, 1972). Some examples may be chosen from among the exotica in which anthropologists delight.

Among the Banaro, marriage involves several socially sanctioned sexual partnerships. When a woman is married, she is initiated into intercourse by the sib-friend of her groom's father. After bearing a child by this man, she begins to have intercourse with her husband. She also has an institutionalized partnership with the sib-friend of her husband. A man's partners include his wife, the wife of his sib-friend, and the wife of his

The realm of human sex, gender, and procreation has been subjected to, and changed by, relentless social activity for millennia. Sex as we know it — gender identity, sexual desire and fantasy, concepts of childhood — is itself a social product. We need to understand the relations of its production, and forget, for awhile, about food, clothing, automobiles, and transistor radios. In most Marxist tradition, and even in Engels' book, the concept of the "second aspect of material life" has tended to fade into the background, or to be incorporated into the usual notions of "material life." Engels' suggestion has never been followed up and subjected to the refinement which it needs. But he does indicate the existence and importance of the domain of social life which I want to call the sex/gender system.

Other names have been proposed for the sex/gender system. The most common alternatives are "mode of reproduction" and "patriarchy." It may be foolish to quibble about terms, but both of these can lead to confusion. All three proposals have been made in order to introduce a distinction between "economic" systems and "sexual" systems, and to indicate that sexual systems have a certain autonomy and cannot always by explained in terms of economic forces. "Mode of reproduction," for instance, has been proposed in opposition to the more familiar "mode of production." But this terminology links the "economy" to production, and the sexual system

sib-friend's son (Thurnwald, 1916). Multiple intercourse is a more pronounced custom among the Marind Anim. At the time of marriage, the bride has intercourse with all of the members of the groom's clan, the groom coming last. Every major festival is accompanied by a practice known as *otiv-bombari*, in which semen is collected for ritual purposes. A few women have intercourse with many men, and the resulting semen is collected in coconut-shell buckets. A Marind male is subjected to multiple homosexual intercourse during initiation. Among the Etoro, heterosexual intercourse is taboo for between 205 and 260 days a year. In much of New Guinea, men fear copulation and think that it will kill them if they engage in it without magical precautions. Usually, such ideas of feminine pollution express the subordination of women. But symbolic systems contain internal contradictions, whose logical extensions sometimes lead to inversions of the propositions on which a system is based. In New Britain, men's fear of sex is so extreme that rape appears to be feared by men rather than women. Women run after the men, who flee from them, women are the sexual aggressors, and it is bridegrooms who are reluctant. [Rubin] to "reproduction." It reduces the richness of either system, since "productions" and "reproductions" take place in both. Every mode of production involves reproduction — of tools, labor, and social relations. We cannot relegate all of the multi-faceted aspects of social reproduction to the sex system. Replacement of machinery is an example of reproduction in the economy. On the other hand, we cannot limit the sex system to "reproduction" in either the social or biological sense of the term. A sex/gender system is not simply the reproductive moment of a "mode of production." The formation of gender identity is an example of production in the realm of the sexual system. And a sex/gender system involves more than the "relations of procreation," reproduction in the biological sense.

The term "patriarchy" was introduced to distinguish the forces maintaining sexism from other social forces, such as capitalism. But the use of "patriarchy" obscures other distinctions. Its use is analogous to using capitalism to refer to all modes of production, whereas the usefulness of the term "capitalism" lies precisely in that it distinguishes between the different systems by which societies are provisioned and organized. Any society will have some system of "political economy." Such a system may be egalitarian or socialist. It may be class stratified, in which case the oppressed class may consist of serfs, peasants, or slaves. The oppressed class may consist of wage laborers, in which case the system is properly labeled "capitalist." The power of the term lies in its implication that, in fact, there are alternatives to capitalism.

Similarly, any society will have some systematic ways to deal with sex, gender, and babies. Such a system may be sexually egalitarian, at least in theory, or it may be "gender stratified," as seems to be the case for most or all of the known examples. But it is important — even in the face of a depressing history — to maintain a distinction between the human capacity and necessity to create a sexual world, and the empirically oppressive ways in which sexual worlds have been organized. Patriarchy subsumes both meanings into the same term. Sex/gender system, on the other hand, is a neutral term which refers to the domain and indicates that oppression is not inevitable in

that domain, but is the product of the specific social relations which organize it.

Finally, there are gender-stratified systems which are not adequately described as patriarchal. Many New Guinea societies (Enga, Maring, Bena Bena, Huli, Melpa, Kuma, Gahuku-Gama, Fore, Marind Anim, ad nauseum) are viciously oppressive to women. But the power of males in these groups is not founded on their roles as fathers or patriarchs, but on their collective adult maleness, embodied in secret cults, men's houses, warfare, exchange networks, ritual knowledge, and various initiation procedures. Patriarchy is a specific form of male dominance, and the use of the term ought to be confined to the Old Testament-type pastoral nomads from whom the term comes, or groups like them. Abraham was a Patriarch — one old man whose absolute power over wives, children, herds, and dependents was an aspect of the institution of fatherhood, as defined in the social group in which he lived.

Whichever term we use, what is important is to develop concepts to adequately describe the social organization of sexuality and the reproduction of the conventions of sex and gender. We need to pursue the project Engels abandoned when he located the subordination of women in a development within the mode of production.[10] To do this, we can imitate Engels in his method rather than in his results. Engels approached the task of analyzing the "second aspect of material life" by way of an examination of a theory of kinship systems. Kinship systems are and do many things. But they are made up of, and reproduce, concrete forms of socially organized sexuality. Kinship systems are observable and empirical forms of sex/gender systems.

[10]Engels thought that men acquired wealth in the form of herds and, wanting to pass this wealth to their own children, overthrew "mother right" in favor of patrilineal inheritance. "The overthrow of mother right was the *world historical defeat of the female sex*. The man took command in the home also; the woman was degraded and reduced to servitude; she became the slave of his lust and a mere instrument for the production of children" (Engels, *Origin*, 1972, 120–21, italics in original). As has been often pointed out, women do not necessarily have significant social authority in societies practicing matrilineal inheritance. (David Schneider and Kathleen Gough, eds., *Matrilineal Kinship*. Berkeley: U California P, 1961). [Rubin]

KINSHIP

(On the part played by sexuality in the transition from ape to "man")

To an anthropologist, a kinship system is not a list of biological relatives. It is a system of categories and statuses which often contradict actual genetic relationships. There are dozens of examples in which socially defined kinship statuses take precedence over biology. The Nuer custom of "woman marriage" is a case in point. The Nuer define the status of fatherhood as belonging to the person in whose name cattle bridewealth is given for the mother. Thus, a woman can be married to another woman, and be husband to the wife and father of her children, despite the fact that she is not the inseminator (Evans-Pritchard, 107–09).*

In pre-state societies, kinship is the idiom of social interaction, organizing economic, political, and ceremonial, as well as sexual, activity. One's duties, responsibilities, and privileges vis-à-vis others are defined in terms of mutual kinship or lack thereof. The exchange of goods and services, production and distribution, hostility and solidarity, ritual and ceremony, all take place within the organizational structure of kinship. The ubiquity and adaptive effectiveness of kinship has led many anthropologists to consider its invention, along with the invention of language, to have been the developments which decisively marked the discontinuity between semi-human hominids and human beings.

While the idea of the importance of kinship enjoys the status of a first principle in anthropology, the internal workings of kinship systems have long been a focus for intense controversy. Kinship systems vary wildly from one culture to the next. They contain all sorts of bewildering rules which govern whom one may or may not marry. Their internal complexity is dazzling. Kinship systems have for decades provoked the anthropological imagination into trying to explain incest taboos, cross-cousin marriage, terms of descent, relationships of avoidance or forced intimacy, clans and sections, taboos on names — the diverse array of

items found in descriptions of actual kinship systems. In the nineteenth century, several thinkers attempted to write comprehensive accounts of the nature and history of human sexual systems. One of these was *Ancient Society*, by Lewis Henry Morgan. It was this book which inspired Engels to write *The Origin of the Family, Private Property, and the State*. Engels' theory is based upon Morgan's account of kinship and marriage.

In taking up Engels' project of extracting a theory of sex oppression from the study of kinship, we have the advantage of the maturation of ethnology since the nineteenth century. We also have the advantage of a peculiar and particularly appropriate book, Lévi-Strauss' *The Elementary Structures of Kinship*. This is the boldest twentieth-century version of the nineteenth-century project to understand human marriage. It is a book in which kinship is explicitly conceived of as an imposition of cultural organization upon the facts of biological procreation. It is permeated with an awareness of the importance of sexuality in human society. It is a description of society which does not assume an abstract, genderless human subject. On the contrary, the human subject in Lévi-Strauss' work is always either male or female, and the divergent social destinies of the two sexes can therefore be traced. Since Lévi-Strauss sees the essence of kinship systems to lie in an exchange of women between men, he constructs an implicit theory of sex oppression. Aptly, the book is dedicated to the memory of Lewis Henry Morgan.

"Vile and precious merchandise" — Monique Wittig

The Elementary Structures of Kinship is a grand statement on the origin and nature of human society. It is a treatise on the kinship systems of approximately one-third of the ethnographic globe. Most fundamentally, it is an attempt to discern the structural principles of kinship. Lévi-Strauss argues that the application of these principles (summarized in the last chapter of *Elementary Structures*) to kinship data reveals an intelligible logic to the taboos and marriage rules which have perplexed and mystified Western anthropologists. He constructs a chess game of

---

*E. E. Evans-Pritchard, *Kinship and Marriage Among the Nuer*. London: Oxford UP, 1951.

such complexity that it cannot be recapitulated here. But two of his chess pieces are particularly relevant to women — the "gift" and the incest taboo, whose dual articulation adds up to his concept of the exchange of women.

The Elementary Structures is in part a radical gloss on another famous theory of primitive social organization, Mauss' *Essay on the Gift*. It was Mauss who first theorized as to the significance of one of the most striking features of primitive societies: the extent to which giving, receiving, and reciprocating gifts dominates social intercourse. In such societies, all sorts of things circulate in exchange — food, spells, rituals, words, names, ornaments, tools, and powers.

> Your own mother, your own sister, your own pigs, your own yams that you have piled up, you may not eat. Other people's mothers, other people's sister, other people's pigs, other people's yams that they have piled up, you may eat. (Arapesh, cited in Lévi-Strauss, 27)*

In a typical gift transaction, neither party gains anything. In the Trobriand Islands, each household maintains a garden of yams and each household eats yams. But the yams a household grows and the yams it eats are not the same. At harvest time, a man sends the yams he has cultivated to the household of his sister; the household in which he lives is provisioned by his wife's brother (Malinowski).** Since such a procedure appears to be a useless one from the point of view of accumulation or trade, its logic has been sought elsewhere. Mauss proposed that the significance of gift giving is that it expresses, affirms, or creates a social link between the partners of an exchange. Gift giving confers upon its participants a special relationship of trust, solidarity, and mutual aid. One can solicit a friendly relationship in the offer of a gift; acceptance implies a willingness to return a gift and a confirmation of the relationship. Gift exchange may also be the idiom of competition and rivalry. There are many examples in which one person humiliates another by giving more than can

be reciprocated. Some political systems, such as the Big Man systems of Highland New Guinea, are based on exchange which is unequal on the material plane. An aspiring Big Man wants to give away more goods than can be reciprocated. He gets his return in political prestige.

Although both Mauss and Lévi-Strauss emphasize the solidary[11] aspects of gift exchange, the other purposes served by gift giving only strengthen the point that it is an ubiquitous means of social commerce. Mauss proposed that gifts were the threads of social discourse, the means by which such societies were held together in the absence of specialized governmental institutions. "The gift is the primitive way of achieving the peace that in civil society is secured by the state. . . . Composing society, the gift was the liberation of culture" (Sahlins, 169, 175).†

Lévi-Strauss adds to the theory of primitive reciprocity the idea that marriages are a most basic form of gift exchange, in which it is women who are the most precious of gifts. He argues that the incest taboo should best be understood as a mechanism to insure that such exchanges take place between families and between groups. Since the existence of incest taboos is universal, but the content of their prohibitions variable, they cannot be explained as having the aim of preventing the occurrence of genetically close matings. Rather, the incest taboo imposes the social aim of exogamy and alliance upon the biological events of sex and procreation. The incest taboo divides the universe of sexual choice into categories of permitted and prohibited sexual partners. Specifically, by forbidding unions within a group it enjoins marital exchange between groups.

> The prohibition on the sexual use of a daughter or a sister compels them to be given in marriage to another man, and at the same time it establishes a right to the daughter or sister of this other man. . . . The woman whom one does not take is, for that very reason, offered up. (Lévi-Strauss, *Elementary Structures*, 51)

> The prohibition of incest is less a rule prohibiting marriage with the mother, sister, or daughter, than a

*Claude Lévi-Strauss, *The Elementary Structures of Kinship*. Boston: Beacon, 1969.
**Bronislaw Malinowski, *The Sexual Life of Savages*. London: Routledge, 1929.

†Marshall Sahlins, *Stone Age Economics*. Chicago: Aldine, 1972.
[11]Stemming from communal interests.

rule obliging the mother, sister, or daughter to be given to others. It is the supreme rule of the gift. . . . (Ibid.: 481)

The result of a gift of women is more profound than the result of other gift transactions, because the relationship thus established is not just one of reciprocity, but one of kinship. The exchange partners have become affines, and their descendents will be related by blood: "Two people may meet in friendship and exchange gifts and yet quarrel and fight in later times, but intermarriage connects them in a permanent manner" (Best, cited in Lévi-Strauss, *Elementary Structures*, 481). As is the case with other gift giving, marriages are not always so simply activities to make peace. Marriages may be highly competitive, and there are plenty of affines who fight each other. Nevertheless, in a general sense the argument is that the taboo on incest results in a wide network of relations, a set of people whose connections with one another are a kinship structure. All other levels, amounts, and directions of exchange — including hostile ones — are ordered by this structure. The marriage ceremonies recorded in the ethnographic literature are moments in a ceaseless and ordered procession in which women, children, shells, words, cattle names, fish, ancestors, whale's teeth, pigs, yams, spells, dances, mats, etc., pass from hand to hand, leaving as their tracks the ties that bind. Kinship is organization, and organization gives power. But who is organized?

If it is women who are being transacted, then it is the men who give and take them who are linked, the woman being a conduit of a relationship rather than a partner to it.[12] The exchange of women does not necessarily imply that women are objectified, in the modern sense, since objects in the primitive world are imbued with highly personal qualities. But it does imply a distinction between gift and giver. If women are the gifts, then it is men who are the exchange partners. And it is the partners, not the presents, upon whom reciprocal exchange confers its quasi-mystical power of social linkage. The relations of such a system are such that women are in no position to realize the benefits of their own circulation. As long as the relations specify that men exchange women, it is men who are the beneficiaries of the product of such exchanges — social organization.

The total relationship of exchange which constitutes marriage is not established between a man and a woman, but between two groups of men, and the woman figures only as one of the objects in the exchange, not as one of the partners. . . . This remains true even when the girl's feelings are taken into consideration, as, moreover, is usually the case. In acquiescing to the proposed union, she precipitates or allows the exchange to take place, she cannot alter its nature. . . . (Lévi-Strauss in ibid.: 115)[13]

To enter into a gift exchange as a partner, one must have something to give. If women are for men to dispose of, they are in no position to give themselves away.

"What woman," mused a young Northern Melpa man, "is ever strong enough to get up and say, 'Let us make *moka*, let us find wives and pigs, let us give our daughters to men, let us wage war, let us kill our enemies!' No indeed not!. . . they are little rubbish things who stay at home simply, don't you see?" (Strathern, 161)*

What women indeed! The Melpa women of whom the young man spoke can't get wives, they *are* wives, and what they get are husbands, an entirely different matter. The Melpa women can't give their daughters to men, because they do not have the same rights in their daughters that their male kin have, rights of bestowal (although *not* of ownership).

<hr/>

[12]"What, would you like to marry your sister? What is the matter with you? Don't you want a brother-in-law? Don't you realize that if you marry another man's sister and another man marries your sister, you will have at least two brothers-in-law, while if you marry your own sister you will have none? With whom will you hunt, with whom will you garden, whom will you go visit?" (Arapesh, cited in Lévi-Strauss, *Elementary Structures,* 485). [Rubin]

[13]This analysis of society as based on bonds between men by means of women makes the separatist responses of the women's movement thoroughly intelligible. Separatism can be seen as a mutation in social structure, as an attempt to form social groups based on unmediated bonds between women. It can also be seen as a radical denial of men's "rights" in women, and as a claim by women of rights in themselves. [Rubin]

*Marilyn Strathern, *Women in Between*. New York: Seminar, 1972.

The "exchange of women" is a seductive and powerful concept. It is attractive in that it places the oppression of women within social systems, rather than in biology. Moreover, it suggests that we look for the ultimate locus of women's oppression within the traffic in women, rather than within the traffic in merchandise. It is certainly not difficult to find ethnographic and historical examples of trafficking in women. Women are given in marriage, taken in battle, exchanged for favors, sent as tribute, traded, bought, and sold. Far from being confined to the "primitive" world, these practices seem only to become more pronounced and commercialized in more "civilized" societies. Men are of course also trafficked — but as slaves, hustlers, athletic stars, serfs, or as some other catastrophic social status, rather than as men. Women are transacted as slaves, serfs, and prostitutes, but also simply as women. And if men have been sexual subjects — exchangers — and women sexual semi-objects — gifts — for much of human history, then many customs, clichés, and personality traits seem to make a great deal of sense (among others, the curious custom by which a father gives away the bride).

The "exchange of women" is also a problematic concept. Since Lévi-Strauss argues that the incest taboo and the results of its application constitute the origin of culture, it can be deduced that the world historical defeat of women occurred with the origin of culture, and is a prerequisite of culture. If his analysis is adopted in its pure form, the feminist program must include a task even more onerous than the extermination of men; it must attempt to get rid of culture and substitute some entirely new phenomena on the face of the earth. However, it would be a dubious proposition at best to argue that if there were no exchange of women there would be no culture, if for no other reason than that culture is, by definition, inventive. It is even debatable that "exchange of women" adequately describes all of the empirical evidence of kinship systems. Some cultures, such as the Lele and the Luma, exchange women explicitly and overtly. In other cultures, the exchange of women can be inferred. In some — particularly those hunters and gatherers excluded from Lévi-Strauss's sample — the efficacy of the concept becomes altogether questionable. What are we to make of a concept which seems so useful and yet so difficult?

The "exchange of women" is neither a definition of culture nor a system in and of itself. The concept is an acute, but condensed, apprehension of certain aspects of the social relations of sex and gender. A kinship system is an imposition of social ends upon a part of the natural world. It is therefore "production" in the most general sense of the term: a molding, a transformation of objects (in this case, people) to and by a subjective purpose (for this sense of production, see Marx, 80–99).* It has its own relations of production, distribution, and exchange, which include certain "property" forms in people. These forms are not exclusive, private property rights, but rather different sorts of rights that various people have in other people. Marriage transactions — the gifts and material which circulate in the ceremonies marking a marriage — are a rich source of data for determining exactly who has which rights in whom. It is not difficult to deduce from such transactions that in most cases women's rights are considerably more residual than those of men.

Kinship systems do not merely exchange women. They exchange sexual access, genealogical statuses, lineage names and ancestors, rights and *people* — men, women and children — in concrete systems of social relationships. These relationships always include certain rights for men, others for women. "Exchange of women" is a shorthand for expressing that the social relations of a kinship system specify that men have certain rights in their female kin, and that women do not have the same rights either to themselves or to their male kin. In this sense, the exchange of women is a profound perception of a system in which women do not have full rights to themselves. The exchange of women becomes an obfuscation if it is seen as cultural necessity, and when it is used as the single tool with which an analysis of a particular kinship system is approached.

If Lévi-Strauss is correct in seeing the exchange of women as a fundamental principle of kinship, the subordination of women can be seen as a product of the relationships by which sex and gender are organized and produced. The economic oppression of women is derivative and secondary.

*Karl Marx, *Pre-Capitalist Economic Formations*. New York: International, 1971.

But there is an "economics" of sex and gender, and what we need is a political economy of sexual systems. We need to study each society to determine the exact mechanisms by which particular conventions of sexuality are produced and maintained. The "exchange of women" is an initial step toward building an arsenal of concepts with which sexual systems can be described.

DEEPER INTO THE LABYRINTH

More concepts can be derived from an essay by Lévi-Strauss, "The Family," in which he introduces other considerations into his analysis of kinship. In *The Elementary Structures of Kinship*, he describes rules and systems of sexual combination. In "The Family," he raises the issue of the preconditions necessary for marriage systems to operate. He asks what sort of "people" are required by kinship systems, by way of an analysis of the sexual division of labor.

Although every society has some sort of division of tasks by sex, the assignment of any particular task to one sex or the other varies enormously. In some groups, agriculture is the work of women, in others, the work of men. Women carry the heavy burdens in some societies, men in others. There are even examples of female hunters and warriors, and of men performing child-care tasks. Lévi-Strauss concludes from a survey of the division of labor by sex that it is not a biological specialization, but must have some other purpose. This purpose, he argues, is to insure the union of men and women by making the smallest viable economic unit contain at least one man and one woman.

> The very fact that it [the sexual division of labor] varies endlessly according to the society selected for consideration shows that . . . it is the mere fact of its existence which is mysteriously required, the form under which it comes to exist being utterly irrelevant, at least from the point of view of any natural necessity . . . the sexual division of labor is nothing else than a device to institute a reciprocal state of dependency between the sexes. (Lévi-Strauss, 347–48)*

The division of labor by sex can therefore be seen as a "taboo": a taboo against the sameness of men and women, a taboo dividing the sexes into two mutually exclusive categories, a taboo which exacerbates the biological differences between the sexes and thereby *creates* gender. The division of labor can also be seen as a taboo against sexual arrangements other than those containing at least one man and one woman, thereby enjoining heterosexual marriage.

The argument in "The Family" displays a radical questioning of all human sexual arrangements, in which no aspect of sexuality is taken for granted as "natural" (Hertz constructs a similar argument for a thoroughly cultural explanation of the denigration of left-handedness).** Rather, all manifest forms of sex and gender are seen as being constituted by the imperatives of social systems. From such a perspective, even *The Elementary Structures of Kinship* can be seen to assume certain preconditions. In purely logical terms, a rule forbidding some marriages and commanding others presupposes a rule enjoining marriage. And marriage presupposes individuals who are disposed to marry.

It is of interest to carry this kind of deductive enterprise even further than Lévi-Strauss does, and to explicate the logical structure which underlies his entire analysis of kinship. At the most general level, the social organization of sex rests upon gender, obligatory heterosexuality, and the constraint of female sexuality.

Gender is a socially imposed division of the sexes. It is a product of the social relations of sexuality. Kinship systems rest upon marriage. They therefore transform males and females into "men" and "women," each an incomplete half which can only find wholeness when united with the other. Men and women are, of course, different. But they are not as different as day and night, earth and sky, yin and yang, life and death. In fact, from the standpoint of nature, men and women are closer to each other than either is to anything else — for instance, mountains, kangaroos, or coconut palms. The idea that men and women are more different from one another than

---

*Claude Lévi-Strauss, "The Family," in H. Shapiro, ed., *Man, Culture, and Society*. London: Oxford UP, 1971.

**Robert Hertz, *Death and the Right Hand*. Glencoe, IL: Free Press, 1960.

either is from anything else must come from somewhere other than nature. Furthermore, although there is an average difference between males and females on a variety of traits, the range of variation of those traits shows considerable overlap. There will always be some women who are taller than some men, for instance, even though men are on the average taller than women. But the idea that men and women are two mutually exclusive categories must arise out of something other than a nonexistent "natural" opposition.[14] Far from being an expression of natural differences, exclusive gender identity is the suppression of natural similarities. It requires repression: in men, of whatever is the local version of "feminine" traits; in women, of the local definition of "masculine" traits. The division of the sexes has the effect of repressing some of the personality characteristics of virtually everyone, men and women. The same social system which oppresses women in its relations of exchange, oppresses everyone in its insistence upon a rigid division of personality.

Furthermore, individuals are engendered in order that marriage be guaranteed. Lévi-Strauss comes dangerously close to saying that heterosexuality is an instituted process. If biological and hormonal imperatives were as overwhelming as popular mythology would have them, it would hardly be necessary to insure heterosexual unions by means of economic interdependency. Moreover, the incest taboo presupposes a prior, less articulate taboo on homosexuality. A prohibition against *some* heterosexual unions assumes a taboo against *non*-heterosexual unions. Gender is not only an identification with one sex; it also entails that sexual desire be directed toward the other sex. The sexual division of labor is implicated in both aspects of gender — male and female it creates them, and it creates them heterosexual. The suppression of the homosexual component of human sexuality, and by corollary, the oppression of homosexuals, is therefore a product of the same system whose rules and relations oppress women.

In fact, the situation is not so simple, as is obvious when we move from the level of generalities to the analysis of specific sexual systems. Kinship systems do not merely encourage heterosexuality to the detriment of homosexuality. In the first place, specific forms of heterosexuality may be required. For instance, some marriage systems have a rule of obligatory cross-cousin[15] marriage. A person in such a system is not only heterosexual, but "cross-cousin-sexual." If the rule of marriage further specifies matrilateral cross-cousin marriage, then a man will be "mother's-brother's-daughter-sexual" and a woman will be "father's-sister's-son-sexual."

On the other hand, the very complexities of a kinship system may result in particular forms of institutionalized homosexuality. In many New Guinea groups, men and women are considered to be so inimical to one another that the period spent by a male child *in utero* negates his maleness. Since male life force is thought to reside in semen, the boy can overcome the malevolent effects of his fetal history by obtaining and consuming semen. He does so through a homosexual partnership with an older male kinsman.

In kinship systems where bridewealth determines the statuses of husband and wife, the simple prerequisites of marriage and gender may be overridden. Among the Azande, women are monopolized by older men. A young man of means may, however, take a boy as wife while he waits to come of age. He simply pays a bridewealth (in spears) for the boy, who is thereby turned into a wife (Evans-Pritchard).* In Dahomey, a woman could turn herself into a husband if she possessed the necessary bridewealth (Herskovitz, 1937).**

The institutionalized "transvesticism" of the Mohave permitted a person to change from one sex to the other. An anatomical man could become a woman by means of a special ceremony, and an anatomical woman could in the same way become a man. The transvestite then took a wife or husband of her/his own anatomical

---

[14]"The woman shall not wear that which pertaineth unto a man, neither shall a man put on a woman's garment: for all that do so *are* abominated unto the LORD thy God" (Deuteronomy, 22:5; emphasis not mine). [Rubin]

[15]Child of one's mother's brother or father's sister (the child of one's father's brother or mother's sister is an ortho cousin).

*E. E. Evans-Pritchard, "Sexual Inversion among the Azande," *American Anthropologist* 72 (1970): 1428–34.

**Melville Herskovitz, "A Note on 'Woman-Marriage' in Dahomey," *Africa* 10.3 (1937): 335–41.

sex and opposite social sex. These marriages, which we would label homosexual, were heterosexual ones by Mohave standards, unions of opposite socially defined sexes. By comparison with our society, this whole arrangement permitted a great deal of freedom. However, a person was not permitted to be some of both genders — he/she could be either male or female, but not a little of each.

In all of the above examples, the rules of gender division and obligatory heterosexuality are present even in their transformations. These two rules apply equally to the constraint of both male and female behavior and personality. Kinship systems dictate some sculpting of the sexuality of both sexes. But it can be deduced from *The Elementary Structures of Kinship* that more constraint is applied to females when they are pressed into the service of kinship than to males. If women are exchanged, in whatever sense we take the term, marital debts are reckoned in female flesh. A woman must become the sexual partner of some man to whom she is owed as return on a previous marriage. If a girl is promised in infancy, her refusal to participate as an adult would disrupt the flow of debts and promises. It would be in the interests of the smooth and continuous operation of such a system if the woman in question did not have too many ideas of her own about whom she might want to sleep with. From the standpoint of the system, the preferred female sexuality would be one which responded to the desire of others, rather than one which actively desired and sought a response.

This generality, like the ones about gender and heterosexuality, is also subject to considerable variation and free play in actual systems. The Lele and the Kuma provide two of the clearest ethnographic examples of the exchange of women. Men in both cultures are perpetually engaged in schemes which necessitate that they have full control over the sexual destinies of their female kinswomen. Much of the drama in both societies consists in female attempts to evade the sexual control of their kinsmen. Nevertheless, female resistance in both cases is severely circumscribed.

One last generality could be predicted as a consequence of the exchange of women under a system in which rights to women are held by men. What would happen if our hypothetical woman not only refused the man to whom she was promised, but asked for a woman instead? If a single refusal were disruptive, a double refusal would be insurrectionary. If each woman is promised to some man, neither has a right to dispose of herself. If two women managed to extricate themselves from the debt nexus, two other women would have to be found to replace them. As long as men have rights in women which women do not have in themselves, it would be sensible to expect that homosexuality in women would be subject to more suppression than in men.

In summary, some basic generalities about the organization of human sexuality can be derived from an exegesis of Lévi-Strauss's theories of kinship. These are the incest taboo, obligatory heterosexuality, and an asymmetric division of the sexes. The asymmetry of gender — the difference between exchanger and exchanged — entails the constraint of female sexuality. Concrete kinship systems will have more specific conventions, and these convention vary a great deal. While particular socio-sexual systems vary, each one is specific, and individuals within it will have to conform to a finite set of possibilities. Each new generation must learn and become its sexual destiny, each person must be encoded with its appropriate status within the system. It would be extraordinary for one of us to calmly assume that we would conventionally marry a mother's brother's daughter, or a father's sister's son. Yet there are groups in which such a marital future is taken for granted.

Anthropology, and descriptions of kinship systems, do not explain the mechanisms by which children are engraved with the conventions of sex and gender. Psychoanalysis, on the other hand, is a theory about the reproduction of kinship. Psychoanalysis describes the residue left within individuals by their confrontation with the rules and regulations of sexuality of the societies to which they are born.

PSYCHOANALYSIS AND ITS DISCONTENTS

The battle between psychoanalysis and the women's and gay movements has become legendary. In part, this confrontation between sexual revolutionaries and the clinical establishment has been due to the evolution of psychoanalysis in the United States, where clinical tradition has fetishized anatomy. The child is thought to travel through its organismic stages until it reaches its anatomical destiny and the missionary position. Clinical practice has often seen its mission as the repair of individuals who somehow have become derailed en route to their "biological" aim. Transforming moral law into scientific law, clinical practice has acted to enforce sexual convention upon unruly participants. In this sense, psychoanalysis has often become more than a theory of the mechanisms of the reproduction of sexual arrangements; it has been one of those mechanisms. Since the aim of the feminist and gay revolts is to dismantle the apparatus of sexual enforcement, a critique of psychoanalysis has been in order.

But the rejection of Freud by the women's and gay movements has deeper roots in the rejection by psychoanalysis of its own insights. Nowhere are the effects on women of male-dominated social systems better documented than within the clinical literature. According to the Freudian orthodoxy, the attainment of "normal" femininity extracts severe costs from women. The theory of gender acquisition could have been the basis of a critique of sex roles. Instead, the radical implications of Freud's theory have been radically repressed. This tendency is evident even in the original formulations of the theory, but it has been exacerbated over time until the potential for a critical psychoanalytic theory of gender is visible only in the symptomatology of its denial — an intricate rationalization of sex roles as they are. It is not the purpose of this paper to conduct a psychoanalysis of the psychoanalytic unconscious; but I do hope to demonstrate that it exists. Moreover, the salvage of psychoanalysis from its own motivated repression is not for the sake of Freud's good name. Psychoanalysis contains a unique set of concepts for understanding men, women, and sexuality. It is a theory of sexuality in human society. Most importantly, psychoanalysis provides a decryption of the mechanisms by which the sexes are divided and deformed, of how bisexual, androgynous infants are transformed into boys and girls.[16] Psychoanalysis is a feminist theory *manqué*. . . .

WOMEN UNITE TO OFF THE OEDIPAL RESIDUE OF CULTURE

The precision of the fit between Freud and Lévi-Strauss is striking. Kinship systems require a division of the sexes. The Oedipal phase divides the sexes. Kinship systems include sets of rules governing sexuality. The Oedipal crisis is the assimilation of these rules and taboos. Compulsory heterosexuality is the product of kinship. The Oedipal phase constitutes heterosexual desire. Kinship rests on a radical difference between the rights of men and women. The Oedipal complex confers male rights upon the boy, and forces the girl to accommodate herself to her lesser rights.

This fit between Lévi-Strauss and Freud is by implication an argument that our sex/gender system is still organized by the principles outlined by Lévi-Strauss, despite the entirely nonmodern character of his data base. The more recent data on which Freud bases his theories testifies to the endurance of these sexual structures. If my reading of Freud and Lévi-Strauss is accurate, it suggests that the feminist movement must attempt to resolve the Oedipal crisis of culture by reorganizing the domain of sex and gender in such a way that each individual's Oedipal experience would be less destructive. The dimensions of such a task are difficult to imagine, but at least certain conditions would have to be met.

[16]"In studying women we cannot neglect the methods of a science of the mind, a theory that attempts to explain how women become women and men, men. The borderline between the biological and the social which finds expression in the family is the land psychoanalysis sets out to chart, the land where sexual distinction originates." (Juliet Mitchell, *Women's Estate*. New York: Vintage, 1971, 167)

"What is the object of psychoanalysis? . . . but the '*effects*,' prolonged into the surviving adult, of the extraordinary adventure which from birth the liquidation of the Oedipal phase transforms a small animal conceived by a man and a woman into a small human child . . . the 'effects' still present in the survivors of the forced 'humanization' of the small human animal into a *man* or a *woman*. . . ." (Louis Althusser, "Freud and Lacan," *New Left Review* 55 (1971): 57, 59; italics in original) [Rubin]

Several elements of the Oedipal crisis would have to be altered in order that the phase not have such disastrous effects on the young female ego. The Oedipal phase institutes a contradiction in the girl by placing irreconcilable demands upon her. On the one hand, the girl's love for the mother is induced by the mother's job of child care. The girl is then forced to abandon this love because of the female sex role — to belong to a man. If the sexual division of labor were such that adults of both sexes cared for children equally, primary object choice would be bisexual. If heterosexuality were not obligatory, this early love would not have to be suppressed, and the penis would not be overvalued. If the sexual property system were reorganized in such a way that men did not have overriding rights in women (if there was no exchange of women) and if there were no gender, the entire Oedipal drama would be a relic. In short, feminism must call for a revolution in kinship.

The organization of sex and gender once had functions other than itself — it organized society. Now, it only organizes and reproduces itself. The kinds of relationships of sexuality established in the dim human past still dominate our sexual lives, our ideas about men and women, and the ways we raise our children. But they lack the functional load they once carried. One of the most conspicuous features of kinship is that it has been systematically stripped of its functions — political, economic, educational, and organizational. It has been reduced to its barest bones — *sex and gender*.

Human sexual life will always be subject to convention and human intervention. It will never be completely "natural," if only because our species is social, cultural, and articulate. The wild profusion of infantile sexuality will always be tamed. The confrontation between immature and helpless infants and the developed social life of their elders will probably always leave some residue of disturbance. But the mechanisms and aims of this process need not be largely independent of conscious choice. Cultural evolution provides us with the opportunity to seize control of the means of sexuality, reproduction, and socialization, and to make conscious decisions to liberate human sexual life from the archaic relationships which deform it. Ultimately, a thoroughgoing feminist revolution would liberate more than women. It would liberate forms of sexual expression, and it would liberate human personality from the straitjacket of gender.

"Daddy, daddy, you bastard, I'm through." — *Sylvia Plath*

In the course of this essay I have tried to construct a theory of women's oppression by borrowing concepts from anthropology and psychoanalysis. But Lévi-Strauss and Freud write within an intellectual tradition produced by a culture in which women are oppressed. The danger in my enterprise is that the sexism in the tradition of which they are a part tends to be dragged in with each borrowing. "We cannot utter a single destructive proposition which has not already slipped into the form, the logic, and the implicit postulations of precisely what it seeks to contest" (Derrida, 1972:250).[17] And what slips in is formidable. Both psychoanalysis and structural anthropology are, in one sense, the most sophisticated ideologies of sexism around.[18]

For instance, Lévi-Strauss sees women as being like words, which are misused when they are not "communicated" and exchanged. On the last page of a very long book, he observes that

[17]See p. 915 (Derrida, "Structure, Sign, and Play," originally published in *The Structuralist Controversy: The Languages of Criticism and the Science of Man*. Baltimore: Johns Hopkins, 1972).

[18]Parts of Wittig's *Les Guérillères* (1973) appear to be tirades against Lévi-Strauss and Lacan. For instance:

> Has he not indeed written, power and the possession of women, leisure and the enjoyment of women? He writes that you are currency, an item of exchange. He writes, barter, barter, possession and acquisition of women and merchandise. Better for you to see your guts in the sun and utter the death rattle than to live a life that anyone can appropriate. What belongs to you on this earth? Only death. No power on earth can take that away from you. And — consider explain tell yourself — if happiness consists in the possession of something, then hold fast to this sovereign happiness — to die. (Monique Wittig, *Les Guérillères*. New York: Avon, 1973:115–16; see also 106–07; 113–14; 134)

The awareness of French feminists of Lévi-Strauss and Lacan is most clearly evident in a group called "Psychoanalyse et Politique" which defined its task as a feminist use and critique of Lacanian psychoanalysis. [Rubin] this creates something of a contradiction in women, since women are at the same time "speakers" and "spoken." His only comment on this contradiction is this:

> But woman could never become just a sign and nothing more, since even in a man's world she is still a person, and since insofar as she is defined as a sign she must be recognized as a generator of signs. In the matrimonial dialogue of men, woman is never purely what is spoken about; for if women in general represent a certain category of signs, destined to a certain kind of communication, each woman preserves a particular value arising from her talent, before and after marriage, for taking her part in a duet. In contrast to words, which have wholly become signs, woman has remained at once a sign and a value. *This explains why the relations between the sexes have preserved that affective richness, ardour and mystery which doubtless originally permeated the entire universe of human communications.* (Lévi-Strauss, *Elementary Structures*, 496; my italics)

This is an extraordinary statement. Why is he not, at this point, denouncing what kinship systems do to women, instead of presenting one of the greatest rip-offs of all time as the root of romance?

A similar insensitivity is revealed within psychoanalysis by the inconsistency with which it assimilates the critical implications of its own theory. For instance, Freud did not hesitate to recognize that his findings posed a challenge to conventional morality:

> We cannot avoid observing with critical eyes, and we have found that it is impossible to give our support to conventional sexual morality or to approve highly of the means by which society attempts to arrange the practical problems of sexuality in life. *We can demonstrate with ease that what the world calls its code of morals demands more sacrifices than it is worth*, and that its behavior is neither dictated by honesty nor instituted with wisdom. (Freud, 376–77; my emphasis)*

Nevertheless, when psychoanalysis demonstrates with equal facility that the ordinary components of feminine personality are masochism, self-hatred, and passivity,[19] a similar judgment is *not* made.

*Sigmund Freud, *A General Introduction to Psychoanalysis*. Garden City, NY, 1943.

[19]"Every woman adores a fascist." — Sylvia Plath. [Rubin]

Instead, a double standard of interpretation is employed. Masochism is bad for men, essential to women. Adequate narcissism is necessary for men, impossible for women. Passivity is tragic in man, while lack of passivity is tragic in a woman.

It is this double standard which enables clinicians to try to accommodate women to a role whose destructiveness is so lucidly detailed in their own theories. It is the same inconsistent attitude which permits therapists to consider lesbianism as a problem to be cured, rather than as the resistance to a bad situation that their own theory suggests.[20]

There are points within the analytic discussions of femininity where one might say, "This is oppression of women," or "We can demonstrate with ease that what the world calls femininity demands more sacrifices than it is worth." It is precisely at such points that the implications of the theory are ignored, and are replaced with formulations whose purpose is to keep those implications firmly lodged in the theoretical unconscious. It is at these points that all sorts of mysterious chemical substances, joys in pain, and biological aims are substituted for a critical assessment of the costs of femininity. These substitutions are the symptoms of theoretical repression, in that they are not consistent with the usual canons of psychoanalytic argument. The extent to which these rationalizations of femininity go against the grain of psychoanalytic logic is strong evidence for the extent of the need to suppress the radical and feminist implications of the theory of femininity

[20]One clinician, Charlotte Wolff (*Love Between Women.* New York: St. Martin's, 1971) has taken the psychoanalytic theory of womanhood to its logical extreme and proposed that lesbianism is a healthy response to female socialization.

> Women who do not rebel against the status of object have declared themselves defeated as persons in their own right. (Wolff, 65)

> The lesbian girl is the one who, by all means at her disposal, will try to find a place of safety inside and outside the family, through her fight for equality with the male. She will not, like other women, play up to him: indeed, she despises the very idea of it. (Ibid.:59)

> The lesbian was and is unquestionably in the avant-garde of the fight for equality of the sexes, and for the psychical liberation of women. (Ibid.:66)

It is revealing to compare Wolff's discussion with the articles on lesbianism in Marmor, 1965. [Rubin]

(Deutsch's[21] discussions are excellent examples of this process of substitution and repression).

The argument which must be woven in order to assimilate Lévi-Strauss and Freud into feminist theory is somewhat tortuous. I have engaged it for several reasons. First, while neither Lévi-Strauss nor Freud questions the undoubted sexism endemic to the systems they describe, the questions which ought to be posed are blindingly obvious. Secondly, their work enables us to isolate sex and gender from "mode of production," and to counter a certain tendency to explain sex oppression as a reflex of economic forces. Their work provides a framework in which the full weight of sexuality and marriage can be incorporated into an analysis of sex oppression. It suggests a conception of the women's movement as analogous to, rather than isomorphic with, the working-class movement, each addressing a different source of human discontent. In Marx's vision, the working-class movement would do more than throw off the burden of its own exploitation. It also had the potential to change society, to liberate humanity, to create a classless society. Perhaps the women's movement has the task of effecting the same kind of social change for a system of which Marx had only an imperfect apperception. Something of this sort is implicit in Wittig (1973) — the dictatorship of the Amazon *guérillères* is a temporary means for achieving a genderless society.

The sex/gender system is not immutably oppressive and has lost much of its traditional function. Nevertheless, it will not wither away in the absence of opposition. It still carries the social burden of sex and gender, of socializing the young, and of providing ultimate propositions about the nature of human beings themselves. And it serves economic and political ends other than those it was originally designed to further. The sex/gender system must be reorganized through political action.

Finally, the exegesis of Lévi-Strauss and Freud suggests a certain vision of feminist politics and the feminist utopia. It suggests that we

should not aim for the elimination of men, but for the elimination of the social system that creates sexism and gender. I personally find a vision of an Amazon matriarchate, in which men are reduced to servitude or oblivion (depending on the possibilities for parthenogenetic reproduction), distasteful and inadequate. Such a vision maintains gender and the division of the sexes. It is a vision which simply inverts the arguments of those who base their case for inevitable male dominance on ineradicable and *significant* biological differences between the sexes. But we are not only oppressed *as* women, we are oppressed by having to *be* women, or men as the case may be. I personally feel that the feminist movement must dream of even more than the elimination of the oppression of women. It must dream of the elimination of obligatory sexualities and sex roles. The dream I find most compelling is one of an androgynous and genderless (though not sexless) society, in which one's sexual anatomy is irrelevant to who one is, what one does, and with whom one makes love.

THE POLITICAL ECONOMY OF SEX

It would be nice to be able to conclude here with the implications for feminism and gay liberation of the overlap between Freud and Lévi-Strauss. But I must suggest, tentatively, a next step on the agenda: a Marxist analysis of sex/gender systems. Sex/gender systems are not ahistorical emanations of the human mind; they are products of historical human activity.

We need, for instance, an analysis of the evolution of sexual exchange along the lines of Marx's discussion in *Capital* of the evolution of money and commodities. There is an economics and a politics to sex/gender systems which is obscured by the concept of "exchange of women." For instance, a system in which women are exchangeable only for one another has different effects on women than one in which there is a commodity equivalent for women.

> That marriage in simple societies involves an "exchange" is a somewhat vague notion that has often confused the analysis of social systems. The extreme case is the exchange of "sisters," formerly practiced in parts of Australia and Africa. Here

[21]Helene Deutsch (1884–1982), American psychoanalyst, author of *The Psychology of Women* (1944).

the term has the precise dictionary meaning of "to be received as an equivalent for," "to give and receive reciprocally." From quite a different standpoint the virtually universal incest prohibition means that marriage systems necessarily involve "exchanging" siblings for spouses, giving rise to a reciprocity that is purely notational. But in most societies marriage is mediated by a set of intermediary transactions. If we see these transactions as simply implying immediate or long-term reciprocity, then the analysis is likely to be blurred. . . . The analysis is further limited if one regards the passage of property simply as a symbol of the transfer of rights, for then the nature of the objects handed over . . . is of little importance. . . . Neither of these approaches is wrong; both are inadequate. (Goody and Tambiah, 1973:2)*

There are systems in which there is no equivalent for a woman. To get a wife, a man must have a daughter, a sister, or other female kinswoman in whom he has a right of bestowal. He must have control over some female flesh. The Lele and Kuma are cases in point. Lele men scheme constantly in order to stake claims in some as yet unborn girl, and scheme further to make good their claims. A Kuma girl's marriage is determined by an intricate web of debts, and she has little say in choosing her husband. A girl is usually married against her will, and her groom shoots an arrow into her thigh to symbolically prevent her from running away. The young wives almost always do run away, only to be returned to their new husbands by an elaborate conspiracy enacted by their kin and affines.

In other societies, there is an equivalent for women. A woman can be converted into bridewealth,[22] and bridewealth can be in turn converted into a woman. The dynamics of such systems vary accordingly, as does the specific kind of pressure exerted upon women. The marriage of a Melpa woman is not a return for a previous debt. Each transaction is self-contained, in that the payment of a bridewealth in pigs and shells will cancel the debt. The Melpa woman therefore has more latitude in choosing her husband than does her

Kuma counterpart. On the other hand, her destiny is linked to bridewealth. If her husband's kin are slow to pay, her kin may encourage her to leave him. On the other hand, if her consanguineal kin are satisfied with the balance of payments, they may refuse to back her in the event that she wants to leave her husband. Moreover, her male kinsmen use the bridewealth for their own purposes, in *moka* exchange and for their own marriages. If a woman leaves her husband, some or all of the bridewealth will have to be returned. If, as is usually the case, the pigs and shells have been distributed or promised, her kin will be reluctant to back her in the event of marital discord. And each time a woman divorces and remarries, her value in bridewealth tends to depreciate. On the whole, her male consanguines will lose in the event of a divorce, unless the groom has been delinquent in his payments. While the Melpa woman is freer as a new bride than a Kuma woman, the bridewealth system makes divorce difficult or impossible (Strathern, *Women in Between,* 1972).

In some societies, like the Nuer, bridewealth can only be converted into brides. In others, bridewealth can be converted into something else, like political prestige. In this case, a woman's marriage is implicated in a political system. In the Big Man systems of Highland New Guinea, the material which circulates for women also circulates in the exchanges on which political power is based. Within the political system, men are in constant need of valuables to disburse, and they are dependent upon input. They depend not only upon their immediate partners, but upon the partners of their partners, to several degrees of remove. If a man has to return some bridewealth he may not be able to give it to someone who planned to give it to someone else who intended to use it to give a feast upon which his status depends. Big Men are therefore concerned with the domestic affairs of others, whose relationship with them may be extremely indirect. There are cases in which headmen intervene in marital disputes involving indirect trading partners in order that *moka* exchanges not be disrupted. The weight of this entire system may come to rest upon one woman kept in a miserable marriage.

In short, there are other questions to ask of a marriage system than whether or not it exchanges

*Jack Goody and S. J. Tambiah, *Bridewealth and Dowry.* Cambridge: Cambridge UP, 1973.

[22]Property that must be given in exchange for a woman (opposite of dowry, property which is given together with a woman).

women. Is the woman traded for a woman, or is there an equivalent? Is this equivalent only for women, or can it be turned into something else? If it can be turned into something else, is it turned into political power or wealth? On the other hand, can bridewealth be obtained only in marital exchange, or can it be obtained from elsewhere? Can women be accumulated through amassing wealth? Can wealth be accumulated by disposing of women? Is a marriage system part of a system of stratification?[23]

These last questions point to another task for a political economy of sex. Kinship and marriage are always parts of total social systems, and are always tied into economic and political arrangements.

> Lévi-Strauss . . . rightly argues that the structural implications of a marriage can only be understood if we think of it as one item in a whole series of transactions between kin groups. So far, so good. But in none of the examples which he provides in his book does he carry this principle far enough. The reciprocities of kinship obligation are not merely symbols of alliance; they are also economic transactions, political transactions, charters to rights of domicile and land use. No useful picture of "how a kinship system works" can be provided unless these several aspects or implications of the kinship organization are considered simultaneously. (Leach, 90)[*]

Among the Kachin, the relationship of a tenant to a landlord is also a relationship between a son-in-law and a father-in-law. "The procedure for acquiring land rights of any kind is in almost all cases tantamount to marrying a woman from the lineage of the lord" (ibid.: 88). In the Kachin system, bridewealth moves from commoners to aristocrats, women moving in the opposite direction.

> From an economic aspect the effect of matrilateral cross-cousin marriage is that, on balance, the headman's lineage constantly pays wealth to the chief's lineage in the form of bridewealth. The payment can also, from an analytical point of view, be regarded as a rent paid to the senior landlord by the tenant. The most important part of this payment is

in the form of consumer goods — namely cattle. The chief converts this perishable wealth into imperishable prestige through the medium of spectacular feasting. The ultimate consumers of the goods are in this way original producers, namely, the commoners who attend the feast. (Ibid.: 89)

In another example, it is traditional in the Trobriands for a man to send a harvest gift — *urigubu* — of yams to his sister's household. For the commoners, this amounts to a simple circulation of yams. But the chief is polygamous, and marries a woman from each subdistrict within his domain. Each of these subdistricts therefore sends *urigubu* to the chief, providing him with a bulging storehouse out of which he finances feasts, craft production, and *kula* expeditions. This "fund of power" underwrites the political system and forms the basis for chiefly power (Malinowski).[**]

In some systems, position in a political hierarchy and position in a marriage system are intimately linked. In traditional Tonga, women married up in rank. Thus, low-ranking lineages would send women to higher ranking lineages. Women of the highest lineage were married into the "house of Fiji," a lineage defined as outside the political system. If the highest ranking chief gave his sister to a lineage other than one which had no part in the ranking system, he would no longer be the highest ranking chief. Rather, the lineage of his sister's son would outrank his own. In times of political rearrangement, the demotion of the previous high-ranking lineage was formalized when it gave a wife to a lineage which it had formerly outranked. In traditional Hawaii, the situation was the reverse. Women married down, and the dominant lineage gave wives to junior lines. A paramount[24] would either marry a sister or obtain a wife from Tonga. When a junior lineage usurped rank, it formalized its position by giving a wife to its former senior line.

There is even some tantalizing data suggesting that marriage systems may be implicated in the evolution of social strata, and perhaps in the

---

[23]Another line of inquiry would compare bridewealth systems to dowry systems. Many of these questions are treated in Goody and Tambiah, 1973. [Rubin]

[*]Edmund Leach, *Rethinking Anthropology.* New York: Humanities, 1971.

[**]Bronislaw Malinowski, "The Primitive Economics of the Trobriand Islanders," in T. Harding and B. Wallace, eds., *Cultures of the Pacific.* New York: Free Press, 1970.

[24]Overlord.

development of early states. The first round of the political consolidation which resulted in the formation of a state in Madagascar occurred when one chief obtained title to several autonomous districts through the vagaries of marriage and inheritance (Henry Wright, personal communication). In Samoa, legends place the origin of the paramount title — the *Tafa'ifa* — as a result of intermarriage between ranking members of four major lineages. My thoughts are too speculative, my data too sketchy, to say much on this subject. But a search ought to be undertaken for data which might demonstrate how marriage systems intersect with large-scale political processes like state-making. Marriage systems might be implicated in a number of ways: in the accumulation of wealth and the maintenance of differential access to political and economic resources; in the building of alliances; in the consolidation of high-ranking persons into a single closed stratum of endogamous[25] kin.

These examples — like the Kachin and the Trobriand ones — indicate that sexual systems cannot, in the final analysis, be understood in complete isolation. A full-bodied analysis of women in a single society, or throughout history, must take *everything* into account: the evolution of commodity forms in women, systems of land tenure, political arrangements, subsistence technology, etc. Equally important, economic and political analyses are incomplete if they do not consider women, marriage, and sexuality. Traditional concerns of anthropology and social science — such as the evolution of social stratification and the origin of the state — must be reworked to include the implications of matrilateral cross-cousin marriages, surplus extracted in the form of daughters, the conversion of female labor into male wealth, the conversion of female lives into marriage alliances, the contribution of marriage to political power, and the transformations which all of these varied aspects of society have undergone in the course of time.

This sort of endeavor is, in the final analysis, exactly what Engels tried to do in his effort to weave a coherent analysis of so many of the diverse aspects of social life. He tried to relate men and women, town and country, kinship and state, forms of property, systems of land tenure, convertibility of wealth, forms of exchange, the technology of food production, and forms of trade, to name a few, into a systematic historical account. Eventually someone will have to write a new version of *The Origin of the Family, Private Property and the State*, recognizing the mutual interdependence of sexuality, economics, and politics without underestimating the full significance of each in human society.

---

[25]Marrying within a lineage to a close relative.

Eve Kosofsky Sedgwick
b. 1950

Few would have guessed from Eve Kosofsky Sedgwick's 1975 doctoral dissertation, published as The Coherence of Gothic Conventions *in 1980, that she was to be one of the founders of gay and lesbian studies in America, nor that her 1989 MLA talk "Jane Austen and the Masturbating Girl" (published in 1991 in* Critical Inquiry*) would be singled out for attack by right-wing columnist Roger Kimball as a prime example of "tenured radicalism." Eve Sedgwick was born in Dayton, Ohio, and educated at Cornell and Yale. Her strikingly original work on homosocial desire began from lectures she gave while teaching women's studies at Boston University. Sedgwick writes: "When I began work on* Between Men: English Literature and Male Homosocial Desire *(1986), I saw myself as working mainly in the context of feminist literary criticism and theory. By the time I published* Epistemology of the

Closet in 1990, it was unmistakably clear that lesbian/gay criticism was a going concern in its own right. I see my work as being strongly marked by a queer politics that is at once antiseparatist and antiassimilationist; by a methodology that draws on deconstruction among other techniques; and by writerly experimentation." A poet as well as a critic, Sedgwick has taught writing and literature at Hamilton College, Boston University, Amherst College, and Duke University; she is currently profes- sor of English at the Graduate Center of the City University of New York. Her most recent books are Tendencies *(1993),* Fat Art, Thin Art *(1994),* Novel Gazing: Queer Readings in Fiction *(1997),* A Dialogue on Love *(1999), and* Touching Feeling: Affect, Pedagogy, Performativity *(2003). The fol- lowing selections are from the introductions to* Between Men *and* Epistemology of the Closet.

From *Between Men*

INTRODUCTION

i. Homosocial Desire

The subject of this book is a relatively short, recent, and accessible passage of English culture, chiefly as embodied in the mid-eighteenth- to mid-nineteenth-century novel. The attraction of the period to theorists of many disciplines is obvious: condensed, self-reflective, and widely influential change in economic, ideological, and gender arrangements. I will be arguing that con- comitant changes in the structure of the contin- uum of male "homosocial desire" were tightly, often causally bound up with the other more visi- ble changes; that the emerging pattern of male friendship, mentorship, entitlement, rivalry, and hetero- and homosexuality was in an intimate and shifting relation to class; and that no element of that pattern can be understood outside of its rela- tion to women and the gender system as a whole.

"Male homosocial desire": the phrase in the title of this study is intended to mark both discriminations and paradoxes. "Homosocial desire," to begin with, is a kind of oxymoron. "Homosocial" is a word occasionally used in his- tory and the social sciences, where it describes social bonds between persons of the same sex; it is a neologism, obviously formed by analogy with "homosexual," and just as obviously meant to be distinguished from "homosexual." In fact, it is applied to such activities as "male bonding," which

may, as in our society, be characterized by intense homophobia, fear and hatred of homosexuality.[1] To draw the "homosocial" back into the orbit of "desire," of the potentially erotic, then, is to hypothesize the potential unbrokenness of a con- tinuum between homosocial and homosexual — a continuum whose visibility, for men, in our soci- ety, is radically disrupted. It will become clear, in the course of my argument, that my hypothesis of

[1]The notion of "homophobia" is itself fraught with diffi- culties. To begin with, the word is etymologically nonsensi- cal. A more serious problem is that the linking of fear and hatred in the "-phobia" suffix, and in the word's usage, does tend to prejudge the question of the cause of homosexual oppression: it is attributed to fear, as opposed to (for example) a desire for power, privilege, or material goods. An alternative term that is more suggestive of collective, structurally inscribed, perhaps materially based oppression is "heterosex- ism." This study will, however, continue to use "homopho- bia," for three reasons. First, it will be an important concern here to question, rather than to reinforce, the presumptively symmetrical opposition between homo- and heterosexuality, which seems to be implicit in the term "heterosexism." Second, the etiology of individual people's attitudes toward male homosexuality will not be a focus of discussion. And third, the ideological and thematic treatments of male homo- sexuality to be discussed from the late eighteenth century onward do combine fear and hatred in a way that is appropri- ately called phobic. For a good summary of social science research on the concept of homophobia, see [Stephen M.] Morin and [Ellen] Garfinkle, "Male Homophobia" [in *Gayspeak: Gay Male and Lesbian Communication*. Ed. James W. Chesebro. New York: Pilgrim Press, 1981, pp. 117–29]. [Sedgwick]

the unbrokenness of this continuum is not a *genetic* one — I do not mean to discuss genital homosexual desire as "at the root of" other forms of male homosociality — but rather a strategy for making generalizations about, and marking historical differences in, the *structure* of men's relations with other men. "Male homosocial desire" is the name this book will give to the entire continuum.

I have chosen the word "desire" rather than "love" to mark the erotic emphasis because, in literary critical and related discourse, "love" is more easily used to name a particular emotion, and "desire" to name a structure; in this study, a series of arguments about the structural permutations of social impulses fuels the critical dialectic. For the most part, I will be using "desire" in a way analogous to the psychoanalytic use of "libido" — not for a particular affective state or emotion, but for the affective or social force, the glue, even when its manifestation is hostility or hatred or something less emotively charged, that shapes an important relationship. How far this force is properly sexual (what, historically, it means for something to be "sexual") will be an active question.

The title is specific about *male* homosocial desire partly in order to acknowledge from the beginning (and stress the seriousness of) a limitation of my subject; but there is a more positive and substantial reason, as well. It is one of the main projects of this study to explore the ways in which the shapes of sexuality, and what *counts* as sexuality, both depend on and affect historical power relationships.[2] A corollary is that in a society where men and women differ in their access to power, there will be important gender differences, as well, in the structure and constitution of sexuality.

For instance, the diacritical opposition between the "homosocial" and the "homosexual" seems to be much less thorough and dichotomous for women, in our society, than for men. At this particular historical moment, an intelligible continuum of aims, emotions, and valuations links lesbianism with the other forms of women's attention to women: the bond of mother and daughter, for instance, the bond of sister and sister, women's friendship, "networking," and the active struggles of feminism.[3] The continuum is crisscrossed with deep discontinuities — with much homophobia, with conflicts of race and class — but its intelligibility seems now a matter of simple common sense. However agonistic the politics, however conflicted the feelings, it seems at this moment to make an obvious kind of sense to say that women in our society who love women, women who teach, study, nurture, suckle, write about, march for, vote for, give jobs to, or otherwise promote the interests of other women, are pursuing congruent and closely related activities. Thus the adjective "homosocial" as applied to women's bonds (by, for example, historian Carroll Smith-Rosenberg)[4] need not be pointedly dichotomized as against "homosexual"; it can intelligibly denominate the entire continuum.

The apparent simplicity — the unity — of the continuum between "women loving women" and "women promoting the interests of women," extending over the erotic, social, familial, economic, and political realms, would not be so striking if it were not in strong contrast to the arrangement among males. When Ronald Reagan and Jesse Helms get down to serious logrolling on "family policy," they are men promoting men's interests. (In fact, they embody Heidi Hartmann's definition of patriarchy: "relations between men, which have a material base, and which, though hierarchical, establish or create interdependence and solidarity among men that enable them to dominate women.")[5] Is their bond in any way congruent with the bond of a loving gay male couple? Reagan and Helms would say no — disgustedly. Most gay couples would say no — disgustedly.

[2] For a good survey of the background to this assertion, see Jeffrey Weeks, *Sex, Politics and Society: The Regulation of Sexuality since 1800* (London: Longman, 1981), pp. 1–18. [Sedgwick]

[3] Adrienne Rich describes these bonds as forming a "lesbian continuum," in her essay, "Compulsory Heterosexuality and Lesbian Existence," in Catherine R. Stimpson and Ethel Spector Person, eds., *Women, Sex and Sexuality*, (Chicago: U Chicago P, 1980), pp. 62–91; especially pp. 79–82. [Sedgwick]

[4] "The Female World of Love and Ritual," in [Nancy F]. Cott and [Elizabeth] Pleck, eds., *A Heritage of Their Own*, New Haven: Yale UP, 1977, pp. 311–42; the usage appears on, e.g., pp. 316, 317. [Sedgwick]

[5] "The Unhappy Marriage of Marxism and Feminism: Towards a More Progressive Union," in Lydia Sargent, ed., *Women and Revolution* (Boston: South End Press, 1981), pp. 1–41; quotation is from p. 14. [Sedgwick]

But why not? Doesn't the continuum between "men-loving-men" and "men-promoting-the-interests-of men" have the same intuitive force that it has for women?

Quite the contrary: much of the most useful recent writing about patriarchal structures suggests that "obligatory heterosexuality" is built into male-dominated kinship systems, or that homophobia is a *necessary* consequence of such patriarchal institutions as heterosexual marriage.[6] Clearly, however convenient it might be to group together all the bonds that link males to males, and by which males enhance the status of males — usefully symmetrical as it would be, that grouping meets with a prohibitive structural obstacle. From the vantage point of our own society, at any rate, it has apparently been impossible to imagine a form of patriarchy that was not homophobic. Gayle Rubin writes, for instance, "The suppression of the homosexual component of human sexuality, and by corollary, the oppression of homosexuals, is . . . a product of the same system whose rules and relations oppress women."[7]

The historical manifestations of this patriarchal oppression of homosexuals have been savage and nearly endless. Louis Crompton makes a detailed case for describing the history as genocidal.[8] Our own society is brutally homophobic; and the homophobia directed against both males and females is not arbitrary or gratuitous, but tightly knit into the texture of family, gender, age, class, and race relations. Our society could not cease to be homophobic and have its economic and political structures remain unchanged.

Nevertheless, it has yet to be demonstrated that, because most patriarchies structurally include homophobia, therefore patriarchy structurally *requires* homophobia. K. J. Dover's recent study, *Greek Homosexuality*, seems to give a strong counter example in classical Greece. Male homosexuality, according to Dover's evidence, was a widespread, licit, and very influential part of the culture. Highly structured along lines of class, and within the citizen class along lines of age, the pursuit of the adolescent boy by the older man was described by stereotypes that we associate with romantic heterosexual love (conquest, surrender, the "cruel fair," the absence of desire in the love object), with the passive part going to the boy. At the same time, however, because the boy was destined in turn to grow into manhood, the assignment of roles was not permanent.[9] Thus the love relationship, while temporarily oppressive to the object, had a strongly educational functions; Dover quotes Pausanias in Plato's *Symposium* as saying "that it would be right for him [the boy] to perform any service for one who improves him in mind and character."[10] Along with its erotic component, then, this was a bond of mentorship; the boys were apprentices in the ways and virtues of Athenian citizenship, whose privileges they inherited. These privileges included the power to command the labor of slaves of both sexes, and of women of any class including their own. "Women and slaves belonged and lived together," Hannah Arendt writes. The system of sharp class and gender subordination was a necessary part of what the male culture valued most in itself: "Contempt for laboring originally [arose] out of a passionate striving for freedom from necessity and a no less passionate impatience with every effort that left no trace, no monument, no great work worthy of remembrance";[11] so the contemptible labor was left to women and slaves.

The example of the Greeks demonstrates, I think, that while heterosexuality is necessary for the maintenance of any patriarchy, homophobia, against males at any rate, is not. In fact, for the Greeks, the continuum between "men loving men" and "men promoting the interests of men"

---

[6]See, for example, Gayle Rubin, "The Traffic in Women," in Reyne Reiter, ed., *Toward an Anthropology of Women* (New York: Monthly Review Press, 1975), pp. 182–83. [Sedgwick] See p. 1664.

[7]See Rubin, p. 180. [Sedgwick] See p. 1675.

[8]Louis Crompton, "Gay Genocide: From Leviticus to Hitler" in *The Gay Academic*, ed. Louie Crew (Palm Springs, CA: ETC Publications, 1978) 67–91; but see chapter 5 for a discussion of the limitations of "genocide" as an understanding of the fate of homosexual men. [Sedgwick]

[9]On this, see Jean Baker Miller, *Towards a New Psychology of Women* (Boston: Beacon Press, 1976), ch. 1. [Sedgwick]

[10]K. J. Dover, *Greek Homosexuality* (New York: Random House, 1980), p. 91. [Sedgwick]

[11]Hannah Arendt, *The Human Condition* (Chicago: U Chicago P, 1958), p. 83, quoted in Adrienne Rich, *On Lies, Secrets and Silence* (New York: Norton, 1979) p. 206. [Sedgwick]

appears to have been quite seamless. It is as if, in our terms, there were no perceived discontinuity between the male bonds at the Continental Baths and the male bonds at the Bohemian Grove[12] or in the board room or Senate cloakroom.

It is clear, then, that there is an asymmetry in our present society between, on the one hand, the relatively continuous relation of female homosocial and homosexual bonds, and, on the other hand, the radically discontinuous relation of male homosocial and homosexual bonds. The example of the Greeks (and of other, tribal cultures, such as the New Guinea "Sambia" studied by G. H. Herdt) shows, in addition, that the structure of homosocial continuums is culturally contingent, not an innate feature of either "maleness" or "femaleness." Indeed, closely tied though it obviously is to questions of male vs. female power, the

[12]On the Bohemian Grove, an all male summer camp for American ruling-class men, see G. William Domhoff, *The Bohemian Grove and Other Retreats* (New York: Harper and Row, 1974); and a more vivid, although homophobic, account, John van der Zee, *The Greatest Men's Party on Earth: Inside the Bohemian Grove* (New York: Harcourt, 1974). [Sedgwick]

explanation will require a more exact mode of historical categorization than "patriarchy," as well, since patriarchal power structures (in Hartmann's sense) characterize both Athenian and American societies. Nevertheless, we may take as an explicit axiom that the historically differential shapes of male and female homosociality — much as they themselves may vary over time — will always be articulations and mechanisms of the enduring inequality of power between women and men.

Why should the different shapes of the homosocial continuum be an interesting question? Why should it be a *literary* question? Its importance for the practical politics of the gay movement as a minority rights movement is already obvious from the recent history of strategic and philosophical differences between lesbians and gay men. In addition, it is theoretically interesting partly as a way of approaching a larger question of "sexual politics": what does it mean — what difference does it make — when a social or political relationship is sexualized? if the relation of homosocial to homosexual bonds is so shifty, then what theoretical framework do we have for drawing any links between sexual and power relationships?

From *Epistemology of the Closet*

AXIOM 6: THE RELATION OF GAY STUDIES TO DEBATES ON THE LITERARY CANON IS, AND HAD BEST BE, TORTUOUS.

Early on in the work on *Epistemology of the Closet,* in trying to settle on a literary text that would provide a first example for the kind of argument I meant the book to enable, I found myself circling around a text of 1891, a narrative that in spite of its relative brevity has proved a durable and potent centerpiece of gay male intertexuality and indeed has provided a durable and potent physical icon for gay male desire. It tells the story of a young Englishman famous for an

extreme beauty of face and figure that seems to betray his aristocratic origin — an origin marked, however, also by mystery and class misalliance. If the gorgeous youth gives his name to the book and stamps his bodily image on it, the narrative is nonetheless more properly the story of a male triangle: a second, older man is tortured by a desire for the youth for which he can find no direct mode of expression, and a third man, emblem of suavity and the world, presides over the dispensation of discursive authority as the beautiful youth murders the tortured lover and is himself, in turn, by the novel's end ritually killed.

But maybe, I thought, one such text would offer an insufficient basis for cultural hypothesis.

Might I pick two? It isn't yet commonplace to read *Dorian Gray* and *Billy Budd* by one another's light, but that can only be a testimony to the power of accepted English and American literary canons to insulate and deform the reading of politically important texts. In any gay male canon the two contemporaneous experimental works must be yoked together as overarching gateway texts of our modern period, and the conventionally obvious differences between them of style, literary positioning, national origin, class ethos, structure, and the thematics must cease to be taken for granted and must instead become newly salient in the context of their startling erotic congruence. The book of the beautiful male English body foregrounded on an international canvas; the book of its inscription and evocation through a trio of male figures — the lovely boy, the tormented desirer, the deft master of the rules of their discourse; the story in which the lover is murdered by the boy and the boy is himself sacrificed; the deftly magisterial recounting that finally frames, preserves, exploits, and desublimates the male bodily image: *Dorian Gray* and *Billy Budd* are both that book.

The year 1891 is a good moment to which to look for a cross section of the inaugural discourses of modern homo/heterosexuality — in medicine and psychiatry, in language and law, in the crisis of female status, in the career of imperialism. *Billy Budd* and *Dorian Gray* are among the texts that have set the terms for a modern homosexual identity. And in the Euro-American culture of this past century it has been notable that foundational texts of modern gay culture — *A la recherche du temps perdu* and *Death in Venice*, for instance, along with *Dorian Gray* and *Billy Budd* — have often been the identical texts that mobilized and promulgated the most potent images and categories for (what is now visible as) the canon of homophobic mastery.

Neither *Dorian Gray* nor *Billy Budd* is in the least an obscure text. Both are available in numerous paperback editions, for instance; and, both conveniently short, each differently canonical within a different national narrative, both are taught regularly in academic curricula. As what they are taught, however, and as what canonized, comes so close to disciplining the reading permitted of each that even the contemporaneity of the two texts (*Dorian Gray* was published as a book the year *Billy Budd* was written) may startle. That every major character in the archetypal American "allegory of good and evil" is English; that the archetypal English fin-de-siècle "allegory of art and life" was a sufficiently American event to appear in a Philadelphia publisher's magazine nine months before it became a London book — the canonic regimentation that effaces these international bonds has how much the more scope to efface the intertext and the intersexed. How may the strategy of a new canon operate in this space?

Contemporary discussions of the question of the literary canon tend to be structured either around the possibility of change, of rearrangement and reassignment of texts, within one overarching master-canon of literature — the strategy of adding Mary Shelley to the Norton Anthology — or, more theoretically defensible at the moment, around a vision of an exploding master-canon whose fracture would produce, or at least leave room for, a potentially infinite plurality of mini-canons, each specified as to its thematic or structural or authorial coverage: francophone Canadian or Inuit canons, for instance; clusters of magical realism or national allegory; the blues tradition; working-class narrative; canons of the sublime or the self-reflexive; Afro-Caribbean canons; canons of Anglo-American women's writing.

In fact, though, the most productive canon effects that have been taking place in recent literary studies have occurred, not from within the mechanism either of the master-canon or of a post-fractural plurality of canons, but through an interaction between these two models of the canon. In this interaction the new pluralized mini-canons have largely failed to dislodge the master-canon from its empirical centrality in such institutional practices as publishing and teaching, although they have made certain specific works and authors newly available for inclusion in the master-canon. Their more important effect, however, has been to challenge, if not the empirical centrality, then the conceptual anonymity of the master-canon. The most notorious instance of this has occurred with feminist studies in literature, which by on the one hand confronting the master-canon with alternative canons of women's literature, and on the other hand reading rebelliously within the master-canon, has not only somewhat rearranged the table of contents for the master-canon but, more important, given it a title. If it is still in important respects *the* master-canon it nevertheless cannot now escape naming itself with every syllable also *a* particular canon, a canon of mastery, in this case of men's mastery over, and over against, women. Perhaps never again need women — need, one hopes, anybody — feel greeted by the Norton Anthology of mostly white men's Literature with the implied insolent salutation, "I'm nobody. Who are you?"

This is an encouraging story of female canon-formation, working in a sort of pincers movement with a process of feminist canon-*naming,* that has been in various forms a good deal told by now. How much the cheering clarity of this story is indebted, however, to the scarifying coarseness and visibility with which women and men are, in most if not all societies, distinguished publicly and once and for all from one another emerges only when attempts are made to apply the same model to that very differently structured though closely related form of oppression, modern homophobia. It is, as we have seen, only recently — and, I am arguing, only very incompletely and raggedly, although to that extent violently and brutally — that a combination of discursive forces have carved out, for women and for men, a possible though intensively proscribed homosexual identity in Euro-American culture. To the extent that such an identity is traceable, there is clearly the possibility, now being realized within literary criticism, for assembling alternative canons of lesbian and gay male writing *as* minority canons, as a literature of oppression and resistance and survival and heroic making. This modern view of lesbians and gay men as a distinctive minority population is of course importantly anachronistic in relation to earlier writing, however; and even in relation to modern writing it seems to falter in important ways in the implicit analysis it offers of the mechanisms of homophobia and of same-sex desire. It is with these complications that the relation between lesbian and gay literature as a minority canon, and the process of making salient the homosocial, homosexual, and homophobic strains and torsions in the already existing master-canon, becomes especially revealing.

It's revealing only, however, for those of us for whom relations within and among canons are active relations of thought. From the keepers of a dead canon we hear a rhetorical question — that is to say, a question posed with the arrogant intent of maintaining ignorance. Is there, as Saul Bellow put it, a Tolstoi of the Zulus? Has there been, ask the defenders of a monocultural curriculum, not intending to stay for an answer, has there ever yet been a Socrates of the Orient, an African American Proust, a female Shakespeare? However assaultive or fatuous, in the context of the current debate the question has not been unproductive. To answer it in good faith has been to broach inquiries across a variety of critical fronts: into the canonical or indeed world-historic texts of non–Euro-American cultures, to begin with, but also into the nonuniversal functions of literacy and the literary, into the contingent and uneven secularization and sacralization of an aesthetic realm, into the relations of public to private in the ranking of genres, into the cult of the individual author and the organization of liberal arts education as an expensive form of masterpiece theatre.

Moreover, the flat insolent question teases by the very difference of its resonance with different projects of inquiry: it stimulates or irritates or reveals differently in the context of oral or written cultures; of the colonized or the colonizing, or cultures that have had both experiences; of peoples concentrated or in diaspora; of traditions partially internal or largely external to a dominant culture of the latter twentieth century.

From the point of view of this relatively new and inchoate academic presence, then, the gay studies movement, what distinctive soundings are to be reached by posing the question our way — and staying for an answer? Let's see how it sounds.

> Has there ever been a gay Socrates?
> Has there ever been a gay Shakespeare?
> Has there ever been a gay Proust?

Does the Pope wear a dress? If these questions startle, it is not least as tautologies. A short answer, though a very incomplete one, might be that not only have there been a gay Socrates, Shakespeare, and Proust but that their names are Socrates, Shakespeare, Proust; and, beyond that, legion — dozens or hundreds of the most centrally canonic figures in what the monoculturalists are pleased to consider "our" culture, as indeed, always in different forms and senses, in every other.

What's now in place, in contrast, in most scholarship and most curricula is an even briefer response to questions like these: Don't ask. Or, less laconically: You shouldn't know. The vast preponderance of scholarship and teaching, accordingly, even among liberal academics, does simply neither ask nor know. At the most expansive, there is a series of dismissals of such questions on the grounds that:

1. Passionate language of same-sex attraction was extremely common during whatever period is under discussion — and therefore must have been completely meaningless. Or

2. Same-sex genital relations may have been perfectly common during the period under discussion — but since there was no language about them, *they* must have been completely meaningless. Or

3. Attitudes about homosexuality were intolerant back then, unlike now — so people probably didn't do anything. Or

4. Prohibitions against homosexuality didn't exist back then, unlike now — so if people did anything, it was completely meaningless. Or

5. The word "homosexuality" wasn't coined until 1869 — so everyone before then was heterosexual. (Of course, heterosexuality has always existed.) Or

6. The author under discussion is certified or rumored to have had an attachment to someone of the other sex — so their feelings about people of their own sex must have been completely meaningless. Or (under a perhaps somewhat different rule of admissible evidence)

7. There is no actual proof of homosexuality, such as sperm taken from the body of another man or a nude photograph with another woman — so the author may be assumed to have been ardently and exclusively heterosexual. Or (as a last resort)

8. The author or the author's important attachments may very well have been

homosexual — but it would be provincial to let so insignificant a fact make any difference at all to our understanding of any serious project of life, writing, or thought.

These responses reflect, as we have already seen, some real questions of sexual definition and historicity. But they only reflect them and don't reflect *on* them: the family resemblance among this group of extremely common responses comes from their closeness to the core grammar of *Don't ask; You shouldn't know*. It didn't happen; it doesn't make any difference; it didn't mean anything; it doesn't have interpretive consequences. Stop asking just here; stop asking just now; we know in advance the kind of difference that would be made by the invocation of *this* difference; it makes no difference; it doesn't mean. The most openly repressive project of censorship, such as William Bennett's[1] literally murderous opposition to serious AIDS education in schools on the grounds that it would communicate a tolerance for the lives of homosexuals, are, through this mobilization of the powerful mechanism of the open secret, made perfectly congruent with the smooth, dismissive knowingness of the urbane and the pseudo-urbane.

And yet the absolute canonical centrality of the list of authors about whom one might think to ask these questions — What was the structure, function, historical surround of same-sex love in and for Homer or Plato or Sappho? What, then, about Euripides or Virgil? If a gay Marlowe, what about Spenser or Milton? Shakespeare? Byron? But what about Shelley? Montaigne, Leopardi . . . ? Leonardo, Michelangelo, but . . . ? Beethoven? Whitman, Thoreau, Dickinson (Dickinson?), Tennyson, Wilde, Woolf, Hopkins, but Brontë? Wittgenstein, but . . . Nietzsche? Proust, Musil, Kafka, Cather, but . . . Mann? James, but . . . Lawrence? Eliot? but . . . Joyce? The very centrality of this list and its seemingly almost infinite elasticity suggest that no one *can* know *in advance* where the limits of a gay-centered inquiry are to be drawn, or where a gay theorizing

---

[1]William Bennett was secretary of education in the George H. W. Bush administration (1988–1992).

of and through even the hegemonic high culture of the Euro-American tradition may need or be able to lead. The emergence, even within the last year or two, of nascent but ambitious programs and courses in gay and lesbian studies, at schools including those of the Ivy League, may now make it possible for the first time to ask these difficult questions from within the very heart of the empowered cultural institutions to which they pertain, as well as from the marginal and endangered institutional positions from which, for so long, the most courageous work in this area has emanated.

Furthermore, as I have been suggesting, the violently contradictory and volatile energies that every morning's newspaper proves to us are circulating even at this moment, in our society, around the issues of homo/heterosexual definition show over and over again how preposterous is anybody's urbane pretense at having a clear, simple story to tell about the outlines and meanings of what and who are homosexual and heterosexual. To be gay, or to be potentially classifiable as gay — that is to say, *to be sexed or gendered* — in this system is to come under the radically overlapping aegises of a universalizing discourse of acts or bonds and at the same time of a minoritizing discourse of kinds of persons. Because of the double binds implicit in the space overlapped by universalizing and minoritizing models, the stakes in matters of definitional control are extremely high.

Obviously, this analysis suggests as one indispensable approach to the traditional Euro-American canon a pedagogy that could treat it neither as something quite exploded nor as something quite stable. A canon seen to be genuinely unified by the maintenance of a particular tension of homo/heterosexual definition can scarcely be dismantled; but neither can it ever be treated as the repository of reassuring "traditional" truths that could be made matter for any settled consolidation or congratulation. Insofar as the problematics of homo-heterosexual definition, in an intensely homophobic culture, are seen to be precisely internal to the central nexuses of that culture, this canon must always be treated as a loaded one. Considerations of the canon, it becomes clear, while vital in themselves cannot take the place of questions of pedagogic relations within and around the canon. Canonicity itself then seems the necessary wadding of pious obliviousness that allows for the transmission from one generation to another of texts that have the potential to dismantle the impacted foundations upon which a given culture rests.

Steven Kruger

b. 1958

Steven Kruger did his doctorate at Stanford on medieval theories of dreaming and medieval dream poetry, publishing the results as Dreaming in the Middle Ages *(1992). In the 1980s and early 1990s, Kruger turned to thinking about contemporary gay/lesbian writing, particularly on the topic of HIV/AIDS; this led to* AIDS Narratives: Gender and Sexuality, Fiction and Science *(1996), which uses feminist and queer theory to analyze a wide range of discourses — political, scientific, and journalistic, as well as fictional — that developed in the early years of the AIDS crisis. His more recent work has continued to look at questions of identity — race and religion, as well as gender and sexuality — in both contemporary and medieval contexts. His* Approaching the Millennium *(1997, co-edited with Deborah R. Geis) brings together a variety of scholarly perspectives on Tony Kushner's influential play,* Angels in America. *Queering the Middle Ages (2001, co-edited with Glenn Burger) presents essays that bring the perspectives of gender and sexuality theory to medieval sites and texts. His forthcoming book is* The Spectral Jew: Embodiment and Conversion in Medieval Europe *(2005).* *"Claiming the Pardoner," in which Kruger turns back to medieval materials with gender and queer theory — and AIDS — still in mind, appeared originally in* Exemplaria *(1994), from which it is reprinted here.*

Claiming the Pardoner: Toward a Gay Reading of Chaucer's Pardoner's Tale[1]

In memory of Donald R. Howard, Arturo Islas, and John J. Winkler

I. THE PARDONER, 1990

At a crucial point in Allen Barnett's recent short story "Philostorgy, Now Obscure,"[2] Chaucer's Pardoner suddenly and unexpectedly appears.[3] The story's main character, Preston, returns home "[a]fter the doctor had given him his diagnosis" of AIDS (45) and begins to clean his apartment with a vengeance (45–46):

> He took blinds from the windows and soaked them in the tub. He took books from their shelves and wiped them with a damp rag. He polished brass and waxed wood and relined shelves with new paper

till the apartment was astringent with the smell of powder cleanser and bleach.

Preston's housecleaning comes at the center of a story that navigates complexly back and forth between memories of the past, a present transformed by AIDS, and imaginations of the future, and the scene of cleaning functions in a complicated manner within the nexus of past, present, and future. It represents a wishful if futile attempt to deny AIDS, to cleanse the present of the tinges of disease; but it also provides Preston with an initial way, however oblique, to face his diagnosis. "[A]n addictive tonic that kept him going for three days" (46), it serves almost as a medicine that moves Preston forward into his new life. The movement forward, however, involves a confrontation with the past, and specifically a gay past whose meaning AIDS has irrevocably changed. The cleaning house entailed by Preston's diagnosis forces him to come to terms with the artifacts of his former life, and these in turn, as if by an inexorable logic, lead him back to thoughts of disease and death. Caught up in this circular movement, Preston tries to expurgate the past, "empt[ying]" his "closets" ruthlessly (46):

> Bureau drawers gave up a T-shirt proclaiming SO MANY MEN, SO LITTLE TIME, old jock straps, unmatched socks, silk shirts and silk underwear he wouldn't be caught dead in. He had once read an article by a journalist whose neighbor had died of

---

[1] Earlier versions of this paper were presented at the Graduate Center of the City University of New York and the Spring 1992 meeting of the Medieval Academy; questions and comments at each event helped shape the essay's final form. I am especially indebted to suggestions made by Sara Blair, Barbara Bowen, Sherron Knopp, Charles Molesworth, Anthony O'Brien, Judith Raiskin, Ron Scapp, and Martin Stevens, and by the anonymous readers for *Exemplaria*. [Kruger]

[2] *Philostorgy* is a term (now obscure) that means "natural affection."

[3] The story was originally published in the *New Yorker* and subsequently included, in revised form, in Barnett's collection of short stories, *The Body and Its Dangers* (New York: St. Martin's Press, 1990), 34–61. I quote from the revised version, giving page numbers parenthetically in my text. [Kruger]

AIDS. The writer had described the contents of the dead man's garbage, reducing an entire life to a leather vest, chaps, and sex toys. Writing about the clothes was more invasive than wearing them would have been, he thought. And he thought about what people would find cleaning out his own apartment.

Preston's cleaning here prepares for a future, more final "cleaning out," and the confrontation of the past it involves, the gesture of "emptying closets," functions complicatedly — on the one hand, echoing the "coming out of the closet" of gay and lesbian liberation, while, on the other, discarding just those objects that, like Preston's old T-shirt, "proclaim" a gay life enabled by "coming out." Preston (and Barnett) stray dangerously close here to the homophobic moralizing equation of a certain gay "lifestyle," with its "leather vest[s], chaps, and sex toys," to disease and death, even as they, in an opposite movement, protest against "reducing an entire life" to such artifacts. The urgent question here is whether anything of a past gay life like Preston's can be salvaged now that AIDS has retrospectively rewritten that past, and rewritten it in terms disturbingly similar to those of homophobic moralizing.

At first Preston's answer seems to be no. Even though "his college notebooks slowed the process [of cleaning] down, as if there should be a reason to stave off their destruction, as if there was something in them he might have forgotten and needed learning again," these too are finally judged as "useless scribbles" (46), to be gotten rid of along with drafts of poems that are now only embarrassments (46–47):

> Better to throw it all away than to have someone find it, lay claim to it, or reduce his life to it. . . . Preston ripped the pages from their black bindings, then burned them in the sink like love letters after a divorce till there was nothing left but ash and smoke that hovered near the ceiling and made the fire alarm scream like a banshee. He needed to do the same with old friends, affect their memory of him, introduce himself anew and say, "This is me now."

But the products of his past intellectual life do give Preston pause, seeming perhaps to offer some wisdom for the present,[4] and Preston does

[4]An important role is played elsewhere in the story by Preston's encounter with an old college professor, and by his

save certain objects. What is salvaged, however, cannot remain untouched by the present; Preston's memory of it, like his old friends' "memory of him,"[5] must be made new, transformed by the experience of illness (47):

> Some things he saved: letters from friends, and two papers he had written in college, one on the Pardoner from *The Canterbury Tales*, and one on Walt Whitman. "The first angry homosexual," he had written about the Pardoner, "the first camp sensibility in English literature." And then there was Whitman's vision of love between two men, almost a civic duty, and one that had flourished for a while. The latter paper he had turned in late with a note to the teacher, "I have gotten a disease in a Whitmanesque fashion, perhaps a hazard from the kind of research I have been doing lately." Something had made the glands in his legs swell up till it was impossible to walk. "Are you homosexual?" the school doctor asked, having seen the same infection in the gay neighborhood where his practice was. "Well, now that you mention it," Preston replied.

"How much space should the past be given in a one-bedroom apartment?" (46). Barnett provides an answer to this question that is finally complex, involving both the stripping away of the past and its reconstruction, the reaffirmation of connections to old friends and lovers but also the reforging of those connections in the face of radical change ("This is me now"). He especially emphasizes the need to discover and claim a particular, complicated gay history — one that includes both Whitman and the Pardoner, celebrating Whitman's "vision of love . . . that had flourished for a while" alongside the Pardoner's anger, and a "camp sensibility" that is a certain alternative to anger.[6] Such a history is complexly related to the

memories of classes on Augustine's *Confessions;* see especially 49–51. [Kruger]

[5]Preston's readjustment of relations with old friends and lovers is at the center of Barnett's story. [Kruger]

[6]Compare H. Marshall Leicester, Jr., *The Disenchanted Self: Representing the Subject in the Canterbury Tales* (Berkeley: University of California Press, 1990), 39–40:

[T]his particular Pardoner goes out of his way to stage his abuses and make them even more blatant than those of his historically attested compeers. The same is true of his physical and sexual peculiarities. I take it that such things as his immediate echoing of the Host's "manly" oath "by Seint Ronyan" present moment, with Whitman's joyous "vision" paradoxically bound up in the experience of disease, and the Pardoner's anger providing Preston with a model for his own angry response to the diagnosis of AIDS, a historical correlative to the "banshee" scream of the fire alarm set off as the products of a former life are converted to "ash and smoke."

Giving the Pardoner a central place in Preston's life history, Barnett points up the urgency of historical claiming at a moment in gay life when, under the pressure of AIDS, past, present, and future have all been radically transformed. While recognizing that the recent gay past with its "Whitmanesque" legacy no longer "flourishes" and can no longer be seen free of the specter of disease — and even as he strips away the artifacts of that past — Barnett's Preston salvages "Whitman's vision of love between two men." But Barnett also suggests that the openly liberatory history of Whitman and the "Whitmanesque" is not enough in the face of AIDS. Preston reaches beyond Whitman to claim the Pardoner and his anger, as though the pressures of the present echo the historical conditions that first produced "angry homosexual[s]," as though the response to AIDS needs to tap the anger and "camp sensibility" generated by centuries of homophobia. Preston looks to the violence of the past out of the violence of the present to claim a voice that might angrily challenge or campily subvert the legacies of homophobia.

2. APPROACHING THE PARDONER

Barnett's invocation of the Pardoner does not stand alone in recent gay men's culture. Other striking gay readings of Chaucer include Pier Paolo Pasolini's *The Canterbury Tales* (1971) and Robert Glück's enigmatic short story "Chaucer" (1982), which mixes equal parts of Chaucer, Pasolini, and Hollywood Boulevard.[7] Both of these works focus attention on Chaucer's Pardoner, claiming him as a certain kind of "ancestor" and writing the *Canterbury Tales* into a history of gay subversion and resistance.[8]

Taking as their starting point the current moment in gay culture, such acts of claiming, though "historical" in that they participate in writing a certain gay history, are not necessarily "historicist." That is, they claim a certain identity with historical figures — in the case of Barnett's story, the fictional Pardoner read as "first angry homosexual" and "first camp sensibility" — but they do not as a matter of course concern themselves with a particularized understanding of the past, with what separates us from Chaucer, with the subtle or grand changes one might trace in writing a "history of sexuality." To arrive at a more fully historicized gay reading, we would need to look to recent work in the history of homosexuality like that of John Boswell and Brigitte Spreitzer[9] and to the recent elaboration of

[7]Robert Glück, *Elements of a Coffee Service* (San Francisco: Four Seasons Foundations, 1982), 50–54. Glück's story and Pasolini's film, along with, for instance, Pasolini's *Decameron*, Melvin Dixon's *Vanishing Rooms*, and George Whitmore's *The Confessions of Danny Slocum* (the latter two rewriting, though in very different ways, Dante and his classical and Christian predecessors), participate in a claiming and revision of medieval texts by gay male writers that I hope to treat more fully elsewhere. [Kruger]

[8]On the claiming of "ancestors" and its problematic relation to a historicist and social-constructionist understanding of sexuality, see Diana Fuss, *Essentially Speaking: Feminism, Nature and Difference* (New York: Routledge, 1989), 106:

essentialists argue that the Foucauldian reading of sexuality as a social construct rather than a natural essence must inevitably pose a threat to a politics based on the continuity of a shared homosexual tradition. It is argued . . . that the strict social constructionist approach "denies us a history that allows us to name Plato, Michelangelo and Sappho as our ancestors" . . . and it is charged that such academic theorizing fails to speak to the lived experience and self-conceptions of most members of the gay and lesbian communities.[Kruger]

[9]John Boswell, *Christianity, Social Tolerance, and Homosexuality: Gay People in Western Europe from the Beginning of the Christian Era to the Fourteenth Century* (Chicago: University of Chicago Press, 1980); Brigitte Spreitzer, *Die stumme Sünde: Homosexualität im Mittelalter, mit einem Textanhang*, Göppinger Arbeiten zur Germanistik 498 (Göppingen: Kümmerle, 1988). [Kruger]

and his announced preference for jolly wenches in every town though babies starve for it . . . have in common the tactic of calling attention to the sexual oddity the *General Prologue* notes so emphatically by deliberately shamming exaggerated virility. This is a form of camp in which the hypermasculinity is as much a put-on as the mock demonism of what Patterson calls his "gross and deliberate parody of sinfulness." [Kruger] "queer theory"[10] with its (Foucauldian) aware-ness of the changing social construction of sexual categories. Several Chaucerians, most notably Carolyn Dinshaw, H. Marshall Leicester, and Glenn Burger, have begun to move in this direc-tion in their readings of the Pardoner, and I hope that my discussion represents another step in elaborating this kind of reading.[11] It is important, still, not to forget the power of a reading like Barnett's — a bold claiming of the past for present ends — and to recognize that our own readings, however historicized, are always in some sense a response to the current moment.

What I want, then, to do in this essay is stage a negotiation between myself as a gay man living in 1992 to whom Barnett's invocation of Chaucer speaks powerfully and personally, and myself as a medievalist trained in a certain kind of close reading and a certain brand of historicism. I am concerned here to navigate between Chaucer's text, a historical understanding of the late-medieval construction of male homosexuality and of homophobia, and my own contemporary position, my own political stances and needs. Those needs include the need for a rediscovered or reconstructed gay history, and the ultimate question at issue for me here is what role Chaucer's Pardoner might play in the writing of such a history.

There are two main objections one might raise to Barnett's use of the Pardoner. First, can we really call the Pardoner a "homosexual," given the depiction of the character, given that the specific category "homosexual" was not available until long after the Middle Ages (1869), and given the claim of various historians that "homosexual iden-tity" (as opposed to "homosexual behavior") first arose in Western Europe in the nineteenth (or eighteenth or seventeenth) century?[12] Second, even if we *can* argue that the Pardoner is the fourteenth-century equivalent of a gay man, do we really want what we get in claiming him?

To take the second question first: Despite the occasional sympathetic reading of Chaucer's Pardoner, Chaucerians still largely follow Kittredge in seeing the Pardoner as "an aban-doned wretch," "the one lost soul among the Canterbury Pilgrims."[13] Such a view is not to be ascribed only to the critics' homophobia (though neither should we discount homophobia as an important force operating in readings of the tale);[14] Chaucer gives the critics, in the Pardoner's own words, ample ammunition for character assassination. To embrace the Pardoner, to claim the Pardoner as somehow our own, is not just to embrace a gay ancestor — if that is what he is — but also to take to ourselves a self-proclaimed hypocrite and cheat, and, worse yet, to make our-selves (as we identify with the Pardoner) the tar-get of the strong, and violent, hatred of the tale's conclusion (the Host's verbal, but almost physi-cal, attack on the Pardoner). The Pardoner may be

[10]For a sampling of the kinds of questions central to "queer theory," and for an explanation of at least one rationale for the use of the term, see Teresa de Lauretis, ed., "Queer Theory: Lesbian and Gay Sexualities," *Differences: A Journal of Feminist Cultural Studies* 3.2 (Summer 1991); and see the essays collected by Diana Fuss, *Inside/Out: Lesbian Theories, Gay Theories* (New York: Routledge, 1991). Such work, and that of critics like Eve Kosofsky Sedgwick, Jonathan Dollimore, and David Halperin, consistently emphasizes an awareness of the historical situatedness of sexuality. [Kruger]

[11]Carolyn Dinshaw, *Chaucer's Sexual Poetics* (Madison: University of Wisconsin Press, 1989), 156–84; Leicester, *Disenchanted Self*, 35–64 and 161–94; and Glenn Burger, "Kissing the Pardoner," *PMLA* 107 (1992): 1142–56. Burger's article, published after my essay was largely com-plete, makes especially productive use of recent critical and theoretical work concerned with re-evaluating gender, sexual-ity, and their interrelationships; it also responds to both Dinshaw and Leicester. [Kruger]

[12]For a brief summary of this "social constructionist," his-torical view, and of the disagreement over when precisely to date the "birth" of a "homosexual identity," see Fuss, *Essentially Speaking*, 107–8. Fuss quotes the phrases "homo-sexual identity" and "homosexual behavior" from Jeffrey Weeks, *Coming Out: Homosexual Politics in Britain from the Nineteenth Century to the Present* (London: Quartet, 1977). [Kruger]

[13]George Lyman Kittredge, *Chaucer and His Poetry* (Cambridge: Harvard University Press, 1915), 21 and 180. Also see 211: "The most abandoned character among the Canterbury Pilgrims is the Pardoner." [Kruger]

[14]Such homophobia was recognized especially clearly in Donald R. Howard's 1984 MLA talk, "The Sexuality of Chaucer's Pardoner." I am indebted to Thomas C. Moser, Jr., for providing me with a copy of Howard's corrected transcript for the talk. [Kruger]

intended by Chaucer to be the medieval equivalent of a gay man, but if so he is a character written out of homophobia; can we claim the Pardoner's gayness without implicating ourselves in that homophobia — without supporting the homophobic movements of the text and without making ourselves their object? Here, I think Barnett does well to focus on the Pardoner's *anger* and "camp sensibility" — those things in the character that might resist or challenge homophobia — rather than uncritically to embrace the whole character. Similarly, feminists might claim those elements of the Wife of Bath that resist patriarchy, while still recognizing that the Wife is a creation of patriarchy, and herself implicated in patriarchal ways of thinking.

But of course there is also a prior question: Can we even speak of the Pardoner as a "homosexual"? The definition of the Pardoner's sexuality has been an important issue in Chaucer criticism at least since Walter Clyde Curry argued (in 1919) that the Pardoner "carries upon his body and has stamped upon his mind and character the marks of what is known to mediaeval physiognomists as a *eunuchus ex nativitate.*"[15,16] One strain of readings follows Curry in defining the Pardoner according to medieval medical, psychological, and spiritual categories. Thus, Robert Miller agrees with Curry's basic diagnosis, but insists on reading the Pardoner allegorically, as the *eunuchus non Dei*[17] "sinning vigorously against the Holy Ghost."[18] Another group of readings explains the Pardoner's physical and psychic peculiarities by appealing to modern medicine and psychoanalysis: Daniel Silvia has proposed that the Pardoner suffers from Klinefelter's syndrome;[19] Beryl Rowland suggests that he is a "testicular pseudo-hermaphrodite of the feminine type";[20] and, in perhaps the most sweeping (but also most confusing) diagnosis, Eric Stockton claims that he is "a manic depressive with traces of anal eroticism, and a pervert with a tendency toward alcoholism."[21]

In recent years, much of the debate about the Pardoner's sexuality has centered particularly on the question of his homosexuality, which seems to have been first proposed in the 1940s, though the idea is, I think, also hinted at in earlier criticism.[22] Since Monica McAlpine's influential 1980 article, "The Pardoner's Homosexuality and How It Matters," the view of the Pardoner as a homosexual has been especially prominent. The evidence McAlpine brings forward strikes me as largely convincing, and other work on medieval homosexuality would support her argument that the Pardoner should be viewed "as a possible homosexual."[23] Thus, as John Boswell has shown, the "hare," to which the Pardoner is compared, is associated consistently in medieval

---

[15]Walter Clyde Curry, *Chaucer and the Mediaeval Sciences*, revised ed. (New York: Barnes and Noble, 1960), 59. [Kruger]

[16]Latin for "eunuch from his birth," a person whose sexual organs do not develop naturally, often as a result of chromosomal abnormalities such as Klinefelter's syndrome (mentioned below).

[17]Latin for "eunuch not for God," as opposed to those who castrated themselves as part of their divine mission, such as the Patristic father Origen, or the eunuch converted by Philip in Acts 8: 27–38.

[18]Robert P. Miller, "Chaucer's Pardoner, the Scriptural Eunuchs, and the Pardoner's Tale," *Speculum* 30 (1955): 180–99; I quote from the reprinted article in Richard J. Schoeck and Jerome Taylor, eds., *Chaucer Criticism* (Notre Dame: University of Notre Dame Press, 1960), 1:226, 231. [Kruger]

[19]See Donald R. Howard, *Chaucer: His Life, His Works, His World* (New York: E. P. Dutton 1987), 489 and 614n. [Kruger]

[20]Beryl Rowland, "Animal Imagery and the Pardoner's Abnormalities," *Neophilologus* 48 (1964): 58. See also Rowland's more recent treatment, "Chaucer's Idea of the Pardoner," *Chaucer Review* 14 (1979): 140–54. [Kruger]

[21]Eric W. Stockton, "The Deadliest Sin in *The Pardoner's Tale,*" *Tennessee Studies in Literature* 6 (1961): 47. [Kruger]

[22]C. David Benson, *Chaucer's Drama of Style: Poetic Variety and Contrast in the Canterbury Tales* (Chapel Hill: The University of North Carolina Press, 1986), 159n9, attributes the first critical suggestions of the Pardoner's homosexuality to Muriel Bowden, *A Commentary on the General Prologue of the Canterbury Tales* (New York: Macmillan, 1948), 274; and Gordon H. Gerould, *Chaucerian Essays* (1952; rpt. New York: Russell & Russell, 1968), 59. Earlier hints at the Pardoner's sexual "queerness" include perhaps Kittredge's stress on the word "abandoned," with its strong sexual connotations. [Kruger]

[23]Monica E. McAlpine, "The Pardoner's Homosexuality and How It Matters," *PMLA* 95 (1980): 8–22, at 8. [Kruger]

writings with homosexual activity, particularly anal intercourse:[24]

> The hare, for example, is said to grow a new anus each year, so that he has the same number of openings as the number of years he has lived. Hence the prohibition against eating the hare represents a rejection of pederasty.[25]

> They say that the hare of the nobler sex bears the little hares in the womb. Can it be that a bizarre nature has made him a hermaphrodite? . . . Effeminate men who violate the laws of nature are thus said to imitate hares, offending against the highest majesty of nature.[26]

But while many critics have adopted a reading of the Pardoner as a homosexual, many others remain skeptical. C. David Benson argues "the weakness of th[e] entire approach" that would diagnose "the Pardoner's sexual condition," though he himself suggests that the Pardoner may best be read as an effeminate *hetero*sexual like Absolon in the *Miller's Tale*.[27] Richard Firth Green, in an article entitled "The Sexual Normality of Chaucer's Pardoner," essentially concurs, proposing for the Pardoner "a more ordinary sexual life," "ordinary in everything, perhaps, but its debilitating [and

feminizing] excesses."[28] In a very different vein, Donald Howard has — I think largely out of a desire to dissociate the Pardoner's sinfulness from the attribution of homosexuality, and out of a recognition of the implicit homophobia of some other readings of the Pardoner[29] — consistently emphasized the *anomalies* of the Pardoner's sexuality, refusing to identify Chaucer's character simply as a eunuch or a homosexual or any other easily-defined type. In Howard's words.

> The Pardoner . . . is *feminoid* in a starkly physical way — his voice, his hair, his beard are involved. . . . [H]e is a mystery, an enigma — sexually anomalous, hermaphroditic, menacing, contradictory.[30]

Certainly Chaucer wants to raise questions about the Pardoner's sexuality. The most explicit definition of the character's sexual identity after all presents us with alternatives rather than with one clear identification: "I trowe he were a geldyng or a mare" (I.691).[31] And if we are inclined to read the Pardoner as a homosexual, we must

[24]Boswell, *Christianity, Social Tolerance, and Homosexuality*, 137–38, 142, 253, 306, 317, and 356–57. Also see Edward C. Schweitzer, Jr., "Chaucer's Pardoner and the Hare," *ELN* 4 (1967): 247–50. Interestingly, in at least one exegetical treatment, the hare is also taken as standing for the Jews (Schweitzer, 250). Further, the goat, to which the Pardoner is also compared, could be associated with hermaphroditism; see Rowland, "Animal Imagery," 58. Both hare and goat are more generally attached to lechery; see, for instance, D. W. Robertson, Jr., *A Preface to Chaucer: Studies in Medieval Perspectives* (Princeton: Princeton University Press, 1962), 255: "one common medieval device for illustrating lechery is to depict a man riding on a goat and either carrying or pursuing a rabbit." [Kruger]

[25]Clement of Alexandria, *Paedagogus* 2.10, cited in Boswell, *Christianity, Social Tolerance, and Homosexuality*, 356–57. [Kruger]

[26]Alexander Neckam, *De naturis rerum* 134, cited in Boswell, *Christianity, Social Tolerance, and Homosexuality*, 306. [Kruger]

[27]C. David Benson, "Chaucer's Pardoner: His Sexuality and Modern Critics," *Mediaevalia* 8 (1982): 337–49; the quotations are from 338, while the comparison to Absolon is on 345. [Kruger]

[28]Richard Firth Green "The Sexual Normality of Chaucer's Pardoner," *Mediaevalia* 8 (1982): 351–58; the quotations are from 357. Green cites the phrase " a more ordinary sexual life" from Benson, "Chaucer's Pardoner," 345. [Kruger]

[29]See especially Howard's 1984 MLA talk, "The Sexuality of Chaucer's Pardoner," a response to McAlpine and Benson, as well as the comments in *Chaucer: His Life, His Works, His World*, 489 (and notes ad loc.). The following is from the transcript of the MLA talk, 5–6:

> Many critics want the Pardoner to be homosexual, and some want it desperately. I think one reason is that it *defuses* the Pardoner: Chaucer meant him to be a sinister, alarming figure and meant his effect on us to be disturbing and unforgettable. But this is too much for some readers, and they want to neutralize or trivialize the figure by saying he's drunk or queer or sick, when in fact he's evil, possibly damned. Another motive is that some men want to be reassured that any two disagreeable males seen together must be queer. . . . Homophobia can produce extremes of intolerance and persecution, but in the academic world it more often produces articles. Homophobia has characterized some articles on Chaucer's Pardoner. [Kruger]

[30]Donald R. Howard, *The Idea of the Canterbury Tales* (Berkeley: University of California Press, 1976), 344–45. [Kruger]

[31]All citations of Chaucer are from *The Riverside Chaucer*, 3d ed., ed. Larry D. Benson et al. (Boston: Houghton Mifflin, 1987) with fragment and line numbers or, for *Troilus and Criseyde*, book and line numbers, given in my text. [Kruger]

find some way to account for remarks made by him that seem explicitly heterosexual (and heterosexist). Interrupting the Wife of Bath, he claims, "I was aboute to wedde a wyf; allas!" (III.166); and, introducing himself to the other pilgrims before his tale, he boasts, "I wol . . . have a joly wenche in every toun" (VI.452–53).[32] Given the difficulties of the text, our imperfect understanding of medieval ideas about sexuality, our awareness (following Foucault) of how historically contingent constructions of sexuality are, and given the current consideration, in such writers as Fuss and Butler,[33] of what precisely constitutes identity, and particularly sexual identity (whether this is somehow "essential," socially constructed, discursive, performative), we should be careful not to speak too confidently about the sexual identities of the past, or to project our own notions of sexuality back onto subjects distant from (and perhaps inaccessible to) us.

[32]One might indeed argue that the expression of a heterosexual drive is not inconsistent with medieval ideas about homosexuality: at least sometimes in medieval discussions, homosexual activity is seen as related to a generally increased sex drive and loss of sexual control. The homosexual poses a threat to women as well as other men. Thus, in discussing Muslim sexual abuses, Guibert of Nogent (*Gesta dei per francos*) suggests (cited in Boswell, *Christianity, Social Tolerance, and Homosexuality*, 208):

> Although it is allowed the wretches, in their opinion, to have many women, this is accounted little by them unless the value of such filth is also sullied by uncleanliness with men.

And Jacques de Vitry, in his *Oriental History*, argues that Muhammad (ibid., 281),

> the enemy of nature, popularized the vice of sodomy among his people, who sexually abuse not only both genders but even animals and have for the most part become like mindless horses or mules. . . . Sunk, dead, and buried in the filth of obscene desire, pursuing like animals the lusts of the flesh, they can resist no vices but are miserably enslaved to and ruled by carnal passions, often without even being roused by desire; they consider it meritorious to stimulate the most sordid desires.

Also see R. I. Moore, *The Formation of a Persecuting Society: Power and Deviance in Western Europe, 950–1250* (Oxford: Basil Blackwell, 1987), 91–94. Alternatively, one may read the Pardoner's claims of heterosexual interest, with Leicester, as "a form of camp in which the hypermasculinity is . . . a put-on" (*Disenchanted Self*, 39). [Kruger]

[33]See, for instance, Fuss, *Essentially Speaking*, and Judith Butler, *Gender Trouble: Feminism and the Subversion of Identity* (London: Routledge, 1990). [Kruger]

I am not, in other words, concerned to "prove" the Pardoner's (indeed unprovable) homosexuality; but I am convinced that Chaucer wants us to see, as part of the Pardoner's sexual "queerness," the possibility of homosexuality. And I am convinced that reading the *Pardoner's Tale* with medieval ideas about male homosexuality in mind can generate new and exciting interpretations of the Chaucerian text.

3. MEDIEVAL HOMOPHOBIA AND THE PARDONER

Barnett's claiming of the Pardoner as "the first angry homosexual" evokes a gay history responsive to the anger of the current moment, but it neglects any specific confrontation with medieval history. A richer, if more difficult, act of claiming would situate itself in relation to both the current moment and the alterity of the Middle Ages, recognizing that the Pardoner is at least partly created out of heterosexism and homophobia, and is not just a gay ancestor to be embraced. The specific historical contexts of a text like Chaucer's, especially the particularity of late medieval sexual practices and ideas about sexuality,[34] would inform such an act of claiming. Thus, while the reading of the *Pardoner's Tale* that I wish to open here participates in a contemporary project like Barnett's concerned with writing lesbians and gay men back into a history where they too often remain absent, it also attempts to historicize the Pardoner, considering how one constellation of common medieval ideas about male homosexuality might shape an approach to Chaucer's text.

In medieval treatments of sexuality and homosexuality, linguistic and literary questions are often at issue. As Dinshaw has recently argued, acts of writing and reading are, for the Middle Ages, often depicted in a sexualized way, with

[34]For one of the most recent contributions in this area, see John W. Baldwin, "Five Discourses on Desire: Sexuality and Gender in Northern France around 1200," *Speculum* 66 (1991): 797–819, esp. 818–19, on homosexuality ("Only on one conclusion were the five voices unequivocal in agreement: that homosexual and bestial expressions of desire are totally reprehensible" [818]). [Kruger]

the female body a common figure for the text, and with the dressing and undressing of that body common emblems of writing and of allegorical interpretation.[35] Procreative sexuality and fecundity are crucial metaphors for meaningful literature, and the most common medieval figure for allegory — "the letter covers the spirit as the chaff covers the grain"[36] — participates in this metaphoric constellation. In the formulation of Robert Holcot, "a grain sown in its covering of chaff will not as well and quickly germinate as it would if the chaff were removed. In the same way a mystical and obscure teaching will not be so fruitful as a nude one, although it may delight the curious very much more."[37]

Given such a sexualized way of theorizing literature, it is not surprising that errors or distortions in writing or reading are often described in sexual terms, and that homosexuality is often associated with linguistic "perversion." When Hermann of Cologne, a Jew who converted to Christianity in the twelfth century, speaks of his former interpretive "blindness" (that is, his Judaism), he revealingly uses a language of perversion that, while not limited to specifically sexual senses, certainly includes them.[38] And, conversely, when homosexuality is described, it is often treated as interpretive "blindness" and

linguistic abuse.[39] In the words of the most famous, and one of the most thoroughgoing, medieval attacks on "sodomy," Alain de Lille's *Plaint of Nature*:[40]

> The active sex shudders in disgrace as it sees itself degenerate into the passive sex. A man turned woman blackens the fair name of his sex. The witchcraft of Venus turns him into a hermaphrodite. He is subject and predicate: one and the same term is given a double application. Man here extends too far the laws of grammar. Becoming a barbarian in grammar, he disclaims the manhood given him by nature. . . .
>
> That man, in whose case a simple conversion in an Art causes Nature's laws to come to naught, is pushing logic too far. He hammers on an anvil which issues no seeds. The very hammer itself shudders in horror of its anvil. He imprints on no matter the stamp of a parent-stem: rather his ploughshare scores a barren strand.[41]

The barrenness of perverse sexuality, and particularly homosexual activity, is here affiliated with a

[35]Dinshaw, *Chaucer's Sexual Poetics*. [Kruger]

[36]From the Preface to the Canticle ascribed to St. Gregory (PL 79:471 ff.); cited in Robertson, *Preface*, 58. [Kruger]

[37]From Robert Holcot, *Super librum Ecclesiastici* (Venice, 1509), 3v; cited in Robertson, *Preface*, 335–36. [Kruger]

[38]Hermann of Cologne (Hermannus quondam Judaeus), *Opusculum de conversione sua*, ed. Gerlinde Niemeyer, MGH, Quellen zur Geistesgeschichte des Mittelalters, 4 (Weimar: Hermann Böhlaus Nachfolger, 1963). See, for instance, Hermann's comment on his (unconverted) reading of certain Biblical passages: "sinistra ea qualibet interpretatione pervertebam" (chapter 9, 97) [I perverted them by some left-handed interpretation]. The textual "perversion" here is clearly and closely linked to sexual temptation, used by the Jews (and the devil acting through them) to try to prevent Hermann's conversion (see especially the immediately following sections of the text, chapter 10).

For a reading of "perversion's lost histories" especially useful for the links it draws between sexual perversion and racial difference, see Jonathan Dollimore, *Sexual Dissidence: Augustine to Wilde, Freud to Foucault* (Oxford: Clarendon Press, 1991), 103–65. [Kruger]

[39]See, for instance, the frequent appeal to the metaphor of "caecitas" in Peter Damian's *Liber Gomorrhianus*, PL 145:159–90. Boswell briefly discusses this text, *Christianity, Social Tolerance, and Homosexuality*, 210–12, and he translates Pope Leo IX's response to the *Liber*, 365–66. [Kruger]

[40]On the *De planctu Naturae*, and its (sexualized) use of the grammatical metaphor, see John Alford, "The Grammatical Metaphor: A Survey of Its Use in the Middle Ages," *Speculum* 57 (1982): 728–60; Jan Ziolkowski, *Alan of Lille's Grammar of Sex* (Cambridge: Medieval Academy, 1985); and Thomas C. Moser, Jr., "The Latin Love Lyric in English Manuscripts: 1150–1325," Ph.D. diss., Stanford University, 1987, 99–116. [Kruger]

[41]I cite Alan of Lille, *Plaint of Nature*, trans. James J. Sheridan (Toronto: PIMS, 1980), meter 1, 67–69. Also see Alan's prose 4 (Nature's actual complaint [136–37]):

> This great multitude of men monsters are scattered hither and thither over the whole expanse of earth and from contact with their spell, chastity itself is bewitched. Of those men who subscribe to Venus' procedures in grammar, some closely embrace those of masculine gender only, others, those of feminine gender, others, those of common, or epicene gender. Some, indeed, as though belonging to the heteroclite class, show variations in deviation by reclining with those of female gender in Winter and those of masculine gender in Summer. There are some, who in the disputations in Venus' school of logic in their conclusions reach a law of interchangeability of subject and predicate. There are those who take the part of the subject and cannot function as predicate. There are some who function as predicates only but have no desire to have the subject term duly submit to them. [Kruger]

linguistic barrenness, with the inability to produce the "fruyt" of meaning, and with an unproductive entrapment in the "chaff" of ungrammatical, non-sensical language. Like others (for instance, Jews and heretics)[42] who are seen as unable properly to orchestrate meaning in texts — to move from the literal "chaff" to the spiritual "fruyt" — those practicing "sodomy" are strongly associated with the body rather than the spirit, and with bodies debased particularly by their conversion of the masculine to the feminine:

> You try to be smooth and hairless below
> So that your temple there might be like that of a
> woman,
> So that in defiance of nature you might become a
> girl.
> You have declared war on nature with your filth.
> . . .
> Your Venus is sterile and fruitless,
> And highly injurious to womankind.
> When a male mounts a male in so reprobate a fash-
> ion,
> A monstrous Venus imitates a woman.[43]

[42]Jews appear at interesting moments in the *Pardoner's Tale*, when the first of the Pardoner's false relics is described at length (VI.350–71), and when attention is focused on the figurative rending of the body of Christ through the use of oaths ("Oure blissed Lordes body they totere—/Hem thoughte that Jewes rente hym noght ynough" [VI.474–75]). In each case, a bodily corruption is associated with Judaism, and (in the first case implicitly, in the second case explicitly) tied back into the Jews' repudiation of Christ that, in medieval Christian thought, is seen as both their essential interpretive error (a massive misreading of the typology of the "Old" Testament) and the source of a distance from spiritual truth frequently figured as immersion in the literal/material and associated with the supposed degenerate quality of Jewish bodies (bleedings, male menstruation, etc.) and the supposed attacks by Jews on (holy) Christian bodies. [Kruger]

[43]From "Ganymede and Helen," an anonymous twelfth-century poem, translated in Boswell, *Christianity, Social Tolerance, and Homosexuality*, 381–89; I cite passages from 386–87. For similar material, see St. John Chrysostom, Commentary on Romans (*In Epistolam ad Romanos*), Homily 4, and Peter Cantor, *De vitio sodomitico*, both translated in Boswell, 359–62 and 375–78. In medieval literary texts from a wide variety of cultures, the accusation of male homosexual behavior is closely associated with a loss of masculinity and an imputation of femininity; see, for instance, Marie de France's "Lanval," *The Lais of Marie de France*, trans. Robert Hanning and Joan Ferrante (Durham: The Labyrinth Press, 1982), 112–13, and *Gíslasaga*, *The Saga of Gisli*, trans. George Johnston (Toronto: University of Toronto Press, 1963), 3–4. [Kruger]

The homophobic constriction I briefly sketch here — and which I hope elsewhere to elaborate more fully — is particularly suggestive for a reading of the *Pardoner's Tale*. We might in fact describe the world of that tale in the terms of the homophobic construction, that is, as a world in which the female is excluded but parodied by men, and in which the abandonment of "proper" heterosexual behavior points up abuses of language closely linked to literalness and to a deep involvement in and debasement of body.

First of all, in what has surprisingly been given little attention by the critics, the *Pardoner's Tale* is (along with the *Canon's Yeoman's Tale*) the only one of the *Canterbury Tales* that focuses solely on male characters. Though the Pardoner boasts about his own success with women and his own almost-marriage, in the story he tells — the exemplum of the three rioters — women are evoked only to be excluded. Thus, when the female appears at the center of the story, in the haunting words of the old man —

> "on the ground, which is my moodres gate,
> I knokke with my staf, bothe erly and late,
> And seye 'Leeve mooder, leet me in!'"
>
> VI.729–31

— it figures only as absence, only as an origin and terminus inaccessible to the characters of the tale. And while the scene of the tavern — with its

> tombesteres
> Fetys and smale, and yonge frutesteres,
> Syngeres with harpes, baudes, wafereres,
> Whiche been the verray develes officeres
>
> VI.477–80

— is at first a strongly feminized realm of "lech-erye" (VI.481), when it comes to the actual account of the rioters, the female figures used to set the tavern scene have disappeared.

The tavern itself is thus tainted by an open display of female sexuality explicitly associated with moral depravity, and that taint cannot but adhere to the main inhabitants of the tavern, the three rioters, Still, insofar as their particular actions are described, these men move in an all-male world, encountering taverner, young boy, and old man, responding to the demise of their "felawe" (VI.672), searching for Death figured as a male "theef" (VI.675). Strikingly, the relationship among the three is depicted in terms familiar from Chaucer's representation of male homosocial relations in several of the other tales, that is, in the terms of sworn brotherhood (VI.702–4).[44] In the *Pardoner's Tale*, as in most of the other tales where this relationship of male bonding occurs, it proves to be unstable. But the instability of that relationship is, in the other tales (notably the Knight's and Shipman's), consistently tied to its competition with heterosexual attraction. Indeed, in the *Knight's Tale*, we discover the strength of the sworn bond between Palamon and Arcite only as that bond is threatened by the love each knight suddenly feels for Emily.[45] In the *Pardoner's Tale*, on the other hand, no such competition of homosocial and heterosexual loyalties exists; the object of desire that splits the brotherhood apart is not a woman, but rather the gold that is ultimately the death of all three men. The sexual is not, however, excluded from the scene of death: when two of the rioters plot the death of the third — enacting in the pairing of two against one a parody of the heterosexual triangles of tales like the Knight's and the fabliaux — they do so in language that strongly evokes the description of heterosexual activity elsewhere in the *Tales*:

"Now," quod the firste, "thou woost wel we be
    tweye,
And two of us shul strenger be than oon.
Looke whan that he is set, that right anoon
Arys as though thou woldest with hym pleye,

And I shal ryve hym thurgh the sydes tweye
Whil that thou strogelest with hym as in game,
And with thy daggere looke thou do the same;
And thanne shal al this gold departed be,
My deere freend, bitwixen me and thee.
Thanne may we bothe oure lustes all fulfille,
And pleye at dees right at oure owene wille."
                VI.824–34

"Lustes," "wille," "game," and "pleye" are all words commonly used by Chaucer in depicting sexual "play," and the verb "struggle" is used elsewhere in the *Tales* only in sexual contexts.[46] At the heart of the Pardoner's exemplum, we find a physical penetration, a violent parody of sexual intercourse, that leads not to renewed life, or even to the rich and easy life of "pleye at dees" anticipated by the rioters, but rather to a stark and sterile death.

The turning of potentially fruitful "play" into destructive "struggle" follows inexorably in the exemplum from the rioters' consistent attachment to the physical and their consistent failure to read beyond the literal level; the depiction of the rioters thus again clearly parallels the medieval homophobic construction of male homosexuality. The rioters' brotherhood is formed out of a misunderstanding of the personification of Death, and their quest is thoroughly informed by this

---

[44] On "male homosocial desire," see Eve Kosofsky Sedgwick, *Between Men: English Literature and Male Homosocial Desire* (New York: Columbia University Press, 1985). For a discussion of Chaucer's depiction of "sworn brotherhood" in the larger social context of late fourteenth-century England, see Paul Strohm, *Social Chaucer* (Cambridge: Harvard University Press, 1989), 96–102. Strohm discusses the *Pardoner's Tale* briefly on 97. [Kruger] For Sedgwick, see p. 1684.

[45] See Palamon's speech at I.1129 ff. Only in the *Friar's Tale* of the corrupt summoner does the sworn brotherhood remain intact and only there is it, as in the *Pardoner's Tale*, unrelated to heterosexual desire. This is perhaps especially significant in that the tale is an attack on the Pardoner's travelling companion, the Summoner. [Kruger]

[46] "Pleye" is used to describe the (physical) flirtation of Nicholas and Alison toward the beginning of the *Miller's Tale* (I.3273), as well as the sexual act itself in the *Merchant's Tale*:

    "A man may do no synne with his wyf,
    Ne hurte hymselven with his owene knyf,
    For we han leve to pleye us by the lawe."
                IV.1839–41

"Game" can connote amorous play, as in the *Monk's Tale* (VII.2288) and *Troilus and Criseyde* (II.38). "Struggle," while not so clearly sexual, appears elsewhere in Chaucer only in sexual contexts: it is used in the *Man of Law's Tale* to describe Custance's resistance to sexual assault (II.921), and, most memorably, in the denouement of the *Merchant's Tale*, as a substitute description for the sex act performed in the pear tree:

    "Was no thing bet, to make yow to see,
    Than strugle with a man upon a tree.
    God woot, I dide it in ful good entente."
    "Strugle?" quod he, "Ye, algate in it wente!"
                V.2373–76

These, along with the instance in the *Pardoner's Tale*, are the only occurrences of the word in Chaucer. [Kruger]

misunderstanding. Their ultimate error, the inability to recognize the gold treasure as itself equivalent to death, also represents a failure of allegorical reading. Firmly tied to the physical world of the tavern, of eating and drinking, of treasure and rat poison, involved in the body and its debasement even in their closest approach to spiritual discourse (as they unwittingly echo a Christian understanding of Jesus's sacrifice) —

> And many a grisly ooth thanne han they sworn,
> And Cristes blessed body they torente —
> Deeth shal be deed, if that they may hym hente!
> VI.708–10

— the rioters enact, in the destruction of their own bodies, the death associated with the purely literal.[47] The absence of the feminine from the scene of action, except as it is evoked in the rioters' violent parody of heterosexuality, emphasizes the absence of fertile, spiritual reading figured so often in the Middle Ages through the dressing and undressing of the female body.

The exemplum of the *Pardoner's Tale* thus deploys a common medieval constellation of ideas about male homosexuality: an exclusion of the female, with heterosexual behavior replaced by a homosocial parody of procreative sexuality; a failure of reading; an involvement in and debasement of body. A similar set of ideas is evoked by the larger performance of the Pardoner, in which the exemplum is framed by a diatribe against the "tavern sins" (false oaths, gambling, gluttony), and that in turn is framed by the Pardoner's self-revelation. The whole of this performance can be read, like the exemplum at its center, as a drama of reading, an exploration of allegory and allegoresis; in this drama, reading is again closely linked to sexual issues, to the body, and specifically to the feminized body of the Pardoner himself.

The "gentil Pardoner" (1.669), from his introduction in the *General Prologue*, is consistently associated with the physical, and with a particularly feminized physicality; his concern with

fashion, his high voice, his long, smooth, yellow hair, his beardlessness — all lead to the conclusion that he is at least devoid of the properly masculine ("a geldyng") and perhaps fully feminine ("a mare," 1.691; see 1.669–91). Describing his preaching, the Pardoner himself foregrounds his physical being, focusing attention on the different bodily parts that become prominent in his public appearances:

> Thanne peyne I me to strecche forth the nekke,
> And est and west upon the peple I bekke,
> As dooth a dowve sittynge on a berne.
> Myne handes and my tonge goon so yerne
> That it is joye to se my bisynesse. VI.395–99

> Thanne wol I stynge hym with my tonge smerte
> In prechyng. VI.413–14

None of the other male pilgrims, and only the Wife of Bath among the women, describes him- or herself in such strongly physical terms, and as so clearly the object of the public gaze. And, as in the exemplum, physicality is here again closely tied up with questions of reading, misreading, linguistic fraud: the Pardoner's foregrounded body plays an integral role in the deception of his audiences. The strong association of the Pardoner with false relics additionally emphasizes the physical, and particularly the way in which bodies that might serve holy purposes — as might the Pardoner's own body, were he a different kind of preacher — can instead become part of an elaborate art of deception. Just as the rioters' oaths debase, by tearing apart, the holy body of Christ, the Pardoner's misuse of the institution of relics profanes the holy bodies of the saints.

But the Pardoner's larger performance raises different and more difficult questions than does the exemplum he tells. Unlike the three rioters of his story, the Pardoner shows himself aware of the linguistic and interpretive distortions in which he is involved; indeed, he celebrates these. Where the rioters are unable to escape their literalism, to move out of the realm of the physical to grasp spiritual meaning, the Pardoner is very much in control of meaning, self-consciously crafting his sermonizing as allegorical and moral. In the exemplum, a fatal misreading occurs in the rioters' insistently literal interpretation of what needs to be seen spiritually, but in the Pardoner's own

---

[47]In the vastly influential formulation of 2 Corinthians 3:6: "Littera enim occidit, Spiritus autem vivificat." [Kruger] In the King James Version, "For the letter killeth, but the spirit giveth life."

use of the false relics we have an inverse problem, a situation in which what is really only material is presented as though it in fact had spiritual efficacy. The Pardoner's whole performance plays self-consciously with the relations of the material to the spiritual: presenting himself to his audiences, and finally to the Canterbury pilgrims themselves, as a spiritually efficacious force, he nonetheless also reveals to the pilgrims his status as "a ful vicious man" (VI.459).

The Pardoner, in Chaucer's portrayal, appears as especially dangerous because, while implicated in the same debasement of body and meaning as the three rioters, depicted like them in the terms of medieval homophobia, he shows himself to be much more fully in control of body and meaning than they are. And unlike the rioters, whose "immorality" of nature and of behavior mirror each other, the Pardoner, while self-confessedly "vicious," behaves in ways that may in fact have fruitful moral outcomes. In his own most succinctly self-aware formulation:

> "But though myself be gilty in that synne,
> Yet kan I maken oother folk to twynne
> From avarice and soore to repente." VI.429–31

As has been recognized by many critics, the Pardoner's performance consistently foregrounds the question of what happens when a moral role is played by an immoral figure (a question confronted elsewhere by medieval authors in a wide range of texts; for instance, in the Lollard and anti-Lollard debates of the late fourteenth century and in the first story of Boccaccio's *Decameron*).[48,49]

As presented by the Pardoner, the story of the rioters' misreadings in fact becomes a powerful allegory of what happens when people do not move beyond physical attachments, when they refuse to attend to the spiritual; as such, it should function to turn its audience away from the material world. The Pardoner deploys the medieval homophobic construction in his tale to provide a warning about the dangers of a sterile "sodomitical" relation to the world. If the central portions of the Pardoner's performance — the exemplum framed by the diatribe against the "tavern sins" — stood alone, they would unquestionably constitute, for medieval Christianity, a "moral tale" (VI.460). But the Pardoner's insistent self-presentation, the insistent foregrounding of his sinfulness, viciousness, physicality, and verbal trickery — and specifically the way he is implicated in the very homophobic construction deployed to moralizing ends in the exemplum — prevents such a comfortable reading.[50]

---

[48]The "disparity between motive and act" (Howard, *Idea*, 352) has been an important issue in recent criticism of the *Pardoner's Tale*. Alan J. Fletcher, "The Topical Hypocrisy of Chaucer's Pardoner," *ChauR* 25 (1990): 110–26, connects this issue particularly with the Wycliffite controversy contemporary with the writing of the *Pardoner's Tale* (113), as does Peggy Knapp, *Chaucer and the Social Contest* (London: Routledge, 1990), 77–84. The larger argument in both Knapp and Fletcher — that the tale should be read in the context of Lollard and anti-Lollard debate — has perhaps some connection to the question of sexuality, since, as both Boswell and Spreitzer make clear, heresy, in medieval discourse, is often associated with homosexuality. As Fletcher suggests in his brief discussion of "gelding or mare," "aberrant sexual behavior was a standard accusation in heresy charges" (120).

Robert O. Payne, "Rhetoric in Chaucer: Chaucer's Realization of Himself as Rhetor," in *Medieval Eloquence: Studies in the Theory and Practice of Medieval Rhetoric*, ed. James J. Murphy (Berkeley: University of California Press, 1978), 270–87, raises the question "can a corrupt officer perform a good service?" (274) in relation to a different tradition — the rhetorical. Martin Stevens and Kathleen Falvey, "Substance, Accident, and Transformations: A Reading of the *Pardoner's Tale*," *ChauR* 17 (1982): 142–58, take up Payne's suggestion, though they arrive at a very different conclusion — "that [for Chaucer] art and morality are inextricably linked" (156). [Kruger]

[49]The Lollards were an early (pre-Luther) Protestant reform movement in England 1380–1430, followers of John Wycliffe. They were somewhat in favor under Richard II, Chaucer's patron, but violently persecuted after the accession of Henry IV.

[50]In Lee W. Patterson's view, "Chaucerian Confession: Penitential Literature and the Pardoner," *Medievalia et Humanistica* 7 (1976): 153–73, the focusing of attention on the Pardoner's body is itself an instance of a literal-minded misreading (167):

> But the Pardoner egoistically misreads himself, and, like the rioters of his tale, takes letter for spirit, fleshly understanding for spiritual. . . . [H]is obsessive self-regard is directed not to his sinful acts but to his physically-maimed body. Ashamed of his literal eunuchry, he hides behind a far more shameful spiritual sterility; fearing exposure to his companions, he mocks the judgment of God; his sorrow is not *de amissione patriae celetis, et multiplici offensa Creatoris* but simply *de ipso*; and his hatred is not *vilitatis peccati* but for the vileness of his body. [Kruger]

His own debased body, placed parodically in the holy role of preacher, strongly calls attention to itself, and, as a consequence, his whole performance twists itself into paradoxes and conundrums instead of "straight" meaning. How can the straightforward Christian doctrine of the tale be recognized through the strange, feminized body and self-admittedly corrupt motives of the Pardoner? Even in the Pardoner's most orthodox preaching against gluttony and the other sins, when he speaks in the voice of St. Paul or Pope Innocent III on the sins of "throte" (VI.517) and "bely" (VI.534), how can the moral message, the spirit of the teaching, overcome the image of the corrupt teacher and his own gluttonous body?

Paradoxically, the Pardoner presents a perfect allegory of the dangers of not reading spiritually, but then, by framing this with his vivid self-confession, forces his audience away from a spiritual reading, away from submitting to the moral force of the sermon. The reader or listener is, in essence, backed into an untenable position — either to accept the Pardoner's teaching, ignoring the depravity of the teacher, or reject that teaching, turning away from what is in fact good Christian doctrine. This is the conundrum faced by the other pilgrims at the end of the tale, and the reason why, for his performance to be complete, the Pardoner must demand a direct response from them, must ask them (literally) to buy into his performance. The whole tale builds up to the point where the stark and visceral power of the exemplum — its dark and frightening "proof" of the dangers of materialism — can be baldly confronted by the Pardoner's own materialism; this point of high tension comes when the Pardoner demands a monetary "offering" from the other pilgrims. He here forces a decisive reading of his performance — either a rejection of it or a buying into it — that in fact has been made impossible by the performance itself. The tale has conspired to confound a reading that is either material or spiritual, that focuses either just on the sinful body of the Pardoner or just on the moral doctrine of his preaching. The coup de grâce in the confrontation of material and spiritual that structures the tale comes in the Pardoner's final promise of a spiritual reward in exchange for a material offering that is itself payment for spiritual guidance provided by someone openly celebrating his own material corruptions.

4. RESISTING HOMOPHOBIA

If, in the exemplum proper, Chaucer signals the dangers of literal misreading by deploying a medieval homophobic construction that associates a male exclusion and parodying of the female with excessive, debased physicality and a failure of interpretation, his deployment of a similar construction in the broader forum of the tale forces a standoff between spiritual reading and a need to respond to the Pardoner's insistent and provocative materiality — the impulse to reject even good teaching given a knowledge of the teacher's depravity. In one way, then, the tale finally reconfirms the homophobic construction that it employs: the performance of the Pardoner — this feminized man, deeply involved in body and grotesquely distorting the proper uses of language — forcefully dramatizes a fear of the loss of that meaningful signification so often affiliated, in the Middle Ages, with heterosexual fecundity. And in the final homosocial encounter of the tale, the Pardoner's challenge to the Host and the Host's angry response to the Pardoner, this fear is at least ostensibly put to rest and a heterosexual hegemony reestablished. The Host bypasses the Pardoner's linguistic constructions, refusing to respond in any direct way to what the Pardoner has said. He sidesteps the interpretive impasse to which the Pardoner's audience(s) have been brought, and launches instead an ad hominem attack couched in the terms of medieval homophobia: he associates the Pardoner with a debased physicality ("thyn olde breech" [VI.948], "with thy fundement depeint" [VI.950]), and calls attention to the proper site of his masculinity ("I wolde I hadde thy coillons in myn hond" [VI.952]) only to perform a verbal emasculation ("Lat kutte hem of" [VI.954]). In doing so, he reduces the Pardoner to speechlessness, gathering the fecund power of language to himself in a verbal act that constructs the Pardoner as outside the realm of proper masculinity even as it consolidates masculine potency for the Host himself; Harry Bailly not only promises to deprive the Pardoner of his (perhaps nonexistent) "coillons" but at the same time suggests himself as the proper bearer of their power — "Lat kutte hem of, I wol thee helpe hem carie" (VI.954). With the Pardoner thus silenced and rendered abject, the Knight can step in and smooth things over, reaffirming the social order that depends on a certain kind of communication and signification, and that has been so deeply challenged by the Pardoner's speech.

But the tale's conclusion can be read less reassuringly for the heterosexual project of signification and for the security of heterosexual self-definition over against the (homophobically constructed) medieval idea of male homosexuality, and it is such a reading that I most wish to advance here. If the Pardoner's danger lies largely in his ability to confound proper procedures of signification and interpretation, then the Host's response — especially in its rejection of any allegorical or spiritual reading of the Pardoner's performance — testifies to the Pardoner's continuing power. In his attack on the Pardoner, the Host in fact could not stand farther from Christian spirituality, and he here fully involves himself in the debased physical world presented by the Pardoner as his own:

> "Nay, nay!" quod he, "thanne have I Cristes curs!
> Lat be," quod he, "it shal nat be, so theech!
> Thou woldest make me kisse thyn olde breech,
> And swere it were a relyk of a seint,
> Though it were with thy fundement depeint!
> But, by the croys which that Seint Eleyne fond,
> I wolde I hadde thy coillons in myn hond
> In stide of relikes or of seintuarie.
> Lat kutte hem of, I wol thee heple hem carie;
> They shul be shryned in an hogges toord!"
> This Pardoner answerde nat a word;
> So wrooth he was, no word ne wolde he seye.
> "Now," quod oure Hoost, "I wol no lenger pleye
> With thee, ne with noon other angry man."
>
> VI.946–59

The angry language here strongly connects the Host to his "angry" opponent, involving itself in the physical debasement of the Pardoner's false relics and queer body even as it rejects these. The Host's language is violent, but, like the language of the rioters in the tale's exemplum, it evokes the sexual: "kisse thyn olde breech," "I wolde I hadde thy coillons in myn hand," "I wol

no lenger pleye / With thee." Though reduced to silence, the Pardoner here perhaps gains a certain kind of victory. In the Host's revulsion, in what we might read as a moment of homosexual panic,[51] the Host is drawn strongly away from the spiritual and strongly into the circle of the Pardoner's body. The knight's final act of reconciliation, while bringing the Pardoner back into the sanctioned realm of the pilgrimage, also brings the Host to "kisse" the Pardoner.[52] In any case, the complex challenges posed by the Pardoner's performance do not permit an easy reassertion of the dominant medieval paradigm of moral (allegorical) literature. The Host's response merely bypasses these challenges, and indeed represents a refusal to read spiritually; it does not put the Pardoner's paradoxical performance to rest. The dilemma of reading that the Pardoner poses for the other pilgrims is never solved; it hangs heavily over many of the tales that follow it.[53]

Chaucer thus admits in the standoff between Pardoner and Host the possibility that an angry homosexual voice might present real challenges to dominant heterosexual paradigms. Even so, of course, the Pardoner's "victory" is in part a (darker) reaffirmation of homophobia: we might hear in the conclusion of the tale the dominant voices of medieval culture lamenting what might happen if the power of language were allowed to those who could not or would not play by the rules. The Pardoner's confounding of processes of representation and interpretation, while Chaucer gives voice to it, is not something he celebrates, though certainly he recognizes (indeed creates) its power.

[51]On the "difficult and contested definition" (19) of "homosexual panic," see Eve Kosofsky Sedgwick, *Epistemology of the Closet* (Berkeley: University of California Press, 1990), 19–21 and 182–212. Here, Sedgwick rethinks in certain ways her earlier use of the term in *Between Men.* [Kruger] For Sedgwick, see pp. 1684 and 1687.

[52]For a fine reading of the complexities of the kiss, see Burger, "Kissing the Pardoner"; Burger also notes the ways in which the final confrontation of Host and Pardoner implicates the Host in "exactly what the pardoner stands accused of representing" (1146). [Kruger]

[53]I am thinking here of the Ellesmere order, and particularly the ways in which the tales of Fragment VII take up literary questions raised by the *Pardoner's Tale.* [Kruger]

Still, we — gay men and lesbians, queers, anti-heterosexist critics and historians — can read the text *against* what might have been the homophobic intentions of its author, celebrating rather than condemning the Pardoner and his disruption of the heterosexual constructions of dominant medieval culture. As the classicist John J. Winkler suggests in a different context:

> [T]he larger methodological issue is whether readers should simply be trying to reproduce that author's meaning (if he had one — that is, if he had *one*) as the goal. Should we concede that much authority to the writers we read? If our critical faculties are placed only in the service of recovering and reanimating an author's meaning, then we have already committed ourselves to the premises and protocols of the past — past structures of cultural violence and their descendants in the bedrooms and mean streets and school curricula of the present. This above all we must not do. The ambiguities and contradictions within the sexual ideology of *D[alphnis] and C[hloe]* — whether they derive from the author's intention or from internal inconsistencies in the dominant cultural discourse of his age — afford us an opportunity to become resisting readers in the complex guerilla fighting of cultural studies. . . . and an occasion to struggle against the tacit, conventional, and violent embrace in which we are held by the past.[54]

While Chaucer himself may present the Pardoner's "anger" and "camp sensibility" only as dangerous, only as threatening to the heterosexual model of writing and reading so central to medieval culture, we can lay claim to that threat and advance it. Most crucially, we need to show how the Pardoner's challenge to medieval heterosexist notions of signification — and Chaucer's anxiety about that challenge — lays bare the constructed nature of those notions. The very act of containing the Pardoner — the verbal violence that needs to be done to silence him — reveals the violent force needed to contain the queer; it simultaneously reveals the force, the effort needed to construct and maintain the dominance of what Harry Bailly represents. While heterosexuality elsewhere in the *Canterbury Tales*, and in medieval culture more generally, relentlessly defines itself as natural, the movement of the *Pardoner's Tale* — and especially the final movement to repress the queer — reveals the artificiality, the unnatural and violent constructedness, of heterosexual paradigms.

What do we finally get in claiming the Pardoner? In reading the *Pardoner's Tale* from a late-twentieth-century queer perspective, we at least regain for ourselves a piece of the history of homophobia, a sense of the particular medieval voicings of revulsion against persons of queer sexuality, and a sense of the kinds of issues at stake in that revulsion. Further, reading texts like the *Pardoner's Tale* as part of a process of writing queers (and women and Jews) back into the Middle Ages, we can begin to understand the ways in which a dominant medieval European culture — self-defined as Christian, heterosexual, masculinist — depended for its self-definition upon a rigorous writing-out of Judaism and Islam, of women's experience, of the sexually other. Our own historical accounts, insofar as they replicate and support the dominant view of a Middle Ages that is "naturally," effortlessly, monolithically Christian, masculinist, and heterosexual, erase the particular sites of struggle at which the female, Jewish, "heretical," queer resisted silencing even as they were brought to silence. Claiming the Pardoner, we can intervene at one such site to locate and excavate the operations of medieval homophobia, and to hear, in however muted and distorted a fashion, the queer presences against which that homophobia was anxiously erected.

[54]John J. Winkler, *The Constraints of Desire: The Anthropology of Sex and Gender in Ancient Greece* (London: Routledge, 1990), 126. Also see Alan Bray, *Homosexuality in Renaissance England* (London: Gay Men's Press, 1982), 11:

> This book should be judged, firstly, by its capacity to explain the many fragments from the past bearing on homosexuality which are now coming to light, and secondly, by its ability to illuminate the world around us as history has given us it and — this above all else — to play a part in changing it. [Kruger]

Judith Butler

b. 1956

Judith Butler's first training in philosophy took place at the synagogue in her hometown of Cleveland, Ohio. She attended Bennington College and then Yale University, where she received her B.A. in philosophy in 1978 and her Ph.D. in 1984. She taught at Wesleyan and at Johns Hopkins Universities before becoming Chancellor Professor of rhetoric and comparative literature at the University of California at Berkeley. Butler has written extensively on questions of identity politics, gender, and sexuality. Her books include Subjects of Desire *(1987),* Gender Trouble: Feminism and the Subversion of Identity *(1989),* Bodies That Matter: On the Discursive Limits of "Sex" *(1993),* The Psychic Life of Power: Theories in Subjection *(1997),* Precarious Life: The Powers of Mourning and Violence *(2004) and* Undoing Gender *(2004). Her Wellek Library lectures have been published as* Antigone's Claim: Kinship Between Life and Death *(2000); her Spinoza lectures have been published as* Giving an Account of Oneself: A Critique of Ethical Violence *(2003). Originally given as a lecture in 1989 at a conference on homosexuality at Yale, "Imitation and Gender Insubordination" is reprinted from* Inside/Out: Lesbian Theories, Gay Theories, *edited by Diana Fuss (New York: Routledge, 1991).*

Imitation and Gender Insubordination

So what is this divided being introduced into language through gender? It is an impossible being, it is a being that does not exist, an ontological joke.
— MONIQUE WITTIG[1]

Beyond physical repetition and the psychical or metaphysical repetition, is there an ontological repetition? ... This ultimate repetition, this ultimate theatre, gathers everything in a certain way; and in another way, it destroys everything; and in yet another way, it selects from everything.
— GILLES DELEUZE[2]

TO THEORIZE AS A LESBIAN?

At first I considered writing a different sort of essay, one with a philosophical tone: the "being" of being homosexual. The prospect of *being* anything, even for pay, has always produced in me a certain anxiety, for "to be" gay, "to be" lesbian seems to be more than a simple injunction to become who or what I already am. And in no way does it settle the anxiety for me to say that this is "part" of what I am. To write or speak *as a lesbian* appears a paradoxical appearance of this "I," one which feels neither true nor false. For it is a production, usually in response to a request, to come out or write in the name of an identity which, once produced, sometimes functions as a politically efficacious phantasm. I'm not at ease with "lesbian theories, gay theories," for as I've argued elsewhere,[3] identity categories tend to be instruments of regulatory regimes, whether as the normalizing categories of oppressive structures or as the rallying points for a liberatory contestation of that very oppression. This is not to say that I will not appear at political occasions under the sign of lesbian, but that I would like to have it permanently unclear what precisely that

---

[1]"The Mark of Gender," *Feminist Issues* 5 no. 2 (1985): 6. [Butler]

[2]*Différence et répétition* (Paris: PUF, 1986), 374; my translation. [Butler]

[3]*Gender Trouble: Feminism and the Subversion of Identity* (New York and London: Routledge, 1990). [Butler]

sign signifies. So it is unclear how it is that I can contribute to this book and appear under its title, for it announces a set of terms that I propose to contest. One risk I take is to be recolonized by the sign under which I write, and so it is this risk that I seek to thematize. To propose that the invocation of identity is always a risk does not imply that resistance to it is always or only symptomatic of a self-inflicted homophobia. Indeed, a Foucaultian perspective might argue that the affirmation of "homosexuality" is itself an extension of a homophobic discourse. And yet "discourse," he writes on the same page, "can be both an instrument and an effect of power, but also a hindrance, a stumbling-block, a point of resistance and a starting point for an opposing strategy."[4]

So I am skeptical about how the "I" is determined as it operates under the title of the lesbian sign, and I am no more comfortable with its homophobic determination than with those normative definitions offered by other members of the "gay or lesbian community." I'm permanently troubled by identity categories, consider them to be invariable stumbling-blocks, and understand them, even promote them, as sites of necessary trouble. In fact, if the category were to offer no trouble, it would cease to be interesting to me: it is precisely the *pleasure* produced by the instability of those categories which sustains the various erotic practices that make me a candidate for the category to begin with. To install myself within the terms of an identity category would be to turn against the sexuality that the category purports to describe; and this might be true for any identity category which seeks to control the very eroticism that it claims to describe and authorize, much less "liberate."

And what's worse, I do not understand the notion of "theory," and am hardly interested in being cast as its defender, much less in being signified as part of an elite gay/lesbian theory crowd that seeks to establish the legitimacy and domestication of gay/lesbian studies within the academy. Is there a pregiven distinction between theory, politics, culture, media? How do those divisions operate to quell a certain intertextual writing that might well generate wholly different epistemic maps? But I am writing here now: is it too late? Can this writing, can any writing, refuse the terms by which it is appropriated even as, to some extent, that very colonizing discourse enables or produces this stumbling block, this resistance? How do I relate the paradoxical situation of this dependency and refusal?

If the political task is to show that theory is never merely *theoria,* in the sense of disengaged contemplation, and to insist that it is fully political (*phronesis*[5] or even *praxis*), then why not simply call this operation *politics,* or some necessary permutation of it?

I have begun with confessions of trepidation and a series of disclaimers, but perhaps it will become clear that *disclaiming,* which is no simple activity, will be what I have to offer as a form of affirmative resistance to a certain regulatory operation of homophobia. The discourse of "coming out" has clearly served its purposes, but what are its risks? And here I am not speaking of unemployment or public attack or violence, which are quite clearly and widely on the increase against those who are perceived as "out" whether or not of their own design. Is the "subject" who is "out" free of its subjection and finally in the clear? Or could it be that the subjection that subjectivates the gay or lesbian subject in some ways continues to oppress, or oppresses most insidiously, once "outness" is claimed? What or who is it that is "out," made manifest and fully disclosed, when and if I reveal myself as lesbian? What is it that is now known, anything? What remains permanently concealed by the very linguistic act that offers up the promise of a transparent revelation of sexuality? Can sexuality even remain sexuality once it submits to a criterion of transparency and disclosure, or does it perhaps cease to be sexuality precisely when the semblance of full explicitness is achieved?[6] Is sexuality of any kind even

⁴Michel Foucault, *The History of Sexuality, Vol. I,* trans. Robert Hurley (New York: Random House, 1980), 101. [Butler]

⁵Practical understanding.
⁶Here I would doubtless differ from the very fine analysis of Hitchcock's *Rope* offered by D. A. Miller in this volume. [Butler] See D. A. Miller, "Anal Rope." *Inside/Out: Lesbian Theories, Gay Theories,* ed. Diana Fuss (New York: Routledge, 1991), pp. 119–41.

possible without that opacity designated by the unconscious, which means simply that the conscious "I" who would reveal its sexuality is perhaps the last to know the meaning of what it says?

To claim that this is what I *am* is to suggest a provisional totalization of this "I." But if the I can so determine itself, then that which it excludes in order to make that determination remains constitutive of the determination itself. In other words, such a statement presupposes that the "I" exceeds its determination, and even produces that very excess in and by the act which seeks to exhaust the semantic field of that "I." In the act which would disclose the true and full content of that "I," a certain radical *concealment* is thereby produced. For it is always finally unclear what is meant by invoking the lesbian-signifier, since its signification is always to some degree out of one's control, but also because its *specificity* can only be demarcated by exclusions that return to disrupt its claim to coherence. What, if anything, can lesbians be said to share? And who will decide this question, and in the name of whom? If I claim to be a lesbian, I "come out" only to produce a new and different "closet." The "you" to whom I come out now has access to a different region of opacity. Indeed, the locus of opacity has simply shifted: before, you did not know whether I "am," but now you do not know what that means, which is to say that the copula[7] is empty, that it cannot be substituted for with a set of descriptions.[8] And perhaps that is a situation to be valued. Conventionally, one comes out *of* the closet (and yet, how often is it the case that we are "outted" when we are young and without resources?); so we are out of the closet, but into what? what new unbounded spatiality? the room, the den, the attic, the basement, the house, the bar, the university, some new enclosure whose door, like Kafka's door,[9] produces the expectation of a fresh air and a light of illumination that never arrives? Curiously, it is the figure of the closet that produces this expectation, and which guarantees its dissatisfaction. For being "out" always depends to some extent on being "in"; it gains its meaning only within that polarity. Hence, being "out" must produce the closet again and again in order to maintain itself as "out." In this sense, *outness* can only produce a new opacity; and *the closet* produces the promise of a disclosure that can, by definition, never come. Is this infinite postponement of the disclosure of "gayness," produced by the very act of "coming out," to be lamented? Or is this very deferral of the signified *to be valued*, a site for the production of values, precisely because the term now takes on a life that cannot be, can never be, permanently controlled?

It is possible to argue that whereas no transparent or full revelation is afforded by "lesbian" and "gay," there remains a political imperative to use these necessary errors or category mistakes, as it were (what Gayatri Spivak might call "catachrestic"[10] operations: to use a proper name improperly[11]), to rally and represent an oppressed political constituency. Clearly, I am not legislating against the use of the term. My question is simply: which use will be legislated, and what play will there be between legislation and use such that the instrumental uses of "identity" do not become regulatory imperatives? If it is already true that "lesbians" and "gay men" have been traditionally designated as impossible identities, errors of classification, unnatural disasters within juridico-medical discourses, or, what perhaps amounts to the same, the very paradigm of what calls to be classified, regulated, and controlled, then perhaps these sites of disruption, error, confusion, and trouble can be the very rallying points for a certain resistance to classification and to identity as such.

[7] Refers to the verb "to be," used with a predicate noun or adjective.

[8] For an example of "coming out" that is strictly unconfessional and which, finally, offers no content for the category of lesbian, see Barbara Johnson's deftly constructed "Sula Passing: No Passing" presentation at UCLA, May 1990. [Butler]

[9] Butler refers to the parable of the law in *The Trial* by Franz Kafka.

[10] Rhetorical term for an outrageous play on words.

[11] Gayatri Chakravorty Spivak, "Displacement and the Discourse of Woman." In *Displacement: Derrida and After*, ed. Mark Krupnick (Bloomington: Indiana University Press, 1983). [Butler]

The question is not one of *avowing* or *disavowing* the category of lesbian or gay, but, rather, why it is that the category becomes the site of this "ethical" choice? What does it mean to *avow* a category that can only maintain its specificity and coherence by performing a prior set of *disavowals?* Does this make "coming out" into the avowal of disavowal, that is, a return to the closet under the guise of an escape? And it is not something like heterosexuality or bisexuality that is disavowed by the category, but a set of identificatory and practical crossings between these categories that renders the discreteness of each equally suspect. Is it not possible to maintain and pursue heterosexual identifications and aims within homosexual practice, and homosexual identifications and aims within heterosexual practices? If a sexuality is to be disclosed, what will be taken as the true determinant of its meaning: the phantasy structure, the act, the orifice, the gender, the anatomy? And if the practice engages a complex interplay of all of those, which one of these erotic dimensions will come to stand for the sexuality that requires them all? Is it the *specificity* of a lesbian experience or lesbian desire or lesbian sexuality that lesbian theory needs to elucidate? Those efforts have only and always produced a set of contests and refusals which should by now make it clear that there is no necessarily common element among lesbians, except perhaps that we all know something about how homophobia works against women — although, even then, the language and the analysis we use will differ.

To argue that there might be a *specificity* to lesbian sexuality has seemed a necessary counterpoint to the claim that lesbian sexuality is just heterosexuality once removed, or that it is derived, or that it does not exist. But perhaps the claim of specificity, on the one hand, and the claim of derivativeness or non-existence, on the other, are not as contradictory as they seem. Is it not possible that lesbian sexuality is a process that reinscribes the power domains that it resists, that it is constituted in part from the very heterosexual matrix that it seeks to displace, and that its specificity is to be established, not *outside* or *beyond* that reinscription or reiteration, but in the very modality and effects of that reinscription. In other words, the negative constructions of lesbianism

as a fake or a bad copy can be occupied and reworked to call into question the claims of heterosexual priority. In a sense I hope to make clear in what follows, lesbian sexuality can be understood to redeploy its "derivativeness" in the service of displacing hegemonic heterosexual norms. Understood in this way, the political problem is not to establish the specificity of lesbian sexuality over and against its derivativeness, but to turn the homophobic construction of the bad copy against the framework that privileges heterosexuality as origin, and so "derive" the former from the latter. This description requires a reconsideration of imitation, drag, and other forms of sexual crossing that affirm the internal complexity of a lesbian sexuality constituted in part within the very matrix of power that it is compelled both to reiterate and to oppose.

ON THE BEING OF GAYNESS AS NECESSARY DRAG

The professionalization of gayness requires a certain performance and production of a "self" which is the *constituted effect* of a discourse that nevertheless claims to "represent" that self as a prior truth. When I spoke at the conference on homosexuality in 1989,[12,13] I found myself telling my friends beforehand that I was off to Yale to be

[12]The conference on homosexuality at Yale, at which this essay was given as an oral presentation in somewhat different form.

[13]Let me take this occasion to apologize to the social worker at that conference who asked a question about how to deal with those clients with AIDS who turned to Bernie Segal and others for the purposes of psychic healing. At the time, I understood this questioner to be suggesting that such clients were full of self-hatred because they were trying to find the causes of AIDS in their own selves. The questioner and I appear to agree that any effort to locate the responsibility for AIDS in those who suffer from it is politically and ethically wrong. I thought the questioner, however, was prepared to tell his clients that they were self-hating, and I reacted strongly (too strongly) to the paternalistic prospect that this person was going to pass judgment on someone who was clearly not only suffering, but already passing judgment on him or herself. To call another person self-hating is itself an act of power that calls for some kind of scrutiny, and I think in response to someone who is already dealing with AIDS, that is perhaps the last thing one needs to hear. I also happened to have a

a lesbian, which of course didn't mean that I wasn't one before, but that somehow then, as I spoke in that context, I *was* one in some more thorough and totalizing way, at least for the time being. So I *am* one, and my qualifications are even fairly unambiguous. Since I was sixteen, being a lesbian is what I've been. So what's the anxiety, the discomfort? Well, it has something to do with that redoubling, the way I can say, I'm going to Yale to be a lesbian; a lesbian is what I've been being for so long. How is it that I can both "be" one, and yet endeavor to be one at the same time? When and where does my being a lesbian come into play, when and where does this playing a lesbian constitute something like what I am? To say that I "play" at being one is not to say that I am not one "really"; rather, how and where I play at being one is the way in which that "being" gets established, instituted, circulated, and confirmed. This is not a performance from which I can take radical distance, for this is deep-seated play, psychically entrenched play, *and this "I" does not play its lesbianism as a role*. Rather, it is through the repeated play of this sexuality that the "I" is insistently reconstituted as a lesbian "I"; paradoxically, it is precisely the *repetition* of that play that establishes as well the *instability* of the very category that it constitutes. For if the "I" is a site of repetition, that is, if the "I" only achieves the semblance of identity through a

certain repetition of itself, then the I is always displaced by the very repetition that sustains it. In other words, does or can the "I" ever repeat itself, cite itself, faithfully, or is there always a displacement from its former moment that establishes the permanently non-self-identical status of that "I" or its "being lesbian"? What "performs" does not exhaust the "I"; it does not lay out in visible terms the comprehensive content of that "I," for if the performance is "repeated," there is always the question of what differentiates from each other the moments of identity that are repeated. And if the "I" is the effect of a certain repetition, one which produces the semblance of a continuity or coherence, then there is no "I" that precedes the gender that it is said to perform; the repetition, and the failure to repeat, produce a string of performances that constitute and contest the coherence of that "I."

But *politically*, we might argue, isn't it quite crucial to insist on lesbian and gay identities precisely because they are being threatened with erasure and obliteration from homophobic quarters? Isn't the above theory *complicitous* with those political forces that would obliterate the possibility of gay and lesbian identity? Isn't it "no accident" that such theoretical contestations of identity emerge within a political climate that is performing a set of similar obliterations of homosexual identities through legal and political means?

The question I want to raise in return is this: ought such threats of obliteration dictate the terms of the political resistance to them, and if they do, do such homophobic efforts to that extent win the battle from the start? There is no question that gays and lesbians are threatened by the violence of public erasure, but the decision to counter that violence must be careful not to reinstall another in its place. Which version of lesbian or gay ought to be rendered visible, and which internal exclusions will that rendering visible institute? Can the visibility of identity *suffice* as a political strategy, or can it only be the starting point for a strategic intervention which calls for a transformation of policy? Is it not a sign of despair over public politics when identity becomes its own policy, bringing with it those who would "police" it from various sides? And this is not a call to return to silence or invisibility,

friend who sought out advice from Bernie Segal, not with the belief that there is an exclusive or even primary psychic cause or solution for AIDS, but that there might be a psychic contribution to be made to surviving with AIDS. Unfortunately, I reacted quickly to this questioner, and with some anger. And I regret now that I didn't have my wits about me to discuss the distinctions with him that I have just laid out.

Curiously, this incident was invoked at a CLAGS (Center for Lesbian and Gay Studies) meeting at CUNY sometime in December of 1989 and, according to those who told me about it, my angry denunciation of the social worker was taken to be symptomatic of the political insensitivity of a "theorist" in dealing with someone who is actively engaged in AIDS work. That attribution implies that I do not do AIDS work, that I am not politically engaged, and that the social worker in question does not read theory. Needless to say, I was reacting angrily on behalf of an absent friend with AIDS who sought out Bernie Segal and company. So as I offer this apology to the social worker, I wait expectantly that the CLAGS member who misunderstood me will offer me one in turn. [Butler] but, rather, to make use of a category that can be called into question, made to account for what it excludes. That any consolidation of identity requires some set of differentiations and exclusions seems clear. But which ones ought to be valorized? That the identity-sign I use now has its purposes seems right, but there is no way to predict or control the political uses to which that sign will be put in the future. And perhaps this is a kind of openness, regardless of its risks, that ought to be safeguarded for political reasons. If the rendering visible of lesbian/gay identity now presupposes a set of exclusions, then perhaps part of what is necessarily excluded is *the future uses of the sign*. There is a political necessity to use some sign now, and we do, but how to use it in such a way that its futural significations are not *foreclosed?* How to use the sign and avow its temporal contingency at once?

In avowing the sign's strategic provisionality (rather than its strategic essentialism), that identity can become a site of contest and revision, indeed, take on a future set of significations that those of us who use it now may not be able to foresee. It is in the safeguarding of the future of the political signifiers — preserving the signifier as a site of rearticulation — that Laclau and Mouffe discern its democratic promise.

Within contemporary U.S. politics, there are a vast number of ways in which lesbianism in particular is understood as precisely that which cannot or dare not *be*. In a sense, Jesse Helms's attack on the NEA for sanctioning representations of "homoeroticism" focuses various homophobic fantasies of what gay men are and do on the work of Robert Mapplethorpe.[14] In a sense, for Helms, gay men exist as objects of prohibition; they are, in his twisted fantasy, sadomasochistic exploiters of children, the paradigmatic exemplars of "obscenity"; in a sense, the lesbian is not even produced within this discourse as a prohibited object. Here it becomes important to recognize that oppression works not merely through acts of overt prohibition, but covertly, through the constitution of viable subjects and through the corollary constitution of a domain of unviable (un)subjects — *abjects,* we might call them — who are neither named nor prohibited within the economy of the law. Here oppression works through the production of a domain of unthinkability and unnameability. Lesbianism is not explicitly prohibited in part because it has not even made its way into the thinkable, the imaginable, that grid of cultural intelligibility that regulates the real and the nameable. How, then, to "be" a lesbian in a political context in which the lesbian does not exist? That is, in a political discourse that wages its violence against lesbianism in part by excluding lesbianism from discourse itself? To be prohibited explicitly is to occupy a discursive site from which something like a reverse-discourse can be articulated; to be implicitly proscribed is not even to qualify as an object of prohibition.[15] And though homosexualities of all kinds in this present climate are being erased, reduced, and (then) reconstituted as sites of radical homophobic fantasy, it is important to retrace the different routes by which the unthinkability of homosexuality is being constituted time and again.

It is one thing to be erased from discourse, and yet another to be present within discourse as an abiding falsehood. Hence, there is a political imperative to render lesbianism visible, but how is that to be done outside or through existing regulatory regimes? Can the exclusion from ontology itself become a rallying point for resistance?

Here is something like a confession which is meant merely to thematize the impossibility of confession: As a young person, I suffered for a long time, and I suspect many people have, from being told, explicitly or implicitly, that what I "am" is a copy, an imitation, a derivative example, a shadow of the real. Compulsory heterosexuality

---

[14]See my "The Force of Fantasy: Feminism, Mapplethorpe, and Discursive Excess," *Differences* 2, no. 2 (Summer 1990). Since the writing of this essay, lesbian artists and representations have also come under attack. [Butler]

[15]It is this particular ruse of erasure which Foucault for the most part fails to take account of in his analysis of power. He almost always presumes that power takes place through discourse as its instrument, and that oppression is linked with subjection and subjectivation, that is, that it is installed as the formative principle of the identity of subjects. [Butler]

sets itself up as the original, the true, the authentic; the norm that determines the real implies that "being" lesbian is always a kind of miming, a vain effort to participate in the phantasmatic plenitude of naturalized heterosexuality which will always and only fail.[16] And yet, I remember quite distinctly when I first read in Esther Newton's *Mother Camp: Female Impersonators in America*[17] that drag is not an imitation or a copy of some prior and true gender; according to Newton, drag enacts the very structure of impersonation by which *any gender* is assumed. Drag is not the putting on of a gender that belongs properly to some other group, i.e. an act of *ex*propriation or *ap*propriation that assumes that gender is the rightful property of sex, that "masculine" belongs to "male" and "feminine" belongs to "female." There is no "proper" gender, a gender proper to one sex rather than another, which is in some sense that sex's cultural property. Where that notion of the "proper" operates, it is always and only *improperly* installed as the effect of a compulsory system. Drag constitutes the mundane way in which genders are appropriated, theatricalized, worn, and done; it implies that all gendering is a kind of impersonation and approximation. If this is true, it seems, there is no original or primary gender that drag imitates, but *gender is a kind of imitation for which there is no original;* in fact, it is a kind of imitation that produces the very notion of the original as an *effect* and consequence of the imitation itself. In other words, the naturalistic effects of heterosexualized genders are produced through imitative strategies; what they imitate is a phantasmatic ideal of heterosexual identity, one that is produced by the imitation as its effect. In this sense, the "reality" of heterosexual identities is performatively constituted through an imitation that sets itself up as the origin and the ground of all imitations. In other words, heterosexuality is always in the process of imitating and approximating its own phantasmatic idealization of itself — *and failing.* Precisely because it is bound to fail, and yet endeavors to succeed, the project of heterosexual identity is propelled into an endless repetition of itself. Indeed, in its efforts to naturalize itself as the original, heterosexuality must be understood as a compulsive and compulsory repetition that can only produce the *effect* of its own originality; in other words, compulsory heterosexual identities, those ontologically consolidated phantasms of "man" and "woman," are theatrically produced effects that posture as grounds, origins, the normative measure of the real.[18]

[16]Although miming suggests that there is a prior model which is being copied, it can have the effect of exposing that prior model as purely phantasmatic. In Jacques Derrida's "The Double Session" in *Dissemination,* trans. Barbara Johnson (Chicago: University of Chicago Press, 1981), he considers the textual effect of the mime in Mallarmé's "Mimique." There Derrida argues that the mime does not imitate or copy some prior phenomenon, idea, or figure, but constitutes — some might say *performatively* — the phantasm of the original in and through the mime:

He represents nothing, imitates nothing, does not have to conform to any prior referent with the aim of achieving adequation or verisimilitude. One can here foresee an objection: since the mime imitates nothing, reproduces nothing, opens up in its origin the very thing he is tracing out, presenting, or producing, he must be the very movement of truth. Not, of course, truth in the form of adequation between the representation and the present of the thing itself, or between the imitator and the imitated, but truth as the present unveiling of the present. . . . But this is not the case. . . . We are faced then with mimicry imitating nothing; faced, so to speak, with a double that couples no simple, a double that nothing anticipates, nothing at least that is not itself already double. There is no simple reference. . . . This speculum reflects no reality: it produces mere "reality-effects." . . . In this speculum with no reality, in this mirror of a mirror, a difference or dyad does exist, since there are mimes and phantoms. But it is a difference without reference, or rather reference without a referent, without any first or last unit, a ghost that is the phantom of no flesh . . . (206). [Butler]

[17]Esther Newton, *Mother Camp: Female Impersonators in America* (Chicago: University of Chicago Press, 1972). [Butler]

[18]In a sense, one might offer a redescription of the above in Lacanian terms. The sexual "positions" of heterosexually differentiated "man" and "woman" are part of the *Symbolic,* that is, an ideal embodiment of the Law of sexual difference which constitutes the object of imaginary pursuits, but which is always thwarted by the "real." These symbolic positions for Lacan are by definition impossible to occupy even as they are impossible to resist as the structuring telos of desire. I accept the former point, and reject the latter one. The imputation of universal necessity to such positions simply encodes compulsory heterosexuality at the level of the Symbolic, and the "failure" to achieve it is implicitly lamented as a source of heterosexual pathos. [Butler] See the introduction to Psychoanalytic Theory, p. 1111.

Reconsider then the homophobic charge that queens and butches and femmes are imitations of the heterosexual real. Here "imitation" carries the meaning of "derivative" or "secondary," a copy of an origin which is itself the ground of all copies, but which is itself a copy of nothing. Logically, this notion of an "origin" is suspect, for how can something operate as an origin if there are no secondary consequences which retrospectively confirm the originality of that origin? The origin requires its derivations in order to affirm itself as an origin, for origins only make sense to the extent that they are differentiated from that which they produce as derivatives. Hence, if it were not for the notion of the homosexual *as* copy, there would be no construct of heterosexuality *as* origin. Heterosexuality here presupposes homosexuality. And if the homosexual *as* copy *precedes* the heterosexual as *origin,* then it seems only fair to concede that the copy comes before the origin, and that homosexuality is thus the origin, and heterosexuality the copy.

But simple inversions are not really possible. For it is only *as* a copy that homosexuality can be argued to *precede* heterosexuality as the origin. In other words, the entire framework of copy and origin proves radically unstable as each position inverts into the other and confounds the possibility of any stable way to locate the temporal or logical priority of either term.

But let us then consider this problematic inversion from a psychic/political perspective. If the structure of gender imitation is such that the imitat*ed* is to some degree produced — or, rather, *re*produced — by imitation (see again Derrida's inversion and displacement of mimesis in "The Double Session"), then to claim that gay and lesbian identities are implicated in heterosexual norms or in hegemonic culture generally is not to *derive* gayness from straightness. On the contrary, *imitation* does not copy that which is prior, but produces and *inverts* the very terms of priority and derivativeness. Hence, if gay identities are implicated in heterosexuality, that is not the same as claiming that they are determined or derived from heterosexuality, and it is not the same as claiming that that heterosexuality is the only cultural network in which they are implicated. These are, quite literally, *inverted* imitations, ones which invert the order of imitated and imitation, and which, in the process, expose the fundamental dependency of "the origin" on that which it claims to produce as its secondary effect.

What follows if we concede from the start that gay identities as derivative inversions are in part defined in terms of the very heterosexual identities from which they are differentiated? If heterosexuality is an impossible imitation of itself, an imitation that performatively constitutes itself as the original, then the imitative parody of "heterosexuality" — when and where it exists in gay cultures — is always and only an imitation of an imitation, a copy of a copy, for which there is no original. Put in yet a different way, the parodic or imitative effect of gay identities works neither to copy nor to emulate heterosexuality, but rather, to expose heterosexuality as an incessant and *panicked* imitation of its own naturalized idealization. That heterosexuality is always in the act of elaborating itself is evidence that it is perpetually at risk, that is, that it "knows" its own possibility of becoming undone: hence, its compulsion to repeat which is at once a foreclosure of that which threatens its coherence. That it can never eradicate that risk attests to its profound dependency upon the homosexuality that it seeks fully to eradicate and never can or that it seeks to make second, but which is always already there as a prior possibility.[19] Although this failure of naturalized heterosexuality might constitute a source of pathos for heterosexuality itself — what its theorists often refer to as its constitutive malaise — it can become an occasion for a subversive and proliferating parody of gender norms in which the very claim to originality and to the real is shown to be the effect of a certain kind of naturalized gender mime.

It is important to recognize the ways in which heterosexual norms reappear within gay identities, to affirm that gay and lesbian identities are not only structured in part by dominant heterosexual frames, but that they are *not* for that reason

[19]Of course, it is Eve Kosofsky Sedgwick's *Epistemology of the Closet* (Berkeley: University of California Press, 1990) which traces the subtleties of this kind of panic in Western heterosexual epistemes. [Butler] See Sedgwick p. 1687.

determined by them. They are running commentaries on those naturalized positions as well, parodic replays and resignifications of precisely those heterosexual structures that would consign gay life to discursive domains of unreality and unthinkability. But to be constituted or structured in part by the very heterosexual norms by which gay people are oppressed is not, I repeat, to be claimed or determined by those structures. And it is not necessary to think of such heterosexual constructs as the pernicious intrusion of "the straight mind," one that must be rooted out in its entirety. In a way, the presence of heterosexual constructs and positionalities in whatever form in gay and lesbian identities presupposes that there is a gay and lesbian repetition of straightness, a racapitulation of straightness — which is itself a repetition and recapitulation of its own ideality — within its own terms, a site in which all sorts of resignifying and parodic repetitions become possible. The parodic replication and resignification of heterosexual constructs within non-heterosexual frames brings into relief the utterly constructed status of the so-called original, but it shows that heterosexuality only constitutes itself as the original through a convincing act of repetition. The more that "act" is expropriated, the more the heterosexual claim to originality is exposed as illusory.

Although I have concentrated in the above on the reality-effects of gender practices, performances, repetitions, and mimes, I do not mean to suggest that drag is a "role" that can be taken on or taken off at will. There is no volitional subject behind the mime who decides, as it were, which gender it will be today. On the contrary, the very possibility of becoming a viable subject requires that a certain gender mime be already under way. The "being" of the subject is no more self-identical than the "being" of any gender; in fact, coherent gender, achieved through an apparent repetition of the same, produces as its *effect* the illusion of a prior and volitional subject. In this sense, gender is not a performance that a prior subject elects to do, but gender is *performative* in the sense that it constitutes as an effect the very subject it appears to express. It is a *compulsory* performance in the sense that acting out of line with heterosexual norms brings with it ostracism, punishment, and violence, not to mention the transgressive pleasures produced by those very prohibitions.

To claim that there is no performer prior to the performed, that the performance is performative, that the performance constitutes the appearance of a "subject" as its effect is difficult to accept. This difficulty is the result of a predisposition to think of sexuality and gender as "expressing" in some indirect or direct way a psychic reality that precedes it. The denial of the *priority* of the subject, however, is not the denial of the subject; in fact, the refusal to conflate the subject with the psyche marks the psychic as that which exceeds the domain of the conscious subject. This psychic excess is precisely what is being systematically denied by the notion of a volitional "subject" who elects at will which gender and/or sexuality to be at any given time and place. It is this excess which erupts within the intervals of those repeated gestures and acts that construct the apparent uniformity of heterosexual positionalities, indeed which compels the repetition itself, and which guarantees its perpetual failure. In this sense, it is this excess which, within the heterosexual economy, implicitly includes homosexuality, that perpetual threat of a disruption which is quelled through a reenforced repetition of the same. And yet, if repetition is the way in which power works to construct the illusion of a seamless heterosexual identity, if heterosexuality is compelled to *repeat itself* in order to establish the illusion of its own uniformity and identity, then this is an identity permanently at risk, for what if it fails to repeat, or if the very exercise of repetition is redeployed for a very different performative purpose? If there is, as it were, always a compulsion to repeat, repetition never fully accomplishes identity. That there is a need for a repetition at all is a sign that identity is not self-identical. It requires to be instituted again and again, which is to say that it runs the risk of becoming *de*-instituted at every interval.

So what is this psychic excess, and what will constitute a subversive or *de*-instituting repetition? First, it is necessary to consider that sexuality always exceeds any given performance, presentation, or narrative which is why it is not possible to derive or read off a sexuality from any given gender presentation. And sexuality may be said to exceed any definitive narrativization. Sexuality is never fully "expressed" in a performance or practice; there will be passive and butchy femmes, femmy and aggressive butches, and both of those, and more, will turn out to describe more or less anatomically stable "males" and "females." There are no direct expressive or causal lines between sex, gender, gender presentation, sexual practice, fantasy and sexuality. None of those terms captures or determines the rest. Part of what constitutes sexuality is precisely that which does not appear and that which, to some degree, can never appear. This is perhaps the most fundamental reason why sexuality is to some degree always closeted, especially to the one who would express it through acts of self-disclosure. That which is excluded for a given gender presentation to "succeed" may be precisely what is played out sexually, that is, an "inverted" relation, as it were, between gender and gender presentation, and gender presentation and sexuality. On the other hand, both gender presentation and sexual practices may corollate such that it appears that the former "expresses" the latter, and yet both are jointly constituted by the very sexual possibilities that they exclude.

This logic of inversion gets played out interestingly in versions of lesbian butch and femme gender stylization. For a butch can present herself as capable, forceful, and all-providing, and a stone butch may well seek to constitute her lover as the exclusive site of erotic attention and pleasure. And yet, this "providing" butch who seems *at first* to replicate a certain husband-like role, can find herself caught in a logic of inversion whereby that "providingness" turns to a self-sacrifice, which implicates her in the most ancient trap of feminine self-abnegation. She may well find herself in a situation of radical need, which is precisely what she sought to locate, find, and fulfill in her femme lover. In effect, the butch inverts into the femme or remains caught up in the specter of that inversion, or takes pleasure in it.[20]

On the other hand, the femme who, as Amber Hollibaugh has argued, "orchestrates" sexual exchange,[21] may well eroticize a certain dependency only to learn that the very power to orchestrate that dependency exposes her own incontrovertible power, at which point she inverts into a butch or becomes caught up in the specter of that inversion, or perhaps delights in it.

PSYCHIC MIMESIS

What stylizes or forms an erotic style and/or a gender presentation — and that which makes such categories inherently unstable — is a set of *psychic identifications* that are not simple to describe. Some psychoanalytic theories tend to construe identification and desire as two mutually exclusive relations to love objects that have been lost through prohibition and/or separation. Any intense emotional attachment thus divides into either wanting to have someone or wanting to be that someone, but never both at once. It is important to consider that identification and desire can coexist, and that their formulation in terms of mutually exclusive oppositions serves a heterosexual matrix. But I would like to focus attention on yet a different construal of that scenario, namely, that "wanting to be" and "wanting to have" can operate to differentiate mutually exclusive positionalities internal to lesbian erotic exchange. Consider that identifications are always made in response to loss of some kind, and that they involve a certain *mimetic practice* that seeks to incorporate the lost love within the very "identity" of the one who remains. This was Freud's thesis in "Mourning and Melancholia" in 1917 and continues to inform contemporary psychoanalytic discussions of identification.[22]

For psychoanalytic theorists Mikkel Borch-Jacobsen and Ruth Leys, however, identification

[20]Butler's argument here recapitulates Hegel's paradox of the master and the slave, in which the master, in his dependency, becomes in effect the slave to his slaves.

[21]Amber Hollibaugh and Cherríe Moraga, "What We're Rollin Around in Bed With: Sexual Silences in Feminism," in *Powers of Desire: The Politics of Sexuality,* ed. Ann Snitow, Christine Stansell, and Sharon Thompson (New York: Monthly Review Press, 1983), 394–405. [Butler]

[22]Mikkel Borch-Jacobsen, *The Freudian Subject* (Stanford: Stanford University Press, 1988); for citations of Ruth Leys's work, see the following two notes. [Butler]

and, in particular, identificatory mimetism, *precedes* "identity" and constitutes identity as that which is fundamentally "other to itself." The notion of this Other *in* the self, as it were, implies that the self/Other distinction is *not* primarily external (a powerful critique of ego psychology follows from this); the self is from the start radically implicated in the "Other." This theory of primary mimetism differs from Freud's account of melancholic incorporation. In Freud's view, which I continue to find useful, incorporation — a kind of psychic miming — is a response to, and refusal of, *loss*. Gender as the site of such psychic mimes is thus constituted by the variously gendered Others who have been loved and lost, where the loss is suspended through a melancholic and imaginary incorporation (and preservation) of those Others into the psyche. Over and against this account of psychic mimesis by way of incorporation and melancholy, the theory of primary mimetism argues an even stronger position in favor of the non-self-identity of the psychic subject. Mimetism is not motivated by a drama of loss and wishful recovery, but appears to precede and constitute desire (and motivation) itself; in this sense, mimetism would be prior to the possibility of loss and the disappointments of love.

Whether loss or mimetism is primary (perhaps an undecidable problem), the psychic subject is nevertheless constituted internally by differentially gendered Others and is, therefore, never, as a gender, self-identical.

In my view, the self only becomes a self on the condition that it has suffered a separation (grammar fails us here, for the "it" only becomes differentiated through that separation), a loss which is suspended and provisionally resolved through a melancholic incorporation of some "Other." That "Other" installed in the self thus establishes the permanent incapacity of that "self" to achieve self-identity; it is as it were always already disrupted by that Other; the disruption of the Other at the heart of the self is the very condition of that self's possibility.[23]

Such a consideration of psychic identification would vitiate the possibility of any stable set of typologies that explain or describe something like gay or lesbian identities. And any effort to supply one — as evidenced in Kaja Silverman's recent inquiries into male homosexuality — suffer from simplification, and conform, with alarming ease, to the regulatory requirements of diagnostic epistemic regimes. If incorporation in Freud's sense in 1914 is an effort to *preserve* a lost and loved object and to refuse or postpone the recognition of loss and, hence, of grief, then to become *like* one's mother or father or sibling or other early "lovers" may be an act of love and/or a hateful effort to replace or displace. How would we "typologize" the ambivalence at the heart of mimetic incorporations such as these?[24]

How does this consideration of psychic identification return us to the question, what constitutes a subversive repetition? How are troublesome identifications apparent in cultural practices? Well, consider the way in which heterosexuality naturalizes itself through setting up certain illusions of continuity between sex, gender, and desire. When Aretha Franklin sings, "you make me feel like a natural woman," she seems at first to suggest that some natural potential of her biological sex is actualized by her participation in the cultural position of "woman" as object of heterosexual recognition. Something in her "sex" is thus expressed by her "gender" which is then

---

Political, eds. Judith Butler and Joan W. Scott (New York and London: Routledge, 1992). For Leys, a primary mimetism or suggestibility requires that the "self" from the start is constituted by its incorporations; the effort to differentiate oneself from that by which one is constituted is, of course, impossible, but it does entail a certain "incorporative violence," to use her term. The violence of identification is in this way in the service of an effort at differentiation, to take the place of the Other who is, as it were, installed at the foundation of the self. That this replacement, which seeks to be a displacement, fails, and must repeat itself endlessly, becomes the trajectory of one's psychic career. [Butler]

[24]Here again, I think it is the work of Ruth Leys which will clarify some of the complex questions of gender constitution that emerge from a close psychoanalytic consideration of imitation and identification. Her forthcoming book manuscript will doubtless galvanize this field: *The Subject of Imitation*. [Butler]

---

[23]For a very fine analysis of primary mimetism with direct implications for gender formation, see Ruth Leys, "The Real Miss Beauchamp: The History and Sexual Politics of the Multiple Personality Concept," in *Feminists Theorize the*

fully known and consecrated within the heterosexual scene. There is no breakage, no discontinuity between "sex" as biological facticity and essence, or between gender and sexuality. Although Aretha appears to be all too glad to have her naturalness confirmed, she also seems fully and paradoxically mindful that that confirmation is never guaranteed, that the effect of naturalness is only achieved as a consequence of that moment of heterosexual recognition. After all, Aretha sings, you make me feel *like* a natural woman, suggesting that this is a kind of metaphorical substitution, an act of imposture, a kind of sublime and momentary participation in an ontological illusion produced by the mundane operation of heterosexual drag.

But what if Aretha were singing to me? Or what if she were singing to a drag queen whose performance somehow confirmed her own?

How do we take account of these kinds of identifications? It's not that there is some kind of *sex* that exists in hazy biological form that is somehow *expressed* in the gait, the posture, the gesture; and that some sexuality then expresses both that apparent gender or that more or less magical sex. If gender is drag, and if it is an imitation that regularly produces the ideal it attempts to approximate, then gender is a performance that *produces* the illusion of an inner sex or essence or psychic gender core; it *produces* on the skin, through the gesture, the move, the gait (that array of corporeal theatrics understood as gender presentation), the illusion of an inner depth. In effect, one way that gender gets naturalized is through being constructed as an inner psychic or physical *necessity*. And yet, it is always a surface sign, a signification on and with the public body that produces this illusion of an inner depth, necessity or essence that is somehow magically, causally expressed.

To dispute the psyche as *inner depth,* however, is not to refuse the psyche altogether. On the contrary, the psyche calls to be rethought precisely as a compulsive repetition, as that which conditions and disables the repetitive performance of identity. If every performance repeats itself to institute the effect of identity, then every repetition requires an interval between the acts, as it were, in which risk and excess threaten to disrupt the identity being constituted. The unconscious is this

excess that enables and contests every performance, and which never fully appears within the performance itself. The psyche is not "in" the body, but in the very signifying process through which that body comes to appear; it is the lapse in repetition as well as its compulsion, precisely what the performance seeks to deny, and that which compels it from the start.

To locate the psyche within this signifying chain as the instability of all iterability[25] is not the same as claiming that it is inner core that is awaiting its full and liberatory expression. On the contrary, the psyche is the permanent failure of expression, a failure that has its values, for it impels repetition and so reinstates the possibility of disruption. What then does it mean to pursue disruptive repetition within compulsory heterosexuality?

Although compulsory heterosexuality often presumes that there is first a sex that is expressed through a gender and then through a sexuality, it may now be necessary fully to invert and displace that operation of thought. If a regime of sexuality mandates a compulsory performance of sex, then it may be only through that performance that the binary system of gender and the binary system of sex come to have intelligibility at all. It may be that the very categories of sex, of sexual identity, of gender are produced or maintained in the *effects* of this compulsory performance, effects which are disingenuously renamed as causes, origins, disingenuously lined up within a causal or expressive sequence that the heterosexual norm produces to legitimate itself as the origin of all sex. How then to expose the causal lines as retrospectively and performatively produced fabrications, and to engage gender itself as an inevitable fabrication, to fabricate gender in terms which reveal every claim to the origin, the inner, the true, and the real as nothing other than the effects of *drag,* whose subversive possibilities ought to be played and replayed to make the "sex" of gender into a site of insistent political play? Perhaps this will be a matter of working sexuality *against* identity, even against gender, and of letting that which cannot fully appear in any performance persist in its disruptive promise.

[25]See the introduction to Structuralism and Deconstruction, p. 828.

Martha Nussbaum

b. 1947

Martha Nussbaum was born in 1947 in New York City. She attended Wellesley College and studied acting at New York University before taking her B.A. there in 1969. She completed her doctorate in classical philology at Harvard University in 1975 and went on to teach philosophy, classics, and literature at Brown University. After her appointment as Ernst Freund Distinguished Service Professor of Law and Ethics at the University of Chicago, she taught in the philosophy and classics departments, the Law School, the Divinity School, and the College. Her many books have included Love's Knowledge *(1990),* Poetic Justice: The Literary Imagination and Public Life *(1995),* Sex and Social Justice *(1999),* Women and Human Development: The Capabilities Approach *(2000),* The Fragility of Goodness: Luck and Ethics in Greek Tragedy and Philosophy *(2001),* Upheavals of Thought: The Intelligence of Emotions *(2001), and* Hiding from Humanity: Disgust, Shame, and the Law *(2004).*

Nussbaum's ferocious response to Judith Butler came in a 1999 review of Excitable Speech *in the* New Republic, *and attacked her as an ethical philosopher who cynically sidestepped the issues she uncovered. It caused a furor in academic circles, some viewing the attack as personal rivalry, others as an overdue assault on an overinflated reputation.*

From *The Professor of Parody*

The idea of gender as performance is Butler's most famous idea, and so it is worth pausing to scrutinize it more closely. She introduced the notion intuitively, in *Gender Trouble*, without invoking theoretical precedent. Later she denied that she was referring to quasi-theatrical performance, and associated her notion instead with Austin's account of speech acts in *How to Do Things with Words*.[1] Austin's linguistic category of "performatives" is a category of linguistic utterances that function, in and of themselves, as actions rather than as assertions. . . .

Butler's point is presumably this: when we act and speak in a gendered way, we are not simply reporting on something that is already fixed in the world, we are actively constituting it, replicating it, and reinforcing it. By behaving as if there were male and female "natures," we co-create the social fiction that these natures exist. They are never there apart from our deeds; we are always making them be there. At the same time, by carrying out these performances in a slightly different manner, a parodic manner, we can perhaps unmake them just a little.

Thus the one place for agency in a world constrained by hierarchy is in the small opportunities we have to oppose gender roles every time they take shape. When I find myself doing femaleness, I can turn it around, poke fun at it, do it a little bit differently. Such reactive and parodic performances, in Butler's view, never destabilize the larger system. She doesn't envisage mass movements of resistance or campaigns for political reform; only personal acts carried out by a small

[1]See J. L. Austin, p. 679.

number of knowing actors. Just as actors with a bad script can subvert it by delivering the bad lines oddly, so too with gender: the script remains bad, but the actors have a tiny bit of freedom. . . .

What precisely does Butler offer when she counsels subversion? She tells us to engage in parodic performances, but she warns us that the dream of escaping altogether from the oppressive structures is just a dream: it is within the oppressive structures that we must find little spaces for resistance, and this resistance cannot hope to change the overall situation. And here lies a dangerous quietism.

If Butler means only to warn us against the dangers of fantasizing an idyllic world in which sex raises no serious problems, she is wise to do so. Yet frequently she goes much further. She suggests that the institutional structures that ensure the marginalization of lesbians and gay men in our society, and the continued inequality of women, will never be changed in a deep way; and so our best hope is to thumb our noses at them, and to find pockets of personal freedom within them. "Called by an injurious name, I come into social being, and because I have a certain inevitable attachment to my existence, because a certain narcissism takes hold of any term that confers existence, I am led to embrace the terms that injure me because they constitute me socially." In other words: I cannot escape the humiliating structures without ceasing to be, so the best I can do is mock, and use the language of subordination stingingly. In Butler, resistance is always imagined as personal, more or less private, involving no unironic, organized public action for legal or institutional change.

Isn't this like saying to a slave that the institution of slavery will never change, but you can find ways of mocking it and subverting it, finding your personal freedom within those acts of carefully limited defiance? Yet it is a fact that the institution of slavery can be changed, and was changed — but not by people who took a Butler-like view of the possibilities. It was changed because people did not rest content with parodic performance: they demanded, and to some extent they got, social upheaval. It is also a fact that the institutional structures that shape women's lives have changed. The law of rape, still defective, has at least improved; the law of sexual harassment exists, where it did not exist before; marriage is no longer regarded as giving men monarchical control over women's bodies. These things were changed by feminists who would not take parodic performance as their answer, who thought that power, where bad, should, and would, yield before justice.

Butler not only eschews such a hope, she takes pleasure in its impossibility. She finds it exciting to contemplate the alleged immovability of power, and to envisage the ritual subversions of the slave who is convinced that she must remain such. She tells us — this is the central thesis of *The Psychic Life of Power*[2] — that we all eroticize the power structures that oppress us, and can thus find sexual pleasure only within their confines. It seems to be for that reason that she prefers the sexy acts of parodic subversion to any lasting material or institutional change. Real change would so uproot our psyches that it would make sexual satisfaction impossible. Our libidos are the creation of the bad enslaving forces, and thus necessarily sadomasochistic in structure.

Well, parodic performance is not so bad when you are a powerful tenured academic in a liberal university. But here is where Butler's focus on the symbolic, her proud neglect of the material side of life, becomes a fatal blindness. For women who are hungry, illiterate, disenfranchised, beaten, raped, it is not sexy or liberating to reenact, however parodically, the conditions of hunger, illiteracy, disenfranchisement, beating, and rape. Such women prefer food, schools, votes, and the integrity of their bodies. I see no reason to believe that they long sadomasochistically for a return to the bad state. If some individuals cannot live without the sexiness of domination, that seems sad, but it is not really our business. But when a major theorist tells women in desperate conditions that life offers them only bondage, she purveys a cruel lie, and a lie that flatters evil by giving it much more power than it actually has. . . .

---

[2]*The Psychic Life of Power: Theories in Subjection* is a 1997 book by Judith Butler.

Lauren Berlant

b. 1957

Lauren Berlant received her Ph.D. at Cornell University and is currently the director of the Center for Gender Studies and professor of English at the University of Chicago. Berlant's studies of popular culture concentrate on the dual fantasies of nationhood and citizenship, and the ways that an individual's affective bonds to race, gender, and sexual communities help to identify the self in relationship to the state and to other citizens. Berlant's objects of historical and psychoanalytic study range from political and legal discourses to popular culture throughout the nineteenth and twentieth centuries. Her publications include The Anatomy of National Fantasy: Hawthorne, Utopia, and Everyday Life *(1991),* The Queen of America Goes to Washington City: Essays on Sex and Citizenship *(1997), and* The Female Complaint: The Unfinished Business of Sentimentality in American Culture *(2004). She has edited collections on compassion and on the Monica Lewinsky affair, as well as a celebrated issue of* Critical Inquiry *in winter 1998, from which the following collaboration with Michael Warner is excerpted. This journal issue was later expanded into a collection of essays published as* Intimacy *in 2000.*

Michael Warner

b. 1958

One of the few queer theorists to graduate from Oral Roberts University, Michael Warner survived to take his M.A. at the University of Wisconsin and his doctorate at Johns Hopkins. After teaching at Northwestern University, Warner moved on to Rutgers, where he is now professor of English. His interests are split between social theory and queer culture, and the institutional history of literature and criticism in America. Warner has written The Letters of the Republic: Publication and the Public Sphere in Eighteenth-Century America *(1990),* The Trouble with Normal *(2000), and* Publics and Counterpublics *(2002), and has edited* Fear of a Queer Planet: Queer Politics and Social Theory *(1993). Warner's other works include* The Origins of Literary Studies in America *(ed., with Gerald Graff, 1988) and* The English Literatures of America, 1500 to 1800 *(ed., with Myra Jehlen, 1997). He writes on AIDS and queer theory for both* The Village Voice *and academic journals. The following essay, "Sex in Public," appeared originally in* Critical Inquiry.

Sex in Public

1. THERE IS NOTHING MORE PUBLIC THAN PRIVACY

A paper titled "Sex in Public" teases with the obscurity of its object and the twisted aim of its narrative. In this paper we will be talking not about the sex people already have clarity about, nor identities and acts, nor a wildness in need of derepression; but rather about sex as it is mediated by publics.[1] Some of these publics have an obvious relation to sex: pornographic cinema, phone sex, "adult" markets for print, lap dancing. Others are organized around sex, but not necessarily sex *acts* in the usual sense: queer zones and other worlds estranged from heterosexual culture, but also more tacit scenes of sexuality like official national culture, which depends on a notion of privacy to cloak its sexualization of national membership.

The aim of this paper is to describe what we want to promote as the radical aspirations of queer culture building: not just a safe zone for queer sex but the changed possibilities of identity, intelligibility, publics, culture, and sex that appear when the heterosexual couple is no longer the referent or the privileged example of sexual culture. Queer social practices like sex and theory try to unsettle the garbled but powerful norms

supporting that privilege — including the project of normalization that has made heterosexuality hegemonic — as well as those material practices that, though not explicitly sexual, are implicated in the hierarchies of property and propriety that we will describe as heteronormative.[2] We open with two scenes of sex in public.

Scene 1

In 1993 *Time* magazine published a special issue about immigration called "The New Face of America."[3] The cover girl of this issue was morphed via computer from head shots representing a range of U.S. immigrant groups: an amalgam of "Middle Eastern," "Italian," "African," "Vietnamese," "Anglo-Saxon," "Chinese," and "Hispanic" faces. The new face of America is supposed to represent what the model citizen will look like when, in the year 2004, it is projected, there is no longer a white statistical

---

[1] On public sex in the standard sense, see Pat Califia, *Public Sex: The Culture of Radical Sex* (Pittsburgh, 1994). On acts and identities, see Janet E. Halley, "The Status/Conduct Distinction in the 1993 Revisions to Military Antigay Policy: A Legal Archaeology," *GLQ* 3 (1996): 159–252. The classic political argument for sexual derepression as a condition of freedom is put forth in Herbert Marcuse, *Eros and Civilization: A Philosophical Inquiry into Freud* (Boston, 1966). In contemporary prosex thought inspired by volume 1 of Michel Foucault's *The History of Sexuality*, the denunciation of "erotic injustice and sexual oppression" is situated less in the freedom of individuals than in analyses of the normative and coercive relations between specific "populations" and the institutions created to manage them (Gayle Rubin, "Thinking Sex: Notes for a Radical Theory of the Politics of Sexuality," in *Pleasure and Danger: Exploring Female Sexuality*, ed. Carole S. Vance [Boston, 1984], p. 275). See also Michel Foucault, *The History of Sexuality: An Introduction*, vol. 1 of *The History of Sexuality*, trans. Robert Hurley (New York, 1978). [Berlant and Warner]

[2] By heteronormativity we mean the institutions, structures of understanding, and practical orientations that make heterosexuality seem not only coherent — that is, organized as a sexuality — but also privileged. Its coherence is always provisional, and its privilege can take several (sometimes contradictory) forms: unmarked, as the basic idiom of the personal and the social; or marked as a natural state; or projected as an ideal or moral accomplishment. It consists less of norms that could be summarized as a body of doctrine than of a sense of rightness produced in contradictory manifestations — often unconscious, immanent to practice or to institutions. Contexts that have little visible relation to sex practice, such as life narrative and generational identity, can be heteronormative in this sense, while in other contexts forms of sex between men and women might *not* be heteronormative. Heteronormativity is thus a concept distinct from heterosexuality. One of the most conspicuous differences is that it has no parallel, unlike heterosexuality, which organizes homosexuality as its opposite. Because homosexuality can never have the invisible, tacit, society-founding rightness that heterosexuality has, it would not be possible to speak of "homonormativity" in the same sense. See Michael Warner, "Fear of a Queer Planet," *Social Text*, no. 29 (1991): 3–17. [Berlant and Warner]

[3] See *Time*, special issue, "The New Face of America," Fall 1993. This analysis reworks materials in Lauren Berlant, *The Queen of America Goes to Washington City: Essays on Sex and Citizenship* (Durham, N.C., 1997), pp. 200–208. [Berlant and Warner]

majority in the United States. Naked, smiling, and just off-white, *Time*'s divine Frankenstein aims to organize hegemonic optimism about citizenship and the national future. *Time*'s theory is that by the twenty-first century interracial reproductive sex will have taken place in the United States on such a mass scale that racial difference itself will be finally replaced by a kind of family feeling based on blood relations. In the twenty-first century, *Time* imagines, hundreds of millions of hybrid faces will erase American racism altogether: the nation will become a happy racial monoculture made up of "one (mixed) blood."[4]

The publication of this special issue caused a brief flurry of interest but had no important effects; its very banality calls us to understand the technologies that produce its ordinariness. The fantasy banalized by the image is one that reverberates in the law and in the most intimate crevices of everyday life. Its explicit aim is to help its public process the threat to "normal" or "core" national culture that is currently phrased as "the problem of immigration."[5] But this crisis image of immigrants is also a *racial mirage* generated by a white-dominated society, supplying a specific phobia to organize its public so that a more substantial discussion of exploitation in the United States can be avoided and then remaindered to the part of collective memory sanctified not by nostalgia but by mass aversion. Let's call this the amnesia archive. The motto above the door is Memory Is the Amnesia You Like.

But more than exploitation and racism are forgotten in this whirl of projection and suppression. Central to the transfiguration of the immigrant into a nostalgic image to shore up core national culture and allay white fears of minoritization is something that cannot speak its name, though its signature is everywhere: national heterosexuality.

National heterosexuality is the mechanism by which a core national culture can be imagined as a sanitized space of sentimental feeling and immaculate behavior, a space of pure citizenship. A familial model of society displaces the recognition of structural racism and other systemic inequalities. This is not entirely new: the family form has functioned as a mediator and metaphor of national existence in the United States since the eighteenth century.[6] We are arguing that its contemporary deployment increasingly supports the governmentality of the welfare state by separating the aspirations of national belonging from the critical culture of the public sphere and from political citizenship.[7] Immigration crises have also previously produced feminine icons that function as prostheses for the state — most famously, the Statue of Liberty, which symbolized seamless immigrant assimilation to the metaculture of the United States. In *Time*'s face it is not symbolic femininity but practical heterosexuality that guarantees the monocultural nation.

The nostalgic family values covenant of contemporary American politics stipulates a privatization of citizenship and sex in a number of ways. In law and political ideology, for example, the fetus and the child have been spectacularly elevated to the place of sanctified nationality. The state now sponsors stings and legislation to purify

[4]For a treatment of the centrality of "blood" to U.S. nationalist discourse, see Bonnie Honig, *Democracy and the Foreigner*. Princeton: Princeton UP, 2001. [Berlant and Warner]

[5]See, for example, William J. Bennett, *The De-Valuing of America: The Fight for Our Culture and Our Children* (New York, 1992); Peter Brimelow, *Alien Nation: Common Sense about America's Immigration Disaster* (New York, 1995); and William A. Henry III, *In Defense of Elitism* (New York, 1994). [Berlant and Warner]

[6]On the family form in national rhetoric, see Jay Fliegelman, *Prodigals and Pilgrims: The American Revolution against Patriarchal Authority, 1750–1800* (Cambridge, 1982), and Shirley Samuels, *Romances of the Republic: Women, the Family, and Violence in the Literature of the Early American Nation* (New York, 1996). On fantasies of genetic assimilation, see Robert S. Tilton, *Pocahontas: The Evolution of an American Narrative* (Cambridge, 1994), pp. 9–33, and Elise Lemire, "Making Miscegenation" (Ph.D. diss., Rutgers University, 1996). [Berlant and Warner]

[7]The concept of welfare state governmentality has a growing literature. For a concise statement, see Jürgen Habermas, "The New Obscurity: The Crisis of the Welfare State and the Exhaustion of Utopian Energies," *The New Conservatism: Cultural Criticism and the Historians Debate*, trans. Shierry Weber Nicholsen (Cambridge, Mass., 1989), pp. 48–70. Michael Warner has discussed the relation between this analysis and queer culture in his "Something Queer about the Nation-State," in *After Political Correctness: The Humanities and Society in the 1990s*, ed. Christopher Newfield and Ronald Strickland (Boulder, Colo., 1995), pp. 361–71. [Berlant and Warner]

the internet on behalf of children. New welfare and tax "reforms" passed under the cooperation between the Contract with America and Clintonian familialism seek to increase the legal and economic privileges of married couples and parents.[8] Vouchers and privatization rezone education as the domain of parents rather than citizens. Meanwhile, senators such as Ted Kennedy and Jesse Helms support amendments that refuse federal funds to organizations that "promote, disseminate, or produce materials that are obscene or that depict or describe, in a patently offensive way, sexual or excretory activities or organs, including but not limited to obscene depictions of sadomasochism, homo-eroticism, the sexual exploitation of children, or individuals engaged in sexual intercourse."[9] These developments, though distinct, are linked in the way they organize a hegemonic national public around sex. But because this sex public officially claims to act only in order to protect the zone of heterosexual privacy, the institutions of economic privilege and social reproduction informing its practices and organizing its ideal world are protected by the spectacular demonization of any represented sex.

Scene 2

In October 1995, the New York City Council passed a new zoning law by a forty-one to nine vote. The Zoning Test Amendment covers adult book and video stores, eating and drinking establishments, theaters, and other businesses. It allows these businesses only in certain areas zoned as nonresidential, most of which turn out to be on the waterfront. Within the new reserved districts, adult businesses are disallowed within five hundred feet of another adult establishment or within five hundred feet of a house of worship, school, or day-care center. They are limited to one per lot and in size to ten thousand square feet. Signs are limited in size, placement, and illumination. All other adult businesses are required to close within a year. Of the estimated 177 adult businesses in the city, all but 28 may have to close under this law. Enforcement of the bills is entrusted to building inspectors.

A court challenge against the bill was brought by a coalition that also fought it in the political process, formed by anticensorship groups such as the New York Civil Liberties Union (NYCLU), Feminists for Free Expression, People for the American Way, and the National Coalition Against Censorship as well as gay and lesbian organizations such as the Lambda Legal Defense Fund, the Empire State Pride Agenda, and the AIDS Prevention Action League. (An appeal was still pending as of July 1997.) These latter groups joined the anticensorship groups for a simple reason: the impact of rezoning on businesses catering to queers, especially to gay men, will be devastating. All five of the adult businesses on Christopher Street will be shut down, along with the principal venues where men meet men for sex. None of these businesses have been targets of local complaints. Gay men have come to take for granted the availability of explicit sexual materials, theaters, and clubs. That is how they have learned to find each other; to map a commonly accessible world; to construct the architecture of queer space in a homophobic environment; and, for the last fifteen years, to cultivate a collective ethos of safer sex. All of that is about to change. Now, gay men who want sexual materials or who want to meet other men for sex will have two choices: they can cathect[10] the privatized virtual public of phone sex and the internet; or they can travel to small, inaccessible, little-trafficked, badly lit areas, remote from public transportation and from any residences, mostly on the waterfront, where heterosexual porn users will also be relocated and where the risk of violence will consequently be higher.[11] In either

---

[8] Berlant and Warner may be referring to the "Child Tax Credit" for parents raising children under 17, not restricted to heterosexual parents. The 1998 Republican proposal to eliminate the "marriage penalty" was passed by Congress in 1999 but vetoed by President Clinton; another version was voted into law later under George W. Bush.

[9] *Congressional Record*, 101st Cong., 1st sess., 1989, 135, pt. 134:12967. [Berlant and Warner] Kennedy and Helms are chosen as the most liberal and most reactionary members of the Senate.

[10] In Freudian terminology, to cathect is to invest emotional energy (libido) in some activity.

[11] Political geography in this way produces systematic effects of violence. Queers are forced to find each other in

case, the result will be a sense of isolation and diminished expectations for queer life, as well as an attenuated capacity for political community. The nascent lesbian sexual culture, including the Clit Club and the only video rental club catering to lesbians, will also disappear. The impact of the sexual purification of New York will fall unequally on those who already have fewest publicly accessible resources.

2. NORMATIVITY AND SEXUAL CULTURE

Heterosexuality is not a thing. We speak of heterosexual culture rather than heterosexuality because that culture never has more than a provisional unity.[12] It is neither a single Symbolic nor a single ideology nor a unified set of shared beliefs.[13] The conflicts between these strands are seldom more than dimly perceived in practice, where the

givenness of male-female sexual relations is part of the ordinary rightness of the world, its fragility masked in shows of solemn rectitude. Such conflicts have also gone unrecognized in theory, partly because of the metacultural work of the very category of heterosexuality, which consolidates as *a sexuality* widely differing practices, norms, and institutions; and partly because the sciences of social knowledge are themselves so deeply anchored in the process of normalization to which Foucault attributes so much of modern sexuality.[14] Thus when we say that the contemporary United States is saturated by the project of constructing national heterosexuality, we do not mean that national heterosexuality is anything like a simple monoculture. Hegemonies are nothing if not elastic alliances, involving dispersed and contradictory strategies for self-maintenance and reproduction.

Heterosexual culture achieves much of its metacultural intelligibility through the ideologies and institutions of intimacy. We want to argue here that although the intimate relations of private personhood appear to be the realm of sexuality itself, allowing "sex in public" to appear like matter out

---

untrafficked areas because of the combined pressures of propriety, stigma, the closet, and state regulation such as laws against public lewdness. The same areas are known to gay-bashers and other criminals. And they are disregarded by police. The effect is to make both violence and police neglect seem like natural hazards, voluntarily courted by queers. As the 1997 documentary film *Licensed to Kill* illustrates, antigay violence has been difficult to combat by legal means: victims are reluctant to come forward in any public and prosecutorial framework, while bashers can appeal to the geographic circumstances to implicate the victims themselves. The legal system has helped to produce the violence it is called upon to remedy. [Berlant and Warner] One may get the false impression that the 1995 zoning amendment was directed primarily against gay and lesbian establishments; in fact the overwhelming majority of adult businesses relocated were topless bars and peepshows patronized primarily by heterosexual males.

[12]See Eve Kosofsky Sedgwick, *Epistemology of the Closet* (Berkeley, 1992). [Berlant and Warner] See Sedgwick p. 1687.

[13]Gay and lesbian theory, especially in the humanities, frequently emphasizes psychoanalytic or psychoanalytic-style models of subject-formation, the differences among which are significant and yet all of which tend to elide the difference between the categories male/female and the process and project of heteronormativity. Three propositional paradigms are relevant here: those that propose that human identity itself is fundamentally organized by gender identifications that are hardwired into infants; those that equate the clarities of gender identity with the domination of a relatively coherent and vertically stable "straight" ideology; and those that focus on a phallocentric Symbolic order that produces gendered subjects who live out the destiny of their positioning in it. The psychoanalytic and philosophical insights and limits of these

models (which, we feel, underdescribe the practices, institutions, and incongruities of heteronormativity) require further engagement. For the time being, these works stand in as the most challenging relevant archive: Judith Butler, *Bodies that Matter: On the Discursive Limits of "Sex"* (New York, 1993); Luce Irigaray, *Speculum of the Other Woman*, trans. Gillian C. Gill (Ithaca, N.Y., 1985) and *This Sex Which Is Not One*, trans. Catherine Porter and Carolyn Burke (Ithaca, N.Y., 1985); Teresa de Lauretis, *The Practice of Love: Lesbian Sexuality and Perverse Desire* (Bloomington, Ind., 1994): Kaja Silverman, *Male Subjectivity at the Margins* (New York, 1992); and Monique Wittig, *The Straight Mind and Other Essays* (Boston, 1992). Psychoanalytic work on sexuality does not always match acts and inclinations to natural or constructed "identity": see, for example, Leo Bersani, *Homos* (Cambridge, Mass., 1995) and "Is the Rectum a Grave?" in *AIDS: Cultural Analysis/Cultural Activism*, ed. Douglas Crimp (Cambridge, Mass., 1988). [Berlant and Warner]

[14]The notion of metaculture we borrow from Greg Urban. See Greg Urban, *A Discourse-Centered Approach to Culture: Native South American Myths and Rituals* (Austin, Tex., 1991) and *Noumenal Community: Myth and Reality in an Amerindian Brazilian Society* (Austin, Tex., 1996). On normalization, see Foucault, *Discipline and Punish: The Birth of the Prison*, trans. Alan Sheridan (New York, 1979), pp. 184–85 and *The History of Sexuality*, p. 144. Foucault derives his argument here from the revised version of Georges Canguilhem, *The Normal and the Pathological*, trans. Carolyn R. Fawcett and Robert S. Cohen (New York, 1991). [Berlant and Warner]

of place, intimacy is itself publicly mediated, in several senses. First, its conventional spaces presuppose a structural differentiation of "personal life" from work, politics, and the public sphere.[15] Second, the normativity of heterosexual culture links intimacy only to the institutions of personal life, making them the privileged institutions of social reproduction, the accumulation and transfer of capital, and self-development. Third, by making sex seem irrelevant or merely personal, heteronormative conventions of intimacy block the building of nonnormative or explicit public sexual cultures. Finally, those conventions conjure a mirage: a home base of prepolitical humanity from which citizens are thought to come into political discourse and to which they are expected to return in the (always imaginary) future after political conflict. Intimate life is the endlessly cited *elsewhere* of political public discourse, a promised haven that distracts citizens from the unequal conditions of their political and economic lives, consoles them for the damaged humanity of mass society, and shames them for any divergence between their lives and the intimate sphere that is alleged to be simple personhood.

Ideologies and institutions of intimacy are increasingly offered as a vision of the good life for the destabilized and struggling citizenry of the United States, the only (fantasy) zone in which a future might be thought and willed, the only (imaginary) place where good citizens might be produced away from the confusing and unsettling distractions and contradictions of capitalism and politics. Indeed, one of the unforeseen paradoxes of national-capitalist privatization has been that citizens have been led through heterosexual culture to identify both themselves *and their politics* with privacy. In the official public, this involves making sex private; reintensifying blood as a psychic base for identification; replacing state mandates for social justice with a privatized ethics of responsibility, charity, atonement, and "values";

and enforcing boundaries between moral persons and economic ones.[16]

A complex cluster of sexual practices gets confused, in heterosexual culture, with the love plot of intimacy and familialism that signifies belonging to society in a deep and normal way. Community is imagined through scenes of intimacy, coupling, and kinship; a historical relation to futurity is restricted to generational narrative and reproduction.[17] A whole field of social relations becomes intelligible as heterosexuality, and this privatized sexual culture bestows on its sexual

[16]On privatization and intimacy politics, see Berlant, *The Queen of America Goes to Washington City*, pp. 1–24 and "Feminism and the Institutions of Intimacy," in *The Politics of Research*, ed. E. Ann Kaplan and George Levine (New Brunswick, N.J., 1997), pp. 143–61; Honig, *No Place Like Home*; and Rosalind Pollack Petchesky, "The Body as Property: A Feminist Re-vision," in *Conceiving the New World Order: The Global Politics of Reproduction*, ed. Faye D. Ginsburg and Rayna Rapp (Berkeley, 1995), pp. 387–406. On privatization and national-capitalism, see David Harvey, *The Condition of Postmodernity: An Enquiry into the Origins of Cultural Change* (Oxford, 1989), and Mike Davis, *City of Quartz: Excavating the Future in Los Angeles* (New York, 1992). [Berlant and Warner]

[17]This language for community is a problem for gay historiography. In otherwise fine and important studies such as Esther Newton's *Cherry Grove, Fire Island: Sixty Years in America's First Gay and Lesbian Town* (Boston, 1993), or Elizabeth Lapovsky Kennedy and Madeline D. Davis's *Boots of Leather, Slippers of Gold: The History of a Lesbian Community* (New York, 1993), or even George Chauncey's *Gay New York: Gender, Urban Culture, and the Makings of the Gay Male World, 1890–1940* (New York, 1994), community is imagined as whole-person, face-to-face relations — local, experiential, proximate, and saturating. But queer worlds seldom manifest themselves in such forms. Cherry Grove — a seasonal resort depending heavily on weekend visits by New Yorkers — may be typical less of a "gay and lesbian town" than of the way queer sites are specialized spaces in which transits can project alternative worlds. John D'Emilio's *Sexual Politics, Sexual Communities: The Making of a Homosexual Minority in the United States, 1940–1970* is an especially interesting example of the imaginative power of the idealization of a local community for queers: the book charts the separate tracks of political organizing and local scenes such as bar life, showing that when the "movement" and the "subculture" began to converge in San Francisco, the result was a new formation with a new utopian appeal: "A 'community,'" D'Emilio writes, "was in fact forming around a shared sexual orientation" (John D'Emilio, *Sexual Politics, Sexual Communities: The Making of a Homosexual Minority in the United States, 1940–1970* [Chicago, 1983], p. 195). D'Emilio (wisely) keeps scare quotes around "community" in the very sentence declaring it to exist in fact. [Berlant and Warner]

[15]Here we are influenced by Eli Zaretsky, *Capitalism, the Family, and Personal Life* (New York, 1986), and Stephanie Coontz, *The Social Origins of Private Life: A History of American Families, 1600–1900* (London, 1988), though heteronormativity is a problem not often made visible in Coontz's work. [Berlant and Warner]

practices a tacit sense of rightness and normalcy. This sense of rightness — embedded in things and not just in sex — is what we call heteronormativity. Heteronormativity is more than ideology, or prejudice, or phobia against gays and lesbians; it is produced in almost every aspect of the forms and arrangements of social life: nationality, the state, and the law; commerce; medicine; and education; as well as in the conventions and affects of narrativity, romance, and other protected spaces of culture. It is hard to see these fields as heteronormative because the sexual culture straight people inhabit is so diffuse, a mix of languages they are just developing with premodern notions of sexuality so ancient that their material conditions feel hardwired into personhood.

But intimacy has not always had the meaning it has for contemporary heteronormative culture. Along with Foucault and other historians, the classicist David Halperin, for example, has shown that in ancient Athens sex was a transitive act rather than a fundamental dimension of personhood or an expression of intimacy. The verb for having sex appears on a late antique list of things that are not done in regard to or through others: "namely, speaking, singing, dancing, fist-fighting, competing, hanging oneself, dying, being crucified, diving, finding a treasure, having sex, vomiting, moving one's bowels, sleeping, laughing, crying, talking to the gods, and the like."[18] Halperin points out that the inclusion of fucking on this list shows that sex is not here "knit up in a web of mutuality."[19] In contrast, modern heterosexuality is supposed to refer to relations of intimacy and identification with other persons, and sex acts are supposed to be the most intimate communication of them all.[20] The sex act shielded by the zone of privacy is the affectional nimbus that heterosexual culture protects and from which it abstracts its model of ethics, but this utopia of social belonging is also supported and extended by acts less commonly recognized as part of sexual culture: paying taxes, being disgusted, philandering, bequeathing, celebrating a holiday, investing for the future, teaching, disposing of a corpse, carrying wallet photos, buying economy size, being nepotistic, running for president, divorcing, or owning anything "His" and "Hers."

The elaboration of this list is a project for further study. Meanwhile, to make it and to laugh at it is not immediately to label any practice as oppressive, uncool, or definitive. We are describing a constellation of practices that everywhere disperses heterosexual privilege as a tacit but central organizing index of social membership. Exposing it inevitably produces what we have elsewhere called a "wrenching sense of recontextualization," as its subjects, even its gay and lesbian subjects, begin to piece together how it is that social and economic discourses, institutions, and practices that don't feel especially sexual or familial collaborate to produce an extremely narrow context for living.[21] Heterosexual culture cannot recognize, validate, sustain, incorporate, or remember much of what people know and experience about the cruelty of normal culture even to the people who identify with it.

But that cruelty does not go unregistered. Intimacy, for example, has a whole public environment of therapeutic genres dedicated to witnessing the constant failure of heterosexual ideologies and institutions. Every day, in many countries now, people testify to their failure to

[18]Artemidorus, *Oneirocritica* 1.2, quoted in David M. Halperin, "Sex before Sexuality: Pederasty, Politics, and Power in Classical Athens," in *Hidden from History: Reclaiming the Gay and Lesbian Past*, ed. Martin Bauml Duberman, Martha Vicinus, and Chauncey (New York, 1989), p. 49. [Berlant and Warner]

[19]Halperin, "Sex before Sexuality," p. 49. [Berlant and Warner] Halperin's literal reading of Artemidorus has been criticized by other classical scholars for its lack of, among other things, a sense of humor.

[20]Studies of intimacy that do not assume this "web of mutuality," either as the self-evident nature of intimacy or as a human value, are rare. Roland Barthes's *A Lover's*

Discourse: Fragments, trans. Richard Howard (New York, 1978), and Niklas Luhmann's *Love as Passion*, trans. Jeremy Gaines and Doris L. Jones (Cambridge, Mass., 1986) both try, in very different ways, to describe analytically the production of intimacy. More typical is Anthony Gidden's attempt to theorize intimacy as "pure relationship" in *The Transformation of Intimacy: Sexuality, Love, and Eroticism in Modern Societies* (Cambridge, 1992). There, ironically, it is "the gays who are the pioneers" in separating the "pure relationship" of love from extraneous institutions and contexts such as marriage and reproduction. [Berlant and Warner]

[21]Berlant and Warner. "What Does Queer Theory Teach Us about X?" *PMLA* 110 (May 1995): 345. [Berlant and Warner]

sustain or be sustained by institutions of privacy on talk shows, in scandal journalism, even in the ordinary course of mainstream journalism addressed to middlebrow culture. We can learn a lot from these stories of love plots that have gone astray: about the ways quotidian violence is linked to complex pressures from money, racism, histories of sexual violence, cross-generational tensions. We can learn a lot from listening to the increasing demands on love to deliver the good life it promises. And we can learn from the extremely punitive responses that tend to emerge when people seem not to suffer enough for their transgressions and failures.

Maybe we would learn too much. Recently, the proliferation of evidence for heterosexuality's failings has produced a backlash against talk-show therapy. It has even brought William Bennett[22] to the podium; but rather than confessing his transgressions or making a complaint about someone else's, we find him calling for boycotts and for the suppression of heterosexual therapy culture altogether. Recognition of heterosexuality's daily failures agitates him as much as queerness. "We've forgotten that civilization depends on keeping some of this stuff under wraps," he said. "This is a tropism toward the toilet."[23]

But does civilization need to cover its ass? Or does heterosexual culture actually secure itself through banalizing intimacy? Does belief that normal life is actually possible require amnesia and the ludicrous stereotyping of a bottom-feeding culture apparently inadequate to intimacy? On these shows no one ever blames the ideology and institutions of heterosexuality. Every day, even the talk-show hosts are newly astonished to find that people who are committed to hetero intimacy are nevertheless unhappy. After all is said and done, the prospects and promises of heterosexual culture still represent the optimism for optimism, a hope to which people apparently have already pledged their consent — at least in public.

Recently, Biddy Martin has written that some queer social theorists have produced a reductive and pseudoradical antinormativity by actively repudiating the institutions of heterosexuality that have come to oversaturate the social imaginary. She shows that the kinds of arguments that crop up in the writings of people like Andrew Sullivan are not just right-wing fantasies. "In some queer work," she writes, "the very fact of attachment has been cast as only punitive and constraining because already socially constructed. . . . Radical anti-normativity throws out a lot of babies with a lot of bathwater. . . . An enormous fear of ordinariness or normalcy results in superficial accounts of the complex imbrication of sexuality with other aspects of social and psychic life, and in far too little attention to the dilemmas of the average people that we also are."[24]

We think our friend Biddy might be referring to us, although in this segment she cites no one in particular. We would like to clarify the argument. To be against heteronormativity is not to be against norms. To be against the processes of normalization is not to be afraid of ordinariness. Nor is it to advocate the "existence without limit" she sees as produced by bad Foucauldians ("EH," p. 123). Nor is it to decide that sentimental identifications with family and children are waste or garbage, or make people into waste or garbage. Nor is it to say that any sex called "lovemaking" isn't lovemaking; whatever the ideological or historical burdens of sexuality have been, they have not excluded, and indeed may have entailed, the ability of sex to count as intimacy and care. What we have been arguing here is that the space of cultural sex has become obnoxiously cramped from doing the work of maintaining a normal metaculture. When Biddy Martin calls us to recognize ourselves as "average people," to relax from an artificially stimulated "fear of normalcy," the image of average personhood appears to be simply descriptive ("EH," p. 123). But its averageness is also normative, in exactly the sense that Foucault meant by "normalization": not the imposition of an alien will, but a distribution around a statistically

[22]Neoconservative pundit, secretary of education under Ronald Reagan, author of moralistic tracts such as *A Book of Virtues* (1993).

[23]Bennett, quoted in Maureen Dowd, "Talk Is Cheap," *New York Times*, 26 Oct. 1995, p. A25. [Berlant and Warner]

[24]Biddy Martin, "Extraordinary Homosexuals and the Fear of Being Ordinary," *Differences* 6 (Summer–Fall 1994): 123; hereafter abbreviated "EH." [Berlant and Warner]

imagined norm. This deceptive appeal of the average remains heteronormative, measuring deviance from the mass. It can also be consoling, an expression of a utopian desire for conflicted personhood. But this desire cannot be satisfied in the current conditions of privacy. People feel that the price they must pay for social membership and a relation to the future is identification with the heterosexual life narrative; that they are individually responsible for the rages, instabilities, ambivalences, and failures they experience in their intimate lives, while the fractures of the contemporary United States shame and sabotage them everywhere. Heterosexuality involves so many practices that are not sex that a world in which this hegemonic cluster would not be dominant is, at this point, unimaginable. We are trying to bring that world into being.

3. QUEER COUNTERPUBLICS

By queer culture we mean a world-making project, where "world," like "public," differs from community or group because it necessarily includes more people than can be identified, more spaces than can be mapped beyond a few reference points, modes of feeling that can be learned rather than experienced as a birthright. The queer world is a space of entrances, exits, unsystematized lines of acquaintance, projected horizons, typifying examples, alternate routes, blockages, incommensurate geographies.[25] World making, as much in the mode of dirty talk as of print-mediated representation, is dispersed through incommensurate registers, by

[25]In some traditions of social theory, the process of world making as we describe it here is seen as common to all social actors. See for example, Alfred Schutz's emphasis on the practices of typification and projects of action involved in ordinary knowledge of the social in *The Phenomenology of the Social World*, trans. George Walsh and Frederick Lehnert (Evanston, Ill., 1967). Yet in most contexts the social world is understood, not as constructed by reference to types or projects, but as an instantiated whole in a form capable of reproducing itself. The family, the state, a neighborhood, the human species, or institutions such as school and church — such images of social being share an appearance of plenitude seldom approached in contexts of queer world making. However much the latter might resemble the process of world construction in ordinary contexts, queer worlds do not have the power to represent a taken-for-granted social existence. [Berlant and Warner]

definition *unrealizable* as community or identity. Every cultural form, be it a novel or an after-hours club or an academic lecture, indexes a virtual social world, in ways that range from a repertoire of styles and speech genres to referential metaculture. A novel like Andrew Holleran's *Dancer from the Dance* relies much more heavily on referential metaculture than does an after-hours club that survives on word of mouth and may be a major scene because it is only barely coherent *as* a scene. Yet for all their differences, both allow for the concretization of a queer counterpublic. We are trying to promote this world-making project, and a first step in doing so is to recognize that queer culture constitutes itself in many ways other than through the official publics of opinion culture and the state, or through the privatized forms normally associated with sexuality. Queer and other insurgents have long striven, often dangerously or scandalously, to cultivate what good folks used to call criminal intimacies. We have developed relations and narratives that are only recognized as intimate in queer culture: girlfriends, gal pals, fuckbuddies, tricks. Queer culture has learned not only how to sexualize these and other relations, but also to use them as a context for witnessing intense and personal affect while elaborating a public world of belonging and transformation. Making a queer world has required the development of kinds of intimacy that bear no necessary relation to domestic space, to kinship, to the couple form, to property, or to the nation. These intimacies *do* bear a necessary relation to a counterpublic — an indefinitely accessible world conscious of its subordinate relation. They are typical both of the inventiveness of queer world making and of the queer world's fragility.

Nonstandard intimacies would seem less criminal and less fleeting if, as used to be the case, normal intimacies included everything from consorts to courtiers, friends, amours, associates, and co-conspirators.[26] Along with the sex it legitimates,

[26]See, for example, Alan Bray, "Homosexuality and the Signs of Male Friendship in Elizabethan England," *History Workshop* 29 (Spring 1990): 1–19; Laurie J. Shannon, "Emilia's Argument: Friendship and 'Human Title' in *The Two Noble Kinsmen*," ELH 64 (Fall 1997); and *Passions of the Renaissance*, trans. Arthur Goldhammer, ed. Roger Chartier, vol. 3 of *A History of Private Life*, ed. Philippe Ariès and Georges Duby (Cambridge, Mass., 1989). [Berlant and Warner]

intimacy has been privatized; the discourse contexts that narrate true personhood have been segregated from those that represent citizens, workers, or professionals.

This transformation in the cultural forms of intimacy is related both to the history of the modern public sphere and to the modern discourse of sexuality as a fundamental human capacity. In *The Structural Transformation of the Public Sphere*, Habermas shows that the institutions and forms of domestic intimacy made private people private, members of the public sphere of private society rather than the market or the state. Intimacy grounded abstract, disembodied citizens in a sense of universal humanity.[27] In *The History of Sexuality*, Foucault describes the personalization of sex from the other direction: the confessional and expert discourses of civil society continually posit an inner personal essence, equating this true personhood with sex and surrounding that sex with dramas of secrecy and disclosure.[28] There is an instructive convergence here in two thinkers who otherwise seem to be describing different planets.[29] Habermas overlooks the administrative and normalizing dimensions of privatized sex in sciences of social knowledge because he is interested in the norm of a critical relation between state and civil society. Foucault overlooks the critical culture that might enable transformation of sex and other private relations; he wants to show that modern epistemologies of sexual personhood, far from bringing sexual publics into being, are techniques of isolation; they identify persons as normal or perverse, for the purpose of medicalizing or otherwise administering them as individuals. Yet both Habermas and Foucault point to the way a hegemonic public has founded itself by a privatization of sex and the sexualization of private personhood. Both identify the conditions in which sexuality seems like a property of subjectivity rather than a publicly or counterpublicly accessible culture.

Like most ideologies, that of normal intimacy may never have been an accurate description of how people actually live. It was from the beginning mediated not only by a structural separation of economic and domestic space but also by opinion culture, correspondence, novels, and romances; Rousseau's *Confessions* is typical both of the ideology and of its reliance on mediation by print and by new, hybrid forms of life narrative. Habermas notes that "subjectivity, as the innermost core of the private, was always oriented to an audience,"[30] adding that the structure of this intimacy includes a fundamentally contradictory relation to the economy:

> To the autonomy of property owners in the market corresponded a self-presentation of human beings in the family. The latter's intimacy, apparently set free from the constraint of society, was the seal on the truth of a private autonomy exercised in competition. Thus it was a private autonomy denying its economic origins . . . that provided the bourgeois family with its consciousness of itself.[31]

This structural relation is no less normative for being imperfect in practice. Its force is to prevent the recognition, memory, elaboration, or institutionalization of all the nonstandard intimacies that people have in everyday life. Affective life slops over onto work and political life; people have key self-constitutive relations with strangers and acquaintances; and they have eroticism, if not sex, outside of the couple form. These border intimacies give people tremendous pleasure. But when that pleasure is called sexuality, the spillage of eroticism into everyday social life seems transgressive in a way that provokes normal aversion, a hygienic recoil even as contemporary consumer and media cultures increasingly trope toiletward, splattering the matter of intimate life at the highest levels of national culture.

In gay male culture, the principal scenes of criminal intimacy have been tearooms, streets, sex clubs, and parks — a tropism toward the public

---

[27]For Habermas on the public sphere, see pp. 1212–13.
[28]For Foucault, see p. 1627.
[29]On the relation between Foucault and Habermas, we take inspiration from Tom McCarthy, *Ideals and Illusions* (Cambridge, Mass., 1991), pp. 43–75. [Berlant and Warner]

[30]Habermas, *The Structural Transformation of the Public Sphere: An Inquiry into a Category of Bourgeois Society*, trans. Thomas Burger and Frederick Lawrence (Cambridge, Mass., 1991), p. 49. [Berlant and Warner]
[31]Ibid., p. 46. [Berlant and Warner]

toilet.[32] Promiscuity is so heavily stigmatized as nonintimate that it is often called anonymous, whether names are used or not. One of the most commonly forgotten lessons of AIDS is that this promiscuous intimacy turned out to be a lifesaving public resource. Unbidden by experts, gay people invented safer sex; and, as Douglas Crimp wrote in 1987

we were able to invent safe sex because we have always known that sex is not, in an epidemic or not, limited to penetrative sex. Our promiscuity taught us many things, not only about the pleasures of sex, but about the great multiplicity of those pleasures. It is that psychic preparation, that experimentation, that conscious work on our own sexualities that has allowed many of us to change our sexual behaviors — something that brutal "behavioral therapies" tried unsuccessfully for over a century to force us to do — very quickly and very dramatically. . . . All those who contend that gay male promiscuity is merely sexual *compulsion* resulting from fear of intimacy are now faced with very strong evidence against their prejudices. . . . Gay male promiscuity should be seen instead as a positive model of how sexual pleasures might be pursued by and granted to everyone if those pleasures were not confined within the narrow limits of institutionalized sexuality.[33]

AIDS is a special case, and this method of sexual culture has been typically male. But sexual practice is only one kind of counterintimacy. More important is the critical practical knowledge that allows such relations to count as intimate, to be not empty release or transgression but a common language of self-cultivation, shared knowledge, and the exchange of inwardness.

Queer culture has found it necessary to develop this knowledge in mobile sites of drag, youth culture, music, dance, parades, flaunting, and cruising — sites whose mobility makes them possible but also renders them hard to recognize as world making because they are so fragile and ephemeral. They are paradigmatically trivialized as "lifestyle." But to understand them only as self-expression or as a demand for recognition would be to misrecognize the fundamentally unequal material conditions whereby the institutions of social reproduction are coupled to the forms of hetero culture.[34] Contexts of queer world making depend on parasitic and fugitive elaboration through gossip, dance clubs, softball leagues, and the phone-sex ads that increasingly are the commercial support for print-mediated left culture in general.[35] Queer is difficult to entextualize *as* culture.

This is particularly true of intimate culture. Heteronormative forms of intimacy are supported, as we have argued, not only by overt referential discourse such as love plots and sentimentality but materially, in marriage and family law, in the architecture of the domestic, in the zoning of work and politics. Queer culture, by contrast, has almost no institutional matrix for its counterintimacies. In the absence of marriage and the rituals that organize life around matrimony, improvisation is always necessary for the speech act of pledging, or the narrative practice of dating, or for such apparently noneconomic economies as joint checking. The heteronormativity in such practices may seem weak and indirect. After all, same-sex couples have sometimes

---

[32]On the centrality of semipublic spaces like tearooms, bathrooms, and bathhouses to gay male life, see Chauncey, *Gay New York*, and Lee Edelman, "Tearooms and Sympathy, or, Epistemology of the Water Closet," in *Nationalisms and Sexualities*, ed. Andrew Parker et al. (New York, 1992), pp. 263–84. The spaces of both gay and lesbian semipublic sexual practices are investigated in *Mapping Desire: Geographies of Sexualities*, ed. David Bell and Gill Valentine (New York, 1995). [Berlant and Warner]

[33]Douglas Crimp, "How to Have Promiscuity in an Epidemic," *October*, no. 43 (Winter 1987): 253. [Berlant and Warner]

[34]The notion of a demand for recognition has been recently advanced by a number of thinkers as a way of understanding multicultural politics. See, for example, Axel Honneth, *The Struggle for Recognition: The Moral Grammar of Social Conflicts*, trans. Joel Anderson (Cambridge, 1995), or *Multiculturalism: Examining the Politics of Recognition*, ed. Amy Gutmann (Princeton, N.J., 1994). We are suggesting that although queer politics does contest the terrain of recognition, it cannot be conceived as a politics of recognition *as opposed to* an issue of distributive justice; this is the distinction proposed in Nancy Fraser's "From Redistribution to Recognition? Dilemmas of Justice in a 'Postsocialist' Age," *New Left Review*, no. 212 (July–Aug. 1995): 68–93; rept. in her *Justice Interruptus: Critical Reflections on the "Postsocialist" Condition* (New York, 1997). [Berlant and Warner]

[35]See Sedgwick, *Epistemology of the Closet*, and Yvonne Zipter, *Diamonds Are a Dyke's Best Friend: Reflections, Reminiscence, and Reports from the Field on the Lesbian National Pastime* (Ithaca, N.Y., 1988). [Berlant and Warner] For Sedgwick See p. 1687.

been able to invent versions of such practices. But they have done so only by betrothing themselves to the couple form and its language of personal significance, leaving untransformed the material and ideological conditions that divide intimacy from history, politics, and publics. The queer project we imagine is not just to destigmatize those average intimacies, not just to give access to the sentimentality of the couple for persons of the same sex, and definitely not to certify as properly private the personal lives of gays and lesbians.[36] Rather, it is to support forms of affective, erotic, and personal living that are public in the sense of accessible, available to memory, and sustained through collective activity.

Because the heteronormative culture of intimacy leaves queer culture especially dependent on ephemeral elaborations in urban space and print culture, queer publics are also peculiarly vulnerable to initiatives such as Mayor Rudolph Giuliani's new zoning law. The law aims to restrict any counterpublic sexual culture by regulating its economic conditions; its effects will reach far beyond the adult businesses it explicitly controls. The gay bars on Christopher Street draw customers from people who come there because of its sex trade. The street is cruiser because of the sex shops. The boutiques that sell freedom rings and "Don't Panic" T-shirts do more business for the same reasons. Not all of the thousands who migrate or make pilgrimages to Christopher Street use the porn shops, but all benefit from the fact that some do. After a certain point, a quantitative change is a qualitative change. A critical mass develops. The street becomes queer. It develops a dense, publicly accessible sexual culture. It therefore becomes a base for nonporn businesses, like

the Oscar Wilde Bookshop. And it becomes a political base from which to pressure politicians with a gay voting bloc.[37]

No group is more dependent on this kind of pattern in urban space than queers. If we could not concentrate a publicly accessible culture somewhere, we would always be outnumbered and overwhelmed. And because what brings us together is sexual culture, there are very few places in the world that have assembled much of a queer population without a base in sex commerce, and even those that do exist, such as the lesbian culture in Northampton, Massachusetts, are stronger because of their ties to places like the West Village, Dupont Circle, West Hollywood, and the Castro. Respectable gays like to think that they owe nothing to the sexual subculture they think of as sleazy. But their success, their way of living, their political rights, and their very identities would never have been possible but for the existence of the public sexual culture they now despise. Extinguish it, and almost all *out* gay or queer culture will wither on the vine. No one knows this connection better than the right. Conservatives would not so flagrantly contradict their stated belief in a market free from government interference if they did not see this kind of hyper regulation as an important victory.

The point here is not that queer politics needs more free-market ideology, but that heteronormative forms, so central to the accumulation and reproduction of capital, also depend on heavy interventions in the regulation of capital. One of the most disturbing fantasies in the zoning scheme, for example, is the idea that an urban locale is a community of shared interests based on residence and property. The ideology of the neighborhood is politically unchallengeable in the current debate, which is dominated by a fantasy that sexual subjects only reside, that the space relevant to sexual politics is the neighborhood. But a district like Christopher Street is not

[36]Such a politics is increasingly recommended within the gay movement. See, for example, Andrew Sullivan, *Same-Sex Marriage, Pro and Con* (New York, 1997); Michelangelo Signorile, *Life Outside: The Signorile Report on Gay Men, Sex, Drugs, Muscles, and the Passages of Life* (New York, 1997); Gabriel Rotello, *Sexual Ecology: AIDS and the Destiny of Gay Men* (New York, 1997); William N. Eskridge, Jr. *The Case for Same-Sex Marriage: From Sexual Liberty to Civilized Commitment* (New York, 1996); *Same-Sex Marriage: The Moral and Legal Degate*, ed. Robert M. Baird and Stuart E. Rosenbaum (Amherst, N.Y., 1996); and Mark Strasser, *Legally Wed: Same-Sex Marriage and the Constitution* (Ithaca, N.Y., 1997). [Berlant and Warner]

[37]Nearly a decade later, the fear expressed by Berlant and Warner here and elsewhere that Giuliani's zoning law would seriously affect the queer culture of Greenwich Village seems exaggerated; indeed, the nonresidential "meatpacking district" at the waterfront north of the Village, to which many adult businesses relocated, has filled with trendy restaurants and small theatres, and has become highly trafficked and safe.

just a neighborhood affair. The local character of the neighborhood depends on the daily presence of thousands of nonresidents. Those who actually live in the West Village should not forget their debt to these mostly queer pilgrims. And we should not make the mistake of confusing the class of citizens with the class of property owners. Many of those who hang out on Christopher Street — typically young, queer, and African American — couldn't possibly afford to live there. Urban space is always a host space. The right to the city extends to those who use the city.[38] It is not limited to property owners. It is not because of a fluke in the politics of zoning that urban space is so deeply misrecognized; normal sexuality requires such misrecognitions, including their economic and legal enforcement, in order to sustain its illusion of humanity.

4. TWEAKING AND THWACKING

Queer social theory is committed to sexuality as an inescapable category of analysis, agitation, and refunctioning. Like class relations, which in this moment are mainly visible in the polarized embodiments of identity forms, heteronormativity is a fundamental motor of social organization in the United States, a founding condition of unequal and exploitative relations throughout even straight society. Any social theory that miscomprehends this participates in their reproduction.

The project of thinking about sex in public does not only engage sex when it is disavowed or suppressed. Even if sex practice is not the object domain of queer studies, sex is everywhere present. But where is the tweaking, thwacking, thumping, sliming, and rubbing you might have expected — or dreaded — in a paper on sex? We close with two scenes that might have happened on the same day in our wanderings around the city. One afternoon, we were riding with a young straight couple we know, in their station wagon. Gingerly, after much circumlocution, they

brought the conversation around to vibrators. These are people whose reproductivity governs their lives, their aspirations, and their relations to money and entailment, mediating their relations to everyone and everything else. But the woman in this couple had recently read an article in a women's magazine about sex toys and other forms of nonreproductive eroticism. She and her husband did some mail-order shopping and have become increasingly involved in what from most points of view would count as queer sex practices; their bodies have become disorganized and exciting to them. They said to us: you're the only people we can talk to about this; to all our straight friends this would make us perverts. In order not to feel like perverts, they had to make *us* into a kind of sex public.

Later, the question of aversion and perversion came up again. This time we were in a bar that on most nights is a garden-variety leather bar, but that, on Wednesday nights, hosts a sex performance event called "Pork." Shows typically include spanking, flagellation, shaving, branding, laceration, bondage, humiliation, wrestling — you know, the usual: amateur, everyday practitioners strutting for everyone else's gratification, not unlike an academic conference. This night, word was circulating that the performance was to be erotic vomiting. This sounded like an appetite spoiler, and the thought of leaving early occurred to us but was overcome by a simple curiosity: what would the foreplay be like? Let's stay until it gets messy. Then we can leave.

A boy, twentyish, very skateboard, comes on the low stage at one end of the bar, wearing lycra shorts and a dog collar. He sits loosely in a restraining chair. His partner comes out and tilts the bottom's head up to the ceiling, stretching out his throat. Behind them is an array of foods. The top begins pouring milk down the boy's throat, then food, then more milk. It spills over, down his chest and onto the floor. A dynamic is established between them in which they carefully keep at the threshold of gagging. The bottom struggles to keep taking in more than he really can. The top is careful to give him just enough to stretch his capacities. From time to time a baby bottle is offered as a respite, but soon the rhythm intensifies. The boy's stomach is beginning to rise and pulse, almost convulsively.

[38]The phrase "the right to the city" is Henri Lefebvre's, from his *Le Droit à la ville* (Paris, 1968); trans. Eleonore Kofman and Elizabeth Lebas, under the title "The Right to the City," *Writings on Cities* (Oxford, 1996), pp. 147–59. See also Manuel Castells, *The City and the Grassroots* (Berkeley, 1983). [Berlant and Warner]

It is at this point that we realize we cannot leave, cannot even look away. No one can. The crowd is transfixed by the scene of intimacy and display, control and abandon, ferocity and abjection. People are moaning softly with admiration, then whistling, stomping, screaming encouragements. They have pressed forward in a compact and intimate group. Finally, as the top inserts two, then three fingers in the bottom's throat, insistently offering his own stomach for the repeated climaxes, we realize that we have never seen such a display of trust and violation. We are breathless. But, good academics that we are, we also have some questions to ask. Word had gone around that the boy is straight. We want to know: What does that mean in this context? How did you discover that this is what you want to do? How did you find a male top to do it with? How did you come to do it in a leather bar? Where else do you do this? How do you feel about your new partners, this audience?

We did not get to ask these questions, but we have others that we can pose now, about these scenes where sex appears more sublime than narration itself, neither redemptive nor transgressive, moral nor immoral, hetero nor homo, nor sutured to any axis of social legitimation. We have been arguing that sex opens a wedge to the transformation of those social norms that require only its static intelligibility or its deadness as source of meaning.[39]

In these cases, though, paths through publicity led to the production of nonheteronormative bodily contexts. They intended nonheteronormative worlds because they refused to pretend that privacy was their ground; because they were forms of sociability that unlinked money and family from the scene of the good life; because they made sex the consequence of public mediations and collective self-activity in a way that made for unpredicted pleasures; because, in turn, they attempted to make a context of support for their practices; because their pleasures were not purchased by a redemptive pastoralism of sex, nor by mandatory amnesia about failure, shame, and aversion.[40]

We are used to thinking about sexuality as a form of intimacy and subjectivity, and we have just demonstrated how limited that representation is. But the heteronormativity of U.S. culture is not something that can be easily rezoned or disavowed by individual acts of will, by a subversiveness imagined only as personal rather than as the basis of public-formation, nor even by the lyric moments that interrupt the hostile cultural narrative that we have been staging here. Remembering the utopian wish behind normal intimate life, we also want to remember that we aren't married to it.

---

[39]On deadness as an affect and aspiration of normative social membership, see Berlant, "Live Sex Acts (Parental Advisory: Explicit Material)," *The Queen of America Goes to Washington City,* pp. 59–60, 79–81. [Berlant and Warner]

[40]The classic argument against the redemptive sex pastoralism of normative sexual ideology is made in Bersani, "Is the Rectum a Grave?"; on redemptive visions more generally, see his *The Culture of Redemption* (Cambridge, Mass., 1990). [Berlant and Warner]

Judith Halberstam

b. 1961

As a young tomboy, Judith Halberstam states she was often misrecognized as a boy, and now, as a post-Butlerian theorist of genders and sexualities, she sees these moments of misrecognition as key to the formation of a mind-set that resists performing within the male/female gender binary. Halberstam studied English at the University of California at Berkeley, where she received a B.A., followed by an M.A. and Ph.D. in English literature at the University of Minnesota at Minneapolis. She has been a professor at the State University of New York at Purchase, University of California at San Diego and at Santa Cruz, and is currently a professor and the director of the Center for Feminist Research at the University of Southern California. Halberstam is the author of Skin Shows: Gothic Horror and the Technology of Monsters (1995), Female Masculinity (1998), The Drag King Book (1999, with photographer Del LaGrace Volcano), and In a Queer Time and Place: Transgender Bodies, Subcultural Lives (2005), in addition to many journal articles. In her work, which is based on historical studies of gender performance from the Victorian era to the present day, Halberstam seeks to create a new vernacular for gender hybridities that escapes the residual binarism that exists in both medical and popular discussions of transgendered, transsexual, homosexual, and "bisexual" people. Unlike Judith Butler, who interprets male and female categories as perpetually suspect, Halberstam rather sees these categories as ways of making nameable behaviors which would otherwise remain outside language, and therefore outside cultural recognition. The following essay is from Halberstam's Introduction to Female Masculinity.

From the Introduction to *Female Masculinity*

Masculinity without Men

What's the use of being a little boy if you are going to grow up to be a man?
— GERTRUDE STEIN, *Everybody's Autobiography* (1937)

THE REAL THING

What is "masculinity"? This has been probably the most common question that I have faced over the past five years while writing on the topic of female masculinity. If masculinity is not the social and cultural and indeed political expression of maleness, then what is it? I do not claim to have any definitive answer to this question, but I do have a few proposals about why masculinity must not and cannot and should not reduce down to the male body and its effects. I also venture to assert that although we seem to have a difficult time defining masculinity, as a society we have little trouble in recognizing it, and indeed we spend massive amounts of time and money ratifying and supporting the versions of masculinity that we enjoy and trust; many of these "heroic masculinities" depend absolutely on the subordination of alternative masculinities. I claim in this book that far from being an imitation of maleness, female masculinity actually affords us a glimpse of how masculinity is constructed as masculinity. In other words, female masculinities are framed as the rejected scraps of dominant masculinity in order that male masculinity may appear to be the real thing. But what we understand as heroic masculinity has been produced by and across both male and female bodies.

This opening chapter does not simply offer a conventional theoretical introduction to the enterprise of conceptualizing masculinity without men; rather, it attempts to compile the myths and fantasies about masculinity that have ensured that masculinity and maleness are profoundly difficult to pry apart. I then offer, by way of a preliminary attempt to re-imagine masculinity, numerous examples of alternative masculinities in fiction, film, and lived experience. These examples are mostly queer and female, and they show clearly how important it is to recognize alternative masculinities when and where they emerge. Throughout this introduction, I detail the many ways in which female masculinity has been blatantly ignored both in the culture at large and within academic studies of masculinity. This widespread indifference to female masculinity, I suggest, has clearly ideological motivations and has sustained the complex social structures that wed masculinity to maleness and to power and domination. I firmly believe that a sustained examination of female masculinity can make crucial interventions within gender studies, cultural studies, queer studies, and mainstream discussions of gender in general.

Masculinity in this society inevitably conjures up notions of power and legitimacy and privilege; it often symbolically refers to the power of the state and to uneven distributions of wealth. Masculinity seems to extend outward into patriarchy and inward into the family; masculinity represents the power of inheritance, the consequences of the traffic in women, and the promise of social privilege. But, obviously, many other lines of identification traverse the terrain of masculinity, dividing its power into complicated differentials of class, race, sexuality, and gender. If what we call "dominant masculinity" appears to be a naturalized relation between maleness and power, then it makes little sense to examine men for the contours of that masculinity's social construction. Masculinity, this book will claim, becomes legible as masculinity where and when it leaves the white male middle-class body. Arguments about excessive masculinity tend to focus on black bodies (male and female), latino/a bodies, or working-class bodies, and insufficient masculinity is all too often figured by Asian bodies or upper-class bodies; these stereotypical constructions of variable masculinity mark the process by which masculinity becomes dominant in the sphere of white middle-class maleness. But all too many studies that currently attempt to account for the power of white masculinity recenter this white male body by concentrating all their analytical efforts on detailing the forms and expressions of white male dominance. Numerous studies of Elvis, white male youth, white male feminism, men and marriage, and domestications of maleness amass information about a subject whom we know intimately and ad nauseam. This study professes a degree of indifference to the whiteness of the male and the masculinity of the white male and the project of naming his power: male masculinity figures in my project as a hermeneutic, and as a counterexample to the kinds of masculinity that seem most informative about gender relations and most generative of social change. This book seeks Elvis only in the female Elvis impersonator Elvis Herselvis; it searches for the political contours of masculine privilege not in men but in the lives of aristocratic European cross-dressing women in the 1920s; it describes the details of masculine difference by comparing not men and women but butch lesbians and female-to-male transsexuals; it examines masculinity's iconicity not in the male matinee idol but in a history of butches in cinema; it finds, ultimately, that the shapes and forms of modern masculinity are best showcased within female masculinity.

How else to begin a book on female masculinity but by deposing one of the most persistent of male heroes: Bond, James Bond. To illustrate my point that modern masculinity is most easily recognized as female masculinity, consider the James Bond action film, in which male masculinity very often appears as only a shadow of a more powerful and convincing alternative masculinity. In *Goldeneye* (1995), for example, Bond battles the usual array of bad guys: Commies, Nazis, mercenaries, and a superaggressive violent femme type. He puts on his usual performance of debonair action adventure hero, and he has his usual supply of gadgetry to aid him — a retractable belt, a bomb disguised as a pen, a laser weapon watch, and so on. But there's something curiously lacking in *Goldeneye*, namely, credible masculine power. Bond's boss, M, is a noticeably butch older woman who calls Bond a dinosaur and chastises him for being a misogynist and a sexist. His secretary, Miss Moneypenny, accuses him of sexual harassment, his male buddy betrays him and calls him a dupe, and ultimately women seem not to go for his charms — bad suits and lots of sexual innuendo — which seem as old and as ineffective as his gadgets.

Masculinity, in this rather actionless film, is primarily prosthetic and, in this and countless other action films, has little if anything to do with biological maleness and signifies more often as a technical special effect. In *Goldeneye* it is M who most convincingly performs masculinity, and she does so partly by exposing the sham of Bond's own performance. It is M who convinces us that sexism and misogyny are not necessarily part and parcel of masculinity, even though historically it has become difficult, if not impossible, to untangle masculinity from the oppression of women. The action adventure hero should embody an extreme version of normative masculinity, but instead we find that excessive masculinity turns into a parody or exposure of the norm. Because masculinity tends to manifest as natural gender itself, the action flick, with its emphases on prosthetic extension, actually undermines the heterosexuality of the hero even as it extends his masculinity. So, in *Goldeneye*, for example, Bond's masculinity is linked not only to a profoundly unnatural form of masculine embodiment but also to gay masculinities. In the scene in which Bond goes to pick up his newest set of gadgets, a campy and almost queeny science nerd gives Bond his brand-new accessories and demonstrates each one with great enthusiasm. It is no accident that the science nerd is called Agent Q. We might read Agent Q as a perfect model of the interpenetration of queer and dominant regimes — Q is precisely an agent, a queer subject who exposes the workings of dominant heterosexual masculinity. The gay masculinity of Agent Q and the female masculinity of M provide a remarkable representation of the absolute dependence of dominant masculinities on minority masculinities.

When you take his toys away, Bond has very little propping up his performance of masculinity. Without the slick suit, the half smile, the cigarette lighter that transforms into a laser gun, our James is a hero without the action or the adventure. The masculinity of the white male, what we might call "epic masculinity," depends absolutely, as any Bond flick demonstrates, on a vast subterranean network of secret government groups, well-funded scientists, the army, and an endless supply of both beautiful bad babes and beautiful good babes, and finally it relies heavily on an immediately recognizable "bad guy." The "bad guy" is a standard generic feature of epic masculinity narratives: think only of *Paradise Lost* and its eschatological separation between God and Devil; Satan, if you like, is the original bad guy. Which is not to say that the bad guy's masculinity bars him from the rewards of male privilege — on the contrary, bad guys may also look like winners, but they just tend to die more quickly. Indeed, there is currently a line of clothing called Bad Boy that revels in the particular power of the bad guy and reveals how quickly transgression adds up to nothing more than consumerism in the sphere of the white male. Another line of clothing that indulges in the consumer potential of male rebellion is No Fear gear. This label features advertisements with skydiving, surfing, car-racing men who show their manliness by wearing the No Fear logo and practicing death-defying stunts in their leisure time. To test how domesticated this label actually is, we have only to imagine what No Fear might mean for women. It might mean learning how to shoot a gun or working out or taking up a martial art, but it would hardly translate into skydiving. Obviously, then, No Fear is a luxury and can in no way be equated with any form of social rebellion.

There is also a long literary and cinematic history that celebrates the rebellion of the male. If James Stewart, Gregory Peck, and Fred Astaire represent a few faces of good-guy appeal, James Dean, Marlon Brando, and Robert De Niro represent the bad-guy appeal, and really it becomes quite hard to separate one group from the other. Obviously, bad-boy representations in the 1950s captured something of a white working-class rebellion against middle-class society and against particular forms of domestication, but today's rebel without a cause is tomorrow's investment banker, and male rebellion tends toward respectability as the rewards for conformity quickly come to outweigh the rewards for social rebellion. To paraphrase Gertrude Stein, what's the point of being a rebel boy if you are going to grow up to be a man? Obviously, where and when rebellion ceases to be white middle-class male rebellion (individualized and localized within the lone male or even generalized into the boy gang) and becomes class rebellion or race rebellion, a very different threat emerges.

TOMBOYS

What happens when boy rebellion is located not in the testosterone-induced pout of the hooligan but in the sneer of the tomboy? Tomboyism generally describes an extended childhood period of female masculinity. If we are to believe general accounts of childhood behavior, tomboyism is quite common for girls and does not generally give rise to parental fears. Because comparable cross-identification behaviors in boys do often give rise to quite hysterical responses, we tend to believe that female gender deviance is much more tolerated than male gender deviance.[1] I am not sure that tolerance in such matters can be measured or at any rate that responses to childhood gender behaviors necessarily tell us anything concrete about the permitted parameters of adult male and female gender deviance. Tomboyism tends to be associated with a "natural" desire for the greater freedoms and mobilities enjoyed by boys. Very often it is read as a sign of independence and self-motivation, and tomboyism may even be encouraged to the extent that it remains comfortably linked to a stable sense of a girl identity. Tomboyism is punished, however, when it appears to be the sign of extreme male identification (taking a boy's name or refusing girl clothing of any type) and when it threatens to extend beyond childhood and into adolescence.[2] Teenage tomboyism presents a problem and tends to be subject to the most severe efforts to reorient. We could say that tomboyism is tolerated as long as the child remains prepubescent; as soon as puberty begins, however, the full force of gender conformity descends on the girl. Gender conformity is pressed onto all girls, not just tomboys, and this is where it becomes hard to uphold the notion that male femininity presents a greater threat to social and familial stability than female masculinity. Female adolescence represents the crisis of coming of age as a girl in a male-dominated society. If adolescence for boys represents a rite of passage (much celebrated in Western literature in the form of the bildungsroman), and an ascension to some version (however attenuated) of social power, for girls, adolescence is a lesson in restraint, punishment, and repression. It is in the context of female adolescence that the tomboy instincts of millions of girls are remodeled into compliant forms of femininity.

That any girls do emerge at the end of adolescence as masculine women is quite amazing. The growing visibility and indeed respectability of lesbian communities to some degree facilitate the emergence of masculine young women. But as even a cursory survey of popular cinema confirms, the image of the tomboy can be tolerated only within a narrative of blossoming womanhood; within such a narrative, tomboyism represents a resistance to adulthood itself rather than to adult femininity. In both the novel and film versions of the classic tomboy narrative *The Member of the Wedding*, by Carson McCullers,[3] tomboy Frankie Addams fights a losing battle against womanhood, and the text locates womanhood or femininity as a crisis of representation that confronts the heroine with unacceptable life options. As her brother's wedding approaches, Frankie Addams pronounces herself mired in a realm of unbelonging, outside the symbolic partnership of the wedding but also alienated from belonging in almost every category that might describe her. McCullers writes: "It happened that green and crazy summer when Frankie was twelve years old. This was the summer when for a long time she had not been a member. She belonged to no club and was a member of nothing in the world. Frankie was an unjoined person who hung around in doorways, and she was afraid."[4] McCullers positions Frankie on the verge of adolescence ("when Frankie was twelve years old") and in the midst of an enduring state of being "unjoined": "She belonged to no club and was a member of nothing in the world." While childhood in general

[1]For an extension of this discussion of tomboys see my article "Oh Bondage Up Yours: Female Masculinity and the Tomboy," in *Sissies and Tomboys: A CLAGS Reader* (New York: New York University Press, 1999). [Halberstam]

[2]For more on the punishment of tomboys see Phyllis Burke, *Gender Shock: Exploding the Myths of Male and Female* (New York: Anchor Books, 1996). Burke analyzes some recent case histories of so-called GID or Gender Identity Disorder, in which little girls are carefully conditioned out of male behavior and into exceedingly constrictive forms of femininity. [Halberstam]

[3]*The Member of the Wedding*, novel (1946) and play (1950) by (Lula) Carson (Smith) McCullers (1917–1967), filmed in 1952 by Fred Zinnemann. "Berenice" Sadie Brown is the African American maid who is the other important female character.

[4]Carson McCullers, *The Member of the Wedding* (1946; reprint, New York: Bantam, 1973), 1. [Halberstam]

may qualify as a period of "unbelonging," for the boyish girl arriving on the doorstep of womanhood, her status as "unjoined" marks her out for all manner of social violence and opprobrium. As she dawdles in the last light of childhood, Frankie Addams has become a tomboy who "hung around in doorways, and she was afraid."

As a genre, the tomboy film, as I show in chapter 6, "Looking Butch," suggests that the categories available to women for racial, gendered, and sexual identification are simply inadequate. In her novel, McCullers shows this inadequacy to be a direct result of the tyranny of language — a structure that fixes people and things in place artificially but securely. Frankie tries to change her identity by changing her name: "Why is it against the law to change your name?" she asks Berenice (107). Berenice answers: "Because things accumulate around your name," and she stresses that without names, confusion would reign and "the whole world would go crazy." But Berenice also acknowledges that the fixity conferred by names also traps people into many different identities, racial as well as gendered: "We all of us somehow caught. . . . And maybe we wants to widen and bust free. But no matter what we do we still caught" (113). Frankie thinks that naming represents the power of definition, and name changing confers the power to reimagine identity, place, relation, and even gender. "I wonder if it is against the law to change your name," says Frankie, "Or add to it. . . . Well I don't care. . . . F. Jasmine Addams"(15).

Psychoanalysis posits a crucial relationship between language and desire such that language structures desire and expresses therefore both the fullness and the futility of human desire — full because we always desire, futile because we are never satisfied. Frankie in particular understands desire and sexuality to be the most regimented forms of social conformity — we are supposed to desire only certain people and only in certain ways, but her desire does not work that way, and she finds herself torn between longing and belonging. Because she does not desire in conventional ways, Frankie seeks to avoid desire altogether. Her struggle with language, her attempts to remake herself through naming and remake the world with a new order of being, are

ultimately heroic, but unsuccessful. McCullers's pessimism has to do with a sense of the overwhelming "order of things," an order that cannot be affected by the individual, and works through things as basic as language, and forces nonmembers into memberships they cannot fulfill.

My book refuses the futility long associated with the tomboy narrative and instead seizes on the opportunity to recognize and ratify differently gendered bodies and subjectivities. Moving from the nineteenth century to the present and examining diaries, court cases, novels, letters, films, performances, events, critical essays, videos, news items, and testimonies, this book argues for the production of new taxonomies, what Eve K. Sedgwick humorously called "nonce taxonomies" in *Epistemology of the Closet*, classifications of desire, physicality, and subjectivity that attempt to intervene in hegemonic processes of naming and defining. Nonce taxonomies are categories that we use daily to make sense of our worlds but that work so well that we actually fail to recognize them. In this book, I attempt to bring some of the nonce taxonomies of female masculinity into view, and I detail the histories of the suppression of these categories. Here, and in the rest of the book, I am using the topic of female masculinity to explore a queer subject position that can successfully challenge hegemonic models of gender conformity. Female masculinity is a particularly fruitful site of investigation because it has been vilified by heterosexist and feminist/womanist programs alike; unlike male femininity, which fulfills a kind of ritual function in male homosocial cultures, female masculinity is generally received by hetero- and homo-normative cultures as a pathological sign of misidentification and maladjustment, as a longing to be and to have a power that is always just out of reach. Within a lesbian context, female masculinity has been situated as the place where patriarchy goes to work on the female psyche and reproduces misogyny within femaleness. There have been to date remarkably few studies or theories about the inevitable effects of a fully articulated female masculinity on a seemingly fortified male masculinity. Sometimes female masculinity coincides with the excesses of male supremacy, and sometimes it codifies a unique form of social rebellion; often female masculinity is the sign of sexual alterity, but occasionally it marks heterosexual variation; sometimes female masculinity marks the place of pathology, and every now and then it represents the healthful alternative to what are considered the histrionics of conventional femininities.

I want to carefully produce a model of female masculinity that remarks on its multiple forms but also calls for new and self-conscious affirmations of different gender taxonomies. Such affirmations begin not by subverting masculine power or taking up a position against masculine power but by turning a blind eye to conventional masculinities and refusing to engage. Frankie Addams, for example, constitutes her rebellion not in opposition to the law but through indifference to the law: she recognizes that it may be against the law to change one's name or add to it, but she also has a simple response to such illegal activity: "Well, I don't care." I am not suggesting in this book that we follow the futile path of what Foucault calls "saying no to power," but I am asserting that power may inhere within different forms of refusal: "Well, I don't care."

QUEER METHODOLOGIES

This book deploys numerous methodologies in order to pursue the multiple forms of gender variance presented within female masculinity. On account of the interdisciplinary nature of my project, I have had to craft a methodology out of available disciplinary methods. Deploying what I would call a "queer methodology," I have used some combination of textual criticism, ethnography, historical survey, archival research, and the production of taxonomies. I call this methodology "queer" because it attempts to remain supple enough to respond to the various locations of information on female masculinity and betrays a certain disloyalty to conventional disciplinary methods. Obviously, I could have produced methodological consistency by confining myself to literary texts, but the queer methodology used here, then, typifies just one of the forms of refusal that I discussed in my last section.

Although some of the most informative work on alternative sexual communities has come in the form of ethnography, and although autobiographies

and narrative histories tend to be the material that we turn to for information on sexual identities, there is nonetheless some disagreement among queer scholars about how we should collect and interpret such information on sexual identity. Indeed, some of the most bitter and long-lasting disagreements within queer studies have been about disciplinarity and methodology. Whereas some cultural studies proponents have argued that social science methods of collecting, collating, and presenting sexual data through surveys and other methods of social research tend to rediscover the sexual systems they already know rather than finding out about those they do not, social science proponents argue that cultural studies scholars do not pay enough attention to the material realities of queer life. And while there has been plenty of discussion in the academy about the need for interdisciplinary work, there has been far less support for such work in the university at large. A project such as this one, therefore, risks drawing criticism from historians for not providing a proper history, from literary critics for not focusing on literary texts, and from social scientists for not deploying the traditional tools of social science research. While I take full responsibility for all the errors I may make in my attempts to produce readings and histories and ethnography, I also recognize that this book exemplifies the problem confronted by queer studies itself: How do we forge queer methodologies while as scholars we reside in traditional departments?

At least one method of sex research that I reject in creating a queer methodology is the traditional social science project of surveying people and expecting to squeeze truth from raw data. In a review essay in the *New York Review of Books* about a series of new sex surveys, R. C. Lewontin comments on the difficulty associated with this social science approach to sexuality: "Given the social circumstances of sexual activity, there seems no way to find out what people do 'in the bedroom' except to ask them. But the answers they give cannot be put to the test of incredulity."[5] Lewontin suggests that people tend

[5] R. C. Lewontin, "Sex, Lies, and Social Science," *New York Review of Books* 42, no. 7 (20 April 1995): 24. [Halberstam]

not to be truthful when it comes to reporting on their own sexual behavior (men exaggerate and women downplay, for example), and there are no ways to make allowances for personal distortion within social science methods. Furthermore, social scientists seem not to be concerned with the high levels of untruth in relation to sexuality but spend all their energy on solving methodological problems. Ultimately, Lewontin claims — and I think he has a point — social science surveys are "demonstrations of what their planners already believed they knew to be true" (25). At a time when the humanities are under severe scrutiny and attack, it is important to point to the reliance of social science methods on strategies such as narrative analysis, interpretation, and speculation. As Lewontin says in his conclusion: "How then can there be a social science? The answer surely is to be less ambitious and stop trying to make sociology into a natural science although it is, indeed, the study of natural objects" (29). This is not to say, however, that traditional social science research methods such as questionnaires are never appropriate. Indeed, there are certain questions that can be answered only by survey methods in the realm of sexuality (i.e., how many lesbians are using dental dams? What age-groups or social classes do these lesbians belong to?), but all too often surveys are used to try to gather far less factual information, and all subtlety tends to be lost.[6]

There is some irony in the apparent impossibility of applying traditional social science methods to the study of sex because as queer sociologists are all too quick to point out, many of the theoretical systems that we use to talk about sex, such as social constructionism, come from sociology. In a recent "queer" issue of *Sociological Theory*, a group of sociologists attempted to account for the currently strained relations between sociological theory and queer theory. Steven Epstein pointed out that sociology asserted that sexuality was socially constructed and indeed that "without seeking to minimize the importance of other disciplines, I would suggest that neither queer theory nor lesbian and gay studies in general could be imagined in their present forms without the contributions of sociological theory."[7] Arlene Stein and Ken Plummer continue Epstein's line of inquiry and add a critique of the present state of queer theory:

> Queer theorists . . . appreciate the extent to which the texts of literature and mass culture shape sexuality, but their weakness is that they rarely, if ever, move beyond the text. There is a dangerous tendency for the new queer theorists to ignore "real" queer life as it is materially experienced across the world, while they play with the free-floating signifiers of texts.[8]

In an effort to restore sociology to its proper place within the study of sexuality, Stein and Plummer have reinvested here in a clear and verifiable difference between the real and the textual, and they designate textual analysis as a totally insular activity with no referent, no material consequences, and no intellectual gain. But as Lewontin's review suggested, it is precisely this belief in the real and the material as separate from the represented and the textual that creates the problems of survey analysis. To be fair, Stein and Plummer are clearly not suggesting merely a

[6]Thanks to Esther Newton for making this point and suggesting when and how survey methods are useful. For an example of the kinds of questions used in sex surveys see John Gagnon et al., *Sex in America* (Boston: Little Brown, 1994). This particular volume is remarkable because the explicit questions it asks about the kinds of sex people were having focus obsessively on the couple, and the study links certain activities definitively to certain identities. So, for example, questions about anal sex are directed only at male/female and male/male couples because anal sex is defined as "when a man's penis is inside his partner's anus or rectum" (260). There are no questions directed specifically at female/female couples and no questions about sex toys or use of dildos or hands in this section. [Halberstam] A "dental dam" is a sort of condom to protect against sexually transmitted diseases during oral sex.

[7]Steven Epstein, "A Queer Encounter: Sociology and the Study of Sexuality," *Sociological Theory* 12, no. 2 (July 1994): 189. [Halberstam]

[8]Arlene Stein and Ken Plummer, " 'I Can't Even Think Straight' ": Queer Theory and the Missing Revolution in Sociology," *Sociological Theory* 12, no. 2 (July 1994): 184. [Halberstam]

quantitative approach to the study of sexuality and queer subcultures, but they do, on some level, seem to have re-created some essential divide between the truth of sexual behavior and the fiction of textual analysis.

The answer to the problem of how to study sexuality, I am trying to suggest, must lie to some extent in an interdisciplinary approach that can combine information culled from people with information culled from texts. So, whereas Cindy Patton, for example, in "Tremble Hetero Swine," remarks with dismay on the dominance of "textually based forms of queer theory," we must question whether there is a form of queer theory or sexual theory that is not textually based.[9] Isn't a sexual ethnographer studying texts? And doesn't a social historian collate evidence from texts? Sometimes the texts are oral histories, sometimes they might be interview material, sometimes they might be fiction or autobiography, but given our basic formulation of sex as "private," something that happens when other people are not around, there is no way to objectively observe "in the bedroom." Conversely, readings of texts also require historical contexts and some relation to the lived experience of subjects. The text-based methodologies err on the side of abstraction, and the sociological studies err on the side of overly rationalizing sexual behavior. Finally, although some have criticized literary or cultural studies approaches to identity construction as apolitical or ahistorical, theories that tie the history of sexuality unproblematically to economics or the movement of capital tend to produce exactly the linear narratives of rational progress and modernization that sexuality seems to resist.

A queer methodology, in a way, is a scavenger methodology that uses different methods to collect and produce information on subjects who have been deliberately or accidentally excluded from traditional studies of human behavior. The queer methodology attempts to combine methods that are often cast as being at odds with each other, and it refuses the academic compulsion toward disciplinary coherence. Although this book will be immediately recognizable as a work of cultural studies, it will not shy away from the more empirical methods associated with ethnographic research.

CONSTRUCTING MASCULINITIES

Within cultural studies itself, masculinity has recently become a favorite topic. I want to try here to account for the growing popularity of a body of work on masculinity that evinces absolutely no interest in masculinity without men. I first noticed the unprecedented interest in masculinity in April 1994 when the DIA Center for the Performing Arts convened a group of important intellectuals to hold forth on the topic of masculinities. On the opening night of this event, one commentator wondered, "Why masculinity, why now?" Several others, male critics and scholars, gave eloquent papers about their memories of being young boys and about their relationships with their fathers. The one lesbian on the panel, a poet, read a moving poem about rape. At the end of the evening, only one panelist had commented on the limitations of a discussion of masculinity that interpreted "masculinity" as a synonym for men or maleness.[10] This lonely intervention highlighted the gap between mainstream discussions of masculinity and men and ongoing queer discussions about masculinity, which extend far beyond the male body. Indeed, in answer to the naive question that began the evening, "Why masculinities, why now?" one might state: Because masculinity in the 1990s has finally been recognized as, at least in part, a construction by female- as well as male-born people.[11]

[9]Cindy Patton, "Tremble Hetero Swine," in *Fear of a Queer Planet: Queer Politics and Social Theory*, ed. Michael Warner (Minneapolis: University of Minnesota Press, 1993), 165. [Halberstam]

[10]The conference papers were collected in a volume called *Constructing Masculinity*, ed. Maurice Berger, Brian Wallis, and Simon Watson (New York: Routledge, 1996), and the one intervention on behalf of nonmale masculinities was made by Eve Kosofsky Sedgwick. [Halberstam]

[11]I am using the terms "female born" and "male born" to indicate a social practice of assigning one of two genders to babies at birth. My terminology suggests that these assignations may not hold for the lifetime of the individual, and it suggests from the outset that binary gender continues to dominate our cultural and scientific notions of gender but that individuals inevitably fail to find themselves in only one of two options. [Halberstam]

The anthology that the conference produced provides more evidence of the thoroughgoing association that the editors have made between masculinity and maleness. The title page features a small photographic illustration of a store sign advertising clothing as "Fixings for Men." This illustration has been placed just below the title, *Constructing Masculinity*, and forces the reader to understand the construction of masculinity as the outfitting of males within culture. The introduction to the volume attempts to diversify this definition of masculinity by using Judith Butler's and Eve Sedgwick's contributions to suggest that the anthology recognizes the challenges made by gays, lesbians, and queers to the terms of gender normativity. The editors insist that masculinity is multiple and that "far from just being about men, the idea of masculinity engages, inflects, and shapes everyone."[12] The commitment to the representation of masculinity as multiple is certainly borne out in the first essay in the volume, by Eve Sedgwick, in which she proposes that masculinity may have little to do with men, and is somewhat extended by Butler's essay "Melancholy Gender." But Sedgwick also critiques the editors for having proposed a book and a conference on masculinity that remain committed to linking masculinity to maleness. Although the introduction suggests that the editors have heeded Sedgwick's call for gender diversity, the rest of the volume suggests otherwise. There are many fascinating essays in this anthology, but there are no essays specifically on female masculinity. Although gender-queer images by Loren Cameron and Cathy Opie adorn the pages of the book, the text contains no discussions of these images. The book circles around discussions of male icons such as Clint Eastwood and Steven Seagal; it addresses the complex relations between fathers and sons; it examines topics such as how science defines men and masculinity and the law. The volume concludes with an essay by Stanley Aronowitz titled "My Masculinity," an autobiographically inflected consideration of various forms of male power.

None of my analysis here is to say that this is an uninteresting anthology or that the essays are

somehow wrong or misguided, but I am trying to point out that the editorial statement at the beginning of the volume is less a prologue to what follows and more of an epilogue that describes what a volume on masculinity *should* do as opposed to what the anthology does do. Even when the need for an analysis of female masculinity has been acknowledged, in other words, it seems remarkably difficult to follow through on. What is it then that, to paraphrase Eve Sedgwick's essay, makes it so difficult *not* to presume an essential relation between masculinity and men?[13]

By beginning with this examination of the *Constructing Masculinity* conference and anthology, I do not want to give the impression that the topic of female masculinities must always be related to some larger topic, some more general set of masculinities that has been, and continues to be, about men. Nor do I want to suggest that gender theory is the true origin of gender knowledges. Rather, this conference and book merely emphasize the lag between community knowledges and practices and academic discourses.[14] I believe it is both helpful and important to contextualize a discussion of female and lesbian masculinities in direct opposition to a more generalized discussion of masculinity within cultural studies that seems intent on insisting that masculinity remain the property of male bodies. The continued refusal in Western society to admit ambiguously gendered bodies into functional social relations (evidenced, for example, by our continued use of either/or bathrooms, either women or men) is, I will claim, sustained by a conservative and protectionist attitude by men in general toward masculinity. Such an attitude has

[13]More and more journals are putting together special issues on masculinity, but I have yet to locate a single special issue with a single essay about female masculinity. The latest journal announcement that found its way to me was from *The Velvet Light Trap: A Critical Journal of Film and Television*. They announced an issue on "New Masculinities" that featured essays titled "The 'New Masculinity' in *Tootsie*." "On Fathers and Sons, Sex and Death," "Male Melodrama and the Feeling Man," and so forth. This is not to say that such topics are not interesting, only that the "new masculinities" sound remarkably like the old ones. See *The Velvet Light Trap*, "New Masculinities," no. 38 (Fall 1996). [Halberstam]

[14]Berger, Wallis, and Watson, *Constructing Masculinity*. [Halberstam]

[12]Berger, Wallis, and Watson, introduction to *Constructing Masculinity*, 7. [Halberstam]

been bolstered by a more general disbelief in female masculinity. I can only describe such disbelief in terms of a failure in a collective imagination: in other words, female-born people have been making convincing and powerful assaults on the coherence of male masculinity for well over a hundred years; what prevents these assaults from taking hold and accomplishing the diminution of the bonds between masculinity and men? Somehow, despite multiple images of strong women (such as bodybuilder Bev Francis or tennis player Martina Navratilova), of cross-identifying women (Radclyffe Hall or Ethel Smyth), of masculine-coded public figures (Janet Reno), of butch superstars (k. d. lang), of muscular and athletic women (Jackie Joyner-Kersee), of female-born transgendered people (Leslie Feinberg), there is still no general acceptance or even recognition of masculine women and boyish girls. This book addresses itself to this collective failure to imagine and ratify the masculinity produced by, for, and within women.

In case my concerns about the current discussions of masculinity in cultural studies sound too dismissive, I want to look in an extended way at what happens when academic discussions of male masculinity take place to the exclusion of discussions of more wide-ranging masculinities. While it may seem that I am giving an inordinate amount of attention to what is after all just one intervention into current discussions, I am using one book as representative of a whole slew of other studies of masculinity that replicate the intentions and the mistakes of this one. In an anthology called *Boys: Masculinities in Contemporary Culture*, edited by Paul Smith for a Cultural Studies series, Smith suggests that masculinity must always be thought of "in the plural" as masculinities "defined and cut through by differences and contradictions of all sorts."[15] The plurality of masculinities for Smith encompasses a dominant white masculinity that is crisscrossed by its others, gay, bisexual, black, Asian, and Latino masculinities. Although the recognition

of a host of masculinities makes sense, Smith chooses to focus on dominant white masculinity to the exclusion of the other masculinities he has listed. Smith, predictably, warns the reader not to fall into the trap of simply critiquing dominant masculinity or simply celebrating minority masculinities, and then he makes the following foundational statement:

And it may well be the case, as some influential voices often tell us, that masculinity or masculinities are in some real sense not the exclusive "property" of biologically male subjects — it's true that many female subjects lay claim to masculinity as their property. Yet in terms of cultural and political *power*, it still makes a difference when masculinity coincides with biological maleness. (4)

What is immediately noticeable to me here is the odd attribution of immense power to those "influential voices" who keep telling us that masculinity is not the property of men. There is no naming of these influential voices, and we are left supposing that "influence" has rendered the "female masculinity theorists" so powerful that names are irrelevant: these voices, one might suppose, are hegemonic. Smith goes on to plead with the reader, asking us to admit that the intersection of maleness and masculinity does "still" make a difference. His appeal here to common sense allows him to sound as if he is trying to reassert some kind of rationality to a debate that is spinning off into totally inconsequential discussions. Smith is really arguing that we must turn to dominant masculinity to begin deconstructing masculinity because it is the equation of maleness plus masculinity that adds up to social legitimacy. As I argued earlier in this chapter, however, precisely because white male masculinity has obscured all other masculinities, we have to turn away from its construction to bring other more mobile forms of masculinity to light. Smith's purpose in his reassertion of the difference that male masculinity makes is to uncover the "cultural and political *power*" of this union in order to direct our attention to the power of patriarchy. The second part of the paragraph makes this all too clear:

Biological men — male-sexed beings — are after all, in varying degrees, the bearers of privilege and power within the systems against which women

[15]Paul Smith, ed., *Boys: Masculinities in Contemporary Culture* (Boulder, Colo.: Westview Press, 1996), 3. [Halberstam]

still struggle. The privilege and power are, of course, different for different men, endlessly diversified through the markers of class, nation, race, sexual preference and so on. But I'd deny that there are any men who are entirely outside of the ambit, let's say, of power and privilege *in relation to women*. In that sense it has to be useful to our thinking to recall that masculinities are not only a function of dominant notions of masculinity and not constituted solely in resistant notions of "other" masculinities. In fact, masculinities exist inevitably in relation to what feminisms have construed as the system of patriarchy and patriarchal relations.[16]

The most noticeable feature of this paragraph is the remarkable stability of the terms "women" and "men." Smith advances here a slightly old-fashioned feminism that understands women as endlessly victimized within systems of male power. Woman, within such a model, is the name for those subjects within patriarchy who have no access to male power and who are regulated and confined by patriarchal structures. But what would Smith say to Monique Wittig's claim that lesbians are not women because they are not involved in the heterosexual matrix that produces sexual differences as a power relation? What can Smith add to Judith Butler's influential theory of "gender trouble," which suggests that "gender is a copy with no original" and that dominant sexualities and genders are in some sense imbued with a pathetic dependence on their others that puts them perpetually at risk? What would Smith say to Jacob Hale's claim that the genders we use as reference points in gender theory fall far behind community productions of alternative genderings?[17] Are butch dykes women? Are male transvestites men? How does gender variance disrupt the flow of powers presumed by patriarchy in

relations between men and women? Smith, in other words, cannot take female masculinity into account because he sees it as inconsequential and secondary to much more important questions about male privilege. Again, this sounds more like a plaintive assertion that men *do* still access male power within patriarchy (don't they?), and it conveniently ignores the ways in which gender relations are scrambled where and when gender variance comes into play.

Smith's attempt to shore up male masculinity by dismissing the importance of other masculinities finds further expression in his attempt to take racialized masculinities into consideration. His introductory essay opens with a meditation on the complications of the O.J. Simpson case, and Smith wonders at the way popular discourse on the O.J. case sidesteps issues of masculinity and male domination in favor of race. When he hears a black male caller to a radio talk show link O.J.'s case to an ongoing conspiracy against black men in this country, Smith ponders: "His spluttering about the attempted genocide of black men reminded me, somehow, that another feature of the O.J. case was the way it had started with the prosecution trying to establish the relevance of O.J.'s record as a wife beater" (Smith, *Boys*, 1). Noting that the callers to the talk show did not have much to say about this leads Smith to wonder whether race can constitute a collective identity but masculinity cannot, and finally he suggests that although "it might be difficult to talk about race in this country, it is even more difficult to talk about masculinity" (1). If you are a white man, it is probably extremely difficult to talk about either race or masculinity let alone both at the same time. But, of course, race and masculinity, especially in the case of O.J., are not separable into tidy categories. Indeed, one might say that the caller's "spluttering" about conspiracies against black men constituted a far more credible race analysis in this case than Smith's articulation of the relations between race and masculinity. For Smith, masculinity in the case of O.J. constitutes a flow of domination that comes up against his blackness as a flow of subordination. There is no discussion here of the injustices of the legal system, the role of class and money in the trial, or the complicated history of relations

[16]Paul Smith, introduction to *Boys: Masculinities in Contemporary Culture*, 4–5. [Halberstam]

[17]See Monique Wittig, "The Straight Mind," in *The Straight Mind and Other Essays* (Boston: Beacon Press, 1992); Judith Butler, "Imitation and Gender Insubordination," in *Inside/Out: Lesbian Theories, Gay Theories*, ed., Diana Fuss (New York: Routledge, 1991), 13–31; Jacob Hale, "Are Lesbians Women?" *Hypatia* 11, no. 2 (spring 1996): 94–121. [Halberstam]

between black men and white women. Smith uses O.J. as shorthand for a model that is supposed to suggest power and disempowerment in the same location.

I am taking so much time and effort to discount Smith's introduction to *Boys* because there is a casualness to his essay that both indicates his lack of any real investment in the project of alternative masculinities and suggests an unwillingness to think through the messy identifications that make up contemporary power relations around gender, race, and class. The book that Smith introduces also proves to have nothing much to offer to new discussions of masculinity, and we quickly find ourselves, from the opening essay on, in the familiar territory of men, boys, and their fathers. The first essay, for example, by Fred Pfeil, "A Buffalo, New York Story," tells a pitiful tale about father-son relations in the 1950s. In one memorable moment from the memoir, he (Fred) and Dad have cozied up on the couch to watch *Bonanza* while Mom and Sis are doing the dishes in the kitchen. Boy asks Dad "why bad guys were always so stupid," and Dad laughs and explains "because they were bad" (10). The story goes on to detail the innocent young boy's first brushes with his male relatives' racism and his own painful struggle with car sickness. Besides taking apart the dynamics of fathers and sons cozying up together to watch *Bonanza*, there most certainly are a multitude of important things to say about men and masculinity in patriarchy, but Smith and some of his contributors choose not to say them. We could be producing ethnographies on the aggressive and indeed protofascist masculinities produced by male sports fans.[18] Much work still remains to be done on the socialization (or lack thereof) of young men in high schools, on (particularly rich white male) domestic abusers, on the new sexism embodied by "sensitive men," on the men who participate in the traffic in mail-order brides and sex tourism (including a study of privileged white gay masculinity). But studies in male masculinity are predictably not so interested in taking apart the patriarchal bonds between white maleness and privilege; they are much more concerned to detail the fragilities of male socialization, the pains of manhood, and the fear of female empowerment.[19]

Because I have criticized Smith for his apparent lack of investment in the project of producing alternative masculinities, let me take a moment to make my own investments clear. Although I make my own masculinity the topic of my last chapter, it seems important to state that this book is an attempt to make my own female masculinity plausible, credible, and real. For a large part of my life, I have been stigmatized by a masculinity that marked me as ambiguous and illegible. Like many other tomboys, I was mistaken for a boy throughout my childhood, and like many other tomboy adolescents, I was forced into some semblance of femininity for my teenage years. When gender-ambiguous children are constantly challenged about their gender identity, the chain of misrecognitions can actually produce a new recognition: in other words, to be constantly mistaken for a boy, for many tomboys, can contribute to the production of a masculine identity. It was not until my midtwenties that I finally found a word for my particular gender configuration: butch. In my final chapter, "Raging Bull (Dyke)," I address the ways in which butches manage to affirm their masculinity despite the multiple sites in which that masculinity is challenged, denied, threatened, and violated.

THE BATHROOM PROBLEM

If three decades of feminist theorizing about gender has thoroughly dislodged the notion that anatomy is destiny, that gender is natural, and that male and female are the only options, why do we still operate in a world that assumes that people who are not male are female, and people who

[18]Indeed, one such ethnography has been carried out, but significantly it took English soccer hooligans as its topic. See Bill Buford's remarkable *Among the Thugs* (New York: Norton, 1992). A similar work on American male fans would be extremely useful. [Halberstam]

[19]For verification of such topics of concern just check out the men's sections that are popping up in your local bookstores. More specifically see the work of Michael Kimmel and Victor Seidler: Michael Kimmel, *Manhood in America: A Cultural History* (New York: Free Press, 1996); Victor J. Seidler, *Unreasonable Men: Masculinity and Social Theory* (New York: Routledge, 1994). [Halberstam]

are not female are male (and even that people who are not male are not people!). If gender has been so thoroughly defamiliarized, in other words, why do we not have multiple gender options, multiple gender categories, and real-life nonmale and nonfemale options for embodiment and identification? In a way, gender's very flexibility and seeming fluidity is precisely what allows dimorphic gender to hold sway. Because so few people actually match any given community standards for male or female, in other words, gender can be imprecise and therefore multiply relayed through a solidly binary system. At the same time, because the definitional boundaries of male and female are so elastic, there are very few people in any given public space who are completely unreadable in terms of their gender.

Ambiguous gender, when and where it does appear, is inevitably transformed into deviance, thirdness, or a blurred version of either male or female. As an example, in public bathrooms for women, various bathroom users tend to fail to measure up to expectations of femininity, and those of us who present in some ambiguous way are routinely questioned and challenged about our presence in the "wrong" bathroom. For example, recently, on my way to give a talk in Minneapolis, I was making a connection at Chicago's O'Hare airport. I strode purposefully into the women's bathroom. No sooner had I entered the stall than someone was knocking at the door: "Open up, security here!" I understood immediately what had happened. I had, once again, been mistaken for a man or a boy, and some woman had called security. As soon as I spoke, the two guards at the bathroom stall realized their error, mumbled apologies, and took off. On the way home from the same trip, in the Denver airport, the same sequence of events was repeated. Needless to say, the policing of gender within the bathroom is intensified in the space of the airport, where people are literally moving through space and time in ways that cause them to want to stabilize some boundaries (gender) even as they traverse others (national). However, having one's gender challenged in the women's rest room is a frequent occurrence in the lives of many androgynous or masculine women; indeed, it is so frequent that one wonders whether the category "woman,"

when used to designate public functions, is completely outmoded.[20]

It is no accident, then, that travel hubs become zones of intense scrutiny and observation. But gender policing within airport bathrooms is merely an intensified version of a larger "bathroom problem." For some gender-ambiguous women, it is relatively easy to "prove" their right to use the women's bathroom — they can reveal some decisive gender trait (a high voice, breasts), and the challenger will generally back off. For others (possibly low-voiced or hairy or breastless people), it is quite difficult to justify their presence in the women's bathroom, and these people may tend to use the men's bathroom, where scrutiny is far less intense. Obviously, in these bathroom confrontations, the gender-ambiguous person first appears as not-woman ("You are in the wrong bathroom!"), but then the person appears as something actually even more scary, not-man ("No, I am not," spoken in a voice recognized as not-male). Not-man and not-woman, the gender-ambiguous bathroom user is also not androgynous or in-between; this person is gender deviant.

For many gender deviants, the notion of passing is singularly unhelpful. Passing as a narrative assumes that there is a self that masquerades as another kind of self and does so successfully; at various moments, the successful pass may cohere into something akin to identity. At such a moment, the passer has *become*. What of a biological female who presents as butch, passes as male in some circumstances and reads as butch in

---

[20]The continued viability of the category "woman" has been challenged in a variety of academic locations already: Monique Wittig, most notably, argued that "lesbians are not women" in her essay "The Straight Mind," 121. Wittig claims that because lesbians are refusing primary relations to men, they cannot occupy the position "woman." In another philosophical challenge to the category "woman," transgender philosopher Jacob Hale uses Monique Wittig's radical claim to theorize the possibility of gendered embodiments that exceed male and female (see Jacob Hale, "Are Lesbians Women?" *Hypatia* II, no. 2 [spring 1996]). Elsewhere, Cheshire Calhoun suggests that the category "woman" may actually "operate as a lesbian closet" (see Cheshire Calhoun, "The Gender Closet: Lesbian Disappearance under the Sign 'Women,'" *Feminist Studies* 21, no. 1 [spring 1995]: 7–34). [Halberstam]

others, and considers herself not to be a woman but maintains distance from the category "man"? For such a subject, identity might best be described as a process with multiple sites for becoming and being. To understand such a process, we would need to do more than map psychic and physical journeys between male and female and within queer and straight space; we would need, in fact, to think in fractal terms and about gender geometries. Furthermore, I argue in chapter 4, in my discussion of the stone butch, when and where we discuss the sexualities at stake in certain gender definitions, very different identifications between sexuality, gender, and the body emerge. The stone butch, for example, in her self-definition as a non-feminine, sexually untouchable female, complicates the idea that lesbians share female sexual practices or women share female sexual desires or even that masculine women share a sense of what animates their particular masculinities.

I want to focus on what I am calling "the bathroom problem" because I believe it illustrates in remarkably clear ways the flourishing existence of gender binarism despite rumors of its demise. Furthermore, many normatively gendered women have no idea that a bathroom problem even exists and claim to be completely ignorant about the trials and tribulations that face the butch woman who needs to use a public bathroom. But queer literature is littered with references to the bathroom problem, and it would not be an exaggeration to call it a standard feature of the butch narrative. For example, Leslie Feinberg provides clear illustrations of the dimensions of the bathroom problem in *Stone Butch Blues*. In this narrative of the life of the he-she factory worker, Jess Goldberg, Jess recounts many occasions in which she has to make crucial decisions about whether she can afford to use the women's bathroom. On a shopping outing with some drag queens, Jess tells Peaches: "I gotta use the bathroom. God, I wish I could wait, but I can't." Jess takes a deep breath and enters the ladies room:

> Two women were freshening their makeup in front of the mirror.
> One glanced at the other and finished applying her lipstick. "Is that a man or a woman?" She said to her friend as I passed them.

The other woman turned to me. "This is the woman's bathroom," she informed me.

I nodded. "I know."

I locked the stall door behind me. Their laughter cut me to the bone.

"You don't really know if that is a man or not," one woman said to the other. "We should call security to make sure."

I flushed the toilet and fumbled with my zipper in fear. Maybe it was just an idle threat. Maybe they really would call security. I hurried out of the bathroom as soon as I heard both women leave.[21]

For Jess, the bathroom represents a limit to her ability to move around in the public sphere. Her body, with its needs and physical functions, imposes a limit on her attempts to function normally despite her variant gender presentation. The women in the rest room, furthermore, are depicted as spiteful, rather than fearful. They toy with Jess by calling into question her right to use the rest room and threatening to call the police. As Jess puts it: "They never would have made fun of a guy like that." In other words, if the women were truly anxious for their safety, they would not have toyed with the intruder, and they would not have hesitated to call the police. Their casualness about calling security indicates that they know Jess is a woman but want to punish her for her inappropriate self-presentation.

Another chronicle of butch life, *Throw It to the River*, by Nice Rodriguez, a Filipina-Canadian writer, also tells of the bathroom encounter. In a story called "Every Full Moon," Rodriguez tells a romantic tale about a butch bus conductor called Remedios who falls in love with a former nun called Julianita. Remedios is "muscular around the arms and shoulders," and her "toughness allows her to bully anyone who will not pay the fare."[22] She aggressively flirts with Julianita until Julianita agrees to go to a movie with Remedios. To prepare for her date, Remedios dresses herself up, carefully flattening out her chest with Band-Aids over the nipples: "She bought a white shirt in Divisoria just for this date. Now she worries

[21]Leslie Feinberg, *Stone Butch Blues: A Novel* (Ithaca, N.Y.: Firebrand, 1993), 59. [Halberstam]
[22]Nice Rodriguez, *Throw It to the River* (Toronto, Canada: Women's Press, 1993), 25–26. [Halberstam]

that the cloth may be too thin and transparent, and that Julianita will be turned off when her nipples protrude out like dice" (33). With her "well-ironed jeans," her smooth chest, and even a man's manicure, Remedios heads out for her date. However, once out with Julianita, Remedios, now dressed in her butch best, has to be careful about public spaces. After the movie, Julianita rushes off to the washroom, but Remedios waits outside for her:

> She has a strange fear of ladies rooms. She wishes there was another washroom somewhere between the mens' and the ladies' for queers like her. Most of the time she holds her pee — sometimes as long as half a day — until she finds a washroom where the users are familiar with her. Strangers take to her unkindly, especially elder women who inspect her from head to toe. (40–41)

Another time, Remedios tells of being chased from a ladies' room and beaten by a bouncer. The bathroom problem for Remedios and for Jess severely limits their ability to circulate in public spaces and actually brings them into contact with physical violence as a result of having violated a cardinal rule of gender: one must be readable at a glance. After Remedios is beaten for having entered a ladies' room, her father tells her to be more careful, and Rodriguez notes: "She realized that being cautious means swaying her hips and parading her boobs when she enters any ladies room" (30).

If we use the paradigm of the bathroom as a limit of gender identification, we can measure the distance between binary gender schema and lived multiple gendered experiences. The accusation "you're in the wrong bathroom" really says two different things. First, it announces that your gender seems at odds with your sex (your apparent masculinity or androgyny is at odds with your supposed femaleness); second, it suggests that single-gender bathrooms are only for those who fit clearly into one category (male) or the other (female). Either we need open access bathrooms or multigendered bathrooms, or we need wider parameters for gender identification. The bathroom, as we know it, actually represents the crumbling edifice of gender in the twentieth century. The frequency with which gender-deviant "women" are mistaken for men in public bathrooms suggests that a large number of feminine women spend a large amount of time and energy policing masculine women. Something very different happens, of course, in the men's public toilet, where the space is more likely to become a sexual cruising zone than a site for gender repression. Lee Edelman, in an essay about the interpenetration of nationalism and sexuality, argues that "the institutional men's room constitutes a site at which the zones of public and private cross with a distinctive psychic charge."[23] The men's room, in other words, constitutes both an architecture of surveillance and an incitement to desire, a space of homosocial interaction and of homoerotic interaction.

So, whereas men's rest rooms tend to operate as a highly charged sexual space in which sexual interactions are both encouraged and punished, women's rest rooms tend to operate as an arena for the enforcement of gender conformity. Sex-segregated bathrooms continue to be necessary to protect women from male predations but also produce and extend a rather outdated notion of a public-private split between male and female society. The bathroom is a domestic space beyond the home that comes to represent domestic order, or a parody of it, out in the world. The women's bathroom accordingly becomes a sanctuary of enhanced femininity, a "little girl's room" to which one retreats to powder one's nose or fix one's hair. The men's bathroom signifies as the extension of the public nature of masculinity — it is precisely not domestic even though the names given to the sexual function of the bathroom — such as cottage or tearoom — suggest it is a parody of the domestic. The codes that dominate within the women's bathroom are primarily gender codes; in the men's room, they are sexual codes. Public sex versus private gender, openly sexual versus discreetly repressive, bathrooms beyond the home take on the proportions of a gender factory.

Marjorie Garber comments on the liminality of the bathroom in *Vested Interests* in a chapter

[23]Lee Edelman, "Tearooms and Sympathy, or The Epistemology of the Water Closet," in *Homographesis: Essays in Gay Literary and Cultural Theory* (New York: Routledge, 1994), 158. [Halberstam]

on the perils and privileges of cross-dressing. She discusses the very different modes of passing and cross-dressing for cross-identified genetic males and females, and she observes that the rest room is a "potential waterloo" for both female-to-male (FTM) and male-to-female (MTF) cross-dressers and transsexuals.[24] For the FTM, the men's room represents the most severe test of his ability to pass, and advice frequently circulates within FTM communities about how to go unnoticed in male-only spaces. Garber notes: "The cultural paranoia of being caught in the ultimately wrong place, which may be inseparable from the pleasure of "passing" in that same place, depends in part on the same cultural binarism, the idea that gender categories are sufficiently uncomplicated to permit self-assortment into one of the two 'rooms' without deconstructive reading" (47). It is worth pointing out here (if only because Garber does not) that the perils for passing FTMS in the men's room are very different from the perils of passing MTFS in the women's room. On the one hand, the FTM in the men's room is likely to be less scrutinized because men are not quite as vigilant about intruders as women for obvious reasons. On the other hand, if caught, the FTM may face some version of gender panic from the man who discovers him, and it is quite reasonable to expect and fear violence in the wake of such a discovery. The MTF, by comparison, will be more scrutinized in the women's room but possibly less open to punishment if caught. Because the FTM ventures into male territory with the potential threat of violence hanging over his head, it is crucial to recognize that the bathroom problem is much more than a glitch in the machinery of gender segregation and is better described in terms of the violent enforcement of our current gender system.

[24]Marjorie Garber, *Vested Interests: Cross-Dressing and Cultural Anxiety* (New York: Routledge, 1992), 47. Obviously Garber's use of the term "waterloo" makes a pun out of the drama of bathroom surveillance. Although the pun is clever and even amusing, it is also troubling to see how often Garber turns to punning in her analyses. The constant use of puns throughout the book has the overall effect of making gender crossing sound like a game or at least trivializes the often life-or-death processes involved in cross-identification. This is not to say gender can never be a "laughing matter" and must always be treated seriously but only to question the use of the pun here as a theoretical method. [Halberstam]

Garber's reading of the perilous use of rest rooms by both FTMS and MTFS develops out of her introductory discussion of what Lacan calls "urinary segregation."[25] Lacan used the term to describe the relations between identities and signifiers, and he ultimately used the simple diagram of the rest room signs "Ladies" and "Gentlemen" to show that within the production of sexual difference, primacy is granted to the signifier over that which it signifies; in more simple terms, naming confers, rather than reflects, meaning.[26] In the same way, the system of urinary segregation creates the very functionality of the categories "men" and "women." Although rest room signs seem to serve and ratify distinctions that already exist, in actual fact these markers produce identifications within these constructed categories. Garber latches on to the notion of "urinary segregation" because it helps her to describe the processes of cultural binarism within the production of gender; for Garber, transvestites and transsexuals challenge this system by resisting the literal translation of the signs "Ladies" and "Gentlemen." Garber uses the figures of the transvestite and the transsexual to show the obvious flaws and gaps in a binary gender system; the transvestite, as interloper, creates a third space of possibility within which all binaries become unstable. Unfortunately, as in all attempts to break a binary by producing a third term, Garber's third space tends to stabilize the other two. In "Tearooms and Sympathy," Lee Edelman also turns to Lacan's term "urinary segregation," but Edelman uses Lacan's diagram to mark heterosexual anxiety "about the potential inscriptions of homosexual desire and about the possibility of knowing or recognizing whatever might constitute 'homosexual difference'" (160). Whereas for Garber it is the transvestite who marks the instability of the markers "Ladies" and Gentlemen," for Edelman it is not the passing transvestite but the passing homosexual.

Both Garber and Edelman, interestingly enough, seem to fix on the men's room as the site

[25]See Lacan, p. 1132.
[26]"The Agency of the Letter in the Unconscious," in *Ecrits: A Selection*, trans. Alan Sheridan (New York: Norton, 1977), 151. [Halberstam]

of these various destabilizing performances. As I am arguing here, however, focusing exclusively on the drama of the men's room avoids the much more complicated theater of the women's room. Garber writes of urinary segregation: "For transvestites and transsexuals, the 'men's room' problem is really a challenge to the way in which such cultural binarism is read" (14). She goes on to list some cinematic examples of the perils of urinary segregation and discusses scenes from *Tootsie* (1982), *Cabaret* (1972), and the *Female Impersonator Pageant* (1975). Garber's examples are odd illustrations of what she calls "the men's room problem" if only because at least one of her examples (*Tootsie*) demonstrates gender policing in the women's room. Also, Garber makes it sound as if vigorous gender policing happens in the men's room while the women's room is more of a benign zone for gender enforcement. She notes: "In fact, the urinal has appeared in a number of fairly recent films as a marker of the ultimate 'difference' — or studied indifference" (14). Obviously, Garber is drawing a parallel here between the conventions of gender attribution within which the penis marks the "ultimate difference"; however, by not moving beyond this remarkably predictable description of gender differentiation, Garber overlooks the main distinction between gender policing in the men's room and in the women's room. Namely, in the women's room, it is not only the MTF but *all* gender-ambiguous females who are scrutinized, whereas in the men's room, biological men are rarely deemed out of place. Garber's insistence that there is "a third space of possibility" occupied by the transvestite has closed down the possibility that there may be a fourth, fifth, sixth, or one hundredth space beyond the binary. The "women's room problem" (as opposed to the "men's room problem") indicates a multiplicity of gender displays even within the supposedly stable category of "woman."

So what gender are the hundreds of female-born people who are consistently not read as female in the women's room? And because so many women clearly fail the women's room test, why have we not begun to count and name the genders that are clearly emerging at this time? One could answer this question in two ways: On the one hand, we do not name and notice new genders because as a society we are committed to maintaining a binary gender system. On the other hand, we could also say that the failure of "male" and "female" to exhaust the field of gender variation actually ensures the continued dominance of these terms. Precisely because virtually nobody fits the definitions of male and female, the categories gain power and currency from their impossibility. In other words, the very flexibility and elasticity of the terms "man" and "woman" ensures their longevity. To test this proposition, look around any public space and notice how few people present formulaic versions of gender and yet how few are unreadable or totally ambiguous. The "It's Pat" character on a *Saturday Night Live* skit dramatized the ways in which people insist on attributing gender in terms of male or female on even the most undecidable characters.[27] The "It's Pat" character produced laughs by consistently sidestepping gender fixity — Pat's partner had a neutral name, and everything Pat did or said was designed to be read either way. Of course, the enigma that Pat represented could have been solved very easily; Pat's coworkers could simply have asked Pat what gender s/he was or preferred. This project on female masculinity is designed to produce more than two answers to that question and even to argue for a concept of "gender preference" as opposed to compulsory gender binarism. The human potential for incredibly precise classifications has been demonstrated in multiple arenas; why then do we settle for a paucity of classifications when it comes to gender? A system of gender preferences would allow for gender neutrality until such a time when the child or young adult announces his or her or its gender. Even if we could not let go of a binary gender system, there are still ways to make gender optional — people could come out as a gender in the way they come out as a sexuality. The point here is that there are many ways to depathologize gender variance and to account for the multiple genders that we already produce and sustain. Finally, as I suggested in relation to Garber's

[27]*It's Pat* was extended into a 1994 film of that title, directed by Adam Bernstein, written by Julia Sweeney and (uncredited) Quentin Tarantino. [Halberstam]

arguments about transvestism, "thirdness" merely balances the binary system and, furthermore, tends to homogenize many different gender variations under the banner of "other."

It is remarkably easy in this society not to look like a woman. It is relatively difficult, by comparison, not to look like a man: the threats faced by men who do not gender conform are somewhat different than for women. Unless men are consciously trying to look like women, men are less likely than women to fail to pass in the rest room. So one question posed by the bathroom problem asks, what makes femininity so approximate and masculinity so precise? Or to pose the question with a different spin, why is femininity easily impersonated or performed while masculinity seems resilient to imitation? Of course, this formulation does not easily hold and indeed quickly collapses into the exact opposite: why is it, in the case of the masculine woman in the bathroom, for example, that one finds the limits of femininity so quickly, whereas the limits of masculinity in the men's room seem fairly expansive?

We might tackle these questions by thinking about the effects, social and cultural, of reversed gender typing. In other words, what are the implications of male femininity and female masculinity? One might imagine that even a hint of femininity sullies or lowers the social value of maleness while all masculine forms of femaleness should result in an elevation of status.[28] My bathroom example alone proves that this is far from true. Furthermore, if we think of popular

examples of approved female masculinity like a buffed Linda Hamilton in *Terminator* 2 (1991) or a lean and mean Sigourney Weaver in *Aliens*, it is not hard to see that what renders these performances of female masculinity quite tame is their resolute heterosexuality. Indeed, in *Alien Resurrection* (1997), Sigourney Weaver combines her hard body with some light flirtation with co-star Winona Ryder and her masculinity immediately becomes far more threatening and indeed "alien." In other words, when and where female masculinity conjoins with possibly queer identities, it is far less likely to meet with approval. Because female masculinity seems to be at its most threatening when coupled with lesbian desire, in this book I concentrate on queer female masculinity almost to the exclusion of heterosexual female masculinity. I have no doubt that heterosexual female masculinity menaces gender conformity in its own way, but all too often it represents an acceptable degree of female masculinity as compared to the excessive masculinity of the dyke. It is important when thinking about gender variations such as male femininity and female masculinity not simply to create another binary in which masculinity always signifies power; in alternative models of gender variation, female masculinity is not simply the opposite of female femininity, nor is it a female version of male masculinity. Rather, as we shall see in some of the artwork and gender performances to follow, very often the unholy union of femaleness and masculinity can produce wildly unpredictable results.

[28]Susan Bordo argues this in "Reading the Male Body," *Michigan Quarterly Review* 32, no. 4 (Fall 1993). She writes: "When masculinity gets 'undone' in this culture, the deconstruction nearly always lands us in the territory of the degraded; when femininity gets symbolically undone, the result is an immense elevation of status" (721). [Halberstam]

9

POSTCOLONIALISM AND ETHNIC STUDIES

This chapter links together postcolonial and ethnic studies, two key theoretical positions. Postcolonialism deals with the contemporary literatures and cultures of nations today that once formed part of overseas European empires; ethnic studies addresses the literatures and cultures of minority groups such as African Americans, Latinos, Asians, and others operating within a majority culture whose leaders are primarily whites of European origin. We will be analyzing the relations of power and knowledge, politics and aesthetics, among these groups, groups that in both cases are marked for race, nationality, or ethnicity. In both postcolonial and ethnic studies, the same theorists — Marx and Gramsci, Foucault and Derrida — will provide our foundations. In both cases we will consider the way we form imaginary communities to which we are ourselves attached, or create in our imagination for those whom we exclude from our own community. And in both areas of study parallel questions have emerged: whether the use of the metropolitan language/white dialect robs the subaltern/black of his/her culture, and whether literary theory itself, with its origins in European thought, is too "white" to be useful in the cultural struggles in which ethnic and postcolonial scholars are engaged.

This is not a mere marriage of convenience, then, and indeed, it may be hard to distinguish postcolonial writing from that of minority groups inhabiting European countries, who may be primarily citizens from these former colonies or their descendants.[1] The most significant minority groups living in the United States may not, as in Europe, have been connected with overseas colonies; instead they are likely to have become American citizens by an analogous process of internal colonization, which proceeded through absorption or immigration. Native Americans, French Creoles, and Mexicans were absorbed as their vast territories were annexed to the expanding nation, while Africans and Europeans immigrated (by brute force, in the case of African slaves, or compelled by starvation and persecution, in the case of

---

[1]Similar distinctions between the periphery and the metropolis can be significant within areas that were never colonies as such, such as Scotland's position within the United Kingdom.

most European ethnics). Nationality interacts with ethnicity, so there will be differences between the cultural stance of Jamaicans of African origin living in Jamaica, where they form the majority, and those living as minorities in Brixton, South London, or in the borough of Queens in New York. All three groups, however, may consider themselves as living in the African diaspora.[2]

IMPERIALISM AND DECOLONIZATION

Imperialism as a military adventure began at the dawn of human history, or even perhaps before it, since the very first recorded annals speak of how the rulers of Egypt, Mesopotamia, and China extended their power by conquest over neighboring peoples. The Bible records Israel both as an imperial state and as a colony, a conquering nation under David, whose empire was later conquered by Babylon, and then for good measure by Persia, Greece, and Rome. Rome, whose Mediterranean empire may have seemed universal, split in two and then fell in its turn, replaced in Europe by a Holy Roman Empire, and in Asia successively by the Caliphate of the Arabs, the Khanate of the Moguls and the Sultanate of the Ottomans. Off the stage of the Eurasian land mass, we are more dimly aware of how the Aztecs wiped out the Mayas in the Americas, or how Songhai displaced Mali in Central Africa. Some of these conquerors left subjected peoples with their own rulers and cultures, appointing a military garrison and a tax-gatherer as the only oppressive forces; others imposed new laws and religions, in effect a new culture; still others pursued wars of annihilation, holocausts of long ago.

But what most of us mean by the age of imperialism began around 1500 as European sailors after voyages of discovery laid claim to huge inhabited territories in Asia and the Americas, despoiling the aboriginal peoples of their wealth, infecting them with virulent diseases, enslaving them or forcing their escape into the hinterland. Portugal and Spain were the first world powers to succeed at this strategy, though by the seventeenth century they shared the stage with rival powers — Holland, France, and Great Britain — and began to decline. The eighteenth century saw wars primarily fought to obtain by conquest lucrative overseas possessions, although by this point the primary advantage of empire was in securing wealth through trade, as colonies produced raw materials and became captive markets for manufactured goods produced at the seat of empire. In the nineteenth century the great European powers scrambled to divide up Africa amongst them, with England and France taking the vast heart of the continent, with smaller pieces for Portugal

---

[2]Exactly what status a group needs to have in order to constitute a recognized "minority" worth studying seems to be a question of local interests and politics. Programs in "African American Studies" exist on many campuses throughout the country, but at Queens College, where I teach, most students of color are descended not from American slaves but are rather immigrants from former colonies in the Caribbean, and our program marks that difference by being called "Africana Studies." (Similarly, we have a "Latin American Area Studies" program rather than one in Chicano Studies because the Spanish-speaking groups in the borough are not primarily from Mexico.) Queens College also has an old and well-funded program in Italian Studies, reflecting, among other things, its founders' wish to counter the tendency of ethnic Italians to enter manual trades rather than the learned professions, and more recently has added institutes studying Asian American and modern Greek cultures.

and Spain, Belgium, Italy, and Germany. At its height around 1900, the British Empire, with possessions nearly everywhere, counted over 400 million subjects of the Crown living on about 25 percent of the earth's landmass, compared with the 35 million inhabitants of the British Isles who lived on less than 0.2 percent.

Although some colonies separated by an ocean from the seat of empire broke away through insurgencies and wars of liberation and became independent nations as early as the eighteenth century, it was not until the twentieth century that the great European empires broke up and worldwide decolonization occurred. After World War I, the losers, particularly the Ottoman and Austrian empires, were chopped up into smaller states, whose governance was often given "in trust" to one or another of the victorious countries (e.g., Lebanon and Syria to France, Palestine and Iraq to Great Britain). But after World War II, even the victors gave up the vast majority of their colonies, sometimes voluntarily, sometimes after bloody wars of insurgency, with the result that the United Nations organization, formed in 1945 by 51 states, grew to the nearly 200 states it is today.[3] Whether the new nations formed by decolonization then became truly independent is a debatable point, though, particularly because of the polarization of the world through the second half of the twentieth century toward either the United States or the Soviet Union, the two nuclear superpowers. The "Cold War" was fought not only through the buildup of huge arsenals, but through hot stretches of proxy war between the superpowers fought out primarily between or within these new states. It was often hard to distinguish between this kind of proxy war and a war of national liberation fought against a Western democracy with the aid of tactical support by communist powers.[4] One classic example was the civil war that broke out in Angola, after it had achieved independence from Portugal in 1974, between factions allied with the Soviet Union and those with the West, although one should remember that, in this and other "proxy" wars, the nations or factions involved have their own interests at stake and may not think of themselves as proxies for the Great Powers.

For as long as the Cold War lasted, about half a century, the West spoke of a "Free World" of allied industrialized nations including the United States and Canada, the European democracies, and Japan; and a "Communist World" of industrial nations allied with Soviet Russia and mainland China. Decolonization produced a "Third World" of unaligned "developing" nations in Central and South America, Africa, and Asia, many of them former European colonies. Around 1990, at the end of the Cold War era, which coincidentally was also the end of the era of grand theory, the distinctions between the three worlds began to dissolve, as victorious global

---

[3]A few dozen colonies, mainly small islands, still exist, and a classic colonial war between rival claimants of territory occurred as recently as 1982 between Britain and Argentina over the ownership of the Falkland Islands (called Las Malvinas by Argentina).

[4]The classic case of this category mistake was Vietnam, whose insurgency against the colonial power of France was taken by American leaders to be a strategic move by China in the Cold War, one that would inevitably lead by a "domino effect" to the loss to the Western alliance, one after another, of its neighboring countries. Failing to understand the deep hostility of the Vietnamese to China, which for millennia had been the hegemonic power in the region, the United States intervened, prolonging the war by a decade, escalating the bloodshed, and directly or indirectly causing millions of deaths not only in Vietnam but in neighboring Laos and Cambodia.

capitalism stretched its tentacles everywhere (for a discussion of the era of grand theory, see above, p. vi). Global communism ceased to be a coherent force as the Soviet Union itself splintered into over a dozen separate states, while its satellite nations joined Europe and even NATO. Meanwhile the economic split between "developed" countries pursuing manufactures and "developing" nations supplying agricultural products and other raw materials has been at least partly effaced. Over the past two decades, Europe and America have come to support fewer industrial jobs, which have moved to countries such as Mexico, India, and Singapore, where a worker's pay is a fraction of what it is in the West, and recently it has become possible to "outsource" to other countries the jobs of knowledge workers (such as computer technicians and radiologists). Today it seems to be multinational corporations, capable of moving capital and creating jobs anywhere in the world, that are calling the shots, rather than the imperial nation-states that began to compete with each other for power and wealth over five hundred years ago.

Having come thus far with this familiar narrative, one needs to reflect on its characteristic pitfalls. One is that it takes a particular subject position: that of the imperialists, the colonial Powers That Were. It is their motives, their agency, that form the basis of the narrative, rather than those of the peoples whom they ruled. We have viewed the situation from the perspective of those making voyages of discovery and conquest, not of those on whose shores they landed. Each of the peoples who lived on each of those shores has another story to tell, though, and it is a story that reads very differently. Those of us who have read Chinua Achebe's *Things Fall Apart* often become aware that the story of how the lives of men and women of Nigeria are affected by the invasion of English Christian culture is both unfamiliar and too familiar — unfamiliar because we are unused to the perspective, too familiar because it is the obverse of Joseph Conrad's *Heart of Darkness*.

Another unexamined assumption of the conventional narrative is that political independence marks the end of colonial status. For most former colonies, independence may be only the beginning of the end, since colonial structures, political, economic, and cultural, usually continue long after the European viceroy closes down his office and departs. To perpetuate these structures is to perpetuate one's subaltern status, but to tear them down before others have been readied is to invite chaos. As Ama Ata Adoo put it, "Applied to Africa, India, and some other parts of the world, [the concept of the] 'postcolonial' is not only a fiction but a most pernicious fiction, a cover-up of a dangerous period in our people's lives."[5]

Another dangerous assumption is the limitation of colonialism to a single standard scenario, like that of the British Raj, in which a European power sends military force and a bureaucracy to take over and administer an extraterritorial land. In this

[5]Quoted in Padmini Mongia ed., *Contemporary Postcolonial Theory: A Reader* (London: Arnold, 1997), p. 1. One needs to add that some overseas former colonies have not sought independence but rather have been annexed to the mother country, such as French Guyana, which is legally part of France, an extraterritorial department where the euro is the official currency. Similarly, the Hawaiian islands, once a colony of the United States, were admitted to the union as the fiftieth state. Puerto Rico, perhaps the most culturally significant of the remaining colonies of the United States, seems for the present to have rejected both statehood and separation as an independent nation.

sense the United States has been a colonial power very briefly and only in very limited areas. But in another sense the expansion of the United States, from the colonies originally implanted by Britain on the Atlantic seaboard to its present compass, including most of the fertile lands on the North American continent, has taken place by a sort of internal colonization, annexing by war or by purchase lands inhabited by Native Americans, by French Creoles in Louisiana, and by Spanish colonialists in Florida and the southwest from Texas to California. In these territories no movement of decolonization seems likely to occur.[6]

Furthermore, one needs to take account of another analogue of colonization that occurs through forced migrations, particularly the transfer of millions of Africans as slaves to the colonies in the Americas and the Caribbean. Migrations can be "forced" by economic conditions as easily as by brute physical power, and it may be useful to extend the analogy beyond internal colonization to immigrant groups with a different coherent culture. Here might be considered, among others, the Irish, Italian, German, and Eastern Europeans who populated the American cities and hinterland beginning in the 1840s; the vast numbers of middle class East Indian immigrants who migrated to work in the infrastructure of Caribbean and African colonies under the British Empire, most of whom remained after decolonization; and the former colonials from the Maghreb, Central Africa, or Southeast Asia who have migrated to France, or the Caribbean Islanders, Africans, and South Asians who have migrated to England. The large communities of guest workers from Turkey and other Islamic countries in present-day Germany are a related example.

In terms of this history, "postcolonial" literature and culture might be defined as the literature of the countries that, in the nineteenth and twentieth centuries were administered by the United States, Great Britain, France, and other European countries, particularly on the Indian subcontinent, in northern and central Africa, southeast Asia, and Central and South America. Postcolonial criticism has focused on both the literatures developed by these nations, which are sometimes — as in the case of the works of Chinua Achebe, Salman Rushdie, and Naguib Mahfouz — written in European languages and sometimes not, and on white European responses to colonialism in texts by such familiar authors as Rudyard Kipling, Joseph Conrad, E. M. Forster, George Orwell, and Albert Camus.[7] However, like other cultural critics, postcolonial theorists enjoy examining texts outside the standard literary genres, and frequently examine phenomena that are analogically related to those encountered in former European colonies. These include the writings and cultural productions of aboriginal groups (such as the Native Americans

[6]A similar internal colonization of Eurasian lands annexed by Russia occurred over roughly the same period, with decolonization occurring rapidly after 1989. The present insurgency in Chechnya seems to be a war of liberation conducted by a people whose attempt to set up their own state is being opposed rather than encouraged by the new Russian government, as it did with the Ukraine, Georgia, and Armenia.

[7]These writers are all white Europeans, but in addition one needs to consider the agonistic relationship of different colonial populations with one another. The novelist V. S. Naipaul, for example, is not a white European, being descended from Indians imported by Great Britain to form a middle-class infrastructure in Caribbean islands. But Naipaul is so much less sympathetic to the ruling cadres of African and Asian former colonies than most white writers are that postcolonial scholars tend to lump him with patronizing Europeans like Conrad. See in particular *A Bend in the River*.

or the Maoris in New Zealand), marginalized groups that have been included within a nation as the result of its border wars (such as Latinos who became citizens of the United States as a result of its wars and treaties with Mexico), and immigrant groups, willing or otherwise (including African American descendants of slaves in the Unites States and guest-workers in Europe). It should go without saying that the histories, legal status, and cultural relations of these groups with the dominant culture differ from one another, and that it is dangerous to import ideas taken from a cultural study of one group into that of another without carefully examining their applicability. But the theoretical questions that animate postcolonial studies are nevertheless very much a part of the discourse of African American studies, Latino/a studies, Asian studies, and other ethnically oriented components of the cultural studies movements.

THEORIZING NATIONALITY AND ETHNICITY: BENEDICT ANDERSON

All the groups and formations of which the theorists in this chapter will speak are versions of what the anthropologist Benedict Anderson has called "imagined communities." There are real communities of limited size and scope — the people of a village who all know one another, your classmates and colleagues, your fellow congregants at your church — but races, ethnic groups, nations, are all communities that, despite their tremendous hold on us, exist only in our minds. Anderson cites the French philosopher Ernest Renan, who ironically remarked that "it is of the essence of a nation that all its individuals have lots of things in common that they have forgotten." As a particular form of imagined community, the nation is limited and sovereign. The nation

> is imagined as *limited* because even the largest of them encompassing perhaps a billion living human beings, has finite, if elastic boundaries, beyond which lie other nations. No nation imagines itself coterminous with mankind. . . . It is imagined as *sovereign* because the concept was born in an age in which Enlightenment and Revolution were destroying the legitimacy of the divinely-ordained, hierarchical dynastic realm. Coming to maturity at a stage of human history when even the most devout adherents of any universal religion were inescapably confronted with the living pluralism of such religions, and the allomorphism between each faith's ontological claims and territorial stretch, nations dream of being free, and, if under God, directly so. The gage and emblem of this freedom is the sovereign state. Finally, it is imagined as a *community*, because, regardless of the actual inequality and exploitation that may prevail in each, the nation is always conceived as a deep, horizontal comradeship. Ultimately it is this fraternity that makes it possible, over the past two centuries, for so many millions of people, not so much to kill, as willingly to die for such limited imaginings.

The chapter from *Imagined Communities* that we have included is "The Origins of National Consciousness," in which Anderson speculates about the connection between the age of print culture, which began in the middle of the eighteenth century throughout Europe, and what he considers its two political consequences: the development of the "idea of the nation" within the individual Frenchman or Britisher, and the beginnings of the development of European empires whose common languages would extend the reach of the imagined national community.

THE PREHISTORY OF POSTCOLONIALISM

The resistance to colonialism began centuries ago, as one might expect, with colonialism itself, long before postcolonial theory became a recognized academic discipline. And the writings of popular resistance leaders like Mohandas K. Gandhi and Kwame Nkrumah were naturally inspirational to their followers in India and Africa. The period after World War II provoked many intellectuals who had been born in colonies just achieving their freedom to try to understand the political and psychological burdens of emerging nations, of whom three of the most important are Albert Memmi, Aimé Césaire, and Frantz Fanon.

Albert Memmi was born in 1920 in Tunis to Jewish Arabic-speaking parents. Memmi fought in World War II and was imprisoned during 1943–45 in a labor camp. He later taught at a lycée in Tunis. Following the decolonization of Tunisia, he moved to France, where he married, got his doctorate, and had a career as novelist and psychologist; he became a professor at the University of Paris/Nanterre. His major work in this field is *The Colonizer and the Colonized* (1957), which came out one year after the decolonization of Tunisia and during the tremendous violence of the Algerian war of independence. It featured Memmi's unique cultural perspective, which was neither Arab nor entirely French. Although most of the Jews of Tunis generally assimilated culturally to the dominant French, Memmi himself joined the decolonization movement of the Arabs. Memmi's book is about the social and psychological consequences of colonialism for both the natives and the European colonizers. The Arabs of Tunisia were tempted to assimilate culturally to France, as a way of rising in the world (only as far as the colonizers would allow, of course). Those who do not assimilate are even worse off. All the colonized are excluded from real politics, they may become apathetic, or may find a source of self-esteem in religion or in revolutionary politics, or in some combination. Revolt, according to Memmi, is not a final solution: even decolonization is only a stage in the evolution of the alienation of the colonized. The colonizers have their own problems. Psychologically they consider themselves exiles, although there is nothing preventing them from returning to their homeland. The exile is purely positional: in the colony they may have achieved a position of importance, whereas back in France they would return to mediocrity; in the colony their salaries are high and prices are low, and a return to France would lower their financial status. Most important of all is self-esteem: the colonizers are of the top caste when in North Africa, with servants to bully, feeling above any member of the majority Arab population no matter how accomplished.

Aimé Césaire was born in Martinique in 1913, was educated there and at the prestigious Lycée Louis-le-Grand in Paris, where he came under the influence of Leopold Senghor, founder of the négritude movement, whose purpose was to bolster the cultural self-image of Africans everywhere. After founding a journal for students of African descent, Césaire returned to Martinique where he taught school along with his wife. After World War II, Martinique along with the other French colonies in the Americas — Guyane, Guadeloupe — were not made independent countries but were instead converted into *departements* of France, the equivalent of statehood. Césaire, a member of the Communist party, was in 1945 elected mayor of Fort-de-France, the capital of Martinique, and a delegate in the representative assembly. In 1950 he published his "Discourse on Colonialism," which compares colonialism with Nazism as a racist ideology. Césaire is perhaps most famous for his play *Une Tempête* (1968), a take-off on Shakespeare's *Tempest* in which Caliban accuses Prospero of forcing him to believe in his own monstrosity as a result of the wizard's lies and spells.

Like Césaire, Frantz Fanon (1925–1961) was born in Martinique and, after fighting with the Free French army during 1943–45, was educated in France in medicine and psychiatry. His experience with racism in France led him to write *Black Skin, White Masks* (1952), which lays out the idea of cultural binarism, explicating the way white French identity is constituted by contrast with the black- and brown-skinned peoples who have come to France from the colonies. For Fanon, the pervasive racism comes from the culture as a whole, and particularly from the language, which equates blackness with evil. Thus in striving to succeed in Francophone society, the black colonial needs to internalize a sign-system that alienates him from himself. Fanon moved to Algeria in the early 1950s, becoming the head of psychiatry at the hospital at Blida-Joinville, where his patients included both Arab revolutionaries and the French colonial officials who fought against, and often tortured, those revolutionaries. Fanon resigned his post in 1956 in order to work actively for the Algerian revolution, which succeeded in ousting France but whose outcome disappointed Fanon. In 1961, as he lay dying of leukemia, Fanon published his most influential book, *The Wretched of the Earth*, which is a critique both of colonialism and of the emergent nationalism that generally followed decolonization. For Fanon, the irony of decolonization was that, for the most part, the lot of the peasants who were most deeply oppressed during the imperial period, and who shed their blood during the insurgency, was not materially improved by decolonization. The underclass were encouraged to focus their feelings on nationalist enthusiasm by the real winners of the revolution, those bourgeois Arabs and blacks who most closely identified with the culture of the European oppressors. Fanon felt that the revolutions that had freed Africa from its European overlords would be incomplete until the new nations were led by *fellahin* (peasants) from the lower depths of the class structure, and he counseled "total revolution," uncompromising violence, until that end could be achieved.

THEORIZING THE COLONIAL: SAID, SPIVAK, BHABHA

The book that is generally considered to have launched the growing field of postcolonial theory is Edward Said's *Orientalism* (1978). Said takes off from Michel Foucault's position that as knowledge is in itself a way of exercising power, so discourses become a weapon of imperial and international politics. In this light Said presents the Western study of the Orient in the nineteenth century (limiting himself almost exclusively to the Near East here) as one of the ways Europe found to dominate that region. Said treats the scholarship into Near Eastern languages, cultures, and social structures as an archive that he mines for the Western ways of "knowing" the East that become a way of asserting the superiority of the West. For example, Edward Lane's 1836 book on the manners and customs of the Egyptians of his own day presents that culture in the form of descriptions that are "sadomasochistic colossal tidbits: the self-mutilation of dervishes, the cruelty of judges, the blending of religion with licentiousness among Muslims, the excess of libidinous passions, and so on" (162). Even fields that might seem utterly neutral, the comparative study of language, can be used to disparage the culture of the Near East. Said shows how Ernest Renan's philological treatise on the evolution of human languages takes the "organic" development of the Indo-European languages as the norm, with each new language — Sanskrit, Greek, Latin, French — developing new energies as it buds off from its predecessor. By contrast the Oriental Semitic languages (Hebrew, Aramaic, Arabic) are seen as "inorganic, essentially unregenerative . . . , ossified" (143). In effect the vital, energetic West is contrasted with the played-out and regressive East. In particular, Said witheringly critiques the Western image of the Oriental as "irrational, depraved (fallen), childlike, 'different,'" which has allowed the West to define itself as "rational, virtuous, mature, 'normal'" (40). Western students of Oriental literature and culture, from artists to professors of language and history, have helped to create this self-affirming vision, which in turn has been used to justify the domination of the Arab and other Asian peoples by European governments, the marginalization of their languages and cultures, and the uprooting of their institutions. For Said, the cultural practices and forms of knowledge typical of Orientalism have not vanished with the official colonial regimes. As a Palestinian theorist, Said views his own attempt to understand the cultural work of Orientalism as a site of resistance to the hegemony of Western values and ideas.

Said's argument in *Orientalism* also has the defects of its virtues. Even more than Foucault's own "archeological" investigations into prisons and madhouses, Said presents Orientalism as a historical phenomenon tied causally to European imperialism, but his examples widen out so far as to contradict his conclusion. In the first place, Orientalism seems to have always existed: Said cites Aeschylus's representation of the Persians as effeminate and depraved, or Dante's placement of Mohammed in the *Inferno* not among the prophets of God but among the Christian heretics. Examples so many centuries removed from the European imperialist enterprise seem less connected with the British and French takeover of Arab lands than part of a timeless universal ethnocentrism in which cultures treat their antagonists as "others" who represent lower forms of life. An anti-Said could certainly collect from Eastern writings equivalent examples of "Occidentalism."

In the second place, Orientalism, as an unchanging ideology held over several centuries throughout the West, fails to explain why the policy of the British Raj became increasingly repressive of Indian culture during the nineteenth century[8] or

[8]For a recent account of this see Gauri Viswanathan, *Masks of Conquest* (New York: Columbia University Press, 1989). Other specific problems with Said's historical understanding are outlined in Moore-Gilbert, p. 45ff.

why the extensive Orientalist research by German scholars was never connected with any political move toward empire in the Near East. In general Said's notion of a "latent" Orientalism, universal within Western culture, expands to become the disparaging basis not only for imperialism but for the occasional resistance within the West to the project of imperialism (not only Arabophile scholarship like that of Sir Richard Burton, but also narratives by Kipling, Conrad, Orwell, and Forster that sometimes attack or satirize the blind stupidity and cruelty of the imperial administration). This comfortless vision may leave no one a place to stand, not even, perhaps, the Western-educated Said himself.

The notion of postcolonial studies as constituting a site of resistance appears as well in theorists who are less taken with Foucault's methodology of cultural study than Said is. Gayatri Chakravorti Spivak, born in Calcutta, did a dissertation on Yeats under Paul de Man and found fame as the first English translator of Jacques Derrida's *Of Grammatology* (1967, translated 1976). Spivak's version of postcolonialism prefers the deconstructive mode as a way of questioning the binarisms and exposing the misunderstandings of language and signification set up within colonial discourse. She has called herself a "gadfly" and her chosen mode of discourse is critique. Her tendency when she looks at a piece of discourse is to ask in effect "What gets left out, what is silenced, when we look at things *this* way?" Spivak sees herself as a Marxist and as a feminist, but is usually found to be boring away from within at the blind spots of these theories. In the introduction it was shown how Spivak's analysis of "subaltern studies" as practiced by Marxist social historians in India silences or occludes the female subject by shaping their question in terms of a dialogue between (male-dominated) Western and (male-dominated) Asian characterizations of social institutions. This works the other way round as well: giving the female voice may silence the subaltern.

In "Three Women's Texts and a Critique of Imperialism," included in this chapter, Spivak trains the lens of deconstructive analysis on women's writing, and finds that giving voice to the feminine entails the silencing or occlusion of the colonized subject. *Jane Eyre*, which Spivak calls a "cult text of feminism," empowers Brontë's titular heroine at the expense of her "dark double" Bertha Mason, who, though specified as being from a wealthy Creole family, is staged as the colonial Caliban, mute except for a horrid laugh, on the borderline between the human and the animal. On the other side, Brontë's feminism sponsors the imperialist mission Jane considered for herself before heeding the preternatural call of Rochester; the life of "active goodness" of which she dreamed looking out from Thornfield took the form of attending upon the missionary St. John Rivers and going forth to the East to convert the heathen in Calcutta. Jean Rhys's *Wide Sargasso Sea*, a reinscription of *Jane Eyre*, gets a little closer to the silenced colonized subject by placing at the center the white creole woman, called Antoinette in the text, through whom we can understand what it feels like to become the colonial Caliban, even as she finds reflections of herself in the darker natives of her own sex, her black friend Tia and her maid Christophine.

Spivak finds the strongest critique of imperialism in Mary Shelley's *Frankenstein*, which may seem strange since on a literal level (as Spivak herself points out), the narrative approves of bringing Western civilization to the East:

Victor's admired friend Clerval is presented as studying Eastern languages in order to take up the white man's burden where Arabic or Persian are spoken. There is even a passive colonial subject in the Arabian girl Safie. To get her reading, Spivak is forced to allegorize the central story through the metaphorical lens of colonialism. In this reading the Monster, whose speech and literacy are accidental developments, becomes the colonial Caliban, the occluded subject whom Frankenstein creates just as the colonial governors seek to create the empire's colonized subjects, but from whose demands for companionship and autonomy the master recoils with fear and horror. What seems to Spivak most honest about this vision is how uncompromising it is: the Monster and Frankenstein cannot be reconciled; neither can absorb the other into his vision of the self, so that the Caliban and the Prospero can only destroy each other.

Bombay-born Homi Bhabha, like Spivak, is interested in probing and problematizing Said's binaries of East/West using the deconstructive tools of Derrida and Lacan. For Bhabha, the problem with Said's analysis is the way in which it restricts itself to analyzing the consciousness of Europeans vis-à-vis the Orient, with little attention to the way in which colonized peoples are implicated in this relationship. Bhabha sees the experience of colonial peoples as creating a hybridity of perspective, a split consciousness in which the individual identifies simultaneously with his or her own people and with the colonial power. This hybridity or liminality (existing on the borderline) is not necessarily an undesirable state: It is, as Bhabha sees it, part of the postmodern condition. It is the situation not only of the colonial subject but of minority groups like African Americans and, to one extent or another, of every inhabitant of the globe. Bhabha's book, *Locations of Culture*, presents his view of the connections between minority and postcolonial literature as sites of resistance. While W. E. B. Du Bois a century ago had understood "double consciousness" to be an inevitable condition of the souls of black folk, Bhabha understands it as inevitable for us all.

The complexities of the doubled relationships of the imperialist and the colonized subaltern, whose mimicry of the imperialist includes both flattery and a kind of mockery, are central to Bhabha's breakthrough essay, "Signs Taken for Wonders." The title of the essay itself contains a dry mock of the phrase "signs and wonders," which appears many times in the Hebrew Bible in terms of the mighty acts God performed for the liberation of the Israelites in Egypt. Bhabha's scene of signs outside Delhi in 1817 is all about the opposite of liberation, it is about enslavement, particularly how the technologies of imperialism can be used to remake the colonial subject in the image of the English ruler by importing the English book. The hope, as Macaulay would later put it explicitly, is that cheap or free Bibles imparting the English language and the spiritual comforts of Christianity ultimately will undermine native Indian languages and religions. Using missionary records, Bhabha portrays an Indian convert, Anund Messeh, bringing the Gospel (which God "gave long ago to the Sahibs") to his countrymen. His audience, apparently respectful and ingratiating, compete to be the quickest to learn and the best teachers of this Word, but in copying the Sahibs they very much remain themselves. They insist on their own customs, including the separation of castes, and refuse the very notion of taking communion because when the Word is made flesh it becomes abhorrent, since "the Europeans eat cow's flesh and this will never do for us."

Bhabha juxtaposes to this scene a pair of other scenes later in the history of imperialism. The first is of Conrad's Marlow, going up the Congo toward the heart of darkness, where he questions his faith in the Western mission, finding relief from his spiritual vertigo when he comes upon another sort of "bible" devoted to the Western technology of imperialism, a book on navigation (Towson's *Seamanship*). The second is of the postcolonial Caribbean/Indian writer V. S. Naipaul, who, during his own voyage to England to take up the life of an expatriate writer, discovers that another English book, in his case Conrad's *Heart of Darkness*, sets a high bar for any performance of his own: "Conrad . . . had been everywhere before me." Messeh, Marlow, Naipaul: all turn away from the messy, mocking, imitative colonial world toward the enlightened truth of the Western Bible, Western Science, Western Literature.

As Bhabha sums it up

> The discovery of the English book establishes both a measure of mimesis and a mode of civil authority and order. If these scenes, as I have narrated them, suggest the triumph of the writ of colonialist power, then it must be conceded that the wily letter of the law inscribes a much more ambivalent text of authority. For it is in between the edict of Englishness and the assault of the dark unruly spaces of the earth, through an act of repetition, that the colonial text emerges uncertainly. . . . The colonial presence is always ambivalent, split between its appearance as original and authoritative and its articulation as repetition and difference.

THEORIZING MINORITY LITERATURE: DELEUZE AND GUATTARI

Disadvantaged minority groups perforce write what French critics Gilles Deleuze and Felix Guattari call "minor literature." In "What Is a Minor Literature?" Deleuze and Guattari take time from their study of novelist Franz Kafka to theorize about the special character his writing derived from his being a Jew in Prague, writing not in Yiddish or Hebrew (the languages of his ethnic group) nor in Czech (the language of a majority of the natives of Prague) but in German (the language of the Austro-Hungarian elite who ruled the province of Bohemia). This language, when used by a Prague Jew, is "deterritorialized" — it speaks not for a country or province but rather for people of a diaspora living as an Other in a land not their own. Within such minor literatures "everything . . . is political" and "everything takes on a collective value" as every observation speaks about the hegemonic society from the perspective of the silenced members of the minority (p. 1778). Deleuze and Guattari conclude paradoxically that there is no major literature except minor literature, for poetic value resides precisely in the tensions inherent in using the language of the oppressors to speak for the oppressed. Deleuze and Guattari explicitly compare Kafka's Prague German with "what blacks in America today are able to do with the English language."

AFRICANISM: RACISM HERE AND ABROAD

Just as Edward Said coined the term "Orientalism" to refer to the ways in which darker colonial people are characterized as the Other in the works of European writers; Toni Morrison uses the term "Africanism" in a parallel way to refer to the literal and figurative "blackness" whites found in the new world, and the ways they represented that "blackness."

Morrison sees Africanism as pervasive: it appears not only in texts like *Uncle Tom's Cabin* and *Huckleberry Finn* that feature important black characters, but in texts that have only minor roles for blacks or none at all, even texts in which race and slavery are never mentioned.[9] Morrison feels that every major work of American literature was shaped in part by the fact that, in the midst of a republic dedicated to freedom, there was a large population held in total subjection. The motif of the Forest in a work like *The Scarlet Letter*, for example, brings up the dialectic between savagery and civilization. Morrison is in effect asking whether Hawthorne's vision of the Savage could avoid being affected by the idea of the Savage that whites projected onto blacks, an idea that was derived in part from their own savage treatment of their human property. In fact it is Morrison's contention that all the major themes in which critics have sought the unity of American literature, "individualism, masculinity, the conflict between social engagement and historical isolation, an acute and ambiguous moral problematics, the juxtaposition of innocence with figures representing death and hell" draw their mythic strength from the dark Other within the American body politic. Africanism is thus to be found everywhere in white public discourse; "encoded or implicit, indirect or overt, the linguistic responses to an Africanistic presence complicate the texts, sometimes contradicting them entirely."

Morrison's method of reading can be enormously revealing, but it may need to be employed with some tact. Africans were surely not the only group constituted as "Other" in American society and represented as the "Other" in American literature. European colonists had encountered the Native Americans as friendly or hostile cohabitants of the continent long before African slavery was institutionalized, and it has been well documented how the encounter with the Native American reshaped the imagination of Europe and of those Europeans who had migrated to America. And from the mid-nineteenth century, the new migrant (from Europe or Asia) began to serve as a representation of the Other to native-born Americans a few generations removed from their own immigration.

Within British (as opposed to American) literature, ethnic and racial otherness operates with similar complexities. Within medieval and early modern literature the English defined themselves predominantly against outsiders like Jews or Moors, peoples that loomed large in the English imagination given their tiny populations in English society.[10] From the eighteenth century, as England was taking its pre-eminent

---

[9]At the same time, Morrison is painfully aware that the blackness of some of the most important African characters in American literature — including Ahab's servant Pip in Melville's *Moby-Dick*, the slave girl Nancy Till in Willa Cather's *Sapphira and the Slave Girl*, Melanctha in Gertrude Stein's *Three Women* — appears to be a subject taboo to the polite practitioners of literary criticism.

[10]It would be a mistake to leave out the Irish as the Other within British Literature, usually seen as comically feckless rather than sinister, from a colony England acquired long before India.

place in the colonization of Africa and South Asia, the racial Other became African or Indian, often portrayed as the childlike object of European benevolence and Enlightenment rationality, or as the female object of forbidden desire, a dark body constructed by masculine fantasy.

A British version of Morrison's "Africanism" inspires the Nigerian novelist Chinua Achebe's resistant reading of Conrad's *Heart of Darkness* (p. 1783). This is a text often celebrated by white readers for its liberal exposure of the hideous face under the benevolent mask of colonialism, as it portrays Kurtz, the apostle of European enlightenment, degenerating into a mad, genocidal tyrant. Achebe finds it hard to concur, arguing that, whatever its liberal political position on the imperial mission, Conrad denies to the Africans that he portrays the humanity — well-intentioned or self-centered — that he accords even the slimiest of the Europeans. The natives of the Congo are a mere exotic spectacle, appearing out of or disappearing into the bush, yelling like savages or dying silently but picturesquely near the coastal forts. But they are not imagined as people, for which reason Achebe feels that *Heart of Darkness* is an "offensive and deplorable book" and Conrad himself "a bloody racist." Achebe is expressing here the bitterness with which the African views the white liberal position on British imperialism, which allowed England to deprive hundreds of millions of darker-skinned men and women of their political and economic freedom so long as that imperial rule was just and humane by European standards.

But is that an inevitable position? Wilson Harris, another colonial novelist of African descent (from Guyana) argues that Conrad was writing, not out of Enlightenment optimism, as Achebe suggested, but rather out of a profound despair arising from his sense that the "sacred human" order "may come to shelter the greatest evil." Harris calls *Heart of Darkness* a "frontier novel," by which he means one that interprets and translates between the European societies that had been transformed by their imperialist mission and the African, Asian, and American societies that had become hybrid mixtures of native and European social and mental structures. Harris is deeply aware of the way black Caribbean writers like himself and African writers like Wole Soyinka have used Conrad, along with other European texts, in generating a fertile postcolonial literature. And he hints that Achebe has a deep need to misread Conrad in order to make imaginative space for himself, a site of resistance from which he can speak.

THE MASTER'S LANGUAGE, THE MASTER'S TOOLS

One key political question that troubles postcolonial theory is about the language in which postcolonial literature should be written. There are in Africa dozens, perhaps hundreds, of indigenous languages, as opposed to the handful of "metropolitan" languages of the imperialists, including English, French, and Arabic. Can African writers be truly African, can they be true to their ethnic identities, while using the languages of imperialism? "Is it right that a man should abandon his mother tongue for someone else's? It looks like a dreadful betrayal."

That question was Chinua Achebe's, but finally Achebe concluded that, despite the fact that no one uses a second language as well as the native tongue, there is no other practical solution. He himself does not have the time to learn the other six or seven ethnic languages in his own native Nigeria, much less all the other languages of Africa, so that if there is to be an African literature that can be read all over Africa and the rest of the world, it can be written only in the metropolitan languages. Achebe suggests, though, that Africans writing in English will — because they have something new to say — change English into something that is at least partly African: "The price a world language must pay is submission to many kinds of use. . . . The English language will be able to carry the weight of my African experience. But it will have to be a new English, still in full communion with its ancestral home but altered to suit its new African surroundings."[11]

After writing and publishing his first important works in English, the Kenyan novelist Ngugi wa Thiong'o eventually came down on the other side from Achebe, and around 1976 began to write his fiction in his native Gikuyu instead. "Europhonism, Universities, and the Magic Fountain," presents the most complex and far-reaching arguments for his personal decision, although ultimately it rests upon an organic theory of culture. For Ngugi, the soil and the people of Africa can be the only basis for African culture, and an educational system that explicitly ignores and implicitly disparages the ethnic languages of Africa's villagers is one that cuts Africa's intellectuals off from their culture, leaving them rootless, incapable of understanding each other or themselves. And although he finds much to admire in the literature Africans have written in English, Ngugi has a sense that too much energy has gone into imitating European models — an energy that he feels invigorates European languages and cultures without giving anything back to Africa. Worse: it is a Europhone literature, and not a genuinely African literature.

What inspires Ngugi most intensely now, one suspects, two dozen years after he began writing in Gikuyu, is the threat of spiritual death from the homogenized universal commercial culture that derives from globalism — what Benjamin Barber has called "McWorld" — which threatens by its very ubiquity to engulf and destroy every vestige of local culture. Ngugi's increasingly desperate appeal to African writers is to return to the languages of their childhood as the "magic fountain" of an authentic cultural life. To a theorist like Bhabha, of course, this crucial "debate" between Achebe and Ngugi would be only more evidence of "liminality": the way postcolonial writers negotiate the threshold between two worlds.[12] Similar linguistic issues come up within ethnic studies: Chicana writers like Sandra Cisneros have to decide whether to write in English or in their own regional dialect of American Spanish, or in both, and African American writers need to decide just how intensely they want to evoke the special qualities of African American vernacular.

[11]Chinua Achebe, "The African Writer and the English Language," from *Morning Yet on Creation Day* (New York: Doubleday, 1975), pp. 91–103.

[12]It may seem obvious that it would be more "politically correct" to use a native language than a Europhone language, but that may depend on precisely which native language one speaks. In *The Great Railway Bazaar* (1975), Paul Theroux encounters on a train a group of Tamil speakers from the southernmost tip of India who resent being addressed in Hindi, the local language of New Delhi, the capital far to the north. They insist on using English, because the language of the former oppressor has the virtue of equalizing the status of their province and the capital.

The special liminality of Chicano/Chicana culture is evoked brilliantly in the late Gloria Anzaldúa's "La conciencia de la mestiza: Towards a New Consciousness"; the essay is written in a mixture of English and Spanish, which monolingual readers should try to penetrate as well as they can without recourse to the supplied notes, at least at first, to get a sense of the way her language expresses the continuous movement of her discourse across the permeable borderlands. Anzaldúa portrays herself as a *nahual* — a magical shape-shifter who can transform herself into "a tree, a coyote, another person." A *mestiza* is literally a half-breed: Anzaldúa not only finds herself on the boundary between languages, she feels simultaneously the pull of the different races that have gone into her gene pool: the native Americans of Mexico, the Spaniards, the African slaves with whom they intermarried, the "gringo" Americans stemming from Northern Europe. Her spiritual vision reflects all these roots: she recognizes from Africa "Eshu, Yoruba god of indeterminacy," sees the Aztec mother goddess Coatlapopeuh blend in with the Virgin of Guadalupe. If all these elements could live together in peace, the consciousness of the *mestiza* would be richer and fuller than any pure-blood culture, but there is an internal quarrel that leaves her alienated within herself: "commonly held beliefs of the white culture attack commonly held beliefs of the Mexican culture, and both attack commonly held beliefs of the indigenous culture." And the attack is not only internal: everywhere the half-breed is despised by the pureblood, and, since Anzaldúa is a lesbian as well, she has a sense of being an outcast by sexuality as well as race. Despite this sense of alienation, similar to what Fanon described in North African culture, Anzaldúa's stance is an attempt at inclusiveness and balance. She understands the pull of violence but for her the "proudly defiant" attitude of the "counterstance" defines one in terms of what one is against, and she does not want an identity merely borrowed from the oppressor; she wants "to act and not react." In the long run, the conflict might lead to violence, or to a withdrawal from the dominant culture, or there might be some more complex accommodation that will occur, when we realize that no one is pure, that we are all complex mixtures, that we all share the consciousness of the *mestiza: el dia de la Chicana.*

DIALOGUE: JAMESON AND AHMAD ON THIRD WORLD LITERATURE

An even more complex dilemma appears in the dialogue between Fredric Jameson and Aijaz Ahmad on Third World literature that originally appeared in the pages of *Social Text.* The problem with which Jameson begins is one related to the debate at the time over the Western literary canon and the extent to which it could and should be opened to include previously ignored writing by women and ethnic minorities. One problem with gaining equivalent traction for contemporary Third World writing is that its insistent social realism reminds Western readers of writers of over a century ago, like Dreiser and Zola, and its production today suggests that it is being written not for them at all but for another kind of reader, a naive Third World reader not yet ready for modernist, much less postmodernist texts. The other problem is that the Third World novel, by taking the literary form of national allegory, transgresses the Western split between the political and the personal: *"the story of the private individual destiny is always an allegory of the embattled situation of the public third world culture and society"* (italics Jameson's). Jameson may have solved, to his satisfaction, the question of the resistance of the West to Third World writing, but for Ahmad — who is like Jameson a Marxist theorist indebted to Gramsci and the Frankfurt School — there is a different sort of resistance, and in fact a personal as well as a theoretical problem here: "I realized that what was being theorized was, among many other things, myself. . . ."

But Ahmad's response is not merely personal: what he wants to point out is the way Jameson is essentializing the Third World as the Other of the West — a sophisticated equivalent of saying "all you darkies look alike to us." As Ahmad points out, they don't look alike to each other because they aren't alike: each new nation has had a different history with a different relationship to metropolitan cultures, so there is no single "public third world culture" and no single "embattled situation." Ahmad wants to get rid of the entire "three worlds" metaphor, in fact. Because if we are all living in one world today, not a hierarchy of three where it can be taken for granted that it is the aesthetic sensibility of the West that matters, then the question Jameson starts with can be turned on its head. Perhaps we should be asking how the Western canon of literature looks in the eyes of traditional Urdu aesthetics.

In the final response of Jameson to Ahmad, there is a bit of backpedaling — he has a sense, probably unusual for Jameson, of having missed some of the complexity of the questions he raised. But Jameson insists on the perhaps deplorable fact that living in one world does not make us all equal: Western power (the power of finance more than the power of its weaponry) is going to skew inevitably whose vision of humanity and society becomes dominant, and whose aesthetics dominate that arena. It does not seem an accident that the most influential writers of the Third World, like Gabriel Garcia Marquez, Chinua Achebe, and Salman Rushdie, are those modernists or postmodernists whose aesthetic is closest to our own. But it also doesn't seem an accident that it is Jameson, the Marxist born in the West, who calls attention to that fact, or that Jameson and Ahmad seem divided less by ideology than by location.

DIALOGUE: BAKER ON GATES

The response of Houston Baker Jr. to the early work of Henry Louis Gates Jr. is also an internecine quarrel, but here the quarreling family consists of theorists of African American literature, and the quarrel is quite a bit like that of theorists in general about whether to emphasize the language of literature or its social basis. Gates arrived on the scene as the scholar whose mission it was to adapt the fashionable theories of structuralism and deconstruction to the study of African American literature. Where Saussure and the structuralists had stressed the arbitrary relation of the signifier and the signified, where Derrida had stressed the free play of the signifier, Gates stressed "signifying" — an African American locution for language at play, what might be called free play, as it was developed by the enslaved and the formerly enslaved to ensnare the listener, to speak truth to power, or to trick the more mighty opponent. Gates published his credo emphasizing the semiotic issues in African American writing as "Preface to Blackness: Texts and Pretexts" in the important Dexter Fisher/Robert B. Stepto collection, *Afro-American Literature: The Reconstruction of Instruction* (1979). As Gates was to put it in "Criticism in de Jungle" (1981), "The challenge of black literary criticism is to derive principles of literary criticism from the black tradition itself, as defined in the idiom of critical theory but also in the idiom which constitutes the 'language of blackness,' the signifyin(g) difference which makes the black tradition our very own."

This emphasis on the free play of the signifier struck other African American literary theorists, like Houston Baker, as a way to cut literary forms off from the specific social origins that produce human consciousness, a consciousness that can create such forms and respond to them. In the selection from *Blues, Ideology and Afro-American Literature*, Baker quotes Gates and responds from his Marxist perspective: literature, as a form of ideology, can have no history that can be cut off or isolated from the history of the social formation that produces it.

Many quarrels within literary theory are dialogues of the deaf, but the one between Baker and Gates was not. Instead of digging in their heels, each responded by narrowing the distance between their two stances. As Theodore Mason has put it, "While Gates could be seen as moving from theory towards literary nationalism (to put it crudely), Baker could be seen as moving from a profoundly nationalistic cultural base toward a revision of that position complicated by an engagement with language and with theory. Consequently, by the end of the [twentieth century], both Gates and Baker, for all their differences, early and late, could be seen as occupying relatively similar positions." (Michael Groden, Martin Kreiswirth, and Imre Szeman, ed., *Johns Hopkins Guide to Literary Theory and Criticism*, 2005, p. 18.)

How similar may appear from the selection in this chapter, "Writing, 'Race,' and the Difference It Makes." In this essay, Gates examines the history of doubt, expressed by freeborn Englishmen and slaveowners, as to whether people of African origin were truly human (that is, possessed of reason, the Enlightenment criterion of humanity) and able to be subjects as well as objects of discourse. Some seventeenth-century philosophers held that the "Negro" was not human at all, while Hume and Kant placed the African at the bottom of the human scale on the Great Chain of Being. The poems of Phillis Wheatley, a young African girl whose master had taught her to read and write both English and Latin, offended Thomas Jefferson's prejudice that blacks should be unable to write poetry, though it is not clear whether his contemptuous opinion — "the compositions published under her name are below the dignity of criticism" — was meant to dismiss the poems on the ground of quality, Wheatley's authorship, or both. To keep them from establishing their humanity through participation in the world of letters, slaves were forbidden to learn to write or read. Thus the slave narratives of African Americans, such as Frederick Douglass, William Wells Brown, and dozens of others, were assertions of their transgressive existence as subjects.

But Gates argues that "black people . . . have not been 'liberated' from racism by their writings. . . . Black writing . . . served not to obliterate the difference of 'race,' . . . rather, the inscription of the black voice in Western literatures has preserved those very cultural differences to be imitated and revised in a separate Western literary tradition, a tradition of black difference." For Gates, the African American writer is torn between two traditions: the written tradition of Western European culture into which African slaves were forcibly transplanted, and what he calls the "talking book" or the "speakerly text," the oral tradition of Africa that survives in the songs, legends, and stories of the people. In creating in 1996 his prestigious *Norton Anthology of African American Literature*, Gates not only included work songs and blues, legends and stories, but a cassette tape as well so that the "reader" can listen to the texts as performed.

One might ask, though, whether Gates may have come too far toward Baker, whether he may be slanting the African American canon by privileging texts with the strongest roots in the African oral traditions at the expense of those that, written in an English indistinguishable from that of the oppressor, exploit the "double consciousness" that W. E. B. Du Bois felt was the inevitable lot of the African American. Should we prefer Paul Laurence Dunbar's dialect poems, such as "Little Brown Baby" and "When Malindy Sings," as Howells[13] did, or his poems written in standard English, like "We Wear the Mask"? It seems clear that Gates values the "speakerly text" derived from the oral tradition, over a dense and "writerly" tradition of African American literature, represented by James Baldwin and Ralph Ellison, that pays allegiance to one particular white master — Henry James. When a minority group is identified with a particular mode of writing, it inevitably marginalizes those in that minority who write otherwise. This may be the key danger inherent in the attempt to essentialize some particular version of "blackness" as the core of the African American tradition.

DIALOGUE: IS THEORY WHITE?

The same sort of issue underlies Barbara Christian's provocation piece, "The Race for Theory," and the responses that it evoked. Published in 1988 in an issue of *Feminist Studies* devoted to feminism and deconstruction, Christian's disturbingly heartfelt discourse expresses the pain of a scholar and critic who had devoted her life to elucidating and promoting the status of literature by African American women, and who views her life's work as marginalized by a change in fashion within the academy. The theoretical revolution that broke over departments of literature starting in the late 1970s produced, along with a great deal of stimulating discourse, considerable acrimony, particularly among professors for whom "close reading" of poetic texts was the beginning and end of literary study, and among traditional scholars pursuing answers to literary-historical questions. The academy is a hierarchy in

---

[13]William Dean Howells (1837–1920), American novelist, editor of *Harper's Magazine*, who had reviewed Dunbar's first book of poems and actively promoted his talent.

which status is based on the presumed importance of one's work, and to the extent that prestige was being conferred on theorists, together with the perquisites that went with prestige — fellowships, professorial chairs, the chance to train the best students — less would be left for traditional scholars and critics. It may not be exactly a zero-sum game, where one person's winnings must be another's losses, but it is close.[14] Theory could be a real threat to one's research projects.

Christian's narrative makes it clear that her early work had been energized by the attention that was newly being paid both to feminism and to the African American studies movement, but that attention had shifted to applications of "high theory," particularly interpretive theory based on poststructuralist thinkers like Derrida and de Man, and French feminist thinkers about gender whose ideas are based on neo-Freudian analysts like Lacan. Christian does not name specific names of those applying high theory to African American literature, but it would be surprising if she did not have male theorists like Houston Baker Jr. in mind, or white theorists like Barbara Johnson who applied Lacan to Zora Neale Hurston. The name that seems most clearly unspoken, perhaps, is that of Henry Louis Gates Jr., who after unearthing in 1981 the first novel published by an African American woman — *Our Nig* [1859], by Harriet E. Wilson — rocketed to fame within white academia by becoming the first African American scholar to apply high theory to black literature.

Part of the problem, Christian argues, is that she finds theory "prescriptive." Here she clearly is worried about repeating her own history with the "Black Arts Movement" of the 1960s, which attempted to judge texts by African Americans according to their participation in a posited essence of blackness, an essence that tended to exclude works by black women. But she never explains why French poststructuralist theory should be prescriptive in the same way the highly political Black Arts group had been, and the reader may come away thinking, ironically, that it is Christian who has become politically prescriptive, because for her the problem with theory is that it is too white and too male, even when practiced by women and persons of color.

Christian's attack on theory drew a wide range of responses, including Michael Awkward's "Appropriative Gestures," which argued that African American scholars and critics would do their work best if they took over whatever tools were needed to do their job, regardless of the color, gender, and nationality of the inventors. Awkward approves of Christian's efforts to move the literary work of African American women closer to the center of the canon, where they will affect the lives of their readers, but he argues that this end will be poorly served by isolating such texts from contemporary theoretical methods. "If the literature of black women is . . . to gain the respect it doubtlessly deserves as an ideologically and aesthetically complex, analytically rich literary tradition within an increasingly theoretical

[14]Possibly worse than a zero-sum game, if, as Louis Menand has shown, federal and state governments since 1975 have been cutting the funds available for higher education, with the cuts disproportionately centered in the arts and humanities. As the flow of grant money dried up, the academy became more and more competitive, which increased the desperation for ambitious scholars to become affiliated to whatever movement was the "flavor of the month."

academy, it will require that its critics . . . master the discourse of contemporary literary theory." And as African American critics become prominent in the canon of theory, theory itself will cease to be "white."

Deborah E. McDowell's response to this controversy in "Recycling" is fascinating, particularly because McDowell is *herself* one of the foremost African American scholars doing theory within the academy. Her much earlier essay, "New Directions for Black Feminist Criticism," although sympathetic to the sense of marginalization that provoked critics like Barbara Smith and Barbara Christian, sought to escape the divisiveness of the standard binaries: black versus white, women versus men, lesbian versus heterosexual, and it urged black scholars to approach their tasks using any and all available methodologies. In "Recycling," McDowell seems to have circled back to a more defensive posture against the reach of poststructuralist theory. She does not take the view that "theory is white" as such — she knows that black theorists are using it without losing touch with their own identities or the cultural significance of the texts they treat. But she is troubled by the way the move to valorize texts by black female authors seems always to take place under the aegis of white men (Marx, Derrida, Lacan, and the other usual suspects) and to evade the particulars of black female experience. McDowell's "counterhistory" suggests that poststructural theory, with its proclamations of the loss of stable meaning and the death of the author, may be liberating when it destabilizes ancient and unquestioned dogmas about literature and culture, the "great tradition" of dead white males, but to the extent that it installs a different "great tradition" of white male theorists, it can have the unintended result of undermining the best efforts of black feminist scholarship today. And she quotes Rey Chow — whom we shall discuss shortly — to the effect that the very same kind of undermining takes place with respect to the literature of the third world as well.

The fact is that African American feminist criticism is by no means the only one that senses a rivalry with theory: the same kind of conflict exists between practitioners of postcolonial studies and practitioners of postcolonial theory. Bart Moore-Gilbert's excellent study, *Postcolonial Theory: Contexts, Practices, Politics*, spends the first chapter outlining the deep divisions — divisions that he thinks can ultimately be bridged — between the high theorists with which this chapter began and scholars of postcolonial literatures. Some of the causes of the conflict are fairly superficial, like the annoyance with the arcane vocabulary of poststructural theory, and some may primarily reflect resentment over the academic success of theorists like Said and Spivak. But other issues are harder to dismiss: scholars like Stephen Slemon and Helen Tiffin argue that theorists like Bhabha evade "the real politics of the postcolonial predicament as a consequence of their obsession with 'a set of philosophical questions whose cultural and historical specificity within postmodern Anglo-American culture is rarely admitted.' "[15] Aijaz Ahmad, from his own Marxist perspective, views postcolonial theory as aloof and hyperintellectual, preferring a

[15]Stephen Slemon and Helen Tiffin, Introduction to *After Europe*, xi, quoted in Moore-Gilbert, pp. 20–21.

textual to a material engagement with the forces of repression, and isolated from the struggles for liberation still going on in the poorest of the former colonies.[16] To the extent that this is an ethical challenge to the theorists, it can often be answered with biography: Edward Said was, until his recent death from leukemia, a tireless advocate of the Palestinian people in their quest for autonomy and statehood, and Gayatri Spivak, for at least the last ten years, has been involved in creating and training "barefoot schools" for the women of rural India. Nevertheless one could claim that there is a split between theory and practice here, between the Foucauldian theorist of Orientalism and the Palestinian advocate, between the deconstructor of subaltern studies and the benefactor of Indian women. So in postcolonial studies, as with ethnic studies, the question remains: Is theory white?

Rey Chow's difficult but rewarding essay, "The Interruption of Referentiality," takes the blunt question "Is theory white?" to what are probably its sublimest heights. At the outset of her argument, Chow very abstractly delineates a certain rhetorical move that, at this point, should be rather familiar to us. A critic studying a "particular group, identity, or ethnic culture" gestures toward Western theory in order to reject it. You can call the identity group "African American women," if you like, but because it really doesn't matter which group, Chow abstractly calls it X. But what Chow means by Western theory isn't just any old theory: Chow specifically excludes historical, sociological, anthropological theories that quickly get down to cases: she is talking about poststructuralist theories such as those of Lacan, Foucault, and Derrida, which tend to question the nature of meaning as referentiality (in which a signifier points to a signified) and instead refer meaning to differences in a chain of signifiers. Deconstructive theory destabilizes the standard Western hierarchies valorizing "man" over "woman," "white" over "black," "heterosexual" over "homosexual," and so on, which is why studies of marginalized identity groups want to gesture toward theory. But by destabilizing meaning as reference, theory also calls into question the stability of the identity group, which is why they want to resist or reject theory.

> In the face of the practical struggles that go on daily against different forms of social injustice, it is, for many, unacceptable to declare, in accordance with poststructuralist theoretical logic, that these versions of X do not exist. Yet the alternative — the insistence that they are real . . . , that their empirical existence is absolutely incontestable, and that they are thus a core from which to stage resistance to the virtual claims of high theory — is equally untenable because it is theoretically naive.

The dizzying paradox into which Chow's logic draws us explains why critics studying X keep making that same rhetorical move, and also why that move somehow always fails to work. It explains how come all the "new projects of articulating alternative identities, cultures, and group formations often seem so predictable in the end" with their endless talk of ambivalence, hybridity, disruptiveness, resistance: the rhetoric of poststructuralism homogenizes all cultural differences into a mishmash of *différance*.

---

[16]Aijaz Ahmad, Introduction to *In Theory*, p. 3.

Selected Bibliography

Achebe, Chinua. *Hopes and Impediments*. London: Doubleday, 1988.

———. "The African Writer and the English Language." *Morning Yet on Creation Day*. New York: Doubleday, 1975.

Ahmad, [Mohammed] Aijaz. *In Theory: Classes, Nations, Literatures*. London: Verso, 1992.

Anderson, Benedict. *Imagined Communities: Reflections on the Origin and Spread of Nationalism*. New York: Verso, 1983.

Anzaldúa, Gloria. *Borderlands/La Frontera*. San Francisco: Aunt Lute, 1999.

Appiah, Kwame Anthony. *In My Father's House: Africa in the Philosophy of Culture*. London: Methuen, 1992.

Ashcroft, Bill, Gareth Griffiths, and Helen Tiffin, eds. *The Empire Writes Back: Theory and Practice in Post-Colonial Literatures*. London: Routledge, 1989.

Awkward, Michael. *Negotiating Difference: Race, Gender, and the Politics of Positionality*. Chicago: University of Chicago Press, 1995.

Bahri, Deepika. *Coming to Terms with the "Postcolonial": Between the Lines*. Philadelphia: Temple University Press, 1996.

Baker, Houston A., Jr. *Blues, Ideology, and Afro-American Literature: A Vernacular Theory*. Chicago: University of Chicago Press, 1984.

Baker, Houston A., Jr., and Patricia Redmond, eds. *Afro-American Literary Study in the 1990s*. Chicago: University of Chicago Press, 1989.

Bhabha, Homi K., *The Location of Culture*. New York: Routledge, 1994.

———, ed., *Nation and Narration*. New York: Routledge, 1990.

Brantlinger, Patrick. *Rule of Darkness: British Literature and Imperialism, 1830–1914*. Ithaca: Cornell University Press, 1988.

Césaire, Aimé. *Un tempête*. Paris: Seuil, 1969.

Chow, Rey. *Writing Diaspora: Tactics of Intervention in Contemporary Cultural Studies*. Bloomington: Indiana University Press, 1993.

Christian, Barbara. *Black Feminist Criticism*. New York: Pergamon, 1985.

Deleuze, Gilles, and Félix Guattari. *Kafka: Toward a Minor Literature*. Minneapolis: University of Minnesota Press, 1986.

Fanon, Frantz. *Black Skin, White Masks*. New York: Grove Press, 1967.

———. *The Wretched of the Earth*. New York: Grove Press, 1961.

Gates, Henry Louis. *Black Literature and Literary Theory*. New York: Methuen, 1984.

———. *Loose Canons: Notes on the Culture Wars*. New York: Oxford University Press, 1992.

———. *The Signifying Monkey: A Theory of African-American Literary Criticism*. New York: Oxford University Press, 1988.

———, ed., *"Race," Writing, and Difference*. Chicago: University of Chicago Press, 1986.

Gilroy, Paul. *The Black Atlantic: Modernity and Double Consciousness*. Cambridge: Harvard University Press, 1993.

Harris, Wilson. *Selected Essays*. New York: Routledge, 1999.

Jameson, Fredric. *The Geopolitical Aesthetic: Cinema and Space in the World System*. Bloomington: Indiana University Press, 1992.

———. "Third World Literature in the Era of Multinational Capitalism." *Social Text* 15 (1986): 65–88.

Jameson, Fredric, and Masao Miyoshi, eds. *The Cultures of Globalization*. Durham: Duke University Press, 1998.

Loomba, Ania, ed. *Colonialism/Postcolonialism*. New York: Routledge, 1998.

McDowell, Deborah. *The Changing Same: Black Women's Literature, Criticism, and Theory*. Bloomington: Indiana University Press, 1995.

Memmi, Albert. *The Colonizer and the Colonized*. Boston: Beacon Press, 1965.

Menand, Louis. "What Are Universities For?" *Harper's* 283 (December 1991): 47–56.

Mohanty, Chandra Talpade, Ann Russo, and Lourdes Torres, eds. *Third World Women and the Politics of Feminism*. Bloomington: Indiana University Press, 1991.

Mongia, Padmini, ed. *Contemporary Postcolonial Theory: A Reader*. London: Arnold, 1997.

Moore-Gilbert, Bart, Gareth Stanton, and Willy Maley, eds. *Postcolonial Criticism*. London: Longman, 1997.

Morrison, Toni. *Playing in the Dark: Whiteness and the Literary Imagination*. Cambridge: Harvard University Press, 1992.

Naipaul, V. S. *The Middle Passage*. London: Deutsch, 1962.

Ngugi wa Thiong'o. *Decolonising the Mind: The Politics of Language*. London: James Currey, 1989.

———. *Moving the Centre: The Struggle for Cultural Freedom*. London: James Currey, 1993.

———. *Penpoints, Gunpoints, and Dreams: Towards a Critical Theory of the Arts and the State in Africa*. New York: Oxford University Press, 1998.

Riquelme, John P. "Location and Home in Beckett, Bhabha, Fanon, and Heidegger." *Centennial Review* 42, no. 3 (1998): 541–68.

Rushdie, Salman. *Imaginary Homelands: Essays and Criticism, 1981–1991*. London: Penguin, 1991.

Said, Edward. *Orientalism*. New York: Vintage, 1979.

———. *The World, the Text, and the Critic*. Cambridge: Harvard University Press, 1983.

———. *Culture and Imperialism*. New York: Vintage, 1994.

Sharpe, Jenny. "Is the United States Postcolonial? Transnationalism, Immigration, and Race." *Diaspora* 4, no. 2 (Fall 1995): 181–99.

Slemon, Stephen, and Helen Tiffin, eds. *After Europe: Critical Theory and Post-Colonial Writing*. Mundelstrup: Dangaroo Press, 1990.

Soyinka, Wole. *Myth, Literature and the African World*. Cambridge: Cambridge University Press, 1990.

Spillers, Hortense J. "Who Cuts the Borders? Some Readings on 'America.'" In *Comparative American Identities: Race, Sex, and Nationality in the Modern Text*, ed. Hortense J. Spillers. New York: Routledge, 1991.

Spivak, Gayatri Chakravorti. *In Other Worlds: Essays in Cultural Politics*. London: Methuen, 1987.

———. "Can the Subaltern Speak?" *Marxism and the Interpretation of Culture*, ed. Cary Nelson and Lawrence Grossberg. Urbana: University of Illinois Press, 1988.

———. *A Critique of Post-Colonial Reason: Toward a History of the Vanishing Present*. Cambridge: Harvard University Press, 1999.

Trinh, T. Minh-Ha, *Woman, Native, Other: Writing Postcoloniality and Feminism*. Bloomington: Indiana University Press, 1989.

West, Cornel. *Race Matters*. Boston: Beacon Press, 1993.

Williams, Patrick, and Laura Chrisman, eds. *Colonial Discourse and Post-Colonial Theory*. New York: Harvester Wheatsheaf, 1993.

Gilles Deleuze

b. 1925

Félix Guattari

1930–1992

Gilles Deleuze was born in Paris in 1925 and was educated at the Sorbonne under Jean-Paul Sartre before undertaking an academic career in philosophy and literature. Félix Guattari was born in 1930 in the Parisian suburb of Villeneuve-les-Sablons and trained to become a psychoanalyst in the new style of Jacques Lacan. They met in 1968, when Paris erupted in demonstrations led by its radical intelligentsia. The result of the meeting was a series of collaborations in which (as Deleuze recalls) "everything became possible, even if we failed." Together they wrote Anti-Oedipus *(1972), the first volume of* Capitalism and Schizophrenia, *a political critique of Freudian psychology arguing that the unconscious is a social and political domain rather than merely a private memory bank. Their sequel was* A Thousand Plateaux *(1980, translated 1987), which presented the political distinction between the center and the margin as a psychological version of the eternal conflict between civilization and nomadism. (For Deleuze and Guattari the various arts and sciences are either "royalist" or "nomadic" in character.) They published* Kafka: Toward a Minor Literature, *from which this selection is taken, in 1975 and their final collaboration,* What Is Philosophy? *in 1991 (translated 1994). Gilles Deleuze is currently professor of philosophy at Université de Paris VIII at Saint-Denis. His solo works include* Nietzsche and Philosophy *(1983),* Kant's Critical Philosophy *(1985),* Foucault *(1988),* Cinema *(2 volumes, 1986 and 1989),* Difference and Repetition *(1994), and* Essays Critical and Clinical *(1997). Félix Guattari, for forty years a psychoanalyst at the Clinique de la Borde at Cour-Cheverny, died in 1992.*

What Is a Minor Literature?

The problem of expression is staked out by Kafka[1] not in an abstract and universal fashion but in relation to those literatures that are considered minor, for example, the Jewish literature of Warsaw and Prague. A minor literature doesn't come from a minor language; it is rather that which a minority constructs within a major language. But the first characteristic of minor literature in any case is that in it language is affected with a high coefficient of deterritorialization. In

Translated by Dana Polan.

[1]Franz Kafka (1883–1924) was a Jew and a native of Prague, currently the capital of the Czech Republic but before 1918 the capital of the province of Bohemia in the Austro-Hungarian Empire. Kafka was a lawyer and civil servant who in his spare time wrote surrealistic narratives. His works defy literal interpretation, and critics have often tried to read them as allegories of his own psychological conflicts or as philosophical fables about man's relationship to an obscure and distant God. During his lifetime, Kafka published two novellas, *The Metamorphosis* (1915) and *In the Penal Colony* (1919), and two collections of stories, *A Country Doctor* (1919) and *The Hunger Artist* (1924). His novels were edited and published after his death: *The Trial* in 1925, *The Castle* in 1926, and

Amerika in 1927. As a Prague Jew, Kafka spoke Czech (the native language of the Bohemian population), German (the language of the Austro-Hungarian administration), and Yiddish (a dialect of Middle High German — medieval German — spoken by Eastern European Jews) and was learning Hebrew at the time of his death. He wrote exclusively in German.

this sense, Kafka marks the impasse that bars access to writing for the Jews of Prague and turns their literature into something impossible — the impossibility of not writing, the impossibility of writing in German, the impossibility of writing otherwise.[2] The impossibility of not writing because national consciousness, uncertain or oppressed, necessarily exists by means of literature ("The literary struggle has its real justification at the highest possible levels"). The impossibility of writing other than in German is for the Prague Jews the feeling of an irreducible distance from their primitive Czech territoriality. And the impossibility of writing in German is the deterritorialization of the German population itself, an oppressive minority that speaks a language cut off from the masses, like a "paper language" or an artificial language; this is all the more true for the Jews who are simultaneously a part of this minority and excluded from it, like "gypsies who have stolen a German child from its crib." In short, Prague German is a deterritorialized language, appropriate for strange and minor uses. (This can be compared in another context to what blacks in America today are able to do with the English language.)

The second characteristic of minor literatures is that everything in them is political. In major literatures, in contrast, the individual concern (familial, marital, and so on) joins with other no less individual concerns, the social milieu serving as a mere environment or a background; this is so much the case that none of these Oedipal intrigues are specifically indispensable or absolutely necessary but all become as one in a large space. Minor literature is completely different; its cramped space forces each individual intrigue to connect immediately to politics. The individual concern thus becomes all the more necessary, indispensable, magnified, because a whole other story is vibrating within it. In this way, the family triangle connects to other triangles — commercial, economic, bureaucratic, juridical — that determine its values. When Kafka indicates that one of the goals of a minor literature is the "purification of the conflict that opposes father and son and the possibility of discussing that conflict," it isn't a question of an Oedipal phantasm but of a political program. "Even though something is often thought through calmly, one still does not reach the boundary where it connects up with similar things, one reaches the boundary soonest in politics, indeed, one even strives to see it before it is there, and often sees this limiting boundary everywhere. . . . What in great literature goes on down below, constituting a not indispensable cellar of the structure, here takes place in the full light of day, what is there a matter of passing interest for a few, here absorbs everyone no less than as a matter of life and death."[3]

The third characteristic of minor literature is that in it everything takes on a collective value. Indeed, precisely because talent isn't abundant in a minor literature, there are no possibilities for an individuated enunciation that would belong to this or that "master" and that could be separated from a collective enunciation. Indeed, scarcity of talent is in fact beneficial and allows the conception of something other than a literature of masters; what each author says individually already constitutes a common action, and what he or she says or does is necessarily political, even if others aren't in agreement. The political domain has contaminated every statement (énoncé). But above all else, because collective or national consciousness is "often inactive in external life and always in the process of breakdown," literature finds itself positively charged with the role and function of collective, and even revolutionary, enunciation. It is literature that produces an active solidarity in spite of skepticism; and if the writer is in the margins or completely outside his or her fragile community, this situation allows the writer all the more the possibility to express another possible community and to forge the means for another consciousness and another

[2]See letter to Max Brod of June 1921, in Franz Kafka, *Letters to Friends, Family and Editors*, trans. Richard and Clara Winston (New York: Schocken Books, 1977): 289, and the commentaries in Klaus Wagenbach, *Franz Kafka: Pictures of a Life*, Arthur S. Wensiger (New York: Pantheon, 1984), 84. [Deleuze and Guattari]

[3]Franz Kafka, entry for 25 December 1911 in *The Diaries of Franz Kafka*, trans. Joseph Kresh (New York: Schocken Books, 1948), 194. [Deleuze and Guattari]

sensibility; just as the dog of "Investigations"[4] calls out in his solitude to *another science*. The literary machine thus becomes the relay for a revolutionary machine-to-come, not at all for ideological reasons but because the literary machine alone is determined to fill the conditions of a collective enunciation that is lacking elsewhere in this milieu: *literature is the people's concern*.[5] It is certainly in these terms that Kafka sees the problem. The message doesn't refer back to an enunciating subject who would be its cause, no more than to a subject of the statement (*sujet d'énoncé*) who would be its effect. Undoubtedly, for a while, Kafka thought according to these traditional categories of the two subjects, the author and the hero, the narrator and the character, the dreamer and the one dreamed of.[6] But he will quickly reject the role of the narrator, just as he will refuse an author's or master's literature, despite his admiration for Goethe. Josephine the mouse renounces the individual act of singing in order to melt into the collective enunciation of "the immense crowd of the heroes of [her] people." A movement from the individuated animal to the pack or to a collective multiplicity — seven canine musicians. In "The Investigations of a Dog," the expressions of the solitary researcher tend toward the assemblage (*agencement*) of a collective enunciation of the canine species even if this collectivity is no longer or not yet given. There isn't a subject; *there are only collective assemblages of enunciation*, and literature expresses these acts insofar as they're not imposed from without and insofar as they exist only as diabolical powers to come or revolutionary forces to be constructed. Kafka's solitude opens him up to everything going on in history today. The letter K no longer designates a narrator or a character but an assemblage that becomes all the more machine-like, an agent that becomes all the more collective because an individual is locked into it in his or her solitude (it is only in connection to a subject that something individual would be separable from the collective and would lead its own life).

The three characteristics of minor literature are the deterritorialization of language, the connection of the individual to a political immediacy, and the collective assemblage of enunciation. We might as well say that minor no longer designates specific literatures but the revolutionary conditions for every literature within the heart of what is called great (or established) literature. Even he who has the misfortune of being born in the country of a great literature must write in its language, just as a Czech Jew writes in German, or an Ouzbekian writes in Russian. Writing like a dog digging a hole, a rat digging its burrow. And to do that, finding his own point of underdevelopment, his own *patois*, his own third world, his own desert. There has been much discussion of the questions "What is a marginal literature?" and "What is a popular literature, a proletarian literature?" The criteria are obviously difficult to establish if one doesn't start with a more objective concept — that of minor literature. Only the possibility of setting up a minor practice of major language from within allows one to define popular literature, marginal literature, and so on.[7] Only in this way can literature really become a collective machine of expression and really be able to treat and develop its contents. Kafka emphatically declares that a minor literature is much more able to work over its material.[8] Why this machine of

---

[4]An allusion to Kafka's satirical story, "Investigations of a Dog" (1922).

[5]Kafka, *Diaries*, 193: "[L]iterature is less a concern of literary history, than of the people." [Deleuze and Guattari]

[6]See "Wedding Preparations in the Country," in Kafka, *Complete Stories* (New York: Schocken Books, 1971): "And so long as you say 'one' instead of 'I,' there's nothing in it" (p. 53). And the two subjects appear several pages later: "I don't even need to go to the country myself, it isn't necessary. I'll send my clothed body," while the narrator stays in bed like a bug or a beetle (p. 55). No doubt, this is one of the origins of Gregor's becoming-beetle in "The Metamorphosis" (in the same way, Kafka will give up going to meet Felice [Felice Bauer, Kafka's off-again on-again fiancée] and will prefer to stay in bed). But in "The Metamorphosis," the animal takes on all the value of a true becoming and no longer has any of the stagnancy of a subject of enunciation. [Deleuze and Guattari]

[7]See Michel Ragon, *Histoire de la littérature prolétarienne en France* (Paris: Albin Michel, 1974), on the difficulty of criteria and on the need to use a concept of a "secondary zone literature." [Deleuze and Guattari]

[8]Kafka, *Diaries*, 25 December 1911, 193: "A small nation's memory is not smaller than the memory of a large one and so can digest the existing material more thoroughly." [Deleuze and Guattari]

expression, and what is it? We know that it is in a relation of multiple deterritorializations with language; it is the situation of the Jews who have dropped the Czech language at the same time as the rural environment, but it is also the situation of the German language as a "paper language." Well, one can go even farther; one can push this movement of deterritorialization of expression even farther. But there are only two ways to do this. One way is to artificially enrich this German, to swell it up through all the resources of symbolism, of oneirism,[9] of esoteric sense, of a hidden signifier. This is the approach of the Prague school, Gustav Meyrink and many others, including Max Brod.[10, 11] But this attempt implies a desperate attempt at symbolic reterritorialization, based in archetypes, Kabbala,[12] and alchemy, that accentuates its break from the people and will find its political result only in Zionism and such things as the "dream of Zion." Kafka will quickly choose the other way, or, rather, he will invent another way. He will opt for the German language of Prague as it is and in its very poverty. Go always farther in the direction of deterritorialization, to the point of sobriety. Since the language is arid, make it vibrate with a new intensity. Oppose a purely intensive usage of language to all symbolic or even significant or simply signifying usages of it. Arrive at a perfect and unformed expression, a materially intense expression. (For these two possible paths, couldn't we find the same alternatives, under other conditions, in Joyce and Beckett?[13] As Irishmen, both of them live within the genial conditions of a minor literature. That is the glory of this sort of minor literature — to be the revolutionary force for all literature. The utilization of English and of every language in Joyce. The utilization of English and French in Beckett. But the former never stops

operating by exhilaration and overdetermination and brings about all sorts of worldwide reterritorializations. The other proceeds by dryness and sobriety, a willed poverty, pushing deterritorialization to such an extreme that nothing remains but intensities.)

How many people today live in a language that is not their own? Or no longer, or not yet, even know their own and know poorly the major language that they are forced to serve? This is the problem of immigrants, and especially of their children, the problem of minorities, the problem of a minor literature, but also a problem for all of us: how to tear a minor literature away from its own language, allowing it to challenge the language and making it follow a sober revolutionary path? How to become a nomad and an immigrant and a gypsy in relation to one's own language? Kafka answers: steal the baby from its crib, walk the tightrope. . . .[14]

Let's return to the situation in the Hapsburg empire. The breakdown and fall of the empire increases the crisis, accentuates everywhere movements of deterritorialization, and invites all sorts of complex reterritorializations — archaic, mythic, or symbolist. At random, we can cite the following among Kafka's contemporaries: Einstein and his deterritorialization of the representation of the universe (Einstein teaches in Prague, and the physicist Philipp Frank gives conferences there with Kafka in attendance); the Austrian dodecaphonists[15] and their deterritorialization of musical representation (the cry that is Marie's death in *Wozzeck*, or Lulu's, or the echoed *si* that seems to us to follow a musical path similar in certain ways to what Kafka is doing); the expressionist cinema and its

---

[9]Writing that conveys the feeling of the dream state.

[10]Max Brod was Kafka's friend and literary executor, who assembled Kafka's novels for publication.

[11]See the excellent chapter "Prague at the turn of the century," in Wagenbach, *Franz Kafka*, on the situation of the German language in Czechoslovakia and on the Prague school. [Deleuze and Guattari]

[12]Collective term for Jewish mystical writings.

[13]James Joyce (1882–1941) and Samuel Beckett (1906–1989) were writers born in or near Dublin who lived and worked in Paris.

[14]In the next short section, omitted here, Deleuze and Guattari discuss some psycholinguistic aspects of minor literature.

[15]Viennese composer Arnold Schoenberg, and his disciples Alban Berg and Anton von Webern. They wrote dodecaphonic or twelve-tone music, avoiding a home key by using equally all the notes of the chromatic scale. Deleuze and Guattari refer in detail to Berg's emotionally intense operas written in this style, to *Lulu* (based on *Spring's Awakening* and *Pandora's Box* by playwright Franz Wedekind) and his earlier *Wozzeck* (based on a George Buechner play), at the climax of which the single note B (*si* in the French nomenclature) is repeatedly and obsessively played.

double movement of deterritorialization and reterritorialization of the image (Robert Weine, who has a Czech background; Fritz Lang, born in Vienna; Paul Wegener and his utilization of Prague themes).[16] Of course, we should mention Viennese psychoanalysis and Prague school linguistics.[17] What is the specific situation of the Prague Jews in relation to the "four languages"? The vernacular language for these Jews who have come from a rural milieu is Czech, but the Czech language tends to be forgotten and repressed; as for Yiddish, it is often disdained or viewed with suspicion — it *frightens*, as Kafka tells us. German is the vehicular language of the towns, a bureaucratic language of the state, a commercial language of exchange (but English has already started to become indispensable for this purpose). The German language — but this time, Goethe's German — has a cultural and referential function (as does French to a lesser degree). As a mythic language, Hebrew is connected with the start of Zionism and still possesses the quality of an active dream. For each of these languages, we need to evaluate the degrees of territoriality, deterritorialization, and reterritorialization. Kafka's own situation: he is one of the few Jewish writers in Prague to understand and speak Czech (and this language will have a great importance in his relationship with Milena).[18] German plays precisely the double role of vehicular and cultural language, with Goethe always on the horizon (Kafka also knows

French, Italian, and probably a bit of English). He will not learn Hebrew until later. What is complicated is Kafka's relation to Yiddish; he sees it less as a sort of linguistic territoriality for the Jews than as a nomadic movement of deterritorialization that reworks German language. What fascinates him in Yiddish is less a language of a religious community than that of a popular theater (he will become patron and impresario for the traveling theater of Isak Lowy).[19] The manner in which Kafka, in a public meeting, presented Yiddish to a rather hostile Jewish bourgeois audience is completely remarkable: Yiddish is a language that frightens more than it invites disdain, "dread mingled with a certain fundamental distaste"; it is a language that is lacking a grammar and that is filled with vocables that are fleeting, mobilized, emigrating, and turned into nomads that interiorize "relations of force." It is a language that is grafted onto Middle-High German and that so reworks the German language from within that one cannot translate it into German without destroying it; one can understand Yiddish only by "feeling it" in the heart. In short, it is a language where minor utilizations will carry you away: "Then you will come to feel the true unity of Yiddish and so strongly that it will frighten you, yet it will no longer be fear of Yiddish but of yourselves. Enjoy this self-confidence as much as you can!"[20]

Kafka does not opt for a reterritorialization through the Czech language. Nor toward a hyper-cultural usage of German with all sorts of oneiric or symbolic or mythic flights (even Hebrew-ifying ones), as was the case with the Prague school. Nor toward an oral, popular Yiddish. Instead, using the path that Yiddish opens up to him, he takes it in such way as to convert it into a unique and solitary form of writing. Since Prague German is deterritorialized to several degrees, he will always take it farther, to a greater degree of intensity, but in the

[16]Einstein's special theory of relativity destroyed the idea of absolute space (or time). Philipp Frank (1884–1966), a life-long friend of Einstein, succeeded him as professor of physics at the German University of Prague in 1912. The expressionist silent film directors named were the creators of the horror film: Robert Wiene (1880–1938) is best known for *The Cabinet of Doctor Caligari* (1920), Fritz Lang (1890–1976) for *Metropolis* (1927), and Paul Wegener (1874–1948) for *The Golem* (1920).

[17]On the Prague Circle and its role in linguistics, see *Change*, No. 3 (1969) and 10 (1972). (It is true that the Prague circle was only formed in 1925. But in 1920, Jakobson came to Prague where there was already a Czech movement directed by Mathesius and connected with Anton Marty, who had taught in the German university system. From 1902 to 1905, Kafka followed the courses given by Marty, a disciple of Brentano, and participated in Brentanoist meetings.) [Deleuze and Guattari]

[18]Milena Jesenska, a Czech journalist and translator with whom Kafka had a stormy, passionate love affair.

[19]On Kafka's connections to Lowy and Yiddish theater, see Brod, *Franz Kafka: A Biography* (New York: Schocken Books, 1960), 110–16, and Wagenbach, *Franz Kafka*, 163–67. In this mime theater, there must have been many bent heads and straightened heads. [Deleuze and Guattari]

[20]"An Introductory Talk on the Yiddish Language," trans. Ernst Kaiser and Eithne Wilkins in Franz Kafka, *Dearest Father* (New York: Schocken Books, 1954), 381–86. [Deleuze and Guattari]

direction of a new sobriety, a new and unexpected modification, a pitiless rectification, a straightening of the head. Schizo politeness, a drunkenness caused by water.[21] He will make the German language take flight on a line of escape. He will feed himself on abstinence; he will tear out of Prague German all the qualities of underdevelopment that it has tried to hide; he will make it cry with an extremely sober and rigorous cry. He will pull from it the barking of the dog, the cough of the ape, and the bustling of the beetle. He will turn syntax into a cry that will embrace the rigid syntax of this dried-up German. He will push it toward a deterritorialization that will no longer be saved by culture or by myth, that will be an absolute deterritorialization, even if it is slow, sticky, coagulated. To bring language slowly and progressively to the desert. To use syntax in order to cry, to give a syntax to the cry.

There is nothing that is major or revolutionary except the minor. To hate all languages of masters. Kafka's fascination for servants and employees (the same thing in Proust in relation to servants, to their language). What interests him even more is the possibility of making his own language — assuming that it is unique, that it is a major language or has been — a minor utilization. To be a sort of stranger *within* his own language; this is the situation of Kafka's Great Swimmer.[22] Even when it is unique, a language remains a mixture, a schizophrenic mélange, a Harlequin costume in which very different functions of language and distinct centers of power are played out, blurring what can be said and what can't be said; one function will be played off against the other, all the degrees of territoriality and relative deterritorialization will be played out. Even when major, a language is open to an intensive utilization that makes it take flight along creative lines of escape which, no matter how slowly, no matter how cautiously, can now form an absolute deterritorialization.

All this inventiveness, not only lexically, since the lexical matters little, but sober syntactical invention, simply to write like a dog (but a dog can't write — exactly, exactly). It's what Artaud did with French — cries, gasps; what Celine did with French, following another line, one that was exclamatory to the highest degree. Celine's syntactic evolution went from *Voyage* to *Death on the Credit Plan*, then from *Death on the Credit Plan* to *Guignol's Band*. (After that, Celine had nothing more to talk about except his own misfortunes; in other words, he had no longer any desire to write, only the need to make money. And it always ends like that, language's lines of escape: silence, the interrupted, the interminable, or even worse. But until that point, what a crazy creation, what a writing machine! Celine was so applauded for *Voyage* that he went even further in *Death on the Credit Plan* and then in the prodigious *Guignol's Band* where language is nothing more than intensities. He spoke with a kind of "minor music." Kafka, too, is a minor music, a different one, but always made up of deterritorialized sounds, a language that moves head over heels and away.) These are the true minor authors. An escape for language, for music, for writing. What we call pop — pop music, pop philosophy, pop writing — Worterflucht.[23] To make use of the polylingualism of one's own language, to make a minor or intensive use of it, to oppose the oppressed quality of this language to its oppressive quality, to find points of nonculture or underdevelopment, linguistic Third World zones by which a language can escape, an animal enters into things, an assemblage comes into play. How many styles or genres or literary movements, even very small ones, have only one single dream: to assume a major function in language, to offer themselves as a sort of state language, an official language (for example, psychoanalysis today, which would like to be a master of the signifier, or metaphor, of wordplay). Create the opposite dream: know how to create a becoming-minor. (Is there a hope for philosophy, which for a long time has been an official, referential genre? Let us profit from this moment in which antiphilosophy is trying to be a language of power.)

[21]A magazine editor will declare that Kafka's prose has "the air of the cleanliness of a child who takes care of himself" (see Wagenbach, *Franz Kafka*, 82). [Deleuze and Guattari]

[22]"The Great Swimmer" is undoubtedly one of the most Beckett-like of Kafka's texts: "I have to well admit that I am in my own country and that, in spite of all my efforts, I don't understand a word of the language that you are speaking." [Deleuze and Guattari]

[23]German for "language's lines of escape," as in the previous paragraph.

Chinua Achebe

b. 1930

Albert Chinualumogu Achebe was born in 1930 in Ogidi, Nigeria. He attended Government College in Umuahia from 1944 to 1947 and University College in Ibadan from 1948 to 1953. He went on to receive a B.A. from London University in 1953 and studied broadcasting at the British Broadcasting Corporation in London in 1956. Chinua Achebe is considered to be one of the founders of new Nigerian literature, as well as one of the finest Nigerian novelists to date. He is also a much-celebrated examiner of the European-African, black-white connection and, in this selection, is sharply and controversially critical of Joseph Conrad. He has been a literature professor at the University of Massachusetts at Amherst, the University of Connecticut at Storrs, and the University of Nigeria. He currently teaches at Bard College. His novels include Things Fall Apart *(1958),* Arrow of God *(1964),* A Man of the People *(1964),* Anthills of the Savannah *(1988), and* Hopes and Impediments *(1988). His most recent book is* Home and Exile *(2000). The following essay was published in the* Massachusetts Review *(1977).*

An Image of Africa

It was a fine autumn morning at the beginning of this academic year such as encouraged friendliness to passing strangers. Brisk youngsters were hurrying in all directions, many of them obviously freshmen in their first flush of enthusiasm. An older man, going the same way as I, turned and remarked to me how very young they came these days. I agreed. Then he asked me if I was a student too. I said no, I was a teacher. What did I teach? African literature. Now that was funny, he said, because he never had thought of Africa as having that kind of stuff, you know. By this time I was walking much faster. "Oh well," I heard him say finally, behind me, "I guess I have to take your course to find out."

A few weeks later I received two very touching letters from high school children in Yonkers, New York, who — bless their teacher — had just read *Things Fall Apart*. One of them was particularly happy to learn about the customs and superstitions of an African tribe.

I propose to draw from these rather trivial encounters rather heavy conclusions which at first sight might seem somewhat out of proportion to them: But only at first sight.

The young fellow from Yonkers, perhaps partly on account of his age but I believe also for much deeper and more serious reasons, is obviously unaware that the life of his own tribesmen in Yonkers, New York, is full of odd customs and superstitions and, like everybody else in his culture, imagines that he needs a trip to Africa to encounter those things.

The other person being fully my own age could not be excused on the grounds of his years. Ignorance might be a more likely reason; but here again I believe that something more willful than a mere lack of information was at work. For did not that erudite British historian and Regius Professor at Oxford, Hugh Trevor-Roper, pronounce a few years ago that African history did not exist?[1]

If there is something in these utterances more than youthful experience, more than a lack of factual knowledge, what is it? Quite simply it is the desire — one might indeed say the need — in

[1]The remark of Trevor-Roper (1914–2003), in a BBC talk of November 1963, was: "Perhaps in the future there will be some African history to teach. But at present there is none, or very little: there is only the history of Europe in Africa."

Western psychology to set Africa up as a foil in Europe, a place of negations at once remote and vaguely familiar in comparison with which Europe's own state of spiritual grace will be manifest.

This need is not new: which should relieve us of considerable responsibility and perhaps make us even willing to look at this phenomenon dispassionately. I have neither the desire nor, indeed, the competence to do so with the tools of the social and biological sciences. But, I can respond, as a novelist, to one famous book of European fiction, Joseph Conrad's *Heart of Darkness*, which better than any other work I know displays that Western desire and need which I have just spoken about. Of course, there are whole libraries of books devoted to the same purpose, but most of them are so obvious and so crude that few people worry about them today. Conrad, on the other hand, is undoubtedly one of the great stylists of modern fiction and a good storyteller into the bargain. His contribution therefore falls automatically into a different class — permanent literature — read and taught and constantly evaluated by serious academics. *Heart of Darkness* is indeed so secure today that a leading Conrad scholar has numbered it "among the half-dozen greatest short novels in the English language."[2] I will return to this critical opinion in due course because it may seriously modify my earlier suppositions about who may or may not be guilty in the things of which I will now speak.

Heart of Darkness projects the image of Africa as "the other world," the antithesis of Europe and therefore of civilization, a place where a man's vaunted intelligence and refinement are finally mocked by triumphant bestiality. The book opens on the River Thames, tranquil, resting peacefully "at the decline of day after ages of good service done to the race that peopled its banks." But the actual story takes place on the River Congo, the very antithesis of the Thames. The River Congo is quite decidedly not a River Emeritus.[3] It has rendered no service and enjoys no old-age pension.

We are told that "going up that river was like travelling back to the earliest beginning of the world."

Is Conrad saying then that these two rivers are very different, one good, the other bad? Yes, but that is not the real point. What actually worries Conrad is the lurking hint of kinship, of common ancestry. For the Thames, too, "has been one of the dark places of the earth." It conquered its darkness, of course, and is now at peace. But if it were to visit its primordial relative, the Congo, it would run the terrible risk of hearing grotesque, suggestive echoes of its own forgotten darkness, and of falling victim to an avenging recrudescence of the mindless frenzy of the first beginnings.

I am not going to waste your time with examples of Conrad's famed evocation of the African atmosphere. In the final consideration it amounts to no more than a steady, ponderous, fake-ritualistic repetition of two sentences, one about silence and the other about frenzy. An example of the former is "It was the stillness of an implacable force brooding over an inscrutable intention" and of the latter, "The steamer toiled along slowly on the edge of a black and incomprehensible frenzy." Of course, there is a judicious change of adjective from time to time so that instead of "inscrutable," for example, you might have "unspeakable," etc., etc.

The eagle-eyed English critic, F. R. Leavis,[4] drew attention nearly thirty years ago to Conrad's "adjectival insistence upon inexpressible and incomprehensible mystery." That insistence must not be dismissed lightly, as many Conrad critics have tended to do, as a mere stylistic flaw. For it raises serious questions of artistic good faith. When a writer, while pretending to record scenes, incidents and their impact, is in reality engaged in inducing hypnotic stupor in his readers through a bombardment of emotive words and other forms of trickery, much more has to be at stake than stylistic felicity. Generally, normal readers are well armed to detect and resist such underhanded activity. But Conrad chose his subject well — one which was guaranteed not to put him in conflict with the psychological predisposition of his

[2]Albert J. Guerard, Introduction to *Heart of Darkness* (New York: New American Library, 1950), p. 9. [Achebe]

[3]"Emeritus" is a title usually conferred on a professor who is retired from teaching.

[4]See Leavis, p. 650; the quotation is from *The Great Tradition*.

readers or raise the need for him to contend with their resistance. He chose the role of purveyor of comforting myths.

The most interesting and revealing passages in *Heart of Darkness* are, however, about people. I must quote a long passage from the middle of the story in which representatives of Europe in a steamer going down the Congo encounter the denizens of Africa:

> We were wanderers on a prehistoric earth, on an earth that wore the aspect of an unknown planet. We could have fancied ourselves the first of men taking possession of an accursed inheritance, to be subdued at the cost of profound anguish and of excessive toil. But suddenly, as we struggled round a bend, there would be a glimpse of rush walls, of peaked grass-roofs, a burst of yells, a whirl of black limbs, a mass of hands clapping, of feet stamping, of bodies swaying, of eyes rolling, under the droop of heavy and motionless foliage. The steamer toiled along slowly on the edge of a black and incomprehensible frenzy. The prehistoric man was cursing us, praying to us, welcoming us — who could tell? We were cut off from the comprehension of our surroundings; we glided past like phantoms, wondering and secretly appalled, as sane men would be before an enthusiastic outbreak in a madhouse. We could not remember because we were travelling in the night of first ages, of those ages that are gone, leaving hardly a sign — and no memories.
>
> The earth seemed unearthly. We are accustomed to look upon the shackled form of a conquered monster, but there — there you could look at a thing monstrous and free. It was unearthly, and the men were — No, they were not inhuman. Well, you know, that was the worst of it — this suspicion of their not being inhuman. It would come slowly to one. They howled and leaped, and spun, and made horrid faces; but what thrilled you was just the thought of your remote kinship with this wild and passionate uproar. Ugly. Yes, it was ugly enough; but if you were man enough you would admit to yourself that there was in you just the faintest trace of a response to the terrible frankness of that noise, a dim suspicion of there being a meaning in it which you — you so remote from the night of first ages — could comprehend.

Herein lies the meaning of *Heart of Darkness* and the fascination it holds over the Western mind: "What thrilled you was just the thought of their humanity — like yours. . . . Ugly."

Having shown us Africa in the mass, Conrad then zeros in on a specific example, giving us one of his rare descriptions of an African who is not just limbs or rolling eyes:

> And between whiles I had to look after the savage who was fireman. He was an improved specimen; he could fire up a vertical boiler. He was there below me, and, upon my word, to look at him was as edifying as seeing a dog in a parody of breeches and a feather hat, walking on his hind legs. A few months of training had done for that really fine chap. He squinted at the steam gauge and at the water gauge with an evident effort of intrepidity — and he had filed his teeth, too, the poor devil, and the wool of his pate shaved into queer patterns, and three ornamental scars on each of his cheeks. He ought to have been clapping his hands and stamping his feet on the bank, instead of which he was hard at work, a thrall to strange witchcraft, full of improving knowledge.

As everybody knows, Conrad is a romantic on the side. He might not exactly admire savages clapping their hands and stamping their feet but they have at least the merit of being in their place, unlike this dog in a parody of breeches. For Conrad, things (and persons) being in their place is of the utmost importance.

Towards the end of the story, Conrad lavishes great attention quite unexpectedly on an African woman who has obviously been some kind of mistress to Mr. Kurtz and now presides (if I may be permitted a little imitation of Conrad) like a formidable mystery over the inexorable imminence of his departure:

> She was savage and superb, wild-eyed and magnificent. . . . She stood looking at us without a stir and like the wilderness itself, with an air of brooding over an inscrutable purpose.

This Amazon is drawn in considerable detail, albeit of a predictable nature, for two reasons. First, she is in her place and so can win Conrad's special brand of approval; and second, she fulfills a structural requirement of the story; she is a savage counterpart to the refined, European woman with whom the story will end:

> She came forward, all in black with a pale head, floating towards me in the dusk. She was in mourning. . . . She took both my hands in hers and murmured, "I had heard you were coming." . . . She

had a mature capacity for fidelity, for belief, for suffering.

The difference in the attitude of the novelist to these two women is conveyed in too many direct and subtle ways to need elaboration. But perhaps the most significant difference is the one implied in the author's bestowal of human expression to the one and the withholding of it from the other. It is clearly not part of Conrad's purpose to confer language on the "rudimentary souls" of Africa. They only "exchanged short grunting phrases" even among themselves but mostly they were too busy with their frenzy. There are two occasions in the book, however, when Conrad departs somewhat from his practice and confers speech, even English speech, on the savages. The first occurs when cannibalism gets the better of them:

> "Catch 'im," he snapped, with a bloodshot widening of his eyes and a flash of sharp white teeth — "catch 'im. Give 'im to us." "To you, eh?" I asked; "what would you do with them?" "Eat 'im!" he said curtly. . . .

The other occasion is the famous announcement:

> Mistah Kurtz — he dead.

At first sight, these instances might be mistaken for unexpected acts of generosity from Conrad. In reality, they constitute some of his best assaults. In the case of the cannibals, the incomprehensible grunts that had thus far served them for speech suddenly proved inadequate for Conrad's purpose of letting the European glimpse the unspeakable craving in their hearts. Weighing the necessity for consistency in the portrayal of the dumb brutes against the sensational advantages of securing their conviction by clear, unambiguous evidence issuing out of their own mouth, Conrad chose the latter. As for the announcement of Mr. Kurtz's death by the "insolent black head of the doorway," what better or more appropriate *finis*[5] could be written to the horror story of that wayward child of civilization who willfully had given his soul to the powers of darkness and "taken a high seat amongst the devils of the land" than the proclamation of his physical death by the forces he had joined?

[5]Latin for "end."

It might be contended, of course, that the attitude to the African in *Heart of Darkness* is not Conrad's but that of his fictional narrator, Marlow, and that far from endorsing it Conrad might indeed be holding it up to irony and criticism. Certainly, Conrad appears to go to considerable pains to set up layers of insulation between himself and the moral universe of his story. He has, for example, a narrator behind a narrator. The primary narrator is Marlow but his account is given to us through the filter of a second, shadowy person. But if Conrad's intention is to draw a *cordon sanitaire*[6] between himself and the moral and psychological malaise of his narrator, his care seems to me totally wasted because he neglects to hint however subtly or tentatively at an alternative frame of reference by which we may judge the actions and opinions of his characters. It would not have been beyond Conrad's power to make that provision if he had thought it necessary. Marlow seems to me to enjoy Conrad's complete confidence — a feeling reinforced by the close similarities between their careers.

Marlow comes through to us not only as a witness of truth, but one holding those advanced and humane views appropriate to the English liberal tradition which required all Englishmen of decency to be deeply shocked by atrocities in Bulgaria or the Congo of King Leopold of the Belgians or wherever. Thus Marlow is able to toss out such bleeding-heart sentiments as these:

> They were all dying slowly — it was very clear. They were not enemies, they were not criminals, they were nothing earthly now — nothing but black shadows of disease and starvation, lying confusedly in the greenish gloom. Brought from all the recesses of the coast in all the legality of time contracts, lost in uncongenial surroundings, fed on unfamiliar food, they sickened, became inefficient, and were then allowed to crawl away and rest.

The kind of liberalism espoused here by Marlow/Conrad touched all the best minds of the age in England, Europe, and America. It took different forms in the minds of different people but almost always managed to sidestep the ultimate

[6]Maintain a healthy distance — literally, a quarantine line (French).

question of equality between white people and black people. That extraordinary missionary, Albert Schweitzer, who sacrificed brilliant careers in music and theology in Europe for a life of service to Africans in much the same area as Conrad writes about, epitomizes the ambivalence. In a comment which I have often quoted but must quote one last time Schweitzer says: "The African is indeed my brother but my junior brother." And so he proceeded to build a hospital appropriate to the needs of junior brothers with standards of hygiene reminiscent of medical practice in the days before the germ theory of disease came into being. Naturally, be became a sensation in Europe and America. Pilgrims flocked, and I believe still flock even after he has passed on, to witness the prodigious miracle in Lamberene, on the edge of the primeval forest.

Conrad's liberalism would not take him quite as far as Schweitzer's, though. He would not use the word "brother" however qualified; the farthest he would go was "kinship." When Marlow's African helmsman falls down with a spear in his heart he gives his white master one final disquieting look.

> And the intimate profundity of that look he gave me when he received his hurt remains to this day in my memory — like a claim of distant kinship affirmed in a supreme moment.

It is important to note that Conrad, careful as ever with his words, is not talking so much about *distant kinship* as about someone *laying a claim* on it. The black man lays a claim on the white man which is well-nigh intolerable. It is the laying of this claim which frightens and at the same time fascinates Conrad, ". . . the thought of their humanity — like yours. . . . Ugly."

The point of my observations should be quite clear by now, namely, that Conrad was a bloody racist. That this simple truth is glossed over in criticism of his work is due to the fact that white racism against Africa is such a normal way of thinking that its manifestations go completely undetected. Students of *Heart of Darkness* will often tell you that Conrad is concerned not so much with Africa as with the deterioration of one European mind caused by solitude and sickness. They will point out to you that Conrad is, if anything, less charitable to the Europeans in the story than he is to the natives. A Conrad student told me in Scotland last year that Africa is merely a setting for the disintegration of the mind of Mr. Kurtz.

Which is partly the point: Africa as setting and backdrop which eliminates the African as human factor. Africa as a metaphysical battlefield devoid of all recognizable humanity, into which the wandering European enters at his peril. Of course, there is a preposterous and perverse kind of arrogance in thus reducing Africa to the role of props for the breakup of one petty European mind. But that is not even the point. The real question is the dehumanization of Africa and Africans which this age-long attitude has fostered and continues to foster in the world. And the question is whether a novel which celebrates this dehumanization, which depersonalizes a portion of the human race, can be called a great work of art. My answer is: No, it cannot. I would not call that man an artist, for example, who composes an eloquent instigation to one people to fall upon another and destroy them. No matter how striking his imagery or how beautiful his cadences fall such a man is no more a great artist than another may be called a priest who reads the mass backwards or a physician who poisons his patients. All those men in Nazi Germany who lent their talent to the service of virulent racism whether in science, philosophy, or the arts have generally and rightly been condemned for their perversions. The time is long overdue for taking a hard look at work of creative artists who apply their talent, alas often considerable as in the case of Conrad, to set people against people. This, I take it, is what Yevtushenko is after when he tells us that a poet cannot be a slave trader at the same time, and gives the striking example of Arthur Rimbaud who was fortunately honest enough to give up any pretenses to poetry when he opted for slave trading. For poetry surely can only be on the side of man's deliverance and not his enslavement; for the brotherhood and unity of all mankind and against the doctrines of Hitler's master races or Conrad's "rudimentary souls."

Last year was the 50th anniversary of Conrad's death. He was born in 1857, the very year in which the first Anglican missionaries were arriving among my own people in Nigeria. It was certainly not his fault that he lived his life at a time when the reputation of the black man was at a particularly low level. But even after due allowances have been made for all the influences of contemporary prejudice on his sensibility, there remains still in Conrad's attitude a residue of antipathy to black people which his peculiar psychology alone can explain. His own account of his first encounter with a black man is very revealing:

> A certain enormous buck nigger encountered in Haiti fixed my conception of blind, furious, unreasoning rage, as manifested in the human animal to the end of my days. Of the nigger I used to dream for years afterwards.

Certainly, Conrad had a problem with niggers. His inordinate love of that word itself should be of interest to psychoanalysts. Sometimes his fixation on blackness is equally interesting as when he gives us this brief description:

> A black figure stood up, strode on long black legs, waving long black arms.[7]

as though we might expect a black figure striding along on black legs to have *white* arms! But so unrelenting is Conrad's obsession.

As a matter of interest Conrad gives us in *A Personal Record* what amounts to a companion piece to the buck nigger of Haiti. At the age of sixteen Conrad encountered his first Englishman in Europe. He calls him "my unforgettable Englishman" and describes him in the following manner:

> [his] calves exposed to the public gaze . . . dazzled the beholder by the splendor of their marble-like condition and their rich tone of young ivory. . . . The light of a headlong, exalted satisfaction with the world of men . . . illumined his face . . . and triumphant eyes. In passing he cast a glance of kindly curiosity and a friendly gleam of big, sound, shiny teeth . . . his white calves twinkled sturdily.[8]

Irrational love and irrational hate jostling together in the heart of that tormented man. But whereas

irrational love may at worst engender foolish acts of indiscretion, irrational hate can endanger the life of the community. Naturally, Conrad is a dream for psychoanalytic critics. Perhaps the most detailed study of him in this direction is by Bernard C. Meyer, M.D. In this lengthy book, Dr. Meyer follows every conceivable lead (and sometimes inconceivable ones) to explain Conrad. As an example, he gives us long disquisitions on the significance of hair and hair-cutting in Conrad. And yet not even one word is spared for his attitude to black people. Not even the discussion of Conrad's anti-Semitism was enough to spark off in Dr. Meyer's mind those other dark and explosive thoughts. Which only leads one to surmise that Western psychoanalysts must regard the kind of racism displayed by Conrad as absolutely normal despite the profoundly important work done by Frantz Fanon[9] in the psychiatric hospitals of French Algeria.

Whatever Conrad's problems were, you might say he is now safely dead. Quite true. Unfortunately, his heart of darkness plagues us still. Which is why an offensive and totally deplorable book can be described by a serious scholar as "among the half dozen greatest short novels in the English language," and why it is today perhaps the most commonly prescribed novel in the twentieth-century literature courses in our own English Department here. Indeed the time is long overdue for a hard look at things.

There are two probable grounds on which what I have said so far may be contested. The first is that it is no concern of fiction to please people about whom it is written. I will go along with that. But I am not talking about pleasing people. I am talking about a book which parades in the most vulgar fashion prejudices and insults from which a section of mankind has suffered untold agonies and atrocities in the past and continues to do so in many ways and many places today. I am talking about a story in which the very humanity of black people is called in question. It seems to me totally inconceivable that great art or even good art could possibly reside in such unwholesome surroundings.

[7]Jonah Raskin, *The Mythology of Imperialism* (New York: Random House, 1971), p. 143. [Achebe]

[8]Bernard C. Meyer, M.D., *Joseph Conrad: A Psychoanalytic Biography* (Princeton, N.J.: Princeton University Press, 1967), p. 30. [Achebe]

[9]For more on Fanon, see the introduction to this chapter, p. 1760.

Secondly, I may be challenged on the grounds of actuality. Conrad, after all, sailed down the Congo in 1890 when my own father was still a babe in arms, and recorded what he saw. How could I stand up in 1975, fifty years after his death and purport to contradict him? My answer is that as a sensible man I will not accept just any traveller's tales solely on the grounds that I have not made the journey myself. I will not trust the evidence even of a man's very eyes when I suspect them to be as jaundiced as Conrad's. And we also happen to know that Conrad was, in the words of his biographer, Bernard C. Meyer, "notoriously inaccurate in the rendering of his own history."[10]

But more important by far is the abundant testimony about Conrad's savages which we could gather if we were so inclined from other sources and which might lead us to think that these people must have had other occupations besides merging into the evil forest or materializing out of it simply to plague Marlow and his dispirited band. For as it happened, soon after Conrad had written his book an event of far greater consequence was taking place in the art world of Europe. This is how Frank Willett, a British art historian, describes it:

> Gauguin had gone to Tahiti, the most extravagant individual act of turning to a non-European culture in the decades immediately before and after 1900, when European artists were avid for new artistic experiences, but it was only about 1904–5 that African art began to make its distinctive impact. One piece is still identifiable; it is a mask that had been given to Maurice Vlaminck in 1905. He records that Derain was "speechless" and "stunned" when he saw it, bought it from Vlaminck and in turn showed it to Picasso and Matisse, who were also greatly affected by it. Ambroise Vollard then borrowed it and had it cast in bronze. . . . The revolution of twentieth century art was under way![11]

The mask in question was made by other savages living just north of Conrad's River Congo. They have a name, the Fang people, and are without a doubt among the world's greatest masters of the sculptured form. As you might have guessed, the event to which Frank Willett refers marked the beginning of cubism and the infusion of new life into European art that had run completely out of strength.

The point of all this is to suggest that Conrad's picture of the people of the Congo seems grossly inadequate even at the height of their subjection to the ravages of King Leopold's International Association for the Civilization of Central Africa. Travellers with closed minds can tell us little except about themselves. But even those not blinkered, like Conrad, with xenophobia, can be astonishingly blind.

Let me digress a little here. One of the greatest and most intrepid travellers of all time, Marco Polo, journeyed to the Far East from the Mediterranean in the thirteenth century and spent twenty years in the court of Kublai Khan in China. On his return to Venice he set down in his book entitled *Description of the World* his impressions of the peoples and places and customs he had seen. There are at least two extraordinary omissions in his account. He says nothing about the art of printing unknown as yet in Europe but in full flower in China. He either did not notice it at all or if he did, failed to see what use Europe could possibly have for it. Whatever reason, Europe had to wait another hundred years for Gutenberg. But even more spectacular was Marco Polo's omission of any reference to the Great Wall of China nearly 4,000 miles long and already more than 1,000 years old at the time of his visit. Again, he may not have seen it; but the Great Wall of China is the only structure built by man which is visible from the moon![12] Indeed, travellers can be blind.

As I said earlier, Conrad did not originate the image of Africa which we find in his book. It was and is the dominant image of Africa in the Western imagination and Conrad merely brought the peculiar gifts of his own mind to bear on it. For reasons which can certainly use close psychological inquiry, the West seems to suffer deep anxieties about the precariousness of its civilization and to have a need for constant reassurance

---

[10]Meyer, p. 30. [Achebe]
[11]Frank Willett, *African Art* (New York: Praeger, 1971), pp. 35–36. [Achebe]

[12]About the omission of the Great Wall of China I am indebted to *The Journey of Marco Polo* as recreated by artist Michael Foreman, published by *Pegasus* Magazine, 1974. [Achebe]

by comparing it with Africa. If Europe, advancing in civilization, could cast a backward glance periodically at Africa trapped in primordial barbarity, it could say with faith and feeling: There go I but for the grace of God. Africa is to Europe as the picture is to Dorian Gray — a carrier onto whom the master unloads his physical and moral deformities so that he may go forward, erect and immaculate. Consequently, Africa is something to be avoided just as the picture has to be hidden away to safeguard the man's jeopardous integrity. Keep away from Africa, or else! Mr. Kurtz of *Heart of Darkness* should have heeded that warning and the prowling horror in his heart would have kept its place, chained to its lair. But he foolishly exposed himself to the wild irresistible allure of the jungle and lo! the darkness found him out.

In my original conception of this talk I had thought to conclude it nicely on an appropriately positive note in which I would suggest from my privileged position in African and Western culture some advantages the West might derive from Africa once it rid its mind of old prejudices and began to look at Africa not through a haze of distortions and cheap mystification but quite simply as a continent of people — not angels, but not rudimentary souls either — just people, often highly gifted people and often strikingly successful in their enterprise with life and society. But as I thought more about the stereotype image, about its grip and pervasiveness, about the willful tenacity with which the West holds it to its heart; when I thought of your television and the cinema and newspapers, about books read in schools and out of school, of churches preaching to empty pews about the need to send help to the heathen in Africa, I realized that no easy optimism was possible. And there is something totally wrong in offering bribes to the West in return for its good opinion of Africa. Ultimately, the abandonment of unwholesome thoughts must be its own and only reward. Although I have used the word *willful* a few times in this talk to characterize the West's view of Africa it may well be that what is happening at this stage is more akin to reflex action than calculated malice. Which does not make the situation more, but less, hopeful. Let me give you one last and really minor example of what I mean.

Last November the *Christian Science Monitor* carried an interesting article written by its Education Editor on the serious psychological and learning problems faced by little children who speak one language at home and then go to school where something else is spoken. It was a wide-ranging article taking in Spanish-speaking children in this country, the children of migrant Italian workers in Germany, the quadrilingual phenomenon in Malaysia, and so on. And all this while the article speaks unequivocally about *language*. But then out of the blue sky comes this:

> In London there is an enormous immigration of children who speak Indian or Nigerian dialects, or some other native language.[13]

I believe that the introduction of *dialects*, which is technically erroneous in the context, is almost a reflex action caused by an instinctive desire of the writer to downgrade the discussion to the level of Africa and India. And this is quite comparable to Conrad's withholding of language from his rudimentary souls. Language is too grand for these chaps; let's give them dialects. In all this business a lot of violence is inevitably done to words and their meaning. Look at the phrase "native language" in the above excerpt. Surely the only native language possible in London is Cockney English. But our writer obviously means something else — something Indians and Africans speak.

Perhaps a change will come. Perhaps this is the time when it can begin, when the high optimism engendered by the breathtaking achievements of Western science and industry is giving way to doubt and even confusion. There is just the possibility that Western man may begin to look seriously at the achievements of other people. I read in the papers the other day a suggestion that what America needs at this time is somehow to bring back the extended family. And I saw in my mind's eye future African Peace Corps Volunteers coming to help you set up the system.

Seriously, although the work which needs to be done may appear too daunting, I believe that it is not one day too soon to begin. And where better than at a University?

[13]*Christian Science Monitor*, Nov. 25, 1974, p. 11. [Achebe]

Toni Morrison

b. 1931

The most widely respected and read African American novelist of our time, winner of the 1993 Nobel Prize for Literature, was born Chloe Anthony Wofford, in Loraine, Ohio, in 1931. She was educated at Howard University and at Cornell, from which she received an M.A. in English in 1955. Morrison taught English at Texas Southern University and at Howard, where her students included Claude Brown and Stokely Carmichael. In 1964 she left teaching and began working as an editor for Random House, writing fiction in her spare time. Her novels include The Bluest Eye *(1970),* Sula *(1974),* Song of Solomon *(1977), and* Tar Baby *(1981); she achieved her highest fame and critical success with* Beloved *(1987), which won the Pulitzer Prize for fiction. Her most recent books are* Jazz *(1993),* Birth of a Nation'Hood: Gaze, Script, and Spectacle in the O. J. Simpson Case *(co-ed., 1997),* Paradise *(1998),* The Big Box *(1999), and* Love *(2003). Morrison is also writing a series of illustrated children's books (*The Big Box, The Book of Mean People, *etc.) under the collective title* Who's Got Game? *In 1984 Morrison was appointed to the Albert Schweitzer Chair in Letters at the State University of New York at Albany. The present selection is from Morrison's first book of literary criticism,* Playing in the Dark: Whiteness and the Literary Imagination *(1992).*

From *Playing in the Dark: Whiteness and the Literary Imagination*

I have been thinking for some time now about the validity or vulnerability of a certain set of assumptions conventionally accepted among literary historians and critics and circulated as "knowledge." This "knowledge" holds that traditional, canonical American literature is free of, uninformed by, and unshaped by the four-hundred-year-old presence of first Africans and then African Americans in the United States. It assumes that this presence — which shaped the body politic, the Constitution, and the entire history of the culture — has had no significant place or consequence in the origin and development of that culture's literature. Moreover, it assumes that the characteristics of our national literature emanate from a particular "Americanness" that is separate from and unaccountable to this presence. There seems to be a more or less tacit agreement among literary scholars that because American literature has been clearly the preserve of white male views, genius, and power, those views, genius, and power are removed from and without relationship to the presence of black people in the United States — a population that antedated every American writer of renown and was perhaps the most furtively radical, impinging force on the country's literature.

I am convinced that the contemplation of this black presence is central to any understanding of our national literature and should not be relegated to the margins of the literary imagination. Furthermore, American literature distinguishes itself as a coherent entity because of and in reference to this unsettled and unsettling population. I have begun to wonder whether the major, much celebrated themes of American literature — individualism, masculinity, the conflict between social engagement and historical isolation, an acute and ambiguous moral problematic, the juxtaposition of innocence with figures representing death and hell — are not in fact responses to a dark, abiding, signing Africanistic presence. The coded language and purposeful restriction by which the newly formed nation dealt with the racial disingenuousness and moral frailty at its heart are maintained in its literature, even through the twentieth century. A real or fabricated Africanistic presence has been crucial to writers' sense of their Americanness. And it shows: through significant and underscored omissions, startling contradictions, heavily nuanced conflicts, and the way their work is peopled with the signs and bodies of this presence.

My curiosity has developed into a still-informal study of what I am calling American Africanism. It is an investigation into the ways in which a nonwhite, Africanistic presence was constructed in the United States, and the imaginative uses this fabricated presence served. I am using the term "Africanism" as a term for the denotative and connotative blackness African peoples have come to signify, as well as the entire range of views, assumptions, readings, and misreadings that characterize these peoples in Eurocentric eyes. It is important to recognize the lack of restraint attached to the uses of this trope. As a disabling virus within literary discourse, Africanism has become, in the Eurocentric tradition favored by American education, both a way of talking about and a way of policing matters of class, sexual license and repression, the formation and exercise of power, ethics, and accountability.

What Africanism became and how it functioned in the literary imagination are of paramount interest because it may be possible to discover, through a close look at literary "blackness," the nature and even the source of literary "whiteness." What is it *for*? What parts do the invention and development of "whiteness" play in the construction of what is described as an "American"? If this inquiry of mine ever comes to maturity, it may provide me access to a coherent reading of American literature, a reading that is not completely available to me now — at least, I suspect, because of the studied indifference of literary criticism to these matters.

One likely reason for the paucity of critical material on this large and compelling subject is that in matters of race, silence and evasion have historically ruled literary discourse. Evasion has fostered another, substitute language in which the issues are encoded and made unavailable for open debate. The situation is aggravated by the anxiety that breaks into discourse on race. It is further complicated by the fact that ignoring race is understood to be a graceful, liberal, even generous habit. To notice is to recognize an already discredited difference; to maintain its invisibility through silence is to allow the black body a shadowless participation in the dominant cultural body. Following this logic, every well-bred instinct argues against noticing and forecloses adult discourse. It is just this concept of literary and scholarly *moeurs* (which functions smoothly in literary criticism, but neither makes nor receives credible claims in other disciplines) that has terminated the shelf life of some once extremely well-regarded American authors and blocked access to the remarkable insights some of their works contain.

Another reason for this ornamental vacuum in literary discourse is the pattern of thinking about racialism asymmetrically, in terms of its consequences on its victims alone. A good deal of time and intelligence have been invested in exposing racialism and its horrific effects on its objects. The result has been constant, if erratic, efforts to legislate preventive regulations. There have also been powerful and persuasive attempts to analyze the origin of racialism itself, contesting the assumption that it is an inevitable and permanent part of all social landscapes. I do not wish to disparage these inquiries in any way. It is precisely because of them that any progress has been accomplished in matters of racial discourse. But I do want to see that well-established study joined by another, equally important: the effect of racialism on those who perpetuate it. It seems to me both poignant and striking how the effect of racialism on the subject has been avoided and left unanalyzed. The scholarship that looks into the mind, the imagination, and the behavior of slaves is valuable; equally so is a serious intellectual examination of what racial ideology did and does to the mind, the imagination, the behavior of the master.

National literatures, like writers, get along as best they can and with what they can. Yet they do seem to end up describing and inscribing what is really on the national mind. For the most part, literature of the United States has taken as its concern the architecture of a *new white man*. If I am disenchanted with the indifference of literary criticism toward examining the nature of that concern, I do have a last resort: the writers themselves.

What happens when literature tries to imagine an Africanistic Other? What does the inclusion of Africans and African Americans do to and for the work? As a reader, I had always assumed that nothing "happens." That Africans and their descendants are *there* in no sense that matters; that when they are *there*, they are decorative displays of the facile writer's technical expertise. I assumed that since the author was not Africanistic, the appearance of Africanistic characters or narrative or idiom in his or her work could never be *about* anything other than the "normal," unracialized, illusory, white world that provides the backdrop for the work. Certainly no American fiction of the sort I am discussing was ever written *for* black people, any more than *Uncle Tom's Cabin* was written for Uncle Tom to read or be persuaded by. As a writer reading, I realized the obvious: that the subject of the dream is the dreamer. The fabrication of an Africanistic persona was reflexive; it was an extraordinary meditation on the self, a powerful exploration of the fears and desires that reside in the writerly consciousness, an astonishing revelation of longing, of terror, of perplexity, of shame, of magnanimity.

Rereading canonical American literature as a writer provided me an access to it unavailable to me before I began to write. It was as though I had been looking at a fishbowl, seeing the glide and flick of the golden scales, the green tip, and bolt of white careening back from the gills, the castles at the bottom, surrounded by pebbles and tiny, intricate fronds of green, the barely disturbed water, the flecks of waste and food, the tranquil bubbles traveling to the surface — and suddenly I saw the bowl itself, the structure transparently, invisibly, permitting the ordered life it contained to exist in the larger world. In other words, I began to rely on my knowledge of how books get written, how language arrives, on my sense of how and why writers abandon or take on certain aspects of their project. I began to rely on my understanding of what the linguistic struggle requires of writers and what they make of the surprise that is the inevitable, necessary concomitant of the act of creation. What became transparent were the self-evident ways Americans chose to talk about themselves through and within a sometimes allegorical, sometimes metaphorical, but always choked representation of an Africanistic presence.

Young America distinguished itself by pressing with full awareness toward a future, a freedom, a kind of human dignity believed to be unprecedented in the world. A whole tradition of "universal" yearnings collapsed into that well-fondled phrase "The American Dream." While the immigrants' dream deserves the exhaustive scrutiny it has received in the scholarly disciplines and the arts, it is just as important to know what these people were rushing from as it is to know what they were hastening to. If the New World fed dreams, what was the Old World reality that whetted the appetite for them? And how might that reality caress and grip the shaping of a new one?

The flight from the Old World to the New is generally understood to be a flight from oppression and limitation to freedom and possibility. In fact, for some the escape was a flight from license — from a society perceived to be unacceptably permissive, ungodly, and undisciplined. For those fleeing for reasons other than religious ones, however, constraint and limitation impelled the journey. The Old World offered these emigrants only poverty, prison, social ostracism, and not infrequently death. There was, of course, another group of immigrants who came for the adventures possible in founding a colony for rather than against one or another mother country or fatherland. And of course there were the merchants, who came for the cash.

To all of these people, the attraction was of the "clean slate" variety, a once-in-a-lifetime opportunity not only to be born again, but to be born again in new clothes, as it were: the new setting would provide new raiments of self. The New World offered the vision of a limitless future that gleamed more brightly against the constraint, dissatisfaction, and turmoil being left behind. A promise genuinely promising. With luck and endurance one could discover freedom, find a way to make God's law manifest in Man, or end up rich as a prince. The desire for freedom is preceded by oppression; a yearning for God's law is born of the detestation of man's license and corruption; the glamour of riches is in thrall to poverty, hunger, and debt.

There was much more to make the trip worth the risk. The habit of genuflection would be replaced by the thrill of command. Power — control of one's own destiny — would replace the powerlessness felt before the gates of class, caste, and cunning persecution. One could move from discipline and punishment to disciplining and punishing; from being socially ostracized to becoming an arbiter of social rank. One could be released from a useless, binding, repulsive past into a kind of historylessness — a blank page waiting to be inscribed. Much was to be written there: noble impulses were made into law and appropriated for a national tradition, but so were base ones, learned and elaborated in the rejected and rejecting homeland.

The body of literature produced by the young nation is one place it inscribed these fears, forces, and hopes. It is difficult to read the literature of young America without being struck by how antithetical it is to our modern conception of the "American Dream," how pronounced is the absence of that term's elusive mixture of hope, realism, materialism, and promise. Coming from a people who made much of their "newness" — their potential, their freedom, their innocence — it is striking how dour, how troubled, how frightened, and how haunted the early, founding literature truly is.

We have words and labels for this haunting — "gothic," "romantic," "sermonic," "Puritan" — whose sources are, of course, to be found in the literature of the world from which they fled. And the strong affinity between the nineteenth-century American psyche and gothic romance has, rightly, been much remarked upon. It is not surprising that a young country, repelled by Europe's moral and social disorder and swooning in a fit of desire and rejection, would devote its talents to reproducing in its own literature the typology of diabolism from which its citizens and their fathers had escaped. After all, one way to benefit from the lessons of earlier mistakes and past misfortunes was to record them — in inoculation against their repetition, as it were.

Romance was the form in which this uniquely American prophylaxis was played out. Long after it had faded in Europe, romance remained the cherished expression of young America. What was there in American romanticism that made it so attractive to Americans as a battle plain upon which to fight, to engage, to imagine their demons?

It has been suggested that romance is an evasion of history, and thus perhaps attractive to a people trying to erase the recent past. But I am more persuaded by arguments that find in it the head-on encounter with very real, very pressing historical forces and the contradictions inherent in them, as these come to be experienced by writers. Romance, an exploration of anxiety imported from the shadows of European culture, made possible the embrace — sometimes safe, other times risky — of some quite specific, understandably human, American fears: the fear of being outcast, of failing, of powerlessness; of boundarylessness, of Nature unbridled and crouched for attack; of the absence of so-called civilization; of loneliness, of aggression both external and internal. In short, the terror of human freedom — the thing they coveted most of all. Romance offered writers not less but more; not a narrow historical canvas but a wide historical one; not escape but engagement. It offered platforms for moralizing and fabulation, and for the imaginative entertainment of violence, sublime incredibility, and terror — whose most significant, overweening ingredient was darkness, with all the connotative value it contained.

There is no romance free of what Melville called "the power of blackness," especially not in a country in which there was a resident population, already black, upon which the imagination could articulate the fears, the dilemmas, the divisions that obsessed it historically, morally, metaphysically, and socially. This slave population seemed to volunteer itself as objects for meditation on the lure and elusiveness of human freedom, on the outcast's terror and his dread of failure, of powerlessness, Nature without limits, inborn loneliness, internal aggression, evil, sin, greed . . . ; in other words, on human freedom in all terms except those of human potential and the rights of man.

And yet the rights of man, an organizing principle upon which the nation was founded, was inevitably, and especially, yoked to Africanism. Its history and origin are permanently allied with another seductive concept — the hierarchy of race. As the sociologist Orlando Patterson has noted, we should not be surprised that the Enlightenment could accommodate slavery; we should be surprised if it could not. The concept of freedom did not emerge in a vacuum. Nothing highlighted — or perhaps, in fact, created — freedom as slavery did.

In that construction of blackness and enslavement could be found not only the not-free but also the projection of the not-me. The result was a playground for the imagination. And what rose up out of collective needs to allay internal fears and rationalize external exploitation was an Africanism — a fabricated brew of darkness, otherness, alarm, and desire — that is uniquely American. (There also exists a European Africanism with its counterpart in its own colonial literature.)

What I wish to examine is how the image of reined-in, bound, suppressed, and repressed darkness became objectified in American literature as an Africanistic persona. I want to show how the duties of that persona — duties of mirroring and embodying and exorcism — are demanded and displayed throughout much of the national literature and help provide its distinguishing characteristics.

I pointed out that cultural identities are formed and informed by a nation's literature. What seemed to be on the "mind" of the literature of the United States was the self-conscious but highly problematic construction of the American as a new white man. Emerson's call for that new man, "The American Scholar," indicates the deliberateness of the construction, the conscious necessity for establishing difference. But the writers who responded to this call, accepting or rejecting it, did not look solely to Europe to establish a reference for difference. There was a very theatrical difference underfoot. Writers were able to celebrate or deplore an identity — already existing or rapidly taking form — that was elaborated through racial difference. That difference provided a huge trove of signs, symbols, and agencies for organizing, separating, and consolidating identity along valuable lines of interest.

The historian Bernard Bailyn has provided us with an extraordinary investigation of European settlers in the act of becoming Americans. Particularly relevant is a description in his *Voyagers to the West.* One long passage from that book will help to clarify and underscore the salient aspects of this American character I have been describing:

William Dunbar, seen through his letters and diary, appears to be more fictional than real. . . . He . . . was a man in his early twenties who appeared suddenly in the Mississippi wilderness to stake out a claim to a large parcel of land, then disappeared to the Caribbean to return leading a battalion of "wild" slaves with whose labor alone he built an estate where before there had been nothing but trees and uncultivated soil. He was . . . complex . . . and . . . part of a violent biracial world whose tensions could lead in strange directions. For this wilderness planter was a scientist, who would later correspond with Jefferson on science and exploration, a Mississippi planter whose contributions to the American Philosophical Society . . . included linguistics, archeology, hydrostatics, astronomy, and climatology, and whose geographical explorations were reported in widely known publications. . . . An exotic figure in the plantation world of early Mississippi . . . he imported into that raw, half-savage world the niceties of European culture: not chandeliers and costly rugs, but books, surveyor's equipment of the finest kind, and the latest instruments of science.

Dunbar was . . . educated first by tutors at home, then at the university in Aberdeen where his interest in mathematics, astronomy, and belles-lettres took mature shape. What happened to him after his return home and later in London, where he circulated with young intellectuals, what propelled, or led, him out of the metropolis on the first leg of his long voyage west is not known. But whatever his motivation may have been, in April 1771, aged only twenty-two, Dunbar appeared in Philadelphia. . . .

Ever eager for gentility, this well-educated product of the Scottish enlightenment and of London's sophistication — this bookish young *littérateur* and scientist, who, only five years earlier, had been corresponding about scientific problems — about "Dean Swifts beatitudes," about the "virtuous and happy life," and about the Lord's commandment that mankind should "love one another" — was strangely insensitive to the suffering of those who served him. In July 1776 he recorded not the independence of the American colonies from Britain, but the suppression of an alleged conspiracy for freedom by slaves on his own plantation. . . .

Dunbar, the young *érudit*, the Scottish scientist and man of letters, was no sadist. His plantation regime was, by the standards of the time, mild; he clothed and fed his slaves decently, and frequently relented in his more severe punishments. But 4,000 miles from the sources of culture, alone on the far periphery of British civilization where physical survival was a daily struggle, where ruthless exploitation was a way of life, and where disorder, violence, and human degradation were commonplace, he had triumphed by successful adaptation. Endlessly enterprising and resourceful, his finer sensibilities dulled by the abrasions of frontier life, and feeling within himself a sense of authority and autonomy he had not known before, a force that flowed from his absolute control over the lives of others, he emerged a distinctive new man, a borderland gentleman, a man of property in a raw, half-savage world.

In this portrait, this narrative of William Dunbar, some elements, some pairings and interdependencies, are particularly noteworthy. First, the historical connection between the Enlightenment and the institution of slavery — the rights of man and his enslavement. Second, the relationship of Dunbar's education and his new world enterprise. His education was exceptionally cultivated and included the latest thoughts on theology and science — in an effort perhaps to make them mutually accountable, to make each support the other. He is a product not only of "the Scottish enlightenment" but also of "London's sophistication." He reads Swift, discusses the Christian commandment to "love one another," and is described as "strangely" insensitive to the suffering of his slaves. On July 12, 1776, he records with astonishment and hurt the slave rebellion on his plantation: "Judge my surprise. . . . Of what avail is kindness and good usage when rewarded by such ingratitude." "Constantly bewildered," Bailyn goes on, "by his slaves' behavior . . . [Dunbar] recovered two runaways and 'condemned them to receive 500 lashes each at five dif[feren]t times, and to carry a chain & log fixt to the ancle.'" I take this to be a succinct portrait of the process by which the American as new, white, and male was constituted. It is a formation that has several attractive consequences, all of which are referred to in Bailyn's summation of Dunbar's character and located in how Dunbar feels "within himself" — "a power, a sense of freedom he had not known before." But what had he "known before"? Fine education, London sophistication, theological and scientific thought. None of these, one gathers, could provide him with the authority and autonomy Mississippi planter life did. His "sense" is a "force" that "flows": not a willed domination, a thought-out, calculated choice, but rather a kind of natural resource, already present, a Niagara Falls waiting to spill over as soon as he is in a position to possess "absolute control over the lives of others." And once he has moved into that position, he is resurrected as a new man, a distinctive man, a different man. Whatever his social status in London, in the New World he is a gentleman. More gentle; more man. Why? Because the site of his transformation is within rawness. He is backgrounded by savagery.

Autonomy, newness, difference, authority, absolute power: these are the major themes and concerns of American literature, and each one is made possible, shaped, and activated by a complex awareness and use of a constituted Africanism that, deployed as rawness and savagery, provided the staging ground and arena for the elaboration of the quintessential American identity.

Autonomy — freedom — translates into the much championed and revered "individualism"; newness translates into "innocence"; distinctiveness becomes difference and strategies for maintaining it; authority becomes a romantic, conquering "heroism" and "virility" and raises the problematics of wielding absolute power over the lives of others. These four are made possible, finally, by the fifth: absolute power called forth and acted out against, upon, and within a natural and mental landscape conceived of as a "raw, half-savage world."

Why "raw and savage"? Because it is peopled by a nonwhite indigenous population? Perhaps. But certainly because there is readily at hand a bound and unfree, rebellious but serviceable black population by which Dunbar and all white men are enabled to measure these privileging and privileged differences.

Eventually individualism will lead to a prototype of Americans as solitary, alienated malcontents. What, one wants to ask, are Americans alienated from? What are Americans always so insistently innocent of? Different from? And over whom is absolute power held, from whom withheld, to whom distributed?

Answers to these questions lie in the potent and ego-reinforcing presence of an Africanistic population. The new white male can now persuade himself that savagery is "out there": that the lashes ordered (five hundred, applied five times, equals twenty-five hundred) are not one's own savagery; that repeated and dangerous breaks for freedom are "puzzling" confirmations of black irrationality; that the combination of Dean Swift's beatitudes and a life of regularized violence is civilized; that, if sensibilities are dulled enough, the rawness remains external.

The imaginative and historical terrain upon which early American writers journey is in very large measure shaped and determined by the presence of the racial Other. Statements to the contrary insisting upon the meaninglessness of race to American identity are themselves full of meaning. The world does not become raceless or will not become unracialized by assertion. The act of enforcing racelessness in literary discourse is itself a racial act. Pouring rhetorical acid on the fingers of a black hand may indeed destroy the prints, but not the hand. Besides, what happens, in that violent, self-serving act of erasure, to the hands, the fingers, the fingerprints of the one who does the pouring? Do they remain acid-free? The literature itself suggests otherwise.

Explicit or implicit, the Africanistic presence is a deep and abiding one that serves the literary imagination as both a visible and an invisible mediating force. So that even and especially, when American texts are not "about" Africanistic presences, or characters, or narrative, or idiom, their shadows hover there, implied, signified, as boundaries. It is no accident and no mistake that immigrant populations (and much immigrant literature) understood their "Americanness" as an opposition to the resident population. Race, in fact, now functions as a metaphor so necessary to the construction of "Americanness" that it rivals the old pseudoscientific and class-informed racialisms whose dynamics we are more used to deciphering.

As a means of transacting the whole process of Americanization while burying its particular racial ingredients, this Africanistic presence may be something the United States cannot do without. For in this part of the twentieth century, the word *American* contains its profound association with race. This is not true of *Canadian* or *English*. To identify someone as *South African* is to say very little; we need the adjective "white" or "black" or "colored" to make our meaning clear. In the United States it is quite the reverse. *American* means *white*, and Africanistic people struggle to make the terms applicable to themselves with ethnicity and hyphens. Americans did not have an immanent nobility from which to wrest and against which to define an identity of national virtue while continuing to covet aristocratic license and luxury. The American nation negotiated both its disdain and its envy in the same way Dunbar did: through a self-reflexive contemplation of fabricated, mythological Africanism. For Dunbar, and for American writers generally, this Africanistic Other became the means of thinking about the body, mind, chaos, kindness, and love; became the occasion for exercises in the absence of restraint, the presence of restraint, the contemplation of freedom, of aggression; for the exploration of ethics and morality, for meeting the obligations of the social contract, for bearing the cross of religion and following out the ramifications of power.

Reading and charting the emergence of an Africanistic persona in the development of a national literature is both a fascinating project and an urgent one, if the history and criticism of our literature are to become coherent. Emerson's plea for intellectual independence was like the offer of an empty plate that writers could fill with nourishment from an indigenous kitchen. The language was, of course, to be English, but the content of the language, its subject, was to be deliberately, insistently un-English and anti-European, insofar as it rhetorically repudiated an adoration of the Old World and defined the past as corrupt and indefensible.

The necessity for establishing difference stemmed not only from the Old World but from a difference within the New. What was distinctive in the New was, first of all, its claim to freedom and, second, the presence of the unfree at the heart of the democratic experiment — the critical absence of democracy, its echo, its shadow, its silence, and its silent force in the political and intellectual activity of some not-Americans. The distinguishing features of the not-Americans were their slave status, their social status — and their color. It is conceivable that the first would have self-destructed in a variety of ways had it not been for the last. These slaves, unlike many others in the world's history, were visible to a fault. And they had inherited, among other things, a long history of the "meaning" of color. It was not simply that this slave population had a distinctive color; it was that this color "meant" something. This "meaning" had been named and deployed by scholars from at least the moment, in the eighteenth century, when other and sometimes the same scholars investigated both the natural history and the inalienable rights of man — that is to say, human freedom.

One supposes that if Africans all had three eyes, or one ear, the significance of that difference from the smaller but conquering European invaders would also have been found to have "meaning." In any case, the subjective nature of ascribing value and meaning to color cannot be questioned this late in the twentieth century. What matters is the alliance of "visually rendered ideas with linguistic utterances," which leads us to the social and political nature of received knowledge.

Knowledge, however mundane and utilitarian, creates linguistic images and cultural practices. Responding to culture — clarifying, explicating, valorizing, translating, transforming, critiquing — is what artists everywhere do, and this is especially true of writers involved in the development of a literature at the founding of a new nation. Whatever were their personal and formally "political" responses to the "problem" inherent in the contradiction of a free republic deeply committed to a slave population, nineteenth-century writers were mindful of the presence of these blacks. More importantly, they addressed, in more or less passionate ways, their views on that difficult presence.

Awareness of this slave population did not confine itself to the personal encounters writers may have had. The publication of slave narratives was a nineteenth-century publication boom. The discussion of slavery and freedom filled the press, as well as the campaigns and policies of political parties and elected government. One would have to have been isolated indeed to be unaware of the most explosive issue in the nation. How could one speak of profit, economy, labor, progress, suffragism, Christianity, the frontier, the formation of new states, the acquisition of new lands, education, transportation (freight and passengers), neighborhoods, quarters, the military — practically anything a country concerns itself with — without having as a referent, at the heart of the discourse, at the heart definition, the presence of Africans and their descendants?

It was not possible. And it did not happen. What did happen, frequently, was an effort to talk about these things with a vocabulary designed to disguise the subject. This did not always succeed, and in the work of many writers disguise was never intended. But the consequence was a master narrative that spoke *for* the African and his descendants, or *of* him. The legislator's narrative could not coexist with a response from the Africanistic persona.

Whatever popularity the slave narratives had — and they inspired abolitionists and converted antiabolitionists — the slaves' own narrative, while freeing the narrator in many ways, did not destroy the master narrative. That latter narrative could accommodate many shifts, could make any number of adjustments to keep itself intact. Silence from and about the subject was the order of the day. Some of the silences were broken and some maintained by authors who lived with and within the policing narrative. I am interested in the strategies for maintaining the silence and for breaking it. How did the founding writers of young America create and employ an Africanistic presence and persona? How does excavating these pathways lead to fresher, more profound analyses of what they contain and how they contain it?

Let me take one example: a major American novel that is both an example and a critique of romance as a genre. If we supplement our reading of *Huckleberry Finn*, expand it, move beyond its clutch of sentimental nostrums about lighting out to the territory, river gods, and the fundamental innocence of Americanness; if we incorporate into our reading the novel's combative critique of antebellum America, thus shedding much light on the problems created by traditional readings too shy to linger over the implications of the Africanistic presence at its center, it seems to be another, somehow fuller novel. We understand that at a certain level, the critique of class and race is there, although disguised or enhanced through a combination of humor, adventure, and the naive.

Twain's readers are free to dismiss the novel's combative, contestatory qualities and focus on its celebration of savvy innocence, while voicing polite embarrassment at the symptomatic racial attitude it espouses. Early criticism, those reappraisals in the fifties that led to the canonization of *Huckleberry Finn* as a great novel, missed or dismissed the social quarrel because the work appears to have fully assimilated the ideological assumptions of its society and culture; because it is narrated in the voice and controlled by the gaze of a child without status — an outsider, marginal and already "othered" by the middle-class society he loathes and seems never to envy; and because the novel masks itself in the comic, the parody and exaggeration of the tall tale.

In this young but street-smart innocent, Huck, who is virginally uncorrupted by bourgeois yearnings, fury, and helplessness, Mark Twain inscribes the critique of slavery and the pretensions of the would-be middle class, the resistance to the loss of Eden, and the difficulty of becoming that oxymoron, "a social individual." The agency for Huck's struggle, however, is the nigger Jim, and it is absolutely necessary that the term *nigger* be inextricable from Huck's deliberations about who and what he himself is. Or, more precisely, is not. The major controversies about the greatness or near-greatness of *Huckleberry Finn* as an American (or even "world") novel exist as controversies because they forgo a close examination of the interdependence of slavery and freedom, of Huck's growth and Jim's serviceability within it, and even of Twain's inability to continue, to explore the journey into free territory.

The critical controversy focuses on the collapse of the so-called "fatal" ending of the novel. It has been suggested that the ending is a brilliant finesse that returns Tom Sawyer to center stage where he should be. That it is a brilliant play on the dangers and limitations of romance. That it is a valuable learning experience for Jim and for Huck for which we and they should be grateful. That it is a sad and confused ending to a book that the author, after a long blocked period, did not know what to do with and so changed it back to a child's story out of disgust. What is not stressed is that there is no way, given the confines of the novel, for Huck to mature into a moral human being in America without Jim, and therefore that to let Jim go free, to let him *not* miss the mouth of the Ohio River and passage into free territory, would be to abandon the whole premise of the book.

Neither Huck nor Twain can tolerate in imaginative terms Jim freed. To do so would blast the predilection from its mooring. Thus the "fatal" ending becomes an elaborate deferment of a necessary and necessarily unfree Africanistic character's escape, because freedom has no meaning to Huck or the novel without the specter of enslavement, the anodyne to individualism, the yardstick of absolute power over the life of another: the signed, marked, informing, and mutating presence of a black slave. The novel addresses at every point in its structural edifice, and lingers over in every fissure, the slave's body and personality: the way it spoke, what passion, legal or illicit, it was prey to, what pain it could endure, what limits, if any, there were to its suffering, what possibilities there were for forgiveness, for compassion, for love.

Two things strike us in this novel: the apparently limitless store of love and compassion the black man has for his white masters, and his assumptions that the whites are indeed what they say they are — superior and adult. This representation of Jim as the visible Other can be read as white yearning for forgiveness and love, but the yearning is made possible only when it is understood that the black man has recognized his inferiority (not as a slave but as a black) and despised it; that, as Jim is made to, he has permitted his persecutors to torment and humiliate him, and responds to the torment and humiliation with boundless love. The humiliation Huck and Tom subject Jim to is baroque, endless, foolish, mind-softening — and it comes *after* we have experienced Jim as an adult, a caring father, and a sensitive man. If Jim had been a white ex-convict befriended by Huck, the ending could not have been imagined or written because it would not have been possible for two children to play so painfully with the life of a white man (regardless of his class, education, or fugitiveness) once he had been revealed to us as a moral adult. Jim's slave status makes the "play and deferment" possible, and also actualizes, in its style and mode of narration, the significance of slavery to the achievement (in actual terms) of freedom. Jim seems unassertive, loving, irrational, passionate, dependent, inarticulate (except for the "talks" he and Huck have, long sweet talks we are not privy to. What did you talk about, Huck?). What should solicit our attention is not what Jim *seems*, but what Twain, Huck, and especially Tom need from him. *Huckleberry Finn* is indeed "great," because in its structure, in what hell it puts its readers through at the end, the frontal debate it forces, it simulates and describes the parasitical nature of white freedom.

My suggestion that Africanism has come to have a metaphysical necessity should in no way be understood to imply that it has lost its ideological one. There is still much ill-gotten gain to reap from rationalizing power grabs and clutches with inferences of inferiority and the ranking of differences. There is still much national solace in continuing dreams of democratic egalitarianism to be gained by hiding class conflict, rage, and impotence in figurations of race. And there is quite a lot of juice to be extracted from plummy reminiscences of "individualism" and "freedom" if the tree upon which such fruit hangs is a black population forced to serve as freedom's polar opposite. "Individualism" is foregrounded and believed in when its background is stereotyped, enforced dependency. "Freedom" (to move, to earn, to learn, to be allied with a powerful center, to narrate the world) can be relished more deeply cheek by jowl with the bound and the unfree, the economically oppressed, the marginalized, the

silenced. The ideological dependence on racialism is intact.

Surely, it will be said, white Americans have considered questions of morality and ethics, the supremacy of mind and the vulnerability of body, the blessings and liabilities of progress and modernity, without reference to the situation of its black population. Where, it will be asked, does one find the record that such a referent was part of these deliberations?

My answer to this question is another one: In what public discourse can the reference to black people be said not to exist? It is there in every moment of the nation's mightiest struggles. The presence of black people not only lies behind the framing of the Constitution, it is also in the battle over enfranchising unpropertied citizens, women, and the illiterate. In the construction of a free and public school system, in the balancing of representation in legislative bodies, in jurisprudence and the legal definitions of justice. In theological discourse, in the memoranda of banking houses, in the concept of Manifest Destiny and the narrative that accompanies the initiation of every immigrant into the community of American citizenship.

The literature of the United States, like its history, illustrates and represents the transformations of biological, ideological, and metaphysical concepts of racial differences. But literature has an additional concern and subject matter: the private imagination interacting with the external world it inhabits. Literature redistributes and mutates in figurative language the social conventions of Africanism. In minstrelsy, a layer of blackness applied to a white face released it from law. Just as entertainers, through blackface, could render permissible topics that would otherwise have been taboo, so American writers have been able to employ an imagined Africanistic persona to articulate and imaginatively act out the forbidden in American culture.

Encoded or implicit, indirect or overt, the linguistic responses to an Africanisitic presence complicate the texts, sometimes contradicting them entirely. They can serve as allegorical fodder for the contemplation of Eden, expulsion, and the availability of grace. They provide paradox, ambiguity; they reveal omissions, repetitions, disruptions, polarities, reifications, violence. In other words, they give the texts a deeper, richer, more complex life than the sanitized one commonly presented to us. It would be a pity if criticism of this literature continued to shellac these

texts, immobilizing their complexities and power beneath its tight, reflecting surface. It would be a pity if the criticism remained too polite or too fearful to notice a disrupting darkness before its eyes.

Edward W. Said
1935–2003

Although his early writings focused on the usefulness of Continental philosophy and interdisciplinary approaches to literary studies, Edward W. Said's work increasingly dealt with questions of the relation of literary criticism to international politics. Said was born in 1935 in Jerusalem, and attended Western schools in Jerusalem, Cairo, and Massachusetts before receiving degrees at Princeton and Harvard. Beginning in 1963 he was a professor of English and comparative literature at Columbia University and a visiting professor at Yale, Stanford, Harvard, and Johns Hopkins Universities. From the late 1980s until his death, Said often appeared on news programs as a moderate and articulate spokesman for the Palestinian people. His book Orientalism *(1978) was a runner-up for a National Book Award for criticism. His other books include* Joseph Conrad and the Fiction of Autobiography *(1966),* Beginnings: Intention and Method *(1975),* The Question of Palestine *(1979),* The World, the Text, and the Critic *(1983),* After the Last Sky: Palestinian Lives *(1986),* Blaming the Victims *(1988),* Culture and Imperialism *(1993),* Peace and Its Discontents *(1996),* Covering Islam *(1997),* Reflections on Exile *(2000),* Parallels and Paradoxes *(2002, with Daniel Barenboim), and* Humanism and Democratic Criticism *and* From Oslo to Iraq *(both published posthumously in 2004). The following selection is from the introduction to* Orientalism.

From the Introduction to *Orientalism*

II

I have begun with the assumption that the Orient is not an inert fact of nature. It is not merely *there*, just as the Occident itself is not just *there* either. We must take seriously Vico's[1] great observation that men make their own history, that what they can know is what they have made, and extend it to geography: as both geographical and cultural

entities — to say nothing of historical entities — such locales, regions, geographical sectors as "Orient" and "Occident" are manmade. Therefore as much as the West itself, the Orient is an idea that has a history and a tradition of thought, imagery, and vocabulary that have given it reality and presence in and for the West. The two geographical entities thus support and to an extent reflect each other.

Having said that, one must go on to state a number of reasonable qualifications. In the first place, it would be wrong to conclude that the Orient was *essentially* an idea, or a creation with

[1]The *Scienza nuova* (1725) of Italian philosopher Giambattista Vico (1668–1744) presented a theory of historical evolution of cultures.

no corresponding reality. When Disraeli said in his novel *Tancred* that the East was a career,[2] he meant that to be interested in the East was something bright young Westerners would find to be an all-consuming passion; he should not be interpreted as saying that the East was *only* a career for Westerners. There were — and are — cultures and nations whose location is in the East, and their lives, histories, and customs have a brute reality obviously greater than anything that could be said about them in the West. About that fact this study of Orientalism has very little to contribute, except to acknowledge it tacitly. But the phenomenon of Orientalism as I study it here deals principally, not with a correspondence between Orientalism and Orient, but with the internal consistency of Orientalism and its ideas about the Orient (the East as career) despite or beyond any correspondence, or lack thereof, with a "real" Orient. My point is that Disraeli's statement about the East refers mainly to that created consistency, that regular constellation of ideas as that pre-eminent thing about the Orient, and not to its mere being, as Wallace Stevens's phrase has it.[3]

A second qualification is that ideas, cultures, and histories cannot seriously be understood or studied without their force, or more precisely their configurations of power, also being studied. To believe that the Orient was created — or, as I call it, "Orientalized" — and to believe that such things happen simply as a necessity of the imagination, is to be disingenuous. The relationship between Occident and Orient is a relationship of power, of domination, of varying degrees of a complex hegemony, and is quite accurately indicated in the title of K. M. Panikkar's classic *Asia and Western Dominance*.[4] The Orient was Orientalized not only because it was discovered to be "Oriental" in all those ways considered commonplace by an average nineteenth-century European, but also because it *could be* — that is,

submitted to being — *made* Oriental. There is very little consent to be found, for example, in the fact that Flaubert's encounter with an Egyptian courtesan produced a widely influential model of the Oriental woman; she never spoke of herself, she never represented her emotions, presence, or history. *He* spoke for and represented her. He was foreign, comparatively wealthy, male, and these were historical facts of domination that allowed him not only to posses Kuchuk Hanem physically but to speak for her and tell his readers in what way she was "typically Oriental." My argument is that Flaubert's situation of strength in relation to Kuchuk Hanem was not an isolated instance. It fairly stands for the pattern of relative strength between East and West, and the discourse about the Orient that it enabled.[5]

This brings us to a third qualification. One ought never to assume that the structure of Orientalism is nothing more than a structure of lies or of myths which, were the truth about them to be told, would simply blow away. I myself believe that Orientalism is more particularly valuable as a sign of European-Atlantic power over the Orient than it is as a veridic discourse about the Orient (which is what, in its academic or scholarly form, it claims to be). Nevertheless, what we must respect and try to grasp is the sheer knitted-together strength of Orientalist discourse, its very close ties to the enabling socio-economic and political institutions, and its redoubtable durability. After all, any system of ideas that can remain unchanged as teachable wisdom (in academies, books, congresses, universities, foreign-service institutes) from the period of Ernest Renan[6] in the late 1840s until the present in the United States must be something more formidable than a mere collection of lies. Orientalism, therefore, is not an airy European fantasy about the Orient, but a created body of theory and practice in which, for

[2]British prime minister and novelist Benjamin Disraeli (1804–1871) wrote *Tancred* as part of his Condition of England trilogy in 1847.
[3]The author is referring to Wallace Stevens's poem "Of Mere Being" (1955).
[4]K. M. Panikkar, *Asia and Western Dominance* (London: George Allen & Unwin, 1959). [Said]

[5]As Said explains later, Kutchuk Hanem was an Egyptian dancer and courtesan with whom Gustave Flaubert slept during his 1859 tour of Greece and the Middle East. Said argues that the experience influenced Flaubert's portraits of oriental women like Salammbô and Salomé as visions of escapist sexual fantasy.
[6]Ernest Renan (1823–1892) won the Prix Volney for his 1847 *General History of the Semitic Languages*, a work Said characterizes as racist and reductive.

many generations, there has been a considerable material investment. Continued investment made Orientalism, as a system of knowledge about the Orient, an accepted grid for filtering through the Orient into Western consciousness, just as that same investment multiplied — indeed, made truly productive — the statements proliferating out from Orientalism into the general culture.

Gramsci[7] has made the useful analytic distinction between civil and political society in which the former is made up of voluntary (or at least rational and noncoercive) affiliations like schools, families, and unions, the latter of state institutions (the army, the police, the central bureaucracy) whose role in the polity is direct domination. Culture, of course, is to be found operating within civil society, where the influence of ideas, of institutions, and of other persons works not through domination but by what Gramsci calls consent. In any society not totalitarian, then, certain cultural forms predominate over others, just as certain ideas are more influential than others; the form of this cultural leadership is what Gramsci has identified as *hegemony*, an indispensable concept for any understanding of cultural life in the industrial West. It is hegemony, or rather the result of cultural hegemony at work, that gives Orientalism the durability and the strength I have been speaking about so far. Orientalism is never far from what Denys Hay has called the idea of Europe,[8] a collective notion identifying "us" Europeans as against all "those" non-Europeans, and indeed it can be argued that the major component in European culture is precisely what made that culture hegemonic both in and outside Europe: the idea of European identity as a superior one in comparison with all the non-European peoples and cultures. There is in addition the hegemony of European ideas about the Orient, themselves reiterating European superiority over Oriental backwardness, usually overriding the possibility that a more independent, or more skeptical, thinker might have had different views on the matter.

In a quite constant way, Orientalism depends for its strategy on this flexible *positional* superiority, which puts the Westerner in a whole series of possible relationships with the Orient without ever losing him the relative upper hand. And why should it have been otherwise, especially during the period of extraordinary European ascendancy from the late Renaissance to the present? The scientist, the scholar, the missionary, the trader, or the soldier was in, or thought about, the Orient because he *could be there*, or could think about it, with very little resistance on the Orient's part. Under the general heading of knowledge of the Orient, and within the umbrella of Western hegemony over the Orient during the period from the end of the eighteenth century, there emerged a complex Orient suitable for study in the academy, for display in the museum, for reconstruction in the colonial office, for theoretical illustration in anthropological, biological, linguistic, racial, and historical theses about mankind and the universe, for instances of economic and sociological theories of development, revolution, cultural personality, national or religious character. Additionally, the imaginative examination of things Oriental was based more or less exclusively upon a sovereign Western consciousness out of whose unchallenged centrality an Oriental world emerged, first according to general ideas about who or what was an Oriental, then according to a detailed logic governed not simply by empirical reality but by a battery of desires, repressions, investments, and projections. If we can point to great Orientalist works of genuine scholarship like Silvestre de Sacy's *Chrestomathie arabe* or Edward William Lane's *Account of the Manners and Customs of the Modern Egyptians*,[9] we need also to note that Renan's and Gobineau's[10] racial ideas came out

[7]See the introduction to Marxist Criticism, p. 1206.
[8]Denys Hay, *Europe: The Emergence of an Idea*, 2nd ed. (Edinburgh: Edinburgh University Press, 1968). [Said]

[9]Baron Antoine Isaac Silvestre de Sacy (1758–1838), French Arabist, published his influential anthology *Chrestomathie arabe* (3 Vols.) in 1806. Edward William Lane (1801–1876), scholar of oriental languages, published his *Account of the Manners and Customs of the Modern Egyptians* in 1836.
[10]Joseph Arthur, comte de Gobineau (1816–1882), was a French sociologist, whose most important work, *The Moral and Intellectual Diversity of Races* (1854), stated the thesis of Nordic racial superiority espoused by composer Richard Wagner and adopted by Adolf Hitler.

of the same impulse, as did a great many Victorian pornographic novels (see the analysis by Steven Marcus of "The Lustful Turk"[11]).

And yet, one must repeatedly ask oneself whether what matters in Orientalism is the general group of ideas overriding the mass of material — about which who could deny that they were shot through with doctrines of European superiority, various kinds of racism, imperialism, and the like, dogmatic views of "the Oriental" as a kind of ideal and unchanging abstraction? — or the much more varied work produced by almost uncountable individual writers, whom one would take up as individual instances of authors dealing with the Orient. In a sense the two alternatives, general and particular, are really two perspectives on the same material: in both instances one would have to deal with pioneers in the field like William Jones, with great artists like Nerval or Flaubert.[12] And why would it not be possible to employ both perspectives together, or one after the other? Isn't there an obvious danger of distortion (of precisely the kind that academic Orientalism has always been prone to) if either too general or too specific a level of description is maintained systematically?

My two fears are distortion and inaccuracy, or rather the kind of inaccuracy produced by too dogmatic a generality and too positivistic a localized focus. In trying to deal with these problems I have tried to deal with three main aspects of my own contemporary reality that seem to me to point the way out of the methodological or perspectival difficulties I have been discussing, difficulties that might force one, in the first instance, into writing a coarse polemic on so unacceptably general a level of description as not to be worth the effort, or in the second instance, into writing so detailed and atomistic a series of analyses as to lose all track of the general lines of force informing the field, giving it its special cogency. How

[11]Steven Marcus, *The Other Victorians: A Study of Sexuality and Pornography in Mid-Nineteenth Century England* (1966; reprint ed., New York: Bantam Books, 1967), pp. 200–19. [Said]
[12]Sir William Jones (1746–1794) translated Arabic and Sanskrit poetry in the 1780s and 1790s. Gérard de Nerval (1808–1855) was a French symbolist poet who wrote *Le Voyage en orient* in 1851.

then to recognize individuality and to reconcile it with its intelligent, and by no means passive or merely dictatorial, general and hegemonic context?

III

I mentioned three aspects of my contemporary reality: I must explain and briefly discuss them now, so that it can be seen how I was led to a particular course of research and writing.

1. *The distinction between pure and political knowledge.* It is very easy to argue that knowledge about Shakespeare or Wordsworth is not political whereas knowledge about contemporary China or the Soviet Union is. My own formal and professional designation is that of "humanist," a title which indicates the humanities as my field and therefore the unlikely eventuality that there might be anything political about what I do in that field. Of course, all these labels and terms are quite unnuanced as I use them here, but the general truth of what I am pointing to is, I think, widely held. One reason for saying that a humanist who writes about Wordsworth, or an editor whose specialty is Keats, is not involved in anything political is that what he does seems to have no direct political effect upon reality in the everyday sense. A scholar whose field is Soviet economics works in a highly charged area where there is much government interest, and what he might produce in the way of studies or proposals will be taken up by policymakers, government officials, institutional economists, intelligence experts. The distinction between "humanists" and persons whose work has policy implications, or political significance, can be broadened further by saying that the former's ideological color is a matter of incidental importance to politics (although possibly of great moment to his colleagues in the field, who may object to his Stalinism or fascism or too easy liberalism), whereas the ideology of the latter is woven directly into his material — indeed, economics, politics, and sociology in the modern academy are ideological sciences — and therefore taken for granted as being "political."

Nevertheless the determining impingement on most knowledge produced in the contemporary

West (and here I speak mainly about the United States) is that it be nonpolitical, that is, scholarly, academic, impartial, above partisan or small-minded doctrinal belief. One can have no quarrel with such an ambition in theory, perhaps, but in practice the reality is much more problematic. No one has ever devised a method for detaching the scholar from the circumstances of life, from the fact of his involvement (conscious or unconscious) with a class, a set of beliefs, a social position, or from the mere activity of being a member of a society. These continue to bear on what he does professionally, even though naturally enough his research and its fruits do attempt to reach a level of relative freedom from the inhibitions and the restrictions of brute, everyday reality. For there is such a thing as knowledge that is less, rather than more, partial than the individual (with his entangling and distracting life circumstances) who produces it. Yet this knowledge is not therefore automatically nonpolitical.

Whether discussions of literature or of classical philology are fraught with — or have unmediated — political significance is a very large question that I have tried to treat in some detail elsewhere.[13] What I am interested in doing now is suggesting how the general liberal consensus that "true" knowledge is fundamentally nonpolitical (and conversely, that overtly political knowledge is not "true" knowledge) obscures the highly if obscurely organized political circumstances obtaining when knowledge is produced. No one is helped in understanding this today when the adjective "political" is used as a label to discredit any work for daring to violate the protocol of pretended suprapolitical objectivity. We may say, first, that civil society recognizes a gradation of political importance in the various fields of knowledge. To some extent the political importance given a field comes from the possibility of its direct translation into economic terms; but to a greater extent political importance comes from the closeness of a field to ascertainable sources of power in political society. Thus an economic study of long-term Soviet energy potential and its effect on military capability is likely to be commissioned by the Defense Department, and thereafter to acquire a kind of political status impossible for a study of Tolstoi's early fiction financed in part by a foundation. Yet both works belong in what civil society acknowledges to be a similar field, Russian studies, even though one work may be done by a very conservative economist, the other by a radical literary historian. My point here is that "Russia" as a general subject matter has political priority over nicer distinctions such as "economics" and "literary history," because political society in Gramsci's sense reaches into such realms of civil society as the academy and saturates them with significance of direct concern to it.

I do not want to press all this any further on general theoretical grounds: it seems to me that the value and credibility of my case can be demonstrated by being much more specific, in the way, for example, Noam Chomsky has studied the instrumental connection between the Vietnam War and the notion of objective scholarship as it was applied to cover state-sponsored military research.[14] Now because Britain, France, and recently the United States are imperial powers, their political societies impart to their civil societies a sense of urgency, a direct political infusion as it were, where and whenever matters pertaining to their imperial interests abroad are concerned. I doubt that it is controversial, for example, to say that an Englishman in India or Egypt in the later nineteenth century took an interest in those countries that was never far from their status in his mind as British colonies. To say this may seem quite different from saying that all academic knowledge about India and Egypt is somehow tinged and impressed with, violated by, the gross political fact — and yet *that is what I am saying* in this study of Orientalism. For if it is true that no production of knowledge in the human sciences can ever ignore or disclaim its author's involvement as a human subject in his own circumstances, then it must also be true that for a European or American studying the Orient there can be no

[13]See my book *The World, the Text, and the Critic* (Cambridge, Mass.: Harvard University Press, 1983). [Said]

[14]Principally in his *American Power and the New Mandarins: Historical and Political Essays* (New York: Pantheon Books, 1969) and *For Reasons of State* (New York: Pantheon Books, 1973). [Said]

disclaiming the main circumstances of *his* actuality: that he comes up against the Orient as a European or American first, as an individual second. And to be a European or an American in such a situation is by no means an inert fact. It meant and means being aware, however dimly, that one belongs to a power with definite interests in the Orient, and more important, that one belongs to a part of the earth with a definite history of involvement in the Orient almost since the time of Homer.

Put in this way, these political actualities are still too undefined and general to be really interesting. Anyone would agree to them without necessarily agreeing also that they mattered very much, for instance, to Flaubert as he wrote *Salammbô*, or to H. A. R. Gibb as he wrote *Modern Trends in Islam*.[15] The trouble is that there is too great a distance between the big dominating fact, as I have described it, and the details of everyday life that govern the minute discipline of a novel or a scholarly text as each is being written. Yet if we eliminate from the start any notion that "big" facts like imperial domination can be applied mechanically and deterministically to such complex matters as culture and ideas, then we will begin to approach an interesting kind of study. My idea is that European and then American interest in the Orient was political according to some of the obvious historical accounts of it that I have given here, but that it was the culture that created that interest, that acted dynamically along with brute political, economic, and military rationales to make the Orient the varied and complicated place that it obviously was in the field I call Orientalism.

Therefore, Orientalism is not a mere political subject matter or field that is reflected passively by culture, scholarship, or institutions; nor is it a large and diffuse collection of texts about the Orient; nor is it representative and expressive of some nefarious "Western" imperialist plot to hold down the "Oriental" world. It is rather a *distribution* of geopolitical awareness into aesthetic, scholarly, economic, sociological, historical, and philological texts; it is an *elaboration* not only of a basic geographical distinction (the world is made up of two unequal halves, Orient and Occident) but also of a whole series of "interests" which, by such means as scholarly discovery, philological reconstruction, psychological analysis, landscape and sociological description, it not only creates but also maintains; it *is*, rather than expresses, a certain *will* or *intention* to understand, in some cases to control, manipulate, even to incorporate, what is a manifestly different (or alternative and novel) world; it is, above all, a discourse that is by no means in direct, corresponding relationship with political power in the raw, but rather is produced and exists in an uneven exchange with various kinds of power, shaped to a degree by the exchange with power political (as with a colonial or imperial establishment), power intellectual (as with reigning sciences like comparative linguistics or anatomy, or any of the modern policy sciences), power cultural (as with orthodoxies and canons of taste, texts, values), power moral (as with ideas about what "we" do and what "they" cannot do or understand as "we" do). Indeed, my real argument is that Orientalism is — and does not simply represent — a considerable dimension of modern political-intellectual culture, and as such has less to do with the Orient than it does with "our" world.

Because Orientalism is a cultural and a political fact, then, it does not exist in some archival vacuum; quite the contrary, I think it can be shown that what is thought, said, or even done about the Orient follows (perhaps occurs within) certain distinct and intellectually knowable lines. Here too a considerable degree of nuance and elaboration can be seen working as between the broad superstructural pressures and the details of composition, the facts of textuality. Most humanistic scholars are, I think, perfectly happy with the notion that texts exist in contexts, that there is such a thing as intertextuality, that the pressures of conventions, predecessors, and rhetorical styles limit what Walter Benjamin once called the "overtaxing of the productive person in the name of . . . the principle of 'creativity,'" in which the poet is believed on his own, and out of his pure mind, to have brought forth his work.[16] Yet

[15] In this 1947 text Sir Hamilton Gibb wrote of the Muslim "rejection of rationalist modes of thought."

[16] Walter Benjamin, *Charles Baudelaire: A Lyric Poet in the Era of High Capitalism*, trans. Harry Zohn (London: New Left Books, 1973), p. 71. [Said]

there is a reluctance to allow that political, institutional, and ideological constraints act in the same manner on the individual author. A humanist will believe it to be an interesting fact to any interpreter of Balzac that he was influenced in the *Comédie humaine* by the conflict between Geoffroy Saint-Hilaire and Cuvier,[17] but the same sort of pressure on Balzac of deeply reactionary monarchism is felt in some vague way to demean his literary "genius" and therefore to be less worth serious study. Similarly — as Harry Bracken has been tirelessly showing — philosophers will conduct their discussions of Locke, Hume, and empiricism without ever taking into account that there is an explicit connection in these classic writers between their "philosophic" doctrines and racial theory, justifications of slavery, or arguments for colonial exploitation.[18] These are common enough ways by which contemporary scholarship keeps itself pure.

Perhaps it is true that most attempts to rub culture's nose in the mud of politics have been crudely iconoclastic; perhaps also the social interpretation of literature in my own field has simply not kept up with the enormous technical advances in detailed textual analysis. But there is no getting away from the fact that literary studies in general, and American Marxist theorists in particular, have avoided the effort of seriously bridging the gap between the superstructural and the base levels in textual, historical scholarship;[19] on another occasion I have gone so far as to say that the literary-cultural establishment as a whole has declared the serious study of imperialism and culture off limits.[20] For Orientalism brings one up

directly against that question — that is, to realizing that political imperialism governs an entire field of study, imagination, and scholarly institutions — in such a way as to make its avoidance an intellectual and historical impossibility. Yet there will always remain the perennial escape mechanism of saying that a literary scholar and a philosopher, for example, are trained in literature and philosophy respectively, not in politics or ideological analysis. In other words, the specialist argument can work quite effectively to block the larger and, in my opinion, the more intellectually serious perspective.

Here it seems to me there is a simple two-part answer to be given, at least so far as the study of imperialism and culture (or Orientalism) is concerned. In the first place, nearly every nineteenth-century writer (and the same is true enough of writers in earlier periods) was extraordinarily well aware of the fact of empire: this is a subject not very well studied, but it will not take a modern Victorian specialist long to admit that liberal cultural heroes like John Stuart Mill, Arnold, Carlyle, Newman, Macaulay, Ruskin, George Eliot, and even Dickens had definite views on race and imperialism, which are quite easily to be found at work in their writing. So even a specialist must deal with the knowledge that Mill, for example, made it clear in *On Liberty* and *Representative Government* that his views there could not be applied to India (he was an India Office functionary for a good deal of his life, after all) because the Indians were civilizationally, if not racially, inferior. The same kind of paradox is to be found in Marx, as I try to show in this book. In the second place, to believe that politics in the form of imperialism bears upon the production of literature, scholarship, social theory, and history writing is by no means equivalent to saying that culture is therefore a demeaned or denigrated thing. Quite the contrary: my whole point is to say that we can better understand the persistence and the durability of saturating hegemonic systems like culture when we realize that their internal constraints upon writers and thinkers were *productive*, not unilaterally inhibiting. It is this idea that Gramsci, certainly, and Foucault and Raymond Williams in their very different ways have been trying to illustrate. Even one or two

[17]Étienne Geoffroy Saint-Hilaire (1772–1844), French naturalist, collaborated with paleontologist Baron Georges Cuvier (1769–1832) on five works of natural history published in the first decade of the nineteenth century. The two later quarrelled furiously over biological principle. Cuvier was a functionalist who believed that invariant species were specialized by nature for their ecological niches. Saint-Hilaire, on the contrary, thought that all organisms stemmed from one original structure, and that there were many rudimentary organs that betrayed a long-term evolution of organisms from one mode of functioning to another.

[18]Harry Bracken, "Essence, Accident and Race," *Hermathena* 116 (Winter 1973): 81–96. [Said]

[19]See Raymond Williams on base and superstructure, pp. 1272.

[20]In an interview published in *Diacritics* 6, no. 3 (Fall 1976): 38. [Said]

pages by Williams on "the uses of the Empire" in *The Long Revolution* tell us more about nineteenth-century cultural richness than many volumes of hermetic textual analyses.[21]

Therefore I study Orientalism as a dynamic exchange between individual authors and the large political concerns shaped by the three great empires — British, French, American — in whose intellectual and imaginative territory the writing was produced. What interests me most as a scholar is not the gross political verity but the detail, as indeed what interests us in someone like Lane or Flaubert or Renan is not the (to him) indisputable truth that Occidentals are superior to Orientals, but the profoundly worked over and modulated evidence of his detailed work within the very wide space opened up by that truth. One need only remember that Lane's *Manners and Customs of the Modern Egyptians* is a classic of historical and anthropological observation because of its style, its enormously intelligent and brilliant details, not because of its simple reflection of racial superiority, to understand what I am saying here.

The kind of political questions raised by Orientalism, then, are as follows; What other sorts of intellectual, aesthetic, scholarly, and cultural energies went into the making of an imperialist tradition like the Orientalist one? How did philology, lexicography, history, biology, political and economic theory, novel-writing, and lyric poetry come to the service of Orientalism's broadly imperialist view of the world? What changes, modulations, refinements, even revolutions take place within Orientalism? What is the meaning of originality, of continuity, of individuality, in this context? How does Orientalism transmit or reproduce itself from one epoch to another? In fine, how can we treat the cultural, historical phenomenon of Orientalism as a kind of *willed human work* — not of mere unconditioned ratiocination — in all its historical complexity, detail, and worth without at the same time losing sight of the alliance between cultural work, political tendencies, the state, and the specific realities of domination? Governed by such

concerns a humanistic study can responsibly address itself to politics *and* culture. But this is not to say that such a study establishes a hard-and-fast rule about the relationship between knowledge and politics. My argument is that each humanistic investigation must formulate the nature of that connection in the specific context of the study, the subject matter, and its historical circumstances.

2. *The methodological question.* In a previous book I gave a good deal of thought and analysis to the methodological importance for work in the human sciences of finding and formulating a first step, a point of departure, a beginning principle.[22] A major lesson I learned and tried to present was that there is no such thing as a merely given, or simply available, starting point: beginnings have to be made for each project in such a way as to *enable* what follows from them. Nowhere in my experience has the difficulty of this lesson been more consciously lived (with what success — or failure — I cannot really say) than in this study of Orientalism. The idea of beginning, indeed the act of beginning, necessarily involves an act of delimitation by which something is cut out of a great mass of material, separated from the mass, and made to stand for, as well as be, a starting point, a beginning; for the student of texts one such notion of inaugural delimitation is Louis Althusser's idea of the *problematic*, a specific determinate unity of a text, or group of texts, which is something given rise to by analysis.[23] Yet in the case of Orientalism (as opposed to the case of Marx's texts, which is what Althusser studies) there is not simply the problem of finding a point of departure, or problematic, but also the question of designating which texts, authors, and periods are the ones best suited for study.

It has seemed to me foolish to attempt an encyclopedic narrative history of Orientalism, first of all because if my guiding principle was to be "the European idea of the Orient" there would be virtually no limit to the material I would have had to deal with; second, because the narrative model

[21]Raymond Williams, *The Long Revolution* (London: Chatto & Windus, 1961), pp. 66–7. [Said]

[22]In my *Beginnings: Intention and Method* (New York: Basic Books, 1975). [Said.]

[23]Louis Althusser, *For Marx*, trans. Ben Brewster (New York: Pantheon Books, 1969), pp. 65–7. [Said]

itself did not suit my descriptive and political interests; third, because in such books as Raymond Schwab's *La Renaissance orientale*, Johann Fück's *Die Arabischen Studien in Europa bis in den Anfang des 20. Jahrhunderts*, and more recently, Dorothee Metlitzki's *The Matter of Araby in Medieval England*[24] there already exist encyclopedic works on certain aspects of the European-Oriental encounter such as make the critic's job, in the general political and intellectual context I sketched above, a different one.

There still remained the problem of cutting down a very fat archive to manageable dimensions, and more important, outlining something in the nature of an intellectual order within that group of texts without at the same time following a mindlessly chronological order. My starting point therefore has been the British, French, and American experience of the Orient taken as a unit, what made that experience possible by way of historical and intellectual background, what the quality and character of the experience has been. For reasons I shall discuss presently I limited that already limited (but still inordinately large) set of questions to the Anglo-French-American experience of the Arabs and Islam, which for almost a thousand years together stood for the Orient. Immediately upon doing that, a large part of the Orient seemed to have been eliminated — India, Japan, China, and other sections of the Far East — not because these regions were not important (they obviously have been) but because one could discuss Europe's experience of the Near Orient, or of Islam, apart from its experience of the Far Orient. Yet at certain moments of that general European history of interest in the East, particular parts of the Orient like Egypt, Syria, and Arabia cannot be discussed without also studying Europe's involvement in the more distant parts, of which Persia and India are the most important; a notable case in point is the connection between Egypt and India so far as

eighteenth- and nineteenth-century Britain was concerned. Similarly the French role in deciphering the Zend-Avesta,[25] the pre-eminence of Paris as a center of Sanskrit studies during the first decade of the nineteenth century, the fact that Napoleon's interest in the Orient was contingent upon his sense of the British role in India: all these Far Eastern interests directly influenced French interest in the Near East, Islam, and the Arabs.

Britain and France dominated the Eastern Mediterranean from about the end of the seventeenth century on. Yet my discussion of that domination and systematic interest does not do justice to (*a*) the important contributions to Orientalism of Germany, Italy, Russia, Spain, and Portugal and (*b*) the fact that one of the important impulses toward the study of the Orient in the eighteenth century was the revolution in Biblical studies[26] stimulated by such variously interesting pioneers as Bishop Lowth, Eichhorn, Herder, and Michaelis. In the first place, I had to focus rigorously upon the British-French and later the American material because it seemed inescapably true not only that Britain and France were the pioneer nations in the Orient and in Oriental studies, but that these vanguard positions were held by virtue of the two greatest colonial networks in pre-twentieth-century history; the American Oriental position since World War II has fit — I think, quite self-consciously — in the places excavated by the two earlier European powers. Then, too, I believe that the sheer quality, consistency, and mass of British, French, and American writing on the Orient lifts it above the doubtless crucial work done in Germany, Italy, Russia, and elsewhere. But I think it is also true that the major steps in Oriental scholarship were first taken in either Britain and France, then elaborated upon

[24]Raymond Schwab, *La Renaissance orientale* (Paris: Payot, 1950); Johann W. Fück, *Die Arabischen Studien in Europa bis in den Anfang des 20. Jahrhunderts* (Leipzig: Otto Harrassowitz, 1955); Dorothee Metlitzki, *The Matter of Araby in Medieval England* (New Haven, Conn.: Yale University Press, 1977). [Said]

[25]The "bible" of the Zoroastrian religion, sacred to the Parsees.

[26]Said alludes to the "higher criticism" of the late eighteenth and nineteenth centuries which, taking the Bible as created by men (however inspired) rather than by God, sought to understand the biblical texts as products of the near eastern societies of the first millenium B.C.E. and the two subsequent centuries. This in turn led to intense study of near eastern languages, customs, geography, and history as a means of illuminating the chief documents of Western European religion.

by Germans. Silvestre de Sacy, for example, was not only the first modern and institutional European Orientalist, who worked on Islam, Arabic literature, the Druze religion, and Sassanid Persia; he was also the teacher of Champollion[27] and of Franz Bopp, the founder of German comparative linguistics. A similar claim of priority and subsequent pre-eminence can be made for William Jones and Edward William Lane.

In the second place — and here the failings of my study of Orientalism are amply made up for — there has been some important recent work on the background in Biblical scholarship to the rise of what I have called modern Orientalism. The best and the most illuminatingly relevant is E. S. Shaffer's impressive *"Kubla Khan" and The Fall of Jersualem*,[28] an indispensable study of the origins of Romanticism, and of the intellectual activity underpinning a great deal of what goes on in Coleridge, Browning, and George Eliot. To some degree Shaffer's work refines upon the outlines provided in Schwab, by articulating the material of relevance to be found in the German Biblical scholars and using that material to read, in an intelligent and always interesting way, the work of three major British writers. Yet what is missing in the book is some sense of the political as well as ideological edge given the Oriental material by the British and French writers I am principally concerned with; in addition, unlike Shaffer I attempt to elucidate subsequent developments in academic as well as literary Orientalism that bear on the connection between British and French Orientalism on the one hand and the rise of an explicitly colonial-minded imperialism on the other. Then too, I wish to show how all these earlier matters are reproduced more or less in American Orientalism after the Second World War.

[27]Jean François Champollion (1790–1832) was a French archaeologist who worked out the grammar and lexicon of the ancient Egyptian hieroglyphic language by deciphering the Rosetta Stone. The stone is a black basalt slab discovered by Napoleon's troops in 1799; about two thousand years earlier, it had been inscribed with a royal decree in three scripts: hieroglyphic and demotic Egyptian and Greek.
[28]E. S. Shaffer, *"Kubla Khan" and The Fall of Jerusalem: The Mythological School in Biblical Criticism and Secular Literature, 1770–1880* (Cambridge: Cambridge University Press, 1975). [Said]

Nevertheless there is a possibly misleading aspect to my study, where, aside from an occasional reference, I do not exhaustively discuss the German developments after the inaugural period dominated by Sacy. Any work that seeks to provide an understanding of academic Orientalism and pays little attention to scholars like Steinthal, Müller, Becker, Goldziher, Brockelmann, Nöldeke — to mention only a handful — needs to be reproached, and I freely reproach myself. I particularly regret not taking more account of the great scientific prestige that accrued to German scholarship by the middle of the nineteenth century, whose neglect was made into a denunciation of insular British scholars by George Eliot. I have in mind Eliot's unforgettable portrait of Mr. Casaubon in *Middlemarch*. One reason Casaubon cannot finish his Key to All Mythologies is, according to his young cousin Will Ladislaw, that he is unacquainted with German scholarship. For not only has Casaubon chosen a subject "as changing as chemistry: new discoveries are constantly making new points of view": he is undertaking a job similar to a refutation of Paracelsus because "he is not an Orientalist, you know."[29]

Eliot was not wrong in implying that by about 1830, which is when *Middlemarch* is set, German scholarship had fully attained its European pre-eminence. Yet at no time in German scholarship during the first two-thirds of the nineteenth century could a close partnership have developed between Orientalists and a protracted, sustained *national* interest in the Orient. There was nothing in Germany to correspond to the Anglo-French presence in India, the Levant, North Africa. Moreover, the German Orient was almost exclusively a scholarly, or at least a classical, Orient: it was made the subject of lyrics, fantasies, and even novels, but it was never actual, the way Egypt and Syria were actual for Chauteaubriand, Lane, Lamartine, Burton, Disraeli, or Nerval. There is some significance in the fact that the two most renowned German works on the Orient, Goethe's *Westöstlicher Diwan* and Friedrich Schlegel's *Über die Sprache und Weisheit der*

[29]George Eliot, *Middlemarch: A Study of Provincial Life* (1872; reprint ed., Boston: Houghton Mifflin Co., 1956), p. 164. [Said]

Indier,[30] were based respectively on a Rhine journey and on hours spent in Paris libraries. What German Oriental scholarship did was to refine and elaborate techniques whose application was to texts, myths, ideas, and languages almost literally gathered from the Orient by imperial Britain and France.

Yet what German Orientalism had in common with Anglo-French and later American Orientalism was a kind of intellectual *authority* over the Orient within Western culture. This authority must in large part be the subject of any description of Orientalism, and it is so in this study. Even the name *Orientalism* suggests a serious, perhaps ponderous style of expertise; when I apply it to modern American social scientists (since they do not call themselves Orientalists, my use of the word is anomalous), it is to draw attention to the way Middle East experts can still draw on the vestiges of Orientalism's intellectual position in nineteenth-century Europe.

There is nothing mysterious or natural about authority. It is formed, irradiated, disseminated; it is instrumental, it is persuasive; it has status, it establishes canons of taste and value; it is virtually indistinguishable from certain ideas it dignifies as true, and from traditions, perceptions, and judgments it forms, transmits, reproduces. Above all, authority can, indeed must, be analyzed. All these attributes of authority apply to Orientalism, and much of what I do in this study is to describe both the historical authority in and the personal authorities of Orientalism.

My principal methodological devices for studying authority here are what can be called *strategic location*, which is a way of describing the author's position in a text with regard to the Oriental material he writes about, and *strategic formation*, which is a way of analyzing the relationship between texts and the way in which groups of texts, types of texts, even textual genres,

acquire mass, density, and referential power among themselves and thereafter in the culture at large. I use the notion of strategy simply to identify the problem every writer on the Orient has faced: how to get hold of it, how to approach it, how not to be defeated or overwhelmed by its sublimity, its scope, its awful dimensions. Everyone who writes about the Orient must locate himself vis-à-vis the Orient; translated into his text, this location includes the kind of narrative voice he adopts, the type of structure he builds, the kinds of images, themes, motifs that circulate in his text — all of which add up to deliberate ways of addressing the reader, containing the Orient, and finally, representing it or speaking in its behalf. None of this takes place in the abstract, however. Every writer on the Orient (and this is true even of Homer) assumes some Oriental precedent, some previous knowledge of the Orient, to which he refers and on which he relies. Additionally, each work on the Orient *affiliates* itself with other works, with audiences, with institutions, with the Orient itself. The ensemble of relationships between works, audiences, and some particular aspects of the Orient therefore constitutes an analyzable formation — for example, that of philological studies, of anthologies of extracts from Oriental literature, of travel books, of Oriental fantasies — whose presence in time, in discourse, in institutions (schools, libraries, foreign services) gives it strength and authority.

It is clear, I hope, that my concern with authority does not entail analysis of what lies hidden in the Orientalist text, but analysis rather of the text's surface, its exteriority to what it describes. I do not think that this idea can be overemphasized. Orientalism is premised upon exteriority, that is, on the fact that the Orientalist, poet or scholar, makes the Orient speak, describes the Orient, renders its mysteries plain for and to the West. He is never concerned with the Orient except as the first cause of what he says. What he says and writes, by virtue of the fact that it is said or written, is meant to indicate that the Orientalist is outside the Orient, both as an existential and as a moral fact. The principal product of this exteriority is of course representation: as early as Aeschylus's play *The Persians* the Orient is

---

[30]Goethe's *Westöstliche Diwan* (1819; the title is untranslatable: the first word is German for "Western/Eastern," the second is Persian for the audience-chamber where the Sultan meets with his court) consists of lyrics imitated from the fourteenth-century Persian poet Hafiz; it is not a scientific treatise like the younger Schlegel's *On the Languages and Learning of India* (1808).

transformed from a very far distant and often threatening Otherness into figures that are relatively familiar (in Aeschylus's case, grieving Asiatic women). The dramatic immediacy of representation in *The Persians* obscures the fact that the audience is watching a highly artificial enactment of what a non-Oriental has made into a symbol for the whole Orient. My analysis of the Orientalist text therefore places emphasis on the evidence, which is by no means invisible, for such representations *as representations*, not as "natural" depictions of the Orient. This evidence is found just as prominently in the so-called truthful text (histories, philological analyses, political treatises) as in the avowedly artistic (i.e., openly imaginative) text. The things to look at are style, figures of speech, setting, narrative devices, historical and social circumstances, *not* the correctness of the representation nor its fidelity to some great original. The exteriority of the representation is always governed by some version of the truism that if the Orient could represent itself, it would; since it cannot, the representation does the job, for the West, and *faute de mieux*,[31] for the poor Orient. "Sie können sich nicht vertreten, sie müssen vertreten werden," as Marx wrote in *The Eighteenth Brumaire of Louis Bonaparte*.[32]

Another reason for insisting upon exteriority is that I believe it needs to be made clear about cultural discourse and exchange within a culture that what is commonly circulated by it is not "truth" but representations. It hardly needs to be demonstrated again that language itself is a highly organized and encoded system, which employs many devices to express, indicate, exchange messages and information, represent, and so forth. In any instance of at least written language, there is no such thing as a delivered presence, but a *re-presence*, or a representation. The value, efficacy, strength, apparent veracity of a written statement about the Orient therefore relies very little, and cannot instrumentally depend, on the Orient as such. On the contrary, the written statement is a presence to the reader by virtue of its having excluded, displaced, made supererogatory any such *real thing* as "the Orient." Thus all of Orientalism stands forth and away from the Orient: that Orientalism makes sense at all depends more on the West than on the Orient, and this sense is directly indebted to various Western techniques of representation that make the Orient visible, clear, "there" in discourse about it. And these representations rely upon institutions, traditions, conventions, agreed-upon codes of understanding for their effects, not upon a distant and amorphous Orient.

The difference between representations of the Orient before the last third of the eighteenth century and those after it (that is, those belonging to what I call modern Orientalism) is that the range of representation expanded enormously in the later period. It is true that after William Jones and Anquetil-Duperron,[33] and after Napoleon's Egyptian expedition, Europe came to know the Orient more scientifically, to live in it with greater authority and discipline than ever before. But what mattered to Europe was the expanded scope and the much greater refinement given its techniques for receiving the Orient. When around the turn of the eighteenth century the Orient definitively revealed the age of its languages — thus outdating Hebrew's divine pedigree — it was a group of Europeans who made the discovery, passed it on to other scholars, and preserved the discovery in the new science of Indo-European philology. A new powerful science for viewing the linguistic Orient was born, and with it, as Foucault has shown in *The Order of Things*, a whole web of related scientific interests. Similarly William Beckford,[34] Byron, Goethe, and Hugo restructured the Orient by their art and made its colors, lights, and people visible through their images, rhythms, and motifs. At most, the "real" Orient provoked a writer to his vision; it very rarely guided it.

[31]For want of better.

[32]"They cannot represent themselves: they must be represented." Marx's statement about the class of small peasant proprietors in *The Eighteenth Brumaire of Louis Bonaparte*.

[33]Abraham Hyacinthe Anquetil-Duperron (1731–1805), French orientalist, author of *Zend-Avesta* (1771, 3 vols.), a life of Zoroaster and a collection of Zoroastrian writings.

[34]William Beckford (1760–1844), English author of *The History of the Caliph Vathek* (1782 in French, translated in 1786), an oriental-Gothic tale.

Orientalism responded more to the culture that produced it than to its putative object, which was also produced by the West. Thus the history of Orientalism has both an internal consistency and a highly articulated set of relationships to the dominant culture surrounding it. My analyses consequently try to show the field's shape and internal organization, its pioneers, patriarchal authorities, canonical texts, doxological ideas, exemplary figures, its followers, elaborators, and new authorities; I try also to explain how Orientalism borrowed and was frequently informed by "strong" ideas, doctrines, and trends ruling the culture. Thus there was (and is) a linguistic Orient, a Freudian Orient, a Spenglerian Orient, a Darwinian Orient, a racist Orient — and so on. Yet never has there been such a thing as a pure, or unconditional, Orient; similarly, never has there been a nonmaterial form of Orientalism, much less something so innocent as an "idea" of the Orient. In this underlying conviction and in its ensuing methodological consequences do I differ from scholars who study the history of ideas. For the emphases and the executive form, above all the material effectiveness, of statements made by Orientalist discourse are possible in ways that any hermetic history of ideas tends completely to scant. Without those emphases and that material effectiveness Orientalism would be just another idea, whereas it is and was much more than that. Therefore I set out to examine not only scholarly works but also works of literature, political tracts, journalistic texts, travel books, religious and philological studies. In other words, my hybrid perspective is broadly historical and "anthropological," given that I believe all texts to be worldly and circumstantial in (of course) ways that vary from genre to genre, and from historical period to historical period.

Yet unlike Michel Foucault, to whose work I am greatly indebted, I do believe in the determining imprint of individual writers upon the otherwise anonymous collective body of texts constituting a discursive formation like Orientalism. The unity of the large ensemble of texts I analyze is due in part to the fact that they frequently refer to each other: Orientalism is after all a system for citing works and authors. Edward William Lane's *Manners and Customs of the Modern Egyptians* was read and cited by such diverse figures as Nerval, Flaubert, and Richard Burton.[35] He was an authority whose use was an imperative for anyone writing or thinking about the Orient, not just about Egypt: when Nerval borrows passages verbatim from *Modern Egyptians* it is to use Lane's authority to assist him in describing village scenes in Syria, not Egypt. Lane's authority and the opportunities provided for citing him discriminately as well as indiscriminately were there because Orientalism could give his text the kind of distributive currency that he acquired. There is no way, however, of understanding Lane's currency without also understanding the peculiar features of *his* text; this is equally true of Renan, Sacy, Lamartine, Schlegel, and a group of other influential writers. Foucault believes that in general the individual text or author counts for very little; empirically, in the case of Orientalism (and perhaps nowhere else) I find this not to be so. Accordingly my analyses employ close textual readings whose goal is to reveal the dialectic between individual text or writer and the complex collective formation to which his work is a contribution.

Yet even though it includes an ample selection of writers, this book is still far from a complete history or general account of Orientalism. Of this failing I am very conscious. The fabric of as thick a discourse as Orientalism has survived and functioned in Western society because of its richness: all I have done is to describe parts of that fabric at certain moments, and merely to suggest the existence of a larger whole, detailed, interesting, dotted with fascinating figures, texts, and events. I have consoled myself with believing that this book is one installment of several, and hope there are scholars and critics who might want to write others. There is still a general essay to be written on imperialism and culture; other studies would go more deeply into the connection between Orientalism and pedagogy, or into Italian, Dutch, German, and Swiss Orientalism, or into the dynamic between scholarship and imaginative writing, or into the relationship

[35]Sir Richard Francis Burton (1821–1890), known for his African explorations as well as his sixteen-volume translation of *The Arabian Nights* (1885–88).

between administrative ideas and intellectual discipline. Perhaps the most important task of all would be to undertake studies in contemporary alternatives to Orientalism, to ask how one can study other cultures and peoples from a libertarian, or a nonrepressive and nonmanipulative, perspective. But then one would have to rethink the whole complex problem of knowledge and power. These are all tasks left embarrassingly incomplete in this study.

The last, perhaps self-flattering, observation on method that I want to make here is that I have written this study with several audiences in mind. For students of literature and criticism, Orientalism offers a marvelous instance of the interrelations between society, history, and textuality; moreover, the cultural role played by the Orient in the West connects Orientalism with ideology, politics, and the logic of power, matters of relevance, I think, to the literary community. For contemporary students of the Orient, from university scholars to policymakers, I have written with two ends in mind: one, to present their intellectual genealogy to them in a way that has not been done; two, to criticize — with the hope of stirring

discussion — the often unquestioned assumptions on which their work for the most part depends. For the general reader, this study deals with matters that always compel attention, all of them connected not only with Western conceptions and treatments of the Other but also with the singularly important role played by Western culture in what Vico called the world of nations. Lastly, for readers in the so-called Third World, this study proposes itself as a step towards an understanding not so much of Western politics and of the non-Western world in those politics as of the *strength* of Western cultural discourse, a strength too often mistaken as merely decorative or "superstructural." My hope is to illustrate the formidable structure of cultural domination and, specifically for formerly colonized peoples, the dangers and temptations of employing this structure upon themselves or upon others.[36]

[36]Said's third aspect "of my contemporary reality" (see p. 1804), omitted in this selection, is "the personal dimension," his own experience as "a child growing up in two British colonies."

Benedict Anderson

b. 1936

Benedict Richard O'Gorman Anderson was born in Kunming, China, to James O'Gorman, an officer in the Imperial Maritime Customs, and Veronica Beatrice Mary Anderson. He began school in 1941 in California. He received his B.A. in classics at Cambridge University in England before pursuing a Ph.D. in Indonesian studies in the government department at Cornell University, where he taught political science. During this time, his studies led him to Jakarta in 1961. In 1966, he published a report about the previous year's coup and massacres that indicated the uprising was instigated not by the communists, but by disgruntled army officers. This report, known as the "Cornell Paper," caused Anderson to be barred indefinitely from Indonesia. He was exiled to Thailand, where he spent a few years before returning to Cornell, where he is currently a professor of international studies. Based on observations of southeastern Asia and of the development of the United Nations, Anderson theorizes that the nation itself is an "imagined political community that is imagined as both inherently limited and sovereign." He argues that Creole states (New World nations) were the first to develop a concept of nationhood because the shared language and customs with their parent countries forced a conceptualization of national boundaries beyond the racial or linguistic. His books include Java in a Time of Revolution *(1972),* Imagined Communities: Reflections on the Origin and Spread of Nationalism *(1983),* Literature and Politics in Siam in the American Era *(1986),* Language and Power: Exploring Political Cultures in Indonesia *(1990), and* Spectres of Comparison *(1998). The following selection is excerpted from* Imagined Communities.

The Origins of National Consciousness

If the development of print-as-commodity is the key to the generation of wholly new ideas of simultaneity, still, we are simply at the point where communities of the type "horizontal-secular, transverse-time" become possible. Why, within that type, did the nation become so popular? The factors involved are obviously complex and various. But a strong case can be made for the primacy of capitalism.

As already noted, at least 20,000,000 books had already been printed by 1500,[1] signalling the onset of Benjamin's "age of mechanical reproduction."[2] If manuscript knowledge was scarce and arcane lore, print knowledge lived by reproducibility and dissemination.[3] If, as [Lucien Paul Victor] Febvre and [Henri-Jean] Martin believe, possibly as many as 200,000,000 volumes had been manufactured by 1600, it is no wonder that Francis Bacon believed that print had changed "the appearance and state of the world."[4]

One of the earlier forms of capitalist enterprise, book-publishing, felt all of capitalism's restless search for markets. The early printers established branches all over Europe: "in this way a veritable 'international' of publishing houses, which ignored national [sic] frontiers, was created."[5] And since the years 1500–1550 were a period of exceptional European prosperity, publishing shared in the general boom. "More than at any other time" it was "a great industry under the control of wealthy capitalists."[6] Naturally, "book-sellers were primarily concerned to make a profit and to sell their products, and consequently they sought out first and foremost those works which were of interest to the largest possible number of their contemporaries."[7]

The initial market was literate Europe, a wide but thin stratum of Latin-readers. Saturation of this market took about a hundred and fifty years. The determinative fact about Latin — aside from its sacrality — was that it was a language of bilinguals. Relatively few were born to speak it and even fewer, one imagines, dreamed in it. In the sixteenth century the proportion of bilinguals within the total population of Europe was quite small; very likely no larger than the proportion in the world's population today, and — proletarian

---

[1] The population of that Europe where print was then known was about 100,000,000. Lucien Febvre and Henri-Jean Martin, *The Coming of the Book,* (New Left, 1976), pp. 248–49. [Anderson]

[2] Emblematic is Marco Polo's *Travels,* which remained largely unknown till its first printing in 1559. *The Travels of Marco Polo,* trans. and ed. William Marsden (London and New York: Everyman, 1945), p. xiii. [Anderson]

[3] See Walter Benjamin's *The Work of Art in an Age of Mechanical Reproduction,* p. 1233.

[4] Quoted in Elizabeth Eisenstein, "Some Conjectures about the Impact of Printing on Western Society and Thought: A Preliminary Report," *Journal of Modern History* 40 (1968): 56. [Anderson] It was in *Novum Organum* (1620) that Bacon said that "printing, gunpowder, and the magnetic compass" had changed the world.

[5] Febvre and Martin, *The Coming of the Book,* p. 122. (The original text, however, speaks simply of "par-dessus les frontières." *L'Apparition du livre,* [Paris: Michel, 1958], p. 184.) [Anderson]

[6] Ibid., p. 187. The original text speaks of "puissants" (powerful) rather than "wealthy" capitalists. *L'Apparition,* p. 281. [Anderson]

[7] "Hence the introduction of printing was in this respect a stage on the road to our present society of mass consumption and standardisation." Ibid., pp. 259–60. (The original text has "une civilisation de masse et de standardisation," which may be better rendered "standardised, mass civilization." *L'Apparition,* p. 394). [Anderson]

internationalism notwithstanding — in the centuries to come. Then and now the bulk of mankind is monoglot. The logic of capitalism thus meant that once the elite Latin market was saturated, the potentially huge markets represented by the monoglot masses would beckon. To be sure, the Counter-Reformation encouraged a temporary resurgence of Latin-publishing, but by the mid-seventeenth century the movement was in decay, and fervently Catholic libraries replete. Meantime, a Europe-wide shortage of money made printers think more and more of peddling cheap editions in the vernaculars.[8]

The revolutionary vernacularizing thrust of capitalism was given further impetus by three extraneous factors, two of which contributed directly to the rise of national consciousness. The first, and ultimately the least important, was a change in the character of Latin itself. Thanks to the labors of the Humanists in reviving the broad literature of pre-Christian antiquity and spreading it through the print-market, a new appreciation of the sophisticated stylistic achievements of the ancients was apparent among the trans-European intelligentsia. The Latin they now aspired to write became more and more Ciceronian, and, by the same token, increasingly removed from ecclesiastical and everyday life. In this way it acquired an esoteric quality quite different from that of Church Latin in medieval times. For the older Latin was not arcane because of its subject matter or style, but simply because it was written at all, i.e. because of its status as *text*. Now it became arcane because of what was written, because of the language-in-itself.

Second was the impact of the Reformation, which, at the same time, owed much of its success to print-capitalism. Before the age of print, Rome easily won every war against heresy in Western Europe because it always had better internal lines of communication than its challengers. But when in 1517 Martin Luther nailed his theses to the chapel-door in Wittenberg, they were printed up in German translation, and "within 15 days [had been] seen in every part of the country."[9] In the

two decades 1520–1540 three times as many books were published in German as in the period 1500–1520, an astonishing transformation to which Luther was absolutely central. His works represented no less than one third of *all* German-language books sold between 1518 and 1525. Between 1522 and 1546, a total of 430 editions (whole or partial) of his Biblical translations appeared. "We have here for the first time a truly mass readership and a popular literature within everybody's reach."[10] In effect, Luther became the first best-selling author *so known*. Or, to put it another way, the first writer who could "sell" his *new* books on the basis of his name.[11]

Where Luther led, others quickly followed, opening the colossal religious propaganda war that raged across Europe for the next century. In this titanic "battle for men's minds," Protestantism was always fundamentally on the offensive, precisely because it knew how to make use of the expanding vernacular print-market being created by capitalism, while the Counter-Reformation defended the citadel of Latin. The emblem for this is the Vatican's *Index Librorum Prohibitorum* — to which there was no Protestant counterpart — a novel catalogue made necessary by the sheer volume of printed subversion. Nothing gives a better sense of this siege mentality than François I's panicked 1535 ban on the printing of *any* books in his realm — on pain of death by hanging! The reason for both the ban and its unenforceability was that by then his realm's eastern borders were ringed with Protestant states and cities producing a massive stream of smugglable print. To take Calvin's Geneva alone: between 1533 and 1540 only 42 editions were published there, but the numbers swelled to 527 between 1550 and 1564, by which latter date no less than 40 separate printing-presses were working overtime.[12]

[8]Ibid., p. 195. [Anderson]
[9]Ibid., pp. 289–90. [Anderson]

[10]Ibid., pp. 291–95. [Anderson]
[11]From this point it was only a step to the situation in seventeenth-century France where Corneille, Molière, and La Fontaine could sell their manuscript tragedies and comedies directly to publishers, who bought them as excellent investments in view of their authors' market reputations. Ibid., p. 161. [Anderson]
[12]Ibid., pp. 310–15. [Anderson]

The coalition between Protestantism and print-capitalism, exploiting cheap popular editions, quickly created large new reading publics — not least among merchants and women, who typically knew little or no Latin — and simultaneously mobilized them for politico-religious purposes. Inevitably, it was not merely the Church that was shaken to its core. The same earthquake produced Europe's first important non-dynastic, non-city states in the Dutch Republic and the Commonwealth of the Puritans. (François I's panic was as much political as religious.)

Third was the slow, geographically uneven, spread of particular vernaculars as instruments of administrative centralization by certain well-positioned would-be absolutist monarchs. Here it is useful to remember that the universality of Latin in medieval Western Europe never corresponded to a universal political system. The contrast with Imperial China, where the reach of the mandarinal bureaucracy and of painted characters largely coincided, is instructive. In effect, the political fragmentation of Western Europe after the collapse of the Western Empire meant that no sovereign could monopolize Latin and make it his-and-only-his language-of-state, and thus Latin's religious authority never had a true political analogue.

The birth of administrative vernaculars predated both print and the religious upheaval of the sixteenth century, and must therefore be regarded (at least initially) as an independent factor in the erosion of the sacred imagined community. At the same time, nothing suggests that any deep-seated ideological, let alone proto-national, impulses underlay this vernacularization where it occurred. The case of "England" — on the northwestern periphery of Latin Europe — is here especially enlightening. Prior to the Norman Conquest, the language of the court, literary and administrative, was Anglo-Saxon. For the next century and a half virtually all royal documents were composed in Latin. Between about 1200 and 1350 this state-Latin was superseded by Norman French. In the meantime, a slow fusion between this language of a foreign ruling class and the Anglo-Saxon of the subject population produced Early English. The fusion made it possible for the new language to take its turn, after 1362, as the language of the courts — and for the opening of Parliament.

Wycliffe's vernacular *manuscript* Bible followed in 1382.[13] It is essential to bear in mind that this sequence was a series of "state," not "national," languages; and that the state concerned covered at various times not only today's England and Wales, but also portions of Ireland, Scotland *and France*. Obviously, huge elements of the subject populations knew little or nothing of Latin, Norman French, or Early English.[14] Not till almost a century *after* Early English's political enthronement was London's power swept out of "France."

On the Seine, a similar movement took place, if at a slower pace. As Bloch wryly puts it, "French, that is to say a language which, since it was regarded as merely a corrupt form of Latin, took several centuries to raise itself to literary dignity,"[15] only became the official language of the courts of justice in 1539, when François I issued the Edict of Villers-Cotterêts.[16] In other dynastic realms Latin survived much longer — under the Habsburgs well into the nineteenth century. In still others, "foreign" vernaculars took over: in the eighteenth century the languages of the Romanov court were French and German.[17]

In every instance, the "choice" of language appears as a gradual, unselfconscious, pragmatic, not to say haphazard development. As such, it was utterly different from the selfconscious language policies pursued by nineteenth-century dynasts confronted with the rise of hostile popular linguistic-nationalisms. One clear sign of the difference is that the old administrative languages were *just that*: languages used by and for officialdoms for their own inner convenience. There was no idea of systematically imposing the language on the dynasts' various subject

[13]Seton-Watson, *Nations and States*, pp. 28–29; Bloch, *Feudal Society*, I, p. 25. [Anderson]

[14]We should not assume that administrative vernacular unification was immediately or fully achieved. It is unlikely that the Guyenne ruled from London was ever primarily administered in Early English. [Anderson]

[15]Marc Bloch, *Feudal Society*, I (Chicago: U Chicago P, 1961), p. 98. [Anderson]

[16]Hugh Seton-Watson, *Nations and States: An Enquiry into the Origins of Nations and the Politics of Nationalism* (Boulder: Westview, 1977), p. 48. [Anderson]

[17]Ibid., p. 83. [Anderson]

populations.[18] Nonetheless, the elevation of these vernaculars to the status of languages-of-power, where, in one sense, they were competitors with Latin (French in Paris, [Early] English in London), made its own contribution to the decline of the imagined community of Christendom.

At bottom, it is likely that the esotericization of Latin, the Reformation, and the haphazard development of administrative vernaculars are significant, in the present context, primarily in a negative sense — in their contributions to the dethronement of Latin. It is quite possible to conceive of the emergence of the new imagined national communities without any one, perhaps all, of them being present. What, in a positive sense, made the new communities imaginable was a half-fortuitous, but explosive, interaction between a system of production and productive relations (capitalism), a technology of communications (print), and the fatality of human linguistic diversity.[19]

The element of fatality is essential. For whatever superhuman feats capitalism was capable of, it found in death and languages two tenacious adversaries.[20] Particular languages can die or be wiped out, but there was and is no possibility of humankind's general linguistic unification. Yet this mutual incomprehensibility was historically of only slight importance until capitalism and print created monoglot mass reading publics.

While it is essential to keep in mind an idea of fatality, in the sense of a *general* condition of irremediable linguistic diversity, it would be a mistake to equate this fatality with that common element in nationalist ideologies which stresses the primordial fatality of *particular* languages and their association with *particular* territorial units. The essential thing is the *interplay* between fatality, technology, and capitalism. In pre-print Europe, and, of course, elsewhere in the world, the diversity of spoken languages, those languages that for their speakers were (and are) the warp and woof of their lives, was immense; so immense, indeed, that had print-capitalism sought to exploit each potential oral vernacular market, it would have remained a capitalism of petty proportions. But these varied idiolects were capable of being assembled, within definite limits, into print-languages far fewer in number. The very arbitrariness of any system of signs for sounds facilitated the assembling process.[21] (At the same time, the more ideographic[22] the signs, the vaster the potential assembling zone. One can detect a sort of descending hierarchy here from algebra through Chinese and English, to the regular syllabaries of French or Indonesian.) Nothing served to "assemble" related vernaculars more than capitalism, which, within the limits imposed by grammars and syntaxes, created mechanically reproduced print-languages capable of dissemination through the market.[23]

---

[18]An agreeable confirmation of this point is provided by François I, who, as we have seen, banned all printing of books in 1535 and made French the language of his courts four years later! [Anderson]

[19]It was not the first "accident" of its kind. Febvre and Martin note that while a visible bourgeoisie already existed in Europe by the late thirteenth century, paper did not come into general use until the end of the fourteenth. Only paper's smooth plane surface made the mass reproduction of texts and pictures possible — and this did not occur for still another seventy-five years. But paper was not a European invention. It floated in from another history — China's — through the Islamic world. *The Coming of the Book*, pp. 22, 30, and 45. [Anderson]

[20]We still have no giant multinationals in the world of publishing. [Anderson] True in 1983 but true no longer: multinationals dominate book publishing today. Bertelsmann A.G., based in Germany, owns the American group Random House, Inc.; Rupert Murdoch's News Corp owns the international HarperCollins, based in the U.S.A. and the U.K., and much else; the book you hold, published by Bedford/St.Martin's is a division of Von Holtzbrinck of Stuttgart, Germany, an honor it shares with Farrar, Straus and Giroux and Henry Holt.

[21]For a useful discussion of this point, see S. H. Steinberg, *Five Hundred Years of Printing*, chapter 5. That the sign *ough* is pronounced differently in the words although, bough, lough, rough, cough, and hiccough, shows both the idiolectic variety out of which the now-standard spelling of English emerged, and the ideographic quality of the final product. [Anderson]

[22]An ideograph is a single character symbolizing an idea, as in Chinese.

[23]I say "nothing served . . . more than capitalism" advisedly. Both Steinberg and Eisenstein come close to theomorphizing "print" *qua* print as the genius of modern history. Febvre and Martin never forget that behind print stand printers and publishing firms. It is worth remembering in this context that although printing was invented first in China, possibly 500 years before its appearance in Europe, it had no major, let alone revolutionary impact — precisely because of the absence of capitalism there. [Anderson]

These print-languages laid the bases for national consciousnesses in three distinct ways. First and foremost, they created unified fields of exchange and communication below Latin and above the spoken vernaculars. Speakers of the huge variety of Frenches, Englishes, or Spanishes, who might find it difficult or even impossible to understand one another in conversation, became capable of comprehending one another via print and paper. In the process, they gradually became aware of the hundreds of thousands, even millions, of people in their particular language-field, and at the same time that *only those* hundreds of thousands, or millions, so belonged. These fellow-readers, to whom they were connected through print, formed, in their secular, particular, visible invisibility, the embryo of the nationally imagined community.

Second, print-capitalism gave a new fixity to language, which in the long run helped to build that image of antiquity so central to the subjective idea of the nation. As Febvre and Martin remind us, the printed book kept a permanent form, capable of virtually infinite reproduction, temporally and spatially. It was no longer subject to the individualizing and "unconsciously modernizing" habits of monastic scribes. Thus, while twelfth-century French differed markedly from that written by Villon[24] in the fifteenth, the rate of change slowed decisively in the sixteenth. "By the 17th century languages in Europe had generally assumed their modern forms."[25] To put it another way, for three centuries now these stabilized print-languages have been gathering a darkening varnish; the words of our seventeenth-century forebears are accessible to us in a way that to Villon his twelfth-century ancestors were not.

Third, print-capitalism created languages-of-power of a kind different from the older administrative vernaculars. Certain dialects inevitably were "closer" to each print-language and dominated their final forms. Their disadvantaged cousins, still assimilable to the emerging print-language, lost caste, above all because they were unsuccessful (or only relatively successful) in insisting on their own print-form. "Northwestern German" became Platt Deutsch, a largely spoken, thus sub-standard, German, because it was assimilable to print-German in a way that Bohemian spoken-Czech was not. High German, the King's English, and, later, Central Thai, were correspondingly elevated to a new politico-cultural eminence. (Hence the struggles in late-twentieth-century Europe by certain "sub-"nationalities to change their subordinate status by breaking firmly into print — and radio.)

It remains only to emphasize that in their origins, the fixing of print-languages and the differentiation of status between them were largely unselfconscious processes resulting from the explosive interaction between capitalism, technology and human linguistic diversity. But as with so much else in the history of nationalism, once "there," they could become formal models to be imitated, and, where expedient, consciously exploited in a Machiavellian spirit. Today, the Thai government actively discourages attempts by foreign missionaries to provide its hill-tribe minorities with their own transcription-systems and to develop publications in their own languages: the same government is largely indifferent to what these minorities *speak*. The fate of the Turkic-speaking peoples in the zones incorporated into today's Turkey, Iran, Iraq, and the USSR is especially exemplary.[26] A family of spoken languages, once everywhere assemblable, thus comprehensible, within an Arabic orthography, has lost that unity as a result of conscious manipulations. To heighten Turkish-Turkey's national consciousness at the expense of any wider Islamic identification, Atatürk imposed compulsory

[24]François Villon (1431–1465?), the best known French poet of the Middle Ages (*The Legacy*, 1456; *The Testament*, 1461).
[25]*The Coming of the Book*, p. 319. Cf. *L'Apparition*, p. 477: "Au XVIIe siècle, les langues nationales apparaissent un peu partout cristallisées." [Anderson]

[26]With the breakup of the Soviet Union, these Turkic-speaking peoples of Central Asia are located today in the new nations of Uzbekistan, Turkmenistan, Tajikistan, Kyrgyzstan, and Kazakhstan. Their Turkic languages were originally written in Arabic script, then the Cyrillic alphabet used for Russian; today the Latin alphabet is coming into fashion as these nations break ties with Russia and look west toward Europe.

romanization.[27] The Soviet authorities followed suit, first with an anti-Islamic, anti-Persian compulsory romanization, then, in Stalin's 1930s, with a Russifying compulsory Cyrillicization.[28]

We can summarize the conclusions to be drawn from the argument thus far by saying that the convergence of capitalism and print technology on the fatal diversity of human language created the possibility of a new form of imagined community, which in its basic morphology set the stage for the modern nation. The potential stretch of these communities was inherently limited, and, at the same time, bore none but the most fortuitous relationship to existing political boundaries (which were, on the whole, the highwater marks of dynastic expansionisms).

Yet it is obvious that while today almost all modern self-conceived nations — and also nation-

states — have "national print-languages," many of them have these languages in common, and in others only a tiny fraction of the population "uses" the national language in conversation or on paper. The nation-states of Spanish America or those of the "Anglo-Saxon family" are conspicuous examples of the first outcome; many ex-colonial states, particularly in Africa, of the second. In other words, the concrete formation of contemporary nation-states is by no means isomorphic with the determinate reach of particular print-languages. To account for the discontinuity-in-connectedness between print-languages, national consciousness, and nation-states, it is necessary to turn to the large cluster of new political entities that sprang up in the Western hemisphere between 1776 and 1838, all of which self-consciously defined themselves as nations, and, with the interesting exception of Brazil, as (non-dynastic) republics. For not only were they historically the first such states to emerge on the world stage, and therefore inevitably provided the first real models of what such states should "look like," but their numbers and contemporary births offer fruitful ground for comparative enquiry.

[27]Hans Kohn, *The Age of Nationalism: The First Era of Global History* (New York: Harper; 1962), p. 108. It is probably only fair to add that Kemal also hoped thereby to align Turkish nationalism with the modern, romanized civilization of Western Europe. [Anderson]

[28]Seton-Watson, *Nations and States*, p. 317. [Anderson]

Ngugi wa Thiong'o
b. 1938

Born in Kenya of Gikuyu descent in an area known at the time as the "White Highlands," Ngugi was educated at Makerere University in Kampala, Uganda, and then at the University of Leeds. His early novels, Weep Not, Child *(1964),* The River Between *(1965), and* A Grain of Wheat *(1967) describe the struggle he felt as a young man attempting to reconcile Gikuyu and Western cultural, educational, and religious traditions. While teaching at Makerere University and then at the University of Nairobi, Ngugi wrote theoretical works such as* The Black Hermit *(1968) and* Homecoming: Essays on African and Caribbean Literature, Culture and Politics *(1972). During this time, he began to feel his work had become, in his words, "intellectual dithering," and that he wanted to reach not just Western academics, but Gikuyu people on the community level. In the 1970s, this commitment led him to start several community theater projects whose plays sharply criticized the postcolonial government and depicted the struggle of a people to define themselves as a nation under the stress of political transition and corruption. In 1977, after the publication of the novel* Petals of Blood, *the Kenyan government arrested Ngugi for his involvement with these theaters. While in prison, he became convinced of the need for a body of truly African literature and wrote the entirety of his first novel in Gikuyu,* Devil on the Cross *(1980), on prison toilet paper. Though he was eventually released, he lost his university positions and his family was harassed until 1982, when they left Kenya. Ngugi has been in exile ever since in the United States. In 1986, he wrote his "farewell to English,"* Decolonizing the Mind: The Politics of Language in African Literature *(1986), in which he further develops the theory that Western language is the internal colonizer that the African must reject. His works since have been written exclusively in Gikuyu. He is currently professor of comparative literature at New York University. The following lecture was delivered at Cambridge University in May 1999.*

Europhonism, Universities, and the Magic Fountain: The Future of African Literature and Scholarship[1]

I was lucky, in preparing for this lecture, to come across one of Eric Ashby's books, *African Universities and Western Tradition*, and a cursory reading brought a sense of recognition. I noticed the irony in the way the book had crossed my life while also embodying a number of my concerns. The book was the Godkin lectures he gave at Harvard University in 1964. It was the year I graduated from Makerere College with a University of London honors degree in English. It was also the year that William Heinemann brought out a hardcover edition of my novel, *Weep Not, Child*, written in English, obviously a product of my five years at Makerere. My novel and I were products of the kind of universities which Eric Ashby was talking about and whose social function was "to produce men and women with the standards of public service and capacity for leadership which self rule requires" (20),[2] in short a governing elite in the expected new political dispensation following the end of the Second World War.

The colleges were established in the fifties, the culmination of a series of committees and recommendations going back to the 1925 advisory committee that years later metamorphosed into the Asquith Committee and the Inter-University Council for Higher Education. But the vision of a modern university in Africa did not begin in the twentieth century with these official committees but rather in the nineteenth century with James Africanus Beale Horton in 1868 and Edward Blyden in 1872. Both Horton and Blyden were of African descent, both from Sierra Leone, and they clearly wanted the best for Africa. Nevertheless, their two visions were different. According to Ashby, Horton wanted to introduce into Africa "undiluted Western education" and "there was no place in his scheme of higher education for the incorporation of African languages, history or culture." The way to African modernity lay by way of the Greek classics and European languages and culture. Blyden on the other hand wanted to free higher education in Africa from "despotic Europeanizing which had warped and crushed the Negro mind" (qtd. in Ashby 13). Writing in 1883 Blyden said:

> All our traditions and experiences are connected with a foreign race. We have no poetry but that of

[1] Ashby Lecture given at Clare Hall, Cambridge, May 1999. I would like to thank Miss Total Gajarawala for her research into this paper. [Ngugi]
[2] Eric Ashby, *African Universities and Western Tradition* (Cambridge: Harvard University Press, 1964).

our taskmasters. The songs which live in our ears and are often on our lips are the songs we heard sung by those who shouted while we groaned and lamented. They sang of their history, which was the history of our degradation. They recited their triumphs, which contained the records of our humiliation. To our great misfortune, we learned their prejudices and their passions, and thought we had their aspirations and their power. (qtd. in Blyden 91)[3]

He wanted a system of education which rejected all the errors and falsehoods about the African and, while he wanted the Greek and Latin classics as part of the curricula for his visions of an African university, he also wanted African languages to be an integral part of it. J. E. Casely Hayford of Ghana, then Gold Coast, was to go further than Blyden and in his *Ethiopia Unbound* of 1911 he too articulated a vision of an African university in which the medium of instruction would be an African language and to meet the needs of the relevant material scholars would be employed to translate books into African languages.

When eventually Universities were set up in Africa following the recommendations of the Asquith committee — Ibadan in 1948, University of Gold Coast in 1948, Makerere University College in 1950 — it was the Horton vision which triumphed, except that where Greek and Latin had been envisioned as the foundation of excellence, English took over as the foundation of that excellence. At the risk of simplification I shall call this the Horton-Asquith model to contrast it with the Blyden-Hayford model.

What divided the Horton-Asquith model and the Blyden-Casely Hayford vision were clearly not their disagreements about the need for excellence in the pursuit of higher education but rather the way of achieving it and the question of African languages was central. In the Horton-Asquith model African languages were relegated to the periphery and in the Blyden-Hayford model they would occupy a central place in the scheme of things. Periphery or the center, that was the great divide and the implications of which model failed to make the grade and which eventually occupied the center still haunt African

[3]Edward Wilmot Blyden, *Christianity, Islam and the Negro Race* (1887; Chesapeake, NY: ECA, 1990), p. 91.

scholarship and politics. In short, the answer to the question as to whether African languages occupy center stage or the periphery is still relevant as Africa struggles for a more equitable place in the economic and political map of the global community of the twenty-first century.

In most of my publications, principally in *Decolonizing the Mind*; *Penpoints, Gunpoints and Dreams*; and *Writers in Politics*, I have tried to argue that the language question is so crucial because language occupies a significant position in the entire hierarchy of the organization of wealth, power, and values in a society. Let me summarize the argument. Language is a product of a community in its economic, political, and cultural evolution in time and space. In their very negotiation with nature and with one another humans give birth to a system of communication whose highest expression and development is the signs which we come to give the name of language. But language is also the producer of a community, for it is language after all which enables humans to negotiate effectively their way into and out of nature and indeed that which makes possible their multifaceted evolution. It is in that very negotiation that a community comes to know itself as a specific community different from others. This is because in doing similar things over a similar natural environment within similar regulations which govern what is extracted from nature, how it is extracted and how it is shared out, such a community develops knowledges which are passed from generation to generation and which becomes the basis of their future actions and the stuff of their way of life. Every community has a way of life: a way of what, how, and when it negotiates with nature, with one another, with other communities, with self and the universe. Language carries the cultural universe of the community and in that universe also resides the entire body of values held by that community. Every community of humans with a given particularity has notions of what is right and wrong, of the bad and the good, of the ugly and the beautiful, in short a system of ethics and aesthetics the entirety of which, with associated feelings, emotions and attitudes, forms the basis of their identity or their being for themselves.

In his *Science of Logic* and in *The Phenomenology of Spirit* as indeed in all his works, Hegel, the nineteenth-century German philosopher, often talks of the notions of being and becoming, making the distinction between Being in itself and Being for itself, notions which Jean Paul Sartre plays with in *Being and Nothingness*, further talking about Being for others.[4] We can think of Being in itself as when an entity exists objectively undifferentiated as opposed to being for itself when it becomes aware of itself as an entity. Language is what most helps in the movement of a community from the state of being in itself to a state of being for itself and this self-awareness is what gives the community its spiritual strength to keep on reproducing its being as it continually renews itself in culture, in its power relations, and in its negotiations with its entire environment. It is its culture which enables a community to imagine and re-imagine itself in history. And that is why a culture is to a community what a flower is to a plant. A flower is very beautiful, very colorful, often very delicate. But it is the flower which often readily defines the identity of so many plants. Most important it is the flower which is the carrier of the seeds which make possible the reproduction of the roots and trunks of that plant. Kill the tree trunk and even the roots but retain the seeds and the tree can reproduce itself. It can, if you like, re-imagine itself. Language which is the carrier of culture is the ultimate and the most primary means of imagination.

Empire builders have always known that and in trying to shape how the dominated imagined their future they clearly saw the importance of delinking the elites of the dominated communities from their languages and literally transplanting their minds in the languages of the imperial center. And where the traditional elite resisted the transplant because they were too rooted in their languages and cultures, the empire builders simply manufactured a new elite through a massive cultural surgery carried out in the theaters of the new schools and colleges. The aim, realized or not, was to turn the elite into beings for others even in their conception of themselves. Examples

abound and we do not even have to go to the special case of plantation slavery where whole communities were delinked from the languages of their original homes. Colonial India will do.

India, because of its centrality in the making of modern Britain, became a social laboratory with the results later exported to other colonies. And so, the words of Thomas Babington Macaulay who as a member of the Supreme Council of India (1834–38) helped reform the colony's education system as well as drawing its penal code have a special significance. You remember that in the famous minute on Indian education he had visions of the English language producing "a class of persons, Indian in blood and color, but English in taste, in opinions, in morals, and in intellect." Note that this was not for the aesthetic pleasure of disinterested cultural engineering but rather, this class of persons "may be interpreters between us and the people we govern."[5] Exactly eighty-seven years later, Macaulay's words were to be repeated in colonial Kenya by the then British Governor, Sir Phillip Mitchell. In outlining a policy for English-language dominance in African education literally as a moral crusade to supplement the armed crusade against the Mau Mau guerrilla army, he saw this new language education as bringing about a "civilized state in which the values and standards are to be the values and standards of Britain, in which every one, whatever his origins, has an interest and a part." In both instances, Macaulay's India in nineteenth-century and Mitchell's Kenya in the twentieth century, the context was colonial and the aim was clear. Just as in the military realm the colonial powers had carved out a native army simultaneously alienated from the people whence they came and collaborative with the forces of their own conquest, the same would be true in the realm of the mind: create from the governed an intellectual army both alienated and collaborative. You create a being not for itself but being for others and therefore against its own being.

Thus the Horton-Asquith model had a whole colonial tradition and theory behind it and it was

---

[4]For Hegel, see p. 369; for Sartre, see p. 659.

[5]From Thomas Babington Macaulay, "Minute of 2 February 1835 on Indian Education" in *Macaulay: Prose and Poetry* (Cambridge: Harvard University Press, 1957), 721–29.

the model which was inherited almost unaltered in the era of independence. It was the products of this model, a Macaulayite system of education, who spread out to fill the vacant places of white judges, prosecutors, defense lawyers, lawmakers, governors, military leaders, and heads of departments of education. What an inheritance for Africa! It was an interesting twist of historical fate, that those nurtured in the colonial mold should hold the key in molding the new nations in the military, educational and economic realms. It is ironic and interesting to compare the position of the elites who, before the set-up of the Asquith colleges in Africa, were educated in London, Paris, and Washington. They lit the fires of nationalism and pan-Africanism and the politics of cultural identities as in the concepts of negritude and African personality. Whether they spoke African languages or not, they still paid homage to them as in the case of Nyerere translating the works of Shakespeare into Kiswahili or Kwame Nkrumah setting up the Bureau of African Languages or Birago Diop and Cheikh Diop stressing the centrality of African languages in the self-emancipation of Africa.[6] But the products of the Asquith colleges embraced the English language with an almost religious fervor as the language of modernization and respect in the global community. In various ways they argued and sought to convince themselves that English was now an African language.

The result is really a paradox. Systems of education entrusted by the new nations to research ideas of emancipating and modernizing Africa and for which process the new nations invest a good percent of their GNP now bring up brilliant intellects in every field of modern learning and yet they cannot put even a summary of what they have acquired in any African language. There is no doubt that these colleges, particularly in their heydays, have produced a remarkable scholarship. African scholars, whose first degrees were acquired in the colleges of the Horton-Asquith model, are to be found in major universities in Africa and Abroad. But they are clearly alienated intellects, exiles at home and abroad, or exiles in search of a place they can truly claim as their own. In the context of the collective social body, they become beings for others, at the very least beings against themselves, against the very soil that gave birth to them. African-language communities pay for intellects which cannot put a single idea, even about agriculture or health or business, or democracy, or finance, into the very languages which gave them birth. This great paradox of African scholarship in general is best mirrored in the particular case of the production of African literature.

Because English was so central to all aspects of learning in the new colleges, the English Departments were very prestigious and quite frankly it is difficult to quite express in words the tremendous prestige with which a good performance in English was held. Students of English were the elite of the elite and a first-class degree in English was simply the first among equals. The history of English Literature, described in an apt phrase originally coined by Professor Abiola Irele as ranging from Spenser to Spender, was at the center of that curriculum. Since all the new colleges were largely external affiliates of the University of London, they virtually offered the same history, the same authors, whether one went to the English Department at Makerere in Uganda or Ibadan in Nigeria, and that is why in the Ashby description of the rise of these universities I could see myself so clearly. I was definitely a product of the Horton-Asquith model, as were indeed nearly all the pioneering writers of the fifties and sixties. They were products of the English Department and often their initial inspirations were triggered by the admiration or disagreements with the models they read, a practice Clark-Bedekeremo once again described as *The Example of Shakespeare*.

A cursory glance at some of the early titles of African fiction tells the story. Achebe's *Things Fall Apart* and also *No Longer at Ease* from Yeats's "Second Coming" and Eliot's "Journey of the Magi." The title of my own first published novel, *Weep Not, Child*, was taken from Walt Whitman. And I am sure that within the narratives

[6]Nyerere is Julius Nyerere (1922–1999), president of Tanzania 1965–1985. Nkrumah (1909–1972) was president of Ghana 1960–1966. Birago Diop (1906–1989) was a Senegalese poet and storyteller (native language Wolof). Cheikh Anta Diop (1923–1986) was a Senegalese historian and linguist.

or poetry it is possible to hear echoes of Thomas Hardy, Dickens, D. H. Lawrence, Joseph Conrad, T. S. Eliot, and Ezra Pound. In his essay "Named for Victoria, Queen of England," Chinua Achebe tells us that his initial motivation to write came from his encounter with some appalling novels about Africa including Joyce Cary's *Mister Johnson*, and he decided "that the story we had to tell could not be told for us by anybody else no matter how gifted or well intentioned." But here I am not so much concerned with the impact of the models as the language in which we produced our reaction to those models.

It is quite ironic that while one of the biggest achievements of the Horton-Asquith model was the production of an African literature in English it was a literature often motivated by the Blydenian vision of positive affirmation of the African image:

> In all English speaking countries [Blyden had written in 1883], the mind of the intelligent Negro child revolts against the descriptions given in elementary books — geographies, travels, novels, histories — of the negro, but though he experiences an instinctive revulsion from the caricatures and misrepresentations, he is obliged to continue, as he grows in years, to study such pernicious teachings. After leaving school he finds the same things in newspapers in quasi-scientific works, and after a while — saepe cadendo[7] — they begin to seem the proper things to say about his race, and he accepts what, at first, his unbiased feelings naturally and indignantly repelled. Such is the effect of repetition. . . . Having embraced, or at least assented to these errors and falsehoods about himself, he concludes that his only hope of rising in the scale of respectable manhood is to strive after whatever is most unlike himself and most alien to his taste. [qtd. in Ngugi, *Writers in Politics*, 1981, 1997]

The words and the sentiments are echoed in a statement by one of the early products of the new colleges. "If I were God," Chinua Achebe wrote in 1963 in the famous essay "The Novelist as a Teacher," "I would regard as the very worst our

acceptance, for whatever reason, of racial inferiority" and he went on to define his role as a writer as that of an educator trying to help "my society regain belief in itself and put away the complexes of the years of denigration and self-denigration."

Thus this literature had two contradictory tendencies. It was often motivated and driven by the nationalistic and racial pride inherent in assumptions of the Blyden model, and yet its models were often the English authors read in class. Written in a European language it has nevertheless come to be the nearest thing to a common pan-African heritage. When Wole Soyinka won the Nobel Prize for Literature, his achievement and recognition were celebrated in many parts of Africa, Kenya for instance. Names of writers like Chinua Achebe, Ama Ata Aidoo, Kwei Armah are known and respected in the four corners of the continent.[8] Because of the models of its inspiration, the nineteenth-century Victorian novel with its natural realism and linear narrative structure for instance, the literature, and particularly the narratives tend to be conservative, almost imitative in form and yet very pertinent in their descriptions of the concerns of twentieth-century Africa. Even in form it feels different and in novative compared with the models of its imitation.

What gives it this innovative sense? It cannot be the models which inspired it either in anger or pleasure. And this brings us to another paradox. For what gives it that innovative difference is surely its relationship to African languages and the great heritage of orature in those languages. These languages are a reservoir of images, proverbs, riddles, and ballads, stories from which this literature in European languages draws freely and often creatively. Among the Ibo, Achebe wrote in *Things Fall Apart*, the proverb is like the palm wine with which words are eaten.

These languages are the magic fountain from which African Literature in English or French or Portuguese draws and which give it a perpetual youthfulness. The paleness arising from its

---

[7]Blyden is quoting the last words of the Latin proverb (ascribed to Hugh Latimer and Giordano Bruno, among others) "Gutta cavat lapidem non vi sed saepe cadendo" — drops of water hollow out the stone, not through force but by frequent falling.

[8]Ama Ata Aidoo (b. 1942) is a poet, Ayi Kwei Armah (b. 1939), a novelist, both from Ghana.

imitation and the use of European languages to represent the real-life speech of the characters is immediately refreshed in color by the stamina and blood it draws from African languages.

All this — its pan-African reach, its racial pride, its championing of human and democratic values — is the most positive side of what now I call Europhone African Literature. Its Europhonity is of course a direct product of the Horton model and so whatever is positive in it would justify Horton's hope that the great achievements of the classics and Western civilization would generate excellence in the African recipients.

But Europhonism has no language or cultural universe of its own. The literature it generates — Europhone Literature — is given identity in the market place of all writings in European tongues by all the reservoir of images in African life and languages. It has therefore a negative, almost parasitic side to it. Like a leech it sucks blood and stamina from African languages and it never gives anything back to the people who created the languages and the orature from which it draws so freely to give it that identity in the market place of world-wide writings in European tongues.

The two tendencies inherent in Europhone African literature are actually true of all the scholarship produced by the Horton-Asquith model. There is the creative tendency. The scholarship takes away from the African heritage and produces great works on many aspects of African history and landscape most of which are now to be found in libraries all over the world. But there is also the parasitic aspect to this scholarship which knows only how to take away but never how to give anything back to the languages and peoples on whose behalf it makes its claim in the global community of scholarship in the arts, sciences, and technology. Knowledges of Africa, the results of extensive research, invention, and discoveries about Africa, by the sons and daughters of the continent, are actually stored in European-language granaries.

We can now see the implications of the Horton-Asquith model. A people can be deprived of wealth and even power. But one of the worst deprivations is the means of perceiving all that, articulating it, and therefore developing a vision

and a strategy for fighting it out. We can of course blame it on colonialism and I have done my share of blaming in many of my publications, but remember that we cannot accuse colonialism of failing to do what it was clearly not meant to do. Colonialism and colonial models were never meant to develop the colonies for the benefit of the colonized. And that is why I think it is time that African scholarship and the university begin to question the Horton-Asquith model and its legacy of language policy and practice.

I have said elsewhere how I find it very contradictory in Africa today and elsewhere in the academies of the world to hear of scholars of African realities who do not know a word of the languages of the environment of which they are experts. Do you think that Cambridge here would give me a job as Professor of French Literature if I confessed that I did not know a word of French? And yet schools in Africa and abroad are peopled by experts — whether African or not, whether sympathetic to the African cause or not, whether progressive or not — who do not have to demonstrate any acquaintance let alone expertise in any African language. They hold chairs and produce Ph.D.'s without the requirement of an African language. It is difficult to blame this on institutions abroad when they are merely taking the lead from the practice of African universities. The result is the marginalization of African languages in the academy at home. They do not control their own home turf because tongues from Europe rule their home base.

But the same holds true for African languages at the global level. The culture and thought of the twentieth-century global community is largely dominated by a handful of European languages. Even the UNO and its agencies assume the centrality of European languages in international relations. Thus African languages become invisible intellectually and politically at home and abroad. They are forced to assume a kind of intellectual and political death.

In this respect I find the words of Haunani Kay Trask[9] on the death of languages frighteningly

[9]Trask (b. 1949) is professor of Hawaiian Studies at the University of Hawaii.

pertinent. In her book, *From a Native Daughter* she argues that indigenous languages replaced by colonial ones result in the creation of dead languages. But what is dead or lost is not the language but the people who once spoke it and transmitted their mother tongues to succeeding generations. Everywhere it is as if European languages have come shouting the often-quoted words from *Bhagavad Gita*:[10]

I am become death The shatterer of worlds

We think of death too narrowly in terms of physical disappearance. Death comes in many forms and there is the equally devastating cultural death and we Africans already provide a good example of such a possibility.

Over the last four hundred years we have seen Africans in the West lose their names completely so that our existence is in terms of Jones, James, Jones, and Janes. Now every achievement in sports, in academia, in the sciences and the arts goes to reinforce European naming systems and cultural personality. Language is of course the most basic of naming systems. With the loss of our languages will come the loss of our entire naming system and every historical intervention no matter how revolutionary will thence be within an European naming system, enhancing its capacities for ill or good. Thus in whatever she or he does, they will be performing their being for the enrichment of the cultural personality of white Europe.

For me the question of language goes to the heart of the very being and existence of the African or for that matter any community deprived of its language. That is why I now regard Europhonism as the most dangerous intellectual system for the development of Africa. Its logic is the complete wiping off of the African personality in the global cultural map. We simply become one of several branches in the European language system and the only struggle is for the recognition of equal worth of all the cultural branches of a European global whole.

Perhaps it is time that African scholars seriously took another look at the Blyden vision. The Blyden-Hayford model rejects the assumptions underlying the relationship of Africa to the world which equates knowledge, modernity, modernization, civilization, progress, development — whatever the name — to an acquisition of European tongues. There are hundreds of languages in Africa and the world, each of which is a unique store of memories and thoughts and experiences which are of benefit to human life. It is true that the current revolutions in information technologies daily shrink the globe into McLuhan's global village.[11] But they also open possibilities of expansion of the human community. Academic and other cultural institutions should be among the first to sensitize the world community to the existence and reality of knowledge in diverse languages of the world. There are of course practical difficulties in implementing policies that realize fully plurality and diversity of languages but there should be conscious efforts by various disciplines to recognize the existence of knowledge in languages from places other than Europe and find ways of tapping into the knowledges thereby contained and in the process help in the dialogue among languages. Dialogue among languages is definitely one way of giving back to any language from which we draw sustenance. There are moves in that direction. In 1966 I attended a conference in Barcelona, Spain, organized in part by International PEN[12] and which came with the Universal Declaration of Human Rights based on the recognition of the need for equality and dialogue among languages big and small.

But for Africa the question of languages goes beyond that of simply sensitizing the world to the plurality of languages and it goes to the very heart of our being and existence. And that is why I have always taken it that the main challenge is to African scholars and writers and universities to act as pathfinders. It is this consciousness that

[10]"The Song of God," Sanskrit poem, one of the core texts of Hinduism, written between the fifth and second centuries B.C.E., spoken by Krishna to Arjuna as part of the epic *Mahabharata*.

[11]Marshall McLuhan (1911–1980), Canadian theorist of communications, proposed in *Understanding Media* (1964) that with the speed of radio and television, the world was becoming like a village, hearing news and rumors at the same time.
[12]Worldwide association of writers based in London formed to foster freedom of expression.

made me turn to Gikuyu language for my creative endeavor and now I cannot go back. I work at New York University and I have just finished the fourth draft of a one thousand one hundred and forty-two page novel in the Gikuyu language tentatively titled *Murogi wa Kagoogo*, in English, *The Wizard of the Crow*. I have also founded a journal with the help of New York University in the Gikuyu language and in which I publish papers on every aspect of development, hoping that the journal will act as an inspiration for more journals in African languages. Then I see a very exciting possibility for mutual exchange among such journals making it possible through translations [to have] a genuine dialogue among African languages. There is also the conference on Literature and African Languages due in Asmara, Eritrea, in January at the beginning of the new millennium. The conference which brings together writers from every country in Africa who write in African languages and scholars who want to confront the question of African languages and knowledge and scholarship should be the first of many in the first century of the new millennium to raise the visibility of African languages and to celebrate the fact that [despite] all the odds stacked against them African languages have refused to go away.

I started by quoting from the Godwin lectures which Eric Ashby gave in Harvard. The book he published in 1964 opens with two quotations. One of these is taken from a dispatch from the Governor General of India in 1934 in which he declares that the education they intend to impose on India is that of the sciences, arts, philosophy, and literature of Europe, in short, European knowledge, a kind of Horton model. The other is from the 1959 charter of the University of Ghana. By then Ghana was independent and the charter saw the university as taking its place among the foremost universities in the world. As a great seat of African learning it would give leadership to African thought, scholarship, and development. That lofty ideal is still shared by many African institutions and scholars. But the question of African languages is primary to that leadership in thought, scholarship, and development, and I hope that all the African scholars and writers will heed the call. Let us go back to the magic fountain and draw that which gives power and knowledge to the real agents of social change in the continent — the ordinary man and woman who probably only speaks his or her language. When African writers reject Europhonism as the only way of performing their being, they will bring about genuine revolution in their literature in both content and form. Then we can draw from whatever sources elsewhere to add to that fountain instead of always drawing from it and taking away. We shall link with the globe without delinking from our worlds. It is then that Africa will say with Martin Carter of Guyana:

> I come from the nigger yard of yesterday
> Leaping from the oppressor's hate
> And the scorn of myself.
> I come to the world with scars upon my soul
> Wounds on my body fury in my hands.
> I turn to the histories of men and the lives of the peoples.
> I examine the shower of sparks the wealth of the dreams.
> I am pleased with the glories and sad with the sorrows, rich with the riches, poor with the loss
> From the nigger yard of yesterday I come with my burden
> To the world of tomorrow I turn with my strength.[13]

I believe now more than ever that Africa must use its languages and peoples as a strength with which it can leap into tomorrow. African scholars and writers must lead the way as we enter the twenty-first century.

[13]From *Poems of Succession* (London: New Beacon, 1977), 39.

❖ DIALOGUE BETWEEN FREDRIC JAMESON AND AIJAZ AHMAD

Fredric Jameson

b. 1934

The following excerpted selection, "Third World Literature in the Era of Multinational Capitalism," appeared first in Social Text *in autumn 1986. The question Jameson addresses is why so few Third World writers were becoming widely read in the West at a time when the canon was opening to European and American women and ethnic minorities. One problem, Jameson suggests, is the insistent social realism of most Third World writing, which resembles the naturalistic literature of a century ago, such as that of Dreiser and Zola. The other problem is that Third World novels are shaped as allegories in which the protagonists' struggle stands for that of their society. Jameson's analysis in terms of literary style and genre was to provoke a sharp response by the poet and theorist Aijaz Ahmad (see pp. 1831–34). Jameson's reply to Ahmad can be found on pp. 1834–36. (For biographical information on Jameson, see p. 1290.)*

Aijaz Ahmad

b. 1945

Born in India in the last years of British colonial rule, Aijaz Ahmad was a "child of nationalism," subject to the political tensions of independent India but deeply influenced by British literature and culture. He has been professorial fellow at the Nehru Memorial Museum and Library in New Delhi, India, and professor of political sciences at York University in Ontario, Canada. He currently holds the Khan Abdul Ghaffar Khan Chair in the Academy for Third World Studies in Jamia Milia Islamia University in New Delhi. A poet as well as a political thinker, he is the author of Lineages of the Present: Ideological and Political Genealogies of Contemporary South Asia *(1996),* On Communalism and Globalization: Offensives of the Far Right *(2002), and* Afghanistan, Iraq and the Imperialism of Our Time *(2004), which have focused anthropological attention on current instances of neocolonialism.*

In his controversial 1992 book, In Theory: Classes, Nations, Literatures *(1992), Ahmad criticizes much postcolonial theory as a Western invention that homogenizes the developing world, erasing the unique political behaviors and attitudes that arise in each nation. According to Ahmad, there was a distinct rise in nationalistic behavior in "Third World" countries following World War II as an impulse against the process of globalization, and Western postcolonial theory is often guilty of erasing the individual identities that these nations have struggled to preserve. In the following selection from* In Theory, *originally printed in* Social Text *in the fall of 1987, Ahmad takes on his fellow Marxist Fredric Jameson, whose argument that Third World novels operate as national allegories struck Ahmad as theorizing out of their individual existence literary texts from the developing world — including his own.*

FREDRIC JAMESON

From *Third-World Literature in the Era of Multinational Capitalism*

Many arguments can be made for the importance and interest of non-canonical forms of literature such as that of the third world,[1] but one is peculiarly self-defeating because it borrows the weapons of the adversary: the strategy of trying to prove that these texts are as "great" as those of the canon itself. The object is then to show that, to take an example from another non-canonical form, Dashiell Hammett is really as great as Dostoyevsky, and therefore can be admitted. This is to attempt dutifully to wish away all traces of that "pulp" format which is constitutive of sub-genres, and it invites immediate failure insofar as any passionate reader of Dostoyevsky will know at once, after a few pages, that those kinds of satisfactions are not present. Nothing is to be gained by passing over in silence the radical difference of non-canonical texts. The third-world novel will not offer the satisfactions of Proust or Joyce; what is more damaging than that, perhaps, is its tendency to remind us of outmoded stages of our own first-world cultural development and to cause us to conclude that "they are still writing novels like Dreiser or Sherwood Anderson."

A case could be built on this kind of discouragement, with its deep existential commitment to a rhythm of modernist innovation if not fashion-changes; but it would not be a moralizing one — a historicist one, rather, which challenges our imprisonment in the present of postmodernism and calls for a reinvention of the radical difference of *our own* cultural past and its now seemingly old-fashioned situations and novelties.

But I would rather argue all this a different way, at least for now[2]: these reactions to third-world texts are at one and the same time perfectly natural, perfectly comprehensible, *and* terribly parochial. If the purpose of the canon is to restrict our aesthetic sympathies, to develop a range of rich and subtle perceptions which can be exercised only on the occasion of a small but choice body of texts, to discourage us from reading anything else or from reading those things in different ways, then it is humanly impoverishing. Indeed our want of sympathy for these often unmodern third-world texts is itself frequently but a disguise for some deeper fear of the affluent about the way people actually live in other parts of the world — a way of life that still has little in common with daily life in the American suburb. There is nothing particularly disgraceful in having lived a sheltered life, in never having had to confront the difficulties, the complications and the frustrations of urban living, but it is nothing to be particularly proud of either. Moreover, a limited experience of life normally does not make for a wide range of sympathies with very different kinds of people (I'm thinking of differences that range from gender and race all the way to those of social class and culture).

The way in which all this affects the reading process seems to be as follows: as western readers whose tastes (and much else) have been formed by our own modernisms, a popular or socially realistic third-world novel tends to come before us, not immediately, but as though already-read. We sense, between ourselves and this alien text, the presence of another reader, of the Other reader, for whom a narrative, which strikes us as conventional or naive, has a freshness of information and a social interest that we cannot share. The fear and the resistance I'm evoking has to do, then, with the sense of our own non-coincidence with that Other reader, so different from ourselves; our sense that to coincide in any adequate way with that Other "ideal reader" — that is to say, to read this text adequately — we would have to give up a great deal that is individually precious to us and

---

[1] I have argued elsewhere for the importance of mass culture and science fiction. See "Reification and Utopia in Mass Culture," *Social Text* no. 1 (1979), 130–148. [Jameson]

[2] The essay was written for an immediate occasion — the third memorial lecture in honor of my late colleague and friend Robert C. Elliot at the University of California, San Diego. It is essentially reprinted as given. [Jameson]

acknowledge an existence and a situation unfamiliar and therefore frightening — one that we do not know and prefer *not* to know. . . .

. . . Let me now, by way of a sweeping hypothesis, try to say what all third-world cultural productions seem to have in common and what distinguishes them radically from analogous cultural forms in the first world. All third-world texts are necessarily, I want to argue, allegorical, and in a very specific way: they are to be read as what I will call *national allegories*, even when, or perhaps I should say, particularly when their forms develop out of predominantly western machineries of representation, such as the novel. Let me try to state this distinction in a grossly oversimplified way: one of the determinants of capitalist culture, that is, the culture of the western realist and modernist novel, is a radical split between the private and the public, between the poetic and the political, between what we have come to think of as the domain of sexuality and the unconscious and that of the public world of classes, of the economic, and of secular political power: in other words, Freud versus Marx. Our numerous theoretical attempts to overcome this great split only reconfirm its

existence and its shaping power over our individual and collective lives. We have been trained in a deep cultural conviction that the lived experience of our private existences is somehow incommensurable with the abstractions of economic science and political dynamics. Politics in our novels therefore is, according to Stendhal's canonical formulation, a "pistol shot in the middle of a concert."

I will argue that, although we may retain for convenience and for analysis such categories as the subjective and the public or political, the relations between them are wholly different in third-world culture. Third-world texts, even those which are seemingly private and invested with a properly libidinal dynamic — necessarily project a political dimension in the form of national allegory: *the story of the private individual destiny is always an allegory of the embattled situation of the public third-world culture and society.* Need I add that it is precisely this very different ratio of the political to the personal which makes such texts alien to us at first approach, and consequently, resistant to our conventional western habits of reading? . . .

AIJAZ AHMAD

From *Jameson's Rhetoric of Otherness and the "National Allegory"*

There is doubtless a personal, somewhat existential side to my encounter with this text, which is best clarified at the outset. I have been reading Jameson's work now for roughly fifteen years, and at least some of what I know about the literatures and cultures of Western Europe and the US comes from him; and because I am a marxist, I had always thought of us, Jameson and myself, as birds of the same feather even though we never quite flocked together. But, then, when I was on the fifth page of this text (specifically, on the sentence

starting with "All third-world texts are necessarily . . ." etc.), I realized that what was being theorized was, among many other things, myself. Now, I was born in India and I am a Pakistani citizen; I write poetry in Urdu, a language not commonly understood among US intellectuals. So, I said to myself: *"All? . . . necessarily?"* It felt odd. Matters got much more curious, however. For, the farther I read the more I realized, with no little chagrin, that the man whom I had for so long, so affectionately, even though from a physical distance, taken as a comrade was, in his own opinion, my civilizational Other. It was not a good feeling. . . .

III

I have said already that if one believes in the Three Worlds Theory, hence in a "third world" defined exclusively in terms of "the experience of colonialism and imperialism," then the primary ideological formation available to a leftwing intellectual shall be that of nationalism; it will then be possible to assert, surely with very considerable exaggeration but nonetheless, that "all third-world texts are necessarily . . . *national allegories*" (emphases in the original). This exclusive emphasis on the nationalist ideology is there even in the opening paragraph of Jameson's text where the only choice for the "third world" is said to be between its "nationalisms" and a "global American postmodernist culture." Is there no other choice? Could not one join the "second world," for example? There used to be, in the marxist discourse, a thing called socialist and/or communist culture which was neither nationalist nor postmodernist. Has that vanished from our discourse altogether, even as the name of a desire?

Jameson's haste in totalizing historical phenomena in terms of binary oppositions (nationalism/postmodernism, in this case) leaves little room for the fact, for instance, that the only nationalisms in the so-called third world which have been able to resist US cultural pressure and have actually produced any alternatives are the ones which are already articulated to and assimilated within the much larger field of socialist political practice. Virtually all others have had no difficulty in reconciling themselves with what Jameson calls "global American postmodernist culture"; in the singular and sizeable case of Iran (which Jameson forbids us to mention on the grounds that it is "predictable" that we shall do so), the anti-communism of the Islamic nationalists has produced not social regeneration but clerical fascism. Nor does the absolutism of that opposition (postmodernism/nationalism) permit any space for the simple idea that nationalism itself is not some unitary thing with some pre-determined essence and value. There are hundreds of nationalisms in Asia and Africa today; some are progressive, others are not. Whether or not a nationalism will produce a progressive cultural practice depends, to put it in Gramscian terms, upon the political character of the power bloc which takes hold of it and utilizes it, as a material force, in the process of constituting its own hegemony. There is neither theoretical ground nor empirical evidence to support the notion that bourgeois nationalisms of the so-called third world will have any difficulty with postmodernism; they *want* it.

Yet, there *is* a very tight fit between the Three Worlds Theory, the over-valorization of the nationalist ideology, and the assertion that "national allegory" is the primary, even exclusive, form of narrativity in the so-called third world. If this "third world" is *constituted* by the singular "experience of colonialism and imperialism," and if the only possible response is a nationalist one, then what else is there that is more urgent to narrate than this "experience"; in fact, there is *nothing else* to narrate. For, if societies here are defined not by relations of production but by relations of intra-national domination; if they are forever suspended outside the sphere of conflict between capitalism (first world) and socialism (second world); if the motivating force for history here is neither class formation and class struggle nor the multiplicities of intersecting conflicts based upon class, gender, nation, race, region and so on, but the unitary "experience" of national oppression (if one is merely the *object* of history, the Hegelian slave) then what else *can* one narrate but that national oppression? Politically, we are Calibans, all. Formally, we are fated to be in the poststructuralist world of repetition with difference; the same allegory, the nationalist one, re-written, over and over again, until the end of time: "all third-world texts are necessarily . . ."

IV

But one could start with a radically different premise, namely the proposition that we live not in three worlds but in one; that this world includes the experience of colonialism and imperialism on both sides of Jameson's global divide (the "experience" of imperialism is a central fact of all aspects of life inside the US from ideological formation to the utilization of the social surplus in military-industrial complexes); that societies in formations of backward capitalism are as much constituted by the division of classes as are societies in the advanced capitalist countries; that socialism is not restricted to something called the second world but is simply the name of a resistance that saturates the globe today, as capitalism itself does; that the different parts of the capitalist system are to be known not in terms of a binary opposition but as a contradictory unity, with differences, yes, but also with profound overlaps. One immediate consequence for literary theory would be that the unitary search for "a theory of cognitive aesthetics for third-world literature" would be rendered impossible, and one would have to forego the idea of a meta-narrative that encompasses all the fecundity of real narratives in the so-called third world. Conversely, many of the questions that one would ask about, let us say, Urdu or Bengali traditions of literature may turn out to be rather similar to the questions one has asked previously about English/American literatures. By the same token, a *real* knowledge of those other traditions may force US literary theorists to ask questions about their own tradition which they have heretofore not asked.

Jameson claims that one cannot proceed from the premise of a real unity of the world "without falling back into some general liberal and humanistic universalism." That is a curious idea, coming from a marxist. One should have thought that the world was united not by liberalist ideology — that the world was not at all constituted in the realm of an Idea, be it Hegelian or humanist — but by the global operation of a single mode of production, namely the capitalist one, and the global resistance to this mode, a resistance which is itself unevenly developed in different parts of the globe. Socialism, one should have thought, was not by any means limited to the so-called second world (the socialist countries) but a global phenomenon, reaching into the farthest rural communities in Asia, Africa and Latin America, not to speak of individuals and groups within the United States. What gives the world its unity, then, is not a humanist ideology but the ferocious

struggle of capital and labor which is now strictly and fundamentally global in character. The prospect of a socialist revolution has receded so much from the practical horizon of so much of the metropolitan left that the temptation for the US left intelligentsia is to forget the ferocity of that basic struggle which in our time transcends all others. The advantage of coming from Pakistan, in my own case, is that the country is saturated with capitalist commodities, bristles with US weaponry, borders on China, the Soviet Union and Afghanistan, suffers from a proliferation of competing nationalisms, and is currently witnessing the first stage in the consolidation of the communist movement. It is difficult, coming from there, to forget that primary motion of history which gives to our globe its contradictory unity: a notion that has nothing to do with liberal humanism.

As for the specificity of cultural difference, Jameson's theoretical conception tends, I believe, in the opposite direction, namely, that of homogenization. Difference between the first world and the third is absolutized as an Otherness, but the enormous cultural heterogeneity of social formations within the so-called third world is submerged within a singular identity of "experience." Now, countries of Western Europe and North America have been deeply tied together over roughly the last two hundred years; capitalism itself is so much older in these countries; the cultural logic of late capitalism[1] is so strongly operative in these metropolitan formations; the circulation of cultural products among them is so immediate, so extensive, so brisk that one could sensibly speak of a certain cultural homogeneity among them. But Asia, Africa, and Latin America? Historically, these countries were never so closely tied together; Peru and India simply do not have a common history of the sort that Germany and France, or Britain and the United States, have; not even the singular "experience of colonialism and imperialism" has been in specific ways the same or similar in, say, India and Namibia. These various countries, from the

[1] *The Cultural Logic of Late Capitalism* is the subtitle of Jameson's book on postmodernism. An essay by Jameson on postmodernism appears in Chapter 10, p. 1956.

three continents, have been assimilated into the global structure of capitalism not as a single cultural ensemble but highly differentially, each establishing its own circuits of (unequal) exchange with the metropolis, each acquiring its own very distinct class formations. Circuits of exchange among them are rudimentary at best; an average Nigerian who is literate about his own country would know infinitely more about England and the United States than about any country of Asia or Latin America or indeed about most countries of Africa. The kind of circuits that bind the cultural complexes of the advanced capitalist countries simply do not exist among countries of backward capitalism, and capitalism itself, which is dominant but not altogether universalized, does not yet have the same power of homogenization in its cultural logic in most of these countries, except among the urban bourgeoisie.

Of course, great cultural similarities also exist among countries that occupy analogous positions in the global capitalist system, and there are similarities in many cases that have been bequeathed by the similarities of socio-economic structures in the pre-capitalist past. The point is not to construct a typology that is simply the obverse of Jameson's, but rather to define the material basis for a fair degree of cultural homogenization among the advanced capitalist countries and the lack of that kind of homogenization in the rest of the capitalist world. In context, therefore, one is doubly surprised at Jameson's absolute insistence upon difference and the relation of otherness between the first world and the third, and his equally insistent idea that the "experience" of the "third world" could be contained and communicated within a single narrative form.

By locating capitalism in the first world and socialism in the second, Jameson's theory freezes and de-historicizes the global space within which struggles between these great motivating forces actually take place. And, by assimilating the enormous heterogeneities and productivities of our life into a single Hegelian metaphor of the master/slave relation, this theory reduces us to an ideal-type and demands from us that we narrate ourselves through a form commensurate with that ideal-type. To say that all third-world texts are necessarily this or that is to say, in effect, that any text originating within that social space which is *not* this or that is not a "true" narrative. It is in this sense above all, that the category of "third-world literature" which is the site of this operation, with the "national allegory" as its metatext as well as the mark of its constitution and difference, is, to my mind, epistemologically an impossible category.

FREDRIC JAMESON

A Brief Response

I can understand many of Aijaz Ahmad's reactions to my essay without, finally, losing the feeling that it was worth doing and that these things were worth saying. The essay was intended as an intervention into a "first-world" literary and critical situation, in which it seemed important to me to stress the loss of certain literary functions and intellectual commitments in the contemporary American scene. It seemed useful to dramatize that loss by showing the constitutive presence of those things — what I called narrative allegory (namely the coincidence of the personal story and the "tale of the tribe," as still in Spenser)[1] and also the political role of the cultural intellectual — in

[1]Jameson's point is that Spenser's epic *The Faerie Queene* (1594) is simultaneously a knightly romance and an allegory about England.

other parts of the world. To be sure, one then returns to show that US literature also includes its own "third-world" cultures (which escape the categories in which one describes hegemonic culture); and equally clearly, the classical cultures of the East (for example) are no more to be thought of as third-world cultures than the English Renaissance is to be thought of as a first-world one.

As for such categories, they are meant to stimulate the perception of difference by imposing comparisons and comparative operations that do not always suggest themselves automatically in our present academic division of labor, where Lu Xun[2] belongs to Chinese departments and Ousmane[3] (if to anything) to French departments. I believe that we have every interest in developing a kind of comparative cultural study (on the model, say, of Barrington Moore's comparative sociology) in which such disparate texts are juxtaposed, not to turn both into "the same thing," but rather with a view towards establishing radical *situational* difference in cultural production and meanings.

The methodological problem is that such differences can only be established within some larger preestablished identity: if there is nothing in common between two cultural situations, then clearly the establishment of difference is both pointless and given in advance. What this means is that if Identity and Difference are fixed and eternal opposites, we have either a ceaseless alternation, or a set of intolerable choices: presumably there would be no great advantage gained by junking the category of "third world" if the result is that North America then becomes "the same" as the subcontinent, say. But nothing is to be done with sheer random difference either, which either leaves us back in Boasian anthropology or in the empiricist history of "one damned thing after another." The claim of the dialectic as a distinct mode of thought is to set categories like those of Identity and Difference in motion, so that the inevitable starting point is ultimately transformed beyond recognition; whether this claim can be honored cannot, of course, be decided in advance.

A great many other important issues are raised in this paper, which I can scarcely touch on now, let alone answer. The concept of "national allegory," for example, was not meant as an endorsement of nationalism, although I believe that a certain nationalism does not always play an exclusively negative and harmful role in some socialist revolutions.

As for the term "first world," I hope it is not necessary to say that the priority it implies is not a social one (the burden of my paper was to argue virtually the opposite position), nor is it an intellectual one (particularly given our Roman eclecticism[4] — currently expanding, I'm happy to say, to include a keen interest in contemporary Indian theory), nor is it even, God knows, a matter of production: it is based, far more even than military power, on the fact that American bankers hold the levers of the world system. As for one's feeling that this system, late capitalism, is the supreme unifying force of contemporary history, such a belief — which has been characterized as "monotheism" by some — confirms the descriptions of the *Grundrisse*[5] and does seem to me to correspond to a fact of life. I don't, however, see how my argument can be taken for an endorsement of this gravitational force, which it would be well, however, to take into account if one plans to try to resist it.

I think I can detect some final implication here that "theory" is, in the very nature of the beast, repressive and an exercise of power — although I can't be sure whether Aijaz Ahmad would endorse the full "theoretical" form of this particular position about theory. My own feeling is that such anxiety is particularly misplaced in a

---

[2]Pen name of Zhou Shuren (1881–1936), considered the father of modern Chinese literature.

[3]Ousmane Sembène (b. 1923), Senegalese novelist, poet, film director.

[4]Jameson is gesturing toward the fact that the Roman Empire allowed its subjugated states to keep their own customs as long as they paid their taxes.

[5]Marx's "Critique of Political Economy," a massive manuscript that precedes and underlies *Capital*, not published until 1939, a selection from which appears at pp. 410–11.

situation in which the "role" of the intellectual (and the very category itself) has never been less influential and in which anti-intellectualism is deeply ingrained in the very spirit of the culture. It seems to me much more productive to insist, as he also does, on the way in which we are all *situated* and determined socially and ideologically by our multiple class positions — something I hope I never seemed to deny. But even speaking from that position (as I could not but do), I still think my intervention was a positive and progressive one, whose implications (on any number of levels) include: the necessity for teaching third-world literatures; the recognition of the challenge they pose to even the most advanced contemporary theory; the need for a *relational* way of thinking global culture (such that we cannot henceforth think "first-world" literature in isolation from that of other global spaces); the proposal for a comparative study of cultural situations (which I have been clearer about here, perhaps, but for which my code word, in the essay in question, was the slogan, "mode of production"); and finally, the suggestion (which Ahmad seems to endorse) that when we get done with all that we may want to entertain the possibility that we also need a (new) theory of second-world culture as well.

Gayatri Spivak

b. 1942

The chief spokesperson for "subaltern studies," Gayatri Chakravorty Spivak was born in Calcutta and educated at the University of Calcutta and at Cornell University. Her translation of and introduction to Jacques Derrida's Of Grammatology *(1967) made her a national figure, and her critical method continues to feature the deconstructive turn. But she is even more widely known today as a postcolonial theorist from a global feminist Marxist perspective. Her social commitments are not merely theoretical: Professor Spivak is active in rural literacy teacher training on the grassroots level in India and Bangladesh. Spivak was the Andrew W. Mellon Professor of English at the University of Pittsburgh before becoming Avalon Professor at Columbia University in 1991. Spivak's books include* Myself I Must Remake: The Life and Poetry of W. B. Yeats *(1974),* In Other Worlds: Essays in Cultural Politics *(1988),* Selected Subaltern Studies *(ed., 1988),* The Post-Colonial Critic *(1990),* Outside in the Teaching Machine *(1993),* A Critique of Postcolonial Reason: Toward a History of the Vanishing Present *(1999), and* Death of a Discipline *(2003). Her work in progress includes a book of essays on identity. The present selection, originally published in* Critical Inquiry *12 (Autumn 1985), is here included because of its important place in the history of postcolonial theory. Over the twenty years since it was first published, however, Spivak has changed her position on many of the issues she raised here, and the interested reader must be referred to the revised version, which appears in her* Critique of Postcolonial Reason *(1999), pp. 112–48.*

Three Women's Texts and a Critique of Imperialism

It should not be possible to read nineteenth-century British literature without remembering that imperialism, understood as England's social mission, was a crucial part of the cultural representation of England to the English. The role of literature in the production of cultural representation should not be ignored. These two obvious "facts" continue to be disregarded in the reading of nineteenth-century British literature. This itself attests to the continuing success of the imperialist project, displaced and dispersed into more modern forms.

If these "facts" were remembered, not only in the study of British literature but in the study of the literatures of the European colonizing cultures of the great age of imperialism, we would produce a narrative, in literary history, of the "worlding" of what is now called "the Third World." To consider the Third World as distant cultures, exploited but with rich intact literary heritages waiting to be recovered, interpreted, and curricularized in English translation fosters the emergence of "the Third World" as a signifier that allows us to forget that "worlding," even as it expands the empire of the literary discipline.[1]

It seems particularly unfortunate when the emergent perspective of feminist criticism reproduces the axioms of imperialism. A basically isolationist admiration for the literature of the female subject in Europe and Anglo-America establishes the high feminist norm. It is supported and operated by an information-retrieval approach to "Third-World" literature which often employs a deliberately "non-theoretical" methodology with self-conscious rectitude.

In this essay, I will attempt to examine the operation of the "worlding" of what is today "the Third World" by what has become a cult text of feminism: *Jane Eyre*.[2] I plot the novel's reach and grasp, and locate its structural motors. I read *Wide Sargasso Sea* as *Jane Eyre's* reinscription and *Frankenstein* as an analysis — even a deconstruction — of a "worlding" such as *Jane Eyre's*.[3]

I need hardly mention that the object of my investigation is the printed book, not its "author." To make such a distinction is, of course, to ignore the lessons of deconstruction. A deconstructive critical approach would loosen the binding of the book, undo the opposition between verbal text and the biography of the named subject "Charlotte Brontë," and see the two as each other's "scene of writing." In such a reading, the life that writes itself as "my life" is as much a production in psychosocial space (other names can be found) as the book that is written by the holder of that named life — a book that is then consigned to what *is* most often recognized as genuinely "social": the world of publication and distribution.[4] To touch Brontë's "life" in such a way, however, would be too risky here. We must rather strategically take shelter in an essentialism which, not wishing to lose the important advantages won by U.S. mainstream feminism, will continue to honor the suspect binary oppositions — book and author, individual and history — and start with an assurance of the following sort: my readings here do not seek to undermine the excellence of the individual artist. If even minimally successful, the readings will incite a degree of rage against the imperialist

---

[2]See Charlotte Brontë, *Jane Eyre* (New York, 1960); all further references to this work, abbreviated *JE*, will be included in the text. [Spivak]

[3]See Jean Rhys, *Wide Sargasso Sea* (Harmondsworth, 1996); all further references to this work, abbreviated *WSS*, will be included in the text. And see Mary Shelley, *Frankenstein; or, the Modern Prometheus* (New York, 1965); all further references to this work, abbreviated *F*, will be included in the text. [Spivak]

[4]I have tried to do this in my essay "Unmaking and Making in *To the Lighthouse*," in *Women and Language in Literature and Society*, ed. Sally McConnell-Ginet, Ruth Borker, and Nelly Furman (New York, 1980), pp. 310–27. [Spivak]

[1]My notion of the "worlding of a world" upon what must be assumed to be uninscribed earth is a vulgarization of Martin Heidegger's idea; see "The Origin of the Work of Art," *Poetry, Language, Thought*, trans. Albert Hofstadter (New York, 1977), pp. 17–87. [Spivak] For Heidegger, see p. 611.

narrativization of history, that it should produce so abject a script for her. I provide these assurances to allow myself some room to situate feminist individualism in its historical determination rather than simply to canonize it as feminism as such.

Sympathetic U.S. feminists have remarked that I do not do justice to Jane Eyre's subjectivity. A word of explanation is perhaps in order. The broad strokes of my presuppositions are that what is at stake, for feminist individualism in the age of imperialism, is precisely the making of human beings, the constitution and "interpellation" of the subject not only as individual but as "individualist."[5] This stake is represented on two registers: childbearing and soul making. The first is domestic-society-through-sexual-reproduction cathected[6] as "companionate love"; the second is the imperialist project cathected as civil-society-through-social-mission. As the female individualist, not-quite/not-male, articulates herself in shifting relationship to what is at stake, the "native female" as such (*within* discourse, *as* a signifier) is excluded from any share in this emerging norm.[7] If we read this account from an isolationist perspective in a "metropolitan" context, we see nothing there but the psychobiography of the militant female subject. In a reading such as mine, in contrast, the effort is to wrench oneself away from the mesmerizing focus of the "subject-constitution" of the female individualist.

To develop further the notion that my stance need not be an accusing one, I will refer to a passage from Roberto Fernández Retamar's "Caliban."[8] José Enrique Rodó had argued in 1900 that the model for the Latin American intellectual in relationship to Europe could be Shakespeare's Ariel.[9] In 1971 Retamar, denying the possibility of an identifiable "Latin American Culture," recast the model as Caliban. Not surprisingly, this powerful exchange still excludes any specific consideration of the civilizations of the Maya, the Aztecs, the Incas, or the smaller nations of what is now called Latin America. Let us note carefully that, at this stage of my argument, this "conversation" between Europe and Latin America (without a specific consideration of the political economy of the "worlding" of the "native") provides a sufficient thematic description of our attempt to confront the ethnocentric and reverse-ethnocentric benevolent double bind (that is, considering the "native" as object for enthusiastic information-retrieval and thus denying its own "worlding") that I sketched in my opening paragraphs.

In a moving passage in "Caliban," Retamar locates both Caliban and Ariel in the postcolonial intellectual:

> There is no real Ariel–Caliban polarity: both are slaves in the hands of Prospero, the foreign magician. But Caliban is the rude and unconquerable master of the island, while Ariel, a creature of the air, although also a child of the isle, is the intellectual.

> The deformed Caliban — enslaved, robbed of his island, and taught the language by Prospero — rebukes him thus: "You taught me language, and my profit on't/ Is, I know how to curse." ["C," pp. 28, 11]

---

[5] As always, I take my formula from Louis Althusser, "Ideology and Ideological State Apparatuses (Notes towards an Investigation)," *Lenin and Philosophy and Other Essays*, trans. Ben Brewster (New York, 1971), pp. 127–86. For an acute differentiation between the individual and individualism, see V. N. Vološinov, *Marxism and the Philosophy of Language*, trans. Ladislav Matejka, and I. R. Titunik, *Studies in Language*, vol. 1 (New York, 1973), pp. 93–94 and 152–53. For a "straight" analysis of the roots and ramifications of English "individualism," see C. B. MacPherson, *The Political Theory of Possessive Individualism: Hobbes to Locke* (Oxford, 1962). I am grateful to Jonathan Rée for bringing this book to my attention and for giving a careful reading of all but the very end of the present essay. [Spivak] For Althusser, see p. 1263.

[6] In Freudian terminology, to cathect is to invest emotional energy (libido) in some way.

[7] I am constructing an analogy with Homi Bhabha's powerful notion of "not-quite/not white" in his "Of Mimicry and Man: The Ambiguity of Colonial Discourse," *October* 28 (Spring 1984): 132. I should also add that I use the word "native" here in reaction to the term "Third-World Woman." It cannot, of course, apply with equal historical justice to both the West Indian and the Indian contexts nor to contexts of imperialism by transportation. [Spivak]

[8] See Roberto Fernández Retamar, "Caliban: Notes towards a Discussion of Culture in Our America," trans. Lynn Garafola, David Arthur McMurray, and Robert Márquez, *Massachusetts Review* 15 (Winter–Spring 1974): 7–72; all further references to this work, abbreviated "C," will be included in the text. [Spivak]

[9] See José Enrique Rodó, *Ariel*, ed. Gordon Brotherston (Cambridge, 1967). [Spivak]

As we attempt to unlearn our so-called privilege as Ariel and "seek from [a certain] Caliban the honor of a place in his rebellious and glorious ranks," we do not ask that our students and colleagues should emulate us but that they should attend to us ("C," p. 72). If, however, we are driven by a nostalgia for lost origins, we too run the risk of effacing the "native" and stepping forth as "the real Caliban," of forgetting that he is a name in a play, an inaccessible blankness circumscribed by an interpretable text.[10] The stagings of Caliban work alongside the narrativization of history: claiming to *be* Caliban legitimizes the very individualism that we must persistently attempt to undermine from within.

Elizabeth Fox-Genovese, in an article on history and women's history, shows us how to define the historical moment of feminism in the West in terms of female access to individualism.[11] The battle for female individualism plays itself out within the larger theater of the establishment of meritocratic individualism, indexed in the aesthetic field by the ideology of "the creative imagination." Fox-Genovese's presupposition will guide us into the beautifully orchestrated opening of *Jane Eyre*.

It is a scene of the marginalization and privatization of the protagonist: "There was no possibility of taking a walk that day. . . . Out-door exercise was now out of the question. I was glad of it," Brontë writes (*JE*, p. 9). The movement continues as Jane breaks the rules of the appropriate topography of withdrawal. The family at the center withdraws into the sanctioned architectural space of the withdrawing room or drawing room; Jane inserts herself — "I slipped in" — into the margin — "A small breakfast-room *adjoined* the drawing room" (*JE*, p. 9; my emphasis).

The manipulation of the domestic inscription of space within the upwardly mobilizing currents of the eighteenth- and nineteenth-century bourgeoisie in England and France is well known. It

seems fitting that the place to which Jane withdraws is not only not the withdrawing room but also not the dining room, the sanctioned place of family meals. Nor is it the library, the appropriate place for reading. The breakfast room "contained a book-case" (*JE*, p. 9). As Rudolph Ackerman wrote in his *Repository* (1823), one of the many manuals of taste in circulation in nineteenth-century England, these low bookcases and stands were designed to "contain all the books that may be desired for a sitting-room without reference to the library."[12] Even in this already triply off-center place, "having drawn the red moreen curtain nearly close, I [Jane] was shrined in double retirement" (*JE*, pp. 9–10).

Here in Jane's self-marginalized uniqueness, the reader becomes her accomplice: the reader and Jane are united — both are reading. Yet Jane still preserves her odd privilege, for she continues never quite doing the proper thing in its proper place. She cares little for reading what is *meant* to be read: the "letter-press." *She* reads the pictures. The power of this singular hermeneutics[13] is precisely that it can make the outside inside. "At intervals, while turning over the leaves of my book, I studied the aspect of that winter afternoon." Under "the clear panes of glass," the rain no longer penetrates, "the drear November day" is rather a one-dimensional "aspect" to be "studied," not decoded like the "letter-press" but, like pictures, deciphered by the unique creative imagination of the marginal individualist (*JE*, p. 10).

Before following the track of this unique imagination, let us consider the suggestion that the progress of *Jane Eyre* can be charted through a sequential arrangement of the family/counter-family dyad. In the novel, we encounter, first, the Reeds as the legal family and Jane, the late Mr. Reed's sister's daughter, as the representative of a near incestuous counter-family; second, the Brocklehursts, who run the school Jane is sent to, as the legal family and Jane, Miss Temple, and Helen Burns as a counter-family that falls short because it is only a community of women; third,

[10]For an elaboration of "an inaccessible blankness circumscribed by an interpretable text," see my "Can the Subaltern Speak?" *Interpretation of Culture*, eds. Cary Nelson and Lawrence Grossberg (Urbana, Ill., 1988). [Spivak]

[11]See Elizabeth Fox-Genovese, "Placing Women's History in History," *New Left Review* 133 (May–June 1982): 5–29. [Spivak]

[12]Rudolph Ackerman, *The Repository of Arts, Literature, Commerce, Manufactures, Fashions, and Politics* (London, 1823), p. 310. [Spivak]

[13]Mode of interpretation.

Rochester and the mad Mrs. Rochester as the legal family and Jane and Rochester as the illicit counter-family. Other items may be added to the thematic chain in this sequence: Rochester and Céline Varens as structurally functional counter-family; Rochester and Blanche Ingram as dissimulation of legality — and so on. It is during this sequence that Jane is moved from the counter-family to the family-in-law. In the next sequence, it is Jane who restores full family status to the as-yet-incomplete community of siblings, the Riverses. The final sequence of the book is a *community of families*, with Jane, Rochester, and their children at the center.

In terms of the narrative energy of the novel, how is Jane moved from the place of the counter-family to the family-in-law? It is the active ideology of imperialism that provides the discursive field.

(My working definition of "discursive field" must assume the existence of discrete "systems of signs" at hand in the socius,[14] each based on a specific axiomatics. I am identifying these systems as discursive fields. "Imperialism as social mission" generates the possibility of one such axiomatics. How the individual artist taps the discursive field at hand with a sure touch, if not with transhistorical clairvoyance, in order to make the narrative structure move I hope to demonstrate through the following example. It is crucial that we extend our analysis of this example beyond the minimal diagnosis of "racism.")

Let us consider the figure of Bertha Mason, a figure produced by the axiomatics of imperialism. Through Bertha Mason, the white Jamaican Creole, Brontë renders the human/animal frontier as acceptably indeterminate, so that a good greater than the letter of the Law can be broached. Here is the celebrated passage, given in the voice of Jane:

In the deep shade, at the further end of the room, a figure ran backwards and forwards. What it was, whether beast or human being, one could not . . . tell: it grovelled, seemingly, on all fours; it snatched and growled like some strange wild animal: but it was covered with clothing, and a quantity of dark, grizzled hair, wild as a mane, hid its head and face. [*JE*, p. 295]

[14]Individual considered as a unit of society.

In a matching passage, given in the voice of Rochester speaking *to* Jane, Brontë presents the imperative for a shift beyond the Law as divine injunction rather than human motive. In the terms of my essay, we might say that this is the register not of mere marriage or sexual reproduction but of Europe and its not-yet-human Other, of soul making. The field of imperial conquest is here inscribed as Hell:

"One night I had been awakened by her yells . . . it was a fiery West Indian night. . . .

" 'This life,' said I at last, 'is hell! — this is the air — those are the sounds of the bottomless pit! *I have a right* to deliver myself from it if I can. . . . Let me break away, and go home to God!' . . .

"A wind fresh from Europe blew over the ocean and rushed through the open casement: the storm broke, streamed, thundered, blazed, and the air grew pure. . . . It was true Wisdom that consoled me in that hour, and showed me the right path. . . .

"The sweet wind from Europe was still whispering in the refreshed leaves, and the Atlantic was thundering in glorious liberty. . . .

" 'Go,' said Hope, 'and live again in Europe. . . . You have done all that God and Humanity require of you.' " [*JE*, pp. 310–11; my emphasis]

It is the unquestioned ideology of imperialist axiomatics, then, that conditions Jane's move from the counter-family set to the set of the family-in-law. Marxist critics such as Terry Eagleton have seen this only in terms of the ambiguous *class* position of the governess.[15] Sandra Gilbert and Susan Gubar, on the other hand, have seen Bertha Mason only in psychological terms, as Jane's dark double.[16]

I will not enter the critical debates that offer themselves here. Instead, I will develop the suggestion that nineteenth-century feminist individualism could conceive of a "greater" project than access to the closed circle of the nuclear family. This is the project of soul making beyond "mere"

[15]See Terry Eagleton, *Myths of Power: A Marxist Study of the Brontës* (London, 1975); this is one of the general presuppositions of his book. [Spivak]
[16]See Sandra M. Gilbert and Susan Gubar, *The Madwoman in the Attic: The Woman Writer and the Nineteenth-Century Literary Imagination* (New Haven, Conn., 1979), pp. 360–62. [Spivak] For Gilbert and Gubar, see p. 1531.

sexual reproduction. Here the native "subject" is not almost an animal but rather the object of what might be termed the terrorism of the categorical imperative.

I am using "Kant" in this essay as a metonym for the most flexible ethical moment in the European eighteenth century. Kant words the categorical imperative, conceived as the universal moral law given by pure reason, in this way: "In all creation every thing one chooses and over which one has any power, may be used *merely as means*; man alone, and with him every rational creature, is an *end in himself.*" It is thus a moving displacement of Christian ethics from religion to philosophy. As Kant writes: "With this agrees very well the possibility of such a command as: *Love God above everything, and thy neighbor as thyself.* For as a command it requires respect for a law which *commands love* and does not leave it to our own arbitrary choice to make this our principle."[17]

The "categorical" in Kant cannot be adequately represented in determinately grounded action. The dangerous transformative power of philosophy, however, is that its formal subtlety can be travestied in the service of the state. Such a travesty in the case of the categorical imperative can justify the imperialist project by producing the following formula: *make* the heathen into a human so that he can be treated as an end in himself.[18] This project is presented as a sort of tangent in *Jane Eyre*, a tangent that escapes the closed circle of the *narrative* conclusion. The tangent narrative is the story of St. John Rivers, who is granted the important task of concluding the *text.*

At the novel's end, the *allegorical* language of Christian psychobiography — rather than the textually constituted and seemingly *private* grammar of the creative imagination which we noted in the novel's opening — marks the inaccessibility of the imperialist project as such to the nascent "feminist" scenario. The concluding passage of *Jane Eyre* places St. John Rivers within the fold of *Pilgrim's Progress.*[19] Eagleton pays no attention to this but accepts the novel's ideological lexicon, which establishes St. John Rivers' heroism by identifying a life in Calcutta with an unquestioning choice of death. Gilbert and Gubar, by calling *Jane Eyre* "Plain Jane's Progress," see the novel as simply replacing the male protagonist with the female. They do not notice the distance between sexual reproduction and soul making, both actualized by the unquestioned idiom of imperialist presuppositions evident in the last part of *Jane Eyre*:

> Firm, faithful, and devoted, full of energy, and zeal, and truth, [St. John Rivers] labours for his race. . . . His is the sternness of the warrior Greatheart, who guards his pilgrim convoy from the onslaught of Apollyon. . . . His is the ambition of the high master-spirit[s] . . . who stand without fault before the throne of God; who share the last mighty victories of the Lamb; who are called, and chosen, and faithful. [*JE*, p. 455]

Earlier in the novel, St. John Rivers himself justifies the project: "My vocation? My great work? . . . My hopes of being numbered in the band who have merged all ambitions in the glorious one of bettering their race — of carrying knowledge into the realms of ignorance — of substituting peace for war — freedom for bondage — religion for superstition — the hope of heaven for the fear of hell?" (*JE*, p. 376). Imperialism and its territorial and subject-constituting project are a violent deconstruction of these oppositions.

[17] Immanuel Kant, *Critique of Practical Reason, The "Critique of Pure Reason," the "Critique of Practical Reason" and Other Ethical Treatises, the "Critique of Judgement,"* trans. J. M. D. Meiklejohn et al. (Chicago, 1952), pp. 328, 326. [Spivak]

[18] I have tried to justify the reduction of sociohistorical problems to formulas or propositions in my essay "Can the Subaltern Speak?" The "travesty" I speak of does not befall the Kantian ethic in its purity as an accident but rather exists within its lineaments as a possible supplement. On the register of the human being as child rather than heathen, my formula can be found, for example, in "What Is Enlightenment?" in Kant, *"Foundations of the Metaphysics of Morals," "What Is Enlightenment?" and a Passage from "The Metaphysics of Morals,"* trans. and ed. Lewis White Beck (Chicago, 1950). I have profited from discussing Kant with Jonathan Rée. [Spivak]

[19] The inset quotation from *Jane Eyre* below alludes to Part II of Bunyan's *Pilgrim's Progress* (1684), the sequel in which Christian's wife, Christiana, follows in her husband's path.

When Jean Rhys, born on the Caribbean island of Dominica, read *Jane Eyre* as a child, she was moved by Bertha Mason: "I thought I'd try to write her a life."[20] *Wide Sargasso Sea*, the slim novel published in 1965, at the end of Rhys' long career, is that "life."

I have suggested that Bertha's function in *Jane Eyre* is to render indeterminate the boundary between human and animal and thereby to weaken her entitlement under the spirit if not the letter of the Law. When Rhys rewrites the scene in *Jane Eyre* where Jane hears "a snarling, snatching sound, almost like a dog quarrelling" and then encounters a bleeding Richard Mason (*JE*, p. 210), she keeps Bertha's humanity, indeed her sanity as critic of imperialism, intact. Grace Poole, another character originally in *Jane Eyre*, describes the incident to Bertha in *Wide Sargasso Sea*: "So you don't remember that you attacked this gentleman with a knife? . . . I didn't hear all he said except 'I cannot interfere legally between yourself and your husband.' It was when he said 'legally' that you flew at him'" (*WSS*, p. 150). In Rhys' retelling, it is the dissimulation that Bertha discerns in the word "legally" — not an innate bestiality — that prompts her violent *reaction*.

In the figure of Antoinette, whom in *Wide Sargasso Sea* Rochester violently renames Bertha, Rhys suggests that so intimate a thing as personal and human identity might be determined by the politics of imperialism. Antoinette, as a white Creole child growing up at the time of emancipation in Jamaica,[21] is caught between the English imperialist and the black native. In recounting Antoinette's development, Rhys reinscribes some thematics of Narcissus.

There are, noticeably, many images of mirroring in the text. I will quote one from the first section. In this passage, Tia is the little black servant girl who is Antoinette's close companion: "We had eaten the same food, slept side by side, bathed in the same river. As I ran, I thought, I will live with Tia and I will be like her. . . . When I was close I saw the jagged stone in her hand but I did not see her throw it. . . . We stared at each other, blood on my face, tears on hers. It was as if I saw myself. Like in a looking glass" (*WSS*, p. 38).

A progressive sequence of dreams reinforces this mirror imagery. In its second occurrence, the dream is partially set in a *hortus conclusus*, or "enclosed garden" — Rhys uses the phrase (*WSS*, p. 50) — a Romance rewriting of the Narcissus topos as the place of encounter with Love.[22] In the enclosed garden, Antoinette encounters not Love but a strange threatening voice that says merely "in here," inviting her into a prison which masquerades as the legalization of love (*WSS*, p. 50).

In Ovid's *Metamorphoses*, Narcissus' madness is disclosed when he recognizes his Other as his self: "Iste ego sum."[23] Rhys makes Antoinette see her *self* as her Other, Brontë's Bertha. In the last section of *Wide Sargasso Sea*, Antoinette acts out *Jane Eyre's* conclusion and recognizes herself as the so-called ghost in Thornfield Hall: "I went into the hall again with the tall candle in my hand. It was then that I saw her — the ghost. The woman with streaming hair. She was surrounded by a gilt frame but I knew her" (*WSS*, p. 154). The gilt frame encloses a mirror: as Narcissus' pool reflects the selfed Other, so this "pool" reflects the Othered self. Here the dream sequence ends, with an invocation of none other than Tia, the Other that could not be selfed, because the fracture of imperialism rather than the Ovidian pool intervened. (I will return to this difficult point.) "That was the third time I had my dream, and it ended. . . . I called 'Tia' and jumped and woke" (*WSS*, p. 155). It is now, at the very end of the book, that Antoinette/Bertha can say: "Now at last I know why I was brought here and what I have to do" (*WSS*, pp. 155–56). We can read this as her having been brought into the England of Brontë's novel: "This cardboard house" — a

[20]Jean Rhys, in an interview with Elizabeth Vreeland, quoted in Nancy Harrison, *Jean Rhys and the Novel as Women's Text* (Chapel Hill: University of North Carolina P, 1988). This is an excellent, detailed study of Rhys. [Spivak]
[21]Jamaica's slaves were emancipated in 1834.

[22]See Louise Vinge, *The Narcissus Theme in Western European Literature Up to the Early Nineteenth Century*, trans. Robert Dewsnap et al. (Lund, 1967), chap. 5. [Spivak]
[23]For a detailed study of this text, see John Brenkman, "Narcissus in the Text," *Georgia Review* 30 (Summer 1976): 293–327. [Spivak]

book between cardboard covers — "where I walk at night is not England" (*WSS*, p. 148). In this fictive England, she must play out her role, act out the transformation of her "self" into that fictive Other, set fire to the house and kill herself, so that Jane Eyre can become the feminist individualist heroine of British fiction. I must read this as an allegory of the general epistemic violence of imperialism, the construction of a self-immolating colonial subject for the glorification of the social mission of the colonizer. At least Rhys sees to it that the woman from the colonies is not sacrificed as an insane animal for her sister's consolation.

Critics have remarked that *Wide Sargasso Sea* treats the Rochester character with understanding and sympathy.[24] Indeed, he narrates the entire middle section of the book. Rhys makes it clear that he is a victim of the patriarchal inheritance law of entailment rather than of a father's natural preference for the firstborn: in *Wide Sargasso Sea*, Rochester's situation is clearly that of a younger son dispatched to the colonies to buy an heiress. If in the case of Antoinette and her identity, Rhys utilizes the thematics of Narcissus, in the case of Rochester and his patrimony, she touches on the thematics of Oedipus. (In this she has her finger on our "historical moment." If, in the nineteenth century, subject-constitution is represented as childbearing and soul making, in the twentieth century psychoanalysis allows the West to plot the itinerary of the subject from Narcissus [the "imaginary"] to Oedipus [the "symbolic"]. This subject, however, is the normative male subject. In Rhys' reinscription of these themes, divided between the female and the male protagonist, feminism and a critique of imperialism become complicit.)

In place of the "wind from Europe" scene, Rhys substitutes the scenario of a suppressed letter to a father, a letter which would be the "correct" explanation of the tragedy of the book.[25] "I thought about the letter which should have been written to England a week ago. Dear Father . . ." (*WSS*, p. 57). This is the first instance: the letter not written. Shortly afterward:

> Dear Father. The thirty thousand pounds have been paid to me without question or condition. No provision made for her (that must be seen to). . . . I will never be a disgrace to you or to my dear brother the son you love. No begging letters, no mean requests. None of the furtive shabby manoeuvres of a younger son. I have sold my soul or you have sold it, and after all is it such a bad bargain? The girl is thought to be beautiful, she is beautiful. And yet . . . [*WSS*, p. 59]

This is the second instance: the letter not sent. The formal letter is uninteresting; I will quote only a part of it:

> Dear Father, we have arrived from Jamaica after an uncomfortable few days. This little estate in the Windward Islands is part of the family property and Antoinette is much attached to it. . . . All is well and has gone according to your plans and wishes. I dealt of course with Richard Mason. . . . He seemed to become attached to me and trusted me completely. This place is very beautiful but my illness has left me too exhausted to appreciate it fully. I will write again in a few days' time. [*WSS*, p. 63]

And so on.

Rhys' version of the Oedipal exchange is ironic, not a closed circle. We cannot know if the letter actually reaches its destination. "I wondered how they got their letters posted," the Rochester figures muses. "I folded mine and put it into a drawer of the desk. . . . There are blanks in my mind that cannot be filled up" (*WSS*, p. 64). It is as if the text presses us to note the analogy between letter and mind.

Rhys denies to Brontë's Rochester the one thing that is supposed to be secured in the Oedipal relay: the Name of the Father, or the patronymic. In *Wide Sargasso Sea*, the character corresponding to Rochester has no name. His writing of the

---

[24]See, e.g., Thomas F. Staley, *Jean Rhys: A Critical Study* (Austin, Tex. 1979), pp. 108–16; it is interesting to note Staley's masculinist discomfort with this and his consequent dissatisfaction with Rhys' novel. [Spivak] *Iste ego sum* is Latin for "I am that man." The phrase is from Ovid, *Metamorphoses* 3: 463.

[25]I have tried to relate castration and suppressed letters in my "The Letter As Cutting Edge," in *Literature and Psychoanalysis; The Question of Reading: Otherwise*, ed. Shoshana Felman (New Haven, Conn., 1981), pp. 208–26. [Spivak]

final version of the letter to his father is supervised, in fact, by an image of the *loss* of the patronymic: "There was a crude bookshelf made of three shingles strung together over the desk and I looked at the books, Byron's poems, novels by Sir Walter Scott, *Confessions of an Opium Eater* . . . and on the last shelf, *Life and Letters of* . . . The rest was eaten away" (*WSS*, p. 63).

Wide Sargasso Sea marks with uncanny clarity the limits of its own discourse in Christophine, Antoinette's black nurse. We may perhaps surmise the distance between *Jane Eyre* and *Wide Sargasso Sea* by remarking that Christophine's unfinished story is the tangent to the latter narrative, as St. John Rivers' story is to the former. Christophine is not a native of Jamaica; she is from Martinique. Taxonomically, she belongs to the category of the good servant rather than that of the pure native. But within these borders, Rhys creates a powerfully suggestive figure.

Christophine is the first interpreter and named speaking subject in the text. "The Jamaican ladies had never approved of my mother, 'because she pretty like pretty self' Christophine said," we read in the book's opening paragraph (*WSS*, p. 15). I have taught this book five times, once in France, once to students who had worked on the book with the well-known Caribbean novelist Wilson Harris, and once at a prestigious institute where the majority of the students were faculty from other universities. It is part of the political argument I am making that all these students blithely stepped over this paragraph without asking or knowing what Christophine's patois, so-called incorrect English, might mean.

Christophine is, of course, a commodified person. "She was your father's wedding present to me" explains Antoinette's mother, "one of his presents" (*WSS*, p. 18). Yet Rhys assigns her some crucial functions in the text. It is Christophine who judges that black ritual practices are culture-specific and cannot be used by whites as cheap remedies for social evils, such as Rochester's lack of love for Antoinette. Most important, it is Christophine alone whom Rhys allows to offer a hard analysis of Rochester's actions, to challenge him in a face-to-face

encounter. The entire extended passage is worthy of comment. I quote a brief extract:

"She is Creole girl, and she have the sun in her. Tell the truth now. She don't come to your house in this place England they tell me about, she don't come to your beautiful house to beg you to marry with her. No, it's you come all the long way to her house — it's you beg her to marry. And she love you and she give you all she have. Now you say you don't love her and you break her up. What you do with her money, eh?" [And then Rochester, the white man, comments silently to himself] Her voice was still quiet but with a hiss in it when she said "money." [*WSS*, p. 130]

Her analysis is powerful enough for the white man to be afraid: "I no longer felt dazed, tried, half hypnotized, but alert and wary, ready to defend myself" (*WSS*, p. 130).

Rhys does not, however, romanticize individual heroics on the part of the oppressed. When the Man refers to the forces of Law and Order, Christophine recognizes their power. This exposure of civil inequality is emphasized by the fact that, just before the Man's successful threat, Christophine had invoked the emancipation of slaves in Jamaica by proclaiming: "No chain gang, no tread machine, no dark jail either. This is free country and I am free woman" (*WSS*, p. 131).

As I mentioned above, Christophine is tangential to this narrative. She cannot be contained by a novel which rewrites a canonical English text within the European novelistic tradition in the interest of the white Creole rather than the native. No perspective *critical* of imperialism can turn the Other into a self, because the project of imperialism has always already historically refracted what might have been the absolutely Other into a domesticated Other that consolidates the imperialist self.[26] The Caliban of Retamar, caught between Europe and Latin America, reflects this predicament. We can read Rhys' reinscription of Narcissus as a thematization of the same problematic.

Of course, we cannot know Jean Rhys' feelings in the matter. We can, however, look at the

[26]This is the main argument of my "Can the Subaltern Speak?" [Spivak]

scene of Christophine's inscription in the text. Immediately after the exchange between her and the Man, well before the conclusion, she is simply driven out of the story, with neither narrative nor characterological explanation or justice. "'Read and write I don't know. Other things I know.' She walked away without looking back" (*WSS*, p. 133).

Indeed, if Rhys rewrites the madwoman's attack on the Man by underlining of the misuse of "legality," she cannot deal with the passage that corresponds to St. John Rivers' own justification of his martyrdom, for it has been displaced into the current idiom of modernization and development. Attempts to construct the "Third-World Woman" as a signifier remind us that the hegemonic definition of literature is itself caught within the history of imperialism. A full literary reinscription cannot easily flourish in the imperialist fracture or discontinuity, covered over by an alien legal system masquerading as Law as such, an alien ideology established as only Truth, and a set of human sciences busy establishing the "native" as self-consolidating Other.

In the Indian case at least, it would be difficult to find an ideological clue to the planned epistemic violence of imperialism merely by rearranging curricula or syllabi within existing norms of literary pedagogy. For a later period of imperialism — when the constituted colonial subject has firmly taken hold — straightforward experiments of comparison can be undertaken, say, between the functionally witless India of *Mrs. Dalloway*, on the one hand, and literary texts produced in India in the 1920s, on the other. But the first half of the nineteenth century resists questioning through literature or literary criticism in the narrow sense, because both are implicated in the project of producing Ariel. To reopen the fracture without succumbing to a nostalgia for lost origins, the literary critic must turn to the archives of imperial governance.

In conclusion, I shall look briefly at Mary Shelley's *Frankenstein*, a text of nascent feminism that remains cryptic, I think, simply because it does not speak the language of feminist individualism which we have come to hail as the language of high feminism within English literature. It is interesting that Barbara Johnson's brief study

tries to rescue this recalcitrant text for the service of feminist autobiography.[27] Alternatively, George Levine reads *Frankenstein* in the context of the creative imagination and the nature of the hero. He sees the novel as a book about its own writing and about writing itself, a Romantic allegory of reading within which Jane Eyre as unselfconscious critic would fit quite nicely.[28]

I propose to take *Frankenstein* out of this arena and focus on it in terms of that sense of English cultural identity which I invoked at the opening of this essay. Within that focus we are obliged to admit that, although *Frankenstein* is ostensibly about the origin and evolution of man in our society, it does not deploy the axiomatics of imperialism.

Let me say at once that there is plenty of incidental imperialist sentiment in *Frankenstein*. My point, within the argument of this essay, is that the discursive field of imperialism does not produce unquestioned ideological correlatives for the narrative structuring of the book. The discourse of imperialism surfaces in a curiously powerful way in Shelley's novel, and I will later discuss the moment at which it emerges.

Frankenstein is not a battleground of male and female individualism articulated in terms of sexual reproduction (family and female) and social subject-production (race and male). That binary opposition is undone in Victor Frankenstein's laboratory — an artificial womb where both projects are undertaken simultaneously, though the terms are never openly spelled out. Frankenstein's apparent antagonist is God himself as Maker of Man, but this real competitor is also woman as the maker of children. It is not just that his dream of the death of mother and bride and the actual death of his bride are associated with the visit of his monstrous homoerotic "son" to his bed. On a much more overt level, the monster is a bodied "corpse," unnatural because bereft of a determinable childhood: "No father had watched my infant days, no mother had blessed me with

[27] See Barbara Johnson, "My Monster/My Self," *Diacritics* 12 (Summer 1982): 2–10. [Spivak]

[28] See George Levine, *The Realistic Imagination: English Fiction from Frankenstein to Lady Chatterley* (Chicago, 1981), pp. 23–35. [Spivak]

smiles and caresses; or if they had, all my past was now a blot, a blind vacancy in which I distinguished nothing" (*F*, pp. 57, 115). It is Frankenstein's own ambiguous and miscued understanding of the real motive for the monster's vengefulness that reveals his own competition with woman as maker:

> I created a rational creature and was bound towards him to assure, as far as was in my power, his happiness and well-being. This was my duty, but there was another still paramount to that. My duties towards the beings of my own species had greater claims to my attention because they included a greater proportion of happiness or misery. Urged by this view, I refused, and I did right in refusing, to create a companion for the first creature. [*F*, p. 206]

It is impossible not to notice the accents of transgression inflecting Frankenstein's demolition of his experiment to create the future Eve. Even in the laboratory, the woman-in-the-making is not a bodied corpse but " a human being." The (il)logic of the metaphor bestows on her a prior existence which Frankenstein aborts, rather than an anterior death which he reembodies: "The remains of the half-finished creature, whom I had destroyed, lay scattered on the floor, and I almost felt as if I had mangled the living flesh of a human being" (*F*, p. 163).

In Shelley's view, man's hubris as soul maker both usurps the place of God and attempts — vainly — to sublate woman's physiological prerogative.[29] Indeed, indulging a Freudian fantasy here, I could urge that, if to give and withhold to/from the mother a phallus is *the* male fetish, then to give and withhold to/from the man a womb might be the female fetish.[30] The icon of the sublimated womb in man is surely his productive brain, the box in the head.

In the judgment of classical psychoanalysis, the phallic mother exists only by virtue of the castration-anxious son; in *Frankenstein's* judgment, the hysteric father (Victor Frankenstein gifted with his laboratory — the womb of theoretical reason) cannot produce a daughter. Here the language of racism — the dark side of imperialism understood as social mission — combines with the hysteria of masculism into the idiom of (the withdrawal of) sexual reproduction rather than subject-constitution. The roles of masculine and feminine individualists are hence reversed and displaced. Frankenstein cannot produce a "daughter" because "she might become ten thousand times more malignant than her mate . . . [and because] one of the first results of those sympathies for which the demon thirsted would be children, and a race of devils would be propagated upon the earth who might make the very existence of the species of man a condition precarious and full of terror" (*F*, p. 158). This particular narrative strand also launches a thoroughgoing critique of the eighteenth-century European discourses on the origin of society through (Western Christian) man.[31] Should I mention that, much like Jean-Jacques Rousseau's remark in his *Confessions*, Frankenstein declares himself to be "by birth a Genevese" (*F*, p. 31)?

In this overtly didactic text, Shelley's point is that social engineering should not be based on pure, theoretical, or natural-scientific reason alone, which is her implicit critique of the utilitarian vision of an engineered society. To this end, she presents in the first part of her deliberately schematic story three characters, childhood friends, who seem to represent Kant's three-part conception of the human subject: Victor Frankenstein, the forces of theoretical reason or "natural philosophy"; Henry Clerval, the forces of practical reason or "the moral relations of things"; and Elizabeth Lavenza, that aesthetic judgment — "the aerial creation of the poets" — which,

[29]Consult the publications of the Feminist International Network for the best overview of the current debate on reproductive technology. [Spivak]

[30]For the male fetish, see Sigmund Freud, "Fetishism," *The Standard Edition of the Complete Psychological Works of Sigmund Freud*, ed. and trans. James Strachey et al., 24 vols. (London, 1953–74), 21: 152–57. For a more "serious" Freudian study of *Frankenstein*, see Mary Jacobus, "Is There a Woman in This Text?" *New Literary History* 14 (Autumn 1982): 117–41. My "fantasy" would of course be disproved by the "fact" that it is more difficult for a woman to assume the position of fetishist than for a man; see Mary Ann Doane, "Film and the Masquerade: Theorising the Female Spectator," *Screen* 23 (Sept./Oct. 1982): 74–87. [Spivak]

[31]Spivak is gesturing at the relationship between the "state of nature" argument in Rousseau's *Social Contract* and Frankenstein's imagined state of war between the races of men and monsters.

according to Kant, is "a suitable mediating link connecting the realm of the concept of nature and that of the concept of freedom . . . (which) promotes . . . *moral* feeling" (*F*, pp. 37, 36).[32]

This three-part subject does not operate harmoniously in *Frankenstein*. That Henry Clerval, associated as he is with practical reason, should have as his "design . . . to visit India, in the belief that he had in his knowledge of its various languages, and in the views he had taken of its society, the means of materially assisting the progress of European colonization and trade" is proof of this, as well as part of the incidental imperialist sentiment that I speak of above (*F*, pp. 151–52). I should perhaps point out that the language here is entrepreneurial rather than missionary:

> He came to the university with the design of making himself complete master of the Oriental languages, as thus he should open a field for the plan of life he had marked out for himself. Resolved to pursue no inglorious career, he turned his eyes towards the East as affording scope for his spirit of enterprise. The Persian, Arabic, and Sanskrit languages engaged his attention. [*F*, pp. 66–67]

But it is of course Victor Frankenstein, with his strange itinerary of obsession with natural philosophy, who offers the strongest demonstration that the multiple perspectives of the three-part Kantian subject cannot cooperate harmoniously. Frankenstein creates a putative human subject out of natural philosophy alone. According to his own miscued summation: "In a fit of enthusiastic madness I created a rational creature" (*F*, p. 206). It is not at all farfetched to say that Kant's categorical imperative can most easily be mistaken for the hypothetical imperative — a command to ground in cognitive comprehension what can be apprehended only by moral will — by putting natural philosophy in the place of practical reason.

I should hasten to add here that just as readings such as this one do not necessarily accuse Charlotte Brontë the named individual of harboring imperialist sentiments, so also they do not necessarily commend Mary Shelley the named

individual for writing a successful Kantian allegory. The most I can say is that it is possible to read these texts, within the frame of imperialism and the Kantian ethical moment, in a politically useful way. Such an approach presupposes that a "disinterested" reading attempts to render transparent the interests of the hegemonic readership. (Other "political" readings — for instance, that the monster is the nascent working class — can also be advanced.)

Frankenstein is built in the established epistolary tradition of multiple frames. At the heart of the multiple frames, the narrative of the monster (as reported by Frankenstein to Robert Walton, who then recounts it in a letter to his sister) is of his almost learning, clandestinely, to be human. It is invariably noticed that the monster reads *Paradise Lost* as true history. What is not so often noticed is that he also reads Plutarch's *Lives*, "the histories of the first founders of the ancient republics," which he compares to "the patriarchal lives of my protectors" (*F*, pp. 123, 124). And his *education* comes through "Volney's *Ruins of Empires*," which he purported to be a prefiguration of the French Revolution, published after the event and after the author had rounded off his theory with practice (*F*, p. 113). It is an attempt at an enlightened universal secular, rather than a Eurocentric Christian, history, written from the perspective of a narrator "from below," somewhat like the attempts of Eric Wolf or Peter Worsley in our own time.[33]

---

[32]Kant, *Critique of Judgement*, trans. J. H. Bernard (New York, 1951), p. 39. [Spivak]

[33]See [Constantin François Chasseboeuf de Volney], *The Ruins; or, Meditations on the Revolutions of Empires*, trans. pub. (London, 1811). Johannes Fabian has shown us the manipulation of time in "new" secular histories of a similar kind; see *Time and the Other: How Anthropology Makes Its Object* (New York, 1983). See also Eric R. Wolf, *Europe and the People without History* (Berkeley and Los Angeles, 1982), and Peter Worsley, *The Third World*, 2d ed. (Chicago, 1973); I am grateful to Dennis Dworkin for bringing the latter book to my attention. The most striking ignoring of the monster's education through Volney is in Gilbert's otherwise brilliant "Horror's Twin: Mary Shelley's Monstrous Eve," *Feminist Studies* 4 (June 1980): 48–73. Gilbert's essay reflects the absence of race-determinations in a certain sort of feminism. Her present work has most convincingly filled in this gap; see, e.g., her recent piece on H. Rider Haggard's *She* ("Rider Haggard's Heart of Darkness," *Partisan Review* 50, no. 3 [1983]: 444–53. [Spivak]

This Caliban's education in (universal secular) humanity takes place through the monster's eavesdropping on the instruction of an Ariel — Safie, the Christianized "Arabian" to whom "a residence in Turkey was abhorrent" (*F*, p. 121). In depicting Safie, Shelley uses some commonplaces of eighteenth-century liberalism that are shared by many today: Safie's Muslim father was a victim of (bad) Christian religious prejudice and yet was himself a wily and ungrateful man not as morally refined as her (good) Christian mother. Having tasted the emancipation of woman, Safie could not go home. The confusion between "Turk" and "Arab" has its counterpart in present-day confusion about Turkey and Iran as "Middle Eastern" but not "Arab."

Although we are a far cry here from the unexamined and covert axiomatics of imperialism in *Jane Eyre*, we will gain nothing by celebrating the time-bound pieties that Shelley, as the daughter of two antievangelicals, produces. It is more interesting for us that Shelley differentiates the Other, works at the Caliban/Ariel distinction, and *cannot* make the monster identical with the proper recipient of these lessons. Although he had "heard of the discovery of the American hemisphere and *wept with Safie* over the helpless fate of its original inhabitants," Safie cannot reciprocate his attachment. When she first catches sight of him, "Safie, unable to attend to her friend [Agatha], rushed out of the cottage" (*F*, pp. 114, [my emphasis], 129).

In the taxonomy of characters, the Muslim-Christian Safie belongs with Rhys' Antoinette/Bertha. And indeed, like Christophine the good servant, the subject created by the fiat of natural philosophy is the tangential unresolved moment in *Frankenstein*. The simple suggestion that the monster is human inside but monstrous outside and only provoked into vengefulness is clearly not enough to bear the burden of so great a historical dilemma.

At one moment, in fact, Shelley's Frankenstein does try to tame the monster, to humanize him by bringing him within the circuit of the Law. He "repair[s] to a criminal judge in the town and . . . relate[s his] history briefly but with firmness" — the first and disinterested version of the narrative of Frankenstein — "marking the dates with accuracy and never deviating into invective or exclamation. . . . When I had concluded my narration I said, 'This is the being whom I accuse and for whose seizure and punishment I call upon you to exert your whole power. It is your duty as a magistrate'" (*F*, pp. 189, 190). The sheer social reasonableness of the mundane voice of Shelley's "Genevan magistrate" reminds us that the absolutely Other cannot be selfed, that the monster has "properties" which will not be contained by "proper" measures:

"I will exert myself [he says], and if it is in my power to seize the monster, be assured that he shall suffer punishment proportionate to his crimes. But I fear, from what you have yourself described to be his properties, that this will prove impracticable; and thus, while every proper measure is pursued, you should make up your mind to disappointment." [*F*, p. 190]

In the end, as is obvious to most readers, distinctions of human individuality themselves seem to fall away from the novel. Monster, Frankenstein, and Walton seem to become each others' relays. Frankenstein's story comes to an end in death; Walton concludes his own story within the frame of his function as letter writer. In the *narrative* conclusion, he is the natural philosopher who learns from Frankenstein's example. At the end of the *text*, the monster, having confessed his guilt toward his maker and ostensibly intending to immolate himself, is borne away on an ice raft. We do not see the conflagration of his funeral pile — the self-immolation is not consummated in the text: he too cannot be contained by the text. In terms of narrative logic, he is "lost in darkness and distance" (*F*, p. 211) — these are the last words of the novel — into an existential temporality that is coherent with neither the territorializing individual imagination (as in the opening of *Jane Eyre*) nor the authoritative scenario of Christian psychobiography (as at the end of Brontë's work). The very relationship between sexual reproduction and social subject-production — the dynamic nineteenth-century topos of feminism-in-imperialism — remains problematic within the limits of Shelley's text and, paradoxically, constitutes its strength.

Earlier, I offered a reading of woman as womb holder in *Frankenstein*. I would now suggest that there is a framing woman in the book who is neither tangential, nor encircled, nor yet encircling. "Mrs. Saville," "excellent Margaret," "beloved Sister" are her address and kinship inscriptions (*F*, pp. 15, 16, 22). She is the occasion, though not the protagonist, of the novel. She is the feminine *subject* rather than the female individualist: she is the irreducible *recipient*-function of the letters that constitute *Frankenstein*. I have commented on the singular appropriative hermeneutics of the reader reading with Jane in the opening pages of *Jane Eyre*. Here the reader must read with Margaret Saville in the crucial sense that she must *intercept* the recipient-function, read the letters *as* recipient, in order for the novel to exist.[34] Margaret Saville does not respond to close the text as frame. The frame is thus simultaneously not a frame, and the monster can step "beyond the text" and be "lost in darkness." Within the allegory of our reading, the place of both the English lady and the unnamable monster are left open by this great flawed text. It is satisfying for a postcolonial reader to consider this a noble resolution for a nineteenth-century English novel. This is all the more striking because, on the anecdotal level, Shelley herself abundantly "identifies" with Victor Frankenstein.[35]

I must myself close with an idea that I cannot establish within the limits of this essay. Earlier I contended that *Wide Sargasso Sea* is necessarily bound by the reach of the European novel. I suggested that, in contradistinction, to reopen the epistemic fracture of imperialism without succumbing to a nostalgia for lost origins, the critic must turn to the archives of imperialist governance. I have not turned to those archives in these pages. In my current work, by way of a modest and inexpert "reading" of "archives," I try to extend, outside the reach of the European novelistic tradition, the most powerful suggestion in *Wide Sargasso Sea*: that *Jane Eyre* can be read as the orchestration and staging of the self-immolation of Bertha Mason as "good wife." The power of that suggestion remains unclear if we remain insufficiently knowledgeable about the history of the legal manipulation of widow-sacrifice in the entitlement of the British government in India. I would hope that an informed critique of imperialism, granted some attention from readers in the First World, will at least expand the frontiers of the politics of reading.

---

[34]"A letter is always and *a priori* intercepted, . . . the 'subjects' are neither the senders nor the receivers of messages. . . . The letter is constituted . . . by its interception" (Jacques Derrida, "Discussion," after Claude Rabant, "Il n'a aucune chance de l'entendre," in *Affranchissement: Du transfert et de la lettre*, ed. René Major [Paris, 1981], p. 106; my translation). Margaret Saville is not made to appropriate the reader's "subject" into the signature of her own "individuality." [Spivak]

[35]The most striking "internal evidence" is the admission in the "Author's Introduction" that, after dreaming of the yet-unnamed Victor Frankenstein figure and being terrified (through, yet not quite through, him) by the monster in a scene she later reproduced in Frankenstein's story, Shelley began her tale "on the morrow . . . with the words 'It was on a dreary night of November'"(*F*, p. xi). Those are the opening words of chapter 5 of the finished book, where Frankenstein begins to recount the actual making of his monster (see *F*, p. 56). [Spivak]

Gloria Anzaldúa

1942–2004

Gloria Anzaldúa was born in 1942 in Jesus Maria of the Valley, Texas, to a family of Mexican immigrants. The only person from her neighborhood to achieve a college degree, a B.A. from Pan American University, she went on to receive an M.A. in English and education from the University of Texas. Anzaldúa began teaching a bilingual preschool program for the children of migrant farm workers, and then taught mentally and emotionally handicapped students. At the University of Texas at Austin, Vermont College of Norwich University, and San Francisco State University, she taught courses in feminism, Chicano Studies, and creative writing. Her book Borderlands/La Frontera: The New Mestiza *(1987) was a radical combination of Spanish and English poetry, memoir, and historical analysis, and became the basis for academic attention to Chicano literature, language, and culture. As a lesbian feminist and the bilingual daughter of Mexican parents, Anzaldúa theorizes the necessity of self-fashioning and finding new identities separate from those offered by society. She edited the collections* Making Face, Making Soul/Haciendo Caras: Creative and Critical Perspectives by Feminists of Color *(1989) and* This Bridge We Call Home: Radical Visions for Transformation *(2002, with Analouise Keating), and wrote* La Prieta *(1997) and a number of books for children. She died in 2004 from a diabetes-related illness, just weeks from completing her Ph.D. at the University of California at Santa Cruz. The following essay, "La conciencia de la mestiza: Towards a New Consciousness," appears in* Borderlands/La Frontera.

La conciencia de la mestiza: Towards a New Consciousness

> *Por la mujer de mi raza*
> *hablará el espíritu.*[1]

Jose Vasconcelos, Mexican philosopher, envisaged *una raza mestiza, una mezcla de razas afines, una raza de color — la primera raza síntesis del globo*. He called it a cosmic race, *la raza cósmica*, a fifth race embracing the four major races of the world.[2] Opposite to the theory of the pure Aryan, and to the policy of racial purity that white America practices, his theory is one of inclusivity. At the confluence of two or more genetic streams, with chromosomes constantly "crossing over," this mixture of races, rather than resulting in an inferior being, provides hybrid progeny, a mutable, more malleable species with a rich gene pool. From this racial, ideological, cultural and biological cross-pollinization, an "alien" consciousness is presently in the making — a new *mestiza* consciousness, *una conciencia de mujer*. It is a consciousness of the Borderlands.

UNA LUCHA DE FRONTERAS/ A STRUGGLE OF BORDERS

> Because I, a *mestiza*,
> continually walk out of one culture
> and into another,
> because I am in all cultures at the same time,

[1]This is my own "take-off" on Jose Vasconcelos' idea. Jose Vasconcelos, *La Raza Cósmica: Missión de la Raza Ibero–Americana* (México: Aguilar S.A. de Ediciones, 1961). [Anzaldúa]

[2]Vasconcelos. [Anzaldúa]

alma entre dos mundos, tres, cuatro,
me zumba la cabeza con lo contradictorio.
Estoy norteada por todas las voces que me hablan
simultáneamente.

The ambivalence from the clash of voices results in mental and emotional states of perplexity. Internal strife results in insecurity and indecisiveness. The *mestiza*'s dual or multiple personality is plagued by psychic restlessness.

In a constant state of mental nepantilism, an Aztec word meaning torn between ways, *la mestiza* is a product of the transfer of the cultural and spiritual values of one group to another. Being tricultural, monolingual, bilingual or multilingual, speaking a patois, and in a state of perpetual transition, the *mestiza* faces the dilemma of the mixed breed: which collectivity does the daughter of a darkskinned mother listen to?

El choque de un alma atrapado entre el mundo del espíritu y el mundo de la técnica a veces la deja entullada. Cradled in one culture, sandwiched between two cultures, straddling all three cultures and their value systems, *la mestiza* undergoes a struggle of flesh, a struggle of borders, an inner war. Like all people, we perceive the version of reality that our culture communicates. Like others having or living in more than one culture, we get multiple, often opposing messages. The coming together of two self-consistent but habitually incompatible frames of reference[3] causes *un choque*, a cultural collision.

Within us and within *la cultura chicana*, commonly held beliefs of the white culture attack commonly held beliefs of the Mexican culture, and both attack commonly held beliefs of the indigenous culture. Subconsciously, we see an attack on ourselves and our beliefs as a threat and we attempt to block with a counterstance.

But it is not enough to stand on the opposite river bank, shouting questions, challenging patriarchical, white conventions. A counterstance locks one into a duel of oppressor and oppressed; locked in mortal combat, like the cop and the criminal, both are reduced to a common denominator of violence. The counterstance refutes the dominant culture's views and beliefs, and, for this, it is proudly defiant. All reaction is limited by, and dependent on, what it is reacting against. Because the counterstance stems from a problem with authority — outer as well as inner — it's a step towards liberation from cultural domination. But it is not a way of life. At some point, on our way to a new consciousness, we will have to leave the opposite bank, the split between the two mortal combatants somehow healed so that we are on both shores at once and, at once, see through serpent and eagle eyes. Or perhaps we will decide to disengage from the dominant culture, write it off altogether as a lost cause, and cross the border into a wholly new and separate territory. Or we might go another route. The possibilities are numerous once we decide to act and not react.

A TOLERANCE FOR AMBIGUITY

These numerous possibilities leave *la mestiza* floundering in uncharted seas. In perceiving conflicting information and points of view, she is subjected to a swamping of her psychological borders. She has discovered that she can't hold concepts or ideas in rigid boundaries. The borders and walls that are supposed to keep the undesirable ideas out are entrenched habits and patterns of behavior; these habits and patterns are the enemy within. Rigidity means death. Only by remaining flexible is she able to stretch the psyche horizontally and vertically. *La mestiza* constantly has to shift out of habitual formations; from convergent thinking, analytical reasoning that tends to use rationality to move toward a single goal (a Western mode), to divergent thinking,[4] characterized by movement away from set patterns and goals and toward a more whole perspective, one that includes rather than excludes.

The new *mestiza* copes by developing a tolerance for contradictions, a tolerance for ambiguity. She learns to be an Indian in Mexican culture, to be Mexican from an Anglo point of view. She learns to juggle cultures. She has a plural personality, she operates in a pluralistic mode — nothing is thrust

[3]Arthur Koestler termed this "bisociation." Albert Rothenberg, *The Creative Process in Art, Science, and Other Fields* (Chicago, IL: University of Chicago Press, 1979), 12. [Anzaldúa]

[4]In part, I derive my definitions for "convergent" and "divergent" thinking from Rothenberg, 12–13. [Anzaldúa]

out, the good, the bad and the ugly, nothing rejected, nothing abandoned. Not only does she sustain contradictions, she turns the ambivalence into something else.

She can be jarred out of ambivalence by an intense, and often painful, emotional event which inverts or resolves the ambivalence. I'm not sure exactly how. The work takes place underground — subconsciously. It is work that the soul performs. That focal point or fulcrum, that juncture where the *mestiza* stands, is where phenomena tend to collide. It is where the possibility of uniting all that is separate occurs. This assembly is not one where severed or separated pieces merely come together. Nor is it a balancing of opposing powers. In attempting to work out a synthesis, the self has added a third element which is greater than the sum of its severed parts. That third element is a new consciousness — a *mestiza* consciousness — and though it is a source of intense pain, its energy comes from a continual creative motion that keeps breaking down the unitary aspect of each new paradigm.

En unas pocas centurias, the future will belong to the *mestiza*. Because the future depends on the breaking down of paradigms, it depends on the straddling of two or more cultures. By creating a new mythos — that is, a change in the way we perceive reality, the way we see ourselves and the ways we behave — la mestiza creates a new consciousness.

The work of *mestiza* consciousness is to break down the subject-object duality that keeps her a prisoner and to show in the flesh and through the images in her work how duality is transcended. The answer to the problem between the white race and the colored, between males and females, lies in healing the split that originates in the very foundation of our lives, our culture, our languages, our thoughts. A massive uprooting of dualistic thinking in the individual and collective consciousness is the beginning of a long struggle, but one that could, in our best hopes, bring us to the end of rape, of violence, of war.

LA ENCRUCIJADA/THE CROSSROADS

A chicken is being sacrificed
    at a crossroads, a simple mound of earth

a mud shrine for *Eshu*,
    Yoruba god of indeterminacy,
who blesses her choice of path.
    She begins her journey.

Su cuerpo es una bocacalle. La mestiza has gone from being the sacrificial goat to becoming the officiating priestess at the crossroads.

As a *mestiza* I have no country, my homeland cast me out; yet all countries are mine because I am every woman's sister or potential lover. (As a lesbian I have no race, my own people disclaim me; but I am all races because there is the queer of me in all races.) I am cultureless because, as a feminist, I challenge the collective cultural/religious male-derived beliefs of Indo-Hispanics and Anglos; yet I am cultured because I am participating in the creation of yet another culture, a new story to explain the world and our participation in it, a new value system with images and symbols that connect us to each other and to the planet. *Soy un amasamiento*, I am an act of kneading, of uniting and joining that not only has produced both a creature of darkness and a creature of light, but also a creature that questions the definitions of light and dark and gives them new meanings.

We are the people who leap in the dark, we are the people on the knees of the gods. In our flesh, (r)evolution works out the clash of cultures. It makes us crazy constantly, but if the center holds, we've made some kind of evolutionary step forward. *Nuestra alma el trabajo*, the opus, the great alchemical work; spiritual *mestizaje*, a "morphogenesis,"[5] an inevitable unfolding. We have become the quickening serpent movement.

Indigenous like corn, like corn, the *mestiza* is a product of crossbreeding, designed for preservation under a variety of conditions. Like an ear of corn — a female seed-bearing organ — the

[5]To borrow chemist Ilya Prigogine's theory of "dissipative structures." Prigogine discovered that substances interact not in predictable ways as it was taught in science, but in different and fluctuating ways to produce new and more complex structures, a kind of birth he called "morphogenesis," which created unpredictable innovations. Harold Gilliam, "Searching for a New World View," *This World* (January, 1981), 23. [Anzaldúa]

mestiza is tenacious, tightly wrapped in the husks of her culture. Like kernels she clings to the cob; with thick stalks and strong brace roots, she holds tight to the earth — she will survive the crossroads.

Lavando y remojando el maíz en agua de cal, despojando el pellejo. Moliendo, mixteando, amasando, haciendo tortillas de masa.[6] She steeps the corn in lime, it swells, softens. With stone roller on *metate*, she grinds the corn, then grinds again. She kneads and moulds the dough, pats the round balls into *tortillas*.

We are the porous rock in the stone *metate*
squatting on the ground.
We are the rolling pin, *el maíz y agua,*
la masa harina. Somos el amasijo.
Somos lo molido en el metate.
We are the *comal* sizzling hot,
the hot *tortilla*, the hungry mouth.
We are the coarse rock.
We are the grinding motion,
the mixed potion, *somos el molcajete.*
We are the pestle, the *comino, ajo, pimienta,*
We are the *chile colorado,*
the green shoot that cracks the rock.
We will abide.

EL CAMINO DE LA MESTIZA/ THE *MESTIZA* WAY

Caught between the sudden contraction, the breath sucked in and the endless space, the brown woman stands still, looks at the sky. She decides to go down, digging her way along the roots of trees. Sifting through the bones, she shakes them to see if there is any marrow in them. Then, touching the dirt to her forehead, to her tongue, she takes a few bones, leaves the rest in their burial place.

She goes through her backpack, keeps her journal and address book, throws away the muni-bart metromaps. The coins are heavy and they go next, then the greenbacks flutter through the air. She keeps her knife, can opener and eyebrow pencil. She puts bones, pieces of bark, *hierbas*, eagle feather, snake-skin, tape recorder, the rattle and drum in her pack and she sets out to become the complete *tolteca*.

[6]Corn tortillas are of two types, the smooth uniform ones made in a tortilla press and usually bought at a tortilla factory or supermarket, and *gorditas*, made by mixing *masa* with lard or shortening or butter (my mother sometimes puts in bits of bacon or *chicharrones*). [Anzaldúa]

Her first step is to take inventory. *Despojando, desgranando, quitando paja.* Just what did she inherit from her ancestors? This weight on her back — which is the baggage from the Indian mother, which the baggage from the Spanish father, which the baggage from the Anglo?

Pero es difícil differentiating between *lo heredado, lo adquirido, lo impuesto.* She puts history through a sieve, winnows out the lies, looks at the forces that we as a race, as women, have been a part of. *Luego bota lo que no vale, los desmientos, los desencuentos, el embrutec-imiento. Aguarda el juicio, hondo y enraízado, de la gente antigua.* This step is a conscious rupture with all oppressive traditions of all cultures and religions. She communicates that rupture, documents the struggle. She reinterprets history and, using new symbols, she shapes new myths. She adopts new perspectives toward the dark-skinned, women and queers. She strengthens her tolerance (and intolerance) for ambiguity. She is willing to share, to make herself vulnerable to foreign ways of seeing and thinking. She surren-ders all notions of safety, of the familiar. Deconstruct, construct. She becomes a *nahual*, able to transform herself into a tree, a coyote, into another person. She learns to transform the small "I" into the total Self. *Se hace moldeadora de su alma. Según la concepción que tiene de sí misma, así será.*

QUE NO SE NOS OLVIDE LOS HOMBRES

"Tú no sirves pa' nada —
you're good for nothing.
Eres pura vieja."

"You're nothing but a woman" means you are defective. Its opposite is to be *un macho*. The mod-ern meaning of the word "machismo," as well as the concept, is actually an Anglo invention. For men like my father, being "macho" meant being strong enough to protect and support my mother and us, yet being able to show love. Today's macho has doubts about his ability to feed and protect his family. His "machismo" is an adap-tation to oppression and poverty and low self-esteem. It is the result of hierarchical male dominance. The Anglo, feeling inadequate and inferior and powerless, displaces or transfers these feelings to the Chicano by shaming him. In the Gringo world, the Chicano suffers from excessive humility and self-effacement, shame of self and self-deprecation. Around Latinos he suffers from a sense of language inadequacy and its accompanying discomfort; with Native Americans he suffers from a racial amnesia which ignores our common blood, and from guilt because the Spanish part of him took their land and oppressed them. He has an excessive compensatory hubris when around Mexicans from the other side. It overlays a deep sense of racial shame.

The loss of a sense of dignity and respect in the macho breeds a false machismo which leads him to put down women and even to brutalize them. Coexisting with his sexist behavior is a love for the mother which takes precedence over that of all others. Devoted son, macho pig. To wash down the shame of his acts, of his very being, and to handle the brute in the mirror, he takes to the bottle, the snort, the needle and the fist.

Though we "understand" the root causes of male hatred and fear, and the subsequent wounding of women, we do not excuse, we do not condone and we will no longer put up with it. From the men of our race, we demand the admission/ acknowledgement/disclosure/testimony that they wound us, violate us, are afraid of us and of our power. We need them to say they will begin to eliminate their hurtful put-down ways. But more than the words, we demand acts. We say to them: we will develop equal power with you and those who have shamed us.

It is imperative that *mestizas* support each other in changing the sexist elements in the Mexican-Indian culture. As long as woman is put down, the Indian and the Black in all of us is put down. The struggle of the *mestiza* is above all a feminist one. As long as *los hombres* think they have to *chingar mujeres* and each other to be men, as long as men are taught that they are superior and therefore culturally favored over *la mujer*, as long as to be a *vieja* is a thing of derision, there can be no real healing of our psyches. We're halfway there — we have such love of the Mother, the good mother. The first step is to unlearn the *puta/virgen* dichotomy and to see *Coatlapopeuh — Coatlicue* in the Mother, *Guadalupe.*

Tenderness, a sign of vulnerability, is so feared that it is showered on women with verbal abuse and blows. Men, even more than women, are fettered to gender roles. Women at least have had the guts to break out of bondage. Only gay men have had the courage to expose themselves to the woman inside them and to challenge the current masculinity. I've encountered a few scattered and isolated gentle straight men, the beginnings of a new breed, but they are confused, and entangled with sexist behaviors that they have not been able to eradicate. We need a new masculinity and the new man needs a movement.

Lumping the males who deviate from the general norm with man, the oppressor, is a gross injustice. *Asombra pensar que nos hemos quedado en ese pozo oscuro donde el mundo encierra a las lesbianas. Asombra pensar que hemos, como femenistas y lesbianas, cerrado nuestros corazónes a los hombres, a nuestros hermanos los jotos, desheredados y marginales como nosotros.* Being the supreme crossers of cultures, homosexuals have strong bonds with the queer white, Black, Asian, Native American, Latino and with the queer in Italy, Australia and the rest of the planet. We come from all colors, all classes, all races, all time periods. Our role is to link people with each other — the Blacks with Jews with Indians with Asians with whites with extraterrestrials. It is to transfer ideas and information from one culture to another. Colored homosexuals have more knowledge of other cultures; have always been at the forefront (although sometimes in the closet) of all liberation struggles in this country; have suffered more injustices and have survived them despite all odds. Chicanos need to acknowledge the political and artistic contributions of their queer. People, listen to what your *jotería* is saying.

The *mestizo* and the queer exist at this time and point on the evolutionary continuum for a purpose. We are a blending that proves that all blood is intricately woven together, and that we are spawned out of similar souls.

SOMOS UNA GENTA

Hay tantísimas fronteras
que dividen a la gente,
pero por cada frontera
existe también un puente.   — GINA VALDÉS[7]

Divided Loyalties

Many women and men of color do not want to have any dealings with white people. It takes too much time and energy to explain to the downwardly mobile, white middle-class women that it's okay for us to want to own "possessions," never having had any nice furniture on our dirt floors or "luxuries" like washing machines. Many feel that whites should help their own people rid themselves of race hatred and fear first. I, for one, choose to use some of my energy to serve as mediator. I, think we need to allow whites to be our allies. Through our literature, art, *corridos* and folktales we must share our history with them so when they set up committees to help Big Mountain Navajos or the Chicano farmworkers or *los Nicaragüenses* they won't turn people away because of their racial fears and ignorances. They will come to see that they are not helping us but following our lead.

Individually, but also as a racial entity, we need to voice our needs. We need to say to white society: we need you to accept the fact that Chicanos are different, to acknowledge your rejection and negation of us. We need you to own the fact that you looked upon us as less than human, that you stole our lands, our personhood, our self-respect. We need you to make public restitution: to say that, to compensate for your own sense of defectiveness, you strive for power over us, you erase our history and our experience because it makes you feel guilty — you'd rather forget your brutish acts. To say you've split yourself from minority groups, that you disown us, that your dual consciousness splits off parts of yourself, transferring the "negative" parts onto us. (Where there is persecution of minorities, there is shadow projection. Where there is violence and war, there is repression of shadow.) To say that you are afraid of us, that to put distance

[7]Gina Valdés, *Puentes y Fronteras: Coplas Chicanas* (Los Angeles, CA: Castle Lithograph, 1982), 2. [Anzaldúa]

between us, you wear the mask of contempt. Admit that Mexico is your double, that she exists in the shadow of this country, that we are irrevocably tied to her. Gringo, accept the doppelganger in your psyche. By taking back your collective shadow the intracultural split will heal. And finally, tell us what you need from us.

BY YOUR TRUE FACES WE WILL KNOW YOU

I am visible — see this Indian face — yet I am invisible. I both blind them with my beak nose and am their blind spot. But I exist, we exist. They'd like to think I have melted in the pot. But I haven't, we haven't.

The dominant white culture is killing us slowly with its ignorance. By taking away our self-determination, it has made us weak and empty. As a people we have resisted and we have taken expedient positions, but we have never been allowed to develop unencumbered — we have never been allowed to be fully ourselves. The whites in power want us people of color to barricade ourselves behind our separate tribal walls so they can pick us off one at a time with their hidden weapons; so they can whitewash and distort history. Ignorance splits people, creates prejudices. A misinformed people is a subjugated people.

Before the Chicano and the undocumented worker and the Mexican from the other side can come together, before the Chicano can have unity with Native Americans and other groups, we need to know the history of their struggle and they need to know ours. Our mothers, our sisters and brothers, the guys who hang out on street corners, the children in the playgrounds, each of us must know our Indian lineage, our afro-*mestisaje*, our history of resistance.

To the immigrant *mexicano* and the recent arrivals we must teach our history. The 80 million *mexicanos* and the Latinos from Central and South America must know of our struggles. Each one of us must know basic facts about Nicaragua, Chile and the rest of Latin America. The Latinoist movement (Chicanos, Puerto Ricans, Cubans and other Spanish-speaking people working together to combat racial discrimination in the market place) is good but it is not enough. Other than a common culture we will have nothing to hold us together. We need to meet on a broader communal ground.

The struggle is inner: Chicano, *indio*, American Indian, *mojado, mexicano*, immigrant Latino, Anglo in power, working class Anglo, Black, Asian — our psyches resemble the bordertowns and are populated by the same people. The struggle has always been inner, and is played out in the outer terrains. Awareness of our situation must come before inner changes, which in turn come before changes in society. Nothing happens in the "real" world unless it first happens in the images in our heads.

El día de la Chicana

> I will not be shamed again
> Nor will I shame myself.

I am possessed by a vision: that we Chicanas and Chicanos have taken back or uncovered our true faces, our dignity and self-respect. It's a validation vision.

Seeing the Chicana anew in light of her history I seek an exoneration, a seeing through the fictions of white supremacy, a seeing of ourselves in our true guises and not as the false racial personality that has been given to us and that we have given to ourselves. I seek our woman's face, our true features, the positive and the negative seen clearly, free of the tainted biases of male dominance. I seek new images of identity, new beliefs about ourselves, our humanity and worth no longer in question.

Estamos viviendo en la noche de la Raza, un tiempo cuando el trabajo se hace a lo quieto, en el oscuro. El día cuando aceptamos tal y como somos y para en donde vamos y porque — ese día será el día de la Raza. Yo tengo el compromiso de expresar mi visión, mi sensibilidad, mi percepción de la revalidación de la gente mexicana, su mérito, estimación, honra, aprecio y validez.

On December 2nd when my sun goes into my first house, I celebrate *el día de la Chicana y el Chicano*. On that day I clean my altars, light my *Coatlalopeuh* candle, burn sage and copal, take *el baño para espantar basura*, sweep my house. On that day I bare my soul, make myself vulnerable to friends and family by expressing my feelings. On that day I affirm who we are.

On that day I look inside our conflicts and our basic introverted racial temperament. I identify our needs, voice them. I acknowledge that the self and the race have been wounded. I recognize the need to take care of our personhood, of our racial self. On that day I gather the splintered and disowned parts of *la gente mexicana* and hold them in my arms. *Todas las partes de nosotros valen.*

On that day I say, "Yes, all you people wound us when you reject us. Rejection strips us of self-worth; our vulnerability exposes us to shame. It is our innate identity you find wanting. We are ashamed that we need your good opinion, that we need your acceptance. We can no longer camouflage our needs, can no longer let defenses and fences sprout around us. We can no longer withdraw. To rage and look upon you with contempt is to rage and be contemptuous of ourselves. We can no longer blame you, nor disown the white parts, the male parts, the pathological parts, the queer parts, the vulnerable parts. Here we are weaponless with open arms, with only our magic. Let's try it our way, the *mestiza* way, the Chicana way, the woman way.

On that day, I search for our essential dignity as a people, a people with a sense of purpose — to belong and contribute to something greater than our *pueblo*. On that day I seek to recover and reshape my spiritual identity. *¡Anímate! Raza, a celebrar el día de la Chicana.*

El retorno

> All movements are accomplished in six stages, and the seventh brings return. — I CHING[8]

Tanto tiempo sin verte casa mía,
mi cuna, mi hondo nido de la huerta.
— "SOLEDAD"[9]

[8] Richard Wilhelm, *The I Ching or Book of Changes*, trans. Cary F. Baynes (Princeton, NJ: Princeton University Press, 1950), 98. [Anzaldúa]

[9] "Soledad" is sung by the group Haciendo Punto en Otro Son. [Anzaldúa]

I stand at the river, watch the curving, twisting serpent, a serpent nailed to the fence where the mouth of the Rio Grande empties into the Gulf.

I have come back. *Tanto dolor me costó el alejamiento.* I shade my eyes and look up. The bone beak of a hawk slowly circling over me, checking me out as potential carrion. In its wake a little bird flickering its wings, swimming sporadically like a fish. In the distance the expressway and the slough of traffic like an irritated sow. The sudden pull in my gut, *la tierra, los aguaceros.* My land, *el viento soplando la arena, el lagartijo debajo de un nopalito. Me acuerdo como era antes. Una región desértica de vasta llanuras, costeras de baja altura, de escasa lluvia, de chaparrales formados por mesquites y huizaches.* If I look real hard I can almost see the Spanish fathers who were called "the cavalry of Christ" enter this valley riding their burros, see the clash of cultures commence.

Tierra natal. This is home, the small towns in the Valley, *los pueblitos* with chicken pens and goats picketed to mesquite shrubs. *En las colonias* on the other side of the tracks, junk cars line the front yards of hot pink and lavender-trimmed houses — Chicano architecture we call it, self-consciously. I have missed the TV shows where hosts speak in half and half, and where awards are given in the category of Tex-Mex music. I have missed the Mexican cemeteries blooming with artificial flowers, the fields of aloe vera and red pepper, rows of sugar cane, of corn hanging on the stalks, the cloud of *polvareda* in the dirt roads behind a speeding truck, *el sabor de tamales de rez y venado.* I have missed *la yequa colorada* gnawing the wooden gate of her stall, the smell of horse flesh from Carito's corrals. *He hecho menos las noches calientes sin aire, noches de linternas y lechuzas* making holes in the night.

I still feel the old despair when I look at the unpainted, dilapidated, scrap lumber houses consisting mostly of corrugated aluminum. Some of the poorest people in the U.S. live in the Lower Rio Grande Valley, an arid and semi-arid land of irrigated farming, intense sunlight and heat, citrus groves next to chaparral and cactus. I walk through the elementary school I attended so long ago, that remained segregated until recently. I remember how the white teachers used to punish us for being Mexican.

How I love this tragic valley of South Texas, as Ricardo Sánchez calls it; this borderland between the Nueces and the Rio Grande. This land has survived possession and ill-use by five countries: Spain, Mexico, the Republic of Texas, the Confederacy, and the U.S. again. It has survived Anglo-Mexican blood feuds, lynchings, burnings, rapes, pillage.

Today I see the Valley still struggling to survive. Whether it does or not, it will never be as I remember it. The borderlands depression that was set off by the 1982 peso devaluation in Mexico resulted in the closure of hundreds of Valley businesses. Many people lost their homes, cars, land. Prior to 1982, U.S. store owners thrived on retail sales to Mexicans who came across the borders for groceries and clothes and appliances. While goods on the U.S. side have become 10, 100, 1000 times more expensive for Mexican buyers, goods on the Mexican side have become 10, 100, 1000 times cheaper for Americans. Because the Valley is heavily dependent on agriculture and Mexican retail trade, it has the highest unemployment rates along the entire border region; it is the Valley that has been hardest hit.[10]

"It's been a bad year for corn," my brother, Nune, says. As he talks, I remember my father scanning the sky for a rain that would end the drought, looking up into the sky, day after day, while the corn withered on its stalk. My father has been dead for 29 years, having worked himself to death. The life span of a Mexican farm laborer is 56 — he lived to be 38. It shocks me that I am older than he. I, too, search the sky for rain. Like the ancients, I worship the rain god and the maize goddess, but unlike my father I have recovered their names. Now for rain (irrigation) one offers not a sacrifice of blood, but of money.

[10]Out of the twenty-two border counties in the four border states, Hidalgo County (named for Father Hidalgo who was shot in 1810 after instigating Mexico's revolt against Spanish rule under the banner of *la Virgen de Guadalupe*) is the most poverty-stricken county in the nation as well as the largest home base (along with Imperial in California) for migrant farmworkers. It was here that I was born and raised, I am amazed that both it and I have survived. [Anzaldúa]

"Farming is in a bad way," my brother says. "Two to three thousand small and big farmers went bankrupt in this country last year. Six years ago the price of corn was $8.00 per hundred pounds," he goes on. "This year it is $3.90 per hundred pounds." And, I think to myself, after taking inflation into account, not planting anything puts you ahead.

I walk out to the back yard, stare at *los rosales de mamá*. She wants me to help her prune the rose bushes, dig out the carpet grass that is choking them. *Mamagrande Ramona también tenía rosales*. Here every Mexican grows flowers. If they don't have a piece of dirt, they use car tires, jars, cans, shoe boxes. Roses are the Mexican's favorite flower. I think, how symbolic — thorns and all.

Yes, the Chicano and Chicana have always taken care of growing things and the land. Again I see the four of us kids getting off the school bus, changing into our work clothes, walking into the field with Papí and Mamí, all six of us bending to the ground. Below our feet, under the earth lie the watermelon seeds. We cover them with paper plates, putting *terremotes* on top of the plates to keep them from being blown away by the wind. The paper plates keep the freeze away. Next day or the next, we remove the plates, bare the tiny green shoots to the elements. They survive and grow, give fruit hundreds of times the size of the seed. We water them and hoe them. We harvest them. The vines dry, rot, are plowed under. Growth, death, decay, birth. The soil prepared again and again, impregnated, worked on. A constant changing of forms, *renacimientos de la tierra madre*.

> This land was Mexican once
> was Indian always
> and is.
> And will be again.

Barbara Christian

1943–2000

Born on St. Thomas in the U.S. Virgin Islands in 1943, Barbara Christian was educated at Marquette University and did her doctoral work at Columbia. During the 1960s, while teaching at City College in New York, Christian was deeply involved in the Black Liberation movement and the opposition to the Vietnam War. In 1971, Christian took a position at the University of California at Berkeley. Christian called academic attention to African American women like Zora Neale Hurston, Alice Walker, and Toni Morrison, moving them from special-interest status to a more central position within academic and popular circles of readership in America. Works by these authors had been criticized according to the rubrics of Eurocentric masculinist literary analysis, according to Christian, who helped to develop a Black Feminist Criticism that could understand this literature on its own terms. Christian died of cancer in 2000 at the age of fifty-six. Her books include Black Women Novelists: The Development of a Tradition, 1892–1976 *(1980),* Black Feminist Criticism: Perspectives on Black Women Writers *(1985),* From the Inside Out: Afro-American Women's Literary Tradition and the State *(1987), and* Alice Walker's "The Color Purple" and Other Works: A Critical Commentary *(1988).*

In the following essay, "The Race for Theory," excerpted from Gender and Theory: Dialogues on Feminist Criticism *(1989), Christian argues that the academic race to theorize African American women's writing has often eclipsed the theoretical implications of the literature itself. Her argument that theory was "white" created a controversy within the African American academy; two thoughtful responses, by Michael Awkward and Deborah McDowell, follow the selection.*

The Race for Theory

I have seized this occasion to break the silence among those of us, critics, as we are now called, who have been intimidated, devalued by what I call the race for theory. I have become convinced that there has been a takeover in the literary world by Western philosophers from the old literary élite, the neutral humanists. Philosophers have been able to effect such a takeover because so much of the literature of the West has become pallid, laden with despair, self-indulgent, and disconnected. The New Philosophers, eager to understand a world that is today fast escaping their political control, have redefined literature so that the distinctions implied by that term, that is, the distinctions between everything written and those things written to evoke feeling as well as to express thought, have been blurred. They have changed literary critical language to suit their own purposes as philosophers, and they have reinvented the meaning of theory.

My first response to this realization was to ignore it. Perhaps, in spite of the egocentrism of this trend, some good might come of it. I had, I felt, more pressing and interesting things to do, such as reading and studying the history and literature of black women, a history that had been totally ignored, a contemporary literature bursting with originality, passion, insight, and beauty. But unfortunately it is difficult to ignore this new takeover, since theory has become a commodity which helps determine whether we are hired or promoted in academic institutions — worse, whether we are heard at all. Due to this new orientation, works (a word which evokes labor) have become texts. Critics are no longer concerned with literature, but with other critics' texts, for the critic yearning for attention has displaced the writer and has conceived of himself as the center. Interestingly in the first part of this century, at least in England and America, the critic was usually also a writer of poetry, plays, or novels. But today, as a new generation of professionals develops, he or she is increasingly an academic. Activities such as teaching or writing one's response to specific works of literature have,

among this group, become subordinated to one primary thrust, that moment when one creates a theory, thus fixing a constellation of ideas for a time at least, a fixing which no doubt will be replaced in another month or so by somebody else's competing theory as the race accelerates. Perhaps because those who have effected the takeover have the power (although they deny it) first of all to be published, and thereby to determine the ideas which are deemed valuable, some of our most daring and potentially radical critics (and by *our* I mean black, women, third world) have been influenced, even co-opted, into speaking a language and defining their discussion in terms alien to and opposed to our needs and orientation. At least so far, the creative writers I study have resisted this language.

For people of color have always theorized — but in forms quite different from the Western form of abstract logic. And I am inclined to say that our theorizing (and I intentionally use the verb rather than the noun) is often in narrative forms, in the stories we create, in riddles and proverbs, in the play with language, since dynamic rather than fixed ideas seem more to our liking. How else have we managed to survive with such spiritedness the assault on our bodies, social institutions, countries, our very humanity? And women, at least the women I grew up around, continuously speculated about the nature of life through pithy language that unmasked the power relations of their world. It is this language, and the grace and pleasure with which they played with it, that I find celebrated, refined, critiqued in the works of writers like Morrison and Walker. My folk, in other words, have always been in a race for theory — though more in the form of the hieroglyph, a written figure which is both sensual and abstract, both beautiful and communicative. In my own work I try to illuminate and explain these hieroglyphs, which is, I think, an activity quite different from the creating of the hieroglyphs themselves. As the Buddhists would say, the finger pointing at the moon is not the moon.

In this discussion, however, I am more concerned with the issue raised by my first use of the term, the race for theory, in relation to its academic hegemony, and possibly of its inappropriateness to the energetic emerging literatures in the world today. The pervasiveness of this academic hegemony is an issue continually spoken about — but usually in hidden groups, lest we, who are disturbed by it, appear ignorant to the reigning academic elite. Among the folk who speak in muted tones are people of color, feminists, radical critics, creative writers, who have struggled for much longer than a decade to make their voices, their various voices, heard, and for whom literature is not an occasion for discourse among critics but is necessary nourishment for their people and one way by which they come to understand their lives better. Clichéd though this may be, it bears, I think, repeating here.

The race for theory, with its linguistic jargon, its emphasis on quoting its prophets, its tendency towards "Biblical" exegesis, its refusal even to mention specific works of creative writers, far less contemporary ones, its preoccupations with mechanical analyses of language, graphs, algebraic equations, its gross generalizations about culture, has silenced many of us to the extent that some of us feel we can no longer discuss our own literature, while others have developed intense writing blocks and are puzzled by the incomprehensibility of the language set adrift in literary circles. There have been, in the last year, any number of occasions on which I had to convince literary critics who have pioneered entire new areas of critical inquiry that they did have something to say. Some of us are continually harassed to invent wholesale theories regardless of the complexity of the literature we study. I, for one, am tired of being asked to produce a black feminist literary theory as if I were a mechanical man. For I believe such theory is prescriptive — it ought to have some relationship to practice. Since I can count on one hand the number of people attempting to be black feminist literary critics in the world today, I consider it presumptuous of me to invent a theory of how we ought to read. Instead, I think we need to read the works of our writers in our various ways and remain open to the intricacies of the intersection of language,

class, race, and gender in the literature. And it would help if we share our process, that is, our practice, as much as possible since, finally, our work is a collective endeavor.

The insidious quality of this race for theory is symbolized for me by the very name of this special issue — Minority Discourse — a label which is borrowed from the reigning theory of the day and is untrue to the literatures being produced by our writers, for many of our literatures (certainly Afro-American literature) are central, not minor, and by the titles of many of the articles, which illuminate language as an assault on the other, rather than as possible communication, and play with, or even affirmation of another. I have used the passive voice in my last sentence construction, contrary to the rules of Black English, which like all languages has a particular value system, since I have not placed responsibility on any particular person or group. But that is precisely because this new ideology has become so prevalent among us that it behaves like so many of the other ideologies with which we have had to contend. It appears to have neither head nor center. At the least, though, we can say that the terms "minority" and "discourse" are located firmly in a Western dualistic or "binary" frame which sees the rest of the world as minor, and tries to convince the rest of the world that it *is* major, usually through force and then through language, even as it claims many of the ideas that we, its "historical" other, have known and spoken about for so long. For many of us have never conceived of ourselves only as somebody's *other*.

Let me not give the impression that by objecting to the race for theory I ally myself with or agree with the neutral humanists who see literature as pure expression and will not admit to the obvious control of its production, value, and distribution by those who have power, who deny, in other words, that literature is, of necessity, political. I am studying an entire body of literature that has been denigrated for centuries by such terms as *political*. For an entire century Afro-American writers, from Charles Chesnutt in the nineteenth century through Richard Wright in the 1930s, Imamu Baraka in the 1960s, Alice Walker in the 1970s, have protested the literary hierarchy of dominance which declares when literature is literature, when literature is great, depending on what it thinks is to its advantage. The Black Arts Movement of the 1960s, out of which Black Studies, the Feminist Literary Movement of the 1970s, and Women's Studies grew, articulated precisely those issues, which came *not* from the declarations of the New Western philosophers but from these groups' reflections on their own lives. That Western scholars have long believed their ideas to be universal has been strongly opposed by many such groups. Some of my colleagues do not see black critical writers of previous decades as eloquent enough. Clearly they have not read Wright's "Blueprint for Negro Writing," Ellison's *Shadow and Act*, Chesnutt's resignation from being a writer, or Alice Walker's "In Search of Zora Neale Hurston." There are two reasons for this general ignorance of what our writer-critics have said. One is that black writing has been generally ignored in this country. Since we, as Toni Morrison has put it, are seen as a discredited people, it is no surprise, then, that our creations are also discredited, but this is also due to the fact that until recently dominant critics in the Western World have also been creative writers who have had access to the upper middle class institutions of education and until recently our writers have decidedly been excluded from these institutions and in fact have often been opposed to them. Because of the academic world's general ignorance about the literature of black people and of women, whose work too has been discredited, it is not surprising that so many of our critics think that the position arguing that literature is political begins with these New Philosophers. Unfortunately, many of our young critics do not investigate the reasons *why* that statement — literature is political — is now acceptable when before it was not; nor do we look to our own antecedents for the sophisticated arguments upon which we can build in order to change the tendency of any established Western idea to become hegemonic.

For I feel that the new emphasis on literary critical theory is as hegemonic as the world which it attacks. I see the language it creates as one which mystifies rather than clarifies our condition, making it possible for a few people who know that particular language to control the critical scene — that language surfaced, interestingly enough, just when the literature of peoples of color, of black women, of Latin Americans, of Africans began to move to "the center." Such words as *center* and *periphery* are themselves instructive. *Discourse, canon, texts*, words as latinate as the tradition from which they come, are quite familiar to me. Because I went to a Catholic Mission school in the West Indies I must confess that I cannot hear the word "canon" without smelling incense, that the word "text" immediately brings back agonizing memories of Biblical exegesis, that "discourse" reeks for me of metaphysics forced down my throat in those courses that traced *world* philosophy from Aristotle through Thomas Aquinas to Heidegger. "Periphery" too is a word I heard throughout my childhood, for if anything was seen as being at the periphery, it was those small Caribbean islands which had neither land mass nor military power. Still I noted how intensely important this periphery was, for U.S. troops were continually invading one island or another if any change in political control even seemed to be occurring. As I lived among folk for whom language was an absolutely necessary way of validating our existence, I was told that the minds of the world lived only in the small continent of Europe. The metaphysical language of the New Philosophy, then, I must admit, is repulsive to me and is one reason why I raced from philosophy to literature, since the latter seemed to me to have the possibilities of rendering the world as large and as complicated as I experienced it, as sensual as I knew it was. In literature I sensed the possibility of the integration of feeling/knowledge, rather than the split between the abstract and the emotional in which Western philosophy inevitably indulged.

Now I am being told that philosophers are the ones who write literature, that authors are dead, irrelevant, mere vessels through which their narratives ooze, that they do not work nor have they the faintest idea what they are doing; rather they produce texts as disembodied as the angels. I am frankly astonished that scholars who call themselves Marxists or post-Marxists could seriously use such metaphysical language even as they attempt to deconstruct the philosophical tradition from which their language comes. And as a student of literature, I am appalled by the sheer ugliness of the language, its lack of clarity, its unnecessarily complicated sentence constructions, its lack of pleasurableness, its alienating quality. It is the kind of writing for which composition teachers would give a freshman a resounding F.

Because I am a curious person, however, I postponed readings of black women writers I was working on and read some of the prophets of this new literary orientation. These writers did announce their dissatisfaction with some of the cornerstone ideas of their own tradition, a dissatisfaction with which I was born. But in their attempt to change the orientation of Western scholarship, they, as usual, concentrated on themselves and were not in the slightest interested in the worlds they had ignored or controlled. Again I was supposed to know *them*, while they were not at all interested in knowing *me*. Instead they sought to "deconstruct" the tradition to which they belonged even as they used the same forms, style, language of that tradition, forms which necessarily embody its values. And increasingly as I read them and saw their substitution of their philosophical writings for literary ones, I began to have the uneasy feeling that their folk were not producing any literature worth mentioning. For they always harkened back to the masterpieces of the past, again reifying the very texts they said they were deconstructing. Increasingly, as *their* way, *their* terms, *their* approaches remained central and became the means by which one defined literary critics, many of my own peers who had previously been concentrating on dealing with the other side of the equation, the reclamation and discussion of past and *present* third world literatures, were diverted into continually discussing the new literary theory.

From my point of view as a critic of contemporary Afro-American women's writing, this orientation is extremely problematic. In attempting to find the deep structures in the literary tradition, a major preoccupation of the new New Criticism, many of us have become obsessed with the nature of reading itself to the extent that we have stopped writing about literature being written today. Since I am slightly paranoid, it has begun to occur to me that the literature being produced *is* precisely one of the reasons why this new philosophical-literary-critical theory of relativity is so prominent. In other words, the literature of blacks, women of South America and Africa, etc., as overtly "political" literature was being preempted by a new Western concept which proclaimed that reality does not exist, that everything is relative, and that every text is silent about something — which indeed it must necessarily be.

There is, of course, much to be learned from exploring how we know what we know, how we read what we read, an exploration which, of necessity, can have no end. But there also has to be a "what," and that "what," when it is even mentioned by the new philosophers, are texts of the past, primarily Western male texts, whose norms are again being transferred onto third world, female texts as theories of reading proliferate. Inevitably a hierarchy has now developed between what is called theoretical criticism and practical criticism, as mind is deemed superior to matter. I have no quarrel with those who wish to philosophize about how we know what we know. But I do resent the fact that this particular orientation is so privileged and has diverted so many of us from doing the first readings of the literature being written today as well as of past works about which nothing has been written. I note, for example, that there is little work done on Gloria Naylor, that most of Alice Walker's works have not been commented on — despite the rage around *The Color Purple* — that there has yet to be an in-depth study of Frances Harper, the nineteenth-century abolitionist poet and novelist. If our emphasis on theoretical criticism continues, critics of the future may have to reclaim the writers we are now ignoring, that is, if they are even aware these artists exist.

I am particularly perturbed by the movement to exalt theory, as well, because of my own adult history. I was an active member of the Black Arts Movement of the sixties and know how dangerous theory can become. Many today may not be aware of this, but the Black Arts Movement tried to create Black Literary Theory and in doing so became prescriptive. My fear is that when Theory is not rooted in practice, it becomes prescriptive, exclusive, élitish.

An example of this prescriptiveness is the approach the Black Arts Movement took towards language. For it, blackness resided in the use of black talk which they defined as hip urban language. So that when Nikki Giovanni reviewed Paule Marshall's *Chosen Place, Timeless People*, she criticized the novel on the grounds that it was not black, for the language was too elegant, too white. Blacks, she said, did not speak that way. Having come from the West Indies where we do, some of the time, speak that way, I was amazed by the narrowness of her vision. The emphasis on *one way* to be black resulted in the works of Southern writers being seen as non-black since the black talk of Georgia does not sound like the black talk of Philadelphia. Because the ideologues, like Baraka, come from the urban centers they tended to privilege their way of speaking, thinking, writing, and to condemn other kinds of writing as not being black enough. Whole areas of the canon were assessed according to the dictum of the Black Arts Nationalist point of view, as in Addison Gayle's *The Way of the New World*, while other works were ignored because they did not fit the scheme of cultural nationalism. Older writers like Ellison and Baldwin were condemned because they saw that the intersection of Western and African influences resulted in a new Afro-American culture, a position with which many of the Black Nationalist ideologues disagreed. Writers were told that writing love poems was not being black. Further examples abound.

It is true that the Black Arts Movement resulted in a necessary and important critique both of previous Afro-American literature and of the white-established literary world. But in attempting to take over power, it, as Ishmael Reed satirizes so well in *Mumbo Jumbo*, became much like its opponent, monolithic and downright repressive.

It is this tendency towards the monolithic, monotheistic, etc., which worries me about the race for theory. Constructs like the *center* and the *periphery* reveal that tendency to want to make the world less complex by organizing it according to one principle, to fix it through an idea which is really an ideal. Many of us are particularly sensitive to monolithism since one major element of

ideologies of dominance, such as sexism and racism, is to dehumanize people by stereotyping them, by denying them their variousness and complexity. Inevitably, monolithism becomes a metasystem, in which there is a controlling ideal, especially in relation to pleasure. Language as one form of pleasure is immediately restricted, and becomes heavy, abstract, prescriptive, monotonous.

Variety, multiplicity, eroticism are difficult to control. And it may very well be that these are the reasons why writers are often seen as *persona non grata* by political states, whatever form they take, since writers/artists have a tendency to refuse to give up their way of seeing the world and of playing with possibilities; in fact, their very expression relies on that insistence. Perhaps that is why creative literature, even when written by politically reactionary people, can be so freeing, for in having to embody ideas and recreate the world, writers cannot merely produce "one way."

The characteristics of the Black Arts Movement are, I am afraid, being repeated again today, certainly in the other area to which I am especially tuned. In the race for theory, feminists, eager to enter the halls of power, have attempted their own prescriptions. So often I have read books on feminist literary theory that restrict the definition of what *feminist* means and overgeneralize about so much of the world that most women as well as men are excluded. Nor seldom do feminist theorists take into account the complexity of life — that women are of many races and ethnic backgrounds with different histories and cultures and that as a rule women belong to different classes that have different concerns. Seldom do they note these distinctions, because if they did they could not articulate a theory. Often as a way of clearing themselves they do acknowledge that women of color, for example, do exist, then go on to do what they were going to do anyway, which is to invent a theory that has little relevance for us.

That tendency towards monolithism is precisely how I see the French feminist theorists. They concentrate on the female body as the means to creating a female language, since language, they say, is male and necessarily conceives of woman as other. Clearly many of them have been irritated by the theories of Lacan for whom language is phallic. But suppose there are peoples in the world whose language was invented primarily in relation to women, who after all are the ones who relate to children and teach language. Some Native American languages, for example, use female pronouns when speaking about non-gender specific activity. Who knows who, according to gender, created languages. Further, by positing the body as the source of everything French feminists return to the old myth that biology determines everything and ignore the fact that gender is a social rather than a biological construct.

I could go on critiquing the positions of French feminists who are themselves more various in their points of view than the label which is used to describe them, but that is not my point. What I am concerned about is the authority this school now has in feminist scholarship — the way it has become *authoritative discourse*, monologic, which occurs precisely because it does have access to the means of promulgating its ideas. The Black Arts Movement was able to do this for a time because of the political movements of the 1960s — so too with the French feminists who could not be inventing "theory" if a space had not been created by the Women's Movement. In both cases, both groups posited a theory that excluded many of the people who made that space possible. Hence one of the reasons for the surge of Afro-American women's writing during the 1970s and its emphasis on sexism in the black community is precisely that when the ideologues of the 1960s said *black*, they meant *black male*.

I and many of my sisters do not see the world as being so simple. And perhaps that is why we have not rushed to create abstract theories. For we know there are countless women of color, both in America and in the rest of the world to whom our singular ideas would be applied. There is, therefore, a caution we feel about pronouncing black feminist theory that might be seen as a decisive statement about Third World women. This is not to say we are not theorizing. Certainly our literature is an indication of the ways in which our theorizing, of necessity, is based on our multiplicity of experiences.

There is at least one other lesson I learned from the Black Arts Movement. One reason for its monolithic approach had to do with its desire to destroy the power which controlled black people, but it was a power which many of its ideologues wished to achieve. The nature of our context today is such that an approach which desires power singlemindedly must of necessity become like that which it wishes to destroy. Rather than wanting to change the whole model, many of us want to be at the center. It is this point of view that writers like June Jordan and Audre Lorde continually critique even as they call for empowerment, as they emphasize the fear of difference among us and our need for leaders rather than a reliance on ourselves.

For one must distinguish the desire for power from the need to become empowered — that is, seeing oneself as capable of and having the right to determine one's life. Such empowerment is partially derived from a knowledge of history. The Black Arts Movement did result in the creation of Afro-American Studies as a concept, thus giving it a place in the university where one might engage in the reclamation of Afro-American history and culture and pass it on to others. I am particularly concerned that institutions such as Black Studies and Women's Studies, fought for with such vigor and at some sacrifice, are not often seen as important by many of our black or women scholars precisely because the old hierarchy of traditional departments is seen as superior to these "marginal" groups. Yet, it is in this context that many others of us are discovering the extent of our complexity, the interrelationships of different areas of knowledge in relation to a distinctly Afro-American or female experience. Rather than having to view our world as subordinate to others, or rather than having to work as if we were hybrids, we can pursue ourselves as subjects.

My major objection to the race for theory, as some readers have probably guessed by now, really hinges on the question, "for whom are we doing what we are doing when we do literary criticism?" It is, I think, the central question today especially for the few of us who have infiltrated the academy enough to be wooed by it. The answer to that question determines what orientation we take in our work, the language we use, the purposes for which it is intended.

I can only speak for myself. But what I write and how I write is done in order to save my own life. And I mean that literally. For me literature is a way of knowing that I am not hallucinating, that whatever I feel/know *is*. It is an affirmation that sensuality is intelligence, that sensual language is language that makes sense. My response, then, is directed to those who write what I read and to those who read what I read — put concretely — to Toni Morrison and to people who read Toni Morrison (among whom I would count few academics). That number is increasing, as is the readership of Walker and Marshall. But in no way is the literature Morrison, Marshall, or Walker create supported by the academic world. Nor given the political context of our society, do I expect that to change soon. For there is no reason, given who controls these institutions, for them to be anything other than threatened by these writers.

My readings do presuppose a need, a desire among folk who like me also want to save their own lives. My concern, then, is a passionate one, for the literature of people who are not in power has always been in danger of extinction or of co-optation, not because we do not theorize, but because what we can even imagine, far less who we can reach, is constantly limited by societal structures. For me, literary criticism is promotion as well as understanding, a response to the writer to whom there is often no response, to folk who need the writing as much as they need anything. I know, from literary history, that writing disappears unless there is a response to it. Because I write about writers who are now writing, I hope to help ensure that their tradition has continuity and survives.

So my "method," to use a new "lit. crit." word, is not fixed but relates to what I read and to the historical context of the writers I read *and* to the many critical activities in which I am engaged, which may or may not involve writing. It is a learning from the language of creative writers, which is one of surprise, so that I might discover what language I might use. For my language is very much based on what I read and how it affects me, that is, on the surprise that comes from reading something that compels you to read differently, as I believe literature does. I, therefore, have no set method, another prerequisite of the new theory, since for me every work suggests a new approach. As risky as that might seem, it is, I believe, what intelligence means — a tuned sensitivity to that which is alive and therefore cannot be known until it is known. Audre Lorde puts it in a far more succinct and sensual way in her essay "Poetry Is Not a Luxury":

> As they become known to and accepted by us, our feelings and the honest exploration of them become sanctuaries and spawning grounds for the most radical and daring of ideas. They become a safe-house for that difference so necessary to change and the conceptualization of any meaningful action. Right now, I could name at least ten ideas I would have found intolerable or incomprehensible and frightening, except as they came after dreams and poems. This is not idle fantasy, but a disciplined attention to the true meaning of "it feels right to me." We can train ourselves to respect our feelings and to transpose them into a language so they can be shared. And where that language does not yet exist, it is our poetry which helps to fashion it. Poetry is not only dream and vision; it is the skeleton architecture of our lives. It lays the foundations for a future of change, a bridge across our fears of what has never been before.[1]

[1]Audre Lord, *Sister Outsider* (Trumansburg, N.Y.: The Crossing Press, 1984), 37.

Michael Awkward

b. 1959

In his memoir, Scenes of Instruction *(1999), Michael Awkward recounts how, as a young African American boy at a predominantly white elementary school in Philadelphia, severely scarred by a burn and embarrassed both by academic success and his often inebriated single mother, he desperately sought a role for himself in his family, his schools, and in society. Calling his mother "the most complicated text I have ever read or ever will read," he credits her with his lifelong desire to explore the lives of African American women. As a feminist theorist, particularly of African American literature, Awkward highlights the pitfalls of identity politics that attend theories of race and gender. He received his B.A. from Brandeis University, followed by an M.A. and Ph.D. at the University of Pennsylvania. In 1986, he joined the faculty of the University of Michigan and headed Michigan's Center for Afro-American and African Studies for three years. He returned to the University of Pennsylvania to direct the Center for the Study of Black Literature and Culture, and then, in 2003, joined Emory University's English department. He is the author of* Inspiriting Influences: Tradition, Revision, and Afro-American Women's Novels *(1989) and* Negotiating Difference: Race, Gender and the Politics of Positionality *(1995). The following essay is excerpted from "Appropriative Gestures: Theory and Afro-American Literary Criticism," originally published in the 2000 collection,* African American Literary Theory.

Deborah E. McDowell

b. 1951

Deborah E. McDowell is one of the leading voices of African American literature and women's studies. Born in Birmingham, Alabama, McDowell received her B.A. from the Tuskegee Institute (1972) and her graduate degrees in American and Afro-American literature from Purdue University. She has taught at Colby College, where she was tenured as associate professor of English. Since 1987, she has been Alice Griffin Professor of American and African American English at the University of Virginia. McDowell's publications include studies of the work of Alice Walker, Toni Morrison, Dorothy West, and Jesse Redmon Fauset, and she is the general editor of the Black Women Writers Series. *Her recent publications include* Slavery and the Literary Imagination *(ed., with Arnold Ramparsad, 1989), and* The Changing Same *(1995), a study of generational connections among black women novelists. Her autobiography is* Leaving Pipe Shop: Memories of Kin *(1996).*

"Recycling: Race, Gender and the Practice of Theory" responds to both Barbara Christian and Michael Awkward, and, in a way, to her own earlier work, since it revises somewhat McDowell's former position on race and theory. The entire essay from which this selection is taken originally appeared in Studies in Historical Change, *edited by Ralph Cohen (1992).*

MICHAEL AWKWARD

From *Appropriative Gestures: Theory and Afro-American Literary Criticism*

Barbara Christian's "The race for theory" leaves no doubt in the mind of its readers that the esteemed black feminist critic is — in the words of the controversial Steven Knapp and Walter Benn Michaels essay — against theory. Christian's reaction to theory, however, differs from that of Knapp and Michaels, who seek to discredit theory by discussing what they argue are its fallacious oppositions — meaning/intent, knowledge/belief. She also differs from Afro-American critic Joyce Joyce, who discusses what she views as the ideologically deficient theoretical practice of several black critics in order to demonstrate an incompatibility between practical Afrocentric criticism and contemporary literary theory.[1] For Christian neither systematically attacks what she believes are the inadequacies of its most basic tenets nor attempts to address in specific ways what she holds are the flawed critical practices of Afro-Americanist uses of theory. Instead, Christian asserts that theory is a putatively radical enterprise which has done little to change the *status quo* or advance our comprehension of the processes of literary production, and that its ideologically radial practitioners have been "co-opted into speaking a language and defining their discussion in terms alien to and opposed to our needs and orientation."[2]

The particulars of Christian's attacks on theory certainly are not original, nor are they, I believe, particularly persuasive. By condemning the discourse of literary theory, calling those who employ theoretical paradigms "critic[s] yearning for attention," and implying that literary theory had gained a significant hold on our attention primarily because "so much of the literature of the

West has become pallid, laden with despair, self-indulgent and disconnected," Christian rehearses old arguments which, frankly, I am not interested in addressing. I am aware of no evidence which convincingly suggests that today's literary critics are, as a group, any more egotistical than their predecessors, or that figurations of despair historically have proven any less *analytically* provocative than those of any other psychological/emotional state. What I am interested in exploring — and arguing against — are Christian's specific reasons for viewing as counterproductive the theoretical practice of black feminist criticism and other non-hegemonic — non-white male — schools of literary analysis. For I believe that the strategies of reading which she deplores offer the Afrocentric critic a means of more fully and adequately decoding the black literary text and canon than what the critic Daniel O'Hara might call the "fly-by-the-seat-of-one's-pants"[3] approach Christian advances at the end of her essay as a corrective to "the race for theory."

Christian characterizes her own critical practice as an effort to save the emerging, under-appreciated Afro-American woman's text from the types of critical marginality and canonical oblivion that had previously been the fate of early- and mid-twentieth century products of black female imaginations. Clearly, Christian's preservatory impulses are commendable and historically well founded. Despite the inroads some Afro-American women's texts have made in small areas in the canon, black women's literature still does not assume the prominent place in courses and criticism that those who devote a great deal of scholarly attention to it feel it merits. I do not, then, object to the tenets which inform Christian's critical practice, nor do I feel that it is correct to

---

[1] See Knapp and Michaels 1985, and Joyce 1987. [Awkward] Steven Knapp and Walter Benn Michaels, "Against Theory," in *Against Theory: Literary Studies and the New Pragmatism*, edited by W. J. T. Mitchell (Chicago: University of Chicago Press, 1985). James Joyce, "The Black Canon" in *New Literary History* 18.2 (1987): 335–44.

[2] See Christian, p. 1859.

[3] In Mitchell 1985: 37. [Awkward] See "For and Against Theory" in *Against Theory*, n. 1.

dismiss out of hand the works of those scholars in the field which are not obviously informed by post-structuralist theories. The types of re-readings of neglected black women's texts and "first readings" of new works to which Christian has devoted herself can be, when performed in the energetic manner with which she approaches her work, quite helpful to our understanding of what she has called "the development of the tradition" of black women's literature. What I do object to where Christian's discussion of Afro-American critical engagement of literary theory is concerned is her consistent refusal to acknowledge that its employment by several clearly Afrocentric critics has indeed deepened our received knowledge of the textual production of black writers.

Christian sees literary theory as a coercive hegemonic force which has begun to poison the discourse of "some of our most daring and potentially radical critics (and by *our* I mean black, women, third world)"[4] whose adoption of post-structuralist modes of reading suggests that they "have been influenced, even co-opted" by a hegemonic critical discourse. While here, as at most points in her essay, she is unwilling to name victims or villains, Christian suggests that, as an enterprise, literary theory has corrupted a previously methodologically sound black feminist criticism, forcing its practitioners either into silence or into the defensive postures of black female natives invaded by an alien, white, phallocentric critical discourse that they employ against their will and better judgment. While the imagery she uses resonates with historically significant indignation — the black female critic as pure Afrocentric maiden corrupted by an institutionally all-powerful white male post-structuralist theory — Christian's representation of theoretically informed black female (and other non-caucasian and/or male) critics as "co-opted" can only be read as an attack on their personal integrity and recent work. She apparently cannot even conceive of the possibility that these critics *choose* to employ theory because they believe it offers provocative means of discussing the texts of non-hegemonic groups, that theory indeed

is viewed by them as useful in the critical analysis of the literary products of "the other."

Further, Christian's "resistance to theory" leads her to overstate her claims about a purely descriptive, non-theoretical stage of black feminist criticism. One of its earlier and most eloquent statements, Barbara Smith's groundbreaking essay "Toward a Black Feminist Criticism," is essentially a theoretical — if not post-structuralist — discussion of critical practice and textual production.[5] In this much-anthologized essay, Smith — like all theorists — prescriptively asserts what she believes ought to be the informing principles of the critics she wants to persuade. She defines the limits of the black feminist interpretive project, telling aspiring black feminist critics how Afro-American women's texts ought to be read and suggesting what sorts of findings such readings ought to uncover. Smith says: "Beginning with a primary commitment to exploring how both sexual and racial politics and Black and female identity are inextricable elements in Black women's writings, she would also work from the assumption that Black women writers constitute an identifiable literary tradition. . . . [S]he would think and write out of her own identity and not try to graft the ideas or methodology of white/male literary thought upon the precious materials of Black women's art."[6]

While post-structuralist theorists might intervene here and censure Smith's overdetermined collision of biology and ideology — Smith assumes that the black feminist critic will necessarily be a black woman, that whites and black men are incapable of offering the types of analyses she advocates because they "are of course ill-equipped to deal [simultaneously] with the subtleties of racial [and sexual] politics"[7] — it is in her move from theory to practice that contemporary critical theory could be most helpful to her project. For Smith problematically believes that her (now generally accepted) theoretical suggestions — that one analyze in black women's

<hr/>

[4]See Christian, p. 1859.

[5]For Barbara Smith, see p. 1600.

[6]See Smith, p. 1604.

[7]For a fuller discussion of this collision of biology and ideology in black feminist criticism, see my 1988 essay "Race, gender, and the politics of reading," *Black American Literature Forum*, 22.1 (1988): 5–27. [Awkward]

texts figurations of the relationships between race, gender and class, as well as demonstrate the contours of the black woman's literary tradition — will lead necessarily to critical acts such as her still-controversial reading of Toni Morrison's *Sula* as a lesbian novel. Unlike Deborah McDowell, who in "New Directions for Black Feminist Criticism" argues that the problems with Smith's analysis result from a lack of a precise definition of the term "lesbian" and from the fact that Smith's "'innovative' analysis is pressed to the service of an individual political persuasion"[8] I feel that the problems with Smith's critical manuevers lie in her lack of awareness of the contemporary literary theories that Christian devalues. Combined with her own convincingly articulated black feminist approach, an engagement of reader-response theory and theories about the textual construction of gendered/ideological readers might have led Smith to be even more innovative. Rather than arguing that Morrison's is a black lesbian text (a reading to which Morrison herself forcefully objected in a recent interview[9]), she might instead have offered a theory of a *black lesbian reader*. Rather than involving herself needlessly and unprofitably in discussions of authorial intent,[10] Smith might have focused on the *effects on the reader* of *Sula*'s clear and consistent critique of heterosexual institutions, on the text's progressive "lesbianization" of the reader. Whether Morrison *intends* this is, to a certain extent, beside the point;

the point of Smith's theorizing is that such a process does — or at least *can* — indeed occur as a necessary function of careful, ideologically informed reading of Morrison's novel. The problem with the move from practical theory to theoretical practice in "Toward a Black Feminist Criticism" is not, as Christian's perspectives suggest, Smith's attempt to "overgeneralize," to *theorize*, about the process of reading, but her insufficient awareness of advances in reader-response theory that would have allowed her to discuss in a more convincing manner her perceptions of the effects of reading Morrison's novel.

My own intent here is not to discredit Smith's essay, which I believe remains the most influential work in the area of black feminist criticism. Rather, it is to suggest the misconceptions that mar Christian's three most forcefully articulated arguments against a black feminist engagement of literary theory: 1) that black feminist criticism and literary theory are essentially incompatible enterprises; 2) that post-structuralism is the cause of (premature) attempts at black feminist literary theory; and 3) that black feminist literary theory has not — and should not have — emerged before the practice of reading black women's texts is more firmly established. Clearly, Smith's essay — and its careful analysis — serves to challenge the general applicability to black feminist criticism of Christian's suppositions. For Smith's 1977 essay (however problematically) *theorizes* despite its lack of a clearly informed awareness of deconstruction, reader-response theory, semiotics, or any of what Smith terms "the ideas or methodology of white/male literary thought," and does so *while* bemoaning the paucity of black feminist critical acts. Despite an obviously antagonistic relationship to white/male hegemony, Smith believes, like the villainous post-structuralist theorists of Christian's essay, that she can offer a prescription, a theory, of how most profitably to read literary texts.

Unlike Smith, Christian is concerned primarily not with theorizing about profitable means by which to approach Afro-American women's literature, but with "help[ing to] ensure that [the black woman's literary] tradition has continuity and survives" by offering "first readings" of new works by Afro-American women. As a consequence, she

[8]Deborah McDowell, "New Directions for Black Feminist Criticism," in *The New Feminist Criticism*, edited by Elaine Showalter (New York: Pantheon, 1985).

[9]In her interview collected in Tate 1983, Morrison asserts — obviously with Smith's comments in mind: "Nobody ever talked about friendship between women unless it was homosexual, and there is no homosexuality in *Sula*" (p. 118). [Awkward] Claudia Tate, ed., *Black Women Writers at Work* (New York: Continuum, 1983).

[10]The problems with Smith's discussion of *Sula* are most glaringly manifested in her attempts to distinguish between textual meaning and authorial intent. She argues that despite the novel's "consistently critical stance toward the heterosexual institutions of male-female relationships, marriage, and the family" (p. 175), Morrison's failure to "approach . . . her subject with the consciousness that a lesbian relationship was at least a possibility for her characters" results from the novelist's overdetermined "heterosexual assumptions [that] can veil what may logically be expected to occur in a work" (p. 181). [Awkward] See Smith, pp. 1605 and 1608.

perceives as quite problematic the insistence that black feminist critics devise theoretical ways of approaching the Afro-American woman's literary tradition. She says:

> Some of us are continually harassed to invent wholesale theories regardless of the complexity of the literature we study. I, for one, am tired of being asked to produce a black feminist literary theory as if I were a mechanical man. For I believe such theory is prescriptive — it ought to have some relationship to practice. Since I can count on one hand the number of people attempting to be black feminist literary critics in the world today, I consider it presumptuous of me to invent a theory of how we ought to read.[11]

Certainly Christian's anger is justified if, as she suggests, the requests she has received to offer theoretical models adequate to a discussion of black women's literature have indeed taken the form of intellectual harassment. But she can argue that critical practice in the last fifteen years has not adequately prepared the way for new the-

[11]See Christian, p. 1860.

ories of black women's textual production only by being as restrictive in her definition of "black feminist literary critics" as she accuses feminist literary theorists of being when they define the term "feminist." (Are black feminist critics only black women? If so, they number much more than a handful. Can a gendered and/or racial other learn the ideology, speak the discourse, of "black feminist literary critics"? If not, how should we label such essential works on black women writers as Robert Hemenway's biography of Zora Neale Hurston, Barbara Johnson's essays on Hurston, Calvin Hernton's *The Sexual Mountain* and *Black Women Writers*?) A multitude of readings — by black and white women and men — have appeared in journals, collections of essays, and books that analyze black women's texts in terms of "the intricacies of the intersection of language, class, race, and gender," enough at least to suggest to Christian, as it has to other black female critics, that black feminist criticism has reached an appropriate time in its history to begin theorizing about its practice and the literary production of Afro-American woman writers.

DEBORAH E. MCDOWELL

From *Recycling: Race, Gender, and the Practice of Theory*

GENDERING AFRICAN-AMERICAN THEORY

We can observe such strategies of dominance [of theory over literary analysis] in *Gender and Theory*, a recent anthology edited by Linda Kauffman. Kauffman tries studiously to prevent a reproduction of the simplistic divisions and antagonisms between black and white, male and female, "theory" and "politics." She explains in her introduction that while the title — *Gender and Theory* — posits a couple . . . the essays are arranged to permit men to respond to the essays by women and vice versa. That "structure is

designed . . . to draw attention to such dichotomies in order to displace them by dissymmetry and dissonance."[1] Despite that goal, these very oppositions are evident nonetheless.

In fact, we could argue that if theory is often to "practice-politics" what Europe is to America, what white is to black, what straight is to gay, in Kauffman's anthology, theory is to practice what black male is to black female. This reductive accounting has entered the contemporary critical

[1]*Gender and Theory*, ed. Linda Kauffman (New York, 1989), p. 2. [McDowell]

record and has constructed black women as categorically resistant to theory. To be sure, some black women have indeed helped to foster this perception and to encourage the metonymic strategy of choosing the name of any black woman to summarize the critical position of all.[2]

"Race" in Kauffman's anthology is constructed once again as synonymous with "blackness." Barbara Christian's "The Race for Theory" and Michael Awkward's response, "Appropriative Gestures: Theory and Afro-American Literary Criticism," are placed at the very end of the volume and thus apart from the preceding pairs of essays, none of which interrogates the racial inflections of "gender and theory." The racial opposition coordinates with a gendered opposition between male and female and a gendered opposition between theory and practice.

The question Kauffman poses in her introduction — "In what ways are Afro-American theory and Afro-American feminism complementary, and what ways are they antagonistic?" — gets answered in the two concluding essays: "Afro-American theory" is gendered male and Afro-American feminism is gendered female, and they function effectively as structural polarities. Such a seemingly innocent structure has already quickly decided its conclusion: Michael Awkward's response to Barbara Christian calls for a "theory" to her "practice."

One of the strengths of Awkward's response to Christian lies in its implicit recognition that poststructuralist theory cannot be homogenized, nor can it stand synecdochically for all theory. Although it is clear that he thinks Christian has missed the theoretical mark, he asserts that Barbara Smith's "Toward a Black Feminist Criticism" was "essentially a theoretical statement" "if not [a] post-structuralist discussion of critical practice and textual production." Smith's essay, he goes on to say, "theorizes despite its lack of a clearly informed awareness of deconstruction, reader-response theory, [and] semiotics."[3]

Here, Awkward's vocabulary — "if not" and "lack of " — essentially negates whatever value he initially assigns to Smith's essay, which is structured as the negative of the positive — poststructuralism, the sole frame of reference. In an uncritical assertion of the synonymity between black women writers and "black women" as critics, Awkward offers a cautionary note: "If this field [black women's literature] is to continue to make inroads into the canon, if it is to gain the respect it doubtlessly deserves as an ideologically rich literary tradition, within an increasingly theoretical academy, it will require that its critics continue to move beyond description and master the discourse of contemporary theory."[4] If, as Awkward suggests, "black women's literature still does not assume the prominent place in courses and criticism" that it merits, I would ask whether that marginality can be explained exclusively by the lack of theorizing on the part of black women or rather whether that marginalization is often structured into the very theories that Awkward wants black women to master. Again, my point should not be read as a simplistic rejection of theory, as it is narrowly associated with poststructuralist projects, but as a call for a more searching examination of the processes and procedures of marginalizing any historically subjugated knowledge.

Awkward's essay does more than close Kauffman's volume; it performs a kind of closure, or functions as a kind of "final word," which extends far beyond the boundaries of the collection, *Gender and Theory*. He leaves intact the clichéd and unstudied distinctions between "theory" and "practice," represented by Paul de Man and Barbara Christian, respectively.[5] It is

[2]Such a perception derives in large part from the wasteful battle waged on the pages of *New Literary History* 18 (1987). See Joyce Ann Joyce, "The Black Canon: Reconstructing Black American Literary Criticism"; Henry Louis Gates, Jr., " 'What's Love Got to Do with It?': Critical Theory, Integrity, and the Black Idiom"; Houston A. Baker, Jr., "In Dubious Battle"; and Joyce Ann Joyce, "Who the Cap Fit': Unconsciousness and Unconscionableness in the Criticism of Houston A. Baker, Jr., and Henry Louis Gates, Jr." Christian's "The Race for Theory" added significantly to that perception. [McDowell]

[3]See Awkward, p. 1869.

[4]Michael Awkward, "Appropriative Gestures: Theory and Afro-American Literary Criticism," in Kauffman, *Gender and Theory*, p. 243. [McDowell]

[5]In the final section of his essay, omitted here, Awkward quotes from Paul de Man's *The Resistance to Theory* (1986).

paradoxical and ironic that an essay that privileges poststructuralist theory and extols de Man,
relies on an uncritical construction of theory as
an autonomous entity with semantic stability
and immanent properties that separate it from
practice. It is all the more ironic that such a
dichotomy should dominate in an essay that valorizes a body of theory that emerged to blur such
inherited and unmediated oppositions. But such
dichotomies mark a difference and issue a set of
limits — social limits — with implications that
extend beyond the academic realm. In identifying with Paul de Man, Awkward consolidates his
own critical authority against Barbara
Christian's, making theory a province shared
between men.

NOTES TOWARD A COUNTERHISTORY

Where might we go from here? I would start with
the forthright assertion that the challenge of any
discourse identifying itself as black feminist is
not necessarily or most immediately to vindicate
itself as theory but to resist the theory-practice
dichotomy as at once too broad and too simple to
capture the range and diversity of contemporary
critical projects, including the range and diversity
in the contributions of black women to that discourse. A far more valuable and necessary project
would proceed from the commonplace assumption that no consideration of *any* intellectual project is complete without an understanding of the
process of that project's formation. And thus any
responsible accounting of the work of black
women in literary studies would have to provide
a history of its emergence and to consider that
emergence first on its own terms.

Of course, part of the historical accounting of
recent critical production is well under way, but
unfortunately it leaves questions of the relations
between race and critical discourse largely unexplored. A counterhistory, a more urgent history,
would bring theory and practice into a productive tension that would force a re-evaluation of
each side. But that history could not be written
without considering the determining, should I
say the overdetermining, influences of institutional life out of which all critical utterances
emerge.

It follows, then, that we would have to submit
to careful scrutiny the past two decades, which
witnessed the uncanny convergence and confluence of significant historical moments, all contributing to the present shape and contours of
literary studies. These are: the emergence of a
second renaissance of black women writing to
public acclaim; a demographic shift that brought
the first generation of black intellectuals into the
halls of predominantly white, male, and elitist
institutions; the institutionalization and decline of
Afro-American studies and Women's Studies;
and the rising command in the United States
academy of poststructuralism, regarded as a synonym for theory.

Our historical narrative would have to dramatize the process by which deconstruction
came to stand synecdochically for poststructuralist theory, its dominion extending from the
pages of arcane journals of critical theory to the
pages of such privileged arbiters of culture as
the *New York Times Magazine* and *New York
Review of Books*, to the less illustrious pages of
Time and *Newsweek*.[6] The analysis would have
to explore how deconstruction became associated as much with an ideological position as a
revitalizing and energetic intellectual project at
roughly the same time that a few black women,
following Barbara Smith's challenge, began to
articulate a position identified as black feminist
criticism. Smith focused on recuperating the
writings of black women for critical examination and establishing reading strategies attentive
to the intersections of gender, race, and class in
their work.[7]

[6]Jonathan Arac, Wlad Godzich, and Wallace Martin
described the spread of deconstruction in their preface to *The
Yale Critics* (Minneapolis, 1987). In his estimation, "critics
doing the new work most respected by a professionally
authoritative screening group have drawn heavily from the
Yale critics. In thirty-five essays that recently reached the
Editorial Committee of *PMLA*, the American critics most
cited were Miller . . . de Man, Bloom, Hartman and Derrida."
Yet another and related sign of their powerful sway, Martin
observed, was deconstruction's spread "from elite private
institutions to public institutions," embracing "much more of
the United States" and enrolling much "broader student bodies." [McDowell]
[7]Barbara Smith, "Toward a Black Feminist Criticism."
[McDowell] For Smith, see p. 1600.

If we were to isolate the salient terms of black feminist criticism and poststructuralist theory for this historical narrative, they might run as follows:

1. While black feminist criticism was asserting the significance of black women's experience, poststructuralism was dismantling the authority of experience.
2. While black feminist criticism was calling for nonhostile interpretations of black women's writings, poststructuralism was calling interpretation into question.
3. While black feminist criticism required that these interpretations be grounded in historical context, deconstruction denied history any authoritative value and truth claims, and read context as just another text.
4. While the black woman as author was central to the efforts of black feminist writers to construct a canon of new as well as unknown black women writers, poststructuralism had already rendered such efforts naive by asking, post-Foucault, "What Is an Author?" (1969) and trumpeting post–Roland Barthes, "The Death of the Author" (1968).[8]
5. While black feminist critics and Afro-Americanists more generally were involved in recuperating a canon of writers, a critical vocabulary emerged that subordinated texts and traditions to textuality.

But the salient terms of these admittedly tendentious synopses would also have to reveal some useful correspondences. Both black feminist criticism and deconstruction see the regulation and exclusion of the marginal as essential to maintaining hegemonic structures. Both describe the structural and hierarchical relations between the margins and the center. Our narrative might then pause to ponder how these two reading strategies came to be perceived as antithetical. How their specific *units* of critical interest came to be polarized and assigned an order of intellectual value that drew on a racist and sexist schema with heavy implications and investments in the sociopolitical arrangements of our time.

[8] For Foucault, see p. 904; for Barthes, see p. 874.

CHOOSING SIDES

What viable position can be taken in this context? We might begin to assert a provisional conclusion: When the writings of black women and other critics of color are excluded from the category of theory, it must be partly because theory has been reduced to a very particular practice. Since that reduction has been widely accepted, a great many ways of talking about literature have been excluded and a variety of discursive moves and strategies disqualified, in Terry Eagleton's words, as "invalid, illicit, noncritical."[9]

The value of Eagleton's discussion of literary theory lies mainly in its understanding of how critical discourse is institutionalized. In that process, the power arrogated to some to police language, to determine that "certain statements must be excluded because they do not conform to what is acceptably sayable," cannot be denied.[10] The critical language of black women is represented, with few exceptions, as outside the bounds of the acceptably sayable and is heard primarily as an illicit and noncritical variety of critical discourse defined in opposition to theory. Its definition and identity continue to be constructed in contemporary critical discourses, all of which must be recognized, distinguished, and divided from each other in the academy's hierarchical system of classifying and organizing knowledge. To be sure, the discourses that exist at any given historical juncture compete with each other for dominance and meaning, compete with each other for status as knowledge, but we must be constantly on guard for what Biodun Jeyifo is right to term a *misrecognition* of theory, although this misrecognition has "achieved the status of that naturalization and transparency to which all ideologies aspire and which only the most hegemonic achieve."[11]

[9] Terry Eagleton, *Literary Theory: An Introduction* (Minneapolis, 1983), p. 203. [McDowell]
[10] Ibid. [McDowell]
[11] Biodun Jeyifo, "Literary Theory and Theories of Decolonization." Unpublished manuscript. Also see his "On Eurocentric Critical Theory: Some Paradigms from the Texts and Sub-Texts of Post-Colonial Writing," in Helen Tiffin and Stephen Slemon, eds., *After Europe: Critical Theory, Post-Colonial Writing* (Sydney, 1989). [McDowell]

Given this *misrecognition* of theory and the privileged status it enjoys, even in moments of embattlement, it is readily understandable why some black feminists and other women of color in the academy would argue for the rightful *recognition* of their work as theory. While I would not presume to speak for or issue directives to "women of color," which would, in any case, assume a false and coherent totality, I openly share my growing skepticism, about the tactical advantages of this position.

I am far more interested, for the moment, in joining the growing number of critics — many of them Third World — who have begun to ask the difficult questions about the material conditions of institutional life and to view theory, in its narrow *usages* (rather than in any intrinsic properties to be assigned to it), as an ideological category associated with the politically dominant. It is important that such a statement *not* be read as a resistance to "theory," but one that inquires into why that category is so reductively defined, and especially why its common definitions exclude so many marginalized groups within the academy. Such is Barbara Christian's point in "The Race for Theory," although in their rush to contain her inquiry, critics missed those aspects of value in her critique.

The question that Christian raises about the reassertions of racially coded territorial assumptions and imperatives implied in the distinction between theory and practice is echoed in the writings of a growing number of students of minority and postcolonial discourses. For example, Rey Chow addresses the problem of "the asymmetrical structure between the 'West' as dominating subject and the 'nonWest' or 'Third World' as the oppressed 'other.'" She argues that "contrary to the absolute difference that is often claimed *for* the 'Third World' . . . the work of a twentieth-century Chinese intellectual foretells much that is happening in the contemporary 'Western' theoretical scene."[12] Chow's observations go far beyond and far deeper than a plea for a liberal pluralist position here, beyond a plea for "equal time." Neither she, nor the growing number of Third World intellectuals who have begun to interrogate the uses to which theory has been put for the past twenty years, is so naive as to suggest that the power of theory's gravitational field can be so simply and reactively resisted.[13] Most of us know that the debate over the uses and abuses of theory, formulated as such, followed by a growing demand to choose sides, is sterile and boring. But more importantly, it diverts us from the more difficult pursuit of understanding how theory has been *made* into an exclusively Western phenomenon inextricably attached to the view that it does not and cannot exist outside a Western orbit.

That view is especially apparent in what Edward Said refers to as a "maddening new critical shorthand" that "makes us no less susceptible to the dangers of received authority from canonical works and authors than we ever were. We make lackluster references to Nietzsche, Freud, Lacan as if the name alone carried enough value to override any objection or to settle any quarrel."[14] Said's list of names requires others who are said to embody the most popular terms of critical opprobrium. I am concerned to note that often these are the names of black American women. Their assignment to the political, the empirical, the historical camps helps to construct an identity, a subjectivity for black feminist thinking among the general critical discourses of our time. That identity has so far been anything but fluctuating. It has been solidly fixed to a reference schemata and a racial stigmata that we have seen before.

---

[12]Rey Chow, " 'It's You, and Not Me': Domination and 'Othering' in Theorizing the 'Third World,' " in *Coming to Terms: Feminism, Theory, Politics*, ed. Elizabeth Week (New York, 1989), p. 161. [McDowell]

[13]For Chow, see p. 1909.
[14]Edward Said, *The World, the Text, and the Critic* (New York, 1983). [McDowell]

Homi K. Bhabha

b. 1949

Homi Bhabha was born into the Parsi community of Bombay and grew up in the shade of the Fire Temple. Bhabha received a B.A. from Bombay University, and an M.A., M.Phil., and D.Phil. from Christ Church, Oxford University. Bhabha has taught at the University of Sussex, Princeton University, the University of Pennsylvania, Dartmouth College, and the University of Chicago. He is currently Anne F. Rothenberg Professor of English and American Literature at Harvard University. Bhabha has edited the essay collection Nation and Narration *(1990) and is the author of* The Location of Culture *(1994), along with many articles and interviews. The following selection, "Signs Taken for Wonders," originally appeared in* Critical Inquiry *in 1985 and was reprinted in* The Location of Culture.*

Signs Taken for Wonders:[1] Questions of Ambivalence and Authority under a Tree Outside Delhi, May 1817

A remarkable peculiarity is that they (the English) always write the personal pronoun I with a capital letter. May we not consider this Great I as an unintended proof how much an Englishman thinks of his own consequence?
— ROBERT SOUTHEY, *Letters from England*

I would like to thank Stephan Feuchtwang for his sustaining advice, Gayatri Spivak for suggesting that I should further develop my concept of colonial mimicry; Parveen Adams for her impeccable critique of the text; and Jacqueline Bhabha, whose political engagement with the discriminatory nature of British immigration and nationality law has convinced me of the modesty of the theoretical enterprise. [Bhabha]

[1] Bhabha's title duplicates the title of a 1983 book by comparatist Franco Moretti, but given that the "English book" is the Bible, it seems rather to point to a biblical phrase, "signs and wonders" (probably a hendiadys for "wondrous signs") that appears about thirty times throughout the Old and New Testaments. Hendiadys (Greek for "one by means of two") is a figure of speech in which two words, joined by "and," are actually joined in a more intimate way (one of the nouns, usually the second, is secretly being used as an adjective). As when Edmund says to Edgar in *King Lear*: "I have told you what I have seen and heard but faintly, nothing like the image

There is a scene in the cultural writings of English colonialism which repeats so insistently after the early nineteenth century — and, through that repetition, so triumphantly *inaugurates* a literature of empire — that I am bound to repeat it once more. It is the scenario, played out in the wild and wordless wastes of colonial India, Africa, the Caribbean, of the sudden, fortuitous discovery of the English book. It is, like all myths of origin, memorable for its balance between epiphany and enunciation. The discovery of the book is, at once, a moment of originality and authority, as well as a process of displacement that, paradoxically, makes the presence of the book wondrous to the extent to which it is repeated, translated, misread, displaced. It is with the emblem of the English book — "signs taken for wonders" — as

and horror of it." (where "image and horror" = "horrible image"). Or Lady Macbeth: "To be the same in thine own act and valour/As thou art in desire." (act and valor = valorous act.)

an insignia of colonial authority and a signifier of colonial desire and discipline, that I want to begin this essay.

In the first week of May 1817, Anund Messeh, one of the earliest Indian catechists, made a hurried and excited journey from his mission in Meerut to a grove of trees just outside Delhi.

He found about 500 people, men, women and children, seated under the shade of the trees, and employed, as had been related to him, in reading and conversation. He went up to an elderly looking man, and accosted him, and the following conversation passed.

"Pray who are all these people? and whence come they?" "We are poor and lowly, and we read and love this book." — "What is that book?" "The book of God!" — "Let me look at it, if you please." Anund, on opening the book, perceived it to be the Gospel of our Lord, translated into the Hindoostanee Tongue, many copies of which seemed to be in the possession of the party: some were PRINTED, others WRITTEN by themselves from the printed ones. Anund pointed to the name of Jesus, and asked, "Who is that?" "That is God! He gave us this book." — "Where did you obtain it?" "An Angel from heaven gave it us, at Hurdwar fair." — "An Angel?" "Yes, to us he was God's Angel: but he was a man, a learned Pundit."[2] (Doubtless these translated Gospels must have been the books distributed, five or six years ago, at Hurdwar by the Missionary.) "The written copies we write ourselves, having no other means of obtaining more of this blessed word." — "These books," said Anund, "teach the religion of the European Sahibs. It is THEIR book; and they printed it in our language, for our use." "Ah! no," replied the stranger, "that cannot be, for they eat flesh." — "Jesus Christ," said Anund, "teaches that it does not signify what a man eats or drinks. EATING is nothing before God. *Not that which entereth into a man's mouth defileth him, but that which cometh out of the mouth, this defileth a man:* for vile things come forth from the heart. *Out of the heart proceed evil thoughts, murders, adulteries, fornications, thefts; and these are the things that defile.*"[3]

[2]The original meaning, which arrives in English in the seventeenth century, is a Hindu learned in Sanskrit.
[3]The Biblical quotation is from Mark 7: 15–23. Since upper-caste Hindus (Brahmins) are vegetarians, Jesus's thesis about the unimportance of dietary laws is as revolutionary to the Indians as it was to the Jews of his own day.

"That is true; but how can it be the European Book, when we believe that it is God's gift to us? He sent it to us at Hurdwar." "God gave it long ago to the Sahibs, and THEY sent it to us." . . . The ignorance and simplicity of many are very striking, never having heard of a printed book before; and its very appearance was to them miraculous. A great stir was excited by the gradual increasing information hereby obtained, and all united to acknowledge the superiority of the doctrines of this Holy Book to every thing which they had hitherto heard or known. An indifference to the distinctions of Caste soon manifested itself; and the interference and tyrannical authority of the Brahmins became more offensive and contemptible. At last, it was determined to separate themselves from the rest of their Hindoo Brethren; and to establish a party of their own choosing, four or five, who could read the best, to be the public teachers from this newly-acquired Book. . . . Anund asked them, "Why are you all dressed in white?" "The people of God should wear white raiment," was the reply, "as a sign that they are clean, and rid of their sins." — Anund observed, "You ought to be BAPTIZED, in the name of the Father, and of the Son, and of the Holy Ghost. Come to Meerut: there is a Christian Padre there; and he will shew you what you ought to do." They answered, "Now we must go home to the harvest; but, as we mean to meet once a year, perhaps the next year we may come to Meerut." . . . I explained to them the nature of the Sacrament and of Baptism; in answer to which, they replied, "We are willing to be baptized, but we will never take the Sacrament. To all the other customs of Christians we are willing to conform, but not to the Sacrament, because the Europeans eat cow's flesh, and this will never do for us." To this I answered, "This WORD is of God, and not of men; and when HE makes your hearts to understand, then you will PROPERLY comprehend it." They replied, "If all our country will receive this Sacrament, then will we." I then observed, "The time is at hand, when all the countries will receive this WORD!" They replied, "True!"[4]

Almost a hundred years later, in 1902, Joseph Conrad's Marlow, traveling in the Congo, in the night of the first ages, without a sign and no memories, cut off from the comprehension of his

[4]*Missionary Register,* Church Missionary Society, London, Jan. 1818, pp. 18–19; all further references to this work, abbreviated *MR,* will be included in the text, with dates and page numbers in parentheses. [Bhabha]

surroundings, desperately in need of a deliberate belief, comes upon Towson's (or Towser's) *Inquiry into Some Points of Seamanship.*

> Not a very enthralling book; but at the first glance you could see there a singleness of intention, an honest concern for the right way of going to work, which made these humble pages, thought out so many years ago, luminous with another than a professional light. . . . I assure you to leave off reading was like tearing myself away from the shelter of an old and solid friendship. . . .

"It must be this miserable trader — this intruder," exclaimed the manager, looking back malevolently at the place we had left. "He must be English," I said.[5]

Half a century later, a young Trinidadian discovers that same volume of Towson's in that very passage from Conrad and draws from it a vision of literature and a lesson of history. "The scene," writes V. S. Naipaul,[6]

> answered some of the political panic I was beginning to feel.
>
> To be a colonial was to know a kind of security; it was to inhabit a fixed world. And I suppose that in my fantasy I had seen myself coming to England as to some purely literary region, where, untrammeled by the accidents of history or background, I could make a romantic career for myself as a writer. But in the new world I felt that ground move below me. . . . Conrad . . . had been everywhere before me. Not as a man with a cause, but a man offering . . . a vision of the world's half-made societies . . . where always "something inherent in the necessities of successful action . . . carried with it the moral degradation of the idea." Dismal but deeply felt: a kind of truth and half a consolation.[7]

Written as they are in the name of the father and the author, these texts of the civilizing mission immediately suggest the triumph of the colonialist moment in early English Evangelism and modern English literature. The discovery of the book installs the sign of appropriate representation: the word of God, truth, art creates the conditions for a beginning, a practice of history and narrative. But the institution of the Word in the wilds is also an *Entstellung*,[8] a process of displacement, distortion, dislocation, repetition[9] — the dazzling light of literature sheds only areas of darkness. Still the idea of the English book is presented as universally adequate: like the "metaphoric writing of the West," it communicates "the immediate vision of the thing, freed from the discourse that accompanied it, or even encumbered it."[10]

Shortly before the discovery of the book, Marlow interrogates the odd, inappropriate, "colonial" transformation of a textile into an uncertain textual sign, possibly a fetish:

> Why? Where did he get it? Was it a badge — an ornament — a charm — a propitiatory act? Was there any idea at all connected with it? It looked startling round his black neck, this bit of white thread from beyond the seas.[11]

Such questions of the historical act of enunciation, which carry a political intent, are lost, a few pages later, in the myth of origins and discovery. The immediate vision of the book figures those ideological correlatives of the Western sign — empiricism, idealism, mimeticism, monoculturalism (to use Edward Said's term) — that sustain a

[5] Joseph Conrad, *Heart of Darkness*, ed. Paul O'Prey (Harmondsworth, 1983), pp. 71, 72. [Bhabha] Bhabha is later to refer to Conrad's international origins: "a Polish émigré, deeply influenced by Gustave Flaubert, writing about Africa, produces an English classic."

[6] Vidiadhar Surajprasad Naipaul (b. 1932) was born on Trinidad, where his father had come as an indentured servant, was educated at Oxford, and has had a four-decade career as a novelist and writer, culminating in the Nobel Prize for literature in 2001. Because of his defense of Western, particularly British, institutions over those that evolved in former colonies after decolonization, Naipaul is a frequent target of postcolonial theorists.

[7] V. S. Naipaul, "Conrad's Darkness," *The Return of Eva Perón* (New York, 1974), p. 233. [Bhabha]

[8] Freud's word for an ego defense, usually translated "displacement."

[9] Overall effect of the dream-work: the latent thoughts are transformed into a manifest formation in which they are not easily recognizable. They are not only transposed, as it were, into another key, but *they are also distorted in such a fashion that only an effort of interpretation can reconstitute them*" (J. Laplanche and J. B. Pontalis, *The Language of PsychoAnalysis*, trans. Donald Nicholson-Smith [London, 1980], p. 124; my emphasis). See also Samuel Weber's excellent chapter "Metapsychology Set Apart," *The Legend of Freud* (Minneapolis, 1982), pp. 32–60. [Bhabha]

[10] Jacques Derrida, *Dissemination*, trans. Barbara Johnson (Chicago, 1981), pp. 189–90; all further references to this work, abbreviated *D*, will be included in the text. [Bhabha]

[11] Conrad, *Heart of Darkness*, p. 45. [Bhabha]

tradition of English "national" authority. It is, significantly, a normalizing myth whose organic and revisionary narrative is also the history of that nationalist discipline of Commonwealth history and its equally expansionist epigone, Commonwealth literature. Their versions of traditional, academicist wisdom moralize the conflictual moment of colonialist intervention into that constitutive chain of exemplum and imitation, what Friedrich Nietzsche describes as the monumental history beloved of "gifted egoists and visionary scoundrels."[12] For despite first appearances, a repetition of the episodes of the book reveals that they represent important moments in the historical transformation and discursive transfiguration of the colonial text and context.

Anund Messeh's riposte to the natives who refuse the sacrament — "the time is at hand when all countries *will* receive this WORD" (my emphasis) — is both firmly and timely spoken in 1817. For it represents a shift away from the "orientalist" educational practice of, say, Warren Hastings[13] and the much more interventionist and "interpellative" ambition of Charles Grant[14] for a culturally and linguistically homogeneous English India. It was with Grant's election to the board of the East India Company in 1794 and to Parliament in 1802, and through his energetic espousal of the Evangelical ideals of the Clapham sect, that the East India Company reintroduced a "pious clause" into its charter for 1813. By 1817 the Church Missionary Society ran sixty-one schools, and in 1818 it commissioned the Burdwan Plan, a central plan of education for instruction in the English language. The aim of the plan anticipates, almost to the word, Thomas Macaulay's infamous 1835 "Minute on Education": "to form a body of well instructed labourers, competent in their proficiency in English to act as Teachers, Translators, and Compilers of useful works for the masses of the people."[15] Anund Messeh's lifeless repetition of chapter and verse, his artless technique of translation, participate in one of the most artful technologies of colonial power. In the same month that Anund Messeh discovered the miraculous effects of the book outside Delhi — May 1817 — a correspondent of the Church Missionary Society wrote to London describing the method of English education at Father John's mission in Tranquebar:

> The principal method of teaching them the English language would be by giving them English phrases and sentences, with a translation for them to commit to memory. These sentences might be so arranged as to teach them whatever sentiments the instructor should choose. They would become, in short, attached to the Mission; and though first put into the school from worldly motives alone, should any of them be converted, accustomed as they are to the language, manners and climate of the country, they might soon be prepared for a great usefulness in the cause of religion. . . . In this way the Heathens themselves might be made the instruments of pulling down their own religion, and of erecting in its ruins the standards of the Cross. [*MR*, May 1817, p. 187]

Marlow's ruminative closing statement, "He must be English," acknowledges at the heart of darkness, in Conrad's *fin de siècle*[16] malaise which Ian Watt so thoroughly describes, the particular debt that both Marlow and Conrad owe to the ideals of English "liberty" and its liberal-conservative culture.[17] Caught as he is — between the madness of "prehistoric" Africa and the unconscious desire to repeat the traumatic intervention of modern colonialism within the compass of a seaman's yarn — Towson's manual provides Marlow with a singleness of intention. It is the book of work that turns delirium into the discourse of civil address. For the ethic of work, as

[12]Friedrich Nietzsche, *Untimely Meditations*, trans. R. J. Hollingdale (Cambridge, 1983), p. 71. [Bhabha]

[13]Hastings (1732–1818) was the first governor-general of India (1773–86), who respected the Hindu scriptures and employed learned Brahmins to shape the law that would apply to the British Raj.

[14]Grant (1746–1823) was a merchant working in India 1763–90 (contemporary with Hastings); on his return to Britain he rose within the East India Corporation to chairman of the board, and forcefully promoted evangelical missionary activity in India.

[15]Thomas Babington Macaulay, "Minute on Education," quoted in Elmer H. Cutts, "The Background of Macaulay's Minute," *American Historical Review* 58 (July 1953): 839. [Bhabha]

[16]French for "end of the [nineteenth] century."

[17]See Ian Watt, *Conrad in the Nineteenth Century* (Berkeley and Los Angeles, 1979), chap. 4, pt. 1. [Bhabha]

Conrad was to exemplify in "Tradition" (1918), provides a sense of right conduct and honor achievable only through the acceptance of those "customary" norms which are the signs of culturally cohesive "civil" communities.[18] These aims of the civilizing mission, endorsed in the "idea" of British imperialism and enacted on the red sections of the map,[19] speak with a peculiarly English authority based upon the *customary practice* on which both English common law and the English national language rely for their effectivity and appeal.[20] It is the ideal of English civil discourse that permits Conrad to entertain the ideological ambivalences that riddle his narratives. It is under its watchful eye that he allows the fraught text of late nineteenth-century imperialism to implode within the practices of early modernism. The devastating effects of such an encounter are not only contained in an (un)common yarn; they are concealed in the propriety of a civil "lie" told to the Intended (the complicity of the customary?): "The horror! The horror!" must not be repeated in the drawing-rooms of Europe.

It is to preserve the peculiar sensibility of what he understands as a tradition of civility that Naipaul "translates" Conrad, from Africa to the Caribbean, in order to transform the despair of postcolonial history into an appeal for the autonomy of art. The more fiercely he believes that "the wisdom of the heart ha[s] no concern with the erection or demolition of theories," the more convinced he becomes of the unmediated nature of the Western book — "the words it pronounces have the value of acts of integrity."[21] The values that such a perspective generates for his own work, and for the once colonized world it chooses to represent and evaluate, are visible in the hideous panorama that some of his titles provide: *The Loss of El Dorado*, *The Mimic Men*, *An Area of Darkness*, *A Wounded Civilization*, *The Overcrowded Barracoon*.

The discovery of the English book establishes both a measure of mimesis and a mode of civil authority and order. If these scenes, as I've narrated them, suggest the triumph of the writ of colonialist power, then it must be conceded that the wily letter of the law inscribes a much more ambivalent text of authority. For it is in between the edict of Englishness and the assault of the dark unruly spaces of the earth, through an act of repetition, that the colonial text emerges uncertainly. Anund Messeh disavows the natives' disturbing questions as he returns to repeat the now questionable "authority" of Evangelical dicta; Marlow turns away from the African jungle to recognize, in retrospect, the peculiarly "English" quality of the discovery of the book; Naipaul turns his back on the hybrid half-made colonial world to fix his eye on the universal domain of English literature. What we witness is neither an untroubled, innocent dream of England nor a "secondary revision" of the nightmare of India, Africa, the Caribbean. What is "English" in these discourses of colonial power cannot be represented as a plenitude or a "full" presence; it is determined by its belatedness. As a signifier of authority, the English book acquires its meaning *after* the traumatic scenario of colonial difference, cultural or racial, returns the eye of power to some prior, archaic image or identity. Paradoxically, however, such an image can neither be "original" — by virtue of the act of repetition that constructs it — nor "identical" — by virtue of the difference that defines it. Consequently, the colonial presence is always ambivalent, split between its appearance as original and authoritative and its articulation as repetition and difference.

It is this ambivalence that makes the boundaries of colonial "positionality" — the division of self/other — and the question of colonial power — the differentiation of colonizer/colonized — different from both the Hegelian master/slave dialectic[22] or the phenomenological projection of

[18]See Conrad, "Tradition," *Notes on Life and Letters* (London, 1925), pp. 194–201. [Bhabha]

[19]In the first half of the twentieth century, maps conventionally colored red the United Kingdom and all the countries that formed part of the British Empire or Commonwealth.

[20]See John Barrell's excellent chapter "The Language Properly So-called: The Authority of Common Usage," *English Literature in History, 1730–1780: An Equal Wide Survey* (New York, 1983), pp. 110–75. [Bhabha]

[21]Conrad, quoted in Naipaul, "Conrad's Darkness," p. 236. [Bhabha]

[22]See Hegel, p. 369.

Otherness. It is a *différance*[23] produced within the act of enunciation as a specifically colonial articulation of those two disproportionate sites of colonial discourse and power: the colonial scene as the invention of historicity, mastery, mimesis or as the "other scene" of *Entstellung*, displacement, fantasy, psychic defence, and an "open" textuality. Such a display of difference produces a mode of authority that is agonistic (rather than antagonistic). Its discriminatory effects are visible in those split subjects of the racist stereotype — the simian Negro, the effeminate Asiatic male — which ambivalently fix identity as the fantasy of difference.[24] To recognize the *différance* of the colonial presence is to realize that the colonial text occupies that space of double inscription, hallowed — no, hollowed — by Jacques Derrida:

> whenever any writing both marks and goes back over its mark with an undecidable stroke . . . [this] double mark escapes the pertinence or authority of truth: it does not overturn it but rather inscribes it within its play as one of its functions or parts. This displacement does not take place, has not taken place once as an *event*. It does not occupy a simple place. It does not take place *in* writing. This dislocation (is what) writes/is written. [*D*, p. 193]

How can the question of authority, the power and presence of the English, be posed in the interstices of a double inscription? I have no wish to replace an idealist myth — the metaphoric English book — with a historicist one — the colonialist project of English civility. Such a reductive reading would deny what is obvious, that the representation of colonial authority depends less on a universal symbol of English identity than on its productivity as a sign of difference. Yet in my use of "English" there is a "transparency" of reference that registers a certain obvious presence: the Bible translated into Hindi, propagated by Dutch or native catechists, is still the English book; a Polish émigré, deeply influenced by Gustave Flaubert, writing about Africa, produces an English classic. What is there about such a process

of visibility and recognition that never fails to be an authoritative acknowledgement without ceasing to be a "spacing between desire and fulfillment, between perpetuation and its recollection . . . [a] medium [which] has nothing to do with a center" (*D*, p. 212)?

This question demands a departure from Derrida's objectives in "The Double Session"; a turning away from the vicissitudes of interpretation in the mimetic act of reading to the question of the effects of power, the inscription of strategies of individuation and domination in those "dividing practices" which construct the colonial space — a departure from Derrida which is also a return to those moments in his essay when he acknowledges the problematic of "presence" as a certain quality of discursive transparency which he describes as "the production of *mere* reality-effects" or "the effect of content" or as the problematic relation between the "medium of writing and the determination of each textual unit." In the rich ruses and rebukes with which he shows up the "false appearance of the present," Derrida fails to decipher the specific and determinate system of *address* (not referent) that is signified by the "effect of content" (see *D*, pp. 173–85). It is precisely such a strategy of address — the *immediate presence* of the English — that engages the questions of authority that I want to raise. When the ocular metaphors of presence refer to the process by which content is fixed as an "effect of the present," we encounter not plenitude but the structured gaze of power whose objective is authority, whose "subjects" are historical.

The reality effect constructs a mode of address in which a complementarity of meaning — not a correspondential notion of truth, as anti-realists insist — produces the moment of discursive transparency. It is the moment when, "under the false appearance of the present," the semantic seems to prevail over the syntactic, the signified over the signifier. Contrary to current avant-garde orthodoxy, however, the transparent is neither simply the triumph of the "imaginary" capture of the subject in realist narrative nor the ultimate interpellation of the individual by ideology. It is not a proposal that you cannot positively refuse. It is better described, I suggest, as a form of the *disposal* of those discursive signs

---

[23]Bhabha is alluding to Jacques Derrida's essay "Differance," in this volume on pp. 932–49.

[24]See my "The Other Question — The Stereotype and Colonial Discourse," *Screen* 24 (Nov.–Dec. 1983): 18–36. [Bhabha]

of presence/the present within the strategies that articulate the range of meanings from "dispose to disposition." Transparency is the action of the distribution and arrangement of differential spaces, positions, knowledges in relation to each other, relative to a differential, not inherent, sense of order. This effects a regulation of spaces and places that is authoritatively assigned; it puts the addressee into the proper frame or condition for some action or result. Such a mode of governance addresses itself to a form of conduct that is achieved through a reality effect that equivocates between the sense of disposal, as the bestowal of a frame of reference, and disposition, as mental inclination, a frame of mind. Such equivocation allows neither an equivalence of the two sites of disposal nor their division as self/other, subject/object. Transparency achieves an effect of authority in the present (and an authoritative presence) through a process similar to what Michel Foucault describes as "an effect of finalisation, relative to an objective." Without its necessary attribution to a subject that makes a prohibitory law, thou shalt or thou shalt not.[25]

The place of difference and otherness, or the space of the adversarial, within such a system of "disposal" as I've proposed, is never entirely on the outside or implacably oppositional. It is a pressure, and a presence, that acts constantly, if unevenly, along the entire boundary of authorization, that is, on the surface between what I've called disposal-as-bestowal and disposition-as-inclination. The contour of difference is agonistic, shifting, splitting, rather like Freud's description of the system of consciousness which occupies a position in space lying on the borderline between outside and inside, a surface of protection, reception, and projection.[26] The power play of presence is lost if its transparency is treated naively as the nostalgia for plenitude that should be flung repeatedly into the abyss — *mise*

en abîme — from which its desire is born. Such theoreticist anarchism cannot intervene in the agonistic space of authority where

> the true and the false are separated and specific effects of power [are] attached to the true, it being understood also that it is not a matter of a battle "on behalf" of the truth, but of a battle about the status of truth and the economic and political role it plays.[27]

It is precisely to intervene in such a battle for the *status* of the truth that it becomes crucial to examine the *presence* of the English book. For it is this *surface* that stabilizes the agonistic colonial space; it is its *appearance* that regulates the ambivalence between origin and *Entstellung*, discipline and desire, mimesis and repetition.

Despite appearances, the text of transparency inscribes a double vision: the field of the "true" emerges as a visible effect of knowledge/power only after the regulatory and displacing division of the true and the false. From this point of view, discursive "transparency" is best read in the photographic sense in which a transparency is also always a negative, processed into visibility through the technologies of reversal, enlargement, lighting, editing, projection, not a source but a re-source of light. Such a bringing to light is never a prevision; it is always a question of the provision of visibility as a capacity, a strategy, an agency but also in the sense in which the prefix pro(vision) might indicate an elision of sight, delegation, substitution, contiguity, in place of . . . what?

This is the question that brings us to the ambivalence of the presence of authority, peculiarly visible in its colonial articulation. For if transparency signifies discursive closure — intention, image, author — it does so through a disclosure of its *rules of recognition* — those social texts of epistemic, ethnocentric, nationalist intelligibility which cohere in the address of authority as the "present," the voice of modernity. The acknowledgement of authority depends upon the immediate — unmediated — visibility of its rules of recognition as the unmistakable referent of historical necessity. In the doubly inscribed

[25]Michel Foucault, "The Confession of the Flesh," *Power/Knowledge: Selected Interviews and Other Writings, 1972–1977*, ed. Colin Gordon, trans. Gordon et al. (New York, 1980), p. 204. [Bhabha]

[26]See Sigmund Freud, *Beyond the Pleasure Principle*, trans. and ed. James Strachey (London, 1974), pp. 18–25. [Bhabha]

[27]Foucault, "Truth and Power," *Power/Knowledge*, p. 132. [Bhabha]

space of colonial representation where the presence of authority — the English book — is also a question of its repetition and displacement, where transparency is *technē*,[28] the immediate visibility of such a régime of recognition is resisted. Resistance is not necessarily an oppositional act of political intention, nor is it the simple negation or exclusion of the "content" of an other culture, as a difference once perceived. It is the effect of an ambivalence produced within the rules of recognition of dominating discourses as they articulate the signs of cultural difference and reimplicate them within the deferential relations of colonial power — hierarchy, normalization, marginalization, and so forth. For domination is achieved through a process of disavowal that denies the *différance* of colonialist power — the chaos of its intervention as *Entstellung*, its dislocatory presence — in order to preserve the authority of its identity in the universalist narrative of nineteenth-century historical and political evolutionism.

The exercise of colonialist authority, however, requires the production of differentiations, individuations, identity effects through which discriminatory practices can map out subject populations that are tarred with the visible and transparent mark of power. Such a mode of subjection is distinct from what Foucault describes as "power through transparency": the reign of opinion, after the late eighteenth century, which could not tolerate areas of darkness and sought to exercise power through the mere fact of things being known and people seen in an immediate, collective gaze.[29] What radically differentiates the exercise of colonial power is the unsuitability of the Enlightenment assumption of collectivity and the eye that beholds it. For Jeremy Bentham[30] (as Michel Perrot[31] points out), the small group is representative of the whole society — the part is

already the whole. Colonial authority requires modes of discrimination (cultural, racial, administrative . . .) that disallow a stable unitary assumption of collectivity. The "part" (which must be the colonialist foreign body) must be representative of the "whole" (conquered country), but the right of representation is based on its radical difference. Such doublethink is made viable only through the strategy of disavowal just described, which requires a theory of the "hybridization" of discourse and power that is ignored by Western post-structuralists who engage in the battle for "power" as the purists of difference.

The discriminatory effects of the discourse of cultural colonialism, for instance, do not simply or singly refer to a "person," or to a dialectical power struggle between self and Other, or to a discrimination between mother culture and alien cultures. Produced through the strategy of disavowal, the *reference* of discrimination is always to a process of splitting as the condition of subjection: a discrimination between the mother culture and its bastards, the self and its doubles, where the trace of what is disavowed is not repressed but repeated as something *different* — a mutation, a hybrid. It is such a partial and double force that is more than the mimetic but less than the symbolic, that disturbs the visibility of the colonial presence and makes the recognition of its authority problematic. To be authoritative, its rules of recognition must reflect consensual knowledge or opinion; to be powerful, these rules of recognition must be breached in order to represent the exorbitant objects of discrimination that lie beyond its purview. Consequently, if the unitary (and essentialist) reference to race, nation, or cultural tradition is essential to preserve the presence of authority as an immediate mimetic effect, such essentialism must be exceeded in the articulation of "differentiatory," discriminatory identities.

To demonstrate such an "excess" is not merely to celebrate the joyous power of the signifier. Hybridity is the sign of the productivity of colonial power, its shifting forces and fixities; it is the name for the strategic reversal of the process of domination through disavowal (that is, the production of discriminatory identities that secure

[28]Greek for "art;" see Derrida, "Differance," p. 943.
[29]Foucault, "The Eye of Power," *Power/Knowledge*, p. 154; and see pp. 152–56. [Bhabha]
[30]English utilitarian philosopher (1748–1832).
[31]Probably Bhabha means Michelle Perrot, French cultural historian of the Annales school, author of "L'Inspecteur Bentham" and editor of *Le Panoptique* (1977), a French edition of Bentham's writings on the model prison, the Panopticon, that he proposed in 1787.

the "pure" and original identity of authority). Hybridity is the revaluation of the assumption of colonial identity through the repetition of discriminatory identity effects. It displays the necessary deformation and displacement of all sites of discrimination and domination. It unsettles the mimetic or narcissistic demands of colonial power but reimplicates its identifications in strategies of subversion that turn the gaze of the discriminated back upon the eye of power. For the colonial hybrid is the articulation of the ambivalent space where the rite of power is enacted on the site of desire, making its objects at once disciplinary and disseminatory — or, in my mixed metaphor, a negative transparency. If discriminatory effects enable the authorities to keep an eye on them, their proliferating difference evades that eye, escapes that surveillance. Those discriminated against may be instantly recognized, but they also force a recognition of the immediacy and articulacy of authority — a disturbing effect that is familiar in the repeated hesitancy afflicting the colonialist discourse when it contemplates its discriminated subjects: the *inscrutability* of the Chinese, the *unspeakable* rites of the Indians, the *indescribable* habits of the Hottentots. It is not that the voice of authority is at a loss for words. It is, rather, that the colonial discourse has reached that point when, faced with the hybridity of its objects, the *presence* of power is revealed as something other than what its rules of recognition assert.

If the effect of colonial power is seen to be the *production* of hybridization rather than the noisy command of colonialist authority or the silent repression of native traditions, then an important change of perspective occurs. It reveals the ambivalence at the source of traditional discourses on authority and enables a form of subversion, founded on that uncertainty, that turns the discursive conditions of dominance into the grounds of intervention. It is traditional academic wisdom that the presence of authority is properly established through the nonexercise of private judgment and the exclusion of reasons, in conflict with the authoritative reason. The recognition of authority, however, requires a validation of its source that must be immediately, even intuitively, apparent — "You have that in your countenance which I would fain call master"[32] — and held in common (rules of recognition). What is left unacknowledged is the paradox of such a demand for proof and the resulting ambivalence for positions of authority. If, as Steven Lukes rightly says, the acceptance of authority excludes any evaluation of the content of an utterance, and if its source, which must be acknowledged, disavows both conflicting reasons and personal judgment, then can the "signs" or "marks" of authority be anything more than "empty" presences of strategic devices?[33] Need they be any the less effective because of that? Not less effective but effective in a different form, would be our answer.

Tom Nairn reveals a basic ambivalence between the symbols of English imperialism which could not help "looking universal" and a "hollowness [that] sounds through the English imperialist mind in a thousand forms: in Rider Haggard's necrophilia, in Kipling's moments of gloomy doubt, . . . in the gloomy cosmic truth of Forster's Marabar caves."[34] Nairn explains this "imperial delirium" as the disproportion between the grandiose rhetoric of English imperialism and the *real* economic and political situation of late Victorian England. I would like to suggest that these crucial moments in English literature are not simply crises of England's own making. They are also the signs of a discontinuous history, an estrangement of the English book. They mark the disturbance of its authoritative representations by the uncanny forces of race, sexuality, violence, cultural and even climatic differences which emerge in the colonial discourse as the mixed and split texts of hybridity. If the appearance of the English book is read as a production of colonial hybridity, then it no longer simply commands authority. It gives rise to a series of *questions of authority* that, in my bastardized repetition, must sound strangely familiar:

> Was it a badge — an ornament — a charm — a propitiatory act? Was there any idea at all connected

[32] Alludes to Kent's line spoken to Lear in *King Lear* I.iv.
[33] See Steven Lukes, "Power and Authority," in *A History of Sociological Analysis*, ed. Tom Bottomore and Robert Nisbet (New York, 1978), pp. 633–76. [Bhabha]
[34] Tom Nairn, *The Break-Up of Britain: Crisis and Neo-Nationalism* (London, 1981), p. 265. [Bhabha]

with it? It looked startling in this black neck of the woods, this bit of white writing from beyond the seas.

In repeating the scenario of the English book, I hope I have succeeded in representing a colonial difference: it is the effect of uncertainty that afflicts the discourse of power, an uncertainty that estranges the familiar symbol of English "national" authority and emerges from its colonial appropriation as the sign of its difference. Hybridity is the name of this displacement of value from symbol to sign that causes the dominant discourse to split along the axis of its power to be representative, authoritative. Hybridity represents that ambivalent "turn" of the discriminated subject into the terrifying, exorbitant object of paranoid classification — a disturbing questioning of the images and presences of authority. To grasp the ambivalence of hybridity, it must be distinguished from an inversion that would suggest that the originary is, really, only the "effect" of an *Entstellung*. Hybridity has no such perspective of depth or truth to provide: it is not a third term that resolves the tension between two cultures, or the two scenes of the book, in a dialectical play of "recognition." The displacement from symbol to sign creates a crisis for any concept of authority based on a system of recognition: colonial specularity, doubly inscribed, does not produce a mirror where the self apprehends itself; it is always the split screen of the self and its doubling, the hybrid.

These metaphors are very much to the point, because they suggest that colonial hybridity is not a *problem* of genealogy or identity between two *different* cultures which can then be resolved as an issue of cultural relativism. Hybridity is a *problematic* of colonial representation and individuation that reverses the effects of the colonialist disavowal, so that other "denied" knowledges enter upon the dominant discourse and estrange the basis of its authority — its rules of recognition. Again, it must be stressed, it is not simply the *content* of disavowed knowledges — be they forms of cultural Otherness or traditions of colonialist treachery — that return to be acknowledged as counterauthorities. For the resolution of conflicts between authorities, civil discourse always maintains an adjudicative procedure.

What is irremediably estranging in the presence of the hybrid — in the revaluation of the symbol of national authority as the sign of colonial difference — is that the difference of cultures can no longer be identified or evaluated as objects of epistemological or moral contemplation: they are not simply *there* to be seen or appropriated.

Hybridity reverses the *formal* process of disavowal so that the violent dislocation, the *Entstellung* of the act of colonization, becomes the *conditionality* of colonial discourse. The presence of colonialist authority is no longer immediately visible; its discriminatory identifications no longer have their authoritative reference to this culture's cannibalism or that people's perfidy. As an articulation of displacement and dislocation, it is now possible to identify "the cultural" as a disposal of power, a negative transparency that comes to be agonistically constructed *on the boundary* between frame of reference/frame of mind. It is crucial to remember that the colonial construction of the cultural (the site of the civilizing mission) through the process of disavowal is authoritative to the extent to which it is structured around the ambivalence of splitting, denial, repetition — strategies of defence that mobilize culture as an open-textured, warlike strategy whose aim "is rather a continued agony than a total disappearance of the pre-existing culture."[35] To see the cultural not as the *source* of conflict — *different* cultures — but as the *effect* of discriminatory practices — the production of cultural *differentiation* as signs of authority — changes its value and its rules of recognition. What is preserved is the visible surfaces of its artefacts — the mere *visibility* of the symbol, as a fleeting immediacy. Hybridity intervenes in the exercise of authority not merely to indicate the impossibility of its identity but to represent the unpredictability of its presence. The book retains its presence, but it is no longer a representation of an essence; it is now a partial presence, a (strategic) device in a specific colonial engagement, an appurtenance of authority.

This partializing process of hybridity is best described as a metonymy of presence. It shares

[35]Frantz Fanon, *Toward the African Revolution*, trans. Haakon Chevalier (Harmondsworth, 1967), p. 44. [Bhabha]

Sigmund Freud's valuable insight into the strategy of disavowal as the persistence of the narcissistic demand in the acknowledgement of difference.[36] This, however, exacts a price, for the existence of two contradictory knowledges (multiple beliefs) splits the ego (or the discourse) into two psychical attitudes, and forms of knowledge, toward the external world. The first of these takes reality into consideration while the second replaces it with a product of desire. What is remarkable is that these two contradictory objectives always represent a "partiality" in the construction of the fetish object, at once a substitute for the phallus and a mark of its absence. There is an important difference between fetishism and hybridity. The fetish reacts to the change in the value of the phallus by fixing on an object *prior to the perception of difference*, an object that can metaphorically substitute for its presence while registering the difference. So long as it fulfills the fetishistic ritual, the object can look like anything (or nothing!). The hybrid object, however, retains the actual semblance of the authoritative symbol but revalues its presence by resisting it as the signifier of *Entstellung — after the intervention of difference*. It is the power of this strange metonymy of presence to so disturb the systematic (and systemic) construction of discriminatory knowledges that the cultural, once recognized as the medium of authority, becomes virtually unrecognizable. Culture, as a colonial space of intervention and agonism, as the trace of the displacement of symbol to sign, can be transformed by the unpredictable and partial desire of hybridity. Deprived of their full presence, the knowledges of cultural authority may be articulated with forms of "native" knowledges or faced with those discriminated subjects that they must rule but can no longer represent. This may lead, as in the case of the natives outside Delhi, to questions of authority that the authorities — the Bible included — cannot answer. Such a process is not the deconstruction of a cultural system from the margins of its own aporia nor, as in Derrida's "Double Session," the mime that haunts mimesis. The display of hybridity — its peculiar "replication" —

terrorizes authority with the *ruse* of recognition, its mimicry, its mockery.

Such a reading of colonial authority profoundly unsettles the demand that figures at the center of the originary myth of colonialist power. It is the demand that *the space it occupies be unbounded*, its reality *coincident* with the emergence of an imperialist narrative and history, its discourse *nondialogic*, its enunciation *unitary*, unmarked by the trace of difference — a demand that is recognizable in a range of justificatory Western "civil" discourses where the presence of the "colony" often alienates its own language of liberty and reveals its universalist concepts of labor and property as particular, post-Enlightenment ideological and technological practices. Consider, for example: Locke's notion of the wasteland of Carolina — "Thus in the beginning all the World was *America*"; Montesquieu's emblem of the wasteful and disorderly life and labor in despotic societies — "When the savages of Louisiana are desirous of fruit, they cut the tree to the root, and gather the fruit"; Grant's belief in the impossibility of law and history in Muslim and Hindu India — "where treasons and revolutions are continual; by which the insolent and abject frequently change places"; or the contemporary Zionist myth of the neglect of Palestine — "of a *whole* territory," Said writes, "essentially unused, unappreciated, misunderstood . . . *to be made* useful, appreciated, understandable."[37]

What renders this demand of colonial power impossible is precisely the point at which the question of authority emerges. For the unitary voice of command is interrupted by questions that arise from these heterogeneous sites and circuits of power which, though momentarily "fixed" in the authoritative alignment of subjects, must continually be represented in the production of terror or fear — the paranoid threat from the

[36]See Freud, *An Outline of Psycho-Analysis*, trans. and ed. Strachey (London, 1973), pp. 59–61. [Bhabha]

[37]John Locke, "The Second Treatise of Government," *Two Treatises of Government* (New York, 1965), p. 343, par. 49; Baron de Montesquieu, *The Spirit of the Laws*, trans. Thomas Nugent (New York, 1949), p. 57; Charles Grant, "Observations on the State of Society among the Asiatic Subjects of Great Britain," *Sessional Papers of the East India Company* 10, no. 282 (1812–13): 70; Edward W. Said, *The Question of Palestine* (New York, 1979), p. 85. [Bhabha]

hybrid is finally uncontainable because it breaks down the symmetry and duality of self/Other, inside/outside. In the productivity of power, the boundaries of authority — its reality effects — are always besieged by "the other scene" of fixations and phantoms. We can now understand the link between the psychic and political that is suggested in Frantz Fanon's figure of speech: the colon[38] is an exhibitionist, because his *preoccupation* with security makes him "remind the native out loud that there he alone is master."[39] The native, caught in the chains of colonialist command, achieves a "pseudo-petrification" which further incites and excites him, thus making the settler-native boundary an anxious and ambivalent one. What then presents itself as the subject of authority in the discourse of colonial power is, in fact, a desire that so exceeds the original authority of the book and the immediate visibility of its metaphoric writing that we are bound to ask: What does colonial power want? My answer is only partially in agreement with Lacan's *vel*[40] or Derrida's veil or hymen. For the desire of colonial discourse *is* a splitting of hybridity that is *less than one and double*; and if that sounds enigmatic, it is because its explanation has to wait upon the authority of those canny questions that the natives put, so insistently, to the English book.

The native questions quite literally turn the origin of the book into an enigma. First: *How can the word of God come from the flesh-eating mouths of the English?* — a question that faces the unitary and universalist assumption of authority with the cultural difference of its historical moment of enunciation. And later: *How can it be the* European *Book, when we believe that it is God's gift to us? He sent it to Hurdwar.* This is not merely an illustration of what Foucault would call the capillary effects of the microtechnics of power. It reveals the penetrative power — *both* psychic and social — of the technology of the printed word in early nineteenth-century rural India. Imagine the scene: the Bible, perhaps translated into a North Indian dialect like Brigbhasha, handed out free or for one rupee within a culture where usually only caste Hindus would possess a copy of the Scriptures, and received in awe by the natives as both a novelty and a household deity. Contemporary missionary records reveal that, in Middle India alone, by 1815 we could have witnessed the spectacle of the Gospel "doing its own work," as the Evangelicals put it, in at least eight languages and dialects, with a first edition of between one thousand and ten thousand copies in each translation (see *MR*, May 1816, pp. 181–82). It is the force of these colonialist practices that produces that discursive tension between Anund Messeh, whose address *assumes* its authority, and the natives who question the English presence and seek a culturally differentiated, "colonial" authority *to* address.

The subversive character of the native questions will be realized only once we recognize the strategic disavowal of cultural/historical difference in Anund Messeh's Evangelical discourse. Having introduced the *presence* of the English and their *intercession* — "God gave [the Book] long ago to the Sahibs, and THEY sent it to us" — he then disavows that political/linguistic "imposition" by attributing the intervention of the Church to the power of God and the received authority of chapter and verse. What is being disavowed is not entirely visible in Anund Messeh's contradictory statements, at the level of the "enounced." What he, as well as the English Bible-in-disguise, must conceal are their particular enunciatory conditions — that is, the design of the Burdwan Plan to deploy "natives" to destroy native culture and religion. This is done through the repeated

[38]French for "colonialist."

[39]Fanon, *The Wretched of the Earth*, trans. Constance Farrington (Harmondsworth, 1969), p. 42. [Bhabha]

[40]*Vel* is Latin for an exclusive "or": A or B, and never both. In *The Four Fundamental Concepts of Psychoanalysis*, Lacan introduces the concept of the "*vel*" as the choice by which the subject is alienated from the self. At the fall into language, the subject has to choose between meaning (the big Other, language) and being (the subject): The choice splits the subject: when one chooses being, the subject disappears into non-meaning; when one chooses meaning, the part of meaning that corresponds to the subject disappears, into the unconscious. Later Bhabha will allude to Seminar XI, in which Lacan illustrates the *vel* with the highwayman's line, "Your money or your life." Choosing your money doesn't mean you get to live to spend your money, but no matter what you choose, you don't get to keep everything. So the fall into language is always accompanied by a sense of loss.

production of a teleological narrative of Evangelical witness: eager conversions, bereft Brahmins, and Christian gatherings. The descent from God to the English is both linear and circular: "This WORD is of God, and not of men; and when HE makes your hearts to understand, then you will PROPERLY comprehend." The historical "evidence" of Christianity is plain for all to see, Indian Evangelists would have argued, with the help of William Paley's *Evidences of Christianity* (1791), the most important missionary manual throughout the nineteenth century. The miraculous authority of colonial Christianity, they would have held, lies precisely in its being both English and universal, empirical and uncanny, for "ought we not rather to expect that such a Being on occasions of peculiar importance, may interrupt the order which he had appointed?"[41] The Word, no less theocratic than logocentric, would have certainly borne absolute witness to the gospel of Hurdwar had it not been for the rather tasteless fact that most Hindus were vegetarian!

By taking their stand on the grounds of dietary law, the natives resist the miraculous equivalence of God and the English. They introduce the practice of colonial cultural differentiation *as an* indispensable *enunciative function* in the discourse of authority — a function Foucault describes as linked to "a 'referential' that . . . forms the place, the condition, the field of emergence, the *authority to differentiate* between individuals or objects, states of things and relations that are brought into play by the statement itself; it defines the possibilities of appearance and delimitation."[42] Through the natives' strange questions, it is possible to see, with historical hindsight, what they resisted in questioning the presence of the English — as religious mediation and as a cultural and linguistic medium. What is the value of English in the offering of the Hindi Bible? It is the creation of a print technology calculated to produce a visual effect that will not "look like the work of foreigners"; it is the decision

to produce simple, abridged tracts of the plainest narrative that may inculcate the habit of "private, solitary reading," as a missionary wrote in 1816, so that the natives may resist the Brahmin's "monopoly of knowledge" and lessen their dependence on their own religious and cultural traditions; it is the opinion of the Reverend Donald Corrie that "on learning English they acquire ideas quite new, and of the first importance, respecting God and his government" (*MR*, July 1816, p. 193; Nov. 1816, pp. 444–45; Mar. 1816, pp. 106–7). It is the shrewd view of an unknown native, in 1819:

> For instance, I take a book of yours and read it awhile and whether I become a Christian or not, I leave the book in my family: after my death, my son, conceiving that I would leave nothing useless or bad in my house, will look into the book, understand its contents, consider that his father left him that book, and become a Christian. [*MR*, Jan. 1819, p. 27]

When the natives demand an Indianized Gospel, they are using the powers of hybridity to resist baptism and to put the project of conversion in an impossible position. Any adaptation of the Bible was forbidden by the evidences of Christianity, for, as the bishop of Calcutta preached in his Christmas sermon in 1815: "I mean that it is a Historical Religion: the History of the whole dispensation is before us from the creation of the world to the present hour: and it is throughout consistent with itself and with the attributes of God" (*MR*, Jan. 1817, p. 31). Their stipulation that only mass conversion would persuade them to take the sacrament touches on a tension between missionary zeal and the East India Company Statutes for 1814 which strongly advised against such proselytizing. When they make these intercultural, hybrid demands, the natives are both challenging the boundaries of discourse and subtly changing its terms by setting up another specifically colonial space of power/knowledge. And they do this under the eye of authority, through the production of "partial" knowledges and positionalities in keeping with my earlier, more general explanation of hybridity. Such objects of knowledges make the signifiers of authority enigmatic in a way that is "less than one and double." They change their conditions of

---

[41]William Paley, quoted in D. L. LeMahieu, *The Mind of William Paley: A Philosopher and His Age* (Lincoln, Nebr., 1976), p. 97. [Bhabha]

[42]Foucault, *The Archaeology of Knowledge*, trans. A. M. Sheridan Smith (London, 1972), p. 91; my emphasis. [Bhabha]

recognition while maintaining their visibility; they introduce a lack that is then represented as a doubling or mimicry. This mode of discursive disturbance is a sharp practice, rather like that of the perfidious barbers in the bazaars of Bombay who do not mug their customers with the blunt Lacanian *vel* "Your money or your life," leaving them with nothing. No, these wily oriental thieves, with far greater skill, pick their clients' pockets and cry out, "How the master's face shines!" and then, in a whisper, "But he's lost his mettle!"

And this traveler's tale, told by a native, is an emblem of that form of splitting — less than one and double — that I have suggested for the reading of the ambivalence of colonial cultural texts. In estranging the word of God from the English medium, the natives' questions dispense the logical order of the discourse of authority — "These books . . . teach the religion of the European Sahibs. It is THEIR Book; and they printed it in our language, for our use." The natives expel the copula, or middle term, of the Evangelical "power = knowledge" equation, which then disarticulates the structure of the God-Englishman equivalence. Such a crisis in the positionality and propositionality of colonialist authority destabilizes the sign of authority. For by alienating "English" as the middle term, the presence of authority is freed of a range of ideological correlates — for instance, intentionality, originality, authenticity, cultural normativity. The Bible is now ready for a specific colonial appropriation. On the one hand, its paradigmatic presence as the Word of God is assiduously preserved: it is only to the direct quotations from the Bible that the natives give their unquestioning approval — "True!" The expulsion of the copula, however, empties the presence of its syntagmatic supports — codes, connotations, and cultural associations that give it contiguity and continuity — that make its presence culturally and politically authoritative.

In this sense, then, it may be said that the *presence* of the book has acceded to the logic of the signifier and has been "separated," in Lacan's use of the term, from "itself." If, on one side, its authority, or some symbol or meaning of it, is maintained — willy-nilly, *less than one* — then,

on the other, it fades. It is at the point of its fading that the signifier of presence gets caught up in an alienating strategy of doubling or repetition. Doubling repeats the fixed and empty presence of authority by articulating it syntagmatically with a range of differential knowledges and positionalities that both estrange its "identity" and produce new forms of knowledge, new modes of differentiation, new sites of power. In the case of the colonial discourse, these syntagmatic appropriations of presence confront it with those contradictory and threatening differences of its enunciative function that had been disavowed. In their repetition, these disavowed knowledges return to make the presence of authority uncertain. This may take the form of multiple or contradictory beliefs, as in some forms of native knowledges: "We are willing to be baptized, but we will never take the Sacrament." Or they may be forms of mythic explanation that refuse to acknowledge the agency of the Evangelicals: "An Angel from heaven gave it [the Bible] us at Hurdwar fair." Or they may be the fetishistic repetition of litany in the face of an unanswerable challenge to authority: for instance, Anund Messeh's *"Not that which entereth into a man's mouth defileth him, but that which cometh out of the mouth."*

In each of these cases we see a colonial doubling which I've described as a strategic displacement of value through a process of the metonymy of presence. It is through this partial process, represented in its enigmatic, inappropriate signifiers — stereotypes, jokes, multiple and contradictory beliefs, the "native" Bible — that we begin to get a sense of a specific space of cultural colonial discourse. It is a "separate" space, a space of *separation* — less than one and double — which has been systematically denied by both colonialists and nationalists who have sought authority in the authenticity of "origins." It is precisely as a separation from origins and essences that this colonial space is constructed. It is separate, in the sense in which the French psychoanalyst Victor Smirnoff describes the separateness of the fetish as a "separateness that makes the fetish easily available, so that the subject can make use of it in his own way and establish it in an order of things that frees it from any subordination."[43]

The metonymic strategy produces the signifier of colonial *mimicry* as the affect of hybridity — at once a mode of appropriation and of resistance, from the disciplined to the desiring. As the discriminated object, the metonym of presence becomes the support of an authoritarian voyeurism, all the better to exhibit the eye of power. Then, as discrimination turns into the assertion of the hybrid, the insignia of authority becomes a mask, a mockery. After our experience of the native interrogation, it is difficult to agree entirely with Fanon that the psychic choice is to "turn white or disappear."[44] There is the more ambivalent, third choice: camouflage, mimicry, black skins/white masks. "Mimicry reveals something in so far as it is distinct from what might be called an *itself* that is behind. The effect of mimicry," writes Lacan, "is camouflage, in the strictly technical sense. It is not a question of harmonizing with the background but, against a mottled background, of being mottled — exactly like the technique of camouflage practiced in human warfare."[45]

Read as a masque of mimicry, Anund Messeh's tale emerges as a *question* of colonial authority, an agonistic space. To the extent to which discourse is a form of defensive warfare, mimicry marks those moments of civil disobedience within the discipline of civility: signs of spectacular resistance. When the words of the master become the site of hybridity — the warlike sign of the native — then we may not only read between the lines but even seek to change the often coercive reality that they so lucidly contain. It is with the strange sense of a hybrid history that I want to end.

Despite Anund Messeh's miraculous evidence, "native Christians were never more than vain phantoms" as J. A. Dubois wrote in 1815,

after twenty-five years in Madras. Their parlous partial state caused him particular anxiety,

> for in embracing the Christian religion they never entirely renounce their superstitions towards which they always keep a secret bent . . . there is no *unfeigned, undisguised* Christian among these Indians. [*MR*, Nov. 1816, p. 212]

And what of the native discourse? Who can tell? The Reverend Mr. Corrie, the most eminent of the Indian evangelists, warned that

> till they came under the English Government, they have not been accustomed to assert the nose upon their face their own. . . . This temper prevails, more or less, in the converted. [*MR*, Mar. 1816, pp. 106–7]

Archdeacon Potts, in handing over charge to the Reverend J. P. Sperschneider in July 1818, was a good deal more worried:

> If you urge them with their gross and unworthy misconceptions of the nature and will of God or the monstrous follies of their fabulous theology, they will turn it off with a sly civility perhaps, or with a popular and careless proverb. [*MR*, Sept. 1818, p. 375]

Was it in the spirit of such sly civility that the native Christians parried so long with Anund Messeh and then, at the mention of baptism, politely excused themselves: "Now we must go home to the harvest. . . . perhaps the next year we may come to Meerut."

And what is the significance of the Bible? Who knows?

Three years before the native Christians received the Bible at Hurdwar, a schoolmaster named Sandappan wrote from southern India, asking for a Bible:

> Rev. Fr. Have mercy upon me. I am amongst so many craving beggars for the Holy Scriptures the chief craving beggar. The bounty of the bestowers of this treasure is so great I understand, that even this book is read in rice and salt-markets. [*MR*, June 1813, pp. 221–22]

But, in the same year — 1817 — as the miracle outside Delhi, a much-tried missionary wrote in some considerable rage:

> Still everyone would gladly receive a Bible. And why? That he may store it up as a curiosity; sell it

[43]Victor N. Smirnoff, "The Fetishistic Transaction," in *Psychoanalysis in France*, ed. Serge Lebovici and Daniel Widlöcher (New York, 1980), p. 307. [Bhabha]

[44]See Fanon, "The Negro and Psychopathology," *Black Skin, White Masks*, trans. Charles Lam Markmann (New York, 1967). [Bhabha]

[45]Jacques Lacan, *The Four Fundamental Concepts of Psycho-analysis*, ed. Jacques-Alain Miller, trans. Alan Sheridan (New York, 1978), p. 99. [Bhabha]

for a few pice; or use it for waste paper. . . . Some have been bartered in the markets. . . . If these remarks are at all warranted then an indiscriminate distribution of the scriptures, to everyone who may say he wants a Bible, can be little less than a waste of time, a waste of money and a waste of expectations. For while the public are hearing of so many Bibles distributed, they expect to hear soon of a correspondent number of conversions. [*MR*, May 1817, p. 186]

Henry Louis Gates Jr.
b. 1950

Henry Louis Gates Jr. was born in Keyser, West Virginia, and received his bachelor's degree in history from Yale University. At age twenty, he hitchhiked through Africa on a Carnegie Foundation fellowship. In 1973 Gates studied at Clare College, Cambridge University, where his tutor, the African writer Wole Soyinka, shifted Gates's interests from history to literature, particularly to the ways in which African mythology and folktales inform the literature of Africa and the American diaspora. Upon completing his Ph.D. in English literature at Cambridge in 1979, Gates was appointed to a professorship at Yale, where he had been teaching since 1976. Gates's initial groundbreaking publication was the reprinting in 1983 of the first novel by a black woman, Harriet Wilson's Our Nig *(1859). Gates has continued his recovery of "lost" texts by black Americans in the Schomberg Library of Nineteenth-Century Black Women's Writings, of which he is series editor. In 1987 he published two books,* Figures in Black: Words, Signs, and the Racial Self, *and* The Signifying Monkey: Towards a Theory of Afro-American Literature, *which together established his reputation as one of the premier black theorists in the country, but also attracted animated response from those whose work stressed material culture rather than semiotics and style. Drawing on his work with Soyinka in African mythology, Gates's poststructuralist approach to African American literature defines its particular way of "signifying" as being based on an inherited oral tradition. His work is equally concerned with the continuities between African and African American modes of reader-response and interpretation. Gates has taught at Yale, Cornell, and Duke Universities, and is currently W. E. B. Du Bois Professor of the Humanities and chairman of the department of African and African American Studies at Harvard University. His recent books include* Loose Canons: Notes on the Culture Wars *(1992),* Speaking of Race, Speaking of Sex: Hate Speech, Civil Rights, and Civil Liberties *(1994),* The Future of the Race *(with Cornel West, 1996),* The Norton Anthology of African American Literature *(general editor, with Nelly Y. McKay, 1996; second edition 2004),* Thirteen Ways of Looking at a Black Man *(1997),* The African American Century *(2000),* The Trials of Phillis Wheatley *(2003), and* America Behind the Color Line *(2004). His autobiography is* Colored People: A Memoir *(1994). The present selection, which was first published in* Critical Inquiry *in 1985, is reprinted from* Loose Canons.

Writing, "Race," and the Difference It Makes

The truth is that, with the fading of the Renaissance ideal through progressive stages of specialism, leading to intellectual emptiness, we are left with a potentially suicidal movement among "leaders of the profession," while, at the same time, the profession sprawls, without its old center, in helpless disarray.

One quickly cited example is the professional organization, the Modern Language Association. . . . A glance at its thick program for its last meeting shows a massive increase and fragmentation into more than 500 categories! I cite a few examples: . . . "The Trickster Figure in Chicano and Black Literature." . . . Naturally, the progressive trivialization of topics has made these meetings a laughingstock in the national press.

— W. JACKSON BATE

. . . language, for the individual consciousness, lies on the borderline between oneself and the other. The word in language is half someone else's. It becomes "one's own" only when the speaker populates it with his own intention, his own accent, when he appropriates the word, adapting it to his own semantic and expressive intention. Prior to this moment of appropriation, the word does not exist in a neutral and impersonal language (it is not, after all, out of a dictionary that the speaker gets his words!), but rather it exists in other people's mouths, in other people's contexts, serving other people's intentions: it is from there that one must take the word, and make it "one's own."

— MIKHAIL BAKHTIN

They cannot represent themselves; they must be represented.

— MARX

I

Of what import is "race" as a meaningful category in the study of literature and the shaping of critical theory? If we attempt to answer this question by examining the history of Western literature and its criticism, our initial response would ostensibly be "nothing," or at the very least, "nothing explicitly." Indeed, until the past decade or so, even the most subtle and sensitive literary critics would most probably have argued that, except for aberrant moments in the history of criticism, "race" has been brought to bear upon the study of literature in no apparent way. The Western literary tradition, after all, and the canonical texts that comprise this splendid tradition, has been defined since Eliot as a more-or-less closed set of works that somehow speak to, or respond to, the "human condition" and to each other in formal patterns of repetition and revision.[1] And while judgment is subject to the moment and indeed does reflect temporal-specific presuppositions, certain works seem to transcend value judgments of the moment, speaking irresistibly to the "human condition." The question of the place of texts written by "the Other" (be that odd metaphor defined as African, Arabic, Chinese, Latin American, female, or Yiddish authors) in the proper study of "literature," "Western literature," or "comparative literature" has, until recently, remained an unasked question, suspended or silenced by a discourse in which the "canonical" and the "non-canonical" stand as the ultimate opposition. "Race," in much of the thinking about the proper study of literature in this century, has been an invisible quality, present implicitly at best.

This was not always the case, of course. By the middle of the nineteenth century, "national spirit" and "historical period" had become widely accepted metaphors within theories of the nature and function of literature which argued that the principal value in a "great" work of literary art resided in the extent to which these categories were *reflected* in that work of art. Montesquieu's *Esprit des lois* had made a culture's formal social institution the repository of its "guiding spirit," while Vico's *Principii d'una scienza nuova* had read literature against a complex pattern of

[1] Gates alludes to T. S. Eliot's "Tradition and the Individual Talent"; see p. 537.

historical cycles.[2] The two Schlegels managed rather deftly to bring to bear upon the interpretation of literature "both national spirit and historical period," as Walter Jackson Bate has shown.[3] But it was Taine who made the implicit explicit by postulating "race, moment, and *milieu*" as positivistic criteria through which any work could be read, and which, by definition, any work reflected. Taine's *History of English Literature* is the great foundation upon which subsequent nineteenth-century notions of "national literatures" would be constructed.[4]

What Taine called "race" was the source of all structures of feeling. To "track the root of man," he wrote, "is to consider the race itself, . . . the structure of his character and mind, his general processes of thought and feeling, . . . the irregularity and revolutions of his conception, which arrest in him the birth of fair dispositions and harmonious forms, the disdain of appearances, the desire for truth, the attachment for bare and abstract ideas, which develop in him conscience, at the expense of all else." In "race," Taine concluded, was predetermined "a particularity inseparable from all the motions of his intellect and his heart. Here lie the grand causes, for they are the universal and permanent causes, . . . indestructible, and finally infallibly supreme." "Poetries," as Taine put it, and all other forms of social expression, "are in fact only the imprints stamped by their seal."

"Race," for Taine was "the first and richest source of these master faculties from which historical events take their rise;" it was a "community of blood and intellect which to this day binds its off-shoots together." Lest we misunderstand the *naturally* determining role of "race," Taine concluded that it "is no simple spring but a kind of lake, a deep reservoir wherein other springs have, for a multitude of centuries, discharged their several streams."

Taine's originality lay not in these ideas about the nature and role of race, but in their almost "scientific" application to the history of literature. These ideas about race were received from the Enlightenment, if not from the Renaissance. By midpoint in the nineteenth century, ideas of irresistible racial differences were commonly held: when Abraham Lincoln invited a small group of black leaders to the White House in 1862 to share with them his ideas about returning all blacks in America to Africa, his argument turned upon these "natural" differences. "You and we are different races," he said. "We have between us a broader difference than exists between any other two races." Since this sense of difference was never to be bridged, Lincoln concluded, the slaves and the ex-slaves should be returned to their own. The growth of canonical "national" literatures was coterminous with the shared assumption among intellectuals that "race" was a "thing," an ineffaceable quantity, which irresistibly determined the shape and contour of thought and feelings as surely as it did the shape and contour of human anatomy.

How did the great movement away from "race, moment, and *milieu*" and toward the language of the text in the 1920s and 1930s in the Practical Criticism movement at Cambridge[5] and the New Criticism movement at Yale affect this category of "race" in the reading of literature? Race, along with all sorts of other unseemly or untoward notions about the composition of the literary work of art, was bracketed or suspended. Race, within these theories of literature to which we are all heir, was rendered *implicit* in the elevation of ideas of canonical *cultural* texts that comprise the Western tradition in Eliot's simultaneous order, with a simultaneous existence. History, *milieu*, and

[2]Charles-Louis de Secondat Montesquieu (1689–1755), a French philosopher, wrote *De l'esprit des lois (On the Spirit of the Laws)* in 1749. Giambattista Vico (1668–1744), an Italian philosopher, wrote *Principii d'una scienza nuova intorno alla natura delle nazioni (Principles of a New Science of Nations)*, proposing a cyclical theory of history in 1725; the work is generally referred to as the *Scienza nuova.*

[3]August Wilhelm (1767–1845) and Friedrich von Schlegel (1772–1829) were German philologists, theorists of the Romantic movement.

[4]The *Histoire de la littérature anglaise* (1863) of Hippolyte Taine (1828–1893) accounted for national literatures in terms of a scheme involving ethnicity, environment, and history: *race, milieu, moment.*

[5]The "Practical Criticism movement at Cambridge" refers to the British branch of New Criticism pioneered by I. A. Richards and William Empson. See the introduction to Formalisms, p. 754.

even moment were brought to bear upon the interpretation of literature through philology and etymology: the dictionary — in the Anglo-American tradition, the *Oxford English Dictionary* — was the castle in which Taine's criteria took refuge. Once the concept of value became encased in the belief in a canon of texts whose authors purportedly shared a "common culture" inherited from *both* the Greco-Roman and the Judeo-Christian traditions, no one need speak of matters of "race" since "the race" of these authors was "the same." One not heir to these traditions was, by definition, of another "race." This logic was impenetrable.

Despite their beliefs in the unassailable primacy of language in the estimation of a work of literature, however, both I. A. Richards and Allen Tate,[6] in separate prefaces to books of poems by black authors, paused to wonder aloud about the black faces of the authors, and the import this had upon the reading of their texts. The often claimed "racism" of the Southern Agrarians,[7] while an easily identifiable target, was only an explicit manifestation of presuppositions that formed a large segment of the foundation upon which formalism was built. The citizens of the republic of literature, in other words, were all white, and mostly male. Difference, if difference obtained at all, was a difference obliterated by the "simultaneity" of Eliot's "tradition." Eliot's fiction of tradition, for the writer of a culture of color, was the literary equivalent of the "grandfather clause." So, in response to Robert Penn Warren's statement in "Pondy Woods" — "Nigger, your breed ain't metaphysical" — Sterling A. Brown wrote, "Cracker, your breed ain't exegetical." The Signifyin(g) pun deconstructed the "racialism" inherent in these claims of tradition.

II

"Race" as a meaningful criterion within the biological sciences has long been recognized to be a fiction. When we speak of the "white race" or the "black race," the "Jewish race" or the "Aryan race," we speak in misnomers, biologically, and in metaphors, more generally. Nevertheless, our conversations are replete with usages of *race* which have their sources in the dubious pseudo-science of the eighteenth and nineteenth centuries. One need only flip through the pages of the *New York Times* to find headlines such as "Brown University President Sees School Racial Problems," or "Sensing Racism, Thousands March in Paris." In a lead editorial of its March 29, 1985, number, "The Lost White Tribe," the *Times* notes that while "racism is not unique to South Africa," we must condemn that society because "Betraying the religious tenets underlying Western culture, it has made race the touchstone of political rights." Eliot's "dissociation of sensibility," caused in large part by the "fraternal" atrocities of World War I, and then by the inexplicable and insane murder of European Jews two decades later, the *Times* editorial echoes. (For millions of people who originated outside Europe, however, this dissociation of sensibility had its origins in colonialism and human slavery.) *Race*, in these usages, pretends to be an objective term of classification, when in fact it is a trope.[8]

The sense of difference defined in popular usages of the term *race* has been used both to describe and *inscribe* differences of language, belief system, artistic tradition, "gene pool," and all sorts of supposedly "natural" attributes such as rhythm, athletic ability, cerebration, usury, and fidelity. The relation between "racial character" and these sorts of "characteristics" has been inscribed through tropes of race, lending to even supposedly "innocent" descriptions of cultural tendencies and differences the sanction of God, biology, or the natural order. "Race consciousness," Zora Neale Hurston wrote, "is a deadly explosive on the tongues of men." I even heard a member of the House of Lords in 1973 describe

[6] John Orley Allen Tate (1899–1979) was a Kentucky-born poet and critic whose *Reason in Madness* (1941) allied him with the group of other Southern critics (including Cleanth Brooks, Robert Penn Warren, John Crowe Ransom) who led the American wing of "New Criticism." See the introduction to Formalisms, p. 754.

[7] Social philosophy of the 1930s, hostile to both Marxism and corporate capitalism, espoused primarily by Southern intellectuals. Tate contributed an essay, "Remarks on the Southern Religion" to *I'll Take My Stand: The South and the Agrarian Tradition by Twelve Southerners* (1930).

[8] Gates may be alluding to the fact that the word "race" originates with the Latin *radix*, "root."

the differences between Irish Protestants and Catholics in terms of their "distinct and clearly definable differences of race."

"You mean to say that you can tell them apart?" I asked incredulously.

"Of course," responded the lord. "Any Englishman can."

Race has become a trope of ultimate, irreducible difference between cultures, linguistic groups, or practitioners of specific belief systems, who more often than not have fundamentally opposed economic interests. Race is the ultimate trope of difference because it is so very arbitrary in its application. The sanction of biology contained in sexual difference, simply put, does not and can never obtain when one is speaking of "racial difference." Yet, we carelessly use language in such a way as to *will* this sense of *natural* difference into our formulations. To do so is to engage in a pernicious act of language, one which exacerbates the complex problem of cultural or "ethnic" difference, rather than assuages or redresses it. This is especially the case at a time when racism has become fashionable, once again. That, literally every day, scores of people are killed in the name of differences ascribed to "race" only makes even more imperative this gesture to "deconstruct," if you will, the ideas of difference inscribed in the trope of race, to take discourse itself as our common subject to be explicated to reveal the latent relations of power and knowledge inherent in popular and academic usages of "race." When twenty-five thousand people feel compelled to gather on the Rue de Rivoli in support of the antiracist "Ne touche pas à mon pote" movement,[9] when thousands of people willingly accept arrest to protest apartheid, when Iran and Iraq feel justified in murdering the other's citizens because of their "race," when Beirut stands as a museum of shards and pieces reflecting degrees of horror impossible to comprehend, the gesture that we make here seems local and tiny.

There is a curious dialectic between formal language use and the inscription of metaphorical

[9]The slogan of an antiracist movement founded in Paris in the 1980s by Harlem Désir was "Touche pas mon pote," colloquial French for "Don't touch my pal."

"racial" differences. At times, as Nancy Stepan expertly shows in *The Idea of Race in Science*, these metaphors have sought a universal and transcendent sanction in biological science. Western writers in French, Spanish, German, Portuguese, and English have sought to make literal these rhetorical figures of "race," to make them natural, absolute, essential. In doing so, they have *inscribed* these differences as fixed and finite categories which they merely report or draw upon for authority. But it takes little reflection to recognize that these pseudoscientific categories are themselves figures of thought. Who has seen a black or red person, a white, yellow, or brown? These terms are arbitrary constructs, not reports of reality. But language is not only the medium of this often pernicious tendency, it is its *sign*. Language use signifies the difference between cultures and their possession of power, spelling the difference between subordinate and superordinate, between bondsman and lord. Its call into use is simultaneous with the shaping of an economic order in which the cultures of color have been dominated in several important senses by Western Judeo-Christian, Greco-Hellenic cultures and their traditions. To use contemporary theories of criticism to explicate these modes of inscription is to demystify large and obscure ideological relations and indeed theory itself. It would be useful here to consider a signal example of the black tradition's confinement and delimitation by the commodity of writing. For literacy, as I hope to demonstrate, could be the most pervasive emblem of capitalist commodity functions.

III

Where better to test this thesis than in the example of the black tradition's first poet in English, the African slave girl Phillis Wheatley. Let us imagine a scene:

One bright morning in the spring of 1772, a young African girl walked demurely into the courthouse at Boston, to undergo an oral examination, the results of which would determine the direction of her life and work. Perhaps she was shocked upon entering the appointed room. For there, gathered in a semicircle, sat eighteen of Boston's most notable citizens. Among them was

John Erving, a prominent Boston merchant; the Reverend Charles Chauncey, pastor of the Tenth Congregational Church and a son of Cotton Mather; and John Hancock, who would later gain fame for his signature on the Declaration of Independence. At the center of this group would have sat His Excellency, Thomas Hutchinson, governor of the colony, with Andrew Oliver, his lieutenant governor, close by his side.

Why had this august group been assembled? Why had it seen fit to summon this young African girl, scarcely eighteen years old, before it? This group of "the most respectable characters in *Boston*," as it would later define itself, had assembled to question the African adolescent closely on the slender sheaf of poems that the young woman claimed to have written by herself. We can only speculate on the nature of the questions posed to the fledgling poet. Perhaps they asked her to explain for all to hear exactly who were the Greek and Latin gods and poets alluded to so frequently in her work. Or perhaps they asked her to conjugate a verb in Latin, or even to translate randomly selected passages from the Latin, which she and her master, John Wheatley, claimed that she "had made some progress in." Or perhaps they asked her to recite from memory key passages from the texts of Milton and Pope, the two poets by whom the African claimed to be most directly influenced. We do not know.

We do know, however, that the African poet's responses were more than sufficient to prompt the eighteen august gentlemen to compose, sign, and publish a two-paragraph "Attestation," an open letter "To the Publick" that prefaces Phillis Wheatley's book, and which reads in part:

> We whose Names are underwritten, do assure the World, that the poems specified in the following Page, were (as we verily believe) written by Phillis, a young Negro Girl, who was but a few Years since, brought an uncultivated Barbarian from *Africa*, and has ever since been, and now is, under the Disadvantage of serving as a Slave in a Family in this Town. She has been examined by some of the best judges, and is thought qualified to write them.

So important was this document in securing a publisher for Phillis's poems that it forms the signal element in the prefatory matter printed in the opening pages of her *Poems on Various Subjects, Religious and Moral*, published at London in 1773.

Without the published "Attestation," Wheatley's publisher claimed, few would believe that an African could possibly have written poetry all by herself. As the eighteen put the matter clearly in their letter, "Numbers would be ready to suspect they were not really the Writings of Phillis." Phillis's master, John Wheatley, and Phillis had attempted to publish a similar volume in 1770 at Boston, but Boston publishers had been incredulous. Three years later, "Attestation" in hand, Phillis and her mistress's son, Nathaniel Wheatley, sailed for England, where they completed arrangements for the publication of a volume of her poems, with the aid of the Countess of Huntington and the Earl of Dartmouth.

This curious anecdote, surely one of the oddest oral examinations on record, is only a tiny part of a larger, and even more curious, episode in the eighteenth century's Enlightenment. At least since 1600, Europeans had wondered aloud whether or not the African "species of men," as they most commonly put it, *could* ever create formal literature, could ever master the "arts and sciences." If they could, the argument ran, then the African variety of humanity and the European variety were fundamentally related. If not, then it seemed clear that the African was destined by nature to be a slave.

Determined to discover the answer to this crucial quandary, several Europeans and Americans undertook experiments in which young African slaves were tutored and trained along with white children. Phillis Wheatley was merely one result of such an experiment. Francis Williams, a Jamaican who took the B.A. at the University of Cambridge before 1730; Jacobus Capitein, who earned several degrees in Holland; Wilhelm Amo, who took the doctorate degree in philosophy at Halle; and Ignatius Sancho, who became a friend of Sterne's and who published a volume of letters in 1782 — these were just a few of the black subjects of such "experiments." The published writings of these black men and one woman, who wrote in Latin, Dutch, German, and English, were seized upon both by pro- and antislavery proponents as proof that their arguments were sound.

So widespread was the debate over "the nature of the African" between 1730 and 1830 that not until the Harlem Renaissance would the work of black writers be as extensively reviewed as it was in the eighteenth century. Phillis Wheatley's list of reviewers includes Voltaire, Thomas Jefferson, George Washington, Samuel Rush, and James Beatty, to name only a few.[10] Francis Williams's work was analyzed by no less than David Hume and Immanuel Kant. Hegel, writing in the *Philosophy of History* in 1813, used the writings of these Africans as the sign of their innate inferiority. The list of commentators is extensive, amounting to a "Who's Who" of the French, English, and American Enlightenment.

Why was the *creative writing* of the African of such importance to the eighteenth century's debate over slavery? I can briefly outline one thesis: After Descartes, *reason* was privileged, or valorized, among all other human characteristics. Writing, especially after the printing press became so widespread, was taken to be the *visible* sign of reason. Blacks were "reasonable," and hence "men," if — and only if — they demonstrated mastery of the "arts and sciences," the eighteenth century's formula for writing. So, while the Enlightenment is famous for establishing its existence upon the human ability to reason, it simultaneously used the absence and presence of "reason" to delimit and circumscribe the very humanity of the cultures and people of color which Europeans had been "discovering" since the Renaissance. The urge toward the systematization of all human knowledge, by which we characterize the Enlightenment, led directly to the relegation of black people to a lower rung on the Great Chain of Being, an eighteenth-century construct that arranged all of creation on a vertical scale from animals and plants and insects through humans to the angels and God himself.

By 1750, the chain had become individualized; the human scale slid from "the lowliest Hottentot" (black south Africans) to "glorious Milton and Newton." If blacks could write and publish imaginative literature, then they could, in effect, take a few Giant Steps up the Chain of Being, in a pernicious game of "Mother, May I?" As the Reverend James W. C. Pennington, an ex-slave who wrote a slave narrative and who was a prominent black abolitionist, summarized this curious idea in his prefatory note "To the Reader" that authorized Ann Plato's 1841 book of essays, biographies, and poems: "The history of the arts and sciences is the history of individuals, of individual nations." Only by publishing books such as Plato's, he argued, could blacks demonstrate "the fallacy of that stupid theory, *that nature has done nothing but fit us for slaves, and that art cannot unfit us for slavery!*"

IV

The relation between what, for lack of a better term, I shall call the "nonwhite" writer and the French, Portuguese, Spanish, and English languages and literatures manifests itself in at least two ways of interest to theorists of literature and literary history. I am thinking here of what in psychoanalytic criticism is sometimes called "the other," and more especially of this "other" as the subject and object in literature. What I mean by citing these two overworked terms is precisely this: how blacks are figures in literature, and also how blacks *figure*, as it were, literature of their own making.

These two poles of a received opposition have been formed, at least since the early seventeenth century, by an extraordinary *subdiscourse* of the European philosophies of aesthetic theory and language. The two subjects, often in marginal ways, have addressed directly the supposed relation among "race," defined variously as language use and "place in nature." Human beings wrote books. Beautiful books were reflections of sublime genius. Sublime genius was the province of the European.

Blacks, and other people of color, could not "write." "Writing," these writers argued, stood alone among the fine arts as the most salient repository of "genius," the visible sign of reason itself. In this subordinate role, however, "writing," although secondary to "reason," was nevertheless the *medium* of reason's expression. They

[10]"Samuel Rush" may be Benjamin Rush (1745–1813), Pennsylvania-born scientist and abolitionist; "James Beatty" may be James Beattie (1735–1803), Scottish poet and philosopher.

knew reason by its writing, by its representations. This representation could assume the spoken or the written form. And while several superb scholars gave priority to the *spoken* as the privileged of the pair, in their writings about blacks, at least, Europeans privileged *writing* as the principal measure of Africans' "humanity," their "capacity for progress," their very place in "the great chain of being."

This system of signs is arbitrary. Key words, such as *capacity*, which became a metaphor for cranial size, reflect the predominance of "scientific" discourse in metaphysics. That "reason," moreover, could be seen to be "natural" was the key third term of a homology which, in practice, was put to pernicious uses. The transformation of writing from an activity of mind into a commodity not only reflects larger mercantile relations between Africa and Europe but is also the subject I wish to explore here. Let me retrace, in brief, the history of this idea, of the relationship of the absence of "writing" and the absence of "humanity" in European letters of 1600.

We must understand this correlation of use and *presence* in language if we are to begin to learn how to read, for example, the slave's narrative within what Geoffrey H. Hartman calls its "text-milieu." The slave narratives, taken together, represent the attempt of blacks to *write themselves into being*. What a curious idea: Through the mastery of formal Western languages, the presupposition went, a black person could posit a full and sufficient self, as an act of self-creation through the medium of language. Accused of having no collective history by Hegel, blacks effectively responded by publishing hundreds of individual histories which functioned as the part standing for the whole. As Ralph Ellison defined this relation, "We tell ourselves our individual stories so as to become aware of our *general* story."

Writing as the visible sign of Reason, at least since the Renaissance in Europe, had been consistently invoked in Western aesthetic theory in the discussion of the enslavement and status of the black. The origin of this received association of political salvation and artistic genius can be traced at least to the seventeenth century. What we arrive at by extracting a rather black and slender thread from among the philosophical discourses of the Enlightenment is a reading of another side of the philosophy of enlightenment, indeed its nether side. Writing in *The New Organon* in 1620, Sir Francis Bacon, confronted with the problem of classifying the people of color which a seafaring Renaissance Europe had "discovered," turned to the arts as the ultimate measure of a race's place in nature. "Again," he wrote, "let a man only consider what a difference there is between the life of men in the most civilized province of Europe, and in the wildest and most barbarous districts of New India; he will feel it be great enough to justify the saying that 'man is a god to man,' not only in regard to aid and benefit, but also by comparison of condition. And this difference comes not from soil, not from climate, not from race, but from the arts." Eleven years later, Peter Heylyn, in his *Little Description of the Great World*, used Bacon's formulation to relegate the blacks to a subhuman status: Black Africans, he wrote, lacked completely "the use of Reason which is peculiar unto man; [they are] of little Wit; and destitute of all arts and sciences; prone to luxury, and for the greatest part Idolators." All subsequent commentaries on the matter were elaborations upon Heylyn's position.

By 1680, Heylyn's key words, *reason* and *wit*, had been reduced to "reading and writing," as Morgan Godwyn's summary of received opinion attests:

> [A] disingenuous and unmanly *Position* had been formed; and privately (and as it were *in the dark*) handed to and again, which is this, That the Negro's though in their figure they carry some resemblances of manhood, yet are indeed *no* men. . . . the consideration of the shape and figure of our Negro's Bodies, their Limbs and members; their Voice and Countenance, in all things according with other mens; together with their *Risibility* and *Discourse* (man's Peculiar Faculties) should be sufficient Conviction. How should they otherwise be capable of *Trades*, and other no less manly imployments; as also of *Reading and Writing*, or show so much Discretion in management of Business; . . . but wherein (we know) that many of our own People are *deficient*, were they not truly Men?

Such a direct correlation of political rights and literacy helps us to understand both the transformation of writing into a commodity and the sheer burden of received opinion that motivated the black slave to seek his or her text. As well, it defined the "frame" against which each black text would be read. The following 1740 South Carolina statute was concerned to make it impossible for black literacy mastery even to occur:

> *And whereas* the having of slaves taught to write, or suffering them to be employed in writing, may be attending with great inconveniences;
>
> *Be it enacted*, that all and every person and persons whatsoever, who shall hereafter teach, or cause any slave or slaves to be taught to write, or shall use or employ any slave as a scribe in any manner of writing whatsoever, hereafter taught to write; every such person or persons shall, for every offense, forfeit the sum of one hundred pounds current money.

Learning to read and to write, then, was not only difficult, it was a violation of a law. That Frederick Douglass, Thomas Smallwood, William Wells Brown, Moses Grandy, James Pennington, and John Thompson, among numerous others,[11] all rendered statements about the direct relation between freedom and discourse not only as central scenes of instruction but also as repeated fundamental structures of their very rhetorical strategies only emphasizes the dialectical relation of black texts to a "context," defined here as *"other,"* racist texts, against which the slave's narrative, by definition, was forced to react.

By 1705, a Dutch explorer, William Bosman, had encased Peter Heylyn's bias into a myth which the Africans he had "discovered" had purportedly related to him. It is curious insofar as it justifies human slavery. According to Bosman, the blacks "tell us that in the beginning God created Black as well as White men; thereby giving the Blacks the first Election, who chose Gold, and left the Knowledge of Letters to the White. God granted their request, but being incensed at their Avarice, resolved that the Whites should ever be their masters, and they obliged to wait on them as their slaves." Bosman's fabrication, of course, was a myth of origins designed to sanction through mythology a political order created by Europeans. It was David Hume, writing at midpoint in the

eighteenth century, who gave to Bosman's myth the sanction of Enlightenment philosophical reasoning.

In a major essay, "Of National Characters" (1748), Hume discussed the "characteristics" of the world's major division of human beings. In a footnote added to his original text in 1753 (the margins of his discourse), Hume posited with all of the authority of philosophy the fundamental identity of complexion, character, and intellectual capacity. "I am apt to suspect the negroes," he wrote,

> and in general all the other species of men (for there are four or five different kinds) to be naturally inferior to the whites. There never was a civilized nation of any other complexion than white, nor even any individual eminent either in action or speculation. No ingenious manufacturers amongst them, *no arts, no sciences*. . . . Such a uniform and constant difference could not happen, in so many countries and ages, if *nature* had not made our original distinction betwixt these breeds of men. Not to mention our colonies, there are Negroe slaves dispersed all over Europe, of which none ever discovered any symptoms of ingenuity; . . . In Jamaica, indeed they talk of one negroe as a man of parts and learning [Francis Williams, the Cambridge-educated poet who wrote verse in Latin]; but 'tis likely he is admired for very slender accomplishments, like a parrot who speaks a few words plainly.

Hume's opinion on the subject, as we might expect, became prescriptive.

Writing in 1764, in his *Observations on the Feelings of the Beautiful and the Sublime*, Immanuel Kant elaborated upon Hume's essay in a fourth section entitled "Of National Characters, as far as They Depend upon the Distinct Feeling of the Beautiful and the Sublime." Kant first claimed that "So fundamental is the difference between [the black and white] races of man, and it appears to be as great in regard to mental capacities as in color." Kant, moreover, was one of the earliest major European philosophers to conflate "color" with "intelligence," a determining relation he posited with dictatorial surety. The excerpt bears citation:

> . . . Father Labat reports that a Negro carpenter, whom he reproached for haughty treatment toward

---

[11]Frederick Douglass and the rest were authors of slave narratives.

his wives, answered: "You whites are indeed fools, for first you make great concessions to your wives, and afterward you complain when they drive you mad." And it might be that there were something in this which perhaps deserved to be considered; but in short, this fellow was *quite black* from head to foot, a clear proof that what he said was stupid. (emphasis added)

The correlation of "blackness" and "stupidity" Kant posited as if self-evident.

Writing in "Query XIV" of *Notes on the State of Virginia*, Thomas Jefferson maintained that "Never yet could I find that a black had uttered a thought above the level of plain narration, never see even an elementary trait of painting or sculpture." Of Wheatley, the first black person to publish a book of poetry in England, Jefferson the critic wrote, "Misery is often the parent of the most affecting touches in poetry. Among the blacks is misery enough, God knows, but not poetry. . . . The compositions published under her name are below the dignity of criticism."

In that same year (1785), Kant, basing his observations on the absence of published writing among blacks, noted as if simply obvious that "Americans [Indians] and blacks are lower in their mental capacities than all other races." Again, Hegel, echoing Hume and Kant, noted the absence of history among black people and derided them for failing to develop indigenous African scripts, or even to master the art of writing in modern languages.

Hegel's strictures on the African about the absence of "history" presume a crucial role of *memory* — a collective, cultural memory — in the estimation of civilization. Metaphors of the "childlike" nature of the slaves, of the masked, puppetlike "personality" of the black, all share this assumption about the absence of memory. Mary Langdon, in her 1855 novel *Ida May: A Story of Things Actual and Possible*, wrote that "but then they *are* mere children. . . . You seldom hear them say much about anything that's past, if they only get enough to eat and drink at the present moment." Without writing, there could exist no *repeatable* sign of the workings of reason, of mind. Without memory or mind, there could exist no history. Without history, there could exist no "humanity," as defined consistently from Vico to Hegel. As William Gilmore Simms[12] argued at the middle of the nineteenth century:

> [If one can establish] that the negro intellect is fully equal to that of the white race . . . you not only take away the best argument for keeping him in subjection, but you take away the possibility of doing so. *Prima facie*, however, the fact that he *is* a slave, is conclusive against the argument for his freedom, as it is against his equality of claim in respect of intellect. . . . Whenever the negro shall be fully fit for freedom, he will make himself free, and no power on earth can prevent him.

V

Ironically, Anglo-African writing arose as a response to allegations of its absence. Black people responded to these profoundly serious allegations about their "nature" as directly as they could: they wrote books, poetry, autobiographical narratives. Political and philosophical discourse were the predominant forms of writing. Among these, autobiographical "deliverance" narratives were the most common, and the most accomplished. Accused of lacking a formal and collective history, blacks published individual histories which, taken together, were intended to narrate, in segments, the larger yet fragmented history of blacks in Africa, now dispersed throughout a cold New World. The narrated, descriptive "eye" was put into service as a literary form to posit both the individual "I" of the black author and the collective "I" of the race. Text created author, and black authors, it was hoped, would create, or re-create, the image of the race in European discourse. The very *face* of the race, representations of the features of which are common in all sorts of writings about blacks at this time, was contingent upon the recording of the black *voice*. Voice presupposes a face but also seems to have been thought to determine the contours of the black face.

The recording of an "authentic" black voice, a voice of deliverance from the deafening discursive silence which an enlightened Europe cited as

[12]Gilmore Simms (1806–1870) is best known as the author of *The Yemasee* (1835), a romance influenced by Walter Scott about the conflict between the Carolina colonists and the native Yemasee tribe.

proof of the absence of the African's humanity, was the millennial instrument of transformation through which the African would become the European, the slave become the ex-slave, the brute animal become the human being. So central was this idea to the birth of the black literary tradition in the eighteenth century that five of the earliest slave narratives draw upon the figure of the voice in the text as crucial "scenes of instruction" in the development of the slave on the road to freedom. James Gronniosaw in 1770, John Marrant in 1785, Ottobah Cugoano in 1787, Olaudah Equiano in 1789, and John Jea in 1815 — all drew upon the trope of the talking book. Gronniosaw's usage bears citing here especially because it repeats Kant's correlation of physical — and, as it were, metaphysical — characteristics:

> My master used to read prayers in public to the ship's crew every Sabbath day; and when I first saw him read, I was never so surprised in my life, as when I saw the book talk to my master, for I thought it did, as I observed him to look upon it, and move his lips. I wished it would do so with me. As soon as my master had done reading, I followed him to the place where he put the book, being mightily delighted with it, and when nobody saw me, I opened it, and put my ear down close upon it, in great hope that it would say something to me; but I was very sorry, and greatly disappointed, when I found that it would not speak. This thought immediately presented itself to me, that every body and every thing despised me because I was black.

Even for this black author, his own mask of black humanity was a negation, a sign of absence. Gronniosaw accepted his role as a nonspeaking would-be subject and the absence of his common humanity with the European.

That the figure of the talking book recurs in these five black eighteenth-century texts says much about the degree of presupposition and intertextuality in early black letters, more than we heretofore thought. Equally important, however, this figure itself underscores the received correlation between silence and blackness which we have been tracing, as well as the urgent need to make the text speak, the process by which the slave marked his distance from the master. The voice in the text was truly a millennial voice for the African person of letters in the eighteenth century, for it was that very voice of deliverance and of redemption which would signify a new order for the black.

These narrators, linked by revision of a trope into the very first black chain of signifiers, implicitly signify upon another "chain," the metaphorical Great Chain of Being. Blacks were most commonly represented on the chain either as the "lowest" of the human races, or as first cousin to the ape. Since writing, according to Hume, was the ultimate sign of difference between animal and human, these writers implicitly were Signifyin(g) upon the figure of the chain itself, simply by publishing autobiographies that were indictments of the received order of Western culture, of which slavery, to them, by definition stood as the most salient sign. The writings of Gronniosaw, Marrant, Equiano, Cugoano, and Jea served as a critique of the sign of the Chain of Being and the black person's figurative "place" on the chain. This chain of black signifiers, regardless of their intent or desire, made the first political gesture in the Anglo-African literary tradition "simply" by the act of writing, a collective act that gave birth to the black literary tradition and defined it as the "other's chain," the chain of black being as black people themselves would have it. Making the book speak, then, constituted a motivated, and political, engagement with and condemnation of Europe's fundamental figure of domination, the Great Chain of Being.

The trope of the talking book is not a trope of the presence of voice at all, but of its absence. To speak of a "silent voice" is to speak in an oxymoron. There is no such thing as a silent voice. Furthermore, as Juliet Mitchell has put the matter, there is something untenable about the attempt to represent what is not there, to represent that which is *missing* or absent. Given that this is what these five black authors sought to do, we are justified in wondering aloud if the sort of subjectivity that they sought could be realized through a process that was so very ironic from the outset. Indeed, how can the black subject posit a full and sufficient self in a language in which blackness is a sign of absence? Can writing, the very "difference" it makes and marks, mask the blackness of the black face that addresses the text of Western letters, in a voice that "speaks English" in an idiom that contains the irreducible element of cultural difference that shall always separate the white voice from the black? Black people, we know, have not been "liberated" from racism by their writings, and they accepted a false premise by assuming that racism would be destroyed once white racists became convinced that we were human, too. Writing stood as a complex "certificate of humanity," as Paulin J. Hountondji put it. Black writing, and especially the literature of the slave, served not to obliterate the difference of "race," as a would-be white man such as Gronniosaw so ardently desired; rather, the inscription of the black voice in Western literatures has preserved those very cultural differences to be imitated and revised in a separate Western literary tradition, a tradition of black difference.

Blacks, as we have seen, tried to write themselves out of slavery, a slavery even more profound than mere physical bondage. Accepting the challenge of the great white Western tradition, black writers wrote as if their lives depended upon it — and, in a curious sense, their lives did, the "life" of "the race" in Western discourse. But if blacks accepted this challenge, we also accepted its premises, premises in which perhaps lay concealed a trap. What trap might this be? Let us recall the curious case of M. Edmond Laforest.

In 1915, Edmond Laforest, a prominent member of the Haitian literary movement called La Ronde, made of his death a symbolic, if ironic, statement of the curious relation of the "non-Western" writer to the act of writing in a modern language. M. Laforest, with an inimitable, if fatal, flair for the grand gesture, stood upon a bridge, calmly tied a Larousse dictionary[13] around his neck, then proceeded to leap to his death by drowning. While other black writers, before and after M. Laforest, have suffocated as artists beneath the weight of various modern languages, Laforest chose to make his death an emblem of this relation of indenture.

It is the challenge of the black tradition to critique this relation of indenture, an indenture that obtains for our writers and for our critics. We must master, as Derrida wrote, "how to speak the other's language without renouncing (our) own." When we attempt to appropriate, by inversion, *race* as a term for an essence, as did the Negritude movement, for example ("We feel, therefore we are," as Senghor argued of the African), we yield too much, such as the basis of a shared humanity. Such gestures, as Anthony Appiah has observed, are futile and dangerous because of their further inscription of new and bizarre stereotypes. How do we meet Derrida's challenge in the discourse of criticism? The Western critical tradition has a canon, just as does the Western literary tradition. Whereas I once thought it our most important gesture to *master* the canon of criticism, to *imitate* and *apply* it, I now believe that we must turn to the black tradition itself to arrive at theories of criticism indigenous to our literatures. Alice Walker's revision of a parable of white interpretation written in 1836 by Rebecca Cox Jackson, a Shaker eldress and black visionary, makes this point most tellingly. Jackson, who like John Jea claimed to have been taught to read by the Lord, wrote in her autobiography that she dreamed that a "white man" came to her house to teach her how to *interpret* and "understand" the word of God, now that God had taught her to read:

> A white man took me by my right hand and led me on the north side of the room, where sat a square table. On it lay a book open. And he said to me, "Thou shall be instructed in this book, from Genesis to Revelations." And then he took me on the west side, where stood a table. And it looked like the first. And said, "Yea, thou shall be instructed from the beginning of creation to the end of time." And then he took me on the east side of the room also, where stood a table and book like the two first, and said, "I will instruct thee — yea, thou shall be instructed from the beginning of all things to the end of all things. Yea, thou shall be well instructed. I will instruct."

> And then I awoke, and I saw him as plain as I did in my dream. And after that he taught me daily. And when I would be reading and come to a hard word, I would see him standing by my side and he would teach me the word right. And often, when I would be in meditation and looking into things which was hard to understand, I would find him by me, teaching and giving me understanding. And oh, his labor and care which he had with me often

<hr/>

[13]The Larousse is the standard French dictionary-encyclopedia.

caused me to weep bitterly, when I would see my great ignorance and the great trouble he had to make me understand eternal things. For I was so buried in the depth of the tradition of my forefathers, that it did seem as if I never could be dug up.

In response to Jackson's relation of interpretive indenture to a "white man," Alice Walker, writing in *The Color Purple*, records an exchange between Celie and Shug about turning away from "the old white man," which soon turns into a conversation about the elimination of "man" as a mediator between a woman and "everything":

... You have to git man off your eyeball, before you can see anything a'tall.

Man corrupt everything, say Shug. He on your box of grits, in your head, and all over the radio. He try to make you think he everywhere. Soon as you think he everywhere, you think he God. But he ain't. Whenever you trying to pray, and man plot himself on the other end of it, tell him to git lost, say Shug.

Celie and Shug's omnipresent "man," of course, echoes the black tradition's epithet for the white power structure, "the man."

For non-Western, so-called noncanonical critics, getting the "man off your eyeball" means using the most sophisticated critical theories and methods generated by the Western tradition to reappropriate and to define our own "colonial" discourses. We must use these theories and methods insofar as these are relevant and applicable to the study of our own literatures. The danger in doing so, however, is best put, again by Anthony Appiah in his definition of what he calls the "Naipaul fallacy"[14]: "It is not necessary to show that African literature is fundamentally the same as European literature in order to show that it can be treated with the same tools. ... Nor should we endorse a more sinister line ... : the post-colonial legacy which requires us to show that African literature is worthy of study precisely (but only) because it is fundamentally the same as European literature." We *must* not, Appiah concludes, "ask the reader to understand Africa by embedding it in European culture."

We must, of course, analyze the ways in which writing relates to "race," how attitudes toward racial differences generate and structure literary texts by us *and* about us; we must determine how critical methods can effectively disclose the traces of racial difference in literature; but we must also understand how certain forms of difference and the *languages* we employ to define those supposed "differences" not only reinforce each other but tend to create and maintain each other. Similarly, and as importantly, we must analyze the language of contemporary criticism itself, recognizing that hermeneutical systems, especially, are not "universal," "color-blind," or "apolitical," or "neutral." Whereas some critics wonder aloud, as Appiah notes, about such matters as whether or not "a structuralist poetics is inapplicable in Africa because structuralism is European," the concern of the "Third World" critic should properly be to understand the ideological subtext which any critical theory reflects and embodies, and what relation this subtext bears to the production of meaning. No critical theory — be that Marxism, feminism, poststructuralism, Nkrumah's consciencism, or whatever — escapes the specificity of value and ideology, no matter how mediated these may be. To attempt to appropriate our own discourses using Western critical theory "uncritically" is to substitute one mode of neocolonialism for another. To begin to do this in my own tradition, theorists have turned to the black vernacular tradition — to paraphrase Rebecca Cox Jackson, to dig into the depths of the tradition of our foreparents — to isolate the signifying black difference through which to theorize about the so-called Discourse of the Other.

[14]V[idiadhar] S[urajprasad] Naipaul (b. 1932), a Trinidad-born, Oxford-educated novelist and journalist whose works chronicle racism, corruption, and violence in the new nations of Africa and the Caribbean ruled by blacks, is a favorite object of odium to Africanist cultural critics such as Gates and Appiah.

❖ DIALOGUE BETWEEN HENRY LOUIS GATES JR. AND HOUSTON A. BAKER JR.

Henry Louis Gates Jr.
b. 1950

In "Text and Pretext," Henry Louis Gates Jr. articulates his differences with those he calls the "race and superstructure" critics — Stephen Henderson, Addison Gayle, and Houston Baker Jr. — who gauge the value of African American literature by ideology rather than literary quality, particularly the degree to which particular texts conform to an essentialized vision of Blackness. (For biographical information on Gates, see p. 1890.)

Houston A. Baker Jr.
b. 1943

Houston A. Baker Jr. aims to determine the aesthetics of an Afro-American literary tradition, which he believes must be based on different criteria from those underlying the Anglo-American tradition. Born in Kentucky, Baker received a B.A. in English from Howard University and did his doctoral work at UCLA. He has taught at Yale (1968–69) and the University of Virginia (1970–73), where he became a full professor in 1973. Since 1974, Baker has been a professor at the University of Pennsylvania where he is head of the Center for the Study of Black Literature and Culture. In addition to collections of poetry and edited books, Baker has also published critical and theoretical studies, including Long Black Song: Essays in Black American Literature and Culture *(1972);* A Many-Colored Coat of Dreams: The Poetry of Countee Cullen *(1974);* The Journey Back: Issues in Black Literature and Criticism *(1980);* Blues, Ideology, and Afro-American Literature: A Vernacular Theory *(1984);* Modernism and the Harlem Renaissance *(1987),* Workings of the Spirit *(1991), and* Black Studies, Rap, and the Academy *(1993); his most recent books are* Turning South Again *(2001), and the Averitt lectures published as* Critical Memory *(2001). The selection below, from* Blues, Ideology, and Afro-American Literature, *articulates Baker's disagreement with the early theories of Henry Louis Gates Jr.: his insistence that any semiotic study of black literature be grounded in the material culture from which its language and its literature derive.*

HENRY LOUIS GATES JR.

From *Preface to Blackness: Text and Pretext*

In the first essay of *Long Black Song, Essays in Black American Literature and Culture*,[1] Houston Baker proffers the considerable claim that black culture, particularly as "measured" through black folklore and literature, serves in intent and effect as an "index" of repudiation not only of white Western values and white Western culture but of white Western literature as well. "In fact," he writes, "it is to a great extent the culture theorizing of whites that has made for a separate and distinctive black American culture. That is to say, one index of the distinctiveness of black American culture is the extent to which it repudiates the culture theorizing of the white Western world." Repudiation, he continues, "is characteristic of black American folklore; and this is one of the most important factors in setting black American literature apart from white American literature." Further, "Black folklore and the black American literary tradition that grew out of it reflect a culture that is distinctive both of white American and of African culture, and therefore neither can provide valid standards by which black American folklore and literature may be judged." A text becomes "blacker," it surely follows, to the extent that it serves as an "index of repudiation." Here we find an ironic response to Harold Bloom's *Anxiety of Influence* in what we could characterize as an "Animosity of Influence."

Baker discusses this notion of influence between black and white American culture at length. "Call it black, Afro-American, Negro," he writes, "the fact remains that there is a fundamental, qualitative difference between it and white American culture." The bases of this "fundamental, qualitative difference" are, first, that "black American culture was developed orally or musically for many years"; second, that "black American culture was never characterized by a collective ethos"; and, finally, that

"one of [black American culture's] most salient characteristics is an index of repudiation." Oral, collectivistic, and repudiative, he concludes, "each of these aspects helps to distinguish black American culture from white American culture."

These tenets suggest that there must be an arbitrary relation between a sign and its referent; indeed, that all meaning is culture-bound. Yet what we find elaborated here are rather oversimplified, basically political, criteria, which are difficult to verify, partly because they are not subject to *verbal* analysis (that is, can this sense of *difference* be measured through the literary uses of language?), partly because the *thematic* analytical tools employed seem to be useful primarily for black naturalist novels or for the mere paraphrasing of poetry, partly because the matter of influence is almost certainly too subtle to be traced in other than close textual readings, and finally because his three bases of "fundamental, qualitative difference" seem to me too unqualified. There is so much more to Jean Toomer, Zora Hurston, Langston Hughes, Sterling Brown, Ralph Ellison, Leon Forrest, Ishmael Reed, Toni Morrison, and Alice Walker than their "index of repudiation," whatever that is. Besides, at least Toomer, Ellison, and Reed have taken care to discuss the complex matter of literary ancestry, in print and without. It is one of the ironies of the study of black literature that our critical activity is, almost by definition, a comparative one, since many of our writers seem to be influenced by Western masters, writing in English as well as outside it, as they are by indigenous, Afro-American oral or even written forms. That the base for our literature is an oral one is certainly true; but, as Millman Parry and Albert Lord have amply demonstrated,[2] so is the base of the whole of Western literature, commencing with

---

[1]*Long Black Song* (Charlottesville: Univ. of Virginia Press, 1972). [Gates]

[2]Lord, *The Singer of Tales* (Cambridge: Harvard Univ. Press, 1960). [Gates]

the Hebrews and the Greeks. Nevertheless, Baker does not suggest any critical tools for explicating the oral tradition in our literature, such as the formulaic studies so common to the subject. Nor does he suggest how folklore is displaced in literature, even though, like Henderson, he does see it at "the base of the black literary tradition." That black culture is characterized by a collective ethos most definitely demands some qualification, since our history, literary and extraliterary, often turns on a tension, a dialectic, between the private perceptions of the individual and the white public perceptions of that same individual.

Nor does Baker's thought-provoking contention of the deprivation of the American frontier stand to prove this thesis:

> When the black American reads Frederick Jackson Turner's *The Frontier in American History*, he feels no regret over the end of the Western frontier. To black America, *frontier* is an alien word; for, in essence, all frontiers established by the white psyche have been closed to the black man. Heretofore, later, few have been willing to look steadily at America's past and acknowledge that the black man was denied his part in the frontier and his share of the nation's wealth.

Yet, at least Ralph Ellison has written extensively on the fact of the frontier (physical and metaphysical) and its centrality to his sensibility. Further, Ishmael Reed uses the frontier again and again as a central trope.

Part of the problem here is not only Baker's exclusive use of thematic analysis to attempt to delineate a literary tradition but also his implicit stance that literature functions primarily as a cultural artifact, as a repository for ideas. "It is impossible to comprehend the process of transcribing cultural values," he says (in his essay "Racial Wisdom and Richard Wright's *Native Son*"), "without an understanding of the changes that have characterized both the culture as a whole and the lives of its individual transcribers." Further, "Black American literature has a human immediacy and a pointed relevance which are obscured by the overingenious methods of the New Criticism, or any other school that attempts to talk of works of art as though they had no creators or of sociohistorical factors as though they

did not filter through the lives of individual human beings." Here we find the implicit thesis in *Long Black Song*, the rather Herderian notion of literature as primarily the reflection of ideas and experiences outside of it. It is not, of course, that literature is unrelated to culture, to other disciplines, or even to other arts; it is not that words and usage somehow exist in a vacuum or that the literary work of art occupies an ideal or reified, privileged status, the province of some elite cult of culture. It is just that the literary work of art is a system of signs that may be decoded with various methods, all of which assume the fundamental unity of form and content and all of which demand close reading. Only the rare critic, such as Michael G. Cooke, Nathan A. Scott, or Sherley Williams, has made of thematic analysis the subtle tool that intelligent, sensitive reading requires. Baker seems to be reading black texts in a particular fashion for other than literary purposes. In *Singers of Daybreak: Studies in Black American Literature*,[3] he suggests these purposes. "What lies behind the neglect of black American literature," he asserts, "is not a supportable body of critical criteria that includes a meaningful definition of *utile* and *dulce*, but a refusal to believe that blacks possess the humanity requisite for the production of works of art." Baker finds himself shadowboxing with the ghostly judgments of Jefferson on Phillis Wheatley and Ignatius Sancho; his blows are often telling, but his opponent's feint is deadly. . . .

What is wrong with employing race and superstructure as critical premises? This critical activity sees language and literature as reflections of "Blackness." It postulates "Blackness" as an entity, rather than as metaphor or sign. Thus, the notion of a signified *black* element in literature retains a certain impressiveness insofar as it exists in some mystical kingdom halfway between a fusion of psychology and religion on the one hand and the Platonic Theory of Ideas on the other. Reflections of this "Blackness" are

---

[3]*Singers of Daybreak: Studies in Black American Literature* (Washington, D.C.: Howard Univ. Press, 1974). [Gates]

more or less "literary" according to the ideological posture of the critic. Content is primary over form and indeed is either divorced completely from form, in terms of genesis and normative value, or else is merely facilitated by form as a means to an end. In this criticism, rhetorical value judgments are closely related to social values. This method reconstitutes "message," when what is demanded is a deconstruction of a literary system.

HOUSTON A. BAKER JR.

From *Blues, Ideology, and Afro-American Literature*

Henry Louis Gates's "Preface to Blackness: Text and Pretext" . . . commences with the notion that the criticism of Afro-American literature (prior to 1975) rested on a mistake. This mistake, according to Gates, consisted in the assumption that a "determining formal relation" exists between "literature" and "social institutions."

> The idea of a determining formal relation between literature and social institutions does not in itself explain the sense of urgency that has, at least since the publication in 1760 of *A Narrative of the Uncommon Sufferings and Surprising Deliverance of Briton Hammon, A Negro Man*, characterized nearly the whole of Afro-American writing. This idea has often encouraged a posture that belabors the social and documentary status of black art, and indeed the earliest discrete examples of written discourse by slave and ex-slave came under a scrutiny not primarily literary. [p. 44]

For Gates, "social institutions" is an omnibus category equivalent to Stepto's "nonliterary structures." Such institutions include the philosophical musings of the Enlightenment on the "African Mind," eighteenth-century debates concerning the African's place in the great chain of being, the politics of abolitionism, or (more recently) the economics, politics, and sociology of the Afro-American liberation struggle in the twentieth century. Gates contends that Afro-American literature has repeatedly been interpreted and evaluated according to criteria derived from such "institutions."

As a case in point, he surveys the critical response that marked the publication of Phillis Wheatley's *Poems on Various Subjects, Religious and Moral*, discovering that "almost immediately after its publication in London in 1773," the black Boston poet's collection became "the international antislavery movement's most salient argument for the African's innate mental equality" (p. 46). Gates goes on to point out that "literally scores of public figures" provided prefatory signatures, polemical reviews, or "authenticating" remarks dedicated to proving that Wheatley's verse was (or was not, as the case may be) truly the product of an African imagination. Such responses were useless in the office of criticism, however, because "virtually no one," according to Gates, "discussed . . . [Wheatley's collection] as poetry" (p. 46). Hence, "The documentary status of black art assumed priority over mere [?] literary judgment; criticism rehearsed content to justify one notion of origins or another" (p. 46).

Thomas Jefferson's condemnation (on "extraliterary" grounds) of Wheatley and of the black eighteenth-century epistler Ignatius Sancho set an influential model for the discussion of Afro-American literature that, in Gates's view, "exerted a prescriptive influence over the criticism of the writings of blacks for the next 150 years" (p. 46). Jefferson's recourse to philosophical, political, religious, economic, and other cultural systems for descriptive and evaluative terms in which to discuss black writing was, in short, a *mistake* that has been replicated through the decades by both white and Afro-American commentators. William Dean Howells, the writers of the Harlem Renaissance, and, most recently, according to Gates, spokesmen for the Black Aesthetic have repeated the critical offense of Jefferson: They have assumed there is, in fact, a determining formal relation between literature and other cultural institutions and that various dimensions of these other institutions constitute areas of knowledge relevant to literary criticism.

Gates says a thunderous no to such assumptions. As he reviews the "prefaces" affixed to various Afro-American texts through the decades, he finds no useful criteria for the practice of literary criticism. He discovers only introductory remarks that are "pretexts" for discussing African humanity or for displaying "artifacts of the sable mind" (p. 49), or for chronicling the prefacer's own "attitude toward being black in white America" (p. 65).

Like Larry Neal,[1] Gates concludes that such "pretexts" and the lamentable critical situation they imply are functions of the powerful influence of "race" as a variable in all spheres of American intellectual endeavor related to Afro-America. And like Neal, he states that racial considerations have substituted for "class" as a category in the thinking of those who have attempted to criticize Afro-American literature, resulting in what he calls "race and superstructure" criticism: "blacks borrowed whole the Marxist notion of base and superstructure and made of it, if you will, race and superstructure" (p. 56). Gates also believes that Afro-American creative writers have fallen prey to the mode of thought that marks "race and superstructure" criticism. For these writers have shaped their work on polemical, documentary lines designed to prove the equality of Afro-Americans or to argue a case for their humanity. In the process, they have neglected the "literary" engagement that results in true art.

[1]Neal (1937–1981) was a leader of the Black Arts movement, author of many plays and screenplays, and editor, with LeRoi Jones (a.k.a. Amiri Baraka), of the polemical anthology *Black Fire* (1968).

What, then, is the path that leads beyond the critical and creative failings of the past? According to Gates, it lies in a semiotic understanding of literature as a "system" of signs that stand in an "arbitrary" relationship to social reality (pp. 64–68). Having drawn a semiotic circle around literature, however, he moves rapidly to disclaim the notion that literature as a "system" is radically distinct from other domains of culture:

> It is not, of course, that literature is unrelated to culture, to other disciplines, or even to other arts; it is not that words and usage somehow exist in a vacuum or that the literary work of art occupies an ideal or reified, privileged status, the province of some elite cult of culture. It is just that the literary work of art is a system of signs that may be decoded with various methods, all of which assume the fundamental unity of form and content and all of which demand close reading. [p. 64]

The epistemology on which this description rests is stated as follows:

> . . . perceptions of reality are in no sense absolute; reality is a function of our senses. Writers present models of reality, rather than a description of it, though obviously the two may be related variously. In fact, fiction often contributes to cognition by providing models that highlight the nature of things precisely by their failure to coincide with it. Such certainly is the case in science fiction. [p. 66]

The semiotic notion of literature and culture implied by Gates seems to combine positivism (reality as a "function of our senses") with an ontology of signs that suggests they are somehow "natural" or "inherent" to human beings. If "reality" is, indeed, a function of our senses (surely an extraordinarily semiotically naive proposition), then observation and study of human physiological capacities should yield some comprehension of a subject's "reality." In truth, it is never brute physiological processes in themselves that interest Gates, but rather the operation of such processes under the conditions of "models" of cognition, which, of course, is a very different matter. If one begins, not with the phenomenal, but with the cognitive, then one is required to ask: How are cognitive "models" conceived, articulated, and transmitted in human cultures? Certainly one of the obvious answers here is *not* that human beings are *endowed* with a "system of signs," but rather that *models of cognition are conceived in, articulated through, and transmitted by language.* And like other systems of culture, language *is* a "social institution." Hence, if cognitive "models" of "fiction" differ from those of other spheres of human behavior, they do so not because fiction is somehow discontinuous with social institutions. In fact, it is the attempt to understand the coextensiveness of language as a social institution and literature as a system within it that constitutes a defining project of literary-theoretical study in our day.

When, therefore, Gates proposes metaphysical and behavioral models that suggest that literature, or even a single text (p. 67), exists as a structured "world" ("a system of signs") that can be comprehended without reference to "social institutions," he is misguided in his claims, appearing only vaguely aware of recent developments in literary study, symbolic anthropology, linguistics, the psychology of perception, and other related areas of intellectual inquiry. He seems, in fact, to have adopted, without qualification, a theory of the literary sign (of the "word" in a literary text) that presupposes a privileged status for the creative writer: "The black writer is the point of consciousness of his language" (p. 67). What this assertion means to Gates is that a writer is more capable than others in society of producing a "complex structure of meanings" — a linguistic structure that (presumably) corresponds more closely than those produced by nonwriters to the organizing principles by which a group's world view operates in consciousness (p. 67).

How can a writer achieve this end unless he is fully aware of language *as a social institution* and of the relationship language bears to other institutions that create, shape, maintain, and transmit a society's "organizing principles"? Surely Gates does not want to suggest that the mind of the writer is an autonomous semantic domain where complex structures are conceived and maintained "nonlinguistically." On the other hand, if such structures of meaning are, in fact, "complex" *because* they are linguistically maintained, then so are similar structures conceived by nonwriters.

That is to say, Gates renders but small service to the office of theoretical distinction when he

states that "a poem is above all atemporal and must cohere at a symbolic level, if it coheres at all" (p. 60), or when he posits that "literature approaches its richest development when its 'presentational symbolism' (as opposed by Suzanne Langer to its 'literal discourse') cannot be reduced to the form of a literal proposition" (p. 66). The reason such sober generalities contribute little to an understanding of literature, of course, is that Gates provides no informed notion of the nature of "literal discourse." He fails to admit both its social-institutional status and its fundamental existence as a symbolic system.

On what basis, then, except a somewhat naive belief in the explanatory power of semiotics can Gates suggest a radical disjunction between literature and other modes of linguistic behavior in a culture? The critic who attempted to pattern his work on Gates's model would find himself confronted by a theory of language, literature, and culture that suggests that "literary" meanings are conceived in a nonsocial, noninstitutional manner by the "point of consciousness" of a language and maintained and transmitted, without an agent, within a closed circle of "intertextuality" (p. 68). It does seem, therefore, that despite his disclaimer, Gates feels "literature is unrelated to culture." For culture consists in the interplay of various human symbolic systems, an interplay that is essential to the production and comprehension of meaning. Gates's independent literary domain, which produces meanings from some mysteriously nonsocial, noninstitutional medium, bears no relationship to such a process. . . .

Gates's formulations, however, imply an ideal critic whose readings would summon knowledge only from the *literary system* of Afro-America. The semantics endorsed by his ideal critic would *not* be those of a culture. They would be the specially consecrated meanings of an intertextual world of "written art."

The emphasis on close reading (p. 64) in Gates's formulations, therefore, might justifiably be designated a call for a *closed* reading of selected Afro-American written texts. In fact, Gates implies that the very defining criteria of a culture may be extrapolated from selected written, literary texts rather than vice versa (p. 62). For example, if any Afro-American literary artist has entertained the notion of "frontier," then he feels that "frontier" as a notion must have defining force in Afro-America culture (pp. 63–64). Only by ignoring the mass or vernacular level of Afro-America and holding up the "message" of literary works of art by, say, Ralph Ellison and Ishmael Reed as normative utterances in Afro-American culture can Gates support such a claim. His claim is thus a function of a privileged status granted to the writer and an elite status bestowed on the literary uses of language (p. 62).

But if it is true that scholarly investigations of an Afro-American expressive tradition must begin at a vernacular level — at the level of the "forms of things unknown" — then Gates's claim that "frontier" has defining force in Afro-America would have to be supported by the testimony of, say, the blues, work songs, or early folktales of Afro-America. And emphasis on "frontier," in the sense suggested by Frederick Jackson Turner, is scarcely discernible in such cultural manifestations of Afro-America.

Gates, however, is interested only in what *writers* (as "points of consciousness") have to say, and he seems to feel no obligation to turn to Afro-American folklore. In fact, when he comments on Henderson's formulations on Afro-American folk language,[2] or vernacular, he reveals not only a lack of interest in folk processes but also profound misconceptions about the nature of Afro-American language itself.

[2]Stephen E. Henderson (1925–1997), associated with the Black Aesthetic movement, was author of *The Militant Black Writer in Africa and the United States* (1969), and *Understanding the New Black Poetry: Black Speech and Black Music as Poetic References* (1973).

Rey Chow

b. 1957

Born in Hong Kong and educated at British colonial and American institutions, Rey Chow received her Ph.D. in modern thought and literature from Stanford University. She taught at the University of Minnesota and the University of California at Irvine before becoming Andrew W. Mellon Professor of the Humanities at Brown University. Her many publications, which have been widely anthologized and translated into major Asian and European languages, include Woman and Chinese Modernity: The Politics of Reading between West and East *(1991),* Writing Diaspora: Tactics of Intervention in Contemporary Cultural Studies *(1993),* Primitive Passions: Visuality, Sexuality, Ethnography, and Contemporary Chinese Cinema *(1995),* Ethics After Idealism: Theory-Culture-Ethnicity-Reading *(1998), and* The Protestant Ethic and the Spirit of Capitalism *(2002). She is also the editor of the collection* Modern Chinese Literary and Cultural Studies in the Age of Theory: Reimagining a Field *(2001). A new book,* The Age of the World Target: Self-Referentiality in War, Theory, and Comparative Work, *will be published in 2006. The following essay, "The Interruption of Referentiality: Poststructuralism and the Conundrum of Critical Multiculturalism," was originally published in the winter 2002 issue of* The South Atlantic Quarterly.

The Interruption of Referentiality:
Poststructuralism and the Conundrum
of Critical Multiculturalism

In the increasingly globalized realm of theoretical discourse, a habitual move may be readily discerned in critical discussions regarding marginalized groups and non-Western cultures: the critic makes a gesture toward Western theory, but only in such a way as to advance the point that such theory is inadequate, negligent, and Eurocentric. As a consequence, what legitimates concern for the particular group, identity, or ethnic culture under discussion (which for the purposes of this essay I will simply call *X*) is its historical, cultural, gendered difference, which becomes, in terms of the theoretical strategies involved, the basis for the claim of opposition and resistance. Epistemologically, what is specific to *X* — that is, local, history-bound, culturally unique — is imagined to pose a certain challenge to Western theory; hence the frequent adoption of the vocabulary of contestation, disruption, critique, and so forth. I refrain from references to particular authors whose works fall into such critical patterns because the point is not to show individuals up for their theoretical shortcomings.[1] Rather, it would be more productive to delineate a general picture of the predicament we face collectively as scholars whose intellectual lives have been deeply affected both by the presence of theory and by the reactions to theory in the past few decades.

I use the term *theory* to mark the paradigm shift introduced by poststructuralism, whereby the study of language, literature, and cultural forms becomes irrevocably obligated to attend to the semiotic operations involved in the production of meanings, meanings that can no longer be assumed to be natural. Obviously there are other types of theories that have had great impact on large numbers of academic intellectuals — one thinks of the cultural writings of the Frankfurt School critics,

various forms of historicisms, or sociological and anthropological theories, for instance — but it is arguably poststructuralism, with its tenacious attention to the materiality of human signification, that has generated some of the most far-reaching ramifications for the ways we approach questions of objectivity and questions of subjectivity alike.

The one indisputable accomplishment of poststructuralist theory in the past several decades has been its systematic unsettling of the stability of meaning, its interruption of referentiality. If such meaning had never been entirely stable even in pretheory days, what poststructuralist theory provides is a metalanguage in which it (meaning) can now be defined anew as a repetitive effect produced in the chain of signification in the form of an exact but illusory correspondence between signifier and signified. While referentiality as such may continue to exist, for the new metalanguage it is the movements in the realm of signification that matter, that command critical interest as the (shifting) basis for meaning. Henceforth, *meaning* is a term that occurs within scare quotes. With the emphasis on material signifiers comes the determining function of difference — to be further differentiated as both differing and deferring — which would from now on take the place of sameness and identity as the condition for signification. Ferdinand de Saussure's summary statements may be conveniently recalled here: "In language there are only differences. Even more important: a difference generally implies positive terms between which the difference is set up; but in language there are only differences *without positive terms.*" "*Language is a form and not a substance.*"[2] The foregrounding of differencing

---

[1] Barbara Christian's "The Race for Theory" (see p. 1859) and its responses are in this tradition.

[2] Ferdinand de Saussure, *Course in General Linguistics*, intro. Jonathan Culler, ed. Charles Bally and Albert Sechehaye in collaboration with Albert Reidlinger, trans. Wade Baskin (Glasgow: Collins, 1974), 120, 122; emphases in the original. [Chow] For Saussure, see p. 841.

means that it is no longer possible to speak casually about any anchorage for meaning. If intelligibility itself is now understood as the effect of a movement of differencing, a movement that always involves delays and deferrals, then no longer can the old-fashioned belief in epistemological groundedness hold. In its stead the conception of (linguistic) identity becomes structurally defined, with (linguistic) signifiers mutually dependent on one another for the generation of what makes sense. Rather than being that which follows identity, difference now precedes identity. It is difference that creates an object of study.

It is necessary, in any consideration of the vicissitudes of theory, to acknowledge the substantial impact made by poststructuralism's landmark demotion and refusal of referentiality. The exercise of bracketing referentiality is enormously useful because adherence to referentiality has often led to a conservative clinging to a "reality" that is presumed to exist, in some unchanging manner, independently of language and signification. This a priori real world is, moreover, often given the authority of what authenticates, of what bestows the value of transcendental truth on language and signification. The dismantling of such a metaphysics of presence is hence most effective in disciplines in which the presumption of a factographic form of knowing has traditionally gone uncontested (as in some practices of history, for instance), but it is groundbreaking also in areas in which the naturalness of an object of knowledge — such as literature, for instance — has seldom been put into question. By intensifying our awareness of (linguistic) signification as first and foremost *self-referential*, poststructuralist theory opens a way for the ingrained ideological presuppositions behind such practices of knowledge production to be rethought.

From these fundamental revelations of poststructuralism, many critics have gone on pragmatically to explore differencing and its liberating egalitarianism in various social and historical contexts. They do so, for instance, by translating the open-endedness of linguistic signification into the fluidity of the human subject. When transplanted into the tradition of individualism, significatory differencing quite logically means the multiplication of selves. Nowadays, what is commonly referred to as identity politics typically takes as its point of departure the problematizing and critiquing of essentialist notions that are attached to personhood, subjectivity, and identity formation.[3] Such branching off from high theory into democratic investigations of selfhood (through a thematization of differencing) is in many cases justifiable, but it has also left certain problems intact. In this regard I think it is important not simply to practice antiessentialist differencing ad infinitum but also to reconsider such a practice in conjunction with the rejection of referentiality that lies at the origins of poststructuralism. Exactly what is being thrown out when referentiality is theoretically rejected? I hope the significance of this point will become clear as I move through my arguments, for it bears on what I think is the conundrum in the critical study of marginalized groups and non-Western cultures today.

To begin, let me briefly revisit the question of how poststructuralist theory has methodologically radicalized the very production not only of the subject but also of the notion of an object of study. Albeit discussed much less frequently these days (simply because objectivity itself, it is assumed, can no longer be assumed), the issues that surround this topic remain instructive.

Consider the discipline of literature, for which one ongoing concern on which poststructuralist theory has helped to shed light is the problem of literariness, of what is specific to literature. At one level, this is of course precisely a question about referentiality. What is literature all about? To what does it refer? What reality does it represent? Old-fashioned though it may sound, such a preoccupation with literariness has surprising affinities with the contemporary cultural politics that clusters around identity. Let us retrace some of the well-known attempts at approaching this problem.

Marx's and Engels's discussion of literary writing and aesthetic representation provides a good

[3]The greatly influential work of Judith Butler is exemplary in this regard. [Chow] See Butler, p. 1707.

instance of this because it is contextualized in their more general concern for social revolution and radical political practice. In their exchanges with authors seeking advice on writing fiction, Marx and Engels, we remember, made some rather startling statements.[4] Albeit theoretically forward looking, they were careful to warn these writers against turning literature into socialist propaganda in which fictional characters simply become mouthpieces for revolutionary doctrines. "The solution of the problem," writes Engels, "must become manifest from the situation and the action themselves without being expressly pointed out and . . . the author is not obliged to serve the reader on a platter the future historical resolution of the social conflicts which he describes."[5] Embedded in these brief remarks is an intuitive sense that theoretical and literary discourses are distinguished from each other by an essential articulatory difference, and that literary discourse, which specializes in indirection, can only become dull and mediocre should one turn it into a platform for direct proletarian pronouncements. Even where the subject matter cries out for justice to be done on some people's behalf, literary writing, they suggest, tends to accomplish its task more effectively when it does not explicitly solicit the reader's sympathy as such. In literature, the modus operandi is not to speak about something expressly even when one feels one

must, in a manner quite opposite the clarity and forthrightness of theoretical argumentation. "The more the opinions of the author remain hidden, the better for the work of art";[6] in other words, a very different kind of power for producing change is in play. David Craig summarizes this point succinctly: "Surely, if literature affects action or changes someone's life, it is not by handing out a recipe for the applying but rather by disturbing us emotionally, mentally, because it *finds* us . . . , so that, after a series of such experiences and along with others that work with it, we feel an urge to 'do something' or at least to ask ourselves the question (the great question put by Chernyshevsky, Lenin, and Silone): 'What is to be done?' "[7]

What remains illuminating in these discussions is a perception of the work of indirection that seemed, to Marx and Engels at least, to be the unique characteristic of literary discourse; this is remarkable especially in light of their political belief in asserting the necessity to reform and revolutionize society, a belief that, in discursive terms, would be more in line with direct, straightforward, clear-cut expression — the very antithesis of their observations about literary writing. As political theorists, Marx and Engels nonetheless recognized that literary production could not be reduced to a mechanical mirroring of some reality out there, and that whatever literature is "about," such referentiality occurs, by definition, in a refracted manner rather than by straightforward declaration.[8]

In subsequent debates it was the critics who were overtly concerned with form (rather than with politics) who would continue the elaboration of this observation of literature-as-indirection, even though indirection was now theorized in different terms. For instance, the Russian Formalists' effort in defining the defamiliarizing

[4]For useful discussions of the problematic of (aesthetic) reflection in Marxist theory, see, for instance, Pierre Macherey, *A Theory of Literary Production*, trans. Geoffrey Wall (London: Routledge, 1978), and Terry Eagleton, *Criticism and Ideology* (London: Verso, 1978). For related discussions, see Henri Arvon, *Marxist Esthetics*, trans. Helen R. Lane, intro. Fredric Jameson (Ithaca: Cornell University Press, 1973); *Marxism and Art: Essays Classic and Contemporary*, selected and with historical and critical commentary by Maynard Solomon (New York: Knopf, 1973); and Theodor Adorno, Walter Benjamin, Ernst Bloch, Bertolt Brecht, and Georg Lukács, *Aesthetics and Politics*, afterword by Fredric Jameson, trans. Ronald Taylor (London: Verso, 1980), as well as the essays in David Craig, ed., *Marxists on Literature: An Anthology* (New York: Penguin, 1975). [Chow]

[5]Friedrich Engels, "Letter to Minna Kautsky," in Craig, *Marxists on Literature*, 268. See also chaps. 8, 9 (Marx's and Engels's letters to Lasalle), and 13 (Engels's letter to Margaret Harkness), all reprinted from Karl Marx and Friedrich Engels, *Selected Correspondence* (Moscow: n.p., n.d.). [Chow]

[6]Engels, "Letter to Margaret Harkness," in Craig, *Marxists on Literature*, 270. [Chow]

[7]David Craig, introduction to Craig, *Marxists on Literature*, 22. [Chow]

[8]Pierre Macherey's discussion of Lenin's reading of Leo Tolstoy (and the question of reflection in Tolstoy's works) remains one of the most illuminating accounts in this regard. See Macherey, *Theory of Literary Production*, 105–35, 299–323. [Chow]

capacity of art and literature — of art's capacity for presenting something familiar in such a manner as to call attention to its "artfulness," or its capacity for taking readers by surprise through the process of de-formation — can in retrospect be understood as an attempt to identify, perhaps to construct, a kind of rupture and distance from within a conventional discourse, so that the shock and alienating effect produced can be described as what is specific to art and literary expression.[9] Such shock and alienation, again, are not a matter of direct expression but, rather, of a sensitively perceived differential — the more implicitly the differential is grasped, the greater the effect of artfulness and literariness — so much so that the art object itself takes on only secondary importance.

In the Anglo-American world the literary-theoretical avant-garde of the twentieth century was represented by New Criticism, which specializes in the discernment of a literary work's specificity through close reading.[10] The contradiction between the aim and the practice of New Criticism has been well noted. Between the nostalgic desire to produce a complete, intrinsic reading that would exemplify the literary work as a self-sufficient world with rules that apply only to itself,[11] on the one hand, and the ambiguous open-endedness of meaning that results ironically from such desire-in-practice, on the other, lies the aporia that becomes, for a deconstructive critic such as Paul de Man, New Criticism's unwitting self-undoing. De Man demonstrates this by reintroducing the dimension of temporality — hence of postponements, deferrals, and belatedness — in the process of coming to terms with literary discourse: "The temporal factor, so persistently forgotten, should remind us that the form is never anything but a process on its way to completion."[12] Whereas New Criticism is still invested in a kind of time-less reading of the work of literature, a reading that circumvents temporality by the ideological projection of the work's organic wholeness, deconstruction would distinguish its comparable interest in literary specificity by underscoring the effects of time as manifested through the negative momentum of language. In de Man's hands, the previous attempts to get at literature's indirectness culminate in a sophisticated reformulation by way of the originary constitutive role of temporal difference, one that consistently undermines textual presence and plenitude.[13] If literature is indirect, defamiliarizing, ambiguous, ironic, allegorical, and so forth — if, in other words, it is never straight-forwardly referential — it is because human linguistic signification itself is always already mediated by the slow but indismissible labor of temporality.

But the perception of time alone does not necessarily account for the derailing of reference. One is reminded of the great humanist literary critic Erich Auerbach,[14] for instance, for whom the noticeable temporal shifts in modernist literary representation, shifts he describes with animation and verve, nonetheless do not challenge the basic idea that there exists something common to all of our lives even in the midst of diversities.[15] From a poststructuralist, difference-oriented perspective, this statement from the end of Auerbach's *Mimesis* is quite astonishing,

[9]See Shklovsky, p. 774.

[10]For New Criticism, see p. 749.

[11]See John Bender and David E. Wellbery, "Rhetoricality: On the Modernist Return of Rhetoric," in *The Ends of Rhetoric: History, Theory, Practice*, ed. John Bender and David E. Wellbery (Stanford, Calif.: Stanford University Press, 1990), 3–39. The authors see modernist rhetoricality, with its emphasis on the groundlessness of truth, as a legacy of Friedrich Nietzsche. [Chow]

[12]Paul de Man, "Form and Intent in the American New Criticism," "The Rhetoric of Temporality," and "The Dead-End of Formalist Criticism," in *Blindness and Insight: Essays in the Rhetoric of Contemporary Criticism*, 2d ed., rev., intro. Wlad Godzich (Minneapolis: University of Minnesota Press, 1983), 20–35, 187–228, 299–45. The quotation is on p. 31. [Chow]

[13]See the introduction to Structuralism and Deconstruction, p. 835.

[14]For Auerbach, see p. 702.

[15]Erich Auerbach, *Mimesis: The Representation of Reality in Western Literature*, trans. Willard R. Trask (Princeton, N.J.: Princeton University Press, 1953). See especially his perceptive discussion of Virginia Woolf, in whose work, as he notes, external events often have only the vaguest contours while the rich and sensitively registered internal time of the characters has led to the abdication of authorial objectivity and hegemony. [Chow]

particularly in view of the sensitive close readings he has performed:

> The more it is exploited, the more the elementary things which our lives have in common come to light. The more numerous, varied, and simple the people are who appear as subjects of such random moments, the more effectively must what they have in common shine forth. In this unprejudiced and exploratory type of representation we cannot but see to what an extent — below the surface conflicts — the differences between men's ways of life and forms of thought have already lessened. The strata of societies and their different ways of life have become inextricably mingled. There are no longer even exotic peoples. A century ago (in Mérimée for example), Corsicans or Spaniards were still exotic; today the term would be quite unsuitable for Pearl Buck's Chinese peasants.[16]

In spite of his grasp of the changes in literary, representational time, referentiality itself is not a problem for Auerbach because he remains convinced of a universal something called human reality. Mimesis is simply a way of accessing it; accessibility itself is not an issue.

The contribution made by poststructuralist theory, then, lies not merely in its articulation of temporality but also in its insistence that time does not coincide with itself. This recurrent slippage and intrinsic irreconcilability — between speaking and writing, between sign and meaning, and between fiction and reality — allows deconstructionist critics to assert that deconstruction is a rigorously historical process. As Geoff Bennington writes, "Deconstruction, insofar as it insists on the necessary non-coincidence of the present with itself, is in fact in some senses the most historical of discourses imaginable."[17] For Marian Hobson, the point of deconstruction-as-history is precisely that identity is never possible and that such impossibility is itself plural: "It is trace, track, which makes identity impossible. But this impossibility is itself plural, not simple. It is not a straight negative — not simple, identical,

non-identity. Trace, lack of self-coincidence, is on the contrary a plurality of impossibilities, a disjunction of negatives."[18] If conventional practices of history may be criticized on the basis of a premature projection of the referent, deconstruction's response is that history resides, rather, in the permanently self-undermining process of differentiation, a process that, by the sheer force of its logic, need not have an end in sight.

This potential alliance between the lack of (temporal and ontological) self-presence and differentiation-as-historicity is one major reason poststructuralism has left such indelible imprints on those areas of knowledge production that do not at first seem to have much to do with semiotics or, for that matter, with the revamping of metalanguages, but that are intimately linked to empirical issues such as culture and group identity. It is not difficult to see that the basic tenets of structuralist linguistics and semiotics — difference, identity, value, arbitrariness, convention, and systematicity — carry within them connotations that have resonances well beyond the terrain of a narrow sense of language. With the bracketing of the object of knowledge and the foregrounding of the process of signification, as introduced by poststructuralism, it is inevitable that the certitude of the identities involved — epistemological, subjective, or collective — can no longer be safely taken for granted. It is not surprising, therefore, that one of the most prevalent uses of the poststructuralist metalanguage of differencing is to be found in areas in which existential identity is most at stake: multiculturalism, postcoloniality, and ethnicity.[19]

If this is the case, how is it that in these areas of study there is currently also a persistent refrain that non-Western subjects and subject matters are "oppositional" and "resistant" to Western theory? About fifteen to twenty years ago, even though

---

[16] Ibid., 552. [Chow]

[17] Geoff Bennington, "Demanding History," in *Post-structuralism and the Question of History*, ed. Derek Attridge, Geoff Bennington, and Robert Young (New York: Cambridge University Press, 1987), 17. [Chow]

[18] Marian Hobson, "History Traces," in Attridge, Bennington, and Young, *Post-structuralism and the Question of History*, 102–3. [Chow]

[19] I discuss this in greater detail in "The Secrets of Ethnic Abjection," in *Traces* 2 (2001): 53–77. A few passages from that essay have been incorporated with modifications into the present one. [Chow]

the same ambivalent gesture toward the West might have been made, theory itself was not an issue. Nowadays, as can be surmised from journals, conferences, anthologies, and single-author publications, not only are more trendy topics such as transgender politics, Asian pop music, Third World urban geography, or cultural translation obligated to gesture toward one kind of Western theory or another; even the study of ancient ethnic poems and narratives must, in order to argue the case of their uniqueness, their beyond-comparison status, somehow demonstrate an awareness of the background of Western theoretical issues. If all this is testimony to the hegemony enjoyed by Western theory, why are claims of resistance and opposition at the same time so adamant?

If the exploration of literary difference was in order to ground literary specificity — that is, to define literature as an object with its essential attributes, attributes that make literature definitively unlike anything else — then one of the consequences of such exploration is, ironically, the dissipation of this "object" altogether. From the nineteenth-century perception of its essence (in Marx and Engels) as indirection to the late-twentieth-century assertion (by deconstructionist critics) of its noncoincidence with itself, the object of literariness seems to have become theoretically unsustainable exactly at the moment of its concrete definition: it "is" what it always is not. If the ongoing efforts to define literary difference have brought to light all that has been repressed, neglected, or ignored, such efforts have also shown how literature does not and cannot stop at the mere restoration or redemption of such difference. Inevitably, difference as such will continue to fragment and dismantle whatever specificity that may have been established through it, once again rendering the goal of stable objectification impossible.

Permanent differentiation and permanent impermanence: these are the key features of post-structuralist theoretical practice as we find it today. The example of literature has simply demonstrated the Pyrrhic victory[20] of the scientific or social scientific attempt to produce an object of

[20]An apparent victory that is actually a defeat.

knowledge by way of differencing. If literariness is that which tends to disappear into something else at the moment of its being objectified, then literature is, ultimately, a historically mobile, changing relationship (of writing) rather than a concrete essence. Might this lesson about literariness be extended beyond the discipline of literature?

Consider now the study of X, those areas that, as I mentioned at the beginning, often attain visibility by gesturing toward and resisting Western theory at the same time. As in the case of literariness, we may set out to define X as an object with certain attributes. But we already know from the example of literariness that such an attempt at discovering the specificity of X will lead first to the process of differencing and eventually to the dissipation of X itself as a stable referent. Should we then say that, ultimately, X as such does not exist, that X, like literariness, is a permanently shifting, non-self-identical relationship? What might be the implications of proclaiming, let us say, that African American, Asian American, and gay and lesbian specificities do not exist? Such proclamations are, to be sure, intolerable to many, but it is perhaps less because these "people" really do exist than because the theoretical claim for their existence is inseparable from the hierarchical politics of race, class, gender, and ethnicity that structure Western and non-Western societies alike. In the face of the practical struggles that go on daily against different forms of social injustice, it is, for many, unacceptable to declare, in accordance with poststructuralist theoretical logic, that these versions of X do not exist. Yet the alternative — the insistence that they are real, that they are out there, that their empirical existence is absolutely incontestable, and that they are thus a core from which to stage resistance to the virtual claims of high theory — is equally untenable because it is theoretically naive.

The conundrum we face today in the wake of theory may thus be described as follows: In their attempts to argue the specificity of their objects of study, critics of marginalized historical areas often must rhetorically assert their resistance to or distrust of Western theory. But what exactly is the nature of that which they are resisting and distrusting? As these critics try to defend the viability of their proposed objects, they are compelled, against their own proclaimed beliefs, to set into motion precisely the poststructuralist operation of differencing, of making essentialist categories of identity disintegrate. Indeed, differencing is often the very weapon with which they mount their criticisms of Western theory. While they criticize Western theory, then, these critics are meanwhile implementing the bracketing of anchored, referential meanings that constitutes one of contemporary Western theory's most profound influences. Since there is nothing inherent in the methodological mechanism of structural differentiation that calls for resistance or differentiation at a level beyond the chain of signification, the objects to which these critics cling — in resistance — inevitably dissipate over time in a manner similar to that in which the object of literariness dissipates. To truly argue for resistance, they would in fact need to go against or abandon altogether the very theoretical premises (of poststructuralist differencing) on which they make their criticisms in the first place.[21]

Put in a different way, the attempt to argue the specificity of X as such, even as it discredits Western theory, tends to reproduce the very terms — and the very problems — that once surrounded the theoretical investigation of literariness. Like literature, X is often constructed (negatively) as what defamiliarizes, what departs from conventional expectations, what disrupts the norm, and so forth, terms that are invested in constructing specificity by way of differentiation. Like the attempt to define literariness also, the attempt to define X seems doomed to destroy its own object in the process of objectification. More disturbing still, if representation of X as such is recognizable in these similar theoretical terms, does it not mean that there is no essential difference between X and high theory — that the articulation of X, however historically specific it may be, is somehow already *within* the trajectory mapped out by high theory?

This is the juncture at which a rethinking of poststructuralist theory is in order, not once

again by way of temporal differencing but, more significantly, by way of reexamining theory's interruption of referentiality. By bracketing referentiality, separating it from the signified, and making the signified part of the chain of signification and an effect produced by the play of signifiers, poststructuralism has devised an epistemological framework in which what lies "outside" can be recoded as what is inside. There is hence no outside to the text. At the same time, however, this also means that poststructuralism really does not offer a way of thinking about any outside except by reprogramming it into part of an ongoing interior (chain) condition. This is not exactly the same as saying that poststructuralism is a closed system of permutations; rather, it is simply that its mechanism of motility, which provides a set of terms that redefines referentiality effectively as the illusion produced by the play of temporal differences, also tends to preclude any other way of getting at the outside than by directing it inward. My point, then, is this: rather than systematicity per se (which was the problem characteristic of structuralism), the problem here is perhaps none other than temporality rendered as nonpresence.

Although it constitutes what is arguably poststructuralism's most radical intervention in European thought, the notion of time's noncoincidence with itself may nevertheless have a substantially contrary set of reverberations once we go beyond the parameters of Europe. Where otherness stands as an empirical and a cultural as well as a theoretical issue, the assertion of temporal disjunction as such (as an absolute force that structures all signification) may coincide, or become complicit, with the anthropological problematic that Johannes Fabian has called, in his well-known phrase, the denial of coevalness — *"a persistent and systematic tendency to place the referent(s) of anthropology in a Time other than the present of the producer of anthropological discourse."*[22]

---

[21]For a succinct critique of the contradictions that accompany poststructuralist theory and that have had a profound impact on the multiculturalist trends in the humanities, see Masao Miyoshi, "Ivory Tower in Escrow," *boundary 2* 27.1 (2000), in particular 39–50. [Chow]

[22]Johannes Fabian, *Time and the Other: How Anthropology Makes Its Object* (New York: Columbia University Press, 1983), 31; emphasis in the original. [Chow] To put Fabian's point crudely, anthropologists' discourse about "primitive" peoples implicitly suggests that they somehow belong to a time earlier than that of the observer.

In other words, whereas the insistence on the noncoincidence of the present with itself may indeed be a revolutionary charge within the philosophical and epistemological terrains from which poststructuralism stems, such an insistence, when seen in light of Europe's history with its colonized others, may turn out to be no more than another current of what Fabian calls allochronic discourse, in which other peoples who are our contemporaries are discursively confined each to their culture gardens/ethnic ghettos, in the name, precisely, of difference. Be it temporal, ontological, linguistic, or identitarian, noncoincidence can hardly be considered groundbreaking in the global circuits of colonialism and imperialism because the non-Western others are already, by definition, classified as noncoincident, discontinuous, and fundamentally different (from populations in the West, from the times and languages of Western ethnographers). To emphasize noncoincidence as such is thus merely to reify and raise to the level of metalanguage a rather conventional anthropological attitude toward the other's otherness — which is often unproblematically upheld as a fact — without actually confronting the conditions that enable such assumptions of noncoincidence to stand in the first place. Referring to the relevance of Fabian's work for the study of colonial America, for instance, Carlos Alonso comments on one such manifestation of the (principle of) noncoincidence inherent to the rhetoric of temporality — the expression of amazement: "Europe's rhetoric of amazement vis-à-vis America . . . necessitates the ceaseless deferral of total cognitive mastery. But rather than being deployed in order to maintain an irreducible alterity, the European figuration of the New World as new posited a continuity between itself and the new territories that made possible European appropriation of the recently discovered lands while simultaneously affirming their exoticism."[23]

Let me push my point one step further: the definition of time as non-coincidental with itself, I would like to suggest, means that poststructuralism ultimately does not offer any viable way of

thinking about an *act of exclusion* except by recoding it as a (passive) *condition of exteriority*. Once recoded (in the form of an "always already"), this condition is channeled into an existing interior in such a manner as to become part of this interior's infinite series of differentiations over time, always open ended and incomplete, always ready for further differentiation to be sure, yet never again directed at the primary, originary moment involving the as yet unresolved outside. At the level of metalanguage, this outside, or what has been banished there, is none other than referentiality, which must henceforth live the life of the exiled, the exotic, and the exorcised — that which is barred once and for all from entering, from migrating into the interior of, the chain of signification.

It follows that when one is dealing with sexual, cultural, and ethnic others, it is always considered premature in poststructuralist theory to name and identify such references as such; instead, deconstruction's preferred benevolent gesture is to displace and postpone these others to a utopian, unrealizable realm, to a spectral dimension whose radicalness lies precisely in its spectrality, the fact that it cannot materialize *in the present*. Again, Alonso's observations about the discursive place occupied by America in the European imagination during the colonial epoch are pointedly on the mark. From being perceived as novel, he writes, America gradually shifted into the position of the future:

> Almost imperceptibly, the coevalness that the narrative of newness required was replaced by a narrative paradigm in which America occupied a position of *futurity* vis-à-vis the Old World. This transformation from novelty to futurity was significant because, among other things, it created the conditions for a permanent exoticization of the New World — the sort that cannot be undermined or dissolved by actual experience or objective analysis: safely ensconced in an always postponed future, America could become the object of a ceaselessly regenerating discourse of mystification and perpetual promise.[24]

This inability to deal with the other except by temporal displacement returns us to the scenario

[23]Carlos J. Alonso, *The Burden of Modernity: The Rhetoric of Cultural Discourse in Spanish America* (New York: Oxford University Press, 1998), 7. [Chow]

[24]Ibid., 8; emphasis in the original. [Chow]

with which I began this essay. When scholars of marginalized groups and non-Western subjects rely on notions of resistance and opposition (to Western theory) in their attempts to argue the specificity of X, they are unwittingly reproducing the epistemological conundrum by which the specificity of an object of study is conceived of in terms of a differential — a differential, moreover, that has to be included in the chain of signification in order to be recognized. However, by virtue of its mechanism of postponement and displacement, this kind of logic implies the eventual dissolution of the object without being able to address *how* X presents not just a condition (exteriority) that has always already existed but more importantly an active politics of exclusion and discrimination. Within the bounds of this logic, the more resistive and oppositional (that is, on the outside) X is proclaimed to be, the more inevitably it is to lose its specificity (that is, become incorporated) in the larger framework of the systematic production of differences, while the circumstances that make this logic possible (that is, that enable it to unfold and progress as a self-regulating interior) remain unchallenged. This is one reason why so many new projects of articulating alternative identities, cultures, and group formations often seem so predictable in the end. Whether the topic under discussion is a particular ethnic work or the identity of an ethnic person, what has become predictable is precisely the invocation of "ambivalence," "multiplicity," "hybridity," "heterogeneity," "disruptiveness," "resistance," and the like, and no matter how new an object of study may appear to be, it is bound to lose its novelty once the play of temporal difference is set into motion. The moves permitted by the rules of the originary exclusion — the difference that makes the difference, as it were — have already been exhausted, and critics dealing with X can only repeatedly run up against the incommensurability between the experience of temporality as self-deconstruction (with its radical theoretical nuances) and the experience of temporality as allochronism (with its racialist anthropological ramifications).

In sum, contemporary uses of poststructuralist theory have tended to adopt poststructuralism's solution, differencing, without sufficiently reflecting on its flip side, its circumvention of exclusion. Yet contemporary issues of identity and cultural conflict almost invariably involve the politics of exclusion. Can these mutually incompatible states of affairs be reconciled with each other? How can they be reconciled? Can specificity be imagined in terms other than a naturalized differential, an automatized discontinuity? Are there perhaps forms of closure, limits, and references that should not be prematurely disavowed, because the act of disavowing them inevitably becomes a self-contradictory move, leading only to a theoretical impasse? (That is, the act of reprogramming everything as part of an interior inevitably becomes an act to exclude, with what is excluded being, first and foremost, the assertion of the violence of exclusion itself.)

The reference that is social injustice — itself a type of differential but a differential hierarchized with value — cannot be as easily postponed or displaced, because the mechanisms of postponement and displacement do not by themselves address the hierarchical or discriminatory nature of the differential involved. As a result, however permanently the issue may be deferred, the originary differential of inequality will not and cannot go away. The kind of theoretical mechanism that works by dissolving specificities into differences is therefore incapable of addressing the concerns implied here, because there is nothing inherent in such a mechanism that would necessitate the recognition of the inequality and injustice that may indeed, for lack of a better term, be "out there" yet that may not be immediately or entirely incorporable into the chain of signification. Referentiality, reformulated in this manner, may in the end require us to accept it precisely as the limit, the imperfect, irreducible difference that is not pure difference but difference thoroughly immersed in and corrupted by the errors and delusions of history.

For similar reasons, an awareness of historical asymmetries of power, aggression, social antagonism, inequality of representation, and their like cannot simply be accomplished through an adherence to the nebulous concept of resistance and opposition. That concept itself is often constituted with the logic of differentiation — of disruption and departure — within a theoretical framework whose success lies precisely in its perennial capacity for including and absorbing that which is on the outside. Resistance that imagines itself as purely premised on the outside is thus a futile exercise in the wake of poststructuralist theory. In its stead, it would be more productive to let referentiality interrupt, to reopen the poststructuralist closure on this issue, to acknowledge the inevitability of reference even in the most avant-garde of theoretical undertakings, and to demand a thorough reassessment of an originary act of repudiation/exclusion in terms that can begin to address the "scandal of domination and exploitation of one part of mankind by another."[25]

[25]Fabian, *Time and the Other*, x. In Miyoshi's terms, this would mean restoring the hitherto discredited function of so-called metanarratives: "The academics' work in this marketized world . . . is to learn and watch problems in as many sites as they can keep track of, not in any specific areas, nations, races, ages, genders, or cultures, but in all areas, nations, races, ages, genders, and cultures. In other words, far from abandoning the master narratives, the critics and scholars in the humanities must restore the public rigor of the metanarratives" ("Ivory Tower in Escrow," 49). [Chow]

10

THEORIZING POSTMODERNISM

What is postmodernism? How can we understand what it means to be "post"? One place to start is with definitions of *postmodernism* and the allied term, *postmodernity*, such as the deft characterizations of Terry Eagleton:

> Postmodernity is a style of thought which is suspicious of classical notions of truth, reason, identity, and objectivity, of the idea of universal progress or emancipation, of single frameworks, grand narratives or ultimate grounds of explanation. Against these Enlightenment norms, it sees the world as contingent, ungrounded, diverse, unstable, indeterminate, a set of disunified cultures or interpretations which breed a degree of skepticism about the objectivity of truth, history and norms, the givenness of natures and the coherence of identities. . . . Postmodernism is a style of culture . . . , a depthless, decentred, ungrounded, self-reflexive, playful, derivative, eclectic, pluralistic art which blurs the boundaries between "high" and "popular" cultures, as well as between art and everyday experience. (*The Illusions of Postmodernism*, vii)

Complicated as this may seem, it's quite a bit more complicated than that. "Postmodern" artistic creations are defined as a style system relative to modern artistic creations, but precisely what modernism means and how the distinction is drawn depends quite a bit on whether one is talking about prose fiction or drama or poetry, architecture or painting, longhair music or pop.

Many of the roots and branches of contemporary postmodern literary and cultural theory have already been discussed elsewhere, in chapters on deconstruction, Lacanian psychology, Marxism, gender theory, cultural studies, and postcolonialism. So here we can draw together some of the interconnections, cooperative and competitive, between these sets of ideas, for like the blind men with the elephant, each of these modes of theory will explain postmodernism differently. Theorizing postmodernism from the perspective of deconstruction, we would naturally emphasize the epistemological crisis in the representation of life by language, the breakdown of the distinction between words and things, the widening suspicion of the binary logic imposed by language on the world of experience. Lacanian psychology will view postmodernism in terms of its portrait of the human mind. It would reject as naive the modernist version of the mind — a solitary self creating the world in terms of its own unique vision, such as we see in Virginia Woolf. This for Lacan is the imaginary self-image formed during the Mirror Stage. The Lacanian version of the "self" is in fact deeply postmodern in character: a shifting, unstable subject position created in each of us by our fall into language. Theorists of gender or race or nationality would view postmodern culture as subverting the Enlightenment essentialization of "human nature," as a "universal" that is not universal at all, since this essence happens to be male, heterosexual, white, and of Western European origin. Marxists would tend to view postmodernism as a by-product of postindustrial capitalism, with its focus on consumerism rather than forms of production. It is not an accident, however, that the topic of postmodernism is of particular concern to thinkers influenced by Marx, who are likely to feel the need to explain any trend washed up by history, particularly a trend within which history itself is in danger of being washed up. Fortunately, Marxists are likely to disagree as much with each other as with non-Marxists, and all postmodern thinkers tend to be suspicious, not only of "Enlightenment norms" but also of other forms of postmodern thought. For some of the theorists in this chapter, postmodernism is a dreadful state into which we have fallen; for others, it is a turn into a liberating climate of thought. For some people, postmodernism means a liberation from the movement of history into an eclectic stylistic framework where rules of art no longer apply — and confine. And there are some people, like myself, who think that postmodernism may be something we will look back upon, like Dada, as a premature rebellion against modernist styles and cultural icons whose influence was becoming oppressive.

First, in what is bound to be a whirlwind tour of a huge subject, it seems important to take a brief look back at the history of the word *postmodern*. The *Oxford English Dictionary* finds the first usage of *postmodernism* in its contemporary sense in writing about architecture after World War II, by architects like Robert Venturi and Philip Johnson who were critical of the distant, abstract "modern" architecture of the Bauhaus and the International Style associated with Le Corbusier, Walter Gropius, and Mies van der Rohe, and searching for a new style that would celebrate pleasure rather than inspire respect and awe.[1] But as Hans Bertens has written, the term *postmodernism* begins to enter a continuous debate around the 1960s, in writings by poets and critics comparing post–World War II literature with the masterpieces of modernism written between 1918 and 1939. Poets like Charles Olson used the term *postmodern* to refer to a poetry of immediate experience that could restore human beings to their sensual place within nature, instead of imprisoning them in the conceptual structures of Western culture. Striking a similar note without actually using the term, the late Susan Sontag called for a literary criticism that would also celebrate the sensual pleasures of poetry, demanding an "erotics of art" to replace the hermeneutics of the Freudians and the New Critics, who busied themselves searching out the hidden meanings in symbolically encoded texts.[2]

[1] In different senses, the word has a much longer history than that, going back to the 1870s, and appearing in a book title in 1926 (Bertens, 20).

[2] See "Against Interpretation" in this book, p. 740.

One key early theorist of postmodernism was Ihab Hassan, who viewed exemplary texts of contemporary literature as descendants of a subversive strain "coiled within modernism," stemming from the disruptive rejection of language as representation in Mallarmé and Rimbaud. These poets, Hassan argues, led to the iconoclastic works of Alfred Jarry, André Breton and the Dadaists, and to the antihumanistic texts of Kafka and Beckett, and from there to the literary avant-garde of the 1960s, including Robbe-Grillet and his fellow practitioners of the most experimental branch of French fiction, the *nouveau roman*. Leslie Fiedler, also writing in the 1960s, focuses on America rather than Europe, but Fiedler views postmodernism as an opposition to modernism rather than as an extension of one side of it. His new age centers on popular literature serving a "post-white" and "post-male" youth culture that has turned against whiteness and masculinity. This literature is antirationalistic, aimed at pleasure, and parodic of canonical texts, turning them into "vaudeville and burlesque." Nor does Fiedler seek his antimodern novel among the refined aporias of the *nouveau roman*, which are too anemic, too highbrow, and probably simply too French for his vision, but in early Barth, Pynchon, and Vonnegut, whose bawdy ramshackle texts lean on the conventions of subliterary genres like the thriller, the mystery story, or science fiction.

But mentioning only architecture and literature would distort the reach of the postmodern aesthetic in every other line of creative work: in music the minimalism of John Cage, the trance music of Philip Glass, the oneiric invocations of George Crumb, and postmodern pop music like that of Kraftwerk and Beck; in dance, the archly ironic styles of Pilobolus, Pina Bausch, Douglas Dunn, Meredith Monk; the pop creations of Andy Warhol, the dark conceptual sculptures of Joseph Beuys, the witty environments of Red Grooms, the entrancing video installations of Bill Viola.

What seems obvious from this listing, already hinted at in the Eagleton quotation, is the diversity and eclecticism of postmodern art. While it is hard to know exactly how the artistic scene appeared to people of earlier times, there seems to have been, at least from the middle of the eighteenth century until relatively recent times, a dominant style system, and, though not every creative artist was necessarily working within it, the highest prestige, within an aesthetic system dominated by the value of originality, derived from advancing its possibilities. Art produced within that style system has to be brought to what seems a peak of perfection, and shortly thereafter, perhaps, to a point of exhaustion, before the style system is abandoned for another, related system. Realist fiction in English (Trollope and Eliot and James) seemed to lead to naturalist fiction (Hardy and Dreiser) which led to modernist fiction (Joyce and Woolf). Realistic painting seemed to lead to impressionist painting, and then to abstract expressionism in the form of blots (Jackson Pollack) or of diagrams (Piet Mondrian). Baroque music seemed to lead naturally to the classical style, then to romantic and postromantic music.[3] But by some point during the twentieth century — different points for art, for music, and for literature — the whole idea of a single

---

[3] To take one example in detail: the "classical" style in Western music, exploiting a new system of tonality based on the "tempered" scale, runs from Johann Christian Bach through Haydn and early Beethoven, coming to a peak with Mozart. Early in the nineteenth century, "romantic" composers like Schubert and Beethoven began to exploit ambiguities in the system of tonality (enharmonic key changes), or to violate the expectations generated by the tonal system by adding dissonant notes that do not belong

dominant style system, led by an avant-garde of creative artists representing "the new" for that particular time, became a less and less useful description of what was going on within any of these major genres.[4] Fredric Jameson suggests that there was something oppressive about "the immense weight of seventy or eighty years of classical modernism. . . . The writers and artists of the present day will no longer be able to invent new styles and worlds — they've already been invented; only a limited number of combinations are possible; the unique ones have been thought of already."[5]

To put your finger on what all the incredibly diverse style systems in different art forms have in common requires soaring up to a very high level of generality. One key issue is what Linda Hutcheon calls "the presence of the past." Whereas the modernists followed Ezra Pound's precept "Make It New," postmodern creative personalities, aware perhaps that Pound was merely adapting a phrase from Confucius, prefer to make it old. They revisit the history of design, not out of a sense of emulation or even nostalgia (the way the Parisian Pantheon copied the original in Rome), but in a spirit of playful allusion and re-interpretation. "Parody," Hutcheon writes, "is a perfect postmodern form . . . for it paradoxically both incorporates and challenges that which it parodies."[6] For example, Philip Johnson's 1984 ATT Building in New York [now the Sony Building] caps a modernist skyscraper with a roof line inspired by an eighteenth-century Chippendale style broken-pediment desk, and continues these parodic quotations of eighteenth-century Enlightenment elegance within the grand lobby and throughout the interiors.

In narrative fiction, postmodern texts may be equally playful, using the techniques of modernist fiction while discarding its enabling assumptions. In texts like Barth's "Lost in the Funhouse," or Nabokov's *Pale Fire*, narrative technique becomes the self-conscious, self-reflexive vehicle for exploring the limits and paradoxes of storytelling itself. Robert Coover's *Briar Rose*, for example, retells and retells the familiar fairytale story of Sleeping Beauty, telling it from the point of view of Beauty, or the Prince, or the Evil Fairy; starting at the beginning or near the end; playing off the simple German version collected by the Brothers Grimm,

---

to the home key (chromaticism). By the end of the nineteenth century expressive chromaticism had gone so far (in Strauss and Mahler) that it exhausted the possibility of further play within the tonal system. This led to a new style system pioneered by Arnold Schönberg and Alban Berg: atonal music avoided any sense of a home key by treating equally each of the twelve notes of the tempered scale. But logical as the move from Mahler to Schönberg was, there was no general agreement to follow in that direction, and in particular Stravinsky seems to have experimented with just about everything, moving like a musical Picasso through a series of eclectic styles (some of which involved a revisiting of the past, either through primitivism, in his tone poem *The Rite of Spring*, or through neoclassicism, in the opera *Oedipus Rex*).

[4]Lyotard argues that "laughing at" the former avant-gardes in art is a mistake, because to heal the cultural neurosis of the present we need to understand our artistic past the way a psychiatric patient needs to understand and work through his own history. But his general position is that the former idea of an avant-garde no longer works.

[5]See Jameson, p. 1959.

[6]Some of Hutcheon's other generalizations apply only to particular cultural forms, such as her contention that postmodernism is "liminal," skating the fine line between fact and fiction. This may be true of many postmodern narratives—like her main example, Jerzy Kosinski's *Blind Date*, or Tim O'Brien's *The Things We Carried*. But it not only does not apply generally to postmodern narrative, it isn't even clear what such a claim might mean applied to postmodern architecture or postmodern music.

against the more literary French version of Charles Perrault, and against the brutal and outrageous Italian version of Giambattista Basile. One episode even explores (in ways we are not usually permitted in fairytales) what a castle full of people who have been sleeping for a hundred years without bathing is going to smell like. Ultimately the story, which started out as part of each of its reader's worlds, becomes a witty world of its own, a world of absurdly motionless women and absurdly dynamic men that reflects our own world as in a distorting mirror.

But postmodern fiction's wit may also turn serious, as it revisits history critically rather than playfully. J. M. Coetzee's novel *Foe* appears to be a historical fiction narrated by a female castaway who joins Robinson Crusoe and Friday on their island, escaping with them to England. Because it takes place partly in the fictional world Daniel Defoe created, and partly in Defoe's own world, Coetzee's novel plays with the boundaries of fact, fiction, and metafiction.[7] *Foe* alters and continues Defoe's story in ways that make us conscious, not only of the racism and imperialism that for centuries permitted English voyagers to enslave people of color around the world, but also of the patriarchal system that allows the merchant and writer Daniel Defoe to expropriate the narrative written by the female castaway. Part of Coetzee's point is that fiction like *Robinson Crusoe* became an element within the sense of the destiny of the British empire, which in turn inspired a history of which Coetzee, a white male South African, is deeply ashamed. We can find similar moves to revise fictional or historical texts in postmodern novels like Rhys's *Wide Sargasso Sea*, Pynchon's *Mason and Dixon*, Rushdie's *Midnight's Children*, and Doctorow's *Ragtime*.

This historical critique is described by French theorist Jean-François Lyotard in terms of the disengagement of postmodernity from what he calls the "metanarratives" which dominated Western thought through the modernist period.[8] By *metanarrative*, Lyotard means a story that we tell to organize history, one that predicts the future as well as helps us understand the past. And history is seen teleologically, as moving toward a desired end. The Christian metanarrative sees the world as a series of stages: after the Fall, humanity lives in a state of sin; at a key moment God comes to earth to redeem us through grace; after the crucifixion, humanity lives on awaiting the creation of a new heaven and earth, when time will end and eternity begin. The Enlightenment metanarrative is about the liberation of knowledge and science from superstition and religion, followed by the widening spread of literacy, the outbreak of material progress, the development of commerce and industry, leading, in the future, to ever greater material comforts, longer lives, and so on. The Marxist metanarrative is about history shaping itself through revolution, where the bourgeois revolution that displaced the feudal world will be followed, at some time in the future, by a proletarian revolution that will displace capitalism and usher in a rational society. These metanarratives not only help us understand the past and map out

---

[7]*Robinson Crusoe* (1719) was itself loosely based on the real-life adventures of Alexander Selkirk, who spent four years alone on an island off the coast of Chile, as related in Woodes Rogers's *Cruising Voyage* (1712).

[8]Confusingly, metanarratives are also sometimes referred to as "grand narratives" and "master-narratives."

the future, they serve the function of giving legitimacy to social action. Christians feel empowered to convert nonbelievers by force so they can share eternal life in the end time. Enlightened Europeans are obliged by their sense of humanity to change by any means necessary the social structures of the "primitive" peoples whom they encounter, bringing them into accord with the progressive spirit of modernity. Marxists obey the laws of history by destroying petit-bourgeois groups whose interests are felt to clash with those of the proletariat.

In "Defining the Postmodern," Lyotard argues that all these metanarratives legitimate through a vision of progress, and it is precisely that vision of progress, particularly development "through arts, technology, knowledge and liberty," about which people have become skeptical in the last few decades. If the Enlightenment metanarrative of emancipation through technology leads to Auschwitz, with its mechanization of death and annihilation of the non-Aryan body, we are right to be skeptical. Since World War II, Lyotard thinks, science and technology have become disengaged from the Enlightenment metanarrative, and researchers no longer care whether their discoveries will signify anything for humanity, but are nevertheless continuing to accumulate data and objects of knowledge out of some robotic "autonomous force." And as the world, or knowledge about the world, becomes ever more complex, it becomes ever more difficult to live in.

Lyotard's vision of the collapse of the metanarratives makes a kind of sense: one can understand why, as a French Marxist who experienced the collapse of communism in Europe, Lyotard would be eager to believe that humanity had become skeptical about metanarratives of progress. Many who are not French Marxists have begun to share the same skepticism.

On the other hand, the past decade has proven that technological, informational, and political progress is a fiction that has not entirely lost its charms. That science has become so complex that it is difficult to understand except by specialists is a longstanding complaint, but one that does not prevent scientists from inventing technologies that ordinary people put to use without necessarily understanding them. And the accumulated data on the Internet, quantitatively overwhelming when considered in the abstract, has given those with access to it greater control of available knowledge, including knowledge they use for the simple tasks of living. The United States is currently governed by people who seem to believe in the Enlightenment metanarrative of modernization and liberty, and who have used this metanarrative to legitimate a pre-emptive war in Iraq, hoping that democracy there will spread throughout the Arab world. (But of course there are competing versions of progress: we have not forgotten the existence of a large cadre, living perhaps far off in Afghanistan or perhaps in the housing complex next door, who have adopted a Jihadist metanarrative of Islam regaining its purity from the defiling filth of Western modernity.) Lyotard may have issued a death certificate for metanarratives too quickly.

For another French Marxist, Jean Baudrillard, the real death is the "death of the real" that proceeds from the prevalence of simulacra (unreal objects) and simulations (unreal signifiers). In an early book, *The System of Objects* (1968), Baudrillard had argued that capitalism since the end of World War II had been morphing into a new form, one based on consumption rather than production, in that the satisfactions and self-definition that used to come from work were now coming from leisure time activities. In theory this could be liberating: though alienated at work, and dependent upon capitalist bosses for their jobs, citizens could achieve satisfying self-definition through their own freely informed choices at play. In reality, though, workers are manipulated by images from mass media advertising creating desires for particular profitable forms of consumption. Jeans, for example, were at one time a way of opting out of the planned obsolescence of fashion; today we have "designer jeans" within the fashion system, and every teenager has to have the latest color and cut. What is called "popular music" has nothing to do with what is spontaneously created, but instead is manufactured to be a profitable consumer item, where the "singers" may be lip-synching the words, and where even the revolutionary lyrics of gangsta rap are co-opted to support the capitalist system. Choices are still available between different consumer goods, but capitalism through its control of media has taken over the process of defining their meaning. Since 1968 Baudrillard has extended his arguments about the destruction of the real. His argument in "Simulations" (1983) is that, while societies have always created simulated versions of the real (e.g., maps of a territory) as a necessary way of understanding the world, postmodern capitalism has inundated our mass society with third and fourth degree simulacra: objects that hide the absence of the real, and objects that have no reference to anything real but instead constitute a simulated form of reality itself. But these created simulacra are "hyperreal" — more real than any reality could be, and thus suck the life out of actual events.

Almost everything seen on television might be viewed as hyperreal simulacra, but Baudrillard singles out the 1975 PBS documentary series "An American Family," because it is larger-than-life fact rather than fiction, and because of the hypocritical pretense that the presence of the camera does not disturb, even provoke, the events it records. His take seems a prescient analysis of the current fad of "reality TV" here and elsewhere in the West, since the contest-shows masquerade as pumped-up versions of work, dating, or vacation camping, and since the audience is encouraged to become involved with the nonprofessional actors who participate in the contests precisely as though they were characters in a fiction.

There is always a political side to simulacra, but Baudrillard finds a rich lode analyzing the simulated nature of international public events. The "space race" to put a man into earth orbit or onto the moon was a simulacrum Baudrillard analyzes as a substitute or proxy for nuclear war between the United States and the Soviet Union (a pleasant substitute, for those of us who lived through it). Similarly, the Vietnam War of 1963–75 was a surrogate for nuclear war with China. President Nixon's bombing of Hanoi in December 1972, as a symbolic manifestation of American military power prior to the withdrawal from Vietnam, was a simulation that killed thousands of real people, even though it was known in advance that it would not affect the course of the war.[9] Reading recent American foreign adventures through Baudrillard can be very rewarding. On the other hand, we may be less convinced by

---

[9]Baudrillard doesn't let the French off the hook either — he points to the parallels between the Hanoi bombing and the so-called Battle of Algiers of 1960.

some of his historical examples, such as his notion that the Watergate affair was merely a simulation that allowed capitalism to replace Richard Nixon with a more palatable Republican leader.

One question we may want to ask about Baudrillard is about his own implicit position outside the world of make-believe he describes. He describes the ideological power wielded by the postmodern elite as being so pervasive and potent that it sucks all the reality out of life, but that makes it hard to account for the clarity of his own satiric vision, or the bounciness of his prose. If Baudrillard had gotten outside, and seen through, postmodern ideology, then isn't it a nightmare from which we can all wake up?

The aesthetic factors Fredric Jameson identifies with postmodernism are similar to those of Hutcheon; both of them see the "presence of the past," and what for Hutcheon is the postmodern's formal insistence on parody becomes in Jameson a fixation with pastiche. Like Baudrillard, Jameson reads postmodernism as ideology, specifically the ideology of late postindustrial consumer capitalism, global in scope and reach, an information society producing social relations with cordiality but without depth. Today we seem shallow even to ourselves and may wonder whether those hidden depths of self people felt in the past, and struggled to penetrate, with Freud or Kierkegaard, were just illusion. The distinction between elite and popular culture has been erased, and the popular arts present the past, sometimes as nostalgic pastiche, mixing sympathy with irony, as in *American Graffiti*, sometimes as a re-creation of forms pleasurably recollected from a time before postmodernity (cheap science fiction film serials, lovingly recreated in *Star Wars*, or 1940s film noir, recreated in *Body Heat*). Such films reproduce "the form history takes in an age that has forgotten how to think historically in the first place."[10] Here images from the past coalesce with the images of the present, fed to us through daily television news programs, which we take in quickly and as quickly forget. We become disoriented in time in the same way and for the same reasons that we become disoriented in space within postmodern architecture like the Weston Bonaventure hotel, in Jameson's brilliant (and accurate) analysis of the experience.

As a Marxist, Jameson ought to be outraged by an age where class consciousness cannot develop because of our vague, tentative relations with neighbors and co-workers, and because everyone of every income level consumes the same sets of images. And he ought to be despondent at a scene where history has been forgotten, where future progress is therefore impossible to envision except in the sense that we can have more of what we already have. By the time he wrote his magnum opus on the subject, *Postmodernism, or The Cultural Logic of Late Capitalism*, Jameson had indeed worked up an appropriate sense of gloom. Possibly this was because by 1991, with the breakup of the Soviet Union and the re-introduction of capitalism into China, it had become clear that the Marxist state was headed for the dustbin of history, whatever the vitality of Marxism as a mode of cultural analysis. But in his early lectures on postmodernism, it is not merely that Jameson ultimately suggests an

[10]Jameson, *Postmodernism, or The Cultural Logic of Late Capitalism*, ix.

escape route — that contemporary culture might give scope for resisting postindustrial capitalism. His tone suggests that he is not only attuned to the kaleidoscopic imagery and oneiric disorientation of the postmodern world, but to a certain extent caught up in its pleasures.

One of the few self-proclaimed socialists to embrace the postmodern world is Donna Haraway, whose "Cyborg Manifesto" is to postmodernism what "The Laugh of the Medusa" was to Lacanian psychology. Haraway takes us first on a journey down two blind alleys. One is the socialist feminism of Catherine MacKinnon, in which the sexual objectification of women is equated with the alienation of labor. The other is contemporary identity politics, the politics of difference and of differential victimization, in which individuals falling into not-white, not-male, not-Anglo, and not-straight categories find themselves in smaller and smaller groupings seeking voice and redress. Haraway's revolutionary move is to ally rather than to divide, to include rather than exclude, to see humans at one with beasts and with mechanisms, particularly the computers on which we have all become increasingly dependent. Animal rights activists will cheer the former but Haraway's key theoretical purchase is gained by seeing ourselves as already cyborgs, cybernetic organisms like the humanoid robots of *Blade Runner*. Wires may not run under our skin, but we are given mobility by airplanes and automobiles, as well as legs; we communicate through telephones and TVs as well as mouths; we extend the speed of our thinking with computers and our capacity for storing knowledge in libraries, hard disks, and the Internet, as well as in that meat computer between our ears.

What makes this vision both feminist and revolutionary is its riposte to the notion that women must be subjugated because anatomy is destiny, because nature trumps culture. If it is part of the "nature" of humanity to use tools to extend its strength, speed, and intelligence, it becomes impossible to essentialize the sexes in physical terms. As cyborgs, furthermore, our "anatomy" can no longer be confined to our protoplasm. And work need not be alienating, as long as we can become one with the machines that lend us power and expression, and that allow us to integrate ourselves with networks of other cyborgs. Haraway is wary of creating imaginary utopias that make us unwilling to fight against economic or political repression, but she has no doubt that the way to freedom lies in the future rather than a posited primitive past. Patriarchy may have begun when the Great Goddess was dethroned by Zeus, but there is no going back there, and in any case, as Haraway says: "I would rather be a cyborg than a goddess."

Greater ambivalence about the postmodern condition is displayed in two essays by African American theorists Cornel West and bell hooks, although West decidedly sees the glass as half empty while hooks sees it as half full. West has no doubt that there are creative black Americans operating in a postmodern idiom: he mentions the novelist Ishmael Reed in his first paragraph and devotes much of the eighth paragraph to a listing of significant African American painters, poets, and novelists working in postmodern modes. What West is less sure about is the significance of these creators in relation to popular black culture, which he views as based on a tradition of improvisational self-projection, aimed at resistance against white domination. The venues here are not the arts and letters in the traditional sense: they involve rhetoric, sports, and music (jazz, rock, and rap), in which African Americans excel by the projection of the self, in a risky tightrope walk that courts abject failure in achieving inspired success. This resistance against white domination can take shape as a sermon by Martin Luther King, a slam-dunk by Julius Irving, a solo by Charlie Parker. In contrast, West sees the "highbrow" world of writers, artists, and intellectuals as marginal to black culture, lacking "any organic link with most of black life," and imitative of a postmodern scene developed by white Europe and America. Indeed, even the world of popular music is culturally suspect for West, since it is dominated by multinational corporations seeking crossover material that will be acceptable to white America and Europe, and thus willing to sacrifice black authenticity in the process.

In "Postmodern Blackness" — which explicitly seems to be responding to West's suspicion about contemporary black writers and intellectuals — hooks radically questions the assumptions West makes about black identity, with hooks adopting a postmodern critique of identity politics. For people like West, there is a single black identity: creative artists and writers are either in tune with it or they are not. For hooks, there was indeed a "specific history . . . of African Americans"; nevertheless, as postmodern theory suggests, there are "multiple experiences of black identity that are the lived conditions which make diverse cultural production possible." As a result of their individual "lived conditions," blacks can be "nationalist or assimilationist, black-identified or white-identified." To say that one is more authentic than another is to essentialize black identity, a move that implicitly buys into the racial metanarrative that was one factor in the cruel history of black America. And she suggests that the postmodern decentering of "highbrow" culture allows for a dialogue with the urban underclass that would have been far more difficult under the regime of modernism. Even so, hooks gives only two cheers for postmodernism. She finds herself "on the outside of the discourse looking in," well aware how much postmodernist theory tends to ignore the black experience. And she identifies some of the crucial moments of the black power movements of the 1960s with the modernist politics of identity. One might add that some of the masterpieces of African American literature that helped to create black identity or reflect black experience, from *Their Eyes Were Watching God* to *Invisible Man*, were written in the modernist style-system with intricate structures of symbol and allusion. Giving up on modernism can be hard to do.

Giving up on modernity is even harder for Jürgen Habermas. A Marxist social thinker from the Frankfurt school, Habermas has sought a way to recuperate the enlightenment ideal of a just and rational society within the context of late capitalism. Writing at a time when rhetoric and discourse are seen as the prime constituents of reality rather than as verbal veils of material conditions, Habermas takes Marxism through the "linguistic turn." Progress, for Habermas, would come not just from material progress and organizational reform, but from a purification of public discourse.

Habermas's theory of social discourse owes a great deal to Wittgenstein, to Gadamer, and to J. L. Austin, whose ideas he adopted and against whom he reacted.

His theory presumes that public discourse by government officials, corporation executives, union leaders, occurs within a framework that makes certain idealizing assumptions ("validity claims") about real-life utterances: that what we say is understandable, that its objective propositional content is true, that the speaker is sincere, and that it is appropriate for the speaker to be performing the speech-act. Obviously these assumptions do not hold for all, or even most, real-life utterances. Nonetheless, the attainment of any consensus needed for public action depends on these validity claims. Genuine consensus can be built provided all the participants in a dialogue have a fair share in the discourse, are allowed freely to assert or question any claim that is made, and are able to express attitudes, feelings, and intentions, without being dominated, materially or ideologically, by another speaker. In such a dialogue people attempt to persuade one another not by authority or by false claims of scientific rationality but by the force of the better argument. Habermas knows that such a situation is counterfactual, that contemporary society throws up hundreds of barriers to the production of what he calls "legitimate consensus." But he argues that we cannot give up on it any more than we can give up on the just society of which Marx and Adorno dreamed.

With this melioristic general program for social discourse and social organization, Habermas views postmodern philosophy as a grotesque mistake, prematurely drawing the curtain on the "modern project" of progress and enlightenment. The radical critique of reason, which Habermas identifies with Michel Foucault and Jacques Derrida, is an anarchistic rhetoric that leads to quietism and despair. Such anarchism is implicitly conservative: it leaves us stuck in a hopeless solipsism, when what is needed for taking on the alienating conditions of late capitalism and the power of the interventionist state is a discourse that can build toward legitimate consensus. Just as radicals from the left and right can become indistinguishable, in Habermas's view the "young conservatives" of postmodernism are effectively allied with the pre-Enlightenment position of the "old conservatives" who reject the Enlightenment's idealistic view that the common people can be trusted with political power.[11]

Habermas's diagnosis of the cultural scene follows from his sense that the Enlightenment saw the emancipation of humanity as dependent on its ability to integrate knowledge of the physical world, social and moral understanding, and aesthetic experience. Beginning around the middle of the nineteenth century, however, the arenas of theoretical, practical, and aesthetic knowledge split off from one another, and moved individually toward progress through expertise exercised by scientists and technologists, legal and social thinkers, and creative writers, artists, and composers, each working in separate spheres. The aesthetic realm was validated by creative professionals and experienced critics. To attain the highest esteem, a work of art in any genre had to be original, even avant-garde, but it was no longer obliged to represent and shed light on the life-world of the people. The result was a greater and greater separation of aesthetic creativity from the culture as a whole, a gap that

[11]Habermas's "old conservatives" include Leo Strauss, the University of Chicago professor who was the guru of the group today called the neo-cons (political figures like Paul Wolfowitz, journalists like William Kristol).

was filled by commodity entertainment. In a sense the progressive crisis and failure of the avant-garde since World War II might be taken as a good sign, together with the growing interest of educators from the academy in representations that have genuine resonance within popular culture. But for the project of Enlightenment to be completed, it would require a reintegration of social, moral, and scientific knowledge with aesthetic experience. It is a tall order for which Habermas does not cherish unrealistic hopes — but one he cannot abandon either.

As I hinted earlier, my own suspicion is that Habermas is right to consider modernity an unfinished project that has been disrupted but not derailed by the cultural politics of postmodernism, which may be a phase rather than a permanent feature of the landscape, and neither as pervasive nor as ineluctable as its most pessimistic analysts have feared. Probably the most heartening recent innovation for an unreconstructed humanist like Habermas, though, is the Internet, the quintessentially postmodern institution, which has re-created the world of the eighteenth-century coffeehouse in cyberspace, as an essentially unrestricted public sphere for political discussion and general communication, where discourse is messy, sometimes savage, but has not been filtered by the power of money.

And forty years after we made the turn into the postmodern condition, the culture we live in turns out to be very resilient; indeed the media have changed more than the content. Narratives still signify, though the most significant ones may be films or even television shows with excellent writers (*The Simpsons*, *The Sopranos*) rather than novels. Poetry is still important, though the texts that most move us may be pop songs with excellent writers (*Jacques Brel*, *Bob Dylan*, *The Clash*, *Eminem*) rather than poetry published in slim volumes or little magazines. And the "death of the author" may be have been announced prematurely, when anyone who likes can publish novels on their websites, and anyone who likes can read them.

Finally, theorizing postmodernism is something we have been doing in this chapter, but in a more general sense it is something we have been doing for most of this book. We began Part II of *The Critical Tradition* by considering the Formalism that had become widespread around the middle of the twentieth century — with the critical method, that is, that had been created, intentionally or otherwise, to explicate the masterpieces of modernism. Theory since the 1970s has been about the instability of the text and of the psyche, the paradoxes of historical perspective, the aporias of gender and race and class, the mysteries of global and local culture — in short, it has been all about the postmodern condition. The journey we have made rightly ends here. But the journey of our culture and the ways of critically considering it go on.

Selected Bibliography

Baudrillard, Jean. *Selected Writings,* ed. Mark Poster. Stanford: Stanford University Press, 1988.
———. *Simulations*, trans. Paul Foss, Paul Patton, and Philip Beitschman. New York: Semiotexte, 1983.
Bauman, Zygmunt. *Postmodernity and Its Discontents*. New York: NYU Press, 1997.
Bertens, Johannes Willem. *The Idea of the Postmodern: A History*. New York: Routledge, 1995.

Best, Steven, and Douglas Kellner. *The Postmodern Turn*. New York: Guilford Press, 1997.

Bové, Paul, ed. *Early Postmodernism: Foundational Essays*. Durham: Duke University Press, 1995.

Danto, Arthur Coleman. *After the End of Art: Contemporary Art and the Pale of History*. Princeton: Princeton University Press, 1997.

Eagleton, Terry. *The Illusions of Postmodernism*. Cambridge: Blackwell, 1996.

Fiedler, Leslie. "Cross the Border, Close the Gap." In *Postmodernism: A Reader*, ed. Patricia Waugh. New York: Routledge, 1992.

Habermas, Jürgen. *The Philosophical Discourse of Modernity: Twelve Lectures*. Cambridge: MIT Press, 1987.

————. *The Theory of Communicative Action*, trans. Thomas McCarthy. Boston: Beacon, 1987.

Haraway, Donna Jeanne. *Simians, Cyborgs and Women: The Reinvention of Nature*. New York: Routledge, 1991.

Hassan, Ihab Habib. *The Postmodern Turn: Essays in Postmodern Theory and Culture*. Columbus: Ohio State University Press, 1987.

hooks, bell. *Yearnings: Race, Gender, and Cultural Politics*. Boston: South End Press, 1990.

Hutcheon, Linda. *A Poetics of Postmodernism: History, Theory, Fiction*. New York: Routledge, 1988.

Huyssen, Andreas. *After the Great Divide: Modernism, Mass Culture, Postmodernism*. Bloomington: Indiana University Press, 1986.

Jameson, Fredric. *Postmodernism, or The Cultural Logic of Late Capitalism*. Durham: Duke University Press, 1991.

————. *The Cultural Turn: Selected Essays on Postmodernism 1983–1998*. London: Verso, 1998.

Lyotard, Jean François. *The Postmodern Condition: A Report on Knowledge*, trans. Geoffrey Bennington and Brian Massumi. Minneapolis: University of Minnesota Press, 1984.

McClary, Susan. *Conventional Wisdom: The Content of Musical Form*. Berkeley: University of California Press, 2000.

McHale, Brian. *Constructing Postmodernism*. London and New York: Routledge, 1992.

Murphy, Richard John. *Theorizing the Avant-Garde*. New York: Cambridge University Press, 1999.

Natoli, Joseph, and Linda Hutcheon, eds. *A Postmodern Reader*. Albany: State University of New York Press, 1993.

Olson, Charles. "Preliminary Images." In *Early Postmodernism: Foundational Essays*, edited by Paul Bové. Durham: Duke University Press, 1995.

Richter, David H. "Murder in Jest: Serial Homicide in the Postmodern Detective Story," *Journal of Narrative Technique* 8 (1989): 117–32.

Rorty, Richard. *Contingency, Irony, and Solidarity*. New York: Cambridge University Press, 1989.

Sontag, Susan. *Against Interpretation*. New York: Farrar, Straus and Giroux, 1966.

Spanos, William V. *Repetitions: The Postmodern Occasion in Literature and Culture*. Baton Rouge: Louisiana State University Press, 1987.

Waugh, Patricia, ed. *Postmodernism: A Reader*. New York: Routledge, 1992.

West, Cornel. "Black Culture and Postmodernism." In *A Postmodern Reader*, ed. Joseph Natoli and Linda Hutcheon. Albany: State University of New York Press, 1993.

Jean-François Lyotard

b. 1924

Born in Versailles, Lyotard considered becoming a Dominican monk but entered the Sorbonne instead. In 1952, he began to teach philosophy at a secondary school in Constantine, Algeria, and then in various French academies. In the late 1950s, Lyotard became a prominent member of the anti-Stalinist group Socialisme ou Barbarie, a group of left-wing French intellectuals that formed in response to the Hungarian uprising of 1956. By the time he received his doctorate in 1971, Lyotard's first book Phenomenology *(1954) was already in its seventh edition. He taught in the faculty of philosophy at the University of Paris at Nanterre, then moved to the University of Paris at Vincennes, where he taught from 1972 to 1984. In 1981, he was a founder, and then first president, of the International College of Philosophy. Of the more than forty books Lyotard has written, those most familiar to postmodern theorists include* Discours, figure *(1971),* Economie libidinale *(1974),* The Postmodern Condition: A Report on Knowledge *(1979),* The Differend *(1984),* Heidegger and the Jews *(1988),* Inhuman *(1988),* Lessons on the Analytic of the Sublime *(1991),* Postmodern Explained *(1992),* Postmodern Fables *(1997),* Chambre sourde *(1998), and* The Confession of Augustine *(2001). In his work on postmodernism, Lyotard urges experimental discourse, rather than searches for truth, as all knowledge structures, such as metanarratives, cease to have meaning. He argues that the search for knowledge will become the primary focus of the postmodern age, and that the search for information will become the major stake for global economic and political power. The following essay, "Defining the Postmodern," was published in* Postmodernism (ICA Documents 4) *in 1986.*

Defining the Postmodern

I should like to make only a small number of observations, in order to point to — and not at all to resolve — some problems surrounding the term "postmodern." My aim is not to close the debate, but to open it, to allow it to develop by avoiding certain confusions and ambiguities, as far as this is possible.

There are many debates implied by, and implicated in, the term "postmodern." I will distinguish three of them.

First, the opposition between postmodernism and modernism, or the Modern Movement (1910–45), in architectural theory. According to Paolo Portoghesi (*Dell'architectura moderna*[1]),

there is a rupture or break, and this break would be the abrogation of the hegemony of Euclidean geometry, which was sublimated in the plastic poetry of the movement known as De Stijl,[2] for example. According to Victorio Grigotti, another Italian architect, the difference between the two periods is characterized by what is possibly a more interesting fissure. There is no longer any close linkage between the architectural project and socio-historical progress in the realization of human emancipation on the larger scale. Postmodern architecture is condemned to generate a multiplicity of small transformations in the space it inherits, and to give up the project of a last rebuilding of the

Translated by Geoff Bennington.
[1] The actual title of Portoghesi's 1980 book is *Dopo l'architettura moderna* (*After Modern Architecture*).

[2] Artistic movement in the 1920s dedicated to harmonious abstract painting whose most celebrated member was Piet Mondrian (1872–1944).

whole space occupied by humanity. In this sense, a perspective is opened in the larger landscape.

In this account there is no longer a horizon of universalization, of general emancipation before the eyes of postmodern man, or in particular, of the postmodern architect. The disappearance of this idea of progress within rationality and freedom would explain a certain tone, style or modus which is specific to postmodern architecture. I would say a sort of *bricolage*: the high frequency of quotations of elements from previous styles or periods (classical or modern), giving up the consideration of environment, and so on.

Just a remark about this aspect. The "post-", in the term "postmodernist" is in this case to be understood in the sense of a simple succession, of a diachrony of periods, each of them clearly identifiable. Something like a conversion, a new direction after the previous one. I should like to observe that this idea of chronology is totally modern. It belongs to Christianity, Cartesianism, Jacobinism.[3] Since we are beginning something completely new, we have to re-set the hands of the clock at zero. The idea of modernity is closely bound up with this principle that it is possible and necessary to break with tradition and to begin a new way of living and thinking. Today we can presume that this "breaking" is, rather, a manner of forgetting or repressing the past. That's to say of repeating it. Not overcoming it.

I would say that the quotation of elements of past architectures in the new one seems to me to be the same procedure as the use of remains coming from past life in the dream-work as described by Freud, in the *Interpretation of Dreams*. This use of repetition or quotation, be it ironical or not, cynical or not, can be seen in the trends dominating contemporary painting, under the name of "transavantgardism" (Achille Bonito Oliva) or under the name of neo-expressionism. I'll come back to this question in my third point.

The second point. A second connotation of the term "postmodern," and I admit that I am at least partly responsible for the misunderstanding associated with this meaning.

The general idea is a trivial one. One can note a sort of decay in the confidence placed by the two last centuries in the idea of progress. This idea of progress as possible, probable or necessary was rooted in the certainty that the development of the arts, technology, knowledge and liberty would be profitable to mankind as a whole. To be sure, the question of knowing which was the subject truly victimized by the lack of development — whether it was the poor, the worker, the illiterate — remained open during the 19th and 20th centuries. There were disputes, even wars, between liberals, conservatives and leftists over the very name of the subject we are to help to become emancipated. Nevertheless, all the parties concurred in the same belief that enterprises, discoveries and institutions are legitimate only insofar as they contribute to the emancipation of mankind.

After two centuries, we are more sensitive to signs that signify the contrary. Neither economic nor political liberalism, nor the various Marxisms, emerge from the sanguinary last two centuries free from the suspicion of crimes against mankind. We can list a series of proper names (names of places, persons and dates) capable of illustrating and founding our suspicion. Following Theodor Adorno, I use the name of Auschwitz to point out the irrelevance of empirical matter, the stuff of recent past history, in terms of the modern claim to help mankind to emancipate itself.[4] What kind of thought is able to sublate (*Aufheben*) Auschwitz in a general (either empirical or speculative) process towards a universal emancipation? So there is a sort of sorrow in the *Zeitgeist*. This can express itself by reactive or reactionary attitudes or by utopias, but never by a positive orientation offering a new perspective.

---

[3]Christians believe in a spiritual rebirth and a new being, and Jacobins (radical revolutionaries) also believe in destroying the old society down to its roots before re-creating a new society. Lyotard's reference to "Cartesianism" may refer to the radical skepticism of René Descartes in the *Discourse on Method* (1637), where he resolves to doubt whatever can be doubted, radically destroying the world of quotidian belief before building up a new world based on what is certain.

[4]Lyotard is probably not simply referring to Adorno's best known saying: "To write poetry after Auschwitz is barbaric"; he is referring to his statement in *Negative Dialectics* (1966) to the effect that Auschwitz has become a new categorical imperative, in the sense that humanity has been given the task of so arranging their way of thinking that nothing of the kind can ever happen again. It is unthinkable to him that it could be "sublated" (transcended), that Auschwitz could have been a *necessary* step in the dialectical conflict leading ultimately to a utopia.

The development of techno-sciences has become a means of increasing disease, not of fighting it. We can no longer call this development by the old name of progress. This development seems to be taking place by itself, by an autonomous force or "motricity." It doesn't respond to a demand coming from human needs. On the contrary, human entities (individual or social) seem always to be destabilized by the results of this development. The intellectual results as much as the material ones. I would say that mankind is in the condition of running after the process of accumulating new objects of practice and thought. In my view it is a real and obscure question to determine the reason of this process of complexification. It's something like a destiny towards a more and more complex condition. Our demands for security, identity and happiness, coming from our condition as living beings and even social beings appear today irrelevant in the face of this sort of obligation to complexify, mediate, memorize and synthesize every object, and to change its scale. We are in this techno-scientific world like Gulliver: sometimes too big, sometimes too small, never at the right scale. Consequently, the claim for simplicity, in general, appears today that of a barbarian.

From this point, it would be necessary to consider the division of mankind into two parts: one part confronted with the challenge of complexity; the other with the terrible ancient task of survival. This is a major aspect of the failure of the modern project (which was, in principle, valid for mankind as a whole).

The third argument is more complex, and I shall present it as briefly as possible. The question of postmodernity is also the question of the expressions of thought: art, literature, philosophy, politics. You know that in the field of art for example, and more especially the plastic arts, the dominant idea is that the big movement of avant-gardism is over.

There seems to be general agreement about laughing at the avant-gardes, considered as the expression of an obsolete modernity. I don't like the term avant-garde any more than anyone else, because of its military connotations.[5] Nevertheless I would like to observe that the very process of avant-gardism in painting was in reality a long, obstinate and highly responsible investigation of the presuppositions implied in modernity. The right approach, in order to understand the work of painters from, say, Manet to Duchamp or Barnett Newman is to compare their work with the anamnesis[6] which takes place in psychoanalytical therapy. Just as the patient elaborates his present trouble by freely associating the more imaginary, immaterial, irrelevant bits with past situations, so discovering hidden meanings of his life, we can consider the work of Cézanne, Picasso, Delaunay, Kandinsky, Klee, Mondrian, Malevitch and finally Duchamp[7] as a working through[8] — what Freud called *Durcharbeitung* — operated by modernity on itself. If we give up this responsibility, it is certain that we are condemned to repeat, without any displacement, the modern neurosis, the Western schizophrenia, paranoia, and so on. This being granted, the "post-" of postmodernity does not mean a process of coming back or flashing back, feeding back, but of *ana*-lysing, *ana*-mnesing, of reflecting.

[5]The avant-garde (French for vanguard) was literally the body of troops that would make first contact with the enemy.
[6]Work of remembering.
[7]Lyotard takes us through a quick history of stages in avant-garde modern European art from late impressionism through surrealism and abstract expressionism.
[8]Freud's word for the process by which psychoanalytic patients reinvent themselves by reinvesting their energies in new objects after traumatic losses; this could come after "remembrance" and "repetition" — the discussion of the past with the analyst.

Jean Baudrillard

b. 1929

Born in France's Champagne capital of Reims, this poststructuralist, post-Marxist sociologist and theorist was the son of civil servants and grandson of peasant farmers, the first in his family to attend university. He began his career teaching German in a lycée before completing his doctoral thesis in sociology under Marxist philosopher Henri Lefebvre. In 1966, he began teaching at the University of Paris at Nanterre. During this time, he was associated with Roland Barthes, whose ideas deeply influenced Baudrillard's first book, The System of Objects *(1968). After reading the work of Marshall McLuhan, Baudrillard began to see the symbolic representations of culture in mass media to be the basis for performing sociological analysis. After the student revolt at Nanterre in 1968, he wrote for a typical journal of the time,* Utopie, *using Marxist analysis to critique the symbols of capitalism. He eventually came to regard Marxism itself a symbolist ideology produced by the mass culture of capitalism, and to lose his oppositional stance against mass media and technology. His later works discuss the extreme reproducibility of images and sounds through electronic media forms, creating, in Baudrillard's terminology, a culture of the "hyperreal." He became maître-assistant (assistant professor) at Nanterre from 1970 to 1987. He is currently professor of philosophy of culture and media criticism at the European Graduate School in Saas-Fee, Switzerland. His books include* Consumer Society *(1970),* For a Critique of the Political Economy of the Sign *(1972),* The Mirror of Production *(1973),* In the Shadow of the Silent Majorities *(1983),* Simulations *(1983),* Forget Foucault *(1987),* Simulacra and Simulations *(1988),* Seduction *(1990),* The Illusion of the End *(1992),* The Gulf War Did Not Take Place *(1995),* The Perfect Crime *(1996),* America *(1998),* The Spirit of Terrorism *(2001),* Screened Out *(2002), and* Passwords *(2003). The following essay is taken from* Simulations.

From *The Precession*[1] *of Simulacra*

> *The simulacrum is never that which conceals the truth — it is the truth which conceals that there is none.*
> *The simulacrum is true.* —ECCLESIASTES[2]

If we were able to take as the finest allegory of simulation the Borges tale[3] where the cartographers of the Empire draw up a map so detailed that it ends up exactly covering the territory (but where the decline of the Empire sees this map

Translated by Paul Foss and Paul Patton.

[1]Baudrillard's title hinges on a scientific term that refers to the "wobble" of anything spinning that is also acted on by an outside force (including gravity). For example the axis of the earth's rotation wobbles very slowly (the period is 18,600 years), so that different stars have been (and in due course will be) in the position now held by Polaris. One of the proofs of Einstein's theory of relativity was its correct predictions about the precession in the orbit of Mercury. Possibly Baudrillard's point is that the ability to map our world depends on such imperceptible phenomena.

[2]Ecclesiastes is a biblical book containing worldly, sometimes cynical wisdom, but nothing remotely resembling this particular text is to be found there.

[3]"On Exactitude in Science" (1960), by Jorge Luis Borges (1899–1986).

become frayed and finally ruined, a few shreds still discernible in the deserts — the metaphysical beauty of this ruined abstraction, bearing witness to an Imperial pride and rotting like a carcass, returning to the substance of the soil, rather as an aging double ends up being confused with the real thing) — then this fable has come full circle for us, and now has nothing but the discrete charm of second-order simulacra.[4]

Abstraction today is no longer that of the map, the double, the mirror or the concept. Simulation is no longer that of a territory, a referential being or a substance. It is the generation by models of a real without origin or reality: a hyperreal. The territory no longer precedes the map, nor survives it. Henceforth, it is the map that precedes the territory — PRECESSION OF SIMULACRA — it is the map that engenders the territory and if we were to revive the fable today, it would be the territory

[4]Cf. J. Baudrillard, *L'Echange symbolique et la mort,* ("L'Ordre des simulacres"), Paris, Gallimard, 1975. [Baudrillard]

whose shreds are slowly rotting across the map. It is the real, and not the map, whose vestiges subsist here and there, in the deserts which are no longer those of the Empire, but our own. *The desert of the real itself.*

In fact, even inverted, the fable is useless. Perhaps only the allegory of the Empire remains. For it is with the same Imperialism that present-day simulators try to make the real, all the real, coincide with their simulation models. But it is no longer a question of either maps or territory. Something has disappeared: the sovereign difference between them that was the abstraction's charm. For it is the difference which forms the poetry of the map and the charm of the territory, the magic of the concept and the charm of the real. This representational imaginary, which both culminates in and is engulfed by the cartographer's mad project of an ideal coextensivity between the map and the territory, disappears with simulation — whose operation is nuclear and genetic, and no longer specular and discursive. With it goes all of metaphysics. No more mirror of being and appearances, of the real and its concept. No more imaginary coextensivity: rather, genetic miniaturization is the dimension of simulation. The real is produced from miniaturized units, from matrices, memory banks and command models — and with these it can be reproduced an indefinite number of times. It no longer has to be rational, since it is no longer measured against some ideal or negative instance. It is nothing more than operational. In fact, since it is no longer enveloped by an imaginary, it is no longer real at all. It is a hyperreal, the product of an irradiating synthesis of combinatory models in a hyperspace without atmosphere.

In this passage to a space whose curvature is no longer that of the real, nor of truth, the age of simulation thus begins with a liquidation of all referentials — worse: by their artificial resurrection in systems of signs, a more ductile material than meaning, in that it lends itself to all systems of equivalence, all binary oppositions and all combinatory algebra. It is no longer a question of imitation, nor of reduplication, nor even of parody. It is rather a question of substituting signs of the real for the real itself, that is, an operation to deter every real process by its operational double,

a metastable, programmatic, perfect descriptive machine which provides all the signs of the real and short-circuits all its vicissitudes. Never again will the real have to be produced — this is the vital function of the model in a system of death, or rather of anticipated resurrection which no longer leaves any chance even in the event of death. A hyperreal henceforth sheltered from the imaginary, and from any distinction between the real and the imaginary, leaving room only for the orbital recurrence of models and the simulated generation of difference.

THE DIVINE IRREFERENCE OF IMAGES

To dissimulate is to feign not to have what one has. To simulate is to feign to have what one hasn't. One implies a presence, the other an absence. But the matter is more complicated, since to simulate is not simply to feign: "Someone who feigns an illness can simply go to bed and make believe he is ill. Some[one] who simulates an illness produces in himself some of the symptoms." (Littré)[5] Thus, feigning or dissimulating leaves the reality principle intact: the difference is always clear, it is only masked; whereas simulation threatens the difference between "true" and "false," between "real" and "imaginary." Since the simulator produces "true" symptoms, is he ill or not? He cannot be treated objectively either as ill, or as not-ill. Psychology and medicine stop at this point, before a thereafter undiscoverable truth of the illness. For if any symptom can be "produced," and can no longer be accepted as a fact of nature, then every illness may be considered as simulatable and simulated, and medicine loses its meaning since it only knows how to treat "true" illnesses by their objective causes. Psychosomatics evolves in a dubious way on the edge of the illness principle. As for psychoanalysis, it transfers the symptom from the organic to the unconscious order: once again, the latter is held to be true, more true than the former — but why should simulation stop at the portals of the unconscious? Why couldn't the "work" of the unconscious be

[5]Paul-Maximilien-Emile Littré (1801–1888) translated the works of science of the classical period, and compiled (1854) a dictionary of medicine and surgery, from which the quotation is taken.

"produced" in the same way as any other symptom in classical medicine? Dreams already are.[6]

The alienist,[7] of course, claims that "for each form of the mental alienation there is a particular order in the succession of symptoms, of which the simulator is unaware and in the absence of which the alienist is unlikely to be deceived." This (which dates from 1865) in order to save at all cost the truth principle, and to escape the spectre raised by simulation — namely that truth, reference and objective causes have ceased to exist. What can medicine do with something which floats on either side of illness, on either side of health, or with the reduplication of illness in a discourse that is no longer true or false? What can psychoanalysis do with the reduplication of the discourse of the unconscious in a discourse of simulation that can never be unmasked, since it isn't false either?[8]

What can the army do with simulators? Traditionally, following a direct principle of identification, it unmasks and punishes them. Today, it can reform an excellent simulator as though he were equivalent to a "real" homosexual, heartcase or lunatic. Even military psychology retreats from the Cartesian clarities and hesitates to draw the distinction between true and false, between the "produced" symptom and the authentic symptom. "If he acts crazy so well, then he must be mad." Nor is it mistaken: in the sense that all lunatics are simulators, and this lack of distinction is the worst from of subversion. Against it classical reason armed itself with all its categories. But it is this today which again outflanks them, submerging the truth principle.

Outside of medicine and the army, favored terrains of simulation, the affair goes back to religion and the simulacrum of divinity: "I forbad any simulacrum in the temples because the divinity that breathes life into nature cannot be represented."[9] Indeed it can. But what becomes of the divinity when it reveals itself in icons, when it is multiplied in simulacra? Does it remain the supreme authority, simply incarnated in images as a visible theology? Or is it volatilized into simulacra which alone deploy their pomp and power of fascination — the visible machinery of icons being substituted for the pure and intelligible Idea of God? This is precisely what was feared by the Iconoclasts, whose millennial quarrel is still with us today.[10] Their rage to destroy images rose precisely because they sensed this omnipotence of simulacra, this facility they have of effacing God from the consciousness of men, and the overwhelming, destructive truth which they suggest: that ultimately there has never been any God, that only the simulacrum exists, indeed that God himself has only ever been his own simulacrum. Had they been able to believe that images only occulted or masked the Platonic Idea of God, there would have been no reason to destroy them. One can live with the idea of a distorted truth. But their metaphysical despair came from the idea that the images concealed nothing at all, and that in fact they were not images, such as the original model would have made them, but actually perfect simulacra forever radiant with their own fascination. But this death of the divine referential has to be exorcised at all cost.

It can be seen that the iconoclasts, who are often accused of despising and denying images, were in fact the ones who accorded them their actual worth, unlike the iconolaters, who saw in them only reflections and were content to venerate God at one remove. But the converse can also be said, namely that the iconolaters were the most

---

[6]Baudrillard's point is that the "truth principle," the explanatory power of medicine as positive science, is weakened by the existence of psychosomatic symptoms in a simulating sufferer, because each disease becomes two diseases, one produced by physical, the other by psychological causes. Since dreams are psychological symptoms for the psychoanalyst, Baudrillard speculates that they too can be produced by the simulating psyche.

[7]Early term for a psychoanalyst.

[8]And which is not susceptible to resolution in transference. It is the entanglement of these two discourses which makes psychoanalysis interminable. [Baudrillard]

[9]The quotation is not from the Bible, but reflects Baudrillard's rationale for the second commandment, at Exodus 20:4, against idolatry: that a simulacrum eventually supplants the original.

[10]Cf. M. Perniola, "Icones, Visions, Simulacres," *Traverses/10*, p. 39. [Baudrillard] In the Byzantine empire of the eighth and ninth centuries, certain emperors ordered the destruction of all pictorial representations of God. Protestant leaders of the sixteenth century, like Calvin and Zwingli, also favored the destruction of religious art seen as idolatrous. Iconoclasm continues in the Islamic world.

modern and adventurous minds, since underneath the idea of the apparition of God in the mirror of images, they already enacted his death and his disappearance in the epiphany of his representations (which they perhaps knew no longer represented anything, and that they were purely a game, but that this was precisely the greatest game — knowing also that it is dangerous to unmask images, since they dissimulate the fact that there is nothing behind them).

This was the approach of the Jesuits, who based their politics on the virtual disappearance of God and on the worldly and spectacular manipulation of consciences — the evanescence of God in the epiphany of power — the end of transcendence, which no longer serves as alibi for a strategy completely free of influences and signs. Behind the baroque of images hides the grey eminence[11] of politics.

Thus perhaps at stake has always been the murderous capacity of images, murderers of the real, murderers of their own model as the Byzantine icons could murder the divine identity. To this murderous capacity is opposed the dialectical capacity of representations as visible and intelligible mediation of the Real. All of Western faith and good faith was engaged in this wager on representation: that a sign could refer to the depth of meaning, that a sign could *exchange* for meaning and that something could guarantee this exchange — God, of course. But what if God himself can be simulated, that is to say, reduced to the signs which attest his existence? Then the whole system becomes weightless, it is no longer anything but a gigantic simulacrum — not unreal, but a simulacrum, never again exchanging for what is real, but exchanging in itself, in an uninterrupted circuit without reference or circumference.

So it is with simulation, insofar as it is opposed to representation. The latter starts from the principle that the sign and the real are equivalent (even if this equivalence is utopian, it is a fundamental axiom). Conversely, simulation starts from the *utopia* of this principle of equivalence, *from the radical negation of the sign as value*, from the sign as reversion and death sentence of every reference. Whereas representation tries to absorb simulation by interpreting it as false representation, simulation envelops the whole edifice of representation as itself a simulacrum.

This would be the successive phases of the image:

— it is the reflection of a basic reality
— it masks and perverts a basic reality
— it masks the *absence* of a basic reality
— it bears no relation to any reality whatever: it is its own pure simulacrum.

In the first case, the image is a *good* appearance — the representation is of the order of sacrament. In the second, it is an *evil* appearance — of the order of malefice. In the third, it *plays at being* an appearance — it is of the order of sorcery. In the fourth, it is no longer in the order of appearance at all, but of simulation.

The transition from signs which dissimulate something to signs which dissimulate that there is nothing, marks the decisive turning point. The first implies a theology of truth and secrecy (to which the notion of ideology still belongs). The second inaugurates an age of simulacra and simulation, in which there is no longer any God to recognize his own, nor any last judgment to separate true from false, the real from its artificial resurrection, since everything is already dead and risen in advance.

When the real is no longer what it used to be, nostalgia assumes its full meaning. There is a proliferation of myths of origin and signs of reality; of second-hand truth, objectivity and authenticity. There is an escalation of the true, of the lived experience; a resurrection of the figurative where the object and substance have disappeared. And there is a panic-stricken production of the real and the referential, above and parallel to the panic of material production: this is how simulation appears in the phase that concerns us — a strategy of the real, neo-real and hyperreal whose universal double is a strategy of deterrence. . . .[12]

---

[11]The term "grey eminence" (*eminence grise*) originates in Father Joseph, the Capuchin monk who was confessor to Cardinal Richelieu, and who was thought to be the true center of power during the reign of Louis XIII.

[12]Baudrillard here hints at something he will discuss at length later, the way in which proxy conflicts of various kinds (including the Vietnam War) serve as simulations standing for but deterring the nuclear war between the United States and the USSR.

HYPERREAL AND IMAGINARY

Disneyland is a perfect model of all the entangled orders of simulation. To begin with it is a play of illusions and phantasms: Pirates, the Frontier, Future World, etc. This imaginary world is supposed to be what makes the operation successful. But what draws the crowds is undoubtedly much more the social microcosm, the miniaturized and *religious* revelling in real America, in its delights and drawbacks. You park outside, queue up inside, and are totally abandoned at the exit. In this imaginary world the only phantasmagoria is in the inherent warmth and affection of the crowd, and in that sufficiently excessive number of gadgets used there to specifically maintain the multitudinous affect. The contrast with the absolute solitude of the parking lot — a veritable concentration camp — is total. Or rather: inside, a whole range of gadgets magnetize the crowd into direct flows — outside, solitude is directed onto a single gadget: the automobile. By an extraordinary coincidence (one that undoubtedly belongs to the peculiar enchantment of this universe), this deep-frozen infantile world happens to have been conceived and realized by a man who is himself now cryogenized: Walt Disney, who awaits his resurrection at minus 180 degrees centigrade.[13]

The objective profile of America, then, may be traced throughout Disneyland, even down to the morphology of individuals and the crowd. All its values are exalted here, in miniature and comic strip form. Embalmed and pacified. Whence the possibility of an ideological analysis of Disneyland (L. Marin does it well in *Utopies, jeux d'espaces*): digest of the American way of life, panegyric to American values, idealized transposition of a contradictory reality. To be sure. But this conceals something else, and that "ideological" blanket exactly serves to cover over a *third-order simulation*: Disneyland is there to conceal the fact that it is the "real" country, all of

[13] It is merely an urban legend that Walt Disney (1901–1965) had his body cryogenically preserved in the hope of being resuscitated some day. In fact his body was cremated and his ashes rest at Forest Lawn cemetery. It is unclear whether Baudrillard actually believes the urban legend or whether it merely served as a useful image connected with Disneyland's intended resurrection-effect, to turn the adult visitor into a child again.

"real" America, which *is* Disneyland (just as prisons are there to conceal the fact that it is the social in its entirety, in its banal omnipresence, which is carceral). Disneyland is presented as imaginary in order to make us believe that the rest is real, when in fact all of Los Angeles and the America surrounding it are no longer real, but of the order of the hyperreal and of simulation. It is no longer a question of a false representation of reality (ideology), but of concealing the fact that the real is no longer real, and thus of saving the reality principle.

The Disneyland imaginary is neither true nor false; it is a deterrence machine set up in order to rejuvenate in reverse the fiction of the real. Whence the debility, the infantile degeneration of this imaginary. It is meant to be an infantile world, in order to make us believe that the adults are elsewhere, in the "real" world, and to conceal the fact that real childishness is everywhere, particularly amongst those adults who go there to act the child in order to foster illusions as to their real childishness.

Moreover, Disneyland is not the only one. Enchanted Village, Magic Mountain, Marine World: Los Angeles is encircled by these "imaginary stations" which feed reality, reality-energy, to a town whose mystery is precisely that it is nothing more than a network of endless, unreal circulation — a town of fabulous proportions, but without space or dimensions. As much as electrical and nuclear power stations, as much as film studios, this town, which is nothing more than an immense script and a perpetual motion picture, needs this old imaginary made up of childhood signals and faked phantasms for its sympathetic nervous system.

POLITICAL INCANTATION

Watergate. Same scenario as Disneyland (an imaginary effect concealing that reality no more exists outside than inside the bounds of the artificial perimeter): though here it is a scandal effect concealing that there is no difference between the facts and their denunciation (identical methods are employed by the CIA and the *Washington Post* journalists). Same operation, though this time tending towards scandal as a means to regenerate a moral and political principle, towards the imaginary as a means to regenerate a reality principle in distress.

The denunciation of scandal always pays homage to the law. And Watergate above all succeeded in imposing the idea that Watergate *was* a scandal — in this sense it was an extraordinary operation of intoxication. The reinjection of a large dose of political morality on a global scale. It could be said along with Bourdieu that: "The specific character of every relation of force is to dissimulate itself as such, and to acquire all its force only because it is so dissimulated," understood as follows: capital, which is immoral and unscrupulous, can only function behind a moral superstructure, and whoever regenerates this public morality (by indignation, denunciation, etc.) spontaneously furthers the order of capital, as did the *Washington Post* journalists.

But this is still only the formula of ideology, and when Bourdieu enunciates it, he takes "relation of force" to mean the *truth* of capitalist domination, and he *denounces* this relation of force as itself a *scandal* — he therefore occupies the same deterministic and moralistic position as the *Washington Post* journalists. He does the same job of purging and reviving moral order, an order of truth wherein the genuine symbolic violence of the social order is engendered, well beyond all relations of force, which are only its indifferent and shifting configuration in the moral and political consciousness of men.

All that capital asks of us is to receive it as rational or to combat it in the name of rationality, to receive it as moral or to combat it in the name of morality. For they are *identical*, meaning *they can be read another way*: before, the task was to dissimulate scandal; today, the task is to conceal the fact that there is none.

Watergate is not a scandal: this is what must be said at all cost, for this is what every one is concerned to conceal, this dissimulation masking a strengthening of morality, a moral panic as we approach the primal (mise en) scène of capital: its instantaneous cruelty, its incomprehensible ferocity, its fundamental immorality — this is what is scandalous, unaccountable for in that system of moral and economic equivalence which remains the axiom of leftist thought, from Enlightenment theory to communism. Capital doesn't give a damn about the idea of the contract which is imputed to it — it is a monstrous unprincipled undertaking, nothing more. Rather, it is "enlightened" thought which seeks to control capital by imposing rules on it. And all that recrimination which replaced revolutionary thought today comes down to reproaching capital for not following the rules of the game. "Power is unjust, its justice is a class justice, capital exploits us, etc." — as if capital were linked by a contract to the society it rules. It is the left which holds out the mirror of equivalence, hoping that capital will fall for this phantasmagoria of the social contract and fulfill its obligation towards the whole of society (at the same time, no need for revolution: it is enough that capital accept the rational formula of exchange).

Capital in fact has never been linked by a contract to the society it dominates. It is a sorcery of the social relation, it is a *challenge to society* and should be responded to as such. It is not a scandal to be denounced according to moral and economic rationality, but a challenge to take up according to symbolic law.

THE END OF THE PANOPTICON[14]

It is again to this ideology of the lived experience, of exhumation, of the real in its fundamental banality, in its radical authenticity, that the American TV-verité[15] experiment on the Loud family in 1971 refers:[16] 7 months of uninterrupted shooting, 300 hours of direct non-stop broadcasting, without script or scenario, the odyssey of a family, its dramas, its joys, ups and downs — in brief, a "raw" historical document, and the "best thing ever on television, comparable, at the level of our daily

[14]Prison building designed by English philosopher Jeremy Bentham (1748–1832); its key feature was that every inmate could be seen at all times by the guard. Michel Foucault discusses the Panopticon in his book, *Discipline and Punish*, mentioned by Baudrillard later.

[15]Baudrillard plays on the French word for "documentary film," *cinéma-verité*, literally "film-truth."

[16]Baudrillard's topic is *An America Family*, a twelve-part documentary covering the daily life of an affluent Santa Barbara family, William and Pat Loud and their five children, which was shot by Allan and Susan Raymond beginning in 1971. During filming the marriage of the Louds broke up, and the film also "outed" the family's gay son, Lance. The program was first aired by the public television network in 1973.

existence, to the film of the lunar landing." Things are complicated by the fact that this family came apart during the shooting: a crisis flared up, the Louds went their separate ways, etc. Whence that insoluble controversy: was TV responsible? What would have happened *if TV hadn't been there.*

More interesting is the phantasm of filming the Louds *as if TV wasn't there.* The producer's trump card was to say: "They lived as if we weren't there." An absurd, paradoxical formula — neither true, nor false: but utopian. The "as if *we* weren't there" is equivalent to "as if *you* were there." It is this utopia, this paradox that fascinated 20 million viewers, much more than the "perverse" pleasure of prying. In this "truth" experiment, it is neither a question of secrecy nor of perversion, but of a kind of thrill of the real, or of an aesthetics of the hyperreal, a thrill of vertiginous and phony exactitude, a thrill of aliena- tion and of magnification, of distortion in scale, of excessive transparency all at the same time. The joy in an excess of meaning, when the bar of the sign slips below the regular water line of meaning: the non-signifier is elevated by the camera angle. Here the real can be seen to have never existed (but "as if you were there"), without the distance which pro- duces perspective space and our depth vision (but "more true than nature"). Joy in the microscopic simulation which transforms the real into the hyper- real. (This is also a little like what happens in porno, where fascination is more metaphysical than sexual.)

This family was in any case already some- what hyperreal by its very selection: a typical, California-housed, 3-garage, 5-children, well-to- do professional upper middle class ideal American family with an ornamental housewife. In a way, it is this statistical perfection which dooms it to death. This ideal heroine of the American way of life is chosen, as in sacrificial rites, to be glorified and to die under the fiery glare of the studio lights, a modern fatum. For the heavenly fire no longer strikes depraved cities, it is rather the lens which cuts through ordinary reality like a laser, putting it to death. "The Louds: simply a family who agreed to deliver themselves into the hands of television, and to die from it," said the pro- ducer. So it is really a question of a sacrificial process, of a sacrificial spectacle offered to 20 million Americans. The liturgical drama of a mass society.

TV-verité. Admirable ambivalent terms: does it refer to the truth of this family, or to the truth of TV? In fact, it is TV which is the Loud's truth, it is it which is true, it is it which renders true. A truth which is no longer the reflexive truth of the mirror, nor the perspective truth of the panoptic system and of the gaze, but the manipulative truth of the test which probes and interrogates, of the laser which touches and then pierces, of computer cards which retain your punched-out sequences, of the genetic code which regulates your combinations, of cells which inform your sensory universe. It is to this kind of truth that the Loud family is subjected by the TV medium, and in this sense it really amounts to a death sentence (but is it still a question of truth?).

The end of the panoptic system. The eye of TV is no longer the source of an absolute gaze, and the ideal of control is no longer that of trans- parency. The latter still presupposes an objective space (that of the Renaissance) and the omnipo- tence of a despotic gaze. This is still, if not a sys- tem of confinement, at least a system of scrutiny. No longer subtle, but always in a position of exte- riority, playing on the opposition between seeing and being seen, even if the focal point of the panopticon may be blind.

It is entirely different when with the Louds "You no longer watch TV, TV watches you (live)," or again: "You no longer listen to *Pas de Panique, Pas de Panique* listens to you" — switching over from the panoptic apparatus of surveillance (of *Discipline and Punish*) to a system of deterrence, where the distinction between active and passive is abolished. No longer is there any imperative to submit to the model, or to the gaze. "YOU are the model!" "YOU are the majority!" Such is the slope of a hyperrealist sociality, where the real is con- fused with the model, as in the statistic operation, or with the medium, as in the Loud's operation. Such is the later stage of development of the social relation, our own, which is no longer one of persuasion (the classical age of propaganda, ideo- logy, publicity, etc.) but one of dissuasion or deterrence: "YOU are news, you are the social, the event is you, you are involved, you can use your voice, etc." A turnabout of affairs by which it becomes impossible to locate an instance of the model, of power, of the gaze, of the medium itself, since *you* are always already on the other side. No more subject, focal point, center or periphery: but pure flexion or circular inflection. No more violence or surveillance: only "information," secret virulence, chain reaction, slow implosion and simulacra of spaces where the real-effect again comes into play.

We are witnessing the end of perspective and panoptic space (which remains a moral hypothesis bound up with every classical analysis of the "objective" essence of power), and hence the *very abolition of the spectacular*. Television, in the case of the Louds for example, is no longer a spectacular medium. We are no longer in the society of spectacle which the situationists talked about, nor in the specific types of alienation and repression which this implied. The medium itself is no longer identifiable as such, and the merging of the medium and the message (McLuhan[17]) is the first great formula of this new age. There is no

longer any medium in the literal sense: it is now intangible, diffuse and diffracted in the real, and it can no longer even be said that the latter is distorted by it.

Such immixture, such a viral, endemic, chronic, alarming presence of the medium, without our being able to isolate its effects — spectralized, like those publicity holograms sculptured in empty space with laser beams, the event filtered by the medium — the dissolution of TV into life, the dissolution of life into TV — an indiscernible chemical solution: we are all Louds, doomed not to invasion, to pressure, to violence and to blackmail by the media and the models, but to their induction, to their infiltration, to their illegible violence.

But we must be careful of the negative twist discourse gives this: it is a question neither of an illness nor of a viral complaint. Rather, we must think of the media as if they were, in outer orbit,

---

[17]The medium/message confusion, of course, is a correlative of the confusion between sender and receiver, thus sealing the disappearance of all the dual, polar structures which formed the discursive organization of language, referring to the celebrated grid of functions in Jacobson, the organization of all determinate articulation of meaning. "Circular" discourse must be taken literally: that is, it no longer goes from one point to the other but describes a circle that *indistinctly* incorporates the positions of transmitter and receiver, henceforth unlocatable as such. Thus there is no longer any instance of power, any transmitting authority — power is something that circulates and whose source can no longer be located, a cycle in which the positions of dominator and the dominated interchange in an endless reversion which is also the end of power in its classical definition. The circularization of power, knowledge and discourse brings every localization of instances and poles to an end. Even in psychoanalytic interpretation, the "power" of the interpreter does not come from any external authority, but from the interpreted themselves. This changes everything, for we can always ask the traditional holders of power where they get their power from. Who made you Duke? The King. And who made the King? God. God alone does not reply. But to the question: who made the psychoanalyst? the analyst quite easily replies: You. Thus is expressed, by an inverse simulation, the passage from the "analyzed" to the "analyzand," from active to passive, which only goes to describe the swirling, mobile effect of the poles, its effect of circularity in which power is lost, is dissolved, is resolved into complete manipulation (this is no longer of the order of the directive authority and the gaze, but of the order of personal contact and commutation). See, also, the State/family circularity secured by the floating and metastatic regulation of images of the social and the private. (J. Donzelot, *The Policing of Families*)

From now on, it is impossible to ask the famous question: "From what position do you speak?" — "How do you know?" — "From where do you get the power?," without immediately getting the reply: "But it is *of* (from) you that I speak" — meaning, it is you who speaks, it is you who knows, power is you. A gigantic circonvolution, circumlocution of the spoken word, which amounts to irredeemable blackmail and irremovable deterrence of the subject supposed to speak, but left without a word to say, responseless, since to questions asked can come the inevitable reply: but *you are* the reply, or: your question is already an answer, etc. — the whole sophistical stranglehold of word-tapping, forced confession disguised as free expression, trapping the subject in his own questioning, the precession of the reply about the question (the whole violence of interpretation in there, and the violence of the conscious or unconscious self-management of "speech").

This simulacrum of inversion or involution of poles, this clever subterfuge which is the secret of the whole discourse of manipulation and hence, today, in every domain, the secret of all those new powers sweeping clean the stage of power, forging the assumption of all speech from which comes that fantastic silent majority characteristic of our times — all this undoubtedly began in the political sphere with the democratic simulacrum, that is to say with the substitution of the instance of the people for the instance of God as source of power, and the substitution of power as *representation* for power as *emanation*. An anti-Copernican revolution: no longer any transcendent instance nor any sun nor any luminous source of power and knowledge — everything comes from and returns to the people. It is [through] this magnificent *recycling* that the universal simulacrum of manipulation, from the scenario of mass suffrage to present-day and illusory opinion polls, begins to be installed. [Baudrillard] a sort of genetic code which controls the mutation of the real into the hyperreal, just as the other, micromolecular code controls the passage of the signal from a representative sphere of meaning to the genetic sphere of the programmed signal.[18]

The whole traditional mode of causality is brought into question: the perspective, deterministic mode, the "active," critical mode, the analytical mode — the distinction between cause and effect, between active and passive, between subject and object, between ends and means. It is in this mode that it can be said: TV watches us, TV alienates us, TV manipulates us, TV informs us. . . . Throughout all this one is dependent on the analytical conception whose vanishing point is the horizon between reality and meaning.

On the contrary, we must imagine TV on the DNA model, as an effect in which the opposing poles of determination vanish according to a nuclear contraction or retraction of the old polar schema which has always maintained a minimal distance between a cause and an effect, between the subject and an object: precisely, the meaning gap, the discrepancy, the difference, the smallest possible margin of error, irreducible under penalty of reabsorption in an aleatory[19] and indeterminable process which discourse can no longer even account for, since it is itself a determinable order.

It is this gap which vanishes in the genetic coding process, where indeterminacy is less a product of molecular randomness than a product of the abolition, pure and simple, of the *relation*. In the process of molecular control, which "goes" from the DNA nucleus to the "substance" it "informs," there is no more traversing of an effect, of an energy, of a determination, of any message. "Order, signal, impulse, message": all these attempt to render the matter intelligible to us, but by analogy, retranscribing in terms of inscription,

vector, decoding, a dimension of which we know nothing — it is no longer even a "dimension," or perhaps it is the fourth (that which is defined, however, in Einsteinian relativity, by the absorption of the distinct poles of space and time). In fact, this whole process only makes sense to us in the negative form. But nothing separates one pole from the other, the initial from the terminal: there is just a sort of contraction into each other, a fantastic telescoping, a collapsing of the two traditional poles into one another: an IMPLOSION — an absorption of the radiating model of causality, of the differential mode of determination, with its positive and negative electricity — an implosion of meaning. *This is where simulation begins.*

Everywhere, in whatever political, biological, psychological, media domain, where the distinction between poles can no longer be maintained, one enters into simulation, and hence into absolute manipulation — not passivity, but the *non-distinction of active and passive.* DNA realizes this aleatory reduction at the level of the living substance. Television itself, in the example of the Louds, also attains this *indefinite* limit where the family *vis-à-vis* TV is no more or less active or passive than is a living substance *vis-à-vis* its molecular code. In both there is only a nebula indecipherable into its simple elements, indecipherable as to its truth.

ORBITAL AND NUCLEAR[20]

. . . Yet, despite this deterrence by the orbital authority — the nuclear code or molecular — events continue at ground level, mishaps are increasingly more numerous, despite the global process of contiguity and simultaneity of data. But, subtly, these events no longer make any sense; they are nothing more than a duplex effect of simulation at the summit. The best example must be the Vietnam war, since it was at the crossroads of a maximal historical or "revolutionary" stake and

[18]Baudrillard is analogizing the television/life relationship to the DNA/organism relationship. DNA carries information that codes the organism, and in that sense is a simulacrum for the organism; mutations in the DNA cause changes in the organism. Similarly, Baudrillard argues, television gives the viewer a picture of life, a simulacrum that is translated into a vision of human meaning that controls how people live.

[19]Aleatory means "random" (*aleator* is Latin for diceplayer).

[20]Here Baudrillard explores the idea of war as theater, where the simulacra are proxy conflicts within the 1946–1989 Cold War between the United States and the USSR, with China as a third major player. In an omitted section, Baudrillard considers the "orbital" space race in which the United States and USSR competed in a proxy war to put a man into Earth orbit and then onto the moon.

the installation of this deterrent authority. What sense did that war make, if not that its unfolding sealed the end of history in the culminating and decisive event of our age?

Why did such a difficult, long and arduous war vanish overnight as if by magic?

Why didn't the American defeat (the greatest reversal in its history) have any internal repercussions? If it had truly signified a setback in the planetary strategy of the USA, it should have necessarily disturbed the internal balance of the American political system. But no such thing happened.

Hence something else took place. Ultimately this war was only a crucial episode in a peaceful coexistence. It marked the advent of China to peaceful coexistence. The long sought-after securing and concretizing of China's non-intervention, China's apprenticeship in a global *modus vivendi*, the passing from a strategy of world revolution to one of a sharing of forces and empires, the transition from a radical alternative to political alternation in a now almost settled system (normalization of Peking-Washington relations): all this was the stake of the Vietnam war, and in that sense, the USA pulled out of Vietnam but they won the war.

And the war "spontaneously" came to an end when the objective had been attained. This is why it was de-escalated, demobilized so easily.[21]

The effects of this same remolding are legible in the field. The war lasted as long as there remained unliquidated elements irreducible to healthy politics and a discipline of power, even a communist one. When finally the war passed from the resistance to the hands of regular Northern

troops, it could stop: it had attained its objective. Thus the stake was a political relay. When the Vietnamese proved they were no longer bearers of an unpredictable subversion, it could be handed over to them. That this was a communist order wasn't fundamentally serious: it had proved itself, it could be trusted. They are even more effective than capitalists in liquidating "primitive" precapitalist and antiquated structures.

Same scenario as in the Algerian war.[22]

The other aspect of this war and of all wars since: behind the armed violence, the murderous antagonism between adversaries — which seems a matter of life and death, and which is played as such (otherwise you could never send out people to get smashed up in this kind of trouble), behind this simulacrum of a struggle to death and of ruthless global stakes, the two adversaries are fundamentally as one against that other, unnamed, never mentioned thing, whose objective outcome in war, with equal complicity between the two adversaries, is total liquidation. It is tribal, communal, precapitalist structures, every form of exchange, language and symbolic organization which must be abolished. Their murder is the object of war — and in its immense spectacular contrivance of death, war is only the medium of this process of terrorist rationalization by the social — the murder through which sociality can be founded, no matter what allegiance, communist or capitalist. The total complicity or division of labor between two adversaries (who can even make huge sacrifices to reach that) for the very purpose of remolding and domesticating social relations.

"The North Vietnamese were advised to countenance a scenario of the liquidation of the American presence through which, of course, honor must be preserved."

The scenario: the extremely heavy bombardment of Hanoi. The intolerable nature of this

[21]Baudrillard's theory is that the 1963–1975 Vietnam War had to continue as long as the United States was convinced that its Vietcong opponents were proxies for China, and that defeat in Vietnam would mean defeat by China throughout Asia. As soon as President Nixon reached a separate settlement with China, and control of the war passed to North Vietnam, ideology became irrelevant, the proxy aspect of the Vietnam War vanished, the war itself became a merely local conflict that could be quickly settled. The heavy bombing of Hanoi just before the withdrawal of U.S. forces was a different simulacrum intended for home consumption: the images of the bombing (which would cost many lives but would not change the political situation) would mitigate the appearance that the United States had been defeated.

[22]Like the U.S./Vietnam War, the Algerian war of independence (1954–1962) posed a Western colonial government against a populist independence movement. Baudrillard's interpretation of the 1962 endgame of the war would emphasize the mutation of the popular Algerian movement (the FLN) into an official political party under Ahmed Ben Bella and Houari Boumedienne, and the willingness of France to relinquish its colony to a government that would take power and repress the remnants of its populist base.

bombing should not conceal the fact that it was only a simulacrum to allow the Vietnamese to seem to countenance a compromise and Nixon to make the Americans swallow the retreat of their forces. The game was already won, nothing was objectively at stake but the credibility of the final montage.

Moralists about war, champions of war's exalted values should not be greatly upset: a war is not any the less heinous for being a mere simulacrum — the flesh suffers just the same, and the dead ex-combatants count as much there as in other wars. That objective is always amply accomplished, like that of the partitioning of territories and of disciplinary sociality. What no longer exists is the adversity of adversaries, the reality of antagonistic causes, the ideological seriousness of war — also the reality of defeat or victory, war being a process whose triumph lies quite beyond these appearances.

Jürgen Habermas

b. 1929

Jürgen Habermas, the most significant social philosopher in Germany and the Marxist most quoted by liberal humanists, was born in Düsseldorf and educated at the Universities of Göttingen and Zurich before taking his Ph.D. at Bonn in 1954. He taught at the University of Marburg and at Heidelberg before moving in 1964 to the Institute for Social Research at Frankfurt, where, as professor of philosophy, he was Theodor Adorno's assistant at the end of Adorno's career. Since 1981, Habermas has been director of the Max Planck Institute for Social Science at Starnberg; he also teaches at Northwestern University. Habermas has published nearly thirty books, including Knowledge and Human Interests *(1968),* Toward a Rational Society *(1971),* Legitimation Crisis *(1971),* Communication and the Evolution of Society *(1979),* The Philosophical Discourse of Modernity *(1985),* Autonomy and Solidarity *(1986),* On the Logic of the Social Sciences *(1988),* The New Conservatism: Cultural Criticism and the Historians' Debate *(1989),* Moral Consciousness and Communicative Action *(1990),* The Structural Transformation of the Public Sphere: An Inquiry into a Category of Bourgeois Society *(1991),* Remarks on Discourse Ethics *(1993),* Between Facts and Norms *(1996), and* The Pragmatics of Communication *(1998). Habermas's most recent work has taken up international politics:* The Postnational Constellation *(2001),* Religion and Rationality: Essays of Reason, God, and Modernity *(2002), and* Philosophy in a Time of Terror *(with Jacques Derrida, 2003). In 2004, Habermas won philosophy's equivalent of the Nobel, the Kyoto Prize; his acceptance speech was on "The Public Role of Religion in a Secular Context." The following essay, "Modernity versus Postmodernity" originated as a talk on the occasion of Habermas's acceptance of the Adorno prize awarded by the city of Frankfurt in 1980.*

Modernity versus Postmodernity

Last year, architects were admitted to the Biennial in Venice, following painters and filmmakers. The note sounded at this first Architecture Biennial was one of disappointment. I would describe it by saying that those who exhibited in Venice formed an avant-garde of reversed fronts. I mean that they sacrificed the tradition of modernity in order to make room for a new historicism. Upon this occasion, a critic of the German newspaper, *Frankfurter Allgemeine Zeitung*, advanced a thesis whose significance reaches beyond this particular event; it is a diagnosis of our times: "Postmodernity definitely presents itself as Antimodernity." This statement describes an emotional current of our times which has penetrated all spheres of intellectual life. It has placed on the agenda theories of post-enlightenment, postmodernity, even of posthistory.

From history we know the phrase:

"The Ancients and the Moderns"[1]

Let me begin by defining these concepts. The term "modern" has a long history, one which has been investigated by Hans Robert Jauss.[2] The word "modern" in its Latin form "modernus" was used for the first time in the late 5th century in order to distinguish the present, which had become officially Christian, from the Roman and pagan past. With varying content, the term "modern" again and again expresses the consciousness of an epoch that relates itself to the past of antiquity, in order to view itself as the result of a transition from the old to the new.

Some writers restrict this concept of "modernity" to the Renaissance, but this is historically too narrow. People considered themselves modern during the period of Charles the Great, in the 12th century, as well as in France of the late 17th century, at the time of the famous "Querelle des Anciens et des Modernes." This is to say, the term "modern" appeared and reappeared exactly during those periods in Europe when the consciousness of a new epoch formed itself through a renewed relationship to the ancients — whenever, moreover, antiquity was considered a model to be recovered through some kind of imitation.

The spell which the classics of the ancient world cast upon the spirit of later times was first dissolved with the ideals of the French Enlightenment. Specifically, the idea of being "modern" by looking back to the ancients changed with the belief, inspired by modern science, in the infinite progress of knowledge and in the infinite advance towards social and moral betterment. Another form of modernist consciousness was formed in the wake of this change. The romantic modernist sought to oppose the antique ideals of the classicists; he looked for a new historical epoch, and found it in the idealized Middle Ages. However, this new ideal age, established early in the 19th century, did not remain a fixed ideal. In the course of the 19th century, there emerged out

This essay was delivered as a James Lecture of The New York Institute for the Humanities at New York University on March 5, 1981. It had been delivered first in German in September 1980 when Habermas was awarded the Theodor W. Adorno prize by the city of Frankfurt. [Publisher's note]

Translated by Seyla Ben-Habib.

[1]Habermas refers primarily to the seventeenth-century debate (usually termed the *querelle des anciens et des modernes*) over whether the classical poets like Homer and Sophocles, Virgil and Seneca, were still the finest writers, or whether modern writers, admittedly building upon the ancients' achievements, had surpassed them. Dryden's "An Essay of Dramatic Poesy," p. 163, is one version of this argument; Swift's satirical "Battle of the Books" (1704) is another.

[2]Jauss is a prominent German literary historian and critic involved in "the aesthetics of reception," a type of criticism related to reader-response criticism in this country. For a discussion of "modern" see Jauss, *Ästhetische Normen und geschichtliche Reflexion in der Querelle des Anciens et des Modernes* (Munich, 1964). For a reference in English see Jauss, "History of Art and Pragmatic History," *Toward an Aesthetic of Reception*, trans. Timothy Bahti (Minneapolis: University of Minnesota Press, 1982), pp. 46–8. [Hal Foster, ed.] For Jauss, see p. 981.

of this romantic spirit that radicalized consciousness of modernity which freed itself from all specific historical ties. This most recent modernism simply makes an abstract opposition between tradition and the present; and we are, in a way, still the contemporaries of that kind of aesthetic modernity which first appeared in the midst of the 19th century. Since then, the distinguishing mark of works which count as modern is "the new" which will be overcome and made obsolete through the novelty of the next style. But, while that which is merely "stylish" will soon become outmoded, that which is modern preserves a secret tie to the classical. Of course, whatever can survive time has always been considered to be a classic. But the emphatically modern document no longer borrows this power of being a classic from the authority of a past epoch; instead, a modern work becomes a classic because it has once been authentically modern. Our sense of modernity creates its own self-enclosed canons of being classic. In this sense we speak, e.g., in view of the history of modern art, of classical modernity. The relation between "modern" and "classical" has definitely lost a fixed historical reference.

THE DISCIPLINE OF AESTHETIC MODERNITY

The spirit and discipline of aesthetic modernity assumed clear contours in the work of Baudelaire. Modernity then unfolded in various avant-garde movements, and finally reached its climax in the Café Voltaire[3] of the dadaists, and in surrealism. Aesthetic modernity is characterized by attitudes which find a common focus in a changed consciousness of time. This time consciousness expresses itself through metaphors of the vanguard and the avant-garde. The avant-garde understands itself as invading unknown territory, exposing itself to the dangers of sudden, of shocking encounters, conquering an as yet unoccupied future. The avant-garde must find a direction in a landscape into which no one seems to have yet ventured.

But these forward gropings, this anticipation of an undefined future and the cult of the new, mean in fact the exaltation of the present. The new time consciousness, which enters philosophy in the writings of Bergson, does more than express the experience of mobility in society, acceleration in history, of discontinuity in everyday life. The new value placed on the transitory, the elusive, and the ephemeral, the very celebration of dynamism, discloses the longing for an undefiled, an immaculate and stable present.

This explains the rather abstract language in which the modernist temper has spoken of the "past." Individual epochs lose their distinct forces. Historical memory is replaced by the heroic affinity of the present with the extremes of history: a sense of time wherein decadence immediately recognizes itself in the barbaric, the wild and the primitive. We observe the anarchistic intention of blowing up the continuum of history, and we can account for it in terms of the subversive force of this new aesthetic consciousness. Modernity revolts against the normalizing functions of tradition; modernity lives on the experience of rebelling against all that is normative. This revolt is one way to neutralize the standards of both, morality and utility. This aesthetic consciousness continuously stages a dialectical play between secrecy and public scandal; it is addicted to the fascination of that horror which accompanies the act of profaning, and is yet always in flight from the trivial results of profanation.

On the other hand, the time consciousness articulated in avant-garde art is not simply ahistorical; it is directed against what might be called a false normativity in history. The modern, avant-garde spirit has sought, instead, to use the past in a different way; it disposes over those pasts which have been made available by the objectifying scholarship of historicism, but it opposes at the same time a neutralized history, which is locked up in the museum of historicism.

Drawing upon the spirit of surrealism, Walter Benjamin constructs the relationship of modernity to history, in what I would call a posthistoricist attitude. He reminds us of the

---

[3]In 1915 the avant-garde antiwar artists (including Tristan Tzara and Hans Arp) who were to form the core of the dadaist movement met in neutral Switzerland at the Café Voltaire in Zurich. *Cabaret Voltaire* became the title of the periodical in which they circulated their collective productions and manifestos. In the 1920s surrealism developed out of the dadaist movement.

self-understanding of the French Revolution: "The Revolution cited ancient Rome, just as fashion cites an antiquated dress. Fashion has a scent for what is current, whenever this moves within the thicket of what was once." This is Benjamin's concept of the *Jetztzeit*, of the present as a moment of revelation; a time, in which splinters of a messianic presence are enmeshed. In this sense, for Robespierre, the antique Rome was a past laden with momentary revelations.[4]

Now, this spirit of aesthetic modernity has recently begun to age. It has been recited once more in the 1960s; after the 1970s, however, we must admit to ourselves that this modernism arouses a much fainter response today than it did fifteen years ago. Octavio Paz, a fellow traveller of modernity, noted already in the middle of the 1960s that "the avant-garde of 1967 repeats the deeds and gestures of those of 1917. We are experiencing the end of the idea of modern art." The work of Peter Bürger has since taught us to speak of "post-avant-garde" art; this term is chosen to indicate the failure of the surrealist rebellion.[5] But, what is the meaning of this failure? Does it signal a farewell to modernity? Thinking more generally, does the existence of a post-avant-garde mean there is a transition to that broader phenomenon called postmodernity?

This is in fact how Daniel Bell, the most brilliant of the American neoconservatives, interprets matters. In his book, *The Cultural Contradictions of Capitalism*, Bell argues that the crises of the developed societies of the West are to be traced back to a split between culture and society. Modernist culture has come to penetrate the values of everyday life; the life-world[6] is infected by modernism. Because of the forces of modernism, the principle of unlimited self-realization, the demand for authentic self-experience and the subjectivism of a hyperstimulated sensitivity have come to be dominant. This temperament unleashes hedonistic motives irreconcilable with the discipline of professional life in society, Bell says. Moreover, modernist culture is altogether incompatible with the moral basis of a purposive rational conduct of life. In this manner, Bell places the burden of responsibility for the dissolution of the Protestant ethic (a phenomenon which has already disturbed Max Weber), on the "adversary culture." Culture, in its modern form, stirs up hatred against the conventions and virtues of an everyday life, which has become rationalized under the pressures of economic and administrative imperatives.

I would call your attention to a complex wrinkle in this view. The impulse of modernity, we are told on the other hand, is exhausted; anyone who considers himself avant-garde can read his own death warrant. Although the avant-garde is still considered to be expanding, it is supposedly no longer creative. Modernism is dominant but dead. For the neoconservative, the question then arises: how can norms arise in society which will limit libertinism, reestablish the ethic of discipline and work? What new norms will put a brake on the levelling caused by the social welfare state, so that the virtues of individual competition for achievement can again dominate? Bell sees a religious revival to be the only solution. Religious faith tied to a faith in tradition will provide individuals with clearly defined identities, and with existential security.

CULTURAL MODERNITY AND SOCIETAL MODERNIZATION

One can certainly not conjure up by magic the compelling beliefs which command authority. Analyses like Bell's, therefore, only result in an attitude which is spreading in Germany no less than here in the States: an intellectual and political confrontation with the carriers of cultural modernity. I cite Peter Steinfels, an observer of the new style which the neoconservatives have imposed upon the intellectual scene in the 1970s.

---

[4]See Benjamin, "Theses on the Philosophy of History," *Illuminations*, trans. Harry Zohn (New York: Schocken, 1969), p. 261. [Hal Foster, ed.] *Jetztzeit* is literally "nowtime"; for Benjamin, see p. 1238. Maximilien Robespierre (1758–1794), the leader of the most radical wing of the Jacobin party during the French Revolution, appealed to the "republican virtue" of ancient Athens and Rome as justifications for the Reign of Terror.

[5]For Paz on the avant-garde see in particular *Children of the Mire: Modern Poetry from Romanticism to the Avant-Garde* (Cambridge: Harvard University Press, 1974), pp. 148–64. For Bürger see *Theory of the Avant-Garde* (Minneapolis: University of Minnesota Press, Fall 1983). [Hal Foster, ed.]

[6]Ordinary day-to-day lived experience.

The struggle takes the form of exposing every manifestation of what could be considered an oppositionist mentality and tracing its "logic" so as to link it to various forms of extremism: drawing the connection between modernism and nihilism . . . between government regulation and totalitarianism, between criticism or arms expenditures and subservience to communism, between Women's liberation or homosexual rights and the destruction of the family . . . between the Left generally and terrorism, anti-semitism, and fascism. . . .[7]

The *ad hominem* approach and the bitterness of these intellectual accusations have also been trumpeted loudly in Germany. They should not be explained so much in terms of the psychology of neoconservative writers; rather, they are rooted in the analytical weaknesses of neoconservative doctrine itself.

Neoconservatism shifts onto cultural modernism the uncomfortable burdens of a more or less successful capitalist modernization of the economy and society. The neoconservative doctrine blurs the relationship between the welcomed process of societal modernization on the one hand, and the lamented cultural development on the other. The neoconservative does not uncover the economic and social causes for the altered attitudes towards work, consumption, achievement, and leisure. Consequently, he attributes all of the following — hedonism, the lack of social identification, the lack of obedience, narcissism, the withdrawal from status and achievement competition — to the domain of "culture." In fact, however, culture is intervening in the creation of all these problems in only a very indirect and mediated fashion.

In the neoconservative view, those intellectuals who still feel themselves committed to the project of modernity are then presented as taking the place of those unanalyzed causes. The mood which feeds neoconservatism today in no way originates from the discontents about the antinomian[8] consequences of a culture breaking from the museums into the stream of ordinary life. These discontents have not been called into life by modernist intellectuals. They are rooted in deep seated reactions against the process of *societal* modernization. Under the pressures of the dynamics of economic growth and the organizational accomplishments of the state, this social modernization penetrates deeper and deeper into previous forms of human existence. I would describe this subordination of the life-worlds under the system's imperatives as a matter of disturbing the communicative infrastructure of everyday life.

Thus, for example, neo-populist protests only bring to expression in pointed fashion a widespread fear regarding the destruction of the urban and natural environment, and of forms of human sociability. There is a certain irony about these protests in terms of neoconservatism. The tasks of passing on a cultural tradition, of social integration, and of socialization require the adherence to a criterion of communicative rationality. The occasions for protest and discontent originate exactly when spheres of communicative action, centered on the reproduction and transmission of values and norms, are penetrated by a form of modernization guided by standards of economic and administrative rationality; however, those very spheres are dependent on quite different standards of rationalization — on the standards of what I would call communicative rationality.[9] But, neoconservative doctrines turn our attention precisely away from such societal processes: they project the causes, which they do not bring to light, onto the plane of a subversive culture and its advocates.

To be sure, cultural modernity generates its own aporias[10] as well. Independently from the consequences of *societal* modernization, and from *within the perspective of cultural* development itself, there originate motives for doubting the project of modernity. Having dealt with a feeble kind of criticism of modernity — that of

[7] Peter Steinfels, *The Neoconservatives* (New York: Simon and Schuster, 1979), p. 65. [Hal Foster, ed.]

[8] Rejecting social rules.

[9] For Habermas's notion of "communicative rationality," which entails rational unforced mutual argumentation between agents, see p. 1213. His point is that modern economic and political systems treat individuals as the passive objects of discourse, to be manipulated from above, and that no one should be surprised that those individuals no longer feel attached to the norms of a society in which they cannot meaningfully participate.

[10] Perplexing difficulties.

neoconservatism — let me now move our discussion of modernity and its discontents into a different domain that touches on these aporias of cultural modernity, issues which often serve only as a pretense for those positions (which either call for a postmodernity, or recommend a return to some form of premodernity or which throw modernity radically overboard).

THE PROJECT OF ENLIGHTENMENT

The idea of modernity is intimately tied to the development of European art; but what I call "the project of modernity" comes only into focus when we dispense with the usual concentration upon art. Let me start a different analysis by recalling an idea from Max Weber. He characterized cultural modernity as the separation of the substantive reason expressed in religion and metaphysics into three autonomous spheres. They are: science, morality and art. These came to be differentiated because the unified world conceptions of religion and metaphysics fell apart. Since the 18th century, the problems inherited from these older world-views could be rearranged so as to fall under specific aspects of validity: truth, normative rightness, authenticity and beauty. They could then be handled as questions of knowledge, or of justice and morality, or of taste. Scientific discourse, theories of morality, jurisprudence, the production and criticism of art, could in turn be institutionalized. Each domain of culture could be made to correspond to cultural professions, in which problems could be dealt with as the concern of special experts. This professionalized treatment of the cultural tradition brings to the fore the intrinsic structures of each of the three dimensions of culture. There appear the structures of cognitive-instrumental, moral-practical, and of aesthetic-expressive rationality, each of these under the control of specialists who seem more adept at being logical in these particular ways than other people are. As a result, the distance has grown between the culture of the experts and that of the larger public. What accrues to culture through specialized treatment and reflexion does not immediately and necessarily become the property of everyday praxis. With cultural rationalization of this sort, the threat increases that the life-world, whose traditional substance has already been devalued, will become more and more impoverished.

The project of modernity formulated in the 18th century by the philosophers of the Enlightenment consisted in their efforts to develop objective science, universal morality and law, and autonomous art, according to their inner logic. At the same time, this project intended to release the cognitive potentials of each of these domains to set them free from their esoteric forms. The Enlightenment philosophers wanted to utilize this accumulation of specialized culture for the enrichment of everyday life, that is to say, for the rational organization of everyday social life.

Enlightenment thinkers of the cast of mind of Condorcet still had the extravagant expectation that the arts and the sciences would promote not only the control of natural forces, but would also further understanding of the world and of the self, would promote moral progress, the justice of institutions, and even the happiness of human beings. The 20th century has shattered this optimism. The differentiation of science, morality, and art has come to mean the autonomy of the segments treated by the specialist and at the same time letting them split off from the hermeneutics of everyday communication. This splitting off is the problem that has given rise to those efforts to "negate" the culture of expertise. But the problem won't go away: should we try to hold on to the *intentions* of the Enlightenment, feeble as they may be, or should we declare the entire project of modernity a lost cause? I now want to return to the problem of artistic culture, having explained why, historically, that aesthetic modernity is a part only of cultural modernity in general.

THE FALSE PROGRAMS OF THE NEGATION OF CULTURE

Greatly oversimplifying, I would say in the history of modern art one can detect a trend toward ever greater autonomy in the definition and practice of art. The category of "beauty" and the domain of beautiful objects were first constituted in the Renaissance. In the course of the 18th century, literature, the fine arts and music were institutionalized as activities independent from sacred and courtly life. Finally, around the middle of the 19th century an aestheticist conception of art emerged, which encouraged the artist to produce his work according to the distinct consciousness of art for art's sake. The autonomy of the aesthetic sphere could then become a deliberate project: the talented artist could lend authentic expression to those experiences he had in encountering his own de-centered subjectivity, detached from the constraints of routinized cognition and everyday action.

In the mid-19th century, in painting and literature, a movement began which Octavio Paz finds epitomized already in the art criticism of Baudelaire. Color, lines, sounds and movement ceased to serve primarily the cause of representation; the media of expression and the techniques of production themselves became the aesthetic object. Theodor W. Adorno could therefore begin his *Aesthetic Theory* with the following sentence: "It is now taken for granted that nothing which concerns art can be taken for granted any more: neither art itself, nor art in its relationship to the whole, nor even the right of art to exist." And this is what surrealism then denied: *das Existenzrecht der Kunst als Kunst*.[11] To be sure, surrealism would not have challenged the right of art to exist, if modern art no longer had advanced a promise of happiness concerning its own relationship "to the whole" of life. For Schiller,[12] such a promise was delivered by aesthetic intuition, but not fulfilled by it. Schiller's *Letters on the Aesthetic Education of Man* speak to us of a utopia reaching beyond art itself. But by the time of Baudelaire, who repeated this *promesse de bonheur*,[13] via art, the utopia of reconciliation with society had gone sour. A relation of opposites had come into being; art had become a critical mirror, showing the irreconcilable nature of the aesthetic and the social world. This modernist transformation was all the more painfully realized, the more art alienated itself from life and withdrew into the untouchableness of complete autonomy. Out of such emotional currents finally gathered those explosive energies which

unloaded themselves in the surrealist attempt to blow up the autarkical sphere of art and to force a reconciliation of art and life.

But all those attempts to level art and life, fiction and praxis, appearance and reality to one plane; the attempts to remove the distinction between artifact and object of use, between conscious staging and spontaneous excitement; the attempts to declare everything to be art and everyone to be artist, to retract all criteria and to equate aesthetic judgment with the expression of subjective experiences — all these undertakings have proved themselves to be sort of nonsense experiments. These experiments have served to bring back to life, and to illuminate all the more glaringly, exactly those structures of art which they were meant to dissolve. They gave a new legitimacy, as an end in itself, to appearance as the medium of fiction, to the transcendence of the art work over society, to the concentrated and planned character of artistic production as well as to the special cognitive status of judgements of taste. The radical attempt to negate art has ended up ironically by giving due exactly to these categories through which Enlightenment aesthetics had circumscribed its object domain. The surrealists waged the most extreme warfare, but two mistakes in particular destroyed their revolt. First, when the containers of an autonomously developed cultural sphere are shattered, the contents get dispersed. Nothing remains from a desublimated meaning or a destructed form; an emancipatory effect does not follow.

Their second mistake has more important consequences. In everyday communication, cognitive meanings, moral expectations, subjective expressions and evaluations must relate to one another. Communication processes need a cultural tradition covering all spheres — cognitive, moral-practical and expressive. A rationalized everyday life, therefore, could hardly be saved from cultural impoverishment through breaking open a single cultural sphere — art — and so providing access to just one of the specialized knowledge complexes. The surrealist revolt would have replaced only one abstraction.

In the sphere of theoretical knowledge and morality as well, there are parallels to this failed attempt of what we might call the false negation

[11]The right of art to exist as art.
[12]For Friedrich von Schiller, see p. 298.
[13]French for "promise of happiness."

of culture. Only they are less pronounced. Since the days of the Young Hegelians, there has been talk about the negation of philosophy. Since Marx, the question of the relationship of theory and practice has been posed. However, Marxist intellectuals joined a social movement; and only at its peripheries were there sectarian attempts to carry out a program of the negation of philosophy similar to the surrealist program to negate art. A parallel to the surrealist mistakes becomes visible in these programs when one observes the consequences of dogmatism and of moral rigorism.

A reified everyday praxis can be cured only by creating unconstrained interaction of the cognitive with the moral-practical and the aesthetic-expressive elements.[14] Reification cannot be overcome by forcing just one of those highly stylized cultural spheres to open up and become more accessible. Instead, we see under certain circumstances a relationship emerge between terroristic activities and the over-extension of any one of these spheres into other domains: examples would be tendencies to aestheticize politics, or to replace politics by moral rigorism or to submit it to the dogmatism of a doctrine. These phenomena should not lead us, however, into denouncing the intentions of the surviving Enlightenment tradition as intentions rooted in a "terroristic reason."[15] Those who lump together the very project of modernity with the state of consciousness and

the spectacular action of the individual terrorist are no less short-sighted than those who would claim that the incomparably more persistent and extensive bureaucratic terror practiced in the dark, in the cellars of the military and secret police, and in camps and institutions, is the *raison d'être* of the modern state, only because this kind of administrative terror makes use of the coercive means of modern bureaucracies.

ALTERNATIVES

I think that instead of giving up modernity and its project as a lost cause, we should learn from the mistakes of those extravagant programs which have tried to negate modernity. Perhaps the types of reception of art may offer an example which at least indicates the direction of a way out.

Bourgeois art had two expectations at once from its audiences. On the one hand, the layman who enjoyed art should educate himself to become an expert. On the other hand, he should also behave as a competent consumer who uses art and relates aesthetic experiences to his own life problems. This second, and seemingly harmless, manner of experiencing art has lost its radical implications, exactly because it had a confused relation to the attitude of being expert and professional.

To be sure, artistic production would dry up, if it were not carried out in the form of a specialized treatment of autonomous problems, and if it were to cease to be the concern of experts who do not pay so much attention to exoteric questions. Both artists and critics accept thereby the fact that such problems fall under the spell of what I earlier called the "inner logic" of a cultural domain. But this sharp delineation, this exclusive concentration on one aspect of validity alone, and the exclusion of aspects of truth and justice, breaks down as soon as aesthetic experience is drawn into an individual life history and is absorbed into ordinary life. The reception of art by the layman, or by the "everyday expert," goes in a rather different direction than the reception of art by the professional critic.

Albrecht Wellmer has drawn my attention to one way that an aesthetic experience which is not framed around the experts' critical judgements of taste can have its significance altered: as soon as

[14]For Habermas, the Enlightenment project was an integration of the individual lifeworld with the spheres of knowledge, morality, and art. But in the course of the nineteenth century these spheres (as science, jurisprudence, and aesthetics) became "reified" (made into "things") as the separate domains of experts, with limited access by ordinary individuals. The radical experiments with aesthetics (represented by dadaism and surrealism) were an attempt to break down the barriers to individual discourse in just one of these spheres (art) while leaving the others untouched. His point here is that progress toward the Enlightenment ideal can only occur when all these spheres become simultaneously accessible to the lifeworld of the individual, and that when one of these spheres is used as a tool to pry open the others, the result is different forms of "terrorism."

[15]The phrase "to aestheticize politics" echoes Benjamin's famous formulation of the false social program of the fascists in "The Work of Art in the Age of Mechanical Reproduction." Habermas's criticism here of Enlightenment critics seems directed less at Adorno and Max Horkheimer than at the contemporary *nouveaux philosophes* (Bernard-Henri Lèvy, etc.) and their German and American counterparts. [Hal Foster, ed.]

such an experience is used to illuminate a life-historical situation and is related to life problems, it enters into a language game which is no longer that of the aesthetic critic. The aesthetic experience then not only renews the interpretation of our needs in whose light we perceive the world. It permeates as well our cognitive significations and our normative expectations and changes the manner in which all these moments refer to one another. Let me give an example of this process.

This manner of receiving and relating to art is suggested in the first volume of the work *The Aesthetics of Resistance* by the German-Swedish writer Peter Weiss. Weiss describes the process of reappropriating art by presenting a group of politically motivated, knowledge-hungry workers in 1937 in Berlin.[16] These were young people, who, through an evening high school education, acquired the intellectual means to fathom the general and the social history of European art. Out of the resilient edifice of the objective mind, embodied in works of art which they saw again and again in the museums in Berlin, they started removing their own chips of stone, which they gathered together and reassembled in the context of their own milieu. This milieu was far removed from that of traditional education as well as from the then existing regime. These young workers went back and forth between the edifice of European art and their own milieu until they were able to illuminate both.

In examples like this which illustrate the reappropriation of the expert's culture from the standpoint of the life-world, we can discern an element which does justice to the intentions of the hopeless surrealist revolts, perhaps even more to Brecht's and Benjamin's interests in how art works, which lost their aura, could yet be received in illuminating ways.[17] In sum, the project of modernity has not yet been fulfilled. And the reception of art is only one of at least three of its aspects. The project aims at a differentiated relinking of modern culture with an everyday praxis that still depends on vital heritages, but would be impoverished through mere traditionalism. This new connection, however, can only be established under the condition that societal modernization will also be steered in a different direction. The life-world has to become able to develop institutions out of itself which set limits to the internal dynamics and to the imperatives of an almost autonomous economic system and its administrative complements.

If I am not mistaken, the chances for this today are not very good. More or less in the entire Western world, a climate has developed that furthers capitalist modernization processes as well as trends critical of cultural modernism. The disillusionment with the very failures of those programs that called for the negation of art and philosophy has come to serve as a pretense for conservative positions. Let me briefly distinguish the antimodernism of the young conservatives from the premodernism of the old conservatives and from the postmodernism of the neoconservatives.

The *Young Conservatives* recapitulate the basic experience of aesthetic modernity. They claim as their own the revelations of a decentered subjectivity, emancipated from the imperatives of work and usefulness, and with this experience they step outside the modern world. On the basis of modernistic attitudes, they justify an irreconcilable anti-modernism. They remove into the sphere of the far away and the archaic the spontaneous powers of imagination, of self-experience and of emotionality. To instrumental reason, they juxtapose in Manichean fashion a principle only accessible through evocation, be it the will to power or sovereignty, Being or the Dionysiac force of the poetical. In France this line leads from Bataille via Foucault to Derrida.[18]

[16]The reference is to the novel *Die Ästhetik des Widerstands* (1975–8) by the author perhaps best known here for his 1965 play *Marat/Sade*. The work of art "reappropriated" by the workers is the Pergamon altar, emblem of power, classicism and rationality. [Hal Foster, ed.] The Pergamon Altar is a magnificent architectural structure, with a frieze of sculptures almost 400 feet long, from a temple of Zeus built at Bergama in the second century B.C.E. It was acquired by Imperial Germany in the late nineteenth century and placed in a museum in Berlin, where it symbolized the striving for power of the Kaisers and, later, the Nazis — hence the fantasy that Weiss attaches to it.

[17]For Brecht and Benjamin, see pp. 1232 and 1249.

[18]For Foucault and Derrida, see pp. 904 and 914. Georges Bataille (1897–1962), avant-garde author of *Story of the Eye, The Tears of Eros*, and many other works, is the literary "terrorist" link between the dadaists and surrealists of the 1920s and the poststructuralists Habermas deplores; among other things, he started the journal *Critique*, which published the early work of Barthes, Foucault, and Derrida.

The *Old Conservatives* do not allow themselves to be contaminated by cultural modernism. They observe the decline of substantive reason, the differentiation of science, morality and art, the modern world view and its merely procedural rationality, with sadness and recommend a withdrawal to a position *anterior* to modernity.

Neo-Aristotelianism, in particular, enjoys a certain success today. In view of the problematic of ecology, it allows itself to call for a cosmological ethic. As belonging to this school, which originates with Leo Strauss, one can count for example the interesting works of Hans Jonas and Robert Spaemann.[19]

Finally, the *Neoconservatives* welcome the development of modern science, as long as this only goes beyond its sphere to carry forward technical progress, capitalist growth and rational administration. Moreover, they recommend a politics of defusing the explosive content of cultural modernity. According to one thesis, science, when properly understood, has become irrevocably meaningless for the orientation of the life-world. A further thesis is that politics must be kept as far aloof as possible from the demands of moral-practical justification. And a third thesis asserts the pure immanence of art, disputes that it has a utopian content, and points to its illusory character in order to limit the aesthetic experience to privacy.

[19]Leo Strauss (1899–1973), political philosopher at the University of Chicago, was the intellectual father of the "neoconservative" movement. Hans Jonas (1903–1993), moral philosopher associated with the New School, author of *The Imperative of Responsibility* (1974), an attempt to craft morality for a technological age. Robert Spaemann (b. 1927), professor of moral and religious philosophy at the University of Salzburg, author of *Happiness and Benevolence*.

One could name here the early Wittgenstein, Carl Schmitt of the middle period, and Gottfried Benn of the late period. But with the decisive confinement of science, morality and art to autonomous spheres separated from the life-world and administered by experts, what remains from the project of cultural modernity is only what we would have if we were to give up the project of modernity altogether. As a replacement one points to traditions, which, however, are held to be immune to demands of (normative) justification and validation.

This typology is like any other, of course, a simplification; but it may not prove totally useless for the analysis of contemporary intellectual and political confrontations. I fear that the ideas of anti-modernity, together with an additional touch of premodernity, are becoming popular in the circles of alternative culture. When one observes the transformations of consciousness within political parties in Germany, a new ideological shift (*Tendenzwende*) becomes visible. And this is the alliance of postmodernists with premodernists. It seems to me that there is no party in particular that monopolizes the abuse of intellectuals and the position of neoconservatism. I therefore have good reason to be thankful for the liberal spirit in which the city of Frankfurt offers me a prize bearing the name of Theodor Adorno.[20] Adorno, a most significant son of this city, who as philosopher and writer has stamped the image of the intellectual in our country in incomparable fashion; even more, who has become the very image of emulation for the intellectual.

[20]For Adorno, see p. 1254. This text was originally Habermas's lecture on receiving the Adorno prize awarded by the city of Frankfurt.

Fredric Jameson

b. 1934

In "Postmodernism and Consumer Society," Marxist critic Fredric Jameson locates postmodernism as the cultural form taken by contemporary capitalism, in which we are primarily shoppers rather than workers, defined not by what work we do but by what we choose to buy from a global marketplace. (For biographical information on Jameson, see p. 1290.)

Postmodernism and Consumer Society

The concept of postmodernism is not widely accepted or even understood today. Some of the resistance to it may come from the unfamiliarity of the works it covers, which can be found in all the arts: the poetry of John Ashbery, for instance, as well as the much simpler talk poetry that came out of the reaction against complex, ironic, academic modernist poetry in the 1960s; the reaction against modern architecture and in particular against the monumental buildings of the International Style; the pop buildings and decorated sheds celebrated by Robert Venturi in his manifesto *Learning from Las Vegas*; Andy Warhol, pop art and the more recent Photorealism; in music, the moment of John Cage but also the later synthesis of classical and "popular" styles found in composers like Philip Glass and Terry Riley, and also punk and new wave rock with such groups as The Clash, Talking Heads and the Gang of Four; in film, everything that comes out of Godard — contemporary vanguard film and video — as well as a whole new style of commercial or fiction films, which has its equivalent in contemporary novels, where the works of William Burroughs, Thomas Pynchon and Ishmael Reed on the one hand, and the French new novel[1] on the other, are also to be numbered among the varieties of what can be called postmodernism.

This list would seem to make two things clear at once. First, most of the postmodernisms mentioned above emerge as specific reactions against the established forms of high modernism, against this or that dominant high modernism which conquered the university, the museum, the art gallery network and the foundations. Those formerly subversive and embattled styles — Abstract Expressionism; the great modernist poetry of Pound, Eliot or Wallace Stevens; the International Style (Le Corbusier, Gropius, Mies van der Rohe); Stravinsky; Joyce, Proust and Mann — felt to be scandalous or shocking by our grandparents are, for the generation which arrives at the gate in the 1960s, felt to be the establishment and the enemy — dead, stifling, canonical, the reified monuments one has to destroy to do anything new. This means that there will be as many different forms of postmodernism as there were high modernisms in place, since the former are at least initially specific and local reactions against those models. That obviously does not make the job of describing postmodernism as a coherent thing any easier, since the unity of this new impulse — if it has one — is given not in itself but in the very modernism it seeks to displace.

The second feature of this list of postmodernisms is the effacement of some key boundaries or separations, most notably the erosion of the older distinction between high culture and so-called mass or popular culture. This is perhaps the most distressing development of all from an academic standpoint, which has traditionally had a vested interest in preserving a realm of high or elite culture against the surrounding environment of philistinism, of schlock and kitsch,[2] of TV series and *Reader's Digest* culture, and in transmitting difficult and complex skills of reading, listening and seeing to its initiates. But many of the newer postmodernisms have been fascinated precisely by that whole landscape of advertising and motels, of the Las Vegas strip, of the Late Show and B-grade Hollywood film, of so-called paraliterature with its airport paperback categories of the gothic and the romance, the popular biography, the murder mystery and the science fiction or fantasy novel. They no longer "quote" such "texts" as a Joyce might have done, or a Mahler; they incorporate them, to the point where the line between high art and commercial forms seems increasingly difficult to draw.

A rather different indication of this effacement of the older categories of genre and discourse can

---

[1]Jameson means the experimental *nouveau roman* of Butor, Duras, and Robbe-Grillet.

[2]*Schlock* denotes mere garbage; *kitsch*, on the other hand, is lovingly detailed and crafted art that is in terrible taste. *Philistinism* denotes indifference to the arts in general.

be found in what is sometimes called contemporary theory. A generation ago there was still a technical discourse of professional philosophy — the great systems of Sartre or the phenomenologists,[3] the work of Wittgenstein or analytical or common language philosophy[4] — alongside which one could still distinguish that quite different discourse of the other academic disciplines — of political science, for example, or sociology or literary criticism. Today, increasingly, we have a kind of writing simply called "theory" which is all or none of those things at once. This new kind of discourse, generally associated with France and so-called French theory, is becoming widespread and marks the end of philosophy as such. Is the work of Michel Foucault, for example, to be called philosophy, history, social theory or political science? It's undecidable, as they say nowadays, and I will suggest that such "theoretical discourse" is also to be numbered among the manifestations of postmodernism.

Now I must say a word about the proper use of this concept: it is not just another word for the description of a particular style. It is also, at least in my use, a periodizing concept whose function is to correlate the emergence of new formal features in culture with the emergence of a new type of social life and a new economic order — what is often euphemistically called modernization, post-industrial or consumer society, the society of the media or the spectacle, or multinational capitalism. This new moment of capitalism can be dated from the post-war boom in the United States in the late 1940s and early 1950s or, in France, from the establishment of the Fifth Republic in 1958. The 1960s are in many ways the key transitional period, a period in which the new international order (neo-colonialism, the Green Revolution, computerization and electronic information) is at one and the same time set in place and is swept and shaken by its own internal contradictions and by external resistance. I want here to sketch a few of the ways in which

the new postmodernism expresses the inner truth of that newly emergent social order of late capitalism, but will have to limit the description to only two of its significant features, which I will call pastiche and schizophrenia; they will give us a chance to sense the specificity of the postmodernist experience of space and time respectively.

PASTICHE ECLIPSES PARODY

One of the most significant features or practices in postmodernism today is pastiche. I must first explain this term (from the language of the visual arts), which people generally tend to confuse with or assimilate to that related verbal phenomenon called parody. Both pastiche and parody involve the imitation or, better still, the mimicry of other styles and particularly of the mannerisms and stylistic twitches of other styles. It is obvious that modern literature in general offers a very rich field for parody, since the great modern writers have all been defined by the invention or production of rather unique styles: think of the Faulknerian long sentence or of D. H. Lawrence's characteristic nature imagery; think of Wallace Stevens' peculiar way of using abstractions; think also of mannerisms of the philosophers, of Heidegger for example, or Sartre; think of the musical styles of Mahler or Prokofiev. All of these styles, however different from one another, are comparable in this: each is quite unmistakable; once one of them is learned, it is not likely to be confused with something else.

Now parody capitalizes on the uniqueness of these styles and seizes on their idiosyncrasies and eccentricities to produce an imitation which mocks the original. I won't say that the satiric impulse is conscious in all forms of parody: in any case, a good or great parodist has to have some secret sympathy for the original, just as a great mimic has to have the capacity to put himself/herself in the place of the person imitated. Still, the general effect of parody is — whether in sympathy or with malice — to cast ridicule on the private nature of these stylistic mannerisms and their excessiveness and eccentricity with respect to the way people normally speak or write. So there remains somewhere behind all parody the feeling that there is a linguistic norm in contrast

---

[3]The particular phenomenologists Jameson probably has in mind are the ones that influenced Jean-Paul Sartre: his own teacher, Martin Heidegger, and Heidegger's teacher, Edmond Husserl.

[4]Exemplified in this book by the work of J. L. Austin; see p. 679.

to which the styles of the great modernists can be mocked.

But what would happen if one no longer believed in the existence of normal language, of ordinary speech, of the linguistic norm (the kind of clarity and communicative power celebrated by Orwell in his famous essay "Politics and the English Language," say)? One could think of it in this way: perhaps the immense fragmentation and privatization of modern literature — its explosion into a host of distinct private styles and mannerisms — foreshadows deeper and more general tendencies in social life as a whole. Supposing that modern art and modernism — far from being a kind of specialized aesthetic curiosity — actually anticipated social developments along these lines; supposing that in the decades since the emergence of the great modern styles society had itself begun to fragment in this way, each group coming to speak a curious private language of its own, each profession developing its private code or idiolect,[5] and finally each individual coming to be a kind of linguistic island, separated from everyone else? But then in that case, the very possibility of any linguistic norm in terms of which one could ridicule private languages and idiosyncratic styles would vanish, and we would have nothing but stylistic diversity and heterogeneity.

That is the moment at which pastiche appears and parody has become impossible. Pastiche is, like parody, the imitation of a peculiar or unique style, the wearing of a stylistic mask, speech in a dead language: but it is a neutral practice of such mimicry, without parody's ulterior motive, without the satirical impulse, without laughter, without that still latent feeling that there exists something *normal* compared with which what is being imitated is rather comic. Pastiche is blank parody, parody that has lost its sense of humor: pastiche is to parody what that curious thing, the modern practice of a kind of blank irony, is to what Wayne Booth calls the stable and comic ironies of the eighteenth century.[6]

[5] The word *idiolect* usually denotes those aspects of language that are peculiar to a single individual; a profession would have a jargon, or perhaps a dialect.

[6] Wayne C. Booth, *The Rhetoric of Irony* (Chicago, 1975). [Jameson]

THE DEATH OF THE SUBJECT

But now we need to introduce a new piece into this puzzle, which may help to explain why classical modernism is a thing of the past and why postmodernism should have taken its place. This new component is what is generally called the "death of the subject" or, to say it in more conventional language, the end of individualism as such. The great modernisms were, as we have said, predicated on the invention of a personal, private style, as unmistakable as your fingerprint, as incomparable as your own body. But this means that the modernist aesthetic is in some way organically linked to the conception of a unique self and private identity, a unique personality and individuality, which can be expected to generate its own unique vision of the world and to forge its own unique, unmistakable style.

Yet today, from any number of distinct perspectives, the social theorists, the psychoanalysts, even the linguists, not to speak of those of us who work in the area of culture and cultural and formal change, are all exploring the notion that this kind of individualism and personal identity is a thing of the past; that the old individual or individualist subject is "dead"; and that one might even describe the concept of the unique individual and the theoretical basis of individualism as ideological. There are in fact two positions on all this, one of which is more radical than the other. The first one is content to say: yes, once upon a time, in the classic age of competitive capitalism, in the heyday of the nuclear family and the emergence of the bourgeoisie as the hegemonic social class, there was such a thing as individualism, as individual subjects. But today, in the age of corporate capitalism, of the so-called organization man, of bureaucracies in business as well as in the state, of demographic explosion — today, that older bourgeois individual subject no longer exists.

Then there is a second position, the more radical of the two — what one might call the poststructuralist position. It adds: not only is the bourgeois individual subject a thing of the past, it is also a myth; it never really existed in the first place; there have never been autonomous subjects of that type. Rather, this construct is merely a philosophical and cultural mystification which sought to persuade people that they "had" individual subjects and possessed some unique personal identity.

For our purposes, it is not particularly important to decide which of these positions is correct (or rather, which is more interesting and productive). What we have to retain from all this is rather an aesthetic dilemma: because if the experience and the ideology of the unique self, an experience and ideology which informed the stylistic practice of classical modernism, is over and done with, then it is no longer clear what the artists and writers of the present period are supposed to be doing. What is clear is merely that the older models — Picasso, Proust, T. S. Eliot — do not work any more (or are positively harmful), since nobody has that kind of unique private world and style to express any longer. And this is perhaps not merely a "psychological" matter: we also have to take into account the immense weight of seventy or eighty years of classical modernism itself. This is yet another sense in which the writers and artists of the present day will no longer be able to invent new styles and worlds — they've already been invented; only a limited number of combinations are possible; the unique ones have been thought of already. So the weight of the whole modernist aesthetic tradition — now dead — also "weighs like a nightmare on the brain of the living," as Marx said in another context.[7]

Hence, once again, pastiche: in a world in which stylistic innovation is no longer possible, all that is left is to imitate dead styles, to speak through the masks and with the voices of the styles in the imaginary museum. But this means that contemporary or postmodernist art is going to be about art itself in a new kind of way; even more, it means that one of its essential messages will involve the necessary failure of art and the aesthetic, the failure of the new, the imprisonment in the past.

THE NOSTALGIA MODE

As this may seem very abstract, I want to give a few examples, one of which is so omnipresent

[7]Marx said that "the tradition of all dead generations weighs like a nightmare on the brains of the living" in "The Eighteenth Brumaire of Louis Napoleon" (1852).

that we rarely link it with the kinds of developments in high art discussed here. This particular practice of pastiche is not high-cultural but very much within mass culture, and it is generally known as the "nostalgia film" (what the French neatly call la mode rétro — retrospective styling). We must conceive of this category in the broadest way. Narrowly, no doubt, it consists merely of films about the past and about specific generational moments of that past. Thus, one of the inaugural films in this new "genre" (if that's what it is) was Lucas's American Graffiti, which in 1973 set out to recapture all the atmosphere and stylistic peculiarities of the 1950s United States: the United States of the Eisenhower era. Polanski's great film Chinatown (1974) does something similar for the 1930s, as does Bertolucci's The Conformist (1969) for the Italian and European context of the same period, the fascist era in Italy; and so forth. We could go on listing these films for some time. But why call them pastiche? Are they not, rather, work in the more traditional genre known as the historical film — work which can more simply be theorized by extrapolating that other well-known form, the historical novel?

I have my reasons for thinking that we need new categories for such films. But let me first add some anomalies: supposing I suggested that Star Wars (George Lucas, 1977) is also a nostalgia film. What could that mean? I presume that we can agree that this is not a historical film about our own intergalactic past. Let me put it somewhat differently: one of the most important cultural experiences of the generations that grew up from the 1930s to the 1950s was the Saturday afternoon serial of the Buck Rogers type — alien villains, true American heroes, heroines in distress, the death ray or the doomsday box, and the cliff-hanger at the end whose miraculous solution was to be witnessed next Saturday afternoon. Star Wars reinvents this experience in the form of a pastiche; there is no point to a parody of such serials, since they are long extinct. Far from being a pointless satire of such dead forms, Star Wars satisfies a deep (might I even say repressed?) longing to experience them again: it is a complex object in which on some first level children and adolescents can take the adventures straight, while the adult public is able to gratify a deeper and more properly nostalgic desire to return to that older period and to live its strange old aesthetic artefacts through once again. This film is thus *metonymically* a historical or nostalgia film. Unlike *American Graffiti*, it does not reinvent a picture of the past in its lived totality; rather, by reinventing the feel and shape of characteristic art objects of an older period (the serials), it seeks to reawaken a sense of the past associated with those objects. *Raiders of the Lost Ark* (1981), meanwhile, occupies an intermediary position here: on some level it is about the 1930s and 1940s, but in reality it too conveys that period metonymically through its own characteristic adventure stories (which are no longer ours).

Now let me discuss another anomaly which may take us further towards understanding nostalgia films in particular and pastiche generally. This one involves a recent film called *Body Heat* (Lawrence Kasdan, 1981), which, as has abundantly been pointed out by the critics, is a kind of distant remake of *Double Indemnity* (1944). (The allusive and elusive plagiarism of older plots is, of course, also a feature of pastiche.) Now *Body Heat* is technically not a nostalgia film, since it takes place in a contemporary setting, in a little Florida village near Miami. On the other hand, this technical contemporaneity is most ambiguous indeed: the credits — always our first cue — are all lettered in a 1930s Art-Deco style which cannot but trigger nostalgic reactions (first to *Chinatown*, no doubt, and then beyond it to some more historical referent). Then the very style of the hero himself is ambiguous: William Hurt is a new star but has nothing of the distinctive style of the preceding generation of male superstars like Steve McQueen or Jack Nicholson, or rather, his persona here is a kind of mix of their characteristics with an older role of the type generally associated with Clark Gable. So here too there is a faintly archaic feel to all this. This spectator begins to wonder why this story, which could have been situated anywhere, is set in a small Florida town, in spite of its contemporary reference. One begins to realize after a while that the small town setting has a crucial strategic function: it allows the film to do without most of the signals and references which we might associate with the contemporary world, with consumer society — the appliances and artefacts, the high rises, the object world of late capitalism. Technically, then, its objects (its cars, for instance) are 1980s products, but everything in the film conspires to blur that immediate contemporary reference and to make it possible to receive this too as nostalgia work — as a narrative set in some indefinable nostalgic past, an eternal 1930s, say, beyond history. It seems to me exceedingly symptomatic to find the very style of nostalgia films invading and colonizing even those movies today which have contemporary settings, as though, for some reason, we were unable today to focus our own present, as though we had become incapable of achieving aesthetic representations of our own current experience. But if that is so, then it is a terrible indictment of consumer capitalism itself — or, at the very least, an alarming and pathological symptom of a society that has become incapable of dealing with time and history.

So now we come back to the question of why the nostalgia film or pastiche is to be considered different from the older historical novel or film. I should also include in this discussion the major literary example of all this, to my mind: the novels of E. L. Doctorow — *Ragtime*, with its turn-of-the-century atmosphere, and *Loon Lake*, for the most part about our 1930s. But these are, in my opinion, historical novels in appearance only. Doctorow is a serious artist and one of the few genuinely left or radical novelists at work today. It is no disservice to him, however, to suggest that his narratives do not represent our historical past so much as they represent our ideas or cultural stereotypes about that past. Cultural production has been driven back inside the mind, within the monadic subject: it can no longer look directly out of its eyes at the real world for the referent but must, as in Plato's cave, trace its mental images of the world on its confining walls. If there is any realism left here, it is a "realism" which springs from the shock of grasping that confinement and of realizing that, for whatever peculiar reasons, we seem condemned to seek the historical past through our own pop images and stereotypes about the past, which itself remains forever out of reach.

POSTMODERNISM AND THE CITY

Now, before I try to offer a somewhat more positive conclusion, I want to sketch the analysis of a full-blown postmodern building — a work which is in many ways uncharacteristic of that postmodern architecture whose principal names are Robert Venturi, Charles Moore, Michael Graves and more recently Frank Gehry, but which to my mind offers some very striking lessons about the originality of postmodernist space. Let me amplify the figure which has run through the preceding remarks, and make it even more explicit: I am proposing the notion that we are here in the presence of something like a mutation in built space itself. My implication is that we ourselves, the human subjects who happen into this new space, have not kept pace with that evolution; there has been a mutation in the object, unaccompanied as yet by any equivalent mutation in the subject; we do not yet possess the perceptual equipment to match this new hyperspace, as I will call it, in part because our perceptual habits were formed in that older kind of space I have called the space of high modernism. The newer architecture — like many of the other cultural products I have evoked in the preceding remarks — therefore stands as something like an imperative to grow new organs to expand our sensoria and our bodies to some new, as yet unimaginable, perhaps ultimately impossible, dimensions.

The Bonaventure Hotel

The building whose features I will enumerate here is the Westin Bonaventure Hotel, built in the new Los Angeles downtown by the architect and developer John Portman, whose other works include the various Hyatt Regencies, the Peachtree Center in Atlanta, and the Renaissance Center in Detroit. I must mention the populist aspect of the rhetorical defence of postmodernism against the elite (and utopian) austerities of the great architectural modernisms: it is generally affirmed that these newer buildings are popular works on the one hand; and that they respect the vernacular of the American city fabric on the other. That is to say that they no longer attempt, as did the masterworks and monuments of high modernism, to insert a different, distinct, an elevated, a new utopian language into the tawdry and commercial sign-system of the surrounding city, but on the contrary, seek to speak that very language, using its lexicon and syntax, that has been emblematically "learned from Las Vegas."

On the first of these counts, Portman's Bonaventure fully confirms the claim: it is a popular building, visited with enthusiasm by locals and tourists alike (although Portman's other buildings are even more successful in this respect). The populist insertion into the city fabric is, however, another matter, and it is with this that we will begin. There are three entrances to the Bonaventure: one from Figueroa, and the other two by way of elevated gardens on the other side of the hotel, which is built into the remaining slope of the former Beacon Hill. None of these is anything like the old hotel marquee, or the monumental *porte-cochère*[8] with which the sumptuous buildings of yesteryear were wont to stage your passage from city street to the older interior. The entryways of the Bonaventure are, as it were, lateral and rather backdoor affairs: the gardens in the back admit you to the sixth floor of the towers, and even there you must walk down one flight to find the elevator by which you gain access to the lobby. Meanwhile, what one is still tempted to think of as the front entry, on Figueroa, admits you, baggage and all, onto the second-story balcony, from which you must take an escalator down to the main registration desk. More about these elevators and escalators in a moment. What I first want to suggest about these curiously unmarked ways-in is that they seem to have been imposed by some new category of closure governing the inner space of the hotel itself (and this over and above the material constraints under which Portman had to work). I believe that, with a certain number of other characteristic postmodern buildings, such as the Beaubourg in Paris, or the Eaton Center in Toronto, the Bonaventure aspires to being a total space, a complete world, a kind of miniature city (and I would want to add that to this new total space corresponds a new

[8]An entranceway with a large overhang allowing people to enter from a coach (or automobile) without getting wet from the rain.

collective practice, a new mode in which individuals move and congregate, something like the practice of a new and historically original kind of hyper-crowd). In this sense, then, the mini-city of Portman's Bonaventure ideally ought not to have entrances at all (since the entryway is always the seam that links the building to the rest of the city that surrounds it), for it does not wish to be a part of the city, but rather its equivalent and its replacement or substitute. That is, however, obviously not possible or practical, hence the deliberate downplaying and reduction of the entrance function to its bare minimum. But this disjunction from the surrounding city is very different from that of the great monuments of the International Style: there, the act of disjunction was violent, visible and had a very real symbolic significance — as in Le Corbusier's great *pilotis*,[9] whose gesture radically separates the new utopian space of the modern from the degraded and fallen city fabric, which it thereby explicitly repudiates (although the gamble of the modern was that this new utopian space, in the virulence of its Novum, would fan out and transform that eventually by the power of its new spatial language). The Bonaventure, however, is content to "let the fallen city fabric continue to be in its being" (to parody Heidegger); no further effects — no larger protopolitical utopian transformation — are either expected or desired.

This diagnosis is, to my mind, confirmed by the great reflective glass skin of the Bonaventure, whose function might first be interpreted as developing a thematics of reproductive technology. Now, on a second reading, one would want to stress the way in which the glass skin repels the city outside; a repulsion for which we have analogies in those reflective sunglasses which make it impossible for your interlocutor to see your own eyes and thereby achieve a certain aggressivity towards and power over the Other. In a similar way, the glass skin achieves a peculiar and placeless dissociation of the Bonaventure from its neighborhood: it is not even an exterior, inasmuch as when you seek to look at the hotel's outer walls you cannot see the hotel itself, but only the distorted images of everything that surrounds it.

Now I want to say a few words about escalators and elevators. Given their very real pleasures in Portman's architecture — particularly these last, which the artist has termed "gigantic kinetic sculptures" and which certainly account for much of the spectacle and the excitement of the hotel interior, especially in the Hyatts, where like great Japanese lanterns or gondolas they ceaselessly rise and fall — and given such a deliberate marking and foregrounding in their own right, I believe one has to see such "people movers" (Portman's own term, adapted from Disney) as something a little more meaningful than mere functions and engineering components. We know in any case that recent architectural theory has begun to borrow from narrative analysis in other fields, and to attempt to see our physical trajectories through such buildings as virtual narratives or stories, as dynamic paths and narrative paradigms which we as visitors are asked to fulfil and to complete with our own bodies and movements. In the Bonaventure, however, we find a dialectical heightening of this process. It seems to me that not only do the escalators and elevators here henceforth replace movement, but also and above all designate themselves as new reflexive signs and emblems of movement proper (something which will become evident when we come to the whole question of what remains of older forms of movement in this building, most notably walking itself). Here the narrative stroll has been underscored, symbolized, reified and replaced by a transportation machine which becomes the allegorical signifier of that older promenade we are no longer allowed to conduct on our own. This is a dialectical intensification of the autoreferentiality of all modern culture, which tends to turn upon itself and designate its own cultural production as its content.

I am more at a loss when it comes to conveying the thing itself, the experience of space you undergo when you step off such allegorical devices into the lobby or atrium, with its great central column, surrounded by a miniature lake, the whole positioned between the four symmetrical residential towers with their elevators, and surrounded by rising balconies capped by a kind

[9]Exterior supporting columns that allow the actual usable space of the building to be lifted off the ground.

of greenhouse roof at the sixth level. I am tempted to say that such space makes it impossible for us to use the language of volume or volumes any longer, since these last are impossible to seize. Hanging streamers indeed suffuse this empty space in such a way as to distract systematically and deliberately from whatever form it might be supposed to have; while a constant busyness gives the feeling that emptiness is here absolutely packed, that it is an element within which you yourself are immersed, without any of that distance that formerly enabled the perception of perspective or volume. You are in this hyperspace up to your eyes and your body; and if it seemed to you before that the suppression of depth observable in postmodern painting or literature would necessarily be difficult to achieve in architecture itself, perhaps you may now be willing to see this bewildering immersion as its formal equivalent in the new medium.

Yet escalator and elevator are also, in this context, dialectical opposites; and we may suggest that the glorious movement of the elevator gondolas is also a dialectical compensation for this filled space of the atrium — it gives us the chance of a radically different, but complementary, spatial experience: that of rapidly shooting up through the ceiling and outside, along one of the four symmetrical towers, with the referent, Los Angeles itself, spread out breathtakingly and even alarmingly before us. But even this vertical movement is contained: the elevator lifts you to one of those revolving cocktail lounges, in which you, seated, are again passively rotated about and offered a contemplative spectacle of the city itself, now transformed into its own images by the glass windows through which you view it.

Let me quickly conclude all this by returning to the central space of the lobby itself (with the passing observation that the hotel rooms are visibly marginalized: the corridors in the residential sections are low-ceilinged and dark, most depressingly functional indeed, while one understands that the rooms — frequently redecorated — are in the worst taste). The descent is dramatic enough, plummeting back down through the roof to splash down in the lake; what happens when you get there is something else, which I can only try to characterize as milling confusion, something like

the vengeance this space takes on those who still seek to walk through it. Given the absolute symmetry of the four towers, it is quite impossible to get your bearings in this lobby; recently, color coding and directional signals have been added in a pitiful, rather desperate and revealing attempt to restore the co-ordinates of an older space. I will take as the most dramatic practical result of this spatial mutation the notorious dilemma of the shopkeepers on the various balconies: it has been obvious, since the very opening of the hotel in 1977, that nobody could ever find any of these stores, and even if you located the appropriate boutique, you would be most unlikely to be as fortunate a second time; as a consequence, the commercial tenants are in despair and all the merchandise is marked down to bargain prices. When you recall that Portman is a businessman as well as an architect, and a millionaire developer, an artist who is at one and the same time a capitalist in his own right, you cannot but feel that here too something of a "return of the repressed" is involved.

So I come finally to my principal point here, that this latest mutation in space — postmodern hyperspace — has finally succeeded in transcending the capacities of the individual human body to locate itself, to organize its immediate surroundings perceptually, and to map cognitively its position in a mappable external world. And I have already suggested that this alarming disjunction between the body and its built environment — which is to the initial bewilderment of the older modernism as the velocities of spacecraft are to those of the automobile — can itself stand as the symbol and analogue of that even sharper dilemma, which is the incapacity of our minds, at least at present, to map the great global, multinational and decentered communicational network in which we find ourselves caught as individual subjects.

The New Machine

But as I am anxious that Portman's space not be perceived as something either exceptional or seemingly marginalized and leisure-specialized on the order of Disneyland, I would like in passing to juxtapose this complacent and entertaining (although bewildering) leisure-time space with its analogue in a very different area, namely the space of postmodern warfare, in particular as Michael Herr evokes it in his great book on the experience of Vietnam, *Dispatches*. The extraordinary linguistic innovations of this work may be considered postmodern in the eclectic way in which its language impersonally fuses a whole range of contemporary collective idiolects, most notably rock language and black language, but the fusion is dictated by problems of content. This first terrible postmodernist war cannot be recounted in any of the traditional paradigms of the war novel or movie — indeed, that breakdown of all previous narrative paradigms is, along with the breakdown of any shared language through which a veteran might convey such experience, among the principal subjects of the book and may be said to open up the place of a whole new reflexivity. Benjamin's account of Baudelaire,[10] and of the emergence of modernism from a new experience of city technology which transcends all the older habits of bodily perception, is both singularly relevant here and singularly antiquated, in the light of this new and virtually unimaginable quantum leap in technological alienation:

> He was a moving-target-survivor subscriber, a true child of the war, because except for the rare times when you were pinned or stranded the system was geared to keep you mobile, if that was what you thought you wanted. As a technique for staying alive it seemed to make as much sense as anything, given naturally that you were there to begin with and wanted to see it close; it started out sound and straight but it formed a cone as it progressed, because the more you moved the more you saw, the more you saw besides death and mutilation you risked, and the more you risked of that the more you would have to let go of one day as a "survivor." Some of us moved around the war like crazy people until we couldn't see which way the run was taking us anymore, only the war all over its surface with occasional, unexpected penetration. As long as we could have choppers like taxis it took real exhaustion or depression near shock or a

dozen pipes of opium to keep us even apparently quiet, we'd still be running around inside our skins like something was after us, ha, ha, La Vida Loca. In the months after I got back the hundreds of helicopters I'd flown in began to draw together until they'd formed a collective meta-chopper, and in my mind it was the sexiest thing going; saver-destroyer, provider-waster, right hand-left hand, nimble, fluent, canny and human; hot steel, grease, jungle-saturated canvas webbing, sweat cooling and warming up again, cassette rock and roll in one ear and door-gun fire in the other, fuel, heat, vitality and death, death itself, hardly an intruder.[11]

In this new machine, which does not, like the older modernist machinery of the locomotive or the airplane, represent motion, but which can only be represented *in motion*, something of the mystery of the new postmodernist space is concentrated.

THE AESTHETIC OF CONSUMER SOCIETY

Now I must try, in conclusion, to characterize the relationship of cultural production of this kind to social life in this country today. This will also be the moment to address the principal objection to concepts of postmodernism of the type I have sketched here: namely that all the features we have enumerated are not new at all but abundantly characterized modernism proper or what I call high modernism. Was not Thomas Mann, after all, interested in the idea of pastiche, and is not "The Oxen of the Sun" chapter of *Ulysses* its most obvious realization? Can Flaubert, Mallarmé and Gertrude Stein not be included in an account of postmodernist temporality? What is so new about all of this? Do we really need the concept of postmodernism?

One kind of answer to this question would raise the whole issue of periodization and of how a historian (literary or other) posits a radical break between two henceforth distinct periods. I must limit myself to the suggestion that radical breaks between periods do not generally

---

[10]Walter Benjamin's essays on Baudelaire had recently been translated as *Charles Baudelaire: A Lyric Poet in the Era of High Capitalism* (London: Verso, 1983).

[11]Michael Herr, *Dispatches* (New York, 1977), pp. 8–9. [Jameson]

involve complete changes of content but rather the restructuring of a certain number of elements already given: features that in an earlier period or system were subordinate now become dominant, and features that had been dominant again become secondary.[12] In this sense, everything we have described here can be found in earlier periods and most notably within modernism proper. My point is that until the present day those things have been secondary or minor features of modernist art, marginal rather than central, and that we have something new when they become the central features of cultural production.

But I can argue this more concretely by turning to the relationship between cultural production and social life generally. The older or classical modernism was an oppositional art; it emerged within the business society of the gilded age as scandalous and offensive to the middle-class public — ugly, dissonant, bohemian, sexually shocking. It was something to make fun of (when the police were not called in to seize the books or close the exhibitions): an offence to good taste and to common sense, or, as Freud and Marcuse would have put it, a provocative challenge to the reigning reality- and performance-principles of early twentieth-century middle-class society. Modernism in general did not go well with overstuffed Victorian furniture, with Victorian moral taboos, or with the conventions of polite society. This is to say that whatever the explicit political content of the great high modernisms, the latter were always in some mostly implicit ways dangerous and explosive, subversive within the established order.

If then we suddenly return to the present day, we can measure the immensity of the cultural changes that have taken place. Not only are Joyce and Picasso no longer weird and repulsive, they have become classics and now look rather realistic to us. Meanwhile, there is very little in either the form or the content of contemporary art that contemporary society finds intolerable and scandalous. The most offensive forms of this art — punk rock, say, or what is called sexually explicit material — are all taken in its stride by society, and they are commercially successful, unlike the productions of the older high modernism. But this means that even if contemporary art has all the same formal features as the older modernism, it has still shifted its position fundamentally within our culture. For one thing, commodity production and in particular our clothing, furniture, buildings and other artefacts are now intimately tied in with styling changes which derive from artistic experimentation; our advertising, for example, is fed by modernism in all the arts and inconceivable without. For another, the classics of high modernism are now part of the so-called canon and are taught in schools and universities — which at once empties them of any of their older subversive power. Indeed, one way of marking the break between the periods and of dating the emergence of postmodernism is precisely to be found there: at the moment (the early 1960s, one would think) in which the position of high modernism and its dominant aesthetics become established in the academy and are henceforth felt to be academic by a whole new generation of poets, painters and musicians.

But one can also come at the break from the other side, and describe it in terms of periods of recent social life. As I have suggested, Marxists and non-Marxists alike have come around to the general feeling that at some point following World War Two a new kind of society began to emerge (variously described as post-industrial society, multinational capitalism, consumer society, media society and so forth). New types of consumption; planned obsolescence; an ever more rapid rhythm of fashion and styling changes; the penetration of advertising, television and the media generally to a hitherto unparalleled degree throughout society; the replacement of the old tension between city and country, center and province, by the suburb and by universal standardization; the growth of the great networks of superhighways and the arrival of automobile culture — these are some of the features which would seem to mark a radical break with that older pre-war society in which high modernism was still an underground force.

---

[12]The process of change within literary history Jameson describes here is similar to that argued by Yuri Tynyanov and other Russian Formalists; see pp. 753–54. Jameson was one of the first American theorists to appreciate the Russian Formalists and to analyze their achievements in *The Prison House of Language* (1972).

I believe that the emergence of postmodernism is closely related to the emergence of this new moment of late consumer or multinational capitalism. I believe also that its formal features in many ways express the deeper logic of this particular social system. I will only be able, however, to show this for one major theme: namely the disappearance of a sense of history, the way in which our entire contemporary social system has little by little begun to lose its capacity to retain its own past, has begun to live in a perpetual present and in a perpetual change that obliterates traditions of the kind which all earlier social information have had, in one way or another, to preserve. Think only of the media exhaustion of news: of how Nixon and, even more so, Kennedy, are figures from a now distant past. One is tempted to say that the very function of the news media is to relegate such recent historical experiences as rapidly as possible into the past. The informational function of the media would thus be to help us forget, to serve as the very agents and mechanisms for our historical amnesia.

But in that case the two features of postmodernism on which I have dwelt here — the transformation of reality into images, the fragmentation of time into a series of perpetual presents — are both extraordinarily consonant with this process. My own conclusion here must take the form of a question about the critical value of the newer art. There is some agreement that the older modernism functioned against its society in ways which are variously described as critical, negative, contestatory, subversive, oppositional and the like. Can anything of the sort be affirmed about postmodernism and its social moment? We have seen that there is a way in which postmodernism replicates or reproduces — reinforces — the logic of consumer capitalism; the more significant question is whether there is also a way in which it resists that logic. But that is a question we must leave open.

Donna Haraway

b. 1944

The woman who "would rather be a cyborg than a goddess" was born in Denver, where she attended Catholic schools, then Colorado College, where she studied zoology and philosophy, along with English. On a Fulbright fellowship, she then traveled to Paris to study philosophies of evolution. She earned a Ph.D. in biology from Yale in 1972, writing her dissertation on the functions of metaphor in shaping research in developmental biology in the twentieth century. After teaching women's studies and general science at the University of Hawaii, she went on to Johns Hopkins University; she is now professor in the History of Consciousness Program at the University of California at Santa Cruz. Haraway uses the metaphor of the cyborg to discuss the relationship of self to others in high-tech postmodern culture. As the binaries such as truth/illusion, male/female, and mind/body are challenged by the possibilities of technology, Haraway argues, we become unable to think of ourselves according to these categories or even as merely biological beings. Her books include Crystals, Fabrics, and Fields: Metaphors That Shape Embryos *(1976),* Primate Visions: Gender, Race and Nature in the World of Modern Science *(1990),* Simians, Cyborgs, and Women: The Reinvention of Nature *(1991),* Modest_Witness@Second_Millennium.FemaleMan©_Meets_OncoMouse™: Feminism and Technoscience *(1996), and* The Companion Species Manifesto: Dogs, People, and Significant Otherness *(2003). An earlier version of Haraway's "manifesto for cyborgs" originally appeared in* Socialist Review *in 1985; appearing below is the revised version that first appeared in* Simians, Cyborgs, and Women.

A Cyborg Manifesto: Science, Technology, and Socialist-Feminism in the Late Twentieth Century[1]

AN IRONIC DREAM OF A COMMON LANGUAGE FOR WOMEN IN THE INTEGRATED CIRCUIT

This chapter is an effort to build an ironic political myth faithful to feminism, socialism, and materialism. Perhaps more faithful as blasphemy is faithful, than as reverent worship and identification. Blasphemy has always seemed to require taking things very seriously. I know no better stance to adopt from within the secular-religious, evangelical traditions of United States politics, including the politics of socialist feminism. Blasphemy protects one from the moral majority within, while still insisting on the need for community. Blasphemy is not apostasy. Irony is about contradictions that do not resolve into larger wholes, even dialectically, about the tension of holding incompatible things together because both or all are necessary and true. Irony is about

humor and serious play. It is also a rhetorical strategy and a political method, one I would like to see more honored within socialist-feminism. At the center of my ironic faith, my blasphemy, is the image of the cyborg.

A cyborg is a cybernetic organism, a hybrid of machine and organism, a creature of social reality as well as a creature of fiction. Social reality is lived social relations, our most important political constructions, a world-changing fiction. The international women's movements have constructed "women's experience," as well as uncovered or discovered this crucial collective object. This experience is a fiction and fact of the most crucial, political kind. Liberation rests on the construction of the consciousness, the imaginative apprehension, of oppression, and so of possibility. The cyborg is a matter of fiction and lived experience that changes what counts as women's experience in the late twentieth century. This is a struggle over

[1]Research was funded by an Academic Senate Faculty Research Grant from the University of California, Santa Cruz. An earlier version of the paper on genetic engineering appeared as "Lieber Kyborg als Göttin: für eine sozialistisch-feministische Unterwanderung der Gentechnologie," in Bernd-Peter Lange and Anna Marie Stuby, eds, Berlin: Argument-Sonderband 105, 1984, pp 66–84. The cyborg manifesto grew from my "New machines, new bodies, new communities: political dilemmas of a cyborg feminist," "The Scholar and the Feminist X: The Question of Technology," Conference, Barnard College, April 1983.

The people associated with the History of Consciousness Board of UCSC have had an enormous influence on this paper, so that it feels collectively authored more than most, although those I cite may not recognize their ideas. In particular, members of graduate and undergraduate feminist theory, science, and politics, and theory and methods courses contributed to the cyborg manifesto. Particular debts here are due Hilary Klein (1989), Paul Edwards (1985). Lisa Lowe (1986), and James Clifford (1985).

Parts of the paper were my contribution to a collectively developed session, "Poetic Tools and Political Bodies: Feminist Approaches to High Technology Culture," 1984 California American Studies Association, with History of Consciousness graduate students Zoe Sofoulis, "Jupiter

space"; Katie King, "The pleasures of repetition and the limits of identification in feminist science fiction: reimaginations of body after the cyborg"; and Chela Sandoval, "The construction of subjectivity and oppositional consciousness in feminist film and video." Sandoval's (n.d.) theory of oppositional consciousness was published as "Women respond to racism: A Report on the National Women's Studies Association Conference." For Sofoulis's semiotic-psychoanalytic readings of nuclear culture, see Sofia (1984). King's unpublished papers ("Questioning tradition: canon formation and the veiling of power"; "Gender and genre: reading the science fiction of Joanna Russ"; "Varley's Titan and Wizard: feminist parodies of nature, culture, and hardware") deeply informed the cyborg manifesto.

Barbara Epstein, Jeff Escoffier, Rusten Hogness, and Jaye Miler gave extensive discussion and editorial help. Members of the Silicon Valley Research Project of UCSC and participants in SVRP conferences and workshops were very important, especially Rick Gordon, Linda Kimball, Nancy Snyder, Langdon Winner, Judith Stacey, Linda Lim, Patricia Fernandez-Kelly, and Judith Gregory. Finally, I was to thank Nancy Hartsock for years of friendship and discussion on feminist theory and feminist science fiction. I also thank Elizabeth Bird for my favorite political button: "Cyborgs for Earthly Survival." [Haraway] life and death, but the boundary between science fiction and social reality is an optical illusion.

Contemporary science fiction is full of cyborgs — creatures simultaneously animal and machine, who populate worlds ambiguously natural and crafted. Modern medicine is also full of cyborgs, of couplings between organism and machine, each conceived as coded devices, in an intimacy and with a power that was not generated in the history of sexuality. Cyborg "sex" restores some of the lovely replicative baroque of ferns and invertebrates (such nice organic prophylactics against heterosexism). Cyborg replication is uncoupled from organic reproduction. Modern production seems like a dream of cyborg colonization work, a dream that makes the nightmare of Taylorism[2] seem idyllic. And modern war is a cyborg orgy, coded by C^3I, command-control-communication-intelligence, an \$84 billion item in 1984's US defence budget. I am making an argument for the cyborg as a fiction mapping our social and bodily reality and as an imaginative resource suggesting some very fruitful couplings. Michel Foucault's biopolitics[3] is a flaccid premonition of cyborg politics, a very open field.

By the late twentieth century, our time, a mythic time, we are all chimeras,[4] theorized and fabricated hybrids of machine and organism; in short, we are cyborgs. The cyborg is our ontology; it gives us our politics. The cyborg is a condensed image of both imagination and material reality, the two joined centers structuring any possibility of historical transformation. In the traditions of "Western" science and politics — the tradition of racist, male-dominant capitalism; the tradition of progress; the tradition of the appropriation of nature as resource for the productions of culture; the tradition of reproduction of the self from the reflections of the other — the relation between organism and machine has been a border war. The stakes in the border war have been the territories of production, reproduction, and imagination. This chapter is an argument for *pleasure* in the confusion of boundaries and for *responsibility* in their construction. It is also an effort to contribute to socialist-feminist culture and theory in a postmodernist, non-naturalist mode and in the utopian tradition of imagining a world without gender, which is perhaps a world without genesis, but maybe also a world without end. The cyborg incarnation is outside salvation history. Nor does it mark time on an oedipal calendar, attempting to heal the terrible cleavages of gender in an oral symbiotic utopia or post-oedipal apocalypse. As Zoe Sofoulis argues in her unpublished manuscript on Jacques Lacan, Melanie Klein, and nuclear culture, *Lacklein*, the most terrible and perhaps the most promising monsters in cyborg worlds are embodied in non-oedipal narratives with a different logic of repression, which we need to understand for our survival.

The cyborg is a creature in a post-gender world; it has no truck with bisexuality, pre-oedipal symbiosis, unalienated labor, or other seductions to organic wholeness through a final appropriation of all the powers of the parts into a higher unity.[5] In a sense, the cyborg has no origin story in the Western sense — a "final" irony since the cyborg is also the awful apocalyptic *telos*[6] of the "West's" escalating dominations of abstract individuation, an ultimate self untied at last from all dependency, a man in space. An origin story in the "Western," humanist sense depends on the myth of original unity, fullness, bliss and terror, represented by the phallic mother from whom all humans must separate, the task of individual-development and of history, the twin potent

---

[2]Management of labor practices, based on time and motion studies, named for Frederick Winslow Taylor (1856–1915), who published *Principles of Scientific Management* in 1911.

[3]Foucault appears to have coined the term *biopolitics* in his 1975–76 seminar published as "Society Must Be Defended" (2003), and it specifically dealt with the relationship between racism, eugenics, and public health in the late nineteenth century; it was later expanded to cover all relations between sex and state power.

[4]A chimera was a monstrous hybrid of different animals; Haraway uses the term to include other forms of hybridity, including our connections with machines we use for work and self-expression.

[5]Haraway cites disparate myths of organic unity: In Plato's *Symposium*, Aristophanes posits that humans were originally bisexual till the male and female halves were cut apart; Freud posits a period prior to the Oedipal conflict when children are at one with their parents and sexually polymorphous; Marx posits a state of nature when labor was not alienated.

[6]Greek for "end" or "purpose."

myths inscribed most powerfully for us in psychoanalysis and Marxism. Hilary Klein has argued that both Marxism and psychoanalysis, in their concepts of labor and of individuation and gender formation, depend on the plot of original unity out of which difference must be produced and enlisted in a drama of escalating domination of woman/nature. The cyborg skips the step of original unity, of identification with nature in the Western sense. This is its illegitimate promise that might lead to subversion of its teleology as star wars.

The cyborg is resolutely committed to partiality, irony, intimacy, and perversity. It is oppositional, utopian, and completely without innocence. No longer structured by the polarity of public and private, the cyborg defines a technological polis based partly on a revolution of social relations in the *oikos*, the household. Nature and culture are reworked; the one can no longer be the resource for appropriation or incorporation by the other. The relationships for forming wholes from parts, including those of polarity and hierarchical domination, are at issue in the cyborg world. Unlike the hopes of Frankenstein's monster,[7] the cyborg does not expect its father to save it through a restoration of the garden; that is, through the fabrication of a heterosexual mate, through its completion in a finished whole, a city and cosmos. The cyborg does not dream of community on the model of the organic family, this time without the oedipal project. The cyborg would not recognize the Garden of Eden; it is not made of mud and cannot dream of returning to dust. Perhaps that is why I want to see if cyborgs can subvert the apocalypse of returning to nuclear dust in the manic compulsion to name the Enemy. Cyborgs are not reverent; they do not remember the cosmos. They are wary of holism, but needy for connection — they seem to have a natural feel for united front politics,[8] but without the vanguard party. The main trouble with cyborgs, of course, is that they are the illegitimate offspring of militarism and patriarchal capitalism, not to mention state socialism. But illegitimate offspring are often exceedingly unfaithful to their origins. Their fathers, after all, are inessential.

I will return to the science fiction of cyborgs at the end of this chapter, but now I want to signal three crucial boundary breakdowns that make the following political-fictional (political-scientific) analysis possible. By the late twentieth century in United States scientific culture, the boundary between human and animal is thoroughly breached. The last beachheads of uniqueness have been polluted if not turned into amusement parks — language, tool use, social behavior, mental events, nothing really convincingly settles the separation of human and animal. And many people no longer feel the need for such a separation; indeed, many branches of feminist culture affirm the pleasure of connection of human and other living creatures. Movements for animal rights are not irrational denials of human uniqueness; they are a clear-sighted recognition of connection across the discredited breach of nature and culture. Biology and evolutionary theory over the last two centuries have simultaneously produced modern organisms as objects of knowledge and reduced the line between humans and animals to a faint trace re-etched in ideological struggle or professional disputes between life and social science. Within this framework, teaching modern Christian creationism should be fought as a form of child abuse.

Biological-determinist ideology is only one position opened up in scientific culture for arguing the meanings of human animality. There is much room for radical political people to contest the meanings of the breached boundary.[9] The cyborg appears in myth precisely where the boundary between human and animal is transgressed. Far from signalling a walling off of people from other living beings, cyborgs signal disturbingly and

[7]In Mary Shelley's *Frankenstein* (1818), the monster (who has read Milton's *Paradise Lost*) asks Victor Frankenstein to create a mate for him, just as God created a mate for Adam in the Garden of Eden.

[8]In socialist political theory, a temporary union between liberal and radical workers' movements that will defeat the conservatives; the "vanguard party" is the party of the radical workers that will ultimately gain control.

[9]Useful references to left and/or feminist radical science movements and theory and to biological/biotechnical issues include: Bleier (1984, 1986), Harding (1986), Fausto-Sterling (1985), Gould (1981), Hubbard et al. (1982), Keller (1985), Lewontin et al. (1984), *Radical Science Journal* (became *Science as Culture* in 1987), 26 Freegrove Road, London N7 9RQ; *Science for the People*, 897 Main St., Cambridge, MA 02139. [Haraway]

pleasurably tight coupling. Bestiality has a new status in this cycle of marriage exchange.

The second leaky distinction is between animal-human (organism) and machine. Pre-cybernetic machines could be haunted; there was always the specter of the ghost in the machine.[10] This dualism structured the dialogue between materialism and idealism that was settled by a dialectical progeny, called spirit or history, according to taste. But basically machines were not self-moving, self-designing, autonomous. They could not achieve man's dream, only mock it. They were not man, an author to himself, but only a caricature of that masculinist reproductive dream. To think they were otherwise was paranoid. Now we are not so sure. Late twentieth-century machines have made thoroughly ambiguous the difference between natural and artificial, mind and body, self-developing and externally designed, and many other distinctions that used to apply to organisms and machines. Our machines are disturbingly lively, and we ourselves frighteningly inert.

Technological determination is only one ideological space opened up by the reconceptions of machine and organism as coded texts through which we engage in the play of writing and reading the world.[11] "Textualization" of everything in poststructuralist, postmodernist theory has been damned by Marxists and socialist feminists for its utopian disregard for the lived relations of domination that ground the "play" of arbitrary reading.[12] It is certainly true that postmodernist strategies, like my cyborg myth, subvert myriad organic wholes (for example, the poem, the primitive culture, the biological organism). In short, the certainty of what counts as nature — a source of insight and promise of innocence — is undermined, probably fatally. The transcendent authorization of interpretation is lost, and with it the ontology grounding "Western" epistemology. But the alternative is not cynicism or faithlessness, that is, some version of abstract existence, like the

[10]In *The Concept of Mind* (1949), philosopher Gilbert Ryle uses the term "ghost in the machine" to denote the belief that there is an independent "mind" inside the brain that gives commands to make the body do its work, like a captain at the helm of a ship, as opposed to viewing mind as the collective coordinating functions of the brain.

[11]Starting points for left and/or feminist approaches to technology and politics include: Cowan (1983), Rothschild (1983), Traweek (1988), Young and Levidow (1981, 1985), Weizenbaum (1976), Winner (1977, 1986), Zimmerman (1983), Athanasiou (1987), Cohn (1987a, 1987b), Winograd and Flores (1986), Edwards (1985). *Global Electronics Newsletter*, 867 West Dana St. #204, Mountain View, CA 94041; *Processed World*, 55 Sutter St., San Francisco, CA 94104; ISIS, Women's International Information and Communication Service, PO Box 50 (Cornavin), 1211 Geneva 2, Switzerland, and Via Santa Maria Dell'Anima 30, 00186 Rome, Italy. Fundamental approaches to modern social studies of science that do not continue the liberal mystification that it all started with Thomas Kuhn, include: Knorr-Cetina (1981), Knorr-Cetina and Mulkay (1983), Latour and Woolgar (1979), Young (1979). The 1984 Directory of the Network for the Ethnographic Study of Science, Technology, and Organizations lists a wide range of people and projects crucial to better radical analysis; available from NESSTO, PO Box 11442, Stanford, CA 94305. [Haraway]

[12]A provocative, comprehensive argument about the politics and theories of "postmodernism" is made by Fredric Jameson (1984), who argues that postmodernism is not an option, a style among others, but a cultural dominant requiring radical reinvention of left politics from within; there is no longer any place from without that gives meaning to the comforting fiction of critical distance. Jameson also makes clear why one cannot be for or against postmodernism, an essentially moralist move. My position is that feminists (and others) need continuous cultural reinvention, postmodernist critique, and historical materialism; only a cyborg would have a chance. The old dominations of white capitalist patriarchy seem nostalgically innocent now: they normalized heterogeneity, into man and woman, white and black, for example. "Advanced capitalism" and postmodernism release heterogeneity without a norm, and we are flattened, without subjectivity, which requires depth, even unfriendly and drowning depths. It is time to write *The Death of the Clinic*. The clinic's methods required bodies and works; we have texts and surfaces. Our dominations don't work by medicalization and normalization any more; they work by networking, communications redesign, stress management. Normalization gives way to automation, utter redundancy. Michel Foucault's *Birth of the Clinic* (1963), *History of Sexuality* (1976), and *Discipline and Punish* (1975) name a form of power at its moment of implosion. The discourse of biopolitics gives way to technobabble, the language of the spliced substantive; no noun is left whole by the multinationals. These are their names, listed from one issue of *Science*. Tech-Knowledge, Genentech, Allergen, Hybritech, Compupro, Genen-cor, Syntex, Allelix, Agrigenetics Corp., Syntro, Codon, Repligen, MicroAngelo from Scion Corp., Percom Data, Inter Systems, Cyborg Corp., Statcom Corp., Intertec. If we are imprisoned by language, then escape from that prison-house requires language poets, a kind of cultural restriction enzyme to cut the code; cyborg heteroglossia is one form of radical cultural politics. For cyborg poetry, see Perloff (1984); Fraser (1984). For feminist modernist/postmodernist "cyborg" writing, see HOW(ever), 871 Corbett Ave., San Francisco, CA 94131. [Haraway]

accounts of technological determinism destroying "man" by the "machine" or "meaningful political action" by the "text." Who cyborgs will be is a radical question; the answers are a matter of survival. Both chimpanzees and artefacts have politics, so why shouldn't we (de Waal, 1982; Winner, 1980)?

The third distinction is a subset of the second: the boundary between physical and non-physical is very imprecise for us. Pop physics books on the consequences of quantum theory and the indeterminacy principle[13] are a kind of popular scientific equivalent to Harlequin romances as a marker of radical change in American white heterosexuality: they get it wrong, but they are on the right subject. Modern machines are quintessentially microelectronic devices: they are everywhere and they are invisible. Modern machinery is an irreverent upstart god, mocking the Father's ubiquity and spirituality. The silicon chip is a surface for writing; it is etched in molecular scales disturbed only by atomic noise, the ultimate interference for nuclear scores.[14] Writing, power, and technology are old partners in Western stories of the origin of civilization, but miniaturization has changed our experience of mechanism. Miniaturization has turned out to be about power; small is not so much beautiful as pre-eminently dangerous, as in cruise missiles. Contrast the TV sets of the 1950s or the news cameras of the 1970s with the TV wrist bands or hand-sized video cameras now advertised. Our best machines are made of sunshine; they are all light and clean because they are nothing but signals, electromagnetic waves, a section of a spectrum, and these machines are eminently portable, mobile — a matter of immense human pain in Detroit and Singapore. People are nowhere near so fluid, being both material and opaque. Cyborgs are ether, quintessence.

The ubiquity and invisibility of cyborgs is precisely why these sunshine-belt machines are so deadly. They are as hard to see politically as materially. They are about consciousness — or its simulation.[15] They are floating signifiers moving in pickup trucks across Europe, blocked more effectively by the witch-weavings of the displaced and so unnatural Greenham women,[16] who read the cyborg webs of power so very well, than by the militant labor of older masculinist politics, whose natural constituency needs defence jobs. Ultimately the "hardest" science is about the realm of greatest boundary confusion, the realm of pure number, pure spirit, C^3I, cryptography, and the preservation of potent secrets. The new machines are so clean and light. Their engineers are sun-worshippers mediating a new scientific revolution associated with the night dream of post-industrial society. The diseases evoked by these clean machines are "no more" than the minuscule coding changes of an antigen in the immune system, "no more" than the experience of stress. The nimble fingers of "Oriental" women, the old fascination of little Anglo-Saxon Victorian girls with doll's houses, women's enforced attention to the small take on quite new dimensions in this world. There might be a cyborg Alice[17] taking account of these new dimensions. Ironically, it might be the unnatural cyborg women making chips in Asia and spiral dancing in Santa Rita jail[18] whose constructed unities will guide effective oppositional strategies.

So my cyborg myth is about transgressed boundaries, potent fusions, and dangerous possibilities which progressive people might explore as one part of needed political work. One of my

[15]Baudrillard (1983). Jameson (1984, p. 66) points out that Plato's definition of the simulacrum is the copy for which there is no original, i.e., the world of advanced capitalism, of pure exchange. See *Discourse* 9 (Spring/Summer 1987) for a special issue on technology (cybernetics, ecology, and the postmodern imagination). [Haraway] For Baudrillard, see p. 1935.

[16]Starting in 1981, the stationing of nuclear cruise missiles by the United States on its air force base at Greenham Common (southwest of London) was successfully protested by residents, primarily women. By 1991 the missiles were all removed (the Cold War was also over).

[17]Haraway refers to Lewis Carroll's *Alice in Wonderland* (1865), in which Alice became very small when she ate from one side of a special mushroom.

[18]A practice at once both spiritual and political that linked guards and arrested anti-nuclear demonstrators in the Alameda County jail in California in the early 1980s. [Haraway]

[13]Quantum theory allows one to specify only the probability that an atomic particle is in a given place; its position is indeterminate. Haraway may also be alluding to Werner Karl Heisenberg's "uncertainty principle," which states that the more strictly one specifies an atomic particle's mass the less strictly one can specify its velocity (and vice versa).

[14]Haraway's point is that the limit to the memory capacity of a silicon chip is set by the interference that would be caused by electrons moving to random quantum states.

premises is that most American socialists and feminists see deepened dualisms of mind and body, animal and machine, idealism and materialism in the social practices, symbolic formulations, and physical artefacts associated with "high technology" and scientific culture. From *One-Dimensional Man* (Marcuse, 1964) to *The Death of Nature* (Merchant, 1980), the analytic resources developed by progressives have insisted on the necessary domination of technics and recalled us to an imagined organic body to integrate our resistance. Another of my premises is that the need for unity of people trying to resist world-wide intensification of domination has never been more acute. But a slightly perverse shift of perspective might better enable us to contest for meanings, as well as for other forms of power and pleasure in technologically mediated societies.

From one perspective, a cyborg world is about the final imposition of a grid of control on the planet, about the final abstraction embodied in a Star Wars apocalypse waged in the name of defence, about the final appropriation of women's bodies in a masculinist orgy of war (Sofia, 1984). From another perspective, a cyborg world might be about lived social and bodily realities in which people are not afraid of their joint kinship with animals and machines, not afraid of permanently partial identities and contradictory standpoints. The political struggle is to see from both perspectives at once because each reveals both dominations and possibilities unimaginable from the other vantage point. Single vision produces worse illusions than double vision or many-headed monsters. Cyborg unities are monstrous and illegitimate; in our present political circumstances, we could hardly hope for more potent myths for resistance and recoupling. I like to imagine LAG, the Livermore Action Group, as a kind of cyborg society, dedicated to realistically converting the laboratories that most fiercely embody and spew out the tools of technological apocalypse, and committed to building a political form that actually manages to hold together witches, engineers, elders, perverts, Christians, mothers, and Leninists long enough to disarm the state. Fission Impossible is the name of the affinity group in my town. (Affinity: related not by blood but by choice, the appeal of one chemical nuclear group for another, avidity.)[19]

THE INFORMATICS OF DOMINATION

In this attempt at an epistemological and political position, I would like to sketch a picture of possible unity, a picture indebted to socialist and feminist principles of design. The frame for my sketch is set by the extent and importance of rearrangements in world-wide social relations tied to science and technology. I argue for a politics rooted in claims about fundamental changes in the nature of class, race, and gender in an emerging system of world order analogous in its novelty and scope to that created by industrial capitalism; we are living through a movement from an organic, industrial society to a polymorphous, information system — from all work to all play, a deadly game. Simultaneously material and ideological, the dichotomies may be expressed in the following chart of transitions from the comfortable old hierarchical dominations to the scary new networks I have called the informatics of domination:

Representation	Simulation
Bourgeois novel, realism	Science fiction, postmodernism
Organism	Biotic component
Depth, integrity	Surface, boundary

[19]For ethnographic accounts and political evaluations, see Epstein (1991), Sturgeon (1986). Without explicit irony, adopting the spaceship earth/whole earth logo of the planet photographed from space, set off by the slogan "Love Your Mother," the May 1987 Mothers and Others Day action at the nuclear weapons testing facility in Nevada none the less took account of the tragic contradictions of views of the earth. Demonstrators applied for official permits to be on the land from officers of the Western Shoshone tribe, whose territory was invaded by the US government when it built the nuclear weapons test group in the 1950s. Arrested for trespassing, the demonstrators argued that the police and weapons facility personnel, without authorization from the proper officials, were the trespassers. One affinity group at the women's action called themselves the Surrogate Others; and in solidarity with the creatures forced to tunnel in the same ground with the bomb, they enacted a cyborgian emergence from the constructed body of a large, non-heterosexual desert worm. [Haraway]

Heat	Noise
Biology as clinical practice	Biology as inscription
Physiology	Communications engineering
Small group	Subsystem
Perfection	Optimization
Eugenics	Population Control
Decadence, *Magic Mountain*	Obsolescence, *Future Shock*
Hygiene	Stress Management
Microbiology, tuberculosis	Immunology, AIDS
Organic division of labor	Ergonomics / cybernetics of labor
Functional specialization	Modular construction
Reproduction	Replication
Organic sex role specialization	Optimal genetic strategies
Biological determinism	Evolutionary inertia, constraints
Community ecology	Ecosystem
Racial chain of being	Neo-imperialism, United Nations humanism
Scientific management in home / factory	Global factory / Electronic cottage
Family / Market / Factory	Women in the Integrated Circuit
Family wage	Comparable worth
Public / Private	Cyborg citizenship
Nature / Culture	Fields of difference
Co-operation	Communications enhancement
Freud	Lacan
Sex	Genetic engineering
Labor	Robotics
Mind	Artificial Intelligence
Second World War	Star Wars
White Capitalist Patriarchy	Informatics of Domination

This list suggests several interesting things.[20] First, the objects on the right-hand side cannot be coded as "natural," a realization that subverts naturalistic coding for the left-hand side as well. We cannot go back ideologically or materially. It's not just that "god" is dead; so is the "goddess." Or both are revivified in the worlds charged with microelectronic and biotechnological politics. In relation to objects like biotic components, one must think not in terms of essential properties, but in terms of design, boundary constraints, rates of flows, systems logics, costs of lowering constraints. Sexual reproduction is one kind of reproductive strategy among many, with costs and benefits as a function of the system environment. Ideologies of sexual reproduction can no longer reasonably call on notions of sex and sex role as organic aspects in natural objects like organisms and families. Such reasoning will be unmasked as irrational, and ironically corporate executives reading *Playboy* and anti-porn radical feminists will make strange bedfellows in jointly unmasking the irrationalism.

Likewise for race, ideologies about human diversity have to be formulated in terms of frequencies of parameters, like blood groups or intelligence scores. It is "irrational" to invoke concepts like primitive and civilized. For liberals and radicals, the search for integrated social systems gives way to a new practice called "experimental ethnography" in which an organic object dissipates in attention to the play of writing. At the level of ideology, we see translations of racism and colonialism into languages of development and under-development, rates and constraints of modernization. Any objects or persons can be reasonably thought of in terms of disassembly and reassembly; no "natural" architectures constrain system design. The financial districts in all the world's cities, as well as the export-processing and free-trade zones, proclaim this elementary

[20]This chart was published in 1985. My previous efforts to understand biology as a cybernetic command-control discourse and organisms as "natural-technical objects of knowledge" were Haraway (1979, 1983, 1984). The 1979 version of this dichotomous chart appears in this vol., ch. 3; for a 1989 version, see ch. 10. The differences indicate shifts in argument. [Haraway]

fact of "late capitalism." The entire universe of objects that can be known scientifically must be formulated as problems in communications engineering (for the managers) or theories of the text (for those who would resist). Both are cyborg semiologies.

One should expect control strategies to concentrate on boundary conditions and interfaces, on rates of flow across boundaries — and not on the integrity of natural objects. "Integrity" or "sincerity" of the Western self gives way to decision procedures and expert systems. For example, control strategies applied to women's capacities to give birth to new human beings will be developed in the languages of population control and maximization of goal achievement for individual decision-makers. Control strategies will be formulated in terms of rates, costs of constraints, degrees of freedom. Human beings, like any other component or subsystem, must be localized in a system architecture whose basic modes of operation are probabilistic, statistical. No objects, spaces, or bodies are sacred in themselves; any component can be interfaced with any other if the proper standard, the proper code, can be constructed for processing signals in a common language. Exchange in this world transcends the universal translation effected by capitalist markets that Marx analyzed so well. The privileged pathology affecting all kinds of components in this universe is stress — communications breakdown (Hogness, 1983). The cyborg is not subject to Foucault's biopolitics; the cyborg simulates politics, a much more potent field of operations.

This kind of analysis of scientific and cultural objects of knowledge which have appeared historically since the Second World War prepares us to notice some important inadequacies in feminist analysis which has proceeded as if the organic, hierarchical dualisms ordering discourse in "the West" since Aristotle still ruled. They have been cannibalized, or as Zoe Sofia (Sofoulis) might put it, they have been "techno-digested." The dichotomies between mind and body, animal and human, organism and machine, public and private, nature and culture, men and women, primitive and civilized are all in question ideologically. The actual situation of women is their integration/exploitation into a world system of production/reproduction and communication called the informatics of domination. The home, workplace, market, public arena, the body itself — all can be dispersed and interfaced in nearly infinite, polymorphous ways, with large consequences for women and others — consequences that themselves are very different for different people and which make potent oppositional international movements difficult to imagine and essential for survival. One important route for reconstructing socialist-feminist politics is through theory and practice addressed to the social relations of science and technology, including crucially the systems of myth and meanings structuring our imaginations. The cyborg is a kind of disassembled and reassembled, postmodern collective and personal self. This is the self feminists must code.

Communications technologies and biotechnologies are the crucial tools recrafting our bodies. These tools embody and enforce new social relations for women world-wide. Technologies and scientific discourses can be partially understood as formalizations, i.e., as frozen moments, of the fluid social interactions constituting them, but they should also be viewed as instruments for enforcing meanings. The boundary is permeable between tool and myth, instrument and concept, historical systems of social relations and historical anatomies of possible bodies, including objects of knowledge. Indeed, myth and tool mutually constitute each other.

Furthermore, communications sciences and modern biologies are constructed by a common move — *the translation of the world into a problem of coding*, a search for a common language in which all resistance to instrumental control disappears and all heterogeneity can be submitted to disassembly, reassembly, investment, and exchange.

In communications sciences, the translation of the world into a problem in coding can be illustrated by looking at cybernetic (feedback-controlled) systems theories applied to telephone technology, computer design, weapons deployment, or data base construction and maintenance. In each case, the solution to the key questions rests on a theory of language and control; the key operation is determining the rates, directions, and probabilities of flow of a quantity called information. The world is subdivided by boundaries differentially permeable to information. Information is just that kind of quantifiable element (unit, basis of unity) which allows universal translation, and so unhindered instrumental power (called effective communication). The biggest threat to such power is interruption of communication. Any system breakdown is a function of stress. The fundamentals of this technology can be condensed into the metaphor C^3I, command-control-communication-intelligence, the military's symbol for its operations theory.

In modern biologies, the translation of the world into a problem in coding can be illustrated by molecular genetics, ecology, sociobiological evolutionary theory, and immunobiology. The organism has been translated into problems of genetic coding and read-out. Biotechnology, a writing technology, informs research broadly.[21] In a sense, organisms have ceased to exist as objects of knowledge, giving way to biotic components, i.e., special kinds of information-processing devices. The analogous moves in ecology could be examined by probing the history and utility of the concept of the ecosystem. Immunobiology and associated medical practices are rich exemplars of the privilege of coding and recognition systems as objects of knowledge, as constructions of bodily reality for us. Biology here is a kind of cryptography. Research is necessarily a kind of intelligence activity. Ironies abound. A stressed system goes awry; its communication processes break down; it fails to recognize the difference between self and other.[22] Human babies with baboon hearts evoke national ethical perplexity — for animal rights activists at least as much as for the guardians of human purity. In the US gay men and intravenous drug users are the "privileged" victims of an awful immune system disease that marks (inscribes on the body) confusion of boundaries and moral pollution (Treichler, 1987).[23]

But these excursions into communications sciences and biology have been at a rarefied level; there is a mundane, largely economic reality to support my claim that these sciences and technologies indicate fundamental transformations in the structure of the world for us. Communications technologies depend on electronics. Modern states, multinational corporations, military power, welfare state apparatuses, satellite systems, political processes, fabrication of our imaginations, labor-control systems, medical constructions of our bodies, commercial pornography, the international division of labor, and religious evangelism depend intimately upon electronics. Microelectronics is the technical basis of simulacra; that is, of copies without originals.

Microelectronics mediates the translations of labor into robotics and word processing, sex into genetic engineering and reproductive technologies, and mind into artificial intelligence and decision procedures. The new biotechnologies concern more than human reproduction. Biology as a powerful engineering science for redesigning materials and processes has revolutionary implications for industry, perhaps most obvious today in areas of fermentation, agriculture, and energy. Communications sciences and biology are constructions of natural-technical objects of knowledge in which the difference between machine and organism is thoroughly blurred; mind, body, and tool are on very intimate terms. The "multinational" material organization of the production and reproduction of daily life and the symbolic organization of the production and reproduction of culture and imagination seem equally implicated. The boundary-maintaining images of base and superstructure, public and

[21]For progressive analyses and action on the biotechnology debates: *GeneWatch, a Bulletin of the Committee for Responsible Genetics*, 5 Doane St., 4th Floor, Boston, MA 02109; Genetic Screening Study Group (formerly the Sociobiology Study Group of Science for the People), Cambridge, MA; Wright (1982, 1986); Yoxen (1983). [Haraway]

[22]In autoimmune diseases (e.g., juvenile diabetes, multiple sclerosis, rheumatoid arthritis) the body attacks its own tissues, misperceiving them as invading "others."

[23]Haraway refers to the fact that HIV is transmitted at sites where fluids from bodies, normally separate, meet. Anal intercourse and intravenous drug use were forms of "moral pollution" first isolated as leading to the spread of AIDS. Haraway's biopolitical scheme omits the fourth "privileged" group among whom AIDS first appeared: hospital patients who received donated blood.

private, or material and ideal never seemed more feeble.

I have used Rachel Grossman's (1980) image of women in the integrated circuit to name the situation of women in a world so intimately restructured through the social relations of science and technology.[24] I used the odd circumlocution, "the social relations of science and technology," to indicate that we are not dealing with a technological determinism, but with a historical system depending upon structured relations among people. But the phrase should also indicate that science and technology provide fresh sources of power, that we need fresh sources of analysis and political action (Latour, 1984). Some of the rearrangements of race, sex, and class rooted in high-tech-facilitated social relations can make socialist-feminism more relevant to effective progressive politics.

THE "HOMEWORK ECONOMY" OUTSIDE "THE HOME"

The "New Industrial Revolution" is producing a new world-wide working class, as well as new sexualities and ethnicities. The extreme mobility of capital and the emerging international division of labor are intertwined with the emergence of new collectivities, and the weakening of familiar groupings. These developments are neither gender- nor race-neutral. White men in advanced industrial societies have become newly vulnerable to permanent job loss, and women are not disappearing from the job rolls at the same rates as men. It is not simply that women in Third World countries are the preferred labor force for the science-based multinationals in the export-processing sectors, particularly in electronics. The picture is more systematic and involves reproduction, sexuality, culture, consumption, and production. In the prototypical Silicon Valley, many women's lives have been structured around employment in electronics-dependent jobs, and their intimate realities include serial heterosexual monogamy, negotiating childcare, distance from extended kin or most other forms of traditional community, a high likelihood of loneliness and extreme economic vulnerability as they age. The ethnic and racial diversity of women in Silicon Valley structures a microcosm of conflicting differences in culture, family, religion, education, and language.

Richard Gordon has called this new situation the "homework economy."[25] Although he includes the phenomenon of literal homework emerging in connection with electronics assembly, Gordon intends "homework economy" to name a restructuring of work that broadly has the characteristics formerly ascribed to female jobs, jobs literally done only by women. Work is being redefined as both literally female and feminized, whether performed by men or women. To be feminized means to be made extremely vulnerable; able to be disassembled, reassembled, exploited as a reserve labor force; seen less as workers than as servers; subjected to time arrangements on and off the paid job that make a mockery of a limited work day; leading an existence that always borders on being obscene, out of place, and reducible to sex. Deskilling is an old strategy newly applicable to formerly privileged workers. However, the homework economy does not refer only to large-scale deskilling, nor does it deny that new areas of high skill are emerging, even for women and men previously excluded from skilled employment. Rather, the concept indicates that factory, home, and market are integrated on a new scale and that the places of women are crucial — and need to be analyzed for differences among women and for meanings for relations between men and women in various situations.

[24]Starting references for "women in the integrated circuit": D'Onofrio-Flores and Pfafflin (1982), Fernandez-Kelly (1983), Fuentes and Ehrenreich (1983), Grossman (1980), Nash and Fernandez-Kelly (1983), Ong (1987), Science Policy Research unit (1982). [Haraway]

[25]For the "homework economy outside the home" and related arguments: Gordon (1983); Gordon and Kimball (1985); Stacey (1987); Reskin and Hartmann (1986); *Women and Poverty* (1984); S. Rose (1986); Collins (1982); Burr (1982); Gregory and Nussbaum (1982); Piven and Coward (1982); Microelectronics Group (1980); Stallard et al. (1983) which includes a useful organization and resource list. [Haraway]

The homework economy as a world capitalist organizational structure is made possible by (not caused by) the new technologies. The success of the attack on relatively privileged, mostly white, men's unionized jobs is tied to the power of the new communications technologies to integrate and control labor despite extensive dispersion and decentralization. The consequences of the new technologies are felt by women both in the loss of the family (male) wage (if they ever had access to this white privilege) and in the character of their own jobs, which are becoming capital-intensive; for example, office work and nursing.

The new economic and technological arrangements are also related to the collapsing welfare state and the ensuing intensification of demands on women to sustain daily life for themselves as well as for men, children, and old people. The feminization of poverty — generated by dismantling the welfare state, by the homework economy where stable jobs become the exception, and sustained by the expectation that women's wages will not be matched by a male income for the support of children — has become an urgent focus. The causes of various women-headed households are a function of race, class, or sexuality; but their increasing generality is a ground for coalitions of women on many issues. That women regularly sustain daily life partly as a function of their enforced status as mothers is hardly new; the kind of integration with the overall capitalist and progressively war-based economy is new. The particular pressure, for example, on US black women, who have achieved an escape from (barely) paid domestic service and who now hold clerical and similar jobs in large numbers, has large implications for continued enforced black poverty *with* employment. Teenage women in industrializing areas of the Third World increasingly find themselves the sole or major source of a cash wage for their families, while access to land is ever more problematic. These developments must have major consequences in the psychodynamics and politics of gender and race.

Within the framework of three major stages of capitalism (commercial/early industrial, monopoly, multinational) — tied to nationalism, imperialism, and multinationalism, and related to Jameson's three dominant aesthetic periods of realism, modernism, and postmodernism — I would argue that specific forms of families dialectically relate to forms of capital and to its political and cultural concomitants. Although lived problematically and unequally, ideal forms of these families might be schematized as (1) the patriarchal nuclear family, structured by the dichotomy between public and private and accompanied by the white bourgeois ideology of separate spheres and nineteenth-century Anglo-American bourgeois feminism; (2) the modern family mediated (or enforced) by the welfare state and institutions like the family wage, with a flowering of a feminist heterosexual ideologies, including their radical versions represented in Greenwich Village around the First World War; and (3) the "family" of the homework economy with its oxymoronic structure of women-headed households and its explosion of feminisms and the paradoxical intensification and erosion of gender itself. This is the context in which the projections for world-wide structural unemployment stemming from the new technologies are part of the picture of the homework economy. As robotics and related technologies put men out of work in "developed" countries and exacerbate failure to generate male jobs in Third World "development," and as the automated office becomes the rule even in labor-surplus countries, the feminization of work intensifies. Black women in the United States have long known what it looks like to face the structural underemployment ("feminization") of black men, as well as their own highly vulnerable position in the wage economy. It is no longer a secret that sexuality, reproduction, family, and community life are interwoven with this economic structure in myriad ways which have also differentiated the situations of white and black women. Many more women and men will contend with similar situations, which will make cross-gender and race alliances on issues of basic life support (with or without jobs) necessary, not just nice.

The new technologies also have a profound effect on hunger and on food production for subsistence world-wide. Rae Lessor Blumberg (1983) estimates that women produce about 50 percent of the world's subsistence food.[26] Women are excluded generally from benefiting from the increased high-tech commodification of food and energy crops, their days are made more arduous because their responsibilities to provide food do not diminish, and their reproductive situations are made more complex. Green Revolution technologies interact with other high-tech industrial production to alter gender divisions of labor and differential gender migration patterns.

The new technologies seem deeply involved in the forms of "privatization" that Ros Petchesky (1981) has analyzed, in which militarization, right-wing family ideologies and policies, and intensified definitions of corporate (and state) property as private synergistically interact.[27] The new communications technologies are fundamental to the eradication of "public life" for everyone. This facilitates the mushrooming of a permanent high-tech military establishment at the cultural and economic expense of most people, but especially of women. Technologies like video games and highly miniaturized televisions seem crucial to production of modern forms of "private life." The culture of video games is heavily orientated to individual competition and extraterrestrial warfare. High-tech, gendered imaginations are produced here, imaginations that can contemplate destruction of the planet and a sci-fi escape from its consequences. More than our imaginations is militarized; and the other realities of electronic and nuclear warfare are inescapable. These are the technologies that promise ultimate mobility and perfect exchange — and incidentally enable tourism, that perfect practice of mobility and exchange, to emerge as one of the world's largest single industries.

The new technologies affect the social relations of both sexuality and of reproduction, and not always in the same ways. The close ties of sexuality and instrumentality, of views of the body as a kind of private satisfaction- and utility-maximizing machine, are described nicely in sociobiological origin stories that stress a genetic calculus and explain the inevitable dialectic of domination of male and female gender roles.[28] These sociobiological stories depend on a high-tech view of the body as a biotic component or cybernetic communications system. Among the many transformations of reproductive situations is the medical one, where women's bodies have boundaries newly permeable to both "visualization" and "intervention." Of course, who controls the interpretation of bodily boundaries in medical hermeneutics is a major feminist issue. The speculum[29] served as an icon of women's claiming their bodies in the 1970s; that handcraft tool is inadequate to express our needed body politics in the negotiation of reality in the practices of cyborg reproduction. Self-help is not enough. The technologies of visualization recall the important cultural practice of hunting with the camera and the deeply predatory nature of a photographic consciousness.[30] Sex, sexuality, and reproduction are central actors in high-tech myth systems structuring our imaginations of personal and social possibility.

[26]The conjunction of the Green Revolution's social relations with biotechnologies like plant genetic engineering makes the pressures on land in the Third World increasingly intense. AID's estimates (*New York Times*, 14 October 1984) used at the 1984 World Food Day are that in Africa, women produce about 90 percent of rural food supplies, about 60–80 percent in Asia, and provide 40 percent of agricultural labour in the Near East and Latin America. Blumberg charges that world organizations' agricultural politics, as well as those of multinationals and national governments in the Third World, generally ignore fundamental issues in the sexual division of labor. The present tragedy of famine in Africa might owe as much to male supremacy as to capitalism, colonialism, and rain patterns. More accurately, capitalism and racism are usually structurally male dominant. See also Blumberg (1981); Hacker (1984); Hacker and Bovit (1981); Busch and Lacy (1983); Wilfred (1982); Sachs (1983); International Fund for Agricultural Development (1985); Bird (1984). [Haraway]

[27]See also Enloe (1983a, b). [Haraway]

[28]For a feminist version of this logic, see Hrdy (1981). For an analysis of scientific women's story-telling practices, especially in relation to sociobiology in evolutionary debates around child abuse and infanticide, see this vol., ch. 5. [Haraway]

[29]A surgical instrument used in a pelvic examination to hold apart the sides of the vagina to allow one to view the uterus. Feminists of the 1970s recommended that women examine their own bodies, including pelvic self-examinations, as a step toward raising their consciousness as women.

[30]For the moment of transition of hunting with guns to hunting with cameras in the construction of popular meanings of nature for an American urban immigrant public, see Haraway (1984–5, 1989b), Nash (1979), Sontag (1977), Preston (1984). [Haraway]

Another critical aspect of the social relations of the new technologies is the reformulation of expectations, culture, work, and reproduction for the large scientific and technical work-force. A major social and political danger is the formation of a strongly bimodal social structure, with the masses of women and men of all ethnic groups, but especially people of color, confined to a homework economy, illiteracy of several varieties, and general redundancy and impotence, controlled by high-tech repressive apparatuses ranging from entertainment to surveillance and disappearance. An adequate socialist-feminist politics should address women in the privileged occupational categories, and particularly in the production of science and technology that constructs scientific-technical discourses, processes, and objects.[31]

This issue is only one aspect of enquiry into the possibility of a feminist science, but it is important. What kind of constitutive role in the production of knowledge, imagination, and practice can new groups doing science have? How can these groups be allied with progressive social and political movements? What kind of political accountability can be constructed to tie women together across the scientific-technical hierarchies separating us? Might there be ways of developing feminist science/technology politics in alliance with anti-military science facility conversion action groups? Many scientific and technical workers in Silicon Valley, the high-tech cowboys included, do not want to work on military science.[32] Can these personal preferences and cultural tendencies be welded into progressive politics among this professional middle class in which women, including women of colour, are coming to be fairly numerous?

WOMEN IN THE INTEGRATED CIRCUIT

Let me summarize the picture of women's historical locations in advanced industrial societies, as

these positions have been restructured partly through the social relations of science and technology. If it was ever possible ideologically to characterize women's lives by the distinction of public and private domains — suggested by images of the division of working-class life into factory and home, of bourgeois life into market and home, and of gender existence into personal and political realms — it is now a totally misleading ideology, even to show how both terms of these dichotomies construct each other in practice and in theory. I prefer a network ideological image, suggesting the profusion of spaces and identities and the permeability of boundaries in the personal body and in the body politic. "Networking" is both a feminist practice and a multinational corporate strategy — weaving is for oppositional cyborgs.

So let me return to the earlier image of the informatics of domination and trace one vision of women's "place" in the integrated circuit, touching only a few idealized social locations seen primarily from the point of view of advanced capitalist societies: Home, Market, Paid Work Place, State, School, Clinic-Hospital, and Church. Each of these idealized spaces is logically and practically implied in every other locus, perhaps analogous to a holographic photograph. I want to suggest the impact of the social relations mediated and enforced by the new technologies in order to help formulate needed analysis and practical work. However, there is no "place" for women in these networks, only geometrics of difference and contradiction crucial to women's cyborg identities. If we learn how to read these webs of power and social life, we might learn new couplings, new coalitions. There is no way to read the following list from a standpoint of "identification," of a unitary self. The issue is dispersion. The task is to survive in the diaspora.

Home: Women-headed households, serial monogamy, flight of men, old women alone, technology of domestic work, paid homework, reemergence of home sweat-shops, home-based businesses and telecommuting, electronic cottage, urban homelessness, migration, module architecture, reinforced (simulated) nuclear family, intense domestic violence.

[31]For guidance for thinking about the political/cultural/racial implications of the history of women doing science in the United States see: Haas and Perucci (1984); Hacker (1981); Keller (1983); National Science Foundation (1988); Rossiter (1982); Schiebinger (1987); Haraway (1989b). [Haraway]

[32]Markoff and Siegel (1983). High Technology Professionals for Peace and Computer Professionals for Social Responsibility are promising organizations. [Haraway]

Market: Women's continuing consumption work, newly targeted to buy the profusion of new production from the new technologies (especially as the competitive race among industrialized and industrializing nations to avoid dangerous mass unemployment necessitates finding ever bigger new markets for ever less clearly needed commodities); bimodal buying power, coupled with advertising targeting of the numerous affluent groups and neglect of the previous mass markets; growing importance of informal markets in labor and commodities parallel to high-tech, affluent market structures; surveillance systems through electronic funds transfer; intensified market abstraction (commodification) of experience, resulting in ineffective utopian or equivalent cynical theories of community; extreme mobility (abstraction) of marketing/financing systems; interpenetration of sexual and labor markets; intensified sexualization of abstracted and alienated consumption.

Paid Work Place: Continued intense sexual and racial division of labor, but considerable growth of membership in privileged occupational categories for many white women and people of color; impact of new technologies on women's work in clerical, service, manufacturing (especially textiles), agriculture, electronics; international restructuring of the working classes; development of new time arrangements to facilitate the homework economy (flex time, part time, over time, no time); homework and out work; increased pressures for two-tiered wage structures; significant numbers of people in cash-dependent populations world-wide with no experience or no further hope of stable employment; most labor "marginal" or "feminized."

State: Continued erosion of the welfare state; decentralizations with increased surveillance and control; citizenship by telematics; imperialism and political power broadly in the form of information rich/information poor differentiation; increased high-tech militarization increasingly opposed by many social groups; reduction of civil service jobs as a result of the growing capital intensification of office work, with implications for occupational mobility for women of color; growing privatization of material and ideological life and culture; close integration of privatization and militarization, the high-tech forms of bourgeois capitalist personal and public life; invisibility of different social groups to each other, linked to psychological mechanisms of belief in abstract enemies.

School: Deepening coupling of high-tech capital needs and public education at all levels, differentiated by race, class, and gender; managerial classes involved in educational reform and refunding at the cost of remaining progressive educational democratic structures for children and teachers; education for mass ignorance and repression in technocratic and militarized culture; growing anti-science mystery cults in dissenting and radical political movements; continued relative scientific illiteracy among white women and people of color; growing industrial direction of education (especially higher education) by science-based multinationals (particularly in electronics- and biotechnology-dependent companies); highly educated, numerous élites in a progressively bimodal society.

Clinic-hospital: Intensified machine-body relations; renegotiations of public metaphors which channel personal experience of the body, particularly in relation to reproduction, immune system functions, and "stress" phenomena; intensification of reproductive politics in response to world historical implications of women's unrealized, potential control of their relation to reproduction; emergence of new, historically specific diseases; struggles over meanings and means of health in environments pervaded by high technology products and processes; continuing feminization of health work; intensified struggle over state responsibility for health; continued ideological role of popular health movements as a major form of American politics.

Church: Electronic fundamentalist "super-saver" preachers solemnizing the union of electronic capital and automated fetish gods; intensified importance of churches in resisting the militarized state; central struggle over women's meanings and authority in religion; continued relevance of spirituality, intertwined with sex and health, in political struggle.

The only way to characterize the informatics of domination is as a massive intensification of insecurity and cultural impoverishment, with common failure of subsistence networks for the most vulnerable. Since much of this picture interweaves with the social relations of science and technology, the urgency of a socialist-feminist politics addressed to science and technology is plain. There is much now being done, and the grounds for political work are rich. For example, the efforts to develop forms of collective struggle for women in paid work, like SEIU's District 925,[33] should be a high priority for all of us. These efforts are profoundly tied to technical restructuring of labor processes and reformations of working classes. These efforts also are providing understanding of a more comprehensive kind of labor organization, involving community, sexuality, and family issues never privileged in the largely white male industrial unions.

The structural rearrangements related to the social relations of science and technology evoke strong ambivalence. But it is not necessary to be ultimately depressed by the implications of late twentieth-century women's relation to all aspects of work, culture, production of knowledge, sexuality, and reproduction. For excellent reasons, most Marxisms see domination best and have trouble understanding what can only look like false consciousness and people's complicity in their own domination in late capitalism. It is crucial to remember that what is lost, perhaps especially from women's points of view, is often virulent forms of oppression, nostalgically naturalized in the face of current violation. Ambivalence towards the disrupted unities mediated by high-tech culture requires not sorting consciousness into categories of "clear-sighted critique grounding a solid political epistemology" versus "manipulated false consciousness," but subtle understanding of emerging pleasures, experiences, and powers with serious potential for changing the rules of the game.

There are grounds for hope in the emerging bases for new kinds of unity across race, gender, and class, as these elementary units of socialist-feminist analysis themselves suffer protean transformations. Intensifications of hardship experienced world-wide in connection with the social

relations of science and technology are severe. But what people are experiencing is not transparently clear, and we lack sufficiently subtle connections for collectively building effective theories of experience. Present efforts — Marxist, psychoanalytic, feminist, anthropological — to clarify even "our" experience are rudimentary.

I am conscious of the odd perspective provided by my historical position — a PhD in biology for an Irish Catholic girl was made possible by Sputnik's[34] impact on US national science-education policy. I have a body and mind as much constructed by the post-Second World War arms race and cold war as by the women's movements. There are more grounds for hope in focusing on the contradictory effects of politics designed to produce loyal American technocrats, which also produced large numbers of dissidents, than in focusing on the present defeats.

The permanent partiality of feminist points of view has consequences for our expectations of forms of political organization and participation. We do not need a totality in order to work well. The feminist dream of a common language, like all dreams for a perfectly true language, of perfectly faithful naming of experience, is a totalizing and imperialist one. In that sense, dialectics too is a dream language, longing to resolve contradiction. Perhaps, ironically, we can learn from our fusions with animals and machines how not to be Man, the embodiment of Western logos. From the point of view of pleasure in these potent and taboo fusions, made inevitable by the social relations of science and technology, there might indeed be a feminist science.

CYBORGS: A MYTH OF POLITICAL IDENTITY

I want to conclude with a myth about identity and boundaries which might inform late twentieth-century political imaginations. I am indebted in this story to writers like Joanna Russ, Samuel R.

[33]Service Employees International Union's office workers' organization in the US. [Haraway]

[34]Sputnik was the name of the first satellite launched into Earth's orbit by the Soviet Union in October 1957. The U.S. government, stunned by its rival's achievement, poured money not only directly into the space race but into science education through the National Science Foundation and the National Defense Education Act.

Delany, John Varley, James Tiptree, Jr, Octavia Butler, Monique Wittig, and Vonda McIntyre.[35] These are our story-tellers exploring what it means to be embodied in high-tech worlds. They are theorists for cyborgs. Exploring conceptions of bodily boundaries and social order, the anthropologist Mary Douglas (1966, 1970) should be credited with helping us to consciousness about how fundamental body imagery is to world view, and so to political language. French feminists like Luce Irigaray and Monique Wittig, for all their differences, know how to write the body; how to weave eroticism, cosmology, and politics from imagery of embodiment, and especially for Wittig, from imagery of fragmentation and reconstitution of bodies.[36]

American radical feminists like Susan Griffin, Audre Lorde, and Adrienne Rich have profoundly affected our political imaginations — and perhaps restricted too much what we allow as a friendly body and political language.[37] They insist on the organic, opposing it to the technological. But their symbolic systems and the related positions of ecofeminism and feminist paganism, replete with organicisms, can only be understood in Sandoval's terms as oppositional ideologies fitting the late twentieth century. They would simply bewilder anyone not preoccupied with the machines and consciousness of late capitalism. In that sense they are part of the cyborg world. But there are also great riches for feminists in explicitly embracing the possibilities inherent in the breakdown of clean distinctions between organism and machine and similar distinctions structuring the Western self. It is the simultaneity of breakdowns that cracks the matrices of domination and opens geometric possibilities. What might be learned from personal and political "technological" pollution? I look briefly at two overlapping groups of texts for their insight into the construction of a potentially helpful cyborg myth: constructions of women of color and monstrous selves in feminist science fiction.

Earlier I suggested that "women of color" might be understood as a cyborg identity, a potent subjectivity synthesized from fusions of outsider identities and in the complex political-historical layerings of her "biomythography," *Zami* (Lorde, 1982; King, 1987a, 1987b). There are material and cultural grids mapping this potential. Audre Lorde (1984) captures the tone in the title of her *Sister Outsider*. In my political myth, Sister Outsider is the offshore woman, whom US workers, female and feminized, are supposed to regard as the enemy preventing their solidarity, threatening their security. Onshore, inside the boundary of the United States, Sister Outsider is a potential amidst the races and ethnic identities of women manipulated for division, competition, and exploitation in the same industries. "Women of color" are the preferred labor force for the science-based industries, the real women for whom the world-wide sexual market, labor market, and politics of reproduction kaleidoscope into daily life. Young Korean women hired in the sex industry and in electronics assembly are recruited from high schools, educated for the integrated circuit. Literacy, especially in English, distinguishes the "cheap" female labor so attractive to the multinationals.

Contrary to orientalist stereotypes of the "oral primitive," literacy is a special mark of women of color, acquired by US black women as well as men through a history of risking death to learn and to teach reading and writing. Writing has a special significance for all colonized groups. Writing has been crucial to the Western myth of the distinction between oral and written cultures, primitive and civilized mentalities, and more recently to the erosion of that distinction in "postmodernist" theories attacking the phallogocentrism of the West, with

[35]King (1984). An abbreviated list of feminist science fiction underlying themes of this essay: Octavia Butler, *Wild Seed, Mind of My Mind, Kindred, Survivor*; Suzy McKee Charnas, *Motherliness*; Samuel R. Delany, the Nevèrÿon series; Anne McCaffery, *The Ship Who Sang, Dinosaur Planet*; Vonda McIntyre, *Superluminal, Dreamsnake*; Joanna Russ, *Adventures of Alix, The Female Man*; James Tiptree, Jr., *Star Songs of an Old Primate, Up the Walls of the World*; John Varley, *Titan, Wizard, Demon*. [Haraway]

[36]French feminisms contribute to cyborg heteroglossia. Burke (1981); Irigaray (1977, 1979); Marks and de Courtivron (1980); *Signs* (Autumn 1981); Wittig (1973); Duchen (1986). For English translation of some currents of francophone feminism see *Feminist Issues: A Journal of Feminist Social and Political Theory*, 1980. [Haraway]

[37]But all these poets are very complex, not least in their treatment of themes of lying and erotic, decentred collective and personal identities. Griffin (1978), Lorde (1984), Rich (1978). [Haraway]

its worship of the monotheistic, phallic, authoritative, and singular work, the unique and perfect name.[38] Contests for the meanings of writing are a major form of contemporary political struggle. Releasing the play of writing is deadly serious. The poetry and stories of US women of color are repeatedly about writing, about access to the power to signify; but this time that power must be neither phallic nor innocent. Cyborg writing must not be about the Fall, the imagination of a once-upon-a-time wholeness before language, before writing, before Man. Cyborg writing is about the power to survive, not on the basis of original innocence, but on the basis of seizing the tools to mark the world that marked them as other.

The tools are often stories, retold stories, versions that reverse and displace the hierarchical dualisms of naturalized identities. In retelling origin stories, cyborg authors subvert the central myths of origin of Western culture. We have all been colonized by those origin myths, with their longing for fulfilment in apocalypse. The phallogocentric origin stories most crucial for feminist cyborgs are built into the literal technologies — technologies that write the world, biotechnology and microelectronics — that have recently textualized our bodies as code problems on the grid of C^3I. Feminist cyborg stories have the task of recoding communication and intelligence to subvert command and control.

Figuratively and literally, language politics pervade the struggles of women of color; and stories about language have a special power in the rich contemporary writing by US women of color. For example, retellings of the story of the indigenous woman Malinche, mother of the mestizo "bastard" race of the new world, master of languages, and mistress of Cortés, carry special meaning for Chicana constructions of identity.[39] Cherríe Moraga (1983) in *Loving in the War Years* explores the themes of identity when one never possessed the original language, never told the original story, never resided in the harmony of legitimate heterosexuality in the garden of culture, and so cannot base identity on a myth or a fall from innocence and right to natural names, mother's or father's.[40] Moraga's writing, her superb literacy, is presented in her poetry as the same kind of violation as Malinche's mastery of the conqueror's language — a violation, an illegitimate production, that allows survival. Moraga's language is not "whole"; it is self-consciously spliced, a chimera of English and Spanish, both conqueror's languages. But it is this chimeric monster, without claim to an original language before violation, that crafts the erotic, competent, potent identities of women of color. Sister Outsider hints at the possibility of world survival not because of her innocence, but because of her ability to live on the boundaries, to write without the founding myth of original wholeness, with its inescapable apocalypse of final return to a deathly oneness that Man has imagined to be the innocent and all-powerful Mother, freed at the End from another spiral of appropriation by her son. Writing marks Moraga's body, affirms it as the body of a woman of color, against the possibility of passing into the unmarked category of the Anglo father or into the orientalist myth of "original illiteracy" of a

[38]Derrida (1976, especially part II); Lévi-Strauss (1961, especially "The Writing Lesson"); Gates (1985); Kahn and Neumaier (1985); Ong (1982); Kramarae and Treichler (1985). [Haraway] Haraway here and elsewhere appeals to the thought of Jacques Derrida, particularly his discussion of the way Western culture has traditionally privileged presence over absence, speech over writing, the masculine over the feminine (see p. 830). "Phallogocentrism" is a coinage by Hélène Cixous connecting these privileged categories (see p. 1645).

[39]Hernando Cortés (1485–1547) was the Spanish conqueror of Mexico. Malinche, his long-term mistress, also known as Doña Marina, was the daughter of a noble Aztec family who had been sold into slavery and later given to Cortés. Skilled in languages, she assisted in Cortés's negotiations with Aztec leaders. Malinche is a very ambivalent character in Mexican culture, admired as one who assisted in the development of Christian culture and reviled as a collaborator with the conqueror because she is perceived to have turned her back on her own culture.

[40]The sharp relation of women of color to writing as theme and politics can be approached through: Program for "The Black Woman and the Diaspora: Hidden Connections and Extended Acknowledgments," An International Literary Conference, Michigan State University, October 1985; Evans (1984); Christian (1985); Carby (1987); Fisher (1980); *Frontiers* (1980, 1983); Kingston (1977); Lerner (1973); Giddings (1985); Moraga and Anzaldúa (1981); Morgan (1984). Anglophone European and Euro-American women have also crafted special relations to their writing as a potent sign: Gilbert and Gubar (1979), Russ (1983). [Haraway]

mother that never was. Malinche was mother here, not Eve before eating the forbidden fruit. Writing affirms Sister Outsider, not the Woman-before-the-Fall-into-Writing needed by the phallogocentric Family of Man.

Writing is pre-eminently the technology of cyborgs, etched surfaces of the late twentieth century. Cyborg politics is the struggle for language and the struggle against perfect communication, against the one code that translates all meaning perfectly, the central dogma of phallogocentrism. That is why cyborg politics insist on noise and advocate pollution, rejoicing in the illegitimate fusions of animal and machine. These are the couplings which make Man and Woman so problematic, subverting the structure of desire, the force imagined to generate language and gender, and so subverting the structure and modes of reproduction of "Western" identity, of nature and culture, of mirror and eye, slave and master, body and mind. "We" did not originally choose to be cyborgs, but choice grounds a liberal politics and epistemology that imagines the reproduction of individuals before the wider replications of "texts."

From the perspective of cyborgs, freed of the need to ground politics in "our" privileged position of the oppression that incorporates all other dominations, the innocence of the merely violated, the ground of those closer to nature, we can see powerful possibilities. Feminisms and Marxisms have run aground on Western epistemological imperatives to construct a revolutionary subject from the perspective of a hierarchy of oppressions and/or a latent position of moral superiority, innocence, and greater closeness to nature. With no available original dream of a common language or original symbiosis promising protection from hostile "masculine" separation, but written into the play of a text that has no finally privileged reading or salvation history, to recognize "oneself" as fully implicated in the world, frees us of the need to root politics in identification, vanguard parties, purity, and mothering. Stripped of identity, the bastard race teaches about the power of the margins and the importance of a mother like Malinche. Women of color have transformed her from the evil mother of masculinist fear into the originally literate mother who teaches survival.

This is not just literary deconstruction, but liminal transformation. Every story that begins with original innocence and privileges the return to wholeness imagines the drama of life to be individuation, separation, the birth of the self, the tragedy of autonomy, the fall into writing, alienation; that is, war, tempered by imaginary respite in the bosom of the Other. These plots are ruled by a reproductive politics — rebirth without flaw, perfection, abstraction. In this plot women are imagined either better or worse off, but all agree they have less selfhood, weaker individuation, more fusion to the oral, to Mother, less at stake in masculine autonomy. But there is another route to having less at stake in masculine autonomy, a route that does not pass through Woman, Primitive, Zero, the Mirror Stage and its imaginary.[41] It passes through women and other present-tense, illegitimate cyborgs, not of Woman born, who refuse the ideological resources of victimization so as to have a real life. These cyborgs are the people who refuse to disappear on cue, no matter how many times a "Western" commentator remarks on the sad passing of another primitive, another organic group done in by "Western" technology, by writing.[42] These real-life cyborgs (for example, the Southeast Asian village women workers in Japanese and US electronics firms described by Aihwa Ong) are actively rewriting the texts of their bodies and societies. Survival is the stakes in this play of readings.

To recapitulate, certain dualisms have been persistent in Western traditions; they have all been systemic to the logics and practices of domination of women, people of color, nature, workers, animals — in short, domination of all constituted as others, whose task is to mirror the self. Chief among

[41]Haraway alludes to Lacan's stages of development; see above pp. 1112–13.

[42]The convention of ideologically taming militarized high technology by publicizing its applications to speech and motion problems of the disabled/differently abled takes on a special irony in monotheistic, patriarchal, and frequently anti-semitic culture when computer-generated speech allows a boy with no voice to chant the Haftorah at his bar mitzvah. See Sussman (1986). Making the always context-relative social definitions of "ableness" particularly clear, military high-tech has a way of making human beings disabled by definition, a perverse aspect of much automated battlefield and Star Wars R&D. See Welford (1 July 1986). [Haraway]

these troubling dualisms are self/other, mind/body, culture/nature, male/female, civilized/primitive, reality/appearance, whole/part, agent/resource, maker/made, active/passive, right/wrong, truth/illusion, total/partial, God/man. The self is the One who is not dominated, who knows that by the service of the other, the other is the one who holds the future, who knows that by the experience of domination, which gives the lie to the autonomy of the self. To be One is to be autonomous, to be powerful, to be God; but to be One is to be an illusion, and so to be involved in a dialectic of apocalypse with the other. Yet to be other is to be multiple, without clear boundary, frayed, insubstantial. One is too few, but two are too many.

High-tech culture challenges these dualisms in intriguing ways. It is not clear who makes and who is made in the relation between human and machine. It is not clear what is mind and what body in machines that resolve into coding practices. In so far as we know ourselves in both formal discourse (for example, biology) and in daily practice (for example, the homework economy in the integrated circuit), we find ourselves to be cyborgs, hybrids, mosaics, chimeras. Biological organisms have become biotic systems, communications devices like others. There is no fundamental, ontological separation in our formal knowledge of machine and organism, of technical and organic. The replicant Rachel in the Ridley Scott film *Blade Runner* stands as the image of a cyborg culture's fear, love, and confusion.

One consequence is that our sense of connection to our tools is heightened. The trance state experienced by many computer users has become a staple of science-fiction film and cultural jokes. Perhaps paraplegics and other severely handicapped people can (and sometimes do) have the most intense experiences of complex hybridization with other communication devices.[43] Anne McCaffrey's prefeminist *The Ship Who Sang* (1969) explored the consciousness of a cyborg, hybrid of girl's brain and complex machinery, formed after the birth of a severely handicapped child. Gender, sexuality, embodiment, skill: all were reconstituted in the

story. Why should our bodies end at the skin, or include at best other beings encapsulated by skin? From the seventeenth century till now, machines could be animated — given ghostly souls to make them speak or move or to account for their orderly development and mental capacities. Or organisms could be mechanized — reduced to body understood as resource of mind. These machine/organism relationships are obsolete, unnecessary. For us, in imagination and in other practice, machines can be prosthetic devices, intimate components, friendly selves. We don't need organic holism to give impermeable wholeness, the total woman and her feminist variants (mutants?). Let me conclude this point by a very partial reading of the logic of the cyborg monsters of my second group of texts, feminist science fiction.

The cyborgs populating feminist science fiction make very problematic the statuses of man or woman, human, artefact, member of a race, individual entity, or body. Katie King clarifies how pleasure in reading these fictions is not largely based on identification. Students facing Joanna Russ for the first time, students who have learned to take modernist writers like James Joyce or Virginia Woolf without flinching, do not know what to make of *The Adventures of Alyx* or *The Female Man*, where characters refuse the reader's search for innocent wholeness while granting the wish for heroic quests, exuberant eroticism, and serious politics. *The Female Man* is the story of four versions of one genotype, all of whom meet, but even taken together do not make a whole, resolve the dilemmas of violent moral action, or remove the growing scandal of gender. The feminist science fiction of Samuel R. Delany, especially *Tales of Nevèrÿon*, mocks stories of origin by redoing the neolithic revolution, replaying the founding moves of Western civilization to subvert their plausibility. James Tiptree, Jr., an author whose fiction was regarded as particularly manly until her "true" gender was revealed,[44] tells tales of reproduction based on non-mammalian technologies like alternation of generations of male brood pouches and male nurturing. John Varley constructs a supreme cyborg in his arch-feminist

[43]James Clifford (1985, 1988) argues persuasively for recognition of continuous cultural reinvention, the stubborn non-disappearance of those "marked" by Western imperializing practices. [Haraway]

[44]Tiptree was the pen name of Alice B. Sheldon (1915–1987).

exploration of Gaea, a mad goddess-planet-trickster-old woman-technological device on whose surface an extraordinary array of post-cyborg symbioses are spawned. Octavia Butler writes of an African sorceress pitting her powers of transformation against the genetic manipulations of her rival (*Wild Seed*), of time warps that bring a modern US black woman into slavery where her actions in relation to her white master-ancestor determine the possibility of her own birth (*Kindred*), and of the illegitimate insights into identity and community of an adopted cross-species child who came to know the enemy as self (*Survivor*). In *Dawn* (1987), the first installment of a series called *Xenogenesis*, Butler tells the story of Lilith Iyapo, whose personal name recalls Adam's first and repudiated wife and whose family name marks her status as the widow of the son of Nigerian immigrants to the US. A black woman and a mother whose child is dead, Lilith mediates the transformation of humanity through genetic exchange with extra-terrestrial lovers/rescuers/destroyers/genetic engineers, who reform earth's habitats after the nuclear holocaust and coerce surviving humans into intimate fusion with them. It is a novel that interrogates reproductive, linguistic, and nuclear politics in a mythic field structured by late twentieth-century race and gender.

Because it is particularly rich in boundary transgressions, Vonda McIntyre's *Superluminal* can close this truncated catalogue of promising and dangerous monsters who help redefine the pleasures and politics of embodiment and feminist writing. In a fiction where no character is "simply" human, human status is highly problematic. Orca,[45] a genetically altered diver, can speak with killer whales and survive deep ocean conditions, but she longs to explore space as a pilot, necessitating bionic implants jeopardizing her kinship with the divers and cetaceans. Transformations are effected by virus vectors carrying a new developmental code, by transplant surgery, by implants of microelectronic devices, by analogue doubles, and other means. Laenea becomes a pilot by accepting a heart implant and a host of other alterations allowing survival in

transit at speeds exceeding that of light. Radu Dracul survives a virus-caused plague in his outerworld planet to find himself with a time sense that changes the boundaries of spatial perception for the whole species. All the characters explore the limits of language; the dream of communicating experience; and the necessity of limitation, partiality, and intimacy even in this world of protean transformation and connection. *Superluminal* stands also for the defining contradictions of a cyborg world in another sense; it embodies textually the intersection of feminist theory and colonial discourse in the science fiction I have alluded to in this chapter. This is a conjunction with a long history that many "First World" feminists have tried to repress, including myself in my readings of *Superluminal* before being called to account by Zoe Sofoulis, whose different location in the world system's informatics of domination made her acutely alert to the imperialist moment of all science fiction cultures, including women's science fiction. From an Australian feminist sensitivity, Sofoulis remembered more readily McIntyre's role as writer of the adventures of Captain Kirk and Spock in TV's *Star Trek* series than her rewriting the romance in *Superluminal*.

Monsters have always defined the limits of community in Western imaginations. The Centaurs and Amazons[46] of ancient Greece established the limits of the centered polis of the Greek male human by their disruption of marriage and boundary pollutions of the warrior with animality and woman. Unseparated twins and hermaphrodites were the confused human material in early modern France who grounded discourse on the natural and supernatural, medical and legal, portents and diseases —all crucial to establishing modern identity.[47] The evolutionary and behavioral sciences of monkeys and apes have marked the multiple boundaries of late twentieth-century industrial identities. Cyborg monsters in feminist science fiction define quite different political possibilities and

---

[45]The scientific name for the killer whale is *Orcinus orca*.

[46]According to Greek legends, centaurs were combinations of man and horse; the Amazons were a society composed only of women whose warriors cut off one breast in order to be able to wield the bow.

[47]DuBois (1982), Daston and Park (n.d.), Park and Daston (1981). The noun *monster* shares its root with the verb *to demonstrate*. [Haraway]

limits from those proposed by the mundane fiction of Man and Woman.

There are several consequences to taking seriously the imagery of cyborgs as other than our enemies. Our bodies, ourselves; bodies are maps of power and identity. Cyborgs are no exception. A cyborg body is not innocent; it was not born in a garden; it does not seek unitary identity and so generate antagonistic dualisms without end (or until the world ends); it takes irony for granted. One is too few, and two is only one possibility. Intense pleasure in skill, machine skill, ceases to be a sin, but an aspect of embodiment. The machine is not an *it* to be animated, worshipped, and dominated. The machine is us, our processes, an aspect of our embodiment. We can be responsible for machines; *they* do not dominate or threaten us. We are responsible for boundaries; we are they. Up till now (once upon a time), female embodiment seemed to be given, organic, necessary; and female embodiment seemed to mean skill in mothering and its metaphoric extensions. Only by being out of place could we take intense pleasure in machines, and then with excuses that this was organic activity after all, appropriate to females. Cyborgs might consider more seriously the partial, fluid, sometimes aspect of sex and sexual embodiment. Gender might not be global identity after all, even if it has profound historical breadth and depth.

The ideologically charged question of what counts as daily activity, as experience, can be approached by exploiting the cyborg image. Feminists have recently claimed that women are given to dailiness, that women more than men somehow sustain daily life, and so have a privileged epistemological position potentially. There is a compelling aspect to this claim, one that makes visible unvalued female activity and names it as the ground of life. But *the* ground of life? What about all the ignorance of women, all the exclusions and failures of knowledge and skill? What about men's access to daily competence, to knowing how to build things, to take them apart, to play? What about other embodiments? Cyborg gender is a local possibility taking a global vengeance. Race, gender, and capital require a cyborg theory of wholes and parts. There is no drive in cyborgs to produce total theory, but there is an intimate experience of boundaries, their construction and deconstruction. There is a myth system waiting to become a political language to ground one way of looking at science and technology and challenging the informatics of domination — in order to act potently.

One last image: organisms and organismic, holistic politics depend on metaphors of rebirth and invariably call on the resources of reproductive sex. I would suggest that cyborgs have more to do with regeneration and are suspicious of the reproductive matrix and of most birthing. For salamanders, regeneration after injury, such as the loss of a limb, involves regrowth of structure and restoration of function with the constant possibility of twinning or other odd topographical productions at the site of former injury. The regrown limb can be monstrous, duplicated, potent. We have all been injured, profoundly. We require regeneration, not rebirth, and the possibilities for our reconstitution include the Utopian dream of the hope for a monstrous world without gender.

Cyborg imagery can help express two crucial arguments in this essay: first, the production of universal, totalizing theory is a major mistake that misses most of reality, probably always, but certainly now; and second, taking responsibility for the social relations of science and technology means refusing an anti-science metaphysics, a demonology of technology, and so means embracing the skillful task of reconstructing the boundaries of daily life, in partial connection with others, in communication with all of our parts. It is not just that science and technology are possible means of great human satisfaction, as well as a matrix of complex dominations. Cyborg imagery can suggest a way out of the maze of dualisms in which we have explained our bodies and our tools to ourselves. This is a dream not of a common language, but of a powerful infidel heteroglossia. It is an imagination of a feminist speaking in tongues to strike fear into the circuits of the supersavers of the new right.[48] It means both building and destroying machines, identities, categories, relationships, space stories. Though both are bound in the spiral dance, I would rather be a cyborg than a goddess.

[48]At the time of the writing of this essay, the "new right" were the followers of Ronald Reagan and Margaret Thatcher.

Works Cited

Athanasiou, Tom (1987). "High Tech Politics: The Case of Artificial Intelligence," *Socialist Review* 92: 7–35.

Baudrillard, Jean (1983). *Simulations*, New York: Semiotext(e).

Bleier, Ruth (1984). *Science and Gender*, New York: Pergamon.

———— (1986). *Feminist Approaches to Science*, New York: Pergamon.

Blumberg, Rae Lessor (1981). *Stratification: Socioeconomic and Sexual Inequality*, Boston: Brown.

———— (1983). "A General Theory of Sex Stratification," paper delivered to Sociology Board, University of California at Santa Cruz.

Burke, Carolyn (1981). "Irigaray through the Looking Glass," *Feminist Studies* 7.2: 288–306.

Burr, Sara G. (1982). "Women and Work" in Barbara K. Haber, ed., *The Women's Annual 1981*, Boston: G. K. Hall.

Busch, Lawrence, and William Lacy (1983). *Science, Agriculture and the Politics of Research*, Boulder, CO: Westview.

Carby, Hazel (1987). *Reconstructing Womanhood*, New York: Oxford UP.

Christian, Barbara (1985). *Black Feminist Criticism*, New York: Pergamon.

Clifford, James (1985). "On Ethnographic Allegory," in James Clifford and George Marcus, eds., *Writing Culture*, Berkeley: U California P.

———— (1988). *The Predicament of Culture*, Cambridge, MA: Harvard UP.

Cohn, Carol (1987a). "Nuclear Language, and How We Learned to Pat the Bomb," *Bulletin of Atomic Scientists*: 17–24.

———— (1987b). "Sex and Death in the Rational World of Defense Intellectuals," *Signs* 12.4: 687–718.

Collins, Patricia (1982). "Third World Women in America," in Barbara K. Haber, ed., *The Women's Annual 1981*, Boston: G. K. Hall.

Cowan Ruth Schwartz (1983). *More Work for Mother*, New York: Basic Books.

Daston, Lorraine, and Katherine Park (n.d.). "Hermaphrodites in Renaissance France," unpublished paper.

Derrida, Jacques (1976). *Of Grammatology*, Baltimore: Johns Hopkins UP.

de Waal, Frans (1982). *Chimpanzee Power: Power and Sex among the Apes*, New York: Harper and Row.

D'Onofrio-Flores, Pamela, and Sheila Pfafflin, eds. (1982). *Scientific Technological Change and the Role of Women in Development*, Boulder: Westview.

Douglas, Mary (1966). *Purity and Danger*, London: Routledge and Kegan Paul.

———— (1970). *Natural Symbols*, London: Cresset Press.

DuBois, Page (1982). *Centaurs and Amazons*, Ann Arbor: U Michigan Pr.

Duchen, Claire (1986). *Feminism in France from May 68 to Mitterand*, London: Routledge.

Edwards, Paul (1985). "Border Wars: The Science and Politics of Artificial Intelligence," *Radical America*, 19.6:39–52.

Enloe, Cynthia (1983). *Does Khaki Become You? The Militarization of Women's Lives*, Boston: South End.

Epstein, Barbara (1991). *Political Protest and Cultural Revolution*, Berkeley: U California P.

Evans, Mari, ed. (1984). *Black Women Writers: A Critical Evaluation*, Garden City, NY: Doubleday/Anchor.

Fausto-Sterling, Anne (1985). *Myths of Gender: Biological Theories about Women and Men*, New York: Basic.

Fernandez-Kelly, Maria Patricia (1983). *For We Are Sold, I and My People*, Albany NY: SUNY Press.

Fisher, Dexter, ed. (1980). *The Third Woman: Minority Women Writers of the U.S.*, Boston: Houghton Mifflin.

Fraser, Kathleen (1984). *Something (Even Human Voices, in the Foreground, a Lake)*. Berkeley, CA: Kelsey St. Press.

Fuentes, Annette, and Barbara Ehrenreich (1983). *Women in the Global Factory*, Boston: South End.

Gates, Henry Louis (1985). "Writing, 'Race,' and the Difference It Makes," *Critical Inquiry* 12.1:1–20.

Giddings, Paula (1985). *When and Where I Enter*, Toronto: Bantam.

Gilbert, Sandra, and Susan Gubar (1979). *The Madwoman in the Attic*, New Haven: Yale UP.

Gordon, Linda (1983). *Women's Body, Women's Rights*, New York: Viking.

Gordon, Richard, and Linda Kimball (1985). *Heroes of Their Own Lives*, New York: Viking Penguin.

Gould, Stephen J. (1981). *Mismeasure of Man*, New York: Norton.

Gregory, Judith, and Karen Nussbaum (1982). "Race against Time: Automation of the Office," *Office: Technology and People* 1:197–236.

Griffin, Susan (1978). *Woman and Nature: The Roaring Inside Her*, New York: Harper & Row.

Grossman, Rachel (1980). "Women's Place in the Integrated Circuit," *Radial America* 14.1:29–50.

Haas, Violet, and Carolyn Perucci, eds. (1984). *Women in Scientific and Engineering Professions*, Ann Arbor: U Michigan P.

Hacker, Sally (1981). "The Culture of Engineering: Women, Workplace, and Machine," *Women's Studies International Quarterly* 4.3:341–53.

—— (1984). "Doing It the Hard Way," Paper delivered at the California American Studies Association, Pomona.

Hacker, Sally, and Liza Bovit (1981). "Agriculture to Agribusiness," paper delivered at Society for the History of Technology, Milwaukee.

Haraway, Donna (1979). "The Biological Enterprise," *Radical History Review* 20:206–37.

—— (1983). "Signs of Dominance," *Studies in the History of Biology* 6: 129–219.

—— (1984). "Class, Race, Sex, Scientific Objects of Knowledge," in Haas and Perucci (1984): 212–29.

—— (1984–5). "Teddy Bear Patriarchy," *Social Text* 11:20–64.

—— (1989b). *Primate Visions: Gender, Race and Nature in the World of Modern Science*, New York: Routledge.

Harding, Sandra (1986). *The Science Question in Feminism*, Ithaca: Cornell UP.

Hogness, E. Rusten (1983). "Why Stress? A Look at the Making of Stress 1936–56," unpublished paper available from the author, 4437 Mill Creek Road, Healdsburg, CA 95448.

Hrdy, Sarah Blaffer (1981). *The Woman That Never Evolved*, Cambridge: Harvard UP.

Hubbard, Ruth, Mary Sue Henefin, and Barbara Smith, eds. (1982). *Biological Woman: The Convenient Myth*, Cambridge, MA: Schenckman.

International Fund for Agriculture Development (1985). *IFAD Experience Relating to Rural Women 1977–84*, Rome: IFAD, 37.

Irigaray, Luce (1977). *Ce sex qui n'en est pas un*, Paris: Minuit.

Jameson, Fredric (1984). "Postmodernism, or The Cultural Logic of Late Capitalism," *New Left Review* 146:53–92.

Kahn, Douglas, and Diane Neumaier, eds. (1985). *Cultures in Contention*, Seattle: Real Comet.

Keller, Evelyn Fox (1983). *A Feeling for the Organism*, San Francisco: Freeman.

—— (1985). *Reflections on Gender and Science*, New Haven: Yale UP.

King, Katie (1984). "The Pleasure of Repetition," paper delivered at California American Studies Association, Pomona.

—— (1987a). *Canons without Innocence*, University of California at Santa Cruz Ph.D. Thesis.

—— (1987b). *The Passing Dreams of Choice*, book prospectus, University of Maryland at College Park.

Kingston, Maxine Hong (1977). *The Woman Warrior*, New York: Knopf.

Klein, Hilary (1989). "Marxism, Psychoanalysis, and Mother Nature," *Feminist Studies* 15.2:255–78.

Knorr-Cetina, Karin (1981). *The Manufacture of Knowledge*, Oxford: Pergamon.

Knorr-Cetina, Karin, and Michael Mulkay, eds. (1983). *Science Observed*, Beverly Hills: Sage.

Kramerae, Cheris, and Paula Treichler (1985). *A Feminist Dictionary*, Boston: Pandora.

Latour, Bruno (1984). *Les Microbes, guerre et paix, suivi des irréductions*, Paris: Métailié.

Latour, Bruno, and Steve Woolgar (1979). *Laboratory Life*, Beverly Hills: Sage.

Lerner, Gerda, ed. (1973). *Black Women in White America*, New York: Vintage.

Lewontin et al. (1984). *Not in Our Genes: Biology, Ideology and Human Nature*, New York: Pantheon.

Lorde, Audre (1982). *Zami*, Trumansburg, NY: Crossing.

—— (1984). *Sister Outsider*, Trumansburg, NY: Crossing.

Lowe, Lisa (1986). "French Literary Orientalism," University of California Santa Cruz Ph.D. thesis.

McCaffrey, Anne (1969). *The Ship Who Sang*, New York: Ballantine.

Marcuse, Herbert (1964). *One-Dimensional Man*, Boston: Beacon.

Markoff, John, and Lenny Siegel (1983). "Military Micros." Paper delivered at Silicon Valley Research Project Conference, University of California Santa Cruz.

Marks, Elaine, and Isabelle de Courtivron (1980). *New French Feminism*, Amherst: U Massachusetts P.

Merchant, Carolyn (1980). *The Death of Nature: Women, Ecology, and the Scientific Revolution*, New York: Harper and Row.

Microelectronics Group (1980). *Microelectronics: Capitalist Technology and the Working Class*, London: CSE.

Moraga, Cherríe (1983). *Loving in the War Years*, Boston: South End.

Moraga, Cherríe, and Gloria Anzaldúa (1981). *This Bridge Called My Back*, Watertown: Persephone.

Morgan, Robin, ed. (1984). *Sisterhood Is Global*, Garden City NY: Doubleday/Anchor.

Nash, June, and Maria Patricia Fernandez-Kelly (1983). *Women and Men and the International Division of Labor*, Albany: State U of NY P.

Nash, Roderick (1979). "The Exporting and Importing of Nature," *Perspectives in American History* 3: 517–60.

National Science Foundation (1988). *Women and Minorities in Science and Engineering*, Washington, D.C.: NSF.

Ong, Aihwa (1987). *Spirits of Resistance and Capitalist Discipline: Factory Workers in Malaysia*, Albany: State U of NY P.

Ong, Walter (1982). *Orality and Literacy*, New York: Methuen.

Park, Katherine, and Lorraine J. Daston (1981). "Unnatural Conceptions: The Study of Monsters in 16th and 17th Century France and England," *Past and Present* 92: 20–54.

Perloff, Marjorie (1984). "Dirty Language and Scramble Systems," *Sulfur* 11:178–83.

Petchesky, Rosalind (1981). "Abortion, Anti-Feminism and the Rise of the New Right," *Feminist Studies* 7.2: 206–46.

Piven, Frances Fox, and Richard Coward (1982). *The New Class War*, New York: Pantheon.

Preston, Douglas (1984). "Shooting in Paradise," *Natural History* 93.12: 14–19.

Reskin, Barbara F., and Heidi Hartmann, eds. (1986). *Women's Work, Men's Work*, Washington, D.C.: National Academy of Sciences.

Rich, Adrienne (1978). *The Dream of a Common Language*, New York: Norton.

Rose, Stephen (1986). *The American Profile Poster*, New York: Pantheon.

Rossiter, Margaret (1982). *Women Scientists in America*, Baltimore: Johns Hopkins UP.

Rothschild, Joan, ed. (1983). *Machina ex Dea: Feminist Perspectives on Technology*, New York: Pergamon.

Russ, Joanna (1983). *How to Suppress Women's Writing*, Austin: U Texas P.

Sachs, Carolyn (1983). *The Invisible Farmers*, Totowa NJ: Rowman and Allenheld.

Schiebinger, Londa (1987). "The History and Philosophy of Women in Science," *Signs* 12.2: 305–32.

Science Policy Research Unit (1982). *Microelectronics and Women's Employment in Britain*, University of Sussex.

Sofia, Zoe (1984). "Exterminating Fetuses: Abortion, Disarmament, and the Sexosemiotics of Extraterrestrialism," *Diacritics* 14.2: 47–59.

Sontag, Susan (1977). *On Photography*, New York: Dell.

Stacey, Judith (1987). "Sexism by a Subtler Name? Postindustrial Conditions and Postfeminist Consciousness," *Social Review* 96: 7–28.

Stallard, Karin, Barbara Ehrenreich, and Holly Sklar (1983). *Poverty in the American Dream*, Boston: South End.

Sturgeon, Noel (1986). "Feminism, Anarchism, and Non-Violent Direct Actions Politics," University of California Santa Cruz Ph.D. Qualifying Essay.

Sussman, Vic (1986). "Personal Tech: Technology Lends a Hand," *The Washington Post Magazine*, 9 November: 45–56.

Traweek, Sharon (1988). *Beamtimes and Lifetimes: The World of High Energy Physics*, Cambridge: Harvard UP.

Treichler, Paula (1987). "AIDS, Homophobia and Biomedical Discourse," *October* 43: 31–70.

Weitzenbaum, Joseph (1976). *Computer Power and Human Reason*, San Francisco: Freeman.

Welford, John Noble (1 July 1986). "Pilot's Helmet Helps Interpret High Speed World," *New York Times*, pp. 21, 24.

Wilfred, Denis (1982). "Capital and Agriculture: A Review of Marxian Problematics," *Studies in Political Economy* 7: 127–54.

Winner, Langdon (1977). *Autonomous Technology*, Cambridge: MIT Press.

——— (1980). "Do Artifacts Have Politics?" *Daedalus* 109.1:121–36.

——— (1986). *The Whale and the Reactor*, Chicago: U Chicago Pr.

Winograd, Terry, and Fernando Flores (1986). *Understanding Computers and Cognition*, Norwood, NJ: Ablex.

Wittig, Monique (1973). *The Lesbian Body*, trans. David LeVay, New York: Avon.

Wright, Susan (1982). "Recombinant DNA: The Status of Hazards and Controls," *Environment* 24:6: 12–20, 51–53.

———— (1986). "Recombinant DNA Technology and Its Social Transformation," *Osiris* 2nd series, 2: 303–60.

Young, Robert M. (1979). "Interpreting the Production of Science," *New Scientist* 29: 1026–8.

Young, Robert M., and Les Levidow, eds (1981, 1985). *Science, Technology and the Labour Process*, 2 vols., London: CSE and Free Association Books.

Yoxen, Edward (1983). *The Gene Business*, New York: Harper and Row.

Zimmerman, Jan (1983). *The Technological Woman: Interfacing with Tomorrow*, New York: Praeger.

Linda Hutcheon

b. 1947

Linda Hutcheon was born in Toronto into an Italian-Canadian family. She earned a B.A. in modern languages from the University of Toronto, an M.A. in romance studies from Cornell University, and a Ph.D. in comparative literature from Toronto. She began to teach English at McMaster University in Hamilton, Ontario. During this time, she published Narcissistic Narrative: The Metafictional Paradox *(1980),* Formalism and the Freudian Aesthetic: The Example of Charles Mauron *(1984), and* A Theory of Parody: The Teachings of Twentieth-Century Art Forms *(1985). In 1988, she joined the comparative literature program at the University of Toronto, where she currently is a professor. While at Toronto, she has published a number of books on postmodernism and postmodern art, including* A Poetics of Postmodernism: History, Theory, Fiction *(1988),* The Canadian Postmodern: A Study of Contemporary English-Canadian Fiction *(1988),* Leonard Cohen and His Writing *(1989),* The Politics of Postmodernism *(1989),* Splitting Images: Contemporary Canadian Ironies *(1991), and* Irony's Edge: The Theory and Politics of Irony *(1994). With her husband, Michael Hutcheon, a physician, she has written two of her most interdisciplinary works on artistic representations of disease,* Opera: Desire, Disease, Death *(1996) and* Bodily Charm: Living Opera *(2000). In 2000, she served as president of the Modern Language Association. Hutcheon is one of the few feminist theorists who openly embraces postmodern theory. By arguing that "postmodernism is political," Hutcheon insists on the practical ends of postmodern theory, particularly in the lives of ethnic minorities and women. The following essay, "Theorizing the Postmodern: Toward a Poetics," originally appeared in* A Poetics of Postmodernism.

Theorizing the Postmodern: Toward a Poetics

I

Clearly, then, the time has come to theorize the term [postmodernism], if not to define it, before it fades from awkward neologism to derelict cliché without ever attaining to the dignity of a cultural concept.
— IHAB HASSAN

Of all the terms bandied about in both current cultural theory and contemporary writing on the arts, postmodernism must be the most over- and under-defined. It is usually accompanied by a grand flourish of negativized rhetoric: we hear of discontinuity, disruption, dislocation, decentring, indeterminacy, and antitotalization. What all of these words literally do (precisely by their disavowing prefixes — *dis*, *de*, *in*, *anti*) is incorporate that which they aim to contest — as does, I suppose, the term *post*modernism itself. I point to this simple verbal fact in order to begin "theorizing" the cultural enterprise to which we seem to have given such a provocative label. Given all the confusion and vagueness associated with the term itself (see Paterson 1986), I would like to begin by arguing that, for me, postmodernism is a contradictory phenomenon, one that uses and abuses, installs and then subverts, the very concepts it challenges — be it in architecture, literature, painting, sculpture, film, video, dance, TV, music, philosophy, aesthetic theory, psychoanalysis, linguistics, or historiography. These are some of the realms from which my "theorizing" will proceed, and my examples will always be specific, because what I want to avoid are those polemical generalizations — often by those inimical to postmodernism: Jameson (1984a), Eagleton (1985), Newman (1985) — that leave us guessing about just what it is that is being called postmodernist, though never in doubt as to its undesirability. Some assume a generally accepted "tacit definition" (Caramello 1983); others locate the beast by temporal (after 1945? 1968? 1970? 1980?) or economic signposting. But in as pluralist and fragmented a culture as that of the western world today, such designations are not terribly useful if they intend to generalize about all the vagaries of our culture. After all, what does television's "Dallas" have in common with the architecture of Ricardo Bofill? What does John Cage's music share with a play (or film) like *Amadeus*?

In other words, postmodernism cannot simply be used as a synonym for the contemporary (cf. Kroker and Cook 1986). And it does not really describe an international cultural phenomenon, for it is primarily European and American (North and South). Although the concept of *modernism* is largely an Anglo-American one (Suleiman 1986), this should not limit the poetics of *postmodernism* to that culture, especially since those who would argue that very stand are usually the ones to find room to sneak in the French *nouveau roman*[1] (A. Wilde 1981; Brooke-Rose 1981; Lodge 1977). And almost everyone (e.g. Barth 1980) wants to be sure to include what Severo Sarduy (1974) has labelled — not postmodern — but "neo-baroque" in a Spanish culture where "modernism" has a rather different meaning.[2]

I offer instead, then, a specific, if polemical, start from which to operate: as a cultural activity that can be discerned in most art forms and many currents of thought today, what I want to call postmodernism is fundamentally contradictory, resolutely historical, and inescapably political. Its contradictions may well be those of late capitalist society, but whatever the cause, these contradictions are certainly manifest in the important postmodern concept of "the presence of the past." This was the title given to the 1980 Venice Biennale which marked the institutional recognition of postmodernism in architecture. Italian

---

[1]French for "new novel," a genre that flourished in the 1960s, characterized by radical experimentation with temporal perspective and point of view. Its practitioners include Michel Butor, Marguerite Duras, Jean Ricardou, and Alain Robbe-Grillet.

[2]The neo-baroque is a peculiarly Latin American movement, flourishing in the 1980s, that critiques Western modernity; its practitioners include José Lezama Lima, Martin Adán, Nestor Perlongher, and Severo Sarduy.

architect Paolo Portoghesi's (1983) analysis of the twenty facades of the "Strada Novissima" — whose very newness lay paradoxically in its historical parody — shows how architecture has been rethinking modernism's purist break with history. This is not a nostalgic return; it is a critical revisiting, an ironic dialogue with the past of both art and society, a recalling of a critically shared vocabulary of architectural forms. "The past whose presence we claim is not a golden age to be recuperated," argues Portoghesi (1983, 26). Its aesthetic forms and its social formations are problematized by critical reflection. The same is true of the postmodernist rethinking of figurative painting in art and historical narrative in fiction and poetry (see Perloff 1985, 155–71): it is always a critical reworking, never a nostalgic "return." Herein lies the governing role of irony in postmodernism. Stanley Tigerman's dialogue with history in his projects for family houses modelled on Raphael's palatial Villa Madama is an ironic one: his miniaturization of the monumental forces a rethinking of the social function of architecture — both then and now.

Because it is contradictory and works within the very systems it attempts to subvert, postmodernism can probably not be considered a new paradigm (even in some extension of the Kuhnian sense of the term).[3] It has not replaced liberal humanism, even if it has seriously challenged it. It may mark, however, the site of the struggle of the emergence of something new. The manifestations in art of this struggle may be those almost undefinable and certainly bizarre works like Terry Gilliam's film, *Brazil*. The postmodern ironic rethinking of history is here textualized in the many general parodic references to other movies: *A Clockwork Orange*, *1984*, Gilliam's own *Time Bandits* and Monty Python sketches, and Japanese epics, to name but a few. The more specific parodic recalls range from *Star Wars'* Darth Vader to the Odessa Steps sequence of Eisenstein's *Battleship Potemkin*.[4] In *Brazil*, however, the famous shot of the baby carriage on the steps is replaced by one of a floor cleaner, and the result is to reduce epic tragedy to the bathos of the mechanical and debased. Along with this ironic reworking of the history of film comes a temporal historical warp: the movie is set, we are told, at 8:49 AM, sometime in the twentieth century. The decor does not help us identify the time more precisely. The fashions mix the absurdly futuristic with 1930s styling; an oddly old-fashioned and dingy setting belies the omnipresence of computers — though even they are not the sleekly designed creatures of today. Among the other typically postmodern contradictions in this movie is the co-existence of heterogeneous filmic genres: fantasy Utopia and grim dystopia; absurd slapstick comedy and tragedy (the Tuttle/Buttle mix-up); the romantic adventure tale and the political documentary.

While all forms of contemporary art and thought offer examples of this kind of postmodernist contradiction, this book (like most others on the subject) will be privileging the novel genre, and one form in particular, a form that I want to call "historiographic metafiction." By this I mean those well-known and popular novels which are both intensely self-reflexive and yet paradoxically also lay claim to historical events and personages: *The French Lieutenant's Woman, Midnight's Children, Ragtime, Legs, G., Famous Last Words*.[5] In most of the critical work on postmodernism, it is narrative — be it in literature, history, or theory — that has usually been the major focus of attention. Historiographic metafiction incorporates all three of these domains: that

---

[3]In *The Structure of Scientific Revolutions* (1970), Thomas Kuhn used the term *paradigm* in a sense that meant the collection of beliefs shared by a community of scientists that allows them to agree on how problems are to be understood and approached. Kuhn's theory was that "normal" science operates within such paradigms, and that scientific "revolutions" are episodes during which the shared paradigm no longer holds sway, and disagreement is rife over the most fundamental topics, until a new paradigm is established and "normal" scientific research can again proceed. Hutcheon is using Kuhn's term in an "extended" sense that includes style systems in the arts.

[4]Eisenstein's 1925 classic film features a sequence in which armed Czarist troops march down a long flight of steps leading to the port of Odessa, shooting the innocent civilians who flee before them. The climactic episode involves a mother with a baby carriage; the mother is shot and the baby carriage goes hurtling down the steps out of control.

[5]Novels respectively by John Fowles (1969), Salman Rushdie (1980), E. L. Doctorow (1975), William Kennedy (1975), John Berger (1972), and Timothy Findlay (1981).

is, its theoretical self-awareness of history and fiction as human constructs (historio*graphic meta*fiction) is made the grounds for its rethinking and reworking of the forms and contents of the past. This kind of fiction has often been noticed by critics, but its paradigmatic quality has been passed by: it is commonly labelled in terms of something else — for example as "midfiction" (A. Wilde 1981) or "paramodernist" (Malmgren 1985). Such labeling is another mark of the inherent contradictoriness of historiographic metafiction, for it always works *within* conventions in order to subvert them. It is not just metafictional; nor is it just another version of the historical novel or the non-fictional novel. Gabriel García Márquez's *One Hundred Years of Solitude* has often been discussed in exactly the contradictory terms that I think define postmodernism. For example Larry McCaffery sees it as both metafictionally self-reflexive and yet speaking to us powerfully about real political and historical realities: "It has thus become a kind of model for the contemporary writer, being self-conscious about its literary heritage and about the limits of mimesis . . . but yet managing to reconnect its readers to the world outside the page" (1982, 264). What McCaffery here adds as almost an afterthought at the end of his book, *The Metafictional Muse*, is in many ways my starting point.

Most theorists of postmodernism who see it as a "cultural dominant" (Jameson 1984a, 56) agree that it is characterized by the results of late capitalist dissolution of bourgeois hegemony and the development of mass culture (see Jameson 1984a [via Lefebvre 1968]; Russell 1980a; Egbert 1970; Calinescu 1977). I would agree and, in fact, argue that the increasing uniformization of mass culture is one of the totalizing forces that postmodernism exists to challenge. Challenge, but not deny. But it does seek to assert difference, not homogeneous identity. Of course, the very concept of difference could be said to entail a typically postmodern contradiction: "difference," unlike "otherness," has no exact opposite against which to define itself. Thomas Pynchon allegorizes otherness in *Gravity's Rainbow* through the single, if anarchic, "we-system" that exists as the counterforce of the totalizing "They-system" (though also implicated in it). Postmodern difference or rather differences, in the plural, are always multiple and provisional.

Postmodern culture, then, has a contradictory relationship to what we usually label our dominant, liberal humanist culture. It does not deny it, as some have asserted (Newman 1985, 42; Palmer 1977, 364). Instead, it contests it from within its own assumptions. Modernists like Eliot and Joyce have usually been seen as profoundly humanistic (e.g. Stern 1971, 26) in their paradoxical desire for stable aesthetic and moral values, even in the face of their realization of the inevitable absence of such universals. Postmodernism differs from this, not in its humanistic contradictions, but in the provisionality of its response to them: it refuses to posit any structure or what Lyotard (1984a) calls master narrative — such as art or myth — which, for such modernists, would have been consolatory.[6] It argues that such systems are indeed attractive, perhaps even necessary; but this does not make them any the less illusory. For Lyotard, postmodernism is characterized by exactly this kind of incredulity toward master or metanarratives: those who lament the "loss of meaning" in the world or in art are really mourning the fact that knowledge is no longer primarily narrative knowledge of this kind (1984a, 26). This does not mean that knowledge somehow disappears. There is no radically new paradigm here, even if there is change.

It is no longer big news that the master narratives of bourgeois liberalism are under attack. There is a long history of many such skeptical sieges to positivism and humanism, and today's footsoldiers of theory — Foucault, Derrida, Habermas, Vattimo,[7] Baudrillard — follow in the footsteps of Nietzsche, Heidegger, Marx, and Freud, to name but a few, in their attempts to challenge the empiricist, rationalist, humanist assumptions of our cultural systems, including those of science (Graham 1982, 148; Toulmin 1972). Foucault's early rethinking of the history of ideas in terms of an "archaeology" (in *The Order of Things*, 1970; *The Archaeology of*

[6]For Lyotard, see p. 1933.
[7]Gianni Vattimo (b.1936), author of *The End of Modernity* (1985). For Foucault, see p. 904; for Derrida, see p. 914; for Habermas, see p. 1946. For Nietzsche, see p. 435; for Heidegger, see p. 611; for Marx, see p. 397; for Freud, see p. 497.

Knowledge, 1972) that might stand outside the universalizing assumptions of humanism is one such attempt, whatever its obvious weaknesses. So is Derrida's more radical contesting of Cartesian and Platonic views of the mind as a system of closed meanings (see B. Harrison 1985, 6). Like Gianni Vattimo's *pensiero debole* (weak thought) (1983; 1985), these challenges characteristically operate in clearly paradoxical terms, knowing that to claim epistemological authority is to be caught up in what they seek to displace. The same applies to Habermas's work, though it often appears somewhat less radical in its determined desire to work from within the system of "Enlightenment" rationality and yet manage to critique it at the same time. This is what Lyotard has attacked as just another totalizing narrative (1984b). And Jameson (1984b) has argued that both Lyotard and Habermas are resting their arguments on different but equally strong legitimizing "narrative archetypes."

This game of meta-narrative one-upmanship could go on and on, since arguably Jameson's Marxism leaves him vulnerable too. But this is not the point. What is important in all these internalized challenges to humanism is the interrogating of the notion of consensus. Whatever narratives or systems that once allowed us to think we could unproblematically and universally define public agreement have now been questioned by the acknowledgement of differences — in theory and in artistic practice. In its most extreme formulation, the result is that consensus becomes the illusion of consensus, whether it be defined in terms of minority (educated, sensitive, élitist) or mass (commercial, popular, conventional) culture, for *both* are manifestations of late capitalist, bourgeois, informational, postindustrial society, a society in which social reality is structured by discourses (in the plural) — or so postmodernism endeavors to teach.

What this means is that the familiar humanist separation of art and life (or human imagination and order *versus* chaos and disorder) no longer holds. Postmodernist contradictory art still installs that order, but it then uses it to demystify our everyday processes of structuring chaos, of imparting or assigning meaning (D'Haen 1986, 225). For example, within a positivistic frame of reference, photographs could be accepted as neutral representations, as technological windows on the world. In the postmodern photos of Heribert Berkert or Ger Dekkers, they still represent (for they cannot avoid reference) but what they represent is self-consciously shown to be highly filtered by the discursive and aesthetic assumptions of the camera-holder (D. Davis 1977). While not wanting to go as far as Morse Peckham (1965) and argue that the arts are somehow "biologically" necessary for social change, I would like to suggest that, in its very contradictions, postmodernist art (like Brecht's epic theater)[8] might be able to dramatize and even provoke change from within. It is not that the modernist world was "a world in need of mending" and the postmodernist one "beyond repair" (A. Wilde 1981, 131). Postmodernism works to show that all repairs are human constructs, but that, from that very fact, they derive their value as well as their limitation. All repairs are both comforting and illusory. Postmodernist interrogations of humanist certainties live within this kind of contradiction.

Perhaps it is another inheritance from the 1960s to believe that challenging and questioning are positive values (even if solutions to problems are not offered), for the knowledge derived from such inquiry may be the only possible condition of change. In the late 1950s in *Mythologies* (1973), Roland Barthes had prefigured this kind of thinking in his Brechtian challenges to all that is "natural" or "goes without saying" in our culture — that is, all that is considered universal and eternal, and therefore unchangeable. He suggested the need to question and demystify first, and then work for change.[9] The 1960s were the time of ideological formation for many of the postmodernist thinkers and artists of the 1980s and it is now that we can see the results of that formation.

Perhaps, as some have argued, the 1960s themselves (that is, at the time) produced no enduring innovation in aesthetics, but I would argue that they did provide the background, though not the definition, of the postmodern (cf. Bertens 1986, 17), for they were crucial in developing a different

---

[8]For Brecht, see p. 1249.
[9]For a sample of Barthes's *Striptease*, see p. 869.

concept of the possible function of art, one that would contest the "Arnoldian" or humanist moral view with its potentially élitist class bias (see R. Williams 1960, xiii). One of the functions of art in mass culture, argued Susan Sontag, would be to "modify consciousness" (1967, 304). And many cultural commentators since have argued that the energies of the 1960s have changed the framework and structure of how we consider art (e.g. Wasson 1974). The conservatism of the late 1970s and 1980s may have their impact when the thinkers and artists being formed now begin to produce their work (cf. McCaffery 1982), but to call Foucault or Lyotard a neoconservative — as did Habermas (1983, 14) — is historically and ideologically inaccurate (see too Calinescu 1986, 246; Giddens 1981, 17).

The political, social, and intellectual experience of the 1960s helped make it possible for postmodernism to be seen as what Kristeva calls "writing-as-experience-of-limits" (1980a, 137): limits of language, of subjectivity, of sexual identity, and we might also add: of systematization and uniformization. This interrogating (and even pushing) of limits has contributed to the "crisis in legitimation" that Lyotard and Habermas see (differently) as part of the postmodern condition. It has certainly meant a rethinking and putting into question of the bases of our western modes of thinking that we usually label, perhaps rather too generally, as liberal humanism.

II

What is the postmodern scene? Baudrillard's excremental culture? Or a final homecoming to a technoscape where a "body without organs" (Artaud), a "negative space" (Rosalind Krauss), a "pure implosion" (Lyotard), a "looking away" (Barthes) or an "aleatory mechanism" (Serres) is now first nature and thus the terrain of a new political refusal? — ARTHUR KROKER AND DAVID COOK

What precisely, though, is being challenged by postmodernism? First of all, institutions have come under scrutiny: from the media to the university, from museums to theaters. Much postmodern dance, for instance, contests theatrical space by moving out into the street. Sometimes it is overtly measured by the clock, thereby foregrounding the unspoken conventions of theatrical time (see Pops 1984, 59). Make-believe or illusionist conventions of art are often bared in order to challenge the institutions in which they find a home — and a meaning. Similarly Michael Asher sandblasted a wall of the Toselli Gallery in Milan in 1973 to reveal the plaster beneath. This was his "work of art," one that collapsed together the "work" and the gallery so as to reveal at once their collusion and the strong but usually unacknowledged power of the gallery's invisibility as a dominant (and dominating) cultural institution (see Kibbins 1983).

The important contemporary debate about the margins and the boundaries of social and artistic conventions (see Culler 1983, 1984) is also the result of a typically postmodern transgressing of previously accepted limits: those of particular arts, of genres, of art itself. Rauschenberg's narrative (or discursive) work, *Rebus*, or Cy Twombly's series on Spenserian texts, or Shosaku Arakawa's poster-like pages of *The Mechanism of Meaning* are indicative of the fruitful straddling of the borderline between the literary and visual arts. As early as 1969, Theodore Ziolkowski had noted that the

> new arts are so closely related that we cannot hide complacently behind the arbitrary walls of self-contained disciplines: poetics inevitably gives way to general aesthetics, considerations of the novel move easily to the film, while the new poetry often has more in common with contemporary music and art than with the poetry of the past. (1969, 113)

The years since have only verified and intensified this perception. The borders between literary genres have become fluid: who can tell anymore what the limits are between the novel and the short story collection (Alice Munro's *Lives of Girls and Women*), the novel and the long poem (Michael Ondaatje's *Coming Through Slaughter*), the novel and autobiography (Maxine Hong Kingston's *China Men*), the novel and history (Salman Rushdie's *Shame*), the novel and biography (John Banville's *Kepler*)? But, in any of these examples, the conventions of the two genres are played off against each other; there is no simple, unproblematic merging.

In Carlos Fuentes's *The Death of Artemio Cruz*, the title already points to the ironic inversion of biographical conventions: it is the death, not the life, that will be the focus. The subsequent narrative complications of three voices (first-, second-, and third-person) and three tenses (present, future, past) disseminate but also reassert (in a typically postmodernist way) the enunciative situation or discursive context of the work. The traditional verifying third-person past tense voice of history and realism is both installed and undercut by the others. In other works, like Italian writer Giorgio Manganelli's *Amore*, the genres of theoretical treatise, literary dialogue, and novel are played off against one another (see Lucente 1986, 317). Eco's *The Name of the Rose* contains at least three major registers of discourse: the literary-historical, the theological-philosophical, and the popular-cultural (de Lauretis 1985, 16), thereby paralleling Eco's own three areas of critical activity.

The most radical boundaries crossed, however, have been those between fiction and non-fiction and — by extension — between art and life. In the March 1986 issue of *Esquire* magazine, Jerzy Kosinski published a piece in the "Documentary" section called "Death in Cannes," a narrative of the last days and subsequent death of French biologist, Jacques Monod. Typically postmodern, the text refuses the omniscience and omnipresence of the third person and engages instead in a dialogue between a narrative voice (which both is and is not Kosinski's) and a projected reader. Its viewpoint is avowedly limited, provisional, personal. However, it also works (and plays) with the conventions of both literary realism and journalistic facticity: the text is accompanied by photographs of the author and the subject. The commentary uses these photos to make us, as readers, aware of our expectations of both narrative and pictorial interpretation, including our naive but common trust in the representational veracity of photography. One set of photos is introduced with: "I bet the smiling picture was taken last, I always bet on a happy ending" (1986, 82), but the subsequent prose section ends with: "look at the pictures if you must but . . . don't bet on them. Bet on the worth of a word" (82). But we come to learn later that there are events — like Monod's death — that are beyond both words and pictures.

Kosinski calls this postmodern form of writing "autofiction": "fiction" because all memory is fictionalizing; "auto" because it is, for him, "a literary genre, generous enough to let the author adopt the nature of his fictional protagonist — not the other way around" (1986, 82). When he "quotes" Monod, he tells the fictive and questioning reader that it is in his own "*autolingua* — the inner language of the storyteller" (86). In his earlier novel, *Blind Date*, Kosinski had used Monod's death and the text of his *Chance and Necessity* as structuring concepts in the novel: from both, he learned of our need to rid ourselves of illusions of totalizing explanations and systems of ethics. But it is not just this kind of historiographic metafiction that challenges the life/art borders or that plays on the margins of genre. Painting and sculpture, for instance, come together with similar impact in some of the three-dimensional canvasses of Robert Rauschenberg and Tom Wesselman (see D'Haen 1986 and Owens 1980b). And, of course, much has been made of the blurring of the distinctions between the discourses of theory and literature in the works of Jacques Derrida and Roland Barthes — or somewhat less fashionably, if no less provocatively, in some of the writing of Ihab Hassan (1975; 1980a) and Zulfikar Ghose (1983). Rosalind Krauss has called this sort of work "paraliterary" and sees it as challenging both the concept of the "work of art" and the separation of that concept from the domain of the academic critical establishment: "The paraliterary space is the space of debate, quotation, partisanship, betrayal, reconciliation; but it is not the space of unity, coherence, or resolution that we think of as constituting the work of art" (1980, 37). This is the space of the postmodern.

In addition to being "borderline" inquiries, most of these postmodernist contradictory texts are also specifically parodic in their intertextual relation to the traditions and conventions of the genres involved. When Eliot recalled Dante or Virgil in *The Waste Land*, one sensed a kind of wishful call to continuity beneath the fragmented echoing. It is precisely this that is contested in postmodern parody where it is often ironic discontinuity that is revealed at the heart of continuity, difference at the heart of similarity (Hutcheon

1985). Parody is a perfect postmodern form, in some senses, for it paradoxically both incorporates and challenges that which it parodies. It also forces a reconsideration of the idea of origin or originality that is compatible with other postmodern interrogations of liberal humanist assumptions. While *theorists* like Jameson (1983, 114–19) see this loss of the modernist unique, individual style as a negative, as an imprisoning of the text in the past through pastiche, it has been seen by postmodern *artists* as a liberating challenge to a definition of subjectivity and creativity that has for too long ignored the role of history in art and thought. On Rauschenberg's use of reproduction and parody in his work, Douglas Crimp writes: "The fiction of the creating subject gives way to the frank confiscation, quotation, excerptation, accumulation and repetition of already existing images. Notions of originality, authenticity and presence . . . are undermined" (1983, 53). The same is true of the fiction of John Fowles or the music of George Rochberg. As Foucault noted, the concepts of subjective consciousness and continuity that are now being questioned are tied up with an entire set of ideas that have been dominant in our culture until now: "the point of creation, the unity of a work, of a period, of a theme . . . the mark of originality and the infinite wealth of hidden meanings" (1972, 230).

Another consequence of this far-reaching postmodern inquiry into the very nature of subjectivity is the frequent challenge to traditional notions of perspective, especially in narrative and painting. The perceiving subject is no longer assumed to a coherent, meaning-generating entity. Narrators in fiction become either disconcertingly multiple and hard to locate (as in D. M. Thomas's *The White Hotel*) or resolutely provisional and limited — often undermining their own seeming omniscience (as in Salman Rushdie's *Midnight's Children*). In Charles Russell's terms, with postmodernism we start to encounter and are challenged by "an art of shifting perspective, of double self-consciousness, of local and extended meaning" (1980a, 192).

As Foucault and others have suggested, linked to this contesting of the unified and coherent subject is a more general questioning of *any* totalizing or homogenizing system. Provisionality and heterogeneity contaminate any neat attempts at unifying coherence (formal or thematic). Historical and narrative continuity and closure are contested, but again, from within. The teleology of art forms — from fiction to music — is both suggested and transformed. The center no longer completely holds. And, from the decentered perspective, the "marginal" and what I will be calling the "ex-centric" (be it in class, race, gender, sexual orientation, or ethnicity) take on new significance in the light of the implied recognition that our culture is not really the homogeneous monolith (that is middle-class, male, heterosexual, white, western) we might have assumed. The concept of alienated otherness (based on binary oppositions that conceal hierarchies) gives way, as I have argued, to that of differences, that is to the assertion, not of centralized sameness, but of decentralized community — another postmodern paradox. The local and the regional are stressed in the face of mass culture and a kind of vast global informational village that McLuhan could only have dreamed of.[10] Culture (with a capital C and in the singular) has become cultures (uncapitalized and plural), as documented at length by our social scientists. And this appears to be happening in spite of — and, I would argue, maybe even because of — the homogenizing impulse of the consumer society of late capitalism: yet another postmodern contradiction.

In attempting to define what he called the "trans-avant-garde," Italian art critic Achille Bonito Oliva found he had to talk of differences as much as similarities from country to country (1984, 71–3): it would seem that the "presence of the past" depends on the local and culture-specific nature of each past. The questioning of the universal and totalizing in the name of the local and particular does not automatically entail the end of all consensus. As Victor Burgin reminds us: "*Of course* moralities and histories are 'relative,' but this does not mean they do not *exist*" (1986, 198). Postmodernism is careful

[10]Marshall McLuhan (1911–1980), Canadian theorist of communications, proposed in *Understanding Media* (1964) that with the speed of radio and television, the world was becoming like a village, hearing news and rumors at the same time.

not to make the marginal into a new center, for it knows, in Burgin's words, that "[what] have expired are the absolute guarantees issued by over-riding metaphysical systems" (198). Any certainties we do have are what he calls "positional," that is, derived from complex networks of local and contingent conditions.

In this sort of context, different kinds of texts will take on value — the ones that operate what Derrida calls "breaches or infractions" — for it is they that can lead us to suspect the very concept of "art" (1981a, 69). In Derrida's words, such artistic practices seem "to mark and to organize a structure of resistance to the philosophical conceptuality that allegedly dominated and comprehended them, whether directly, or whether through categories derived from this philosophical fund, the categories of esthetics, rhetoric, or traditional criticism" (69). Of course, Derrida's own texts belong solely to neither philosophical nor literary discourse, though they partake of both in a deliberately self-reflexive and contradictory (postmodern) manner.

Derrida's constant self-consciousness about the status of his own discourse raises another question that must be faced by anyone — like myself — writing on postmodernism. From what position can one "theorize" (even self-consciously) a disparate, contradictory, multivalent, current cultural phenomenon? Stanley Fish (1986) has wittily pointed out the "anti-foundationalist" paradox that I too find myself in when I comment on the importance of Derrida's critical self-consciousness. In Fish's ironic terms: "Ye shall know that truth is not what it seems and *that* truth shall set you free."[11] Barthes, of course, had seen the same danger earlier as he watched (and helped) demystification become part of the *doxa*[12] (1977, 166). Similarly Christopher Norris has noted that in textualizing all forms of knowledge, deconstruction theory often, in its very unmasking of rhetorical strategies, itself still lays claim to the status of "theoretical knowledge" (1985, 22). Most postmodern theory, however, realizes this paradox or contradiction. Rorty, Baudrillard, Foucault, Lyotard, and others seem to imply that

any knowledge cannot escape complicity with some meta-narrative, with the fictions that render possible any claim to "truth," however provisional. What they add, however, is that *no* narrative can be a natural "master" narrative: there are no natural hierarchies; there are only those we construct. It is this kind of self-implicating questioning that should allow postmodernist theorizing to challenge narratives that do presume to "master" status, without necessarily assuming that status for itself.

Postmodern art similarly asserts and then deliberately undermines such principles as value, order, meaning, control, and identity (Russell 1985, 247) that have been the basic premises of bourgeois liberalism. Those humanistic principles are still operative in our culture, but for many they are no longer seen as eternal and unchallengeable. The contradictions of both postmodern theory and practice are positioned within the system and yet work to allow its premises to be seen as fictions or as ideological structures. This does not necessarily destroy their "truth" value, but it does define the conditions of that "truth." Such a process reveals rather than conceals the tracks of the signifying systems that constitute our world — that is, systems constructed by us in answer to our needs. However important these systems are, they are not natural, given, or universal. The very limitations imposed by the postmodern view are also perhaps ways of opening new doors: perhaps now we can better study the interrelations of social, aesthetic, philosophical, and ideological constructs. In order to do so, postmodernist critique must acknowledge its own position as an ideological one (Newman 1985, 60). I think the formal and thematic contradictions of postmodern art and theory work to do just that: to call attention to both what is being contested and what is being offered as a critical response to that, and to do so in a self-aware way that admits its own provisionality. In Barthesian terms (1972, 256), it is criticism which would include in its own discourse an implicit (or explicit) reflection upon itself.

In writing about these postmodern contradictions, then, I clearly would not want to fall into the trap of suggesting any "transcendental identity" (Radhakrishnan 1983, 33) or essence for

[11]Fish is intentionally misquoting the Gospel of John 8:32.
[12]Received opinion.

postmodernism. Instead, I see it as an ongoing cultural process or activity, and I think that what we need, more than a fixed and fixing definition, is a "poetics," an open, ever-changing theoretical structure by which to order both our cultural knowledge and our critical procedures. This would not be a poetics in the structuralist sense of the word, but would go beyond the study of literary discourse to the study of cultural practice and theory. As Tzvetan Todorov realized, in a later expanding and translating of his 1968 *Introduction to Poetics*: "Literature is inconceivable outside a typology of discourses" (1981a, 71). Art and theory about art (and culture) should both be part of a poetics of postmodernism. Richard Rorty has posited the existence of "poetic" moments "as occurring periodically in many different areas of culture — science, philosophy, painting and politics, as well as the lyric and the drama" (1984b, 4). But this is no coincidental moment; it is made, not found. As Rorty explains (23n):

> it is a mistake to think that Derrida, or anybody else, "recognized" problems about the nature of textuality or writing which had been ignored by the tradition. What he did was to think up ways of speaking which made old ways of speaking optional, and thus more or less dubious.

It is both a way of speaking — a discourse — and a cultural process involving the expressions of thought (Lyotard 1986, 125) that a poetics would seek to articulate.

A poetics of postmodernism would not posit any relation of causality or identity either among the arts or between art and theory. It would merely offer, as provisional hypotheses, perceived overlappings of concern, here specifically with regard to the contradictions that I see as characterizing postmodernism. It would be a matter of reading literature through its surrounding theoretical discourses (Cox 1985, 57), rather than as continuous with theory. It would not mean seeing literary theory as a particularly imperialistic intellectual practice that has overrun art (H. White 1978b, 261); nor would it mean blaming self-reflexive art for having created an "ingrown" theory wherein "specific critical and literary trends [have] buttressed each other into a hegemonic network" (Chénetier 1985, 654). The

interaction of theory and practice in postmodernism is a complex one of shared responses to common provocations. There are also, of course, many postmodern artists who double as theorists — Eco, Lodge, Bradbury, Barth, Rosler, Burgin — though they have rarely become the major theorists or apologists of their own work, as the *nouveaux romanciers* (from Robbe-Grillet to Ricardou) and surfictionists (Federman and Sukenick especially) have tended to do.[13] What a poetics of postmodernism would articulate is less the theories of Eco in relation to *The Name of the Rose* than the overlappings of concern between, for instance, the contradictory form of the writing of theory in Lyotard's *Le Différend* (1983) and that of a novel like Peter Ackroyd's *Hawksmoor*. Their sequentially ordered sections are equally disrupted by a particularly dense network of interconnections and intertexts, and each enacts or performs, as well as theorizes, the paradoxes of continuity and disconnection, of totalizing interpretation and the impossibility of final meaning. In Lyotard's own words:

> A postmodern artist or writer is in the position of a philosopher: the text he writes, the work he produces are not in principle governed by preestablished rules, and they cannot be judged according to a determining judgment, by applying familiar categories to the text or to the work. Those rules and categories are what the work of *art itself is looking for*. (1984b, 81)

III

To analyze discourses is to hide and reveal contradictions; it is to show the play that they set up within it; it is to manifest how it can express them, embody them, or give them a temporary appearance. — MICHEL FOUCAULT

Jameson has listed "theoretical discourse" among the manifestations of postmodernism (1983, 112) and this would include, not only the obvious Marxist, feminist, and poststructuralist philosophical and literary theory, but also analytic

---

[13]Raymond Federman coined the term "surfiction" for his own minimalist type of postmodern fiction published by the Fiction Collective, which include *Double or Nothing* (1971) and *Take It or Leave It* (1976); Ronald Sukenick is the author of surfictions titled *Up* (1968), *Out* (1973) and *98.6* (1975).

philosophy, psychoanalysis, linguistics, historiography, sociology, and other areas. Recently critics have begun to notice the similarities of concern between various kinds of theory and current literary discourse, sometimes to condemn (Newman 1985, 118), sometimes merely to describe (Hassan 1986). With novels like Ian Watson's *The Embedding* around, it is not surprising that the link would be made. I do not at all think, however, that this has contributed to any "inflation of discourse" at the expense of historical contextualization (Newman 1985, 10), primarily because historiography is itself taking part in what LaCapra has called a "reconceptualization of culture in terms of collective discourses" (1985a, 46). By this, he does not mean to imply that historians no longer concern themselves with "archivally based documentary realism," but only that, within the discipline of history, there is also a growing concern with redefining intellectual history as "the study of social meaning as historically constituted" (46) (see too H. White 1973; 1980; 1981; 1984). This is exactly what historiographic metafiction is doing: Graham Swift's *Waterland*, Rudy Wiebe's *The Temptations of Big Bear*, Ian Watson's *Chekhov's Journey*.

In the past, of course, history has often been used in novel criticism, though usually as a model of the realistic pole of representation. Postmodern fiction problematizes this model to query the relation of both history to reality and reality to language. In Lionel Gossman's terms:

> Modern history and modern literature [I would say *post*modern in both cases] have both rejected the ideal of representation that dominated them for so long. Both now conceive of their work as exploration, testing, creation of new meanings, rather than as disclosure or revelation of meanings already in some sense "there," but not immediately perceptible. (1978, 38–9)

The view that postmodernism relegates history to "the dustbin of an obsolete episteme, arguing gleefully that history does not exist except as text" (Huyssen 1981, 35) is simply wrong. History is not made obsolete: it is, however, being rethought — as a human construct. And in arguing that *history* does not exist except as text, it does not stupidly and "gleefully" deny that the *past* existed, but only that its accessibility to us now is entirely conditioned by textuality. We cannot know the past except through its texts: its documents, its evidence, even its eye-witness accounts are *texts*. Even the institutions of the past, its social structures and practices, could be seen, in one sense, as social texts. And postmodern novels — *The Scorched-Wood People, Flaubert's Parrot, Antichthon, The White Hotel* — teach us about both this fact and its consequences.

Along with the obvious and much publicized case of postmodern architecture (Jencks 1977; 1980a; 1980b), it has been (American) black and (general) feminist theory and practice that have been particularly important in this postmodernist refocusing on historicity, both formally (largely through parodic intertextuality) and thematically. Works like Ishmael Reed's *Mumbo Jumbo*, Maxine Hong Kingston's *China Men*, and Gayl Jones's *Corregidora* have gone far to expose — very self-reflexively — the myth- or illusion-making tendencies of historiography. They have also linked racial and/or gender difference to questions of discourse and of authority and power that are at the heart of the postmodernist enterprise in general and, in particular, of both black theory and feminism. All are theoretical discourses that have their roots in a reflection on actual praxis and continue to derive their critical force from their conjunction with that social and aesthetic practice (on feminism, see de Lauretis 1984, 184). It is true that, as Susan Suleiman (1986, 268, n. 12) acutely noted, literary discussions of postmodernism often appear to exclude the work of women (and, one might add, often of blacks as well), even though female (and black) explorations of narrative and linguistic form have been among the most contesting and radical. Certainly women and Afro-American artists' use of parody to challenge the male white tradition from within, to use irony to implicate and yet to critique, is distinctly paradoxical and postmodernist. Both black and feminist thought have shown how it is possible to move theory out of the ivory tower and into the larger world of social praxis, as theorists like Said (1983) have been advocating. Women have helped develop the postmodern valuing of the margins and the ex-centric as a way out of the power problematic of centers and of male/female oppositions (Kamuf 1982). Certainly Susan Swan's *The Biggest Modern Woman of the World*, a biographical metafiction about a real (and, by definition, ex-centric) giantess, would suggest precisely this in its opposition to what the protagonist sees as "emblem fatigue": "an affliction peculiar to giants [or women or blacks or ethnics] who are always having to shoulder giant expectations from normal folk" (1983, 139).

Lately there have been other critical works which have come close to articulating the kind of poetics I think we need, though all offer a somewhat more limited version. But they too have investigated the overlappings of concern between current philosophical and literary theory and practice. Evan Watkins's *The Critical Act: Criticism and Community* aims to derive a theory of literature that can "elicit from recent poetry in particular the means of talking about and talking back to developments in theory" (1978, x). His model, however, is one of "dialectical reciprocity" that often implies a causal relationship (12) that the sort of poetics I envisage would avoid.

David Carroll's fine study, *The Subject in Question: The Languages of Theory and the Strategies of Fiction* (1982), is somewhat more limited than a general poetics of postmodernism would be, for it focuses on the aporias and contradictions specifically in the work of Jacques Derrida and Claude Simon in order to study the limitations of both theory and fiction in examining the problem of history, limitations that are made evident by the revealing confrontation of theory with practice. As I see it, however, a poetics would not seek to place itself in a position *between* theory and practice (1982, 2) on the question of history, but rather would seek a position *within* both. A work like Peter Uwe Hohendahl's *The Institution of Criticism* (1982), while limited to the German context, is useful here in showing the kind of question that a poetics positioned within both theory and practice must ask, especially regarding the norms and standards of *criticism* — the autonomous institution that mediates theory and practice in the field of literary studies.

Allen Thiher's *Words in Reflection: Modern Language Theory and Postmodern Fiction* comes closest to defining a poetics in that it studies some current theories together with contemporary literary practice in order to show what he feels to be a major "displacement in the way we think and, perhaps more important, write the past" (1984, 189). However, this lucid and thorough study limits itself to modern language theory and linguistically self-reflexive metafiction and posits a kind of influence model (of theory over fiction) that a poetics of postmodernism would not be willing to do. Rather than separating theory from practice, it would seek to integrate them and would organize itself around issues (narrative, representation, textuality, subjectivity, ideology, and so on) that both theory and art problematize and continually reformulate in paradoxical terms. (See all of Part II.)

First, however, any poetics of postmodernism should come to terms with the immense amount of material that has already been written on the subject of postmodernism in all fields. The debate invariably begins over the meaning of the prefix, "post" — a four-letter word if ever there was one. Does it have negative a ring of supersession and rejection as many contend (Barth 1980; Moser 1984)? I would argue that, as is most clear perhaps in postmodern architecture, the "Post Position" (Culler 1982a, 81) signals its contradictory dependence on and independence from that which temporally preceded it and which literally made it possible. Postmodernism's relation to modernism is, therefore, typically contradictory. It marks neither a simple and radical break from it nor a straightforward continuity with it: it is both and neither. And this would be the case in aesthetic, philosophical, or ideological terms.

Of the many arguments mounted on either side of the modernist/postmodernist debate, let me here consider only one in detail, a recent and influential one, that of Terry Eagleton in his 1985 article, "Capitalism, Modernism and Postmodernism." In fact, much of what is offered here is repeated in other theorizing on postmodernism. Like many before him (both defenders and detractors), Eagleton separates practice and theory, choosing to argue primarily in abstract theoretical terms and almost seeming deliberately to avoid mention of exactly what kind of aesthetic practice is actually being talked about. This strategy, however clever and certainly convenient, leads only to endless confusion. My first response to his article, for instance, was that, from the descriptive theorizing alone, Eagleton, like Jameson (1983; 1984a), must mean something quite different from what I do by postmodernism in art. Yet they both make passing references to architecture, and so I suppose I must presume, though I cannot prove from their texts, that we are all indeed talking of the same kind of artistic manifestation. And so, I will proceed on that assumption.

I want to look at each of Eagleton's eight major points in the light of the specific postmodern artistic practice I have been discussing, for I think that his absolutist binary thinking — that makes postmodernism into the negative and opposite of modernism — negates much of the complexity of that art. His theory is neat, but maybe too neat. For example can the historical and discursive contextualizing of Doctorow's *Ragtime* really be considered dehistoricized and devoid of historical memory? It may alter received historical opinion but it does not evade the notions of historicity or historical determination. Is the highly individualized and problematic voice of Saleem Sinai in *Midnight's Children* really to be dubbed "depthless" and "without style"? Is that novel (or are Coover's *The Public Burning* or Doctorow's *The Book of Daniel*) to be seriously labelled as empty of political content? Yet Eagleton asserts all of this — minus the examples — as defining what he calls postmodernism (1985, 61).

He continues. And I would again ask: in Findley's *Famous Last Words*, does the obvious "performativity" of the text really "replace truth" (Eagleton 1985, 63) or does it, rather, question *whose* notion of truth gains power and authority over others and then examine the process of how it does so? The Brechtian involvement of the reader — both textualized (Quinn) and extratextual (us) — is something Eagleton appears to approve of in the modernist "revolutionary" avant-garde. But it is also a very postmodern strategy, and here leads to the acknowledgement, not of truth, but of truths in the plural, truths that are socially, ideologically, and historically conditioned. Eagleton sees that postmodernism dissolves modernist boundaries,

but sees this as a negative, an act of becoming "coextensive with commodified life itself" (68). But historiographic metafiction like Puig's *Kiss of the Spider Woman* works precisely to combat any aestheticist fetishing of art by *refusing* to bracket exactly what Eagleton wants to see put *back* into art: "the referent or real historical world" (67). What such fiction also does, however, is problematize both the nature of the referent and its relation to the real, historical world by its paradoxical combination of metafictional self-reflexivity with historical subject matter. How, then, could Cortázar's *A Manual for Manuel* be reduced to celebrating "kitsch" (68)? Is all art that introduces non-high art forms (here, those of journalism and the spy story) by definition kitsch? What Eagleton (like Jameson — 1984a — before him) seems to ignore is the subversive potential of irony, parody, and humor in contesting the universalizing pretensions of "serious" art.

Eagleton broadens the scope of his attack on postmodernism by describing it as "confidently post-metaphysical" (70). The one thing which the provisional, contradictory postmodernist enterprise is *not* is "confidently" anything. A novel like Banville's *Doctor Copernicus* does not confidently accept that things are things as Eagleton asserts. Its entire formal and thematic energy is founded in its philosophical problematizing of the nature of reference, of the relation of word to thing, of discourse to experience. Postmodern texts like *The White Hotel* or *Kepler* do not confidently disintegrate and banish the humanist subject either, though Eagleton says postmodernism (in his theoretical terms) does. They *do* disturb humanist certainties about the nature of the self and of the role of consciousness and Cartesian reason (or positivistic science), but they do so by inscribing that subjectivity and only then contesting it.

I have deliberately discussed each of Eagleton's eight points in terms of specific examples in order to illustrate the dangers of separating neat theory from messy practice. A poetics of postmodernism must deal with *both* and can theorize only on the basis of all the forms of postmodern discourse available to it. As Nicholas Zurbrugg (1986, 71) has argued, too many of the theorists of postmodernism have simplified and misread the complexities and creative potential of postmodern cultural practices by predicating their theories on a very partial sampling. For example the constant complaint that postmodernism is either ahistorical or, if it uses history, that it does so in a naive and nostalgic way, just will not stand up in the light of actual novels such as those listed above or films like *Crossroads* or *Zelig*. What starts to look naive, by contrast, is the reductive belief that any recall of the past must, by definition, be sentimental nostalgia or antiquarianism. What postmodernism does, as its very name suggests, is confront and contest any modernist discarding *or* recuperating of the past in the name of the future. It suggests no search for transcendent timeless meaning, but rather a re-evaluation of and a dialogue with the past in the light of the present. We could call this, once again, "the presence of the past" or perhaps its "present-ification" (Hassan 1983). It does not deny the *existence* of the past; it does question whether we can ever *know* that past other than through its textualized remains.

However, the binary oppositions that are usually set up in the writing on postmodernism — between past and present, modern and postmodern, and so on — should probably be called into question, if only because, like the rhetoric of rupture (*dis*continuity, *de*centering, and so on), *post*modernism literally names and constitutes its own paradoxical identity, and does so in an uneasy contradictory relationship of constant slippage. So much that has been written on this subject has physically taken the form of opposing columns, usually labelled modernist versus postmodernist (see Hassan 1975, 1980b; cf. Lethen 1986, 235–6). But this is a structure that implicitly denies the mixed, plural, and contradictory nature of the postmodern enterprise.

Whether this complexity is a result of our particularly contradictory age, caught between "myths of totality" and "ideologies of fracture" (Hassan 1980a, 191) is another question. Surely many ages could be so described. Whatever the cause, a poetics of postmodernism should try to come to grips with some of the obvious paradoxes in both theory and practice. Let me offer just a few more examples: one would be the contradiction or

irony of Lyotard's (1984a) obviously meta-narrative theory of postmodernism's incredulity to meta-narrative (see Lacoue-Labarthe 1984) or of Foucault's early anti-totalizing epistemic totalizations. These are typically paradoxical: they are the masterful denials of mastery, the cohesive attacks on cohesion, the essentializing challenges to essences, that characterize postmodern theory. Similarly historiographic metafiction — like postmodern painting, sculpture, and photography — inscribes and only then subverts its mimetic engagement with the world. It does not reject it (cf. Graff 1979); nor does it merely accept it (cf. Butler 1980, 93; A. Wilde 1981, 170). But it does change irrevocably any simple notions of realism or reference by directly confronting the discourse of art with the discourse of history.

A further postmodern paradox that this particular kind of fiction enacts is to be found in its bridging of the gap between élite and popular art, a gap which mass culture has no doubt broadened. Many have noted postmodernism's attraction to popular art forms (Fiedler 1975; Tani 1984) such as the detective story (Fowles's *A Maggot*) or the western (Doctorow's *Welcome to Hard Times* or Thomas Berger's *Little Big Man*). But what has not been dealt with is the paradox of novels like *The French Lieutenant's Woman* or *The Name of the Rose* themselves being at once popular best-sellers and objects of intense academic study. I would argue that, as typically postmodernist contradictory texts, novels like these parodically use and abuse the conventions of both popular and élite literature, and do so in such a way that they can actually *use* the invasive culture industry to challenge its own commodification processes from within.[14] And, in addition, if élitist culture has indeed been fragmented into specialist disciplines, as many have argued, then hybrid novels like these work both to address and to subvert that fragmentation through their pluralizing recourse to the discourses of history, sociology, theology, political science, economics, philosophy, semiotics, literature, literary criticism, and so on. Historiographic metafiction

[14]Hutcheon is alluding to Horkheimer and Adorno's attack on the culture industry's commodification of art; see above, p. 1254.

clearly acknowledges that it is a complex institutional and discursive network of élite, official, mass, popular cultures that postmodernism operates in.

What we seem to need, then, is some way of talking about our culture which is neither "unificatory" nor "contradictionist" in a Marxist dialectical sense (Ruthven 1984, 32). The visible paradoxes of the postmodern do not mask any hidden unity which analysis can reveal. Its irreconcilable incompatibilities are the very bases upon which the problematized discourses of postmodernism emerge (see Foucault 1977, 151). The differences that these contradictions foreground should not be dissipated. While unresolved paradoxes may be unsatisfying to those in need of absolute and final answers, to postmodernist thinkers and artists they have been the source of intellectual energy that has provoked new articulations of the postmodern condition. Despite the obvious danger, they do not appear to have brought on what LaCapra has called a "lemming-like fascination for discursive impasses" (1985a, 141) that might threaten to undermine *any* working concept of "theorizing." The model of contradictions offered here — while admittedly only another model — would hope to open up any poetics of postmodernism to plural, contestatory elements without necessarily reducing or recuperating them. In order to try to avoid the tempting trap of co-option, what is necessary is the acknowledging of the fact that such a position is itself an ideology, one that is profoundly implicated in that which it seeks to theorize. Criticism, as Barthes reminded us, is "essentially an activity, i.e., a series of intellectual acts profoundly committed to the historical and subjective existence (they are the same) of the man [sic] who performs them" (1972, 257).

In other words, we cannot exempt our own "discriminating scholarly discourse" as Douwe Fokkema would like (1986a, 2), for it too is as institutionalized as the fiction or the painting or the philosophy or the history it would pretend to scrutinize. Within such a "postmodernist" ideology, all a poetics of postmodernism would do would be self-consciously to enact the metalinguistic contradiction of being inside and outside, complicitous and distanced, inscribing and contesting its own provisional formulations. Such an enterprise would obviously not yield any universal truths but, then again, that would not be what it sought to do. To move from the desire and expectation of sure and single meaning to a recognition of the value of differences and even contradictions might be a tentative first step to accepting responsibility for both art and theory *as signifying processes*. In other words, maybe we could begin to study the implications of both our *making* and our *making sense* of our culture.

Works Cited

Barth, John (1980). "The Literature of Replenishment: Postmodern Fiction," *The Atlantic* 245, 1: 65–71.

Barthes, Roland (1972). *Critical Essays*, trans. Richard Howard, Evanston: Northwestern UP.

———— (1977). *Image Music Text*, trans. Stephen Heath, New York: Hill & Wang.

Bertens, Hans (1986). "The Postmodern *Weltanschauung* and Its Relation with Modernism: An Introductory Survey" in Fokkema and Bertens (1986): 9–51.

Brooke-Rose, Christine (1981). *A Rhetoric of the United States in Narrative and Structure, Especially of the Fantastic*, Cambridge and New York: Cambridge UP.

Burgin, Victor (1986). *The End of Art Theory: Criticism and Postmodernity*, Atlantic Highlands, NJ: Humanities Press International.

Butler, Christopher (1980). *After the Wake: An Essay on the Contemporary Avant-Garde*, Oxford: Oxford UP.

Calinescu, Matei (1977). *Faces of Modernity*, Bloomington: Indiana UP.

———— (1986). "Postmodernism and Some Paradoxes of Periodization," in Fokkema and Bertens (1986): 239–54.

Canary, Robert H., and Kozicki, Henry (eds) (1978). *The Writing of History: Literary Form and Historical Understanding*, Madison: U Wisconsin Pr.

Carroll, David (1982). *The Subject in Question*, Chicago: U Chicago Pr.

Chénetier, Marc (1985). "Charting Contemporary American Fiction: A View from Abroad," *New Literary History* 16, 3: 653–69.

Cox, Christoph (1985). "Barthes, Borges, Foucault, Utopia," *Subjects/Objects* 3: 55–69.

Crimp, Douglas (1983). "On the Museum's Ruins," in Foster (1983): 43–56.

Culler, Jonathan (1982a). "Structuralism and Grammatology," in Spanos, Bové, and O'Hara (1982): 75–86.

——— (1983, 1984). "At the Boundaries: Barthes and Derrida," in Sussman (1983, 1984): 23–41.

Cunliffe, Marcus (ed.) (1975). *American Literature since 1900*, London: Sphere.

Davis, Douglas (1977). *Artculture: Essays on the Post-Modern*, New York: Harper & Row.

de Lauretis, Teresa (1984). *Alice Doesn't: Feminism, Semiotics, Cinema*, Bloomington: Indiana UP.

Derrida, Jacques (1981a). *Positions*, trans. Alan Bass, Chicago: U Chicago Pr.

D'Haen, Theo (1983). *Text to Reader: A Communicative Approach to Fowles, Barth, Cortázar and Boon*, Amsterdam: John Benjamins.

——— (1986). "Postmodernism in American Fiction and Art," in Fokkema and Bertens (1986): 211–31.

Eagleton, Terry (1985). "Capitalism, Modernism and Postmodernism," *New Life Review* 152: 60–73.

Egbert, Donald D. (1970). *Social Radicalism and the Arts*, New York: Knopf.

Fiedler, Leslie (1975). "Cross the Border—Close that Gap: Post-modernism," in Cunliffe (1975): 344–66.

Fish, Stanley (1986). "Critical Self-Consciousness or Can We Know What We Are Doing?" lecture, McMaster University, Ontario.

Fokkema, Douwe (1986a). "Preliminary Remarks," in Fokkema and Bertens (1986): 1–8.

Fokkema, Douwe, and Bertens, Hans (eds.) (1986). *Approaching Postmodernism*, Amsterdam and Philadelphia: John Benjamins.

Foster, Hal (ed.) (1983). *The Anti-Aesthetic: Essays on Postmodern Culture*, Port Townsend, WA: Bay Press.

Foucault, Michel (1977). *Language, Counter-Memory, Practice*, trans. Donald F. Bouchard and Sherry Simon, Ithaca: Cornell UP.

Garvin, Harry R. (ed.) (1980). *Romanticism, Modernism, Postmodernism*, Lewisburg, PA: Bucknell UP; London: Associated UP.

Ghose, Zulfikar (1983). *The Fiction of Reality*, London: Macmillan.

Giddens, Anthony (1981). "Modernism and Post-Modernism," *New German Critique* 22:15–18.

Gossman, Lionel (1978). "History and Literature: Reproduction or Signification," in Canary and Kozicki (1978): 3–39.

Graff, Gerald (1979). *Literature Against Itself*, Chicago: U Chicago Pr.

Graham, Joseph F. (1982). "Critical Persuasion: In Response to Stanley Fish" in Spanos, Bové, and O'Hara (1982): 147–58.

Habermas, Jürgen (1983). "Modernity—An Incomplete Project," in Foster (1983): 3–15.

Harrison, Bernard (1985). "Deconstructing Derrida," *Comparative Criticism* 7: 3–24.

Hassan, Ihab (1971a). *Liberations: New Essays on the Humanities in Revolution*, Middletown, CT: Wesleyan UP.

——— (1975). *Paracriticisms: Seven Speculations of the Times*. Urbana: U Illinois Pr.

——— (1980a). *The Right Promethean Fire: Imagination, Science and Cultural Change*, Urbana: U Illinois Pr.

——— (1983). "Postmodernism: A Vanishing Horizon," paper to Modern Language Association, New York.

——— (1986). "Pluralism in Postmodern Perspective," *Critical Inquiry* 12, 3: 503–20.

Hohendahl, Peter Uwe (1982). *The Institution of Criticism*, Ithaca: Cornell UP.

Hutcheon, Linda (1985). *Narcissistic Narrative: The Metafictional Paradox*, Waterloo, Ont: Wilfrid Laurier UP.

Huyssen, Andreas (1981). "The Search for Tradition: Avant-Garde and Postmodernism in the 1970s," *New German Critique* 22: 23–40.

Jameson, Fredric (1983). "Postmodernism and Consumer Society," in Foster (1983): 111–25.

——— (1984a). "Postmoderism, Or The Cultural Logic of Late Capitalism," *New Left Review* 146: 53–92.

——— (1984b). "Forward," in Lyotard (1984a): vii–xxi.

Jencks, Charles (1977). *The Language of Post-Modern Architecture*, London: Academy.

Kamuf, Penny (1982). "Replacing Feminist Criticism," *Diacritics* 12, 2: 42–47.

Kibbins, Gary (1983). "The Enduring of the Artsystem," *Open Letter* 5th series, 5–6: 126–39.

Kosinski, Jerzy (1986). "Death in Cannes," *Esquire* March: 81–89.

Krauss, Rosalind (1980). "Poststructuralism and the 'Paraliterary,'" *October* 13: 36–40.

Kristeva, Julia (1980a). "Postmodernism?" in Garvin (1980): 136–41.

Kroker, Arthur, and Cook, David (1986). *The Postmodern Scene: Excremental Culture and Hyper-Aesthetics*, Montreal: New World Perspectives.

LaCapra, Dominick (1985a). *History and Criticism*, Ithaca: Cornell UP.

Lacoue-Labarthe, Philippe (1984). "Talks," trans. Christopher Fynsk, *Diacritics* 14, 3: 24–37.

Lefebvre, Henri (1968). *La Vie quotidienne dans le monde moderne*, Paris: Gallimard.

Lethen, Helmut (1986). "Modernism Cut in Half: The Exclusion of the Avant-garde and the Debate on Postmodernism," in Fokkema and Bertens (1986): 233–8.

Lodge, David (1977). *The Modes of Modern Writing: Metaphor, Metonymy and the Typology of Modern Literature*, London: Edward Arnold.

Lucente, Gregory L. (1986). *Beautiful Fables: Self-Consciousness in Italian Narrative from Manzoni to Calvino*, Baltimore and London: Johns Hopkins UP.

Lyotard, Jean-François (1983). *Le Differend*, Paris: Minuit.

———— (1984a). *The Postmodern Condition: A Report on Knowledge*, trans. Geoff Bennington and Brian Massumi, Minneapolis: U Minnesota Pr.

———— (1984b). "Answering the Question: What Is Postmodernism?" trans. Regis Durand, in Lyotard (1984a): 71–82.

———— (1986). *Le Postmoderne expliqué aux enfants: Correspondence 1982–1985*, Paris: Galilée.

McCaffery, Larry (1982). *The Metafictional Muse*, Pittsburgh: U Pittsburgh Pr.

Malmgren, Carl Darryl (1985). *Fictional Space in the Modernist and Postmodernist American Novel*, Lewisburg, PA: Bucknell UP.

Moreno, César Fernàndez (ed.) (1974). *América Latina en su Literatura*, 2nd ed., Buenos Aires: Siglo XXI.

Moser, Walter (1984). "Mode-Moderne-Postmoderne," *Etudes Françaises* 20, 2: 29–48.

Newman, Charles (1985). *The Post-Modern Aura: The Act of Fiction in an Age of Inflation*, Evanston, IL: Northwestern UP.

Norris, Christopher (1985). *The Contest of the Faculties: Philosophy and Theory after Deconstruction*, London and New York: Methuen.

Oliva, Achille Bonito (1984). "La trans-avanguardia," *Il Verri* n. 1–2, 7th series: 56–79.

Owens, Craig (1980b). "The Allegorical Impulse: Toward a Theory of Postmodernism, Part II," *October* 13: 59–80.

Palmer, Richard E. (1977). "Postmodernity and Hermeneutics," *Boundary 2* 5, 2: 363–93.

Paterson, Janet (1986). "Le Roman 'postmoderne': mise au point et perspectives," *Canadian Review of Comparative Literature* 13, 2; 238–55.

Perloff, Marjorie (1985). *The Dance of the Intellect: Studies in the Poetry of the Pound Tradition*, Cambridge: Cambridge UP.

Pops, Martin (1984). *Home Remedies*, Amherst: U Massachusetts Pr.

Portoghesi, Paolo (1983). *Postmodern: The Architecture of the Postindustial Society*, New York: Rizzoli.

Radhakrishnan, Rajagoplan (1983). "The Post-Modern Event and the End of Logocentrism," *Boundary 2* 12, 1: 33–60.

Rorty, Richard (1984b). "Deconstruction and Circumvention," *Critical Inquiry* 11, 1: 1–23.

Russell, Charles (1980a). "The Context of the Concept," in Garvin (1980): 181–93.

———— (1985). *Poets, Prophets, and Revolutionaries: The Literary Avant-garde from Rimbaud through Postmodernism*, New York and Oxford: Oxford UP.

Ruthven, K. K. (1984). *Feminist Literary Studies: An Introduction*, Cambridge: Cambridge UP.

Said, Edward (1983). *The World, the Text, and the Critic*, Cambridge: Harvard UP.

Sarduy, Severo (1974). "El barroco y el neobarroco," in Moreno (1974): 167–84.

Sontag, Susan (1967). *Against Interpretation and Other Essays*, New York: Dell.

Spanos, William V., Bové, Paul A., and O'Hara, Daniel (eds.) (1982). *The Question of Textuality*, Bloomington, Indiana UP.

Stern, Daniel (1971). "The Mysterious New Novel," in Hassan (1971a): 22–37.

Suleiman, Susan Rubin (1986). "Naming a Difference: Reflections on 'Modernism versus Postmodernism' in Literature," in Fokkema and Bertens (1986): 255–70.

Sussman, Herbert L. (ed.) (1983, 1984). *At the Boundaries*, Boston: Northeastern UP.

Swan, Susan (1983). *The Biggest Modern Woman of the World*, Toronto: Lester & Orpen Dennys.

Tani, Stefano (1984). *The Doomed Detective*, Carbondale: Southern Illinois UP.

Thiher, Allen (1984). *Words in Reflection: Modern Language Theory and Postmodern Fiction*, Chicago: U Chicago Pr.

Todorov, Tzvetan (1981a). *Introduction to Poetics*, trans. Richard Howard, Minneapolis: U Minnesota Pr.

Toulmin, Stephen (1972). *Human Understanding*, Princeton, NJ: Princeton UP.

Vattimo, Gianni (1983). "Dialettica, differenza, pensiero debole," in Vattimo and Rovatti (1983): 12–28.

———— (1985). *La fine della modernità: Nichilismo ed ermeneutica nella cultura post-moderna*, Milano: Garzanti.

Vattimo, Gianni, and Rovatti, Pier Aldo (eds.) (1983). *Il Pensiero Debole*, Milano: Feltrinelli.

Wasson, Richard (1974). "From Priest to Prometheus: Culture and Criticism in the Post-Modernist Period," *Journal of Modern Literature* 3, 5: 1188–1202.

Watkins, Evan (1978). *The Critical Act: Criticism and Community*, New Haven: Yale UP.

White, Hayden (1978b). *Tropics of Discourse*, Baltimore: Johns Hopkins UP.

———— (1980). "The Value of Narrativity in the Representation of Reality," *Critical Inquiry* 7, 1: 5–27.

———— (1981). "The Narrativization of Real Events," *Critical Inquiry* 7, 4: 793–8.

———— (1984). "The Question of Narrative in Contemporary Historical Theory," *History and Theory* 23, 1: 1–33.

Wilde, Alan (1981). *Horizons of Assent: Modernism, Postmodernism, and the Ironic Imagination*, Baltimore: Johns Hopkins UP.

Williams, Raymond (1960). *Culture and Society 1780–1950*. Garden City, NY: Doubleday.

Ziolkowski, Theodore (1969). "Toward a Post-Modern Aesthetics?" *Mosaic* 2, 4: 112–19.

Zurbrugg, Nicholas (1986). "Postmodernity, *Métaphore manquée*, and the Myth of the Trans-avant-garde," *SubStance* 48: 68–90.

bell hooks

b. 1952

Gloria Watkins, who writes under the pseudonym of bell hooks, was born in Kentucky and educated at all-black public schools. She received her bachelor's degree from Stanford University and attended Yale University before receiving her Ph.D. from the University of California at Santa Cruz. Her radical cultural and literary theory, which is based almost equally on race, class, and gender, never strays far from her experience of growing up within an oppressed culture in the South and her experience of negotiating the conflict between that background and the largely white academic culture in which she has found an honored place. Hooks was an associate professor for three years in the African American studies department at Yale before moving to City College of New York, where she helped heal the politically riven Africana studies program. Since 1995, hooks has been Distinguished Professor of English at CCNY and at the City University Graduate Center. Hooks has published over thirty books including Ain't I a Woman: Black Women and Feminism *(1981),* Feminist Theory: From Margin to Center *(1984), and* Yearning: Race, Gender and Cultural Politics *(1990). Her latest works include* Outlaw Culture: Resisting Representations *(1994),* Art on My Mind: Visual Politics *(1995),* Killing Rage: Ending Racism *(1995),* Bone Black: Memories of Girlhood *(1996),* Reel to Real: Race, Sex, and Class in the Movies *(1996),* Remembered Rapture: The Writer at Work *(1999),* Communion: The Female Search for Love *(2002),* Rock My Soul: Black People and Self-Esteem *(2003), and* We Real Cool: Black Men and Masculinity *(2004). The following essay is a chapter in* Yearnings *(1989).*

Postmodern Blackness

Postmodernist discourses are often exclusionary even as they call attention to, appropriate even, the experience of "difference" and "Otherness" to provide oppositional political meaning, legitimacy, and immediacy when they are accused of lacking concrete relevance. Very few African-American intellectuals have talked or written about postmodernism. At a dinner party I talked about trying to grapple with the significance of postmodernism for contemporary black experience. It was one of those social gatherings where only one other black person was present. The setting quickly became a field of contestation. I was told by the other black person that I was wasting my time, that "this stuff does not relate in any way to what's happening with black people." Speaking in the presence of a group of white onlookers, staring at us as though this encounter were staged for their benefit, we engaged in a passionate discussion about black experience. Apparently, no one sympathized with my insistence that racism is perpetuated when blackness is associated solely with concrete gut level experience conceived as either opposing or having no connection to abstract thinking and the production of critical theory. The idea that there is no meaningful connection between black experience and critical thinking about aesthetics or culture must be continually interrogated.

My defense of postmodernism and its relevance to black folks sounded good, but I worried that I lacked conviction, largely because I approach the subject cautiously and with suspicion.

Disturbed not so much by the "sense" of postmodernism but by the conventional language used when it is written or talked about and by those who speak it, I find myself on the outside of the discourse looking in. As a discursive practice it is dominated primarily by the voices of white male intellectuals and/or academic elites who speak to and about one another with coded familiarity. Reading and studying their writing to understand postmodernism in its multiple manifestations, I appreciate it but feel little inclination to ally myself with the academic hierarchy and exclusivity pervasive in the movement today.

Critical of most writing on postmodernism, I perhaps am more conscious of the way in which the focus on "Otherness and difference" that is often alluded to in these works seems to have little concrete impact as an analysis or standpoint that might change the nature and direction of postmodernist theory. Since much of this theory has been constructed in reaction to and against high modernism, there is seldom any mention of black experience or writings by black people in this work, specifically black women (though in more recent work one may see a reference to Cornel West, the black male scholar who has most engaged postmodernist discourse). Even if an aspect of black culture is the subject of postmodern critical writing, the works cited will usually be those of black men. A work that comes immediately to mind is Andrew Ross's chapter "Hip, and the Long Front of Color" in *No Respect: Intellectuals and Popular Culture*; while it is an interesting reading, it constructs black culture as though black women have had no role in black cultural production. At the end of Meaghan Morris' discussion of postmodernism in her collection of essays *The Pirate's Fiance: Feminism and Postmodernism*, she provides a bibliography of works by women, identifying them as important contributions to a discourse on postmodernism that offer new insight as well as challenging male theoretical hegemony. Even though many of the works do not directly address postmodernism, they address similar concerns. There are no references to works by black women.

The failure to recognize a critical black presence in the culture and in most scholarship and writing on postmodernism compels a black reader, particularly a black female reader, to interrogate her interest in a subject where those who discuss and write about it seem not to know black women exist or even to consider the possibility that we might be somewhere writing or saying something that should be listened to, or producing art that should be seen, heard, approached with intellectual seriousness. This is especially the case with works that go on and on about the way in which postmodernist discourse has opened up a theoretical terrain where "difference and Otherness" can be considered legitimate issues in the academy. Confronting both the absence of recognition of black female presence that much postmodernist theory re-inscribes and the resistance on the part of most black folks to hearing about real connection between postmodernism and black experience, I enter a discourse, a practice, where there may be no ready audience for my words, no clear listener, uncertain then, that my voice can or will be heard.

During the sixties, [the] black power movement was influenced by perspectives that could easily be labeled modernist. Certainly many of the ways black folks addressed issues of identity conformed to a modernist universalizing agenda. There was little critique of patriarchy as a master narrative among black militants. Despite the fact that black power ideology reflected a modernist sensibility, these elements were soon rendered irrelevant as militant protest was stifled by a powerful, repressive postmodern state. The period directly after the black power movement was a time when major news magazines carried articles with cocky headlines like "Whatever Happened to Black America?" This response was an ironic reply to the aggressive, unmet demand by decentered, marginalized black subjects who had at least momentarily successfully demanded a hearing, who had made it possible for black liberation to be on the national political agenda. In the wake of the black power movement, after so many rebels were slaughtered and lost, many of these voices were silenced by a repressive state; others became inarticulate. It has become necessary to find new avenues to transmit the messages of black liberation struggle, new ways to talk about racism and other politics of domination. Radical postmodernist practice, most powerfully conceptualized as a "politics of difference," should incorporate the voices of displaced, marginalized, exploited, and oppressed black people. It is sadly ironic that the contemporary discourse which talks the most about heterogeneity, the decentered subject, declaring breakthroughs that allow

recognition of Otherness, still directs its critical voice primarily to a specialized audience that shares a common language rooted in the very master narratives it claims to challenge. If radical postmodernist thinking is to have a transformative impact, then a critical break with the notion of "authority" as "mastery over" must not simply be a rhetorical device. It must be reflected in habits of being, including styles of writing as well as chosen subject matter. Third world nationals, elites, and white critics who passively absorb white supremacist thinking, and therefore never notice or look at black people on the streets or at their jobs, who render us invisible with their gaze in all areas of daily life, are not likely to produce liberatory theory that will challenge racist domination, or promote a breakdown in traditional ways of seeing and thinking about reality, ways of constructing aesthetic theory and practice. From a different standpoint, Robert Storr[1] makes a similar critique in the global issue of *Art in America* when he asserts:

> To be sure, much postmodernist critical inquiry has centered precisely on the issues of "difference" and "Otherness." On the purely theoretical plane the exploration of these concepts has produced some important results, but in the absence of any sustained research into what artists of color and others outside the mainstream might be up to, such discussions become rootless instead of radical. Endless second guessing about the latent imperialism of intruding upon other cultures only compounded matters, preventing or excusing these theorists from investigating what black, Hispanic, Asian and Native American artists were actually doing.

Without adequate concrete knowledge of and contact with the nonwhite "Other," white theorists may move in discursive theoretical directions that are threatening and potentially disruptive of that critical practice which would support radical liberation struggle.

The postmodern critique of "identity," though relevant for renewed black liberation struggle, is often posed in ways that are problematic. Given a pervasive politics of white supremacy which seeks to prevent the formation of radical black

[1]Senior curator at the Museum of Modern Art in New York 1990–2002, now professor of art history at New York University.

subjectivity, we cannot cavalierly dismiss a concern with identity politics. Any critic exploring the radical potential of postmodernism as it relates to racial difference and racial domination would need to consider the implications of a critique of identity for oppressed groups. Many of us are struggling to find new strategies of resistance. We must engage decolonization as a critical practice if we are to have meaningful chances of survival even as we must simultaneously cope with the loss of political grounding which made radical activism more possible. I am thinking here about the postmodernist critique of essentialism as it pertains to the construction of "identity" as one example.

Postmodern theory that is not seeking to simply appropriate the experience of "Otherness" to enhance the discourse or to be radically chic should not separate the "politics of difference" from the politics of racism. To take racism seriously one must consider the plight of underclass people of color, a vast majority of whom are black. For African-Americans our collective condition prior to the advent of postmodernism and perhaps more tragically expressed under current postmodern conditions has been and is characterized by continued displacement, profound alienation, and despair. Writing about blacks and postmodernism, Cornel West describes our collective plight:

> There is increasing class division and differentiation, creating on the one hand a significant black middle-class, highly anxiety-ridden, insecure, willing to be co-opted and incorporated into the powers that be, concerned with racism to the degree that it poses constraints on upward social mobility; and, on the other, a vast and growing black underclass, an underclass that embodies a kind of walking nihilism of pervasive drug addiction, pervasive alcoholism, pervasive homicide, and an exponential rise in suicide. Now because of the deindustrialization, we also have a devastated black industrial working class. We are talking here about tremendous hopelessness.

This hopelessness creates longing for insight and strategies for change that can renew spirits and reconstruct grounds for collective black liberation struggle. The overall impact of postmodernism is that many other groups now share with black folks a sense of deep alienation, despair, uncertainty, loss of a sense of grounding even if it is not informed by shared circumstance. Radical postmodernism calls attention to those shared sensibilities which cross the boundaries of class, gender, race, etc., that could be fertile ground for the construction of empathy — ties that would promote recognition of common commitments, and serve as a base for solidarity and coalition.

Yearning is the word that best describes a common psychological state shared by many of us, cutting across boundaries of race, class, gender, and sexual practice. Specifically, in relation to the post-modernist deconstruction of "master" narratives, the yearning that wells in the hearts and minds of those whom such narratives have silenced is the longing for critical voice. It is no accident that "rap" has usurped the primary position of rhythm and blues music among young black folks as the most desired sound or that it began as a form of "testimony" for the underclass. It has enabled underclass black youth to develop a critical voice, as a group of young black men told me, a "common literacy." Rap projects a critical voice, explaining, demanding, urging. Working with this insight in his essay "Putting the Pop Back into Postmodernism," Lawrence Grossberg comments:

> The postmodern sensibility appropriates practices as boasts that announce their own — and consequently our own — existence, like a rap song boasting of the imaginary (or real — it makes no difference) accomplishments of the rapper. They offer forms of empowerment not only in the face of nihilism but precisely through the forms of nihilism itself: an empowering nihilism, a moment of positivity through the production and structuring of affective relations.

Considering that it is as subject one comes to voice, then the postmodernist focus on the critique of identity appears at first glance to threaten and close down the possibility that this discourse and practice will allow those who have suffered the crippling effects of colonization and domination to gain or regain a hearing. Even if this sense of threat and the fear it evokes are based on a misunderstanding of the postmodernist political project, they nevertheless shape responses. It never surprises me when black folks respond to the critique of essentialism, especially when it denies the validity of identity politics by saying, "Yeah, it's easy to give up identity, when you got one." Should we not be suspicious of postmodern critiques of the "subject" when they surface at a historical moment when many subjugated people feel themselves coming to voice for the first time. Though an apt and oftentimes appropriate comeback, it does not really intervene in the discourse in a way that alters and transforms.

Criticisms of directions in postmodern thinking should not obscure insights it may offer that open up our understanding of African-American experience. The critique of essentialism encouraged by postmodernist thought is useful for African-Americans concerned with reformulating outmoded notions of identity. We have too long had imposed upon us from both the outside and the inside a narrow, constricting notion of blackness. Postmodern critiques of essentialism which challenge notions of universality and static overdetermined identity within mass culture and mass consciousness can open up new possibilities for the construction of self and the assertion of agency.

Employing a critique of essentialism allows African-Americans to acknowledge the way in which class mobility has altered collective black experience so that racism does not necessarily have the same impact on our lives. Such a critique allows us to affirm multiple black identities, varied black experience. It also challenges colonial imperialist paradigms of black identity which represent blackness one-dimensionally in ways that reinforce and sustain white supremacy. This discourse created the idea of the "primitive" and promoted the notion of an "authentic" experience, seeing as "natural" those expressions of black life which conformed to a pre-existing pattern or stereotype. Abandoning essentialist notions would be a serious challenge to racism. Contemporary African-American resistance struggle must be rooted in a process of decolonization that continually opposes re-inscribing notions of "authentic" black identity. This critique should not be made synonymous with a dismissal of the struggle of oppressed and exploited peoples to make ourselves subjects. Nor should it deny that in certain circumstances this experience affords us a privileged critical location from which to speak. This is not a re-inscription of modernist master narratives of authority which privilege some voices by denying voice to others. Part of our struggle for radical black subjectivity is the quest to find ways to construct self and identity that are oppositional and liberatory. The unwillingness to critique essentialism on the part of many African-Americans is rooted in the fear that it will cause folks to lose sight of the specific history and experience of African-Americans and the unique sensibilities and culture that arise from that experience. An adequate response to this concern is to critique essentialism while emphasizing the significance of "the authority of experience." There is a radical difference between a repudiation of the idea that there is a black "essence" and recognition of the way black identity has been specifically constituted in the experience of exile and struggle.

When black folks critique essentialism, we are empowered to recognize multiple experiences of black identity that are the lived conditions which make diverse cultural productions possible. When this diversity is ignored, it is easy to see black folks as falling into two categories: nationalist or assimilationist, black-identified or white-identified. Coming to terms with the impact of postmodernism for black experience, particularly as it changes our sense of identity, means that we must and can rearticulate the basis for collective bonding. Given the various crises facing African-Americans (economic, spiritual, escalating racial violence, etc.), we are compelled by circumstance to reassess our relationship to popular culture and resistance struggle. Many of us are as reluctant to face this task as many non-black postmodern thinkers who focus theoretically on the issue of "difference" are to confront the issue of race and racism.

Music is the cultural product created by African-Americans that has most attracted postmodern theorists. It is rarely acknowledged that there is far greater censorship and restriction of other forms of cultural production by black folks — literary, critical writing, etc. Attempts on the part of editors and publishing houses to control and manipulate the representation of black culture, as well as the desire to promote the creation of products that will attract the widest audience, limit in a crippling and stifling way the kind of work many black folks feel we can do and still receive recognition. Using myself as an example, that creative writing I do which I consider to be most reflective of a postmodern oppositional sensibility, work that is abstract, fragmented, non-linear narrative, is constantly rejected by editors and publishers. It does not conform to the type of writing they think black women should be doing or the type of writing they believe will sell. Certainly I do not think I am the only black person engaged in forms of cultural production, especially experimental ones, who is constrained by the lack of an audience for certain kinds of work. It is important for postmodern thinkers and theorists to constitute themselves as an audience for such work. To do this they must assert power and privilege within the space of critical writing to open up the field so that it will be more inclusive. To change the exclusionary practice of postmodern critical discourse is to enact a postmodernism of resistance. Part of this intervention entails black intellectual participation in the discourse.

In his essay "Postmodernism and Black America," Cornel West suggests that black intellectuals "are marginal — usually languishing at the interface of Black and white cultures or thoroughly ensconced in Euro-American settings." He cannot see this group as potential producers of radical postmodernist thought. While I generally agree with this assessment, black intellectuals must proceed with the understanding that we are not condemned to the margins. The way we work and what we do can determine whether or not what we produce will be meaningful to a wider audience, one that includes all classes of black people. West suggest that black intellectuals lack "any organic link with most of Black life" and that this "diminishes their value to Black resistance." This statement bears traces of essentialism. Perhaps we need to focus more on those black intellectuals, however rare our presence, who do not feel this lack and whose work is primarily directed towards the enhancement of black critical consciousness and the strengthening of our collective capacity to engage in meaningful resistance struggle. Theoretical ideas and critical thinking need not be transmitted solely in written work or solely in the academy. While I work in a predominantly white institution, I remain intimately and passionately engaged with black community. It's not like I'm going to talk about writing and thinking about postmodernism with other academics and/or intellectuals and not discuss these ideas with underclass non-academic black folks who are family, friends, and comrades. Since I have not broken the ties that bind me to underclass poor black community, I have seen that knowledge, especially that which enhances daily life and strengthens our capacity to survive, can be shared. It means that critics, writers, and academics have to give the same critical attention to nurturing and cultivating our ties to black community that we give to writing articles, teaching, and lecturing. Here again I am really talking about cultivating habits of being that reinforce awareness that knowledge can be disseminated and shared on a number of fronts. The extent to which knowledge is made available, accessible, etc. depends on the nature of one's political commitments.

Postmodern culture with its decentered subject can be the space where ties are severed or it can provide the occasion for new and varied forms of bonding. To some extent, ruptures, surfaces, contextuality, and a host of other happenings create gaps that make space for oppositional practices which no longer require intellectuals to be confined by narrow separate spheres with no meaningful connection to the world of the everyday. Much postmodern engagement with culture emerges from the yearning to do intellectual work that connects with habits of being, forms of artistic expression, and aesthetics that inform the daily life of writers and scholars as well as a mass population. On the terrain of culture, one can participate in critical dialogue with the uneducated poor, the black underclass who are thinking about aesthetics. One can talk about what we are seeing, thinking, or listening to; a space is there for critical exchange. It's exciting to think, write, talk about, and create art that reflects passionate engagement with popular culture, because this may very well be "the" central future location of resistance struggle, a meeting place where new and radical happenings can occur.

Cornel West

b. 1953

Combining the radicalism of the Black Panthers with the performance skills of the African American clergy, Cornel West has long been a major force in American cultural politics. Born in Tulsa in 1953, West was raised in a Baptist family that moved to California, where he was deeply influenced by the social activism of the Black Panthers but repudiated their violence. He completed his B.A. at Harvard University in three years, magna cum laude, and received his Ph.D. in philosophy from Princeton University in 1980. Eight years later, he returned to Princeton University as director of the African-American Studies Program. In 1993, he took up a position at Harvard University, which ended in a very public dispute with university president Lawrence Summers in 2002. He is currently once again at Princeton, where he is Class of 1943 Professor of Religion. West is the author of many books on philosophy and theology, race and politics, including Prophetic Fragments *(1988),* The American Evasion of Philosophy *(1989),* The Ethical Dimensions of Marxist Thought *(1991), the best-selling* Race Matters *(1994),* Keeping Faith *(1994),* Prophesy Deliverance *(2002), and* Democracy Matters *(2004). In addition, West has appeared in the films* The Matrix Reloaded *(2003) and* The Matrix Revolutions *(2004) as "Councillor West" and has recently put out a hip-hop album entitled* Sketches of My Culture. *The essay "Postmodernism and Black America" originally appeared in* Zeta *magazine in 1987.*

Postmodernism and Black America

What is postmodernism? How are we to understand the postmodernism debate now raging in our cultural periodicals? And what does this debate have to do with the crisis in Black America?

In the popular mind, postmodernism is associated with the return of the decorative and ornamental, as in the eclecticism of Robert Venturi, Charles Jencks, and Philip Johnson in architecture; the unsettling strategies of John Barth, Ishmael Reed, and Thomas Pynchon in literature; and the self-reflexive photography of Barbara Kruger and Martha Rosler.

In the academic mind, postmodernism is usually viewed as a French intellectual product that highlights a world of fragments bereft of human will — a world of flashing images, quick information, and consumer activities that promotes historical amnesia and fosters political apathy. In such a world ironic consciousness becomes the badge of sophistication, social hope the naive stance of a bygone era.

These impressionistic perceptions in the popular and academic mind fixate on symptomatic emblems and therefore miss a crucial feature: *the growing diversity and complexity of Afro-American cultural production.* On the one hand, the popular mind rightly notes that postmodernism is primarily American, initiated among architects and later taken up by painters, poets, novelists, photographers, and literary critics who revolted against the domesticated, diluted modernism of the museum, academy, architectural firms, and galleries. On the other hand, the academic mind correctly sees that contemporary French philosophers and critics focusing on difference, marginality, and otherness are central to the postmodernism debate. Yet this debate has remained largely silent about a fundamental difference, race.

Some of this silence has to do with the reluctance of most Black critics to intervene due to a healthy dose of intellectual suspicion — yet the postmodernism debate is principally a battle over how we conceive of culture and, most importantly, how we interpret the current crisis in our society and muster resources to alleviate it. Every conception of postmodernism presupposes some notions of the modern and modernism — such as when they began, when they peaked, why they declined, how they ended, and what comes after. Therefore, to insert race in the postmodernism debate is to question how we understand the modern and modernism in light of race. Talking about race in the making of the modern world means talking about European colonialism and trans-Atlantic imperialism.

THE DECLINE OF EUROPE

The postmodernism debate consists of reflections about how to live, think, and act in a world that no longer rests on European hegemony and domination. So it is not surprising to see European intellectual self-confidence shattering in such exemplary strategies as the demystifying of European cultural predominance, the destruction of European metaphysical systems, and the deconstruction of European philosophical edifices. In this way, a historical condition for the postmodernism debate is the end of the age of Europe (1492–1945).

With the emergence of the U.S. as supreme world power and the collapse of European colonialism in Asia and Africa, distinctive issues of the postmodernism debate surface: the relation of high and popular culture, the effectiveness of opposition in politics and culture, the possibilities for a post-European world. These issues involve the cultural and political agency of peoples of color owing to the centrality of race in the U.S. and the decolonization process in the Third World. Yet this agency tends to be downplayed or ignored in much of the postmodernism debate because of the taming

of Black political opposition and the marginalized status of Black cultural resistance. In this sense, it is not just racial parochialism that circumscribes postmodernism debate, but the larger political and cultural contexts which permit this parochialism to flourish. If there is one basic lesson to learn from the history of race relations in the U.S., it is that only sustained efforts can thwart deeply ingrained racism. When social movements wane, the political status quo and cultural atmosphere reverts, re-rendering most black people powerless and invisible. This holds even in the time of Bill Cosby and Michael Jackson — and especially in the academy and the highbrow art world that thrive on tokenism in the name of illusory inclusivity.

DOWN-PLAYING BLACK CULTURE

Yet one aim of the postmodernism debate in the academic and highbrow art world is to promote inclusion, diversity, and heterogeneity. How is it that this aim seems undermined by the perceptions and practices of its interlocutors? Could it be that this debate that highlights ideas of difference, marginality, and otherness actually marginalizes people of difference and otherness? If so, how and why does this occur?

Postmodernism debate downplays Black culture for three basic reasons. First, U.S. critics lack interest in and are ignorant of most Black highbrow and popular cultural production. How else can we account for the grand talents yet modest successes of Emma Amos, Camille Billops, Melvin Edwards, Sam Gilliam, Alvin Loving, Howardena Pindell, and Betye Saar?[1] The reward system and sources of social recognition they honor prevent critics from taking seriously and hence promoting most Afro-American artists. Second, too few Black critics make powerful cases for the many marginal Afro-American artists. For the resulting peripheralization of black culture to occur at a time when the works of such masters as Toni Morrison and Samuel Delaney

[1]West is suggesting that whites are unlikely to have heard of these important postmodern African American artists, whose work hangs in major museums throughout the United States, because they have not been given the visibility in the media accorded to postmodern white artists. Most have websites where their work can be viewed online.

and such innovators as Alice Walker, Spike Lee, and Clarence Major flourish is a shame. Last, Black critics have often shunned the debate entirely due to its predominant white male academic composition. Why should black critics enter such a limited discourse when other matters call? The persuasive response is that this debate raises fundamental issues with which every serious critic should be grappling. The problem with the debate is not the issues as much as the way the issues are formulated and addressed. And one important issue postmodernism debate raises is the relation between popular culture and resistance.

CULTURE AND RESISTANCE

Undeniably U.S. mass culture is disproportionately influenced by Black people, especially in popular music, linguistic innovation, and athletics. Owing to both a particular African heritage and specific Euro-American oppressions, Black American cultural production has focused on performance and pageantry, style and spectacle with innovations in music and sermons rooted in Black religious practices and innovations in sports rooted in Black male-bonding networks that flaunt machismo, promote camaraderie, and, in some cases, lead to financial success. Black religious practices — the indigenous cradle of Afro-American culture — principally attempt to provide hope and sustain sanity in light of the absurdity of being Black in America and the absurdity of transplanted European moderns casting America in the role of the promised land. The Black religious ideological response was often to recast America as Egypt; and the concrete, everyday response to institutionalized terrorism — be it slavery or Jim-Crowism — was to use weapons of kinetic orality, passionate physicality, and combative spirituality to survive and dream of freedom. By kinetic orality, I mean dynamic repetitive and energetic rhetorical styles that cement communities, e.g., antiphonal call-and-response and linguistic innovations which accent fluid, improvisational identities that promote survival at almost any cost, e.g., Ellison's Rhinehart,[2] Trickster, and

[2]Rhinehart is a trickster figure in Ralph Ellison's *Invisible Man* (1952).

Brer Rabbit tales (opportunist, hustling styles). By passionate physicality, I mean bodily stylizations of the world by means of syncopations and polyrhythms that assert somebodiness in a society in which body lacks no public worth other than as a purely laboring metabolism. And by combative spirituality, I mean a sense of historical patience, subversive joy, and daily perseverance in an apparently hopeless and meaningless historical situation.

Black cultural practices emerge out of acknowledging the ragged edges of necessity constructed by white supremacist practices in North America during the age of Europe. These ragged edges of not being able to eat, not to have shelter, not to have health care, are infused into the strategies of Black cultural practice. Of course, all people have undergone social misery, yet people of African descent in the U.S. have done so in the most prosperous country in the world.

A distinctive feature of Black style is a projection of the self in performance. This is not simply a self-investment and self-improvement in music, rhetoric, and athletics; it also acknowledges radical contingency and even solicits challenge and danger. It is a spectacular self-imposed form of risk-ridden execution — be it a Charlie Parker solo, a Sarah Vaughn rendition, Muhammed Ali footwork and Jab (shuffle), a Martin Luther King, Jr. sermon, a Bill Cosby routine, a Julius Irving dunk shot, a Prince spectacle, or a James Brown (or Michael Jackson) dance performance. This feature not only results from what some anthropologists have called the African deification of accident — the *sense* of perennially being on a slippery tightrope — it also comes from the highly precarious historical situations in which Black people actually do find themselves. And with political and economic avenues usually blocked, Black resistance was channeled into culture.

CULTURE AS COMMODITY

Ironically, Black American culture has surfaced owing to three basic reasons. First, Black music — spirituals, gospels, blues, jazz, soul — is the unique cultural product created by Americans of any hue and so as the globalization of American culture escalated, Black music was given a vast international exposure. Second, as the consumption cycle of advanced multi-national corporate capitalism was speeded up, cultural production became more and more mass commodity production with stress not only on the new and fashionable, but also on the exotic and primitive. Black cultural products have served as a major source for European and Euro-American exotic interests that sometimes even issue from a healthy critique of the mechanistic, puritanical, utilitarian, and productivist aspects of modern life. Yet as Black cultural products become the commodified possession of Euro-Americans, they play a new role. For example, they speak less of the Black sense of absurdity in America and more of the universal values of love applicable to Blacks and whites alike. Needless to say, the sheer size of the white consumer market motivates Blacks to "crossover" by paying more attention to white tastes and sensibilities. Some crossover artists preserved their cultural integrity, e.g., Sly Stone in the 1960s, and Luther Vandross and Anita Baker in the 1980s. Yet the temptation to de-Africanize style and dilute Black culture for commercial success is often irresistible.

Thirdly, Black culture became identified with the first mass youth culture, a growing world consumer market since the 1950s. This youth culture responded to the eclipse of first world utopian energies and waning alternative political options by associating transcendence with music and sexual liberation. Given the European and Euro-American identification of Africans and Afro-Americans with sexual licentiousness and liberation, Black music became a symbol and facilitator of white sexual freedom. And with the sexualization of the advertising industry — an industry that now specializes in recycling recent past Black music hits — much of Black popular music can now be accepted by both rebellious youth and the cultural mainstream.

BLACK CULTURAL RESISTANCE

What then is the oppositional potential of black cultural practice and to what extent can we sensibly designate some of them postmodern? Of the three major forms of Black cultural products — musical, sermonic, and athletic — certainly the latter is the most incorporated and co-opted. Sermons, still far removed from most white observation and consumption, are limited to ecclesiastical and denominational constituencies making it difficult for ecumenical figures to remain rooted in Black institutional life yet attract people from outside their own constituencies. Yet when such figures do emerge — King, Malcolm X, Jackson[3] — they can generate tremendous energy due to the paucity of articulate and charismatic spokespersons on the American left and the potentially positive role charismatic leaders can play in empowering people to believe in themselves and act in unity against the powers that be.

Black music — packaged in radios or videos, records or live performances — helps keep alive some sense of the agency and creativity of oppressed people. Yet this sense is so vague and so far removed from organized political resistance that one must conclude that most of Black music here and abroad has simply become a major means by which U.S. record companies have colonized the leisure time of eager consumers — including me. Yet since Black music is so integral to Black life in America, it is difficult to imagine a Black resistance movement in which Black music does not play an important role.

What of literary artists, painters, and other Black intellectuals? Have I unduly neglected them? Are they possible producers of postmodern products, thereby making the terms partly relevant to Black life? Granted I have spent most of my time on Black mass culture. But this is because my interest in Black resistance leads me to look for the possible momentum of common Black people who suffer, work, and long for social freedom. The configuration of Black culture is such that literary artists, painters, and other intellectuals (mainly in the academy) are marginal — usually languishing at the interface of Black and white cultures or thoroughly ensconced in Euro-American settings. This lack of any organic link with most of Black life diminishes their value to Black resistance, no matter how militant their individual stances may

[3]West refers here to Jesse L. Jackson (b. 1941), African American minister, civil rights leader, and politician.

be. Their oppositional value exists primarily as dedicated teachers to anxiety-ridden students. In short, Black middle-class artists and intellectuals may play crucial roles, yet in a meditation on postmodernism and Black America, one must end rather than begin with their predicament since — given their material interests, professional ambitions, and cultural dispositions — they are most apt to uncritically emulate major moves in the Eurocentric postmodernism debate.

Alternative Contents

7. FORMALISM

8. HERMENEUTICS

14. QUEER THEORY

15. RACE AND ETHNICITY STUDIES

16. READER RESPONSE CRITICISM

17. RHETORICAL THEORY

18. STRUCTURALISM AND SEMIOTICS

Acknowledgments *(continued from page iv)*

Art:

Diego Rodriguez Velázquez, *Las Meninas*, 1656. Museo del Prado, Madrid, Spain. Erich Lessing/Art Resources, N.Y.

Text:

Chinua Achebe. "An Image of Africa," from *Hopes and Impediments* by Chinua Achebe, copyright © 1988 by Chinua Achebe. Used by permission of Doubleday, a division of Random House, Inc. Reprinted by permission of Harold Ober Associates Incorporated.

Aijaz Ahmad, "Jameson's Rhetoric of Otherness and the 'National Allegory,'" in *Social Text*, Volume 17, No. 4, pp. 3–4, 8–11. Copyright, 1987, Duke University Press. All rights reserved. Used by permission of the publisher.

Dante Alighieri, "Letter to Can Grande della Scala," Reprinted from *Literary Criticism of Dante Alighieri,* translated and edited by Robert S. Haller by permission of the University of Nebraska Press. Copyright © 1973 by the University of Nebraska Press. Copyright © renewed 2001 by the University of Nebraska Press. Reprinted by permission of the publisher.

Louis Althusser, "Ideology and Ideological State Apparatuses," from *Lenin and Philosophy, and Other Essays.* (London: New Left Books, 1971). Reprinted by permission of Verso Books.

Benedict Anderson, "The Origins of National Consciousness," from *Imagined Communities.* (London: Verso Books, 1991). Reprinted by permission of Verso Books.

Gloria Anzaldúa, "La conciencia de la mestiza: Towards a New Consciousness," from *Making Face, Making Soul: Haciendo Caras.* Copyright © 1990 edited by Gloria Anzaldúa. Reprinted by permission of Aunt Lute Books.

Aristotle, *Poetics* reprinted from *Aristotle's Poetics: A Translation and Commentary for Students of Literature* by Leon Golden and O. B. Hardison Jr., by permission of the publisher, Florida State University Press/University Presses of Florida, Tallahassee.

Nancy Armstrong, "Some Call It Fiction: On the Politics of Domesticity," from *The Other Perspective in Gender and Culture: Rewriting Women and the Symbolic,* by Nancy Armstrong, ed. Juliet Flower MacConnell. Copyright © 1990 Columbia University Press. Reprinted with permission of the publisher.

Erich Auerbach, "Odysseus' Scar," from *Mimesis.* © 1953 Princeton University Press, 1981 renewed Princeton University Press, 2003 paperback edition. Reprinted by permission of Princeton University Press.

John L. Austin, Reprinted by permission of the publisher from *How to Do Things with Words* by John L. Austin, edited by J. O. Urmson and Marina Sbisa, pp. 1–11, 94–108, Cambridge, Mass.: Harvard University Press, Copyright © 1962, 1975 by the President and Fellows of Harvard College.

Michael Awkward. "Appropriative Gestures: Theory and Afro-American Literary Criticism," from *Gender and Theory: Dialogues on Feminist Criticism.* Ed. Linda Kauffman.

(Oxford: Basil Blackwell, 1988). Reprinted by permission of Blackwell Publishing.

Houston A. Baker Jr., Excerpts from "Blues, Ideology, and Afro-American Literature," from *Blues, Ideology and Afro-American Theory.* Copyright © 1987 by The University of Chicago. Reprinted by permission of the author and The University of Chicago Press.

Mikhail Bakhtin, Excerpts from "Discourse in the Novel," from the *Dialogic Imagination: Four Essays* by M. M. Bakhtin, edited by Michael Holquist, translated by Caryl Emerson and Michael Holquist. Copyright © 1981. By permission of the University of Texas Press. Table from *Problems of Dostoevsky's Poetics* by Mikhail Bakhtin, translated by Caryl Emerson, published by the University of Minnesota Press, Minneapolis. Copyright © 1984 by the University of Minnesota. Reprinted by permission.

Roland Barthes, "The Death of the Author" and "From Work to Text" from *Image/Music/Text* by Roland Barthes, translated by Stephen Heath. English translation copyright © 1977 by Stephen Heath. Reprinted by permission of Hill and Wang, a division of Farrar, Straus and Giroux, L.L.C. "Striptease" from *Mythologies* by Roland Barthes, translated by Annette Lavers. Translation copyright © 1972 by Jonathan Cape Ltd. Reprinted by permission of Hill and Wang, a division of Farrar, Straus and Giroux, L.L.C. Reprinted by permission of The Random House Group Ltd. "The Structuralist Activity," from *Critical Essays.* Translated by Richard Howard. Evanston: Northwestern University Press, 1972, pp. 213–20. Reprinted by permission of the publisher.

Jean Baudrillard, "The Precession of Simulacra," from *Simulations.* Trans. Paul Foss, Paul Patton, and Philip Beitchman. Ed. by Sylvere Lotringer. (New York: Semiotext(e), 1983): 1–13, 23–30, 49–58, 66–70, plus notes on pp. 75–79. Reprinted with permission.

Nina Baym, "Melodramas of Beset Manhood: How Theories of American Fiction Exclude Women Authors," *American Quarterly* 33:2 (1981), 123–39. © The American Studies Association. Reprinted with permission of The Johns Hopkins University Press.

Simone de Beauvoir, From *The Second Sex* by Simone de Beauvoir, translated by H. M. Parshley, copyright 1952 and renewed 1980 by Alfred A. Knopf, a division of Random House, Inc. Used by permission of Alfred A. Knopf, a division of Random House, Inc.

Walter Benjamin, "The Work of Art in the Age of Mechanical Reproduction" from *Illuminations,* copyright © 1968 by Hannah Arendt, reprinted by permission of Harcourt, Inc.

Lauren Berlant and Michael Warner, "Sex in Public," from *Critical Inquiry* 24 (Winter 1998). Copyright © 1998 by the University of Chicago. Reprinted by permission of the authors and the University of Chicago Press.

Homi K. Bhabha, Copyright © 1994 From "Signs Taken for Wonders: Questions of Ambivalence and Authority under a Tree Outside Delhi, May 1817," from *The Location of Culture* by Homi K. Bhabha. Reproduced by permission of Routledge/Taylor & Francis Books, Inc. Reprinted with permission of the author.

Harold Bloom, "Pages 5–16," from *The Anxiety of Influence: A Theory of Poetry 2e* by Harold Bloom, copyright © 1997 by Oxford University Press, Inc. Used by permission of Oxford University Press, Inc.

Wayne Booth, "Control of Distance in Jane Austen's *Emma*," from *The Rhetoric of Fiction.* Copyright © 1961, 1983 by the University of Chicago. Reprinted by permission of the author and the University of Chicago Press.

Pierre Bourdieu, Reprinted by permission of the publisher from *Distinction: A Social Critique of the Judgment of Taste* by Pierre Bourdieu, translated by Richard Nice, p. 107, Cambridge, Mass.: Harvard University Press, Copyright © 1984 by the President and Fellows of Harvard College and Routledge and Kegan Paul, Ltd.

Bertolt Brecht, "The Popular and the Realistic," from *Brecht on Theatre,* edited and translated by John Willett. Translation copyright © 1964, renewed 1992 by John Willett. Reprinted by permission of Hill and Wang, a division of Farrar, Straus and Giroux, L.L.C. Reprinted by permission of Methuen Publishing Limited.

Cleanth Brooks, "Irony as Principle of Structure," from *Literary Opinion in America,* edited by Morton Dauwen Zobel. Reprinted by permission of the author. "My Credo." First published in *The Kenyon Review,* Winter 1951, OS Vol. XIII, No. 1, Copyright *The Kenyon Review.* Reprinted by permission of *The Kenyon Review.*

Peter Brooks, "Freud's Masterplot," in *Yale French Studies* 55/56 (1977). Copyright © 1977 by *Yale French Studies.* Reprinted by permission of the publisher.

Lawrence Buell, "The Ecocritical Insurgency," from *New Literary History.* Copyright © 1999 by The University of Virginia. By permission of Lawrence Buell.

Kenneth Burke, "Literature as Equipment for Living," from *The Philosophy of Literary Form,* 3rd ed. rev., by Kenneth Burke. Copyright © 1973 by the Regents of the University of California. Reprinted by permission of the University of California Press. "Symbolic Action in a Poem by Keats," from *A Grammar of Motives* by Kenneth Burke. Copyright © 1969 Kenneth Burke and by the Regents of the University of California. Reprinted by permission of the University of California Press.

Judith Butler, Copyright © 1991 From "Imitation and Gender Insubordination," from *Inside/Out: Lesbian Theories, Gay Theories,* by Judith Butler/edited by Diana Fuss. Reproduced by permission of Routledge/Taylor & Francis Books, Inc. Reprinted with permission of the author.

Michel de Certeau, "Walking in the City," from *The Practice of Everyday Life,* translated by Stephen Rendall. Copyright © 1984 by the Regents of the University of California. Reprinted by permission of the University of California Press.

Rey Chow, "The Interruption of Referentiality: Poststructuralism and the Conundrum of Critical Multiculturalism," in *South Atlantic Quarterly,* Volume 101, No. 1, pp. 171–86. Copyright, 2002, Duke University Press. All rights reserved. Used by permission of the publisher.

Barbara Christian, "The Race for Theory," from *Cultural Critique* (Spring 1987) pp. 51–63. Copyright © 1987 by the University of Minnesota. Reprinted by permission of the University of Minnesota Press.

Hélène Cixous, "The Laugh of the Medusa," translated by Keith Cohen & Paula Cohen, reprinted from *Signs I* (1976) by permission of the translators, the author, and the University of Chicago Press. Copyright © 1976 by the University of Chicago Press.

Jonathan Culler, "Reading as a Woman," from *On Deconstruction: Theory and Criticism after Structuralism,* by Jonathan Culler. Copyright © 1982 by Cornell University. Used by permission of the publisher, Cornell University Press.

Gilles Deleuze and Félix Guattari, "What Is a Minor Literature?" from *Kafka: Toward a Minor Literature,* translated by Dana Polan. Copyright © 1986 by the University of Minnesota. Originally published as *Kafka: Pour une literature mineure.* Copyright © 1975 by Les Éditions de Minuit, Paris. Reprinted by permission of the University of Minnesota Press.

Paul de Man, "Semiology and Rhetoric" from *Diacritics* 3:3 (Fall 1973). Reprinted by permission of the Johns Hopkins University Press.

Jacques Derrida, "Differance," from *Speech and Phenomena and Other Essays on Husserl's Theory of Signs.* Translated by David B. Allison. Evanston: Northwestern University Press, 1979, pp. 129–60. Reprinted by permission of the publisher. "Structure, Sign, and Play in the Discourse of the Human Sciences," from *The Structuralist Controversy: The Languages of Criticism and the Science of Man,* edited by Richard Macksey and Eugenio Donato, published by the Johns Hopkins University Press. Reprinted by permission of the publisher.

Terry Eagleton, "Categories for a Materialist Criticism," from *Criticism and Ideology: A Study in Marxist Literary Theory.* (Verso/NLB, 1976). Reprinted with permission of Verso Books. Copyright © 1987 From "Response" from *Men in Feminism* by Terry Eagleton/edited by Alice Jardine and Paul Smith. Reproduced by permission of Routledge/Taylor & Francis Books, Inc. Reprinted with permission of the author.

Umberto Eco, "The Myth of Superman," translated by Natalie Chilton from *The Role of the Reader: Explorations in the Semiotics of Texts* by Umberto Eco. Reprinted by permission of Indiana University Press.

T. S. Eliot, "Tradition and the Individual Talent," from *Selected Works* by T. S. Eliot. Published by Faber and Faber Ltd. Reprinted for distribution in Canada by permission of Faber and Faber Ltd.

Judith Fetterley, "Introduction: On the Politics of Literature" from *The Resisting Reader: A Feminist Approach to American Fiction* by Judith Fetterley. Copyright © by Judith Fetterley. Published by Indiana University Press. Reprinted by permission of Indiana University Press.

Stanley Fish, "How to Recognize a Poem When You See One" reprinted by permission of the publisher from *Is There a Text in This Class?: The Authority of Interpretive Communities* by Stanley Fish, pp. 322–37, Cambridge, Mass.: Harvard University Press, Copyright © 1980 by the President and Fellows of Harvard College.

Michel Foucault, "What Is an Author?" Reprinted from Michel Foucault, "What Is an Author?" in *Language, Counter-Memory, Practice: Selected Essays and Interviews*. Edited by Donald F. Bouchard. Copyright © 1977 by Cornell University. Used by permission of the publisher, Cornell University Press. "Las Meninas," chapter 1 of *The Order of Things: An Archaeology of the Human Sciences*, copyright © 1970 Random House; original French edition copyright © 1966 by Éditions Gallímard. Reprinted by permission of the Estate of Michel Foucault and Georges Borchardt, Inc. Excerpt from *The History of Sexuality*, Volume I. An Introduction by Michel Foucault, translated by Robert Hurley, copyright © 1978 Random House; original French edition copyright © 1976 Éditions Gallímard. Reprinted by permission of the Estate of Michel Foucault and Georges Borchardt, Inc.

Sigmund Freud, Excerpt from "The Dream-Work" from *The Interpretation of Dreams*. Translated by A. A. Brill. New York: Modern Library, 1950. Reprinted by permission of the estate of A. A. Brill. "Medusa's Head" from *The Collected Papers*, Volume 2 by Sigmund Freud. Authorized translation under the supervision of Joan Riviere. Published by Basic Books, Inc. by arrangement with the Hogarth Press, Ltd. and the Institute of Psycho-Analysis, London. Reprinted by permission of Basic Books, a member of Perseus Books, L.L.C. From Sigmund Freud © Copyrights, The Institute of Psycho-Analysis and The Hogarth Press for permission to quote from *The Standard Edition of the Complete Psychological Works of Sigmund Freud* translated and edited by James Strachey. Reprinted by permission of The Random House Group Ltd. "The Relation of the Poet to Daydreaming," from *The Collected Papers*, Volume 4 by Sigmund Freud. Authorized translation under the supervision of Joan Riviere. Published by Basic Books, Inc. by arrangement with The Hogarth Press, Ltd. and The Institute of Psycho-Analysis, London. Reprinted by permission of Basic Books, a member of Perseus Books, L.L.C. Reprinted by permission of The Random House Group Ltd. "The Uncanny" from *The Collected Papers*, Volume 4 by Sigmund Freud. Authorized translation under the supervision of Joan Riviere. Published by Basic Books, Inc. by arrangement with the Hogarth Press, Ltd. and the Institute of Psycho-Analysis, London. Reprinted by permission of Basic Books, a member of Perseus Books, L.L.C. From Sigmund Freud © Copyrights, The Institute of Psycho-Analysis and The Hogarth Press for permission to quote from *The Standard Edition of the Complete Psychological Works of Sigmund Freud* translated and edited by James Strachey. Reprinted by permission of The Random House Group Ltd.

Northrop Frye, "The Archetypes of Literature" from *Fables of Identity: Studies in Poetic Mythology*, copyright © 1963 by Harcourt, Inc. and renewed 1991 by Jane Widdicombe.

Hans Georg Gadamer, "The Elevation of the Historicity of Understanding to the Status of Hermeneutical Principle," from *Truth and Method*. Copyright second review edition © 1989 by the Crossroad Publishing Company. Reprinted by permission of The Continuum International Publishing Group.

Henry Louis Gates Jr., "Writing, 'Race,' and the Difference it Makes," from *Loose Canons: Notes on the Cultural Wars* by Henry Louis Gates Jr., copyright © 1992 by Henry Louis Gates Jr. Used by permission of Oxford University Press, Inc. "Preface to Blackness: Text and Pretext," Reprinted by permission of the Modern Language Association of America from *Afro-American Literature: The Reconstruction of Instruction*. Copyright © 1978.

Clifford Geertz, "Thick Description: Toward an Interpretive Theory of Culture," from *The Interpretation of Cultures* by Clifford Geertz. Copyright © 1973 by Basic Books, Inc. Reprinted by permission of Basic Books, a member of Perseus Books, L.L.C.

Sandra M. Gilbert and Susan Gubar, "Infection in the Sentence: The Woman Writer and the Anxiety of Authorship," from *The Madwoman in the Attic: The Woman Writer and the Nineteenth Century Literary Imagination* by Sandra Gilbert and Susan Gubar, published by Yale University Press. Copyright © 1979 Yale University Press. Reprinted by permission of Yale University Press.

Stephen Greenblatt, Introduction and "*King Lear* and Harsnett's 'Devil Fiction,'" from the special issue of *Genre: The Power of Forms in the English Renaissance*, edited by Stephen Greenblatt. Copyright © 1982 by the University of Oklahoma. Reprinted by permission.

John Guillory, excerpt from *Cultural Capital: The Problem of Literary Canon Formation*. Copyright © 1993 by the University of Chicago. Reprinted by permission of the author and the University of Chicago Press.

Jürgen Habermas, "Modernity versus Postmodernity." This article appeared originally in *New German Critique* 22 (Winter, 1981). Reprinted by permission of the publisher.

Judith Halberstam, "An Introduction to Female Masculinity," in *Female Masculinity*, pp. 1–29. Copyright, 1998, Duke University Press. All rights reserved. Used by permission of the publisher.

Stuart Hall, "Cultural Studies: Two Paradigms," from *Media, Culture and Society*, Vol. 2. Reproduced with permission from Stuart Hall, *Media, Culture and Society*, © Sage Publications, 1980, by permission of Sage Publications Ltd.

Donna Haraway, "A Cyborg Manifesto: Science, Technology, and Socialist-Feminism in the Late Twentieth Century," from *Simians, Cyborgs and Women: The Reinvention of Nature* (Taylor & Francis: 1991). Reprinted by permission of the author.

Georg Wilhelm Friedrich Hegel, "Introduction to the Philosophy of Fine Art." Reprinted with the permission of Scribner, a Division of Simon & Schuster Adult Publishing Group, from *Hegel: Selections*, edited by J. Lowenberg. Copyright © 1929 by Charles Scribner's Sons; copyright renewed 1957. All rights reserved.

Martin Heidegger, "Hölderlin and the Essence of Poetry." Reprinted from *Existence and Being* by Martin Heidegger, translated by Douglas Scott, introduction by Werner Brock, published by Henry Regnery, 1949.

Guy Hocquenghem, "Homosexual Desire [excerpt only]," in *Homosexual Desire*, pp. 121–32. Copyright, 1993, Duke University Press. All rights reserved. Used by permission of the publisher.

Norman N. Holland, "The Question: Who Reads What How?" from *5 Readers Reading* by Norman N. Holland, published by Yale University Press. Copyright © 1975 Yale University. Reprinted by permission of Yale University Press.

bell hooks, "Postmodern Blackness," from *Yearning: Race, Gender, and Cultural Politics.* Boston: South End Press, 1990. Reprinted by permission of the publisher. From Toronto: Between the Lines Publishing, Copyright © 1990. Reprinted by permission of the publisher.

Horace, "The Art of Poetry," from *Satires and Epistles of Horace,* edited and translated by Smith Palmer Bovie. Copyright © 1959 by the University of Chicago. Reprinted by permission of the translator and the University of Chicago Press.

Max Horkheimer and Theodor W. Adorno, "The Culture Industry: Enlightenment as Mass Deception," from *Dialectic of Enlightenment.* Translated by John Cumming. Copyright © English translation 1972 by Herder and Herder Inc. Reprinted by permission of The Continuum International Publishing Group.

Linda Hutcheon, Copyright © 1988 from "Theorizing the Postmodern: Toward a Poetics" from *A Poetics of Postmodernism: History, Theory, Fiction* by Linda Hutcheon. Reproduced by permission of Routledge/Taylor & Francis Books, Inc. Reprinted with permission of the author.

Wolfgang Iser, "The Reading Process: A Phenomenological Approach," from *The Implied Reader,* published by the Johns Hopkins University Press. Reprinted by permission of the publisher.

Roman Jakobson, "Linguistics and Poetics," from *Style in Language.* Ed. Thomas Sebeok. Copyright © 1960. Reprinted by permission of MIT Press.

Fredric Jameson, From *The Political Unconscious: Narrative as a Socially Symbolic Act,* by Fredric Jameson. Copyright © 1981 by Cornell University. Used by permission of the publisher, Cornell University Press. "Postmodernism and Consumer Society," from *The Cultural Turn: Selected Writings on the Postmodern, 1983–1998.* (Verso Books, 1998). Reprinted by permission of Verso Books. "Third World Literature in the Era of Multinational Capitalism," in *Social Text,* Volume 15, No. 3, pp. 65–66, 69. Copyright, 1986, *Social Text.* All rights reserved. Used by permission of the publisher. "A Brief Response [excerpt only]," in *Social Text,* Volume 17, No. 1, pp. 26–27. Copyright, 1987, Duke University Press. All rights reserved. Used by permission of the publisher.

Hans Robert Jauss, ["The Three Horizons of Reading,"] from "The Poetic Text within the Change of Horizons of Reading: The Example of Baudelaire's 'Spleen II,'" in *Toward an Aesthetic of Reception.* Copyright © 1982 by the University of Minnesota. Reprinted by permission of the University of Minnesota Press.

Carl Gustav Jung, "On the Relation of Analytical Psychology to Poetry," from *The Collected Works of C. G. Jung,* translated by R. F. C. Hull, Bollingen Series XX, Vol. 15. © Copyright 1966 by Princeton University Press. Jung, C. G., *The Collected Works of C. G. Jung.* 1977 Princeton University Press. Reprinted by permission of Princeton University Press. "The Principle Archetypes," from *The Collected Works of C. G. Jung,* translated by R. F. C. Hull, Bollingen Series XX, Vol. 9. © Copyright 1959 Princeton University Press. Jung, C. G., *The Collected Works of C. G. Jung.* 1977 Princeton University Press. Reprinted by permission of Princeton University Press.

Immanuel Kant, Excerpt from *Critique of Judgment.* Reprinted and edited with the permission of The Free Press, a Division of Simon & Schuster Adult Publishing Group, from *Critique of Judgment* by Immanuel Kant, translated by J. H. Bernard. Copyright © 1951 by Hafner Press; copyright renewed 1979. All rights reserved.

Laura Kipnis, Copyright © 1992 From "(Male) Desire and (Female) Disgust: Reading *Hustler,*" from *Cultural Studies,* by Laura Kipnis/Ed. Grossberg et al. Reproduced by permission of Routledge/Taylor & Francis Books, Inc. Reprinted with permission of the author.

Annette Kolodny, "Dancing through the Minefield: Some Observations on the Theory, Practice, and Politics of a Feminist Literary Criticism." Copyright © 1979 by Annette Kolodny; all rights reserved. Reprinted by permission of the author.

Julia Kristeva, "Women's Time," translated by Alice Jardine and Harry Blake. *Signs: Journal of Women in Culture and Society,* 1981. Vol. 7, no. 1. © 1981 by The University of Chicago. Reprinted by permission of the author and The University of Chicago Press.

Stephen F. Kruger, "Claiming the Pardoner: Toward a Gay Reading of Chaucer's *Pardoner's Tale,*" from *Exemplaria: A Journal of Theory in Medieval and Renaissance Studies* 6:1 (Spring 1994). Copyright © 1994 by Pegasus Press. Reproduced by permission.

Jacques Lacan, "The Mirror Stage as Formative of the Function of the I" and "The Agency of the Letter in the Unconscious or Reason Since Freud" by Jacques Lacan, translated by Alan Sheridan, from *Écrits: A Selection* by Jacques Lacan, translated by Alan Sheridan. Copyright © 1966 by Editions du Seuil. English translation copyright © 1977 by Tavistock Publications. Used by permission of W. W. Norton & Company, Inc. "The Meaning of the Phallus," from *Feminine Sexuality* by Jacques Lacan, edited by Juliet Mitchell & J. Rose, translated by Jacqueline Rose. Copyright © 1982 by Jacqueline Rose. Copyright © 1966, 1968, 1975 by Editions de Seuil. Copyright 1975 by Le Graphe. Used by permission of W. W. Norton & Company, Inc.

Jay Ladin, "'So Anthracite, to live': Emily Dickinson and American Literary History," *Emily Dickinson Journal* 13:1 (2004), 19–21. © The Johns Hopkins University Press. Reprinted with permission of The Johns Hopkins University Press.

F. R. Leavis, from *The Great Tradition* by F. R. Leavis, published by Chatto & Windus. Reprinted by permission of The Random House Group Ltd.

Frank Lentricchia, *Ariel and the Police.* © 1988. Reprinted by permission of The University of Wisconsin Press.

Claude Lévi-Strauss. "The Structural Study of Myth," from *Structural Anthropology,* Volume I by Claude Lévi-Strauss. English translation copyright © 1963 by Basic

Books, Inc. Reprinted by permission of Basic Books, a member of Perseus Books, L.L.C.

Lawrence Lipking, "The Practice of Theory." Reprinted by permission of the Modern Language Association of America from *ADE Bulletin 76*. Copyright © 1983.

Georg Lukács, "The Ideology of Modernism" [pp. 17–46] from *Realism in Our Time: Literature and the Class Struggle*. Copyright © 1962 by Merlin Press Ltd. Introduction copyright © 1964 by George Steiner. Reprinted by permission of the Merlin Press, PO Box 30705, London WC2E 8QD, *www.merlinpress.co.uk*. Reprinted by permission of HarperCollins Publishers Inc.

Jean-François Lyotard, "Defining the Postmodern," from *Postmodernism*, pp. 6–7 *ICA Documents 4*. Geoff Bennington, translator. Copyright © 1986 by Institute of Contemporary Arts Publications. We have made diligent efforts to contact the copyright holder to obtain permission to reprint this selection. If you have information that would help us, please write to Bedford/St. Martin's, 75 Arlington Street, Boston, MA 02116.

Karl Marx, "Consciousness Derived from Material Conditions," from *The German Ideology* by Karl Marx. Reprinted by permission of International Publishers Co., New York. "The Alienation of Labor," translated by Richard Hooker. Copyright © 1996. We have made diligent efforts to contact the copyright holder to obtain permission to reprint this selection. If you have information that would help us, please write to Bedford/St. Martin's, 75 Arlington Street, Boston, MA 02116.

Deborah McDowell, from "Recycling: Race, Gender, and the Practice of Theory," ed. Ralph Cohen. *Studies in Historical Change*. Copyright © 1992 by the University of Virginia Press. Reprinted with permission of the University of Virginia Press.

Toril Moi, "Women Writing and Writing About Women" by Toril Moi, from *Sexual/Textual Politics: Feminist Literary Theory*. Copyright © 1994 by Routledge. Reprinted by permission of Taylor & Francis Group Ltd.

Meaghan Morris, "Things to Do with Shopping Centres," from *Grafts: Feminist Cultural Criticism*. Ed. Susan Sheridan. (Verso Books, 1989). Reprinted by permission of Verso Books.

Toni Morrison, from *Playing in the Dark: Whiteness and the Literary Imagination*. Reprinted by permission of International Creative Management, Inc. Copyright © 1992 by Toni Morrison.

Laura Mulvey, "Visual Pleasure and Narrative Cinema," from *Screen* 16:3 (1975). Reprinted with permission of the author.

Friedrich Nietzsche. From *Birth of Tragedy and the Case of Wagner* by Friedrich Nietzsche, translated by Walter Kauffman, copyright © 1967 by Walter Kauffman. Used by permission of Random House, Inc. From *Twilight of the Idols: Or, How to Philosophize with a Hammer; The Anti-Christ* by Friedrich Nietzsche, translated by R. J. Hollingdale (Penguin Classics, 1968), pp. 72–74, 78–79, 81–82. Copyright © R. J. Hollingdale, 1968. Reproduced by permission of Penguin Books Ltd. "On Truth and Lie in an Extra-Moral Sense," translated by Harry Heuser. Copyright © 2005 Bedford/St. Martin's. Reprinted by permission of the translator.

Ngugi wa Thiong'o. "Euphonism, Universities, and the Magic Fountain: The Future of African Literature and Scholarship," from *Research in African Literatures*, Spring 2000, vol. 31, issue 1. Copyright © 2000 Indiana University Press.

Martha Nussbaum, Excerpts from "The Professor of Parody," *New Republic*. V. 220, no. 8. Excerpted by permission of *The New Republic*, copyright © 1999, *The New Republic*, L.L.C.

James Phelan, "Data, Danda, and Disagreement." *Diacritics* 13:2 (1983), 39–45. © The Johns Hopkins University Press. Reprinted with permission of The Johns Hopkins University Press.

Christine de Pisan. From "La Querelle de la Rose": Letters and Documents edited and translated by Joseph L. Baird and John R. Kane. Copyright © 1978 by the University of North Carolina Press. Published for the North Carolina Studies in the Romance Languages and Literatures, no. 199. Used by permission of the publisher.

Plato, from *Plato: Phaedrus, Ion, Gorgias, and Symposium, with Passages from the Republic and Laws*, by Lane Cooper. Copyright © 1938 by Lane Cooper. Used by permission of the publisher, Cornell University Press.

Plotinus, "On the Intellectual Beauty," from *Plotinus: The Enneads*, edited by B. S. Page, translation by Stephen Mackenna. Published by Faber and Faber Ltd. Reprinted with permission of the publisher.

Vladimir Propp. Excerpt from "The Morphology of the Folktale," originally published in *Readings in Russian Poetics*. Edited and translated by Ladislaw Matejka and Krystyna Pomorska. (Cambridge: MIT Press, 1978): 94–114. Reprinted by permission of Ladislaw Matejka.

Peter Rabinowitz, "Who Is Reading?" and "Rules of Reading," pages 20–46 from *Before Reading: Narrative Conventions and the Politics of Interpretation* by Peter J. Rabinowitz. Copyright © 1986 by Peter J. Rabinowitz. Used by permission of the author.

I. A. Richards, "The Two Uses of Language" and "Poetry and Beliefs" from *Principles of Literary Criticism*, copyright © 1925 by Harcourt, Inc. Reprinted by permission of the publisher.

Gayle Rubin, "The Traffic in Women: Notes on the 'Political Economy' of Sex," from *Toward an Anthropology of Women*. Rayna Reiter, ed. Copyright © 1975 by *Monthly Review Press*. Reprinted by permission of the author. All rights reserved.

Edward Said, From *Orientalism* by Edward W. Said, copyright © 1978 by Edward W. Said. Used by permission of Pantheon Books, a division of Random House, Inc.

Jean-Paul Sartre, "Why Write?" from *What Is Literature?* by Jean-Paul Sartre, translated by Bernard Frechtman. Reprinted by permission of The Philosophical Library, New York.

Ferdinand de Saussure, "Nature of the Linguistic Sign," pages 65–70 plus pages 114–127 from *Course in General Linguistics* by Ferdinand de Saussure. Reprinted by permission of The Philosophical Library, New York.

Elaine Scarry. "On Vivacity: The Difference between Daydreaming and Imagining-Under-Authorial-Instruction,"

Representations, Vol 52, No. 1: 1–26. © 1995, The Regents of the University of California. All rights reserved. Used by permission. Reprinted by permission of the author. For elaborations of the ideas in this essay please see Elaine Scarry's *Dreaming by the Book*, Princeton: Princeton University Press, 2001.

Friedrich von Schiller, from "On Naïve and Sentimental Poetry," from *Two Essays by Friedrich von Schiller*, translated by Julias A. Elias. Copyright © 1966 by Frederick Ungar Publishing Company. Reprinted by permission of the publisher.

Eve Kosofsky Sedgwick. Excerpt from *Epistemology of the Closet*, pages 48–54. Copyright © 1990 by the Regents of the University of California. Reprinted by permission of the University of California Press. "Introduction: Homosocial Desire," from *Between Men: English Literature and Male Homosocial Desire*, by Eve Kosofsky Sedgwick. Copyright © 1985 Columbia University Press. Reprinted with permission of the publisher.

Victor Shklovsky, "Art as Technique," reproduced from *Russian Formalist Criticism: Four Essays* translated and with an introduction by Lee T. Lemon and Marion J. Reis by permission of the University of Nebraska Press. Copyright © 1965 by the University of Nebraska Press. Copyright © renewed 1993 by the University of Nebraska Press. Reprinted by permission of the publisher.

Elaine Showalter, Copyright © 1987 "Critical Cross-Dressing: Male Feminists and the Woman of the Year," and "In Reply," from *Men in Feminism* by Elaine Showalter/Eds. Alice Jardine and Paul Smith. Reproduced by permission of Routledge/Taylor & Francis Books, Inc. Reprinted with permission of the author.

Barbara Smith, "Toward a Black Feminist Criticism," from *The Truth That Never Hurts*. Copyright © 1998 by Barbara Smith. Reprinted by permission of Rutgers University Press.

Barbara Herrnstein Smith, "Contingencies of Value," from *Critical Inquiry* 10:1 (1983). Copyright © 1983 by the University of Chicago. Reprinted by permission of the author and the University of Chicago Press.

Susan Sontag, "Against Interpretation," from *Against Interpretation* by Susan Sontag. Copyright © 1964, 1966, renewed 1994 by Susan Sontag. Reprinted by permission of Farrar, Straus and Giroux, L.L.C.

Gayatri Chakravorty Spivak, from "Introduction" to *Selected Subaltern Studies*. Reproduced by permission of Oxford University Press India, New Delhi. From "Three Women's Texts and a Critique of Imperialism," from *Critical Inquiry*, 12:1 (Autumn 1985). Reprinted by permission of the author.

Germaine de Staël, "Essays on Fictions" and "On Women Writers," from *An Extraordinary Woman*, by Germaine de Staël, ed. Vivian Folkenflik. Copyright © 1987 Columbia University Press. Reprinted with permission of the publisher.

Leo Tolstoy, Excerpt from "What Is Art?" from *Kreutzer Sonata and Other Stories,* by Leo Tolstoy. Copyright © Oxford University Press 1998. By permission of Oxford University Press.

Mark Turner, "Poetry: Metaphor and the Conceptual Context of Invention," in *Poetics Today,* Volume 11, No. 3, pp. 463–82. Copyright, 1990, Porter Institute for Poetics and Semiotics, Tel Aviv University. All rights reserved. Used by permission of the publisher.

Cornel West, "Postmodernism and Black America," from *Zeta Magazine* 1 (1987): 27–29. Reprinted by permission of the author.

Hayden White, "The Historical Text as Literary Artifact," originally published in *Clio* 3:3 (1974). Reprinted by permission of publisher.

Raymond Williams, Excerpt from *Marxism and Literature.* Copyright © Oxford University Press 1977. By permission of Oxford University Press. From *Culture and Society 1780–1950*, by Raymond Williams. Copyright © 1958 Columbia University Press. Reprinted with permission of the publisher.

Edmund Wilson, "Dickens: The Two Scrooges" from *The Wound and the Bow* by Edmund Wilson. Copyright © 1978 by Edmund Wilson. Reprinted by permission of Farrar, Straus and Giroux, L.L.C.

W. K. Wimsatt and Monroe C. Beardsley, "The Intentional Fallacy," from *The Verbal Icon* by William K. Wimsatt and Monroe Beardsley. Copyright © 1954 by the University Press of Kentucky. Copyright renewed 1982 by Margaret H. Wimsatt. Reprinted by permission.

Monique Wittig, "One Is Not Born a Woman," from *The Straight Mind* by Monique Wittig. Copyright © 1992 by Monique Wittig. Reprinted by permission of Beacon Press, Boston.

Virginia Woolf, "Shakespeare's Sister," "Austen–Brontë–Eliot," and "The Androgynous Vision" from *A Room of One's Own* by Virginia Woolf, copyright © 1929 by Harcourt, Inc. and renewed 1957 by Leonard Woolf. Reprinted by permission of the publisher.

Slavoj Žižek, "Courtly Love, or, Woman as Thing," from *The Metastases of Enjoyment.* (London: Verso Books, 1994) Reprinted by permission of Verso Books.

Lisa Zunshine, "Theory of Mind and Experimental Representations of Fictional Consciousness," from *Narrative* Vol. 11, No. 3 (October 2003): 270–87. Reprinted with permission of The Ohio State University Press. All rights reserved.

Index

Algorithms: in Lacan, 1115, 1154

Alienation: in Barthes, 876; in Benjamin, 1241; in Lacan, 1113; in Lukács, 1229; in Marx, 398, 400–03, 405, 1969; in Wittig, 1641

Allegories of reading: in De Man, 888–90; in Lipking, 898

Allegory, 742; in Benjamin, 1229, 1231; in Christine de Pisan, 130; in Dante, 120, 122; in Eagleton, 1597; in Eco, 956; in Jameson, 1834–35; in Jung, 553; in Lukács, 1229–30; in Sidney, 143, 150; in Sontag, 741

Allochronic discourse: in Fabian, 1917–18

Alonso, Carlow, 1917

Alterity: in Butler, 1717; in Cixous, 1649, 1651, 1654–55; in Derrida, 945; in Irigaray, 1613; in Jauss, 987

Alternative cinema, 1173

Alternative hegemony: in Jameson, 1297; in Williams, 1280, 1282

Althusser, Louis, 12, 976, 1111–14, 1200, 1206–08, 1210, 1277, 1291, 1295, 1299–1300, 1306, 1323, 1325, 1404, 1411–13, 1415, 1512, 1677, 1808, 1838; biography, 1263–64; *Ideology and Ideological State Apparatuses,* **1264–72;** *Reading Capital,* 1206

Altieri, Charles, 1554

Ambiguity, 161, 739, 969; in Anzaldúa, 1851; in Aristotle, 80; in Peter Brooks, 1165; in Dante, 121; in Empson, 754, 758; in Fish, 966; in New Criticism, 750; in Pope, 198; in Rabinowitz, 1052

American Dream, 1794

Ammons, A. R., 1159, 1439

Amo, Wilhelm, 1895

Amphion, 337

Anacreon, 227, 328, 1067, 1073

Anagnorisis. *See* Recognition

Anagogy: in Dante, 122

Anal phase: in Freud, 1107, 1110, 1112

Analysis: in Arnold, 416; in Coleridge, 327; in Freud, 1109; in Shelley, 344, 346

Anamorphosis: in Lacan, 1186

Ancients vs. moderns: in Dryden, 165–68, 172, 175, 180; in Johnson, 215–16; in Schiller, 301–02; in Swift, 160

Anderson, Benedict, 1037, 1758; biography, 1814; **"The Origins of National Consciousness," 1815–20**

Anderson, Sherwood, 1830; "I Want to Know Why," 972, 1036, 1041

Andrewes, Lancelot, 535

Androgyny, 1614; in Cixous, 1616, 1649; in Showalter, 1511; in Woolf, 598, 1511

Ang, Ien, 1323

Angel in the house: in Gilbert and Gubar, 1536

Anglo-American feminist literary criticism. *See* Feminist literary criticism

Anima: in Jung, 543, 556–60, 562–63, 1124

Animus: in Jung, 543, 556–57, 559–60, 562

Annales school, 1326, 1329, 1449

Anquetil-Duperron, Abraham Hyacinthe, 1812

Anthropology: in Frye, 696–97, 699; in Geertz, 1368; in Lévi-Strauss, 860

Anticipation: in Iser, 1005–07, 1012

Anti-Semitism, 1624, 1700

Antonioni, Michelangelo, 744

Anxiety of authorship, 1533; in Gilbert and Gubar, 1511, 1532, 1533–43, 1595

Anxiety of influence: in Bloom, 1111, 1158–59, 1534; in Eliot, 536; in Gilbert and Gubar, 1111

Anxiety, spatial: in Gilbert and Gubar, 1539–44

Anzaldúa, Gloria, 1768, 1775; and liminality, 1768; biography, 1850; **"La concienza de la mestiza," 1850–58**

Aphanisis, 1150; in Lacan, 1116

Aphasia, 1130

Apollinaire, Guillaume, 825, 988

Apollo, 437; in Nietzsche, 439–41, 443, 448

Aporia, 836, 1295; and deconstruction, 836

Appiah, Kwame Anthony, 1476, 1901–02

Application: as horizon, in Jauss, 985

Appreciation: aesthetic, in Jauss, 986

Apuleius, 156

Aquinas, St. Thomas, 120, 903, 1026, 1861

Archaeology: in Foucault, 1328; in Lévi-Strauss, 863

Archaic (cultural formations): in Williams, 1283, 1305

Arché-écriture: in Derrida, 829

Archetypes, 5, 1780, anima, 543; animus, 543; in Baym, 1528; in Eco, 952; in Frye, 691–92, 696–98, 700, 896; in Jung, 542, 552, 556–59, 561, 563–64, 861; in Plotinus, 112, 115, 118; mask, 543; quest, 543; shadow, 543; spirit, 543. *See also* specific archetypes: Anima; Animus; Night-sea-journey; Shadow; Spirit

Archilochus, 39–40, 86, 104, 106, 444–45

Architectonic: in Sidney, 133, 140

Architecture, 1920–23; in Benjamin, 1247; in Hegel, 372, 380, 383; in Jameson, 1956, 1961–64; in Lyotard 1924

Arendt, Hannah, 612, 1686

Aries, Philippe, 1326, 1729

Ariosto, Ludovico, 237, 340, 356, 509; *Orlando Furioso,* 138, 357, 360

Aristophanes, 61, 166, 168–69, 172, 186, 338, 493

Aristotle, 1, 4, 6–8, 11–12, 25, 55–58, 82–83, 95, 131–33, 155, 157, 161–62, 166–67, 169–71, 175, 201, 203, 208, 211, 221, 242, 247, 312, 372, 412, 477, 479, 491, 576, 639, 695, 732, 740, 759–60, 808, 813, 822, 880, 897, 906, 911, 951, 1017, 1064, 1144, 1162, 1219, 1266, 1331, 1396, 1475, 1549, 1861; *De Anima,* 1061; materialism, 55; *Metaphysics,* 121, 123; *Nicomachean Ethics,* 145; **Poetics, 59–81,** 139–40, 143, 145, 148–49, 153, 161, 167, 175, 223, 412, 434, 448, 746, 770, 952, 962, 1006, 1161–62, 1164, 1396; *Politics,* 58; *Posterior Analytics,* 56; problematic method, 55; *Rhetoric,* 73, 1080; style, 76

Armah, Ayi Kwei, 1825

Armstrong, Nancy, 1330, 1515; biography, 1418; *Desire and Domestic Fiction,* 1330, 1420; development of female domain, 1425–29; female discourse as site of power, 1429–32; **"Some Call It Fiction: On the Politics of Domesticity," 1418–32**

Arnheim, Rudolf, 1240–41, 1245

Arnold, Matthew, 1, 96, 483, 650–51, 814, 1159, 1435, 1617, 1807; biography, 412; *Culture and Anarchy,* 412; "Dover Beach," 801; elitism, 413; *Essays in Criticism,* 412; **"The Function of Criticism at the Present Time," 415–29;** holistic method, 413; **"The Study of Poetry," 429–34**

Aron, Raymond, 660

Aronowitz, Stanley, 1301

Arrian, 101

Art: in Arnold, 412; in Benjamin, 1233, 1235, 1238, 1244; in Coleridge, 329; in Dryden, 179, 187; in Du Bois, 567, 569, 572–74; in Emerson, 386, 395; in Freud, 1109; in Frye, 693; in Hegel, 371, 373, 375, 377–78, 381; in Horace, 90, 92; in Hume, 238; in James, 466, 470; in Johnson, 215, 222; in Jung, 544, 548; in Kant, 247–49, 264, 271; in Longinus, 95–96, 98, 100; in Marx, 398–99, 403, 410–11; in Nietzsche, 435, 437, 439, 446, 447; in Plato, 1, 27, 40, 45, 232; in Plotinus, 4, 109, 111, 118; in Pope, 199–201, 204; in Potebnya, 751; in Schiller, 301; in Shklovsky, 775; in Sidney, 144, 155; in Wilde, 479, 478–96; in Williams, 1287; popular, 7; powers, 1; properties, 1; rules of, 2; sources, 1; uses, 1; value, 4; value of, for Plato, 27. *See also* Nature

Art for art's sake: in Nietzsche, 461

Artaud, Antonin, 738, 1117, 1782

Artisanal production: in Eagleton, 1308; in Mulvey, 1173. *See also* Author; Poet

Artist, 1–2, 7; in Baym, 1529–30; in Brecht, 1252; in De Man, 883; in Eliot, 537; in Emerson, 386; in Freud, 1109; in Frye, 695; in James, 467, 475; in Jung, 551, 553; in Kant, 250; in Longinus, 96; in Nietzsche, 437, 441, 459–60; in Plotinus, 109, 111, 114; in Sartre, 665; in Sidney, 134

Artistic autonomy: in Bourdieu, 1401

Ashbery, John, 1061, 1076, 1086, 1159, 1957

Ashby, Eric, 1821, 1828

Asperger syndrome, 1091

Assimilation, 1759

Associationism, 320–21

Astell, Mary, 191

Asyndeton, 1350

Atget, Eugène, 1238

Attitude: in Richards, 769

Auden, W.H., 696, 1083, 1249, 1929

Audience, 2–3, 5–8, 962; in Aristotle, 7, 68, 70, 72, 962; in Behn, 190, 196; in Benjamin, 1235–36, 1239–40, 1244, 1246; in Bleich, 963, 971; in Booth, 973; in Brecht, 1250, 1252–54; in Culler, 963, 968; in Dryden, 161–62, 170, 174, 176–77, 179–81, 186; in Eco, 963, 968; in Fish, 973; in Freud, 498, 514, 1109–10; in Genette, 963; in Greenblatt, 1445, 1447; in Holland, 963, 969–70, 973, 1018; in Horace, 82, 86, 88–89, 962; in Hume, 231, 240,

242, 249; in Iser, 973; in James, 466; in Jauss, 973, 976; in Johnson, 211, 213, 220, 223–24, 226–27; in Kant, 249; in Kolodny, 1505; in Longinus, 95, 97, 100; in Mulvey, 1174, 1176, 1180; in New Criticism, 755, 963; in Nietzsche, 447; in Plato, 42, 962; in Poulet, 973; in Rabinowitz, 1043–54; in rhetorical theory, 5; in Richards, 963; in Rosenblatt, 969–70; in Said, 1811; in Staël, 287, 292; in structuralism, 963, 968; in Wilde, 493. *See also* Reader

Auerbach, Erich, 1092, 1101, 1390, 1913, 1914; biography, 702; **"Odysseus' Scar," 704–17**

Auerbach, Nina, 1596

Augustine, 120, 702, 729, 1026, 1131; City of God, 1393

Aura (Benjamin), 1202, 1235–36, 1240, 1242, 1249, 1955

Austen, Jane, 475, 598, 600, 602–03, 606, 651–55, 658, 1003, 1032, 1101, 1338, 1419–20, 1429, 1435, 1504, 1511, 1530, 1533, 1537–40, 1546, 1549; *Emma,* 989–1001, 1053, 1429; *Mansfield Park,* 999; *Northanger Abbey,* 1385, 1420; *Persuasion,* 992–94, 999, 1034; *Sense and Sensibility,* 1054

Austin, J. L., 576, 876, 885, 888, 1188, 1212–13, 1719, 1930, 1958; biography, 679; *How to Do Things with Words,* **681–90**

Authenticity: in Benjamin, 1234–36; in Heidegger, 612; in Lukács, 1228. *See also* Artist; Poet

Author: in Burke, 634; in Freud, 1109; in Horace, 88; in James, 467; in Longinus, 95; in Wimsatt and Beardsley, 811, 814; as transcendental signified, in Gilbert and Gubar, 1546; death of, in Foucault, 833; in Bakhtin, 588; in Barthes, 875–80; in Lipking, 894; in McDowell, 1773; in Rabinowitz, 965, 1045; in Said, 1811; determined by history, 8; in Coleridge, 328; in Foucault, 904–14

Author-function: in Foucault, 833, 908, 910, 912, 914

Authorial audience (Rabinowitz), 1043–46, 1049–50, 1052–54

Authorial commentary (Booth), 964

Authorial ideology (Eagleton), 1208, 1308, 1314, 1316–19

Authorial intention, 1048, 1869. *See also* Intention

Authorial voice: in Gilbert and Gubar, 1547

Authoritative discourse (Bakhtin), 580–82, 585. *See also* Monological discourse

Authority: in Baym, 1530, 1532; in Benjamin, 1243; in Cixous, 1655; in Gilbert and Gubar, 1532; in Greenblatt, 1447; in Said, 1811

Autism, 1090–93

Auto-eroticism, 1174

Autonomous complex: in Jung, 549, 551

Autonomy: in Eagleton, 1311; in Greenblatt, 1444; in Williams, 1276

Autrui (the absolutely Other): in Levinas, 933, 945

Avant-garde, 1173, 1923–24, 1931–32, 1936, 1948–50, 1955, 1999, 2004

Avenarius, Richard, 777

Awkward, Michael, 1772; **Appropriative Gestures, 1867–70;** biography, 1866

Ayer, A. J., 679, 834

Baader-Meinhoff Gang, 1574
Babbitt, Irving, 534
Bach, Johann Sebastian, 248
Bach, Johann Christian, 1923
Bachelard, Gaston, 892; *Poetics of Space,* 1542
Bacon, Sir Francis, 348–49, 359, 361, 907, 1815, 1897
Bahti, Timothy, 836
Bailyn, Bernard, 1795–96
Baker, Houston, 1769–70, 1772, 1871, 1903–05; biography, 1903; *Blues, Ideology, and Afro-American Literature, 1906–09;* literature as cultural artifact, 1905
Bakhtin, Mikhail Mikhailovich, 15–17, 20–22, 95–96, 575–78, 718, 1296, 1322, 1324, 1424, 1488–89, 1891; biography, 575–78; grotesque body, 1324; **"Heteroglossia in the Novel,"** 588–95; *Rabelais and His World,* 575, 1424; **"The Topic of the Speaking Person,"** 578–88
Baldwin, James, 1771, 1863
Balibar, Etienne, 1188, 1303
Balzac, Honore de, 483, 489, 492, 606, 702, 832, 874–75, 877, 881, 907, 1049, 1211, 1225, 1251–52, 1292, 1294, 1298, 1319, 1589, 1807; *Illusions Perdues,* 483; *La Peau de chagrin,* 1167; *Père Goriot,* 968
Bambara, Toni Cade: *Gorilla My Love,* 1606
Baraka, Imamu Amiri (aka Leroi Jones), 1860, 1863, 1907
Barbauld, Anna Laetitia, 1420, 1502, 1508
Barber, Benjamin, 1767
Barnes, Djuna, 657
Barnes, Margaret Ayer: *Edna His Wife,* 1047
Barnett, Allen: "Philostorgy, Now Obscure," 1692–94
Baroque, 1923
Barrie, James: *Peter Pan,* 950
Barry, Philip: *Holiday,* 1056
Barth, John, 1923–24, 1993, 2001, 2003, 2006–07, 2015
Barth, Karl, 1264
Barthes, Roland, 660, 738, 745, 822, 832–33, 835, 837–39, 884, 985, 1030, 1111, 1116, 1162–63, 1171, 1347, 1455, 1461, 1546, 1727, 1873, 1937, 1955, 1996–98, 2000, 2006–07, biography, 868; **"The Death of the Author,"** 874–78; **"From Work to Text,"** 878–82; move to post-structuralism, 832; *Mythologies,* 832, 1323; *S/Z,* 832; *The Pleasure of the Text,* 833, 968; **"Striptease"** 869–71; **"The Structuralist Activity,"** 871–74
Base (Grundlage), 1199, 1206, 1208, 1273–77; in Marx, 1233; in Said, 1807; in Foucault, 1629; in Williams, 1272, 1407. *See also* Superstructure *(Uberbau)*
Basile, Giambattista, 1925
Bataille, George, 879, 944, 1354, 1955
Bate, Walter Jackson, 1157, 1891, 1892
Bateson, Gregory, 817
Baudelaire, Charles, 483, 699, 817, 822, 824, 875, 877, 975, 988, 1202, 1455, 1949, 1953, 1965; *Spleen,* 982
Baudrillard, Jean, 13, 1300–01, 1467, 1926–28, 1972, 1989, 1995, 1997, 2000; biography, 1936–37; imagery and simulations, 1938–40; on America as Disneyland, 1941; on

television as panopticon, 1942–45; on Vietnam, 1945–47; on Watergate, 1942; **"The Precession of Simulacra,"** 1936–46
Baym, Nina, 972, 1508; biography, 1519; **"Melodramas of Beset Manhood,"** 1520–30
Beardsley, Monroe C., 887, 963, 1053; biography, 810; **"The Intentional Fallacy,"** 811–18
Beaumont, Francis, 175, 184, 307
Beaumont, Francis and John Fletcher: *The Maid's Tragedy,* 196; *Philaster,* 184
Beauty, as ideal form, 4; in Aristotle, 64; in Arnold, 421, 430; in Benjamin, 1236; in Dryden, 178; in Du Bois, 570, 572–73; in Emerson, 386–88, 392, 395; in Habermas, 1952; in Hegel, 373, 383; in Horace, 86; in Hume, 232, 234, 236–37, 239, 242; in James, 474; in Kant, 247–49, 251–56, 259–62, 269, 371, 665; in Keats, 330–31; in Nietzsche, 444; in Longinus, 96; in Plotinus, 4, 109, 111–12, 115–16, 118–19; in Pope, 200, 203; in Richards, 765, 767, 774; in Sartre, 665; in Shelley, 361; in Sidney, 151, 157; in Wordsworth, 312. *See also* Sublime
Beauvoir, Simone de, 598, 659, 1504, 1535, 1543, 1545, 1547, 1581, 1613–14, 1638–39; biography, 673; *The Second Sex,* 673, 676–79
Beckett, Samuel, 742, 904, 1041, 1222, 1225, 1232, 1780, 1923
Beckford, William, 1812
Beethoven, Ludwig van, 1050, 1235, 1256, 1372, 1690, 1923
Behaviorism, 319
Behn, Aphra, 598, 1503; biography, 189–90; *The Dutch Lover,* 189–91; **"An Epistle to the Reader,"** 192–95; *The Lucky Chance,* 190; *Oroonoko,* 189–90, **Preface to *The Lucky Chance,*** 195–98; *The Rover,* 190
Being: in Derrida, 916, 924; in Heidegger, 618, 917; in Plato, 11; in Plotinus, 113, 114, 116; in Sartre, 662
Being There: in Heidegger. See *Dasein*
Beliefs: in Booth, 964; in Rabinowitz, 1043, 1046; in Richards, 766, 770–71, 774
Belinsky, Vissarion, 750
Bell, Daniel, 1301, 1950
Bellini, Giovanni, 490
Bellow, Saul, 1689; *Henderson the Rain King,* 1526
Bely, Andrei, 750, 776–77
Ben Bella, Ahmed, 1946
Benda, Julien, 672
Benedict, Ruth: *Patterns of Culture,* 699
Benjamin, Walter, 738, 745, 1100, 1163, 1167, 1202–05, 1208–09, 1212, 1214, 1228–32, 1254–55, 1307, 1322, 1455, 1460, 1470, 1596, 1806, 1815, 1912, 1949–50, 1954–55, 1965; biography, 1232; **"The Work of Art in the Age of Mechanical Reproduction,"** 1203, **1233–49**
Benn, Gottfried, 1222, 1225–26, 1232, 1956
Bennett, Tony, 751, 976
Bennett, William, 1472, 1475, 1477–78, 1690, 1728
Bennington, Geoff, 1914
Bentham, Jeremy, 1344–45, 1882, 1942; *Panopticon,* 1355

Cather, Willa, 1527, 1690; *O Pioneers*, 1528; *Sapphira and the Slave Girl*, 1765; *The Song of the Lark*, 1527

Cathexis: in Peter Brooks, 1169; in Freud, 510, 1107

Catullus, Caius Valerius, 307, 354

Caudwell, Christopher, 1208

Causality: in Aristotle, 6; in Kant, 258; in Foucault, 1328

Cavell, Stanley, 1373

Celine, Louis Ferdinand, 1782

Cellini, Benvenuto, 487

Certeau, Michel de, 1322–24, 1332–33, 1455, 1461; and urban practices, 1345–47, 1350–51; biography, 1342; city as text, 1343–47, 1350–51; city place-names, 1352–53; *The Practice of Everyday Life*, 1334; urban legends, 1355; urban practices, 1354; **"Walking in the City," 1343–54**

Cervantes, Miguel de, 592–93; Don Quixote, 51, 54, 193, 468, 991

Césaire, Aimé, 1759–60, 1775; *Une Tempête*, 1760

Cézanne, Paul, 1936

Chain of signification: in Lacan, 1134–35, 1141–43. *See also* Signifier

Champollion, Jean-Francois, 1138

Chanson de Roland, 432, 950, 951

Chapman, George, 393

Character: in Aristotle, 56–57, 63–64, 67, 69; in Booth, 964, 991–92; in Brecht, 1240; in Dryden, 177, 181, 183, 186; in Eco, 952, 954; in Emerson, 388; in Freud, 1109–10; in Frye, 695; in Holland, 1016; in Horace, 86; in Iser, 1010; in James, 463, 470; in Leavis, 653; in Lukács, 1221, 1223; in Neo-Aristotelianism, 760; in Johnson, 210, 214, 217, 219, 221, 228–29; in Woolf, 602; in Wordsworth, 308

Chase, Cynthia, 835

Chase, Richard, 1509, 1525–26, 1529

Chateaubriand, Francois René, 492, 879, 1810

Chatman, Seymour, 855, 1047

Chaucer, Geoffrey, 121, 125, 142, 150, 206, 226, 228, 358–59, 393, 396, 399, 413, 756, 1109, 1337, 1537, 1623–24; *The Pardoner's Tale*, 1692–1706; Troilus and Criseyde, 155

Chekhov, Anton, 490

Chernishevsky, Nikolai Gavrilovich, 750, 1059, 1912

Chesnutt, Charles, 1860–61

Chesterfield, Philip Dormer Stanhope, Earl of, 1308

Chicago, Judy, 1534

Chicano culture: in Anzaldúa, 1856–58

Chladni, Ernst, 454, 731–32

Chomsky, Noam, 820–21, 837, 977, 1113, 1333, 1473, 1805

Chopin, Kate, 1508, 1552; *The Awakening*, 1515

Chora (Kristeva), 1116–17, 1565

Chorus: in Aristotle, 62, 67, 72, in Dryden 169, 171, 183; in Horace, 88, 90; in Nietzsche, 436, 448, in Plato, 42, in Shelley 348

Chow, Rey, 1773, 1874; and identity politics, 1774; aporias of poststructural theory, 1915–19; biography, 1909; **"The Interruption of Referentiality" 1910–19;** referentiality

and identity politics, 1910–11; referentiality and literariness, 1911–15

Christian, Barbara, 1771, 1773, 1869, 1871, 1874, 1910; biography, 1858; **"The Race for Theory," 1859–66.**

Christie, Agatha: *The A.B.C. Murders*, 1053; *The Mystery of the Blue Train*, 1053–54

Christine de Pisan, 1503, 1508; biography, 124–25; Book of the City of Ladies, 124, 125; Epistre au Dieu d'Amours, 129; **La Querelle de la Rose 126–31**

Cibber, Colley, 226

Cicero, Marcus Tullius, 12, 105, 141–42, 144, 148, 157, 164, 169, 242, 349, 425, 1134, 1816

Cinema: in Mulvey, 1117–18, 1172–80; in Sontag, 743–44, in Zunshine 1093

Cisneros, Sandra, 1767

Cixous, Hélène, 500, 598, 1503, 1516, 1612–13, 1616, 1624, 1984; biography, 1643; **"The Laugh of the Medusa,"** 1613, **1643–55**

Clare, John, 1205

Class and class struggle, 1546, 1915; in Beauvoir, 674; in Bourdieu, 1334; in Brecht, 1251; in Horace, 83; in Jameson, 1296, 1299, 1301; in Kipnis, 1324, 1485–90, 1492, 1494, 1497, 1500; in Marx, 6, 1665; in Morris, 1459; in Williams, 1275, 1290

Classic, 1525, 1528–29; in Arnold, 431; in Frye, 696; in Gadamer, 726–28; in Hegel, 371, 377–83; in Leavis, 653

Claudel, Paul, 676–77, 1398, 1581

Clausewitz, Karl von, 1629

Clement of Alexandria, 906

Cleveland, John, 164, 172

Clifford, James L., 1986

Clinamen: in Bloom, 1533

Clinton, Bill, 1326

Cocteau, Jean: *The Blood of a Poet*, 743

Codes: in Barthes, 819

Coetzee, J. M., 1925

Coffin, Charles M., 816

Cognitive theory, 976–77, 1057, 1061, 1073–74, 1076, 1090–91, 1093, 1095–99, 1102–03, 1833. *See also* Scarry; Turner; Zunshine

Cohen, Hermann, 575, 718

Colenso, John William, 483

Coleridge, Mary Elizabeth: "The Other Side of the Mirror," 1535

Coleridge, Samuel Taylor, 7, 247, 306, 331, 333–34, 342, 364, 366, 384–85, 417, 598, 607, 609–10, 634, 641, 654, 696, 754, 769, 807–08, 814–15, 817, 1157–58, 1504, 1542, 1810; *Biographia Literaria*, 305, 319, **325–30**, 641; biography, 319; *Christabel and Other Poems*, 319; *Lyrical Ballads*, 319, 326; "The Rime of the Ancient Mariner," 1156; **"Shakespeare's Judgment Equal to His Genius," 323–25**

Collective enunciation (Deleuze and Guattari), 1778

Collective unconscious (Jung): 552, 556, 558, 562

Collingwood, R. G., 1321, 1331, 1384, 1386–87

Collins, Wilkie, 653, *The Woman in White*, 1325

Collins, William, 340

Colonial discourse: in Bhabha, 1880, 1883–84, 1888; in Haraway, 1987; in Spivak, 1762

Colonialism, 1756–60, 1763, 1766, 1826, 1832–33, 1875, 1878, 1882, 1893, 1917; and authority, 1764; cultural legacies, 1756; political legacies, 1756; psychological consequences, 1759; social consequences, 1759

Colonization, internal: 1753; by Russia, 1757; by the USA, 1757

Comedy, 161, 413; in Aristotle, 55, 59, 62–63, 65, 81; in Bakhtin, 588–94; in Behn, 194; in Booth, 990, 993, 996, 999; in Dante, 122–23; in Dryden, 170, 172, 174, 179–81, 186; in Frye, 692, 698; in Horace, 86, 90, 167; in Johnson, 211–12, 219–24, 228–29; in Longinus, 103; in Schiller, 299; in Shelley, 352–53; in Sidney, 146–47, 151, 156; in Staël, 288; in White, 1330

Common sense: in Hume, 236; in Kant, 249, 261

Communication: in Bakhtin, 578; in Jakobson, 822; in Habermas, 1951; in Tolstoy, 52, 768

Communism, 397, 634, 660, 1201, 1293, 1299

Communities, imaginary, 1753, 1758, 1820; in Behn 190; in Frye, 700

Competence and performance. *See* Langue and parole

Compulsory heterosexuality, 1712; in Rubin, 1615, 1676–78. *See also* Heteronormativity

Comte, August, 678

Concept: in Nietzsche, 454–459

Concretization: in Iser and Jauss, 973, 984, 986, 1002

Condell, Henry, 220

Condensation, (ego defense): 1113, 1115, 1144; in Freud, 498, 501–05, 508–09; in Lacan, 1139

Condorcet, Jean-Antoine, Marquis de, 1952

Confucius, 1924

Congreve, William, 230, 463; *Love for Love*, 230; *The Old Bachelor*, 230

Connotation: in Cleanth Brooks, 800

Conrad, Joseph, 651, 652, 656, 658, 1292, 1419, 1757, 1825, 1879; *Heart of Darkness*, 1419, 1756, 1764, 1766, 1784–90, 1876, 1878; *Lord Jim*, 1211, 1296; *Nostromo*, 1211; *A Personal Record*, 1788

Conscious mind: in Freud, 546, 1107; in Jung, 549, 560. *See also* Unconscious

Consciousness: in Althusser, 1266; in Derrida, 916, 942–43; in Freud, 917; in Hegel, 11, 370, 374; in Iser, 1004, 1008, 1014; in Leavis, 657; in Lukács, 1221; in Marx, 397–99, 404, 406–10; in Nietzsche, 436; in Sartre, 670; in Wimsatt and Beardsley, 812; in Williams, 1273

Constant, Benjamin, 288

Constatives, 1213; in Austin, 680–86, 1188–89, 1212–13. *See also* Performatives

Constraints: on interpretation, in Turner, 1087; in Zunshine, 1090, 1093

Consumption, 1922; in Barthes, 881; in Bourdieu, 1399; in Eagleton, 1309; in Jameson, 1301; in Morris, 1453

Content: in De Man, 883; in Horkheimer and Adorno, 1261

Content: in Brooks, 757; in Hegel, 375–78; in Jung, 550; in Jameson, 1209, 1305; in Lukács, 1219; in Russian formalism, 752; in Sontag, 740–43, 745; latent, 739. *See also* Subject-matter

Context: in Cleanth Brooks, 800–01, 804

Contingency: in Herrnstein Smith, 246; in Foucault, 1328

Continuity of scenes: in Dryden, 185

Convention: in Frye, 695; in Horace, 88

Conventions, 161, 1555; in Dryden, 167; in Fish, 1028; in Horace, 83, 88; in Johnson, 211; in Rabinowitz, 1047; in Staël, 290. *See also* Rules

Cooke, Michael, 1905

Coomaraswamy, Ananda K., 812

Cooper, James Fenimore, 543, 1337, 1509, 1526–27

Coover, Robert, 1924, 2004

Copernicus, Nicholas, 1142

Corneille, Pierre, 160–61, 168, 171, 175, 177–183, 187, 223, 234, 728, 813, 1816; *Polyeucte*, 244

Correspondences: in Adorno, 1203; in Benjamin, 1202, 1203; in Frye, 700; in Goldmann, 1205; in Williams, 1205

Counterculture, 1280, 1301

Coupure (Foucault), 1327–28

Courtly love, 1181–97

Cowley, Abraham, 166, 307

Cowper, William, 340, 1158

Craig, David, 1912

Crane, Hart, 639

Crane, Ronald Salmon, 9–10, 756, 759–60, 807, 822, 1266; **"The Critical Monism of Cleanth Brooks,"** 807–10

Crawford, F. Marion, 481; *Mr. Isaacs*, 483

Creativity, 2, 6–7; in Aristotle, 57, 412; in Arnold, 415–17, 421, 428; in Baym, 1529; in Bely, 777; in Benjamin, 1233; in Burke, 639; in Coleridge, 321, 641; in Foucault, 906; in Freud, 509–14, 531, 1109; in Gilbert and Gubar, 1548; in Iser, 1003; in Jung, 544, 548–53; in Kant, 249, 271; in Leavis, 655–57; in Longinus, 97; in mimetic theories, 3; in Nietzsche, 447; in Plotinus, 110–11, 114, 115; in Pope, 199; in Rich, 1513; in Sartre, 662, 664; in Shelley, 359; in Shklovsky, 777; in Sidney, 138; in Wordsworth, 311, 415. *See also* Genius; Imagination

Crews, Frederick C.: *The Sins of the Fathers*, 1109

Criteria of value: in Dryden, 164

Critical practice: in New Criticism, 755

Criticism: archetypal, 7, 9, 1159; biographical, 7, 9; cultural, 750; deconstructionist, 759; ethical, 9; evolution of, 6; expressive, 2, 4–5, 7, 9; feminist, 759, 1111, 1504; formalist, 3, 6–8, 882, 1159, 1162, 1444; Freudian, 739, 1109; historical, 9, 749; history of, 2; in Arnold, 412, 415–17, 420–21, 423–28, 430; in Baym, 1528; in Benjamin, 1244; in Bloom, 1159; in Burke, 639, 648; in De Man, 891; in Eliot, 538; in Frye, 693, 695–97, 699; in Greenblatt, 1444; in Horace, 93; in Sontag, 739; in Wordsworth, 415; Lacanian, 1114; Marxist, 8, 739, 759;

mimetic, 2, 6, 9; objective, 4; psychoanalytic, 7, 9, 546, 742, 1109–10, 1171; reader-response, 10, 1110; rhetorical, 2, 3, 5, 8–9, 95; sociological, 7, 9; structuralist, 750, 1162; thematic, 757

Criticism of life: in Arnold, 413, 430

Croce, Benedetto, 109, 756, 812, 1331

Cronenberg, David: *M. Butterfly*, 1194–96

Cross-dressing, 1617, 1625, 1710, 1736; and bathrooms; in Halberstam, 1746–51, in Sidney, 134. *See also* Drag

Crowne, John: *City Politicks*, 196; *Sir Courtly Nice*, 196

Cruising: and homosexuality, 1662

Cugoano, Ottobah, 1900

Cullen, Countee, 566, 571

Culler, Jonathan, 819, 824, 825, 838, 1046, 1505, 1514, 1592, 1596, 2003; biography, 1579; literary competence, 1047, **"Reading as a Woman," 1579–90**

Cult value (Benjamin): 1237–1240, 1248. *See also* Aura

Cultural capital, 1473, 1484; in Bourdieu, 1334, 1338, 1400, 1403; in Guillory, 1335, 1477

Cultural field (Bourdieu), 1333

Cultural institutions: in Williams, 1282

Cultural materialism, 1323; in Williams, 1206, 1330

Cultural poetics. *See* New Historicism

Cultural production, 1476; in Bourdieu, 1334; in Guillory, 1483; in Williams, 1278

Cultural studies, 8, 702, **1342–1501,** 1452, 1736, 1742, 1744, 1758, 1921; and Marxism, 1404–11; and structuralism, 1411–17; beginnings 1404–09

Culture, 1043, 1331, 1921; as discourse, in Armstrong 1419–22; as symbolic system, in Geertz, 1366, 1373–75; definitions, in Geertz, 1367–71, 1383; formations, in Williams, 1280–82; in Anzaldúa, 1851; in Arnold, 412, 414, 424; in De Man, 883; in Foucault, 904, 907, 914; in Greenblatt, 1445; in Guillory, 1335, 1473, 1481; in Herrnstein Smith, 245; in Horkheimer and Adorno, 1255; in Lacan, 1130; in Leavis, 650–51; in Lévi-Strauss, 918, 919; in Nietzsche, 451; in Rabinowitz, 1055; in Said, 1807; in Sontag, 744; in Staël, 296–97; in Trilling, 1523; in Wilde, 493; in Williams, 364, 1273, 1405–07; in Wimsatt and Beardsley, 814; Latino, 1474; minority, 1474; postcolonial, 1757; practices, 1419, 1811–13; revolutions, 1303, 1423

Culture and literature: in Baker, 1904; in Baym, 1521; in Burke, 648; in Nietzsche, 449, 451; in Sontag, 738; in Williams, 365–67; in Wilson, 1201. *See also* Anthropology; Society and literature

Culture industry: in Horkheimer and Adorno, 1204, 1255–62

Culture of the school: in Guillory, 1472–76, 1481–82

Curtius, Robert, 702

Curtiz: *Casablanca,* 1177

Cuvier, Georges, 911, 1807

Cyberculture, 1338

Cyborg: in Haraway, 1928–29, 1967–73, 1975, 1979–80, 1983–88, 1990

Dadaism, 1246, 1247, 1260, 1923, 1949

Daedalus, 1343

Danda (Pepper): in Phelan, 967, 1031–33; in Rabinowitz, 1045, 1054

Dante Alighieri, 5, 136, 144, 159, 345, 348–49, 356–59, 386, 395, 413, 450, 540, 614, 702, 745, 817, 852, 891, 963, 1026, 1181, 1259, 1475, 1598, 1694, 1998; biography, 120; *Divine Comedy,* 703; *Inferno,* 356, 433, 531, 540, 852, 1069, 1761; **"Letter to Can Grande della Scala," 121–24,** 741; *Paradiso,* 356; *Purgatorio,* 783, 1069

Darwin, Charles, 413, 1367, 1640, 1813

Dasein, 613; in Heidegger, 611, 619–20, 1219, 1355

Daudet, Alphonse, 482

Davies, Sarah Emily, 602, 609

Davis, Kathleen, 1427

Davis, Lennard, 1420

Davis, Robert Con, 1114

Davis, Walter, 11

Day, Thomas: *Sandford and Merton,* 277

Daydreaming: in Freud, 497, 509–14; in Lukács, 1220; in Scarry, 1059–61, 1072–75

De Graef, Ortwin, 836

De Man, Paul, 12, 826, 835–41, 894, 977, 1159, 1762, 1772, 1871–72, 1913; and salvational poetics, 836; biography, 882; *Semiology and Rhetoric,* **882–93;** wartime collaboration, 836–37

De Quincey, Thomas, 606, 1844

Death instinct: in Freud, 1167, 1169; in Lacan, 1127

Decolonization, 1757–60, 1877; economic effects, 1756; history, 1755; political effects, 1755. *See also* Colonization; Imperialism

Deconstruction, 17, 19–21, 826–37, 882–94, 915–949, 976, 978, 1081, 1099, 1134, 1326, 1433, 1516, 1594, 1620, 1769, 1771, 1837, 1841, 1861–62, 1869, 1871–73, 1885, 1906, 1913–14, 1917–18, 1921; and binaries, 1774; and feminism, 1514; and left politics, 836; and literary criticism, 834; and literature, 834; and New Criticism, 834; and politics, 837; and referentiality, 1914; as critical toolkit, 837; as mode of close reading, 826; at Yale, 835; in Baym, 1530; in Bhabha, 1879–1880; in Butler, 1621, 1711, 1714; in Cixous, 1614; in Culler, 1506, 1591; in De Man, 835, 891–94; in Derrida, 918; in Freud, 1168; in Gates, 1894; in Lipking, 902–03; in Spivak, 1837; politics of, 836

Decorum, 161; in Dryden, 172, 177–79, 182; in Horace, 85, 88–89; in Johnson, 211; in Sidney, 134, 156

Defamiliarization: 1913, in Culler, 824; in Iser, 1010; in Russian formalism, 751; in Shklovsky, 751, 778–83

Defense mechanisms, 9, 739; in Bloom, 1159; in Freud, 504, 1107, 1109, 1115, 1157; in Holland, 970, 1021. *See also* names of specific defenses: Condensation; Displacement; Repression; Symbolization; etc.

Defoe, Daniel, 190, 653, 964, 1207, 1315, 1419, 1925; *Moll Flanders,* 1100; *Robinson Crusoe,* 767; Journal of the Plague Year, 487

Division of labor: in Marx, 407

Dixon, Thomas, Jr.: *The Leopard's Spots,* 1051

Döblin, Alfred, 1221

Dobrolyubov, Nikolai, 750

Doctorow, E. L., 1925, 1961, 1994, 2004–05

Dollimore, Jonathan, 1695

Domestic fiction: in Armstrong, 1420

Dominance, 1206, 1276–79, 1281, 1283, 1285–86, 1293, 1299, 1301, 1304–05, 1308, 1317–18

Dominio (rule): in Gramsci, 1276, 1803

Don Giovanni (Mozart-da Ponte), 1051

Donne, John, 173, 307, 535–36, 641, 651–52, 694, 755, 803, 816, 818, 853, 1541; "The Bait," 1081; "The Canonization," 809

Dos Passos, John, 1221, 1523; *U.S.A.,* 1050

Dostoevsky, Fyodor, 53, 435, 489, 577, 582, 584, 594, 595, 623, 626, 631, 703, 1056, 1227, 1830; *The Brothers Karamazov,* 998; *Crime and Punishment,* 1044, 1053; *The Idiot,* 1044

Double: in Freud, 521–23, 530

Double consciousness (Du Bois), 567, 1763, 1771

Double inscription (*dedoublement*): in Bhabha, 1880

Doublethink: in Bhabha, 1882

Double-voiced: in Bakhtin, 580–81, 584, 586–87. *See also* Dialogism; Heteroglossia

Doubrovsky, Serge, 1056

Douglas, Ann, 1586

Douglas, Mary, 1491, 1494–95

Douglas, Norman, 655

Douglass, Frederick, 1770, 1898

Doyle, Arthur Conan, 855

Drag, 1710, 1713, 1718. *See also* Cross-dressing

Drama, 95, 160, 349; in Dryden, 165, 173; in Hegel, 372; in Johnson, 218, 220, 224; in Nietzsche, 436; in Schiller, 302; in Shelley, 351–52; in Sontag, 744; in Wilde, 485; in Wordsworth, 314

Dramatic ratio: in Burke, 640

Dreams: in Freud, 5, 436, 497–509, 512–13, 520, 522, 528, 1107, 1109, 1140, 1164; in Jung, 558, 562; in Nietzsche, 436–37, 439, 442, 445

Dream-work in Freud, 500–09

Dreiser, Theodore, 1201, 1523, 1768, 1829, 1830, 1923; *Sister Carrie,* 1211

Dreyer, Carl, 1241

Droysen, Johann Gustav, 725

Dryden, John, 5–6, 96, 191, 194, 196, 198, 205, 210, 223, 285, 307, 340, 536; *Alexander's Feast,* 204; biography, 160; **Essay of Dramatic Poesy,** 134; **163–88;** 1948; *Fables,* 207

Du Bellay, Joachim, 1352

Du Bois, W. E. B., 1433, 1763, 1771; biography, 565, 567; **"Criteria for Negro Art,"** 569–75;

double consciousness, 565; *The Souls of Black Folk,* 565, **567–69**

Ducasse, Curt, 814

Duchamp, Marcel, 1936

Ducrot, Oswald, 1188–89

Duerrenmatt, Friedrich: *The Visit,* 1021

Duhamel, Georges, 1246

Dumas, Alexandre, 475, 881; *The Three Musketeers,* 952; *Le Vicomte de Bragelonne,* 484

Dunbar, Paul Laurence, 566, 571, 1771

Dunbar, Robin, 1102–03

Dunbar, William, 1795–97

Duras, Marguerite, 1957, 1993

Durkheim, Emile, 860, 1411

Durrell, Lawrence, 657

Dworkin, Andrea, 1494, 1501, 1639

Dworkin, Ronald, 1056

Eagleton, Terry, 651, 756, 1044, 1049, 1052, 1116, 1198, 1207–09, 1211–12, 1307, 1470, 1514, 1591, 1594–96, 1840–41, 1873, 1921, 1923, 1933, 2003–04, 2007; biography, 1307; **"Categories for a Materialist Criticism,"** **1308–19;** *Criticism and Ideology,* 1208; *The Rape of Clarissa,* 1209; *Saint Oscar,* 1209

Eberhart, Richard, 1157

Ecclesiastes, 1937

Eco, Umberto, 825–26, 838, 950, 1055, 1305, 1998, 2001; biography, 950; **"The Myth of Superman,"** **950–61**

Ecocriticism, 1336–37, 1339–40, 1433–34, 1436, 1438–40; and anthropocentrism, 1440; and cultural studies, 1440; and deconstructionism, 1438; and evolutionary biology, 1437; and gender, 1440–41; and literary representation, 1437; and science studies, 1436; and poststructuralism, 1438; and urban landscapes, 1439; as movement, 1434; canon, 1434; methodologies, 1434

Ecology, in Certeau, 1345

Écriture féminine, 1572, 1576, 1597, 1613; in Christian, 1863, 1864; in Cixous, 1643, 1644, 1645, 1647, 1648, 1649, 1652; in Woolf, 597. *See also* Feminist literary criticism; Writing

Edelman, Lee, 1617, 1731, 1749

Edgeworth, Maria, 1426, 1428, 1549

Education: in Bourdieu, 1334, 1399, 1400

Education of women: in Wollstonecraft, 276

Education in Africa: in Ngugi, 1821, 1822

Educational field: in Bourdieu, 1333

Effect: aesthetic, in Iser, 986; in Horkheimer and Adorno, 1258; in rhetorical theories, 7

Effects of poetry: in Pope, 203; in Sidney, 136, 140, 142, 146

Ego, 1110; in Freud, 497–98, 504, 512, 522–23, 1108–09, 1123, 1144, 1146; in Jung, 549, 554–56, 561; in Lacan, 1114, 1126; in Lawrence, 657

Ego ideal, in Mulvey, 1175–76

Ego-defenses in Freud, 497, 1144

Eidolon: in Plato, 4

Eidos: in Derrida, 916; in Neo-Aristotelianism, 760

Eikhenbaum, Boris, 753

Einstein, Albert, 1780

Eisler, Hanns, 1252

Ekphrasis, 978

Ekstasis, 95; in Jung, 553; in Nietzsche, 440; in Pope, 202; in Schopenhauer, 440

Elegy, 1319; in Dante, 123; in Sidney, 147

Eliot, George (Mary Ann Evans), 474, 482, 598, 600, 602, 604, 606, 651–53, 655, 658, 836, 1504, 1530, 1536–39, 1549, 1554, 1807, 1810, 1923; *Daniel Deronda,* 484; *Middlemarch,* 604, 656, 1552, 1810; *Romola,* 484; "Silly Novels by Lady Novelists," 1532

Eliot, Thomas Stearns, 7, 16, 597–98, 622, 652, 657, 694, 743, 750, 754–55, 801, 809, 816–17, 963, 1157, 1222, 1690, 1825, 1891, 1893, 1957, 1960, 1995, 1998; biography, 534–35; *The Cocktail Party,* 534; criticism, 534; *Four Quartets,* 534; modernism, 534–35; *Murder in the Cathedral,* 534; *Prufrock and Other Observations,* 534; **"Tradition and the Individual Talent,"** 535, **537–41,** 755; *The Waste Land,* 534, 809

Ellis, Havelock, 1624

Ellison, Ralph, 1771, 1861, 1863, 1897, 1904–05, 1909; *Invisible Man,* 1930, 2017

Ellmann, Mary, 598, 1041, 1504–06, 1550, 1551, 1585; *Thinking about Women,* 1603

Elohist, 710, 711; author of "Sacrifice of Isaac," 707

Emergent (cultural formations): in Williams, 1206, 1283–86, 1288–89, 1300. *See also* Dominant; Residual

Emerson, Ralph Waldo, 479, 1159, 1432, 1797; "The American Scholar," 1795; biography, 384; *Essays,* 384; idealism, 384, 385; metaphysics, 384; **"The Poet,"** 385–96

Emes (minimal components of a symbol system), 821–22, 832; in Geertz, 1373; in Lacan, 1134

Emotions: in Aristotle, 71; in Booth, 992; in Eliot, 540–41; in Jung, 544; in Richards, 766, 769–70; in Sartre, 668; in Shelley, 347; in Wordsworth, 316. *See also* Feelings; Passion

Empedocles, 60, 93, 620, 1143, 1160

Empire. *See* Colonialism; Imperialism

Empiricism, 1877; in Aristotle, 56; in Lévi-Strauss, 830

Emplotment: in White, 1386

Empson, William, 121, 633, 650, 754–55, 757–58, 763, 966, 1167, 1892; *Seven Types of Ambiguity,* 755

Ending. *See* Denouement

Engels, Friedrich, 397, 400, 1200, 1208, 1274–75, 1299, 1615, 1667–70, 1683, 1911–12, 1915

Enlightenment, 982, 1157, 1327, 1423, 1472, 1758, 1766, 1770, 1795–96, 1882, 1885, 1892, 1895–98, 1906, 1921–22, 1924–26, 1930–32, 1942, 1948, 1952–54, 1996

Ennius, 89

Enthousiasmós: in Plato, 27, 41–42, 46. *See also* Inspiration

Enthusiasm: in Wordsworth, 311

Epic, 95, 345, 349, 753, 810; in Aristotle, 59, 62, 71–72, 76–77, 81; in Arnold, 432; in Bakhtin, 588–91; in Benjamin, 1247;

in Dryden, 165, 173; in Frye, 696; in Hegel, 372; in Hume, 241; in Lukács, 1218; in Nietzsche, 445; in Propp, 787, 793; in Schiller, 299, 302; in Sidney, 148

Epic theatre (Brecht), 1309

Epictetus, 585

Epicurus, 242

Epimenides, 1377

Epistemé: in Derrida, 915, 924; in Foucault, 833, 904, 1322, 1326–28, 1366; in Lévi-Strauss, 921

Epistemology: in Plato, 27

Equiano, Olaudah, 1900

Erasmus, Desiderius, 149, 208, 1148, 1344

Erikson, Erik, 1019, 1542

Erlich, Victor, 750

Erotic identity: in Mulvey, 1175–78, 1708. *See also* Sexual identity

Eschenbach, Wolfram von: *Parsifal,* 955

Essentialism, 1707, 1769; in Christian, 1772; in hooks, 2012–13

Essentially contested concepts: in W. B. Gallie, 1382

Estrangement: in Benjamin, 1241; in Marx, 400–05

Etherege, George, 189; *The Man of Mode,* 196

Ethics and literature: 11–12; in Bakhtin, 582; in Behn, 192–93, 195, 197; in Booth, 993, 998, 1000–01, 1048; in Christine de Pisan, 127–31, 128; in Dante, 123; in Hegel, 373; in Hume, 232–33, 243; in James, 463, 466, 474; in Johnson, 213–14, 221; in Jung, 557; in Kant, 248, 254, 259; in Leavis, 651, 655; in Lukács, 1227; in Nietzsche, 452; in Pope, 207; in Rabinowitz, 1051; in Sartre, 671; in Shelley, 351–52, 361; in Sidney, 138, 140, 143; in Staël, 288–89, 291–92; in Wilde, 477; in Wimsatt and Beardsley, 812; in Wordsworth, 308, 316–18

Ethnic studies, 1753; African American, 1758; Asian, 1754, 1758; Chicano, 1754; Greek, 1754; Italian, 1754; Latino, 1758

Ethnicity, 1753–54, 1797, 1892, 1914–15

Ethnocentricism: in Spivak, 1838

Ethnography, 1368

Euripides, 41, 68, 71, 72, 76, 79, 153, 156, 166, 168, 172, 217, 351, 436, 448, 494, 666, 768, 1038, 1582, 1690; *The Bacchae,* 445; *Electra,* 108; *Hyppolitus,* 684; *Iphigenia at Aulis,* 69; *Iphigenia at Tauris,* 67, 69–71; *Medea,* 68, 70, 80, 170; *Orestes,* 69, 80

Europhonism (Ngugi), 1767, 1821, 1826–28

Evaluation: in Baym, 1521; in Booth, 964; in Jakobson, 853; in James, 471; in Lipking, 903; social function, 246. *See also* Canon; Taste; Value

Evans-Pritchard, E. E., 1615, 1670, 1675

Evidence: external, 814, 816; internal, 814, 816

Evolution: in Peter Brooks, 1169; in Freud 523; in Frye, 694, 698; in Gadamer, 730; in Hegel, 376, 383; in Nietzsche, 439, 444, 449, 454; in Propp, 787; in Russian formalism, 754; in Saussure, 844, 851; in Tolstoy, 52; in Zunshine, 1091, 1100, 1103

Exchange of women, 820; in Halberstam, 1736; in Rubin, 1615, 1670–74, 1676, 1678, 1680–83

Exegesis: in Jauss, 982; in Lacan, 1148; in Propp, 792; in Wilde, 483; in Wimsatt and Beardsley, 818. *See also* Interpretation

Exhibition value: in Benjamin, 1237–38. *See also* Cult value

Existence: in Heidegger, 616–21; in Sartre, 659

Existentialism, 1115, 1127; in Beauvoir, 673; in Sartre, 659, 972

Expectations: in Iser, 986, 1004, 1007, 1009

Experience: in Hume, 232–33, 236, 239, 241; in Iser, 1008–12, 1014; in Kant, 261; in Nietzsche, 437, 454, 459

Explication: in Jameson, 1291; in New Criticism, 754, 757

Expression, 8, 740, 814; in Croce, 812; in Dewey, 111; in Dryden, 164; in Eliot, 537; in Emerson, 386, 391; in Foucault, 904, 909; in Freud, 501, 507–09, 512, 521, 525–26, 529; in Hegel, 376, 378; in Hume, 237; in James, 469, 472; in Jung, 549; in Lipking, 902; in Longinus, 111; in Plotinus, 115; in Pope, 204; in Schiller, 301; in Tolstoy, 52; in Wilde, 492; in Wimsatt and Beardsley, 811, 814; in Woolf, 606

Expressionism, 1258, 1260, 1923, 1935–36

Extraversion: in Jung, 548

Fabian, Johannes, 1847, 1916, 1919

Fable: in Johnson, 223; in Shklovsky, 779; in Sidney, 153

Fabula, 1161; in Peter Brooks, 1164, 1166–67, 1169; in Shklovsky, 751

Fairy tale, in Propp, 756–769, 785, 790

Fame: in Horace, 85, 91; in Longinus, 106

Family: in Foucault, 1631, 1635–36

Fancy: in Coleridge, 321–22, 326, 329; in Dryden, 164; in Emerson, 386; in Johnson, 211, 217, 224; in Sidney, 151; in Staël, 286; in Wordsworth, 305. *See also* Imagination

Fanon, Frantz: 1534, 1759, 1768, 1775–76, 1788, 1884, 1886, 1889; *Black Skins, White Masks,* 1889; cultural binarism, 1760

Fantasies, 9, 1173, 1611, 1712; in Freud, 497–99, 510–14, 519, 523, 527–28, 530; in Holland, 970; in Jung, 552; in Schiller, 300

Fascism, 1204, 1223, 1233, 1237, 1248–49, 1293

Faulkner, William, 1037, 1056, 1170, 1220, 1222, 1225, 1339, 1523; *A Rose for Emily,* 1015, 1022, 1037, 1041; *The Bear,* 1439; *The Sound and the Fury,* 965

Fauset, Jessie, 571

Febvre, Lucien Paul Victor, 1815

Feeling: in Eliot, 540; in Hegel, 382; in Jung, 562; in New Criticism, 755; in Richards, 754, 771; in Russian formalism, 752; in Tolstoy, 54; in Wordsworth, 305, 308, 312, 315, 317–18. *See also* Emotion

Feidelson, Charles, 1509, 1525

Felman, Shoshana, 1114, 1582, 1589

Female experience: in Culler, 1580–81

Female language, 1571

Female monster: in Gilbert and Gubar, 1536–37

Female reader: in Culler, 1583, 1586, 1587; in Felman, 1582; in Fetterley, 1035, 1583; in Showalter, 1583; in Spivak, 1582

Female social domain: in Armstrong, 1425–29

Femininity, 1547, 1613–14, 1616, 1621–22, 1644–46, 1649–50; in Cixous, 1644, 1649–50; in Freud, 1613; in Gilbert and Gubar, 1548; in Kristeva, 1565

Feminism (social movement), 903, 976, 978, 1099, 1112, 1117–18, 1173, 1305, 1326, 1337, 1433, 1503–04, 1511, 1611–13, 1617, 1625, 1643, 1685, 1762, 1771–72, 1837–39, 1843, 1845, 1847–48, 1850, 1861, 1871, 1902, 1929; and deconstruction, 1514; and homophobia, 1600–05; and identity, 1641; and individualism, 1839; and Lacan, 1116; and Marxism, 1514; and motherhood, 1576–78; and psychoanalysis, 1514; and racism, 1600–05; and socialism, 1568; black, 1773; French; in Armstrong, 1425, 1431–32; Beauvoir, 673–78; in Behn, 191, 194, 196; in Christine de Pisan, 125; in Haraway, 1968, 1983; in Kipnis, 1324; in Kolodny, 1559; in Kristeva, 1116; in Morris, 1324, 1453, 1455–57; in Rabinowitz, 1049; in Rubin, 1680; in Sedgwick, 1689; in Spivak, 1838–39; in Staël, 286, 294–97; in Wittig, 1637–41, in Woolf, 597; lesbian, 1513; male, 1514; radical, 1486, 1570–75

Feminist aesthetics: in Gilbert and Gubar, 1548

Feminist literary criticism, 963, **1502–1610**, 1625, 1863, 1987; and critique, 1503, 1551; and gender theory, 1515; definitions, 1502; evolution, 1503; in Kipnis, 1455–56, 1485; in Kolodny, 1558; in Morris, 1453

Femme: in Butler, 1716. *See also* Butch

Femme fatale, 1192

Fénelon, François de Salignac de la Mothe, 235

Ferenczi, Sandor, 533, 1625, 1663; theories about homosexuality, 1657–59

Fetishism, 1154, 1177–80, 1613

Fetterley, Judith, 971–72, 1035, 1049, 1118, 1505–06, 1515, 1593; biography, 1035; *The Resisting Reader,* **1035–41**

Feudalism, 1299; in Eagleton, 1313

Feuerbach, Ludwig, 1264–65, 1271, 1274

Feyerabend, Paul, 612

Fiction: in Armstrong, 1419; in Baym, 1530; in Coleridge, 322; in Foucault, 914; in Freud, 498, 529–32; in Hume, 236; in James, 470, 472; in Samuel Johnson, 212, 214, 219, 224, 226; in Richards, 766, 772; in Sidney, 151; in Sontag, 744

Fiedler, Leslie, 1524, 1527, 1583, 1923, 1933, 2005, 2007

Field: in Bourdieu. *See* Cultural field; Economic field, etc.; in Lacan. *See* Imaginary; Real; Symbolic

Fielding, Henry, 285, 288, 588, 592, 964, 1000–01, 1315, 1419; *Tom Jones,* 210, 285, 291, 654, 1007

Figural representation: in Auerbach, 703

Figures of speech: in De Man, 885; in Johnson, 222; in Longinus, 96, 100; in New Criticism, 750; in Pope, 203; in Sidney, 157; in White, 1394; in Wordsworth, 309–10. *See also* Tropes; and individual figures as Metaphor; Simile; etc.

Theory of Sexuality, 1174, 1186; *Totem and Taboo*, 1143, 1149; **"The Uncanny,"** **514–32.** *See also* Psychoanalytic theory
Freud, Anna, 1126
Friedman, Norman, 9–10, 759
Frigidity, 1155. *See also* Aphanisis
Fromm, Erich, 1254
Fromm, Harold, 1337
Frontier: as American theme, in Baym, 1520–25, 1530
Frost, Robert, 1435
Frye, Northrop, 1, 5, 121, 543, 760, 822, 896, 1008, 1046, 1073, 1291, 1331, 1385, 1388–1390; *Anatomy of Criticism,* 691, 1210, 1384, 1386; **"The Archetypes of Literature,"** **693–701;** biography, 691; *Fables of Identity,* 691; *The Great Code,* 691
Fück, Johann W., 1809
Furman, Nelly, 1557
Fuss, Diane, 1698

Gadamer, Hans-Georg, 577, 612, 974, 976, 982, 984, 1001, 1212, 1291; biography, 718; *Truth and Method,* **721–37**
Galen, 1329
Galileo, 55, 816, 911–12
Gallagher, Catherine, 1330
Gallie, W.B., 1382
Gallop, Jane, 1514, 1592, 1612
Galsworthy, John, 609
Gance, Abel, 1235, 1239
Gandhi, Mohandas, 1759
Gaps: in Iser, 1005–07
Garber, Marjorie, 1750
Garbo, Greta, 1176
García Márquez, Gabriel, 1769, 1995
Garth, Samuel, 207
Garvey, Marcus, 566
Gasché, Rodolphe, 834
Gaskell, Elizabeth, 653, 655, 1530; *The Life of Charlotte Brontë,* 1072
Gates, Henry Louis, 1769, 1772, 1871, 1906, 1984; and history of racism, 1770–71; and oral traditions, 1771; and signifying, 1770; biography, 1890; **"Preface to Blackness,"** **1904–06;** race as trope of difference, 1894; theory of language, 1908; **"Writing, 'Race,' and the Difference It Makes,"** **1891–1903**
Gautier, Theophile, 483
Gay and lesbian studies, 1691
Gay canon: in Sedgwick, 1690
Gay culture, 1688; in Kruger, 1694
Gay history: in Kruger, 1623
Gay identity, 1620, 1711, 1712; in Butler, 1710; in Sedgwick, 1687, 1689, 1691
Gay liberation, 1618; in Rubin, 1680
Gay literature: in Sedgwick, 1689

Gay marriage, 1623
Gay studies, 1433
Gayle, Addison, 1863, 1903
Gaze: in Mulvey, 1117–19, 1174–80; in Žižek, 1185
Geertz, Clifford, 1320, 1322, 1326, 1331–32, 1449, 1551, 1561; biography, 1366; Marmusha raid, 1376–77; **"Thick Description: Toward an Interpretive Theory of Culture,"** **1367–83**
Gehry, Frank, 1962
Gellert, Christian Fürchtegott, 447
Gender, 1, 1043, 1516, 1611, 1612, 1616–18, 1620–21, 1625, 1707, 1710, 1713–18, 1870, 1921; and creativity, 603; and culture, 1421; and history, 600; and language, 123, 1507; and race, 1512; and reading, 1430, 1558; as binary system, 1625; as performance, 1621, 1713, 1715, 1718; as social construction, 1617; essentialism, 1620; in Armstrong, 1424; in Baym, 1521, 1528; in Behn, 191, 197; in Chow, 1915; in Foucault, 1329; in Halberstam, 1746; in Haraway, 1974; in Lacan, 1133; in Sidney, 134–35; in Staël, 293, 296–97; in Wittig, 1616
Gender identity: in Halberstam, 1622; in Rubin, 1675
Gender studies, 1326, 1503, **1611–1752.** *See also* Queer Theory
Gender theory, 1330, 1516, 1616, 1617, 1625
Genealogy: in Foucault, 1327, 1328
General ideology: in Eagleton, 1308, 1313–19
General introduction, 1–22
General mode of production: in Eagleton, 1308, 1310–13, 1315–18
General nature: in Johnson, 211, 216, 217, 218, 305; in Wordsworth, 313
Genesis of poetry: in Wordsworth, 305
Genêt, Jean, 666, 1167, 1581, 1650, 1660
Genetic structuralism, 1205, 1407–08
Genette, Gérard, 825–26, 839, 884–85, 920, 963, 968, 1116, 1171, 1175, 1643; *Figures,* 1162
Genius, 2, 199, 963, 1896; in Arnold, 416; in Benjamin, 1233; in Christine de Pisan, 128; in Coleridge, 322, 324–25, 329; in Dryden, 166, 173, 185; in Emerson, 386–88, 391, 396; in Foucault, 913; in Horace, 82, 90, 92; in Hume, 232, 236, 240, 242; in James, 468; in Johnson, 216, 227; in Kant, 249, 271–72; in Leavis, 655–56, 658; in Longinus, 100, 103, 107; in Nietzsche, 447; in Plotinus, 110; in Pope, 198–200; in Schiller, 299; in Sidney, 134, 155; in Sontag, 743; in Staël, 286–88, 290; in Woolf, 600, 603–05. *See also* Imagination
Genovese, Eugene, 1297
Genre, 5, 161, 1331; in Aristotle, 56, 59, 62, 72, 83, 412; in Bakhtin, 589, 592; in Barthes, 879; in Behn, 190, 192, 193; in Dante, 122, 123; in Dryden, 180; in Eagleton, 1317; in Foucault, 904; in Frye, 692; 696, 760; in Greenblatt, 1443, 1445; in Hegel, 372; in Horace, 83, 86; in Hume, 242; in Johnson, 211, 219–20; in Lukács, 1229; in New Criticism, 756; in Nietzsche, 447; in Propp, 793; in

Genre [*cont.*]
Russian formalism, 754; in Rabinowitz, 1055; in Schiller, 299; in Sidney, 133–34, 139, 140, 146; in Staël, 287. *See also* names of individual genres: Comedy; Romance; Satire; Tragedy; etc.

Gentner, Dedre, 1084

Geoffroy Saint-Hilaire, Etienne, 1807

Georg, Stefan, 613

Gesamtkunstwerk, 1257

Gestalt, 1124

Ghirlandaio, Domenico, 1059, 1400

Ghost story, 1068

Gibb, H. A. R.: *Modern Trends in Islam*, 1806

Gibbon, Edward, 285, 340, 359, 466, 606, 1330, 1385, 1396; *Decline and Fall of the Roman Empire*, 1023

Gibson, J. J., 1062–67, 1072

Gide, André, 1147, 1221, 1232; *The Counterfeiters*, 1232

Gilbert, Sandra, 606, 1034, 1111, 1502, 1509, 1511, 1545, 1547, 1549, 1556, 1588, 1612, 1840, 1841, 1847; anxiety over space, 1539–44; political implications, 1545; biography, 1531; **"Infection in the Sentence," 1532–44**

Gilbert, William Schwenck, 476

Gilgamesh, 1100, 1433

Gilman, Charlotte Perkins, 1505, 1508, 1540, 1580; "The Yellow Wallpaper," 1543–44, 1556

Gioacchino da Fiore, 1393

Giovanni, Nikki, 1512, 1863

Girard, René: *Violence and the Sacred*, 1570–73

Gissing, George, 1292, 1298; *The Odd Women*, 1592

Giuliani, Rudolph, 1732

Givenness (Scarry), 1071, 1075

Glasgow, Ellen, 1527

Glaspell, Susan Keating, 1505; *A Jury of Her Peers*, 1558

Glass, Philip, 1923, 1957, 1989

Globalization: 1564, 1767

Glotfelty, Cheryll, 1337

Gnostics, 109

Gobineau, Joseph Arthur, 1803

Godard, Jean-Luc, 744, 1118, 1957

Gödel, Kurt, 829

Godwin, William, 275–76, 344; *Caleb Williams*, 291

Goethe, Johann Wolfgang von, 298–300, 416–18, 424, 477, 486, 508, 615, 648, 702, 705–06, 812, 815, 888, 1136, 1779, 1781, 1812; *Faust,* 548, 550, 1235; *Iphigenia on Tauris,* 298, 422; *The Sorrows of Young Werther,* 285, 292, 299, 301, 342, 491, 1170; *West-Ostlicher Diwan,* 1810; *Wilhelm Meisters Lehrjahre,* 1136

Gogol, Nikolai, 54, 582, 623, 775, 781; "The Nose," 751

Golden age of poetry: in Peacock, 337–38

Goldmann, Lucien, 1205–06, 1323, 1407–08, 1412, 1563

Goldsmith, Oliver, 340, 1337

Goliardic poetry, 130

Gombrich, Ernst, 1008–09

Goncourt: Edmond de: *Chérie*, 473;

Goodman, Nelson, 1080

Gordon, Caroline, 964

Gorgias, 26

Gorky, Maxim, 784

Gospel according to John, 1081–82, 1086–87

Gothic novel, 476; in Foucault, 911; in Wordsworth, 309

Gouldner, Alvin, 1478

Graff, Gerald, 8, 1030, 1052

Grammar: in De Man, 885, 886, 888; in Peirce, 886; in Sidney, 138

Grammatology: in Derrida, 942

Gramsci, Antonio, 18–21, 1206, 1276–79, 1322–25, 1340, 1404, 1408–09, 1415–17, 1421–22, 1472, 1479–83, 1629, 1753, 1769, 1803, 1805, 1807, 1832

Grand narratives, 18, 21, 1921. *See also* Metanarratives

Grandy, Moses, 1898

Grant, Charles, 1878, 1885

Gray, Thomas, 304, 310, 340, 800, 809–10

Greenblatt, Stephen, 1320–22, 1330, 1452; biography, 1442; **Introduction to** *The Power of Forms in the English Renaissance* **1443–45;** **"King Lear** *and Harsnett's 'Devil-Fiction,'"* **1445–48;** *Shakespearean Negotiations,* 1329

Gregory, John: *A Father's Legacy to His Daughters*, 281

Greimas, A. J., 832, 839, 884, 1162, 1210, 1295, 1349

Griffith, D. W., 744

Grigotti, Victorio, 1934

Grimke, Angeline Weld, 1609

Gronniosaw, James, 1900–01

Grooms, Red, 1923

Gropius, Walter, 1922, 1957

Grundlage. See Base

Guattari, Félix, 1764, 1775; biography, 1777; **"What Is a Minor Literature," 1777–83**

Gubar, Susan, 606, 1034, 1111, 1502, 1509, 1556, 1612; biography, 1531; **"Infection in the Sentence," 1532–44**

Guha, Rajanit, 17

Guillory, John, 1336; biography, 1471; crisis of the humanities, 1477–78, 1480–81; *Cultural Capital,* **1472–84**

Gutenberg, Johann, 1789

Gynocriticism: in Gilbert and Gubar, 1583; in Showalter, 1503, 1583

H. D. (Hilda Doolittle), 1533, 1540

Habermas, Jürgen, 1204, 1212–15, 1255, 1305, 1723, 1730, 1930–33, 1995–97, 2007; and anti-modernity, 1955–56; and domains of culture, 1952; biography, 1947; discourse theory, 1212–13; *Knowledge and Human Interests,* 1305; modernity and aesthetics, 1949–50; modernity and history, 1948–49; **"Modernity versus Postmodernity," 1947–55;** *The Philosophical Discourse of Modernity,* 1213; theory of the public sphere, 1212

Habitus, 1333, 1473; in Bourdieu, 1333–34, 1399, 1401–02; in Geertz, 1372

Haggard, H. Rider: *King Solomon's Mines*, 481; *She*, 481, 1847

Halberstam, Judith, 1621–22; bathrooms and cross-dressing, 1751, 1746–51; biography, 1734–35; *Female Masculinity, 1735–52;* tomboyism, 1737–40

Hall, Stuart, 1323; biography, 1404; *Cultural Studies: Two Paradigms,* **1404–18**

Hallam, Arthur Henry, 1620

Halperin, David, 1625–26, 1695, 1727

Hamartia (tragic flaw): in Aristotle, 57, 67

Hammett, Dashiell, 649, 1830

Hamsun, Knut: *Hunger*, 782

Happiness: in Kant, 253

Haraway, Donna, 1929, 1933; biography, 1967; *A Cyborg Manifesto,* **1967–90;** cyborgs and traditional boundaries, 1968–70; information and domination, 1973–77; utopias in feminist science fiction, 1982–88; women and technology, 1977–82

Hardy, Thomas 651, 655, 800, 1063, 1065, 1067–68, 1073, 1313, 1435, 1825, 1923; *Far from the Madding Crowd*, 1060; *Jude the Obscure*, 1582; *The Mayor of Casterbridge*, 1579, 1582; *The Return of the Native,* 543, 1060; *Tess of the D'Urbervilles*, 1065–66, 1069–71, 1074–75

Harlem Renaissance, 566, 1907

Harris, Bertha, 1605

Harris, James "Hermes," 9

Harris, Wilson, 1766, 1844

Harris, Zellig, 1113

Harsnett, Samuel: *Declaration of Egregious Popish Impostures*, 1321, 1329, 1445–46

Hartman, Geoffrey, 1, 834, 836, 1073, 1158, 1159, 1384, 1394, 1579, 1593, 1872, 1897

Haskell, Molly, 1176

Hassan, Ihab, 1923, 1933, 1993, 1998, 2002, 2005, 2007–08

Hastings, Warren, 1878

Hauptmann, Gerhard, 552

Hawks, Howard: *The Big Sleep*, 1177

Hawthorne, Nathaniel, 470, 1037, 1109, 1520, 1523, 1527, 1586; "The Birthmark," 1037; *The Scarlet Letter*, 1509, 1527, 1765

Hay, Denys, 1803

Haydn, Joseph, 1923

Haydon, Benjamin, 333

Hayford, J. E. Casely, 1822

Haywood, Eliza, 1515

Hazlitt, Thomas, 330

Heaney, Seamus, 1063, 1065

Hegel, Georg Wilhelm Friedrich, 11, 50, 300, 397–98, 400, 613, 702, 724–25, 827, 830–31, 874, 934, 940–41, 944, 1152, 1181, 1188, 1199, 1206, 1212, 1217, 1220, 1223, 1237, 1255, 1271, 1300–01, 1326, 1385, 1393–94, 1451, 1823, 1832, 1834, 1879, 1896–97, 1899; *Aesthetics*, 370; biography, 369; dialectic, 371; holistic thought, 370;

"Introduction to the Philosophy of Art," 373–84, 1240; *Logic*, 369; *Phenomenology of Spirit*, 369–370, 1112; *The Philosophy of Right*, 369

Hegemony, 1206, 1276–83, 1297, 1301, 1313–14, 1323, 1337, 1419, 1832; in Eagleton, 1314; in Foucault, 1422, 1628; in Gramsci, 1421, 1482, 1803; in Guillory, 1475; in Said, 1802–03; in Williams, 1206, 1277. *See also* Dominance; Subordination

Heidegger, Martin, 478, 577, 611–12, 650, 659, 662, 673, 702, 718–19, 721–22, 724, 729–30, 827, 829–31, 837, 901, 917, 933, 940, 946–49, 957, 1143, 1148, 1189, 1213, 1219–20, 1223, 1225, 1227, 1230, 1475, 1597, 1837, 1861, 1934, 1958, 1963, 1995; *Being and Time*, 611, 659, 722, 937; biography, 611–12; **"Hölderlin and the Essence of Poetry,"** 614–22

Heilbrun, Carolyn, 1535, 1582

Heilman, Robert B., 754, 759

Heisenberg, Werner Karl, 1972

Helms, Jesse, 1712

Hemenway, Robert, 1870

Heminges, John, 220

Hemingway, 801, 1023, 1098, 1597; *A Farewell to Arms*, 1036–37, 1041, 1095, 1584; "Big Two-Hearted River," 1439; *For Whom the Bell Tolls*, 1527; *The Sun Also Rises*, 968

Henderson, Stephen, 1903, 1905, 1909

Hendiadys, 1875

Heraclitus, 386, 452, 541, 946

Herbert, George, 535, 967

Herder, Johann Gottfried von, 725, 1905

Herman, David, 1099–1100

Hermaphrodism, 1632, 1697

Hermeneutic circle, 22, 721, 729–30, 966

Hermeneutic code: in Barthes, 1162

Hermeneutics, 903, 982, 1001, 1922; historical, 986; in Bakhtin, 578; in Gadamer, 718–37; in Jauss, 984–88; in Lipking, 895; in Sontag, 741, 745; literary, 987; theological, 987. *See also* Exegesis; Interpretation

Hernadi, Paul, 1090, 1099

Hernton, Calvin, 1870

Herodotus, 65, 99, 106, 137, 144, 338, 350, 458, 486, 525, 532

Herr, Michael, 1965

Hesiod, 33, 39–40, 101, 106, 136, 159, 1566

Heteroglossia (Bakhtin): 587–89, 591–93. *See also* Dialogism

Heteronormativity (Berlant and Warner), 1622–23, 1722–27, 1729, 1731. *See also* Compulsory heterosexuality

Heterosexuality, 1119, 1176, 1611, 1616–17, 1633, 1690–91, 1710, 1713–18; and patriarchy, 1686; defined in opposition to homosexuality, 1620

Heylin, Peter, 1897

Heyward, DuBose: *Porgy*, 573

Hicks, Granville, 1200

Hieroglyph, 1024

High modernism, 1957, 1965–66, 2010. *See also* Modernism

in Shelley, 349, 357; in Herrnstein Smith, 245, in Wordsworth, 307, 311, 313

Humanism: in Barthes, 877; in Williams, 1308

Humanities, curriculum, and crisis; in Guillory, 1335, 1481–82

Humboldt: Wilhelm von, 299

Hume, David, 5, 199, 248–49, 320, 340, 359, 400, 1073, 1262, 1807, 1896, 1898, 1900; biography, 231; **"Of the Standard of Taste," 234–44;** skepticism of, 231

Humours: in Dryden, 166, 180, 184, 186; in Hume, 242; in Keats, 333; in Shelley, 353

Hurston, Zora Neale, 1512, 1603–04, 1609, 1772, 1858, 1861, 1870, 1893, 1904; *Their Eyes Were Watching God*, 1439, 1515, 1930

Husserl, Edmund, 611–12, 659, 718, 735, 827, 838–39, 914, 925, 942, 946, 954, 984, 1004, 1372, 1958

Hustler, 1324–25, 1485–88, 1490–93, 1495–1501; anti-Semitism, 1501; misogyny, 1501

Hutcheon, Linda, 1924, 1928, 1933; biography, 1992; **"Theorizing the Postmodern: Toward a Poetics," 1992–2007**

Hutcheson, Francis, 231

Huxley, Aldous, 334, 1242

Huysman, J. K.: *Against Nature*, 1066–67, 1070, 1073

Hybridity, 1774, 1883–84, 1889; in Anzaldúa, 1850; in Bhabha, 1763, 1882–87, 1889; in Chow, 1918; in Haraway, 1969

Hyman, Stanley Edgar, 1016

Hypnosis: in Scarry, 1073

Hypothesis testing: in Fish, 1033

Hysteria, 1126, 1566–67; hysterical subject, in Foucault, 1619, 1633, 1636

I (Lacanian subject): in Butler, 1708–09, 1711; in Lacan, 1122–24, 1126–28, 1162, 1175. *See also* Ego; Subject

Iamblichus, 388

Id: in Freud, 1107, 1109, 1114, 1123, 1146, 1151; in Lacan, 1126

Idea: in Arnold, 429; in Hegel, 371, 376–77, 383; in Kant, 250; in Plato, 4, 232; in Plotinus, 111–12, 115; in Schiller, 301, 303; in Sidney, 143

Idealism, 1877; in Plato, 4

Idealism, 1228; in Emerson, 389, 391; in Keats, 330; in Plato, 25, 26, 28; in Plotinus, 4; in Shelley, 344, 345

Ideas: in Kant, 266; in Plotinus, 109

Identification: in Iser, 1012; in Lacan, 1124; in Mulvey, 1176; in Poulet, 1013

Identity: categories, 1707–08, 1916; in Berlant and Warner, 1621; in Bhabha, 1882–83; in Butler, 1707–08, 1710; in Culler, 1590; in Halberstam, 1621; in Morris, 1459

Identity politics, 1625, 1866, 1918, 1929–30, 2012; and post-structuralism; in Chow, 1915; in Butler, 1711; in Chow, 1910–11; in hooks, 2013; in Smith, 1600–05

Identity theme: in Holland, 970, 1019

Ideologeme, 822, 1298; in Jameson, 1291, 1298, 1304

Ideological state apparatuses: in Althusser, 1266; in Eagleton, 1313; in Williams, 1282

Ideology, 6, 1277, 1287–88, 1295–96, 1513, 1612; collective consciousness, 1200; false consciousness, 1200, 1204, 1256; in Ahmad, 1833; in Althusser, 1264–66, 1269–70; in Arnold, 413; in Baker, 1770; in Bakhtin, 578, 580, 582, 584; in Baudrillard, 1941–42; in Brecht, 1251; in Eagleton, 1310–11, 1313, 1316; in Eco, 960–61; in Fetterley, 972; in Foucault, 913, 1632; in Gilbert and Gubar, 1512, 1547; in Goldmann, 1205; in Greenblatt, 1444, 1447; in Guillory, 1481; in Hall, 1411; in Horkheimer and Adorno, 1256, 1261, 1262; in Kolodny, 1561; in Lukács, 1219, 1221, 1223, 1226–27; in Marx, 398–99, 409; in New Historicism, 1449; in Rabinowitz, 965, 1055; in Williams, 1273, 1277; in Wittig, 1637; in Žižek, 1119; Marxist concept, 1200, 1202, 1207; religious, 1271. *See also* Aesthetic ideology; Authorial ideology; General ideology; etc.

Ideology of form (Jameson), 1292, 1304–05

Illocutionary utterance (Austin), 680, 685–90, 888, 893, 1213

Image, 102, 750; in Baym, 1528; in Benjamin, 1230; in Bloom, 1157; in Burke, 635; in De Man, 888; in Dryden, 169; in Eliot, 540; in Foucault, 1361; in Frye, 697; in Heilman, 758; in James, 469; in Jung, 551–53; in Lacan, 1112–13; in Nietzsche, 436; in Plotinus, 114–15, 117; in Potebnya, 775; in Scarry, 1075; in Shklovsky, 775–77, 781; in Sidney, 143. *See also* Symbol

Image schemas: in Turner, 1082–84, 1087

Imagery: archetypal, 5; in Burke, 638; in Johnson, 215; in Longinus, 98; in Pope, 198; in Shelley, 349; in Sidney, 148; in Wordsworth, 314

Imaginary (Lacanian field), 1112, 1114–15, 1124, 1128, 1144, 1152, 1172, 1265, 1922, 1941; in Baudrillard, 1938; in Bhabha, 1880; in Butler, 1717; in Cixous, 1644; in Guillory, 1480; in Jameson, 1295; in Mulvey, 1172–73, 1175, 1177; in Spivak, 1843; in Wittig, 1639–40

Imagination, 5, 7; and gender, 1510; in Benjamin, 1236; in Bloom, 1157; in Brecht, 1252; in Cixous, 1648; in Coleridge, 319, 321–22, 325, 329, 754, 814; in Collingwood, 1386; in Dryden, 164, 182; in Eco, 956; in Emerson, 385, 392, 394; in Freud, 509–14, 521, 529–31; in Hegel, 379, 383; in Horkheimer and Adorno, 1259; in Hume, 236, 238–39, 241, 243; in Iser, 1002, 1004–05, 1007, 1014; in James, 468; in Johnson, 213, 215, 218, 223; in Jung, 562; in Kant, 249, 251, 259, 261, 263–64, 266–68, 271–73, 320; in Keats, 330–31; in Lipking, 902; in Marx, 406, 409, 411; in New Criticism, 756; in Nietzsche, 441; in Ngugi, 1823; in Pope, 200; in Sartre, 665, 1072; in Scarry, 1058, 1063–64, 1067–68; in Schiller, 302–03; in Shelley, 344, 346–48, 351, 354, 360; in Sidney, 143, 150; in Spivak, 1848; in Staël, 286–87; in Turner, 1087; in Wimsatt and Beardsley, 813; in Woolf, 600, 605; in Wordsworth, 305, 307, 316; primary, 321, 325; productive, 321; secondary, 321, 325. *See also* Fancy; Genius

Imago: in Freud, 1124; in Lacan, 1124, 1127

Imitation, 2–5, 7, 11, 199, 740; and ecocriticism, 1438–39; in Aristotle, 4, 6–7, 57, 59, 61, 63, 65, 76, 78, 82, 740; in Auerbach, 702–17; in Barthes, 872, 881; in Bhabha, 1879, 1881; in Butler, 1620–21, 1710, 1712–14, 1718; in Coleridge, 325; in Derrida, 1714; in Dryden, 162, 167, 172, 175–77, 179; in Emerson, 389; in Hegel, 374; in Horace, 82, 84, 87, 90; in Jauss, 975; in Johnson, 211, 214–15, 217, 224, 227, 229; in Kant, 273; in Kolodny, 1560; in Lipking, 902; in Longinus, 106; in Marxist criticism, 1201–02; in Neo-Aristotelianism, 759; in Nietzsche, 451; in Plato, 4, 6, 27, 30–31, 33–34, 57, 111, 740; in Plotinus, 4, 109, 111; in Pope, 201, 205; in Propp, 789; in Scarry, 1061, 1066, 1070–71; in Shelley, 347, 350, 353; in Sidney, 132, 139, 143–45, 155; in Staël, 288, 290; in Wilde, 486–91, 495; in Wimsatt and Beardsley, 811. *See also* Representation

Immasculation (Fetterley), 972, 1039, 1118, 1593

Imperialism, 1761–62, 1766, 1804, 1807, 1810, 1813, 1828, 1832–33, 1837–49, 1879, 1883, 1917; and aboriginal cultures, 1757–58; and imagined communities, 1759; and native languages, 1766, 1822, 1824; history, 1754; in Bhabha, 1763–64; in hooks, 2013; in Said, 1807; motives, 1754; narratives, 1756–57; resistance, 1759; Victorians' views, 1807. *See also* Colonialism

Impersonality: and poetry, 7; in Eliot, 756

Implied author: in Booth, 964, 996

Impressionism, 1923, 1936

Incest: in Peter Brooks, 1170; in Foucault, 1635–36; in Freud, 1143; in Kipnis 1494; in Lacan, 1149; in Lévi-Strauss, 918–19, 1128; in Rubin, 1672, 1675–76, 1681

Indeterminacy: in Iser, 1005, 1007–08, 1010; in Jauss, 986; in Lipking, 901

Individualism, 365, 436, 638, 898, 914, 1452, 1489, 1765, 1791, 1796–97, 1799–1800, 1838–40, 1845, 1958

Industrial Revolution, 364, 1205, 1211, 1327, 1567, 1976

Infantile sexuality: in Freud, 1107, 1624; in Rubin, 1678

Infection: in Tolstoy, 50, 52

Influence: in Bloom, 1156–57; in Leavis, 653, 656–57; in Longinus, 106

Information theory, 1131

Ingarden, Roman, 973, 979, 1001–05

Inside views (Booth), 991

Inspiration: in Arnold, 416; in Emerson, 392; in Longinus, 95, 101, 106; in Plato, 27, 41, 117; in Plotinus, 110, 116, 117; in Poulet, 973; in Sartre, 664; in Shelley, 345, 360, 362; in Sidney, 139; in Wimsatt and Beardsley, 811. See also *Enthousiasmós*

Instincts: in Freud, 1107, 1166; in Jung, 551; in Richards, 766

Institutionon for Social Research. *See* Frankfurt School

Instruction: in Dryden, 166; in Horace, 91; in James, 466; in Johnson, 217, 219, 221, 225; in rhetorical theory, 5; in Sidney, 133, 148; in Staël, 287; in Wordsworth, 305. *See also* Delight; Didacticism

Insurgency (colonial), 1755, 1757, 1760

Integrated circuit: in Haraway, 1977, 1980, 1983, 1986

Integrity, 814; in Woolf, 604–05

Intellect: in Nietzsche, 452–53

Intellectual-Principle: in Plotinus, 112, 114, 118–19

Intention: in Barthes, 880; in De Man, 887; in Fish, 966, 1023; in Iser, 1004, 1010; in Jung, 548; in Lipking, 902; in Lukács, 1219; in New Criticism, 756, 1321; in Peter Brooks, 1167; in Plotinus, 111; in Rabinowitz, 1045; in Sartre, 667–68; in Wimsatt and Beardsley, 811, 814, 818

Intentional fallacy: in Burke, 634; in Wimsatt and Beardsley, 811–18

Intentionality, levels: in Dennett, 1101; in Zunshine, 1096–99

Internally persuasive discourse: in Bakhtin, 580, 582–84

Interpellation: in Althusser, 1268–70; in Bhabha, 1880; in Spivak, 1838

Interpretation: in Aquinas, 120; in Barthes, 877, 880, 1162; in Bourdieu, 1399; in Culler, 825; in De Man, 883, 888; in Derrida, 925–26; in Fish, 966, 1024–25, 1027, 1032; in Foucault, 906; in Freud, 506, 509, 1110; in Frye, 701; in Gadamer, 722; in Geertz, 1368, 1373–75, 1377, 1379–83; in Greenblatt, 1444; in Holland, 1016, 1017; in Iser, 1006, 1010; in Jameson, 1291; in Jauss, 982–85, 987; in Lacan, 1148; in Lipking, 897; in McKeon, 11; in New Criticism, 756, 758; in Nietzsche, 916; in Rabinowitz, 1048; in Richards, 773; in Sontag, 739, 741, 742, 743, 745; in Zunshine, 1094. *See also* Exegesis; Hermeneutics

Interpretive communities: in Fish, 967, 1022–23, 1027–30, 1032, 1044, 1047, 1052, 1054; in Rabinowitz, 965, 1044, 1047, 1052

Interpretive conventions: in Culler, 824; in Rabinowitz, 1055

Interpretive strategies: in Fish, 1027, 1032; in Kolodny, 1555

Intertextuality: in Bakhtin, 575; in Barthes, 987–88; in Gates, 1900, 1908; in Guillory 1476; in Hutcheon, 2001; in Kristeva 1572; in Said, 1806

Intoxication: in Nietzsche, 437, 439–40, 459–60

Introversion: in Jung, 548

Intuition: in Croce, 812; in Kant, 249, 252, 262–63, 267–68, 271, 273; in Keats, 330; in Nietzsche, 438, 452; in Plotinus, 109; in Wordsworth, 313

Invention: in Sidney, 138; in Turner, 1077

Irigaray, Luce, 598, 1112, 1506, 1516, 1548, 1611–13, 1624, 1725, 1983; *Speculum of the Other Woman*, 1587

Irony, 739, 1394; in Booth, 995–96, 998; in Cleanth Brooks, 758, 800–01, 804, 808; in Frye, 692; in Iser, 1011; in Leavis, 654–56; in New Criticism, 750; in Plato, 26–27; in Robert Penn Warren, 758; in White, 1330

Irving Washington: *Rip Van Winkle*, 1036–37, 1041–43

Iser, Wolfgang, 660, 718, 962, 972, 985–86, 988, 1022, 1052; biography, 1001; **"The Reading Process: A Phenomenological Approach,"** 1002–14

Iteration: in Derrida, 925; in Eco, 957, 959

Ivanov, Vyacheslav, 776, 784

Jackson, Jesse, 2018
Jackson, Rebecca Cox, 1901–02
Jacobinism, 1935
Jacobs, Carol, 836
Jacobus, Mary, 1512, 1514, 1545–49, 1582
Jahvist, 710
Jakobson, Roman, 750, 752, 822, 824, 826, 839, 852, 859, 884, 983, 1130, 1136, 1168, 1348, 1384, 1395, 1781, 1944; biography, 852; **"Linguistics and Poetics," 852–59**
James, Henry, 334, 481, 534, 622, 626, 651–52, 656, 658, 964, 989, 994–95, 1001, 1036, 1209, 1509, 1523, 1527, 1580, 1620, 1690, 1771, 1923; **"The Art of Fiction," 464–75;** biography, 462; *The Bostonians,* 1036, 1038, 1042, 1585; expressive criticism, 463; *An International Episode,* 473; theories of fiction, 462; *The Turn of the Screw,* 1043
James, William, 565, 679, 777
James, Vanessa: *Fire and the Ice,* 1053
Jameson, Fredric, 13, 661, 1022, 1118, 1198, 1207, 1209–12, 1263, 1322, 1562, 1768–69, 1775, 1829–34, 1912, 1924, 1928, 1933, 1956, 1958–59, 1965–66, 1971–72, 1978, 1990, 1993, 1995–96, 1999, 2001, 2004, 2007; as cultural critic, 1211; biography, 1290; end of modernist subjectivity, 1959–60; location of postmodernism, 1957–58; Marxism and Form, 1209–10, 1296; pastiche and parody, 1958–59; *The Political Unconscious,* 1210–11, **1291–1306;** postmodern architecture, 1962–65; postmodernism and capitalism, 1965–67; **"postmodernism and Consumer Society," 1956–65;** postmodernism and nostalgia, 1961; *Postmodernism, or The Cultural Logic of Late Capitalism,* 1833; **"Third World Literature in the Era of Multinational Capitalism," 1830–31, 1834–6**
Jardine, Alice, 1563, 1565, 1569, 1571, 1597
Jarrell, Randall: "Eighth Air Force," 805–06
Jarry, Alfred, 1246, 1923
Jaspers, Karl, 612, 718
Jauss, Hans Robert, 660, 718, 972, 1001, 1047, 1948; biography, 981, **"[The Three Horizons of Reading]," 982–89**
Jea, John, 1900–01
Jean de Meun, 125–26
Jean Paul (Johann Paul Friedrich Richter), 588, 593–94
Jefferson, Thomas, 1770, 1896, 1899, 1905–06
Jencks, Charles, 2015
Jesenska, Milena, 1781
Jespersen, Otto, 1130
Jews, 95, 102, 375, 707, 712
Jeyifo, Biodun, 1873
Joan of Arc, 125, 126
Johnson, Samuel, 5–6, 231, 285, 304–05, 317, 415, 652, 893, 1199, 1295, 1308; biography, 210; *Irene,* 415; *Lives of the Poets,* 415; "London," 754; moralism, 210; **"Preface to Shakespeare,"** 134, **216–30,** 413; *Rambler* No. 4, **212–15,** 285; 465, 606, 751; *Rasselas,* **215–16;** rhetorical principles, 210; tragic vision, 211; universalizing perspective, 211; "The Vanity of Human Wishes," 754

Johnson, Barbara, 835, 1772, 1845, 1870
Johnson, Mark, 1082
Johnson, Philip, 1922, 1924, 2015
Jonas, Hans, 1956
Jones, Ann Rosalind, 1516
Jones, Ernest, 1150; *Hamlet and Oedipus,* 1109
Jones, Sir William, 1804, 1810, 1812
Jonson, Ben, 160, 162, 169, 175, 180, 184, 191, 194, 227, 536, 622, 653; *The Alchemist,* 180–81, 194; *Bartholomew Fair,* 180; *Catiline,* 176, 182; *Discoveries,* 168; *Epicoene,* 180–81, 184–87; *Every Man in His Humour,* 184; *Every Man out of His Humour,* 204; *The Magnetic Lady,* 178; *Sejanus,* 176; *Volpone,* 182, 991
Jordan, June, 1864
Jordan, Neil: *The Crying Game,* 1192, 1194, 1196–97
Jouissance, 832, 1196; in Barthes, 832, 881, 969; in De Man, 893; in Kristeva, 1566; in Lacan, 1187
Joyce, James, 463, 612, 622, 651, 657, 699, 956, 963, 1048, 1218, 1220–21, 1225, 1232; *Finnegans Wake,* 825, 1374, 1565; *Ulysses,* 1011, 1218, 1650, 1690, 1780, 1830, 1957, 1966, 1986, 1995
Joyce, Joyce Ann, 1867, 1871
Judgment, critical, 9; in Arnold, 428; in Baym, 1521; in Booth, 993–94; in Dryden, 172, 182, 184, 187; in Eliot, 538; in Frye, 694; in Hume, 232–33, 235, 238, 241; in Johnson, 217; in Jung, 545; in Kant, 247, 249, 251–52, 254–56, 258–59, 261–63, 265, 268–70; in Leavis, 652; in Pope, 200, 202, 205, 207; in Wimsatt and Beardsley, 814. *See also* Taste
Jung, Carl Gustav, 5, 9, 497, 498, 691, 698, 701, 772, 861, 1124; biography, 542; **"On the Relation of Analytical Psychology to Poetry," 544–54; "The Principal Archetypes," 554–64**
Juvenal, 160, 169, 299, 338, 362; *Satires,* 154, 157, 174

Kafka, Franz, 623, 664, 742, 905, 1052, 1203, 1212, 1220, 1222, 1226–27, 1230–31, 1690, 1764, 1775, 1777–82, 1923; *The Castle,* 1227; "Investigations of a Dog," 1779; *The Metamorphosis,* 1167, 1779; *The Trial,* 1054, 1227, 1709
Kamuf, Peggy, 1514, 1587, 1590, 1592
Kandinsky, Wassily, 1356
Kant, Immanuel, 96, 199, 298–300, 319–20, 342, 344, 385, 452, 454, 555, 643, 664, 681, 724, 1078, 1113, 1188–89, 1258, 1262, 1334, 1386, 1402–03, 1770, 1777, 1841, 1846–47, 1896, 1898–1900; biography, 247; *Critique of Judgment,* **251–74,** 281, 826, 1189, 1190; *Critique of Practical Reason,* 258, 1187; *Critique of Pure Reason,* 247, 319, 953; *Metaphysic of Morals,* 259
Kaplan, Cora, 1547
Kauffman, Linda, 1870
Kazin, Alfred, 1201
Keast, William Rea, 759
Keats, John, 364, 366–67, 540, 601, 638–39, 641, 643–44, 696, 767, 853, 857, 1035, 1040, 1060, 1159, 1804; biography,

853–59; in Johnson, 218, 220, 222, 226, 229; in Kant, 271; in Kristeva, 1116; in Lacan, 1112–13, 1115, 1130, 1132, 1147; in Leavis, 657; in Lévi-Strauss, 920; in Lipking, 901–02; in Longinus, 97; in Neo-Aristotelianism, 760; in New Criticism, 757–58; in Ngugi, 1822–23; in Nietzsche, 437–38, 453, 454; in Plato, 26; in Pope, 203; in poststructuralism, 8; in Richards, 754, 764; in Russian formalism, 751–52; in Sartre, 664; in Saussure, 827, 842, 847–50, 938; in Shelley, 345, 347–48, 353; in Shklovsky, 776; in Sidney, 159; in the Sophists, 26; in structuralism, 819, 822; in Williams, 1288; in Wimsatt and Beardsley, 812, 814–16; in Woolf, 606; in Wordsworth, 306–12, 314, 317

Langue and parole, 820, 823, 832, 861–62; in Jameson, 1291, 1297, 1298; in Lacan, 1131; in Lévi-Strauss, 863, 868

Lanser, Susan Sniader, 1515

Lardner, Ring: "Haircut," 965

Latent content: in Freud, 497–98, 742, 1109; in Holland, 970

Lauretis, Teresa de, 1118, 1611, 1695, 1725

Lautréamont, Lucien-Isidore Ducasse, Comte de, 853, 1117

Law: in Sidney, 138, 141

Lawrence, D. H., 597, 639, 650–51, 655–58, 675–77, 743, 766, 1038, 1505, 1581, 1597, 1690, 1825

Le Corbusier (Charles-Edouard Jeanneret), 1922, 1957, 1963

Leach, Edmund, 1682

Learning: in Eliot, 539; in Pope, 202, 207

Leavis, F. R., 651, 1405, 1435, 1509, 1784; biography, 650; *The Great Tradition,* 651, **652–59**

Leavis, Q. D., 650, 654

Lee, Spike, 2017

Legitimation: in Bourdieu, 1443

Leibniz, Gottfried Wilhelm, 555

Leitch, Vincent, 1337

Lenin, Vladimir Ilych, 1912

Lentricchia, Frank, 1322; biography, 1448; *Ariel and the Police,* **1447–52**

Lenz, Jakob Michael: *The Tutor,* 1636

Leonardo da Vinci, 1129, 1690

Leontius of Byzantium, 479

Lermontov, Mikhail: *A Hero of Our Time,* 584

Leroi-Ladurie, Emmanuel, 1326

Lesage, Alain-René, 92

Lesbian continuum: in Adrienne Rich, 1617, 1685

Lesbian culture, 1637: in Anzaldúa, 1852, in Wittig, 1616

Lesbianism, 1513, 1600–02, 1605–10, 1617–18, 1621, 1625, 1689, 1709–12; and psychoanalysis, 1679; definitions, 1608; in Barbara Smith, 1600; in Butler, 1707. *See also* Homosexuality; Queer Theory

Leskov, Nikolai, 784

Lessing, Doris, 1537, 1557

Lessing, Gotthold Ephraim, 453, 1067; *Nathan the Wise,* 302

Levinas, Emmanuel, 838, 933, 937, 945–46

Levine, George, 1845

Lévi-Strauss, Claude, 12, 543, 750, 753, 785, 822–24, 826, 830–31, 839–40, 859–62, 872–74, 917–19, 983, 1113,

1124, 1128, 1162, 1323, 1331, 1354, 1374, 1384, 1391, 1411–13, 1416, 1563, 1577, 1597, 1615, 1636, 1663–65, 1670–80, 1682, 1984; biography, 859; **"The Structural Study of Myth,"** 860–68, 1292–93

Lewis, R. W. B., 1509, 1525

Lewis, Sinclair: *Babbitt,* 648

Lewontin, Richard, 1740–41

Leys, Ruth, 1716

Liberal humanism, 1261, 1315

Libido, 1127, 1155, 1175, 1179, 1648, 1652, 1654; in Freud, 1107, 1111; in Frye, 700

Lichtenstein, Heinz, 1014

Life-world (Jauss), 987

Liminality, 1767; in Anzaldúa, 1768; in Bhabha, 1763. *See also* Hybridity

Lincoln, Abraham, 16, 566, 1892

Linguistics, 1151; historical, 854; in Jakobson, 852; in Lacan, 1131; in Lévi-Strauss, 861

Lipking, Lawrence, 1596; biography, 893; **"The Practice of Theory,"** **893–903**

Lippi, Fra Filippo, 1400

Lispector, Clarice, 1614

Literacy, 1311

Literariness: in Chow, 1911, 1913, 1915–16

Literary ancestry: in Gates, 1904

Literary anthropology: in Iser, 1002

Literary competence: in Kolodny, 1554

Literary criticism: in Eagleton, 1318

Literary discourse: in Engels, 1912

Literary economy: in Aristotle, 81

Literary evolution. *See* Literary history

Literary hermeneutics: in Jauss, 988

Literary history, 1338: in Armstrong, 1419; in Bakhtin, 582, 586; in Baym, 1520, 1524; in Bloom, 1534; in Brecht, 1252; in Frye, 696, 699; in Gates, 1891; in Greenblatt, 1444; in Iser, 974; in Jameson, 1303–04; in Jauss, 973, 981; in Kolodny, 1553–60; in Leavis, 653; in Lipking, 895, 901; in Marxist criticism, 754; in Russian Formalism, 753; in Wimsatt and Beardsley, 811. *See also* History and literature

Literary language: in Fish, 1024

Literary mode of production: in Eagleton, 1308–19

Literature: African American, 1770–71; and homophobia, 1690; and referentiality, 1911; and revolution, 1778; and society, 635, 1510; as ideology, 1906; as system, 752–54; effects, 1; in Arnold, 412, 416, 428; in Baker, 1906; in Barthes, 872, 878–80; in Brecht, 1250; in Burke, 634–35, 646, 648; in De Man, 882–83, 891; in Eagleton, 1315; in Foucault, 908; in Freud, 1110; in Frye, 693; in Greenblatt, 1444; in Johnson, 226; in Lacan, 1116; in Leavis, 652; in McDowell, 1773; in Russian formalism, 752; in Sartre, 671, in Scarry, 1074; in Showalter, 1510; inscribed in language, 1; linguistic basis, 1769–70; paternity, 1534; postcolonial, 1757; social basis, 1769–70; "Third World," 1768–69

Livy (Titus Livius), 144, 350

Locke, Alain, 566, 1602

Locke, John, 319, 359, 1069, 1061, 1807, 1885; *Essay Concerning Human Understanding*, 319, 1062–63, 1069

Locutionary utterance: in Austin, 680, 685–90, 1213

Logical positivism, 679, 1132

Logocentrism, 1614

Logos: in Derrida, 927, 929–31

Longfellow, Henry Wadsworth, 853; *The Song of Hiawatha*, 859

Longinus, 95, 208, 812, 977; identity of, 95; influence of, 96; method of, 95; **"On the Sublime,"** 97–108

Longus: *Daphnis and Chloë*, 1150

Lord, Albert, 1904

Lorde, Audre, 1609, 1864–65, 1983, 1990

Love and Death (Woody Allen), 1056

Lovejoy, Arthur, 1450

Lowes, John Livingston, 815

Lu Xun, 1835

Lucan, 351, 357; *Pharsalia*, 225

Lucretius, 139, 354, 357, 439

Lud, Ned, 1429

Lukács, Georg, 1049, 1170, 1198, 1200–03, 1208–09, 1251, 1255, 1407, 1553, 1912; biography, 1217; *History and Class Consciousness*, 1217; **"The Ideology of Modernism,"** 1201, 1217, **1218–31**

Luther, Martin, 1816

Lynch, David: *Wild at Heart*, 1191

Lyotard, Jean-François, 1924–26, 1933, 1995–97, 2000–01, 2005, 2007–08; biography, 1933; **"Defining the Postmodern,"** 1933–35

Lyric, 95, 985; as drama, 811; in Cleanth Brooks, 802; in Dryden, 165; in Hegel, 372; in Schiller, 302; in Sidney, 151, 157; in Wordsworth, 314. *See also* Poetry; Verse

Lyrical intuition: in Croce, 756

Lysias, 26

Mabinogion, 888

Macaulay, Thomas Babington, 466, 1330, 1763, 1807, 1823–24, 1878

Macherey, Pierre, 1207, 1208, 1210, 1264, 1912

Machiavelli, Niccolo, 12, 353, 1630; *Clitia*, 243

Machismo: in Anzaldúa, 1853

MacKinnon, Catherine, 1929

Maclean, Norman, 759

MacLeish, Archibald, 811

Madonna studies, 1325, 1339

Madwoman: in Gilbert and Gubar, 1536–37

Maecenas, 82

Magnitude: in Aristotle, 64–65, 77, 81, 1164; in Kant, 265, 267–69; in Plotinus, 112

Mahfouz, Naguib, 1757

Mahler, Gustav, 1924, 1957–58

Mailer, Norman, 1504–05, 1581–82, 1585; *An American Dream*, 1036–38, 1041–42

Mailloux, Steven, 1044, 1047, 1049, 1055

Makarie. *See* Goethe

Malcolm X, 2018

Male bonding: in Sedgwick, 1687

Male chauvinism: in Baym, 1521. *See also* Misogyny

Malebranche, Nicholas, 1258

Malinche, 1984–85

Malinowski, Bronislaw, 856, 1331, 1348, 1375, 1377, 1379, 1671

Mallarmé, Stephane, 852, 872, 875, 881, 1117, 1237, 1923, 1965

Malory, Sir Thomas: *Morte d'Arthur*, 226, 692

Malraux, André, 677

Malthus, Thomas Robert, 400, 1632

Malthusian couple: in Foucault, 1619, 1633

Mandeville, John, 487

Manet, Edouard, 1936

Manifest content: in Freud, 497, 500–01, 503, 505, 741, 1109; in Holland, 970. *See also* Latent content

Manley, Delariviere, 1515

Mann, Thomas, 623, 655, 742, 1218, 1690, 1957, 1965; *Death in Venice*, 1662; *Doctor Faustus*, 1223, 1229; *Lotte in Weimar*, 1218

Mansfield, Katherine, 1001

Maps of literary theory: Abrams, 3, 8, 10, 12; Crane, 9–10; Friedman, 9–10; McKeon, 11–12

Mapplethorpe, Robert, 1489, 1712

Marcus, Steven, 1804

Marcuse, Herbert, 1199, 1212, 1216, 1254–55, 1623, 1722, 1966, 1973, 1990

Marlowe, Christopher, 536, 1158, 1690

Marmontel, Jean-Francois: *Moral Tales*, 291

Marnie (Alfred Hitchcock), 1178–79

Marrant, John, 1900

Marriage and sexuality: in Foucault, 1633–34

Marryat, Frederick, 653

Marsh, Robert C., 759

Marshall, Paule, 1863, 1865

Martial (Marcus Valerius Martialis), 164, 168

Martin, Biddy, 1728

Marvell, Andrew, 651, 701, 801, 803, 817–18, 853

Marx, Groucho, 1155

Marx, Karl, 6, 8, 285, 371, 397–401, 633, 741–42, 884, 911, 914, 1188, 1198–1201, 1206–08, 1212–16, 1232–33, 1263–66, 1270, 1272–76, 1287, 1299, 1301, 1303–04, 1306, 1322, 1326–27, 1334, 1367, 1385, 1393, 1404, 1449, 1451, 1614–15, 1641, 1665, 1673, 1753, 1773, 1807–08, 1812, 1831, 1891, 1911–12, 1915, 1931, 1954, 1960, 1969, 1995; **"The Alienation of Labor,"** 400–06; *Capital*, 397, 1302, 1680; *The Communist Manifesto*, 397; *A Contribution to the Critique of Political Economy* (the

Grundrisse), 1272; "The Eighteenth Brumaire of Louis Bonaparte," 1273, 1387, 1812; *The German Ideology,* 397, **406–10,** 1421, 1835; **"On Greek Art in Its Time,"** **410–11;** reputation in America, 1198; *Theories on Surplus Value,* 1276; *Theses on Feuerbach,* 1408, 1421

Marx, Leo: *The Machine in the Garden,* 1437

Marxism, 12, 841, 871, 874, 878–80, 903, 912, 972, 976, 978, 1119, 1274, 1287, 1296, 1305, 1323, 1325, 1337, 1383, 1450, 1769, 1861, 1902, 1921–22, 1925, 1930, 1937, 1970, 1990, 1996; and feminism, 1514; dialectical method, 1324; in Ahmad, 1831; in Baker, 1770; in Jameson, 1291, 1831; in Rubin, 1665; in Wittig, 1640–42

Marxist literary criticism, 754, 836, 965, 971, **1198–1319,** 1516, 1546, 1559, 1594–95

Masaccio, Tommaso, 1059

Masculinities, 1622; alternative, 1746; and ethnicity, 1621; and misogyny, 1736; and performance, 1622; and power, 1736; and race, 1621; as cultural construct, 1742–44; as performance, 1737; as social construction, 1736–37; female, 1735–41, 1743–49, 1751–52; gay, 1746; in Halberstam, 1621, 1735–52; in Woolf, 610

Masefield, John, 571

Masochism, 1625; and homosexuality, 1660–61; in Deleuze, 1183; in Žižek, 1184, 1196. *See also* Sadism

Mason, Theodore, 1770

Mass audience: in Horkheimer and Adorno, 1257, 1262

Mass culture, 1261; as ideology, 1204; in Guillory, 1483; in Horkheimer and Adorno, 1204, 1256, 1258, 1261; in Jameson, 1830

Mass media, 1338

Massinger, Philip, 535–36

Master narrative, in Bhabha, 1327; in hooks, 2013, in Jameson, 1294. *See also* Grand narratives; Metanarratives

Master trope: in New Criticism, 758

Masturbation: in Foucault, 1619, 1631–33

Material of art: in Plotinus, 111

Materialism: in Aristotle, 4; in Marx, 397–98, 400–03, 406–07, 409–11

Matisse, Henri, 1059–61, 1065, 1789

Matthiessen, F. O., 817, 1522

Maupassant, Guy de, 54, 482

Mauriac, François, 1148

Mauss, Marcel, 923–24, 1323, 1672

McCoy, Richard, 1325

McCullers, Carson: *The Member of the Wedding,* 1622, 1738–39

McDowell, Deborah, 1513, 1515, 1773, 1869; biography, 1866, **"Recycling," 1870–75**

McKeon, Richard, 11–12, 759

McLuhan, Marshall, 1827, 1999

Mead, Margaret, 1374

Meaning: in Chow, 1774, 1910; in Croce, 813; in Lipking, 894; in Wimsatt and Beardsley, 811

Means of imitation: in Aristotle, 60

Means of production: in Marx, 405, 407–08

Mechanical reproduction: in Benjamin, 1233–37, 1239–41, 1244; in Horkheimer and Adorno, 1259, 1263;

Méconnaissance (misrecognition), 1115, 1140, 1154; in Althusser, 1268; in Lacan, 1114, 1127, 1147, 1150, 1174; in McDowell, 1873–74

Mediation: in Marxist criticism, 1202–05

Medusa, 499, 533

Medvedev, P. N., 576

Melmoth, Sebastian. *See* Wilde

Melville, Herman, 836; 975, 1523, 1525, 1586, 1620, 1794; *Billy Budd,* 1687–88; *Moby-Dick,* 1440, 1765

Memmi, Albert: *The Colonizer and the Colonized,* 1759, 1776

Menand, Louis, 1772

Menander, 168, 338

Mencius, 1132

Mendelssohn, Moses, 254

Mentalités, histoire de, 1325

Meredith, George, 334, 335, 483, 655; *The Egoist,* 1582

Merezhkovsky, Dmitri, 750, 776, 779

Merleau-Ponty, Maurice, 1006, 1101, 1344

Mestiza consciousness: in Anzaldúa, 1768, 1850–53, 1855–0057

Metacommentary: in Jameson, 1209

Metalinguistic aspect of language; in Barthes, 871; in Certeau, 1349; in Jakobson, 856, 858, 882

Metanarratives, 1919, 1925–26, 1930, 1934, 1995, 2005. See also Grand narratives; Master narratives

Metaphor, 750, 825, 835, 852, 880, 883–84, 888–93, 927–30, 977, 1137, 1143, 1168, 1327, 1337, 1394; in Aristotle, 74–77, 80; in Barthes, 880; in Baym, 1529; in Booth, 994; in Cleanth Brooks, 799, 806; in Peter Brooks, 1161, 1169; in De Man, 888–91, 893; in Derrida, 916, 929; in Dryden, 172; in Freud, 1107; in Hume, 236; in Jakobson, 1130; in Lacan, 1112–15, 1136, 1141–42, 1148; in Longinus, 100; in Potebnya, 750–51; in Shelley, 345, 347; in Sidney, 158; in Turner, 1077–80, 1087; in White, 1330, 1392; in Wimsatt and Beardsley, 816. *See also* Figures of speech; Tropes

Metaphysics: in Derrida, 916–17, 919, 924, 927, 946–47; in Kant, 247; in New Criticism, 757; in Plato, 4; in Plotinus, 109; in Sidney, 133

Metatheoretical hypotheses: in Phelan, 1033–34

Meter: 229; in Aristotle, 61, 63, 77; in Peter Brooks, 1165; in Coleridge, 321, 328; in Dryden, 164; in Emerson, 387; in Horace, 85, 89; in Johnson, 229; in Pope, 198; in Shelley, 349; in Sidney, 140, 146, 149, 158; in Wordsworth, 307, 310–11, 314, 316

Methods: critical, 6; dialectical, 11–12; in Barthes, 878; in Burke, 649; logistic, 11–12; operational, 11–12; problematic, 11–12

Metlitzki, Dorothee: *Matter of Araby*, 1809

Metonymy, 835, 879, 889–92, 977, 1327, 1394; in Peter Brooks, 1162; in Genette, 885; in Jakobson, 1130; in Lacan, 1113, 1115, 1136–37, 1139, 1141–42, 1148, 1165, 1168; in Saussure, 851; in White, 1330

Metropolis vs. periphery, 1753

Meyrink, Gustav, 1780

Michaels, Walter Benn, 1048, 1867

Michelangelo Buonarroti, 232, 1077, 1690, 1694

Michelet, Jules, 1387, 1394–96

Middleton, Thomas, 535, 755

Mies van der Rohe, Ludwig, 1922, 1957

Mill, John Stuart, 1510, 1547, 1807

Millennial studies, 1338

Miller, Christopher, 1483

Miller, George, 978

Miller, Henry, 657, 1504, 1581–82

Miller, J. Hillis, 834, 835, 1049, 1164

Miller, Jacques-Alain, 1180

Miller, Nancy, 1514, 1592, 1595

Millett, Kate, 598, 1038, 1504, 1506, 1545, 1547, 1551, 1581, 1582

Milton, John, 232, 236, 299, 309, 310, 340, 345–46, 349, 353, 357, 392, 395, 413, 432, 536, 635, 651–52, 694, 891, 1022, 1294, 1302, 1554, 1690, 1895–96; "Comus," 701; "Lycidas," 634, 1158; *Paradise Lost*, 302, 330–31, 360, 433, 753, 987, 1315–16, 1538, 1555, 1558, 1847, 1970

Mimesis. *See* Imitation

Mind: conscious, 6, 9; in Hegel, 370; in Hume, 238; in Kant, 247, 249, 259, 264, 267, 269, 271; unconscious, 5–6, 9, 12. *See also* Unconscious

Minimal units in structuralism. *See* Emes; Ideologeme; Morpheme; Phoneme; etc.

Minor literature (Deleuze and Guattari), 1764, 1777–81

Minority status: and local politics, 1754

Minority writing, 1753

Mirror-stage (Lacan), 1112, 1114–15, 1123–28, 1268, 1922, 1985

Mise en abîme: in Bhabha, 1881. *See also* Aporia

Misogyny, 1486–87, 1500, 1503; in Black male writers, 1600–05; in *Hustler,* 1499

Misreading: in Bloom, 1111, 1156–57, 1160; in Holland, 1016; in Pope, 207; in Richards, 1018

Misrecognition. See *Méconnaisance*

Mitchell, Juliet, 1677, 1900

Mitchell, Margaret: *Gone with the Wind,* 1045

Miyazaki, Hayao, 1064, 1067

Miyoshi, Masao, 1916

Modern Language Association, 622

Modernism, 1830, 1921–24, 1930, 1932, 1934, 1949–51, 1955–57, 1960, 1962, 1964–67, 1978, 1993–94, 2003–04, 2007, 2015–16; and postcolonialism, 1769; in Adorno, 1203; in Auerbach, 703; in Eliot, 535–36; in Jameson,

1957, 1959; in Lukács, 1201, 1220, 1223–24, 1226–27, 1229–32; in Woolf, 597–98

Modernity: in Barthes, 876, 878, 881; in Bhabha, 1881; in Habermas, 1214, 1947–54; in Kristeva, 1577; in Morris, 1452, 1457–58, 1461, 1469–70; in Ngugi, 1821, 1827; in Wilde, 484, 495

Modes of thought, 11

Moers, Ellen, 1509, 1513, 1556; *Literary Women*, 1603

Moi, Toril, 1117, 1209, 1502, 1509, 1512; biography, 1545; *Sexual/Textual Politics,* **1545–50**

Molière, 51, 54, 180, 187, 302, 856, 1226, 1636, 1816

Mondrian, Piet, 872–73, 1923, 1934, 1936

Monk, Meredith, 1923

Monod, Jacques, 1998

Monologism: in Bakhtin, 576. *See also* Dialogism

Monroe, Marilyn, 1176

Montaigne, Michel de, 702, 1329, 1690

Montesquieu, Robert de, 1885, 1891

Montgomery, Robert: *Lady in the Lake*, 1185

Montherlant, Henri de, 675–77, 1225, 1581

Montrose, Louis, 1445

Monumental history: (Nietzsche) 1564–65, 1878

Moore, George, 655

Moore, Marianne, 16, 1157

Moore, Thomas Sturge, 898

Moore-Gilbert, Bart, 1773

Moravia: Alberto, 1221

More, Paul Elmer, 750;

More, Sir Thomas, 142, 225; *Utopia*, 1344

Moretti, Franco, 1875

Morocco (Josef von Sternberg), 1178

Morpheme, 821, 862

Morris, Charles W., 754

Morris, Meaghan, 1323, 1324, 1452, 2010; biography, 1452; **"Things to Do with Shopping Centres,"** **1452–70**

Morris, William, 479, 494

Morrison, Toni, 1512, 1602, 1604, 1765–66, 1776, 1791, 1858–59, 1861, 1865–66, 1869, 1904, 2016; *Beloved*, 1515; biography, 1791; *Playing in the Dark,* **1791–1801**; *Sula,* 1605–08, 1869

Motifs, 3; in Propp, 786, 790, 792, 795; in Veselovsky, 751

Motives: in Burke, 639

Mouffe, Chantal, 1415, 1712

Mozart, Wolfgang Amadeus, 1260, 1923

Mudie's Library, 1312

Mukarovsky, Jan, 750

Multiculturalism, 1472–74, 1476–77, 1479, 1481–83, 1914

Mulvey, Laura, 1117–1118; **"Visual Pleasure and Narrative Cinema,"** **1172–80**

Murry, John Middleton, 1001

Music, 7; classical, 1923; in Foucault, 910; in Frye, 697; in Hegel, 372, 381–83; in Horace, 88; in Kant, 259; in Lukács, 1227; in Nietzsche, 435–36, 439, 445, 449, 451; in Pope, 201; in Sidney, 149; in Wilde, 478

Musil, Robert, 1220–23, 1225–27, 1230, 1232, 1625, 1660–61, 1690; *Young Törless*, 1625, 1660–61
Mussolini, Benito, 609
Mysticism: in Plotinus, 109, 110
Myth: in Aristotle, 79; in Barthes, 869–70; in Baym, 1525–29; in Bhabha, 1877–78, 1881; in Bloom, 1159; in Eco, 951, 953, 956, 960; in Freud, 513, 520, 533; in Frye, 691, 695–96, 698, 700, 1386; in Jung, 542, 552, 558–59; in Lévi-Strauss, 823, 860–67, 920–21; in Moers, 1510; in Morris, 1454; in Wagner, 436; of origin, 1877–78, 1885, 1940
Myth criticism, 903; in Jameson, 1291
Mythemes, 822–24, 862–64; in Lévi-Strauss, 922

NAACP, 566, 571
Nabokov, Vladimir, 612, 622–23, 1089, 1924; *Lolita*, 1043, 1044
Naipaul, V. S., 1757, 1764, 1776, 1877, 1879, 1902
Nairn, Tom, 1883
Naïve (artist) in Schiller, 299–300, 302–03, 331, 442, 548, 699. *See also* Sentimental
Napoleon, 1045
Narcissism, 1175, 1183, 1645, 1653, 1655; in Freud, 523, 526, 1127, 1679; in Jung, 546; in Lacan, 1127
Narratee (Gerald Prince), 968–69, 1046
Narration: in Peter Brooks, 1163; in Dryden, 167, 177–78; in Johnson, 222; in Lukács, 1218; in Sidney, 151
Narrative: in Aristotle, 77; in Peter Brooks, 1111, 1161–62, 1164, 1167, 1171; in Eco, 825, 951–54, 959–60; in Frye, 697–98; in James, 470; in Jauss, 985; in Schiller, 302; in White, 1385. See also Sjužet
Narrative audience (Rabinowitz): 965
Narrative psychotherapy, 1331; in White, 1388, 1389
Narrative theory, 1099, 1161
Narrator: in Booth, 996, 1000
National allegory: in Jameson, 1832
National consciousness: in Anderson, 1819; in Deleuze and Guattari, 1778
Nationalism, 1758; and Fanon, 1760; and print culture, 1819–20; in Ahmad, 1832; in Du Bois, 569; in Kristeva, 1563–64
Nationality, 1753–54, 1776
Naturalism, 1923; in Lukács, 1224, 1226–27, 1230
Nature: and culture, 830; in Baym, 1528–29; in Benjamin, 1236; in Coleridge, 325, 329; in Dryden, 166, 169–70, 172, 176; in ecocriticism, 1337; in Emerson, 386–87, 389, 392; in Hegel, 370, 373–374, 377; in Horace, 86, 92; in Hume, 237, 242; in Jung, 561; in Kant, 248–49, 253, 263–64, 266–71, 273; in Lévi-Strauss, 830, 918–19; in Longinus, 98; in Nietzsche, 441, 443; in Plato, 232; in Plotinus, 111–12, 114, 118; in Pope, 198, 200–03, 206, 208; in Richards, 774; in Johnson, 211, 213, 215, 217, 219–20, 225–26, 228; in Schiller, 299–302; in Sidney, 138, 145; in Staël, 290; in Wilde, 479, 478–96; in Wordsworth, 308, 312–14, 316; writing, 1337. *See also* Art; Culture

Neal, Larry, 1907
Negation: in Heidegger, 621
Negative capability: in Eliot, 539; in Keats, 330–31, 333
Negative dialectic: in Adorno, 1204
Négritude, 1759
Negro art: in Du Bois, 566, 569
Neo-Aristotelianism, 8, 749, 752, 756, 759, 807, 903, 1306; aesthetics, 759; disputes with New Criticism, 759; later generations, 759; origins, 759; positivism of, 760
Neo-conservative, 1950–51, 1956, 1997
Neo-Platonism: 25; in Plotinus, 109
Nerval, Gérard de, 818, 1804, 1810, 1813
Neural science, 977
Neurosis: in Freud, 506, 509, 545
New class (managerial-professional): in Guillory, 1335, 1477
New Criticism, 7–8, 635, 739, 749–50, 752, 754, 756, 759, 763, **764–74, 797–819,** 807, 826, 834, 875, 883–84, 893, 895–96, 901, 903, 964, 1021, 1081, 1321, 1337, 1433–34, 1444, 1525, 1905, 1913, 1922; and tropes, 834; decline and fall, 758; disdain of professionalism, 758
New Historicism, 8, 702, 836, 1320–1322, 1325, 1329–1334, 1336, 1338, **1419–32,** 1433, **1442–52,** 1516
Newman, Barnett, 1936
Newman, John Henry, Cardinal, 606, 1807
Newton, Esther, 1713
Newton, Isaac, 160, 178, 912, 1896
Newton, Judith Lowder, 1329–30, 1514
Ngugi wa Thiong'o, 1767; biography, 1820–21; "Europhonism, Native Languages and the Magic Fountain," **1821–29**
Niagara Movement, 566
Niebelungenlied, 950
Nietzsche, Friedrich, 478, 522, 546, 612–13, 736, 741, 827, 830–31, 833, 838, 840, 882, 886, 890–91, 905, 916–17, 925, 933, 942–46, 949, 1157, 1213, 1327, 1385, 1564, 1589, 1652, 1690, 1777, 1874, 1878, 1913, 1995; biography, 435; *The Birth of Tragedy from the Spirit of Music,* 435, **439–52;** *The Genealogy of Morals,* 1157; "**On Truth and Lie in an Extra-Moral Sense,**" **452–59;** philosophical style, 435; *Thus Spake Zarathustra,* 435, 548, 550; *Twilight of the Idols,* **459–62**
Nightingale, Florence, 602
Night-Sea-Journey: in Jung, 543
Nixon, Richard, 1927, 1946, 1967
Nkrumah, Kwame, 566, 1759, 1824, 1902
Nom-du-Père: in Lacan, 1112–13
Nonnus: *Dionysiaca,* 339
Normative rules, 820
Norris, Christopher, 831, 2000
Norwid, Cyprian, 853
Noumena: in Kant, 320
Nouveau roman, 1923, 1957, 1993
Novel: in Bakhtin, 578, 581, 584; in Peter Brooks, 1171; in Coleridge, 328; in Eco, 952; in Foucault, 911; in Iser,

discourse, 1612; in Anzaldúa, 1851; in Cixous, 1645, 1646, 1650; in Fetterley, 1037; in Gilbert and Gubar, 1536, 1547–48; in Halberstam, 1739; in Haraway, 1974; in Kipnis, 1496; in Millett, 1504; in Moi, 1547–48; in Rubin, 1614, 1664, 1669, 1680; in Sedgwick, 1687; in Wittig, 1638; in Woolf, 605. *See also* Misogyny; Sexism

Patronage, 1310

Patterson, Orlando, 1795

Payn, James: *By Proxy*, 481

Paz, Octavio, 1950, 1953

Peacock, Thomas Love, 345, 352, 655, 1394; biography, 334; *The Four Ages of Poetry,* **335–44**

Peckham, Morse, 1020

Pedagogy and poststructuralism: in Lipking, 894–903

Pederasty, 1632; in classical Athens, 1616

Peirce, Charles Sanders, 820, 886, 1390

Penelope, Julia, 1508

Penis envy, 1115, 1149, 1154, 1569–70, 1612–13, 1653

Penitence: in Foucault, 1631, 1635

Pennington, James W. C., 1896

Pensée sauvage: in Lévi-Strauss, 868

Penthouse Magazine, 1324, 1487–88, 1495–96, 1498

Pepper, Stephen, 967, 1031

Perception: in Kant, 247; in Scarry, 1059–60;

Performative: in Austin, 680, 683–85, 688–89, 1188–89, 1213; in Barthes, 876; in Butler, 1611, 1621–22, 1719; in Hutcheon, 2004. *See also* Constative

Periodization: historical, in Jameson, 1965

Peripeteia. *See* Reversal

Perlocutionary utterance: in Austin, 680, 685, 687–90, 888, 1213

Perrault, Charles, 1925

Perrot, Michelle, 1882

Persistence (Scarry): 1073–75

Personal unconscious: in Jung, 552, 556–57, 563. *See also* Unconscious

Personality: in Eliot, 536–37, 540; in Holland, 1016

Perversity, in Foucault, 1625, 1632, 1634, 1636; in Žižek, 1188

Peterloo massacre, 1330, 1431

Petrarch (Francesco Petrarca), 136, 234, 244, 329, 356, 358–59, 585

Petronius Arbiter, 165, 169, 208, 328, 335, 702–03

Petry, Ann: *The Street*, 1602

Phallic mother, 1149, 1152, 1154

Phallic phase, 1107, 1149–50

Phallocentrism, 1173, 1589, 1614, 1644, 1646, in Cixous, 1648–49, 1655; in Mulvey, 1172–73

Phallogocentrism, 1116, 1984; in Cixous, 1645, 1650; in Gilbert and Gubar, 1548–49; in Haraway, 1985

Phallus (Lacan), 1112, 1115, 1145, 1149, 1152–55, 1172–73, 1187–88, 1594, 1612–14, 1647, 1649–50, 1654–55; in Bhabha, 1885

Pharmakon: in Derrida, 927–28

Phatic (aspect of language): in Austin, 685–86; in Certeau, 1347

Phelan, James, 759, 826, 967, 1042, 1103; biography, 1031; **"Data, Danda, and Disagreement," 1031–35**

Pheme: in Austin, 686

Phenomena: in Kant, 264

Phenomenology, 903, 946; in Eco, 954; in Gadamer, 721–37; in Iser, 1003; in Kolodny, 1560; in Poulet, 1012; in Sartre, 659–660

Philo of Alexandria, 95, 741

Philosophy, 6; in Arnold, 429; in Dryden, 166; in Frye, 693; in Sidney, 133, 136, 141–42, 144–46, 149

Phoneme, 821, 828, 842, 847–48, 855, 857, 862–63, 872, 934

Phonetic writing: in Derrida, 934

Phonetics: in Austin, 685–86; in Shklovsky, 783

Phonology: in Aristotle, 73

Photography: in Benjamin, 1234, 1237–39, 1245

Piaget, Jean, 1091

Picasso, Pablo, 1244, 1260, 1789, 1924, 1936, 1960, 1966

Pictorialism: in Horace, 91

Piercy, Marge, 1539

Piero della Francesca, 1400

Pindar, 148, 338, 417

Pinker, Steven, 1102

Pinsky, Robert, 1069

Pinter, Harold, 534

Pirandello, Luigi, 1240–41

Piscator, Edwin, 1252

Pity and fear: in Aristotle, 63, 66–68, 73, 175; in Eco, 951; in Longinus, 101

Plath, Sylvia, 1041, 1535, 1537, 1540, 1544, 1678

Plato, 1, 4, 6, 11, 25, 55, 57, 66, 83, 90, 95, 99, 105–06, 109, 114, 116, 132–33, 136, 141, 145–46, 148, 150, 152–53, 232, 242, 247, 328, 344–45, 349, 356, 370–71, 386, 393, 413, 435, 447, 477, 480, 583, 661, 700, 740, 760, 827, 830–31, 834, 915, 918, 926–30, 942, 963, 973, 976, 1017, 1145, 1157, 1263, 1268, 1327, 1473, 1475, 1481, 1542, 1565, 1613, 1690, 1694, 1961, 1972; *Apology*, 813; consistency of, 27; dialectical method, 55; epistemology, 27; imitation in, 27; influence of, 25; *Ion*, **38–46,** 110; *Phaedrus,* 27–28, **46–50,** 117, 134, 137, 153, 391, 827, 831, 915, 926, 928–30, 1109; politics in, 26; rationalism, 27; *Republic*, 111, 134, 137, 356, 447, 494, 547, 930, 931; *Republic* **Book X, 30–38;** Socratic dialogues of, 59; *Symposium*, 134, 153, 929, 1168, 1686, 1969; *Timaeus*, 116, 1116; value of art, 26

Plato, Ann, 1896

Plautus, 85, 89, 156, 168, 172, 174; *Amphitrio*, 156; *Menaechmi*, 227

Play (also free-play, *jeu, Spiel*), 8; in Arnold, 420–21; in Barthes, 879, 881; in Butler, 1621, 1709, 1711, 1718; in Cixous, 1649; in Derrida, 829, 834–35, 915, 923, 925, 935, 938, 946, 949, 1134, 1769; in Freud, 510–11, 513; in Gates, 1770; in Heidegger, 615; in Kant, 249, 259, 261–63; in Lacan, 1134; in Lévi-Strauss, 830, 924–25; in Nietzsche, 916; in Plato, 831; in Sartre, 665–72

Postmodern art, 1936

Postmodernism, 1920–2019; and African American culture, 1929–30, 2010; and artistic play, 1924; and capitalism, 1922; and conservatism, 1931–32; and contemporary theory, 1932; and historical critique, 1925–26; and Marxism, 1928–29; and metanarratives, 1935; and postcolonialism, 1769; and reflexivity, 1924; and simulacra, 1926; and style systems, 1935; and technology, 1929, 1936; as ideology, 1928; as style system, 1921; defined, 1921; earliest applications, 1922–23; in Ahmad, 1832; in Habermas, 1213, 1214; in Haraway, 1967–90; in hooks, 2008–13; in Hutcheon, 1993, 2004; in Jameson, 1830, 1957, 1965; in Morris, 2010, in West, 2014–18

Postmodernity, 1763, 1921, 1925, 1928, 1936, 1948, 1950, 1952, 1954; and alienation, 1927; defined, 1921

Poststructuralism, 8, 894, 896, 900–01, 903, 1214, 1333, 1563, 1595, 1773, 1869, 1871, 1873, 1902; in Chow, 1774, 1910, 1916; in Lipking, 900, 902; influence, in Chow, 1914, 1919

Potebnya, Alexander, 750–51, 775, 779, 781

Poulantzas, Nicos, 1302

Poulet, Georges, 661, 972–73, 1012–13

Pound, Ezra, 16, 534, 536, 743, 750, 1157, 1159; 1825, 1924, 1957, 2008

Power: in Bourdieu, 1333; in Butler, 1708, 1710, 1715–16; in Cixous, 1645, 1648, 1654; in Foucault, 1449, 1619; in Greenblatt, 1443, 1445–46, 1449; in Mulvey, 1176–79; in Wollstonecraft, 277

Power/knowledge (*pouvoir-savoir*): in Bhabha, 1881, 1888; in Foucault, 1322, 1326, 1422, 1611, 1613, 1619, 1627–36, 1688; defined, 1629; in Said, 1802, 1805, 1808

Powys, T. F., 653

Practical language: in Shklovsky, 777–78, 784

Practices: in Bourdieu, 1333; in Certeau, 1333; in Morris, 1465

Pratt, Mary Louise, 1045, 1047, 1056, 1478

Praxiteles, 489

Preconscious, 1107

Preintentions: in Husserl, 1004; in Iser, 1005; in Jauss, 984

Prejudice: in Gadamer, 719–20, 724–26; in Hume, 233, 240–41; in Johnson, 216–17

Presence: in Derrida, 828, 915–16, 924–25, 935, 937–38, 941–42, 944; in Heidegger, 917, 942, 947

Presentism, 1436

Priapus, 1153

Priestley, J. B., 653

Primal scene: in Peter Brooks, 1170; in Mulvey, 1174

Primary process: in Freud, 497–98, 1108–09. *See also* Secondary process

Prince, Gerald, 963, 968, 1046–47

Principle of sufficient reason: in Nietzsche, 454

Principles (McKeon): actional, 11; comprehensive, 11; reflexive, 11; simple, 11

Print culture, 1758; in Anderson, 1815–17, 1820

Pritchett, V. S., 1594

Privacy: in Berlant/Warner, 1724

Proairetic code: in Barthes, 1162

Probability: in Aristotle, 66, 69, 73, 78, 80; in Dryden, 168, 176, 178–79, 182; in Horace, 86, 91; in Johnson, 213, 215, 218, 223; in Sidney, 143

Process: as Aristotelian principle, 4

Production: in Eagleton, 1309

Professional-managerial class. *See* New class: in Guillory

Projection: in Freud, 1107

Proletarian writing: in Williams, 1285

Promiscuity: in Berlant and Warner, 1731

Property: in Marx, 400–01, 405, 407

Propp, Vladimir Yakovlevich, 752–53, 785, 832, 872, 1161–62; biography, 785; *[Fairy Tale Transformations],* **785–97**

Prosody: in Jakobson, 858; in Pope, 198, 204

Protagoras of Abdera, 33, 73

Proust, Marcel, 537, 610, 622, 626, 663, 702–03, 834–35, 838, 875, 880–85, 888–93, 905, 977, 981, 1058, 1060, 1062–69, 1162, 1171, 1228, 1620, 1639, 1659, 1662, 1689–90, 1782, 1830, 1957, 1960; *Remembrance of Things Past*, 835, 890–91, 1064, 1069–71, 1073

Psalms of David, 137

Pseudostatements: in Austin, 681; in Cleanth Brooks, 801; in Frye, 694; in Richards, 739, 754

Psychic censor: in Freud, 497–98, 504–06, 508, 523

Psychoanalysis, 12, 860, 903, 912, 1016, 1019–20, 1116, 1123, 1128, 1140, 1145, 1150, 1152, 1224, 1244, 1331, 1486, 1576, 1612, 1660, 1739, 1781; and feminism, 1514; and gender, 1624; and patriarchy, 1676–77; in Barthes, 878; in Baudrillard, 1938, 1939; in Kristeva, 1565; in Lacan, 1184; in queer theory, 1725; in Rubin, 1665; political uses, 1172; theory, 1173, 1612

Psychoanalytic criticism, 1048, **1106–97;** 1516, 1546, 1559, 1922; in Jameson, 1291

Psychology: in Frye, 695, 699; in Hume, 231, 233, 237; in Jung, 544, 550, 554–55; in Kant, 247, 249; in Leavis, 656; in Richards, 764; in Edmund Wilson, 626, 630

Public sphere: in Habermas, 1204

Publication: in Horace, 83

Publishing industry: effect on literary scene, 7

Purposiveness without purpose (Kant): 248, 257–60, 262, 264–65, 665

Pushkin, Alexander, 20, 54, 789; *Eugene Onegin*, 584, 622, 783

Pynchon, Thomas, 1923, 1925, 1957, 1995, 2015

Pythagoras, 33, 136

Qualitative criticism: in Longinus, 95

Quality: in Kant, 248, 251

Queen, Ellery: *The Tragedy of X*, 1047

Queer culture: and zoning laws; in Anzaldúa, 1854; in Berlant and Warner, 1622, 1722, 1724–25, 1729, 1732–33; queer ethnology: in Halberstam, 1742; sex practices: in Berlant and Warner, 1733, 1734

Skinner, B. F., 1368
Sklar, Martin J., 1301
Slave narratives, 1770
Slavery, 1795–96, 1798–1800
Slemon, Stephen, 1773
Smallwood, Thomas, 1898
Smirnoff, Victor, 1888
Smith, Adam, 231, 334, 400, 1665; *The Wealth of Nations*, 1199
Smith, Barbara, 1502, 1773, 1868, 1871; biography, 1600; racism, sexism, homophobia, 1600–05; *Sula* as lesbian novel, 1605–08, **"Toward a Black Feminist Criticism," 1600–10**
Smith, Barbara Herrnstein, 1022, 1048, 1056, 1163; biography, 245; **"Contingencies of Value," 245–46**
Smith, Henry Nash, 1509, 1525, 1528
Smollett, Tobias, 588
Social feminism: in Kolodny, 1562; in Kristeva, 1567; in Nussbaum, 1720
Society, 1, 6, 12; in Ahmad, 1832; in Arnold, 416; in Baym, 1528, 1529; in Eco, 957; in Jung, 564; in Marx, 411; in Shelley, 347, 348; in Staël, 286; in Wordsworth, 313
Society and literature, 742, 1325; in Adorno, 1203; in Arnold, 413, 416; in Baym, 1526; in Benjamin, 1233, 1244; in Cleanth Brooks, 805; in Burke, 638, 645, 648; in Cixous, 1644; in Du Bois, 569; in Eco, 957, 959; in ecocriticism, 1440; in Eagleton, 1310; in Foucault, 908; in Frye, 696; in Gates, 1906; in James, 468; in Jauss, 975; in Marx, 397; in Russian formalism, 751; in Shelley, 345, 350–51, 353, 355, 358; in Trilling, 1525; in Edmund Wilson, 623–28, 630; in Wordsworth, 308
Sociology of consumption: in Morris, 1454–55
Sociology of literature, 971, 1294
Socius: in Spivak, 1840
Socrates, 26, 436–37, 447, 827, 831, 838, 926–31, 1689
Sodomy, 1632
Sokal, Alan, 1338
Sollers, Philippe, 879
Sontag, Susan, 1922; **"Against Interpretation," 740–45;** as cultural conduit, 738; biography, 738
Sophists, 6, 8, 26, 479, 918
Sophocles, 61–62, 72, 79, 81, 98, 154, 166, 168, 172, 323, 338, 354, 417, 436, 447–48, 614, 1948; *Ajax*, 142; *Antigone*, 69, 372; *Oedipus the King*, 58, 66, 68–71, 78, 170, 352; *Philoctetes*, 352, 1219; *Tereus*, 70
Sophrosyne: in Sidney, 140
Source (vehicle of metaphor): in Turner, 1024–25, 1027–30, 1037, 1072–73, 1078–83, 1085–87
Southey, Robert, 319, 334, 341–342, 361
Southworth, Emma D. E. N., 1508, 1520
Souvestre and Allain: *Fantomas*, 959
Sovereignty: in Foucault, 1628
Soyinka, Wole, 1513, 1766, 1776, 1825, 1890
Spacks, Patricia Meyer, 1513, 1556; *The Female Imagination*, 1534, 1603

Spaltung (splitting), 1152
Spatial form: in Frye, 697; in Lévi-Strauss, 864
Speaking person: in Bakhtin, 578–586
Spectacle: in Aristotle, 56, 63, 64, 68
Speech: in Cixous, 1647, in Derrida, 828, 928, 934; in Plato, 929–930
Speech act theory: 576, 1212–13; in Austin, 679, 681–91; in Certeau, 1347; in De Man, 883, 885, 888
Speech genres: in Bakhtin, 590–91, 594
Spence, Donald, 1389
Spencer, Herbert, 258, 413, 487, 777, 784
Spender, Stephen, 1824
Spengemann, William C., 1522
Spengler, Oswald, 648, 1300, 1385, 1813
Spenser, Edmund, 229, 351, 356, 361, 388, 651, 817, 1294, 1325, 1558, 1690, 1824, 1834; 1158; *The Faerie Queene*, 357, 753, 1533; *The Shepherd's Calendar*, 155
Spiller, Robert E., 1522
Spinoza, Baruch, 943, 1270–71, 1306, 1578
Spirit: in Emerson, 386, 388; in Hegel, 370, 372–74, 376, 378, 381–83; in Jung, 559; in Kant, 250, 271; in Plotinus, 112; in Schiller, 300
Spitzer, Leo, 702, 983
Spivak, Gayatri Chakravorty, 17–18, 20–21, 1049, 1582, 1592, 1709, 1762–63, 1773–74, 1776, 1836–47, 1849, 1875; and deconstruction, 1762; and feminism, 1762; and Marxism, 1762; axiomatics of imperialism, 1840, 1845, 1848; biography, 1836; **"Three Women's Texts and a Critique of Imperialism," 1837–50**
Springer, Mary Doyle, 759
Spurgeon: Caroline, 697
St. Augustine, 131, 585; *Confessions*, 1693
St. Jerome, 909–10
St. Paul, 131, 713, 1041
Staël, Germaine de: 1503; biography, 285, **"Essay on Fictions," 287–93; "On Women Writers," 293–97**
Stalin, Josef, 660, 750, 1038, 1130, 1208, 1250, 1582
Starobinski, Jean, 1134
State apparatus: in Althusser, 1629; in Foucault, 1628, 1629
Stein, Gertrude, 622, 1456, 1513, 1549, 1735, 1737, 1965; *Three Women*, 1765
Steinbeck, John: *In Dubious Battle*, 1050
Steinfels, Peter, 1951
Stendhal (Marie-Henri Beyle), 675–77, 702, 907, 1225, 1504, 1581, 1831; *The Charterhouse of Parma*, 669; *The Red and the Black*, 951
Stepan, Nancy, 1894
Stephen, Leslie, 597, 653
Sternberg, Josef von, 1118, 1177–78
Sterne, Laurence, 299, 320, 588, 592–94, 606, 653, 964, 1895; *Tristram Shandy*, 751, 991, 1002, 1167; *A Sentimental Journey*, 291
Stevens, Wallace, 612, 1157, 1159, 1435, 1957; *Of Mere Being*, 1802

Stevenson: Robert Louis, 473; *The Black Arrow*, 481; *Dr. Jekyll and Mr. Hyde*, 481, 489, 490; *Treasure Island*, 473
Stimpson, Catharine, 1535
Stoll, Edgar, 697, 811
Stoppard, Tom: *Rosencrantz and Guildenstern Are Dead*, 1044
Stout, Rex: Nero Wolfe stories, 958
Stowe, Harriet Beecher, 1508; *Uncle Tom's Cabin*, 53, 572, 1520, 1586, 1765
Stramm, August, 1246
Strauss, David Friedrich, 369, 413, 425
Strauss, Leo, 730, 1137, 1931, 1956
Stravinsky, Igor, 1203, 1323, 1924, 1957;
Structural linguistics, 820, 822, 854, 1113; in Lévi-Strauss, 863
Structural Marxism, 1205
Structuralism, 6, 8, 692, 753, **819–961**, 963, 968, 976, 978, 983, 985, 987, 1056, 1133, 1151, 1295, 1326, 1337, 1433, 1555, 1563, 1769, 1902, 1914, 1916; and anthropology, 823; as activity, 822; decline, 826; in Barthes, 832, 871; in Frye, 692; in Kolodny, 1559; in Lévi-Strauss, 922, in Lipking, 899; in Rubin, 1665; logistic method, 1324. *See also* Semiotics
Structure: in Barthes, 871–72; in Cleanth Brooks, 804; in Peter Brooks, 1161, 1165; in Burke, 636; in Coleridge, 322; in Derrida, 915, 916, 917, 924; in Eco, 951, 954, 956, 960, 961; in Foucault, 905; in Frye, 694, 696; in Greenblatt, 1444; in Leavis, 657; in Lévi-Strauss, 867, 921; in Lipking, 894; in Propp, 785; in Ransom, 757; in Sartre, 668. *See also* Form
Structures of feeling (Williams), 1286–90
Strunk, Janet, 134
Style, 6, 161; feminine, 1613; in Aristotle, 75–77, 80; in Booth, 994; in Dante, 123; in Dryden, 164; in Holland, 1019; in Horace, 91, 95; in Johnson, 216, 221; in Lacan, 1115; in Leavis, 655; in Longinus, 95, 99–100, 103; in Lukács, 1218–19; in Pope, 203; in Wordsworth, 304, 307, 309, 315
Style system, 1921–24; in Horkheimer and Adorno, 1259–61
Stylistics, 824, 982–83, 1022–23, 1031, 1033
Subaltern, 1753, 1756, 1762–63, 1774, 1836
Subaltern studies, 17–19, 21, 1762
Subject, 1333; in Althusser, 1266, 1268; in Derrida, 941; in Eco, 954; in Foucault, 905, 910, 913, 1326, 1366; in Hume, 232, 236; in Jung, 563; in Kant, 247, 251–52, 254, 258; in Lacan, 1114–15, 1126, 1131, 1135, 1142, 1152–53; in Lévi-Strauss, 921; in Nietzsche, 436, 445, 446, 891; in Sartre, 663; formation, in queer theory, 1725
Subjectivity: in Kant, 256; in Lukács, 1221; in Sartre, 664, 665
Subject-matter: in Dryden, 164; in James, 463, 471
Sublimation: in Bloom, 1158; in Lacan, 1187
Sublime: 1438; in Arnold, 413; in Cleanth Brooks, 800; in Dante, 123; in Eliot, 540; in Emerson, 392; in Hegel, 377;

in Hume, 242; in Johnson, 226; in Kant, 249, 263–64, 266–70; in Longinus, 95–98, 100–03, 105–06; in Plotinus, 118; in Schiller, 302
Sublime object: in Žižek, 1119
Subordination, 1206, 1277–79, 1293, 1308, 1311, 1317
Substance: in Hegel, 370, 372, 377
Suckling, Sir John, 165, 184
Suetonius, 486, 858
Suffering: in Aristotle, 67–68
Suleiman, Susan, 1044
Sundquist, Eric, 1530
Sunset Boulevard (Billy Wilder), 1177
Superego: in Freud, 499, 1108, 1110, 1124, 1150
Superreader: in Barthes, 987
Superstructure *(uberbau)*, 1205–06; in Marx, 1233, 1273–77, 1279; in Said, 1806–07; in Williams, 1272. *See also* Base
Supplement: in Derrida, 830, 923; in Lévi-Strauss, 923
Surplus value: in Marx, 1615, 1666
Surrealism, 1125, 1936, 1949, 1953
Surrey, Henry Howard, Earl of, 155
Surveillance: in Baudrillard, 1943–44; in Certeau, 1346; in Foucault, 1631
Suspense: in Booth, 995–96
Swedenborg, Emmanuel, 384, 386, 394;
Swift, Jonathan, 160, 214, 299, 1133, 1294, 1796; *Battle of the Books*, 1948; *Gulliver's Travels*, 1133
Symbol, 750, 819–20, 823, 832, 867, 1780; in Blackmur, 758; in Cleanth Brooks, 800, 804, 806; in Eagleton, 1317; in Emerson, 389, 390, 394; in Freud, 546; in Frye, 692, 695; in Greenblatt, 1445; in Jung, 544, 546, 550, 552, 558; in Lacan, 1112; in Robert Penn Warren, 758; in Wilde, 492; in Wimsatt and Beardsley, 817
Symbolic (Lacanian field), 1151, 1172–73, 1175, 1178–79; Berlant and Warner, 1725; in Butler, 1714; in Cixous, 1644, 1647, 1649, 1652; in Lacan, 1112–13, 1115–17; in Mulvey, 1172, 1177; in Spivak, 1843
Symbolic (mode of art): in Hegel, 371, 377, 380, 383
Symbolic action: in Burke, 633, 636, 638–39, 642, 648, 1294; in Jameson, 1291, 1295, 1299, 1304
Symbolism, 776; Freudian, 743; in Cleanth Brooks, 804; in Lukács, 1226; in Nietzsche, 435; in Sontag, 743
Symbolization (ego defense): in Freud, 1107; in Lacan, 1113
Synchronic and diachronic: in Barthes, 871; in Jakobson, 853, 854; in Jauss, 975 in Lévi-Strauss, 863, 867
Synecdoche, 825, 887, 1350, 1394; in White, 1330
Synolon: in Neo-Aristotelianism, 760
Syntagmata. *See* Paradigmata and syntagmata
Syntax, 820–21, 823; in Aristotle, 73, 74; in Barthes, 1162; in De Man, 886, 887; in Derrida, 917; in Lacan, 1113; in Lipking, 897; in Todorov, 1162; in Wimsatt and Beardsley, 814
Synthesis: in Arnold, 416; in Shelley, 344, 346
Syzygy: in Jung, 543

Tacit knowledge: in Rabinowitz, 965

Tacitus, 233, 242, 289, 486, 727

Taine, Hippolyte, 6, 285, 623, 630, 1394, 1449–50, 1892

Talking book: in Gates, 1900

Tannen, Deborah: *You Just Don't Understand*, 1508

Tardieu, Jean, 1137

Target (tenor of metaphor): in Turner, 1078–87, 1092

Tasso, Torquato, 351, 356–57, 361

Taste, 5, 7, 242; in Behn, 190; in Bourdieu, 1334, 1398–1403; in Dryden, 162–63; in Emerson, 385; in Frye, 694; in Horace, 89, 93; in Hume, 232–38, 241–42; in James, 471–72; in Kant, 248, 250–52, 254–62, 271; in Longinus, 108; in Plato, 232; in Pope, 200, 203, 205, 207–08; in Johnson, 230; in Shelley, 347; in Staël, 289; in Wordsworth, 307, 311–12, 316. *See also* Judgment; Value

Tate, Allen, 754, 756, 758, 964, 1892

Taxonomy, 1327

Tchaikovsky, 875

Technē: in Plato, 45; in Derrida, 943; in Bhabha, 1882

Technique: in Booth, 990; in Leavis, 657; in Russian formalism, 752

Technology: in Benjamin, 1249; in Foucault, 1628, 1634, 1636

Teena, Brandon, 1622

Tel Quel, 836, 939

Television and postmodernity, 1927

Temporality: in De Man, 1913; in Kristeva, 1566

Temporalization: in Derrida, 936, 941

Tennenhouse, Leonard, 1422

Tennyson, Alfred, Lord, 496, 535, 571, 601, 608, 651, 692, 694, 809, 817, 824, 1159, 1542, 1620, 1690

Tension: in Tate, 758

Terence, 123, 142, 168–69, 171–72, 242–43, 307; *Adelphi*, 172; *Andria*, 170; *Eunuch*, 156, 168, 171–72, 178, 186; *The Self-Tormentor*, 153, 171

Text, 8–10; in Barthes, 878, 880, 882; in Bleich, 1021; in Fish, 966, 1030; in Foucault, 904, 910, 912; in Holland, 1019, 1021; in Iser, 1002, 1004, 1005, 1009, 1012; in Jameson, 1295; in Lacan, 1114; in Rabinowitz, 1052; in Said, 1811; in Wimsatt and Beardsley, 816

Textual analysis, 982

Textual criticism: in Lipking, 897

Textuality, 8; and deconstruction, 836; in Bhabha, 1880; in Peter Brooks, 1111, 1170

Texture: in Coleridge, 322; in Ransom, 757

Thackeray, Anne, Lady Ritchie, 469

Thackeray, William Makepeace, 464, 588, 606, 651, 653, 655, 1596; *Henry Esmond*, 484; *The Newcomes*, 489; *Vanity Fair*, 489, 543

Theme, 3, 6, 739; in Cleanth Brooks, 799, 806; in Burke, 635; in New Criticism, 755; in Veselovsky, 751

Theocritus, 155, 354

Theories: literary, 2

Theory: 2; and pedagogy, 894–96; as cultural capital, 1336; as

hegemonic discourse, 1861, 1862, 1865; in Leavis, 652; in Lipking, 903; in McDowell, 1873; postcolonial, 1757; resistance to, 1915. *See also* Criticism

Theory and race: in Awkward, 1772–73, 1867–70; in Christian, 1772, 1859–65; in McDowell, 1773, 1870–74

Theory of mind: in Zunshine, 1089–96, 1098–99, 1101–02, 1104–05

"There": in Plotinus, 113, 114

Theroux, Paul, 1767

Thespis, 89

Thick description: in Geertz, 1332

Thiong'o. *See* Ngugi wa Thiong'o

Third World, 1768–69, 1775–76, 1779, 1782, 1814, 1829–37, 1847, 1864, 1874, 1902, 1915, 1977–79, 2011, 2016; as product of decolonization, 1755; discourse, in Spivak, 1838; literatures, as national allegory, 1831–36

Thompson, E. P., 1323, 1330, 1404–05, 1408–09, 1413; *Making of the English Working Class*, 1330, 1420, 1431

Thompson, Stith, 752–53

Thomson, James, 299, 853

Thoreau, Henry David, 384, 1375, 1432, 1526, 1690; *Walden*, 1441

Thoth (Egyptian god of writing), 926

Thought: in Aristotle, 56, 63–64, 73; in Dryden, 164, 173; in Emerson, 387; in Horace, 90; in Longinus, 100; in Neo-Aristotelianism, 760

Thucydides, 106, 338, 1396

Thurber, James: "The Secret Life of Walter Mitty," 1052

Tiffin, Helen, 1773

Tillich, Paul, 612

Tillotson, Kathleen, 1012

Tillyard, E. M. W., 811, 814

Titchborne Claimant (Arthur Orton), 1325

To Have and Have Not (Howard Hawks), 1176, 1177

Tocqueville, Alexis de, 1262, 1387, 1394–95

Todd, Janet, 1595

Todorov, Tzvetan, 750, 826, 832, 836, 841, 884–85, 1043, 1047, 1116, 1161–62, 1164–65, 1169, 1171, 1188, 1350, 1643

Toklas, Alice B., 1513

Tolstoy, Count Leo, 13, 50, 51, 52, 477, 577, 582, 604, 610, 703, 768, 778, 779, 1049, 1251, 1252, 1256, 1689, 1805, 1912; *Anna Karenina*, 51; *The Death of Ivan Ilych*, 1219; "Kholstomer," 779, 780, 783; *Resurrection*, 781; *War and Peace*, 51, 780–81, 1049, 1054, 1056; **"What Is Art?"** **52–55**

Tomashevsky, Boris, 752

Tomboyism: in Halberstam, 1737–40

Toomer, Jean, 1904

Totalitarianism, 1300, 1301, 1573

Totalization: in Jameson, 1300

Touchstone: in Arnold, 432–34, in Heidegger, 612

Tourneur, Cyril, 541

Toynbee, Arnold, 1385

Trace: in Certeau, 1347; in Derrida, 925, 933, 939–40, 942–48, 1135

Tradition: female, 1508–09; in Arnold, 429, 430; in Bakhtin, 582; in Benjamin, 1235, 1236; in Bloom, 1158; in Cixous, 1646; in Eagleton, 1317; in Eco, 959; in Eliot, 536, 537, 538, 539, 541, 755; in Foucault, 906, 909, 910; in Frye, 691; in Gadamer, 720, 730–31; in Holland, 1017; in Horace, 82, 86, 87; in Jakobson, 853; in Leavis, 651, 653–54, 658; in Showalter, 1511; in Williams, 1280–81; in Woolf, 606; literary, 6. *See also* History and literature; Literary history

Tragedy, 161; definition, 63; development in Aristotle, 62; in Aristotle, 56–59, 62, 67, 81, 760; in Benjamin, 1247; in Bloom, 1158; in Coleridge, 323; in Dante, 122; in Dryden, 167–68, 173, 175–76, 180; in Frye, 692, 699; in Greenblatt, 1443; in Hegel, 372; in Holland, 1017; in Horace, 83, 89–90; in Hume, 241; in Johnson, 211, 219–20, 222, 224, 228–29; in Longinus, 98; in Nietzsche, 435–36, 439, 442, 444, 447–48, 450, 452; in Plato, 32, 34; in Richards, 772; in Schiller, 299; in Shelley, 352–53, 359; in Sidney, 134, 139, 146–47, 155–56; in Staël, 288; in White, 1330

Tragicomedy: in Booth, 998; in Dryden, 175; in Sidney, 156

Traherne, Thomas, 535

Trajan, 714

Transaction: in Holland, 970

Transcendental dialectic: in Hegel, 371. *See also* Dialectic

Transcendental signifier. *See* Phallus

Transference: in Lacan, 1149

Transformation: in Propp, 786–87, 791, 793–96

Transformational grammar, 1023

Transgender, 1621–22; in Halberstam, 1735; in Rubin, 1675–76

Transsexuality, 1617; in Halberstam, 1736

Trask, Haunani Kay, 1826, 1827

Trevelyan, George Macaulay, 600

Trevor-Roper, Hugh, 1783

Trilling, Lionel, 1, 633, 738, 1201, 1509, 1523–25, 1530, 1580

Trollope, Anthony, 465–66, 651–52, 655, 1318, 1923

Tropes, 1330; in Peter Brooks, 1165; in Lacan, 1144. *See also* Figures of speech; Metaphor; Metonymy; etc.

Trotsky, Leon: *Literature and Revolution,* 1200–01

Truffaut: *Day for Night,* 1191; Francois, 744

Truth: in Aristotle, 57; in Arnold, 424, 434; in Coleridge, 328; in Dryden, 168, 170; in Hegel, 374; in James, 466, 474; in Keats, 331–32; in Nietzsche, 453–55, 457; in Plato, 57; in Shelley, 345, 349; in Sidney, 150–51; in Wilde, 480, 478–96. *See also* Realism; Verisimilitude

Turgenev, Ivan Sergeievich: 471, 779; *Fathers and Sons,* 489

Turner, Frederick Jackson, 1509, 1909; *The Frontier in American History,* 1905

Turner, J. M. W., 491–92

Turner, Mark, 977, 1090; "Poetry: Metaphor and the Conceptual Context of Invention," 1077–91

Twain, Mark (Samuel Clemens): *Huckleberry Finn,* 1509, 1623, 1765, 1799, 1800

Tylor, E. B., 1367

Tynyanov, Yuri, 576, 752–53, 1966

Types and tokens: in Derrida, 828

Typology: biblical, 1023

Tyutchev, Fyodor, 775

Tzara, Tristan, 1949

Uberbau. *See* Superstructure

Uncanny: in Freud, 498–99, 514–32; in Žižek, 1160, 1165–66, 1182, 1184, 1190

Unconscious, 1137, 1709; in Freud, 497–98, 502, 504, 507, 512, 518, 523–24, 526, 533, 546, 1107–08, 1111, 1138, 1140, 1142, 1145, 1151; in Frye, 698; in Jung, 542, 549, 553–54, 558–59, 562–63; in Lacan, 1105, 1112–13, 1115, 1130, 1140, 1146

Understanding: aesthetic, 987; in Coleridge, 329; in Hume, 236, 241; in Jauss, 983, 985–86; in Kant, 251, 262–63, 267, 272–73; in Schiller, 299–300

Unities of drama: in Dryden, 184; in Johnson, 211, 222; in Pope, 203

Unity, 223, 814; in Aristotle, 64, 77, 81; in Bakhtin, 578; in Cleanth Brooks, 808; in Coleridge, 329; in Foucault, 909; in Frye, 695; in Hegel, 376, 378, 381; in Horace, 87; in Kant, 269; in Neo-Aristotelianism, 760; in Plotinus, 109, 111, 114, 116; in Schiller, 301, 303

Unity of action: in Aristotle, 161; in Behn, 194; in Dryden, 161, 167–68, 175–76, 181–82, 185; in Samuel Johnson, 223–24; in Sidney, 134

Unity of place: in Behn, 194; in Corneille, 161; in Dryden, 161, 167–68, 175, 182, 185; in Johnson, 223–24; in Sidney, 134, 155

Unity of time: in Aristotle, 62, 161; in Behn, 194; in Corneille, 161; in Dryden, 161, 167, 175, 182, 185; in Johnson, 211, 223–24; in Sidney, 134, 155–56

Universality: in Aristotle, 65; in Johnson, 211; in Kant, 248, 255–57, 263; in Sidney, 143

Unpacking, 13

Unpleasure: in Mulvey, 1174, 1177, 1179. *See also* Pleasure

Unreliable narrator: in Booth, 964, 1011

Updike, John, 13; *Rabbit, Run,* 1526

Utility: in Horace, 85; in Kant, 248

Valentinus, 1159

Valéry, Paul, 622, 875, 884, 1233–34, 1245, 1308; "Au platane," 1135

Value of poetry: in Dryden, 166; in Plato, 35; in Johnson, 216; in Sidney, 148. *See also* Taste

Values: in Booth, 964, 998, 999, 1000

Van Dine, S. S., 1053

Van Ghent, Dorothy, 1594–95

Van Gogh, Vincent, 669

Vasconcelos, José, 1850